2005–2006 Edition

International Income Taxation

Code and Regulations
Selected Sections

As of June 1, 2005

Coordinating Editor

RICHARD CRAWFORD PUGH
Distinguished Professor of Law, University of San Diego

Contributing Editors

CHARLES H. GUSTAFSON
Professor of Law, Georgetown University

ROBERT J. PERONI
Parker C. Fielder Regents Professor in Tax Law
University of Texas

CCH INCORPORATED
Chicago
A WoltersKluwer Company

This publication is designed to provide accurate and authoritative information in regard to the subject matter covered. It is sold with the understanding that the publisher is not engaged in rendering legal, accounting, or other professional service. If legal advice or other expert assistance is required, the services of a competent professional person should be sought.

ISBN 0-8080-1308-4

©2005, **CCH** INCORPORATED

4025 W. Peterson Ave.
Chicago, IL 60646-6085
1 800 248 3248
http://tax.cchgroup.com

No claim is made to original government works; however, within this Product or Publication, the following are subject to CCH's copyright: (1) the gathering, compilation, and arrangement of such government materials; (2) the magnetic translation and digital conversion of data, if applicable; (3) the historical, statutory and other notes and references; and (4) the commentary and other materials.

All Rights Reserved

Printed in the United States of America

Preface

This volume represents an effort to collect the principal Code sections relating to the United States taxation of the income from international trade and investment, both inbound and outbound. Also included are the significant final, temporary, and proposed regulations associated with these Code sections. The volume is intended to serve as a convenient reference tool for lawyers, accountants, teachers, students, and others who work in this area. The volume reflects the state of the law and regulations as of June 1, 2005. Suggestions from users as to additions and deletions that would increase the usefulness of the volume would be greatly appreciated.

Richard Crawford Pugh
Charles H. Gustafson
Robert J. Peroni

June 2005

Contents

Internal Revenue Code, Selected Sections	1
Income Tax Regulations, Selected Sections	1001
Indexes	
Index to Code.....................................	2601
Index to Regulations	2701

Internal Revenue Code

INTERNAL REVENUE CODE OF 1986

SUBTITLE A—INCOME TAXES

CHAPTER 1—NORMAL TAXES AND SURTAXES

SUBCHAPTER A—DETERMINATION OF TAX LIABILITY

PART I—TAX ON INDIVIDUALS

[Sec. 1]

SECTION 1. TAX IMPOSED.

[Sec. 1(a)]

(a) MARRIED INDIVIDUALS FILING JOINT RETURNS AND SURVIVING SPOUSES.—There is hereby imposed on the taxable income of—

(1) every married individual (as defined in section 7703) who makes a single return jointly with his spouse under section 6013, and

(2) every surviving spouse (as defined in section 2(a)),

a tax determined in accordance with the following table:

If taxable income is:	The tax is:
Not over $36,900	15% of taxable income.
Over $36,900 but not over $89,150	$5,535, plus 28% of the excess over $36,900.
Over $89,150 but not over $140,000	$20,165, plus 31% of the excess over $89,150.
Over $140,000 but not over $250,000	$35,928.50, plus 36% of the excess over $140,000.
Over $250,000	$75,528.50, plus 39.6% of the excess over $250,000.

[Sec. 1(b)]

(b) HEADS OF HOUSEHOLDS.—There is hereby imposed on the taxable income of every head of a household (as defined in section 2(b)) a tax determined in accordance with the following table:

If taxable income is:	The tax is:
Not over $29,600	15% of taxable income.
Over $29,600 but not over $76,400	$4,440, plus 28% of the excess over $29,600.
Over $76,400 but not over $127,500	$17,544, plus 31% of the excess over $76,400.
Over $127,500 but not over $250,000	$33,385, plus 36% of the excess over $127,500.
Over $250,000	$77,485, plus 39.6% of the excess over $250,000.

[Sec. 1(c)]

(c) UNMARRIED INDIVIDUALS (OTHER THAN SURVIVING SPOUSES AND HEADS OF HOUSEHOLDS).—There is hereby imposed on the taxable income of every individual (other than a surviving spouse as defined in section 2(a) or the head of a household as defined in section 2(b)) who is not a married individual (as defined in section 7703) a tax determined in accordance with the following table:

If taxable income is:	The tax is:
Not over $22,100	15% of taxable income.
Over $22,100 but not over $53,500	$3,315, plus 28% of the excess over $22,100.
Over $53,500 but not over $115,000	$12,107, plus 31% of the excess over $53,500.
Over $115,000 but not over $250,000	$31,172, plus 36% of the excess over $115,000.
Over $250,000	$79,772, plus 39.6% of the excess over $250,000.

[Sec. 1(d)]

(d) MARRIED INDIVIDUALS FILING SEPARATE RETURNS.—There is hereby imposed on the taxable income of every married individual (as defined in section 7703) who does not make a single return jointly with his spouse under section 6013, a tax determined in accordance with the following table:

If taxable income is:	The tax is:
Not over $18,450	15% of taxable income.
Over $18,450 but not over $44,575	$2,767.50, plus 28% of the excess over $18,450.
Over $44,575 but not over $70,000	$10,082.50, plus 31% of the excess over $44,575.
Over $70,000 but not over $125,000	$17,964.25, plus 36% of the excess over $70,000.
Over $125,000	$37,764.25, plus 39.6% of the excess over $125,000.

[Sec. 1(e)]

(e) ESTATES AND TRUSTS.—There is hereby imposed on the taxable income of—

    (1) every estate, and

    (2) every trust,

taxable under this subsection a tax determined in accordance with the following table:

If taxable income is:	The tax is:
Not over $1,500	15% of taxable income.
Over $1,500 but not over $3,500	$225, plus 28% of the excess over $1,500.
Over $3,500 but not over $5,500	$785, plus 31% of the excess over $3,500.
Over $5,500 but not over $7,500	$1,405, plus 36% of the excess over $5,500.
Over $7,500	$2,125, plus 39.6% of the excess over $7,500.

[Sec. 1(f)]

(f) PHASEOUT OF MARRIAGE PENALTY IN 15-PERCENT BRACKET; ADJUSTMENTS IN TAX TABLES SO THAT INFLATION WILL NOT RESULT IN TAX INCREASES.—

    (1) IN GENERAL.—Not later than December 15 of 1993, and each subsequent calendar year, the Secretary shall prescribe tables which shall apply in lieu of the tables contained in subsections (a), (b), (c), (d), and (e) with respect to taxable years beginning in the succeeding calendar year.

    (2) METHOD OF PRESCRIBING TABLES.—The table which under paragraph (1) is to apply in lieu of the table contained in subsection (a), (b), (c), (d), or (e), as the case may be, with respect to taxable years beginning in any calendar year shall be prescribed—

        (A) except as provided in paragraph (8), by increasing the minimum and maximum dollar amounts for each rate bracket for which a tax is imposed under such table by the cost-of-living adjustment for such calendar year,

        (B) by not changing the rate applicable to any rate bracket as adjusted under subparagraph (A), and

        (C) by adjusting the amounts setting forth the tax to the extent necessary to reflect the adjustments in the rate brackets.

    (3) COST-OF-LIVING ADJUSTMENT.—For purposes of paragraph (2), the cost-of-living adjustment for any calendar year is the percentage (if any) by which—

        (A) the CPI for the preceding calendar year, exceeds

        (B) the CPI for calendar year 1992.

    (4) CPI FOR ANY CALENDAR YEAR.—For purposes of paragraph (3), the CPI for any calendar year is the average of the Consumer Price Index as of the close of the 12-month period ending on August 31 of such calendar year.

    (5) CONSUMER PRICE INDEX.—For purposes of paragraph (4), the term "Consumer Price Index" means the last Consumer Price Index for all-urban consumers published by the Department of Labor. For purposes of the preceding sentence, the revision of the Consumer Price Index which is most consistent with the Consumer Price Index for calendar year 1986 shall be used.

    (6) ROUNDING.—

        (A) IN GENERAL.—If any increase determined under paragraph (2)(A), section 63(c)(4), section 68(b)(2) or section 151(d)(4) is not a multiple of $50, such increase shall be rounded to the next lowest multiple of $50.

(B) TABLE FOR MARRIED INDIVIDUALS FILING SEPARATELY.—In the case of a married individual filing a separate return, subparagraph (A) (other than with respect to sections 63(c)(4) and 151(d)(3)(A)) shall be applied by substituting "$25" for"$50" each place it appears.

* * *

(8) ELIMINATION OF MARRIAGE PENALTY IN 15-PERCENT BRACKET.—With respect to taxable years beginning after December 31, 2003, in prescribing the tables under paragraph (1)—

(A) the maximum taxable income in the 15-percent rate bracket in the table contained in subsection (a) (and the minimum taxable income in the next higher taxable income bracket in such table) shall be 200 percent of the maximum taxable income in the 15-percent rate bracket in the table contained in subsection (c) (after any other adjustment under this subsection), and

(B) the comparable taxable income amounts in the table contained in subsection (d) shall be ½ of the amounts determined under subparagraph (A).

* * *

[Sec. 1(h)]

(h) MAXIMUM CAPITAL GAINS RATE.—

(1) IN GENERAL.—If a taxpayer has a net capital gain for any taxable year, the tax imposed by this section for such taxable year shall not exceed the sum of—

(A) a tax computed at the rates and in the same manner as if this subsection had not been enacted on the greater of—

(i) taxable income reduced by the net capital gain, or

(ii) the lesser of—

(I) the amount of taxable income taxed at a rate below 25 percent; or

(II) taxable income reduced by the adjusted net capital gain;

(B) 5 percent (0 percent in the case of taxable years beginning after 2007) of so much of the adjusted net capital gain (or, if less, taxable income) as does not exceed the excess (if any) of—

(i) the amount of taxable income which would (without regard to this paragraph) be taxed at a rate below 25 percent, over

(ii) the taxable income reduced by the adjusted net capital gain;

(C) 15 percent of the adjusted net capital gain (or, if less, taxable income) in excess of the amount on which a tax is determined under subparagraph (B);

(D) 25 percent of the excess (if any) of—

(i) the unrecaptured section 1250 gain (or, if less, the net capital gain (determined without regard to paragraph (11))), over

(ii) the excess (if any) of—

(I) the sum of the amount on which tax is determined under subparagraph (A) plus the net capital gain, over

(II) taxable income; and

(E) 28 percent of the amount of taxable income in excess of the sum of the amounts on which tax is determined under the preceding subparagraphs of this paragraph.

(2) NET CAPITAL GAIN TAKEN INTO ACCOUNT AS INVESTMENT INCOME.—For purposes of this subsection, the net capital gain for any taxable year shall be reduced (but not below zero) by the amount which the taxpayer takes into account as investment income under section 163(d)(4)(B)(iii).

(3) ADJUSTED NET CAPITAL GAIN.—For purposes of this subsection, the term "adjusted net capital gain" means the sum of—

(A) net capital gain (determined without regard to paragraph (11)) reduced (but not below zero) by the sum of—

(i) unrecaptured section 1250 gain, and

(ii) 28-percent rate gain, plus

(B) qualified dividend income (as defined in paragraph (11)).

(4) 28-PERCENT RATE GAIN.—For purposes of this subsection, the term "28-percent rate gain" means the excess (if any) of—

    (A) the sum of—

        (i) collectibles gain; and

        (ii) section 1202 gain, over

    (B) the sum of—

        (i) collectibles loss;

        (ii) the net short-term capital loss, and

        (iii) the amount of long-term capital loss carried under section 1212(b)(1)(B) to the taxable year.

(5) COLLECTIBLES GAIN AND LOSS.—For purposes of this subsection—

    (A) IN GENERAL.—The terms "collectibles gain" and "collectibles loss" mean gain or loss (respectively) from the sale or exchange of a collectible (as defined in section 408(m) without regard to paragraph (3) thereof) which is a capital asset held for more than 1 year but only to the extent such gain is taken into account in computing gross income and such loss is taken into account in computing taxable income.

    (B) PARTNERSHIPS, ETC.—For purposes of subparagraph (A), any gain from the sale of an interest in a partnership, S corporation, or trust which is attributable to unrealized appreciation in the value of collectibles shall be treated as gain from the sale or exchange of a collectible. Rules similar to the rules of section 751 shall apply for purposes of the preceding sentence.

(6) UNRECAPTURED SECTION 1250 GAIN.—For purposes of this subsection—

    (A) IN GENERAL.—The term "unrecaptured section 1250 gain" means the excess (if any) of—

        (i) the amount of long-term capital gain (not otherwise treated as ordinary income) which would be treated as ordinary income if section 1250(b)(1) included all depreciation and the applicable percentage under section 1250(a) were 100 percent, over

        (ii) the excess (if any) of—

            (I) the amount described in paragraph (4)(B); over

            (II) the amount described in paragraph (4)(A).

    (B) LIMITATION WITH RESPECT TO SECTION 1231 PROPERTY.—The amount described in subparagraph (A)(i) from sales, exchanges, and conversions described in section 1231(a)(3)(A) for any taxable year shall not exceed the net section 1231 gain (as defined in section 1231(c)(3)) for such year.

(7) SECTION 1202 GAIN.—For purposes of this subsection, the term "section 1202 gain" means the excess of—

    (A) the gain which would be excluded from gross income under section 1202 but for the percentage limitation in section 1202(a), over

    (B) the gain excluded from gross income under section 1202.

(8) COORDINATION WITH RECAPTURE OF NET ORDINARY LOSSES UNDER SECTION 1231.—If any amount is treated as ordinary income under section 1231(c), such amount shall be allocated among the separate categories of net section 1231 gain (as defined in section 1231(c)(3)) in such manner as the Secretary may by forms or regulations prescribe.

(9) REGULATIONS.—The Secretary may prescribe such regulations as are appropriate (including regulations requiring reporting) to apply this subsection in the case of sales and exchanges by pass-thru entities and of interests in such entities.

(10) PASS-THRU ENTITY DEFINED.—For purposes of this subsection, the term "pass-thru entity" means—

    (A) a regulated investment company;

    (B) a real estate investment trust;

    (C) an S corporation;

    (D) a partnership;

(E) an estate or trust;

(F) a common trust fund; and

(G) a qualified electing fund (as defined in section 1295).

(11) DIVIDENDS TAXED AS NET CAPITAL GAIN.—

(A) IN GENERAL.—For purposes of this subsection, the term "net capital gain" means net capital gain (determined without regard to this paragraph) increased by qualified dividend income.

(B) QUALIFIED DIVIDEND INCOME.—For purposes of this paragraph—

(i) IN GENERAL.—The term "qualified dividend income" means dividends received during the taxable year from—

(I) domestic corporations, and

(II) qualified foreign corporations.

(ii) CERTAIN DIVIDENDS EXCLUDED.—Such term shall not include—

(I) any dividend from a corporation which for the taxable year of the corporation in which the distribution is made, or the preceding taxable year, is a corporation exempt from tax under section 501 or 521,

(II) any amount allowed as a deduction under section 591 (relating to deduction for dividends paid by mutual savings banks, etc.), and

(III) any dividend described in section 404(k).

* * *

(C) QUALIFIED FOREIGN CORPORATIONS.—

(i) IN GENERAL.—Except as otherwise provided in this paragraph, the term "qualified foreign corporation" means any foreign corporation if—

(I) such corporation is incorporated in a possession of the United States, or

(II) such corporation is eligible for benefits of a comprehensive income tax treaty with the United States which the Secretary determines is satisfactory for purposes of this paragraph and which includes an exchange of information program.

(ii) DIVIDENDS ON STOCK READILY TRADABLE ON UNITED STATES SECURITIES MARKET.—A foreign corporation not otherwise treated as a qualified foreign corporation under clause (i) shall be so treated with respect to any dividend paid by such corporation if the stock with respect to which such dividend is paid is readily tradable on an established securities market in the United States.

(iii) EXCLUSION OF DIVIDENDS OF CERTAIN FOREIGN CORPORATIONS.—Such term shall not include any foreign corporation which for the taxable year of the corporation in which the dividend was paid, or the preceding taxable year, is a passive foreign investment company (as defined in section 1297).

(iv) COORDINATION WITH FOREIGN TAX CREDIT LIMITATION.—Rules similar to the rules of section 904(b)(2)(B) shall apply with respect to the dividend rate differential under this paragraph.

* * *

[Sec. 1(i)]

(i) RATE REDUCTIONS AFTER 2000.—

(1) 10-PERCENT RATE BRACKET.—

(A) IN GENERAL.—In the case of taxable years beginning after December 31, 2000—

(i) the rate of tax under subsections (a), (b), (c), and (d) on taxable income not over the initial bracket amount shall be 10 percent, and

(ii) the 15 percent rate of tax shall apply only to taxable income over the initial bracket amount but not over the maximum dollar amount for the 15-percent rate bracket.

(B) INITIAL BRACKET AMOUNT.—For purposes of this paragraph, the initial bracket amount is—

(i) $14,000 in the case of subsection (a),

(ii) $10,000 in the case of subsection (b), and

(iii) ½ the amount applicable under clause (i) (after adjustment, if any, under subparagraph (C)) in the case of subsections (c) and (d).

(C) INFLATION ADJUSTMENT.—In prescribing the tables under subsection (f) which apply with respect to taxable years beginning in calendar years after 2003—

(i) the cost-of-living adjustment shall be determined under subsection (f)(3) by substituting "2002" for "1992" in subparagraph (B) thereof, and

(ii) the adjustments under clause (i) shall not apply to the amount referred to in subparagraph (B)(iii).

If any amount after adjustment under the preceding sentence is not a multiple of $50, such amount shall be rounded to the next lowest multiple of $50.

(D) COORDINATION WITH ACCELERATION OF 10 PERCENT RATE BRACKET BENEFIT FOR 2001.—This paragraph shall not apply to any taxable year to which section 6428 applies.

(2) REDUCTIONS IN RATES AFTER JUNE 30, 2001.—In the case of taxable years beginning in a calendar year after 2000, the corresponding percentage specified for such calendar year in the following table shall be substituted for the otherwise applicable tax rate in the tables under subsections (a), (b), (c), (d), and (e).

In the case of taxable years beginning during calendar year:	*The corresponding percentages shall be substituted for the following percentages:*			
	28%	*31%*	*36%*	*39.6%*
2001	27.5%	30.5%	35.5%	39.1%
2002	27.0%	30.0%	35.0%	38.6%
2003 and thereafter	25.0%	28.0%	33.0%	35.0%

(3) ADJUSTMENT OF TABLES.—The Secretary shall adjust the tables prescribed under subsection (f) to carry out this subsection.

[Sec. 2]

SEC. 2. DEFINITIONS AND SPECIAL RULES.

* * *

[Sec. 2(d)]

(d) NONRESIDENT ALIENS.—In the case of a nonresident alien individual, the taxes imposed by sections 1 and 55 [relating to the alternative minimum tax] shall apply only as provided by section 871 or 877.

* * *

PART II—TAX ON CORPORATIONS

[Sec. 11]

SEC. 11. TAX IMPOSED.

[Sec. 11(a)]

(a) CORPORATIONS IN GENERAL.—A tax is hereby imposed for each taxable year on the taxable income of every corporation.

[Sec. 11(b)]

(b) AMOUNT OF TAX.—

(1) IN GENERAL.—The amount of the tax imposed by subsection (a) shall be the sum of—

(A) 15 percent of so much of the taxable income as does not exceed $50,000,

(B) 25 percent of so much of the taxable income as exceeds $50,000 but does not exceed $75,000,

(C) 34 percent of so much of the taxable income as exceeds $75,000 but does not exceed $10,000,000, and

(D) 35 percent of so much of the taxable income as exceeds $10,000,000.

In the case of a corporation which has taxable income in excess of $100,000 for any taxable year, the amount of tax determined under the preceding sentence for such taxable year shall be increased by the lesser of (i) 5 percent of such excess, or (ii) $11,750. In the case of a corporation which has taxable income in excess of $15,000,000, the amount of the tax determined under the foregoing provisions of this paragraph shall be increased by an additional amount equal to the lesser of (i) 3 percent of such excess, or (ii) $100,000.

(2) CERTAIN PERSONAL SERVICE CORPORATIONS NOT ELIGIBLE FOR GRADUATED RATES.—Notwithstanding paragraph (1), the amount of the tax imposed by subsection (a) on the taxable income of a qualified personal service corporation (as defined in section 448(d)(2)) shall be equal to 35 percent of the taxable income.

[Sec. 11(c)]

(c) EXCEPTIONS.—Subsection (a) shall not apply to a corporation subject to a tax imposed by—

(1) section 594 (relating to mutual savings banks conducting life insurance business),

(2) subchapter L (sec. 801 and following, relating to insurance companies), or

(3) subchapter M (sec. 851 and following, relating to regulated investment companies and real estate investment trusts).

[Sec. 11(d)]

(d) FOREIGN CORPORATIONS.—In the case of a foreign corporation, the taxes imposed by subsection (a) and section 55 [relating to the alternative minimum tax] shall apply only as provided by section 882.

PART IV—CREDITS AGAINST TAX

Subpart B—Foreign Tax Credit, Etc.

[Sec. 27]

SEC. 27. TAXES OF FOREIGN COUNTRIES AND POSSESSIONS OF THE UNITED STATES; POSSESSION TAX CREDIT.

[Sec. 27(a)]

(a) FOREIGN TAX CREDIT.—The amount of taxes imposed by foreign countries and possessions of the United States shall be allowed as a credit against the tax imposed by this chapter to the extent provided in section 901.

[Sec. 27(b)]

(b) SECTION 936 CREDIT.—In the case of a domestic corporation, the amount provided by section 936 (relating to Puerto Rico and possession tax credit) shall be allowed as a credit against the tax imposed by this chapter.

[Sec. 30A]

SEC. 30A. PUERTO RICO ECONOMIC ACTIVITY CREDIT.

[Sec. 30A(a)]

(a) ALLOWANCE OF CREDIT.—

(1) IN GENERAL.—Except as otherwise provided in this section, if the conditions of both paragraph (1) and paragraph (2) of subsection (b) are satisfied with respect to a qualified domestic corporation, there shall be allowed as a credit against the tax imposed by this chapter an amount equal to the portion of the tax which is attributable to the taxable income, from sources without the United States, from—

(A) the active conduct of a trade or business within Puerto Rico, or

(B) the sale or exchange of substantially all of the assets used by the taxpayer in the active conduct of such trade or business.

In the case of any taxable year beginning after December 31, 2001, the aggregate amount of taxable income taken into account under the preceding sentence (and in applying subsection (d)) shall not exceed the adjusted base period income of such corporation, as determined in the same manner as under section 936(j).

(2) QUALIFIED DOMESTIC CORPORATION.—For purposes of paragraph (1), the term "qualified domestic corporation" means a domestic corporation—

(A) which is an existing credit claimant with respect to Puerto Rico, and

(B) with respect to which section 936(a)(4)(B) does not apply for the taxable year.

(3) SEPARATE APPLICATION.—For purposes of determining—

(A) whether a taxpayer is an existing credit claimant with respect to Puerto Rico, and

(B) the amount of the credit allowed under this section,

this section (and so much of section 936 as relates to this section) shall be applied separately with respect to Puerto Rico.

[Sec. 30A(b)]

(b) CONDITIONS WHICH MUST BE SATISFIED.—The conditions referred to in subsection (a) are—

(1) 3-YEAR PERIOD.—If 80 percent or more of the gross income of the qualified domestic corporation for the 3-year period immediately preceding the close of the taxable year (or for such part of such period immediately preceding the close of such taxable year as may be applicable) was derived from sources within a possession (determined without regard to section 904(f)).

(2) TRADE OR BUSINESS.—If 75 percent or more of the gross income of the qualified domestic corporation for such period or such part thereof was derived from the active conduct of a trade or business within a possession.

[Sec. 30A(c)]

(c) CREDIT NOT ALLOWED AGAINST CERTAIN TAXES.—The credit provided by subsection (a) shall not be allowed against the tax imposed by—

(1) section 59A (relating to environmental tax),

(2) section 531 (relating to the tax on accumulated earnings),

(3) section 541 (relating to personal holding company tax), or

(4) section 1351 (relating to recoveries of foreign expropriation losses).

[Sec. 30A(d)]

(d) LIMITATIONS ON CREDIT FOR ACTIVE BUSINESS INCOME.—The amount of the credit determined under subsection (a) for any taxable year shall not exceed the sum of the following amounts:

(1) 60 percent of the sum of—
(A) the aggregate amount of the qualified domestic corporation's qualified possession wages for such taxable year, plus
(B) the allocable employee fringe benefit expenses of the qualified domestic corporation for such taxable year.
(2) The sum of—
(A) 15 percent of the depreciation allowances for the taxable year with respect to short-life qualified tangible property,
(B) 40 percent of the depreciation allowances for the taxable year with respect to medium-life qualified tangible property, and
(C) 65 percent of the depreciation allowances for the taxable year with respect to long-life qualified tangible property.
(3) If the qualified domestic corporation does not have an election to use the method described in section 936(h)(5)(C)(ii) (relating to profit split) in effect for the taxable year, the amount of the qualified possession income taxes for the taxable year allocable to non-sheltered income.

[Sec. 30A(e)]

(e) ADMINISTRATIVE PROVISIONS.—For purposes of this title—
(1) the provisions of section 936 (including any applicable election thereunder) shall apply in the same manner as if the credit under this section were a credit under section 936(a)(1)(A) for a domestic corporation to which section 936(a)(4)(A) applies,
(2) the credit under this section shall be treated in the same manner as the credit under section 936, and
(3) a corporation to which this section applies shall be treated in the same manner as if it were a corporation electing the application of section 936.

[Sec. 30A(f)]

(f) DENIAL OF DOUBLE BENEFIT.—Any wages or other expenses taken into account in determining the credit under this section may not be taken into account in determining the credit under section 41.

[Sec. 30A(g)]

(g) DEFINITIONS.—For purposes of this section, any term used in this section which is also used in section 936 shall have the same meaning given such term by section 936.

[Sec. 30A(h)]

(h) APPLICATION OF SECTION.—This section shall apply to taxable years beginning after December 31, 1995, and before January 1, 2006.

Subpart C—Refundable Credits

[Sec. 33]

SEC. 33. TAX WITHHELD AT SOURCE ON NONRESIDENT ALIENS AND FOREIGN CORPORATIONS.

There shall be allowed as a credit against the tax imposed by this subtitle the amount of tax withheld at source under subchapter A of chapter 3 (relating to withholding of tax on nonresident aliens and on foreign corporations).

PART VI—ALTERNATIVE MINIMUM TAX

[Sec. 55]

SEC. 55. ALTERNATIVE MINIMUM TAX IMPOSED.

[Sec. 55(a)]

(a) GENERAL RULE.—There is hereby imposed (in addition to any other tax imposed by this subtitle) a tax equal to the excess (if any) of—
(1) the tentative minimum tax for the taxable year, over
(2) the regular tax for the taxable year.

[Sec. 55(b)]

(b) TENTATIVE MINIMUM TAX.—For purposes of this part—

(1) AMOUNT OF TENTATIVE TAX.—

(A) NONCORPORATE TAXPAYERS.—

(i) IN GENERAL.—In the case of a taxpayer other than a corporation, the tentative minimum tax for the taxable year is the sum of—

(I) 26 percent of so much of the taxable excess as does not exceed $175,000, plus

(II) 28 percent of so much of the taxable excess as exceeds $175,000.

The amount determined under the preceding sentence shall be reduced by the alternative minimum tax foreign tax credit for the taxable year.

(ii) TAXABLE EXCESS.—For purposes of this subsection, the term "taxable excess" means so much of the alternative minimum taxable income for the taxable year as exceeds the exemption amount.

(iii) MARRIED INDIVIDUAL FILING SEPARATE RETURN.—In the case of a married individual filing a separate return, clause (i) shall be applied by substituting "$87,500" for "$175,000" each place it appears. For purposes of the preceding sentence, marital status shall be determined under section 7703.

(B) CORPORATIONS.—In the case of a corporation, the tentative minimum tax for the taxable year is—

(i) 20 percent of so much of the alternative minimum taxable income for the taxable year as exceeds the exemption amount, reduced by

(ii) the alternative minimum tax foreign tax credit for the taxable year.

(2) ALTERNATIVE MINIMUM TAXABLE INCOME.—The term "alternative minimum taxable income" means the taxable income of the taxpayer for the taxable year—

(A) determined with the adjustments provided in section 56 and section 58, and

(B) increased by the amount of the items of tax preference described in section 57.

If a taxpayer is subject to the regular tax, such taxpayer shall be subject to the tax imposed by this section (and, if the regular tax is determined by reference to an amount other than taxable income, such amount shall be treated as the taxable income of such taxpayer for purposes of the preceding sentence).

(3) MAXIMUM RATE OF TAX ON NET CAPITAL GAIN OF NONCORPORATE TAXPAYERS.—The amount determined under the first sentence of paragraph (1)(A)(i) shall not exceed the sum of—

(A) the amount determined under such first sentence computed at the rates and in the same manner as if this paragraph had not been enacted on the taxable excess reduced by the lesser of—

(i) the net capital gain; or

(ii) the sum of—

(I) the adjusted net capital gain, plus

(II) the unrecaptured section 1250 gain, plus

(B) 5 percent (0 percent in the case of taxable years beginning after 2007) of so much of the adjusted net capital gain (or, if less, taxable excess) as does not exceed an amount equal to the excess described in section 1(h)(1)(B), plus

(C) 15 percent of the adjusted net capital gain (or, if less, taxable excess) in excess of the amount on which tax is determined under subparagraph (B), plus

(D) 25 percent of the amount of taxable excess in excess of the sum of the amounts on which tax is determined under the preceding subparagraphs of this paragraph.

Terms used in this paragraph which are also used in section 1(h) shall have the respective meanings given such terms by section 1(h) but computed with the adjustments under this part.

[Sec. 55(c)]

(c) REGULAR TAX.—

(1) IN GENERAL.—For purposes of this section, the term "regular tax" means the regular tax liability for the taxable year (as defined in section 26(b)) reduced by the foreign tax credit allowable under section 27(a), the section 936 credit allowable under section 27(b), and the Puerto Rico economic activity credit under section 30A. Such terms shall not include any increase in tax under section 49(b) or 50(a) or subsection (j) or (k) of section 42.

(2) COORDINATION WITH INCOME AVERAGING FOR FARMERS AND FISHERMEN.—Solely for purposes of this section, section 1301 (relating to averaging of farm and fishing income) shall not apply in computing the regular tax.

(3) CROSS REFERENCES.—

For provisions providing that certain credits are not allowable against the tax imposed by this section, see sections 26(a), 29(b)(6), 30(b)(3), and 38(c).

[Sec. 55(d)]

(d) EXEMPTION AMOUNT.—For purposes of this section—

(1) EXEMPTION AMOUNT FOR TAXPAYERS OTHER THAN CORPORATIONS.—In the case of a taxpayer other than a corporation, the term "exemption amount" means—

(A) $45,000 ($58,000 in the case of taxable years beginning in 2003, 2004, and 2005) in the case of—

(i) a joint return, or

(ii) a surviving spouse,

(B) $33,750 ($40,250 in the case of taxable years beginning in 2003, 2004, and 2005) in the case of an individual who—

(i) is not a married individual, and

(ii) is not a surviving spouse,

(C) 50 percent of the dollar amount applicable under paragraph (1)(A) in the case of a married individual who files a separate return, and

(D) $22,500 in the case of an estate or trust.

For purposes of this paragraph, the term "surviving spouse" has the meaning given to such term by section 2(a), and marital status shall be determined under section 7703.

(2) CORPORATIONS.—In the case of a corporation, the term "exemption amount" means $40,000.

(3) PHASE-OUT OF EXEMPTION AMOUNT.—The exemption amount of any taxpayers shall be reduced (but not below zero) by an amount equal to 25 percent of the amount by which the alternative minimum taxable income of the taxpayer exceeds—

(A) $150,000 in the case of a taxpayer described in paragraph (1)(A) or (2),

(B) $112,500 in the case of a taxpayer described in paragraph (1)(B), and

(C) $75,000 in the case of a taxpayer described in subparagraph (C) or (D) of paragraph (1).

In the case of a taxpayer described in paragraph (1)(C), alternative minimum taxable income shall be increased by the lesser of (i) 25 percent of the excess of alternative minimum taxable income (determined without regard to this sentence) over the minimum amount of such income (as so determined) for which the exemption amount under paragraph (1)(C) is zero, or (ii) such exemption amount (determined without regard to this paragraph).

[Sec. 55(e)]

(e) EXEMPTION FOR SMALL CORPORATIONS.—

(1) IN GENERAL.—

(A) $7,500,000 GROSS RECEIPTS TEST.—The tentative minimum tax of a corporation shall be zero for any taxable year if the corporation's average annual gross receipts for all 3-taxable-year periods ending before such taxable year does not exceed $7,500,000. For purposes of the preceding sentence, only taxable years beginning after December 31, 1993, shall be taken into account.

(B) $5,000,000 GROSS RECEIPTS TEST FOR FIRST 3-YEAR PERIOD.—Subparagraph (A) shall be applied by substituting "$5,000,000" for "$7,500,000" for the first 3-taxable-year period (or portion thereof) of the corporation which is taken into account under subparagraph (A).

(C) FIRST TAXABLE YEAR CORPORATION IN EXISTENCE.—If such taxable year is the first taxable year that such corporation is in existence, the tentative minimum tax of such corporation for such year shall be zero.

(D) SPECIAL RULES.—For purposes of this paragraph, the rules of paragraphs (2) and (3) of section 448(c) shall apply.

(2) PROSPECTIVE APPLICATION OF MINIMUM TAX IF SMALL CORPORATION CEASES TO BE SMALL.—In the case of a corporation whose tentative minimum tax is zero for any prior taxable year by reason of paragraph (1), the application of this part for taxable years beginning with the first taxable year such corporation ceases to be described in paragraph (1) shall be determined with the following modifications:

(A) Section 56(a)(1) (relating to depreciation) and section 56(a)(5) (relating to pollution control facilities) shall apply only to property placed in service on or after the change date.

(B) Section 56(a)(2) (relating to mining exploration and development costs) shall apply only to costs paid or incurred on or after the change date.

(C) Section 56(a)(3) (relating to treatment of long-term contracts) shall apply only to contracts entered into on or after the change date.

(D) Section 56(a)(4) (relating to alternative net operating loss deduction) shall apply in the same manner as if, in section 56(d)(2), the change date were substituted for "January 1, 1987" and the day before the change date were substituted for "December 31, 1986" each place it appears.

(E) Section 56(g)(2)(B) (relating to limitation on allowance of negative adjustments based on adjusted current earnings) shall apply only to prior taxable years beginning on or after the change date.

(F) Section 56(g)(4)(A) (relating to adjustment for depreciation to adjusted current earnings) shall not apply.

(G) Subparagraphs (D) and (F) of section 56(g)(4) (relating to other earnings and profits adjustments and depletion) shall apply in the same manner as if the day before the change date were substituted for "December 31, 1989" each place it appears therein.

(3) EXCEPTION.—The modifications in paragraph (2) shall not apply to—

(A) any item acquired by the corporation in a transaction to which section 381 applies, and

(B) any property the basis of which in the hands of the corporation is determined by reference to the basis of the property in the hands of the transferor, if such item or property was subject to any provision referred to in paragraph (2) while held by the transferor.

(4) CHANGE DATE.—For purposes of paragraph (2), the change date is the first day of the first taxable year for which the taxpayer ceases to be described in paragraph (1).

(5) LIMITATION ON USE OF CREDIT FOR PRIOR YEAR MINIMUM TAX LIABILITY.—In the case of a taxpayer whose tentative minimum tax for any taxable year is zero by reason of paragraph (1), section 53(c) shall be applied for such year by reducing the amount otherwise taken into account under section 53(c)(1) by 25 percent of so much of such amount as exceeds $25,000. Rules similar to the rules of section 38(c)(3)(B) shall apply for purposes of the preceding sentence.

[Sec. 56]

SEC. 56. ADJUSTMENTS IN COMPUTING ALTERNATIVE MINIMUM TAXABLE INCOME.

* * *

[Sec. 56(g)]

(g) ADJUSTMENTS BASED ON ADJUSTED CURRENT EARNINGS.—

(1) IN GENERAL.—The alternative minimum taxable income of any corporation for any taxable year shall be increased by 75 percent of the excess (if any) of—

(A) the adjusted current earnings of the corporation, over

(B) the alternative minimum taxable income (determined without regard to this subsection and the alternative tax net operating loss deduction).

(2) ALLOWANCE OF NEGATIVE ADJUSTMENTS.—

(A) IN GENERAL.—The alternative minimum taxable income for any corporation of any taxable year shall be reduced by 75 percent of the excess (if any) of—

(i) the amount referred to in subparagraph (B) of paragraph (1), over

(ii) the amount referred to in subparagraph (A) of paragraph (1).

(B) LIMITATION.—The reduction under subparagraph (A) for any taxable year shall not exceed the excess (if any) of—

(i) the aggregate increases in alternative minimum taxable income under paragraph (1) for prior taxable years, over

(ii) the aggregate reductions under subparagraph (A) of this paragraph for prior taxable years.

(3) ADJUSTED CURRENT EARNINGS.—For purposes of this subsection, the term "adjusted current earnings" means the alternative minimum taxable income for the taxable year—

(A) determined with the adjustments provided in paragraph (4), and

(B) determined without regard to this subsection and the alternative tax net operating loss deduction.

(4) ADJUSTMENTS.—In determining adjusted current earnings, the following adjustments shall apply:

* * *

(B) INCLUSION OF ITEMS INCLUDED FOR PURPOSES OF COMPUTING EARNINGS AND PROFITS.—

(i) IN GENERAL.—In the case of any amount which is excluded from gross income for purposes of computing alternative minimum taxable income but is taken into account in determining the amount of earnings and profits—

(I) such amount shall be included in income in the same manner as if such amount were includible in gross income for purposes of computing alternative minimum taxable income, and

(II) the amount of such income shall be reduced by any deduction which would have been allowable in computing alternative minimum taxable income if such amount were includible in gross income.

The preceding sentence shall not apply in the case of any amount excluded from gross income under section 108 (or the corresponding provisions of prior law) or under section 139A or 1357. In the case of any insurance company taxable under section 831(b), this clause shall not apply to any amount not described in section 834(b).

* * *

(C) DISALLOWANCE OF ITEMS NOT DEDUCTIBLE IN COMPUTING EARNINGS AND PROFITS.—

(i) IN GENERAL.—A deduction shall not be allowed for any item if such item would not be deductible for any taxable year for purposes of computing earnings and profits.

(ii) SPECIAL RULE FOR CERTAIN DIVIDENDS.—

(I) IN GENERAL.—Clause (i) shall not apply to any deduction allowable under section 243 or 245 for any dividend which is a 100-percent dividend or which is received from a 20-percent owned corporation (as defined in section

243(c)(2)), but only to the extent such dividend is attributable to income of the paying corporation which is subject to tax under this chapter (determined after the application of sections 30A, 936 (including subsections (a)(4), (i), and (j) thereof) and 921).

(II) 100-PERCENT DIVIDEND.—For purposes of subclause (I), the term "100 percent dividend" means any dividend if the percentage used for purposes of determining the amount allowable as a deduction under section 243 or 245 with respect to such dividend is 100 percent.

(iii) TREATMENT OF TAXES ON DIVIDENDS FROM 936 CORPORATIONS.—

(I) IN GENERAL.—For purposes of determining the alternative minimum foreign tax credit, 75 percent of any withholding or income tax paid to a possession of the United States with respect to dividends received from a corporation eligible for the credit provided by section 936 shall be treated as a tax paid to a foreign country by the corporation receiving the dividend.

(II) LIMITATION.—If the aggregate amount of the dividends referred to in subclause (I) for any taxable year exceeds the excess referred to in paragraph (1), the amount treated as tax paid to a foreign country under subclause (I) shall not exceed the amount which would be so treated without regard to this subclause multiplied by a fraction the numerator of which is the excess referred to in paragraph (1) and the denominator of which is the aggregate amount of such dividends.

(III) TREATMENT OF TAXES IMPOSED ON 936 CORPORATION.—For purposes of this clause, taxes paid by any corporation eligible for the credit provided by section 936 to a possession of the United States shall be treated as a withholding tax paid with respect to any dividend paid by such corporation to the extent such taxes would be treated as paid by the corporation receiving the dividend under rules similar to the rules of section 902 (and the amount of any such dividend shall be increased by the amount so treated).

(IV) SEPARATE APPLICATION OF FOREIGN TAX CREDIT LIMITATIONS.—In determining the alternative minimum foreign tax credit, section 904(d) shall be applied as if dividends from a corporation eligible for the credit provided by section 936 were a separate category of income referred to in a subparagraph of section 904(d)(1).

(V) COORDINATION WITH LIMITATION ON 936 CREDIT.—Any reference in this clause to a dividend received from a corporation eligible for the credit provided by section 936 shall be treated as a reference to the portion of any such dividend for which the dividends received deduction is disallowed under clause (i) after the application of clause (ii)(I).

(VI) APPLICATION TO SECTION 30A CORPORATIONS.—References in this clause to section 936 shall be treated as including references to section 30A.

(iv) SPECIAL RULE FOR CERTAIN DIVIDENDS RECEIVED BY CERTAIN COOPERATIVES.—In the case of a cooperative described in section 927(a)(4), clause (i) shall not apply to any amount allowable as a deduction under section 245(c).

(v) DEDUCTION FOR DOMESTIC PRODUCTION.—Clause (i) shall not apply to any amount allowable as a deduction under section 199.

(vi) SPECIAL RULE FOR CERTAIN DISTRIBUTIONS FROM CONTROLLED FOREIGN CORPORATIONS.—Clause (i) shall not apply to any deduction allowable under section 965.

* * *

[Sec. 59]

SEC. 59. OTHER DEFINITIONS AND SPECIAL RULES.

[Sec. 59(a)]

(a) ALTERNATIVE MINIMUM TAX FOREIGN TAX CREDIT.—For purposes of this part—

(1) IN GENERAL.—The alternative minimum tax foreign tax credit for any taxable year shall be the credit which would be determined under section 27(a) for such taxable year if—

(A) the pre-credit tentative minimum tax were the tax against which such credit was taken for purposes of section 904 for the taxable year and all prior taxable years beginning after December 31, 1986,

(B) section 904 were applied on the basis of alternative minimum taxable income instead of taxable income, and

(C) the determination of whether any income is high-taxed income for purposes of section 904(d)(2) were made on the basis of the applicable rate specified in subparagraph (A)(i) or (B)(i) of section 55(b)(1) (whichever applies) in lieu of the highest rate of tax specified in section 1 or 11 (whichever applies).

(2) PRE-CREDIT TENTATIVE MINIMUM TAX.—For purposes of this subsection, the term "pre-credit tentative minimum tax" means—

(A) in the case of a taxpayer other than a corporation, the amount determined under the first sentence of section 55(b)(1)(A)(i), or

(B) in the case of a corporation, the amount determined under section 55(b)(1)(B)(i).

(3) ELECTION TO USE SIMPLIFIED SECTION 904 LIMITATION.—

(A) IN GENERAL.—In determining the alternative minimum tax foreign tax credit for any taxable year to which an election under this paragraph applies—

(i) subparagraph (B) of paragraph (1) shall not apply, and

(ii) the limitation of section 904 shall be based on the proportion which—

(I) the taxpayer's taxable income (as determined for purposes of the regular tax) from sources without the United States (but not in excess of the taxpayer's entire alternative minimum taxable income), bears to

(II) the taxpayer's entire alternative minimum taxable income for the taxable year.

(B) ELECTION.—

(i) IN GENERAL.—An election under this paragraph may be made only for the taxpayer's first taxable year which begins after December 31, 1997, and for which the taxpayer claims an alternative minimum tax foreign tax credit.

(ii) ELECTION REVOCABLE ONLY WITH CONSENT.—An election under this paragraph, once made, shall apply to the taxable year for which made and all subsequent taxable years unless revoked with the consent of the Secretary.

[Sec. 59(b)]

(b) MINIMUM TAX NOT TO APPLY TO INCOME ELIGIBLE FOR CREDITS UNDER SECTION 30A OR 936.—In the case of any corporation for which a credit is allowable for the taxable year under section 30A or 936, alternative minimum taxable income shall not include any income with respect to which a credit is determined under section 30A or 936.

* * *

SUBCHAPTER B—COMPUTATION OF TAXABLE INCOME

PART I—DEFINITION OF GROSS INCOME, ADJUSTED GROSS INCOME, TAXABLE INCOME, ETC.

[Sec. 61]

SEC. 61. GROSS INCOME DEFINED.

[Sec. 61(a)]

(a) GENERAL DEFINITION.—Except as otherwise provided in this subtitle, gross income means all income from whatever source derived, including (but not limited to) the following items:

(1) Compensation for services, including fees, commissions, fringe benefits, and similar items;

(2) Gross income derived from business;

(3) Gains derived from dealings in property;

(4) Interest;

(5) Rents;

(6) Royalties;

(7) Dividends;

(8) Alimony and separate maintenance payments;

(9) Annuities;

(10) Income from life insurance and endowment contracts;

(11) Pensions;

(12) Income from discharge of indebtedness;

(13) Distributive share of partnership gross income;

(14) Income in respect of a decedent; and

(15) Income from an interest in an estate or trust.

* * *

[Sec. 63]

SEC. 63. TAXABLE INCOME DEFINED.

[Sec. 63(a)]

(a) IN GENERAL.—Except as provided in subsection (b), for purposes of this subtitle, the term "taxable income" means gross income minus the deductions allowed by this chapter (other than the standard deduction).

* * *

PART II—ITEMS SPECIFICALLY INCLUDED IN GROSS INCOME

[Sec. 78]

SEC. 78. DIVIDENDS RECEIVED FROM CERTAIN FOREIGN CORPORATIONS BY DOMESTIC CORPORATIONS CHOOSING FOREIGN TAX CREDIT.

If a domestic corporation chooses to have the benefits of subpart A of part III of subchapter N (relating to foreign tax credit) for any taxable year, an amount equal to the taxes deemed to be paid by such corporation under section 902(a) (relating to credit for corporate stockholder in foreign corporation) or under section 960(a)(1) (relating to taxes paid by foreign corporation) for such taxable year shall be treated for purposes of this title (other than section 245) as a dividend received by such domestic corporation from the foreign corporation.

PART III—ITEMS SPECIFICALLY EXCLUDED FROM GROSS INCOME

Caution: Code Sec. 114, below, has been repealed, subject to the transitional rules of Sec. 101(d)-(f) of the American Jobs Creation Act of 2004, below.

[Sec. 114]

SEC. 114. EXTRATERRITORIAL INCOME.

[Sec. 114(a)]

(a) EXCLUSION.—Gross income does not include extraterritorial income.

[Sec. 114(b)]

(b) EXCEPTION.—Subsection (a) shall not apply to extraterritorial income which is not qualifying foreign trade income as determined under subpart E of part III of subchapter N.

[Sec. 114(c)]

(c) Disallowance of Deductions.—

(1) In general.—Any deduction of a taxpayer allocated under paragraph (2) to extraterritorial income of the taxpayer excluded from gross income under subsection (a) shall not be allowed.

(2) Allocation.—Any deduction of the taxpayer properly apportioned and allocated to the extraterritorial income derived by the taxpayer from any transaction shall be allocated on a proportionate basis between—

(A) the extraterritorial income derived from such transaction which is excluded from gross income under subsection (a), and

(B) the extraterritorial income derived from such transaction which is not so excluded.

[Sec. 114(d)]

(d) Denial of Credits for Certain Foreign Taxes.—Notwithstanding any other provision of this chapter, no credit shall be allowed under this chapter for any income, war profits, and excess profits taxes paid or accrued to any foreign country or possession of the United States with respect to extraterritorial income which is excluded from gross income under subsection (a).

[Sec. 114(e)]

(e) Extraterritorial Income.—For purposes of this section, the term "extraterritorial income" means the gross income of the taxpayer attributable to foreign trading gross receipts (as defined in section 942) of the taxpayer.

AMERICAN JOBS CREATION ACT OF 2004 SEC. 101(d)-(f), TRANSITIONAL RULE

[Sec. 101]

* * *

(d) Transitional Rule for 2005 and 2006.—

(1) In general.—In the case of transactions during 2005 or 2006, the amount includible in gross income by reason of the amendments made by this section shall not exceed the applicable percentage of the amount which would have been so included but for this subsection.

(2) Applicable percentage.—For purposes of paragraph (1), the applicable percentage shall be as follows:

(A) For 2005, the applicable percentage shall be 20 percent.

(B) For 2006, the applicable percentage shall be 40 percent.

(e) Revocation of Election To Be Treated as Domestic Corporation.—If, during the 1-year period beginning on the date of the enactment of this Act [October 22, 2004], a corporation for which an election [to be treated as a domestic corporation] is in effect under section 943(e) of the Internal Revenue Code of 1986 revokes such election, no gain or loss shall be recognized with respect to property treated as transferred under clause (ii) of section 943(e)(4)(B) of such Code to the extent such property—

(1) was treated as transferred under clause (i) thereof, or

(2) was acquired during a taxable year to which such election applies and before May 1, 2003, in the ordinary course of its trade or business.

The Secretary of the Treasury (or such Secretary's delegate) may prescribe such regulations as may be necessary to prevent the abuse of the purposes of this subsection.

(f) Binding Contracts.—The amendments made by this section shall not apply to any transaction in the ordinary course of a trade or business which occurs pursuant to a binding contract—

(1) which is between the taxpayer and a person who is not a related person (as defined in section 943(b)(3) of such Code, as in effect on [October 21, 2004,] the day before the date of the enactment of this Act), and

(2) which is in effect on September 17, 2003, and at all times thereafter.

For purposes of this subsection, a binding contract shall include a purchase option, renewal option, or replacement option which is included in such contract and which is enforceable against the seller or lessor.

[Sec. 275]

SEC. 275. CERTAIN TAXES.

[Sec. 275(a)]

(a) GENERAL RULE.—No deduction shall be allowed for the following taxes:

* * *

(4) Income, war profits, and excess profits taxes imposed by the authority of any foreign country or possession of the United States if—

(A) the taxpayer chooses to take to any extent the benefits of section 901, or

(B) such taxes are paid or accrued with respect to foreign trade income (within the meaning of section 923(b)) of a FSC.

* * *

[Sec. 119]

SEC. 119. MEALS OR LODGING FURNISHED FOR THE CONVENIENCE OF THE EMPLOYER.

[Sec. 119(a)]

(a) MEALS AND LODGING FURNISHED TO EMPLOYEE, HIS SPOUSE, AND HIS DEPENDENTS, PURSUANT TO EMPLOYMENT.—There shall be excluded from gross income of an employee the value of any meals or lodging furnished to him, his spouse, or any of his dependents by or on behalf of his employer for the convenience of the employer, but only if—

(1) in the case of meals, the meals are furnished on the business premises of the employer, or

(2) in the case of lodging, the employee is required to accept such lodging on the business premises of his employer as a condition of his employment.

* * *

[Sec. 119(c)]

(c) EMPLOYEES LIVING IN CERTAIN CAMPS.—

(1) IN GENERAL.—In the case of an individual who is furnished lodging in a camp located in a foreign country by or on behalf of his employer, such camp shall be considered to be part of the business premises of the employer.

(2) CAMP.—For purposes of this section, a camp constitutes lodging which is—

(A) provided by or on behalf of the employer for the convenience of the employer because the place at which such individual renders services is in a remote area where satisfactory housing is not available on the open market,

(B) located, as near as practicable, in the vicinity of the place at which such individual renders services, and

(C) furnished in a common area (or enclave) which is not available to the public and which normally accommodates 10 or more employees.

* * *

PART IV—TAX EXEMPTION REQUIREMENTS FOR STATE AND LOCAL BONDS

Subpart B—Requirements Applicable to All State and Local Bonds

[Sec. 149]

SEC. 149. BONDS MUST BE REGISTERED TO BE TAX EXEMPT; OTHER REQUIREMENTS.

[Sec. 149(a)]

(a) BONDS MUST BE REGISTERED TO BE TAX EXEMPT.—

* * *

(3) SPECIAL RULES.—

(A) BOOK ENTRIES PERMITTED.—For purposes of paragraph (1), a book entry bond shall be treated as in registered form if the right to the principal of, and stated interest on, such bond may be transferred only through a book entry consistent with regulations prescribed by the Secretary.

(B) NOMINEES.—The Secretary shall prescribe such regulations as may be necessary to carry out the purpose of paragraph (1) where there is a nominee or chain of nominees.

* * *

PART VI—ITEMIZED DEDUCTIONS FOR INDIVIDUALS AND CORPORATIONS

[Sec. 162]

SEC. 162. TRADE OR BUSINESS EXPENSES.

[Sec. 162(a)]

(a) IN GENERAL.—There shall be allowed as a deduction all the ordinary and necessary expenses paid or incurred during the taxable year in carrying on any trade or business, including—

* * *

(2) traveling expenses (including amounts expended for meals and lodging other than amounts which are lavish or extravagant under the circumstances) while away from home in the pursuit of a trade or business; and

* * *

[Sec. 162(c)]

(c) ILLEGAL BRIBES, KICKBACKS, AND OTHER PAYMENTS.—

(1) ILLEGAL PAYMENTS TO GOVERNMENT OFFICIALS OR EMPLOYEES.—No deduction shall be allowed under subsection (a) for any payment made, directly or indirectly, to an official or employee of any government, or of any agency or instrumentality of any government, if the payment constitutes an illegal bribe or kickback or, if the payment is to an official or employee of a foreign government, the payment is unlawful under the Foreign Corrupt Practices Act of 1977. The burden of proof in respect of the issue, for the purposes of this paragraph, as to whether a payment constitutes an illegal bribe or kickback (or is unlawful under the Foreign Corrupt Practices Act of 1977) shall be upon the Secretary to the same extent as he bears the burden of proof under section 7454 (concerning the burden of proof when the issue relates to fraud).

* * *

[Sec. 162(f)]

(f) FINES AND PENALTIES.—No deduction shall be allowed under subsection (a) for any fine or similar penalty paid to a government for the violation of any law.

* * *

Internal Revenue Code of 1986

[Sec. 162(j)]

(j) CERTAIN FOREIGN ADVERTISING EXPENSES.—

(1) IN GENERAL.—No deduction shall be allowed under subsection (a) for any expenses of an advertisement carried by a foreign broadcast undertaking and directed primarily to a market in the United States. This paragraph shall apply only to foreign broadcast undertakings located in a country which denies a similar deduction for the cost of advertising directed primarily to a market in the foreign country when placed with a United States broadcast undertaking.

(2) BROADCAST UNDERTAKING.—For purposes of paragraph (1), the term "broadcast undertaking" includes (but is not limited to) radio and television stations.

* * *

[Sec. 163]

SEC. 163. INTEREST.

* * *

[Sec. 163(e)]

(e) ORIGINAL ISSUE DISCOUNT.—

(1) IN GENERAL.—In the case of any debt instrument issued after July 1, 1982, the portion of the original issue discount with respect to such debt instrument which is allowable as a deduction to the issuer for any taxable year shall be equal to the aggregate daily portions of the original issue discount for days during such taxable year.

(2) DEFINITIONS AND SPECIAL RULES.—For purposes of this subsection—

(A) DEBT INSTRUMENT.—The term "debt instrument" has the meaning given such term by section 1275(a)(1).

(B) DAILY PORTIONS.—The daily portion of the original issue discount for any day shall be determined under section 1272(a) (without regard to paragraph (7) thereof and without regard to section 1273(a)(3)).

(C) SHORT-TERM OBLIGATIONS.—In the case of an obligor of a short-term obligation (as defined in section 1283(a)(1)(A)) who uses the cash receipts and disbursements method of accounting, the original issue discount (and any other interest payable) on such obligation shall be deductible only when paid.

(3) SPECIAL RULE FOR ORIGINAL ISSUE DISCOUNT ON OBLIGATION HELD BY RELATED FOREIGN PERSON.—

(A) IN GENERAL.—If any debt instrument having original issue discount is held by a related foreign person, any portion of such original issue discount shall not be allowable as a deduction to the issuer until paid. The preceding sentence shall not apply to the extent that the original issue discount is effectively connected with the conduct by such foreign related person of a trade or business within the United States unless such original issue discount is exempt from taxation (or is subject to a reduced rate of tax) pursuant to a treaty obligation of the United States.

(B) SPECIAL RULE FOR CERTAIN FOREIGN ENTITIES.—

(i) IN GENERAL.—In the case of any debt instrument having original issue discount which is held by a related foreign person which is a controlled foreign corporation (as defined in section 957) or a passive foreign investment company (as defined in section 1297), a deduction shall be allowable to the issuer with respect to such original issue discount for any taxable year before the taxable year in which paid only to the extent such original issue discount is includible (determined without regard to properly allocable deductions and qualified deficits under section 952(c)(1)(B)) during such prior taxable year in the gross income of a United States person who owns (within the meaning of section 958(a)) stock in such corporation.

(ii) SECRETARIAL AUTHORITY.—The Secretary may by regulation exempt transactions from the application of clause (i), including any transaction which is entered into by a payor in the ordinary course of a trade or business in which the payor is predominantly engaged.

(C) RELATED FOREIGN PERSON.—For purposes of subparagraph (A), the term "related foreign person" means any person—

(i) who is not a United States person, and

(ii) who is related (within the meaning of section 267(b)) to the issuer.

(4) EXCEPTIONS.—This subsection shall not apply to any debt instrument described in—

(A) subparagraph (D) of section 1272(a)(2) (relating to obligations issued by natural persons before March 2, 1984), and

(B) subparagraph (E) of section 1272(a)(2) (relating to loans between natural persons).

(5) SPECIAL RULES FOR ORIGINAL ISSUE DISCOUNT ON CERTAIN HIGH YIELD OBLIGATIONS.—

(A) IN GENERAL.—In the case of an applicable high yield discount obligation issued by a corporation—

(i) no deduction shall be allowed under this chapter for the disqualified portion of the original issue discount on such obligation, and

(ii) the remainder of such original issue discount shall not be allowable as a deduction until paid.

For purposes of this paragraph, rules similar to the rules of subsection (i)(3)(B) shall apply in determining the amount of the original issue discount and when the original issue discount is paid.

(B) DISQUALIFIED PORTION TREATED AS STOCK DISTRIBUTION FOR PURPOSES OF DIVIDEND RECEIVED DEDUCTION.—

(i) IN GENERAL.—Solely for purposes of sections 243, 245, 246, and 246A, the dividend equivalent portion of any amount includible in gross income of a corporation under section 1272(a) in respect of an applicable high yield discount obligation shall be treated as a dividend received by such corporation from the corporation issuing such obligation.

(ii) DIVIDEND EQUIVALENT PORTION.—For purposes of clause (i), the dividend equivalent portion of any amount includible in gross income under section 1272(a) in respect of an applicable high yield discount obligation is the portion of the amount so includible—

(I) which is attributable to the disqualified portion of the original issue discount on such obligation, and

(II) which would have been treated as a dividend if it had been a distribution made by the issuing corporation with respect to stock in such corporation.

(C) DISQUALIFIED PORTION.—

(i) IN GENERAL.—For purposes of this paragraph, the disqualified portion of the original issue discount on any applicable high yield discount obligation is the lesser of—

(I) the amount of such original issue discount, or

(II) the portion of the total return on such obligation which bears the same ratio to such total return as the disqualified yield on such obligation bears to the yield to maturity on such obligation.

(ii) DEFINITIONS.—For purposes of clause (i), the term "disqualified yield" means the excess of the yield to maturity on the obligation over the sum referred to subsection (i)(1)(B) plus 1 percentage point, and the term "total return" is the amount which would have been the original issue discount on the obligation if interest described in the parenthetical in section 1273(a)(2) were included in the stated redemption price at maturity.

(D) EXCEPTION FOR S CORPORATIONS.—This paragraph shall not apply to any obligation issued by any corporation for any period for which such corporation is an S corporation.

(E) EFFECT ON EARNINGS AND PROFITS.—This paragraph shall not apply for purposes of determining earnings and profits; except that, for purposes of determining the dividend equivalent portion of any amount includible in gross income under section 1272(a) in respect of an applicable high yield discount obligation, no reduction shall be made for any amount attributable to the disqualified portion of any original issue discount on such obligation.

(F) CROSS REFERENCE.—

For definition of applicable high yield discount obligation, see subsection (i).

(6) CROSS REFERENCES.—

For provision relating to deduction of original issue discount on tax-exempt obligation, see section 1288.

For special rules in the case of the borrower under certain loans for personal use, see section 1275(b).

[Sec. 163(f)]

(f) DENIAL OF DEDUCTION FOR INTEREST ON CERTAIN OBLIGATIONS NOT IN REGISTERED FORM.—

(1) IN GENERAL.—Nothing in subsection (a) or in any other provision of law shall be construed to provide a deduction for interest on any registration-required obligation unless such obligation is in registered form.

(2) REGISTRATION-REQUIRED OBLIGATION.—For purposes of this section—

(A) IN GENERAL.—The term "registration-required obligation" means any obligation (including any obligation issued by a governmental entity) other than an obligation which—

(i) is issued by a natural person,

(ii) is not of a type offered to the public,

(iii) has a maturity (at issue) of not more than 1 year, or

(iv) is described in subparagraph (B).

(B) CERTAIN OBLIGATIONS NOT INCLUDED.—An obligation is described in this subparagraph if—

(i) there are arrangements reasonably designed to ensure that such obligation will be sold (or resold in connection with the original issue) only to a person who is not a United States person, and

(ii) in the case of an obligation not in registered form—

(I) interest on such obligation is payable only outside the United States and its possessions, and

(II) on the face of such obligation there is a statement that any United States person who holds such obligation will be subject to limitations under the United States income tax laws.

(C) AUTHORITY TO INCLUDE OTHER OBLIGATIONS.—Clauses (ii) and (iii) of subparagraph (A), and subparagraph (B), shall not apply to any obligation if—

(i) in the case of—

(I) subparagraph (A), such obligation is of a type which the Secretary has determined by regulations to be used frequently in avoiding Federal taxes, or

(II) subparagraph (B), such obligation is of a type specified by the Secretary in regulations, and

(ii) such obligation is issued after the date on which the regulations referred to in clause (i) take effect.

(3) BOOK ENTRIES PERMITTED, ETC.—For purposes of this subsection, rules similar to the rules of section 149(a)(3) shall apply.

* * *

[Sec. 163(i)]

(i) APPLICABLE HIGH YIELD DISCOUNT OBLIGATION.—

(1) IN GENERAL.—For purposes of this section, the term "applicable high yield discount obligation" means any debt instrument if—

(A) the maturity date of such instrument is more than 5 years from the date of issue,

(B) the yield to maturity on such instrument equals or exceeds the sum of—

(i) the applicable Federal rate in effect under section 1274(d) for the calendar month in which the obligation is issued, plus

(ii) 5 percentage points, and

(C) such instrument has significant original issue discount.

For purposes of subparagraph (B)(i), the Secretary may by regulation permit a rate to be used with respect to any debt instrument which is higher than the applicable Federal rate if the taxpayer establishes to the satisfaction of the Secretary that such higher rate is based on the same principles as the applicable Federal rate and is appropriate for the term of the instrument.

(2) SIGNIFICANT ORIGINAL ISSUE DISCOUNT.—For purposes of paragraph (1)(C), a debt instrument shall be treated as having significant original issue discount if—

(A) the aggregate amount which would be includible in gross income with respect to such instrument for periods before the close of any accrual period (as defined in section 1272(a)(5)) ending after the date 5 years after the date of issue, exceeds—

(B) the sum of—

(i) the aggregate amount of interest to be paid under the instrument before the close of such accrual period, and

(ii) the product of the issue price of such instrument (as defined in sections 1273(b) and 1274(a)) and its yield to maturity.

(3) SPECIAL RULES.—For purposes of determining whether a debt instrument is an applicable high yield discount obligation—

(A) any payment under the instrument shall be assumed to be made on the last day permitted under the instrument, and

(B) any payment to be made in the form of another obligation of the issuer (or a related person within the meaning of section 453(f)(1) shall be assumed to be made when such obligation is required to be paid in cash or in property other than such obligation).

Except for purposes of paragraph (1)(B), any reference to an obligation in subparagraph (B) of this paragraph shall be treated as including a reference to stock.

(4) DEBT INSTRUMENT.—For purposes of this subsection, the term "debt instrument" means any instrument which is a debt instrument as defined in section 1275(a).

(5) REGULATIONS.—The Secretary shall prescribe such regulations as may be appropriate to carry out the purposes of this subsection and subsection (e)(5), including—

(A) regulations providing for modifications to the provisions of this subsection and subsection (e)(5) in the case of varying rates of interest, put or call options, indefinite maturities, contingent payments, assumptions of debt instruments, conversion rights, or other circumstances where such modifications are appropriate to carry out the purposes of this subsection and subsection (e)(5), and

(B) regulations to prevent avoidance of the purposes of this subsection and subsection (e)(5) through the use of issuers other than C corporations, agreements to borrow amounts due under the debt instrument, or other arrangements.

[Sec. 163(j)]

(j) LIMITATION ON DEDUCTION FOR INTEREST ON CERTAIN INDEBTEDNESS.—

(1) LIMITATION.—

(A) IN GENERAL.—If this subsection applies to any corporation for any taxable year, no deduction shall be allowed under this chapter for disqualified interest paid or accrued by such corporation during such taxable year. The amount disallowed under the preceding sentence shall not exceed the corporation's excess interest expense for the taxable year.

(B) DISALLOWED AMOUNT CARRIED TO SUCCEEDING TAXABLE YEAR.—Any amount disallowed under subparagraph (A) for any taxable year shall be treated as disqualified interest paid or accrued in the succeeding taxable year (and clause (ii) of paragraph (2)(A) shall not apply for purposes of applying this subsection to the amount so treated).

(2) CORPORATIONS TO WHICH SUBSECTION APPLIES.—

(A) IN GENERAL.—This subsection shall apply to any corporation for any taxable year if—

(i) such corporation has excess interest expense for such taxable year, and

(ii) the ratio of debt to equity of such corporation as of the close of such taxable year (or on any other day during the taxable year as the Secretary may by regulations prescribe) exceeds 1.5 to 1.

(B) EXCESS INTEREST EXPENSE.—

(i) IN GENERAL.—For purposes of this subsection, the term "excess interest expense" means the excess (if any) of—

(I) the corporation's net interest expense, over

(II) the sum of 50 percent of the adjusted taxable income of the corporation plus any excess limitation carryforward under clause (ii).

(ii) EXCESS LIMITATION CARRYFORWARD.—If a corporation has an excess limitation for any taxable year, the amount of such excess limitation shall be an excess limitation carryforward to the 1st succeeding taxable year and to the 2nd and 3rd succeeding taxable years to the extent not previously taken into account under this clause. The amount of such a carryforward taken into account for any such succeeding taxable year shall not exceed the excess interest expense for such succeeding taxable year (determined without regard to the carryforward from the taxable year of such excess limitation).

(iii) EXCESS LIMITATION.—For purposes of clause (ii), the term "excess limitation" means the excess (if any) of—

(I) 50 percent of the adjusted taxable income of the corporation, over

(II) the corporation's net interest expense.

(C) RATIO OF DEBT TO EQUITY.—For purposes of this paragraph, the term "ratio of debt to equity" means the ratio which the total indebtedness of the corporation bears to the sum of its money and all other assets reduced (but not below zero) by such total indebtedness. For purposes of the preceding sentence—

(i) the amount taken into account with respect to any asset shall be the adjusted basis thereof for purposes of determining gain,

(ii) the amount taken into account with respect to any indebtedness with original issue discount shall be its issue price plus the portion of the original issue discount previously accrued as determined under the rules of section 1272 (determined without regard to subsection (a)(7) or (b)(4) thereof), and

(iii) there shall be such other adjustments as the Secretary may by regulations prescribe.

(3) DISQUALIFIED INTEREST.—For purposes of this subsection, the term "disqualified interest" means—

(A) any interest paid or accrued by the taxpayer (directly or indirectly) to a related person if no tax is imposed by this subtitle with respect to such interest,

(B) any interest paid or accrued by the taxpayer with respect to any indebtedness to a person who is not a related person if—

(i) there is a disqualified guarantee of such indebtedness, and

(ii) no gross basis tax is imposed by this subtitle with respect to such interest, and

(C) any interest paid or accrued (directly or indirectly) by a taxable REIT subsidiary (as defined in section 856(l)) of a real estate investment trust to such trust.

(4) RELATED PERSON.—For purposes of this subsection—

(A) IN GENERAL.—Except as provided in subparagraph (B), the term "related person" means any person who is related (within the meaning of section 267(b) or 707(b)(1)) to the taxpayer.

(B) SPECIAL RULE FOR CERTAIN PARTNERSHIPS.—

(i) IN GENERAL.—Any interest paid or accrued to a partnership which (without regard to this subparagraph) is a related person shall not be treated as paid or accrued to a related person if less than 10 percent of the profits and capital interests in such partnership are held by persons with respect to whom no tax is imposed by this subtitle on such interest. The preceding sentence shall not apply to any interest allocable to any partner in such partnership who is a related person to the taxpayer.

(ii) SPECIAL RULE WHERE TREATY REDUCTION.—If any treaty between the United States and any foreign country reduces the rate of tax imposed by this subtitle on a partner's share of any interest paid or accrued to a partnership, such partner's interests in such partnership shall, for purposes of clause (i), be treated as held in part by a tax-exempt person and in part by a taxable person under rules similar to the rules of paragraph (5)(B).

(5) SPECIAL RULES FOR DETERMINING WHETHER INTEREST IS SUBJECT TO TAX.—

(A) TREATMENT OF PASS-THRU ENTITIES.—In the case of any interest paid or accrued to a partnership, the determination of whether any tax is imposed by this subtitle on such interest shall be made at the partner level. Rules similar to the rules of the preceding sentence shall apply in the case of any pass-thru entity other than a partnership and in the case of tiered partnerships and other entities.

(B) INTEREST TREATED AS TAX-EXEMPT TO EXTENT OF TREATY REDUCTION.—If any treaty between the United States and any foreign country reduces the rate of tax imposed by this subtitle on any interest paid or accrued by the taxpayer, such interest shall be treated as interest on which no tax is imposed by this subtitle to the extent of the same proportion of such interest as—

(i) the rate of tax imposed without regard to such treaty, reduced by the rate of tax imposed under the treaty, bears to

(ii) the rate of tax imposed without regard to the treaty.

(6) OTHER DEFINITIONS AND SPECIAL RULES.—For purposes of this subsection—

(A) ADJUSTED TAXABLE INCOME.—The term "adjusted taxable income" means the taxable income of the taxpayer—

(i) computed without regard to—

(I) any deduction allowable under this chapter for the net interest expense,

(II) the amount of any net operating loss deduction under section 172, and

(III) any deduction allowable for depreciation, amortization, or depletion, and

(ii) computed with such other adjustments as the Secretary may by regulations prescribe.

(B) NET INTEREST EXPENSE.—The term "net interest expense" means the excess (if any) of—

(i) the interest paid or accrued by the taxpayer during the taxable year, over

(ii) the amount of interest includible in the gross income of such taxpayer for such taxable year.

The Secretary may by regulations provide for adjustments in determining the amount of net interest expense.

(C) TREATMENT OF AFFILIATED GROUP.—All members of the same affiliated group (within the meaning of section 1504(a)) shall be treated as 1 taxpayer.

(D) DISQUALIFIED GUARANTEE.—

(i) IN GENERAL.—Except as provided in clause (ii), the term "disqualified guarantee" means any guarantee by a related person which is—

(I) an organization exempt from taxation under this subtitle, or

(II) a foreign person.

(ii) EXCEPTIONS.—The term "disqualified guarantee" shall not include a guarantee—

(I) in any circumstances identified by the Secretary by regulation, where the interest on the indebtedness would have been subject to a net basis tax if the interest had been paid to the guarantor, or

(II) if the taxpayer owns a controllng interest in the guarantor.

For purposes of subclause (II), except as provided in regulations, the term "a controlling interest" means direct or indirect ownership of at least 80 percent of the total voting power and value of all classes of stock of a corporation, or 80 percent of the profit and capital interests in any other entity. For purposes of the preceding sentence, the rules of paragraphs (1) and (5) of section 267(c) shall apply; except that such rules shall also apply to interest in entities other than corporations.

(iii) GUARANTEE.—Except as provided in regulations, the term "guarantee" includes any arrangement under which a person (directly or indirectly through an entity or otherwise) assures, on a conditional or unconditional basis, the payment of another person's obligation under any indebtedness.

(E) GROSS BASIS AND NET BASIS TAXATION.—

(i) GROSS BASIS TAX.—The term "gross basis tax" means any tax imposed by this subtitle which is determined by reference to the gross amount of any item of income without any reduction for any deduction allowed by this subtitle.

(ii) NET BASIS TAX.—The term "net basis tax" means any tax imposed by this subtitle which is not a gross basis tax.

(7) COORDINATION WITH PASSIVE LOSS RULES, ETC.—This subsection shall be applied before sections 465 and 469.

(8) REGULATIONS.—The Secretary shall prescribe such regulations as may be appropriate to carry out the purposes of this subsection, including—

(A) such regulations as may be appropriate to prevent the avoidance of the purposes of this subsection,

(B) regulations providing such adjustments in the case of corporations which are members of an affiliated group as may be appropriate to carry out the purposes of this subsection, and

(C) regulations for the coordination of this subsection with section 884.

* * *

Sec. 163(j)(6)(B)

[Sec. 164]

SEC. 164. TAXES.

[Sec. 164(a)]

(a) GENERAL RULE.—Except as otherwise provided in this section, the following taxes shall be allowed as a deduction for the taxable year within which paid or accrued:

(1) State and local, and foreign, real property taxes.

(2) State and local personal property taxes.

(3) State and local, and foreign, income, war profits, and excess profits taxes.

(4) The GST tax imposed on income distributions.

(5) The environmental tax imposed by section 59A.

In addition, there shall be allowed as a deduction State and local, and foreign, taxes not described in the preceding sentence which are paid or accrued within the taxable year in carrying on a trade or business or an activity described in section 212 (relating to expenses for production of income). Notwithstanding the preceding sentence, any tax (not described in the first sentence of this subsection) which is paid or accrued by the taxpayer in connection with an acquisition or disposition of property shall be treated as part of the cost of the acquired property or, in the case of a disposition, as a reduction in the amount realized on the disposition.

[Sec. 164(b)]

(b) DEFINITIONS AND SPECIAL RULES.—For purposes of this section—

(1) PERSONAL PROPERTY TAXES.—The term "personal property tax" means an ad valorem tax which is imposed on an annual basis in respect of personal property.

(2) STATE OR LOCAL TAXES.—A State or local tax includes only a tax imposed by a State, a possession of the United States, or a political subdivision of any of the foregoing, or by the District of Columbia.

(3) FOREIGN TAXES.—A foreign tax includes only a tax imposed by the authority of a foreign country.

(4) SPECIAL RULES FOR GST TAX.—

(A) IN GENERAL.—The GST tax imposed on income distributions is—

(i) the tax imposed by section 2601, and

(ii) any State tax described in section 2604,

but only to the extent such tax is imposed on a transfer which is included in the gross income of the distributee and to which section 666 does not apply.

(B) SPECIAL RULE FOR TAX PAID BEFORE DUE DATE.—Any tax referred to in subparagraph (A) imposed with respect to a transfer occurring during the taxable year of the distributee (or, in the case of a taxable termination, the trust) which is paid not later than the time prescribed by law (including extensions) for filing the return with respect to such transfer shall be treated as having been paid on the last day of the taxable year in which the transfer was made.

(5) GENERAL SALES TAXES.—For purposes of subsection (a)—

(A) ELECTION TO DEDUCT STATE AND LOCAL SALES TAXES IN LIEU OF STATE AND LOCAL INCOME TAXES.—

(i) IN GENERAL.—At the election of the taxpayer for the taxable year, subsection (a) shall be applied—

(I) without regard to the reference to State and local income taxes, and

(II) as if State and local general sales taxes were referred to in a paragraph thereof.

(B) DEFINITION OF GENERAL SALES TAX.—The term "general sales tax" means a tax imposed at one rate with respect to the sale at retail of a broad range of classes of items.

(C) SPECIAL RULES FOR FOOD, ETC.—In the case of items of food, clothing, medical supplies, and motor vehicles—

(i) the fact that the tax does not apply with respect to some or all of such items shall not be taken into account in determining whether the tax applies with respect to a broad range of classes of items, and

(ii) the fact that the rate of tax applicable with respect to some or all of such items is lower than the general rate of tax shall not be taken into account in determining whether the tax is imposed at one rate.

(D) ITEMS TAXED AT DIFFERENT RATES.—Except in the case of a lower rate of tax applicable with respect to an item described in subparagraph (C), no deduction shall be allowed under this paragraph for any general sales tax imposed with respect to an item at a rate other than the general rate of tax.

(E) COMPENSATING USE TAXES.—A compensating use tax with respect to an item shall be treated as a general sales tax. For purposes of the preceding sentence, the term "compensating use tax" means, with respect to any item, a tax which—

(i) is imposed on the use, storage, or consumption of such item, and

(ii) is complementary to a general sales tax, but only if a deduction is allowable under this paragraph with respect to items sold at retail in the taxing jurisdiction which are similar to such item.

(F) SPECIAL RULE FOR MOTOR VEHICLES.—In the case of motor vehicles, if the rate of tax exceeds the general rate, such excess shall be disregarded and the general rate shall be treated as the rate of tax.

(G) SEPARATELY STATED GENERAL SALES TAXES.—If the amount of any general sales tax is separately stated, then, to the extent that the amount so stated is paid by the consumer (other than in connection with the consumer's trade or business) to the seller, such amount shall be treated as a tax imposed on, and paid by, such consumer.

(H) AMOUNT OF DEDUCTION MAY BE DETERMINED UNDER TABLES.—

(i) IN GENERAL.—At the election of the taxpayer for the taxable year, the amount of the deduction allowed under this paragraph for such year shall be—

(I) the amount determined under this paragraph (without regard to this subparagraph) with respect to motor vehicles, boats, and other items specified by the Secretary, and

(II) the amount determined under tables prescribed by the Secretary with respect to items to which subclause (I) does not apply.

(ii) REQUIREMENTS FOR TABLES.—The tables prescribed under clause (i)—

(I) shall reflect the provisions of this paragraph,

(II) shall be based on the average consumption by taxpayers on a State-by-State basis (as determined by the Secretary) of items to which clause (i)(I) does not apply, taking into account filing status, number of dependents, adjusted gross income, and rates of State and local general sales taxation, and

(III) need only be determined with respect to adjusted gross incomes up to the applicable amount (as determined under section 68(b)).

(I) APPLICATION OF PARAGRAPH.—This paragraph shall apply to taxable years beginning after December 31, 2003, and before January 1, 2006.

* * *

[Sec. 165]

SEC. 165. LOSSES.

[Sec. 165(a)]

(a) GENERAL RULE.—There shall be allowed as a deduction any loss sustained during the taxable year and not compensated for by insurance or otherwise.

* * *

[Sec. 165(c)]

(c) LIMITATION ON LOSSES OF INDIVIDUALS.—In the case of an individual, the deduction under subsection (a) shall be limited to—

(1) losses incurred in a trade or business;

(2) losses incurred in any transaction entered into for profit, though not connected with a trade or business; and

(3) except as provided in subsection (h) [relating to casualty gains and losses], losses of property not connected with a trade or business or a transaction entered into for profit, if such losses arise from fire, storm, shipwreck, or other casualty, or from theft.

* * *

[Sec. 165(g)]

(g) WORTHLESS SECURITIES.—

(1) GENERAL RULE.—If any security which is a capital asset becomes worthless during the taxable year, the loss resulting therefrom shall, for purposes of this subtitle, be treated as a loss from the sale or exchange, on the last day of the taxable year, of a capital asset.

(2) SECURITY DEFINED.—For purposes of this subsection, the term "security" means—

(A) a share of stock in a corporation;

(B) a right to subscribe for, or to receive, a share of stock in a corporation; or

(C) a bond, debenture, note, or certificate, or other evidence of indebtedness, issued by a corporation or by a government or political subdivision thereof, with interest coupons or in registered form.

* * *

[Sec. 165(j)]

(j) DENIAL OF DEDUCTION FOR LOSSES ON CERTAIN OBLIGATIONS NOT IN REGISTERED FORM.—

(1) IN GENERAL.—Nothing in subsection (a) or in any other provision of law shall be construed to provide a deduction for any loss sustained on any registration-required obligation unless such obligation is in registered form (or the issuance of such obligation was subject to tax under section 4701).

(2) DEFINITIONS.—For purposes of this subsection—

(A) REGISTRATION-REQUIRED OBLIGATION.—The term "registration-required obligation" has the meaning given to such term by section 163(f)(2) except that clause (iv) of subparagraph (A), and subparagraph (B), of such section shall not apply.

(B) REGISTERED FORM.—The term "registered form" has the same meaning as when used in section 163(f).

(3) EXCEPTIONS.—The Secretary may, by regulations, provide that this subsection and section 1287 shall not apply with respect to obligations held by any person if—

(A) such person holds such obligations in connection with a trade or business outside the United States,

(B) such person holds such obligations as a broker dealer (registered under Federal or State law) for sale to customers in the ordinary course of his trade or business,

(C) such person complies with reporting requirements with respect to ownership, transfers, and payments as the Secretary may require, or

(D) such person promptly surrenders the obligation to the issuer for the issuance of a new obligation in registered form,

but only if such obligations are held under arrangements provided in regulations or otherwise which are designed to assure that such obligations are not delivered to any United States person other than a person described in subparagraph (A), (B), or (C).

* * *

SEC. 166. BAD DEBTS.

(a) GENERAL RULE.—

(1) WHOLLY WORTHLESS DEBTS.—There shall be allowed as a deduction any debt which becomes worthless within the taxable year.

(2) PARTIALLY WORTHLESS DEBTS.—When satisfied that a debt is recoverable only in part, the Secretary may allow such debt, in an amount not in excess of the part charged off within the taxable year, as a deduction.

(b) AMOUNT OF DEDUCTION.—For purposes of subsection (a), the basis for determining the amount of the deduction for any bad debt shall be the adjusted basis provided in section 1011 for determining the loss from the sale or other disposition of property.

[Sec. 166(c)—Repealed]

(d) NONBUSINESS DEBTS.—

(1) GENERAL RULE.—In the case of a taxpayer other than a corporation—
　(A) subsection (a) shall not apply to any nonbusiness debt; and
　(B) where any nonbusiness debt becomes worthless within the taxable year, the loss resulting therefrom shall be considered a loss from the sale or exchange, during the taxable year, of a capital asset held for not more than 1 year.

(2) NONBUSINESS DEBT DEFINED.—For purposes of paragraph (1), the term "nonbusiness debt" means a debt other than—
　(A) a debt created or acquired (as the case may be) in connection with a trade or business of the taxpayer; or
　(B) a debt the loss from the worthlessness of which is incurred in the taxpayer's trade or business.

(e) WORTHLESS SECURITIES.—This section shall not apply to a debt which is evidenced by a security as defined in section 165(g)(2)(C).

* * *

SEC. 168. ACCELERATED COST RECOVERY SYSTEM.

* * *

(g) ALTERNATIVE DEPRECIATION SYSTEM FOR CERTAIN PROPERTY.—

(1) IN GENERAL.—In the case of—
　(A) any tangible property which during the taxable year is used predominantly outside the United States,
　(B) any tax-exempt use property,
　(C) any tax-exempt bond financed property,
　(D) any imported property covered by an Executive order under paragraph (6), and
　(E) any property to which an election under paragraph (7) applies,
the depreciation deduction provided by section 167(a) shall be determined under the alternative depreciation system.

* * *

(4) EXCEPTION FOR CERTAIN PROPERTY USED OUTSIDE UNITED STATES.—Subparagraph (A) of paragraph (1) shall not apply to—

(A) any aircraft which is registered by the Administrator of the Federal Aviation Agency and which is operated to and from the United States or is operated under contract with the United States;

(B) rolling stock which is used within and without the United States and which is—

(i) of a rail carrier subject to part A of subtitle IV of title 49, or

(ii) of a United States person (other than a corporation described in clause (i)) but only if the rolling stock is not leased to one or more foreign persons for periods aggregating more than 12 months in any 24-month period;

(C) any vessel documented under the laws of the United States which is operated in the foreign or domestic commerce of the United States;

(D) any motor vehicle of a United States person (as defined in section 7701(a)(30)) which is operated to and from the United States;

(E) any container of a United States person which is used in the transportation of property to and from the United States;

(F) any property (other than a vessel or an aircraft of a United States person which is used for the purpose of exploring for, developing, removing, or transporting resources from the outer Continental Shelf (within the meaning of section 2 of the Outer Continental Shelf Lands Act, as amended and supplemented; (43 U.S.C. 1331));

(G) any property which is owned by a domestic corporation (other than a corporation which has an election in effect under section 936) or by a United States citizen (other than a citizen entitled to the benefits of section 931 or 933) and which is used predominantly in a possession of the United States by such a corporation or such a citizen, or by a corporation created or organized in, or under the law of, a possession of the United States;

(H) any communications satellite (as defined in section 103(3) of the Communications Satellite Act of 1962, 47 U.S.C. 702(3)), or any interest therein, of a United States person;

(I) any cable, or any interest therein, of a domestic corporation engaged in furnishing telephone service to which section 168(i)(10)(C) applies (or of a wholly owned domestic subsidiary of such a corporation), if such cable is part of a submarine cable system which constitutes part of a communication link exclusively between the United States and one or more foreign countries;

(J) any property (other than a vessel or an aircraft) of a United States person which is used in international or territorial waters within the northern portion of the Western Hemisphere for the purpose of exploring for, developing, removing, or transporting resources from ocean waters or deposits under such waters;

(K) any property described in section 48(l)(3)(A)(ix) (as in effect on the day before the date of the enactment of the Revenue Reconciliation Act of 1990) which is owned by a United States person and which is used in international or territorial waters to generate energy for use in the United States; and

(L) any satellite (not described in subparagraph (H)) or other spacecraft (or any interest therein) held by a United States person if such satellite or other spacecraft was launched from within the United States.

For purposes of subparagraph (J), the term "northern portion of the Western Hemisphere" means the area lying west of the 30th meridian west of Greenwich, east of the international dateline, and north of the Equator, but not including any foreign country which is a country of South America.

* * *

[Sec. 176]

SEC. 176. PAYMENTS WITH RESPECT TO EMPLOYEES OF CERTAIN FOREIGN CORPORATIONS.

In the case of a domestic corporation, there shall be allowed as a deduction amounts (to the extent not compensated for) paid or incurred pursuant to an agreement entered into under section 3121(l) with respect to services performed by United States citizens employed by foreign subsidiary corporations. Any reimbursement of any amount previously allowed as a deduction under this section shall be included in gross income for the taxable year in which received.

[Sec. 197]

SEC. 197. AMORTIZATION OF GOODWILL AND CERTAIN OTHER INTANGIBLES.

[Sec. 197(a)]

(a) GENERAL RULE.—A taxpayer shall be entitled to an amortization deduction with respect to any amortizable section 197 intangible. The amount of such deduction shall be determined by amortizing the adjusted basis (for purposes of determining gain) of such intangible ratably over the 15-year period beginning with the month in which such intangible was acquired.

[Sec. 197(b)]

(b) NO OTHER DEPRECIATION OR AMORTIZATION DEDUCTION ALLOWABLE.—Except as provided in subsection (a), no depreciation or amortization deduction shall be allowable with respect to any amortizable section 197 intangible.

[Sec. 197(c)]

(c) AMORTIZABLE SECTION 197 INTANGIBLE.—For purposes of this section—

(1) IN GENERAL.—Except as otherwise provided in this section, the term "amortizable section 197 intangible" means any section 197 intangible—

(A) which is acquired by the taxpayer after the date of the enactment of this section, and

(B) which is held in connection with the conduct of a trade or business or an activity described in section 212.

(2) EXCLUSION OF SELF-CREATED INTANGIBLES, ETC.—The term "amortizable section 197 intangible" shall not include any section 197 intangible—

(A) which is not described in subparagraph (D), (E), or (F) of subsection (d)(1), and

(B) which is created by the taxpayer.

This paragraph shall not apply if the intangible is created in connection with a transaction (or series of related transactions) involving the acquisition of assets constituting a trade or business or substantial portion thereof.

(3) ANTI-CHURNING RULES.—

For exclusion of intangibles acquired in certain transactions, see subsection (f)(9).

[Sec. 197(d)]

(d) SECTION 197 INTANGIBLE.—For purposes of this section—

(1) IN GENERAL.—Except as otherwise provided in this section, the term "section 197 intangible" means—

(A) goodwill,

(B) going concern value,

(C) any of the following intangible items:

(i) workforce in place including its composition and terms and conditions (contractual or otherwise) of its employment,

(ii) business books and records, operating systems, or any other information base (including lists or other information with respect to current or prospective customers),

(iii) any patent, copyright, formula, process, design, pattern, knowhow, format, or other similar item,

(iv) any customer-based intangible,

(v) any supplier-based intangible, and

(vi) any other similar item,

(D) any license, permit, or other right granted by a governmental unit or an agency or instrumentality thereof,

(E) any covenant not to compete (or other arrangement to the extent such arrangement has substantially the same effect as a covenant not to compete) entered into in connection with an acquisition (directly or indirectly) of an interest in a trade or business or substantial portion thereof, and

(F) any franchise, trademark, or trade name.

(2) CUSTOMER-BASED INTANGIBLE.—

(A) IN GENERAL.—The term "customer-based intangible" means—

(i) composition of market,

(ii) market share, and

(iii) any other value resulting from future provision of goods or services pursuant to relationships (contractual or otherwise) in the ordinary course of business with customers.

(B) SPECIAL RULE FOR FINANCIAL INSTITUTIONS.—In the case of a financial institution, the term "customer-based intangible" includes deposit base and similar items.

(3) SUPPLIER-BASED INTANGIBLE.—The term "supplier-based intangible" means any value resulting from future acquisitions of goods or services pursuant to relationships (contractual or otherwise) in the ordinary course of business with suppliers of goods or services to be used or sold by the taxpayer.

[Sec. 197(e)]

(e) EXCEPTIONS.—For purposes of this section, the term "section 197 intangible" shall not include any of the following:

(1) FINANCIAL INTERESTS.—Any interest—

(A) in a corporation, partnership, trust, or estate, or

(B) under an existing futures contract, foreign currency contract, notional principal contract, or other similar financial contract.

(2) LAND.—Any interest in land.

(3) COMPUTER SOFTWARE.—

(A) IN GENERAL.—Any—

(i) computer software which is readily available for purchase by the general public, is subject to a nonexclusive license, and has not been substantially modified, and

(ii) other computer software which is not acquired in a transaction (or series of related transactions) involving the acquisition of assets constituting a trade or business or substantial portion thereof.

(B) COMPUTER SOFTWARE DEFINED.—For purposes of subparagraph (A), the term "computer software" means any program designed to cause a computer to perform a desired function. Such term shall not include any data base or similar item unless the data base or item is in the public domain and is incidental to the operation of otherwise qualifying computer software.

(4) CERTAIN INTERESTS OR RIGHTS ACQUIRED SEPARATELY.—Any of the following not acquired in a transaction (or series of related transactions) involving the acquisition of assets constituting a trade business or substantial portion thereof:

(A) Any interest in a film, sound recording, video tape, book, or similar property.

(B) Any right to receive tangible property or services under a contract or granted by a governmental unit or agency or instrumentality thereof.

(C) Any interest in a patent or copyright.

(D) To the extent provided in regulations, any right under a contract (or granted by a governmental unit or an agency or instrumentality thereof) if such right—

(i) has a fixed duration of less than 15 years, or

(ii) is fixed as to amount and, without regard to this section, would be recoverable under a method similar to the unit-of-production method.

(5) INTERESTS UNDER LEASES AND DEBT INSTRUMENTS.—Any interest under—

(A) an existing lease of tangible property, or

(B) except as provided in subsection (d)(2)(B), any existing indebtedness.

(6) MORTGAGE SERVICING.—Any right to service indebtedness which is secured by residential real property unless such right is acquired in a transaction (or series of related transactions) involving the acquisition of assests (other than rights described in this paragraph) constituting a trade or business or substantial portion thereof.

(7) CERTAIN TRANSACTION COSTS.—Any fees for professional services, and any transaction costs, incurred by parties to a transaction with respect to which any portion of the gain or loss is not recognized under part III of subchapter C.

[Sec. 197(f)]

(f) SPECIAL RULES.—

* * *

(3) TREATMENT OF AMOUNTS PAID PURSUANT TO COVENANTS NOT TO COMPETE, ETC.—Any amount paid or incurred pursuant to a covenant or arrangement referred to in subsection (d)(1)(E) shall be treated as an amount chargeable to capital account.

(4) TREATMENT OF FRANCHISES, ETC.—

(A) FRANCHISE.—The term "franchise" has the meaning given to such term by section 1253(b)(1).

(B) TREATMENT OF RENEWALS.—Any renewal of a franchise, trademark, or trade name (or of a license, a permit, or other right referred to in subsection (d)(1)(D)) shall be treated as an acquisition. The preceding sentence shall only apply with respect to costs incurred in connection with such renewal.

(C) CERTAIN AMOUNTS NOT TAKEN INTO ACCOUNT.—Any amount to which section 1253(d)(1) applies shall not be taken into account under this section.

* * *

(7) TREATMENT AS DEPRECIABLE.—For purposes of this chapter, any amortizable section 197 intangible shall be treated as property which is of a character subject to the allowance for depreciation provided in section 167.

* * *

[Sec. 199]

SEC. 199. INCOME ATTRIBUTABLE TO DOMESTIC PRODUCTION ACTIVITIES.

[Sec. 199(a)]

(a) ALLOWANCE OF DEDUCTION.—

(1) IN GENERAL.—There shall be allowed as a deduction an amount equal to 9 percent of the lesser of—

(A) the qualified production activities income of the taxpayer for the taxable year, or

(B) taxable income (determined without regard to this section) for the taxable year.

(2) PHASEIN.—In the case of any taxable year beginning after 2004 and before 2010, paragraph (1) and subsections (d)(1) and (d)(6) shall be applied by substituting for the percentage contained therein the transition percentage determined under the following table:

For taxable years beginning in:	The transition percentage is:
2005 or 2006	3
2007, 2008, or 2009	6

INCOME TAX—DOMESTIC PRODUCTION ACTIVITIES

[Sec. 199(b)]

(b) DEDUCTION LIMITED TO WAGES PAID.—

(1) IN GENERAL.—The amount of the deduction allowable under subsection (a) for any taxable year shall not exceed 50 percent of the W-2 wages of the employer for the taxable year.

(2) W-2 WAGES.—For purposes of paragraph (1), the term "W-2 wages" means the sum of the aggregate amounts the taxpayer is required to include on statements under paragraphs (3) and (8) of section 6051(a) with respect to employment of employees of the taxpayer during the calendar year ending during the taxpayer's taxable year.

(3) ACQUISITIONS AND DISPOSITIONS.—The Secretary shall provide for the application of this subsection in cases where the taxpayer acquires, or disposes of, the major portion of a trade or business or the major portion of a separate unit of a trade or business during the taxable year.

[Sec. 199(c)]

(c) QUALIFIED PRODUCTION ACTIVITIES INCOME.—For purposes of this section—

(1) IN GENERAL.—The term "qualified production activities income" for any taxable year means an amount equal to the excess (if any) of—

(A) the taxpayer's domestic production gross receipts for such taxable year, over

(B) the sum of—

(i) the cost of goods sold that are allocable to such receipts,

(ii) other deductions, expenses, or losses directly allocable to such receipts, and

(iii) a ratable portion of other deductions, expenses, and losses that are not directly allocable to such receipts or another class of income.

(2) ALLOCATION METHOD.—The Secretary shall prescribe rules for the proper allocation of items of income, deduction, expense, and loss for purposes of determining income attributable to domestic production activities.

(3) SPECIAL RULES FOR DETERMINING COSTS.—

(A) IN GENERAL.—For purposes of determining costs under clause (i) of paragraph (1)(B), any item or service brought into the United States shall be treated as acquired by purchase, and its cost shall be treated as not less than its value immediately after it entered the United States. A similar rule shall apply in determining the adjusted basis of leased or rented property where the lease or rental gives rise to domestic production gross receipts.

(B) EXPORTS FOR FURTHER MANUFACTURE.—In the case of any property described in subparagraph (A) that had been exported by the taxpayer for further manufacture, the increase in cost or adjusted basis under subparagraph (A) shall not exceed the difference between the value of the property when exported and the value of the property when brought back into the United States after the further manufacture.

(4) DOMESTIC PRODUCTION GROSS RECEIPTS.—

(A) IN GENERAL.—The term "domestic production gross receipts" means the gross receipts of the taxpayer which are derived from—

(i) any lease, rental, license, sale, exchange, or other disposition of—

(I) qualifying production property which was manufactured, produced, grown, or extracted by the taxpayer in whole or in significant part within the United States,

(II) any qualified film produced by the taxpayer, or

(III) electricity, natural gas, or potable water produced by the taxpayer in the United States,

(ii) construction performed in the United States, or

Sec. 199(c)(4)(A)(ii)

(iii) engineering or architectural services performed in the United States for construction projects in the United States.

(B) EXCEPTIONS.—Such term shall not include gross receipts of the taxpayer which are derived from—

(i) the sale of food and beverages prepared by the taxpayer at a retail establishment, and

(ii) the transmission or distribution of electricity, natural gas, or potable water.

(5) QUALIFYING PRODUCTION PROPERTY.—The term "qualifying production property" means—

(A) tangible personal property,

(B) any computer software, and

(C) any property described in section 168(f)(4).

(6) QUALIFIED FILM.—The term "qualified film" means any property described in section 168(f)(3) if not less than 50 percent of the total compensation relating to the production of such property is compensation for services performed in the United States by actors, production personnel, directors, and producers. Such term does not include property with respect to which records are required to be maintained under section 2257 of title 18, United States Code.

(7) RELATED PERSONS.—

(A) IN GENERAL.—The term "domestic production gross receipts" shall not include any gross receipts of the taxpayer derived from property leased, licensed, or rented by the taxpayer for use by any related person.

(B) RELATED PERSON.—For purposes of subparagraph (A), a person shall be treated as related to another person if such persons are treated as a single employer under subsection (a) or (b) of section 52 or subsection (m) or (o) of section 414, except that determinations under subsections (a) and (b) of section 52 shall be made without regard to section 1563(b).

[Sec. 199(d)]

(d) DEFINITIONS AND SPECIAL RULES.—

(1) APPLICATION OF SECTION TO PASS-THRU ENTITIES.—

(A) IN GENERAL.—In the case of an S corporation, partnership, estate or trust, or other pass-thru entity—

(i) subject to the provisions of paragraphs (2) and (3), this section shall be applied at the shareholder, partner, or similar level, and

(ii) the Secretary shall prescribe rules for the application of this section, including rules relating to—

(I) restrictions on the allocation of the deduction to taxpayers at the partner or similar level, and

(II) additional reporting requirements.

(B) APPLICATION OF WAGE LIMITATION.—Notwithstanding subparagraph (A)(i), for purposes of applying subsection (b), a shareholder, partner, or similar person which is allocated qualified production activities income from an S corporation, partnership, estate, trust, or other pass-thru entity shall also be treated as having been allocated W-2 wages from such entity in an amount equal to the lesser of—

(i) such person's allocable share of such wages (without regard to this subparagraph), as determined under regulations prescribed by the Secretary, or

(ii) 2 times 9 percent of the qualified production activities income allocated to such person for the taxable year.

(2) APPLICATION TO INDIVIDUALS.—In the case of an individual, subsection (a)(1)(B) shall be applied by substituting "adjusted gross income" for "taxable income". For purposes of the preceding sentence, adjusted gross income shall be determined—

(A) after application of sections 86, 135, 137, 219, 221, 222, and 469, and

(B) without regard to this section.

(3) Patrons of agricultural and horticultural cooperatives.—

(A) In general.—If any amount described in paragraph (1) or (3) of section 1385(a)—

(i) is received by a person from an organization to which part I of subchapter T applies which is engaged—

(I) in the manufacturing, production, growth, or extraction in whole or significant part of any agricultural or horticultural product, or

(II) in the marketing of agricultural or horticultural products, and

(ii) is allocable to the portion of the qualified production activities income of the organization which, but for this paragraph, would be deductible under subsection (a) by the organization and is designated as such by the organization in a written notice mailed to its patrons during the payment period described in section 1382(d),

then such person shall be allowed a deduction under subsection (a) with respect to such amount. The taxable income of the organization shall not be reduced under section 1382 by reason of any amount to which the preceding sentence applies.

(B) Special rules.—For purposes of applying subparagraph (A), in determining the qualified production activities income which would be deductible by the organization under subsection (a)—

(i) there shall not be taken into account in computing the organization's taxable income any deduction allowable under subsection (b) or (c) of section 1382 (relating to patronage dividends, per-unit retain allocations, and nonpatronage distributions), and

(ii) in the case of an organization described in subparagraph (A)(i)(II), the organization shall be treated as having manufactured, produced, grown, or extracted in whole or significant part any qualifying production property marketed by the organization which its patrons have so manufactured, produced, grown, or extracted.

(4) Special rule for affiliated groups.—

(A) In general.—All members of an expanded affiliated group shall be treated as a single corporation for purposes of this section.

(B) Expanded affiliated group.—For purposes of this section, the term "expanded affiliated group" means an affiliated group as defined in section 1504(a), determined—

(i) by substituting "50 percent" for "80 percent" each place it appears, and

(ii) without regard to paragraphs (2) and (4) of section 1504(b).

(C) Allocation of deduction.—Except as provided in regulations, the deduction under subsection (a) shall be allocated among the members of the expanded affiliated group in proportion to each member's respective amount (if any) of qualified production activities income.

(5) Trade or business requirement.—This section shall be applied by only taking into account items which are attributable to the actual conduct of a trade or business.

(6) Coordination with minimum tax.—The deduction under this section shall be allowed for purposes of the tax imposed by section 55; except that for purposes of section 55, the deduction under subsection (a) shall be 9 percent of the lesser of—

(A) qualified production activities income (determined without regard to part IV of subchapter A), or

(B) alternative minimum taxable income (determined without regard to this section) for the taxable year.

In the case of an individual, subparagraph (B) shall be applied by substituting "adjusted gross income" for "alternative minimum taxable income". For purposes of the preceding sentence, adjusted gross income shall be determined in the same manner as provided in paragraph (2).

PART VIII—SPECIAL DEDUCTIONS FOR CORPORATIONS

[Sec. 243]

SEC. 243. DIVIDENDS RECEIVED BY CORPORATIONS.

[Sec. 243(a)]

(a) GENERAL RULE.—In the case of a corporation, there shall be allowed as a deduction an amount equal to the following percentages of the amount received as dividends from a domestic corporation which is subject to taxation under this chapter:

(1) 70 percent, in the case of dividends other than dividends described in paragraph (2) or (3);

(2) 100 percent, in the case of dividends received by a small business investment company operating under the Small Business Investment Act of 1958 (15 U.S.C. 661 and following); and

(3) 100 percent, in the case of qualifying dividends (as defined in subsection (b)(1)).

[Sec. 243(b)]

(b) QUALIFYING DIVIDENDS.—

(1) IN GENERAL.—For purposes of this section, the term "qualifying dividend" means any dividend received by a corporation—

(A) if at the close of the day on which such dividend is received, such corporation is a member of the same affiliated group as the corporation distributing such dividend, and

(B) if—

(i) such dividend is distributed out of the earnings and profits of a taxable year of the distributing corporation which ends after December 31, 1963, for which an election under section 1562 was not in effect, and on each day of which the distributing corporation and the corporation receiving the dividend were members of such affiliated group, or

(ii) such dividend is paid by a corporation with respect to which an election under section 936 is in effect for the taxable year in which such dividend is paid.

* * *

[Sec. 243(e)]

(e) CERTAIN DIVIDENDS FROM FOREIGN CORPORATIONS.—For purposes of subsection (a) and for purposes of section 245, any dividend from a foreign corporation from earnings and profits accumulated by a domestic corporation during a period with respect to which such domestic corporation was subject to taxation under this chapter (or corresponding provisions of prior law) shall be treated as a dividend from a domestic corporation which is subject to taxation under this chapter.

[Sec. 245]

SEC. 245. DIVIDENDS RECEIVED FROM CERTAIN FOREIGN CORPORATIONS.

[Sec. 245(a)]

(a) DIVIDENDS FROM 10-PERCENT OWNED FOREIGN CORPORATIONS.—

(1) IN GENERAL.—In the case of dividends received by a corporation from a qualified 10-percent owned foreign corporation, there shall be allowed as a deduction an amount equal to the percent (specified in section 243 for the taxable year) of the U.S.-source portion of such dividends.

(2) QUALIFIED 10-PERCENT OWNED FOREIGN CORPORATION.—For purposes of this subsection, the term "qualified 10-percent owned foreign corporation" means any foreign corporation (other than a passive foreign investment company) if at least 10 percent of the stock of such corporation (by vote and value) is owned by the taxpayer.

Sec. 199(d)(7)

(3) U.S.-SOURCE PORTION.—For purposes of this subsection, the U.S.-source portion of any dividend is an amount which bears the same ratio to such dividends as—

(A) the post-1986 undistributed U.S. earnings, bears to

(B) the total post-1986 undistributed earnings.

(4) POST-1986 UNDISTRIBUTED EARNINGS.—For purposes of this subsection, the term "post-1986 undistributed earnings" has the meaning given to such term by section 902(c)(1).

(5) POST-1986 UNDISTRIBUTED U.S. EARNINGS.—For purposes of this subsection, the term "post-1986 undistributed U.S. earnings" means the portion of the post-1986 undistributed earnings which is attributable to—

(A) income of the qualified 10-percent owned foreign corporation which is effectively connected with the conduct of a trade or business within the United States and subject to tax under this chapter, or

(B) any dividend received (directly or through a wholly owned foreign corporation) from a domestic corporation at least 80 percent of the stock of which (by vote and value) is owned (directly or through such wholly owned foreign corporation) by the qualified 10-percent owned foreign corporation.

(6) SPECIAL RULE.—If the 1st day on which the requirements of paragraph (2) are met with respect to any foreign corporation is in a taxable year of such corporation beginning after December 31, 1986, the post-1986 undistributed earnings and the post-1986 undistributed U.S. earnings of such corporation shall be determined by only taking into account periods beginning on and after the 1st day of the 1st taxable year in which such requirements are met.

(7) COORDINATION WITH SUBSECTION (b).—Earnings and profits of any qualified 10-percent owned foreign corporation for any taxable year shall not be taken into account under this subsection if the deduction provided by subsection (b) would be allowable with respect to dividends paid out of such earnings and profits.

(8) DISALLOWANCE OF FOREIGN TAX CREDIT.—No credit shall be allowed under section 901 for any taxes paid or accrued (or treated as paid or accrued) with respect to the United States-source portion of any dividend received by a corporation from a qualified 10-percent-owned foreign corporation.

(9) COORDINATION WITH SECTION 904.—For purposes of section 904, the U.S.-source portion of any dividend received by a corporation from a qualified 10-percent owned foreign corporation shall be treated as from sources in the United States.

(10) COORDINATION WITH TREATIES.—If—

(A) any portion of a dividend received by a corporation from a qualified 10-percent-owned foreign corporation would be treated as from sources in the United States under paragraph (9),

(B) under a treaty obligation of the United States (applied without regard to this subsection), such portion would be treated as arising from sources outside the United States, and

(C) the taxpayer chooses the benefits of this paragraph,

this subsection shall not apply to such dividend (but subsections (a), (b), and (c) of section 904 and sections 902, 907, and 960 shall be applied separately with respect to such portion of such dividend).

(11) COORDINATION WITH SECTION 1248.—For purposes of this subsection, the term "dividend" does not include any amount treated as a dividend under section 1248.

[Sec. 245(b)]

(b) CERTAIN DIVIDENDS RECEIVED FROM WHOLLY OWNED FOREIGN SUBSIDIARIES.—

(1) IN GENERAL.—In the case of dividends described in paragraph (2) received from a foreign corporation by a domestic corporation which, for its taxable year in which such dividends are received, owns (directly or indirectly) all of the outstanding stock of such foreign corporation, there shall be allowed as a deduction (in lieu of the deduction provided by subsection (a)) an amount equal to 100 percent of such dividends.

(2) ELIGIBLE DIVIDENDS.—Paragraph (1) shall apply only to dividends which are paid out of the earnings and profits of a foreign corporation for a taxable year during which—

(A) all of its outstanding stock is owned (directly or indirectly) by the domestic corporation to which such dividends are paid; and

(B) all of its gross income from all sources is effectively connected with the conduct of a trade or business within the United States.

* * *

[Sec. 246]

SEC. 246. RULES APPLYING TO DEDUCTIONS FOR DIVIDENDS RECEIVED.

* * *

[Sec. 246(d)]

(d) DIVIDENDS FROM A DISC OR FORMER DISC.—No deduction shall be allowed under section 243 in respect of a dividend from a corporation which is a DISC or former DISC (as defined in section 992(a)) to the extent such dividend is paid out of the corporation's accumulated DISC income or previously taxed income, or is a deemed distribution pursuant to section 995(b)(1).

[Sec. 246(e)]

(e) CERTAIN DISTRIBUTIONS TO SATISFY REQUIREMENTS.—No deduction shall be allowed under section 243(a) with respect to a dividend received pursuant to a distribution described in section 936(h)(4).

PART IX—ITEMS NOT DEDUCTIBLE

[Sec. 263]

SEC. 263. CAPITAL EXPENDITURES.

[Sec. 263(a)]

(a) GENERAL RULE.—No deduction shall be allowed for—

(1) Any amount paid out for new buildings or for permanent improvements or betterments made to increase the value of any property or estate. This paragraph shall not apply to—

(A) expenditures for the development of mines or deposits deductible under section 616,

(B) research and experimental expenditures deductible under section 174,

(C) soil and water conservation expenditures deductible under section 175,

(D) expenditures by farmers for fertilizer, etc., deductible under section 180,

(E) expenditures for removal of architectural and transportation barriers to the handicapped and elderly which the taxpayer elects to deduct under section 190,

(F) expenditures for tertiary injectants with respect to which a deduction is allowed under section 193;

(G) expenditures for which a deduction is allowed under section 179;

(H) expenditures for which a deduction is allowed under section 179A; or

(I) expenditures for which a deduction is allowed under section 179B.

(2) Any amount expended in restoring property or in making good the exhaustion thereof for which an allowance is or has been made.

[Sec. 263(c)]

(c) INTANGIBLE DRILLING AND DEVELOPMENT COSTS IN THE CASE OF OIL AND GAS WELLS AND GEOTHERMAL WELLS.—Notwithstanding subsection (a), and except as provided in subsection (i), regulations shall be prescribed by the Secretary under this subtitle corresponding to the regulations which granted the option to deduct as expenses intangible drilling and development costs in the case of oil and gas wells and which were recognized and approved by the Congress in House Concurrent Resolution 50, Seventy-ninth Congress. Such regulations shall also grant the option to deduct as expenses intangible drilling and development costs in the case of wells drilled for any geothermal deposit (as defined in section 613(e)(2)) to the same extent and in the same manner as such expenses are deductible in the case of oil and gas wells. This subsection shall not apply with respect to any costs to which any deduction is allowed under section 59(e) or 291.

* * *

[Sec. 263(i)]

(i) SPECIAL RULES FOR INTANGIBLE DRILLING AND DEVELOPMENT COSTS INCURRED OUTSIDE THE UNITED STATES.—In the case of intangible drilling and development costs paid or incurred with respect to an oil, gas, or geothermal well located outside the United States—

(1) subsection (c) shall not apply, and

(2) such costs shall—

(A) at the election of the taxpayer, be included in adjusted basis for purposes of computing the amount of any deduction allowable under section 611 (determined without regard to section 613), or

(B) if subparagraph (A) does not apply, be allowed as a deduction ratably over the 10-taxable year period beginning with the taxable year in which such costs were paid or incurred.

This subsection shall not apply to costs paid or incurred with respect to a nonproductive well.

[Sec. 267]

SEC. 267. LOSSES, EXPENSES, AND INTEREST WITH RESPECT TO TRANSACTIONS BETWEEN RELATED TAXPAYERS.

[Sec. 267(a)]

(a) IN GENERAL.—

(1) DEDUCTION FOR LOSSES DISALLOWED.—No deduction shall be allowed in respect of any loss from the sale or exchange of property, directly or indirectly, between persons specified in any of the paragraphs of subsection (b). The preceding sentence shall not apply to any loss of the distributing corporation (or the distributee) in the case of a distribution in complete liquidation.

(2) MATCHING OF DEDUCTION AND PAYEE INCOME ITEM IN THE CASE OF EXPENSES AND INTEREST.—If—

(A) by reason of the method of accounting of the person to whom the payment is to be made, the amount thereof is not (unless paid) includible in the gross income of such person, and

(B) at the close of the taxable year of the taxpayer for which (but for this paragraph) the amount would be deductible under this chapter, both the taxpayer and the person to whom the payment is to be made are persons specified in any of the paragraphs of subsection (b),

then any deduction allowable under this chapter in respect of such amount shall be allowable as of the day as of which such amount is includible in the gross income of the person to whom the payment is made (or, if later, as of the day on which it would be so allowable but for this paragraph). For purposes of this paragraph, in the case of a personal service corporation (within the meaning of section 441(i)(2)), such corporation and any employee-owner (within the meaning of section 269A(b)(2), as modified by section 441(i)(2)) shall be treated as persons specified in subsection (b).

(3) PAYMENTS TO FOREIGN PERSONS

(A) IN GENERAL.—The Secretary shall by regulations apply the matching principle of paragraph (2) in cases in which the person to whom the payment is to be made is not a United States person.

(B) SPECIAL RULE FOR CERTAIN FOREIGN ENTITIES.—

(i) IN GENERAL.—Notwithstanding subparagraph (A), in the case of any item payable to a controlled foreign corporation (as defined in section 957) or a passive foreign investment company (as defined in section 1297), a deduction shall be allowable to the payor with respect to such amount for any taxable year before the taxable year in which paid only to the extent that an amount attributable to such item is includible (determined without regard to properly allocable deductions and qualified deficits under section 952(c)(1)(B)) during such prior taxable year in the gross income of a United States person who owns (within the meaning of section 958(a)) stock in such corporation.

(ii) SECRETARIAL AUTHORITY.—The Secretary may by regulation exempt transactions from the application of clause (i), including any transaction which is entered into by a payor in the ordinary course of a trade or business in which the payor is predominantly engaged and in which the payment of the accrued amounts occurs within 8½ months after accrual or within such other period as the Secretary may prescribe.

[Sec. 267(b)]

(b) RELATIONSHIPS.—The persons referred to in subsection (a) are:

(1) Members of a family, as defined in subsection (c)(4);

(2) An individual and a corporation more than 50 percent in value of the outstanding stock of which is owned, directly or indirectly, by or for such individual;

(3) Two corporations which are members of the same controlled group (as defined in subsection (f));

(4) A grantor and a fiduciary of any trust;

(5) A fiduciary of a trust and a fiduciary of another trust, if the same person is a grantor of both trusts;

(6) A fiduciary of a trust and a beneficiary of such trust;

(7) A fiduciary of a trust and a beneficiary of another trust, if the same person is a grantor of both trusts;

(8) A fiduciary of a trust and a corporation more than 50 percent in value of the outstanding stock of which is owned, directly or indirectly, by or for the trust or by or for a person who is a grantor of the trust;

(9) A person and an organization to which section 501 (relating to certain educational and charitable organizations which are exempt from tax) applies and which is controlled directly or indirectly by such person or (if such person is an individual) by members of the family of such individual;

(10) A corporation and a partnership if the same persons own—

(A) more than 50 percent in value of the outstanding stock of the corporation, and

(B) more than 50 percent of the capital interest, or the profits interest, in the partnership;

(11) An S corporation and another S corporation if the same persons own more than 50 percent in value of the outstanding stock of each corporation;

(12) An S corporation and a C corporation, if the same persons own more than 50 percent in value of the outstanding stock of each corporation; or

(13) Except in the case of a sale or exchange in satisfaction of a pecuniary bequest, an executor of an estate and a beneficiary of such estate.

[Sec. 267(c)]

(c) CONSTRUCTIVE OWNERSHIP OF STOCK.—For purposes of determining, in applying subsection (b), the ownership of stock—

(1) Stock owned, directly or indirectly, by or for a corporation, partnership, estate, or trust shall be considered as being owned proportionately by or for its shareholders, partners, or beneficiaries;

(2) An individual shall be considered as owning the stock owned, directly or indirectly, by or for his family;

(3) An individual owning (otherwise than by the application of paragraph (2)) any stock in a corporation shall be considered as owning the stock owned, directly or indirectly, by or for his partner;

(4) The family of an individual shall include only his brothers and sisters (whether by the whole or half blood), spouse, ancestors, and lineal descendants; and

(5) Stock constructively owned by a person by reason of the application of paragraph (1) shall, for the purpose of applying paragraph (1), (2), or (3), be treated as actually owned by such person, but stock constructively owned by an individual by reason of the application of paragraph (2) or (3) shall not be treated as owned by him for the purpose of again applying either of such paragraphs in order to make another the constructive owner of such stock.

[Sec. 267(d)]

(d) AMOUNT OF GAIN WHERE LOSS PREVIOUSLY DISALLOWED.—If—

(1) in the case of a sale or exchange of property to the taxpayer a loss sustained by the transferor is not allowable to the transferor as a deduction by reason of subsection (a) (1) (or by reason of section 24 (b) of the Internal Revenue Code of 1939); and

(2) after December 31, 1953, the taxpayer sells or otherwise disposes of such property (or of other property the basis of which in his hands is determined directly or indirectly by reference to such property) at a gain,

then such gain shall be recognized only to the extent that it exceeds so much of such loss as is properly allocable to the property sold or otherwise disposed of by the taxpayer. This subsection applies with respect to taxable years ending after December 31, 1953. This subsection shall not apply if the loss sustained by the transferor is not allowable to the transferor as a deduction by reason of section 1091 (relating to wash sales) or by reason of section 118 of the Internal Revenue Code of 1939.

[Sec. 267(e)]

(e) SPECIAL RULES FOR PASS-THRU ENTITIES.—

(1) IN GENERAL.—In the case of any amount paid or incurred by, to, or on behalf of, a pass-thru entity, for purposes of applying subsection (a)(2)—

(A) such entity,

(B) in the case of—

(i) a partnership, any person who owns (directly or indirectly) any capital interest or profits interest of such partnership, or

(ii) an S corporation, any person who owns (directly or indirectly) any of the stock of such corporation,

(C) any person who owns (directly or indirectly) any capital interests or profits interest of a partnership in which such entity owns (directly or indirectly) any capital interest or profits interest, and

(D) any person related (within the meaning of subsection (b) of this section or section 707(b)(1) to a person described in subparagraph (B) or (C),

shall be treated as persons specified in a paragraph of subsection (b). Subparagraph (C) shall apply to a transaction only if such transaction is related either to the operations of the partnership described in such subparagraph or to an interest in such partnership.

(2) PASS-THRU ENTITY.—For purposes of this section, the term "pass-thru entity" means—

(A) a partnership, and

(B) an S corporation.

(3) CONSTRUCTIVE OWNERSHIP IN THE CASE OF PARTNERSHIPS.—For purposes of determining ownership of a capital interest or profits interest of a partnership, the principles of subsection (c) shall apply, except that—

(A) paragraph (3) of subsection (c) shall not apply, and

(B) interests owned (directly or indirectly) by or for a C corporation shall be considered as owned by or for any shareholder only if such shareholder owns (directly or indirectly) 5 percent or more in value of the stock of such corporation.

(4) SUBSECTION (A)(2) NOT TO APPLY TO CERTAIN GUARANTEED PAYMENTS OF PARTNERSHIPS.—In the case of any amount paid or incurred by a partnership, subsection (a)(2) shall not apply to the extent that section 707(c) applies to such amount.

(5) EXCEPTION FOR CERTAIN EXPENSES AND INTEREST OF PARTNERSHIPS OWNING LOW-INCOME HOUSING.—

(A) IN GENERAL.—This subsection shall not apply with respect to qualified expenses and interest paid or incurred by a partnership owning low-income housing to—

(i) any qualified 5-percent or less partner of such partnership, or

(ii) any person related (within the meaning of subsection (b) of this section or section 707(b)(1)) to any qualified 5-percent or less partner of such partnership.

(B) QUALIFIED 5-PERCENT OR LESS PARTNER.—For purposes of this paragraph, the term "qualified 5-percent or less partner" means any partner who has (directly or indirectly) an interest of 5 percent or less in the aggregate capital and profits interests of the partnership but only if—

(i) such partner owned the low-income housing at all times during the 2-year period ending on the date such housing was transferred to the partnership, or

(ii) such partnership acquired the low-income housing pursuant to a purchase, assignment, or other transfer from the Department of Housing and Urban Development or any State or local housing authority.

For purposes of the preceding sentence, a partner shall be treated as holding any interest in the partnership which is held (directly or indirectly) by any person related (within the meaning of subsection (b) of this section or section 707(b)(1)) to such partner.

(C) QUALIFIED EXPENSES AND INTEREST.—For purpose of this paragraph, the term "qualified expenses and interest" means any expense or interest incurred by the partnership with respect to low-income housing held by the partnership but—

(i) only if the amount of such expense or interest (as the case may be) is unconditionally required to be paid by the partnership not later than 10 years after the date such amount was incurred, and

(ii) in the case of such interest, only if such interest is incurred at an annual rate not in excess of 12 percent.

(D) LOW-INCOME HOUSING.—For purposes of this paragraph, the term "low-income housing" means—

(i) any interest in property described in clause (i), (ii), (iii), or (iv) of section 1250(a)(1)(B), and

(ii) any interest in a partnership owning such property.

(6) CROSS REFERENCE.—

For additional rules relating to partnerships, see section 707(b).

[Sec. 267(f)]

(f) CONTROLLED GROUP DEFINED; SPECIAL RULES APPLICABLE TO CONTROLLED GROUPS.—

(1) CONTROLLED GROUP DEFINED.—For purposes of this section, the term "controlled group" has the meaning given to such term by section 1563(a), except that—

(A) "more than 50 percent" shall be substituted for "at least 80 percent" each place it appears in section 1563(a), and

(B) the determination shall be made without regard to subsections (a)(4) and (e)(3)(C) of section 1563.

(2) DEFERRAL (RATHER THAN DENIAL) OF LOSS FROM SALE OR EXCHANGE BETWEEN MEMBERS.—In the case of any loss from the sale or exchange of property which is between members of the same controlled group and to which subsection (a)(1) applies (determined without regard to this paragraph but with regard to paragraph (3))—

(A) subsections (a)(1) and (d) shall not apply to such loss, but

(B) such loss shall be deferred until the property is transferred outside such controlled group and there would be recognition of loss under consolidated return principles or until such other time as may be prescribed in regulations.

(3) LOSS DEFERRAL RULES NOT TO APPLY IN CERTAIN CASES.—

(A) TRANSFER TO DISC.—For purposes of applying subsection (a)(1), the term "controlled group" shall not include a DISC.

(B) CERTAIN SALES OF INVENTORY.—Except to the extent provided in regulations prescribed by the Secretary, subsection (a)(1) shall not apply to the sale or exchange of property between members of the same controlled group (or persons described in subsection (b)(10)) if—

(i) such property in the hands of the transferor is property described in section 1221(a)(1),

(ii) such sale or exchange is in the ordinary course of the transferor's trade or business,

(iii) such property in the hands of the transferee is property described in section 1221(a)(1), and

(iv) the transferee or the transferor is a foreign corporation.

(C) CERTAIN FOREIGN CURRENCY LOSSES.—To the extent povided in regulations, subsection (a)(1) shall not apply to any loss sustained by a member of a controlled group on the repayment of a loan made to another member of such group if such loan is payable in a foreign currency or is denominated in such a currency and such loss is attributable to a reduction in value of such foreign currency.

(4) DETERMINATION OF RELATIONSHIP RESULTING IN DISALLOWANCE OF LOSS, FOR PURPOSES OF OTHER PROVISIONS.—For purposes of any other section of this title which refers to a relationship which would result in a disallowance of losses under this section, deferral under paragraph (2) shall be treated as disallowance.

* * *

[Sec. 269]

SEC. 269. ACQUISITIONS MADE TO EVADE OR AVOID INCOME TAX.

[Sec. 269(a)]

(a) IN GENERAL.—If—

(1) any person or persons acquire, or acquired on or after October 8, 1940, directly or indirectly, control of a corporation, or

(2) any corporation acquires, or acquired on or after October 8, 1940, directly or indirectly, property of another corporation, not controlled, directly or indirectly, immediately before such acquisition, by such acquiring corporation or its stockholders, the basis of which property, in the hands of the acquiring corporation, is determined by reference to the basis in the hands of the transferor corporation,

and the principal purpose for which such acquisition was made is evasion or avoidance of Federal income tax by securing the benefit of a deduction, credit, or other allowance which such person or corporation would not otherwise enjoy, then the Secretary may disallow such deduction, credit, or other allowance. For purposes of paragraphs (1) and (2), control means the ownership of stock possessing at least 50 percent of the total combined voting power of all classes of stock entitled to vote or at least 50 percent of the total value of shares of all classes of stock of the corporation.

[Sec. 269(b)]

(b) CERTAIN LIQUIDATIONS AFTER QUALIFIED STOCK PURCHASES.—

(1) IN GENERAL.—If—

(A) there is a qualified stock purchase by a corporation of another corporation,

(B) an election is not made under section 338 with respect to such purchase,

(C) the acquired corporation is liquidated pursuant to a plan of liquidation adopted not more than 2 years after the acquisition date, and

(D) the principal purpose for such liquidation is the evasion or avoidance of Federal income tax by securing the benefit of a deduction, credit, or other allowance which the acquiring corporation would not otherwise enjoy,

then the Secretary may disallow such deduction, credit, or other allowance.

(2) MEANING OF TERMS.—For purposes of paragraph (1), the terms "qualified stock purchase" and "acquisition date" have the same respective meanings as when used in section 338.

[Sec. 269(c)]

(c) POWER OF SECRETARY TO ALLOW DEDUCTION, ETC., IN PART.—In any case to which subsection (a) or (b) applies the Secretary is authorized—

(1) to allow as a deduction, credit, or allowance any part of any amount disallowed by such subsection, if he determines that such allowance will not result in the evasion or avoidance of Federal income tax for which the acquisition was made; or

(2) to distribute, apportion, or allocate gross income, and distribute, apportion, or allocate the deductions, credits, or allowances the benefit of which was sought to be secured, between or among the corporations, or properties, or parts thereof, involved, and to allow such deductions, credits, or allowances so distributed, apportioned, or allocated, but to give effect to such allowance only to such extent as he determines will not result in the evasion or avoidance of Federal income tax for which the acquisition was made; or

(3) to exercise his powers in part under paragraph (1) and in part under paragraph (2).

[Sec. 269B]

SEC. 269B. STAPLED ENTITIES.

[Sec. 269B(a)]

(a) GENERAL RULE.—Except as otherwise provided by regulations, for purposes of this title—

(1) if a domestic corporation and a foreign corporation are stapled entities, the foreign corporation shall be treated as a domestic corporation,

(2) in applying section 1563, stock in a second corporation which constitutes a stapled interest with respect to stock of a first corporation shall be treated as owned by such first corporation, and

(3) in applying subchapter M for purposes of determining whether any stapled entity is a regulated investment company or a real estate investment trust, all entities which are stapled entities with respect to each other shall be treated as 1 entity.

[Sec. 269B(b)]

(b) SECRETARY TO PRESCRIBE REGULATIONS.—The Secretary shall prescribe such regulations as may be necessary to prevent avoidance or evasion of Federal income tax through the use of stapled entities. Such regulations may include (but shall not be limited to) regulations providing the extent to which 1 of such entities shall be treated as owning the other entity (to the extent of the stapled interest) and regulations providing that any tax imposed on the foreign corporation referred to in subsection (a)(1) may, if not paid by such corporation, be collected from the domestic corporation referred to in such subsection or the shareholders of such foreign corporation.

[Sec. 269B(c)]

(c) DEFINITIONS.—For purposes of this section—

(1) ENTITY.—The term "entity" means any corporation, partnership, trust, association, estate, or other form of carrying on a business or activity.

(2) STAPLED ENTITIES.—The term "stapled entities" means any group of 2 or more entities if more than 50 percent in value of the beneficial ownership in each of such entities consists of stapled interests.

(3) STAPLED INTERESTS.—Two or more interests are stapled interests if, by reason of form of ownership, restrictions on transfer, or other terms or conditions, in connection with the transfer of 1 of such interests the other such interests are also transferred or required to be transferred.

Income Tax—Entertainment Expenses

[Sec. 269B(d)]

(d) SPECIAL RULE FOR TREATIES.—Nothing in section 894 or 7852(d) or in any other provision of law shall be construed as permitting an exemption, by reason of any treaty obligation of the United States heretofore or hereafter entered into, from the provisions of this section.

[Sec. 269B(e)]

(e) SUBSECTION (a)(1) NOT TO APPLY IN CERTAIN CASES.—

(1) IN GENERAL.—Subsection (a)(1) shall not apply if it is established to the satisfaction of the Secretary that the domestic corporation and the foreign corporation referred to in such subsection are foreign owned.

(2) FOREIGN OWNED.—For purposes of paragraph (1), a corporation is foreign owned if less than 50 percent of—

(A) the total combined voting power of all classes of stock of such corporation entitled to vote, and

(B) the total value of the stock of the corporation,

is held directly (or indirectly through applying paragraphs (2) and (3) of section 958(a) and paragraph (4) of section 318(a)) by United States persons (as defined in section 7701(a)(30)).

[Sec. 274]

SEC. 274. DISALLOWANCE OF CERTAIN ENTERTAINMENT, ETC., EXPENSES.

* * *

[Sec. 274(c)]

(c) CERTAIN FOREIGN TRAVEL.—

(1) IN GENERAL.—In the case of any individual who travels outside the United States away from home in pursuit of a trade or business or in pursuit of an activity described in section 212, no deduction shall be allowed under section 162 or section 212 for that portion of the expenses of such travel otherwise allowable under such section which, under regulations prescribed by the Secretary, is not allocable to such trade or business or to such activity.

(2) EXCEPTION.—Paragraph (1) shall not apply to the expenses of any travel outside the United States away from home if—

(A) such travel does not exceed one week, or

(B) the portion of the time of travel outside the United States away from home which is not attributable to the pursuit of the taxpayer's trade or business or an activity described in section 212 is less than 25 percent of the total time on such travel.

(3) DOMESTIC TRAVEL EXCLUDED.—For purposes of this subsection, travel outside the United States does not include any travel from one point in the United States to another point in the United States.

* * *

[Sec. 274(h)]

(h) ATTENDANCE AT CONVENTIONS, ETC.—

(1) IN GENERAL.—In the case of any individual who attends a convention, seminar, or similar meeting which is held outside the North American area, no deduction shall be allowed under section 162 for expenses allocable to such meeting unless the taxpayer establishes that the meeting is directly related to the active conduct of his trade or business and that, after taking into account in the manner provided by regulations prescribed by the Secretary—

(A) the purpose of such meeting and the activities taking place at such meeting,

(B) the purposes and activities of the sponsoring organizations or groups,

(C) the residences of the active members of the sponsoring organization and the places at which other meetings of the sponsoring organization or groups have been held or will be held, and

(D) such other relevant factors as the taxpayer may present, it is as reasonable for the meeting to be held outside the North American area as within the North American area.

(2) CONVENTIONS ON CRUISE SHIPS.—In the case of any individual who attends a convention, seminar, or other meeting which is held on any cruise ship, no deduction shall be allowed under section 162 for expenses allocable to such meeting, unless the taxpayer meets the requirements of paragraph (5) and establishes that the meeting is directly related to the active conduct of his trade or business and that—

(A) the cruise ship is a vessel registered in the United States; and

(B) all ports of call of such cruise ship are located in the United States or in possessions of the United States.

With respect to cruises beginning in any calendar year, not more than $2,000 of the expenses attributable to an individual attending one or more meetings may be taken into account under section 162 by reason of the preceding sentence.

(3) DEFINITIONS.—For purposes of this subsection—

(A) NORTH AMERICAN AREA.—The term "North American area" means the United States, its possessions, and the Trust Territory of the Pacific Islands, and Canada and Mexico.

(B) CRUISE SHIP.—The term "cruise ship" means any vessel sailing within or without the territorial waters of the United States.

(4) SUBSECTION TO APPLY TO EMPLOYER AS WELL AS TO TRAVELER.—

(A) Except as provided in subparagraph (B), this subsection shall apply to deductions otherwise allowable under section 162 to any person, whether or not such person is the individual attending the convention, seminar, or similar meeting.

(B) This subsection shall not deny a deduction to any person other than the individual attending the convention, seminar, or similar meeting with respect to any amount paid by such person to or on behalf of such individual if includible in the gross income of such individual. The preceding sentence shall not apply if the amount is required to be included in any information return filed by such person under part III of subchapter A of chapter 61 and is not so included.

(5) REPORTING REQUIREMENTS.—No deduction shall be allowed under section 162 for expenses allocable to attendance at a convention, seminar, or similar meeting on any cruise ship unless the taxpayer claiming the deduction attaches to the return of tax on which the deduction is claimed—

(A) a written statement signed by the individual attending the meeting which includes—

(i) information with respect to the total days of the trip, excluding the days of transportation to and from the cruise ship port, and the number of hours of each day of the trip which such individual devoted to scheduled business activities,

(ii) a program of the scheduled business activities of the meeting, and

(iii) such other information as may be required in regulations prescribed by the Secretary; and

(B) a written statement signed by an officer of the organization or group sponsoring the meeting which includes—

(i) a schedule of business activities of each day of the meeting,

(ii) the number of hours which the individual attending the meeting attended such scheduled business activities, and

(iii) such other information as may be required in regulations prescribed by the Secretary.

(6) TREATMENT OF CONVENTIONS IN CERTAIN CARIBBEAN COUNTRIES.—

(A) IN GENERAL.—For purposes of this subsection, the term "North American area" includes, with respect to any convention, seminar, or similar meeting, any beneficiary country if (as of the time such meeting begins)—

(i) there is in effect a bilateral or multilateral agreement described in subparagraph (C) between such country and the United States providing for the exchange of information between the United States and such country, and

(ii) there is not in effect a finding by the Secretary that the tax laws of such country discriminate against conventions held in the United States.

(B) BENEFICIARY COUNTRY.—For purposes of this paragraph, the term "beneficiary country" has the meaning given to such term by section 212(a)(1)(A) of the Caribbean Basin Economic Recovery Act; except that such term shall include Bermuda.

(C) AUTHORITY TO CONCLUDE EXCHANGE OF INFORMATION AGREEMENTS.—

(i) IN GENERAL.—The Secretary is authorized to negotiate and conclude an agreement for the exchange of information with any beneficiary country. Except as provided in clause (ii), an exchange of information agreement shall provide for the exchange of such information (not limited to information concerning nationals or residents of the United States or the beneficiary country) as may be necessary or appropriate to carry out and enforce the tax laws of the United States and the beneficiary country (whether criminal or civil proceedings), including information which may otherwise be subject to nondisclosure provisions of the local law of the beneficiary country such as provisions respecting bank secrecy and bearer shares. The exchange of information agreement shall be terminable by either country on reasonable notice and shall provide that information received by either country will be disclosed only to persons or authorities (including courts and administrative bodies) involved in the administration or oversight of, or in the determination of appeals in respect of, taxes of the United States or the beneficiary country and will be used by such persons or authorities only for such purposes.

(ii) NONDISCLOSURE OF QUALIFIED CONFIDENTIAL INFORMATION SOUGHT FOR CIVIL TAX PURPOSES.—An exchange of information agreement need not provide for the exchange of qualified confidential information which is sought only for civil tax purposes if—

(I) the Secretary of the Treasury, after making all reasonable efforts to negotiate an agreement which includes the exchange of such information, determines that such an agreement cannot be negotiated but that the agreement which was negotiated will significantly assist in the administration and enforcement of the tax laws of the United States, and

(II) the President determines that the agreement as negotiated is in the national security interest of the United States.

(iii) QUALIFIED CONFIDENTIAL INFORMATION DEFINED.—For purposes of this subparagraph, the term "qualified confidential information" means information which is subject to the nondisclosure provisions of any local law of the beneficiary country regarding bank secrecy or ownership of bearer shares.

(iv) CIVIL TAX PURPOSES.—For purposes of this subparagraph, the determination of whether information is sought only for civil tax purposes shall be made by the requesting party.

(D) COORDINATION WITH OTHER PROVISIONS.—Any exchange of information agreement negotiated under subparagraph (C) shall be treated as an income tax convention for purposes of section 6103(k)(4). The Secretary may exercise his authority under subchapter A of chapter 78 to carry out any obligation of the United States under an agreement referred to in subparagraph (C).

(E) DETERMINATIONS PUBLISHED IN THE FEDERAL REGISTER.—The following shall be published in the Federal Register—

(i) any determination by the President under subparagraph (C)(ii) (including the reasons for such determination),

(ii) any determination by the Secretary under subparagraph (C)(ii) (including the reasons for such determination), and

(iii) any finding by the Secretary under subparagraph (A)(ii) (and any termination thereof).

(7) SEMINARS, ETC. FOR SECTION 212 PURPOSES.—No deduction shall be allowed under section 212 for expenses allocable to a convention, seminar, or similar meeting.

* * *

CARIBBEAN BASIN ECONOMIC RECOVERY ACT OF 1983

[Sec. 212]

SEC. 212. BENEFICIARY COUNTRY.

(a) DEFINITIONS; TERMINATION OF DESIGNATION

(1) For purposes of this chapter—

(A) The term "beneficiary country" means any country listed in subsection (b) of this section with respect to which there is in effect a proclamation by the President designating such country as a beneficiary country for purposes of this chapter. Before the President designates any country as a beneficiary country for purposes of this chapter, he shall notify the House of Representatives and the Senate of his intention to make such designation, together with the considerations entering into such decision.

(B) The term "entered" means entered, or withdrawn from warehouse for consumption, in the customs territory of the United States.

(C) The term "HTS" means Harmonized Tariff Schedule of the United States.

(D) The term "NAFTA" means the North American Free Trade Agreement entered into between the United States, Mexico, and Canada on December 17, 1992.

(E) The terms "WTO" and "WTO member" have the meanings given those terms in section 3501 of this title.

(2) If the President has designated any country as a beneficiary country for purposes of this chapter, he shall not terminate such designation (either by issuing a proclamation for that purpose or by issuing a proclamation which has the effect of terminating such designation) unless, at least sixty days before such termination, he has notified the House of Representatives and the Senate and has notified such country of his intention to terminate such designation, together with the considerations entering into such decision.

(b) COUNTRIES ELIGIBLE FOR DESIGNATION AS BENEFICIARY COUNTRIES; CONDITIONS

In designating countries as "beneficiary countries" under this chapter the President shall consider only the following countries and territories or successor political entities:

Anguilla	Haiti
Antigua and Barbuda	Honduras
Bahamas, The	Jamaica
Barbados	Montserrat
Belize	Netherlands Antilles
Cayman Islands	Nicaragua
Costa Rica	Panama
Dominica	Saint Christopher-Nevis
Dominican Republic	Saint Lucia
El Salvador	Saint Vincent and the Grenadines
Grenada	Surinam
Guatemala	Trinidad and Tobago
Guyana	Turks and Caicos Islands
	Virgin Islands, British

In addition, the President shall not designate any country a beneficiary country under this chapter—

(1) if such country is a Communist country;

(2) if such country—

(A) has nationalized, expropriated or otherwise seized ownership or control of property owned by a United States citizen or by a corporation, partnership, or association which is 50 per centum or more beneficially owned by United States citizens,

(B) has taken steps to repudiate or nullify—

(i) any existing contract or agreement with, or

(ii) any patent, trademark, or other intellectual property of,

a United States citizen or a corporation, partnership, or association which is 50 per centum or more beneficially owned by United States citizens, the effect of which is to nationalize, expropriate, or otherwise seize ownership or control of property so owned, or

(C) has imposed or enforced taxes or other exactions, restrictive maintenance or operational conditions, or other measures with respect to property so owned, the effect of which is to nationalize, expropriate, or otherwise seize ownership or control of such property, unless the President determines that—

(i) prompt, adequate, and effective compensation has been or is being made to such citizen, corporation, partnership, or association,

(ii) good-faith negotiations to provide prompt, adequate, and effective compensation under the applicable provisions of international law are in progress, or such country is otherwise taking steps to discharge its obligations under international law with respect to such citizen, corporation, partnership, or association, or

(iii) a dispute involving such citizen, corporation, partnership, or association, over compensation for such a seizure has been submitted to arbitration under the provisions of the Convention for the Settlement of Investment Disputes, or in another mutually agreed upon forum, and

promptly furnishes a copy of such determination to the Senate and House of Representatives;

(3) if such country fails to act in good faith in recognizing as binding or in enforcing arbitral awards in favor of United States citizens or a corporation, partnership or association which is 50 per centum or more beneficially owned by United States citizens, which have been made by arbitrators appointed for each case or by permanent arbitral bodies to which the parties involved have submitted their dispute;

(4) if such country affords preferential treatment to the products of a developed country, other than the United States, which has, or is likely to have, a significant adverse effect on United States commerce, unless the President has received assurances satisfactory to him that such preferential treatment will be eliminated or that action will be taken to assure that there will be no such significant adverse effect, and he reports those assurances to the Congress;

(5) if a government-owned entity in such country engages in the broadcast of copyrighted material, including films or television material, belonging to United States copyright owners without their express consent;

(6) unless such country is a signatory to a treaty, convention, protocol, or other agreement regarding the extradition of United States citizens; and

(7) if such country has not or is not taking steps to afford internationally recognized worker rights (as defined in section 2467(4) of this title) to workers in the country (including any designated zone in that country).

Paragraphs (1), (2), (3), (5), and (7) shall not prevent the designation of any country as a beneficiary country under this Act if the President determines that such designation will be in the national economic or security interest of the United States and reports such determination to the Congress with his reasons therefor.

(c) FACTORS DETERMINING DESIGNATION

In determining whether to designate any country a beneficiary country under this chapter, the President shall take into account—

(1) an expression by such country of its desire to be so designated;

(2) the economic conditions in such country, the living standards of its inhabitants, and any other economic factors which he deems appropriate;

(3) the extent to which such country has assured the United States it will provide equitable and reasonable access to the markets and basic commodity resources of such country;

(4) the degree to which such country follows the accepted rules of international trade provided for under the WTO Agreement and the multilateral trade agreements (as such terms are defined in paragraphs (9) and (4), respectively, of section 3501 of this title);

(5) the degree to which such country uses export subsidies or imposes export performance requirements or local content requirements which distort international trade;

(6) the degree to which the trade policies of such country as they relate to other beneficiary countries are contributing to the revitalization of the region;

(7) the degree to which such country is undertaking self-help measures to promote its own economic development;

(8) whether or not such country has taken or is taking steps to afford to workers in that country (including any designated zone in that country) internationally recognized worker rights;

(9) the extent to which such country provides under its law adequate and effective means for foreign nationals to secure, exercise, and enforce exclusive rights in intellectual property, including patent, trademark, and copyright rights;

(10) the extent to which such country prohibits its nationals from engaging in the broadcast of copyrighted material, including films or television material, belonging to United States copyright owners without their express consent; and

(11) the extent to which such country is prepared to cooperate with the United States in the administration of the provisions of this chapter.

(d) Omitted

(e) WITHDRAWAL OR SUSPENSION OF DUTY-FREE TREATMENT TO SPECIFIC ARTICLES

(1)(A) The President may, after the requirements of subsection (a)(2) of this section and paragraph (2) have been met—

>> (i) withdraw or suspend the designation of any country as a beneficiary country, or

>> (ii) withdraw, suspend, or limit the application of duty-free treatment under this chapter to any article of any country,

if, after such designation, the President determines that as a result of changed circumstances such country would be barred from designation as a beneficiary country under subsection (b) of this section.

> (B) The President may, after the requirements of subsection (a)(2) and paragraph (2) have been met

>> (i) withdraw or suspend the designation of any country as a CBTPA beneficiary country; or

>> (ii) withdraw, suspend, or limit the application of preferential treatment under section 2703(b)(2) and (3) of this title to any article of any country,

if, after such designation, the President determines that, as a result of changed circumstances, the performance of such country is not satisfactory under the criteria set forth in section 2703(b)(5)(B) of this title.

(2)(A) The President shall publish in the Federal Register notice of the action the President proposes to take under paragraph (1) at least 30 days prior to taking such action.

> (B) The United States Trade Representative shall, within the 30-day period beginning on the date on which the President publishes under subparagraph (A) notice of proposed action—

>> (i) accept written comments from the public regarding such proposed action,

>> (ii) hold a public hearing on such proposed action, and

>> (iii) publish in the Federal Register—

>>> (I) notice of the time and place of such hearing prior to the hearing, and

>>> (II) the time and place at which such written comments will be accepted.

(3) If preferential treatment under section 2703(b)(2) and (3) of this title is withdrawn, suspended, or limited with respect to a CBTPA beneficiary country, such country shall not be deemed to be a "party" for the purposes of applying section 2703(b)(5)(C) of this title to imports of articles for which preferential treatment has been withdrawn, suspended, or limited with respect to such country.

(f) REPORTING REQUIREMENTS

(1) IN GENERAL.—Not later than December 31, 2001, and every 2 years thereafter during the period this chapter is in effect, the United States Trade Representative shall submit to Congress a report regarding the operation of this chapter, including—

(A) with respect to subsections (b) and (c), the results of a general review of beneficiary countries based on the considerations described in such subsections; and

(B) the performance of each beneficiary country or CBTPA beneficiary country, as the case may be, under the criteria set forth in section 2703(b)(5)(B) of this title.

(2) PUBLIC COMMENT.—Before submitting the report described in paragraph (1), the United States Trade Representative shall publish a notice in the Federal Register requesting public comments on whether beneficiary countries are meeting the criteria listed in section 2703(b)(5)(B) of this title.

[Caribbean Basin Economic Recovery Act of 1983, P.L. 98-67, has been codified at 19 U.S.C. 2702.]

[Sec. 275]

SEC. 275. CERTAIN TAXES.

[Sec. 275(a)]

(a) GENERAL RULE.—No deduction shall be allowed for the following taxes:

* * *

(4) Income, war profits, and excess profits taxes imposed by the authority of any foreign country or possession of the United States if—

(A) the taxpayer chooses to take to any extent the benefits of section 901, or

(B) such taxes are paid or accrued with respect to foreign trade income (within the meaning of section 923(b)) of a FSC.

* * *

SUBCHAPTER C—CORPORATE DISTRIBUTIONS AND ADJUSTMENTS

PART I—DISTRIBUTIONS BY CORPORATIONS

Subpart A—Effects on Recipients

[Sec. 301]

SEC. 301. DISTRIBUTIONS OF PROPERTY.

[Sec. 301(a)]

(a) IN GENERAL.—Except as otherwise provided in this chapter, a distribution of property (as defined in section 317(a)) made by a corporation to a shareholder with respect to its stock shall be treated in the manner provided in subsection (c).

[Sec. 301(b)]

(b) AMOUNT DISTRIBUTED.—

(1) GENERAL RULE.—For purposes of this section, the amount of any distribution shall be the amount of money received, plus the fair market value of the other property received.

(2) REDUCTION FOR LIABILITIES.—The amount of any distribution determined under paragraph (1) shall be reduced (but not below zero) by—

(A) the amount of any liability of the corporation assumed by the shareholder in connection with the distribution, and

(B) the amount of any liability to which the property received by the shareholder is subject immediately before, and immediately after, the distribution.

(3) DETERMINATION OF FAIR MARKET VALUE.—For purposes of this section, fair market value shall be determined as of the date of the distribution.

[Sec. 301(c)]

(c) AMOUNT TAXABLE.—In the case of a distribution to which subsection (a) applies—

(1) AMOUNT CONSTITUTING DIVIDEND.—That portion of the distribution which is a dividend (as defined in section 316) shall be included in gross income.

(2) AMOUNT APPLIED AGAINST BASIS.—That portion of the distribution which is not a dividend shall be applied against and reduce the adjusted basis of the stock.

(3) AMOUNT IN EXCESS OF BASIS.—

(A) IN GENERAL.—Except as provided in subparagraph (B), that portion of the distribution which is not a dividend, to the extent that it exceeds the adjusted basis of the stock, shall be treated as gain from the sale or exchange of property.

(B) DISTRIBUTIONS OUT OF INCREASE IN VALUE ACCRUED BEFORE MARCH 1, 1913.—That portion of the distribution which is not a dividend, to the extent that it exceeds the adjusted basis of the stock and to the extent that it is out of increase in value accrued before March 1, 1913, shall be exempt from tax.

[Sec. 301(d)]

(d) BASIS.—The basis of property received in a distribution to which subsection (a) applies shall be the fair market value of such property.

[Sec. 301(e)]

(e) SPECIAL RULE FOR CERTAIN DISTRIBUTIONS RECEIVED BY 20 PERCENT CORPORATE SHAREHOLDER.—

(1) IN GENERAL.—Except to the extent otherwise provided in regulations, solely for purposes of determining the taxable income of any 20 percent corporate shareholder (and its adjusted basis in the stock of the distributing corporation), section 312 shall be applied with respect to the distributing corporation as if it did not contain subsections (k) and (n) thereof.

(2) 20 PERCENT CORPORATE SHAREHOLDER.—For purposes of this subsection, the term "20 percent corporate shareholder" means, with respect to any distribution, any corporation which owns (directly or through the application of section 318)—

(A) stock in the corporation making the distribution possessing at least 20 percent of the total combined voting power of all classes of stock entitled to vote, or

(B) at least 20 percent of the total value of all stock of the distributing corporation (except nonvoting stock which is limited and preferred as to dividends),

but only if, but for this subsection, the distributee corporation would be entitled to a deduction under section 243, 244, or 245 with respect to such distribution.

(3) APPLICATION OF SECTION 312(n)(7) NOT AFFECTED.—The reference in paragraph (1) to subsection (n) of section 312 shall be treated as not including a reference to paragraph (7) of such subsection.

(4) REGULATIONS.—The Secretary shall prescribe such regulations as may be necessary or appropriate to carry out the purposes of this subsection.

* * *

[Sec. 302]

SEC. 302. DISTRIBUTIONS IN REDEMPTION OF STOCK.

[Sec. 302(a)]

(a) GENERAL RULE.—If a corporation redeems its stock (within the meaning of section 317 (b)), and if paragraph (1), (2), (3), or (4) of subsection (b) applies, such redemption shall be treated as a distribution in part or full payment in exchange for the stock.

[Sec. 302(b)]

(b) REDEMPTIONS TREATED AS EXCHANGES.—

(1) REDEMPTIONS NOT EQUIVALENT TO DIVIDENDS.—Subsection (a) shall apply if the redemption is not essentially equivalent to a dividend.

(2) SUBSTANTIALLY DISPROPORTIONATE REDEMPTION OF STOCK.—

(A) IN GENERAL.—Subsection (a) shall apply if the distribution is substantially disproportionate with respect to the shareholder.

(B) LIMITATION.—This paragraph shall not apply unless immediately after the redemption the shareholder owns less than 50 percent of the total combined voting power of all classes of stock entitled to vote.

(C) DEFINITIONS.—For purposes of this paragraph, the distribution is substantially disproportionate if—

(i) the ratio which the voting stock of the corporation owned by the shareholder immediately after the redemption bears to all of the voting stock of the corporation at such time,

is less than 80 percent of—

(ii) the ratio which the voting stock of the corporation owned by the shareholder immediately before the redemption bears to all of the voting stock of the corporation at such time.

For purposes of this paragraph, no distribution shall be treated as substantially disproportionate unless the shareholder's ownership of the common stock of the corporation (whether voting or nonvoting) after and before redemption also meets the 80 percent requirement of the preceding sentence. For purposes of the preceding sentence, if there is more than one class of common stock, the determinations shall be made by reference to fair market value.

(D) SERIES OF REDEMPTIONS.—This paragraph shall not apply to any redemption made pursuant to a plan the purpose or effect of which is a series of redemptions resulting in a distribution which (in the aggregate) is not substantially disproportionate with respect to the shareholder.

(3) TERMINATION OF SHAREHOLDER'S INTEREST.—Subsection (a) shall apply if the redemption is in complete redemption of all of the stock of the corporation owned by the shareholder.

(4) REDEMPTION FROM NONCORPORATE SHAREHOLDER IN PARTIAL LIQUIDATION.—Subsection (a) shall apply to a distribution if such distribution is—

(A) in redemption of stock held by a shareholder who is not a corporation, and

(B) in partial liquidation of the distributing corporation.

(5) APPLICATION OF PARAGRAPHS.—In determining whether a redemption meets the requirements of paragraph (1), the fact that such redemption fails to meet the requirements of paragraph (2), (3), or (4) shall not be taken into account. If a redemption meets the requirements of paragraph (3) and also the requirements of paragraph (1), (2), or (4), then so much of subsection (c) (2) as would (but for this sentence) apply in respect of the acquisition of an interest in the corporation within the 10-year period beginning on the date of the distribution shall not apply.

[Sec. 302(c)]

(c) CONSTRUCTIVE OWNERSHIP OF STOCK.—

(1) IN GENERAL.—Except as provided in paragraph (2) of this subsection, section 318 (a) shall apply in determining the ownership of stock for purposes of this section.

(2) FOR DETERMINING TERMINATION OF INTEREST.—

(A) In the case of a distribution described in subsection (b) (3), section 318 (a) (1) shall not apply if—

(i) immediately after the distribution the distributee has no interest in the corporation (including an interest as officer, director, or employee), other than an interest as a creditor,

(ii) the distributee does not acquire any such interest (other than stock acquired by bequest or inheritance) within 10 years from the date of such distribution, and

(iii) the distributee, at such time and in such manner as the Secretary by regulations prescribes, files an agreement to notify the Secretary of any acquisition described in clause (ii) and to retain such records as may be necessary for the application of this paragraph.

If the distributee acquires such an interest in the corporation (other than by bequest or inheritance) within 10 years from the date of the distribution, then the periods of limitation provided in sections 6501 and 6502 on the making of an assessment and the collection by levy or a proceeding in court shall, with respect to any deficiency (including interest and additions to the tax) resulting from such acquisition, include one year immediately following the date on which the distributee (in accordance with regulations prescribed by the Secretary) notifies the Secretary of such acquisition; and such assessment and collection may be made notwithstanding any provision of law or rule of law which otherwise would prevent such assessment and collection.

(B) Subparagraph (A) of this paragraph shall not apply if—

(i) any portion of the stock redeemed was acquired, directly or indirectly, within the 10-year period ending on the date of the distribution by the distributee from a person the ownership of whose stock would (at the time of distribution) be attributable to the distributee under section 318(a), or

(ii) any person owns (at the time of the distribution) stock the ownership of which is attributable to the distributee under section 318(a) and such person acquired any stock in the corporation, directly or indirectly, from the distributee within the 10-year period ending on the date of the distribution, unless such stock so acquired from the distributee is redeemed in the same transaction.

The preceding sentence shall not apply if the acquisition (or, in the case of clause (ii), the disposition) by the distributee did not have as one of its principal purposes the avoidance of Federal income tax.

(C) SPECIAL RULE FOR WAIVERS BY ENTITIES.—

(i) IN GENERAL.—Subparagraph (A) shall not apply to a distribution to any entity unless—

(I) such entity and each related person meet the requirements of clauses (i), (ii), and (iii) of subparagraph (A), and

(II) each related person agrees to be jointly and severally liable for any deficiency (including interest and additions to tax) resulting from an acquisition described in clause (ii) of subparagraph (A).

In any case to which the preceding sentence applies, the second sentence of subparagraph (A) and subparagraph (B)(ii) shall be applied by substituting "distributee or any related person" for "distributee" each place it appears.

(ii) DEFINITIONS.—For purposes of this subparagraph—

(I) the term "entity" means a partnership, estate, trust, or corporation; and

(II) the term "related person" means any person to whom ownership of stock in the corporation is (at the time of the distribution) attributable under section 318(a)(1) if such stock is further attributable to the entity under section 318(a)(3).

[Sec. 302(d)]

(d) REDEMPTIONS TREATED AS DISTRIBUTIONS OF PROPERTY.—Except as otherwise provided in this subchapter, if a corporation redeems its stock (within the meaning of section 317 (b)), and if subsection (a) of this section does not apply, such redemption shall be treated as a distribution of property to which section 301 applies.

[Sec. 302(e)]

(e) PARTIAL LIQUIDATION DEFINED.—

(1) IN GENERAL.—For purposes of subsection (b)(4), a distribution shall be treated as in partial liquidation of a corporation if—

(A) the distribution is not essentially equivalent to a dividend (determined at the corporate level rather than at the shareholder level), and

(B) the distribution is pursuant to a plan and occurs within the taxable year in which the plan is adopted or within the succeeding taxable year.

(2) TERMINATION OF BUSINESS.—The distributions which meet the requirements of paragraph (1)(A) shall include (but shall not be limited to) a distribution which meets the requirements of subparagraphs (A) and (B) of this paragraph:

(A) The distribution is attributable to the distributing corporation's ceasing to conduct, or consists of the assets of, a qualified trade or business.

(B) Immediately after the distribution, the distributing corporation is actively engaged in the conduct of a qualified trade or business.

(3) QUALIFIED TRADE OR BUSINESS.—For purposes of paragraph (2), the term "qualified trade or business" means any trade or business which—

(A) was actively conducted throughout the 5-year period ending on the date of the redemption, and

(B) was not acquired by the corporation within such period in a transaction in which gain or loss was recognized in whole or in part.

(4) REDEMPTION MAY BE PRO RATA.—Whether or not a redemption meets the requirements of subparagraphs (A) and (B) of paragraph (2) shall be determined without regard to whether or not the redemption is pro rata with respect to all of the shareholders of the corporation.

(5) TREATMENT OF CERTAIN PASS-THRU ENTITIES.—For purposes of determining under subsection (b)(4) whether any stock is held by a shareholder who is not a corporation, any stock held by a partnership, estate, or trust shall be treated as if it were actually held proportionately by its partners or beneficiaries.

* * *

[Sec. 304]

SEC. 304. REDEMPTION THROUGH USE OF RELATED CORPORATIONS.

[Sec. 304(a)]

(a) TREATMENT OF CERTAIN STOCK PURCHASES.—

(1) ACQUISITION BY RELATED CORPORATION (OTHER THAN SUBSIDIARY).—For purposes of sections 302 and 303, if—

(A) one or more persons are in control of each of two corporations, and

(B) in return for property, one of the corporations acquires stock in the other corporation from the person (or persons) so in control,

then (unless paragraph (2) applies) such property shall be treated as a distribution in redemption of the stock of the corporation acquiring such stock. To the extent that such distribution is treated as a distribution to which section 301 applies, the transferor and the acquiring corporation shall be treated in the same manner as if the transferor had transferred the stock so acquired to the acquiring corporation in exchange for stock of the acquiring corporation in a transaction to which section 351(a) applies, and then the acquiring corporation had redeemed the stock it was treated as issuing in such transaction.

(2) ACQUISITION BY SUBSIDIARY.—For purposes of sections 302 and 303, if—

(A) in return for property, one corporation acquires from a shareholder of another corporation stock in such other corporation, and

(B) the issuing corporation controls the acquiring corporation,

then such property shall be treated as a distribution in redemption of the stock of the issuing corporation.

[Sec. 304(b)]

(b) SPECIAL RULES FOR APPLICATION OF SUBSECTION (a).—

(1) RULE FOR DETERMINATIONS UNDER SECTION 302(b).—In the case of any acquisition of stock to which subsection (a) of this section applies, determinations as to whether the acquisition is, by reason of section 302(b), to be treated as a distribution in part or full payment in exchange for the stock shall be made by reference to the stock of the issuing corporation. In applying section 318(a) (relating to constructive ownership of stock) with respect to section 302(b) for purposes of this paragraph, sections 318(a)(2)(C) and 318(a)(3)(C) shall be applied without regard to the 50 percent limitation contained therein.

(2) AMOUNT CONSTITUTING DIVIDEND.—In the case of any acquisition of stock to which subsection (a) applies, the determination of the amount which is a dividend (and the source thereof) shall be made as if the property were distributed—

(A) by the acquiring corporation to the extent of its earnings and profits, and

(B) then by the issuing corporation to the extent of its earnings and profits.

(3) COORDINATION WITH SECTION 351.—

(A) PROPERTY TREATED AS RECEIVED IN REDEMPTION.—Except as otherwise provided in this paragraph, subsection (a) (and not section 351 and not so much of sections 357 and 358 as relates to section 351) shall apply to any property received in a distribution described in subsection (a).

(B) CERTAIN ASSUMPTIONS OF LIABILITY, ETC.—

(i) IN GENERAL.—In the case of an acquisition described in section 351, subsection (a) shall not apply to any liability—

(I) assumed by the acquiring corporation, or

(II) to which the stock is subject,

if such liability was incurred by the transferor to acquire the stock. For purposes of the preceding sentence, the term "stock" means stock referred to in paragraph (1)(B) or (2)(A) of subsection (a).

(ii) EXTENSION OF OBLIGATIONS, ETC.—For purposes of clause (i), an extension, renewal, or refinancing of a libility which meets the requirements of clause (i) shall be treated as meeting such requirements.

(iii) CLAUSE (i) DOES NOT APPLY TO STOCK ACQUIRED FROM RELATED PERSON EXCEPT WHERE COMPLETE TERMINATION.—Clause (i) shall apply only to stock acquired by the transferor from a person—

(I) none of whose stock is attributable to the transferor under section 318(a) (other than paragraph (4) thereof), or

(II) who satisfies rules similar to the rules of section 302(c)(2) with respect to both the acquiring and the issuing corporations (determined as if such person were a distributee of each such corporation).

(C) DISTRIBUTIONS INCIDENT TO FORMATION OF BANK HOLDING COMPANIES.—If—

(i) pursuant to a plan, control of a bank is acquired and within 2 years after the date on which such control is acquired, stock constituting control of such bank is transferred to a BHC in connection with its formation,

(ii) incident to the formation of the BHC there is a distribution of property described in subsection (a), and

(iii) the shareholders of the BHC who receive distributions of such property do not have control of such BHC,

then, subsection (a) shall not apply to any securities received by a qualified minority shareholder incident to the formation of such BHC. For purposes of this subparagraph, any assumption of (or acquisition of stock subject to) a liability under subparagraph (B) shall not be treated as a distribution of property.

(D) DEFINITIONS AND SPECIAL RULE.—For purposes of subparagraph (C) and this subparagraph—

(i) QUALIFIED MINORITY SHAREHOLDER.—The term "qualified minority shareholder" means any shareholder who owns less than 10 percent (in value) of the stock of the BHC. For purposes of the preceding sentence, the rules of paragraph (3) of subsection (c) shall apply.

(ii) BHC.—The term "BHC" means a bank holding company (within the meaning of section 2(a) of the Bank Holding Company Act of 1956).

(iii) SPECIAL RULE IN CASE OF BHC's FORMED BEFORE 1985.—In the case of a BHC which is formed before 1985, clause (i) of subparagraph (C) shall not apply.

Income Tax—Related Corporations

(4) TREATMENT OF CERTAIN INTRAGROUP TRANSACTIONS.—

(A) IN GENERAL.—In the case of any transfer described in subsection (a) of stock from 1 member of an affiliated group to another member of such group, proper adjustments shall be made to—

(i) the adjusted basis of any intragroup stock, and

(ii) the earnings and profits of any member of such group,

to the extent necessary to carry out the purposes of this section.

(B) DEFINITIONS.—For purposes of this paragraph—

(i) AFFILIATED GROUP.—The term "affiliated group" has the meaning given such term by section 1504(a).

(ii) INTRAGROUP STOCK.—The term "intragroup stock" means any stock which—

(I) is in a corporation which is a member of an affiliated group, and

(II) is held by another member of such group.

(5) ACQUISITIONS BY FOREIGN CORPORATIONS.—

(A) IN GENERAL.—In the case of any acquisition to which subsection (a) applies in which the acquiring corporation is a foreign corporation, the only earnings and profits taken into account under paragraph (2)(A) shall be those earnings and profits—

(i) which are attributable (under regulations prescribed by the Secretary) to stock of the acquiring corporation owned (within the meaning of section 958(a)) by a corporation or individual which is—

(I) a United States shareholder (within the meaning of section 951(b)) of the acquiring corporation, and

(II) the transferor or a person who bears a relationship to the transferor described in section 267(b) or 707(b), and

(ii) which were accumulated during the period or periods such stock was owned by such person while the acquiring corporation was a controlled foreign corporation.

(B) REGULATIONS.—The Secretary shall prescribe such regulations as are appropriate to carry out the purposes of this paragraph.

(6) AVOIDANCE OF MULTIPLE INCLUSIONS, ETC.—In the case of any acquisition to which subsection (a) applies in which the acquiring corporation or the issuing corporation is a foreign corporation, the Secretary shall prescribe such regulations as are appropriate in order to eliminate a multiple inclusion of any item in income by reason of this subpart and to provide appropriate basis adjustments (including modifications to the application of sections 959 and 961).

[Sec. 304(c)]

(c) CONTROL.—

(1) IN GENERAL.—For purposes of this section, control means the ownership of stock possessing at least 50 percent of the total combined voting power of all classes of stock entitled to vote, or at least 50 percent of the total value of shares of all classes of stock. If a person (or persons) is in control (within the meaning of the preceding sentence) of a corporation which in turn owns at least 50 percent of the total combined voting power of all stock entitled to vote of another corporation, or owns at least 50 percent of the total value of the shares of all classes of stock of another corporation, then such person (or persons) shall be treated as in control of such other corporation.

(2) STOCK ACQUIRED IN THE TRANSACTION.—For purposes of subsection (a)(1)—

(A) GENERAL RULE.—Where 1 or more persons in control of the issuing corporation transfer stock of such corporation in exchange for stock of the acquiring corporation, the stock of the acquiring corporation received shall be taken into account in determining whether such person or persons are in control of the acquiring corporation.

Sec. 304(c)(2)(A)

(B) DEFINITION OF CONTROL GROUP.—Where 2 or more persons in control of the issuing corporation transfer stock of such corporation to acquiring corporation and, after the transfer, the transferors are in control of the acquiring corporation, the person or persons in control of each corporation shall include each of the persons who so transfer stock.

(3) CONSTRUCTIVE OWNERSHIP.—

(A) IN GENERAL.—Section 318(a) (relating to constructive ownership of stock) shall apply for purposes of determining control under this section.

(B) MODIFICATION OF 50-PERCENT LIMITATIONS IN SECTION 318.—For purposes of subparagraph (A)—

(i) paragraph (2)(C) of section 318(a) shall be applied by substituting "5 percent" for "50 percent", and

(ii) paragraph (3)(C) of section 318(a) shall be applied—

(I) by substituting "5 percent" for "50 percent", and

(II) in any case where such paragraph would not apply but for subclause (I), by considering a corporation as owning the stock (other than stock in such corporation) owned by or for any shareholder of such corporation in that proportion which the value of the stock which such shareholder owned in such corporation bears to the value of all stock in such corporation.

Subpart B—Effects on Corporation

[Sec. 311]

SEC. 311. TAXABILITY OF CORPORATION ON DISTRIBUTION.

[Sec. 311(a)]

(a) GENERAL RULE.—Except as provided in subsection (b), no gain or loss shall be recognized to a corporation on the distribution (not in complete liquidation) with respect to its stock of—

(1) its stock (or rights to acquire its stock), or

(2) property.

[Sec. 311(b)]

(b) DISTRIBUTIONS OF APPRECIATED PROPERTY.—

(1) IN GENERAL.—If—

(A) a corporation distributes property (other than an obligation of such corporation) to a shareholder in a distribution to which subpart A applies, and

(B) the fair market value of such property exceeds its adjusted basis (in the hands of the distributing corporation),

then gain shall be recognized to the distributing corporation as if such property were sold to the distributee at its fair market value.

(2) TREATMENT OF LIABILITIES.—Rules similar to the rules of section 336(b) shall apply for purposes of this subsection.

(3) SPECIAL RULE FOR CERTAIN DISTRIBUTIONS OF PARTNERSHIP OR TRUST INTERESTS.—If the property distributed consists of an interest in a partnership or trust, the Secretary may by regulations provide that the amount of the gain recognized under paragraph (1) shall be computed without regard to any loss attributable to property contributed to the partnership or trust for the principal purpose of recognizing such loss on the distribution.

[Sec. 312]

SEC. 312. EFFECT ON EARNINGS AND PROFITS.

* * *

[Sec. 312(k)]

(k) EFFECT OF DEPRECIATION ON EARNINGS AND PROFITS.—

(1) GENERAL RULE.—For purposes of computing the earnings and profits of a corporation for any taxable year beginning after June 30, 1972, the allowance for depreciation (and amortization, if any) shall be deemed to be the amount which would be allowable for such year if the straight line method of depreciation had been used for each taxable year beginning after June 30, 1972.

(2) EXCEPTION.—If for any taxable year a method of depreciation was used by the taxpayer which the Secretary has determined results in a reasonable allowance under section 167(a) and which is the unit-of-production method or other method not expressed in a term of years, then the adjustment to earnings and profits for depreciation for such year shall be determined under the method so used (in lieu of the straight line method).

(3) EXCEPTION FOR TANGIBLE PROPERTY.—

(A) IN GENERAL.—Except as provided in subparagraph (B), in the case of tangible property to which section 168 applies, the adjustment to earnings and profits for depreciation for any taxable year shall be determined under the alternative depreciation system (within the meaning of section 168(g)(2)).

(B) TREATMENT OF AMOUNTS DEDUCTIBLE UNDER SECTION 179, 179A, or 179B.—For purposes of computing the earnings and profits of a corporation, any amount deductible under section 179, 179A, or 179B shall be allowed as a deduction ratably over the period of 5 taxable years (beginning with the taxable year for which such amount is deductible under section 179, 179A, or 179B, as the case may be).

(4) CERTAIN FOREIGN CORPORATIONS.—The provisions of paragraph (1) shall not apply in computing the earnings and profits of a foreign corporation for any taxable year for which less than 20 percent of the gross income from all sources of such corporation is derived from sources within the United States.

(5) BASIS ADJUSTMENT NOT TAKEN INTO ACCOUNT.—In computing the earnings and profits of a corporation for any taxable year, the allowance for depreciation (and amortization, if any) shall be computed without regard to any basis adjustment under section 50(c).

* * *

Subpart C—Definitions; Constructive Ownership of Stock

[Sec. 316]

SEC. 316. DIVIDEND DEFINED.

[Sec. 316(a)]

(a) GENERAL RULE.—For purposes of this subtitle, the term "dividend" means any distribution of property made by a corporation to its shareholders—

(1) out of its earnings and profits accumulated after February 28, 1913, or

(2) out of its earnings and profits of the taxable year (computed as of the close of the taxable year without diminution by reason of any distributions made during the taxable year), without regard to the amount of the earnings and profits at the time the distribution was made.

Except as otherwise provided in this subtitle, every distribution is made out of earnings and profits to the extent thereof, and from the most recently accumulated earnings and profits. To the extent that any distribution is, under any provision of this subchapter, treated as a distribution of property to which section 301 applies, such distribution shall be treated as a distribution of property for purposes of this subsection.

[Sec. 316(b)]

(b) SPECIAL RULES.—

(1) CERTAIN INSURANCE COMPANY DIVIDENDS.—The definition in subsection (a) shall not apply to the term "dividend" as used in subchapter L in any case where the reference is to dividends of insurance companies paid to policyholders as such.

(2) DISTRIBUTIONS BY PERSONAL HOLDING COMPANIES.—

(A) In the case of a corporation which—

(i) under the law applicable to the taxable year in which the distribution is made, is a personal holding company (as defined in section 542), or

(ii) for the taxable year in respect of which the distribution is made under section 563(b) (relating to dividends paid after the close of the taxable year), or section 547 (relating to deficiency dividends), or the corresponding provisions of prior law, is a personal holding company under the law applicable to such taxable year,

the term "dividend" also means any distribution of property (whether or not a dividend as defined in subsection (a)) made by the corporation to its shareholders, to the extent of its undistributed personal holding company income (determined under section 545 without regard to distributions under this paragraph) for such year.

(B) For purposes of subparagraph (A), the term "distribution of property" includes a distribution in complete liquidation occurring within 24 months after the adoption of a plan of liquidation, but—

(i) only to the extent of the amounts distributed to distributees other than corporate shareholders, and

(ii) only to the extent that the corporation designates such amounts as a dividend distribution and duly notifies such distributees of such designation, under regulations prescribed by the Secretary, but

(iii) not in excess of the sum of such distributees' allocable share of the undistributed personal holding company income for such year, computed without regard to this subparagraph or section 562(b).

(3) DEFICIENCY DIVIDEND DISTRIBUTIONS BY A REGULATED INVESTMENT COMPANY OR REAL ESTATE INVESTMENT TRUST.—The term "dividend" also means any distribution of property (whether or not a dividend as defined in subsection (a)) which constitutes a "deficiency dividend" as defined in section 860(f).

[Sec. 317]

SEC. 317. OTHER DEFINITIONS.

[Sec. 317(a)]

(a) PROPERTY.—For purposes of this part, the term "property" means money, securities, and any other property; except that such term does not include stock in the corporation making the distribution (or rights to acquire such stock).

* * *

[Sec. 318]

SEC. 318. CONSTRUCTIVE OWNERSHIP OF STOCK.

[Sec. 318(a)]

(a) GENERAL RULE.—For purposes of those provisions of this subchapter to which the rules contained in this section are expressly made applicable—

(1) MEMBERS OF FAMILY.—

(A) IN GENERAL.—An individual shall be considered as owning the stock owned, directly or indirectly, by or for—

(i) his spouse (other than a spouse who is legally separated from the individual under a decree of divorce or separate maintenance), and

(ii) his children, grandchildren, and parents.

(B) EFFECT OF ADOPTION.—For purposes of subparagraph (A) (ii), a legally adopted child of an individual shall be treated as a child of such individual by blood.

(2) ATTRIBUTION FROM PARTNERSHIPS, ESTATES, TRUSTS, AND CORPORATIONS.—

(A) FROM PARTNERSHIPS AND ESTATES.—Stock owned, directly or indirectly, by or for a partnership or estate shall be considered as owned proportionately by its partners or beneficiaries.

(B) FROM TRUSTS.—

(i) Stock owned, directly or indirectly, by or for a trust (other than an employees' trust described in section 401(a) which is exempt from tax under section 501(a)) shall be considered as owned by its beneficiaries in proportion to the actuarial interest of such beneficiaries in such trust.

(ii) Stock owned, directly or indirectly, by or for any portion of a trust of which a person is considered the owner under subpart E of part I of subchapter J (relating to grantors and others treated as substantial owners) shall be considered as owned by such person.

(C) FROM CORPORATIONS.—If 50 percent or more in value of the stock in a corporation is owned, directly or indirectly, by or for any person, such person shall be considered as owning the stock owned, directly or indirectly, by or for such corporation, in that proportion which the value of the stock which such person so owns bears to the value of all the stock in such corporation.

(3) ATTRIBUTION TO PARTNERSHIPS, ESTATES, TRUSTS, AND CORPORATIONS.—

(A) TO PARTNERSHIPS AND ESTATES.—Stock owned, directly or indirectly, by or for a partner or a beneficiary of an estate shall be considered as owned by the partnership or estate.

(B) TO TRUSTS.—

(i) Stock owned, directly or indirectly, by or for a beneficiary of a trust (other than an employees' trust described in section 401(a) which is exempt from tax under section 501 (a)) shall be considered as owned by the trust, unless such beneficiary's interest in the trust is a remote contingent interest. For purposes of this clause, a contingent interest of a beneficiary in a trust shall be considered remote if, under the maximum exercise of discretion by the trustee in favor of such beneficiary, the value of such interest, computed actuarially, is 5 percent or less of the value of the trust property.

(ii) Stock owned, directly or indirectly, by or for a person who is considered the owner of any portion of a trust under subpart E of part I of subchapter J (relating to grantors and others treated as substantial owners) shall be considered as owned by the trust.

(C) TO CORPORATIONS.—If 50 percent or more in value of the stock in a corporation is owned, directly or indirectly, by or for any person, such corporation shall be considered as owning the stock owned, directly or indirectly, by or for such person.

(4) OPTIONS.—If any person has an option to acquire stock, such stock shall be considered as owned by such person. For purposes of this paragraph, an option to acquire such an option, and each one of a series of such options, shall be considered as an option to acquire such stock.

(5) OPERATING RULES.—

(A) IN GENERAL.—Except as provided in subparagraphs (B) and (C), stock constructively owned by a person by reason of the application of paragraph (1), (2), (3), or (4), shall, for purposes of applying paragraphs (1), (2), (3), and (4), be considered as actually owned by such person.

(B) MEMBERS OF FAMILY.—Stock constructively owned by an individual by reason of the application of paragraph (1) shall not be considered as owned by him for purposes of again applying paragraph (1) in order to make another the constructive owner of such stock.

(C) PARTNERSHIPS, ESTATES, TRUSTS, AND CORPORATIONS.—Stock constructively owned by a partnership, estate, trust, or corporation by reason of the application of paragraph (3) shall not be considered as owned by it for purposes of applying paragraph (2) in order to make another the constructive owner of such stock.

(D) OPTION RULE IN LIEU OF FAMILY RULE.—For purposes of this paragraph, if stock may be considered as owned by an individual under paragraph (1) or (4), it shall be considered as owned by him under paragraph (4).

(E) S CORPORATION TREATED AS PARTNERSHIP.—For purposes of this subsection—

(i) an S corporation shall be treated as a partnership, and

(ii) any shareholder of the S corporation shall be treated as a partner of such partnership.

The preceding sentence shall not apply for purposes of determining whether stock in the S corporation is constructively owned by any person.

* * *

PART II—CORPORATE LIQUIDATIONS

Subpart A—Effects on Recipients

[Sec. 331]

SEC. 331. GAIN OR LOSS TO SHAREHOLDERS IN CORPORATE LIQUIDATIONS.

[Sec. 331(a)]

(a) DISTRIBUTIONS IN COMPLETE LIQUIDATION TREATED AS EXCHANGES.—Amounts received by a shareholder in a distribution in complete liquidation of a corporation shall be treated as in full payment in exchange for the stock.

[Sec. 331(b)]

(b) NONAPPLICATION OF SECTION 301.—Section 301 (relating to effects on shareholder of distributions of property) shall not apply to any distribution of property (other than a distribution referred to in paragraph (2)(B) of section 316(b)), in complete liquidation.

* * *

[Sec. 332]

SEC. 332. COMPLETE LIQUIDATIONS OF SUBSIDIARIES.

[Sec. 332(a)]

(a) GENERAL RULE.—No gain or loss shall be recognized on the receipt by a corporation of property distributed in complete liquidation of another corporation.

[Sec. 332(b)]

(b) LIQUIDATIONS TO WHICH SECTION APPLIES.—For purposes of this section, a distribution shall be considered to be in complete liquidation only if—

(1) the corporation receiving such property was, on the date of the adoption of the plan of liquidation, and has continued to be at all times until the receipt of the property, the owner of stock (in such other corporation) meeting the requirements of section 1504(a)(2); and either

(2) the distribution is by such other corporation in complete cancellation or redemption of all its stock, and the transfer of all the property occurs within the taxable year; in such case the adoption by the shareholders of the resolution under which is authorized the distribution of all the assets of such corporation in complete cancellation or redemption of all its stock shall be considered an adoption of a plan of liquidation, even though no time for the completion of the transfer of the property is specified in such resolution; or

(3) such distribution is one of a series of distributions by such other corporation in complete cancellation or redemption of all its stock in accordance with a plan of liquidation under which the transfer of all the property under the liquidation is to be completed within 3 years from the close of the taxable year during which is made the first of the series of distributions under the plan, except that if such transfer is not completed within such period, or if the taxpayer does not continue qualified under paragraph (1) until the completion of such transfer, no distribution under the plan shall be considered a distribution in complete liquidation.

If such transfer of all the property does not occur within the taxable year, the Secretary may require of the taxpayer such bond, or waiver of the statute of limitations on assessment and collection, or both, as he may deem necessary to insure, if the transfer of the property is not completed within such 3-year period, or if the taxpayer does not continue qualified under paragraph (1) until the completion of such transfer, the assessment and collection of all income taxes then imposed by law for such taxable year or subsequent taxable years, to the extent attributable to property so received. A distribution otherwise constituting a distribution in complete liquidation within the meaning of this subsection shall not be considered as not constituting such a distribution merely because it does not constitute a distribution or liquidation within the meaning of the corporate law under which the distribution is made; and for purposes of this subsection a transfer of property of such other corporation to the taxpayer shall not be considered as not constituting a distribution (or one of a series of distributions) in complete cancellation or redemption of all the stock of such other corporation, merely because the carrying out of the plan involves (A) the transfer under the plan to the taxpayer by such other corporation of property, not attributable to shares owned by the taxpayer, on an exchange described in section 361, and (B) the complete cancellation or redemption under the plan, as a result of exchanges described in section 354, of the shares not owned by the taxpayer.

[Sec. 332(c)]

(c) DEDUCTIBLE LIQUIDATING DISTRIBUTIONS OF REGULATED INVESTMENT COMPANIES AND REAL ESTATE INVESTMENT TRUSTS.—If a corporation receives a distribution from a regulated investment company or a real estate investment trust which is considered under subsection (b) as being in complete liquidation of such company or trust, then, notwithstanding any other provision of this chapter, such corporation shall recognize and treat as a dividend from such company or trust an amount equal to the deduction for dividends paid allowable to such company or trust by reason of such distribution.

[Sec. 332(d)]

(d) RECOGNITION OF GAIN ON LIQUIDATION OF CERTAIN HOLDING COMPANIES.—

(1) IN GENERAL.—In the case of any distribution to a foreign corporation in complete liquidation of an applicable holding company—

(A) subsection (a) and section 331 shall not apply to such distribution, and

(B) such distribution shall be treated as a distribution to which section 301 applies.

(2) APPLICABLE HOLDING COMPANY.—For purposes of this subsection:

(A) IN GENERAL.—The term "applicable holding company" means any domestic corporation—

(i) which is a common parent of an affiliated group,

(ii) stock of which is directly owned by the distributee foreign corporation,

(iii) substantially all of the assets of which consist of stock in other members of such affiliated group, and

(iv) which has not been in existence at all times during the 5 years immediately preceding the date of the liquidation.

(B) AFFILIATED GROUP.—For purposes of this subsection, the term "affiliated group" has the meaning given such term by section 1504(a) (without regard to paragraphs (2) and (4) of section 1504(b)).

(3) COORDINATION WITH SUBPART F.—If the distributee of a distribution described in paragraph (1) is a controlled foreign corporation (as defined in section 957), then notwith-

standing paragraph (1) or subsection (a), such distribution shall be treated as a distribution to which section 331 applies.

(4) REGULATIONS.—The Secretary shall provide such regulations as appropriate to prevent the abuse of this subsection, including regulations which provide, for the purposes of clause (iv) of paragraph (2)(A), that a corporation is not in existence for any period unless it is engaged in the active conduct of a trade or business or owns a significant ownership interest in another corporation so engaged.

[Sec. 334]

SEC. 334. BASIS OF PROPERTY RECEIVED IN LIQUIDATIONS.

[Sec. 334(a)]

(a) GENERAL RULE.—If property is received in a distribution in complete liquidation, and if gain or loss is recognized on receipt of such property, then the basis of the property in the hands of the distributee shall be the fair market value of such property at the time of the distribution.

[Sec. 334(b)]

(b) LIQUIDATION OF SUBSIDIARY.—

(1) IN GENERAL.—If property is received by a corporate distributee in a distribution in a complete liquidation to which section 332 applies (or in a transfer described in section 337(b)(1)), the basis of such property in the hands of such distributee shall be the same as it would be in the hands of the transferor; except that the basis of such property in the hands of such distributee shall be the fair market value of the property at the time of the distribution—

(A) in any case in which gain or loss is recognized by the liquidating corporation with respect to such property, or

(B) in any case in which the liquidating corporation is a foreign corporation, the corporate distributee is a domestic corporation, and the corporate distributee's aggregate adjusted bases of property described in section 362(e)(1)(B) which is distributed in such liquidation would (but for this subparagraph) exceed the fair market value of such property immediately after such liquidation.

(2) CORPORATE DISTRIBUTEE.—For purposes of this subsection, the term "corporate distributee" means only the corporation which meets the stock ownership requirements specified in section 332(b).

Subpart B—Effects on Corporation

[Sec. 336]

SEC. 336. GAIN OR LOSS RECOGNIZED ON PROPERTY DISTRIBUTED IN COMPLETE LIQUIDATION.

[Sec. 336(a)]

(a) GENERAL RULE.—Except as otherwise provided in this section or section 337, gain or loss shall be recognized to a liquidating corporation on the distribution of property in complete liquidation as if such property were sold to the distributee at its fair market value.

[Sec. 336(b)]

(b) TREATMENT OF LIABILITIES.—If any property distributed in the liquidation is subject to a liability or the shareholder assumes a liability of the liquidating corporation in connection with the distribution, for purposes of subsection (a) and section 337, the fair market value of such property shall be treated as not less than the amount of such liability.

[Sec. 336(c)]

(c) EXCEPTION FOR LIQUIDATIONS WHICH ARE PART OF A REORGANIZATION.—For provision providing that this subpart does not apply to distributions in pursuance of a plan of reorganization, see section 361(c)(4).

[Sec. 336(d)]

(d) LIMITATIONS ON RECOGNITION OF LOSS.—

(1) NO LOSS RECOGNIZED IN CERTAIN DISTRIBUTIONS TO RELATED PERSONS.—

(A) IN GENERAL.—No loss shall be recognized to a liquidating corporation on the distribution of any property to a related person (within the meaning of section 267) if—

(i) such distribution is not pro rata, or

(ii) such property is disqualified property.

(B) DISQUALIFIED PROPERTY.—For purposes of subparagraph (A), the term "disqualified property" means any property which is acquired by the liquidating corporation in a transaction to which section 351 applied, or as a contribution to capital, during the 5-year period ending on the date of the distribution. Such term includes any property if the adjusted basis of such property is determined (in whole or in part) by reference to the adjusted basis of property described in the preceding sentence.

(2) SPECIAL RULE FOR CERTAIN PROPERTY ACQUIRED IN CERTAIN CARRYOVER BASIS TRANSACTIONS.—

(A) IN GENERAL.—For purposes of determining the amount of loss recognized by any liquidating corporation on any sale, exchange, or distribution of property described in subparagraph (B), the adjusted basis of such property shall be reduced (but not below zero) by the excess (if any) of—

(i) the adjusted basis of such property immediately after its acquisition by such corporation, over

(ii) the fair market value of such property as of such time.

(B) DESCRIPTION OF PROPERTY.—

(i) IN GENERAL.—For purposes of subparagraph (A), property is described in this subparagraph if—

(I) such property is acquired by the liquidating corporation in a transaction to which section 351 applied or as a contribution to capital, and

(II) the acquisition of such property by the liquidating corporation was part of a plan a principal purpose of which was to recognize loss by the liquidating corporation with respect to such property in connection with the liquidation.

Other property shall be treated as so described if the adjusted basis of such other property is determined (in whole or in part) by reference to the adjusted basis of property described in the preceding sentence.

(ii) CERTAIN ACQUISITIONS TREATED AS PART OF PLAN.—For purposes of clause (i), any property described in clause (i)(I) acquired by the liquidated corporation after the date 2 years before the date of the adoption of the plan of complete liquidation shall, except as provided in regulations, be treated as acquired as part of a plan described in clause (i)(II).

(C) RECAPTURE IN LIEU OF DISALLOWANCE.—The Secretary may prescribe regulations under which, in lieu of disallowing a loss under subparagraph (A) for a prior taxable year, the gross income of the liquidating corporation for the taxable year in which the plan of complete liquidation is adopted shall be increased by the amount of the disallowed loss.

(3) SPECIAL RULE IN CASE OF LIQUIDATION TO WHICH SECTION 332 APPLIES.—In the case of any liquidation to which section 332 applies, no loss shall be recognized to the liquidating corporation on any distribution in such liquidation. The preceding sentence shall apply to any distribution to the 80-percent distributee only if subsection (a) or (b)(1) of section 337 applies to such distribution.

[Sec. 336(e)]

(e) CERTAIN STOCK SALES AND DISTRIBUTIONS MAY BE TREATED AS ASSET TRANSFERS.—Under regulations prescribed by the Secretary, if—

(1) a corporation owns stock in another corporation meeting the requirements of section 1504(a)(2), and

(2) such corporation sells, exchanges, or distributes all of such stock,

an election may be made to treat such sale, exchange, or distribution as a disposition of all of the assets of such other corporation, and no gain or loss shall be recognized on the sale, exchange, or distribution of such stock.

[Sec. 337]

SEC. 337. NONRECOGNITION FOR PROPERTY DISTRIBUTED TO PARENT IN COMPLETE LIQUIDATION OF SUBSIDIARY.

[Sec. 337(a)]

(a) IN GENERAL.—No gain or loss shall be recognized to the liquidating corporation on the distribution to the 80-percent distributee of any property in a complete liquidation to which section 332 applies.

[Sec. 337(b)]

(b) TREATMENT OF INDEBTEDNESS OF SUBSIDIARY, ETC.—

(1) INDEBTEDNESS OF SUBSIDIARY TO PARENT.—If—

(A) a corporation is liquidated in a liquidation to which section 332 applies, and

(B) on the date of the adoption of the plan of liquidation, such corporation was indebted to the 80-percent distributee.

for purposes of this section and section 336, any transfer of property to the 80-percent distributee in satisfaction of such indebtedness shall be treated as a distribution to such distributee in such liquidation.

(2) TREATMENT OF TAX-EXEMPT DISTRIBUTEE.—

(A) IN GENERAL.—Except as provided in subparagraph (B), paragraph (1) and subsection (a) shall not apply where the 80-percent distributee is an organization (other than a cooperative described in section 521) which is exempt from the tax imposed by this chapter.

(B) EXCEPTION WHERE PROPERTY WILL BE USED IN UNRELATED BUSINESS.—

(i) IN GENERAL.—Subparagraph (A) shall not apply to any distribution of property to an organization described in section 511(a)(2) if, immediately after such distribution, such organization uses such property in an activity the income from which is subject to tax under 511(a).

(ii) LATER DISPOSITION OR CHANGE IN USE.—If any property to which clause (i) applied is disposed of by the organization acquiring such property, notwithstanding any other provision of law, any gain (not in excess of the amount not recognized by reason of clause (i)) shall be included in such organization's unrelated business taxable income. For purposes of the preceding sentence, if such property ceases to be used in an activity referred to in clause (i), such organization shall be treated as having disposed of such property on the date of such cessation.

[Sec. 337(c)]

(c) 80-PERCENT DISTRIBUTEE.—For purposes of this section, the term "80-percent distributee" means only the corporation which meets the 80-percent stock ownership requirements specified in section 332(b). For purposes of this section, the determination of whether any corporation is an 80-percent distributee shall be made without regard to any consolidated return regulation.

[Sec. 337(d)]

(d) REGULATIONS.—The Secretary shall prescribe such regulations as may be necessary or appropriate to carry out the purposes of the amendments made by subtitle D of title VI of the Tax Reform Act of 1986, including—

(1) regulations to ensure that such purposes may not be circumvented through the use of any provision of law or regulations (including the consolidated return regulations and part

III of this subchapter) or through the use of a regulated investment company, real estate investment trust, or tax exempt entity, and

(2) regulations providing for appropriate coordination of the provisions of this section with the provisions of this title relating to taxation of foreign corporations and their shareholders.

[Sec. 338]

SEC. 338. CERTAIN STOCK PURCHASES TREATED AS ASSET ACQUISITIONS.

[Sec. 338(a)]

(a) GENERAL RULE.—For purposes of this subtitle, if a purchasing corporation makes an election under this section (or is treated under subsection (e) as having made such an election), then, in the case of any qualified stock purchase, the target corporation—

(1) shall be treated as having sold all of its assets at the close of the acquisition date at fair market value in a single transaction, and

(2) shall be treated as a new corporation which purchased all of the assets referred to in paragraph (1) as of the beginning of the day after the acquisition date.

[Sec. 338(b)]

(b) BASIS OF ASSETS AFTER DEEMED PURCHASE.—

(1) IN GENERAL.—For purposes of subsection (a), the assets of the target corporation shall be treated as purchased for an amount equal to the sum of—

(A) the grossed-up basis of the purchasing corporation's recently purchased stock, and

(B) the basis of the purchasing corporation's nonrecently purchased stock.

(2) ADJUSTMENT FOR LIABILITIES AND OTHER RELEVANT ITEMS.—The amount described in paragraph (1) shall be adjusted under regulations prescribed by the Secretary for liabilities of the target corporation and other relevant items.

(3) ELECTION TO STEP-UP THE BASIS OF CERTAIN TARGET STOCK.—

(A) IN GENERAL.—Under regulations prescribed by the Secretary, the basis of the purchasing corporation's nonrecently purchased stock shall be the basis amount determined under subparagraph (B) of this paragraph if the purchasing corporation makes an election to recognize gain as if such stock were sold on the acquisition date for an amount equal to the basis amount determined under subparagraph (B).

(B) DETERMINATION OF BASIS AMOUNT.—For purposes of subparagraph (A), the basis amount determined under this subparagraph shall be an amount equal to the grossed-up basis determined under subparagraph (A) of paragraph (1) multiplied by a fraction—

(i) the numerator of which is the percentage of stock (by value) in the target corporation attributable to the purchasing corporation's nonrecently purchased stock, and

(ii) the denominator of which is 100 percent minus the percentage referred to in clause (i).

(4) GROSSED-UP BASIS.—For purposes of paragraph (1), the grossed-up basis shall be an amount equal to the basis of the corporation's recently purchased stock, multiplied by a fraction—

(A) the numerator of which is 100 percent, minus the percentage of stock (by value) in the target corporation attributable to the purchasing corporation's nonrecently purchased stock, and

(B) the denominator of which is the percentage of stock (by value) in the target corporation attributable to the purchasing corporation's recently purchased stock.

(5) ALLOCATION AMONG ASSETS.—The amount determined under paragraphs (1) and (2) shall be allocated among the assets of the target corporation under regulations prescribed by the Secretary.

(6) DEFINITIONS OF RECENTLY PURCHASED STOCK AND NONRECENTLY PURCHASED STOCK.—For purposes of this subsection—

(A) RECENTLY PURCHASED STOCK.—The term "recently purchased stock" means any stock in the target corporation which is held by the purchasing corporation on the acquisition date and which was purchased by such corporation during the 12-month acquisition period.

(B) NONRECENTLY PURCHASED STOCK.—The term "nonrecently purchased stock" means any stock in the target corporation which is held by the purchasing corporation on the acquisition date and which is not recently purchased stock.

[Sec. 338(d)]

(d) PURCHASING CORPORATION; TARGET CORPORATION; QUALIFIED STOCK PURCHASE.—For purposes of this section—

(1) PURCHASING CORPORATION.—The term "purchasing corporation" means any corporation which makes a qualified stock purchase of stock of another corporation.

(2) TARGET CORPORATION.—The term "target corporation" means any corporation the stock of which is acquired by another corporation in a qualified stock purchase.

(3) QUALIFIED STOCK PURCHASE.—The term "qualified stock purchase" means any transaction or series of transactions in which stock (meeting the requirements of section 1504(a)(2)) of 1 corporation is acquired by another corporation by purchase during the 12-month acquisition period.

[Sec. 338(e)]

(e) DEEMED ELECTION WHERE PURCHASING CORPORATION ACQUIRES ASSET OF TARGET CORPORATION.—

(1) IN GENERAL.—A purchasing corporation shall be treated as having made an election under this section with respect to any target corporation if, at any time during the consistency period, it acquires any asset of the target corporation (or a target affiliate).

(2) EXCEPTIONS.—Paragraph (1) shall not apply with respect to any acquisition by the purchasing corporation if—

(A) such acquisition is pursuant to a sale by the target corporation (or the target affiliate) in the ordinary course of its trade or business,

(B) the basis of the property acquired is determined (wholly) by reference to the adjusted basis of such property in the hands of the person from whom acquired,

(C) such acquisition was before September 1, 1982, or

(D) such acquisition is described in regulations prescribed by the Secretary and meets such conditions as such regulations may provide.

(3) ANTI-AVOIDANCE RULE.—Whenever necessary to carry out the purpose of this subsection and subsection (f), the Secretary may treat stock acquisitions which are pursuant to a plan and which meet the requirements of section 1504(a)(2) as qualified stock purchases.

[Sec. 338(f)]

(f) CONSISTENCY REQUIRED FOR ALL STOCK ACQUISITIONS FROM SAME AFFILIATED GROUP.—If a purchasing corporation makes qualified stock purchases with respect to the target corporation and 1 or more target affiliates during any consistency period, then (except as otherwise provided in subsection (e))—

(1) any election under this section with respect to the first such purchase shall apply to each other such purchase, and

(2) no election may be made under this section with respect to the second or subsequent such purchase if such an election was not made with respect to the first such purchase.

[Sec. 338(g)]

(g) ELECTION.—

(1) WHEN MADE.—Except as otherwise provided in regulations, an election under this section shall be made not later than the 15th day of the 9th month, beginning after the month in which the acquisition date occurs.

(2) MANNER.—An election by the purchasing corporation under this section shall be made in such manner as the Secretary shall by regulations prescribe.

(3) ELECTION IRREVOCABLE.—An election by a purchasing corporation under this section, once made, shall be irrevocable.

[Sec. 338(h)]

(h) DEFINITIONS AND SPECIAL RULES.—For purposes of this section—

(1) 12-MONTH ACQUISITION PERIOD.—The term "12-month acquisition period" means the 12-month period beginning with the date of the first acquisition by purchase of stock included in a qualified stock purchase (or, if any of such stock was acquired in an acquisition which is a purchase by reason of subparagraph (C) of paragraph (3), the date on which the acquiring corporation is first considered under section 318(a) (other than paragraph (4) thereof) as owning stock owned by the corporation from which such acquisition was made).

(2) ACQUISITION DATE.—The term "acquisition date" means, with respect to any corporation, the first day on which there is a qualified stock purchase with respect to the stock of such corporation.

(3) PURCHASE.—

(A) IN GENERAL.—The term "purchase" means any acquisition of stock, but only if—

(i) the basis of the stock in the hands of the purchasing corporation is not determined (I) in whole or in part by reference to the adjusted basis of such stock in the hands of the person from whom acquired, or (II) under section 1014(a) (relating to property acquired from a decedent),

(ii) the stock is not acquired in an exchange to which section 351, 354, 355, or 356 applies and is not acquired in any other transaction described in regulations in which the transferor does not recognize the entire amount of the gain or loss realized on the transaction, and

(iii) the stock is not acquired from a person the ownership of whose stock would, under section 318(a) (other than paragraph (4) thereof), be attributed to the person acquiring such stock.

(B) DEEMED PURCHASE UNDER SUBSECTION (a).—The term "purchase" includes any deemed purchase under subsection (a)(2). The acquisition date for a corporation which is deemed purchased under subsection (a)(2) shall be determined under regulations prescribed by the Secretary.

(C) CERTAIN STOCK ACQUISITIONS FROM RELATED CORPORATIONS.—

(i) IN GENERAL.—Clause (iii) of subparagraph (A) shall not apply to an acquisition of stock from a related corporation if at least 50 percent in value of the stock of such related corporation was acquired by purchase (within the meaning of subparagraphs (A) and (B)).

(ii) CERTAIN DISTRIBUTIONS.—Clause (i) of subparagraph (A) shall not apply to an acquisition of stock described in clause (i) of this subparagraph if the corporation acquiring such stock—

(I) made a qualified stock purchase of stock of the related corporation, and

(II) made an election under this section (or is treated under subsection (e) as having made such an election) with respect to such qualified stock purchase.

(iii) RELATED CORPORATION DEFINED.—For purposes of this subparagraph, a corporation is a related corporation if stock owned by such corporation is treated (under section 318(a) other than paragraph (4) thereof) as owned by the corporation acquiring the stock.

(4) CONSISTENCY PERIOD.—

(A) IN GENERAL.—Except as provided in subparagraph (B), the term "consistency period" means the period consisting of—

(i) the 1-year period before the beginning of the 12-month acquisition period for the target corporation,

(ii) such acquisition period (up to and including the acquisition date), and

(iii) the 1-year period beginning on the day after the acquisition date.

(B) EXTENSION WHERE THERE IS PLAN.—The period referred to in subparagraph (A) shall also include any period during which the Secretary determines that there was in effect a plan to make a qualified stock purchase plus 1 or more other qualified stock purchases (or asset acquisitions described in subsection (e)) with respect to the target corporation or any target affiliate.

(5) AFFILIATED GROUP.—The term "affiliated group" has the meaning given to such term by section 1504(a) (determined without regard to the exceptions contained in section 1504(b)).

(6) TARGET AFFILIATE.—

(A) IN GENERAL.—A corporation shall be treated as a target affiliate of the target corporation if each of such corporations was, at any time during so much of the consistency period as ends on the acquisition date of the target corporation, a member of an affiliated group which had the same common parent.

(B) CERTAIN FOREIGN CORPORATIONS, ETC.—Except as otherwise provided in regulations (and subject to such conditions as may be provided in regulations)—

(i) the term "target affiliate" does not include a foreign corporation, a DISC, or a corporation to which an election under section 936 applies, and

(ii) stock held by a target affiliate in a foreign corporation or a domestic corporation which is a DISC or described in section 1248(e) shall be excluded from the operation of this section.

(7) [Repealed.]

(8) ACQUISITIONS BY AFFILIATED GROUP TREATED AS MADE BY 1 CORPORATION.—Except as provided in regulations prescribed by the Secretary, stock and asset acquisitions made by members of the same affiliated group shall be treated as made by 1 corporation.

(9) TARGET NOT TREATED AS MEMBER OF AFFILIATED GROUP.—Except as otherwise provided in paragraph (10) or in regulations prescribed under this paragraph, the target corporation shall not be treated as a member of an affiliated group with respect to the sale described in subsection (a)(1).

(10) ELECTIVE RECOGNITION OF GAIN OR LOSS BY TARGET CORPORATION, TOGETHER WITH NONRECOGNITION OF GAIN OR LOSS ON STOCK SOLD BY SELLING CONSOLIDATED GROUP.—

(A) IN GENERAL.—Under regulations prescribed by the Secretary, an election may be made under which if—

(i) the target corporation was, before the transaction, a member of the selling consolidated group, and

(ii) the target corporation recognizes gain or loss with respect to the transaction as if it sold all of its assets in a single transaction,

then the target corporation shall be treated as a member of the selling consolidated group with respect to such sale, and (to the extent provided in regulations) no gain or loss will be recognized on stock sold or exchanged in the transaction by members of the selling consolidated group.

(B) SELLING CONSOLIDATED GROUP.—For purposes of subparagraph (A), the term "selling consolidated group" means any group of corporations which (for the taxable period which includes the transaction)—

(i) includes the target corporation, and

(ii) files a consolidated return.

To the extent provided in regulations, such term also includes any affiliated group of corporations which includes the target corporation (whether or not such group files a consolidated return).

(C) INFORMATION REQUIRED TO BE FURNISHED TO THE SECRETARY.—Under regulations, where an election is made under subparagraph (A), the purchasing corporation and the common parent of the selling consolidated group shall, at such times and in such manner as may be provided in regulations, furnish to the Secretary the following information:

(i) The amount allocated under subsection (b)(5) to goodwill or going concern value.

(ii) Any modification of the amount described in clause (i).

(iii) Any other information as the Secretary deems necessary to carry out the provisions of this paragraph.

(11) ELECTIVE FORMULA FOR DETERMINING FAIR MARKET VALUE.—For purposes of subsection (a)(1), fair market value may be determined on the basis of a formula provided in regulations prescribed by the Secretary which takes into account liabilities and other relevant items.

(12) [Repealed.]

(13) TAX ON DEEMED SALE NOT TAKEN INTO ACCOUNT FOR ESTIMATED TAX PURPOSES.—For purposes of section 6655, tax attributable to the sale described in subsection (a)(1) shall not be taken into account. The preceding sentence shall not apply with respect to a qualified stock purchase for which an election is made under paragraph (10).

(14) [Stricken.]

(15) COMBINED DEEMED SALE RETURN.—Under regulations prescribed by the Secretary, a combined deemed sale return may be filed by all target corporations acquired by a purchasing corporation on the same acquisition date if such target corporations were members of the same selling consolidated group (as defined in subparagraph (B) of paragraph (10)).

(16) COORDINATION WITH FOREIGN TAX CREDIT PROVISIONS.—Except as provided in regulations, this section shall not apply for purposes of determining the source or character of any item for purposes of subpart A of part III of subchapter N of this chapter (relating to foreign tax credit). The preceding sentence shall not apply to any gain to the extent such gain is includible in gross income as a dividend under section 1248 (determined without regard to any deemed sale under this section by a foreign corporation).

[Sec. 338(i)]

(i) REGULATIONS.—The Secretary shall prescribe such regulations as may be necessary or appropriate to carry out the purposes of this section, including—

(1) regulations to ensure that the purpose of this section to require consistency of treatment of stock and asset sales and purchases may not be circumvented through the use of any provision of law or regulations (including the consolidated return regulations) and

(2) regulations providing for the coordination of the provisions of this section with the provision of this title relating to foreign corporations and their shareholders.

Subpart D—Definition and Special Rule

[Sec. 346]

SEC. 346. DEFINITION AND SPECIAL RULE.

[Sec. 346(a)]

(a) COMPLETE LIQUIDATION.—For purposes of this subchapter, a distribution shall be treated as in complete liquidation of a corporation if the distribution is one of a series of distributions in redemption of all of the stock of the corporation pursuant to a plan.

* * *

PART III—CORPORATE ORGANIZATIONS AND REORGANIZATIONS

Subpart A—Corporate Organizations

[Sec. 351]

SEC. 351. TRANSFER TO CORPORATION CONTROLLED BY TRANSFEROR.

[Sec. 351(a)]

(a) GENERAL RULE.—No gain or loss shall be recognized if property is transferred to a corporation by one or more persons solely in exchange for stock in such corporation and immediately after the exchange such person or persons are in control (as defined in section 368(c)) of the corporation.

[Sec. 351(b)]

(b) RECEIPT OF PROPERTY.—If subsection (a) would apply to an exchange but for the fact that there is received, in addition to the stock permitted to be received under subsection (a), other property or money, then—

(1) gain (if any) to such recipient shall be recognized, but not in excess of—

(A) the amount of money received, plus

(B) the fair market value of such other property received; and

(2) no loss to such recipient shall be recognized.

[Sec. 351(c)]

(c) SPECIAL RULES WHERE DISTRIBUTION TO SHAREHOLDERS.—

(1) IN GENERAL.—In determining control for purposes of this section, the fact that any corporate transferor distributes part or all of the stock in the corporation which it receives in the exchange to its shareholders shall not be taken into account.

(2) SPECIAL RULE FOR SECTION 355.—If the requirements of section 355 (or so much of section 356 as relates to section 355) are met with respect to a distribution described in paragraph (1), then, solely for purposes of determining the tax treatment of the transfers of property to the controlled corporation by the distributing corporation, the fact that the shareholders of the distributing corporation dispose of part or all of the distributed stock, or the fact that the corporation whose stock was distributed issues additional stock, shall not be taken into account in determining control for purposes of this section.

[Sec. 351(d)]

(d) SERVICES, CERTAIN INDEBTEDNESS, AND ACCRUED INTEREST NOT TREATED AS PROPERTY.—For purposes of this section, stock issued for—

(1) services,

(2) indebtedness of the transferee corporation which is not evidenced by a security, or

(3) interest on indebtedness of the transferee corporation which accrued on or after the beginning of the transferor's holding period for the debt,

shall not be considered as issued in return for property.

[Sec. 351(e)]

(e) EXCEPTIONS.—This section shall not apply to—

(1) TRANSFER OF PROPERTY TO AN INVESTMENT COMPANY.—A transfer of property to an investment company. For purposes of the preceding sentence, the determination of whether a company is an investment company shall be made—

(A) by taking into account all stock and securities held by the company, and

(B) by treating as stock and securities—

(i) money,

(ii) stocks and other equity interests in a corporation, evidences of indebtedness, options, forward or futures contracts, notional principal contracts and derivatives,

(iii) any foreign currency,

(iv) any interest in a real estate investment trust, a common trust fund, a regulated investment company, a publicly-traded partnership (as defined in section 7704(b)) or any other equity interest (other than in a corporation) which pursuant to its terms or any other arrangement is readily convertible into, or exchangeable for, any asset described in any preceding clause, this clause or clause (v) or (viii),

(v) except to the extent provided in regulations prescribed by the Secretary, any interest in a precious metal, unless such metal is used or held in the active conduct of a trade or business after the contribution,

(vi) except as otherwise provided in regulations prescribed by the Secretary, interests in any entity if substantially all of the assets of such entity consist (directly or indirectly) of any assets described in any preceding clause or clause (viii),

(vii) to the extent provided in regulations prescribed by the Secretary, any interest in any entity not described in clause (vi), but only to the extent of the value of such interest that is attributable to assets listed in clauses (i) through (v) or clause (viii), or

(viii) any other asset specified in regulations prescribed by the Secretary.

The Secretary may prescribe regulations that, under appropriate circumstances, treat any asset described in clauses (i) through (v) as not so listed.

(2) TITLE 11 OR SIMILAR CASE.—A transfer of property of a debtor pursuant to a plan while the debtor is under the jurisdiction of a court in a title 11 or similar case (within the meaning of section 368(a)(3)(A)), to the extent that the stock received in the exchange is used to satisfy the indebtedness of such debtor.

[Sec. 351(f)]

(f) TREATMENT OF CONTROLLED CORPORATION.—If—

(1) property is transferred to a corporation (hereinafter in this subsection referred to as the "controlled corporation") in an exchange with respect to which gain or loss is not recognized (in whole or in part) to the transferor under this section, and

(2) such exchange is not in pursuance of a plan of reorganization,

section 311 shall apply to any transfer in such exchange by the controlled corporation in the same manner as if such transfer were a distribution to which subpart A of part I applies.

[Sec. 351(g)]

(g) NONQUALIFIED PREFERRED STOCK NOT TREATED AS STOCK.—

(1) IN GENERAL.—In the case of a person who transfers property to a corporation and receives nonqualified preferred stock—

(A) subsection (a) shall not apply to such transferor, and

(B) if (and only if) the transferor receives stock other than nonqualified preferred stock—

(i) subsection (b) shall apply to such transferor; and

(ii) such nonqualified preferred stock shall be treated as other property for purposes of applying subsection (b).

(2) NONQUALIFIED PREFERRED STOCK.—For purposes of paragraph (1)—

(A) IN GENERAL.—The term "nonqualified preferred stock" means preferred stock if—

(i) the holder of such stock has the right to require the issuer or a related person to redeem or purchase the stock,

(ii) the issuer or a related person is required to redeem or purchase such stock,

(iii) the issuer or a related person has the right to redeem or purchase the stock and, as of the issue date, it is more likely than not that such right will be exercised, or

(iv) the dividend rate on such stock varies in whole or in part (directly or indirectly) with reference to interest rates, commodity prices, or other similar indices.

(B) LIMITATIONS.—Clauses (i), (ii), and (iii) of subparagraph (A) shall apply only if the right or obligation referred to therein may be exercised within the 20-year period beginning on the issue date of such stock and such right or obligation is not subject to a contingency which, as of the issue date, makes remote the likelihood of the redemption or purchase.

(C) EXCEPTIONS FOR CERTAIN RIGHTS OR OBLIGATIONS.—

(i) IN GENERAL.—A right or obligation shall not be treated as described in clause (i), (ii), or (iii) of subparagraph (A) if—

(I) it may be exercised only upon the death, disability, or mental incompetency of the holder, or

(II) in the case of a right or obligation to redeem or purchase stock transferred in connection with the performance of services for the issuer or a related person (and which represents reasonable compensation), it may be exercised only upon the holder's separation from service from the issuer or a related person.

(ii) EXCEPTION.—Clause (i)(I) shall not apply if the stock relinquished in the exchange, or the stock acquired in the exchange is in—

(I) a corporation if any class of stock in such corporation or a related party is readily tradable on an established securities market or otherwise, or

(II) any other corporation if such exchange is part of a transaction or series of transactions in which such corporation is to become a corporation described in subclause (I).

(3) DEFINITIONS.—For purposes of this subsection—

(A) PREFERRED STOCK.—The term "preferred stock" means stock which is limited and preferred as to dividends and does not participate in corporate growth to any significant extent. Stock shall not be treated as participating in corporate growth to any significant extent unless there is a real and meaningful likelihood of the shareholder actually participating in the earnings and growth of the corporation.

(B) RELATED PERSON.—A person shall be treated as related to another person if they bear a relationship to such other person described in section 267(b) or 707(b).

(4) REGULATIONS.—The Secretary may prescribe such regulations as may be necessary or appropriate to carry out the purposes of this subsection and sections 354(a)(2)(C), 355(a)(3)(D), and 356(e). The Secretary may also prescribe regulations, consistent with the treatment under this subsection and such sections, for the treatment of nonqualified preferred stock under other provisions of this title.

[Sec. 351(h)]

(h) CROSS REFERENCES.—

(1) For special rule where another party to the exchange assumes a liability, see section 357.

(2) For the basis of stock or property received in an exchange to which this section applies, see sections 358 and 362.

(3) For special rule in the case of an exchange described in this section but which results in a gift, see section 2501 and following.

(4) For special rule in the case of an exchange described in this section but which has the effect of the payment of compensation by the corporation or by a transferor, see section 61(a)(1).

(5) For coordination of this section with section 304, see section 304(b)(3).

Subpart B—Effects on Shareholders and Security Holders

[Sec. 354]

SEC. 354. EXCHANGES OF STOCK AND SECURITIES IN CERTAIN REORGANIZATIONS.

[Sec. 354(a)]

(a) GENERAL RULE.—

(1) IN GENERAL.—No gain or loss shall be recognized if stock or securities in a corporation a party to a reorganization are, in pursuance of the plan of reorganization, exchanged solely for stock or securities in such corporation or in another corporation a party to the reorganization.

(2) LIMITATIONS.—

(A) EXCESS PRINCIPAL AMOUNT.—Paragraph (1) shall not apply if—

(i) the principal amount of any such securities received exceeds the principal amount of any such securities surrendered, or

(ii) any such securities are received and no such securities are surrendered.

(B) PROPERTY ATTRIBUTABLE TO ACCRUED INTEREST.—Neither paragraph (1) nor so much of section 356 as relates to paragraph (1) shall apply to the extent that any stock (including nonqualified preferred stock, as defined in section 351(g)(2)), securities, or other property received is attributable to interest which has accrued on securities on or after the beginning of the holder's holding period.

(C) NONQUALIFIED PREFERRED STOCK.—

(i) IN GENERAL.—Nonqualified preferred stock (as defined in section 351(g)(2)) received in exchange for stock other than nonqualified preferred stock (as so defined) shall not be treated as stock or securities.

(ii) RECAPITALIZATIONS OF FAMILY-OWNED CORPORATIONS.—

(I) IN GENERAL.—Clause (i) shall not apply in the case of a recapitalization under section 368(a)(1)(E) of a family-owned corporation.

(II) FAMILY-OWNED CORPORATION.—For purposes of this clause, except as provided in regulations, the term "family-owned corporation" means any corporation which is described in clause (i) of section 447(d)(2)(C) throughout the 8-year period beginning on the date which is 5 years before the date of the recapitalization. For purposes of the preceding sentence, stock shall not be treated as owned by a family member during any period described in section 355(d)(6)(B).

(III) EXTENSION OF STATUTE OF LIMITATIONS.—The statutory period for the assessment of any deficiency attributable to a corporation failing to be a family-owned corporation shall not expire before the expiration of 3 years after the date the Secretary is notified by the corporation (in such manner as the Secretary may prescribe) of such failure, and such deficiency may be assessed before the expiration of such 3-year period notwithstanding the provisions of any other law or rule of law which would otherwise prevent such assessment.

(3) CROSS REFERENCES.—

(A) For treatment of the exchange if any property is received which is not permitted to be received under this subsection (including nonqualified preferred stock and an excess principal amount of securities received over securities surrendered, but not including property to which paragraph (2)(B) applies), see section 356.

(B) For treatment of accrued interest in the case of an exchange described in paragraph (2)(B), see section 61.

[Sec. 354(b)]

(b) EXCEPTION.—

(1) IN GENERAL.—Subsection (a) shall not apply to an exchange in pursuance of a plan of reorganization within the meaning of subparagraph (D) or (G) of section 368(a)(1), unless—

(A) the corporation to which the assets are transferred acquires substantially all of the assets of the transferor of such assets; and

(B) the stock, securities, and other properties received by such transferor, as well as the other properties of such transferor, are distributed in pursuance of the plan of reorganization.

(2) CROSS REFERENCE.—

For special rules for certain exchanges in pursuance of plans of reorganization within the meaning of subparagraph (D) or (G) of section 368(a)(1), see section 355.

* * *

[Sec. 355]

SEC. 355. DISTRIBUTION OF STOCK AND SECURITIES OF A CONTROLLED CORPORATION.

[Sec. 355(a)]

(a) EFFECT ON DISTRIBUTEES.—

(1) GENERAL RULE.—If—

(A) a corporation (referred to in this section as the "distributing corporation")

(i) distributes to a shareholder, with respect to its stock, or

(ii) distributes to a security holder, in exchange for its securities,

solely stock or securities of a corporation (referred to in this section as "controlled corporation") which it controls immediately before the distribution,

(B) the transaction was not used principally as a device for the distribution of the earnings and profits of the distributing corporation or the controlled corporation or both (but the mere fact that subsequent to the distribution stock or securities in one or more of such corporations are sold or exchanged by all or some of the distributees (other than pursuant to an arrangement negotiated or agreed upon prior to such distribution) shall not be construed to mean that the transaction was used principally as such a device),

(C) the requirements of subsection (b) (relating to active businesses) are satisfied, and

(D) as part of the distribution, the distributing corporation distributes—

(i) all of the stock and securities in the controlled corporation held by it immediately before the distribution, or

(ii) an amount of stock in the controlled corporation constituting control within the meaning of section 368 (c), and it is established to the satisfaction of the Secretary that the retention by the distributing corporation of stock (or stock and securities) in the controlled corporation was not in pursuance of a plan having as one of its principal purposes the avoidance of Federal income tax,

then no gain or loss shall be recognized to (and no amount shall be includible in the income of) such shareholder or security holder on the receipt of such stock or securities.

(2) NON PRO RATA DISTRIBUTIONS, ETC.—Paragraph (1) shall be applied without regard to the following:

(A) whether or not the distribution is pro rata with respect to all of the shareholders of the distributing corporation,

(B) whether or not the shareholder surrenders stock in the distributing corporation, and

(C) whether or not the distribution is in pursuance of a plan of reorganization (within the meaning of section 368(a)(1)(D)).

(3) LIMITATIONS.—

(A) EXCESS PRINCIPAL AMOUNT.—Paragraph (1) shall not apply if—

(i) the principal amount of the securities in the controlled corporation which are received exceeds the principal amount of the securities which are surrendered in connection with such distribution, or

(ii) securities in the controlled corporation are received and no securities are surrendered in connection with such distribution.

(B) STOCK ACQUIRED IN TAXABLE TRANSACTIONS WITHIN 5 YEARS TREATED AS BOOT.—For purposes of this section (other than paragraph (1)(D) of this subsection) and so much of section 356 as relates to this section, stock of a controlled corporation acquired by the distributing corporation by reason of any transaction—

(i) which occurs within 5 years of the distribution of such stock, and

(ii) in which gain or loss was recognized in whole or in part,

shall not be treated as stock of such controlled corporation, but as other property.

(C) PROPERTY ATTRIBUTABLE TO ACCRUED INTEREST.—Neither paragraph (1) nor so much of section 356 as relates to paragraph (1) shall apply to the extent that any stock (including nonqualified preferred stock, as defined in section 351(g)(2)), securities, or other property received is attributable to interest which has accrued on securities on or after the beginning of the holder's holding period.

(D) NONQUALIFIED PREFERRED STOCK.—Nonqualified preferred stock (as defined in section 351(g)(2)) received in a distribution with respect to stock other than nonqualified preferred stock (as so defined) shall not be treated as stock or securities.

(4) CROSS REFERENCES.—

(A) For treatment of the exchange if any property is received which is not permitted to be received under this subsection (including nonqualified preferred stock and an excess principal amount of securities received over securities surrendered, but not including property to which paragraph (3)(C) applies), see section 356.

(B) For treatment of accrued interest in the case of an exchange described in paragraph (3)(C), see section 61.

[Sec. 355(b)]

(b) REQUIREMENTS AS TO ACTIVE BUSINESS.—

(1) IN GENERAL.—Subsection (a) shall apply only if either—

(A) the distributing corporation, and the controlled corporation (or, if stock of more than one controlled corporation is distributed, each of such corporations), is engaged immediately after the distribution in the active conduct of a trade or business, or

(B) immediately before the distribution, the distributing corporation had no assets other than stock or securities in the controlled corporations and each of the controlled corporations is engaged immediately after the distribution in the active conduct of a trade or business.

(2) DEFINITION.—For purposes of paragraph (1), a corporation shall be treated as engaged in the active conduct of a trade or business if and only if—

(A) it is engaged in the active conduct of a trade or business, or substantially all of its assets consist of stock and securities of a corporation controlled by it (immediately after the distribution) which is so engaged,

(B) such trade or business has been actively conducted throughout the 5-year period ending on the date of the distribution,

(C) such trade or business was not acquired within the period described in subparagraph (B) in a transaction in which gain or loss was recognized in whole or in part, and

(D) control of a corporation which (at the time of acquisition of control) was conducting such trade or business—

(i) was not acquired by any distributee corporation directly (or through 1 or more corporations, whether through the distributing corporation or otherwise) within the period described in subparagraph (B) and was not acquired by the distributing corporation directly (or through 1 or more corporations) within such period, or

(ii) was so acquired by any such corporation within such period, but, in each case in which such control was so acquired, it was so acquired, only by reason of transactions in which gain or loss was not recognized in whole or in part, or only by reason of such transactions combined with acquisitions before the beginning of such period.

For purposes of subparagraph (D), all distributee corporations which are members of the same affiliated group (as defined in section 1504(a) without regard to section 1504(b)) shall be treated as 1 distributee corporation.

[Sec. 355(c)]

(c) TAXABILITY OF CORPORATION ON DISTRIBUTION.—

(1) IN GENERAL.—Except as provided in paragraph (2), no gain or loss shall be recognized to a corporation on any distribution to which this section (or so much of section 356 as relates to this section) applies and which is not in pursuance of a plan of reorganization.

(2) DISTRIBUTION OF APPRECIATED PROPERTY.—

(A) IN GENERAL.—If—

(i) in a distribution referred to in paragraph (1), the corporation distributes property other than qualified property, and

(ii) the fair market value of such property exceeds its adjusted basis (in the hands of the distributing corporation),

then gain shall be recognized to the distributing corporation as if such property were sold to the distributee at its fair market value.

(B) QUALIFIED PROPERTY.—For purposes of subparagraph (A), the term "qualified property" means any stock or securities in the controlled corporation.

(C) TREATMENT OF LIABILITIES.—If any property distributed in the distribution referred to in paragraph (1) is subject to a liability or the shareholder assumes a liability of the distributing corporation in connection with the distribution, then, for purposes of subparagraph (A), the fair market value of such property shall be treated as not less than the amount of such liability.

(3) COORDINATION WITH SECTIONS 311 AND 336(A).—Sections 311 and 336(a) shall not apply to any distribution referred to in paragraph (1).

[Sec. 355(d)]

(d) RECOGNITION OF GAIN ON CERTAIN DISTRIBUTIONS OF STOCK OR SECURITIES IN CONTROLLED CORPORATION.—

(1) IN GENERAL.—In the case of a disqualified distribution, any stock or securities in the controlled corporation shall not be treated as qualified property for purposes of subsection (c)(2) of this section or section 361(c)(2).

(2) DISQUALIFIED DISTRIBUTION.—For purposes of this subsection, the term "disqualified distribution" means any distribution to which this section (or so much of section 356 as relates to this section) applies if, immediately after the distribution—

(A) any person holds disqualified stock in the distributing corporation which constitutes a 50-percent or greater interest in such corporation, or

(B) any person holds disqualified stock in the controlled corporation (or, if stock of more than 1 controlled corporation is distributed, in any controlled corporation) which constitutes a 50-percent or greater interest in such corporation.

(3) DISQUALIFIED STOCK.—For purposes of this subsection, the term "disqualified stock" means—

(A) any stock in the distributing corporation acquired by purchase after October 9, 1990, and during the 5-year period ending on the date of the distribution, and

(B) any stock in any controlled corporation—

(i) acquired by purchase after October 9, 1990, and during the 5-year period ending on the date of the distribution, or

(ii) received in the distribution to the extent attributable to distributions on—

(I) stock described in subparagraph (A), or

(II) any securities in the distributing corporation acquired by purchase after October 9, 1990, and during the 5-year period ending on the date of the distribution.

(4) 50-PERCENT OR GREATER INTEREST.—For purposes of this subsection, the term "50-percent or greater interest" means stock possessing at least 50 percent of the total combined voting power of all classes of stock entitled to vote or at least 50 percent of the total value of shares of all classes of stock.

(5) PURCHASE.—For purposes of this subsection—

(A) IN GENERAL.—Except as otherwise provided in this paragraph, the term "purchase" means any acquisition but only if—

(i) the basis of the property acquired in the hands of the acquirer is not determined (I) in whole or in part by reference to the adjusted basis of such property in the hands of the person from whom acquired, or (II) under section 1014(a), and

(ii) the property is not acquired in an exchange to which section 351, 354, 355, or 356 applies.

(B) CERTAIN SECTION 351 EXCHANGES TREATED AS PURCHASES.—The term "purchase" includes any acquisition of property in an exchange to which section 351 applies to the extent such property is acquired in exchange for—

(i) any cash or cash item,

(ii) any marketable stock or security, or

(iii) any debt of the transferor.

(C) CARRYOVER BASIS TRANSACTIONS.—If—

(i) any person acquires property from another person who acquired such property by purchase (as determined under this paragraph with regard to this subparagraph), and

(ii) the adjusted basis of such property in the hands of such acquirer is determined in whole or in part by reference to the adjusted basis of such property in the hands of such other person,

such acquirer shall be treated as having acquired such property by purchase on the date it was so acquired by such other person.

(6) SPECIAL RULE WHERE SUBSTANTIAL DIMINUTION OF RISK.—

(A) IN GENERAL.—If this paragraph applies to any stock or securities for any period, the running of any 5-year period set forth in subparagraph (A) or (B) of paragraph (3) (whichever applies) shall be suspended during such period.

(B) PROPERTY TO WHICH SUSPENSION APPLIES.—This paragraph applies to any stock or securities for any period during which the holder's risk of loss with respect to such stock or securities, or with respect to any portion of the activities of the corporation, is (directly or indirectly) substantially diminished by—

(i) an option,

(ii) a short sale,

(iii) any special class of stock, or

(iv) any other device or transaction.

(7) AGGREGATION RULES.—

(A) IN GENERAL.—For purposes of this subsection, a person and all persons related to such person (within the meaning of section 267(b) or 707(b)(1)) shall be treated as one person.

(B) PERSONS ACTING PURSUANT TO PLANS OR ARRANGEMENTS.—If two or more persons act pursuant to a plan or arrangement with respect to acquisitions of stock or securities in the distributing corporation or controlled corporation, such persons shall be treated as one person for purposes of this subsection.

(8) ATTRIBUTION FROM ENTITIES.—

(A) IN GENERAL.—Paragraph (2) of section 318(a) shall apply in determining whether a person holds stock or securities in any corporation (determined by substituting "10 percent" for "50 percent" in subparagraph (C) of such paragraph (2) and by treating any reference to stock as including a reference to securities).

(B) DEEMED PURCHASE RULE.—If—

(i) any person acquires by purchase an interest in any entity, and

(ii) such person is treated under subparagraph (A) as holding any stock or securities by reason of holding such interest,

such stock or securities shall be treated as acquired by purchase by such person on the later of the date of the purchase of the interest in such entity or the date such stock or securities are acquired by purchase by such entity.

(9) REGULATIONS.—The Secretary shall prescribe such regulations as may be necessary to carry out the purposes of this subsection, including—

(A) regulations to prevent the avoidance of the purposes of this subsection through the use of related persons, intermediaries, pass-thru entities, options, or other arrangements, and

(B) regulations modifying the definition of the term "purchase".

[Sec. 355(e)]

(e) RECOGNITION OF GAIN ON CERTAIN DISTRIBUTIONS OF STOCK OR SECURITIES IN CONNECTION WITH ACQUISITIONS.—

(1) GENERAL RULE.—If there is a distribution to which this subsection applies, any stock or securities in the controlled corporation shall not be treated as qualified property for purposes of subsection (c)(2) of this section or section 361(c)(2).

(2) DISTRIBUTIONS TO WHICH SUBSECTION APPLIES.—

(A) IN GENERAL.—This subsection shall apply to any distribution—

(i) to which this section (or so much of section 356 as relates to this section) applies, and

(ii) which is part of a plan (or series of related transactions) pursuant to which 1 or more persons acquire directly or indirectly stock representing a 50-percent or greater interest in the distributing corporation or any controlled corporation.

(B) PLAN PRESUMED TO EXIST IN CERTAIN CASES.—If 1 or more persons acquire directly or indirectly stock representing a 50-percent or greater interest in the distributing corporation or any controlled corporation during the 4-year period beginning on the date which is 2 years before the date of the distribution, such acquisition shall be treated as pursuant to a plan described in subparagraph (A)(ii) unless it is established that the distribution and the acquisition are not pursuant to a plan or series of related transactions.

(C) CERTAIN PLANS DISREGARDED.—A plan (or series of related transactions) shall not be treated as described in subparagraph (A)(ii) if, immediately after the completion of such plan or transactions, the distributing corporation and all controlled corporations are members of a single affiliated group (as defined in section 1504 without regard to subsection (b) thereof).

(D) COORDINATION WITH SUBSECTION (d).—This subsection shall not apply to any distribution to which subsection (d) applies.

(3) SPECIAL RULES RELATING TO ACQUISITIONS.—

(A) CERTAIN ACQUISITIONS NOT TAKEN INTO ACCOUNT.—Except as provided in regulations, the following acquisitions shall not be taken into account in applying paragraph (2)(A)(ii):

(i) The acquisition of stock in any controlled corporation by the distributing corporation.

(ii) The acquisition by a person of stock in any controlled corporation by reason of holding stock or securities in the distributing corporation.

(iii) The acquisition by a person of stock in any successor corporation of the distributing corporation or any controlled corporation by reason of holding stock or securities in such distributing or controlled corporation.

(iv) The acquisition of stock in the distributing corporation or any controlled corporation to the extent that the percentage of stock owned directly or indirectly in such corporation by each person owning stock in such corporation immediately before the acquisition does not decrease.

This subparagraph shall not apply to any acquisition if the stock held before the acquisition was acquired pursuant to a plan (or series of related transactions) described in paragraph (2)(A)(ii).

(B) ASSET ACQUISITIONS.—Except as provided in regulations, for purposes of this subsection, if the assets of the distributing corporation or any controlled corporation are acquired by a successor corporation in a transaction described in subparagraph (A), (C), or (D) of section 368(a)(1) or any other transaction specified in regulations by the Secretary, the shareholders (immediately before the acquisition) of the corporation acquiring such assets shall be treated as acquiring stock in the corporation from which the assets were acquired.

(4) DEFINITION AND SPECIAL RULES.—For purposes of this subsection—

(A) 50-PERCENT OR GREATER INTEREST.—The term "50-percent or greater interest" has the meaning given such term by subsection (d)(4).

(B) DISTRIBUTIONS IN TITLE 11 OR SIMILAR CASE.—Paragraph (1) shall not apply to any distribution made in a title 11 or similar case (as defined in section 368(a)(3)).

(C) AGGREGATION AND ATTRIBUTION RULES.—

(i) AGGREGATION.—The rules of paragraph (7)(A) of subsection (d) shall apply.

(ii) ATTRIBUTION.—Section 318(a)(2) shall apply in determining whether a person holds stock or securities in any corporation. Except as provided in regulations, section 318(a)(2)(C) shall be applied without regard to the phrase "50 percent or more in value" for purposes of the preceding sentence.

(D) SUCCESSORS AND PREDECESSORS.—For purposes of this subsection, any reference to a controlled corporation or a distributing corporation shall include a reference to any predecessor or successor of such corporation.

(E) STATUTE OF LIMITATIONS.—If there is a distribution to which paragraph (1) applies—

(i) the statutory period for the assessment of any deficiency attributable to any part of the gain recognized under this subsection by reason of such distribution shall not expire before the expiration of 3 years from the date the Secretary is notified by the taxpayer (in such manner as the Secretary may by regulations prescribe) that such distribution occurred, and

(ii) such deficiency may be assessed before the expiration of such 3-year period notwithstanding the provisions of any other law or rule of law which would otherwise prevent such assessment.

(5) REGULATIONS.—The Secretary shall prescribe such regulations as may be necessary to carry out the purposes of this subsection, including regulations—

(A) providing for the application of this subsection where there is more than 1 controlled corporation,

(B) treating 2 or more distributions as 1 distribution where necessary to prevent the avoidance of such purposes, and

(C) providing for the application of rules similar to the rules of subsection (d)(6) where appropriate for purposes of paragraph (2)(B).

[Sec. 355(f)]

(f) SECTION NOT TO APPLY TO CERTAIN INTRAGROUP DISTRIBUTIONS.—Except as provided in regulations, this section (or so much of section 356 as relates to this section) shall not apply to the distribution of stock from 1 member of an affiliated group (as defined in section 1504(a)) to another member of such group if such distribution is part of a plan (or series of related transactions) described in subsection (e)(2)(A)(ii) (determined after the application of subsection (e)).

[Sec. 356]

SEC. 356. RECEIPT OF ADDITIONAL CONSIDERATION.

[Sec. 356(a)]

(a) GAIN ON EXCHANGES.—

(1) RECOGNITION OF GAIN.—If—

(A) section 354 or 355 would apply to an exchange but for the fact that

(B) the property received in the exchange consists not only of property permitted by section 354 or 355 to be received without the recognition of gain but also of other property or money,

then the gain, if any, to the recipient shall be recognized, but in an amount not in excess of the sum of such money and the fair market value of such other property.

(2) TREATMENT AS DIVIDEND.—If an exchange is described in paragraph (1) but has the effect of the distribution of a dividend (determined with the application of section 318(a)), then there shall be treated as a dividend to each distributee such an amount of the gain recognized under paragraph (1) as is not in excess of his ratable share of the undistributed earnings and profits of the corporation accumulated after February 28, 1913. The remainder, if any, of the gain recognized under paragraph (1) shall be treated as gain from the exchange of property.

[Sec. 356(b)]

(b) ADDITIONAL CONSIDERATION RECEIVED IN CERTAIN DISTRIBUTIONS.—If—

(1) section 355 would apply to a distribution but for the fact that

(2) the property received in the distribution consists not only of property permitted by section 355 to be received without the recognition of gain, but also of other property or money,

then an amount equal to the sum of such money and the fair market value of such other property shall be treated as a distribution of property to which section 301 applies.

[Sec. 356(c)]

(c) LOSS.—If—

(1) section 354 would apply to an exchange, or section 355 would apply to an exchange or distribution, but for the fact that

(2) the property received in the exchange or distribution consists not only of property permitted by section 354 or 355 to be received without the recognition of gain or loss, but also of other property or money,

then no loss from the exchange or distribution shall be recognized.

[Sec. 356(d)]

(d) SECURITIES AS OTHER PROPERTY.—For purposes of this section—

(1) IN GENERAL.—Except as provided in paragraph (2), the term "other property" includes securities.

(2) EXCEPTIONS.—

(A) SECURITIES WITH RESPECT TO WHICH NONRECOGNITION OF GAIN WOULD BE PERMITTED.—The term "other property" does not include securities to the extent that, under section 354 or 355, such securities would be permitted to be received without the recognition of gain.

(B) GREATER PRINCIPAL AMOUNT IN SECTION 354 EXCHANGE.—If—

(i) in an exchange described in section 354 (other than subsection (c) thereof), securities of a corporation a party to the reorganization are surrendered and securities of any corporation a party to the reorganization are received, and

(ii) the principal amount of such securities received exceeds the principal amount of such securities surrendered,

then, with respect to such securities received, the term "other property" means only the fair market value of such excess. For purposes of this subparagraph and subparagraph (C), if no securities are surrendered, the excess shall be the entire principal amount of the securities received.

(C) GREATER PRINCIPAL AMOUNT IN SECTION 355 TRANSACTION.—If, in an exchange or distribution described in section 355, the principal amount of the securities in the controlled corporation which are received exceeds the principal amount of the securities in the distributing corporation which are surrendered, then, with respect to such securities received, the term "other property" means only the fair market value of such excess.

[Sec. 356(e)]

(e) NONQUALIFIED PREFERRED STOCK TREATED AS OTHER PROPERTY.—For purposes of this section—

(1) IN GENERAL.—Except as provided in paragraph (2), the term "other property" includes nonqualified preferred stock (as defined in section 351(g)(2)).

(2) EXCEPTION.—The term "other property" does not include nonqualified preferred stock (as so defined) to the extent that, under section 354 or 355, such preferred stock would be permitted to be received without the recognition of gain.

[Sec. 356(f)]

(f) EXCHANGES FOR SECTION 306 STOCK.—Notwithstanding any other provision of this section, to the extent that any of the other property (or money) is received in exchange for section 306 stock, an amount equal to the fair market value of such other property (or the amount of such money) shall be treated as a distribution of property to which section 301 applies.

[Sec. 356(g)]

(g) TRANSACTIONS INVOLVING GIFT OR COMPENSATION.—

For special rules for a transaction described in section 354, 355, or this section, but which—

(1) results in a gift, see section 2501 and following, or

(2) has the effect of the payment of compensation, see section 61(a)(1).

[Sec. 357]

SEC. 357. ASSUMPTION OF LIABILITY.

[Sec. 357(a)]

(a) GENERAL RULE.—Except as provided in subsections (b) and (c), if—

(1) the taxpayer receives property which would be permitted to be received under section 351 or 361 without the recognition of gain if it were the sole consideration, and

(2) as part of the consideration, another party to the exchange assumes a liability of the taxpayer,

then such assumption shall not be treated as money or other property, and shall not prevent the exchange from being within the provisions of section 351 or 361, as the case may be.

[Sec. 357(b)]

(b) TAX AVOIDANCE PURPOSE.—

(1) IN GENERAL.—If, taking into consideration the nature of the liability and the circumstances in the light of which the arrangement for the assumption was made, it appears that the principal purpose of the taxpayer with respect to the assumption described in subsection (a)—

(A) was a purpose to avoid Federal income tax on the exchange, or

(B) if not such purpose, was not a bona fide business purpose,

then such assumption (in the total amount of the liability assumed pursuant to such exchange) shall, for purposes of section 351 or 361 (as the case may be), be considered as money received by the taxpayer on the exchange.

(2) BURDEN OF PROOF.—In any suit or proceeding where the burden is on the taxpayer to prove such assumption is not to be treated as money received by the taxpayer, such burden shall not be considered as sustained unless the taxpayer sustains such burden by the clear preponderance of the evidence.

[Sec. 357(c)]

(c) LIABILITIES IN EXCESS OF BASIS.—

(1) IN GENERAL.—In the case of an exchange—

(A) to which section 351 applies, or

(B) to which section 361 applies by reason of a plan of reorganization within the meaning of section 368(a)(1)(D) with respect to which stock or securities of the corporation to which the assets are transferred are distributed in a transaction which qualifies under section 355,

if the sum of the amount of the liabilities assumed exceeds the total of the adjusted basis of the property transferred pursuant to such exchange, then such excess shall be considered as a gain from the sale or exchange of a capital asset or of property which is not a capital asset, as the case may be.

(2) EXCEPTIONS.—Paragraph (1) shall not apply to any exchange—

(A) to which subsection (b)(1) of this section applies, or

(B) which is pursuant to a plan of reorganization within the meaning of section 368(a)(1)(G) where no former shareholder of the transferor corporation receives any consideration for his stock.

(3) CERTAIN LIABILITIES EXCLUDED.—

(A) IN GENERAL.—If a taxpayer transfers, in an exchange to which section 351 applies, a liability the payment of which either—

(i) would give rise to a deduction, or

(ii) would be described in section 736(a),

then, for purposes of paragraph (1), the amount of such liability shall be excluded in determining the amount of liabilities assumed.

(B) EXCEPTION.—Subparagraph (A) shall not apply to any liability to the extent that the incurrence of the liability resulted in the creation of, or an increase in, the basis of any property.

[Sec. 357(d)]

(d) DETERMINATION OF AMOUNT OF LIABILITY ASSUMED.—

(1) IN GENERAL.—For purposes of this section, section 358(d), section 358(h), section 362(d), section 368(a)(1)(C), and section 368(a)(2)(B), except as provided in regulations—

(A) a recourse liability (or portion thereof) shall be treated as having been assumed if, as determined on the basis of all facts and circumstances, the transferee has agreed to, and is expected to, satisfy such liability (or portion), whether or not the transferor has been relieved of such liability; and

(B) except to the extent provided in paragraph (2), a nonrecourse liability shall be treated as having been assumed by the transferee of any asset subject to such liability.

(2) EXCEPTION FOR NONRECOURSE LIABILITY.—The amount of the nonrecourse liability treated as described in paragraph (1)(B) shall be reduced by the lesser of—

(A) the amount of such liability which an owner of other assets not transferred to the transferee and also subject to such liability has agreed with the transferee to, and is expected to, satisfy, or

(B) the fair market value of such other assets (determined without regard to section 7701(g)).

(3) REGULATIONS.—The Secretary shall prescribe such regulations as may be necessary to carry out the purposes of this subsection and section 362(d). The Secretary may also prescribe regulations which provide that the manner in which a liability is treated as assumed under this subsection is applied, where appropriate, elsewhere in this title.

[Sec. 358]

SEC. 358. BASIS TO DISTRIBUTEES.

[Sec. 358(a)]

(a) GENERAL RULE.—In the case of an exchange to which section 351, 354, 355, 356, or 361 applies—

(1) NONRECOGNITION PROPERTY.—The basis of the property permitted to be received under such section without the recognition of gain or loss shall be the same as that of the property exchanged—

(A) decreased by—

(i) the fair market value of any other property (except money) received by the taxpayer,

(ii) the amount of any money received by the taxpayer, and

(iii) the amount of loss to the taxpayer which was recognized on such exchange, and

(B) increased by—

(i) the amount which was treated as a dividend, and

(ii) the amount of gain to the taxpayer which was recognized on such exchange (not including any portion of such gain which was treated as a dividend).

(2) OTHER PROPERTY.—The basis of any other property (except money) received by the taxpayer shall be its fair market value.

[Sec. 358(b)]

(b) ALLOCATION OF BASIS.—

(1) IN GENERAL.—Under regulations prescribed by the Secretary, the basis determined under subsection (a)(1) shall be allocated among the properties permitted to be received without the recognition of gain or loss.

(2) SPECIAL RULE FOR SECTION 355.—In the case of an exchange to which section 355 (or so much of section 356 as relates to section 355) applies, then in making the allocation under paragraph (1) of this subsection, there shall be taken into account not only the property so permitted to be received without the recognition of gain or loss, but also the stock or securities (if any) of the distributing corporation which are retained, and the allocation of basis shall be made among all such properties.

[Sec. 358(c)]

(c) SECTION 355 TRANSACTIONS WHICH ARE NOT EXCHANGES.—For purposes of this section, a distribution to which section 355 (or so much of section 356 as relates to section 355) applies shall be treated as an exchange, and for such purposes the stock and securities of the distributing corporation which are retained shall be treated as surrendered, and received back, in the exchange.

[Sec. 358(d)]

(d) ASSUMPTION OF LIABILITY.—

(1) IN GENERAL.—Where, as part of the consideration to the taxpayer, another party to the exchange assumed a liability of the taxpayer, such assumption shall, for purposes of this section, be treated as money received by the taxpayer on the exchange.

(2) EXCEPTION.—Paragraph (1) shall not apply to the amount of any liability excluded under section 357(c)(3).

[Sec. 358(e)]

(e) EXCEPTION.—This section shall not apply to property acquired by a corporation by the exchange of its stock or securities (or the stock or securities of a corporation which is in control of the acquiring corporation) as consideration in whole or in part for the transfer of the property to it.

[Sec. 358(f)]

(f) DEFINITION OF NONRECOGNITION PROPERTY IN CASE OF SECTION 361 EXCHANGE.—For purposes of this section, the property permitted to be received under section 361 without the recognition of gain or loss shall be treated as consisting only of stock or securities in another corporation a party to the reorganization.

[Sec. 358(g)]

(g) ADJUSTMENTS IN INTRAGROUP TRANSACTIONS INVOLVING SECTION 355.—In the case of a distribution to which section 355 (or so much of section 356 as relates to section 355) applies and which involves the distribution of stock from 1 member of an affiliated group (as defined in section 1504(a) without regard to subsection (b) thereof) to another member of such group, the Secretary may, notwithstanding any other provision of this section, provide adjustments to the adjusted basis of any stock which—

(1) is in a corporation which is a member of such group, and

(2) is held by another member of such group, to appropriately reflect the proper treatment of such distribution.

[Sec. 358(h)]

(h) SPECIAL RULES FOR ASSUMPTION OF LIABILITIES TO WHICH SUBSECTION (D) DOES NOT APPLY.—

(1) IN GENERAL.—If, after application of the other provisions of this section to an exchange or series of exchanges, the basis of property to which subsection (a)(1) applies exceeds the fair market value of such property, then such basis shall be reduced (but not below such fair market value) by the amount (determined as of the date of the exchange) of any liability—

(A) which is assumed by another person as part of the exchange, and

(B) with respect to which subsection (d)(1) does not apply to the assumption.

(2) EXCEPTIONS.—Except as provided by the Secretary, paragraph (1) shall not apply to any liability if—

(A) the trade or business with which the liability is associated is transferred to the person assuming the liability as part of the exchange, or

(B) substantially all of the assets with which the liability is associated are transferred to the person assuming the liability as part of the exchange.

(3) LIABILITY.—For purposes of this subsection, the term "liability" shall include any fixed or contingent obligation to make payment, without regard to whether the obligation is otherwise taken into account for purposes of this title.

Subpart C—Effects on Corporations

[Sec. 361]
SEC. 361. NONRECOGNITION OF GAIN OR LOSS TO CORPORATIONS; TREATMENT OF DISTRIBUTIONS.

[Sec. 361(a)]

(a) GENERAL RULE.—No gain or loss shall be recognized to a corporation if such corporation is a party to a reorganization and exchanges property, in pursuance of the plan of reorganization, solely for stock or securities in another corporation a party to the reorganization.

[Sec. 361(b)]

(b) EXCHANGES NOT SOLELY IN KIND.—

(1) GAIN.—If subsection (a) would apply to an exchange but for the fact that the property received in exchange consists not only of stock or securities permitted by subsection (a) to be received without the recognition of gain, but also of other property or money, then—

(A) PROPERTY DISTRIBUTED.—If the corporation receiving such other property or money distributes it in pursuance of the plan of reorganization, no gain to the corporation shall be recognized from the exchange, but

(B) PROPERTY NOT DISTRIBUTED.—If the corporation receiving such other property or money does not distribute it in pursuance of the plan of reorganization, the gain, if any, to the corporation shall be recognized.

The amount of gain recognized under subparagraph (B) shall not exceed the sum of the money and the fair market value of the other property so received which is not so distributed.

(2) LOSS.—If subsection (a) would apply to an exchange but for the fact that the property received in exchange consists not only of property permitted by subsection (a) to be received without the recognition of gain or loss, but also of other property or money, then no loss from the exchange shall be recognized.

(3) TREATMENT OF TRANSFERS TO CREDITORS.—For purposes of paragraph (1), any transfer of the other property or money received in the exchange by the corporation to its creditors in connection with the reorganization shall be treated as a distribution in pursuance of the plan of reorganization. The Secretary may prescribe such regulations as may be necessary to prevent avoidance of tax through abuse of the preceding sentence or subsection (c)(3). In the case of a reorganization described in section 368(a)(1)(D) with respect to which stock or securities of the corporation to which the assets are transferred are distributed in a transaction which qualifies under section 355, this paragraph shall apply only to the extent that the sum of the money and the fair market value of other property transferred to such creditors does not exceed the adjusted bases of such assets transferred.

[Sec. 361(c)]

(c) TREATMENT OF DISTRIBUTIONS.—

(1) IN GENERAL.—Except as provided in paragraph (2), no gain or loss shall be recognized to a corporation a party to a reorganization on the distribution to its shareholders of property in pursuance of the plan of reorganization.

(2) DISTRIBUTIONS OF APPRECIATED PROPERTY.—

(A) IN GENERAL.—If—

(i) in a distribution referred to in paragraph (1), the corporation distributes property other than qualified property, and

(ii) the fair market value of such property exceeds its adjusted basis (in the hands of the distributing corporation),

then gain shall be recognized to the distributing corporation as if such property were sold to the distributee at its fair market value.

(B) QUALIFIED PROPERTY.—For purposes of this subsection, the term "qualified property" means—

(i) any stock in (or right to acquire stock in) the distributing corporation or obligation of the distributing corporation, or

(ii) any stock in (or right to acquire stock in) another corporation which is a party to the reorganization or obligation of another corporation which is such a party if such stock (or right) or obligation is received by the distributing corporation in the exchange.

(C) TREATMENT OF LIABILITIES.—If any property distributed in the distribution referred to in paragraph (1) is subject to a liability or the shareholder assumes a liability of the distributing corporation in connection with the distribution, then, for purposes of subparagraph (A), the fair market value of such property shall be treated as not less than the amount of such liability.

(3) TREATMENT OF CERTAIN TRANSFERS TO CREDITORS.—For purposes of this subsection, any transfer of qualified property by the corporation to its creditors in connection with the reorganization shall be treated as a distribution to its shareholders pursuant to the plan of reorganization.

(4) COORDINATION WITH OTHER PROVISIONS.—Section 311 and subpart B of part II of this subchapter shall not apply to any distribution referred to in paragraph (1).

(5) CROSS REFERENCE.—

For provision providing for recognition of gain in certain distributions, see section 355(d).

[Sec. 362]

SEC. 362. BASIS TO CORPORATIONS.

[Sec. 362(a)]

(a) PROPERTY ACQUIRED BY ISSUANCE OF STOCK OR AS PAID-IN SURPLUS.—If property was acquired on or after June 22, 1954, by a corporation—

(1) in connection with a transaction to which section 351 (relating to transfer of property to corporation controlled by transferor) applies, or

(2) as paid-in surplus or as a contribution to capital,

then the basis shall be the same as it would be in the hands of the transferor, increased in the amount of gain recognized to the transferor on such transfer.

[Sec. 362(b)]

(b) TRANSFERS TO CORPORATIONS.—If property was acquired by a corporation in connection with a reorganization to which this part applies, then the basis shall be the same as it would be in the hands of the transferor, increased in the amount of gain recognized to the transferor on such transfer. This subsection shall not apply if the property acquired consists of stock or securities in a corporation a party to the reorganization, unless acquired by the exchange of stock or securities of the transferee (or of a corporation which is in control of the transferee) as the consideration in whole or in part for the transfer.

[Sec. 362(c)]

(c) SPECIAL RULE FOR CERTAIN CONTRIBUTIONS TO CAPITAL.—

(1) PROPERTY OTHER THAN MONEY.—Notwithstanding subsection (a)(2), if property other than money—

(A) is acquired by a corporation, on or after June 22, 1954, as a contribution to capital, and

(B) is not contributed by a shareholder as such,

then the basis of such property shall be zero.

(2) MONEY.—Notwithstanding subsection (a)(2), if money—

(A) is received by a corporation, on or after June 22, 1954, as a contribution to capital, and

(B) is not contributed by a shareholder as such,

then the basis of any property acquired with such money during the 12-month period beginning on the day the contribution is received shall be reduced by the amount of such contribution. The excess (if any) of the amount of such contribution over the amount of the reduction under the preceding sentence shall be applied to the reduction (as of the last day of the period specified in the preceding sentence) of the basis of any other property held by the taxpayer. The particular properties to which the reductions required by this paragraph shall be allocated shall be determined under regulations prescribed by the Secretary.

[Sec. 362(d)]

(d) LIMITATION ON BASIS INCREASE ATTRIBUTABLE TO ASSUMPTION OF LIABILITY.—

(1) IN GENERAL.—In no event shall the basis of any property be increased under subsection (a) or (b) above the fair market value of such property (determined without regard to section 7701(g)) by reason of any gain recognized to the transferor as a result of the assumption of a liability.

(2) TREATMENT OF GAIN NOT SUBJECT TO TAX.—Except as provided in regulations, if—

(A) gain is recognized to the transferor as a result of an assumption of a nonrecourse liability by a transferee which is also secured by assets not transferred to such transferee; and

(B) no person is subject to tax under this title on such gain,

then, for purposes of determining basis under subsections (a) and (b), the amount of gain recognized by the transferor as a result of the assumption of the liability shall be determined as if the liability assumed by the transferee equaled such transferee's ratable portion of such liability determined on the basis of the relative fair market values (determined without regard to section 7701(g)) of all of the assets subject to such liability.

[Sec. 362(e)]

(e) LIMITATIONS ON BUILT-IN LOSSES.—

(1) LIMITATION ON IMPORTATION OF BUILT-IN LOSSES.—

(A) IN GENERAL.—If in any transaction described in subsection (a) or (b) there would (but for this subsection) be an importation of a net built-in loss, the basis of each property described in subparagraph (B) which is acquired in such transaction shall (notwithstanding subsections (a) and (b)) be its fair market value immediately after such transaction.

(B) PROPERTY DESCRIBED.—For purposes of subparagraph (A), property is described in this subparagraph if—

(i) gain or loss with respect to such property is not subject to tax under this subtitle in the hands of the transferor immediately before the transfer, and

(ii) gain or loss with respect to such property is subject to such tax in the hands of the transferee immediately after such transfer.

In any case in which the transferor is a partnership, the preceding sentence shall be applied by treating each partner in such partnership as holding such partner's proportionate share of the property of such partnership.

(C) IMPORTATION OF NET BUILT-IN LOSS.—For purposes of subparagraph (A), there is an importation of a net built-in loss in a transaction if the transferee's aggregate adjusted bases of property described in subparagraph (B) which is transferred in such transaction would (but for this paragraph) exceed the fair market value of such property immediately after such transaction.

(2) LIMITATION ON TRANSFER OF BUILT-IN LOSSES IN SECTION 351 TRANSACTIONS.—

(A) IN GENERAL.—If—

(i) property is transferred by a transferor in any transaction which is described in subsection (a) and which is not described in paragraph (1) of this subsection, and

(ii) the transferee's aggregate adjusted bases of such property so transferred would (but for this paragraph) exceed the fair market value of such property immediately after such transaction, then, notwithstanding subsection (a), the transferee's aggregate adjusted bases of the property so transferred shall not exceed the fair market value of such property immediately after such transaction.

(B) ALLOCATION OF BASIS REDUCTION.—The aggregate reduction in basis by reason of subparagraph (A) shall be allocated among the property so transferred in proportion to their respective built-in losses immediately before the transaction.

(C) ELECTION TO APPLY LIMITATION TO TRANSFEROR'S STOCK BASIS.—

(i) IN GENERAL.—If the transferor and transferee of a transaction described in subparagraph (A) both elect the application of this subparagraph—

(I) subparagraph (A) shall not apply, and

(II) the transferor's basis in the stock received for property to which subparagraph (A) does not apply by reason of the election shall not exceed its fair market value immediately after the transfer.

(ii) ELECTION.—An election under clause (i) shall be included with the return of tax for the taxable year in which the transaction occurred, shall be in such form and manner as the Secretary may prescribe, and, once made, shall be irrevocable.

Subpart D—Special Rule; Definitions

[Sec. 367]

SEC. 367. FOREIGN CORPORATIONS.

[Sec. 367(a)]

(a) TRANSFERS OF PROPERTY FROM THE UNITED STATES.—

(1) GENERAL RULE.—If, in connection with any exchange described in section 332, 351, 354, 356, or 361, a United States person transfers property to a foreign corporation, such foreign corporation shall not, for purposes of determining the extent to which gain shall be recognized on such transfer, be considered to be a corporation.

(2) EXCEPTION FOR CERTAIN STOCK OR SECURITIES.—Except to the extent provided in regulations, paragraph (1) shall not apply to the transfer of stock or securities of a foreign corporation which is a party to the exchange or a party to the reorganization.

(3) EXCEPTION FOR TRANSFERS OF CERTAIN PROPERTY USED IN THE ACTIVE CONDUCT OF A TRADE OR BUSINESS.—

(A) IN GENERAL.—Except as provided in regulations prescribed by the Secretary, paragraph (1) shall not apply to any property transferred to a foreign corporation for use by such foreign corporation in the active conduct of a trade or business outside of the United States.

(B) PARAGRAPH NOT TO APPLY TO CERTAIN PROPERTY.—Except as provided in regulations prescribed by the Secretary, subparagraph (A) shall not apply to any—

(i) property described in paragraph (1) or (3) of section 1221(a) (relating to inventory and copyrights, etc.),

(ii) installment obligations, accounts receivable, or similar property,

(iii) foreign currency or other property denominated in foreign currency,

(iv) intangible property (within the meaning of section 936(h)(3)(B)), or

(v) property with respect to which the transferor is a lessor at the time of the transfer, except that this clause shall not apply if the transferee was the lessee.

(C) TRANSFER OF FOREIGN BRANCH WITH PREVIOUSLY DEDUCTED LOSSES.—Except as provided in regulations prescribed by the Secretary, subparagraph (A) shall not apply to gain realized on the transfer of the assets of a foreign branch of a United States person to a foreign corporation in an exchange described in paragraph (1) to the extent that—

(i) the sum of losses—

(I) which were incurred by the foreign branch before the transfer, and

(II) with respect to which a deduction was allowed to the taxpayer, exceeds

(ii) the sum of—

(I) any taxable income of such branch for a taxable year after the taxable year in which the loss was incurred and through the close of the taxable year of the transfer, and

(II) the amount which is recognized under section 904(f)(3) on account of the transfer.

Any gain recognized by reason of the preceding sentence shall be treated for purposes of this chapter as income from sources outside the United States having the same character as such losses had.

(4) SPECIAL RULE FOR TRANSFER OF PARTNERSHIP INTERESTS.—Except as provided in regulations prescribed by the Secretary, a transfer by a United States person of an interest in a partnership to a foreign corporation in an exchange described in paragraph (1) shall, for purposes of this subsection, be treated as a transfer to such corporation of such person's pro rata share of the assets of the partnership.

(5) PARAGRAPHS (2) AND (3) NOT TO APPLY TO CERTAIN SECTION 361 TRANSACTIONS.—Paragraphs (2) and (3) shall not apply in the case of an exchange described in subsection (a) or (b) of section 361. Subject to such basis adjustments and such other conditions as shall be provided in regulations, the preceding sentence shall not apply if the transferor corporation is controlled (within the meaning of section 368(c)) by 5 or fewer domestic corporations. For purposes of the preceding sentence, all members of the same affiliated group (within the meaning of section 1504) shall be treated as 1 corporation.

(6) SECRETARY MAY EXEMPT CERTAIN TRANSACTIONS FROM APPLICATION OF THIS SUBSECTION.—Paragraph (1) shall not apply to the transfer of any property which the Secretary, in order to carry out the purposes of this subsection, designates by regulation.

[Sec. 367(b)]

(b) OTHER TRANSFERS.—

(1) EFFECT OF SECTION TO BE DETERMINED UNDER REGULATIONS.—In the case of any exchange described in section 332, 351, 354, 355, 356, or 361 in connection with which there is no transfer of property described in subsection (a)(1), a foreign corporation shall be considered to be a corporation except to the extent provided in regulations prescribed by the Secretary which are necessary or appropriate to prevent the avoidance of Federal income taxes.

(2) REGULATIONS RELATING TO SALE OR EXCHANGE OF STOCK IN FOREIGN CORPORATIONS.—The regulations prescribed pursuant to paragraph (1) shall include (but shall not be limited to) regulations dealing with the sale or exchange of stock or securities in a foreign corporation by a United States person, including regulations providing—

(A) the circumstances under which—

(i) gain shall be recognized currently, or amounts included in gross income currently as a dividend, or both, or

(ii) gain or other amounts may be deferred for inclusion in the gross income of a shareholder (or his successor in interest) at a later date, and

(B) the extent to which adjustments shall be made to earnings and profits, basis of stock or securities, and basis of assets.

[Sec. 367(c)]

(c) TRANSACTIONS TO BE TREATED AS EXCHANGES.—

(1) SECTION 355 DISTRIBUTION.—For purposes of this section, any distribution described in section 355 (or so much of section 356 as relates to section 355) shall be treated as an exchange whether or not it is an exchange.

(2) CONTRIBUTION OF CAPITAL TO CONTROLLED CORPORATIONS.—For purposes of this chapter, any transfer of property to a foreign corporation as a contribution to the capital of such corporation by one or more persons who, immediately after the transfer, own (within the

meaning of section 318) stock possessing at least 80 percent of the total combined voting power of all classes of stock of such corporation entitled to vote shall be treated as an exchange of such property for stock of the foreign corporation equal in value to the fair market value of the property transferred.

[Sec. 367(d)]

(d) SPECIAL RULES RELATING TO TRANSFERS OF INTANGIBLES.—

(1) IN GENERAL.—Except as provided in regulations prescribed by the Secretary, if a United States person transfers any intangible property (within the meaning of section 936(h)(3)(B)) to a foreign corporation in an exchange described in section 351 or 361—

(A) subsection (a) shall not apply to the transfer of such property, and

(B) the provisions of this subsection shall apply to such transfer.

(2) TRANSFER OF INTANGIBLES TREATED AS TRANSFER PURSUANT TO SALE OF CONTINGENT PAYMENTS.—

(A) IN GENERAL.—If paragraph (1) applies to any transfer, the United States person transferring such property shall be treated as—

(i) having sold such property in exchange for payments which are contingent upon the productivity, use, or disposition of such property, and

(ii) receiving amounts which reasonably reflect the amounts which would have been received—

(I) annually in the form of such payments over the useful life of such property, or

(II) in the case of a disposition following such transfer (whether direct or indirect), at the time of the disposition.

The amounts taken into account under clause (ii) shall be commensurate with the income attributable to the intangible.

(B) EFFECT ON EARNINGS AND PROFITS.—For purposes of this chapter, the earnings and profits of a foreign corporation to which the intangible property was transferred shall be reduced by the amount required to be included in the income of the transferor of the intangible property under subparagraph (A)(ii).

(C) AMOUNTS RECEIVED TREATED AS ORDINARY INCOME.—For purposes of this chapter, any amount included in gross income by reason of this subsection shall be treated as ordinary income. For purposes of applying section 904(d), any such amount shall be treated in the same manner as if such amount were a royalty.

(3) REGULATIONS RELATING TO TRANSFERS OF INTANGIBLES TO PARTNERSHIPS.—The Secretary may provide by regulations that the rules of paragraph (2) also apply to the transfer of intangible property by a United States person to a partnership in circumstances consistent with the purposes of this subsection.

[Sec. 367(e)]

(e) TREATMENT OF DISTRIBUTIONS DESCRIBED IN SECTION 355 OR LIQUIDATIONS UNDER SECTION 332.—

(1) DISTRIBUTIONS DESCRIBED IN SECTION 355.—In the case of any distribution described in section 355 (or so much of section 356 as relates to section 355) by a domestic corporation to a person who is not a United States person, to the extent provided in regulations, gain shall be recognized under principles similar to the principles of this section.

(2) LIQUIDATIONS UNDER SECTION 332.—In the case of any liquidation to which section 332 applies, except as provided in regulations, subsections (a) and (b)(1) of section 337 shall not apply where the 80-percent distributee (as defined in section 337(c)) is a foreign corporation.

[Sec. 367(f)]

(f) OTHER TRANSFERS.—To the extent provided in regulations, if a United States person transfers property to a foreign corporation as paid-in surplus or as a contribution to capital (in a transaction not otherwise described in this section), such transfer shall be treated as a sale or exchange for an amount equal to the fair market value of the property transferred, and the transferor shall recognize as gain the excess of—

(1) the fair market value of the property so transferred, over

(2) the adjusted basis (for purposes of determining gain) of such property in the hands of the transferor.

[Sec. 368]

SEC. 368. DEFINITIONS RELATING TO CORPORATE REORGANIZATIONS.

[Sec. 368(a)]

(a) REORGANIZATION.—

(1) IN GENERAL.—For purposes of parts I and II and this part, the term "reorganization" means—

(A) a statutory merger or consolidation;

(B) the acquisition by one corporation, in exchange solely for all or a part of its voting stock (or in exchange solely for all or a part of the voting stock of a corporation which is in control of the acquiring corporation), of stock of another corporation if, immediately after the acquisition, the acquiring corporation has control of such other corporation (whether or not such acquiring corporation had control immediately before the acquisition);

(C) the acquisition by one corporation, in exchange solely for all or a part of its voting stock (or in exchange solely for all or a part of the voting stock of a corporation which is in control of the acquiring corporation), of substantially all of the properties of another corporation, but in determining whether the exchange is solely for stock the assumption by the acquiring corporation of a liability of the other shall be disregarded;

(D) a transfer by a corporation of all or a part of its assets to another corporation if immediately after the transfer the transferor, or one or more of its shareholders (including persons who were shareholders immediately before the transfer), or any combination thereof, is in control of the corporation to which the assets are transferred; but only if, in pursuance of the plan, stock or securities of the corporation to which the assets are transferred are distributed in a transaction which qualifies under section 354, 355, or 356;

(E) a recapitalization;

(F) a mere change in identity, form, or place of organization of one corporation, however effected; or

(G) a transfer by a corporation of all or part of its assets to another corporation in a title 11 or similar case; but only if, in pursuance of the plan, stock or securities of the corporation to which the assets are transferred are distributed in a transaction which qualifies under section 354, 355, or 356.

(2) SPECIAL RULES RELATING TO PARAGRAPH (1).—

(A) REORGANIZATIONS DESCRIBED IN BOTH PARAGRAPH (1)(C) AND PARAGRAPH (1)(D).—If a transaction is described in both paragraph (1)(C) and paragraph (1)(D), then, for purposes of this subchapter (other than for purposes of subparagraph (C)), such transaction shall be treated as described only in paragraph (1)(D).

(B) ADDITIONAL CONSIDERATION IN CERTAIN PARAGRAPH (1)(C) CASES.—If—

(i) one corporation acquires substantially all of the properties of another corporation,

(ii) the acquisition would qualify under paragraph (1)(C) but for the fact that the acquiring corporation exchanges money or other property in addition to voting stock, and

(iii) the acquiring corporation acquires, solely for voting stock described in paragraph (1)(C), property of the other corporation having a fair market value which is at least 80 percent of the fair market value of all of the property of the other corporation,

then such acquisition shall (subject to subparagraph (A) of this paragraph) be treated as qualifying under paragraph (1)(C). Solely for the purpose of determining whether clause

(iii) of the preceding sentence applies, the amount of any liability assumed by the acquiring corporation shall be treated as money paid for the property.

(C) TRANSFERS OF ASSETS OR STOCK TO SUBSIDIARIES IN CERTAIN PARAGRAPH (1)(A), (1)(B), (1)(C), AND (1)(G) CASES.—A transaction otherwise qualifying under paragraph (1)(A), (1)(B), or (1)(C) shall not be disqualified by reason of the fact that part or all of the assets or stock which were acquired in the transaction are transferred to a corporation controlled by the corporation acquiring such assets or stock. A similar rule shall apply to a transaction otherwise qualifying under paragraph (1)(G) where the requirements of subparagraphs (A) and (B) of section 354(b)(1) are met with respect to the acquisition of the assets.

(D) USE OF STOCK OF CONTROLLING CORPORATION IN PARAGRAPH (1)(A) AND (1)(G) CASES.—The acquisition by one corporation, in exchange for stock of a corporation (referred to in this subparagraph as "controlling corporation") which is in control of the acquiring corporation, of substantially all of the properties of another corporation shall not disqualify a transaction under paragraph (1)(A) or (1)(G) if—

(i) no stock of the acquiring corporation is used in the transaction, and

(ii) in the case of a transaction under paragraph (1)(A), such transaction would have qualified under paragraph (1)(A) had the merger been into the controlling corporation.

(E) STATUTORY MERGER USING VOTING STOCK OF CORPORATION CONTROLLING MERGED CORPORATION.—A transaction otherwise qualifying under paragraph (1)(A) shall not be disqualified by reason of the fact that stock of a corporation (referred to in this subparagraph as the "controlling corporation") which before the merger was in control of the merged corporation is used in the transaction, if—

(i) after the transaction, the corporation surviving the merger holds substantially all of its properties and of the properties of the merged corporation (other than stock of the controlling corporation distributed in the transaction); and

(ii) in the transaction, former shareholders of the surviving corporation exchanged, for an amount of voting stock of the controlling corporation, an amount of stock in the surviving corporation which constitutes control of such corporation.

(F) CERTAIN TRANSACTIONS INVOLVING 2 OR MORE INVESTMENT COMPANIES.—

(i) If immediately before a transaction described in paragraph (1) (other than subparagraph (E) thereof), 2 or more parties to the transaction were investment companies, then the transaction shall not be considered to be a reorganization with respect to any such investment company (and its shareholders and security holders) unless it was a regulated investment company, a real estate investment trust, or a corporation which meets the requirements of clause (ii).

(ii) A corporation meets the requirements of this clause if not more than 25 percent of the value of its total assets is invested in the stock and securities of any one issuer and not more than 50 percent of the value of its total assets is invested in the stock and securities of 5 or fewer issuers. For purposes of this clause, all members of a controlled group of corporations (within the meaning of section 1563(a)) shall be treated as one issuer. For purposes of this clause, a person holding stock in a regulated investment company, a real estate investment trust, or an investment company which meets the requirements of this clause shall, except as provided in regulations, be treated as holding its proportionate share of the assets held by such company or trust.

(iii) For purposes of this subparagraph the term "investment company" means a regulated investment company, a real estate investment trust, or a corporation 50 percent or more of the value of whose total assets are stock and securities and 80 percent or more of the value of whose total assets are assets held for investment. In making the 50-percent and 80-percent determinations under the preceding sentence, stock and securities in any subsidiary corporation shall be disregarded and the parent corporation shall be deemed to own its ratable share of the subsidiary's assets, and a corporation shall be considered a subsidiary if the parent owns 50 percent or more of the combined voting power of all classes of stock entitled to vote, or 50 percent or more of the total value of shares of all classes of stock outstanding.

(iv) For purposes of this subparagraph, in determining total assets there shall be excluded cash and cash items (including receivables), Government securities, and, under regulations prescribed by the Secretary, assets acquired (through incurring indebtedness or otherwise) for purposes of meeting the requirements of clause (ii) or ceasing to be an investment company.

(v) This subparagraph shall not apply if the stock of each investment company is owned substantially by the same persons in the same proportions.

(vi) If an investment company which does not meet the requirements of clause (ii) acquires assets of another corporation, clause (i) shall be applied to such investment company and its shareholders and security holders as though its assets had been acquired by such other corporation. If such investment company acquires stock of another corporation in a reorganization described in section 368(a)(1)(B), clause (i) shall be applied to the shareholders of such investment company as though they had exchanged with such other corporation all of their stock in such company for stock having a fair market value equal to the fair market value of their stock of such investment company immediately after the exchange. For purposes of section 1001, the deemed acquisition or exchange referred to in the two preceding sentences shall be treated as a sale or exchange of property by the corporation and by the shareholders and security holders to which clause (i) is applied.

(vii) For purposes of clauses (ii) and (iii), the term "securities" includes obligations of State and local governments, commodity futures contracts, shares of regulated investment companies and real estate investment trusts, and other investments constituting a security within the meaning of the Investment Company Act of 1940 (15 U.S.C. 80a-2(36)).

(G) DISTRIBUTION REQUIREMENT FOR PARAGRAPH (1)(C).—

(i) IN GENERAL.—A transaction shall fail to meet the requirements of paragraph (1)(C) unless the acquired corporation distributes the stock, securities, and other properties it receives, as well as its other properties, in pursuance of the plan of reorganization. For purposes of the preceding sentence, if the acquired corporation is liquidated pursuant to the plan of reorganization, any distribution to its creditors in connection with such liquidation shall be treated as pursuant to the plan of reorganization.

(ii) EXCEPTION.—The Secretary may waive the application of clause (i) to any transaction subject to any conditions the Secretary may prescribe.

(H) SPECIAL RULES FOR DETERMINING WHETHER CERTAIN TRANSACTIONS ARE QUALIFIED UNDER PARAGRAPH (1)(D).—For purposes of determining whether a transaction qualifies under paragraph (1)(D)—

(i) in the case of a transaction with respect to which the requirements of subparagraphs (A) and (B) of section 354(b)(1) are met, the term "control" has the meaning given such term by section 304(c), and

(ii) in the case of a transaction with respect to which the requirements of section 355 (or so much of section 356 as relates to section 355) are met, the fact that the shareholders of the distributing corporation dispose of part or all of the distributed stock, or the fact that the corporation whose stock was distributed issues additional stock, shall not be taken into account.

(3) ADDITIONAL RULES RELATING TO TITLE 11 AND SIMILAR CASES.—

(A) TITLE 11 OR SIMILAR CASE DEFINED.—For purposes of this part, the term "title 11 or similar case" means—

(i) a case under title 11 of the United States Code, or

(ii) a receivership, foreclosure, or similar proceeding in a Federal or State court.

(B) TRANSFER OF ASSETS IN A TITLE 11 OR SIMILAR CASE.—In applying paragraph (1)(G), a transfer of the assets of a corporation shall be treated as made in a title 11 or similar case if and only if—

(i) any party to the reorganization is under the jurisdiction of the court in such case, and

(ii) the transfer is pursuant to a plan of reorganization approved by the court.

(C) REORGANIZATIONS QUALIFYING UNDER PARAGRAPH (1)(G) AND ANOTHER PROVISION.—If a transaction would (but for this subparagraph) qualify both—

(i) under subparagraph (G) of paragraph (1), and

(ii) under any other subparagraph of paragraph (1) or under section 332 or 351,

then, for purposes of this subchapter (other than section 357(c)(1)), such transaction shall be treated as qualifying only under subparagraph (G) of paragraph (1).

(D) AGENCY RECEIVERSHIP PROCEEDINGS WHICH INVOLVE FINANCIAL INSTITUTIONS.—For purposes of subparagraphs (A) and (B), in the case of a receivership, foreclosure, or similar proceeding before a Federal or State agency involving a financial institution referred to in section 581 or 591, the agency shall be treated as a court.

(E) APPLICATION OF PARAGRAPH (2)(E)(ii).—In the case of a title 11 or similar case, the requirement of clause (ii) of paragraph (2)(E) shall be treated as met if—

(i) no former shareholder of the surviving corporation received any consideration for his stock, and

(ii) the former creditors of the surviving corporation exchanged, for an amount of voting stock of the controlling corporation, debt of the surviving corporation which had a fair market value equal to 80 percent or more of the total fair market value of the debt of the surviving corporation.

[Sec. 368(b)]

(b) PARTY TO A REORGANIZATION.—For purposes of this part, the term "a party to a reorganization" includes—

(1) a corporation resulting from a reorganization, and

(2) both corporations, in the case of a reorganization resulting from the acquisition by one corporation of stock or properties of another.

In the case of a reorganization qualifying under paragraph (1)(B) or (1)(C) of subsection (a), if the stock exchanged for the stock or properties is stock of a corporation which is in control of the acquiring corporation, the term "a party to a reorganization" includes the corporation so controlling the acquiring corporation. In the case of a reorganization qualifying under paragraph (1)(A), (1)(B), (1)(C), or (1)(G) of subsection (a) by reason of paragraph (2)(C) of subsection (a), the term "a party to a reorganization" includes the corporation controlling the corporation to which the acquired assets or stock are transferred. In the case of a reorganization qualifying under paragraph (1)(A) or (1)(G) of subsection (a) by reason of paragraph (2)(D) of that subsection, the term "a party to a reorganization" includes the controlling corporation referred to in such paragraph (2)(D). In the case of a reorganization qualifying under subsection (a)(1)(A) by reason of subsection (a)(2)(E), the term "party to a reorganization" includes the controlling corporation referred to in subsection (a)(2)(E).

[Sec. 368(c)]

(c) CONTROL DEFINED.—For purposes of part I (other than section 304), part II, this part, and part V, the term "control" means the ownership of stock possessing at least 80 percent of the total combined voting power of all classes of stock entitled to vote and at least 80 percent of the total number of shares of all other classes of stock of the corporation.

PART VI—TREATMENT OF CERTAIN CORPORATE INTERESTS AS STOCK OR INDEBTEDNESS

[Sec. 385]

SEC. 385. TREATMENT OF CERTAIN INTERESTS IN CORPORATIONS AS STOCK OR INDEBTEDNESS.

[Sec. 385(a)]

(a) AUTHORITY TO PRESCRIBE REGULATIONS.—The Secretary is authorized to prescribe such regulations as may be necessary or appropriate to determine whether an interest in a corporation is to be treated for purposes of this title as stock or indebtedness (or as in part stock and in part indebtedness).

[Sec. 385(b)]

(b) FACTORS.—The regulations prescribed under this section shall set forth factors which are to be taken into account in determining with respect to a particular factual situation whether a debtor-creditor relationship exists or a corporation-shareholder relationship exists. The factors so set forth in the regulations may include among other factors:

(1) whether there is a written unconditional promise to pay on demand or on a specified date a sum certain in money in return for an adequate consideration in money or money's worth, and to pay a fixed rate of interest,

(2) whether there is subordination to or preference over any indebtedness of the corporation,

(3) the ratio of debt to equity of the corporation,

(4) whether there is convertibility into the stock of the corporation, and

(5) the relationship between holdings of stock in the corporation and holdings of the interest in question.

* * *

SUBCHAPTER E—ACCOUNTING PERIODS AND METHODS OF ACCOUNTING

PART I—ACCOUNTING PERIODS

[Sec. 441]

SEC. 441. PERIOD FOR COMPUTATION OF TAXABLE INCOME.

* * *

[Sec. 441(h)]

(h) TAXABLE YEAR OF FSC'S AND DISC'S.—

(1) IN GENERAL.—For purposes of this subtitle, the taxable year of any FSC or DISC shall be the taxable year of that shareholder (or group of shareholders with the same 12-month taxable year) who has the highest percentage of voting power.

(2) SPECIAL RULE WHERE MORE THAN ONE SHAREHOLDER (OR GROUP) HAS HIGHEST PERCENTAGE.—If 2 or more shareholders (or groups) have the highest percentage of voting power under paragraph (1), the taxable year of the FSC or DISC shall be the same 12-month period as that of any such shareholder (or group).

(3) SUBSEQUENT CHANGES OF OWNERSHIP.—The Secretary shall prescribe regulations under which paragraphs (1) and (2) shall apply to a change of ownership of a corporation after the taxable year of the corporation has been determined under paragraph (1) or (2) only if such change is a substantial change of ownership.

(4) VOTING POWER DETERMINED.—For purposes of this subsection, voting power shall be determined on the basis of total combined voting power of all classes of stock of the corporation entitled to vote.

PART II—METHODS OF ACCOUNTING

Subpart A—Methods of Accounting in General

[Sec. 446]

SEC. 446. GENERAL RULE FOR METHODS OF ACCOUNTING.

[Sec. 446(a)]

(a) GENERAL RULE.—Taxable income shall be computed under the method of accounting on the basis of which the taxpayer regularly computes his income in keeping his books.

[Sec. 446(b)]

(b) EXCEPTIONS.—If no method of accounting has been regularly used by the taxpayer, or if the method used does not clearly reflect income, the computation of taxable income shall be made under such method as, in the opinion of the Secretary, does clearly reflect income.

[Sec. 446(c)]

(c) PERMISSIBLE METHODS.—Subject to the provisions of subsections (a) and (b), a taxpayer may compute taxable income under any of the following methods of accounting—

    (1) the cash receipts and disbursements method;

    (2) an accrual method;

    (3) any other method permitted by this chapter; or

    (4) any combination of the foregoing methods permitted under regulations prescribed by the Secretary.

[Sec. 446(d)]

(d) TAXPAYER ENGAGED IN MORE THAN ONE BUSINESS.—A taxpayer engaged in more than one trade or business may, in computing taxable income, use a different method of accounting for each trade or business.

[Sec. 446(e)]

(e) REQUIREMENT RESPECTING CHANGE OF ACCOUNTING METHOD.—Except as otherwise expressly provided in this chapter, a taxpayer who changes the method of accounting on the basis of which he regularly computes his income in keeping his books shall, before computing his taxable income under the new method, secure the consent of the Secretary.

[Sec. 446(f)]

(f) FAILURE TO REQUEST CHANGE OF METHOD OF ACCOUNTING.—If the taxpayer does not file with the Secretary a request to change the method of accounting, the absence of the consent of the Secretary to a change in the method of accounting shall not be taken into account—

    (1) to prevent the imposition of any penalty, or the addition of any amount to tax, under this title, or

    (2) to diminish the amount of such penalty or addition to tax.

Subpart D—Inventories

[Sec. 475]

SEC. 475. MARK TO MARKET ACCOUNTING METHOD FOR DEALERS IN SECURITIES.

* * *

[Sec. 475(c)]

(c) DEFINITIONS.—For purposes of this section—

    (1) DEALER IN SECURITIES DEFINED.—The term "dealer in securities" means a taxpayer who—

        (A) regularly purchases securities from or sells securities to customers in the ordinary course of a trade or business; or

        (B) regularly offers to enter into, assume, offset, assign or otherwise terminate positions in securities with customers in the ordinary course of a trade or business.

    (2) SECURITY DEFINED.—The term "security" means any—

        (A) share of stock in a corporation;

        (B) partnership or beneficial ownership interest in a widely held or publicly traded partnership or trust;

        (C) note, bond, debenture, or other evidence of indebtedness;

        (D) interest rate, currency, or equity notional principal contract;

(E) evidence of an interest in, or a derivative financial instrument in, any security described in subparagraph (A), (B), (C), or (D), or any currency, including any option, forward contract, short position, and any similar financial instrument in such a security or currency; and

(F) position which—

(i) is not a security described in subparagraph (A), (B), (C), (D), or (E),

(ii) is a hedge with respect to such a security, and

(iii) is clearly identified in the dealer's records as being described in this subparagraph before the close of the day on which it was acquired or entered into (or such other time as the Secretary may by regulations prescribe).

Subparagraph (E) shall not include any contract to which section 1256(a) applies.

* * *

PART III—ADJUSTMENTS

[Sec. 482]

SEC. 482. ALLOCATION OF INCOME AND DEDUCTIONS AMONG TAXPAYERS.

In any case of two or more organizations, trades, or businesses (whether or not incorporated, whether or not organized in the United States, and whether or not affiliated) owned or controlled directly or indirectly by the same interests, the Secretary may distribute, apportion, or allocate gross income, deductions, credits, or allowances between or among such organizations, trades, or businesses, if he determines that such distribution, apportionment, or allocation is necessary in order to prevent evasion of taxes or clearly to reflect the income of any of such organizations, trades, or businesses. In the case of any transfer (or license) of intangible property (within the meaning of section 936(h)(3)(B)), the income with respect to such transfer or license shall be commensurate with the income attributable to the intangible.

[Sec. 483]

SEC. 483. INTEREST ON CERTAIN DEFERRED PAYMENTS.

[Sec. 483(a)]

(a) AMOUNT CONSTITUTING INTEREST.—For purposes of this title, in the case of any payment—

(1) under any contract for the sale or exchange of any property, and

(2) to which this section applies,

there shall be treated as interest that portion of the total unstated interest under such contract which, as determined in a manner consistent with the method of computing interest under section 1272(a), is properly allocable to such payment.

[Sec. 483(b)]

(b) TOTAL UNSTATED INTEREST.—For purposes of this section, the term "total unstated interest" means, with respect to a contract for the sale or exchange of property, an amount equal to the excess of—

(1) the sum of the payments to which this section applies which are due under the contract, over

(2) the sum of the present values of such payments and the present values of any interest payments due under the contract.

For purposes of the preceding sentence, the present value of a payment shall be determined under the rules of section 1274(b)(2) using a discount rate equal to the applicable Federal rate determined under section 1274(d).

[Sec. 483(c)]

(c) PAYMENTS TO WHICH SUBSECTION (a) APPLIES.—

(1) IN GENERAL.—Except as provided in subsection (d), this section shall apply to any payment on account of the sale or exchange of property which constitutes part or all of the sales price and which is due more than 6 months after the date of such sale or exchange under a contract—

(A) under which some or all of the payments are due more than 1 year after the date of such sale or exchange, and

(B) under which there is total unstated interest.

(2) TREATMENT OF OTHER DEBT INSTRUMENTS.—For purposes of this section, a debt instrument of the purchaser which is given in consideration for the sale or exchange of property shall not be treated as a payment, and any payment due under such debt instrument shall be treated as due under the contract for the sale or exchange.

(3) DEBT INSTRUMENT DEFINED.—For purposes of this subsection, the term "debt instrument" has the meaning given such term by section 1275(a)(1).

[Sec. 483(d)]

(d) EXCEPTIONS AND LIMITATIONS.—

(1) COORDINATION WITH ORIGINAL ISSUE DISCOUNT RULES.—This section shall not apply to any debt instrument for which an issue price is determined under section 1273(b) (other than paragraph (4) thereof) or section 1274.

(2) SALES PRICES OF $3,000 OR LESS.—This section shall not apply to any payment on account of the sale or exchange of property if it can be determined at the time of such sale or exchange that the sales price cannot exceed $3,000.

(3) CARRYING CHARGES.—In the case of the purchaser, the tax treatment of amounts paid on account of the sale or exchange of property shall be made without regard to this section if any such amounts are treated under section 163(b) as if they included interest.

(4) CERTAIN SALES OF PATENTS.—In the case of any transfer described in section 1235(a) (relating to sale or exchange of patents), this section shall not apply to any amount contingent on the productivity, use, or disposition of the property transferred.

[Sec. 483(e)]

(e) MAXIMUM RATE OF INTEREST ON CERTAIN TRANSFERS OF LAND BETWEEN RELATED PARTIES.—

(1) IN GENERAL.—In the case of any qualified sale, the discount rate used in determining the total unstated interest rate under subsection (b) shall not exceed 6 percent, compounded semiannually.

(2) QUALIFIED SALE.—For purposes of this subsection, the term "qualified sale" means any sale or exchange of land by an individual to a member of such individual's family (within the meaning of section 267(c)(4)).

(3) $500,000 LIMITATION.—Paragraph (1) shall not apply to any qualified sale between individuals made during any calendar year to the extent that the sales price for such sale (when added to the aggregate sale price for prior qualified sales between such individuals during the calendar year) exceeds $500,000.

(4) NONRESIDENT ALIEN INDIVIDUALS.—Paragraph (1) shall not apply to any sale or exchange if any party to such sale or exchange is a nonresident alien individual.

[Sec. 483(f)]

(f) REGULATIONS.—The Secretary shall prescribe such regulations as may be necessary or appropriate to carry out the purposes of this section including regulations providing for the application of this section in the case of—

(1) any contract for the sale or exchange of property under which the liability for, or the amount or due date of, a payment cannot be determined at the time of the sale or exchange, or

(2) any change in the liability for, or the amount or due date of, any payment (including interest) under a contract for the sale or exchange of property.

[Sec. 483(g)]

(g) CROSS REFERENCES.—

(1) For treatment of assumptions, see section 1274(c)(4).

Income Tax—Surplus Accumulations

(2) For special rules for certain transactions where stated principal amount does not exceed $2,800,000, see section 1274A.

(3) For special rules in the case of the borrower under certain loans for personal use, see section 1275(b).

SUBCHAPTER G—CORPORATIONS USED TO AVOID INCOME TAX ON SHAREHOLDERS

PART I—CORPORATIONS IMPROPERLY ACCUMULATING SURPLUS

[Sec. 531]

SEC. 531. IMPOSITION OF ACCUMULATED EARNINGS TAX.

In addition to other taxes imposed by this chapter, there is hereby imposed for each taxable year on the accumulated taxable income (as defined in section 535) of each corporation described in section 532, an accumulated earnings tax equal to 15 percent of the accumulated taxable income.

[Sec. 532]

SEC. 532. CORPORATIONS SUBJECT TO ACCUMULATED EARNINGS TAX.

[Sec. 532(a)]

(a) GENERAL RULE.—The accumulated earnings tax imposed by section 531 shall apply to every corporation (other than those described in subsection (b)) formed or availed of for the purpose of avoiding the income tax with respect to its shareholders or the shareholders of any other corporation, by permitting earnings and profits to accumulate instead of being divided or distributed.

[Sec. 532(b)]

(b) EXCEPTIONS.—The accumulated earnings tax imposed by section 531 shall not apply to—

(1) a personal holding company (as defined in section 542),

(2) a foreign personal holding company (as defined in section 552),

(3) a corporation exempt from tax under subchapter F (section 501 and following), or

(4) a passive foreign investment company (as defined in section 1297).

[Sec. 532(c)]

(c) APPLICATION DETERMINED WITHOUT REGARD TO NUMBER OF SHAREHOLDERS.—The application of this part to a corporation shall be determined without regard to the number of shareholders of such corporation.

[Sec. 533]

SEC. 533. EVIDENCE OF PURPOSE TO AVOID INCOME TAX.

[Sec. 533(a)]

(a) UNREASONABLE ACCUMULATION DETERMINATIVE OF PURPOSE.—For purposes of section 532, the fact that the earnings and profits of a corporation are permitted to accumulate beyond the reasonable needs of the business shall be determinative of the purpose to avoid the income tax with respect to shareholders, unless the corporation by the preponderance of the evidence shall prove to the contrary.

[Sec. 533(b)]

(b) HOLDING OR INVESTMENT COMPANY.—The fact that any corporation is a mere holding or investment company shall be prima facie evidence of the purpose to avoid the income tax with respect to shareholders.

Sec. 533(b)

SEC. 534. BURDEN OF PROOF.

(a) GENERAL RULE.—In any proceeding before the Tax Court involving a notice of deficiency based in whole or in part on the allegation that all or any part of the earnings and profits have been permitted to accumulate beyond the reasonable needs of the business, the burden of proof with respect to such allegation shall—

(1) if notification has not been sent in accordance with subsection (b), be on the Secretary, or

(2) if the taxpayer has submitted the statement described in subsection (c), be on the Secretary with respect to the grounds set forth in such statement in accordance with the provisions of such subsection.

(b) NOTIFICATION BY SECRETARY.—Before mailing the notice of deficiency referred to in subsection (a), the Secretary may send by certified mail or registered mail a notification informing the taxpayer that the proposed notice of deficiency includes an amount with respect to the accumulated earnings tax imposed by section 531.

(c) STATEMENT BY TAXPAYER.—Within such time (but not less than 30 days) after the mailing of the notification described in subsection (b) as the Secretary may prescribe by regulations, the taxpayer may submit a statement of the grounds (together with facts sufficient to show the basis thereof) on which the taxpayer relies to establish that all or any part of the earnings and profits have not been permitted to accumulate beyond the reasonable needs of the business.

(d) JEOPARDY ASSESSMENT.—If pursuant to section 6861 (a) a jeopardy assessment is made before the mailing of the notice of deficiency referred to in subsection (a), for purposes of this section such notice of deficiency shall, to the extent that it informs the taxpayer that such deficiency includes the accumulated earnings tax imposed by section 531, constitute the notification described in subsection (b), and in that event the statement described in subsection (c) may be included in the taxpayer's petition to the Tax Court.

SEC. 535. ACCUMULATED TAXABLE INCOME.

(a) DEFINITION.—For purposes of this subtitle, the term "accumulated taxable income" means the taxable income, adjusted in the manner provided in subsection (b), minus the sum of the dividends paid deduction (as defined in section 561) and the accumulated earnings credit (as defined in subsection (c)).

(b) ADJUSTMENTS TO TAXABLE INCOME.—For purposes of subsection (a), taxable income shall be adjusted as follows:

(1) TAXES.—There shall be allowed as a deduction Federal income and excess profits taxes and income, war profits, and excess profits taxes of foreign countries and possessions of the United States (to the extent not allowable as a deduction under section 275(a)(4)), accrued during the taxable year or deemed to be paid by a domestic corporation under section 902(a) or 960(a)(1) for the taxable year, but not including the accumulated earnings tax imposed by section 531, the personal holding company tax imposed by section 541, or the taxes imposed by corresponding sections of a prior income tax law.

(2) CHARITABLE CONTRIBUTIONS.—The deduction for charitable contributions provided under section 170 shall be allowed without regard to section 170(b)(2).

(3) SPECIAL DEDUCTIONS DISALLOWED.—The special deductions for corporations provided in part VIII (except section 248) of subchapter B (section 241 and following, relating to the deduction for dividends received by corporations, etc.) shall not be allowed.

(4) NET OPERATING LOSS.—The net operating loss deduction provided in section 172 shall not be allowed.

(5) CAPITAL LOSSES.—

(A) IN GENERAL.—Except as provided in subparagraph (B), there shall be allowed as a deduction an amount equal to the net capital loss for the taxable year (determined without regard to paragraph (7)(A)).

(B) RECAPTURE OF PREVIOUS DEDUCTIONS FOR CAPITAL GAINS.—The aggregate amount allowable as a deduction under subparagraph (A) for any taxable year shall be reduced by the lesser of—

(i) the nonrecaptured capital gains deductions, or

(ii) the amount of the accumulated earnings and profits of the corporation as of the close of the preceding taxable year.

(C) NONRECAPTURED CAPITAL GAINS DEDUCTIONS.—For purposes of subparagraph (B), the term "nonrecaptured capital gains deductions" means the excess of—

(i) the aggregate amount allowable as a deduction under paragraph (6) for preceding taxable years beginning after July 18, 1984, over

(ii) the aggregate of the reductions under subparagraph (B) for preceding taxable years.

(6) NET CAPITAL GAINS.—

(A) IN GENERAL.—There shall be allowed as a deduction—

(i) the net capital gain for the taxable year (determined with the application of paragraph (7)), reduced by

(ii) the taxes attributable to such net capital gain.

(B) ATTRIBUTABLE TAXES.—For purposes of subparagraph (A), the taxes attributable to the net capital gain shall be an amount equal to the difference between—

(i) the taxes imposed by this subtitle (except the tax imposed by this part) for the taxable year, and

(ii) such taxes computed for such year without including in taxable income the net capital gain for the taxable year (determined without the application of paragraph (7)).

(7) CAPITAL LOSS CARRYOVERS.—

(A) UNLIMITED CARRYFORWARD.—The net capital loss for any taxable year shall be treated as a short-term capital loss in the next taxable year.

(B) SECTION 1212 INAPPLICABLE.—No allowance shall be made for the capital loss carryback or carryforward provided in section 1212.

(8) SPECIAL RULES FOR MERE HOLDING OR INVESTMENT COMPANIES.—In the case of a mere holding or investment company—

(A) CAPITAL LOSS DEDUCTION, ETC., NOT ALLOWED.—Paragraphs (5) and (7)(A) shall not apply.

(B) DEDUCTION FOR CERTAIN OFFSETS.—There shall be allowed as a deduction the net short-term capital gain for the taxable year to the extent such gain does not exceed the amount of any capital loss carryover to such taxable year under section 1212 (determined without regard to paragraph (7)(B)).

(C) EARNINGS AND PROFITS.—For purposes of subchapter C, the accumulated earnings and profits at any time shall not be less than they would be if this subsection had applied to the computation of earnings and profits for all taxable years beginning after July 18, 1984.

Sec. 535(b)(8)(C)

(9) SPECIAL RULE FOR CAPITAL GAINS AND LOSSES OF FOREIGN CORPORATIONS.—In the case of a foreign corporation, paragraph (6) shall be applied by taking into account only gains and losses which are effectively connected with the conduct of a trade or business within the United States and are not exempt from tax under treaty.

[Sec. 535(c)]

(c) ACCUMULATED EARNINGS CREDIT.—

(1) GENERAL RULE.—For purposes of subsection (a), in the case of a corporation other than a mere holding or investment company the accumulated earnings credit is (A) an amount equal to such part of the earnings and profits for the taxable year as are retained for the reasonable needs of the business, minus (B) the deduction allowed by subsection (b)(6). For purposes of this paragraph, the amount of the earnings and profits for the taxable year which are retained is the amount by which the earnings and profits for the taxable year exceed the dividends paid deduction (as defined in section 561) for such year.

(2) MINIMUM CREDIT.—

(A) IN GENERAL.—The credit allowable under paragraph (1) shall in no case be less than the amount by which $250,000 exceeds the accumulated earnings and profits of the corporation at the close of the preceding taxable year.

(B) CERTAIN SERVICE CORPORATIONS.—In the case of a corporation the principal function of which is the performance of services in the field of health, law, engineering, architecture, accounting, actuarial science, performing arts, or consulting, subparagraph (A) shall be applied by substituting "$150,000" for "$250,000".

(3) HOLDING AND INVESTMENT COMPANIES.—In the case of a corporation which is a mere holding or investment company, the accumulated earnings credit is the amount (if any) by which $250,000 exceeds the accumulated earnings and profits of the corporation at the close of the preceding taxable year.

(4) ACCUMULATED EARNINGS AND PROFITS.—For purposes of paragraphs (2) and (3), the accumulated earnings and profits at the close of the preceding taxable year shall be reduced by the dividends which under section 563(a) (relating to dividends paid after the close of the taxable year) are considered as paid during such taxable year.

(5) CROSS REFERENCE.—

For denial of credit provided in paragraph (2) or (3) where multiple corporations are formed to avoid tax, see section 1551, and for limitation on such credit in the case of certain controlled corporations, see section 1561.

[Sec. 535(d)]

(d) INCOME DISTRIBUTED TO UNITED STATES-OWNED FOREIGN CORPORATION RETAINS UNITED STATES CONNECTION.—

(1) IN GENERAL.—For purposes of this part, if 10 percent or more of the earnings and profits of any foreign corporation for any taxable year—

(A) is derived from sources within the United States, or

(B) is effectively connected with the conduct of a trade or business within the United States,

any distribution out of such earnings and profits (and any interest payment) received (directly or through 1 or more other entities) by a United States-owned foreign corporation shall be treated as derived by such corporation from sources within the United States.

Caution: *Code Sec. 535(d)(2), below, is effective for tax years on or before December 31, 2006.*

(2) UNITED STATES-OWNED FOREIGN CORPORATION.—The term "United States-owned foreign corporation" has the meaning given to such term by section 904(g)(6).

Caution: *Code Sec. 535(d)(2), below, is effective for tax years beginning after December 31, 2006.*

(2) UNITED STATES-OWNED FOREIGN CORPORATION.—The term "United States-owned foreign corporation" has the meaning given to such term by section 904(h)(6).

[Sec. 536]

SEC. 536. INCOME NOT PLACED ON ANNUAL BASIS.

Section 443(b) (relating to computation of tax on change of annual accounting period) shall not apply in the computation of the accumulated earnings tax imposed by section 531.

[Sec. 537]

SEC. 537. REASONABLE NEEDS OF THE BUSINESS.

[Sec. 537(a)]

(a) GENERAL RULE.—For purposes of this part, the term "reasonable needs of the business" includes—

(1) the reasonably anticipated needs of the business,
(2) the section 303 redemption needs of the business, and
(3) the excess business holdings redemption needs of the business.

[Sec. 537(b)]

(b) SPECIAL RULES.—For purposes of subsection (a)—

(1) SECTION 303 REDEMPTION NEEDS.—The term "section 303 redemption needs" means, with respect to the taxable year of the corporation in which a shareholder of the corporation died or any taxable year thereafter, the amount needed (or reasonably anticipated to be needed) to make a redemption of stock included in the gross estate of the decedent (but not in excess of the maximum amount of stock to which section 303(a) may apply).

(2) EXCESS BUSINESS HOLDINGS REDEMPTION NEEDS.—The term "excess business holdings redemption needs" means the amount needed (or reasonably anticipated to be needed) to redeem from a private foundation stock which—

(A) such foundation held on May 26, 1969 (or which was received by such foundation pursuant to a will or irrevocable trust to which section 4943(c)(5) applies), and

(B) constituted excess business holdings on May 26, 1969, or would have constituted excess business holdings as of such date if there were taken into account (i) stock received pursuant to a will or trust described in subparagraph (A), and (ii) the reduction in the total outstanding stock of the corporation which would have resulted solely from the redemption of stock held by the private foundation.

(3) OBLIGATIONS INCURRED TO MAKE REDEMPTIONS.—In applying paragraphs (1) and (2), the discharge of any obligation incurred to make a redemption described in such paragraphs shall be treated as the making of such redemption.

(4) PRODUCT LIABILITY LOSS RESERVES.—The accumulation of reasonable amounts for the payment of reasonably anticipated product liability losses (as defined in section 172(f)), as determined under regulations prescribed by the Secretary, shall be treated as accumulated for the reasonably anticipated needs of the business.

(5) NO INFERENCE AS TO PRIOR TAXABLE YEARS.—The application of this part to any taxable year before the first taxable year specified in paragraph (1) shall be made without regard to the fact that distributions in redemption coming within the terms of such paragraphs were subsequently made.

PART II—PERSONAL HOLDING COMPANIES

[Sec. 541]

SEC. 541. IMPOSITION OF PERSONAL HOLDING COMPANY TAX.

In addition to other taxes imposed by this chapter, there is hereby imposed for each taxable year on the undistributed personal holding company income (as defined in section 545) of every personal holding company (as defined in section 542) a personal holding company tax equal to 15 percent of the undistributed personal holding company income.

[Sec. 542]

SEC. 542. DEFINITION OF PERSONAL HOLDING COMPANY.

[Sec. 542(a)]

(a) GENERAL RULE.—For purposes of this subtitle, the term "personal holding company" means any corporation (other than a corporation described in subsection (c)) if—

(1) ADJUSTED ORDINARY GROSS INCOME REQUIREMENT.—At least 60 percent of its adjusted ordinary gross income (as defined in section 543(b)(2)) for the taxable year is personal holding company income (as defined in section 543(a)), and

(2) STOCK OWNERSHIP REQUIREMENT.—At any time during the last half of the taxable year more than 50 percent in value of its outstanding stock is owned, directly or indirectly, by or for not more than 5 individuals. For purposes of this paragraph, an organization described in section 401(a), 501(c)(17), or 509(a) or a portion of a trust permanently set aside or to be used exclusively for the purposes described in section 642(c) or a corresponding provision of a prior income tax law shall be considered an individual.

[Sec. 542(b)]

(b) CORPORATIONS FILING CONSOLIDATED RETURNS.—

(1) GENERAL RULE.—In the case of an affiliated group of corporations filing or required to file a consolidated return under section 1501 for any taxable year, the adjusted ordinary gross income requirement of subsection (a)(1) of this section shall, except as provided in paragraphs (2) and (3), be applied for such year with respect to the consolidated adjusted ordinary gross income and the consolidated personal holding company income of the affiliated group. No member of such an affiliated group shall be considered to meet such adjusted ordinary gross income requirement unless the affiliated group meets such requirement.

(2) INELIGIBLE AFFILIATED GROUP.—Paragraph (1) shall not apply to an affiliated group of corporations if—

(A) any member of the affiliated group of corporations (including the common parent corporation) derived 10 percent or more of its adjusted ordinary gross income for the taxable year from sources outside the affiliated group, and

(B) 80 percent or more of the amount described in subparagraph (A) consists of personal holding company income (as defined in section 543).

For purposes of this paragraph, section 543 shall be applied as if the amount described in subparagraph (A) were the adjusted ordinary gross income of the corporation.

(3) EXCLUDED CORPORATIONS.—Paragraph (1) shall not apply to an affiliated group of corporations if any member of the affiliated group (including the common parent corporation) is a corporation excluded from the definition of personal holding company under subsection (c).

(4) CERTAIN DIVIDEND INCOME RECEIVED BY A COMMON PARENT.—In applying paragraph (2)(A) and (B), personal holding company income and adjusted ordinary gross income shall not include dividends received by a common parent corporation from another corporation if—

(A) the common parent corporation owns, directly or indirectly, more than 50 percent of the outstanding voting stock of such other corporation, and

(B) such other corporation is not a personal holding company for the taxable year in which the dividends are paid.

(5) CERTAIN DIVIDEND INCOME RECEIVED FROM A NONINCLUDIBLE LIFE INSURANCE COMPANY.—In the case of an affiliated group of corporations filing or required to file a consolidated return under section 1501 for any taxable year, there shall be excluded from consolidated personal holding company income and consolidated adjusted ordinary gross income for purposes of this part dividends received by a member of the affiliated group from a life insurance company taxable under section 801 that is not a member of the affiliated group solely by reason of the application of paragraph (2) of subsection (b) of section 1504.

[Sec. 542(c)]

(c) EXCEPTIONS.—The term "personal holding company" as defined in subsection (a) does not include—

(1) a corporation exempt from tax under subchapter F (sec. 501 and following);

(2) a bank as defined in section 581, or a domestic building and loan association within the meaning of section 7701(a)(19);

(3) a life insurance company;

(4) a surety company;

(5) a foreign corporation,

(6) a lending or finance company if—

(A) 60 percent or more of its ordinary gross income (as defined in section 543(b)(1)) is derived directly from the active and regular conduct of a lending or finance business;

(B) the personal holding company income for the taxable year (computed without regard to income described in subsection (d)(3) and income derived directly from the active and regular conduct of a lending or finance business, and computed by including as personal holding company income the entire amount of the gross income from rents, royalties, produced film rents, and compensation for use of corporate property by shareholders) is not more than 20 percent of the ordinary gross income;

(C) the sum of the deductions which are directly allocable to the active and regular conduct of its lending or finance business equals or exceeds the sum of—

(i) 15 percent of so much of the ordinary gross income derived therefrom as does not exceed $500,000, plus

(ii) 5 percent of so much of the ordinary gross income derived therefrom as exceeds $500,000; and

(D) the loans to a person who is a shareholder in such company during the taxable year by or for whom 10 percent or more in value of its outstanding stock is owned directly or indirectly (including, in the case of an individual, stock owned by members of his family as defined in section 544(a)(2)), outstanding at any time during such year do not exceed $5,000 in principal amount;

(7) a small business investment company which is licensed by the Small Business Administration and operating under the Small Business Investment Act of 1958 (15 U.S.C. 661 and following) and which is actively engaged in the business of providing funds to small business concerns under that Act. This paragraph shall not apply if any shareholder of the small business investment company owns at any time during the taxable year directly or indirectly (including, in the case of an individual, ownership by the members of his family as defined in section 544(a)(2)) a 5 per centum or more proprietary interest in a small business concern to which funds are provided by the investment company or 5 per centum or more in value of the outstanding stock of such concern; and

(8) a corporation which is subject to the jurisdiction of the court in a title 11 or similar case (within the meaning of section 368(a)(3)(A)) unless a major purpose of instituting or continuing such case is the avoidance of the tax imposed by section 541.

[Sec. 542(d)]

(d) SPECIAL RULES FOR APPLYING SUBSECTION (c)(6).—

(1) LENDING OR FINANCE BUSINESS DEFINED.—

(A) IN GENERAL.—Except as provided in subparagraph (B), for purposes of subsection (c)(6), the term "lending or finance business" means a business of—

(i) making loans,

(ii) purchasing or discounting accounts receivable, notes, or installment obligations,

(iii) rendering services or making facilities available in connection with activities described in clauses (i) and (ii) carried on by the corporation rendering services or making facilities available, or

(iv) rendering services or making facilities available to another corporation which is engaged in the lending or finance business (within the meaning of this paragraph), if such services or facilities are related to the lending or finance business (within such meaning) of such other corporation and such other corporation and the corporation rendering services or making facilities available are members of the same affiliated group (as defined in section 1504).

(B) EXCEPTIONS.—For purposes of subparagraph (A), the term "lending or finance business" does not include the business of—

(i) making loans, or purchasing or discounting accounts receivable, notes, or installment obligations, if (at the time of the loan, purchase, or discount) the remaining maturity exceeds 144 months; unless—

(I) the loans, notes, or installment obligations are evidenced or secured by contracts of conditional sale, chattel mortgages, or chattel lease agreements arising out of the sale of goods or services in the course of the borrower's or transferor's trade or business, or

(II) the loans, notes, or installment obligations are made or acquired by the taxpayer and meet the requirements of subparagraph (C), or

(ii) making loans evidenced by, or purchasing, certificates of indebtedness issued in a series, under a trust indenture, and in registered form or with interest coupons attached.

For purposes of clause (i), the remaining maturity shall be treated as including any period for which there may be a renewal or extension under the terms of an option exercisable by the borrower.

(C) INDEFINITE MATURITY CREDIT TRANSACTIONS.—For purposes of subparagraph (B)(i), a loan, note, or installment obligation meets the requirements of this subparagraph if it is made under an agreement—

(i) under which the creditor agrees to make loans or advances (not in excess of an agreed upon maximum amount) from time to time to or for the account of the debtor upon request, and

(ii) under which the debtor may repay the loan or advance in full or in installments.

(2) BUSINESS DEDUCTIONS.—For purposes of subsection (c)(6)(C), the deductions which may be taken into account shall include only—

(A) deductions which are allowable only by reason of section 162 or section 404, except there shall not be included any such deduction in respect of compensation for personal services rendered by shareholders (including members of the shareholder's family as described in section 544(a)(2)), and

(B) deductions allowable under section 167, and deductions allowable under section 164 for real property taxes, but in either case only to the extent that the property with respect to which such deductions are allowable is used directly in the active and regular conduct of the lending or finance business.

(3) INCOME RECEIVED FROM CERTAIN AFFILIATED CORPORATIONS.—For purposes of subsection (c)(6)(B), in the case of a lending or finance company which meets the requirements of subsection (c)(6)(A), there shall not be treated as personal holding company income the lawful income received from a corporation which meets the requirements of subsection (c)(6) and which is a member of the same affiliated group (as defined in section 1504) of which such company is a member.

Income Tax—Personal Holding Companies

[Sec. 543]

SEC. 543. PERSONAL HOLDING COMPANY INCOME.

[Sec. 543(a)]

(a) GENERAL RULE.—For purposes of this subtitle, the term "personal holding company income" means the portion of the adjusted ordinary gross income which consists of:

(1) DIVIDENDS, ETC.—Dividends, interest, royalties (other than mineral, oil, or gas royalties or copyright royalties), and annuities. This paragraph shall not apply to—

(A) interest constituting rent (as defined in subsection (b)(3)),

(B) interest on amounts set aside in a reserve fund under section 511 or 607 of the Merchant Marine Act, 1936 (46 U.S.C. App 1161 or 1177),

(C) active business computer software royalties (within the meaning of subsection (d)), and

(D) interest received by a broker or dealer (within the meaning of section 3(a)(4) or (5) of the Securities and Exchange Act of 1934) in connection with—

(i) any securities or money market instruments held as property described in section 1221(a)(1),

(ii) margin accounts, or

(iii) any financing for a customer secured by securities or money market instruments.

(2) RENTS.—The adjusted income from rents; except that such adjusted income shall not be included if—

(A) such adjusted income constitutes 50 percent or more of the adjusted ordinary gross income, and

(B) the sum of—

(i) the dividends paid during the taxable year (determined under section 562),

(ii) the dividends considered as paid on the last day of the taxable year under section 563(d) (as limited by the second sentence of section 563(b)), and

(iii) the consent dividends for the taxable year (determined under section 565),

equals or exceeds the amount, if any, by which the personal holding company income for the taxable year (computed without regard to this paragraph and paragraph (6), and computed by including as personal holding company income copyright royalties and the adjusted income from mineral, oil, and gas royalties) exceeds 10 percent of the ordinary gross income.

(3) MINERAL, OIL, AND GAS ROYALTIES.—The adjusted income from mineral, oil, and gas royalties; except that such adjusted income shall not be included if—

(A) such adjusted income constitutes 50 percent or more of the adjusted ordinary gross income,

(B) the personal holding company income for the taxable year (computed without regard to this paragraph, and computed by including as personal holding company income copyright royalties and the adjusted income from rents) is not more than 10 percent of the ordinary gross income, and

(C) the sum of the deductions which are allowable under section 162 (relating to trade or business expenses) other than—

(i) deductions for compensation for personal services rendered by the shareholders, and

(ii) deductions which are specifically allowable under sections other than section 162,

equals or exceeds 15 percent of the adjusted ordinary gross income.

(4) COPYRIGHT ROYALTIES.—Copyright royalties; except that copyright royalties shall not be included if—

(A) such royalties (exclusive of royalties received for the use of, or right to use, copyrights or interests in copyrights on works created in whole, or in part, by any shareholder) constitute 50 percent or more of the ordinary gross income,

(B) the personal holding company income for the taxable year computed—

Sec. 543(a)(4)(B)

(i) without regard to copyright royalties, other than royalties received for the use of, or right to use, copyrights or interests in copyrights in works created in whole, or in part, by any shareholder owning more than 10 percent of the total outstanding capital stock of the corporation,

(ii) without regard to dividends from any corporation in which the taxpayer owns at least 50 percent of all classes of stock entitled to vote and at least 50 percent of the total value of all classes of stock and which corporation meets the requirements of this subparagraph and subparagraphs (A) and (C), and

(iii) by including as personal holding company income the adjusted income from rents and the adjusted income from mineral, oil, and gas royalties,

is not more than 10 percent of the ordinary gross income, and

(C) the sum of the deductions which are properly allocable to such royalties and which are allowable under section 162, other than—

(i) deductions for compensation for personal services rendered by the shareholders,

(ii) deductions for royalties paid or accrued, and

(iii) deductions which are specifically allowable under sections other than section 162,

equals or exceeds 25 percent of the amount by which the ordinary gross income exceeds the sum of the royalties paid or accrued and the amounts allowable as deductions under section 167 (relating to depreciation) with respect to copyright royalties.

For purposes of this subsection, the term "copyright royalties" means compensation, however designated, for the use of, or the right to use, copyrights in works protected by copyright issued under title 17 of the United States Code and to which copyright protection is also extended by the laws of any country other than the United States of America by virtue of any international treaty, convention, or agreement, or interests in any such copyrighted works, and includes payments from any person for performing rights in any such copyrighted work and payments (other than produced film rents as defined in paragraph (5)(B)) received for the use of, or right to use, films. For purposes of this paragraph, the term "shareholder" shall include any person who owns stock within the meaning of section 544. This paragraph shall not apply to active business computer software royalties.

(5) PRODUCED FILM RENTS.—

(A) Produced film rents; except that such rents shall not be included if such rents constitute 50 percent or more of the ordinary gross income.

(B) For purposes of this section, the term "produced film rents" means payments received with respect to an interest in a film for the use of, or right to use, such film, but only to the extent that such interest was acquired before substantial completion of production of such film. In the case of a producer who actively participates in the production of the film, such term includes an interest in the proceeds or profits from the film, but only to the extent such interest is attributable to such active participation.

(6) USE OF CORPORATE PROPERTY BY SHAREHOLDER.—

(A) Amounts received as compensation (however designated and from whomever received) for the use of, or the right to use, tangible property of the corporation in any case where, at any time during the taxable year, 25 percent or more in value of the outstanding stock of the corporation is owned, directly or indirectly, by or for an individual entitled to the use of the property (whether such right is obtained directly from the corporation or by means of a sublease or other arrangement).

(B) Subparagraph (A) shall apply only to a corporation which has personal holding company income in excess of 10 percent of its ordinary gross income.

(C) For purposes of the limitation in subparagraph (B), personal holding company income shall be computed—

(i) without regard to subparagraph (A) or paragraph (2),

(ii) by excluding amounts received as compensation for the use of (or right to use) intangible property (other than mineral, oil, or gas royalties or copyright royalties) if a substantial part of the tangible property used in connection with such intangible property is owned by the corporation and all such tangible and intangible property is used in the active conduct of a trade or business by an individual or individuals described in subparagraph (A), and

(iii) by including copyright royalties and adjusted income from mineral, oil, and gas royalties.

(7) PERSONAL SERVICE CONTRACTS.—

(A) Amounts received under a contract under which the corporation is to furnish personal services; if some person other than the corporation has the right to designate (by name or by description) the individual who is to perform the services, or if the individual who is to perform the services is designated (by name or by description) in the contract; and

(B) amounts received from the sale or other disposition of such a contract.

This paragraph shall apply with respect to amounts received for services under a particular contract only if at some time during the taxable year 25 percent or more in value of the outstanding stock of the corporation is owned, directly or indirectly, by or for the individual who has performed, is to perform, or may be designated (by name or by description) as the one to perform, such services.

(8) ESTATES AND TRUSTS.—Amounts includible in computing the taxable income of the corporation under part I of subchapter J (sec. 641 and following, relating to estates, trusts, and beneficiaries).

[Sec. 543(b)]

(b) DEFINITIONS.—For purposes of this part—

(1) ORDINARY GROSS INCOME.—The term "ordinary gross income" means the gross income determined by excluding—

(A) all gains from the sale or other disposition of capital assets, and

(B) all gains (other than those referred to in subparagraph (A)) from the sale or other disposition of property described in section 1231(b).

(2) ADJUSTED ORDINARY GROSS INCOME.—The term "adjusted ordinary gross income" means the ordinary gross income adjusted as follows:

(A) RENTS.—From the gross income from rents (as defined in the second sentence of paragraph (3) of this subsection) subtract the amount allowable as deductions for—

(i) exhaustion, wear and tear, obsolescence, and amortization of property other than tangible personal property which is not customarily retained by any one lessee for more than three years,

(ii) property taxes,

(iii) interest, and

(iv) rent,

to the extent allocable, under regulations prescribed by the Secretary, to such gross income from rents. The amount subtracted under this subparagraph shall not exceed such gross income from rents.

(B) MINERAL ROYALTIES, ETC.—From the gross income from mineral, oil, and gas royalties described in paragraph (4), and from the gross income from working interests in an oil or gas well, subtract the amount allowable as deductions for—

(i) exhaustion, wear and tear, obsolescence, amortization, and depletion,

(ii) property and severance taxes,

(iii) interest, and

(iv) rent,

to the extent allocable, under regulations prescribed by the Secretary, to such gross income from royalties or such gross income from working interests in oil or gas wells. The amount subtracted under this subparagraph with respect to royalties shall not exceed the gross income from such royalties, and the amount subtracted under this subparagraph with respect to working interests shall not exceed the gross income from such working interests.

(C) INTEREST.—There shall be excluded—

(i) interest received on a direct obligation of the United States held for sale to customers in the ordinary course of trade or business by a regular dealer who is making a primary market in such obligations, and

(ii) interest on a condemnation award, a judgment, and a tax refund.

(D) CERTAIN EXCLUDED RENTS.—From the gross income consisting of compensation described in subparagraph (D) of paragraph (3) subtract the amount allowable as deductions for the items described in clauses (i), (ii), (iii), and (iv) of subparagraph (A) to the extent allocable, under regulations prescribed by the Secretary, to such gross income. The amount subtracted under this subparagraph shall not exceed such gross income.

(3) ADJUSTED INCOME FROM RENTS.—The term "adjusted income from rents" means the gross income from rents, reduced by the amount subtracted under paragraph (2)(A) of this subsection. For purposes of the preceding sentence, the term "rents" means compensation, however designated, for the use of, or right to use, property, and the interest on debts owed to the corporation, to the extent such debts represent the price for which real property held primarily for sale to customers in the ordinary course of its trade or business was sold or exchanged by the corporation; but such term does not include—

(A) amounts constituting personal holding company income under subsection (a)(6),

(B) copyright royalties (as defined in subsection (a)(4)),

(C) produced film rents (as defined in subsection (a)(5)(B)),

(D) compensation, however designated, for the use of, or the right to use, any tangible personal property manufactured or produced by the taxpayer, if during the taxable year the taxpayer is engaged in substantial manufacturing or production of tangible personal property of the same type, or

(E) active business computer software royalties (as defined in subsection (d)).

(4) ADJUSTED INCOME FROM MINERAL, OIL, AND GAS ROYALTIES.—The term "adjusted income from mineral, oil, and gas royalties" means the gross income from mineral, oil, and gas royalties (including production payments and overriding royalties), reduced by the amount subtracted under paragraph (2)(B) of this subsection in respect of such royalties.

[Sec. 543(c)]

(c) GROSS INCOME OF INSURANCE COMPANIES OTHER THAN LIFE INSURANCE COMPANY.—In the case of an insurance company other than a life insurance company, the term "gross income" as used in this part means the gross income, as defined in section 832(b)(1), increased by the amount of losses incurred, as defined in section 832(b)(5), and the amount of expenses incurred, as defined in section 832(b)(6), and decreased by the amount deductible under section 832(c)(7) (relating to tax-free interest).

[Sec. 543(d)]

(d) ACTIVE BUSINESS COMPUTER SOFTWARE ROYALTIES.—

(1) IN GENERAL.—For purposes of this section, the term "active business computer software royalties" means any royalties—

(A) received by any corporation during the taxable year in connection with the licensing of computer software, and

(B) with respect to which the requirements of paragraphs (2), (3), (4), and (5) are met.

(2) ROYALTIES MUST BE RECEIVED BY CORPORATION ACTIVELY ENGAGED IN COMPUTER SOFTWARE BUSINESS.—The requirements of this paragraph are met if the royalties described in paragraph (1)—

(A) are received by a corporation engaged in the active conduct of the trade or business of developing, manufacturing, or producing computer software, and

(B) are attributable to computer software which—

(i) is developed, manufactured, or produced by such corporation (or its predecessor) in connection with the trade or business described in subparagraph (A), or

(ii) is directly related to such trade or business.

(3) ROYALTIES MUST CONSTITUTE AT LEAST 50 PERCENT OF INCOME.—The requirements of this paragraph are met if the royalties described in paragraph (1) constitute at least 50 percent of the ordinary gross income of the corporation for the taxable year.

(4) DEDUCTIONS UNDER SECTIONS 162 AND 174 RELATING TO ROYALTIES MUST EQUAL OR EXCEED 25 PERCENT OF ORDINARY GROSS INCOME.—

(A) IN GENERAL.—The requirements of this paragraph are met if—

(i) the sum of the deductions allowable to the corporation under sections 162, 174, and 195 for the taxable year which are properly allocable to the trade or business described in paragraph (2) equals or exceeds 25 percent of the ordinary gross income of such corporation for such taxable year, or

(ii) the average of such deductions for the 5-taxable year period ending with such taxable year equals or exceeds 25 percent of the average ordinary gross income of such corporation for such period.

If a corporation has not been in existence during the 5-taxable year period described in clause (ii), then the period of existence of such corporation shall be substituted for such 5-taxable year period.

(B) DEDUCTIONS ALLOWABLE UNDER SECTION 162.—For purposes of subparagraph (A), a deduction shall not be treated as allowable under section 162 if it is specifically allowable under another section.

(C) LIMITATION ON ALLOWABLE DEDUCTIONS.—For purposes of subparagraph (A), no deduction shall be taken into account with respect to compensation for personal services rendered by the 5 individual shareholders holding the largest percentage (by value) of the outstanding stock of the corporation. For purposes of the preceding sentence—

(i) individuals holding less than 5 percent (by value) of the stock of such corporation shall not be taken into account, and

(ii) stock deemed to be owned by a shareholder solely by attribution from a partner under section 544(a)(2) shall be disregarded.

(5) DIVIDENDS MUST EQUAL OR EXCEED EXCESS OF PERSONAL HOLDING COMPANY INCOME OVER 10 PERCENT OF ORDINARY GROSS INCOME.—

(A) IN GENERAL.—The requirements of this paragraph are met if the sum of—

(i) the dividends paid during the taxable year (determined under section 562),

(ii) the dividends considered as paid on the last day of the taxable year under section 563(d) (as limited by the second sentence of section 563(b)), and

(iii) the consent dividends for the taxable year (determined under section 565),

equals or exceeds the amount, if any, by which the personal holding company income for the taxable year exceeds 10 percent of the ordinary gross income of such corporation for such taxable year.

(B) COMPUTATION OF PERSONAL HOLDING COMPANY INCOME.—For purposes of this paragraph, personal holding company income shall be computed—

(i) without regard to amounts described in subsection (a)(1)(C),

(ii) without regard to interest income during any taxable year—

(I) which is in the 5-taxable year period beginning with the later of the 1st taxable year of the corporation or the 1st taxable year in which the corporation conducted the trade or business described in paragraph (2)(A), and

(II) during which the corporation meets the requirements of paragraphs (2), (3), and (4), and

(iii) by including adjusted income from rents and adjusted income from mineral, oil, and gas royalties (within the meaning of paragraphs (2) and (3) of subsection (a)).

Sec. 543(d)(5)(B)(iii)

(6) SPECIAL RULES FOR AFFILIATED GROUP MEMBERS.—

(A) IN GENERAL.—In any case in which—

(i) the taxpayer receives royalties in connection with the licensing of computer software, and

(ii) another corporation which is a member of the same affiliated group as the taxpayer meets the requirements of paragraphs (2), (3), (4), and (5) with respect to such computer software,

the taxpayer shall be treated as having met such requirements.

(B) AFFILIATED GROUP.—For purposes of this paragraph, the term "affiliated group" has the meaning given such term by section 1504(a).

[Sec. 544]

SEC. 544. RULES FOR DETERMINING STOCK OWNERSHIP.

[Sec. 544(a)]

(a) CONSTRUCTIVE OWNERSHIP.—For purposes of determining whether a corporation is a personal holding company, insofar as such determination is based on stock ownership under section 542(a)(2), section 543(a)(7), section 543(a)(6) or section 543(a)(4)—

(1) STOCK NOT OWNED BY INDIVIDUAL.—Stock owned, directly or indirectly, by or for a corporation, partnership, estate, or trust shall be considered as being owned proportionately by its shareholders, partners, or beneficiaries.

(2) FAMILY AND PARTNERSHIP OWNERSHIP.—An individual shall be considered as owning the stock owned, directly or indirectly, by or for his family or by or for his partner. For purposes of this paragraph, the family of an individual includes only his brothers and sisters (whether by the whole or half blood), spouse, ancestors, and lineal descendants.

(3) OPTIONS.—If any person has an option to acquire stock, such stock shall be considered as owned by such person. For purposes of this paragraph, an option to acquire such an option, and each one of a series of such options, shall be considered as an option to acquire such stock.

(4) APPLICATION OF FAMILY-PARTNERSHIP AND OPTION RULES.—Paragraphs (2) and (3) shall be applied—

(A) for purposes of the stock ownership requirement provided in section 542(a)(2), if, but only if, the effect is to make the corporation a personal holding company;

(B) for purposes of section 543(a)(7) (relating to personal service contracts), of section 543(a)(6) (relating to the use of property by shareholders), or of section 543(a)(4) (relating to copyright royalties), if, but only if, the effect is to make the amounts therein referred to includible under such paragraph as personal holding company income.

(5) CONSTRUCTIVE OWNERSHIP AS ACTUAL OWNERSHIP.—Stock constructively owned by a person by reason of the application of paragraph (1) or (3) shall, for purposes of applying paragraph (1) or (2), be treated as actually owned by such person; but stock constructively owned by an individual by reason of the application of paragraph (2) shall not be treated as owned by him for purposes of again applying such paragraph in order to make another the constructive owner of such stock.

(6) OPTION RULE IN LIEU OF FAMILY AND PARTNERSHIP RULE.—If stock may be considered as owned by an individual under either paragraph (2) or (3) it shall be considered as owned by him under paragraph (3).

[Sec. 544(b)]

(b) CONVERTIBLE SECURITIES.—Outstanding securities convertible into stock (whether or not convertible during the taxable year) shall be considered as outstanding stock—

(1) for purposes of the stock ownership requirement provided in section 542(a)(2), but only if the effect of the inclusion of all such securities is to make the corporation a personal holding company;

(2) for purposes of section 543(a)(7) (relating to personal service contracts), but only if the effect of the inclusion of all such securities is to make the amounts therein referred to includible under such paragraph as personal holding company income;

(3) for purposes of section 543(a)(6) (relating to the use of property by shareholders), but only if the effect of the inclusion of all such securities is to make the amounts therein referred to includible under such paragraph as personal holding company income; and

(4) for purposes of section 543(a)(4) (relating to copyright royalties), but only if the effect of the inclusion of all such securities is to make the amounts therein referred to includible under such paragraph as personal holding company income.

The requirement in paragraphs (1), (2), (3), and (4) that all convertible securities must be included if any are to be included shall be subject to the exception that, where some of the outstanding securities are convertible only after a later date than in the case of others, the class having the earlier conversion date may be included although the others are not included, but no convertible securities shall be included unless all outstanding securities having a prior conversion date are also included.

[Sec. 545]

SEC. 545. UNDISTRIBUTED PERSONAL HOLDING COMPANY INCOME.

[Sec. 545(a)]

(a) DEFINITION.—For purposes of this part, the term "undistributed personal holding company income" means the taxable income of a personal holding company adjusted in the manner provided in subsections (b), (c), and (d), minus the dividends paid deduction as defined in section 561. In the case of a personal holding company which is a foreign corporation, not more than 10 percent in value of the outstanding stock of which is owned (within the meaning of section 958(a)) during the last half of the taxable year by United States persons, the term "undistributed personal holding company income" means the amount determined by multiplying the undistributed personal holding company income (determined without regard to this sentence) by the percentage in value of its outstanding stock which is the greatest percentage in value of its outstanding stock so owned by United States persons on any one day during such period.

[Sec. 545(b)]

(b) ADJUSTMENTS TO TAXABLE INCOME.—For the purposes of subsection (a), the taxable income shall be adjusted as follows:

(1) TAXES.—There shall be allowed as a deduction Federal income and excess profits taxes and income, war profits and excess profits taxes of foreign countries and possessions of the United States (to the extent not allowable as a deduction under section 275(a)(4)), accrued during the taxable year or deemed to be paid by a domestic corporation under section 902(a) or 960(a)(1) for the taxable year, but not including the accumulated earnings tax imposed by section 531, the personal holding company tax imposed by section 541, or the taxes imposed by corresponding sections of a prior income tax law.

(2) CHARITABLE CONTRIBUTIONS.—The deduction for charitable contributions provided under section 170 shall be allowed, but in computing such deduction the limitations in section 170(b)(1)(A), (B), and (D) shall apply, and section 170(b)(2) and (d)(1) shall not apply. For purposes of this paragraph, the term "contribution base" when used in section 170(b)(1) means the taxable income computed with the adjustments (other than the 10-percent limitation) provided in section 170(b)(2) and (d)(1) and without deduction of the amount disallowed under paragraph (6) of this subsection.

(3) SPECIAL DEDUCTIONS DISALLOWED.—The special deductions for corporations provided in part VIII (except section 248) of subchapter B (section 241 and following, relating to the deduction for dividends received by corporations, etc.) shall not be allowed.

(4) NET OPERATING LOSS.—The net operating loss deduction provided in section 172 shall not be allowed, but there shall be allowed as a deduction the amount of the net operating loss (as defined in section 172 (c)) for the preceding taxable year computed without the deductions provided in part VIII (except section 248) of subchapter B.

(5) NET CAPITAL GAINS.—There shall be allowed as a deduction the net capital gain for the taxable year, minus the taxes imposed by this subtitle attributable to such excess. The taxes attributable to such net capital gain shall be an amount equal to the difference between—

(A) the taxes imposed by this subtitle (except the tax imposed by this part) for such year, and

(B) such taxes computed for such year without including such net capital gain in taxable income.

(6) EXPENSES AND DEPRECIATION APPLICABLE TO PROPERTY OF THE TAXPAYER.—The aggregate of the deductions allowed under section 162 (relating to trade or business expenses) and section 167 (relating to depreciation), which are allocable to the operation and maintenance of property owned or operated by the corporation, shall be allowed only in an amount equal to the rent or other compensation received for the use of, or the right to use, the property, unless it is established (under regulations prescribed by the Secretary) to the satisfaction of the Secretary—

(A) that the rent or other compensation received was the highest obtainable, or, if none was received, that none was obtainable;

(B) that the property was held in the course of a business carried on bona fide for profit; and

(C) either that there was reasonable expectation that the operation of the property would result in a profit, or that the property was necessary to the conduct of the business.

(7) SPECIAL RULE FOR CAPITAL GAINS AND LOSSES OF FOREIGN CORPORATIONS.—In the case of a foreign corporation, paragraph (5) shall be applied by taking into account only gains and losses which are effectively connected with the conduct of a trade or business within the United States and are not exempt from tax under treaty.

[Sec. 545(c)]

(c) CERTAIN FOREIGN CORPORATIONS.—In the case of a foreign corporation all of the outstanding stock of which during the last half of the taxable year is owned by nonresident alien individuals (whether directly or indirectly through foreign estates, foreign trusts, foreign partnerships, or other foreign corporations), the taxable income for purposes of subsection (a) shall be the income which constitutes personal holding company income under section 543(a)(7), reduced by the deductions attributable to such income, and adjusted, with respect to such income, in the manner provided in subsection (b).

[Sec. 546]

SEC. 546. INCOME NOT PLACED ON ANNUAL BASIS.

Section 443 (b) (relating to computation of tax on change of annual accounting period) shall not apply in the computation of the personal holding company tax imposed by section 541.

[Sec. 547]

SEC. 547. DEDUCTION FOR DEFICIENCY DIVIDENDS.

[Sec. 547(a)]

(a) GENERAL RULE.—If a determination (as defined in subsection (c)) with respect to a taxpayer establishes liability for personal holding company tax imposed by section 541 (or by a corresponding provision of a prior income tax law) for any taxable year, a deduction shall be allowed to the taxpayer for the amount of deficiency dividends (as defined in subsection (d)) for the purpose of determining the personal holding company tax for such year, but not for the purpose of determining interest, additional amounts, or assessable penalties computed with respect to such personal holding company tax.

[Sec. 547(b)]

(b) RULES FOR APPLICATION OF SECTION.—

(1) ALLOWANCE OF DEDUCTION.—The deficiency dividend deduction shall be allowed as of the date the claim for the deficiency dividend deduction is filed.

(2) CREDIT OR REFUND.—If the allowance of a deficiency dividend deduction results in an overpayment of personal holding company tax for any taxable year, credit or refund with respect to such overpayment shall be made as if on the date of the determination 2 years remained before the expiration of the period of limitation on the filing of claim for refund for the taxable year to which the overpayment relates. No interest shall be allowed on a credit or refund arising from the application of this section.

[Sec. 547(c)]

(c) DETERMINATION.—For purposes of this section, the term "determination" means—

(1) a decision by the Tax Court or a judgment, decree, or other order by any court of competent jurisdiction, which has become final;

(2) a closing agreement made under section 7121; or

(3) under regulations prescribed by the Secretary, an agreement signed by the Secretary and by, or on behalf of, the taxpayer relating to the liability of such taxpayer for personal holding company tax.

[Sec. 547(d)]

(d) DEFICIENCY DIVIDENDS.—

(1) DEFINITION.—For purposes of this section, the term "deficiency dividends" means the amount of the dividends paid by the corporation on or after the date of the determination and before filing claim under subsection (e), which would have been includible in the computation of the deduction for dividends paid under section 561 for the taxable year with respect to which the liability for personal holding company tax exists, if distributed during such taxable year. No dividends shall be considered as deficiency dividends for purposes of subsection (a) unless distributed within 90 days after the determination.

(2) EFFECT ON DIVIDENDS PAID DEDUCTION.—

(A) FOR TAXABLE YEAR IN WHICH PAID.—Deficiency dividends paid in any taxable year (to the extent of the portion thereof taken into account under subsection (a) in determining personal holding company tax) shall not be included in the amount of dividends paid for such year for purposes of computing the dividends paid deduction for such year and succeeding years.

(B) FOR PRIOR TAXABLE YEAR.—Deficiency dividends paid in any taxable year (to the extent of the portion thereof taken into account under subsection (a) in determining personal holding company tax) shall not be allowed for purposes of section 563 (b) in the computation of the dividends paid deduction for the taxable year preceding the taxable year in which paid.

[Sec. 547(e)]

(e) CLAIM REQUIRED.—No deficiency dividend deduction shall be allowed under subsection (a) unless (under regulations prescribed by the Secretary) claim therefor is filed within 120 days after the determination.

[Sec. 547(f)]

(f) SUSPENSION OF STATUTE OF LIMITATIONS AND STAY OF COLLECTION.—

(1) SUSPENSION OF RUNNING OF STATUTE.—If the corporation files a claim, as provided in subsection (e), the running of the statute of limitations provided in section 6501 on the making of assessments, and the bringing of distraint or a proceeding in court for collection, in respect of the deficiency and all interest, additional amounts, or assessable penalties, shall be suspended for a period of 2 years after the date of the determination.

(2) STAY OF COLLECTION.—In the case of any deficiency with respect to the tax imposed by section 541 established by a determination under this section—

(A) the collection of the deficiency and all interest, additional amounts, and assessable penalties shall, except in cases of jeopardy, be stayed until the expiration of 120 days after the date of the determination, and

(B) if claim for deficiency dividend deduction is filed under subsection (e), the collection of such part of the deficiency as is not reduced by the deduction for deficiency dividends provided in subsection (a) shall be stayed until the date the claim is disallowed (in whole or in part), and if disallowed in part collection shall be made only with respect to the part disallowed.

No distraint or proceeding in court shall be begun for the collection of an amount the collection of which is stayed under subparagraph (A) or (B) during the period for which the collection of such amount is stayed.

[Sec. 547(g)]

(g) DEDUCTION DENIED IN CASE OF FRAUD, ETC.—No deficiency dividend deduction shall be allowed under subsection (a) if the determination contains a finding that any part of the deficiency is due to fraud with intent to evade tax, or to wilful failure to file an income tax return within the time prescribed by law or prescribed by the Secretary in pursuance of law.

PART IV—DEDUCTION FOR DIVIDENDS PAID

[Sec. 561]

SEC. 561. DEFINITION OF DEDUCTION FOR DIVIDENDS PAID.

[Sec. 561(a)]

(a) GENERAL RULE.—The deduction for dividends paid shall be the sum of—

(1) the dividends paid during the taxable year,

(2) the consent dividends for the taxable year (determined under section 565), and

(3) in the case of a personal holding company, the dividend carryover described in section 564.

[Sec. 561(b)]

(b) SPECIAL RULES APPLICABLE.—In determining the deduction for dividends paid, the rules provided in section 562 (relating to rules applicable in determining dividends eligible for dividends paid deduction) and section 563 (relating to dividends paid after the close of the taxable year) shall be applicable.

[Sec. 562]

SEC. 562. RULES APPLICABLE IN DETERMINING DIVIDENDS ELIGIBLE FOR DIVIDENDS PAID DEDUCTION.

[Sec. 562(a)]

(a) GENERAL RULE.—For purposes of this part, the term "dividend" shall, except as otherwise provided in this section, include only dividends described in section 316 (relating to definition of dividends for purposes of corporate distributions).

[Sec. 562(b)]

(b) DISTRIBUTIONS IN LIQUIDATION.—

(1) Except in the case of a personal holding company described in section 542—

(A) in the case of amounts distributed in liquidation, the part of such distribution which is properly chargeable to earnings and profits accumulated after February 28, 1913, shall be treated as a dividend for purposes of computing the dividends paid deduction, and

(B) in the case of a complete liquidation occurring within 24 months after the adoption of a plan of liquidation, any distribution within such period pursuant to such plan shall, to the extent of the earnings and profits (computed without regard to capital losses) of the corporation for the taxable year in which such distribution is made, be treated as a dividend for purposes of computing the dividends paid deduction.

For purposes of subparagraph (A), a liquidation includes a redemption of stock to which section 302 applies. Except to the extent provided in regulations, the preceding sentence shall not apply in the case of any mere holding or investment company which is not a regulated investment company.

(2) In the case of a complete liquidation of a personal holding company occurring within 24 months after the adoption of a plan of liquidation, the amount of any distribution within such period pursuant to such plan shall be treated as a dividend for purposes of computing

the dividends paid deduction, to the extent that such amount is distributed to corporate distributees and represents such corporate distributees' allocable share of the undistributed personal holding company income for the taxable year of such distribution computed without regard to this paragraph and without regard to subparagraph (B) of section 316(b)(2).

[Sec. 562(c)]

(c) PREFERENTIAL DIVIDENDS.—The amount of any distribution shall not be considered as a dividend for purposes of computing the dividends paid deduction, unless such distribution is pro rata, with no preference to any share of stock as compared with other shares of the same class, and with no preference to one class of stock as compared with another class except to the extent that the former is entitled (without reference to waivers of their rights by shareholders) to such preference. In the case of a distribution by a regulated investment company to a shareholder who made an initial investment of at least $10,000,000 in such company, such distribution shall not be treated as not being pro rata or as being preferential solely by reason of an increase in the distribution by reason of reductions in administrative expenses of the company.

[Sec. 562(d)]

(d) DISTRIBUTIONS BY A MEMBER OF AN AFFILIATED GROUP.—In the case where a corporation which is a member of an affiliated group of corporations filing or required to file a consolidated return for a taxable year is required to file a separate personal holding company schedule for such taxable year, a distribution by such corporation to another member of the affiliated group shall be considered as a dividend for purposes of computing the dividends paid deduction if such distribution would constitute a dividend under the other provisions of this section to a recipient which is not a member of an affiliated group.

[Sec. 562(e)]

(e) SPECIAL RULES FOR REAL ESTATE INVESTMENT TRUSTS.—In the case of a real estate investment trust, in determining the amount of dividends under section 316 for purposes of computing the dividends paid deduction, the earnings and profits of such trust for any taxable year beginning after December 31, 1980, shall be increased by the total amount of gain (if any) on the sale or exchange of real property by such trust during such taxable year.

[Sec. 563]

SEC. 563. RULES RELATING TO DIVIDENDS PAID AFTER CLOSE OF TAXABLE YEAR.

[Sec. 563(a)]

(a) ACCUMULATED EARNINGS TAX.—In the determination of the dividends paid deduction for purposes of the accumulated earnings tax imposed by section 531, a dividend paid after the close of any taxable year and on or before the 15th day of the third month following the close of such taxable year shall be considered as paid during such taxable year.

[Sec. 563(b)]

(b) PERSONAL HOLDING COMPANY TAX.—In the determination of the dividends paid deduction for purposes of the personal holding company tax imposed by section 541, a dividend paid after the close of any taxable year and on or before the 15th day of the third month following the close of such taxable year shall, to the extent the taxpayer elects in its return for the taxable year, be considered as paid during such taxable year. The amount allowed as a dividend by reason of the application of this subsection with respect to any taxable year shall not exceed either—

(1) The undistributed personal holding company income of the corporation for the taxable year, computed without regard to this subsection, or

(2) 20 percent of the sum of the dividends paid during the taxable year, computed without regard to this subsection.

[Sec. 563(c)]

(c) DIVIDENDS CONSIDERED AS PAID ON LAST DAY OF TAXABLE YEAR.—For the purpose of applying section 562(a), with respect to distributions under subsection (a) or (b) of this section, a distribution made after the close of a taxable year and on or before the 15th day of the third month following the close of the taxable year shall be considered as made on the last day of such taxable year.

[Sec. 564]

SEC. 564. DIVIDEND CARRYOVER.

[Sec. 564(a)]

(a) GENERAL RULE.—For purposes of computing the dividends paid deduction under section 561, in the case of a personal holding company the dividend carryover for any taxable year shall be the dividend carryover to such taxable year, computed as provided in subsection (b), from the two preceding taxable years.

[Sec. 564(b)]

(b) COMPUTATION OF DIVIDEND CARRYOVER.—The dividend carryover to the taxable year shall be determined as follows:

(1) For each of the 2 preceding taxable years there shall be determined the taxable income computed with the adjustments provided in section 545 (whether or not the taxpayer was a personal holding company for either of such preceding taxable years), and there shall also be determined for each such year the deduction for dividends paid during such year as provided in section 561 (but determined without regard to the dividend carryover to such year).

(2) There shall be determined for each such taxable year whether there is an excess of such taxable income over such deduction for dividends paid or an excess of such deduction for dividends paid over such taxable income, and the amount of each such excess.

(3) If there is an excess of such deductions for dividends paid over such taxable income for the first preceding taxable year, such excess shall be allowed as a dividend carryover to the taxable year.

(4) If there is an excess of such deduction for dividends paid over such taxable income for the second preceding taxable year, such excess shall be reduced by the amount determined in paragraph (5), and the remainder of such excess shall be allowed as a dividend carryover to the taxable year.

(5) The amount of the reduction specified in paragraph (4) shall be the amount of the excess of the taxable income, if any, for the first preceding taxable year over such deduction for dividends paid, if any, for the first preceding taxable year.

[Sec. 565]

SEC. 565. CONSENT DIVIDENDS.

[Sec. 565(a)]

(a) GENERAL RULE.—If any person owns consent stock (as defined in subsection (f)(1)) in a corporation on the last day of the taxable year of such corporation, and such person agrees, in a consent filed with the return of such corporation in accordance with regulations prescribed by the Secretary, to treat as a dividend the amount specified in such consent, the amount so specified shall, except as provided in subsection (b), constitute a consent dividend for purposes of section 561 (relating to the deduction for dividends paid).

[Sec. 565(b)]

(b) LIMITATIONS.—A consent dividend shall not include—

(1) an amount specified in a consent which, if distributed in money, would constitute, or be part of, a distribution which would be disqualified for purposes of the dividends paid deduction under section 562(c) (relating to preferential dividends), or

(2) an amount specified in a consent which would not constitute a dividend (as defined in section 316) if the total amounts specified in consents filed by the corporation had been distributed in money to shareholders on the last day of the taxable year of such corporation.

[Sec. 565(c)]

(c) EFFECT OF CONSENT.—The amount of a consent dividend shall be considered, for purposes of this title—

(1) as distributed in money by the corporation to the shareholder on the last day of the taxable year of the corporation, and

(2) as contributed to the capital of the corporation by the shareholder on such day.

[Sec. 565(d)]

(d) CONSENT DIVIDENDS AND OTHER DISTRIBUTIONS.—If a distribution by a corporation consists in part of money or other property, the entire amount specified in the consents and the amount of such money or other property shall be considered together for purposes of applying this title.

[Sec. 565(e)]

(e) NONRESIDENT ALIENS AND FOREIGN CORPORATIONS.—In the case of a consent dividend which, if paid in money would be subject to the provisions of section 1441 (relating to withholding of tax on nonresident aliens) or section 1442 (relating to withholding of tax on foreign corporations), this section shall not apply unless the consent is accompanied by money, or such other medium of payment as the Secretary may by regulations authorize, in an amount equal to the amount that would be required to be deducted and withheld under sections 1441 or 1442 if the consent dividend had been, on the last day of the taxable year of the corporation, paid to the shareholder in money as a dividend. The amount accompanying the consent shall be credited against the tax imposed by this subtitle on the shareholder.

[Sec. 565(f)]

(f) DEFINITIONS.—

(1) CONSENT STOCK.—Consent stock, for purposes of this section, means the class or classes of stock entitled, after the payment of preferred dividends, to a share in the distribution (other than in complete or partial liquidation) within the taxable year of all the remaining earnings and profits, which share constitutes the same proportion of such distribution regardless of the amount of such distribution.

(2) PREFERRED DIVIDENDS.—Preferred dividends, for purposes of this section, means a distribution (other than in complete or partial liquidation), limited in amount, which must be made on any class of stock before a further distribution (other than in complete or partial liquidation) of earnings and profits may be made within the taxable year.

PART III—SALES AND EXCHANGES

[Sec. 631]

SEC. 631. GAIN OR LOSS IN THE CASE OF TIMBER, COAL, OR DOMESTIC IRON ORE.

* * *

[Sec. 631(b)]

(b) DISPOSAL OF TIMBER.—In the case of the disposal of timber held for more than 1 year before such disposal, by the owner thereof under any form or type of contract by virtue of which such owner either retains an economic interest in such timber or makes an outright sale of such timber, the difference between the amount realized from the disposal of such timber and the adjusted depletion basis thereof, shall be considered as though it were a gain or loss, as the case may be, on the sale of such timber. In determining the gross income, the adjusted gross income, or the taxable income of the lessee, the deductions allowable with respect to rents and royalties shall be determined without regard to the provisions of this subsection. In the case of disposal of timber with a retained economic interest, the date of disposal of such timber shall be deemed to be the date such timber is cut, but if payment is made to the owner under the contract before such timber is cut the owner may elect to treat the date of such payment as the date of disposal of such timber. For purposes of this subsection, the term "owner" means any person who owns an interest in such timber, including a sublessor and a holder of a contract to cut timber.

[Sec. 631(c)]

(c) DISPOSAL OF COAL OR DOMESTIC IRON ORE WITH A RETAINED ECONOMIC INTEREST.—In the case of the disposal of coal (including lignite), or iron ore mined in the United States, held for more than 1 year before such disposal, by the owner thereof under any form of contract by virtue of which such owner retains an economic interest in such coal or iron ore, the difference between the amount realized from the disposal of such coal or iron ore and the adjusted depletion basis thereof plus the deductions disallowed for the taxable year under section 272 shall be considered as though it were a gain or loss, as the case may be, on the sale of such coal or iron ore. If for the taxable year of such gain or loss the maximum rate of tax imposed by this chapter on any net capital gain is less than such maximum rate for ordinary income, such owner shall not be entitled to the allowance for percentage depletion provided in section 613 with respect to such coal or iron ore. This subsection shall not apply to income realized by any owner as a co-adventurer, partner, or principal in the mining of such coal or iron ore, and the word "owner" means any person who owns an economic interest in coal or iron ore in place, including a sublessor. The date of disposal of such coal or iron ore shall be deemed to be the date such coal or iron ore is mined. In determining the gross income, the adjusted gross income, or the taxable income of the lessee, the deductions allowable with respect to rents and royalties shall be determined without regard to the provisions of this subsection. This subsection shall have no application, for purposes of applying subchapter G, relating to corporations used to avoid income tax on shareholders (including the determinations of the amount of the deductions under section 535(b)(6) or section 545(b)(5)). This subsection shall not apply to any disposal of iron ore or coal—

(1) to a person whose relationship to the person disposing of such iron ore or coal would result in the disallowance of losses under section 267 or 707(b), or

(2) to a person owned or controlled directly or indirectly by the same interests which own or control the person disposing of such iron ore or coal.

PART V—CONTINENTAL SHELF AREAS

[Sec. 638]

SEC. 638. CONTINENTAL SHELF AREAS.

For purposes of applying the provisions of this chapter (including sections 861(a)(3) and 862(a)(3) in the case of the performance of personal services) with respect to mines, oil and gas wells, and other natural deposits—

(1) the term "United States" when used in a geographical sense includes the seabed and subsoil of those submarine areas which are adjacent to the territorial waters of the United States and over which the United States has exclusive rights, in accordance with international law, with respect to the exploration and exploitation of natural resources; and

(2) the terms "foreign country" and "possession of the United States" when used in a geographical sense include the seabed and subsoil of those submarine areas which are adjacent to the territorial waters of the foreign country or such possession and over which the foreign country (or the United States in case of such possession) has exclusive rights, in accordance with international law, with respect to the exploration and exploitation of natural resources, but this paragraph shall apply in the case of a foreign country only if it exercises, directly or indirectly, taxing jurisdiction with respect to such exploration or exploitation.

No foreign country shall, by reason of the application of this section, be treated as a country contiguous to the United States.

SUBCHAPTER J—ESTATES, TRUSTS, BENEFICIARIES, AND DECEDENTS

PART I—ESTATES, TRUSTS, AND BENEFICIARIES

Subpart E—Grantors and Others Treated as Substantial Owners

[Sec. 679]

SEC. 679. FOREIGN TRUSTS HAVING ONE OR MORE UNITED STATES BENEFICIARIES.

[Sec. 679(a)]

(a) TRANSFEROR TREATED AS OWNER.—

(1) IN GENERAL.—A United States person who directly or indirectly transfers property to a foreign trust (other than a trust described in section 6048(a)(3)(B)(ii)) shall be treated as the owner for his taxable year of the portion of such trust attributable to such property if for such year there is a United States beneficiary of any portion of such trust.

(2) EXCEPTIONS.—Paragraph (1) shall not apply—

(A) TRANSFERS BY REASON OF DEATH.—To any transfer by reason of the death of the transferor.

(B) TRANSFERS AT FAIR MARKET VALUE.—To any transfer of property to a trust in exchange for consideration of at least the fair market value of the transferred property. For purposes of the preceding sentence, consideration other than cash shall be taken into account at its fair market value.

(3) CERTAIN OBLIGATIONS NOT TAKEN INTO ACCOUNT UNDER FAIR MARKET VALUE EXCEPTION.—

(A) IN GENERAL.—In determining whether paragraph (2)(B) applies to any transfer by a person described in clause (ii) or (iii) of subparagraph (C), there shall not be taken into account—

(i) except as provided in regulations, any obligation of a person described in subparagraph (C), and

(ii) to the extent provided in regulations, any obligation which is guaranteed by a person described in subparagraph (C).

(B) TREATMENT OF PRINCIPAL PAYMENTS ON OBLIGATION.—Principal payments by the trust on any obligation referred to in subparagraph (A) shall be taken into account on and after the date of the payment in determining the portion of the trust attributable to the property transferred.

(C) PERSONS DESCRIBED.—The persons described in this subparagraph are—

(i) the trust,

(ii) any grantor, owner, or beneficiary of the trust, and

(iii) any person who is related (within the meaning of section 643(i)(2)(B)) to any grantor, owner, or beneficiary of the trust.

(4) SPECIAL RULES APPLICABLE TO FOREIGN GRANTOR WHO LATER BECOMES A UNITED STATES PERSON.—

(A) IN GENERAL.—If a nonresident alien individual has a residency starting date within 5 years after directly or indirectly transferring property to a foreign trust, this section and section 6048 shall be applied as if such individual transferred to such trust on the residency starting date an amount equal to the portion of such trust attributable to the property transferred by such individual to such trust in such transfer.

(B) TREATMENT OF UNDISTRIBUTED INCOME.—For purposes of this section, undistributed net income for periods before such individual's residency starting date shall be taken into account in determining the portion of the trust which is attributable to property transferred by such individual to such trust but shall not otherwise be taken into account.

(C) RESIDENCY STARTING DATE.—For purposes of this paragraph, an individual's residency starting date is the residency starting date determined under section 7701(b)(2)(A).

(5) OUTBOUND TRUST MIGRATIONS.—If—

(A) an individual who is a citizen or resident of the United States transferred property to a trust which was not a foreign trust, and

(B) such trust becomes a foreign trust while such individual is alive,

then this section and section 6048 shall be applied as if such individual transferred to such trust on the date such trust becomes a foreign trust an amount equal to the portion of such trust attributable to the property previously transferred by such individual to such trust. A rule similar to the rule of paragraph (4)(B) shall apply for purposes of this paragraph.

[Sec. 679(b)]

(b) TRUSTS ACQUIRING UNITED STATES BENEFICIARIES.—If—

(1) subsection (a) applies to a trust for the transferor's taxable year, and

(2) subsection (a) would have applied to the trust for his immediately preceding taxable year but for the fact that for such preceding taxable year there was no United States beneficiary for any portion of the trust,

then, for purposes of this subtitle, the transferor shall be treated as having income for the taxable year (in addition to his other income for such year) equal to the undistributed net income (at the close of such immediately preceding taxable year) attributable to the portion of the trust referred to in subsection (a).

[Sec. 679(c)]

(c) TRUSTS TREATED AS HAVING A UNITED STATES BENEFICIARY.—

(1) IN GENERAL.—For purposes of this section, a trust shall be treated as having a United States beneficiary for the taxable year unless—

(A) under the terms of the trust, no part of the income or corpus of the trust may be paid or accumulated during the taxable year to or for the benefit of a United States person, and

(B) if the trust were terminated at any time during the taxable year, no part of the income or corpus of such trust could be paid to or for the benefit of a United States person.

(2) ATTRIBUTION OF OWNERSHIP.—For purposes of paragraph (1), an amount shall be treated as paid or accumulated to or for the benefit of a United States person if such amount is paid to or accumulated for a foreign corporation, foreign partnership, or foreign trust or estate, and—

(A) in the case of a foreign corporation, such corporation is a controlled foreign corporation (as defined in section 957(a)),

(B) in the case of a foreign partnership, a United States person is a partner of such partnership, or

(C) in the case of a foreign trust or estate, such trust or estate has a United States beneficiary (within the meaning of paragraph (1)).

(3) CERTAIN UNITED STATES BENEFICIARIES DISREGARDED.—A beneficiary shall not be treated as a United States person in applying this section with respect to any transfer of property to foreign trust if such beneficiary first became a United States person more than 5 years after the date of such transfer.

[Sec. 679(d)]

(d) REGULATIONS.—The Secretary shall prescribe such regulations as may be necessary or appropriate to carry out the purposes of this section.

Subpart F—Miscellaneous

⤳ *Caution: Code Sec. 684, below, applies to transfers on or before December 31, 2009.*

[Sec. 684]

SEC. 684. RECOGNITION OF GAIN ON CERTAIN TRANSFERS TO CERTAIN FOREIGN TRUSTS AND ESTATES.

[Sec. 684(a)]

(a) IN GENERAL.—Except as provided in regulations, in the case of any transfer of property by a United States person to a foreign estate or trust, for purposes of this subtitle, such transfer shall be treated as a sale or exchange for an amount equal to the fair market value of the property transferred, and the transferor shall recognize as gain the excess of—

(1) the fair market value of the property so transferred, over

(2) the adjusted basis (for purposes of determining gain) of such property in the hands of the transferor.

[Sec. 684(b)]

(b) EXCEPTION.—Subsection (a) shall not apply to a transfer to a trust by a United States person to the extent that any person is treated as the owner of such trust under section 671.

[Sec. 684(c)]

(c) TREATMENT OF TRUSTS WHICH BECOME FOREIGN TRUSTS.—If a trust which is not a foreign trust becomes a foreign trust, such trust shall be treated for purposes of this section as having transferred, immediately before becoming a foreign trust, all of its assets to a foreign trust.

⇒ *Caution: Code Sec. 684, below, as amended by the Economic Growth and Tax Relief Reconciliation Act of 2001, P.L. 107-16, applies to transfers after December 31, 2009.*

[Sec. 684]

SEC. 684. RECOGNITION OF GAIN ON CERTAIN TRANSFERS TO CERTAIN FOREIGN TRUSTS AND ESTATES AND NONRESIDENT ALIENS.

[Sec. 684(a)]

(a) IN GENERAL.—Except as provided in regulations, in the case of any transfer of property by a United States person to a foreign estate or trust or to a nonresident alien, for purposes of this subtitle, such transfer shall be treated as a sale or exchange for an amount equal to the fair market value of the property transferred, and the transferor shall recognize as gain the excess of—

(1) the fair market value of the property so transferred, over

(2) the adjusted basis (for purposes of determining gain) of such property in the hands of the transferor.

[Sec. 684(b)]

(b) EXCEPTIONS.—

(1) TRANSFERS TO CERTAIN TRUSTS.—Subsection (a) shall not apply to a transfer to a trust by a United States person to the extent that any United States person is treated as the owner of such trust under section 671.

(2) LIFETIME TRANSFERS TO NONRESIDENT ALIENS.—Subsection (a) shall not apply to a lifetime transfer to a nonresident alien.

[Sec. 684(c)]

(c) TREATMENT OF TRUSTS WHICH BECOME FOREIGN TRUSTS.—If a trust which is not a foreign trust becomes a foreign trust, such trust shall be treated for purposes of this section as having transferred, immediately before becoming a foreign trust, all of its assets to a foreign trust.

SUBCHAPTER K—PARTNERS AND PARTNERSHIPS

PART I—DETERMINATION OF TAX LIABILITY

[Sec. 701]

SEC. 701. PARTNERS, NOT PARTNERSHIP, SUBJECT TO TAX.

A partnership as such shall not be subject to the income tax imposed by this chapter. Persons carrying on business as partners shall be liable for income tax only in their separate or individual capacities.

[Sec. 702]

SEC. 702. INCOME AND CREDITS OF PARTNER.

[Sec. 702(a)]

(a) GENERAL RULE.—In determining his income tax, each partner shall take into account separately his distributive share of the partnership's—

(1) gains and losses from sales or exchanges of capital assets held for not more than 1 year,

(2) gains and losses from sales or exchanges of capital assets held for more than 1 year,

(3) gains and losses from sales or exchanges of property described in section 1231 (relating to certain property used in a trade or business and involuntary conversions),

(4) charitable contributions (as defined in section 170(c)),

(5) dividends with respect to which section 1(h)(11) or part VIII of subchapter B applies,

(6) taxes, described in section 901, paid or accrued to foreign countries and to possessions of the United States,

(7) other items of income, gain, loss, deduction, or credit, to the extent provided by regulations prescribed by the Secretary, and

(8) taxable income or loss, exclusive of items requiring separate computation under other paragraphs of this subsection.

[Sec. 702(b)]

(b) CHARACTER OF ITEMS CONSTITUTING DISTRIBUTIVE SHARE.—The character of any item of income, gain, loss, deduction, or credit included in a partner's distributive share under paragraphs (1) through (7) of subsection (a) shall be determined as if such item were realized directly from the source from which realized by the partnership, or incurred in the same manner as incurred by the partnership.

* * *

[Sec. 703]

SEC. 703. PARTNERSHIP COMPUTATIONS.

[Sec. 703(a)]

(a) INCOME AND DEDUCTIONS.—The taxable income of a partnership shall be computed in the same manner as in the case of an individual except that—

(1) the items described in section 702(a) shall be separately stated, and

(2) the following deductions shall not be allowed to the partnership:

* * *

(B) the deduction for taxes provided in section 164(a) with respect to taxes, described in section 901, paid or accrued to foreign countries and to possessions of the United States,

* * *

[Sec. 703(b)]

(b) ELECTIONS OF THE PARTNERSHIP.—Any election affecting the computation of taxable income derived from a partnership shall be made by the partnership, except that any election under—

* * *

(3) section 901 (relating to taxes of foreign countries and possessions of the United States),

shall be made by each partner separately.

[Sec. 704]

SEC. 704. PARTNER'S DISTRIBUTIVE SHARE.

[Sec. 704(a)]

(a) EFFECT OF PARTNERSHIP AGREEMENT.—A partner's distributive share of income, gain, loss, deduction, or credit shall, except as otherwise provided in this chapter, be determined by the partnership agreement.

[Sec. 704(b)]

(b) DETERMINATION OF DISTRIBUTIVE SHARE.—A partner's distributive share of income, gain, loss, deduction, or credit (or item thereof) shall be determined in accordance with the partner's interest in the partnership (determined by taking into account all facts and circumstances), if—

(1) the partnership agreement does not provide as to the partner's distributive share of income, gain, loss, deduction, or credit (or item thereof), or

(2) the allocation to a partner under the agreement of income, gain, loss, deduction, or credit (or item thereof) does not have substantial economic effect.

* * *

[Sec. 706]

SEC. 706. TAXABLE YEARS OF PARTNER AND PARTNERSHIP.

[Sec. 706(a)]

(a) YEAR IN WHICH PARTNERSHIP INCOME IS INCLUDIBLE.—In computing the taxable income of a partner for a taxable year, the inclusions required by section 702 and section 707(c) with respect to a partnership shall be based on the income, gain, loss, deduction, or credit of the partnership for any taxable year of the partnership ending within or with the taxable year of the partner.

[Sec. 706(b)]

(b) TAXABLE YEAR.—

(1) PARTNERSHIP'S TAXABLE YEAR.—

(A) PARTNERSHIP TREATED AS TAXPAYER.—The taxable year of a partnership shall be determined as though the partnership were a taxpayer.

(B) TAXABLE YEAR DETERMINED BY REFERENCE TO PARTNERS.—Except as provided in subparagraph (C), a partnership shall not have a taxable year other than—

(i) the majority interest taxable year (as defined in paragraph (4)),

(ii) if there is no taxable year described in clause (i), the taxable year of all the principal partners of the partnership, or

(iii) if there is no taxable year described in clause (i) or (ii), the calendar year unless the Secretary by regulations prescribes another period.

(C) BUSINESS PURPOSE.—A partnership may have a taxable year not described in subparagraph (B) if it establishes, to the satisfaction of the Secretary, a business purpose therefor. For purposes of this subparagraph, any deferral of income to partners shall not be treated as a business purpose.

(2) PARTNER'S TAXABLE YEAR.—A partner may not change to a taxable year other than that of a partnership in which he is a principal partner unless he establishes, to the satisfaction of the Secretary, a business purpose therefor.

(3) PRINCIPAL PARTNER.—For the purpose of this subsection, a principal partner is a partner having an interest of 5 percent or more in partnership profits or capital.

(4) MAJORITY INTEREST TAXABLE YEAR; LIMITATION ON REQUIRED CHANGES.—

(A) MAJORITY INTEREST TAXABLE YEAR DEFINED.—For purposes of paragraph (1)(B)(i)—

(i) IN GENERAL.—The term "majority interest taxable year" means the taxable year (if any) which, on each testing day, constituted the taxable year of 1 or more partners having (on such day) an aggregate interest in partnership profits and capital of more than 50 percent.

(ii) TESTING DAYS.—The testing days shall be—

(I) the 1st day of the partnership taxable year (determined without regard to clause (i)), or

(II) the days during such representative period as the Secretary may prescribe.

(B) FURTHER CHANGE NOT REQUIRED FOR 3 YEARS.—Except as provided in regulations necessary to prevent the avoidance of this section, if, by reason of paragraph (1)(B)(i), the taxable year of a partnership is changed, such partnership shall not be required to change to another taxable year for either of the 2 taxable years following the year of change.

* * *

[Sec. 707]

SEC. 707. TRANSACTIONS BETWEEN PARTNER AND PARTNERSHIP.

* * *

[Sec. 707(b)]

(b) CERTAIN SALES OR EXCHANGES OF PROPERTY WITH RESPECT TO CONTROLLED PARTNERSHIPS.—

(1) LOSSES DISALLOWED.—No deduction shall be allowed in respect of losses from sales or exchanges of property (other than an interest in the partnership), directly or indirectly, between—

(A) a partnership and a person owning, directly or indirectly, more than 50 percent of the capital interest, or the profits interest, in such partnership, or

(B) two partnerships in which the same persons own, directly or indirectly, more than 50 percent of the capital interests or profits interests.

In the case of a subsequent sale or exchange by a transferee described in this paragraph, section 267(d) shall be applicable as if the loss were disallowed under section 267(a)(1). For purposes of section 267(a)(2), partnerships described in subparagraph (B) of this paragraph shall be treated as persons specified in section 267(b).

* * *

PART II—CONTRIBUTIONS, DISTRIBUTIONS, AND TRANSFERS

Subpart A—Contributions to a Partnership

[Sec. 721]

SEC. 721. NONRECOGNITION OF GAIN OR LOSS ON CONTRIBUTION.

* * *

[Sec. 721(c)]

(c) REGULATIONS RELATING TO CERTAIN TRANSFERS TO PARTNERSHIPS.—The Secretary may provide by regulations that subsection (a) shall not apply to gain realized on the transfer of property to a partnership if such gain, when recognized, will be includible in the gross income of a person other than a United States person.

* * *

SUBCHAPTER N—TAX BASED ON INCOME FROM SOURCES WITHIN OR WITHOUT THE UNITED STATES

PART I—DETERMINATION OF SOURCES OF INCOME

[Sec. 861]

SEC. 861. INCOME FROM SOURCES WITHIN THE UNITED STATES.

[Sec. 861(a)]

(a) GROSS INCOME FROM SOURCES WITHIN UNITED STATES.—The following items of gross income shall be treated as income from sources within the United States:

(1) INTEREST.—Interest from the United States or the District of Columbia, and interest on bonds, notes, or other interest-bearing obligations of noncorporate residents or domestic corporations, not including—

(A) interest from a resident alien individual or domestic corporation, if such individual or corporation meets the 80-percent foreign business requirements of subsection (c)(1),

(B) interest—

(i) on deposits with a foreign branch of a domestic corporation or a domestic partnership if such branch is engaged in the commercial banking business, and

(ii) on amounts satisfying the requirements of subparagraph (B) of section 871(i)(3) which are paid by a foreign branch of a domestic corporation or a domestic partnership, and

(C) in the case of a foreign partnership, which is predominantly engaged in the active conduct of a trade or business outside the United States, any interest not paid by a trade or business engaged in by the partnership in the United States and not allocable to income which is effectively connected (or treated as effectively connected) with the conduct of a trade or business in the United States.

(2) DIVIDENDS.—The amount received as dividends—

(A) from a domestic corporation other than a corporation which has an election in effect under section 936, or

(B) from a foreign corporation unless less than 25 percent of the gross income from all sources of such foreign corporation for the 3-year period ending with the close of its taxable year preceding the declaration of such dividends (or for such part of such period as the corporation has been in existence) was effectively connected (or treated as effectively connected other than income described in section 884(d)(2)) with the conduct of a trade or business within the United States; but only in an amount which bears the same ratio to such dividends as the gross income of the corporation for such period which was effectively connected (or treated as effectively connected other than income described in section 884(d)(2)) with the conduct of a trade or business within the United States bears to its gross income from all sources; but dividends (other than dividends for which a deduction is allowable under section 245(b)) from a foreign corporation shall, for purposes of subpart A of part III (relating to foreign tax credit), be treated as income from sources without the United States to the extent (and only to the extent) exceeding the amount which is 100/70th of the amount of the deduction allowable under section 245 in respect of such dividends, or

(C) from a foreign corporation to the extent that such amount is required by section 243(e) (relating to certain dividends from foreign corporations) to be treated as dividends from a domestic corporation which is subject to taxation under this chapter, and to such extent subparagraph (B) shall not apply to such amount, or

(D) from a DISC or former DISC (as defined in section 992(a)) except to the extent attributable (as determined under regulations prescribed by the Secretary) to qualified export receipts described in section 993(a)(1) (other than interest and gains described in section 995(b)(1)).

In the case of any dividend from a 20-percent owned corporation (as defined in section 243(c)(2)), subparagraph (B) shall be applied by substituting "100/80th" for "100/70th".

(3) PERSONAL SERVICES.—Compensation for labor or personal services performed in the United States; except that compensation for labor or services performed in the United States shall not be deemed to be income from sources within the United States if—

(A) the labor or services are performed by a nonresident alien individual temporarily present in the United States for a period or periods not exceeding a total of 90 days during the taxable year,

(B) such compensation does not exceed $3,000 in the aggregate, and

(C) the compensation is for labor or services performed as an employee of or under a contract with—

(i) a nonresident alien, foreign partnership, or foreign corporation, not engaged in trade or business within the United States, or

(ii) an individual who is a citizen or resident of the United States, a domestic partnership, or a domestic corporation, if such labor or services are performed for an office or place of business maintained in a foreign country or in a possession of the United States by such individual, partnership, or corporation.

In addition, compensation for labor or services performed in the United States shall not be deemed to be income from sources within the United States if the labor or services are performed by a nonresident alien individual in connection with the individual's temporary presence in the United States as a regular member of the crew of a foreign vessel engaged in transportation between the United States and a foreign country or a possession of the United States.

(4) RENTALS AND ROYALTIES.—Rentals or royalties from property located in the United States or from any interest in such property, including rentals or royalties for the use of or for the privilege of using in the United States patents, copyrights, secret processes and formulas, good will, trade-marks, trade brands, franchises, and other like property.

(5) DISPOSITION OF UNITED STATES REAL PROPERTY INTEREST.—Gains, profits, and income from the disposition of a United States real property interest (as defined in section 897(c)).

(6) SALE OR EXCHANGE OF INVENTORY PROPERTY.—Gains, profits, and income derived from the purchase of inventory property (within the meaning of section 865(i)(1)) without the United States (other than within a possession of the United States) and its sale or exchange within the United States.

(7) Amounts received as underwriting income (as defined in section 832(b)(3)) derived from the issuing (or reinsuring) of any insurance or annuity contract—

(A) in connection with property in, liability arising out of an activity in, or in connection with the lives or health of residents of, the United States, or

(B) in connection with risks not described in subparagraph (A) as a result of any arrangement whereby another corporation receives a substantially equal amount of premiums or other consideration in respect to issuing (or reinsuring) any insurance or annuity contract in connection with property in, liability arising out of activity in, or in connection with the lives or health of residents of, the United States.

(8) SOCIAL SECURITY BENEFITS.—Any social security benefit (as defined in section 86(d)).

[Sec. 861(b)]

(b) TAXABLE INCOME FROM SOURCES WITHIN UNITED STATES.—From the items of gross income specified in subsection (a) as being income from sources within the United States there shall be deducted the expenses, losses, and other deductions properly apportioned or allocated thereto and a ratable part of any expenses, losses, or other deductions which cannot definitely be allocated to some item or class of gross income. The remainder, if any, shall be included in full as taxable income from sources within the United States. In the case of an individual who does not itemize deductions, an amount equal to the standard deduction shall be considered a deduction which cannot definitely be allocated to some item or class of gross income.

[Sec. 861(c)]

(c) FOREIGN BUSINESS REQUIREMENTS.—

(1) FOREIGN BUSINESS REQUIREMENTS.—

(A) IN GENERAL.—An individual or corporation meets the 80-percent foreign business requirements of this paragraph if it is shown to the satisfaction of the Secretary that at least 80 percent of the gross income from all sources of such individual or corporation for the testing period is active foreign business income.

(B) ACTIVE FOREIGN BUSINESS INCOME.—For purposes of subparagraph (A), the term "active foreign business income" means gross income which—

(i) is derived from sources outside the United States (as determined under this subchapter) or, in the case of a corporation, is attributable to income so derived by a subsidiary of such corporation, and

(ii) is attributable to the active conduct of a trade or business in a foreign country or possession of the United States by the individual or corporation (or by a subsidiary).

For purposes of this subparagraph, the term "subsidiary" means any corporation in which the corporation referred to in this subparagraph owns (directly or indirectly) stock meeting the requirements of section 1504(a)(2) (determined by substituting "50 percent" for "80 percent" each place it appears).

(C) TESTING PERIOD.—For purposes of this subsection, the term "testing period" means the 3-year period ending with the close of the taxable year of the individual or corporation preceding the payment (or such part of such period as may be applicable). If the individual or corporation has no gross income for such 3-year period (or part thereof), the testing period shall be the taxable year in which the payment is made.

Income Tax—Sources of Income

(2) LOOK-THRU WHERE RELATED PERSON RECEIVES INTEREST.—

(A) IN GENERAL.—In the case of interest received by a related person from a resident alien individual or domestic corporation meeting the 80-percent foreign business requirements of paragraph (1), subsection (a)(1)(A) shall apply only to a percentage of such interest equal to the percentage which—

(i) the gross income of such individual or corporation for the testing period from sources outside the United States (as determined under this subchapter), is of

(ii) the total gross income of such individual or corporation for the testing period.

(B) RELATED PERSON.—For purposes of this paragraph, the term "related person" has the meaning given such term by section 954(d)(3), except that—

(i) such section shall be applied by substituting "the individual or corporation making the payment" for "controlled foreign corporation" each place it appears, and

(ii) such section shall be applied by substituting "10 percent or more" for "more than 50 percent" each place it appears.

[Sec. 861(d)]

(d) SPECIAL RULE FOR APPLICATION OF SUBSECTION (a)(2)(B).—For purposes of subsection (a)(2)(B), if the foreign corporation has no gross income from any source for the 3-year period (or part thereof) specified, the requirements of such subsection shall be applied with respect to the taxable year of such corporation in which the payment of the dividend is made.

[Sec. 861(e)]

(e) INCOME FROM CERTAIN RAILROAD ROLLING STOCK TREATED AS INCOME FROM SOURCES WITHIN THE UNITED STATES.—

(1) GENERAL RULE.—For purposes of subsection (a) and section 862(a), if—

(A) a taxpayer leases railroad rolling stock which is section 1245 property (as defined in section 1245(a)(3)) to a domestic common carrier by railroad or a corporation which is controlled, directly or indirectly, by one or more such common carriers, and

(B) the use under such lease is expected to be use within the United States,

all amounts includible in gross income by the taxpayer with respect to such railroad rolling stock (including gain from sale or other disposition of such railroad rolling stock) shall be treated as income from sources within the United States. The requirements of subparagraph (B) of the preceding sentence shall be treated as satisfied if the only expected use outside the United States is use by a person (whether or not a United States person) in Canada or Mexico on a temporary basis which is not expected to exceed a total of 90 days in any taxable year.

(2) PARAGRAPH (1) NOT TO APPLY WHERE LESSOR IS A MEMBER OF CONTROLLED GROUP WHICH INCLUDES A RAILROAD.—Paragraph (1) shall not apply to a lease between two members of the same controlled group of corporations (as defined in section 1563) if any member of such group is a domestic common carrier by railroad or a switching or terminal company all of whose stock is owned by one or more domestic common carriers by railroad.

(3) DENIAL OF FOREIGN TAX CREDIT.—No credit shall be allowed under section 901 for any payments to foreign countries with respect to any amount received by the taxpayer with respect to railroad rolling stock which is subject to paragraph (1).

[Sec. 861(f)]

(f) CROSS REFERENCE.—

For treatment of interest paid by the branch of a foreign corporation, see section 884(f).

[Sec. 862]

SEC. 862. INCOME FROM SOURCES WITHOUT THE UNITED STATES.

[Sec. 862(a)]

(a) GROSS INCOME FROM SOURCES WITHOUT UNITED STATES.—The following items of gross income shall be treated as income from sources without the United States:

(1) interest other than that derived from sources within the United States as provided in section 861 (a) (1);

(2) dividends other than those derived from sources within the United States as provided in section 861 (a) (2);

(3) compensation for labor or personal services performed without the United States;

(4) rentals or royalties from property located without the United States or from any interest in such property, including rentals or royalties for the use of or for the privilege of using without the United States patents, copyrights, secret processes and formulas, good will, trade-marks, trade brands, franchises, and other like properties;

(5) gains, profits, and income from the sale or exchange of real property located without the United States;

(6) gains, profits, and income derived from the purchase of inventory property (within the meaning of section 865(i)(1)) within the United States and its sale or exchange without the United States;

(7) underwriting income other than that derived from sources within the United States as provided in section 861(a)(7); and

(8) gains, profits, and income from the disposition of a United States real property interest (as defined in section 897(c)) when the real property is located in the Virgin Islands.

[Sec. 862(b)]

(b) TAXABLE INCOME FROM SOURCES WITHOUT UNITED STATES.—From the items of gross income specified in subsection (a) there shall be deducted the expenses, losses, and other deductions properly apportioned or allocated thereto, and a ratable part of any expenses, losses, or other deductions which cannot definitely be allocated to some item or class of gross income. The remainder, if any, shall be treated in full as taxable income from sources without the United States. In the case of an individual who does not itemize deductions, an amount equal to the standard deduction shall be considered a deduction which cannot definitely be allocated to some item or class of gross income.

[Sec. 863]

SEC. 863. SPECIAL RULES FOR DETERMINING SOURCE.

[Sec. 863(a)]

(a) ALLOCATION UNDER REGULATIONS.—Items of gross income, expenses, losses, and deductions, other than those specified in sections 861 (a) and 862 (a), shall be allocated or apportioned to sources within or without the United States, under regulations prescribed by the Secretary. Where items of gross income are separately allocated to sources within the United States, there shall be deducted (for the purpose of computing the taxable income therefrom) the expenses, losses, and other deductions properly apportioned or allocated thereto and a ratable part of other expenses, losses, or other deductions which cannot definitely be allocated to some item or class of gross income. The remainder, if any, shall be included in full as taxable income from sources within the United States.

[Sec. 863(b)]

(b) INCOME PARTLY FROM WITHIN AND PARTLY FROM WITHOUT THE UNITED STATES.—In the case of gross income derived from sources partly within and partly without the United States, the taxable income may first be computed by deducting the expenses, losses, or other deductions apportioned or allocated thereto and a ratable part of any expenses, losses, or other deductions which cannot definitely be allocated to some item or class of gross income; and the portion of such taxable income attributable to sources within the United States may be determined by processes or formulas of general apportionment prescribed by the Secretary. Gains, profits, and income—

(1) from services rendered partly within and partly without the United States,

(2) from the sale or exchange of inventory property (within the meaning of section 865(i)(1)) produced (in whole or in part) by the taxpayer within and sold or exchanged without the United States, or produced (in whole or in part) by the taxpayer without and sold or exchanged within the United States, or

(3) derived from the purchase of inventory property (within the meaning of section 865(i)(1))

shall be treated as derived partly from sources within and partly from sources without the United States.

[Sec. 863(c)]

(c) SOURCE RULE FOR CERTAIN TRANSPORTATION INCOME.—

(1) TRANSPORTATION BEGINNING AND ENDING IN THE UNITED STATES.—All transportation income attributable to transportation which begins and ends in the United States shall be treated as derived from sources within the United States.

(2) OTHER TRANSPORTATION HAVING UNITED STATES CONNECTION.—

(A) IN GENERAL.—50 percent of all transportation income attributable to transportation which—

(i) is not described in paragraph (1), and

(ii) begins or ends in the United States,

shall be treated as from sources in the United States.

(B) SPECIAL RULE FOR PERSONAL SERVICE INCOME.—Subparagraph (A) shall not apply to any transportation income which is income derived from personal services performed by the taxpayer, unless such income is attributable to transportation which—

(i) begins in the United States and ends in a possession of the United States, or

(ii) begins in a possession of the United States and ends in the United States.

In the case of transportation income derived from, or in connection with, a vessel, this subparagraph shall only apply if the taxpayer is a citizen or resident alien.

(3) TRANSPORTATION INCOME.—For purposes of this subsection, the term "transportation income" means any income derived from, or in connection with—

(A) the use (or hiring or leasing for use) of a vessel or aircraft, or

(B) the performance of services directly related to the use of a vessel or aircraft.

For purposes of the preceding sentence, the term "vessel or aircraft" includes any container used in connection with a vessel or aircraft.

[Sec. 863(d)]

(d) SOURCE RULES FOR SPACE AND CERTAIN OCEAN ACTIVITIES.—

(1) IN GENERAL.—Except as provided in regulations, any income derived from a space or ocean activity—

(A) if derived by a United States person, shall be sourced in the United States, and

(B) if derived by a person other than a United States person, shall be sourced outside the United States.

(2) SPACE OR OCEAN ACTIVITY.—For purposes of paragraph (1)—

(A) IN GENERAL.—The term "space or ocean activity" means—

(i) any activity conducted in space, and

(ii) any activity conducted on or under water not within the jurisdiction (as recognized by the United States) of a foreign country, possession of the United States, or the United States.

Such term includes any activity conducted in Antarctica.

(B) EXCEPTION FOR CERTAIN ACTIVITIES.—The term "space or ocean activity" shall not include—

(i) any activity giving rise to transportation income (as defined in section 863(c)),

(ii) any activity giving rise to international communications income (as defined in subsection (e)(2)), and

(iii) any activity with respect to mines, oil and gas wells, or other natural deposits to the extent within the United States or any foreign country or possession of the United States (as defined in section 638).

For purposes of applying section 638, the jurisdiction of any foreign country shall not include any jurisdiction not recognized by the United States.

[Sec. 863(e)]

(e) INTERNATIONAL COMMUNICATIONS INCOME.—

(1) SOURCE RULES.—

(A) UNITED STATES PERSONS.—In the case of any United States person, 50 percent of any international communications income shall be sourced in the United States and 50 percent of such income shall be sourced outside the United States.

(B) FOREIGN PERSONS.—

(i) IN GENERAL.—Except as provided in regulations or clause (ii), in the case of any person other than a United States person, any international communications income shall be sourced outside the United States.

(ii) SPECIAL RULE FOR INCOME ATTRIBUTABLE TO OFFICE OR FIXED PLACE OF BUSINESS IN THE UNITED STATES.—In the case of any person (other than a United States person) who maintains an office or other fixed place of business in the United States, any international communications income attributable to such office or other fixed place of business shall be sourced in the United States.

(2) DEFINITION.—For purposes of this section, the term "international communications income" includes all income derived from the transmission of communications or data from the United States to any foreign country (or possession of the United States) or from any foreign country (or possession of the United States) to the United States.

[Sec. 864]

SEC. 864. DEFINITIONS AND SPECIAL RULES.

[Sec. 864(a)]

(a) PRODUCED.—For purposes of this part, the term "produced" includes created, fabricated, manufactured, extracted, processed, cured, or aged.

[Sec. 864(b)]

(b) TRADE OR BUSINESS WITHIN THE UNITED STATES.—For purposes of this part, part II, and chapter 3, the term "trade or business within the United States" includes the performance of personal services within the United States at any time within the taxable year, but does not include—

(1) PERFORMANCE OF PERSONAL SERVICES FOR FOREIGN EMPLOYER.—The performance of personal services—

(A) for a nonresident alien individual, foreign partnership, or foreign corporation, not engaged in trade or business within the United States, or

(B) for an office or place of business maintained in a foreign country or in a possession of the United States by an individual who is a citizen or resident of the United States or by a domestic partnership or a domestic corporation,

by a nonresident alien individual temporarily present in the United States for a period or periods not exceeding a total of 90 days during the taxable year and whose compensation for such services does not exceed in the aggregate $3,000.

(2) TRADING IN SECURITIES OR COMMODITIES.—

(A) STOCKS AND SECURITIES.—

(i) IN GENERAL.—Trading in stocks or securities through a resident broker, commission agent, custodian, or other independent agent.

(ii) TRADING FOR TAXPAYER'S OWN ACCOUNT.—Trading in stocks or securities for the taxpayer's own account, whether by the taxpayer or his employees or through a resident broker, commission agent, custodian, or other agent, and whether or not any such employee or agent has discretionary authority to make decisions in effecting the transactions. This clause shall not apply in the case of a dealer in stocks or securities.

(B) COMMODITIES.—

(i) IN GENERAL.—Trading in commodities through a resident broker, commission agent, custodian, or other independent agent.

(ii) TRADING FOR TAXPAYER'S OWN ACCOUNT.—Trading in commodities for the taxpayer's own account, whether by the taxpayer or his employees or through a resident broker, commission agent, custodian, or other agent, and whether or not any such employee or agent has discretionary authority to make decisions in effecting the transactions. This clause shall not apply in the case of a dealer in commodities.

(iii) LIMITATION.—Clauses (i) and (ii) shall apply only if the commodities are of a kind customarily dealt in on an organized commodity exchange and if the transaction is of a kind customarily consummated at such place.

(C) LIMITATION.—Subparagraphs (A)(i) and (B)(i) shall apply only if, at no time during the taxable year, the taxpayer has an office or other fixed place of business in the United States through which or by the direction of which the transactions in stocks or securities, or in commodities, as the case may be, are effected.

[Sec. 864(c)]

(c) EFFECTIVELY CONNECTED INCOME, ETC.—

(1) GENERAL RULE.—For purposes of this title—

(A) In the case of a nonresident alien individual or a foreign corporation engaged in trade or business within the United States during the taxable year, the rules set forth in paragraphs (2), (3), (4), (6), and (7) shall apply in determining the income, gain, or loss which shall be treated as effectively connected with the conduct of a trade or business within the United States.

(B) Except as provided in paragraph (6) or (7) or in section 871(d) or sections 882(d) and (e), in the case of a nonresident alien individual or a foreign corporation not engaged in trade or business within the United States during the taxable year, no income, gain, or loss shall be treated as effectively connected with the conduct of a trade or business within the United States.

(2) PERIODICAL, ETC., INCOME FROM SOURCES WITHIN UNITED STATES—FACTORS.—In determining whether income from sources within the United States of the types described in section 871(a)(1), section 871(h), section 881(a), or section 881(c) or whether gain or loss from sources within the United States from the sale or exchange of capital assets, is effectively connected with the conduct of a trade or business within the United States, the factors taken into account shall include whether—

(A) the income, gain, or loss is derived from assets used in or held for use in the conduct of such trade or business, or

(B) the activities of such trade or business were a material factor in the realization of the income, gain, or loss.

In determining whether an asset is used in or held for use in the conduct of such trade or business or whether the activities of such trade or business were a material factor in realizing an item of income, gain, or loss, due regard shall be given to whether or not such asset or such income, gain, or loss was accounted for through such trade or business.

(3) OTHER INCOME FROM SOURCES WITHIN UNITED STATES.—All income, gain, or loss from sources within the United States (other than income, gain, or loss to which paragraph (2) applies) shall be treated as effectively connected with the conduct of a trade or business within the United States.

(4) INCOME FROM SOURCES WITHOUT UNITED STATES.—

(A) Except as provided in subparagraphs (B) and (C), no income, gain, or loss from sources without the United States shall be treated as effectively connected with the conduct of a trade or business within the United States.

(B) Income, gain, or loss from sources without the United States shall be treated as effectively connected with the conduct of a trade or business within the United States by a nonresident alien individual or a foreign corporation if such person has an office or other fixed place of business within the United States to which such income, gain, or loss is attributable and such income, gain, or loss—

(i) consists of rents or royalties for the use of or for the privilege of using intangible property described in section 862(a)(4) derived in the active conduct of such trade or business;

(ii) consists of dividends or interest, and either is derived in the active conduct of a banking, financing, or similar business within the United States or is received by a corporation the principal business of which is trading in stocks or securities for its own account; or

(iii) is derived from the sale or exchange (outside the United States) through such office or other fixed place of business of personal property described in section 1221(a)(1), except that this clause shall not apply if the property is sold or exchanged for use, consumption, or disposition outside the United States and an office or other fixed place of business of the taxpayer in a foreign country participated materially in such sale.

Any income or gain which is equivalent to any item of income or gain described in clause (i), (ii), or (iii) shall be treated in the same manner as such item for purposes of this subparagraph.

(C) In the case of a foreign corporation taxable under part I or part II of subchapter L, any income from sources without the United States which is attributable to its United States business shall be treated as effectively connected with the conduct of a trade or business within the United States.

(D) No income from sources without the United States shall be treated as effectively connected with the conduct of a trade or business within the United States if it either—

(i) consists of dividends, interest, or royalties paid by a foreign corporation in which the taxpayer owns (within the meaning of section 958(a)), or is considered as owning (by applying the ownership rules of section 958(b)), more than 50 percent of the total combined voting power of all classes of stock entitled to vote, or

(ii) is subpart F income within the meaning of section 952(a).

(5) RULES FOR APPLICATION OF PARAGRAPH (4)(B).—For purposes of subparagraph (B) of paragraph (4)—

(A) in determining whether a nonresident alien individual or a foreign corporation has an office or other fixed place of business, an office or other fixed place of business of an agent shall be disregarded unless such agent (i) has the authority to negotiate and conclude contracts in the name of the nonresident alien individual or foreign corporation and regularly exercises that authority or has a stock of merchandise from which he regularly fills orders on behalf of such individual or foreign corporation, and (ii) is not a general commission agent, broker, or other agent of independent status acting in the ordinary course of his business,

(B) income, gain, or loss shall not be considered as attributable to an office or other fixed place of business within the United States unless such office or fixed place of business is a material factor in the production of such income, gain, or loss and such office or fixed place of business regularly carries on activities of the type from which such income, gain, or loss is derived, and

(C) the income, gain, or loss which shall be attributable to an office or other fixed place of business within the United States shall be the income, gain, or loss properly allocable thereto, but, in the case of a sale or exchange described in clause (iii) of such subparagraph, the income which shall be treated as attributable to an office or other fixed place of business within the United States shall not exceed the income which would be derived from sources within the United States if the sale or exchange were made in the United States.

(6) TREATMENT OF CERTAIN DEFERRED PAYMENTS, ETC.—For purposes of this title, in the case of any income or gain of a nonresident alien individual or a foreign corporation which—

(A) is taken into account for any taxable year, but

(B) is attributable to a sale or exchange of property or the performance of services (or any other transaction) in any other taxable year, the determination of whether such income or gain is taxable under section 871(b) or 882 (as the case may be) shall be made as if such income or gain were taken into account in such other taxable year and without regard to the requirement that the taxpayer be engaged in a trade or business within the United States during the taxable year referred to in subparagraph (A).

(7) TREATMENT OF CERTAIN PROPERTY TRANSACTIONS.—For purposes of this title, if—

(A) any property ceases to be used or held for use in connection with the conduct of a trade or business within the United States, and

(B) such property is disposed of within 10 years after such cessation,

the determination of whether any income or gain attributable to such disposition is taxable under section 871(b) or 882 (as the case may be) shall be made as if such sale or exchange occurred immediately before such cessation and without regard to the requirement that the taxpayer be engaged in a trade or business within the United States during the taxable year for which such income or gain is taken into account.

[Sec. 864(d)]

(d) TREATMENT OF RELATED PERSON FACTORING INCOME.—

(1) IN GENERAL.—For purposes of the provisions set forth in paragraph (2), if any person acquires (directly or indirectly) a trade or service receivable from a related person, any income of such person from the trade or service receivable so acquired shall be treated as if it were interest on a loan to the obligor under the receivable.

(2) PROVISIONS TO WHICH PARAGRAPH (1) APPLIES.—The provisions set forth in this paragraph are as follows:

(A) Section 904 (relating to limitation on foreign tax credit).

(B) Subpart F of part III of this subchapter (relating to controlled foreign corporations).

(3) TRADE OR SERVICE RECEIVABLE.—For purposes of this subsection, the term "trade or service receivable" means any account receivable or evidence of indebtedness arising out of—

(A) the disposition by a related person of property described in section 1221(a)(1), or

(B) the performance of services by a related person.

(4) RELATED PERSON.—For purposes of this subsection, the term "related person" means—

(A) any person who is a related person (within the meaning of section 267(b)), and

(B) any United States shareholder (as defined in section 951(b)) and any person who is a related person (within the meaning of section 267(b)) to such a shareholder.

(5) CERTAIN PROVISIONS NOT TO APPLY.—

(A) CERTAIN EXCEPTIONS.—The following provisions shall not apply to any amount treated as interest under paragraph (1) or (6):

(i) Subparagraph (A)(iii)(II), (B)(ii), and (C)(iii)(II) of section 904(d)(2) (relating to exceptions for export financing interest).

(ii) Subparagraph (A) of section 954(b)(3) (relating to exception where foreign base company income is less than 5 percent or $1,000,000).

(iii) Subparagraph (B) of section 954(c)(2) (relating to certain export financing).

(iv) Clause (i) of section 954(c)(3)(A) (relating to certain income received from related persons).

(B) SPECIAL RULES FOR POSSESSIONS.—An amount treated as interest under paragraph (1) shall not be treated as income described in subparagraph (A) or (B) of section

936(a)(1) unless such amount is from sources within a possession of the United States (determined after the application of paragraph (1)).

(6) SPECIAL RULE FOR CERTAIN INCOME FROM LOANS OF A CONTROLLED FOREIGN CORPORATION.—Any income of a controlled foreign corporation (within the meaning of section 957(a)) from a loan to a person for the purpose of financing—

 (A) the purchase of property described in section 1221(a)(1) of a related person, or

 (B) the payment for the performance of services by a related person,

shall be treated as interest described in paragraph (1).

(7) EXCEPTION FOR CERTAIN RELATED PERSONS DOING BUSINESS IN SAME FOREIGN COUNTRY.—Paragraph (1) shall not apply to any trade or service receivable acquired by any person from a related person if—

 (A) the person acquiring such receivable and such related person are created or organized under the laws of the same foreign country and such related person has a substantial part of its assets used in its trade or business located in such same foreign country, and

 (B) such related person would not have derived any foreign base company income (as defined in section 954(a), determined without regard to section 954(b)(3)(A)), or any income effectively connected with the conduct of a trade or business within the United States, from such receivable if it had been collected by such related person.

(8) REGULATIONS.—The Secretary shall prescribe such regulations as may be necessary to prevent the avoidance of the provisions of this subsection or section 956(b)(3).

[Sec. 864(e)]

(e) RULES FOR ALLOCATING INTEREST, ETC.—For purposes of this subchapter—

(1) TREATMENT OF AFFILIATED GROUPS.—The taxable income of each member of an affiliated group shall be determined by allocating and apportioning interest expense of each member as if all members of such group were a single corporation.

(2) GROSS INCOME METHOD MAY NOT BE USED FOR INTEREST.—All allocations and apportionments of interest expense shall be made on the basis of assets rather than gross income.

(3) TAX-EXEMPT ASSETS NOT TAKEN INTO ACCOUNT.—For purposes of allocating and apportioning any deductible expense, any tax-exempt asset (and any income from such an asset) shall not be taken into account. A similar rule shall apply in the case of the portion of any dividend (other than a qualifying dividend as defined in section 243(b)) equal to the deduction allowable under section 243 or 245(a) with respect to such dividend and in the case of a like portion of any stock the dividends on which would be so deductible and would not be qualifying dividends (as so defined).

(4) BASIS OF STOCK IN NONAFFILIATED 10-PERCENT OWNED CORPORATIONS ADJUSTED FOR EARNINGS AND PROFITS CHANGES.—

 (A) IN GENERAL.—For purposes of allocating and apportioning expenses on the basis of assets, the adjusted basis of any stock in a nonaffiliated 10-percent owned corporation shall be—

  (i) increased by the amount of the earnings and profits of such corporation attributable to such stock and accumulated during the period the taxpayer held such stock, or

  (ii) reduced (but not below zero) by any deficit in earnings and profits of such corporation attributable to such stock for such period.

 (B) NONAFFILIATED 10-PERCENT OWNED CORPORATION.—For purposes of this paragraph, the term "nonaffiliated 10-percent owned corporation" means any corporation if—

  (i) such corporation is not included in the taxpayer's affiliated group, and

  (ii) members of such affiliated group own 10 percent or more of the total combined voting power of all classes of stock of such corporation entitled to vote.

(C) EARNINGS AND PROFITS OF LOWER TIER CORPORATIONS TAKEN INTO ACCOUNT.—

(i) IN GENERAL.—If, by reason of holding stock in a nonaffiliated 10-percent owned corporation, the taxpayer is treated under clause (iii) as owning stock in another corporation with respect to which the stock ownership requirements of clause (ii) are met, the adjustment under subparagraph (A) shall include an adjustment for the amount of the earnings and profits (or deficit therein) of such other corporation which are attributable to the stock the taxpayer is so treated as owning and to the period during which the taxpayer is treated as owning such stock.

(ii) STOCK OWNERSHIP REQUIREMENTS.—The stock ownership requirements of this clause are met with respect to any corporation if members of the taxpayer's affiliated group own (directly or through the application of clause (iii)) 10 percent or more of the total combined voting power of all classes of stock of such corporation entitled to vote.

(iii) STOCK OWNED THROUGH ENTITIES.—For purposes of this subparagraph, stock owned (directly or indirectly) by a corporation, partnership, or trust shall be treated as being owned proportionately by its shareholders, partners, or beneficiaries. Stock considered to be owned by a person by reason of the application of the preceding sentence, shall, for purposes of applying such sentence, be treated as actually owned by such person.

(D) COORDINATION WITH SUBPART F, ETC.—For purposes of this paragraph, proper adjustment shall be made to the earnings and profits of any corporation to take into account any earnings and profits included in gross income under section 951 or under any other provision of this title and reflected in the adjusted basis of the stock.

(5) AFFILIATED GROUP.—For purposes of this subsection—

(A) IN GENERAL.—Except as provided in subparagraph (B), the term "affiliated group" has the meaning given such term by section 1504 (determined without regard to paragraph (4) of section 1504(b)).

(B) TREATMENT OF CERTAIN FINANCIAL INSTITUTIONS.—For purposes of subparagraph (A), any corporation described in subparagraph (C) shall be treated as an includible corporation for purposes of section 1504 only for purposes of applying such section separately to corporations so described. This subparagraph shall not apply for purposes of paragraph (6).

(C) DESCRIPTION.—A corporation is described in this subparagraph if—

(i) such corporation is a financial institution described in section 581 or 591,

(ii) the business of such financial institution is predominantly with persons other than related persons (within the meaning of subsection (d)(4)) or their customers, and

(iii) such financial institution is required by State or Federal law to be operated separately from any other entity which is not such an institution.

(D) TREATMENT OF BANK HOLDING COMPANIES.—To the extent provided in regulations—

(i) a bank holding company (within the meaning of section 2(a) of the Bank Holding Company Act of 1956), and

(ii) any subsidiary of a financial institution described in section 581 or 591 or of any bank holding company if such subsidiary is predominantly engaged (directly or indirectly) in the active conduct of a banking, financing, or similar business,

shall be treated as a corporation described in subparagraph (C).

(6) ALLOCATION AND APPORTIONMENT OF OTHER EXPENSES.—Expenses other than interest which are not directly allocable or apportioned to any specific income producing activity shall be allocated and apportioned as if all members of the affiliated group were a single corporation.

Internal Revenue Code of 1986

>>>→ *Caution: Code Sec. 864(e)(7), below, is effective for tax years beginning on or before December 31, 2008.*

(7) REGULATIONS.—The Secretary shall prescribe such regulations as may be necessary or appropriate to carry out the purposes of this section, including regulations providing—

(A) for the resourcing of income of any member of an affiliated group or modifications to the consolidated return regulations to the extent such resourcing or modification is necessary to carry out the purposes of this section,

(B) for direct allocation of interest expense incurred to carry out an integrated financial transaction to any interest (or interest-type income) derived from such transaction,

(C) for the apportionment of expenses allocated to foreign source income among the members of the affiliated group and various categories of income described in section 904(d)(1),

(D) for direct allocation of interest expense in the case of indebtedness resulting in a disallowance under section 246A,

(E) for appropriate adjustments in the application of paragraph (3) in the case of an insurance company, and

(F) that this subsection shall not apply for purposes of any provision of this subchapter to the extent the Secretary determines that the application of this subsection for such purposes would not be appropriate.

>>>→ *Caution: Code Sec. 864(e)(7), below, is effective for tax years beginning after December 31, 2008.*

(7) REGULATIONS.—The Secretary shall prescribe such regulations as may be necessary or appropriate to carry out the purposes of this section, including regulations providing—

(A) for the resourcing of income of any member of an affiliated group or modifications to the consolidated return regulations to the extent such resourcing or modification is necessary to carry out the purposes of this section,

(B) for direct allocation of interest expense incurred to carry out an integrated financial transaction to any interest (or interest-type income) derived from such transaction and in other circumstances where such allocation would be appropriate to carry out the purposes of this subsection,

(C) for the apportionment of expenses allocated to foreign source income among the members of the affiliated group and various categories of income described in section 904(d)(1),

(D) for direct allocation of interest expense in the case of indebtedness resulting in a disallowance under section 246A,

(E) for appropriate adjustments in the application of paragraph (3) in the case of an insurance company,

(F) preventing assets or interest expense from being taken into account more than once, and

(G) that this subsection shall not apply for purposes of any provision of this subchapter to the extent the Secretary determines that the application of this subsection for such purposes would not be appropriate.

>>>→ *Caution: Code Sec. 864(f), below, is effective for tax years beginning after December 31, 2008.*

[Sec. 864(f)]

(f) ELECTION TO ALLOCATE INTEREST, ETC. ON WORLDWIDE BASIS.—For purposes of this subchapter, at the election of the worldwide affiliated group—

(1) ALLOCATION AND APPORTIONMENT OF INTEREST EXPENSE.—

(A) IN GENERAL.—The taxable income of each domestic corporation which is a member of a worldwide affiliated group shall be determined by allocating and apportioning interest expense of each member as if all members of such group were a single corporation.

(B) TREATMENT OF WORLDWIDE AFFILIATED GROUP.—The taxable income of the domestic members of a worldwide affiliated group from sources outside the United States shall be determined by allocating and apportioning the interest expense of such domestic members to such income in an amount equal to the excess (if any) of—

(i) the total interest expense of the worldwide affiliated group multiplied by the ratio which the foreign assets of the worldwide affiliated group bears to all the assets of the worldwide affiliated group, over

(ii) the interest expense of all foreign corporations which are members of the worldwide affiliated group to the extent such interest expense of such foreign corporations would have been allocated and apportioned to foreign source income if this subsection were applied to a group consisting of all the foreign corporations in such worldwide affiliated group.

(C) WORLDWIDE AFFILIATED GROUP.—For purposes of this paragraph, the term "worldwide affiliated group" means a group consisting of—

(i) the includible members of an affiliated group (as defined in section 1504(a), determined without regard to paragraphs (2) and (4) of section 1504(b)), and

(ii) all controlled foreign corporations in which such members in the aggregate meet the ownership requirements of section 1504(a)(2) either directly or indirectly through applying paragraph (2) of section 958(a) or through applying rules similar to the rules of such paragraph to stock owned directly or indirectly by domestic partnerships, trusts, or estates.

(2) ALLOCATION AND APPORTIONMENT OF OTHER EXPENSES.—Expenses other than interest which are not directly allocable or apportioned to any specific income producing activity shall be allocated and apportioned as if all members of the affiliated group were a single corporation. For purposes of the preceding sentence, the term "affiliated group" has the meaning given such term by section 1504 (determined without regard to paragraph (4) of section 1504(b)).

(3) TREATMENT OF TAX-EXEMPT ASSETS; BASIS OF STOCK IN NONAFFILIATED 10-PERCENT OWNED CORPORATIONS.—The rules of paragraphs (3) and (4) of subsection (e) shall apply for purposes of this subsection, except that paragraph (4) shall be applied on a worldwide affiliated group basis.

(4) TREATMENT OF CERTAIN FINANCIAL INSTITUTIONS.—

(A) IN GENERAL.—For purposes of paragraph (1), any corporation described in subparagraph (B) shall be treated as an includible corporation for purposes of section 1504 only for purposes of applying this subsection separately to corporations so described.

(B) DESCRIPTION.—A corporation is described in this subparagraph if—

(i) such corporation is a financial institution described in section 581 or 591,

(ii) the business of such financial institution is predominantly with persons other than related persons (within the meaning of subsection (d)(4)) or their customers, and

(iii) such financial institution is required by State or Federal law to be operated separately from any other entity which is not such an institution.

(C) TREATMENT OF BANK AND FINANCIAL HOLDING COMPANIES.—To the extent provided in regulations—

(i) a bank holding company (within the meaning of section 2(a) of the Bank Holding Company Act of 1956 (12 U.S.C. 1841(a)),

(ii) a financial holding company (within the meaning of section 2(p) of the Bank Holding Company Act of 1956 (12 U.S.C. 1841(p)), and

(iii) any subsidiary of a financial institution described in section 581 or 591, or of any such bank or financial holding company, if such subsidiary is predominantly engaged (directly or indirectly) in the active conduct of a banking, financing, or similar business,

shall be treated as a corporation described in subparagraph (B).

(5) ELECTION TO EXPAND FINANCIAL INSTITUTION GROUP OF WORLDWIDE GROUP.—

(A) IN GENERAL.—If a worldwide affiliated group elects the application of this subsection, all financial corporations which—

(i) are members of such worldwide affiliated group, but

(ii) are not corporations described in paragraph (4)(B),

shall be treated as described in paragraph (4)(B) for purposes of applying paragraph (4)(A). This subsection (other than this paragraph) shall apply to any such group in the same manner as this subsection (other than this paragraph) applies to the pre-election worldwide affiliated group of which such group is a part.

(B) FINANCIAL CORPORATION.—For purposes of this paragraph, the term "financial corporation" means any corporation if at least 80 percent of its gross income is income described in section 904(d)(2)(D)(ii) and the regulations thereunder which is derived from transactions with persons who are not related (within the meaning of section 267(b) or 707(b)(1)) to the corporation. For purposes of the preceding sentence, there shall be disregarded any item of income or gain from a transaction or series of transactions a principal purpose of which is the qualification of any corporation as a financial corporation.

(C) ANTI-ABUSE RULES.—In the case of a corporation which is a member of an electing financial institution group, to the extent that such corporation—

(i) distributes dividends or makes other distributions with respect to its stock after the date of the enactment of this paragraph to any member of the pre-election worldwide affiliated group (other than to a member of the electing financial institution group) in excess of the greater of—

(I) its average annual dividend (expressed as a percentage of current earnings and profits) during the 5-taxable-year period ending with the taxable year preceding the taxable year, or

(II) 25 percent of its average annual earnings and profits for such 5-taxable-year period, or

(ii) deals with any person in any manner not clearly reflecting the income of the corporation (as determined under principles similar to the principles of section 482),

an amount of indebtedness of the electing financial institution group equal to the excess distribution or the understatement or overstatement of income, as the case may be, shall be recharacterized (for the taxable year and subsequent taxable years) for purposes of this paragraph as indebtedness of the worldwide affiliated group (excluding the electing financial institution group). If a corporation has not been in existence for 5 taxable years, this subparagraph shall be applied with respect to the period it was in existence.

(D) ELECTION.—An election under this paragraph with respect to any financial institution group may be made only by the common parent of the pre-election worldwide affiliated group and may be made only for the first taxable year beginning after December 31, 2008, in which such affiliated group includes 1 or more financial corporations. Such an election, once made, shall apply to all financial corporations which are members of the electing financial institution group for such taxable year and all subsequent years unless revoked with the consent of the Secretary.

(E) DEFINITIONS RELATING TO GROUPS.—For purposes of this paragraph—

(i) PRE-ELECTION WORLDWIDE AFFILIATED GROUP.—The term "pre-election worldwide affiliated group" means, with respect to a corporation, the worldwide affiliated group of which such corporation would (but for an election under this paragraph) be a member for purposes of applying paragraph (1).

(ii) ELECTING FINANCIAL INSTITUTION GROUP.—The term "electing financial institution group" means the group of corporations to which this subsection applies separately by reason of the application of paragraph (4)(A) and which includes financial corporations by reason of an election under subparagraph (A).

(F) REGULATIONS.—The Secretary shall prescribe such regulations as may be appropriate to carry out this subsection, including regulations—

Income Tax—Sources of Income 145

(i) providing for the direct allocation of interest expense in other circumstances where such allocation would be appropriate to carry out the purposes of this subsection,

(ii) preventing assets or interest expense from being taken into account more than once, and

(iii) dealing with changes in members of any group (through acquisitions or otherwise) treated under this paragraph as an affiliated group for purposes of this subsection.

(6) ELECTION.—An election to have this subsection apply with respect to any worldwide affiliated group may be made only by the common parent of the domestic affiliated group referred to in paragraph (1)(C) and may be made only for the first taxable year beginning after December 31, 2008, in which a worldwide affiliated group exists which includes such affiliated group and at least 1 foreign corporation. Such an election, once made, shall apply to such common parent and all other corporations which are members of such worldwide affiliated group for such taxable year and all subsequent years unless revoked with the consent of the Secretary.

* * *

[Sec. 865]

SEC. 865. SOURCE RULES FOR PERSONAL PROPERTY SALES.

[Sec. 865(a)]

(a) GENERAL RULE.—Except as otherwise provided in this section, income from the sale of personal property—

(1) by a United States resident shall be sourced in the United States, or

(2) by a nonresident shall be sourced outside the United States.

[Sec. 865(b)]

(b) EXCEPTION FOR INVENTORY PROPERTY.—In the case of income derived from the sale of inventory property—

(1) this section shall not apply, and

(2) such income shall be sourced under the rules of sections 861(a)(6), 862(a)(6), and 863.

Notwithstanding the preceding sentence, any income from the sale of any unprocessed timber which is a softwood and was cut from an area in the United States shall be sourced in the United States and the rules of sections 862(a)(6) and 863(b) shall not apply to any such income. For purposes of the preceding sentence, the term "unprocessed timber" means any log, cant, or similar form of timber.

[Sec. 865(c)]

(c) EXCEPTION FOR DEPRECIABLE PERSONAL PROPERTY.—

(1) IN GENERAL.—Gain (not in excess of the depreciation adjustments) from the sale of depreciable personal property shall be allocated between sources in the United States and sources outside the United States—

(A) by treating the same proportion of such gain as sourced in the United States as the United States depreciation adjustments with respect to such property bear to the total depreciation adjustments, and

(B) by treating the remaining portion of such gain as sourced outside the United States.

(2) GAIN IN EXCESS OF DEPRECIATION.—Gain (in excess of the depreciation adjustments) from the sale of depreciable personal property shall be sourced as if such property were inventory property.

(3) UNITED STATES DEPRECIATION ADJUSTMENTS.—For purposes of this subsection—

(A) IN GENERAL.—The term "United States depreciation adjustments" means the portion of the depreciation adjustments to the adjusted basis of the property which are attributable to the depreciation deductions allowable in computing taxable income from sources in the United States.

(B) SPECIAL RULE FOR CERTAIN PROPERTY.—Except in the case of property of a kind described in section 168(g)(4), if, for any taxable year—

(i) such property is used predominantly in the United States, or

(ii) such property is used predominantly outside the United States,

all of the depreciation deductions allowable for such year shall be treated as having been allocated to income from sources in the United States (or, where clause (ii) applies, from sources outside the United States).

(4) OTHER DEFINITIONS.—For purposes of this subsection—

(A) DEPRECIABLE PERSONAL PROPERTY.—The term "depreciable personal property" means any personal property if the adjusted basis of such property includes depreciation adjustments.

(B) DEPRECIATION ADJUSTMENTS.—The term "depreciation adjustments" means adjustments reflected in the adjusted basis of any property on account of depreciation deductions (whether allowed with respect to such property or other property and whether allowed to the taxpayer or to any other person).

(C) DEPRECIATION DEDUCTIONS.—The term "depreciation deductions" means any deductions for depreciation or amortization or any other deduction allowable under any provision of this chapter which treats an otherwise capital expenditure as a deductible expense.

[Sec. 865(d)]

(d) EXCEPTION FOR INTANGIBLES.—

(1) IN GENERAL.—In the case of any sale of an intangible—

(A) this section shall apply only to the extent the payments in consideration of such sale are not contingent on the productivity, use, or disposition of the intangible, and

(B) to the extent such payments are so contingent, the source of such payments shall be determined under this part in the same manner as if such payments were royalties.

(2) INTANGIBLE.—For purposes of paragraph (1), the term "intangible" means any patent, copyright, secret process or formula, goodwill, trademark, trade brand, franchise, or other like property.

(3) SPECIAL RULE IN THE CASE OF GOODWILL.—To the extent this section applies to the sale of goodwill, payments in consideration of such sale shall be treated as from sources in the country in which such goodwill was generated.

(4) COORDINATION WITH SUBSECTION (c).—

(A) GAIN NOT IN EXCESS OF DEPRECIATION ADJUSTMENTS SOURCED UNDER SUBSECTION (c).—Notwithstanding paragraph (1), any gain from the sale of an intangible shall be sourced under subsection (c) to the extent such gain does not exceed the depreciation adjustments with respect to such intangible.

(B) SUBSECTION (c)(2) NOT TO APPLY TO INTANGIBLES.—Paragraph (2) of subsection (c) shall not apply to any gain from the sale of an intangible.

[Sec. 865(e)]

(e) SPECIAL RULES FOR SALES THROUGH OFFICES OR FIXED PLACES OF BUSINESS.—

(1) SALES BY RESIDENTS.—

(A) IN GENERAL.—In the case of income not sourced under subsection (b), (c), (d)(1)(B) or (3), or (f), if a United States resident maintains an office or other fixed place of business in a foreign country, income from sales of personal property attributable to such office or other fixed place of business shall be sourced outside the United States.

(B) TAX MUST BE IMPOSED.—Subparagraph (A) shall not apply unless an income tax equal to at least 10 percent of the income from the sale is actually paid to a foreign country with respect to such income.

(2) SALES BY NONRESIDENTS.—

(A) IN GENERAL.—Notwithstanding any other provisions of this part, if a nonresident maintains an office or other fixed place of business in the United States, income from any sale of personal property (including inventory property) attributable to such office or other fixed place of business shall be sourced in the United States. The preceding sentence shall not apply for purposes of section 971 (defining export trade corporation).

(B) EXCEPTION.—Subparagraph (A) shall not apply to any sale of inventory property which is sold for use, disposition, or consumption outside the United States if an office or other fixed place of business of the taxpayer in a foreign country materially participated in the sale.

(3) SALES ATTRIBUTABLE TO AN OFFICE OR OTHER FIXED PLACE OF BUSINESS.—The principles of section 864(c)(5) shall apply in determining whether a taxpayer has an office or other fixed place of business and whether a sale is attributable to such an office or other fixed place of business.

[Sec. 865(f)]

(f) STOCK OF AFFILIATES.—If—

(1) a United States resident sells stock in an affiliate which is a foreign corporation,

(2) such sale occurs in a foreign country in which such affiliate is engaged in the active conduct of a trade or business, and

(3) more than 50 percent of the gross income of such affiliate for the 3-year period ending with the close of such affiliate's taxable year immediately preceding the year in which the sale occurred was derived from the active conduct of a trade or business in such foreign country,

any gain from such sale shall be sourced outside the United States. For purposes of paragraphs (2) and (3), the United States resident may elect to treat an affiliate and all other corporations which are wholly owned (directly or indirectly) by the affiliate as one corporation.

[Sec. 865(g)]

(g) UNITED STATES RESIDENT; NONRESIDENT.—For purposes of this section—

(1) IN GENERAL.—Except as otherwise provided in this subsection—

(A) UNITED STATES RESIDENT.—The term "United States resident" means—
(i) any individual who—
(I) is a United States citizen or a resident alien and does not have a tax home (as defined in section 911(d)(3)) in a foreign country, or
(II) is a nonresident alien and has a tax home (as so defined) in the United States, and
(ii) any corporation, trust, or estate which is a United States person (as defined in section 7701(a)(30)).

(B) NONRESIDENT.—The term "nonresident" means any person other than a United States resident.

(2) SPECIAL RULES FOR UNITED STATES CITIZENS AND RESIDENT ALIENS.—For purposes of this section, a United States citizen or resident alien shall not be treated as a nonresident with respect to any sale of personal property unless an income tax equal to a least 10 percent of the gain derived from such sale is actually paid to a foreign country with respect to that gain.

(3) SPECIAL RULE FOR CERTAIN STOCK SALES BY RESIDENTS OF PUERTO RICO.—Paragraph (2) shall not apply to the sale by an individual who was a bona fide resident of Puerto Rico during the entire taxable year of stock in a corporation if—

(A) such corporation is engaged in the active conduct of a trade or business in Puerto Rico, and

(B) more than 50 percent of its gross income for the 3-year period ending with the close of such corporation's taxable year immediately preceding the year in which such sale occurred was derived from the active conduct of a trade or business in Puerto Rico.

For purposes of the preceding sentence, the taxpayer may elect to treat a corporation and all other corporations which are wholly owned (directly or indirectly) by such corporation as one corporation.

[Sec. 865(h)]

(h) TREATMENT OF GAINS FROM SALE OF CERTAIN STOCK OR INTANGIBLES AND FROM CERTAIN LIQUIDATIONS.—

(1) IN GENERAL.—In the case of gain to which this subsection applies—

(A) such gain shall be sourced outside the United States, but

(B) subsections (a), (b), and (c) of section 904 and sections 902, 907, and 960 shall be applied separately with respect to such gain.

(2) GAIN TO WHICH SUBSECTION APPLIES.—This subsection shall apply to—

(A) GAIN FROM SALE OF CERTAIN STOCK OR INTANGIBLES.—Any gain—

(i) which is from the sale of stock in a foreign corporation or an intangible (as defined in subsection (d)(2)) and which would otherwise be sourced in the United States under this section,

(ii) which, under a treaty obligation of the United States (applied without regard to this section), would be sourced outside the United States, and

(iii) with respect to which the taxpayer chooses the benefits of this subsection.

(B) GAIN FROM LIQUIDATION IN POSSESSION.—Any gain which is derived from the receipt of any distribution in liquidation of a corporation—

(i) which is organized in a possession of the United States, and

(ii) more than 50 percent of the gross income of which during the 3-taxable year period ending with the close of the taxable year immediately preceding the taxable year in which the distribution is received from the active conduct of a trade or business in such possession.

[Sec. 865(i)]

(i) OTHER DEFINITIONS.—For purposes of this section—

(1) INVENTORY PROPERTY.—The term "inventory property" means personal property described in paragraph (1) of section 1221(a).

(2) SALE INCLUDES EXCHANGE.—The term "sale" includes an exchange or any other disposition.

(3) TREATMENT OF POSSESSIONS.—Any possession of the United States shall be treated as a foreign country.

(4) AFFILIATE.—The term "affiliate" means a member of the same affiliated group (within the meaning of section 1504(a) without regard to section 1504(b)).

(5) TREATMENT OF PARTNERSHIPS.—In the case of a partnership, except as provided in regulations, this section shall be applied at the partner level.

[Sec. 865(j)]

(j) REGULATIONS.—The Secretary shall prescribe such regulations as may be necessary or appropriate to carry out the purpose of this section, including regulations—

(1) relating to the treatment of losses from sales of personal property,

(2) applying the rules of this section to income derived from trading in futures contracts, forward contracts, options contracts, and other instruments, and

(3) providing that, subject to such conditions (which may include provisions comparable to section 877) as may be provided in such regulations, subsections (e)(1)(B) and (g)(2) shall not apply for purposes of sections 931, 933, and 936.

Income Tax—Sources of Income

[Sec. 865(k)]

(k) Cross References.—

(1) For provisions relating to the characterization as dividends for source purposes of gains from the sale of stock in certain foreign corporations, see section 1248.

(2) For sourcing of income from certain foreign currency transactions, see section 988.

PART II—NONRESIDENT ALIENS AND FOREIGN CORPORATIONS

Subpart A—Nonresident Alien Individuals

[Sec. 871]

SEC. 871. TAX ON NONRESIDENT ALIEN INDIVIDUALS.

[Sec. 871(a)]

(a) Income Not Connected with United States Business—30 Percent Tax.—

(1) Income other than capital gains.—Except as provided in subsection (h), there is hereby imposed for each taxable year a tax of 30 percent of the amount received from sources within the United States by a nonresident alien individual as—

(A) interest (other than original issue discount as defined in section 1273), dividends, rents, salaries, wages, premiums, annuities, compensations, remunerations, emoluments, and other fixed or determinable annual or periodical gains, profits, and income,

(B) gains described in section 631(b) or (c), and gains on transfers described in section 1235 made on or before October 4, 1966,

(C) in the case of—

(i) a sale or exchange of an original issue discount obligation, the amount of the original issue discount accruing while such obligation was held by the nonresident alien individual (to the extent such discount was not theretofore taken into account under clause (ii)), and

(ii) a payment on an original issue discount obligation, an amount equal to the original issue discount accruing while such obligation was held by the nonresident alien individual (except that such original issue discount shall be taken into account under this clause only to the extent such discount was not theretofore taken into account under this clause and only to the extent that the tax thereon does not exceed the payment less the tax imposed by subparagraph (A) thereon), and

(D) gains from the sale or exchange after October 4, 1966, of patents, copyrights, secret processes and formulas, good will, trademarks, trade brands, franchises, and other like property, or of any interest in any such property, to the extent such gains are from payments which are contingent on the productivity, use, or disposition of the property or interest sold or exchanged,

but only to the extent the amount so received is not effectively connected with the conduct of a trade or business within the United States.

(2) Capital gains of aliens present in the United States 183 days or more.—In the case of a nonresident alien individual present in the United States for a period or periods aggregating 183 days or more during the taxable year, there is hereby imposed for such year a tax of 30 percent of the amount by which his gains, derived from sources within the United States, from the sale or exchange at any time during such year of capital assets exceed his losses, allocable to sources within the United States, from the sale or exchange at any time during such year of capital assets. For purposes of this paragraph, gains and losses shall be taken into account only if, and to the extent that, they would be recognized and taken into account if such gains and losses were effectively connected with the conduct of a trade or business within the United States, except that such gains and losses shall be determined without regard to section 1202 and such losses shall be determined without the benefits of the capital loss carryover provided in section 1212. Any gain or loss which is taken into account in determining the tax under paragraph (1) or subsection (b) shall not be taken into account in determining the tax under this paragraph. For purposes of the 183-day requirement of this paragraph, a nonresident alien individual not engaged in trade or business within the United States who has not established a taxable year for any prior period shall be treated as having a taxable year which is the calendar year.

(3) TAXATION OF SOCIAL SECURITY BENEFITS.—For purposes of this section and section 1441—

    (A) 85 percent of any social security benefit (as defined in section 86(d)) shall be included in gross income (notwithstanding section 207 of the Social Security Act), and

    (B) section 86 shall not apply.

For treatment of certain citizens of possessions of the United States, see section 932(c).

[Sec. 871(b)]

(b) INCOME CONNECTED WITH UNITED STATES BUSINESS—GRADUATED RATE OF TAX.—

    (1) IMPOSITION OF TAX.—A nonresident alien individual engaged in trade or business within the United States during the taxable year shall be taxable as provided in section 1 or 55 on his taxable income which is effectively connected with the conduct of a trade or business within the United States.

    (2) DETERMINATION OF TAXABLE INCOME.—In determining taxable income for purposes of paragraph (1), gross income includes only gross income which is effectively connected with the conduct of a trade or business within the United States.

[Sec. 871(c)]

(c) PARTICIPANTS IN CERTAIN EXCHANGE OR TRAINING PROGRAMS.—For purposes of this section, a nonresident alien individual who (without regard to this subsection) is not engaged in trade or business within the United States and who is temporarily present in the United States as a nonimmigrant under subparagraph (F), (J), (M), or (Q) of section 101(a)(15) of the Immigration and Nationality Act, as amended (8 U.S.C. 1101(a)(15)(F), (J), (M), or (Q)), shall be treated as a nonresident alien individual engaged in trade or business within the United States, and any income described in the second sentence of section 1441(b) which is received by such individual shall, to the extent derived from sources within the United States, be treated as effectively connected with the conduct of a trade or business within the United States.

[Sec. 871(d)]

(d) ELECTION TO TREAT REAL PROPERTY INCOME AS INCOME CONNECTED WITH UNITED STATES BUSINESS.—

    (1) IN GENERAL.—A nonresident alien individual who during the taxable year derives any income—

        (A) from real property held for the production of income and located in the United States, or from any interest in such real property, including (i) gains from the sale or exchange of such real property or an interest therein, (ii) rents or royalties from mines, wells, or other natural deposits, and (iii) gains described in section 631(b) or (c), and

        (B) which, but for this subsection, would not be treated as income which is effectively connected with the conduct of a trade or business within the United States,

may elect for such taxable year to treat all such income as income which is effectively connected with the conduct of a trade or business within the United States. In such case, such income shall be taxable as provided in subsection (b)(1) whether or not such individual is engaged in trade or business within the United States during the taxable year. An election under this paragraph for any taxable year shall remain in effect for all subsequent taxable years, except that it may be revoked with the consent of the Secretary with respect to any taxable year.

    (2) ELECTION AFTER REVOCATION.—If an election has been made under paragraph (1) and such election has been revoked, a new election may not be made under such paragraph for any taxable year before the 5th taxable year which begins after the first taxable year for which such revocation is effective, unless the Secretary consents to such new election.

    (3) FORM AND TIME OF ELECTION AND REVOCATION.—An election under paragraph (1), and any revocation of such an election, may be made only in such manner and at such time as the Secretary may by regulations prescribe.

* * *

[Sec. 871(g)]

(g) SPECIAL RULES FOR ORIGINAL ISSUE DISCOUNT.—For purposes of this section and section 881—

(1) ORIGINAL ISSUE DISCOUNT OBLIGATION.—

(A) IN GENERAL.—Except as provided in subparagraph (B), the term "original issue discount obligation" means any bond or other evidence of indebtedness having original issue discount (within the meaning of section 1273).

(B) EXCEPTIONS.—The term "original issue discount obligation" shall not include—

(i) CERTAIN SHORT-TERM OBLIGATIONS.—Any obligation payable 183 days or less from the date of original issue (without regard to the period held by the taxpayer).

(ii) TAX-EXEMPT OBLIGATIONS.—Any obligation the interest on which is exempt from tax under section 103 or under any other provision of law without regard to the identity of the holder.

(2) DETERMINATION OF PORTION OF ORIGINAL ISSUE DISCOUNT ACCRUING DURING ANY PERIOD.—The determination of the amount of the original issue discount which accrues during any period shall be made under the rules of section 1272 (or the corresponding provisions of prior law) without regard to any exception for short-term obligations.

(3) SOURCE OF ORIGINAL ISSUE DISCOUNT.—Except to the extent provided in regulations prescribed by the Secretary, the determination of whether any amount described in subsection (a)(1)(C) is from sources within the United States shall be made at the time of the payment (or sale or exchange) as if such payment (or sale or exchange) involved the payment of interest.

(4) STRIPPED BONDS.—The provisions of section 1286 (relating to the treatment of stripped bonds and stripped coupons as obligations with original issue discount) shall apply for purposes of this section.

[Sec. 871(h)]

(h) REPEAL OF TAX ON INTEREST OF NONRESIDENT ALIEN INDIVIDUALS RECEIVED FROM CERTAIN PORTFOLIO DEBT INVESTMENTS.—

(1) IN GENERAL.—In the case of any portfolio interest received by a nonresident individual from sources within the United States, no tax shall be imposed under paragraph (1)(A) or (1)(C) of subsection (a).

(2) PORTFOLIO INTEREST.—For purposes of this subsection, the term "portfolio interest" means any interest (including original issue discount) which would be subject to tax under subsection (a) but for this subsection and which is described in any of the following subparagraphs:

(A) CERTAIN OBLIGATIONS WHICH ARE NOT REGISTERED.—Interest which is paid on any obligation which—

(i) is not in registered form, and

(ii) is described in section 163(f)(2)(B).

(B) CERTAIN REGISTERED OBLIGATIONS.—Interest which is paid on an obligation—

(i) which is in registered form, and

(ii) with respect to which the United States person who would otherwise be required to deduct and withhold tax from such interest under section 1441(a) receives a statement (which meets the requirements of paragraph (5)) that the beneficial owner of the obligation is not a United States person.

(3) PORTFOLIO INTEREST NOT TO INCLUDE INTEREST RECEIVED BY 10-PERCENT SHAREHOLDERS.—For purposes of this subsection—

(A) IN GENERAL.—The term "portfolio interest" shall not include any interest described in subparagraph (A) or (B) of paragraph (2) which is received by a 10-percent shareholder.

(B) 10-PERCENT SHAREHOLDER.—The term "10-percent shareholder" means—

(i) in the case of an obligation issued by a corporation, any person who owns 10 percent or more of the total combined voting power of all classes of stock of such corporation entitled to vote, or

(ii) in the case of an obligation issued by a partnership, any person who owns 10 percent or more of the capital or profits interest in such partnership.

(C) ATTRIBUTION RULES.—For purposes of determining ownership of stock under subparagraph (B)(i) the rules of section 318(a) shall apply, except that—

(i) section 318(a)(2)(C) shall be applied without regard to the 50-percent limitation therein,

(ii) section 318(a)(3)(C) shall be applied—

(I) without regard to the 50-percent limitation therein; and

(II) in any case where such section would not apply but for subclause (I), by considering a corporation as owning the stock (other than stock in such corporation) which is owned by or for any shareholder of such corporation in that proportion which the value of the stock which such shareholder owns in such corporation bears to the value of all stock in such corporation, and

(iii) any stock which a person is treated as owning after application of section 318(a)(4) shall not, for purposes of applying paragraphs (2) and (3) of section 318(a), be treated as actually owned by such person.

Under regulations prescribed by the Secretary, rules similar to the rules of the preceding sentence shall be applied in determining the ownership of the capital or profits interest in a partnership for purposes of subparagraph (B)(ii).

(4) PORTFOLIO INTEREST NOT TO INCLUDE CERTAIN CONTINGENT INTEREST.—For purposes of this subsection—

(A) IN GENERAL.—Except as otherwise provided in this paragraph, the term 'portfolio interest' shall not include—

(i) any interest if the amount of such interest is determined by reference to—

(I) any receipts, sales or other cash flow of the debtor or a related person,

(II) any income or profits of the debtor or a related person,

(III) any change in value of any property of the debtor or a related person, or

(IV) any dividend, partnership distributions, or similar payments made by the debtor or a related person, or

(ii) any other type of contingent interest that is identified by the Secretary by regulation, where a denial of the portfolio interest exemption is necessary or appropriate to prevent avoidance of Federal income tax.

(B) RELATED PERSON.—The term "related person" means any person who is related to the debtor within the meaning of section 267(b) or 707(b)(1), or who is a party to any arrangement undertaken for a purpose of avoiding the application of this paragraph.

(C) EXCEPTIONS.—Subparagraph (A)(i) shall not apply to—

(i) any amount of interest solely by reason of the fact that the timing of any interest or principal payment is subject to a contingency,

(ii) any amount of interest solely by reason of the fact that the interest is paid with respect to nonrecourse or limited recourse indebtedness,

(iii) any amount of interest all or substantially all of which is determined by reference to any other amount of interest not described in subparagraph (A) (or by reference to the principal amount of indebtedness on which such other interest is paid),

(iv) any amount of interest solely by reason of the fact that the debtor or a related person enters into a hedging transaction to manage the risk of interest rate or currency fluctuations with respect to such interest,

(v) any amount of interest determined by reference to—

(I) changes in the value of property (including stock) that is actively traded (within the meaning of section 1092(d)) other than property described in section 897(c)(1) or (g),

(II) the yield on property described in subclause (I), other than a debt instrument that pays interest described in subparagraph (A), or stock or other property that represents a beneficial interest in the debtor or a related person, or

(III) changes in any index of the value of property described in subclause (I) or of the yield on property described in subclause (II), and

(vi) any other type of interest identified by the Secretary by regulation.

(D) EXCEPTION FOR CERTAIN EXISTING INDEBTEDNESS.—Subparagraph (A) shall not apply to any interest paid or accrued with respect to any indebtedness with a fixed term—

(i) which was issued on or before April 7, 1993, or

(ii) which was issued after such date pursuant to a written binding contract in effect on such date and at all times thereafter before such indebtedness was issued.

(5) CERTAIN STATEMENTS.—A statement with respect to any obligation meets the requirements of this paragraph if such statement is made by—

(A) the beneficial owner of such obligation, or

(B) a securities clearing organization, a bank, or other financial institution that holds customers' securities in the ordinary course of its trade or business.

The preceding sentence shall not apply to any statement with respect to payment of interest on any obligation by any person if, at least one month before such payment, the Secretary has published a determination that any statement from such person (or any class including such person) does not meet the requirements of this paragraph.

(6) SECRETARY MAY PROVIDE SUBSECTION NOT TO APPLY IN CASES OF INADEQUATE INFORMATION EXCHANGE.—

(A) IN GENERAL.—If the Secretary determines that the exchange of information between the United States and a foreign country is inadequate to prevent evasion of the United States income tax by United States persons, the Secretary may provide in writing (and publish a statement) that the provisions of this subsection shall not apply to payments of interest to any person within such foreign country (or payments addressed to, or for the account of, persons within such foreign country) during the period—

(i) beginning on the date specified by the Secretary, and

(ii) ending on the date that the Secretary determines that the exchange of information between the United States and the foreign country is adequate to prevent the evasion of United States income tax by United States persons.

(B) EXCEPTION FOR CERTAIN OBLIGATIONS.—Subparagraph (A) shall not apply to the payment of interest on any obligation which is issued on or before the date of the publication of the Secretary's determination under such subparagraph.

(7) REGISTERED FORM.—For purposes of this subsection, the term "registered form" has the same meaning given such term by section 163(f).

[Sec. 871(i)]

(i) TAX NOT TO APPLY TO CERTAIN INTEREST AND DIVIDENDS.—

(1) IN GENERAL.—No tax shall be imposed under paragraph (1)(A) or (1)(C) of subsection (a) on any amount described in paragraph (2).

(2) AMOUNTS TO WHICH PARAGRAPH (1) APPLIES.—The amounts described in this paragraph are as follows:

(A) Interest on deposits, if such interest is not effectively connected with the conduct of a trade or business within the United States.

(B) A percentage of any dividend paid by a domestic corporation meeting the 80-percent foreign business requirements of section 861(c)(1) equal to the percentage determined for purposes of section 861(c)(2)(A).

(C) Income derived by a foreign central bank of issue from bankers' acceptances.

(D) Dividends paid by a foreign corporation which are treated under section 861(a)(2)(B) as income from sources within the United States.

(3) DEPOSITS.—For purposes of paragraph (2), the term "deposit" means amounts which are—

(A) deposits with persons carrying on the banking business,

(B) deposits or withdrawable accounts with savings institutions chartered and supervised as savings and loan or similar associations under Federal or State law, but only to the extent that amounts paid or credited on such deposits or accounts are deductible under section 591 (determined without regard to sections 265 and 291) in computing the taxable income of such institutions, and

(C) amounts held by an insurance company under an agreement to pay interest thereon.

[Sec. 871(j)]

(j) EXEMPTION FOR CERTAIN GAMBLING WINNINGS.—No tax shall be imposed under paragraph (1)(A) of subsection (a) on the proceeds from a wager placed in any of the following games: blackjack, baccarat, craps, roulette, or big-6 wheel. The preceding sentence shall not apply in any case where the Secretary determines by regulation that the collection of the tax is administratively feasible.

* * *

[Sec. 872]

SEC. 872. GROSS INCOME.

[Sec. 872(a)]

(a) GENERAL RULE.—In the case of a nonresident alien individual, except where the context clearly indicates otherwise, gross income includes only—

(1) gross income which is derived from sources within the United States and which is not effectively connected with the conduct of a trade or business within the United States, and

(2) gross income which is effectively connected with the conduct of a trade or business within the United States.

[Sec. 872(b)]

(b) EXCLUSIONS.—The following items shall not be included in gross income of a nonresident alien individual, and shall be exempt from taxation under this subtitle:

(1) SHIPS OPERATED BY CERTAIN NONRESIDENTS.—Gross income derived by an individual resident of a foreign country from the international operation of a ship or ships if such foreign country grants an equivalent exemption to individual residents of the United States.

(2) AIRCRAFT OPERATION BY CERTAIN NONRESIDENTS.—Gross income derived by an individual resident of a foreign country from the international operation of aircraft if such foreign country grants an equivalent exemption to individual residents of the United States.

(3) COMPENSATION OF PARTICIPANTS IN CERTAIN EXCHANGE OR TRAINING PROGRAMS.—Compensation paid by a foreign employer to a nonresident alien individual for the period he is temporarily present in the United States as a nonimmigrant under subparagraph (F), (J), or (Q) of section 101(a)(15) of the Immigration and Nationality Act, as amended. For purposes of this paragraph, the term "foreign employer" means—

(A) a nonresident alien individual, foreign partnership, or foreign corporation, or

(B) an office or place of business maintained in a foreign country or in a possession of the United States by a domestic corporation, a domestic partnership, or an individual who is a citizen or resident of the United States.

(4) CERTAIN BOND INCOME OF RESIDENTS OF THE RYUKYU ISLANDS OR THE TRUST TERRITORY OF THE PACIFIC ISLANDS.—Income derived by a nonresident alien individual from a series E or series H United States savings bond, if such individual acquired such bond while a resident of the Ryukyu Islands or the Trust Territory of the Pacific Islands.

(5) INCOME DERIVED FROM WAGERING TRANSACTIONS IN CERTAIN PARIMUTUEL POOLS.—Gross income derived by a nonresident alien individual from a legal wagering transaction initiated outside the United States in a parimutuel pool with respect to a live horse race or dog race in the United States.

(6) CERTAIN RENTAL INCOME.—Income to which paragraphs (1) and (2) apply shall include income which is derived from the rental on a full or bareboat basis of a ship or ships or aircraft, as the case may be.

(7) APPLICATION TO DIFFERENT TYPES OF TRANSPORTATION.—The Secretary may provide that this subsection be applied separately with respect to income from different types of transportation.

(8) TREATMENT OF POSSESSIONS.—To the extent provided in regulations, a possession of the United States shall be treated as a foreign country for purposes of this subsection.

[Sec. 873]

SEC. 873. DEDUCTIONS.

[Sec. 873(a)]

(a) GENERAL RULE.—In the case of a nonresident alien individual, the deductions shall be allowed only for purposes of section 871(b) and (except as provided by subsection (b)) only if and to the extent that they are connected with income which is effectively connected with the conduct of a trade or business within the United States; and the proper apportionment and allocation of the deductions for this purpose shall be determined as provided in regulations prescribed by the Secretary.

[Sec. 873(b)]

(b) EXCEPTIONS.—The following deductions shall be allowed whether or not they are connected with income which is effectively connected with the conduct of a trade or business within the United States:

(1) LOSSES.—The deduction allowed by section 165 for casualty or theft losses described in paragraph (2) or (3) of section 165(c), but only if the loss is of property located within the United States.

(2) CHARITABLE CONTRIBUTIONS.—The deduction for charitable contributions and gifts allowed by section 170.

(3) PERSONAL EXEMPTION.—The deduction for personal exemptions allowed by section 151, except that only one exemption shall be allowed under section 151 unless the taxpayer is a resident of a contiguous country or is a national of the United States.

* * *

[Sec. 874]

SEC. 874. ALLOWANCE OF DEDUCTIONS AND CREDITS.

[Sec. 874(a)]

(a) RETURN PREREQUISITE TO ALLOWANCE.—A nonresident alien individual shall receive the benefit of the deductions and credits allowed to him in this subtitle only by filing or causing to be filed with the Secretary a true and accurate return, in the manner prescribed in subtitle F (sec. 6001 and following, relating to procedure and administration), including therein all the information which the Secretary may deem necessary for the calculation of such deductions and credits. This subsection shall not be construed to deny the credits provided by sections 31 and 33 for tax withheld at source or the credit provided by section 34 for certain uses of gasoline and special fuels.

[Sec. 874(b)]

(b) TAX WITHHELD AT SOURCE.—The benefit of the deduction for exemptions under section 151 may, in the discretion of the Secretary, and under regulations prescribed by the Secretary, be received by a nonresident alien individual entitled thereto, by filing a claim therefor with the withholding agent.

[Sec. 874(c)]

(c) FOREIGN TAX CREDIT.—Except as provided in section 906, a nonresident alien individual shall not be allowed the credits against the tax for taxes of foreign countries and possessions of the United States allowed by section 901.

[Sec. 875]

SEC. 875. PARTNERSHIPS; BENEFICIARIES OF ESTATES AND TRUSTS.

For purposes of this subtitle—

(1) a nonresident alien individual or foreign corporation shall be considered as being engaged in a trade or business within the United States if the partnership of which such individual or corporation is a member is so engaged, and

(2) a nonresident alien individual or foreign corporation which is a beneficiary of an estate or trust which is engaged in any trade or business within the United States shall be treated as being engaged in such trade or business within the United States.

[Sec. 876]

SEC. 876. ALIEN RESIDENTS OF PUERTO RICO, GUAM, AMERICAN SAMOA, OR THE NORTHERN MARIANA ISLANDS.

[Sec. 876(a)]

(a) GENERAL RULE.—This subpart shall not apply to any alien individual who is a bona fide resident of Puerto Rico, Guam, American Samoa, or the Northern Mariana Islands during the entire taxable year and such alien shall be subject to the tax imposed by section 1.

[Sec. 876(b)]

(b) CROSS REFERENCES.—

For exclusion from gross income of income derived from sources within—

(1) Guam, American Samoa, and the Northern Mariana Islands, see section 931, and

(2) Puerto Rico, see section 933.

[Sec. 877]

SEC. 877. EXPATRIATION TO AVOID TAX.

[Sec. 877(a)]

(a) TREATMENT OF EXPATRIATES.—

(1) IN GENERAL.—Every nonresident alien individual to whom this section applies and who, within the 10-year period immediately preceding the close of the taxable year, lost United States citizenship shall be taxable for such taxable year in the manner provided in subsection (b) if the tax imposed pursuant to such subsection (after any reduction in such tax under the last sentence of such subsection) exceeds the tax which, without regard to this section, is imposed pursuant to section 871.

(2) INDIVIDUALS SUBJECT TO THIS SECTION.—This section shall apply to any individual if—

(A) the average annual net income tax (as defined in section 38(c)(1)) of such individual for the period of 5 taxable years ending before the date of the loss of United States citizenship is greater than $124,000,

(B) the net worth of the individual as of such date is $2,000,000 or more, or

(C) such individual fails to certify under penalty of perjury that he has met the requirements of this title for the 5 preceding taxable years or fails to submit such evidence of such compliance as the Secretary may require.

In the case of the loss of United States citizenship in any calendar year after 2004, such $124,000 amount shall be increased by an amount equal to such dollar amount multiplied by the cost-of-living adjustment determined under section 1(f)(3) for such calendar year by substituting "2003" for "1992" in subparagraph (B) thereof. Any increase under the preceding sentence shall be rounded to the nearest multiple of $1,000.

Income Tax—Sources of Income **157**

[Sec. 877(b)]

(b) ALTERNATIVE TAX.—A nonresident alien individual described in subsection (a) shall be taxable for the taxable year as provided in section 1 or 55, except that—

(1) the gross income shall include only the gross income described in section 872(a) (as modified by subsection (d) of this section), and

(2) the deductions shall be allowed if and to the extent that they are connected with the gross income included under this section, except that the capital loss carryover provided by section 1212(b) shall not be allowed; and the proper allocation and apportionment of the deductions for this purpose shall be determined as provided under regulations prescribed by the Secretary.

For purposes of paragraph (2), the deductions allowed by section 873(b) shall be allowed; and the deduction (for losses not connected with the trade or business if incurred in transactions entered into for profit) allowed by section 165(c)(2) shall be allowed, but only if the profit, if such transaction had resulted in a profit, would be included in gross income under this section. The tax imposed solely by reason of this section shall be reduced (but not below zero) by the amount of any income, war profits, and excess profits taxes (within the meaning of section 903) paid to any foreign country or possession of the United States on any income of the taxpayer on which tax is imposed solely by reason of this section.

[Sec. 877(c)]

(c) EXCEPTIONS.—

(1) IN GENERAL.—Subparagraphs (A) and (B) of subsection (a)(2) shall not apply to an individual described in paragraph (2) or (3).

(2) DUAL CITIZENS.—

(A) IN GENERAL.—An individual is described in this paragraph if—

(i) the individual became at birth a citizen of the United States and a citizen of another country and continues to be a citizen of such other country, and

(ii) the individual has had no substantial contacts with the United States.

(B) SUBSTANTIAL CONTACTS.—An individual shall be treated as having no substantial contacts with the United States only if the individual—

(i) was never a resident of the United States (as defined in section 7701(b)),

(ii) has never held a United States passport, and

(iii) was not present in the United States for more than 30 days during any calendar year which is 1 of the 10 calendar years preceding the individual's loss of United States citizenship.

(3) CERTAIN MINORS.—An individual is described in this paragraph if—

(A) the individual became at birth a citizen of the United States,

(B) neither parent of such individual was a citizen of the United States at the time of such birth,

(C) the individual's loss of United States citizenship occurs before such individual attains age 18½, and

(D) the individual was not present in the United States for more than 30 days during any calendar year which is 1 of the 10 calendar years preceding the individual's loss of United States citizenship.

[Sec. 877(d)]

(d) SPECIAL RULES FOR SOURCE, ETC.—For purposes of subsection (b)—

(1) SOURCE RULES.—The following items of gross income shall be treated as income from sources within the United States:

(A) SALE OF PROPERTY.—Gains on the sale or exchange of property (other than stock or debt obligations) located in the United States.

Sec. 877(d)(1)(A)

(B) STOCK OR DEBT OBLIGATIONS.—Gains on the sale or exchange of stock issued by a domestic corporation or debt obligations of United States persons or of the United States, a State or political subdivision thereof, or the District of Columbia.

(C) INCOME OR GAIN DERIVED FROM CONTROLLED FOREIGN CORPORATION.—Any income or gain derived from stock in a foreign corporation but only—

(i) if the individual losing United States citizenship owned (within the meaning of section 958(a)), or is considered as owning (by applying the ownership rules of section 958(b)), at any time during the 2-year period ending on the date of the loss of United States citizenship, more than 50 percent of—

(I) the total combined voting power of all classes of stock entitled to vote of such corporation, or

(II) the total value of the stock of such corporation, and

(ii) to the extent such income or gain does not exceed the earnings and profits attributable to such stock which were earned or accumulated before the loss of citizenship and during periods that the ownership requirements of clause (i) are met.

(2) GAIN RECOGNITION ON CERTAIN EXCHANGES.—

(A) IN GENERAL.—In the case of any exchange of property to which this paragraph applies, notwithstanding any other provision of this title, such property shall be treated as sold for its fair market value on the date of such exchange, and any gain shall be recognized for the taxable year which includes such date.

(B) EXCHANGES TO WHICH PARAGRAPH APPLIES.—This paragraph shall apply to any exchange during the 10-year period beginning on the date the individual loses United States citizenship if—

(i) gain would not (but for this paragraph) be recognized on such exchange in whole or in part for purposes of this subtitle,

(ii) income derived from such property was from sources within the United States (or, if no income was so derived, would have been from such sources), and

(iii) income derived from the property acquired in the exchange would be from sources outside the United States.

(C) EXCEPTION.—Subparagraph (A) shall not apply if the individual enters into an agreement with the Secretary which specifies that any income or gain derived from the property acquired in the exchange (or any other property which has a basis determined in whole or part by reference to such property) during such 10-year period shall be treated as from sources within the United States. If the property transferred in the exchange is disposed of by the person acquiring such property, such agreement shall terminate and any gain which was not recognized by reason of such agreement shall be recognized as of the date of such disposition.

(D) SECRETARY MAY EXTEND PERIOD.—To the extent provided in regulations prescribed by the Secretary, subparagraph (B) shall be applied by substituting the 15-year period beginning 5 years before the loss of United States citizenship for the 10-year period referred to therein. In the case of any exchange occurring during such 5 years, any gain recognized under this subparagraph shall be recognized immediately after such loss of citizenship.

(E) SECRETARY MAY REQUIRE RECOGNITION OF GAIN IN CERTAIN CASES.—To the extent provided in regulations prescribed by the Secretary—

(i) the removal of appreciated tangible personal property from the United States, and

(ii) any other occurrence which (without recognition of gain) results in a change in the source of the income or gain from property from sources within the United States to sources outside the United States,

shall be treated as an exchange to which this paragraph applies.

(3) SUBSTANTIAL DIMINISHING OF RISKS OF OWNERSHIP.—For purposes of determining whether this section applies to any gain on the sale or exchange of any property, the running

of the 10-year period described in subsection (a) and the period applicable under paragraph (2) shall be suspended for any period during which the individual's risk of loss with respect to the property is substantially diminished by—

    (A) the holding of a put with respect to such property (or similar property),

    (B) the holding by another person of a right to acquire the property, or

    (C) a short sale or any other transaction.

  (4) TREATMENT OF PROPERTY CONTRIBUTED TO CONTROLLED FOREIGN CORPORATIONS.—

    (A) IN GENERAL.—If—

      (i) an individual losing United States citizenship contributes property during the 10-year period beginning on the date the individual loses United States citizenship to any corporation which, at the time of the contribution, is described in subparagraph (B), and

      (ii) income derived from such property immediately before such contribution was from sources within the United States (or, if no income was so derived, would have been from such sources),

any income or gain on such property (or any other property which has a basis determined in whole or part by reference to such property) received or accrued by the corporation shall be treated as received or accrued directly by such individual and not by such corporation. The preceding sentence shall not apply to the extent the property has been treated under subparagraph (C) as having been sold by such corporation.

    (B) CORPORATION DESCRIBED.—A corporation is described in this subparagraph with respect to an individual if, were such individual a United States citizen—

      (i) such corporation would be a controlled foreign corporation (as defined in 957), and

      (ii) such individual would be a United States shareholder (as defined in section 951(b)) with respect to such corporation.

    (C) DISPOSITION OF STOCK IN CORPORATION.—If stock in the corporation referred to in subparagraph (A) (or any other stock which has a basis determined in whole or part by reference to such stock) is disposed of during the 10-year period referred to in subsection (a) and while the property referred to in subparagraph (A) is held by such corporation, a pro rata share of such property (determined on the basis of the value of such stock) shall be treated as sold by the corporation immediately before such disposition.

    (D) ANTI-ABUSE RULES.—The Secretary shall prescribe such regulations as may be necessary to prevent the avoidance of the purposes of this paragraph, including where—

      (i) the property is sold to the corporation, and

      (ii) the property taken into account under subparagraph (A) is sold by the corporation.

    (E) INFORMATION REPORTING.—The Secretary shall require such information reporting as is necessary to carry out the purposes of this paragraph.

[Sec. 877(e)]

(e) COMPARABLE TREATMENT OF LAWFUL PERMANENT RESIDENTS WHO CEASE TO BE TAXED AS RESIDENTS.—

  (1) IN GENERAL.—Any long-term resident of the United States who—

    (A) ceases to be a lawful permanent resident of the United States (within the meaning of section 7701(b)(6)), or

    (B) commences to be treated as a resident of a foreign country under the provisions of a tax treaty between the United States and the foreign country and who does not waive the benefits of such treaty applicable to residents of the foreign country,

shall be treated for purposes of this section and sections 2107, 2501, and 6039G in the same manner as if such resident were a citizen of the United States who lost United States citizenship on the date of such cessation or commencement.

(2) LONG-TERM RESIDENT.—For purposes of this subsection, the term "long-term resident" means any individual (other than a citizen of the United States) who is a lawful permanent resident of the United States in at least 8 taxable years during the period of 15 taxable years ending with the taxable year during which the event described in subparagraph (A) or (B) of paragraph (1) occurs. For purposes of the preceding sentence, an individual shall not be treated as a lawful permanent resident for any taxable year if such individual is treated as a resident of a foreign country for the taxable year under the provisions of a tax treaty between the United States and the foreign country and does not waive the benefits of such treaty applicable to residents of the foreign country.

(3) SPECIAL RULES.—

(A) EXCEPTIONS NOT TO APPLY.—Subsection (c) shall not apply to an individual who is treated as provided in paragraph (1).

(B) STEP-UP IN BASIS.—Solely for purposes of determining any tax imposed by reason of this subsection, property which was held by the long-term resident on the date the individual first became a resident of the United States shall be treated as having a basis on such date of not less than the fair market value of such property on such date. The preceding sentence shall not apply if the individual elects not to have such sentence apply. Such an election, once made, shall be irrevocable.

(4) AUTHORITY TO EXEMPT INDIVIDUALS.—This subsection shall not apply to an individual who is described in a category of individuals prescribed by regulation by the Secretary.

(5) REGULATIONS.—The Secretary shall prescribe such regulations as may be appropriate to carry out this subsection, including regulations providing for the application of this subsection in cases where an alien individual becomes a resident of the United States during the 10-year period after being treated as provided in paragraph (1).

[Sec. 877(f)]

(f) BURDEN OF PROOF.—If the Secretary establishes that it is reasonable to believe that an individual's loss of United States citizenship would, but for this section, result in a substantial reduction for the taxable year in the taxes on his probable income for such year, the burden of proving for such taxable year that such loss of citizenship did not have for one of its principal purposes the avoidance of taxes under this subtitle or subtitle B shall be on such individual.

[Sec. 877(g)]

(g) PHYSICAL PRESENCE.—

(1) IN GENERAL.—This section shall not apply to any individual to whom this section would otherwise apply for any taxable year during the 10-year period referred to in subsection (a) in which such individual is physically present in the United States at any time on more than 30 days in the calendar year ending in such taxable year, and such individual shall be treated for purposes of this title as a citizen or resident of the United States, as the case may be, for such taxable year.

(2) EXCEPTION.—

(A) IN GENERAL.—In the case of an individual described in any of the following subparagraphs of this paragraph, a day of physical presence in the United States shall be disregarded if the individual is performing services in the United States on such day for an employer. The preceding sentence shall not apply if—

(i) such employer is related (within the meaning of section 267 and 707) to such individual, or

(ii) such employer fails to meet such requirements as the Secretary may prescribe by regulations to prevent the avoidance of the purposes of this paragraph.

Not more than 30 days during any calendar year may be disregarded under this subparagraph.

(B) INDIVIDUALS WITH TIES TO OTHER COUNTRIES.—An individual is described in this subparagraph if—

(i) the individual becomes (not later than the close of a reasonable period after loss of United States citizenship or termination of residency) a citizen or resident of the country in which—

(I) such individual was born,

(II) if such individual is married, such individual's spouse was born, or

(III) either of such individual's parents were born, and

(ii) the individual becomes fully liable for income tax in such country.

(C) MINIMAL PRIOR PHYSICAL PRESENCE IN THE UNITED STATES.—An individual is described in this subparagraph if, for each year in the 10-year period ending on the date of loss of United States citizenship or termination of residency, the individual was physically present in the United States for 30 days or less. The rule of section 7701(b)(3)(D)(ii) shall apply for purposes of this subparagraph.

[Sec. 878]

SEC. 878. FOREIGN EDUCATIONAL, CHARITABLE, AND CERTAIN OTHER EXEMPT ORGANIZATIONS.

For special provisions relating to foreign educational, charitable, and other exempt organizations, see sections 512(a) and 4948.

[Sec. 879]

SEC. 879. TAX TREATMENT OF CERTAIN COMMUNITY INCOME IN THE CASE OF NONRESIDENT ALIEN INDIVIDUALS.

[Sec. 879(a)]

(a) GENERAL RULE.—In the case of a married couple 1 or both of whom are nonresident alien individuals and who have community income for the taxable year, such community income shall be treated as follows:

(1) Earned income (within the meaning of section 911(d)(2)), other than trade or business income and a partner's distributive share of partnership income, shall be treated as the income of the spouse who rendered the personal services,

(2) Trade or business income, and a partner's distributive share of partnership income, shall be treated as provided in section 1402(a)(5),

(3) Community income not described in paragraph (1) or (2) which is derived from the separate property (as determined under the applicable community property law) of one spouse shall be treated as the income of such spouse, and

(4) All other such community income shall be treated as provided in the applicable community property law.

[Sec. 879(b)]

(b) EXCEPTION WHERE ELECTION UNDER SECTION 6013(g) IS IN EFFECT.—Subsection (a) shall not apply for any taxable year for which an election under subsection (g) or (h) of section 6013 (relating to election to treat nonresident alien individual as resident of the United States) is in effect.

[Sec. 879(c)]

(c) DEFINITIONS AND SPECIAL RULES.—For purposes of this section—

(1) COMMUNITY INCOME.—The term "community income" means income which, under applicable community property laws, is treated as community income.

(2) COMMUNITY PROPERTY LAWS.—The term "community property laws" means the community property laws of a State, a foreign country, or a possession of the United States.

(3) DETERMINATION OF MARITAL STATUS.—The determination of marital status shall be made under section 7703(a).

Subpart B—Foreign Corporations

[Sec. 881]

SEC. 881. TAX ON INCOME OF FOREIGN CORPORATIONS NOT CONNECTED WITH UNITED STATES BUSINESS.

[Sec. 881(a)]

(a) IMPOSITION OF TAX.—Except as provided in subsection (c), there is hereby imposed for each taxable year a tax of 30 percent of the amount received from sources within the United States by a foreign corporation as—

(1) interest (other than original issue discount as defined in section 1273), dividends, rents, salaries, wages, premiums, annuities, compensations, remunerations, emoluments, and other fixed or determinable annual or periodical gains, profits, and income,

(2) gains described in section 631(b) or (c),

(3) in the case of—

(A) a sale or exchange of an original issue discount obligation, the amount of the original issue discount accruing while such obligation was held by the foreign corporation (to the extent such discount was not theretofore taken into account under subparagraph (B)), and

(B) a payment on an original issue discount obligation, an amount equal to the original issue discount accruing while such obligation was held by the foreign corporation (except that such original issue discount shall be taken into account under this subparagraph only to the extent such discount was not theretofore taken into account under this subparagraph and only to the extent that the tax thereon does not exceed the payment less the tax imposed by paragraph (1) thereon), and

(4) gains from the sale or exchange after October 4, 1966, of patents, copyrights, secret processes and formulas, good will, trademarks, trade brands, franchises, and other like property, or of any interest in any such property, to the extent such gains are from payments which are contingent on the productivity, use, or disposition of the property or interest sold or exchanged,

but only to the extent the amount so received is not effectively connected with the conduct of a trade or business within the United States.

[Sec. 881(b)]

(b) EXCEPTION FOR CERTAIN POSSESSIONS.—

(1) GUAM, AMERICAN SAMOA, THE NORTHERN MARIANA ISLANDS, AND THE VIRGIN ISLANDS.—For purposes of this section and section 884, a corporation created or organized in Guam, American Samoa, the Northern Mariana Islands, or the Virgin Islands or under the law of any such possession shall not be treated as a foreign corporation for any taxable year if—

(A) at all times during such taxable year less than 25 percent in value of the stock of such corporation is beneficially owned (directly or indirectly) by foreign persons,

(B) at least 65 percent of the gross income of such corporation is shown to the satisfaction of the Secretary to be effectively connected with the conduct of a trade or business in such a possession or the United States for the 3-year period ending with the close of the taxable year of such corporation (or for such part of such period as the corporation or any predecessor had been in existence), and

(C) no substantial part of the income of such corporation is used (directly or indirectly) to satisfy obligations to persons who are not bona fide residents of such a possession or the United States.

(2) COMMONWEALTH OF PUERTO RICO.—

(A) IN GENERAL.—If dividends are received during a taxable year by a corporation—

(i) created or organized in, or under the law of, the Commonwealth of Puerto Rico, and

(ii) with respect to which the requirements of subparagraphs (A), (B), and (C) of paragraph (1) are met for the taxable year, subsection (a) shall be applied for such taxable year by substituting "10 percent" for "30 percent".

(B) APPLICABILITY.—If, on or after the date of the enactment of this paragraph, an increase in the rate of the Commonwealth of Puerto Rico's withholding tax which is generally applicable to dividends paid to United States corporations not engaged in a trade or business in the Commonwealth to a rate greater than 10 percent takes effect, this paragraph shall not apply to dividends received on or after the effective date of the increase.

(3) DEFINITIONS.—

(A) FOREIGN PERSON.—For purposes of paragraph (1), the term "foreign person" means any person other than—

(i) a United States person, or

(ii) a person who would be a United States person if references to the United States in section 7701 included references to a possession of the United States.

(B) INDIRECT OWNERSHIP RULES.—For purposes of paragraph (1), the rules of section 318(a)(2) shall apply except that "5 percent" shall be substituted for "50 percent" in subparagraph (C) thereof.

[Sec. 881(c)]

(c) REPEAL OF TAX ON INTEREST OF FOREIGN CORPORATIONS RECEIVED FROM CERTAIN PORTFOLIO DEBT INVESTMENTS.—

(1) IN GENERAL.—In the case of any portfolio interest received by a foreign corporation from sources within the United States, no tax shall be imposed under paragraph (1) or (3) of subsection (a).

(2) PORTFOLIO INTEREST.—For purposes of this subsection, the term "portfolio interest" means any interest (including original issue discount) which would be subject to tax under subsection (a) but for this subsection and which is described in any of the following subparagraphs:

(A) CERTAIN OBLIGATIONS WHICH ARE NOT REGISTERED.—Interest which is paid on any obligation which is described in section 871(h)(2)(A).

(B) CERTAIN REGISTERED OBLIGATIONS.—Interest which is paid on an obligation—

(i) which is in registered form, and

(ii) with respect to which the person who would otherwise be required to deduct and withhold tax from such interest under section 1442(a) receives a statement which meets the requirements of section 871(h)(5) that the beneficial owner of the obligation is not a United States person.

(3) PORTFOLIO INTEREST SHALL NOT INCLUDE INTEREST RECEIVED BY CERTAIN PERSONS.—For purposes of this subsection, the term "portfolio interest" shall not include any portfolio interest which—

(A) except in the case of interest paid on an obligation of the United States, is received by a bank on an extension of credit made pursuant to a loan agreement entered into in the ordinary course of its trade or business,

(B) is received by a 10-percent shareholder (within the meaning of section 871(h)(3)(B)), or

(C) is received by a controlled foreign corporation from a related person (within the meaning of section 864(d)(4)).

(4) PORTFOLIO INTEREST NOT TO INCLUDE CERTAIN CONTINGENT INTEREST.—For purposes of this subsection, the term "portfolio interest" shall not include any interest which is treated as not being portfolio interest under the rules of section 871(h)(4).

(5) SPECIAL RULES FOR CONTROLLED FOREIGN CORPORATIONS.—

(A) IN GENERAL.—In the case of any portfolio interest received by a controlled foreign corporation, the following provisions shall not apply:

(i) Subparagraph (A) of section 954(b)(3) (relating to exception where foreign base company income is less than 5 percent or $1,000,000).

(ii) Paragraph (4) of section 954(b) (relating to exception for certain income subject to high foreign taxes).

(iii) Clause (i) of section 954(c)(3)(A) (relating to certain income received from related persons).

(B) CONTROLLED FOREIGN CORPORATION.—For purposes of this subsection, the term "controlled foreign corporation" has the meaning given to such term by section 957(a).

(6) SECRETARY MAY CEASE APPLICATION OF THIS SUBSECTION.—Under rules similar to the rules of section 871(h)(6), the Secretary may provide that this subsection shall not apply to payments of interest described in section 871(h)(6).

(7) REGISTERED FORM.—For purposes of this subsection, the term "registered form" has the meaning give such term by section 163(f).

[Sec. 881(d)]

(d) TAX NOT TO APPLY TO CERTAIN INTEREST AND DIVIDENDS.—No tax shall be imposed under paragraph (1) or (3) of subsection (a) on any amount described in section 871(i)(2).

[Sec. 881(e)]

(e) TAX NOT TO APPLY TO CERTAIN DIVIDENDS OF REGULATED INVESTMENT COMPANIES.—

(1) INTEREST-RELATED DIVIDENDS.—

(A) IN GENERAL.—Except as provided in subparagraph (B), no tax shall be imposed under paragraph (1) of subsection (a) on any interest-related dividend (as defined in section 871(k)(1)) received from a regulated investment company.

(B) EXCEPTION.—Subparagraph (A) shall not apply—

(i) to any dividend referred to in section 871(k)(1)(B), and

(ii) to any interest-related dividend received by a controlled foreign corporation (within the meaning of section 957(a)) to the extent such dividend is attributable to interest received by the regulated investment company from a person who is a related person (within the meaning of section 864(d)(4)) with respect to such controlled foreign corporation.

(C) TREATMENT OF DIVIDENDS RECEIVED BY CONTROLLED FOREIGN CORPORATIONS.—The rules of subsection (c)(5)(A) shall apply to any [dividend received by a controlled foreign corporation] (within the meaning of section 957(a)) to the extent such dividend is attributable to interest received by the regulated investment company which is described in clause (ii) of section 871(k)(1)(E) (and not described in clause (i) or (iii) of such section).

(2) SHORT-TERM CAPITAL GAIN DIVIDENDS.—No tax shall be imposed under paragraph (1) of subsection (a) on any short-term capital gain dividend (as defined in section 871(k)(2)) received from a regulated investment company.

[Sec. 881(f)]

(f) CROSS REFERENCE.—

For doubling of tax on corporations of certain foreign countries, see section 891.

For special rules for original issue discount, see section 871(g).

Sec. 881(c)(5)(A)(i)

[Sec. 882]

SEC. 882. TAX ON INCOME OF FOREIGN CORPORATIONS CONNECTED WITH UNITED STATES BUSINESS.

[Sec. 882(a)]

(a) IMPOSITION OF TAX.—

(1) IN GENERAL.—A foreign corporation engaged in trade or business within the United States during the taxable year shall be taxable as provided in section 11, 55, 59A, or 1201(a) on its taxable income which is effectively connected with the conduct of a trade or business within the United States.

(2) DETERMINATION OF TAXABLE INCOME.—In determining taxable income for purposes of paragraph (1), gross income includes only gross income which is effectively connected with the conduct of a trade or business within the United States.

(3) For special tax treatment of gain or loss from the disposition by a foreign corporation of a United States real property interest, see section 897.

[Sec. 882(b)]

(b) GROSS INCOME.—In the case of a foreign corporation, except where the context clearly indicates otherwise, gros income includes only—

(1) gross income which is derived from sources within the United States and which is not effectively connected with the conduct of a trade or business within the United States, and

(2) gross income which is effectively connected with the conduct of a trade or business within the United States.

[Sec. 882(c)]

(c) ALLOWANCE OF DEDUCTIONS AND CREDITS.—

(1) ALLOCATION OF DEDUCTIONS.—

(A) GENERAL RULE.—In the case of a foreign corporation, the deductions shall be allowed only for purposes of subsection (a) and (except as provided by subparagraph (B)) only if and to the extent that they are connected with income which is effectively connected with the conduct of a trade or business within the United States; and the proper apportionment and allocation of the deductions for this purpose shall be determined as provided in regulations prescribed by the Secretary.

(B) CHARITABLE CONTRIBUTIONS.—The deduction for charitable contributions and gifts provided by section 170 shall be allowed whether or not connected with income which is effectively connected with the conduct of a trade or business within the United States.

(2) DEDUCTIONS AND CREDITS ALLOWED ONLY IF RETURN FILED.—A foreign corporation shall receive the benefit of the deductions and credits allowed to it in this subtitle only by filing or causing to be filed with the Secretary a true and accurate return, in the manner prescribed in subtitle F, including therein all the information which the Secretary may deem necessary for the calculation of such deductions and credits. The preceding sentence shall not apply for purposes of the tax imposed by section 541 (relating to personal holding company tax), and shall not be construed to deny the credit provided by section 33 for tax withheld at source or the credit provided by section 34 for certain uses of gasoline.

(3) FOREIGN TAX CREDIT.—Except as provided by section 906, foreign corporations shall not be allowed the credit against the tax for taxes of foreign countries and possessions of the United States allowed by section 901.

(4) CROSS REFERENCE.—

For rule that certain foreign taxes are not to be taken into account in determining deduction or credit, see section 906(b)(1).

[Sec. 882(d)]

(d) ELECTION TO TREAT REAL PROPERTY INCOME AS INCOME CONNECTED WITH UNITED STATES BUSINESS.—

(1) IN GENERAL.—A foreign corporation which during the taxable year derives any income—

(A) from real property located in the United States, or from any interest in such real property, including (i) gains from the sale or exchange of real property or an interest therein, (ii) rents or royalties from mines, wells, or other natural deposits, and (iii) gains described in section 631(b) or (c), and

(B) which, but for this subsection, would not be treated as income effectively connected with the conduct of a trade or business within the United States,

may elect for such taxable year to treat all such income as income which is effectively connected with the conduct of a trade or business within the United States. In such case, such income shall be taxable as provided in subsection (a)(1) whether or not such corporation is engaged in trade or business within the United States during the taxable year. An election under this paragraph for any taxable year shall remain in effect for all subsequent taxable years, except that it may be revoked with the consent of the Secretary with respect to any taxable year.

(2) ELECTION AFTER REVOCATION, ETC.—Paragraphs (2) and (3) of section 871(d) shall apply in respect of elections under this subsection in the same manner and to the same extent as they apply in respect of elections under section 871(d).

[Sec. 882(e)]

(e) INTEREST ON UNITED STATES OBLIGATIONS RECEIVED BY BANKS ORGANIZED IN POSSESSIONS.—In the case of a corporation created or organized in, or under the law of, a possession of the United States which is carrying on the banking business in a possession of the United States, interest on obligations of the United States which is not portfolio interest (as defined in section 881(c)(2)) shall—

(1) for purposes of this subpart, be treated as income which is effectively connected with the conduct of a trade or business within the United States, and

(2) shall be taxable as provided in subsection (a)(1) whether or not such corporation is engaged in trade or business within the United States during the taxable year.

[Sec. 882(f)]

(f) RETURNS OF TAX BY AGENT.—If any foreign corporation has no office or place of business in the United States but has an agent in the United States, the return required under section 6012 shall be made by the agent.

[Sec. 883]

SEC. 883. EXCLUSIONS FROM GROSS INCOME.

[Sec. 883(a)]

(a) INCOME OF FOREIGN CORPORATIONS FROM SHIPS AND AIRCRAFT.—The following items shall not be included in gross income of a foreign corporation, and shall be exempt from taxation under this subtitle:

(1) SHIPS OPERATED BY CERTAIN FOREIGN CORPORATIONS.—Gross income derived by a corporation organized in a foreign country from the international operation of a ship or ships if such foreign country grants an equivalent exemption to corporations organized in the United States.

(2) AIRCRAFT OPERATED BY CERTAIN FOREIGN CORPORATIONS.—Gross income derived by a corporation organized in a foreign country from the international operation of aircraft if such foreign country grants an equivalent exemption to corporations organized in the United States.

(3) RAILROAD ROLLING STOCK OF FOREIGN CORPORATIONS.—Earnings derived from payments by a common carrier for the use on a temporary basis (not expected to exceed a total of 90

days in any taxable year) of railroad rolling stock owned by a corporation of a foreign country which grants an equivalent exemption to corporations organized in the United States.

(4) SPECIAL RULES.—The rules of paragraphs (6), (7), and (8) of section 872(b) shall apply for purposes of this subsection.

(5) SPECIAL RULE FOR COUNTRIES WHICH TAX ON RESIDENCE BASIS.—For purposes of this subsection, there shall not be taken into account any failure of a foreign country to grant an exemption to a corporation organized in the United States if such corporation is subject to tax by such foreign country on a residence basis pursuant to provisions of foreign law which meets such standards (if any) as the Secretary may prescribe.

[Sec. 883(b)]

(b) EARNINGS DERIVED FROM COMMUNICATIONS SATELLITE SYSTEM.—The earnings derived from the ownership or operation of a communications satellite system by a foreign entity designated by a foreign government to participate in such ownership or operation shall be exempt from taxation under this subtitle, if the United States, through its designated entity, participates in such system pursuant to the Communications Satellite Act of 1962 (47 U.S.C. 701 and following).

[Sec. 883(c)]

(c) TREATMENT OF CERTAIN FOREIGN CORPORATIONS.—

(1) IN GENERAL.—Paragraphs (1) or (2) of subsection (a) (as the case may be) shall not apply to any foreign corporation if 50 percent or more of the value of the stock of such corporation is owned by individuals who are not residents of such foreign country or another foreign country meeting the requirements of such paragraph.

(2) TREATMENT OF CONTROLLED FOREIGN CORPORATIONS.—Paragraph (1) shall not apply to any foreign corporation which is a controlled foreign corporation (as defined in section 957(a)).

(3) SPECIAL RULES FOR PUBLICLY TRADED CORPORATIONS.—

(A) EXCEPTION.—Paragraph (1) shall not apply to any corporation which is organized in a foreign country meeting the requirements of paragraph (1) or (2) of subsection (a) (as the case may be) and the stock of which is primarily and regularly traded on an established securities market in such foreign country, another foreign country meeting the requirements of such paragraph, or the United States.

(B) TREATMENT OF STOCK OWNED BY PUBLICLY TRADED CORPORATION.—Any stock in another corporation which is owned (directly or indirectly) by a corporation meeting the requirements of subparagraph (A) shall be treated as owned by individuals who are residents of the foreign country in which the corporation meeting the requirements of subparagraph (A) is organized.

(4) STOCK OWNERSHIP THROUGH ENTITIES.—For purposes of paragraph (1), stock owned (directly or indirectly) by or for a corporation, partnership, trust, or estate shall be treated as being owned proportionately by its shareholders, partners, or beneficiaries. Stock considered to be owned by a person by reason of the application of the preceding sentence shall, for purposes of applying such sentence, be treated as actually owned by such person.

[Sec. 884]

SEC. 884. BRANCH PROFITS TAX.

[Sec. 884(a)]

(a) IMPOSITION OF TAX.—In addition to the tax imposed by section 882 for any taxable year, there is hereby imposed on any foreign corporation a tax equal to 30 percent of the dividend equivalent amount for the taxable year.

[Sec. 884(b)]

(b) DIVIDEND EQUIVALENT AMOUNT.—For purposes of subsection (a), the term "dividend equivalent amount" means the foreign corporation's effectively connected earnings and profits for the taxable year adjusted as provided in this subsection:

(1) REDUCTION FOR INCREASE IN U.S. NET EQUITY.—If—

(A) the U.S. net equity of the foreign corporation as of the close of the taxable year, exceeds

(B) the U.S. net equity of the foreign corporation as of the close of the preceding taxable year,

the effectively connected earnings and profits for the taxable year shall be reduced (but not below zero) by the amount of such excess.

(2) INCREASE FOR DECREASE IN NET EQUITY.—

(A) IN GENERAL.—If—

(i) the U.S. net equity of the foreign corporation as of the close of the preceding taxable year, exceeds

(ii) the U.S. net equity of the foreign corporation as of the close of the taxable year,

the effectively connected earnings and profits for the taxable year shall be increased by the amount of such excess.

(B) LIMITATION.—

(i) IN GENERAL.—The increase under subparagraph (A) for any taxable year shall not exceed the accumulated effectively connected earnings and profits as of the close of the preceding taxable year.

(ii) ACCUMULATED EFFECTIVELY CONNECTED EARNINGS AND PROFITS.—For purposes of clause (i), the term "accumulated effectively connected earnings and profits" means the excess of—

(I) the aggregate effectively connected earnings and profits for preceding taxable years beginning after December 31, 1986, over

(II) the aggregate dividend equivalent amounts determined for such preceding taxable years.

[Sec. 884(c)]

(c) U.S. NET EQUITY.—For purposes of this section—

(1) IN GENERAL.—The term "U.S. net equity" means—

(A) U.S. assets, reduced (including below zero) by

(B) U.S. liabilities.

(2) U.S. ASSETS AND U.S. LIABILITIES.—For purposes of paragraph (1)—

(A) U.S. ASSETS.—The term "U.S. assets" means the money and aggregate adjusted bases of property of the foreign corporation treated as connected with the conduct of a trade or business in the United States under regulations prescribed by the Secretary. For purposes of the preceding sentence, the adjusted basis of any property shall be its adjusted basis for purposes of computing earnings and profits.

(B) U.S. LIABILITIES.—The term "U.S. liabilities" means the liabilities of the foreign corporation treated as connected with the conduct of a trade or business in the United States under regulations prescribed by the Secretary.

(C) REGULATIONS TO BE CONSISTENT WITH ALLOCATION OF DEDUCTIONS.—The regulations prescribed under subparagraphs (A) and (B) shall be consistent with the allocation of deductions under section 882(c)(1).

[Sec. 884(d)]

(d) EFFECTIVELY CONNECTED EARNINGS AND PROFITS.—For purposes of this section—

(1) IN GENERAL.—The term "effectively connected earnings and profits" means earnings and profits (without diminution by reason of any distributions made during the taxable year) which are attributable to income which is effectively connected (or treated as effectively connected) with the conduct of a trade or business within the United States.

(2) EXCEPTION FOR CERTAIN INCOME.—The term "effectively connected earnings and profits" shall not include any earnings and profits attributable to—

(A) income not includible in gross income under paragraph (1) or (2) of section 883(a),

(B) income treated as effectively connected with the conduct of a trade or business within the United States under section 921(d) or 926(b),

(C) gain on the disposition of a United States real property interest described in section 897(c)(1)(A)(ii),

(D) income treated as effectively connected with the conduct of a trade or business within the United States under section 953(c)(3)(C), or

(E) income treated as effectively connected with the conduct of a trade or business within the United States under section 882(e).

Property and liabilities of the foreign corporation treated as connected with such income under regulations prescribed by the Secretary shall not be taken into account in determining the U.S. assets or U.S. liabilities of the foreign corporation.

[Sec. 884(e)]

(e) COORDINATION WITH INCOME TAX TREATIES; ETC.—

(1) LIMITATION ON TREATY EXEMPTION.—No treaty between the United States and a foreign country shall exempt any foreign corporation from the tax imposed by subsection (a) (or reduce the amount thereof) unless—

(A) such treaty is an income tax treaty, and

(B) such foreign corporation is a qualified resident of such foreign country.

(2) TREATY MODIFICATIONS.—If a foreign corporation is a qualified resident of a foreign country with which the United States has an income tax treaty—

(A) the rate of tax under subsection (a) shall be the rate of tax specified in such treaty—

(i) on branch profits if so specified, or

(ii) if not so specified, on dividends paid by a domestic corporation to a corporation resident in such country which wholly owns such domestic corporation, and

(B) any other limitations under such treaty on the tax imposed by subsection (a) shall apply.

(3) COORDINATION WITH WITHHOLDING TAX.—

(A) IN GENERAL.—If a foreign corporation is subject to the tax imposed by subsection (a) for any taxable year (determined after the application of any treaty), no tax shall be imposed by section 871(a), 881(a), 1441, or 1442 on any dividends paid by such corporation out of its earnings and profits for such taxable year.

(B) LIMITATION ON CERTAIN TREATY BENEFITS.—If—

(i) any dividend described in section 861(a)(2)(B) is received by a foreign corporation, and

(ii) subparagraph (A) does not apply to such dividend,

rules similar to the rules of subparagraphs (A) and (B) of subsection (f)(3) shall apply to such dividend.

(4) QUALIFIED RESIDENT.—For purposes of this subsection—

(A) IN GENERAL.—Except as otherwise provided in this paragraph, the term "qualified resident" means, with respect to any foreign country, any foreign corporation which is a resident of such foreign country unless—

(i) 50 percent or more (by value) of the stock of such foreign corporation is owned (within the meaning of section 883(c)(4)) by individuals who are not residents of such foreign country and who are not United States citizens or resident aliens, or

(ii) 50 percent or more of its income is used (directly or indirectly) to meet liabilities to persons who are not residents of such foreign country or citizens or residents of the United States.

(B) SPECIAL RULE FOR PUBLICLY TRADED CORPORATIONS.—A foreign corporation which is a resident of a foreign country shall be treated as a qualified resident of such foreign country if—

(i) the stock of such corporation is primarily and regularly traded on an established securities market in such foreign country, or

(ii) such corporation is wholly owned (either directly or indirectly) by another foreign corporation which is organized in such foreign country and the stock of which is so traded.

(C) CORPORATIONS OWNED BY PUBLICLY TRADED DOMESTIC CORPORATIONS.—A foreign corporation which is a resident of a foreign country shall be treated as a qualified resident of such foreign country if—

(i) such corporation is wholly owned (directly or indirectly) by a domestic corporation, and

(ii) the stock of such domestic corporation is primarily and regularly traded on an established securities market in the United States.

(D) SECRETARIAL AUTHORITY.—The Secretary may, in his sole discretion, treat a foreign corporation as being a qualified resident of a foreign country if such corporation establishes to the satisfaction of the Secretary that such corporation meets such requirements as the Secretary may establish to ensure that individuals who are not residents of such foreign country do not use the treaty between such foreign country and the United States in a manner inconsistent with the purposes of this subsection.

(5) EXCEPTION FOR INTERNATIONAL ORGANIZATIONS.—This section shall not apply to an international organization (as defined in section 7701(a)(18)).

[Sec. 884(f)]

(f) TREATMENT OF INTEREST ALLOCABLE TO EFFECTIVELY CONNECTED INCOME.—

(1) IN GENERAL.—In the case of a foreign corporation engaged in a trade or business in the United States (or having gross income treated as effectively connected with the conduct of a trade or business in the United States), for purposes of this subtitle—

(A) any interest paid by such trade or business in the United States shall be treated as if it were paid by a domestic corporation, and

(B) to the extent that the allocable interest exceeds the interest described in subparagraph (A), such foreign corporation shall be liable for tax under section 881(a) in the same manner as if such excess were interest paid to such foreign corporation by a wholly owned domestic corporation on the last day of such foreign corporation's taxable year.

To the extent provided in regulations, subparagraph (A) shall not apply to interest in excess of the amounts reasonably expected to be allocable interest.

(2) ALLOCABLE INTEREST.—For purposes of this subsection, the term "allocable interest" means any interest which is allocable to income which is effectively connected (or treated as effectively connected) with the conduct of a trade or business in the United States.

(3) COORDINATION WITH TREATIES.—

(A) PAYOR MUST BE QUALIFIED RESIDENT.—In the case of any interest described in paragraph (1) which is paid or accrued by a foreign corporation, no benefit under any treaty between the United States and the foreign country of which such corporation is a resident shall apply unless—

(i) such treaty is an income tax treaty, and

(ii) such foreign corporation is a qualified resident of such foreign country.

(B) RECIPIENT MUST BE QUALIFIED RESIDENT.—In the case of any interest described in paragraph (1) which is received or accrued by any corporation, no benefit under any treaty between the United States and the foreign country of which such corporation is a resident shall apply unless—

> (i) such treaty is an income treaty, and
>
> (ii) such foreign corporation is a qualified resident of such foreign country.

[Sec. 884(g)]

(g) REGULATIONS.—The Secretary shall prescribe such regulations as may be necessary or appropriate to carry out the purposes of this section, including regulations providing for appropriate adjustments in the determination of the dividend equivalent amount in connection with the distribution in such determination as are necessary or appropriate to carry out the purposes of this section.

Subpart C—Tax on Gross Transportation Income

[Sec. 887]

SEC. 887. IMPOSITION OF TAX ON GROSS TRANSPORTATION INCOME OF NONRESIDENT ALIENS AND FOREIGN CORPORATIONS.

[Sec. 887(a)]

(a) IMPOSITION OF TAX.—In the case of any nonresident alien individual or foreign corporation, there is hereby imposed for each taxable year a tax equal to 4 percent of such individual's or corporation's United States source gross transportation income for such taxable year.

[Sec. 887(b)]

(b) UNITED STATES SOURCE GROSS TRANSPORTATION INCOME.—

(1) IN GENERAL.—Except as provided in paragraphs (2) and (3), the term "United States source gross transportation income" means any gross income which is transportation income (as defined in section 863(c)(3)) to the extent such income is treated as from sources in the United States under section 863(c)(2). To the extent provided in regulations, such term does not include any income of a kind to which an exemption under paragraph (1) or (2) of section 883(a) would not apply.

(2) EXCEPTION FOR CERTAIN INCOME EFFECTIVELY CONNECTED WITH BUSINESS IN THE UNITED STATES.—The term "United States source gross transportation income" shall not include any income taxable under section 871(b) or 882.

(3) EXCEPTION FOR CERTAIN INCOME TAXABLE IN POSSESSIONS.—The term "United States source gross transportation income" does not include any income taxable in a possession of the United States under the provisions of this title as made applicable in such possession.

(4) DETERMINATION OF EFFECTIVELY CONNECTED INCOME.—For purposes of this chapter, United States source gross transportation income of any taxpayer shall not be treated as effectively connected with the conduct of a trade or business in the United States unless—

> (A) the taxpayer has a fixed place of business in the United States involved in the earning of United States source gross transportation income, and
>
> (B) substantially all of the United States source gross transportation income (determined without regard to paragraph (2)) of the taxpayer is attributable to regularly scheduled transportation (or, in the case of income from the leasing of a vessel or aircraft, is attributable to a fixed place of business in the United States).

[Sec. 887(c)]

(c) COORDINATION WITH OTHER PROVISIONS.—Any income taxable under this section shall not be taxable under section 871, 881, or 882.

Subpart D—Miscellaneous Provisions

[Sec. 891]

SEC. 891. DOUBLING OF RATES OF TAX ON CITIZENS AND CORPORATIONS OF CERTAIN FOREIGN COUNTRIES.

Whenever the President finds that, under the laws of any foreign country, citizens or corporations of the United States are being subjected to discriminatory or extraterritorial taxes, the President shall so proclaim and the rates of tax imposed by sections 1, 3, 11, 801, 831, 852, 871, and 881 shall, for the taxable year during which such proclamation is made and for each taxable year thereafter, be doubled in the case of each citizen and corporation of such foreign country; but the tax at such doubled rate shall be considered as imposed by such sections as the case may be. In no case shall this section operate to increase the taxes imposed by such sections (computed without regard to this section) to an amount in excess of 80 percent of the taxable income of the taxpayer (computed without regard to the deductions allowable under section 151 and under part VIII of subchapter B). Whenever the President finds that the laws of any foreign country with respect to which the President has made a proclamation under the preceding provisions of this section have been modified so that discriminatory and extraterritorial taxes applicable to citizens and corporations of the United States have been removed, he shall so proclaim, and the provisions of this section providing for doubled rates of tax shall not apply to any citizen or corporation of such foreign country with respect to any taxable year beginning after such proclamation is made.

[Sec. 892]

SEC. 892. INCOME OF FOREIGN GOVERNMENTS AND OF INTERNATIONAL ORGANIZATIONS.

[Sec. 892(a)]

(a) FOREIGN GOVERNMENTS.—

   (1) IN GENERAL.—The income of foreign governments received from—

      (A) investments in the United States in—

         (i) stock, bonds, or other domestic securities owned by such foreign governments, or

         (ii) financial instruments held in the execution of governmental financial or monetary policy, or

      (B) interest on deposits in banks in the United States of moneys belonging to such foreign governments,

shall not be included in gross income and shall be exempt from taxation under this subtitle.

   (2) INCOME RECEIVED DIRECTLY OR INDIRECTLY FROM COMMERCIAL ACTIVITIES.—

      (A) IN GENERAL.—Paragraph (1) shall not apply to any income—

         (i) derived from the conduct of any commercial activity (whether within or outside the United States),

         (ii) received by a controlled commercial entity or received (directly or indirectly) from a controlled commercial entity, or

         (iii) derived from the disposition of any interest in a controlled commercial entity.

      (B) CONTROLLED COMMERCIAL ENTITY.—For purposes of subparagraph (A), the term "controlled commercial entity" means any entity engaged in commercial activities (whether within or outside the United States) if the government—

         (i) holds (directly or indirectly) any interest in such entity which (by value or voting interest) is 50 percent or more of the total of such interests in such entity, or

         (ii) holds (directly or indirectly) any other interest in such entity which provides the foreign government with effective control of such entity.

For purposes of the preceding sentence, a central bank of issue shall be treated as a controlled commercial entity only if engaged in commercial activities within the United States.

(3) TREATMENT AS RESIDENT.—For purposes of this title, a foreign government shall be treated as a corporate resident of its country. A foreign government shall be so treated for purposes of any income tax treaty obligation of the United States if such government grants equivalent treatment to the Government of the United States.

[Sec. 892(b)]

(b) INTERNATIONAL ORGANIZATIONS.—The income of international organizations received from investments in the United States in stocks, bonds, or other domestic securities owned by such international organizations, or from interest on deposits in banks in the United States of moneys belonging to such international organizations, or from any other source within the United States, shall not be included in gross income and shall be exempt from taxation under this subtitle.

[Sec. 892(c)]

(c) REGULATIONS.—The Secretary shall prescribe such regulations as may be necessary or appropriate to carry out the purposes of this section.

[Sec. 893]

SEC. 893. COMPENSATION OF EMPLOYEES OF FOREIGN GOVERNMENTS OR INTERNATIONAL ORGANIZATIONS.

[Sec. 893(a)]

(a) RULE FOR EXCLUSION.—Wages, fees, or salary of any employee of a foreign government or of an international organization (including a consular or other officer, or a nondiplomatic representative), received as compensation for official services to such government or international organization shall not be included in gross income and shall be exempt from taxation under this subtitle if—

(1) such employee is not a citizen of the United States, or is a citizen of the Republic of the Philippines (whether or not a citizen of the United States); and

(2) in the case of an employee of a foreign government, the services are of a character similar to those performed by employees of the Government of the United States in foreign countries; and

(3) in the case of an employee of a foreign government, the foreign government grants an equivalent exemption to employees of the Government of the United States performing similar services in such foreign country.

[Sec. 893(b)]

(b) CERTIFICATE BY SECRETARY OF STATE.—The Secretary of State shall certify to the Secretary of the Treasury the names of the foreign countries which grant an equivalent exemption to the employees of the Government of the United States performing services in such foreign countries, and the character of the services performed by employees of the Government of the United States in foreign countries.

[Sec. 893(c)]

(c) LIMITATION ON EXCLUSION.—Subsection (a) shall not apply to—

(1) any employee of a controlled commercial entity (as defined in section 892(a)(2)(B)), or

(2) any employee of a foreign government whose services are primarily in connection with a commercial activity (whether within or outside the United States) of the foreign government.

[Sec. 894]

SEC. 894. INCOME AFFECTED BY TREATY.

[Sec. 894(a)]

(a) TREATY PROVISIONS.—

(1) IN GENERAL.—The provisions of this title shall be applied to any taxpayer with due regard to any treaty obligation of the United States which applies to such taxpayer.

(2) CROSS REFERENCE.—

For relationship between treaties and this title, see section 7852(d).

[Sec. 894(b)]

(b) PERMANENT ESTABLISHMENT IN UNITED STATES.—For purposes of applying any exemption from, or reduction of, any tax provided by any treaty to which the United States is a party with respect to income which is not effectively connected with the conduct of a trade or business within the United States, a nonresident alien individual or a foreign corporation shall be deemed not to have a permanent establishment in the United States at any time during the taxable year. This subsection shall not apply in respect of the tax computed under section 877(b).

[Sec. 894(c)]

(c) DENIAL OF TREATY BENEFITS FOR CERTAIN PAYMENTS THROUGH HYBRID ENTITIES.—

(1) APPLICATION TO CERTAIN PAYMENTS.—A foreign person shall not be entitled under any income tax treaty of the United States with a foreign country to any reduced rate of any withholding tax imposed by this title on an item of income derived through an entity which is treated as a partnership (or is otherwise treated as fiscally transparent) for purposes of this title if—

(A) such item is not treated for purposes of the taxation laws of such foreign country as an item of income of such person,

(B) the treaty does not contain a provision addressing the applicability of the treaty in the case of an item of income derived through a partnership, and

(C) the foreign country does not impose tax on a distribution of such item of income from such entity to such person.

(2) REGULATIONS.—The Secretary shall prescribe such regulations as may be necessary or appropriate to determine the extent to which a taxpayer to which paragraph (1) does not apply shall not be entitled to benefits under any income tax treaty of the United States with respect to any payment received by, or income attributable to any activities of, an entity organized in any jurisdiction (including the United States) that is treated as a partnership or is otherwise treated as fiscally transparent for purposes of this title (including a common investment trust under section 584, a grantor trust, or an entity that is disregarded for purposes of this title) and is treated as fiscally nontransparent for purposes of the tax laws of the jurisdiction of residence of the taxpayer.

[Sec. 895]

SEC. 895. INCOME DERIVED BY A FOREIGN CENTRAL BANK OF ISSUE FROM OBLIGATIONS OF THE UNITED STATES OR FROM BANK DEPOSITS.

Income derived by a foreign central bank of issue from obligations of the United States or of any agency or instrumentality thereof (including beneficial interests, participations, and other instruments issued under section 302(c) of the Federal National Mortgage Association Charter Act (12 U. S. C. 1717)) which are owned by such foreign central bank of issue, or derived from interest on deposits with persons carrying on the banking business, shall not be included in gross income and shall be exempt from taxation under this subtitle unless such obligations or deposits are held for, or used in connection with, the conduct of commercial banking functions or other commercial activities. For purposes of the preceding sentence the Bank for International Settlements shall be treated as a foreign central bank of issue.

[Sec. 896]

SEC. 896. ADJUSTMENT OF TAX ON NATIONALS, RESIDENTS, AND CORPORATIONS OF CERTAIN FOREIGN COUNTRIES.

[Sec. 896(a)]

(a) IMPOSITION OF MORE BURDENSOME TAXES BY FOREIGN COUNTRY.—Whenever the President finds that—

(1) under the laws of any foreign country, considering the tax system of such foreign country, citizens of the United States not residents of such foreign country or domestic corporations are being subjected to more burdensome taxes, on any item of income received by such citizens or corporations from sources within such foreign country, than taxes

imposed by the provisions of this subtitle on similar income derived from sources within the United States by residents or corporations of such foreign country,

(2) such foreign country, when requested by the United States to do so, has not acted to revise or reduce such taxes so that they are no more burdensome than taxes imposed by the provisions of this subtitle on similar income derived from sources within the United States by residents or corporations of such foreign country, and

(3) it is in the public interest to apply pre-1967 tax provisions in accordance with the provisions of this subsection to residents or corporations of such foreign country,

the President shall proclaim that the tax on such similar income derived from sources within the United States by residents or corporations of such foreign country shall, for taxable years beginning after such proclamation, be determined under this subtitle without regard to amendments made to this subchapter and chapter 3 on or after the date of enactment of this section.

[Sec. 896(b)]

(b) IMPOSITION OF DISCRIMINATORY TAXES BY FOREIGN COUNTRY.—Whenever the President finds that—

(1) under the laws of any foreign country, citizens of the United States or domestic corporations (or any class of such citizens or corporations) are, with respect to any item of income, being subjected to a higher effective rate of tax than are nationals, residents, or corporations of such foreign country (or a similar class of such nationals, residents, or corporations) under similar circumstances;

(2) such foreign country, when requested by the United States to do so, has not acted to eliminate such higher effective rate of tax; and

(3) it is in the public interest to adjust, in accordance with the provisions of this subsection, the effective rate of tax imposed by this subtitle on similar income of nationals, residents, or corporations of such foreign country (or such similar class of such nationals, residents, or corporations),

the President shall proclaim that the tax on similar income of nationals, residents, or corporations of such foreign country (or such similar class of such nationals, residents, or corporations) shall, for taxable years beginning after such proclamation, be adjusted so as to cause the effective rate of tax imposed by this subtitle on such similar income to be substantially equal to the effective rate of tax imposed by such foreign country on such item of income of citizens of the United States or domestic corporations (or such class of citizens or corporations). In implementing a proclamation made under this subsection, the effective rate of tax imposed by this subtitle on an item of income may be adjusted by the disallowance, in whole or in part, of any deduction, credit, or exemption which would otherwise be allowed with respect to that item of income or by increasing the rate of tax otherwise applicable to that item of income.

[Sec. 896(c)]

(c) ALLEVIATION OF MORE BURDENSOME OR DISCRIMINATORY TAXES.—Whenever the President finds that—

(1) the laws of any foreign country with respect to which the President has made a proclamation under subsection (a) have been modified so that citizens of the United States not residents of such foreign country or domestic corporations are no longer subject to more burdensome taxes on the item of income derived by such citizens or corporations from sources within such foreign country, or

(2) the laws of any foreign country with respect to which the President has made a proclamation under subsection (b) have been modified so that citizens of the United States or domestic corporations (or any class of such citizens or corporations) are no longer subject to a higher effective rate of tax on the item of income,

he shall proclaim that the tax imposed by this subtitle on the similar income of nationals, residents, or corporations of such foreign country shall, for any taxable year beginning after such proclamation, be determined under this subtitle without regard to such subsection.

[Sec. 896(d)]

(d) NOTIFICATION OF CONGRESS REQUIRED.—No proclamation shall be issued by the President pursuant to this section unless, at least 30 days prior to such proclamation, he has notified the Senate and the House of Representatives of his intention to issue such proclamation.

[Sec. 896(e)]

(e) IMPLEMENTATION BY REGULATIONS.—The Secretary shall prescribe such regulations as he deems necessary or appropriate to implement this section.

[Sec. 897]

SEC. 897. DISPOSITION OF INVESTMENT IN UNITED STATES REAL PROPERTY.

[Sec. 897(a)]

(a) GENERAL RULE.—

(1) TREATMENT AS EFFECTIVELY CONNECTED WITH UNITED STATES TRADE OR BUSINESS.—For purposes of this title, gain or loss of a nonresident alien individual or a foreign corporation from the disposition of a United States real property interest shall be taken into account—

(A) in the case of a nonresident alien individual, under section 871(b)(1), or

(B) in the case of a foreign corporation, under section 882(a)(1),

as if the taxpayer were engaged in a trade or business within the United States during the taxable year and as if such gain or loss were effectively connected with such trade or business.

(2) MINIMUM TAX ON NONRESIDENT ALIEN INDIVIDUALS.—

(A) IN GENERAL.—In the case of any nonresident alien individual, the taxable excess for purposes of section 55(b)(1)(A) shall not be less than the lesser of—

(i) the individual's alternative minimum taxable income (as defined in section 55(b)(2)) for the taxable year, or

(ii) the individual's net United States real property gain for the taxable year.

(B) NET UNITED STATES REAL PROPERTY GAIN.—For purposes of subparagraph (A), the term "net United States real property gain" means the excess of—

(i) the aggregate of the gains for the taxable year from dispositions of United States real property interests, over

(ii) the aggregate of the losses for the taxable year from dispositions of such interests.

[Sec. 897(b)]

(b) LIMITATION ON LOSSES OF INDIVIDUALS.—In the case of an individual, a loss shall be taken into account under subsection (a) only to the extent such loss would be taken into account under section 165(c) (determined without regard to subsection (a) of this section).

[Sec. 897(c)]

(c) UNITED STATES REAL PROPERTY INTEREST.—For purposes of this section—

(1) UNITED STATES REAL PROPERTY INTEREST.—

(A) IN GENERAL.—Except as provided in subparagraph (B), the term "United States real property interest" means—

(i) an interest in real property (including an interest in a mine, well, or other natural deposit) located in the United States or the Virgin Islands, and

(ii) any interest (other than an interest solely as a creditor) in any domestic corporation unless the taxpayer establishes (at such time and in such manner as the Secretary by regulations prescribes) that such corporation was at no time a United States real property holding corporation during the shorter of—

(I) the period after June 18, 1980, during which the taxpayer held such interest, or

(II) the 5-year period ending on the date of the disposition of such interest.

(B) EXCLUSION FOR INTEREST IN CERTAIN CORPORATIONS.—The term "United States real property interest" does not include any interest in a corporation if—

(i) as of the date of the disposition of such interest, such corporation did not hold any United States real property interests, and

(ii) all of the United States real property interests held by such corporation at any time during the shorter of the periods described in subparagraph (A)(ii)—

(I) were disposed of in transactions in which the full amount of the gain (if any) was recognized, or

(II) ceased to be United States real property interests by reason of the application of this subparagraph to 1 or more other corporations.

(2) UNITED STATES REAL PROPERTY HOLDING CORPORATION.—The term "United States real property holding corporation" means any corporation if—

(A) the fair market value of its United States real property interests equals or exceeds 50 percent of

(B) the fair market value of—

(i) its United States real property interests,

(ii) its interests in real property located outside the United States, plus

(iii) any other of its assets which are used or held for use in a trade or business.

(3) EXCEPTION FOR STOCK REGULARLY TRADED ON ESTABLISHED SECURITIES MARKETS.—If any class of stock of a corporation is regularly traded on an established securities market, stock of such class shall be treated as a United States real property interest only in the case of a person who, at some time during the shorter of the periods described in paragraph (1)(A)(ii), held more than 5 percent of such class of stock.

(4) INTERESTS HELD BY FOREIGN CORPORATIONS AND BY PARTNERSHIPS, TRUSTS, AND ESTATES.— For purpose of determining whether any corporation is a United States real property holding corporation—

(A) FOREIGN CORPORATIONS.—Paragraph (1)(A)(ii) shall be applied by substituting "any corporation (whether foreign or domestic)" for "any domestic corporation".

(B) ASSETS HELD BY PARTNERSHIPS, ETC.—Under regulations prescribed by the Secretary, assets held by a partnership, trust, or estate shall be treated as held proportionately by its partners or beneficiaries. Any asset treated as held by a partner or beneficiary by reason of this subparagraph which is used or held for use by the partnership, trust, or estate in a trade or business shall be treated as so used or held by the partner or beneficiary. Any asset treated as held by a partner or beneficiary by reason of this subparagraph shall be so treated for purposes of applying this subparagraph successively to partnerships, trusts, or estates which are above the first partnership, trust, or estate in a chain thereof.

(5) TREATMENT OF CONTROLLING INTERESTS.—

(A) IN GENERAL.—Under regulations, for purposes of determining whether any corporation is a United States real property holding corporation, if any corporation (hereinafter in this paragraph referred to as the "first corporation") holds a controlling interest in a second corporation—

(i) the stock which the first corporation holds in the second corporation shall not be taken into account,

(ii) the first corporation shall be treated as holding a portion of each asset of the second corporation equal to the percentage of the fair market value of the stock of the second corporation represented by the stock held by the first corporation, and

(iii) any asset treated as held by the first corporation by reason of clause (ii) which is used or held for use by the second corporation in a trade or business shall be treated as so used or held by the first corporation.

Any asset treated as held by the first corporation by reason of the preceding sentence shall be so treated for purposes of applying the preceding sentence successively to corporations which are above the first corporation in a chain of corporations.

(B) CONTROLLING INTEREST.—For purposes of subparagraph (A), the term "controlling interest" means 50 percent or more of the fair market value of all classes of stock of a corporation.

(6) OTHER SPECIAL RULES.—

(A) INTEREST IN REAL PROPERTY.—The term "interest in real property" includes fee ownership and co-ownership of land or improvements thereon, leaseholds of land or improvements thereon, options to acquire land or improvements thereon, and options to acquire leaseholds of land or improvements thereon.

(B) REAL PROPERTY INCLUDES ASSOCIATED PERSONAL PROPERTY.—The term "real property" includes movable walls, furnishings, and other personal property associated with the use of the real property.

(C) CONSTRUCTIVE OWNERSHIP RULES.—For purposes of determining under paragraph (3) whether any person holds more than 5 percent of any class of stock and of determining under paragraph (5) whether a person holds a controlling interest in any corporation, section 318(a) shall apply (except that paragraphs (2)(C) and (3)(C) of section 318(a) shall be applied by substituting "5 percent" for "50 percent").

[Sec. 897(d)]

(d) TREATMENT OF DISTRIBUTIONS BY FOREIGN CORPORATIONS.—

(1) IN GENERAL.—Except to the extent otherwise provided in regulations, notwithstanding any other provision of this chapter, gain shall be recognized by a foreign corporation on the distribution (including a distribution in liquidation or redemption) of a United States real property interest in an amount equal to the excess of the fair market value of such interest (as of the time of the distribution) over its adjusted basis.

(2) EXCEPTIONS.—Gain shall not be recognized under paragraph (1)—
    (A) if—
        (i) at the time of the receipt of the distributed property, the distributee would be subject to taxation under this chapter on a subsequent disposition of the distributed property, and
        (ii) the basis of the distributed property in the hands of the distributee is no greater than the adjusted basis of such property before the distribution, increased by the amount of gain (if any) recognized by the distributing corporation, or
    (B) if such nonrecognition is provided in regulations prescribed by the Secretary under subsection (e)(2).

[Sec. 897(e)]

(e) COORDINATION WITH NONRECOGNITION PROVISIONS.—

(1) IN GENERAL.—Except to the extent otherwise provided in subsection (d) and paragraph (2) of this subsection, any nonrecognition provision shall apply for purposes of this section to a transaction only in the case of an exchange of a United States real property interest for an interest the sale of which would be subject to taxation under this chapter.

(2) REGULATIONS.—The Secretary shall prescribe regulations (which are necessary or appropriate to prevent the avoidance of Federal income taxes) providing—
    (A) the extent to which nonrecognition provisions shall, and shall not, apply for purposes of this section, and
    (B) the extent to which—
        (i) transfers of property in reorganization, and
        (ii) changes in interests in, or distributions from, a partnership, trust, or estate,
shall be treated as sales of property at fair market value.

(3) NONRECOGNITION PROVISION DEFINED.—For purposes of this subsection, the term "nonrecognition provision" means any provision of this title for not recognizing gain or loss.

[Sec. 897(g)]

(g) SPECIAL RULE FOR SALES OF INTEREST IN PARTNERSHIPS, TRUSTS, AND ESTATES.—Under regulations prescribed by the Secretary, the amount of any money, and the fair market value of any property, received by a nonresident alien individual or foreign corporation in exchange for all or part of its interest in a partnership, trust, or estate shall, to the extent attributable to United States real property interests, be considered as an amount received from the sale or exchange in the United States of such property.

[Sec. 897(h)]

(h) SPECIAL RULES FOR CERTAIN INVESTMENT ENTITIES.—For purposes of this section—

(1) LOOK-THROUGH OF DISTRIBUTIONS.—Any distribution by a qualified investment entity to a nonresident alien individual or a foreign corporation shall, to the extent attributable to gain from sales or exchanges by the qualified investment entity of United States real property interests, be treated as gain recognized by such nonresident alien individual or foreign corporation from the sale or exchange of a United States real property interest. Notwithstanding the preceding sentence, any distribution by a REIT with respect to any class of stock which is regularly traded on an established securities market located in the United States shall not be treated as gain recognized from the sale or exchange of a United States real property interest if the shareholder did not own more than 5 percent of such class of stock at any time during the taxable year.

(2) SALE OF STOCK IN DOMESTICALLY CONTROLLED ENTITY NOT TAXED.—The term "United States real property interest" does not include any interest in a domestically controlled qualified investment entity.

(3) DISTRIBUTIONS BY DOMESTICALLY CONTROLLED QUALIFIED INVESTMENT ENTITIES.—In the case of a domestically controlled qualified investment entity, rules similar to the rules of subsection (d) shall apply to the foreign ownership percentage of any gain.

(4) DEFINITIONS.—

(A) QUALIFIED INVESTMENT ENTITY.—

(i) IN GENERAL.—The term "qualified investment entity" means—

(I) any real estate investment trust, and

(II) any regulated investment company.

(ii) TERMINATION.—Clause (i) (II) shall not apply after December 31, 2007.

(B) DOMESTICALLY CONTROLLED.—The term "domestically controlled qualified investment entity" means any qualified investment entity in which at all times during the testing period less than 50 percent in value of the stock was held directly or indirectly by foreign persons.

(C) FOREIGN OWNERSHIP PERCENTAGE.—The term "foreign ownership percentage" means that percentage of the stock of the qualified investment entity which was held (directly or indirectly) by foreign persons at the time during the testing period during which the direct and indirect ownership of stock by foreign persons was greatest.

(D) TESTING PERIOD.—The term "testing period" means whichever of the following periods is the shortest:

(i) the period beginning on June 19, 1980, and ending on the date of the disposition or of the distribution, as the case may be,

(ii) the 5-year period ending on the date of the disposition or of the distribution, as the case may be, or

(iii) the period during which the qualified investment entity was in existence.

[Sec. 897(i)]

(i) ELECTION BY FOREIGN CORPORATION TO BE TREATED AS DOMESTIC CORPORATION.—

(1) IN GENERAL.—If—

(A) a foreign corporation holds a United States real property interest, and

(B) under any treaty obligation of the United States the foreign corporation is entitled to nondiscriminatory treatment with respect to that interest,

then such foreign corporation may make an election to be treated as a domestic corporation for purposes of this section, section 1445, and section 6039C.

(2) REVOCATION ONLY WITH CONSENT.—Any election under paragraph (1), once made, may be revoked only with the consent of the Secretary.

(3) MAKING OF ELECTION.—An election under paragraph (1) may be made only—

(A) if all of the owners of all classes of interests (other than interests solely as a creditor) in the foreign corporation at the time of the election consent to the making of the election and agree that gain, if any, from the disposition of such interest after June 18, 1980, which would be taken into account under subsection (a) shall be taxable notwithstanding any provision to the contrary in a treaty to which the United States is a party, and

(B) subject to such other conditions as the Secretary may prescribe by regulations with respect to the corporation or its shareholders.

In the case of a class of interest (other than an interest solely as a creditor) which is regularly traded on an established securities market, the consent described in subparagraph (A) need only be made by any person if such person held more than 5 percent of such class of interest at some time during the shorter of the periods described in subsection (c)(1)(A)(ii). The constructive ownership rules of subsection (c)(6)(C) shall apply in determining whether a person held more than 5 percent of a class of interest.

(4) EXCLUSIVE METHOD OF CLAIMING NONDISCRIMINATION.—The election provided by paragraph (1) shall be the exclusive remedy for any person claiming discriminatory treatment with respect to this section, section 1445, and section 6039C.

[Sec. 897(j)]

(j) CERTAIN CONTRIBUTIONS TO CAPITAL.—Except to the extent otherwise provided in regulations, gain shall be recognized by a nonresident alien individual or foreign corporation on the transfer of a United States real property interest to a foreign corporation if the transfer is made as paid in surplus or as a contribution to capital, in the amount of the excess of—

(1) the fair market value of such property transferred, over

(2) the sum of—

(A) the adjusted basis of such property in the hands of the transferor, plus

(B) the amount of gain, if any, recognized to the transferor under any other provision at the time of the transfer.

[Sec. 898]

SEC. 898. TAXABLE YEAR OF CERTAIN FOREIGN CORPORATIONS.

[Sec. 898(a)]

(a) GENERAL RULE.—For purposes of this title, the taxable year of any specified foreign corporation shall be the required year determined under subsection (c).

[Sec. 898(b)]

(b) SPECIFIED FOREIGN CORPORATION.—For purposes of this section—

(1) IN GENERAL.—The term "specified foreign corporation" means any foreign corporation—

(A) which is treated as a controlled foreign corporation for any purpose under subpart F of part III of this subchapter, and

(B) with respect to which the ownership requirements of paragraph (2) are met.

(2) OWNERSHIP REQUIREMENTS.—

(A) IN GENERAL.—The ownership requirements of this paragraph are met with respect to any foreign corporation if a United States shareholder owns, on each testing day, more than 50 percent of—

(i) the total voting power of all classes of stock of such corporation entitled to vote, or

(ii) the total value of all classes of stock of such corporation.

(B) OWNERSHIP.—For purposes of subparagraph (A), the rules of subsections (a) and (b) of section 958 shall apply in determining ownership.

(3) UNITED STATES SHAREHOLDER.—The term "United States shareholder" has the meaning given to such term by section 951(b), except that, in the case of a foreign corporation having related person insurance income (as defined in section 953(c)(2)), the Secretary may treat any person as a United States shareholder for purposes of this section if such person is treated as a United States shareholder under section 953(c)(1).

[Sec. 898(c)]

(c) DETERMINATION OF REQUIRED YEAR.—

(1) IN GENERAL.—The required year is—

(A) the majority U.S. shareholder year, or

(B) if there is no majority U.S. shareholder year, the taxable year prescribed under regulations.

(2) 1-MONTH DEFERRAL ALLOWED.—A specified foreign corporation may elect, in lieu of the taxable year under paragraph (1)(A), a taxable year beginning 1 month earlier than the majority U.S. shareholder year.

(3) MAJORITY U.S. SHAREHOLDER YEAR.—

(A) IN GENERAL.—For purposes of this subsection, the term "majority U.S. shareholder year" means the taxable year (if any) which, on each testing day, constituted the taxable year of—

(i) each United States shareholder described in subsection (b)(2)(A), and

(ii) each United States shareholder not described in clause (i) whose stock was treated as owned under subsection (b)(2)(B) by any shareholder described in such clause.

(B) TESTING DAY.—The testing days shall be—

(i) the first day of the corporation's taxable year (determined without regard to this section), or

(ii) the days during such representative period as the Secretary may prescribe.

PART III—INCOME FROM SOURCES WITHOUT THE UNITED STATES

Subpart A—Foreign Tax Credit

[Sec. 901]

SEC. 901. TAXES OF FOREIGN COUNTRIES AND OF POSSESSIONS OF UNITED STATES.

[Sec. 901(a)]

(a) ALLOWANCE OF CREDIT.—If the taxpayer chooses to have the benefits of this subpart, the tax imposed by this chapter shall, subject to the limitation of section 904, be credited with the amounts provided in the applicable paragraph of subsection (b) plus, in the case of a corporation, the taxes deemed to have been paid under sections 902 and 960. Such choice for any taxable year may be made or changed at any time before the expiration of the period prescribed for making a claim for credit or refund of the tax imposed by this chapter for such taxable year. The credit shall not be allowed against any tax treated as a tax not imposed by this chapter under section 26(b).

[Sec. 901(b)]

(b) AMOUNT ALLOWED.—Subject to the limitation of section 904, the following amounts shall be allowed as the credit under subsection (a):

(1) CITIZENS AND DOMESTIC CORPORATIONS.—In the case of a citizen of the United States and of a domestic corporation, the amount of any income, war profits, and excess profits taxes paid or accrued during the taxable year to any foreign country or to any possession of the United States; and

(2) RESIDENT OF THE UNITED STATES OR PUERTO RICO.—In the case of a resident of the United States and in the case of an individual who is a bona fide resident of Puerto Rico during the entire taxable year, the amount of any such taxes paid or accrued during the taxable year to any possession of the United States; and

(3) ALIEN RESIDENT OF THE UNITED STATES OR PUERTO RICO.—In the case of an alien resident of the United States and in the case of an alien individual who is a bona fide resident of Puerto Rico during the entire taxable year, the amount of any such taxes paid or accrued during the taxable year to any foreign country; and

(4) NONRESIDENT ALIEN INDIVIDUALS AND FOREIGN CORPORATIONS.—In the case of any nonresident alien individual not described in section 876 and in the case of any foreign corporation, the amount determined pursuant to section 906; and

(5) PARTNERSHIPS AND ESTATES.—In the case of any person described in paragraph (1), (2), (3), or (4), who is a member of a partnership or a beneficiary of an estate or trust, the amount of his proportionate share of the taxes (described in such paragraph) of the partnership or the estate or trust paid or accrued during the taxable year to a foreign country or to any possession of the United States, as the case may be. Under rules or regulations prescribed by the Secretary, in the case of any foreign trust of which the settlor or another person would be treated as owner of any portion of the trust under subpart E but for section 672(f), [the term "taxes imposed on the trust" includes] the allocable amount of any income, war profits, and excess profits taxes imposed by any foreign country or possession of the United States on the settlor or such other person in respect of trust income.

[Sec. 901(c)]

(c) SIMILAR CREDIT REQUIRED FOR CERTAIN ALIEN RESIDENTS.—Whenever the President finds that—

(1) a foreign country, in imposing income, war profits, and excess profits taxes, does not allow to citizens of the United States residing in such foreign country a credit for any such taxes paid or accrued to the United States or any foreign country, as the case may be, similar to the credit allowed under subsection (b)(3),

(2) such foreign country, when requested by the United States to do so, has not acted to provide such a similar credit to citizens of the United States residing in such foreign country, and

(3) it is in the public interest to allow the credit under subsection (b)(3) to citizens or subjects of such foreign country only if it allows such a similar credit to citizens of the United States residing in such foreign country,

the President shall proclaim that, for taxable years beginning while the proclamation remains in effect, the credit under subsection (b)(3) shall be allowed to citizens or subjects of such foreign country only if such foreign country, in imposing income, war profits, and excess profits taxes, allows to citizens of the United States residing in such foreign country such a similar credit.

[Sec. 901(d)]

(d) TREATMENT OF DIVIDENDS FROM A DISC OR FORMER DISC.—For purposes of this subpart, dividends from a DISC or former DISC (as defined in section 992(a)) shall be treated as dividends from a foreign corporation to the extent such dividends are treated under part I as income from sources without the United States.

[Sec. 901(e)]

(e) FOREIGN TAXES ON MINERAL INCOME.—

(1) REDUCTION IN AMOUNT ALLOWED.—Notwithstanding subsection (b), the amount of any income, war profits, and excess profits taxes paid or accrued during the taxable year to any foreign country or possession of the United States with respect to foreign mineral income from sources within such country or possession which would (but for this paragraph) be allowed under such subsection shall be reduced by the amount (if any) by which—

(A) the amount of such taxes (or, if smaller, the amount of the tax which would be computed under this chapter with respect to such income determined without the deduction allowed under section 613), exceeds

(B) the amount of the tax computed under this chapter with respect to such income.

(2) FOREIGN MINERAL INCOME DEFINED.—For purposes of paragraph (1), the term "foreign mineral income" means income derived from the extraction of minerals from mines, wells, or other natural deposits, the processing of such minerals into their primary products, and the transportation, distribution, or sale of such minerals or primary products. Such term includes, but is not limited to—

(A) dividends received from a foreign corporation in respect of which taxes are deemed paid by the taxpayer under section 902, to the extent such dividends are attributable to foreign mineral income, and

(B) that portion of the taxpayer's distributive share of the income of partnerships attributable to foreign mineral income.

[Sec. 901(f)]

(f) CERTAIN PAYMENTS FOR OIL OR GAS NOT CONSIDERED AS TAXES.—Notwithstanding subsection (b) and sections 902 and 960, the amount of any income, or profits, and excess profits taxes paid or accrued during the taxable year to any foreign country in connection with the purchase and sale of oil or gas extracted in such country is not to be considered as tax for purposes of section 275(a) and this section if—

(1) the taxpayer has no economic interest in the oil or gas to which section 611(a) applies, and

(2) either such purchase or sale is at a price which differs from the fair market value for such oil or gas at the time of such purchase or sale.

[Sec. 901(g)]

(g) CERTAIN TAXES PAID WITH RESPECT TO DISTRIBUTIONS FROM POSSESSIONS CORPORATIONS.—

(1) IN GENERAL.—For purposes of this chapter, any tax of a foreign country or possession of the United States which is paid or accrued with respect to any distribution from a corporation—

(A) to the extent that such distribution is attributable to periods during which such corporation is a possessions corporation, and

(B)(i) if a dividends received deduction is allowable with respect to such distribution under part VIII of subchapter B, or

(ii) to the extent that such distribution is received in connection with a liquidation or other transaction with respect to which gain or loss is not recognized,

shall not be treated as income, war profits, or excess profits taxes paid or accrued to a foreign country or possession of the United States, and no deduction shall be allowed under this title with respect to any amount so paid or accrued.

(2) POSSESSIONS CORPORATION.—For purposes of paragraph (1), a corporation shall be treated as a possessions corporation for any period during which an election under section 936 applied to such corporation, during which section 931 (as in effect on the day before the date of the enactment of the Tax Reform Act of 1976) applied to such corporation, or during which section 957(c) (as in effect on the day before the date of the enactment of the Tax Reform Act of 1986) applied to such corporation.

[Sec. 901(h)]

(h) TAXES PAID WITH RESPECT TO FOREIGN TRADE INCOME.—No credit shall be allowed under this section for any income, war profits, and excess profits taxes paid or accrued with respect to the foreign trade income (within the meaning of section 923(b)) of a FSC, other than section 923(a)(2) non-exempt income (within the meaning of section 927(d)(6)).

[Sec. 901(i)]

(i) TAXES USED TO PROVIDE SUBSIDIES.—Any income, war profits, or excess profits tax shall not be treated as a tax for purposes of this title to the extent—

(1) the amount of such tax is used (directly or indirectly) by the country imposing such tax to provide a subsidy by any means to the taxpayer, a related person (within the meaning of section 482), or any party to the transaction or to a related transaction, and

(2) such subsidy is determined (directly or indirectly) by reference to the amount of such tax, or the base used to compute the amount of such tax.

[Sec. 901(j)]

(j) DENIAL OF FOREIGN TAX CREDIT, ETC., WITH RESPECT TO CERTAIN FOREIGN COUNTRIES.—

(1) IN GENERAL.—Notwithstanding any other provision of this part—

(A) no credit shall be allowed under subsection (a) for any income, war profits, or excess profits taxes paid or accrued (or deemed paid under section 902 or 960) to any country if such taxes are with respect to income attributable to a period during which this subsection applies to such country, and

(B) subsections (a), (b), and (c) of section 904 and sections 902 and 960 shall be applied separately with respect to income attributable to such a period from sources within such country.

(2) COUNTRIES TO WHICH SUBSECTION APPLIES.—

(A) IN GENERAL.—This subsection shall apply to any foreign country—

(i) the government of which the United States does not recognize, unless such government is otherwise eligible to purchase defense articles or services under the Arms Export Control Act,

(ii) with respect to which the United States has severed diplomatic relations,

(iii) with respect to which the United States has not severed diplomatic relations but does not conduct such relations, or

(iv) which the Secretary of State has, pursuant to section 6(j) of the Export Administration Act of 1979, as amended, designated as a foreign country which repeatedly provides support for acts of international terrorisms.

(B) PERIOD FOR WHICH SUBSECTION APPLIES.—This subsection shall apply to any foreign country described in subparagraph (A) during the period—

(i) beginning on the later of—

(I) January 1, 1987, or

(II) 6 months after such country becomes a country described in subparagraph (A), and

(ii) ending on the date the Secretary of State certifies to the Secretary of the Treasury that such country is no longer described in subparagraph (A).

(3) TAXES ALLOWED AS A DEDUCTION, ETC.—Sections 275 and 78 shall not apply to any tax which is not allowable as a credit under subsection (a) by reason of this subsection.

(4) REGULATIONS.—The Secretary shall prescribe such regulations as may be necessary or appropriate to carry out the purposes of this subsection, including regulations which treat income paid through 1 or more entities as derived from a foreign country to which this subsection applies if such income was, without regard to such entities, derived from such country.

(5) WAIVER OF DENIAL.—

(A) IN GENERAL.—Paragraph (1) shall not apply with respect to taxes paid or accrued to a country if the President—

(i) determines that a waiver of the application of such paragraph is in the national interest of the United States and will expand trade and investment opportunities for United States companies in such country; and

(ii) reports such waiver under subparagraph (B).

(B) REPORT.—Not less than 30 days before the date on which a waiver is granted under this paragraph, the President shall report to Congress—

(i) the intention to grant such waiver; and

(ii) the reason for the determination under subparagraph (A)(i).

[Sec. 901(k)]

(k) Minimum Holding Period for Certain Taxes on Dividends.—

(1) Withholding taxes.—

(A) In general.—In no event shall a credit be allowed under subsection (a) for any withholding tax on a dividend with respect to stock in a corporation if—

(i) such stock is held by the recipient of the dividend for 15 days or less during the 31-day period beginning on the date which is 15 days before the date on which such share becomes ex-dividend with respect to such dividend, or

(ii) to the extent that the recipient of the dividend is under an obligation (whether pursuant to a short sale or otherwise) to make related payments with respect to positions in substantially similar or related property.

(B) Withholding tax.—For purposes of this paragraph, the term "withholding tax" includes any tax determined on a gross basis; but does not include any tax which is in the nature of a prepayment of a tax imposed on a net basis.

(2) Deemed paid taxes.—In the case of income, war profits, or excess profits taxes deemed paid under section 853, 902, or 960 through a chain of ownership of stock in 1 or more corporations, no credit shall be allowed under subsection (a) for such taxes if—

(A) any stock of any corporation in such chain (the ownership of which is required to obtain credit under subsection (a) for such taxes) is held for less than the period described in paragraph (1)(A)(i), or

(B) the corporation holding the stock is under an obligation referred to in paragraph (1)(A)(ii).

(3) 45-day rule in the case of certain preference dividends.—In the case of stock having preference in dividends and dividends with respect to such stock which are attributable to a period or periods aggregating in excess of 366 days, paragraph (1)(A)(i) shall be applied—

(A) by substituting "45 days" for "15 days" each place it appears, and

(B) by substituting "91-day period" for "31-day period".

(4) Exception for certain taxes paid by securities dealers.—

(A) In general.—Paragraphs (1) and (2) shall not apply to any qualified tax with respect to any security held in the active conduct in a foreign country of a business as a securities dealer of any person—

(i) who is registered as a securities broker or dealer under section 15(a) of the Securities Exchange Act of 1934,

(ii) who is registered as a Government securities broker or dealer under section 15C(a) of such Act, or

(iii) who is licensed or authorized in such foreign country to conduct securities activities in such country and is subject to bona fide regulation by a securities regulating authority of such country.

(B) Qualified tax.—For purposes of subparagraph (A), the term "qualified tax" means a tax paid to a foreign country (other than the foreign country referred to in subparagraph (A)) if—

(i) the dividend to which such tax is attributable is subject to taxation on a net basis by the country referred to in subparagraph (A), and

(ii) such country allows a credit against its net basis tax for the full amount of the tax paid to such other foreign country.

(C) Regulations.—The Secretary may prescribe such regulations as may be appropriate to carry out this paragraph, including regulations to prevent the abuse of the exception provided by this paragraph and to treat other taxes as qualified taxes.

(5) Certain rules to apply.—For purposes of this subsection, the rules of paragraphs (3) and (4) of section 246(c) shall apply.

(6) TREATMENT OF BONA FIDE SALES.—If a person's holding period is reduced by reason of the application of the rules of section 246(c)(4) to any contract for the bona fide sale of stock, the determination of whether such person's holding period meets the requirements of paragraph (2) with respect to taxes deemed paid under section 902 or 960 shall be made as of the date such contract is entered into.

(7) TAXES ALLOWED AS DEDUCTION, ETC.—Sections 275 and 78 shall not apply to any tax which is not allowable as a credit under subsection (a) by reason of this subsection.

[Sec. 901(l)]

(l) MINIMUM HOLDING PERIOD FOR WITHHOLDING TAXES ON GAIN AND INCOME OTHER THAN DIVIDENDS ETC.—

(1) IN GENERAL.—In no event shall a credit be allowed under subsection (a) for any withholding tax (as defined in subsection (k)) on any item of income or gain with respect to any property if—

(A) such property is held by the recipient of the item for 15 days or less during the 31-day period beginning on the date which is 15 days before the date on which the right to receive payment of such item arises, or

(B) to the extent that the recipient of the item is under an obligation (whether pursuant to a short sale or otherwise) to make related payments with respect to positions in substantially similar or related property.

This paragraph shall not apply to any dividend to which subsection (k) applies.

(2) EXCEPTION FOR TAXES PAID BY DEALERS.—

(A) IN GENERAL.—Paragraph (1) shall not apply to any qualified tax with respect to any property held in the active conduct in a foreign country of a business as a dealer in such property.

(B) QUALIFIED TAX.—For purposes of subparagraph (A), the term "qualified tax" means a tax paid to a foreign country (other than the foreign country referred to in subparagraph (A)) if—

(i) the item to which such tax is attributable is subject to taxation on a net basis by the country referred to in subparagraph (A), and

(ii) such country allows a credit against its net basis tax for the full amount of the tax paid to such other foreign country.

(C) DEALER.—For purposes of subparagraph (A), the term "dealer" means—

(i) with respect to a security, any person to whom paragraphs (1) and (2) of subsection (k) would not apply by reason of paragraph (4) thereof if such security were stock, and

(ii) with respect to any other property, any person with respect to whom such property is described in section 1221(a)(1).

(D) REGULATIONS.—The Secretary may prescribe such regulations as may be appropriate to carry out this paragraph, including regulations to prevent the abuse of the exception provided by this paragraph and to treat other taxes as qualified taxes.

(3) EXCEPTIONS.—The Secretary may by regulation provide that paragraph (1) shall not apply to property where the Secretary determines that the application of paragraph (1) to such property is not necessary to carry out the purposes of this subsection.

(4) CERTAIN RULES TO APPLY.—Rules similar to the rules of paragraphs (5), (6), and (7) of subsection (k) shall apply for purposes of this subsection.

(5) DETERMINATION OF HOLDING PERIOD.—Holding periods shall be determined for purposes of this subsection without regard to section 1235 or any similar rule.

[Sec. 901(m)]

(m) CROSS REFERENCE.—

(1) For deductions of income, war profits, and excess profits taxes paid to a foreign country or a possession of the United States, see sections 164 and 275.

Income Tax—Sources Without U.S. **187**

(2) For right of each partner to make election under this section, see section 703(b).

(3) For right of estate or trust to the credit for taxes imposed by foreign countries and possessions of the United States under this section, see section 642(a).

(4) For reduction of credit for failure of a United States person to furnish certain information with respect to a foreign corporation or partnership controlled by him, see section 6038.

[Sec. 902]

SEC. 902. DEEMED PAID CREDIT WHERE DOMESTIC CORPORATION OWNS 10 PERCENT OR MORE OF VOTING STOCK OF FOREIGN CORPORATION.

[Sec. 902(a)]

(a) TAXES PAID BY FOREIGN CORPORATION TREATED AS PAID BY DOMESTIC CORPORATION.—For purposes of this subpart, a domestic corporation which owns 10 percent or more of the voting stock of a foreign corporation from which it receives dividends in any taxable year shall be deemed to have paid the same proportion of such foreign corporation's post-1986 foreign income taxes as—

    (1) the amount of such dividends (determined without regard to section 78), bears to

    (2) such foreign corporation's post-1986 undistributed earnings.

[Sec. 902(b)]

(b) DEEMED TAXES INCREASED IN CASE OF CERTAIN LOWER TIER CORPORATIONS.—

    (1) IN GENERAL.—If—

        (A) any foreign corporation is a member of a qualified group, and

        (B) such foreign corporation owns 10 percent or more of the voting stock of another member of such group from which it receives dividends in any taxable year,

such foreign corporation shall be deemed to have paid the same proportion of such other member's post-1986 foreign income taxes as would be determined under subsection (a) if such foreign corporation were a domestic corporation.

    (2) QUALIFIED GROUP.—For purposes of paragraph (1), the term "qualified group" means—

        (A) the foreign corporation described in subsection (a), and

        (B) any other foreign corporation if—

            (i) the domestic corporation owns at least 5 percent of the voting stock of such other foreign corporation indirectly through a chain of foreign corporations connected through stock ownership of at least 10 percent of their voting stock,

            (ii) the foreign corporation described in subsection (a) is the first tier corporation in such chain, and

            (iii) such other corporation is not below the sixth tier in such chain.

The term "qualified group" shall not include any foreign corporation below the third tier in the chain referred to in clause (i) unless such foreign corporation is a controlled foreign corporation (as defined in section 957) and the domestic corporation is a United States shareholder (as defined in section 951(b)) in such foreign corporation. Paragraph (1) shall apply to those taxes paid by a member of the qualified group below the third tier only with respect to periods during which it was a controlled foreign corporation.

[Sec. 902(c)]

(c) DEFINITIONS AND SPECIAL RULES.—For purposes of this section—

    (1) POST-1986 UNDISTRIBUTED EARNINGS.—The term "post-1986 undistributed earnings" means the amount of the earnings and profits of the foreign corporation (computed in accordance with sections 964(a) and 986) accumulated in taxable years beginning after December 31, 1986—

        (A) as of the close of the taxable year of the foreign corporation in which the dividend is distributed, and

        (B) without diminution by reason of dividends distributed during such taxable year.

(2) POST-1986 FOREIGN INCOME TAXES.—The term "post-1986 foreign income taxes" means the sum of—

(A) the foreign income taxes with respect to the taxable year of the foreign corporation in which the dividend is distributed, and

(B) the foreign income taxes with respect to prior taxable years beginning after December 31, 1986, to the extent such foreign taxes were not attributable to dividends distributed by the foreign corporation in prior taxable years.

(3) SPECIAL RULE WHERE FOREIGN CORPORATION FIRST QUALIFIES AFTER DECEMBER 31, 1986.—

(A) IN GENERAL.—If the 1st day on which the requirements of subparagraph (B) are met with respect to any foreign corporation is in a taxable year of such corporation beginning after December 31, 1986, the post-1986 undistributed earnings and the post-1986 foreign income taxes of such foreign corporation shall be determined by taking into account only periods beginning on and after the 1st day of the 1st taxable year in which such ownership are met.

(B) REQUIREMENTS.—The requirements of this subparagraph are met with respect to any foreign corporation if—

(i) 10 percent of more of the voting stock of such foreign corporation is owned by a domestic corporation, or

(ii) the requirements of subsection (b)(2) are met with respect to such foreign corporation.

(4) FOREIGN INCOME TAXES.—

(A) IN GENERAL.—The term "foreign income taxes" means any income, war profits, or excess profits taxes paid by the foreign corporation to any foreign country or possession of the United States.

(B) TREATMENT OF DEEMED TAXES.—Except for purposes of determining the amount of the post-1986 foreign income taxes of a sixth tier foreign corporation referred to in subsection (b)(2), the term "foreign income taxes" includes any such taxes deemed to be paid by the foreign corporation under this section.

(5) ACCOUNTING PERIODS.—In the case of a foreign corporation the income, war profits, and excess profits taxes of which are determined on the basis of an accounting period of less than 1 year, the word "year" as used in this subsection shall be construed to mean such accounting period.

(6) TREATMENT OF DISTRIBUTIONS FROM EARNINGS BEFORE 1987.—

(A) IN GENERAL.—In the case of any dividend paid by a foreign corporation out of accumulated profits (as defined in this section as in effect on the day before the date of the enactment of the Tax Reform Act of 1986) for taxable years beginning before the 1st taxable year taken into account in determining the post-1986 undistributed earnings of such corporation—

(i) this section (as amended by the Tax Reform Act of 1986) shall not apply, but

(ii) this section (as in effect on the day before the date of the enactment of such Act) shall apply.

(B) DIVIDENDS PAID FIRST OUT OF POST-1986 EARNINGS.—Any dividend in a taxable year beginning after December 31, 1986, shall be treated as made out of post-1986 undistributed earnings to the extent thereof.

(7) CONSTRUCTIVE OWNERSHIP THROUGH PARTNERSHIPS.—Stock owned, directly or indirectly, by or for a partnership shall be considered as being owned proportionately by its partners. Stock considered to be owned by a person by reason of the preceding sentence shall, for purposes of applying such sentence, be treated as actually owned by such person. The Secretary may prescribe such regulations as may be necessary to carry out the purposes of this paragraph, including rules to account for special partnership allocations of dividends, credits, and other incidents of ownership of stock in determining proportionate ownership.

(8) REGULATIONS.—The Secretary shall provide such regulations as may be necessary or appropriate to carry out the provisions of this section and section 960, including provisions

which provide for the separate application of this section and section 960 to reflect the separate application of section 904 to separate types of income and loss.

[Sec. 902(d)]

(d) CROSS REFERENCES.—

(1) For inclusion in gross income of an amount equal to taxes deemed paid under subsection (a), see section 78.

(2) For application of subsections (a) and (b) with respect to taxes deemed paid in a prior taxable year by a United States shareholder with respect to a controlled foreign corporation, see section 960.

(3) For reduction of credit with respect to dividends paid out of post-1986 undistributed earnings for years for which certain information is not furnished, see section 6038.

[Sec. 903]

SEC. 903. CREDIT FOR TAXES IN LIEU OF INCOME, ETC., TAXES.

For purposes of this part and of sections 164(a) and 275(a), the term "income, war profits, and excess profits taxes" shall include a tax paid in lieu of a tax on income, war profits, or excess profits otherwise generally imposed by any foreign country or by any possession of the United States.

[Sec. 904]

SEC. 904. LIMITATION ON CREDIT.

[Sec. 904(a)]

(a) LIMITATION.—The total amount of the credit taken under section 901(a) shall not exceed the same proportion of the tax against which such credit is taken which the taxpayer's taxable income from sources without the United States (but not in excess of the taxpayer's entire taxable income) bears to his entire taxable income for the same taxable year.

[Sec. 904(b)]

(b) TAXABLE INCOME FOR PURPOSE OF COMPUTING LIMITATION.—

(1) PERSONAL EXEMPTIONS.—For purposes of subsection (a), the taxable income in the case of an individual, estate, or trust shall be computed without any deduction for personal exemptions under section 151 or 642(b).

(2) CAPITAL GAINS.—For purposes of this section—

(A) IN GENERAL.—Taxable income from sources outside the United States shall include gain from the sale or exchange of capital assets only to the extent of foreign source capital gain net income.

(B) SPECIAL RULES WHERE CAPITAL GAIN RATE DIFFERENTIAL.—In the case of any taxable year for which there is a capital gain rate differential—

(i) in lieu of applying subparagraph (A), the taxable income from sources outside the United States shall include gain from the sale or exchange of capital assets only in an amount equal to foreign source capital gain net income reduced by the rate differential portion of foreign source net capital gain,

(ii) the entire taxable income shall include gain from the sale or exchange of capital assets only in an amount equal to capital gain net income reduced by the rate differential portion of net capital gain, and

(iii) for purposes of determining taxable income from sources outside the United States, any net capital loss (and any amount which is a short-term capital loss under section 1212(a)) from sources outside the United States to the extent taken into account in determining capital gain net income for the taxable year shall be reduced by an amount equal to the rate differential portion of the excess of the net capital gain from sources within the United States over net capital gain.

(C) COORDINATION WITH CAPITAL GAINS RATES.—The Secretary may by regulations modify the application of this paragraph and paragraph (3) to the extent necessary to properly reflect any capital gain rate differential under section 1(h) or 1201(a) and the computation of net capital gain.

(3) DEFINITIONS.—For purposes of this subsection—

(A) FOREIGN SOURCE CAPITAL GAIN NET INCOME.—The term "foreign source capital gain net income" means the lesser of—

(i) capital gain net income from sources without the United States, or

(ii) capital gain net income.

(B) FOREIGN SOURCE NET CAPITAL GAIN.—The term "foreign source net capital gain" means the lesser of—

(i) net capital gain from sources without the United States, or

(ii) net capital gain.

(C) SECTION 1231 GAINS.—The term "gain from the sale or exchange of capital assets" includes any gain so treated under section 1231.

(D) CAPITAL GAIN RATE DIFFERENTIAL.—There is a capital gain rate differential for any taxable year if—

(i) in the case of a taxpayer other than a corporation, subsection (h) of section 1 applies to such taxable year, or

(ii) in the case of a corporation, any rate of tax imposed by section 11, 511, or 831(a) or (b) (whichever applies) exceeds the alternative rate of tax under section 1201(a) (determined without regard to the last sentence of section 11(b)(1)).

(E) RATE DIFFERENTIAL PORTION.—

(i) IN GENERAL.—The rate differential portion of foreign source net capital gain, net capital gain, or the excess of net capital gain from sources within the United States over net capital gain, as the case may be, is the same proportion of such amount as—

(I) the excess of the highest applicable tax rate over the alternative tax rate, bears to

(II) the highest applicable tax rate.

(ii) HIGHEST APPLICABLE TAX RATE.—For purposes of clause (i), the term "highest applicable tax rate" means—

(I) in the case of a taxpayer other than a corporation, the highest rate of tax set forth in subsection (a), (b), (c), (d), or (e) of section 1 (whichever applies), or

(II) in the case of a corporation, the highest rate of tax specified in section 11(b).

(iii) ALTERNATIVE TAX RATE.—For purposes of clause (i), the term "alternative tax rate" means—

(I) in the case of a taxpayer other than a corporation, the alternative rate of tax determined under section 1(h), or

(II) in the case of a corporation, the alternative rate of tax under section 1201(a).

(4) COORDINATION WITH SECTION 936.—For purposes of subsection (a), in the case of a corporation, the taxable income shall not include any portion thereof taken into account for purposes of the credit (if any) allowed by section 936 (without regard to subsections (a)(4) and (i) thereof).

[Sec. 904(c)]

(c) CARRYBACK AND CARRYOVER OF EXCESS TAX PAID.—Any amount by which all taxes paid or accrued to foreign countries or possessions of the United States for any taxable year for which the taxpayer chooses to have the benefits of this subpart exceed the limitation under subsection (a) shall be deemed taxes paid or accrued to foreign countries or possessions of the United States in the first preceding taxable year, and in any of the first 10 succeeding taxable years, in that order and to the extent not deemed taxes paid or accrued in a prior taxable year, in the amount by which the limitation under subsection (a) for such preceding or succeeding taxable year exceeds the sum of the taxes paid or accrued to foreign countries or possessions of the United States for such preceding or succeeding taxable year and the amount of the taxes for any taxable year earlier than the current taxable year which shall be deemed to have been paid or accrued in such preceding or subsequent taxable year (whether or not the taxpayer chooses to have the benefits of this subpart with respect to such earlier taxable year). Such amount deemed paid or accrued in any year may be availed of only as a tax credit and not as a deduction and only if the taxpayer for such year chooses to have the benefits of this subpart as to taxes paid or accrued for that year to foreign countries or possessions of the United States.

[Sec. 904(d)]

(d) SEPARATE APPLICATION OF SECTION WITH RESPECT TO CERTAIN CATEGORIES OF INCOME.—

⋙→ *Caution: Code Sec. 904(d)(1), below, is effective for tax years beginning on or before December 31, 2006.*

(1) IN GENERAL.—The provisions of subsections (a), (b), and (c) and sections 902, 907, and 960 shall be applied separately with respect to each of the following items of income:

(A) passive income,

(B) high withholding tax interest,

(C) financial services income,

(D) shipping income,

(E) [Repealed.]

(F) dividends from a DISC or former DISC (as defined in section 992(a)) to the extent such dividends are treated as income from sources without the United States,

(G) taxable income attributable to foreign trade income (within the meaning of section 923(b)),

(H) distributions from a FSC (or former FSC) out of earnings and profits attributable to foreign trade income (within the meaning of section 923(b) or interest or carrying charges (as defined in section 927(d)(1)) derived from a transaction which results in foreign trade income (as defined in section 923(b)), and

(I) income other than income described in any of the preceding subparagraphs.

⋙→ *Caution: Code Sec. 904(d)(1), below, is effective for tax years beginning after December 31, 2006.*

(1) IN GENERAL.—The provisions of subsections (a), (b), and (c) and sections 902, 907, and 960 shall be applied separately with respect to—

(A) passive category income, and

(B) general category income.

⋙→ *Caution: Code Sec. 904(d)(2), below, is effective for tax years beginning on or before December 31, 2006.*

(2) DEFINITIONS AND SPECIAL RULES.—For purposes of this subsection—

(A) PASSIVE INCOME.—

(i) IN GENERAL.—Except as otherwise provided in this subparagraph, the term "passive income" means any income received or accrued by any person which is of a kind which would be foreign personal holding company income (as defined in section 954(c)).

(ii) CERTAIN AMOUNTS INCLUDED.—Except as provided in clause (iii), the term "passive income" includes, except as provided in subparagraph (E)(iii) or paragraph (3)(I), any amount includible in gross income under section 1293 (relating to certain passive foreign investment companies).

(iii) EXCEPTIONS.—The term "passive income" shall not include—

(I) any income described in a subparagraph of paragraph (1) other than subparagraph (A),

(II) any export financing interest, and

(III) any high-taxed income.

(iv) CLARIFICATION OF APPLICATION OF SECTION 864(d)(6).—In determining whether any income is of a kind which would be foreign personal holding company income, the rules of section 864(d)(6) shall apply only in the case of income of a controlled foreign corporation.

(B) HIGH WITHHOLDING TAX INTEREST.—

(i) IN GENERAL.—Except as otherwise provided in this subparagraph, the term "high withholding tax interest" means any interest if—

(I) such interest is subject to a withholding tax of a foreign country or possession of the United States (or other tax determined on a gross basis), and

(II) the rate of such tax applicable to such interest is at least 5 percent.

(ii) EXCEPTION FOR EXPORT FINANCING.—The term "high withholding tax interest" shall not include any export financing interest.

(iii) REGULATIONS.—The Secretary may by regulations provide that—

(I) amounts (not otherwise high withholding tax interest) shall be treated as high withholding tax interest where necessary to prevent avoidance of the purposes of this subparagraph, and

(II) a tax shall not be treated as a withholding tax or other tax imposed on a gross basis if such tax is in the nature of a prepayment of a tax imposed on a net basis.

(C) FINANCIAL SERVICES INCOME.—

(i) IN GENERAL.—Except as otherwise provided in this subparagraph, the term "financial services income" means any income which is received or accrued by any person predominantly engaged in the active conduct of a banking, insurance, financing, or similar business, and which is—

(I) described in clause (ii),

(II) passive income (determined without regard to subclauses (I) and (III) of subparagraph (A)(iii)), or

(III) export financing interest which (but for subparagraph (B)(ii)) would be high withholding tax interest.

(ii) GENERAL DESCRIPTION OF FINANCIAL SERVICES INCOME.—Income is described in this clause if such income is—

(I) derived in the active conduct of a banking, financing, or similar business,

(II) derived from the investment by an insurance company of its unearned premiums or reserves ordinary and necessary for the proper conduct of its insurance business, or

(III) of a kind which would be insurance income as defined in section 953(a) determined without regard to those provisions of paragraph (1)(A) of such section which limit insurance income to income from countries other than the country in which the corporation was created or organized.

(iii) EXCEPTIONS.—The term "financial services income" does not include—

(I) any high withholding tax interest, and

(II) any export financing interest not described in clause (i)(III).

(D) SHIPPING INCOME.—The term "shipping income" means any income received or accrued by any person which is of a kind which would be foreign base company shipping income (as defined in section 954(f)). Such term does not include any financial services income.

(E) NONCONTROLLED SECTION 902 CORPORATION.—

(i) IN GENERAL.—The term "noncontrolled section 902 corporation" means any foreign corporation with respect to which the taxpayer meets the stock ownership requirements of section 902(a) (or, for purposes of applying paragraph (3) or (4), the requirements of section 902(b)). A controlled foreign corporation shall not be treated as a noncontrolled section 902 corporation with respect to any distribution out of its earnings and profits for periods during which it was a controlled foreign corporation.

(ii) TREATMENT OF INCLUSIONS UNDER SECTION 1293.—If any foreign corporation is a non-controlled section 902 corporation with respect to the taxpayer, any inclusion under section 1293 with respect to such corporation shall be treated as a dividend from such corporation.

(F) HIGH-TAXED INCOME.—The term "high-taxed income" means any income which (but for this subparagraph) would be passive income if the sum of—

(i) the foreign income taxes paid or accrued by the taxpayer with respect to such income, and

(ii) the foreign income taxes deemed paid by the taxpayer with respect to such income under section 902 or 960,

exceeds the highest rate of tax specified in section 1 or 11 (whichever applies) multiplied by the amount of such income (determined with regard to section 78). For purposes of the preceding sentence, the term "foreign income taxes" means any income, war profits, or excess profits tax imposed by any foreign country or possession of the United States.

(G) EXPORT FINANCING INTEREST.—For purposes of this paragraph, the term "export financing interest" means any interest derived from financing the sale (or other disposition) for use or consumption outside the United States of any property—

(i) which is manufactured, produced, grown, or extracted in the United States by the taxpayer or a related person, and

(ii) not more than 50 percent of the fair market value of which is attributable to products imported into the United States.

For purposes of clause (ii), the fair market value of any property imported into the United States shall be its appraised value, as determined by the Secretary under section 402 of the Tariff Act of 1930 (19 U.S.C. 1401a) in connection with its importation.

(H) RELATED PERSON.—For purposes of this paragraph, the term "related person" has the meaning given such term by section 954(d)(3), except that such section shall be applied by substituting "the person with respect to whom the determination is being made" for "controlled foreign corporation" each place it appears.

(I) TRANSITIONAL RULE.—For purposes of paragraph (1)—

(i) taxes paid or accrued in a taxable year beginning before January 1, 1987, with respect to income which was described in subparagraph (A) of paragraph (1) (as in effect on the day before the date of the enactment of the Tax Reform Act of 1986) shall be treated as taxes paid or accrued with respect to income described in subparagraph (A) of paragraph (1) (as in effect after such date),

(ii) taxes paid or accrued in a taxable year beginning before January 1, 1987, with respect to income which was described in subparagraph (E) of paragraph (1) (as in effect on the day before the date of the enactment of the Tax Reform Act of 1986) shall be treated as taxes paid or accrued with respect to income described in subparagraph (I) of paragraph (1) (as in effect after such date) except that

(I) such taxes shall be treated as paid or accrued with respect to shipping income to the extent the taxpayer establishes to the satisfaction of the Secretary that such taxes were paid or accrued with respect to such income,

(II) in the case of a person described in subparagraph (C)(i), such taxes shall be treated as paid or accrued with respect to financial services income to the extent the taxpayer establishes to the satisfaction of the Secretary that such taxes were paid or accrued with respect to such income, and

(III) such taxes shall be treated as paid or accrued with respect to high withholding tax interest to the extent the taxpayer establishes to the satisfaction of the Secretary that such taxes were paid or accrued with respect to such income, and

(iii) taxes paid or accrued in a taxable year beginning before January 1, 1987, with respect to income described in any other subparagraph of paragraph (1) (as so in effect before such date) shall be treated as taxes paid or accrued with respect to income described in the corresponding subparagraph of paragraph (1) (as so in effect after such date).

>>>→ *Caution: Code Sec. 904(d)(2), below, is effective for tax years beginning after December 31, 2006.*

(2) DEFINITIONS AND SPECIAL RULES.—For purposes of this subsection—

(A) CATEGORIES.—

(i) PASSIVE CATEGORY INCOME.—The term "passive category income" means passive income and specified passive category income.

(ii) GENERAL CATEGORY INCOME.—The term "general category income" means income other than passive category income.

(B) PASSIVE INCOME.—

(i) IN GENERAL.—Except as otherwise provided in this subparagraph, the term "passive income" means any income received or accrued by any person which is of a kind which would be foreign personal holding company income (as defined in section 954(c)).

(ii) CERTAIN AMOUNTS INCLUDED.—Except as provided in clause (iii), the term "passive income" includes, except as provided in subparagraph (E)(iii) or paragraph (3)(I), any amount includible in gross income under section 1293 (relating to certain passive foreign investment companies).

(iii) EXCEPTIONS.—The term "passive income" shall not include—

(I) any export financing interest, and

(II) any high-taxed income.

(iv) CLARIFICATION OF APPLICATION OF SECTION 864(D)(6).—In determining whether any income is of a kind which would be foreign personal holding company income, the rules of section 864(d)(6) shall apply only in the case of income of a controlled foreign corporation.

(v) SPECIFIED PASSIVE CATEGORY INCOME.—The term "specified passive category income" means—

(I) dividends from a DISC or former DISC (as defined in section 992(a)) to the extent such dividends are treated as income from sources without the United States,

(II) taxable income attributable to foreign trade income (within the meaning of section 923(b)), and

(III) distributions from a FSC (or a former FSC) out of earnings and profits attributable to foreign trade income (within the meaning of section 923(b)) or interest or carrying charges (as defined in section 927(d)(1)) derived from a transaction which results in foreign trade income (as defined in section 923(b)).

(C) TREATMENT OF FINANCIAL SERVICES INCOME AND COMPANIES.—

(i) IN GENERAL.—Financial services income shall be treated as general category income in the case of—

(I) a member of a financial services group,

(II) any other person if such person is predominantly engaged in the active conduct of a banking, insurance, financing, or similar business.

(ii) FINANCIAL SERVICES GROUP.—The term "financial services group" means any affiliated group (as defined in section 1504(a) without regard to paragraphs (2) and (3) of section 1504(b)) which is predominantly engaged in the active conduct of a banking, insurance, financing, or similar business. In determining whether such a group is so engaged, there shall be taken into account only the income of members of the group that are—

(I) United States corporations, or

(II) controlled foreign corporations in which such United States corporations own, directly or indirectly, at least 80 percent of the total voting power and value of the stock.

(iii) PASS-THRU ENTITIES.—The Secretary shall by regulation specify for purposes of this subparagraph the treatment of financial services income received or accrued by partnerships and by other pass-thru entities which are not members of a financial services group.

(D) FINANCIAL SERVICES INCOME.—

(i) IN GENERAL.—Except as otherwise provided in this subparagraph, the term "financial services income" means any income which is received or accrued by any person predominantly engaged in the active conduct of a banking, insurance, financing, or similar business, and which is—

(I) described in clause (ii), or

(II) passive income (determined without regard to subparagraph (B)(iii)(II)).

(ii) GENERAL DESCRIPTION OF FINANCIAL SERVICES INCOME.—Income is described in this clause if such income is—

(I) derived in the active conduct of a banking, financing, or similar business,

(II) derived from the investment by an insurance company of its unearned premiums or reserves ordinary and necessary for the proper conduct of its insurance business, or

(III) of a kind which would be insurance income as defined in section 953(a) determined without regard to those provisions of paragraph (1)(A) of such section which limit insurance income to income from countries other than the country in which the corporation was created or organized.

(iii) [Stricken.]

(E) NONCONTROLLED SECTION 902 CORPORATION.—

(i) IN GENERAL.—The term "noncontrolled section 902 corporation" means any foreign corporation with respect to which the taxpayer meets the stock ownership requirements of section 902(a) (or, for purposes of applying paragraph (3) or (4), the requirements of section 902(b)). A controlled foreign corporation shall not be treated as a noncontrolled section 902 corporation with respect to any distribution out of its earnings and profits for periods during which it was a controlled foreign corporation.

(ii) TREATMENT OF INCLUSIONS UNDER SECTION 1293.—If any foreign corporation is a non-controlled section 902 corporation with respect to the taxpayer, any inclusion under section 1293 with respect to such corporation shall be treated as a dividend from such corporation.

(F) HIGH-TAXED INCOME.—The term "high-taxed income" means any income which (but for this subparagraph) would be passive income if the sum of—

(i) the foreign income taxes paid or accrued by the taxpayer with respect to such income, and

(ii) the foreign income taxes deemed paid by the taxpayer with respect to such income under section 902 or 960,

exceeds the highest rate of tax specified in section 1 or 11 (whichever applies) multiplied by the amount of such income (determined with regard to section 78). For purposes of the preceding sentence, the term "foreign income taxes" means any income, war profits, or excess profits tax imposed by any foreign country or possession of the United States.

Sec. 904(d)(2)(F)(ii)

(G) EXPORT FINANCING INTEREST.—For purposes of this paragraph, the term "export financing interest" means any interest derived from financing the sale (or other disposition) for use or consumption outside the United States of any property—

(i) which is manufactured, produced, grown, or extracted in the United States by the taxpayer or a related person, and

(ii) not more than 50 percent of the fair market value of which is attributable to products imported into the United States.

For purposes of clause (ii), the fair market value of any property imported into the United States shall be its appraised value, as determined by the Secretary under section 402 of the Tariff Act of 1930 (19 U.S.C. 1401a) in connection with its importation.

(H) TREATMENT OF INCOME TAX BASE DIFFERENCES.—

(i) IN GENERAL.—In the case of taxable years beginning after December 31, 2006, tax imposed under the law of a foreign country or possession of the United States on an amount which does not constitute income under United States tax principles shall be treated as imposed on income described in paragraph (1)(B).

(ii) SPECIAL RULE FOR YEARS BEFORE 2007.—

(I) IN GENERAL.—In the case of taxes paid or accrued in taxable years beginning after December 31, 2004, and before January 1, 2007, a taxpayer may elect to treat tax imposed under the law of a foreign country or possession of the United States on an amount which does not constitute income under United States tax principles as tax imposed on income described in subparagraph (C) or (I) of paragraph (1).

(II) ELECTION IRREVOCABLE.—Any such election shall apply to the taxable year for which made and all subsequent taxable years described in subclause (I) unless revoked with the consent of the Secretary.

(I) RELATED PERSON.—For purposes of this paragraph, the term "related person" has the meaning given such term by section 954(d)(3), except that such section shall be applied by substituting "the person with respect to whom the determination is being made" for "controlled foreign corporation" each place it appears.

(J) TRANSITIONAL RULE.—For purposes of paragraph (1)—

(i) taxes paid or accrued in a taxable year beginning before January 1, 1987, with respect to income which was described in subparagraph (A) of paragraph (1) (as in effect on the day before the date of the enactment of the Tax Reform Act of 1986) shall be treated as taxes paid or accrued with respect to income described in subparagraph (A) of paragraph (1) (as in effect after such date),

(ii) taxes paid or accrued in a taxable year beginning before January 1, 1987, with respect to income which was described in subparagraph (E) of paragraph (1) (as in effect on the day before the date of the enactment of the Tax Reform Act of 1986) shall be treated as taxes paid or accrued with respect to income described in subparagraph (I) of paragraph (1) (as in effect after such date) except that

(I) such taxes shall be treated as paid or accrued with respect to shipping income to the extent the taxpayer establishes to the satisfaction of the Secretary that such taxes were paid or accrued with respect to such income,

(II) in the case of a person described in subparagraph (C)(i), such taxes shall be treated as paid or accrued with respect to financial services income to the extent the taxpayer establishes to the satisfaction of the Secretary that such taxes were paid or accrued with respect to such income, and

(III) such taxes shall be treated as paid or accrued with respect to high withholding tax interest to the extent the taxpayer establishes to the satisfaction of the Secretary that such taxes were paid or accrued with respect to such income, and

(iii) taxes paid or accrued in a taxable year beginning before January 1, 1987, with respect to income described in any other subparagraph of paragraph (1) (as so in effect before such date) shall be treated as taxes paid or accrued with respect to income described in the corresponding subparagraph of paragraph (1) (as so in effect after such date).

(K) TRANSITIONAL RULES FOR 2007 CHANGES.—For purposes of paragraph (1)—

(i) taxes carried from any taxable year beginning before January 1, 2007, to any taxable year beginning on or after such date, with respect to any item of income, shall be treated as described in the subparagraph of paragraph (1) in which such income would be described were such taxes paid or accrued in a taxable year beginning on or after such date, and

(ii) the Secretary may by regulations provide for the allocation of any carryback of taxes with respect to income from a taxable year beginning on or after January 1, 2007, to a taxable year beginning before such date for purposes of allocating such income among the separate categories in effect for the taxable year to which carried.

⇒ *Caution: Code Sec. 904(d)(3), below, is effective for tax years beginning on or before December 31, 2006.*

(3) LOOK-THRU IN CASE OF CONTROLLED FOREIGN CORPORATIONS.—

(A) IN GENERAL.—Except as otherwise provided in this paragraph, dividends, interest, rents, and royalties received or accrued by the taxpayer from a controlled foreign corporation in which the taxpayer is a United States shareholder shall not be treated as income in a separate category.

(B) SUBPART F INCLUSIONS.—Any amount included in gross income under section 951(a)(1)(A) shall be treated as income in a separate category to the extent the amount so included is attributable to income in such category.

(C) INTEREST, RENTS, AND ROYALTIES.—Any interest, rent, or royalty which is received or accrued from a controlled foreign corporation in which the taxpayer is a United States shareholder shall be treated as income in a separate category to the extent it is properly allocable (under regulations prescribed by the Secretary) to income of the controlled foreign corporation in such category.

(D) DIVIDENDS.—Any dividend paid out of the earnings and profits of any controlled foreign corporation in which the taxpayer is a United States shareholder shall be treated as income in a separate category in proportion to the ratio of—

(i) the portion of the earnings and profits attributable to income in such category, to

(ii) the total amount of earnings and profits.

(E) LOOK-THRU APPLIES ONLY WHERE SUBPART F APPLIES.—If a controlled foreign corporation meets the requirements of section 954(b)(3)(A) (relating to de minimis rule) for any taxable year, for purposes of this paragraph, none of its foreign base company income (as defined in section 954(a) without regard to section 954(b)(5)) and none of its gross insurance income (as defined in section 954(b)(3)(C)) for such taxable year shall be treated as income in a separate category, except that this sentence shall not apply to any income which (without regard to this sentence) would be treated as financial services income. Solely for purposes of applying subparagraph (D), passive income of a controlled foreign corporation shall not be treated as income in a separate category if the requirements of section 954(b)(4) are met with respect to such income.

(F) SEPARATE CATEGORY.—For purposes of this paragraph—

(i) IN GENERAL.—Except as provided in clause (ii), the term "separate category" means any category of income described in subparagraph (A), (B), (C), or (D) of paragraph (1).

(ii) COORDINATION WITH HIGH-TAXED INCOME PROVISIONS.—

(I) In determining whether any income of a controlled foreign corporation is in a separate category, subclause (III) of paragraph (2)(A)(iii) shall not apply.

(II) Any income of the taxpayer which is treated as income in a separate category under this paragraph shall be so treated notwithstanding any provision of paragraph (2); except that the determination of whether any amount is high-taxed income shall be made after the application of this paragraph.

(G) DIVIDEND.—For purposes of this paragraph, the term "dividend" includes any amount included in gross income in section 951(a)(1)(B). Any amount included in gross income under section 78 to the extent attributable to amounts included in gross income in section 951(a)(1)(A) shall not be treated as a dividend but shall be treated as included in gross income under section 951(a)(1)(A).

(H) EXCEPTION FOR CERTAIN HIGH WITHHOLDING TAX INTEREST.—This paragraph shall not apply to any amount which—

(i) without regard to this paragraph, is high withholding tax interest (including any amount treated as high withholding tax interest under paragraph (2)(B)(iii)), and

(ii) would (but for this subparagraph) be treated as financial services income under this paragraph.

The amount to which this paragraph does not apply by reason of the preceding sentence shall not exceed the interest or equivalent income of the controlled foreign corporation taken into account in determining financial services income without regard to this subparagraph.

(I) LOOK-THRU APPLIES TO PASSIVE FOREIGN INVESTMENT COMPANY INCLUSION.—If—

(i) a passive foreign investment company is a controlled foreign corporation, and

(ii) the taxpayer is a United States shareholder in such controlled foreign corporation,

any amount included in gross income under section 1293 shall be treated as income in a separate category to the extent such amount is attributable to income in such category.

⇛ *Caution: Code Sec. 904(d)(3), below, is effective for tax years beginning after December 31, 2006.*

(3) LOOK-THRU IN CASE OF CONTROLLED FOREIGN CORPORATIONS.—

(A) IN GENERAL.—Except as otherwise provided in this paragraph, dividends, interest, rents, and royalties received or accrued by the taxpayer from a controlled foreign corporation in which the taxpayer is a United States shareholder shall not be treated as passive category income.

(B) SUBPART F INCLUSIONS.—Any amount included in gross income under section 951(a)(1)(A) shall be treated as passive category income to the extent the amount so included is attributable to passive category income.

(C) INTEREST, RENTS, AND ROYALTIES.—Any interest, rent, or royalty which is received or accrued from a controlled foreign corporation in which the taxpayer is a United States shareholder shall be treated as passive category income to the extent it is properly allocable (under regulations prescribed by the Secretary) to passive category income of the controlled foreign corporation.

(D) DIVIDENDS.—Any dividend paid out of the earnings and profits of any controlled foreign corporation in which the taxpayer is a United States shareholder shall be treated as passive category income in proportion to the ratio of—

(i) the portion of the earnings and profits attributable to passive category income, to

(ii) the total amount of earnings and profits.

(E) LOOK-THRU APPLIES ONLY WHERE SUBPART F APPLIES.—If a controlled foreign corporation meets the requirements of section 954(b)(3)(A) (relating to de minimis rule) for any taxable year, for purposes of this paragraph, none of its foreign base company income (as defined in section 954(a) without regard to section 954(b)(5)) and none of its gross insurance income (as defined in section 954(b)(3)(C)) for such taxable year shall be treated as passive category income, except that this sentence shall not apply to any income which (without regard to this sentence) would be treated as financial services income. Solely for purposes of applying subparagraph (D), passive income of a controlled foreign corporation shall not be treated as passive category income if the requirements of section 954(b)(4) are met with respect to such income.

(F) COORDINATION WITH HIGH-TAXED INCOME PROVISIONS.—

(i) In determining whether any income of a controlled foreign corporation is passive category income, subclause (II) of paragraph (2)(B)(iii) shall not apply.

(ii) Any income of the taxpayer which is treated as passive category income under this paragraph shall be so treated notwithstanding any provision of paragraph (2); except that the determination of whether any amount is high-taxed income shall be made after the application of this paragraph.

(G) DIVIDEND.—For purposes of this paragraph, the term "dividend" includes any amount included in gross income in section 951(a)(1)(B). Any amount included in gross income under section 78 to the extent attributable to amounts included in gross income in section 951(a)(1)(A) shall not be treated as a dividend but shall be treated as included in gross income under section 951(a)(1)(A).

(H) LOOK-THRU APPLIES TO PASSIVE FOREIGN INVESTMENT COMPANY INCLUSION.—If—

(i) a passive foreign investment company is a controlled foreign corporation, and

(ii) the taxpayer is a United States shareholder in such controlled foreign corporation,

any amount included in gross income under section 1293 shall be treated as income in a separate category to the extent such amount is attributable to income in such category.

⟫→ *Caution: Code Sec. 904(d)(4), below, is effective for tax years beginning after December 31, 2002.*

(4) LOOK-THRU APPLIES TO DIVIDENDS FROM NONCONTROLLED SECTION 902 CORPORATIONS.—

(A) IN GENERAL.—For purposes of this subsection, any dividend from a noncontrolled section 902 corporation with respect to the taxpayer shall be treated as income described in a subparagraph of paragraph (1) in proportion to the ratio of—

(i) the portion of earnings and profits attributable to income described in such subparagraph, to

(ii) the total amount of earnings and profits.

(B) EARNINGS AND PROFITS OF CONTROLLED FOREIGN CORPORATIONS.—In the case of any distribution from a controlled foreign corporation to a United States shareholder, rules similar to the rules of subparagraph (A) shall apply in determining the extent to which earnings and profits of the controlled foreign corporation which are attributable to dividends received from a noncontrolled section 902 corporation may be treated as income in a separate category.

(C) SPECIAL RULES.—For purposes of this paragraph—

(i) EARNINGS AND PROFITS.—

(I) IN GENERAL.—The rules of section 316 shall apply.

(II) REGULATIONS.—The Secretary may prescribe regulations regarding the treatment of distributions out of earnings and profits for periods before the taxpayer's acquisition of the stock to which the distributions relate.

(ii) INADEQUATE SUBSTANTIATION.—If the Secretary determines that the proper subparagraph of paragraph (1) in which a dividend is described has not been substantiated, such dividend shall be treated as income described in paragraph (1)(A).

(iii) COORDINATION WITH HIGH-TAXED INCOME PROVISIONS.—Rules similar to the rules of paragraph (3)(F) shall apply for purposes of this paragraph.

(iv) LOOK-THRU WITH RESPECT TO CARRYOVER OF CREDIT.—Rules similar to subparagraph (A) also shall apply to any carryforward under subsection (c) from a taxable year beginning before January 1, 2003, of tax allocable to a dividend from a noncontrolled section 902 corporation with respect to the taxpayer. The Secretary may by regulations provide for the allocation of any carryback of tax allocable to a dividend from a noncontrolled section 902 corporation from a taxable year beginning on or after January 1, 2003, to a taxable year beginning before such date for purposes of allocating such dividend among the separate categories in effect for the taxable year to which carried.

(5) CONTROLLED FOREIGN CORPORATION; UNITED STATES SHAREHOLDER.—For purposes of this subsection—

(A) CONTROLLED FOREIGN CORPORATION.—The term "controlled foreign corporation" has the meaning given such term by section 957 (taking into account section 953(c)).

(B) UNITED STATES SHAREHOLDER.—The term "United States shareholder" has the meaning given such term by section 951(b) (taking into account section 953(c)).

(6) REGULATIONS.—The Secretary shall prescribe such regulations as may be necessary or appropriate for the purposes of this subsection, including regulations—

(A) for the application of paragraph (3) and subsection (f)(5) in the case of income paid (or loans made) through 1 or more entities or between 2 or more chains of entities,

(B) preventing the manipulation of the character of income the effect of which is to avoid the purposes of this subsection, and

(C) providing that rules similar to the rules of paragraph (3)(C) shall apply to interest, rents, and royalties received or accrued from entities which would be controlled foreign corporations if they were foreign corporations.

[Sec. 904(e)—Repealed]

[Sec. 904(f)]

(f) RECAPTURE OF OVERALL FOREIGN LOSS.—

(1) GENERAL RULE.—For purposes of this subpart and section 936, in the case of any taxpayer who sustains an overall foreign loss for any taxable year, that portion of the taxpayer's taxable income from sources without the United States for each succeeding taxable year which is equal to the lesser of—

(A) the amount of such loss (to the extent not used under this paragraph in prior taxable years), or

(B) 50 percent (or such larger percent as the taxpayer may choose) of the taxpayer's taxable income from sources without the United States for such succeeding taxable year,

shall be treated as income from sources within the United States (and not as income from sources without the United States).

(2) OVERALL FOREIGN LOSS DEFINED.—For purposes of this subsection, the term "overall foreign loss" means the amount by which the gross income for the taxable year from sources without the United States (whether or not the taxpayer chooses the benefits of this subpart for such taxable year) for such year is exceeded by the sum of the deductions properly apportioned or allocated thereto, except that there shall not be taken into account—

(A) any net operating loss deduction allowable for such year under section 172(a), and

(B) any—

(i) foreign expropriation loss for such year, as defined in section 172(h) (as in effect on the day before the date of the enactment of the Revenue Reconciliation Act of 1990), or

(ii) loss for such year which arises from fire, storm, shipwreck, or other casualty, or from theft,

to the extent such loss is not compensated for by insurance or otherwise.

(3) DISPOSITIONS.—

(A) IN GENERAL.—For purposes of this chapter, if property which has been used predominantly without the United States in a trade or business is disposed of during any taxable year—

(i) the taxpayer, notwithstanding any other provision of this chapter (other than paragraph (1)), shall be deemed to have received and recognized taxable income from sources without the United States in the taxable year of the disposition, by reason of such disposition, in an amount equal to the lesser of the excess of the fair market value of such property over the taxpayer's adjusted basis in such property or the remaining amount of the overall foreign losses which were not used under paragraph (1) for such taxable year or any prior taxable year, and

(ii) paragraph (1) shall be applied with respect to such income by substituting "100 percent" for "50 percent".

In determining for purposes of this subparagraph whether the predominant use of any property has been without the United States, there shall be taken into account use during the 3-year period ending on the date of the disposition (or, if shorter, the period during which the property has been used in the trade or business).

(B) DISPOSITION DEFINED AND SPECIAL RULES.—

(i) For purposes of this subsection, the term "disposition" includes a sale, exchange, distribution, or gift of property whether or not gain or loss is recognized on the transfer.

(ii) Any taxable income recognized solely by reason of subparagraph (A) shall have the same characterization it would have had if the taxpayer had sold or exchanged the property.

(iii) The Secretary shall prescribe such regulations as he may deem necessary to provide for adjustments to the basis of property to reflect taxable income recognized solely by reason of subparagraph (A).

(C) EXCEPTIONS.—Notwithstanding subparagraph (B), the term "disposition" does not include—

(i) a disposition of property which is not a material factor in the realization of income by the taxpayer, or

(ii) a disposition of property to a domestic corporation in a distribution or transfer described in section 381(a).

(D) APPLICATION TO CERTAIN DISPOSITIONS OF STOCK IN CONTROLLED FOREIGN CORPORATION.—

(i) IN GENERAL.—This paragraph shall apply to an applicable disposition in the same manner as if it were a disposition of property described in subparagraph (A), except that the exception contained in subparagraph (C)(i) shall not apply.

(ii) APPLICABLE DISPOSITION.—For purposes of clause (i), the term "applicable disposition" means any disposition of any share of stock in a controlled foreign corporation in a transaction or series of transactions if, immediately before such transaction or series of transactions, the taxpayer owned more than 50 percent (by vote or value) of the stock of the controlled foreign corporation. Such term shall not include a disposition described in clause (iii) or (iv), except that clause (i) shall apply to any gain recognized on any such disposition.

(iii) EXCEPTION FOR CERTAIN EXCHANGES WHERE OWNERSHIP PERCENTAGE RETAINED.—A disposition shall not be treated as an applicable disposition under clause (ii) if it is part of a transaction or series of transactions—

(I) to which section 351 or 721 applies, or under which the transferor receives stock in a foreign corporation in exchange for the stock in the controlled foreign corporation and the stock received is exchanged basis property (as defined in section 7701(a)(44)), and

(II) immediately after which, the transferor owns (by vote or value) at least the same percentage of stock in the controlled foreign corporation (or, if the controlled foreign corporation is not in existence after such transaction or series of transactions, in another foreign corporation stock in which was received by the transferor in exchange for stock in the controlled foreign corporation) as the percentage of stock in the controlled foreign corporation which the taxpayer owned immediately before such transaction or series of transactions.

(iv) EXCEPTION FOR CERTAIN ASSET ACQUISITIONS.—A disposition shall not be treated as an applicable disposition under clause (ii) if it is part of a transaction or series of transactions in which the taxpayer (or any member of a controlled group of corporations filing a consolidated return under section 1501 which includes the taxpayer) acquires the assets of a controlled foreign corporation in exchange for the shares of the controlled foreign corporation in a liquidation described in section 332 or a reorganization described in section 368(a)(1).

(v) CONTROLLED FOREIGN CORPORATION.—For purposes of this subparagraph, the term "controlled foreign corporation" has the meaning given such term by section 957.

(vi) STOCK OWNERSHIP.—For purposes of this subparagraph, ownership of stock shall be determined under the rules of subsections (a) and (b) of section 958.

(4) ACCUMULATION DISTRIBUTIONS OF FOREIGN TRUST.—For purposes of this chapter, in the case of amounts of income from sources without the United States which are treated under section 666 (without regard to subsections (b) and (c) thereof if the taxpayer chose to take a deduction with respect to the amounts described in such subsections under section 667(d)(1)(B)) as having been distributed by a foreign trust in a preceding taxable year, that portion of such amounts equal to the amount of any overall foreign loss sustained by the beneficiary in a year prior to the taxable year of the beneficiary in which such distribution is received from the trust shall be treated as income from sources within the United States (and not income from sources without the United States) to the extent that such loss was not used under this subsection in prior taxable years, or in the current taxable year, against other income of the beneficiary.

(5) TREATMENT OF SEPARATE LIMITATION LOSSES.—

(A) IN GENERAL.—The amount of the separate limitation losses for any taxable year shall reduce income from sources within the United States for such taxable year only to the extent the aggregate amount of such losses exceeds the aggregate amount of the separate limitation incomes for such taxable year.

(B) ALLOCATION OF LOSSES.—The separate limitation losses for any taxable year (to the extent such losses do not exceed the separate limitation incomes for such year) shall be allocated among (and operate to reduce) such incomes on a proportionate basis.

(C) RECHARACTERIZATION OF SUBSEQUENT INCOME.—If—

(i) a separate limitation loss from any income category (hereinafter in this subparagraph referred to as "the loss category") was allocated to income from any other category under subparagraph (B), and

(ii) the loss category has income for a subsequent taxable year,

such income (to the extent it does not exceed the aggregate separate limitation losses from the loss category not previously recharacterized under this subparagraph) shall be recharacterized as income from such other category in proportion to the prior reductions under subparagraph (B) in such other category not previously taken into account under this subparagraph. Nothing in the preceding sentence shall be construed as recharacterizing any tax.

(D) SPECIAL RULES FOR LOSSES FROM SOURCES IN THE UNITED STATES.—Any loss from sources in the United States for any taxable year (to the extent such loss does not exceed the separate limitation incomes from such year) shall be allocated among (and operate to reduce) such incomes on a proportionate basis. This subparagraph shall be applied after subparagraph (B).

(E) DEFINITIONS.—For purposes of this paragraph—

(i) INCOME CATEGORY.—The term "income category" means each separate category of income described in subsection (d)(1).

(ii) SEPARATE LIMITATION INCOME.—The term "separate limitation income" means, with respect to any income category, the taxable income from sources outside the United States, separately computed for such category.

(iii) SEPARATE LIMITATION LOSS.—The term "separate limitation loss" means, with respect to any income category, the loss from such category determined under the principles of section 907(c)(4)(B).

(F) DISPOSITIONS.—If any separate limitation loss for any taxable year is allocated against any separate limitation income for such taxable year, except to the extent provided in regulations, rules similar to the rules of paragraph (3) shall apply to any disposition of property if gain from such disposition would be in the income category with respect to which there was such separate limitation loss.

➤➤➤ *Caution: New Code Sec. 904(g), below, is effective for tax years beginning after December 31, 2006.*

[Sec. 904(g)]

(g) RECHARACTERIZATION OF OVERALL DOMESTIC LOSS.—

(1) GENERAL RULE.—For purposes of this subpart and section 936, in the case of any taxpayer who sustains an overall domestic loss for any taxable year beginning after December 31, 2006, that portion of the taxpayer's taxable income from sources within the United States for each succeeding taxable year which is equal to the lesser of—

(A) the amount of such loss (to the extent not used under this paragraph in prior taxable years), or

(B) 50 percent of the taxpayer's taxable income from sources within the United States for such succeeding taxable year,

shall be treated as income from sources without the United States (and not as income from sources within the United States).

(2) OVERALL DOMESTIC LOSS DEFINED.—For purposes of this subsection—

(A) IN GENERAL.—The term "overall domestic loss" means any domestic loss to the extent such loss offsets taxable income from sources without the United States for the taxable year or for any preceding taxable year by reason of a carryback. For purposes of the preceding sentence, the term "domestic loss" means the amount by which the gross income for the taxable year from sources within the United States is exceeded by the sum of the deductions properly apportioned or allocated thereto (determined without regard to any carryback from a subsequent taxable year).

(B) TAXPAYER MUST HAVE ELECTED FOREIGN TAX CREDIT FOR YEAR OF LOSS.—The term "overall domestic loss" shall not include any loss for any taxable year unless the taxpayer chose the benefits of this subpart for such taxable year.

(3) CHARACTERIZATION OF SUBSEQUENT INCOME.—

(A) IN GENERAL.—Any income from sources within the United States that is treated as income from sources without the United States under paragraph (1) shall be allocated among and increase the income categories in proportion to the loss from sources within the United States previously allocated to those income categories.

(B) INCOME CATEGORY.—For purposes of this paragraph, the term "income category" has the meaning given such term by subsection (f)(5)(E)(i).

(4) COORDINATION WITH SUBSECTION (f).—The Secretary shall prescribe such regulations as may be necessary to coordinate the provisions of this subsection with the provisions of subsection (f).

⇶→ *Caution: Former Code Sec. 904(g), below, was redesignated as Code Sec. 904(h), effective for tax years beginning after December 31, 2006.*

[Sec. 904(h)]

(h) SOURCE RULES IN CASE OF UNITED STATES-OWNED FOREIGN CORPORATIONS.—

(1) IN GENERAL.—The following amounts which are derived from a United States-owned foreign corporation and which would be treated as derived from sources outside the United States without regard to this subsection shall, for purposes of this section, be treated as derived from sources within the United States to the extent provided in this subsection:

(A) Any amount included in gross income under—

(i) section 951(a) (relating to amounts included in gross income of United States shareholders), or

(ii) section 1293 (relating to current taxation of income from qualified funds).

(B) Interest.

(C) Dividends.

(2) SUBPART F AND PASSIVE FOREIGN INVESTMENT COMPANY INCLUSIONS.—Any amount described in subparagraph (A) of paragraph (1) shall be treated as derived from sources within the United States to the extent such amount is attributable to income of the United States-owned foreign corporation from sources within the United States.

(3) CERTAIN INTEREST ALLOCABLE TO UNITED STATES SOURCE INCOME.—Any interest which—

(A) is paid or accrued by a United States-owned foreign corporation during any taxable year,

(B) is paid or accrued to a United States shareholder (as defined in section 951(b)) or a related person (within the meaning of section 267(b)) to such a shareholder, and

(C) is properly allocable (under regulations prescribed by the Secretary) to income of such foreign corporation for the taxable year from sources within the United States,

shall be treated as derived from sources within the United States.

(4) DIVIDENDS.—

(A) IN GENERAL.—The United States source ratio of any dividend paid or accrued by a United States-owned foreign corporation shall be treated as derived from sources within the United States.

(B) UNITED STATES SOURCE RATIO.—For purposes of subparagraph (A), the term "United States source ratio" means, with respect to any dividend paid out of the earnings and profits for any taxable year, a fraction—

(i) the numerator of which is the portion of the earnings and profits for such taxable year from sources within the United States, and

(ii) the denominator of which is the total amount of earnings and profits for such taxable year.

(5) EXCEPTION WHERE UNITED STATES-OWNED FOREIGN CORPORATION HAS SMALL AMOUNT OF UNITED STATES SOURCE INCOME.—Paragraph (3) shall not apply to interest paid or accrued during any taxable year (and paragraph (4) shall not apply to any dividends paid out of the earnings and profits for such taxable year) if—

(A) the United States-owned foreign corporation has earnings and profits for such taxable year, and

(B) less than 10 percent of such earnings and profits is attributable to sources within the United States.

For purposes of the preceding sentence, earnings and profits shall be determined without any reduction for interest described in paragraph (3) (determined without regard to subparagraph (C) thereof).

(6) UNITED STATES-OWNED FOREIGN CORPORATION.—For purposes of this subsection, the term "United States-owned foreign corporation" means any foreign corporation if 50 percent or more of—

(A) the total combined voting power of all classes of stock of such corporation entitled to vote, or

(B) the total value of the stock of such corporation,

is held directly (or indirectly through applying paragraphs (2) and (3) of section 958(a) and paragraph (4) of section 318(a)) by United States persons (as defined in section 7701(a)(30)).

(7) DIVIDEND.—For purposes of this subsection, the term "dividend" includes any gain treated as ordinary income under section 1246 or as a dividend under section 1248.

(8) COORDINATION WITH SUBSECTION (f).—This subsection shall be applied before subsection (f).

(9) TREATMENT OF CERTAIN DOMESTIC CORPORATIONS.—For purposes of this subsection—

(A) in the case of interest treated as not from sources within the United States under section 861(a)(1)(A), the corporation paying such interest shall be treated as a United States-owned foreign corporation, and

(B) in the case of any dividend treated as not from sources within the United States under section 861(a)(2)(A), the corporation paying such dividend shall be treated as a United States-owned foreign corporation.

(10) COORDINATION WITH TREATIES.—

(A) IN GENERAL.—If—

(i) any amount derived from a United States-owned foreign corporation would be treated as derived from sources within the United States under this subsection by reason of an item of income of such United States-owned foreign corporation,

(ii) under a treaty obligation of the United States (applied without regard to this subsection and by treating any amount included in gross income under section 951(a)(1) as a dividend), such amount would be treated as arising from sources outside the United States, and

(iii) the taxpayer chooses the benefits of this paragraph,

this subsection shall not apply to such amount to the extent attributable to such item of income (but subsections (a), (b), and (c) of this section and sections 902, 907, and 960 shall be applied separately with respect to such amount to the extent so attributable).

(B) SPECIAL RULE.—Amounts included in gross income under section 951(a)(1) shall be treated as a dividend under subparagraph (A)(ii) only if dividends paid by each corporation (the stock in which is taken into account in determining whether the shareholder is a United States shareholder in the United States-owned foreign corporation), if paid to the United States shareholder, would be treated under a treaty obligation of the United States as arising from sources outside the United States (applied without regard to this subsection).

(11) REGULATIONS.—The Secretary shall prescribe such regulations as may be necessary or appropriate for purposes of this subsection, including—

(A) regulations for the application of this subsection in the case of interest or dividend payments through 1 or more entities, and

(B) regulations providing that this subsection shall apply to interest paid or accrued to any person (whether or not a United States shareholder).

⇒ *Caution: Former Code Sec. 904(h), below, was redesignated as Code Sec. 904(i), effective for tax years beginning after December 31, 2006.*

[Sec. 904(i)]

(i) COORDINATION WITH NONREFUNDABLE PERSONAL CREDITS.—In the case of an individual, for purposes of subsection (a), the tax against which the credit is taken is such tax reduced by the sum of the credits allowable under subpart A of part IV of subchapter A of this chapter (other than sections 23, 24, and 25B). This subsection shall not apply to taxable years beginning during 2000, 2001, 2002, 2003, 2004, or 2005.

»»→ Caution: *Former Code Sec. 904(i), below, was redesignated as Code Sec. 904(j), effective for tax years beginning after December 31, 2006.*

[Sec. 904(j)]

(j) LIMITATION ON USE OF DECONSOLIDATION TO AVOID FOREIGN TAX CREDIT LIMITATIONS.—If 2 or more domestic corporations would be members of the same affiliated group if—

(1) section 1504(b) were applied without regard to the exceptions contained therein, and

(2) the constructive ownership rules of section 1563(e) applied for purposes of section 1504(a),

the Secretary may by regulations provide for resourcing the income of any of such corporations or for modifications to the consolidated return regulations to the extent that such resourcing or modifications are necessary to prevent the avoidance of the provisions of this subpart.

»»→ Caution: *Former Code Sec. 904(j), below, was redesignated as Code Sec. 904(k), effective for tax years beginning after December 31, 2006.*

[Sec. 904(k)]

(k) CERTAIN INDIVIDUALS EXEMPT.—

(1) IN GENERAL.—In the case of an individual to whom this subsection applies for any taxable year—

(A) the limitation of subsection (a) shall not apply,

(B) no taxes paid or accrued by the individual during such taxable year may be deemed paid or accrued under subsection (c) in any other taxable year, and

(C) no taxes paid or accrued by the individual during any other taxable year may be deemed paid or accrued under subsection (c) in such taxable year.

(2) INDIVIDUALS TO WHOM SUBSECTION APPLIES.—This subsection shall apply to an individual for any taxable year if—

(A) the entire amount of such individual's gross income for the taxable year from sources without the United States consists of qualified passive income,

(B) the amount of the creditable foreign taxes paid or accrued by the individual during the taxable year does not exceed $300 ($600 in the case of a joint return), and

(C) such individual elects to have this subsection apply for the taxable year.

(3) DEFINITIONS.—For purposes of this subsection—

(A) QUALIFIED PASSIVE INCOME.—The term "qualified passive income" means any item of gross income if—

(i) such item of income is passive income (as defined in subsection (d)(2)(B) without regard to clause (iii) thereof), and

(ii) such item of income is shown on a payee statement furnished to the individual.

(B) CREDITABLE FOREIGN TAXES.—The term "creditable foreign taxes" means any taxes for which a credit is allowable under section 901; except that such term shall not include any tax unless such tax is shown on a payee statement furnished to such individual.

(C) PAYEE STATEMENT.—The term "payee statement" has the meaning given to such term by section 6724(d)(2).

(D) ESTATES AND TRUSTS NOT ELIGIBLE.—This subsection shall not apply to any estate or trust.

≫→ *Caution: Former Code Sec. 904(k), below, was redesignated as Code Sec. 904(l), effective for tax years beginning after December 31, 2006.*

[Sec. 904(l)]

(l) CROSS REFERENCES.—

(1) For increase of limitation under subsection (a) for taxes paid with respect to amounts received which were included in the gross income of the taxpayer for a prior taxable year as a United States shareholder with respect to a controlled foreign corporation, see section 960(b).

(2) For modification of limitation under subsection (a) for purposes of determining the amount of credit which can be taken against the alternative minimum tax, see section 59(a).

[Sec. 905]

SEC. 905. APPLICABLE RULES.

[Sec. 905(a)]

(a) YEAR IN WHICH CREDIT TAKEN.—The credits provided in this subpart may, at the option of the taxpayer and irrespective of the method of accounting employed in keeping his books, be taken in the year in which the taxes of the foreign country or the possession of the United States accrued, subject, however, to the conditions prescribed in subsection (c). If the taxpayer elects to take such credits in the year in which the taxes of the foreign country or the possession of the United States accrued, the credits for all subsequent years shall be taken on the same basis, and no portion of any such taxes shall be allowed as a deduction in the same or any succeeding year.

[Sec. 905(b)]

(b) PROOF OF CREDITS.—The credits provided in this subpart shall be allowed only if the taxpayer establishes to the satisfaction of the Secretary—

(1) the total amount of income derived from sources without the United States, determined as provided in part I,

(2) the amount of income derived from each country, the tax paid or accrued to which is claimed as a credit under this subpart, such amount to be determined under regulations prescribed by the Secretary, and

(3) all other information necessary for the verification and computation of such credits.

[Sec. 905(c)]

(c) ADJUSTMENTS TO ACCRUED TAXES.—

(1) IN GENERAL.—If—

(A) accrued taxes when paid differ from the amounts claimed as credits by the taxpayer,

(B) accrued taxes are not paid before the date 2 years after the close of the taxable year to which such taxes relate, or

(C) any tax paid is refunded in whole or in part,

the taxpayer shall notify the Secretary, who shall redetermine the amount of the tax for the year or years affected. The Secretary may prescribe adjustments to the pools of post-1986 foreign income taxes and the pools of post-1986 undistributed earnings under sections 902 and 960 in lieu of the redetermination under the preceding sentence.

(2) SPECIAL RULE FOR TAXES NOT PAID WITHIN 2 YEARS.—

(A) IN GENERAL.—Except as provided in subparagraph (B), in making the redetermination under paragraph (1), no credit shall be allowed for accrued taxes not paid before the date referred to in subparagraph (B) of paragraph (1).

(B) TAXES SUBSEQUENTLY PAID.—Any such taxes if subsequently paid—

(i) shall be taken into account—

(I) in the case of taxes deemed paid under section 902 or section 960, for the taxable year in which paid (and no redetermination shall be made under this section by reason of such payment), and

(II) in any other case, for the taxable year to which such taxes relate, and

(ii) shall be translated as provided in section 986(a)(2)(A).

(3) ADJUSTMENTS.—The amount of tax (if any) due on any redetermination under paragraph (1) shall be paid by the taxpayer on notice and demand by the Secretary, and the amount of tax overpaid (if any) shall be credited or refunded to the taxpayer in accordance with subchapter B of chapter 66 (section 6511 et seq.).

(4) BOND REQUIREMENTS.—In the case of any tax accrued but not paid, the Secretary, as a condition precedent to the allowance of the credit provided in this subpart, may require the taxpayer to give a bond, with sureties satisfactory to and approved by the Secretary, in such sum as the Secretary may require, conditioned on the payment by the taxpayer of any amount of tax found due on any such redetermination. Any such bond shall contain such further conditions as the Secretary may require.

(5) OTHER SPECIAL RULES.—In any redetermination under paragraph (1) by the Secretary of the amount of tax due from the taxpayer for the year or years affected by a refund, the amount of the taxes refunded for which credit has been allowed under this section shall be reduced by the amount of any tax described in section 901 imposed by the foreign country or possession of the United States with respect to such refund; but no credit under this subpart, or deduction under section 164, shall be allowed for any taxable year with respect to any such tax imposed on the refund. No interest shall be assessed or collected on any amount of tax due on any redetermination by the Secretary, resulting from a refund to the taxpayer, for any period before the receipt of such refund, except to the extent interest was paid by the foreign country or possession of the United States on such refund for such period.

[Sec. 906]

SEC. 906. NONRESIDENT ALIEN INDIVIDUALS AND FOREIGN CORPORATIONS.

[Sec. 906(a)]

(a) ALLOWANCE OF CREDIT.—A nonresident alien individual or a foreign corporation engaged in trade or business within the United States during the taxable year shall be allowed a credit under section 901 for the amount of any income, war profits, and excess profits taxes paid or accrued during the taxable year (or deemed, under section 902, paid or accrued during the taxable year) to any foreign country or possession of the United States with respect to income effectively connected with the conduct of a trade or business within the United States.

[Sec. 906(b)]

(b) SPECIAL RULES.—

(1) For purposes of subsection (a) and for purposes of determining the deductions allowable under sections 873(a) and 882(c), in determining the amount of any tax paid or accrued to any foreign country or possession there shall not be taken into account any amount of tax to the extent the tax so paid or accrued is imposed with respect to income from sources within the United States which would not be taxed by such foreign country or possession but for the fact that—

(A) in the case of a nonresident alien individual, such individual is a citizen or resident of such foreign country or possession, or

(B) in the case of a foreign corporation, such corporation was created or organized under the law of such foreign country or possession or is domiciled for tax purposes in such country or possession.

(2) For purposes of subsection (a), in applying section 904 the taxpayer's taxable income shall be treated as consisting only of the taxable income effectively connected with the taxpayer's conduct of a trade or business within the United States.

(3) The credit allowed pursuant to subsection (a) shall not be allowed against any tax imposed by section 871(a) (relating to income of nonresident alien individual not connected with United States business) or 881 (relating to income of foreign corporations not connected with United States business).

(4) For purposes of sections 902(a) and 78, a foreign corporation choosing the benefits of this subpart which receives dividends shall, with respect to such dividends, be treated as a domestic corporation.

(5) No credit shall be allowed under this section for any income, war profits, and excess profits taxes paid or accrued with respect to the foreign trade income (within the meaning of section 923(b)) of a FSC.

(6) For purposes of section 902, any income, war profits, and excess profits taxes paid or accrued (or deemed paid or accrued) to any foreign country or possession of the United States with respect to income effectively connected with the conduct of a trade or business within the United States shall not be taken into account, and any accumulated profits attributable to such income shall not be taken into account.

(7) No credit shall be allowed under this section against the tax imposed by section 884.

[Sec. 907]

SEC. 907. SPECIAL RULES IN CASE OF FOREIGN OIL AND GAS INCOME.

[Sec. 907(a)]

(a) REDUCTION IN AMOUNT ALLOWED AS FOREIGN TAX UNDER SECTION 901.—In applying section 901, the amount of any oil and gas extraction taxes paid or accrued (or deemed to have been paid) during the taxable year which would (but for this subsection) be taken into account for purposes of section 901 shall be reduced by the amount (if any) by which the amount of such taxes exceeds the product of—

(1) the amount of the foreign oil and gas extraction income for the taxable year,

(2) multiplied by—

(A) in the case of a corporation, the percentage which is equal to the highest rate of tax specified under section 11(b), or

(B) in the case of an individual, a fraction the numerator of which is the tax against which the credit under section 901(a) is taken and the denominator of which is the taxpayer's entire taxable income.

[Sec. 907(b)]

(b) FOREIGN TAXES ON FOREIGN OIL RELATED INCOME.—For purposes of this subtitle, in the case of taxes paid or accrued to any foreign country with respect to foreign oil related income, the term "income, war profits, and excess profits taxes" shall not include any amount paid or accrued after December 31, 1982, to the extent that the Secretary determines that the foreign law imposing such amount of tax is structured, or in fact operates, so that the amount of tax imposed with respect to foreign oil related income will generally be materially greater, over a reasonable period of time, than the amount generally imposed on income that is neither foreign oil related income nor foreign oil and gas extraction income. In computing the amount not treated as tax under this subsection, such amount shall be treated as a deduction under the foreign law.

[Sec. 907(c)]

(c) FOREIGN INCOME DEFINITIONS AND SPECIAL RULES.—For purposes of this section—

(1) FOREIGN OIL AND GAS EXTRACTION INCOME.—The term "foreign oil and gas extraction income" means the taxable income derived from sources without the United States and its possessions from—

(A) the extraction (by the taxpayer or any other person) of minerals from oil or gas wells, or

(B) the sale or exchange of assets used by the taxpayer in the trade or business described in subparagraph (A).

Such term does not include any dividend or interest income which is passive income (as defined in section 904(d)(2)(A)).

(2) FOREIGN OIL RELATED INCOME.—The term "foreign oil related income" means the taxable income derived from sources outside the United States and its possessions from—

(A) the processing of minerals extracted (by the taxpayer or by any other person) from oil or gas wells into their primary products,

(B) the transportation of such minerals or primary products,

(C) the distribution or sale of such minerals or primary products,

(D) the disposition of assets used by the taxpayer in the trade or business described in subparagraph (A), (B), or (C), or

(E) the performance of any other related service.

Such term does not include any dividend or interest income which is passive income (as defined in section 904(d)(2)(A)).

(3) DIVIDENDS, INTEREST, PARTNERSHIP DISTRIBUTION, ETC.—The term "foreign oil and gas extraction income" and the term "foreign oil related income" include—

(A) dividends and interest from a foreign corporation in respect of which taxes are deemed paid by the taxpayer under section 902,

(B) amounts with respect to which taxes are deemed paid under section 960(a), and

(C) the taxpayer's distributive share of the income of partnerships.[,]

to the extent such dividends, interest, amounts, or distributive share is attributable to foreign oil and gas extraction income, or to foreign oil related income, as the case may be; except that interest described in subparagraph (A) shall not be taken into account in computing foreign oil and gas extraction income but shall be taken into account in computing foreign oil-related income.

(4) RECAPTURE OF FOREIGN OIL AND GAS EXTRACTION LOSSES BY RECHARACTERIZING LATER EXTRACTION INCOME.—

(A) IN GENERAL.—That portion of the income of the taxpayer for the taxable year which (but for this paragraph) would be treated as foreign oil and gas extraction income shall be treated as income (from sources without the United States) which is not foreign oil and gas extraction income to the extent of the excess of—

(i) the aggregate amount of foreign oil extraction losses for preceding taxable years beginning after December 31, 1982, over

(ii) so much of such aggregate amount as was recharacterized under this subparagraph for preceding taxable years beginning after December 31, 1982.

(B) FOREIGN OIL EXTRACTION LOSS DEFINED.—

(i) IN GENERAL.—For purposes of this paragraph, the term "foreign oil extraction loss" means the amount by which—

(I) the gross income for the taxable year from sources without the United States and its possessions (whether or not the taxpayer chooses the benefits of this subpart for such taxable year) taken into account in determining the foreign oil and gas extraction income for such year, is exceeded by

(II) the sum of the deductions properly apportioned or allocated thereto.

(ii) NET OPERATING LOSS DEDUCTION NOT TAKEN INTO ACCOUNT.—For purposes of clause (i), the net operating loss deduction allowable for the taxable year under section 172(a) shall not be taken into account.

(iii) EXPROPRIATION AND CASUALTY LOSSES NOT TAKEN INTO ACCOUNT.—For purposes of clause (i), there shall not be taken into account—

(I) any foreign expropriation loss (as defined in section 172(h) (as in effect on the day before the date of the enactment of the Revenue Reconciliation Act of 1990)) for the taxable year, or

(II) any loss for the taxable year which arises from fire, storm, shipwreck, or other casualty, or from theft,

to the extent such loss is not compensated for by insurance or otherwise.

(5) OIL AND GAS EXTRACTION TAXES.—The term "oil and gas extraction taxes" means any income, war profits, and excess profits tax paid or accrued (or deemed to have been paid under section 902 or 960) during the taxable year with respect to foreign oil and gas extraction income (determined without regard to paragraph (4)) or loss which would be taken into account for purposes of section 901 without regard to this section.

[Sec. 907(d)]

(d) DISREGARD OF CERTAIN POSTED PRICES, ETC.—For purposes of this chapter, in determining the amount of taxable income in the case of foreign oil and gas extraction income, if the oil or gas is disposed of, or is acquired other than from the government of a foreign country, at a posted price (or other pricing arrangement) which differs from the fair market value for such oil or gas, such fair market value shall be used in lieu of such posted price (or other pricing arrangement).

[Sec. 907(f)]

(f) CARRYBACK AND CARRYOVER OF DISALLOWED CREDITS.—

(1) IN GENERAL.—If the amount of the oil and gas extraction taxes paid or accrued during any taxable year exceeds the limitation provided by subsection (a) for such taxable year (hereinafter in this subsection referred to as the "unused credit year"), such excess shall be deemed to be oil and gas extraction taxes paid or accrued in the first preceding taxable year, and in any of the first 10 succeeding taxable year, in that order and to the extent not deemed tax paid or accrued in a prior taxable year by reason of the limitation imposed by paragraph (2). Such amount deemed paid or accrued in any taxable year may be availed of only as a tax credit and not as a deduction and only if the taxpayer for such year chooses to have the benefits of this subpart as to taxes paid or accrued for that year to foreign countries or possessions.

(2) LIMITATION.—The amount of the unused oil and gas extraction taxes which under paragraph (1) may be deemed paid or accrued in any preceding or succeeding taxable year shall not exceed the lesser of—

(A) the amount by which the limitation provided by subsection (a) for such taxable year exceeds the sum of—

(i) the oil and gas extraction taxes paid or accrued during such taxable year, plus

(ii) the amounts of the oil and gas extraction taxes which by reason of this subsection are deemed paid or accrued in such taxable year and are attributable to taxable years preceding the unused credit year; or

(B) the amount by which the limitation provided by section 904 for such taxable year exceeds the sum of—

(i) the taxes paid or accrued (or deemed to have been paid under section 902 or 960) to all foreign countries and possessions of the United States during such taxable year,

(ii) the amount of such taxes which were deemed paid or accrued in such taxable year under section 904(c) and which are attributable to taxable years preceding the unused credit year, plus

(iii) the amount of the oil and gas extraction taxes which by reason of this subsection are deemed paid or accrued in such taxable year and are attributable to taxable years preceding the unused credit year.

(3) SPECIAL RULES.—

(A) In the case of any taxable year which is an unused credit year under this subsection and which is an unused credit year under section 904(c), the provisions of this subsection shall be applied before section 904(c).

(B) For purposes of determining the amount of taxes paid or accrued in any taxable year which may be deemed paid or accrued in a preceding or succeeding taxable year under section 904(c), any tax deemed paid or accrued in such preceding or succeeding taxable year under this subsection shall be considered to be tax paid or accrued in such preceding or succeeding taxable year.

Sec. 907(f)(3)(B)

[Sec. 908]

SEC. 908. REDUCTION OF CREDIT FOR PARTICIPATION IN OR COOPERATION WITH AN INTERNATIONAL BOYCOTT.

[Sec. 908(a)]

(a) IN GENERAL.—If a person, or a member of a controlled group (within the meaning of section 993(a)(3)) which includes such person, participates in or cooperates with an international boycott during the taxable year (within the meaning of section 999(b)), the amount of the credit allowable under section 901 to such person, or under section 902 or 960 to United States shareholders of such person, for foreign taxes paid during the taxable year shall be reduced by an amount equal to the product of—

    (1) the amount of the credit which, but for this section, would be allowed under section 901 for the taxable year, multiplied by

    (2) the international boycott factor (determined under section 999).

[Sec. 908(b)]

(b) APPLICATION WITH SECTIONS 275(a)(4) and 78.—Section 275(a)(4) and section 78 shall not apply to any amount of taxes denied credit under subsection (a).

Subpart B—Earned Income of Citizens or Residents of United States

[Sec. 911]

SEC. 911. CITIZENS OR RESIDENTS OF THE UNITED STATES LIVING ABROAD.

[Sec. 911(a)]

(a) EXCLUSION FROM GROSS INCOME.—At the election of a qualified individual (made separately with respect to paragraphs (1) and (2)), there shall be excluded from the gross income of such individual, and exempt from taxation under this subtitle, for any taxable year—

    (1) the foreign earned income of such individual, and

    (2) the housing cost amount of such individual.

[Sec. 911(b)]

(b) FOREIGN EARNED INCOME.—

    (1) DEFINITION.—For purposes of this section—

        (A) IN GENERAL.—The term "foreign earned income" with respect to any individual means the amount received by such individual from sources within a foreign country or countries which constitute earned income attributable to services performed by such individual during the period described in subparagraph (A) or (B) of subsection (d)(1), whichever is applicable.

        (B) CERTAIN AMOUNTS NOT INCLUDED IN FOREIGN EARNED INCOME.—The foreign earned income for an individual shall not include amounts—

            (i) received as a pension or annuity,

            (ii) paid by the United States or an agency thereof to an employee of the United States or an agency thereof,

            (iii) included in gross income by reason of section 402(b) (relating to taxability of beneficiary of nonexempt trust) or section 403(c) (relating to taxability of beneficiary under a nonqualified annuity), or

            (iv) received after the close of the taxable year following the taxable year in which the services to which the amounts are attributable are performed.

    (2) LIMITATION ON FOREIGN EARNED INCOME.—

        (A) IN GENERAL.—The foreign earned income of an individual which may be excluded under subsection (a)(1) for any taxable year shall not exceed the amount of foreign earned income computed on a daily basis at an annual rate equal to the exclusion amount for the calendar year in which such taxable year begins.

(B) ATTRIBUTION TO YEAR IN WHICH SERVICES ARE PERFORMED.—For purposes of applying subparagraph (A), amounts received shall be considered received in the taxable year in which the services to which the amounts are attributable are performed.

(C) TREATMENT OF COMMUNITY INCOME.—In applying subparagraph (A) with respect to amounts received from services performed by a husband or wife which are community income under community property laws applicable to such income, the aggregate amount which may be excludable from the gross income of such husband and wife under subsection (a)(1) for any taxable year shall equal the amount which would be so excludable if such amounts did not constitute community income.

(D) EXCLUSION AMOUNT.—

(i) IN GENERAL.—The exclusion amount for any calendar year is the exclusion amount determined in accordance with the following table (as adjusted by clause (ii)):

For calendar year—	The exclusion amount is—
1998	$72,000
1999	74,000
2000	76,000
2001	78,000
2002 and thereafter	80,000

(ii) INFLATION ADJUSTMENT.—In the case of any taxable year beginning in a calendar year after 2007, the $80,000 amount in clause (i) shall be increased by an amount equal to the product of—

(I) such dollar amount, and

(II) the cost-of-living adjustment determined under section 1(f)(3) for the calendar year in which the taxable year begins, determined by substituting "2006" for "1992" in subparagraph (B) thereof.

If any increase determined under the preceding sentence is not a multiple of $100, such increase shall be rounded to the next lowest multiple of $100.

[Sec. 911(c)]

(c) HOUSING COST AMOUNT.—For purposes of this section—

(1) IN GENERAL.—The term "housing cost amount" means an amount equal to the excess of—

(A) the housing expenses of an individual for the taxable year, over

(B) an amount equal to the product of—

(i) 16 percent of the salary (computed on a daily basis) of an employee of the United States who is compensated at a rate equal to the annual rate paid for step 1 of grade GS–14, multiplied by

(ii) the number of days of such taxable year within the applicable period described in subparagraph (A) or (B) of subsection (d)(1).

(2) HOUSING EXPENSES.—

(A) IN GENERAL.—The term "housing expenses" means the reasonable expenses paid or incurred during the taxable year by or on behalf of an individual for housing for the individual (and, if they reside with him, for his spouse and dependents) in a foreign country. The term—

(i) includes expenses attributable to the housing (such as utilities and insurance), but

(ii) does not include interest and taxes of the kind deductible under section 163 or 164 or any amount allowable as a deduction under section 216(a).

Housing expenses shall not be treated as reasonable to the extent such expenses are lavish or extravagant under the circumstances.

(B) SECOND FOREIGN HOUSEHOLD.—

(i) IN GENERAL.—Except as provided in clause (ii), only housing expenses incurred with respect to that abode which bears the closest relationship to the tax home of the individual shall be taken into account under paragraph (1).

(ii) SEPARATE HOUSEHOLD FOR SPOUSE AND DEPENDENTS.—If an individual maintains a separate abode outside the United States for his spouse and dependents and they do not reside with him because of living conditions which are dangerous, unhealthful, or otherwise adverse, then—

(I) the words "if they reside with him" in subparagraph (A) shall be disregarded, and

(II) the housing expenses incurred with respect to such abode shall be taken into account under paragraph (1).

(3) SPECIAL RULES WHERE HOUSING EXPENSES NOT PROVIDED BY EMPLOYER.—

(A) IN GENERAL.—To the extent the housing cost amount of any individual for any taxable year is not attributable to employer provided amounts, such amount shall be treated as a deduction allowable in computing adjusted gross income to the extent of the limitation of subparagraph (B).

(B) LIMITATION.—For purposes of subparagraph (A), the limitation of this subparagraph is the excess of—

(i) the foreign earned income of the individual for the taxable year, over

(ii) the amount of such income excluded from gross income under subsection (a) for the taxable year.

(C) 1-YEAR CARRYOVER OF HOUSING AMOUNTS NOT ALLOWED BY REASON OF SUBPARAGRAPH (B).—

(i) IN GENERAL.—The amount not allowable as a deduction for any taxable year under subparagraph (A) by reason of the limitation of subparagraph (B) shall be treated as a deduction allowable in computing adjusted gross income for the succeeding taxable year (and only for the succeeding taxable year) to the extent of the limitation of clause (ii) for such succeeding taxable year.

(ii) LIMITATION.—For purposes of clause (i), the limitation of this clause for any taxable year is the excess of—

(I) the limitation of subparagraph (B) for such taxable year, over

(II) amounts treated as a deduction under subparagraph (A) for such taxable year.

(D) EMPLOYER PROVIDED AMOUNTS.—For purposes of this paragraph, the term "employer provided amounts" means any amount paid or incurred on behalf of the individual by the individual's employer which is foreign earned income included in the individual's gross income for the taxable year (without regard to this section).

(E) FOREIGN EARNED INCOME.—For purposes of this paragraph, an individual's foreign earned income for any taxable year shall be determined without regard to the limitation of subparagraph (A) of subsection (b)(2).

[Sec. 911(d)]

(d) DEFINITIONS AND SPECIAL RULES.—For purposes of this section—

(1) QUALIFIED INDIVIDUAL.—The term "qualified individual" means an individual whose tax home is in a foreign country and who is—

(A) a citizen of the United States and establishes to the satisfaction of the Secretary that he has been a bona fide resident of a foreign country or countries for an uninterrupted period which includes an entire taxable year, or

(B) a citizen or resident of the United States and who, during any period of 12 consecutive months, is present in a foreign country or countries during at least 330 full days in such period.

(2) EARNED INCOME.—

(A) IN GENERAL.—The term "earned income" means wages, salaries, or professional fees, and other amounts received as compensation for personal services actually rendered, but does not include that part of the compensation derived by the taxpayer for personal services rendered by him to a corporation which represents a distribution of earnings or profits rather than a reasonable allowance as compensation for the personal services actually rendered.

(B) TAXPAYER ENGAGED IN TRADE OR BUSINESS.—In the case of a taxpayer engaged in a trade or business in which both personal services and capital are material income-producing factors, under regulations prescribed by the Secretary, a reasonable allowance as compensation for the personal services rendered by the taxpayer, not in excess of 30 percent of his share of the net profits of such trade or business, shall be considered as earned income.

(3) TAX HOME.—The term "tax home" means, with respect to any individual, such individual's home for purposes of section 162(a)(2) (relating to traveling expenses while away from home). An individual shall not be treated as having a tax home in a foreign country for any period for which his abode is within the United States.

(4) WAIVER OF PERIOD OF STAY IN FOREIGN COUNTRY.—Notwithstanding paragraph (1), an individual who—

(A) is a bona fide resident of, or is present in, a foreign country for any period,

(B) leaves such foreign country after August 31, 1978—

(i) during any period during which the Secretary determines, after consultation with the Secretary of State or his delegate, that individuals were required to leave such foreign country because of war, civil unrest, or similar adverse conditions in such foreign country which precluded the normal conduct of business by such individuals, and

(ii) before meeting the requirements of such paragraph (1), and

(C) establishes to the satisfaction of the Secretary that such individual could reasonably have been expected to have met such requirements but for the conditions referred to in clause (i) of subparagraph (B),

shall be treated as a qualified individual with respect to the period described in subparagraph (A) during which he was a bona fide resident of, or was present in, the foreign country, and in applying subsections (b)(2)(A) and (c)(1)(B)(ii) with respect to such individual, only the days within such period shall be taken into account.

(5) TEST OF BONA FIDE RESIDENCE.—If—

(A) an individual who has earned income from sources within a foreign country submits a statement to the authorities of that country that he is not a resident of that country, and

(B) such individual is held not subject as a resident of that country to the income tax of that country by its authorities with respect to such earnings,

then such individual shall not be considered a bona fide resident of that country for purposes of paragraph (1)(A).

(6) DENIAL OF DOUBLE BENEFITS.—No deduction or exclusion from gross income under this subtitle or credit against the tax imposed by this chapter (including any credit or deduction for the amount of taxes paid or accrued to a foreign country or possession of the United States) shall be allowed to the extent such deduction, exclusion, or credit is properly allocable to or chargeable against amounts excluded from gross income under subsection (a).

(7) AGGREGATE BENEFIT CANNOT EXCEED FOREIGN EARNED INCOME.—The sum of the amount excluded under subsection (a) and the amount deducted under subsection (c)(3)(A) for the taxable year shall not exceed the individual's foreign earned income for such year.

(8) LIMITATION ON INCOME EARNED IN RESTRICTED COUNTRY.—

(A) IN GENERAL.—If travel (or any transaction in connection with such travel) with respect to any foreign country is subject to the regulations described in subparagraph (B) during any period—

(i) the term "foreign earned income" shall not include any income from sources within such country attributable to services performed during such period,

(ii) the term "housing expenses" shall not include any expenses allocable to such period for housing in such country or for housing of the spouse or dependents of the taxpayer in another country while the taxpayer is present in such country, and

(iii) an individual shall not be treated as a bona fide resident of, or as present in, a foreign country for any day during which such individual was present in such country during such period.

(B) REGULATIONS.—For purposes of this paragraph, regulations are described in this subparagraph if such regulations—

(i) have been adopted pursuant to the Trading With the Enemy Act (50 U.S.C. App. 1 et seq.), or the International Emergency Economic Powers Act (50 U.S.C. 1701 et seq.), and

(ii) include provisions generally prohibiting citizens and residents of the United States from engaging in transactions related to travel to, from, or within a foreign country.

(C) EXCEPTION.—Subparagraph (A) shall not apply to any individual during any period in which such individual's activities are not in violation of the regulations described in subparagraph (B).

(9) REGULATIONS.—The Secretary shall prescribe such regulations as may be necessary or appropriate to carry out the purposes of this section, including regulations providing rules—

(A) for cases where a husband and wife each have earned income from sources outside the United States, and

(B) for married individuals filing separate returns.

[Sec. 911(e)]

(e) ELECTION.—

(1) IN GENERAL.—An election under subsection (a) shall apply to the taxable year for which made and to all subsequent taxable years unless revoked under paragraph (2).

(2) REVOCATION.—A taxpayer may revoke an election made under paragraph (1) for any taxable year after the taxable year for which such election was made. Except with the consent of the Secretary, any taxpayer who makes such a revocation for any taxable year may not make another election under this section for any subsequent taxable year before the 6th taxable year after the taxable year for which such revocation was made.

[Sec. 911(f)]

(f) CROSS REFERENCES.—

For administrative and penal provisions relating to the exclusions provided for in this section, see sections 6001, 6011, 6012(c), and the other provisions of subtitle F.

[Sec. 912]

SEC. 912. EXEMPTION FOR CERTAIN ALLOWANCES.

The following items shall not be included in gross income, and shall be exempt from taxation under this subtitle:

(1) FOREIGN AREAS ALLOWANCES.—In the case of civilian officers and employees of the Government of the United States, amounts received as allowances or otherwise (but not amounts received as post differentials) under—

(A) chapter 9 of title I of the Foreign Service Act of 1980,

(B) section 4 of the Central Intelligence Agency Act of 1949, as amended (50 U. S. C., sec. 403e),

(C) title II of the Overseas Differentials and Allowances Act, or

(D) subsection (e) or (f) of the first section of the Administrative Expenses Act of 1946, as amended, or section 22 of such Act.

(2) COST-OF-LIVING ALLOWANCES.—In the case of civilian officers or employees of the Government of the United States stationed outside the continental United States (other than Alaska), amounts (other than amounts received under title II of the Overseas Differentials and Allowances Act) received as cost-of-living allowances in accordance with regulations approved by the President (or in the case of judicial officers or employees of the United States, in accordance with rules similar to such regulations).

(3) PEACE CORPS ALLOWANCES.—In the case of an individual who is a volunteer or volunteer leader within the meaning of the Peace Corps Act and members of his family, amounts received as allowances under section 5 or 6 of the Peace Corps Act other than amounts received as—

(A) termination payments under section 5(c) or section 6(1) of such Act,

(B) leave allowances,

(C) if such individual is a volunteer leader training in the United States, allowances to members of his family, and

(D) such portion of living allowances as the President may determine under the Peace Corps Act as constituting basic compensation.

Subpart D—Possessions of the United States

[Sec. 931]

SEC. 931. INCOME FROM SOURCES WITHIN GUAM, AMERICAN SAMOA, OR THE NORTHERN MARIANA ISLANDS.

[Sec. 931(a)]

(a) GENERAL RULE.—In the case of an individual who is a bona fide resident of a specified possession during the entire taxable year, gross income shall not include—

(1) income derived from sources within any specified possession, and

(2) income effectively connected with the conduct of a trade or business by such individual within any specified possession.

[Sec. 931(b)]

(b) DEDUCTIONS, ETC. ALLOCABLE TO EXCLUDED AMOUNTS NOT ALLOWABLE.—An individual shall not be allowed—

(1) as a deduction from gross income any deductions (other than the deduction under section 151, relating to personal exemptions), or

(2) any credit,

properly allocable or chargeable against amounts excluded from gross income under this section.

[Sec. 931(c)]

(c) SPECIFIED POSSESSION.—For purposes of this section, the term "specified possession" means Guam, American Samoa, and the Northern Mariana Islands.

[Sec. 931(d)]

(d) EMPLOYEES OF THE UNITED STATES.—Amounts paid for services performed as an employee of the United States (or any agency thereof) shall be treated as not described in paragraph (1) or (2) of subsection (a).

[Sec. 932]

SEC. 932. COORDINATION OF UNITED STATES AND VIRGIN ISLANDS INCOME TAXES.

[Sec. 932(a)]

(a) TREATMENT OF UNITED STATES RESIDENTS.—

(1) APPLICATION OF SUBSECTION.—This subsection shall apply to an individual for the taxable year if—

(A) such individual—

(i) is a citizen or resident of the United States (other than a bona fide resident of the Virgin Islands during the entire taxable year), and

(ii) has income derived from sources within the Virgin Islands, or effectively connected with the conduct of a trade or business within such possession, for the taxable year, or

(B) such individual files a joint return for the taxable year with an individual described in subparagraph (A).

(2) FILING REQUIREMENT.—Each individual to whom this subsection applies for the taxable year shall file his income tax return for the taxable year with both the United States and the Virgin Islands.

(3) EXTENT OF INCOME TAX LIABILITY.—In the case of an individual to whom this subsection applies in a taxable year for purposes of so much of this title (other than this section and section 7654) as relates to the taxes imposed by this chapter, the United States shall be treated as including the Virgin Islands.

[Sec. 932(b)]

(b) PORTION OF UNITED STATES TAX LIABILITY PAYABLE TO THE VIRGIN ISLANDS.—

(1) IN GENERAL.—Each individual to whom subsection (a) applies for the taxable year shall pay the applicable percentage of the taxes imposed by this chapter for such taxable year (determined without regard to paragraph (3)) to the Virgin Islands.

(2) APPLICABLE PERCENTAGE.—

(A) IN GENERAL.—For purposes of paragraph (1), the term "applicable percentage" means the percentage which Virgin Islands adjusted gross income bears to adjusted gross income.

(B) VIRGIN ISLANDS ADJUSTED GROSS INCOME.—For purposes of subparagraph (A), the term "Virgin Islands adjusted gross income" means adjusted gross income determined by taking into account only income derived from sources within the Virgin Islands and deductions properly apportioned or allocable thereto.

(3) AMOUNTS PAID ALLOWED AS CREDIT.—There shall be allowed as a credit against the tax imposed by this chapter for the taxable year an amount equal to the taxes required to be paid to the Virgin Islands under paragraph (1) which are so paid.

[Sec. 932(c)]

(c) TREATMENT OF VIRGIN ISLANDS RESIDENTS.—

(1) APPLICATION OF SUBSECTION.—This subsection shall apply to an individual for the taxable year if—

(A) such individual is a bona fide resident of the Virgin Islands during the entire taxable year, or

(B) such individual files a joint return for the taxable year with an individual described in subparagraph (A).

(2) FILING REQUIREMENT.—Each individual to whom this subsection applies for the taxable year shall file an income tax return for the taxable year with the Virgin Islands.

(3) EXTENT OF INCOME TAX LIABILITY.—In the case of an individual to whom this subsection applies in a taxable year for purposes of so much of this title (other than this section and section 7654) as relates to the taxes imposed by this chapter, the Virgin Islands shall be treated as including the United States.

(4) RESIDENTS OF THE VIRGIN ISLANDS.—In the case of an individual—

(A) who is a bona fide resident of the Virgin Islands during the entire taxable year,

(B) who, on his return of income tax to the Virgin Islands, reports income from all sources and identifies the source of each item shown on such return, and

(C) who fully pays his tax liability referred to in section 934(a) to the Virgin Islands with respect to such income, for purposes of calculating income tax liability to the United States, gross income shall not include any amount included in gross income on such return, and allocable deductions and credits shall not be taken into account.

[Sec. 932(d)]

(d) SPECIAL RULE FOR JOINT RETURNS.—In the case of a joint return, this section shall be applied on the basis of the residence of the spouse who has the greater adjusted gross income (determined without regard to community property laws) for the taxable year.

[Sec. 932(e)]

(e) SPECIAL RULE FOR APPLYING SECTION TO TAX IMPOSED IN VIRGIN ISLANDS.—In applying this section for purposes of determining income tax liability incurred to the Virgin Islands, the provisions of this section shall not be affected by the provisions of Federal law referred to in section 934(a).

[Sec. 933]

SEC. 933. INCOME FROM SOURCES WITHIN PUERTO RICO.

The following items shall not be included in gross income and shall be exempt from taxation under this subtitle:

(1) RESIDENT OF PUERTO RICO FOR ENTIRE TAXABLE YEAR.—In the case of an individual who is a bona fide resident of Puerto Rico during the entire taxable year, income derived from sources within Puerto Rico (except amounts received for services performed as an employee of the United States or any agency thereof); but such individual shall not be allowed as a deduction from his gross income any deductions (other than the deduction under section 151, relating to personal exemptions), or any credit, properly allocable to or chargeable against amounts excluded from gross income under this paragraph.

(2) TAXABLE YEAR OF CHANGE OF RESIDENCE FROM PUERTO RICO.—In the case of an individual citizen of the United States who has been a bona fide resident of Puerto Rico for a period of at least 2 years before the date on which he changes his residence from Puerto Rico, income derived from sources therein (except amounts received for services performed as an employee of the United States or any agency thereof) which is attributable to that part of such period of Puerto Rican residence before such date; but such individual shall not be allowed as a deduction from his gross income any deductions (other than the deduction for personal exemptions under section 151), or any credit, properly allocable to or chargeable against amounts excluded from gross income under this paragraph.

[Sec. 934]

SEC. 934. LIMITATION ON REDUCTION IN INCOME TAX LIABILITY INCURRED TO THE VIRGIN ISLANDS.

[Sec. 934(a)]

(a) GENERAL RULE.—Tax liability incurred to the Virgin Islands pursuant to this subtitle, as made applicable in the Virgin Islands by the Act entitled "An Act making appropriations for the naval service for the fiscal year ending June 30, 1922, and for other purposes", approved July 12, 1921 (48 U. S. C. 1397), or pursuant to section 28(a) of the Revised Organic Act of the Virgin Islands, approved July 22, 1954 (48 U. S. C. 1642), shall not be reduced or remitted in any way, directly or indirectly, whether by grant, subsidy, or other similar payment, by any law enacted in the Virgin Islands, except to the extent provided in subsection (b).

[Sec. 934(b)]

(b) REDUCTIONS PERMITTED WITH RESPECT TO CERTAIN INCOME.—

(1) IN GENERAL.—Except as provided in paragraph (2), subsection (a) shall not apply with respect to so much of the tax liability referred to in subsection (a) as is attributable to income derived from sources within the Virgin Islands or income effectively connected with the conduct of a trade or business within the Virgin Islands.

(2) EXCEPTION FOR LIABILITY PAID BY CITIZENS OR RESIDENTS OF THE UNITED STATES.—Paragraph (1) shall not apply to any liability payable to the Virgin Islands under section 932(b).

(3) SPECIAL RULE FOR NON-UNITED STATES INCOME OF CERTAIN FOREIGN CORPORATIONS.—

(A) IN GENERAL.—In the case of a qualified foreign corporation, subsection (a) shall not apply with respect to so much of the tax liability referred to in subsection (a) as is attributable to income which is derived from sources outside the United States and which is not effectively connected with the conduct of a trade or business within the United States.

(B) QUALIFIED FOREIGN CORPORATION.—For purposes of subparagraph (A), the term "qualified foreign corporation" means any foreign corporation if less than 10 percent of—

(i) the total voting power of the stock of such corporation, and

(ii) the total value of the stock of such corporation,

is owned or treated as owned (within the meaning of section 958) by 1 or more United States persons.

(4) DETERMINATION OF INCOME SOURCE, ETC.—The determination as to whether income is derived from sources within the United States or is effectively connected with the conduct of a trade or business within the United States shall be made under regulations prescribed by the Secretary.

[Sec. 936]

SEC. 936. PUERTO RICO AND POSSESSION TAX CREDIT.

[Sec. 936(a)]

(a) ALLOWANCE OF CREDIT.—

(1) IN GENERAL.—Except as otherwise provided in this section, if a domestic corporation elects the application of this section and if the conditions of both subparagraph (A) and subparagraph (B) of paragraph (2) are satisfied, there shall be allowed as a credit against the tax imposed by this chapter an amount equal to the portion of the tax which is attributable to the sum of—

(A) the taxable income, from sources without the United States, from—

(i) the active conduct of a trade or business within a possession of the United States, or

(ii) the sale or exchange of substantially all of the assets used by the taxpayer in the active conduct of such trade or business, and

(B) the qualified possession source investment income.

(2) CONDITIONS WHICH MUST BE SATISFIED.—The conditions referred to in paragraph (1) are:

>>>→ *Caution: Code Sec. 936(a)(2)(A), below, is effective for tax years on or before December 31, 2006.*

(A) 3-YEAR PERIOD.—If 80 percent or more of the gross income of such domestic corporation for the 3-year period immediately preceding the close of the taxable year (or for such part of such period immediately preceding the close of such taxable year as may be applicable) was derived from sources within a possession of the United States (determined without regard to section 904(f)); and

>>>→ *Caution: Code Sec. 936(a)(2)(A), below, is effective for tax years beginning after December 31, 2006.*

(A) 3-YEAR PERIOD.—If 80 percent or more of the gross income of such domestic corporation for the 3-year period immediately preceding the close of the taxable year (or for such part of such period immediately preceding the close of such taxable year as may be applicable) was derived from sources within a possession of the United States (determined without regard to subsections (f) and (g) of section 904); and

(B) TRADE OR BUSINESS.—If 75 percent or more of the gross income of such domestic corporation for such period or such part thereof was derived from the active conduct of a trade or business within a possession of the United States.

(3) CREDIT NOT ALLOWED AGAINST CERTAIN TAXES.—The credit provided by paragraph (1) shall not be allowed against the tax imposed by—

(A) section 59A (relating to environmental tax),

(B) section 531 (relating to the tax on accumulated earnings),

(C) section 541 (relating to personal holding company tax), or

(D) section 1351 (relating to recoveries of foreign expropriation losses).

(4) LIMITATIONS ON CREDIT FOR ACTIVE BUSINESS INCOME.—

(A) IN GENERAL.—The amount of the credit determined under paragraph (1) for any taxable year with respect to income referred to in subparagraph (A) thereof shall not exceed the sum of the following amounts:

(i) 60 percent of the sum of—

(I) the aggregate amount of the possession corporation's qualified possession wages for such taxable year, plus

(II) the allocable employee fringe benefit expenses of the possession corporation for the taxable year.

(ii) The sum of—

(I) 15 percent of the depreciation allowances for the taxable year with respect to short-life qualified tangible property;

(II) 40 percent of the depreciation allowances for the taxable year with respect to medium-life qualified tangible property, and

(III) 65 percent of the depreciation allowances for the taxable year with respect to long-life qualified tangible property.

(iii) If the possession corporation does not have an election to use the method described in subsection (h)(5)(C)(ii) (relating to profit split) in effect for the taxable year, the amount of qualified possession income taxes for the taxable year allocable to nonsheltered income.

(B) ELECTION TO TAKE REDUCED CREDIT.—

(i) IN GENERAL.—If an election under this subparagraph applies to a possession corporation for any taxable year—

(I) subparagraph (A), and the provisions of subsection (i), shall not apply to such possession corporation for such taxable year, and

(II) the credit determined under paragraph (1) for such taxable year with respect to income referred to in subparagraph (A) thereof shall be the applicable percentage of the credit which would otherwise have been determined under such paragraph with respect to such income.

Notwithstanding subclause (I), a possession corporation to which an election under this subparagraph applies shall be entitled to the benefits of subsection (i)(3)(B) for taxes allocable (on a pro rata basis) to taxable income the tax on which is not offset by reason of this subparagraph.

(ii) APPLICABLE PERCENTAGE.—The term "applicable percentage" means the percentage determined in accordance with the following table:

In the case of taxable years beginning in:	The percentage is:
1994	60
1995	55
1996	50
1997	45
1998 and thereafter	40

(iii) ELECTION.—

(I) IN GENERAL.—An election under this subparagraph by any possession corporation may be made only for the corporation's first taxable year beginning after December 31, 1993, for which it is a possession corporation.

(II) PERIOD OF ELECTION.—An election under this subparagraph shall apply to the taxable year for which made and all subsequent taxable years unless revoked.

(III) AFFILIATED GROUPS.—If, for any taxable year, an election is not in effect for any possession corporation which is a member of an affiliated group, any election under this subparagraph for any other member of such group is revoked for such taxable year and all subsequent taxable years. For purposes of this subclause, members of an affiliated group shall be determined without regard to the exceptions contained in section 1504(b) and as if the constructive ownership rules of section 1563(e) applied for purposes of section 1504(a). The Secretary may prescribe regulations to prevent the avoidance of this subclause through deconsolidation or otherwise.

(C) CROSS REFERENCE.—

For definitions and special rules applicable to this paragraph, see subsection (i).

[Sec. 936(b)]

(b) AMOUNTS RECEIVED IN UNITED STATES.—In determining taxable income for purposes of subsection (a), there shall not be taken into account as income from sources without the United States any gross income which was received by such domestic corporation within the United States, whether derived from sources within or without the United States. This subsection shall not apply to any amount described in subsection (a)(1)(A)(i) received from a person who is not a related person (within the meaning of subsection (h)(3) but without regard to subparagraphs (D)(ii) and (E)(i) thereof) with respect to the domestic corporation.

[Sec. 936(c)]

(c) TREATMENT OF CERTAIN FOREIGN TAXES.—For purposes of this title, any tax of a foreign country or a possession of the United States which is paid or accrued with respect to taxable income which is taken into account in computing the credit under subsection (a) shall not be treated as income, war profits, or excess profits taxes paid or accrued to a foreign country or possession of the United States, and no deduction shall be allowed under this title with respect to any amounts so paid or accrued.

[Sec. 936(d)]

(d) DEFINITIONS AND SPECIAL RULES.—For purposes of this section—

(1) POSSESSION.—The term "possession of the United States" includes the Commonwealth of Puerto Rico, and the Virgin Islands.

(2) QUALIFIED POSSESSION SOURCE INVESTMENT INCOME.—The term "qualified possession source investment income" means gross income which—

(A) is from sources within a possession of the United States in which a trade or business is actively conducted, and

(B) the taxpayer establishes to the satisfaction of the Secretary is attributable to the investment in such possession (for use therein) of funds derived from the active conduct of a trade or business in such possession, or from such investment,

less the deductions properly apportioned or allocated thereto.

(3) CARRYOVER BASIS PROPERTY.—

(A) IN GENERAL.—Income from the sale or exchange of any asset the basis of which is determined in whole or in part by reference to its basis in the hands of another person shall not be treated as income described in subparagraph (A) or (B) of subsection (a)(1).

(B) EXCEPTION FOR POSSESSIONS CORPORATIONS, ETC.—For purposes of subparagraph (A), the holding of any asset by another person shall not be taken into account if throughout the period for which such asset was held by such person section 931, this section, or section 957(c) (as in effect on the day before the date of the enactment of the Tax Reform Act of 1986) applied to such person.

(4) INVESTMENT IN QUALIFIED CARIBBEAN BASIN COUNTRIES.—

(A) IN GENERAL.—For purposes of paragraph (2)(B), an investment in a financial institution shall, subject to such conditions as the Secretary may prescribe by regulations, be treated as for use in Puerto Rico to the extent used by such financial institution (or by the Government Development Bank for Puerto Rico or the Puerto Rico Economic Development Bank)—

(i) for investment, consistent with the goals and purposes of the Caribbean Basin Economic Recovery Act, in—

(I) active business assets in a qualified Caribbean Basin country, or

(II) development projects in a qualified Caribbean Basin country, and

(ii) in accordance with a specific authorization granted by the Commissioner of Financial Institutions of Puerto Rico pursuant to regulations issued by such Commissioner.

A similar rule shall apply in the case of a direct investment in the Government Development Bank for Puerto Rico or the Puerto Rico Economic Development Bank.

(B) QUALIFIED CARIBBEAN BASIN COUNTRY.—For purposes of this subsection, the term "qualified Caribbean Basin country" means any beneficiary country (within the meaning of section 212(a)(1)(A) of the Caribbean Basin Economic Recovery Act) which meets the requirements of clauses (i) and (ii) of section 274(h)(6)(A) and the Virgin Islands.

(C) ADDITIONAL REQUIREMENTS.—Subparagraph (A) shall not apply to any investment made by a financial institution (or by the Government Development Bank for Puerto Rico or the Puerto Rico Economic Development Bank) unless—

(i) the person in whose trade or business such investment is made (or such other recipient of the investment) and the financial institution or such Bank certify to the Secretary and the Commissioner of Financial Institutions of Puerto Rico that the proceeds of the loan will be promptly used to acquire active business assets or to make other authorized expenditures, and

(ii) the financial institution (or the Government Development Bank for Puerto Rico or the Puerto Rico Economic Development Bank) and the recipient of the investment funds agree to permit the Secretary and the Commissioner of Financial Institutions of Puerto Rico to examine such of their books and records as may be necessary to ensure that the requirements of this paragraph are met.

(D) REQUIREMENT FOR INVESTMENT IN CARIBBEAN BASIN COUNTRIES.—

(i) IN GENERAL.—For each calendar year, the government of Puerto Rico shall take such steps as may be necessary to ensure that at least $100,000,000 of qualified Caribbean Basin country investments are made during such calendar year.

(ii) QUALIFIED CARIBBEAN BASIN COUNTRY INVESTMENT.—For purposes of clause (i), the term "qualified Caribbean Basin country investment" means any investment if—

(I) the income from such investment is treated as qualified possession source investment income by reason of subparagraph (A), and

(II) such investment is not (directly or indirectly) a refinancing of a prior investment (whether or not such prior investment was a qualified Caribbean Basin country investment).

[Sec. 936(e)]

(e) ELECTION.—

(1) PERIOD OF ELECTION.—The election provided in subsection (a) shall be made at such time and in such manner as the Secretary may by regulations prescribe. Any such election shall apply to the first taxable year for which such election was made and for which the domestic corporation satisfied the conditions of subparagraphs (A) and (B) of subsection

(a)(2) and for each taxable year thereafter until such election is revoked by the domestic corporation under paragraph (2). If any such election is revoked by the domestic corporation under paragraph (2), such domestic corporation may make a subsequent election under subsection (a) for any taxable year thereafter for which such domestic corporation satisfies the conditions of subparagraphs (A) and (B) of subsection (a)(2) and any such subsequent election shall remain in effect until revoked by such domestic corporation under paragraph (2).

(2) REVOCATION.—An election under subsection (a)—

(A) may be revoked for any taxable year beginning before the expiration of the 9th taxable year following the taxable year for which such election first applies only with the consent of the Secretary; and

(B) may be revoked for any taxable year beginning after the expiration of such 9th taxable year without the consent of the Secretary.

[Sec. 936(f)]

(f) LIMITATION ON CREDIT FOR DISC'S AND FSC'S.—No credit shall be allowed under this section to a corporation for any taxable year—

(1) for which it is a DISC or former DISC, or

(2) in which it owns at any time stock in a—

(A) DISC or former DISC, or

(B) FSC or former FSC.

[Sec. 936(g)]

(g) EXCEPTION TO ACCUMULATED EARNINGS TAX.—

(1) For purposes of section 535, the term "accumulated taxable income" shall not include taxable income entitled to the credit under subsection (a).

(2) For purposes of section 537, the term "reasonable needs of the business" includes assets which produce income eligible for the credit under subsection (a).

[Sec. 936(h)]

(h) TAX TREATMENT OF INTANGIBLE PROPERTY INCOME.—

(1) IN GENERAL.—

(A) INCOME ATTRIBUTABLE TO SHAREHOLDERS.—The intangible property income of a corporation electing the application of this section for any taxable year shall be included on a pro rata basis in the gross income of all shareholders of such electing corporation at the close of the taxable year of such electing corporation as income from sources within the United States for the taxable year of such shareholder in which or with which the taxable year of such electing corporation ends.

(B) EXCLUSION FROM THE INCOME OF AN ELECTING CORPORATION.—Any intangible property income of a corporation electing the application of this section which is included in the gross income of a shareholder of such corporation by reason of subparagraph (A) shall be excluded from the gross income of such corporation.

(2) FOREIGN SHAREHOLDERS; SHAREHOLDERS NOT SUBJECT TO TAX.—

(A) IN GENERAL.—Paragraph (1)(A) shall not apply with respect to any shareholder—

(i) who is not a United States person, or

(ii) who is not subject to tax under this title on intangible property income which would be allocated to such shareholder (but for this subparagraph).

(B) TREATMENT OF NONALLOCATED INTANGIBLE PROPERTY INCOME.—For purposes of this subtitle, intangible property income of a corporation electing the application of this section which is not included in the gross income of a shareholder of such corporation by reason of subparagraph (A)—

(i) shall be treated as income from sources within the United States, and

(ii) shall not be taken into account under subsection (a)(2).

(3) INTANGIBLE PROPERTY INCOME.—For purposes of this subsection—

(A) IN GENERAL.—The term "intangible property income" means the gross income of a corporation attributable to any intangible property other than intangible property which has been licensed to such corporation since prior to 1948 and is in use by such corporation on the date of the enactment of this subparagraph.

(B) INTANGIBLE PROPERTY.—The term "intangible property" means any—

(i) patent, invention, formula, process, design, pattern, or knowhow;

(ii) copyright, literary, musical, or artistic composition;

(iii) trademark, trade name, or brand name;

(iv) franchise, license, or contract;

(v) method, program, system, procedure, campaign, survey, study, forecast, estimate, customer list, or technical data; or

(vi) any similar item,

which has substantial value independent of the services of any individual.

(C) EXCLUSION OF REASONABLE PROFIT.—The term "intangible property income" shall not include any portion of the income from the sale, exchange or other disposition of any product, or from the rendering of services, by a corporation electing the application of this section which is determined by the Secretary to be a reasonable profit on the direct and indirect costs incurred by such electing corporation which are attributable to such income.

(D) RELATED PERSON.—

(i) IN GENERAL.—A person (hereinafter referred to as the "related person") is related to any person if—

(I) the related person bears a relationship to such person specified in section 267(b) or section 707(b)(1), or

(II) the related person and such person are members of the same controlled group of corporations.

(ii) SPECIAL RULE.—For purposes of clause (i), section 267(b) and section 707(b)(1) shall be applied by substituting "10 percent" for "50 percent".

(E) CONTROLLED GROUP OF CORPORATIONS.—The term "controlled group of corporations" has the meaning given to such term by section 1563(a), except that—

(i) "more than 10 percent" shall be substituted for "at least 80 percent" and "more than 50 percent" each place either appears in section 1563(a), and

(ii) the determination shall be made without regard to subsections (a)(4), (b)(2), and (e)(3)(C) of section 1563.

(4) DISTRIBUTIONS TO MEET QUALIFICATION REQUIREMENTS.—

(A) IN GENERAL.—If the Secretary determines that a corporation does not satisfy a condition specified in subparagraph (A) or (B) of subsection (a)(2) for any taxable year by reason of the exclusion from gross income under paragraph (1)(B), such corporation shall nevertheless be treated as satisfying such condition for such year if it makes a pro rata distribution of property after the close of such taxable year to its shareholders (designated at the time of such distribution as a distribution to meet qualification requirements) with respect to their stock in an amount which is equal to—

(i) if the condition of subsection (a)(2)(A) is not satisfied, that portion of the gross income for the period described in subsection (a)(2)(A)—

(I) which was not derived from sources within a possession, and

(II) which exceeds the amount of such income for such period which would enable such corporation to satisfy the condition of subsection (a)(2)(A),

(ii) if the condition of subsection (a)(2)(B) is not satisfied, that portion of the gross income for such period—

(I) which was not derived from the active conduct of a trade or business within a possession, and

(II) which exceeds the amount of such income for such period which would enable such corporation to satisfy the conditions of subsection (a)(2)(B), or

(iii) if neither of such conditions is satisfied, that portion of the gross income which exceeds the amount of gross income for such period which would enable such corporation to satisfy the conditions of subparagraphs (A) and (B) of subsection (a)(2).

(B) EFFECTIVELY CONNECTED INCOME.—In the case of a shareholder who is a nonresident alien individual or a foreign corporation, trust, or estate, any distribution described in subparagraph (A) shall be treated as income which is effectively connected with the conduct of a trade or business conducted through a permanent establishment of such shareholder within the United States.

(C) DISTRIBUTION DENIED IN CASE OF FRAUD OR WILLFUL NEGLECT.—Subparagraph (A) shall not apply to a corporation if the determination of the Secretary described in subparagraph (A) contains a finding that the failure of such corporation to satisfy the conditions in subsection (a)(2) was due in whole or in part to fraud with intent to evade tax or willful neglect on the part of such corporation.

(5) ELECTION OUT.—

(A) IN GENERAL.—The rules contained in paragraphs (1) through (4) do not apply for any taxable year if an election pursuant to subparagraph (F) is in effect to use one of the methods specified in subparagraph (C).

(B) ELIGIBILITY.—

(i) REQUIREMENT OF SIGNIFICANT BUSINESS PRESENCE.—An election may be made to use one of the methods specified in subparagraph (C) with respect to a product or type of service only if an electing corporation has a significant business presence in a possession with respect to such product or type of service. An election may remain in effect with respect to such product or type of service for any subsequent taxable year only if such electing corporation maintains a significant business presence in a possession with respect to such product or type of service in such subsequent taxable year. If an election is not in effect for a taxable year because of the preceding sentence, the electing corporation shall be deemed to have revoked the election on the first day of such taxable year.

(ii) DEFINITION.—For purposes of this subparagraph, an electing corporation has a "significant business presence" in a possession for a taxable year with respect to a product or type of service if:

(I) the total production costs (other than direct material costs and other than interest excluded by regulations prescribed by the Secretary) incurred by the electing corporation in the possession in producing units of that product sold or otherwise disposed of during the taxable year by the affiliated group to persons who are not members of the affiliated group are not less than 25 percent of the difference between (a) the gross receipts from sales or other dispositions during the taxable year by the affiliated group to persons who are not members of the affiliated group of such units of the product produced, in whole or in part, by the electing corporation in the possession, and (b) the direct material costs of the purchase of materials for such units of that product by all members of the affiliated group from persons who are not members of the affiliated group; or

(II) no less than 65 percent of the direct labor costs of the affiliated group for units of the product produced during the taxable year in whole or in part by the electing corporation or for the type of service rendered by the electing corporation during the taxable year, is incurred by the electing corporation and is compensation for services performed in the possession; or

(III) with respect to purchases and sales by an electing corporation of all goods not produced in whole or in part by any member of the affiliated group and sold by the electing corporation to persons other than members of the affiliated group, no less than 65 percent of the total direct labor costs of the affiliated group in connection with all purchases and sales of such goods sold during the taxable year by such electing corporation is incurred by such electing corporation and is compensation for services performed in the possession.

Notwithstanding satisfaction of one of the foregoing tests, an electing corporation shall not be treated as having a significant business presence in a possession with respect to a product produced in whole or in part by the electing corporation in the possession, for purposes of an election to use the method specified in subparagraph (C)(ii), unless such product is manufactured or produced in the possession by the electing corporation within the meaning of subsection (d)(1)(A) of section 954.

(iii) SPECIAL RULES.—

(I) An electing corporation which produces a product or renders a type of service in a possession on the date of the enactment of this clause is not required to meet the significant business presence test in a possession with respect to such product or type of service for its taxable years beginning before January 1, 1986.

(II) For purposes of this subparagraph, the costs incurred by an electing corporation or any other member f the affiliated group in connection with contract manufacturing by a person other than a member of the affiliated group, or in connection with a similar arrangement thereto, shall be treated as direct labor costs of the affiliated group and shall not be treated as production costs incurred by the electing corporation in the possession or as direct material costs or as compensation for services performed in the possession, except to the extent as may be otherwise provided in regulations prescribed by the Secretary.

(iv) REGULATIONS.—The Secretary may prescribe regulations setting forth:

(I) an appropriate transitional (but not in excess of three taxable years) significant business presence test for commencement in a possession of operations with respect to products or types of service after the date of the enactment of this clause and not described in subparagraph (B)(iii)(I),

(II) a significant business presence test for other appropriate cases, consistent with the tests specified in subparagraph (B)(ii),

(III) rules for the definition of a product or type of service, and

(IV) rules for treating components produced in whole or in part by a related person as materials, and the costs (including direct labor costs) related thereto as a cost of materials, where there is an independent resale price for such components or where otherwise consistent with the intent of the substantial business presence tests.

(C) METHODS OF COMPUTATION OF TAXABLE INCOME.—If an election of one of the following methods is in effect pursuant to subparagraph (F) with respect to a product or type of service, an electing corporation shall compute its income derived from the active conduct of a trade or business in a possession with respect to such product or type of service in accordance with the method which is elected.

(i) COST SHARING.—

(I) PAYMENT OF COST SHARING.—If an election of this method is in effect, the electing corporation must make a payment for its share of the cost (if any) of product area research which is paid or accrued by the affiliated group during that taxable year. Such share shall not be less than the same proportion of 110 percent of the cost of such product area research which the amount of "possession sales" bears to the amount of "total sales" of the affiliated group. The cost of product area research paid or accrued solely by the electing corporation in a taxable year (excluding amounts paid directly or indirectly to or on behalf of related persons and excluding amounts paid under any cost sharing agreements with related persons) will reduce (but not below zero) the amount of the electing corporation's cost sharing payment under this method for that year. In the case of intangible property described in subsection (h)(3)(B)(i) which the electing corporation is treated as owning under subclause (II), in no event shall the payment required under this subclause be less than the inclusion or payment which would be required under section 367(d)(2)(A)(ii) or section 482 if the electing corporation were a foreign corporation.

(a) PRODUCT AREA RESEARCH.—For purposes of this section, the term "product area research" includes (notwithstanding any provision to the contrary) the research, development and experimental costs, losses, expenses and other related deductions—including amounts paid or accrued for the performance of research or similar activities by another person; qualified research expenses within the meaning of section 41(b); amounts paid or accrued for the use of, or the right to use, research or any of the items specified in subsection (h)(3)(B)(i); and a proper allowance for amounts incurred for the acquisition of any of the items specified in subsection (h)(3)(B)(i)—which are properly apportioned or allocated to the same product area as that in which the electing corporation conducts its activities, and a ratable part of any such costs, losses, expenses and other deductions which cannot definitely be allocated to a particular product area.

(b) AFFILIATED GROUP.—For purposes of this subsection, the term "affiliated group" shall mean the electing corporation and all other organizations, trades or businesses (whether or not incorporated, whether or not organized in the United States, and whether or not affiliated) owned or controlled directly or indirectly by the same interests, within the meaning of section 482.

(c) POSSESSION SALES.—For purposes of this section, the term "possession sales" means the aggregate sales or other dispositions for the taxable year to persons who are not members of the affiliated group by members of the affiliated group of products produced, in whole or in part, by the electing corporation in the possession which are in the same product area as is used for determining the amount of product area research, and of services rendered, in whole or in part, in the possession in such product area to persons who are not members of the affiliated group.

(d) TOTAL SALES.—For purposes of this section, the term "total sales" means the aggregate sales or other dispositions for the taxable year to persons who are not members of the affiliated group by members of the affiliated group of all products in the same product area as is used for determining the amount of product area research, and of services rendered in such product area to persons who are not members of the affiliated group.

(e) PRODUCT AREA.—For purposes of this section, the term "product area" shall be defined by reference to the three-digit classification of the Standard Industrial Classification code. The Secretary may provide for the aggregation of two or more three-digit classifications where appropriate, and for a classification system other than the Standard Industrial Classification code in appropriate cases.

(II) EFFECT OF ELECTION.—For purposes of determining the amount of its gross income derived from the active conduct of a trade or business in a possession with respect to a product produced by, or type of service rendered by, the electing corporation for a taxable year, if an election of this method is in effect, the electing corporation shall be treated as the owner (for purposes of obtaining a return thereon) of intangible property described in subsection (h)(3)(B)(i) which is related to the units of the product produced, or type of service rendered, by the electing corporation. Such electing corporation shall not be treated as the owner (for purposes of obtaining a return thereon) of any intangible property described in subsection (h)(3)(B)(ii) through (v) (to the extent not described in subsection (h)(3)(B)(i)) or of any other nonmanufacturing intangible. Notwithstanding the preceding sentence, an electing corporation shall be treated as the owner (for purposes of obtaining a return thereon) of (a) intangible property which was developed solely by such corporation in a possession and is owned by such corporation, (b) intangible property described in subsection (h)(3)(B)(i) acquired by such corporation from a person who was not related to such corporation (or to any person related to such corporation) at the time of, or in connection with, such acquisition, and (c) any intangible property described in subsection (h)(3)(B)(ii) through (v) (to the extent not described in subsection (h)(3)(B)(i)) and other nonmanufacturing intangibles which relate to sales of units of products, or services rendered, to unrelated persons for ultimate consumption or use in the possession in which the electing corporation conducts its trade or business.

(III) PAYMENT PROVISIONS.—

(a) The cost sharing payment determined under subparagraph (C)(i)(I) for any taxable year shall be made to the person or persons specified in subparagraph (C)(i)(IV)(a) not later than the time prescribed by law for filing the electing corporation's return for such taxable year (including any extensions thereof). If all or part of such payment is not timely made, the amount of the cost sharing payment required to be paid shall be increased by the amount of interest that would have been due under section 6601(a) had the portion of the cost sharing payment that is not timely made been an amount of tax imposed by this title and had the last date prescribed for payment been the due date of the electing corporations return (determined without regard to any extension thereof). The amount by which a cost sharing payment determined under subparagraph (C)(i)(I) is increased by reason of the preceding sentence shall not be treated as a cost sharing payment or as interest. If failure to make timely payment is due in whole or in part to fraud or willful neglect, the electing corporation shall be deemed to have revoked the election made under subparagraph (A) on the first day of the taxable year for which the cost sharing payment was required.

(b) For purposes of this title, any tax of a foreign country or possession of the United States which is paid or accrued with respect to the payment or receipt of a cost sharing payment determined under subparagraph (C)(i)(I) or of an amount of increase referred to in subparagraph (C)(i)(III)(a) shall not be treated as income, war profits, or excess profits taxes paid or accrued to a foreign country or possession of the United States, and no deduction shall be allowed under this title with respect to any amounts of such tax so paid or accrued.

(IV) SPECIAL RULES.—

(a) The amount of the cost sharing payment determined under subparagraph (C)(i)(I), and any increase in the amount thereof in accordance with subparagraph (C)(i)(III)(a), shall not be treated as income of the recipient, but shall reduce the amount of the deductions (and the amount of reductions in earnings and profits) otherwise allowable to the appropriate domestic member or members (other than an electing corporation) of the affiliated group, or, if there is no such domestic member, to the foreign member or members of such affiliated group as the Secretary may provide under regulations.

(b) If an election of this method is in effect, the electing corporation shall determine its intercompany pricing under the appropriate section 482 method, provided, however, that an electing corporation shall not be denied use of the resale price method for purposes of such intercompany pricing merely because the reseller adds more than an insubstantial amount to the value of the product by the use of intangible property.

(c) The amount of qualified research expenses, within the meaning of section 41, of any member of the controlled group of corporations (as defined in section 41(f)) of which the electing corporation is a member shall not be affected by the cost sharing payment required under this method.

(ii) PROFIT SPLIT.—

(I) GENERAL RULE.—If an election of this method is in effect, the electing corporation's taxable income derived from the active conduct of a trade or business in a possession with respect to units of a product produced or type of service rendered, in whole or in part, by the electing corporation shall be equal to 50 percent of the combined taxable income of the affiliated group (other than foreign affiliates) derived from covered sales of units of the product produced or type of service rendered, in whole or in part, by the electing corporation in a possession.

(II) COMPUTATION OF COMBINED TAXABLE INCOME.—Combined taxable income shall be computed separately for each product produced or type of service rendered, in whole or in part, by the electing corporation in a possession. Combined taxable income shall be computed (notwithstanding any provision to the contrary) for each such product or type of service rendered by deducting from the gross income of the affiliated group (other than foreign affiliates) derived from covered sales of such product or type of service all expenses, losses, and other deductions properly apportioned or allocated to gross income from such sales or services, and a ratable part of all expenses, losses, or other deductions which cannot definitely be allocated to some item or class of gross income, which are incurred by the affiliated group (other than foreign affiliates). Notwithstanding any other provision to the contrary, in computing the combined taxable income for each such product or type of service rendered, the research, development, and experimental costs, expenses and related deductions for the taxable year which would otherwise be apportioned or allocated to the gross income of the affiliated group (other than foreign affiliates) derived from covered sales of such product produced or type of service rendered, in whole or in part, by the electing corporation in a possession, shall not be less than the same proportion of the amount of the share of product area research determined under subparagraph (C)(i)(I) (without regard to the third and fourth sentences thereof, by substituting "120 percent" for "110 percent" in the second sentence thereof) in the product area which includes such product or type of service, that such gross income from the product or type of service bears to such gross income from all products and types of services, within such product area, produced or rendered, in whole or part, by the electing corporation in a possession.

(III) DIVISION OF COMBINED TAXABLE INCOME.—50 percent of the combined taxable income computed as provided in subparagraph (C)(ii)(II) shall be allocated to the electing corporation. Combined taxable income, computed without regard to the last sentence of subparagraph (C)(ii)(II), less the amount allocated to the electing corporation, under the preceding sentence, shall be allocated to the appropriate domestic member or members (other than any electing corporation) of the affiliated group and shall be treated as income from sources within the United States, or, if there is no such domestic member, to a foreign member or members of such affiliated group as the Secretary may provide under regulations.

(IV) COVERED SALES.—For purposes of this paragraph, the term "covered sales" means sales by members of the affiliated group (other than foreign affiliates) to persons who are not members of the affiliated group or to foreign affiliates.

(D) UNRELATED PERSON.—For purposes of this paragraph, the term "unrelated person" means any person other than a person related within the meaning of paragraph (3)(D) to the electing corporation.

(E) ELECTING CORPORATION.—For purposes of this subsection, the term "electing corporation" means a domestic corporation for which an election under this section is in effect.

(F) TIME AND MANNER OF ELECTION; REVOCATION.—

(i) IN GENERAL.—An election under subparagraph (A) to use one of the methods under subparagraph (C) shall be made only on or before the due date prescribed by law (including extensions) for filing the tax return of the electing corporation for its first taxable year beginning after December 31, 1982. If an election of one of such methods is made, such election shall be binding on the electing corporation and such method must be used for each taxable year thereafter until such election is revoked by the electing corporation under subparagraph (F)(iii). If any such election is revoked by the electing corporation under subparagraph (F)(iii), such electing corporation may make a subsequent election under subparagraph (A) only with the consent of the Secretary.

(ii) MANNER OF MAKING ELECTION.—An election under subparagraph (A) to use one of the methods under subparagraph (C) shall be made by filing a statement to such effect with the return referred to in subparagraph (F)(i) or in such other manner as the Secretary may prescribe by regulations.

(iii) REVOCATION.—

(I) Except as provided in subparagraph (F)(iii)(II), an election may be revoked for any taxable year only with the consent of the Secretary.

(II) An election shall be deemed revoked for the year in which the electing corporation is deemed to have revoked such election under subparagraph (B)(i) or (C)(i)(III)(a).

(iv) AGGREGATION.—

(I) Where more than one electing corporation in the affiliated group produces any product or renders any services in the same product area, all such electing corporations must elect to compute their taxable income under the same method under subparagraph (C).

(II) All electing corporations in the same affiliated group that produce any products or render any services in the same product area may elect, subject to such terms and conditions as the Secretary may prescribe by regulations, to compute their taxable income from export sales under a different method from that used for all other sales and services. For this purpose, export sales means all sales by the electing corporation of products to foreign persons for use or consumption outside the United States and its possessions, provided such products are manufactured or produced in the possession within the meaning of subsection (d)(1)(A) of section 954, and further provided (except to the extent otherwise provided by regulations) the income derived by such foreign person on resale of such products (in the same state or in an altered state) is not included in foreign base company income for purposes of section 954(a).

(III) All members of an affiliated group must consent to an election under this subsection at such time and in such manner as shall be prescribed by the Secretary by regulations.

(6) TREATMENT OF CERTAIN SALES MADE AFTER JULY 1, 1982.—

(A) IN GENERAL.—For purposes of this section, in the case of a disposition of intangible property made by a corporation after July 1, 1982, any gain or loss from such disposition shall be treated as gain or loss from sources within the United States to which paragraph (5) does not apply.

(B) EXCEPTION.—Subparagraph (A) shall not apply to any disposition by a corporation of intangible property if such disposition is to a person who is not a related person to such corporation.

(C) PARAGRAPH DOES NOT AFFECT ELIGIBILITY.—This paragraph shall not apply for purposes of determining whether the corporation meets the requirements of subsection (a)(2).

(7) SECTION 864(e)(1) NOT TO APPLY.—This subsection shall be applied as if section 864(e)(1) (relating to treatment of affiliated groups) had not been enacted.

(8) REGULATIONS.—The Secretary shall prescribe such regulations as may be necessary or appropriate to carry out the purposes of this subsection, including rules for the application of this subsection to income from leasing of products to unrelated persons.

[Sec. 936(i)]

(i) DEFINITIONS AND SPECIAL RULES RELATING TO LIMITATIONS OF SUBSECTION (A)(4).—

(1) QUALIFIED POSSESSION WAGES.—For purposes of this section—

(A) IN GENERAL.—The term "qualified possession wages" paid or incurred by the possession corporation during the taxable year in connection with the active conduct of a trade or business within a possession of the United States to any employee for services performed in such possession, but only if such services are performed while the principal place of employment of such employee is within such possession.

(B) LIMITATION ON AMOUNT OF WAGES TAKEN INTO ACCOUNT.—

(i) IN GENERAL.—The amount of wages which may be taken into account under subparagraph (A) with respect to any employee for any taxable year shall not exceed 85 percent of the contribution and benefit base determined under section 230 of the Social Security Act for the calendar year in which such taxable year begins.

(ii) TREATMENT OF PART-TIME EMPLOYEES, ETC.—If—

(I) any employee is not employed by the possession corporation on a substantially full-time basis at all times during the taxable year, or

(II) the principal place of employment of any employee with the possession corporation is not within a possession at all times during the taxable year,

the limitation applicable under clause (i) with respect to such employee shall be the appropriate portion (as determined by the Secretary) of the limitation which would otherwise be in effect under clause (i).

(C) TREATMENT OF CERTAIN EMPLOYEES.—The term "qualified possession wages" shall not include any wages paid to employees who are assigned by the employer to perform services for another person, unless the principal trade or business of the employer is to make employees available for temporary periods to other persons in return for compensation. All possession corporations treated as 1 corporation under paragraph (5) shall be treated as 1 employer for purposes of the preceding sentence.

(D) WAGES.—

(i) IN GENERAL.—Except as provided in clause (ii), the term "wages" has the meaning given to such term by subsection (b) of section 3306 (determined without regard to any dollar limitation contained in such section). For purposes of the preceding sentence, such subsection (b) shall be applied as if the term "United States" included all possessions of the United States.

(ii) SPECIAL RULE FOR AGRICULTURAL LABOR AND RAILWAY LABOR.—In any case to which subparagraph (A) or (B) of paragraph (1) of section 51(h) applies, the term "wages" has the meaning given to such term by section 51(h)(2).

(2) ALLOCABLE EMPLOYEE FRINGE BENEFIT EXPENSES.—

(A) IN GENERAL.—The allocable employee fringe benefit expenses of any possession corporation for any taxable year is an amount which bears the same ratio to the amount determined under subparagraph (B) for such taxable year as—

(i) the aggregate amount of the possession corporation's qualified possession wages for such taxable year, bears to

(ii) the aggregate amount of the wages paid or incurred by such possession corporation during such taxable year.

In no event shall the amount determined under the preceding sentence exceed 15 percent of the amount referred to in clause (i).

(B) EXPENSES TAKEN INTO ACCOUNT.—For purposes of subparagraph (A), the amount determined under this subparagraph for any taxable year is the aggregate amount allowable as a deduction under this chapter to the possession corporation for such taxable year with respect to—

(i) employer contributions under a stock bonus, pension, profit-sharing, or annuity plan,

(ii) employer-provided coverage under any accident or health plan for employees, and

(iii) the cost of life or disability insurance provided to employees.

Any amount treated as wages under paragraph (1)(D) shall not be taken into account under this subparagraph.

(3) TREATMENT OF POSSESSION TAXES.—

(A) AMOUNT OF CREDIT FOR POSSESSION CORPORATIONS NOT USING PROFIT SPLIT.—

(i) IN GENERAL.—For purposes of subsection (a)(4)(A)(iii), the amount of the qualified possession income taxes for any taxable year allocable to nonsheltered income shall be an amount which bears the same ratio to the possession income taxes for such taxable year as—

(I) the increase in the tax liability of the possession corporation under this chapter for the taxable year by reason of subsection (a)(4)(A) (without regard to clause (iii) thereof), bears to

(II) the tax liability of the possession corporation under this chapter for the taxable year determined without regard to the credit allowable under this section.

(ii) LIMITATION ON AMOUNT OF TAXES TAKEN INTO ACCOUNT.—Possession income taxes shall not be taken into account under clause (i) for any taxable year to the extent that the amount of such taxes exceeds 9 percent of the amount of the taxable income for such taxable year.

(B) DEDUCTION FOR POSSESSION CORPORATIONS USING PROFIT SPLIT.—Notwithstanding subsection (c), if a possession corporation is not described in subsection (a)(4)(A)(iii) for the taxable year, such possession corporation shall be allowed a deduction for such taxable year in an amount which bears the same ration to the possession income taxes for such taxable year as—

(i) the increase in the tax liability of the possession corporation under this chapter for the taxable year by reason of subsection (a)(4)(A), bears to

(ii) the tax liability of the possession corporation under this chapter for the taxable year determined without regard to the credit allowable under this section.

In determining the credit under subsection (a) and in applying the preceding sentence, taxable income shall be determined without regard to the preceding sentence.

(C) POSSESSION INCOME TAXES.—For purposes of this paragraph, the term "possession income taxes" means any taxes of a possession of the United States which are treated as not being income, war profits, or excess profits taxes paid or accrued to a possession of the United States by reason of subsection (c).

(4) DEPRECIATION RULES.—For purposes of this section—

(A) DEPRECIATION ALLOWANCES.—The term "depreciation allowances" means the depreciation deductions allowable under section 167 to the possession corporation.

(B) CATEGORIES OF PROPERTY.—

(i) QUALIFIED TANGIBLE PROPERTY.—The term "qualified tangible property" means any tangible property used by the possession corporation in a possession of the United States in the active conduct of a trade or business within such possession.

(ii) SHORT-LIFE QUALIFIED TANGIBLE PROPERTY.—The term "short-life qualified tangible property" means any qualified tangible property to which section 168 applies and which is 3-year property or 5-year property for purposes of such section.

(iii) MEDIUM-LIFE QUALIFIED TANGIBLE PROPERTY.—The term "medium-life qualified tangible property" means any qualified tangible property to which section 168 applies and which is 7-year property or 10-year property for purposes of such section.

(iv) LONG-LIFE QUALIFIED TANGIBLE PROPERTY.—The term "long-life qualified tangible property" means any qualified tangible property to which section 168 applies and which is not described in clause (ii) or (iii).

(v) TRANSITIONAL RULE.—In the case of any qualified tangible property to which section 168 (as in effect on the day before the date of the enactment of the Tax Reform Act of 1986) applies, any reference in this paragraph to section 168 shall be treated as a reference to such section as so in effect.

(5) ELECTION TO COMPUTE CREDIT ON CONSOLIDATED BASIS.—

(A) IN GENERAL.—Any affiliated group may elect to treat all possession corporations which would be members of such group but for section 1504(b)(3) or (4) as 1 corporation for purposes of this section. The credit determined under this section with respect to such 1 corporation shall be allocated among such possession corporations in such manner as the Secretary may prescribe.

(B) ELECTION.—An election under subparagraph (A) shall apply to the taxable year for which made and all succeeding taxable years unless revoked with the consent of the Secretary.

(6) POSSESSION CORPORATION.—The term "possession corporation" means a domestic corporation for which the election provided in subsection (a) is in effect.

[Sec. 936(j)]

(j) TERMINATION.—

(1) IN GENERAL.—Except as otherwise provided in this subsection, this section shall not apply to any taxable year beginning after December 31, 1995.

(2) TRANSITION RULES FOR ACTIVE BUSINESS INCOME CREDIT.—Except as provided in paragraph (3)—

(A) ECONOMIC ACTIVITY CREDIT.—In the case of an existing credit claimant—

(i) with respect to a possession other than Puerto Rico, and

(ii) to which subsection (a)(4)(B) does not apply,

the credit determined under subsection (a)(1)(A) shall be allowed for taxable years beginning after December 31, 1995, and before January 1, 2002.

(B) SPECIAL RULE FOR REDUCED CREDIT.—

(i) IN GENERAL.—In the case of an existing credit claimant to which subsection (a)(4)(B) applies, the credit determined under subsection (a)(1)(A) shall be allowed for taxable years beginning after December 31, 1995, and before January 1, 1998.

(ii) ELECTION IRREVOCABLE AFTER 1997.—An election under subsection (a)(4)(B)(iii) which is in effect for the taxpayer's last taxable year beginning before 1997 may not be revoked unless it is revoked for the taxpayer's first taxable year beginning in 1997 and all subsequent taxable years.

(C) ECONOMIC ACTIVITY CREDIT FOR PUERTO RICO.—For economic activity credit for Puerto Rico, see section 30A.

(3) ADDITIONAL RESTRICTED CREDIT.—

(A) IN GENERAL.—In the case of an existing credit claimant—

(i) the credit under subsection (a)(1)(A) shall be allowed for the period beginning with the first taxable year after the last taxable year to which subparagraph (A) or (B) of paragraph (2), whichever is appropriate, applied and ending with the last taxable year beginning before January 1, 2006, except that

(ii) the aggregate amount of taxable income taken into account under subsection (a)(1)(A) for any such taxable year shall not exceed the adjusted base period income of such claimant.

(B) COORDINATION WITH SUBSECTION (a)(4).—The amount of income described in subsection (a)(1)(A) which is taken into account in applying subsection (a)(4) shall be such income as reduced under this paragraph.

(4) ADJUSTED BASE PERIOD INCOME.—For purposes of paragraph (3)—

(A) IN GENERAL.—The term "adjusted base period income" means the average of the inflation-adjusted possession incomes of the corporation for each base period year.

(B) INFLATION-ADJUSTED POSSESSION INCOME.—For purposes of subparagraph (A), the inflation-adjusted possession income of any corporation for any base period year shall be an amount equal to the sum of—

(i) the possession income of such corporation for such base period year, plus

(ii) such possession income multiplied by the inflation adjustment percentage for such base period year.

(C) INFLATION ADJUSTMENT PERCENTAGE.—For purposes of subparagraph (B), the inflation adjustment percentage for any base period year means the percentage (if any) by which—

(i) the CPI for 1995, exceeds

(ii) the CPI for the calendar year in which the base period year for which the determination is being made ends.

For purposes of the preceding sentence, the CPI for any calendar year is the CPI (as defined in section 1(f)(5)) for such year under section 1(f)(4).

(D) INCREASE IN INFLATION ADJUSTMENT PERCENTAGE FOR GROWTH DURING BASE YEARS.—The inflation adjustment percentage (determined under subparagraph (C) without regard to this subparagraph) for each of the 5 taxable years referred to in paragraph (5)(A) shall be increased by—

(i) 5 percentage points in the case of a taxable year ending during the 1-year period ending on October 13, 1995;

(ii) 10.25 percentage points in the case of a taxable year ending during the 1-year period ending on October 13, 1994;

(iii) 15.76 percentage points in the case of a taxable year ending during the 1-year period ending on October 13, 1993;

(iv) 21.55 percentage points in the case of a taxable year ending during the 1-year period ending on October 13, 1992; and

(v) 27.63 percentage points in the case of a taxable year ending during the 1-year period ending on October 13, 1991.

(5) BASE PERIOD YEAR.—For purposes of this subsection—

(A) IN GENERAL.—The term "base period year" means each of 3 taxable years which are among the 5 most recent taxable years of the corporation ending before October 14, 1995, determined by disregarding—

(i) one taxable year for which the corporation had the largest inflation-adjusted possession income, and

(ii) one taxable year for which the corporation had the smallest inflation-adjusted possession income.

(B) CORPORATIONS NOT HAVING SIGNIFICANT POSSESSION INCOME THROUGHOUT 5-YEAR PERIOD.—

(i) IN GENERAL.—If a corporation does not have significant possession income for each of the most recent 5 taxable years ending before October 14, 1995, then, in lieu of applying subparagraph (A), the term "base period year" means only those taxable years (of such 5 taxable years) for which the corporation has significant possession income; except that, if such corporation has significant possession income for 4 of such 5 taxable years, the rule of subparagraph (A)(ii) shall apply.

(ii) SPECIAL RULE.—If there is no year (of such 5 taxable years) for which a corporation has significant possession income—

(I) the term "base period year" means the first taxable year ending on or after October 14, 1995, but

(II) the amount of possession income for such year which is taken into account under paragraph (4) shall be the amount which would be determined if such year were a short taxable year ending on September 30, 1995.

(iii) SIGNIFICANT POSSESSION INCOME.—For purposes of this subparagraph, the term "significant possession income" means possession income which exceeds 2 percent of the possession income of the taxpayer for the taxable year (of the period of 6 taxable years ending with the first taxable year ending on or after October 14, 1995) having the greatest possession income.

(C) ELECTION TO USE ONE BASE PERIOD YEAR.—

(i) IN GENERAL.—At the election of the taxpayer, the term "base period year" means—

(I) only the last taxable year of the corporation ending in calendar year 1992, or

(II) a deemed taxable year which includes the first ten months of calendar year 1995.

(ii) BASE PERIOD INCOME FOR 1995.—In determining the adjusted base period income of the corporation for the deemed taxable year under clause (i)(II), the possession income shall be annualized and shall be determined without regard to any extraordinary item.

(iii) ELECTION.—An election under this subparagraph by any possession corporation may be made only for the corporation's first taxable year beginning after December 31, 1995, for which it is a possession corporation. The rules of subclauses (II) and (III) of subsection (a)(4)(B)(iii) shall apply to the election under this subparagraph.

(D) ACQUISITIONS AND DISPOSITIONS.—Rules similar to the rules of subparagraphs (A) and (B) of section 41(f)(3) shall apply for purposes of this subsection.

(6) POSSESSION INCOME.—For purposes of this subsection, the term "possession income" means, with respect to any possession, the income referred to in subsection (a)(1)(A) determined with respect to that possession. In no event shall possession income be treated as being less than zero.

(7) SHORT YEARS.—If the current year or a base period year is a short taxable year, the application of this subsection shall be made with such annualizations as the Secretary shall prescribe.

(8) SPECIAL RULES FOR CERTAIN POSSESSIONS.—

(A) IN GENERAL.—In the case of an existing credit claimant with respect to an applicable possession, this section (other than the preceding paragraphs of this subsection) shall apply to such claimant with respect to such applicable possession for taxable years beginning after December 31, 1995, and before January 1, 2006.

(B) APPLICABLE POSSESSION.—For purposes of this paragraph, the term "applicable possession" means Guam, American Samoa, and the Commonwealth of the Northern Mariana Islands.

(9) EXISTING CREDIT CLAIMANT.—For purposes of this subsection—

(A) IN GENERAL.—The term "existing credit claimant" means a corporation—

(i)(I) which was actively conducting a trade or business in a possession on October 13, 1995, and

(II) with respect to which an election under this section is in effect for the corporation's taxable year which includes October 13, 1995, or

(ii) which acquired all of the assets of a trade or business of a corporation which—

(I) satisfied the requirements of subclause (I) of clause (i) with respect to such trade or business, and

(II) satisfied the requirements of subclause (II) of clause (i).

(B) NEW LINES OF BUSINESS PROHIBITED.—If, after October 13, 1995, a corporation which would (but for this subparagraph) be an existing credit claimant adds a substantial new line of business (other than in an acquisition described in subparagraph (A)(ii)), such corporation shall cease to be treated as an existing credit claimant as of the close of the taxable year ending before the date of such addition.

(C) BINDING CONTRACT EXCEPTION.—If, on October 13, 1995, and at all times thereafter, there is in effect with respect to a corporation a binding contract for the acquisition of assets to be used in, or for the sale of assets to be produced from, a trade or business, the corporation shall be treated for purposes of this paragraph as actively conducting such trade or business on October 13, 1995. The preceding sentence shall not apply if such trade or business is not actively conducted before January 1, 1996.

(10) SEPARATE APPLICATION TO EACH POSSESSION.—For purposes of determining—

(A) whether a taxpayer is an existing credit claimant, and

(B) the amount of the credit allowed under this section,

this subsection (and so much of this section as relates to this subsection) shall be applied separately with respect to each possession.

Subpart E—Qualifying Foreign Trade Income

⋙→ *Caution: Code Sec. 941, below, is repealed for transactions after December 31, 2004. For transitional rules applicable to Code Sec. 114, see Act Sec. 101(d)-(f) of the American Jobs Creation Act of 2004 on page 17.*

[Sec. 941]

SEC. 941. QUALIFYING FOREIGN TRADE INCOME.

[Sec. 941(a)]

(a) QUALIFYING FOREIGN TRADE INCOME.—For purposes of this subpart and section 114—

(1) IN GENERAL.—The term "qualifying foreign trade income" means, with respect to any transaction, the amount of gross income which, if excluded, will result in a reduction of the taxable income of the taxpayer from such transaction equal to the greatest of—

(A) 30 percent of the foreign sale and leasing income derived by the taxpayer from such transaction,

(B) 1.2 percent of the foreign trading gross receipts derived by the taxpayer from the transaction, or

(C) 15 percent of the foreign trade income derived by the taxpayer from the transaction.

In no event shall the amount determined under subparagraph (B) exceed 200 percent of the amount determined under subparagraph (C).

(2) ALTERNATIVE COMPUTATION.—A taxpayer may compute its qualifying foreign trade income under a subparagraph of paragraph (1) other than the subparagraph which results in the greatest amount of such income.

(3) LIMITATION ON USE OF FOREIGN TRADING GROSS RECEIPTS METHOD.—If any person computes its qualifying foreign trade income from any transaction with respect to any property under paragraph (1)(B), the qualifying foreign trade income of such person (or any related person) with respect to any other transaction involving such property shall be zero.

(4) RULES FOR MARGINAL COSTING.—The Secretary shall prescribe regulations setting forth rules for the allocation of expenditures in computing foreign trade income under paragraph (1)(C) in those cases where a taxpayer is seeking to establish or maintain a market for qualifying foreign trade property.

(5) PARTICIPATION IN INTERNATIONAL BOYCOTTS, ETC.—Under regulations prescribed by the Secretary, the qualifying foreign trade income of a taxpayer for any taxable year shall be reduced (but not below zero) by the sum of—

(A) an amount equal to such income multiplied by the international boycott factor determined under section 999, and

(B) any illegal bribe, kickback, or other payment (within the meaning of section 162(c)) paid by or on behalf of the taxpayer directly or indirectly to an official, employee, or agent in fact of a government.

[Sec. 941(b)]

(b) FOREIGN TRADE INCOME.—For purposes of this subpart—

(1) IN GENERAL.—The term "foreign trade income" means the taxable income of the taxpayer attributable to foreign trading gross receipts of the taxpayer.

(2) SPECIAL RULE FOR COOPERATIVES.—In any case in which an organization to which part I of subchapter T applies which is engaged in the marketing of agricultural or horticultural products sells qualifying foreign trade property, in computing the taxable income of such cooperative, there shall not be taken into account any deduction allowable under subsection (b) or (c) of section 1382 (relating to patronage dividends, per-unit retain allocations, and nonpatronage distributions).

[Sec. 941(c)]

(c) FOREIGN SALE AND LEASING INCOME.—For purposes of this section—

(1) IN GENERAL.—The term "foreign sale and leasing income" means, with respect to any transaction—

(A) foreign trade income properly allocable to activities which—

(i) are described in paragraph (2)(A)(i) or (3) of section 942(b), and

(ii) are performed by the taxpayer (or any person acting under a contract with such taxpayer) outside the United States, or

(B) foreign trade income derived by the taxpayer in connection with the lease or rental of qualifying foreign trade property for use by the lessee outside the United States.

(2) SPECIAL RULES FOR LEASED PROPERTY.—

(A) SALES INCOME.—The term "foreign sale and leasing income" includes any foreign trade income derived by the taxpayer from the sale of property described in paragraph (1)(B).

(B) LIMITATION IN CERTAIN CASES.—Except as provided in regulations, in the case of property which—

(i) was manufactured, produced, grown, or extracted by the taxpayer, or

(ii) was acquired by the taxpayer from a related person for a price which was not determined in accordance with the rules of section 482,

the amount of foreign trade income which may be treated as foreign sale and leasing income under paragraph (1)(B) or subparagraph (A) of this paragraph with respect to any transaction involving such property shall not exceed the amount which would have been determined if the taxpayer had acquired such property for the price determined in accordance with the rules of section 482.

(3) SPECIAL RULES.—

(A) EXCLUDED PROPERTY.—Foreign sale and leasing income shall not include any income properly allocable to excluded property described in subparagraph (B) of section 943(a)(3) (relating to intangibles).

(B) ONLY DIRECT EXPENSES TAKEN INTO ACCOUNT.—For purposes of this subsection, any expense other than a directly allocable expense shall not be taken into account in computing foreign trade income.

Income Tax—Foreign Trade Income

⇒ *Caution: Code Sec. 942, below, is repealed for transactions after December 31, 2004. For transitional rules applicable to Code Sec. 114, see Act Sec. 101(d)-(f) of the American Jobs Creation Act of 2004 on page 17.*

[Sec. 942]

SEC. 942. FOREIGN TRADING GROSS RECEIPTS.

[Sec. 942(a)]

(a) FOREIGN TRADING GROSS RECEIPTS.—

(1) IN GENERAL.—Except as otherwise provided in this section, for purposes of this subpart, the term "foreign trading gross receipts" means the gross receipts of the taxpayer which are—

(A) from the sale, exchange, or other disposition of qualifying foreign trade property,

(B) from the lease or rental of qualifying foreign trade property for use by the lessee outside the United States,

(C) for services which are related and subsidiary to—

(i) any sale, exchange, or other disposition of qualifying foreign trade property by such taxpayer, or

(ii) any lease or rental of qualifying foreign trade property described in subparagraph (B) by such taxpayer,

(D) for engineering or architectural services for construction projects located (or proposed for location) outside the United States, or

(E) for the performance of managerial services for a person other than a related person in furtherance of the production of foreign trading gross receipts described in subparagraph (A), (B), or (C).

Subparagraph (E) shall not apply to a taxpayer for any taxable year unless at least 50 percent of its foreign trading gross receipts (determined without regard to this sentence) for such taxable year is derived from activities described in subparagraph (A), (B), or (C).

(2) CERTAIN RECEIPTS EXCLUDED ON BASIS OF USE; SUBSIDIZED RECEIPTS EXCLUDED.—The term "foreign trading gross receipts" shall not include receipts of a taxpayer from a transaction if—

(A) the qualifying foreign trade property or services—

(i) are for ultimate use in the United States, or

(ii) are for use by the United States or any instrumentality thereof and such use of qualifying foreign trade property or services is required by law or regulation, or

(B) such transaction is accomplished by a subsidy granted by the government (or any instrumentality thereof) of the country or possession in which the property is manufactured, produced, grown, or extracted.

(3) ELECTION TO EXCLUDE CERTAIN RECEIPTS.—The term "foreign trading gross receipts" shall not include gross receipts of a taxpayer from a transaction if the taxpayer elects not to have such receipts taken into account for purposes of this subpart.

[Sec. 942(b)]

(b) FOREIGN ECONOMIC PROCESS REQUIREMENTS.—

(1) IN GENERAL.—Except as provided in subsection (c), a taxpayer shall be treated as having foreign trading gross receipts from any transaction only if economic processes with respect to such transaction take place outside the United States as required by paragraph (2).

(2) REQUIREMENT.—

(A) IN GENERAL.—The requirements of this paragraph are met with respect to the gross receipts of a taxpayer derived from any transaction if—

(i) such taxpayer (or any person acting under a contract with such taxpayer) has participated outside the United States in the solicitation (other than advertising), the negotiation, or the making of the contract relating to such transaction, and

(ii) the foreign direct costs incurred by the taxpayer attributable to the transaction equal or exceed 50 percent of the total direct costs attributable to the transaction.

(B) ALTERNATIVE 85-PERCENT TEST.—A taxpayer shall be treated as satisfying the requirements of subparagraph (A)(ii) with respect to any transaction if, with respect to each of at least 2 subparagraphs of paragraph (3), the foreign direct costs incurred by such taxpayer attributable to activities described in such subparagraph equal or exceed 85 percent of the total direct costs attributable to activities described in such subparagraph.

(C) DEFINITIONS.—For purposes of this paragraph—

(i) TOTAL DIRECT COSTS.—The term "total direct costs" means, with respect to any transaction, the total direct costs incurred by the taxpayer attributable to activities described in paragraph (3) performed at any location by the taxpayer or any person acting under a contract with such taxpayer.

(ii) FOREIGN DIRECT COSTS.—The term "foreign direct costs" means, with respect to any transaction, the portion of the total direct costs which are attributable to activities performed outside the United States.

(3) ACTIVITIES RELATING TO QUALIFYING FOREIGN TRADE PROPERTY.—The activities described in this paragraph are any of the following with respect to qualifying foreign trade property—

(A) advertising and sales promotion,

(B) the processing of customer orders and the arranging for delivery,

(C) transportation outside the United States in connection with delivery to the customer,

(D) the determination and transmittal of a final invoice or statement of account or the receipt of payment, and

(E) the assumption of credit risk.

(4) ECONOMIC PROCESSES PERFORMED BY RELATED PERSONS.—A taxpayer shall be treated as meeting the requirements of this subsection with respect to any sales transaction involving any property if any related person has met such requirements in such transaction or any other sales transaction involving such property.

[Sec. 942(c)]

(c) EXCEPTION FROM FOREIGN ECONOMIC PROCESS REQUIREMENT.—

(1) IN GENERAL.—The requirements of subsection (b) shall be treated as met for any taxable year if the foreign trading gross receipts of the taxpayer for such year do not exceed $5,000,000.

(2) RECEIPTS OF RELATED PERSONS AGGREGATED.—All related persons shall be treated as one person for purposes of paragraph (1), and the limitation under paragraph (1) shall be allocated among such persons in a manner provided in regulations prescribed by the Secretary.

(3) SPECIAL RULE FOR PASS-THRU ENTITIES.—In the case of a partnership, S corporation, or other pass-thru entity, the limitation under paragraph (1) shall apply with respect to the partnership, S corporation, or entity and with respect to each partner, shareholder, or other owner.

⇒ *Caution: Code Sec. 943, below, is repealed for transactions after December 31, 2004. For transitional rules applicable to Code Sec. 114, see Act Sec. 101(d)-(f) of the American Jobs Creation Act of 2004 on page 17.*

[Sec. 943]

SEC. 943. OTHER DEFINITIONS AND SPECIAL RULES.

[Sec. 943(a)]

(a) QUALIFYING FOREIGN TRADE PROPERTY.—For purposes of this subpart—

(1) IN GENERAL.—The term "qualifying foreign trade property" means property—

    (A) manufactured, produced, grown, or extracted within or outside the United States,

    (B) held primarily for sale, lease, or rental, in the ordinary course of trade or business for direct use, consumption, or disposition outside the United States, and

    (C) not more than 50 percent of the fair market value of which is attributable to—

        (i) articles manufactured, produced, grown, or extracted outside the United States, and

        (ii) direct costs for labor (determined under the principles of section 263A) performed outside the United States.

For purposes of subparagraph (C), the fair market value of any article imported into the United States shall be its appraised value, as determined by the Secretary under section 402 of the Tariff Act of 1930 (19 U.S.C. 1401a) in connection with its importation, and the direct costs for labor under clause (ii) do not include costs that would be treated under the principles of section 263A as direct labor costs attributable to articles described in clause (i).

(2) U.S. TAXATION TO ENSURE CONSISTENT TREATMENT.—Property which (without regard to this paragraph) is qualifying foreign trade property and which is manufactured, produced, grown, or extracted outside the United States shall be treated as qualifying foreign trade property only if it is manufactured, produced, grown, or extracted by—

    (A) a domestic corporation,

    (B) an individual who is a citizen or resident of the United States,

    (C) a foreign corporation with respect to which an election under subsection (e) (relating to foreign corporations electing to be subject to United States taxation) is in effect, or

    (D) a partnership or other pass-thru entity all of the partners or owners of which are described in subparagraph (A), (B), or (C).

Except as otherwise provided by the Secretary, tiered partnerships or pass-thru entities shall be treated as described in subparagraph (D) if each of the partnerships or entities is directly or indirectly wholly owned by persons described in subparagraph (A), (B), or (C).

(3) EXCLUDED PROPERTY.—The term "qualifying foreign trade property" shall not include—

    (A) property leased or rented by the taxpayer for use by any related person,

    (B) patents, inventions, models, designs, formulas, or processes whether or not patented, copyrights (other than films, tapes, records, or similar reproductions, and other than computer software (whether or not patented), for commercial or home use), goodwill, trademarks, trade brands, franchises, or other like property,

    (C) oil or gas (or any primary product thereof),

    (D) products the transfer of which is prohibited or curtailed to effectuate the policy set forth in paragraph (2)(C) of section 3 of Public Law 96-72, or

    (E) any unprocessed timber which is a softwood.

For purposes of subparagraph (E), the term "unprocessed timber" means any log, cant, or similar form of timber.

(4) PROPERTY IN SHORT SUPPLY.—If the President determines that the supply of any property described in paragraph (1) is insufficient to meet the requirements of the domestic economy, the President may by Executive order designate the property as in short supply. Any property so designated shall not be treated as qualifying foreign trade property during the period beginning with the date specified in the Executive order and ending with the date specified in an Executive order setting forth the President's determination that the property is no longer in short supply.

[Sec. 943(b)]

(b) OTHER DEFINITIONS AND RULES.—For purposes of this subpart—

    (1) TRANSACTION.—

        (A) IN GENERAL.—The term "transaction" means—

(i) any sale, exchange, or other disposition,

(ii) any lease or rental, and

(iii) any furnishing of services.

(B) GROUPING OF TRANSACTIONS.—To the extent provided in regulations, any provision of this subpart which, but for this subparagraph, would be applied on a transaction-by-transaction basis may be applied by the taxpayer on the basis of groups of transactions based on product lines or recognized industry or trade usage. Such regulations may permit different groupings for different purposes.

(2) UNITED STATES DEFINED.—The term "United States" includes the Commonwealth of Puerto Rico. The preceding sentence shall not apply for purposes of determining whether a corporation is a domestic corporation.

(3) RELATED PERSON.—A person shall be related to another person if such persons are treated as a single employer under subsection (a) or (b) of section 52 or subsection (m) or (o) of section 414, except that determinations under subsections (a) and (b) of section 52 shall be made without regard to section 1563(b).

(4) GROSS AND TAXABLE INCOME.—Section 114 shall not be taken into account in determining the amount of gross income or foreign trade income from any transaction.

[Sec. 943(c)]

(c) SOURCE RULE.—Under regulations, in the case of qualifying foreign trade property manufactured, produced, grown, or extracted within the United States, the amount of income of a taxpayer from any sales transaction with respect to such property which is treated as from sources without the United States shall not exceed—

(1) in the case of a taxpayer computing its qualifying foreign trade income under section 941(a)(1)(B), the amount of the taxpayer's foreign trade income which would (but for this subsection) be treated as from sources without the United States if the foreign trade income were reduced by an amount equal to 4 percent of the foreign trading gross receipts with respect to the transaction, and

(2) in the case of a taxpayer computing its qualifying foreign trade income under section 941(a)(1)(C), 50 percent of the amount of the taxpayer's foreign trade income which would (but for this subsection) be treated as from sources without the United States.

[Sec. 943(d)]

(d) TREATMENT OF WITHHOLDING TAXES.—

(1) IN GENERAL.—For purposes of section 114(d), any withholding tax shall not be treated as paid or accrued with respect to extraterritorial income which is excluded from gross income under section 114(a). For purposes of this paragraph, the term "withholding tax" means any tax which is imposed on a basis other than residence and for which credit is allowable under section 901 or 903.

(2) EXCEPTION.—Paragraph (1) shall not apply to any taxpayer with respect to extraterritorial income from any transaction if the taxpayer computes its qualifying foreign trade income with respect to the transaction under section 941(a)(1)(A).

[Sec. 943(e)]

(e) ELECTION TO BE TREATED AS DOMESTIC CORPORATION.—

(1) IN GENERAL.—An applicable foreign corporation may elect to be treated as a domestic corporation for all purposes of this title if such corporation waives all benefits to such corporation granted by the United States under any treaty. No election under section 1362(a) may be made with respect to such corporation.

(2) APPLICABLE FOREIGN CORPORATION.—For purposes of paragraph (1), the term "applicable foreign corporation" means any foreign corporation if—

(A) such corporation manufactures, produces, grows, or extracts property in the ordinary course of such corporation's trade or business, or

(B) substantially all of the gross receipts of such corporation are foreign trading gross receipts.

(3) PERIOD OF ELECTION.—

(A) IN GENERAL.—Except as otherwise provided in this paragraph, an election under paragraph (1) shall apply to the taxable year for which made and all subsequent taxable years unless revoked by the taxpayer. Any revocation of such election shall apply to taxable years beginning after such revocation.

(B) TERMINATION.—If a corporation which made an election under paragraph (1) for any taxable year fails to meet the requirements of subparagraph (A) or (B) of paragraph (2) for any subsequent taxable year, such election shall not apply to any taxable year beginning after such subsequent taxable year.

(C) EFFECT OF REVOCATION OR TERMINATION.—If a corporation which made an election under paragraph (1) revokes such election or such election is terminated under subparagraph (B), such corporation (and any successor corporation) may not make such election for any of the 5 taxable years beginning with the first taxable year for which such election is not in effect as a result of such revocation or termination.

(4) SPECIAL RULES.—

(A) REQUIREMENTS.—This subsection shall not apply to an applicable foreign corporation if such corporation fails to meet the requirements (if any) which the Secretary may prescribe to ensure that the taxes imposed by this chapter on such corporation are paid.

(B) EFFECT OF ELECTION, REVOCATION, AND TERMINATION.—

(i) ELECTION.—For purposes of section 367, a foreign corporation making an election under this subsection shall be treated as transferring (as of the first day of the first taxable year to which the election applies) all of its assets to a domestic corporation in connection with an exchange to which section 354 applies.

(ii) REVOCATION AND TERMINATION.—For purposes of section 367, if—

(I) an election is made by a corporation under paragraph (1) for any taxable year, and

(II) such election ceases to apply for any subsequent taxable year,

such corporation shall be treated as a domestic corporation transferring (as of the 1st day of the first such subsequent taxable year to which such election ceases to apply) all of its property to a foreign corporation in connection with an exchange to which section 354 applies.

(C) ELIGIBILITY FOR ELECTION.—The Secretary may by regulation designate one or more classes of corporations which may not make the election under this subsection.

[Sec. 943(f)]

(f) RULES RELATING TO ALLOCATIONS OF QUALIFYING FOREIGN TRADE INCOME FROM SHARED PARTNERSHIPS.—

(1) IN GENERAL.—If—

(A) a partnership maintains a separate account for transactions (to which this subpart applies) with each partner,

(B) distributions to each partner with respect to such transactions are based on the amounts in the separate account maintained with respect to such partner, and

(C) such partnership meets such other requirements as the Secretary may by regulations prescribe,

then such partnership shall allocate to each partner items of income, gain, loss, and deduction (including qualifying foreign trade income) from any transaction to which this subpart applies on the basis of such separate account.

(2) SPECIAL RULES.—For purposes of this subpart, in the case of a partnership to which paragraph (1) applies—

(A) any partner's interest in the partnership shall not be taken into account in determining whether such partner is a related person with respect to any other partner, and

(B) the election under section 942(a)(3) shall be made separately by each partner with respect to any transaction for which the partnership maintains separate accounts for each partner.

[Sec. 943(g)]

(g) EXCLUSION FOR PATRONS OF AGRICULTURAL AND HORTICULTURAL COOPERATIVES.—Any amount described in paragraph (1) or (3) of section 1385(a)—

(1) which is received by a person from an organization to which part I of subchapter T applies which is engaged in the marketing of agricultural or horticultural products, and

(2) which is allocable to qualifying foreign trade income and designated as such by the organization in a written notice mailed to its patrons during the payment period described in section 1382(d),

shall be treated as qualifying foreign trade income of such person for purposes of section 114. The taxable income of the organization shall not be reduced under section 1382 by reason of any amount to which the preceding sentence applies.

[Sec. 943(h)]

(h) SPECIAL RULE FOR DISCS.—Section 114 shall not apply to any taxpayer for any taxable year if, at any time during the taxable year, the taxpayer is a member of any controlled group of corporations (as defined in section 927(d)(4), as in effect before the date of the enactment of this subsection) of which a DISC is a member.

Subpart F—Controlled Foreign Corporations

[Sec. 951]

SEC. 951. AMOUNTS INCLUDED IN GROSS INCOME OF UNITED STATES SHAREHOLDERS.

[Sec. 951(a)]

(a) AMOUNTS INCLUDED.—

(1) IN GENERAL.—If a foreign corporation is a controlled foreign corporation for an uninterrupted period of 30 days or more during any taxable year, every person who is a United States shareholder (as defined in subsection (b)) of such corporation and who owns (within the meaning of section 958(a)) stock in such corporation on the last day, in such year, on which such corporation is a controlled foreign corporation shall include in his gross income, for his taxable year in which or with which such taxable year of the corporation ends—

(A) the sum of—

(i) his pro rata share (determined under paragraph (2)) of the corporation's subpart F income for such year,

(ii) his pro rata share (determined under section 955(a)(3) as in effect before the enactment of the Tax Reduction Act of 1975) of the corporation's previously excluded subpart F income withdrawn from investment in less developed countries for such year, and

(iii) his pro rata share (determined under section 955(a)(3)) of the corporation's previously excluded subpart F income withdrawn from foreign base company shipping operations for such year; and

(B) the amount determined under section 956 with respect to such shareholder for such year (but only to the extent not excluded from gross income under section 959(a)(2)).

(2) PRO RATA SHARE OF SUBPART F INCOME.—The pro rata share referred to in paragraph (1)(A)(i) in the case of any United States shareholder is the amount—

(A) which would have been distributed with respect to the stock which such shareholder owns (within the meaning of section 958(a)) in such corporation if on the last day, in its taxable year, on which the corporation is a controlled foreign corporation it had distributed pro rata to its shareholders an amount (i) which bears the same ratio to its subpart F income for the taxable year, as (ii) the part of such year during which the corporation is a controlled foreign corporation bears to the entire year, reduced by

(B) the amount of distributions received by any other person during such year as a dividend with respect to such stock, but only to the extent of the dividend which would have been received if the distribution by the corporation had been the amount (i) which bears the same ratio to the subpart F income of such corporation for the taxable year, as (ii) the part of such year during which such shareholder did not own (within the meaning of section 958(a)) such stock bears to the entire year. For purposes of subparagraph (B), any gain included in the gross income of any person as a dividend under section 1248 shall be treated as a distribution received by such person with respect to the stock involved.

(3) LIMITATION ON PRO RATA SHARE OF PREVIOUSLY EXCLUDED SUBPART F INCOME WITHDRAWN FROM INVESTMENT.—For purposes of paragraph (1)(A)(iii), the pro rata share of any United States shareholder of the previously excluded subpart F income of a controlled foreign corporation withdrawn from investment in foreign base company shipping operations shall not exceed an amount—

(A) which bears the same ratio to his pro rata share of such income withdrawn (as determined under section 955(a)(3)) for the taxable year, as

(B) the part of such year during which the corporation is a controlled foreign corporation bears to the entire year.

[Sec. 951(b)]

(b) UNITED STATES SHAREHOLDER DEFINED.—For purposes of this subpart, the term "United States shareholder" means, with respect to any foreign corporation, a United States person (as defined in section 957(c)) who owns (within the meaning of section 958(a)), or is considered as owning by applying the rules of ownership of section 958(b), 10 percent or more of the total combined voting power of all classes of stock entitled to vote of such foreign corporation.

[Sec. 951(c)]

(c) FOREIGN TRADE INCOME NOT TAKEN INTO ACCOUNT.—

(1) IN GENERAL.—The foreign trade income of a FSC and any deductions which are apportioned or allocated to such income shall not be taken into account under this subpart.

(2) FOREIGN TRADE INCOME.—For purposes of this subsection, the term "foreign trade income" has the meaning given such term by section 923(b), but does not include section 923(a)(2) non-exempt income (within the meaning of section 927(d)(6)).

[Sec. 951(d)]

(d) COORDINATION WITH PASSIVE FOREIGN INVESTMENT COMPANY PROVISIONS.—If, but for this subsection, an amount would be included in the gross income of a United States shareholder for any taxable year both under subsection (a)(1)(A)(i) and under section 1293 (relating to current taxation of income from certain passive foreign investment companies), such amount shall be included in the gross income of such shareholder only under subsection (a)(1)(A).

[Sec. 952]

SEC. 952. SUBPART F INCOME DEFINED.

[Sec. 952(a)]

(a) IN GENERAL.—For purposes of this subpart, the term "subpart F income" means, in the case of any controlled foreign corporation, the sum of—

(1) insurance income (as defined under section 953),

(2) the foreign base company income (as determined under section 954),

(3) an amount equal to the product of—

(A) the income of such corporation other than income which—

(i) is attributable to earnings and profits of the foreign corporation included in the gross income of a United States person under section 951 (other than by reason of this paragraph), or

(ii) is described in subsection (b),

multiplied by

(B) the international boycott factor (as determined under section 999),

(4) the sum of the amounts of any illegal bribes, kickbacks, or other payments (within the meaning of section 162(c)) paid by or on behalf of the corporation during the taxable year of the corporation directly or indirectly to an official, employee, or agent in fact of a government, and

(5) the income of such corporation derived from any foreign country during any period during which section 901(j) applies to such foreign country.

The payments referred to in paragraph (4) are payments which would be unlawful under the Foreign Corrupt Practices Act of 1977 if the payor were a United States person. For purposes of paragraph (5), the income described therein shall be reduced, under regulations prescribed by the Secretary, so as to take into account deductions (including taxes) properly allocable to such income.

[Sec. 952(b)]

(b) EXCLUSION OF UNITED STATES INCOME.—In the case of a controlled foreign corporation, subpart F income does not include any item of income from sources within the United States which is effectively connected with the conduct by such corporation of a trade or business within the United States unless such item is exempt from taxation (or is subject to a reduced rate of tax) pursuant to a treaty obligation of the United States. For purposes of the preceding sentence, income described in paragraph (2) or (3) of section 921(d) shall be treated as derived from sources within the United States. For purposes of this subsection, any exemption (or reduction) with respect to the tax imposed by section 884 shall not be taken into account.

[Sec. 952(c)]

(c) LIMITATION.—

(1) IN GENERAL.—

(A) SUBPART F INCOME LIMITED TO CURRENT EARNINGS AND PROFITS.—For purposes of subsection (a), the subpart F income of any controlled foreign corporation for any taxable year shall not exceed the earnings and profits of such corporation for such taxable year.

(B) CERTAIN PRIOR YEAR DEFICITS MAY BE TAKEN INTO ACCOUNT.—

(i) IN GENERAL.—The amount included in the gross income of any United States shareholder under section 951(a)(1)(A)(i) for any taxable year and attributable to a qualified activity shall be reduced by the amount of such shareholder's pro rata share of any qualified deficit.

(ii) QUALIFIED DEFICIT.—The term "qualified deficit" means any deficit in earnings and profits of the controlled foreign corporation for any prior taxable year which began after December 31, 1986, and for which the controlled foreign corporation was a controlled foreign corporation; but only to the extent such deficit—

(I) is attributable to the same qualified activity as the activity giving rise to the income being offset, and

(II) has not previously been taken into account under this subparagraph.

In determining the deficit attributable to qualified activities described in clause (iii)(III) or (IV), deficits in earnings and profits (to the extent not previously taken into account under this section) for taxable years beginning after 1962 and before 1987 also shall be taken into account. In the case of the qualified activity described in clause (iii)(II), the rule of the preceding sentence shall apply, except that "1982" shall be substituted for "1962".

(iii) QUALIFIED ACTIVITY.—For purposes of this paragraph, the term "qualified activity" means any activity giving rise to—

Income Tax—Controlled Foreign Corporations

(I) foreign base company oil related income,

(II) foreign base company sales income,

(III) foreign base company services income,

(IV) in the case of a qualified insurance company, insurance income or foreign personal holding company income, or

(V) in the case of a qualified financial institution, foreign personal holding company income.

(iv) PRO RATA SHARE.—For purposes of this paragraph, the shareholder's pro rata share of any deficit for any prior taxable year shall be determined under rules similar to rules under section 951(a)(2) for whichever of the following yields the smaller share:

(I) the close of the taxable year, or

(II) the close of the taxable year in which the deficit arose.

(v) QUALIFIED INSURANCE COMPANY.—For purposes of this subparagraph, the term "qualified insurance company" means any controlled foreign corporation predominantly engaged in the active conduct of an insurance business in the taxable year and in the prior taxable years in which the deficit arose.

(vi) QUALIFIED FINANCIAL INSTITUTION.—For purposes of this paragraph, the term "qualified financial institution" means any controlled foreign corporation predominantly engaged in the active conduct of a banking, financing, or similar business in the taxable year and in the prior taxable year in which the deficit arose.

(vii) SPECIAL RULES FOR INSURANCE INCOME.—

(I) IN GENERAL.—An election may be made under this clause to have section 953(a) applied for purposes of this title without regard to the same country exception under paragraph (1)(A) thereof. Such election, once made, may be revoked only with the consent of the Secretary.

(II) SPECIAL RULES FOR AFFILIATED GROUPS.—In the case of an affiliated group of corporations (within the meaning of section 1504 but without regard to section 1504(b)(3) and by substituting "more than 50 percent" for "at least 80 percent" each place it appears), no election may be made under subclause (I) for any controlled foreign corporation unless such election is made for all other controlled foreign corporations who are members of such group and who were created or organized under the laws of the same country as such controlled foreign corporation. For purposes of clause (v), in determining whether any controlled corporation described in the preceding sentence is a qualified insurance company, all such corporations shall be treated as 1 corporation.

(C) CERTAIN DEFICITS OF MEMBER OF THE SAME CHAIN OF CORPORATIONS MAY BE TAKEN INTO ACCOUNT.—

(i) IN GENERAL.—A controlled foreign corporation may elect to reduce the amount of its subpart F income for any taxable year which is attributable to any qualified activity by the amount of any deficit in earnings and profits of a qualified chain member for a taxable year ending with (or within) the taxable year of such controlled foreign corporation to the extent such deficit is attributable to such activity. To the extent any deficit reduces subpart F income under the preceding sentence, such deficit shall not be taken into account under subparagraph (B).

(ii) QUALIFIED CHAIN MEMBER.—For purposes of this subparagraph, the term "qualified chain member" means, with respect to any controlled foreign corporation, any other corporation which is created or organized under the laws of the same foreign country as the controlled foreign corporation but only if—

(I) all the stock of such other corporation (other than directors' qualifying shares) is owned at all times during the taxable year in which the deficit arose (directly or through 1 or more corporations other than the common parent) by such controlled foreign corporation, or

(II) all the stock of such controlled foreign corporation (other than directors' qualifying shares) is owned at all times during the taxable year in which the deficit arose (directly or through 1 or more corporations other than the common parent) by such other corporation.

(iii) COORDINATION.—This subparagraph shall be applied after subparagraphs (A) and (B).

(2) RECHARACTERIZATION IN SUBSEQUENT TAXABLE YEARS.—If the subpart F income of any controlled foreign corporation for any taxable year was reduced by reason of paragraph (1)(A), any excess of the earnings and profits of such corporation for any subsequent taxable year over the subpart F income of such foreign corporation for such taxable year shall be recharacterized as subpart F income under rules similar to the rules applicable under section 904(f)(5).

(3) SPECIAL RULE FOR DETERMINING EARNINGS AND PROFITS.—For purposes of this subsection, earnings and profits of any controlled foreign corporation shall be determined without regard to paragraphs (4), (5), and (6) of section 312(n). Under regulations, the preceding sentence shall not apply to the extent it would increase earnings and profits by an amount which was previously distributed by the controlled foreign corporation.

[Sec. 953]

SEC. 953. INSURANCE INCOME.

[Sec. 953(a)]

(a) INSURANCE INCOME.—

(1) IN GENERAL.—For purposes of section 952(a)(1), the term "insurance income" means any income which—

(A) is attributable to the issuing (or reinsuring) of an insurance or annuity contract, and

(B) would (subject to the modifications provided by subsection (b)) be taxed under subchapter L of this chapter if such income were the income of a domestic insurance company.

(2) EXCEPTION.—Such term shall not include any exempt insurance income (as defined in subsection (e)).

[Sec. 953(b)]

(b) SPECIAL RULES.—For purposes of subsection (a)—

(1) The following provisions of subchapter L shall not apply:

(A) The small life insurance company deduction.

(B) Section 805(a)(5) (relating to operations loss deduction).

(C) Section 832(c)(5) (relating to certain capital losses).

(2) The items referred to in—

(A) section 803(a)(1) (relating to gross amount of premiums and other considerations),

(B) section 803(a)(2) (relating to net decrease in reserves),

(C) section 805(a)(2) (relating to net increase [in] reserves), and

(D) section 832(b)(4) (relating to premiums earned on insurance contracts),

shall be taken into account only to the extent they are in respect of any reinsurance or the issuing of any insurance or annuity contract described in subsection (a)(1).

(3) Reserves for any insurance or annuity contract shall be determined in the same manner as under section 954(i).

(4) All items of income, expenses, losses, and deductions shall be properly allocated or apportioned under regulations prescribed by the Secretary.

Income Tax—Controlled Foreign Corporations

[Sec. 953(c)]

(c) SPECIAL RULE FOR CERTAIN CAPTIVE INSURANCE COMPANIES.—

(1) IN GENERAL.—For purposes only of taking into account related person insurance income—

(A) the term "United States shareholder" means, with respect to any foreign corporation, a United States person (as defined in section 957(c)) who owns (within the meaning of section 958(a)) any stock of the foreign corporation,

(B) the term "controlled foreign corporation" has the meaning given to such term by section 957(a) determined by substituting "25 percent or more" for "more than 50 percent", and

(C) the pro rata share referred to in section 951(a)(1)(A)(i) shall be determined under paragraph (5) of this subsection.

(2) RELATED PERSON INSURANCE INCOME.—For purposes of this subsection, the term "related person insurance income" means any insurance income (within the meaning of subsection (a)) attributable to a policy of insurance or reinsurance with respect to which the person (directly or indirectly) insured is a United States shareholder in the foreign corporation or a related person to such a shareholder.

(3) EXCEPTIONS.—

(A) CORPORATIONS NOT HELD BY INSUREDS.—Paragraph (1) shall not apply to any foreign corporation if at all times during the taxable year of such foreign corporation—

(i) less than 20 percent of the total combined voting power of all classes of stock of such corporation entitled to vote, and

(ii) less than 20 percent of the total value of such corporation,

is owned (directly or indirectly under the principles of section 883(c)(4)) by persons who are (directly or indirectly) insured under any policy of insurance or reinsurance issued by such corporation or who are related persons to any such person.

(B) DE MINIMIS EXCEPTION.—Paragraph (1) shall not apply to any foreign corporation for a taxable year of such corporation if the related person insurance income (determined on a gross basis) of such corporation for such taxable year is less than 20 percent of its insurance income (as so determined) for such taxable year determined without regard to those provisions of subsection (a)(1) which limit insurance income to income from countries other than the country in which the corporation was created or organized.

(C) ELECTION TO TREAT INCOME AS EFFECTIVELY CONNECTED.—Paragraph (1) shall not apply to any foreign corporation for any taxable year if—

(i) such corporation elects (at such time and in such manner as the Secretary may prescribe)—

(I) to treat its related person insurance income for such taxable year as income effectively connected with the conduct of a trade or business in the United States, and

(II) to waive all benefits (other than with respect to section 884) with respect to related person insurance income granted by the United States under any treaty between the United States and any foreign country, and

(ii) such corporation meets such requirements as the Secretary shall prescribe to ensure that the tax imposed by this chapter on such income is paid.

An election under this subparagraph made for any taxable year shall not be effective if the corporation (or any predecessor thereof) was a disqualified corporation for the taxable year for which the election was made or for any prior taxable year beginning after 1986.

(D) SPECIAL RULES FOR SUBPARAGRAPH (C).—

(i) PERIOD DURING WHICH ELECTION IN EFFECT.—

(I) IN GENERAL.—Except as provided in subclause (II), any election under subparagraph (C) shall apply to the taxable year for which made and all subsequent taxable years unless revoked with the consent of the Secretary.

(II) TERMINATION.—If a foreign corporation which made an election under subparagraph (C) for any taxable year is a disqualified corporation for any subsequent taxable year, such election shall not apply to any taxable year beginning after such subsequent taxable year.

(ii) EXEMPTION FROM TAX IMPOSED BY SECTION 4371.—The tax imposed by section 4371 shall not apply with respect to any related person insurance income treated as effectively connected with the conduct of a trade or business within the United States under subparagraph (C).

(E) DISQUALIFIED CORPORATION.—For purposes of this paragraph the term "disqualified corporation" means, with respect to any taxable year, any foreign corporation which is a controlled foreign corporation for an uninterrupted period of 30 days or more during such taxable year (determined without regard to this subsection) but only if a United States shareholder (determined without regard to this subsection) owns (within the meaning of section 958(a)) stock in such corporation at some time during such taxable year.

(4) TREATMENT OF MUTUAL INSURANCE COMPANIES.—In the case of a mutual insurance company—

(A) this subsection shall apply,

(B) policyholders of such company shall be treated as shareholders, and

(C) appropriate adjustments in the application of this subpart shall be made under regulations prescribed by the Secretary.

(5) DETERMINATION OF PRO RATA SHARE.—

(A) IN GENERAL.—The pro rata share determined under this paragraph for any United States shareholder is the lesser of—

(i) the amount which would be determined under paragraph (2) of section 951(a) if—

(I) only related person insurance income were taken into account,

(II) stock owned (within the meaning of section 958(a)) by United States shareholders on the last day of the taxable year were the only stock in the foreign corporation, and

(III) only distributions received by United States shareholders were taken into account under subparagraph (B) of such paragraph (2), or

(ii) the amount which would be determined under paragraph (2) of section 951(a) if the entire earnings and profits of the foreign corporation for the taxable year were subpart F income.

(B) COORDINATION WITH OTHER PROVISIONS.—The Secretary shall prescribe regulations providing for such modifications to the provisions of this subpart as may be necessary or appropriate by reason of subparagraph (A).

(6) RELATED PERSON.—For purposes of this subsection—

(A) IN GENERAL.—Except as provided in subparagraph (B), the term "related person" has the meaning given such term by section 954(d)(3).

(B) TREATMENT OF CERTAIN LIABILITY INSURANCE POLICIES.—In the case of any policy of insurance covering liability arising from services performed as a director, officer, or employee of a corporation or as a partner or employee of a partnership, the person performing such services and the entity for which such services are performed shall be treated as related persons.

(7) COORDINATION WITH SECTION 1248.—For purposes of section 1248, if any person is (or would be but for paragraph (3)) treated under paragraph (1) as a United States shareholder with respect to any foreign corporation which would be taxed under subchapter L if it were a domestic corporation and which is (or would be but for paragraph (3)) treated under paragraph (1) as a controlled foreign corporation—

(A) such person shall be treated as meeting the stock ownership requirements of section 1248(a)(2) with respect to such foreign corporation, and

(B) such foreign corporation shall be treated as a controlled foreign corporation.

(8) REGULATIONS.—The Secretary shall prescribe such regulations as may be necessary to carry out the purposes of this subsection, including—

(A) regulations preventing the avoidance of this subsection through cross insurance arrangements or otherwise, and

(B) regulations which may provide that a person will not be treated as a United States shareholder under paragraph (1) with respect to any foreign corporation if neither such person (nor any related person to such person) is (directly or indirectly) insured under any policy of insurance or reinsurance issued by such foreign corporation.

[Sec. 953(d)]

(d) ELECTION BY FOREIGN INSURANCE COMPANY TO BE TREATED AS DOMESTIC CORPORATION.—

(1) IN GENERAL.—If—

(A) a foreign corporation is a controlled foreign corporation (as defined in section 957(a) by substituting "25 percent or more" for "more than 50 percent" and by using the definition of United States shareholder under 953(c)(1)(A)),

(B) such foreign corporation would qualify under part I or II of subchapter L for the taxable year if it were a domestic corporation,

(C) such foreign corporation meets such requirements as the Secretary shall prescribe to ensure that the taxes imposed by this chapter on such foreign corporation are paid, and

(D) such foreign corporation makes an election to have this paragraph apply and waives all benefits to such corporation granted by the United States under any treaty,

for purposes of this title, such corporation shall be treated as a domestic corporation.

(2) PERIOD DURING WHICH ELECTION IS IN EFFECT.—

(A) IN GENERAL.—Except as provided in subparagraph (B), an election under paragraph (1) shall apply to the taxable year for which made and all subsequent taxable years unless revoked with the consent of the Secretary.

(B) TERMINATION.—If a corporation which made an election under paragraph (1) for any taxable year fails to meet the requirements of subparagraphs (A), (B), and (C), of paragraph (1) for any subsequent taxable year, such election shall not apply to any taxable year beginning after such subsequent taxable year.

(3) TREATMENT OF LOSSES.—If any corporation treated as a domestic corporation under this subsection is treated as a member of an affiliated group for purposes of chapter 6 (relating to consolidated returns), any loss of such corporation shall be treated as a dual consolidated loss for purposes of section 1503(d) without regard to paragraph (2)(B) thereof.

(4) EFFECT OF ELECTION.—

(A) IN GENERAL.—For purposes of section 367, any foreign corporation making an election under paragraph (1) shall be treated as transferring (as of the 1st day of the 1st taxable year to which such election applies) all of its assets to a domestic corporation in connection with an exchange to which section 354 applies.

(B) EXCEPTION FOR PRE-1988 EARNINGS AND PROFIT.—

(i) IN GENERAL.—Earnings and profits of the foreign corporation accumulated in taxable years beginning before January 1, 1988, shall not be included in the gross income of the persons holding stock in such corporation by reason of subparagraph (A).

(ii) TREATMENT OF DISTRIBUTIONS.—For purposes of this title, any distribution made by a corporation to which an election under paragraph (1) applies out of earnings and profits accumulated in taxable years beginning before January 1, 1988, shall be treated as a distribution made by a foreign corporation.

(iii) CERTAIN RULES TO CONTINUE TO APPLY TO PRE-1988 EARNINGS.—The provisions specified in clause (iv) shall be applied without regard to paragraph (1), except that, in the case of a corporation to which an election under paragraph (1) applies, only earnings and profits accumulated in taxable years beginning before January 1, 1988, shall be taken into account.

    (iv) SPECIFIED PROVISIONS.—The provisions specified in this clause are:

     (I) Section 1248 (relating to gain from certain sales or exchanges of stock in certain foreign corporations).

     (II) Subpart F of part III of subchapter N to the extent such subpart relates to earnings invested in United States property or amounts referred to in clause (ii) or (iii) of section 951(a)(1)(A).

     (III) Section 884 to the extent the foreign corporation reinvested 1987 earnings and profits in United States assets.

  (5) EFFECT OF TERMINATION.—For purposes of section 367, if—

   (A) an election is made by a corporation under paragraph (1) for any taxable year, and

   (B) such election ceases to apply for any subsequent taxable year,

such corporation shall be treated as a domestic corporation transferring (as of the 1st day of such subsequent taxable year) all of its property to a foreign corporation in connection with an exchange to which section 354 applies.

  (6) ADDITIONAL TAX ON CORPORATION MAKING ELECTION.—

   (A) IN GENERAL.—If a corporation makes an election under paragraph (1), the amount of tax imposed by this chapter for the 1st taxable year to which such election applies shall be increased by the amount determined under subparagraph (B).

   (B) AMOUNT OF TAX.—The amount of tax determined under this paragraph shall be equal to the lesser of—

    (i) ¾ of 1 percent of the aggregate amount of capital and accumulated surplus of the corporation as of December 31, 1987, or

    (ii) $1,500,000.

[Sec. 953(e)]

(e) EXEMPT INSURANCE INCOME.—For purposes of this section—

 (1) EXEMPT INSURANCE INCOME DEFINED.—

  (A) IN GENERAL.—The term "exempt insurance income" means income derived by a qualifying insurance company which—

   (i) is attributable to the issuing (or reinsuring) of an exempt contract by such company or a qualifying insurance company branch of such company, and

   (ii) is treated as earned by such company or branch in its home country for purposes of such country's tax laws.

  (B) EXCEPTION FOR CERTAIN ARRANGEMENTS.—Such term shall not include income attributable to the issuing (or reinsuring) of an exempt contract as the result of any arrangement whereby another corporation receives a substantially equal amount of premiums or other consideration in respect of issuing (or reinsuring) a contract which is not an exempt contract.

  (C) DETERMINATIONS MADE SEPARATELY.—For purposes of this subsection and section 954(i), the exempt insurance income and exempt contracts of a qualifying insurance company or any qualifying insurance company branch of such company shall be determined separately for such company and each such branch by taking into account—

   (i) in the case of the qualifying insurance company, only items of income, deduction, gain, or loss, and activities of such company not properly allocable or attributable to any qualifying insurance company branch of such company, and

   (ii) in the case of a qualifying insurance company branch, only items of income, deduction, gain, or loss and activities properly allocable or attributable to such branch.

(2) EXEMPT CONTRACT.—

(A) IN GENERAL.—The term "exempt contract" means an insurance or annuity contract issued or reinsured by a qualifying insurance company or qualifying insurance company branch in connection with property in, liability arising out of activity in, or the lives or health of residents of, a country other than the United States.

(B) MINIMUM HOME COUNTRY INCOME REQUIRED.—

(i) IN GENERAL.—No contract of a qualifying insurance company or of a qualifying insurance company branch shall be treated as an exempt contract unless such company or branch derives more than 30 percent of its net written premiums from exempt contracts (determined without regard to this subparagraph)—

(I) which cover applicable home country risks, and

(II) with respect to which no policyholder, insured, annuitant, or beneficiary is a related person (as defined in section 954(d)(3)).

(ii) APPLICABLE HOME COUNTRY RISKS.—The term "applicable home country risks" means risks in connection with property in, liability arising out of activity in, or the lives or health of residents of, the home country of the qualifying insurance company or qualifying insurance company branch, as the case may be, issuing or reinsuring the contract covering the risks.

(C) SUBSTANTIAL ACTIVITY REQUIREMENTS FOR CROSS BORDER RISKS.—A contract issued by a qualifying insurance company or qualifying insurance company branch which covers risks other than applicable home country risks (as defined in subparagraph (B)(ii)) shall not be treated as an exempt contract unless such company or branch, as the case may be—

(i) conducts substantial activity with respect to an insurance business in its home country, and

(ii) performs in its home country substantially all of the activities necessary to give rise to the income generated by such contract.

(3) QUALIFYING INSURANCE COMPANY.—The term "qualifying insurance company" means any controlled foreign corporation which—

(A) is subject to regulation as an insurance (or reinsurance) company by its home country, and is licensed, authorized, or regulated by the applicable insurance regulatory body for its home country to sell insurance, reinsurance, or annuity contracts to persons other than related persons (within the meaning of section 954(d)(3)) in such home country,

(B) derives more than 50 percent of its aggregate net written premiums from the issuance or reinsurance by such controlled foreign corporation and each of its qualifying insurance company branches of contracts—

(i) covering applicable home country risks (as defined in paragraph (2)) of such corporation or branch, as the case may be, and

(ii) with respect to which no policyholder, insured, annuitant, or beneficiary is a related person (as defined in section 954(d)(3)),

except that in the case of a branch, such premiums shall only be taken into account to the extent such premiums are treated as earned by such branch in its home country for purposes of such country's tax laws, and

(C) is engaged in the insurance business and would be subject to tax under subchapter L if it were a domestic corporation.

(4) QUALIFYING INSURANCE COMPANY BRANCH.—The term "qualifying insurance company branch" means a qualified business unit (within the meaning of section 989(a)) of a controlled foreign corporation if—

(A) such unit is licensed, authorized, or regulated by the applicable insurance regulatory body for its home country to sell insurance, reinsurance, or annuity contracts to persons other than related persons (within the meaning of section 954(d)(3)) in such home country, and

(B) such controlled foreign corporation is a qualifying insurance company, determined under paragraph (3) as if such unit were a qualifying insurance company branch.

(5) LIFE INSURANCE OR ANNUITY CONTRACT.—For purposes of this section and section 954, the determination of whether a contract issued by a controlled foreign corporation or a qualified business unit (within the meaning of section 989(a)) is a life insurance contract or an annuity contract shall be made without regard to sections 72(s), 101(f), 817(h), and 7702 if—

(A) such contract is regulated as a life insurance or annuity contract by the corporation's or unit's home country, and

(B) no policyholder, insured, annuitant, or beneficiary with respect to the contract is a United States person.

(6) HOME COUNTRY.—For purposes of this subsection, except as provided in regulations—

(A) CONTROLLED FOREIGN CORPORATION.—The term "home country" means, with respect to a controlled foreign corporation, the country in which such corporation is created or organized.

(B) QUALIFIED BUSINESS UNIT.—The term "home country" means, with respect to a qualified business unit (as defined in section 989(a)), the country in which the principal office of such unit is located and in which such unit is licensed, authorized, or regulated by the applicable insurance regulatory body to sell insurance, reinsurance, or annuity contracts to persons other than related persons (as defined in section 954(d)(3)) in such country.

(7) ANTI-ABUSE RULES.—For purposes of applying this subsection and section 954(i)—

(A) the rules of section 954(h)(7) (other than subparagraph (B) thereof) shall apply,

(B) there shall be disregarded any item of income, gain, loss, or deduction of, or derived from, an entity which is not engaged in regular and continuous transactions with persons which are not related persons,

(C) there shall be disregarded any change in the method of computing reserves a principal purpose of which is the acceleration or deferral of any item in order to claim the benefits of this subsection or section 954(i),

(D) a contract of insurance or reinsurance shall not be treated as an exempt contract (and premiums from such contract shall not be taken into account for purposes of paragraph (2)(B) or (3)) if—

(i) any policyholder, insured, annuitant, or beneficiary is a resident of the United States and such contract was marketed to such resident and was written to cover a risk outside the United States, or

(ii) the contract covers risks located within and without the United States and the qualifying insurance company or qualifying insurance company branch does not maintain such contemporaneous records, and file such reports, with respect to such contract as the Secretary may require,

(E) the Secretary may prescribe rules for the allocation of contracts (and income from contracts) among 2 or more qualifying insurance company branches of a qualifying insurance company in order to clearly reflect the income of such branches, and

(F) premiums from a contract shall not be taken into account for purposes of paragraph (2)(B) or (3) if such contract reinsures a contract issued or reinsured by a related person (as defined in section 954(d)(3)).

For purposes of subparagraph (D), the determination of where risks are located shall be made under the principles of section 953.

(8) COORDINATION WITH SUBSECTION (C).—In determining insurance income for purposes of subsection (c), exempt insurance income shall not include income derived from exempt contracts which cover risks other than applicable home country risks.

(9) REGULATIONS.—The Secretary shall prescribe such regulations as may be necessary or appropriate to carry out the purposes of this subsection and section 954(i).

(10) APPLICATION.—This subsection and section 954(i) shall apply only to taxable years of a foreign corporation beginning after December 31, 1998, and before January 1, 2007, and to taxable years of United States shareholders with or within which any such taxable year of such foreign corporation ends. If this subsection does not apply to a taxable year of a foreign

corporation beginning after December 31, 2006 (and taxable years of United States shareholders ending with or within such taxable year), then, notwithstanding the preceding sentence, subsection (a) shall be applied to such taxable years in the same manner as it would if the taxable year of the foreign corporation began in 1998.

(11) CROSS REFERENCE.—For income exempt from foreign personal holding company income, see section 954(i).

[Sec. 954]

SEC. 954. FOREIGN BASE COMPANY INCOME.

[Sec. 954(a)]

(a) FOREIGN BASE COMPANY INCOME.—For purposes of section 952(a)(2), the term "foreign base company income" means for any taxable year the sum of—

(1) the foreign personal holding company income for the taxable year (determined under subsection (c) and reduced as provided in subsection (b)(5)),

(2) the foreign base company sales income for the taxable year (determined under subsection (d) and reduced as provided in subsection (b)(5)),

(3) the foreign base company services income for the taxable year (determined under subsection (e) and reduced as provided in subsection (b)(5)),

(4) [Stricken.]

(5) the foreign base company oil related income for the taxable year (determined under subsection (g) and reduced as provided in subsection (b)(5)).

[Sec. 954(b)]

(b) EXCLUSIONS AND SPECIAL RULES.—

(1) [Repealed]

(2) [Repealed]

(3) DE MINIMIS, ETC., RULES.—For purposes of subsection (a) and section 953—

(A) DE MINIMIS RULE.—If the sum of foreign base company income (determined without regard to paragraph (5)) and the gross insurance income for the taxable year is less than the lesser of—

(i) 5 percent of gross income, or

(ii) $1,000,000,

no part of the gross income for the taxable year shall be treated as foreign base company income or insurance income.

(B) FOREIGN BASE COMPANY INCOME AND INSURANCE INCOME IN EXCESS OF 70 PERCENT OF GROSS INCOME.—If the sum of the foreign base company income (determined without regard to paragraph (5)) and the gross insurance income for the taxable year exceeds 70 percent of gross income, the entire gross income for the taxable year shall, subject to the provisions of paragraphs (4) and (5), be treated as foreign base company income or insurance income (whichever is appropriate).

(C) GROSS INSURANCE INCOME.—For purposes of subparagraphs (A) and (B), the term "gross insurance income" means any item of gross income taken into account in determining insurance income under section 953.

(4) EXCEPTION FOR CERTAIN INCOME SUBJECT TO HIGH FOREIGN TAXES.—For purposes of subsection (a) and section 953, foreign base company income and insurance income shall not include any item of income received by a controlled foreign corporation if the taxpayer establishes to the satisfaction of the Secretary that such income was subject to an effective rate of income tax imposed by a foreign country greater than 90 percent of the maximum rate of tax specified in section 11. The preceding sentence shall not apply to foreign base company oil-related income described in subsection (a)(5).

(5) DEDUCTIONS TO BE TAKEN INTO ACCOUNT.—For purposes of subsection (a), the foreign personal holding company income, the foreign base company sales income, the foreign base company services income, and the foreign base company oil related income shall be reduced,

under regulations prescribed by the Secretary, so as to take into account deductions (including taxes) properly allocable to such income. Except to the extent provided in regulations prescribed by the Secretary, any interest which is paid or accrued by the controlled foreign corporation to any United States shareholder in such corporation (or any controlled foreign corporation related to such a shareholder) shall be allocated first to foreign personal holding company income which is passive income (within the meaning of section 904(d)(2)) of such corporation to the extent thereof. The Secretary may, by regulations, provide that the preceding sentence shall apply also to interest paid or accrued to other persons.

(6) FOREIGN BASE COMPANY OIL RELATED INCOME NOT TREATED AS ANOTHER KIND OF BASE COMPANY INCOME.—Income of a corporation which is foreign base company oil related income shall not be considered foreign base company income of such corporation under paragraph (2), or (3) of subsection (a).

[Sec. 954(c)]

(c) FOREIGN PERSONAL HOLDING COMPANY INCOME.—

(1) IN GENERAL.—For purposes of subsection (a)(1), the term "foreign personal holding company income" means the portion of the gross income which consists of:

(A) DIVIDENDS, ETC.—Dividends, interest, royalties, rents, and annuities.

(B) CERTAIN PROPERTY TRANSACTIONS.—The excess of gains over losses from the sale or exchange of property—

(i) which gives rise to income described in subparagraph (A) (after application of paragraph (2)(A)) other than property which gives rise to income not treated as foreign personal holding company income by reason of subsection (h) or (i) for the taxable year,

(ii) which is an interest in a trust, partnership, or REMIC, or

(iii) which does not give rise to any income.

Gains and losses from the sale or exchange of any property which, in the hands of the controlled foreign corporation, is properly described in section 1221(a)(1) shall not be taken into account under this subparagraph.

(C) COMMODITIES TRANSACTIONS.—The excess of gains over losses from transactions (including futures, forward, and similar transactions) in any commodities. This subparagraph shall not apply to gains or losses which—

(i) arise out of commodity hedging transactions (as defined in paragraph (4)(A)) [(5)(A)],

(ii) are active business gains or losses from the sale of commodities, but only if substantially all of the controlled foreign corporation's commodities are property described in paragraph (1), (2), or (8) of section 1221(a), or

(iii) are foreign currency gains or losses (as defined in section 988(b)) attributable to any section 988 transactions.

(D) FOREIGN CURRENCY GAINS.—The excess of foreign currency gains over foreign currency losses (as defined in section 988(b)) attributable to any section 988 transactions. This subparagraph shall not apply in the case of any transaction directly related to the business needs of the controlled foreign corporation.

(E) INCOME EQUIVALENT TO INTEREST.—Any income equivalent to interest, including income from commitment fees (or similar amounts) for loans actually made.

(F) INCOME FROM NOTIONAL PRINCIPAL CONTRACTS.—Net income from notional principal contracts. Any item of income, gain, deduction, or loss from a notional principal contract entered into for purposes of hedging any item described in any preceding subparagraph shall not be taken into account for purposes of this subparagraph but shall be taken into account under such other subparagraph.

(G) PAYMENTS IN LIEU OF DIVIDENDS.—Payments in lieu of dividends which are made pursuant to an agreement to which section 1058 applies.

(I) [(H)] PERSONAL SERVICE CONTRACTS.—

(i) Amounts received under a contract under which the corporation is to furnish personal services if—

(I) some person other than the corporation has the right to designate (by name or by description) the individual who is to perform the services, or

(II) the individual who is to perform the services is designated (by name or by description) in the contract, and

(ii) amounts received from the sale or other disposition of such a contract.

This subparagraph shall apply with respect to amounts received for services under a particular contract only if at some time during the taxable year 25 percent or more in value of the outstanding stock of the corporation is owned, directly or indirectly, by or for the individual who has performed, is to perform, or may be designated (by name or by description) as the one to perform, such services.

(2) EXCEPTION FOR CERTAIN AMOUNTS.—

(A) RENTS AND ROYALTIES DERIVED IN ACTIVE BUSINESS.—Foreign personal holding company income shall not include rents and royalties which are derived in the active conduct of a trade or business and which are received from a person other than a related person (within the meaning of subsection (d)(3)). For purposes of the preceding sentence, rents derived from leasing an aircraft or vessel in foreign commerce shall not fail to be treated as derived in the active conduct of a trade or business if, as determined under regulations prescribed by the Secretary, the active leasing expenses are not less than 10 percent of the profit on the lease.

(B) CERTAIN EXPORT FINANCING.—Foreign personal holding company income shall not include any interest which is derived in the conduct of a banking business and which is export financing interest (as defined in section 904(d)(2)(G)).

(C) EXCEPTION FOR DEALERS.—Except as provided by regulations, in the case of a regular dealer in property which is property described in paragraph (1)(B), forward contracts, option contracts, or similar financial instruments (including notional principal contracts and all instruments referenced to commodities), there shall not be taken into account in computing foreign personal holding company income—

(i) any item of income, gain, deduction, or loss (other than any item described in subparagraph (A), (E), or (G) of paragraph (1)) from any transaction (including hedging transactions and transactions involving physical settlement) entered into in the ordinary course of such dealer's trade or business as such a dealer, and

(ii) if such dealer is a dealer in securities (within the meaning of section 475), any interest or dividend or equivalent amount described in subparagraph (E) or (G) of paragraph (1) from any transaction (including any hedging transaction or transaction described in section 956(c)(2)(J)) entered into in the ordinary course of such dealer's trade or business as such a dealer in securities, but only if the income from the transaction is attributable to activities of the dealer in the country under the laws of which the dealer is created or organized (or in the case of a qualified business unit described in section 989(a), is attributable to activities of the unit in the country in which the unit both maintains its principal office and conducts substantial business activity).

(3) CERTAIN INCOME RECEIVED FROM RELATED PERSONS.—

(A) IN GENERAL.—Except as provided in subparagraph (B), the term "foreign personal holding company income" does not include—

(i) dividends and interest received from a related person which (I) is a corporation created or organized under the laws of the same foreign country under the laws of which the controlled foreign corporation is created or organized, and (II) has a substantial part of its assets used in its trade or business located in such same foreign country, and

(ii) rents and royalties received from a corporation which is a related person for the use of, or the privilege of using, property within the country under the laws of which the controlled foreign corporation is created or organized.

To the extent provided in regulations, payments made by a partnership with 1 or more corporate partners shall be treated as made by such corporate partners in proportion to their respective interests in the partnership.

(B) EXCEPTION NOT TO APPLY TO ITEMS WHICH REDUCE SUBPART F INCOME.—Subparagraph (A) shall not apply in the case of any interest, rent, or royalty to the extent such interest, rent, or royalty reduces the payor's subpart F income or creates (or increases) a deficit which under section 952(c) may reduce the subpart F income of the payor or another controlled foreign corporation.

(C) EXCEPTION FOR CERTAIN DIVIDENDS.—Subparagraph (A)(i) shall not apply to any dividend with respect to any stock which is attributable to earnings and profits of the distributing corporation accumulated during any period during which the person receiving such dividend did not hold such stock either directly, or indirectly through a chain of one or more subsidiaries each of which meets the requirements of subparagraph (A)(i).

(4) LOOK-THRU RULE FOR CERTAIN PARTNERSHIP SALES.—

(A) IN GENERAL.—In the case of any sale by a controlled foreign corporation of an interest in a partnership with respect to which such corporation is a 25-percent owner, such corporation shall be treated for purposes of this subsection as selling the proportionate share of the assets of the partnership attributable to such interest. The Secretary shall prescribe such regulations as may be appropriate to prevent abuse of the purposes of this paragraph, including regulations providing for coordination of this paragraph with the provisions of subchapter K.

(B) 25-PERCENT OWNER.—For purposes of this paragraph, the term "25-percent owner" means a controlled foreign corporation which owns directly 25 percent or more of the capital or profits interest in a partnership. For purposes of the preceding sentence, if a controlled foreign corporation is a shareholder or partner of a corporation or partnership, the controlled foreign corporation shall be treated as owning directly its proportionate share of any such capital or profits interest held directly or indirectly by such corporation or partnership.

(5) DEFINITION AND SPECIAL RULES RELATING TO COMMODITY TRANSACTIONS.—

(A) COMMODITY HEDGING TRANSACTIONS.—For purposes of paragraph (1)(C)(i), the term "commodity hedging transaction" means any transaction with respect to a commodity if such transaction—

(i) is a hedging transaction as defined in section 1221(b)(2), determined—

(I) without regard to subparagraph (A)(ii) thereof,

(II) by applying subparagraph (A)(i) thereof by substituting "ordinary property or property described in section 1231(b)" for "ordinary property", and

(III) by substituting "controlled foreign corporation" for "taxpayer" each place it appears, and

(ii) is clearly identified as such in accordance with section 1221(a)(7).

(B) TREATMENT OF DEALER ACTIVITIES UNDER PARAGRAPH (1)(C).—Commodities with respect to which gains and losses are not taken into account under paragraph (2)(C) in computing a controlled foreign corporation's foreign personal holding company income shall not be taken into account in applying the substantially all test under paragraph (1)(C)(ii) to such corporation.

(C) REGULATIONS.—The Secretary shall prescribe such regulations as are appropriate to carry out the purposes of paragraph (1)(C) in the case of transactions involving related parties.

[Sec. 954(d)]

(d) FOREIGN BASE COMPANY SALES INCOME.—

(1) IN GENERAL.—For purposes of subsection (a)(2), the term "foreign base company sales income" means income (whether in the form of profits, commissions, fees, or otherwise) derived in connection with the purchase of personal property from a related person and its sale to any person, the sale of personal property to any person on behalf of a related

person, the purchase of personal property from any person and its sale to a related person, or the purchase of personal property from any person on behalf of a related person where—

　(A) the property which is purchased (or in the case of property sold on behalf of a related person, the property which is sold) is manufactured, produced, grown, or extracted outside the country under the laws of which the controlled foreign corporation is created or organized, and

　(B) the property is sold for use, consumption, or disposition outside such foreign country, or, in the case of property purchased on behalf of a related person, is purchased for use, consumption, or disposition outside such foreign country.

For purposes of this subsection, personal property does not include agricultural commodities which are not grown in the United States in commercially marketable quantities.

　(2) CERTAIN BRANCH INCOME.—For purposes of determining foreign base company sales income in situations in which the carrying on of activities by a controlled foreign corporation through a branch or similar establishment outside the country of incorporation of the controlled foreign corporation has substantially the same effect as if such branch or similar establishment were a wholly owned subsidiary corporation deriving such income, under regulations prescribed by the Secretary the income attributable to the carrying on of such activities of such branch or similar establishment shall be treated as income derived by a wholly owned subsidiary of the controlled foreign corporation and shall constitute foreign base company sales income of the controlled foreign corporation.

　(3) RELATED PERSON DEFINED.—For purposes of this section, a person is a related person with respect to a controlled foreign corporation, if—

　　(A) such person is an individual, corporation, partnership, trust, or estate which controls, or is controlled by, the controlled foreign corporation, or

　　(B) such person is a corporation, partnership, trust, or estate which is controlled by the same person or persons which control the controlled foreign corporation.

For purposes of the preceding sentence, control means, with respect to a corporation, the ownership, directly or indirectly, of stock possessing more than 50 percent of the total voting power of all classes of stock entitled to vote or of the total value of stock of such corporation. In the case of a partnership, trust, or estate, control means the ownership, directly or indirectly, more than 50 percent (by value) of the beneficial interests in such partnership, trust, or estate. For purposes of this paragraph, rules similar to the rules of section 958 shall apply.

　(4) SPECIAL RULE FOR CERTAIN TIMBER PRODUCTS.—For purposes of subsection (a)(2), the term "foreign base company sales income" includes any income (whether in the form of profits, commissions, fees, or otherwise) derived in connection with—

　　(A) the sale of any unprocessed timber referred to in section 865(b), or

　　(B) the milling of any such timber outside the United States.

Subpart G shall not apply to any amount treated as subpart F income by reason of this paragraph.

[Sec. 954(e)]

(e) FOREIGN BASE COMPANY SERVICES INCOME.—

　(1) IN GENERAL.—For purposes of subsection (a)(3), the term "foreign base company services income" means income (whether in the form of compensation, commissions, fees, or otherwise) derived in connection with the performance of technical, managerial, engineering, architectural, scientific, skilled, industrial, commercial, or like services which—

　　(A) are performed for or on behalf of any related person (within the meaning of subsection (d)(3)), and

　　(B) are performed outside the country under the laws of which the controlled foreign corporation is created or organized.

　(2) EXCEPTION.—Paragraph (1) shall not apply to income derived in connection with the performance of services which are directly related to—

　　(A) the sale or exchange by the controlled foreign corporation of property manufactured, produced, grown, or extracted by it and which are performed before the time of the sale or exchange, or

(B) an offer or effort to sell or exchange such property.

Paragraph (1) shall also not apply to income which is exempt insurance income (as defined in section 953(e)) or which is not treated as foreign personal holding income by reason of subsection (c)(2)(C)(ii), (h), or (i).

[Sec. 954(f)—Stricken]

[Sec. 954(g)]

(g) FOREIGN BASE COMPANY OIL RELATED INCOME.—For purposes of this section—

(1) IN GENERAL.—Except as otherwise provided in this subsection, the term "foreign base company oil related income" means foreign oil related income (within the meaning of paragraphs (2) and (3) of section 907(c)) other than income derived from a source within a foreign country in connection with—

(A) oil or gas which was extracted from an oil or gas well located in such foreign country, or

(B) oil, gas, or a primary product of oil or gas which is sold by the foreign corporation or a related person for use or consumption within such country or is loaded in such country on a vessel or aircraft as fuel for such vessel or aircraft.

Such term shall not include any foreign personal holding company income (as defined in subsection (c)).

(2) PARAGRAPH (1) APPLIES ONLY WHERE CORPORATION HAS PRODUCED 1,000 BARRELS PER DAY OR MORE.—

(A) IN GENERAL.—The term "foreign base company oil related income" shall not include any income of a foreign corporation if such corporation is not a large oil producer for the taxable year.

(B) LARGE OIL PRODUCER.—For purposes of subparagraph (A), the term "large oil producer" means any corporation if, for the taxable year or for the preceding taxable year, the average daily production of foreign crude oil and natural gas of the related group which includes such corporation equaled or exceeded 1,000 barrels.

(C) RELATED GROUP.—The term "related group" means a group consisting of the foreign corporation and any other person who is a related person with respect to such corporation.

(D) AVERAGE DAILY PRODUCTION OF FOREIGN CRUDE OIL AND NATURAL GAS.—For purposes of this paragraph, the average daily production of foreign crude oil or natural gas of any related group for any taxable year (and the conversion of cubic feet of natural gas into barrels) shall be determined under rules similar to the rules of section 613A except that only crude oil or natural gas from a well located outside the United States shall be taken into account.

[Sec. 954(h)]

(h) SPECIAL RULE FOR INCOME DERIVED IN THE ACTIVE CONDUCT OF BANKING, FINANCING, OR SIMILAR BUSINESSES.—

(1) IN GENERAL.—For purposes of subsection (c)(1), foreign personal holding company income shall not include qualified banking or financing income of an eligible controlled foreign corporation.

(2) ELIGIBLE CONTROLLED FOREIGN CORPORATION.—For purposes of this subsection—

(A) IN GENERAL.—The term "eligible controlled foreign corporation" means a controlled foreign corporation which—

(i) is predominantly engaged in the active conduct of a banking, financing, or similar business, and

(ii) conducts substantial activity with respect to such business.

(B) PREDOMINANTLY ENGAGED.—A controlled foreign corporation shall be treated as predominantly engaged in the active conduct of a banking, financing, or similar business if—

(i) more than 70 percent of the gross income of the controlled foreign corporation is derived directly from the active and regular conduct of a lending or finance business from transactions with customers which are not related persons,

(ii) it is engaged in the active conduct of a banking business and is an institution licensed to do business as a bank in the United States (or is any other corporation not so licensed which is specified by the Secretary in regulations), or

(iii) it is engaged in the active conduct of a securities business and is registered as a securities broker or dealer under section 15(a) of the Securities Exchange Act of 1934 or is registered as a Government securities broker or dealer under section 15C(a) of such Act (or is any other corporation not so registered which is specified by the Secretary in regulations).

(3) QUALIFIED BANKING OR FINANCING INCOME.—For purposes of this subsection—

(A) IN GENERAL.—The term "qualified banking or financing income" means income of an eligible controlled foreign corporation which—

(i) is derived in the active conduct of a banking, financing, or similar business by—

(I) such eligible controlled foreign corporation, or

(II) a qualified business unit of such eligible controlled foreign corporation,

(ii) is derived from one or more transactions—

(I) with customers located in a country other than the United States, and

(II) substantially all of the activities in connection with which are conducted directly by the corporation or unit in its home country, and

(iii) is treated as earned by such corporation or unit in its home country for purposes of such country's tax laws.

(B) LIMITATION ON NONBANKING AND NONSECURITIES BUSINESSES.—No income of an eligible controlled foreign corporation not described in clause (ii) or (iii) of paragraph (2)(B) (or of a qualified business unit of such corporation) shall be treated as qualified banking or financing income unless more than 30 percent of such corporation's or unit's gross income is derived directly from the active and regular conduct of a lending or finance business from transactions with customers which are not related persons and which are located within such corporation's or unit's home country.

(C) SUBSTANTIAL ACTIVITY REQUIREMENT FOR CROSS BORDER INCOME.—The term "qualified banking or financing income" shall not include income derived from 1 or more transactions with customers located in a country other than the home country of the eligible controlled foreign corporation or a qualified business unit of such corporation unless such corporation or unit conducts substantial activity with respect to a banking, financing, or similar business in its home country.

(D) DETERMINATIONS MADE SEPARATELY.—For purposes of this paragraph, the qualified banking or financing income of an eligible controlled foreign corporation and each qualified business unit of such corporation shall be determined separately for such corporation and each such unit by taking into account—

(i) in the case of the eligible controlled foreign corporation, only items of income, deduction, gain, or loss and activities of such corporation not properly allocable or attributable to any qualified business unit of such corporation, and

(ii) in the case of a qualified business unit, only items of income, deduction, gain, or loss and activities properly allocable or attributable to such unit.

(E) DIRECT CONDUCT OF ACTIVITIES.—For purposes of subparagraph (A)(ii)(II), an activity shall be treated as conducted directly by an eligible controlled foreign corporation or qualified business unit in its home country if the activity is performed by employees of a related person and—

(i) the related person is an eligible controlled foreign corporation the home country of which is the same as the home country of the corporation or unit to which subparagraph (A)(ii)(II) is being applied,

(ii) the activity is performed in the home country of the related person, and

(iii) the related person is compensated on an arm's-length basis for the performance of the activity by its employees and such compensation is treated as earned by such person in its home country for purposes of the home country's tax laws.

(4) LENDING OR FINANCE BUSINESS.—For purposes of this subsection, the term "lending or finance business" means the business of—

(A) making loans,

(B) purchasing or discounting accounts receivable, notes, or installment obligations,

(C) engaging in leasing (including entering into leases and purchasing, servicing, and disposing of leases and leased assets),

(D) issuing letters of credit or providing guarantees,

(E) providing charge and credit card services, or

(F) rendering services or making facilities available in connection with activities described in subparagraphs (A) through (E) carried on by—

(i) the corporation (or qualified business unit) rendering services or making facilities available, or

(ii) another corporation (or qualified business unit of a corporation) which is a member of the same affiliated group (as defined in section 1504, but determined without regard to section 1504(b)(3)).

(5) OTHER DEFINITIONS.—For purposes of this subsection—

(A) CUSTOMER.—The term "customer" means, with respect to any controlled foreign corporation or qualified business unit, any person which has a customer relationship with such corporation or unit and which is acting in its capacity as such.

(B) HOME COUNTRY.—Except as provided in regulations—

(i) CONTROLLED FOREIGN CORPORATION.—The term "home country" means, with respect to any controlled foreign corporation, the country under the laws of which the corporation was created or organized.

(ii) QUALIFIED BUSINESS UNIT.—The term "home country" means, with respect to any qualified business unit, the country in which such unit maintains its principal office.

(C) LOCATED.—The determination of where a customer is located shall be made under rules prescribed by the Secretary.

(D) QUALIFIED BUSINESS UNIT.—The term "qualified business unit" has the meaning given such term by section 989(a).

(E) RELATED PERSON.—The term "related person" has the meaning given such term by subsection (d)(3).

(6) COORDINATION WITH EXCEPTION FOR DEALERS.—Paragraph (1) shall not apply to income described in subsection (c)(2)(C)(ii) of a dealer in securities (within the meaning of section 475) which is an eligible controlled foreign corporation described in paragraph (2)(B)(iii).

(7) ANTI-ABUSE RULES.—For purposes of applying this subsection and subsection (c)(2)(C)(ii)—

(A) there shall be disregarded any item of income, gain, loss, or deduction with respect to any transaction or series of transactions one of the principal purposes of which is qualifying income or gain for the exclusion under this section, including any transaction or series of transactions a principal purpose of which is the acceleration or deferral of any item in order to claim the benefits of such exclusion through the application of this subsection,

(B) there shall be disregarded any item of income, gain, loss, or deduction of an entity which is not engaged in regular and continuous transactions with customers which are not related persons,

(C) there shall be disregarded any item of income, gain, loss, or deduction with respect to any transaction or series of transactions utilizing, or doing business with—

(i) one or more entities in order to satisfy any home country requirement under this subsection, or

(ii) a special purpose entity or arrangement, including a securitization, financing, or similar entity or arrangement,

if one of the principal purposes of such transaction or series of transactions is qualifying income or gain for the exclusion under this subsection, and

(D) a related person, an officer, a director, or an employee with respect to any controlled foreign corporation (or qualified business unit) which would otherwise be treated as a customer of such corporation or unit with respect to any transaction shall not be so treated if a principal purpose of such transaction is to satisfy any requirement of this subsection.

(8) REGULATIONS.—The Secretary shall prescribe such regulations as may be necessary or appropriate to carry out the purposes of this subsection, subsection (c)(1)(B)(i), subsection (c)(2)(C)(ii), and the last sentence of subsection (e)(2).

(9) APPLICATION.—This subsection, subsection (c)(2)(C)(ii), and the last sentence of subsection (e)(2) shall apply only to taxable years of a foreign corporation beginning after December 31, 1998, and before January 1, 2007, and to taxable years of United States shareholders with or within which any such taxable year of such foreign corporation ends.

[Sec. 954(i)]

(i) SPECIAL RULE FOR INCOME DERIVED IN THE ACTIVE CONDUCT OF INSURANCE BUSINESS.—

(1) IN GENERAL.—For purposes of subsection (c)(1), foreign personal holding company income shall not include qualified insurance income of a qualifying insurance company.

(2) QUALIFIED INSURANCE INCOME.—The term "qualified insurance income" means income of a qualifying insurance company which is—

(A) received from a person other than a related person (within the meaning of subsection (d)(3)) and derived from the investments made by a qualifying insurance company or a qualifying insurance company branch of its reserves allocable to exempt contracts or of 80 percent of its unearned premiums from exempt contracts (as both are determined in the manner prescribed under paragraph (4)), or

(B) received from a person other than a related person (within the meaning of subsection (d)(3)) and derived from investments made by a qualifying insurance company or a qualifying insurance company branch of an amount of its assets allocable to exempt contracts equal to—

(i) in the case of property, casualty, or health insurance contracts, one-third of its premiums earned on such insurance contracts during the taxable year (as defined in section 832(b)(4)), and

(ii) in the case of life insurance or annuity contracts, 10 percent of the reserves described in subparagraph (A) for such contracts.

(3) PRINCIPLES FOR DETERMINING INSURANCE INCOME.—Except as provided by the Secretary, for purposes of subparagraphs (A) and (B) of paragraph (2)—

(A) in the case of any contract which is a separate account-type contract (including any variable contract not meeting the requirements of section 817), income credited under such contract shall be allocable only to such contract, and

(B) income not allocable under subparagraph (A) shall be allocated ratably among contracts not described in subparagraph (A).

(4) METHODS FOR DETERMINING UNEARNED PREMIUMS AND RESERVES.—For purposes of paragraph (2)(A)—

(A) PROPERTY AND CASUALTY CONTRACTS.—The unearned premiums and reserves of a qualifying insurance company or a qualifying insurance company branch with respect to property, casualty, or health insurance contracts shall be determined using the same methods and interest rates which would be used if such company or branch were subject to tax under subchapter L, except that—

(i) the interest rate determined for the functional currency of the company or branch, and which, except as provided by the Secretary, is calculated in the same manner as the Federal mid-term rate under section 1274(d), shall be substituted for the applicable Federal interest rate, and

(ii) such company or branch shall use the appropriate foreign loss payment pattern.

(B) LIFE INSURANCE AND ANNUITY CONTRACTS.—

(i) IN GENERAL.—Except as provided in clause (ii), the amount of the reserve of a qualifying insurance company or qualifying insurance company branch for any life insurance or annuity contract shall be equal to the greater of—

(I) the net surrender value of such contract (as defined in section 807(e)(1)(A)), or

(II) the reserve determined under paragraph (5).

(ii) RULING REQUEST, ETC.—The amount of the reserve under clause (i) shall be the foreign statement reserve for the contract (less any catastrophe, deficiency, equalization, or similar reserves), if, pursuant to a ruling request submitted by the taxpayer or as provided in published guidance, the Secretary determines that the factors taken into account in determining the foreign statement reserve provide an appropriate means of measuring income.

(C) LIMITATION ON RESERVES.—In no event shall the reserve determined under this paragraph for any contract as of any time exceed the amount which would be taken into account with respect to such contract as of such time in determining foreign statement reserves (less any catastrophe, deficiency, equalization, or similar reserves).

(5) AMOUNT OF RESERVE.—The amount of the reserve determined under this paragraph with respect to any contract shall be determined in the same manner as it would be determined if the qualifying insurance company or qualifying insurance company branch were subject to tax under subchapter L, except that in applying such subchapter—

(A) the interest rate determined for the functional currency of the company or branch, and which, except as provided by the Secretary, is calculated in the same manner as the Federal mid-term rate under section 1274(d), shall be substituted for the applicable Federal interest rate,

(B) the highest assumed interest rate permitted to be used in determining foreign statement reserves shall be substituted for the prevailing State assumed interest rate, and

(C) tables for mortality and morbidity which reasonably reflect the current mortality and morbidity risks in the company's or branch's home country shall be substituted for the mortality and morbidity tables otherwise used for such subchapter.

The Secretary may provide that the interest rate and mortality and morbidity tables of a qualifying insurance company may be used for 1 or more of its qualifying insurance company branches when appropriate.

(6) DEFINITIONS.—For purposes of this subsection, any term used in this subsection which is also used in section 953(e) shall have the meaning given such term by section 953.

[Sec. 955]

SEC. 955. WITHDRAWAL OF PREVIOUSLY EXCLUDED SUBPART F INCOME FROM QUALIFIED INVESTMENT.

[Sec. 955(a)]

(a) GENERAL RULES.—

(1) AMOUNT WITHDRAWN.—For purposes of this subpart, the amount of previously excluded subpart F income of any controlled foreign corporation withdrawn from investment in foreign base company shipping operations for any taxable year is an amount equal to the decrease in the amount of qualified investments in foreign base company shipping operations of the controlled foreign corporation for such year, but only to the extent that the amount of such decrease does not exceed an amount equal to—

(A) the sum of the amounts excluded under section 954(b)(2) from the foreign base company income of such corporation for all prior taxable years beginning before 1987, reduced by

(B) the sum of the amounts of previously excluded subpart F income withdrawn from investment in foreign base company shipping operations of such corporation determined under this subsection for all prior taxable years.

(2) DECREASE IN QUALIFIED INVESTMENTS.—For purposes of paragraph (1), the amount of the decrease in qualified investments in foreign base company shipping operations of any controlled foreign corporation for any taxable year is the amount by which—

(A) the amount of qualified investments in foreign base company shipping operations of the controlled foreign corporation as of the close of the last taxable year beginning before 1987 (to the extent such amounts exceed the sum of the decreases in qualified investments determined under this paragraph for prior taxable years beginning after 1986), exceeds

(B) the amount of qualified investments in foreign base company shipping operations of the controlled foreign corporation at the close of the taxable year,

to the extent that the amount of such decrease does not exceed the sum of the earnings and profits for the taxable year and the earnings and profits accumulated for prior taxable years beginning after December 31, 1975, and the amount of previously excluded subpart F income invested in less developed country corporations described in section 955(c)(2) (as in effect before the enactment of the Tax Reduction Act of 1975) to the extent attributable to earnings and profits accumulated for taxable years beginning after December 31, 1962. For purposes of this paragraph, if qualified investments in foreign base company shipping operations are disposed of by the controlled foreign corporation during the taxable year, the amount of the decrease in qualified investments in foreign base company shipping operations of such controlled foreign corporation for such year shall be reduced by an amount equal to the amount (if any) by which the losses on such dispositions during such year exceed the gains on such dispositions during such year.

(3) PRO RATA SHARE OF AMOUNT WITHDRAWN.—In the case of any United States shareholder, the pro rata share of the amount of previously excluded subpart F income of any controlled foreign corporation withdrawn from investment in foreign base company shipping operations for any taxable year is his pro rata share of the amount determined under paragraph (1).

[Sec. 955(b)]

(b) QUALIFIED INVESTMENTS IN FOREIGN BASE COMPANY SHIPPING OPERATIONS.—

(1) IN GENERAL.—For purposes of this subpart, the term "qualified investments in foreign base company shipping operations" means investments in—

(A) any aircraft or vessel used in foreign commerce, and

(B) other assets which are used in connection with the performance of services directly related to the use of any such aircraft or vessel.

Such term includes, but is not limited to, investments by a controlled foreign corporation in stock or obligations of another controlled foreign corporation which is a related person (within the meaning of section 954(d)(3)) and which holds assets described in the preceding sentence, but only to the extent that such assets are so used.

(2) QUALIFIED INVESTMENTS BY RELATED PERSONS.—For purposes of determining the amount of qualified investments in foreign base company shipping operations, an investment (or a decrease in investment) in such operations by one or more controlled foreign corporations may, under regulations prescribed by the Secretary, be treated as an investment (or a decrease in investment) by another corporation which is a controlled foreign corporation and is a related person (as defined in section 954(d)(3)) with respect to the corporation actually making or withdrawing the investment.

(3) SPECIAL RULE.—For purposes of this subpart, a United States shareholder of a controlled foreign corporation may, under regulations prescribed by the Secretary, elect to make the determinations under subsection (a)(2) of this section and under subsection (g) of section 954 as of the close of the years following the years referred to in such subsections, or as of the close of such longer period of time as such regulations may permit, in lieu of on the

last day of such years. Any election under this paragraph made with respect to any taxable year shall apply to such year and to all succeeding taxable years unless the Secretary consents to the revocation of such election.

(4) AMOUNT ATTRIBUTABLE TO PROPERTY.—The amount taken into account under this subpart with respect to any property described in paragraph (1) shall be its adjusted basis, reduced by any liability to which such property is subject.

(5) INCOME EXCLUDED UNDER PRIOR LAW.—Amounts invested in less developed country corporations described in section 955(c)(2) (as in effect before the enactment of the Tax Reduction Act of 1975) shall be treated as qualified investments in foreign base company shipping operations and shall not be treated as investments in less developed countries for purposes of section 951(a)(1)(A)(ii).

[Sec. 956]

SEC. 956. INVESTMENT OF EARNINGS IN UNITED STATES PROPERTY.

[Sec. 956(a)]

(a) GENERAL RULE.—In the case of any controlled foreign corporation, the amount determined under this section with respect to any United States shareholder for any taxable year is the lesser of—

(1) the excess (if any) of—

(A) such shareholder's pro rata share of the average of the amounts of United States property held (directly or indirectly) by the controlled foreign corporation as of the close of each quarter of such taxable year, over

(B) the amount of earnings and profits described in section 959(c)(1)(A) with respect to such shareholder, or

(2) such shareholder's pro rata share of the applicable earnings of such controlled foreign corporation.

The amount taken into account under paragraph (1) with respect to any property shall be its adjusted basis as determined for purposes of computing earnings and profits, reduced by any liability to which the property is subject.

[Sec. 956(b)]

(b) SPECIAL RULES.—

(1) APPLICABLE EARNINGS.—For purposes of this section, the term "applicable earnings" means, with respect to any controlled foreign corporation, the sum of—

(A) the amount (not including a deficit) referred to in section 316(a)(1) to the extent such amount was accumulated in prior taxable years, and

(B) the amount referred to in section 316(a)(2),

but reduced by distributions made during the taxable year and by earnings and profits described in section 959(c)(1).

(2) SPECIAL RULE FOR U.S. PROPERTY ACQUIRED BEFORE CORPORATION IS A CONTROLLED FOREIGN CORPORATION.—In applying subsection (a) to any taxable year, there shall be disregarded any item of United States property which was acquired by the controlled foreign corporation before the first day on which such corporation was treated as a controlled foreign corporation. The aggregate amount of property disregarded under the preceding sentence shall not exceed the portion of the applicable earnings of such controlled foreign corporation which were accumulated during periods before such first day.

(3) SPECIAL RULE WHERE CORPORATION CEASES TO BE CONTROLLED FOREIGN CORPORATION.—If any foreign corporation ceases to be a controlled foreign corporation during any taxable year—

(A) the determination of any United States shareholder's pro rata share shall be made on the basis of stock owned (within the meaning of section 958(a)) by such shareholder on the last day during the taxable year on which the foreign corporation is a controlled foreign corporation,

(B) the average referred to in subsection (a)(1)(A) for such taxable year shall be determined by only taking into account quarters ending on or before such last day, and

(C) in determining applicable earnings, the amount taken into account by reason of being described in paragraph (2) of section 316(a) shall be the portion of the amount so described which is allocable (on a pro rata basis) to the part of such year during which the corporation is a controlled foreign corporation.

[Sec. 956(c)]

(c) UNITED STATES PROPERTY DEFINED.—

(1) IN GENERAL.—For purposes of subsection (a), the term "United States property" means any property acquired after December 31, 1962, which is—

(A) tangible property located in the United States;

(B) stock of a domestic corporation;

(C) an obligation of a United States person; or

(D) any right to the use in the United States of—

(i) a patent or copyright,

(ii) an invention, model, or design (whether or not patented),

(iii) a secret formula or process, or

(iv) any other similar property right,

which is acquired or developed by the controlled foreign corporation for use in the United States.

(2) EXCEPTIONS.—For purposes of subsection (a), the term "United States property" does not include—

(A) obligations of the United States, money, or deposits with—

(i) any bank (as defined by section 2(c) of the Bank Holding Company Act of 1956 (12 U.S.C. 1841(c)), without regard to subparagraphs (C) and (G) of paragraph (2) of such section), or

(ii) any corporation not described in clause (i) with respect to which a bank holding company (as defined by section 2(a) of such Act) or financial holding company (as defined by section 2(p) of such Act) owns directly or indirectly more than 80 percent by vote or value of the stock of such corporation;

(B) property located in the United States which is purchased in the United States for export to, or use in, foreign countries;

(C) any obligation of a United States person arising in connection with the sale or processing of property if the amount of such obligation outstanding at no time during the taxable year exceeds the amount which would be ordinary and necessary to carry on the trade or business of both the other party to the sale or processing transaction and the United States person had the sale or processing transaction been made between unrelated persons;

(D) any aircraft, railroad rolling stock, vessel, motor vehicle, or container used in the transportation of persons or property in foreign commerce and used predominantly outside the United States;

(E) an amount of assets of an insurance company equivalent to the unearned premiums or reserves ordinary and necessary for the proper conduct of its insurance business attributable to contracts which are not contracts described in section 953(a)(1);

(F) the stock or obligations of a domestic corporation which is neither a United States shareholder (as defined in section 951(b)) of the controlled foreign corporation, nor a domestic corporation, 25 percent or more of the total combined voting power of which, immediately after the acquisition of any stock in such domestic corporation by the controlled foreign corporation, is owned, or is considered as being owned, by such United States shareholders in the aggregate;

(G) any movable property (other than a vessel or aircraft) which is used for the purpose of exploring for, developing, removing, or transporting resources from ocean waters or under such waters when used on the Continental Shelf of the United States;

(H) an amount of assets of the controlled foreign corporation equal to the earnings and profits accumulated after December 31, 1962, and excluded from subpart F income under section 952(b);

(I) to the extent provided in regulations prescribed by the Secretary, property which is otherwise United States property which is held by a FSC and which is related to the export activities of such FSC;

(J) deposits of cash or securities made or received on commercial terms in the ordinary course of a United States or foreign person's business as a dealer in securities or in commodities, but only to the extent such deposits are made or received as collateral or margin for (i) a securities loan, notional principal contract, options contract, forward contract, or futures contract, or (ii) any other financial transaction in which the Secretary determines that it is customary to post collateral or margin;

(K) an obligation of a United States person to the extent the principal amount of the obligation does not exceed the fair market value of readily marketable securities sold or purchased pursuant to a sale and repurchase agreement or otherwise posted or received as collateral for the obligation in the ordinary course of its business by a United States or foreign person which is a dealer in securities or commodities;

(L) securities acquired and held by a controlled foreign corporation in the ordinary course of its business as a dealer in securities if—

(i) the dealer accounts for the securities as securities held primarily for sale to customers in the ordinary course of business, and

(ii) the dealer disposes of the securities (or such securities mature while held by the dealer) within a period consistent with the holding of securities for sale to customers in the ordinary course of business; and

(M) an obligation of a United States person which—

(i) is not a domestic corporation, and

(ii) is not—

(I) a United States shareholder (as defined in section 951(b)) of the controlled foreign corporation, or

(II) a partnership, estate, or trust in which the controlled foreign corporation, or any related person (as defined in section 954(d)(3)), is a partner, beneficiary, or trustee immediately after the acquisition of any obligation of such partnership, estate, or trust by the controlled foreign corporation.

For purposes of subparagraphs (J), (K), and (L), the term "dealer in securities" has the meaning given such term by section 475(c)(1), and the term "dealer in commodities" has the meaning given such term by section 475(e), except that such term shall include a futures commission merchant.

(3) CERTAIN TRADE OR SERVICE RECEIVABLES ACQUIRED FROM RELATED UNITED STATES PERSONS.—

(A) IN GENERAL.—Notwithstanding paragraph (2) (other than subparagraph (H) thereof), the term "United States property" includes any trade or service receivable if—

(i) such trade or service receivable is acquired (directly or indirectly) from a related person who is a United States person, and

(ii) the obligor under such receivable is a United States person.

(B) DEFINITIONS.—For purposes of this paragraph, the term "trade or service receivable" and "related person" have the respective meanings given to such terms by section 864(d).

[Sec. 956(d)]

(d) PLEDGES AND GUARANTEES.—For purposes of subsection (a), a controlled foreign corporation shall, under regulations prescribed by the Secretary, be considered as holding an obligation of a United States person if such controlled foreign corporation is a pledgor or guarantor of such obligation.

[Sec. 956(e)]

(e) REGULATIONS.—The Secretary shall prescribe such regulations as may be necessary to carry out the purposes of this section, including regulations to prevent the avoidance of the provisions of this section through reorganizations or otherwise.

[Sec. 956A—Repealed]

[Sec. 957]

SEC. 957. CONTROLLED FOREIGN CORPORATIONS; UNITED STATES PERSONS.

[Sec. 957(a)]

(a) GENERAL RULE.—For purposes of this subpart, the term "controlled foreign corporation" means any foreign corporation if more than 50 percent of—

(1) the total combined voting power of all classes of stock of such corporation entitled to vote, or

(2) the total value of the stock of such corporation,

is owned (within the meaning of section 958(a)), or is considered as owned by applying the rules of ownership of section 958(b), by United States shareholders on any day during the taxable year of such foreign corporation.

[Sec. 957(b)]

(b) SPECIAL RULE FOR INSURANCE.—For purposes only of taking into account income described in section 953(a) (relating to insurance income), the term "controlled foreign corporation" includes not only a foreign corporation as defined by subsection (a) but also one of which more than 25 percent of the total combined voting power of all classes of stock (or more than 25 percent of the total value of the stock) is owned (within the meaning of section 958(a)), or is considered as owned by applying the rules of ownership of section 958(b), by United States shareholders on any day during the taxable year of such corporation, if the gross amount of premiums or other consideration in respect of the reinsurance or the issuing of insurance or annuity contracts described in section 953(a)(1) exceeds 75 percent of the gross amount of all premiums or other consideration in respect of all risks.

[Sec. 957(c)]

(c) UNITED STATES PERSON.—For purposes of this subpart, the term "United States person" has the meaning assigned to it by section 7701(a)(30) except that—

(1) with respect to a corporation organized under the laws of the Commonwealth of Puerto Rico, such term does not include an individual who is a bona fide resident of Puerto Rico, if a dividend received by such individual during the taxable year from such corporation would, for purposes of section 933(1), be treated as income derived from sources within Puerto Rico, and

(2) with respect to a corporation organized under the laws of Guam, American Samoa, or the Northern Mariana Islands—

(A) 80 percent or more of the gross income of which for the 3-year period ending at the close of the taxable year (or for such part of such period as such corporation or any predecessor has been in existence) was derived from sources within such a possession or was effectively connected with the conduct of a trade or business in such a possession, and

(B) 50 percent or more of the gross income of which for such period (or part) was derived from the active conduct of a trade or business within such a possession,

such term does not include an individual who is a bona fide resident of Guam, American Samoa, or the Northern Mariana Islands.

For purposes of subparagraph (A) and (B) of paragraph (2), the determination as to whether income was derived from the active conduct of a trade or business within a possession shall be made under regulations prescribed by the Secretary.

[Sec. 958]

SEC. 958. RULES FOR DETERMINING STOCK OWNERSHIP.

[Sec. 958(a)]

(a) DIRECT AND INDIRECT OWNERSHIP.—

(1) GENERAL RULE.—For purposes of this subpart (other than section 960(a)(1)), stock owned means—

(A) stock owned directly, and

(B) stock owned with the application of paragraph (2).

(2) STOCK OWNERSHIP THROUGH FOREIGN ENTITIES.—For purposes of subparagraph (B) of paragraph (1), stock owned, directly or indirectly, by or for a foreign corporation, foreign partnership, or foreign trust or foreign estate (within the meaning of section 7701(a)(31)) shall be considered as being owned proportionately by its shareholders, partners, or beneficiaries. Stock considered to be owned by a person by reason of the application of the preceding sentence shall, for purposes of applying such sentence, be treated as actually owned by such person.

(3) SPECIAL RULE FOR MUTUAL INSURANCE COMPANIES.—For purposes of applying paragraph (1) in the case of a foreign mutual insurance company, the term "stock" shall include any certificate entitling the holder to voting power in the corporation.

[Sec. 958(b)]

(b) CONSTRUCTIVE OWNERSHIP.—For purposes of sections 951(b), 954(d)(3), 956(c)(2), and 957, section 318(a) (relating to constructive ownership of stock) shall apply to the extent that the effect is to treat any United States person as a United States shareholder within the meaning of section 951(b), to treat a person as a related person within the meaning of section 954(d)(3), to treat the stock of a domestic corporation as owned by a United States shareholder of the controlled foreign corporation for purposes of section 956(c)(2), or to treat a foreign corporation as a controlled foreign corporation under section 957, except that—

(1) In applying paragraph (1)(A) of section 318(a), stock owned by a nonresident alien individual (other than a foreign trust or foreign estate) shall not be considered as owned by a citizen or by a resident alien individual.

(2) In applying subparagraphs (A), (B), and (C) of section 318(a)(2), if a partnership, estate, trust, or corporation owns, directly or indirectly, more than 50 percent of the total combined voting power of all classes of stock entitled to vote of a corporation, it shall be considered as owning all the stock entitled to vote.

(3) In applying subparagraph (C) of section 318(a)(2), the phrase "10 percent" shall be substituted for the phrase "50 percent" used in subparagraph (C).

(4) Subparagraphs (A), (B), and (C) of section 318(a)(3) shall not be applied so as to consider a United States person as owning stock which is owned by a person who is not a United States person.

Paragraphs (1) and (4) shall not apply for purposes of section 956(c)(2) to treat stock of a domestic corporation as not owned by a United States shareholder.

[Sec. 959]

SEC. 959. EXCLUSION FROM GROSS INCOME OF PREVIOUSLY TAXED EARNINGS AND PROFITS.

[Sec. 959(a)]

(a) EXCLUSION FROM GROSS INCOME OF UNITED STATES PERSONS.—For purposes of this chapter, the earnings and profits of a foreign corporation attributable to amounts which are, or have been, included in the gross income of a United States shareholder under section 951(a) shall not, when—

(1) such amounts are distributed to, or

(2) such amounts would, but for this subsection, be included under section 951(a)(1)(B) in the gross income of,

such shareholder (or any other United States person who acquires from any person any portion of the interest of such United States shareholder in such foreign corporation, but only to the extent of such portion, and subject to such proof of the identity of such interest as the Secretary may by regulations prescribe) directly, or indirectly through a chain of ownership described under section 958(a), be again included in the gross income of such United States shareholder (or of such other United States person). The rules of subsection (c) shall apply for purposes of paragraph (1) of this subsection and the rules of subsection (f) shall apply for purposes of paragraph (2) of this subsection.

[Sec. 959(b)]

(b) EXCLUSION FROM GROSS INCOME OF CERTAIN FOREIGN SUBSIDIARIES.—For purposes of section 951(a), the earnings and profits of a controlled foreign corporation attributable to amounts which are, or have been, included in the gross income of a United States shareholder under section 951(a), shall not, when distributed through a chain of ownership described under section 958(a), be also included in the gross income of another controlled foreign corporation in such chain for purposes of the application of section 951(a) to such other controlled foreign corporation with respect to such United States shareholder (or to any other United States shareholder who acquires from any person any portion of the interest of such United States shareholder in the controlled foreign corporation, but only to the extent of such portion, and subject to such proof of identity of such interest as the Secretary may prescribe by regulations).

[Sec. 959(c)]

(c) ALLOCATION OF DISTRIBUTIONS.—For purposes of subsections (a) and (b), section 316(a) shall be applied by applying paragraph (2) thereof, and then paragraph (1) thereof—

(1) first to the aggregate of—

(A) earnings and profits attributable to amounts included in gross income under section 951(a)(1)(B) (or which would have been included except for subsection (a)(2) of this section), and

(B) earnings and profits attributable to amounts included in gross income under section 951(a)(1)(C) (or which would have been included except for subsection (a)(3) of this section),

with any distribution being allocated between earnings and profits described in subparagraph (A) and earnings and profits described in subparagraph (B) proportionately on the basis of the respective amounts of such earnings and profits,

(2) then to earnings and profits attributable to amounts included in gross income under section 951(a)(1)(A) (but reduced by amounts not included under subparagraph (B) or (C) of section 951(a)(1) because of the exclusions in paragraphs (2) and (3) of subsection (a) of this section), and

(3) then to other earnings and profits.

References in this subsection to section 951(a)(1)(C) and subsection (a)(3) shall be treated as references to such provisions as in effect on the day before the date of the enactment of the Small Business Job Protection Act of 1996.

[Sec. 959(d)]

(d) DISTRIBUTIONS EXCLUDED FROM GROSS INCOME NOT TO BE TREATED AS DIVIDENDS.—Except as provided in section 960(a)(3), any distribution excluded from gross income under subsection (a) shall be treated, for purposes of this chapter, as a distribution which is not a dividend; except that such distributions shall immediately reduce earnings and profits.

[Sec. 959(e)]

(e) COORDINATION WITH AMOUNTS PREVIOUSLY TAXED UNDER SECTION 1248.—For purposes of this section and section 960(b), any amount included in the gross income of any person as a dividend by reason of subsection (a) or (f) of section 1248 shall be treated as an amount included in the gross income of such person (or, in any case to which section 1248(e) applies, of the domestic corporation referred to in section 1248(e)(2)) under section 951(a)(1)(A).

[Sec. 959(f)]

(f) ALLOCATION RULES FOR CERTAIN INCLUSIONS.—

(1) IN GENERAL.—For purposes of this section, amounts that would be included under subparagraph (B) of section 951(a)(1) (determined without regard to this section) shall be treated as attributable first to earnings described in subsection (c)(2), and then to earnings described in subsection (c)(3).

(2) TREATMENT OF DISTRIBUTIONS.—In applying this section, actual distributions shall be taken into account before amounts that would be included under section 951(a)(1)(B) (determined without regard to this section).

[Sec. 960]

SEC. 960. SPECIAL RULES FOR FOREIGN TAX CREDITS.

[Sec. 960(a)]

(a) TAXES PAID BY A FOREIGN CORPORATION.—

(1) DEEMED PAID CREDIT.—For purposes of subpart A of this part, if there is included under section 951(a) in the gross income of a domestic corporation any amount attributable to earnings and profits of a foreign corporation which is a member of a qualified group (as defined in section 902(b)) with respect to the domestic corporation, then, except to the extent provided in regulations, section 902 shall be applied as if the amount so included were a dividend paid by such foreign corporation (determined by applying section 902(c) in accordance with section 904(d)(3)(B)).

(2) TAXES PREVIOUSLY DEEMED PAID BY DOMESTIC CORPORATION.—If a domestic corporation receives a distribution from a foreign corporation, any portion of which is excluded from gross income under section 959, the income, war profits, and excess profits taxes paid or deemed paid by such foreign corporation to any foreign country or to any possession of the United States in connection with the earnings and profits of such foreign corporation from which such distribution is made shall not be taken into account for purposes of section 902, to the extent such taxes were deemed paid by a domestic corporation under paragraph (1) for any prior taxable year.

(3) TAXES PAID BY FOREIGN CORPORATION AND NOT PREVIOUSLY DEEMED PAID BY DOMESTIC CORPORATION.—Any portion of a distribution from a foreign corporation received by a domestic corporation which is excluded from gross income under section 959(a) shall be treated by the domestic corporation as a dividend, solely for purposes of taking into account under section 902 any income, war profits, or excess profits taxes paid to any foreign country or to any possession of the United States, on or with respect to the accumulated profits of such foreign corporation from which such distribution is made, which were not deemed paid by the domestic corporation under paragraph (1) for any prior taxable year.

[Sec. 960(b)]

(b) SPECIAL RULES FOR FOREIGN TAX CREDIT IN YEAR OF RECEIPT OF PREVIOUSLY TAXED EARNINGS AND PROFITS.—

(1) INCREASE IN SECTION 904 LIMITATION.—In the case of any taxpayer who—

(A) either (i) chose to have the benefits of subpart A of this part for a taxable year beginning after September 30, 1993, in which he was required under section 951(a) to include any amount in his gross income, or (ii) did not pay or accrue for such taxable year any income, war profits, or excess profits taxes to any foreign country or to any possession of the United States,

(B) chooses to have the benefits of subpart A of this part for any taxable year in which he receives 1 or more distributions or amounts which are excludable from gross income under section 959(a) and which are attributable to amounts included in his gross income for taxable years referred to in subparagraph (A), and

(C) for the taxable year in which such distributions or amounts are received, pays, or is deemed to have paid, or accrues income, war profits, or excess profits taxes to a foreign country or to any possession of the United States with respect to such distributions or amounts, the limitation under section 904 for the taxable year in which such distributions or amounts are received shall be increased by the lesser of the amount of such taxes paid, or deemed paid, or accrued with respect to such distributions or amounts or the amount in the excess limitation account as of the beginning of such taxable year.

(2) EXCESS LIMITATION ACCOUNT.—

(A) ESTABLISHMENT OF ACCOUNT.—Each taxpayer meeting the requirements of paragraph (1)(A) shall establish an excess limitation account. The opening balance of such account shall be zero.

(B) INCREASES IN ACCOUNT.—For each taxable year beginning after September 30, 1993, the taxpayer shall increase the amount in the excess limitation account by the excess (if any) of—

(i) the amount by which the limitation under section 904(a) for such taxable year was increased by reason of the total amount of the inclusions in gross income under section 951(a) for such taxable year, over

(ii) the amount of any income, war profits, and excess profits taxes paid, or deemed paid, or accrued to any foreign country or possession of the United States which were allowable as a credit under section 901 for such taxable year and which would not have been allowable but for the inclusions in gross income described in clause (i).

Proper reductions in the amount added to the account under the preceding sentence for any taxable year shall be made for any increase in the credit allowable under section 901 for such taxable year by reason of a carryback if such increase would not have been allowable but for the inclusions in gross income described in clause (i).

(C) DECREASES IN ACCOUNT.—For each taxable year beginning after September 30, 1993, for which the limitation under section 904 was increased under paragraph (1), the taxpayer shall reduce the amount in the excess limitation account by the amount of such increase.

(3) DISTRIBUTIONS OF INCOME PREVIOUSLY TAXED IN YEARS BEGINNING BEFORE OCTOBER 1, 1993.—If the taxpayer receives a distribution or amount in a taxable year beginning after September 30, 1993, which is excluded from gross income under section 959(a) and is attributable to any amount included in gross income under section 951(a) for a taxable year beginning before October 1, 1993, the limitation under section 904 for the taxable year in which such amount or distribution is received shall be increased by the amount determined under this subsection as in effect on the day before the date of the enactment of the Revenue Reconciliation Act of 1993.

(4) CASES IN WHICH TAXES NOT TO BE ALLOWED AS DEDUCTION.—In the case of any taxpayer who—

(A) chose to have the benefits of subpart A of this part for a taxable year in which he was required under section 951(a) to include in his gross income an amount in respect of a controlled foreign corporation, and

(B) does not choose to have the benefits of subpart A of this part for the taxable year in which he receives a distribution or amount which is excluded from gross income under section 959(a) and which is attributable to earnings and profits of the controlled foreign corporation which was included in his gross income for the taxable year referred to in subparagraph (A),

no deduction shall be allowed under section 164 for the taxable year in which such distribution or amount is received for any income, war profits, or excess profits taxes paid or accrued to any foreign country or to any possession of the United States on or with respect to such distribution or amount.

(5) INSUFFICIENT TAXABLE INCOME.—If an increase in the limitation under this subsection exceeds the tax imposed by this chapter for such year, the amount of such excess shall be deemed an overpayment of tax for such year.

[Sec. 961]

SEC. 961. ADJUSTMENTS TO BASIS OF STOCK IN CONTROLLED FOREIGN CORPORATIONS AND OF OTHER PROPERTY.

[Sec. 961(a)]

(a) INCREASE IN BASIS.—Under regulations prescribed by the Secretary, the basis of a United States shareholder's stock in a controlled foreign corporation, and the basis of property of a United States shareholder by reason of which he is considered under section 958(a)(2) as owning stock of a controlled foreign corporation, shall be increased by the amount required to be included in his gross income under section 951(a) with respect to such stock or with respect to such property, as the case may be, but only to the extent to which such amount was included in the gross income of such United States shareholder. In the case of a United States shareholder who has made an election under section 962 for the taxable year, the increase in basis provided by this subsection shall not exceed an amount equal to the amount of tax paid under this chapter with respect to the amounts required to be included in his gross income under section 951(a).

[Sec. 961(b)]

(b) REDUCTION IN BASIS.—

(1) IN GENERAL.—Under regulations prescribed by the Secretary, the adjusted basis of stock or other property with respect to which a United States shareholder or a United States person receives an amount which is excluded from gross income under section 959(a) shall be reduced by the amount so excluded. In the case of a United States shareholder who has made an election under section 962 for any prior taxable year, the reduction in basis provided by this paragraph shall not exceed an amount equal to the amount received which is excluded from gross income under section 959(a) after the application of section 962(d).

(2) AMOUNT IN EXCESS OF BASIS.—To the extent that an amount excluded from gross income under section 959(a) exceeds the adjusted basis of the stock or other property with respect to which it is received, the amount shall be treated as gain from the sale or exchange of property.

[Sec. 961(c)]

(c) BASIS ADJUSTMENTS IN STOCK HELD BY FOREIGN CORPORATION.—Under regulations prescribed by the Secretary, if a United States shareholder is treated under section 958(a)(2) as owning any stock in a controlled foreign corporation which is actually owned by another controlled foreign corporation, adjustments similar to the adjustments provided by subsections (a) and (b) shall be made to the basis of such stock in the hands of such other controlled foreign corporation, but only for the purposes of determining the amount included under section 951 in the gross income of such United States shareholder (or any other United States shareholder who acquires from any person any portion of the interest of such United States shareholder by reason of which such shareholder was treated as owning such stock, but only to the extent of such portion, and subject to such proof of identity of such interest as the Secretary may prescribe by regulations).

[Sec. 962]

SEC. 962. ELECTION BY INDIVIDUALS TO BE SUBJECT TO TAX AT CORPORATE RATES.

[Sec. 962(a)]

(a) GENERAL RULE.—Under regulations prescribed by the Secretary, in the case of a United States shareholder who is an individual and who elects to have the provisions of this section apply for the taxable year—

(1) the tax imposed under this chapter on amounts which are included in his gross income under section 951(a) shall (in lieu of the tax determined under sections 1 and 55) be an amount equal to the tax which would be imposed under sections 11 and 55 if such amounts were received by a domestic corporation, and

(2) for purposes of applying the provisions of section 960 (relating to foreign tax credit) such amounts shall be treated as if they were received by a domestic corporation.

[Sec. 962(b)]

(b) ELECTION.—An election to have the provisions of this section apply for any taxable year shall be made by a United States shareholder at such time and in such manner as the Secretary shall prescribe by regulations. An election made for any taxable year may not be revoked except with the consent of the Secretary.

[Sec. 962(c)]

(c) PRO RATION OF EACH SECTION 11 BRACKET AMOUNT.—For purposes of applying subsection (a)(1), the amount in each taxable income bracket in the tax table in section 11(b) shall not exceed an amount which bears the same ratio to such bracket amount as the amount included in the gross income of the United States shareholder under section 951(a) for the taxable year bears to such shareholder's pro rata share of the earnings and profits for the taxable year of all controlled foreign corporations with respect to which such shareholder includes any amount in gross income under section 951(a).

[Sec. 962(d)]

(d) SPECIAL RULE FOR ACTUAL DISTRIBUTIONS.—The earnings and profits of a foreign corporation attributable to amounts which were included in the gross income of a United States shareholder under section 951(a) and with respect to which an election under this section applied shall, when such earnings and profits are distributed, notwithstanding the provisions of section 959(a)(1), be included in gross income to the extent that such earnings and profits so distributed exceed the amount of tax paid under this chapter on the amounts to which such election applied.

[Sec. 964]

SEC. 964. MISCELLANEOUS PROVISIONS.

[Sec. 964(a)]

(a) EARNINGS AND PROFITS.—Except as provided in section 312(k)(4), for purposes of this subpart the earnings and profits of any foreign corporation, and the deficit in earnings and profits of any foreign corporation, for any taxable year shall be determined according to rules substantially similar to those applicable to domestic corporations, under regulations prescribed by the Secretary. In determining such earnings and profits, or the deficit in such earnings and profits, the amount of any illegal bribe, kickback, or other payment (within the meaning of section 162(c)) shall not be taken into account to decrease such earnings and profits or to increase such deficit. The payments referred to in the preceding sentence are payments which would be unlawful under the Foreign Corrupt Practices Act of 1977 if the payor were a United States person.

[Sec. 964(b)]

(b) BLOCKED FOREIGN INCOME.—Under regulations prescribed by the Secretary, no part of the earnings and profits of a controlled foreign corporation for any taxable year shall be included in earnings and profits for purposes of sections 952, 955, and 956, if it is established to the satisfaction of the Secretary that such part could not have been distributed by the controlled foreign corporation to United States shareholders who own (within the meaning of section 958(a)) stock of such controlled foreign corporation because of currency or other restrictions or limitations imposed under the laws of any foreign country.

[Sec. 964(c)]

(c) RECORDS AND ACCOUNTS OF UNITED STATES SHAREHOLDERS.—

(1) RECORDS AND ACCOUNTS TO BE MAINTAINED.—The Secretary may by regulations require each person who is, or has been, a United States shareholder of a controlled foreign corporation to maintain such records and accounts as may be prescribed by such regulations as necessary to carry out the provisions of this subpart and subpart G.

(2) TWO OR MORE PERSONS REQUIRED TO MAINTAIN OR FURNISH THE SAME RECORDS AND ACCOUNTS WITH RESPECT TO THE SAME FOREIGN CORPORATION.—Where, but for this paragraph, two or more United States persons would be required to maintain or furnish the same records and accounts as may by regulations be required under paragraph (1) with respect to the same controlled foreign corporation for the same period, the Secretary may by regulations provide

that the maintenance or furnishing of such records and accounts by only one such person shall satisfy the requirements of paragraph (1) for such other persons.

[Sec. 964(d)]

(d) TREATMENT OF CERTAIN BRANCHES.—

(1) IN GENERAL.—For purposes of this chapter, section 6038, section 6046, and such other provisions as may be specified in regulations—

(A) a qualified insurance branch of a controlled foreign corporation shall be treated as a separate foreign corporation created under the laws of the foreign country with respect to which such branch qualifies under paragraph (2), and

(B) except as provided in regulations, any amount directly or indirectly transferred or credited from such branch to one or more other accounts of such controlled foreign corporation shall be treated as a dividend paid to such controlled foreign corporation.

(2) QUALIFIED INSURANCE BRANCH.—For purposes of paragraph (1), the term "qualified insurance branch" means any branch of a controlled foreign corporation which is licensed and predominantly engaged on a permanent basis in the active conduct of an insurance business in a foreign country if—

(A) separate books and accounts are maintained for such branch,

(B) the principal place of business of such branch is in such foreign country,

(C) such branch would be taxable under subchapter L if it were a separate domestic corporation, and

(D) an election under this paragraph applies to such branch.

An election under this paragraph shall apply to the taxable year for which made and all subsequent taxable years unless revoked with the consent of the Secretary.

(3) REGULATIONS.—The Secretary shall prescribe such regulations as may be necessary or appropriate to carry out the purposes of this subsection.

[Sec. 964(e)]

(e) GAIN ON CERTAIN STOCK SALES BY CONTROLLED FOREIGN CORPORATIONS TREATED AS DIVIDENDS.—

(1) IN GENERAL.—If a controlled foreign corporation sells or exchanges stock in any other foreign corporation, gain recognized on such sale or exchange shall be included in the gross income of such controlled foreign corporation as a dividend to the same extent that it would have been so included under section 1248(a) if such controlled foreign corporation were a United States person. For purposes of determining the amount which would have been so includible, the determination of whether such other foreign corporation was a controlled foreign corporation shall be made without regard to the preceding sentence.

(2) SAME COUNTRY EXCEPTION NOT APPLICABLE.—Clause (i) of section 954(c)(3)(A) shall not apply to any amount treated as a dividend by reason of paragraph (1).

(3) CLARIFICATION OF DEEMED SALES.—For purposes of this subsection, a controlled foreign corporation shall be treated as having sold or exchanged any stock if, under any provision of this subtitle, such controlled foreign corporation is treated as having gain from the sale or exchange of such stock.

[Sec. 965]

SEC. 965. TEMPORARY DIVIDENDS RECEIVED DEDUCTION.

[Sec. 965(a)]

(a) DEDUCTION.—

(1) IN GENERAL.—In the case of a corporation which is a United States shareholder and for which the election under this section is in effect for the taxable year, there shall be allowed as a deduction an amount equal to 85 percent of the cash dividends which are received during such taxable year by such shareholder from controlled foreign corporations.

(2) DIVIDENDS PAID INDIRECTLY FROM CONTROLLED FOREIGN CORPORATIONS.—If, within the taxable year for which the election under this section is in effect, a United States shareholder receives a cash distribution from a controlled foreign corporation which is excluded from gross income under section 959(a), such distribution shall be treated for purposes of this section as a cash dividend to the extent of any amount included in income by such United States shareholder under section 951(a)(1)(A) as a result of any cash dividend during such taxable year to—

(A) such controlled foreign corporation from another controlled foreign corporation that is in a chain of ownership described in section 958(a), or

(B) any other controlled foreign corporation in such chain of ownership, but only to the extent of cash distributions described in section 959(b) which are made during such taxable year to the controlled foreign corporation from which such United States shareholder received such distribution.

[Sec. 965(b)]

(b) LIMITATIONS.—

(1) IN GENERAL.—The amount of dividends taken into account under subsection (a) shall not exceed the greater of—

(A) $500,000,000,

(B) the amount shown on the applicable financial statement as earnings permanently reinvested outside the United States, or

(C) in the case of an applicable financial statement which fails to show a specific amount of earnings permanently reinvested outside the United States and which shows a specific amount of tax liability attributable to such earnings, the amount equal to the amount of such liability divided by 0.35.

The amounts described in subparagraphs (B) and (C) shall be treated as being zero if there is no such statement or such statement fails to show a specific amount of such earnings or liability, as the case may be.

(2) DIVIDENDS MUST BE EXTRAORDINARY.—The amount of dividends taken into account under subsection (a) shall not exceed the excess (if any) of—

(A) the dividends received during the taxable year by such shareholder from controlled foreign corporations, over

(B) the annual average for the base period years of—

(i) the dividends received during each base period year by such shareholder from controlled foreign corporations,

(ii) the amounts includible in such shareholder's gross income for each base period year under section 951(a)(1)(B) with respect to controlled foreign corporations, and

(iii) the amounts that would have been included for each base period year but for section 959(a) with respect to controlled foreign corporations.

The amount taken into account under clause (iii) for any base period year shall not include any amount which is not includible in gross income by reason of an amount described in clause (ii) with respect to a prior taxable year. Amounts described in subparagraph (B) for any base period year shall be such amounts as shown on the most recent return filed for such year; except that amended returns filed after June 30, 2003, shall not be taken into account.

(3) REDUCTION OF BENEFIT IF INCREASE IN RELATED PARTY INDEBTEDNESS.—The amount of dividends which would (but for this paragraph) be taken into account under subsection (a) shall be reduced by the excess (if any) of—

(A) the amount of indebtedness of the controlled foreign corporation to any related person (as defined in section 954(d)(3)) as of the close of the taxable year for which the election under this section is in effect, over

(B) the amount of indebtedness of the controlled foreign corporation to any related person (as so defined) as of the close of October 3, 2004.

All controlled foreign corporations with respect to which the taxpayer is a United States shareholder shall be treated as 1 controlled foreign corporation for purposes of this paragraph.

(4) REQUIREMENT TO INVEST IN UNITED STATES.—Subsection (a) shall not apply to any dividend received by a United States shareholder unless the amount of the dividend is invested in the United States pursuant to a domestic reinvestment plan which—

(A) is approved by the taxpayer's president, chief executive officer, or comparable official before the payment of such dividend and subsequently approved by the taxpayer's board of directors, management committee, executive committee, or similar body, and

(B) provides for the reinvestment of such dividend in the United States (other than as payment for executive compensation), including as a source for the funding of worker hiring and training, infrastructure, research and development, capital investments, or the financial stabilization of the corporation for the purposes of job retention or creation.

[Sec. 965(c)]

(c) DEFINITIONS AND SPECIAL RULES.—For purposes of this section—

(1) APPLICABLE FINANCIAL STATEMENT.—The term "applicable financial statement" means, with respect to a United States shareholder, the most recently audited financial statement (including notes and other documents which accompany such statement) which includes such shareholder—

(A) which is certified on or before June 30, 2003, as being prepared in accordance with generally accepted accounting principles, and

(B) which is used for the purposes of a statement or report—

(i) to creditors,

(ii) to shareholders, or

(iii) for any other substantial nontax purpose.

In the case of a corporation required to file a financial statement with the Securities and Exchange Commission, such term means the most recent such statement filed on or before June 30, 2003.

(2) BASE PERIOD YEARS.—

(A) IN GENERAL.—The base period years are the 3 taxable years—

(i) which are among the 5 most recent taxable years ending on or before June 30, 2003, and

(ii) which are determined by disregarding—

(I) 1 taxable year for which the sum of the amounts described in clauses (i), (ii), and (iii) of subsection (b)(2)(B) is the largest, and

(II) 1 taxable year for which such sum is the smallest.

(B) SHORTER PERIOD.—If the taxpayer has fewer than 5 taxable years ending on or before June 30, 2003, then in lieu of applying subparagraph (A), the base period years shall include all the taxable years of the taxpayer ending on or before June 30, 2003.

(C) MERGERS, ACQUISITIONS, ETC.—

(i) IN GENERAL.—Rules similar to the rules of subparagraphs (A) and (B) of section 41(f)(3) shall apply for purposes of this paragraph.

(ii) SPIN-OFFS, ETC.—If there is a distribution to which section 355 (or so much of section 356 as relates to section 355) applies during the 5-year period referred to in subparagraph (A)(i) and the controlled corporation (within the meaning of section 355) is a United States shareholder—

(I) the controlled corporation shall be treated as being in existence during the period that the distributing corporation (within the meaning of section 355) is in existence, and

(II) for purposes of applying subsection (b)(2) to the controlled corporation and the distributing corporation, amounts described in subsection

Income Tax—Controlled Foreign Corporations

(b)(2)(B) which are received or includible by the distributing corporation or controlled corporation (as the case may be) before the distribution referred to in subclause (I) from a controlled foreign corporation shall be allocated between such corporations in proportion to their respective interests as United States shareholders of such controlled foreign corporation immediately after such distribution.

Subclause (II) shall not apply if neither the controlled corporation nor the distributing corporation is a United States shareholder of such controlled foreign corporation immediately after such distribution.

(3) DIVIDEND.—The term "dividend" shall not include amounts includible in gross income as a dividend under section 78, 367, or 1248. In the case of a liquidation under section 332 to which section 367(b) applies, the preceding sentence shall not apply to the extent the United States shareholder actually receives cash as part of the liquidation.

(4) COORDINATION WITH DIVIDENDS RECEIVED DEDUCTION.—No deduction shall be allowed under section 243 or 245 for any dividend for which a deduction is allowed under this section.

(5) CONTROLLED GROUPS.—

(A) IN GENERAL.—All United States shareholders which are members of an affiliated group filing a consolidated return under section 1501 shall be treated as one United States shareholder.

(B) APPLICATION OF $500,000,000 LIMIT.—All corporations which are treated as a single employer under section 52(a) shall be limited to one $500,000,000 amount in subsection (b)(1)(A), and such amount shall be divided among such corporations under regulations prescribed by the Secretary.

(C) PERMANENTLY REINVESTED EARNINGS.—If a financial statement is an applicable financial statement for more than 1 United States shareholder, the amount applicable under subparagraph (B) or (C) of subsection (b)(1) shall be divided among such shareholders under regulations prescribed by the Secretary.

[Sec. 965(d)]

(d) DENIAL OF FOREIGN TAX CREDIT; DENIAL OF CERTAIN EXPENSES.—

(1) FOREIGN TAX CREDIT.—No credit shall be allowed under section 901 for any taxes paid or accrued (or treated as paid or accrued) with respect to the deductible portion of—

(A) any dividend, or

(B) any amount described in subsection (a)(2) which is included in income under section 951(a)(1)(A).

No deduction shall be allowed under this chapter for any tax for which credit is not allowable by reason of the preceding sentence.

(2) EXPENSES.—No deduction shall be allowed for expenses properly allocated and apportioned to the deductible portion described in paragraph (1).

(3) DEDUCTIBLE PORTION.—For purposes of paragraph (1), unless the taxpayer otherwise specifies, the deductible portion of any dividend or other amount is the amount which bears the same ratio to the amount of such dividend or other amount as the amount allowed as a deduction under subsection (a) for the taxable year bears to the amount described in subsection (b)(2)(A) for such year.

[Sec. 965(e)]

(e) INCREASE IN TAX ON INCLUDED AMOUNTS NOT REDUCED BY CREDITS, ETC.—

(1) IN GENERAL.—Any tax under this chapter by reason of nondeductible CFC dividends shall not be treated as tax imposed by this chapter for purposes of determining—

(A) the amount of any credit allowable under this chapter, or

(B) the amount of the tax imposed by section 55.

Subparagraph (A) shall not apply to the credit under section 53 or to the credit under section 27(a) with respect to taxes attributable to such dividends.

(2) LIMITATION ON REDUCTION IN TAXABLE INCOME, ETC.—

(A) IN GENERAL.—The taxable income of any United States shareholder for any taxable year shall in no event be less than the amount of nondeductible CFC dividends received during such year.

(B) COORDINATION WITH SECTION 172.—The nondeductible CFC dividends for any taxable year shall not be taken into account—

(i) in determining under section 172 the amount of any net operating loss for such taxable year, and

(ii) in determining taxable income for such taxable year for purposes of the 2nd sentence of section 172(b)(2).

(3) NONDEDUCTIBLE CFC DIVIDENDS.—For purposes of this subsection, the term "nondeductible CFC dividends" means the excess of the amount of dividends taken into account under subsection (a) over the deduction allowed under subsection (a) for such dividends.

[Sec. 965(f)]

(f) ELECTION.—The taxpayer may elect to apply this section to—

(1) the taxpayer's last taxable year which begins before the date of the enactment of this section, or

(2) the taxpayer's first taxable year which begins during the 1-year period beginning on such date.

Such election may be made for a taxable year only if made before the due date (including extensions) for filing the return of tax for such taxable year.

Subpart G—Export Trade Corporations

[Sec. 970]

SEC. 970. REDUCTION OF SUBPART F INCOME OF EXPORT TRADE CORPORATIONS.

[Sec. 970(a)]

(a) EXPORT TRADE INCOME CONSTITUTING FOREIGN BASE COMPANY INCOME.—

(1) IN GENERAL.—In the case of a controlled foreign corporation (as defined in section 957) which for the taxable year is an export trade corporation, the subpart F income (determined without regard to this subpart) of such corporation for such year shall be reduced by an amount equal to so much of the export trade income (as defined in section 971(b)) of such corporation for such year as constitutes foreign base company income (as defined in section 954), but only to the extent that such amount does not exceed whichever of the following amounts is the lesser:

(A) an amount equal to 1½ times so much of the export promotion expenses (as defined in section 971(d)) of such corporation for such year as is properly allocable to the export trade income which constitutes foreign base company income of such corporation for such year, or

(B) an amount equal to 10 percent of so much of the gross receipts for such year (or, in the case of gross receipts arising from commissions, fees, or other compensation for its services, so much of the gross amount upon the basis of which such commissions, fees, or other compensation is computed) accruing to such export trade corporation from the sale, installation, operation, maintenance, or use of property in respect of which such corporation derives export trade income as is properly allocable to the export trade income which constitutes foreign base company income of such corporation for such year.

The allocations with respect to export trade income which constitutes foreign base company income under subparagraphs (A) and (B) shall be made under regulations prescribed by the Secretary.

(2) OVERALL LIMITATION.—The reduction under paragraph (1) for any taxable year shall not exceed an amount which bears the same ratio to the increase in the investments in export trade assets (as defined in section 971(c)) of such corporation for such year as the export

trade income which constitutes foreign base company income of such corporation for such year bears to the entire export trade income of such corporation for such year.

[Sec. 970(b)]

(b) INCLUSION OF CERTAIN PREVIOUSLY EXCLUDED AMOUNTS.—Each United States shareholder of a controlled foreign corporation which for any prior taxable year was an export trade corporation shall include in his gross income under section 951(a)(1)(A)(ii), as an amount to which section 955 (relating to withdrawal of previously excluded subpart F income from qualified investment) applies, his pro rata share of the amount of decrease in the investments in export trade assets of such corporation for such year, but only to the extent that his pro rata share of such amount does not exceed an amount equal to—

(1) his pro rata share of the sum of (A) the amounts by which the subpart F income of such corporation was reduced for all prior taxable years under subsection (a), and (B) the amounts not included in subpart F income (determined without regard to this subpart) for all prior taxable years by reason of the treatment (under section 972 as in effect before the date of the enactment of the Tax Reform Act of 1976) of two or more controlled foreign corporations which are export trade corporations as a single controlled foreign corporation, reduced by

(2) the sum of the amounts which were included in his gross income under section 951(a)(1)(A)(ii) under the provisions of this subsection for all prior taxable years.

[Sec. 970(c)]

(c) INVESTMENTS IN EXPORT TRADE ASSETS.—

(1) AMOUNT OF INVESTMENTS.—For purposes of this section, the amount taken into account with respect to any export trade asset shall be its adjusted basis, reduced by any liability to which the asset is subject.

(2) INCREASE IN INVESTMENTS IN EXPORT TRADE ASSETS.—For purposes of subsection (a), the amount of increase in investments in export trade assets of any controlled foreign corporation for any taxable year is the amount by which—

(A) the amount of such investments at the close of the taxable year, exceeds

(B) the amount of such investments at the close of the preceding taxable year.

(3) DECREASE IN INVESTMENTS IN EXPORT TRADE ASSETS.—For purposes of subsection (b), the amount of decrease in investments in export trade assets of any controlled foreign corporation for any taxable year is the amount by which—

(A) the amount of such investments at the close of the preceding taxable year (reduced by an amount equal to the amount of net loss sustained during the taxable year with respect to export trade assets), exceeds

(B) the amount of such investments at the close of the taxable year.

(4) SPECIAL RULE.—A United States shareholder of an export trade corporation may, under regulations prescribed by the Secretary, make the determinations under paragraphs (2) and (3) as of the close of the 75th day after the close of the years referred to in such paragraphs in lieu of on the last day of such years. A United States shareholder of an export trade corporation may, under regulations prescribed by the Secretary, make the determinations under paragraphs (2) and (3) with respect to export trade assets described in section 971(c)(3) as of the close of the years following the years referred to in such paragraphs, or as of the close of such longer period of time as such regulations may permit, in lieu of on the last day of such years and in lieu of on the day prescribed in the preceding sentence. Any election under this paragraph made with respect to any taxable year shall apply to such year and to all succeeding taxable years unless the Secretary consents to the revocation of such election.

[Sec. 971]

SEC. 971. DEFINITIONS.

[Sec. 971(a)]

(a) EXPORT TRADE CORPORATIONS.—For purposes of this subpart, the term "export trade corporation" means—

(1) IN GENERAL.—A controlled foreign corporation (as defined in section 957) which satisfies the following conditions:

(A) 90 percent or more of the gross income of such corporation for the 3-year period immediately preceding the close of the taxable year (or such part of such period subsequent to the effective date of this subpart during which the corporation was in existence) was derived from sources without the United States, and

(B) 75 percent or more of the gross income of such corporation for such period constituted gross income in respect of which such corporation derived export trade income.

(2) SPECIAL RULE.—If 50 percent or more of the gross income of a controlled foreign corporation in the period specified in subsection (a)(1)(A) is gross income in respect of which such corporation derived export trade income in respect of agricultural products grown in the United States, it may qualify as an export trade corporation although it does not meet the requirements of subsection (a)(1)(B).

(3) LIMITATION.—No controlled foreign corporation may qualify as an export trade corporation for any taxable year beginning after October 31, 1971, unless it qualified as an export trade corporation for any taxable year beginning before such date. If a corporation fails to qualify as an export trade corporation for a period of any 3 consecutive taxable years beginning after such date, it may not qualify as an export trade corporation for any taxable year beginning after such period.

[Sec. 971(b)]

(b) EXPORT TRADE INCOME.—For the purposes of this subpart the term "export trade income" means net income from—

(1) the sale to an unrelated person for use, consumption, or disposition outside the United States of export property (as defined in subsection (e)), or from commissions, fees, compensation, or other income from the performance of commercial, industrial, financial, technical, scientific, managerial, engineering, architectural, skilled, or other services in respect of such sales or in respect of the installation or maintenance of such export property;

(2) commissions, fees, compensation, or other income from commercial, industrial, financial, technical, scientific, managerial, engineering, architectural, skilled, or other services performed in connection with the use by an unrelated person outside the United States of patents, copyrights, secret processes and formulas, goodwill, trademarks, trade brands, franchises, and other like property acquired or developed and owned by the manufacturer, producer, grower, or extractor of export property in respect of which the export trade corporation earns export trade income under paragraph (1);

(3) commissions, fees, rentals, or other compensation or income attributable to the use of export property by an unrelated person or attributable to the use of export property in the rendition of technical, scientific, or engineering services to an unrelated person; and

(4) interest from export trade assets described in subsection (c)(4).

For purposes of paragraph (3), if a controlled foreign corporation receives income from an unrelated person attributable to the use of export property in the rendition of services to such unrelated person together with income attributable to the rendition of other services to such unrelated person, including personal services, the amount of such aggregate income which shall be considered to be attributable to the use of the export property shall (if such amount cannot be established by reference to transactions between unrelated persons) be that part of such aggregate income which the cost of the export property consumed in the rendition of such services (including a reasonable allowance for depreciation) bears to the total costs and expenses attributable to such aggregate income.

[Sec. 971(c)]

(c) EXPORT TRADE ASSETS.—For purposes of this subpart, the term "export trade assets" means—

(1) working capital reasonably necessary for the production of export trade income,

(2) inventory of export property held for use, consumption, or disposition outside the United States,

(3) facilities located outside the United States for the storage, handling, transportation, packaging, or servicing of export property, and

(4) evidences of indebtedness executed by persons, other than related persons, in connection with payment for purchases of export property for use, consumption, or disposition outside the United States, or in connection with the payment for services described in subsections (b)(2) and (3).

[Sec. 971(d)]

(d) EXPORT PROMOTION EXPENSES.—For purposes of this subpart, the term "export promotion expenses" means the following expenses paid or incurred in the receipt or production of export trade income—

(1) a reasonable allowance for salaries or other compensation for personal services actually rendered for such purpose,

(2) rentals or other payments for the use of property actually used for such purpose,

(3) a reasonable allowance for the exhaustion, wear and tear, or obsolescence of property actually used for such purpose, and

(4) any other ordinary and necessary expenses of the corporation to the extent reasonably allocable to the receipt or production of export trade income.

No expense incurred within the United States shall be treated as an export promotion expense within the meaning of the preceding sentence, unless at least 90 percent of each category of expenses described in such sentence is incurred outside the United States.

[Sec. 971(e)]

(e) EXPORT PROPERTY.—For purposes of this subpart, the term "export property" means any property or any interest in property manufactured, produced, grown, or extracted in the United States.

[Sec. 971(f)]

(f) UNRELATED PERSON.—For purposes of this subpart, the term "unrelated person" means a person other than a related person as defined in section 954(d)(3).

Subpart I—Admissibility of Documentation Maintained in Foreign Countries

[Sec. 982]

SEC. 982. ADMISSIBILITY OF DOCUMENTATION MAINTAINED IN FOREIGN COUNTRIES.

[Sec. 982(a)]

(a) GENERAL RULE.—If the taxpayer fails to substantially comply with any formal document request arising out of the examination of the tax treatment of any item (hereinafter in this section referred to as the "examined item") before the 90th day after the date of the mailing of such request on motion by the Secretary, any court having jurisdiction of a civil proceeding in which the tax treatment of the examined item is an issue shall prohibit the introduction by the taxpayer of any foreign-based documentation covered by such request.

[Sec. 982(b)]

(b) REASONABLE CAUSE EXCEPTION.—

(1) IN GENERAL.—Subsection (a) shall not apply with respect to any documentation if the taxpayer establishes that the failure to provide the documentation as requested by the Secretary is due to reasonable cause.

(2) FOREIGN NONDISCLOSURE LAW NOT REASONABLE CAUSE.—For purposes of paragraph (1), the fact that a foreign jurisdiction would impose a civil or criminal penalty on the taxpayer (or any other person) for disclosing the requested documentation is not reasonable cause.

[Sec. 982(c)]

(c) FORMAL DOCUMENT REQUEST.—For purposes of this section—

(1) FORMAL DOCUMENT REQUEST.—The term "formal document request" means any request (made after the normal request procedures have failed to produce the requested

documentation) for the production of foreign-based documentation which is mailed by registered or certified mail to the taxpayer at his last known address and which sets forth—

(A) the time and place for the production of the documentation,

(B) a statement of the reason the documentation previously produced (if any) is not sufficient,

(C) a description of the documentation being sought, and

(D) the consequences to the taxpayer of the failure to produce the documentation described in subparagraph (C).

(2) PROCEEDING TO QUASH.—

(A) IN GENERAL.—Notwithstanding any other law or rule of law, any person to whom a formal document request is mailed shall have the right to begin a proceeding to quash such request not later than the 90th day after the day such request was mailed. In any such proceeding, the Secretary may seek to compel compliance with such request.

(B) JURISDICTION.—The United States district court for the district in which the person (to whom the formal document request is mailed) resides or is found shall have jurisdiction to hear any proceeding brought under subparagraph (A). An order denying the petition shall be deemed a final order which may be appealed.

(C) SUSPENSION OF 90-DAY PERIOD.—The running of the 90-day period referred to in subsection (a) shall be suspended during any period during which a proceeding brought under subparagraph (A) is pending.

[Sec. 982(d)]

(d) DEFINITIONS AND SPECIAL RULES.—For purposes of this section—

(1) FOREIGN-BASED DOCUMENTATION.—The term "foreign-based documentation" means any documentation which is outside the United States and which may be relevent or material to the tax treatment of the examined item.

(2) DOCUMENTATION.—The term "documentation" includes books and records.

(3) AUTHORITY TO EXTEND 90-DAY PERIOD.—The Secretary, and any court having jurisdiction over a proceeding under subsection (c)(2), may extend the 90-day period referred to in subsection (a).

[Sec. 982(e)]

(e) SUSPENSION OF STATUTE OF LIMITATIONS.—If any person takes any action as provided in subsection (c)(2), the running of any period of limitations under section 6501 (relating to the assessment and collection of tax) or under section 6531 (relating to criminal prosecutions) with respect to such person shall be suspended for the period during which the proceeding under such subsection, and appeals therein, are pending.

Subpart J—Foreign Currency Transactions

[Sec. 985]

SEC. 985. FUNCTIONAL CURRENCY.

[Sec. 985(a)]

(a) IN GENERAL.—Unless otherwise provided in regulations, all determinations under this subtitle shall be made in the taxpayer's functional currency.

[Sec. 985(b)]

(b) FUNCTIONAL CURRENCY.—

(1) IN GENERAL.—For purposes of this subtitle, the term "functional currency" means—

(A) except as provided in subparagraph (B), the dollar, or

(B) in the case of a qualified business unit, the currency of the economic environment in which a significant part of such unit's activities are conducted and which is used by such unit in keeping its books and records.

(2) FUNCTIONAL CURRENCY WHERE ACTIVITIES PRIMARILY CONDUCTED IN DOLLARS.—The functional currency of any qualified business unit shall be the dollar if activities of such unit are primarily conducted in dollars.

(3) ELECTION.—To the extent provided in regulations, the taxpayer may elect to use the dollar as the functional currency for any qualified business unit if—

    (A) such unit keeps its books and records in dollars, or

    (B) the taxpayer uses a method of accounting that approximates a separate transactions method.

Any such election shall apply to the taxable year for which made and all subsequent taxable years unless revoked with the consent of the Secretary.

(4) CHANGE IN FUNCTIONAL CURRENCY TREATED AS A CHANGE IN METHOD OF ACCOUNTING.—Any change in the functional currency shall be treated as a change in the taxpayer's method of accounting for purposes of section 481 under procedures to be established by the Secretary.

[Sec. 986]

SEC. 986. DETERMINATION OF FOREIGN TAXES AND FOREIGN CORPORATION'S EARNINGS AND PROFITS.

[Sec. 986(a)]

(a) FOREIGN INCOME TAXES.—

    (1) TRANSLATION OF ACCRUED TAXES.—

        (A) IN GENERAL.—For purposes of determining the amount of the foreign tax credit, in the case of a taxpayer who takes foreign income taxes into account when accrued, the amount of any foreign income taxes (and any adjustment thereto) shall be translated into dollars by using the average exchange rate for the taxable year to which such taxes relate.

        (B) EXCEPTION FOR CERTAIN TAXES.—Subparagraph (A) shall not apply to any foreign income taxes—

            (i) paid after the date 2 years after the close of the taxable year to which such taxes relate, or

            (ii) paid before the beginning of the taxable year to which such taxes relate.

        (C) EXCEPTION FOR INFLATIONARY CURRENCIES.—Subparagraph (A) shall not apply to any foreign income taxes the liability for which is denominated in any inflationary currency (as determined under regulations).

        (D) ELECTIVE EXCEPTION FOR TAXES PAID OTHER THAN IN FUNCTIONAL CURRENCY.—

            (i) IN GENERAL.—At the election of the taxpayer, subparagraph (A) shall not apply to any foreign income taxes the liability for which is denominated in any currency other than in the taxpayer's functional currency.

            (ii) APPLICATION TO QUALIFIED BUSINESS UNITS.—An election under this subparagraph may apply to foreign income taxes attributable to a qualified business unit in accordance with regulations prescribed by the Secretary.

            (iii) ELECTION.—Any such election shall apply to the taxable year for which made and all subsequent taxable years unless revoked with the consent of the Secretary.

        (E) SPECIAL RULE FOR REGULATED INVESTMENT COMPANIES.—In the case of a regulated investment company which takes into account income on an accrual basis, subparagraphs (A) through (D) shall not apply and foreign income taxes paid or accrued with respect to such income shall be translated into dollars using the exchange rate as of the date the income accrues.

        (F) CROSS REFERENCE.—

For adjustments where tax is not paid within 2 years, see section 905(c).

(2) TRANSLATION OF TAXES TO WHICH PARAGRAPH (1) DOES NOT APPLY.—For purposes of determining the amount of the foreign tax credit, in the case of any foreign income taxes to which subparagraph (A) or (E) of paragraph (1) does not apply—

(A) such taxes shall be translated into dollars using the exchange rates as of the time such taxes were paid to the foreign country or possession of the United States, and

(B) any adjustment to the amount of such taxes shall be translated into dollars using—

(i) except as provided in clause (ii), the exchange rate as of the time when such adjustment is paid to the foreign country or possession, or

(ii) in the case of any refund or credit of foreign income taxes, using the exchange rate as of the time of the original payment of such foreign income taxes.

(3) AUTHORITY TO PERMIT USE OF AVERAGE RATES.—To the extent prescribed in regulations, the average exchange rate for the period (specified in such regulations) during which the taxes or adjustment is paid may be used instead of the exchange rate as of the time of such payment.

(4) FOREIGN INCOME TAXES.—For purposes of this subsection, the term "foreign income taxes" means any income, war profits, or excess profits taxes paid or accrued to any foreign country or to any possession of the United States.

[Sec. 986(b)]

(b) EARNINGS AND PROFITS AND DISTRIBUTIONS.—For purposes of determining the tax under this subtitle—

(1) of any shareholder of any foreign corporation, the earnings and profits of such corporation shall be determined in the corporation's functional currency, and

(2) in the case of any United States person, the earnings and profits determined under paragraph (1) (when distributed, deemed distributed, or otherwise taken into account under this subtitle) shall (if necessary) be translated into dollars using the appropriate exchange rate.

[Sec. 986(c)]

(c) PREVIOUSLY TAXED EARNINGS AND PROFITS.—

(1) IN GENERAL.—Foreign currency gain or loss with respect to distributions of previously taxed earnings and profits (as described in section 959 or 1293(c)) attributable to movements in exchange rates between the times of deemed and actual distribution shall be recognized and treated as ordinary income or loss from the same source as the associated income inclusion.

(2) DISTRIBUTIONS THROUGH TIERS.—The Secretary shall prescribe regulations with respect to the treatment of distributions of previously taxed earnings and profits through tiers of foreign corporations.

[Sec. 987]

SEC. 987. BRANCH TRANSACTIONS.

In the case of any taxpayer having 1 or more qualified business units with a functional currency other than the dollar, taxable income of such taxpayer shall be determined—

(1) by computing the taxable income or loss separately for each such unit in its functional currency,

(2) by translating the income or loss separately computed under paragraph (1) at the appropriate exchange rate, and

(3) by making proper adjustments (as prescribed by the Secretary) for transfers of property between qualified business units of the taxpayer having different functional currencies, including—

(A) treating post-1986 remittances from each such unit as made on a pro rata basis out of post-1986 accumulated earnings, and

(B) treating gain or loss determined under this paragraph as ordinary income or loss, respectively, and sourcing such gain or loss by reference to the source of the income giving rise to post-1986 accumulated earnings.

Income Tax—Foreign Currency Transactions

[Sec. 988]

SEC. 988. TREATMENT OF CERTAIN FOREIGN CURRENCY TRANSACTIONS.

[Sec. 988(a)]

(a) GENERAL RULE.—Notwithstanding any other provisions of this chapter—

(1) TREATMENT AS ORDINARY INCOME OR LOSS.—

(A) IN GENERAL.—Except as otherwise provided in this section, any foreign currency gain or loss attributable to a section 988 transaction shall be computed separately and treated as ordinary income or loss (as the case may be).

(B) SPECIAL RULE FOR FORWARD CONTRACTS, ETC.—Except as provided in regulations, a taxpayer may elect to treat any foreign currency gain or loss attributable to a forward contract, a futures contract, or option described in subsection (c)(1)(B)(iii) which is a capital asset in the hands of the taxpayer and which is not a part of a straddle (within the meaning of section 1092(c), without regard to paragraph (4) thereof) as capital gain or loss (as the case may be) if the taxpayer makes such election and identifies such transaction before the close of the day on which such transaction is entered into (or such earlier time as the Secretary may prescribe).

(2) GAIN OR LOSS TREATED AS INTEREST FOR CERTAIN PURPOSES.—To the extent provided in regulations, any amount treated as ordinary income or loss under paragraph (1) shall be treated as interest income or expense (as the case may be).

(3) SOURCE.—

(A) IN GENERAL.—Except as otherwise provided in regulations, in the case of any amount treated as ordinary income or loss under paragraph (1) (without regard to paragraph (1)(B)), the source of such amount shall be determined by reference to the residence of the taxpayer or the qualified business unit of the taxpayer on whose books the asset, liability, or item of income or expense is properly reflected.

(B) RESIDENCE.—For purposes of this subpart—

(i) IN GENERAL.—The residence of any person shall be—

(I) in the case of an individual, the country in which such individual's tax home (as defined in section 911(d)(3)) is located,

(II) in the case of any corporation, partnership, trust, or estate which is a United States person (as defined in section 7701(a)(30)), the United States, and

(III) in the case of any corporation, partnership, trust, or estate which is not a United States person, a country other than the United States.

If an individual does not have a tax home (as so defined), the residence of such individual shall be the United States if such individual is a United States citizen or a resident alien and shall be a country other than the United States if such individual is not a United States citizen or a resident alien.

(ii) EXCEPTION.—In the case of a qualified business unit of any taxpayer (including an individual), the residence of such unit shall be the country in which the principal place of business of such qualified business unit is located.

(iii) SPECIAL RULE FOR PARTNERSHIPS.—To the extent provided in regulations, in the case of a partnership, the determination of residence shall be made at the partner level.

(C) SPECIAL RULE FOR CERTAIN RELATED PARTY LOANS.—Except to the extent provided in regulations, in the case of a loan by a United States person or a related person to a 10-percent owned foreign corporation which is denominated in a currency other than the dollar and bears interest at a rate at least 10 percentage points higher than the Federal mid-term rate (determined under section 1274(d)) at the time such loan is entered into, the following rules shall apply:

(i) For purposes of section 904 only, such loan shall be marked to market on an annual basis.

(ii) Any interest income earned with respect to such loan for the taxable year shall be treated as income from sources within the United States to the extent of any loss attributable to clause (i).

For purposes of this subparagraph, the term "related person" has the meaning given such term by section 954(d)(3), except that such section shall be applied by substituting "United States person" for "controlled foreign corporation" each place such term appears.

(D) 10-PERCENT OWNED FOREIGN CORPORATION.—The term "10-percent owned foreign corporation" means any foreign corporation in which the United States person owns directly or indirectly at least 10 percent of the voting stock.

[Sec. 988(b)]

(b) FOREIGN CURRENCY GAIN OR LOSS.—For purposes of this section—

(1) FOREIGN CURRENCY GAIN.—The term "foreign currency gain" means any gain from a section 988 transaction to the extent such gain does not exceed gain realized by reason of changes in exchange rates on or after the booking date and before the payment date.

(2) FOREIGN CURRENCY LOSS.—The term "foreign currency loss" means any loss from a section 988 transaction to the extent such loss does not exceed the loss realized by reason of changes in exchange rates on or after the booking date and before the payment date.

(3) SPECIAL RULE FOR CERTAIN CONTRACTS, ETC.—In the case of any section 988 transaction described in subsection (c)(1)(B)(iii), any gain or loss from such transaction shall be treated as foreign currency gain or loss (as the case may be).

[Sec. 988(c)]

(c) OTHER DEFINITIONS.—For purposes of this section—

(1) SECTION 988 TRANSACTION.—

(A) IN GENERAL.—The term "section 988 transaction" means any transaction described in subparagraph (B) if the amount which the taxpayer is entitled to receive (or is required to pay) by reason of such transaction—

(i) is denominated in terms of a nonfunctional currency, or

(ii) is determined by reference to the value of 1 or more nonfunctional currencies.

(B) DESCRIPTION OF TRANSACTIONS.—For purposes of subparagraph (A), the following transactions are described in this subparagraph:

(i) The acquisition of a debt instrument or becoming the obligor under a debt instrument.

(ii) Accruing (or otherwise taking into account) for purposes of this subtitle any item of expense or gross income or receipts which is to be paid or received after the date on which so accrued or taken into account.

(iii) Entering into or acquiring any forward contract, futures contract, option, or similar financial instrument.

The Secretary may prescribe regulations excluding from the application of clause (ii) any class of items the taking into account of which is not necessary to carry out the purposes of this section by reason of the small amounts or short periods involved, or otherwise.

(C) SPECIAL RULES FOR DISPOSITION OF NONFUNCTIONAL CURRENCY.—

(i) IN GENERAL.—In the case of any disposition of any nonfunctional currency—

(I) such disposition shall be treated as a section 988 transaction, and

(II) any gain or loss from such transaction shall be treated as foreign currency gain or loss (as the case may be).

(ii) NONFUNCTIONAL CURRENCY.—For purposes of this section, the term "nonfunctional currency" includes coin or currency, and nonfunctional currency denominated demand or time deposits or similar instruments issued by a bank or other financial institution.

(D) EXCEPTION FOR CERTAIN INSTRUMENTS MARKED TO MARKET.—

(i) IN GENERAL.—Clause (iii) of subparagraph (B) shall not apply to any regulated futures contract or nonequity option which would be marked to market under section 1256 if held on the last day of the taxable year.

(ii) ELECTION OUT.—

(I) IN GENERAL.—The taxpayer may elect to have clause (i) not apply to such taxpayer. Such an election shall apply to contracts held at any time during the taxable year for which such election is made or any succeeding taxable year unless such election is revoked with the consent of the Secretary.

(II) TIME FOR MAKING ELECTION.—Except as provided in regulations, an election under subclause (I) for any taxable year shall be made on or before the 1st day of such taxable year (or, if later, on or before the 1st day during such year on which the taxpayer holds a contract described in clause (i)).

(III) SPECIAL RULE FOR PARTNERSHIPS, ETC.—In the case of a partnership, an election under subclause (I) shall be made by each partner separately. A similar rule shall apply in the case of an S corporation.

(iii) TREATMENT OF CERTAIN PARTNERSHIPS.—This subparagraph shall not apply to any income or loss of a partnership for any taxable year if such partnership made an election under subparagraph (E)(iii)(V) for such year or any preceding year.

(E) SPECIAL RULES FOR CERTAIN FUNDS.—

(i) IN GENERAL.—In the case of a qualified fund, clause (iii) of subparagraph (B) shall not apply to any instrument which would be marked to market under section 1256 if held on the last day of the taxable year (determined after the application of clause (iv)).

(ii) SPECIAL RULE WHERE ELECTING PARTNERSHIP DOES NOT QUALIFY.—If any partnership made an election under clause (iii)(V) for any taxable year and such partnership has a net loss for such year or any succeeding year from instruments referred to in clause (i), the rules of clauses (i) and (iv) shall apply to any such loss year whether or not such partnership is a qualified fund for such year.

(iii) QUALIFIED FUND DEFINED.—For purposes of this subparagraph, the term "qualified fund" means any partnership if—

(I) at all times during the taxable year (and during each preceding taxable year to which an election under subclause (V) applied), such partnership has at least 20 partners and no single partner owns more than 20 percent of the interests in the capital or profits of the partnership,

(II) the principal activity of such partnership for such taxable year (and each such preceding taxable year) consists of buying and selling options, futures, or forwards with respect to commodities,

(III) at least 90 percent of the gross income of the partnership for the taxable year (and for each such preceding taxable year) consisted of income or gains described in subparagraph (A), (B), or (G) of section 7704(d)(1) or gain from the sale or disposition of capital assets held for the production of interest or dividends,

(IV) no more than a de minimis amount of the gross income of the partnership for the taxable year (and each such preceding taxable year) was derived from buying and selling commodities, and

(V) an election under this subclause applies to the taxable year.

An election under subclause (V) for any taxable year shall be made on or before the 1st day of such taxable year (or, if later, on or before the 1st day during such year on which the partnership holds an instrument referred to in clause (i)). Any such election shall apply to the taxable year for which made and all succeeding taxable years unless revoked with the consent of the Secretary.

(iv) TREATMENT OF CERTAIN CURRENCY CONTRACTS.—

(I) IN GENERAL.—Except as provided in regulations, in the case of a qualified fund, any bank forward contract, any foreign currency futures contract traded on a foreign exchange, or to the extent provided in regulations any similar instrument, which is not otherwise a section 1256 contract shall be treated as a section 1256 contract for purposes of section 1256.

(II) GAINS AND LOSSES TREATED AS SHORT-TERM.—In the case of any instrument treated as a section 1256 contract under subclause (I), subparagraph (A) of section 1256(a)(3) shall be applied by substituting "100 percent" for "40 percent" (and subparagraph (B) of such section shall not apply).

(v) SPECIAL RULES FOR CLAUSE (iii)(I).—

(I) CERTAIN GENERAL PARTNERS.—The interest of a general partner in the partnership shall not be treated as failing to meet the 20-percent ownership requirements of clause (iii)(I) for any taxable year of the partnership if, for the taxable year of the partner in which such partnership taxable year ends, such partner (and each corporation filing a consolidated return with such partner) had no ordinary income or loss from a section 988 transaction which is foreign currency gain or loss (as the case may be).

(II) TREATMENT OF INCENTIVE COMPENSATION.—For purposes of clause (iii)(I), any income allocable to a general partner as incentive compensation based on profits rather than capital shall not be taken into account in determining such partner's interest in the profits of the partnership.

(III) TREATMENT OF TAX-EXEMPT PARTNERS.—Except as provided in regulations, the interest of a partner in the partnership shall not be treated as failing to meet the 20-percent ownership requirements of clause (iii)(I) if none of the income of such partner from such partnership is subject to tax under this chapter (whether directly or through 1 or more pass-thru entities).

(IV) LOOK-THRU RULE.—In determining whether the requirements of clause (iii)(I) are met with respect to any partnership, except to the extent provided in regulations, any interest in such partnership held by another partnership shall be treated as held proportionately by the partners in such other partnership.

(vi) OTHER SPECIAL RULES.—For purposes of this subparagraph—

(I) RELATED PERSONS.—Interest in the partnership held by persons related to each other (within the meaning of sections 267(b) and 707(b)) shall be treated as held by 1 person.

(II) PREDECESSORS.—References to any partnership shall include a reference to any predecessor thereof.

(III) INADVERTENT TERMINATIONS.—Rules similar to the rules of section 7704(e) shall apply.

(IV) TREATMENT OF CERTAIN DEBT INSTRUMENTS.—For purposes of clause (iii)(IV), any debt instrument which is a section 988 transaction shall be treated as a commodity.

(2) BOOKING DATE.—The term "booking date" means—

(A) in the case of a transaction described in paragraph (1)(B)(i), the date of acquisition or on which the taxpayer becomes the obligor, or

(B) in the case of a transaction described in paragraph (1)(B)(ii), the date on which accrued or otherwise taken into account.

(3) PAYMENT DATE.—The term "payment date" means the date on which the payment is made or received.

(4) DEBT INSTRUMENT.—The term "debt instrument" means a bond, debenture, note, or certificate or other evidence of indebtedness. To the extent provided in regulations, such term shall include preferred stock.

(5) SPECIAL RULES WHERE TAXPAYER TAKES OR MAKES DELIVERY.—If the taxpayer takes or makes delivery in connection with any section 988 transaction described in paragraph (1)(B)(iii), any gain or loss (determined as if the taxpayer sold the contract, option, or instrument on the date on which he took or made delivery for its fair market value on such date) shall be recognized in the same manner as if such contract, option, or instrument were so sold.

[Sec. 988(d)]

(d) TREATMENT OF 988 HEDGING TRANSACTIONS.—

(1) IN GENERAL.—To the extent provided in regulations, if any section 988 transaction is part of a 988 hedging transaction, all transactions which are part of such 988 hedging transaction shall be integrated and treated as a single transaction or otherwise treated consistently for purposes of this subtitle. For purposes of the preceding sentence, the determination of whether any transaction is a section 988 transaction shall be determined without regard to whether such transaction would otherwise be marked-to-market under Section 475 or 1256 and such term shall not include any transaction with respect to which an election is made under subsection (a)(1)(B). Sections 475, 1092, and 1256 shall not apply to a transaction covered by this subsection.

(2) 988 HEDGING TRANSACTION.—For purposes of paragraph (1), the term "988 hedging transaction" means any transaction—

(A) entered into by the taxpayer primarily—

(i) to manage risk of currency fluctuations with respect to property which is held or to be held by the taxpayer, or

(ii) to manage risk of currency fluctuations with respect to borrowings made or to be made, or obligations incurred or to be incurred, by the taxpayer, and

(B) identified by the Secretary or the taxpayer as being a 988 hedging transaction.

[Sec. 988(e)]

(e) APPLICATION TO INDIVIDUALS.—

(1) IN GENERAL.—The preceding provisions of this section shall not apply to any section 988 transaction entered into by an individual which is a personal transaction.

(2) EXCLUSION FOR CERTAIN PERSONAL TRANSACTIONS.—If—

(A) nonfunctional currency is disposed of by an individual in any transaction, and

(B) such transaction is a personal transaction,

no gain shall be recognized for purposes of this subtitle by reason of changes in exchange rates after such currency was acquired by such individual and before such disposition. The preceding sentence shall not apply if the gain which would otherwise be recognized on the transaction exceeds $200.

(3) PERSONAL TRANSACTIONS.—For purposes of this subsection, the term "personal transaction" means any transaction entered into by an individual, except that such term shall not include any transaction to the extent that expenses properly allocable to such transaction meet the requirements of—

(A) section 162 (other than traveling expenses described in subsection (a)(2) thereof), or

(B) section 212 (other than that part of section 212 dealing with expenses incurred in connection with taxes).

[Sec. 989]

SEC. 989. OTHER DEFINITIONS AND SPECIAL RULES.

[Sec. 989(a)]

(a) QUALIFIED BUSINESS UNIT.—For purposes of this subpart, the term "qualified business unit" means any separate and clearly identified unit of a trade or business of a taxpayer which maintains separate books and records.

[Sec. 989(b)]

(b) APPROPRIATE EXCHANGE RATE.—Except as provided in regulations, for purposes of this subpart, the term "appropriate exchange rate" means—

(1) in the case of an actual distribution of earnings and profits, the spot rate on the date such distribution is included in income,

(2) in the case of an actual or deemed sale or exchange of stock in a foreign corporation treated as a dividend under section 1248, the spot rate on the date the deemed dividend is included in income,

(3) in the case of any amounts included in income under section 951(a)(1)(A) or 1293(a), the averaged exchange rate for the taxable year of the foreign corporation, or

(4) in the case of any other qualified business unit of a taxpayer, the average exchange rate for the taxable year of such qualified business unit.

For purposes of the preceding sentence, any amount included in income under section 951(a)(1)(B) shall be treated as an actual distribution made on the last day of the taxable year for which such amount was so included.

[Sec. 989(c)]

(c) REGULATIONS.—The Secretary shall prescribe such regulations as may be necessary or appropriate to carry out the purposes of this subpart, including regulations—

(1) setting forth procedures to be followed by taxpayers with qualified business units using a net worth method of accounting before the enactment of this subpart,

(2) limiting the recognition of foreign currency loss on certain remittances from qualified business units,

(3) providing for the recharacterization of interest and principal payments with respect to obligations denominated in certain hyperinflationary currencies,

(4) providing for alternative adjustments to the application of section 905(c),

(5) providing for the appropriate treatment of related party transactions (including transactions between qualified business units of the same taxpayer), and

(6) setting forth procedures for determining the average exchange rate for any period.

PART IV—DOMESTIC INTERNATIONAL SALES CORPORATIONS

Subpart A—Treatment of Qualifying Corporations

[Sec. 991]

SEC. 991. TAXATION OF A DOMESTIC INTERNATIONAL SALES CORPORATION.

For purposes of the taxes imposed by this subtitle upon a DISC (as defined in section 992(a)), a DISC shall not be subject to the taxes imposed by this subtitle.

[Sec. 992]

SEC. 992. REQUIREMENTS OF A DOMESTIC INTERNATIONAL SALES CORPORATION.

[Sec. 992(a)]

(a) DEFINITION OF "DISC" AND "FORMER DISC".—

(1) DISC.—For purposes of this title, the term "DISC" means, with respect to any taxable year, a corporation which is incorporated under the laws of any State and satisfies the following conditions for the taxable year:

(A) 95 percent or more of the gross receipts (as defined in section 993(f)) of such corporation consist of qualified export receipts (as defined in section 993(a)),

(B) the adjusted basis of the qualified export assets (as defined in section 993(b)) of the corporation at the close of the taxable year equals or exceeds 95 percent of the sum of the adjusted basis of all assets of the corporation at the close of the taxable year,

(C) such corporation does not have more than one class of stock and the par or stated value of its outstanding stock is at least $2,500 on each day of the taxable year,

(D) the corporation has made an election pursuant to subsection (b) to be treated as a DISC and such election is in effect for the taxable year, and

(E) such corporation is not a member of any controlled group of which a FSC is a member.

(2) STATUS AS DISC AFTER HAVING FILED A RETURN AS A DISC.—The Secretary shall prescribe regulations setting forth the conditions under and the extent to which a corporation which has filed a return as a DISC for a taxable year shall be treated as a DISC for such taxable year for all purposes of this title, notwithstanding the fact that the corporation has failed to satisfy the conditions of paragraph (1).

(3) "FORMER DISC".—For purposes of this title, the term "former DISC" means, with respect to any taxable year, a corporation which is not a DISC for such year but was a DISC in a preceding taxable year and at the beginning of the taxable year has undistributed previously taxed income or accumulated DISC income.

[Sec. 992(b)]

(b) ELECTION.—

(1) ELECTION.—

(A) An election by a corporation to be treated as a DISC shall be made by such corporation for a taxable year at any time during the 90-day period immediately preceding the beginning of the taxable year, except that the Secretary may give his consent to the making of an election at such other times as he may designate.

(B) Such election shall be made in such manner as the Secretary shall prescribe and shall be valid only if all persons who are shareholders in such corporation on the first day of the first taxable year for which such election is effective consent to such election.

(2) EFFECT OF ELECTION.—If a corporation makes an election under paragraph (1), then the provisions of this part shall apply to such corporation for the taxable year of the corporation for which made and for all succeeding taxable years and shall apply to each person who at any time is a shareholder of such corporation for all periods on or after the first day of the first taxable year of the corporation for which the election is effective.

(3) TERMINATION OF ELECTION.—

(A) REVOCATION.—An election under this subsection made by any corporation may be terminated by revocation of such election for any taxable year of the corporation after the first taxable year of the corporation for which the election is effective. A termination under this paragraph shall be effective with respect to such election—

(i) for the taxable year in which made, if made at any time during the first 90 days of such taxable year, or

(ii) for the taxable year following the taxable year in which made, if made after the close of such 90 days,

and for all succeeding taxable years of the corporation. Such termination shall be made in such manner as the Secretary shall prescribe by regulations.

(B) CONTINUED FAILURE TO BE DISC.—If a corporation is not a DISC for each of any 5 consecutive taxable years of the corporation for which an election under this subsection is effective, the election shall be terminated and not be in effect for any taxable year of the corporation after such 5th year.

[Sec. 992(c)]

(c) DISTRIBUTIONS TO MEET QUALIFICATION REQUIREMENTS.—

(1) IN GENERAL.—Subject to the conditions provided by paragraph (2), a corporation which for a taxable year does not satisfy a condition specified in paragraph (1)(A) (relating to gross receipts) or (1)(B) (relating to assets) of subsection (a) shall nevertheless be deemed to satisfy such condition for such year if it makes a pro rata distribution of property after the close of the taxable year to its shareholders (designated at the time of such distribution as a distribution to meet qualification requirements) with respect to their stock in an amount which is equal to—

(A) if the condition of subsection (a)(1)(A) is not satisfied, the portion of such corporation's taxable income attributable to its gross receipts which are not qualified export receipts for such year,

(B) if the condition of subsection (a)(1)(B) is not satisfied, the fair market value of those assets which are not qualified export assets on the last day of such taxable year, or

(C) if neither of such conditions is satisfied, the sum of the amounts required by subparagraphs (A) and (B).

(2) REASONABLE CAUSE FOR FAILURE.—The conditions under paragraph (1) shall be deemed satisfied in the case of a distribution made under such paragraph—

(A) if the failure to meet the requirements of subsection (a)(1)(A) or (B), and the failure to make such distribution prior to the date on which made, are due to reasonable cause; and

(B) the corporation pays, within the 30-day period beginning with the day on which such distribution is made, to the Secretary, if such corporation makes such distribution after the 15th day of the 9th month after the close of the taxable year, an amount determined by multiplying (i) the amount equal to $4\frac{1}{2}$ percent of such distribution, by (ii) the number of its taxable years which begin after the taxable year with respect to which such distribution is made and before such distribution is made. For purposes of this title, any payment made pursuant to this paragraph shall be treated as interest.

(3) CERTAIN DISTRIBUTIONS MADE WITHIN $8\frac{1}{2}$ MONTHS AFTER CLOSE OF TAXABLE YEAR DEEMED FOR REASONABLE CAUSE.—A distribution made on or before the 15th day of the 9th month after the close of the taxable year shall be deemed for reasonable cause for purposes of paragraph 2(A) if—

(A) at least 70 percent of the gross receipts of such corporation for such taxable year consist of qualified export receipts, and

(B) the adjusted basis of the qualified export assets held by the corporation on the last day of each month of the taxable year equals or exceeds 70 percent of the sum of the adjusted basis of all assets held by the corporation on such day.

[Sec. 992(d)]

(d) INELIGIBLE CORPORATIONS.—The following corporations shall not be eligible to be treated as a DISC—

(1) a corporation exempt from tax by reason of section 501,

(2) a personal holding company (as defined in section 542),

(3) a financial institution to which section 581 applies,

(4) an insurance company subject to the tax imposed by subchapter L,

(5) a regulated investment company (as defined in section 851(a)),

(6) a China Trade Act corporation receiving the special deduction provided in section 941(a), or

(7) an S corporation.

[Sec. 992(e)]

(e) COORDINATION WITH PERSONAL HOLDING COMPANY PROVISIONS IN CASE OF CERTAIN PRODUCED FILM RENTS.—If—

(1) a corporation (hereinafter in this subsection referred to as "subsidiary") was established to take advantage of the provisions of this part, and

(2) a second corporation (hereinafter in this subsection referred to as "parent") throughout the taxable year owns directly at least 80 percent of the stock of the subsidiary,

then, for purposes of applying subsection (d)(2) and section 541 (relating to personal holding company tax) to the subsidiary for the taxable year, there shall be taken into account under section 543(a)(5) (relating to produced film rents) any interest in a film acquired by the parent and transferred to the subsidiary as if such interest were acquired by the subsidiary at the time it was acquired by the parent.

SEC. 993. DEFINITIONS.

[Sec. 993(a)]

(a) QUALIFIED EXPORT RECEIPTS.—

(1) GENERAL RULE.—For purposes of this part, except as provided by regulations under paragraph (2), the qualified export receipts of a corporation are—

(A) gross receipts from the sale, exchange, or other disposition of export property,

(B) gross receipts from the lease or rental of export property, which is used by the lessee of such property outside the United States,

(C) gross receipts for services which are related and subsidiary to any qualified sale, exchange, lease, rental, or other disposition of export property by such corporation,

(D) gross receipts from the sale, exchange, or other disposition of qualified export assets (other than export property),

(E) dividends (or amounts includible in gross income under section 951) with respect to stock of a related foreign export corporation (as defined in subsection (e)),

(F) interest on any obligation which is a qualified export asset,

(G) gross receipts for engineering or architectural services for construction projects located (or proposed for location) outside the United States, and

(H) gross receipts for the performance of managerial services in furtherance of the production of other qualified export receipts of a DISC.

(2) EXCLUDED RECEIPTS.—The Secretary may under regulations designate receipts from the sale, exchange, lease, rental, or other disposition of export property, and from services, as not being receipts described in paragraph (1) if he determines that such sale, exchange, lease, rental, or other disposition, or furnishing of services—

(A) is for ultimate use in the United States;

(B) is accomplished by a subsidy granted by the United States or any instrumentality thereof;

(C) is for use by the United States or any instrumentality thereof where the use of such export property or services is required by law or regulation.

For purposes of this part, the term "qualified export receipts" does not include receipts from a corporation which is a DISC for its taxable year in which the receipts arise and which is a member of a controlled group (as defined in paragraph (3)) which includes the recipient corporation.

(3) DEFINITION OF CONTROLLED GROUP.—For purposes of this part, the term "controlled group" has the meaning assigned to the term "controlled group of corporations" by section 1563(a), except that the phrase "more than 50 percent" shall be substituted for the phrase "at least 80 percent" each place it appears therein, and section 1563(b) shall not apply.

[Sec. 993(b)]

(b) QUALIFIED EXPORT ASSETS.—For purposes of this part, the qualified export assets of a corporation are—

(1) export property (as defined in subsection (c));

(2) assets used primarily in connection with the sale, lease, rental, storage, handling, transportation, packaging, assembly, or servicing of export property, or the performance of engineering or architectural services described in subparagraph (G) of subsection (a)(1) or managerial services in furtherance of the production of qualified export receipts described in subparagraphs (A), (B), (C), and (G) of subsection (a)(1);

(3) accounts receivable and evidences of indebtedness which arise by reason of transactions of such corporation or of another corporation which is a DISC and which is a member of a controlled group which includes such corporation described in subparagraph (A), (B), (C), (D), (G), or (H), of subsection (a)(1);

(4) money, bank deposits, and other similar temporary investments, which are reasonably necessary to meet the working capital requirements of such corporation;

(5) obligations arising in connection with a producer's loan (as defined in subsection (d));

(6) stock or securities of a related foreign export corporation (as defined in subsection (e));

(7) obligations issued, guaranteed, or insured, in whole or in part, by the Export-Import Bank of the United States or the Foreign Credit Insurance Association in those cases where such obligations are acquired from such Bank or Association or from the seller or purchaser of the goods or services with respect to which such obligations arose;

(8) obligations issued by a domestic corporation organized solely for the purpose of financing sales of export property pursuant to an agreement with the Export-Import Bank of the United States under which such corporation makes export loans guaranteed by such bank; and

(9) amounts (other than reasonable working capital) on deposit in the United States that are utilized during the period provided for in, and otherwise in accordance with, regulations prescribed by the Secretary to acquire other qualified export assets.

[Sec. 993(c)]

(c) EXPORT PROPERTY.—

(1) IN GENERAL.—For purposes of this part, the term "export property" means property—

(A) manufactured, produced, grown, or extracted in the United States by a person other than a DISC,

(B) held primarily for sale, lease, or rental, in the ordinary course of trade or business, by, or to, a DISC, for direct use, consumption, or disposition outside the United States, and

(C) not more than 50 percent of the fair market value of which is attributable to articles imported into the United States.

In applying subparagraph (C), the fair market value of any article imported into the United States shall be its appraised value, as determined by the Secretary under section 402 of the Tariff Act of 1930 (19 U.S.C. 1401a) in connection with its importation.

(2) EXCLUDED PROPERTY.—For purposes of this part, the term "export property" does not include—

(A) property leased or rented by a DISC for use by any member of a controlled group (as defined in subsection (a)(3)) which includes the DISC,

(B) patents, inventions, models, designs, formulas, or processes, whether or not patented, copyrights (other than films, tapes, records, or similar reproductions, for commercial or home use), good will, trademarks, trade brands, franchises, or other like property,

(C) products of a character with respect to which a deduction for depletion is allowable (including oil, gas, coal, or uranium products) under section 613 or 613A,

(D) products the export of which is prohibited or curtailed under section 7(a) of the Export Administration Act of 1979 to effectuate the policy set forth in paragraph (2)(C) of section 3 of such Act (relating to the protection of the domestic economy), or

(E) any unprocessed timber which is a softwood.

Subparagraph (C) shall not apply to any commodity or product at least 50 percent of the fair market value of which is attributable to manufacturing or processing, except that subparagraph (C) shall apply to any primary product from oil, gas, coal, or uranium. For purposes of the preceding sentence, the term "processing" does not include extracting or handling, packing, packaging, grading, storing, or transporting. For purposes of subparagraph (E), the term "unprocessed timber" means any log, cant, or similar form of timber.

(3) PROPERTY IN SHORT SUPPLY.—If the President determines that the supply of any property described in paragraph (1) is insufficient to meet the requirements of the domestic economy, he may by Executive order designate the property as in short supply. Any property so designated shall be treated as property not described in paragraph (1) during the period beginning with the date specified in the Executive order and ending with the date specified in an Executive order setting forth the President's determination that the property is no longer in short supply.

[Sec. 993(d)]

(d) PRODUCER'S LOANS.—

(1) IN GENERAL.—An obligation, subject to the rules provided in paragraphs (2) and (3), shall be treated as arising out of a producer's loan if—

(A) the loan, when added to the unpaid balance of all other producer's loans made by the DISC, does not exceed the accumulated DISC income at the beginning of the month in which the loan is made;

(B) the obligation is evidenced by a note (or other evidence of indebtedness) with a stated maturity date not more than 5 years from the date of the loan;

(C) the loan is made to a person engaged in the United States in the manufacturing, production, growing, or extraction of export property determined without regard to subparagraph (C) or (D) of subsection (c)(2), (referred to hereinafter as the "borrower"); and

(D) at the time of such loan it is designated as a producer's loan.

(2) LIMITATION.—An obligation shall be treated as arising out of a producer's loan only to the extent that such loan, when added to the unpaid balance of all other producer's loans to the borrower outstanding at the time such loan is made, does not exceed an amount determined by multiplying the sum of—

(A) the amount of the borrower's adjusted basis determined at the beginning of the borrower's taxable year in which the loan is made, in plant, machinery, and equipment, and supporting production facilities in the United States;

(B) the amount of the borrower's property held primarily for sale, lease, or rental, to customers in the ordinary course of trade or business, at the beginning of such taxable year; and

(C) the aggregate amount of the borrower's research and experimental expenditures (within the meaning of section 174) in the United States during all preceding taxable years beginning after December 31, 1971,

by the percentage which the borrower's receipts, during the 3 taxable years immediately preceding the taxable year (but not including any taxable year commencing prior to 1972) in which the loan is made, from the sale, lease, or rental outside the United States of property which would be export property (determined without regard to subparagraph (C) or (D) of subsection (c)(2)) if held by a DISC is of the gross receipts during such 3 taxable years from the sale, lease, or rental of property held by such borrower primarily for sale, lease, or rental to customers in the ordinary course of the trade or business of such borrower.

(3) INCREASED INVESTMENT REQUIREMENT.—An obligation shall be treated as arising out of a producer's loan in a taxable year only to the extent that such loan, when added to the unpaid balance of all other producer's loans to the borrower made during such taxable year, does not exceed an amount equal to—

(A) the amount by which the sum of the adjusted basis of assets described in paragraph (2)(A) and (B) on the last day of the taxable year in which the loan is made exceeds the sum of the adjusted basis of such assets on the first day of such taxable year; plus

(B) the aggregate amount of the borrower's research and experimental expenditures (within the meaning of section 174) in the United States during such taxable year.

(4) SPECIAL LIMITATION IN THE CASE OF DOMESTIC FILM MAKER.—

(A) IN GENERAL.—In the case of a borrower who is a domestic film maker and who incurs an obligation to a DISC for the making of a film, and such DISC is engaged in the trade or business of selling, leasing, or renting films which are export property, the limitation described in paragraph (2) may be determined (to the extent provided under regulations prescribed by the Secretary) on the basis of—

(i) the sum of the amounts described in subparagraphs (A), (B), and (C) thereof plus reasonable estimates of all such amounts to be incurred at any time by the borrower with respect to films which are commenced within the taxable year in which the loan is made, and

(ii) the percentage which, based on the experience of producers of similar films, the annual receipts of such producers from the sale, lease, or rental of such films outside the United States is of the annual gross receipts of such producers from the sale, lease, or rental of such films.

(B) DOMESTIC FILM MAKER.—For purposes of this paragraph, a borrower is a domestic film maker with respect to a film if—

(i) such borrower is a United States person within the meaning of section 7701(a)(30), except that with respect to a partnership, all of the partners must be United States persons, and with respect to a corporation, all of its officers and at least a majority of its directors must be United States persons;

(ii) such borrower is engaged in the trade or business of making the film with respect to which the loan is made;

(iii) the studio, if any, used or to be used for the taking of photographs and the recording of sound incorporated into such film is located in the United States;

(iv) the aggregate playing time of portions of such film photographed outside the United States does not or will not exceed 20 percent of the playing time of such film; and

(v) not less than 80 percent of the total amount paid or to be paid for services performed in the making of such film is paid or to be paid to persons who are United States persons at the time such services are performed or consists of amounts which are fully taxable by the United States.

(C) SPECIAL RULES FOR APPLICATION OF SUBPARAGRAPH (B)(v).—For purposes of clause (v) of subparagraph (B)—

(i) there shall not be taken into account any amount which is contingent upon receipts or profits of the film and which is fully taxable by the United States (within the meaning of clause (ii)); and

(ii) any amount paid or to be paid to a United States person, to a non-resident alien individual, or to a corporation which furnishes the services of an officer or employee to the borrower with respect to the making of a film, shall be treated as fully taxable by the United States only if the total amount received by such person, individual, officer, or employee for services performed in the making of such films is fully included in gross income for purposes of this chapter.

[Sec. 993(e)]

(e) RELATED FOREIGN EXPORT CORPORATION.—In determining whether a corporation (hereinafter in this subsection referred to as "the domestic corporation") is a DISC—

(1) FOREIGN INTERNATIONAL SALES CORPORATION.—A foreign corporation is a related foreign export corporation if—

(A) stock possessing more than 50 percent of the total combined voting power of all classes of stock entitled to vote is owned directly by the domestic corporation,

(B) 95 percent or more of such foreign corporation's gross receipts for its taxable year ending with or within the taxable year of the domestic corporation consists of qualified export receipts described in subparagraphs (A), (B), (C), and (D) of subsection (a)(1) and interest on any obligation described in paragraphs (3) and (4) of subsection (b), and

(C) the adjusted basis of the qualified export assets (described in paragraphs (1), (2), (3), and (4) of subsection (b)) held by such foreign corporation at the close of such taxable year equals or exceeds 95 percent of the sum of the adjusted basis of all assets held by it at the close of such taxable year.

(2) REAL PROPERTY HOLDING COMPANY.—A foreign corporation is a related foreign export corporation if—

(A) stock possessing more than 50 percent of the total combined voting power of all classes of stock entitled to vote is owned directly by the domestic corporation, and

(B) its exclusive function is to hold real property for the exclusive use (under a lease or otherwise) of the domestic corporation.

(3) ASSOCIATED FOREIGN CORPORATION.—A foreign corporation is a related foreign export corporation if—

(A) less than 10 percent of the total combined voting power of all classes of stock entitled to vote of such foreign corporation is owned (within the meaning of section 1563(d) and (e)) by the domestic corporation or by a controlled group of corporations (within the meaning of section 1563) of which the domestic corporation is a member, and

(B) the ownership of stock or securities in such foreign corporation by the domestic corporation is determined (under regulations prescribed by the Secretary) to be reasonably in furtherance of a transaction or transactions giving rise to qualified export receipts of the domestic corporation.

[Sec. 993(f)]

(f) GROSS RECEIPTS.—For purposes of this part, the term "gross receipts" means the total receipts from the sale, lease, or rental of property held primarily for sale, lease, or rental in the ordinary course of trade or business, and gross income from all other sources. In the case of commissions on the sale, lease, or rental of property, the amount taken into account for purposes of this part as gross receipts shall be the gross receipts on the sale, lease, or rental of the property on which such commissions arose.

[Sec. 993(g)]

(g) UNITED STATES DEFINED.—For purposes of this part, the term "United States" includes the Commonwealth of Puerto Rico and the possessions of the United States.

[Sec. 994]

SEC. 994. INTER-COMPANY PRICING RULES.

[Sec. 994(a)]

(a) IN GENERAL.—In the case of a sale of export property to a DISC by a person described in section 482, the taxable income of such DISC and such person shall be based upon a transfer price which would allow such DISC to derive taxable income attributable to such sale (regardless of the sales price actually charged) in an amount which does not exceed the greatest of—

(1) 4 percent of the qualified export receipts on the sale of such property by the DISC plus 10 percent of the export promotion expenses of such DISC attributable to such receipts.

(2) 50 percent of the combined taxable income of such DISC and such person which is attributable to the qualified export receipts on such property derived as the result of a sale by the DISC plus 10 percent of the export promotion expenses of such DISC attributable to such receipts, or

(3) taxable income based upon the sale price actually charged (but subject to the rules provided in section 482).

[Sec. 994(b)]

(b) RULES FOR COMMISSIONS, RENTALS, AND MARGINAL COSTING.—The Secretary shall prescribe regulations setting forth—

(1) rules which are consistent with the rules set forth in subsection (a) for the application of this section in the case of commissions, rentals, and other income, and

(2) rules for the allocation of expenditures in computing combined taxable income under subsection (a)(2) in those cases where a DISC is seeking to establish or maintain a market for export property.

[Sec. 994(c)]

(c) EXPORT PROMOTION EXPENSES.—For purposes of this section, the term "export promotion expenses" means those expenses incurred to advance the distribution or sale of export property for use, consumption, or distribution outside of the United States, but does not include income taxes. Such expenses shall also include freight expenses to the extent of 50 percent of the cost of shipping export property aboard airplanes owned and operated by United States persons or ships documented under the laws of the United States in those cases where law or regulations does not require that such property be shipped aboard such airplanes or ships.

Subpart B—Treatment of Distributions to Shareholders

[Sec. 995]

SEC. 995. TAXATION OF DISC INCOME TO SHAREHOLDERS.

[Sec. 995(a)]

(a) GENERAL RULE.—A shareholder of a DISC or former DISC shall be subject to taxation on the earnings and profits of a DISC as provided in this chapter, but subject to the modifications of this subpart.

[Sec. 995(b)]

(b) DEEMED DISTRIBUTIONS.—

(1) DISTRIBUTIONS IN QUALIFIED YEARS.—A shareholder of a DISC shall be treated as having received a distribution taxable as a dividend with respect to his stock in an amount which is equal to his pro rata share of the sum (or, if smaller, the earnings and profits for the taxable year) of—

(A) the gross interest derived during the taxable year from producer's loans,

(B) the gain recognized by the DISC during the taxable year on the sale or exchange of property, other than property which in the hands of the DISC is a qualified export asset, previously transferred to it in a transaction in which gain was not recognized in whole or in part, but only to the extent that the transferor's gain on the previous transfer was not recognized,

(C) the gain (other than the gain described in subparagraph (B)) recognized by the DISC during the taxable year on the sale or exchange of property (other than property which in the hands of the DISC is stock in trade or other property described in section 1221(a)(1)) previously transferred to it in a transaction in which gain was not recognized in whole or in part, but only to the extent that the transferor's gain on the previous transfer was not recognized and would have been treated as ordinary income if the property had been sold or exchanged rather than transferred to the DISC,

(D) 50 percent of the taxable income of the DISC for the taxable year attributable to military property.[,]

(E) the taxable income of the DISC attributable to qualified export receipts of the DISC for the taxable year which exceed $10,000,000,

(F) the sum of—

(i) in the case of a shareholder which is a C corporation, one-seventeenth of the excess of the taxable income of the DISC for the taxable year, before reduction for any distributions during the year, over the sum of the amounts deemed distributed for the taxable year under subparagraphs (A), (B), (C), (D), and (E),

(ii) an amount equal to $16/17$ of the excess referred to in clause (i) multiplied by the international boycott factor determined under section 999, and

(iii) any illegal bribe, kickback, or other payment (within the meaning of section 162(c)) paid by or on behalf of the DISC directly or indirectly to an official, employee, or agent in fact of a government, and

(G) the amount of foreign investment attributable to producer's loans (as defined in subsection (d)) of a DISC for the taxable year.

Distributions described in this paragraph shall be deemed to be received on the last day of the taxable year of the DISC in which the income was derived. In the case of a distribution described in subparagraph (G), earnings and profits for the taxable year shall include accumulated earnings and profits.

(2) DISTRIBUTIONS UPON DISQUALIFICATION.—

(A) A shareholder of a corporation which revoked its election to be treated as a DISC or failed to satisfy the conditions of section 992(a)(1) for a taxable year shall be deemed to have received (at the time specified in subparagraph (B)) a distribution taxable as a dividend equal to his pro rata share of the DISC income of such corporation accumulated during the immediately preceding consecutive taxable years for which the corporation was a DISC.

(B) Distributions described in subparagraph (A) shall be deemed to be received in equal installments on the last day of each of the 10 taxable years of the corporation following the year of the termination or disqualification described in subparagraph (A) (but in no case over more than twice the number of immediately preceding consecutive taxable years during which the corporation was a DISC).

(3) TAXABLE INCOME ATTRIBUTABLE TO MILITARY PROPERTY.—

(A) IN GENERAL.—For purposes of paragraph (1)(D), taxable income of a DISC for the taxable year attributable to military property shall be determined by only taking into account—

(i) the gross income of the DISC for the taxable year which is attributable to military property, and

(ii) the deductions which are properly apportioned or allocated to such income.

(B) MILITARY PROPERTY.—For purposes of subparagraph (A), the term "military property" means any property which is an arm, ammunition, or implement of war designated in the munitions list published pursuant to section 38 of the Arms Export Control Act (22 U.S.C. 2778).

(4) AGGREGATION OF QUALIFIED EXPORT RECEIPTS.—

(A) IN GENERAL.—For purposes of applying paragraph (1)(E), all DISC's which are members of the same controlled group shall be treated as a single corporation.

(B) ALLOCATION.—The dollar amount under paragraph (1)(E) shall be allocated among the DISC's which are members of the same controlled group in a manner provided in regulations prescribed by the Secretary.

[Sec. 995(c)]

(c) GAIN ON DISPOSITION OF STOCK IN A DISC.—

(1) IN GENERAL.—If—

(A) a shareholder disposes of stock in a DISC or former DISC any gain recognized on such disposition shall be included in gross income as a dividend to the extent provided in paragraph (2), or

(B) stock of a DISC or former DISC is disposed of in a transaction in which the separate corporate existence of the DISC or former DISC is terminated other than by a mere change in place of organization, however effected, any gain realized on the disposition of such stock in the transaction shall be recognized notwithstanding any other provision of this title to the extent provided in paragraph (2) and to the extent so recognized shall be included in gross income as a dividend.

(2) AMOUNT INCLUDED.—The amounts described in paragraph (1) shall be included in gross income as a dividend to the extent of the accumulated DISC income of the DISC or former DISC which is attributable to the stock disposed of and which was accumulated in taxable years of such corporation during the period or periods the stock disposed of was held by the shareholder which disposed of such stock.

[Sec. 995(d)]

(d) FOREIGN INVESTMENT ATTRIBUTABLE TO DISC EARNINGS.—For the purposes of this part—

(1) IN GENERAL.—The amount of foreign investment attributable to producer's loans of a DISC for a taxable year shall be the smallest of—

(A) the net increase in foreign assets by members of the controlled group (as defined in section 993(a)(3)) which includes the DISC,

(B) the actual foreign investment by domestic members of such group, or

(C) the amount of outstanding producer's loans by such DISC to members of such controlled group.

(2) NET INCREASE IN FOREIGN ASSETS.—The term "net increase in foreign assets" of a controlled group means the excess of—

(A) the amount incurred by such group to acquire assets (described in section 1231(b)) located outside the United States over,

(B) the sum of—

(i) the depreciation with respect to assets of such group located outside the United States;

(ii) the outstanding amount of stock or debt obligations of such group issued after December 31, 1971, to persons other than the United States persons or any member of such group;

(iii) one-half the earnings and profits of foreign members of such group and foreign branches of domestic members of such group;

(iv) one-half the royalties and fees paid by foreign members of such group to domestic members of such group; and

(v) the uncommitted transitional funds of the group as determined under paragraph (4).

For purposes of this paragraph, assets which are qualified export assets of a DISC (or would be qualified export assets if owned by a DISC) shall not be taken into account. Amounts described in this paragraph (other than in subparagraphs (B)(ii) and (v)) shall be taken into account only to the extent they are attributable to taxable years beginning after December 31, 1971.

(3) ACTUAL FOREIGN INVESTMENT.—The term "actual foreign investment" by domestic members of a controlled group means the sum of—

(A) contributions to capital of foreign members of the group by domestic members of the group after December 31, 1971,

(B) the outstanding amount of stock or debt obligations of foreign members of such group (other than normal trade indebtedness) issued after December 31, 1971, to domestic members of such group,

(C) amounts transferred by domestic members of the group after December 31, 1971, to foreign branches of such members, and

(D) one-half the earnings and profits of foreign members of such group and foreign branches of domestic members of such group for taxable years beginning after December 31, 1971.

As used in this subsection, the term "domestic member" means a domestic corporation which is a member of a controlled group (as defined in section 993(a)(3)), and the term "foreign member" means a foreign corporation which is a member of such a controlled group.

(4) UNCOMMITTED TRANSITIONAL FUNDS.—The uncommitted transitional funds of the group shall be an amount equal to the sum of—

(A) the excess of—

(i) the amount of stock or debt obligations of domestic members of such group outstanding on December 31, 1971, and issued on or after January 1, 1968, to persons other than United States persons or any members of such group, but only to the extent the taxpayer establishes that such amount constitutes a long-term borrowing for purposes of the foreign direct investment program, over

(ii) the net amount of actual foreign investment by domestic members of such group during the period that such stock or debt obligations have been outstanding; and

(B) the amount of liquid assets to the extent not included in subparagraph (A) held by foreign members of such group and foreign branches of domestic members of such group on October 31, 1971, in excess of their reasonable working capital needs on such date.

For purposes of this paragraph, the term "liquid assets" means money, bank deposits (not including time deposits), and indebtedness of 2 years or less to maturity on the date of acquisition; and the actual foreign investment shall be determined under paragraph (3) without regard to the date in subparagraph (A) of such paragraph and without regard to subparagraph (D) of such paragraph.

(5) SPECIAL RULE.—Under regulations prescribed by the Secretary the determinations under this subsection shall be made on a cumulative basis with proper adjustments for amounts previously taken into account.

[Sec. 995(e)]

(e) CERTAIN TRANSFERS OF DISC ASSETS.—If—

(1) a corporation owns, directly or indirectly, all of the stock of a subsidiary and a DISC,

(2) the subsidiary has been engaged in the active conduct of a trade or business (within the meaning of section 355(b)) throughout the 5-year period ending on the date of the transfer and continues to be so engaged thereafter, and

(3) during the taxable year of the subsidiary in which its stock is transferred and its preceding taxable year, such trade or business gives rise to qualified export receipts of the subsidiary and the DISC,

then, under such terms and conditions as the Secretary by regulations shall prescribe, transfers of assets, stock, or both, will be deemed to be a reorganization within the meaning of section 368, a transaction to which section 355 applies, an exchange of stock to which section 351 applies, or a combination thereof. The preceding sentence shall apply only to the extent that the transfer or transfers involved are for the purpose of preventing the separation of the ownership of the stock in the DISC from the ownership of the trade or business which (during the base period) produced the export gross receipts of the DISC.

[Sec. 995(f)]

(f) INTEREST ON DISC-RELATED DEFERRED TAX LIABILITY.—

(1) IN GENERAL.—A shareholder of a DISC shall pay for each taxable year interest in an amount equal to the product of—

(A) the shareholder's DISC-related deferred tax liability for such year, and

(B) the base period T-bill rate.

(2) SHAREHOLDER'S DISC-RELATED DEFERRED TAX LIABILITY.—For purposes of this subsection—

(A) IN GENERAL.—The term "shareholder's DISC-related deferred tax liability" means, with respect to any taxable year of a shareholder of a DISC, the excess of—

(i) the amount which would be the tax liability of the shareholder for the taxable year if the deferred DISC income of such shareholder for such taxable year were included in gross income as ordinary income, over

(ii) the actual amount of the tax liability of such shareholder for such taxable year.

Determinations under the preceding sentence shall be made without regard to carrybacks to such taxable year.

(B) ADJUSTMENTS FOR LOSSES, CREDITS, AND OTHER ITEMS.—The Secretary shall prescribe regulations which provide such adjustments—

(i) to the accounts of the DISC, and

(ii) to the amount of any carryover or carryback of the shareholder,

as may be necessary or appropriate in the case of net operating losses, credits, and carryovers, and carrybacks of losses and credits.

(C) TAX LIABILITY.—The term "tax liability" means the amount of the tax imposed by this chapter for the taxable year reduced by credits allowable against such tax (other than credits allowable under sections 31, 32, and 34).

(3) DEFERRED DISC INCOME.—For purposes of this subsection—

(A) IN GENERAL.—The term "deferred DISC income" means, with respect to any taxable year of a shareholder, the excess of—

(i) the shareholder's pro rata share of accumulated DISC income (for periods after 1984) of the DISC as of the close of the computation year, over

(ii) the amount of the distributions-in-excess-of-income for the taxable year of the DISC following the computation year.

(B) COMPUTATION YEAR.—For purposes of applying subparagraph (A) with respect to any taxable year of a shareholder, the computation year is the taxable year of the DISC which ends with (or within) the taxable year of the shareholder which precedes the taxable year of the shareholder for which the amount of deferred DISC income is being determined.

(C) DISTRIBUTIONS-IN-EXCESS-OF-INCOME.—For purposes of subparagraph (A), the term "distributions-in-excess-of-income" means, with respect to any taxable year of a DISC, the excess (if any) of—

(i) the amount of actual distributions to the shareholder out of accumulated DISC income, over

(ii) the shareholder's pro rata share of the DISC income for such taxable year.

(4) BASE PERIOD T-BILL RATE.—For purposes of this subsection, the term "base period T-bill rate" means the annual rate of interest determined by the Secretary to be equivalent to the average of the 1-year constant maturity Treasury yields, as published by the Board of Governors of the Federal Reserve System, for the 1-year period ending on September 30 of the calendar year ending with (or of the most recent calendar year ending before) the close of the taxable year of the shareholder.

(5) SHORT YEARS.—The Secretary shall prescribe such regulations as may be necessary for the application of this subsection to short years of the DISC, the shareholder, or both.

(6) PAYMENT AND ASSESSMENT AND COLLECTION OF INTEREST.—The interest accrued during any taxable year which a shareholder is required to pay under paragraph (1) shall be treated, for purposes of this title, as interest payable under section 6601 and shall be paid by the shareholder at the time the tax imposed by this chapter for such taxable year is required to be paid.

(7) DISC INCLUDES FORMER DISC.—For purposes of this subsection, the term "DISC" includes a former DISC.

[Sec. 995(g)]

(g) TREATMENT OF TAX-EXEMPT SHAREHOLDERS.—If any organization described in subsection (a)(2) or (b)(2) of section 511 (or any other person otherwise subject to tax under section 511) is a shareholder in a DISC—

(1) any amount deemed distributed to such shareholder under subsection (b),

(2) any actual distribution to such shareholder which under section 996 is treated as out of accumulated DISC income, and

(3) any gain which is treated as a dividend under subsection (c),

shall be treated as derived from the conduct of an unrelated trade or business (and the modifications of section 512(b) shall not apply). The rules of the preceding sentence shall apply also for purposes of determining any such shareholder's DISC-related deferred tax liability under subsection (f).

[Sec. 996]

SEC. 996. RULES FOR ALLOCATION IN THE CASE OF DISTRIBUTIONS AND LOSSES.

[Sec. 996(a)]

(a) RULES FOR ACTUAL DISTRIBUTIONS AND CERTAIN DEEMED DISTRIBUTIONS.—

(1) IN GENERAL.—Any actual distribution (other than a distribution described in paragraph (2) or to which section 995(c) applies) to a shareholder by a DISC (or former DISC) which is made out of earnings and profits shall be treated as made—

(A) first, out of previously taxed income, to the extent thereof,

(B) second, out of accumulated DISC income, to the extent thereof, and

(C) finally, out of other earnings and profits.

(2) QUALIFYING DISTRIBUTIONS.—Any actual distribution made pursuant to section 992(c) (relating to distributions to meet qualification requirements), and any deemed distribution

pursuant to section 995(b)(1)(G) (relating to foreign investment attributable to producer's loans), shall be treated as made—

(A) first, out of accumulated DISC income, to the extent thereof,

(B) second, out of the earnings and profits described in paragraph (1)(C), to the extent thereof, and

(C) finally, out of previously taxed income.

In the case of any amount of any actual distribution to a C corporation made pursuant to section 992(c) which is required to satisfy the condition of section 992(a)(1)(A), the preceding sentence shall apply to $^{16}/_{17}$ths of such amount, and paragraph (1) shall apply to the remaining $^{1}/_{17}$th of such amount.

(3) EXCLUSION FROM GROSS INCOME.—Amounts distributed out of previously taxed income shall be excluded by the distributee from gross income except for gains described in subsection (e)(2), and shall reduce the amount of the previously taxed income.

[Sec. 996(b)]

(b) ORDERING RULES FOR LOSSES.—If for any taxable year a DISC, or a former DISC, incurs a deficit in earnings and profits, such deficit shall be chargeable—

(1) first, to earnings and profits described in subsection (a)(1)(C), to the extent thereof,

(2) second, to accumulated DISC income, to the extent thereof, and

(3) finally, to previously taxed income, except that a deficit in earnings and profits shall not be applied against accumulated DISC income which has been determined is to be deemed distributed to the shareholders (pursuant to section 995(b)(2)(A)) as a result of a revocation of election or other disqualification.

[Sec. 996(c)]

(c) PRIORITY OF DISTRIBUTIONS.—Any actual distribution made during a taxable year shall be treated as being made subsequent to any deemed distribution made during such year. Any actual distribution made pursuant to section 992(c) (relating to distributions to meet qualification requirements) shall be treated as being made before any other actual distributions during the taxable year.

[Sec. 996(d)]

(d) SUBSEQUENT EFFECT OF PREVIOUS DISPOSITION OF DISC STOCK.—

(1) SHAREHOLDER PREVIOUSLY TAXED INCOME ADJUSTMENT.—If—

(A) gain with respect to a share of stock of a DISC or former DISC is treated under section 995(c) as a dividend or as ordinary income, and

(B) any person subsequently receives an actual distribution made out of accumulated DISC income, or a deemed distribution made pursuant to section 995(b)(2), with respect to such share,

such person shall treat such distribution in the same manner as a distribution from previously taxed income to the extent that (i) the gain referred to in subparagraph (A), exceeds (ii) any other amounts with respect to such share which were treated under this paragraph as made from previously taxed income. In applying this paragraph with respect to a share of stock in a DISC or former DISC, gain on the acquisition of such share by the DISC or former DISC or gain on a transaction prior to such acquisition shall not be considered gain referred to in subparagraph (A).

(2) CORPORATE ADJUSTMENT UPON REDEMPTION.—If section 995(c) applies to a redemption of stock in a DISC or former DISC, the accumulated DISC income shall be reduced by an amount equal to the gain described in section 995(c) with respect to such stock which is (or has been) treated as ordinary income, except to the extent distributions with respect to such stock have been treated under paragraph (1).

[Sec. 996(e)]

(e) ADJUSTMENT TO BASIS.—

(1) ADDITIONS TO BASIS.—Amounts representing deemed distributions as provided in section 995(b) shall increase the basis of the stock with respect to which the distribution is made.

(2) REDUCTIONS OF BASIS.—The portion of an actual distribution made out of previously taxed income shall reduce the basis of the stock with respect to which it is made, and to the extent that it exceeds the adjusted basis of such stock, shall be treated as gain from the sale or exchange of property. In the case of stock includible in the gross estate of a decedent for which an election is made under section 2032 (relating to alternate valuation), this paragraph shall not apply to any distribution made after the date of the decedent's death and before the alternate valuation date provided by section 2032.

[Sec. 996(f)]

(f) DEFINITIONS OF DIVISIONS OF EARNINGS AND PROFITS.—For purposes of this part:

(1) DISC INCOME.—The earnings and profits derived by a corporation during a taxable year in which such corporation is a DISC, before reduction for any distributions during the year, but reduced by amounts deemed distributed under section 995(b)(1), shall constitute the DISC income for such year. The earnings and profits of a DISC for a taxable year include any amounts includible in such DISC's gross income pursuant to section 951(a) for such year. Accumulated DISC income shall be reduced by deemed distributions under section 995(b)(2).

(2) PREVIOUSLY TAXED INCOME.—Earnings and profits deemed distributed under section 995(b) for a taxable year shall constitute previously taxed income for such year.

(3) OTHER EARNINGS AND PROFITS.—The earnings and profits for a taxable year which are described in neither paragraph (1) nor (2) shall constitute the other earnings and profits for such year.

[Sec. 996(g)]

(g) EFFECTIVELY CONNECTED INCOME.—In the case of a shareholder who is a nonresident alien individual or a foreign corporation, trust, or estate, gains referred to in section 995(c) and all distributions out of accumulated DISC income including deemed distributions shall be treated as gains and distributions which are effectively connected with the conduct of a trade or business conducted through a permanent establishment of such shareholder within the United States and which are derived from sources within the United States.

[Sec. 997]

SEC. 997. SPECIAL SUBCHAPTER C RULES.

For purposes of applying the provisions of subchapter C of chapter 1, any distribution in property to a corporation by a DISC or former DISC which is made out of previously taxed income or accumulated DISC income shall—

(1) be treated as a distribution in the same amount as if such distribution of property were made to an individual, and

(2) have a basis, in the hands of the recipient corporation, equal to the amount determined under paragraph (1).

PART V—INTERNATIONAL BOYCOTT DETERMINATIONS

[Sec. 999]

SEC. 999. REPORTS BY TAXPAYERS; DETERMINATIONS.

[Sec. 999(a)]

(a) INTERNATIONAL BOYCOTT REPORTS BY TAXPAYERS.—

(1) REPORT REQUIRED.—If any person, or a member of a controlled group (within the meaning of section 993(a)(3)) which includes that person, has operations in, or related to—

(A) a country (or with the government, a company, or a national of a country) which is on the list maintained by the Secretary under paragraph (3), or

(B) any other country (or with the government, a company, or a national of that country) in which such person or such member had operations during the taxable year if such person (or, if such person is a foreign corporation, any United States shareholder of that corporation) knows or has reason to know that participation in or cooperation with an international boycott is required as a condition of doing business within such country or with such government, company, or national,

that person or shareholder (within the meaning of section 951(b)) shall report such operations to the Secretary at such time and in such manner as the Secretary prescribes, except that in the case of a foreign corporation such report shall be required only of a United States shareholder (within the meaning of such section) of such corporation.

(2) PARTICIPATION AND COOPERATION; REQUEST THEREFOR.—A taxpayer shall report whether he, a foreign corporation of which he is a United States shareholder, or any member of a controlled group which includes the taxpayer or such foreign corporation has participated in or cooperated with an international boycott at any time during the taxable year, or has been requested to participate in or cooperate with such a boycott, and, if so, the nature of any operation in connection with which there was participation in or cooperation with such boycott (or there was a request to participate or cooperate).

(3) LIST TO BE MAINTAINED.—The Secretary shall maintain and publish not less frequently than quarterly a current list of countries which require or may require participation in or cooperation with an international boycott (within the meaning of subsection (b)(3)).

[Sec. 999(b)]

(b) PARTICIPATION IN OR COOPERATION WITH AN INTERNATIONAL BOYCOTT.—

(1) GENERAL RULE.—If the person or a member of a controlled group (within the meaning of section 993(a)(3)) which includes the person participates in or cooperates with an international boycott in the taxable year, all operations of the taxpayer or such group in that country and in any other country which requires participation in or cooperation with the boycott as a condition of doing business within that country, or with the government, a company, or a national of that country, shall be treated as operations in connection with which such participation or cooperation occurred, except to the extent that the person can clearly demonstrate that a particular operation is a clearly separate and identifiable operation in connection with which there was no participation in or cooperation with an international boycott.

(2) SPECIAL RULE.—

(A) NONBOYCOTT OPERATIONS.—A clearly separate and identifiable operation of a person, or of a member of the controlled group (within the meaning of section 993(a)(3)) which includes that person, in or related to any country within the group of countries referred to in paragraph (1) shall not be treated as an operation in or related to a group of countries associated in carrying out an international boycott if the person can clearly demonstrate that he, or that such member, did not participate in or cooperate with the international boycott in connection with that operation.

(B) SEPARATE AND IDENTIFIABLE OPERATIONS.—A taxpayer may show that different operations within the same country, or operations in different countries, are clearly separate and identifiable operations.

(3) DEFINITION OF BOYCOTT PARTICIPATION AND COOPERATION.—For purposes of this section, a person participates in or cooperates with an international boycott if he agrees—

(A) as a condition of doing business directly or indirectly within a country or with the government, a company, or a national of a country—

(i) to refrain from doing business with or in a country which is the object of the boycott or with the government, companies, or nationals of that country;

(ii) to refrain from doing business with any United States person engaged in trade in a country which is the object of the boycott or with the government, companies, or nationals of that country;

(iii) to refrain from doing business with any company whose ownership or management is made up, all or in part, of individuals of a particular nationality, race, or religion, or to remove (or refrain from selecting) corporate directors who are individuals of a particular nationality, race, or religion; or

(iv) to refrain from employing individuals of a particular nationality, race, or religion; or

(B) as a condition of the sale of a product to the government, a company, or a national of a country, to refrain from shipping or insuring that product on a carrier owned, leased, or operated by a person who does not participate in or cooperate with an international boycott (within the meaning of subparagraph (A)).

(4) COMPLIANCE WITH CERTAIN LAWS.—This section shall not apply to any agreement by a person (or such member)—

(A) to meet requirements imposed by a foreign country with respect to an international boycott if United States law or regulations, or an Executive Order, sanctions participation in, or cooperation with, that international boycott,

(B) to comply with a prohibition on the importation of goods produced in whole or in part in any country which is the object of an international boycott, or

(C) to comply with a prohibition imposed by a country on the exportation of products obtained in such country to any country which is the object of an international boycott.

[Sec. 999(c)]

(c) INTERNATIONAL BOYCOTT FACTOR.—

(1) INTERNATIONAL BOYCOTT FACTOR.—For purposes of sections 908(a), 952(a)(3), and 995(b)(1)(F)(ii), the international boycott factor is a fraction, determined under regulations prescribed by the Secretary, the numerator of which reflects the world-wide operations of a person (or, in the case of a controlled group (within the meaning of section 993(a)(3)) which includes that person, of the group) which are operations in or related to a group of countries associated in carrying out an international boycott in or with which that person or a member of that controlled group has participated or cooperated in the taxable year, and the denominator of which reflects the world-wide operations of that person or group.

(2) SPECIFICALLY ATTRIBUTABLE TAXES AND INCOME.—If the taxpayer clearly demonstrates that the foreign taxes paid and income earned for the taxable year are attributable to specific operations, then, in lieu of applying the international boycott factor for such taxable year, the amount of the credit disallowed under section 908(a), the addition to subpart F income under section 952(a)(3), and the amount of deemed distribution under section 995(b)(1)(F)(ii) for the taxable year, if any, shall be the amount specifically attributable to the operations in which there was participation in or cooperation with an international boycott under section 999(b)(1).

(3) WORLD-WIDE OPERATIONS.—For purposes of this subsection, the term "world-wide operations" means operations in or related to countries other than the United States.

[Sec. 999(d)]

(d) DETERMINATION WITH RESPECT TO PARTICULAR OPERATIONS.—Upon a request made by the taxpayer, the Secretary shall issue a determination with respect to whether a particular operation of the person, or of a member of a controlled group which includes that person, constitutes participation in or cooperation with an international boycott. The Secretary may issue such a determination in advance of such operation in cases which are of such a nature that an advance determination is possible and appropriate under the circumstances. If the request is made before the operation is commenced, or before the end of a taxable year in which the operation is carried out, the Secretary may decline to issue such a determination before the close of the taxable year.

[Sec. 999(e)]

(e) PARTICIPATION OR COOPERATION BY RELATED PERSONS.—If a person controls (within the meaning of section 304(c)) a corporation—

(1) participation in or cooperation with an international boycott by such corporation shall be presumed to be such participation or cooperation by such person, and

Sec. 999(b)(3)(A)(iii)

(2) participation in or cooperation with such a boycott by such person shall be presumed to be such participation or cooperation by such corporation.

[Sec. 999(f)]

(f) WILLFUL FAILURE TO REPORT.—Any person (within the meaning of section 6671(b)) required to report under this section who willfully fails to make such report shall, in addition to other penalties provided by law, be fined not more than $25,000, imprisoned for not more than one year, or both.

SUBCHAPTER O—GAIN OR LOSS ON DISPOSITION OF PROPERTY

PART III—COMMON NONTAXABLE EXCHANGES

[Sec. 1031]

SEC. 1031. EXCHANGE OF PROPERTY HELD FOR PRODUCTIVE USE OR INVESTMENT.

* * *

[Sec. 1031(h)]

(h) SPECIAL RULES FOR FOREIGN REAL AND PERSONAL PROPERTY.—For purposes of this section—

(1) REAL PROPERTY.—Real property located in the United States and real property located outside the United States are not property of a like kind.

(2) PERSONAL PROPERTY.—

(A) IN GENERAL.—Personal property used predominantly within the United States and personal property used predominantly outside the United States are not property of a like kind.

(B) PREDOMINANT USE.—Except as provided in subparagraph (C) and (D), the predominant use of any property shall be determined based on—

(i) in the case of the property relinquished in the exchange, the 2-year period ending on the date of such relinquishment, and

(ii) in the case of the property acquired in the exchange, the 2-year period beginning on the date of such acquisition.

(C) PROPERTY HELD FOR LESS THAN 2 YEARS.—Except in the case of an exchange which is part of a transaction (or series of transactions) structured to avoid the purposes of this subsection—

(i) only the periods the property was held by the person relinquishing the property (or any related person) shall be taken into account under subparagraph (B)(i), and

(ii) only the periods the property was held by the person acquiring the property (or any related person) shall be taken into account under subparagraph (B)(ii).

(D) SPECIAL RULE FOR CERTAIN PROPERTY.—Property described in any subparagraph of section 168(g)(4) shall be treated as used predominantly in the United States.

PART IV—SPECIAL RULES

[Sec. 1058]

SEC. 1058. TRANSFER OF SECURITIES UNDER CERTAIN AGREEMENTS.

[Sec. 1058(a)]

(a) GENERAL RULE.—In the case of a taxpayer who transfers securities (as defined in section 1236(c)) pursuant to an agreement which meets the requirements of subsection (b), no gain or loss shall be recognized on the exchange of such securities by the taxpayer for an obligation under such agreement, or on the exchange of rights under such agreement by that taxpayer for securities identical to the securities transferred by that taxpayer.

[Sec. 1058(b)]

(b) AGREEMENT REQUIREMENTS.—In order to meet the requirements of this subsection, an agreement shall—

(1) provide for the return to the transferor of securities identical to the securities transferred;

(2) require that payments shall be made to the transferor of amounts equivalent to all interest, dividends, and other distributions which the owner of the securities is entitled to receive during the period beginning with the transfer of the securities by the transferor and ending with the transfer of identical securities back to the transferor;

(3) not reduce the risk of loss or opportunity for gain of the transferor of the securities in the securities transferred; and

(4) meet such other requirements as the Secretary may by regulation prescribe.

[Sec. 1058(c)]

(c) BASIS.—Property acquired by a taxpayer described in subsection (a), in a transaction described in that subsection, shall have the same basis as the property transferred by that taxpayer.

[Sec. 1059A]

SEC. 1059A. LIMITATION ON TAXPAYER'S BASIS OR INVENTORY COST IN PROPERTY IMPORTED FROM RELATED PERSONS.

[Sec. 1059A(a)]

(a) IN GENERAL.—If any property is imported into the United States in a transaction (directly or indirectly) between related persons (within the meaning of section 482), the amount of any costs—

(1) which are taken into account in computing the basis or inventory cost of such property by the purchaser, and

(2) which are also taken into account in computing the customs value of such property,

shall not, for purposes of computing such basis or inventory cost for purposes of this chapter, be greater than the amount of such costs taken into account in computing such customs value.

[Sec. 1059A(b)]

(b) CUSTOMS VALUE; IMPORT.—For purposes of this section—

(1) CUSTOMS VALUE.—The term "customs value" means the value taken into account for purposes of determining the amount of any customs duties or any other duties which may be imposed on the importation of any property.

(2) IMPORT.—Except as provided in regulations, the term "import" means the entering, or withdrawal from warehouse, for consumption.

SUBCHAPTER P—CAPITAL GAINS AND LOSSES

PART III—GENERAL RULES FOR DETERMINING CAPITAL GAINS AND LOSSES

[Sec. 1221]

SEC. 1221. CAPITAL ASSET DEFINED.

[Sec. 1221(a)]

(a) IN GENERAL.—For purposes of this subtitle, the term "capital asset" means property held by the taxpayer (whether or not connected with his trade or business), but does not include—

(1) stock in trade of the taxpayer or other property of a kind which would properly be included in the inventory of the taxpayer if on hand at the close of the taxable year, or property held by the taxpayer primarily for sale to customers in the ordinary course of his trade or business;

Income Tax—Capital Gains, Losses

(2) property, used in his trade or business, of a character which is subject to the allowance for depreciation provided in section 167, or real property used in his trade or business;

(3) a copyright, a literary, musical, or artistic composition, a letter or memorandum, or similar property, held by—

(A) a taxpayer whose personal efforts created such property,

(B) in the case of a letter, memorandum, or similar property, a taxpayer for whom such property was prepared or produced, or

⇾ *Caution: Code Sec. 1221(a)(3)(C), below, applies to estates of decedents dying on or before December 31, 2009.*

(C) a taxpayer in whose hands the basis of such property is determined, for purposes of determining gain from a sale or exchange, in whole or part by reference to the basis of such property in the hands of a taxpayer described in subparagraph (A) or (B);

⇾ *Caution: Code Sec. 1221(a)(3)(C), below, applies to estates of decedents dying after December 31, 2009.*

(C) a taxpayer in whose hands the basis of such property is determined (other than by reason of section 1022), for purposes of determining gain from a sale or exchange, in whole or part by reference to the basis of such property in the hands of a taxpayer described in subparagraph (A) or (B);

(4) accounts or notes receivable acquired in the ordinary course of trade or business for services rendered or from the sale of property described in paragraph (1);

(5) a publication of the United States Government (including the Congressional Record) which is received from the United States Government or any agency thereof, other than by purchase at the price at which it is offered for sale to the public, and which is held by—

(A) a taxpayer who so received such publication, or

(B) a taxpayer in whose hands the basis of such publication is determined, for purposes of determining gain from a sale or exchange, in whole or in part by reference to the basis of such publication in the hands of a taxpayer described in subparagraph (A);

(6) any commodities derivative financial instrument held by a commodities derivatives dealer, unless—

(A) it is established to the satisfaction of the Secretary that such instrument has no connection to the activities of such dealer as a dealer, and

(B) such instrument is clearly identified in such dealer's records as being described in subparagraph (A) before the close of the day on which it was acquired, originated, or entered into (or such other time as the Secretary may by regulations prescribe);

(7) any hedging transaction which is clearly identified as such before the close of the day on which it was acquired, originated, or entered into (or such other time as the Secretary may by regulations prescribe); or

(8) supplies of a type regularly used or consumed by the taxpayer in the ordinary course of a trade or business of the taxpayer.

[Sec. 1221(b)]

(b) DEFINITIONS AND SPECIAL RULES.—

(1) COMMODITIES DERIVATIVE FINANCIAL INSTRUMENTS.—For purposes of subsection (a)(6)—

(A) COMMODITIES DERIVATIVES DEALER.—The term "commodities derivatives dealer" means a person which regularly offers to enter into, assume, offset, assign, or terminate positions in commodities derivative financial instruments with customers in the ordinary course of a trade or business.

(B) COMMODITIES DERIVATIVE FINANCIAL INSTRUMENT.—

(i) IN GENERAL.—The term "commodities derivative financial instrument" means any contract or financial instrument with respect to commodities (other than a share of stock in a corporation, a beneficial interest in a partnership or trust, a note, bond, debenture, or other evidence of indebtedness, or a section 1256 contract (as defined in section 1256(b))), the value or settlement price of which is calculated by or determined by reference to a specified index.

(ii) SPECIFIED INDEX.—The term "specified index" means any one or more or any combination of—

(I) a fixed rate, price, or amount, or

(II) a variable rate, price, or amount,

which is based on any current, objectively determinable financial or economic information with respect to commodities which is not within the control of any of the parties to the contract or instrument and is not unique to any of the parties' circumstances.

(2) HEDGING TRANSACTION.—

(A) IN GENERAL.—For purposes of this section, the term "hedging transaction" means any transaction entered into by the taxpayer in the normal course of the taxpayer's trade or business primarily—

(i) to manage risk of price changes or currency fluctuations with respect to ordinary property which is held or to be held by the taxpayer,

(ii) to manage risk of interest rate or price changes or currency fluctuations with respect to borrowings made or to be made, or ordinary obligations incurred or to be incurred, by the taxpayer, or

(iii) to manage such other risks as the Secretary may prescribe in regulations.

(B) TREATMENT OF NONIDENTIFICATION OR IMPROPER IDENTIFICATION OF HEDGING TRANSACTIONS.—Notwithstanding subsection (a)(7), the Secretary shall prescribe regulations to properly characterize any income, gain, expense, or loss arising from a transaction—

(i) which is a hedging transaction but which was not identified as such in accordance with subsection (a)(7), or

(ii) which was so identified but is not a hedging transaction.

(3) REGULATIONS.—The Secretary shall prescribe such regulations as are appropriate to carry out the purposes of paragraph (6) and (7) of subsection (a) in the case of transactions involving related parties.

[Sec. 1222]

SEC. 1222. OTHER TERMS RELATING TO CAPITAL GAINS AND LOSSES.

For purposes of this subtitle—

(1) SHORT-TERM CAPITAL GAIN.—The term "short-term capital gain" means gain from the sale or exchange of a capital asset held for not more than 1 year, if and to the extent such gain is taken into account in computing gross income.

(2) SHORT-TERM CAPITAL LOSS.—The term "short-term capital loss" means loss from the sale or exchange of a capital asset held for not more than 1 year, if and to the extent that such loss is taken into account in computing taxable income.

(3) LONG-TERM CAPITAL GAIN.—The term "long-term capital gain" means gain from the sale or exchange of a capital asset held for more than 1 year, if and to the extent such gain is taken into account in computing gross income.

(4) LONG-TERM CAPITAL LOSS.—The term "long-term capital loss" means loss from the sale or exchange of a capital asset held for more than 1 year, if and to the extent that such loss is taken into account in computing taxable income.

(5) NET SHORT-TERM CAPITAL GAIN.—The term "net short-term capital gain" means the excess of short-term capital gains for the taxable year over the short-term capital losses for such year.

(6) NET SHORT-TERM CAPITAL LOSS.—The term "net short-term capital loss" means the excess of short-term capital losses for the taxable year over the short-term capital gains for such year.

(7) NET LONG-TERM CAPITAL GAIN.—The term "net long-term capital gain" means the excess of long-term capital gains for the taxable year over the long-term capital losses for such year.

(8) NET LONG-TERM CAPITAL LOSS.—The term "net long-term capital loss" means the excess of long-term capital losses for the taxable year over the long-term capital gains for such year.

(9) CAPITAL GAIN NET INCOME.—The term "capital gain net income" means the excess of the gains from sales or exchanges of capital assets over the losses from such sales or exchanges.

(10) NET CAPITAL LOSS.—The term "net capital loss" means the excess of the losses from sales or exchanges of capital assets over the sum allowed under section 1211. In the case of a corporation, for the purpose of determining losses under this paragraph, amounts which are short-term capital losses under section 1212 shall be excluded.

(11) NET CAPITAL GAIN.—The term "net capital gain" means the excess of the net long-term capital gain for the taxable year over the net short-term capital loss for such year.

For purposes of this subtitle, in the case of futures transactions in any commodity subject to the rules of a board of trade or commodity exchange, the length of the holding period taken into account under this section or under any other section amended by section 1402 of the Tax Reform Act of 1976 shall be determined without regard to the amendments made by subsections (a) and (b) of such section 1402.

PART IV—SPECIAL RULES FOR DETERMINING CAPITAL GAINS AND LOSSES

[Sec. 1231]

SEC. 1231. PROPERTY USED IN THE TRADE OR BUSINESS AND INVOLUNTARY CONVERSIONS.

[Sec. 1231(a)]

(a) GENERAL RULE.—

(1) GAINS EXCEED LOSSES.—If—

(A) the section 1231 gains for any taxable year, exceed

(B) the section 1231 losses for such taxable year,

such gains and losses shall be treated as long-term capital gains or long-term capital losses, as the case may be.

(2) GAINS DO NOT EXCEED LOSSES.—If—

(A) the section 1231 gains for any taxable year, do not exceed

(B) the section 1231 losses for such taxable year,

such gains and losses shall not be treated as gains and losses from sales or exchanges of capital assets.

(3) SECTION 1231 GAINS AND LOSSES.—For purposes of this subsection—

(A) SECTION 1231 GAIN.—The term "section 1231 gain" means—

(i) any recognized gain on the sale or exchange of property used in the trade or business, and

(ii) any recognized gain from the compulsory or involuntary conversion (as a result of destruction in whole or in part, theft or seizure, or an exercise of the power of requisition or condemnation or the threat or imminence thereof) into other property or money of—

(I) property used in the trade or business, or

(II) any capital asset which is held for more than 1 year and is held in connection with a trade or business or a transaction entered into for profit.

(B) SECTION 1231 LOSS.—The term "section 1231 loss" means any recognized loss from a sale or exchange or conversion described in subparagraph (A).

(4) SPECIAL RULES.—For purposes of this subsection—

(A) In determining under this subsection whether gains exceed losses—

(i) the section 1231 gains shall be included only if and to the extent taken into account in computing gross income, and

(ii) the section 1231 losses shall be included only if and to the extent taken into account in computing taxable income, except that section 1211 shall not apply.

(B) Losses (including losses not compensated for by insurance or otherwise) on the destruction, in whole or in part, theft or seizure, or requisition or condemnation of—

(i) property used in the trade or business, or

(ii) capital assets which are held for more than 1 year and are held in connection with a trade or business or a transaction entered into for profit,

shall be treated as losses from a compulsory or involuntary conversion.

(C) In the case of any involuntary conversion (subject to the provisions of this subsection but for this sentence) arising from fire, storm, shipwreck, or other casualty, or from theft, of any—

(i) property used in the trade or business, or

(ii) any capital asset which is held for more than 1 year and is held in connection with a trade or business or a transaction entered into for profit,

this subsection shall not apply to such conversion (whether resulting in gain or loss) if during the taxable year the recognized losses from such conversions exceed the recognized gains from such conversions.

[Sec. 1231(b)]

(b) DEFINITION OF PROPERTY USED IN THE TRADE OR BUSINESS.—For purposes of this section—

(1) GENERAL RULE.—The term "property used in the trade or business" means property used in the trade or business, of a character which is subject to the allowance for depreciation provided in section 167, held for more than 1 year, and real property used in the trade or business, held for more than 1 year, which is not—

(A) property of a kind which would properly be includible in the inventory of the taxpayer if on hand at the close of the taxable year,

(B) property held by the taxpayer primarily for sale to customers in the ordinary course of his trade or business,

(C) a copyright, a literary, musical, or artistic composition, a letter or memorandum, or similar property, held by a taxpayer described in paragraph (3) of section 1221(a), or

(D) a publication of the United States Government (including the Congressional Record) which is received from the United States Government, or any agency thereof, other than by purchase at the price at which it is offered for sale to the public, and which is held by a taxpayer described in paragraph (5) of section 1221(a).

(2) TIMBER, COAL, OR DOMESTIC IRON ORE.—Such term includes timber, coal, and iron ore with respect to which section 631 applies.

(3) LIVESTOCK.—Such term includes—

(A) cattle and horses, regardless of age, held by the taxpayer for draft, breeding, dairy, or sporting purposes, and held by him for 24 months or more from the date of acquisition, and

(B) other livestock, regardless of age, held by the taxpayer for draft, breeding, dairy, or sporting purposes, and held by him for 12 months or more from the date of acquisition.

Such term does not include poultry.

(4) UNHARVESTED CROP.—In the case of an unharvested crop on land used in the trade or business and held for more than 1 year, if the crop and the land are sold or exchanged (or compulsorily or involuntarily converted) at the same time and to the same person, the crop shall be considered as "property used in the trade or business."

* * *

Income Tax—Capital Gains, Losses

[Sec. 1235]

SEC. 1235. SALE OR EXCHANGE OF PATENTS.

[Sec. 1235(a)]

(a) GENERAL.—A transfer (other than by gift, inheritance, or devise) of property consisting of all substantial rights to a patent, or an undivided interest therein which includes a part of all such rights, by any holder shall be considered the sale or exchange of a capital asset held for more than 1 year, regardless of whether or not payments in consideration of such transfer are—

(1) payable periodically over a period generally coterminous with the transferee's use of the patent, or

(2) contingent on the productivity, use, or disposition of the property transferred.

[Sec. 1235(b)]

(b) "HOLDER"DEFINED.—For purposes of this section, the term "holder" means—

(1) any individual whose efforts created such property, or

(2) any other individual who has acquired his interest in such property in exchange for consideration in money or money's worth paid to such creator prior to actual reduction to practice of the invention covered by the patent, if such individual is neither—

(A) the employer of such creator, nor

(B) related to such creator (within the meaning of subsection (d)).

[Sec. 1235(c)]

(c) EFFECTIVE DATE.—This section shall be applicable with regard to any amounts received, or payments made, pursuant to a transfer described in subsection (a) in any taxable year to which this subtitle applies, regardless of the taxable year in which such transfer occurred.

[Sec. 1235(d)]

(d) RELATED PERSONS.—Subsection (a) shall not apply to any transfer, directly or indirectly, between persons specified within any one of the paragraphs of section 267(b) or persons described in section 707(b); except that, in applying section 267(b) and (c) and section 707(b) for purposes of this section—

(1) the phrase "25 percent or more" shall be substituted for the phrase "more than 50 percent" each place it appears in section 267(b) or 707(b), and

(2) paragraph (4) of section 267(c) shall be treated as providing that the family of an individual shall include only his spouse, ancestors, and lineal descendants.

[Sec. 1235(e)]

(e) CROSS REFERENCE.—

For special rule relating to nonresident aliens, see section 871(a).

[Sec. 1236]

SEC. 1236. DEALERS IN SECURITIES.

* * *

[Sec. 1236(c)]

(c) DEFINITION OF SECURITY.—For purposes of this section, the term "security" means any share of stock in any corporation, certificate of stock or interest in any corporation, note, bond, debenture, or evidence of indebtedness, or any evidence of an interest in or right to subscribe to or purchase any of the foregoing.

* * *

[Sec. 1239]

SEC. 1239. GAIN FROM SALE OF DEPRECIABLE PROPERTY BETWEEN CERTAIN RELATED TAXPAYERS.

[Sec. 1239(a)]

(a) TREATMENT OF GAIN AS ORDINARY INCOME.—In the case of a sale or exchange of property, directly or indirectly, between related persons, any gain recognized to the transferor shall be treated as ordinary income if such property is, in the hands of the transferee, of a character which is subject to the allowance for depreciation provided in section 167.

[Sec. 1239(b)]

(b) RELATED PERSONS.—For purposes of subsection (a), the term "related persons" means—

(1) a person and all entities which are controlled entities with respect to such person,

(2) a taxpayer and any trust in which such taxpayer (or his spouse) is a beneficiary, unless such beneficiary's interest in the trust is a remote contingent interest (within the meaning of section 318(a)(3)(B)(i)), and

(3) except in the case of a sale or exchange in satisfaction of a pecuniary bequest, an executor of an estate and a beneficiary of such estate.

[Sec. 1239(c)]

(c) CONTROLLED ENTITY DEFINED.—

(1) GENERAL RULE.—For purposes of this section, the term "controlled entity" means, with respect to any person—

(A) a corporation more than 50 percent of the value of the outstanding stock of which is owned (directly or indirectly) by or for such person,

(B) a partnership more than 50 percent of the capital interest or profits interest in which is owned (directly or indirectly) by or for such person, and

(C) any entity which is a related person to such person under paragraph (3), (10), (11), or (12) of section 267(b).

(2) CONSTRUCTIVE OWNERSHIP.—For purposes of this section, ownership shall be determined in accordance with rules similar to the rules under section 267(c) (other than paragraph (3) thereof).

* * *

[Sec. 1239(e)]

(e) PATENT APPLICATIONS TREATED AS DEPRECIABLE PROPERTY.—For purposes of this section, a patent application shall be treated as property which, in the hands of the transferee, is of a character which is subject to the allowance for depreciation provided in section 167.

[Sec. 1248]

SEC. 1248. GAIN FROM CERTAIN SALES OR EXCHANGES OF STOCK IN CERTAIN FOREIGN CORPORATIONS.

[Sec. 1248(a)]

(a) GENERAL RULE.—If—

(1) a United States person sells or exchanges stock in a foreign corporation, and

(2) such person owns, within the meaning of section 958(a), or is considered as owning by applying the rules of ownership of section 958(b), 10 percent or more of the total combined voting power of all classes of stock entitled to vote of such foreign corporation at any time during the 5-year period ending on the date of the sale or exchange when such foreign corporation was a controlled foreign corporation (as defined in section 957),

then the gain recognized on the sale or exchange of such stock shall be included in the gross income of such person as a dividend, to the extent of the earnings and profits of the foreign corporation attributable (under regulations prescribed by the Secretary) to such stock which were accumulated in taxable years of such foreign corporation beginning after December 31, 1962, and during the period or periods the stock sold or exchanged was held by such person while such foreign corporation was a controlled foreign corporation. For purposes of this section, a United States person shall be treated as having sold or exchanged any stock if, under any provision of this subtitle, such person is treated as realizing gain from the sale or exchange of such stock.

[Sec. 1248(b)]

(b) LIMITATION ON TAX APPLICABLE TO INDIVIDUALS.—In the case of an individual, if the stock sold or exchanged is a capital asset (within the meaning of section 1221) and has been held for more than 1 year, the tax attributable to an amount included in gross income as a dividend under subsection (a) shall not be greater than a tax equal to the sum of—

(1) a pro rata share of the excess of—

(A) the taxes that would have been paid by the foreign corporation with respect to its income had it been taxed under this chapter as a domestic corporation (but without allowance for deduction of, or credit for, taxes described in subparagraph (B)), for the period or periods the stock sold or exchanged was held by the United States person in taxable years beginning after December 31, 1962, while the foreign corporation was a controlled foreign corporation, adjusted for distributions and amounts previously included in gross income of a United States shareholder under section 951, over

(B) the income, war profits, or excess profits taxes paid by the foreign corporation with respect to such income; and

(2) an amount equal to the tax that would result by including in gross income, as gain from the sale or exchange of a capital asset held for more than 1 year, an amount equal to the excess of (A) the amount included in gross income as a dividend under subsection (a), over (B) the amount determined under paragraph (1).

[Sec. 1248(c)]

(c) DETERMINATION OF EARNINGS AND PROFITS.—

(1) IN GENERAL.—Except as provided in section 312(k)(4), for purposes of this section the earnings and profits of any foreign corporation for any taxable year shall be determined according to rules substantially similar to those applicable to domestic corporations, under regulations prescribed by the Secretary.

(2) EARNINGS AND PROFITS OF SUBSIDIARIES OF FOREIGN CORPORATIONS.—If—

(A) subsection (a) or (f) applies to a sale, exchange, or distribution by a United States person of stock of a foreign corporation and, by reason of the ownership of the stock sold or exchanged, such person owned within the meaning of section 958(a)(2) stock of any other foreign corporation; and

(B) such person owned, within the meaning of section 958(a), or was considered as owning by applying the rules of ownership of section 958(b), 10 percent or more of the total combined voting power of all classes of stock entitled to vote of such other foreign corporation at any time during the 5-year period ending on the date of the sale or exchange when such other foreign corporation was a controlled foreign corporation (as defined in section 957),

then, for purposes of this section, the earnings and profits of the foreign corporation the stock of which is sold or exchanged which are attributable to the stock sold or exchanged shall be deemed to include the earnings and profits of such other foreign corporation which—

(C) are attributable (under regulations prescribed by the Secretary) to the stock of such other foreign corporation which such person owned within the meaning of section 958(a)(2) (by reason of his ownership within the meaning of section 958(a)(1)(A) of the stock sold or exchanged) on the date of such sale or exchange (or on the date of any sale or exchange of the stock of such other foreign corporation occurring during the 5-year period ending on the date of the sale or exchange of the stock of such foreign corporation, to the extent not otherwise taken into account under this section but not in excess of the fair market value of the stock of such other foreign corporation sold or exchanged over the basis of such stock (for determining gain) in the hands of the transferor); and

(D) were accumulated in taxable years of such other corporation beginning after December 31, 1962, and during the period or periods—

(i) such other corporation was a controlled foreign corporation, and

(ii) such person owned within the meaning of section 958(a) the stock of such other foreign corporation.

[Sec. 1248(d)]

(d) EXCLUSIONS FROM EARNINGS AND PROFITS.—For purposes of this section, the following amounts shall be excluded, with respect to any United States person, from the earnings and profits of a foreign corporation.

(1) AMOUNTS INCLUDED IN GROSS INCOME UNDER SECTION 951.—Earnings and profits of the foreign corporation attributable to any amount previously included in the gross income of such person under section 951, with respect to the stock sold or exchanged, but only to the extent the inclusion of such amount did not result in an exclusion of an amount from gross income under section 959.

(2) [Stricken]

(3) LESS DEVELOPED COUNTRY CORPORATIONS UNDER PRIOR LAW.—Earnings and profits of a foreign corporation which were accumulated during any taxable year beginning before January 1, 1976, while such corporation was a less developed country corporation under section 902(d) as in effect before the enactment of the Tax Reduction Act of 1975.

(4) UNITED STATES INCOME.—Any item includible in gross income of the foreign corporation under this chapter—

(A) for any taxable year beginning before January 1, 1967, as income derived from sources within the United States of a foreign corporation engaged in trade or business within the United States, or

(B) for any taxable year beginning after December 31, 1966, as income effectively connected with the conduct by such corporation of a trade or business within the United States.

This paragraph shall not apply with respect to any item which is exempt from taxation (or is subject to a reduced rate of tax) pursuant to a treaty obligation of the United States.

(5) FOREIGN TRADE INCOME.—Earnings and profits of the foreign corporation attributable to foreign trade income of a FSC other than foreign trade income which—

(A) is section 923(a)(2) non-exempt income (within the meaning of section 927(d)(6)), or

(B) would not (but for section 923(a)(4)) be treated as exempt foreign trade income.

For purposes of the preceding sentence, the terms "foreign trade income" and "exempt foreign trade income" have the respective meanings given such terms by section 923.

(6) AMOUNTS INCLUDED IN GROSS INCOME UNDER SECTION 1293.—Earnings and profits of the foreign corporation attributable to any amount previously included in the gross income of such person under section 1293 with respect to the stock sold or exchanged, but only to the extent the inclusion of such amount did not result in an exclusion of an amount under section 1293(c).

[Sec. 1248(e)]

(e) SALES OR EXCHANGES OF STOCK IN CERTAIN DOMESTIC CORPORATIONS.—Except as provided in regulations prescribed by the Secretary, if—

(1) a United States person sells or exchanges stock of a domestic corporation, and

(2) such domestic corporation was formed or availed of principally for the holding, directly or indirectly, of stock of one or more foreign corporations,

such sale or exchange shall, for purposes of this section, be treated as a sale or exchange of the stock of the foreign corporation or corporations held by the domestic corporation.

[Sec. 1248(f)]

(f) NONRECOGNITION TRANSACTIONS.—Except as provided in regulations prescribed by the Secretary—

(1) IN GENERAL.—If—

(A) a domestic corporation satisfies the stock ownership requirements of subsection (a)(2) with respect to a foreign corporation, and

(B) such domestic corporation distributes stock of such foreign corporation in a distribution to which section 311(a), 337, 355(c)(1), or 361(c)(1) applies,

then, notwithstanding any other provision of this subtitle, an amount equal to the excess of the fair market value of such stock over its adjusted basis in the hands of the domestic corporation shall be included in the gross income of the domestic corporation as a dividend to the extent of the earnings and profits of the foreign corporation attributable (under regulations prescribed by the Secretary) to such stock which were accumulated in taxable years of such foreign corporation beginning after December 31, 1962, and during the period or periods the stock was held by such domestic corporation while such foreign corporation was a controlled foreign corporation. For purposes of subsections (c)(2), (d), and (h), a distribution of stock to which this subsection applies shall be treated as a sale of stock to which subsection (a) applies.

(2) EXCEPTION FOR CERTAIN DISTRIBUTIONS.—In the case of any distribution of stock of a foreign corporation, paragraph (1) shall not apply if such distribution is to a domestic corporation—

(A) which is treated under this section as holding such stock for the period for which the stock was held by the distributing corporation, and

(B) which, immediately after the distribution, satisfies the stock ownership requirements of subsection (a)(2) with respect to such foreign corporation.

(3) APPLICATION TO CASES DESCRIBED IN SUBSECTION (e).—To the extent that earnings and profits are taken into account under this subsection, they shall be excluded and not taken into account for purposes of subsection (e).

[Sec. 1248(g)]

(g) EXCEPTIONS.—This section shall not apply to—

(1) distributions to which section 303 (relating to distributions in redemption of stock to pay death taxes) applies; or

(2) any amount to the extent that such amount is, under any other provision of this title, treated as—

(A) a dividend (other than an amount treated as a dividend under subsection (f)),

(B) ordinary income, or

(C) gain from the sale of an asset held for not more than 1 year.

[Sec. 1248(h)]

(h) TAXPAYER TO ESTABLISH EARNINGS AND PROFITS.—Unless the taxpayer establishes the amount of the earnings and profits of the foreign corporation to be taken into account under subsection (a) or (f), all gain from the sale or exchange shall be considered a dividend under subsection (a) or (f), and unless the taxpayer establishes the amount of foreign taxes to be taken into account under subsection (b), the limitation of such subsection shall not apply.

[Sec. 1248(i)]

(i) TREATMENT OF CERTAIN INDIRECT TRANSFERS.—

(1) IN GENERAL.—If any shareholder of a 10-percent corporate shareholder of a foreign corporation exchanges stock of the 10-percent corporate shareholder for stock of the foreign corporation, such 10-percent corporate shareholder shall recognize gain in the same manner as if the stock of the foreign corporation received in such exchange had been—

(A) issued to the 10-percent corporate shareholder, and

(B) then distributed by the 10-percent corporate shareholder to such shareholder in redemption or liquidation (whichever is appropriate).

The amount of gain recognized by such 10-percent corporate shareholder under the preceding sentence shall not exceed the amount treated as a dividend under this section.

(2) 10-PERCENT CORPORATE SHAREHOLDER DEFINED.—For purposes of this subsection, the term "10-percent corporate shareholder" means any domestic corporation which, as of the

day before the exchange referred to in paragraph (1), satisfies the stock ownership requirements of subsection (a)(2) with respect to the foreign corporation.

[Sec. 1248(j)]

(j) CROSS REFERENCE.—

For provision excluding amounts previously taxed under this section from gross income when subsequently distributed, see section 959(e).

[Sec. 1249]

SEC. 1249. GAIN FROM CERTAIN SALES OR EXCHANGES OF PATENTS, ETC., TO FOREIGN CORPORATIONS.

[Sec. 1249(a)]

(a) GENERAL RULE.—Gain from the sale or exchange after December 31, 1962, of a patent, an invention, model, or design (whether or not patented), a copyright, a secret formula or process, or any other similar property right to any foreign corporation by any United States person (as defined in section 7701(a)(30)) which controls such foreign corporation shall, if such gain would (but for the provisions of this subsection) be gain from the sale or exchange of a capital asset or of property described in section 1231, be considered as ordinary income.

[Sec. 1249(b)]

(b) CONTROL.—For purposes of subsection (a), control means, with respect to any foreign corporation, the ownership, directly or indirectly, of stock possessing more than 50 percent of the total combined voting power of all classes of stock entitled to vote. For purposes of this subsection, the rules for determining ownership of stock prescribed by section 958 shall apply.

[Sec. 1253]

SEC. 1253. TRANSFERS OF FRANCHISES, TRADEMARKS, AND TRADE NAMES.

[Sec. 1253(a)]

(a) GENERAL RULE.—A transfer of a franchise, trademark, or trade name shall not be treated as a sale or exchange of a capital asset if the transferor retains any significant power, right, or continuing interest with respect to the subject matter of the franchise, trademark, or trade name.

[Sec. 1253(b)]

(b) DEFINITIONS.—For purposes of this section—

(1) FRANCHISE.—The term "franchise" includes an agreement which gives one of the parties to the agreement the right to distribute, sell, or provide goods, services, or facilities, within a specified area.

(2) SIGNIFICANT POWER, RIGHT, OR CONTINUING INTEREST.—The term "significant power, right, or continuing interest" includes, but is not limited to, the following rights with respect to the interest transferred:

(A) A right to disapprove any assignment of such interest, or any part thereof.

(B) A right to terminate at will.

(C) A right to prescribe the standards of quality of products used or sold, or of services furnished, and of the equipment and facilities used to promote such products or services.

(D) A right to require that the transferee sell or advertise only products or services of the transferor.

(E) A right to require that the transferee purchase substantially all of his supplies and equipment from the transferor.

(F) A right to payments contingent on the productivity, use, or disposition of the subject matter of the interest transferred, if such payments constitute a substantial element under the transfer agreement.

(3) TRANSFER.—The term "transfer" includes the renewal of a franchise, trademark, or trade name.

[Sec. 1253(c)]

(c) TREATMENT OF CONTINGENT PAYMENTS BY TRANSFEROR.—Amounts received or accrued on account of a transfer, sale, or other disposition of a franchise, trademark, or trade name which are contingent on the productivity, use, or disposition of the franchise, trademark, or trade name transferred shall be treated as amounts received or accrued from the sale or other disposition of property which is not a capital asset.

[Sec. 1253(d)]

(d) TREATMENT OF PAYMENTS BY TRANSFEREE.—

(1) CONTINGENT SERIAL PAYMENTS.—

(A) IN GENERAL.—Any amount described in subparagraph (B) which is paid or incurred during the taxable year on account of a transfer, sale, or other disposition of a franchise, trademark, or trade name shall be allowed as a deduction under section 162(a) (relating to trade or business expenses).

(B) AMOUNTS TO WHICH PARAGRAPH APPLIES.—An amount is described in this subparagraph if it—

(i) is contingent on the productivity, use, or disposition of the franchise, trademark, or trade name, and

(ii) is paid as part of a series of payments—

(I) which are payable not less frequently than annually throughout the entire term of the transfer agreement, and

(II) which are substantially equal in amount (or payable under a fixed formula).

(2) OTHER PAYMENTS.—Any amount paid or incurred on account of a transfer, sale, or other disposition of a franchise, trademark, or trade name to which paragraph (1) does not apply shall be treated as an amount chargeable to capital account.

(3) RENEWALS, ETC.—For purposes of determining the term of a transfer agreement under this section, there shall be taken into account all renewal options (and any other period for which the parties reasonably expect the agreement to be renewed).

PART V—SPECIAL RULES FOR BONDS AND OTHER DEBT INSTRUMENTS

Subpart A—Original Issue Discount

[Sec. 1271]

SEC. 1271. TREATMENT OF AMOUNTS RECEIVED ON RETIREMENT OR SALE OR EXCHANGE OF DEBT INSTRUMENTS.

[Sec. 1271(a)]

(a) GENERAL RULE.—For purposes of this title—

(1) RETIREMENT.—Amounts received by the holder on retirement of any debt instrument shall be considered as amounts received in exchange therefor.

(2) ORDINARY INCOME ON SALE OR EXCHANGE WHERE INTENTION TO CALL BEFORE MATURITY.—

(A) IN GENERAL.—If at the time of original issue there was an intention to call a debt instrument before maturity, any gain realized on the sale or exchange thereof which does not exceed an amount equal to—

(i) the original issue discount, reduced by

(ii) the portion of original issue discount previously includible in the gross income of any holder (without regard to subsection (a)(7) or (b)(4) of section 1272 (or the corresponding provisions of prior law)),

shall be treated as ordinary income.

(B) EXCEPTIONS.—This paragraph (and paragraph (2) of subsection (c)) shall not apply to—

(i) any tax-exempt obligation, or

(ii) any holder who has purchased the debt instrument at a premium.

(3) CERTAIN SHORT-TERM GOVERNMENT OBLIGATIONS.—

(A) IN GENERAL.—On the sale or exchange of any short-term Government obligation, any gain realized which does not exceed an amount equal to the ratable share of the acquisition discount shall be treated as ordinary income.

(B) SHORT-TERM GOVERNMENT OBLIGATION.—For purposes of this paragraph, the term "short-term Government obligation" means any obligation of the United States or any of its possessions, or of a State or any political subdivision thereof, or of the District of Columbia, which has a fixed maturity date not more than 1 year from the date of issue. Such term does not include any tax-exempt obligation.

(C) ACQUISITION DISCOUNT.—For purposes of this paragraph, the term "acquisition discount" means the excess of the stated redemption price at maturity over the taxpayer's basis for the obligation.

(D) RATABLE SHARE.—For purposes of this paragraph, except as provided in subparagraph (E) the ratable share of the acquisition discount is an amount which bears the same ratio to such discount as—

(i) the number of days which the taxpayer held the obligation, bears to

(ii) the number of days after the date the taxpayer acquired the obligation and up to (and including) the date of its maturity.

(E) ELECTION OF ACCRUAL ON BASIS OF CONSTANT INTEREST RATE.—At the election of the taxpayer with respect to any obligation, the ratable share of the aquisition discount is the portion of the acquisition discount accruing while the taxpayer held the obligation determined (under regulations prescribed by the Secretary) on the basis of—

(i) the taxpayer's yield to maturity based on the taxpayer's cost of acquiring the obligation, and

(ii) compounding daily.

An election under this subparagraph, once made with respect to any obligation, shall be irrevocable.

(4) CERTAIN SHORT-TERM NONGOVERNMENT OBLIGATIONS.—

(A) IN GENERAL.—On the sale or exchange of any short-term nongovernment obligation, any gain realized which does not exceed an amount equal to the ratable share of the original issue discount shall be treated as ordinary income.

(B) SHORT-TERM NONGOVERNMENT OBLIGATION.—For purposes of this paragraph, the term "short-term nongovernment obligation" means any obligation which—

(i) has a fixed maturity date not more than 1 year from the date of the issue, and

(ii) is not a short-term Government obligation (as defined in paragraph (3)(B) without regard to the last sentence thereof).

(C) RATABLE SHARE.—For purposes of this paragraph, except as provided in subparagraph (D), the ratable share of the original issue discount is an amount which bears the same ratio to such discount as—

(i) the number of days which the taxpayer held the obligation, bears to

(ii) the number of days after the date of original issue and up to (and including) the date of its maturity.

(D) ELECTION OF ACCRUAL ON BASIS OF CONSTANT INTEREST RATE.—At the election of the taxpayer with respect to any obligation, the ratable share of the original issue discount is the portion of the original issue discount accruing while the taxpayer held the obligation determined (under regulations prescribed by the Secretary) on the basis of—

(i) the yield to maturity based on the issue price of the obligation, and

(ii) compounding daily.

Any election under this subparagraph, once made with respect to any obligation, shall be irrevocable.

[Sec. 1271(b)]

(b) EXCEPTION FOR CERTAIN OBLIGATIONS.—

(1) IN GENERAL.—This section shall not apply to—

(A) any obligation issued by a natural person before June 9, 1997, and

(B) any obligation issued before July 2, 1982, by an issuer which is not a corporation and is not a government or political subdivision thereof.

(2) TERMINATION.—Paragraph (1) shall not apply to any obligation purchased (within the meaning of section 1272(d)(1)) after June 8, 1997.

* * *

[Sec. 1272]

SEC. 1272. CURRENT INCLUSION IN INCOME OF ORIGINAL ISSUE DISCOUNT.

[Sec. 1272(a)]

(a) ORIGINAL ISSUE DISCOUNT ON DEBT INSTRUMENTS ISSUED AFTER JULY 1, 1982, INCLUDED IN INCOME ON BASIS OF CONSTANT INTEREST RATE.—

(1) GENERAL RULE.—For purposes of this title, there shall be included in the gross income of the holder of any debt instrument having original issue discount issued after July 1, 1982, an amount equal to the sum of the daily portions of the original issue discount for each day during the taxable year on which such holder held such debt instrument.

(2) EXCEPTIONS.—Paragraph (1) shall not apply to—

(A) TAX-EXEMPT OBLIGATIONS.—Any tax-exempt obligation.

(B) UNITED STATES SAVINGS BONDS.—Any United States savings bond.

(C) SHORT-TERM OBLIGATIONS.—Any debt instrument which has a fixed maturity date not more than 1 year from the date of issue.

(D) OBLIGATIONS ISSUED BY NATURAL PERSONS BEFORE MARCH 2, 1984.—Any obligation issued by a natural person before March 2, 1984.

(E) LOANS BETWEEN NATURAL PERSONS.—

(i) IN GENERAL.—Any loan made by a natural person to another natural person if—

(I) such loan is not made in the course of a trade or business of the lender, and

(II) the amount of such loan (when increased by the outstanding amount of prior loans by such natural person to such other natural person) does not exceed $10,000.

(ii) CLAUSE (i) NOT TO APPLY WHERE TAX AVOIDANCE A PRINCIPAL PURPOSE.—Clause (i) shall not apply if the loan has as 1 of its principal purposes the avoidance of any Federal tax.

(iii) TREATMENT OF HUSBAND AND WIFE.—For purposes of this subparagraph, a husband and wife shall be treated as 1 person. The preceding sentence shall not apply where the spouses lived apart at all times during the taxable year in which the loan is made.

(3) DETERMINATION OF DAILY PORTIONS.—For purposes of paragraph (1), the daily portion of the original issue discount on any debt instrument shall be determined by allocating to each day in any accrual period its ratable portion of the increase during such accrual period in the adjusted issue price of the debt instrument. For purposes of the preceding sentence, the increase in the adjusted issue price for any accrual period shall be an amount equal to the excess (if any) of—

(A) the product of—

(i) the adjusted issue price of the debt instrument at the beginning of such accrual period, and

(ii) the yield to maturity (determined on the basis of compounding at the close of each accrual period and properly adjusted for the length of the accrual period), over

(B) the sum of the amounts payable as interest on such debt instrument during such accrual period.

(4) ADJUSTED ISSUE PRICE.—For purposes of this subsection, the adjusted issue price of any debt instrument at the beginning of any accrual period is the sum of—

(A) the issue price of such debt instrument, plus

(B) the adjustments under this subsection to such issue price for all periods before the first day of such accrual period.

(5) ACCRUAL PERIOD.—Except as otherwise provided in regulations prescribed by the Secretary, the term "accrual period" means a 6-month period (or shorter period from the date of original issue of the debt instrument) which ends on a day in the calendar year corresponding to the maturity date of the debt instrument or the date 6 months before such maturity date.

(6) DETERMINATION OF DAILY PORTIONS WHERE PRINCIPAL SUBJECT TO ACCELERATION.—

(A) IN GENERAL.—In the case of any debt instrument to which this paragraph applies, the daily portion of the original issue discount shall be determined by allocating to each day in any accrual period its ratable portion of the excess (if any) of—

(i) the sum of (I) the present value determined under subparagraph (B) of all remaining payments under the debt instrument as of the close of such period, and (II) the payments during the accrual period of amounts included in the stated redemption price of the debt instrument, over

(ii) the adjusted issue price of such debt instrument at the beginning of such period.

(B) DETERMINION OF PRESENT VALUE.—For purposes of subparagraph (A), the present value shall be determined on the basis of—

(i) the original yield to maturity (determined on the basis of compounding at the close of each accrual period and properly adjusted for the length of the accrual period),

(ii) events which have occurred before the close of the accrual period, and

(iii) a prepayment assumption determined in the manner prescribed by regulations.

(C) DEBT INSTRUMENTS TO WHICH PARAGRAPH APPLIES.—This paragraph applies to—

(i) any regular interest in a REMIC or qualified mortgage held by a REMIC,

(ii) any other debt instrument if payments under such debt instrument may be accelerated by reason of prepayments of other obligations securing such debt instrument (or, to the extent provided in regulations, by reason of other events), or

(iii) any pool of debt instruments the yield on which may be affected by reason of prepayments (or to the extent provided in regulations, by reason of other events).

To the extent provided in regulations prescribed by the Secretary, in the case of a small business engaged in the trade or business of selling tangible personal property at retail, clause (iii) shall not apply to debt instruments incurred in the ordinary course of such trade or business while held by such business.

(7) REDUCTION WHERE SUBSEQUENT HOLDER PAYS ACQUISITION PREMIUM.—

(A) REDUCTION.—For purposes of this subsection, in the case of any purchase after its original issue of a debt instrument to which this subsection applies, the daily portion for any day shall be reduced by an amount equal to the amount which would be the daily portion for such day (without regard to this paragraph) multiplied by the fraction determined under subparagraph (B).

(B) DETERMINATION OF FRACTION.—For purposes of subparagraph (A), the fraction determined under this subparagraph is a fraction—

(i) the numerator of which is the excess (if any) of—

(I) the cost of such debt instrument incurred by the purchaser, over

(II) the issue price of such debt instrument, increased by the portion of original issue discount previously includible in the gross income of any holder (computed without regard to this paragraph), and

(ii) the denominator of which is the sum of the daily portions for such debt instrument for all days after the date of such purchase and ending on the stated maturity date (computed without regard to this paragraph).

[Sec. 1272(b)]

(b) RATABLE INCLUSION RETAINED FOR CORPORATE DEBT INSTRUMENTS ISSUED BEFORE JULY 2, 1982.—

(1) GENERAL RULE.—There shall be included in the gross income of the holder of any debt instrument issued by a corportion after May 27, 1969, and before July 2, 1982—

(A) the ratable monthly portion of original issue discount, multiplied by

(B) the number of complete months (plus any fractional part of a month determined under paragraph (3)) such holder held such debt instrument during the taxable year.

(2) DETERMINATION OF RATABLE MONTHLY PORTION.—Except as provided in paragraph (4), the ratable monthly portion of original issue discount shall equal—

(A) the original issue discount, divided by

(B) the number of complete months from the date of original issue to the stated maturity date of the debt instrument.

(3) MONTH DEFINED.—For purposes of this subsection—

(A) COMPLETE MONTH.—A complete month commences with the date of original issue and the corresponding day of each succeeding calendar month (or the last day of a calendar month in which there is no corresponding day).

(B) TRANSFERS DURING MONTH.—In any case where a debt instrument is acquired on any day other than a day determined under subparagraph (A), the ratable monthly portion of original issue discount for the complete month (or partial month) in which such acquisition occurs shall be allocated between the transferor and the transferee in accordance with the number of days in such complete (or partial) month each held the debt instrument.

(4) REDUCTION WHERE SUBSEQUENT HOLDER PAYS ACQUISITION PREMIUM.—

(A) REDUCTION.—For purposes of this subsection, the ratable monthly portion of original issue discount shall not include its share of the acquisition premium.

(B) SHARE OF ACQUISITION PREMIUM.—For purposes of subparagraph (A), any month's share of the acquisition premium is an amount (determined at the time of the purchase) equal to—

(i) the excess of—

(I) the cost of such debt instrument incurred by the holder, over

(II) the issue price of such debt instrument, increased by the portion of original issue discount previously includible in the gross income of any holder (computed without regard to this paragraph),

(ii) divided by the number of complete months (plus any fractional part of a month) from the date of such purchase to the stated maturity date of such debt instrument.

[Sec. 1272(c)]

(c) EXCEPTIONS.—This section shall not apply to any holder—

(1) who has purchased the debt instrument at a premium, or

(2) which is a life insurance company to which section 811(b) applies.

* * *

[Sec. 1273]

SEC. 1273. DETERMINATION OF AMOUNT OF ORIGINAL ISSUE DISCOUNT.

[Sec. 1273(a)]

(a) GENERAL RULE.—for purposes of this subpart—

(1) IN GENERAL.—The term "original issue discount" means the excess (if any) of—

(A) the stated redemption price at maturity, over

(B) the issue price.

(2) STATED REDEMPTION PRICE AT MATURITY.—The term "stated redemption price at maturity" means the amount fixed by the last modification of the purchase agreement and includes interest and other amounts payable at that time (other than any interest based on a fixed rate, and payable unconditionally at fixed periodic intervals of 1 year or less during the entire term of the debt instrument).

(3) ¼ OF 1 PERCENT DE MINIMIS RULE.—If the original issue discount determined under paragraph (1) is less than—

(A) ¼ of 1 percent of the stated redemption price at maturity, multiplied by

(B) the number of complete years to maturity,

then the original issue discount shall be treated as zero.

[Sec. 1273(b)]

(b) ISSUE PRICE.—For purposes of this subpart—

(1) PUBLICLY OFFERED DEBT INSTRUMENTS NOT ISSUED FOR PROPERTY.—In the case of any issue of debt instruments—

(A) publicly offered, and

(B) not issued for property,

the issue price is the initial offering price to the public (excluding bond houses and brokers) at which price a substantial amount of such debt instruments was sold.

(2) OTHER DEBT INSTRUMENTS NOT ISSUED FOR PROPERTY.—In the case of any isssue of debt instruments not issued for property and not publicly offered, the issue price of each such instrument is the price paid by the first buyer of such debt instrument.

(3) DEBT INSTRUMENTS ISSUED FOR PROPERTY WHERE THERE IS PUBLIC TRADING.—In the case of a debt instrument which is issued for property and which—

(A) is part of an issue a portion of which is traded on an established securities market, or

(B)(i) is issued for stock or securities which are traded on an established securities market, or

(ii) to the extent provided in regulations, is issued for property (other than stock or securities) of a kind regularly traded on an established market,

the issue price of such debt instrument shall be the fair market value of such property.

(4) OTHER CASES.—Except in any case—

(A) to which paragraph (1), (2), or (3) of this subsection applies, or

(B) to which section 1274 applies,

the issue price of a debt instrument which is issued for property shall be the stated redemption price at maturity.

(5) PROPERTY.—In applying this subsection, the term "property" includes services and the right to use property, but such term does not include money.

[Sec. 1273(c)]

(c) SPECIAL RULES FOR APPLYING SUBSECTION (b).—for purposes of subsection (b)—

(1) INITIAL OFFERING PRICE; PRICE PAID BY THE FIRST BUYER.—The terms "initial offering price" and "price paid by the first buyer" include the aggregate payments made by the purchaser under the purchase agreement, including modifications thereof.

(2) TREATMENT OF INVESTMENT UNITS.—In the case of any debt instrument and an option, security, or other property issued together as an investment unit—

(A) the issue price for such unit shall be determined in accordance with the rules of this subsection and subsection (b) as if it were a debt instrument,

(B) the issue price determined for such unit shall be allocated to each element of such unit on the basis of the relationship of the fair market value of such element to the fair market value of all elements in such unit, and

(C) the issue price of any debt instrument included in such unit shall be the portion of the issue price of the unit allocated to the debt instrument under subparagraph (B).

[Sec. 1274]

SEC. 1274. DETERMINATION OF ISSUE PRICE IN THE CASE OF CERTAIN DEBT INSTRUMENTS ISSUED FOR PROPERTY.

[Sec. 1274(a)]

(a) IN GENERAL.—In the case of any debt instrument to which this section applies, for purposes of this subpart, the issue price shall be—

(1) where there is adequate stated interest, the stated principal amount, or

(2) in any other case, the imputed principal amount.

[Sec. 1274(b)]

(b) IMPUTED PRINCIPAL AMOUNT.—For purposes of this section—

(1) IN GENERAL.—Except as provided in paragraph (3), the imputed principal amount of any debt instrument shall be equal to the sum of the present values of all payments due under such debt instrument.

(2) DETERMINATION OF PRESENT VALUE.—For purposes of paragraph (1), the present value of a payment shall be determined in the manner provided by regulations prescribed by the Secretary—

(A) as of the date of the sale or exchange, and

(B) by using a discount rate equal to the applicable Federal rate, compounded semiannually.

(3) FAIR MARKET VALUE RULE IN POTENTIALLY ABUSIVE SITUATIONS.—

(A) IN GENERAL.—In the case of any potentially abusive situation, the imputed principal amount of any debt instrument received in exchange for property shall be the fair market value of such property adjusted to take into account other consideration involved in the transaction.

(B) POTENTIALLY ABUSIVE SITUATION DEFINED.—For purposes of subparagraph (A), the term "potentially abusive situation" means—

(i) a tax shelter (as defined in section 6662(d)(2)(C)(iii)), and

(ii) any other situation which, by reason of—

(I) recent sales transactions,

(II) nonrecourse financing,

(III) financing with a term in excess of the economic life of the property, or

(IV) other circumstances,

is of a type which the Secretary specifies by regulations as having potential for tax avoidance.

[Sec. 1274(c)]

(c) DEBT INSTRUMENTS TO WHICH SECTION APPLIES.—

(1) IN GENERAL.—Except as otherwise provided in this subsection, this section shall apply to any debt instrument given in consideration for the sale or exchange of property if—

(A) the stated redemption price at maturity for such debt instrument exceeds—

(i) where there is adequate stated interest, the stated principal amount, or

(ii) in any other case, the imputed principal amount of such debt instrument determined under subsection (b), and

(B) some or all of the payments due under such debt instrument are due more than 6 months after the date of such sale or exchange.

(2) ADEQUATE STATED INTEREST.—For purposes of this section, there is adequate stated interest with respect to any debt instrument if the stated principal amount for such debt instrument is less than or equal to the imputed principal amount of such debt instrument determined under subsection (b).

(3) EXCEPTIONS.—This section shall not apply to—

(A) SALES FOR $1,000,000 OR LESS OF FARMS BY INDIVIDUALS OR SMALL BUSINESSES.—

(i) IN GENERAL.—Any debt instrument arising from the sale or exchange of a farm (within the meaning of section 6420(c)(2))—

(I) by an individual, estate, or testamentary trust,

(II) by a corporation which as of the date of the sale or exchange is a small business corporation (as defined in section 1244(c)(3)), or

(III) by a partnership which as of the date of the sale or exchange meets requirements similar to those of section 1244(c)(3).

(ii) $1,000,000 LIMITATION.—Clause (i) shall apply only if it can be determined at the time of the sale or exchange that the sales price cannot exceed $1,000,000. For purposes of the preceding sentence, all sales and exchanges which are part of the same transaction (or a series of related transactions) shall be treated as 1 sale or exchange.

(B) SALES OF PRINCIPAL RESIDENCES.—Any debt instrument arising from the sale or exchange by an individual of his principal residence (within the meaning of section 121).

(C) SALES INVOLVING TOTAL PAYMENTS OF $250,000 OR LESS.—

(i) IN GENERAL.—Any debt instrument arising from the sale or exchange of property if the sum of the following amounts does not exceed $250,000:

(I) the aggregate amount of the payments due under such debt instrument and all other debt instruments received as consideration for the sale or exchange, and

(II) the aggregate amount of any other consideration to be received for the sale or exchange.

(ii) CONSIDERATION OTHER THAN DEBT INSTRUMENT TAKEN INTO ACCOUNT AT FAIR MARKET VALUE.—For purposes of clause (i), any consideration (other than a debt instrument) shall be taken into account at its fair market value.

(iii) AGGREGATION OF TRANSACTIONS.—For purposes of this subparagraph, all sales and exchanges which are part of the same transaction (or a series of related transactions) shall be treated as 1 sale or exchange.

(D) DEBT INSTRUMENTS WHICH ARE PUBLICLY TRADED OR ISSUED FOR PUBLICLY TRADED PROPERTY.—Any debt instrument to which section 1273(b)(3) applies.

(E) CERTAIN SALES OF PATENTS.—In the case of any transfer described in section 1235(a) (relating to sale or exchange of patents), any amount contingent on the productivity, use, or disposition of the property transferred.

(F) SALES OR EXCHANGES TO WHICH SECTION 483(e) APPLIES.—Any debt instrument to the extent section 483(e) (relating to certain land transfers between related persons) applies to such instrument.

(4) EXCEPTION FOR ASSUMPTIONS.—If any person—

(A) in connection with the sale or exchange of property, assumes any debt instrument, or

(B) acquires any property subject to any debt instrument,

in determining whether this section or section 483 applies to such debt instrument, such assumption (or such acquisition) shall not be taken into account unless the terms and conditions of such debt instrument are modified (or the nature of the transaction is changed) in connection with the assumption (or acquisition).

[Sec. 1274(d)]

(d) DETERMINATION OF APPLICABLE FEDERAL RATE.—For purposes of this section—

(1) APPLICABLE FEDERAL RATE.—

(A) IN GENERAL.—

In the case of a debt instrument with a term of:	The applicable Federal rate is:
Not over 3 years	The Federal short-term rate.
Over 3 years but not over 9 years	The Federal mid-term rate.
Over 9 years	The Federal long-term rate.

(B) DETERMINATION OF RATES.—During each calendar month, the Secretary shall determine the Federal short-term rate, mid-term rate, and long-term rate which shall apply during the following calendar month.

(C) FEDERAL RATE FOR ANY CALENDAR MONTH.—For purposes of this paragraph—

(i) FEDERAL SHORT-TERM RATE.—The Federal short-term rate shall be the rate determined by the Secretary based on the average market yield (during any 1-month period selected by the Secretary and ending in the calendar month in which the determination is made) on outstanding marketable obligations of the United States with remaining periods to maturity of 3 years or less.

(ii) FEDERAL MID-TERM AND LONG-TERM RATES.—The Federal mid-term and long-term rate shall be determined in accordance with the principles of clause (i).

(D) LOWER RATE PERMITTED IN CERTAIN CASES.—The Secretary may by regulations permit a rate to be used with respect to any debt instrument which is lower than the applicable Federal rate if the taxpayer establishes to the satisfaction of the Secretary that such lower rate is based on the same principles as the applicable Federal rate and is appropriate for the term of such instrument.

(2) LOWEST 3-MONTH RATE APPLICABLE TO ANY SALE OR EXCHANGE.—

(A) IN GENERAL.—In the case of any sale or exchange, the applicable Federal rate shall be the lowest 3-month rate.

(B) LOWEST 3-MONTH RATE.—For purposes of subparagraph (A), the term "lowest 3-month rate" means the lowest of the applicable Federal rates in effect for any month in the 3-calendar-month period ending with the 1st calendar month in which there is a binding contract in writing for such sale or exchange.

(3) TERM OF DEBT INSTRUMENT.—In determining the term of a debt instrument for purposes of this subsection, under regulations prescribed by the Secretary, there shall be taken into account options to renew or extend.

330 Internal Revenue Code of 1986

[Sec. 1274(e)]

(e) 110 PERCENT RATE WHERE SALE-LEASEBACK INVOLVED.—

(1) IN GENERAL.—In the case of any debt instrument to which this subsection applies, the discount rate used under subsection (b)(2)(B) or section 483(b) shall be 110 percent of the applicable Federal rate, compounded semiannually.

(2) LOWER DISCOUNT RATES SHALL NOT APPLY.—Section 1274A shall not apply to any debt instrument to which this subsection applies.

(3) DEBT INSTRUMENTS TO WHICH THIS SUBSECTION APPLIES.—This subsection shall apply to any debt instrument given in consideration for the sale or exchange of any property if, pursuant to a plan, the transferor or any related person leases a portion of such property after such sale or exchange.

Subpart D—Miscellaneous Provisions

[Sec. 1287]

SEC. 1287. DENIAL OF CAPITAL GAIN TREATMENT FOR GAINS ON CERTAIN OBLIGATIONS NOT IN REGISTERED FORM.

[Sec. 1287(a)]

(a) IN GENERAL.—If any registration-required obligation is not in registered form, any gain on the sale or other disposition of such obligation shall be treated as ordinary income (unless the issuance of such obligation was subject to tax under section 4701).

[Sec. 1287(b)]

(b) DEFINITIONS.—For purposes of subsection (a)—

(1) REGISTRATION-REQUIRED OBLIGATION.—The term "registration-required obligation" has the meaning given to such term by section 163(f)(2) except that clause (iv) of subparagraph (A), and subparagraph (B), of such section shall not apply.

(2) REGISTERED FORM.—the term "registered form" has the same meaning as when used in section 163(f).

PART VI—TREATMENT OF CERTAIN PASSIVE FOREIGN INVESTMENT COMPANIES

Subpart A—Interest on Tax Deferral

[Sec. 1291]

SEC. 1291. INTEREST ON TAX DEFERRAL.

[Sec. 1291(a)]

(a) TREATMENT OF DISTRIBUTIONS AND STOCK DISPOSITIONS.—

(1) DISTRIBUTIONS.—If a United States person receives an excess distribution in respect of stock in a passive foreign investment company, then—

(A) the amount of the excess distribution shall be allocated ratably to each day in the taxpayer's holding period for the stock,

(B) with respect to such excess distribution, the taxpayer's gross income for the current year shall include (as ordinary income) only the amounts allocated under subparagraph (A) to—

(i) the current year, or

(ii) any period in the taxpayer's holding period before the 1st day of the 1st taxable year of the company which begins after December 31, 1986, and for which it was a passive foreign investment company, and

(C) the tax imposed by this chapter for the current year shall be increased by the deferred tax amount (determined under subsection (c)).

(2) DISPOSITIONS.—If the taxpayer disposes of stock in a passive foreign investment company, then the rules of paragraph (1) shall apply to any gain recognized on such disposition in the same manner as if such gain were an excess distribution.

(3) DEFINITIONS.—For purposes of this section—

(A) HOLDING PERIOD.—The taxpayer's holding period shall be determined under section 1223; except that—

(i) for purposes of applying this section to an excess distribution, such holding period shall be treated as ending on the date of such distribution, and

(ii) if section 1296 applied to such stock with respect to the taxpayer for any prior taxable year, such holding period shall be treated as beginning on the first day of the first taxable year beginning after the last taxable year for which section 1296 so applied.

(B) CURRENT YEAR.—The term "current year" means the taxable year in which the excess distribution or disposition occurs.

[Sec. 1291(b)]

(b) EXCESS DISTRIBUTION.—

(1) IN GENERAL.—For purposes of this section, the term "excess distribution" means any distribution in respect of stock received during any taxable year to the extent such distribution does not exceed its ratable portion of the total excess distribution (if any) for such taxable year.

(2) TOTAL EXCESS DISTRIBUTION.—For purposes of this subsection—

(A) IN GENERAL.—The term "total excess distribution" means the excess (if any) of—

(i) the amount of the distributions in respect of the stock received by the taxpayer during the taxable year, over

(ii) 125 percent of the average amount received in respect of such stock by the taxpayer during the 3 preceding taxable years (or, if shorter, the portion of the taxpayer's holding period before the taxable year).

For purposes of clause (ii), any excess distribution received during such 3-year period shall be taken into account only to the extent it was included in gross income under subsection (a)(1)(B).

(B) NO EXCESS FOR 1ST YEAR.—The total excess distributions with respect to any stock shall be zero for the taxable year in which the taxpayer's holding period in such stock begins.

(3) ADJUSTMENTS.—Under regulations prescribed by the Secretary—

(A) determinations under this subsection shall be made on a share-by-share basis, except that shares with the same holding period may be aggregated,

(B) proper adjustments shall be made for stock splits and stock dividends,

(C) if the taxpayer does not hold the stock during the entire taxable year, distributions received during such year shall be annualized,

(D) if the taxpayer's holding period includes periods during which the stock was held by another person, distributions received by such other person shall be taken into account as if received by the taxpayer,

(E) if the distributions are received in a foreign currency, determinations under this subsection shall be made in such currency and the amount of any excess distribution determined in such currency shall be translated into dollars,

(F) proper adjustment shall be made for amounts not includible in gross income by reason of section 959(a) or 1293(c), and

(G) if a charitable deduction was allowable under section 642(c) to a trust for any distribution of its income, proper adjustments shall be made for the deduction so allowable to the extent allocable to distributions or gain in respect of stock in a passive foreign investment company.

[Sec. 1291(c)]

(c) DEFERRED TAX AMOUNT.—For purposes of this section—

(1) IN GENERAL.—The term "deferred tax amount" means, with respect to any distribution or disposition to which subsection (a) applies, an amount equal to the sum of—

(A) the aggregate increases in taxes described in paragraph (2), plus

(B) the aggregate amount of interest (determined in the manner provided under paragraph (3)) on such increases in tax.

Any increase in the tax imposed by this chapter for the current year under subsection (a) to the extent attributable to the amount referred to in subparagraph (B) shall be treated as interest paid under section 6601 on the due date for the current year.

(2) AGGREGATE INCREASES IN TAXES.—For purposes of paragraph (1)(A), the aggregate increases in taxes shall be determined by multiplying each amount allocated under subsection (a)(1)(A) to any taxable year (other than any taxable year referred to in subsection (a)(1)(B)) by the highest rate of tax in effect for such taxable year under section 1 or 11, whichever applies.

(3) COMPUTATION OF INTEREST.—

(A) IN GENERAL.—The amount of interest referred to in paragraph (1)(B) on any increase determined under paragraph (2) for any taxable year shall be determined for the period—

(i) beginning on the due date for such taxable year, and

(ii) ending on the due date for the taxable year with or within which the distribution or disposition occurs,

by using the rates and method applicable under section 6621 for underpayments of tax for such period.

(B) DUE DATE.—For purposes of this subsection, the term "due date" means the date prescribed by law (determined without regard to extensions) for filing the return of the tax imposed by this chapter for the taxable year.

[Sec. 1291(d)]

(d) COORDINATION WITH SUBPART B AND C.—

(1) IN GENERAL.—This section shall not apply with respect to any distribution paid by a passive foreign investment company, or any disposition of stock in a passive foreign investment company, if such company is a qualified electing fund with respect to the taxpayer for each of its taxable years—

(A) which begins after December 31, 1986, and for which such company is a passive foreign investment company, and

(B) which includes any portion of the taxpayer's holding period.

Except as provided in section 1296(j), this section also shall not apply if an election under section 1296(k) is in effect for the taxpayer's taxable year. In the case of stock which is marked to market under section 475 or any other provision of this chapter, this section shall not apply, except that rules similar to the rules of section 1296(j) shall apply.

(2) ELECTION TO RECOGNIZE GAIN WHERE COMPANY BECOMES QUALIFIED ELECTING FUND.—

(A) IN GENERAL.—If—

(i) a passive foreign investment company becomes a qualified electing fund with respect to the taxpayer for a taxable year which begins after December 31, 1986,

(ii) the taxpayer holds stock in such company on the first day of such taxable year, and

(iii) the taxpayer establishes to the satisfaction of the Secretary the fair market value of such stock on such first day,

the taxpayer may elect to recognize gain as if he sold such stock on such first day for such fair market value.

(B) ADDITIONAL ELECTION FOR SHAREHOLDER OF CONTROLLED FOREIGN CORPORATIONS.—

(i) IN GENERAL.—If—

(I) a passive foreign investment company becomes a qualified electing fund with respect to the taxpayer for a taxable year which begins after December 1, 1986,

(II) the taxpayer holds stock in such company on the first day of such taxable year, and

(III) such company is a controlled foreign corporation (as defined in section 957(a)),

the taxpayer may elect to include in gross income as a dividend received on such first day an amount equal to the portion of the post-1986 earnings and profits of such company attributable (under regulations prescribed by the Secretary) to the stock in such company held by the taxpayer on such first day. The amount treated as a dividend under the preceding sentence shall be treated as a excess distribution and shall be allocated under subsection (a)(1)(A) only to days during periods taken into account in determining the post-1986 earnings and profits so attributable.

(ii) POST-1986 EARNINGS AND PROFITS.—For purposes of clause (i), the term "post-1986 earnings and profits" means earnings and profits which were accumulated in taxable years of such company beginning after December 31, 1986, and during the period or periods the stock was held by the taxpayer while the company was a passive foreign investment company.

(iii) COORDINATION WITH SECTION 959(e).—For purposes of section 959(e), any amount included in gross income under this subparagraph shall be treated as included in gross income under section 1248(a).

(C) ADJUSTMENTS.—In the case of any stock to which subparagraph (A) or (B) applies.—

(i) the adjusted basis of such stock shall be increased by the gain recognized under subparagraph (A) or the amount treated as a dividend under subparagraph (B), as the case may be, and

(ii) the taxpayer's holding period in such stock shall be treated as beginning on the first day referred to in such subparagraph.

≫→ *Caution: Code Sec. 1291(e), below, applies to estates of decedents dying on or before December 31, 2009.*

[Sec. 1291(e)]

(e) CERTAIN BASIS, ETC., RULES MADE APPLICABLE.—Except to the extent inconsistent with the regulations prescribed under subsection (f), rules similar to the rules of subsections (c), (d), (e), and (f) of section 1246 (as in effect on the day before the date of the enactment of the American Jobs Creation Act of 2004) shall apply for purposes of this section; except that—

(1) the reduction under subsection (e) of such section shall be the excess of the basis determined under section 1014 over the adjusted basis of the stock immediately before the decedent's death, and

(2) such a reduction shall not apply in the case of a decedent who was a nonresident alien at all times during his holding period in the stock.

≫→ *Caution: Code Sec. 1291(e), below, applies to estates of decedents dying after December 31, 2009.*

[Sec. 1291(e)]

(e) CERTAIN BASIS, ETC., RULES MADE APPLICABLE.—Except to the extent inconsistent with the regulations prescribed under subsection (f), rules similar to the rules of subsections (c), (d), and (f) of section 1246 (as in effect on the day before the date of the enactment of the American Jobs Creation Act of 2004) shall apply for purposes of this section.

[Sec. 1291(f)]

(f) RECOGNITION OF GAIN.—To the extent provided in regulations, in the case of any transfer of stock in a passive foreign investment company where (but for this subsection) there is not full recognition of gain, the excess (if any) of—

(1) the fair market value of such stock, over

(2) its adjusted basis,

shall be treated as gain from the sale or exchange of such stock and shall be recognized notwithstanding any provision of law. Proper adjustment shall be made to the basis of any such stock for gain recognized under the preceding sentence.

[Sec. 1291(g)]

(g) COORDINATION WITH FOREIGN TAX CREDIT RULES.—

(1) IN GENERAL.—If there are creditable foreign taxes with respect to any distribution in respect of stock in a passive foreign investment company—

(A) the amount of such distribution shall be determined for purposes of this section with regard to section 78,

(B) the excess distribution taxes shall be allocated ratably to each day in the taxpayer's holding period for the stock, and

(C) to the extent—

(i) that such excess distribution taxes are allocated to a taxable year referred to in subsection (a)(1)(B), such taxes shall be taken into account under section 901 for the current year, and

(ii) that such excess distribution taxes are allocated to any other taxable year, such taxes shall reduce (subject to the principles of section 904(d) and not below zero) the increase in tax determined under subsection (c)(2) for such taxable year by reason of such distribution (but such taxes shall not be taken into account under section 901).

(2) DEFINITIONS.—For purposes of this subsection—

(A) CREDITABLE FOREIGN TAXES.—The term "creditable foreign taxes" means, with respect to any distribution—

(i) any foreign taxes deemed paid under section 902 with respect to such distribution, and

(ii) any withholding tax imposed with respect to such distribution,

but only if the taxpayer chooses the benefits of section 901 and such taxes are creditable under section 901 (determined without regard to paragraph (1)(C)(ii)).

(B) EXCESS DISTRIBUTION TAXES.—The term "excess distribution taxes" means, with respect to any distribution, the portion of the creditable foreign taxes with respect to such distribution which is attributable (on a pro rata basis) to the portion of such distribution which is an excess distribution.

(C) SECTION 1248 GAIN.—The rules of this subsection also shall apply in the case of any gain which but for this section would be includible in gross income as a dividend under section 1248.

Subpart B—Treatment of Qualified Electing Funds

[Sec. 1293]

SEC. 1293. CURRENT TAXATION OF INCOME FROM QUALIFIED ELECTING FUNDS.

[Sec. 1293(a)]

(a) INCLUSION.—

(1) IN GENERAL.—Every United States person who owns (or is treated under section 1298(a) as owning) stock of a qualified electing fund at any time during the taxable year of such fund shall include in gross income—

(A) as ordinary income, such shareholder's pro rata share of the ordinary earnings of such fund for such year, and

(B) as long-term capital gain, such shareholder's pro rata share of the net capital gain of such fund for such year.

(2) YEAR OF INCLUSION.—The inclusion under paragraph (1) shall be for the taxable year of the shareholder in which or with which the taxable year of the fund ends.

[Sec. 1293(b)]

(b) PRO RATA SHARE.—The pro rata share referred to in subsection (a) in the case of any shareholder is the amount which would have been distributed with respect to the shareholder's stock if, on each day during the taxable year of the fund, the fund had distributed to each shareholder a pro rata share of that day's ratable share of the fund's ordinary earnings and net capital gain for such year. To the extent provided in regulations, if the fund establishes to the satisfaction of the Secretary that it uses a shorter period than the taxable year to determine shareholders' interests in the earnings of such fund, pro rata shares may be determined by using such shorter period.

[Sec. 1293(c)]

(c) PREVIOUSLY TAXED AMOUNTS DISTRIBUTED TAX FREE.—If the taxpayer establishes to the satisfaction of the Secretary that any amount distributed by a passive foreign investment company is paid out of earnings and profits of the company which were included under subsection (a) in the income of any United States person, such amount shall be treated, for purposes of this chapter, as a distribution which is not a dividend; except that such distribution shall immediately reduce earnings and profits. If the passive foreign investment company is a controlled foreign corporation (as defined in section 957(a)), the preceding sentence shall not apply to any United States shareholder (as defined in section 951(b)) in such corporation, and, in applying section 959 to any such shareholder, any inclusion under this section shall be treated as an inclusion under section 951(a)(1)(A).

[Sec. 1293(d)]

(d) BASIS ADJUSTMENTS.—The basis of taxpayer's stock in a passive foreign investment company shall be—

(1) increased by any amount which is included in the income of the taxpayer under subsection (a) with respect to such stock, and

(2) decreased by any amount distributed with respect to such stock which is not includible in the income of the taxpayer by reason of subsection (c).

A similar rule shall apply also in the case of any property if by reason of holding such property the taxpayer is treated under section 1298(a) as owning stock in a qualified electing fund.

[Sec. 1293(e)]

(e) ORDINARY EARNINGS.—For purposes of this section—

(1) ORDINARY EARNINGS.—The term "ordinary earnings" means the excess of the earnings and profits of the qualified electing fund for the taxable year over its net capital gain for such taxable year.

(2) LIMITATION ON NET CAPITAL GAIN.—A qualified electing fund's capital gain for any taxable year shall not exceed its earnings and profits for such taxable year.

(3) DETERMINATION OF EARNINGS AND PROFITS.—The earnings and profits of any qualified electing fund shall be determined without regard to paragraphs (4), (5), and (6) of section 312(n). Under regulations, the preceding sentence shall not apply to the extent it would increase earnings and profits by an amount which was previously distributed by the qualified electing fund.

[Sec. 1293(f)]

(f) FOREIGN TAX CREDIT ALLOWED IN THE CASE OF 10-PERCENT CORPORATE SHAREHOLDER.—For purposes of section 960—

(1) any amount included in the gross income under subsection (a) shall be treated as if it were included under section 951(a), and

(2) any amount excluded from gross income under subsection (c) shall be treated in the same manner as amounts excluded from gross income under section 959.

[Sec. 1293(g)]

(g) OTHER SPECIAL RULES.—

(1) EXCEPTION FOR CERTAIN INCOME.—For purposes of determining the amount included in the gross income of any person under this section, the ordinary earnings and net capital gain of a qualified electing fund shall not include any item of income received by such fund if—

(A) such fund is a controlled foreign corporation (as defined in section 957(a)) and such person is a United States shareholder (as defined in section 951(b)) in such fund, and

(B) such person establishes to the satisfaction of the Secretary that—

(i) such income was subject to an effective rate of income tax imposed by a foreign country greater than 90 percent of the maximum rate of tax specified in section 11, or

(ii) such income is—

(I) from sources within the United States,

(II) effectively connected with the conduct by the qualified electing fund of a trade or business in the United States, and

(III) not exempt from taxation (or subject to a reduced rate of tax) pursuant to a treaty obligation of the United States.

(2) PREVENTION OF DOUBLE INCLUSION.—The Secretary shall prescribe such adjustment to the provisions of this section as may be necessary to prevent the same item of income of a qualified electing fund from being included in the gross income of a United States person more than once.

[Sec. 1294]

SEC. 1294. ELECTION TO EXTEND TIME FOR PAYMENT OF TAX ON UNDISTRIBUTED EARNINGS.

[Sec. 1294(a)]

(a) EXTENSION ALLOWED BY ELECTION.—

(1) IN GENERAL.—At the election of the taxpayer, the time for payment of any undistributed PFIC earnings tax liability of the taxpayer for the taxable year shall be extended to the extent and subject to the limitations provided in this section.

(2) ELECTION NOT PERMITTED WHERE AMOUNTS OTHERWISE INCLUDIBLE UNDER SECTION 951.—The taxpayer may not make an election under paragraph (1) with respect to the undistributed PFIC earnings tax liability attributable to a qualified electing fund for the taxable year if any amount is includible in the gross income of the taxpayer under section 951 with respect to such fund for such taxable year.

[Sec. 1294(b)]

(b) DEFINITIONS.—For purposes of this section—

(1) UNDISTRIBUTED PFIC EARNINGS TAX LIABILITY.—The term "undistributed PFIC earnings tax liability" means, in the case of any taxpayer, the excess of—

(A) the tax imposed by this chapter for the taxable year, over

(B) the tax which would be imposed by this chapter for such year without regard to the inclusion in gross income under section 1293 of the undistributed earnings of a qualified electing fund.

(2) UNDISTRIBUTED EARNINGS.—The term "undistributed earnings" means, with respect to any qualified electing fund, the excess (if any) of—

(A) the amount includible in gross income by reason of section 1293(a) for the taxable year, over

(B) the amount not includible in gross income by reason of section 1293(c) for such taxable year.

[Sec. 1294(c)]

(c) TERMINATION OF EXTENSION.—

(1) DISTRIBUTIONS.—

(A) IN GENERAL.—If a distribution is not includible in gross income for the taxable year by reason of section 1293(c), then the extension under subsection (a) for payment of the undistributed PFIC earnings tax liability with respect to the earnings to which such distribution is attributable shall expire on the last date prescribed by law (determined without regard to extensions) for filing the return of tax for such taxable year.

(B) ORDERING RULE.—For purposes of subparagraph (A), a distribution shall be treated as made from the most recently accumulated earnings and profits.

(2) TRANSFERS, ETC.—If—

(A) stock in a passive foreign investment company is transferred during the taxable year, or

(B) a passive foreign investment company ceases to be a qualified electing fund,

all extensions under subsection (a) for payment of undistributed PFIC earnings tax liability attributable to such stock (or, in the case of such a cessation, attributable to any stock in such company) which had not expired before the date of such transfer or cessation shall expire on the last date prescribed by law (determined without regard to extensions) for filing the return of tax for the taxable year in which such transfer or cessation occurs. To the extent provided in regulations, the preceding sentence shall not apply in the case of a transfer in a transaction with respect to which gain or loss is not recognized (in whole or in part), and the transferee in such transaction shall succeed to the treatment under this section of the transferor.

(3) JEOPARDY.—If the Secretary believes that collection of an amount to which an extension under this section relates is in jeopardy, the Secretary shall immediately terminate such extension with respect to such amount, and notice and demand shall be made by him for payment of such amount.

[Sec. 1294(d)]

(d) ELECTION.—The election under subsection (a) shall be made not later than the time prescribed by law (including extensions) for filing the return of tax imposed by this chapter for the taxable year.

[Sec. 1294(e)]

(e) AUTHORITY TO REQUIRE BOND.—Section 6165 shall apply to any extension under this section as though the Secretary were extending the time for payment of the tax.

[Sec. 1294(f)]

(f) TREATMENT OF LOANS TO SHAREHOLDER.—For purposes of this section and section 1293, any loan by a qualified electing fund (directly or indirectly) to a shareholder of such fund shall be treated as a distribution to such shareholder.

[Sec. 1294(g)]

(g) CROSS REFERENCE.—For provisions providing for interest for the period of the extension under this section, see section 6601.

[Sec. 1295]

SEC. 1295. QUALIFIED ELECTING FUND.

[Sec. 1295(a)]

(a) GENERAL RULE.—For purposes of this part, any passive foreign investment company shall be treated as a qualified electing fund with respect to the taxpayer if—

(1) an election by the taxpayer under subsection (b) applies to such company for the taxable year, and

(2) such company complies with such requirements as the Secretary may prescribe for purposes of—

(A) determining the ordinary earnings and net capital gain of such company, and

(B) otherwise carrying out the purposes of this subpart.

[Sec. 1295(b)]

(b) ELECTION.—

(1) IN GENERAL.—A taxpayer may make an election under this subsection with respect to any passive foreign investment company for any taxable year of the taxpayer. Such an election, once made with respect to any company, shall apply to all subsequent taxable years of the taxpayer with respect to such company unless revoked by the taxpayer with the consent of the Secretary.

(2) WHEN MADE.—An election under this subsection may be made for any taxable year at any time on or before the due date (determined with regard to extensions) for filing the return of the tax imposed by this chapter for such taxable year. To the extent provided in regulations, such an election may be made later than as required in the preceding sentence where the taxpayer fails to make a timely election because the taxpayer reasonably believed that the company was not a passive foreign investment company.

Subpart C—Election of Mark to Market for Marketable Stock

[Sec. 1296]

SEC. 1296. ELECTION OF MARK TO MARKET FOR MARKETABLE STOCK.

[Sec. 1296(a)]

(a) GENERAL RULE.—In the case of marketable stock in a passive foreign investment company which is owned (or treated under subsection (g) as owned) by a United States person at the close of any taxable year of such person, at the election of such person—

(1) If the fair market value of such stock as of the close of such taxable year exceeds its adjusted basis, such United States person shall include in gross income for such taxable year an amount equal to the amount of such excess.

(2) If the adjusted basis of such stock exceeds the fair market value of such stock as of the close of such taxable year, such United States person shall be allowed a deduction for such taxable year equal to the lesser of—

(A) the amount of such excess, or

(B) the unreversed inclusions with respect to such stock.

[Sec. 1296(b)]

(b) BASIS ADJUSTMENTS.—

(1) IN GENERAL.—The adjusted basis of stock in a passive foreign investment company—

(A) shall be increased by the amount included in the gross income of the United States person under subsection (a)(1) with respect to such stock, and

(B) shall be decreased by the amount allowed as a deduction to the United States person under subsection (a)(2) with respect to such stock.

(2) SPECIAL RULE FOR STOCK CONSTRUCTIVELY OWNED.—In the case of stock in a passive foreign investment company which the United States person is treated as owning under subsection (g)—

(A) the adjustments under paragraph (1) shall apply to such stock in the hands of the person actually holding such stock but only for purposes of determining the subsequent treatment under this chapter of the United States person with respect to such stock, and

(B) similar adjustments shall be made to the adjusted basis of the property by reason of which the United States person is treated as owning such stock.

[Sec. 1296(c)]

(c) CHARACTER AND SOURCE RULES.—

(1) ORDINARY TREATMENT.—

(A) GAIN.—Any amount included in gross income under subsection (a)(1), and any gain on the sale or other disposition of marketable stock in a passive foreign investment company (with respect to which an election under this section is in effect), shall be treated as ordinary income.

(B) LOSS.—Any—

(i) amount allowed as a deduction under subsection (a)(2), and

(ii) loss on the sale or other disposition of marketable stock in a passive foreign investment company (with respect to which an election under this section is in effect) to the extent that the amount of such loss does not exceed the unreversed inclusions with respect to such stock,

shall be treated as an ordinary loss. The amount so treated shall be treated as a deduction allowable in computing adjusted gross income.

(2) SOURCE.—The source of any amount included in gross income under subsection (a)(1) (or allowed as a deduction under subsection (a)(2)) shall be determined in the same manner as if such amount were gain or loss (as the case may be) from the sale of stock in the passive foreign investment company.

[Sec. 1296(d)]

(d) UNREVERSED INCLUSIONS.—For purposes of this section, the term "unreversed inclusions" means, with respect to any stock in a passive foreign investment company, the excess (if any) of—

(1) the amount included in gross income of the taxpayer under subsection (a)(1) with respect to such stock for prior taxable years, over

(2) the amount allowed as a deduction under subsection (a)(2) with respect to such stock for prior taxable years.

The amount referred to in paragraph (1) shall include any amount which would have been included in gross income under subsection (a)(1) with respect to such stock for any prior taxable year but for section 1291. In the case of a regulated investment company which elected to mark to market the stock held by such company as of the last day of the taxable year preceding such company's first taxable year for which such company elects the application of this section, the amount referred to in paragraph (1) shall include amounts included in gross income under such mark to market with respect to such stock for prior taxable years.

[Sec. 1296(e)]

(e) MARKETABLE STOCK.—For purposes of this section—

(1) IN GENERAL.—The term "marketable stock" means—

(A) any stock which is regularly traded on—

(i) a national securities exchange which is registered with the Securities and Exchange Commission or the national market system established pursuant to section 11A of the Securities and Exchange Act of 1934, or

(ii) any exchange or other market which the Secretary determines has rules adequate to carry out the purposes of this part,

(B) to the extent provided in regulations, stock in any foreign corporation which is comparable to a regulated investment company and which offers for sale or has outstanding any stock of which it is the issuer and which is redeemable at its net asset value, and

(C) to the extent provided in regulations, any option on stock described in subparagraph (A) or (B).

(2) SPECIAL RULE FOR REGULATED INVESTMENT COMPANIES.—In the case of any regulated investment company which is offering for sale or has outstanding any stock of which it is the issuer and which is redeemable at its net asset value, all stock in a passive foreign investment company which it owns directly or indirectly shall be treated as marketable stock for purposes of this section. Except as provided in regulations, similar treatment as marketable

stock shall apply in the case of any other regulated investment company which publishes net asset valuations at least annually.

[Sec. 1296(f)]

(f) TREATMENT OF CONTROLLED FOREIGN CORPORATIONS WHICH ARE SHAREHOLDERS IN PASSIVE FOREIGN INVESTMENT COMPANIES.—In the case of a foreign corporation which is a controlled foreign corporation and which owns (or is treated under subsection (g) as owning) stock in a passive foreign investment company—

(1) this section (other than subsection (c)(2)) shall apply to such foreign corporation in the same manner as if such corporation were a United States person, and

(2) for purposes of subpart F of part III of subchapter N—

(A) any amount included in gross income under subsection (a)(1) shall be treated as foreign personal holding company income described in section 954(c)(1)(A), and

(B) any amount allowed as a deduction under subsection (a)(2) shall be treated as a deduction allocable to foreign personal holding company income so described.

[Sec. 1296(g)]

(g) STOCK OWNED THROUGH CERTAIN FOREIGN ENTITIES.—Except as provided in regulations—

(1) IN GENERAL.—For purposes of this section, stock owned, directly or indirectly, by or for a foreign partnership or foreign trust or foreign estate shall be considered as being owned proportionately by its partners or beneficiaries. Stock considered to be owned by a person by reason of the application of the preceding sentence shall, for purposes of applying such sentence, be treated as actually owned by such person.

(2) TREATMENT OF CERTAIN DISPOSITIONS.—In any case in which a United States person is treated as owning stock in a passive foreign investment company by reason of paragraph (1)—

(A) any disposition by the United States person or by any other person which results in the United States person being treated as no longer owning such stock, and

(B) any disposition by the person owning such stock,

shall be treated as a disposition by the United States person of the stock in the passive foreign investment company.

[Sec. 1296(h)]

(h) COORDINATION WITH SECTION 851(b).—For purposes of section 851(b)(2), any amount included in gross income under subsection (a) shall be treated as a dividend.

⇛→ *Caution: Code Sec. 1296(i), below, will be stricken with respect to estates of decedents dying after December 31, 2009.*

[Sec. 1296(i)]

(i) STOCK ACQUIRED FROM A DECEDENT.—In the case of stock of a passive foreign investment company which is acquired by bequest, devise, or inheritance (or by the decedent's estate) and with respect to which an election under this section was in effect as of the date of the decedent's death, notwithstanding section 1014, the basis of such stock in the hands of the person so acquiring it shall be the adjusted basis of such stock in the hands of the decedent immediately before his death (or, if lesser, the basis which would have been determined under section 1014 without regard to this subsection).

[Sec. 1296(j)]

(j) COORDINATION WITH SECTION 1291 FOR FIRST YEAR OF ELECTION.—

(1) TAXPAYERS OTHER THAN REGULATED INVESTMENT COMPANIES.—

(A) IN GENERAL.—If the taxpayer elects the application of this section with respect to any marketable stock in a corporation after the beginning of the taxpayer's holding period in such stock, and if the requirements of subparagraph (B) are not satisfied, section 1291 shall apply to—

Income Tax—General Provisions

(i) any distributions with respect to, or disposition of, such stock in the first taxable year of the taxpayer for which such election is made, and

(ii) any amount which, but for section 1291, would have been included in gross income under subsection (a) with respect to such stock for such taxable year in the same manner as if such amount were gain on the disposition of such stock.

(B) REQUIREMENTS.—The requirements of this subparagraph are met if, with respect to each of such corporation's taxable years for which such corporation was a passive foreign investment company and which begin after December 31, 1986, and included any portion of the taxpayer's holding period in such stock, such corporation was treated as a qualified electing fund under this part with respect to the taxpayer.

(2) SPECIAL RULES FOR REGULATED INVESTMENT COMPANIES.—

(A) IN GENERAL.—If a regulated investment company elects the application of this section with respect to any marketable stock in a corporation after the beginning of the taxpayer's holding period in such stock, then, with respect to such company's first taxable year for which such company elects the application of this section with respect to such stock—

(i) section 1291 shall not apply to such stock with respect to any distribution or disposition during, or amount included in gross income under this section for, such first taxable year, but

(ii) such regulated investment company's tax under this chapter for such first taxable year shall be increased by the aggregate amount of interest which would have been determined under section 1291(c)(3) if section 1291 were applied without regard to this subparagraph.

Clause (ii) shall not apply if for the preceding taxable year the company elected to mark to market the stock held by such company as of the last day of such preceding taxable year.

(B) DISALLOWANCE OF DEDUCTION.—No deduction shall be allowed to any regulated investment company for the increase in tax under subparagraph (A)(ii).

[Sec. 1296(k)]

(k) ELECTION.—This section shall apply to marketable stock in a passive foreign investment company which is held by a United States person only if such person elects to apply this section with respect to such stock. Such an election shall apply to the taxable year for which made and all subsequent taxable years unless—

(1) such stock ceases to be marketable stock, or

(2) the Secretary consents to the revocation of such election.

[Sec. 1296(l)]

(l) TRANSITION RULE FOR INDIVIDUALS BECOMING SUBJECT TO UNITED STATES TAX.—If any individual becomes a United States person in a taxable year beginning after December 31, 1997, solely for purposes of this section, the adjusted basis (before adjustments under subsection (b)) of any marketable stock in a passive foreign investment company owned by such individual on the first day of such taxable year shall be treated as being the greater of its fair market value on such first day or its adjusted basis on such first day.

Subpart D—General Provisions

[Sec. 1297]

SEC. 1297. PASSIVE FOREIGN INVESTMENT COMPANY.

[Sec. 1297(a)]

(a) IN GENERAL.—For purposes of this part, except as otherwise provided in this subpart, the term "passive foreign investment company" means any foreign corporation if—

(1) 75 percent of more of the gross income of such corporation for the taxable year is passive income, or

(2) the average percentage of assets (as determined in accordance with subsection (e)) held by such corporation during the taxable year which produce passive income or which are held for the production of passive income is at least 50 percent.

[Sec. 1297(b)]

(b) PASSIVE INCOME.—For purposes of this section—

(1) IN GENERAL.—Except as provided in paragraph (2), the term "passive income" means any income which is of a kind which would be foreign personal holding company income as defined in section 954(c).

(2) EXCEPTIONS.—Except as provided in regulations, the term "passive income" does not include any income—

(A) derived in the active conduct of a banking business by an institution licensed to do business as a bank in the United States (or, to the extent provided in regulations, by any other corporation),

(B) derived in the active conduct of an insurance business by a corporation which is predominantly engaged in an insurance business and which would be subject to tax under subchapter L if it were a domestic corporation,

(C) which is interest, a dividend, or a rent or royalty, which is received or accrued from a related person (within the meaning of section 954(d)(3)) to the extent such amount is properly allocable (under regulations prescribed by the Secretary) to income of such related person which is not passive income, or

(D) which is foreign trade income of a FSC or export trade income of an export trade corporation (as defined in section 971).

For purposes of subparagraph (C), the term "related person" has the meaning given such term by section 954(d)(3) determined by substituting "foreign corporation" for "controlled foreign corporation" each place it appears in section 954(d)(3).

[Sec. 1297(c)]

(c) LOOK-THRU IN THE CASE OF 25-PERCENT OWNED CORPORATIONS.—If a foreign corporation owns (directly or indirectly) at least 25 percent (by value) of the stock of another corporation, for purposes of determining whether such foreign corporation is a passive foreign investment company, such foreign corporation shall be treated as if it—

(1) held its proportionate share of the assets of such other corporation, and

(2) received directly its proportionate share of the income of such other corporation.

[Sec. 1297(d)]

(d) SECTION 1247 CORPORATIONS.—For purposes of this part, the term "passive foreign investment company" does not include any foreign investment company to which section 1247 applies.

[Sec. 1297(e)]

(e) EXCEPTION FOR UNITED STATES SHAREHOLDERS OF CONTROLLED FOREIGN CORPORATIONS.—

(1) IN GENERAL.—For purposes of this part, a corporation shall not be treated with respect to a shareholder as a passive foreign investment company during the qualified portion of such shareholder's holding period with respect to stock in such corporation.

(2) QUALIFIED PORTION.—For purposes of this subsection, the term "qualified portion" means the portion of the shareholder's holding period—

(A) which is after December 31, 1997, and

(B) during which the shareholder is a United States shareholder (as defined in section 951(b)) of the corporation and the corporation is a controlled foreign corporation.

(3) NEW HOLDING PERIOD IF QUALIFIED PORTION ENDS.—

(A) IN GENERAL.—Except as provided in subparagraph (B), if the qualified portion of a shareholder's holding period with respect to any stock ends after December 31, 1997, solely for purposes of this part, the shareholder's holding period with respect to such stock shall be treated as beginning as of the first day following such period.

(B) EXCEPTION.—Subparagraph (A) shall not apply if such stock was, with respect to such shareholder, stock in a passive foreign investment company at any time before the qualified portion of the shareholder's holding period with respect to such stock and no election under section 1298(b)(1) is made.

(4) TREATMENT OF HOLDERS OF OPTIONS.—Paragraph (1) shall not apply to stock treated as owned by a person by reason of section 1298(a)(4) (relating to the treatment of a person that has an option to acquire stock as owning such stock) unless such person establishes that such stock is owned (within the meaning of section 958(a)) by a United States shareholder (as defined in section 951(b)) who is not exempt from tax under this chapter.

[Sec. 1297(f)]

(f) METHODS FOR MEASURING ASSETS.—

(1) DETERMINATION USING VALUE.—The determination under subsection (a)(2) shall be made on the basis of the value of the assets of a foreign corporation if—

(A) such corporation is a publicly traded corporation for the taxable year, or

(B) paragraph (2) does not apply to such corporation for the taxable year.

(2) DETERMINATION USING ADJUSTED BASES.—The determination under subsection (a)(2) shall be based on the adjusted bases (as determined for the purposes of computing earnings and profits) of the assets of a foreign corporation if such corporation is not described in paragraph (1)(A) and such corporation—

(A) is a controlled foreign corporation, or

(B) elects the application of this paragraph.

An election under subparagraph (B), once made, may be revoked only with the consent of the Secretary.

(3) PUBLICLY TRADED CORPORATION.—For purposes of this subsection, a foreign corporation shall be treated as a publicly traded corporation if the stock in the corporation is regularly traded on—

(A) a national securities exchange which is registered with the Securities and Exchange Commission or the national market system established pursuant to section 11A of the Securities and Exchange Act of 1934, or

(B) any exchange or other market which the Secretary determines has rules adequate to carry out the purposes of this subsection.

[Sec. 1298]

SEC. 1298. SPECIAL RULES.

[Sec. 1298(a)]

(a) ATTRIBUTION OF OWNERSHIP.—For purposes of this part—

(1) ATTRIBUTION TO UNITED STATES PERSONS.—This subsection—

(A) shall apply to the extent that the effect is to treat stock of a passive foreign investment company as owned by a United States person, and

(B) except to the extent provided in regulations, shall not apply to treat stock owned (or treated as owned under this subsection) by a United States person as owned by any other person.

(2) CORPORATIONS.—

(A) IN GENERAL.—If 50 percent or more in value of the stock of a corporation is owned, directly or indirectly, by or for any person, such person shall be considered as owning the stock owned directly or indirectly by or for such corporation in that proportion which the value of the stock which such person so owns bears to the value of all stock in the corporation.

(B) 50-PERCENT LIMITATION NOT TO APPLY TO PFIC.—For purposes of determining whether a shareholder of a passive foreign investment company is treated as owning stock owned directly or indirectly by or for such company, subparagraph (A) shall be applied without regard to the 50-percent limitation contained therein. Section 1297(e) shall not apply in determining whether a corporation is a passive foreign investment company for purposes of this subparagraph.

(3) PARTNERSHIPS, ETC.—Stock owned, directly or indirectly, by or for a partnership, estate, or trust shall be considered as being owned proportionately by its partners or beneficiaries.

(4) OPTIONS.—To the extent provided in regulations, if any person has an option to acquire stock, such stock shall be considered as owned by such person. For purposes of this paragraph, an option to acquire such an option, and each one of a series of such options, shall be considered as an option to acquire such stock.

(5) SUCCESSIVE APPLICATION.—Stock considered to be owned by a person by reason of the application of paragraph (2), (3), or (4) shall, for purposes of applying such paragraphs, be considered as actually owned by such person.

[Sec. 1298(b)]

(b) OTHER SPECIAL RULES.—For purposes of this part—

(1) TIME FOR DETERMINATION.—Stock held by a taxpayer shall be treated as stock in a passive foreign investment company if, at any time during the holding period of the taxpayer with respect to such stock, such corporation (or any predecessor) was a passive foreign investment company which was not a qualified electing fund. The preceding sentence shall not apply if the taxpayer elects to recognize gain (as of the last day of the last taxable year for which the company was a passive foreign investment company (determined without regard to the preceding sentence)) under rules similar to the rules of section 1291(d)(2).

(2) CERTAIN CORPORATIONS NOT TREATED AS PFIC'S DURING START-UP YEAR.—A corporation shall not be treated as a passive foreign investment company for the first taxable year such corporation has gross income (hereinafter in this paragraph referred to as the "start-up year") if—

(A) no predecessor of such corporation was a passive foreign investment company,

(B) it is established to the satisfaction of the Secretary that such corporation will not be a passive foreign investment company for either of the 1st 2 taxable years following the start-up year, and

(C) such corporation is not a passive foreign investment company for either of the 1st 2 taxable years following the start-up year.

(3) CERTAIN CORPORATIONS CHANGING BUSINESSES.—A corporation shall not be treated as a passive foreign investment company for any taxable year if—

(A) neither such corporation (nor any predecessor) was a passive foreign investment company for any prior taxable year,

(B) it is established to the satisfaction of the Secretary that—

(i) substantially all of the passive income of the corporation for the taxable year is attributable to proceeds from the disposition of 1 or more active trades or businesses, and

(ii) such corporation will not be a passive foreign investment company for either of the 1st 2 taxable years following such taxable year, and

(C) such corporation is not a passive foreign investment company for either of such 2 taxable years.

(4) SEPARATE INTERESTS TREATED AS SEPARATE CORPORATIONS.—Under regulations prescribed by the Secretary, where necessary to carry out the purposes of this part, separate classes of stock (or other interests) in a corporation shall be treated as interests in separate corporations.

(5) APPLICATION OF PART WHERE STOCK HELD BY OTHER ENTITY.—

(A) IN GENERAL.—Under regulations, in any case in which a United States person is treated as owning stock in a passive foreign investment company by reason of subsection (a)—

Income Tax—General Provisions

(i) any disposition by the United States person or the person owning such stock which results in the United States person being treated as no longer owning such stock, or

(ii) any distribution of property in respect of such stock to the person holding such stock,

shall be treated as a disposition by, or distribution to, the United States person with respect to the stock in the passive foreign investment company.

(B) AMOUNT TREATED IN SAME MANNER AS PREVIOUSLY TAXED INCOME.—Rules similar to the rules of section 959(b) shall apply to any amount described in subparagraph (A) and to any amount included in gross income under section 1293(a) (or which would have been so included but for section 951(f)) in respect of stock which the taxpayer is treated as owning under subsection (a).

(6) DISPOSITIONS.—Except as provided in regulations, if a taxpayer uses any stock in a passive foreign investment company as security for a loan, the taxpayer shall be treated as having disposed of such stock.

(7) COORDINATION WITH SECTION 1246.—Section 1246 shall not apply to earnings and profits of any company for any taxable year beginning after December 31, 1986, if such company is a passive foreign investment company for such taxable year.

(8) TREATMENT OF CERTAIN FOREIGN CORPORATIONS OWNING STOCK IN 25-PERCENT OWNED DOMESTIC CORPORATION.—

(A) IN GENERAL.—If—

(i) a foreign corporation is subject to the tax imposed by section 531 (or waives any benefit under any treaty which would otherwise prevent the imposition of such tax), and

(ii) such foreign corporation owns at least 25 percent (by value) of the stock of a domestic corporation,

for purposes of determining whether such foreign corporation is a passive foreign investment company, any qualified stock held by such domestic corporation shall be treated as an asset which does not produce passive income (and is not held for the production of passive income) and any amount included in gross income with respect to such stock shall not be treated as passive income.

(B) QUALIFIED STOCK.—For purposes of subparagraph (A), the term "qualified stock" means any stock in a C corporation which is a domestic corporation and which is not a regulated investment company or real estate investment trust.

(9) TREATMENT OF CERTAIN SUBPART F INCLUSIONS.—Any amount included in gross income under section 951(a)(1)(B) shall be treated as a distribution received with respect to the stock.

[Sec. 1298(c)]

(c) TREATMENT OF STOCK HELD BY POOLED INCOME FUND.—If stock in a passive foreign investment company is owned (or treated as owned under subsection (a)) by a pooled income fund (as defined in section 642(c)(5)) and no portion of any gain from a disposition of such stock may be allocated to income under the terms of the governing instrument of such fund—

(1) section 1291 shall not apply to any gain on a disposition of such stock by such fund if (without regard to section 1291) a deduction would be allowable with respect to such gain under section 642(c)(3),

(2) section 1293 shall not apply with respect to such stock, and

(3) in determining whether section 1291 applies to any distribution in respect of such stock, subsection (d) of section 1291 shall not apply.

[Sec. 1298(d)]

(d) TREATMENT OF CERTAIN LEASED PROPERTY.—For purposes of this part—

(1) IN GENERAL.—Any tangible personal property with respect to which a foreign corporation is the lessee under a lease with a term of at least 12 months shall be treated as an asset actually held by such corporation.

(2) AMOUNT TAKEN INTO ACCOUNT.—

(A) IN GENERAL.—The amount taken into account under section 1296(a)(2) with respect to any asset to which paragraph (1) applies shall be the unamortized portion (as determined under regulations prescribed by the Secretary) of the present value of the payments under the lease for the use of such property.

(B) PRESENT VALUE.—For purposes of subparagraph (A), the present value of payments described in subparagraph (A) shall be determined in the manner provided in regulations prescribed by the Secretary—

(i) as of the beginning of the lease term, and

(ii) except as provided in such regulations, by using a discount rate equal to the applicable Federal rate determined under section 1274(d)—

(I) by substituting the lease term for the term of the debt instrument, and

(II) without regard to paragraph (2) or (3) thereof.

(3) EXCEPTIONS.—This subsection shall not apply in any case where—

(A) the lessor is a related person (as defined in section 954(d)(3)) with respect to the foreign corporation, or

(B) a principal purpose of leasing the property was to avoid the provisions of this part.

[Sec. 1298(e)]

(e) SPECIAL RULES FOR CERTAIN INTANGIBLES.—For purposes of this part—

(1) RESEARCH EXPENDITURES.—The adjusted basis of the total assets of a controlled foreign corporation shall be increased by the research or experimental expenditures (within the meaning of section 174) paid or incurred by such foreign corporation during the taxable year and the preceding 2 taxable years. Any expenditure otherwise taken into account under the preceding sentence shall be reduced by the amount of any reimbursement received by the controlled foreign corporation with respect to such expenditure.

(2) CERTAIN LICENSED INTANGIBLES.—

(A) IN GENERAL.—In the case of any intangible property (as defined in section 936(h)(3)(B)) with respect to which a controlled foreign corporation is a licensee and which is used by such foreign corporation in the active conduct of a trade or business, the adjusted basis of the total assets of such foreign corporation shall be increased by an amount equal to 300 percent of the payments made during the taxable year by such foreign corporation for the use of such intangible property.

(B) EXCEPTIONS.—Subparagraph (A) shall not apply to—

(i) any payments to a foreign person if such foreign person is a related person (as defined in section 954(d)(3)) with respect to the controlled foreign corporation, and

(ii) any payments under a license if a principal purpose of entering into such license was to avoid the provisions of this part.

(3) CONTROLLED FOREIGN CORPORATION.—For purposes of this subsection, the term "controlled foreign corporation" has the meaning given such term by section 957(a).

[Sec. 1298(f)]

(f) REGULATIONS.—The Secretary shall prescribe such regulations as may be necessary or appropriate to carry out the purposes of this part.

SUBCHAPTER Q—READJUSTMENT OF TAX BETWEEN YEARS AND SPECIAL LIMITATIONS

PART VII—RECOVERIES OF FOREIGN EXPROPRIATION LOSSES

[Sec. 1351]

SEC. 1351. TREATMENT OF RECOVERIES OF FOREIGN EXPROPRIATION LOSSES.

[Sec. 1351(a)]

(a) ELECTION.—

(1) IN GENERAL.—This section shall apply only to a recovery, by a domestic corporation subject to the tax imposed by section 11 or 801, of a foreign expropriation loss sustained by such corporation and only if such corporation was subject to the tax imposed by section 11 or 801, as the case may be, for the year of the loss and elects to have the provisions of this section apply with respect to such loss.

(2) TIME, MANNER, AND SCOPE.—An election under paragraph (1) shall be made at such time and in such manner as the Secretary may prescribe by regulations. An election made with respect to any foreign expropriation loss shall apply to all recoveries in respect of such loss.

[Sec. 1351(b)]

(b) DEFINITION OF FOREIGN EXPROPRIATION LOSS.—For purposes of this section, the term "foreign expropriation loss" means any loss sustained by reason of the expropriation, intervention, seizure, or similar taking of property by the government of any foreign country, any political subdivision thereof, or any agency or instrumentality of the foregoing. For purposes of the preceding sentence, a debt which becomes worthless shall, to the extent of any deduction allowed under section 166(a), be treated as a loss.

[Sec. 1351(c)]

(c) AMOUNT OF RECOVERY.—

(1) GENERAL RULE.—The amount of any recovery of a foreign expropriation loss is the amount of money and the fair market value of other property received in respect of such loss, determined as of the date of receipt.

(2) SPECIAL RULE FOR LIFE INSURANCE COMPANIES.—The amount of any recovery of a foreign expropriation loss includes, in the case of a life insurance company, the amount of decrease of any item taken into account under section 807(c), to the extent such decrease is attributable to the release, by reason of such loss, of its liabilities with respect to such item.

[Sec. 1351(d)]

(d) ADJUSTMENT FOR PRIOR TAX BENEFITS.—

(1) IN GENERAL.—That part of the amount of a recovery of a foreign expropriation loss to which this section applies which, when added to the aggregate of the amounts of previous recoveries with respect to such loss, does not exceed the allowable deductions in prior taxable years on account of such loss shall be excluded from gross income for the taxable year of the recovery for purposes of computing the tax under this subtitle; but there shall be added to, and assessed and collected as a part of, the tax under this subtitle for such taxable year an amount equal to the total increase in the tax under this subtitle for all taxable years which would result by decreasing, in an amount equal to such part of the recovery so excluded, the deductions allowable in the prior taxable years on account of such loss. For purposes of this paragraph, if the loss to which the recovery relates was taken into account as a loss from the sale or exchange of a capital asset, the amount of the loss shall be treated as an allowable deduction even though there were no gains against which to allow such loss.

(2) COMPUTATION.—The increase in the tax for each taxable year referred to in paragraph (1) shall be computed in accordance with regulations prescribed by the Secretary. Such regulations shall give effect to previous recoveries of any kind (including recoveries described in section 111, relating to recovery of tax benefit items) with respect to any prior

taxable year, but shall otherwise treat the tax previously determined for any taxable year in accordance with the principles set forth in section 1314(a) (relating to correction of errors). Subject to the provisions of paragraph (3), all credits allowable against the tax for any taxable year, and all carryovers and carrybacks affected by so decreasing the allowable deductions, shall be taken into account in computing the increase in the tax.

(3) FOREIGN TAXES.—For purposes of this subsection, any choice made under subpart A of part III of subchapter N (relating to foreign tax credit) for any taxable year may be changed.

(4) SUBSTITUTION OF CURRENT TAX RATE.—For purposes of this subsection, the rates of tax specified in section 11(b) for the taxable year of the recovery shall be treated as having been in effect for all prior taxable years.

[Sec. 1351(e)]

(e) GAIN ON RECOVERY.—That part of the amount of a recovery of a foreign expropriation loss to which this section applies which is not excluded from gross income under subsection (d)(1) shall be considered for the taxable year of the recovery as gain on the involuntary conversion of property as a result of its destruction or seizure and shall be recognized or not recognized as provided in section 1033.

[Sec. 1351(f)]

(f) BASIS OF RECOVERED PROPERTY.—The basis of property (other than money) received as a recovery of a foreign expropriation loss to which this section applies shall be an amount equal to its fair market value on the date of receipt, reduced by such part of the gain under subsection (e) which is not recognized as provided in section 1033.

[Sec. 1351(g)]

(g) RESTORATION OF VALUE OF INVESTMENTS.—For purposes of this section, if the value of any interest in, or with respect to, property (including any interest represented by a security, as defined in section 165(g)(2))—

(1) which became worthless by reason of the expropriation, intervention, seizure, or similar taking of such property by the government of any foreign country, any political subdivision thereof, or any agency or instrumentality of the foregoing, and

(2) which was taken into account as a loss from the sale or exchange of a captial asset or with respect to which a deduction for a loss was allowed under section 165 or a deduction for a bad debt was allowed under section 166,

is restored in whole or in part by reason of any recovery of money or other property in respect of the property which became worthless, the value so restored shall be treated as property received as a recovery in respect of such loss or such bad debt.

[Sec. 1351(h)]

(h) SPECIAL RULE FOR EVIDENCES OF INDEBTEDNESS.—Bonds or other evidences of indebtedness received as a recovery of a foreign expropriation loss to which this section applies shall not be considered to have any original issue discount within the meaning of section 1273(a).

[Sec. 1351(i)]

(i) ADJUSTMENTS FOR SUCCEEDING YEARS.—For purposes of this subtitle, proper adjustment shall be made, under regulations prescribed by the Secretary, in—

(1) the credit under section 27 (relating to foreign tax credit),

(2) the credit under section 38 (relating to general business credit),

(3) the net operating loss deduction under section 172, or the operations loss deduction under section 810,

(4) the capital loss carryover under section 1212(a), and

(5) such other items as may be specified by such regulations,

for the taxable year of a recovery of a foreign expropriation loss to which this section applies, and for succeeding taxable years, to take into account items changed in making the computations under subsection (d) for taxable years prior to the taxable year of such recovery.

Sec. 1351(d)(3)

SUBCHAPTER R—ELECTION TO DETERMINE CORPORATE TAX ON CERTAIN INTERNATIONAL SHIPPING ACTIVITIES USING PER TON RATE

[Sec. 1352]

SEC. 1352. ALTERNATIVE TAX ON QUALIFYING SHIPPING ACTIVITIES.

In the case of an electing corporation, the tax imposed by section 11 shall be the amount equal to the sum of—

(1) the tax imposed by section 11 determined after the application of this subchapter, and

(2) a tax equal to—

(A) the highest rate of tax specified in section 11, multiplied by

(B) the notional shipping income for the taxable year.

[Sec. 1353]

SEC. 1353. NOTIONAL SHIPPING INCOME.

[Sec. 1353(a)]

(a) IN GENERAL.—For purposes of this subchapter, the notional shipping income of an electing corporation shall be the sum of the amounts determined under subsection (b) for each qualifying vessel operated by such electing corporation.

[Sec. 1353(b)]

(b) AMOUNTS.—

(1) IN GENERAL.—For purposes of subsection (a), the amount of notional shipping income of an electing corporation for each qualifying vessel for the taxable year shall equal the product of—

(A) the daily notional shipping income, and

(B) the number of days during the taxable year that the electing corporation operated such vessel as a qualifying vessel in United States foreign trade.

(2) TREATMENT OF VESSELS THE INCOME FROM WHICH IS NOT OTHERWISE SUBJECT TO TAX.—In the case of a qualifying vessel any of the income from which is not included in gross income by reason of section 883 or otherwise, the amount of notional shipping income from such vessel for the taxable year shall be the amount which bears the same ratio to such shipping income (determined without regard to this paragraph) as the gross income from the operation of such vessel in the United States foreign trade bears to the sum of such gross income and the income so excluded.

[Sec. 1353(c)]

(c) DAILY NOTIONAL SHIPPING INCOME.—For purposes of subsection (b), the daily notional shipping income from the operation of a qualifying vessel is—

(1) 40 cents for each 100 tons of so much of the net tonnage of the vessel as does not exceed 25,000 net tons, and

(2) 20 cents for each 100 tons of so much of the net tonnage of the vessel as exceeds 25,000 net tons.

[Sec. 1353(d)]

(d) MULTIPLE OPERATORS OF VESSEL.—If for any period 2 or more persons are operators of a qualifying vessel, the notional shipping income from the operation of such vessel for such period shall be allocated among such persons on the basis of their respective ownership and charter interests in such vessel or on such other basis as the Secretary may prescribe by regulations.

[Sec. 1354]

SEC. 1354. ALTERNATIVE TAX ELECTION; REVOCATION; TERMINATION.

[Sec. 1354(a)]

(a) IN GENERAL.—A qualifying vessel operator may elect the application of this subchapter.

[Sec. 1354(b)]

(b) TIME AND MANNER; YEARS FOR WHICH EFFECTIVE.—An election under this subchapter—

(1) shall be made in such form as prescribed by the Secretary, and

(2) shall be effective for the taxable year for which made and all succeeding taxable years until terminated under subsection (d).

Such election may be effective for any taxable year only if made before the due date (including extensions) for filing the corporation's return for such taxable year.

[Sec. 1354(c)]

(c) CONSISTENT ELECTIONS BY MEMBERS OF CONTROLLED GROUPS.—An election under subsection (a) by a member of a controlled group shall apply to all qualifying vessel operators that are members of such group.

[Sec. 1354(d)]

(d) TERMINATION.—

(1) BY REVOCATION.—

(A) IN GENERAL.—An election under subsection (a) may be terminated by revocation.

(B) WHEN EFFECTIVE.—Except as provided in subparagraph (C)—

(i) a revocation made during the taxable year and on or before the 15th day of the 3d month thereof shall be effective on the 1st day of such taxable year, and

(ii) a revocation made during the taxable year but after such 15th day shall be effective on the 1st day of the following taxable year.

(C) REVOCATION MAY SPECIFY PROSPECTIVE DATE.—If the revocation specifies a date for revocation which is on or after the day on which the revocation is made, the revocation shall be effective for taxable years beginning on and after the date so specified.

(2) BY PERSON CEASING TO BE QUALIFYING VESSEL OPERATOR.—

(A) IN GENERAL.—An election under subsection (a) shall be terminated whenever (at any time on or after the 1st day of the 1st taxable year for which the corporation is an electing corporation) such corporation ceases to be a qualifying vessel operator.

(B) WHEN EFFECTIVE.—Any termination under this paragraph shall be effective on and after the date of cessation.

(C) ANNUALIZATION.—The Secretary shall prescribe such annualization and other rules as are appropriate in the case of a termination under this paragraph.

[Sec. 1354(e)]

(e) ELECTION AFTER TERMINATION.—If a qualifying vessel operator has made an election under subsection (a) and if such election has been terminated under subsection (d), such operator (and any successor operator) shall not be eligible to make an election under subsection (a) for any taxable year before its 5th taxable year which begins after the 1st taxable year for which such termination is effective, unless the Secretary consents to such election.

[Sec. 1355]

SEC. 1355. DEFINITIONS AND SPECIAL RULES.

[Sec. 1355(a)]

(a) DEFINITIONS.—For purposes of this subchapter—

(1) ELECTING CORPORATION.—The term "electing corporation" means any corporation for which an election is in effect under this subchapter.

(2) ELECTING GROUP; CONTROLLED GROUP.—

(A) ELECTING GROUP.—The term "electing group" means a controlled group of which one or more members is an electing corporation.

(B) CONTROLLED GROUP.—The term "controlled group" means any group which would be treated as a single employer under subsection (a) or (b) of section 52 if paragraphs (1) and (2) of section 52(a) did not apply.

(3) QUALIFYING VESSEL OPERATOR.—The term "qualifying vessel operator" means any corporation—

(A) who operates one or more qualifying vessels, and

(B) who meets the shipping activity requirement in subsection (c).

(4) QUALIFYING VESSEL.—The term "qualifying vessel" means a self-propelled (or a combination self-propelled and non-self-propelled) United States flag vessel of not less than 10,000 deadweight tons used exclusively in the United States foreign trade during the period that the election under this subchapter is in effect.

(5) UNITED STATES FLAG VESSEL.—The term "United States flag vessel" means any vessel documented under the laws of the United States.

(6) UNITED STATES DOMESTIC TRADE.—The term "United States domestic trade" means the transportation of goods or passengers between places in the United States.

(7) UNITED STATES FOREIGN TRADE.—The term "United States foreign trade" means the transportation of goods or passengers between a place in the United States and a foreign place or between foreign places.

(8) CHARTER.—The term "charter" includes an operating agreement.

[Sec. 1355(b)]

(b) OPERATING A VESSEL.—For purposes of this subchapter—

(1) IN GENERAL.—Except as provided in paragraph (2), a person is treated as operating any vessel during any period if such vessel is—

(A) owned by, or chartered (including a time charter) to, the person, and

(B) is in use as a qualifying vessel during such period.

(2) BAREBOAT CHARTERS.—A person is treated as operating and using a vessel that it has chartered out on bareboat charter terms only if—

(A)(i) the vessel is temporarily surplus to the person's requirements and the term of the charter does not exceed 3 years, or

(ii) the vessel is bareboat chartered to a member of a controlled group which includes such person or to an unrelated person who subbareboats or time charters the vessel to such a member (including the owner of the vessel), and

(B) the vessel is used as a qualifying vessel by the person to whom ultimately chartered.

[Sec. 1355(c)]

(c) SHIPPING ACTIVITY REQUIREMENT.—For purposes of this section—

(1) IN GENERAL.—Except as otherwise provided in this subsection, a corporation meets the shipping activity requirement of this subsection for any taxable year only if the requirement of paragraph (4) is met for each of the 2 preceding taxable years.

(2) SPECIAL RULE FOR 1ST YEAR OF ELECTION.—A corporation meets the shipping activity requirement of this subsection for the first taxable year for which the election under section 1354(a) is in effect only if the requirement of paragraph (4) is met for the preceding taxable year.

(3) CONTROLLED GROUPS.—A corporation who is a member of a controlled group meets the shipping activity requirement of this subsection only if such requirement is met determined—

(A) by treating all members of such group as 1 person, and

(B) by disregarding vessel charters between members of such group.

(4) REQUIREMENT.—The requirement of this paragraph is met for any taxable year if, on average during such year, at least 25 percent of the aggregate tonnage of qualifying vessels used by the corporation were owned by such corporation or chartered to such corporation on bareboat charter terms.

[Sec. 1355(d)]

(d) ACTIVITIES CARRIED ON [BY] PARTNERSHIPS, ETC.—In applying this subchapter to a partner in a partnership—

(1) each partner shall be treated as operating vessels operated by the partnership,

(2) each partner shall be treated as conducting the activities conducted by the partnership, and

(3) the extent of a partner's ownership or charter interest in any vessel owned by or chartered to the partnership shall be determined on the basis of the partner's interest in the partnership.

A similar rule shall apply with respect to other pass-thru entities.

[Sec. 1355(e)]

(e) EFFECT OF TEMPORARILY CEASING TO OPERATE A QUALIFYING VESSEL.—

(1) IN GENERAL.—For purposes of subsections (b) and (c), an electing corporation shall be treated as continuing to use a qualifying vessel during any period of temporary cessation if the electing corporation gives timely notice to the Secretary stating—

(A) that it has temporarily ceased to operate the qualifying vessel, and

(B) its intention to resume operating the qualifying vessel.

(2) NOTICE.—Notice shall be deemed timely if given not later than the due date (including extensions) for the corporation's tax return for the taxable year in which the temporary cessation begins.

(3) PERIOD DISREGARD IN EFFECT.—The period of temporary cessation under paragraph (1) shall continue until the earlier of the date on which—

(A) the electing corporation abandons its intention to resume operation of the qualifying vessel, or

(B) the electing corporation resumes operation of the qualifying vessel.

[Sec. 1355(f)]

(f) EFFECT OF TEMPORARILY OPERATING A QUALIFYING VESSEL IN THE UNITED STATES DOMESTIC TRADE.—

(1) IN GENERAL.—For purposes of this subchapter, an electing corporation shall be treated as continuing to use a qualifying vessel in the United States foreign trade during any period of temporary use in the United States domestic trade if the electing corporation gives timely notice to the Secretary stating—

(A) that it temporarily operates or has operated in the United States domestic trade a qualifying vessel which had been used in the United States foreign trade, and

(B) its intention to resume operation of the vessel in the United States foreign trade.

(2) NOTICE.—Notice shall be deemed timely if given not later than the due date (including extensions) for the corporation's tax return for the taxable year in which the temporary cessation begins.

(3) PERIOD DISREGARD IN EFFECT.—The period of temporary use under paragraph (1) continues until the earlier of the date of which—

(A) the electing corporation abandons its intention to resume operations of the vessel in the United States foreign trade, or

(B) the electing corporation resumes operation of the vessel in the United States foreign trade.

(4) NO DISREGARD IF DOMESTIC TRADE USE EXCEEDS 30 DAYS.—Paragraph (1) shall not apply to any qualifying vessel which is operated in the United States domestic trade for more than 30 days during the taxable year.

[Sec. 1355(g)]

(g) REGULATIONS.—The Secretary shall prescribe such regulations as may be necessary or appropriate to carry out the purposes of this section.

[Sec. 1356]

SEC. 1356. QUALIFYING SHIPPING ACTIVITIES.

[Sec. 1356(a)]

(a) QUALIFYING SHIPPING ACTIVITIES.—For purposes of this subchapter, the term "qualifying shipping activities" means—

(1) core qualifying activities,

(2) qualifying secondary activities, and

(3) qualifying incidental activities.

[Sec. 1356(b)]

(b) CORE QUALIFYING ACTIVITIES.—For purposes of this subchapter, the term "core qualifying activities" means activities in operating qualifying vessels in United States foreign trade.

[Sec. 1356(c)]

(c) QUALIFYING SECONDARY ACTIVITIES.—For purposes of this section—

(1) IN GENERAL.—The term "qualifying secondary activities" means secondary activities but only to the extent that, without regard to this subchapter, the gross income derived by such corporation from such activities does not exceed 20 percent of the gross income derived by the corporation from its core qualifying activities.

(2) SECONDARY ACTIVITIES.—The term "secondary activities" means—

(A) the active management or operation of vessels other than qualifying vessels in the United States foreign trade,

(B) the provision of vessel, barge, container, or cargo-related facilities or services to any person,

(C) other activities of the electing corporation and other members of its electing group that are an integral part of its business of operating qualifying vessels in United States foreign trade, including—

(i) ownership or operation of barges, containers, chassis, and other equipment that are the complement of, or used in connection with, a qualifying vessel in United States foreign trade,

(ii) the inland haulage of cargo shipped, or to be shipped, on qualifying vessels in United States foreign trade, and

(iii) the provision of terminal, maintenance, repair, logistical, or other vessel, barge, container, or cargo-related services that are an integral part of operating qualifying vessels in United States foreign trade, and

(D) such other activities as may be prescribed by the Secretary pursuant to regulations.

(3) COORDINATION WITH CORE ACTIVITIES.—

(A) IN GENERAL.—Such term shall not include any core qualifying activities.

(B) NONELECTING CORPORATIONS.—In the case of a corporation (other than an electing corporation) which is a member of an electing group, any core qualifying activities of the corporation shall be treated as qualifying secondary activities (and not as core qualifying activities).

[Sec. 1356(d)]

(d) QUALIFYING INCIDENTAL ACTIVITIES.—For purposes of this section, the term "qualified incidental activities" means shipping-related activities if—

(1) they are incidental to the corporation's core qualifying activities,

(2) they are not qualifying secondary activities, and

(3) without regard to this subchapter, the gross income derived by such corporation from such activities does not exceed 0.1 percent of the corporation's gross income from its core qualifying activities.

[Sec. 1356(e)]

(e) APPLICATION OF GROSS INCOME TESTS IN CASE OF ELECTING GROUP.—In the case of an electing group, subsections (c)(1) and (d)(3) shall be applied as if such group were 1 entity, and the limitations under such subsections shall be allocated among the corporations in such group.

[Sec. 1357]

SEC. 1357. ITEMS NOT SUBJECT TO REGULAR TAX; DEPRECIATION; INTEREST.

[Sec. 1357(a)]

(a) EXCLUSION FROM GROSS INCOME.—Gross income of an electing corporation shall not include its income from qualifying shipping activities.

[Sec. 1357(b)]

(b) ELECTING GROUP MEMBER.—Gross income of a corporation (other than an electing corporation) which is a member of an electing group shall not include its income from qualifying shipping activities conducted by such member.

[Sec. 1357(c)]

(c) DENIAL OF LOSSES, DEDUCTIONS, AND CREDITS.—

(1) GENERAL RULE.—Subject to paragraph (2), each item of loss, deduction (other than for interest expense), or credit of any taxpayer with respect to any activity the income from which is excluded from gross income under this section shall be disallowed.

(2) DEPRECIATION.—

(A) IN GENERAL.—Notwithstanding paragraph (1), the adjusted basis (for purposes of determining gain) of any qualifying vessel shall be determined as if the deduction for depreciation had been allowed.

(B) METHOD.—

(i) IN GENERAL.—Except as provided in clause (ii), the straight-line method of depreciation shall apply to qualifying vessels the income from operation of which is excluded from gross income under this section.

(ii) EXCEPTION.—Clause (i) shall not apply to any qualifying vessel which is subject to a charter entered into before the date of the enactment of this subchapter.

(3) INTEREST.—

(A) IN GENERAL.—Except as provided in subparagraph (B), the interest expense of an electing corporation shall be disallowed in the ratio that the fair market value of such corporation's qualifying vessels bears to the fair market value of such corporation's total assets.

(B) ELECTING GROUP.—In the case of a corporation which is a member of an electing group, the interest expense of such corporation shall be disallowed in the ratio that the fair market value of such corporation's qualifying vessels bears to the fair market value of the electing group[']s total assets.

[Sec. 1358]

SEC. 1358. ALLOCATION OF CREDITS, INCOME, AND DEDUCTIONS.

[Sec. 1358(a)]

(a) QUALIFYING SHIPPING ACTIVITIES.—For purposes of this chapter, the qualifying shipping activities of an electing corporation shall be treated as a separate trade or business activity distinct from all other activities conducted by such corporation.

[Sec. 1358(b)]

(b) EXCLUSION OF CREDITS OR DEDUCTIONS.—

(1) No deduction shall be allowed against the notional shipping income of an electing corporation, and no credit shall be allowed against the tax imposed by section 1352(a)(2).

(2) No deduction shall be allowed for any net operating loss attributable to the qualifying shipping activities of any person to the extent that such loss is carried forward by such person from a taxable year preceding the first taxable year for which such person was an electing corporation.

[Sec. 1358(c)]

(c) TRANSACTIONS NOT AT ARM'S LENGTH.—Section 482 applies in accordance with this subsection to a transaction or series of transactions—

(1) as between an electing corporation and another person, or

(2) as between an [sic] person's qualifying shipping activities and other activities carried on by it.

[Sec. 1359]

SEC. 1359. DISPOSITION OF QUALIFYING VESSELS.

[Sec. 1359(a)]

(a) IN GENERAL.—If any qualifying vessel operator sells or disposes of any qualifying vessel in an otherwise taxable transaction, at the election of such operator, no gain shall be recognized if any replacement qualifying vessel is acquired during the period specified in subsection (b), except to the extent that the amount realized upon such sale or disposition exceeds the cost of the replacement qualifying vessel.

[Sec. 1359(b)]

(b) PERIOD WITHIN WHICH PROPERTY MUST BE REPLACED.—The period referred to in subsection (a) shall be the period beginning one year prior to the disposition of the qualifying vessel and ending—

(1) 3 years after the close of the first taxable year in which the gain is realized, or

(2) subject to such terms and conditions as may be specified by the Secretary, on such later date as the Secretary may designate on application by the taxpayer.

Such application shall be made at such time and in such manner as the Secretary may by regulations prescribe.

[Sec. 1359(c)]

(c) APPLICATION OF SECTION TO NONCORPORATE OPERATORS.—For purposes of this section, the term "qualifying vessel operator" includes any person who would be a qualifying vessel operator were such person a corporation.

[Sec. 1359(d)]

(d) TIME FOR ASSESSMENT OF DEFICIENCY ATTRIBUTABLE TO GAIN.—If a qualifying vessel operator has made the election provided in subsection (a), then—

(1) the statutory period for the assessment of any deficiency, for any taxable year in which any part of the gain is realized, attributable to such gain shall not expire prior to the expiration of 3 years from the date the Secretary is notified by such operator (in such manner as the Secretary may by regulations prescribe) of the replacement qualifying vessel or of an intention not to replace, and

(2) such deficiency may be assessed before the expiration of such 3-year period notwithstanding the provisions of section 6212(c) or the provisions of any other law or rule of law which would otherwise prevent such assessment.

[Sec. 1359(e)]

(e) BASIS OF REPLACEMENT QUALIFYING VESSEL.—In the case of any replacement qualifying vessel purchased by the qualifying vessel operator which resulted in the nonrecognition of any part of the gain realized as the result of a sale or other disposition of a qualifying vessel, the basis shall be the cost of the replacement qualifying vessel decreased in the amount of the gain not so recognized; and if the property purchased consists of more than one piece of property, the basis determined under this sentence shall be allocated to the purchased properties in proportion to their respective costs.

CHAPTER 3—WITHHOLDING OF TAX ON NONRESIDENT ALIENS AND FOREIGN CORPORATIONS

SUBCHAPTER A—NONRESIDENT ALIENS AND FOREIGN CORPORATIONS

[Sec. 1441]

SEC. 1441. WITHHOLDING OF TAX ON NONRESIDENT ALIENS.

[Sec. 1441(a)]

(a) GENERAL RULE.—Except as otherwise provided in subsection (c), all persons, in whatever capacity acting (including lessees or mortgagors of real or personal property, fiduciaries, employers, and all officers and employees of the United States) having the control, receipt, custody, disposal, or payment of any of the items of income specified in subsection (b) (to the extent that any of such items constitutes gross income from sources within the United States), of any nonresident alien individual or of any foreign partnership shall (except as otherwise provided in regulations prescribed by the Secretary under section 874) deduct and withhold from such items a tax equal to 30 percent thereof, except that in the case of any item of income specified in the second sentence of subsection (b), the tax shall be equal to 14 percent of such item.

[Sec. 1441(b)]

(b) INCOME ITEMS.—The items of income referred to in subsection (a) are interest (other than original issue discount as defined in section 1273), dividends, rent, salaries, wages, premiums, annuities, compensations, remunerations, emoluments, or other fixed or determinable annual or periodical gains, profits, and income, gains described in section 631(b) or (c), amounts subject to tax under section 871(a)(1)(C), gains subject to tax under section 871(a)(1)(D), and gains on transfers described in section 1235 made on or before October 4, 1966. The items of income referred to in subsection (a) from which tax shall be deducted and withheld at the rate of 14 percent are amounts which are received by a nonresident alien individual who is temporarily present in the United States as a nonimmigrant under subparagraph (F), (J), (M), or (Q) of section 101(a)(15) of the Immigration and Nationality Act and which are—

(1) incident to a qualified scholarship to which section 117(a) applies, but only to the extent includible in gross income; or

(2) in the case of an individual who is not a candidate for a degree at an educational organization described in section 170(b)(1)(A)(ii), granted by—

(A) an organization described in section 501(c)(3) which is exempt from tax under section 501(a),

(B) a foreign government,

(C) an international organization, or a binational or multinational educational and cultural foundation or commission created or continued pursuant to the Mutual Educational and Cultural Exchange Act of 1961, or

(D) the United States, or an instrumentality or agency thereof, or a State, or a possession of the United States, or any political subdivision thereof, or the District of Columbia,

as a scholarship or fellowship for study, training, or research in the United States.

In the case of a nonresident alien individual who is a member of a domestic partnership, the items of income referred to in subsection (a) shall be treated as referring to items specified in this subsection included in his distributive share of the income of such partnership.

[Sec. 1441(c)]

(c) EXCEPTIONS.—

(1) INCOME CONNECTED WITH UNITED STATES BUSINESS.—No deduction or withholding under subsection (a) shall be required in the case of any item of income (other than compensation for personal services) which is effectively connected with the conduct of a trade or business within the United States and which is included in the gross income of the recipient under section 871(b)(2) for the taxable year.

(2) OWNER UNKNOWN.—The Secretary may authorize the tax under subsection (a) to be deducted and withheld from the interest upon any securities the owners of which are not known to the withholding agent.

(3) BONDS WITH EXTENDED MATURITY DATES.—The deduction and withholding in the case of interest on bonds, mortgages, or deeds of trust or other similar obligations of a corporation, within subsections (a), (b), and (c) of section 1451 (as in effect before its repeal by the Tax Reform Act of 1984) were it not for the fact that the maturity date of such obligations has been extended on or after January 1, 1934, and the liability assumed by the debtor exceeds 27½ percent of the interest, shall not exceed the rate of 27½ percent per annum.

(4) COMPENSATION OF CERTAIN ALIENS.—Under regulations prescribed by the Secretary, compensation for personal services may be exempted from deduction and withholding under subsection (a).

(5) SPECIAL ITEMS.—In the case of gains described in section 631(b) or (c), gains subject to tax under section 871(a)(1)(D), and gains on transfers described in section 1235 made on or before October 4, 1966, the amount required to be deducted and withheld shall, if the amount of such gain is not known to the withholding agent, be such amount, not exceeding 30 percent of the amount payable, as may be necessary to assure that the tax deducted and withheld shall not be less than 30 percent of such gain.

(6) PER DIEM OF CERTAIN ALIENS.—No deduction or withholding under subsection (a) shall be required in the case of amounts of per diem for subsistence paid by the United States Government (directly or by contract) to any nonresident alien individual who is engaged in any program of training in the United States under the Mutual Security Act of 1954, as amended.

(7) CERTAIN ANNUITIES RECEIVED UNDER QUALIFIED PLANS.—No deduction or withholding under subsection (a) shall be required in the case of any amount received as an annuity if such amount is, under section 871(f), exempt from the tax imposed by section 871(a).

(8) ORIGINAL ISSUE DISCOUNT.—The Secretary may prescribe such regulations as may be necessary for the deduction and withholding of the tax on original issue discount subject to tax under section 871(a)(1)(C) including rules for the deduction and withholding of the tax on original issue discount from payments of interest.

(9) INTEREST INCOME FROM CERTAIN PORTFOLIO DEBT INVESTMENTS.—In the case of portfolio interest (within the meaning of 871(h)), no tax shall be required to be deducted and withheld from such interest unless the person required to deduct and withhold tax from such interest knows, or has reason to know, that such interest is not portfolio interest by reason of section 871(h)(3) or (4).

(10) EXCEPTION FOR CERTAIN INTEREST AND DIVIDENDS.—No tax shall be required to be deducted and withheld under subsection (a) from any amount described in section 871(i)(2).

(11) CERTAIN GAMBLING WINNINGS.—No tax shall be required to be deducted and withheld under subsection (a) from any amount exempt from the tax imposed by section 871(a)(1)(A) by reason of section 871(j).

(12) CERTAIN DIVIDENDS RECEIVED FROM REGULATED INVESTMENT COMPANIES.—

(A) IN GENERAL.—No tax shall be required to be deducted and withheld under subsection (a) from any amount exempt from the tax imposed by section 871(a)(1)(A) by reason of section 871(k).

(B) SPECIAL RULE.—For purposes of subparagraph (A), clause (i) of section 871(k)(1)(B) shall not apply to any dividend unless the regulated investment company knows that such dividend is a dividend referred to in such clause. A similar rule shall apply with respect to the exception contained in section 871(k)(2)(B).

[Sec. 1441(d)]

(d) EXEMPTION OF CERTAIN FOREIGN PARTNERSHIPS.—Subject to such terms and conditions as may be provided by regulations prescribed by the Secretary, subsection (a) shall not apply in the case of a foreign partnership engaged in trade or business within the United States if the Secretary determines that the requirements of subsection (a) impose an undue administrative burden and that the collection of the tax imposed by section 871(a) on the members of such partnership who are nonresident alien individuals will not be jeopardized by the exemption.

[Sec. 1441(e)]

(e) ALIEN RESIDENT OF PUERTO RICO.—For purposes of this section, the term "nonresident alien individual" includes an alien resident of Puerto Rico.

[Sec. 1441(f)]

(f) CONTINENTAL SHELF AREAS.—For sources of income derived from, or for services performed with respect to, the exploration or exploitation of natural resources on submarine areas adjacent to the territorial waters of the United States, see section 638.

[Sec. 1441(g)]

(g) CROSS REFERENCE.—

For provision treating 85 percent of social security benefits as subject to withholding under this section, see section 871(a)(3).

[Sec. 1442]

SEC. 1442. WITHHOLDING OF TAX ON FOREIGN CORPORATIONS.

[Sec. 1442(a)]

(a) GENERAL RULE.—In the case of foreign corporations subject to taxation under this subtitle, there shall be deducted and withheld at the source in the same manner and on the same items of income as is provided in section 1441 a tax equal to 30 percent thereof. For purposes of the preceding sentence, the references in section 1441(b) to sections 871(a)(1)(C) and (D) shall be treated as referring to sections 881(a)(3) and (4), the reference in section 1441(c)(1) to section 871(b)(2) shall be treated as referring to section 842 or section 882(a)(2), as the case may be, the reference in section 1441(c)(5) to section 871(a)(1)(D) shall be treated as referring to section 881(a)(4), the reference in section 1441(c)(8) to section 871(a)(1)(C) shall be treated as referring to section 881(a)(3), the references in section 1441(c)(9) to sections 871(h) and 871(h)(3) or (4) shall be treated as referring to sections 881(c) and 881(c)(3) or (4), the reference in section 1441(c)(10) to section 871(i)(2) shall be treated as referring to section 881(d), and the references in section 1441(c)(12) to sections 871(a) and 871(k) shall be treated as referring to sections 881(a) and 881(e) (except that for purposes of applying subparagraph (A) of section 1441(c)(12), as so modified, clause (ii) of section 881(e)(1)(B) shall not apply to any dividend unless the regulated investment company knows that such dividend is a dividend referred to in such clause).

[Sec. 1442(b)]

(b) EXEMPTION.—Subject to such terms and conditions as may be provided by regulations prescribed by the Secretary, subsection (a) shall not apply in the case of a foreign corporation engaged in trade or business within the United States if the Secretary determines that the requirements of subsection (a) impose an undue administrative burden and that the collection of the tax imposed by section 881 on such corporation will not be jeopardized by the exemption.

[Sec. 1442(c)]

(c) EXCEPTION FOR CERTAIN POSSESSIONS CORPORATIONS.—

(1) GUAM, AMERICAN SAMOA, THE NORTHERN MARIANA ISLANDS, AND THE VIRGIN ISLANDS.—For purposes of this section, the term "foreign corporation" does not include a corporation created or organized in Guam, American Samoa, the Northern Mariana Islands, or the Virgin Islands or under the law of any such possession if the requirements of subparagraphs (A), (B), and (C) of section 881(b)(1) are met with respect to such corporation.

(2) COMMONWEALTH OF PUERTO RICO.—

(A) IN GENERAL.—If dividends are received during a taxable year by a corporation—

(i) created or organized in, or under the law of, the Commonwealth of Puerto Rico, and

(ii) with respect to which the requirements of subparagraphs (A), (B), and (C) of section 881(b)(1) are met for the taxable year,

subsection (a) shall be applied for such taxable year by substituting "10 percent" for "30 percent".

(B) APPLICABILITY.—If, on or after the date of the enactment of this paragraph, an increase in the rate of the Commonwealth of Puerto Rico's withholding tax which is generally applicable to dividends paid to United States corporations not engaged in a trade or business in the Commonwealth to a rate greater than 10 percent takes effect, this paragraph shall not apply to dividends received on or after the effective date of the increase.

[Sec. 1444]

SEC. 1444. WITHHOLDING ON VIRGIN ISLANDS SOURCE INCOME.

For purposes of determining the withholding tax liability incurred in the Virgin Islands pursuant to this title (as made applicable to the Virgin Islands) with respect to amounts received from sources within the Virgin Islands by citizens and resident alien individuals of the United States, and corporations organized in the United States, the rate of withholding tax under sections 1441 and 1442 on income subject to tax under section 871(a)(1) or 881 shall not exceed the rate of tax on such income under section 871(a)(1) or 881, as the case may be.

[Sec. 1445]

SEC. 1445. WITHHOLDING OF TAX ON DISPOSITIONS OF UNITED STATES REAL PROPERTY INTERESTS.

[Sec. 1445(a)]

(a) GENERAL RULE.—Except as otherwise provided in this section, in the case of any disposition of a United States real property interest (as defined in section 897(c)) by a foreign person, the transferee shall be required to deduct and withhold a tax equal to 10 percent of the amount realized on the disposition.

[Sec. 1445(b)]

(b) EXEMPTIONS.—

(1) IN GENERAL.—No person shall be required to deduct and withhold any amount under subsection (a) with respect to a disposition if paragraph (2), (3), (4), (5), or (6) applies to the transaction.

(2) TRANSFEROR FURNISHES NONFOREIGN AFFIDAVIT.—Except as provided in paragraph (7), this paragraph applies to the disposition if the transferor furnishes to the transferee an affidavit by the transferor stating, under penalty of perjury, the transferor's United States taxpayer identification number and that the transferor is not a foreign person.

(3) NONPUBLICLY TRADED DOMESTIC CORPORATION FURNISHES AFFIDAVIT THAT INTEREST IN CORPORATION NOT UNITED STATES REAL PROPERTY INTERESTS.—Except as provided in paragraph (7), this paragraph applies in the case of a disposition of any interest in any domestic

corporation if the domestic corporation furnishes to the transferee an affidavit by the domestic corporation stating, under penalty of perjury, that—

(A) the domestic corporation is not and has not been a United States real property holding corporation (as defined in section 897(c)(2)) during the applicable period specified in section 897(c)(1)(A)(ii),

(B) as of the date of the disposition, interests in such corporation are not United States real property interests by reason of section 897(c)(1)(B).

(4) TRANSFEREE RECEIVES QUALIFYING STATEMENT.—

(A) IN GENERAL.—This paragraph applies to the disposition if the transferee receives a qualifying statement at such time, in such manner, and subject to such terms and conditions as the Secretary may by regulations prescribe.

(B) QUALIFYING STATEMENT.—For purposes of subparagraph (A), the term "qualifying statement" means a statement by the Secretary that—

(i) the transferor either—

(I) has reached agreement with the Secretary (or such agreement has been reached by the transferee) for the payment of any tax imposed by section 871(b)(1) or 882(a)(1) on any gain recognized by the transferor on the disposition of the United States real property interest, or

(II) is exempt from any tax imposed by section 871(b)(1) or 882(a)(1) on any gain recognized by the transferor on the disposition of the United States real property interest, and

(ii) the transferor or transferee has satisfied any transferor's unsatisfied withholding liability or has provided adequate security to cover such liability.

(5) RESIDENCE WHERE AMOUNT REALIZED DOES NOT EXCEED $300,000.—This paragraph applies to the disposition if—

(A) the property is acquired by the transferee for use by him as a residence, and

(B) the amount realized for the property does not exceed $300,000.

(6) STOCK REGULARLY TRADED ON ESTABLISHED SECURITIES MARKET.—This paragraph applies if the disposition is of a share of a class of stock that is regularly traded on an established securities market.

(7) SPECIAL RULES FOR PARAGRAPHS (2) AND (3).—Paragraph (2) or (3) (as the case may be) shall not apply to any disposition—

(A) if—

(i) the transferee has actual knowledge that the affidavit referred to in such paragraph is false, or

(ii) the transferee receives a notice (as described in subsection (d)) from a transferor's agent or a transferee's agent that such affidavit is false, or

(B) if the Secretary by regulations requires the transferee to furnish a copy of such affidavit to the Secretary and the transferee fails to furnish a copy of such affidavit to the Secretary at such time and in such manner as required by such regulations.

[Sec. 1445(c)]

(c) LIMITATIONS ON AMOUNT REQUIRED TO BE WITHHELD.—

(1) CANNOT EXCEED TRANSFEROR'S MAXIMUM TAX LIABILITY.—

(A) IN GENERAL.—The amount required to be withheld under this section with respect to any disposition shall not exceed the amount (if any) determined under subparagraph (B) as the transferor's maximum tax liability.

(B) REQUEST.—At the request of the transferor or transferee, the Secretary shall determine, with respect to any disposition, the transferor's maximum tax liability.

(C) REFUND OF EXCESS AMOUNTS WITHHELD.—Subject to such terms and conditions as the Secretary may by regulations prescribe, a transferor may seek and obtain a refund of any amounts withheld under this section in excess of the transferor's maximum tax liability.

(2) AUTHORITY OF SECRETARY TO PRESCRIBE REDUCED AMOUNT.—At the request of the transferor or transferee, the Secretary may prescribe a reduced amount to be withheld under this section if the Secretary determines that to substitute such reduced amount will not jeopardize the collection of the tax imposed by section 871(b)(1) or 882(a)(1).

(3) PROCEDURAL RULES.—

(A) REGULATIONS.—Request for—

(i) qualifying statements under subsection (b)(4),

(ii) determinations of transferor's maximum tax liability under paragraph (1), and

(iii) reductions under paragraph (2) in the amount required to be withheld,

shall be made at the time and manner, and shall include such information, as the Secretary shall prescribe by regulations.

(B) REQUESTS TO BE HANDLED WITHIN 90 DAYS.—The Secretary shall take action with respect to any request described in subparagraph (A) within 90 days after the Secretary receives the request.

[Sec. 1445(d)]

(d) LIABILITY OF TRANSFEROR'S AGENTS OR TRANSFEREE'S AGENTS.—

(1) NOTICE OF FALSE AFFIDAVIT; FOREIGN CORPORATIONS.—If—

(A) the transferor furnishes the transferee an affidavit described in paragraph (2) of subsection (b) or a domestic corporation furnishes the transferee an affidavit described in paragraph (3) of subsection (b), and

(B) in the case of—

(i) any transferor's agent—

(I) such agent has actual knowledge that such affidavit is false, or

(II) in the case of an affidavit described in subsection (b)(2) furnished by a corporation, such corporation is a foreign corporation, or

(ii) any transferee's agent, such agent has actual knowledge that such affidavit is false,

such agent shall so notify the transferee at such time and in such manner as the Secretary shall require by regulations.

(2) FAILURE TO FURNISH NOTICE.—

(A) IN GENERAL.—If any transferor's agent or transferee's agent is required by paragraph (1) to furnish notice, but fails to furnish such notice at such time or times and in such manner as may be required by regulations, such agent shall have the same duty to deduct and withhold that the transferee would have had if such agent had complied with paragraph (1).

(B) LIABILITY LIMITED TO AMOUNT OF COMPENSATION.—An agent's liability under subparagraph (A) shall be limited to the amount of compensation the agent derives from the transaction.

(3) TRANSFEROR'S AGENT.—For purposes of this subsection, the term "transferor's agent" means any person who represents the transferor—

(A) in any negotiation with the transferee or any transferee's agent related to the transaction, or

(B) in settling the transaction.

(4) TRANSFEREE'S AGENT.—For purposes of this subsection, the term "transferee's agent" means any person who represents the transferee—

(A) in any negotiation with the transferor or any transferor's agent related to the transaction, or

(B) in settling the transaction.

(5) SETTLEMENT OFFICER NOT TREATED AS TRANSFEROR'S AGENT.—For purposes of this subsection, a person shall not be treated as a transferor's agent or transferee's agent with respect to any transaction merely because such person performs 1 or more of the following acts:

(A) The receipt and the disbursement of any portion of the consideration for the transaction.

(B) The recording of any document in connection with the transaction.

[Sec. 1445(e)]

(e) SPECIAL RULES RELATING TO DISTRIBUTIONS, ETC., BY CORPORATIONS, PARTNERSHIPS, TRUSTS, OR ESTATES.—

(1) CERTAIN DOMESTIC PARTNERSHIPS, TRUSTS, AND ESTATES.—In the case of any disposition of a United States real property interest as defined in section 897(c) (other than a disposition described in paragraph (4) or (5)) by a domestic partnership, domestic trust, or domestic estate, such partnership, the trustee or such trust, or the executor of such estate (as the case may be) shall be required to deduct and withhold under subsection (a) a tax equal to 35 percent (or, to the extent provided in regulations, 15 percent) of the gain realized to the extent such gain—

(A) is allocable to a foreign person who is a partner or beneficiary of such partnership, trust, or estate, or

(B) is allocable to a portion of the trust treated as owned by a foreign person under subpart E of Part I of subchapter J.

(2) CERTAIN DISTRIBUTIONS BY FOREIGN CORPORATIONS.—In the case of any distribution by a foreign corporation on which gain is recognized under subsection (d) or (e) of section 897, the foreign corporation shall deduct and withhold under subsection (a) a tax equal to 35 percent of the amount of gain recognized on such distribution under such subsection.

(3) DISTRIBUTIONS BY CERTAIN DOMESTIC CORPORATIONS TO FOREIGN SHAREHOLDERS.—If a domestic corporation which is or has been a United States real property holding corporation (as defined in section 897(c)(2)) during the applicable period specified in section 897(c)(1)(A)(ii) distributes property to a foreign person in a transaction to which section 302 or part II of subchapter C applies, such corporation shall deduct and withhold under subsection (a) a tax equal to 10 percent of the amount realized by the foreign shareholder. The preceding sentence shall not apply if, as of the date of the distribution, interests in such corporation are not United States real property interests by reason of section 897(c)(1)(B). Rules similar to the rules of the preceding provisions of this paragraph shall apply in the case of any distribution to which section 301 applies and which is not made out of the earnings and profits of such a domestic corporation.

(4) TAXABLE DISTRIBUTIONS BY DOMESTIC OR FOREIGN PARTNERSHIPS, TRUSTS, OR ESTATES.—A domestic or foreign partnership, the trustee of a domestic or foreign trust, or the executor of a domestic or foreign estate shall be required to deduct and withhold under subsection (a) a tax equal to 10 percent of the fair market value (as of the time of the taxable distribution) of any United States real property interest distributed to a partner of the partnership or a beneficiary of the trust or estate, as the case may be, who is a foreign person in a transaction which would constitute a taxable distribution under the regulations promulgated by the Secretary pursuant to section 897.

(5) RULES RELATING TO DISPOSITIONS OF INTEREST IN PARTNERSHIPS, TRUSTS, OR ESTATES.—To the extent provided in regulations, the transferee of a partnership interest or of a beneficial interest in a trust or estate shall be required to deduct and withhold under subsection (a) a tax equal to 10 percent of the amount realized on the disposition.

(6) REGULATIONS.—The Secretary shall prescribe such regulations as may be necessary to carry out the purposes of this subsection, including regulations providing for exceptions from provisions of this subsection and regulations for the application of this subsection in the case of payments through 1 or more entities.

[Sec. 1445(f)]

(f) DEFINITIONS.—For purposes of this section—

(1) TRANSFEROR.—The term "transferor" means the person disposing of the United States real property interest.

(2) TRANSFEREE.—The term "transferee" means the person acquiring the United States real property interest.

(3) FOREIGN PERSON.—The term "foreign person" means any person other than a United States person.

(4) TRANSFEROR'S MAXIMUM TAX LIABILITY.—The term "transferor's maximum tax liability" means, with respect to the disposition of any interest, the sum of—

(A) the maximum amount which the Secretary determines could be imposed as tax under section 871(b)(1) or 882(a)(1) by reason of the disposition, plus

(B) the amount the Secretary determines to be the transferor's unsatisfied withholding liability with respect to such interest.

(5) TRANSFEROR'S UNSATISFIED WITHHOLDING LIABILITY.—The term "transferor's unsatisfied withholding liability" means the withholding obligation imposed by this section on the transferor's acquisition of the United States real property interest or on the acquisition of a predecessor interest, to the extent such obligation has not been satisfied.

[Sec. 1446]

SEC. 1446. WITHHOLDING TAX ON FOREIGN PARTNERS' SHARE OF EFFECTIVELY CONNECTED INCOME.

[Sec. 1446(a)]

(a) GENERAL RULE.—If—

(1) a partnership has effectively connected taxable income for any taxable year, and

(2) any portion of such income is allocable under section 704 to a foreign partner,

such partnership shall pay a withholding tax under this section at such time and in such manner as the Secretary shall by regulations prescribe.

[Sec. 1446(b)]

(b) AMOUNT OF WITHHOLDING TAX.—

(1) IN GENERAL.—The amount of the withholding tax payable by any partnership under subsection (a) shall be equal to the applicable percentage of the effectively connected taxable income of the partnership which is allocable under section 704 to foreign partners.

(2) APPLICABLE PERCENTAGE.—For purposes of paragraph (1), the term "applicable percentage" means—

(A) the highest rate of tax specified in section 1 in the case of the portion of the effectively connected taxable income which is allocable under section 704 to foreign partners who are not corporations, and

(B) the highest rate of tax specified in section 11(b)(1) in the case of the portion of the effectively connected taxable income which is allocable under section 704 to foreign partners which are corporations.

[Sec. 1446(c)]

(c) EFFECTIVELY CONNECTED TAXABLE INCOME.—For purposes of this section, the term "effectively connected taxable income" means the taxable income of the partnership which is effectively connected (or treated as effectively connected) with the conduct of a trade or business in the United States computed with the following adjustments:

(1) Paragraph (1) [of] section 703(a) shall not apply.

(2) The partnership shall be allowed a deduction for depletion with respect to oil and gas wells but the amount of such deduction shall be determined without regard to sections 613 and 613A.

(3) There shall not be taken into account any item of income, gain, loss, or deduction to the extent allocable under section 704 to any partner who is not a foreign partner.

[Sec. 1446(d)]

(d) TREATMENT OF FOREIGN PARTNERS.—

(1) ALLOWANCE OF CREDIT.—Each foreign partner of a partnership shall be allowed a credit under section 33 for such partner's share of the withholding tax paid by the partnership under this section. Such credit shall be allowed for the partner's taxable year in which (or with which) the partnership taxable year (for which such tax was paid) ends.

(2) CREDIT TREATED AS DISTRIBUTED TO PARTNER.—Except as provided in regulations, a foreign partner's share of any withholding tax paid by the partnership under this section shall be treated as distributed to such partner by such partnership on the earlier of—

(A) the day on which such tax was paid by the partnership, or

(B) the last day of the partnership's taxable year for which such tax was paid.

[Sec. 1446(e)]

(e) FOREIGN PARTNER.—For purposes of this section, the term "foreign partner" means any partner who is not a United States person.

[Sec. 1446(f)]

(f) REGULATIONS.—The Secretary shall prescribe such regulations as may be necessary to carry out the purposes of this section, including—

(1) regulations providing for the application of this section in the case of publicly traded partnerships, and

(2) regulations providing—

(A) that, for purposes of section 6655, the withholding tax imposed under this section shall be treated as a tax imposed by section 11 and any partnership required to pay such tax shall be treated as a corporation, and

(B) appropriate adjustments in applying section 6655 with respect to such withholding tax.

SUBCHAPTER B—APPLICATION OF WITHHOLDING PROVISIONS

[Sec. 1461]

SEC. 1461. LIABILITY FOR WITHHELD TAX.

Every person required to deduct and withhold any tax under this chapter is hereby made liable for such tax and is hereby indemnified against the claims and demands of any person for the amount of any payments made in accordance with the provisions of this chapter.

[Sec. 1462]

SEC. 1462. WITHHELD TAX AS CREDIT TO RECIPIENT OF INCOME.

Income on which any tax is required to be withheld at the source under this chapter shall be included in the return of the recipient of such income, but any amount of tax so withheld shall be credited against the amount of income tax as computed in such return.

[Sec. 1463]

SEC. 1463. TAX PAID BY RECIPIENT OF INCOME.

If—

(1) any person, in violation of the provisions of this chapter, fails to deduct and withhold any tax under this chapter, and

(2) thereafter the tax against which such tax may be credited is paid,

the tax so required to be deducted and withheld shall not be collected from such person; but this section shall in no case relieve such person from liability for interest or any penalties or additions to the tax otherwise applicable in respect of such failure to deduct and withhold.

[Sec. 1464]

SEC. 1464. REFUNDS AND CREDITS WITH RESPECT TO WITHHELD TAX.

Where there has been an overpayment of tax under this chapter, any refund or credit made under chapter 65 shall be made to the withholding agent unless the amount of such tax was actually withheld by the withholding agent.

CHAPTER 6—CONSOLIDATED RETURNS

SUBCHAPTER A—RETURNS AND PAYMENT OF TAX

[Sec. 1501]

SEC. 1501. PRIVILEGE TO FILE CONSOLIDATED RETURNS.

An affiliated group of corporations shall, subject to the provisions of this chapter, have the privilege of making a consolidated return with respect to the income tax imposed by chapter 1 for the taxable year in lieu of separate returns. The making of a consolidated return shall be upon the condition that all corporations which at any time during the taxable year have been members of the affiliated group consent to all the consolidated return regulations prescribed under section 1502 prior to the last day prescribed by law for the filing of such return. The making of a consolidated return shall be considered as such consent. In the case of a corporation which is a member of the affiliated group for a fractional part of the year, the consolidated return shall include the income of such corporation for such part of the year as it is a member of the affiliated group.

[Sec. 1502]

SEC. 1502. REGULATIONS.

The Secretary shall prescribe such regulations as he may deem necessary in order that the tax liability of any affiliated group of corporations making a consolidated return and of each corporation in the group, both during and after the period of affiliation, may be returned, determined, computed, assessed, collected, and adjusted, in such manner as clearly to reflect the income tax liability and the various factors necessary for the determination of such liability, and in order to prevent avoidance of such tax liability. In carrying out the preceding sentence, the Secretary may prescribe rules that are different from the provisions of chapter 1 that would apply if such corporations filed separate returns.

[Sec. 1503]

SEC. 1503. COMPUTATION AND PAYMENT OF TAX.

* * *

[Sec. 1503(d)[c]]

(d)[c] DUAL CONSOLIDATED LOSS.—

(1) IN GENERAL.—The dual consolidated loss for any taxable year of any corporation shall not be allowed to reduce the taxable income of any other member of the affiliated group for the taxable year or any other taxable year.

(2) DUAL CONSOLIDATED LOSS.—For purposes of this section—

(A) IN GENERAL.—Except as provided in subparagraph (B), the term "dual consolidated loss" means any net operating loss of a domestic corporation which is subject to an income tax of a foreign country on its income without regard to whether such income is from sources in or outside of such foreign country, or is subject to such a tax on a residence basis.

(B) SPECIAL RULE WHERE LOSS NOT USED UNDER FOREIGN LAW.—To the extent provided in regulations, the term "dual consolidated loss" shall not include any loss which, under the foreign income tax law, does not offset the income of any foreign corporation.

(3) TREATMENT OF LOSSES OF SEPARATE BUSINESS UNITS.—To the extent provided in regulations, any loss of a separate unit of a domestic corporation shall be subject to the limitations of this subsection in the same manner as if such unit were a wholly owned subsidiary of such corporation.

(4) INCOME ON ASSETS ACQUIRED AFTER THE LOSS.—The Secretary shall prescribe such regulations as may be necessary or appropriate to prevent the avoidance of the purposes of this subsection by contributing assets to the corporation with the dual consolidated loss after such loss was sustained.

* * *

[Sec. 1504]

SEC. 1504. DEFINITIONS.

[Sec. 1504(a)]

(a) AFFILIATED GROUP DEFINED.—For purposes of this subtitle—

(1) IN GENERAL.—The term "affiliated group" means—

(A) 1 or more chains of includible corporations connected through stock ownership with a common parent corporation which is an includible corporation, but only if—

(B)(i) the common parent owns directly stock meeting the requirements of paragraph (2) in at least 1 of the other includible corporations, and

(ii) stock meeting the requirements of paragraph (2) in each of the includible corporations (except the common parent) is owned directly by 1 or more of the other includible corporations.

(2) 80-PERCENT VOTING AND VALUE TEST.—The ownership of stock of any corporation meets the requirements of this paragraph if it—

(A) possesses at least 80 percent of the total voting power of the stock of such corporation, and

(B) has a value equal to at least 80 percent of the total value of the stock of such corporation.

(3) 5 YEARS MUST ELAPSE BEFORE RECONSOLIDATION.—

(A) IN GENERAL.—If—

(i) a corporation is included (or required to be included) in a consolidated return filed by an affiliated group for a taxable year which includes any period after December 31, 1984, and

(ii) such corporation ceases to be a member of such group in a taxable year beginning after December 31, 1984,

with respect to periods after such cessation, such corporation (and any successor of such corporation) may not be included in any consolidated return filed by the affiliated group (or by another affiliated group with the same common parent or a successor of such common parent) before the 61st month beginning after its first taxable year in which it ceased to be a member of such affiliated group.

(B) SECRETARY MAY WAIVE APPLICATION OF SUBPARAGRAPH (A).—The Secretary may waive the application of subparagraph (A) to any corporation for any period subject to such conditions as the Secretary may prescribe.

(4) STOCK NOT TO INCLUDE CERTAIN PREFERRED STOCK.—For purposes of this subsection, the term "stock" does not include any stock which—

(A) is not entitled to vote,

(B) is limited and preferred as to dividends and does not participate in corporate growth to any significant extent,

(C) has redemption and liquidation rights which do not exceed the issue price of such stock (except for a reasonable redemption or liquidation premium), and

(D) is not convertible into another class of stock.

(5) REGULATIONS.—The Secretary shall prescribe such regulations as may be necessary or appropriate to carry out the purposes of this subsection, including (but not limited to) regulations—

(A) which treat warrants, obligations convertible into stock, and other similar interests as stock, and stock as not stock,

(B) which treat options to acquire or sell stock as having been exercised,

(C) which provide that the requirements of paragraph (2)(B) shall be treated as met if the affiliated group, in reliance on a good faith determination of value, treated such requirements as met,

(D) which disregard an inadvertent ceasing to meet the requirements of paragraph (2)(B) by reason of changes in relative values of different classes of stock,

(E) which provide that transfers of stock within the group shall not be taken into account in determining whether a corporation ceases to be a member of an affiliated group, and

(F) which disregard changes in voting power to the extent such changes are disproportionate to related changes in value.

[Sec. 1504(b)]

(b) DEFINITION OF "INCLUDIBLE CORPORATION".—As used in this chapter, the term "includible corporation" means any corporation except—

(1) Corporations exempt from taxation under section 501.

(2) Insurance companies subject to taxation under section 801.

(3) Foreign corporations.

(4) Corporations with respect to which an election under section 936 (relating to possession tax credit) is in effect for the taxable year.

(5) Corporations organized under the China Trade Act, 1922 [repealed for taxable years beginning after December 31, 1977].

(6) Regulated investment companies and real estate investment trusts subject to tax under subchapter M of chapter 1.

(7) A DISC (as defined in section 992(a)(1)).

(8) An S corporation.

* * *

[Sec. 1504(d)]

(d) SUBSIDIARY FORMED TO COMPLY WITH FOREIGN LAW.—In the case of a domestic corporation owning or controlling, directly or indirectly, 100 percent of the capital stock (exclusive of directors' qualifying shares) of a corporation organized under the laws of a contiguous foreign country and maintained solely for the purpose of complying with the laws of such country as to title and operation of property, such foreign corporation may, at the option of the domestic corporation, be treated for the purpose of this subtitle as a domestic corporation.

* * *

SUBCHAPTER B—RELATED RULES

PART II—CERTAIN CONTROLLED CORPORATIONS

[Sec. 1563]

SEC. 1563. DEFINITIONS AND SPECIAL RULES.

[Sec. 1563(a)]

(a) CONTROLLED GROUP OF CORPORATIONS.—For purposes of this part, the term "controlled group of corporations" means any group of—

(1) PARENT-SUBSIDIARY CONTROLLED GROUP.—One or more chains of corporations connected through stock ownership with a common parent corporation if—

(A) stock possessing at least 80 percent of the total combined voting power of all classes of stock entitled to vote or at least 80 percent of the total value of shares of all classes of stock of each of the corporations, except the common parent corporation, is owned (within the meaning of subsection (d)(1)) by one or more of the other corporations; and

(B) the common parent corporation owns (within the meaning of subsection (d)(1)) stock possessing at least 80 percent of the total combined voting power of all classes of stock entitled to vote or at least 80 percent of the total value of shares of all classes of stock of at least one of the other corporations, excluding, in computing such voting power or value, stock owned directly by such other corporations.

(2) BROTHER-SISTER CONTROLLED GROUP.—Two or more corporations if 5 or fewer persons who are individuals, estates, or trusts own (within the meaning of subsection (d)(2)) stock possessing more than 50 percent of the total combined voting power of all classes of stock entitled to vote or more than 50 percent of the total value of shares of all classes of stock of each corporation, taking into account the stock ownership of each such person only to the extent such stock ownership is identical with respect to each such corporation.

(3) COMBINED GROUP.—Three or more corporations each of which is a member of a group of corporations described in paragraph (1) or (2), and one of which—

(A) is a common parent corporation included in a group of corporations described in paragraph (1), and also

(B) is included in a group of corporations described in paragraph (2).

* * *

SUBTITLE B—ESTATE AND GIFT TAXES

CHAPTER 11—ESTATE TAX

SUBCHAPTER B—ESTATES OF NONRESIDENTS NOT CITIZENS

[Sec. 2107]

SEC. 2107. EXPATRIATION TO AVOID TAX.

[Sec. 2107(a)]

(a) TREATMENT OF EXPATRIATES.—A tax computed in accordance with the table contained in section 2001 is hereby imposed on the transfer of the taxable estate, determined as provided in section 2106, of every decedent nonresident not a citizen of the United States if the date of death occurs during a taxable year with respect to which the decedent is subject to tax under section 877(b).

* * *

CHAPTER 12—GIFT TAX

SUBCHAPTER A—DETERMINATION OF TAX LIABILITY

[Sec. 2501]

SEC. 2501. IMPOSITION OF TAX.

[Sec. 2501(a)]

(a) TAXABLE TRANSFERS.—

(1) GENERAL RULE.—A tax, computed as provided in section 2502, is hereby imposed for each calendar year on the transfer of property by gift during such calendar year by any individual, resident or nonresident.

(2) TRANSFERS OF INTANGIBLE PROPERTY.—Except as provided in paragraph (3), paragraph (1) shall not apply to the transfer of intangible property by a nonresident not a citizen of the United States.

(3) EXCEPTION.—

(A) CERTAIN INDIVIDUALS.—Paragraph (2) shall not apply in the case of a donor to whom section 877(b) applies for the taxable year which includes the date of the transfer.

(B) CREDIT FOR FOREIGN GIFT TAXES.—The tax imposed by this section solely by reason of this paragraph shall be credited with the amount of any gift tax actually paid to any foreign country in respect of any gift which is taxable under this section solely by reason of this paragraph.

(4) TRANSFERS TO POLITICAL ORGANIZATIONS.—Paragraph (1) shall not apply to the transfer of money or other property to a political organization (within the meaning of section 527(e)(1)) for the use of such organization.

(5) TRANSFERS OF CERTAIN STOCK.—

(A) IN GENERAL.—In the case of a transfer of stock in a foreign corporation described in subparagraph (B) by a donor to whom section 877(b) applies for the taxable year which includes the date of the transfer—

(i) section 2511(a) shall be applied without regard to whether such stock is situated within the United States, and

(ii) the value of such stock for purposes of this chapter shall be its U.S.-asset value determined under subparagraph (C).

(B) FOREIGN CORPORATION DESCRIBED.—A foreign corporation is described in this subparagraph with respect to a donor if—

(i) the donor owned (within the meaning of section 958(a)) at the time of such transfer 10 percent or more of the total combined voting power of all classes of stock entitled to vote of the foreign corporation, and

(ii) such donor owned (within the meaning of section 958(a)), or is considered to have owned (by applying the ownership rules of section 958(b)), at the time of such transfer, more than 50 percent of—

(I) the total combined voting power of all classes of stock entitled to vote of such corporation, or

(II) the total value of the stock of such corporation.

(C) U.S.-ASSET VALUE.—For purposes of subparagraph (A), the U.S.-asset value of stock shall be the amount which bears the same ratio to the fair market value of such stock at the time of transfer as—

(i) the fair market value (at such time) of the assets owned by such foreign corporation and situated in the United States, bears to

(ii) the total fair market value (at such time) of all assets owned by such foreign corporation.

* * *

SUBTITLE C—EMPLOYMENT TAXES

CHAPTER 21—FEDERAL INSURANCE CONTRIBUTIONS ACT

[Sec. 3121]

SEC. 3121. DEFINITIONS.

* * *

[Sec. 3121(h)]

(h) AMERICAN EMPLOYER.—For purposes of this chapter, the term "American employer" means an employer which is—

(1) the United States or any instrumentality thereof,

(2) an individual who is a resident of the United States,

(3) a partnership, if two-thirds or more of the partners are residents of the United States,

(4) a trust, if all of the trustees are residents of the United States, or

(5) a corporation organized under the laws of the United States or of any State.

* * *

[Sec. 3121(l)]

(l) AGREEMENTS ENTERED INTO BY AMERICAN EMPLOYERS WITH RESPECT TO FOREIGN AFFILIATES.—

(1) AGREEMENT WITH RESPECT TO CERTAIN EMPLOYEES OF FOREIGN AFFILIATE.—The Secretary shall, at the American employer's request, enter into an agreement (in such manner and form as may be prescribed by the Secretary) with any American employer (as defined in subsection (h)) who desires to have the insurance system established by title II of the Social Security Act extended to service performed outside the United States in the employ of any 1 or more of such employer's foreign affiliates (as defined in paragraph (6)) by all employees who are citizens or residents of the United States, except that the agreement shall not apply to any service performed by, or remuneration paid to, an employee if such service or remuneration would be excluded from the term "employment" or "wages", as defined in this section, had the service been performed in the United States. Such agreement may be amended at any time so as to be made applicable, in the same manner and under the same conditions, with respect to any other foreign affiliate of such American employer. Such agreement shall be applicable with respect to citizens or residents of the United States who, on or after the effective date of the agreement, are employees of and perform services outside the United States for any foreign affiliate specified in the agreement. Such agreement shall provide—

(A) that the American employer shall pay to the Secretary, at such time or times as the Secretary may by regulations prescribe, amounts equivalent to the sum of the taxes which would be imposed by sections 3101 and 3111 (including amounts equivalent to the interest, additions to the taxes, additional amounts, and penalties which would be applicable) with respect to the remuneration which would be wages if the services covered by the agreement constituted employment as defined in this section; and

(B) that the American employer will comply with such regulations relating to payments and reports as the Secretary may prescribe to carry out the purposes of this subsection.

(2) EFFECTIVE PERIOD OF AGREEMENT.—An agreement entered into pursuant to paragraph (1) shall be in effect for the period beginning with the first day of the calendar quarter in which such agreement is entered into or the first day of the succeeding calendar quarter, as may be specified in the agreement; except that in case such agreement is amended to include the services performed for any other affiliate and such amendment is executed after the first month following the first calendar quarter for which the agreement is in effect, the agreement shall be in effect with respect to service performed for such other affiliate only after the calendar quarter in which such amendment is executed. Notwithstanding any other provision of this subsection, the period for which any such agreement is effective with respect to any foreign entity shall terminate at the end of any calendar quarter in which the foreign entity, at any time in such quarter, ceases to be a foreign affiliate as defined in paragraph (6).

(3) NO TERMINATION OF AGREEMENT.—No agreement under this subsection may be terminated, either in its entirety or with respect to any foreign affiliate, on or after June 15, 1989.

(4) DEPOSITS IN TRUST FUNDS.—For purposes of section 201 of the Social Security Act, relating to appropriations to the Federal Old-Age and Survivors Insurance Trust Fund and the Federal Disability Insurance Trust Fund, such remuneration—

(A) paid for services covered by an agreement entered into pursuant to paragraph (1) as would be wages if the services constituted employment, and

(B) as is reported to the Secretary pursuant to the provisions of such agreement or of the regulations issued under this subsection,

shall be considered wages subject to the taxes imposed by this chapter.

(5) OVERPAYMENTS AND UNDERPAYMENTS.—

(A) If more or less than the correct amount due under an agreement entered into pursuant to this subsection is paid with respect to any payment of remuneration, proper adjustments with respect to the amounts due under such agreement shall be made, without interest, in such manner and at such times as may be required by regulations prescribed by the Secretary.

(B) If an overpayment cannot be adjusted under subparagraph (A), the amount thereof shall be paid by the Secretary, through the Fiscal Service of the Treasury Department, but only if a claim for such overpayment is filed with the Secretary within two years from the time such overpayment was made.

(6) FOREIGN AFFILIATE DEFINED.—For purposes of this subsection and section 210(a) of the Social Security Act—

(A) IN GENERAL.—A foreign affiliate of an American employer is any foreign entity in which such American employer has not less than a 10-percent interest.

(B) DETERMINATION OF 10-PERCENT INTEREST.—For purposes of subparagraph (A), an American employer has a 10-percent interest in any entity if such employer has such an interest directly (or through one or more entities)—

(i) in the case of a corporation, in the voting stock thereof, and

(ii) in the case of any other entity, in the profits thereof.

(7) AMERICAN EMPLOYER AS SEPARATE ENTITY.—Each American employer which enters into an agreement pursuant to paragraph (1) of this subsection shall, for purposes of this subsection and section 6413(c)(2)(C), relating to special refunds in the case of employees of certain foreign entities, be considered an employer in its capacity as a party to such agreement separate and distinct from its identity as a person employing individuals on its own account.

(8) REGULATIONS.—Regulations of the Secretary to carry out the purposes of this subsection shall be designed to make the requirements imposed on American employers with respect to services covered by an agreement entered into pursuant to this subsection the same, so far as practicable, as those imposed upon employers pursuant to this title with respect to the taxes imposed by this chapter.

* * *

CHAPTER 24—COLLECTION OF INCOME TAX AT SOURCE ON WAGES

SUBCHAPTER A—WITHHOLDING FROM WAGES

[Sec. 3401]

SEC. 3401. DEFINITIONS.

[Sec. 3401(a)]

(a) WAGES.—For purposes of this chapter, the term "wages" means all remuneration (other than fees paid to a public official) for services performed by an employee for his employer, including the cash value of all remuneration (including benefits) paid in any medium other than cash; except that such term shall not include remuneration paid—

* * *

(5) for services by a citizen or resident of the United States for a foreign government or an international organization; or

(6) for such services, performed by a nonresident alien individual, as may be designated by regulations prescribed by the Secretary; or

(8)(A) for services for an employer (other than the United States or any agency thereof)—

(i) performed by a citizen of the United States if, at the time of the payment of such remuneration, it is reasonable to believe that such remuneration will be excluded from gross income under section 911; or

(ii) performed in a foreign country or in a possession of the United States by such a citizen if, at the time of the payment of such remuneration, the employer is required by the law of any foreign country or possession of the United States to withhold income tax upon such remuneration; or

(B) for services for an employer (other than the United States or any agency thereof) performed by a citizen of the United States within a possession of the United States (other than Puerto Rico), if it is reasonable to believe that at least 80 percent of the remuneration to be paid to the employee by such employer during the calendar year will be for such services; or

(C) for services for an employer (other than the United States or any agency thereof) performed by a citizen of the United States within Puerto Rico, if it is reasonable to believe that during the entire calendar year the employee will be a bona fide resident of Puerto Rico; or

(D) for services for the United States (or any agency thereof) performed by a citizen of the United States within a possession of the United States to the extent the United States (or such agency) withholds taxes on such remuneration pursuant to an agreement with such possession;

* * *

[Sec. 3402]

SEC. 3402. INCOME TAX COLLECTED AT SOURCE.

* * *

[Sec. 3402(f)]

(f) WITHHOLDING EXEMPTIONS.—

* * *

(6) EXEMPTION OF CERTAIN NONRESIDENT ALIENS.—Notwithstanding the provisions of paragraph (1), a nonresident alien individual (other than an individual described in section 3401(a)(6)(A) or (B)) shall be entitled to only one withholding exemption.

* * *

[Sec. 3406]

SEC. 3406. BACKUP WITHHOLDING.

[Sec. 3406(a)]

(a) REQUIREMENT TO DEDUCT AND WITHHOLD.—

(1) IN GENERAL.—In the case of any reportable payment, if—

(A) the payee fails to furnish his TIN to the payor in the manner required,

(B) the Secretary notifies the payor that the TIN furnished by the payee is incorrect,

(C) there has been a notified payee underreporting described in subsection (c), or

(D) there has been a payee certification failure described in subsection (d),

then the payor shall deduct and withhold from such payment a tax equal to the product of the fourth lowest rate of tax applicable under section 1(c) and such payment.

(2) SUBPARAGRAPHS (C) AND (D) OF PARAGRAPH (1) APPLY ONLY TO INTEREST AND DIVIDEND PAYMENTS.—Subparagraphs (C) and (D) of paragraph (1) shall apply only to reportable interest or dividend payments.

* * *

[Sec. 3406(g)]

(g) EXCEPTIONS.—

(1) PAYMENTS TO CERTAIN PAYEES.—Subsection (a) shall not apply to any payment made to—

(A) any organization or governmental unit described in subparagraph (B), (C), (D), (E), or (F) of section 6049(b)(4), or

(B) any other person specified in regulations.

(2) AMOUNTS FOR WHICH WITHHOLDING OTHERWISE REQUIRED.—Subsection (a) shall not apply to any amount for which withholding is otherwise required by this title.

Sec. 3401(a)(8)(C)

(3) EXEMPTION WHILE WAITING FOR TIN.—The Secretary shall prescribe regulations for exemptions from the tax imposed by subsection (a) during the period during which a person is waiting for receipt of a TIN.

* * *

SUBTITLE D—MISCELLANEOUS EXCISE TAXES

CHAPTER 39—REGISTRATION-REQUIRED OBLIGATIONS

[Sec. 4701]

SEC. 4701. TAX ON ISSUER OF REGISTRATION-REQUIRED OBLIGATION NOT IN REGISTERED FORM.

[Sec. 4701(a)]

(a) IMPOSITION OF TAX.—In the case of any person who issues a registration-required obligation which is not in registered form, there is hereby imposed on such person on the issuance of such obligation a tax in an amount equal to the product of—

(1) 1 percent of the principal amount of such obligation, multiplied by

(2) the number of calendar years (or portions thereof) during the period beginning on the date of issuance of such obligation and ending on the date of maturity.

[Sec. 4701(b)]

(b) DEFINITIONS.—For purposes of this section—

(1) REGISTRATION-REQUIRED OBLIGATION.—The term "registration-required obligation" has the same meaning as when used in section 163(f), except that such term shall not include any obligation required to be registered under section 149(a).

(2) REGISTERED FORM.—The term "registered form" has the same meaning as when used in section 163(f).

CHAPTER 45—PROVISIONS RELATING TO EXPATRIATED ENTITIES

[Sec. 4985]

SEC. 4985. STOCK COMPENSATION OF INSIDERS IN EXPATRIATED CORPORATIONS.

[Sec. 4985(a)]

(a) IMPOSITION OF TAX.—In the case of an individual who is a disqualified individual with respect to any expatriated corporation, there is hereby imposed on such person a tax equal to—

(1) the rate of tax specified in section 1(h)(1)(C), multiplied by

(2) the value (determined under subsection (b)) of the specified stock compensation held (directly or indirectly) by or for the benefit of such individual or a member of such individual's family (as defined in section 267) at any time during the 12-month period beginning on the date which is 6 months before the expatriation date.

[Sec. 4985(b)]

(b) VALUE.—For purposes of subsection (a)—

(1) IN GENERAL.—The value of specified stock compensation shall be—

(A) in the case of a stock option (or other similar right) or a stock appreciation right, the fair value of such option or right, and

(B) in any other case, the fair market value of such compensation.

(2) DATE FOR DETERMINING VALUE.—The determination of value shall be made—

(A) in the case of specified stock compensation held on the expatriation date, on such date,

(B) in the case of such compensation which is canceled during the 6 months before the expatriation date, on the day before such cancellation, and

(C) in the case of such compensation which is granted after the expatriation date, on the date such compensation is granted.

[Sec. 4985(c)]

(c) TAX TO APPLY ONLY IF SHAREHOLDER GAIN RECOGNIZED.—Subsection (a) shall apply to any disqualified individual with respect to an expatriated corporation only if gain (if any) on any stock in such corporation is recognized in whole or part by any shareholder by reason of the acquisition referred to in section 7874(a)(2)(B)(i) with respect to such corporation.

[Sec. 4985(d)]

(d) EXCEPTION WHERE GAIN RECOGNIZED ON COMPENSATION.—Subsection (a) shall not apply to—

(1) any stock option which is exercised on the expatriation date or during the 6-month period before such date and to the stock acquired in such exercise, if income is recognized under section 83 on or before the expatriation date with respect to the stock acquired pursuant to such exercise, and

(2) any other specified stock compensation which is exercised, sold, exchanged, distributed, cashed-out, or otherwise paid during such period in a transaction in which income, gain, or loss is recognized in full.

[Sec. 4985(e)]

(e) DEFINITIONS.—For purposes of this section—

(1) DISQUALIFIED INDIVIDUAL.—The term "disqualified individual" means, with respect to a corporation, any individual who, at any time during the 12-month period beginning on the date which is 6 months before the expatriation date—

(A) is subject to the requirements of section 16(a) of the Securities Exchange Act of 1934 with respect to such corporation or any member of the expanded affiliated group which includes such corporation, or

(B) would be subject to such requirements if such corporation or member were an issuer of equity securities referred to in such section.

(2) EXPATRIATED CORPORATION; EXPATRIATION DATE.—

(A) EXPATRIATED CORPORATION.—The term "expatriated corporation" means any corporation which is an expatriated entity (as defined in section 7874(a)(2)). Such term includes any predecessor or successor of such a corporation.

(B) EXPATRIATION DATE.—The term "expatriation date" means, with respect to a corporation, the date on which the corporation first becomes an expatriated corporation.

(3) SPECIFIED STOCK COMPENSATION.—

(A) IN GENERAL.—The term "specified stock compensation" means payment (or right to payment) granted by the expatriated corporation (or by any member of the expanded affiliated group which includes such corporation) to any person in connection with the performance of services by a disqualified individual for such corporation or member if the value of such payment or right is based on (or determined by reference to) the value (or change in value) of stock in such corporation (or any such member).

(B) EXCEPTIONS.—Such term shall not include—

(i) any option to which part II of subchapter D of chapter 1 applies, or

(ii) any payment or right to payment from a plan referred to in section 280G(b)(6).

(4) EXPANDED AFFILIATED GROUP.—The term "expanded affiliated group" means an affiliated group (as defined in section 1504(a) without regard to section 1504(b)(3)); except that section 1504(a) shall be applied by substituting "more than 50 percent" for "at least 80 percent" each place it appears.

Sec. 4985(b)(2)(C)

[Sec. 4985(f)]

(f) SPECIAL RULES.—For purposes of this section—

(1) CANCELLATION OF RESTRICTION.—The cancellation of a restriction which by its terms will never lapse shall be treated as a grant.

(2) PAYMENT OR REIMBURSEMENT OF TAX BY CORPORATION TREATED AS SPECIFIED STOCK COMPENSATION.—Any payment of the tax imposed by this section directly or indirectly by the expatriated corporation or by any member of the expanded affiliated group which includes such corporation—

(A) shall be treated as specified stock compensation, and

(B) shall not be allowed as a deduction under any provision of chapter 1.

(3) CERTAIN RESTRICTIONS IGNORED.—Whether there is specified stock compensation, and the value thereof, shall be determined without regard to any restriction other than a restriction which by its terms will never lapse.

(4) PROPERTY TRANSFERS.—Any transfer of property shall be treated as a payment and any right to a transfer of property shall be treated as a right to a payment.

(5) OTHER ADMINISTRATIVE PROVISIONS.—For purposes of subtitle F, any tax imposed by this section shall be treated as a tax imposed by subtitle A.

[Sec. 4985(g)]

(g) REGULATIONS.—The Secretary shall prescribe such regulations as may be necessary or appropriate to carry out the purposes of this section.

SUBTITLE F—PROCEDURE AND ADMINISTRATION

CHAPTER 61—INFORMATION AND RETURNS

SUBCHAPTER A—RETURNS AND RECORDS

PART II—TAX RETURNS OR STATEMENTS

Subpart A—General Requirement

[Sec. 6011]

SEC. 6011. GENERAL REQUIREMENT OF RETURN, STATEMENT, OR LIST.

* * *

[Sec. 6011(c)]

(c) RETURNS, ETC., OF DISCS AND FORMER DISCS AND FSC'S AND FORMER FSC'S.—

(1) RECORDS AND INFORMATION.—A DISC or former DISC or a FSC or former FSC shall for the taxable year—

(A) furnish such information to persons who were shareholders at any time during such taxable year, and to the Secretary, and

(B) keep such records, as may be required by regulations prescribed by the Secretary.

(2) RETURNS.—A DISC shall file for the taxable year such returns as may be prescribed by the Secretary by forms or regulations.

* * *

Internal Revenue Code of 1986

[Sec. 6013]

SEC. 6013. JOINT RETURNS OF INCOME TAX BY HUSBAND AND WIFE.

* * *

[Sec. 6013(g)]

(g) ELECTION TO TREAT NONRESIDENT ALIEN INDIVIDUAL AS RESIDENT OF THE UNITED STATES.—

(1) IN GENERAL.—A nonresident alien individual with respect to whom this subsection is in effect for the taxable year shall be treated as a resident of the United States—

(A) for purposes of chapter 1 for all of such taxable year, and

(B) for purposes of chapter 24 (relating to wage withholding) for payments of wages made during such taxable year.

(2) INDIVIDUALS WITH RESPECT TO WHOM THIS SUBSECTION IS IN EFFECT.—This subsection shall be in effect with respect to any individual who, at the close of the taxable year for which an election under this subsection was made, was a nonresident alien individual married to a citizen or resident of the United States, if both of them made such election to have the benefits of this subsection apply to them.

(3) DURATION OF ELECTION.—An election under this subsection shall apply to the taxable year for which made and to all subsequent taxable years until terminated under paragraph (4) or (5); except that any such election shall not apply for any taxable year if neither spouse is a citizen or resident of the United States at any time during such year.

(4) TERMINATION OF ELECTION.—An election under this subsection shall terminate at the earliest of the following times:

(A) REVOCATION BY TAXPAYERS.—If either taxpayer revokes the election, as of the first taxable year for which the last day prescribed by law for filing the return of tax under chapter 1 has not yet occurred.

(B) DEATH.—In the case of the death of either spouse, as of the beginning of the first taxable year of the spouse who survives following the taxable year in which such death occurred; except that if the spouse who survives is a citizen or resident of the United States who is a surviving spouse entitled to the benefits of section 2, the time provided by this subparagraph shall be as of the close of the last taxable year for which such individual is entitled to the benefits of section 2.

(C) LEGAL SEPARATION.—In the case of the legal separation of the couple under a decree of divorce or of separate maintenance, as of the beginning of the taxable year in which such legal separation occurs.

(D) TERMINATION BY SECRETARY.—At the time provided in paragraph (5).

(5) TERMINATION BY SECRETARY.—The Secretary may terminate any election under this subsection for any taxable year if he determines that either spouse has failed—

(A) to keep such books and records,

(B) to grant such access to such books and records, or

(C) to supply such other information,

as may be reasonably necessary to ascertain the amount of liability for taxes under chapter 1 of either spouse for such taxable year.

(6) ONLY ONE ELECTION.—If any election under this subsection for any two individuals is terminated under paragraph (4) or (5) for any taxable year, such two individuals shall be ineligible to make an election under this subsection for any subsequent taxable year.

[Sec. 6013(h)]

(h) JOINT RETURN, ETC., FOR YEAR IN WHICH NONRESIDENT ALIEN BECOMES RESIDENT OF UNITED STATES.—

(1) IN GENERAL.—If—

(A) any individual is a nonresident alien individual at the beginning of any taxable year but is a resident of the United States at the close of such taxable year,

(B) at the close of such taxable year, such individual is married to a citizen or resident of the United States, and

(C) both individuals elect the benefits of this subsection at the time and in the manner prescribed by the Secretary by regulation,

then the individual referred to in subparagraph (A) shall be treated as a resident of the United States for purposes of chapter 1 for all of such taxable year, and for purposes of chapter 24 (relating to wage withholding) for payments of wages made during such taxable year.

(2) ONLY ONE ELECTION.—If any election under this subsection applies for any 2 individuals for any taxable year, such 2 individuals shall be ineligible to make an election under this subsection for any subsequent taxable year.

PART III—INFORMATION RETURNS

Subpart A—Information Concerning Persons Subject to Special Provisions

[Sec. 6031]

SEC. 6031. RETURN OF PARTNERSHIP INCOME.

[Sec. 6031(a)]

(a) GENERAL RULE.—Every partnership (as defined in section 761(a)) shall make a return for each taxable year, stating specifically the items of its gross income and the deductions allowable by subtitle A, and such other information for the purpose of carrying out the provisions of subtitle A as the Secretary may by forms and regulations prescribe, and shall include in the return the names and addresses of the individuals who would be entitled to share in the taxable income if distributed and the amount of the distributive share of each individual.

* * *

[Sec. 6031(e)]

(e) FOREIGN PARTNERSHIPS.—

(1) EXCEPTION FOR FOREIGN PARTNERSHIP.—Except as provided in paragraph (2), the preceding provisions of this section shall not apply to a foreign partnership.

(2) CERTAIN FOREIGN PARTNERSHIPS REQUIRED TO FILE RETURN.—Except as provided in regulations prescribed by the Secretary, this section shall apply to a foreign partnership for any taxable year if for such year, such partnership has—

(A) gross income derived from sources within the United States, or

(B) gross income which is effectively connected with the conduct of a trade or business within the United States.

The Secretary may provide simplified filing procedures for foreign partnerships to which this section applies.

* * *

[Sec. 6038]

SEC. 6038. INFORMATION WITH RESPECT TO CERTAIN FOREIGN CORPORATIONS.

[Sec. 6038(a)]

(a) REQUIREMENT.—

(1) IN GENERAL.—Every United States person shall furnish, with respect to any foreign business entity which such person controls, such information as the Secretary may prescribe relating to—

(A) the name, the principal place of business, and the nature of business of such entity, and the country under whose laws such entity is incorporated (or organized in the case of a partnership);

(B) in the case of a foreign corporation, its post-1986 undistributed earnings (as defined in section 902(c));

(C) a balance sheet for such entity listing assets, liabilities, and capital;

(D) transactions between such entity and—

(i) such person,

(ii) any corporation or partnership which such person controls, and

(iii) any United States person owning, at the time the transaction takes place—

(I) in the case of a foreign corporation, 10 percent or more of the value of any class of stock outstanding of such corporation, and

(II) in the case of a foreign partnership, at least a 10-percent interest in such partnership; and

(E)(i) in the case of a foreign corporation, a description of the various classes of stock outstanding, and a list showing the name and address of, and number of shares held by, each United States person who is a shareholder of record owning at any time during the annual accounting period 5 percent or more in value of any class of stock outstanding of such foreign corporation, and

(ii) information comparable to the information described in clause (i) in the case of a foreign partnership.

The Secretary may also require the furnishing of any other information which is similar or related in nature to that specified in the preceding sentence or which the Secretary determines to be appropriate to carry out the provisions of this title.

(2) PERIOD FOR WHICH INFORMATION IS TO BE FURNISHED, ETC.—The information required under paragraph (1) shall be furnished for the annual accounting period of the foreign business entity ending with or within the United States person's taxable year. The information so required shall be furnished at such time and in such manner as the Secretary shall prescribe.

(3) LIMITATION.—No information shall be required to be furnished under this subsection with respect to any foreign business entity for any annual accounting period unless the Secretary has prescribed the furnishing of such information on or before the first day of such annual accounting period.

(4) INFORMATION REQUIRED FROM CERTAIN SHAREHOLDERS IN CERTAIN CASES.—If any foreign corporation is treated as a controlled foreign corporation for any purpose under subpart F of part III of subchapter N of chapter 1, the Secretary may require any United States person treated as a United States shareholder of such corporation for any purpose under subpart F to furnish the information required under paragraph (1).

(5) INFORMATION REQUIRED FROM 10-PERCENT PARTNER OF CONTROLLED FOREIGN PARTNERSHIP.—In the case of a foreign partnership which is controlled by United States persons holding at least 10-percent interests (but not by any one United States person), the Secretary may require each United States person who holds a 10-percent interest in such partnership to furnish information relating to such partnership, including information relating to such partner's ownership interests in the partnership and allocations to such partner of partnership items.

[Sec. 6038(b)]

(b) DOLLAR PENALTY FOR FAILURE TO FURNISH INFORMATION.—

(1) IN GENERAL.—If any person fails to furnish, within the time prescribed under paragraph (2) of subsection (a), any information with respect to any foreign business entity required under paragraph (1) of subsection (a), such person shall pay a penalty of $10,000 for each annual accounting period with respect to which such failure exists.

(2) INCREASE IN PENALTY WHERE FAILURE CONTINUES AFTER NOTIFICATION.—If any failure described in paragraph (1) continues for more than 90 days after the day on which the Secretary mails notice of such failure to the United States person, such person shall pay a penalty (in addition to the amount required under paragraph (1)) of $10,000 for each 30-day period (or fraction thereof) during which such failure continues with respect to any annual accounting period after the expiration of such 90-day period. The increase in any penalty under this paragraph shall not exceed $50,000.

[Sec. 6038(c)]

(c) PENALTY OF REDUCING FOREIGN TAX CREDIT.—

(1) IN GENERAL.—If a United States person fails to furnish, within the time prescribed under paragraph (2) of subsection (a), any information with respect to any foreign business entity required under paragraph (1) of subsection (a), then—

(A) in applying section 901 (relating to taxes of foreign countries and possessions of the United States) to such United States person for the taxable year, the amount of taxes (other than taxes reduced under subparagraph (B)) paid or deemed paid (other than those deemed paid under section 904(c)) to any foreign country or possession of the United States for the taxable year shall be reduced by 10 percent, and

(B) in the case of a foreign business entity which is a foreign corporation, in applying sections 902 (relating to foreign tax credit for corporate stockholder in foreign corporation) and 960 (relating to special rules for foreign tax credit) to any such United States person which is a corporation (or to any person who acquires from any other person any portion of the interest of such other person in any such foreign corporation, but only to the extent of such portion) for any taxable year, the amount of taxes paid or deemed paid by each foreign corporation with respect to which such person is required to furnish information during the annual accounting period or periods with respect to which such information is required under paragraph (2) of subsection (a) shall be reduced by 10 percent.

If such failure continues 90 days or more after notice of such failure by the Secretary to the United States person, then the amount of the reduction under this paragraph shall be 10 percent plus an additional 5 percent for each 3-month period, or fraction thereof, during which such failure to furnish information continues after the expiration of such 90-day period.

(2) LIMITATION.—The amount of the reduction under paragraph (1) for each failure to furnish information with respect to a foreign business entity required under subsection (a)(1) shall not exceed whichever of the following amounts is the greater:

(A) $10,000, or

(B) the income of the foreign business entity for its annual accounting period with respect to which the failure occurs.

(3) COORDINATION WITH SUBSECTION (b).—The amount of the reduction which (but for this paragraph) would be made under paragraph (1) with respect to any annual accounting period shall be reduced by the amount of the penalty imposed by subsection (b) with respect to such period.

(4) SPECIAL RULES.—

(A) No taxes shall be reduced under this subsection more than once for the same failure.

(B) For purposes of this subsection and subsection (b), the time prescribed under paragraph (2) of subsection (a) to furnish information (and the beginning of the 90-day period after notice by the Secretary) shall be treated as being not earlier than the last day on which (as shown to the satisfaction of the Secretary) reasonable cause existed for failure to furnish such information.

(C) In applying subsections (a) and (b) of section 902, and in applying subsection (a) of section 960, the reduction provided by this subsection shall not apply for purposes of determining the amount of post-1986 undistributed earnings.

[Sec. 6038(d)]

(d) TWO OR MORE PERSONS REQUIRED TO FURNISH INFORMATION WITH RESPECT TO SAME FOREIGN BUSINESS ENTITY.—Where, but for this subsection, two or more United States persons would be required to furnish information under subsection (a) with respect to the same foreign business entity for the same period, the Secretary may by regulations provide that such information shall be required only from one person. To the extent practicable, the determination of which person shall furnish the information shall be made on the basis of actual ownership of stock.

[Sec. 6038(e)]

(e) DEFINITIONS.—For purposes of this section—

(1) FOREIGN BUSINESS ENTITY.—The term "foreign business entity" means a foreign corporation and a foreign partnership.

(2) CONTROL OF CORPORATION.—A person is in control of a corporation if such person owns stock possessing more than 50 percent of the total combined voting power of all classes of stock entitled to vote, or more than 50 percent of the total value of shares of all classes of

stock, of a corporation. If a person is in control (within the meaning of the preceding sentence) of a corporation which in turn owns more than 50 percent of the total combined voting power of all classes of stock entitled to vote of another corporation, or owns more than 50 percent of the total value of the shares of all classes of stock of another corporation, then such person shall be treated as in control of such other corporation. For purposes of this paragraph, the rules prescribed by section 318(a) for determining ownership of stock shall apply; except that—

(A) subparagraphs (A), (B), and (C) of section 318(a)(3) shall not be applied so as to consider a United States person as owning stock which is owned by a person who is not a United States person, and

(B) in applying subparagraph (C) of section 318(a)(2), the phrase "10 percent" shall be substituted for the phrase "50 percent" used in subparagraph (C).

(3) PARTNERSHIP-RELATED DEFINITIONS.—

(A) CONTROL.—A person is in control of a partnership if such person owns directly or indirectly more than a 50 percent interest in such partnership.

(B) 50-PERCENT INTEREST.—For purposes of subparagraph (A), a 50-percent interest in a partnership is—

(i) an interest equal to 50 percent of the capital interest, or 50 percent of the profits interest, in such partnership, or

(ii) to the extent provided in regulations, an interest to which 50 percent of the deductions or losses of such partnership are allocated.

For purposes of the preceding sentence, rules similar to the rules of section 267(c) (other than paragraph (3)) shall apply.

(C) 10-PERCENT INTEREST.—A 10-percent interest in a partnership is an interest which would be described in subparagraph (B) if "10 percent" were substituted for "50 percent" each place it appears.

(4) ANNUAL ACCOUNTING PERIOD.—The annual accounting period of a foreign business entity is the annual period on the basis of which such foreign business entity regularly computes its income in taxable year of such foreign business entity shall be treated as its annual accounting period.

[Sec. 6038(f)]

(f) CROSS REFERENCES.—

(1) For provisions relating to penalties for violations of this section, see section 7203.

(2) For definition of the term "United States person", see section 7701(a)(30).

[Sec. 6038A]

SEC. 6038A. INFORMATION WITH RESPECT TO CERTAIN FOREIGN-OWNED CORPORATIONS.

[Sec. 6038A(a)]

(a) REQUIREMENT.—If, at any time during a taxable year, a corporation (hereinafter in this section referred to as the "reporting corporation")—

(1) is a domestic corporation, and

(2) is 25-percent foreign-owned,

such corporation shall furnish, at such time and in such manner as the Secretary shall by regulations prescribe, the information described in subsection (b) and such corporation shall maintain (in the location, in the manner, and to the extent prescribed in regulations) such records as may be appropriate to determine the correct treatment of transactions with related parties as the Secretary shall by regulations prescribe (or shall cause another person to so maintain such records).

[Sec. 6038A(b)]

(b) REQUIRED INFORMATION.—For purposes of subsection (a), the information described in this subsection is such information as the Secretary may prescribe by regulations relating to—

Sec. 6038(e)(2)(A)

(1) the name, principal place of business, nature of business, and country or countries in which organized or resident, of each person which—

(A) is a related party to the reporting corporation, and

(B) had any transaction with the reporting corporation during its taxable year,

(2) the manner in which the reporting corporation is related to each person referred to in paragraph (1), and

(3) transactions between the reporting corporation and each foreign person which is a related party to the reporting corporation.

[Sec. 6038A(c)]

(c) DEFINITIONS.—For purposes of this section—

(1) 25-PERCENT FOREIGN-OWNED.—A corporation is 25-percent foreign-owned if at least 25 percent of—

(A) the total voting power of all classes of stock of such corporation entitled to vote, or

(B) the total value of all classes of stock of such corporation,

is owned at any time during the taxable year by 1 foreign person (hereinafter in this section referred to as a "25-percent foreign shareholder").

(2) RELATED PARTY.—The term "related party" means—

(A) any 25-percent foreign shareholder of the reporting corporation,

(B) any person who is related (within the meaning of section 267(b) or 707(b)(1)) to the reporting corporation or to a 25-percent foreign shareholder of the reporting corporation, and

(C) any other person who is related (within the meaning of section 482) to the reporting corporation.

(3) FOREIGN PERSON.—The term "foreign person" means any person who is not a United States person. For purposes of the preceding sentence, the term "United States person" has the meaning given to such term by section 7701(a)(30), except that any individual who is a citizen of any possession of the United States (but not otherwise a citizen of the United States) and who is not a resident of the United States shall not be treated as a United States person.

(4) RECORDS.—The term "records" includes any books, papers, or other data.

(5) SECTION 318 TO APPLY.—Section 318 shall apply for purposes of paragraph (1) and (2), except that—

(A) "10 percent" shall be substituted for "50 percent" in section 318(a)(2)(C), and

(B) subparagraphs (A), (B), and (C) of section 318(a)(3) shall not be applied so as to consider a United States person as owning stock which is owned by a person who is not a United States person.

[Sec. 6038A(d)]

(d) PENALTY FOR FAILURE TO FURNISH INFORMATION OR MAINTAIN RECORDS.—

(1) IN GENERAL.—If a reporting corporation—

(A) fails to furnish (within the time prescribed by regulations) any information described in subsection (b), or

(B) fails to maintain (or cause another to maintain) records as required by subsection (a),

such corporation shall pay a penalty of $10,000 for each taxable year with respect to which such failure occurs.

(2) INCREASE IN PENALTY WHERE FAILURE CONTINUES AFTER NOTIFICATION.—If any failure described in paragraph (1) continues for more than 90 days after the day on which the Secretary mails notice of such failure to the reporting corporation, such corporation shall pay a penalty (in addition to the amount required under paragraph (1)) of $10,000 for each 30-day

period (or fraction thereof) during which such failure continues after the expiration of such 90-day period.

(3) REASONABLE CAUSE.—For purposes of this subsection, the time prescribed by regulations to furnish information or maintain records (and the beginning of the 90-day period after notice by the Secretary) shall be treated as not earlier than the last day on which (as shown to the satisfaction of the Secretary) reasonable cause existed for failure to furnish the information or maintain the records.

[Sec. 6038A(e)]

(e) ENFORCEMENT OF REQUESTS FOR CERTAIN RECORDS.—

(1) AGREEMENT TO TREAT CORPORATION AS AGENT.—The rules of paragraph (3) shall apply to any transaction between the reporting corporation and any related party who is a foreign person unless such related party agrees (in such manner and at such time as the Secretary shall prescribe) to authorize the reporting corporation to act as such related party's limited agent solely for purposes of applying sections 7602, 7603, and 7604 with respect to any request by the Secretary to examine records or produce testimony related to any such transaction or with respect to any summons by the Secretary for such records or testimony. The appearance of persons or production of records by reason of the reporting corporation being such an agent shall not subject such persons or records to legal process for any purpose other than determining the correct treatment under this title of any transaction between the reporting corporation and such related party.

(2) RULES WHERE INFORMATION NOT FURNISHED.—If—

(A) for purposes of determining the correct treatment under this title of any transaction between the reporting corporation and a related party who is a foreign person, the Secretary issues a summons to such corporation to produce (either directly or as agent for such related party) any records or testimony,

(B) such summons is not quashed in a proceeding begun under paragraph (4) and is not determined to be invalid in a proceeding begun under section 7604(b) to enforce such summons, and

(C) the reporting corporation does not substantially comply in a timely manner with such summons and the Secretary has sent by certified or registered mail a notice to such reporting corporation that such reporting corporation has not so substantially complied,

the Secretary may apply the rules of paragraph (3) with respect to such transaction (whether or not the Secretary begins a proceeding to enforce such summons). If the reporting corporation fails to maintain (or cause another to maintain) records as required by subsection (a), and by reason of that failure, the summons is quashed in a proceeding described in subparagraph (B) or the reporting corporation is not able to provide the records requested in the summons, the Secretary may apply the rules of paragraph (3) with respect to any transaction to which the records relate.

(3) APPLICABLE RULES IN CASES OF NONCOMPLIANCE.—If the rules of this paragraph apply to any transaction—

(A) the amount of the deduction allowed under subtitle A for any amount paid or incurred by the reporting corporation to the related party in connection with such transaction, and

(B) the cost to the reporting corporation of any property acquired in such transaction from the related party (or transferred by such corporation in such transaction to the related party),

shall be the amount determined by the Secretary in the Secretary's sole discretion from the Secretary's own knowledge or from such information as the Secretary may obtain through testimony or otherwise.

(4) JUDICIAL PROCEEDINGS.—

(A) PROCEEDINGS TO QUASH.—Notwithstanding any law or rule of law, any reporting corporation to which the Secretary issues a summons referred to in paragraph (2)(A) shall have the right to begin a proceeding to quash such summons not later than the 90th day after such summons was issued. In any such proceeding, the Secretary may seek to compel compliance with such summons.

(B) REVIEW OF SECRETARIAL DETERMINATION OF NONCOMPLIANCE.—Notwithstanding any law or rule of law, any reporting corporation which has been notified by the Secretary that the Secretary has determined that such corporation has not substantially complied with a summons referred to in paragraph (2) shall have the right to begin a proceeding to review such determination not later than the 90th day after the day on which the notice referred to in paragraph (2)(C) was mailed. If such a proceeding is not begun on or before such 90th day, such determination by the Secretary shall be binding and shall not be reviewed by any court.

(C) JURISDICTION.—The United States district court for the district in which the person (to whom the summons is issued) resides or is found shall have jurisdiction to hear any proceeding brought under subparagraph (A) or (B). Any order or other determination in such a proceeding shall be treated as a final order which may be appealed.

(D) SUSPENSION OF STATUTE OF LIMITATIONS.—If the reporting corporation brings an action under subparagraph (A) or (B), the running of any period of limitations under section 6501 (relating to assessment and collection of tax) or under section 6531 (relating to criminal prosecutions) with respect to any affected taxable year shall be suspended for the period during which such proceeding, and appeals therein, are pending. In no event shall any such period expire before the 90th day after the day on which there is a final determination in such proceeding. For purposes of this subparagraph, the term "affected taxable year" means any taxable year if the determination of the amount of tax imposed for such taxable year is affected by the treatment of the transaction to which the summons relates.

[Sec. 6038A(f)]

(f) CROSS REFERENCE.—

For provisions relating to criminal penalties for violation of this section, see section 7203.

[Sec. 6038B]

SEC. 6038B. NOTICE OF CERTAIN TRANSFERS TO FOREIGN PERSONS.

[Sec. 6038B(a)]

(a) IN GENERAL.—Each United States person who—

(1) transfers property to—

(A) a foreign corporation in an exchange described in section 332, 351, 354, 355, 356, or 361, or

(B) a foreign partnership in a contribution described in section 721 or in any other contribution described in regulations prescribed by the Secretary,

(2) makes a distribution described in section 336 to a person who is not a United States person,

shall furnish to the Secretary, at such time and in such manner as the Secretary shall by regulations prescribe, such information with respect to such exchange or distribution as the Secretary may require in such regulations.

[Sec. 6038B(b)]

(b) EXCEPTIONS FOR CERTAIN TRANSFERS TO FOREIGN PARTNERSHIPS; SPECIAL RULE.—

(1) EXCEPTIONS.—Subsection (a)(1)(B) shall apply to a transfer by a United States person to a foreign partnership only if—

(A) the United States person holds (immediately after the transfer) directly or indirectly at least a 10-percent interest (as defined in section 6046A(d)) in the partnership, or

(B) the value of the property transferred (when added to the value of the property transferred by such person or any related person to such partnership or a related partnership during the 12-month period ending on the date of the transfer) exceeds $100,000.

For purposes of the preceding sentence, the value of any transferred property is its fair market value at the time of its transfer.

(2) SPECIAL RULE.—If by reason of an adjustment under section 482 or otherwise, a contribution described in subsection (a)(1) is deemed to have been made, such contribution shall be treated for purposes of this section as having been made not earlier than the date specified by the Secretary.

[Sec. 6038B(c)]

(c) PENALTY FOR FAILURE TO FURNISH INFORMATION.—

(1) IN GENERAL.—If any United States person fails to furnish the information described in subsection (a) at the time and in the manner required by regulations, such person shall pay a penalty equal to 10 percent of the fair market value of the property at the time of the exchange (and, in the case of a contribution described in subsection (a)(1)(B), such person shall recognize gain as if the contributed property had been sold for such value at the time of such contribution).

(2) REASONABLE CAUSE EXCEPTION.—Paragraph (1) shall not apply to any failure if the United States person shows such failure is due to reasonable cause and not to willful neglect.

(3) LIMIT ON PENALTY.—The penalty under paragraph (1) with respect to any exchange shall not exceed $100,000 unless the failure with respect to such exchange was due to intentional disregard.

[Sec. 6038C]

SEC. 6038C. INFORMATION WITH RESPECT TO FOREIGN CORPORATIONS ENGAGED IN U.S. BUSINESS.

[Sec. 6038C(a)]

(a) REQUIREMENT.—If a foreign corporation (hereinafter in this section referred to as the "reporting corporation") is engaged in a trade or business within the United States at any time during a taxable year—

(1) such corporation shall furnish (at such time and in such manner as the Secretary shall by regulations prescribe) the information described in subsection (b), and

(2) such corporation shall maintain (at the location, in the manner, and to the extent prescribed in regulations) such records as may be appropriate to determine the liability of such corporation for tax under this title as the Secretary shall by regulations prescribe (or shall cause another person to so maintain such records).

[Sec. 6038C(b)]

(b) REQUIRED INFORMATION.—For purposes of subsection (a), the information described in this subsection is—

(1) the information described in section 6038A(b), and

(2) such other information as the Secretary may prescribe by regulations relating to any item not directly connected with a transaction for which information is required under paragraph (1).

[Sec. 6038C(c)]

(c) PENALTY FOR FAILURE TO FURNISH INFORMATION OR MAINTAIN RECORDS.—The provisions of subsection (d) of section 6038A shall apply to—

(1) any failure to furnish (within the time prescribed by regulations) any information described in subsection (b), and

(2) any failure to maintain (or cause another to maintain) records as required by subsection (a),

in the same manner as if such failure were a failure to comply with the provisions of section 6038A.

[Sec. 6038C(d)]

(d) ENFORCEMENT OF REQUESTS FOR CERTAIN RECORDS.—

(1) AGREEMENT TO TREAT CORPORATION AS AGENT.—The rules of paragraph (3) shall apply to any transaction between the reporting corporation and any related party who is a foreign person unless such related party agrees (in such manner and at such time as the Secretary

shall prescribe) to authorize the reporting corporation to act as such related party's limited agent solely for purposes of applying sections 7602, 7603, and 7604 with respect to any request by the Secretary to examine records or produce testimony related to any such transaction or with respect to any summons by the Secretary for such records or testimony. The appearance of persons or production of records by reason of the reporting corporation being such an agent shall not subject such persons or records to legal process for any purpose other than determining the correct treatment under this title of any transaction between the reporting corporation and such related party.

(2) RULES WHERE INFORMATION NOT FURNISHED.—If—

(A) for purposes of determining the amount of the reporting corporation's liability for tax under this title, the Secretary issues a summons to such corporation to produce (either directly or as an agent for a related party who is a foreign person) any records or testimony,

(B) such summons is not quashed in a proceeding begun under paragraph (4) of section 6038A(e) (as made applicable by paragraph (4) of this subsection) and is not determined to be invalid in a proceeding begun under section 7604(b) to enforce such summons, and

(C) the reporting corporation does not substantially comply in a timely manner with such summons and the Secretary has sent by certified or registered mail a notice to such reporting corporation that such reporting corporation has not so substantially complied,

the Secretary may apply the rules of paragraph (3) with respect to any transaction or item to which such summons relates (whether or not the Secretary begins a proceeding to enforce such summons). If the reporting corporation fails to maintain (or cause another to maintain) records as required by subsection (a), and by reason of that failure, the summons is quashed in a proceeding described in subparagraph (B) or the reporting corporation is not able to provide the records requested in the summons, the Secretary may apply the rules of paragraph (3) with respect to any transaction or item to which the records relate.

(3) APPLICABLE RULES.—If the rules of this paragraph apply to any transaction or item, the treatment of such transaction (or the amount and treatment of any such item) shall be determined by the Secretary in the Secretary's sole discretion from the Secretary's own knowledge or from such information as the Secretary may obtain through testimony or otherwise.

(4) JUDICIAL PROCEEDINGS.—The provisions of section 6038A(e)(4) shall apply with respect to any summons referred to in paragraph (2)(A); except that subparagraph (D) of such section shall be applied by substituting "transaction or item" for "transaction".

[Sec. 6038C(e)]

(e) DEFINITIONS.—For purposes of this section, the terms "related party", "foreign person", and "records" have the respective meanings given to such terms by section 6038A(c).

[Sec. 6039C]

SEC. 6039C. RETURNS WITH RESPECT TO FOREIGN PERSONS HOLDING DIRECT INVESTMENTS IN UNITED STATES REAL PROPERTY INTERESTS.

[Sec. 6039C(a)]

(a) GENERAL RULE.—To the extent provided in regulations, any foreign person holding direct investments in United States real property interests for the calendar year shall make a return setting forth—

(1) the name and address of such person,

(2) a description of all United States real property interests held by such person at any time during the calendar year, and

(3) such other information as the Secretary may by regulations prescribe.

[Sec. 6039C(b)]

(b) DEFINITION OF FOREIGN PERSONS HOLDING DIRECT INVESTMENTS IN UNITED STATES REAL PROPERTY INTERESTS.—For purposes of this section, a foreign person shall be treated as holding direct investments in United States real property interests during any calendar year if—

(1) such person did not engage in a trade or business in the United States at any time during such calendar year, and

(2) the fair market value of the United States real property interests held directly by such person at any time during such year equals or exceeds $50,000.

[Sec. 6039C(c)]

(c) DEFINITIONS AND SPECIAL RULES.—For purposes of this section—

(1) UNITED STATES REAL PROPERTY INTEREST.—The term "United States real property interest" has the meaning given to such term by section 897(c).

(2) FOREIGN PERSON.—The term "foreign person" means any person who is not a United States person.

(3) ATTRIBUTION OF OWNERSHIP.—For purposes of subsection (b)(2)—

(A) INTERESTS HELD BY PARTNERSHIPS, ETC.—United States real property interests held by a partnership, trust, or estate shall be treated as owned proportionately by its partners or beneficiaries.

(B) INTERESTS HELD BY FAMILY MEMBERS.—United States real property interests held by the spouse or any minor child of an individual shall be treated as owned by such individual.

(4) TIME AND MANNER OF FILING RETURN.—All returns required to be made under this section shall be made at such time and in such manner as the Secretary shall by regulations prescribe.

[Sec. 6039C(d)]

(d) SPECIAL RULE FOR UNITED STATES INTEREST AND VIRGIN ISLANDS INTEREST.—A nonresident alien individual or foreign corporation subject to tax under section 897(a) (and any person required to withhold tax under section 1445) shall pay any tax and file any return required by this title—

(1) to the United States, in the case of any interest in real property located in the United States and an interest (other than an interest solely as a creditor) in a domestic corporation (with respect to the United States) described in section 897(c)(1)(A)(ii), and

(2) to the Virgin Islands, in the case of any interest in real property located in the Virgin Islands and an interest (other than an interest solely as a creditor) in a domestic corporation (with respect to the Virgin Islands) described in section 897(c)(1)(A)(ii).

[Sec. 6039E]

SEC. 6039E. INFORMATION CONCERNING RESIDENT STATUS.

[Sec. 6039E(a)]

(a) GENERAL RULE.—Notwithstanding any other provision of law, any individual who—

(1) applies for a United States passport (or a renewal thereof), or

(2) applies to be lawfully accorded the privilege of residing permanently in the United States as an immigrant in accordance with the immigration laws,

shall include with any such application a statement which includes the information described in subsection (b).

[Sec. 6039E(b)]

(b) INFORMATION TO BE PROVIDED.—Information required under subsection (a) shall include—

(1) the taxpayer's TIN (if any),

(2) in the case of a passport applicant, any foreign country in which such individual is residing,

(3) in the case of an individual seeking permanent residence, information with respect to whether such individual is required to file a return of the tax imposed by chapter 1 for such individual's most recent 3 taxable years, and

(4) such other information as the Secretary may prescribe.

[Sec. 6039E(c)]

(c) PENALTY.—Any individual failing to provide a statement required under subsection (a) shall be subject to a penalty equal to $500 for each such failure, unless it is shown that such failure is due to reasonable cause and not to willful neglect.

[Sec. 6039E(d)]

(d) INFORMATION TO BE PROVIDED TO SECRETARY.—Notwithstanding any other provision of law, any agency of the United States which collects (or is required to collect) the statement under subsection (a) shall—

   (1) provide any such statement to the Secretary, and

   (2) provide to the Secretary the name (and any other identifying information) of any individual refusing to comply with the provisions of subsection (a).

Nothing in the preceding sentence shall be construed to require the disclosure of information which is subject to section 245A of the Immigration and Nationality Act (as in effect on the date of the enactment of this sentence).

[Sec. 6039E(e)]

(e) EXEMPTION.—The Secretary may by regulations exempt any class of individuals from the requirements of this section if he determines that applying this section to such individuals is not necessary to carry out the purposes of this section.

[Sec. 6039G]

SEC. 6039G. INFORMATION ON INDIVIDUALS LOSING UNITED STATES CITIZENSHIP.

[Sec. 6039G(a)]

(a) IN GENERAL.—Notwithstanding any other provision of law, any individual to whom section 877(b) applies for any taxable year shall provide a statement for such taxable year which includes the information described in subsection (b).

[Sec. 6039G(b)]

(b) INFORMATION TO BE PROVIDED.—Information required under subsection (a) shall include—

   (1) the taxpayer's TIN,

   (2) the mailing address of such individual's principal foreign residence,

   (3) the foreign country in which such individual is residing,

   (4) the foreign country of which such individual is a citizen,

   (5) information detailing the income, assets, and liabilities of such individual,

   (6) the number of days during any portion of which that the individual was physically present in the United States during the taxable year, and

   (7) such other information as the Secretary may prescribe.

[Sec. 6039G(c)]

(c) PENALTY.—If—

   (1) an individual is required to file a statement under subsection (a) for any taxable year, and

   (2) fails to file such a statement with the Secretary on or before the date such statement is required to be filed or fails to include all the information required to be shown on the statement or includes incorrect information,

such individual shall pay a penalty of $10,000 unless it is shown that such failure is due to reasonable cause and not to willful neglect.

[Sec. 6039G(d)]

(d) INFORMATION TO BE PROVIDED TO SECRETARY.—Notwithstanding any other provision of law—

(1) any Federal agency or court which collects (or is required to collect) the statement under subsection (a) shall provide to the Secretary—

(A) a copy of any such statement, and

(B) the name (and any other identifying information) of any individual refusing to comply with the provisions of subsection (a),

(2) the Secretary of State shall provide to the Secretary a copy of each certificate as to the loss of American nationality under section 358 of the Immigration and Nationality Act which is approved by the Secretary of State, and

(3) the Federal agency primarily responsible for administering the immigration laws shall provide to the Secretary the name of each lawful permanent resident of the United States (within the meaning of section 7701(b)(6)) whose status as such has been revoked or has been administratively or judicially determined to have been abandoned.

Notwithstanding any other provision of law, not later than 30 days after the close of each calendar quarter, the Secretary shall publish in the Federal Register the name of each individual losing United States citizenship (within the meaning of section 877(a)) with respect to whom the Secretary receives information under the preceding sentence during such quarter.

Subpart B—Information Concerning Transactions With Other Persons

[Sec. 6041]

SEC. 6041. INFORMATION AT SOURCE.

[Sec. 6041(a)]

(a) PAYMENTS OF $600 OR MORE.—All persons engaged in a trade or business and making payment in the course of such trade or business to another person, of rent, salaries, wages, premiums, annuities, compensations, remunerations, emoluments, or other fixed or determinable gains, profits, and income (other than payments to which section 6042(a)(1), 6044(a)(1), 6047(e)[d], 6049(a), or 6050N(a) applies, and other than payments with respect to which a statement is required under the authority of section 6042(a)(2), 6044(a)(2), or 6045), of $600 or more in any taxable year, or, in the case of such payments made by the United States, the officers or employees of the United States having information as to such payments and required to make returns in regard thereto by the regulations hereinafter provided for, shall render a true and accurate return to the Secretary, under such regulations and in such form and manner and to such extent as may be prescribed by the Secretary, setting forth the amount of such gains, profits, and income, and the name and address of the recipient of such payment.

[Sec. 6041(b)]

(b) COLLECTION OF FOREIGN ITEMS.—In the case of collections of items (not payable in the United States) of interest upon the bonds of foreign countries and interest upon the bonds of and dividends from foreign corporations by any person undertaking as a matter of business or for profit the collection of foreign payments of such interest or dividends by means of coupons, checks, or bills of exchange, such person shall make a return according to the forms or regulations prescribed by the Secretary, setting forth the amount paid and the name and address of the recipient of each such payment.

[Sec. 6041(c)]

(c) RECIPIENT TO FURNISH NAME AND ADDRESS.—When necessary to make effective the provisions of this section, the name and address of the recipient of income shall be furnished upon demand of the person paying the income.

[Sec. 6041(d)]

(d) STATEMENTS TO BE FURNISHED TO PERSONS WITH RESPECT TO WHOM INFORMATION IS REQUIRED.—Every person required to make a return under subsection (a) shall furnish to each person with respect to whom such a return is required a written statement showing—

(1) the name, address, and phone number of the information contact of the person required to make such return, and

(2) the aggregate amount of payments to the person required to be shown on the return.

The written statement required under the preceding sentence shall be furnished to the person on or before January 31 of the year following the calendar year for which the return under subsection (a) was required to be made. To the extent provided in regulations prescribed by the Secretary, this subsection shall also apply to persons required to make returns under subsection (b).

[Sec. 6041(e)]

(e) SECTION DOES NOT APPLY TO CERTAIN TIPS.—This section shall not apply to tips with respect to which section 6053(a) (relating to reporting of tips) applies.

[Sec. 6041(f)]

(f) SECTION DOES NOT APPLY TO CERTAIN HEALTH ARRANGEMENTS.—This section shall not apply to any payment for medical care (as defined in section 213(d)) made under—

(1) a flexible spending arrangement (as defined in section 106(c)(2)), or

(2) a health reimbursement arrangement which is treated as employer-provided coverage under an accident or health plan for purposes of section 106.

[Sec. 6041(g)]

(g) NONQUALIFIED DEFERRED COMPENSATION.—Subsection (a) shall apply to—

(1) any deferrals for the year under a nonqualified deferred compensation plan (within the meaning of section 409A(d)), whether or not paid, except that this paragraph shall not apply to deferrals which are required to be reported under section 6051(a)(13) (without regard to any de minimis exception), and

(2) any amount includible under section 409A and which is not treated as wages under section 3401(a).

[Sec. 6042]

SEC. 6042. RETURNS REGARDING PAYMENTS OF DIVIDENDS AND CORPORATE EARNINGS AND PROFITS.

[Sec. 6042(a)]

(a) REQUIREMENT OF REPORTING.—

(1) IN GENERAL.—Every person—

(A) who makes payments of dividends aggregating $10 or more to any other person during any calendar year, or

(B) who receives payments of dividends as a nominee and who makes payments aggregating $10 or more during any calendar year to any other person with respect to the dividends so received,

shall make a return according to the forms or regulations prescribed by the Secretary, setting forth the aggregate amount of such payments and the name and address of the person to whom paid.

(2) RETURNS REQUIRED BY THE SECRETARY.—Every person who makes payments of dividends aggregating less than $10 to any other person during any calendar year shall, when required by the Secretary, make a return setting forth the aggregate amount of such payments, and the name and address of the person to whom paid.

[Sec. 6042(b)]

(b) DIVIDEND DEFINED.—

(1) GENERAL RULE.—For purposes of this section, the term "dividend" means—

(A) any distribution by a corporation which is a dividend (as defined in section 316); and

(B) any payment made by a stockbroker to any person as a substitute for a dividend (as so defined).

(2) EXCEPTIONS.—For purposes of this section, the term "dividend" does not include any distribution or payment—

    (A) to the extent provided in regulations prescribed by the Secretary—

        (i) by a foreign corporation, or

        (ii) to a foreign corporation, a nonresident alien, or a partnership not engaged in a trade or business in the United States and composed in whole or in part of nonresident aliens, or

    (B) except to the extent otherwise provided in regulations prescribed by the Secretary, to any person described in section 6049(b)(4).

(3) SPECIAL RULE.—If the person making any payment described in subsection (a)(1)(A) or (B) is unable to determine the portion of such payment which is a dividend or is paid with respect to a dividend, he shall, for purposes of subsection (a)(1), treat the entire amount of such payment as a dividend or as an amount paid with respect to a dividend.

* * *

[Sec. 6046]

SEC. 6046. RETURNS AS TO ORGANIZATION OR REORGANIZATION OF FOREIGN CORPORATIONS AND AS TO ACQUISITIONS OF THEIR STOCK.

[Sec. 6046(a)]

(a) REQUIREMENT OF RETURN.—

    (1) IN GENERAL.—A return complying with the requirements of subsection (b) shall be made by—

        (A) each United States citizen or resident who becomes an officer or director of a foreign corporation if a United States person (as defined in section 7701(a)(30)) meets the stock ownership requirements of paragraph (2) with respect to such corporation,

        (B) each United States person—

            (i) who acquires stock which, when added to any stock owned on the date of such acquisition, meets the stock ownership requirements of paragraph (2) with respect to a foreign corporation, or

            (ii) who acquires stock which, without regard to stock owned on the date of such acquisition, meets the stock ownership requirements of paragraph (2) with respect to a foreign corporation,

        (C) each person (not described in subparagraph (B)) who is treated as a United States shareholder under section 953(c) with respect to a foreign corporation, and

        (D) each person who becomes a United States person while meeting the stock ownership requirements of paragraph (2) with respect to stock of a foreign corporation.

In the case of a foreign corporation with respect to which any person is treated as a United States shareholder under section 953(c), subparagraph (A) shall be treated as including a reference to each United States person who is an officer or director of such corporation.

    (2) STOCK OWNERSHIP REQUIREMENTS.—A person meets the stock ownership requirements of this paragraph with respect to any corporation if such person owns 10 percent or more of—

        (A) the total combined voting power of all classes of stock of such corporation entitled to vote, or

        (B) the total value of the stock of such corporation.

[Sec. 6046(b)]

(b) FORM AND CONTENTS OF RETURNS.—The returns required by subsection (a) shall be in such form and shall set forth, in respect of the foreign corporation, such information as the Secretary prescribes by forms or regulations as necessary for carrying out the provisions of the income tax laws, except that in the case of persons described only in subsection (a)(1) the information required shall be limited to the names and addresses of persons described in paragraph (2) or (3) of subsection (a).

[Sec. 6046(c)]

(c) OWNERSHIP OF STOCK.—For purposes of subsection (a), stock owned directly or indirectly by a person (including, in the case of an individual, stock owned by members of his family) shall be taken into account. For purposes of the preceding sentence, the family of an individual shall be considered as including only his brothers and sisters (whether by the whole or half blood), spouse, ancestors, and lineal descendants.

[Sec. 6046(d)]

(d) TIME FOR FILING.—Any return required by subsection (a) shall be filed on or before the 90th day after the day on which, under any provision of subsection (a), the United States citizen, resident, or person becomes liable to file such return (or on or before such later day as the Secretary may by forms or regulations prescribe).

[Sec. 6046(e)]

(e) LIMITATION.—No information shall be required to be furnished under this section with respect to any foreign corporation unless such information was required to be furnished under regulations which have been in effect for at least 90 days before the date on which the United States citizen, resident, or person becomes liable to file a return required under subsection (a).

* * *

[Sec. 6046A]

SEC. 6046A. RETURNS AS TO INTERESTS IN FOREIGN PARTNERSHIPS.

[Sec. 6046A(a)]

(a) REQUIREMENT OF RETURN.—Any United States person, except to the extent otherwise provided by regulations—

    (1) who acquires any interest in a foreign partnership,

    (2) who disposes of any portion of his interest in a foreign partnership, or

    (3) whose proportional interest in a foreign partnership changes substantially,

shall file a return. Paragraphs (1) and (2) shall apply to any acquisition or disposition only if the United States person directly or indirectly holds at least a 10-percent interest in such partnership either before or after such acquisition or disposition, and paragraph (3) shall apply to any change only if the change is equivalent to at least a 10-percent interest in such partnership.

[Sec. 6046A(b)]

(b) FORM AND CONTENTS OF RETURN.—Any return required by subsection (a) shall be in such form and set forth such information as the Secretary shall by regulations prescribe.

[Sec. 6046A(c)]

(c) TIME FOR FILING RETURN.—Any return required by subsection (a) shall be filed on or before the 90th day (or on or before such later day as the Secretary may by regulations prescribe) after the day on which the United States person becomes liable to file such return.

[Sec. 6046A(d)]

(d) 10-PERCENT INTEREST.—For purposes of subsection (a), a 10-percent interest in a partnership is an interest described in section 6038(e)(3)(C).

[Sec. 6046A(e)]

(e) CROSS REFERENCE.—

For provisions relating to penalties for violations of this section, see sections 6679 and 7203.

[Sec. 6048]

SEC. 6048. INFORMATION WITH RESPECT TO CERTAIN FOREIGN TRUSTS.

[Sec. 6048(a)]

(a) NOTICE OF CERTAIN EVENTS.—

(1) GENERAL RULE.—On or before the 90th day (or such later day as the Secretary may prescribe) after any reportable event, the responsible party shall provide written notice of such event to the Secretary in accordance with paragraph (2).

(2) CONTENTS OF NOTICE.—The notice required by paragraph (1) shall contain such information as the Secretary may prescribe, including—

(A) the amount of money or other property (if any) transferred to the trust in connection with the reportable event, and

(B) the identity of the trust and of each trustee and beneficiary (or class of beneficiaries) of the trust.

(3) REPORTABLE EVENT.—For purposes of this subsection—

(A) IN GENERAL.—The term "reportable event" means—

(i) the creation of any foreign trust by a United States person,

(ii) the transfer of any money or property (directly or indirectly) to a foreign trust by a United States person, including a transfer by reason of death, and

(iii) the death of a citizen or resident of the United States if—

(I) the decedent was treated as the owner of any portion of a foreign trust under the rules of subpart E of part I of subchapter J of chapter 1, or

(II) any portion of a foreign trust was included in the gross estate of the decedent.

(B) EXCEPTIONS.—

(i) FAIR MARKET VALUE SALES.—Subparagraph (A)(ii) shall not apply to any transfer of property to a trust in exchange for consideration of at least the fair market value of the transferred property. For purposes of the preceding sentence, consideration other than cash shall be taken into account at its fair market value and the rules of section 679(a)(3) shall apply.

(ii) DEFERRED COMPENSATION AND CHARITABLE TRUSTS.—Subparagraph (A) shall not apply with respect to a trust which is—

(I) described in section 402(b), 404(a)(4), or 404A, or

(II) determined by the Secretary to be described in section 501(c)(3).

(4) RESPONSIBLE PARTY.—For purposes of this subsection, the term "responsible party" means—

(A) the grantor in the case of the creation of an inter vivos trust,

(B) the transferor in the case of a reportable event described in paragraph (3)(A)(ii) other than a transfer by reason of death, and

(C) the executor of the decedent's estate in any other case.

[Sec. 6048(b)]

(b) UNITED STATES OWNER OF FOREIGN TRUST.—

(1) IN GENERAL.—If, at any time during any taxable year of a United States person, such person is treated as the owner of any portion of a foreign trust under the rules of subpart E of part I of subchapter J of chapter 1, such person shall be responsible to ensure that—

(A) such trust makes a return for such year which sets forth a full and complete accounting of all trust activities and operations for the year, the name of the United States agent for such trust, and such other information as the Secretary may prescribe, and

(B) such trust furnishes such information as the Secretary may prescribe to each United States person (i) who is treated as the owner of any portion of such trust or (ii) who receives (directly or indirectly) any distribution from the trust.

(2) TRUSTS NOT HAVING UNITED STATES AGENT.—

(A) IN GENERAL.—If the rules of this paragraph apply to any foreign trust, the determination of amounts required to be taken into account with respect to such trust by a United States person under the rules of subpart E of part I of subchapter J of chapter 1 shall be determined by the Secretary.

(B) UNITED STATES AGENT REQUIRED.—The rules of this paragraph shall apply to any foreign trust to which paragraph (1) applies unless such trust agrees (in such manner, subject to such conditions, and at such time as the Secretary shall prescribe) to authorize a United States person to act as such trust's limited agent solely for purposes of applying sections 7602, 7603, and 7604 with respect to—

(i) any request by the Secretary to examine records or produce testimony related to the proper treatment of amounts required to be taken into account under the rules referred to in subparagraph (A), or

(ii) any summons by the Secretary for such records or testimony.

The appearance of persons or production of records by reason of a United States person being such an agent shall not subject such persons or records to legal process for any purpose other than determining the correct treatment under this title of the amounts required to be taken into account under the rules referred to in subparagraph (A). A foreign trust which appoints an [agent] described in this subparagraph shall not be considered to have an office or a permanent establishment in the United States, or to be engaged in a trade or business in the United States, solely because of the activities of such agent pursuant to this subsection.

(C) OTHER RULES TO APPLY.—Rules similar to the rules of paragraphs (2) and (4) of section 6038A(e) shall apply for purposes of this paragraph.

[Sec. 6048(c)]

(c) REPORTING BY UNITED STATES BENEFICIARIES OF FOREIGN TRUSTS.—

(1) IN GENERAL.—If any United States person receives (directly or indirectly) during any taxable year of such person any distribution from a foreign trust, such person shall make a return with respect to such trust for such year which includes—

(A) the name of such trust,

(B) the aggregate amount of the distributions so received from such trust during such taxable year, and

(C) such other information as the Secretary may prescribe.

(2) INCLUSION IN INCOME IF RECORDS NOT PROVIDED.—

(A) IN GENERAL.—If adequate records are not provided to the Secretary to determine the proper treatment of any distribution from a foreign trust, such distribution shall be treated as an accumulation distribution includible in the gross income of the distributee under chapter 1. To the extent provided in regulations, the preceding sentence shall not apply if the foreign trust elects to be subject to rules similar to the rules of subsection (b)(2)(B).

(B) APPLICATION OF ACCUMULATION DISTRIBUTION RULES.—For purposes of applying section 668 in a case to which subparagraph (A) applies, the applicable number of years for purposes of section 668(a) shall be ½ of the number of years the trust has been in existence.

[Sec. 6048(d)]

(d) SPECIAL RULES.—

(1) DETERMINATION OF WHETHER UNITED STATES PERSON MAKES TRANSFER OR RECEIVES DISTRIBUTION.—For purposes of this section, in determining whether a United States person makes a transfer to, or receives a distribution from, a foreign trust, the fact that a portion of such

trust is treated as owned by another person under the rules of subpart E of part I of subchapter J of chapter 1 shall be disregarded.

(2) DOMESTIC TRUSTS WITH FOREIGN ACTIVITIES.—To the extent provided in regulations, a trust which is a United States person shall be treated as a foreign trust for purposes of this section and section 6677 if such trust has substantial activities, or holds substantial property, outside the United States.

(3) TIME AND MANNER OF FILING INFORMATION.—Any notice or return required under this section shall be made at such time and in such manner as the Secretary shall prescribe.

(4) MODIFICATION OF RETURN REQUIREMENTS.—The Secretary is authorized to suspend or modify any requirement of this section if the Secretary determines that the United States has no significant tax interest in obtaining the required information.

(5) UNITED STATES PERSON'S RETURN MUST BE CONSISTENT WITH TRUST RETURN OR SECRETARY NOTIFIED OF INCONSISTENCY.—Rules similar to the rules of section 6034A(c) shall apply to items reported by a trust under subsection (b)(1)(B) and to United States persons referred to in such subsection.

[Sec. 6049]

SEC. 6049. RETURNS REGARDING PAYMENTS OF INTEREST.

[Sec. 6049(a)]

(a) REQUIREMENT OF REPORTING.—Every person—

(1) who makes payments of interest (as defined in subsection (b)) aggregating $10 or more to any other person during any calendar year, or

(2) who receives payments of interest (as so defined) as a nominee and who makes payments aggregating $10 or more during any calendar year to any other person with respect to the interest so received,

shall make a return according to the forms or regulations prescribed by the Secretary, setting forth the aggregate amount of such payments and the name and address of the person to whom paid.

[Sec. 6049(b)]

(b) INTEREST DEFINED.—

(1) GENERAL RULE.—For purposes of subsection (a), the term "interest" means—

(A) interest on any obligation—

(i) issued in registered form, or

(ii) of a type offered to the public,

other than any obligation with a maturity (at issue) of not more than 1 year which is held by a corporation,

(B) interest on deposits with persons carrying on the banking business,

(C) amounts (whether or not designated as interest) paid by a mutual savings bank, savings and loan association, building and loan association, cooperative bank, homestead association, credit union, industrial loan association or bank, or similar organization, in respect of deposits, investment certificates, or withdrawable or repurchasable shares,

(D) interest on amounts held by an insurance company under an agreement to pay interest thereon,

(E) interest on deposits with brokers (as defined in section 6045(c)),

(F) interest paid on amounts held by investment companies (as defined in section 3 of the Investment Company Act of 1940 (15 U.S.C. 80a-3)) and on amounts invested in other pooled funds or trusts, and

(G) to the extent provided in regulations prescribed by the Secretary, any other interest (which is not described in paragraph (2)).

(2) EXCEPTIONS.—For purposes of subsection (a), the term "interest" does not include—

(A) interest on any obligation issued by a natural person,

Sec. 6048(d)(2)

(B) interest on any obligation if such interest is exempt from tax under section 103(a) or if such interest is exempt from tax (without regard to the identity of the holder) under any other provision of this title,

(C) except to the extent otherwise provided in regulations—

(i) any amount paid to any person described in paragraph (4), or

(ii) any amount described in paragraph (5), and

(D) except to the extent otherwise provided in regulations, any amount not described in subparagraph (C) of this paragraph which is income from sources outside the United States or which is paid by—

(i) a foreign government or international organization or any agency or instrumentality thereof.

(ii) a foreign central bank of issue.

(iii) a foreign corporation not engaged in a trade or business in the United States,

(iv) a foreign corporation, the interest payments of which would be exempt from withholding under subchapter A of chapter 3 if paid to a person who is not a United States person, or

(v) a partnership not engaged in a trade or business in the United States and composed in whole of nonresident alien individuals and persons described in clause (i), (ii), or (iii).

(3) PAYMENTS BY UNITED STATES NOMINEES ETC., OF UNITED STATES PERSON.—If, within the United States, a United States person—

(A) collects interest (or otherwise acts as a middleman between the payor and payee) from a foreign person described in paragraph (2)(D) or collects interest from a United States person which is income from sources outside the United States for a second person who is a United States person, or

(B) makes payments of such interest to such second United States person,

notwithstanding paragraph (2)(D), such payment shall be subject to the requirements of subsection (a) with respect to such second United States person.

(4) PERSONS DESCRIBED IN THIS PARAGRAPH.—A person is described in this paragraph if such person is—

(A) a corporation,

(B) an organization exempt from taxation under section 501(a) or an individual retirement plan,

(C) the United States or any wholly owned agency or instrumentality thereof,

(D) a State, the District of Columbia, a possession of the United States, any political subdivision of any of the foregoing, or any wholly owned agency or instrumentality of any one or more of the foregoing,

(E) a foreign government, a political subdivision of a foreign government, or any wholly owned agency or instrumentality of any one or more of the foregoing,

(F) an international organization or any wholly owned agency or instrumentality thereof,

(G) a foreign central bank of issue,

(H) a dealer in securities or commodities required to register as such under the laws of the United States or a State, the District of Columbia, or a possession of the United States,

(I) a real estate investment trust (as defined in section 856),

(J) an entity registered at all times during the taxable year under the Investment Company Act of 1940,

(K) a common trust fund (as defined in section 584(a)), or

(L) any trust which—

(i) is exempt from tax under section 664(c), or

(ii) is described in section 4947(a)(1).

(5) AMOUNTS DESCRIBED IN THIS PARAGRAPH.—An amount is described in this paragraph if such amount—

    (A) is subject to withholding under subchapter A of chapter 3 (relating to withholding of tax on nonresident aliens and foreign corporations) by the person paying such amount, or

    (B) would be subject to withholding under subchapter A of chapter 3 by the person paying such amount but for the fact that—

        (i) such amount is income from sources outside the United States,

        (ii) the payor thereof is exempt from the application of section 1441(a) by reason of section 1441(c) or a tax treaty,

        (iii) such amount is original issue discount (within the meaning of section 1273(a)), or

        (iv) such amount is described in section 871(i)(2).

[Sec. 6049(c)]

(c) STATEMENTS TO BE FURNISHED TO PERSONS WITH RESPECT TO WHOM INFORMATION IS REQUIRED.—

    (1) IN GENERAL.—Every person required to make a return under subsection (a) shall furnish to each person whose name is required to be set forth in such return a written statement showing—

        (A) the name, address, and phone number of the information contact of the person required to make such return, and

        (B) the aggregate amount of payments to, or the aggregate amount includible in the gross income of, the person required to be shown on the return.

    (2) TIME AND FORM OF STATEMENT.—The written statement under paragraph (1)—

        (A) shall be furnished (either in person or in a statement mailing by first-class mail which includes adequate notice that the statement is enclosed) to the person on or before January 31 of the year following the calendar year for which the return under subsection (a) was required to be made, and

        (B) shall be in such form as the Secretary may prescribe by regulations.

[Sec. 6049(d)]

(d) DEFINITIONS AND SPECIAL RULES.—For purposes of this section—

    (1) PERSON.—The term "person" includes any governmental unit and any agency or instrumentality thereof and any international organization and any agency or instrumentality thereof.

    (2) OBLIGATION.—The term "obligation" includes bonds, debentures, notes, certificates, and other evidences of indebtedness.

    (3) PAYMENTS BY GOVERNMENTAL UNITS.—In the case of payments made by any governmental unit or any agency or instrumentality thereof, the officer or employee having control of the payment of interest (or the person appropriately designated for purposes of this section) shall make the returns and statements required by this section.

    (4) FINANCIAL INSTITUTIONS, BROKERS, ETC., COLLECTING INTEREST MAY BE SUBSTITUTED FOR PAYOR.—To the extent and in the manner provided by regulations, in the case of any obligation—

        (A) a financial institution, broker, or other person specified in such regulations which collects interest on such obligation for the payee (or otherwise acts as a middleman between the payor and the payee) shall comply with the requirements of subsections (a) and (c), and

        (B) no other person shall be required to comply with the requirements of subsections (a) and (c) with respect to any interest on such obligation for which reporting is required pursuant to subparagraph (A).

Returns—Information

(5) INTEREST ON CERTAIN OBLIGATIONS MAY BE TREATED ON A TRANSACTIONAL BASIS.—

(A) IN GENERAL.—To the extent and in the manner provided in regulations, this section shall apply with respect to—

(i) any person described in paragraph (4)(A), and

(ii) in the case of any United States savings bonds, any Federal agency making payments thereon,

on any transactional basis rather than on an annual aggregation basis.

(B) SEPARATE RETURNS AND STATEMENTS.—If subparagraph (A) applies to interest on any obligation, the return under subsection (a) and the statement furnished under subsection (c) with respect to such transaction may be made separately, but any such statement shall be furnished to the payee at such time as the Secretary may prescribe by regulations but not later than January 31 of the next calendar year.

(C) STATEMENT TO PAYEE REQUIRED IN CASE OF TRANSACTIONS INVOLVING $10 OR MORE.—In the case of any transaction to which this paragraph applies which involves the payment of $10 or more of interest, a statement of the transaction may be provided to the payee of such interest in lieu of the statement required under subsection (c). Such statement shall be provided during January of the year following the year in which such payment is made.

(6) TREATMENT OF ORIGINAL ISSUE DISCOUNT.—

(A) IN GENERAL.—Original issue discount on any obligation shall be reported—

(i) as if paid at the time it is includible in gross income under section 1272 (except that for such purpose the amount reportable with respect to any subsequent holder shall be determined as if he were the original holder), and

(ii) if section 1272 does not apply to the obligation, at maturity (or, if earlier, on redemption).

In the case of any obligation not in registered form issued before January 1, 1983, clause (ii) and not clause (i) shall apply.

(B) ORIGINAL ISSUE DISCOUNT.—For purposes of this paragraph, the term "original issue discount" has the meaning given to such term by section 1273(a).

(7) INTERESTS IN REMIC'S AND CERTAIN OTHER DEBT INSTRUMENTS.—

(A) IN GENERAL.—For purposes of subsection (a), the term "interest" includes amounts includible in gross income with respect to regular interests in REMIC's (and such amounts shall be treated as paid when includible in gross income under section 860B(b)).

(B) REPORTING TO CORPORATIONS, ETC.—Except as otherwise provided in regulations, in the case of any interest described in subparagraph (A) of this paragraph and any other debt instrument to which section 1272(a)(6) applies, subsection (b)(4) of this section shall be applied without regard to subparagraphs (A), (H), (I), (J), (K), and (L)(i).

(C) ADDITIONAL INFORMATION.—Except as otherwise provided in regulations, any return or statement required to be filed or furnished under this section with respect to interest income described in subparagraph (A) and interest on any other debt instrument to which section 1272(a)(6) applies shall also provide information setting forth the adjusted issue price of the interest to which the return or statement relates at the beginning of each accrual period with respect to which interest income is required to be reported on such return or statement and information necessary to compute accrual of market discount.

(D) REGULATORY AUTHORITY.—The Secretary may prescribe such regulations as are necessary or appropriate to carry out the purposes of this subparagraph, including regulations which require more frequent or more detailed reporting.

Sec. 6049(d)(7)(D)

SUBCHAPTER B—MISCELLANEOUS PROVISIONS

[Sec. 6103]

SEC. 6103. CONFIDENTIALITY AND DISCLOSURE OF RETURNS AND RETURN INFORMATION.

[Sec. 6103(a)]

(a) GENERAL RULE.—Returns and return information shall be confidential, and except as authorized by this title—

(1) no officer or employee of the United States,

(2) no officer or employee of any State, any local law enforcement agency receiving information under subsection (i)(7)(A), any local child support enforcement agency, or any local agency administering a program listed in subsection (l)(7)(D) who has or had access to returns or return information under this section, and

(3) no other person (or officer or employee thereof) who has or had access to returns or return information under subsection (e)(1)(D)(iii), paragraph (6), (12), (16), (19), or (20) of subsection (l), paragraph (2) or (4)(B) of subsection (m), or subsection (n),

shall disclose any return or return information obtained by him in any manner in connection with his service as such an officer or an employee or otherwise or under the provisions of this section. For purposes of this subsection, the term "officer or employee" includes a former officer or employee.

[Sec. 6103(b)]

(b) DEFINITIONS.—For purposes of this section—

(1) RETURN.—The term "return" means any tax or information return, declaration of estimated tax, or claim for refund required by, or provided for or permitted under, the provisions of this title which is filed with the Secretary by, on behalf of, or with respect to any person, and any amendment or supplement thereto, including supporting schedules, attachments, or lists which are supplemental to, or part of, the return so filed.

(2) RETURN INFORMATION.—The term "return information" means—

(A) a taxpayer's identity, the nature, source, or amount of his income, payments, receipts, deductions, exemptions, credits, assets, liabilities, net worth, tax liability, tax withheld, deficiencies, overassessments, or tax payments, whether the taxpayer's return was, is being, or will be examined or subject to other investigation or processing, or any other data, received by, recorded by, prepared by, furnished to, or collected by the Secretary with respect to a return or with respect to the determination of the existence, or possible existence, of liability (or the amount thereof) of any person under this title for any tax, penalty, interest, fine, forfeiture, or other imposition, or offense,

(B) any part of any written determination or any background file document relating to such written determination (as such terms are defined in section 6110(b)) which is not open to public inspection under section 6110,

(C) any advance pricing agreement entered into by a taxpayer and the Secretary and any background information related to such agreement or any application for an advance pricing agreement, and

(D) any agreement under section 7121, and any similar agreement, and any background information related to such an agreement or request for such an agreement,

but such term does not include data in a form which cannot be associated with, or otherwise identify, directly or indirectly, a particular taxpayer. Nothing in the preceding sentence, or in any other provision of law, shall be construed to require the disclosure of standards used or to be used for the selection of returns for examination, or data used or to be used for determining such standards, if the Secretary determines that such disclosure will seriously impair assessment, collection, or enforcement under the internal revenue laws.

* * *

[Sec. 6110]

SEC. 6110. PUBLIC INSPECTION OF WRITTEN DETERMINATIONS.

[Sec. 6110(a)]

(a) GENERAL RULE.—Except as otherwise provided in this section, the text of any written determination and any background file document relating to such written determination shall be open to public inspection at such place as the Secretary may by regulations prescribe.

[Sec. 6110(b)]

(b) DEFINITIONS.—For purposes of this section—

(1) WRITTEN DETERMINATION.—

(A) IN GENERAL.—The term "written determination" means a ruling, determination letter, technical advice memorandum, or Chief Counsel advice.

(B) EXCEPTIONS.—Such term shall not include any matter referred to in subparagraph (C) or (D) of section 6103(b)(2).

* * *

[Sec. 6111]

SEC. 6111. DISCLOSURE OF REPORTABLE TRANSACTIONS.

[Sec. 6111(a)]

(a) IN GENERAL.—Each material advisor with respect to any reportable transaction shall make a return (in such form as the Secretary may prescribe) setting forth—

(1) information identifying and describing the transaction,

(2) information describing any potential tax benefits expected to result from the transaction, and

(3) such other information as the Secretary may prescribe.

Such return shall be filed not later than the date specified by the Secretary.

[Sec. 6111(b)]

(b) DEFINITIONS.—For purposes of this section—

(1) MATERIAL ADVISOR.—

(A) IN GENERAL.—The term "material advisor" means any person—

(i) who provides any material aid, assistance, or advice with respect to organizing, managing, promoting, selling, implementing, insuring, or carrying out any reportable transaction, and

(ii) who directly or indirectly derives gross income in excess of the threshold amount (or such other amount as may be prescribed by the Secretary) for such advice or assistance.

(B) THRESHOLD AMOUNT.—For purposes of subparagraph (A), the threshold amount is—

(i) $50,000 in the case of a reportable transaction substantially all of the tax benefits from which are provided to natural persons, and

(ii) $250,000 in any other case.

(2) REPORTABLE TRANSACTION.—The term "reportable transaction" has the meaning given to such term by section 6707A(c).

[Sec. 6111(c)]

(c) REGULATIONS.—The Secretary may prescribe regulations which provide—

(1) that only 1 person shall be required to meet the requirements of subsection (a) in cases in which 2 or more persons would otherwise be required to meet such requirements,

(2) exemptions from the requirements of this section, and

(3) such rules as may be necessary or appropriate to carry out the purposes of this section.

[Sec. 6114]

SEC. 6114. TREATY-BASED RETURN POSITIONS.

[Sec. 6114(a)]

(a) IN GENERAL.—Each taxpayer who, with respect to any tax imposed by this title, takes the position that a treaty of the United States overrules (or otherwise modifies) an internal revenue law of the United States shall disclose (in such manner as the Secretary may prescribe) such position—

(1) on the return of tax for such tax (or any statement attached to such return), or

(2) if no return of tax is required to be filed, in such form as the Secretary may prescribe.

[Sec. 6114(b)]

(b) WAIVER AUTHORITY.—The Secretary may waive the requirements of subsection (a) with respect to classes of cases for which the Secretary determines that the waiver will not impede the assessment and collection of tax.

CHAPTER 62—TIME AND PLACE FOR PAYING TAX

SUBCHAPTER B—EXTENSIONS OF TIME FOR PAYMENT

[Sec. 6167]

SEC. 6167. EXTENSION OF TIME FOR PAYMENT OF TAX ATTRIBUTABLE TO RECOVERY OF FOREIGN EXPROPRIATION LOSSES.

[Sec. 6167(a)]

(a) EXTENSION ALLOWED BY ELECTION.—If—

(1) a corporation has a recovery of a foreign expropriation loss to which section 1351 applies, and

(2) the portion of the recovery received in money is less than 25 percent of the amount of such recovery (as defined in section 1351(c)) and is not greater than the tax attributable to such recovery,

the tax attributable to such recovery shall, at the election of the taxpayer, be payable in 10 equal installments on the 15th day of the third month of each of the taxable years following the taxable year of the recovery. Such election shall be made at such time and in such manner as the Secretary may prescribe by regulations. If an election is made under this subsection, the provisions of this subtitle shall apply as though the Secretary were extending the time for payment of such tax.

[Sec. 6167(b)]

(b) EXTENSION PERMITTED BY SECRETARY.—If a corporation has a recovery of a foreign expropriation loss to which section 1351 applies and if an election is not made under subsection (a), the Secretary may, upon finding that the payment of the tax attributable to such recovery at the time otherwise provided in this subtitle would result in undue hardship, extend the time for payment of such tax for a reasonable period or periods not in excess of 9 years from the date on which such tax is otherwise payable.

[Sec. 6167(c)]

(c) ACCELERATION OF PAYMENTS.—If—

(1) an election is made under subsection (a),

(2) during any taxable year before the tax attributable to such recovery is paid in full—

(A) any property (other than money) received on such recovery is sold or exchanged, or

(B) any property (other than money) received on any sale or exchange described in subparagraph (A) is sold or exchanged, and

(3) the amount of money received on such sale or exchange (reduced by the amount of the tax imposed under chapter 1 with respect to such sale or exchange), when added to the amount of money—

(A) received on such recovery, and

(B) received on previous sales or exchanges described in subparagraphs (A) and (B) of paragraph (2) (as so reduced),

exceeds the amount of money which may be received under subsection (a)(2), an amount of the tax attributable to such recovery equal to such excess shall be payable on the 15th day of the third month of the taxable year following the taxable year in which such sale or exchange occurs. The amount of such tax so paid shall be treated, for purposes of this section, as a payment of the first unpaid installment or installments (or portion thereof) which become payable under subsection (a) following such taxable year.

[Sec. 6167(d)]

(d) PRORATION OF DEFICIENCY TO INSTALLMENTS.—If an election is made under subsection (a), and a deficiency attributable to the recovery of a foreign expropriation loss has been assessed, the deficiency shall be prorated to such installments. The part of the deficiency so prorated to any installment the date for payment of which has not arrived shall be collected at the same time as, and as part of, such installment. The part of the deficiency so prorated to any installment the date for payment of which has arrived shall be paid upon notice and demand from the Secretary. This subsection shall not apply if the deficiency is due to negligence, to intentional disregard of rules and regulations, or to fraud with intent to evade tax.

[Sec. 6167(e)]

(e) TIME FOR PAYMENT OF INTEREST.—If the time for payment for any amount of tax has been extended under this section, interest payable under section 6601 on any unpaid portion of such amount shall be paid annually at the same time as, and as part of, each installment payment of the tax. Interest, on that part of a deficiency prorated under this section to any installment the date for payment of which has not arrived, for the period before the date fixed for the last installment preceding the assessment of the deficiency, shall be paid upon notice and demand from the Secretary.

[Sec. 6167(f)]

(f) TAX ATTRIBUTABLE TO RECOVERY OF FOREIGN EXPROPRIATION LOSS.—For purposes of this section, the tax attributable to a recovery of a foreign expropriation loss is the sum of—

(1) the additional tax imposed by section 1351(d)(1) on such recovery, and

(2) the amount by which the tax imposed under subtitle A is increased by reason of the gain on such recovery which under section 1351(e) is considered as gain on the involuntary conversion of property.

[Sec. 6167(g)]

(g) FAILURE TO PAY INSTALLMENT.—If any installment under this section is not paid on or before the date fixed for its payment by this section (including any extension of time for the payment of such installment), the unpaid portion of the tax payable in installments shall be paid upon notice and demand from the Secretary.

* * *

CHAPTER 64—COLLECTION

SUBCHAPTER B—RECEIPT OF PAYMENT

[Sec. 6316]

SEC. 6316. PAYMENT BY FOREIGN CURRENCY.

The Secretary is authorized in his discretion to allow payment of taxes in the currency of a foreign country under such circumstances and subject to such conditions as the Secretary may by regulations prescribe.

CHAPTER 66—LIMITATIONS

SUBCHAPTER A—LIMITATIONS ON ASSESSMENT AND COLLECTION

[Sec. 6503]

SEC. 6503. SUSPENSION OF RUNNING OF PERIOD OF LIMITATION.

* * *

[Sec. 6503(c)]

(c) TAXPAYER OUTSIDE UNITED STATES.—The running of the period of limitations on collection after assessment prescribed in section 6502 shall be suspended for the period during which the taxpayer is outside the United States if such period of absence is for a continuous period of at least 6 months. If the preceding sentence applies and at the time of the taxpayer's return to the United States the period of limitations on collection after assessment prescribed in section 6502 would expire before the expiration of 6 months from the date of his return, such period shall not expire before the expiration of such 6 months.

* * *

[Sec. 6503(e)]

(e) EXTENSIONS OF TIME FOR PAYMENT OF TAX ATTRIBUTABLE TO RECOVERIES OF FOREIGN EXPROPRIATION LOSSES.—The running of the period of limitations for collection of the tax attributable to a recovery of a foreign expropriation loss (within the meaning of section 6167(f)) shall be suspended for the period of any extension of time for payment under subsection (a) or (b) of section 6167.

* * *

[Sec. 6503(i)]

(i) EXTENSION OF TIME FOR PAYMENT OF UNDISTRIBUTED PFIC EARNINGS TAX LIABILITY.—The running of any period of limitations for collection of any amount of undistributed PFIC earnings tax liability (as defined in section 1294(b)) shall be suspended for the period of any extension of time under section 1294 for payment of such amount.

* * *

Subchapter B—Limitations on Credit or Refund

[Sec. 6511]

SEC. 6511. LIMITATIONS ON CREDIT OR REFUND.

* * *

[Sec. 6511(d)]

(d) SPECIAL RULES APPLICABLE TO INCOME TAXES.—

* * *

(3) SPECIAL RULES RELATING TO FOREIGN TAX CREDIT.—

(A) SPECIAL PERIOD OF LIMITATION WITH RESPECT TO FOREIGN TAXES PAID OR ACCRUED.—If the claim for credit or refund relates to an overpayment attributable to any taxes paid or accrued to any foreign country or to any possession of the United States for which credit is allowed against the tax imposed by subtitle A in accordance with the provisions of section 901 or the provisions of any treaty to which the United States is a party, in lieu of the 3-year period of limitation prescribed in subsection (a), the period shall be 10 years from the date prescribed by law for filing the return for the year in which such taxes were actually paid or accrued.

(B) EXCEPTION IN THE CASE OF FOREIGN TAXES PAID OR ACCRUED.—In the case of a claim described in subparagraph (A), the amount of the credit or refund may exceed the portion of the tax paid within the period provided in subsection (b) or (c), whichever is applicable, to the extent of the amount of the overpayment attributable to the allowance of a credit for the taxes described in subparagraph (A).

* * *

CHAPTER 68—ADDITIONS TO THE TAX, ADDITIONAL AMOUNTS, AND ASSESSABLE PENALTIES

SUBCHAPTER A—ADDITIONS TO THE TAX AND ADDITIONAL AMOUNTS

PART I—GENERAL PROVISIONS

[Sec. 6652]

SEC. 6652. FAILURE TO FILE CERTAIN INFORMATION RETURNS, REGISTRATION STATEMENTS, ETC.

* * *

[Sec. 6652(f)]

(f) RETURNS REQUIRED UNDER SECTION 6039C.—

(1) IN GENERAL.—In the case of each failure to make a return by section 6039C which contains the information required by such section on the date prescribed therefor (determined with regard to any extension of time for filing), unless it is shown that such failure is due to reasonable cause and not to willful neglect, the amount determined under paragraph (2) shall be paid (upon notice and demand by the Secretary and in the same manner as tax) by the person failing to make such return.

(2) AMOUNT OF PENALTY.—For purposes of paragraph (1), the amount determined under this paragraph with respect to any failure shall be $25 for each day during which such failure continues.

(3) LIMITATION.—The amount determined under paragraph (2) with respect to any person for failing to meet the requirements of section 6039C for any calendar year shall not exceed the lesser of—

(A) $25,000, or

(B) 5 percent of the aggregate of the fair market value of the United States real property interests owned by such person at any time during such year.

For purposes of the preceding sentence, fair market value shall be determined as of the end of the calendar year (or, in the case of any property disposed of during the calendar year, as of the date of such disposition).

* * *

PART II—ACCURACY AND FRAUD-RELATED PENALTIES

[Sec. 6662]

SEC. 6662. IMPOSITION OF ACCURACY-RELATED PENALTY ON UNDERPAYMENTS.

[Sec. 6662(a)]

(a) IMPOSITION OF PENALTY.—If this section applies to any portion of an underpayment of tax required to be shown on a return, there shall be added to the tax an amount equal to 20 percent of the portion of the underpayment to which this section applies.

[Sec. 6662(b)]

(b) PORTION OF UNDERPAYMENT TO WHICH SECTION APPLIES.—This section shall apply to the portion of any underpayment which is attributable to 1 or more of the following:

(1) Negligence or disregard of rules or regulations.

(2) Any substantial understatement of income tax.

(3) Any substantial valuation misstatement under chapter 1.

(4) Any substantial overstatement of pension liabilities.

(5) Any substantial estate or gift tax valuation understatement.

This section shall not apply to any portion of an underpayment on which a penalty is imposed under section 6663.

[Sec. 6662(c)]

(c) NEGLIGENCE.—For purposes of this section, the term "negligence" includes any failure to make a reasonable attempt to comply with the provisions of this title, and the term "disregard" includes any careless, reckless, or intentional disregard.

[Sec. 6662(d)]

(d) SUBSTANTIAL UNDERSTATEMENT OF INCOME TAX.—

(1) SUBSTANTIAL UNDERSTATEMENT.—

(A) IN GENERAL.—For purposes of this section, there is a substantial understatement of income tax for any taxable year if the amount of the understatement for the taxable year exceeds the greater of—

(i) 10 percent of the tax required to be shown on the return for the taxable year, or

(ii) $5,000.

(B) SPECIAL RULE FOR CORPORATIONS.—In the case of a corporation other than an S corporation or a personal holding company (as defined in section 542), there is a substantial understatement of income tax for any taxable year if the amount of the understatement for the taxable year exceeds the lesser of—

(i) 10 percent of the tax required to be shown on the return for the taxable year (or, if greater, $10,000), or

(ii) $10,000,000.

(2) UNDERSTATEMENT.—

(A) IN GENERAL.—For purposes of paragraph (1), the term "understatement" means the excess of—

(i) the amount of the tax required to be shown on the return for the taxable year, over

(ii) the amount of the tax imposed which is shown on the return, reduced by any rebate (within the meaning of section 6211(b)(2)).

The excess under the preceding sentence shall be determined without regard to items to which section 6662A applies.

(B) REDUCTION FOR UNDERSTATEMENT DUE TO POSITION OF TAXPAYER OR DISCLOSED ITEM.—The amount of the understatement under subparagraph (A) shall be reduced by that portion of the understatement which is attributable to—

(i) the tax treatment of any item by the taxpayer if there is or was substantial authority for such treatment, or

(ii) any item if—

(I) the relevant facts affecting the item's tax treatment are adequately disclosed in the return or in a statement attached to the return, and

(II) there is a reasonable basis for the tax treatment of such item by the taxpayer.

For purposes of clause (ii)(II), in no event shall a corporation be treated as having a reasonable basis for its tax treatment of an item attributable to a multiple-party financing transaction if such treatment does not clearly reflect the income of the corporation.

(C) REDUCTION NOT TO APPLY TO TAX SHELTERS.—

(i) IN GENERAL.—Subparagraph (B) shall not apply to any item attributable to a tax shelter.

(ii) TAX SHELTER.—For purposes of clause (i), the term "tax shelter" means—

(I) a partnership or other entity,

(II) any investment plan or arrangement, or

(III) any other plan or arrangement,

if a significant purpose of such partnership, entity, plan, or arrangement is the avoidance or evasion of Federal income tax.

Accuracy and Fraud-Related Penalties

(3) SECRETARIAL LIST.—The Secretary may prescribe a list of positions which the Secretary believes do not meet the 1 or more of the standards specified in paragraph (2)(B)(i), section 6664(d)(2), and section 6694(a)(1). Such list (and any revisions thereof) shall be published in the Federal Register or the Internal Revenue Bulletin.

[Sec. 6662(e)]

(e) SUBSTANTIAL VALUATION MISSTATEMENT UNDER CHAPTER 1.—

(1) IN GENERAL.—For purposes of this section, there is a substantial valuation misstatement under chapter 1 if—

(A) the value of any property (or the adjusted basis of any property) claimed on any return of tax imposed by chapter 1 is 200 percent or more of the amount determined to be the correct amount of such valuation or adjusted basis (as the case may be), or

(B)(i) the price for any property or services (or for the use of property) claimed on any such return in connection with any transaction between persons described in section 482 is 200 percent or more (or 50 percent or less) of the amount determined under section 482 to be the correct amount of such price, or

(ii) the net section 482 transfer price adjustment for the taxable year exceeds the lesser of $5,000,000 or 10 percent of the taxpayer's gross receipts.

(2) LIMITATION.—No penalty shall be imposed by reason of subsection (b)(3) unless the portion of the underpayment for the taxable year attributable to substantial valuation misstatements under chapter 1 exceeds $5,000 ($10,000 in the case of a corporation other than an S corporation or a personal holding company (as defined in section 542)).

(3) NET SECTION 482 TRANSFER PRICE ADJUSTMENT.—For purposes of this subsection—

(A) IN GENERAL.—The term "net section 482 transfer price adjustment" means, with respect to any taxable year, the net increase in taxable income for the taxable year (determined without regard to any amount carried to such taxable year from another taxable year) resulting from adjustments under section 482 in the price for any property or services (or for the use of property).

(B) CERTAIN ADJUSTMENTS EXCLUDED IN DETERMINING THRESHOLD.—For purposes of determining whether the threshold requirements of paragraph (1)(B)(ii) are met, the following shall be excluded:

(i) Any portion of the net increase in taxable income referred to in subparagraph (A) which is attributable to any redetermination of a price if—

(I) it is established that the taxpayer determined such price in accordance with a specific pricing method set forth in the regulations prescribed under section 482 and that the taxpayer's use of such method was reasonable,

(II) the taxpayer has documentation (which was in existence as of the time of filing the return) which sets forth the determination of such price in accordance with such a method and which establishes that the use of such method was reasonable, and

(III) the taxpayer provides such documentation to the Secretary within 30 days of a request for such documentation.

(ii) Any portion of the net increase in taxable income referred to in subparagraph (A) which is attributable to a redetermination of price where such price was not determined in accordance with such a specific pricing method if—

(I) the taxpayer establishes that none of such pricing methods was likely to result in a price that would clearly reflect income, the taxpayer used another pricing method to determine such price, and such other pricing method was likely to result in a price that would clearly reflect income,

(II) the taxpayer has documentation (which was in existence as of the time of filing the return) which sets forth the determination of such price in accordance with such other method and which establishes that the requirements of subclause (I) were satisfied, and

(III) the taxpayer provides such documentation to the Secretary within 30 days of a request for such documentation.

(iii) Any portion of such net increase which is attributable to any transaction solely between foreign corporations unless, in the case of any such corporations, the treatment of such transaction affects the determination of income from sources within the United States or taxable income effectively connected with the conduct of a trade or business within the United States.

(C) SPECIAL RULE.—If the regular tax (as defined in section 55(c)) imposed by chapter 1 on the taxpayer is determined by reference to an amount other than taxable income, such amount shall be treated as the taxable income of such taxpayer for purposes of this paragraph.

(D) COORDINATION WITH REASONABLE CAUSE EXCEPTION.—For purposes of section 6664(c) the taxpayer shall not be treated as having reasonable cause for any portion of an underpayment attributable to a net section 482 transfer price adjustment unless such taxpayer meets the requirements of clause (i), (ii), or (iii) of subparagraph (B) with respect to such portion.

* * *

[Sec. 6662(h)]

(h) INCREASE IN PENALTY IN CASE OF GROSS VALUATION MISSTATEMENTS.—

(1) IN GENERAL.—To the extent that a portion of the underpayment to which this section applies is attributable to one or more gross valuation misstatements, subsection (a) shall be applied with respect to such portion by substituting "40 percent" for "20 percent".

(2) GROSS VALUATION MISSTATEMENTS.—The term "gross valuation misstatements" means—

(A) any substantial valuation misstatement under chapter 1 as determined under subsection (e) by substituting—

(i) "400 percent" for "200 percent" each place it appears,

(ii) "25 percent" for "50 percent", and

(iii) in paragraph (1)(B)(ii)—

(I) "$20,000,000" for "$5,000,000", and

(II) "20 percent" for "10 percent".

(B) any substantial overstatement of pension liabilities as determined under subsection (f) by substituting "400 percent" for "200 percent", and

(C) any substantial estate or gift tax valuation understatement as determined under subsection (g) by substituting "25 percent" for "50 percent".

[Sec. 6663]

SEC. 6663. IMPOSITION OF FRAUD PENALTY.

[Sec. 6663(a)]

(a) IMPOSITION OF PENALTY.—If any part of any underpayment of tax required to be shown on a return is due to fraud, there shall be added to the tax an amount equal to 75 percent of the portion of the underpayment which is attributable to fraud.

[Sec. 6663(b)]

(b) DETERMINATION OF PORTION ATTRIBUTABLE TO FRAUD.—If the Secretary establishes that any portion of an underpayment is attributable to fraud, the entire underpayment shall be treated as attributable to fraud, except with respect to any portion of the underpayment which the taxpayer establishes (by a preponderance of the evidence) is not attributable to fraud.

* * *

Accuracy and Fraud-Related Penalties

[Sec. 6664]

SEC 6664. DEFINITIONS AND SPECIAL RULES.

[Sec. 6664(a)]

(a) UNDERPAYMENT.—For purposes of this part, the term "underpayment" means the amount by which any tax imposed by this title exceeds the excess of—

(1) the sum of—

(A) the amount shown as the tax by the taxpayer on his return, plus

(B) amounts not so shown previously assessed (or collected without assessment), over

(2) the amount of rebates made.

For purposes of paragraph (2), the term "rebate" means so much of an abatement, credit, refund, or other repayment, as was made on the ground that tax imposed was less than the excess of the amount specified in paragraph (1) over the rebates previously made.

[Sec. 6664(b)]

(b) PENALTIES APPLICABLE ONLY WHERE RETURN FILED.—The penalties provided in this part shall apply only in cases where a return of tax is filed (other than a return prepared by the Secretary under the authority of section 6020(b)).

[Sec. 6664(c)]

(c) REASONABLE CAUSE EXCEPTION FOR UNDERPAYMENTS.—

(1) IN GENERAL.—No penalty shall be imposed under section 6662 or 6663 with respect to any portion of an underpayment if it is shown that there was a reasonable cause for such portion and that the taxpayer acted in good faith with respect to such portion.

(2) SPECIAL RULE FOR CERTAIN VALUATION OVERSTATEMENTS.—In the case of any underpayment attributable to a substantial or gross valuation over statement under chapter 1 with respect to charitable deduction property, paragraph (1) shall not apply unless—

(A) the claimed value of the property was based on a qualified appraisal made by a qualified appraiser, and

(B) in addition to obtaining such appraisal, the taxpayer made a good faith investigation of the value of the contributed property.

(3) DEFINITIONS.—For purposes of this subsection—

(A) CHARITABLE DEDUCTION PROPERTY.—The term "charitable deduction property" means any property contributed by the taxpayer in a contribution for which a deduction was claimed under section 170. For purposes of paragraph (2), such term shall not include any securities for which (as of the date of the contribution) market quotations are readily available on an established securities market.

(B) QUALIFIED APPRAISER.—The term "qualified appraiser" means any appraiser meeting the requirements of the regulations prescribed under section 170(a)(1).

(C) QUALIFIED APPRAISAL.—The term "qualified appraisal" means any appraisal meeting the requirements of the regulations prescribed under section 170(a)(1).

[Sec. 6664(d)]

(d) REASONABLE CAUSE EXCEPTION FOR REPORTABLE TRANSACTION UNDERSTATEMENTS.—

(1) IN GENERAL.—No penalty shall be imposed under section 6662A with respect to any portion of a reportable transaction understatement if it is shown that there was a reasonable cause for such portion and that the taxpayer acted in good faith with respect to such portion.

(2) SPECIAL RULES.—Paragraph (1) shall not apply to any reportable transaction understatement unless—

(A) the relevant facts affecting the tax treatment of the item are adequately disclosed in accordance with the regulations prescribed under section 6011,

(B) there is or was substantial authority for such treatment, and

(C) the taxpayer reasonably believed that such treatment was more likely than not the proper treatment.

A taxpayer failing to adequately disclose in accordance with section 6011 shall be treated as meeting the requirements of subparagraph (A) if the penalty for such failure was rescinded under section 6707A(d).

(3) RULES RELATING TO REASONABLE BELIEF.—For purposes of paragraph (2)(C)—

(A) IN GENERAL.—A taxpayer shall be treated as having a reasonable belief with respect to the tax treatment of an item only if such belief—

(i) is based on the facts and law that exist at the time the return of tax which includes such tax treatment is filed, and

(ii) relates solely to the taxpayer's chances of success on the merits of such treatment and does not take into account the possibility that a return will not be audited, such treatment will not be raised on audit, or such treatment will be resolved through settlement if it is raised.

(B) CERTAIN OPINIONS MAY NOT BE RELIED UPON.—

(i) IN GENERAL.—An opinion of a tax advisor may not be relied upon to establish the reasonable belief of a taxpayer if—

(I) the tax advisor is described in clause (ii), or

(II) the opinion is described in clause (iii).

(ii) DISQUALIFIED TAX ADVISORS.—A tax advisor is described in this clause if the tax advisor—

(I) is a material advisor (within the meaning of section 6111(b)(1)) and participates in the organization, management, promotion, or sale of the transaction or is related (within the meaning of section 267(b) or 707(b)(1)) to any person who so participates,

(II) is compensated directly or indirectly by a material advisor with respect to the transaction,

(III) has a fee arrangement with respect to the transaction which is contingent on all or part of the intended tax benefits from the transaction being sustained, or

(IV) as determined under regulations prescribed by the Secretary, has a disqualifying financial interest with respect to the transaction.

(iii) DISQUALIFIED OPINIONS.—For purposes of clause (i), an opinion is disqualified if the opinion—

(I) is based on unreasonable factual or legal assumptions (including assumptions as to future events),

(II) unreasonably relies on representations, statements, findings, or agreements of the taxpayer or any other person,

(III) does not identify and consider all relevant facts, or

(IV) fails to meet any other requirement as the Secretary may prescribe.

SUBCHAPTER B—ASSESSABLE PENALTIES

PART I—GENERAL PROVISIONS

[Sec. 6672]

SEC. 6672. FAILURE TO COLLECT AND PAY OVER TAX, OR ATTEMPT TO EVADE OR DEFEAT TAX.

[Sec. 6672(a)]

(a) GENERAL RULE.—Any person required to collect, truthfully account for, and pay over any tax imposed by this title who willfully fails to collect such tax, or truthfully account for and pay over such tax, or willfully attempts in any manner to evade or defeat any such tax or the payment thereof, shall, in addition to other penalties provided by law, be liable to a penalty equal to the total amount of the tax evaded, or not collected, or not accounted for and paid over. No penalty shall be imposed under section 6653 or part II of subchapter A of chapter 68 for any offense to which this section is applicable.

* * *

[Sec. 6677]

SEC. 6677. FAILURE TO FILE INFORMATION WITH RESPECT TO CERTAIN FOREIGN TRUSTS.

[Sec. 6677(a)]

(a) CIVIL PENALTY.—In addition to any criminal penalty provided by law, if any notice or return required to be filed by section 6048—

(1) is not filed on or before the time provided in such section, or

(2) does not include all the information required pursuant to such section or includes incorrect information,

the person required to file such notice or return shall pay a penalty equal to 35 percent of the gross reportable amount. If any failure described in the preceding sentence continues for more than 90 days after the day on which the Secretary mails notice of such failure to the person required to pay such penalty, such person shall pay a penalty (in addition to the amount determined under the preceding sentence) of $10,000 for each 30-day period (or fraction thereof) during which such failure continues after the expiration of such 90-day period. In no event shall the penalty under this subsection with respect to any failure exceed the gross reportable amount.

[Sec. 6677(b)]

(b) SPECIAL RULES FOR RETURNS UNDER SECTION 6048(b).—In the case of a return required under section 6048(b)—

(1) the United States person referred to in such section shall be liable for the penalty imposed by subsection (a), and

(2) subsection (a) shall be applied by substituting "5 percent" for "35 percent".

[Sec. 6677(c)]

(c) GROSS REPORTABLE AMOUNT.—For purposes of subsection (a), the term "gross reportable amount" means—

(1) the gross value of the property involved in the event (determined as of the date of the event) in the case of a failure relating to section 6048(a),

(2) the gross value of the portion of the trust's assets at the close of the year treated as owned by the United States person in the case of a failure relating to section 6048(b)(1), and

(3) the gross amount of the distributions in the case of a failure relating to section 6048(c).

[Sec. 6677(d)]

(d) REASONABLE CAUSE EXCEPTION.—No penalty shall be imposed by this section on any failure which is shown to be due to reasonable cause and not due to willful neglect. The fact that a foreign jurisdiction would impose a civil or criminal penalty on the taxpayer (or any other person) for disclosing the required information is not reasonable cause.

* * *

[Sec. 6679]

SEC. 6679. FAILURE TO FILE RETURNS, ETC., WITH RESPECT TO FOREIGN CORPORATIONS OR FOREIGN PARTNERSHIPS.

[Sec. 6679(a)]

(a) CIVIL PENALTY.—

(1) IN GENERAL.—In addition to any criminal penalty provided by law, any person required to file a return under section 6046 and [or] 6046A who fails to file such return at the time provided in such section, or who files a return which does not show the information

required pursuant to such section, shall pay a penalty of $10,000, unless it is shown that such failure is due to reasonable cause.

(2) INCREASE IN PENALTY WHERE FAILURE CONTINUES AFTER NOTIFICATION.—If any failure described in paragraph (1) continues for more than 90 days after the day on which the Secretary mails notice of such failure to the United States person, such person shall pay a penalty (in addition to the amount required under paragraph (1)) of $10,000 for each 30-day period (or fraction thereof) during which such failure continues after the expiration of such 90-day period. The increase in any penalty under this paragraph shall not exceed $50,000.

* * *

[Sec. 6686]

SEC. 6686. FAILURE TO FILE RETURNS OR SUPPLY INFORMATION BY DISC OR FSC.

In addition to the penalty imposed by section 7203 (relating to willful failure to file return, supply information, or pay tax) any person required to supply information or to file a return under section 6011(c) who fails to supply such information or file such return at the time prescribed by the Secretary, or who files a return which does not show the information required, shall pay a penalty of $100 for each failure to supply information (but the total amount imposed on the delinquent person for all such failures during any calendar year shall not exceed $25,000) or a penalty of $1,000 for each failure to file a return, unless it is shown that such failure is due to reasonable cause.

[Sec. 6688]

SEC. 6688. ASSESSABLE PENALTIES WITH RESPECT TO INFORMATION REQUIRED TO BE FURNISHED UNDER SECTION 7654.

In addition to any criminal penalty provided by law, any person described in section 7654(a) who is required under section 937(c) or by regulations prescribed under section 7654 to furnish information and who fails to comply with such requirement at the time prescribed by such regulations, unless it is shown that such failure is due to reasonable cause and not to willful neglect, shall pay (upon notice and demand by the Secretary and in the same manner as tax) a penalty of $1,000 for each such failure.

[Sec. 6689]

SEC. 6689. FAILURE TO FILE NOTICE OF REDETERMINATION OF FOREIGN TAX.

[Sec. 6689(a)]

(a) CIVIL PENALTY.—If the taxpayer fails to notify the Secretary (on or before the date prescribed by regulations for giving such notice) of foreign tax redetermination, unless it is shown that such failure is due to reasonable cause and not due to willful neglect, there shall be added to the deficiency attributable to such redetermination an amount (not in excess of 25 percent of the deficiency) determined as follows—

(1) 5 percent of the deficiency if the failure is for not more than 1 month, with

(2) an additional 5 percent of the deficiency for each month (or fraction thereof) during which the failure continues.

[Sec. 6689(b)]

(b) FOREIGN TAX REDETERMINATION DEFINED.—For purposes of this section, the term "foreign tax redetermination" means any redetermination for which a notice is required under subsection (c) of section 905 or paragraph (2) of section 404A(g).

[Sec. 6712]

SEC. 6712. FAILURE TO DISCLOSE TREATY-BASED RETURN POSITIONS.

[Sec. 6712(a)]

(a) GENERAL RULE.—If a taxpayer fails to meet the requirements of section 6114, there is hereby imposed a penalty equal to $1000 ($10,000 in the case of a C corporation) on each such failure.

Crimes

[Sec. 6712(b)]

(b) AUTHORITY TO WAIVE.—The Secretary may waive all or any part of the penalty provided by this section on a showing by the taxpayer that there was reasonable cause for the failure and that the taxpayer acted in good faith.

[Sec. 6712(c)]

(c) PENALTY IN ADDITION TO OTHER PENALTIES.—The penalty imposed by this section shall be in addition to any other penalty imposed by law.

CHAPTER 70—JEOPARDY, RECEIVERSHIPS, ETC.

SUBCHAPTER A—JEOPARDY

PART I—TERMINATION OF TAXABLE YEAR

[Sec. 6851]

SEC. 6851. TERMINATION ASSESSMENTS OF INCOME TAX.

* * *

[Sec. 6851(d)]

(d) DEPARTURE OF ALIEN.—Subject to such exceptions as may, by regulations, be prescribed by the Secretary—

(1) No alien shall depart from the United States unless he first procures from the Secretary a certificate that he has complied with all the obligations imposed upon him by the income tax laws.

(2) Payment of taxes shall not be enforced by any proceedings under the provisions of this section prior to the expiration of the time otherwise allowed for paying such taxes if, in the case of an alien about to depart from the United States, the Secretary determines that the collection of the tax will not be jeopardized by the departure of the alien.

* * *

CHAPTER 75—CRIMES, OTHER OFFENSES, AND FORFEITURES

SUBCHAPTER A—CRIMES

PART I—GENERAL PROVISIONS

⇛ *Caution: A larger fine may be imposed with respect to Code Sec. 7201 under 18 U.S.C. §3571.*

[Sec. 7201]

SEC. 7201. ATTEMPT TO EVADE OR DEFEAT TAX.

Any person who willfully attempts in any manner to evade or defeat any tax imposed by this title or the payment thereof shall, in addition to other penalties provided by law, be guilty of a felony and, upon conviction thereof, shall be fined not more than $100,000 ($500,000 in the case of a corporation), or imprisoned not more than 5 years, or both, together with the costs of prosecution.

⇛ *Caution: A larger fine may be imposed with respect to Code Sec. 7202 under 18 U.S.C. §3571.*

[Sec. 7202]

SEC. 7202. WILLFUL FAILURE TO COLLECT OR PAY OVER TAX.

Any person required under this title to collect, account for, and pay over any tax imposed by this title who willfully fails to collect or truthfully account for and pay over such tax shall, in addition to other penalties provided by law, be guilty of a felony and, upon conviction thereof, shall be fined not more than $10,000, or imprisoned not more than 5 years, or both, together with the costs of prosecution.

[Sec. 7203]

SEC. 7203. WILLFUL FAILURE TO FILE RETURN, SUPPLY INFORMATION, OR PAY TAX.

Any person required under this title to pay any estimated tax or tax, or required by this title or by regulations made under authority thereof to make a return, keep any records, or supply any information, who willfully fails to pay such estimated tax or tax, make such return, keep such records, or supply such information, at the time or times required by law or regulations, shall, in addition to other penalties provided by law, be guilty of a misdemeanor and, upon conviction thereof, shall be fined not more than $25,000 ($100,000 in the case of a corporation), or imprisoned not more than 1 year, or both, together with the costs of prosecution. In the case of any person with respect to whom there is a failure to pay any estimated tax, this section shall not apply to such person with respect to such failure if there is no addition to tax under section 6654 or 6655 with respect to such failure. In the case of a willful violation of any provision of section 6050 I, the first sentence of this section shall be applied by substituting "felony" for "misdemeanor" and "5 years" for "1 year".

CHAPTER 78—DISCOVERY OF LIABILITY AND ENFORCEMENT OF TITLE

SUBCHAPTER D—POSSESSIONS

[Sec. 7654]

SEC. 7654. COORDINATION OF UNITED STATES AND CERTAIN POSSESSION INDIVIDUAL INCOME TAXES.

[Sec. 7654(a)]

(a) GENERAL RULE.—The net collection of taxes imposed by chapter 1 for each taxable year with respect to an individual to whom section 931 or 932(c) applies shall be covered into the Treasury of the specified possession of which such individual is a bona fide resident.

[Sec. 7654(b)]

(b) DEFINITION AND SPECIAL RULE.—For purposes of this section—

(1) NET COLLECTION.—In determining net collections for a taxable year, an appropriate adjustment shall be made for credits allowed against the tax liability and refunds made of income taxes for the taxable year.

(2) SPECIFIED POSSESSION.—The term "specified possession" means Guam, American Samoa, the Northern Mariana Islands, and the Virgin Islands.

[Sec. 7654(c)]

(c) TRANSFERS.—The transfers of funds between the United States and any specified possession required by this section shall be made not less frequently than annually.

[Sec. 7654(d)]

(d) FEDERAL PERSONNEL.—In addition to the amount determined under subsection (a), the United States shall pay to each specified possession at such times and in such manner as determined by the Secretary—

(1) the amount of the taxes deducted and withheld by the United States under chapter 24 with respect to compensation paid to members of the Armed Forces who are stationed in such possession but who have no income tax liability to such possession with respect to such compensation by reason of the Servicemembers Civil Relief Act (50 App. U.S.C. 501 et seq.), and

(2) the amount of the taxes deducted and withheld under chapter 24 with respect to amounts paid for services performed as an employee of the United States (or any agency thereof) in a specified possession with respect to an individual unless section 931 or 932(c) applies.

[Sec. 7654(e)]

(e) REGULATIONS.—The Secretary shall prescribe such regulations as may be necessary to carry out the provisions of this section and sections 931 and 932, including regulations prohibiting

CHAPTER 79—DEFINITIONS

[Sec. 7701]

SEC. 7701. DEFINITIONS.

[Sec. 7701(a)]

* * *

(1) PERSON.—The term "person" shall be construed to mean and include an individual, a trust, estate, partnership, association, company or corporation.

(2) PARTNERSHIP AND PARTNER.—The term "partnership" includes a syndicate, group, pool, joint venture, or other unincorporated organization, through or by means of which any business, financial operation, or venture is carried on, and which is not, within the meaning of this title, a trust or estate or a corporation; and the term "partner" includes a member in such a syndicate, group, pool, joint venture, or organization.

(3) CORPORATION.—The term "corporation" includes associations, joint-stock companies, and insurance companies.

(4) DOMESTIC.—The term "domestic" when applied to a corporation or partnership means created or organized in the United States or under the law of the United States or of any State unless, in the case of a partnership, the Secretary provides otherwise by regulations.

(5) FOREIGN.—The term "foreign" when applied to a corporation or partnership means a corporation or partnership which is not domestic.

* * *

(9) UNITED STATES.—The term "United States" when used in a geographical sense includes only the States and the District of Columbia.

(10) STATE.—The term "State" shall be construed to include the District of Columbia, where such construction is necessary to carry out provisions of this title.

* * *

(18) INTERNATIONAL ORGANIZATION.—The term "international organization" means a public international organization entitled to enjoy privileges, exemptions, and immunities as an international organization under the International Organizations Immunities Act (22 U. S. C. 288-288f).

* * *

(23) TAXABLE YEAR.—The term "taxable year" means the calendar year, or the fiscal year ending during such calendar year, upon the basis of which the taxable income is computed under subtitle A. "Taxable year" means, in the case of a return made for a fractional part of a year under the provisions of subtitle A or under regulations prescribed by the Secretary, the period for which such return is made.

(24) FISCAL YEAR.—The term "fiscal year" means an accounting period of 12 months ending on the last day of any month other than December.

* * *

(30) UNITED STATES PERSON.—The term "United States person" means—
    (A) a citizen or resident of the United States,
    (B) a domestic partnership,
    (C) a domestic corporation,
    (D) any estate (other than a foreign estate, within the meaning of paragraph (31)), and
    (E) any trust if—

(i) a court within the United States is able to exercise primary supervision over the administration of the trust, and

(ii) one or more United States persons have the authority to control all substantial decisions of the trust.

(31) FOREIGN ESTATE OR TRUST.—

(A) FOREIGN ESTATE.—The term "foreign estate" means an estate the income of which, from sources without the United States which is not effectively connected with the conduct of a trade or business within the United States, is not includible in gross income under subtitle A.

(B) FOREIGN TRUST.—The term "foreign trust" means any trust other than a trust described in subparagraph (E) of paragraph (30).

* * *

(39) PERSONS RESIDING OUTSIDE UNITED STATES.—If any citizen or resident of the United States does not reside in (and is not found in) any United States judicial district, such citizen or resident shall be treated as residing in the District of Columbia for purposes of any provision of this title relating to—

(A) jurisdiction of courts, or

(B) enforcement of summons.

* * *

[Sec. 7701(b)]

(b) DEFINITION OF RESIDENT ALIEN AND NONRESIDENT ALIEN.—

(1) IN GENERAL.—For purposes of this title (other than subtitle B)—

(A) RESIDENT ALIEN.—An alien individual shall be treated as a resident of the United States with respect to any calendar year if (and only if) such individual meets the requirements of clause (i), (ii), or (iii):

(i) LAWFULLY ADMITTED FOR PERMANENT RESIDENCE.—Such individual is a lawful permanent resident of the United States at any time during such calendar year.

(ii) SUBSTANTIAL PRESENCE TEST.—Such individual meets the substantial presence test of paragraph (3).

(iii) FIRST YEAR ELECTION.—Such individual makes the election provided in paragraph (4).

(B) NONRESIDENT ALIEN.—An individual is a nonresident alien if such individual is neither a citizen of the United States nor a resident of the United States (within the meaning of subparagraph (A)).

(2) SPECIAL RULES FOR FIRST AND LAST YEAR OF RESIDENCY.—

(A) FIRST YEAR OF RESIDENCY.—

(i) IN GENERAL.—If an alien individual is a resident of the United States under paragraph (1)(A) with respect to any calendar year, but was not a resident of the United States at any time during the preceding calendar year, such alien individual shall be treated as a resident of the United States only for the portion of such calendar year which begins on the residency starting date.

(ii) RESIDENCY STARTING DATE FOR INDIVIDUALS LAWFULLY ADMITTED FOR PERMANENT RESIDENCE.—In the case of an individual who is a lawfully permanent resident of the United States at any time during the calendar year, but does not meet the substantial presence test of paragraph (3), the residency starting date shall be the first day in such calendar year on which he was present in the United States while a lawful permanent resident of the United States.

(iii) RESIDENCY STARTING DATE FOR INDIVIDUALS MEETING SUBSTANTIAL PRESENCE TEST.—In the case of an individual who meets the substantial presence test of paragraph (3) with respect to any calendar year, the residency starting date shall be the first day during such calendar year on which the individual is present in the United States.

(iv) RESIDENCY STARTING DATE FOR INDIVIDUALS MAKING FIRST YEAR ELECTION.—In the case of an individual who makes the election provided by paragraph (4) with respect to any calendar year, the residency starting date shall be the 1st day during such calendar year on which the individual is treated as a resident of the United States under that paragraph.

(B) LAST YEAR OF RESIDENCY.—An alien individual shall not be treated as a resident of the United States during a portion of any calendar year if—

(i) such portion is after the last day in such calendar year on which the individual was present in the United States (or, in the case of an individual described in paragraph (1)(A)(i), the last day on which he was so described),

(ii) during such portion the individual has a closer connection to a foreign country than to the United States, and

(iii) the individual is not a resident of the United States at any time during the next calendar year.

(C) CERTAIN NOMINAL PRESENCE DISREGARDED.—

(i) IN GENERAL.—For purposes of subparagraphs (A)(iii) and (B), an individual shall not be treated as present in the United States during any period for which the individual establishes that he has a closer connection to a foreign country than to the United States.

(ii) NOT MORE THAN 10 DAYS DISREGARDED.—Clause (i) shall not apply to more than 10 days on which the individual is present in the United States.

(3) SUBSTANTIAL PRESENCE TEST.—

(A) IN GENERAL.—Except as otherwise provided in this paragraph, an individual meets the substantial presence test of this paragraph with respect to any calendar year (hereinafter in this subsection referred to as the "current year") if—

(i) such individual was present in the United States on at least 31 days during the calendar year, and

(ii) the sum of the number of days on which such individual was present in the United States during the current year and the 2 preceding calendar years (when multiplied by the applicable multiplier determined under the following table) equals or exceeds 183 days:

In the case of days in:	The applicable multiplier is:
Current year	1
1st preceding year	$1/3$
2nd preceding year	$1/6$

(B) EXCEPTION WHERE INDIVIDUAL IS PRESENT IN THE UNITED STATES DURING LESS THAN ONE-HALF OF CURRENT YEAR AND CLOSER CONNECTION TO FOREIGN COUNTRY IS ESTABLISHED.—An individual shall not be treated as meeting the substantial presence test of this paragraph with respect to any current year if—

(i) such individual is present in the United States on fewer than 183 days during the current year, and

(ii) it is established that for the current year such individual has a tax home (as defined in section 911(d)(3) without regard to the second sentence thereof) in a foreign country and has a closer connection to such foreign country than to the United States.

(C) SUBPARAGRAPH (B) NOT TO APPLY IN CERTAIN CASES.—Subparagraph (B) shall not apply to any individual with respect to any current year if at any time during such year—

(i) such individual had an application for adjustment of status pending, or

(ii) such individual took other steps to apply for status as a lawful permanent resident of the United States.

(D) EXCEPTION FOR EXEMPT INDIVIDUALS OR FOR CERTAIN MEDICAL CONDITIONS.—An individual shall not be treated as being present in the United States on any day if—

(i) such individual is an exempt individual for such day, or

(ii) such individual was unable to leave the United States on such day because of a medical condition which arose while such individual was present in the United States.

(4) FIRST-YEAR ELECTION.—

(A) An alien individual shall be deemed to meet the requirements of this subparagraph if such individual—

(i) is not a resident of the United States under clause (i) or (ii) of paragraph (1)(A) with respect to a calendar year (hereinafter referred to as the "election year"),

(ii) was not a resident of the United States under paragraph (1)(A) with respect to the calendar year immediately preceding the election year,

(iii) is a resident of the United States under clause (ii) of paragraph (1)(A) with respect to the calendar year immediately following the election year, and

(iv) is both—

(I) present in the United States for a period of at least 31 consecutive days in the election year, and

(II) present in the United States during the period beginning with the first day of such 31-day period and ending with the last day of the election year (hereinafter referred to as the "testing period") for a number of days equal to or exceeding 75 percent of the number of days in the testing period (provided that an individual shall be treated for purposes of this subclause as present in the United States for a number of days during the testing period not exceeding 5 days in the aggregate, notwithstanding his absence from the United States on such days).

(B) An alien individual who meets the requirements of subparagraph (A) shall, if he so elects, be treated as a resident of the United States with respect to the election year.

(C) An alien individual who makes the election provided by subparagraph (B) shall be treated as a resident of the United States for the portion of the election year which begins on the 1st day of the earliest testing period during such year with respect to which the individual meets the requirements of clause (iv) of subparagraph (A).

(D) The rules of subparagraph (D)(i) of paragraph (3) shall apply for purposes of determining an individual's presence in the United States under this paragraph.

(E) An election under subparagraph (B) shall be made on the individual's tax return for the election year, provided that such election may not be made before the individual has met the substantial presence test of paragraph (3) with respect to the calendar year immediately following the election year.

(F) An election once made under subparagraph (B) remains in effect for the election year, unless revoked with the consent of the Secretary.

(5) EXEMPT INDIVIDUAL DEFINED.—For purposes of this subsection—

(A) IN GENERAL.—An individual is an exempt individual for any day if, for such day, such individual is—

(i) a foreign government-related individual,

(ii) a teacher or trainee,

(iii) a student, or

(iv) a professional athlete who is temporarily in the United States to compete in a charitable sports event described in section 274(l)(1)(B).

(B) FOREIGN GOVERNMENT-RELATED INDIVIDUAL.—The term "foreign government-related individual" means any individual temporarily present in the United States by reason of—

(i) diplomatic status, or a visa which the Secretary (after consultation with the Secretary of State) determines represents full-time diplomatic or consular status for purposes of this subsection,

(ii) being a full-time employee of an international organization, or

(iii) being a member of the immediate family of an individual described in clause (i) or (ii).

(C) TEACHER OR TRAINEE.—The term "teacher or trainee" means any individual—

(i) who is temporarily present in the United States under subparagraph (J) or (Q) of section 101(15) of the Immigration and Nationality Act (other than as a student), and

(ii) who substantially complies with the requirements for being so present.

(D) STUDENT.—The term "student" means any individual—

(i) who is temporarily present in the United States—

(I) under subparagraph (F) or (M) of section 101(15) of the Immigration and Nationality Act, or

(II) as a student under subparagraph (J) or (Q) of such section 101(15), and

(ii) who substantially complies with the requirements for being so present.

(E) SPECIAL RULES FOR TEACHERS, TRAINEES, AND STUDENTS.—

(i) LIMITATION ON TEACHERS AND TRAINEES.—An individual shall not be treated as an exempt individual by reason of clause (ii) of subparagraph (A) for the current year if, for any 2 calendar years during the preceding 6 calendar years, such person was an exempt person under clause (ii) or (iii) of subparagraph (A). In the case of an individual all of whose compensation is described in section 872(b)(3), the preceding sentence shall be applied by substituting "4 calendar years" for "2 calendar years".

(ii) LIMITATION ON STUDENTS.—For any calendar year after the 5th calendar year for which an individual was an exempt individual under clause (ii) or (iii) of subparagraph (A), such individual shall not be treated as an exempt individual by reason of clause (iii) of subparagraph (A), unless such individual establishes to the satisfaction of the Secretary that such individual does not intend to permanently reside in the United States and that such individual meets the requirements of subparagraph (D)(ii).

(6) LAWFUL PERMANENT RESIDENT.—For purposes of this subsection, an individual is a lawful permanent resident of the United States at any time if—

(A) such individual has the status of having been lawfully accorded the privilege of residing permanently in the United States as an immigrant in accordance with the immigration laws, and

(B) such status has not been revoked (and has not been administratively or judicially determined to have been abandoned).

(7) PRESENCE IN THE UNITED STATES.—For purposes of this subsection—

(A) IN GENERAL.—Except as provided in subparagraph (B), (C), or (D) an individual shall be treated as present in the United States on any day if such individual is physically present in the United States at any time during such day.

(B) COMMUTERS FROM CANADA OR MEXICO.—If an individual regularly commutes to employment (or self-employment) in the United States from a place of residence in Canada or Mexico, such individual shall not be treated as present in the United States on any day during which he so commutes.

(C) TRANSIT BETWEEN 2 FOREIGN POINTS.—If an individual, who is in transit between 2 points outside the United States, is physically present in the United States for less than 24 hours, such individual shall not be treated as present in the United States on any day during such transit.

(D) CREW MEMBERS TEMPORARILY PRESENT.—An individual who is temporarily present in the United States on any day as a regular member of the crew of a foreign vessel engaged in transportation between the United States and a foreign country or a possession of the United States shall not be treated as present in the United States on such day unless such individual otherwise engages in any trade or business in the United States on such day.

(8) ANNUAL STATEMENTS.—The Secretary may prescribe regulations under which an individual who (but for subparagraph (B) or (D) of paragraph (3)) would meet the substantial presence test of paragraph (3) is required to submit an annual statement setting forth the basis on which such individual claims the benefits of subparagraph (B) or (D) of paragraph (3), as the case may be.

(9) TAXABLE YEAR.—

(A) IN GENERAL.—For purposes of this title, an alien individual who has not established a taxable year for any prior period shall be treated as having a taxable year which is the calendar year.

(B) FISCAL YEAR TAXPAYER.—If—

(i) an individual is treated under paragraph (1) as a resident of the United States for any calendar year, and

(ii) after the application of subparagraph (A), such individual has a taxable year other than a calendar year,

he shall be treated as a resident of the United States with respect to any portion of a taxable year which is within such calendar year.

(10) COORDINATION WITH SECTION 877.—If—

(A) an alien individual was treated as a resident of the United States during any period which includes at least 3 consecutive calendar years (hereinafter referred to as the "initial residency period"), and

(B) such individual ceases to be treated as a resident of the United States but subsequently becomes a resident of the United States before the close of the 3rd calendar year beginning after the close of the initial residency period,

such individual shall be taxable for the period after the close of the initial residency period and before the day on which he subsequently became a resident of the United States in the manner provided in section 877(b). The preceding sentence shall apply only if the tax imposed pursuant to section 877(b) exceeds the tax which, without regard to this paragraph, is imposed pursuant to section 871.

(11) REGULATIONS.—The Secretary shall prescribe such regulations as may be necessary or appropriate to carry out the purposes of this subsection.

* * *

[Sec. 7701(d)]

(d) COMMONWEALTH OF PUERTO RICO.—Where not otherwise distinctly expressed or manifestly incompatible with the intent thereof, references in this title to possessions of the United States shall be treated as also referring to the Commonwealth of Puerto Rico.

* * *

[Sec. 7701(l)]

(l) REGULATIONS RELATING TO CONDUIT ARRANGEMENTS.—The Secretary may prescribe regulations recharacterizing any multiple-party financing transaction as a transaction directly among any 2 or more of such parties where the Secretary determines that such recharacterization is appropriate to prevent avoidance of any tax imposed by this title.

* * *

[Sec. 7701(n)]

(n) SPECIAL RULES FOR DETERMINING WHEN AN INDIVIDUAL IS NO LONGER A UNITED STATES CITIZEN OR LONG-TERM RESIDENT.—An individual who would (but for this subsection) cease to be treated as a citizen or resident of the United States shall continue to be treated as a citizen or resident of the United States, as the case may be, until such individual—

(1) gives notice of an expatriating act or termination of residency (with the requisite intent to relinquish citizenship or terminate residency) to the Secretary of State or the Secretary of Homeland Security, and

(2) provides a statement in accordance with section 6039G.

* * *

CHAPTER 80—GENERAL RULES

SUBCHAPTER B—EFFECTIVE DATE AND RELATED PROVISIONS

[Sec. 7852]

SEC. 7852. OTHER APPLICABLE RULES.

* * *

[Sec. 7852(d)]

(d) TREATY OBLIGATIONS.—

(1) IN GENERAL.—For purposes of determining the relationship between a provision of a treaty and any law of the United States affecting revenue, neither the treaty nor the law shall have preferential status by reason of its being a treaty or law.

(2) SAVINGS CLAUSE FOR 1954 TREATIES.—No provision of this title (as in effect without regard to any amendment thereto enacted after August 16, 1954) shall apply in any case where its application would be contrary to any treaty obligation of the United States in effect on August 16, 1954.

* * *

SUBCHAPTER C—PROVISIONS AFFECTING MORE THAN ONE SUBTITLE

[Sec. 7874]

SEC. 7874. RULES RELATING TO EXPATRIATED ENTITIES AND THEIR FOREIGN PARENTS.

[Sec. 7874(a)]

(a) TAX ON INVERSION GAIN OF EXPATRIATED ENTITIES.—

(1) IN GENERAL.—The taxable income of an expatriated entity for any taxable year which includes any portion of the applicable period shall in no event be less than the inversion gain of the entity for the taxable year.

(2) EXPATRIATED ENTITY.—For purposes of this subsection—

(A) IN GENERAL.—The term "expatriated entity" means—

(i) the domestic corporation or partnership referred to in subparagraph (B)(i) with respect to which a foreign corporation is a surrogate foreign corporation, and

(ii) any United States person who is related (within the meaning of section 267(b) or 707(b)(1)) to a domestic corporation or partnership described in clause (i).

(B) SURROGATE FOREIGN CORPORATION.—A foreign corporation shall be treated as a surrogate foreign corporation if, pursuant to a plan (or a series of related transactions)—

(i) the entity completes after March 4, 2003, the direct or indirect acquisition of substantially all of the properties held directly or indirectly by a domestic corporation or substantially all of the properties constituting a trade or business of a domestic partnership,

(ii) after the acquisition at least 60 percent of the stock (by vote or value) of the entity is held—

(I) in the case of an acquisition with respect to a domestic corporation, by former shareholders of the domestic corporation by reason of holding stock in the domestic corporation, or

(II) in the case of an acquisition with respect to a domestic partnership, by former partners of the domestic partnership by reason of holding a capital or profits interest in the domestic partnership, and

(iii) after the acquisition the expanded affiliated group which includes the entity does not have substantial business activities in the foreign country in which, or under the law of which, the entity is created or organized, when compared to the total business activities of such expanded affiliated group.

An entity otherwise described in clause (i) with respect to any domestic corporation or partnership trade or business shall be treated as not so described if, on or before March 4, 2003, such entity acquired directly or indirectly more than half of the properties held directly or indirectly by such corporation or more than half of the properties constituting such partnership trade or business, as the case may be.

(3) COORDINATION WITH SUBSECTION (b).—Paragraph (1) shall not apply to any entity which is treated as a domestic corporation under subsection (b).

[Sec. 7874(b)]

(b) INVERTED CORPORATIONS TREATED AS DOMESTIC CORPORATIONS.—Notwithstanding section 7701(a)(4), a foreign corporation shall be treated for purposes of this title as a domestic corporation if such corporation would be a surrogate foreign corporation if subsection (a)(2) were applied by substituting "80 percent" for "60 percent".

[Sec. 7874(c)]

(c) DEFINITIONS AND SPECIAL RULES.—

(1) EXPANDED AFFILIATED GROUP.—The term "expanded affiliated group" means an affiliated group as defined in section 1504(a) but without regard to section 1504(b)(3), except that section 1504(a) shall be applied by substituting "more than 50 percent" for "at least 80 percent" each place it appears.

(2) CERTAIN STOCK DISREGARDED.—There shall not be taken into account in determining ownership under subsection (a)(2)(B)(ii)—

(A) stock held by members of the expanded affiliated group which includes the foreign corporation, or

(B) stock of such foreign corporation which is sold in a public offering related to the acquisition described in subsection (a)(2)(B)(i).

(3) PLAN DEEMED IN CERTAIN CASES.—If a foreign corporation acquires directly or indirectly substantially all of the properties of a domestic corporation or partnership during the 4-year period beginning on the date which is 2 years before the ownership requirements of subsection (a)(2)(B)(ii) are met, such actions shall be treated as pursuant to a plan.

(4) CERTAIN TRANSFERS DISREGARDED.—The transfer of properties or liabilities (including by contribution or distribution) shall be disregarded if such transfers are part of a plan a principal purpose of which is to avoid the purposes of this section.

(5) SPECIAL RULE FOR RELATED PARTNERSHIPS.—For purposes of applying subsection (a)(2)(B)(ii) to the acquisition of a trade or business of a domestic partnership, except as provided in regulations, all partnerships which are under common control (within the meaning of section 482) shall be treated as 1 partnership.

(6) REGULATIONS.—The Secretary shall prescribe such regulations as may be appropriate to determine whether a corporation is a surrogate foreign corporation, including regulations—

(A) to treat warrants, options, contracts to acquire stock, convertible debt interests, and other similar interests as stock, and

(B) to treat stock as not stock.

[Sec. 7874(d)]

(d) OTHER DEFINITIONS.—For purposes of this section—

(1) APPLICABLE PERIOD.—The term "applicable period" means the period—

(A) beginning on the first date properties are acquired as part of the acquisition described in subsection (a)(2)(B)(i), and

(B) ending on the date which is 10 years after the last date properties are acquired as part of such acquisition.

(2) INVERSION GAIN.—The term "inversion gain" means the income or gain recognized by reason of the transfer during the applicable period of stock or other properties by an expatriated entity, and any income received or accrued during the applicable period by reason of a license of any property by an expatriated entity—

(A) as part of the acquisition described in subsection (a)(2)(B)(i), or

(B) after such acquisition if the transfer or license is to a foreign related person.

Subparagraph (B) shall not apply to property described in section 1221(a)(1) in the hands of the expatriated entity.

(3) FOREIGN RELATED PERSON.—The term "foreign related person" means, with respect to any expatriated entity, a foreign person which—

(A) is related (within the meaning of section 267(b) or 707(b)(1)) to such entity, or

(B) is under the same common control (within the meaning of section 482) as such entity.

[Sec. 7874(e)]

(e) SPECIAL RULES.—

(1) CREDITS NOT ALLOWED AGAINST TAX ON INVERSION GAIN.—Credits (other than the credit allowed by section 901) shall be allowed against the tax imposed by this chapter on an expatriated entity for any taxable year described in subsection (a) only to the extent such tax exceeds the product of—

(A) the amount of the inversion gain for the taxable year, and

(B) the highest rate of tax specified in section 11(b)(1).

For purposes of determining the credit allowed by section 901, inversion gain shall be treated as from sources within the United States.

(2) SPECIAL RULES FOR PARTNERSHIPS.—In the case of an expatriated entity which is a partnership—

(A) subsection (a)(1) shall apply at the partner rather than the partnership level,

(B) the inversion gain of any partner for any taxable year shall be equal to the sum of—

(i) the partner's distributive share of inversion gain of the partnership for such taxable year, plus

(ii) gain recognized for the taxable year by the partner by reason of the transfer during the applicable period of any partnership interest of the partner in such partnership to the surrogate foreign corporation, and

(C) the highest rate of tax specified in the rate schedule applicable to the partner under this chapter shall be substituted for the rate of tax referred to in paragraph (1).

(3) COORDINATION WITH SECTION 172 AND MINIMUM TAX.—Rules similar to the rules of paragraphs (3) and (4) of section 860E(a) shall apply for purposes of subsection (a).

(4) STATUTE OF LIMITATIONS.—

(A) IN GENERAL.—The statutory period for the assessment of any deficiency attributable to the inversion gain of any taxpayer for any pre-inversion year shall not expire before the expiration of 3 years from the date the Secretary is notified by the taxpayer (in such manner as the Secretary may prescribe) of the acquisition described in subsection (a)(2)(B)(i) to which such gain relates and such deficiency may be assessed before the expiration of such 3-year period notwithstanding the provisions of any other law or rule of law which would otherwise prevent such assessment.

(B) PRE-INVERSION YEAR.—For purposes of subparagraph (A), the term "pre-inversion year" means any taxable year if—

(i) any portion of the applicable period is included in such taxable year, and

(ii) such year ends before the taxable year in which the acquisition described in subsection (a)(2)(B)(i) is completed.

[Sec. 7874(f)]

(f) SPECIAL RULE FOR TREATIES.—Nothing in section 894 or 7852(d) or in any other provision of law shall be construed as permitting an exemption, by reason of any treaty obligation of the United States heretofore or hereafter entered into, from the provisions of this section.

[Sec. 7874(g)]

(g) REGULATIONS.—The Secretary shall provide such regulations as are necessary to carry out this section, including regulations providing for such adjustments to the application of this section as are necessary to prevent the avoidance of the purposes of this section, including the avoidance of such purposes through—

(1) the use of related persons, pass-through or other noncorporate entities, or other intermediaries, or

(2) transactions designed to have persons cease to be (or not become) members of expanded affiliated groups or related persons.

Income Tax Regulations

Tax on Individuals

§ 1.1-1. Income tax on individuals.—

* * *

(b) *Citizens or residents of the United States liable to tax.*—In general, all citizens of the United States, wherever resident, and all resident alien individuals are liable to the income taxes imposed by the Code whether the income is received from sources within or without the United States. Pursuant to section 876, a nonresident alien individual who is a bona fide resident of Puerto Rico during the entire taxable year is, except as provided in section 933 with respect to Puerto Rican source income, subject to taxation in the same manner as a resident alien individual. As to tax on nonresident alien individuals, see sections 871 and 877.

(c) *Who is a citizen.*—Every person born or naturalized in the United States and subject to its jurisdiction is a citizen. For other rules governing the acquisition of citizenship, see chapters 1 and 2 of title III of the Immigration and Nationality Act (8 U.S.C. 1401-1459). For rules governing loss of citizenship, see sections 349 to 357, inclusive, of such Act (8 U.S.C. 1481-1489), *Schneider v. Rusk,* (1964) 377 U.S. 163, and Rev. Rul. 70-506, C.B. 1970-2, 1. For rules pertaining to persons who are nationals but not citizens at birth, e.g., a person born in American Samoa, see section 308 of such Act (8 U.S.C. 1408). For special rules applicable to certain expatriates who have lost citizenship with a principal purpose of avoiding certain taxes, see section 877. A foreigner who has filed his declaration of intention of becoming a citizen but who has not yet been admitted to citizenship by a final order of a naturalization court is an alien. [Reg. § 1.1-1.]

☐ [*T.D.* 6161, 2-3-56. *Amended by T.D.* 7117, 5-24-71, *and T.D.* 7332, 12-20-74.]

Tax on Corporations

§ 1.11-1. Tax on corporations.— (a) Every corporation, foreign or domestic, is liable to the tax imposed under section 11 except (1) corporations specifically excepted under such section from such tax: (2) corporations expressly exempt from all taxation under subtitle A of the Code (see section 501); and (3) corporations subject to tax under section 511(a). For taxable years beginning after December 31, 1966, foreign corporations engaged in trade or business in the United States shall be taxable under section 11 only on their taxable income which is effectively connected with the conduct of a trade or business in the United States (see section 882(a)(1)). For definition of the terms "corporations," "domestic," and "foreign," see section 7701(a)(3), (4), and (5), respectively. It is immaterial that a domestic corporation, and for taxable years beginning after December 31, 1966, a foreign corporation engaged in trade or business in the United States, which is subject to the tax imposed by section 11 may derive no income from sources within the United States. The tax imposed by section 11 is payable upon the basis of the returns rendered by the corporations liable thereto, except that in some cases a tax is to be paid at the source of the income. See subchapter A (sections 6001 and following), chapter 61 of the Code, and section 1442.

* * *

[Reg. § 1.11-1.]

☐ [*T.D.* 6161, 2-3-56. *Amended by T.D.* 6237, 6-10-57; *T.D.* 6350, 1-6-59; *T.D.* 6407, 8-14-59; *T.D.* 6610, 8-30-62; *T.D.* 6681, 10-16-63, *T.D.* 7100, 3-19-71, *T.D.* 7181, 4-24-72, *T.D.* 7293, 11-27-73 *and T.D.* 7413, 3-25-76.]

Items Specifically Included in Gross Income

§ 1.78-1. Dividends received from certain foreign corporations by certain domestic corporations choosing the foreign tax credit.—(a) *Taxes deemed paid by certain domestic corporations treated as a section 78 dividend.*—If a domestic corporation chooses to have the benefits of the foreign tax credit under section 901 for any taxable year, an amount which is equal to the foreign income taxes deemed to be paid by such corporation for such year under section 902(a) in accordance with §§ 1.902-1 and 1.902-2, or under section 960(a)(1) in accordance with § 1.960-7, shall, to the extent provided by this section, be treated as a dividend (hereinafter referred to as a section 78 dividend) received by such domestic corporation from the foreign corporation described in section 902(a) in accordance with §§ 1.902-1 and 1.902-2 or section 960(a)(1) in accordance with § 1.960-7, as the case may be. Any reduction under section 907(a) of the foreign income taxes deemed to be paid with respect to foreign oil and gas extraction income does not affect the amount treated as a section 78 dividend. A section 78 dividend shall be treated as a dividend for all purposes of the Code, except that it shall not be treated as a dividend under section 245, relating to dividends received from certain foreign corporations, or increase the earnings and profits of the domestic corporation. For purposes of determining the source of a section 78 dividend in computing the limitation on the foreign tax credit under section 904, see § 1.902-1(h)(1) and the regulations under section 960. For special rules relating to the determination of the foreign tax credit under section 902 with respect to certain minimum distributions received from controlled foreign corporations and the effect of such rules upon the gross-up under section 78, see paragraph (c) of § 1.963-4. For rules respecting the reduction of foreign income taxes under section 6038(b) in applying section 902(a) in accordance with §§ 1.902-1 and 1.902-2 and section 960(a)(1) in accordance with § 1.960-7 where there has been a failure to furnish certain information and for an illustration of the effect of such reduction upon the amount of a section 78 dividend, see paragraph (1) of § 1.6038-2.

(b) *Certain taxes not treated as a section 78 dividend.*—Foreign income taxes deemed paid by a domestic corporation under section 902(a) in accordance with §§ 1.902-1 and 1.902-2 or section 960(a)(1) in accordance with § 1.960-7 shall not, to the extent provided by paragraph (b) of § 1.960-3, be treated as a section 78 dividend where such taxes are imposed on certain distributions from the earnings and profits of a controlled foreign corporation attributable to an amount which is, or has been, included in gross income of the domestic corporation under section 951.

(c) *United Kingdom income tax included in gross income under treaty.*—Any amount of United Kingdom income tax appropriate to a dividend paid by a corporation which is a resident of the United Kingdom shall not be treated as a section 78 dividend by a domestic corporation to the extent that such tax is included in the gross income of such domestic corporation in accordance with Article XIII (1) of the income tax convention between the United States and the United Kingdom, as amended by Article II of the supplementary protocol between such Governments signed on August 19, 1957 (9 UST 1331). See § 507.117 of this chapter, relating to credit against United States tax liability for income tax paid or deemed to have been paid to the United Kingdom.

(d) *Taxable year in which section 78 dividend is received.*—A section 78 dividend shall be considered received in the taxable year of a domestic corporation in which—

(1) The corporation receives the dividend by reason of which there are deemed paid under 902(a) in accordance with §§ 1.902-1 and 1.902-2 the foreign income taxes which give rise to such section 78 dividend, or

(2) The corporation includes in gross income under section 951(a) the amounts by reason of which there are deemed paid under section 960(a)(1) in accordance with § 1.960-7 the foreign income taxes which give rise to such section 78 dividend,

notwithstanding that such foreign income taxes may be carried back or carried over to another taxable year under section 904(d) and are deemed to be paid or accrued in such other taxable year.

(e) *Effective dates for the application of section 78.*—(1) *In general.*—This section shall apply to amounts of foreign income taxes deemed paid under section 902(a) in accordance with §§ 1.902-1 and 1.902-2, or under section 960(a)(1) in accordance with § 1.960-7 by reason of a distribution received by a domestic corporation—

(i) After December 31, 1964, or

(ii) Before January 1, 1965, in a taxable year of such domestic corporation beginning after December 31, 1962, but only to the extent that such distribution is made out of the accumulated profits of a foreign corporation for a taxable year of such foreign corporation beginning after December 31, 1962.

For special rules relating to determination of accumulated profits for such purposes, see regulations under section 902.

(2) *Amounts under section 951 treated as distributions.*—For purposes of this paragraph, any amount attributable to the earnings and profits for the taxable year of a first-tier corporation (as defined in paragraph (b)(1) of § 1.960-1) which is included in the gross income of a domestic corporation under section 951(a) shall be treated as a distribution received by such domestic corporation on the last day in such taxable year on which such first-tier corporation is a controlled foreign corporation.

(f) *Illustrations.*—The application of this section may be illustrated by the examples provided in § 1.902-1, § 1.904-5, § 1.960-3, § 1.960-4 and § 1.963-4. [Reg. § 1.78-1.]

☐ [*T.D.* 6805, 3-8-65. *Amended by T.D.* 7120, 6-3-71, *T.D.* 7481, 4-15-77, *T.D.* 7490, 6-10-77, *T.D.* 7649, 10-17-79 *and T.D.* 7961, 6-20-84.]

Items Specifically Excluded from Gross Income

§ 5f.103-1. Obligations issued after December 31, 1982, required to be in registered form (Temporary).—

* * *

(c) *Registered form.*—(1) *General rule.*—An obligation issued after January 20, 1987, pursuant to a binding contract entered into after January 20, 1987, is in registered form if—

(i) The obligation is registered as to both principal and any stated interest with the issuer (or its agent) and transfer of the obligation may be effected only by surrender of the old instrument and either the reissuance by the issuer of the old instrument to the new holder or the issuance by the issuer of a new instrument to the new holder,

(ii) The right to the principal of, and stated interest on, the obligation may be transferred only through a book entry system maintained by the issuer (or its agent) (as described in paragraph (c)(2) of this section), or

(iii) The obligation is registered as to both principal and any stated interest with the issuer (or its agent) and may be transferred through both of the methods described in subdivisions (i) and (ii).

(2) *Special rule for registration of a book entry obligation.*—An obligation shall be considered transferable through a book entry system if the ownership of an interest in the obligation is required to be reflected in a book entry, whether or not physical securities are issued. A book entry is a record of ownership that identifies the owner of an interest in the obligation.

* * *

[Temporary Reg. § 5f.103-1.]

☐ [*T.D.* 7852, 11-9-82. *Amended by T.D.* 8111, 12-16-86.]

Itemized Deductions for Individuals and Corporations

§ 5f.163-1. Denial of interest deduction on certain obligations issued after December 31, 1982, unless issued in registered form (temporary).—(a) *Denial of deduction generally.*—Interest paid or accrued on a registration-required obligation (as defined in paragraph (b) of this section) shall not be allowed as a deduction under section 163 or any other provision of law unless such obligation is issued in registered form (as defined in § 5f.103-1(c)).

(b) *Registration-required obligation.*—For purposes of this section, the term "registration-required obligation" means any obligation except any one of the following:

(1) An obligation issued by a natural person.

(2) An obligation not of a type offered to the public. The determination as to whether an obligation is not of a type offered to the public shall be based on whether similar obligations are in fact publicly offered or traded.

(3) An obligation that has a maturity at the date of issue of not more than 1 year.

(4) An obligation issued before January 1, 1983. An obligation first issued before January 1, 1983, shall not be considered to have been issued on or after such date merely as a result of the existence of a right on the part of the holder of such obligation to convert such obligation from registered form into bearer form, or as a result of the exercise of such a right.

(5) An obligation described in subparagraph (1) of paragraph (c) (relating to certain obligations issued to foreign persons).

(d) *Effective date.*—The provisions of this section shall apply to obligations issued after December 31, 1982, unless issued on an exercise of a warrant for the conversion of a convertible obligation if such warrant or obligation was offered or sold outside the United States without registration under the Securities Act of 1933 and was issued before August 10, 1982.

(e) *Obligations first issued after December 31, 1982, where the right exists for the holder to convert such obligation from registered form into bearer form.*—[Reserved]

(f) *Examples.*—The application of this section may be illustrated by the following examples:

Example (1). All of the shares of Corporation X are owned by two individuals, A and B. X desires to sell all of its assets to Corporation Y, all of the shares of which are owned by individual C. Following the sale, Corporation X will be completely liquidated. As partial consideration for the Corporation X assets, Corporation Y delivers a promissory note to X, secured by a security interest and mortgage on the acquired assets. The note given by Y to X is not of a type offered to the public.

Example (2). Corporation 2 has a credit agreement with Bank M pursuant to which Corporation Z may borrow amounts not exceeding $10X upon delivery of Z's note to Bank M. The note Z delivers to M is not of a type offered to the public.

Example (3). Individuals D and E operate a retail business through partnership DE. D wishes to loan partnership DE $5X. DE's note evidencing the loan from D is not of a type offered to the public.

Example (4). Individual F owns one-third of the shares of Corporation W. F makes a cash advance to W. W's note evidencing F's cash advance is not of a type offered to the public.

Example (5). Closely-held Corporation R places its convertible debentures with 30 individuals who are United States persons. The offering is not required to be registered under the Securities Act of 1933. Similar debentures are publicly offered and traded. The obligations are not considered of a type not offered to the public.

Example (6). In 1980, Corporation V issued its bonds due in 1986 through an offering registered with the Securities and Exchange Commission. Although the bonds were initially issued in registered form, the terms of the bonds permit a holder, at his option, to convert a bond into bearer form at any time prior to maturity. Similarly, a person who holds a bond in bearer form may, at any time, have the bond converted into registered form.

(i) Assume G bought one of Corporation V's bonds upon the original issuance in 1980. In 1983, G requests that V convert the bond into bearer form. Except for the change from registered to bearer form, the terms of the bond are unchanged. The bond held by G is not considered issued after December 31, 1982, under § 5f.163-1(b)(4).

(ii) Assume H buys one of Corporation V's bonds in the secondary market in 1983. The bond H receives is in registered form, but H requests that V convert the obligation into bearer form. There is no other change in the terms of the instrument. The bond held by H is not considered issued after December 31, 1982, under § 5f.163-1(b)(4).

(iii) Assume the same facts as in (ii) except that in 1984 I purchases H's V Corporation bond, which is in bearer form. I requests V to convert the bond into registered form. There is no other change in the terms of the instrument. In 1985, I requests V to convert the bond bank into bearer form. Again, there is no other change in the terms of the instrument. The bond purchased by I is not considered issued after December 31, 1982, under § 5f.163-1(b)(4).

Example (7). Corporation U wishes to make a public offering of its debentures to United States persons. U issues a master note to Bank N. The terms of the note require that any person who acquires an interest in the note must have such interest reflected in a book entry. Bank N offers for sale interests in the Corporation U note. Ownership interests in the note are reflected on the books of Bank N. Corporation U's debenture is considered issued in registered form.

Example (8). Issuer S wishes to make a public offering of its debt obligations to United States persons. The obligations will have a maturity in excess of one year. On November 1, 1982, the closing on the debt offering occurs. At the closing, the net cash proceeds of the offering are delivered to S, and S delivers a master note to the underwriter of the offering. On January 2, 1983, S delivers the debt obligations to the purchasers, in definitive form and the master note is cancelled. The obligations are not registration-required because they are considered issued before January 1, 1983.

Example (9). In July 1983, Corporation T sells an issue of debt obligations maturing in 1985 to the public in the United States. Three of the obligations of the issue are issued to J in bearer form. The balance of the obligations of the issue are issued in registered form. The terms of the registered and bearer obligations are identical. The obligations issued to J are of a type offered to the public and are registration-required obligations. Since the three obligations are issued in bearer form, T is subject to the tax imposed under section 4701 with respect to the three bearer obligations. In addition, interest paid or accrued on the three bearer obligations is not deductible by T. Moreover, since the issuance of the three bearer obligations is subject to tax under section 4701, J is not prohibited from deducting losses on the obligations under section 165(j) or from treating gain on the obligations as capital gain under section 1232(d). The balance of the obligations in the issue do not give rise to liability for the tax under section 4701, and the deductibility of interest on such obligations is not affected by section 163(f).

Example (10). Broker K acquires a bond issued in 1980 by the United States Treasury through the Bureau of Public Debt. Broker K sells interests in the bond to the public after December 31, 1982. A purchaser may acquire an interest in any interest payment falling due under the bond or an interest in the principal of the bond. The bond is held by Custodian L for the benefit of the persons acquiring these interests. On receipt of interest and principal payments under the bond, Custodian L transfers the amount received to the person whose ownership interest corresponds to the bond component giving rise to the payment. Under section 1232B, each bond component is treated as an obligation issued with original issue discount equal to the excess of the stated redemption price at maturity over the purchase price of the bond component. The interests sold by K are obligations of a type offered to the public. Further, the interests are, in accordance with section 1232B, considered issued after December 31, 1982. Accordingly, the interests are registration-required obligations under § 5f.163-1(b).
[Temporary Reg. § 5f.163-1.]

☐ [*T.D.* 7852, 11-9-82. *Amended by T.D.* 7965, 8-17-84.]

§ 1.163-5. Denial of interest deduction on certain obligations issued after December 31, 1982, unless issued in registered form.—(a) [Reserved]

(b) [Reserved]

(c) *Obligations issued to foreign persons after September 21, 1984.*—(1) *In general.*—A determination of whether an obligation satisfies each of the requirements of this paragraph shall be made on an obligation-by-obligation basis. An obligation issued directly (or through affiliated entities) in bearer form by, or guaranteed by, a United States Government-owned agency or a United States Government-sponsored enterprise, such as the Federal National Mortgage Association, the Federal Home Loan Banks, the Federal Loan Mortgage Corporation, the Farm Credit Administration, and the Student Loan Marketing Association, may not satisfy this paragraph (c). An obligation issued after September 21, 1984 is described in this paragraph if—

(i) There are arrangements reasonably designed to ensure that such obligation will be sold (or resold in connection with its original issuance) only to a person who is not a United States person or who is a United States person that is a financial institution (as defined in § 1.165-12 (c)(1)(v)) purchasing for its own account or for the account of a customer and that agrees to comply with the requirements of section 165 (j)(3)(A), (B), or (C) and the regulations thereunder, and

(ii) In the case of an obligation which is not in registered form—

(A) Interest on such obligation is payable only outside the United States and its possessions, and

(B) Unless the obligation is described in subparagraph (2)(i)(C) of this paragraph or is a temporary global security, the following statement in English either appears on the face of the obligation and on any interest coupons which may be detached therefrom or, if the obligation is evidenced by a book entry, appears in the book or record in which the book entry is made: "Any United States person who holds this obligation will be subject to limitations under the United States income tax laws, including the limitations provided in sections 165(j) and 1287(a) of the Internal Revenue Code." For purposes of this paragraph, the term "temporary global security" means a security which is held for the benefit of the purchasers of the obligations of the issuer and interests in which are exchangeable for securities in definitive registered or bearer form prior to its stated maturity.

(2) *Rules for the application of this paragraph.*—(i) *Arrangements reasonably designed to ensure sale to non-United States persons.*—An obligation will be considered to satisfy paragraph (c)(1)(i) of this section if the conditions of paragraph (c)(2)(i)(A), (B), (C) or (D) of this section are met in connection with the original issuance of the obligation. An exchange of one obligation for another is considered an original issuance if and only if the exchange constitutes a disposition of property for purposes of section 1001 of the Code. However, an exchange of one obligation for another will not be considered a new issuance if the obligation received is identical in all respects to the obligation surrendered in exchange therefor, except that the obligor of the obligation received need not be the same obligor as the obligor of the obligation surrendered. Obligations that meet the conditions of paragraph (c)(2)(i)(A), (B), (C) or (D) of this section may be issued in a single public offering. The preceding sentence does not apply to certificates of deposit issued under the conditions of paragraph (c)(2)(i)(C) of this section by a United States person or by a controlled foreign corporation within the meaning of section 957(a) that is engaged in the active conduct of a banking business within the meaning of section 954(c)(3)(B) as in effect prior to the Tax Reform Act of 1986, and the regulations thereunder. A temporary global security need not satisfy the conditions of paragraph (c)(2)(i)(A), (B) or (C) of this section, but must satisfy the applicable requirements of paragraph (c)(2)(i)(D) of this section.

(A) In connection with the original issuance of an obligation, the obligation is offered for sale or resale only outside of the United States and its possessions, is delivered only outside the United States and its possessions and is not registered under the Securities Act of 1933 because it is intended for distribution to persons who are not United States persons. An obligation will not be considered to be required to be registered under the Securities Act of 1933 if the issuer, in reliance on the written opinion of counsel received prior to the issuance thereof, determines in good faith that the obligation need not be registered under the Securities Act of 1933 for the reason that it is intended for distribution to persons who are not United States persons. Solely for purposes of this subdivision (i)(A), the term "United States person" has the same meaning as it has for purposes of determining whether an obligation is intended for distribution to persons under the Securities Act of 1933. Except as provided in paragraph (c)(3) of this section, this paragraph (c)(2)(i)(A) applies only to obligations issued on or before September 7, 1990.

(B) The obligation is registered under the Securities Act of 1933, is exempt from registration by reason of section 3 or section 4 of such Act, or does not qualify as a security under the Securities Act of 1933; all of the conditions set forth in paragraph (c)(2)(i)(B)(1), (2), (3), (4), and (5) of this section are met with respect to such obligations; and, except as provided in paragraph (c)(3) of this section, the obligation is issued on or before September 7, 1990.

(1) In connection with the original issuance of an obligation in bearer form, the obligation is offered for sale or resale only outside the United States and its possessions.

(2) The issuer does not, and each underwriter and each member of the selling group, if any, covenants that it will not, in connection with the original issuance of the obligation, offer to sell or resell the obligation in bearer form to any person inside the United States or to a United States person unless such United States person is a financial institution as defined in § 1.165-12(c)(v) purchasing for its own account or for the account of a customer, which financial institution, as a condition of the purchase, agrees to provide on delivery of the obligation (or on issuance, if the obligation is not in definitive form) the certificate required under paragraph (c)(2)(i)(B)(4).

(3) In connection with its sale or resale during the original issuance of the obligation in bearer form, each underwriter and each member of the selling group, if any, or the issuer, if there is no underwriter or selling group, sends a confirmation to the purchaser of the bearer obligation stating that the purchaser represents that it is not a United States person or, if it is a United States person, it is a financial institution as defined in § 1.165-12(c)(v) purchasing for its own account or for the account of a customer and that the financial institution will comply with the requirements of section 165(j)(3)(A), (B), or (C) and the regulations thereunder. The confirmation must also state that, if the purchaser is a dealer, it will send similar confirmations to whomever purchases from it.

(4) In connection with the original issuance of the obligation in bearer form it is delivered in definitive form (or issued, if the obligation is not in definitive form) to the person entitled to physical delivery thereof only outside the United States and its possessions and only upon presentation of a certificate signed by such person to the issuer, underwriter, or member of the selling group, which certificate states that the obligation is not being acquired by or on behalf of a United States person, or for offer to resell or for resale to a United States person or any person inside the United States, or, if a beneficial interest in the obligation is being acquired by a United States person, that such person is a financial institu-

tion as defined in § 1.165-12(c)(1)(v) or is acquiring through a financial institution and that the obligation is held by a financial institution that has agreed to comply with the requirements of section 165(j)(3)(A), (B), or (C) and the regulations thereunder and that is not purchasing for offer to resell or for resale inside the United States. When a certificate is provided by a clearing organization, it must be based on statements provided to it by its member organizations. A clearing organization is an entity which is in the business of holding obligations for member organizations and transferring obligations among such members by credit or debit to the account of a member without the necessity of physical delivery of the obligation. For purposes of paragraph (c)(2)(i)(B), the term "delivery" does not include the delivery of an obligation to an underwriter or member of the selling group, if any.

(5) The issuer, underwriter, or member of the selling group does not have actual knowledge that the certificate described in paragraph (c)(2)(i)(B)(4) of this section is false. The issuer, underwriter, or member of the selling group shall be deemed to have actual knowledge that the certificate described in paragraph (c)(2)(i)(B)(4) of this section is false if the issuer, underwriter, or member of the selling group has a United States address for the beneficial owner (other than a financial institution as defined in § 1.165-12(c)(v) that represents that it will comply with the requirements of section 165(j)(3)(A), (B), or (C) and the regulations thereunder) and does not have documentary evidence as described in § 1.6049-5(c)(1) that the beneficial owner is not a United States person.

(C) The obligation is issued only outside the United States and its possessions by an issuer that does not significantly engage in interstate commerce with respect to the issuance of such obligation either directly or through its agent, an underwriter, or a member of the selling group. In the case of an issuer that is a United States person, such issuer may only satisfy the test set forth in this paragraph (c)(2)(i)(C) if—

(1) It is engaged through a branch in the active conduct of a banking business, within the meaning of section 954(c)(3)(B) as in effect before the Tax Reform Act of 1986, and the regulations thereunder, outside the United States;

(2) The obligation is issued outside of the United States by the branch in connection with that trade or business;

(3) The obligation that is so issued is sold directly to the public and is not issued as a part of a larger issuance made by means of a public offering; and

Reg. § 1.163-5(c)(2)(i)(B)(1)

(4) The issuer either maintains documentary evidence as described in subdivision (iii) of A-5 of 35a.9999-4T that the purchaser is not a United States person (provided that the issuer has no actual knowledge that the documentary evidence is false) or on delivery of the obligation the issuer receives a statement signed by the person entitled to physical delivery thereof and stating either that the obligation is not being acquired by or on behalf of a United States person or that, if a beneficial interest in the obligation is being acquired by a United States person, such person is a financial institution as defined in § 1.165-12(c)(v) or is acquiring through a financial institution and the obligation is held by a financial institution that has agreed to comply with the requirements of 165 (j)(3)(A), (B), or (C) and the regulations thereunder and that it is not purchasing for offer to resell or for resale inside the United States (provided that the issuer has no actual knowledge that the statement is false).

In addition, an issuer that is a controlled foreign corporation within the meaning of section 957(a) that is engaged in the active conduct of a banking business outside the United States within the meaning of section 954(c)(3)(B) as in effect before the Tax Reform Act of 1986, and the regulations thereunder, can only satisfy the provisions of this paragraph (c)(2)(i)(C), if it meets the requirements of this paragraph (c)(2)(i)(C)(2), (3) and (4).

(D) The obligation is issued after September 7, 1990, and all of the conditions set forth in this paragraph (c)(2)(i)(D) are met with respect to such obligation.

(1) Offers and sales.—(i) Issuer.— The issuer does not offer or sell the obligation during the restricted period to a person who is within the United States or its possessions or to a United States person.

(ii) Distributors.—(A) The distributor of the obligation does not offer or sell the obligation during the restricted period to a person who is within the United States or its possessions or to a United States person.

(B) The distributor of the obligation will be deemed to satisfy the requirements of paragraph (c)(2)(i)(D)(1)(ii)(A) of this section if the distributor of the obligation covenants that it will not offer or sell the obligation during the restricted period to a person who is within the United States or its possessions or to a United States person; and the distributor of the obligation has in effect, in connection with the offer and sale of the obligation during the restricted period, procedures reasonably designed to ensure that its employees or agents who are directly engaged in selling the obligation are aware that the obligation cannot be offered or sold during the restricted period to a person who is within the United States or its possessions or is a United States person.

*(iii) Certain rules.—*For purposes of paragraph (c)(2)(i)(D)(*1*)(*i*) and (*ii*) of this section:

(A) An offer or sale will be considered to be made to a person who is within the United States or its possessions if the offeror or seller of the obligation has an address within the United States or its possessions for the offeree or buyer of the obligation with respect to the offer or sale.

(B) An offer or sale of an obligation will not be treated as made to a person within the United States or its possessions or to a United States person if the person to whom the offer or sale is made is: An exempt distributor, as defined in paragraph (c)(2)(i)(D)(*5*) of this section; An international organization as defined in section 7701(a)(18) and the regulations thereunder, or a foreign central bank as defined in section 895 and the regulations thereunder, or the foreign branch of a United States financial institution as described in paragraph (c)(2)(i)(D)(*6*)(*i*) of this section.

Paragraph (c)(2)(i)(D)(*1*)(*iii*)(*B*) regarding an exempt distributor will only apply to an offer to the United States office of an exempt distributor, and paragraph (c)(2)(i)(D)(*1*)(*iii*)(*B*) regarding an international organization or foreign central bank will only apply to an offer to an international organization or foreign central bank, if such offer is made directly and specifically to the United States office, organization or bank.

(C) A sale of an obligation will not be treated as made to a person within the United States or its possessions or to a United States person if the person to whom the sale is made is a person described in paragraph (c)(2)(i)(D)(*6*)(*ii*) of this section.

*(2) Delivery.—*In connection with the sale of the obligation during the restricted period, neither the issuer nor any distributor delivers the obligation in definitive form within the United States or its possessions.

*(3) Certification.—(i) In general.—*On the earlier of the date of the first actual payment of interest by the issuer on the obligation or the date of delivery by the issuer of the obligation in definitive form, a certificate is provided to the issuer of the obligation stating that on such date:

(A) The obligation is owned by a person that is not a United States person;

(B) The obligation is owned by a United States person described in paragraph (c)(2)(i)(D)(6) of this section; or

(C) The obligation is owned by a financial institution for purposes of resale during the restricted period, and such financial institution certifies in addition that it has not acquired the obligation for purposes of resale directly or indirectly to a United States person or to a person within the United States or its possessions.

A certificate described in paragraph (c)(2)(i)(D)(3)(i)(A) or (B) of this section may not be given with respect to an obligation that is owned by a financial institution for purposes of resale during the restricted period. For purposes of paragraph (c)(2)(i)(D)(2) and (3) of this section, a temporary global security (as defined in § 1.163-5(c)(1)(ii)(B)) is not considered to be an obligation in definitive form. If the issuer does not make the obligation available for delivery in definitive form within a reasonable period of time after the end of the restricted period, then the obligation shall be treated as not satisfying the requirements of this paragraph (c)(2)(i)(D)(3). The certificate must be signed (or sent, as provided in paragraph (c)(2)(i)(D)(3)(ii) of this section) either by the owner of the obligation or by a financial institution or clearing organization through which the owner holds the obligation, directly or indirectly. For purposes of this paragraph (c)(2)(i)(D)(3), the term "financial institution" means a financial institution described in § 1.165-12(c)(1)(v). When a certificate is provided by a clearing organization, the certificate must be based on statements provided to it by its member organizations. The requirement of this paragraph (c)(1)(D)(3) shall be deemed not to be satisfied with respect to an obligation if the issuer knows or has reason to know that the certificate with respect to such obligation is false. The certificate must be retained by the issuer (and statements by member organizations must be retained by the clearing organization, in the case of certificates based on such statements) for a period of four calendar years following the year in which the certificate is received.

(ii) Electronic certification.—The certificate required by paragraph (c)(2)(i)(D)(3)(i) of this section (including a statement provided to a clearing organization by a member organization) may be provided electronically, but only if the person receiving such electronic certificate maintains adequate records, for the retention period described in paragraph (c)(2)(i)(D)(3)(i) of this section, establishing that such certificate was received in respect of the subject obligation, and only if there is a written agreement entered into prior to the time of certification (including the written membership rules of a clearing organization) to which the sender and recipient are subject, providing that the electronic certificate shall have the effect of a signed certificate described in paragraph (c)(2)(i)(D)(3)(i) of this section.

(iii) Exception for certain obligations.—This paragraph (c)(2)(i)(D)(3) shall not apply, and no certificate shall be required, in the case of an obligation that is sold during the restricted period and that satisfies all of the following requirements:

(A) The interest and principal with respect to the obligation are denominated only in the currency of a single foreign country.

(B) The interest and principal with respect to the obligation are payable only within that foreign country (according to rules similar to those set forth in § 1.163-5(c)(2)(v)).

(C) The obligation is offered and sold in accordance with practices and documentation customary in that foreign country.

(D) The distributor covenants to use reasonable efforts to sell the obligation within that foreign country.

(E) The obligation is not listed, or the subject of an application for listing, on an exchange located outside that foreign country.

(F) The Commissioner has designated that foreign country as a foreign country in which certification under paragraph (c)(2)(i)(D)(3)(i) of this section is not permissible.

(G) The issuance of the obligation is subject to guidelines or restrictions imposed by governmental, banking or securities authorities in that foreign country.

(H) More than 80 percent by value of the obligations included in the offering of which the obligation is a part are offered and sold to non-distributors by distributors maintaining an office located in that foreign country. Foreign currency denominated obligations that are convertible into U.S. dollar denominated obligations or that by their terms are linked to the U.S. dollar in a way which effectively converts the obligations to U.S. dollar denominated obligations do not satisfy the requirements of this paragraph (c)(2)(i)(D)(3)(iii). A foreign currency denominated obligation will not be treated as linked, by its terms, to the U.S. dollar solely because the obligation is the subject of a swap transaction.

(4) Distributor.—For purposes of this paragraph (c)(2)(i)(D), the term "distributor" means:

(i) a person that offers or sells the obligation during the restricted period pursuant to a written contract with the issuer;

(ii) any person that offers or sells the obligation during the restricted period pursuant to a written contract with a person described in paragraph (c)(2)(i)(D)(4)(i); and

(iii) any affiliate that acquires the obligation from another member of its affiliated group for the purpose of offering or selling the obligation during the restricted period, but only if the transferor member of the group is the issuer or a person described in paragraph (c)(2)(i)(D)(4)(i) or (ii) of this section. The terms "affiliate" and "affiliated group" have the same meanings as in section 1504(a) of the Code, but without regard to the exceptions contained in section 1504(b) and substituting "50 percent" for "80 percent" each time it appears.

For purposes of this paragraph (c)(2)(i)(D)(4), a written contract does not include a confirmation or other notice of the transaction.

(5) Exempt distributor.—For purposes of this paragraph (c)(2)(i)(D), the term "exempt distributor" means a distributor that covenants in its contract with the issuer or with a distributor described in paragraph (c)(2)(i)(D)(4)(i) that it is buying the obligation for the purpose of resale in connection with the original issuance of the obligation, and that if it retains the obligation for its own account, it will only do so in accordance with the requirements of paragraph (c)(2)(i)(D)(6) of this section. In the latter case, the covenant will constitute the certificate required under paragraph (c)(2)(i)(D)(6). The provisions of paragraph (c)(2)(i)(D)(7) governing the restricted period for unsold allotments or subscriptions shall apply to any obligation retained for investment by an exempt distributor.

(6) Certain United States persons.—A person is described in this paragraph (c)(2)(i)(D)(6) if the requirements of this paragraph are satisfied and the person is:

(i) The foreign branch of a United States financial institution purchasing for its own account or for resale, or

(ii) A United States person who acquired the obligation through the foreign branch of a United States financial institution and who, for purposes of the certification required in paragraph (c)(2)(i)(D)(3) of this section, holds the obligation through such financial institution on the date of certification.

For purposes of paragraph (c)(2)(i)(D)(6)(ii) of this section, a United States person will be considered to acquire and hold an obligation through the foreign branch of a United States financial institution if the United States person has an account with the United States office of a financial institution, and the transaction is executed by a foreign office of that financial institution, or by the foreign office of another financial institution acting on behalf of that financial institution. This paragraph (c)(2)(i)(D)(6) will apply, however, only if the United States financial institution (or the United States office of a foreign financial institution) holding the obligation provides a certificate to the issuer or distributor selling the obligation within a reasonable time stating that it agrees to comply with the requirements of section 165(j)(3)(A), (B), or (C) and the regulations thereunder. For purposes of this paragraph (c)(2)(i)(D)(6), the term "financial institution" means a financial institution as defined in § 1.165-12(c)(1)(v). As an alternative to the certification required above, a financial institution may provide a blanket certificate to the issuer or distributor selling the obligation stating that the financial institution will comply with the requirements of section 165(j)(3)(A), (B) or (C) and the regulations thereunder. A blanket certificate must be received by the issuer or the distributor in the year of the issuance of the obligation or in either of the preceding two calendar years, and must be retained by the issuer or distributor for at least four years after the end of the last calendar year to which it relates.

(7) Restricted period.—For purposes of this paragraph (c)(2)(i)(D), the restricted period with respect to an obligation begins on the earlier of the closing date (or the date on which the issuer receives the loan proceeds, if there is no closing with respect to the obligation), or the first date on which the obligation is offered to persons other than a distributor. The restricted period with respect to an obligation ends on the expiration of the forty day period beginning on the closing date (or the date on which the issuer receives the loan proceeds, if there is no closing with respect to the obligation). Notwithstanding the preceding sentence, any offer or sale of the obligation by the issuer or a distributor shall be deemed to be during the restricted period if the issuer or distributor holds the obligation as part of an unsold allotment or subscription.

(8) Clearing organization.—For purposes of this paragraph (c)(2)(i)(D), a "clearing organization" is an entity which is in the business of holding obligations for member organizations and transferring obligations among such members by credit or debit to the account of a member without the necessity of physical delivery of the obligation.

Reg. § 1.163-5(c)(2)(i)(D)(8)

(ii) *Special rules.*—An obligation shall not be considered to be described in paragraph (c)(2)(i)(C) of this section if it is—

(A) Guaranteed by a United States shareholder of the issuer;

(B) Convertible into a debt or equity interest in a United States shareholder of the issuer; or

(C) Substantially identical to an obligation issued by a United States shareholder of the issuer.

For purposes of this paragraph (c)(2)(ii), the term "United States shareholder" is defined as it is defined in section 951(b) and the regulations thereunder. For purposes of this paragraph (c)(2)(ii)(C), obligations are substantially identical if the face amount, interest rate, term of the issue, due dates for payments, and maturity date of each is substantially identical to the other.

(iii) *Interstate commerce.*—For purposes of this paragraph, the term "interstate commerce" means trade or commerce in obligations or any transportation or communication relating thereto between any foreign country and the United States or its possessions.

(A) An issuer will not be considered to engage significantly in interstate commerce with respect to the issuance of an obligation if the only activities with respect to which the issuer uses the means or instrumentalities of interstate commerce are activities of a preparatory or auxiliary character that do not involve communication between a prospective purchaser and an issuer, its agent, an underwriter, or member of the selling group if either is inside the United States or its possessions. Activities of a preparatory or auxiliary character include, but are not limited to, the following activities:

(1) Establishment or participation in establishment of policies concerning the issuance of obligations and the allocation of funding by a United States shareholder with respect to obligations issued by a foreign corporation or by a United States office with respect to obligations issued by a foreign branch;

(2) Negotiation between the issuer and underwriters as to the terms and pricing of an issue;

(3) Transfer of funds to an office of an issuer in the United States or its possessions by a foreign branch or to a United States shareholder by a foreign corporation;

(4) Consultation by an issuer with accountants and lawyers or other financial advisors in the United States or its possessions regarding the issuance of an obligation;

(5) Document drafting and printing; and

(6) Provision of payment or delivery instructions to members of the selling group by an issuer's office or agent that is located in the United States or its possessions.

(B) Activities that will not be considered to be of a preparatory or auxiliary character include, but are not limited to, any of the following activities:

(1) Negotiation or communication between a prospective purchaser and an issuer, its agent, an underwriter, or a member of the selling group concerning the sale of an obligation if either is inside the United States or its possessions;

(2) Involvement of an issuer's office, its agent, an underwriter, or a member of the selling group in the United States or its possessions in the offer or sale of a particular obligation, either directly with the prospective purchaser, or through the issuer in a foreign country;

(3) Delivery of an obligation in the United States or its possessions; or

(4) Advertising or otherwise promoting an obligation in the United States or its possessions.

(C) The following examples illustrate the application of this subdivision (iii) of § 1.163-5(c)(2).

Example (1). Foreign corporation A, a corporation organized in and doing business in foreign country Z, and not a controlled foreign corporation within the meaning of section 957(a) that is engaged in the conduct of a banking business within the meaning of section 954(c)(3)(B) as in effect before the Tax Reform Act of 1986, issues its debentures outside the United States. The debentures are not guaranteed by a United States shareholder of A, nor are they convertible into a debt or equity interest of a United States shareholder of A, nor are they substantially identical to an obligation issued by a United States shareholder of A. A consults its accountants and lawyers in the United States for certain securities and tax advice regarding the debt offering. The underwriting and selling group in respect of A's offering is composed entirely of foreign securities firms, some of which are foreign subsidiaries of United States securities firms. A U.S. affiliate of the foreign underwriter communicates payment and delivery instruction to the selling group. All offering circulars for the offering are mailed and delivered outside the United States and its possessions. All debentures are delivered and paid for outside the United States and its possessions. No office located in the United States or in a United States possession is involved in the sale of debentures. Interest on the debentures is payable only outside the United States and its possessions. A is not significantly engaged in interstate commerce with respect to the offering.

Example (2). B, a United States bank, does business in foreign country X through a branch located in X. The branch is a staffed and operating unit engaged in the active conduct of a banking business consisting of one or more of the activities set forth in § 1.954-2(d)(2)(ii). As part of its ongoing business, the branch in X issues negotiable certificates of deposit with a maturity in excess of one year to customers upon request. The certificates of deposit are not guaranteed by a United States shareholder of B, nor are they convertible into a debt or equity interest of a United States shareholder of B, nor are they substantially identical to an obligation issued by a United States shareholder of B. Policies regarding the issuance of negotiable certificates of deposit and funding allocations for foreign branches are set in the United States at B's main office. Branch personnel decide whether to issue a negotiable certificate of deposit based on the guidelines established by the United States offices of B, but without communicating with the United States offices of B with respect to the issuance of a particular obligation. Negotiable certificates of deposits are delivered and paid for outside the United States and its possessions. Interest on the negotiable certificates of deposit is payable only outside the United States and its possessions. B maintains documentary evidence described in § 1.163-5(c)(2)(i)(C)(*4*). After the issuance of negotiable certificates of deposit by the foreign branch of B, the foreign branch sends the funds to a United States branch of B for use in domestic operations. B is not significantly engaged in interstate commerce with respect to the issuance of such obligation.

Example (3). The facts in Example (2) apply except that the foreign branch of B consulted, by telephone, the main office in the United States to request approval of the issuance of the certificate of deposit at a particular rate of interest. The main office granted permission to issue the negotiable certificate of deposit to the customer by a telex sent from the main office of B to the branch in X. B is significantly engaged in interstate commerce with respect to the issuance of the obligation as a result of the involvement of B's United States office in the issuance of the obligation.

Example (4). The facts in Example (2) apply with the additional fact that a customer contacted the foreign branch of B through a telex originating in the United States or its possessions. Subsequent to the telex, the foreign branch issued the negotiable certificate of deposit and recorded it on the books. B is significantly engaged in interstate commerce with respect to the issuance of the obligation as a result of its communication by telex with a customer in the United States.

(iv) *Possessions*.—For purposes of this section, the term "possessions" includes Puerto Rico, the U.S. Virgin Islands, Guam, American Samoa, Wake Island, and Northern Mariana Islands.

(v) *Interest payable outside of the United States*.—Interest will be considered payable only outside the United States and its possessions if payment of such interest can be made only upon presentation of a coupon, or upon making of any other demand for payment, outside of the United States and its possessions to the issuer or a paying agent. The fact that payment is made by a draft drawn on a United States bank account or by a wire or other electronic transfer from a United States account does not affect this result. Interest payments will be considered to be made within the United States if the payments are made by a transfer of funds into an account maintained by the payee in the United States or mailed to an address in the United States, if—

(A) The interest is paid on an obligation issued by either a United States person, a controlled foreign corporation as defined in section 957(a), or a foreign corporation if 50 percent or more of the gross income of the foreign corporation from all sources of the 3-year period ending with the close of its taxable year preceding the original issuance of the obligation (or for such part of the period that the foreign corporation has been in existence) was effectively connected with the conduct of a trade or business within the United States; and

(B) The interest is paid to a person other than—

(*1*) A person who may satisfy the requirements of section 165(j)(3)(A), (B), or (C) and the regulations thereunder; and

(*2*) A financial institution as a step in the clearance of funds and such interest is promptly credited to an account maintained outside the United States for such financial institution or for persons for which the financial institution has collected such interest.

Interest is considered to be paid within the United States and its possessions if a coupon is presented, or a demand for payment is otherwise made, to the issuer or a paying agent (whether a United States or foreign person) in the United States and its possessions even if the funds paid are credited to an account maintained by the payee outside the United States and its possessions. Interest will be considered payable only outside the United States and its possessions notwithstanding that such interest may become payable at the office of the issuer

Reg. § 1.163-5(c)(2)(v)(B)(*2*)

or its United States paying agent under the following conditions: the issuer has appointed paying agents located outside the United States and its possessions with the reasonable expectation that such paying agents will be able to pay the interest in United States dollars, and the full amount of such payment at the offices of all such paying agents is illegal or effectively precluded because of the imposition of exchange controls or other similar restrictions on the full payment or receipt of interest in United States dollars. A lawsuit brought in the United States or its possessions for payment of the obligation or interest thereon as a result of a default shall not be considered to be a demand for payment. For purposes of this subdivision (v), interest includes original issue discount as defined in section 1273(a). Therefore, an amount equal to the original issue discount as defined in section 1273(a) is payable only outside the United States and its possessions. The amount of market discount as defined in section 1278(a) does not affect the amount of interest to be considered payable only outside the United States and its possessions.

(vi) *Rules relating to obligations issued after December 31, 1982 and on or before September 21, 1984.*—Whether an obligation originally issued after December 31, 1982 and on or before September 21, 1984, or an obligation originally issued after September 21, 1984 pursuant to the exercise of a warrant or the conversion of a convertible obligation, which warrant or obligation (including conversion privilege) was issued after December 31, 1982 and on or before September 21, 1984, is described in section 163(f)(2)(B) shall be determined under the rules provided in § 5f.163-1(c) as in effect prior to its removal. Notwithstanding the preceding sentence, an issuer will be considered to satisfy the requirements of section 163(f)(2)(B) with respect to an obligation issued after December 31, 1982 and on or before September 21, 1984 or after September 21, 1984 pursuant to the exercise of a warrant or the conversion of a convertible obligation, which warrant or obligation (including conversion privilege) was issued after December 31, 1982 and on or before September 21, 1984, if the issuer substantially complied with the proposed regulations provided in § 1.163-5(c), which were published in the Federal Register on September 2, 1983 (48 FR 39953) and superseded by temporary regulations published in the Federal Register on August 22, 1984 (49 FR 33228).

(3) *Effective date.*—(i) *In general.*—These regulations apply generally to obligations issued after January 20, 1987. A taxpayer may choose to apply the rules of § 1.163-5(c) with respect to an obligation issued after December 31, 1982 and on or before January 20, 1987. If this choice is made, the rules of § 1.163-5(c) will apply in lieu of § 1.163-5T(c) except that the legend requirement under § 1.163-5(c)(1)(ii)(B) does not apply with respect to a bearer obligation evidenced exclusively by a book entry and that the certification requirement under § 1.163-5T(c)(2)(i)(B)(*4*) applies in lieu of the certification under § 1.163-5(c)(2)(i)(B)(*4*).

(ii) *Special rules.*—If an obligation is originally issued after September 7, 1990 pursuant to the exercise of a warrant or the conversion of a convertible obligation, which warrant or obligation (including conversion privilege) was issued on or before May 10, 1990, then the issuer may choose to apply either the rules of § 1.163-5(c)(2)(i)(A) or § 1.163-5(c)(2)(i)(B), or the rules of § 1.163-5(c)(2)(i)(D). The issuer of an obligation may choose to apply either the rules of § 1.163-5(c)(2)(i)(A) or (B), or the rules of § 1.163-5(c)(2)(i)(D), to an obligation that is originally issued after May 10, 1990, and on or before September 7, 1990. However, any issuer choosing to apply the rules of § 1.163-5(c)(2)(i)(A) must apply the definition of United States person used for such purposes on December 31, 1989, and must obtain any certificates that would have been required under applicable law on December 31, 1989. [Reg. § 1.163-5.]

☐ [T.D. 8110, 12-16-86. Amended by T.D. 8203, 5-19-88; T.D. 8300, 5-9-90 *and* T.D. 8734, 10-6-97 (T.D. 8804 extended the effective date of T.D. 8734 from January 1, 1999, to January 1, 2000; T.D. 8856 further delayed the effective date of T.D. 8734 until January 1, 2001).]

Proposed Regulation

§ 1.163(j)-1. Limitation on deduction for certain interest paid or accrued by a corporation to related persons.—(a) *In general.*— (1) *Deduction for exempt related person interest expense disallowed.*—Except as provided in this section, no deduction shall be allowed for exempt related person interest expense (as defined in § 1.163(j)-2(a)) paid or accrued during the taxable year directly or indirectly by—

(i) A domestic corporation (other than an S corporation as defined in section 1361), or

(ii) Under the special rules described in § 1.163(j)-8, a foreign corporation with income, gain, or loss that is effectively connected (or treated as effectively connected) with the conduct of a trade or business in the United States.

(2) *Limitation on disallowance of deduction.*—The amount of exempt related person interest expense disallowed as a deduction in any taxable year (described hereafter as the year's "disallowed interest expense") shall not

exceed the payor corporation's excess interest expense (as defined in § 1.163(j)-2(b)) for that year.

(3) *Disallowed interest expense carryforward.*—Disallowed interest expense shall be carried forward to the succeeding taxable year (hereafter, a "disallowed interest expense carryforward"). A deduction for disallowed interest expense carryforward may be allowed as provided in paragraph (c) of this section.

(b) *Debt-equity ratio safe harbor test.*—No deduction shall be disallowed under paragraph (a) of this section for exempt related person interest expense paid or accrued in any taxable year in which the payor corporation's debt-equity ratio (determined as provided in § 1.163(j)-3) is less than or equal to 1.5 to 1 on the last day of the taxable year.

(c) *Treatment of disallowed interest expense carryforward.*—(1) *In general.*—A deduction for disallowed interest expense carryforward is allowed in a carryforward year if and to the extent that there is excess limitation (as defined in § 1.163(j)-2(c)) for such year. Any disallowed interest expense carryforward not so deductible shall be carried forward to the succeeding taxable year.

(2) *Effect of debt-equity safe harbor.*—The debt-equity ratio in a carryforward year is not relevant in determining whether disallowed interest expense carryforward is deductible in such year. Rather, disallowed interest expense carryforward is deductible only to the extent of the excess limitation for such year.

(d) *Carryforward of excess limitation.*—If a corporation has excess limitation (as defined in § 1.163(j)-2(c)) for any taxable year, the amount of such excess limitation, reduced by disallowed interest expense carryforward to that year, shall be carried forward to each of the three succeeding taxable years. In each of those years, such carryforward shall reduce, and be reduced by, the amount, if any, of the corporation's excess interest expense for such year computed without regard to the carryforward. The excess limitation carryforward shall reduce, and be reduced by, excess interest expense in a carryforward year without regard to whether the corporation pays or accrues any exempt related person interest expense in that year, or whether the corporation satisfies the debt-equity ratio safe harbor test described in paragraph (b) of this section for that year. If a corporation has carryforwards from more than one taxable year, such carryforwards shall reduce, and be reduced by, excess interest expense in the order in which they arose. For purposes of all the reductions described in this paragraph, excess limitation, excess limitation carryforward, and excess interest expense shall not be reduced below zero. For rules regarding the effect of an adjusted taxable loss with respect to excess limitation carryforward, see § 1.163(j)-2(f)(4)(ii).

(e) *Effect on earnings and profits.*—The disallowance and carryforward of a deduction for interest expense under this section shall not affect whether or when such interest expense reduces earnings and profits of the payor corporation.

(f) *Anti-avoidance rule.*—Arrangements, including the use of partnerships or trusts, entered into with a principal purpose of avoiding the rules of section 163(j) and these regulations shall be disregarded or recharacterized to the extent necessary to carry out the purposes of section 163(j).

(g) *Examples.*—The following examples illustrate the rules of this section.

Example 1—(i) A, a domestic corporation, is a wholly owned subsidiary of F, a foreign corporation. During its taxable year ending December 31, 1990, A has adjusted taxable income of $100, which includes $20 of interest income, and $90 of interest expense, of which $60 is paid or accrued to F. The balance of the interest expense is paid to unrelated persons. Interest paid to F by A is not subject to U.S. tax due to a tax treaty. A does not satisfy the debt-equity ratio safe harbor test in 1990, and has no excess limitation carried forward to that year.

(ii) A's excess interest expense for 1990 is $20, which is the difference between its net interest expense and 50 percent of its adjusted taxable income ($70 − $50 = $20). Since for 1990, the amount of A's exempt related person interest expense ($60) is greater than its excess interest expense ($20), a deduction for $20 of A's exempt related person interest expense is disallowed under paragraph (a) of this section. A's 1990 disallowed interest expense is carried forward to A's succeeding taxable year.

Example 2—(i) The facts are the same as in paragraph (i) of *Example 1*. In 1991, A has $120 of adjusted taxable income, net interest expense of $50, and $20 of disallowed interest expense carried forward from 1990. All of A's interest expense for 1991 is paid to unrelated persons. A does not satisfy the debt-equity ratio safe harbor test in 1991.

(ii) A has excess limitation (as defined in § 1.163(j)-2 (c)) of $10 ($60 (50% of adjusted taxable income) − $50 (net interest expense)) in 1991. In 1991, A may deduct the interest expense paid or accrued in that year to unrelated persons, plus $10 of disallowed interest expense carryforward from 1990. The balance of A's disallowed interest expense carryforward

Prop. Reg. § 1.163(j)-1(g)

from 1990 ($10) is carried forward to A's 1992 taxable year.

Example 3—(i) The facts are the same as in paragraph (i) of *Example 2*. In 1992, A satisfies the debt-equity ratio safe harbor test, has adjusted taxable income of $210, and net interest expense of $100. All A's interest expense for 1992 is paid or accrued to F.

(ii) In 1992, A has excess limitation of $5 ($105 (50% of adjusted taxable income) − $100 (net interest expense)). Applying the principles of paragraph (c) of this section, A's $10 of disallowed interest expense carryforward from 1991 (see *Example 2*, paragraph (ii)) is allowed in 1992 only to the extent of the $5 of excess limitation for that year. The remaining $5 of disallowed interest expense carried forward from 1991 is carried forward to A's 1993 taxable year.

Example 4—(i) The facts are the same as in paragraph (i) of *Example 3*. In 1993, A satisfies the debt-equity ratio safe harbor test, has adjusted taxable income of $100, and has net interest expense of $75, all of which is paid or accrued to F.

(ii) A's excess interest expense for 1993 is $25 ($75 (A's net interest expense) − $50 (50% of its adjusted taxable income)). Applying the principles of paragraphs (a) and (b) of this section, section 163(j) does not disallow a deduction in 1993 for any of A's excess interest expense that is exempt related person interest expense. Under paragraph (c) of this section, A's $5 of disallowed interest expense carryforward from 1992 (see *Example 3*, paragraph (ii)) is not deductible in 1993, and is carried forward to A's 1994 taxable year.

(h) *Cross-references.*—For rules regarding affiliated groups for purposes of section 163(j), see § 1.163(j)-5. For rules limiting the deductibility of disallowed interest expense carryforward and restricting the use of excess limitation carried forward to taxable years after the occurrence of certain corporate transactions, see § 1.163(j)-6. [Prop. Reg. § 1.163(j)-1.]

[Proposed 6-18-91.]

Proposed Regulation

§ 1.163(j)-2. Definitions.—(a) *Exempt related person interest expense.*—The term "exempt related person interest expense" means interest expense that is (or is treated as) paid or accrued by a corporation described in § 1.163(j)-1(a) to a related person (within the meaning of paragraph (g) of this section) if no tax is imposed with respect to such interest under rules provided in § 1.163(j)-4.

(b) *Excess interest expense.*—The term "excess interest expense" means the excess, if any, of a corporation's net interest expense (as defined in paragraph (d) of this section) over the sum of 50 percent of its adjusted taxable income (as defined in paragraph (f) of this section) plus any excess limitation carried forward to the taxable year (under the rules of § 1.163(j)-1(d)). See paragraph (f)(4)(ii) of this section for rules regarding the effect of an adjusted taxable loss on the computation of excess interest expense.

(c) *Excess limitation.*—The term "excess limitation" means the excess, if any, of 50 percent of a corporation's adjusted taxable income (as defined in paragraph (f) of this section) over its net interest expense (as defined in paragraph (d) of this section).

(d) *Net interest expense.*—The term "net interest expense" means the excess, if any, of the amount of interest expense paid or accrued (directly or indirectly) by a corporation during the taxable year over the amount of interest includible (directly or indirectly) in its gross income for such year.

(e) *Interest income and expense.*—(1) *In general.*—Interest income shall generally be determined under section 61 and shall include original issue discount as provided in sections 1272 through 1275 (adjusted, under section 1272(a)(7), for any acquisition premium paid by a subsequent holder), acquisition discount as provided in sections 1281 through 1283, and amounts that are treated as original issue discount under section 1286 (pertaining to stripped bonds). Interest expense shall generally be determined under section 163(a) and shall include original issue discount as provided in section 163(e). Interest expense for a taxable year does not take into account any disallowed interest expense carried forward to that year under the rules of § 1.163(j)-1. Interest income or expense with respect to a debt instrument denominated in a nonfunctional currency (or the payments of which are determined with reference to a nonfunctional currency) shall be determined in accordance with section 988 and the regulations thereunder. For rules regarding the relationship of section 163(j) to other Code provisions under which a deduction for interest expense may be disallowed or deferred, see § 1.163(j)-7.

(2) *Treatment of bond premium and market discount.*—(i) *Bond premium.*—In the case of any bond with respect to which an election made under section 171(c) is in effect, amortizable bond premium (as defined in section 171(b)) shall reduce interest income. Bond premium included in income by the issuer under the principles of § 1.61-12 (or the successor provision thereof) shall reduce interest expense.

(ii) *Market discount.*—Gain treated as ordinary income on the disposition of a market discount bond under section 1276(a) shall be treated as interest income.

(3) *Interest equivalents.*—[RESERVED]

(4) *Interest income of partnerships.*—Interest paid or accrued to a partnership shall be treated under section 163(j) and these regulations (other than paragraph (g) of this section) as paid or accrued to the partners of the partnership in proportion to each partner's distributive share (as defined in section 704) of the partnership's interest income for the taxable year.

(5) *Interest expense of partnerships.*—Interest expense paid or accrued by a partnership and the tax exempt interest expense of a partnership (within the meaning of § 1.163(j)-4) shall be treated for all purposes under section 163(j) and these regulations as paid or accrued by the partners of the partnership in proportion to each partner's distributive share (as defined in section 704) of the partnership's interest expense and tax exempt interest expense, respectively, for the taxable year. Thus, a corporation which is a partner in a partnership shall be treated as paying or accruing its share of the partnership's interest expense, and is treated as the payor of such interest expense.

(6) *Certain substitute payments.*—(i) *In general.*—If pursuant to an agreement meeting the requirements of section 1058(b), there is a transfer of securities (as defined in section 1236(c)) between related persons (within the meaning of paragraph (g) of this section), payments described in section 1058(b)(2) with respect to such transferred securities ("substitute payments") shall be treated as interest expense for purposes of section 163(j) and these regulations.

(ii) *Effective date.*—This paragraph (e)(6) shall be effective with respect to substitute payments paid or accrued after [30 DAYS AFTER DATE THIS PROPOSED REGULATION IS PUBLISHED IN THE FEDERAL REGISTER].

(f) *Adjusted taxable income.*—(1) *In general.*—The term "adjusted taxable income" means a corporation's taxable income for the taxable year, computed without regard to any carryforwards or disallowances under section 163(j), and determined with the modifications described in paragraphs (f)(2) and (f)(3) of this section. A corporation's adjusted taxable income may be a negative amount (*i.e.,* an adjusted taxable loss). See paragraph (f)(4) of this section for rules regarding the effect of an adjusted taxable loss.

(2) *Additions.*—The following amounts shall be added to a corporation's taxable income to determine its adjusted taxable income:

(i) The net interest expense (as defined in paragraph (d) of this section) for the taxable year;

(ii) The net operating loss deduction under section 172;

(iii) Deductions for depreciation under sections 167 and 168;

(iv) Deductions for the amortization of intangibles and other amortized expenditures (*e.g.,* start-up expenditures under section 195 and organizational expenditures under section 248);

(v) Deductions for depletion under section 611;

(vi) Carryovers of excess charitable contributions (within the meaning of section 170(d)(2)), to the extent allowable as a deduction in the taxable year;

(vii) The increase, if any, between the end of the preceding year and the end of the current year in accounts payable (other than interest payable) that are included in the computation of taxable income;

(viii) The decrease, if any, between the end of the preceding taxable year and the end of the current taxable year in accounts receivable (other than interest receivable) that are included in the computation of taxable income;

(ix) Interest which is excluded from gross income under section 103;

(x) The dividends received deduction as provided under section 243 (other than deductions under section 243(a)(3));

(xi) The increase, if any, in the LIFO recapture amount (as defined in section 312(n)(4)(B)) between the end of the preceding taxable year and the end of the current taxable year; and

(xii) Any deduction in the taxable year for capital loss carrybacks or carryovers.

(3) *Subtractions.*—The following amounts shall be subtracted from taxable income to determine adjusted taxable income:

(i) With respect to the sale or disposition of property (including a sale or disposition of property by a partnership), any depreciation, amortization, or depletion deductions which were allowed or allowable for the taxpayer's taxable years beginning after July 10, 1986, with respect to such property;

(ii) With respect to the sale or disposition of stock of a member of a consolidated group that includes the selling corporation, an amount equal to the investment adjustments (as defined under §§ 1.1502-32 and 1.1502-32T) with respect to such stock that are attributable to deductions described in paragraph (f)(3)(i) of this section;

(iii) With respect to the sale or other disposition of an interest in a partnership, an amount equal to the taxpayer's distributive share of deductions described in paragraph (f)(3)(i) of this section with respect to property held by the partnership at the time of such sale or other disposition;

(iv) The decrease, if any, between the end of the preceding taxable year and the end of the current taxable year in accounts payable (other than interest payable) which are included in the computation of the corporation's taxable income;

(v) The increase, if any, between the end of the preceding taxable year and the end of the current taxable year in accounts receivable (other than interest receivable) which are included in the computation of the corporation's taxable income;

(vi) Amounts that would be deductible but for section 265 (regarding expenses and interest relating to tax-exempt income) or 279 (regarding interest on indebtedness incurred by a corporation to acquire stock or assets of another corporation);

(vii) The amount of any charitable contribution (as defined in section 170(c)) made during the taxable year that exceeds the amount deductible in that year by reason of section 170(b)(2);

(viii) The decrease, if any, in the LIFO recapture amount (as defined in section 312(n)(4)(B)) between the end of the preceding taxable year and the end of the current taxable year; and

(ix) The amount of any net capital loss (as defined in section 1222 (10)) for the taxable year.

(4) *Effect of adjusted taxable loss.*—(i) *In general.*—If a payor corporation has an adjusted taxable loss for the taxable year, then its adjusted taxable income shall be treated as zero.

(ii) *Effect on excess limitation carryforward.*—The amount of an adjusted taxable loss reduces excess limitation carryforward for the purpose of determining whether there is excess interest expense for a taxable year.

(iii) *Adjusted taxable loss not carried forward.*—An adjusted taxable loss in one taxable year shall not affect the determination of a corporation's adjusted taxable income for any other taxable year.

(g) *Related persons.*—(1) *In general.*—The term "related person" means any person who is related to the taxpayer within the meaning of sections 267(b) or 707(b)(1). For this purpose, the constructive ownership and attribution rules of section 267(c) shall apply.

(2) *Anti-abuse rule.*—In determining whether persons are related, the substance, rather than the form, of ownership is controlling. Thus, for example, the principles of § 1.957-1(b)(2) shall apply to determine whether an arrangement to shift formal voting power or formal ownership of shares away from any person for the purpose of avoiding the application of section 163(j) shall be given effect.

(3) *When related person status is tested.*—Whether a person is related to a payor corporation under section 163(j) is determined with respect to an item of interest expense when such interest expense accrues. For this purpose (notwithstanding the rules in § 1.163(j)-7), interest expense (including amounts treated as interest under this section) shall be treated as accruing daily under principles similar to section 1272(a). Also for this purpose, interest described in paragraph (e)(5) of this section shall be treated as accrued by a partner as it is accrued, under the principles of the preceding sentence, by the partnership. Changes in the relationship between the payor corporation and the payee after an item of interest expense accrues shall not be taken into account.

(4) *Special rule for certain partnerships.*—(i) *Less than 10 percent of partnership held by tax exempt persons.*—Any interest expense paid or accrued to a partnership directly or indirectly by a payor corporation that (without regard to this paragraph (g)(4)) is related to the partnership within the meaning of this paragraph (g) shall not be treated as paid or accrued to a related person if less than 10 percent of the capital and profits interests in such partnership are held by persons with respect to whom no tax is imposed on such interest by subtitle A of the Internal Revenue Code under rules provided in § 1.163(j)-4. However, the preceding sentence shall not apply to treat as interest paid to an unrelated person any interest that (under rules described in this section) is includible in the gross income of a partner in such a partnership who is itself a related person with respect to the payor of such interest.

(ii) *Reduction of tax by treaty.*—If a treaty between the United States and a foreign country reduces the rate of tax imposed by subtitle A of the Code on a partner's distributive share of any interest paid or accrued to a partnership, such partner's interest in the partnership shall, for purposes of § 1.163(j)-2(g)(4)(i), be treated as held in part by a taxable person and in part by a tax exempt person in accordance with the rules described in § 1.163(j)-4(b).

(5) *Examples.*—The principles of this paragraph (g) are illustrated by the following examples.

Example 1—(i) Fifty-one percent of the total combined voting power and value of domestic corporation A is owned by a domestic tax-exempt corporation, D1; the remainder is owned by foreign corporation F1. F1 is organized under the laws of country Z. Under a U.S. tax treaty with country Z, interest paid by A to F1 is exempt from U.S. tax under the rules of § 1.163(j)-4.

(ii) Under these facts, D1 is related to A under section 267(b)(3) (because D1 and A are members of the same controlled group of corporations, as defined in section 267(f)), and interest payments made by A to D1 are exempt related person interest expense, a deduction for which may be disallowed under section 163(j). F1 is not related to A within the meaning of sections 267(b) or 707(b)(1). Deductions for interest paid by A to F1 are not subject to disallowance under section 163(j).

Example 2—(i) The facts are the same as in paragraph (i) of *Example 1,* except that D1 and F1 each own 50 percent of the vote and value of X's stock.

(ii) Unless the substance of D1's and F1's ownership differs from its form, so that paragraph (g)(2) of this section (regarding abusive ownership structures) applies, none of the interest paid by A to D1 or F1 is subject to disallowance under section 163(j).

Example 3—(i) A, a domestic corporation whose taxable year is the calendar year, is a wholly owned subsidiary of F, a foreign corporation. A is a partner, with a one-third share in the capital and profits interests, of P, a domestic partnership whose taxable year is the calendar year. During its taxable year ending December 31, 1990, and taking into account its interest in P, A has adjusted taxable income of $126.67. A's directly incurred interest income and expense for the taxable year are $20 and $90. Of the $90 of interest expense, $60 is paid or accrued to F.

(ii) P's interest income and interest expense for the taxable year of the partnership ending December 31, 1990, are $20 and $50, respectively. A's share of these amounts (determined under rules described in § 1.163(j)-2) are $6.67 and $16.67, respectively. Of P's $50 interest expense for the taxable year, $20 is paid or accrued to F, and the balance is paid or accrued to persons unrelated to A or to any of the other partners of P.

(iii) Interest paid or treated as paid to F by A is not subject to U.S. tax due to a tax treaty. Taking into account A's investment in the partnership (under rules described in § 1.163(j)-3), A does not satisfy the debt-equity ratio safe harbor test in 1990.

(iv) Under § 1.163(j)-1(a) and paragraphs (e)(4) and (5) of this section, in its taxable year ending December 31, 1990, A is required to take into account the interest income and interest expense it directly incurs, plus its share of P's interest income and interest expense. Thus, A's interest income for 1990 is $26.67, and its interest expense is $106.67. A's excess interest expense for 1990 is $16.67, which is the difference between its net interest expense ($106.67 (interest expense) − $26.67 (interest income) = $80) and 50 percent of its adjusted taxable income ($126.67 × 50% = $63.33).

(v) For 1990, under the rule described in paragraph (e)(5) of this section, the amount of A's exempt related person interest expense is $66.67 ($60 + $6.67 = $66.67). Since that amount is greater than its excess interest expense ($16.67), section 163(j) disallows a deduction for $16.67 of A's interest expense for the taxable year. That disallowed interest expense is carried forward to A's 1991 taxable year.

Example 4—(i) X, a domestic corporation, is wholly owned by Y, a partnership. A treaty between the United States and foreign country U reduces the rate of tax on interest paid to residents of country U from 30 percent (the applicable rate for related person interest under sections 871 and 881 in the absence of a treaty) to 15 percent. Nineteen percent of the capital and profits interests of partnership Y are held by Z, a country U corporation entitled to claim the reduced (treaty) rate of tax on interest income; the balance is held by unrelated persons not exempt from U.S. tax on their distributive shares of interest paid by the corporation to the partnership.

(ii) Under paragraph (g)(4) of this section, less than ten percent (19 percent divided by two (30/15)) of Y's capital and profits interests are treated as held by persons who are tax exempt. Accordingly, all interest paid to partnership Y by corporation X is treated as paid to an unrelated person. [Prop. Reg. § 1.163(j)-2.]

[Proposed 6-18-91.]

Proposed Regulation

§ 1.163(j)-3. Computation of debt-equity ratio.—(a) *In general.*—For purposes of section 163(j), the term "debt-equity ratio" means the ratio that the debt of the corporation bears to the equity of the corporation. For rules defining debt and equity, see paragraphs (b) and (c) of this section. For rules regarding the computation of the debt and equity of an affiliated group or a foreign corporation, see §§ 1.163(j)-5 or 1.163(j)-8, respectively.

(b) *Debt.*—(1) *In general.*—The debt of a corporation means its liabilities determined according to generally applicable tax principles. Thus, the amount taken into account on the issue date with respect to a debt instrument which is not issued at a discount or a premium shall be the issue price. The amount taken into account with respect to any debt with original issue discount shall be its issue price plus the portion of the original issue discount previously accrued as determined under the rules of section 1272 (determined without regard to section 1272(a)(7) or (b)(4)). In addition, with respect to the issuer, unamortized bond premium shall be treated as debt.

(2) *Exclusions.*—Short-term liabilities as defined in paragraph (b)(2)(i) of this section and commercial financing liabilities as defined in paragraph (b)(2)(ii) of this section shall be excluded from characterization as debt.

(i) *Short-term liabilities.*—The term "short-term liabilities" means accrued operating expenses, accrued taxes payable, and any account payable for the first 90 days of its existence provided that no interest is accrued with respect to any portion of such 90 day period.

(ii) *Commercial financing liabilities.*—The term "commercial financing liabilities" means any liability if it—

(A) Is incurred by the obligor under a commercial financing agreement (such as an automobile "floorplan" agreement) to buy an item of inventory;

(B) Is secured by the item;

(C) Is due on or before sale of the item; and

(D) If entered into between related parties, has terms that are comparable to the terms of such financing agreements between unrelated parties in the same (or a similar) industry.

(3) *Liabilities of a partnership.*—In determining the debt of a corporation that owns an interest in a partnership (directly or indirectly through one or more pass-through entities), liabilities of the partnership shall be treated as liabilities incurred directly by each partner in the same manner and proportions that the liabilities of the partnership are treated as shared by its partners under section 752.

(4) *Anti-rollover rule.*—Decreases in a corporation's aggregate debt during the last 90 days of its taxable year shall be disregarded to the extent that the corporation's aggregate debt is increased during the first 90 days of the succeeding taxable year.

(c) *Equity.*—(1) *In general.*—Equity means the sum of money and the adjusted basis of all other assets of the corporation reduced (but not below zero) by the taxpayer's debt (as defined in paragraph (b) of this section). Whether an item constitutes an asset shall be determined according to generally applicable tax principles.

(2) *Treatment of stock of certain nonincludible corporations.*—Under the general rule of paragraph (c)(1) of this section, assets include the adjusted basis of stock of any corporation which is not an includible corporation (as defined under section 1504(b)). The adjusted basis of stock held in a corporation which is not an includible corporation shall be further adjusted under principles similar to those in section 864(e)(4) if the taxpayer (or the members of an affiliated group of which the taxpayer is a member) owns stock in the corporation satisfying the requirements of section 864(e)(4)(B)(ii). Cf. § 1.861-12T(c)(2).

(3) *Reduction in assets for excluded liabilities.*—The amount of a taxpayer's equity under paragraph (c)(1) and (2) of this section shall be reduced (but not below zero) by an amount equal to the amount of liabilities excluded under paragraph (b)(2) of this section.

(4) *Partnership interests owned by a corporation.*—In determining the assets of a corporation that owns an interest in a partnership, the corporation shall treat as an asset the adjusted basis of its partnership interest.

(5) *Anti-avoidance rules.*—(i) *In general.*—An asset of the taxpayer shall be disregarded in computing the taxpayer's debt-equity ratio if the principal purpose for acquiring the asset was to reduce the taxpayer's debt-equity ratio.

(ii) *Anti-stuffing rule.*—In determining a corporation's equity, any transfer of assets made by a related person to the corporation during the last 90 days of its taxable year shall be disregarded to the extent that there is a transfer of the same or similar assets by the corporation to a related person during the first 90 days of the corporation's succeeding taxable year. However, this rule shall not apply to the extent that there is full consideration for a transfer in money or property (as that term is defined in section 317(a)).

(d) *Determining the debt and equity of a non-dollar functional currency OBU.*—In determining the dollar value of liabilities and assets on the books of a qualified business unit that has a functional currency other than the dollar, such liabilities and assets shall be translated at the spot rate on the last day of the taxable year. [Prop. Reg. § 1.163(j)-3.]

[Proposed 6-18-91.]

Proposed Regulation

§ 1.163(j)-4. Interest not subject to tax.—(a) *In general.*—Interest paid or accrued by a corporation under the rules of § 1.163(j)-1 is not subject to tax for purposes of section 163(j) if no U.S. tax is imposed with respect to such interest under subtitle A of the Internal Revenue Code (determined without regard to net operating losses or net operating loss carryovers), taking into account any applicable treaty obligation of the United States. For this purpose, whether interest paid or accrued to a partnership is subject to tax is determined at the partner level.

(b) *Partially exempt interest.*—Interest that is subject to a reduced rate of tax under any treaty obligation of the United States applicable to the recipient shall be treated as in part subject to the statutory tax rate under sections 871 or 881 and in part not subject to tax, based on the proportion that the rate of tax under the treaty bears to the statutory tax rate. Thus, for purposes of section 163(j), if the statutory tax rate is 30 percent, and pursuant to a treaty U.S. tax is instead limited to a rate of 10 percent, two-thirds of such interest shall be considered interest not subject to tax.

(c) *Date for determining whether interest is subject to U.S. tax.*—The determination of whether interest is subject to U.S. tax is made on the date the interest is received or accrued by the payee, whichever is relevant under normally applicable U.S. tax principles for purposes of determining the tax, if any, on the payee.

(d) *Certain interest paid to special entities.*— (1) *Controlled foreign corporations.*—(i) *In general.*—Interest that is paid or accrued to a foreign corporation described in section 957(a) (a "controlled foreign corporation") and that is not otherwise subject to tax under paragraph (a) of this section shall be deemed subject to tax to the extent that such interest is included in the foreign corporation's net foreign personal holding company income under § 1.954-1T(c) and results in an inclusion in the gross income of a United States shareholder under section 951(a)(1)(A)(i) (or would have been included in a United States shareholder's gross income but for an election under § 1.954-1T(d)).

(ii) *Effect of section 952(c)(1)(A) (earnings and profits) limitation.*—For purposes of paragraph (d)(1) of this section, if a controlled foreign corporation's subpart F income for the taxable year is limited under section 952(c)(1)(A), each category of subpart F income described in section 952(a), and, within each such category, each component thereof, shall be treated as reduced ratably.

(iii) *Net foreign personal holding company income.*—To determine whether an item of interest income is included in a controlled foreign corporation's net foreign personal holding company income for the taxable year, the expenses allocable to such interest shall be deemed to bear the same ratio to the total expenses allocable to the controlled foreign corporation's net foreign personal holding company income (determined pursuant to § 1.954-1T(c)) as the amount of such interest bears to the controlled foreign corporation's gross foreign personal holding company income (determined under § 1.954-1T(a)(2)(i)).

(iv) *Related person interest.*—If related person interest is allocated to the item of interest under the provisions of § 1.904-5(c)(2) and paragraph (d)(1)(iii) of this section, and if the United States shareholder receiving such related person interest is subject to United States tax, then, for purposes of paragraph (d)(1)(i) of this section, such allocable related person interest shall be deemed to be net foreign personal holding company income that results in an inclusion under section 951(a)(1)(A)(i).

(v) *Section 78 amount.*—Any foreign taxes that are allocable to an item of interest income satisfying the requirements of paragraph (d)(1)(i) of this section and that are included in a United States shareholder's income under section 78 (or would have been included, but for an election under § 1.954-1T(d)) shall, for purposes of paragraph (d)(1)(i) of this section, be deemed to be net foreign personal holding company income that results in an inclusion under section 951(a)(1)(A)(i).

(2) *Passive foreign investment companies.*—(i) *In general.*—Interest that is not otherwise subject to tax under paragraph (a) of this section, and that is paid or accrued to a passive foreign investment company (as defined in section 1296) that is not a controlled foreign corporation, and which a U.S. person has elected under section 1295 to treat as a qualified electing fund ("QEF"), shall be treated as subject to tax to the extent that such interest is included in the QEF's ordinary earnings (as defined in section 1293(e)(1)) and results in an inclusion in income of such U.S. person under section 1293(a)(1)(A).

(ii) *Ordinary earnings.*—In determining whether an item of interest income is included in the ordinary earnings of a passive foreign investment company, the item shall be reduced by deductions allocable and apportionable to that item under §§ 1.861-8 through 1.861-14T.

(iii) *Section 78 amount.*—Any foreign taxes that are allocable to an item of interest income satisfying the requirements of paragraph (d)(2)(i) of this section and that are included in a U.S. person's income under section 78 pursuant to section 1293(f) shall, for purposes of paragraph (d)(2)(i) of this section, be deemed to be ordinary earnings that are included in the income of a U.S. person under section 1293(a)(1)(A).

(3) *Foreign personal holding companies.*—(i) *In general.*—Interest that is not otherwise subject to tax under paragraph (a) of this section, and that is paid or accrued to a foreign personal holding company (as defined in section 552) that is neither a passive foreign investment company nor a controlled foreign corporation, shall be treated as subject to tax to the extent that such interest is included in the company's undistributed foreign personal holding company income (as defined in section 556) and results in an inclusion in income of a U.S. person under section 551(a).

(ii) *Undistributed foreign personal company income.*—In determining whether an item of interest income is included in the undistributed foreign personal holding company income of a foreign personal holding company, the item shall be reduced by deductions allocable and apportionable to that item under §§ 1.861-8 through 1.861-14T.

(iii) *Effect of distributions.*—Any amount that would be treated as subject to tax by virtue of this paragraph (d)(3) but for a dividends paid deduction under section 561 shall be treated as subject to tax.

(4) *Producer's loan interest paid to a DISC.*—Interest paid or accrued with respect to a DISC (as defined in section 992) that is treated as interest with respect to a producer's loan (as defined in section 993(d)) is treated as subject to U.S. tax if such interest is taxed to the shareholders of the DISC under section 995(b)(1)(A). [Prop. Reg. § 1.163(j)-4.]

[Proposed 6-18-91.]

Proposed Regulation

§ 1.163(j)-5. Affiliated group rules.—(a) *Certain related corporations treated as one taxpayer.*—(1) *Scope.*—This section applies section 163(j) to certain related corporations which are (or are treated as) members of an affiliated group and which under section 163(j)(6)(C) and (7) are treated as a single taxpayer. Paragraphs (a)(2) and (a)(3) of this section describe the corporations that are subject to such treatment. (For purposes of section 163(j) and these regulations, the rules in regulations under section 1502 apply, but unless the context otherwise requires, the term "member" means a corporation that is, or is treated as, a member of an affiliated group under this paragraph (a), and the term "group" refers collectively to the member and the other corporations that are so treated.) Paragraph (a)(4) of this section provides rules that treat a corporation as a member of a single affiliated group if the rules of this paragraph (a) would otherwise cause it to be treated as a member of more than one affiliated group. Paragraph (b) of this section provides rules regarding the computation of items of income, expense, and carryovers under section 163(j) for an affiliated group of corporations if all of the members of such group join in the filing of a single consolidated return for the taxable year under section 1501. Paragraph (c) of this section provides rules for corporations that are not members of consolidated groups which are subject to the rules of § 1.163(j)-5(b). Paragraph (d) of this section provides rules regarding the computation of the debt-equity ratio for purposes of applying the debt-equity ratio safe harbor test described in § 1.163(j)-1(b). Paragraph (e) of this section provides rules regarding the treatment of, and an election pertaining to, assets of certain acquired corporations.

(2) *Affiliated corporations.*—To the extent provided in this section, all the members of an affiliated group (as defined in section 1504(a)) of which a corporation is a member on the last day of its taxable year shall be treated as one taxpayer for purposes of section 163(j) and this section, without regard to whether such affiliated group files a consolidated return pursuant to section 1501.

(3) *Certain unaffiliated corporations.*—(i) *In general.*—If at least 80 percent of the total voting power and total value of the stock of an includible corporation (as defined in section 1504(b)) is owned, directly or indirectly, by another includible corporation, the first corporation shall be treated as a member of an affiliated group that includes the other corporation and its affiliates. The attribution rules of section 318 shall apply for purposes of determining indirect stock ownership under this paragraph (a)(3).

(ii) *Example.*—The principles of this paragraph (a)(3) are illustrated by the following example.

Example. X and Y are wholly owned domestic subsidiaries of F, a foreign corporation. X and Y are not members of an affiliated group under section 1504(a) because F is not itself an includible corporation under section

1504(b)(3). However, under paragraph (a)(3) of this section, X and Y are treated as members of an affiliated group, since, under section 318(a)(3)(C), X is treated as owning indirectly 100 percent of Y, and Y is treated as owning indirectly 100 percent of X.

(4) *Tie-breaker rules.*—If the rules of this paragraph (a) would treat a corporation as a member of more than one affiliated group, then the principles of section 1563(b)(4) and the regulations thereunder shall determine the group of which such corporation shall be treated as a member.

(b) *Operative rules for consolidated groups.*—(1) *In general.*—If all of the members of the affiliated group are members of a single consolidated group for the taxable year, the computations required by section 163(j) and these regulations (other than the computation of the group's debt-equity ratio under paragraph (d) of this section) shall be made in accordance with the rules of this paragraph (b). See paragraph (c) of this section for rules applicable to affiliated groups not described in the preceding sentence.

(2) *Items determined on a consolidated basis.*—The computations required by section 163(j) and these regulations shall be determined for the group on a consolidated basis. For example, the group's taxable income shall be the consolidated taxable income determined under § 1.1502-11 (without regard to any carryforwards or disallowances under section 163(j)), and the group's net interest expense shall be the excess, if any, of the group's aggregate interest expense over the group's aggregate interest income (as provided in §§ 1.163(j)-2(d) and (e)). Similarly, the group's excess interest expense shall be determined by reference to the group's net interest expense, adjusted taxable income, and excess limitation carryforward (as determined under paragraph (b)(5) of this section). Except as provided in paragraphs (b)(5) and (6) of this section, disallowed interest expense carryforwards and excess limitation carryforwards shall also be determined on a consolidated basis.

(3) *Exempt related person interest expense.*—In determining the group's exempt related person interest expense, interest expense shall be treated as paid or accrued to a related person (within the meaning of § 1.163(j)-2(g)) if it would be so treated if paid or accrued to the same payee by any member of the group.

(4) *Deferred intercompany gain.*—For purposes of determining the adjusted taxable income of the group, the following special rules shall apply—

(i) Any gain on a deferred intercompany transaction (including any gain described in § 1.1502-14T(a)) that is restored in accordance with the rules under §§ 1.1502-13(d) or 1.1502-13T(l) shall be subtracted from the group's consolidated taxable income.

(ii) If property is disposed of under § 1.1502-13(e)(2) or (f) or § 1.1502-13T(m), any amount subtracted from the group's consolidated taxable income in a previous taxable year with respect to such property under paragraph (b)(4)(i) of this section shall be added to the group's consolidated taxable income.

(iii) *Example.*—The principles of this paragraph (b)(4) are illustrated by the following example.

Example—(i) On January 1, 1991, X, a member of an affiliated group which files a consolidated return for the calendar year, purchases property for $200 from an unrelated person. X depreciates the property over a 5-year period. On January 1, 1996, when X's basis in the property is $0, X sells the property to Y, another member of the group, for $200, which is the property's fair market value at such time. The sale is a deferred intercompany transaction under § 1.1502-13, and X's gain of $200 is deferred under § 1.1502-13(c). In the hands of Y, the property is once again depreciable over a 5-year period. The group claims a depreciation deduction with respect to the property of $40 in 1996, which results in the restoration of $40 of X's deferred gain under § 1.1502-13T(l) for such year.

(ii) As provided in paragraph (b)(3)(i) of this section, the group's taxable income for 1996 is reduced by $40, the amount of restored gain under § 1.1502-13T(l) with respect to the transferred property. In addition, as provided in § 1.163(j)-2(f)(2)(iii) and paragraph (b)(2) of this section, the group's taxable income for 1996 is increased by $40, the amount of the group's depreciation deduction with respect to the transferred property for such year.

(iii) On January 1, 1997, Y sells the property for $200 to an unrelated person and recognizes gain of $40. The sale results in restoration of $160 of gain under § 1.1502-13T(m) with respect to the earlier transfer of property from X to Y. Thus, Y's sale results in the group's 1997 consolidated taxable income increasing by $200 prior to any adjustment under section 163(j). Under § 1.163(j)-2(f)(3)(i), the consolidated taxable income is reduced by $240 to reflect previous depreciation deductions with respect to such property. In addition, as provided in paragraph (b)(4)(ii) of this section, the consolidated taxable income is increased by $40, the amount subtracted from the group's 1996 consolidated taxable income by virtue of

Prop. Reg. § 1.163(j)-5(b)(4)(iii)

the restoration of $40 of deferred gain in that year.

(5) *Carryforwards to current taxable year.*—The group's disallowed interest expense carryforward or excess limitation carryforwards to the current taxable year shall be the relevant carryforwards from the group's prior taxable years, plus any disallowed interest expense carryforward or excess limitation carryforwards from separate return years permitted to be used by the group under the rules of § 1.163(j)-6.

(6) *Members leaving the group.*—(i) *Disallowed interest expense carryforward.*—A member leaving the group shall carry forward to its separate return years a portion of the group disallowed interest expense carryforward determined as of the end of the last consolidated return year during which the corporation was a member of the group. Such portion shall equal the amount of the group's disallowed interest expense carryforward multiplied by a fraction, the numerator of which is the aggregate amount of exempt related person interest expense paid or accrued by such member during the period when it was a member of the group, and the denominator of which is the aggregate amount of exempt related person interest expense paid or accrued by all members of the group. If a member has pre-affiliation disallowed interest expense carryforward upon entering the group, the amount of such member's disallowed interest expense carryforward shall be treated as exempt related person interest expense of both the member and the group. Further, the group's disallowed interest expense carryforward shall be reduced by the amount allocated to the member. If the member leaves the group during the consolidated return year, rules similar to the rules of § 1.1502-21(b)(2) shall apply.

(ii) *Excess limitation carryforward.*—A member leaving the group shall not carry forward to its separate return years any portion of the group's excess limitation carryforward, and the group's excess limitation carryforward shall not be reduced by virtue of such member's departure from the group. However, if all the members of a consolidated group become members of another consolidated group, the acquired group's excess limitation carryforward shall become excess limitation carryforward of the corporation that was the common parent of the acquired group. For purposes of determining the extent to which this excess limitation carryforward becomes excess limitation carryforward of the acquiring group under paragraph (b)(5) of this section, see § 1.163(j)-6(b).

(7) *Examples.*—The following examples illustrate the principles of this paragraph (b).

Example 1—(i) X, Y, and Z are domestic corporations that are members of a newly formed consolidated group described in paragraph (b) of this section. X owns 100 percent of the stock of Y, and Y owns 80 percent of the stock of Z. F1, a foreign corporation, owns 60 percent of the stock of X. Any interest paid or accrued by X, Y, or Z to F1 is exempt under section 163(j) because it is exempt from U.S. withholding tax under a treaty with F1's country of residence. Such interest (including interest paid by Z) is also paid or accrued to a related person within the meaning of § 1.163(j)-2(g) and paragraph (b)(3) of this section.

(ii) For 1991, the group's first taxable year, X, Y, and Z have the following relevant items of income and expense—

Company	Interest Income	Interest Expense	Exempt Related Person Interest Expense
X	$600	$500	—
Y	200	900	$600
Z	—	200	150
Total	$800	$1,600	$750

(iii) Under § 1.1502-11, the group's consolidated taxable income for the 1991 year is $150. Adjustments to consolidated taxable income total $50, resulting in consolidated adjusted taxable income of $200. The group's net interest expense for 1991 is $800 ($1,600 − $800), and its excess interest expense is $300 ($800 − ($1,000/2)). The group's exempt related person interest expense for 1991 is $750. The group's disallowed interest expense for 1991 is the lesser of its excess interest expense or its exempt related person interest expense, or $300. This $300 is a group disallowed interest expense carryforward to the group's 1992 taxable year.

Example 2—(i) The facts are the same as in *Example 1*. In the group's 1992 taxable year, the members have the following relevant items of income and expense—

Company	Interest Income	Interest Expense	Exempt Related Person Interest Expense
X	$600	$500	$50
Y	200	900	600
Z	—	200	150
Total	$800	$1,600	$800

(ii) Under § 1.1502-11, the group's consolidated taxable income for 1992 is $1,100. Adjustments to consolidated taxable income total $200, resulting in consolidated adjusted taxable income of $1,300. The group's net interest expense for 1992 is $800 ($1,600 − $800), its excess interest expense is $0 ($800 − ($2,100/2)), and it has excess limitation for the year of $250 ($2,100/2 − $800). The group is permitted to deduct all of its current exempt related person interest expense ($800), plus an amount of its disallowed interest expense carryforward from 1991 equal to its 1992 excess limitation, or $250. This leaves a disallowed interest expense carryforward to the group's 1993 taxable year of $50.

Example 3. The facts are the same as in *Example 2*, except that Z leaves the group on December 31, 1992. Under the rules of paragraph (b)(6)(i) of this section, Z's disallowed interest expense carryforward to its 1993 separate return year is equal to the group's remaining carryforward at the end of 1992 ($50), multiplied by a fraction, the numerator of which is $300 (the total amount of exempt related person interest expense paid or accrued by Z while it was a member of the group) and the denominator of which is $1,550 (the total amount of exempt related person interest expense paid or accrued by all members of the group). Thus, Z's carryforward to its 1993 separate return year is $9.68. The XY group's carryforward to its consolidated 1993 taxable year is reduced by that amount, and is therefore $40.32.

(c) *Operative rules for other groups.*—(1) *In general.*—(i) *Group members' computation years.*—This paragraph (c) provides rules for the application of section 163(j) and these regulations to corporations that are members of a group not governed by paragraph (b) of this section. Under this paragraph (c), a corporation that is a group member is required to take into account the items of income, expense, and carryovers that are pertinent under section 163(j) for all group members whose taxable years end with or within the taxable year of the member with respect to which computations are required (hereafter, a "computation year").

(ii) *Treatment of consolidated subgroup.*—If some of the members of a group subject to this paragraph (c) join in filing a consolidated return under section 1501 for a taxable year ("consolidated subgroup"), such consolidated subgroup shall be treated as a single member of the group for purposes of applying this paragraph (c). The consolidated subgroup's items of income, expense and carryover that are pertinent under section 163(j) and these regulations shall be determined on a consolidated group basis, as if the consolidated subgroup were described in paragraph (b) of this section.

(2) *Determination and allocation of group items.*—The computations required to be made under this paragraph (c) shall be made as follows—

(i) *Step 1—Certain items determined separately.*—The exempt related person interest expense, interest income, interest expense, taxable income, and adjustments to taxable income required by § 1.163(j)-2(f), other than the adjustment for net interest expense described in § 1.163(j)-2(f)(2)(i), shall be determined separately for each member of the group.

(ii) *Step 2—Computation of certain group items.*—(A) *Net interest expense.*—The separately determined amounts of interest income and interest expense for each member shall be aggregated and then netted to determine the group's net interest expense.

(B) *Adjusted taxable income.*—To determine the group's adjusted taxable income, the separately determined taxable income of each member and adjustments thereto (other than net interest expense) shall be aggregated, and the amount of the group's net interest expense (as determined under paragraph (c)(2)(ii)(A) of this section) shall be added to such amount.

(C) *Exempt related person interest expense.*—To determine the amount of the group's exempt related person interest expense, the separately determined amounts of exempt related person interest expense for each member shall be aggregated. In making this determination, interest expense shall be treated as paid or accrued to a related person (within the meaning of § 1.163(j)-2(g)) if it would be so treated if paid or accrued to the same payee by any member of the group.

(D) *Excess limitation carryforward.*—To determine the amount of the group's excess limitation carryforward from each of the three prior computation years, the amount of each member's excess limitation carryforward from each of such prior years shall be aggregated.

(E) *Disallowed interest expense carryforward.*—To determine the amount of the group's disallowed interest expense carryforward, the amounts of disallowed interest expense carryforward of each member shall be aggregated.

(iii) *Step 3—Determination of the group's interest deduction.*—(A) *Excess interest expense of the group.*—The group's excess interest expense for the computation year shall be determined by reference to its net interest expense, adjusted taxable income, and excess limitation carryforward (as determined in *Step 2*). The ordering rule of §1.163(j)-1(d) shall apply in determining which, if any, of the group's excess limitation carryforwards from prior years are absorbed in this computation.

(B) *Disallowed interest expense of the group.*—The group's disallowed interest expense for the computation year shall be determined by reference to its exempt related person interest expense and excess interest expense as determined in *Step 2* and *Step 3*, respectively. Disallowed interest expense of the group arising in the computation year shall be allocated to each member based on the following ratio:

$$\frac{\text{Exempt related person interest expense of the member for the computation year}}{\text{Exempt related person interest expense of the group for the computation year.}}$$

(C) *Excess limitation and deduction of disallowed interest expense carryforward.*—(1) *Excess limitation.*—The group's excess limitation for the computation year shall be determined by reference to its net interest expense and adjusted taxable income (as determined in *Step 2*).

(2) *Deduction of disallowed interest expense carryforward.*—The amount of the group's disallowed interest expense carried forward to the current computation year (as determined in *Step 2*) that is deductible therein under §1.163(j)-1(c) shall be determined by reference to the excess limitation of the group. The deduction for such carryforward shall be allocated to each member of the group based on the following ratio:

$$\frac{\text{Disallowed interest expense carryforward of the member from the preceding computation year}}{\text{Disallowed interest expense carryforward of the group from the preceding computation year.}}$$

(iv) *Step 4—Carryforwards to next computation year.*—(A) *Amounts not deductible in the current computation year.*—Each member's disallowed interest expense carryforward to the next computation year shall consist of such member's allocable share of the group's disallowed interest expense for the current year (as determined in *Step 3*), plus such member's allocable share of the group's disallowed interest expense carryforward to the current year that is not deductible in the current year (because such amount exceeds any excess limitation of the group for that year). The group's unused disallowed interest expense carryforward to the current year shall be allocated to each member of the group based on the following ratio:

$$\frac{\text{Disallowed interest expense carryforward of the member from the preceding computation year}}{\text{Disallowed interest expense carryforward of the group from the preceding computation year.}}$$

(B) *Excess limitation carryforward.*—The excess limitation carryforward of the group, if any, from each of the two prior computation years that is not absorbed in the current computation year (as provided in *Step 3*) shall be allocated, by year, to each member of the group (for succeeding computation years) based on the following ratio:

$$\frac{\text{Excess limitation carryforward of the member from the specific prior computation year}}{\text{Excess limitation carryforward of the group from the same prior computation year.}}$$

(The group's excess limitation carryforward from the third prior computation year expires after the current computation year and therefore cannot be carried forward to the next year. See §1.163(j)-1(d).)

(C) *Allocation of remaining excess limitation of the group for the computation year.*—(1) *In general.*—Excess limitation of the group for the computation year remaining after the deduction of disallowed interest expense carryforward to such year is allocated to each member of the group based on the following ratio:

$$\frac{\text{Separate excess limitation for each member of the group for the computation year}}{\text{Total of the separate excess limitations of each member of the group for the computation year.}}$$

(2) *Separate excess limitation.*—The separate excess limitation of each member shall be computed as if the member was not a member of an affiliated group for the computation year. The separate excess limitation of each member shall be determined under the rules of § 1.163(j)-2(c) and before reduction for the amount of any disallowed interest expense carried forward to that year by such member. For purposes of these computations, a member that has net interest income for the computation year has net interest expense of zero, and a member that has excess interest expense for the computation year has separate excess limitation of zero.

(D) *Members leaving a group.*—A member leaving a group shall carry forward to succeeding taxable years any excess limitation or disallowed interest expense allocated to it under this paragraph (c). For rules limiting the use of such carryforwards when such member becomes a member of another affiliated group, or has transferred its assets in a transaction to which section 381(a) applies, see § 1.163(j)-6.

(3) *Examples.*—The following examples illustrate the principles of this paragraph (c).

Example 1. A, B, and C are calendar-year domestic corporations that are members of an affiliated group. *Table 1* depicts amounts determined in *Step 1* for these corporations for their taxable years ending December 31, 1991. Under rules described in paragraph (d) of this section, this group does not satisfy the debt-equity ratio safe harbor test for 1991. Assume, for purposes of this example, that there are no excess limitation carryforwards and no disallowed interest expense carryforwards to the 1991 taxable year for any member of the group.

TABLE 1

	Interest Income	Interest Expense	Taxable Income Before Applying § 163(j)	Adjustments To Taxable Income (Not Including Net Interest Expense)	Exempt Related Person Interest Expense
A	$600.00	$500.00	$50.00	$25.00	$—
B	$200.00	$900.00	$200.00	$75.00	$600.00
C	$—	$200.00	$50.00	$—	$150.00
Total	$800.00	$1,600.00	$300.00	$100.00	$750.00

(a) *Step 2 determinations.* The group's *Step 2* determinations are as follows:

(1) *Net interest expense.* The separately determined interest income and interest expense of A, B, and C are aggregated. Thus, the net interest expense of the group is $800 ($1,600 − $800).

(2) *Adjusted taxable income.* The separately determined taxable income and the separately determined adjustments (other than net interest expense) of A, B, and C are aggregated and added to the group's net interest expense to determine the group's adjusted taxable income of $1,200 ($300 + $100 + $800 = $1,200).

(3) *Exempt related person interest expense.* The separately determined amounts of exempt related person interest expense of A, B, and C are aggregated to determine the group's exempt related person interest expense of $750 ($600 + $150).

(b) *Step 3 determinations.* The group's *Step 3* determinations are as follows:

(1) *Excess interest expense.* The group's excess interest expense is equal to its net interest expense less one-half of its adjusted taxable income (each as determined in *Step 2*) ($800 − (½ × $1,200) = $200).

(2) *Disallowed interest expense.* The group's disallowed interest expense is $200, which is the lesser of its exempt related person interest expense (as determined in *Step 2* ($750)) or its excess interest expense (as determined in this *Step 3* ($200)).

(3) *Disallowed interest expense allocations.* Disallowed interest expense for the computation year shall be allocated among A, B, and C under *Step 3* based on the ratio of each member's exempt related person interest expense to the group's exempt related person interest expense. Since A has no exempt related person interest expense, no disallowed interest expense is allocated to it. Disallowed interest expense of $160 is allocated to B (($600/$750) × $200). Disallowed interest expense of $40 is allocated to C (($150/$750) × $200). Thus, B and C have $160 and $40, respectively, of disallowed interest expense which shall be carried forward to their succeeding taxable years under *Step 4*.

Example 2. The facts are the same as in *Example 1*, and thus B and C have $160 and $40, respectively, of disallowed interest expense carried forward to the computation year ending December 31, 1992. *Table 2* depicts the separately determined items as determined in *Step 1* for the taxable years of A, B, and C ending December 31, 1992. Under rules described in paragraph (d) of this section, this group does not satisfy the debt-equity ratio safe harbor test for 1992.

TABLE 2

	Interest Income	Interest Expense	Taxable Income Before Applying § 163(j)	Adjustments To Taxable Income (Not Including Net Interest Expense)	Exempt Related Person Interest Expense
A	$200.00	$800.00	$400.00	$50.00	$300.00
B	$100.00	$500.00	$600.00	$100.00	$300.00
C	$300.00	$200.00	$500.00	$50.00	$100.00
Total	$600.00	$1,500.00	$1,500.00	$200.00	$700.00

(a) *Step 2 determinations.* For the 1992 computation year, the *Step 2* determinations of A, B, and C are as follows:

(1) *Net interest expense.* The separately determined interest income and interest expense of A, B, and C are aggregated to determine the group's net interest expense of $900 ($1,500 − $600).

(2) *Adjusted taxable income.* The separately determined taxable income and adjustments to taxable income (other than net interest expense) of A, B, and C are aggregated and added to the group's net interest expense to yield the group's adjusted taxable income of $2,600 ($1,500 + $200 + $900 = $2,600).

(3) *Exempt related person interest expense.* Each member's separately determined amounts of exempt related person interest expense are aggregated to determine the group's exempt related person interest expense of $700 ($300 + $300 + $100).

(b) *Step 3 determinations.* The group has excess limitation of $400 in 1992 (($\frac{1}{2}$ × $2,600) (adjusted taxable income) − $900 (net interest expense)). All $200 of the group's disallowed interest expense carried forward to 1992 is deductible by B and C (in accordance with the allocation described in *Step 3*) and reduces the group's excess limitation arising in 1992 to $200 ($400 − $200).

(c) *Step 4 determinations.* Under *Step 4*, A, B, and C must allocate the $200 of remaining excess limitation among themselves based on the ratio that each member's separate excess limitation bears to the sum of the members' separate excess limitations.

(1) *Computation of each member's separate excess limitation.* The separate excess limitation for each member shall be determined separately, as if each member was not a member of an affiliated group. Accordingly, the separate excess limitations of A, B, and C are determined as follows. A has separate excess interest expense of $75 ($600 − ($\frac{1}{2}$ × $1,050)). B has a separate excess limitation of $150 ($\frac{1}{2}$ × $1,100) − $400). C has separate excess limitation of $275 ($\frac{1}{2}$ × $550).

(2) *Allocation of group excess limitation.* Since A has separate excess interest expense rather than separate excess limitation, no excess limitation is allocated to A. The group's excess limitation of $200 is allocated between B and C as follows. B is allocated $70.59 ($200 × ($150/$425)) and C is allocated $129.41 ($200 × ($275/$425)). Thus, B and C will carry forward $70.59 and $129.41 of excess limitation, respectively, to their succeeding taxable years.

Example 3. A, B, and C are domestic corporations that are members of the same affiliated group under the rules of paragraph (a) of this section. Table 3 depicts their *Step 1* determinations for A's taxable year ending September 30, 1990, B's taxable year ending December 31, 1990, and C's taxable year ending January 31, 1991. Assume, for the taxable years illustrated in *Table 3*, that there is no pre-effective date excess limitation carryforward, that (under the rules described in paragraph (d) of this section) the group does not satisfy the debt-equity ratio safe harbor test, and that all interest expense paid by A, B, and C is exempt related person interest expense.

TABLE 3

	Interest Income	Interest Expense	Taxable Income Before Applying § 163(j)	Adjustments To Taxable Income (Not Including Net Interest Expense)	Exempt Related Person Interest Expense
A	$100.00	$500.00	$150.00	$50.00	$500.00
B	$200.00	$600.00	$350.00	$50.00	$600.00
C	$—	$600.00	$300.00	$100.00	$600.00
Total	$300.00	$1,700.00	$800.00	$200.00	$1,700.00

(a) *A's determinations.* With respect to A's computation year ending September 30, 1990, only A is treated as a member of the affiliated group (since for B and C these are pre-effective date years). Therefore, A's disallowed interest expense is $100, which is the lesser of its excess interest expense of $100 ($400 − (½ × $600)) or its exempt related person interest expense ($500). A's disallowed interest expense of $100 is carried forward to A's next computation year.

(b) *B's Step 2 determinations.* For purposes of computing B's disallowed interest expense for its taxable year ending December 31, 1990, only A and B are treated as affiliated group members (since for C this is a pre-effective date year). B's *Step 2* determinations are as follows:

(1) *Net interest expense.* The separately determined interest income and interest expense of A and B are aggregated to determine their net interest expense of $800 (($500 + $600) − ($100 + $200)).

(2) *Adjusted taxable income.* The separately determined taxable income of A and B ($150 + $350) and the separately determined adjustments to their taxable income (other than net interest expense) ($50 + $50) are aggregated and added to their net interest expense (as provided in *Step 2*) ($800) to yield the adjusted taxable income of A and B of $1,400 ($500 + $100 + $800).

(3) *Exempt related person interest expense.* The separately determined amounts of exempt related person interest expense of A and B are aggregated to determine their exempt related person interest expense of $1,100 ($500 + $600).

(c) *B's Step 3 determinations.* B's *Step 3* determinations are as follows:

(1) *Excess interest expense.* The excess interest expense of A and B is $100, which is equal to their net interest expense less one-half of their adjusted taxable income, each as determined in *Step 2* ($800 − (½ × $1,400)).

(2) *Disallowed interest expense.* The disallowed interest expense of A and B is $100, which is the lesser of the exempt related person interest expense of A and B (as determined in *Step 2* ($1,100)) or their excess interest expense (as determined in *Step 3* ($100)).

(3) *Disallowed interest expense allocations.* Disallowed interest expense for the computation year is allocated to B under *Step 3* based on the ratio of B's separate exempt related person interest expense ($600) to the sum of A and B's exempt related person interest expense ($1,100). Thus, the amount of disallowed interest expense allocated to B with respect to its computation year ending December 31, 1990, is $54.55 (($600/$1,100) × $100), which is carried forward to B's next computation year under *Step 4*. Because this is B's computation year, no allocation of disallowed interest expense for the computation year is made to A.

(d) *C's Step 2 determinations.* To compute its disallowed interest for its computation year ending January 31, 1991, C's *Step 2* determinations are as follows:

(1) *Net interest expense.* The separately determined interest income and interest expense of A, B, and C are aggregated. Thus, the net interest expense of A, B, and C is $1,400 ($1,700 − $300).

(2) *Adjusted taxable income.* The separately determined taxable income of A, B, and C ($150 + $350 + $300) and the separately determined adjustments (other than net interest expense) of A, B, and C ($50 + $50 + $100) are aggregated and combined with the net interest expense of A, B, and C ($1,400, as determined in *Step 2*) to yield the adjusted taxable income of A, B, and C of $2,400 ($800 + $200 + $1,400).

(3) *Exempt related person interest expense.* The separately determined amounts of exempt related person interest expense of A, B, and C are aggregated to determine their exempt related person interest expense of $1,700 ($500 + $600 + $600).

(e) *C's Step 3 determinations.* C's *Step 3* determinations for its computation year ending January 31, 1991 are as follows:

(1) *Excess interest expense.* The excess interest expense of A, B, and C is equal to $200, which is the net interest expense of A, B, and C less one-half of their adjusted taxable incomes, each as determined in *Step 2* ($1,400 − (½ × $2,400)).

(2) *Disallowed interest expense.* The disallowed interest expense of A, B, and C is $200, which is the lesser of the sum of the exempt related person interest expense of A, B, and C as determined in *Step 2* ($1,700) or their excess interest expense as determined in this *Step 3* ($200).

(3) *Disallowed interest expense allocations.* For C's computation year ending January 31, 1991, C is allocated disallowed interest expense under *Step 3* based on the ratio that its exempt related person interest expense ($600) bears to the sum of the exempt related person interest expense of A, B, and C ($500 + $600 + $600 = $1,700). The amount of disallowed interest expense allocated to C with respect to that computation year is $70.59 (($600/$1,700) = $200), which is carried forward to C's next computation year under *Step 4*. Because this is C's computation year, no allocation of disallowed interest expense for the computation year is made to A or B.

Prop. Reg. §1.163(j)-5(c)(3)

(d) *Debt-equity ratio of related corporations treated as one taxpayer.*—(1) *In general.*—In the case of an affiliated group subject to the rules of paragraphs (b) or (c) of this section, the debt-equity ratio safe harbor test described in § 1.163(j)-1(b) shall be applied on a group basis. In the case of a consolidated group subject to paragraph (b) of this section, the debt-equity ratio of the group shall be determined by aggregating the separately determined debt and assets (adjusted as described in paragraphs (d)(2) and (3) of this section) of each member of the group as of the last day of the consolidated return year. In the case of an affiliated group subject to the rules of paragraph (c) of this section, the debt-equity ratio of the group shall be determined, with respect to any member's computation year, by aggregating the separately determined debt and assets (adjusted as described in paragraphs (d)(2) and (3) of this section) of each member of the group as of the last day of its taxable year that is included in the computing member's computation year. For rules regarding the special treatment of, and an election pertaining to, assets of certain acquired corporations, see paragraph (e) of this section.

(2) *Adjustments to group members' debt.*—A member's debt shall be reduced by the amount of its liabilities to another member, and by the amount of any other liability which, if included, would result in duplication of amounts in the group's aggregate debt.

(3) *Adjustments to group members' assets.*—The assets of a member of a group shall be adjusted as follows—

(i) Any amount which represents direct or indirect stock ownership in any member of the affiliated group shall be eliminated from total assets of the affiliated group;

(ii) A note or other evidence of indebtedness between members of an affiliated group shall be eliminated as an asset;

(iii) With respect to transactions between members of an affiliated group in which gain or loss is deferred under §§ 1.1502-13, 1.1502-13T, 1.1502-14, or 1.1502-14T, the adjusted basis of any asset involved in such transaction shall be decreased to the extent of deferred intercompany gain, if any, that has not been taken into account; and

(iv) There shall be eliminated from the assets of the affiliated group any other amount which, if included, would result in duplication of the assets of the affiliated group.

(e) *Election to use fixed stock write-off method for certain stock acquisitions.*—(1) *In general.*—Notwithstanding paragraph (d)(3) of this section, in the case of a qualified stock purchase, an election may be made, in the manner described in paragraph (e)(4) of this section, to determine the group's assets in accordance with the following rules—

(i) The stock of the target corporation and target affiliates (other than stock that is described in paragraph (d)(1)(ii) of this section) shall be treated as an asset of the purchasing corporation. The basis of such stock shall be determined under section 1012, and shall be increased by the amount of the liabilities of the target corporation and target affiliates as of the close of the acquisition date. Solely for purposes of this section, these amounts (together, the "special basis") shall be amortized ratably, on a monthly basis, over the applicable fixed stock write-off period (as described in paragraph (e)(5)(vi) of this section), beginning with the first day of the month in which the acquisition date occurs.

(ii) All assets of the target corporation, target affiliates, and any other members of the affiliated group, the stock of which is owned directly or indirectly by the target or a target affiliate, shall be disregarded.

(iii) Adjustments shall be made to the special basis of the stock of the target corporation and target affiliates solely as provided in paragraphs (e)(1)(i) and (e)(2) of this section. Thus, for example, the special basis shall not be adjusted under the rules of § 1.1502-32.

(2) *Post-acquisition adjustments to special basis.*—The following adjustments shall be made to the special basis of the target corporation and target affiliates—

(i) The special basis of the stock of the target corporation and target affiliates shall be increased under the rules of section 358 for any property contributed to such corporations following the acquisition date;

(ii) The special basis of the stock of the target corporation and target affiliates shall be reduced by the fair market value of any property distributed by such corporations. Solely for purposes of the preceding sentence, any transfer of assets by the target corporation, by any target affiliate, or by any corporation that would be a target affiliate but for the fact that it is not an includible corporation, to any member of the affiliated group other than such corporations, shall be deemed to be a distribution that reduces special basis, but only if such transfer qualifies for nonrecognition under any provision of the Code or is an interaffiliate loan; and

(iii) Where an adjustment is made pursuant to paragraphs (e)(2)(i) or (ii) of this section, the special basis shall be adjusted as of the last day of the month which includes the date of the transaction (or the last day of the shareholder's taxable year, whichever comes first), and the adjusted amount shall be amortized over the remaining amortization period.

(3) *Election out of fixed stock write-off method.*—A taxpayer may elect out of the fixed stock write-off method for any year during the amortization period and use the adjusted tax basis of the assets of the target corporation and its target affiliates to determine its debt-equity ratio for that year and all future years.

(4) *Method for making elections.*— (i) *Election to use method.*—An election to use the fixed stock write-off method is made by attaching a statement to the return of the purchasing corporation (including a consolidated return, where appropriate) for the taxable year that includes the acquisition date for the qualified stock purchase. The election must be signed by an authorized official of, and is effective for, each member of the purchasing corporation's affiliated group.

(ii) *Election to cease to use method.*—An election to cease to use the fixed stock write-off method is made by attaching a statement to the return of the purchasing corporation (including a consolidated return, where appropriate) for the taxable year in which the election is to become effective. The election must be signed by an authorized official of, and is effective for, each member of the purchasing corporation's affiliated group.

(5) *Definitions.*—(i) *Qualified stock purchase.*—For purposes of this paragraph (e), the term "qualified stock purchase" means a qualified stock purchase (as defined under section 338(d)(3)) with respect to which no election has been made under section 338(g), but only if the purchase is made by a corporation which is an includible corporation (as defined in section 1504(b)).

(ii) *Target corporation.*—For purposes of this paragraph (e), the term "target corporation" shall mean a target corporation as defined under section 338(d)(2), but only if such corporation is includible within the purchasing corporation's affiliated group for purposes of this section.

(iii) *Target affiliate.*—For purposes of this paragraph (e), the term "target affiliate" shall mean a target affiliate as defined under section 338(h)(6), but only if such corporation is includible within the purchasing corporation's affiliated group for purposes of this section.

(iv) *Purchasing corporation.*—For purposes of this paragraph (e), the term "purchasing corporation" shall mean a purchasing corporation as defined under section 338(d)(1).

(v) *Acquisition date.*—For purposes of this paragraph (e), the term "acquisition date" shall mean the acquisition date as defined under section 338(h)(2).

(vi) *Fixed stock write-off period.*—(A) *In general.*—Except as provided in paragraph (e)(5)(vi)(B) of this section, the applicable "fixed stock write-off period" means 96 months.

(B) *Acquired corporations owning long-lived assets.*—If more than fifty percent, by value, of the assets of the target corporation and any target affiliates on the acquisition date are described in this paragraph (e)(5)(vi)(B), then the applicable "fixed stock write-off period" means 180 months. An asset is described in this paragraph (e)(5)(vi)(B) if—

(1) It is inventory or a non-wasting tangible or intangible asset (*e.g.*, land or goodwill);

(2) In the case of a depreciable asset, it has a recovery period in excess of 25 years;

(3) In the case of a depletable asset, it has a recovery period for purposes of cost depletion in excess of 25 years;

(4) In the case of an amortizable asset, it has an amortization period in excess of 25 years.

Determinations for purposes of this paragraph (e)(5)(vi)(B) shall be made as if the asset were sold on the acquisition date, and cash, cash items, and marketable securities shall be disregarded for all purposes. A purchasing corporation is only entitled to the benefit of this paragraph (e)(5)(vi)(B) if it demonstrates that it satisfies the requirements of this paragraph in a statement attached to its return accompanying its election to use the fixed stock write-off method. Such statement must provide all necessary information, including all appropriate computations.

(6) *Inclusion of target debt notwithstanding use of fixed stock write-off method.*—Debt of the affiliated group includes the liabilities of a target corporation and any target affiliates notwithstanding that the assets of such corporations are determined using the fixed stock write-off method. [Prop. Reg. § 1.163(j)-5.]

[Proposed 6-18-91.]

Proposed Regulation

§ 1.163(j)-6. Limitation on carryforward of tax attributes.—(a) *Disallowed interest expense carryforward.*—(1) *Affiliated groups.*—If a corporation becomes a member of an affiliated group, the amount of any disallowed interest expense carryforward from a non-affiliation year that may be deducted by the members of an affiliated group under § 1.163(j)-5(b) or (c) may not exceed the amount, if any, of the current year's excess limitation of the affiliated group (determined under §§ 1.163(j)-2(c) and 1.163(j)-5(b) or (c)).

(2) *Section 381(a) transactions.*—The amount of any disallowed interest expense carryforward from a non-affiliation year of a transferor or distributor corporation that may be deducted by the transferee or distributee corporation (or the consolidated group of which it is a member) following a transaction described in section 381(a) may not exceed the amount, if any, of the current year's excess limitation (determined under § 1.163(j)-2(c)).

(3) *Section 382 and SRLY.*—For the application of additional limitations governing disallowed interest expense carryovers, see section 382(h) (relating to built-in deductions of loss corporations) and the regulations thereunder (including § 1.1502-91, relating to section 382(h) rules for built-in deductions of consolidated groups) and § 1.1502-15 (relating to separate return limitation year rules for built-in deductions of consolidated groups)).

(4) *Example.*—The provisions of this paragraph (a) are illustrated by the following example.

Example. In 1992, Z, a non-affiliated corporation, becomes a member of a consolidated group. There is no section 382 ownership change. Under § 1.163(j)-1, Z has $3,000 of disallowed interest expense carryforward from separate return limitation years. Under § 1.163(j)-5(b), the consolidated group (including Z) has excess limitation of $2,000 for 1992 (computed without regard to any disallowed interest expense carryforward). In addition, the consolidated group has excess limitation carryforward of $1,000 from 1991. Under paragraph (a)(1) of this section, only $2,000 (the amount of the consolidated group's excess limitation for 1992) of Z's separate return limitation year disallowed interest expense carryforward is deductible in 1992. The remaining $1,000 of Z's disallowed interest expense carryforward is carried forward to subsequent years and remains subject to the limitations described in paragraph (a) of this section.

(b) *Excess limitation carryforward.*—(1) *Affiliated groups.*—(i) *General rule.*—If a corporation becomes a member of an affiliated group, the amount of any excess limitation carryforward from a non-affiliation year that may be used by members of the group under § 1.163(j)-5(b) or (c) may not exceed the excess, if any, of the corporation's separately computed net interest expense over 50 percent of the corporation's separately computed adjusted taxable income.

(ii) *Special rule for acquired groups.*—If all the members of a group, whether or not consolidated, become members of a consolidated group, the amount of the acquired group's excess limitation carryforward (if any) from non-affiliation years that may be used by the consolidated group may not exceed the acquired group's excess interest expense (if any) for the taxable year. For this purpose, the acquired group's excess interest expense for any taxable year equals the excess interest expense of the former members of the acquired group for the taxable year computed as if they were members of a separate affiliated group making computations under § 1.163(j)-5(c).

(2) *Section 381(a) transactions.*—If a corporation transfers or distributes its assets to another corporation in a transaction described in section 381(a) (other than a transaction described in section 368(a)(1)(F)), the excess limitation carryforward, if any, of the transferor or distributor from a non-affiliation year is reduced to zero immediately after the transaction.

(3) *Anti-avoidance rules.*—Solely for purposes of paragraph (b)(1) of this section, in determining the net interest expense of a member of a group, interest expense paid or accrued with respect to loans incurred or assumed by such member in connection with or after becoming a member of the group are disregarded unless the loan proceeds are actually utilized by the member in its pre-affiliation business. For example, if a loan is incurred by one member of the affiliated group with excess limitation carryforward from non-affiliation years, but the proceeds of the loan are actually utilized by another member of the group, the interest expense with respect to the loan is disregarded for purposes of applying paragraph (b)(1) of this section. In addition, interest on a loan used for the acquisition of the stock of a corporation which is incurred by the acquired corporation may be disregarded for purposes of paragraph (b)(1) of this section if the facts indicate that one of the purposes for the acquired corporation's incurring the loan was to avoid the limitation of such paragraph.

(c) *Affiliation and non-affiliation years.*—(1) *In general.*—For purposes of this section, the taxable year of a member of an affiliated group (as defined in § 1.163(j)-5(a)) is an "affiliation year" with respect to another member if the members were members of an affiliated group (whether or not the same affiliated group as the current affiliated group) with each other on the last day of the taxable year. A "non-affiliation year" is any taxable year that is not an affiliation year.

Prop. Reg. § 1.163(j)-6(a)(2)

(2) *Predecessors and successors.*—For purposes of this section, any reference to a corporation or member or the years of a corporation or member includes, as the context may require, a reference to a successor or predecessor (as defined in § 1.1502-1(f)(4)) or to the years of a successor or predecessor.

(3) *Formation of affiliated groups.*—For purposes of determining whether a corporation has become a member of another corporation's affiliated group solely by reason of § 1.163(j)-5(a), corporations (or affiliated groups) with greater value are deemed to acquire corporations (or affiliated groups) with lesser value and the principles of § 1.1502-75(d)(3) (governing "reverse acquisitions") shall apply.

(d) *Anti-duplication rule.*—The same item of income, expense, or carryforward may not be taken into account more than once if inconsistent with the principles of section 163(j) or these regulations. [Prop. Reg. § 1.163(j)-6.]

[Proposed 6-18-91.]

Proposed Regulation

§ 1.163(j)-7. Relationship to other provisions affecting the deductibility of interest.—(a) *Paid or accrued.*—For purposes of section 163(j), interest expense is not considered "paid or accrued" until such interest would be deductible but for such section.

(b) *Coordination of section 163(j) and certain other provisions.*—(1) *Disallowed interest provisions.*—Except as provided under § 1.163(j)-2(f)(3)(vi), interest expense which is permanently disallowed as a deduction (*e.g.* under sections 265 or 279) is not taken into account under section 163(j).

(2) *Deferred interest provisions.*—Provisions which defer the deductibility of interest (such as sections 163(e)(3) and 267(a)(3)) apply before the application of section 163(j).

(3) *At risk rules and passive activity loss provisions.*—Sections 465 and 469 shall be applied before applying section 163(j). There shall be no recomputation of deductions under section 469.

(4) *Capitalized interest expense.*—Provisions that require the capitalization of interest shall be applied before section 163(j). Capitalized interest is not treated as interest for any purpose under section 163(j). See regulations under section 263A(f) for ordering rules that determine whether exempt related person interest expense is capitalized under section 263A(f).

(5) *Reductions under section 246A.*—Section 246A shall be applied before section 163(j). Any reduction in the dividends received deduction under section 246A shall reduce interest expense taken into account under section 163(j).

(c) *Examples.*—The provisions of this section are illustrated by the following examples.

Example 1—(i) In 1990, Z, a domestic corporation that does not satisfy the debt-equity ratio safe harbor test, has $30,000 of interest expense, all of which is paid to related persons, and no interest income. Of Z's interest expense, $10,000 is permanently disallowed under section 265. The remaining $20,000 of interest expense is exempt from tax under the rules of § 1.163(j)-4. Z's adjusted taxable income for the year is $42,000.

(ii) Under paragraph (b)(1) of this section, the $10,000 interest expense that is permanently disallowed is not taken into consideration for purposes of section 163(j). Therefore, in 1990, none of Z's $20,000 interest expense is disallowed under section 163(j) since that amount is less than 50 percent of Z's 1990 adjusted taxable income ($21,000).

Example 2—(i) In 1990, Q, a domestic corporation that does not satisfy the debt-equity ratio safe harbor test, has $80,000 of adjusted taxable income and $60,000 of interest expense, of which $50,000 is exempt related person interest expense. Q has no interest income. Of Q's exempt related person interest expense, $20,000 is not currently deductible under section 267(a)(2). Assume that the $20,000 expense will be allowed as a deduction under section 267(a)(2) in 1991.

(ii) Under paragraph (b)(2) of this section, section 267(a)(2) is applied before section 163(j). Thus, in computing Q's excess interest expense for 1990, the $20,000 is not taken into account. Accordingly, in 1990, Q has no excess interest expense, since its net interest expense of $40,000 ($60,000 − $20,000) is equal to 50 percent of its adjusted taxable income for the taxable year. The $20,000 of interest expense not allowed as a deduction in 1990 under section 267(a)(2) is taken into account under section 163(j) in 1991, the year in which it is allowed as a deduction under section 267(a)(2).

Example 3—(i) For 1990, H, a closely held domestic corporation that does not satisfy the debt-equity ratio safe harbor test, has $2,000 of rental income and $3,000 of deductions consisting of $1,500 of interest expense, all of which is exempt related person interest expense, $600 of rental expense, and $900 of depreciation expense. Under the passive activity loss provisions of section 469, only $2,000 of H's total expenses are allowable as deductions. These consist of $1,000 ($2,000/$3,000 × $1,500) of interest expense, $400 ($2,000/$3,000 × $600) of rental expense, and $600 of depreciation expense ($2,000/$3,000 × $900). No deduction is allowed in 1990 for H's passive activity loss of $1,000, which consists of $500 of interest expense, $200 of rental expense, and $300 of depreciation expense.

(ii) Under paragraph (b)(3) of this section, section 469 is first applied to determine the amount of interest expense allowable as a deduction ($1,000), after which the rules of section 163(j) are applied. Under section 163(j), H's $1,000 of interest expense is allowable to the extent of 50 percent of its adjusted taxable income ($1,600, determined by adding to H's taxable income (zero) its allowable deductions for interest expense ($1,000) and depreciation deductions ($600). Since H's interest expense of $1,000 (determined after applying section 469) exceeds 50 percent of its adjusted taxable income for 1990 ($800), H's excess interest expense of $200 is disallowed under section 163(j). There is no recomputation of deductions under section 469. [Prop. Reg. § 1.163(j)-7.]

[Proposed 6-18-91.]

Proposed Regulation

§ 1.163(j)-8. Application of section 163(j) to certain foreign corporations.—
(a) *Scope.*—A foreign corporation that has income, gain or loss that is effectively connected (or is treated as effectively connected) with the conduct of a trade or business in the United States for the taxable year will be subject to the rules of this section for the taxable year, provided that it has a debt-equity ratio that exceeds 1.5 to 1 on the last day of the taxable year, computed using the definitions of debt and equity under paragraph (e) of this section.

(b) *Disallowed interest expense.*—In computing its effectively connected taxable income for a taxable year, a foreign corporation described in paragraph (a) of this section will not be allowed to deduct interest expense allocated to its effectively connected income that it has paid, or is deemed to have paid, to a related person (as determined under paragraph (d) of this section) if no tax is imposed with respect to such interest as determined under § 1.163(j)-4. The amount of interest expense disallowed under this paragraph (b), however, shall not exceed the corporation's excess interest expense (as defined in paragraph (c)(2) of this section). Any interest expense that is disallowed under this section may be carried forward to a subsequent taxable year of the foreign corporation and allowed in such year to the extent provided in §§ 1.163(j)-1(c) and 1.163(j)-6(a)(2) and (3). See § 1.163(j)-7 for rules relating to the coordination of this section with other provisions of the Code affecting the deductibility of interest.

(c) *Definitions.*—(1) *In general.*—The terms "net interest expense", "adjusted taxable income", "excess interest expense", and "excess limitation" shall have the same meanings as provided elsewhere in these regulations under section 163(j), with the following additions and modifications. All other terms used in this section shall have the same meanings as provided elsewhere in these regulations under section 163(j).

(2) *Net interest expense.*—The net interest expense of a foreign corporation means the excess, if any, of interest expense that is allocated to the effectively connected income of the foreign corporation for the taxable year and that is taken into account under section 163(j) as provided in § 1.163(j)-7, over the amount of interest includible in its effectively connected gross income for the taxable year.

(3) *Adjusted taxable income.*—The adjusted taxable income of a foreign corporation is its effectively connected taxable income that is not exempt from tax by reason of a U.S. income tax treaty, modified by the additions and subtractions provided in § 1.163(j)-2(f) that are attributable to such effectively connected income.

(4) *Excess interest expense.*—The excess interest expense of a foreign corporation is the excess of its net interest expense determined under paragraph (c)(2) of this section over the sum of 50 percent of its adjusted taxable income determined under paragraph (c)(3) of this section plus any excess limitation carryforward determined under §§ 1.163(j)-1(d) and 1.163(j)-6(b)(2).

(5) *Excess limitation.*—The excess limitation of a foreign corporation means the excess, if any, of 50 percent of the adjusted taxable income of the foreign corporation (determined under paragraph (c)(3) of this section), over its net interest expense (determined under paragraph (c)(2) of this section). For rules regarding the carryforward of any excess limitation of a foreign corporation, see §§ 1.163(j)-1(d) and 1.163(j)-6(b)(2).

(d) *Determination of interest paid to a related person.*—For purposes of this section, the amount of interest that is paid, or deemed paid, by a foreign corporation to a related person, as defined in § 1.163(j)-2(g), shall equal the sum of the amount of interest paid by a U.S. trade or business of the foreign corporation under section 884(f)(1)(A) to a person that is related to the foreign corporation and the amount of interest described in section 884(f)(1)(B) ("excess interest" within the meaning of § 1.884-4T(a)).

(e) *Debt-equity ratio.*—For purposes of computing the debt-equity ratio of a foreign corporation subject to the rules of this section, the debt of the foreign corporation shall equal the amount of its worldwide liabilities for purposes of *Step 2* of § 1.882-5, adjusted in accordance with the rules in § 1.163(j)-3(b) without regard to § 1.163(j)-3(b)(3). The equity of the foreign corporation shall equal the amount of its worldwide assets for purposes of *Step 2* of § 1.882-5, adjusted in accordance with the rules in § 1.163(j)-3(c) without regard to § 1.163(j)-3(c)(4), less its worldwide liabilities as determined in the preceding sentence.

(f) *Example.*—The rules of paragraphs (b) through (e) of this section may be illustrated with the following example.

Example. FC, a country X corporation, is engaged in the active conduct of a trade or business in the United States. FP, a country X corporation, owns all the stock of FC. The debt-equity ratio of FC under paragraph (e) of this section is 3:1. FC has $700 of adjusted taxable income under paragraph (c)(3) of this section, and net interest expense of $600 ($600 of interest expense allocated under § 1.882-5 over $0 of effectively connected interest income) under paragraph (c)(2) of this section. Under § 1.884-4T, $500 of FC's allocated interest expense is treated as interest paid by the U.S. trade or business of FC to FP, and $100 of FC's allocated interest expense is treated as if it were paid by a wholly owned domestic corporation to FC. FC and FP are both qualified residents of country X. Under the treaty, the rate of tax on the $500 of interest paid to FP and on FC's $100 of excess interest is reduced from 30 percent to 10 percent. Thus, of the $600 of interest paid or deemed paid by FC to related persons, two-thirds of the interest is treated as tax-exempt, or $400. The excess interest expense of FC is the excess of FC's net interest expense ($600) over 50 percent of FC's adjusted taxable income ($350) or $250. Thus, $250 of the $400 of interest paid by FC to tax-exempt related persons will be disallowed in computing FC's effectively connected taxable income for the taxable year but may be carried over by FC to a subsequent taxable year.

(g) *Coordination with branch profits tax.*—(1) *Effect on effectively connected earnings and profits.*—The disallowance and carryforward of interest expense under this section shall not affect when such interest expense reduces the effectively connected earnings and profits of a foreign corporation, as defined in § 1.884-1T(f).

(2) *Effect on U.S. net equity.*—The disallowance and carryforward of interest expense under this section shall not affect the computation of the U.S. net equity of a foreign corporation, as defined in § 1.884-1T(c).

(3) *Example.*—The principles of this § 1.163(j)-8(g) are illustrated by the following example.

Example. Assume foreign corporation FC uses money that is treated as a U.S. asset under § 1.884-1T(d)(6) in order to pay interest described in paragraph (d) of this section, and that under this section a deduction for such interest expense is disallowed. Assuming that FC's U.S. assets otherwise remain constant during the year, the U.S. assets of FC will have decreased by the amount of money used to pay the interest expense, and the U.S. net equity of FC will be computed accordingly. [Prop. Reg. § 1.163(j)-8.]

[Proposed 6-18-91.]

Special Deductions for Corporations

§ 1.243-3. Certain dividends from foreign corporations.—

* * *

(b) *Establishing separate earnings and profits accounts.*—A foreign corporation shall, for purposes of section 243(d), maintain a separate account for earnings and profits to which it succeeds which were accumulated by a domestic corporation, and such foreign corporation shall treat such earnings and profits as having been accumulated during the accounting periods in which earned by such domestic corporation. Such foreign corporation shall also maintain such a separate account for the earnings and profits, or deficit in earnings and profits, accumulated by it or accumulated by any other corporations to the earnings and profits of which it succeeds.

(c) *Effect of dividends on earnings and profits accounts.*—Dividends paid out of the accumulated earnings and profits (see section 316(a)(1)) of such foreign corporation shall be treated as having been paid out of the most recently accumulated earnings and profits of such corporation. A deficit in an earnings and profits account for any accounting period shall reduce the most recently accumulated earnings and profits for a prior accounting period in such account. If there are no accumulated earnings and profits in an earnings and profits account because of a deficit incurred in a prior accounting period, such deficit must be restored before earnings and profits can be accumulated in a subsequent accounting period. If a dividend is paid out of earnings and profits of a foreign corporation which maintains two or more accounts (established under the provisions of paragraph (b) of this section) with respect to two or more accounting periods ending on the same day, then the portion of such dividend considered as paid out of each account shall be the same proportion of the total dividend as the amount of earnings and profits in that account bears to the sum of the earnings and profits in all such accounts.

* * *

[Reg. § 1.243-3.]

☐ [*T.D.* 6830, 6-22-65. *Amended by T.D.* 9194, 4-6-2005.]

§ 1.245-1. Dividends received from certain foreign corporations.—(a) *General rule.*—(1) A corporation is allowed a deduction under section 245(a) for dividends received from a foreign corporation (other than a foreign personal holding company as defined in section 552) which is subject to taxation under chapter 1 of the Code if, for an uninterrupted period of not less than 36 months ending with the close of the foreign corporation's taxable year in which the dividends are paid, (i) the foreign corporation is engaged in trade or business in the United States, and (ii) 50 percent or more of the foreign corporation's entire gross income is effectively connected with the conduct of a trade or business in the United States by that corporation. If the foreign corporation has been in existence less than 36 months as of the close of the taxable year in which the dividends are paid, then the applicable uninterrupted period to be taken into consideration in lieu of the uninterrupted period of 36 or more months is the entire period such corporation has been in existence as of the close of such taxable year. An uninterrupted period which satisfied the twofold requirement with respect to business activity and gross income may start at a date later than the date on which the foreign corporation first commenced an uninterrupted period of engaging in trade or business within the United States, but the applicable uninterrupted period is in any event the longest uninterrupted period which satisfies such twofold requirement. The deduction under section 245(a) is allowable to any corporation, whether foreign or domestic, receiving dividends from a distributing corporation which meets the requirements of that section.

(2) Any taxable year of a foreign corporation which falls within the uninterrupted period described in section 245(a)(2) shall not be taken into account in applying section 245(a)(2) and this paragraph if the 100 percent dividends received deduction would be allowable under paragraph (b) of this section, whether or not in fact allowed, with respect to any dividends payable, whether or not in fact paid, out of the earnings and profits of such foreign corporation for that taxable year. Thus, in such case the foreign corporation shall be treated as having no earnings and profits for that taxable year for purposes of determining the dividends received deduction allowance under section 245(a) and this paragraph. However, that taxable year may be taken into account for purposes of determining whether the foreign corporation meets the requirements of section 245(a) that, for the uninterrupted period specified therein, the foreign corporation is engaged in trade or business in the United States and meets the 50 percent gross income requirement.

(b) *Dividends from wholly owned foreign subsidiaries.*—(1) A domestic corporation is allowed a deduction under section 245(b) for any taxable year beginning after December 31, 1966, for dividends received from a foreign corporation (other than a foreign personal holding company as defined in section 552) which is subject to taxation under chapter 1 of the Code if—

(i) The domestic corporation owns either directly or indirectly all of the outstanding stock of the foreign corporation during the entire taxable year of the domestic corporation in which the dividends are received, and

(ii) The dividends are paid out of earnings and profits of a taxable year of the foreign corporation during which (*a*) the domestic corporation receiving the dividends owns directly or indirectly throughout such year all of the outstanding stock of the foreign corporation, and (*b*) all of the gross income of the foreign corporation from all sources is effectively connected for that year with the conduct of a trade or business in the United States by that corporation.

* * *

(c) *Rules of application.*—(1) Except as provided in section 246, the deduction provided by section 245 for any taxable year is the sum of the amounts computed under paragraphs (1) and (2) of section 245(a) plus, in the case of a domestic corporation for any taxable year beginning after December 31, 1966, the sum of the amounts computed under section 245(b)(2).

(2) To the extent that a dividend received from a foreign corporation is treated as a dividend from a domestic corporation in accordance with section 243(d) and § 1.243-3, it shall not be treated as a dividend received from a foreign corporation for purposes of this section.

(3) For purposes of section 245(a) and (b), the amount of a distribution shall be determined under subparagraph (B) (without reference to subparagraph (C)) of section 301(b)(1).

(4) In determining from what year's earnings and profits a dividend is treated as having

been distributed for purposes of this section, the principles of paragraph (a) of § 1.316-2 shall apply. A dividend shall be considered to be distributed, first, out of the earnings and profits of the taxable year which includes the date the dividend is distributed, second, out of the earnings and profits accumulated for the immediately preceding taxable year, third, out of the earnings and profits accumulated for the second preceding taxable year, etc. A deficit in an earnings and profits account for any taxable year shall reduce the most recently accumulated earnings and profits for a prior year in such account. If there are no accumulated earnings and profits in an earnings and profits account because of a deficit incurred in a prior year, such deficit must be restored before earnings and profits can be accumulated in a subsequent accounting year. See also paragraph (c) of § 1.243-3 and paragraph (a)(6) of § 1.243-4.

(5) For purposes of this section the gross income of a foreign corporation for any period before its first taxable year beginning after December 31, 1966, which is from sources within the United States shall be treated as gross income which is effectively connected for that period with the conduct of a trade or business in the United States by that corporation.

(6) For the determination of the source of income and the income which is effectively connected with the conduct of a trade or business in the United States, see sections 861 through 864, and the regulations thereunder.

* * *

[Reg. § 1.245-1.]

☐ [*T.D.* 6183, 6-13-56. *Amended by T.D.* 6752, 9-8-64, *T.D.* 6830, 6-22-65 *and T.D.* 7293, 11-27-73.]

Items Not Deductible

§ 1.267(a)-3. Deduction of amounts owed to related foreign persons.— (a) *Purpose and scope.*—This section provides rules under section 267(a)(2) and (3) governing when an amount owed to a related foreign person that is otherwise deductible under Chapter 1 may be deducted. Paragraph (b) of this section provides the general rules, and paragraph (c) of this section provides exceptions and special rules.

(b) *Deduction of amount owed to related foreign person.*—(1) *In general.*—Except as provided in paragraph (c) of this section, section 267(a)(3) requires a taxpayer to use the cash method of accounting with respect to the deduction of amounts owed to a related foreign person. An amount that is owed to a related foreign person and that is otherwise deductible under Chapter 1 thus may not be deducted by the taxpayer until such amount is paid to the related foreign person. For purposes of this section, a related foreign person is any person that is not a United States person within the meaning of section 7701(a)(30), and that is related (within the meaning of section 267(b)) to the taxpayer at the close of the taxable year in which the amount incurred by the taxpayer would otherwise be deductible. Section 267(f) defines "controlled group" for purposes of section 267(b) without regard to the limitations of section 1563(b). An amount is treated as paid for purposes of this section if the amount is considered paid for purposes of section 1441 or section 1442 (including an amount taken into account pursuant to section 884(f)).

(2) *Amounts covered.*—This section applies to otherwise deductible amounts that are of a type described in section 871(a)(1)(A), (B) or (D), or in section 881(a)(1), (2) or (4). The rules of this section also apply to interest that is from sources outside the United States. Amounts other than interest that are from sources outside the United States, and that are not income of a related foreign person effectively connected with the conduct by such related foreign person of a trade or business within the United States, are not subject to the rules of section 267(a)(2) or (3) or this section. See paragraph (c) of this section for rules governing the treatment of amounts that are income of a related foreign person effectively connected with the conduct of a trade or business within the United States by such related foreign person.

(3) *Change in method of accounting.*—A taxpayer that uses a method of accounting other than that required by the rules of this section must change its method of accounting to conform its method to the rules of this section. The taxpayer's change in method must be made pursuant to the rules of section 446(e), the regulations thereunder, and any applicable administrative procedures prescribed by the Commissioner. Because the rules of this section prescribe a method of accounting, these rules apply in the determination of a taxpayer's earnings and profits pursuant to § 1.1312-6(a).

(4) *Examples.*—The provisions of this paragraph (b) may be illustrated by the following examples:

Example 1. (i) FC, a corporation incorporated in Country X, owns 100 percent of the stock of C, a domestic corporation. C uses the accrual method of accounting in computing its income and deductions, and is a calendar year taxpayer. In Year 1, C accrues an amount owed to FC for interest. C makes an actual payment of the amount owed to FC in Year 2.

(ii) Regardless of its source, the interest owed to FC is an amount to which this section applies. Pursuant to the rules of this paragraph (b), the amount owed to FC by C will not be allowable as a deduction in Year 1. Section 267 does not preclude the deduction of this amount in Year 2.

Example 2. (i) RS, a domestic corporation, is the sole shareholder of FSC, a foreign sales corporation. Both RS and FSC use the accrual method of accounting. In Year 1, RS accrues $z owed to FSC for commissions earned by FSC in Year 1. Pursuant to the foreign sales company provisions, sections 921 through 927, a portion of this amount, $x, is treated as effectively connected income of FSC from sources outside the United States. Accordingly, the rules of section 267(a)(3) and paragraph (b) of this section do not apply. See paragraph (c) of this section for the rules governing the treatment of amounts that are effectively connected income of FSC.

(ii) The remaining amount of the commission, $y, is classified as exempt foreign trade income under section 923(a)(3) and is treated as income of FSC from sources outside the United States that is not effectively connected income. This amount is one to which the provisions of this section do not apply, since it is an amount other than interest from sources outside the United States and is not effectively connected income. Therefore, a deduction for $y is allowable to RS as of the day on which it accrues the otherwise deductible amount, without regard to section 267(a)(2) and (a)(3) and the regulations thereunder.

(c) *Exceptions and special rules.*—(1) *Effectively connected income subject to United States tax.*—The provisions of section 267(a)(2) and the regulations thereunder, and not the provisions of paragraph (b) of this section, apply to an amount that is income of the related foreign person that is effectively connected with the conduct of a United States trade or business of such related foreign person. An amount described in this paragraph (c)(1) thus is allowable as a deduction as of the day on which the amount is includible in the gross income of the related foreign person as effectively connected income under sections 872(a)(2) or 882(b) (or, if later, as of the day on which the deduction would be so allowable but for section 267(a)(2)). However, this paragraph (c)(1) does not apply if the related foreign person is exempt from United States income tax on the amount owed, or is subject to a reduced rate of tax, pursuant to a treaty obligation of the United States (such as under an article relating to the taxation of business profits).

(2) *Items exempt from tax by treaty.*—Except with respect to interest, neither paragraph (b) of this section nor section 267(a)(2) or (a)(3) applies to any amount that is income of a related foreign person with respect to which the related foreign person is exempt from United States taxation on the amount owed pursuant to a treaty obligation of the United States (such as under an article relating to the taxation of business profits). Interest that is effectively connected income of the related foreign person under sections 872(a)(2) or 882(b) is an amount covered by paragraph (c)(1) of this section. Interest that is not effectively connected income of the related foreign person is an amount covered by paragraph (b) of this section, regardless of whether the related foreign person is exempt from United States taxation on the amount owed pursuant to a treaty obligation of the United States.

(3) *Items subject to reduced rate of tax by treaty.*—Paragraph (b) of this section applies to amounts that are income of a related foreign person with respect to which the related foreign person claims a reduced rate of United States income tax on the amount owed pursuant to a treaty obligation of the United States (such as under an article relating to the taxation of royalties).

(4) *Amounts owed to a foreign personal holding company, controlled foreign corporation, or passive foreign investment company.*—(i) *Foreign personal holding companies.*—If an amount to which paragraph (b) of this section otherwise applies is owed to a related foreign person that is a foreign personal holding company within the meaning of section 552, then the amount is allowable as a deduction as of the day on which the amount is includible in the income of the foreign personal holding company. The day on which the amount is includible in income is determined with reference to the method of accounting under which the foreign personal holding company computes its taxable income and earnings and profits for purposes of sections 551 through 558. See section 551(c) and the regulations thereunder for the reporting requirements of the foreign personal holding company provisions (sections 551 through 558).

(ii) *Controlled foreign corporations.*—If an amount to which paragraph (b) of this section otherwise applies is owed to a related foreign person that is a controlled foreign corporation within the meaning of section 957, then the amount is allowable as a deduction as of the day on which the amount is includible in the income of the controlled foreign corporation. The day on which the amount is includible in income is determined with reference to the method of accounting under which the controlled foreign corporation computes its taxable income and earnings and profits for purposes of sections 951 through 964. See section 6038 and the regulations thereunder for the reporting requirements of the controlled foreign corporation provisions (sections 951 through 964).

(iii) *Passive foreign investment companies.*—If an amount to which paragraph (b) of this section otherwise applies is owed to a related foreign person that is a passive foreign investment company within the meaning of section 1296, then the amount is allowable as a deduction as of the day on which [the] amount is includible in the income of the passive foreign investment company. The day on which the amount is includible in income is determined with reference to the method of accounting under which the earnings and profits of the passive foreign investment company are computed for purposes of sections 1291 through 1297. See sections 1291 through 1297 and the regulations thereunder for the reporting requirements of the passive foreign investment company provisions. This exception shall apply, however, only if the person that owes the amount at issue has made and has in effect an election pursuant to section 1295 with respect to the passive foreign investment company to which the amount at issue is owed.

(iv) *Examples.*—The rules of this paragraph (c)(4) may be illustrated by the following examples. Application of the provisions of sections 951 through 964 are provided for illustration only, and do not provide substantive rules concerning the operation of those provisions. The principles of these examples apply equally to the provisions of paragraphs (c)(4)(i) through (iii) of this section.

Example 1. P, a domestic corporation, owns 100 percent of the total combined voting power and value of the stock of both FC1 and FC2. P is a calendar year taxpayer that uses the accrual method of accounting in computing its income and deductions. FC1 is incorporated in Country X, and FC2 is incorporated in Country Y. FC1 and FC2 are controlled foreign corporations within the meaning of section 957, and are both calendar year taxpayers. FC1 computes its taxable income and earnings and profits, for purposes of sections 951 through 964, using the accrual method of accounting, while FC2 uses the cash method. In Year 1 FC1 has gross income of $10,000 that is described in section 952(a) ("subpart F income"), and which includes interest owed to FC1 by P that is described in paragraph (b) of this section and that is otherwise allowable as a deduction to P under chapter 1. The interest owed to FC1 is allowable as a deduction to P in Year 1.

Example 2. The facts are the same as in *Example 1,* except that in Year 1 FC1 reports no subpart F income because of the application of section 954(b)(3)(A) (the subpart F de minimis rule). Because the amount owed to FC1 by P is includible in FC1's gross income in Year 1, the interest owed to FC1 is allowable as a deduction to P in Year 1.

Example 3. The facts are the same as in *Example 1.* In Year 1, FC1 accrues interest owed to FC2 that would be allowable as a deduction by FC1 under chapter 1 if FC1 were a domestic corporation. The interest owed to FC2 by FC1 is paid by FC1 in Year 2. Because FC2 uses the cash method of accounting in computing its taxable income for purposes of subpart F, the interest owed by FC1 is allowable as a deduction by FC1 in Year 2, and not in Year 1.

(d) *Effective date.*—The rules of this section are effective with respect to interest that is allowable as a deduction under chapter 1 (without regard to the rules of this section) in taxable years beginning after December 31, 1983, but are not effective with respect to interest that is incurred with respect to indebtedness incurred on or before September 29, 1983, or incurred after that date pursuant to a contract that was binding on that date and at all times thereafter (unless the indebtedness or the contract was renegotiated, extended, renewed, or revised after that date). The regulations in this document issued under section 267 apply to all other deductible amounts that are incurred after July 31, 1989, but do not apply to amounts that are incurred pursuant to a contract that was binding on September 29, 1983 and at all times thereafter (unless the contract was renegotiated, extended, renewed, or revised after that date). [Reg. § 1.267(a)-3.]

☐ [*T.D.* 8465, 12-31-92.]

Proposed Regulation

§ 1.269B-1. Stapled foreign corporations.—(a) *Treatment as a domestic corporation.*—(1) *General rule.*—Except as otherwise provided, if a foreign corporation is a stapled foreign corporation within the meaning of paragraph (b)(1) of this section, such foreign corporation will be treated as a domestic corporation for U.S. Federal income tax purposes. Accordingly, for example, the worldwide income of such corporation will be subject to the tax imposed by section 11. For application of the branch profits tax under section 884, and application of sections 871(a), 881, 1441, and 1442 to dividends and interest paid by a stapled foreign corporation, see §§ 1.884-1(h) and 1.884-4(d).

(2) *Foreign owned exception.*—Paragraph (a)(1) of this section will not apply if a foreign

corporation and a domestic corporation are stapled entities (as provided in paragraph (b) of this section) and such foreign and domestic corporations are foreign owned within the meaning of this paragraph (a)(2). A corporation will be treated as foreign owned if it is established to the satisfaction of the Commissioner that United States persons hold directly (or indirectly applying section 958(a)(2) and (3) and section 318(a)(4)) less than 50 percent of the total combined voting power of all classes of stock entitled to vote and less than 50 percent of the total value of the stock of such corporation. For the consequences of a stapled foreign corporation becoming or ceasing to be foreign owned, therefore converting its status as either a foreign or domestic corporation within the meaning of this paragraph (a)(2), see paragraph (c) of this section.

(b) *Definition of a stapled foreign corporation.*—(1) *General rule.*—A foreign corporation is a stapled foreign corporation if such foreign corporation and a domestic corporation are stapled entities. A foreign corporation and a domestic corporation are stapled entities if more than 50 percent of the aggregate value of each corporation's beneficial ownership consists of interests that are stapled. In the case of corporations with more than one class of stock, it is not necessary for a class of stock representing more than 50 percent of the beneficial ownership of the foreign corporation to be stapled to a class of stock representing more than 50 percent of the beneficial ownership of the domestic corporation, provided that more than 50 percent of the aggregate value of each corporation's beneficial ownership (taking into account all classes of stock) are in fact stapled. Interests are stapled if a transferor of one or more interests in one entity is required, by form of ownership, restrictions on transfer, or other terms or conditions, to transfer interests in the other entity. The determination of whether interests are stapled for this purpose is based on the relevant facts and circumstances, including, but not limited to, the corporations' by-laws, articles of incorporation or association, and stock certificates, shareholder agreements, agreements between the corporations, and voting trusts with respect to the corporations. For the consequences of a foreign corporation's change in status as a stapled foreign corporation (that is not foreign owned) under this paragraph (b)(1), see paragraph (c) of this section.

(2) *Related party ownership rule.*—For purposes of determining whether a foreign corporation is a stapled foreign corporation, the Commissioner may, at his discretion, treat interests that otherwise would be stapled interests as not being stapled if the same person or related persons (within the meaning of section 267(b) or 707(b)) hold stapled interests constituting more than 50 percent of the beneficial ownership of both corporations, and a principal purpose of the stapling of those interests is the avoidance of U.S. income tax. A stapling of interests may have a principal purpose of tax avoidance even though the tax avoidance purpose is outweighed by other purposes when taken together.

(3) *Example.*—The principles of paragraph (b)(1) of this section are illustrated by the following example:

Example. USCo, a domestic corporation, and FCo, a foreign corporation, are publicly traded companies, each having two classes of stock outstanding. USCo's class A shares, which constitute 75% of the value of all beneficial ownership in USCo, are stapled to FCo's class B shares, which constitute 25% of the value of all beneficial ownership in F Co. USCo's class B shares, which constitute 25% of the value of all beneficial ownership in USCo, are stapled to FCo class A shares, which constitute 75% of the value of all beneficial ownership in FCo. Because more than 50% of the aggregate value of the stock of each corporation is stapled to the stock of the other corporation, USCo and FCo are stapled entities within the meaning of section 269B(c)(2).

(c) *Changes in domestic or foreign status.*—The deemed conversion of a foreign corporation to a domestic corporation under section 269B is treated as a reorganization under section 368(a)(1)(F). Similarly, the deemed conversion of a corporation that is treated as a domestic corporation under section 269B to a foreign corporation is treated as a reorganization under section 368(a)(1)(F). For the consequences of a deemed conversion, including the closing of a corporation's taxable year, see §§ 1.367(a)-1T(e), (f) and 1.367(b)-2(f).

(d) *Includible corporation.*—(1) Except as provided in paragraph (d)(2) of this section, a stapled foreign corporation treated as a domestic corporation under section 269B nonetheless will be treated as a foreign corporation in determining whether it is an includible corporation within the meaning of section 1504(b). Thus, for example, a stapled foreign corporation shall not be eligible to join in the filing of a consolidated return under section 1501, and a dividend paid by such corporation shall not constitute a qualifying dividend under section 243(b), unless a valid section 1504(d) election is made with respect to such corporation.

(2) A stapled foreign corporation will be treated as a domestic corporation in determining whether it is an includible corporation under section 1504(b) for purposes of applying §§ 1.904(i)-1 and 1.861-11T(d)(6).

Prop. Reg. § 1.269B-1(b)

(e) *U.S. treaties.*—(1) A stapled foreign corporation that is treated as a domestic corporation under section 269B may not claim an exemption from U.S. income tax or a reduction in U.S. tax rates by reason of any treaty entered into by the United States.

(2) The principles of this paragraph (e) are illustrated by the following example:

Example. FCo, a Country X corporation, is a stapled foreign corporation that is treated as a domestic corporation under section 269B. FCo qualifies as a resident of Country X pursuant to the income tax treaty between the United States and Country X. Under such treaty, the United States is permitted to tax business profits of a Country X resident only to the extent that the business profits are attributable to a permanent establishment of the Country X resident in the United States. While FCo earns income from sources within and without the United States, it does not have a permanent establishment in the United States within the meaning of the relevant treaty. Under paragraph (e)(1) of this section, however, FCo is subject to U.S. Federal income tax on its income as a domestic corporation without regard to the provisions of the U.S.-Country X treaty and therefore without regard to the fact that FCo has no permanent establishment in the United States.

(f) *Tax assessment and collection procedures.*—(1) *In general.*—(i) Any income tax imposed on a stapled foreign corporation by reason of its treatment as a domestic corporation under section 269B (whether such income tax is shown on the stapled foreign corporation's U.S. Federal income tax return or determined as a deficiency in income tax) shall be assessed as the income tax liability of such stapled foreign corporation.

(ii) Any income tax assessed as a liability of a stapled foreign corporation under paragraph (f)(1)(i) of this section shall be considered as having been properly assessed as an income tax liability of the stapled domestic corporation (as defined in paragraph (f)(4)(i) of this section) and all 10-percent shareholders of the stapled foreign corporation (as defined in paragraph (f)(4)(ii) of this section). The date of such deemed assessment shall be the date the income tax liability of the stapled foreign corporation was properly assessed. The Commissioner may collect such income tax from the stapled domestic corporation under the circumstances set forth in paragraph (f)(2) of this section and may collect such income tax from any 10-percent shareholders of the stapled foreign corporation under the circumstances set forth in paragraph (f)(3) of this section.

(2) *Collection from domestic stapled corporation.*—If the stapled foreign corporation does not pay its income tax liability that was properly assessed, the unpaid balance of such income tax or any portion thereof may be collected from the stapled domestic corporation, provided that the following conditions are satisfied:

(i) The Commissioner has issued a notice and demand for payment of such income tax to the stapled foreign corporation in accordance with § 301.6303-1;

(ii) The stapled foreign corporation has failed to pay the income tax by the date specified in such notice and demand;

(iii) The Commissioner has issued a notice and demand for payment of the unpaid portion of such income tax to the stapled domestic corporation in accordance with § 301.6303-1.

(3) *Collection from 10-percent shareholders of the stapled foreign corporation.*—The unpaid balance of the stapled foreign corporation's income tax liability may be collected from a 10-percent shareholder of the stapled foreign corporation, limited to each such shareholder's income tax liability as determined under paragraph (f)(4)(iv) of this section, provided the following conditions are satisfied:

(i) The Commissioner has issued a notice and demand to the stapled domestic corporation for the unpaid portion of the stapled foreign corporation's income tax liability, as provided in paragraph (f)(2)(iii) of this section;

(ii) The stapled domestic corporation has failed to pay the income tax by the date specified in such notice and demand;

(iii) The Commissioner has issued a notice and demand for payment of the unpaid portion of such income tax to such 10-percent shareholder of the stapled foreign corporation in accordance with § 301.6303-1.

(4) *Special rules and definitions.*—For purposes of this paragraph (f), the following rules and definitions apply:

(i) *Stapled domestic corporation.*—A domestic corporation is a *stapled domestic corporation* with respect to a stapled foreign corporation if such domestic corporation and the stapled foreign corporation are stapled entities as described in paragraph (b)(1) of this section.

(ii) *10-percent shareholder.*—A *10-percent shareholder* of a stapled foreign corporation is any person that owned directly 10 percent or more of the total value or total combined voting power of all classes of stock in the stapled foreign corporation for any day of the stapled foreign corporation's taxable year with respect to which the income tax liability relates.

(iii) *10-percent shareholder in the case of indirect ownership of stapled foreign corporation stock.*—[Reserved].

(iv) *Determination of a 10-percent shareholder's income tax liability.*—The income tax liability of a 10-percent shareholder of a stapled foreign corporation, for the income tax of the stapled foreign corporation under section 269B and this section, is determined by assigning an equal portion of the total income tax liability of the stapled foreign corporation for the taxable year to each day in such corporation's taxable year, and then dividing that portion ratably among the shares outstanding for that day on the basis of the relative values of such shares. The liability of any 10-percent shareholder for this purpose is the sum of the income tax liability allocated to the shares held by such shareholder for each day in the taxable year.

(v) *Income tax.*—The term *income tax* means any income tax liability imposed on a domestic corporation under title 26 of the United States Code, including additions to tax, additional amounts, penalties, and interest related to such income tax liability.

(g) *Effective dates.*—(1) Except as provided in this paragraph (g), the provisions of this section are applicable for taxable years that begin after the date the final regulations are published in the Federal Register.

(2) Paragraphs (d)(1) and (f) of this section (except as applied to the collection of tax from any 10-percent shareholder of a stapled foreign corporation that is a foreign person) are applicable beginning on—

(i) July 18, 1984, for any foreign corporation that became stapled to a domestic corporation after June 30, 1983; and

(ii) January 1, 1987, for any foreign corporation that was stapled to a domestic corporation as of June 30, 1983.

(3) Paragraph (d)(2) of this section is applicable for taxable years beginning after July 22, 2003, except that in the case of a foreign corporation that becomes stapled to a domestic corporation on or after July 22, 2003, paragraph (d)(2) of this section applies for taxable years ending on or after July 22, 2003.

(4) Paragraph (e) of this section is applicable beginning on July 18, 1984, except as provided in paragraph (g)(5) of this section.

(5) In the case of a foreign corporation that was stapled to a domestic corporation as of June 30, 1983, which was entitled to claim benefits under an income tax treaty as of that date, and which remains eligible for such treaty benefits, paragraph (e) of this section will not apply to such foreign corporation and for all purposes of the Code such corporation will continue to be treated as a foreign entity. The prior sentence will continue to apply even if such treaty is subsequently modified by protocol, or superseded by a new treaty, so long as the stapled foreign corporation continues to be eligible to claim such treaty benefits. If the treaty benefits to which the stapled foreign corporation was entitled as of June 30, 1983 are terminated, then a deemed conversion of the foreign corporation to a domestic corporation shall occur pursuant to paragraph (c) of this section as of the date of such termination. [Prop. Reg. § 1.269B-1.]

[Proposed 9-7-2004.]

Section 338 Elections

§ 1.338-1. General principles; status of old target and new target.—(a) *In general.*—(1) *Deemed transaction.*—Elections are available under section 338 when a purchasing corporation acquires the stock of another corporation (the target) in a qualified stock purchase. One type of election, under section 338(g), is available to the purchasing corporation. Another type of election, under section 338(h)(10), is, in more limited circumstances, available jointly to the purchasing corporation and the sellers of the stock. (Rules concerning eligibility for these elections are contained in §§ 1.338-2, 1.338-3, and 1.338(h)(10)-1.) Although target is a single corporation under corporate law, if a section 338 election is made, then two separate corporations, old target and new target, generally are considered to exist for purposes of subtitle A of the Internal Revenue Code. Old target is treated as transferring all of its assets to an unrelated person in exchange for consideration that includes the discharge of its liabilities (see § 1.1001-2(a)), and new target is treated as acquiring all of its assets from an unrelated person in exchange for consideration that includes the assumption of those liabilities. (Such transaction is, without regard to its characterization for Federal income tax purposes, referred to as the deemed asset sale and the income tax consequences thereof as the deemed sale tax consequences.) If a section 338(h)(10) election is made, old target is deemed to liquidate following the deemed asset sale.

(2) *Application of other rules of law.*—Other rules of law apply to determine the tax consequences to the parties as if they had actually engaged in the transactions deemed to

occur under section 338 and the regulations thereunder except to the extent otherwise provided in those regulations. See also § 1.338-6(c)(2). Other rules of law may characterize the transaction as something other than or in addition to a sale and purchase of assets; however, the transaction between old and new target must be a taxable transaction. For example, if target is an insurance company for which a section 338 election is made, the deemed asset sale would be characterized and taxed as an assumption-reinsurance transaction under applicable Federal income tax law. See § 1.817-4(d).

(3) *Overview.*—Definitions and special nomenclature and rules for making the section 338 election are provided in § 1.338-2. Qualification for the section 338 election is addressed in § 1.338-3. The amount for which old target is treated as selling all of its assets (the aggregate deemed sale price, or ADSP) is addressed in § 1.338-4. The amount for which new target is deemed to have purchased all its assets (the adjusted grossed-up basis, or AGUB) is addressed in § 1.338-5. Section 1.338-6 addresses allocation both of ADSP among the assets old target is deemed to have sold and of AGUB among the assets new target is deemed to have purchased. Section 1.338-7 addresses allocation of ADSP or AGUB when those amounts subsequently change. Asset and stock consistency are addressed in § 1.338-8. International aspects of section 338 are covered in § 1.338-9. Rules for the filing of returns are provided in § 1.338-10. Eligibility for and treatment of section 338(h)(10) elections is addressed in § 1.338(h)(10)-1.

(b) *Treatment of target under other provisions of the Internal Revenue Code.*—(1) *General rule for subtitle A.*—Except as provided in this section, new target is treated as a new corporation that is unrelated to old target for purposes of subtitle A of the Internal Revenue Code. Thus—

(i) New target is not considered related to old target for purposes of section 168 and may make new elections under section 168 without taking into account the elections made by old target; and

(ii) New target may adopt, without obtaining prior approval from the Commissioner, any taxable year that meets the requirements of section 441 and any method of accounting that meets the requirements of section 446. Notwithstanding § 1.441-1T(b)(2), a new target may adopt a taxable year on or before the last day for making the election under section 338 by filing its first return for the desired taxable year on or before that date.

(2) *Exceptions for subtitle A.*—New target and old target are treated as the same corporation for purposes of—

(i) The rules applicable to employee benefit plans (including those plans described in sections 79, 104, 105, 106, 125, 127, 129, 132, 137, and 220), qualified pension, profit-sharing, stock bonus and annuity plans (sections 401(a) and 403(a)), simplified employee pensions (section 408(k)), tax qualified stock option plans (sections 422 and 423), welfare benefit funds (sections 419, 419A, 512(a)(3), and 4976), and voluntary employee benefit associations (section 501(a)(9) and the regulations thereunder);

(ii) Sections 1311 through 1314 (relating to the mitigation of the effect of limitations), if a section 338(h)(10) election is not made for target;

(iii) Section 108(e)(5) (relating to the reduction of purchase money debt);

(iv) Section 45A (relating to the Indian Employment Credit), section 51 (relating to the Work Opportunity Credit), section 51A (relating to the Welfare to Work Credit), and section 1396 (relating to the Empowerment Zone Act);

(v) Sections 401(h) and 420 (relating to medical benefits for retirees);

(vi) Section 414 (relating to definitions and special rules); and

(vii) Any other provision designated in the Internal Revenue Bulletin by the Internal Revenue Service. See § 601.601(d)(2)(ii) of this chapter. See, for example, § 1.1001-3(e)(4)(i)(F) providing that an election under section 338 does not result in the substitution of a new obligor on target's debt. See also, for example, § 1.1502-77(e)(4), providing that an election under section 338 does not result in a deemed termination of target's existence for purposes of the rules applicable to the agent for a consolidated group.

(3) *General rule for other provisions of the Internal Revenue Code.*—Except as provided in the regulations under section 338 or in the Internal Revenue Bulletin by the Internal Revenue Service (see § 601.601(d)(2)(ii) of this chapter), new target is treated as a continuation of old target for purposes other than subtitle A of the Internal Revenue Code. For example—

(i) New target is liable for old target's Federal income tax liabilities, including the tax liability for the deemed sale tax consequences and those tax liabilities of the other members of any consolidated group that included old target that are attributable to taxable years in which those corporations and old target joined in the same consolidated return (see § 1.1502-6(a));

Reg. § 1.338-1(b)(3)(i)

(ii) Wages earned by the employees of old target are considered wages earned by such employees from new target for purposes of sections 3101 and 3111 (Federal Insurance Contributions Act) and section 3301 (Federal Unemployment Tax Act); and

(iii) Old target and new target must use the same employer identification number.

(c) *Anti-abuse rule.*—(1) *In general.*—The rules of this paragraph (c) apply for purposes of applying the residual method as provided for under the regulations under sections 338 and 1060. The Commissioner is authorized to treat any property (including cash) transferred by old target in connection with the transactions resulting in the application of the residual method (and not held by target at the close of the acquisition date) as, nonetheless, property of target at the close of the acquisition date if the property so transferred is, within 24 months after the deemed asset sale, owned by new target, or is owned, directly or indirectly, by a member of the affiliated group of which new target is a member and continues after the acquisition date to be held or used primarily in connection with one or more of the activities of new target. In addition, the Commissioner is authorized to treat any property (including cash) transferred to old target in connection with the transactions resulting in the application of the residual method (and held by target at the close of the acquisition date) as, nonetheless, not being property of target at the close of the acquisition date if the property so transferred is, within 24 months after the deemed asset sale, not owned by new target but owned, directly or indirectly, by a member of the affiliated group of which new target is a member, or owned by new target but held or used primarily in connection with an activity conducted, directly or indirectly, by another member of the affiliated group of which new target is a member in combination with other property retained by or acquired, directly or indirectly, from the transferor of the property (or a member of the same affiliated group) to old target. For purposes of this paragraph (c)(1), an interest in an entity is considered held or used in connection with an activity if property of the entity is so held or used. The authority of the Commissioner under this paragraph (c)(1) includes the making of any appropriate correlative adjustments (avoiding, to the extent possible, the duplication or omission of any item of income, gain, loss, deduction, or basis).

(2) *Examples.*—The following examples illustrate this paragraph (c):

Example 1. Prior to a qualified stock purchase under section 338, target transfers one of its assets to a related party. The purchasing corporation then purchases the target stock and also purchases the transferred asset from the related party. After its purchase of target, the purchasing corporation and target are members of the same affiliated group. A section 338 election is made. Under an arrangement with the purchaser, the separately transferred asset is used primarily in connection with target's activities. Applying the anti-abuse rule of this paragraph (c), the Commissioner may consider target to own the transferred asset for purposes of applying the residual method under section 338.

Example 2. T owns all the stock of T1. T1 leases intellectual property to T, which T uses in connection with its own activities. P, a purchasing corporation, wishes to buy the T-T1 chain of corporations. P, in connection with its planned purchase of the T stock, contracts to consummate a purchase of all the stock of T1 on March 1 and of all the stock of T on March 2. Section 338 elections are thereafter made for both T and T1. Immediately after the purchases, P, T and T1 are members of the same affiliated group. T continues to lease the intellectual property from T1 and that is the primary use of the intellectual property. Thus, an asset of T, the T1 stock, was removed from T's own assets prior to the qualified stock purchase of the T stock, T1's own assets are used after the deemed asset sale in connection with T's own activities, and the T1 stock is after the deemed asset sale owned by P, a member of the same affiliated group of which T is a member. Applying the anti-abuse rule of this paragraph (c), the Commissioner may, for purposes of application of the residual method under section 338 both to T and to T1, consider P to have bought only the stock of T, with T at the time of the qualified stock purchases of both T and T1 (the qualified stock purchase of T1 being triggered by the deemed sale under section 338 of T's assets) owning T1. The Commissioner accordingly would allocate consideration to T's assets as though the T1 stock were one of those assets, and then allocate consideration within T1 based on the amount allocated to the T1 stock at the T level.

(d) *Next day rule for post-closing transactions.*—If a target corporation for which an election under section 338 is made engages in a transaction outside the ordinary course of business on the acquisition date after the event resulting in the qualified stock purchase of the target or a higher tier corporation, the target and all persons related thereto (either before or after the qualified stock purchase) under section 267(b) or section 707 must treat the transaction for all Federal income tax purposes as occurring at the beginning of the day following the transaction and after the deemed purchase by new target. [Reg. § 1.338-1.]

☐ [*T.D.* 8940, 2-12-2001. *Amended by T.D.* 9002, 6-27-2002.]

§ 1.338-2. Nomenclature and definitions; mechanics of the section 338 election.—(a) *Scope.*—This section prescribes rules relating to elections under section 338.

(b) *Nomenclature.*—For purposes of the regulations under section 338 (except as otherwise provided):

(1) T is a domestic target corporation that has only one class of stock outstanding. Old T refers to T for periods ending on or before the close of T's acquisition date; new T refers to T for subsequent periods.

(2) P is the purchasing corporation.

(3) The P group is an affiliated group of which P is a member.

(4) P1, P2, etc., are domestic corporations that are members of the P group.

(5) T1, T2, etc., are domestic corporations that are target affiliates of T. These corporations (T1, T2, etc.) have only one class of stock outstanding and may also be targets.

(6) S is a domestic corporation (unrelated to P and B) that owns T prior to the purchase of T by P. (S is referred to in cases in which it is appropriate to consider the effects of having all of the outstanding stock of T owned by a domestic corporation.)

(7) A, a U.S. citizen or resident, is an individual (unrelated to P and B) who owns T prior to the purchase of T by P. (A is referred to in cases in which it is appropriate to consider the effects of having all of the outstanding stock of T owned by an individual who is a U.S. citizen or resident. Ownership of T by A and ownership of T by S are mutually exclusive circumstances.)

(8) B, a U.S. citizen or resident, is an individual (unrelated to T, S, and A) who owns the stock of P.

(9) F, used as a prefix with the other terms in this paragraph (b), connotes foreign, rather than domestic, status. For example, FT is a foreign corporation (as defined in section 7701(a)(5)) and FA is an individual other than a U.S. citizen or resident.

(10) CFC, used as a prefix with the other terms in this paragraph (b) referring to a corporation, connotes a controlled foreign corporation (as defined in section 957, taking into account section 953(c)). A corporation identified with the prefix F may be a controlled foreign corporation. (The prefix CFC is used when the corporation's status as a controlled foreign corporation is significant.)

(c) *Definitions.*—For purposes of the regulations under section 338 (except as otherwise provided):

(1) *Acquisition date.*—The term *acquisition date* has the same meaning as in section 338(h)(2).

(2) *Acquisition date assets.*—*Acquisition date assets* are the assets of the target held at the beginning of the day after the acquisition date (but see § 1.338-1(d) (regarding certain transactions on the acquisition date)).

(3) *Affiliated group.*—The term *affiliated group* has the same meaning as in section 338(h)(5). Corporations are affiliated on any day they are members of the same affiliated group.

(4) *Common parent.*—The term *common parent* has the same meaning as in section 1504.

(5) *Consistency period.*—The *consistency period* is the period described in section 338(h)(4)(A) unless extended pursuant to § 1.338-8(j)(1).

(6) *Deemed asset sale.*—The *deemed asset sale* is the transaction described in § 1.338-1(a)(1) that is deemed to occur for purposes of subtitle A of the Internal Revenue Code if a section 338 election is made.

(7) *Deemed sale tax consequences.*—*Deemed sale tax consequences* refers to, in the aggregate, the Federal income tax consequences (generally, the income, gain, deduction, and loss) of the deemed asset sale. Deemed sale tax consequences also refers to the Federal income tax consequences of the transfer of a particular asset in the deemed asset sale.

(8) *Deemed sale return.*—The *deemed sale return* is the return on which target's deemed sale tax consequences are reported that does not include any other items of target. Target files a deemed sale return when a section 338 election (but not a section 338(h)(10) election) is filed for target and target is a member of a selling group (defined in paragraph (c)(16) of this section) that files a consolidated return for the period that includes the acquisition date. See § 1.338-10. If target is an S corporation for the period that ends on the day before the acquisition date and a section 338 election (but not a section 338(h)(10) election) is filed for target, see § 1.338-10(a)(3).

(9) *Domestic corporation.*—A *domestic corporation* is a corporation—

(i) That is domestic within the meaning of section 7701(a)(4) or that is treated as domestic for purposes of subtitle A of the Internal Revenue Code (e.g., to which an election under section 953(d) or 1504(d) applies); and

(ii) That is not a DISC, a corporation described in section 1248(e), or a corporation to which an election under section 936 applies.

(10) *Old target's final return.*—*Old target's final return* is the income tax return of old target for the taxable year ending at the close of the acquisition date that includes the deemed sale tax consequences. However, if a deemed sale return is filed for old target, the deemed sale return is considered old target's final return.

(11) *Purchasing corporation.*—The term *purchasing corporation* has the same meaning as in section 338(d)(1). The purchasing corporation may also be referred to as purchaser. Unless otherwise provided, any reference to the purchasing corporation is a reference to all members of the affiliated group of which the purchasing corporation is a member. See sections 338(h)(5) and (8). Also, unless otherwise provided, any reference to the purchasing corporation is, with respect to a deemed purchase of stock under section 338(a)(2), a reference to new target with respect to its own deemed purchase of stock in another target.

(12) *Qualified stock purchase.*—The term *qualified stock purchase* has the same meaning as in section 338(d)(3).

(13) *Related persons.*—Two persons are related if stock in a corporation owned by one of the persons would be attributed under section 318(a) (other than section 318(a)(4)) to the other.

(14) *Section 338 election.*—A *section 338 election* is an election to apply section 338(a) to target. A section 338 election is made by filing a statement of section 338 election pursuant to paragraph (d) of this section. The form on which this statement is filed is referred to in the regulations under section 338 as the Form 8023, "Elections Under Section 338 For Corporations Making Qualified Stock Purchases."

(15) *Section 338(h)(10) election.*—A section 338(h)(10) election is an election to apply section 338(h)(10) to target. A section 338(h)(10) election is made by making a joint election for target under § 1.338(h)(10)-1 on Form 8023.

(16) *Selling group.*—The *selling group* is the affiliated group (as defined in section 1504) eligible to file a consolidated return that includes target for the taxable period in which the acquisition date occurs. However, a selling group is not an affiliated group of which target is the common parent on the acquisition date.

(17) *Target; old target; new target.*—*Target* is the target corporation as defined in section 338(d)(2). *Old target* refers to target for periods ending on or before the close of target's acquisition date. *New target* refers to target for subsequent periods.

(18) *Target affiliate.*—The term *target affiliate* has the same meaning as in section 338(h)(6) (applied without section 338(h)(6)(B)(i)). Thus, a corporation described in section 338(h)(6)(B)(i) is considered a target affiliate for all purposes of section 338. If a target affiliate is acquired in a qualified stock purchase, it is also a target.

(19) *12-month acquisition period.*—The *12-month acquisition period* is the period described in section 338(h)(1), unless extended pursuant to § 1.338-8(j)(2).

(d) *Time and manner of making election.*—The purchasing corporation makes a section 338 election for target by filing a statement of section 338 election on Form 8023 in accordance with the instructions to the form. The section 338 election must be made not later than the 15th day of the 9th month beginning after the month in which the acquisition date occurs. A section 338 election is irrevocable. See § 1.338(h)(10)-1(c)(2) for section 338(h)(10) elections.

(e) *Special rules for foreign corporations or DISCs.*—(1) *Elections by certain foreign purchasing corporations.*—(i) *General rule.*—A qualifying foreign purchasing corporation is not required to file a statement of section 338 election for a qualifying foreign target before the earlier of 3 years after the acquisition date and the 180th day after the close of the purchasing corporation's taxable year within which a triggering event occurs.

(ii) *Qualifying foreign purchasing corporation.*—A purchasing corporation is a *qualifying foreign purchasing corporation* only if, during the acquisition period of a qualifying foreign target, all the corporations in the purchasing corporation's affiliated group are foreign corporations that are not subject to United States tax.

(iii) *Qualifying foreign target.*—A target is a *qualifying foreign target* only if target and its target affiliates are foreign corporations that, during target's acquisition period, are not subject to United States tax (and will not become subject to United States tax during such period because of a section 338 election). A target affiliate is taken into account for purposes of the preceding sentence only if, during target's 12-month acquisition period, it is or becomes a member of the affiliated group that includes the purchasing corporation.

(iv) *Triggering event.*—A *triggering event* occurs in the taxable year of the qualifying foreign purchasing corporation in which either that corporation or any corporation in its affiliated group becomes subject to United States tax.

(v) *Subject to United States tax.*—For purposes of this paragraph (e)(1), a foreign corporation is considered subject to United States tax—

(A) For the taxable year for which that corporation is required under § 1.6012-2(g) (other than § 1.6012-2(g)(2)(i)(B)(2)) to file a United States income tax return; or

(B) For the period during which that corporation is a controlled foreign corporation, a passive foreign investment company for which an election under section 1295 is in effect, a foreign investment company, or a foreign corporation the stock ownership of which is described in section 552(a)(2).

(2) *Acquisition period.*—For purposes of this paragraph (e), the term *acquisition period* means the period beginning on the first day of the 12-month acquisition period and ending on the acquisition date.

(3) *Statement of section 338 election may be filed by United States shareholders in certain cases.*—The United States shareholders (as defined in section 951(b)) of a foreign purchasing corporation that is a controlled foreign corporation (as defined in section 957 (taking into account section 953(c))) may file a statement of section 338 election on behalf of the purchasing corporation if the purchasing corporation is not required under § 1.6012-2(g) (other than § 1.6012-2(g)(2)(i)(B)(2)) to file a United States income tax return for its taxable year that includes the acquisition date. Form 8023 must be filed as described in the form and its instructions and also must be attached to the Form 5471, "Information Returns Of U.S. Persons With Respect To Certain Foreign Corporations," filed with respect to the purchasing corporation by each United States shareholder for the purchasing corporation's taxable year that includes the acquisition date (or, if paragraph (e)(1)(i) of this section applies to the election, for the purchasing corporation's taxable year within which it becomes a controlled foreign corporation). The provisions of § 1.964-1(c) (including § 1.964-1(c)(7)) do not apply to an election made by the United States shareholders.

(4) *Notice requirement for U.S. persons holding stock in foreign target.*—(i) *General rule.*—If a target subject to a section 338 election was a controlled foreign corporation, a passive foreign investment company, or a foreign personal holding company at any time during the portion of its taxable year that ends on its acquisition date, the purchasing corporation must deliver written notice of the election (and a copy of Form 8023, its attachments and instructions) to—

(A) Each U.S. person (other than a member of the affiliated group of which the purchasing corporation is a member (the purchasing group member)) that, on the acquisition date of the foreign target, holds stock in the foreign target; and

(B) Each U.S. person (other than a purchasing group member) that sells stock in the foreign target to a purchasing group member during the foreign target's 12-month acquisition period.

(ii) *Limitation.*—The notice requirement of this paragraph (e)(4) applies only where the section 338 election for the foreign target affects income, gain, loss, deduction, or credit of the U.S. person described in paragraph (e)(4)(i) of this section under section 551, 951, 1248, or 1293.

(iii) *Form of notice.*—The notice to U.S. persons must be identified prominently as a notice of section 338 election and must—

(A) Contain the name, address, and employer identification number (if any) of, and the country (and, if relevant, the lesser political subdivision) under the laws of which are organized the purchasing corporation and the relevant target (i.e., the target the stock of which the particular U.S. person held or sold under the circumstances described in paragraph (e)(4)(i) of this section);

(B) Identify those corporations as the purchasing corporation and the foreign target, respectively; and

(C) Contain the following declaration (or a substantially similar declaration):

THIS DOCUMENT SERVES AS NOTICE OF AN ELECTION UNDER SECTION 338 FOR THE ABOVE CITED FOREIGN TARGET THE STOCK OF WHICH YOU EITHER HELD OR SOLD UNDER THE CIRCUMSTANCES DESCRIBED IN TREASURY REGULATIONS SECTION 1.338-2(e)(4). FOR POSSIBLE UNITED STATES FEDERAL INCOME TAX CONSEQUENCES UNDER SECTION 551, 951, 1248, OR 1293 OF THE INTERNAL REVENUE CODE OF 1986 THAT MAY APPLY TO YOU, SEE TREASURY REGULATIONS SECTION 1.338-9(b). YOU MAY BE REQUIRED TO ATTACH THE INFORMA-

TION ATTACHED TO THIS NOTICE TO CERTAIN RETURNS.

(iv) *Timing of notice.*—The notice required by this paragraph (e)(4) must be delivered to the U.S. person on or before the later of the 120th day after the acquisition date of the particular target or the day on which Form 8023 is filed. The notice is considered delivered on the date it is mailed to the proper address (or an address similar enough to complete delivery), unless the date it is mailed cannot be reasonably determined. The date of mailing will be determined under the rules of section 7502. For example, the date of mailing is the date of U.S. postmark or the applicable date recorded or marked by a designated delivery service.

(v) *Consequence of failure to comply.*—A statement of section 338 election is not valid if timely notice is not given to one or more U.S. persons described in this paragraph (e)(4). If the form of notice fails to comply with all requirements of this paragraph (e)(4), the section 338 election is valid, but the waiver rule of § 1.338-10(b)(1) does not apply.

(vi) *Good faith effort to comply.*—The purchasing corporation will be considered to have complied with this paragraph (e)(4), even though it failed to provide notice or provide timely notice to each person described in this paragraph (e)(4), if the Commissioner determines that the purchasing corporation made a good faith effort to identify and provide timely notice to those U.S. persons. [Reg. § 1.338-2.]

☐ [T.D. 8940, 2-12-2001.]

§ 1.338-4. Aggregate deemed sale price; various aspects of taxation of the deemed asset sale.—(a) *Scope.*—This section provides rules under section 338(a)(1) to determine the aggregate deemed sale price (ADSP) for target. ADSP is the amount for which old target is deemed to have sold all of its assets in the deemed asset sale. ADSP is allocated among target's assets in accordance with § 1.338-6 to determine the amount for which each asset is deemed to have been sold. When a subsequent increase or decrease is required under general principles of tax law with respect to an element of ADSP, the redetermined ADSP is allocated among target's assets in accordance with § 1.338-7. This § 1.338-4 also provides rules regarding the recognition of gain or loss on the deemed sale of target affiliate stock. Notwithstanding section 338(h)(6)(B)(ii), stock held by a target affiliate in a foreign corporation or in a corporation that is a DISC or that is described in section 1248(e) is not excluded from the operation of section 338.

* * *

(h) *Deemed sale of target affiliate stock.*—(1) *Scope.*—This paragraph (h) prescribes rules relating to the treatment of gain or loss realized on the deemed sale of stock of a target affiliate when a section 338 election (but not a section 338(h)(10) election) is made for the target affiliate. For purposes of this paragraph (h), the definition of domestic corporation in § 1.338-2(c)(9) is applied without the exclusion therein for DISCs, corporations described in section 1248(e), and corporations to which an election under section 936 applies.

(2) *In general.*—Except as otherwise provided in this paragraph (h), if a section 338 election is made for target, target recognizes no gain or loss on the deemed sale of stock of a target affiliate having the same acquisition date and for which a section 338 election is made if—

(i) Target directly owns stock in the target affiliate satisfying the requirements of section 1504(a)(2);

(ii) Target and the target affiliate are members of a consolidated group filing a final consolidated return described in § 1.338-10(a)(1); or

(iii) Target and the target affiliate file a combined return under § 1.338-10(a)(4).

(3) *Deemed sale of foreign target affiliate by a domestic target.*—A domestic target recognizes gain or loss on the deemed sale of stock of a foreign target affiliate. For the proper treatment of such gain or loss, see, e.g., sections 1246, 1248, 1291 et seq., and 338(h)(16) and § 1.338-9.

(4) *Deemed sale producing effectively connected income.*—A foreign target recognizes gain or loss on the deemed sale of stock of a foreign target affiliate to the extent that such gain or loss is effectively connected (or treated as effectively connected) with the conduct of a trade or business in the United States.

* * *

(6) *Deemed sale of DISC target affiliate.*—A foreign or domestic target recognizes gain (but not loss) on the deemed sale of stock of a target affiliate that is a DISC or a former DISC (as defined in section 992(a)) in an amount equal to the lesser of the gain realized or the amount of accumulated DISC income determined with respect to such stock under section 995(c). Such gain is included in gross income as a dividend as provided in sections 995(c)(2) and 996(g).

* * *

(8) *Examples.*—The following examples illustrate this paragraph (h):

* * *

Example 4. (i) T's sole asset, all of the FT1 stock, has a basis of $25 and a fair market value of $150. FT1's sole asset, all of the FT2 stock, has a basis of $75 and a fair market value of $150. FT1 and FT2 each have $50 of accumulated earnings and profits for purposes of section 1248(c) and (d). FT2's assets have a basis of $125 and a fair market value of $150, and their sale would not generate subpart F income under section 951. The sale of the FT2 stock or assets would not generate income effectively connected with the conduct of a trade or business within the United States. FT1 does not have an election in effect under section 953(d) and neither FT1 nor FT2 is a passive foreign investment company.

(ii) P makes a qualified stock purchase of T and makes a section 338 election for T. T's deemed purchase of the FT1 stock results in a qualified stock purchase of FT1 and a section 338 election is made for M. Similarly, FT1's deemed purchase of the FT2 stock results in a qualified stock purchase of FT2 and a section 338 election is made for FT2.

(iii) T recognizes $125 of gain on the deemed sale of the FT1 stock under paragraph (h)(3) of this section. FT1 does not recognize $75 of gain on the deemed sale of the FT2 stock under paragraph (h)(2) of this section. FT2 recognizes $25 of gain on the deemed sale of its assets. The $125 gain T recognizes on the deemed sale of the FT1 stock is included in T's income as a dividend under section 1248, because FT1 and FT2 have sufficient earnings and profits for full recharacterization ($50 of accumulated earnings and profits in FT1, $50 of accumulated earnings and profits in FT2, and $25 of deemed sale earnings and profits in FT2). Section 1.338-9(b). For purposes of sections 901 through 908, the source and foreign tax credit limitation basket of $25 of the recharacterized gain on the deemed sale of the FT1 stock is determined under section 338(h)(16).

[Reg. § 1.338-4.]

☐ [*T.D.* 8940, 2-12-2001.]

§ 1.338-8. Asset and stock consistency.

* * *

(g) *Extension of consistency if dividends qualifying for 100 percent dividends received deduction are paid.*—(1) *General rule for direct acquisitions from target.*—Unless a section 338 election is made for target, the basis rules of paragraph (d) of this section apply to an asset if—

(i) Target recognizes gain (whether or not deferred) on disposition of the asset during the portion of the target consistency period that ends on the target acquisition date;

(ii) The asset is owned, immediately after the asset disposition and on the target acquisition date, by a corporation that acquires stock of target in the qualified stock purchase (or by an affiliate of an acquiring corporation); and

(iii) During the portion of the target consistency period that ends on the target acquisition date, the aggregate amount of dividends paid by target, to which section 243(a)(3) applies, exceeds the greater of—

(A) $250,000; or

(B) 125 percent of the yearly average amount of dividends paid by target, to which section 243(a)(3) applies, during the three calendar years immediately preceding the year in which the target consistency period begins (or, if shorter, the period target was in existence).

(2) *Other direct acquisitions having same effect.*—The basis rules of paragraph (d) of this section also apply to an asset if the effect of a transaction described in paragraph (g)(1) of this section is achieved through any combination of disposition of assets and payment of dividends to which section 243(a)(3) applies (or any other dividends eligible for a 100 percent dividends received deduction). *See* paragraph (h)(4) of this section for additional rules relating to target affiliates that are controlled foreign corporations.

(3) *Indirect acquisitions.*—The principles of paragraph (f) of this section also apply for purposes of this paragraph (g).

(4) *Examples.*—This paragraph (g) may be illustrated by the following examples:

Example 1. Asset acquired from target paying dividends to which section 243(a)(3) applies. (a) The S group does not file a consolidated return. In Year 1, Year 2, and Year 3, T pays dividends to S to which section 243(a)(3) applies of $200,000, $250,000, and $300,000, respectively. On February 1 of Year 4, T sells an asset to P and recognizes gain. On January 1 of Year 5, P makes a qualified stock purchase of T from S. No section 338 election is made for T. During the portion of T's consistency period that ends on T's acquisition date, T pays S dividends to which section 243(a)(3) applies of $1,000,000.

(b) Under paragraph (g)(1) of this section, paragraph (d) of this section applies to the asset. T recognizes gain on disposition of the asset during the portion of T's consistency period that ends on T's acquisition date, the asset is owned by P immediately after the disposition and on T's acquisition date, and T pays dividends described in paragraph (g)(1)(iii) of this section. Consequently, under paragraph (d)(1) of this section, P's basis in the asset is T's adjusted basis in the asset immediately before the sale to P.

(c) If T is a controlled foreign corporation, the results would be the same if T pays dividends in the amount described in paragraph (g)(1)(iii) of this section that qualify for a 100 percent dividends received deduction. See sections 243(e) and 245.

(d) If S and T3 file a consolidated return in which T, T1, and T2 do not join, the results would be the same because the dividends paid by T are still described in paragraph (g)(1)(iii) of this section.

(e) If T, T1, and T2 file a consolidated return in which S and T3 do not join, the results would be the same because the dividends paid by T are still described in paragraph (g)(1)(iii) of this section.

Example 2. Asset disposition by target affiliate achieving same effect. (a) The S group does not file a consolidated return. On February 1 of Year 1, T2 sells an asset to P and recognizes gain. T pays dividends to S described in paragraph (g)(1)(iii) of this section. On January 1 of Year 2, P makes a qualified stock purchase of T from S. No section 338 election is made for T.

(b) Paragraph (g)(1) of this section does not apply to the asset because T did not recognize gain on the disposition of the asset. However, under paragraph (g)(2) of this section, because the asset disposition by T2 and the dividends paid by T achieve the effect of a transaction described in paragraph (g)(1) of this section, the carryover basis rule of paragraph (d)(1) of this section applies to the asset. The effect was achieved because T2 is a lower-tier affiliate of T and the dividends paid by T to S reduce the value to S of T and its lower-tier affiliates.

(c) If T2 is a controlled foreign corporation, the results would be the same because T2 is a lower-tier affiliate of T and the dividends paid by T to S reduce the value to S of T and its lower-tier affiliates.

(d) If P buys an asset from T3, rather than T2, the asset disposition and the dividends do not achieve the effect of a transaction described in paragraph (g)(1) of this section because T3 is not a lower-tier affiliate of T. Thus, the basis rules of paragraph (d) of this section do not apply to the asset. The results would be the same whether or not P also acquires the T3 stock (whether or not in a qualified stock purchase).

Example 3. Dividends by target affiliate achieving same effect. (a) The S group does not file a consolidated return. On February 1 of Year 1, T1 sells an asset to P and recognizes gain. On January 1 of Year 2, P makes a qualified stock purchase of T from S. No section 338 election is made for T. T does not pay dividends to S described in paragraph (g)(1)(iii) of this section. However, T1 pays dividends to T that would be described in paragraph (g)(1)(iii) of this section if T1 were a target.

(b) Paragraph (g)(1) of this section does not apply to the asset because T did not recognize gain on the disposition of the asset and did not pay dividends described in paragraph (g)(1)(iii) of this section. Further, paragraph (g)(2) of this section does not apply because the dividends paid by T1 to T do not reduce the value to S of T and its lower-tier affiliates.

(c) If both S and T own T1 stock and T1 pays dividends to S that would be described in paragraph (g)(1)(iii) of this section if T1 were a target, paragraph (g)(2) of this section would apply because the dividends paid by T1 to S reduce the value to S of T and its lower-tier affiliates. If T, rather than T1, sold the asset to P, the results would be the same. Further, if T and T1 pay dividends to S that, only when aggregated, would be described in paragraph (g)(1)(iii) of this section (if they were all paid by T), the results would be the same.

Example 4. Gain reflected by reason of dividends. (a) S and T file a consolidated return in which T1 and T2 do not join. On February 1 of Year 1, T1 sells an asset to P and recognizes gain. On January 1 of Year 2, P makes a qualified stock purchase of T from S. No section 338 election is made for T. T1 pays dividends to T that would be described in paragraph (g)(1)(iii) of this section if T1 were a target.

(b) The requirements of paragraph (b) of this section are not satisfied because, under paragraph (c)(3) of this section, gain from T1's sale is not reflected in S's basis in the T stock by reason of the dividends paid by T1 to T.

(c) Although the dividends paid by T1 to T do not reduce the value to S of T and its lower-tier affiliates, paragraph (g)(2) of this section applies because the dividends paid by T1 to T are taken into account under §1.1502-32 in determining S's basis in the T stock. Consequently, the carryover basis rule of paragraph (d)(1) of this section applies to the asset.

(h) *Consistency for target affiliates that are controlled foreign corporations.*—(1) *In general.*—This paragraph (h) applies only if target is a domestic corporation. For additional rules that may apply with respect to controlled foreign corporations, see paragraph (g) of this section. The definitions and nomenclature of §1.338-2(b) and (c) and paragraph (e) of this section apply for purposes of this section.

(2) *Income or gain resulting from asset dispositions.*—(i) *General rule.*—Income or gain of a target affiliate that is a controlled foreign corporation from the disposition of an asset is not reflected in the basis of target stock under

paragraph (c) of this section unless the income or gain results in an inclusion under section 951(a)(1)(A), 951(a)(1)(C), 1291 or 1293.

(ii) *Basis of controlled foreign corporation stock.*—If, by reason of paragraph (h)(2)(i) of this section, the carryover basis rules of this section apply to an asset, no increase in basis in the stock of a controlled foreign corporation under section 961(a) or 1293(d)(1), or under regulations issued pursuant to section 1297(b)(5), is allowed to target or a target affiliate to the extent the increase is attributable to income or gain described in paragraph (h)(2)(i) of this section. A similar rule applies to the basis of any property by reason of which the stock of the controlled foreign corporation is considered owned under section 958(a)(2) or 1297(a).

(iii) *Operating rule.*—For purposes of this paragraph (h)(2)—

(A) If there is an income inclusion under section 951 (a)(1)(A) or (C), the shareholder's income inclusion is first attributed to the income or gain of the controlled foreign corporation from the disposition of the asset to the extent of the shareholder's pro rata share of such income or gain; and

(B) Any income or gain under section 1293 is first attributed to the income or gain from the disposition of the asset to the extent of the shareholder's pro rata share of the income or gain.

(iv) *Increase in asset or stock basis.*—(A) If the carryover basis rules under paragraph (h)(2)(i) of this section apply to an asset, and the purchasing corporation disposes of the asset to an unrelated party in a taxable transaction and recognizes and includes in its U.S. gross income or the U.S. gross income of its shareholders the greater of the income or gain from the disposition of the asset by the selling controlled foreign corporation that was reflected in the basis of the target stock under paragraph (c) of this section, or the gain recognized on the asset by the purchasing corporation on the disposition of the asset, then the purchasing corporation or the target or a target affiliate, as appropriate, shall increase the basis of the selling controlled foreign corporation stock subject to paragraph (h)(2)(ii) of this section, as of the date of the disposition of the asset by the purchasing corporation, by the amount of the basis increase that was denied under paragraph (h)(2)(ii) of this section. The preceding sentence shall apply only to the extent that the controlled foreign corporation stock is owned (within the meaning of section 958(a)) by a member of the purchasing corporation's affiliated group.

(B) If the carryover basis rules under paragraph (h)(2)(i) of this section apply to an asset, and the purchasing corporation or the target or a target affiliate, as appropriate, disposes of the stock of the selling controlled foreign corporation to an unrelated party in a taxable transaction and recognizes and includes in its U.S. gross income or the U.S. gross income of its shareholders the greater of the gain equal to the basis increase that was denied under paragraph (h)(2)(ii) of this section, or the gain recognized in the stock by the purchasing corporation or by the target or a target affiliate, as appropriate, on the disposition of the stock, then the purchasing corporation shall increase the basis of the asset, as of the date of the disposition of the stock of the selling controlled foreign corporation by the purchasing corporation or by the target or a target affiliate, as appropriate, by the amount of the basis increase that was denied pursuant to paragraph (h)(2)(i) of this section. The preceding sentence shall apply only to the extent that the asset is owned (within the meaning of section 958(a)) by a member of the purchasing corporation's affiliated group.

(3) *Stock issued by target affiliate that is a controlled foreign corporation.*—The exception to the carryover basis rules of this section provided in paragraph (d)(2)(iii) of this section does not apply to stock issued by a target affiliate that is a controlled foreign corporation. After applying the carryover basis rules of this section to the stock, the basis in the stock is increased by the amount treated as a dividend under section 1248 on the disposition of the stock (or that would have been so treated but for section 1291), except to the extent the basis increase is attributable to the disposition of an asset in which a carryover basis is taken under this section.

(4) *Certain distributions.*—(i) *General rule.*—In the case of a target affiliate that is a controlled foreign corporation, paragraph (g) of this section applies with respect to the target affiliate by treating any reference to a dividend to which section 243(a)(3) applies as a reference to any amount taken into account under § 1.1502-32 in determining the basis of target stock that is—

(A) A dividend;

(B) An amount treated as a dividend under section 1248 (or that would have been so treated but for section 1291); or

(C) An amount included in income under section 951(a)(1)(B).

(ii) *Basis of controlled foreign corporation stock.*—If the carryover basis rules of this section apply to an asset, the basis in the stock of the controlled foreign corporation (or any

Reg. § 1.338-8(h)(4)(ii)

property by reason of which the stock is considered owned under section 958(a)(2)) is reduced (but not below zero) by the sum of any amounts that are treated, solely by reason of the disposition of the asset, as a dividend, amount treated as a dividend under section 1248 (or that would have been so treated but for section 1291), or amount included in income under section 951(a)(1)(B). For this purpose, any dividend, amount treated as a dividend under section 1248 (or that would have been so treated but for section 1291), or amount included in income under section 951(a)(1)(B) is considered attributable first to earnings and profits resulting from the disposition of the asset.

(iii) *Increase in asset or stock basis.*—(A) If the carryover basis rules under paragraphs (g) and (h)(4)(i) of this section apply to an asset, and the purchasing corporation disposes of the asset to an unrelated party in a taxable transaction and recognizes and includes in its U.S. gross income or the U.S. gross income of its shareholders the greater of the gain equal to the basis increase denied in the asset pursuant to paragraphs (g) and (h)(4)(i) of this section, or the gain recognized on the asset by the purchasing corporation on the disposition of the asset, then the purchasing corporation or the target or a target affiliate, as appropriate, shall increase the basis of the selling controlled foreign corporation stock subject to paragraph (h)(4)(ii) of this section, as of the date of the disposition of the asset by the purchasing corporation, by the amount of the basis reduction under paragraph (h)(4)(ii) of this section. The preceding sentence shall apply only to the extent that the controlled foreign corporation stock is owned (within the meaning of section 958(a)) by a member of the purchasing corporation's affiliated group.

(B) If the carryover basis rules under paragraphs (g) and (h)(4)(i) of this section apply to an asset, and the purchasing corporation or the target or a target affiliate, as appropriate, disposes of the stock of the selling controlled foreign corporation to an unrelated party in a taxable transaction and recognizes and includes in its U.S. gross income or the U.S. gross income of its shareholders the greater of the amount of the basis reduction under paragraph (h)(4)(ii) of this section, or the gain recognized in the stock by the purchasing corporation or by the target or a target affiliate, as appropriate, on the disposition of the stock, then the purchasing corporation shall increase the basis of the asset, as of the date of the disposition of the stock of the selling controlled foreign corporation by the purchasing corporation or by the target or a target affiliate, as appropriate, by the amount of the basis increase that was denied pursuant to paragraphs (g) and (h)(4)(i) of this section. The preceding sentence shall apply only to the extent that the asset is owned (within the meaning of section 958(a)) by a member of the purchasing corporation's affiliated group.

(5) *Examples.*—This paragraph (h) may be illustrated by the following examples:

Example 1. Stock of target affiliate that is a CFC. (a) The S group files a consolidated return; however, T2 is a controlled foreign corporation. On December 1 of Year 1, T1 sells the T2 stock to P and recognizes gain. On January 2 of Year 2, P makes a qualified stock purchase of T from S. No section 338 election is made for T.

(b) Under paragraph (b)(1) of this section, paragraph (d) of this section applies to the T2 stock. Under paragraph (h)(3) of this section, paragraph (d)(2)(iii) of this section does not apply to the T2 stock. Consequently, paragraph (d)(1) of this section applies to the T2 stock. However, after applying paragraph (d)(1) of this section, P's basis in the T2 stock is increased by the amount of T1's gain on the sale of the T2 stock that is treated as a dividend under section 1248. Because P has a carryover basis in the T2 stock, the T2 stock is not considered purchased within the meaning of section 338(h)(3) and no section 338 election may be made for T2.

Example 2. Stock of target affiliate CFC; inclusion under subpart F. (a) The S group files a consolidated return; however, T2 is a controlled foreign corporation. On December 1 of Year 1, T2 sells an asset to P and recognizes subpart F income that results in an inclusion in T1's gross income under section 951(a)(1)(A). On January 2 of Year 2, P makes a qualified stock purchase of T from S. No section 338 election is made for T.

(b) Because gain from the disposition of the asset results in an inclusion under section 951(a)(1)(A), the gain is reflected in the basis of the T stock as of T's acquisition date. See paragraph (h)(2)(i) of this section. Consequently, under paragraph (b)(1) of this section, paragraph (d)(1) of this section applies to the asset. In addition, under paragraph (h)(2)(ii) of this section, T1's basis in the T2 stock is not increased under section 961(a) by the amount of the inclusion that is attributable to the sale of the asset.

(c) If, in addition to making a qualified stock purchase of T, P acquires the T2 stock from T1 on January 1 of Year 2, the results are the same for the asset sold by T2. In addition, under paragraph (h)(2)(ii) of this section, T1's basis in the T2 stock is not increased by the amount of the inclusion that is attributable to the gain on the sale of the asset. Further, under paragraph (h)(3) of this section, paragraph (d)(1) of this section applies to the T2 stock. However, after applying paragraph (d)(1) of this section, P's basis in the T2 stock is increased by the amount of T1's gain on the sale of the T2 stock that is treated as a dividend under section 1248. Finally, because P has a carryover basis in the T2 stock, the T2 stock is not considered purchased within the meaning of section 338(h)(3) and no section 338 election may be made for T2.

(d) If P makes a qualified stock purchase of T2 from T1, rather than of T from S, and T1's gain on the sale of T2 is treated as a dividend under section 1248, under paragraph (h)(1) of this section, paragraphs (h)(2) and (3) of this section do not apply because there is no target that is a domestic corporation. Consequently, the carryover basis rules of paragraph do not apply to the asset sold by T2 or the T2 stock.

Example 3. Gain reflected by reason of section 1248 dividend; gain from non-subpart F asset. (a) The S group files a consolidated return; however, T2 is a controlled foreign corporation. In Years 1 through 4, T2 does not pay any dividends to T1 and no amount is included in T1's income under section 951(a)(1)(B). On December 1 of Year 4, T2 sells an asset with a basis of $400,000 to P for $900,000. T2's gain of $500,000 is not subpart F income. On December 15 of Year 4, T1 sells T2, in which it has a basis of $600,000, to P for $1,600,000. Under section 1248, $800,000 of T1's gain of $1,000,000 is treated as a dividend. However, in the absence of the sale of the asset by T2 to P, only $300,000 would have been treated as a dividend under section 1248. On December 30 of Year 4, P makes a qualified stock purchase of T1 from T. No section 338 election is made for T1.

(b) Under paragraph (h)(4) of this section, paragraph (g)(2) of this section applies by reference to the amount treated as a dividend under section 1248 on the disposition of the T2 stock. Because the amount treated as a dividend is taken into account in determining T's basis in the T1 stock under § 1.150232, the sale of the T2 stock and the deemed dividend have the effect of a transaction described in paragraph (g)(1) of this section. Consequently, paragraph (d)(1) of this section applies to the asset sold by T2 to P and P's basis in the asset is $400,000 as of December 1 of Year 4.

(c) Under paragraph (h)(3) of this section, paragraph (d)(1) of this section applies to the T2 stock and P's basis in the T2 stock is $600,000 as of December 15 of Year 4. Under paragraphs (h)(3) and (4)(ii) of this section, however, P's basis in the T2 stock is increased by $300,000 (the amount of T1's gain treated as a dividend under section 1248 ($800,000), other than the amount treated as a dividend solely as a result of the sale of the asset by T2 to P ($500,000)) to $900,000.

* * *

[Reg. § 1.338-8.]

☐ [*T.D.* 8515, 1-12-94. *Amended by T.D.* 8597, 7-12-95 *and T.D.* 8710, 1-22-97. *Redesignated by T.D.* 8858, 1-5-2000. *Amended by T.D.* 8940, 2-12-2001.]

§ 1.338-9. International aspects of section 338.—(a) *Scope.*—This section provides guidance regarding international aspects of section 338. As provided in § 1.338-2(c)(18), a foreign corporation, a DISC, or a corporation for which a section 936 election has been made is considered a target affiliate for all purposes of section 338. In addition, stock described in section 338(h)(6)(B)(ii) held by a target affiliate is not excluded from the operation of section 338.

(b) *Application of section 338 to foreign targets.*—(1) *In general.*—For purposes of subtitle A, the deemed sale tax consequences, as defined in § 1.338-2(c)(7), of a foreign target for which a section 338 election is made (FT), and the corresponding earnings and profits, are taken into account in determining the taxation of FT and FT's direct and indirect shareholders. See, however, section 338(h)(16). For example, the income and earnings and profits of FT are determined, for purposes of sections 551, 951, 1248, and 1293, by taking into account the deemed sale tax consequences.

(2) *Ownership of FT stock on the acquisition date.*—A person who transfers FT stock to the purchasing corporation on FT's acquisition date is considered to own the transferred stock at the close of FT's acquisition date. See, e.g., § 1.951-1(f) (relating to determination of holding period for purposes of sections 951 through 964). If on the acquisition date the purchasing corporation owns a block of FT stock that was acquired before FT's acquisition date, the purchasing corporation is considered to own such block of stock at the close of the acquisition date.

(3) *Carryover FT stock.*—(i) *Definition.*—FT stock is carryover FT stock if—

(A) FT was a controlled foreign corporation within the meaning of section 957 (taking into account section 953(c)) at any time during the portion of the 12-month acquisition period that ends on the acquisition date; and

(B) Such stock is owned as of the beginning of the day after FT's acquisition date by a person other than a purchasing corporation, or by a purchasing corporation if the stock is nonrecently purchased and is not subject to a gain recognition election under § 1.338-5(d).

(ii) *Carryover of earnings and profits.*—The earnings and profits of old FT (and associated foreign taxes) attributable to the carryover FT stock (adjusted to reflect deemed sale tax consequences) carry over to new FT solely for purposes of—

(A) Characterizing an actual distribution with respect to a share of carryover FT stock as a dividend;

(B) Characterizing gain on a post-acquisition date transfer of a share of carryover FT stock as a dividend under section 1248 (if such section is otherwise applicable);

(C) Characterizing an investment of earnings in United States property as income under sections 951(a)(1)(B) and 956 (if such sections are otherwise applicable); and

(D) Determining foreign taxes deemed paid under sections 902 and 960 with respect to the amount treated as a dividend or income by virtue of this paragraph (b)(3)(ii) (subject to the operation of section 338(h)(16)).

(iii) *Cap on carryover of earnings and profits.*—The amount of earnings and profits of old FT taken into account with respect to a share of carryover FT stock is limited to the amount that would have been included in gross income of the owner of such stock as a dividend under section 1248 if—

(A) The shareholder transferred that share to the purchasing corporation on FT's acquisition date for a consideration equal to the fair market value of that share on that date; or

(B) In the case of nonrecently purchased FT stock treated as carryover FT stock, a gain recognition election under section 338(b)(3)(A) applied to that share. For purposes of the preceding sentence, a shareholder that is a controlled foreign corporation is considered to be a United States person, and the principle of section 1248(c)(2)(D)(ii) (concerning a United States person's indirect ownership of stock in a foreign corporation) applies in determining the correct holding period.

(iv) *Post-acquisition date distribution of old FT earnings and profits.*—A post-acquisition date distribution with respect to a share of carryover FT stock is considered to be derived first from earnings and profits derived after FT's acquisition date and then from earnings and profits derived on or before FT's acquisition date.

(v) *Old FT earnings and profits unaffected by post-acquisition date deficits.*—The carryover amount for a share of carryover FT stock is not reduced by deficits in earnings and profits incurred by new FT. This rule applies for purposes of determining the amount of foreign taxes deemed paid regardless of the fact that there are no accumulated earnings and profits. For example, a distribution by new FT with respect to a share of carryover FT stock is treated as a dividend by the distributee to the extent of the carryover amount for that share notwithstanding that new FT has no earnings and profits.

(vi) *Character of FT stock as carryover FT stock eliminated upon disposition.*—A share of FT stock is not considered carryover FT stock after it is disposed of provided that all gain realized on the transfer is recognized at the time of the transfer, or that, if less than all of the realized gain is recognized, the recognized amount equals or exceeds the remaining carryover amount for that share.

(4) *Passive foreign investment company stock.*—Stock that is owned as of the beginning of the day after FT's acquisition date by a person other than a purchasing corporation, or by a purchasing corporation if the FT stock is nonrecently purchased stock not subject to a gain recognition election under § 1.338-5(d), is treated as passive foreign investment company stock to the extent provided in section 1297(b)(1).

(c) *Dividend treatment under section 1248(e).*—The principles of this paragraph (b) apply to shareholders of a domestic corporation subject to section 1248(e).

(d) *Allocation of foreign taxes.*—If a section 338 election is made for target (whether foreign or domestic), and target's taxable year under foreign law (if any) does not close at the end of the acquisition date, foreign income taxes attributable to the foreign taxable income earned by target during such foreign taxable year are allocated to old target and new target. Such allocation is made under the principles of § 1.1502-76(b).

(e) *Operation of section 338(h)(16).*—[Reserved]

(f) *Examples.*—(1) Except as otherwise provided, all corporations use the calendar year as the taxable year, have no earnings and profits (or deficit) accumulated for any taxable year, and have only one class of outstanding stock.

(2) This section may be illustrated by the following examples:

Example 1. Gain recognition election for carryover FT stock. (a) A has owned 90 of the 100 shares of CFCT stock since CFCT was organized on March 13, 1989. P has owned the remaining 10 shares of CFCT stock since CFCT was organized. Those 10 shares constitute nonrecently purchased stock in P's hands within the meaning of section 338(b)(6)(B). On November 1, 1994, P purchases A's 90 shares of CFCT stock for $90,000 and makes a section 338 election for CFCT. P also makes a gain recognition election under section 338(b)(3)(A) and § 1.338-5(d).

(b) CFCT's earnings and profits for its short taxable year ending on November 1, 1994, are $50,000, determined without taking into account the deemed asset sale. Assume A recognizes gain of $81,000 on the sale of the CFCT stock. Further, assume that CFCT recognizes gain of $40,000 by reason of its deemed sale of assets under section 338(a)(1).

(c) A's sale of CFCT stock to P is a transfer to which section 1248 and paragraphs (b)(1) and (2) of this section apply. For purposes of applying section 1248(a) to A, the earnings and profits of CFCT for its short taxable year ending on November 1, 1994, are $90,000 (the earnings and profits for that taxable year as determined under § 1.1248-2(e) ($50,000) plus earnings from the deemed sale ($40,000)). Thus, A's entire gain is characterized as a dividend under section 1248 (but see section 338(h)(16)).

(d) Assume that P recognizes a gain of $9,000 with respect to the 10 shares of nonrecently purchased CFCT stock by reason of the gain recognition election. Because P is treated as selling the nonrecently purchased stock for all purposes of the Internal Revenue Code, section 1248 applies. Thus, under § 1.1248-2(e), $9,000 of the $90,000 of earnings and profits for 1994 are attributable to the block of 10 shares of CFCT stock deemed sold by P at the close of November 1, 1994 ($90,000 × 10/100). Accordingly, P's entire gain on the deemed sale of 10 shares of CFCT stock is included under section 1248(a) in P's gross income as a dividend (but see section 338(h)(16)).

Example 2. No gain recognition election for carryover FT stock. (a) Assume the same facts as in *Example 1*, except that P does not make a gain recognition election.

(b) The 10 shares of nonrecently purchased CFCT stock held by P is carryover FT stock under paragraph (b)(3) of this section. Accordingly, the earnings and profits (and attributable foreign taxes) of old CFCT carry over to new CFCT solely for purposes of that block of 10 shares. The amount of old CFCT's earnings and profits taken into account with respect to that block in the event, for example, of a distribution by new CFCT with respect to that block is the amount of the section 1248 dividend that P would have recognized with respect to that block had it made a gain recognition election under section 338(b)(3)(A). Under the facts of *Example 1*, P would have recognized a gain of $9,000 with respect to that block, all of which would have been a section 1248 dividend ($90,000 × 10/100). Accordingly, the carryover amount for the block of 10 shares of nonrecently purchased CFCT stock is $9,000.

Example 3. Sale of controlled foreign corporation stock prior to and on the acquisition date. (a) X and Y, both U.S. corporations, have each owned 50% of the CFCT stock since 1986. Among CFCT's assets are assets the sale of which would generate subpart F income. On December 31, 1994, X sells its CFCT stock to P. On June 30, 1995, Y sells its CFCT stock to P. P makes a section 338 election for CFCT. In both 1994 and 1995, CFCT has subpart F income resulting from operations.

(b) For taxable year 1994, X and Y are United States shareholders on the last day of CFCT's taxable year, so pursuant to section 951(a)(1)(A) each must include in income its pro rata share of CFCT's subpart F income for 1994. Because P's holding period in the CFCT stock acquired from X does not begin until January 1, 1995, P is not a United States shareholder on the last day of 1994 for purposes of section 951(a)(1)(A) (see § 1.951-1(f)). X must then determine the extent to which section 1248 recharacterizes its gain on the sale of CFCT stock as a dividend.

(c) For the short taxable year ending June 30, 1995, Y is considered to own the CFCT stock sold to P at the close of CFCT's acquisition date. Because the acquisition date is the last day of CFCT's taxable year, Y and P are United States shareholders on the last day of CFCT's taxable year. Pursuant to section 951(a)(1)(A), each must include its pro rata share of CFCT's subpart F income for the short taxable year ending June 30, 1995. This includes any income generated on the deemed sale of CFCT's assets. Y must then determine the extent to which section 1248 recharacterizes its gain on the sale of the CFCT stock as a dividend, taking into account any increase in CFCT's earnings and profits due to the deemed sale of assets.

Example 4. Acquisition of control for purposes of section 951 prior to the acquisition date. FS owns 100% of the FT stock. On July 1, 1994, P buys 60% of the FT stock. On December 31, 1994, P buys the remaining 40% of the FT stock and makes a section 338 election for FT. For tax year 1994, FT has earnings and profits of $1,000 (including earnings resulting from the deemed sale). The section 338 election results in $500 of subpart F income. As a result of the section 338 election, P must include in gross income the following amount under section 951(a)(1)(A) (see § 1.951-[1](b)(2)):

FT's subpart F income for 1994	$500.00
Less: reduction under section 951(a)(2)(A) for period (1-1-94 through 7-1-94) during which FT is not a controlled foreign corporation ($500 × 182/365)	249.32
Subpart F income as limited by section 951(a)(2)(A)	$250.68
P's pro rata share of subpart F income as determined under section 951(a)(2)(A) (60% × 250.68)	$150.41

Example 5. Coordination with section 936. (a) T is a corporation for which a section 936 election has been made. P makes a qualified stock purchase of T and makes a section 338 election for T.

(b) T's deemed sale of assets under section 338 constitutes a sale for purposes of subtitle A of the Internal Revenue Code, including section 936(a)(1)(A)(ii). To the extent that the assets deemed sold are used in the conduct of an active trade or business in a possession for purposes of section 936(a)(1)(A)(i), and assuming all the other conditions of section 936 are satisfied, the income from the deemed sale qualifies for the credit granted by section 936(a). The source of income from the deemed sale is determined as if the assets had actually been sold and is not affected for purposes of section 936 by section 338(h)(16).

(c) Because new T is treated a new corporation for purposes of subtitle A of the Internal Revenue Code, the three year testing period in section 936(a)(2)(A) begins again for new T on the day following T's acquisition date. Thus, if the character or source of old T's gross income disqualified it for the credit under section 936, a fresh start is allowed by a section 338 election. [Reg. § 1.338-9.]

☐ [*T.D.* 8515, 1-12-94. *Redesignated by T.D.* 8858, 1-5-2000. *Amended by T.D.* 8940, 2-12-2001.]

International Tax-Free Exchanges

§ 1.367(a)-1T. Transfers to foreign corporations subject to section 367(a): In general (temporary).—(a) *Purpose and scope of regulations.*—These regulations set forth rules relating to the provisions of section 367(a) concerning certain transfers of property to foreign corporations. This § 1.367(a)-1T provides general rules explaining the effect of section 367(a)(1) and describing the transfers of property that are subject to the rule of that section. Section 1.367(a)-2T provides rules concerning the exception from the rule of section 367(a)(1) for transfers of property to be used in the active conduct of a trade or business outside of the United States. Rules concerning the application of section 367(a)(1) to transfers of stock or securities are provided in § 1.367(a)-3, while § 1.367(a)-4T provides special rules regarding other specified transfers of property. Section 1.367(a)-5T describes types of property that are subject to the rule of section 367(a)(1) regardless of whether they are transferred for use in a trade or business. Section 1.367(a)-6T provides rules concerning the application of section 367(a) to the transfer of a branch with previously deducted losses. Finally, § 1.367(a)-7T contains transitional rules concerning transfers of intangible property to foreign corporations made after June 6, 1984 and before January 1, 1985. Rules explaining the operation of section 367(d), concerning transfers of intangible property pursuant to an exchange described in section 351 or 361, are provided in § 1.367(d)-1T. Rules concerning the reporting requirements of section 6038B are provided in §§ 1.6038B-1 and 1.6038B-1T.

(b) *General rules.*—(1) *Foreign corporation not considered a corporation for purposes of certain transfers.*—If a U.S. person transfers property to a foreign corporation in connection with an exchange described in section 332, 351, 354, 355, 356, or 361, then pursuant to section 367(a)(1) the foreign corporation shall not be considered to be a corporation for purposes of determining the extent to which gain shall be recognized on the transfer. Section 367(a)(1) denies nonrecognition treatment only to transfers of items of property on which gain is realized. Thus, the amount of gain recognized because of section 367(a)(1) is unaffected by the transfer of items of property on which loss is realized (but not recognized). The transfers of property that are subject to section 367(a)(1) are further described in paragraph (c) of this section, and relevant definitions are provided in paragraph (d) of this section.

(2) *Cases in which foreign corporate status is not disregarded.*—Section 367(a)(1) shall not apply, and a foreign corporate transferee shall, thus, be considered to be a corporation, in the case of any of the following:

(i) [Reserved];

(ii) The transfer of property for use in the active conduct of a trade or business outside of the United States in accordance with the rules of §§ 1.367(a)-2T through 1.367(a)-6T; or

(iii) Certain other transfers of property described in §§ 1.367(a)-2T through 1.367(a)-6T.

(3) *Limitation of gain required to be recognized.*—(i) *In general.*—If a U.S. person transfers property to a foreign corporation in a transaction on which gain is required to be recognized under section 367(a) and regulations thereunder, then the gain required to be recognized by the U.S. person shall in no event exceed the gain that would have been recognized on a taxable sale of those items of property if sold individually and without offsetting individual losses against individual gains.

(ii) *Losses.*—No loss may be recognized by reason of the operation of section 367.

(iii) *Ordinary income and capital gain.*—If section 367(a) and regulations thereunder require the recognition of ordinary income and capital gain in excess of the limitation described in paragraph (b)(3)(i) of this section, then the limitation shall be imposed by making proportionate reductions in the amounts of ordinary income and capital gain, regardless of the character of the gain that would have been recognized on a taxable sale of the property.

(4) *Character, source, and adjustments.*—(i) *In general.*—If a U.S. person is required to recognize gain under section 367 upon a transfer of property to a foreign corporation, then—

(A) The character and source of such gain shall be determined as if the property had been disposed of in a taxable exchange with the transferee foreign corporation (unless otherwise provided by regulation); and

(B) Appropriate adjustments to earnings and profits, basis, and other affected items shall be made according to otherwise applicable rules, taking into account the gain recognized because of section 367(a)(1). Any increase in the basis of the property received by the foreign corporation resulting from the application of section 367(a) and section 362(a) or (b) shall be allocated over the transferred property with respect to which gain is recognized in proportion to the amount realized by the U.S. person on the transfer of each item of that property. See paragraph (c)(3) of this section for special rules applicable to transfers of partnership interests.

(ii) *Example.*—The rules of this paragraph (b)(4) are illustrated by the following example.

Example. Domestic corporation DC transfers inventory with a fair market value of $1 million and adjusted basis of $800,000 to foreign corporation FC in an exchange for stock of FC that is described in section 351(a). Title passes within the U.S. Pursuant to section 367(a), DC is required to recognize gain of $200,000 upon the transfer. Under the rule of this paragraph (b)(4), such gain shall be treated as ordinary income (sections 1201 and 1221) from sources within the U.S. (section 861) arising from a taxable exchange with FC. Appropriate adjustments to earnings and profits, basis, etc., shall be made as if the transfer were subject to section 351. Thus, for example, DC's basis in the FC stock received, and FC's basis in the transferred inventory, will each be increased by the $200,000 gain recognized by DC, pursuant to sections 358(a)(1) and 362(a), respectively.

(c) *Transfers described in section 367(a)(1).*—(1) *In general.*—A transfer described in section 367(a)(1) is any transfer of property by a U.S. person to a foreign corporation pursuant to an exchange described in section 332, 351, 354, 355, 356, or 361. Section 367(a)(1) applies to such a transfer whether it is made directly, indirectly, or constructively. Indirect or constructive transfers that are described in section 367(a)(1) include the transfers described in subparagraphs (2) through (7) of this paragraph (c).

(2) *Indirect transfers in certain reorganizations.*—[Reserved.] For further guidance, see § 1.367(a)-3(d).

(3) *Indirect transfers involving partnerships and interests therein.*—(i) *Transfer by partnership treated as transfer by partners.*—(A) *In general.*—If a partnership (whether foreign or domestic) transfers property to a foreign corporation in an exchange described in section 367(a)(1), then a U.S. person that is a partner in the partnership shall be treated as having transferred a proportionate share of the property in an exchange described in section 367(a)(1). A U.S. person's proportionate share of partnership property shall be determined under the rules and principles of section 701 through 761 and the regulations thereunder. The rule of this paragraph (c)(3)(i)(A) is illustrated by the following example.

Example. P is a partnership having five equal general partners, two of whom are United States persons. P transfers property to F, a foreign corporation, in connection with an exchange described in section 351. The exchange includes an indirect transfer of property by the partners to F. The transfers of property attributable to those partners who are United States persons, that is, 40 percent of each asset transferred to F, are transfers described in section 367(a)(1). The gain (if any) recognized on the transfer of 40 percent of each asset to F is attributable to the two partners who are United States persons.

(B) *Special adjustments to basis.*—If a U.S. person is treated under the rule of this paragraph (c)(3)(i) as having transferred a proportionate share of the property of a partnership in an exchange described in section 367(a), and is therefore required to recognize gain upon the transfer, then—

   (1) The U.S. person's basis in the partnership shall be increased by the amount of gain recognized by him;

   (2) Solely for purposes of determining the basis of the partnership in the stock of the transferee foreign corporation, the U.S. person shall be treated as having newly acquired an interest in the partnership (for an amount equal to the gain recognized), permitting the partnership to make an optional adjustment to basis pursuant to sections 743 and 754; and

   (3) The transferee foreign corporation's basis in the property acquired from the partnership shall be increased by the amount of gain recognized by U.S. persons under this paragraph (c)(3)(i).

  (ii) *Transfer of partnership interest treated as transfer of proportionate share of assets.*—(A) *In general.*—If a U.S. person transfers an interest as a partner in a partnership (whether foreign or domestic) in an exchange described in section 367(a)(1), then that person shall be treated as having transferred a proportionate share of the property of the partnership in an exchange described in section 367(a)(1). Accordingly, the applicability of the exception to section 367(a)(1) provided in §1.367(a)-2T shall be determined with reference to the property of the partnership rather than the partnership interest itself. A U.S. person's proportionate share of partnership property shall be determined under the rules and principles of sections 701 through 761 and the regulations thereunder.

  (B) *Special adjustments to basis.*—If a U.S. person is treated under the rule of paragraph (c)(3)(ii)(A) of this section as having transferred a proportionate share of the property of a partnership in an exchange described in section 367(a), and is therefore required to recognize gain upon the transfer, then—

   (1) The U.S. person's basis in the stock of the transferee foreign corporation shall be increased by the amount of gain so recognized by that person;

   (2) The transferee foreign corporation's basis in the transferred partnership interest shall be increased by the amount of gain recognized by the U.S. person; and

   (3) Solely for purposes of determining the partnership's basis in the property held by it, the U.S. person shall be treated as having newly acquired an interest in the partnership (for an amount equal to the gain recognized), permitting the partnership to make an optional adjustment to basis pursuant to sections 743 and 754.

  (C) *Limited partnership interest.*—The transfer by a U.S. person of an interest in a partnership shall not be subject to the rules of paragraph (c)(3)(ii)(A) and (B) if—

   (1) The interest transferred is a limited partnership interest; and

   (2) Such interest is regularly traded on an established securities market.
Instead, the transfer of such an interest shall be treated in the same manner as a transfer of stock or securities. Thus, the consequences of such a transfer shall be determined under the rules of §1.367(a)-3. For purposes of this section, a limited partnership interest is an interest as a limited partner in a partnership that is organized under the laws of any State of the United States or the District of Columbia. Whether such an interest is regularly traded on an established securities market shall be determined under the provisions of paragraph (c)(3)(ii)(D) of this section.

  (D) *Regularly traded on an established securities market.*—*(1) Established securities market.*—For purposes of this paragraph (c)(3)(ii), an established securities market is—

   (i) A national securities exchange which is registered under section 6 of the Securities Exchange Act of 1934 (15 USC 78f);

   (ii) A foreign national securities exchange which is officially recognized, sanctioned, or supervised by governmental authority; and

   (iii) An over-the-counter market. An over-the-counter market is any market reflected by the existence of an inter-dealer quotation system. An inter-dealer quotation system is any system of general circulation to brokers and dealers which regularly disseminates quotations of stock and securities by identified brokers or dealers, other than by quotation sheets which are prepared and distributed by a broker or dealer in the regular course of business and which contain only quotations of such broker or dealer.

  (2) Regularly traded.—A class of interest that is traded on an established securities market is considered to be regularly traded if it is regularly quoted by brokers or dealers making a market in such interests. A class of interests shall be presumed to be regularly traded if the entity has a total of 500 or more interest-holders.

  (4) *Transfers by trusts and estates.*—(i) *In general.*—For purposes of section 367(a), a transfer of property by an estate or trust shall

be treated as a transfer by the entity itself and not as an indirect transfer by its beneficiaries. Thus, a transfer of property by a foreign trust or estate (as defined in section 7701(a)(31)) is not described in section 367(a)(1), regardless of whether the beneficiaries of the trust or estate are U.S. persons. Similarly, a transfer of property by a domestic trust or estate may be described in section 367(a)(1), regardless of whether the beneficiaries of the trust or estate are foreign persons.

(ii) *Grantor trusts.*—A transfer of a portion or all of the assets of a foreign or domestic trust to a foreign corporation in an exchange described in section 367(a)(1) is considered a transfer by any U.S. person who is treated as the owner of any such portion or all of the assets of the trust under sections 671 through 679.

(5) *Termination of election under section 1504(d).*—Section 367(a) applies to the constructive reorganization and transfer of property from a domestic corporation to a foreign corporation that occurs upon the termination of an election under section 1504(d), which permits the treatment of certain contiguous country corporations as domestic corporations. The rule of this paragraph (c)(5) is illustrated by the following example.

Example. Domestic corporation Y previously made a valid election under section 1504(d) to have its wholly owned Canadian subsidiary, C, treated as a domestic corporation. On July 1, 1986, C fails to continue to qualify for the election under section 1504(d). A constructive reorganization described in section 368(a)(1)(D) occurs. The resulting constructive transfer of assets by "domestic" corporation C to Canadian corporation C upon the termination of the election is a transfer of property described in section 367(a)(1).

(6) *Changes in classification of an entity.*—If a foreign entity is classified as an entity other than an association taxable as a corporation for United States tax purposes, and subsequently a change is made in the governing documents, articles, or agreements of the entity so that the entity is thereafter classified as an association taxable as a corporation, the change in classification is considered a transfer of property to a foreign corporation in connection with an exchange described in section 351. For purposes of section 367(a)(1), the transfer of property is considered as made by the persons determined under the rules set forth in paragraph (c)(3) of this section, with respect to partnerships, and paragraph (c)(4)(i) or (ii), with respect to trusts and estates, and the rules of such paragraphs apply in determining whether a transfer described in section 367(a)(1) has been made.

(7) *Contributions to capital.*—For rules with respect to the treatment of a contribution to the capital of a foreign corporation as a transfer described in section 367(a)(1), see section 367(c)(2) and the regulations thereunder.

(d) *Definitions.*—The following definitions apply for purposes of this section and § 1.367(d)-1T.

(1) *United States person.*—The term "United States person" includes those persons described in section 7701(a)(30). The term includes a citizen or resident of the United States, a domestic partnership, a domestic corporation, and any estate or trust other than a foreign estate or trust. (For definitions of these terms, see section 7701 and regulations thereunder.) For purposes of this section, an individual with respect to whom an election has been made under section 6013(g) or (h) is considered to be a resident of the United States while such election is in effect. A nonresident alien or a foreign corporation will not be considered a United States person because of its actual or deemed conduct of a trade or business within the United States during a taxable year.

(2) *Foreign corporation.*—The term "foreign corporation" has the meaning set forth in section 7701(a)(3) and (5) and § 301.7701-5.

(3) *Transfer.*—For purposes of section 367 and regulations thereunder, the term "transfer" means any transaction that constitutes a transfer for purposes of section 332, 351, 354, 355, 356, or 361, as applicable. A person's entering into a bona fide cost-sharing arrangement under § 1.482-2(d)(4) or acquiring rights to intangible property under such an arrangement shall not be considered a transfer of property described in section 367(a)(1). See § 1.6038B-1T(b)(3) for the date on which the transfer is considered to be made.

(4) *Property.*—For purposes of section 367 and regulations thereunder, the term "property" means any item that constitutes property for purposes of section 332, 351, 354, 355, 356, or 361, as applicable.

(5) *Intangible property.*—(i) *In general.*—For purposes of section 367 and regulations thereunder, the term "intangible property" means knowledge, rights, documents, and any other intangible item within the meaning of section 936(h)(3)(B) that constitutes property for purposes of section 332, 351, 354, 355, 356, or 361, as applicable. Such property shall be treated as intangible property for purposes of section 367(a) and (d) and the regulations

thereunder without regard to whether it is used or developed in the United States or in a foreign country and without regard to whether it is used in manufacturing activities or in marketing activities. A working interest in oil and gas properties shall not be considered to be intangible property for purposes of section 367 and the regulations thereunder.

(ii) *Operating intangibles.*—An operating intangible is any intangible property of a type not ordinarily licensed or otherwise transferred in transactions between unrelated parties for consideration contingent upon the licensee's or transferee's use of the property. Examples of operating intangibles may include long-term purchase or supply contracts, surveys, studies, and customer lists.

(iii) *Foreign goodwill or going concern value.*—Foreign goodwill or going concern value is the residual value of a business operation conducted outside of the United States after all other tangible and intangible assets have been identified and valued. For purposes of section 367 and regulations thereunder, the value of the right to use a corporate name in a foreign country shall be treated as foreign goodwill or going concern value.

(iv) *Transitional rule for certain marketing intangibles.*—For transfers occurring after December 31, 1984, and before May 16, 1986, foreign trademarks, tradenames, brandnames, and similar marketing intangibles developed by a foreign branch shall be treated as foreign goodwill or going concern value.

(e) *Close of taxable year in certain section 368(a)(1)(F) reorganizations.*—If a domestic corporation is the transferor corporation in a reorganization described in section 368(a)(1)(F) after March 30, 1987, in which the acquiring corporation is a foreign corporation, then the taxable year of the transferor corporation shall end with the close of the date of the transfer and the taxable year of the acquiring corporation shall end with the close of the date on which the transferor's taxable year would have ended but for the occurrence of the transfer. With regard to the consequences of the closing of the taxable year, see section 381 and the regulations thereunder.

* * *

[Temporary Reg. § 1.367(a)-1T.]

☐ [*T.D.* 8087, 5-15-86. Amended by *T.D.* 8280, 1-12-90 and *T.D.* 8770, 6-18-98.]

§ 1.367(a)-2T. Exception for transfers of property for use in the active conduct of a trade or business (temporary).—(a) *In general.*—Section 367(a)(1) shall not apply to property transferred to a foreign corporation if—

(1) Such property is transferred for use by that corporation in the active conduct of a trade or business outside the United States; and

(2) The U.S. person that transfers the property complies with the reporting requirements of section 6038B and regulations thereunder.

Where these conditions are satisfied, the foreign corporate transferee of the property shall be considered to be a corporation for purposes of determining the extent to which gain or loss is required to be recognized upon the transfer pursuant to section 332, 351, 354 [reserved as to section 355 or so much of section 356 as relates to section 355], 356, or 361. Paragraph (b) of this section provides rules concerning the requirement that property be transferred for use in the active conduct of a trade or business outside of the United States, while paragraph (c) concerns the application of the requirement where the transferee itself retransfers the property. In addition, § 1.367(a)-3T provides rules concerning the treatment of stock or securities transferred to a foreign corporation in an exchange described in section 367(a)(1), and § 1.367(a)-4T provides special rules concerning the treatment of other specified types of property. Finally, §§ 1.367(a)-5T and 1.367(a)-6T provide rules concerning certain transfers of property that are subject to section 367(a)(1) regardless of whether the property is used in the active conduct of a trade or business.

(b) *Active conduct of a trade or business outside the United States.*—(1) *In general.*—Property qualifies for the exception provided by this section if it is transferred to a foreign corporation for use in the active conduct of a trade or business outside of the United States. Therefore, to determine whether property is subject to the exception provided by this section, four factual determinations must be made:

(i) What is the trade or business of the transferee;

(ii) Do the activities of the transferee constitute the active conduct of that trade or business;

(iii) Is the trade or business conducted outside of the United States; and

(iv) Is the transferred property used or held for use in the trade or business?

Rules concerning these four determinations are provided in paragraph (b)(2), (3), (4), and (5) of this section.

(2) *Trade or business.*—Whether the activities of a foreign corporation constitute a trade or business must be determined under all the facts and circumstances. In general, a trade or business is a specific unified group of activities that constitute (or could constitute) an indepen-

dent economic enterprise carried on for profit. For example, the activities of a foreign selling subsidiary could constitute a trade or business if they could be independently carried on for profit, even though the subsidiary acts exclusively on behalf of, and has operations fully integrated with, its parent corporation. To constitute a trade or business, a group of activities must ordinarily include every operation which forms a part of, or a step in, a process by which an enterprise may earn income or profit. In this regard, one or more of such activities may be carried on by independent contractors under the direct control of the foreign corporation. (However, see paragraph (b)(3) of this section.) The group of activities must ordinarily include the collection of income and the payment of expenses. If the activities of a foreign corporation do not constitute a trade or business, then the exception provided by this section does not apply, regardless of the level of activities carried on by the corporation. The following activities are not considered to constitute by themselves a trade or business for purposes of this section:

(i) Any activity giving rise to expenses that would be deductible only under section 212 if the activities were carried on by an individual; or

(ii) The holding for one's own account of investments in stock, securities, land, or other property, including casual sales thereof.

(3) *Active conduct.*—Whether a trade or business is actively conducted must be determined under all the facts and circumstances. In general, a corporation actively conducts a trade or business only if the officers and employees of the corporation carry out substantial managerial and operational activities. A corporation may be engaged in the active conduct of a trade or business even though incidental activities of the trade or business are carried out on behalf of the corporation by independent contractors. In determining whether the officers and employees of the corporation carry out substantial managerial and operational activities, however, the activities of independent contractors shall be disregarded. On the other hand, the officers and employees of the corporation are considered to include the officers and employees of related entities who are made available to and supervised on a day-to-day basis by, and whose salaries are paid by (or reimbursed to the lending related entity by), the transferee foreign corporation. Whether a trade or business that produces rents or royalties is actively conducted shall be determined under the principles of § 1.954-2(d)(1) (but without regard to whether the rents or royalties are received from an unrelated person). The rule of this paragraph (b)(3) is illustrated by the following example.

Example. X, a domestic corporation, and Y, a foreign corporation not related to X, transfer property to Z, a newly formed foreign corporation organized for the purpose of combining the research activities of X and Y. Z contracts all of its operational and research activities to Y for an arm's-length fee. Z's activities do not constitute the active conduct of a trade or business.

(4) *Outside of the United States.*—Whether a foreign corporation conducts a trade or business outside of the United States must be determined under all the facts and circumstances. Generally, the primary managerial and operational activities of the trade or business must be conducted outside the United States and immediately after the transfer the transferred assets must be located outside the United States. Thus, the exception provided by this section would not apply to the transfer of the assets of a domestic business to a foreign corporation if the domestic business continued to operate in the United States after the transfer. In such a case, the primary operational activities of the business would continue to be conducted in the United States. Moreover, the transferred assets would be located in the United States. However, it is not necessary that every item of property transferred be used outside of the United States. As long as the primary managerial and operational activities of the trade or business are conducted outside of the United States and substantially all of the transferred assets are located outside the United States, incidental items of transferred property located in the United States may be considered to have been transferred for use in the active conduct of a trade or business outside of the United States.

(5) *Use in the trade or business.*—Whether property is used or held for use in a trade or business must be determined under all the facts and circumstances. In general, property is used or held for use in a foreign corporation's trade or business if it is—

(i) Held for the principal purpose of promoting the present conduct of the trade or business;

(ii) Acquired and held in the ordinary course of the trade or business; or

(iii) Otherwise held in a direct relationship to the trade or business. Property is considered held in a direct relationship to a trade or business if it is held to meet the present needs of that trade or business and not its anticipated future needs. Thus, property will not be considered to be held in a direct relationship to a trade or business if it is held for

Reg. § 1.367(a)-2T(b)(5)(iii)

the purpose of providing for future diversification into a new trade or business, future expansion of trade or business activities, future plant replacement, or future business contingencies.

(c) *Property transferred by transferee corporation.*—(1) *General rule.*—If a foreign corporation receives property in an exchange described in section 367(a)(1) and as part of the same transaction transfers the property to another person, then the exception provided by this section shall not apply to the initial transfer. For purposes of the preceding sentence, a subsequent transfer within six months of the initial transfer shall be considered to be part of the same transaction, and a subsequent transfer more than six months after the initial transfer may be considered to be part of the same transaction upon the application of step-transaction principles.

(2) *Exception.*—Notwithstanding paragraph (c)(1) of this section, the active conduct exception provided by this section shall apply to the initial transfer if—

(i) The initial transfer is followed by one or more subsequent transfers described in section 351 or 721; and

(ii) Each subsequent transferee is either a partnership in which the preceding transferor is a general partner or a corporation in which the preceding transferor owns common stock; and

(iii) The ultimate transferee uses the property in the active conduct of a trade or business outside the United States.

* * *

[Temporary Reg. § 1.367(a)-2T.]
☐ [T.D. 8087, 5-15-86.]

§ 1.367(a)-3. Treatment of transfers of stock or securities to foreign corporations.—(a) *In general.*—This section provides rules concerning the transfer of stock or securities by a U.S. person to a foreign corporation in an exchange described in section 367(a). In general, a transfer of stock or securities by a U.S. person to a foreign corporation that is described in section 351, 354 (including a reorganization described in section 368(a)(1)(B) and including an indirect stock transfer described in paragraph (d) of this section), 356 or section 361(a) or (b) is subject to section 367(a)(1) and, therefore, is treated as a taxable exchange, unless one of the exceptions set forth in paragraph (b) of this section (regarding transfers of foreign stock or securities) or paragraph (c) of this section (regarding transfers of domestic stock or securities) applies. However, if in an exchange described in section 354, a U.S. person exchanges stock of a foreign corporation in a reorganization described in section 368(a)(1)(E), or a U.S. person exchanges stock of a domestic or foreign corporation for stock of a foreign corporation pursuant to an asset reorganization described in section 368(a)(1)(C), (D) or (F) that is not treated as an indirect stock transfer under paragraph (d) of this section, such section 354 exchange is not a transfer to a foreign corporation subject to section 367(a). See, e.g., paragraph (d)(3) *Example 12*. For rules regarding other indirect or constructive transfers of stock or securities subject to section 367(a), see § 1.367(a)-1T(c). For additional rules relating to an exchange involving a foreign corporation in connection with which there is a transfer of stock, see section 367(b) and the regulations under that section. For additional rules regarding a transfer of stock or securities in an exchange described in section 361(a) or (b), see section 367(a)(5) and any regulations under that section. For rules regarding reporting requirements with respect to transfers described under section 367(a), see section 6038B and the regulations thereunder.

(b) *Transfers by U.S. persons of stock or securities of foreign corporations to foreign corporations.*—(1) *General rule.*—Except as provided in section 367(a)(5), a transfer of stock or securities of a foreign corporation by a U.S. person to a foreign corporation that would otherwise be subject to section 367(a)(1) under paragraph (a) of this section shall not be subject to section 367(a)(1) if either—

(i) *Less than 5-percent shareholder.*—The U.S. person owns less than five percent (applying the attribution rules of section 318, as modified by section 958(b)) of both the total voting power and the total value of the stock of the transferee foreign corporation immediately after the transfer; or

(ii) *5-percent shareholder.*—The U.S. person enters into a five-year gain recognition agreement with respect to the transferred stock or securities as provided in § 1.367(a)-8.

(2) *Certain transfers subject to sections 367(a) and (b).*—(i) *In general.*—A transfer of foreign stock or securities described in section 367(a) or any regulations thereunder as well as in section 367(b) or any regulations thereunder shall be concurrently subject to sections 367(a) and (b) and the regulations thereunder, except to the extent that the transferee foreign corporation is not treated as a corporation under section 367(a)(1). The example in paragraph (b)(2)(ii) of this section illustrates the rules of this paragraph (b)(2). For an illustration of the interaction of the indirect stock transfer rules under section 367(a) (described under paragraph (d) of this section) and the rules of

section 367(b), see paragraph (d)(3) *Example 11* of this section.

(ii) *Example.*—The following example illustrates the provisions of this paragraph (b)(2):

Example. (i) *Facts.* DC, a domestic corporation, owns all of the stock of FC1, a controlled foreign corporation within the meaning of section 957(a). DC's basis in the stock of FC1 is $50, and the value of such stock is $100. The section 1248 amount with respect to such stock is $30. FC2, also a foreign corporation, is owned entirely by foreign individuals who are not related to DC or FC1. In a reorganization described in section 368(a)(1)(B), FC2 acquires all of the stock of FC1 from DC in exchange for 20 percent of the voting stock of FC2. FC2 is not a controlled foreign corporation after the reorganization.

(ii) *Result without gain recognition agreement.* Under the provisions of this paragraph (b), if DC fails to enter into a gain recognition agreement, DC is required to recognize in the year of the transfer the $50 of gain that it realized upon the transfer, $30 of which will be treated as a dividend under section 1248.

(iii) *Result with gain recognition agreement.* If DC enters into a gain recognition agreement under § 1.367(a)-8 with respect to the transfer of FC1 stock, the exchange will also be subject to the provisions of section 367(b) and the regulations thereunder to the extent that it is not subject to tax under section 367(a)(1). In such case, DC will be required to recognize the section 1248 amount of $30 on the exchange of FC1 for FC2 stock. See § 1.367(b)-4(b). The deemed dividend of $30 recognized by DC will increase its basis in the FC1 stock exchanged in the transaction and, therefore, the basis of the FC2 stock received in the transaction. The remaining gain of $20 realized by DC (otherwise recognizable under section 367(a)) in the exchange of FC1 stock will not be recognized if DC enters into a gain recognition agreement with respect to the transfer. (The result would be unchanged if, for example, the exchange of FC1 stock for FC2 stock qualified as a section 351 exchange, or as an exchange described in both sections 351 and 368(a)(1)(B).)

(c) *Transfers by U.S. persons of stock or securities of domestic corporations to foreign corporations.*—(1) *In general.*—Except as provided in section 367(a)(5), a transfer of stock or securities of a domestic corporation by a U.S. person to a foreign corporation that would otherwise be subject to section 367(a)(1) under paragraph (a) of this section shall not be subject to section 367(a)(1) if the domestic corporation the stock or securities of which are transferred (referred to as the U.S. target company) complies with the reporting requirements in paragraph (c)(6) of this section and if each of the following four conditions is met:

(i) Fifty percent or less of both the total voting power and the total value of the stock of the transferee foreign corporation is received in the transaction, in the aggregate, by U.S. transferors (*i.e.*, the amount of stock received does not exceed the 50-percent ownership threshold).

(ii) Fifty percent or less of each of the total voting power and the total value of the stock of the transferee foreign corporation is owned, in the aggregate, immediately after the transfer by U.S. persons that are either officers or directors of the U.S. target company or that are five-percent target shareholders (as defined in paragraph (c)(5)(iii) of this section) (*i.e.*, there is no control group). For purposes of this paragraph (c)(1)(ii), any stock of the transferee foreign corporation owned by U.S. persons immediately after the transfer will be taken into account, whether or not it was received in the exchange for stock or securities of the U.S. target company.

(iii) Either—

(A) The U.S. person is not a five-percent transferee shareholder (as defined in paragraph (c)(5)(ii) of this section); or

(B) The U.S. person is a five-percent transferee shareholder and enters into a five-year agreement to recognize gain with respect to the U.S. target company stock or securities it exchanged in the form provided in § 1.367(a)-8; and

(iv) The active trade or business test (as defined in paragraph (c)(3) of this section) is satisfied.

(2) *Ownership presumption.*—For purposes of paragraph (c)(1) of this section, persons who transfer stock or securities of the U.S. target company in exchange for stock of the transferee foreign corporation are presumed to be U.S. persons. This presumption may be rebutted in accordance with paragraph (c)(7) of this section.

(3) *Active trade or business test.*—(i) *In general.*—The tests of this paragraph (c)(3), collectively referred to as the active trade or business test, are satisfied if:

(A) The transferee foreign corporation or any qualified subsidiary (as defined in paragraph (c)(5)(vii) of this section) or any qualified partnership (as defined in paragraph (c)(5)(viii) of this section) is engaged in an active trade or business outside the United States, within the meaning of § 1.367(a)-2T(b)(2) and (3), for the entire

36-month period immediately before the transfer;

(B) At the time of the transfer, neither the transferors nor the transferee foreign corporation (and, if applicable, the qualified subsidiary or qualified partnership engaged in the active trade or business) have an intention to substantially dispose of or discontinue such trade or business; and

(C) The substantiality test (as defined in paragraph (c)(3)(iii) of this section) is satisfied.

(ii) *Special rules.*—For purposes of paragraphs (c)(3)(i)(A) and (B) of this section, the following special rules apply:

(A) The transferee foreign corporation, a qualified subsidiary, or a qualified partnership will be considered to be engaged in an active trade or business for the entire 36-month period preceding the exchange if it acquires at the time of, or any time prior to, the exchange a trade or business that has been active throughout the entire 36-month period preceding the exchange. This special rule shall not apply, however, if the acquired active trade or business assets were owned by the U.S. target company or any affiliate (within the meaning of section 1504(a) but excluding the exceptions contained in section 1504(b) and substituting "50 percent" for "80 percent" where it appears therein) at any time during the 36-month period prior to the acquisition. Nor will this special rule apply if the principal purpose of such acquisition is to satisfy the active trade or business test.

(B) An active trade or business does not include the making or managing of investments for the account of the transferee foreign corporation or any affiliate (within the meaning of section 1504(a) but excluding the exceptions contained in section 1504(b) and substituting "50 percent" for "80 percent" where it appears therein). (This paragraph (c)(3)(ii)(B) shall not create any inference as to the scope of § 1.367(a)-2T(b)(2) and (3) for other purposes.)

(iii) *Substantiality test.*—(A) *General rule.*—A transferee foreign corporation will be deemed to satisfy the substantiality test if, at the time of the transfer, the fair market value of the transferee foreign corporation is at least equal to the fair market value of the U.S. target company.

(B) *Special rules.*—(*1*) For purposes of paragraph (c)(3)(iii)(A) of this section, the value of the transferee foreign corporation shall include assets acquired outside the ordinary course of business by the transferee foreign corporation within the 36-month period preceding the exchange only if either—

(*i*) Both—

(*A*) At the time of the exchange, such assets or, as applicable, the proceeds thereof, do not produce, and are not held for the production of, passive income as defined in section 1296(b); and

(*B*) Such assets are not acquired for the principal purpose of satisfying the substantiality test; or

(*ii*) Such assets consist of the stock of a qualified subsidiary or an interest in a qualified partnership. See paragraph (c)(3)(iii)(B)(*2*) of this section.

(*2*) For purposes of paragraph (c)(3)(iii)(A) of this section, the value of the transferee foreign corporation shall not include the value of the stock of any qualified subsidiary or the value of any interest in a qualified partnership, held directly or indirectly, to the extent that such value is attributable to assets acquired by such qualified subsidiary or partnership outside the ordinary course of business and within the 36-month period preceding the exchange unless those assets satisfy the requirements in paragraph (c)(3)(iii)(B)(*1*) of this section.

(*3*) For purposes of paragraph (c)(3)(iii)(A) of this section, the value of the transferee foreign corporation shall not include the value of assets received within the 36-month period prior to the acquisition, notwithstanding the special rule in paragraph (c)(3)(iii)(B)(*1*) of this section, if such assets were owned by the U.S. target company or an affiliate (within the meaning of section 1504(a) but without the exceptions under section 1504(b) and substituting "50 percent" for "80 percent" where it appears therein) at any time during the 36-month period prior to the transaction.

(4) *Special rules.*—(i) *Treatment of partnerships.*—For purposes of this paragraph (c), if a partnership (whether domestic or foreign) owns stock or securities in the U.S. target company or the transferee foreign corporation, or transfers stock or securities in an exchange described in section 367(a), each partner in the partnership, and not the partnership itself, is treated as owning and as having transferred, or as owning, a proportionate share of the stock or securities. See § 1.367(a)-1T(c)(3).

(ii) *Treatment of options.*—For purposes of this paragraph (c), one or more options (or an interest similar to an option) will be treated as exercised and thus will be counted as stock for purposes of determining whether the 50percent threshold is exceeded or whether a control group exists if a principal purpose of the issuance or the acquisition of the option (or other interest) was the avoidance of the general rule contained in section 367(a)(1).

(iii) *U.S. target has a vestigial ownership interest in transferee foreign corporation.*—In cases where, immediately after the transfer, the U.S. target company owns, directly or indirectly (applying the attribution rules of sections 267(c)(1) and (5)), stock of the transferee foreign corporation, that stock will not in any way be taken into account (and, thus, will not be treated as outstanding) in determining whether the 50-percent threshold under paragraph (c)(1)(i) of this section is exceeded or whether a control group under paragraph (c)(1)(ii) of this section exists.

(iv) *Attribution rule.*—Except as otherwise provided in this section, the rules of section 318, as modified by the rules of section 958(b), shall apply for purposes of determining the ownership or receipt of stock, securities or other property under this paragraph (c).

(5) *Definitions.*—(i) *Ownership statement.*—An ownership statement is a statement, signed under penalties of perjury, stating—

(A) The identity and taxpayer identification number, if any, of the person making the statement;

(B) That the person making the statement is not a U.S. person (as defined in paragraph (c)(5)(iv) of this section);

(C) That the person making the statement either—

(1) Owns less than 1 percent of the total voting power and total value of a U.S. target company the stock of which is described in Rule 13D-1(d) of Regulation 13D (17 CFR 240.13d-1(d)) (or any rule or regulation to generally the same effect) promulgated by the Securities and Exchange Commission under the Securities and Exchange Act of 1934 (15 USC 78m), and such person did not acquire the stock with a principal purpose to enable the U.S. transferors to satisfy the requirement contained in paragraph (c)(1)(i) of this section; or

(2) Is not related to any U.S. person to whom the stock or securities owned by the person making the statement are attributable under the rules of section 958(b), and did not acquire the stock with a principal purpose to enable the U.S. transferors to satisfy the requirement contained in paragraph (c)(1)(i) of this section;

(D) The citizenship, permanent residence, home address, and U.S. address, if any, of the person making the statement; and

(E) The ownership such person has (by voting power and by value) in the U.S. target company prior to the exchange and the amount of stock of the transferee foreign corporation (by voting power and value) received by such person in the exchange.

(ii) *Five-percent transferee shareholder.*—A five-percent transferee shareholder is a person that owns at least five percent of either the total voting power or the total value of the stock of the transferee foreign corporation immediately after the transfer described in section 367(a)(1). For special rules involving cases in which stock is held by a partnership, see paragraph (c)(4)(i) of this section.

(iii) *Five-percent target shareholder and certain other 5-percent shareholders.*—A five-percent target shareholder is a person that owns at least five percent of either the total voting power or the total value of the stock of the U.S. target company immediately prior to the transfer described in section 367(a)(1). If the stock of the U.S. target company (or any company through which stock of the U.S. target company is owned indirectly or constructively) is described in Rule 13d-1(d) of Regulation 13D (17 CFR 240.13d-1(d)) (or any rule or regulation to generally the same effect), promulgated by the Securities and Exchange Commission under the Securities Exchange Act of 1934 (15 USC 78m), then, in the absence of actual knowledge to the contrary, the existence or absence of filings of Schedule 13-D or 13-G (or any similar schedules) may be relied upon for purposes of identifying five-percent target shareholders (or a five-percent shareholder of a corporation which itself is a five-percent shareholder of the U.S. target company). For special rules involving cases in which U.S. target company stock is held by a partnership, see paragraph (c)(4)(i) of this section.

(iv) *U.S. person.*—For purposes of this section, a U.S. person is defined by reference to § 1.367(a)-1T(d)(1). For application of the rules of this section to stock or securities owned or transferred by a partnership that is a U.S. person, however, see paragraph (c)(4)(i) of this section.

(v) *U.S. transferor.*—A U.S. transferor is a U.S. person (as defined in paragraph (c)(5)(iv) of this section) that transfers stock or securities of one or more U.S. target companies in exchange for stock of the transferee foreign corporation in an exchange described in section 367.

(vi) *Transferee foreign corporation.*—A transferee foreign corporation is the foreign corporation whose stock is received in the exchange by U.S. persons.

(vii) *Qualified subsidiary.*—A qualified subsidiary is a foreign corporation whose stock is at least 80-percent owned (by total voting power and total value), directly or indirectly, by the transferee foreign corporation. However, a corporation will not be treated as a qualified subsidiary if it was affiliated with the U.S. target company (within the meaning of section 1504(a) but without the exceptions under section 1504(b) and substituting "50 percent" for "80 percent" where it appears therein) at any time during the 36-month period prior to the transfer. Nor will a corporation be treated as a qualified subsidiary if it was acquired by the transferee foreign corporation at any time during the 36-month period prior to the transfer for the principal purpose of satisfying the active trade or business test, including the substantiality test.

(viii) *Qualified partnership.*—(A) Except as provided in paragraph (c)(5)(viii)(B) or (C) of this section, a qualified partnership is a partnership in which the transferee foreign corporation—

(1) Has active and substantial management functions as a partner with regard to the partnership business; or

(2) Has an interest representing a 25 percent or greater interest in the partnership's capital and profits.

(B) A partnership is not a qualified partnership if the U.S. target company or any affiliate of the U.S. target company (within the meaning of section 1504(a) but without the exceptions under section 1504(b) and substituting "50 percent" for "80 percent" where it appears therein) held a 5 percent or greater interest in the partnership's capital and profits at any time during the 36-month period prior to the transfer.

(C) A partnership is not a qualified partnership if the transferee foreign corporation's interest was acquired by that corporation at any time during the 36-month period prior to the transfer for the principal purpose of satisfying the active trade or business test, including the substantiality test.

(6) *Reporting requirements of U.S. target company.*—(i) In order for a U.S. person that transfers stock or securities of a domestic corporation to qualify for the exception provided by this paragraph (c) to the general rule under section 367(a)(1), in cases where 10 percent or more of the total voting power or the total value of the stock of the U.S. target company is transferred by U.S. persons in the transaction, the U.S. target company must comply with the reporting requirements contained in this paragraph (c)(6). The U.S. target company must attach to its timely filed U.S. income tax return for the taxable year in which the transfer occurs a statement titled "Section 367(a)—Reporting of Cross-Border Transfer Under Reg. § 1.367(a)-3(c)(6)," signed under penalties of perjury by an officer of the corporation to the best of the officer's knowledge and belief, disclosing the following information—

(A) A description of the transaction in which a U.S. person or persons transferred stock or securities in the U.S. target company to the transferee foreign corporation in a transfer otherwise subject to section 367(a)(1);

(B) The amount (specified as to the percentage of the total voting power and the total value) of stock of the transferee foreign corporation received in the transaction, in the aggregate, by persons who transferred stock or securities of the U.S. target company. For additional information that may be required to rebut the ownership presumption of paragraph (c)(2) of this section in cases where more than 50 percent of either the total voting power or the total value of the stock of the transferee foreign corporation is received in the transaction, in the aggregate, by persons who transferred stock or securities of the U.S. target company, see paragraph (c)(7) of this section;

(C) The amount (if any) of transferee foreign corporation stock owned directly or indirectly (applying the attribution rules of sections 267(c)(1) and (5)) immediately after the exchange by the U.S. target company;

(D) A statement that there is no control group within the meaning of paragraph (c)(1)(ii) of this section;

(E) A list of U.S. persons who are officers, directors or five-percent target shareholders and the percentage of the total voting power and the total value of the stock of the transferee foreign corporation owned by such persons both immediately before and immediately after the transaction; and

(F) A statement that includes the following—

(1) A statement that the active trade or business test described in paragraph (c)(3) of this section is satisfied by the transferee foreign corporation and a description of such business;

(2) A statement that on the day of the transaction, there was no intent on the part of the transferors or the transferee foreign corporation (or any qualified subsidiary or any qualified partnership, if relevant) to substantially dispose of or discontinue its active trade or business; and

(3) A statement that the substantiality test described in paragraph (c)(3)(iii) of this section is satisfied, and documentation that such test is satisfied, including the value of the transferee foreign corporation and the value of the U.S. target company on the day of the transfer, and either one of the following—

(i) A statement demonstrating that the value of the transferee foreign corporation 36 months prior to the acquisition, plus the value of any assets described in paragraph (c)(3)(iii)(B) of this section (including stock) acquired by the transferee foreign corporation within the 36-month period, less the amount of any liabilities acquired during that period, exceeds the value of the U.S. target company on the acquisition date; or

(ii) A statement demonstrating that the value of the transferee foreign corporation on the date of the acquisition, reduced by the value of any assets not described in paragraph (c)(3)(iii)(B) of this section (including stock) acquired by the transferee foreign corporation within the 36-month period, exceeds the value of the U.S. target company on the date of the acquisition.

(ii) For purposes of this paragraph (c)(6), an income tax return will be considered timely filed if such return is filed, together with the statement required by this paragraph (c)(6), on or before the last date for filing a Federal income tax return (taking into account any extensions of time therefor) for the taxable year in which the transfer occurs. If a return is not timely filed within the meaning of this paragraph (c)(6), the District Director may make a determination, based on all facts and circumstances, that the taxpayer had reasonable cause for its failure to file a timely filed return and, if such a determination is made, the requirement contained in this paragraph (c)(6) shall be waived.

(7) *Ownership statements.*—To rebut the ownership presumption of paragraph (c)(2) of this section, the U.S. target company must obtain ownership statements (described in paragraph (c)(5)(i) of this section) from a sufficient number of persons that transfer U.S. target company stock or securities in the transaction that are not U.S. persons to demonstrate that the 50-percent threshold of paragraph (c)(1)(i) of this section is not exceeded. In addition, the U.S. target company must attach to its timely filed U.S. income tax return (as described in paragraph (c)(6)(ii) of this section) for the taxable year in which the transfer occurs a statement, titled "Section 367(a) - Compilation of Ownership Statements under Reg. § 1.367(a)-3(c)," signed under penalties of perjury by an officer of the corporation, disclosing the following information:

(i) The amount (specified as to the percentage of the total voting power and the total value) of stock of the transferee foreign corporation received, in the aggregate, by U.S. transferors;

(ii) The amount (specified as to the percentage of total voting power and total value) of stock of the transferee foreign corporation received, in the aggregate, by foreign persons that filed ownership statements;

(iii) A summary of the information tabulated from the ownership statements, including—

(A) The names of the persons that filed ownership statements stating that they are not U.S. persons;

(B) The countries of residence and citizenship of such persons; and

(C) Each of such person's ownership (by voting power and by value) in the U.S. target company prior to the exchange and the amount of stock of the transferee foreign corporation (by voting power and value) received by such persons in the exchange.

(8) *Certain transfers in connection with performance of services.*—Section 367(a)(1) shall not apply to a domestic corporation's transfer of its own stock or securities in connection with the performance of services, if the transfer is considered to be to a foreign corporation solely by reason of § 1.83-6(d)(1). The transfer may still, however, be reportable under section 6038B. See § 1.6038B-1(b)(2)(i)(A)(4) and (b)(2)(i)(B)(4).

(9) *Private letter ruling option.*—The Internal Revenue Service may, in limited circumstances, issue a private letter ruling to permit the taxpayer to qualify for an exception to the general rule under section 367(a)(1) if—

(i) A taxpayer is unable to satisfy all of the requirements of paragraph (c)(3) of this section relating to the active trade or business test of paragraph (c)(1)(iv) of this section, but such taxpayer meets all of the other requirements contained in paragraphs (c)(1)(i) through (c)(1)(iii) of this section, and such taxpayer is substantially in compliance with the rules set forth in paragraph (c)(3) of this section; or

(ii) A taxpayer is unable to satisfy any requirement of paragraph (c)(1) of this section due to the application of paragraph (c)(4)(iv) of this section. Notwithstanding the preceding sentence, in no event will the Internal Revenue Service rule on the issue of whether the principal purpose of an acquisition was to satisfy the active trade or business test, including the substantiality test.

(10) *Examples.*—This paragraph (c) may be illustrated by the following examples:

Example 1. Ownership presumption. (i) FC, a foreign corporation, issues 51 percent of its stock to the shareholders of S, a domestic corporation, in exchange for their S stock, in a transaction described in section 367(a)(1).

(ii) Under paragraph (c)(2) of this section, all shareholders of S who receive stock of FC in the exchange are presumed to be U.S. persons. Unless this ownership presumption is rebutted, the condition set forth in paragraph (c)(1)(i) of this section will not be satisfied, and the exception in paragraph (c)(1) of this section will not be available. As a result, all U.S. persons that transferred S stock will recognize gain on the exchange. To rebut the ownership presumption, S must comply with the reporting requirements contained in paragraph (c)(7) of this section, obtaining ownership statements (described in paragraph (c)(5)(i) of this section) from a sufficient number of non-U.S. persons who received FC stock in the exchange to demonstrate that the amount of FC stock received by U.S. persons in the exchange does not exceed 50 percent.

Example 2. Filing of gain recognition agreement. (i) The facts are the same as in *Example 1*, except that FC issues only 40 percent of its stock to the shareholders of S in the exchange. FC satisfies the active trade or business test of paragraph (c)(1)(iv) of this section. A, a U.S. person, owns 10 percent of S's stock immediately before the transfer. All other shareholders of S own less than five percent of its stock. None of S's officers or directors owns any stock in FC immediately after the transfer. A will own 15 percent of the stock of FC immediately after the transfer, 4 percent received in the exchange, and the balance being stock in FC that A owned prior to and independent of the transaction. No S shareholder besides A owns five percent or more of FC immediately after the transfer. The reporting requirements under paragraph (c)(6) of this section are satisfied.

(ii) The condition set forth in paragraph (c)(1)(i) of this section is satisfied because, even after application of the presumption in paragraph (c)(2) of this section, U.S. transferors could not receive more than 50 percent of FC's stock in the transaction. There is no control group because five-percent target shareholders and officers and directors of S do not, in the aggregate, own more than 50 percent of the stock of FC immediately after the transfer (A, the sole five-percent target shareholder, owns 15 percent of the stock of FC immediately after the transfer, and no officers or directors of S own any stock of FC immediately after the transfer). Therefore, the condition set forth in paragraph (c)(1)(ii) of this section is satisfied. The facts assume that the condition set forth in paragraph (c)(1)(iv) of this section is satisfied. Thus, U.S. persons that are not five-percent transferee shareholders will not recognize gain on the exchange of S shares for FC shares. A, a five-percent transferee shareholder, will not be required to include in income any gain realized on the exchange in the year of the transfer if he files a 5-year gain recognition agreement (GRA) and complies with section 6038B.

Example 3. Control group. (i) The facts are the same as in *Example 2*, except that B, another U.S. person, is a 5-percent target shareholder, owning 25 percent of S's stock immediately before the transfer. B owns 40 percent of the stock of FC immediately after the transfer, 10 percent received in the exchange, and the balance being stock in FC that B owned prior to and independent of the transaction.

(ii) A control group exists because A and B, each a five-percent target shareholder within the meaning of paragraph (c)(5)(iii) of this section, together own more than 50 percent of FC immediately after the transfer (counting both stock received in the exchange and stock owned prior to and independent of the exchange). As a result, the condition set forth in paragraph (c)(1)(ii) of this section is not satisfied, and all U.S. persons (not merely A and B) who transferred S stock will recognize gain on the exchange.

Example 4. Partnerships. (i) The facts are the same as in *Example 3*, except that B is a partnership (domestic or foreign) that has five equal partners, only two of whom, X and Y, are U.S. persons. Under paragraph (c)(4)(i) of this section, X and Y are treated as the owners and transferors of 5 percent each of the S stock owned and transferred by B and as owners of 8 percent each of the FC stock owned by B immediately after the transfer. U.S. persons that are five-percent target shareholders thus own a total of 31 percent of the stock of FC immediately after the transfer (A's 15 percent, plus X's 8 percent, plus Y's 8 percent).

(ii) Because no control group exists, the condition in paragraph (c)(1)(ii) of this section is satisfied. The conditions in paragraphs (c)(1)(i) and (iv) of this section also are satisfied. Thus, U.S. persons that are not five-percent transferee shareholders will not recognize gain on the exchange of S shares for FC shares. A, X, and Y, each a five-percent transferee shareholder, will not be required to include in income in the year of the transfer any gain realized on the exchange if they file 5-year GRAs and comply with section 6038B.

(11) *Effective date.*—This paragraph (c) applies to transfers occurring after January 29, 1997. However, taxpayers may elect to apply this section in its entirety to all transfers occurring after April 17, 1994, provided that the statute of limitations of the affected tax year or years is open.

(d) *Indirect stock transfers in certain nonrecognition transfers.*—(1) *In general.*—For purposes of this section, a U.S. person who exchanges, under section 354 (or section 356) stock or securities in a domestic or foreign corporation for stock or securities in a foreign corporation in connection with one of the following transactions described in paragraphs (d)(1)(i) through (v) of this section (or who is deemed to make such an exchange under paragraph (d)(1)(vi) of this section) shall be treated as having made an indirect transfer of such stock or securities to a foreign corporation that is subject to the rules of this section, including, for example, the requirement, where applicable, that the U.S. transferor enter into a gain recognition agreement to preserve nonrecognition treatment under section 367(a). If the U.S. person exchanges stock or securities of a foreign corporation, see also section 367(b) and the regulations thereunder. For an example of the concurrent application of the indirect stock transfer rules under section 367(a) and the rules of section 367(b), see, e.g., paragraph (d)(3) *Example 11* of this section.

(i) *Mergers described in sections 368(a)(1)(A) and (a)(2)(D).*—A U.S. person exchanges stock or securities of a corporation (the acquired corporation) for stock or securities of a foreign corporation that controls the acquiring corporation in a reorganization described in sections 368(a)(1)(A) and (a)(2)(D). See, e.g., paragraph (d)(3) *Example 1* of this section.

(ii) *Mergers described in sections 368(a)(1)(A) and (a)(2)(E).*—A U.S. person exchanges stock or securities of a corporation (the acquiring corporation) for stock or securities in a foreign corporation that controls the acquired corporation in a reorganization described in sections 368(a)(1)(A) and (a)(2)(E).

(iii) *Triangular reorganizations described in section 368(a)(1)(B).*—A U.S. person exchanges stock of the acquired corporation for voting stock of a foreign corporation that is in control (as defined in section 368(c)) of the acquiring corporation in connection with a reorganization described in section 368(a)(1)(B). See, e.g., paragraph (d)(3) *Example 4* of this section.

(iv) *Triangular reorganizations described in section 368(a)(1)(C).*—A U.S. person exchanges stock or securities of a corporation (the acquired corporation) for voting stock or securities of a foreign corporation that controls the acquiring corporation in a reorganization described in section 368(a)(1)(C). See, e.g., paragraph (d)(3) *Example 5* of this section (for an example of a triangular section 368(a)(1)(C) reorganization involving domestic acquired and acquiring corporations), and paragraph (d)(3) *Example 7* of this section (for an example involving a domestic acquired corporation and a foreign acquiring corporation). If the acquired corporation is a foreign corporation, see paragraph (d)(3) *Example 11* of this section, and section 367(b) and the regulations thereunder.

(v) *Reorganizations described in sections 368(a)(1)(C) and (a)(2)(C).*—A U.S. person exchanges stock or securities of a corporation (the acquired corporation) for voting stock or securities of a foreign acquiring corporation in a reorganization described in sections 368(a)(1)(C) and (a)(2)(C) (other than a triangular section 368(a)(1)(C) reorganization described in paragraph (d)(1)(iv) of this section). In the case of a reorganization in which some but not all of the assets of the acquired corporation are transferred pursuant to section 368(a)(2)(C), the transaction shall be considered to be an indirect transfer of stock or securities subject to this paragraph (d) only to the extent of the assets so transferred. (Other assets shall be treated as having been transferred in an asset transfer rather than an indirect stock transfer, and such asset transfer would be subject to the other provisions of section 367, including sections 367(a)(1), (3), (5) and (d) if the acquired corporation is a domestic corporation.) See, e.g., paragraph (d)(3) *Example 5B* of this section.

(vi) *Successive transfers of property to which section 351 applies.*—A U.S. person transfers property (other than stock or securities) to a foreign corporation in an exchange described in section 351, and all or a portion of such assets transferred to the foreign corporation by such person are, in connection with the same transaction, transferred to a second corporation that is controlled by the foreign corporation in one or more exchanges described in section 351. For purposes of this paragraph (d)(1) and § 1.367(a)-8, the initial transfer by the U.S. person shall be deemed to be a transfer of stock described in section 354. (Any assets transferred to the foreign corporation that are not transferred by the foreign corporation to a second corporation shall be treated as a transfer of assets subject to the general rules of section 367, including sections 367(a)(1), (3), (5) and (d), and not as an indirect stock transfer under the rules of this paragraph (d).) See, e.g., paragraph (d)(3) *Example 10* and *Example 10A* of this section.

(2) *Special rules for indirect transfers.*—If a U.S. person is considered to make an indirect transfer of stock or securities described in paragraph (d)(1) of this section, the rules of this section and § 1.367(a)-8 shall apply to the transfer. For purposes of applying the rules of this section and § 1.367(a)-8:

(i) *Transferee foreign corporation.*—The transferee foreign corporation shall be the foreign corporation that issues stock or securities to the U.S. person in the exchange.

(ii) *Transferred corporation.*—The transferred corporation shall be the acquiring corporation, except that in the case of a triangular section 368(a)(1)(B) reorganization described in paragraph (d)(1)(iii) of this section, the transferred corporation shall be the acquired corporation; in the case of a triangular section 368(a)(1)(C) reorganization described in paragraph (d)(1)(iv) of this section followed by a section 368(a)(2)(C) transfer or a section 368(a)(1)(C) reorganization followed by a section 368(a)(2)(C) transfer described in paragraph (d)(1)(v) of this section, the transferred corporation shall be the transferee corporation; and in the case of successive section 351 transfers described in paragraph (d)(1)(vi) of this section, the transferred corporation shall be the transferee corporation in the final section 351 transfer. The transferred property shall be the stock or securities of the transferred corporation, as appropriate in the circumstances.

(iii) *Amount of gain.*—The amount of gain that a U.S. person is required to include in income in the event of a disposition (or a deemed disposition) of some or all of the stock or securities of the transferred corporation shall be the proportionate share (as determined under §1.367(a)-8(e)) of the U.S. person's gain realized but not recognized in the initial exchange (or deemed exchange) of stock or securities under section 354.

(iv) *Gain recognition agreements involving multiple parties.*—The U.S. transferor's agreement to recognize gain, as provided in §1.367(a)-8, shall include appropriate provisions, consistent with the principles of these rules, requiring the transferor to recognize gain in the event of a direct or indirect disposition of the stock or assets of the transferred corporation. For example, in the case of a triangular section 368(a)(1)(B) reorganization described in paragraph (d)(1)(iii) of this section, a disposition of the transferred stock shall include an indirect disposition of such stock by the transferee foreign corporation, such as a disposition of such stock by the acquiring corporation or a disposition of the stock of the acquiring corporation by the transferee foreign corporation. See, e.g., paragraph (d)(3) *Example 4* of this section.

(v) *Determination of whether the transferred corporation disposed of substantially all of its assets.*—For purposes of applying §1.367(a)-8(e)(3)(i) to determine whether the transferred corporation has disposed of substantially all of its assets, the following assets shall be taken into account (but only if such assets are not fully taxable under section 367 in the taxable year that includes the indirect transfer)—

(A) In the case of a sections 368(a)(1)(A) and (a)(2)(D) reorganization, and a triangular section 368(a)(1)(C) reorganization described in paragraph (d)(1)(i) or (iv) of this section, respectively, the assets of the acquired corporation;

(B) In the case of a sections 368(a)(1)(A) and (a)(2)(E) reorganization described in paragraph (d)(1)(ii) of this section, the assets of the acquiring corporation immediately prior to the transaction;

(C) In the case of a sections 368(a)(1)(C) and (a)(2)(C) reorganization described in paragraph (d)(1)(v) of this section, the assets of the acquired corporation that are subject to a transfer described in section 368(a)(2)(C); and

(D) In the case of successive section 351 exchanges described in paragraph (d)(1)(vi) of this section, the assets that are both transferred initially to the foreign corporation, and transferred by the foreign corporation to a second corporation.

(vi) *Coordination between asset transfer rules and indirect stock transfer rules.*—If, pursuant to any of the transactions described in paragraph (d)(1) of this section, a domestic corporation transfers (or is deemed to transfer) assets to a foreign corporation (other than in an exchange described in section 354), the rules of section 367, including sections 367(a)(1), (a)(3) and (a)(5), as well as section 367(d), and the regulations thereunder shall apply prior to the application of the rules of this section. However, if a transaction is described in this paragraph (d), section 367(a) shall not apply in the case of a domestic acquired corporation that transfers its assets to a foreign acquiring corporation, to the extent that such assets are retransferred to a domestic corporation in a transfer described in section 368(a)(2)(C) or paragraph (d)(1)(vi) of this section, but only if the domestic transferee's basis in the assets is no greater than the basis that the domestic acquired company had in such assets. See, e.g., paragraph (d)(3) *Example 8* and *Example 10A* of this section.

(3) *Examples.*—The rules of this paragraph (d) and §1.367(a)-8 are illustrated by the following examples:

Example 1. Section 368(a)(1)(A)/ (a)(2)(D) reorganization—(i) *Facts.* F, a foreign corporation, owns all the stock of Newco, a domestic corporation. A, a domestic corporation, owns all of the stock of W, also a domestic corporation. A and W file a consolidated Federal income tax return. A does not own any stock in F (applying the attribution rules of section 318, as modified by section 958(b)). In a reorganization described in sections 368(a)(1)(A) and (a)(2)(D), Newco acquires all of the assets of W, and A receives 40% of the stock of F in an exchange described in section 354.

(ii) *Result.* Pursuant to paragraph (d)(1)(i) of this section, the reorganization is subject to the indirect stock transfer rules. F is treated as the transferee foreign corporation, and Newco is treated as the transferred corporation. Provided that the requirements of paragraph (c)(1) of this section are satisfied, including the requirement that A enter into a five-year gain recognition agreement as described in § 1.367(a)-8, A's exchange of W stock for F stock under section 354 will not be subject to section 367(a)(1). If F disposes (within the meaning of § 1.367(a)-8(e)) of all (or a portion) of Newco's stock within the five-year term of the agreement (and A has not made a valid election under § 1.367(a)-8(b)(1)(vii)), A is required to file an amended return for the year of the transfer and include in income, with interest, the gain realized but not recognized on the initial section 354 exchange. If A has made a valid election under § 1.367(a)-8(b)(1)(vii) to include the amount subject to the gain recognition agreement in the year of the triggering event, A would instead include the gain on its tax return for the taxable year that includes the triggering event, together with interest.

Example 1A. Transferor is a subsidiary in consolidated group—(i) *Facts.* The facts are the same as in *Example 1*, except that A is owned by P, a domestic corporation, and for the taxable year in which the transaction occurred, P, A and W filed a consolidated Federal income tax return.

(ii) *Result.* Even though A is the U.S. transferor, P is required under § 1.367(a)-8(a)(3) to enter into the gain recognition agreement and comply with the requirements under § 1.367(a)-8. In the event that A leaves the P group, A would make the annual certifications required under § 1.367(a)-8(b)(5)(ii). P would remain liable with A under the gain recognition agreement.

Example 2. Taxable inversion pursuant to indirect stock transfer rules—(i) *Facts.* The facts are the same as in *Example 1*, except that A receives more than fifty percent of either the total voting power or the total value of the stock of F in the transaction.

(ii) *Result.* A is required to include in income in the year of the exchange the amount of gain realized on such exchange. See paragraph (c)(1)(i) of this section. If A fails to include the income on its timely-filed return, A will also be liable for the penalty under section 6038B (together with interest and other applicable penalties) unless A's failure to include the income is due to reasonable cause and not willful neglect. See § 1.6038B-1(f).

Example 3. Disposition by U.S. transferred corporation of substantially all of its assets—(i) *Facts.* The facts are the same as in *Example 1*, except that, during the third year of the gain recognition agreement, Newco disposes of substantially all (as described in § 1.367(a)-8(e)(3)(i)) of the assets described in paragraph (d)(2)(v)(A) of this section for cash and recognizes currently all of the gain realized on the disposition.

(ii) *Result.* Under § 1.367(a)-8(e)(3)(i), the gain recognition agreement is generally triggered when the transferred corporation disposes of substantially all of its assets. However, under the special rule contained in § 1.367(a)-8(h)(2), because A and W filed a consolidated Federal income tax return prior to the transaction, and Newco, the transferred corporation, is a domestic corporation, the gain recognition agreement is terminated and has no further effect.

Example 4. Triangular section 368(a)(1)(B) reorganization—(i) *Facts.* F, a foreign corporation, owns all the stock of S, a domestic corporation. U, a domestic corporation, owns all of the stock of Y, also a domestic corporation. U does not own any of the stock of F (applying the attribution rules of section 318, as modified by section 958(b)). In a triangular reorganization described in section 368(a)(1)(B) and paragraph (d)(1)(iii) of this section, S acquires all the stock of Y, and U receives 10% of the voting stock of F.

(ii) *Result.* U's exchange of Y stock for F stock will not be subject to section 367(a)(1), provided that all of the requirements of paragraph (c)(1) are satisfied, including the requirement that U enter into a five-year gain recognition agreement. For purposes of this section, F is treated as the transferee foreign corporation and Y is treated as the transferred corporation. See paragraphs (d)(2)(i) and (ii) of this section. Under paragraph (d)(2)(iv) of this section, the gain recognition agreement would be triggered if F sold all or a portion of the stock of S, or if S sold all or a portion of the stock of Y.

Example 5. Triangular section 368(a)(1)(C) reorganization—(i) *Facts.* F, a foreign corporation, owns all of the stock of R, a domestic corporation that operates an historical business. V, a domestic corporation, owns all of the stock of Z, also a domestic corporation. V does not own any of the stock of F (applying the attribution rules of section 318 as

Reg. § 1.367(a)-3(d)(3)

modified by section 958(b)). In a triangular reorganization described in section 368(a)(1)(C) (and paragraph (d)(1)(iv) of this section), R acquires all of the assets of Z, and V receives 30% of the voting stock of F.

(ii) *Result.* The consequences of the transfer are similar to those described in *Example 1*; V is required to enter into a 5-year gain recognition agreement under § 1.367(a)-8 to secure nonrecognition treatment under section 367(a). Under paragraphs (d)(2)(i) and (ii) of this section, F is treated as the transferee foreign corporation and R is treated as the transferred corporation. In determining whether, in a later transaction, R has disposed of substantially all of its assets under § 1.367(a)-8(e)(3)(i), see paragraph (d)(2)(v)(A) of this section.

Example 5A. Section 368(a)(1)(C) reorganization followed by section 368(a)(2)(C) exchange—(i) *Facts.* The facts are the same as in *Example 5*, except that the transaction is structured as a section 368(a)(1)(C) reorganization, followed by a section 368(a)(2)(C) exchange, and R is a foreign corporation. The following additional facts are present. Z has 3 businesses: Business A with a basis of $10 and a value of $50, Business B with a basis of $10 and a value of $40, and Business C with a basis of $10 and a value of $30. V and Z file a consolidated Federal income tax return and V has a basis of $30 in the Z stock, which has a value of $120. Assume that Businesses A and B consist solely of assets that will satisfy the section 367(a)(3) active trade or business exception; none of Business C's assets will satisfy the exception. Z transfers all 3 businesses to F in exchange for 30 percent of the F stock, which Z distributes to V pursuant to a section 368(a)(1)(C) reorganization. F then contributes Businesses B and C to R pursuant to section 368(a)(2)(C).

(ii) *Result.* The transfer of the Business A assets by Z to F is subject to the general rules under section 367, as such transfer does not constitute an indirect stock transfer. The transfer by Z of the Business B and C assets to F must first be tested under sections 367(a)(1), (3) and (5). Z recognizes $20 of gain on the outbound transfer of the Business C assets, as such assets do not qualify for an exception to section 367(a)(1). The Business B assets, which will be used by R in an active trade or business outside the United States, qualify for the exception under section 367(a)(3) and § 1.367(a)-2T(c)(2). V is deemed to transfer the stock of Z to F in a section 354 exchange subject to the rules of paragraph (d). V must enter into the gain recognition agreement in the amount of $30 to preserve Z's nonrecognition treatment with respect to its transfer of Business B assets. Under paragraphs (d)(2)(i) and (ii) of this section, F is the transferee foreign corporation and R is the transferred corporation.

Example 5B. Section 368(a)(1)(C) reorganization followed by section 368(a)(2)(C) exchange with U.S. transferee—(i) *Facts.* The facts are the same as in *Example 5A*, except that R is a U.S. corporation.

(ii) *Result.* As in *Example 5A*, the outbound transfer of Business A assets to F is subject to section 367(a) and is not affected by the rules of this paragraph (d). The Business B assets qualified for nonrecognition treatment; the Business C assets did not. However, pursuant to paragraph (d)(2)(vi) of this section, the Business C assets are not subject to section 367(a)(1), provided that the basis of the assets in the hands of R is no greater than the basis of the assets in the hands of Z. V is deemed to make an indirect transfer under the rules of this paragraph (d). To preserve nonrecognition treatment under section 367(a), V must enter into a 5-year gain recognition agreement in the amount of $50, the amount of the appreciation in the Business B and C assets, as the transfer of such assets by Z were not taxable under section 367(a)(1) but were treated as an indirect stock transfer.

Example 6. Triangular section 368(a)(1)(C) reorganization followed by 351 exchange—(i) *Facts.* The facts are the same as in *Example 5*, except that, during the fourth year of the gain recognition agreement, R transfers substantially all of the assets received from Z to K, a wholly-owned domestic subsidiary of R, in an exchange described in section 351.

(ii) *Result.* The disposition by R, the transferred corporation, of substantially all of its assets would trigger the gain recognition agreement if the assets were disposed of in a taxable transaction. However, because the assets were transferred in a nonrecognition transaction, such transfer does not trigger the gain recognition agreement if V satisfies the reporting requirements contained in § 1.367(a)-8(g)(3) (which includes the requirement that V amend its gain recognition agreement to reflect the transaction). See also paragraph (d)(2)(iv) of this section. To determine whether substantially all of the assets are disposed of, any assets of Z that were transferred by Z to R and then contributed by R to K are taken into account.

Example 6A. Triangular section 368(a)(1)(C) reorganization followed by section 351 exchange with foreign transferee—(i) *Facts.* The facts are the same as in *Example 6* except that K is a foreign corporation.

(ii) *Result.* This transfer of assets by R to K must be analyzed to determine its effect upon the gain recognition agreement, and such transfer is also an outbound transfer of assets that is taxable under section 367(a)(1) unless the active trade or business exception under section 367(a)(3) applies. If the transfer is fully taxable under section 367(a)(1), the transfer is treated as if the transferred company, R, sold substantially all of its assets. Thus, the gain recognition agreement would be triggered (but see § 1.367(a)-8(b)(3)(ii) for potential offsets to the gain to be recognized). If each asset transferred qualifies for nonrecognition treatment under section 367(a)(3) and the regulations thereunder (which require, under § 1.367(a)-2T(a)(2), the transferor to comply with the reporting requirements under section 6038B), the result is the same as in *Example 6*. If a portion of the assets transferred qualify for nonrecognition treatment under section 367(a)(3) and a portion are taxable under section 367(a)(1) (but such portion does not result in the disposition of substantially all of the assets), the gain recognition agreement will not be triggered if such information is reported as required under § 1.367(a)-8(b)(5) and (e)(3)(i).

Example 7. Concurrent application of asset transfer and indirect stock transfer rules in consolidated return setting—(i) *Facts*. Assume the same facts as in *Example 5*, except that R is a foreign corporation and V and Z file a consolidated return for Federal income tax purposes. The properties of Z consist of Business A assets, with an adjusted basis of $50 and fair market value of $90, and Business B assets, with an adjusted basis of $50 and a fair market value of $110. Assume that the Business A assets do not qualify for the active trade or business exception under section 367(a)(3), but that the Business B assets do qualify for the exception. V's basis in the Z stock is $100, and the value of such stock is $200.

(ii) *Result*. Under paragraph (d)(2)(vi), the assets of Businesses A and B that are transferred to R must be tested under sections 367(a)(3) and (a)(5) prior to consideration of the indirect stock transfer rules of this paragraph (d). Thus, Z must recognize $40 of income under section 367(a)(1) on the outbound transfer of Business A assets. Under § 1.1502-32, because V and Z file a consolidated return, V's basis in its Z stock increases from $100 to $140 as a result of Z's $40 gain. Provided that all of the other requirements under paragraph (c)(1) of this section are satisfied, to qualify for nonrecognition treatment with respect to V's indirect transfer of Z stock, V must enter into a gain recognition agreement in the amount of $60 (the gain realized but not recognized by V in the stock of Z after the $40 basis adjustment). If F sells a portion of its stock in R during the term of the agreement, V will be required to recognize a portion of the $60 gain subject to the agreement. To determine whether R disposes of substantially all of its assets (under § 1.367(a)-8(e)(3)(i)), only the Business B assets will be considered (because the transfer of the Business A assets was taxable to Z under section 367). See paragraph (d)(2)(v)(A) of this section.

Example 7A. Concurrent application without consolidated returns—(i) *Facts*. The facts are the same as in *Example 7*, except that V and Z do not file consolidated income tax returns.

(ii) *Result*. Z would still recognize $40 of gain on the transfer of its Business A assets, and the Business B assets would still qualify for the active trade or business exception under section 367(a)(3). However, V's basis in its stock of Z would not be increased by the amount of Z's gain. V's indirect transfer of stock will be taxable unless V enters into a gain recognition agreement (as described in § 1.367(a)-8) for the $100 of gain realized but not recognized with respect to the stock of Z.

Example 7B. Concurrent application with individual U.S. shareholder—(i) *Facts*. The facts are the same as in *Example 7*, except that V is an individual U.S. citizen.

(ii) *Result*. Section 367(a)(5) would prevent the application of the active trade or business exception under section 367(a)(3). Thus, Z's transfer of assets to R would be fully taxable under section 367(a)(1). Z would recognize $100 of income. V's basis in its stock of Z is not increased by this amount. V is taxable with respect to its indirect transfer of its Z stock unless V enters into a gain recognition agreement in the amount of the $100, the gain realized but not recognized with respect to its Z stock.

Example 7C. Concurrent application with nonresident alien shareholder—(i) *Facts*. The facts are the same as in *Example 7*, except that V is a nonresident alien.

(ii) *Result*. Pursuant to section 367(a)(5), the active trade or business exception under section 367(a)(3) is not available with respect to Z's transfer of assets to R. Thus, Z has $100 of gain with respect to the Business A and B assets. Because V is a nonresident alien, however, V is not subject to section 367(a) with respect to its indirect transfer of Z stock.

Example 8. Concurrent application with section 368(a)(2)(C) Exchange—(i) *Facts*. The facts are the same as in *Example 7*, except that R transfers the Business A assets to M, a wholly-owned domestic subsidiary of R, in an exchange described in section 368(a)(2)(C).

(ii) *Result*. Pursuant to paragraph (d)(2)(vi) of this section, section 367(a)(1) does not apply to Z's transfer of Business A assets to R, because such assets are transferred to M, a domestic corporation. Sections 367(a)(1), (3) and (5), as well as section 367(d), apply to Z's transfer of assets to R to the extent that such assets are not transferred to M. However, the Business B assets qualify for an exception to taxation under section 367(a)(3). Thus, if the requirements of paragraph (c)(1) of this section are satisfied, including the requirement that V enter into a 5-year gain recognition agreement and comply with the requirements of §1.367(a)-8 with respect to the gain realized on the Z stock, $100, the entire transaction qualifies for nonrecognition treatment under section 367(a)(1). See also section 367(a)(5) and any regulations issued thereunder. Under paragraphs (d)(2)(i) and (ii) of this section, the transferee foreign corporation is F and the transferred corporation is M. Pursuant to paragraph (d)(2)(iv) of this section, a disposition by F of the stock of R, or a disposition by R of the stock of M, will trigger the gain recognition agreement. To determine whether substantially all of the assets have been disposed of (as described under §1.367(a)-8(e)(3)(i)), the Business A assets in M and the Business B assets in R must both be considered.

Example 9. Concurrent application of direct and indirect stock transfer rules—(i) *Facts.* F, a foreign corporation, owns all of the stock of O, also a foreign corporation. D, a domestic corporation, owns all of the stock of E, also a domestic corporation, which owns all of the stock of N, also a domestic corporation. Prior to the transactions described in this *Example 9*, D, E and N filed a consolidated income tax return. D has a basis of $100 in the stock of E, which has a fair market value of $160. The N stock has a fair market value of $100, and E has a basis of $60 in such stock. In addition to the stock of N, E owns the assets of Business X. The assets of Business X have a fair market value of $60, and E has a basis of $50 in such assets. Assume that the Business X assets qualify for nonrecognition treatment under section 367(a)(3). D does not own any stock in F (applying the attribution rules of section 318 as modified by section 958(b)). In a triangular reorganization described in section 368(a)(1)(C) and paragraph (d)(1)(iv) of this section, O acquires all of the assets of E, and D exchanges its stock in E for 40% of the voting stock of F.

(ii) *Result.* E's transfer of its assets, including the N stock, must be tested under the general rules of section 367(a) before consideration of D's indirect transfer of the stock of E. E's transfer of the assets of Business X qualify for nonrecognition under section 367(a)(3). E could qualify for nonrecognition treatment with respect to its transfer of N stock if it enters into a gain recognition agreement (and all of the requirements of paragraph (c)(1)(i) of this section are satisfied); however under §1.367(a)-8(f)(2)(i), D, the parent of the consolidated group, must enter into the agreement. O is the transferee foreign corporation; N is the transferred corporation. D may also qualify for nonrecognition with respect to its indirect transfer of the stock of E if it enters into a separate gain recognition agreement with respect to the E stock (and all of the requirements of paragraph (c)(1)(i) of this section are satisfied). As to this transfer, F is the transferee foreign corporation; O is the transferred corporation. The amount of the gain recognition agreement is $60. See also section 367(a)(5) and any regulations issued thereunder.

Example 10. Successive section 351 exchanges—(i) *Facts.* D, a domestic corporation, owns all the stock of X, a controlled foreign corporation that operates an historical business, which owns all the stock of Y, a controlled foreign corporation that also operates an historical business. The properties of D consist of Business A assets, with an adjusted basis of $50 and a fair market value of $90, and Business B assets, with an adjusted basis of $50 and a fair market value of $110. Assume that the Business B assets qualify for the exception under section 367(a)(3) and §1.367(a)-2T(c)(2), but that the Business A assets do not qualify for the exception. In an exchange described in section 351, D transfers the assets of Businesses A and B to X, and, in connection with the same transaction, X transfers the assets of Business B to Y in another exchange described in section 351.

(ii) *Result.* Under paragraph (d)(1)(vi) of this section, this transaction is treated as an indirect stock transfer for purposes of section 367(a), but the transaction is not recharacterized for purposes of section 367(b). Moreover, under paragraph (d)(2)(vi) of this section, the assets of Businesses A and B that are transferred to X must be tested under section 367(a)(3). The Business A assets, which were not transferred to Y, are subject to the general rules of section 367(a), and not the indirect stock transfer rules described in this paragraph (d). D must recognize $40 of income on the outbound transfer of Business A assets. The transfer of the Business B assets is subject to both the asset transfer rules (under section 367(a)(3)) and the indirect stock transfer rules of this paragraph (d) and §1.367(a)-8. Thus, D's transfer of the Business B assets will not be subject to section 367(a)(1) if D enters into a five-year gain recognition agreement with respect to the stock of Y. Under paragraphs (d)(2)(i) and (ii) of this section, X will be treated as the transferee foreign corporation and Y will be treated as the transferred corporation for purposes of applying the terms of the agreement. If X sells all or a portion of the stock of Y during the term of the agreement, D will be required to recognize a proportionate amount of the $60 gain that was realized by D on the initial transfer of the Business B assets.

Example 10A. Successive section 351 exchanges with ultimate domestic transferee—(i) *Facts*. The facts are the same as in *Example 10*, except that Y is a domestic corporation.

(ii) *Result*. As in *Example 10*, D must recognize $40 of income on the outbound transfer of the Business A assets. Although the Business B assets qualify for the exception under section 367(a)(3) (and end up in U.S. corporate solution, in Y), the $60 of gain realized on the Business B assets is nevertheless taxable under paragraphs (c)(1) and (d)(1)(vi) of this section because the transaction is considered to be a transfer by D of stock of a domestic corporation, Y, in which D receives more than 50 percent of the stock of the transferee foreign corporation, X. A gain recognition agreement is not permitted.

Example 11. Concurrent application of indirect stock transfer rules and section 367(b)—(i) *Facts*. F, a foreign corporation, owns all of the stock of Newco, which is also a foreign corporation. P, a domestic corporation, owns all of the stock of S, a foreign corporation that is a controlled foreign corporation within the meaning of section 957(a). P's basis in the stock of S is $50 and the value of S is $100. The section 1248 amount with respect to S stock is $30. In a reorganization described in section 368(a)(1)(C) (and paragraph (d)(1)(iv) of this section), Newco acquires all of the properties of S, and P exchanges its stock in S for 49 percent of the stock of F.

(ii) *Result*. P's exchange of S stock for F stock under section 354 will be taxable under section 367(a) (and section 1248 will be applicable) if P fails to enter into a 5-year gain recognition agreement in accordance with § 1.367(a)-8. Under paragraph (b)(2) of this section, if P enters into a gain recognition agreement, the exchange will be subject to the provisions of section 367(b) and the regulations thereunder as well as section 367(a). Under § 1.367(b)-4(b) of this chapter, P must recognize the section 1248 amount of $30 because P exchanged stock of a controlled foreign corporation, S, for stock of a foreign corporation that is not a controlled foreign corporation, F. The indirect stock transfer rules do not apply with respect to section 367(b). The deemed dividend of $30 recognized by P will increase P's basis in the F stock received in the transaction, and F's basis in the Newco stock. Thus, the amount of the gain recognition agreement is $20 ($50 gain realized on the transfer less the $30 inclusion under section 367(b)). Under paragraphs (d)(2)(i) and (ii) of this section, F is treated as the transferee foreign corporation and Newco is the transferred corporation.

Example 11A. Triangular section 368(a)(1)(C) reorganization involving foreign acquired corporation—(i) *Facts*. Assume the same facts as in *Example 11*, except that P receives 51 percent of the stock of F.

(ii) *Result*. P may still enter into a gain recognition agreement to avoid taxation under section 367(a). Assuming § 1.367(b)-4(b) does not apply, there is no income inclusion under section 367(b), and the amount of the gain recognition agreement is $50.

Example 12. Direct asset reorganization not subject to stock transfer rules—(i) *Facts*. D is a publicly traded domestic corporation. D's assets consist of tangible assets, including stock or securities. In a reorganization described in section 368(a)(1)(F), D becomes a foreign corporation, F.

(ii) *Result*. The reorganization is characterized under § 1.367(a)-1T(f). D's outbound transfer of assets is taxable under section 367(a)(1). Even if any of D's assets would have otherwise qualified for an exception to section 367(a)(1), section 367(a)(5) provides that no exception can apply. The section 368(a)(1)(F) reorganization is not an indirect stock transfer described in paragraph (d) of this section. Moreover, the exchange by D's shareholders of D stock for F stock in an exchange described under section 354 is not an exchange described under section 367(a). See paragraph (a) of this section.

(e) *Effective dates.*—(1) *In general.*—The rules in paragraphs (a), (b) and (d) of this section apply to transfers occurring on or after July 20, 1998. The rules in paragraph (c) of this section with respect to transfers of domestic stock or securities are generally applicable for transfers occurring after January 29, 1997. See § 1.367(a)-3(c)(11). For rules regarding transfers of domestic stock or securities after December 16, 1987, and before January 30, 1997, and transfers of foreign stock or securities after December 16, 1987, and before July 20, 1998, see paragraph (g) of this section.

(2) *Election.*—Notwithstanding paragraphs (e)(1) and (g) of this section, taxpayers may, by timely filing an original or amended return, elect to apply paragraphs (b) and (d) of this section to all transfers of foreign stock or securities occurring after December 16, 1987, and before July 20, 1998, except to the extent that a gain recognition agreement has been triggered prior to July 20, 1998. If an election is made under this paragraph (e)(2), the provisions of § 1.367(a)-3T(g) (see 26 CFR part 1, revised April 1, 1998) shall apply, and, for this purpose, the term *substantial portion* under § 1.367(a)-3T(g)(3)(iii) (see 26 CFR part 1, revised April 1, 1998) shall be interpreted to mean *substantially all* as defined in section

368(a)(1)(C). In addition, if such an election is made, the taxpayer must apply the rules under section 367(b) and the regulations thereunder to any transfers occurring within that period as if the election to apply § 1.367(a)-3(b) and (d) to transfers occurring within that period had not been made, except that in the case of an exchange described in section 351 the taxpayer must apply section 367(b) and the regulations thereunder as if the exchange was described in § 7.367(b)-7 of this chapter (as in effect before February 23, 2000; see 26 CFR part 1, revised as of April 1, 1999). For example, if a U.S. person, pursuant to a section 351 exchange, transfers stock of a controlled foreign corporation in which it is a United States shareholder but does not receive back stock of a controlled foreign corporation in which it is a United States shareholder, the U.S. person must include in income under § 7.367(b)-7 of this chapter (as in effect before February 23, 2000; see 26 CFR part 1, revised as of April 1, 1999) the section 1248 amount attributable to the stock exchanged (to the extent that the fair market value of the stock exchanged exceeds its adjusted basis). Such inclusion is required even though § 7.367(b)-7 of this chapter (as in effect before February 23, 2000; see 26 CFR part 1, revised as of April 1, 1999), by its terms, did not apply to section 351 exchanges.

(f) *Former 10-year gain recognition agreements.*—If a taxpayer elects to apply the rules of this section to all prior transfers occurring after December 16, 1987, any 10-year gain recognition agreement that remains in effect (has not been triggered in full) on July 20, 1998 will be considered by the Internal Revenue Service to be a 5-year gain recognition agreement with a duration of five full taxable years following the close of the taxable year of the initial transfer.

(g) *Transition rules regarding certain transfers of domestic or foreign stock or securities after December 16, 1987, and prior to July 20, 1998.*—(1) *Scope.*—Transfers of domestic stock or securities described under section 367(a) that occurred after December 16, 1987, and prior to April 17, 1994, and transfers of foreign stock or securities described under section 367(a) that occur after December 16, 1987, and prior to July 20, 1998 are subject to the rules contained in section 367(a) and the regulations thereunder, as modified by the rules contained in paragraph (g)(2) of this section. For transfers of domestic stock or securities described under section 367(a) that occurred after April 17, 1994 and before January 30, 1997, see Temporary Income Regulations under section 367(a) in effect at the time of the transfer (§ 1.367(a)-3T(a) and (c), 26 CFR part 1, revised April 1, 1996) and paragraph (c)(11) of this section. For transfers of domestic stock or securities described under section 367(a) that occur after January 29, 1997, see § 1.367(a)-3(c).

(2) *Transfers of domestic or foreign stock or securities: additional substantive rules.*—(i) *Rule for less than 5-percent shareholders.*—Unless paragraph (g)(2)(iii) of this section applies (in the case of domestic stock or securities) or paragraph (g)(2)(iv) of this section applies (in the case of foreign stock or securities), a U.S. transferor that transfers stock or securities of a domestic or foreign corporation in an exchange described in section 367(a) and owns less than 5 percent of both the total voting power and the total value of the stock of the transferee foreign corporation immediately after the transfer (taking into account the attribution rules of section 958) is not subject to section 367(a)(1) and is not required to enter into a gain recognition agreement.

(ii) *Rule for 5-percent shareholders.*—Unless paragraph (g)(2)(iii) or (iv) of this section applies, a U.S. transferor that transfers domestic or foreign stock or securities in an exchange described in section 367(a) and owns at least 5 percent of either the total voting power or the total value of the stock of the transferee foreign corporation immediately after the transfer (taking into account the attribution rules under section 958) may qualify for nonrecognition treatment by filing a gain recognition agreement in accordance with § 1.367(a)-3T(g) in effect prior to July 20, 1998 (see 26 CFR part 1, revised April 1, 1998) for a duration of 5 or 10 years. The duration is 5 years if the U.S. transferor (5-percent shareholder) determines that all U.S. transferors, in the aggregate, own less than 50 percent of both the total voting power and the total value of the transferee foreign corporation immediately after the transfer. The duration is 10 years in all other cases. See, however, § 1.367(a)-3(f). If a 5-percent shareholder fails to properly enter into a gain recognition agreement, the exchange is taxable to such shareholder under section 367(a)(1).

(iii) *Gain recognition agreement option not available to controlling U.S. transferor if U.S. stock or securities are transferred.*—Notwithstanding the provisions of paragraph (g)(2)(ii) of this section, in no event will any exception to section 367(a)(1) apply to the transfer of stock or securities of a domestic corporation where the U.S. transferor owns (applying the attribution rules of section 958) more than 50 percent of either the total voting power or the total value of the stock of the transferee foreign corporation immediately after the transfer (i.e., the use of a gain recognition agreement to qualify for nonrecognition treatment is unavailable in this case).

(iv) *Loss of United States shareholder status in the case of a transfer of foreign stock.*—Notwithstanding the provisions of paragraphs (g)(2)(i) and (ii) of this section, in no event will any exception to section 367(a)(1) apply to the transfer of stock of a foreign corporation in which the U.S. transferor is a United States shareholder (as defined in § 7.367(b)-2(b) of this chapter (as in effect before February 23, 2000; see 26 CFR part 1, revised as of April 1, 1999) or section 953(c)) unless the U.S. transferor receives back stock in a controlled foreign corporation (as defined in section 953(c), section 957(a) or section 957(b)) as to which the U.S. transferor is a United States shareholder immediately after the transfer. [Reg. § 1.367(a)-3.]

☐ [T.D. 8702, 12-27-96. *Amended by* T.D. 8770, 6-18-98 (*corrected* 3-31-99); T.D. 8850, 12-27-99 *and* T.D. 8862, 1-21-2000.]

Proposed Amendments to Regulation

§ 1.367(a)-3. Treatment of transfers of stock or securities to foreign corporations.—

* * *

(a) * * * However, if, in an exchange described in section 354 or 356, a U.S. person exchanges stock of a foreign corporation in a reorganization described in section 368(a)(1)(E), or a U.S. person exchanges stock of a domestic or foreign corporation for stock of a foreign corporation pursuant to an asset reorganization that is not treated as an indirect stock transfer under paragraph (d) of this section, such section 354 or 356 exchange is not a transfer to a foreign corporation subject to section 367(a). See paragraph (d)(3), *Example 16*, of this section. For purposes of this section, an asset reorganization is defined as a reorganization described in section 368(a)(1) involving a transfer of assets under section 361. If, in a transfer described in section 361, a domestic merging corporation transfers stock of a controlling corporation to a foreign surviving corporation in a reorganization described in sections 368(a)(1)(A) and (a)(2)(E), such section 361 transfer is not subject to section 367(a) if the stock of the controlling corporation is provided to the merging corporation by the controlling corporation pursuant to the plan of reorganization; a section 361 transfer of other property, including stock of the controlling corporation not provided by the controlling corporation pursuant to the plan of reorganization, by the domestic merging corporation to the foreign surviving corporation pursuant to such a reorganization is subject to section 367(a). For special basis and holding period rules involving foreign corporations that are parties to certain reorganizations under section 368(a)(1), see § 1.367(b)-13. * * *

(b) * * *

(2) * * *

(i) *In general.*—A transfer of foreign stock or securities described in section 367(a) and the regulations thereunder as well as in section 367(b) and the regulations thereunder shall be subject concurrently to sections 367(a) and (b) and the regulations thereunder, except as provided in paragraph (b)(2)(i)(A) or (B) of this section. See paragraph (d)(3), *Example 11*, of this section.

(A) If a foreign corporation transfers assets to a domestic corporation in a transaction to which § 1.367(b)-3(a) and (b) and the indirect stock transfer rules of paragraph (d) of this section apply, then the section 367(b) rules shall apply prior to the section 367(a) rules. See paragraph (d)(3), *Example 15*, of this section. This paragraph (b)(2)(i)(A) applies only to transactions occurring after the date these regulations are published as final regulations in the Federal Register.

(B) Except as provided in paragraph (b)(2)(i)(A) of this section, section 367(b) and the regulations thereunder shall not apply if the foreign corporation is not treated as a corporation under section 367(a)(1). See paragraph (d)(3), *Example 14*, of this section.

* * *

(c) * * *

(5) * * *

(vi) *Transferee foreign corporation.*—Except as provided in paragraph (d)(1)(iii)(B) of this section, the transferee foreign corporation shall be the foreign corporation that issues stock or securities to the U.S. person in the exchange.

* * *

(d) * * *

(1) * * * For examples of the concurrent application of the indirect stock transfer rules under section 367(a) and the rules of section 367(b), see paragraph (d)(3), *Examples 14* and *15* of this section. For purposes of this paragraph (d), if a corporation acquiring assets in a reorganization described in section 368(a)(1) transfers all or a portion of such assets to a corporation controlled (within the meaning of section 368(c)) by the acquiring corporation as part of the same transaction, the subsequent transfer of assets to the controlled corporation will be referred to as a controlled asset transfer. See section 368(a)(2)(C).

(i) * * * See paragraph (d)(3), *Example 1* of this section for an example of a reorganization described in sections 368(a)(1)(A) and (a)(2)(D) involving domestic acquired and acquiring corporations, and see paragraph (d)(3), *Example 10* of this section for an example involving a domestic acquired corporation and a foreign acquiring corporation.

(ii) * * * See paragraph (d)(3), *Example 2* of this section for an example of a reorganization described in sections 368(a)(1)(A) and (a)(2)(E) involving domestic acquired and acquiring corporations, and see paragraph (d)(3), *Example 11* of this section for an example involving a domestic acquired corporation and a foreign acquiring corporation.

(iii) *Triangular reorganizations described in section 368(a)(1)(B).*—(A) A U.S. person exchanges stock of the acquired corporation for voting stock of a foreign corporation that is in control (as defined in section 368(c)) of the acquiring corporation in a reorganization described in section 368(a)(1)(B). See paragraph (d)(3), *Example 5* of this section.

(B) A U.S. person exchanges stock of the acquired corporation for voting stock of a domestic corporation that is in control (as defined in section 368(c)) of a foreign acquiring corporation in a reorganization described in section 368(a)(1)(B).

(1) For purposes of paragraphs (b) and (c) of this section, the foreign acquiring corporation is considered to be the transferee foreign corporation even though the U.S. transferor receives stock of the domestic controlling corporation in the exchange.

(2) If stock of a foreign acquired corporation is exchanged for the voting stock of a domestic corporation in control of a foreign acquiring corporation, then the exchange will be subject to the rules of paragraph (b) of this section. If the exchanging shareholder is a section 1248 shareholder with respect to the foreign acquired corporation, the indirect transfer will be subject to sections 367(a) and (b) concurrently. For the application of section 367(b) to the exchange, see §§ 1.367(b)-4 and 1.367(b)-13(c).

(3) If stock of a domestic acquired corporation is exchanged for the voting stock of a domestic corporation in control of a foreign acquiring corporation, then the exchange will be subject to the rules of paragraph (c) of this section.

(4) For purposes of applying the gain recognition agreement provisions of paragraph (d)(2) of this section and § 1.367(a)-8, the domestic controlling corporation will be treated as the transferee foreign corporation. Thus, a disposition of foreign acquiring corporation stock by the domestic controlling corporation, or a disposition of acquired corporation stock by the foreign acquiring corporation, will trigger the gain recognition agreement. See paragraph (d)(3), *Example 5A* of this section.

(5) This paragraph (d)(1)(iii)(B) applies only to transactions occurring after the date these regulations are published as final regulations in the Federal Register.

* * *

(v) *Transfers of assets to subsidiaries in certain section 368(a)(1) reorganizations.*—A U.S. person exchanges stock or securities of a corporation (the acquired corporation) for stock or securities of a foreign acquiring corporation in an asset reorganization (other than a triangular section 368(a)(1)(C) reorganization described in paragraph (d)(1)(iv) of this section or a reorganization described in sections 368(a)(1)(A) and (a)(2)(D) or (a)(2)(E) described in paragraphs (d)(1)(i) or (ii) of this section) that is followed by a controlled asset transfer. In the case of a transaction described in this paragraph (d)(1)(v) in which some but not all of the assets of the acquired corporation are transferred in a controlled asset transfer, the transaction shall be considered to be an indirect transfer of stock or securities subject to this paragraph (d) only to the extent of the assets so transferred. The remaining assets shall be treated as having been transferred in an asset transfer rather than an indirect stock transfer, and such asset transfer shall be subject to the other provisions of section 367, including sections 367(a)(1), (3), and (5), and (d) if the acquired corporation is a domestic corporation. See paragraph (d)(3), *Examples 6A* and *6B* of this section.

* * *

(2) * * *

(i) *Transferee foreign corporation.*—Except as provided in paragraph (d)(1)(iii)(B) of this section, the transferee foreign corporation shall be the foreign corporation that issues stock or securities to the U.S. person in the exchange.

(ii) *Transferred corporation.*—The transferred corporation shall be the acquiring corporation, except as provided in this paragraph (d)(2)(ii). In the case of a triangular section 368(a)(1)(B) reorganization described in paragraph (d)(1)(iii) of this section, the transferred corporation shall be the acquired corporation. In the case of an indirect stock transfer described in paragraph (d)(1)(i), (ii), or (iv) of this section followed by a controlled asset transfer, or an indirect stock transfer described in paragraph (d)(1)(v) of this section, the transferred corporation shall be the controlled corporation to which the assets are transferred. In the case of successive section 351 transfers described in paragraph (d)(1)(vi) of this section, the transferred corporation shall be the corporation to which the assets are transferred in the final section 351 transfer. The transferred property shall be the stock or securities of the transferred corporation, as appropriate under the circumstances.

* * *

(v) * * *

(C) In the case of an asset reorganization followed by a controlled asset transfer, as described in paragraph (d)(1)(v) of this section, the assets of the acquired corporation that are transferred to the corporation controlled by the acquiring corporation;

(D) In the case of a triangular reorganization described in section 368(a)(1)(C) followed by a controlled asset transfer, or a reorganization described in sections 368(a)(1)(A) and (a)(2)(D) followed by a controlled asset transfer, the assets of the acquired corporation including those transferred to the corporation controlled by the acquiring corporation;

(E) In the case of a reorganization described in sections 368(a)(1)(A) and (a)(2)(E) followed by a controlled asset transfer, the assets of the acquiring corporation including those transferred to the corporation controlled by the acquiring corporation; and

* * *

(vi) *Coordination between asset transfer rules and indirect stock transfer rules.*—(A) *General rule.*—If, pursuant to any of the transactions described in paragraph (d)(1) of this section, a U.S. person transfers (or is deemed to transfer) assets to a foreign corporation in an exchange described in section 351 or 361, the rules of section 367, including sections 367(a)(1), (a)(3), and (a)(5), as well as section 367(d), and the regulations thereunder shall apply prior to the application of the rules of this section.

(B) *Exceptions.*—(*1*) If a transaction is described in paragraph (d)(2)(vi)(A) of this section, sections 367(a) and (d) shall not apply to the extent a domestic corporation (domestic acquired corporation) transfers its assets to a foreign corporation (foreign acquiring corporation) in an asset reorganization, and such assets (re-transferred assets) are transferred to a domestic corporation (domestic controlled corporation) controlled (within the meaning of section 368(c)) by the foreign acquiring corporation as part of the same transaction, provided that the domestic controlled corporation's basis in such assets is no greater than the basis that the domestic acquired corporation had in such assets and the conditions contained in either of the following paragraphs are satisfied:

(*i*) The domestic acquired corporation is controlled (within the meaning of section 368(c)) by 5 or fewer domestic corporations, appropriate basis adjustments as provided in section 367(a)(5) are made to the stock of the foreign acquiring corporation, and any other conditions as provided in regulations under section 367(a)(5) are satisfied. For purposes of determining whether the domestic acquired corporation is controlled by 5 or fewer domestic corporations, all members of the same affiliated group within the meaning of section 1504 shall be treated as 1 corporation.

(*ii*) The requirements of paragraphs (c)(1)(i), (ii), and (iv), and (c)(6) of this section are satisfied with respect to the indirect transfer of stock in the domestic acquired corporation, and the domestic acquired corporation attaches a statement described in paragraph (d)(2)(vi)(C) of this section to its U.S. income tax return for the taxable year of the transfer.

(*2*) Sections 367(a) and (d) shall not apply to transfers described in paragraph (d)(1)(vi) of this section where a U.S. person transfers assets to a foreign corporation in a section 351 exchange, to the extent that such assets are transferred by such foreign corporation to a domestic corporation in another section 351 exchange, but only if the domestic transferee's basis in the assets is no greater than the basis that the U.S. transferor had in such assets.

(C) *Required statement.*—The statement required by paragraph (d)(2)(vi)(B)(*1*)(*ii*) of this section shall be entitled "Required Statement under § 1.367(a)-3(d) for Assets Transferred to a Domestic Corporation" and shall be signed under penalties of perjury by an authorized officer of the domestic acquired corporation and by an authorized officer of the foreign acquiring corporation. The required statement shall contain a certification that, if the foreign acquiring corporation disposes of any stock of the domestic controlled corporation in a transaction described in paragraph (d)(2)(vi)(D) of this section, the domestic acquired corporation shall recognize gain as described in paragraph (d)(2)(vi)(E)(*1*) of this section. The domestic acquired corporation (or the foreign acquiring corporation on behalf of the domestic acquired corporation) shall file a U.S. income tax return (or an amended U.S. tax return, as the case may be) for the year of the transfer reporting such gain.

(D) *Gain recognition transaction.*—(*1*) A transaction described in this paragraph (d)(2)(vi)(D) is one where a principal purpose of the transfer by the domestic acquired corporation is the avoidance of U.S. tax that would have been imposed on the domestic acquired corporation on the disposition of the re-transferred assets. A transfer may have a principal purpose of tax avoidance even though the tax avoidance purpose is outweighed by other purposes when taken together.

(2) For purposes of paragraph (d)(2)(vi)(D)(1) of this section, a transaction is deemed to have a principal purpose of tax avoidance if the foreign acquiring corporation disposes of any stock of the domestic controlled corporation (whether in a recognition or non-recognition transaction) within 2 years of the transfer. The rule in this paragraph (d)(2)(vi)(D)(2) shall not apply if the domestic acquired corporation (or the foreign acquiring corporation on behalf of the domestic acquired corporation) demonstrates to the satisfaction of the Commissioner that the avoidance of U.S. tax was not a principal purpose of the transaction.

(E) *Amount of gain recognized and other matters.*—*(1)* In the case of a transaction described in paragraph (d)(2)(vi)(D) of this section, solely for purposes of this paragraph (d)(2)(vi)(E), the domestic acquired corporation shall be treated as if, immediately prior to the transfer, it transferred the re-transferred assets, including any intangible assets, directly to a domestic corporation in exchange for stock of such domestic corporation in a transaction that is treated as a section 351 exchange, and immediately sold such stock to an unrelated party for its fair market value in a sale in which it shall recognize gain, if any (but not loss). Any gain recognized by the domestic acquired corporation pursuant to this paragraph (d)(2)(vi)(E) will increase the basis that the foreign acquiring corporation has in the stock of the domestic controlled corporation immediately before the transaction described in paragraph (d)(2)(vi)(D) of this section, but will not increase the basis of the re-transferred assets held by the domestic controlled corporation. Section 1.367(d)-1T(g)(6) shall not apply with respect to any intangible property included in the re-transferred assets described in the preceding sentence.

(2) If additional tax is required to be paid as a result of a transaction described in paragraph (d)(2)(vi)(D) of this section, then interest must be paid on that amount at rates determined under section 6621 with respect to the period between the date prescribed for filing the domestic acquired corporation's income tax return for the year of the transfer and the date on which the additional tax for that year is paid.

(F) *Examples.*—For illustrations of the rules in paragraph (d)(2)(vi) of this section, see paragraph (d)(3), *Examples 6B, 6C, 6D, 9,* and *13A* of this section.

(G) *Effective dates.*—Paragraph (d)(2)(vi) of this section applies only to transactions occurring after the date these regulations are published as final regulations in the Federal Register. See § 1.367(a)-3(d)(2)(vi), as contained in 26 CFR Part 1 revised as of April 1, 2004, for transactions occurring on or after July 20, 1998, until the date these regulations are published as final regulations in the Federal Register.

(3) * * *

Example 2. Section 368(a)(1)(A)/ (a)(2)(E) reorganization—(i) *Facts.* The facts are the same as in *Example 1,* except that Newco merges into W and Newco receives stock of W which it distributes to F in a reorganization described in sections 368(a)(1)(A) and (a)(2)(E). Pursuant to the reorganization, A receives 40 percent of the stock of F in an exchange described in section 354.

(ii) *Result.* The consequences of the transfer are similar to those described in *Example 1.* Pursuant to paragraph (d)(1)(ii) of this section, the reorganization is subject to the indirect stock transfer rules. F is treated as the transferee foreign corporation, and W is treated as the transferred corporation. Provided that the requirements of paragraph (c)(1) of this section are satisfied, including the requirement that A enter into a five-year gain recognition agreement as described in § 1.367(a)-8, A's exchange of W stock for F stock under section 354 will not be subject to section 367(a)(1).

* * *

Example 5A. Triangular section 368(a)(1)(B) reorganization—(i) *Facts.* The facts are the same as in *Example 5,* except that F is a domestic corporation and S is a foreign corporation.

(ii) *Result.* U's exchange of Y stock for stock of F, a domestic corporation in control of S, the foreign acquiring corporation, is treated as an indirect transfer of Y stock to a foreign corporation under paragraph (d)(1)(iii) of this section. U's exchange of Y stock for F stock will not be subject to section 367(a)(1) provided that all of the requirements of paragraph (c)(1) are satisfied, including the requirement that U enter in a five-year gain recognition agreement. In satisfying the 50 percent or less ownership requirements of paragraph (c)(1)(i) and (ii) of this section, U's indirect ownership of S stock (through its direct ownership of F stock) will determine whether the requirement of paragraph (c)(1)(i) is satisfied and will be taken into account in determining whether the requirement of paragraph (c)(1)(ii) is satisfied. See paragraph (c)(4)(iv)). For purposes of applying the gain recognition agreement provisions of paragraph (d)(2) of this section and §1.367(a)-8, F is treated as the transferee foreign corporation. The gain recognition agreement would be triggered if F sold all or a portion of the stock of S, or if S sold all or a portion of the stock of Y.

* * *

Example 6A. Section 368(a)(1)(C) reorganization followed by a controlled asset transfer—(i) *Facts.* The facts are the same as in *Example 6,* except that the transaction is structured as a section 368(a)(1)(C) reorganization, followed by a controlled asset transfer, and R is a foreign corporation. * * * F then contributes Businesses B and C to R in a controlled asset transfer. * * *

* * *

Example 6B. Section 368(a)(1)(C) reorganization followed by a controlled asset transfer to a domestic controlled corporation—(i) *Facts.* The facts are the same as in *Example 6A,* except that R is a domestic corporation.

(ii) *Result.* As in *Example 6A,* the outbound transfer of the Business A assets to F is not affected by the rules of this paragraph (d) and is subject to the general rules under section 367. However, the Business A assets qualify for the section 367(a)(3) active trade or business exception. The Business B and C assets are part of an indirect stock transfer under this paragraph (d) but must first be tested under sections 367(a) and (d). The Business B assets qualify for the active trade or business exception under section 367(a)(3); the Business C assets do not. However, pursuant to paragraph (d)(2)(vi)(B) of this section, the Business C assets are not subject to section 367(a) or (d), provided that the basis of the Business C assets in the hands of R is no greater than the basis of the assets in the hands of Z, and appropriate basis adjustments are made pursuant to section 367(a)(5) to the stock of F held by V. (In this case, no adjustments are required because, pursuant to section 358, V takes a basis of $30 in the stock of F, which is equal to V's proportionate share of the basis in the assets of Z ($30) transferred to F.) V also is deemed to make an indirect transfer of stock under the rules of paragraph (d). To preserve non-recognition treatment under section 367(a), V must enter into a 5-year gain recognition agreement in the amount of $50, the amount of the appreciation in the Business B and C assets, as the transfer of such assets by Z was not taxable under section 367(a)(1) and constituted an indirect stock transfer.

Example 6C. Section 368(a)(1)(C) reorganization followed by a controlled asset transfer to a domestic controlled corporation—(i) *Facts.* The facts are the same as in *Example 6B,* except that Z is owned by individuals, none of whom qualify as five-percent target shareholders with respect to Z within the meaning of paragraph (c)(5)(iii) of this section. The following additional facts are present. No U.S. persons that are either officers or directors of Z own any stock of F immediately after the transfer. F is engaged in an active trade or business outside the United States that satisfies the test set forth in paragraph (c)(3) of this section.

(ii) *Result.* The transfer of the Business A assets is not affected by the rules of this paragraph (d). However, the transfer of such assets is subject to gain recognition under section 367(a)(1), because the section 367(a)(3) active trade or business exception is inapplicable pursuant to section 367(a)(5). The Business B and C assets are part of an indirect stock transfer under this paragraph (d) but must first be tested under sections 367(a) and (d). The transfer of the Business B assets (which otherwise would satisfy the section 367(a)(3) active trade or business exception) generally is subject to section 367(a)(1) pursuant to section 367(a)(5). The transfer of the Business C assets generally is subject to sections 367(a)(1) and (d). However, pursuant to paragraph (d)(2)(vi)(B) of this section, the transfer of the Business B and C assets is not subject to sections 367(a)(1) and (d), provided the basis of the Business B and C assets in the hands of R is no greater than the basis in the hands of Z and certain other requirements are satisfied. Since Z is not controlled within the meaning of section 368(c) by 5 or fewer domestic corporations, the indirect transfer of Z stock must satisfy the requirements of paragraphs (c)(1)(i), (ii), and (iv), and (c)(6) of this section, and Z must attach a statement described in paragraph (d)(2)(vi)(C) of this section to its U.S. income tax return for the taxable year of the transfer. In general, the statement must contain a certification that, if F disposes of the stock of R (in a recognition or nonrecognition transaction) and a principal purpose of the transfer is the avoidance of U.S. tax that would have been imposed on Z on the disposition of the Business B and C assets transferred to R, then Z (or F on behalf of Z) will file a return (or amended return as the case may be) recognizing gain ($50), as if, immediately prior to the reorganization, Z transferred the Business B and C assets to a domestic corporation in exchange for stock in a transaction treated as a section 351 exchange and immediately sold such stock to an unrelated party for its fair market value. A transaction is deemed to have a principal purpose of U.S. tax avoidance if F disposes of R stock within two years of the transfer, unless Z (or F on behalf of Z) can rebut the presumption to the satisfaction of the Commissioner. See paragraph (d)(2)(vi)(D)(*2*) of this section. With respect to the indirect transfer of Z stock, the requirements of paragraphs (c)(1)(i), (ii), and (iv) of this section are satisfied. Thus, assuming Z attaches the statement described in paragraph (d)(2)(vi)(C) of this section to its U.S. income tax return and satisfies the reporting requirements of (c)(6) of this section, the transfer of Business B and C assets is not subject to section 367(a) or (d).

Example 6D. Section 368(a)(1)(C) reorganization followed by a controlled asset transfer to a domestic controlled corporation—(i) *Facts*. The facts are the same as in *Example 6C*, except that the Z shareholders receive 60 percent of the F stock in exchange for their Z stock in the reorganization.

(ii) *Result*. The requirement of paragraph (c)(1)(i) of this section is not satisfied because the Z shareholders that are U.S. persons do not receive 50 percent or less of the total voting power and the total value of the stock of F in the transaction. Accordingly, Z shareholders that are U.S. persons are subject to section 367(a)(1) on their exchange of Z stock for F stock pursuant to the reorganization. For the same reason, the conditions of paragraph (d)(2)(vi)(B)(1)(ii) of this section are not met. Accordingly, the transfer of Business B and C assets is subject to sections 367(a)(1) and (d), even though such assets are re-transferred to R, a domestic corporation. As in *Example 6C*, the transfer of Business A assets, which is not affected by the rules of paragraph (d) of this section, is subject to gain recognition under sections 367(a)(1) and (5).

* * *

Example 9. Concurrent application with a controlled asset transfer—(i) *Facts*. The facts are the same as in *Example 8*, except that R transfers the Business A assets to M, a wholly owned domestic subsidiary of R, in a controlled asset transfer. In addition, V's basis in its Z stock is $90.

(ii) *Result*. Pursuant to paragraph (d)(2)(vi)(B) of this section, sections 367(a) and (d) do not apply to Z's transfer of the Business A assets to R, because such assets are re-transferred to M, a domestic corporation, provided that the basis of the Business A assets in the hands of M is no greater than the basis of the assets in the hands of Z, and certain other requirements are satisfied. Because Z is controlled (within the meaning of section 368(c)) by V, a domestic corporation, appropriate basis adjustments must be made pursuant to section 367(a)(5) to the stock of F held by V. (In this case, no adjustments are required because, pursuant to section 358, V takes a basis of $90 in the stock of F, which is less than V's proportionate share of the basis in the assets of Z ($100) transferred to R.) Section 367(a)(1) does not apply to Z's transfer of its Business B assets to R (which are not re-transferred to M) because such assets qualify for an exception to gain recognition under section 367(a)(3). With respect to the indirect transfer of Z stock, such transfer is not subject to gain recognition under section 367(a)(1) if the requirements of paragraph (c) of this section are satisfied, including the requirement that V enter into a 5-year gain recognition agreement and comply with the requirements of § 1.367(a)-8 with respect to the gain ($100) realized on the Z stock. Under paragraphs (d)(2)(i) and (ii) of this section, the transferee foreign corporation is F and the transferred corporation is M. Pursuant to paragraph (d)(2)(iv) of this section, a disposition by F of the stock of R, or a disposition by R of the stock of M, will trigger the gain recognition agreement. To determine whether an asset disposition constitutes a deemed disposition of the transferred corporation's stock under the rules of § 1.367(a)-8(e)(3)(i), both the Business A assets in M and the Business B assets in R must be considered.

Example 10. Concurrent application in section 368(a)(1)(A)/(a)(2)(D) reorganization—(i) *Facts*. The facts are the same as in *Example 8*, except that R acquires all of the assets of Z in a reorganization described in sections 368(a)(1)(A) and (a)(2)(D). Pursuant to the reorganization, V receives 30 percent of the stock of F in a section 354 exchange.

(ii) *Result*. The consequences of the transaction are similar to those in *Example 8*. The assets of Businesses A and B that are transferred to R must be tested under section 367(a) prior to the consideration of the indirect stock transfer rules of this paragraph (d). The Business B assets qualify for the active trade or business exception under section 367(a)(3). Because the Business A assets do not qualify for the exception, Z must recognize $40 of gain under section 367(a) on the transfer of Business A assets to R. Because V and Z file a consolidated return, V's basis in the stock of Z is increased from $100 to $140 as a result of Z's $40 gain. V's indirect transfer of Z stock will be taxable under section 367(a) unless V enters into a gain recognition agreement in the amount of $60 ($200 value of Z stock less $140 adjusted basis) and the other requirements of paragraph (c)(1) of this section are satisfied.

Example 11. Section 368(a)(1)(A)/(a)(2)(E) reorganization—(i) *Facts*. F, a foreign corporation, owns all the stock of D, a domestic corporation. V, a domestic corporation, owns all the stock of Z, a foreign corporation. V has a basis of $100 in the stock of Z which has a fair market value of $200. D is an operating corporation with assets valued at $100 with a basis of $60. In a reorganization described in sections 368(a)(1)(A) and (a)(2)(E), D merges into Z, and V exchanges its Z stock for 55 percent of the outstanding F stock.

(ii) *Result.* Under paragraph (d)(1)(ii) of this section, V is treated as making an indirect transfer of Z stock to F. V's exchange of Z stock for F stock will be taxable under section 367(a) (and section 1248 will be applicable) if V fails to enter into a 5-year gain recognition agreement in accordance with the requirements of § 1.367(a)-8. Under paragraph (b)(2) of this section, if V enters into a gain recognition agreement, the exchange will be subject to the provisions of section 367(b) and the regulations thereunder as well as section 367(a). Under § 1.367(b)-4(b) of this chapter, however, no income inclusion is required because both F and Z are controlled foreign corporations with respect to which V is a section 1248 shareholder immediately after the exchange. Under paragraphs (d)(2)(i) and (ii) of this section, the transferee foreign corporation is F, and the transferred corporation is Z (the acquiring corporation). If F disposes (within the meaning of § 1.367(a)-8(e)) of all (or a portion) of Z stock within the 5-year term of the agreement (and V has not made a valid election under § 1.367(a)-8(b)(1)(vii)), V is required to file an amended return for the year of the transfer and include in income, with interest, the gain realized but not recognized on the initial section 354 exchange. To determine whether Z (the transferred corporation) disposes of substantially all of its assets, the assets of Z immediately prior to the transaction are taken into account, pursuant to paragraph (d)(2)(v)(B) of this section. Because D is owned by F, a foreign corporation, section 367(a)(5) precludes any assets of D from qualifying for nonrecognition under section 367(a)(3). Thus, D recognizes $40 of gain on the transfer of its assets to Z under section 367(a)(1).

* * *

Example 15. Concurrent application of indirect stock transfer rules and section 367(b)—(i) *Facts.* F, a foreign corporation, owns all of the stock of Newco, a domestic corporation. P, a domestic corporation, owns all of the stock of FC, a foreign corporation. P's basis in the stock of FC is $50 and the value of FC stock is $100. The all earnings and profits amount with respect to the FC stock held by P is $60. See § 1.367(b)-2(d). In a reorganization described in sections 368(a)(1)(A) and (a)(2)(D) (and paragraph (d)(1)(i) of this section), Newco acquires all of the properties of FC, and P exchanges its stock in FC for 20 percent of the stock in F.

(ii) *Result.* Because a domestic corporation, Newco, acquires the assets of a foreign corporation, FC, in an asset reorganization to which § 1.367(b)-3(a) and (b) and the indirect stock rules of paragraph (d) of this section apply, the section 367(b) rules apply before the section 367(a) rules apply. See § 1.367(a)-3(b)(2)(i)(A). Under the rules of section 367(b), P must include in income the all earnings and profits amount of $60 with respect to its FC stock. See § 1.367(b)-3. Although P's exchange of FC stock for F stock under section 354 is an indirect stock transfer, no gain is recognized under section 367(a), because P's basis in the FC stock is increased by the amount ($60) included in income under the rules of section 367(b). See § 1.367(b)-2(e)(3)(ii). Alternatively, if P's all earnings and profits amount were $30, then the amount of the income inclusion and basis adjustment under the rules of section 367(b) would be $30, and the amount of gain subject to section 367(a)(1) would be $20 unless P entered into a 5-year gain recognition agreement in accordance with § 1.367(a)-8.

* * *

(e) * * *

(1) *In general.*—Except as provided in paragraphs (b)(2)(i)(A), (d)(1)(iii)(B), and (d)(2)(vi)(G), or in this paragraph (e), the rules in paragraphs (a), (b), and (d) of this section apply to transfers occurring on or after July 20, 1998. The rules in paragraphs (a) and (d) of this section, as they apply to section 368(a)(1)(A) reorganizations (including reorganizations described in section 368(a)(2)(D) or (E)) involving a foreign acquiring or acquired corporation, apply only to transfers occurring after the date these regulations are published as final regulations in the Federal Register. * * *

* * *

[Prop. Reg. § 1.367(a)-3.]
[Proposed 1-5-2005.]

Proposed Amendments to Regulation

§ 1.367(a)-3. Treatment of transfers of stock or securities to foreign corporations.—(a) *In general.*—* * * However, if, pursuant to section 304(a)(1), a U.S. person is treated as transferring stock of a domestic or foreign corporation to a foreign corporation in exchange for stock of such foreign corporation in a transaction to which section 351(a) applies, such deemed section 351 exchange is not a transfer to a foreign corporation subject to section 367(a). * * *

* * *

(e) *Effective dates.*—(1) *In general.*—The rules in paragraphs (a), (b) and (d) of this section generally apply to transfers occurring on or after July 20, 1998. However, the third sentence of paragraph (a) of this section shall apply to section 304(a)(1) transactions occurring on or after the date these regulations are published as final regulations in the Federal Register. * * *

* * *

[Prop. Reg. § 1.367(a)-3.]

[Proposed 5-25-2005.]

§ 1.367(a)-4T. Special rules applicable to specified transfers of property (temporary).—(a) *In general.*—This section provides special rules for determining the applicability of section 367(a)(1) to specified transfers of property. Paragraph (b) of this section provides a special rule requiring the recapture of depreciation upon the transfer abroad of property previously used in the United States. Paragraphs (c) through (f) of this section provide rules for determining whether certain types of property are transferred for use in the active conduct of a trade or business outside of the United States. Paragraph (g) excepts certain transfers to FSCs from the operation of section 367(a)(1). The treatment of any transfer of property described in this section shall be determined exclusively under the rules of this section.

(b) *Depreciated property used in the U.S.*—(1) *In general.*—If a U.S. person transfers U.S. depreciated property (as defined in paragraph (b)(2) of this section) to a foreign corporation in an exchange described in section 367(a)(1), then that person shall include in its gross income for the taxable year in which the transfer occurs ordinary income equal to the gain realized that would have been includible in the transferor's gross income as ordinary income under section 617(d)(1), 1245(a), 1250(a), 1252(a), or 1254(a), whichever is applicable, if at the time of the transfer the transferor had sold the property at its fair market value. Recapture of depreciation under this paragraph (b) shall be required regardless of whether any exception to section 367(a)(1) (such as the exception for property transferred for use in the active conduct of a foreign trade or business) would otherwise apply to the transfer. However, any applicable exception shall apply with respect to realized gain that is not included in ordinary income pursuant to this paragraph (b).

(2) *U.S. depreciated property.*—U.S. depreciated property subject to the rules of this paragraph (b) is any property that—

(i) Is either mining property (as defined in section 617(f)(2)), section 1245 property (as defined in section 1245(a)(3)), section 1250 property (as defined in section 1250(c)), farm land (as defined in section 1252(a)(2)), or oil, gas, or geothermal property (as defined in section 1254(a)(3)); and

(ii) Has been used in the United States or has qualified as section 38 property by virtue of section 48(a)(2)(B) prior to its transfer.

(3) *Property used within and without the U.S.*—If U.S. depreciated property has been used partly within and partly without the United States, then the amount required to be included in ordinary income pursuant to this paragraph (b) shall be reduced to an amount determined in accordance with the following formula:

$$\text{Full recapture amount} \times \frac{\text{U.S. use}}{\text{Total use}}$$

For purposes of the above fraction, the "full recapture amount" is the amount that would otherwise be included in the transferor's income under paragraph (b)(1) of this section. "U.S. use" is the number of months that the property either was used within the United States or qualiied as section 38 property by virtue of section 48(a)(2)(B), and was subject to depreciation by the transferor or a related person. "Total use" is the total number of months that the property was used (or available for use), and subject to depreciation, by the transferor or a related person. For purposes of this paragraph (b)(3), property shall not be considered to have been in use outside of the United States during any period in which such property was, for purposes of section 48 or 168, treated as property not used predominantly outside the United States pursuant to the provisions of section 48(a)(2)(B). For purposes of this paragraph (b)(3) the term "related person" shall have the meaning set forth in § 1.367(d)-1T(h).

(4) [Reserved.]

(5) *Effective date.*—This paragraph (b) applies to transfers occurring on or after June 16, 1986.

(c) *Property to be leased.*—(1) *Leasing business of transferee.*—Tangible property transferred to a foreign corporation that will be leased to other persons by the foreign corporation shall be considered to be transferred for use in the active conduct of a trade or business outside of the United States only if—

(i) The transferee's leasing of the property constitutes the active conduct of a leasing business;

(ii) The lessee of the property is not expected to, and does not, use the property in the United States; and

(iii) The transferee has need for substantial investment in assets of the type transferred.

The active conduct of a leasing business requires that the employees of the foreign corporation perform substantial marketing, customer service, repair and maintenance, and other substantial operational activities with respect to the transferred property outside of the United States. Tangible property subject to the rules of this paragraph (c) includes real property located outside of the United States. The rules of § 1.367(a)-5T(b) shall apply to transfers of property described in that section regardless of satisfaction of the rules of this paragraph (c).

(2) *De minimis leasing by transferee.*—Tangible property transferred to a foreign corporation that will be leased to other persons by the foreign corporation and that does not satisfy the conditions of paragraph (b)(1) of this section shall, nevertheless, be considered to be transferred for use in the active conduct of a trade or business if either—

(i) The property transferred will be used by the transferee foreign corporation in the active conduct of a trade or business but will be leased during occasional brief periods when the property would otherwise be idle, such as an airplane leased during periods of excess capacity; or

(ii) The property transferred is real property located outside the United States and—

(A) The property will be used primarily in the active conduct of a trade or business of the transferee foreign corporation; and

(B) Not more than ten percent of the square footage of the property will be leased to others.

(d) *Property to be sold.*—Property shall not be considered to be transferred for use in the active conduct of a trade or business and a transfer of stock or securities shall not be excepted from section 367(a)(1) under the rules of § 1.367(a)-3T if, at the time of the transfer, it is reasonable to believe that, in the reasonably foreseeable future, the transferee will sell or otherwise dispose of any material portion of the transferred stock, securities, or other property other than in the ordinary course of business.

(e) *Oil and gas working interests.*—(1) *In general.*—A working interest in oil and gas properties shall be considered to be transferred for use in the active conduct of a trade or business if—

(i) The transfer satisfies the conditions of paragraph (e)(2) of this section;

(ii) At the time of the transfer, the transferee has no intention to farm out or otherwise transfer any part of the transferred working interest; and

(iii) During the first three years after the transfer there are no farmouts or other transfers of any part of the transferred working interest as a result of which the transferee retains less than a 50 percent share of the transferred working interest.

(2) *Active use of working interest.*—Working interests in oil and gas properties shall be considered to be transferred for use in the active conduct of a trade or business if—

(i) The transferor is regularly and substantially engaged in exploration for and extraction of minerals, either directly or through working interests in joint ventures, other than by reason of the property that is transferred;

(ii) The terms of the working interest transferred were actively negotiated among the joint venturers;

(iii) The working interest transferred constitutes at least a five percent working interest;

(iv) Prior to and at the time of the transfer, through its own employees or officers, the transferor was regularly and actively engaged in (A) operating the working interest, or (B) analyzing technical data relating to the activities of the venture;

(v) Prior to and at the time of the transfer, through its own employees or officers, the transferor was regularly and actively involved in decisionmaking with respect to the operations of the venture, including decisions relating to exploration, development, production, and marketing; and

(vi) After the transfer, the transferee foreign corporation will for the foreseeable future satisfy the requirements of subdivisions (iv) and (v) of this paragraph (d)(2).

(3) *Start-up operations.*—Working interests in oil and gas properties that do not satisfy the requirements of paragraph (e)(2) of this section shall, nevertheless, be considered to be transferred for use in the active conduct of a trade or business if—

(i) The working interest was acquired by the transferor immediately prior to the transfer and for the specific purpose of transferring it to the transferee foreign corporation;

(ii) the requirements of paragraph (e)(2)(ii) and (iii) of this section are satisfied; and

(iii) The transferee foreign corporation will for the foreseeable future satisfy the requirements of paragraph (e)(2)(iv) and (v) of this section.

(4) *Other applicable rules.*—Oil and gas interests not described in this paragraph (e) may nonetheless qualify for the exception to section 367(a)(1) contained in § 1.367(a)-2T, relating to

transfers of property for use in the active conduct of a trade or business outside of the United States. However, a mere royalty interest in oil and gas properties will not be treated as transferred for use in the active conduct of a trade or business outside the United States. Moreover, a royalty or similar interest that constitutes intangible property will be subject to the rules of § 1.367(d)-1T, relating to transfers of intangible property.

(f) *Compulsory transfers.*—Property shall be presumed to be transferred for use in the active conduct of a trade or business outside of the United States, if—

(1) The property was previously in use in the country in which the transferee foreign corporation is organized; and

(2) The transfer is either:

(i) Legally required by the foreign government as a necessary condition of doing business in that country; or

(ii) Compelled by a genuine threat of immediate expropriation by the foreign government.

(g) *Relationship to other sections.*—The rules of §§ 1.367(a)-5T, 1.367(a)-6T, and 1.367(d)-1T apply to transfers of property whether or not the property is transferred for use in the active conduct of a trade or business outside the United States. See § 1.367(d)-1T(g)(2)(ii) for a special election with respect to compulsory transfers of intangible property.

(h) *Transfers of certain property to FSCs.*— (1) *In general.*—The provisions of section 367(a) and (d) and the regulations thereunder shall not apply to a transfer of property by a U.S. person to a foreign corporation that constitutes a FSC, as defined in section 922(a), if—

(i) The transferee FSC uses the property to generate exempt foreign trade income, as defined in section 923(a);

(ii) The property is not excluded property, as defined in section 927(a)(2); and

(iii) The property consists of a corporate name or tangible property that is appropriate for use in the operation of a FSC office.

(2) *Exception.*—The general rule in paragraph (g)(1) of this section shall not apply if, within three years after the original transfer, the original transferee FSC (or a subsequent transferee FSC) disposes of the property other than in the ordinary course of business or through a transfer to another FSC. Thus, the U.S. transferor may recognize gain in the taxable year in which the original transfer occurred through the application of section 367 and the regulations thereunder. [Temporary Reg. § 1.367(a)-4T.]

☐ [*T.D.* 8087, 5-15-86. *Amended by T.D.* 8515, 1-12-94.]

§ 1.367(a)-5T. Property subject to section 367(a)(1) regardless of use in trade or business (temporary).—(a) *In general.*—Section 367(a)(1) shall apply to a transfer of property described in this section regardless of whether the property is transferred for use in the active conduct of a trade or business. Certain exceptions to the operation of this rule are provided in this section, and a special gain limitation rule is provided in paragraph (e). A transfer of property described in this section is subject to section 367(a)(1) even if the transfer is a compulsory transfer described in § 1.367(a)-4T(f).

(b) *Inventory, etc.*—Regardless of use in an active trade or business, section 367(a)(1) shall apply to the transfer of—

(1) Stock in trade of the taxpayer or other property of a kind which would properly be included in the inventory of the taxpayer if on hand at the close of the taxable year, or property held by the taxpayer primarily for sale to customers in the ordinary course of its trade or business; and

(2) A copyright, a literary, musical, or artistic composition, a letter or memorandum, or similar property, held by—

(i) A taxpayer whose personal efforts created such property;

(ii) In the case of a letter, memorandum, or similar property, a taxpayer for whom such property was prepared or produced; or

(iii) A taxpayer in whose hands the basis of such property is determined, for purposes of determining gain from a sale or exchange, in whole or part by reference to the basis of such property in the hands of a taxpayer described in subdivision (i) or (ii) of this paragraph (b)(2).

For purposes of this section, the term "inventory" includes raw materials and supplies, partially completed goods, and finished products.

(c) *Installment obligations, etc.*—Regardless of use in an active trade or business, section 367(a)(1) shall apply to the transfer of installment obligations, accounts receivable, or similar property, but only to the extent that the principal amount of any such obligation has not previously been included by the taxpayer in its taxable income.

(d) *Foreign currency, etc.*—(1) *In general.*— Regardless of use in an active trade or business, section 367(a)(1) shall apply to the transfer of foreign currency or other property denominated in foreign currency, including installment obligations, futures contracts, forward contracts, accounts receivable, or any other obligation entitling its payee to receive payment in a currency other than U.S. dollars.

(2) *Exception for certain obligations.*—If transferred property denominated in a foreign currency—

(i) Is denominated in the currency of the country in which the transferee foreign corporation is organized; and

(ii) Was acquired in the ordinary course of the business of the transferor that will be carried on by the transferee foreign corporation,

then section 367(a)(1) shall apply to the transfer only to the extent that gain is required to be recognized with respect to previously realized income reflected in installment obligations subject to paragraph (c) of this section. The rule of this paragraph (d)(2) shall not apply to transfers of foreign currency.

(3) *Limitation of gain required to be recognized.*—If section 367(a)(1) applies to a transfer of property described in this paragraph, then the gain required to be recognized shall be limited to—

(i) The gain realized upon the transfer of property described in this paragraph (d), minus

(ii) Any loss realized as part of the same transaction upon the transfer of property described in this paragraph (d).

This limitation applies in lieu of the rule in § 1.367(a)-1T(b)(1). No loss shall be recognized with respect to property described in this paragraph (d).

(e) *Intangible property.*—Regardless of use in an active trade or business, a transfer of intangible property pursuant to section 332 shall be subject to section 367(a)(1), unless it constitutes foreign goodwill or going concern value, as defined in § 1.367(a)-1T(d)(5)(iii). For rules concerning transfers of intangible property pursuant to section 351 or 361, see section 367(d) and § 1.367(d)-1T.

(f) *Leased tangible property.*—Regardless of use in an active trade or business, section 367(a)(1) shall apply to a transfer of tangible property with respect to which the transferor is a lessor at the time of the transfer, unless—

(1) With respect to property that will not be leased by the transferee to third persons, the transferee was the lessee of the property at the time of the transfer; or

(2) With respect to property that will be leased by the transferee to third persons, the transferee satisfies the conditions set forth in § 1.367(a)-4T(c)(1) or (2). [Temporary Reg. § 1.367(a)-5T.]

☐ [T.D. 8087, 5-15-86.]

§ 1.367(a)-6T. Transfer of foreign branch with previously deducted losses (temporary).—(a) *In general.*—This section provides special rules relating to the transfer of the assets of a foreign branch with previously deducted losses. Paragraph (b) of this section provides generally that such losses must be recaptured by the recognition of the gain realized on the transfer. Paragraph (c) of this section sets forth rules concerning the character of, and limitations on, the gain required to be recognized. Paragraph (d) of this section defines the term "previously deducted losses." Paragraph (e) of this section describes certain reductions that are made to the previously deducted losses before they are taken into income under this section. Finally, paragraph (g) of this section defines the term "foreign branch."

(b) *Recognition of gain required.*—(1) *In general.*—If a U.S. person transfers any assets of a foreign branch to a foreign corporation in an exchange described in section 367(a)(1), then the transferor shall recognize gain equal to—

(i) The sum of the previously deducted branch ordinary losses as defined and reduced in paragraphs (d) and (e) of this section; and

(ii) The sum of the previously deducted branch capital losses as defined and reduced in paragraphs (d) and (e) of this section.

(2) *No active conduct exception.*—The rules of this paragraph (b) shall apply regardless of whether the assets of the foreign branch are transferred for use in the active conduct of a trade or business outside the United States.

(c) *Special rules concerning gain recognized.*—(1) *Character and source of gain.*—The gain described in paragraph (b)(1)(i) of this section shall be treated as ordinary income of the transferor, and the gain described in paragraph (b)(1)(ii) of this section shall be treated as long-term capital gain of the transferor. Gain that is recognized pursuant to the rules of this section shall be treated as income from sources outside the United States. Such recognized gain shall be treated as foreign oil and gas extraction income (as defined in section 907) in the same proportion that previously deducted foreign oil and gas extraction losses bore to the total amount of previously deducted losses.

(2) *Gain limitation.*—For a rule limiting the amount of gain required to be recognized under section 367(a) upon any transfer of property to a foreign corporation, including the transfer of assets of a foreign branch with previously deducted losses, see § 1.367(a)-1T(b)(3).

(3) *Foreign goodwill and going concern value.*—For purposes of this section, the assets of a foreign branch shall include foreign goodwill and going concern value related to the business of the foreign branch, as defined in § 1.367(a)-1T(d)(5)(iii). Thus, gain realized upon the transfer of the foreign goodwill or going concern value of a foreign branch to a foreign corporation will be taken into account in computing the limitation on loss recapture under paragraph (c)(2) of this section.

(4) *Transfers of certain intangible property.*—Gain realized on the transfer of intangible property (computed with reference to the fair market value of the intangible property as of the date of the transfer) that is an asset of a foreign branch shall be taken into account in computing the limitation on loss recapture under paragraph (c)(2) of this section. For rules relating to the crediting of gain recognized under this section against income deemed to arise by operation of section 367(d), see § 1.367(d)-1T(g)(3).

(d) *Previously deducted losses.*—(1) *In general.*—This paragraph (d) provides rules for determining, for purposes of paragraph (b)(1) of this section, the previously deducted losses of a foreign branch any of whose assets are transferred to a foreign corporation in an exchange described in section 367(a)(1). Initially, the two previously deducted losses of a foreign branch for a taxable year are the total ordinary loss ("previously deducted branch ordinary loss") and the total capital loss ("previously deducted branch capital loss") that were realized by the foreign branch in that taxable year (a "branch loss year") prior to the transfer and that were or will be reflected on a U.S. income tax return of the transferor. The previously deducted branch ordinary loss for each branch loss year is reduced by expired net ordinary losses under paragraph (d)(2) of this section, while the previously deducted capital loss for each loss year is reduced by expired net capital losses under paragraph (d)(3) of this section. For each branch loss year, the remaining previously deducted branch ordinary loss and the remaining previously deducted branch capital loss are then reduced, proceeding from the first branch loss year to the last branch loss year, to reflect expired foreign tax credits under paragraph (d)(4) of this section. The reductions are made in the order of the taxable years in which the foreign tax credits arose. Finally, similar reductions are made to reflect expired investment credits under paragraph (d)(5) of this section.

(2) *Reduction by expired net ordinary loss.*—(i) *In general.*—The previously deducted branch ordinary loss for each branch loss year shall be reduced under this paragraph (d)(2) by the amount of any expired net ordinary loss with respect to that branch loss year. Expired net ordinary losses arising in years other than the branch loss year shall reduce the previously deducted branch ordinary loss for the branch loss year only to the extent that the previously deducted branch ordinary loss exceeds the net operating loss, if any, incurred by the transferor in the branch loss year. The previously deducted branch ordinary losses shall be reduced proceeding from the first branch loss year to the last branch loss year. For each branch loss year, expired net operating losses shall be applied to reduce the previously deducted branch ordinary loss for that year in the order in which the expired net ordinary losses arose.

(ii) *Existence of expired net ordinary loss.*—An expired net ordinary loss exists with respect to a branch loss year to the extent that—

(A) The transferor incurred a net operating loss (within the meaning of section 172(c));

(B) That net operating loss arose in the branch loss year or was available for carryover or carryback to the branch loss year under section 172(b)(1);

(C) That net operating loss has neither given rise to a net operating loss deduction (within the meaning of section 172(a)) for any taxable year prior to the year of the transfer, nor given rise to a reduction of any previously deducted branch ordinary loss (pursuant to paragraph (d)(2) of this section) of any foreign branch of the transferor upon a previous transfer to a foreign corporation; and

(D) The period during which the transferor may claim a net operating loss deduction with respect to that net operating loss has expired.

(3) *Reduction by expired net capital loss.*—(i) *In general.*—The previously deducted branch capital loss for each branch loss year shall be reduced under this paragraph (d)(3) by the amount of any expired net capital loss with respect to that branch loss year. Expired net capital losses arising in years other than the branch loss year shall reduce the previously deducted branch capital loss for the branch loss year only to the extent that the previously deducted branch capital loss exceeds the net capital loss, if any, incurred by the transferor in the branch loss year. The previously deducted branch capital losses shall be reduced proceeding from the first branch loss year to the last branch loss year. For each branch loss year, expired net capital losses shall be applied to reduce the previously de-

ducted branch capital loss for that year in the order in which the expired net capital losses arose.

(ii) *Existence of expired net capital loss.*—An expired net capital loss exists with respect to a branch loss year to the extent that—

(A) The transferor incurred a net capital loss (within the meaning of section 1222(10));

(B) That net capital loss arose in the branch loss year or was available for carryover or carryback to the branch loss year under section 1212;

(C) That net capital loss has neither been allowed for any taxable year prior to the year of the transfer, nor given rise to a reduction of any previously deducted branch capital loss (pursuant to paragraph (d)(3) of this section) of any foreign branch of the transferor upon any previous transfer to a foreign corporation; and

(D) The period during which the transferor may claim a capital loss deduction with respect to that net capital loss has expired.

(4) *Reduction for expired foreign tax credits.*—(i) *In general.*—The previously deducted branch ordinary loss and the previously deducted branch capital loss for each branch loss year remaining after the reductions described in paragraph (d)(2) and (3) of this section shall be further reduced under this paragraph (d)(4) proportionately by the amount of any expired foreign tax credit loss equivalent with respect to that branch loss year. The previously deducted branch losses shall be reduced proceeding from the first branch loss year to the last branch loss year. For each branch loss year, expired foreign tax credit loss equivalents shall be applied to reduce the previously deducted branch loss for the year in the order in which the expired foreign tax credits arose.

(ii) *Existence of foreign tax credit loss equivalent.*—A foreign tax credit loss equivalent exists with respect to a branch loss year if—

(A) The transferor paid, accrued, or is deemed under section 902 or 960 to have paid creditable foreign taxes in a taxable year;

(B) The creditable foreign taxes were paid, accrued, or deemed paid in the branch loss year or were available for carryover or carryback to the branch loss year under section 904(c);

(C) No foreign tax credit with respect to the foreign taxes paid, accrued, or deemed paid has been taken because of the operation of section 904(a) or similar limitations provided by the Code or an applicable treaty, and such taxes have not given rise to a reduction (pursuant to this paragraph (d)(5)) of any previously deducted branch loss of the foreign branch for a prior taxable year or of any previously deducted branch losses of any foreign branch of the transferor upon a prior transfer to a foreign corporation; and

(D) The period during which the transferor may claim a foreign tax credit for the foreign taxes paid, accrued, or deemed paid has expired.

(iii) *Amount of foreign tax credit loss equivalent.*—The amount of the foreign tax credit loss equivalent for the branch loss year with respect to the creditable foreign taxes described in paragraph (d)(4)(ii) of this section is the amount of those creditable foreign taxes divided by the highest rate of tax to which the transferor was subject in the loss year.

(5) *Reduction for expired investment credits.*—(i) *In general.*—The previously deducted branch ordinary loss and the previously deducted branch capital loss for each branch loss year shall be further reduced under this paragraph (d)(5) proportionately by the amount of any expired investment credit loss equivalent with respect to that branch year. The previously deducted branch losses shall be reduced proceeding from the first branch loss year to the last branch loss year. For each branch loss year, expired investment credit loss equivalents shall be applied to reduce the previously deducted branch loss for that year in the order in which the expired investment credits were earned.

(ii) *Existence of investment credit loss equivalent.*—An investment credit loss equivalent exists with respect to a branch loss year if—

(A) The transferor earned an investment credit (within the meaning of section 46(a)) in a taxable year;

(B) The investment credit was earned in the branch loss year or was available for carryover or carryback to the branch loss year under section 39;

(C) The investment credit earned by the transferor in the credit year has been denied by section 38(a) or by similar provisions of the Code and has not given rise to a reduction (pursuant to this paragraph (d)(5)) of any previously deducted branch loss of the foreign branch for a preceding taxable year or of the previously deducted losses of any foreign branch of the transferor upon any previous transfer to a foreign corporation; and

(D) The period during which the transferor may claim the investment credit has expired.

Reg. §1.367(a)-6T(d)(5)(ii)(D)

(iii) *Amount of investment tax credit loss equivalent.*—The amount of the investment credit loss equivalent for the branch loss year with respect to the investment credit described in paragraph (d)(5)(ii) of this section is 85 percent of the amount of that investment credit divided by the highest rate of tax to which the transferor was subject in the loss year.

(e) *Amounts that reduce previously deducted losses subject to recapture.*—(1) *In general.*—This paragraph (e) describes five amounts that reduce the sum of the previously deducted branch ordinary losses and the sum of the previously deducted branch capital losses before they are taken into income under paragraph (b) of this section. Amounts representing ordinary income shall be applied to reduce first the sum of the previously deducted branch ordinary losses to the extent thereof, and then the sum of the previously deducted branch capital losses to the extent thereof. Similarly, amounts representing capital gains shall be applied to reduce first the sum of the previously deducted branch capital losses and then the sum of the previously deducted branch ordinary losses.

(2) *Taxable income.*—The previously deducted losses shall be reduced by any taxable income of the foreign branch recognized through the close of the taxable year of the transfer, whether before or after any taxable year in which losses were incurred.

(3) *Amounts currently recaptured under section 904(f)(3).*—The previously deducted losses shall be reduced by the amount recognized under section 904(f)(3) on account of the transfer.

(4) *Gain recognized under section 367(a).*—The previously deducted branch losses shall be reduced by any gain recognized pursuant to section 367(a)(1) (other than by reason of the provisions of this section) upon the transfer of the assets of the foreign branch to the foreign corporation.

(5) *Amounts previously recaptured under section 904(f)(3).*—(i) *In general.*—The previously deducted branch losses shall be reduced by the portion of any amount recognized under section 904(f)(3) upon a previous transfer of property that was attributable to the losses of the foreign branch, provided that the amount did not reduce any gain otherwise required to be recognized under section 367(a)(3)(C) and this section (or Revenue Ruling 78-201, 1978-1 C.B. 91).

(ii) *Portion attributable to the losses of the foreign branch.*—(A) *Branch property.*—The full amount recognized under section 904(f)(3) upon a previous transfer of property of the branch shall be treated as attributable to the losses of the foreign branch.

(B) *Non-branch property.*—The portion of the amount previously recognized under section 904(f)(3) upon a transfer of non-branch property that was attributable to the losses of the foreign branch shall be the sum, over the taxable years in which the transferor sustained an overall foreign loss some portion of which was recaptured on the disposition, of the recaptured portions of those overall foreign losses after multiplication by the following fraction:

$$\frac{\text{Losses of the foreign branch for the year}}{\text{All foreign losses for the year}}$$

For purposes of this fraction, the term "losses of the foreign branch for the year" means the losses of the foreign branch that were taken into account under section 904(f)(2) in determining the amount of the transferor's overall foreign loss for the year, and the term "all foreign losses for the year" means all of the lossses of the transferor that were taken into account under section 904(f)(2).

(6) *Amounts previously recognized under the rules of this section.*—The previously deducted losses shall be reduced by the amounts previously recognized under the rules of this section upon a previous transfer of assets of the foreign branch.

(f) *Example.*—The rules of paragraphs (b) through (e) of this section are illustrated by the following example.

Example. (i) *Facts.* X, a U.S. corporation, is a calendar year taxpayer. On January 1, 1981, X established a branch in foreign country A to manufacture and sell X's products in country A. On July 1, 1986, X organized corporation Y, a country A subsidiary, and transferred to Y all of the assets of its country A branch, including goodwill and going concern value. During the period from January 1, 1981, through July 1, 1986, X's country A branch earned income and incurred losses in the following amounts:

Country A branch

Year	Ordinary income (loss)	Capital gain (loss)
1981	(200)	0
1982	(300)	(100)
1983	(400)	0
1984	200	0
1985	(100)	0
1986	50	0

Reg. § 1.367(a)-6T(d)(5)(iii)

At the time of the transfer of X's country A branch assets to Y, those assets had a fair market value of $2,500 and an adjusted basis of $1,000. For each of the assets, fair market value exceeded adjusted basis. X had no net capital loss or unused investment credit during any taxable year relevant to the transfer. In 1984, X incurred a net operating loss of $400, $200 of which was carried back to prior years. An additional $50 of the 1984 net operating loss was carried over to 1985. The remaining $150 of the 1984 net operating loss was not used in any year prior to the transfer. In 1979, X paid creditable foreign taxes of $330 that could not be claimed as a credit in that year or any earlier year because of section 904. Of those foreign taxes, $100 were carried over and claimed as a credit in 1983, but the remaining $230 were not used in any year prior to the transfer. X was not required to recognize any gain under section 904(f)(3) on account of the 1986 transfer or any prior transfer. X was not required to recognize gain upon the transfer under section 367(a) (other than by reason of the provisions of this section).

(ii) *Previously deducted losses.* The previously deducted losses of X's country A branch are $575 of ordinary losses and $25 of capital losses, computed as follows: Initially, the branch has previously deducted ordinary losses of $1,000 ($200 + $300 + $400 + $100), and previously deducted capital losses of $100. (See paragraph (d)(1) of this section.)

(iii) *Expired losses and credits.* Under the facts of this example, there are no reductions for expired net ordinary losses or expired net capital losses under paragraph (d)(2) or (3) of this section. However, the previously deducted losses are reduced proceeding from the first branch loss year to the last branch loss year to reflect the expired foreign tax credit from 1979. The amount of the foreign tax credit loss equivalent with respect to 1981 is $500 ($230 / .46). It reduces the previously deducted losses for 1981 proportionately. Thus, the previously deducted ordinary loss for 1981 is reduced from $200 to $0. (See paragraph (d)(4) of this section.) The amount of the foreign tax credit loss equivalent with respect to 1982 is $300 ($500 – $200, *i.e.,* $138 / .46). (See paragraph (d)(4)(ii)(C) of this section.) It reduces the previously deducted losses for 1982 proportionately. Thus, the previously deducted ordinary loss for 1982 is reduced from $300 to $75, and the previously deducted capital loss for 1982 is reduced from $100 to $25.

(iv) *Further reductions.* The previously deducted ordinary losses of $575 and the previously deducted capital losses of $25 are reduced by the taxable income earned by the branch prior to the date of the transfer ($250). (See paragraph (e)(2) of this section.) Since that income was ordinary income, it is applied first to reduce the previously deducted ordinary losses of $575 to $325. (See paragraph (e)(1) of this section.)

(v) *Recapture.* Since the gain realized by X upon its transfer of the branch assets to Y exceeds the sum of the previously deducted branch losses as defined and reduced above ($325 + $25), the limitation in paragraph (c)(2) of this section does not apply. Thus, X is required to recognize $325 of ordinary income and $25 of long-term capital gain upon the transfer. (See paragraph (b) and (c)(1) of this section.)

(g) *Definition of foreign branch.*—(1) *In general.*—For purposes of this section, the term "foreign branch" means an integral business operation carried on by a U.S. person outside the United States. Whether the activities of a U.S. person outside the United States constitute a foreign branch operation must be determined under all the facts and circumstances. Evidence of the existence of a foreign branch includes, but is not limited to, the existence of a separate set of books and records, and the existence of an office or other fixed place of business used by employees or officers of the U.S. person in carrying out business activities outside the United States. Activities outside the United States shall be deemed to constitute a foreign branch for purposes of this section if the activities constitute a permanent establishment under the terms of a treaty between the United States and the country in which the activities are carried out. Any U.S. person may be treated as having a foreign branch for purposes of this section, whether that person is a corporation, partnership, trust, estate, or individual.

(2) *More than one branch.*—If a U.S. person carries on more than one branch operation outside the United States, then the rules of this section must be separately applied with respect to each foreign branch that is transferred to a foreign corporation. Thus, the previously deducted losses of one branch may not be offset, for purposes of determining the gain required to be recognized under the rules of this section, by the income of another branch that is also transferred to a foreign corporation. Similarly, the losses of one branch shall not be recaptured upon a transfer of the assets of a separate branch. Whether the foreign activities

of a U.S. person are carried out through more than one branch must be determined under all of the facts and circumstances. In general, a separate branch exists if a particular group of activities is sufficiently integrated to constitute a single business that could be operated as an independent enterprise. For purposes of determining the combination of activities that constitute a branch operation as defined in this paragraph (g), the nominal relationship among those activities shall not be controlling. Factors suggesting that nominally separate business operations constitute a single foreign branch include a substantial identity of products, customers, operational facilities, operational processes, accounting and record-keeping functions, management, employees, distribution channels, or sales and purchasing forces. For examples of the application of the principles of this paragraph (g)(2), see Revenue Ruling 81-82, 1981-1 C.B. 127.

(3) *Consolidated group.*—For purposes of this section, the activities of each of two domestic corporations outside the United States will be considered to constitute a single foreign branch if—

(i) The two corporations are members of the same consolidated group of corporations; and

(ii) The activities of the two corporations in the aggregate would constitute a single foreign branch if conducted by a single corporation.

Notwithstanding the preceding rule of this paragraph (g)(3), gains of a foreign branch of a domestic corporation arising in a year in which that corporation did not file a consolidated return with a second domestic corporation shall not be applied to reduce the previously deducted losses of a foreign branch of the second corporation (but may be applied to reduce such losses of the foreign branch of the first corporation) upon the transfer of the two branches to a foreign corporation, even though the two domestic corporations file a consolidated return for the year in which the transfer occurs and the two branches are considered at that time to constitute a single foreign branch. For an example of the application of the principles of this paragraph (g)(3), see Revenue Ruling 81-89, 1981-1 C.B. 129.

(4) *Property not transferred.*—A U.S. transferor's failure to transfer any property of a foreign branch shall be irrelevant to the determination of the previously deducted losses of the branch subject to recapture under the rules of this section. Thus, if the activities with respect to untransferred property constituted a part of the branch operation under the rules of this paragraph (g), then the losses generated by those activities shall be subject to recapture, notwithstanding the failure to transfer the property. For an example of the application of the principles of this paragraph (g)(4), see Revenue Ruling 80-247, 1980-2 C.B. 127, relating to property abandoned by the U.S. transferor.

(h) *Anti-abuse rule.*—If—

(1) A U.S. person transfers property of a foreign branch to a domestic corporation for a principal purpose of avoiding the effect of this section; and

(2) The domestic corporation thereafter transfers the property of the foreign branch to a foreign corporation,

then, solely for purposes of this section, that U.S. person shall be treated as having transferred the property of the branch directly to the foreign corporation. A U.S. person shall be presumed to have transferred property of a foreign branch for a principal purpose of avoiding the effect of this section if the property is transferred to the domestic corporation less than two years prior to the domestic corporation's transfer of the property to a foreign corporation. This presumption may be rebutted by clear evidence that the subsequent transfer of the property was not contemplated at the time of the initial transfer to the domestic corporation and that avoidance of the effect of this section was not a principal purpose for the transaction. A transfer may have more than one principal purpose.

(i) *Basis adjustments.*—Basis adjustments reflecting gain recognized pursuant to this section shall be made as described in § 1.367(a)-1T(b)(4)(ii). [Temporary Reg. § 1.367(a)-6T.]

☐ [T.D. 8087, 5-15-86.]

§ 1.367(a)-8. Gain recognition agreement requirements.—(a) *In general.*—This section specifies the general terms and conditions for an agreement to recognize gain entered into pursuant to § 1.367(a)-3(b) or (c) to qualify for nonrecognition treatment under section 367(a).

(1) *Filing requirements.*—A transferor's agreement to recognize gain (described in paragraph (b) of this section) must be attached to, and filed by the due date (including extensions) of, the transferor's income tax return for the taxable year that includes the date of the transfer.

(2) *Gain recognition agreement forms.*—Any agreement, certification, or other document required to be filed pursuant to the provisions of this section shall be submitted on such forms as may be prescribed therefor by the

Commissioner (or similar statements providing the same information that is required on such forms). Until such time as forms are prescribed, all necessary filings may be accomplished by providing the required information to the Internal Revenue Service in accordance with the rules of this section.

(3) *Who must sign.*—The agreement to recognize gain must be signed under penalties of perjury by a responsible officer in the case of a corporate transferor, except that if the transferor is a member but not the parent of an affiliated group (within the meaning of section 1504(a)(1)), that files a consolidated Federal income tax return for the taxable year in which the transfer was made, the agreement must be entered into by the parent corporation and signed by a responsible officer of such parent corporation; by the individual, in the case of an individual transferor (including a partner who is treated as a transferor by virtue of § 1.367(a)-1T(c)(3)); by a trustee, executor, or equivalent fiduciary in the case of a transferor that is a trust or estate; and by a debtor in possession or trustee in a bankruptcy case under Title 11, United States Code. An agreement may also be signed by an agent authorized to do so under a general or specific power of attorney.

(b) *Agreement to recognize gain.*—(1) *Contents.*—The agreement must set forth the following information, with the heading "GAIN RECOGNITION AGREEMENT UNDER § 1.367(a)-8", and with paragraphs labeled to correspond with the numbers set forth as follows—

(i) A statement that the document submitted constitutes the transferor's agreement to recognize gain in accordance with the requirements of this section;

(ii) A description of the property transferred as described in paragraph (b)(2) of this section;

(iii) The transferor's agreement to recognize gain, as described in paragraph (b)(3) of this section;

(iv) A waiver of the period of limitations as described in paragraph (b)(4) of this section;

(v) An agreement to file with the transferor's tax returns for the 5 full taxable years following the year of the transfer a certification as described in paragraph (b)(5) of this section;

(vi) A statement that arrangements have been made in connection with the transferred property to ensure that the transferor will be informed of any subsequent disposition of any property that would require the recognition of gain under the agreement; and

(vii) A statement as to whether, in the event all or a portion of the gain recognition agreement is triggered under paragraph (e) of this section, the taxpayer elects to include the required amount in the year of the triggering event rather than in the year of the initial transfer. If the taxpayer elects to include the required amount in the year of the triggering event, such statement must be included with all of the other information required under this paragraph (b), and filed by the due date (including extensions) of the transferor's income tax return for the taxable year that includes the date of the transfer.

(2) *Description of property transferred.*—(i) The agreement shall include a description of each property transferred by the transferor, an estimate of the fair market value of the property as of the date of the transfer, a statement of the cost or other basis of the property and any adjustments thereto, and the date on which the property was acquired by the transferor.

(ii) If the transferred property is stock or securities, the transferor must provide the information contained in paragraphs (b)(2)(ii)(A) through (F) of this section as follows—

(A) The type or class, amount, and characteristics of the stock or securities transferred, as well as the name, address, and place of incorporation of the issuer of the stock or securities, and the percentage (by voting power and value) that the stock (if any) represents of the total stock outstanding of the issuing corporation;

(B) The name, address and place of incorporation of the transferee foreign corporation, and the percentage of stock (by voting power and value) that the U.S. transferor received or will receive in the transaction;

(C) If stock or securities are transferred in an exchange described in section 361(a) or (b), a statement that the conditions set forth in the second sentence of section 367(a)(5) and any regulations under that section have been satisfied, and an explanation of any basis or other adjustments made pursuant to section 367(a)(5) and any regulations thereunder;

(D) If the property transferred is stock or securities of a domestic corporation, the taxpayer identification number of the domestic corporation whose stock or securities were transferred, together with a statement that all of the requirements of § 1.367(a)-3(c)(1) are satisfied;

(E) If the property transferred is stock or securities of a foreign corporation, a statement as to whether the U.S. transferor was a United States shareholder (a U.S. transferor that satisfies the ownership requirements of section 1248(a)(2) or (c)(2)) of the corporation whose stock was exchanged, and, if so, a statement as to whether the U.S. transferor is a United States shareholder with respect to the stock received, and whether any reporting requirements contained in regulations under section 367(b) are applicable, and, if so, whether they have been satisfied; and

(F) If the transaction involved the transfer of assets other than stock or securities and the transaction was subject to the indirect stock transfer rules of § 1.367(a)-3(d), a statement as to whether the reporting requirements under section 6038B have been satisfied with respect to the transfer of property other than stock or securities, and an explanation of whether gain was recognized under section 367(a)(1) and whether section 367(d) was applicable to the transfer of such assets, or whether any tangible assets qualified for nonrecognition treatment under section 367(a)(3) (as limited by section 367(a)(5) and §§ 1.367(a)-4T, 1.367(a)-5T and 1.367(a)-6T).

(3) *Terms of agreement.*—(i) *General rule.*—If prior to the close of the fifth full taxable year (i.e., not less than 60 months) following the close of the taxable year of the initial transfer, the transferee foreign corporation disposes of the transferred property in whole or in part (as described in paragraphs (e)(1) and (2) of this section), or is deemed to have disposed of the transferred property (under paragraph (e)(3) of this section), then, unless an election is made in paragraph (b)(1)(vii) of this section, by the 90th day thereafter the U.S. transferor must file an amended return for the year of the transfer and recognize thereon the gain realized but not recognized upon the initial transfer, with interest. If an election under paragraph (b)(1)(vii) of this section was made, then, if a disposition occurs, the U.S. transferor must include the gain realized but not recognized on the initial transfer in income on its Federal income tax return for the period that includes the date of the triggering event. In accordance with paragraph (b)(3)(iii) of this section, interest must be paid on any additional tax due. (If a taxpayer properly makes the election under paragraph (b)(1)(vii) of this section but later fails to include the gain realized in income, the Commissioner may, in his discretion, include the gain in the taxpayer's income in the year of the initial transfer.)

(ii) *Offsets.*—No special limitations apply with respect to net operating losses, capital losses, credits against tax, or similar items.

(iii) *Interest.*—If additional tax is required to be paid, then interest must be paid on that amount at the rates determined under section 6621 with respect to the period between the date that was prescribed for filing the transferor's income tax return for the year of the initial transfer and the date on which the additional tax for that year is paid. If the election in paragraph (b)(1)(vii) of this section is made, taxpayers should enter the amount of interest due, labelled as "sec. 367 interest" at the bottom right margin of page 1 of the Federal income tax return for the period that includes the date of the triggering event (page 2 if the taxpayer files a Form 1040), and include the amount of interest in their payment (or reduce the amount of any refund due by the amount of the interest). If the election in paragraph (b)(1)(vii) of this section is made, taxpayers should, as a matter of course, include the amount of gain as taxable income on their Federal income tax returns (together with other income or loss items). The amount of tax relating to the gain should be separately stated at the bottom right margin of page 1 of the Federal income tax return (page 2 if the taxpayer files a Form 1040), labelled as "sec. 367 tax."

(iv) *Basis adjustments.*—(A) *Transferee.*—If a U.S. transferor is required to recognize gain under this section on the disposition by the transferee foreign corporation of the transferred property, then in determining for U.S. income tax purposes any gain or loss recognized by the transferee foreign corporation upon its disposition of such property, the transferee foreign corporation's basis in such property shall be increased (as of the date of the initial transfer) by the amount of gain required to be recognized (but not by any tax or interest required to be paid on such amount) by the U.S. transferor. In the case of a deemed disposition of the stock of the transferred corporation described in paragraph (e)(3)(i) of this section, the transferee foreign corporation's basis in the transferred stock deemed disposed of shall be increased by the amount of gain required to be recognized by the U.S. transferor.

(B) *Transferor.*—If a U.S. transferor is required to recognize gain under this section, then the U.S. transferor's basis in the stock of the transferee foreign corporation shall be increased by the amount of gain required to be recognized (but not by any tax or interest required to be paid on such amount).

(C) *Other adjustments.*—Other appropriate adjustments to basis that are consistent with the principles of this paragraph (b)(3)(iv) may be made if the U.S. transferor is required to recognize gain under this section.

(D) *Example.*—The principles of this paragraph (b)(3) are illustrated by the following example:

Example—(i) *Facts.* D, a domestic corporation owning 100 percent of the stock of S, a foreign corporation, transfers all of the S stock to F, a foreign corporation, in an exchange described in section 368(a)(1)(B). The section 1248 amount with respect to the S stock is $0. In the exchange, D receives 20 percent of the voting stock of F. All of the requirements of § 1.367(a)-3(c)(1) are satisfied, and D enters into a five-year gain recognition agreement to qualify for nonrecognition treatment and does not make the election contained in paragraph (b)(1)(vii) of this section. One year after the initial transfer, F transfers all of the S stock to F1 in an exchange described in section 351, and D complies with the requirements of paragraph (g)(2) of this section. Two years after the initial transfer, D transfers its entire 20 percent interest in F's voting stock to a domestic partnership in exchange for an interest in the partnership. Three years after the initial exchange, S disposes of substantially all (as described in paragraph (e)(3)(i) of this section) of its assets in a transaction that would be taxable under U.S. income tax principles, and D is required by the terms of the gain recognition agreement to recognize all the gain that it realized on the initial transfer of the stock of S.

(ii) *Result.* As a result of this gain recognition and paragraph (b)(3)(iv) of this section, D is permitted to increase its basis in the partnership interest by the amount of gain required to be recognized (but not by any tax or interest required to be paid on such amount), the partnership is permitted to increase its basis in the 20 percent voting stock of F, F is permitted to increase its basis in the stock of F1, and F1 is permitted to increase its basis in the stock of S. S, however, is not permitted to increase its basis in its assets for purposes of determining the direct or indirect U.S. tax results, if any, on the sale of its assets.

(4) *Waiver of period of limitation.*—The U.S. transferor must file, with the agreement to recognize gain, a waiver of the period of limitation on assessment of tax upon the gain realized on the transfer. The waiver shall be executed on Form 8838 (Consent to Extend the Time to Assess Tax Under Section 367—Gain Recognition Agreement) and shall extend the period for assessment of such tax to a date not earlier than the eighth full taxable year following the taxable year of the transfer. Such waiver shall also contain such other terms with respect to assessment as may be considered necessary by the Commissioner to ensure the assessment and collection of the correct tax liability for each year for which the waiver is required. The waiver must be signed by a person who would be authorized to sign the agreement pursuant to the provisions of paragraph (a)(3) of this section.

(5) *Annual certification.*—(i) *In general.*—The U.S. transferor must file with its income tax return for each of the five full taxable years following the taxable year of the transfer a certification that the property transferred has not been disposed of by the transferee in a transaction that is considered to be a disposition for purposes of this section, including a disposition described in paragraph (e)(3) of this section. The U.S. transferor must include with its annual certification a statement describing any taxable dispositions of assets by the transferred corporation that are not in the ordinary course of business. The annual certification pursuant to this paragraph (b)(5) must be signed under penalties of perjury by a person who would be authorized to sign the agreement pursuant to the provisions of paragraph (a)(3) of this section.

(ii) *Special rule when U.S. transferor leaves its affiliated group.*—If, at the time of the initial transfer, the U.S. transferor was a member of an affiliated group (within the meaning of section 1504(a)(1)) filing a consolidated Federal income tax return but not the parent of such group, the U.S. transferor will file the annual certification (and provide a copy to the parent corporation) if it leaves the group during the term of the gain recognition agreement, notwithstanding the fact that the parent entered into the gain recognition agreement, extended the statute of limitations pursuant to this section, and remains liable (with other corporations that were members of the group at the time of the initial transfer) under the gain recognition agreement in the case of a triggering event.

(c) *Failure to comply.*—(1) *General rule.*—If a person that is required to file an agreement under paragraph (b) of this section fails to file the agreement in a timely manner, or if a person that has entered into an agreement under paragraph (b) of this section fails at any time to comply in any material respect with the requirements of this section or with the terms of an agreement submitted pursuant hereto, then the initial transfer of property is described in section 367(a)(1) (unless otherwise excepted under the rules of this section) and will be treated as a taxable exchange in the year of the initial transfer (or in the year of the failure to comply if the agreement was filed with a timely-filed (including extensions) original (not amended) return and an election under paragraph (b)(1)(vii) of this section was made). Such a material failure to comply shall extend the period for assessment of tax until three years after the date on which the Internal Revenue Service receives actual notice of the failure to comply.

(2) *Reasonable cause exception.*—If a person that is permitted under § 1.367(a)-3(b) or (c) to enter into an agreement (described in paragraph (b) of this section) fails to file the agreement in a timely manner, as provided in paragraph (a)(1) of this section, or fails to comply in any material respect with the requirements of this section or with the terms of an agreement submitted pursuant hereto, the provisions of paragraph (c)(1) of this section shall not apply if the person is able to show that such failure was due to reasonable cause and not willful neglect and if the person files the agreement or reaches compliance as soon as he becomes aware of the failure. Whether a failure to file in a timely manner, or materially comply, was due to reasonable cause shall be determined by the district director under all the facts and circumstances.

(d) *Use of security.*—The U.S. transferor may be required to furnish a bond or other security that satisfies the requirements of § 301.7101-1 of this chapter if the district director determines that such security is necessary to ensure the payment of any tax on the gain realized but not recognized upon the initial transfer. Such bond or security will generally be required only if the stock or securities transferred are a principal asset of the transferor and the director has reason to believe that a disposition of the stock or securities may be contemplated.

(e) *Disposition (in whole or in part) of stock of transferred corporation.*—(1) *In general.*—(i) *Definition of disposition.*—For purposes of this section, a disposition of the stock of the transferred corporation that triggers gain under the gain recognition agreement includes any taxable sale or any disposition treated as an exchange under this subtitle, (e.g., under sections 301(c)(3)(A), 302(a), 311, 336, 351(b) or section 356(a)(1)), as well as any deemed disposition described under paragraph (e)(3) of this section. It does not include a disposition that is not treated as an exchange, (e.g., under section 302(d) or 356(a)(2)). A disposition of all or a portion of the stock of the transferred corporation by installment sale is treated as a disposition of such stock in the year of the installment sale. A disposition of the stock of the transferred corporation does not include certain transfers treated as nonrecognition transfers (under paragraph (g) of this section) in which the gain recognition agreement is retained but modified, or certain transfers (under paragraph (h) of this section) in which the gain recognition agreement is terminated and has no further effect.

(ii) *Example.*—The provisions of this paragraph (e) are illustrated by the following example:

Example. Interaction between trigger of gain recognition agreement and subpart F rules—(i) *Facts.* A U.S. corporation (USP) owns all of the stock of two foreign corporations, CFC1 and CFC2. USP's section 1248 amount with respect to CFC2 is $30. USP has a basis of $50 in its stock of CFC2; CFC2 has a value of $100. In a transaction described in section 351 and 368(a)(1)(B), USP transfers the stock of CFC2 in exchange for additional stock of CFC1. The transaction is subject to both sections 367(a) and (b). See §§ 1.367(a)-3(b) and 1.367(b)-1(a). To qualify for nonrecognition treatment under section 367(a), USP enters into a 5-year gain recognition agreement for $50 under this section. No election under paragraph 8(b)(1)(vii) of this section is made. USP also complies with the notice requirement under § 1.367(b)-1(c).

(ii) *Trigger of gain recognition agreement with no election.* Assume that in year 2, CFC1 sells the stock of CFC2 for $120, and that there were no distributions by CFC2 prior to the sale. USP must amend its return for the year of the initial transfer and include $50 in income (with interest), $30 of which will be recharacterized as a dividend pursuant to section 1248. As a result, CFC1 has a basis of $100 in CFC2. As a result of the sale of CFC2 stock by CFC1, USP will have $20 of subpart F foreign personal holding company income. See section 951, et. seq., and the regulations thereunder.

(iii) *Trigger of gain recognition agreement with election.* Assume the same facts as in paragraphs (i) and (ii) of this *Example*, except that when USP attached the gain recognition agreement to its timely filed Federal income tax return for the year of the initial transfer, it elected under paragraph (b)(1)(vii) of this section to include the amount of gain realized but not recognized on the initial transfer, $50, in the year of the triggering event rather than in the year of the initial transfer. In such case, the result is the same as in paragraph (e)(1)(ii)(B) of this section, except that USP will include the $50 of gain on its year 2 return, together with interest. For purposes of determining the dividend component, if any, of the $50 inclusion, USP will take into account the section 1248 amount of CFC2 at the time of the disposition in Year 2.

(2) *Partial disposition.*—If the transferee foreign corporation disposes of (or is deemed to dispose of) only a portion of the transferred stock or securities, then the U.S. transferor is

required to recognize only a proportionate amount of the gain realized but not recognized upon the initial transfer of the transferred property. The proportion required to be recognized shall be determined by reference to the relative fair market values of the transferred stock or securities disposed of and retained. Solely for purposes of determining whether the U.S. transferor must recognize income under the agreement described in paragraph (b) of this section, in the case of transferred property (including stock or securities) that is fungible with other property owned by the transferee foreign corporation, a disposition by such corporation of any such property shall be deemed to be a disposition of no less than a ratable portion of the transferred property.

(3) *Deemed dispositions of stock of transferred corporation.*—(i) *Disposition by transferred corporation of substantially all of its assets.*—(A) *In general.*—Unless an exception applies (as described in paragraph (e)(3)(i)(B) of this section), a transferee foreign corporation will be treated as having disposed of the stock or securities of the transferred corporation if, within the term of the gain recognition agreement, the transferred corporation makes a disposition of substantially all (within the meaning of section 368(a)(1)(C)) of its assets (including stock in a subsidiary corporation or an interest in a partnership). If the initial transfer that necessitated the gain recognition agreement was an indirect stock transfer, see § 1.367(a)-3(d)(2)(v). If the transferred corporation is a U.S. corporation, see paragraph (h)(2) of this section.

(B) The transferee foreign corporation will not be deemed to have disposed of the stock of the transferred corporation if the transferred corporation is liquidated into the transferee foreign corporation under sections 337 and 332, provided that the transferee foreign corporation does not dispose of substantially all of the assets formerly held by the transferred corporation (and considered for purposes of the substantially all determination) within the remaining period during which the gain recognition agreement is in effect. A nonrecognition transfer is not counted for purposes of the substantially all determination as a disposition if the transfer satisfies the requirements of paragraph (g)(3) of this section. A disposition does not include a compulsory transfer as described in § 1.367(a)-4T(f) that was not reasonably foreseeable by the U.S. transferor at the time of the initial transfer.

(ii) *U.S. transferor becomes a non-citizen nonresident.*—If a U.S. transferor loses U.S. citizenship or a long-term resident ceases to be taxed as a lawful permanent resident (as defined in section 877(e)(2)), then immediately prior to the date that the U.S. transferor loses U.S. citizenship or ceases to be taxed as a long-term resident, the gain recognition agreement will be triggered as if the transferee foreign corporation disposed of all of the stock of the transferred corporation in a taxable transaction on such date. No additional inclusion is required under section 877, and a gain recognition agreement under section 877 may not be used to avoid taxation under section 367(a) resulting from the trigger of the section 367(a) gain recognition agreement.

(f) *Effect on gain recognition agreement if U.S. transferor goes out of existence.*—(1) *In general.*—If an individual transferor that has entered into an agreement under paragraph (b) of this section dies, or if a U.S. trust or estate that has entered into an agreement under paragraph (b) of this section goes out of existence and is not required to recognize gain as a consequence thereof with respect to all of the stock of the transferee foreign corporation received in the initial transfer and not previously disposed of, then the gain recognition agreement will be triggered unless one of the following requirements is met—

(i) The person winding up the affairs of the transferor retains, for the duration of the waiver of the statute of limitations relating to the gain recognition agreement, assets to meet any possible liability of the transferor under the duration of the agreement;

(ii) The person winding up the affairs of the transferor provides security as provided under paragraph (d) of this section for any possible liability of the transferor under the agreement; or

(iii) The transferor obtains a ruling from the Internal Revenue Service providing for successors to the transferor under the gain recognition agreement.

(2) *Special rule when U.S. transferor is a corporation.*—(i) *U.S. transferor goes out of existence pursuant to the transaction.*—If the transferor is a U.S. corporation that goes out of existence in a transaction in which the transferor's gain would have qualified for nonrecognition treatment under § 1.367(a)-3(b) or (c) had the U.S. transferor remained in existence and entered into a gain recognition agreement, then the gain may generally qualify for nonrecognition treatment only if the U.S. transferor is owned by a single U.S. parent corporation and the U.S. transferor and its parent corporation file a consolidated Federal income tax return for the taxable year that includes the transfer, and the parent of the consolidated group enters into the gain recognition agreement. However, notwithstanding the preceding sentence, a U.S. transferor that was controlled (within the

meaning of section 368(c)) by five or fewer domestic corporations may request a ruling that, if certain conditions prescribed by the Internal Revenue Service are satisfied, the transaction may qualify for nonrecognition treatment.

(ii) *U.S. corporate transferor is liquidated after gain recognition agreement is filed.*—If a U.S. transferor files a gain recognition agreement but is liquidated during the term of the gain recognition agreement, such agreement will be terminated if the liquidation does not qualify as a tax-free liquidation under sections 337 and 332 and the U.S. transferor includes in income any gain from the liquidation. If the liquidation qualifies for nonrecognition treatment under sections 337 and 332, the gain recognition agreement will be triggered unless the U.S. parent corporation and the U.S. transferor file a consolidated Federal income tax return for the taxable year that includes the dates of the initial transfer and the liquidation of the U.S. transferor, and the U.S. parent enters into a new gain recognition agreement and complies with reporting requirements similar to those contained in paragraph (g)(2) of this section.

(g) *Effect on gain recognition agreement of certain nonrecognition transactions.*—(1) *Certain nonrecognition transfers of stock or securities of the transferee foreign corporation by the U.S. transferor.*—If the U.S. transferor disposes of any stock of the transferee foreign corporation in a nonrecognition transfer and the U.S. transferor complies with reporting requirements similar to those contained in paragraph (g)(2) of this section, the U.S. transferor shall continue to be subject to the terms of the gain recognition agreement in its entirety.

(2) *Certain nonrecognition transfers of stock or securities of the transferred corporation by the transferee foreign corporation.*—(i) If, during the period the gain recognition agreement is in effect, the transferee foreign corporation disposes of all or a portion of the stock of the transferred corporation in a transaction in which gain or loss would not be required to be recognized by the transferee foreign corporation under U.S. income tax principles, such disposition will not be treated as a disposition within the meaning of paragraph (e) of this section if the transferee foreign corporation receives (or is deemed to receive), in exchange for the property disposed of, stock in a corporation, or an interest in a partnership, that acquired the transferred property (or receives stock in a corporation that controls the corporation acquiring the transferred property); and the U.S. transferor complies with the requirements of paragraphs (g)(2)(ii) through (iv) of this section.

(ii) The U.S. transferor must provide a notice of the transfer with its next annual certification under paragraph (b)(5) of this section, setting forth—

(A) A description of the transfer;

(B) The applicable nonrecognition provision; and

(C) The name, address, and taxpayer identification number (if any) of the new transferee of the transferred property.

(iii) The U.S. transferor must provide with its next annual certification a new agreement to recognize gain (in accordance with the rules of paragraph (b) of this section) if, prior to the close of the fifth full taxable year following the taxable year of the initial transfer, either—

(A) The initial transferee foreign corporation disposes of the interest (if any) which it received in exchange for the transferred property (other than in a disposition which itself qualifies under the rules of this paragraph (g)(2)); or

(B) The corporation or partnership that acquired the property disposes of such property (other than in a disposition which itself qualifies under the rules of this paragraph (g)(2)); or

(C) There is any other disposition that has the effect of an indirect disposition of the transferred property.

(iv) If the U.S. transferor is required to enter into a new gain recognition agreement, as provided in paragraph (g)(2)(iii) of this section, the U.S. transferor must provide with its next annual certification (described in paragraph (b)(5) of this section) a statement that arrangements have been made, in connection with the nonrecognition transfer, ensuring that the U.S. transferor will be informed of any subsequent disposition of property with respect to which recognition of gain would be required under the agreement.

(3) *Certain nonrecognition transfers of assets by the transferred corporation.*—A disposition by the transferred corporation of all or a portion of its assets in a transaction in which gain or loss would not be required to be recognized by the transferred corporation under U.S. income tax principles, will not be treated as a disposition within the meaning of paragraph (e)(3) of this section if the transferred corporation receives in exchange stock or securities in a corporation or an interest in a partnership that acquired the assets of the transferred corporation (or receives stock in a corporation that controls the corporation acquiring the assets). If the transaction would be treated as a disposi-

tion of substantially all of the transferred corporation's assets, the preceding sentence shall only apply if the U.S. transferor complies with reporting requirements comparable to those of paragraphs (g)(2)(ii) through (iv) of this section, providing for notice, an agreement to recognize gain in the case of a direct or indirect disposition of the assets previously held by the transferred corporation, and an assurance that necessary information will be provided to appropriate parties.

(h) *Transactions that terminate the gain recognition agreement.*—(1) *Taxable disposition of stock or securities of transferee foreign corporation by U.S. transferor.*—(i) If the U.S. transferor disposes of all of the stock of the transferee foreign corporation that it received in the initial transfer in a transaction in which all realized gain (if any) is recognized currently, then the gain recognition agreement shall terminate and have no further effect. If the transferor disposes of a portion of the stock of the transferee foreign corporation that it received in the initial transfer in a taxable transaction, then in the event that the gain recognition agreement is later triggered, the transferor shall be required to recognize only a proportionate amount of the gain subject to the gain recognition agreement that would otherwise be required to be recognized on a subsequent disposition of the transferred property under the rules of paragraph (b)(2) of this section. The proportion required to be recognized shall be determined by reference to the percentage of stock (by value) of the transferee foreign corporation received in the initial transfer that is retained by the United States transferor.

(ii) The rule of this paragraph (h) is illustrated by the following example:

Example. A, a United States citizen, owns 100 percent of the outstanding stock of foreign corporation X. In a transaction described in section 351, A exchanges his stock in X (and other assets) for 100 percent of the outstanding voting and nonvoting stock of foreign corporation Y. A submits an agreement under the rules of this section to recognize gain upon a later disposition. In the following year, A disposes of 60 percent of the fair market value of the stock of Y, thus terminating 60 percent of the gain recognition agreement. One year thereafter, Y disposes of 50 percent of the fair market value of the stock of X. A is required to include in his income in the year of the later disposition 20 percent (40 percent interest in Y multiplied by a 50 percent disposition of X) of the gain that A realized but did not recognize on his initial transfer of X stock to Y.

(2) *Certain dispositions by a domestic transferred corporation of substantially all of its assets.*—If the transferred corporation is a domestic corporation and the U.S. transferor and the transferred corporation filed a consolidated Federal income tax return at the time of the transfer, the gain recognition agreement shall terminate and cease to have effect if, during the term of such agreement, the transferred corporation disposes of substantially all of its assets in a transaction in which all realized gain is recognized currently. If an indirect stock transfer necessitated the filing of the gain recognition agreement, such agreement shall terminate if, immediately prior to the indirect transfer, the U.S. transferor and the acquired corporation filed a consolidated return (or, in the case of a section 368(a)(1)(A) and (a)(2)(E) reorganization described in §1.367(a)-3(d)(1)(ii), the U.S. transferor and the acquiring corporation filed a consolidated return) and the transferred corporation disposes of substantially all of its assets (taking into account §1.367(a)-3(d)(2)(v)) in a transaction in which all realized gain is recognized currently.

(3) *Distribution by transferee foreign corporation of stock of transferred corporation that qualifies under section 355 or section 337.*—If, during the term of the gain recognition agreement, the transferee foreign corporation distributes to the U.S. transferor, in a transaction that qualifies under section 355, or in a liquidating distribution that qualifies under sections 332 and 337, the stock that initially necessitated the filing of the gain recognition agreement (and any additional stock received after the initial transfer), the gain recognition agreement shall terminate and have no further effect, provided that immediately after the section 355 distribution or section 332 liquidation, the U.S. transferor's basis in the transferred stock is less than or equal to the basis that it had in the transferred stock immediately prior to the initial transfer that necessitated the GRA.

(i) *Effective date.*—The rules of this section shall apply to transfers that occur on or after July 20, 1998. For matters covered in this section for periods before July 20, 1998, the corresponding rules of §1.367(a)-3T(g) (see 26 CFR part 1, revised April 1, 1998) and Notice 87-85 ((1987-2 C.B. 395); see §601.601(d)(2)(ii) of this chapter) apply. In addition, if a U.S. transferor entered into a gain recognition agreement for transfers prior to July 20, 1998, then the rules of §1.367(a)-3T(g) (see 26 CFR part 1, revised April 1, 1998) shall continue to apply in lieu of this section in the event of any direct or indirect nonrecognition transfer of the same property. See, also, §1.367(a)-3(f). [Reg. §1.367(a)-8.]

☐ [T.D. 8770, 6-18-98.]

§ 1.367(b)-1. Other transfers.

(a) *Scope.*—The regulations promulgated under section 367(b) (the section 367(b) regulations) set forth rules regarding the proper inclusions and adjustments that must be made as a result of an exchange described in section 367(b) (a section 367(b) exchange). A section 367(b) exchange is any exchange described in section 332, 351, 354, 355, 356 or 361, with respect to which the status of a foreign corporation as a corporation is relevant for determining the extent to which income shall be recognized or for determining the effect of the transaction on earnings and profits, basis of stock or securities, basis of assets, or other relevant tax attributes. Notwithstanding the preceding sentence, a section 367(b) exchange does not include a transfer to the extent the foreign corporation fails to be treated as a corporation by reason of section 367(a)(1). See § 1.367(a)-3(b)(2)(ii) for an illustration of the interaction of section 367(a) and (b).

(b) *General rules.*—(1) *Rules.*—The following general rules apply under the section 367(b) regulations—

(i) A foreign corporation in a section 367(b) exchange is considered to be a corporation and, as a result, all of the related provisions (e.g., section 381) shall apply, except to the extent provided in the section 367(b) regulations; and

(ii) Nothing in the section 367(b) regulations shall permit—

(A) The nonrecognition of income that would otherwise be required to be recognized under another provision of the Internal Revenue Code or the regulations thereunder; or

(B) The recognition of a loss or deduction that would otherwise not be recognized under another provision of the Internal Revenue Code or the regulations thereunder.

(2) *Example.*—The following example illustrates the rules of this paragraph (b):

Example—(i) *Facts.* DC, a domestic corporation, owns 90 percent of P, a partnership. The remaining 10 percent of P is owned by a person unrelated to DC. P owns all of the outstanding stock of FC, a controlled foreign corporation. FC liquidates into P.

(ii) *Result.* FC's liquidation is not a transaction described in section 332. Nothing in the section 367(b) regulations, including § 1.367(b)-2(k), permits FC's liquidation to qualify as a liquidation described in section 332.

(c) *Notice required.*—(1) *In general.*—A notice under this paragraph (c) (section 367(b) notice) must be filed with regard to any person described in paragraph (c)(2) of this section. A section 367(b) notice must be filed in the time and manner described in paragraph (c)(3) of this section and must include the information described in paragraph (c)(4) of this section.

(2) *Persons subject to section 367(b) notice.*—The following persons are described in this paragraph (c)(2)—

(i) A shareholder described in § 1.367(b)-3(b)(1) that realizes income in a transaction described in § 1.367(b)-3(a);

(ii) A shareholder that makes the election described in § 1.367(b)-3(c)(3);

(iii) A shareholder described in § 1.367(b)-4(b)(1)(i)(A)(*1*) or (*2*) that realizes income in a transaction described in § 1.367(b)-4(a); and

(iv) A shareholder that realizes income in a transaction described in § 1.367(b)-5(c) or 1.367(b)-5(d) and that is either—

(A) A section 1248 shareholder of the distributing or controlled corporation; or

(B) A foreign corporation with one or more shareholders that are described in paragraph (c)(2)(iv)(A) of this section.

(3) *Time and manner for filing notice.*—(i) *United States persons described in § 1.367(b)-1(c)(2).*—A United States person described in paragraph (c)(2) of this section must file a section 367(b) notice attached to a timely filed Federal tax return (including extensions) for the person's taxable year in which income is realized in the section 367(b) exchange. In the case of a shareholder that makes the election described in § 1.367(b)-3(c)(3), notification of such election must be sent to the foreign acquired corporation (or its successor in interest) on or before the date the section 367(b) notice is filed, so that appropriate corresponding adjustments can be made in accordance with the rules of § 1.367(b)-2(e).

(ii) *Foreign corporations described in § 1.367(b)-1(c)(2).*—Each United States person listed in this paragraph (c)(3)(ii) must file a section 367(b) notice with regard to a foreign corporation described in paragraph (c)(2) of this section. Such notice must be attached to a timely filed Federal tax return (including extensions) for the United States person's taxable year in which income is realized in the section 367(b) exchange and, if the United States person is required to file a Form 5471 (Information Return of U.S. Persons With Respect To Certain Foreign Corporations), the section 367(b) notice must be attached to the Form 5471. The following persons are listed in this paragraph (c)(3)(ii)—

(A) United States shareholders (as defined in §1.367(b)-3(b)(2)) of foreign corporations described in paragraph (c)(2)(i) of this section; and

(B) Section 1248 shareholders of foreign corporations described in paragraph (c)(2)(iii) or (iv) of this section.

(4) *Information required.*—Except as provided in paragraph (c)(5) of this section, a section 367(b) notice shall include the following information—

(i) A statement that the exchange is a section 367(b) exchange;

(ii) A complete description of the exchange;

(iii) A description of any stock, securities or other consideration transferred or received in the exchange;

(iv) A statement that describes any amount required, under the section 367(b) regulations, to be taken into account as income or loss or as an adjustment to basis, earnings and profits, or other tax attributes as a result of the exchange;

(v) Any information that is or would be required to be furnished with a Federal income tax return pursuant to regulations under section 332, 351, 354, 355, 356, 361 or 368 (whether or not a Federal income tax return is required to be filed), if such information has not otherwise been provided by the person filing the section 367(b) notice;

(vi) Any information required to be furnished with respect to the exchange under sections 6038, 6038A, 6038B, 6038C or 6046, or the regulations under those sections, if such information has not otherwise been provided by the person filing the section 367(b) notice; and

(vii) If applicable, a statement that the shareholder is making the election described in §1.367(b)-3(c)(3). This statement must include—

(A) A copy of the information the shareholder received from the foreign acquired corporation (or its successor in interest) establishing and substantiating the shareholder's all earnings and profits amount with respect to the shareholder's stock in the foreign acquired corporation; and

(B) A representation that the shareholder has notified the foreign acquired corporation (or its successor in interest) that the shareholder is making the election described in §1.367(b)-3(c)(3).

(5) *Abbreviated notice provision for shareholders that make the election described in §1.367(b)-3(c)(3).*—In the case of a foreign acquired corporation that has never had earnings and profits that would result in any shareholder having an all earnings and profits amount, a shareholder making the election described in §1.367(b)-3(c)(3) may satisfy the information requirements of paragraph (c)(4) of this section by filing a section 367(b) notice that includes—

(i) A statement from the foreign acquired corporation (or its successor in interest) that the foreign acquired corporation has never had any earnings and profits that would result in any shareholder having an all earnings and profits amount; and

(ii) The information described in paragraphs (c)(4)(i) through (iii) of this section.

(6) *Supplemental published guidance.*—The section 367(b) notice requirements may be updated or amended by revenue procedure or other published guidance. [Reg. §1.367(b)-1.]

☐ [*T.D.* 8770, 6-18-98. *Amended by T.D.* 8862, 1-21-2000 (*corrected* 11-3-2000).]

Proposed Amendments to Regulation

§1.367(b)-1. Other transfers.

* * *

(c) * * *

(2) * * *

(v) A foreign surviving corporation described in §1.367(b)-7(a);

(vi) A distributing corporation that is subject to the rules of §1.367(b)-8; and

(vii) A controlled corporation that is subject to the rules of §1.367(b)-8.

(3) * * *

(ii) * * *

(A) United States shareholders (as defined in §1.367(b)-3(b)(2)) of foreign corporations described in paragraph (c)(2)(i), (v), (vi), or (vii) of this section; and

* * *

(4) * * *

(iv) A statement that describes any amount (or amounts) required, under the section 367(b) regulations, to be taken into account as income or loss or as an adjustment (including an adjustment under §1.367(b)-7, 1.367(b)-8, or 1.367(b)-9) to basis, earnings and profits, or other tax attributes as a result of the exchange;

(v) Any information that is or would be required to be furnished with a Federal income tax return pursuant to regulations under section 332, 351, 354, 355, 356, 361, 368, or 381 (whether or not a Federal income tax return is required to be filed), if such information has not otherwise been provided by the person filing the section 367(b) notice;

* * *

[Prop. Reg. §1.367(b)-1.]

[Proposed 11-15-2000.]

§ 1.367(b)-2. Definitions and special rules.—(a) *Controlled foreign corporation.*—The term *controlled foreign corporation* means a controlled foreign corporation as defined in section 957 (taking into account section 953(c)).

(b) *Section 1248 shareholder.*—The term *section 1248 shareholder* means any United States person that satisfies the ownership requirements of section 1248(a)(2) or (c)(2) with respect to a foreign corporation.

(c) *Section 1248 amount.*—(1) *Rule.*—The term *section 1248 amount* with respect to stock in a foreign corporation means the net positive earnings and profits (if any) that would have been attributable to such stock and includible in income as a dividend under section 1248 and the regulations thereunder if the stock were sold by the shareholder. In the case of a transaction in which the shareholder is a foreign corporation (foreign shareholder), the following additional rules shall apply—

(i) The foreign shareholder shall be deemed to be a United States person for purposes of this paragraph (c), except that the foreign shareholder shall not be considered a United States person for purposes of determining whether the stock owned by the foreign shareholder is stock of a controlled foreign corporation; and

(ii) The foreign shareholder's holding period in the stock of the foreign corporation shall be determined by reference to the period that the foreign shareholder's section 1248 shareholders held (directly or indirectly) an interest in the foreign corporation. This paragraph (c)(1)(ii) applies in addition to the section 1248 regulations' incorporation of section 1223 holding periods, as modified by § 1.367(b)-4(d) (as applicable).

(2) *Examples.*—The following examples illustrate the rules of this paragraph (c):

Example 1—(i) *Facts*. DC, a domestic corporation, owns all of the outstanding stock of FC1, a controlled foreign corporation (CFC). FC1 owns all of the outstanding stock of FC2, a CFC. DC has always owned all of the stock of FC1, and FC1 has always owned all of the stock of FC2.

(ii) *Result*. Under this paragraph (c), DC's section 1248 amount with respect to its FC1 stock is computed by reference to all of FC1's and FC2's earnings and profits. See section 1248(c)(2). Because FC1's section 1248 shareholder (DC) always indirectly held all of the stock of FC2, FC1's section 1248 amount with respect to its FC2 stock is computed by reference to all of FC2's earnings and profits.

Example 2—(i) *Facts*. DC, a domestic corporation, owns 40 percent of the outstanding stock of FC1, a foreign corporation. The other 60 percent of FC1 stock is owned (directly and indirectly) by foreign persons that are unrelated to DC. FC1 owns all of the outstanding stock of FC2, a foreign corporation. On January 1, 2001, DC purchases the remaining 60 percent of FC1 stock.

(ii) *Result*. Under this paragraph (c), DC's section 1248 amount with respect to its FC1 stock is computed by reference to FC1's and FC2's earnings and profits that accumulated on or after January 1, 2001, the date FC1 and FC2 became controlled foreign corporations (CFCs). See section 1248(a). Because FC1 is not considered a United States person for purposes of determining whether FC2 is a CFC, FC1's section 1248 amount with respect to its FC2 stock is computed by reference to FC2's earnings and profits that accumulated on or after January 1, 2001, the date FC2 became an actual CFC.

Example 3—(i) *Facts*. FC1, a foreign corporation, owns all of the outstanding stock of FC2, a foreign corporation. DC is a domestic corporation that is unrelated to FC1, FC2, and their direct and indirect owners. On January 1, 2001, DC purchases all of the outstanding stock of FC1.

(ii) *Result*. Under this paragraph (c), DC's section 1248 amount with respect to its FC1 stock is computed by reference to FC1's and FC2's earnings and profits that accumulated on or after January 1, 2001, the first day DC held the stock of FC1. See section 1248(a). FC1's section 1248 amount with respect to its FC2 stock is computed by reference to FC2's earnings and profits that accumulated on or after January 1, 2001, the first day FC1's section 1248 shareholder (DC) indirectly held the stock of FC2.

Example 4—(i) *Facts*. DC, a domestic corporation, directly owns all of the outstanding stock of FC1 and FC2, controlled foreign corporations. DC has always owned all of the stock of FC1 and FC2. On January 1, 2001, DC contributes all of the stock of FC2 to FC1 in a nonrecognition exchange that does not require an income inclusion under the section 367(a) or 367(b) regulations. See §§ 1.367(a)-8 and 1.367(b)-4.

(ii) *Result*. Under this paragraph (c), DC's section 1248 amount with respect to its FC1 stock is computed by reference to all of FC1's and FC2's earnings and profits. See section 1248(c)(2). Because FC1's section 1248 shareholder (DC) always held (directly or indirectly) all of the stock of FC2, FC1's section 1248 amount with respect to its FC2 stock is computed by reference to all of FC2's earnings and profits.

(d) *All earnings and profits amount.*—(1) *General rule.*—The term *all earnings and profits amount* with respect to stock in a foreign corporation means the net positive earnings and profits (if any) determined as provided under paragraph (d)(2) of this section and attributable to such stock as provided under paragraph (d)(3) of this section. The all earnings and profits amount shall be determined without regard to the amount of gain that would be realized on a sale or exchange of the stock of the foreign corporation.

(2) *Rules for determining earnings and profits.*—(i) *Domestic rules generally applicable.*—For purposes of this paragraph (d), except as provided in sections 312(k)(4) and (n)(8), 964 and 986, the earnings and profits of a foreign corporation for any taxable year shall be determined according to principles substantially similar to those applicable to domestic corporations.

(ii) *Certain adjustments to earnings and profits.*—Notwithstanding paragraph (d)(2)(i) of this section, for purposes of this paragraph (d), the earnings and profits of a foreign corporation for any taxable year shall not include the amounts specified in section 1248(d). In the case of amounts specified in section 1248(d)(4), the preceding sentence requires that the earnings and profits for any taxable year be decreased by the net positive amount (if any) of earnings and profits attributable to activities described in section 1248(d)(4), and increased by the net reduction (if any) in earnings and profits attributable to activities described in section 1248(d)(4).

(iii) *Effect of section 332 liquidating distribution.*—The all earnings and profits amount with respect to stock of a corporation that distributes all of its property in a liquidation described in section 332 shall be determined without regard to the adjustments prescribed by section 312(a) and (b) resulting from the distribution of such property in liquidation, except that gain or loss realized by the corporation on the distribution shall be taken into account to the extent provided in section 312(f)(1). See § 1.367(b)-3(b)(3)(ii) *Example 3.*

(3) *Amount attributable to a block of stock.*—(i) *Application of section 1248 principles.*—(A) *In general.*—(1) *Rule.*—The all earnings and profits amount with respect to stock of a foreign corporation is determined according to the attribution principles of section 1248 and the regulations thereunder. The attribution principles of section 1248 shall apply without regard to the requirements of section 1248 that are not relevant to the determination of a shareholder's pro rata portion of earnings and profits. Thus, for example, the all earnings and profits amount is determined without regard to whether the foreign corporation was a controlled foreign corporation at any time during the five years preceding the section 367(b) exchange in question, without regard to whether the shareholder owned a 10 percent or greater interest in the stock, and without regard to whether the earnings and profits of the foreign corporation were accumulated in post-1962 taxable years or while the corporation was a controlled foreign corporation.

(2) *Example.*—The following example illustrates the rules of this paragraph (d)(3)(i)(A):

Example—(i) *Facts.* On January 1, 2001, DC, a domestic corporation, purchases 9 percent of the outstanding stock of FC, a foreign corporation. On January 1, 2002, DC purchases an additional 1 percent of FC stock. On January 1, 2003, DC exchanges its stock in FC in a section 367(b) exchange in which DC is required to include the all earnings and profits amount in income. FC was not a controlled foreign corporation during the entire period DC held its FC stock.

(ii) *Result.* The all earnings and profits amount with respect to DC's stock in FC is computed by reference to 9 percent of FC's earnings and profits from January 1, 2001, through December 31, 2001, and by reference to 10 percent of FC's earnings and profits from January 1, 2002, through January 1, 2003.

(B) *Foreign shareholders.*—In the case of a transaction in which the exchanging shareholder is a foreign corporation (foreign shareholder), the following additional rules shall apply—

(1) The attribution principles of section 1248 shall apply without regard to whether the person directly owning the stock is a United States person; and

(2) The foreign shareholder's holding period in the stock of the foreign acquired corporation shall be determined by reference to the period that the foreign shareholder's United States shareholders (as defined in § 1.367(b)-3(b)(2)) held (directly or indirectly) an interest in the foreign acquired corporation. This paragraph (d)(3)(i)(B)(2) applies in addition to the section 1248 regulations' incorporation of section 1223 holding periods, as modified by paragraph (d)(3)(ii) of this section and § 1.367(b)-4(d) (as applicable).

(ii) *Limitation on amounts attributable to holding periods determined under section 1223.*—(A) *Rule.*—In applying the attribution principles of section 1248 and the regulations

Reg. § 1.367(b)-2(d)(3)(ii)(A)

thereunder to determine the all earnings and profits amount with respect to the stock of a foreign corporation, earnings and profits attributable to a section 1223(2) holding period that relates to a period of direct ownership of the stock of the foreign corporation by a non-United States person shall not be included, except to the extent of earnings and profits attributable to a period when the stock of the foreign corporation was indirectly owned by United States shareholders (as defined in § 1.367(b)-3(b)(2)).

(B) *Example.*—The following example illustrates the rules of this paragraph (d)(3)(ii):

Example—(i) *Facts.* (A) FC1 is a foreign corporation. The outstanding stock of FC1 is directly owned by the following unrelated persons: 20 percent by DP, a domestic partnership; 20 percent by DC, a domestic corporation; 20 percent by FC, a foreign corporation that is directly and indirectly owned by foreign persons; 20 percent by FP, a foreign partnership that is equally owned by 2 partners, DI, a United States citizen, and FI, a nonresident alien; and 20 percent by a variety of minority shareholders, none of whom owns, applying the ownership rules of section 958, 10 percent or more of the outstanding stock of FC (the small shareholders).

(B) FC1 owns all of the outstanding stock of FC2, a foreign corporation that is not a controlled foreign corporation subject to the rules of section 953(c). FC2 has net positive earnings and profits. In a reorganization described in section 368(a)(1)(B), DA, a domestic corporation, acquires all of the stock of FC2 from FC1 in exchange for DA voting stock.

(ii) *Result.* (A) Under section 1223(2), DA holds the stock of FC2 with a holding period that includes the period that FC2 was held by FC1. As a result, the rules of this paragraph (d)(3)(ii) apply for purposes of computing DA's all earnings and profits amount.

(B) In applying the attribution principles of section 1248, earnings and profits attributable to a section 1223(2) holding period that refers to a period of direct ownership of the stock of a foreign corporation by a non-United States person are not included, except to the extent the stock of the foreign corporation was indirectly owned by United States shareholders as defined in § 1.367(b)-3(b)(2). Accordingly, DA's all earnings and profits amount does not include the FC2 earnings and profits attributable to FC, FI, and the small shareholders. DA's all earnings and profits amount does include the FC2 earnings and profits attributable to DP, DC, and DI. See § 1.367(b)-2(k) for rules concerning the treatment of partnerships under the section 367(b) regulations.

(iii) *Exclusion of lower-tier earnings.*—In applying the attribution principles of section 1248 and the regulations thereunder to determine the all earnings and profits amount with respect to stock of a foreign corporation, the earnings and profits of subsidiaries of the foreign corporation shall not be taken into account notwithstanding section 1248(c)(2).

(e) *Treatment of deemed dividends.*—(1) *In general.*—In certain circumstances these regulations provide that an exchanging shareholder shall include an amount in income as a deemed dividend. This paragraph provides rules for the treatment of the deemed dividend.

(2) *Consequences of dividend characterization.*—A deemed dividend described in paragraph (e)(1) of this section shall be treated as a dividend for purposes of the Internal Revenue Code. The deemed dividend shall be considered as paid out of the earnings and profits with respect to which the amount of the deemed dividend was determined. Thus, for example, a deemed dividend that is determined by reference to the all earnings and profits amount or the section 1248 amount will never be considered as paid out of (and therefore will never reduce) earnings and profits specified in section 1248(d), because such earnings and profits are excluded in computing the all earnings and profits amount (under paragraph (d)(2)(ii) of this section) and the section 1248 amount (under section 1248(d) and paragraph (c)(1) of this section). If the deemed dividend is determined by reference to the earnings and profits of a foreign corporation that is owned indirectly (i.e., through one or more tiers of intermediate owners) by the person that is required to include the deemed dividend in income, the deemed dividend shall be considered as having been paid by such corporation to such person through the intermediate owners, rather than directly to such person.

(3) *Ordering rules.*—In the case of an exchange of stock in which the exchanging shareholder is treated as receiving a deemed dividend from a foreign corporation, the following ordering rules concerning the timing, treatment, and effect of such a deemed dividend shall apply. See also paragraph (j)(2) of this section.

(i) For purposes of the section 367(b) regulations, the gain realized by an exchanging shareholder shall be determined before increasing (as provided in paragraph (e)(3)(ii) of this section) the basis in the stock of the foreign corporation by the amount of the deemed dividend.

(ii) Except as provided in paragraph (e)(3)(i) of this section, the deemed dividend shall be considered to be received immediately before the exchanging shareholder's receipt of consideration for its stock in the foreign corporation, and the shareholder's basis in the stock exchanged shall be increased by the amount of the deemed dividend. Such basis increase shall be taken into account before determining the gain otherwise recognized on the exchange (for example, under section 356), the basis that the exchanging shareholder takes in the property that it receives in the exchange (under section 358(a)(1)), and the basis that the transferee otherwise takes in the transferred stock (under section 362).

(iii) Except as provided in paragraph (e)(3)(i) of this section, the earnings and profits of the appropriate foreign corporation shall be reduced by the deemed dividend amount before determining the consequences of the recognition of gain in excess of the deemed dividend amount (for example, under section 356(a)(2) or sections 356(a)(1) and 1248).

(4) *Examples.*—The following examples illustrate the rules of this paragraph (e):

Example 1. DC, a domestic corporation, exchanges stock in FC, a foreign corporation, in a section 367(b) exchange in which DC includes the all earnings and profits amount in income as a deemed dividend. Under paragraph (e)(2) of this section, a deemed dividend is treated as a dividend for purposes of the Internal Revenue Code. As a result, if the requirements of section 902 are met, DC may qualify for a deemed paid foreign tax credit with respect to the deemed dividend that it receives from FC.

Example 2. DC, a domestic corporation, exchanges stock in FC1, a foreign corporation that is a controlled foreign corporation, in a transaction in which DC is required to include the section 1248 amount in income as a deemed dividend. A portion of the section 1248 amount is determined by reference to the earnings and profits of FC1 (the upper-tier portion of the section 1248 amount), and the remainder of the section 1248 amount is determined by reference to the earnings and profits of FC2, which is a wholly owned foreign subsidiary of FC1 (the lower-tier portion of the section 1248 amount). Under paragraph (e)(2) of this section, DC computes its deemed paid foreign tax credit as if the lower-tier portion of the section 1248 amount were distributed as a dividend by FC2 to FC1, and as if such portion and the upper-tier portion of the section 1248 amount were then distributed as a dividend by FC1 to DC.

Example 3. DC, a domestic corporation, exchanges stock in FC, a foreign corporation that is a controlled foreign corporation, in a transaction in which DC realizes gain of $100 (prior to the application of the section 367(b) regulations). In connection with the transaction, DC is required to include $40 in income as a deemed dividend under the section 367(b) regulations. In addition to receiving property permitted to be received under section 354 without the recognition of gain, DC also receives cash in the amount of $70. Under paragraph (e)(3) of this section, the $40 deemed dividend increases DC's basis in its FC stock before determining the gain to be recognized under section 356. Thus, in applying section 356, DC is considered to realize $60 of gain on the exchange, all of which is recognized under section 356(a)(1).

(f) *Deemed asset transfer and closing of taxable year in certain section 368(a)(1)(F) reorganizations.*—(1) *Scope.*—This paragraph applies to a reorganization described in section 368(a)(1)(F) in which the transferor corporation is a foreign corporation.

(2) *Deemed asset transfer.*—In a reorganization described in paragraph (f)(1) of this section, there is considered to exist—

(i) A transfer of assets by the foreign transferor corporation to the acquiring corporation in exchange for stock (or stock and securities) of the acquiring corporation and the assumption by the acquiring corporation of the foreign transferor corporation's liabilities;

(ii) A distribution of such stock (or stock and securities) by the foreign transferor corporation to its shareholders (or shareholders and security holders); and

(iii) An exchange by the foreign transferor corporation's shareholders (or shareholders and security holders) of their stock (or stock and securities) for stock (or stock and securities) of the acquiring corporation.

(3) *Other applicable rules.*—For purposes of this paragraph (f), it is immaterial that the applicable foreign or domestic law treats the acquiring corporation as a continuation of the foreign transferor corporation.

(4) *Closing of taxable year.*—In a reorganization described in paragraph (f)(1) of this section, the taxable year of the foreign transferor corporation shall end with the close of the date of the transfer and, except as otherwise required under the Internal Revenue Code (e.g. section 1502 and the regulations thereunder), the taxable year of the acquiring corporation shall end with the close of the date on which the transferor's taxable year would have ended but for the occurrence of the reorganization if—

(i) The acquiring corporation is a domestic corporation; or

(ii) The foreign transferor corporation has effectively connected earnings and profits (as defined in section 884(d)) or accumulated effectively connected earnings and profits (as defined in section 884(b)(2)(B)(ii)).

(g) *Stapled stock under section 269B.*—For rules treating a foreign corporation as a domestic corporation if it and a domestic corporation are stapled entities, see section 269B. The deemed conversion of a foreign corporation to a domestic corporation under section 269B is treated as a reorganization under section 368(a)(1)(F).

(h) *Section 953(d) domestication elections.*—(1) *Effect of election.*—A foreign corporation that elects under section 953(d) to be treated as a domestic corporation shall be treated for purposes of section 367(b) as transferring, as of the first day of the first taxable year for which the election is effective, all of its assets to a domestic corporation in a reorganization described in section 368(a)(1)(F). Notwithstanding paragraph (d) of this section, for purposes of determining the consequences of the reorganization under § 1.367(b)-3, the all earnings and profits amount shall not be considered to include earnings and profits accumulated in taxable years beginning before January 1, 1988.

(2) *Post-election exchanges.*—For purposes of applying section 367(b) to post-election exchanges with respect to a corporation that has made a valid election under section 953(d) to be treated as a domestic corporation, such corporation shall be treated as a domestic corporation as to earnings and profits that were taken into account at the time of the section 953(d) election or which accrue after such election, and shall be treated as a foreign corporation as to earnings and profits accumulated in taxable years beginning before January 1, 1988. Thus, for example, if the section 953(d) corporation subsequently transfers its assets to a domestic corporation (other than another section 953(d) corporation) in a transaction described in section 381(a), the rules of § 1.367(b)-3 shall apply to such transaction to the extent of the section 953(d) corporation's earnings and profits accumulated in taxable years beginning before January 1, 1988.

(i) *Section 1504(d) elections.*—An election under section 1504(d), which permits certain foreign corporations to be treated as domestic corporations, is treated as a transfer of property to a domestic corporation and will generally constitute a reorganization described in section 368(a)(1)(F). However, if an election under section 1504(d) is made with respect to a foreign corporation from the first day of the foreign corporation's existence, then the foreign corporation shall be treated as a domestic corporation, and the section 367(b) regulations will not apply.

(j) *Sections 985 through 989.*—(1) *Change in functional currency of a qualified business unit.*—(i) *Rule.*—If, as a result of a transaction described in section 381(a), a qualified business unit (as defined in section 989(a)) (QBU) has a different functional currency determined under the rules of section 985(b) than it used prior to the transaction, then the QBU shall be deemed to have automatically changed its functional currency immediately prior to the transaction. A QBU that is deemed to change its functional currency pursuant to this paragraph (j) must make the adjustments described in § 1.985-5.

(ii) *Example.*—The following example illustrates the rule of this paragraph (j)(1):

Example—(i) *Facts.* DC, a domestic corporation, owns 100 percent of FC1, a foreign corporation. FC1 owns and operates a qualified business unit (QBU) (B1) in France, whose functional currency is the euro. FC2, an unrelated foreign corporation, owns and operates a QBU (B2) in France, whose functional currency is the dollar. FC2 acquires FC1's assets (including B1) in a reorganization described in section 368(a)(1)(C). As a part of the reorganization, B1 and B2 combine their operations into one QBU. Applying the rules of section 985(b), the functional currency of the combined operations of B1 and B2 is the euro.

(ii) *Result.* FC2's acquisition of FC1's assets is a section 367(b) exchange that is described in section 381(a). Because the functional currency of the combined operations of B1 and B2 after the exchange is the euro, B2 is deemed to have automatically changed its functional currency to the euro immediately prior to the section 367(b) exchange. B2 must make the adjustments described in § 1.985-5.

(2) *Previously taxed earnings and profits.*—(i) *Exchanging shareholder that is a United States person.*—If an exchanging shareholder that is a United States person is required to include in income either the all earnings and profits amount or the section 1248 amount under the provisions of § 1.367(b)-3 or 1.367(b)-4, then immediately prior to the exchange, and solely for the purpose of computing exchange gain or loss under section 986(c), the exchanging shareholder shall be treated as receiving a distribution of previously taxed earnings and profits from the appropriate foreign corporation that is attributable (under the principles of section 1248) to the exchanged stock. If an exchanging shareholder that is a United States person is a distributee in an exchange described in § 1.367(b)-5(c) or (d), then immediately prior to the exchange, and solely

for the purpose of computing exchange gain or loss under section 986(c), the exchanging shareholder shall be treated as receiving a distribution of previously taxed earnings and profits from the appropriate foreign corporation to the extent such shareholder has a diminished interest in such previously taxed earnings and profits after the exchange. The exchange gain or loss recognized under this paragraph (j)(2)(i) will increase or decrease the exchanging shareholder's adjusted basis in the stock of the foreign corporation, including for purposes of computing gain or loss realized with respect to the stock on the transaction. The exchanging shareholder's dollar basis with respect to each account of previously taxed income shall be increased or decreased by the exchange gain or loss recognized.

(ii) *Exchanging shareholder that is a foreign corporation.*—If an exchanging shareholder that is a foreign corporation is required to include in income either the all earnings and profits amount or the section 1248 amount under the provisions of § 1.367(b)-3 or 1.367(b)-4, then, immediately prior to the exchange, the exchanging shareholder shall be treated as receiving a distribution of previously taxed earnings and profits from the appropriate foreign corporation that is attributable (under the principles of section 1248) to the exchanged stock. If an exchanging shareholder that is a foreign corporation is a distributee in an exchange described in § 1.367(b)-5(c) or (d), then the exchanging shareholder shall be treated as receiving (immediately prior to the exchange) a distribution of previously taxed earnings and profits from the appropriate foreign corporation. Such distribution shall be measured by the extent to which the exchanging shareholder's direct or indirect United States shareholders (as defined in section 951(b)) have a diminished interest in such previously taxed earnings and profits after the exchange.

(3) *Other rules.*—See sections 985 through 989 for other currency rules that may apply in connection with a section 367(b) exchange.

(k) *Partnerships, trusts and estates.*—In applying the section 367(b) regulations, stock of a corporation that is owned by a foreign partnership, trust or estate shall be considered as owned proportionately by its partners, owners, or beneficiaries under the principles of § 1.367(e)-1(b)(2). Stock owned by an entity that is disregarded as an entity separate from its owner under § 301.7701-3 is owned directly by the owner of such entity. In applying § 1.367(b)-5(b), the principles of § 1.367(e)-1(b)(2) shall also apply to a domestic partnership, trust or estate. [Reg. § 1.367(b)-2.]

☐ [*T.D.* 8397, 2-25-92. *Amended by T.D.* 8862, 1-21-2000 (*corrected* 11-3-2000).]

Proposed Amendments to Regulation

§ 1.367(b)-2. Definitions and special rules.

* * *

(j) *Sections 985 through 989.*—(1) *Change in functional currency of a qualified business unit.*—(i) *Rule.*—If, as a result of a section 367(b) exchange described in section 381(a) or 312(h), a qualified business unit (as defined in section 989(a)) (QBU) has a different functional currency determined under the rules of section 985(b) than it used prior to the transaction, then the QBU shall be deemed to have automatically changed its functional currency immediately prior to the transaction. A QBU that is deemed to change its functional currency pursuant to this paragraph (j) must make the adjustments described in § 1.985-5.

* * *

(3) *Dividend described in section 243(e).*—Dividend distributions by a foreign corporation out of earnings and profits accumulated by a domestic corporation that are eligible for the dividends received deduction under section 243(e) shall not exceed an amount equal to the U.S. dollar value of the earnings and profits at the time the earnings and profits were accumulated by such domestic corporation. See § 1.367(b)-8(c)(3), *Example 1* and *Example 3*.

(4) *Coordination with § 1.367(b)-8(c)(2).*—Solely for purposes of Chapter 3 of subtitle A of the Internal Revenue Code, dividend distributions by a foreign corporation that are treated under § 1.367(b)-8(c)(2) as U.S. source shall not exceed an amount equal to the U.S. dollar value of the earnings and profits at the time allocated to the foreign corporation. See § 1.367(b)-8(c)(3), *Example 1*.

(5) [Paragraph (j)(3) was redesignated as paragraph (j)(5) and new paragraphs (j)(3) and (j)(4) were added to read as above.]

* * *

(l) *Additional definitions.*—(1) *Foreign income taxes.*—The term *foreign income taxes* has the meaning set forth in § 1.902-1(a)(7).

(2) *Post-1986 undistributed earnings.*—The term *post-1986 undistributed earnings* has the meaning set forth in § 1.902-1(a)(9).

(3) *Post-1986 foreign income taxes.*—The term *post-1986 foreign income taxes* has the meaning set forth in § 1.902-1(a)(8).

(4) *Pre-1987 accumulated profits.*—The term *pre-1987 accumulated profits* means the earnings and profits described in § 1.902-1(a)(10)(i), computed in accordance with the rules of § 1.902-1(a)(10)(ii).

(5) *Pre-1987 foreign income taxes.*—The term *pre-1987 foreign income taxes* has the meaning set forth in § 1.902-1(a)(10)(iii).

(6) *Pre-1987 section 960 earnings and profits.*—The term *pre-1987 section 960 earnings and profits* means the earnings and profits of a foreign corporation accumulated in taxable years beginning before January 1, 1987, computed under § 1.964-1(a) through (e), and translated into the functional currency (as determined under section 985) of the foreign corporation at the spot rate on the first day of the foreign corporation's taxable year beginning after December 31, 1986. For further guidance, see Notice 88-70 (1988-2 C.B. 369, 370) (see also § 601.601(d)(2) of this chapter). The term pre-1987 section 960 earnings and profits does not include earnings and profits that represent previously taxed earnings and profits for purposes of section 959.

(7) *Pre-1987 section 960 foreign income taxes.*—The term *pre-1987 section 960 foreign income taxes* means the foreign income taxes related to pre-1987 section 960 earnings and profits, determined in accordance with the rules of § 1.902-1(a)(10)(iii), except that the U.S. dollar amounts of pre-1987 section 960 foreign income taxes are determined by reference to the exchange rates in effect when the taxes were paid or accrued.

(8) *Earnings and profits.*—The term *earnings and profits* means post-1986 undistributed earnings, pre-1987 accumulated profits, and pre-1987 section 960 earnings and profits.

(9) *Look-through corporation.*—The term *look-through corporation* means a foreign corporation that is subject to the look-through rules of section 904(d)(3) or section 904(d)(4) (as in effect for taxable years beginning after December 31, 2002 (the day before the effective date of section 1105(b) of Public Law 105-34 (111 Stat. 788)) and regulations thereunder.

(10) *Non-look-through 10/50 corporation.*—The term *non-look-through 10/50 corporation* means a noncontrolled section 902 corporation as defined in section 904(d)(2)(E) that is not a look-through corporation.

(11) *Less-than-10%-U.S.-owned foreign corporation.*—The term *less-than-10%-U.S.-owned foreign corporation* means a foreign corporation that is neither a look-through corporation nor a non-look-through 10/50 corporation.

(12) *Separate category.*—The term *separate category* has the meaning set forth in section 904(d)(1), and shall also include any other category of income to which section 904(a), (b), and (c) are applied separately under any other provision of the Internal Revenue Code (e.g., sections 56(g)(4)(C)(iii)(IV), 245(a)(10), 865(h), 901(j), and 904(g)(10)).

(13) *Statutory grouping of earnings and profits.*—The term *statutory grouping of earnings and profits* means the earnings and profits from a specific source or activity that must be determined for purposes of applying a provision of the Internal Revenue Code. Compare § 1.861-8(a)(4) (providing an analogous definition for statutory grouping of gross income).

[Prop. Reg. § 1.367(b)-2.]

[Proposed 11-15-2000.]

§ 1.367(b)-3. Repatriation of foreign corporate assets in certain nonrecognition transactions.—(a) *Scope.*—This section applies to an acquisition by a domestic corporation (the domestic acquiring corporation) of the assets of a foreign corporation (the foreign acquired corporation) in a liquidation described in section 332 or an asset acquisition described in section 368(a)(1).

(b) *Exchange of stock owned directly by a United States shareholder or by certain foreign corporate shareholders.*—(1) *Scope.*—This paragraph (b) applies in the case of an exchanging shareholder that is either—

(i) A United States shareholder of the foreign acquired corporation; or

(ii) A foreign corporation with respect to which there are one or more United States shareholders.

(2) *United States shareholder.*—For purposes of this section (and for purposes of the other section 367(b) regulation provisions that specifically refer to this paragraph (b)(2)), the term *United States shareholder* means any shareholder described in section 951(b) (without regard to whether the foreign corporation is a controlled foreign corporation), and also any shareholder described in section 953(c)(1)(A) (but only if the foreign corporation is a controlled foreign corporation as defined in section 953(c)(1)(B) subject to the rules of section 953(c)).

(3) *Income inclusion.*—(i) *Inclusion of all earnings and profits amount.*—An exchanging shareholder shall include in income as a deemed dividend the all earnings and profits amount with respect to its stock in the foreign acquired corporation. For the consequences of the deemed dividend, see § 1.367(b)-2(e). Notwithstanding § 1.367(b)-2(e), however, a

deemed dividend from the foreign acquired corporation to an exchanging foreign corporate shareholder shall not qualify for the exception from foreign personal holding company income provided by section 954(c)(3)(A)(i), although it may qualify for the look-through treatment provided by section 904(d)(3) if the requirements of that section are met with respect to the deemed dividend.

(ii) *Examples.*—The following examples illustrate the rules of paragraph (b)(3)(i) of this section:

Example 1—(i) *Facts.* DC, a domestic corporation, owns all of the outstanding stock of FC, a foreign corporation. The stock of FC has a value of $100, and DC has a basis of $30 in such stock. The all earnings and profits amount attributable to the FC stock owned by DC is $20, of which $15 is described in section 1248(a) and the remaining $5 is not (for example, because it accumulated prior to 1963). FC has a basis of $50 in its assets. In a liquidation described in section 332, FC distributes all of its property to DC, and the FC stock held by DC is canceled.

(ii) *Result.* Under paragraph (b)(3)(i) of this section, DC must include $20 in income as a deemed dividend from FC. Under section 337(a) FC does not recognize gain or loss in the assets that it distributes to DC, and under section 334(b), DC takes a basis of $50 in such assets. Because the requirements of section 902 are met, DC qualifies for a deemed paid foreign tax credit with respect to the deemed dividend that it receives from FC.

Example 2—(i) *Facts.* DC, a domestic corporation, owns all of the outstanding stock of FC, a foreign corporation. The stock of FC has a value of $100, and DC has a basis of $30 in such stock. The all earnings and profits amount attributable to the FC stock owned by DC is $75. FC has a basis of $50 in its assets. In a liquidation described in section 332, FC distributes all of its property to DC, and the FC stock held by DC is canceled.

(ii) *Result.* Under paragraph (b)(3)(i) of this section, DC must include $75 in income as a deemed dividend from FC. Under section 337(a) FC does not recognize gain or loss in the assets that it distributes to DC, and under section 334(b), DC takes a basis of $50 in such assets. Because the requirements of section 902 are met, DC qualifies for a deemed paid foreign tax credit with respect to the deemed dividend that it receives from FC.

Example 3—(i) *Facts.* DC, a domestic corporation, owns 80 percent of the outstanding stock of FC, a foreign corporation. DC has owned its 80 percent interest in FC since FC was incorporated. The remaining 20 percent of the outstanding stock of FC is owned by a person unrelated to DC (the minority shareholder). The stock of FC owned by DC has a value of $80, and DC has a basis of $24 in such stock. The stock of FC owned by the minority shareholder has a value of $20, and the minority shareholder has a basis of $18 in such stock. FC's only asset is land having a value of $100, and FC has a basis of $50 in the land. Gain on the land would not generate earnings and profits qualifying under section 1248(d) for an exclusion from earnings and profits for purposes of section 1248. FC has earnings and profits of $20 (determined under the rules of § 1.367(b)-2(d)(2)(i) and (ii)), $16 of which is attributable to the stock owned by DC under the rules of § 1.367(b)-2(d)(3). FC subdivides the land and distributes to the minority shareholder land with a value of $20 and a basis of $10. As part of the same transaction, in a liquidation described in section 332, FC distributes the remainder of its land to DC, and the FC stock held by DC and the minority shareholder is canceled.

(ii) *Result.* Under section 336, FC must recognize the $10 of gain it realizes in the land it distributes to the minority shareholder, and under section 331 the minority shareholder recognizes its gain of $2 in the stock of FC. Such gain is included in income by the minority shareholder as a dividend to the extent provided in section 1248 if the minority shareholder is a United States person that is described in section 1248(a)(2). Under § 1.367(b)-2(d)(2)(iii), the $10 of gain recognized by FC increases its earnings and profits for purposes of computing the all earnings and profits amount and, as a result, $8 of such increase (80 percent of $10) is considered to be attributable to the FC stock owned by DC under § 1.367(b)-2(d)(3)(i)(A)(*1*). DC's all earnings and profits amount with respect to its stock in FC is $24 (the $16 of initial all earnings and profits amount with respect to the FC stock held by DC, plus the $8 addition to such amount that results from FC's recognition of gain on the distribution to the minority shareholder). Under paragraph (b)(3)(i) of this section, DC must include the $24 all earnings and profits amount in income as a deemed dividend from FC.

Example 4—(i) *Facts.* DC1, a domestic corporation, owns all of the outstanding stock of DC2, a domestic corporation. DC1 also owns all of the outstanding stock of FC, a foreign corporation. The stock of FC has a value of $100, and DC1 has a basis of $30 in such stock. The assets of FC have a value of $100. The all earnings and profits amount with respect to the FC stock owned by DC1 is $20. In a reorganization described in section 368(a)(1)(D), DC2 acquires all of the assets of FC solely in exchange for DC2 stock. FC distributes the DC2 stock to DC1, and the FC stock held by DC1 is canceled.

(ii) *Result.* DC1 must include $20 in income as a deemed dividend from FC under paragraph (b)(3)(i) of this section. Under section 361, FC does not recognize gain or loss in the assets that it transfers to DC2 or in the DC2 stock that it distributes to DC1, and under section 362(b) DC2 takes a basis in the assets that it acquires from FC equal to the basis that FC had therein. Under § 1.367(b)-2(e)(3)(ii) and section 358(a)(1), DC1 takes a basis of $50 (its $30 basis in the stock of FC, plus the $20 that was treated as a deemed dividend to DC1) in the stock of DC2 that it receives in exchange for the stock of FC. Under § 1.367(b)-2(e)(3)(iii) and section 312(a), the earnings and profits of FC are reduced by the $20 deemed dividend.

Example 5—(i) *Facts.* DC1, a domestic corporation, owns all of the outstanding stock of DC2, a domestic corporation. DC1 also owns all of the outstanding stock of FC1, a foreign corporation. FC1 owns all of the outstanding stock of FC2, a foreign corporation. The all earnings and profits amount with respect to the FC2 stock owned by FC1 is $20. In a reorganization described in section 368(a)(1)(D), DC2 acquires all of the assets and liabilities of FC2 in exchange for DC2 stock. FC2 distributes the DC2 stock to FC1, and the FC2 stock held by FC1 is canceled.

(ii) *Result.* FC1 must include $20 in income as a deemed dividend from FC2 under paragraph (b)(3)(i) of this section. The deemed dividend is treated as a dividend for purposes of the Internal Revenue Code as provided in § 1.367(b)-2(e)(2); however, under paragraph (b)(3)(i) of this section the deemed dividend cannot qualify for the exception from foreign personal holding company income provided by section 954(c)(3)(A)(i), even if the provisions of that section would otherwise have been met in the case of an actual dividend.

Example 6—(i) *Facts.* DC1, a domestic corporation, owns 99 percent of USP, a domestic partnership. The remaining 1 percent of USP is owned by a person unrelated to DC1. DC1 and USP each directly own 9 percent of the outstanding stock of FC, a foreign corporation that is not a controlled foreign corporation subject to the rule of section 953(c). In a reorganization described in section 368(a)(1)(C), DC2, a domestic corporation, acquires all of the assets and liabilities of FC in exchange for DC2 stock. FC distributes to its shareholders DC2 stock, and the FC stock held by its shareholders is canceled.

(ii) *Result.* (A) DC1 and USP are United States persons that are exchanging shareholders in a transaction described in paragraph (a) of this section. As a result, DC1 and USP are subject to the rules of paragraph (b) of this section if they qualify as United States shareholders as defined in paragraph (b)(2) of this section. Alternatively, if they do not qualify as United States shareholders as defined in paragraph (b)(2) of this section, DC1 and USP are subject to the rules of paragraph (c) of this section. Paragraph (b)(2) of this section defines the term United States shareholder to include any shareholder described in section 951(b) (without regard to whether the foreign corporation is a controlled foreign corporation). A shareholder described in section 951(b) is a United States person that is considered to own, applying the rules of section 958(a) and 958(b), 10 percent or more of the total combined voting power of all classes of stock entitled to vote of a foreign corporation. Under section 958(b), the rules of section 318(a), as modified by section 958(b) and the regulations thereunder, apply so that, in general, stock owned directly or indirectly by a partnership is considered as owned proportionately by its partners, and stock owned directly or indirectly by a partner is considered as owned by the partnership. Thus, under section 958(b), DC1 is treated as owning its proportionate share of FC stock held by USP, and USP is treated as owning all of the FC stock held by DC1.

(B) Accordingly, for purposes of determining whether DC1 is a United States shareholder under paragraph (b)(2) of this section, DC1 is considered as owning 99 percent of the 9 percent of FC stock held by USP. Because DC1 also owns 9 percent of FC stock directly, DC1 is considered as owning more than 10 percent of FC stock. DC1 is thus a United States shareholder of FC under paragraph (b)(2) of this section and, as a result, is subject to the rules of paragraph (b) of this section. However, for purposes of determining DC1's all earnings and profits amount, DC1 is not treated as owning the FC stock held by USP. Under § 1.367(b)-2(d)(3), DC1's all earnings and profits amount is determined by reference to the 9 percent of FC stock that it directly owns.

(C) For purposes of determining whether USP is a United States shareholder under paragraph (b)(2) of this section, USP is considered as owning the 9 percent of FC stock held by DC1. Because USP also owns 9 percent of FC stock directly, USP is considered as owning more than 10 percent of FC stock. USP is thus a United States shareholder of FC under paragraph (b)(2) of this section and, as a result, is subject to the rules of paragraph (b) of this section. However, for purposes of determining USP's all earnings and profits amount, USP is not treated as owning the FC shares held by DC1. Under § 1.367(b)-2(d)(3), USP's all earnings and profits amount is determined by reference to the 9 percent of FC stock that it directly owns.

(iii) *Recognition of exchange gain or loss with respect to capital.*—[Reserved]

(4) *Reserved.*—For further guidance concerning section 367(b) exchanges occurring before February 24, 2001, see § 1.367(b)-3T(b)(4).

(c) *Exchange of stock owned by a United States person that is not a United States shareholder.*—(1) *Scope.*—This paragraph (c) applies in the case of an exchanging shareholder that is a United States person not described in paragraph (b)(1)(i) of this section (i.e., a United States person that is not a United States shareholder of the foreign acquired corporation).

(2) *Requirement to recognize gain.*—An exchanging shareholder described in paragraph (c)(1) of this section shall recognize realized gain (but not loss) with respect to the stock of the foreign acquired corporation.

(3) *Election to include all earnings and profits amount.*—In lieu of the treatment prescribed by paragraph (c)(2) of this section, an exchanging shareholder described in paragraph (c)(1) of this section may instead elect to include in income as a deemed dividend the all earnings and profits amount with respect to its stock in the foreign acquired corporation. For the consequences of a deemed dividend, see § 1.367(b)-2(e). Such election may be made only if—

(i) The foreign acquired corporation (or its successor in interest) has provided the exchanging shareholder information to substantiate the exchanging shareholder's all earnings and profits amount with respect to its stock in the foreign acquired corporation; and

(ii) The exchanging shareholder complies with the section 367(b) notice requirement described in § 1.367(b)-1(c), including the specific rules contained therein concerning the time and manner for electing to apply the rules of this paragraph (c)(3).

(4) *De minimis exception.*—This paragraph (c) shall not apply in the case of an exchanging shareholder whose stock in the foreign acquired corporation has a fair market value of less than $50,000 on the date of the section 367(b) exchange.

(5) *Examples.*—The following examples illustrate the rules of this paragraph (c):

Example 1—(i) *Facts.* DC1, a domestic corporation, owns 5 percent of the outstanding stock of FC, a foreign corporation that is not a controlled foreign corporation subject to the rule of section 953(c). Persons unrelated to DC1 own the remaining 95 percent of the outstanding stock of FC. DC1 has owned its 5 percent interest in FC since FC was incorporated. DC1's stock in FC has a basis of $40,000 and a value of $100,000. The all earnings and profits amount with respect to DC1's stock in FC is $50,000. In a reorganization described in section 368(a)(1)(C), DC2, a domestic corporation, acquires all of the assets and liabilities of FC in exchange for DC2 stock. FC distributes DC2 stock to its shareholders, and the FC stock held by its shareholders is canceled.

(ii) *Alternate result 1.* If DC1 does not make the election described in paragraph (c)(3) of this section, then the general rule of paragraph (c)(2) of this section applies and DC1 must recognize its $60,000 gain in the FC stock. Under section 358(a)(1), DC1 has a $100,000 basis (its $40,000 basis in the FC stock, plus the $60,000 recognized gain) in the DC2 stock that it receives in exchange for its FC stock. Because DC1 is not a shareholder described in section 1248(a)(2), section 1248 does not apply to recharacterize any of DC1's gain as a dividend.

(iii) *Alternate result 2.* If DC1 makes a valid election under paragraph (c)(3) of this section, then DC1 must include in income as a deemed dividend the $50,000 all earnings and profits amount with respect to its FC stock. Under § 1.367(b)-2(e)(3) and section 358(a)(1), DC1 has a $90,000 basis (its $40,000 basis in the FC stock, plus the $50,000 that was treated as a deemed dividend to DC1) in the DC2 stock that it receives in exchange for its FC stock. Because DC1 owns less than 10 percent of the voting stock of FC, DC1 does not qualify for a deemed paid foreign tax credit under section 902.

Example 2—(i) *Facts.* The facts are the same as in *Example 1*, except that DC1's stock in FC has a fair market value of $48,000 on the date DC1 receives the DC2 stock.

(ii) *Result.* Because DC1's stock in FC has a fair market value of less than $50,000 on the date of the section 367(b) exchange, the de minimis exception of paragraph (c)(4) of this section applies. As a result, DC1 is not subject to the gain or income inclusion requirements of this paragraph (c).

(d) *Carryover of certain foreign taxes.*—(1) *Rule.*—Excess foreign taxes under section 904(c) allowable to the foreign acquired corporation under section 906 shall carry over to the domestic acquiring corporation and become allowable under section 901, subject to the limitations prescribed by the Internal Revenue Code (for example, sections 383, 904 and 907). The domestic acquiring corporation shall not succeed to any other foreign taxes paid or incurred by the foreign acquired corporation.

(2) *Example.*—The following example illustrates the rules of this paragraph (d):

Example—(i) *Facts.* DC, a domestic corporation owns 100 percent of the outstanding stock of FC, a foreign corporation. FC has net positive earnings and profits, none of which are attributable to DC's FC stock under § 1.367(b)-2(d)(3). FC has paid foreign taxes that are not eligible for credit under section 906. In a liquidation described in section 332, FC distributes all of its property to DC, and the FC stock held by DC is canceled.

(ii) *Result.* The liquidation of FC into DC is a section 367(b) exchange. Thus, DC is subject to the section 367(b) regulations, and must file a section 367(b) notice pursuant to § 1.367(b)-1(c). Pursuant to the provisions of paragraph (d)(1) of this section, the foreign taxes paid by FC do not carryover to DC because FC's foreign taxes are not eligible for credit under section 906.

[Reg. § 1.367(b)-3.]

☐ [*T.D.* 8862, 1-21-2000 (*corrected* 11-3-2000).]

Proposed Amendments to Regulation

§ 1.367(b)-3. Repatriation of foreign corporate assets in certain nonrecognition transactions.

* * *

(e) *Net operating loss and capital loss carryovers.*—A net operating loss or capital loss carryover of the foreign acquired corporation is described in section 381(c)(1) and (c)(3) and thus is eligible to carry over from the foreign acquired corporation to the domestic acquiring corporation only to the extent the underlying deductions or losses were allowable under chapter 1 of subtitle A of the Internal Revenue Code. Thus, only a net operating loss or capital loss carryover that is effectively connected with the conduct of a trade or business within the United States (or that is attributable to a permanent establishment, in the context of an applicable United States income tax treaty) is eligible to be carried over under section 381. For further guidance, see Rev. Rul. 72-421 (1972-2 C.B. 166) (see also § 601.601(d)(2) of this chapter).

(f) *Carryover of earnings and profits.*—Except to the extent otherwise specifically provided (see, e.g., Notice 89-79 (1989-2 C.B. 392) (see also § 601.601(d)(2) of this chapter)), earnings and profits of the foreign acquired corporation that are not included in income as a deemed dividend under the section 367(b) regulations (or deficit in earnings and profits) are eligible to carry over from the foreign acquired corporation to the domestic acquiring corporation under section 381(c)(2) or § 1.367(b)-8(b)(1)(i) only to the extent such earnings and profits (or deficit in earnings and profits) are effectively connected with the conduct of a trade or business within the United States (or are attributable to a permanent establishment, in the context of an applicable United States income tax treaty). All other earnings and profits (or deficit in earnings and profits) of the foreign acquired corporation shall not carry over to the domestic acquiring corporation and, as a result, shall be eliminated. [Prop. Reg. § 1.367(b)-3.]

[Proposed 11-15-2000 (*corrected* 3-12-2001).]

§ 1.367(b)-3T. Repatriation of foreign corporate assets in certain nonrecognition transactions (temporary).—(a) through (b)(3). [Reserved]. For further guidance, see § 1.367(b)-3(a) through (b)(3).

(b)(4) *Election of taxable exchange treatment.*—(i) *Rules.*—(A) *In general.*—In lieu of the treatment prescribed by § 1.367(b)-3(b)(3)(i), an exchanging shareholder described in § 1.367(b)-3(b)(1) may instead elect to recognize the gain (but not loss) that it realizes in the exchange (taxable exchange election). To make a taxable exchange election, the following requirements must be satisfied—

(*1*) The exchanging shareholder (and its direct or indirect owners that would be affected by the election, in the case of an exchanging shareholder that is a foreign corporation) reports the exchange in a manner consistent therewith (see, e.g., sections 954(c)(1)(B)(i), 1001 and 1248);

(*2*) The notification requirements of paragraph (b)(4)(i)(C) of this section are satisfied; and

(*3*) The adjustments described in paragraph (b)(4)(i)(B) of this section are made when the following circumstances are present—

(*i*) The transaction is described in section 332 or is an asset acquisition described in section 368(a)(1), with regard to which one U.S. person owns (directly or indirectly) 100 percent of the foreign acquired corporation; and

(*ii*) The all earnings and profits amount described in § 1.367(b)-3(b)(3)(i) with respect to the exchange exceeds the gain recognized by the exchanging shareholder.

(B) *Attribute reduction.*—(*1*) *Reduction of NOL carryovers.*—The amount by which the all earnings and profits amount exceeds the gain recognized by the exchanging shareholder (the excess earnings and profits amount) shall be applied to reduce the net operating loss carryovers (if any) of the foreign acquired corporation to which the domestic acquiring corporation would otherwise succeed under section 381(a) and (c)(1). See also Rev. Rul. 72-421 (1972-2 C.B. 166) (see § 601.601(d)(2) of this chapter).

(2) *Reduction of capital loss carryovers.*—After the application of paragraph (b)(4)(i)(B)(*1*) of this section, any remaining excess earnings and profits amount shall be applied to reduce the capital loss carryovers (if any) of the foreign acquired corporation to which the domestic acquiring corporation would otherwise succeed under section 381(a) and (c)(3).

(3) *Reduction of basis.*—After the application of paragraph (b)(4)(i)(B)(*2*) of this section, any remaining excess earnings and profits amount shall be applied to reduce (but not below zero) the basis of the assets (other than dollar-denominated money) of the foreign acquired corporation that are acquired by the domestic acquiring corporation. Such remaining excess earnings and profits amount shall be applied to reduce the basis of such assets in the following order: first, tangible depreciable or depletable assets, according to their class lives (beginning with those assets with the shortest class life); second, other non-inventory tangible assets; third, intangible assets that are amortizable; and finally, the remaining assets of the foreign acquired corporation that are acquired by the domestic acquiring corporation. Within each of these categories, if the total basis of all assets in the category is greater than the excess earnings and profits amount to be applied against such basis, the taxpayer may choose to which specific assets in the category the basis reduction first applies.

(C) *Notification.*—The exchanging shareholder shall elect to apply the rules of this paragraph (b)(4)(i) by attaching a statement of its election to its section 367(b) notice. See § 1.367(b)-1(c) for the rules concerning filing a section 367(b) notice.

(D) *Example.*—The following example illustrates the rules of this paragraph (b)(4)(i):

Example—(i) *Facts.* DC, a domestic corporation, owns all of the outstanding stock of FC, a foreign corporation. The stock of FC has a value of $100, and DC has a basis of $80 in such stock. The assets of FC are one parcel of land with a value of $60 and a basis of $30, and tangible depreciable assets with a value of $40 and a basis of $80. FC has no net operating loss carryovers or capital loss carryovers. The all earnings and profits amount with respect to the FC stock owned by DC is $30, of which $19 is described in section 1248(a) and the remaining $11 is not (for example, because it was earned prior to 1963). In a liquidation described in section 332, FC distributes all of its property to DC, and the FC stock held by DC is canceled. Rather than including in income as a deemed dividend the all earnings and profits amount of $30 as provided in § 1.367(b)-3(b)(3)(i), DC instead elects taxable exchange treatment under paragraph (b)(4)(i)(A) of this section.

(ii) *Result.* DC recognizes the $20 of gain it realizes on its stock in FC. Of this $20 amount, $19 is included in income by DC as a dividend pursuant to section 1248(a). (For the source of the remaining $1 of gain recognized by DC, see section 865. For the treatment of the $1 for purposes of the foreign tax credit limitation, see generally section 904(d)(2)(A)(i).) Because the transaction is described in section 332 and because the all earnings and profits amount with respect to the FC stock held by DC ($30) exceeds by $10 the income recognized by DC ($20), the attribute reduction rules of paragraph (b)(4)(i)(B) of this section apply. Accordingly, the $10 excess earnings and profits amount is applied to reduce the basis of the tangible depreciable assets of FC, beginning with those assets with the shortest class lives. Under section 337(a) FC does not recognize gain or loss in the assets that it distributes to DC, and under section 334(b) (which is applied taking into account the basis reduction prescribed by paragraph (b)(4)(i)(A)(*3*) of this section) DC takes a basis of $30 in the land and $70 in the tangible depreciable assets that it receives from FC.

(ii) *Effective date.*—This paragraph (b)(4) applies for section 367(b) exchanges that occur between February 23, 2000 and February 23, 2001.

(c) and (d) [Reserved]. For further guidance, see § 1.367(b)-3(c) through (d). [Temporary Reg. § 1.367(b)-3T.]

☐ [*T.D.* 8863, 1-21-2000.]

§ 1.367(b)-4. Acquisition of foreign corporate stock or assets by a foreign corporation in certain nonrecognition transactions.—(a) *Scope.*—This section applies to an acquisition by a foreign corporation (the foreign acquiring corporation) of the stock or assets of a foreign corporation (the foreign acquired corporation) in an exchange described in section 351 or a reorganization described in section 368(a)(1)(B), (C), (D), (E), (F) or (G). This section applies notwithstanding that the foreign acquiring corporation and the foreign acquired corporation may be the same corporation (such as in a section

368(a)(1)(E) reorganization). See § 1.367(a)-3(b)(2) for additional rules that may apply.

(b) *Income inclusion.*—If an exchange is described in paragraph (b)(1)(i), (2)(i) or (3) of this section, the exchanging shareholder shall include in income as a deemed dividend the section 1248 amount attributable to the stock that it exchanges.

(1) *Exchange that results in loss of status as section 1248 shareholder.*—(i) *Rule.*—An exchange is described in this paragraph (b)(1)(i) if—

(A) Immediately before the exchange, the exchanging shareholder is—

(1) A United States person that is a section 1248 shareholder with respect to the foreign acquired corporation; or

(2) A foreign corporation, and a United States person is a section 1248 shareholder with respect to such foreign corporation and with respect to the foreign acquired corporation; and

(B) Either of the following conditions is satisfied—

(1) Immediately after the exchange, the stock received in the exchange is not stock in a corporation that is a controlled foreign corporation as to which the United States person described in paragraph (b)(1)(i)(A) of this section is a section 1248 shareholder; or

(2) Immediately after the exchange, the foreign acquiring corporation or the foreign acquired corporation (if any, such as in a transaction described in section 368(a)(1)(B) and/or section 351), is not a controlled foreign corporation as to which the United States person described in paragraph (b)(1)(i)(A) of this section is a section 1248 shareholder.

(ii) *Examples.*—The following examples illustrate the rules of this paragraph (b)(1):

Example 1—(i) *Facts.* FC1 is a foreign corporation that is owned, directly and indirectly (applying the ownership rules of section 958), solely by foreign persons. DC is a domestic corporation that is unrelated to FC1. DC owns all of the outstanding stock of FC2, a foreign corporation. Thus, under § 1.367(b)-2(a) and (b), DC is a section 1248 shareholder with respect to FC2, and FC2 is a controlled foreign corporation. Under § 1.367(b)-2(c)(1), the section 1248 amount attributable to the stock of FC2 held by DC is $20. In a reorganization described in section 368(a)(1)(C), FC1 acquires all of the assets and assumes all of the liabilities of FC2 in exchange for FC1 voting stock. The FC1 voting stock received does not represent more than 50 percent of the voting power or value of FC1's stock. FC2 distributes the FC1 stock to DC, and the FC2 stock held by DC is canceled.

(ii) *Result.* FC1 is not a controlled foreign corporation immediately after the exchange. As a result, the exchange is described in paragraph (b)(1)(i) of this section. Under paragraph (b) of this section, DC must include in income, as a deemed dividend from FC2, the section 1248 amount ($20) attributable to the FC2 stock that DC exchanged.

Example 2—(i) *Facts.* The facts are the same as in *Example 1*, except that the voting stock of FC1, which is received by FC2 in exchange for its assets and distributed by FC2 to DC, represents more than 50 percent of the voting power of FC1's stock under the rules of section 957(a).

(ii) *Result.* Paragraph (b)(1)(i) of this section does not apply to require inclusion in income of the section 1248 amount, because FC1 is a controlled foreign corporation as to which DC is a section 1248 shareholder immediately after the exchange.

Example 3—(i) *Facts.* The facts are the same as in *Example 1*, except that FC2 receives and distributes voting stock of FP, a foreign corporation that is in control (within the meaning of section 368(c)) of FC1, instead of receiving and distributing voting stock of FC1.

(ii) *Result.* For purposes of section 367(a), the transfer is an indirect stock transfer subject to section 367(a). See § 1.367(a)-3(d)(1)(iv). Accordingly, DC's exchange of FC2 stock for FP stock under section 354 will be taxable under section 367(a) (and section 1248 will be applicable) if DC fails to enter into a gain recognition agreement in accordance with § 1.367(a)-8. Under § 1.367(a)-3(b)(2), if DC enters into a gain recognition agreement, the exchange will be subject to the provisions of section 367(b) and the regulations thereunder, as well as section 367(a). If FP and FC1 are controlled foreign corporations as to which DC is a (direct or indirect) section 1248 shareholder immediately after the reorganization, then the section 367(b) result is the same as in *Example 2*—that is, paragraph (b)(1)(i) of this section does not apply to require inclusion in income of the section 1248 amount. Under these circumstances, the amount of the gain recognition agreement would equal the amount of the gain realized on the indirect stock transfer. If FP or FC1 is not a controlled foreign corporation as to which DC is a (direct or indirect) section 1248 shareholder immediately after the exchange, then the section 367(b) result is the same as in *Example 1*—that is, DC must include in income, as a deemed dividend from

FC2, the section 1248 amount ($20) attributable to the FC2 stock that DC exchanged. Under these circumstances, the amount of the gain recognition agreement would equal the amount of the gain realized on the indirect stock transfer, less the $20 section 1248 amount inclusion.

Example 4—(i) *Facts.* DC1, a domestic corporation, owns all of the outstanding stock of DC2, a domestic corporation. DC2 owns various assets including all of the outstanding stock of FC2, a foreign corporation. The stock of FC2 has a value of $100, and DC2 has a basis of $30 in such stock. The section 1248 amount attributable to the FC2 stock held by DC2 is $20. DC2 does not own any other stock in a foreign corporation. FC1 is a foreign corporation that is unrelated to DC1, DC2 and FC2. In a reorganization described in section 368(a)(1)(C), FC1 acquires all of the assets and liabilities of DC2 in exchange for FC1 voting stock that represents 20 percent of the outstanding voting stock of FC1. DC2 distributes the FC1 stock to DC1, and the DC2 stock held by DC1 is canceled. DC1 properly files a gain recognition agreement under §1.367(a)-8 to qualify for nonrecognition treatment under section 367(a) with respect to DC2's transfer of the FC2 stock to FC1. See §1.367(a)-8(f)(2).

(ii) *Result.* Pursuant to paragraph (b)(1)(i)(A) of this section, DC2 is the exchanging shareholder that is a section 1248 shareholder with respect to FC2, the foreign acquired corporation. Immediately after the exchange, DC2 is not a section 1248 shareholder with respect to FC1, the corporation whose stock is received in the exchange (because the DC2 stock is canceled). Thus, paragraph (b)(1)(i)(B) of this section is satisfied and, as a result, paragraph (b)(1)(i) of this section applies to DC2's section 361 exchange of FC2 stock. Accordingly, under paragraph (b) of this section, DC2 must include in income, as a deemed dividend from FC2, the section 1248 amount ($20) attributable to the FC2 stock that DC2 exchanges. This result arises without regard to whether FC1 and FC2 are controlled foreign corporations immediately after the exchange. For the tax treatment of DC2's transfer of assets (other than stock) to FC1, see sections 367(a)(1) and (a)(3), and the regulations thereunder. Because the exchange is also described in section 361(a) or (b), see section 367(a)(5) and any regulations thereunder. If any of the assets transferred are intangible assets, see section 367(d) and the regulations thereunder.

(2) *Receipt by exchanging shareholder of preferred or other stock in certain instances.*—(i) *Rule.*—An exchange is described in this paragraph (b)(2)(i) if—

(A) Immediately before the exchange, the foreign acquired corporation and the foreign acquiring corporations are not members of the same affiliated group (within the meaning of section 1504(a), but without regard to the exceptions set forth in section 1504(b), and substituting the words "more than 50" in place of the words "at least 80" in sections 1504(a)(2)(A) and (B));

(B) Immediately after the exchange, a domestic corporation meets the ownership threshold specified by section 902(a) or (b) such that it may qualify for a deemed paid foreign tax credit if it receives a distribution from the foreign acquiring corporation (directly or through tiers); and

(C) The exchanging shareholder receives preferred stock (other than preferred stock that is fully participating with respect to dividends, redemptions and corporate growth) in consideration for common stock or preferred stock that is fully participating with respect to dividends, redemptions and corporate growth, or, in the discretion of the Commissioner or the Commissioner's delegate (and without regard to whether the stock exchanged is common stock or preferred stock), receives stock that entitles it to participate (through dividends, redemption payments or otherwise) disproportionately in the earnings generated by particular assets of the foreign acquired corporation or foreign acquiring corporation.

(ii) *Examples.*—The following examples illustrate the rules of this paragraph (b)(2):

Example 1—(i) *Facts.* FC1 is a foreign corporation. DC is a domestic corporation that is unrelated to FC1. DC owns all of the outstanding stock of FC2, a foreign corporation, and FC2 has no outstanding preferred stock. The value of FC2 is $100 and DC has a basis of $50 in the stock of FC2. Under §1.367(b)-2(c)(1), the section 1248 amount attributable to the stock of FC2 held by DC is $20. In a reorganization described in section 368(a)(1)(B), FC1 acquires all of the stock of FC2 and, in exchange, DC receives FC1 voting preferred stock that constitutes 10 percent of the voting stock of FC1 for purposes of section 902(a). Immediately after the exchange, FC1 and FC2 are controlled foreign corporations and DC is a section 1248 shareholder of FC1 and FC2, so paragraph (b)(1)(i) of this section does not require inclusion in income of the section 1248 amount.

(ii) *Result.* Pursuant to §1.367(a)-3(b)(2), the transfer is subject to both section 367(a) and section 367(b). Under §1.367(a)-3(b)(1), DC will not be subject to tax under section 367(a)(1) if it enters into a gain recognition agreement in accordance with §1.367(a)-8. Even though paragraph (b)(1)(i) of this section does not apply to require inclusion in income by DC of the section 1248 amount, DC must nevertheless include the $20 section 1248 amount in income as a deemed dividend from FC2 under paragraph (b)(2)(i) of this section. Thus, if DC enters into a gain recognition agreement, the amount is $30 (the $50 gain realized less the $20 recognized under section 367(b)). If DC fails to enter into a gain recognition agreement, it must include in income under section 367(a)(1) the $50 of gain realized ($20 of which is treated as a dividend under section 1248). Section 367(b) does not apply in such case.

Example 2—(i) *Facts*. The facts are the same as in *Example 1*, except that DC owns all of the outstanding stock of FC1 immediately before the transaction.

(ii) *Result*. Both section 367(a) and section 367(b) apply to the transfer. Paragraph (b)(2)(i) of this section does not apply to require inclusion of the section 1248 amount. Under paragraph (b)(2)(i)(A) of this section, the transaction is outside the scope of paragraph (b)(2)(i) of this section because FC1 and FC2 are, immediately before the transaction, members of the same affiliated group (within the meaning of such paragraph). Thus, if DC enters into a gain recognition agreement in accordance with § 1.367(a)-8, the amount of such agreement is $50. As in *Example 1*, if DC fails to enter into a gain recognition agreement, it must include in income $50, $20 of which will be treated as a dividend under section 1248.

Example 3—(i) *Facts*. FC1 is a foreign corporation. DC is a domestic corporation that is unrelated to FC1. DC owns all of the outstanding stock of FC2, a foreign corporation. The section 1248 amount attributable to the stock of FC2 held by DC is $20. In a reorganization described in section 368(a)(1)(B), FC1 acquires all of the stock of FC2 in exchange for FC1 voting stock that constitutes 10 percent of the voting stock of FC1 for purposes of section 902(a). The FC1 voting stock received by DC in the exchange carries voting rights in FC1, but by agreement of the parties the shares entitle the holder to dividends, amounts to be paid on redemption, and amounts to be paid on liquidation, that are to be determined by reference to the earnings or value of FC2 as of the date of such event, and that are affected by the earnings or value of FC1 only if FC1 becomes insolvent or has insufficient capital surplus to pay dividends.

(ii) *Result*. Under § 1.367(a)-3(b)(1), DC will not be subject to tax under section 367(a)(1) if it enters into a gain recognition agreement with respect to the transfer of FC2 stock to FC1. Under § 1.367(a)-3(b)(2), the exchange will be subject to the provisions of section 367(b) and the regulations thereunder to the extent that it is not subject to tax under section 367(a)(1). Furthermore, even if DC would not otherwise be required to recognize income under this section, the Commissioner or the Commissioner's delegate may nevertheless require that DC include the $20 section 1248 amount in income as a deemed dividend from FC2 under paragraph (b)(2)(i) of this section.

(3) *Certain recapitalizations*.—An exchange pursuant to a recapitalization under section 368(a)(1)(E) shall be deemed to be an exchange described in this paragraph (b)(3) if the following conditions are satisfied—

(i) During the 24-month period immediately preceding or following the date of the recapitalization, the corporation that undergoes the recapitalization (or a predecessor of, or successor to, such corporation) also engages in a transaction that would be described in paragraph (b)(2)(i) of this section but for paragraph (b)(2)(i)(C) of this section, either as the foreign acquired corporation or the foreign acquiring corporation; and

(ii) The exchange in the recapitalization is described in paragraph (b)(2)(i)(C) of this section.

(c) *Exclusion of deemed dividend from foreign personal holding company income*.—(1) *Rule*.— In the event the section 1248 amount is included in income as a deemed dividend by a foreign corporation under paragraph (b) of this section, such deemed dividend shall not be included as foreign personal holding company income under section 954(c).

(2) *Example*.—The following example illustrates the rule of this paragraph (c):

Example—(i) *Facts*. FC1 is a foreign corporation that is owned, directly and indirectly (applying the ownership rules of section 958), solely by foreign persons. DC is a domestic corporation that is unrelated to FC1. DC owns all of the outstanding stock of FC2, a foreign corporation. FC2 owns all of the outstanding stock of FC3, a foreign corporation. Under § 1.367(b)-2(c)(1), the section 1248 amount attributable to the stock of FC3 held by FC2 is $20. In a reorganization described in section 368(a)(1)(B), FC1 acquires from FC2 all of the stock of FC3 in exchange for FC1 voting stock. The FC1 voting stock received by FC2 does not represent more than 50 percent of the voting power or value of FC1's stock.

(ii) *Result*. FC1 is not a controlled foreign corporation immediately after the exchange. Under paragraph (b)(1) of this section, FC2 must include in income, as a deemed dividend from FC3, the section 1248 amount ($20) attributable to the FC3 stock that FC2 exchanged. The deemed dividend is treated as a dividend for purposes of the Internal Revenue Code as provided in § 1.367(b)-2(e)(2); however, under this paragraph (c) the deemed dividend is not foreign personal holding company income to FC2.

(d) *Rules for subsequent exchanges.*—(1) *In general.*—If income is not required to be included under paragraph (b) of this section in a section 367(b) exchange described in paragraph (a) of this section (non-inclusion exchange) then, for purposes of applying section 367(b) or 1248 to subsequent exchanges and subject to the limitation of § 1.367(b)-2(d)(3)(iii) (in the case of a transaction described in § 1.367(b)-3), the determination of the earnings and profits attributable to an exchanging shareholder's stock received in the non-inclusion exchange shall include a computation that refers to the exchanging shareholder's pro rata interest in the earnings and profits of the foreign acquiring corporation (and, in the case of a stock transfer, the foreign acquired corporation) that accumulate after the non-inclusion exchange, as well as its pro rata interest in the earnings and profits of the foreign acquired corporation that accumulated before the non-inclusion exchange. See also section 1248(c)(2)(D)(ii). The earnings and profits attributable to the stock received by an exchanging shareholder in the non-inclusion exchange shall not include any earnings and profits of the foreign acquiring corporation that accumulated before the non-inclusion exchange. In the case of a non-inclusion exchange in which the exchanging shareholder is a foreign corporation, this paragraph (d)(1) shall also apply for purposes of determining the earnings and profits attributable to the exchanging foreign corporation's shareholders, as well as for purposes of determining the earnings and profits attributable to the exchanging foreign corporation when applying section 964(e) to subsequent sales or exchanges of the stock of the foreign acquiring corporation.

(2) *Subsequent dispositions by a foreign acquiring corporation.*—In the case of an exchange by a foreign acquiring corporation that is subject to section 367(b) or 964(e) and that follows a non-inclusion exchange (as defined in paragraph (d)(1) of this section), the rules of paragraph (d)(1) of this section shall not apply. However, as a result of such a subsequent exchange, proportionate reductions shall be made to the earnings and profits that accumulated before the non-inclusion exchange and that were attributed under paragraph (d)(1) of this section. Such reductions shall be made without regard to whether gain is recognized on the subsequent sale or exchange.

(3) *Examples.*—The following examples illustrate the rules of this section:

Example 1—(i) *Facts.* DC1, a domestic corporation, owns all of the outstanding stock of FC1, a foreign corporation. DC1 has owned all of the stock of FC1 since FC1's formation. FC1 has $20 of earnings and profits, all of which is eligible for inclusion in the section 1248 amount attributable to DC1's stock in FC1. DC2, a domestic corporation, owns all of the outstanding stock of FC2, a foreign corporation. DC2 has owned all of the stock of FC2 since FC2's formation. FC2 has $40 of earnings and profits, all of which is eligible for inclusion in the section 1248 amount attributable to DC2's stock in FC2. DC1 and DC2 are unrelated. In a reorganization described in section 368(a)(1)(B), DC1 transfers all of the stock of FC1 to FC2 in exchange for 40 percent of FC2 stock. DC1 enters into a five-year gain recognition agreement under the provisions of §§ 1.367(a)-3(b) and 1.367(a)-8 with respect to its transfer of FC1 stock to FC2.

(ii) *Result.* (A) DC1's transfer of FC1 to FC2 is not described in paragraph (b)(1)(i), (2)(i), or (3) of this section. As a result, DC1 is not required to include in income the section 1248 amount attributable to its FC1 stock and the rules of paragraph (d)(1) of this section apply. Thus, for purposes of applying section 367(b) or 1248 to subsequent exchanges of FC2 stock, the determination of the earnings and profits attributable to DC1's stock in FC2 will include a computation that refers to 40 percent of the post-reorganization earnings and profits of FC1 and FC2, and that refers to 100 percent of the $20 of pre-reorganization earnings and profits of FC1. The earnings and profits attributable to DC1's stock in FC2 will not include any of the $40 of earnings and profits accumulated by FC2 prior to the transaction. Those earnings and profits are attributable to DC2 under section 1248. However, paragraph (d)(1) of this section does not apply for purposes of applying section 367(b) or 964(e) to subsequent exchanges of FC1 stock by FC2. For these purposes, the determination of the earnings and profits attributable to FC2's stock in FC1 is made under the principles of section 1248 and, as a result, includes a computation that refers to the $20 of earnings and profits attributable to FC2's section 1223(2) holding period in the FC1 stock.

(B) In the event FC2 exchanges FC1 stock in a transaction that is subject to section 367(b) or 964(e), a proportionate reduction must be made to the $20 of earnings and profits that was previously attributed under paragraph (d)(1) of this section to DC1's stock in FC2. Thus, for example, if FC2 sells 50 percent of its FC1 stock (at a time when there have been no other reductions that affect the $20 of FC1 earnings and profits), paragraph (d)(2) of this section requires DC1 to proportionately reduce the $20 of earnings and profits that was previously attributed to its FC2 stock (to $10). This reduction occurs without regard to whether FC2 recognizes gain on its sale of FC1 stock.

Example 2—(i) *Facts*. The facts are the same as in *Example 1*, except that in a reorganization described in section 368(a)(1)(C), FC1 transfers all of its assets to FC2 in exchange for 40 percent of FC2 stock. FC1 then distributes the stock of FC2 to DC1, and the FC1 stock held by DC1 is canceled. None of FC1's assets include stock.

(ii) *Result*. FC2's acquisition of FC1 is not described in paragraph (b)(1)(i), (2)(i), or (3) of this section. As a result, DC1 is not required to include in income the section 1248 amount attributable to its FC1 stock and the rules of paragraph (d)(1) of this section apply. Thus, for purposes of applying section 367(b) or 1248 to subsequent exchanges, the determination of the earnings and profits attributable to DC1's stock in FC2 will include a computation that refers to 40 percent of the post-reorganization earnings and profits of FC2, and that refers to 100 percent of the pre-reorganization earnings and profits of FC1. The earnings and profits attributable to DC1's stock in FC2 will not include any of the $40 of earnings and profits accumulated by FC2 prior to the transaction. Those earnings and profits are attributable to DC2 under section 1248.

Example 3—(i) *Facts*. DC1, a domestic corporation, owns all of the outstanding stock of FC1, a foreign corporation. FC1 owns all of the outstanding stock of FC3, a foreign corporation. DC1 has owned all of the stock of FC1 since FC1's formation, and FC1 has owned all of the stock of FC3 since FC3's formation. FC3 has $20 of earnings and profits, all of which is eligible for inclusion in the section 1248 amount attributable to DC1's stock in FC1 and in the section 1248 amount attributable to FC1's stock in FC3. Such earnings and profits are similarly eligible for inclusion as a dividend attributable to FC1's stock in FC3 under section 964(e). DC2, a domestic corporation, owns all of the outstanding stock of FC2, a foreign corporation. DC2 has owned all of the stock of FC2 since FC2's formation. FC2 has $40 of earnings and profits, all of which is eligible for inclusion in the section 1248 amount attributable to DC2's stock in FC2. DC1 and DC2 are unrelated. In a reorganization described in section 368(a)(1)(B), FC1 transfers all of the stock of FC3 to FC2 in exchange for 40 percent of FC2 stock.

(ii) *Result*. (A) FC1's transfer of FC3 to FC2 is not described in paragraph (b)(1)(i), (2)(i), or (3) of this section. As a result, FC1 is not required to include in income the section 1248 amount attributable to its FC3 stock and the rules of paragraph (d)(1) of this section apply. Thus, for purposes of applying section 367(b) or 1248 to subsequent exchanges of FC1 stock, the determination of the earnings and profits attributable to DC1's stock in FC1 will include a computation that refers to 40 percent of the post-reorganization earnings and profits of FC2 and FC3, and that refers to 100 percent of the $20 of pre-reorganization earnings and profits of FC3. The earnings and profits attributable to FC1's stock in FC2 will not include any of the $40 of earnings and profits accumulated by FC2 prior to the transaction. Those earnings and profits are attributable to DC2 under section 1248. For purposes of applying section 367(b) or 964(e) to subsequent exchanges of FC2 stock, the determination of the earnings and profits attributable to FC1's stock in FC2 will include a computation that refers to 40 percent of the post-reorganization earnings and profits of FC2 and FC3, and that refers to 100 percent of the $20 of pre-reorganization earnings and profits of FC3. The earnings and profits attributable to FC1's interest in FC2 do not include any of the $40 of earnings and profits accumulated by FC2 prior to the transaction. However, paragraph (d)(1) of this section does not apply for purposes of applying section 367(b) or 964(e) to subsequent exchanges of FC3 stock by FC2. For these purposes, the determination of the earnings and profits attributable to FC2's stock in FC3 is made under the principles of section 1248 and, as a result, includes a computation that refers to the $20 of earnings and profits attributable to FC2's section 1223(2) holding period in the FC3 stock.

(B) In the event FC2 exchanges FC3 stock in a transaction that is subject to section 367(b) or 964(e), a proportionate reduction must be made to the $20 of earnings and profits that was previously attributed under paragraph (d)(1) of this section to DC1's stock in FC1 (for purposes of subsequent application of section 367(b) or 1248) as well as to FC1's stock in FC2 (for purposes of subsequent application of section 367(b) or 964(e)). Thus, for example, if FC2 sells 50 percent of its FC3 stock (at a time when there have been no other reductions that affect the $20 of FC3 earnings and profits), paragraph (d)(2) of this section requires DC1 and FC1 to proportionately reduce the $20 of earnings and profits that was previously attributed to their FC1 and FC2 stock, respectively (to $10). These reductions occur without regard to whether FC2 recognizes gain on its sale of FC3 stock.

[Reg. § 1.367(b)-4.]

☐ [*T.D.* 8770, 6-18-98 (*corrected* 3-31-99). Amended by T.D. 8862, 1-21-2000 (*corrected* 11-3-2000).]

Proposed Amendment to Regulation

§ 1.367(b)-4. Acquisition of foreign corporate stock or assets by a foreign corporation in certain nonrecognition transactions.—(a) *Scope.*—* * * However, if pursuant to section 304(a)(1), a foreign acquiring corporation is treated as acquiring the stock of a foreign acquired corporation in a transaction to which section 351(a) applies, such deemed section 351 exchange is not an acquisition subject to section 367(b).

* * *

[Prop. Reg. § 1.367(b)-4.]
[Proposed 5-25-2005.]

§ 1.367(b)-5. Distributions of stock described in section 355.—(a) *In general.*—(1) *Scope.*—This section provides rules relating to a distribution described in section 355 (or so much of section 356 as relates to section 355) and to which section 367(b) applies. For purposes of this section, the terms *distributing corporation*, *controlled corporation*, and *distributee* have the same meaning as used in section 355 and the regulations thereunder.

(2) *Treatment of distributees as exchanging shareholders.*—For purposes of the section 367(b) regulations, all distributees in a transaction described in paragraph (b), (c), or (d) of this section shall be treated as exchanging shareholders that realize income in a section 367(b) exchange.

(b) *Distribution by a domestic corporation.*—(1) *General rule.*—In a distribution described in section 355, if the distributing corporation is a domestic corporation and the controlled corporation is a foreign corporation, the following general rules shall apply—

(i) If the distributee is a corporation, then the controlled corporation shall be considered to be a corporation; and

(ii) If the distributee is an individual, then, solely for purposes of determining the gain recognized by the distributing corporation, the controlled corporation shall not be considered to be a corporation, and the distributing corporation shall recognize any gain (but not loss) realized on the distribution.

(2) *Section 367(e) transactions.*—The rules of paragraph (b)(1) of this section shall not apply to a foreign distributee to the extent gain is recognized under section 367(e)(1) and the regulations thereunder.

(3) *Determining whether distributees are individuals.*—All distributees in a distribution described in paragraph (b)(1) of this section are presumed to be individuals. However, the shareholder identification principles of § 1.367(e)-1(d) (including the reporting procedures in § 1.367(e)-1(d)(2) and (3)) shall apply for purposes of rebutting this presumption.

(4) *Applicable cross-references.*—For rules with respect to a distributee that is a partnership, trust or estate, see § 1.367(b)-2(k). For additional rules relating to a distribution of stock of a foreign corporation by a domestic corporation, see section 1248(f) and the regulations thereunder. For additional rules relating to a distribution described in section 355 by a domestic corporation to a foreign distributee, see section 367(e)(1) and the regulations thereunder.

(c) *Pro rata distribution by a controlled foreign corporation.*—(1) *Scope.*—This paragraph (c) applies to a distribution described in section 355 in which the distributing corporation is a controlled foreign corporation and in which the stock of the controlled corporation is distributed pro rata to each of the distributing corporation's shareholders.

(2) *Adjustment to basis in stock and income inclusion.*—If the distributee's postdistribution amount (as defined in paragraph (e)(2) of this section) with respect to the distributing or controlled corporation is less than the distributee's predistribution amount (as defined in paragraph (e)(1) of this section) with respect to such corporation, then the distributee's basis in such stock immediately after the distribution (determined under the normal principles of section 358) shall be reduced by the amount of the difference. However, the distributee's basis in such stock shall not be reduced below zero, and to the extent the foregoing reduction would have reduced basis below zero, the distributee shall instead include such amount in income as a deemed dividend from such corporation.

(3) *Interaction with § 1.367(b)-2 (e)(3)(ii).*—The basis increase provided in § 1.367(b)-2(e)(3)(ii) shall not apply to a deemed dividend that is included in income pursuant to paragraph (c)(2) of this section.

(4) *Basis redistribution.*—If a distributee reduces the basis in the stock of the distributing or controlled corporation (or has an inclusion with respect to such stock) under paragraph (c)(2) of this section, the distributee shall increase its basis in the stock of the other corporation by the amount of the basis decrease (or deemed dividend inclusion) required by paragraph (c)(2) of this section. However, the distributee's basis in such stock shall not be increased above the fair market value of such stock and shall not be increased to the extent the increase diminishes the dis-

tributee's postdistribution amount with respect to such corporation.

(d) *Non-pro rata distribution by a controlled foreign corporation.*—(1) *Scope.*—This paragraph (d) applies to a distribution described in section 355 in which the distributing corporation is a controlled foreign corporation and in which the stock of the controlled corporation is not distributed pro rata to each of the distributing corporation's shareholders.

(2) *Treatment of certain shareholders as distributees.*—For purposes of the section 367(b) regulations, all persons owning stock of the distributing corporation immediately after a transaction described in paragraph (d)(1) of this section shall be treated as distributees of such stock. For other applicable rules, see paragraph (a)(2) of this section.

(3) *Inclusion of excess section 1248 amount by exchanging shareholder.*—If the distributee's postdistribution amount (as defined in paragraph (e)(2) of this section) with respect to the distributing or controlled corporation is less than the distributee's predistribution amount (as defined in paragraph (e)(1) of this section) with respect to such corporation, then the distributee shall include in income as a deemed dividend the amount of the difference. For purposes of this paragraph (d)(3), if a distributee owns no stock in the distributing or controlled corporation immediately after the distribution, the distributee's postdistribution amount with respect to such corporation shall be zero.

(4) *Interaction with § 1.367(b)-2(e)(3)(ii).*—(i) *Limited application.*—The basis increase provided in § 1.367(b)-2(e)(3)(ii) shall apply to a deemed dividend that is included in income pursuant to paragraph (d)(3) of this section only to the extent that such basis increase does not increase the distributee's basis above the fair market value of such stock and does not diminish the distributee's postdistribution amount with respect to such corporation.

(ii) *Interaction with predistribution amount.*—For purposes of this paragraph (d), the distributee's predistribution amount (as defined in paragraph (e)(1) of this section) shall be determined without regard to any basis increase permitted under paragraph (d)(4)(i) of this section.

(e) *Definitions.*—(1) *Predistribution amount.*—For purposes of this section, the predistribution amount with respect to a distributing or controlled corporation is the distributee's section 1248 amount (as defined in § 1.367(b)-2(c)(1)) computed immediately before the distribution (and after any section 368(a)(1)(D) transfer connected with the section 355 distribution), but only to the extent that such amount is attributable to the distributing corporation and any corporations controlled by it immediately before the distribution (the distributing group) or the controlled corporation and any corporations controlled by it immediately before the distribution (the controlled group), as the case may be, under the principles of §§ 1.1248-1(d)(3), 1.1248-2 and 1.1248-3. However, the predistribution amount with regard to the distributing group shall be computed without taking into account the distributee's predistribution amount with respect to the controlled group.

(2) *Postdistribution amount.*—For purposes of this section, the postdistribution amount with respect to a distributing or controlled corporation is the distributee's section 1248 amount (as defined in § 1.367(b)-2(c)(1)) with respect to such stock, computed immediately after the distribution (but without regard to paragraph (c) or (d) of this section (whichever is applicable)). The postdistribution amount under this paragraph (e)(2) shall be computed before taking into account the effect (if any) of any inclusion under section 356(a) or (b).

(f) *Exclusion of deemed dividend from foreign personal holding company income.*—In the event an amount is included in income as a deemed dividend by a foreign corporation under paragraph (c) or (d) of this section (including amounts received as an intermediate owner under the rule of § 1.367(b)-2(e)(2)), such deemed dividend shall not be included as foreign personal holding company income under section 954(c).

(g) *Examples.*—The following examples illustrate the rules of this section:

Example 1—(i) *Facts.* USS, a domestic corporation, owns 40 percent of the outstanding stock of FD, a controlled foreign corporation (CFC). USS has owned the stock since FD was incorporated, and FD has always been a CFC. USS has a basis of $80 in its FD stock, which has a fair market value of $200. FD owns 100 percent of the outstanding stock of FC, a foreign corporation. FD has owned the stock since FC was incorporated. Neither FD nor FC own stock in any other corporation. FD has earnings and profits of $0 and a fair market value of $250 (not considering its ownership of FC). FC has earnings and profits of $300, none of which is described in section 1248(d), and a fair market value of $250. In a pro rata distribution described in section 355, FD distributes to USS stock in FC worth $100; thereafter, USS's FD stock is worth $100 as well.

(ii) *Result*—(A) FD's distribution is a transaction described in paragraph (c)(1) of this section. Under paragraph (c)(2) of this section, USS must compare its predistribution amounts with respect to FD and FC to its respective postdistribution amounts. Under paragraph (e)(1) of this section, USS's predistribution amount with respect to FD or FC is its section 1248 amount computed immediately before the distribution, but only to the extent such amount is attributable to FD or FC. Under § 1.367(b)-2(c)(1), USS's section 1248 amount computed immediately before the distribution is $120, all of which is attributable to FC. Thus, USS's predistribution amount with respect to FD is $0, and its predistribution amount with respect to FC is $120. These amounts are computed as follows: If USS had sold its FD stock immediately before the transaction, it would have recognized $120 of gain ($200 fair market value − $80 basis). All of the gain would have been treated as a dividend under section 1248, and all of the section 1248 amount would have been attributable to FC (based on USS's pro rata share of FC's earnings and profits (40 percent × $300)).

(B) Under paragraph (e)(2) of this section, USS's postdistribution amount with respect to FD or FC is its section 1248 amount with respect to such corporation, computed immediately after the distribution (but without regard to paragraph (c) of this section). Under § 1.367(b)-2(c)(1), USS's section 1248 amounts computed immediately after the distribution with respect to FD and FC are $0 and $60, respectively. These amounts, which are USS's postdistribution amounts, are computed as follows: Under the normal principles of section 358, USS allocates its $80 predistribution basis in FD between FD and FC according to the stock blocks' relative values, yielding a $40 basis in each block. If USS sold its FD stock immediately after the distribution, none of the resulting gain would be treated as a dividend under section 1248. If USS sold its FC stock immediately after the distribution, it would have a $60 gain ($100 fair market value − $40 basis), all of which would be treated as a dividend under section 1248.

(C) The basis adjustment and income inclusion rules of paragraph (c)(2) of this section apply to the extent of any difference between USS's postdistribution and predistribution amounts. In the case of FD, there is no difference between the two amounts and, as a result, no adjustment or income inclusion is required. In the case of FC, USS's postdistribution amount is $60 less than its predistribution amount. Accordingly, under paragraph (c)(2) of this section, USS is required to reduce its basis in its FC stock from $40 to $0 and include $20 in income as a deemed dividend. Under § 1.367(b)-2(e)(2), the $20 deemed dividend is considered as having been paid by FC to FD, and by FD to USS, immediately prior to the distribution. Under paragraph (f) of this section, the deemed dividend is not included by FD as foreign personal holding company income under section 954(c). Under paragraph (c)(3) of this section, the basis increase provided in § 1.367(b)-2(e)(3)(ii) does not apply with regard to the $20 deemed dividend. Under the rules of paragraph (c)(4) of this section, USS increases its basis in FD by the amount by which it decreased its basis in FC, as well as by the amount of its deemed dividend inclusion ($40 + $40 + $20 = $100).

Example 2—(i) *Facts.* USS1 and USS2, domestic corporations, each own 50 percent of the outstanding stock of FD, a controlled foreign corporation (CFC). USS1 and USS2 have owned their FD stock since it was incorporated, and FD has always been a CFC. USS1 and USS2 each have a basis of $500 in their FD stock, and the fair market value of each block of FD stock is $750. FD owns 100 percent of the outstanding stock of FC, a foreign corporation. FD owned the stock since FC was incorporated. Neither FD nor FC own stock in any other corporation. FD has earnings and profits of $0 and a fair market value of $750 (not considering its ownership of FC). FC has earnings and profits of $500, none of which is described in section 1248(d), and a fair market value of $750. In a non-pro rata distribution described in section 355, FD distributes all of the stock of FC to USS2 in exchange for USS2's FD stock.

(ii) *Result*—(A) FD's distribution is a transaction described in paragraph (d)(1) of this section. Under paragraph (d)(2) of this section, USS1 is considered a distributee of FD stock. Under paragraph (d)(3) of this section, USS1 and USS2 must compare their predistribution amounts with respect to FD and FC stock to their respective postdistribution amounts. Under paragraph (e)(1) of this section, USS1's predistribution amount with respect to FD or FC is USS1's section 1248 amount computed immediately before the distribution, but only to the extent such amount is attributable to FD or FC. USS2's predistribution amount is determined in the same manner. Under § 1.367(b)-2(c)(1), USS1 and USS2 each have a section 1248 amount computed immediately before the distribution of $250, all of which is attributable to FC. Thus, USS1 and USS2 each have a predistribution amount with respect to FD of $0, and each have a predistribution amount with respect to FC of $250. These amounts are computed as follows: If either USS1 or USS2 had sold its FD stock immediately before the transaction, it would have recognized $250 of gain ($750 fair market value −

$500 basis). All of the gain would have been treated as a dividend under section 1248, and all of the section 1248 amount would have been attributable to FC (based on USS1's and USS2's pro rata shares of FC's earnings and profits (50 percent × $500)).

(B) Under paragraph (d)(3) of this section, a distributee that owns no stock in the distributing or controlled corporation immediately after the distribution has a postdistribution amount with regard to that stock of zero. Accordingly, USS2 has a postdistribution amount of $0 with respect to FD and USS1 has a postdistribution amount of $0 with respect to FC. Under paragraph (e)(2) of this section, USS1's postdistribution amount with respect to FD is its section 1248 amount with respect to such corporation, computed immediately after the distribution (but without regard to paragraph (d) of this section). USS2's postdistribution amount with respect to FC is determined in the same manner. Under § 1.367(b)-2(c)(1), USS1's section 1248 amount computed immediately after the distribution with respect to FD is $0 and USS2's section 1248 amount computed immediately after the distribution with respect to FC is $250. These amounts, which are USS1's and USS2's postdistribution amounts, are computed as follows: After the non-pro rata distribution, USS1 owns all the stock of FD and USS2 owns all the stock of FC. If USS1 sold its FD stock immediately after the distribution, none of the resulting $250 gain ($750 fair market value – $500 basis) would be treated as a dividend under section 1248. If USS2 sold its FC stock immediately after the distribution, it would have a $250 gain ($750 fair market value – $500 basis), all of which would be treated as a dividend under section 1248.

(C) The income inclusion rule of paragraph (d)(3) of this section applies to the extent of any difference between USS1's and USS2's postdistribution and predistribution amounts. In the case of USS2, there is no difference between the two amounts with respect to either FD or FC and, as a result, no income inclusion is required. In the case of USS1, there is no difference between the two amounts with respect to its FD stock. However, USS1's postdistribution amount with respect to FC is $250 less than its predistribution amount. Accordingly, under paragraph (d)(3) of this section, USS1 is required to include $250 in income as a deemed dividend. Under § 1.367(b)-2(e)(2), the $250 deemed dividend is considered as having been paid by FC to FD, and by FD to USS1, immediately prior to the distribution. This deemed dividend increases USS1's basis in FD ($500 + $250 = $750). Under paragraph (f) of this section, the deemed dividend is not included by FD as foreign personal holding company income under section 954(c).

[Reg. § 1.367(b)-5.]

☐ [T.D. 8862, 1-21-2000 (corrected 11-3-2000).]

Proposed Amendments to Regulation

§ 1.367(b)-5. Distributions of stock described in section 355.—

* * *

(b) * * *

(1) * * *

(ii) If the distributee is an individual or a tax-exempt entity as described in § 1.337(d)-4(c)(2) then, solely for purposes of determining the gain recognized by the distributing corporation, the controlled corporation shall not be considered to be a corporation, and the distributing corporation shall recognize any gain (but not loss) realized on the distribution.

* * *

(c) * * *

(2) *Adjustment to basis in stock and income inclusion.*—(i) *In general.*—If the distributee's postdistribution amount (as defined in paragraph (e)(2) of this section) with respect to the distributing or controlled corporation is less than the distributee's predistribution amount (as defined in paragraph (e)(1) of this section) with respect to such corporation, then the distributee's basis in such stock immediately after the distribution (determined under the normal principles of section 358) shall be reduced by the amount of the difference. However, the distributee's basis in such stock shall not be reduced below zero, and to the extent the foregoing reduction would have reduced basis below zero, the distributee shall instead include such amount in income as a deemed dividend from such corporation. See, e.g., paragraph (g) *Example 1* of this section.

(ii) *Exception.*—The basis reduction rule of paragraph (c)(2)(i) of this section shall apply only to the extent such reduction increases the distributee's section 1248 amount (as defined in § 1.367(b)-2(c)(1)) with respect to the distributing or controlled corporation; otherwise such basis reduction shall be replaced by the income inclusion rule of paragraph (c)(2)(i) of this section. See, e.g., § 1.367(b)-8(d)(6) *Example 2.*

* * *

(e) * * *

(3) *Divisive D reorganization with a preexisting controlled corporation.*—In the case of a transaction described in § 1.367(b)-8(b)(4), the predistribution amount with respect to a distributing or controlled corporation shall be computed after the allocation of the distributing corporation's earnings and profits de-

scribed in §1.367(b)-8(b)(4)(i)(A) and (b)(4)(ii)(A) (without regard to the parenthetical phrase in §1.367(b)-8(b)(4)(ii)(A)), but before the reduction in the distributing corporation's earnings and profits described in §1.367(b)-8(b)(4)(i)(B). See, e.g., §1.367(b)-8(d)(6) *Example 3* and §1.367(b)-8(e)(7) *Example 3*.

* * *

[Prop. Reg. §1.367(b)-5.]

[Proposed 11-15-2000.]

§1.367(b)-6. Effective dates and coordination rules.—(a) *Effective date.*—(1) *In general.*—Sections 1.367(b)-1 through 1.367(b)-5, and this section, apply to section 367(b) exchanges that occur on or after February 23, 2000.

(2) *Exception.*—A taxpayer may, however, elect to have §§1.367(b)-1 through 1.367(b)-5, and this section, apply to section 367(b) exchanges that occur (or occurred) before February 23, 2000, if the due date for the taxpayer's timely filed Federal tax return (including extensions) for the taxable year in which the section 367(b) exchange occurs (or occurred) is after February 23, 2000. The election under this paragraph (a)(2) will be valid only if—

(i) The electing taxpayer makes the election on a timely filed section 367(b) notice;

(ii) In the case of an exchanging shareholder that is a foreign corporation, the election is made on the section 367(b) notice that is filed by each of its shareholders listed in §1.367(b)-1(c)(3)(ii); and

(iii) The electing taxpayer provides notice of the election to all corporations (or their successors in interest) whose earnings and profits are affected by the election on or before the date the section 367(b) notice is filed.

(b) *Certain recapitalizations described in §1.367(b)-4(b)(3).*—In the case of a recapitalization described in §1.367(b)-4(b)(3) that occurred prior to July 20, 1998, the exchanging shareholder shall include the section 1248 amount on its tax return for the taxable year that includes the exchange described in §1.367(b)-4(b)(3)(i) (and not in the taxable year of the recapitalization), except that no inclusion is required if both the recapitalization and the exchange described in §1.367(b)-4(b)(3)(i) occurred prior to July 20, 1998.

(c) *Use of reasonable method to comply with prior published guidance.*—(1) *Prior exchanges.*—The taxpayer may use a reasonable method to comply with the following prior published guidance to the extent such guidance relates to section 367(b): Notice 88-71 (1988-2 C.B. 374); Notice 89-30 (1989-1 C.B. 670); and Notice 89-79 (1989-2 C.B. 392) (see §601.601(d)(2) of this chapter). This rule applies to section 367(b) exchanges that occur (or occurred) before February 23, 2000, or, if a taxpayer makes the election described in paragraph (a)(2) of this section, for section 367(b) exchanges that occur (or occurred) before the date described in paragraph (a)(2) of this section. This rule also applies to section 367(b) exchanges and distributions described in paragraph (d) of this section.

(2) *Future exchanges.*—Section 367(b) exchanges that occur on or after February 23, 2000, (or, if a taxpayer makes the election described in paragraph (a)(2) of this section, for section 367(b) exchanges that occur on or after the date described in paragraph (a)(2) of this section) are governed by the section 367(b) regulations and, as a result, paragraph (c)(1) of this section shall not apply.

(d) *Effect of removal of attribution rules.*—To the extent that the rules under §§7.367(b)-9 and 7.367(b)-10(h) of this chapter, as in effect prior to February 23, 2000 (see 26 CFR part 1 revised as of April 1, 1999), attributed earnings and profits to the stock of a foreign corporation in connection with an exchange described in section 351, 354, 355, or 356 before February 23, 2000, the foreign corporation shall continue to be subject to the rules of §7.367(b)-12 of this chapter in the event of any subsequent exchanges and distributions with respect to such stock, notwithstanding the fact that such subsequent exchange or distribution occurs on or after the effective date described in paragraph (a) of this section. [Reg. §1.367(b)-6.]

☐ [*T.D.* 8862, 1-21-2000.]

Proposed Amendment to Regulation

§1.367(b)-6. Effective dates and coordination rules.—(a) *Effective date.*—(1) *In general.*—Sections 1.367(b)-1 through 1.367(b)-5, and this section, apply to section 367(b) exchanges that occur on or after the date that is 30 days after the date these regulations are published as final regulations in the Federal Register. For guidance with respect to section 367(b) exchanges that occur prior to the date 30 days after these regulations are published as final regulations in the Federal Register, see §§1.367(b)-1 through 1.367(b)-6 in effect prior to the date 30 days after these regulations are published in the Federal Register (see 26 CFR part 1 revised as of April 1, 2000).

* * *

[Prop. Reg. §1.367(b)-6.]

[Proposed 11-15-2000.]

Proposed Amendment to Regulation

§ 1.367(b)-6. Effective dates and coordination rules.—(a) *Effective date.*—(1) *In general.*—Sections 1.367(b)-1 through 1.367(b)-5, and this section, generally apply to section 367(b) exchanges that occur on or after February 23, 2000. However, the last sentence of paragraph (a) in § 1.367(b)-4 shall apply to section 304(a)(1) transactions occurring on or after the date these regulations are published as final regulations in the Federal Register.

* * *

[Prop. Reg. § 1.367(b)-6.]
[Proposed 5-25-2005.]

Proposed Regulation

§ 1.367(b)-7. Carryover of earnings and profits and foreign income taxes in certain foreign-to-foreign nonrecognition transactions.—(a) *Scope.*—This section applies to an acquisition by a foreign corporation (foreign acquiring corporation) of the assets of another foreign corporation (foreign target corporation) in a transaction described in section 381 (foreign 381 transaction). This section describes the manner and extent to which earnings and profits and foreign income taxes of the foreign acquiring corporation and the foreign target corporation carry over to the surviving foreign corporation (foreign surviving corporation). See § 1.367(b)-9 for special rules governing reorganizations described in section 368(a)(1)(F) and foreign 381 transactions in which either the foreign target corporation or the foreign acquiring corporation is newly created.

(b) *General rules.*—(1) *Non-previously taxed earnings and profits and related taxes.*—Earnings and profits and related foreign income taxes of the foreign acquiring corporation and the foreign target corporation (pre-transaction earnings and pretransaction taxes, respectively) shall carry over to the foreign surviving corporation in the manner described in paragraphs (d), (e), (f), and (g) of this section. Dividend distributions by the foreign surviving corporation (post-transaction distributions) shall be out of earnings and profits and shall reduce related foreign income taxes in the manner described in paragraph (c) of this section.

(2) *Previously taxed earnings and profits.*— [Reserved]

(c) *Ordering rule for post-transaction distributions.*—Dividend distributions out of a foreign surviving corporation's earnings and profits shall be ordered in accordance with the rules of paragraph (c)(1), (2), or (3) of this section, depending on whether the foreign surviving corporation is a look-through corporation, a non-look-through 10/50 corporation, or a less-than-10%-U.S.-owned foreign corporation.

(1) *If foreign surviving corporation is a lookthrough corporation.*—In the case of a foreign surviving corporation that is a look-through corporation, post-transaction distributions shall be first out of the look-through pool (as described in paragraph (d) of this section), second out of the non-look-through pool (as described in paragraph (e)(1) of this section), and third out of the pre-pooling annual layers (as described in paragraph (f)(1) of this section) under an annual last-in, first-out (LIFO) method.

(2) *If foreign surviving corporation is a non-look-through 10/50 corporation.*—In the case of a foreign surviving corporation that is a non-look-through 10/50 corporation, post-transaction distributions shall be first out of the non-look-through pool (as described in paragraph (e)(2) of this section), and second out of the pre-pooling annual layers (as described in paragraph (f)(1) of this section) under the LIFO method.

(3) *If foreign surviving corporation is a less-than-10%-U.S.-owned foreign corporation.*—In the case of a foreign surviving corporation that is a less-than-10%-U.S.-owned corporation, post-transaction distributions shall be out of the pre-pooling annual layers (as described in paragraph (f)(2) of this section) under the LIFO method.

(d) *Look-through pool.*—If the foreign surviving corporation is a look-through corporation, then the look-through pool shall be determined under the rules of this paragraph (d).

(1) *In general.*—(i) *Qualifying earnings and taxes.*—The look-through pool shall consist of the post-1986 undistributed earnings and related post-1986 foreign income taxes of the foreign acquiring corporation and the foreign target corporation that were subject to the look-through provisions of section 904(d)(3) or section 904(d)(4) (as in effect for taxable years beginning after December 31, 2002 (the day before the effective date of section 1105(b) of Public Law 105-34 (111 Stat. 788)) and regulations thereunder.

(ii) *Carryover rule.*—Subject to paragraph (d)(2) of this section, the amounts described in paragraph (d)(1)(i) of this section attributable to the foreign acquiring corporation and the foreign target corporation shall carry over to the foreign surviving corporation and shall be combined on a separate category-by-separate category basis.

(2) *Hovering deficit.*—The rules of this paragraph (d)(2) apply when the foreign acquiring corporation or the foreign target corporation has a deficit in one or more separate categories of post-1986 undistributed earnings described in paragraph (d)(1)(i) of this section immediately prior to the foreign 381 transaction. In the event both the foreign acquiring corporation and the foreign target corporation have a deficit in the same separate category of earnings and profits, such deficits and their related foreign income taxes shall be combined for purposes of applying this paragraph (d)(2). See also paragraphs (g)(1) and (4) of this section (describing other rules applicable to a deficit described in this paragraph (d)(2)).

(i) *Offset rule.*—A deficit in a separate category of earnings and profits described in this paragraph (d)(2) shall offset only earnings and profits accumulated by the foreign surviving corporation after the foreign 381 transaction (post-transaction earnings) in the same separate category of earnings and profits.

(ii) *Related taxes.*—Foreign income taxes that are related to a deficit in a separate category of earnings and profits described in this paragraph (d)(2) shall be added to the foreign surviving corporation's post-1986 foreign income taxes related to that separate category of earnings and profits only after post-transaction earnings in the same separate category have been offset by and exceed the entire amount of the deficit.

(3) *Examples.*—The following examples illustrate the rules of this paragraph (d). The examples presume the following facts: Foreign corporations A and B were both incorporated after December 31, 1986, always have been controlled foreign corporations, and always have had calendar taxable years. None of the shareholders of foreign corporations A and B are required to include any amount in income under § 1.367(b)-4 as a result of the foreign 381 transaction. Foreign corporations A and B (and all of their respective qualified business units as defined in section 989) maintain a "u" functional currency. Finally, unless otherwise stated, any earnings and profits described in section 904(d)(1)(D) and 904(d)(1)(E) (shipping income and 10/50 dividends, respectively) qualified for the high tax exception from subpart F income under section 954(b)(4), and all United States shareholders elected to exclude such earnings and profits from subpart F income under section 954(b)(4) and § 1.954-1(d)(5). The examples are as follows:

Example 1—(i) *Facts.* (A) On December 31, 2001, foreign corporations A and B have the following earnings and profits and foreign income taxes accounts:

Foreign Corporation A Separate Category	E&P	Foreign Taxes
10/50 dividends from FC1, a noncontrolled section 902 corporation	100u	$40
General	300u	$60
	400u	$100

Foreign Corporation B Separate Category	E&P	Foreign Taxes
Shipping	200u	$40
10/50 dividends from FC2, a noncontrolled section 902 corporation	50u	$20
General	300u	$70
	550u	$130

(B) On January 1, 2002, foreign corporation B acquires the assets of foreign corporation A in a reorganization described in section 368(a)(1)(C). Immediately following the foreign 381 transaction, foreign surviving corporation is a controlled foreign corporation (CFC).

(ii) *Result.* Under the rules described in paragraph (d)(1) of this section, foreign surviving corporation has the following earnings and profits and foreign income taxes accounts:

Separate Category	E&P	Foreign Taxes
Shipping	200u	$40
General	600u	$130
10/50 dividends from FC1	100u	$40
10/50 dividends from FC2	50u	$20
	950u	$230

(iii) *Post-transaction distribution.* (A) During 2002, foreign surviving corporation does not accumulate any earnings and profits or pay or accrue any foreign income taxes. On December 31, 2002, foreign surviving corporation distributes 475u to its shareholders. Under the rules described in § 1.902-1(d)(1) and paragraph (c)(1) of this section, the distribution is out of separate categories and reduces foreign income taxes as follows:

Separate Category	E&P	Foreign Taxes
Shipping	100u	$20
General	300u	$65
10/50 dividends from FC1	50u	$20
10/50 dividends from FC2	25u	$10
	475u	$115

(B) The foreign income taxes available to foreign surviving corporation shareholders upon the distribution are subject to the generally applicable rules and limitations, such as those of sections 902 and 904(d).

(C) Immediately after the distribution, foreign surviving corporation has the following earnings and profits and foreign income taxes accounts:

Separate Category	E&P	Foreign Taxes
Shipping	100u	$20
General	300u	$65
10/50 dividends from FC1	50u	$20
10/50 dividends from FC2	25u	$10
	475u	$115

Example 2—(i) *Facts.* (A) On December 31, 2001, foreign corporations A and B have the following earnings and profits and foreign income taxes accounts:

Foreign Corporation A

Separate Category	E&P	Foreign Taxes
Shipping	(100u)	$5
10/50 dividends	400u	$160
General	(200u)	$25
	100u	$190

Foreign Corporation B

Separate Category	E&P	Foreign Taxes
Shipping	100u	$20
General	300u	$60
	400u	$80

(B) On January 1, 2002, foreign corporation B acquires the assets of foreign corporation A in a reorganization described in section 368(a)(1)(C). Immediately following the foreign 381 transaction, foreign surviving corporation is a CFC.

(ii) *Result.* Under the rules described in paragraphs (d)(1) and (2) of this section, foreign surviving corporation has the following earnings and profits and foreign income taxes accounts:

	Earnings & Profits:		Foreign Taxes:	
Separate Category	Positive E&P	Hovering Deficit	Foreign Taxes Available	Foreign Taxes Associated with Hovering Deficit
Shipping	100u	(100u)	$20	$5
10/50 dividends	400u	0u	$160	$0
General	300u	(200u)	$60	$25
	800u	(300u)	$240	$30

(iii) *Post-transaction distribution.* (A) During 2002, foreign surviving corporation does not accumulate any earnings and profits or pay or accrue any foreign income taxes. On December 31, 2002, foreign surviving corporation distributes 400u to its shareholders. Under the rules described in section 904(d)(3) and paragraph (c)(1) of this section, the distribution is out of separate categories and reduces foreign income taxes as follows:

Prop. Reg. §1.367(b)-7(d)(3)

Separate Category	E&P	Foreign Taxes
Shipping	50u	$10
10/50 dividends	200u	$80
General	150u	$30
	400u	$120

(B) The foreign income taxes available to foreign surviving corporation shareholders upon the distribution are subject to the generally applicable rules and limitations, such as those of sections 902 and 904(d).

(C) Immediately after the distribution, foreign surviving corporation has the following earnings and profits and foreign income taxes accounts:

	Earnings & Profits:		Foreign Taxes:	
Separate Category	Positive E&P	Hovering Deficit	Foreign Taxes Available	Foreign Taxes Associated with Hovering Deficit
Shipping	50u	(100u)	$10	$5
10/50 dividends	200u	0u	$80	$0
General	150u	(200u)	$30	$25
	400u	(300u)	$120	$30

(iv) *Post-transaction earnings.* (A) In its taxable year ending on December 31, 2003, foreign surviving corporation accumulates earnings and profits and pays related foreign income taxes as follows:

Separate Category	E&P	Foreign Taxes
Shipping	105u	$20
General	100u	$20
	205u	$40

(B) None of foreign surviving corporation's earnings and profits for its 2003 taxable year qualify as subpart F income as defined in section 952(a). Under the rules described in paragraphs (d) (2) (i) and (ii) of this section, foreign surviving corporation has the following earnings and profits and foreign income taxes accounts on December 31, 2003:

	Earnings & Profits:		Foreign Taxes:	
Separate Category	Positive E&P	Hovering Deficit	Foreign Taxes Available	Foreign Taxes Associated with Hovering Deficit
Shipping	55u	0u	$35	$0
10/50 dividends	200u	0u	$80	$0
General	150u	(100u)	$50	$25
	405u	(100u)	$165	$25

Example 3—(i) *Facts.* The facts are the same as *Example 2* (i), (ii), (iii), and (iv)(A), except that the 105u in the section 904(d)(1)(D) shipping separate category accumulated by foreign surviving corporation during 2003 qualify as subpart F income, all of which is included in income under section 951(a) by United States shareholders (as defined in section 951(b)).

(ii) *Result.* (A) Under the rule described in paragraph (g)(1) of this section, the 100u hovering deficit in the shipping separate category does not reduce foreign surviving corporation's current earnings and profits for purposes of determining subpart F income. Thus, foreign surviving corporation's United States shareholders include their pro rata shares of the 105u in taxable income for the year and are eligible for a deemed paid foreign tax credit under section 960, computed by reference to their pro rata shares of $20.32 (105u subpart F inclusion ÷ (105u + 50u accumulated earnings and profits in the shipping category = 155u) = 0.68% × $30 foreign income taxes in the shipping category = $20.32).

(B) Immediately after the subpart F inclusion and section 960 deemed paid taxes (and taking into account the taxable year 2003 earnings and profits and related taxes in the general category), foreign surviving corporation has the following earnings and profits and foreign income taxes accounts:

Prop. Reg. § 1.367(b)-7(d)(3)

	Earnings & Profits:		Foreign Taxes:	
Separate Category	Positive E&P	Hovering Deficit	Foreign Taxes Available	Foreign Taxes Associated with Hovering Deficit
Shipping	50u	(100u)	$9.68	$5
10/50 dividends	200u	0u	$80.00	$0
General	150u	(100u)	$50.00	$25
	400u	(200u)	$139.68	$30

(C) The 105u included as subpart F income constitutes previously taxed earnings and profits under section 959.

(e) *Non-look-through pool.*—(1) *If foreign surviving corporation is a look-through corporation.*—If the foreign surviving corporation is a look-through corporation, then the non-look-through pool shall be determined under the rules of this paragraph (e)(1).

(i) *Qualifying earnings and taxes.*—The non-look-through pool shall consist of the post-1986 undistributed earnings and related post-1986 foreign income taxes that were accumulated (or treated as accumulated) by the foreign target corporation or the foreign acquiring corporation while it was a non-look-through 10/50 corporation.

(ii) *Carryover rule.*—Subject to paragraph (e)(1)(iii) of this section, the amounts described in paragraph (e)(1)(i) of this section attributable to the foreign acquiring corporation and the foreign target corporation shall carry over to the foreign surviving corporation but shall not be combined. Thus, post-transaction distributions by the foreign surviving corporation out of the non-look-through pool shall be made from the separate amounts attributable to the foreign acquiring corporation and the foreign target corporation on a pro rata basis, and shall reduce a pro rata portion of any related foreign income taxes.

(iii) *Hovering deficit.*—The rules of this paragraph (e)(1)(iii) apply when the foreign acquiring corporation or the foreign target corporation (or both) has a deficit in the post-1986 undistributed earnings described in paragraph (e)(1)(i) of this section immediately prior to the foreign 381 transaction. In the event that this paragraph (e)(1)(iii) applies to a deficit of both the foreign acquiring corporation and the foreign target corporation, the deficits shall not be combined and the rules of this paragraph (e)(1)(iii) shall be applied separately to each of such deficits on a pro rata basis. See also paragraphs (g)(1) and (g)(4) of this section (describing other rules applicable to a deficit described in this paragraph (e)(1)(iii)).

(A) *Offset rule.*—A deficit described in this paragraph (e)(i)(iii) shall offset only post-transaction earnings. The deficit shall offset a pro rata portion of post-transaction earnings accumulated in each separate category of earnings and profits by the foreign surviving corporation.

(B) *Related taxes.*—Foreign income taxes that are related to a deficit described in this paragraph (e)(1)(iii) shall be added to the foreign surviving corporation's post-1986 foreign income taxes (in the applicable segregated portion of the non-look-through pool) only after post-transaction earnings have been offset by and exceed the entire amount of the deficit.

(iv) *Examples.*—The following examples illustrate the rules of this paragraph (e)(1). The examples presume the following facts: Foreign corporation A was a non-look-through 10/50 corporation from its incorporation on January 1, 1995 until December 31, 1997; foreign corporation A became a CFC on January 1, 1998 and has been a CFC since that time. Foreign corporation B has been a non-look-through 10/50 corporation since its incorporation on January 1, 1993. Both foreign corporation A and foreign corporation B always have had calendar taxable years. None of the shareholders of foreign corporation A are required to include any amount in income under § 1.367(b)-4 as a result of the foreign 381 transaction. Foreign corporations A and B (and all of their respective qualified business units as defined in section 989) maintain a "u" functional currency. Finally, any earnings and profits described in section 904(d)(1)(E) (10/50 dividends) qualified for the high tax exception from subpart F income under section 954(b)(4), and all United States shareholders elected to exclude such earnings and profits from subpart F income under section 954(b)(4) and § 1.954-1(d)(5). The examples are as follows:

Example 1—(i) *Facts.* (A) On December 31, 2001, foreign corporations A and B have the following earnings and profits and foreign income taxes accounts:

Foreign Corporation A	E&P	Foreign Taxes
Separate Category:		
10/50 dividends	100u	$40
General	300u	$60
E&P Accumulated as Non-Look-Through 10/50 Corporation:	400u	$100
	800u	$200

Foreign Corporation B	E&P	Foreign Taxes
E&P Accumulated as Non-Look-Through 10/50 Corporation:	200u	$40

(B) On January 1, 2002, foreign corporation B acquires the assets of foreign corporation A in a reorganization described in section 368(a)(1)(C). Immediately following the foreign 381 transaction, foreign surviving corporation is a CFC.

(ii) *Result.* Under the rules described in paragraphs (d)(1), (e)(1)(i), and (e)(1)(ii) of this section, foreign surviving corporation has the following earnings and profits and foreign income taxes accounts:

	E&P	Foreign Taxes
Look-Through Pool Separate Category:		
10/50 dividends	100u	$40
General	300u	$60
Two Side-by-Side Non-Look-Through Pool Amounts:		
Non-look-through pool amount #1 (from Corp A)	400u	$100
Non-look-through pool amount #2 (from Corp B)	200u	$40
	1,000u	$240

(iii) *Post-transaction distribution.* (A) During 2002, foreign surviving corporation does not accumulate any earnings and profits or pay or accrue any foreign income taxes. On December 31, 2002, foreign surviving corporation distributes 700u to its shareholders. Under the rules described in paragraphs (c)(1) and (e)(1)(ii) of this section, the distribution is first out of the look-through pool, then out of the non-look-through pool, as follows:

	E&P	Foreign Taxes
Look-Through Pool Separate Category:		
10/50 dividends	100u	$40
General	300u	$60
Non-Look-Through Pool Amounts:		
Non-look-through pool amount #1	200u	$50
Non-look-through pool amount #2	100u	$20
	700u	$170

(B) The foreign income taxes available to foreign surviving corporation shareholders upon the distribution are subject to the generally applicable rules and limitations, such as those of sections 902 and 904(d).

(C) Immediately after the distribution, foreign surviving corporation has the following earnings and profits and foreign income taxes accounts:

	E&P	Foreign Taxes
Two Side-by-Side Non-Look-Through Pool Amounts:		
Non-look-through pool amount #1	200u	$50
Non-look-through pool amount #2	100u	$20
	300u	$70

Example 2—(i) *Facts.* (A) On December 31, 2001, foreign corporations A and B have the following earnings and profits and foreign income taxes accounts:

Foreign Corporation A	E&P	Foreign Taxes
Look-through Pool Separate Category:		
10/50 dividends	100u	$40
General	300u	$60
E & P Accumulated as Non-Look-Through 10/50 Corporation:	400u	$100
	800u	$200

Foreign Corporation B	E&P	Foreign Taxes
E&P Accumulated as Non-Look-Through 10/50 Corporation:	(200u)	$5

Prop. Reg. § 1.367(b)-7(e)(1)(iv)

(B) On January 1, 2002, foreign corporation B acquires the assets of foreign corporation A in a reorganization described in section 368(a)(1)(C). Immediately following the foreign 381 transaction, foreign surviving corporation is a CFC.

(ii) *Result.* Under the rules described in paragraphs (d)(1), (e)(1)(i), (e)(1)(ii), and (e)(1)(iii) of this section, foreign surviving corporation has the following earnings and profits and foreign income taxes accounts:

	Earnings & Profits:		Foreign Taxes:	
	Positive E&P	Hovering Deficit	Foreign Taxes Available	Foreign Taxes Associated with Hovering Deficit
Look-through Pool Separate Category:				
10/50 dividends	100u		$40	
General	300u		$60	
Two Side-by-Side Non-Look-Through Pool Amounts:				
Non-look-through pool amount #1	400u		$100	
Non-look-through pool amount #2		(200u)		$5
	800u	(200u)	$200	$5

(iii) *Post-transaction distribution.* (A) During 2002, foreign surviving corporation does not accumulate any earnings and profits or pay or accrue any foreign income taxes. On December 31, 2002, foreign surviving corporation distributes 600u to its shareholders. Under the rules described in paragraphs (c)(1) and (e)(1)(ii) of this section, the distribution is first out of the look-through pool, then out of the non-look-through pool, as follows:

	E&P	Foreign Taxes
Look-Through Pool Separate Category:		
10/50 dividends	100u	$40
General	300u	$60
Non-Look-Through Pool Amount:		
Non-look-through pool amount #1	200u	$50
	600u	$150

(B) The foreign income taxes available to foreign surviving corporation shareholders upon the distribution are subject to the generally applicable rules and limitations, such as those of sections 902 and 904(d).

(C) Immediately after the distribution, foreign surviving corporation has the following earnings and profits and foreign income taxes accounts:

	Earnings & Profits:		Foreign Taxes:	
	Positive E&P	Hovering Deficit	Foreign Taxes Available	Foreign Taxes Associated with Hovering Deficit
Two Side-by Side Non-Look-Through Pool Amounts:				
Non-look-through pool amount #1	200u		$50	
Non-look-through pool amount #2		(200u)		$5
	200u	(200u)	$50	$5

(iv) *Post-transaction earnings.* (A) In the taxable year ending on December 31, 2003, foreign surviving corporation accumulates earnings and profits and pays related foreign income taxes as follows:

	E&P	Foreign Taxes
Separate Category:		
10/50 dividends	150u	$60
General	300u	$60
	450u	$120

Prop. Reg. §1.367(b)-7(e)(1)(iv)

(B) None of the earnings and profits qualify as subpart F income as defined in section 952(a). Under the rules described in paragraph (e)(1)(iii)(A) of this section, the 200u deficit in non-look-through pool amount #2 offsets a pro rata portion of the foreign surviving corporation's post-transaction earnings in each separate category. Thus, the 200u deficit offsets 66.66u of section 904(d)(1)(E) 10/50 dividends separate category earnings (33.33% of 200u) and offsets 133.34u of section 904(d)(1)(I) general separate category earnings (66.67% of 200u). Accordingly, foreign surviving corporation has the following earnings and profits and foreign income taxes accounts as of December 31, 2002:

	E&P	Foreign Taxes
Look-Through Pool Separate Category:		
10/50 dividends	83.34u	$60
General	166.66u	$60
Two Side-by-Side Non-Look-Through Pool Amounts:		
Non-look-through pool amount #1	200u	$50
Non-look-through pool amount #2		$5
	450u	$175

(C) Under paragraph (e)(1)(iii)(B) of this section, the $5 of foreign income taxes associated with the non-look-through pool amount #2 hovering deficit are added to foreign surviving corporation's available foreign income taxes because post-transaction earnings have been offset by and exceed the deficit in the non-look-through pool. However, the $5 of foreign income taxes generally will not be reduced or deemed paid unless a foreign tax refund restores a positive balance to the associated earnings pursuant to section 905(c), and thus will be trapped.

(2) *If foreign surviving corporation is a non-look-through 10/50 corporation.*—If the foreign surviving corporation is a non-look-through 10/50 corporation, then the non-look-through pool shall be determined under the rules of this paragraph (e)(2).

(i) *Qualifying earnings and taxes.*—The non-look-through pool shall consist of the post-1986 undistributed earnings and related post-1986 foreign income taxes of the foreign acquiring corporation and the foreign target corporation.

(ii) *Carryover rule.*—Subject to paragraph (e)(2)(iii) of this section, the amounts described in paragraph (e)(2)(i) of this section attributable to the foreign acquiring corporation and the foreign target corporation shall carry over to the foreign surviving corporation and shall be combined as a single separate category of earnings and profits under section 904(d)(1)(E).

(iii) *Hovering deficit.*—The rules of this paragraph (e)(2)(iii) apply when the foreign acquiring corporation or the foreign target corporation (or both) has an aggregate deficit in its post-1986 undistributed earnings described in paragraph (e)(2)(i) of this section immediately prior to the foreign 381 transaction. In the event that both the foreign acquiring corporation and the foreign target corporation have an aggregate deficit in post-1986 undistributed earnings, such deficits and their related foreign income taxes shall be combined for purposes of applying this paragraph (e)(2)(iii). See also paragraphs (g)(1) and (4) of this section (describing other rules applicable to a deficit described in this paragraph (e)(2)(iii)).

(A) *Offset rule.*—A deficit described in this paragraph (e)(2)(iii) shall offset only post-transaction earnings accumulated by the foreign surviving corporation.

(B) *Related taxes.*—Foreign income taxes that are related to a deficit described in this paragraph (e)(2)(iii) shall be added to the foreign surviving corporation's post-1986 foreign income taxes only after post-transaction earnings have been offset by and exceed the entire amount of the deficit.

(iv) *Examples.*—The following examples illustrate the rules of this paragraph (e)(2). The examples presume the following facts: Both foreign corporation A and foreign corporation B always have had calendar taxable years. Foreign corporations A and B (and all of their respective qualified business units as defined in section 989) maintain a "u" functional currency. Finally, any earnings and profits described in section 904(d)(1)(E) (10/50 dividends) qualified for the high tax exception from subpart F income under section 954(b)(4), and all United States shareholders elected to exclude such earnings and profits from subpart F income under section 954(b)(4) and § 1.954-1(d)(5). The examples are as follows:

Example 1—(i) *Facts.* (A) Foreign corporations A and B are and always have been non-look-through 10/50 corporations since they were incorporated in 1995. On December 31, 2001, foreign corporations A and B have the following earnings and profits and foreign income taxes accounts:

Prop. Reg. § 1.367(b)-7(e)(2)(iv)

Foreign Corporation A	E&P	Foreign Taxes
E & P accumulated as non-look-through 10/50 corporation	400u	$100

Foreign Corporation B	E&P	Foreign Taxes
E & P accumulated as non-look-through 10/50 corporation	200u	$40

(B) On January 1, 2002, foreign corporation B acquires the assets of foreign corporation A in a reorganization described in section 368(a)(1)(C). Immediately following the foreign 381 transaction, foreign surviving corporation is a non-look-through 10/50 corporation.

(ii) *Result.* Under the rules described in paragraphs (e)(2)(i) and (ii) of this section, foreign surviving corporation has the following earnings and profits and foreign income taxes accounts:

	E&P	Foreign Taxes
Non-Look-Through Pool:	600u	$140

Example 2—(i) *Facts.* (A) Foreign corporation A is and always has been a CFC since it was incorporated in 1995. Foreign corporation B is and always has been a non-look-through 10/50 corporation since it was incorporated in 1995. Immediately before the foreign 381 transaction (but after application of the rules of § 1.367(b)-4 to foreign corporation A and its shareholders), foreign corporations A and B have the following earnings and profits and foreign income taxes accounts:

Foreign Corporation A Separate Category:	E&P	Foreign Taxes
Passive	(200u)	$10
10/50 dividends	100u	$40
General	300u	$60
	200u	$110

Foreign Corporation B	E&P	Foreign Taxes
E&P accumulated as non-look-through 10/50 corporation:	200u	$30

(B) On January 1, 2002, foreign corporation B acquires the assets of foreign corporation A in a reorganization described in section 368(a)(1)(C). Immediately following the foreign 381 transaction, foreign surviving corporation is a non-look-through 10/50 corporation.

(ii) *Result.* Because neither foreign corporation A nor foreign corporation B has an aggregate deficit in post-1986 undistributed earnings, the rules described in paragraphs (e)(2)(i) and (ii) of this section apply, but the rules described in paragraph (e)(2)(iii) do not. Accordingly, foreign corporation A's net positive earnings and profits of 200u (300u + 100u + (200u)) and its aggregate foreign income taxes of $110 ($10 + $40 + $60) are combined with the earnings and profits and foreign income taxes of foreign corporation B, so that foreign surviving corporation has the following earnings and profits and foreign income taxes accounts:

	E&P	Foreign Taxes
Non-Look-Through Pool:	400u	$140

Example 3—(i) *Facts.* (A) Foreign corporation A is and always has been a CFC since it was incorporated in 1995. Foreign corporation B is and always has been a non-look-through 10/50 corporation since it was incorporated in 1995. On December 31, 2001, foreign corporations A and B have the following earnings and profits and foreign income taxes accounts:

Foreign Corporation A Separate Category:	E&P	Foreign Taxes
Passive	(200u)	$10
10/50 dividends	100u	$40
General	(300u)	$60
	(400u)	$110

Foreign Corporation B	E&P	Foreign Taxes
E&P accumulated as non-look-through 10/50 corporation:	200u	$30

(B) On January 1, 2002, foreign corporation B acquires the assets of foreign corporation A in a reorganization described in section 368(a)(1)(C). Immediately following the foreign 381 transaction, foreign surviving corporation is a non-look-through 10/50 corporation. (Assume that none of the shareholders of foreign corporation A are required to include an amount in income under § 1.367(b)-4 with regard to this transaction.)

(ii) *Result.* Because foreign corporation A has an aggregate deficit in post-1986 undistributed earnings, the rules of paragraph (e)(2)(iii) of this section apply. Accordingly, foreign corporation A's 400u aggregate deficit in earnings and profits ((200u) + 100u + (300u)) carries over as a hovering deficit to foreign surviving corporation, so that foreign surviving corporation has the following earnings and profits and foreign income taxes accounts:

	Earnings & Profits:		Foreign Taxes:	
	Positive E&P	Hovering Deficit	Foreign Taxes Available	Foreign Taxes Associated with Hovering Deficit
Non-Look-Through Pool:	200u	(400u)	$30	$110

(iii) *Post-transaction earnings.* (A) In the taxable year ending on December 31, 2002, foreign surviving corporation accumulates earnings and profits and pays related foreign income taxes as follows:

	E&P	Foreign Taxes
E & P accumulated as non-look-through 10/50 corporation:	500u	$100

(B) Under the rule described in paragraph (e)(2)(iii)(A) of this section, the hovering deficit of 400u in the non-look-through pool offsets 400u of post-transaction earnings. Under the rules of paragraph (e)(2)(iii)(B) of this section, the foreign income taxes related to the hovering deficit are added to foreign surviving corporation's available foreign income taxes because post-transaction earnings have been offset by and exceed the deficit in the non-look-through pool. Accordingly, foreign surviving corporation has the following earnings and profits and foreign income taxes accounts as of December 31, 2002:

	E&P	Foreign Taxes
Non-Look-Through Pool:	300u	$240

(f) *Pre-pooling annual layers.*—(1) *If foreign surviving corporation is a look-through corporation or a non-look-through 10/50 corporation.*— If the foreign surviving corporation is a look-through corporation or a non-look-through 10/50 corporation, the pre-pooling annual layers shall be determined under the rules of this paragraph (f)(1).

(i) *Qualifying earnings and taxes.*—The pre-pooling annual layers shall consist of the pre-1987 accumulated profits and the pre-1987 foreign income taxes of the foreign acquiring corporation and the foreign target corporation.

(ii) *Carryover rule.*—Subject to paragraph (f)(1)(iii) of this section, the amounts described in paragraph (f)(1)(i) of this section attributable to the foreign acquiring corporation and the foreign target corporation shall carry over to the foreign surviving corporation but shall not be combined. Thus, when the foreign acquiring corporation and the foreign target corporation have pre-1987 accumulated profits in the same year and a distribution is made therefrom, the rules of § 1.902-1(b)(2)(ii) and (b)(3) shall apply separately to reduce pre-1987 accumulated profits and pre-1987 foreign income taxes of the foreign acquiring corporation and the foreign target corporation on a pro rata basis. For further guidance, see Rev. Rul. 68-351 (1968-2 C.B. 307); Rev. Rul. 70-373 (1970-2 C.B. 152) (see also § 601.601(d)(2) of this chapter); see also paragraph (g)(2) of this section (governing the reconciliation of taxable years).

(iii) *Deficits.*—The rules of this paragraph (f)(1)(iii) apply when the foreign acquiring corporation or the foreign target corporation (or both) has a deficit in one or more years that comprise its pre-1987 accumulated profits immediately prior to the foreign 381 transaction (see also paragraphs (g)(1) and (g)(4) of this section, describing other rules applicable to a deficit described in this paragraph (f)(1)(iii)).

(A) *Aggregate positive earnings and profits.*—If the foreign acquiring corporation or the foreign target corporation (or both) has an aggregate positive (or zero) amount of pre-1987 accumulated profits, but a deficit in one or more individual years, then the rules otherwise applicable to such deficits shall apply separately to the pre-1987 accumulated profits and related foreign income taxes of such corporation. For further guidance, see Rev. Rul. 74-550 (1974-2 C.B. 209) (see also § 601.601(d)(2) of this chapter); *Champion Int'l Corp. v. Commissioner*, 81 T.C. 424 (1983), acq. in result, 1987-2 C.B. 1; Rev. Rul. 87-72 (1987-2 C.B. 170) (see also § 601.601(d)(2) of this chapter). As a result, no amount in excess of the aggregate positive amount of pre-1987 accumulated profits shall be distributed from the pre-transaction earnings of the foreign acquiring corporation or the foreign target corporation.

Prop. Reg. § 1.367(b)-7(f)(1)(iii)(A)

(B) *Aggregate deficit in earnings and profits.*—If the foreign acquiring corporation or the foreign target corporation (or both) has an aggregate deficit in pre-1987 accumulated profits, then the rules under § 1.902-2(b) shall apply to such deficit (and related foreign income taxes) immediately prior to the transaction, except that the aggregate deficit that is carried forward into the look-through pool (in the case of a foreign surviving corporation that is a look-through corporation) or non-look-through pool (in the case of a foreign surviving corporation that is a non-look-through 10/50 corporation) shall be available to offset only post-transaction earnings accumulated by the foreign surviving corporation.

(iv) *Pre-1987 section 960 earnings and profits and foreign income taxes.*—The pre-1987 section 960 earnings and profits and pre-1987 section 960 foreign income taxes attributable to the foreign acquiring corporation and the foreign target corporation shall carry over to the foreign surviving corporation but shall not be combined. The rules otherwise applicable to such amounts shall apply separately to the pre-1987 section 960 earnings and profits and pre-1987 section 960 foreign income taxes of the foreign acquiring corporation and the foreign target corporation on a pro rata basis. For further guidance, see Notice 88-70 (1988-2 C.B. 369) (see also § 601.601(d)(2) of this chapter).

(v) *Examples.*—The following examples illustrate the rules of this paragraph (f)(1). The examples presume the following facts: foreign corporation A was incorporated in 1998 and was a less-than-10%-U.S.-owned foreign corporation through December 31, 1999. Foreign corporation A became a non-look-through 10/50 corporation on January 1, 2000 and, as a result, began to maintain a pool of post-1986 undistributed earnings on that date. Foreign corporation B was incorporated in 1998 and always has been owned by foreign shareholders (and thus never has met the requirements of section 902(c)(3)(B)). Both foreign corporation A and foreign corporation B always have had calendar taxable years. Foreign corporations A and B (and all of their respective qualified business units as defined in section 989) maintain a "u" functional currency. The examples are as follows:

Example 1—(i) *Facts.* (A) On December 31, 2001, foreign corporations A and B have the following earnings and profits and foreign income taxes accounts:

Foreign Corporation A	*E&P*	*Foreign Taxes*
E & P accumulated as non-look-through 10/50 corporation:	1,000u	$350
1999	400u	160u
1998	100u	5u
	1,500u	

Foreign Corporation B	*E&P*	*Foreign Taxes*
2001	100u	20u
2000	150u	30u
1999	0u	50u
1998	50u	5u
	300u	105u

(B) On January 1, 2002, foreign corporation B acquires the assets of foreign corporation A in a reorganization described in section 368(a)(1)(C). Immediately following the foreign 381 transaction, foreign surviving corporation is a non-look-through 10/50 corporation.

(ii) *Result.* Under the rules described in paragraphs (e)(2)(i), (e)(2)(ii), (f)(1)(i), and (f)(1)(ii) of this section, foreign surviving corporation has the following earnings and profits and foreign income taxes accounts:

	E&P	*Foreign Taxes*
Non-look-through pool	1,000u	$350
2001	100u	20u
2000	150u	30u
Two Side-by-Side Layers of 1999 E & P:		
1999 layer #1 (from Corp A)	400u	160u
1999 layer #2 (from Corp B)	0u	50u
Two Side-by-Side Layers of 1998 E & P:		
1998 layer #1 (from Corp A)	100u	5u
1998 layer #2 (from Corp B)	50u	5u
	1,800u	

(iii) *Post-transaction distribution.* (A) During 2002, foreign surviving corporation does not accumulate any earnings and profits or pay or accrue any foreign income taxes. On December 31, 2002, foreign surviving corporation distributes 1,700u to its shareholders.

Under the rules of paragraph (c)(2) of this section, the distribution is first out of the non-look-through pool, and then out of the pre-pooling annual layers under the LIFO method, as follows:

Distribution	E&P	Foreign Taxes
Non-look-through pool	1,000u	$350
2001	100u	20u
2000	150u	30u
Two Side-by-Side Layers of 1999 E & P:		
1999 layer #1	400u	160u
1999 layer #2	0u	0u
Two Side-by-Side Layers of 1998 E & P:		
1998 layer #1	33.33u (100u in layer ÷ 150u aggregate 1997 earnings = 66.67% × 50u distribution)	1.67u
1998 layer #2	16.67u (50u in layer ÷ 150u aggregate 1997 earnings = 33.33% × 50u distribution)	1.67u
	1,700u	

(B) The foreign income taxes available to foreign surviving corporation shareholders upon the distribution are subject to the generally applicable rules and limitations, such as those of sections 902 and 904(d).

(C) Immediately after the distribution, foreign surviving corporation has the following earnings and profits and foreign income taxes accounts:

	E&P	Foreign Taxes
1999 layer #2	0.00u	50.00u
Two Side-by-Side Layers of 1998 E & P:		
1998 layer #1	66.67u	3.33u
1998 layer #2	33.33u	3.33u
	100.00u	56.66u

(iv) *Post-transaction earnings.* For the taxable year ending on December 31, 2003, foreign surviving corporation accumulates 500u of current earnings and profits and pays $70 in foreign income taxes. As of the close of the 2003 taxable year, foreign surviving corporation has the following earnings and profits and foreign income taxes accounts:

	E&P	Foreign Taxes
E & P accumulated as non-look-through 10/50 corporation	500.00u	$70.00
1999	0.00u	50.00u
Two Side-by-Side Layers of 1998 E & P:		
1998 layer #1	66.67u	3.33u
1998 layer #2	33.33u	3.33u
	600u	

Example 2—(i). *Facts.* (A) On December 31, 2001, foreign corporations A and B have the following earnings and profits and foreign income taxes accounts:

Foreign Corporation A	E&P	Foreign Taxes
E & P accumulated as non-look-though 10/50 corporation	1,000u	$350
1999	100u	20u
1998	(50u)	5u
	1,050u	

Foreign Corporation B	E&P	Foreign Taxes
2001	100u	20u
2000	(50u)	5u
1999	0u	50u
1998	100u	10u
	150u	85u

(B) On January 1, 2002, foreign corporation B acquires the assets of foreign corporation A in a reorganization described in section 368(a)(1)(C). Immediately following the foreign 381 transaction, foreign surviving corporation is a non-look-through 10/50 corporation.

(ii) *Result.* Because foreign corporations A and B have aggregate positive amounts of pre-1987 accumulated profits with a deficit in one or more individual years, the rules of paragraph (f)(1)(iii)(A) of this section apply. Accordingly, after the foreign 381 transaction, foreign surviving corporation has the following earnings and profits and foreign income taxes accounts:

	Earnings & Profits:		Foreign Taxes:	
	Positive E&P	Deficit E&P	Foreign Taxes Available	Foreign Taxes Associated with Deficit E&P
Non-Look-Through 10/50 Pool	1,000u		$350	
2001	100u		20u	
2000		(50u)		5u
Two Side-by-Side Layers of 1999 E & P:				
1999 layer #1 (from foreign corporation A)	100u		20u	
1999 layer #2 (from foreign corporation B)	0u		50u	
Two Side-by-Side Layers of 1998 E & P:				
1998 layer #1 (from foreign corporation A)		(50u)		5u
1998 layer #2 (from foreign corporation B)	100u		10u	
	1,300u	(100u)		10u

(iii) *Post-transaction distribution.* (A) During 2002, foreign surviving corporation does not accumulate any earnings and profits or pay or accrue any foreign income taxes. On December 31, 2002, foreign surviving corporation distributes 1,175u to its shareholders. Under the rules described in paragraphs (c)(2) and (f)(1)(iii)(A) of this section, the distribution is first out of the non-look-through pool, and then out of the pre-pooling annual layers, as follows:

Distribution	E&P	Foreign Taxes
Non-Look-Through 10/50 Amount	1,000u	$350
2001	100u	20u
2000	0u	0u
Two Side-by-Side Layers of 1999 E & P:		
1999 layer #1	50u	20u
1999 layer #2	0u	0u
Two Side-by-Side Layers of 1998 E & P:		
1998 layer #1	0u	0u
1998 layer #2	25u	5u
	1,175u	

(B) Under the rules described in paragraph (f)(1)(iii)(A) of this section, the rules otherwise applicable when a foreign corporation has an aggregate positive (or zero) amount of pre-1987 accumulated profits, but a deficit in one or more individual years, apply separately to the pre-1987 accumulated profits and related foreign income taxes of foreign corporation A and foreign corporation B. As a result, distributions out of the pre-pooling annual layers of foreign corporation A and foreign corporation B can not exceed the aggregate positive amount of pre-1987 accumulated profits of each corporation. Accordingly, only 50u can be distributed from foreign corporation A's pre-pooling annual layers and is out of its 1999 layer #1. Under *Champion Int'l Corp. v. Commissioner,* 81 T.C. 424 (1983), the full 20u of taxes related to 1999 layer #1 is reduced or deemed paid ($20 × (50 ÷ 50)). Under Rev. Rul. 74-550 (1974-2 C.B. 209) (see also § 601.601(d)(2) of this chapter), 100u is distributed from foreign corporation B's 2001 annual layer. Foreign corporation B's deficit in 2000 is then rolled back to offset its 1998 annual layer to reduce earnings in that layer to 50u, 25u of which is distributed (and reduces one-half of that year's foreign income taxes).

(C) The foreign income taxes available to foreign surviving corporation shareholders upon the distribution are subject to the generally applicable rules and limitations, such as those of sections 902 and 904(d).

	E&P	Foreign Taxes
2000	0u	5u
1999 layer #2	0u	50u
Two Side-by-Side Layers of 1998 E & P:		
1998 layer #1	0u	5u
1998 layer #2	25u	5u
	25u	65u

(E) Under the rules described in paragraph (f)(1)(iii)(A) of this section, the 5u, 50u, and 5u of foreign income taxes related to foreign surviving corporation's 2000 layer, 1999 layer #2, and 1998 layer #1, respectively, remain in those layers. These foreign income taxes generally will not be reduced or deemed paid unless a foreign tax refund restores a positive balance to the associated earnings pursuant to section 905(c), and thus will be trapped.

(D) Immediately after the distribution foreign surviving corporation has the following earnings and profits and foreign income taxes accounts:

Example 3—(i) *Facts.* (A) On December 31, 2001, foreign corporations A and B have the following earnings and profits and foreign income taxes accounts:

Foreign Corporation A	E&P	Foreign Taxes
E & P accumulated as non-look-through 10/50 corporation:	1,000u	$350
1999	150u	20u
1998	100u	5u
	1,250u	

Foreign Corporation B	E&P	Foreign Taxes
2001	100u	20u
2000	(250u)	5u
1999	0u	50u
1998	100u	10u
	(50u)	85u

(B) On January 1, 2002, foreign corporation B acquires the assets of foreign corporation A in a reorganization described in section 368(a)(1)(C). Immediately following the foreign 381 transaction, foreign surviving corporation is a non-look-through 10/50 corporation.

(ii) *Result.* (A) Because foreign corporation B has an aggregate deficit in pre-1987 accumulated profits, the rules of paragraph (f)(1)(iii)(B) of this section apply. Accordingly, §1.902-2(b) applies immediately prior to the foreign 381 transaction, except that foreign corporation B's aggregate deficit in pre-1987 accumulated profits is carried forward into the post-1986 undistributed earnings pool and is available to offset only post-transaction earnings accumulated by foreign surviving corporation. Accordingly, after the foreign 381 transaction, foreign surviving corporation has the following earnings and profits and foreign income taxes accounts:

	Earnings & Profits:		Foreign Taxes:	
	Positive E&P	Hovering Deficit	Foreign Taxes Available	Foreign Taxes Associated with Hovering Deficit
Non-Look-Through 10/50 Pool	1,000u	(50u)	$350	$0
2001	0u		20u	
2000	0u		5u	
Two Side-by-Side Layers of 1999 E & P:				
1999 layer #1 (from Corp A)	150u		20u	
1999 layer #2 (from Corp B)	0u		50u	
Two Side-by-Side Layers of 1998 E & P:				
1998 layer #1 (from Corp A)	100u		5u	
1998 layer #2 (from Corp B)	0u		10u	
	1,250u	(50u)		$0

Prop. Reg. §1.367(b)-7(f)(1)(v)

(B) Under paragraph (f)(1)(iii)(B) of this section, the 20u, 5u, 50u, and 10u of foreign income taxes associated with foreign corporation B's earnings and profits for 2001, 2000, 1999 layer #2, and 1998 layer #2, respectively, remain in those layers. These foreign income taxes generally will not be reduced or deemed paid unless a foreign tax refund restores a positive balance to the associated earnings pursuant to section 905(c), and thus will be trapped.

(2) *If foreign surviving corporation is a less-than-10%-U.S.-owned foreign corporation.*—If the foreign surviving corporation is a less-than-10%-U.S.-owned foreign corporation, then the pre-pooling annual layers shall be determined under the rules of this paragraph (f)(2).

(i) *Qualifying earnings and taxes.*—The pre-pooling annual layers shall consist of the pre-1987 accumulated profits and the pre-1987 foreign income taxes of the foreign acquiring corporation and the foreign target corporation. If the foreign acquiring corporation or the foreign target corporation (or both) has post-1986 undistributed earnings or a deficit in post-1986 undistributed earnings, then those earnings or deficits and any related post-1986 foreign income taxes shall be recharacterized as pre-1987 accumulated profits or deficits and pre-1987 foreign income taxes of the foreign acquiring corporation or the foreign target corporation accumulated immediately prior to the foreign 381 transaction.

(ii) *Carryover rule.*—Subject to paragraph (f)(2)(iii) of this section, the amounts described in paragraph (f)(2)(i) of this section attributable to the foreign acquiring corporation and the foreign target corporation shall carry over to the foreign surviving corporation but shall not be combined. Thus, when the foreign acquiring corporation and the foreign target corporation have pre-1987 accumulated profits in the same year and a distribution is made therefrom, the principles of § 1.902-1(b)(2)(ii) and (3) shall apply separately to reduce pre-1987 accumulated profits and pre-1987 foreign income taxes of the foreign acquiring corporation and the foreign target corporation on a pro rata basis. For further guidance, see Rev. Rul. 68-351 (1968-2 C.B. 307); Rev. Rul. 70-373 (1970-2 C.B. 152) (see also § 601.601(d)(2) of this chapter); see also paragraph (g)(2) of this section (governing the reconciliation of taxable years).

(iii) *Deficits.*—The rules of this paragraph (f)(2)(iii) apply when the foreign acquiring corporation or the foreign target corporation (or both) has a deficit in one or more years that comprise its pre-1987 accumulated profits immediately prior to the foreign 381 transaction (and after application of the last sentence of paragraph (f)(2)(i) of this section). See also paragraphs (g)(1) and (4) of this section (describing other rules applicable to a deficit described in this paragraph (f)(2)(iii)).

(A) *Aggregate positive earnings and profits.*—If the foreign acquiring corporation or the foreign target corporation (or both) has an aggregate positive (or zero) amount of pre-1987 accumulated profits, but a deficit in one or more individual years, then the rules otherwise applicable to such deficits shall apply separately to the pre-1987 accumulated profits and related foreign income taxes of such corporation. For further guidance, see Rev. Rul. 74-550 (1974-2 C.B. 209) (see also § 601.601(d)(2) of this chapter); *Champion Int'l Corp. v. Commissioner*, 81 T.C. 424 (1983), acq. in result, 1987-2 C.B. 1; Rev. Rul. 87-72 (1987-2 C.B. 170) (see also § 601.601(d)(2) of this chapter). As a result, no amount in excess of the aggregate positive amount of pre-1987 accumulated profits shall be distributed from the pre-transaction earnings of the foreign acquiring corporation or the foreign target corporation.

(B) *Aggregate deficit in earnings and profits.*—If the foreign acquiring corporation or the foreign target corporation (or both) has an aggregate deficit in pre-1987 accumulated profits, then the rules otherwise applicable to such deficits shall apply separately to the pre-transaction earnings and profits and related taxes of the applicable corporation. See, e.g., sections 316(a) and 381(c)(2)(B). Thus, any aggregate net deficit shall be available to offset only post-transaction earnings accumulated by the foreign surviving corporation.

(iv) *Pre-1987 section 960 earnings and profits and foreign income taxes.*—The pre-1987 section 960 earnings and profits and pre-1987 section 960 foreign income taxes attributable to the foreign acquiring corporation and the foreign target corporation shall carry over to the foreign surviving corporation but shall not be combined. The rules otherwise applicable to such amounts shall apply separately to the pre-1987 section 960 earnings and profits and pre-1987 section 960 foreign income taxes of the foreign acquiring corporation and the foreign target corporation on a pro rata basis. For further guidance, see Notice 88-70 (1988-2 C.B. 369) (see also § 601.601(d)(2) of this chapter).

(v) *Examples.*—The following examples illustrate the rules of this paragraph (f)(2). The examples presume the following facts: Both foreign corporation A and foreign corporation B always have had calendar taxable years. Foreign corporations A and B (and all of their respective qualified business units as defined in section 989) maintain a "u" functional currency. The examples are as follows:

Example 1—(i) *Facts*. (A) Foreign corporations A and B both were incorporated in 1998. Nine percent of the voting stock of foreign corporation A is owned by domestic corporate shareholder C. Nine percent of the voting stock of foreign corporation B is owned by domestic corporate shareholder D. Shareholders C and D are unrelated. The remaining 91% of the voting stock of each foreign corporation is owned by unrelated foreign shareholders. Thus, neither corporation meets the requirements of section 902(c)(3)(B). On December 31, 2001, foreign corporations A and B have the following earnings and profits and foreign income taxes accounts:

Foreign Corporation A	E&P	Foreign Taxes
2001	500u	350u
2000	400u	300u
1999	400u	160u
1998	100u	5u
	1,400u	815u

Foreign Corporation B	E&P	Foreign Taxes
2001	100u	20u
2000	300u	60u
1999	0u	50u
1998	50u	5u
	450u	135u

(B) On January 1, 2002, foreign corporation B acquires the assets of foreign corporation A in a reorganization described in section 368(a)(1)(C). Immediately following the foreign 381 transaction, foreign surviving corporation is a less-than-10%-U.S.-owned foreign corporation that does not meet the requirements of section 902(c)(3)(B).

(ii) *Result*. Under the rules described in paragraphs (f)(2)(i) and (ii) of this section, foreign surviving corporation has the following earnings and profits and foreign income taxes accounts:

	E&P	Foreign Taxes
Two Side-by-Side Layers of 2001 E & P:		
2001 layer #1 (from Corp A)	500u	350u
2001 layer #2 (from Corp B)	100u	20u
Two Side-by-Side Layers of 2000 E & P:		
2000 layer #1 (from Corp A)	400u	300u
2000 layer #2 (from Corp B)	300u	60u
Two Side-by-Side Layers of 1999 E & P:		
1999 layer #1 (from Corp A)	400u	160u
1999 layer #2 (from Corp B)	0u	50u
Two Side-by-Side Layers of 1998 E & P:		
1998 layer #1 (from Corp A)	100u	5u
1998 layer #2 (from Corp B)	50u	5u
	1,850u	950u

(iii) *Post-transaction distribution*. (A) During 2002, foreign surviving corporation does not accumulate any earnings and profits or pay or accrue any foreign income taxes. On December 31, 2002, foreign surviving corporation distributes 600u to its shareholders. Under the rules of paragraph (c)(3) of this section, the distribution is out of pre-pooling annual layers under the LIFO method as follows:

	E&P	Foreign Taxes
Two Side-by-Side Layers of 2001 E & P:		
2001 layer #1 (from Corp A)	500u	350u
2001 layer #2 (from Corp B)	100u	20u
	600u	370u

(B) Foreign surviving corporation's foreign income tax accounts are reduced to reflect the distribution of earnings and profits, see § 1.902-1(a)(10)(iii), notwithstanding that no shareholders are eligible to claim deemed paid foreign income taxes under section 902.

(C) Immediately after the distribution, foreign surviving corporation has the following earnings and profits and foreign income taxes accounts:

	E&P	Foreign Taxes
Two Side-by-Side Layers of 2000 E & P:		
2000 layer #1 (from Corp A)	400u	300u
2000 layer #2 (from Corp B)	300u	60u
Two Side-by-Side Layers of 1999 E & P:		
1999 layer #1 (from Corp A)	400u	160u
1999 layer #2 (from Corp B)	0u	50u
Two Side-by-Side Layers of 1998 E & P:		
1998 layer #1 (from Corp A)	100u	5u
1998 layer #2 (from Corp B)	50u	5u
	1,250u	580u

Example 2—(i) *Facts.* (A) The facts are the same as in *Example 1* (i)(A), except that foreign corporation A met the requirements of section 902(c)(3)(B) on January 1, 2000, when U.S. corporate shareholder C acquired an additional 1% of voting stock for a total ownership interest of 10%; foreign corporation A thereby became a non-look-through 10/50 corporation. On December 31, 2001, foreign corporations A and B have the following earnings and profits and foreign income taxes accounts:

Foreign Corporation A	E&P	Foreign Taxes
E & P Accumulated as Non-Look-Through 10/50 Corporation:	900u	$650
1999	400u	160u
1998	100u	5u
	1,400u	

Foreign Corporation B	E&P	Foreign Taxes
2001	100u	20u
2000	300u	60u
1999	0u	50u
1998	50u	5u
	450u	135u

(B) On January 1, 2002, foreign corporation B acquires the assets of foreign corporation A in a reorganization described in section 368(a)(1)(C). Immediately following the foreign 381 transaction, foreign surviving corporation is a less-than-10%-U.S.-owned foreign corporation that does not meet the requirements of section 902(c)(3)(B).

(ii) *Result.* Under the rules described in paragraphs (f)(2)(i) and (ii) of this section, foreign surviving corporation has the following earnings and profits and foreign income taxes accounts:

	E&P	Foreign Taxes
Two Side-by-Side Layers of 2001 E & P:		
2001 layer #1 (from Corp A's pool)	900u	$650
2001 layer #2 (from Corp B's layer)	100u	20u
2000 (from Corp B):	300u	60u
Two Side-by-Side Layers of 1999 E & P:		
1999 layer #1 (from Corp A)	400u	160u
1999 layer #2 (from Corp B)	0u	50u
Two Side-by-Side Layers of 1998 E & P:		
1998 layer #1 (from Corp A)	100u	5u
1998 layer #2 (from Corp B)	50u	5u
	1,850u	

(iii) *Subsequent ownership change.* On January 1, 2007, USS (a domestic corporation) acquires 100% of the stock of foreign surviving corporation. Under the rules of paragraph (g)(3) of this section, foreign surviving corporation begins to pool its earnings and profits under section 902(c)(3) as of January 1, 2007. Foreign surviving corporation's earnings and profits and foreign income taxes accrued before January 1, 2007 retain their character as pre-1987 accumulated profits and pre-1987 foreign income taxes.

Example 3—(i) *Facts.* (A) The facts are the same as in *Example 2* (i)(A), except that on December 31, 2001, foreign corporations A and B have the following earnings and profits and foreign income taxes accounts:

Foreign Corporation A	E&P	Foreign Taxes
E & P Accumulated as Non-Look-Through 10/50 Corporation:	1,000u	$500
1999	(200u)	10u
1998	400u	5u
	1,200u	

Foreign Corporation B	E&P	Foreign Taxes
2001	300u	20u
2000	(100u)	60u
1999	0u	50u
1998	50u	5u
	250u	135u

(B) On January 1, 2002, foreign corporation B acquires the assets of foreign corporation A in a reorganization described in section 368(a)(1)(C). Immediately following the foreign 381 transaction, foreign surviving corporation is a less-than-10%-U.S.-owned foreign corporation that does not meet the requirements of section 902(c)(3)(B).

(ii) *Result.* Because foreign corporations A and B have aggregate positive amounts of pre-1987 earnings and profits with a deficit in one or more individual years, the rules of paragraph (f)(2)(iii)(A) of this section apply. Accordingly, after the foreign 381 transaction, foreign surviving corporation has the following earnings and profits and foreign income taxes accounts:

	Earnings & Profits:		Foreign Taxes:	
	Positive E&P	Deficit E&P	Foreign Taxes Available	Foreign Taxes Associated with Deficit E&P
Two Side-by-Side Layers of 2001 E & P:				
2001 layer #1 (from Corp A's non-look-through 10/50 pool)	1,000u		$500	
2001 layer #2 (from Corp B's layer)	300u		20u	
2000 (from Corp B)		(100u)		60u
Two Side-by-Side Layers of 1999 E & P:				
1999 layer #1 (from Corp A)		(200u)		10u
1999 layer #2 (from Corp B)	0u		50u	
Two Side-by-Side Layers of 1998 E & P:				
1998 layer #1 (from Corp A)	400u		5u	
1998 layer #2 (from Corp B)	50u		5u	
	1,750u	(300u)		70u

(iii) *Post-transaction distribution.* (A) During 2002, foreign surviving corporation does not accumulate any earnings and profits or pay or accrue any foreign income taxes. On December 31, 2002, foreign surviving corporation distributes 1,300u to its shareholders. Under the rules described in paragraphs (c)(3) and (f)(2)(iii)(A) of this section, the distribution is out of the pre-pooling annual layers, as follows:

	E&P	Foreign Taxes Paid	
Two Side-by-Side Layers of 2001 E & P:			
2001 layer #1	1,000u	$500	
2001 layer #2	250u	20u	
1998 E & P:			
1998 layer #1	50u	1.25u	(25% of 5u taxes)
	1,300u		

(B) Under the rules described in paragraph (f)(2)(iii)(A) of this section, the rules otherwise applicable when a foreign corporation has an aggregate positive (or zero) amount of pre-1987 accumulated profits, but a deficit in one or more individual years, apply separately to the pre-1987 accumulated profits and related foreign income taxes of foreign corporation A and foreign corporation B. As a result, distributions out of the pre-pooling annual layers of foreign corporation A and foreign corporation B cannot exceed the aggregate positive amount of pre-1987 accumulated profits of each corporation. Accordingly, only 1,200u and 250u can be distributed out of foreign corporation A's and foreign corporation B's pre-pooling annual layers, respectively. Thus, 1,250u of the distribution is out of 1,000u of foreign corporation A's 2001 layer #1 and 250u of foreign corporation B's 2001 layer #2. Under the principles of

Prop. Reg. § 1.367(b)-7(f)(2)(v)

§ 1.902-1(b)(3) and *Champion Int'l Corp. v. Commissioner*, 81 T.C. 424 (1983), all of the taxes in each of those respective layers are reduced. Applying Rev. Rul. 74-550 (1974-2 C.B. 209) (see also § 601.601(d)(2) of this chapter), the remaining 50u is distributed from foreign corporation A's 1998 layer #1 (after rolling back the 200u deficit in 1999 layer #1 to reduce earnings in 1998 layer #1 to 200u (400u − 200u)). Thus, after the distribution, 150u remains in the 1998 layer #1 along with 3.75u of foreign income taxes (5u × (150u ÷ 200u)).

(C) Foreign surviving corporation's foreign income tax accounts are reduced to reflect the distribution of earnings and profits, see § 1.902-1(a)(10)(iii), notwithstanding that no shareholders are eligible to claim a credit for deemed paid foreign income taxes under section 902.

(D) Immediately after the distribution foreign surviving corporation has the following earnings and profits and foreign income taxes accounts:

	E&P	Foreign Taxes
2000	0u	60u
Two Side-by-Side Layers of 1999 E & P:		
1999 layer #1	0u	10u
1999 layer #2	0u	50u
Two Side-by-Side Layers of 1998 E & P:		
1998 layer #1	150u	3.75u
1998 layer #2	0u	5u
	150u	128.75u

(E) Under the rules described in paragraph (f)(2)(iii)(A) of this section, the 60u, 10u, 50u, and 5u of foreign income taxes related to foreign surviving corporation's 2000 layer, 1999 layer #1, 1999 layer #2, and 1998 layer #2, respectively, remain in those layers. These foreign income taxes generally will not be reduced or deemed paid unless a foreign tax refund restores a positive balance to the associated earnings pursuant to section 905(c), and thus will be trapped.

Example 4—(i) *Facts*. (A) The facts are the same as in *Example 2* (i)(A), except that on December 31, 2001, foreign corporations A and B have the following earnings and profits and foreign income taxes accounts:

Foreign Corporation A	E&P	Foreign Taxes
E & P Accumulated as Non-Look-Through 10/50 Corporation:	(1,000u)	$20
1999	(200u)	10u
1998	400u	5u
	(800u)	

Foreign Corporation B	E&P	Foreign Taxes
2001	100u	20u
2000	300u	60u
1999	0u	50u
1998	50u	5u
	450u	135u

(B) On January 1, 2002, foreign corporation A acquires the assets of foreign corporation B in a reorganization described in section 368(a)(1)(C). Immediately following the foreign 381 transaction, foreign surviving corporation is a less-than-10%-U.S.-owned foreign corporation.

(ii) *Result*. Because foreign corporation A has an aggregate deficit in pre-1987 earnings and profits, the rules of paragraph (f)(2)(iii)(B) of this section apply and the rules otherwise applicable apply separately to the pre-1987 accumulated profits that carry over to foreign surviving corporation from foreign corporation A. Accordingly, after the foreign 381 transaction, foreign surviving corporation has the following earnings and profits and foreign income taxes accounts:

	Earnings & Profits:		Foreign Taxes:	
	Positive E&P	Deficit E&P	Foreign Taxes Available	Foreign Taxes Associated with Deficit E&P
Two Side-by-Side Layers of 2001 E & P:				
2001 layer #1 (from Corp A)		(1,000u)		$20
2001 layer #2 (from Corp B)	100u		20u	
2000	300u		60u	
Two Side-by-Side Layers of 1999 E & P:				
1999 layer #1 (from Corp A)		(200u)		10u
1999 layer #2 (from Corp B)	0u		50u	
Two Side-by-Side Layers of 1998 E & P:				
1998 layer #1 (from Corp A)	400u		5u	
1998 layer #2 (from Corp B)	50u		5u	
	850u	(1,200u)	140u	

(iii) *Post-transaction distribution.* (A) During 2002, foreign surviving corporation does not accumulate any earnings and profits or pay or accrue any foreign income taxes. On December 31, 2002, foreign surviving corporation distributes 200u to its shareholders. Under the rules described in paragraph (f)(2)(iii)(B) of this section, no distribution can be made out of the pre-1987 accumulated profits of foreign corporation A (and the 800u aggregate deficit is available to offset only post-transaction earnings accumulated by foreign surviving corporation). Thus, the distribution is out of pre-pooling annual layers as follows:

	E&P	Foreign Taxes
2001 layer #2	100u	20u
2000	100u	20u
	200u	40u

(B) Foreign surviving corporation's foreign income tax accounts are reduced to reflect the distribution of earnings and profits, see § 1.902-1(a)(10)(iii), notwithstanding that no shareholders are eligible to claim deemed paid foreign income taxes under section 902.

(g) *Special rules.*—(1) *Treatment of deficit.*—Any deficit described in paragraph (d)(2), (e)(1)(iii), (e)(2)(iii), (f)(1)(iii), or (f)(2)(iii) of this section shall not be taken into account in determining current or accumulated earnings and profits of a foreign surviving corporation, including for purposes of calculating—

(A) The earnings and profits limitation of section 952(c)(1)(A) and (c)(1)(C); and

(B) the amount of the foreign surviving corporation's subpart F income as defined in section 952(a).

(2) *Reconciling taxable years.*—If a foreign acquiring corporation and a foreign target corporation had taxable years ending on different dates, then the pro rata distribution rules of paragraphs (f)(1)(ii) and (f)(2)(ii) of this section shall apply with respect to the taxable years that end within the same calendar year.

(3) *Post-transaction change of status.*—If a foreign surviving corporation that is subject to the rules of paragraph (c)(2) of this section subsequently becomes a look-through corporation, or if a foreign surviving corporation that is subject to the rules of paragraph (c)(3) of this section subsequently becomes a non-look-through 10/50 corporation or a look-through corporation, by reason, for example, of a reorganization, liquidation, or change of ownership, then post-1986 undistributed earnings and post-1986 foreign income taxes that have lost their look-through or pooling character by reason of this section shall not have such look-through or pooling character restored. See, e.g., paragraph (f)(2)(v) *Example 2* of this section.

(4) *Ordering rule for offsetting multiple hovering deficits.*—(i) *Rule.*—A foreign surviving corporation shall apply the deficit rules of paragraphs (d)(2), (e)(1)(iii), (e)(2)(iii), (f)(1)(iii), and (f)(2)(iii) of this section in that order (in the event that more than one of such rules applies to the foreign surviving corporation).

(ii) *Example.*—The following example illustrates the rules of this paragraph (g)(4). The examples presume the following facts: Foreign corporation A was a non-look-through 10/50 corporation from its incorporation on January 1, 1995 until December 31, 1997; foreign corporation A became a CFC on January 1, 1998 and has been a CFC since that time. Foreign corporation B has been a non-look-through 10/50 corporation since its incorporation on January 1, 1993. Foreign corporations A and B always have had calendar taxable years. Foreign corporations A and B (and all of their respective qualified business units as defined in section 989) maintain a "u" functional currency. Finally, any earnings and profits described in section 904(d)(1)(E) (10/50 dividends) qualified for the high tax exception from subpart F income under section 954(b)(4), and all shareholders elected to exclude such earnings and profits from subpart F income under section 954(b)(4) and §1.954-1(d)(5). The example is as follows:

Foreign Corporation A Separate Category:	E&P	Foreign Taxes
10/50 dividends from FC1, a noncontrolled section 902 corporation	100u	$60
General	(300u)	$25
E & P Accumulated as Non-Look-Through 10/50 Corporation:	300u	$100
	100u	$185

Foreign Corporation B	E&P	Foreign Taxes
E & P Accumulated as Non-Look-Through 10/50 Corporation:	(200u)	$50

(B) On January 1, 2002, foreign corporation B acquires the assets of foreign corporation A in a reorganization described in section 368(a)(1)(C). Immediately following the foreign 381 transaction, foreign surviving corporation is a CFC.

Example—(i) *Facts.* (A) On December 31, 2001, foreign corporations A and B have the following earnings and profits and foreign income taxes accounts:

(ii) *Result.* Under the rules described in paragraphs (d)(1), (d)(2), (e)(1)(i), (e)(1)(ii), and (e)(1)(iii) of this section, foreign surviving corporation has the following earnings and profits and foreign income taxes accounts:

	Earnings & Profits:		Foreign Taxes:	
	Positive E&P	Hovering Deficit	Foreign Taxes Available	Foreign Taxes Associated with Hovering Deficit
Look-Through Pool:				
10/50 dividends	100u		$60	
General		(300u)		$25
Two Side-by-Side Non-Look-Through Pool Amounts:				
Non-look-through pool amount #1 (from Corp A)	300u		$100	
Non-look-through pool amount #2 (from Corp B)		(200u)		$50
	400u	(500u)	$160	$75

(iii) *Post-transaction earnings.* (A) In the taxable year ending on December 31, 2002, foreign surviving corporation accumulates earnings and profits and pays related foreign income taxes as follows:

Separate Category	E&P	Foreign Taxes
10/50 dividends from FC1	150u	$40
General	400u	$60
	550u	$100

(B) None of the earnings and profits qualify as subpart F income as defined in section 952(a). Under the rules of paragraph (g)(4)(i) of this section, the rules of paragraph (d)(2) of this section apply before the rules of paragraph (e)(1)(iii) of this section. Accordingly, post-transaction earnings in a separate category are first offset by a hovering deficit in the same separate category in the look-through pool. Thus, foreign surviving corporation's 300u deficit in the section 904(d)(1)(I) general separate category offsets 300u of post-transaction general separate category earnings. After application of paragraph (d)(2) of this section, foreign surviving corporation has the following post-transaction earnings available for further offset by a hovering deficit: 150u in the section 904(d)(1)(E) 10/50 dividends separate category and 100u in the general separate category. Under paragraph (e)(1)(iii) of this section, a deficit in the non-look-through pool offsets a pro rata portion of post-transaction earnings in each separate category. Thus, foreign surviving corporation's 200u deficit in non-look-through pool amount #2 offsets the remaining post-transaction earnings on a pro rata basis (200u × (150u ÷ 250u) = 120u against 10/50 dividends separate category earnings and 200u × (100u ÷

Prop. Reg. §1.367(b)-7(g)(4)(ii)

250u) = 80u against general separate category earnings). Accordingly, foreign surviving corporation has the following earnings and profits and foreign income taxes accounts at the end of 2002:

	E&P	Foreign Taxes
Look-Through Pool Separate Category:		
10/50 dividends	130u	$100
General	20u	$85
Two Side-by-Side Non-Look-Through Pool Amounts:		
Non-look-through pool amount #1	300u	$100
Non-look-through pool amount #2	0u	$50
	450u	$335

(C) Under paragraph (d)(2)(ii) of this section, the $25 of foreign income taxes related to the 300u hovering deficit in the section 904(d)(1)(I) general separate category is added to foreign surviving corporation's post-1986 foreign income taxes in that separate category (because post-transaction earnings in the general separate category have been offset by and exceed the deficit in that category). Under paragraph (e)(1)(iii)(B) of this section, the $50 of foreign income taxes related to the 200u hovering deficit in non-look-through pool amount #2 is added to foreign surviving corporation's post-1986 foreign income taxes for non-look-through pool amount #2 (because post-transaction earnings have been offset by and exceed the deficit in the non-look-through pool). However, the $50 of foreign income taxes generally will not be reduced or deemed paid unless a foreign tax refund restores a positive balance to the associated earnings pursuant to section 905(c), and thus will be trapped.

(5) *Pro rata rule for earnings during transaction year.*—For purposes of offsetting post-transaction earnings of a foreign surviving corporation under the rules described in paragraphs (d)(2), (e)(1)(iii), (e)(2)(iii), (f)(1)(iii), and (f)(2)(iii), the earnings and profits for the taxable year of the foreign surviving corporation in which the transaction occurs shall be deemed to have been accumulated after such transaction in an amount which bears the same ratio to the undistributed earnings and profits of the foreign surviving corporation for such taxable year (computed without regard to any earnings and profits carried over) as the number of days in the taxable year after the date of transaction bears to the total number of days in the taxable year. See, e.g., § 1.381(c)(2)-1(a)(7) *Example 2* (illustrating application of this rule with respect to domestic corporations).

(6) *Nonapplicability of hovering deficit rules to certain transactions.*—(i) *Rule.*—If a principal purpose of a foreign 381 transaction is to gain a tax benefit from affirmative use of the hovering deficit rule described in paragraph (d)(2), (e)(1)(iii), (e)(2)(iii), (f)(1)(iii), or (f)(2)(iii) of this section, then the Commissioner may exercise discretion to apply the principles of § 1.367(b)-9 to such transaction.

(ii) *Example.*—The following example illustrates the rules of this paragraph (h)(6). The example is as follows:

Example—(i) *Facts.* (A) Foreign corporations A and B are and always have been wholly owned subsidiaries of USP, a domestic corporation. Both foreign corporations A and B were incorporated in 1990, and both always have been CFCs using a calendar taxable year. Both foreign corporations A and B (and all of their respective qualified business units as defined in section 989) maintain a "u" functional currency and 1u = US$1 at all times. Any earnings and profits described in section 904(d)(1)(E) (10/50 dividends) qualified for the high tax exception from subpart F income under section 954(b)(4), and USP elected to exclude such earnings and profits from subpart F income under section 954(b)(4) and § 1.954-1(d)(5). On December 31, 2001, foreign corporation A and foreign corporation B have the following earnings and profits and foreign income taxes accounts:

Foreign Corporation A Separate Category	E&P	Foreign Taxes
Passive	(1,000u)	$5
General	200u	$200
	(800u)	$205

Foreign Corporation B Separate Category	E&P	Foreign Taxes
10/50 dividends	5u	$3

(B) On January 1, 2002, foreign corporation B acquires the assets of foreign corporation A in a reorganization described in section 368(a)(1)(C). A principal purpose of the foreign 381 transaction is to gain a tax benefit from affirmative use of the hovering deficit rule described in paragraph (d)(2) of this section. Immediately following the foreign 381 transaction, foreign surviving corporation is a CFC.

(ii) *Result under general rules.* (A) If the rules of paragraphs (d)(1) and (2) of this section were to apply, foreign surviving corporation would have the following earnings and profits and foreign income taxes accounts immediately after the foreign 381 transaction:

	Earnings & Profits:		Foreign Taxes:	
	Positive E&P	Hovering Deficit	Foreign Taxes Available	Foreign Taxes Associated with Hovering Deficit
Passive..............		(1,000u)		$5
10/50 dividends.........	5u		$3	
General.............	200u		$200	
	205u	(1,000u)	$203	$5

(B) Accordingly, if the hovering deficit rules of paragraph (d)(2) of this section were to apply, foreign surviving corporation would be able to pay to USP a dividend of $205 that would carry deemed paid foreign income taxes of $203 under section 902.

(iii) *Result under this paragraph (g)(6).* Because a principal purpose of the foreign 381 transaction was to gain a tax benefit from affirmative use of the hovering deficit rule described in paragraph (d)(2) of this section, the Commissioner may exercise discretion to apply the principles of § 1.367(b)-9 to the transaction. Under the principles of § 1.367(b)-9, the earnings and profits and foreign income taxes accounts of foreign corporation A and foreign corporation B are combined under paragraph (d)(1) of this section without reference to the hovering deficit rule of paragraph (d)(2) of this section. Accordingly, foreign surviving corporation would have the following earnings and profits and foreign income taxes accounts immediately after the transaction:

Separate Category	E&P	Foreign Taxes
Passive...............................	(1,000u)	$5
10/50 dividends...........................	5u	$3
General...............................	200u	$200
	(795u)	$208

(h) *Effective date.*—This section shall apply to section 367(b) exchanges that occur on or after the date 30 days after these regulations are published as final regulations in the Federal Register. [Prop. Reg. § 1.367(b)-7.]

[Proposed 11-15-2000 (*corrected* 3-12-2001).]

Proposed Regulation

§ 1.367(b)-8. Allocation of earnings and profits and foreign income taxes in certain foreign corporate separations.—(a) *Scope.*—This section applies to distributions to which section 355 (or so much of section 356 as relates to section 355) applies, whether or not in connection with a section 368(a)(1)(D) reorganization (D reorganization), in which the distributing corporation or the controlled corporation (or both) is a foreign corporation (foreign divisive transaction). For purposes of this section, the terms distributing corporation and controlled corporation have the same meaning as used in section 355 and the regulations thereunder. Paragraph (b) of this section provides general rules governing the allocation and reduction of a distributing corporation's earnings and profits and foreign income taxes (pre-transaction earnings and pre-transaction taxes, respectively) in foreign divisive transactions. Paragraphs (c), (d), and (e) of this section describe special rules for the application of paragraph (b) of this section to specific situations, depending upon whether the distributing corporation or the controlled corporation (or both the distributing and the controlled corporation) is a foreign corporation.

(b) *General rules.*—(1) *Application of § 1.312-10.*—(i) *In general.*—Pre-transaction earnings of a distributing corporation shall be allocated between the distributing corporation and the controlled corporation in accordance with the rules of § 1.312-10(a) and shall be reduced in accordance with the rules of § 1.312-10(b), except to the extent otherwise provided in this section.

(ii) *Special rules for application of § 1.312-10(b).*—(A) *Distributing corporation.*—The pre-transaction earnings of a distributing corporation shall be reduced without taking into account § 1.312-10(b)(2).

(B) *Controlled corporation.*—Section 1.312-10(b) shall not apply to increase or replace the earnings and profits of a controlled corporation by the amount of any decrease in the pre-transaction earnings of a distributing corporation.

(iii) *Net deficit in pre-transaction earnings.*—Nothing in this section shall permit any portion of the pre-transaction earnings of a distributing corporation that has a net deficit in pre-transaction earnings to be allocated or reduced under paragraph (b)(1)(i) of this section. See § 1.312-10(c). Compare paragraph (b)(2) of this section (requiring an allocation or reduction of a pro rata portion of deficits in statutory groupings of earnings and profits when a distributing corporation has a net positive amount of pre-transaction earnings).

(iv) *Use of net bases.*—All allocations and reductions described in paragraph (b)(1)(i) of this section shall be determined in accordance with the net bases in assets. Net basis shall have the same meaning as under § 1.312-10(a).

(v) *Gain recognized by distributing corporation.*—The pre-transaction earnings that are subject to allocation or reduction under paragraph (b)(1)(i) of this section shall include any increase in earnings and profits from gain recognized or income included by the distributing corporation as a result of the foreign divisive transaction. See, for example, section 367(a) and (e), section 1248(f), and § 1.367(b)-5(b).

(vi) *Coordination with branch profits tax.*—An allocation or reduction in a distributing corporation's pre-transaction earnings under paragraph (b)(1)(i) of this section shall not be out of or reduce effectively connected earnings and profits or non-previously taxed accumulated effectively connected earnings and profits, as defined in section 884. See also § 1.884-2T(d)(5)(iii) (providing that such earnings and profits are not subject to reduction under § 1.312-10(b)).

(2) *Cross-section of earnings and profits.*—Except to the extent provided in paragraphs (b)(1)(iii), (b)(1)(vi), (d)(2)(ii), (d)(4), and (e)(4) of this section and other than any portion attributable to an inclusion under § 1.367(b)-5 or paragraph (d)(2)(i) of this section, an allocation or reduction of pre-transaction earnings described in paragraph (b)(1)(i) of this section shall decrease, on a pro rata basis, the statutory groupings of earnings and profits (or deficits in statutory groupings of earnings and profits) of the distributing corporation. Thus, for example, a pro rata portion of a foreign distributing corporation's separate categories, post-1986 undistributed earnings, and annual layers of pre-1987 accumulated profits and pre-1987 section 960 earnings and profits shall be allocated or reduced.

(3) *Foreign income taxes.*—Pre-transaction taxes of a distributing corporation shall be ratably allocated or reduced only to the extent described in paragraphs (d)(3) and (e)(3) of this section. Thus, a distributing corporation's excess foreign taxes described in section 904(c) shall not be allocated or reduced under this section.

(4) *Divisive D reorganization with a preexisting controlled corporation.*—In the case of a foreign divisive transaction that includes a D reorganization with a controlled corporation that is not newly created (a preexisting controlled corporation), paragraph (b)(1)(i) of this section shall apply in the following manner:

(i) *Calculation of earnings and profits of distributing corporation.*—The pre-transaction earnings of a distributing corporation shall be reduced by the sum of—

(A) The amount of the reduction in the pre-transaction earnings of the distributing corporation as described in § 1.312-10(a) (as determined under this section); and

(B) The amount of the reduction in the pre-transaction earnings of the distributing corporation as described in § 1.312-10(b) (as determined under this section).

(ii) *Calculation of earnings and profits of controlled corporation.*—The amount of earnings and profits of the controlled corporation immediately after the foreign divisive transaction shall equal the sum of—

(A) The amount described in paragraph (b)(4)(i)(A) of this section (except to the extent such amounts are included in income as a deemed dividend pursuant to the foreign divisive transaction or are subject to the rule of § 1.367(b)-3(f)); and

(B) The amount of earnings and profits of the controlled corporation immediately before the foreign divisive transaction.

(c) *Foreign divisive transactions involving a domestic distributing corporation and a foreign controlled corporation.*—(1) *Scope.*—The rules of this paragraph (c) apply to a foreign divisive transaction involving a domestic distributing corporation and a foreign controlled corporation.

(2) *Earnings and profits allocated to a foreign controlled corporation.*—Pre-transaction earnings of a domestic distributing corporation that are allocated to a foreign controlled corporation under the rules described in paragraph (b)(1)(i) of this section shall not be included in the foreign controlled corporation's post-1986 undistributed earnings, pre-1987 accumulated profits, or pre-1987 section 960 earnings and profits. In addition, if a distribution by the domestic distributing corporation out of pre-transaction earnings immediately before the foreign divisive transaction would have been treated as a U.S. source dividend under section 861(a)(2)(A) that would not be exempt from tax under section 871(i)(2)(B) or 881(d), a dis-

tribution out of such earnings and profits by the foreign controlled corporation shall be treated as a U.S. source dividend under section 904(g) and for purposes of Chapter 3 of subtitle A of the Internal Revenue Code. See *Georday Enterprises v. Commissioner*, 126 F.2d 384 (4th Cir. 1942). See also sections 243(e) and 861(a)(2)(C) and §1.367(b)-2(j) for other rules that may apply.

(3) *Examples.*—The following examples illustrate the application of the rules of this section to transactions described in paragraph (c)(1) of this section. The examples presume the following facts: USD is a domestic corporation engaged in manufacturing and shipping activities through Business A and Business B, respectively. FC is a foreign corporation that is wholly owned by USD. USD and FC use calendar taxable years. FC (and all of its qualified business units as defined in section 989) maintains a "u" functional currency and, except as otherwise specified, 1u = US$1 at all times. The examples are as follows:

Example 1—(i) *Facts.* The stock of USD is owned in equal parts by three shareholders, USP (a domestic corporation), USI (a United States citizen), and FP (a foreign corporation). USD owns assets with total net bases of $260 (including $100 attributable to the Business B shipping assets, which have a $160 fair market value). USD has $500 of earnings and profits (that it accumulated). The entire $500 would have been treated as a U.S. source dividend under section 861(a)(2)(A) that would not be exempt from tax under sections 871(i)(2)(B) or 881(d) if distributed by USD immediately before the foreign divisive transaction. On January 1, 2002, USD incorporates FC and transfers to FC the Business B shipping assets. USD then distributes the FC stock pro rata to USP, USI, and FP. The transaction meets the requirements of sections 368(a)(1)(D) and 355.

(ii) Result—(A) *Gain Recognition.* Under section 367(a)(5), USD recognizes gain equal to the difference between the fair market value and USD's adjusted basis in the Business B shipping assets ($160 − $100 = $60).

(B) *Calculation of USD's earnings and profits.* Under paragraph (b)(1)(v) of this section, USD's pre-transaction earnings include any gain recognized or income included as a result of the foreign divisive transaction. As described in this *Example 1* (ii)(A), USD recognizes $60 of gain as a result of the foreign divisive transaction. Accordingly, USD has $560 of pre-transaction earnings ($500 + $60). Under paragraph (b)(1)(i) of this section, USD's pre-transaction earnings are reduced by an amount equal to its pre-transaction earnings times the net bases of the assets transferred to FC divided by the net bases of the assets held by USD immediately before the foreign divisive transaction ($560 × ($160 ÷ $320) = $280). Following this reduction, USD has $280 of earnings and profits ($560 − $280).

(C) *Calculation of FC's earnings and profits.* Under paragraph (b)(1)(i) of this section, the $280 reduction in USD's pre-transaction earnings is allocated to FC. Under §1.367(b)-2(j)(1), the $280 is translated into "u" at the spot rate on January 1, 2002, to 280u. Under paragraph (c)(2) of this section, the 280u is not included as part of FC's post-1986 undistributed earnings, pre-1987 accumulated profits, or section 960 earnings and profits.

(iii) *Post-transaction distribution.* During 2002, FC does not accumulate any earnings and profits or pay or accrue any foreign income taxes. On December 31, 2002, at a time when US$1 = 0.5u, FC distributes 180u (or $360) to its shareholders. Thus, FP, USP, and USI each receive a $120 dividend. See section 989(b)(1). Under paragraph (c)(2) of this section and §1.367(b)-2(j)(4), $93.33 of the distribution to FP is subject to withholding under Chapter 3 of subtitle A of the Internal Revenue Code ($280 ÷ 3 = $93.33). Under section 243(e) and §1.367(b)-2(j)(3), $93.33 of the distribution to USP is eligible for the dividends received deduction. See also section 861(a)(2)(C). Under paragraph (c)(2) of this section, the remaining $26.67 distribution to USP is treated as U.S. source under section 904(g) (and is not eligible for the dividends received deduction under section 243(e)). Under paragraph (c)(2) of this section, the $120 dividend distribution to USI is treated as U.S. source under section 904(g).

Example 2—(i) *Facts.* The stock of USD is owned by the following unrelated persons: 20 percent by USP (a domestic corporation), 20 percent by USI (a United States citizen), and 60 percent by FP (a foreign corporation). FC is a preexisting controlled corporation that was incorporated in 1995 and USD always has owned all of the FC stock. USD owns assets with total net bases of $320 (including $160 attributable to the FC stock), and USD has $500 of earnings and profits. FC has 150u of earnings and profits in the section 904(d)(1)(D) shipping separate category and has $60 of related foreign income taxes. FC's earnings and profits qualified for the high tax exception from subpart F income under section 954(b)(4), and USD elected to exclude the earnings and profits from subpart F income under section 954(b)(4) and §1.954-1(d)(5). On January 1, 2002, USD distributes the stock of FC to its shareholders in a transaction that meets the requirements of section 355. FC is not a controlled foreign corporation after the foreign divisive transaction. On the date of the foreign divisive transaction, the FC stock has a $460 fair market value.

(ii) *Result*—(A) *Gain Recognition.* Under § 1.367(b)-5(b)(1)(ii), USD recognizes gain equal to the difference between the fair market value and USD's adjusted basis in the FC stock distributed to USI. Under § 1.367(e)-1(b)(1), USD recognizes gain equal to the difference between the fair market value and USD's adjusted basis in the FC stock distributed to FP. As a result of the transfers to USI and FP, USD recognizes gain of $240 (4/5 × ($460 − $160)), $120 of which is included in USD's income as a dividend under section 1248(a) and (f)(1) (4/5 × 150u, translated at the spot rate under section 989(b)(2)). Under section 1248(a) and (f)(1), USD includes as a dividend the difference between the fair market value and its adjusted basis in the FC stock distributed to USP to the extent of FC's earnings and profits attributable to the distributed stock. For further guidance, see also Notice 87-64 (1987-2 C.B. 375) (see also § 601.601(d)(2) of this chapter). As a result of this transfer, USD includes a $30 dividend under section 1248(a) and (f)(1) (1/5 × 150u). USD qualifies for a section 902 deemed paid foreign tax credit with respect to its $150 of section 1248 dividends.

(B) *Calculation of USD's earnings and profits.* Under paragraph (b)(1)(v) of this section, USD's pre-transaction earnings include any gain recognized or income included as a result of the foreign divisive transaction. As described in this *Example 2* (ii)(A), USD recognizes and includes a total of $270 of gain and dividend income as a result of the foreign divisive transaction. Accordingly, USD has $770 of pre-transaction earnings ($500 + $270). Under paragraphs (b)(1)(i) and (b)(1)(ii)(A) of this section, USD's pre-transaction earnings are reduced by the amount of the reduction that would have been required if USD had transferred the stock of FC to a new corporation in a D reorganization. Thus, USD's pre-transaction earnings are reduced by an amount equal to its pre-transaction earnings times its net basis in the FC stock divided by the net bases of the assets held by USD immediately before the foreign divisive transaction ($770 × ($430 ÷ $590) = $561.19). Following this reduction, USD has $208.81 of earnings and profits ($770 − $561.19).

(C) *Calculation of FC's earnings and profits.* Under paragraph (b)(1)(ii)(B) of this section, FC's earnings and profits are not increased (or replaced) as a result of the foreign divisive transaction.

Example 3—(i) *Facts.* USP, a domestic corporation, owns all of the stock of USD. FC is a preexisting controlled corporation and USD has owned all of the FC stock since FC was incorporated in 1995. USD owns assets with total net bases of $320 (including $100 attributable to the FC stock and $160 attributable to the Business B shipping assets). USD has $500 of pre-transaction earnings. FC has 150u of earnings and profits in the section 904(d)(1)(D) shipping separate category and has $60 of related foreign income taxes. FC's earnings and profits qualified for the high tax exception from subpart F income under section 954(b)(4), and USD elected to exclude the earnings and profits from subpart F income under section 954(b)(4) and § 1.954-1(d)(5). On January 1, 2002, USD transfers to FC the Business B shipping assets. USD then distributes the FC stock to USP. The transaction meets the requirements of sections 368(a)(1)(D) and 355. USD's transfer of the Business B shipping assets to FC falls within the active trade or business exception to section 367(a)(1) described in § 1.367(a)-2T. Immediately after the foreign divisive transaction, the FC stock has a $460 fair market value. USP and USD meet and comply with the requirements of section 367(a)(5) and 1248(f)(2) (and any regulations thereunder). (Sections 1.367(b)-5(b)(1)(ii) and 1.367(e)-1(b)(1) do not apply with respect to the foreign divisive transaction because the distributee, USP, is a domestic corporation.)

(ii) *Result*—(A) *Calculation of USD's earnings and profits.* Under paragraph (b)(4)(i) of this section, USD's pre-transaction earnings are reduced by the sum of the amounts described in paragraphs (b)(4)(i)(A) and (b)(4)(i)(B) of this section. Under paragraph (b)(4)(i)(A) of this section, USD's pre-transaction earnings are reduced by an amount equal to USD's pre-transaction earnings times the net bases of the assets transferred to FC divided by the total net bases of the assets held by USD immediately before the foreign divisive transaction ($500 × ($160 ÷ $320) = $250). Under paragraph (b)(4)(i)(B) of this section, USD's pre-transaction earnings are reduced by an amount equal to USD's pre-transaction earnings times USD's net basis in the stock of FC (immediately before USD's transfer of the shipping assets) divided by the total net bases of the assets held by USD immediately before the foreign divisive transaction ($500 × ($100 ÷ $320) = $156.25). The sum of the amounts described in paragraphs (b)(4)(i)(A) and (B) of this section is $406.25 ($250 + $156.25). Following the reduction described in paragraph (b)(4)(i) of this section, USD has $93.75 of earnings and profits ($500 − $406.25).

(B) *Calculation of FC's earnings and profits.* Under paragraphs (b)(4)(ii) of this section, the earnings and profits of FC immediately after the foreign divisive transaction are increased by the amount of the reduction in USD's pre-transaction earnings described in paragraph (b)(4)(i)(A) of this section ($250). Under § 1.367(b)-2(j)(1), this $250 is translated into "u" at the spot rate on January 1, 2002, to 250u.

Prop. Reg. § 1.367(b)-8(c)(3)

Under paragraph (c)(2) of this section, the 250u is not included as part of FC's post-1986 undistributed earnings. FC has 400u in earnings and profits (250u + 150u) immediately after the foreign divisive transaction.

(iii) *Post-transaction distribution.* FC does not accumulate any earnings and profits or pay or accrue any foreign income taxes during 2002. On December 31, 2002, FC distributes 100u as a dividend to USP, which has remained its sole shareholder. Under section 989(b)(1), the 100u distribution is translated into US$ at the spot rate on December 31, 2002, to $100. Proportionate parts of the $100 dividend are attributable to the pre-transaction earnings of FC ($37.50 = $100 × (150 ÷ 400)) and USD ($62.50 = $100 × (250 ÷ 400)). See sections 243(e) and 245. Thus, under sections 243(e) and § 1.367(b)-2(j)(3), $62.50 of the distribution is eligible for the dividends received deduction. See also section 861(a)(2)(C). The remaining $37.50 of the distribution (and $15 of related foreign income taxes) is subject to the generally applicable rules concerning dividends paid by foreign corporations.

(d) *Foreign divisive transactions involving a foreign distributing corporation and a domestic controlled corporation.*—(1) *Scope.*—The rules of this paragraph (d) apply to a foreign divisive transaction involving a foreign distributing corporation and a domestic controlled corporation.

(2) *Coordination with § 1.367(b)-3.*— (i) *In general.*—In the case of a foreign divisive transaction that includes a D reorganization, the rules of § 1.367(b)-3 are applicable with respect to the pre-transaction earnings of a foreign distributing corporation that are allocable to a domestic controlled corporation under paragraph (b)(1)(i) of this section.

(ii) *Determination of all earnings and profits amount.*—An all earnings and profits amount inclusion under paragraph (d)(2)(i) of this section shall be computed with respect to the pre-transaction earnings that are allocable to the domestic controlled corporation, without regard to the parenthetical phrase in paragraph (b)(4)(ii)(A) of this section.

(iii) *Interaction with section 358 and § 1.367(b)-2(e)(3)(ii).*—The basis increase provided in § 1.367(b)-2(e)(3)(ii) shall apply to an all earnings and profits amount inclusion under paragraph (d)(2)(i) of this section, subject to the following rules—

(A) Section 358 shall apply to determine the distributee's basis in the foreign distributing and domestic controlled corporation without regard to the all earnings and profits amount inclusion;

(B) After application of the rule in paragraph (d)(2)(iii)(A) of this section, the basis increase provided in § 1.367(b)-2(e)(3)(ii) shall be applied in a manner that attributes such basis increase solely to the exchanging shareholder's stock in the domestic controlled corporation; and

(C) the rule of paragraph (d)(2)(iii)(B) of this section shall apply prior to § 1.367(b)-5(c)(4) and (d)(4).

(iv) *Coordination with § 1.367(b)-3(c).*—In applying the rule of § 1.367(b)-3(c)(2), an exchanging shareholder described in § 1.367(b)-3(c)(1) shall recognize gain with respect to the stock of the domestic controlled corporation after the foreign divisive transaction.

(v) *Special rule for U.S. persons that own foreign distributing corporation stock after a non pro rata distribution.*—[Reserved]

(3) *Foreign income taxes.*—Pre-transaction taxes related to a foreign distributing corporation's pre-transaction earnings that are allocable or are reduced under the rules described in paragraph (b)(1)(i) of this section shall be ratably reduced. Pre-transaction taxes related to a foreign distributing corporation's pre-transaction earnings that are allocable to a domestic controlled corporation under the rules described in paragraph (b)(1)(i) of this section shall not carry over to the domestic controlled corporation. Nothing in this paragraph (d)(3) shall affect the deemed paid taxes that otherwise would accompany an inclusion under § 1.367(b)-5 or paragraph (d)(2)(i) of this section.

(4) *Previously taxed earnings and profits.*— [Reserved]

(5) *Coordination with § 1.367(b)-5.*—See also § 1.367(b)-5(c) and (d) for other rules that may apply to a foreign divisive transaction described in paragraph (d)(1) of this section.

(6) *Examples.*—The following examples illustrate the application of the rules of this section to transactions described in paragraph (d)(1) of this section. The examples presume the following facts: FD is a foreign corporation engaged in manufacturing and shipping activities through Business A and Business B, respectively. Any earnings and profits of FD described in section 904(d)(1)(D) (shipping income) qualified for the high tax exception from subpart F income under section 954(b)(4), and FD'S United States shareholders elected to exclude the earnings and profits from subpart F income under section 954(b)(4) and § 1.954-1(d)(5). USC is a domestic corporation that is wholly owned by FD. FD and USC use

calendar taxable years. FD (and all of its qualified business units as defined in section 989) maintains a "u" functional currency, and 1u = US$1 at all times. The examples are as follows:

Example 1—(i) *Facts.* (A) USP, a domestic corporation, has owned all of the stock of FD since FD's incorporation in 1995. USP's adjusted basis in the FD stock is $100, and the FD stock has a fair market value of $800. FD owns assets with total net bases of 320u (including 160u attributable to the Business B shipping assets), and has the following pre-transaction earnings and pre-transaction taxes accounts:

Separate Category	E&P	Foreign Taxes
General	300u	$60
Shipping	200u	$80
	500u	$140

(B) On January 1, 2002, FD incorporates USC and transfers to USC the Business B shipping assets. FD then distributes the USC stock to USP. The transaction meets the requirements of sections 368(a)(1)(D) and 355. Immediately after the foreign divisive transaction, the FD stock and the USC stock each have a fair market value of $400.

(ii) *Results*—(A) *Calculation of FD's earnings and profits.* Under paragraph (b)(1)(i) of this section, FD's pre-transaction earnings are reduced by an amount equal to its pre-transaction earnings times the net bases of the assets transferred to USC divided by the net bases of the assets held by FD immediately before the foreign divisive transaction (500u × (160u ÷ 320u) = 250u). Following this reduction, FD has 250u of earnings and profits (500u – 250u).

(B) *All earnings and profits amount inclusion.* Under § 1.367(b)-3 and paragraph (d)(2)(i) of this section, USP includes in income as an all earnings and profits amount the pre-transaction earnings of FD that are allocable to USC under paragraph (b)(1)(i) of this section. Thus, USP's all earnings and profits amount inclusion is $250. See also section 989(b)(1) and paragraph (d)(2)(ii) of this section. Under § 1.367(b)-3(b)(3)(i) and § 1.367(b)-2(e), USP includes the all earnings and profits amount as a deemed dividend received from FD immediately before the foreign divisive transaction. Because the requirements of section 902 are met, USP qualifies for a deemed paid foreign tax credit with respect to the deemed dividend that it receives from FD. Under § 1.902-1(d)(1), the $250 deemed dividend is out of FD's separate categories and reduces foreign income taxes as follows:

Separate Category	E&P	Foreign Taxes
General	150u	$30
Shipping	100u	$40
	250u	$70

(C) *Calculation of USP's basis in USC and USC's earnings and profits.* Under paragraph (d)(2)(iii) of this section, the § 1.367(b)-2(e)(3)(ii) basis increase applies with respect to USP's all earnings and profits amount inclusion from FD and is attributed solely to USP's basis in USC (after application of section 358). Accordingly, USP has a $300 basis in the USC stock ($50 section 358 basis, determined by reference to the relative values of USP's FD and USC stock: $100 pre-transaction basis × ($400 ÷ $800) + $250 § 1.367(b)-2(e)(3)(ii) basis increase = $300). Because USP included in income as a deemed dividend under § 1.367(b)-3 and paragraph (d)(2) of this section the pre-transaction earnings of FD that are allocable to USC under paragraph (b)(1)(i) of this section, such earnings and profits are not available to increase USC's earnings and profits. As a result, USC has zero earnings and profits immediately after the foreign divisive transaction.

(D) *Application of § 1.367(b)-5(c).* The basis adjustment and income inclusion rules of § 1.367(b)-5(c)(2) apply if USP's postdistribution amount with respect to FD stock is less than its predistribution amount with respect to FD stock. Under § 1.367(b)-5(e)(1), USP's predistribution amount with respect to FD stock is USP's section 1248 amount attributable to such stock computed immediately before the distribution but after taking into account the allocation of earnings and profits as a result of the D reorganization. Thus, USP's predistribution amount with respect to FD stock is $250 (500u – 250u). See also section 989(b)(2). Under section 358, USP allocates its $100 basis in FD stock between FD stock and USC stock according to the stock blocks' relative values, yielding a $50 ($100 × ($400 ÷ $800)) basis in FD stock. See also paragraph (d)(2)(iii) of this section. Under § 1.367(b)-5(e)(2), USP's postdistribution amount with respect to FD stock is USP's section 1248 amount with respect to such stock, computed immediately after the distribution. Accordingly, USP's

Prop. Reg. § 1.367(b)-8(d)(6)

postdistribution amount with respect to FD stock is $250. Because USP's, postdistribution amount with respect to FD stock is not less than its predistribution amount, USP is not required to make any basis adjustment or include any income under §1.367(b)-5(c).

(E) *FD's earnings and profits after the foreign divisive transaction.* Following the reduction described in this *Example 1* (ii)(A) and (B), FD has the following earnings and profits and foreign income taxes accounts:

Separate Category	E&P	Foreign Taxes
General	150u	$30
Shipping	100u	$40
	250u	$70

Example 2—(i) *Facts*. (A) USP, a domestic corporation, has owned all of the stock of FD since FD's incorporation in 1995. USP's adjusted basis in the FD stock is $400 and the FD stock has a fair market value of $800. USC is a preexisting controlled corporation. FD owns assets with net total bases of 320u (including 160u attributable to the USC stock), and has the following pre-transaction earnings and pre-transaction taxes accounts:

Separate Category	E&P	Foreign Taxes
General	300u	$60
Shipping	200u	$80
	500u	$140

(B) On January 1, 2002, FD distributes the USC stock to USP in a transaction that meets the requirements of section 355. Immediately after the foreign divisive transaction, the FD stock and the USC stock each have a $400 fair market value.

(ii) *Results*—(A) *Calculation of FD's earnings and profits*. Under paragraphs (b)(1)(i) and (b)(1)(ii)(A) of this section, FD's pre-transaction earnings are reduced by the amount of the reduction that would have been required if FD had transferred the stock of USC to a new corporation in a D reorganization. Thus, FD's pre-transaction earnings are reduced by an amount equal to its pre-transaction earnings times its net basis in the USC stock divided by the net bases of the assets held by FD immediately before the foreign divisive transaction (500u × (160u ÷ 320u) = 250u). Following this reduction, FD has 250u of earnings and profits (500u – 250u).

(B) *Calculation of USC's earnings and profits*. Under paragraph (b)(1)(ii)(B) of this section, USC's earnings and profits are not increased (or replaced) as a result of the foreign divisive transaction. As a result, USP is not required to include an amount in income under paragraph (d)(2)(i) of this section.

(C) *Application of §1.367(b)-5(c)*. The basis adjustment and income inclusion rules of §1.367(b)-5(c)(2) apply if USP's postdistribution amount with respect to FD stock is less than its predistribution amount with respect to FD stock. Under §1.367(b)-5(e)(1), USP's predistribution amount with respect to FD stock is USP's section 1248 amount attributable to such stock computed immediately before the distribution. Thus, USP's predistribution amount with respect to FD stock is $400 (the predistribution amount is limited to USP's built-in gain in FD stock immediately before the distribution ($800 – $400)). See also section 989(b)(2). Under section 358, USP allocates its $400 basis in FD stock between FD stock and USC stock according to the stock blocks' relative values, yielding a $200 ($400 × ($400 ÷ $800)) basis in each block. Under §1.367(b)-5(e)(2), USP's postdistribution amount with respect to FD stock is USP's section 1248 amount with respect to such stock, computed immediately after the distribution. Accordingly, USP's postdistribution amount with respect to FD stock is $200 (the postdistribution amount is limited to USP's built-in gain in FD stock immediately after the distribution ($400 – $200)). Because USP's postdistribution amount with respect to FD stock is $200 less than its predistribution amount with respect to such stock ($400 – $200), §1.367(b)-5(c)(2)(i) and (ii) require USP to reduce its basis in FD stock by the $200 difference, but only to the extent such reduction increases USP's section 1248 amount with respect to the FD stock. As a result, USP reduces its basis in the FD stock from $200 to $150 and includes $150 in income as a deemed dividend from FD. Because the requirements of section 902 are met, USP qualifies for a deemed paid foreign tax credit with respect to the deemed dividend that it receives from FD. Under §1.902-1(d)(1), the $150 deemed dividend is out of FD's separate categories and reduces foreign income taxes as follows:

Prop. Reg. §1.367(b)-8(d)(6)

Separate Category	E&P	Foreign Taxes
General	90u	$18
Shipping	60u	$24
	150u	$42

(D) *Basis adjustment.* Under § 1.367(b)-5(c)(3), USP does not increase its basis in FD stock as a result of USP's $150 deemed dividend from FD. Under § 1.367(b)-5(c)(4), USP increases its basis in the USC stock by the amount by which it decreased its basis in the FD stock, as well as by the amount of its deemed dividend inclusion. The § 1.367(b)-5(c)(4) basis increase applies in full because USP's basis in the USC stock is not increased above the fair market value of such stock. Thus, USP increases its basis in USC stock to $400 ($200 + $50 + $150).

(E) *Reduction in FD's statutory groupings of earnings and profits.* Under paragraph (b)(2) of this section, the reduction in FD's pre-transaction earnings that is not attributable to USP's inclusion under § 1.367(b)-5 decreases FD's statutory groupings of earnings and profits on a pro rata basis. Under paragraph (d)(3) of this section, FD's pre-transaction taxes also are ratably reduced. As described in this *Example 2* (ii)(A), the reduction in FD's pre-transaction earnings is 250u. As described in this *Example 2* (ii)(C), 150u of the 250u reduction is attributable to an inclusion under § 1.367(b)-5. As a result, under paragraphs (b)(2) and (d)(3) of this section the remaining 100u reduction in FD's pre-transaction earnings is out of the following separate categories of earnings and profits and foreign income taxes:

Separate Category	E&P	Foreign Taxes
General	60u	$12
Shipping	40u	$16
	100u	$28

(F) *FD's earnings and profits after the foreign divisive transaction.* After the reductions described in this *Example 2* (ii)(C) and (E), FD has the following earnings and profits and foreign income taxes accounts:

Separate Category	E&P	Foreign Taxes
General	150u	$30
Shipping	100u	$40
	250u	$70

Example 3—(i) *Facts.* (A) USP, a domestic corporation, has owned all of the stock of FD since FD's incorporation in 1995. USP's adjusted basis in the FD stock is $400 and the FD stock has a fair market value of $800. USC is a preexisting controlled corporation. FD owns assets with total net bases of 320u (including 160u attributable to the USC stock and 80u attributable to the Business B shipping assets), and has the following pre-transaction earnings and pre-transaction taxes accounts:

Separate Category	E&P	Foreign Taxes
General	300u	$ 60
Shipping	200u	$80
	500u	$140

(B) On January 1, 2002, FD transfers to USC the Business B shipping assets. FD then distributes the USC stock to USP. The transaction meets the requirements of sections 368(a)(1)(D) and 355. Immediately after the foreign divisive transaction, the FD stock has a $200 fair market value and the USC stock has a $600 fair market value.

(ii) *Results*—(A) *Calculation of FD's earnings and profits.* Under paragraph (b)(4)(i) of this section, FD's pre-transaction earnings are reduced by the sum of the amounts described in paragraphs (b)(4)(i)(A) and (B) of this section. Under paragraph (b)(4)(i)(A) of this section, FD's pre-transaction earnings are reduced by an amount equal to FD's pre-transaction earnings times the net bases of the Business B shipping assets transferred to USC divided by the total net bases of the assets held by FD immediately before the foreign divisive transaction (500u × (80u ÷ 320u) = 125u). Under paragraph (b)(4)(i)(B) of this section, FD's pre-transaction earnings are reduced by an amount equal to FD's pre-transaction earnings times FD's net basis in the stock of USC divided by the total net bases of the assets held by FD immediately before the foreign divisive transaction (500u × (160u ÷ 320u) = 250u). The sum of

Prop. Reg. § 1.367(b)-8(d)(6)

the amounts described in paragraphs (b)(4)(i)(A) and (B) of this section is 375u (125u + 250u).

(B) *All earnings and profits amount inclusion.* Under §1.367(b)-3 and paragraph (d)(2)(i) of this section, USP is required to include in income as an all earnings and profits amount the pre-transaction earnings of FD that are allocable to USC under paragraph (b)(1)(i) of this section. Under paragraph (b)(4)(ii)(A) of this section, the 125u of pre-transaction earnings described in paragraph (b)(4)(i)(A) are allocable to USC. Thus, the all earnings and profits amount is $125. See also section 989(b)(1) and paragraph (d)(2)(ii) of this section. Under §§1.367(b)-3(b)(3)(i) and 1.367(b)-2(e), USP includes the all earnings and profits amount as a deemed dividend received from FD immediately before the foreign divisive transaction. Because the requirements of section 902 are met, USP qualifies for a deemed paid foreign tax credit with respect to the deemed dividend that it receives from FD. Under §1.902-1(d)(1), the $125 deemed dividend is out of FD's separate categories and reduces foreign income taxes as follows:

Separate Category	E&P	Foreign Taxes
General	75u	$15
Shipping	50u	$20
	125u	$35

(C) *Calculation of USP's basis in USC and USC's earnings and profits.* Under paragraph (d)(2)(iii) of this section, the §1.367(b)-2(e)(3)(ii) basis increase applies with respect to USP's all earnings and profits amount inclusion and is attributed solely to USP's basis in USC (after application of section 358). Accordingly, USP has a $425 basis in the USC stock ($300 section 358 basis, determined by reference to the relative values of USP's FD and USC stock: $400 pre-transaction basis × ($600 ÷ $800) + $125 §1.367(b)-2(e)(3)(ii) basis increase = $425). Because USP included in income as a deemed dividend under §1.367(b)-3 and paragraph (d)(2) of this section the pre-transaction earnings of FD that are allocable to USC under paragraph (b)(1)(i) of this section, such earnings and profits are not available to increase USC's earnings and profits. As a result, USC's earnings and profits are not increased as a result of the foreign divisive transaction.

(D) *Application of §1.367(b)-5(c).* The basis adjustment and income inclusion rules of §1.367(b)-5(c)(2) apply if USP's postdistribution amount with respect to FD stock is less than its predistribution amount with respect to FD stock. Under §1.367(b)-5(e)(1) and (3), USP's predistribution amount with respect to FD stock is USP's section 1248 amount attributable to such stock computed immediately before the distribution, after the allocation of FD's pre-transaction earnings described in paragraphs (b)(4)(i)(A) and (ii)(A) of this section, but without regard to the reduction in FD's pre-transaction earnings described in paragraph (b)(4)(i)(B) of this section. Thus, USP's predistribution amount with respect to FD stock is $375 ($500 − $125). See also section 989(b)(2). Under section 358, USP allocates its $400 basis in FD stock between FD stock and USC stock according to the stock blocks' relative values, yielding a $100 ($400 × ($200 ÷ $800)) basis in FD stock. See also paragraph (d)(2)(iii) of this section. Under §1.367(b)-5(e)(2), USP's postdistribution amount with respect to FD stock is USP's section 1248 amount with respect to such stock, computed immediately after the distribution. Accordingly, USP's postdistribution amount with respect to FD stock is $100. (While FD has earnings and profits of 125u immediately after the foreign divisive transaction, USP's postdistribution amount is limited to its built-in gain in FD stock immediately after the distribution ($200 − $100).) Because USP's postdistribution amount with respect to FD stock is $275 less than its predistribution amount with respect to such stock ($375 − $100), §1.367(b)-5(c)(2)(i) and (ii) require USP to reduce its basis in FD stock, but only to the extent such reduction increases USP's section 1248 amount with respect to the FD stock. As a result, USP reduces its basis in the FD stock from $100 to $75 and includes $250 in income as a deemed dividend from FD. Because the requirements of section 902 are met, USP qualifies for a deemed paid foreign tax credit with respect to the deemed dividend that it receives from FD. Under §1.902-1(d)(1), the $250 deemed dividend is out of FD's separate categories and reduces foreign income taxes as follows:

Separate Category	E&P	Foreign Taxes
General	150u	$30
Shipping	100u	$40
	250u	$70

Prop. Reg. §1.367(b)-8(d)(6)

(E) *Basis adjustment.* Under § 1.367(b)-5(c)(3), USP does not increase its basis in FD stock as a result of USP's $250 deemed dividend from FD. Under § 1.367(b)-5(c)(4), USP increases its basis in the USC stock by the amount by which it decreased its basis in the FD stock, as well as by the amount of its deemed dividend inclusion, but only up to the fair market value of USP's USC stock. As described in this *Example 3* (ii)(C), USP has already increased its basis in the USC stock to $425. Because the fair market value of FD's USC stock is $600, USP's basis increase under § 1.367(b)-5(c)(4) is limited to $175. See also paragraph (d)(2)(iii)(C) of this section. Thus, USP has a $600 basis in the USC stock immediately after the foreign divisive transaction.

(F) *Reduction in FD's statutory groupings of earnings and profits.* Under paragraph (b)(2) of this section, the reduction in FD's pre-transaction earnings that is not attributable to USP's inclusion under paragraph (d)(2)(i) of this section or § 1.367(b)-5 decrease FD's statutory groupings of earnings and profits on a pro rata basis. Under paragraph (d)(3) of this section, FD's pre-transaction taxes are also ratably reduced. As described in this *Example 3* (ii)(A), the reduction in FD's pre-transaction earnings is 375u. As described in this *Example 3* (ii)(B) and (D), the entire 375u reduction was subject to inclusion as a deemed dividend by USP under paragraph (d)(2)(i) of this section or § 1.367(b)-5. Thus, none of FD's pre-transaction earnings remain to be reduced under paragraph (b)(2) of this section.

(G) *FD's earnings and profits after the foreign divisive transaction.* After the reductions described in this *Example 3* (ii)(B) and (D), FD has the following earnings and profits and foreign income taxes accounts:

Separate Category	E&P	Foreign Taxes
General	75u	$15
Shipping	50u	$20
	125u	$35

(e) *Foreign divisive transactions involving a foreign distributing corporation and a foreign controlled corporation.*—(1) *Scope.*—The rules of this paragraph (e) apply to a foreign divisive transaction involving a foreign distributing corporation and a foreign controlled corporation.

(2) *Earnings and profits of foreign controlled corporation.*—(i) *In general.*—Except to the extent specified in paragraph (e)(2)(ii) of this section, pre-transaction earnings of a foreign distributing corporation that are allocated to a foreign controlled corporation under the rules described in paragraphs (b)(1)(i) and (4) of this section shall carry over to the foreign controlled corporation in accordance with the rules described in § 1.367(b)-7.

(ii) *Special rule for pre-transaction earnings allocated to a newly created controlled corporation.*—Section 1.367(b)-9 shall apply to pre-transaction earnings that are allocated from a foreign distributing corporation to a newly created foreign controlled corporation under the rules described in paragraph (b)(1)(i) of this section.

(3) *Foreign income taxes.*—Pre-transaction taxes related to a foreign distributing corporation's pre-transaction earnings that are allocated or reduced under the rules described in paragraph (b)(1)(i) of this section shall be ratably reduced. Pre-transaction taxes related to a foreign distributing corporation's pre-transaction earnings that are allocated to a foreign controlled corporation under the rules described in paragraph (b)(1)(i) of this section shall carry over to the foreign controlled corporation in accordance with the rules of § 1.367(b)-7. Section 1.367(b)-9 shall apply to pre-transaction taxes that are allocated from a foreign distributing corporation to a newly created foreign controlled corporation under the rules described in paragraph (b)(1)(i) of this section.

(4) *Previously taxed earnings and profits.*—[Reserved]

(5) *Coordination with § 1.367(b)-5.*—See also § 1.367(b)-5(c) and (d) for other rules that may apply to a foreign divisive transaction described in paragraph (e)(1) of this section.

(6) *Examples.*—The following examples illustrate the application of the rules of this section to transactions described in paragraph (e)(1) of this section. The examples presume the following facts: FD is a foreign corporation engaged in manufacturing and shipping activities through Business A and Business B, respectively. FC is a foreign corporation that is wholly owned by FD. Any earnings and profits of FD or FC described in section 904(d)(1)(D) (shipping income) qualified for the high tax exception from subpart F income under section 954(b)(4), and FD's and FC's United States shareholders elected to exclude the earnings and profits from subpart F income under section 954(b)(4) and § 1.954-1(d)(1). FD and FC have calendar taxable years. FD and FC (and all of their respective qualified business units as defined in section 989) maintain a "u" func-

tional currency, and 1u = US$1 at all times. The examples are as follows:

Example 1—(i) *Facts.* (A) USP, a domestic corporation, has owned all of the stock of FD since FD's incorporation in 1995. USP's adjusted basis in the FD stock is $400 and the FD stock has a fair market value of $800. FD owns assets with total net bases of 320u (including 160u attributable to the Business B shipping assets), and has the following pre-transaction earnings and pre-transaction taxes accounts:

Separate Category	E&P	Foreign Taxes
General	300u	$60
Shipping	200u	$80
	500u	$140

(B) On January 1, 2002, FD incorporates FC and transfers to FC the Business B shipping assets. FD then distributes the FC stock to USP. The transaction meets the requirements of sections 368(a)(1)(D) and 355. Immediately after the foreign divisive transaction, the FD stock and the FC stock each have a $400 fair market value.

(ii) *Result*—(A) *Calculation of FD's earnings and profits.* Under paragraph (b)(1)(i) of this section, FD's pre-transaction earnings are reduced by an amount equal to its pre-transaction earnings times the net bases of the assets transferred to FC divided by the net bases of the assets held by FD immediately before the foreign divisive transaction (500u × (160u ÷ 320u) = 250u). Following this reduction, FD has 250u of earnings and profits (500u − 250u).

(B) *Application of § 1.367(b)-5(c).* The basis adjustment and income inclusion rules of § 1.367(b)-5(c)(2) apply if USP's postdistribution amount with respect to FD or FC stock is less than its predistribution amount with respect to such stock. Under § 1.367(b)-5(e)(1), USP's predistribution amount with respect to FD or FC stock is USP's section 1248 amount attributable to such stock computed immediately before the distribution but after taking into account the allocation of earnings and profits as a result of the D reorganization. Thus, USP's predistribution amounts with respect to FD and FC stock are both $200. See also section 989(b)(2) and § 1.1248-1(d)(3). Under section 358, USP allocates its $400 basis in FD stock between FD stock and FC stock according to the stock blocks' relative values, yielding a $200 ($400 × ($400 ÷ $800)) basis in each block. Under § 1.367(b)-5(e)(2), USP's postdistribution amount with respect to FD or FC stock is USP's section 1248 amount with respect to such stock, computed immediately after the distribution. Accordingly, USP's postdistribution amounts with respect to FD and FC stock are both $200. Because USP's postdistribution amounts with respect to FD and FC stock are not less than USP's respective predistribution amounts, USP is not required to make any basis adjustment or include any income under § 1.367(b)-5(c).

(C) *Reduction in FD's statutory groupings of earnings and profits.* Under paragraph (b)(2) of this section, the 250u reduction in FD's pre-transaction earnings decreases FD's statutory groupings of earnings and profits on a pro rata basis. Under paragraph (e)(3) of this section, FD's pre-transaction taxes also are ratably reduced. Accordingly, FD's pre-transaction earnings and pre-transaction taxes are reduced by the following amounts:

Separate Category	E&P	Foreign Taxes
General	150u	$30
Shipping	100u	$40
	250u	$70

(D) *Calculation of FC's earnings and profits.* Under paragraph (e)(2) of this section, the pre-transaction earnings of FD that are allocated to FC under paragraph (b)(1)(i) of this section carry over to FC in accordance with the rules of § 1.367(b)-7, subject to the rule of § 1.367(b)-9. Under paragraph (e)(3) of this section, FD's pre-transaction taxes related to the pre-transaction earnings that are allocated to FC similarly carry over to FC in accordance with the rules of § 1.367(b)-7, subject to the rule of § 1.367(b)-9. As a result, under § 1.367(b)-7(d), FC has the following earnings and profits and foreign income taxes accounts immediately after the foreign divisive transaction:

Separate Category	E&P	Foreign Taxes
General	150u	$30
Shipping	100u	$40
	250u	$70

Example 2—(i) *Facts.* (A) USP, a domestic corporation, has owned all of the stock of FD since FD's incorporation in 1995. USP's adjusted basis in the FD stock is $300 and the FD stock has a fair market value of $1,500. FC is a preexisting controlled corporation and FD has always owned all of the FC stock. FD owns assets with total net bases of 320u (including

Prop. Reg. § 1.368(b)-8(e)(6)

160u attributable to the FC stock). FD and FC have the following earnings and profits and foreign income taxes accounts:

FD:

Separate Category	E&P	Foreign Taxes
General	400u	$50
Passive	(100u)	$6
Shipping	200u	$80
	500u	$136

FC:

Separate Category	E&P	Foreign Taxes
General	600u	$100
Passive	(50u)	$6
Shipping	100u	$40
	650u	$146

(B) On January 1, 2002, FD distributes the FC stock to USP in a transaction that meets the requirements of section 355. Immediately after the foreign divisive transaction, the FD stock and the FC stock each have a $750 fair market value.

(ii) *Result*—(A) *Calculation of FD's earnings and profits.* Under paragraph (b)(1)(i) and (ii)(A) of this section, FD's pre-transaction earnings are reduced by the amount of the reduction that would have been required if FD had transferred the stock of FC to a new corporation in a D reorganization. Thus, FD's pre-transaction earnings are reduced by an amount equal to its pre-transaction earnings times its net basis in the FC stock divided by the net bases of the assets held by FD immediately before the foreign divisive transaction (500u × (160u ÷ 320u) = 250u). Following this reduction, FD has 250u of earnings and profits (500u – 250u).

(B) *Application of § 1.367(b)-5(c).* The basis adjustment and income inclusion rules of § 1.367(b)-5(c) apply if USP's postdistribution amount with respect to FD or FC stock is less than its predistribution amount with respect to such stock. Under § 1.367(b)-5(e)(1), USP's predistribution amount with respect to FD or FC stock is USP's section 1248 amount attributable to such stock computed immediately before the distribution. Thus, USP's predistribution amounts with respect to FD and FC stock are $500 and $650, respectively. See also section 989(b)(2). Under section 358, USP allocates its $300 basis in FD stock between FD stock and FC stock according to the stock blocks' relative values, yielding a $150 ($300 × ($750 ÷ $1,500)) basis in each block. Under § 1.367(b)-5(e)(2), USP's postdistribution amount with respect to FD or FC stock is USP's section 1248 amount with respect to such stock, computed immediately after the distribution. Accordingly, USP's postdistribution amount with respect to FD stock is $250 (500u – 250u), and its postdistribution amount with respect to FC stock is $600 (while FC has 650u of earnings and profits immediately after the foreign divisive transaction, USP's postdistribution amount is limited to its built-in gain in FC stock immediately after the distribution ($750 – $150)). USP's postdistribution amount with respect to both the FD and FC stock is less than its predistribution amount with respect to such stock. This difference is $50 with respect to FC ($650 – $600), and $250 with respect to FD ($500 – $250). Under § 1.367(b)-5(c)(2)(i) and (ii), USP is required to reduce its basis in the FD and FC stock, but only to the extent such reductions increase USP's section 1248 amount with respect to the stock. Accordingly, USP reduces its basis in the FC stock by $50, and thereafter USP has a $100 basis in such stock ($150 – $100). Because a reduction in USP's basis in FD stock would not increase any of USP's section 1248 amount with respect to such stock, USP includes the entire $250 difference between its predistribution and postdistribution amounts with respect to the FD stock as a deemed dividend from FD. Because the requirements of section 902 are met, USP qualifies for a deemed paid foreign tax credit with respect to the deemed dividend that it receives from FD. Under § 1.960-1(i)(4), the 100u deficit in the section 904(d)(1)(A) passive separate category is allocated proportionately against the other separate categories for purposes of computing the deemed paid credit on the distribution. Thus, there are 333.33u (400u – (100u × (400u ÷ 600u))) of available earnings in the section 904(d)(1)(I) general separate category (along with $50 of foreign income taxes) and 166.67u (200u – (100u × (200u ÷ 600u))) of available earnings in the section 904(d)(1)(D) shipping separate category (along with $80 of foreign income taxes). Under § 1.902-1(d)(1), the $250 deemed dividend is out of FD's separate categories and reduces foreign income taxes as follows:

Separate Category	E&P	Foreign Taxes
General	166.67u	$25
Passive	0u	$0
Shipping	83.33u	$40
	250u	$65

(C) *Basis adjustments.* Under § 1.367(b)-5(c)(3), USP does not increase its basis in FD stock as a result of USP's $250 deemed dividend from FD. Under § 1.367(b)-5(c)(4), USP increases its basis in the FD and FC stock by the amount of its basis decrease or deemed dividend inclusion with respect to the other corporation, but only to the extent such basis increase does not diminish USP's postdistribution amount with respect to that other corporation and only to the extent of the other corporation's fair market value. Under these rules, USP increases its basis in the FD stock by the full amount by which it decreased its basis in FC ($150 + $50 = $200). USP does not increase its basis in the FC stock as a result of its deemed dividend from FD because any increase in the FC stock basis would diminish USP's postdistribution amount with respect to such stock.

(D) *FD's earnings and profits after the foreign divisive transaction.* Because the entire $250 reduction in FD's pre-transaction earnings was subject to inclusion under § 1.367(b)-5 (as described in this *Example 2* (ii)(B)), paragraph (b)(2) of this section does not apply. FD has the following earnings and profits and foreign income taxes accounts immediately after the foreign divisive transaction (see § 1.960-1(i)(4)):

Separate Category	E&P	Foreign Taxes
General	233.33u	$25
Passive	(100u)	$6
Shipping	116.67u	$40
	250u	$71

(E) *Calculation of FC's earnings and profits.* Under paragraph (b)(1)(ii)(B) of this section, FC's earnings and profits are not increased (or replaced) as a result of the foreign divisive transaction. FC's earnings and profits also are not reduced because USP was not required to include a deemed dividend out of FC under § 1.367(b)-5.

Example 3—(i) *Facts.* (A) USP, a domestic corporation, has owned all of the stock of FD since FD's incorporation in 1995. USP's adjusted basis in the FD stock is $100 and the FD stock has a fair market value of $2,000. FC is a preexisting controlled corporation and FD has always owned all of the FC stock. FD owns assets with total net bases of 320u (including 100u attributable to the FC stock and 160u attributable to the Business B shipping assets). FD and FC have the following earnings and profits and foreign income taxes accounts:

FD:
Separate Category	E&P	Foreign Taxes
General	300u	$50
10/50 dividends from FC1, a noncontrolled section 902 corporation	100u	$6
Shipping	200u	$80
	600u	$136

FC:
Separate Category	E&P	Foreign Taxes
General	100u	$10
Passive	(50u)	$6
Shipping	100u	$40
	150u	$56

(B) On January 1, 2002, FD transfers to FC the Business B shipping assets. FD then distributes the FC stock to USP. The transaction meets the requirements of sections 368(a)(1)(D) and 355. Immediately after the foreign divisive transaction, the FD stock and the FC stock each have a $1,000 fair market value.

(ii) *Result*—(A) *Calculation of FD's earnings and profits.* Under paragraph (b)(4)(i) of this section, FD's pre-transaction earnings are reduced by the sum of the amounts described in paragraphs (b)(4)(i)(A) and (B) of this section. Under paragraph (b)(4)(i)(A) of this section, FD's pre-transaction earnings are reduced by an amount equal to FD's pre-transaction earnings times the net bases of the Business B shipping assets transferred to FC divided by the total net bases in the assets held by FD immediately before the foreign divisive transaction (600u × (160u ÷ 320u) = 300u). Under paragraph (b)(4)(i)(B) of this section, FD's pre-transaction earnings are reduced by an amount equal to FD's pre-transaction earnings times FD's net bases in the stock of FC divided by the total net bases of the assets held by FD immediately before the foreign divisive transaction (600u × (100u ÷ 320u) = 187.50u). The sum of the amounts described in paragraphs (b)(4)(i)(A) and (B) of this section is 487.50u.

(B) *Application of § 1.367(b)-5(c)*. The basis adjustment and income inclusion rules of § 1.367(b)-5(c)(2) apply if USP's postdistribution amount with respect to FD or FC stock is less than its predistribution amount with respect to such stock. Under § 1.367(b)-5(e)(1) and (3), USP's predistribution amount with respect to FD or FC stock is USP's section 1248 amount attributable to such stock computed immediately before the distribution, after the allocation of FD's pre-transaction earnings described in paragraphs (b)(4)(i)(A) and (ii)(A) of this section, but before the reduction in FD's pre-transaction earnings described in paragraph (b)(4)(i)(B) of this section. Thus, USP's predistribution amounts with respect to FD and FC stock are $300 (600u − 300u) and $450 (150u + 300u), respectively. See also section 989(b)(2). Under section 358, USP allocates its $100 basis in FD stock between FD stock and FC stock according to the stock blocks' relative values, yielding a $50 ($100 × ($1,000 ÷ $2,000)) basis in each block. Under § 1.367(b)-5(e)(2), USP's postdistribution amount with respect to FD or FC stock is USP's section 1248 amount with respect to such stock, computed immediately after the distribution. Accordingly, USP's postdistribution amount with respect to FD stock is $112.50 (600u − 300u − 187.50u), and its postdistribution amount with respect to FC stock is $450 (150u + 300u). Because USP's postdistribution amount with respect to FC stock is not less than its predistribution amount with respect to such stock, the § 1.367(b)-5(c)(2) basis adjustment and income inclusion rules do not apply with respect to the FC stock. Because USP's postdistribution amount with respect to FD stock is $187.50 less than its predistribution amount with respect to such stock ($300 − $112.50), § 1.367(b)-5(c)(2)(i) and (ii) require USP to reduce its basis in FD stock, but only to the extent such reduction increases USP's section 1248 amount with respect to the FD stock. Because a reduction in USP's basis in the FD stock would not increase any of USP's section 1248 amount with respect to such stock, USP includes the entire $187.50 difference between its predistribution and postdistribution amounts with respect to the FD stock as a deemed dividend from FD. Because the requirements of section 902 are met, USP qualifies for a deemed paid foreign tax credit with respect to the deemed dividend that it receives from FD. Under § 1.902-1(d)(1), the $187.50 deemed dividend is out of FD's separate categories and reduces foreign income taxes as follows:

Separate Category	E&P	Foreign Taxes
General	93.75u	$15.63
10/50 dividends from FC1	31.25u	$1.88
Shipping	62.50u	$25
	187.50u	$42.51

(C) *Basis adjustment*. Under § 1.367(b)-5(c)(3), the basis increase provided in § 1.367(b)-2(e)(3)(ii) does not apply with respect to USP's $187.50 deemed dividend from FD. Under § 1.367(b)-5(c)(4), USP increases its basis in the FC stock by the amount of its deemed dividend inclusion from FD, but only to the extent such basis increase does not diminish USP's postdistribution amount with respect to FC stock and only up to the fair market value of the FC stock. Under these rules, USP increases its basis in the FC stock by the full amount of its deemed dividend from FD ($50 + $187.50 = $237.50).

(D) *Reduction in FD's statutory groupings of earnings and profits*. Under paragraph (b)(2) of this section, the reduction in FD's pre-transaction earnings that is not attributable to USP's inclusion under § 1.367(b)-5 decreases FD's statutory groupings of earnings and profits on a pro rata basis. Under paragraph (e)(3) of this section, FD's pre-transaction taxes are also ratably reduced. As described in this *Example 3* (ii)(A), the reduction in FD's pre-transaction earnings is 487.50u. As described in this *Example 3* (ii)(B), 187.50u of the 487.50u reduction is attributable to a deemed dividend inclusion by USP under § 1.367(b)-5. Thus, under paragraphs (b)(2) and (e)(3) of this section, the remaining 300u reduction in FD's pre-transaction earnings and related pre-transaction taxes is out of FD's separate categories and reduces foreign income taxes as follows:

Separate Category	E&P	Foreign Taxes
General	150u	$25
10/50 dividends from FC1	50u	$3
Shipping	100u	$40
	300u	$68

(E) *Calculation of FC's earnings and profits*. Under paragraph (b)(4)(ii) of this section, FC's earnings and profits immediately after the foreign divisive transaction equal the sum of FC's earnings and profits immediately before the foreign divisive transaction, plus the amount of the reduction in FD's earnings and profits described in paragraph (b)(4)(i)(A) of this section, except to the extent such amount was included in income as a deemed dividend pursuant to the foreign divisive transaction. The reduction in FD's earnings and profits described in paragraph (b)(4)(i)(A) of this section is 300u, none of which was included in income by USP as a deemed dividend pursuant to the foreign divisive transaction. Under paragraphs (e)(2) and (3) of this section, the 300u of pre-transaction earnings and related pre-transaction taxes carry over to FC and combine with FC's earnings and profits and foreign income taxes accounts in accordance with the rules described in § 1.367(b)-7. Under § 1.367(b)-7(d), FC has the following earnings and profits and foreign income taxes accounts immediately after the foreign divisive transaction:

Separate Category	E&P	Hovering Deficit	Taxes	Taxes Associated w/ Hovering Deficit
General	250u		$35	
10/50 dividends from FC1	50u		$3	
Passive		(50u)		$6
Shipping	200u		$80	
	500u	(50u)	$118	$6

(F) *FD's earnings and profits after the foreign divisive transaction.* Following the reductions described in this *Example 3* (ii)(B) and (D), FD has the following earnings and profits and foreign income taxes accounts:

Separate Category	E&P	Foreign Taxes
General	56.25u	$9.37
10/50 dividends from FC1	18.75u	$1.12
Shipping	37.50u	$15
	112.50u	$25.49

(f) *Effective date.*—This section shall apply to section 367(b) exchanges that occur on or after the date 30 days after these regulations are published as final regulations in the Federal Register. [Prop. Reg. § 1.367(b)-8.]

[Proposed 11-15-2000 (*corrected* 3-12-2001).]

Proposed Regulation

§ 1.367(b)-9. Special rule for F reorganizations and similar transactions.—
(a) *Scope.*—This section applies to any foreign 381 transaction (as described in § 1.367(b)-7(a)) described in section 368(a)(1)(F) or in which either the foreign target corporation or the foreign acquiring corporation is newly created. This section also applies to any foreign divisive transaction (as described in § 1.367(b)-8(a)) that is described in § 1.367(b)-8(e)(1) and that involves a newly created foreign distributing or foreign controlled corporation.

(b) *Hovering deficit rules inapplicable.*—If a transaction is described in paragraph (a) of this section, a foreign surviving corporation or a newly created controlled corporation shall succeed to earnings and profits, deficits in earnings and profits, and foreign income taxes without regard to the hovering deficit rules of § 1.367(b)-7(d)(2), (e)(1)(iii), (e)(2)(iii), (f)(1)(iii), and (f)(2)(iii). In the case of a foreign divisive transaction, nothing in this section shall affect the application of § 1.367(b)-8(b)(iii).

(c) *Example.*—The following example illustrates the rules of this section:

Example—(i) *Facts.* (A) Foreign corporation A is and always has been a wholly owned subsidiary of USP, a domestic corporation. Foreign corporation A was incorporated in 1990, and always has been a controlled foreign corporation using a calendar taxable year. Foreign corporation A (and all of its respective qualified business units as defined in section 989) maintains a "u" functional currency, and 1u = US$1 at all times. On December 31, 2001, foreign corporation A has the following earnings and profits and foreign income taxes accounts:

Separate Category	E&P	Foreign Taxes
Passive	(1,000u)	$5
General	200u	$200
	(800u)	$205

(B) On January 1, 2002, foreign corporation A moves its place of incorporation from Country 1 to Country 2 in a reorganization described in section 368(a)(1)(F).

(ii) *Result.* Under § 1.367(b)-7(d), as modified by paragraph (b) of this section, foreign surviving corporation has the following earnings and profits and foreign income taxes accounts immediately after the foreign 381 transaction:

Separate Category	E&P	Foreign Taxes
Passive	(1,000u)	$5
General	200u	$200
	(800u)	$205

(d) *Effective date.*—This section shall apply to section 367(b) exchanges that occur on or after the date 30 days after these regulations are published as final regulations in the Federal Register. [Prop. Reg. § 1.367(b)-9.]

[Proposed 11-15-2000.]

§ 1.367(b)-12. Subsequent treatment of amounts attributed or included in income.—(a) *In general.*—This section applies to distributions with respect to, or a disposition of, stock—

(1) To which, in connection with an exchange occurring before February 23, 2000, an amount has been attributed pursuant to § 7.367(b)-9 or 7.367(b)-10 of this chapter (as in effect prior to February 23, 2000, see 26 CFR part 1 revised as of April 1, 1999); or

(2) In respect of which, before February 23, 2000, an amount has been included in income or added to earnings and profits pursuant to § 7.367(b)-7 or 7.367(b)-10 of this chapter (as in effect prior to February 23, 2000, see 26 CFR part 1 revised as of April 1, 1999).

(b) *Applicable rules.*—See § 7.367(b)-12(b) through (e) of this chapter (as in effect prior to January 11, 2001, see 26 CFR part 1 revised as of April 1, 2000) for purposes of applying paragraph (a) of this section.

(c) *Effective date.*—This section applies to distributions or dispositions that occur on or after January 11, 2001. [Reg. § 1.367(b)-12.]

☐ [*T.D.* 8937, 1-10-2001.]

§ 1.367(d)-1T. Transfers of intangible property to foreign corporations (temporary).—(a) *Purpose and scope.*—This section provides rules under section 367(d) concerning transfers of intangible property by U.S. persons to foreign corporations pursuant to section 351 or 361. Paragraph (b) of this section specifies the transfers that are subject to section 367(d) and the rules of this section, while paragraph (c) provides rules concerning the consequences of such a transfer. In general, the U.S. transferor will be treated as receiving annual payments contingent on productivity or use of the transferred property, over the useful life of the property (regardless of whether such payments are in fact made by the transferee). Paragraphs (d), (e), and (f) of this section provide rules for cases in which there is a later direct or indirect disposition of the intangible property transferred. In general, deemed annual license payments will continue if a transfer is made to a related person, while gain must be recognized immediately if the transfer is to an unrelated person. Paragraph (g) of this section provides several special rules, including a rule allowing appropriate adjustments where deemed payments under section 367(d) are not in fact received by the U.S. transferor of the intangible property, and a rule providing for a limited election to treat certain transfers of intangible property as sales at fair market value (in lieu of applying the general useful life-contingent payment rule). In addition, paragraph (g) of this section provides rules coordinating the application of section 367(d) with other relevant Code sections. Paragraph (h) of this section defines the term "related person" for purposes of this section. Finally, paragraph (i) of this section provides the effective date of this section. For rules concerning transfers of intangible property pursuant to section 332, see § 1.367(a)-5T(e). For purposes of determining whether a U.S. person has made a transfer of intangible property that is subject to the rules of section 367(d), the rules of § 1.367(a)-1T(c) shall apply.

(b) *Intangible property subject to section 367(d).*—Section 367(d) and the rules of this section shall apply to the transfer of any intangible property, as defined in § 1.367(a)-1T(d)(5)(i). However, section 367(d) and the rules of this section shall not apply to the transfer of foreign goodwill or going concern value, as defined in § 1.367(a)-1T(d)(5)(iii), or to the transfer of intangible property described in § 1.367(a)-5T(b)(2). However, the transfer of those items to a foreign corporation is subject to the rules set forth in § 1.367(a)-6T, and the transfer of intangible property described in § 1.367(a)-5T(b)(2) is subject to the rules set forth in § 1.367(a)-5T. For a special rule relating to the transfer of operating intangibles, as defined in § 1.367(a)-1T(d)(5)(ii), see paragraph (g)(3) of this section. Transfers of intangible property to foreign corporations pursuant to section 351 or 361 are subject to the rules of this section regardless of whether the property is to be used in the United States, in connection with goods to be sold or consumed in the United States, or in connection with a trade or business outside the United States.

(c) *Deemed payments upon transfer of intangible property to foreign corporation.*—(1) *In general.*—If a U.S. person transfers intangible property that is subject to section 367(d) and the rules of this section to a foreign corporation in an exchange described in section 351 or 361, then such person shall be treated as having transferred that property in exchange for annual payments contingent on the productivity or use of the property. Such person shall, over the useful life of the property, annually include in gross income an amount that represents an appropriate arms-length charge for the use of the property. The appropriate charge shall be determined in accordance with the provisions of section 482 and regulations thereunder. See § 1.482-2(d). The amount of the deemed payment thus calculated shall be reduced by any royalty or other periodic payment made or accrued by the transferee to an unrelated person during that taxable year for the right to use the intangible property. Amounts so included in the transferor's income shall be treated as ordinary income from sources within the United States. For purposes of computing estimated tax payments, deemed payments under this paragraph (c) shall be treated as received by the transferor on the last day of its taxable year.

(2) *Required adjustments.*—The following adjustments shall be made with respect to a U.S. person's recognition of a deemed payment for the use of intangible property under this paragraph (c):

(i) For purposes of chapter 1 of the Code, the earnings and profits of the transferee foreign corporation shall be reduced by the amount of such deemed payment; and

(ii) For purposes of subpart F of part III of subchapter N of the Code, the transferee foreign corporation may treat such deemed payment as an expense (whether or not that amount is actually paid), properly allocated and apportioned to gross income subject to subpart F, in accordance with the provisions of §§ 1.954-1(c) and 1.861-8.

No other special adjustments to earnings and profits, basis, or gross income shall be permitted by reason of the recognition of a deemed payment under this paragraph (c). However, see paragraph (g)(1) of this section for rules permitting the establishment of an account receivable with respect to deemed payments not actually received by the U.S. person.

(3) *Useful life.*—For purposes of this section, the useful life of intangible property is the entire period during which the property has value. However, in no event shall the useful life of an item of intangible property be considered to exceed twenty years. If intangible property derives its value from secrecy or from protections afforded by law, the useful life of such property shall terminate when the property is no longer secret or no longer legally protected.

(4) *Blocked income.*—No deemed payment included in a taxpayer's income under paragraph (c)(1) of this section shall be treated as deferrable income for purposes of applying rules relating to blocked foreign income. See Revenue Ruling 74-351, 1974-2 C.B. 144.

(d) *Subsequent transfer of stock of transferee foreign corporation to unrelated person.*—(1) *Treatment as sale of intangible property.*—If a U.S. person transfers intangible property that is subject to section 367(d) and the rules of this section to a foreign corporation in an exchange described in section 351 or 361, and within the useful life of the intangible property that U.S. transferor subsequently disposes of the stock of the transferee foreign corporation to a person that is not a related person (within the meaning of paragraph (h) of this section), then the U.S. transferor shall be treated as having simultaneously sold the intangible property to the person acquiring the stock of the transferee foreign corporation. The U.S. transferor shall be required to recognize gain (but not loss) from sources within the United States in an amount equal to the difference between the fair market value of the transferred intangible property on the date of the subsequent disposition and the U.S. transferor's former adjusted basis in that property (determined as of the original transfer). If the U.S. transferor's disposition of the stock of the transferee foreign corporation is subject to U.S. tax other than by reason of this paragraph (d), then the amount of gain otherwise required to be recognized with respect to the stock of the transferee foreign corporation shall be reduced by the amount of gain recognized with respect to the intangible property pursuant to this paragraph (d).

(2) *Required adjustments.*—If a U.S. person disposes of the stock of a transferee foreign corporation, and under paragraph (d)(1) of this section is treated as having simultaneously sold intangible property, then, for purposes of computing basis and earnings and profits, the person acquiring the stock of the transferee foreign corporation shall be deemed to have purchased that property at fair market value and to have immediately thereafter contributed it to the transferee foreign corporation in a transaction not covered by section 367(d). Therefore, for purposes of chapter 1 of the Code—

(i) The transferee foreign corporation's basis in the intangible property will be equal to its fair market value (as calculated for purposes of determining the gain required to be recognized by the U.S. transferor);

(ii) The acquiring person's basis in the stock of the transferee foreign corporation shall be determined as if no portion of the consideration given by the acquiring person for the stock is attributable to the intangible property; and

(iii) The earnings and profits of the transferee foreign corporation will not be affected by the transfer of its stock or the deemed transfer to it of the intangible property.

(e) *Subsequent transfer of stock of transferee foreign corporation to related person.*—(1) *Transfer to related U.S. person treated as disposition of intangible property.*—If a U.S. person transfers intangible property that is subject to section 367(d) and the rules of this section to a foreign corporation in an exchange described in section 351 or 361 and, within the useful life of the transferred intangible property, that U.S. transferor subsequently transfers the stock of the transferee foreign corporation to U.S. persons that are related to the transferor within the meaning of paragraph (h) of this section, then the following rules shall apply:

(i) Each such related U.S. person shall be treated as having received (with the stock of the transferee foreign corporation) a right to receive a proportionate share of the contingent annual payments that would otherwise be deemed to be received by the U.S. transferor under paragraph (c) of this section.

(ii) Each such related U.S. person shall, over the useful life of the property, annually include in gross income a proportionate share of the amount that would have been included in the income of the U.S. transferor pursuant to paragraph (c) of this section. Such amounts shall be treated as ordinary income from sources within the United States.

(iii) The amount of income required to be recognized by the U.S. transferor pursuant to the rule of paragraph (d)(1) of this section shall be reduced to the amount determined in accordance with the following formula:

(d)(1) amount × (100% − (e) percentage).

For purposes of the above formula, the "(d)(1) amount" is the income that would otherwise be required to be recognized by the transferor corporation pursuant to paragraph (d)(1) of this section, and the "(e) percentage" is the percentage of the transferor corporation's total deemed rights to receive contingent annual payments under paragraph (c) of this section that is deemed to be transferred to related U.S. persons under the rules of this paragraph (e).

(iv) The rules of paragraphs (d) and (e) of this section shall be reapplied in the case of any later transfer of the stock of the transferee foreign corporation by a related U.S. person that received such stock in a transfer that was subject to the rules of this paragraph (e). For purposes of reapplying the rules of paragraphs (d) and (e), each such related U.S. person shall be treated as a U.S. transferor of intangible property to the transferee foreign corporation (to the extent of the interest attributed to such person pursuant to subdivision (i) of this paragraph (e)(1)).

(2) *Required adjustments.*—If a U.S. person transfers stock of a transferee foreign corporation to a U.S. related person in a transaction that is subject to the rules of paragraph (e)(1) of this section, the following adjustments shall be made:

(i) For purposes of chapter 1 of the Code, the earnings and profits of the transferee foreign corporation shall be reduced by the amount of any payment deemed to be received by a related U.S. person under paragraph (e)(1)(ii) of this section;

(ii) For purposes of subpart F of part III of subchapter N of the Code, the transferee foreign corporation may allocate and apportion such deemed payments (whether or not such payments are actually made) to gross income subject to subpart F to the extent appropriate under the provisions of §§ 1.954-1(c) and 1.861-8;

(iii) For purposes of reapplying the rules of paragraphs (d) and (e) of this section, if the related U.S. person is deemed to have received a right to contingent annual payments for the use of intangible property, then the U.S. related person shall be deemed to have held a proportionate share of the property with a basis equal to a proportionate share of the U.S. transferor's adjusted basis plus the gain, if any, recognized by the U.S. transferor on the earlier transfer of the stock to the U.S. related person, and then to have transferred that proportionate share of the property to the foreign corporation in a transfer subject to section 367(d); and

(iv) If the U.S. transferor is itself required to recognize gain upon the transfer by reason of the operation of paragraphs (d)(1) and (e)(1)(iii) of this section (because stock of the transferee foreign corporation is also transferred to unrelated persons), then those unrelated persons shall be deemed to have purchased a proportionate share of the transferred intangible property at fair market value and immediately contributed that property to the transferee foreign corporation, consistent with the general rule of paragraph (d)(2) of this section concerning transfers of stock to unrelated persons. Therefore, for purposes of chapter 1 of the Code—

(A) Each unrelated person's basis in the stock of the transferee foreign corporation shall be increased to the extent of the gain recognized by the U.S. transferor upon the deemed purchase of intangible property by that person; and

(B) The transferee foreign corporation will receive an increase in its basis in the transferred intangible property equal to the fair market value of that portion of the intangible

Reg. § 1.367(d)-1T(e)(2)(iv)(B)

property deemed to be contributed to the transferee foreign corporation by unrelated persons (as calculated for purposes of determining the gain required to be recognized by the U.S. transferor).

(3) *Transfer to related foreign person not treated as disposition of intangible property.*—If a U.S. person transfers intangible property that is subject to section 367(d) and the rules of this section to a foreign corporation in an exchange described in section 351 or 361, and within the useful life of the transferred intangible property that U.S. transferor subsequently transfers any of the stock of the transferee foreign corporation to one or more foreign persons that are related to the transferor within the meaning of paragraph (h) of this section, then the U.S. transferor shall continue to include in its income the deemed payments described in paragraph (c) of this section in the same manner as if the subsequent transfer of stock had not occurred. The rule of this paragraph (e)(3) shall not apply with respect to the subsequent transfer by the U.S. person of any of the remaining stock to any related U.S. person or unrelated person.

(4) *Proportionate share.*—For purposes of this paragraph (e), any "proportionate share" shall be determined by reference to the fair market value (at the time of the original transfer) of the stock of the transferee foreign corporation that was transferred by the U.S. transferor and the fair market value of all of the stock of the transferee foreign corporation originally received by the U.S. transferor.

(f) *Subsequent disposition of transferred intangible property by transferee foreign corporation.*—(1) *In general.*—If a U.S. person transfers intangible property that is subject to section 367(d) and the rules of this section to a foreign corporation in an exchange described in section 351 or 361, and within the useful life of the intangible property that transferee foreign corporation subsequently disposes of the intangible property to an unrelated person, then—

(i) The U.S. transferor of the intangible property (or any person treated as such pursuant to paragraph (e)(1) of this section) shall be required to recognize gain from U.S. sources (but not loss) in an amount equal to the difference between the fair market value of the transferred intangible property on the date of the subsequent disposition and the U.S. transferor's former adjusted basis in that property (determined as of the original transfer); and

(ii) the U.S. transferor shall be required to recognize a deemed payment under paragraph (c) of this section for that part of its taxable year that the intangible property was held by the transferee foreign corporation and thereafter shall not be required to recognize any further deemed payments under paragraph (c) or (e)(1) of this section with respect to the transferred intangible property disposed of by the transferee foreign corporation.

(2) *Required adjustments.*—If a U.S. transferor is required to recognize gain under paragraph (f)(1) of this section, then—

(i) For purposes of chapter 1 of the Code, the earnings and profits of the transferee foreign corporation shall be reduced by the amount of gain required to be recognized; and

(ii) The U.S. transferor's recognition of gain will permit the establishment of an account receivable from the transferee foreign corporation, in accordance with paragraph (g)(1) of this section.

(3) *Subsequent transfer of intangible property to related person.*—The requirement that a U.S. person recognize gain under paragraph (c) or (e) of this section shall not be affected by the transferee foreign corporation's subsequent disposition of the transferred intangible property to a related person. For purposes of any required adjustments, and of any accounts receivable created under paragraph (g)(1) of this section, the related person that receives the intangible property shall be treated as the transferee foreign corporation.

(g) *Special rules.*—(1) *Establishment of accounts receivable.*—(i) *In general.*—If a U.S. person is required to recognize income under the provisions of paragraph (c), (e), or (f) of this section, and the amount deemed to be received is not actually paid by the transferee foreign corporation, then the U.S. person may establish an account receivable from the transferee foreign corporation equal to the amount deemed paid that was not actually paid. A separate account receivable must be established for each taxable year in which payments deemed to be received are not actually made. Payments received from the transferee foreign corporation must be designated as payments upon a particular account and must be deducted from that account. Accounts receivable under this paragraph (g)(1) may be established and paid without further U.S. income tax consequences to the U.S. transferor or the transferee foreign corporation. No interest shall be paid or accrued on an account receivable created under this paragraph (g)(1), nor shall any bad debt deduction be allowed under section 166 with respect to any failure to receive payment on an account.

(ii) *Unpaid receivable treated as contribution to capital.*—If any portion of an account receivable established under this paragraph (g)(1) remains unpaid as of the last day of the third taxable year following the taxable year to which the account relates, then—

    (A) Such portion shall be deemed to have been paid on that date; and

    (B) The U.S. person shall be deemed to have contributed an equivalent amount to the capital of the foreign corporation, and the U.S. person's basis in the stock of the foreign corporation shall, therefore, be increased by that amount.

  (2) *Election to treat transfer as sale.*—A U.S. person that transfers intangible property to a foreign corporation in a transaction subject to section 367(d) may elect to recognize income in accordance with the rules of this paragraph (g)(2), if—

    (i) The intangible property transferred constitutes an operating intangible, as defined in § 1.367(a)-1T(d)(5)(ii); or

    (ii) The transfer of the intangible property is either legally required by the government of the country in which the transferee corporation is organized as a condition of doing business in that country, or compelled by a genuine threat of immediate expropriation by the foreign government; or

    (iii)(A) The U.S. person transferred the intangible property to the foreign corporation within three months of the organization of that corporation and as part of the original plan of capitalization of that corporation;

    (B) Immediately after the transfer, the U.S. person owns at least 40 percent but not more than 60 percent of the total voting power and total value of the stock of the transferee foreign corporation;

    (C) Immediately after the transfer, at least 40 percent of the total voting power and total value of the stock of the transferee foreign corporation is owned by foreign persons unrelated to the U.S. person;

    (D) Intangible property constitutes at least 50 percent of the fair market value of the property transferred to the foreign corporation by the U.S. transferor; and

    (E) The transferred intangible property will be used in the active conduct of a trade or business outside of the United States within the meaning of § 1.367(a)-2T and will not be used in connection with the manufacture or sale of products in or for use or consumption in the United States.

A person that makes the election under this paragraph (g)(2) shall not be subject to the provisions of paragraphs (c) through (f) of this section. Such person shall instead recognize in the year of the transfer ordinary income from sources within the United States in an amount equal to the difference between the fair market value of the intangible property transferred and its adjusted basis. A U.S. person shall make an election under this paragraph (g)(2) by notifying the Internal Revenue Service of the election in accordance with the requirements of section 6038B and regulations thereunder, and subsequently including the appropriate amounts in gross income in a timely filed tax return for the year of the transfer.

  (3) *Intangible property transferred from branch with previously deducted losses.*—If income is required to be recognized under section 904(f)(3) and the regulations thereunder or under § 1.367(a)-6T upon the transfer of intangible property of a foreign branch that had previously deducted losses, then the income recognized under those sections with respect to that property shall be credited against amounts that would otherwise be required to be recognized with respect to that same property under paragraphs (c) through (f) of this section in either the current or future taxable years. The amount recognized under section 904(f)(3) or § 1.367(a)-6T with respect to the transferred intangible property shall be determined in accordance with the following formula:

$$\text{Loss recapture income} \times \frac{\text{gain from intangibles}}{\text{gain from all branch assets}}$$

For purposes of the above formula, the "loss recapture income" is the total amount required to be recognized by the U.S. transferor pursuant to section 904(f)(3) or § 1.367(a)-6T. The "gain from intangibles" is the total amount of gain realized by the U.S. transferor pursuant to section 904(f)(3) and § 1.367(a)-6T upon the transfer of items of intangible property that are subject to section 367(d). ("Gain from intangibles" does not include gain realized upon the transfer of property described in § 1.367(a)-5T(b)(2), foreign goodwill or going concern value, or intangible property with respect to which the taxpayer has made the election provided for in § 1.367(d)-1T(g)(2).) The "gain from all branch assets" is the total amount of gain realized by the transferor upon the transfer of items of property of the branch in which gain is realized. The fraction shall not exceed 1.

  (4) *Coordination with section 482.*—(i) *In general.*—Section 367(d) and the rules of this section shall not apply in the case of an actual sale or license of intangible property by a U.S. person to a foreign corporation. If an adjustment under section 482 is required with respect to an actual sale or license of intangible property, then section 367(d) and the rules of this section shall not apply with respect to the required adjustment. If a U.S. person transfers

intangible property to a related foreign corporation without consideration, or in exchange for stock or securities of the transferee in a transaction described in section 351 or 361, no sale or license subject to adjustment under section 482 will be deemed to have occurred. Instead, the U.S. person shall be treated as having made a transfer of the intangible property that is subject to section 367(d).

(ii) *Sham licenses and sales.*—For purposes of paragraph (g)(4)(i) of this section, a purported sale or license of intangible property may be disregarded, and treated as a transfer subject to section 367(d) and the rules of this section, if—

(A) The purported sale or license is made to a foreign corporation in which the transferor holds (or is acquiring) an interest; and

(B) The terms of the purported sale or license differ so greatly from the economic substance of the transaction or the terms that would obtain between unrelated persons that the purported sale or license is a sham.

The terms of a purported sale or license, for purposes of applying the rule of this paragraph (g)(4)(ii), shall be determined by reference not only to the nominal terms of the agreement but also to the actual practice of the parties under that agreement. A sale or license of intangible property shall not be disregarded under this paragraph (g)(4)(ii) solely because other property of an integrated business is simultaneously transferred to the foreign corporation by the U.S. transferor in a transaction described in section 367(a)(1) or any statutory or regulatory exception to section 367(a)(1).

(5) *Determination of fair market value.*—For purposes of determining the gain required to be recognized immediately under paragraph (d), (f) or (g)(2) or this section, the fair market value of transferred property shall be the single payment arm's-length price that would be paid for the property by an unrelated purchaser determined in accordance with the principles of section 482 and regulations thereunder. The allocation of a portion of the purchase price to intangible property agreed to by the parties to the transaction shall not necessarily be controlling for this purpose.

(6) *Anti-abuse rule.*—If a U.S. person—

(i) Transfers intangible property to a domestic corporation with a principal purpose of avoiding the effect of section 367(d) and the rules of this section; and

(ii) Thereafter transfers the stock of that domestic corporation to a related foreign corporation,

then solely for purposes of section 367(d) that U.S. person shall be treated as having transferred the intangible property directly to the foreign corporation. A U.S. person shall be presumed to have transferred intangible property for a principal purpose of avoiding the effect of section 367(d) if the property is transferred to the domestic corporation less than two years prior to the transfer of the stock of that domestic corporation to a foreign corporation. The presumption created by the previous sentence may be rebutted by clear evidence that the subsequent transfer of the stock of the domestic transferee corporation was not contemplated at the time the intangible property was transferred to that corporation and that avoidance of section 367(d) and the rules of this section was not a principal purpose of the transaction. A transfer may have more than one principal purpose.

(h) *Related person.*—For purposes of this section, persons are considered to be related if—

(1) They are partners or partnerships described in section 707(b)(1) of the Code; or

(2) They are related within the meaning of section 267(b), (c), and (f) of the Code, except that—

(i) "10 percent or more" shall be substituted for "more than 50 percent" each place it appears; and

(ii) Section 1563 shall apply (for purposes of section 267(f)), without regard to section 1563(b)(2).

(i) *Effective date.*—Except as specifically provided to the contrary elsewhere in this section, this section applies to transfers occurring after December 31, 1984. [Temporary Reg. § 1.367(d)-1T.]

□ [*T.D.* 8087, 5-15-86. Amended by *T.D.* 8770, 6-18-98.]

§ 1.367(e)-1. Distributions described in section 367(e)(1).—(a) *Purpose and scope.*—This section provides rules for recognition (and nonrecognition) of gain by a domestic corporation (distributing corporation) on a distribution of stock or securities of a corporation (controlled corporation) to foreign persons that is described in section 355. Paragraph (b) of this section contains the general rule that gain is recognized on the distribution to the extent stock or securities of controlled are distributed to foreign persons. Paragraph (c) of this section provides an exception to the gain recognition rule for distributions of stock or securities of a domestic corporation. Paragraph (d) of this section contains rules for determining whether distributees of stock or securities in a section 355 distribution are qualified U.S. persons. Paragraph (e) of this section cross-references section 6038B for certain reporting obligations. Finally, paragraph (f) of this section specifies the effective date of this section.

(b) *Gain recognition.*—(1) *General rule.*—If a domestic corporation makes 1a distribution of stock or securities of a corporation that qualifies for nonrecognition under section 355 to a person who is not a qualified U.S. person, then, except as provided in paragraph (c) of this section, the distributing corporation shall recognize gain (but not loss) on the distribution under section 367(e)(1). A distributing corporation shall not recognize gain under this section with respect to a section 355 distribution to a qualified U.S. person. For purposes of this section, a qualified U.S. person is—

(A) A citizen or resident of the United States; or

(B) A domestic corporation.

(2) *Stock owned through partnerships, disregarded entities, trusts, and estates.*—For purposes of this section, distributing corporation stock or securities owned by or for a partnership (whether foreign or domestic) are owned proportionately by its partners. A partner's proportionate share of the stock or securities of the distributing corporation shall be equal to the partner's distributive share of the gain that would have been recognized had the partnership sold the stock or securities (at a taxable gain) immediately before the distribution. The partner's distributive share of gain shall be determined under the rules and principles of sections 701 through 761 and the regulations thereunder. For purposes of this section, stock or securities owned by or for an entity that is disregarded as an entity separate from its owner (disregarded entity) under §301.7701-3 of this chapter are owned directly by the owner of such disregarded entity. For purposes of this section, stock or securities owned by or for a trust or estate (whether foreign or domestic) are owned proportionately by the persons who would be treated as owning such stock or securities under section 318(a)(2)(A) and (B). In applying section 318(a)(2)(B)(i), if a trust includes interests that are not actuarially ascertainable, all such interests shall be considered to be owned by foreign persons. In a case where an interest holder in a partnership, a disregarded entity, trust, or estate that (directly or indirectly) owns stock of the distributing corporation is itself a partnership, disregarded entity, trust, or estate, the rules of this paragraph (b)(2) apply to such interest holder.

(3) *Gain computation.*—Gain recognized under paragraph (b)(1) of this section shall be equal to the excess of the fair market value of the stock or securities distributed to persons who are not qualified U.S. persons (determined as of the time of the distribution) over the distributing corporation's adjusted basis in the stock or securities distributed to such distributees. For purposes of the preceding sentence, the distributing corporation's adjusted basis in each unit of each class of stock or securities distributed to a distributee shall be equal to the distributing corporation's total adjusted basis in all of the units of the respective class of stock or securities owned immediately before the distribution, divided by the total number of units of the class of stock or securities owned immediately before the distribution.

(4) *Treatment of distributee.*—If the distribution otherwise qualifies for nonrecognition under section 355, each distributee shall be considered to have received stock or securities in a distribution qualifying for nonrecognition under section 355, even though the distributing corporation may recognize gain on the distribution under this section. Thus, the distributee shall not be considered to have received a distribution described in section 301 or a distribution in an exchange described in section 302(b) upon the receipt of the stock or securities of the controlled corporation, and the domestic distributing corporation shall have no withholding responsibilities under section 1441. Except where section 897(e)(1) and the regulations thereunder cause gain to be recognized by the distributee, the basis of the distributed domestic or foreign corporation stock in the hands of the foreign distributee shall be the basis of the distributed stock determined under section 358 without any increase for any gain recognized by the domestic corporation on the distribution.

(c) *Nonrecognition of gain.*—A domestic distributing corporation shall not recognize gain under paragraph (b)(1) of this section on the distribution of stock or securities of a domestic corporation.

(d) *Determining whether distributees are qualified U.S. persons.*—(1) *General rule—presumption of foreign status.*—Except as provided in paragraphs (d)(2) and (3) of this section, all distributions of stock or securities in a distribution described in section 355 in which the distributing corporation is domestic and the controlled corporation is foreign are presumed to be to persons who are not qualified U.S. persons, as defined in paragraph (b)(1) of this section.

(2) *Non-publicly traded distributing corporations.*—If the class of stock or securities of the distributing corporation (in respect to which stock or securities of the controlled corporation are distributed) is not regularly traded

on a qualified exchange or other market (as defined in paragraph (d)(4) of this section), then the distributing corporation may only rebut the presumption contained in paragraph (d)(1) of this section by identifying the qualified U.S. persons to which controlled corporation stock or securities were distributed and by certifying the amount of stock or securities that were distributed to the qualified U.S. persons.

(3) *Publicly traded distributing corporations.*—If the class of stock or securities of the distributing corporation (in respect to which stock or securities of the controlled corporation are distributed) is regularly traded on a qualified exchange or other market (as defined in paragraph (d)(4) of this section), then the distributing corporation may only rebut the presumption contained in paragraph (d)(1) of this section as described in this paragraph (d)(3).

(i) *Five percent shareholders.*—A publicly traded distributing corporation may only rebut the presumption contained in paragraph (d)(1) of this section with respect to distributees that are five percent shareholders of the class of stock or securities of the distributing corporation (in respect to which stock or securities of the controlled corporation are distributed) by identifying the qualified U.S. persons to which controlled corporation stock or securities were distributed and by certifying the amount of stock or securities that were distributed to the qualified U.S. persons. A five percent shareholder is a distributee who is required under U.S. securities laws to file with the Securities and Exchange Commission (SEC) a Schedule 13D or 13G under 17 CFR 240.13d-1 or 17 CFR 240.13d-2, and provide a copy of same to the distributing corporation under 17 CFR 240.13d-7.

(ii) *Other distributees.*—A distributing corporation that has made a distribution described in paragraph (d)(3) of this section may rebut the presumption contained in paragraph (d)(1) of this section with respect to distributees that are not five percent shareholders (as defined in this paragraph (d)(3)) by relying on and providing a reasonable analysis of shareholder records and other relevant information that demonstrates a number of distributees that are qualified U.S. persons. Taxpayers may rely on such analysis, unless it is subsequently determined that there are actually fewer distributees who are qualified U.S. persons than were demonstrated in the analysis.

(4) *Qualified exchange or other market.*—For purposes of paragraph (d) of this section, the term qualified exchange or other market means, for any taxable year—

(i) A national securities exchange which is registered with the SEC or the national market system established pursuant to section 11A of the Securities Exchange Act of 1934 (15 U.S.C. 78f); or

(ii) A foreign securities exchange that is regulated or supervised by a governmental authority of the country in which the market is located and which has the following characteristics—

(A) The exchange has trading volume, listing, financial disclosure, and other requirements designed to prevent fraudulent and manipulative acts and practices, to remove impediments to and perfect the mechanism of a free and open market, and to protect investors; and the laws of the country in which the exchange is located and the rules of the exchange ensure that such requirements are actually enforced; and

(B) The rules of the exchange ensure active trading of listed stocks.

(e) *Reporting under section 6038B.*—See the regulations under section 6038B for reporting requirements for distributions under this section.

(f) *Effective date.*—This section shall be applicable to distributions occurring in taxable years ending after August 8, 1999. [Reg. § 1.367(e)-1.]

☐ [*T.D.* 8834, 8-6-99 (*corrected* 3-2-2000).]

Proposed Amendment to Regulation

§ 1.367(e)-1. Distributions described in section 367(e)(1).—(a) * * * See § 1.367(b)-8(c)(3) for an example illustrating the interaction of § 1.367(e)-1 with other sections of the Internal Revenue Code (such as sections 367(b) and 1248).

* * *

[Proposed 11-15-2000.]

§ 1.367(e)-2. Distributions described in section 367(e)(2).—(a) *Purpose and scope.*—(1) *In general.*—This section provides rules requiring gain and loss recognition by a corporation on its distribution of property to a foreign corporation in a complete liquidation described in section 332. Paragraph (b)(1) of this section contains the general rule that gain and loss are recognized when a domestic corporation makes a distribution of property in complete liquidation under section 332 to a foreign corporation that meets the stock ownership requirements of section 332(b) with respect to stock in the domestic corporation. Paragraph (b)(2) of this section provides the only exceptions to the gain and loss recognition rule of paragraph (b)(1) of this section. Paragraph (b)(3) of this section refers to other consequences of distributions described in paragraphs (b)(1) and (2) of this section. Paragraph (c)(1) of this section contains the general rule that gain and loss are not recognized when a foreign corporation makes a distribution of property in complete liquidation under section 332 to a foreign corporation that meets the stock ownership requirements of section 332(b) with respect to stock in the foreign liquidating corporation. Paragraph (c)(2) of this section provides the only exceptions to the nonrecognition rule of paragraph (c)(1) of this section. Paragraph (c)(3) of this section refers to other consequences of distributions described in paragraphs (c)(1) and (2) of this section. Paragraph (d) of this section contains an anti-abuse rule. Finally, paragraph (e) of this section specifies the effective date for the rules of this section. The rules of this section are issued pursuant to the authority conferred by section 367(e)(2).

(2) *Nonapplicability of section 367(a).*—Section 367(a) shall not apply to a complete liquidation described in section 332 by a domestic liquidating corporation into a foreign corporation that meets the stock ownership requirements of section 332(b).

(b) *Distribution by a domestic corporation.*—(1) *General rule.*—(i) *Recognition of gain and loss.*—If a domestic corporation (domestic liquidating) makes a distribution of property in complete liquidation under section 332 to a foreign corporation (foreign distributee) that meets the stock ownership requirements of section 332(b) with respect to stock in the domestic liquidating corporation, then—

(A) Pursuant to section 367(e)(2), section 337(a) and (b)(1) shall not apply; and

(B) The domestic liquidating corporation shall recognize gain or loss on the distribution of property to the foreign distributee, except as provided in paragraph (b)(2) of this section.

(ii) *Operating rules.*—(A) *General rule.*—Except as provided in paragraphs (b)(1)(ii)(B) and (C) of this section, the rules contained in section 336 will apply to the gain and loss recognized pursuant to this section.

(B) *Overall loss limitation.*—(1) *Overall loss limitation rule.*—Loss in excess of gain from the distribution shall not be recognized. If realized losses exceed recognized losses, the losses shall be recognized on a pro rata basis with respect to the realized loss attributable to each distributed loss asset in the category of assets (i.e., capital or ordinary) to which the realized but unrecognized loss relates. For additional limitations on the recognition of losses, see, e.g., section 1211.

(2) *Example.*—The following example illustrates the overall loss limitation rule, the pro rata loss allocation method, and the general capital loss limitation rule in section 1211(a):

Example. F, a foreign corporation, owns all stock of US1, a domestic corporation. US1 owns the following capital assets: Asset A, which has a fair market value of $100 and an adjusted basis of $40; Asset B, which has a fair market value of $60 and an adjusted basis of $80; and, Asset C, which has a fair market value of $40 and an adjusted basis of $100. US1 also owns the following business assets that will generate ordinary income (or loss) upon disposition: Asset D, which has a fair market value of $100 and an adjusted basis of $40; Asset E, which has a fair market value of $60 and an adjusted basis of $100; and, Asset F, which has a fair market value of $40 and an adjusted basis of $80. US1 liquidates into F and distributes all assets to F in liquidation. None of the assets qualify for nonrecognition under paragraph (b)(2) of this section. US1's total realized capital loss is $80, but it may only recognize $60 of that loss. See section 1211(a). US1's total realized ordinary loss is $80, but it may only recognize $60 of that loss. See paragraph (b)(1)(ii)(B)(*1*) of this section. US1 will allocate $15 (60 × .25) of the recognized capital loss to Asset B and will allocate the remaining $45 (60 × .75) of recognized capital loss to Asset C. See paragraph (b)(1)(ii)(B)(*1*) of this section. US1 will allocate $30 (60 × .50) of the recognized ordinary loss to Asset E and will allocate the remaining $30 (60 × .50) to Asset F. See paragraph (b)(1)(ii)(B)(*1*) of this section.

(C) *Special rules for built-in gains and losses attributable to property received in liquidations and reorganizations.*—Built-in losses attributable to property received in a transaction described in sections 332 or 361 (during the two-year period ending on the date of the distribution in liquidation covered by this section) shall not offset gain from property not received in the same transaction. Built-in gains attributable to property received in a transaction described in sections 332 or 361 (during the two-year period ending on the date of the distribution in liquidation covered by this section) shall not be offset by a loss from property not received in the same transaction. Built-in gain or loss is that amount of gain or loss on property that existed at the time the domestic liquidating corporation acquired such property. See sections 336(d) and 382 for additional limitations on the recognition of losses.

(iii) *Distribution of partnership interest.*—(A) *General rule.*—If a domestic corporation distributes a partnership interest (whether foreign or domestic) in a distribution described in paragraph (b)(1)(i) of this section, then for purposes of applying this section the domestic liquidating corporation shall be treated as having distributed a proportionate share of partnership property. Accordingly, the applicability of the recognition rules of paragraphs (b)(1)(i) and (ii) of this section, and of any exception to recognition provided in this section shall be determined with reference to the partnership property, rather than to the partnership interest itself. Where the partnership property includes an interest in a lower-tier partnership, the applicability of any exception with respect to the interest in the lower-tier partnership shall be determined with reference to the lower-tier partnership property. In the case of multiple tiers of partnerships, the applicability of an exception shall be determined with reference to the property of each partnership, applying the rule contained in the preceding sentence. A domestic liquidating corporation's proportionate share of partnership property shall be determined under the rules and principles of sections 701 through 761 and the regulations thereunder.

(B) *Gain or loss calculation.*—[Reserved]

(C) *Basis adjustments.*—The foreign distributee corporation's basis in the distributed partnership interest shall be equal to the domestic liquidating corporation's basis in such partnership interest immediately prior to the distribution, increased by the amount of gain and reduced by the amount of loss recognized by the domestic liquidating corporation on the distribution of the partnership interest. Solely for purposes of sections 743 and 754, the foreign distributee corporation shall be treated as having purchased the partnership interest for an amount equal to the foreign corporation's adjusted basis therein.

(D) *Publicly traded partnerships.*—The distribution by a domestic liquidating corporation of an interest in a publicly traded partnership that is treated as a corporation for U.S. income tax purposes under section 7704(a) shall not be subject to the rules of paragraphs (b)(1)(iii)(A) and (B) of this section. Instead, the distribution of such an interest shall be treated in the same manner as a distribution of stock. Thus, a transfer of an interest in a publicly traded partnership that is treated as a U.S. corporation for U.S. income tax purposes shall be treated in the same manner as stock in a domestic corporation, and a transfer of an interest in a publicly traded partnership that is treated as a foreign corporation for U.S. income tax purposes shall be treated in the same manner as stock in a foreign corporation.

(2) *Exceptions.*—(i) *Distribution of property used in a U.S. trade or business.*—(A) *Conditions for nonrecognition.*—A domestic liquidating corporation shall not recognize gain or loss under paragraph (b)(1) of this section on its distribution of property (including inventory) used by the domestic liquidating corporation in the conduct of a trade or business within United States, if—

(1) The foreign distributee corporation, immediately thereafter and for the ten-year period beginning on the date of the distribution of such property, uses the property in the conduct of a trade or business within the United States;

(2) The domestic liquidating corporation attaches the statement described in paragraph (b)(2)(i)(C) of this section to its U.S. income tax returns for the taxable years that include the distributions in liquidation; and

(3) The foreign distributee corporation attaches a copy of the property description contained in paragraph (b)(2)(i)(C)(2) of this section to its U.S. income tax return for the tax year that includes the date of distribution.

(B) *Qualifying property.*—Property is used by the foreign distributee corporation in the conduct of a trade or business in the United States within the meaning of this paragraph (b)(2)(i) only if all income from the use of the property and all income or gain from the sale or exchange of the property would be subject to taxation under section 882(a) as effectively connected income. Also, stock held by a dealer as inventory or for sale in the ordinary course of its trade or business shall be treated as inventory and not as stock in the hands of both the domestic liquidating corporation and the distributee foreign corporation. Notwithstanding the foregoing, the exception provided in this paragraph (b)(2)(i) shall not apply to intangibles described in section 936(h)(3)(B).

(C) *Required statement.*—The statement required by paragraph (b)(2)(i)(A) of this section shall be entitled "Required Statement under § 1.367(e)-2(b)(2)(i)" and shall be prepared by the domestic liquidating corporation and signed under penalties of perjury by an authorized officer of the domestic liquidating corporation and by an authorized officer of the foreign distributee corporation. The statement shall contain the following items:

(1) Declaration and certification.—A declaration that the distribution to the foreign distributee corporation is one to which the rules of this paragraph (b)(2)(i) apply and a certification that the domestic liquidating corporation and the foreign distributee corporation agree to all of the terms and conditions set forth in this paragraph (b)(2)(i).

Reg. § 1.367(e)-2(b)(1)(iii)(B)

(2) Property description.—A description of all property distributed by the domestic liquidating corporation (irrespective of whether the property qualifies for nonrecognition). Such description shall be entitled "Master Property Description" and shall identify the property that continues to be used by the foreign distributee corporation in the conduct of a trade or business within the United States, including the location, adjusted basis, estimated fair market value, a summary of the method (including appraisals if any) used for determining such value, and the date of distribution of such items of property. The description shall also identify the property excepted from gain recognition under paragraphs (b)(2)(ii) and (iii) of this section.

(3) Distributee identification.—An identification of the foreign distributee corporation, including its name and address, taxpayer identification number, residence, and place of incorporation.

(4) Treaty benefits waiver.—With respect to property entitled to nonrecognition pursuant to this paragraph (b)(2)(i), a declaration by the foreign distributee corporation that it irrevocably waives any right under any treaty (whether or not currently in force at the time of the liquidation) to sell or exchange any item of such property without U.S. income taxation or at a reduced rate of taxation, or to derive income from the use of any item of such property without U.S. income taxation or at a reduced rate of taxation.

(5) Statute of limitations extension.—An agreement by the domestic liquidating corporation and the foreign distributee corporation to extend the statute of limitations on assessments and collections (under section 6501) with respect to the domestic liquidating corporation on the distribution of each item of property until three years after the date on which all such items of property have ceased to be used in a trade or business within the United States, but in no event shall the extension be for a period longer than 13 years from the filing of the original U.S. income tax return for the taxable year of the last distribution of any such item of property. The agreement to extend the statute of limitation shall be executed on a Form 8838, "Consent to Extend the Time to Assess Tax Under Section 367—Gain Recognition Agreement."

(D) *Failure to file statement.*—If a domestic liquidating corporation that would otherwise qualify for nonrecognition on the distribution of property under this paragraph (b)(2)(i) fails to file the statement described in paragraph (b)(2)(i)(C) of this section or files a statement that does not comply with the requirements of paragraph (b)(2)(i)(C) of this section, the Commissioner may treat the domestic liquidating corporation as if it had claimed nonrecognition under this paragraph (b)(2)(i) and met all the requirements of paragraph (b)(2)(i)(C) of this section, if such treatment is necessary to prevent the domestic liquidating corporation or the foreign distributee corporation from otherwise deriving a tax benefit by such failure.

(E) *Operating rules.*—By the domestic liquidating corporation's claiming nonrecognition under this paragraph (b)(2)(i) and filing a statement described in paragraph (b)(2)(i)(C) of this section, the domestic liquidating corporation and the foreign distributee corporation agree to be subject to the rules of this paragraph (b)(2)(i)(E).

(1) Gain or loss recognition by the foreign distributee corporation.—*(i) Taxable dispositions.*—If, within the ten-year period from the date of a distribution of qualifying property, the foreign distributee corporation disposes of any qualifying property in a transaction subject to tax under section 882(a), then the foreign distributee corporation shall recognize such gain (or loss) and properly report it on a timely filed U.S. income tax return. If the foreign distributee corporation recognizes gain (or loss) under this paragraph (b)(2)(i)(E)(*1*)(*i*) and properly reports such gain (or loss) on its U.S. income tax return, then the domestic liquidating corporation shall not recognize gain attributable to such property under paragraph (b)(2)(i)(E)(*2*) of this section.

(ii) Other triggering events.—If, within the ten-year period from the date of distribution, any qualifying property ceases to be used by the foreign distributee corporation in the conduct of a trade or business in the United States (other than by reason of a taxable disposition described in paragraph (b)(2)(i)(E)(*1*)(*i*) of this section, a nontriggering event described in paragraph (b)(2)(i)(E)(*4*) of this section, or a nontriggering transfer described in paragraph (b)(2)(i)(E)(*5*) of this section), then the foreign distributee corporation shall recognize gain (but not loss) attributable to such property and properly report it on a timely filed U.S. income tax return. If the foreign distributee corporation properly reports gain under this paragraph (or if such qualified property is not gain property on the date that it ceases to be used in the foreign distributee corporation's U.S. trade or business), then the domestic liquidating corporation shall not recognize gain attributable to such property under paragraph (b)(2)(i)(E)(*2*) of this section. The gain recog-

Reg. § 1.367(e)-2(b)(2)(i)(E)(*1*)(ii)

nized under this paragraph (b)(2)(i)(E)(1)(ii) shall be an amount equal to the fair market value of the property on the date it ceases to be used in the foreign distributee corporation's U.S. trade or business less the foreign distributee corporation's adjusted basis in such property.

(2) Gain recognition by the domestic liquidating corporation.—(i) General rule.—If, within the ten-year period from the date of distribution, any qualifying property described in paragraph (b)(2)(i)(B) of this section ceases to be used by the foreign distributee corporation (or a qualifying transferee described in paragraph (b)(2)(i)(E)(5) of this section) in the conduct of a trade or business in the United States for any reason (including but not limited to the sale or exchange of such property or the removal of the property from conduct of the trade or business), then, except to the extent gain (or loss) is recognized under paragraph (b)(1)(i)(E)(1) of this section, the domestic liquidating corporation shall recognize the gain (but not loss) realized but not recognized upon the initial distribution of such item of property. The domestic liquidating corporation shall recognize gain pursuant to this paragraph (b)(2)(i)(E)(2)(i) on the amended U.S. income tax return described in paragraph (b)(2)(i)(E)(2)(ii) of this section.

(ii) Amended return.—If gain recognition is required pursuant to paragraph (b)(2)(i)(E)(2)(i) of this section, the foreign distributee corporation shall file an amended U.S. income tax return on behalf of the domestic liquidating corporation for the year of the distribution of such item of property. On the amended return, the domestic liquidating corporation may use any losses (or credits) existing in the year of the distribution to offset the gain recognized pursuant to paragraph (b)(2)(i)(E)(2)(i) of this section (or the tax thereon), provided that the losses (or credits) were otherwise available in the year distribution and were not used in another year. The amended return shall be filed no later than the due date (including extensions) for the return of the foreign distributee corporation for the taxable year in which the property ceases to be used by the foreign distributee corporation in the conduct of a trade or business in the United States.

(iii) Interest.—If the domestic liquidating corporation owes additional tax pursuant to paragraph (b)(2)(i)(E)(2)(i) of this section for the year of liquidation, then interest must be paid on that amount at the rates determined under section 6621. The interest due will be calculated from the due date of the domestic liquidating corporation's U.S. income tax return for the year of the distribution to the date on which the additional tax for that year is paid.

(iv) Joint and several liability.—The foreign distributee corporation shall be jointly and severally liable for any tax owed by the domestic liquidating corporation as a result of the application of this section, and shall succeed to the domestic liquidating corporation's agreement to extend the statute of limitations on assessments and collections under section 6501.

(3) Schedule for property no longer used in a U.S. trade or business.—If qualifying property (other than inventory) ceases to be used by the foreign distributee corporation in the conduct of a U.S. trade or business in the ten-year period beginning on the date of distribution of such property from the domestic liquidating corporation to the foreign distributee corporation, then the foreign distributee corporation shall list on a separate schedule (attached to its U.S. income tax return for the year of cessation) all such qualifying property. For purposes of this paragraph (b)(2)(i)(E)(3), property ceases to be used in a U.S. trade or business whenever such property is sold, exchanged, or otherwise removed from the U.S. trade or business, irrespective of whether the domestic liquidating corporation filed an amended return under paragraph (b)(2)(i)(E)(2) of this section, and irrespective of whether the property ceases to be used in the foreign distributee corporation's U.S. trade or business by virtue of a nontriggering event described in paragraph (b)(2)(i)(E)(4) of this section or a nontriggering transfer described in paragraph (b)(2)(i)(E)(5) of this section.

(4) Nontriggering events.—(i) Conversions, certain exchanges, and abandonment.—Gain (or loss) under this paragraph (b)(2)(i)(E) shall not be triggered if qualifying property described in paragraph (b)(2)(i)(B) of this section is involuntarily converted into, or exchanged for, similar qualifying property used in the conduct of a trade or business in the United States, to the extent such conversion or exchange qualifies for nonrecognition under sections 1033 or 1031. Also, the abandonment or disposal of worthless or obsolete property shall not trigger gain (or loss) under this paragraph (b)(2)(i)(E).

(ii) Amendment to Master Property Description.—If the foreign distributee corporation acquires replacement property by virtue of a conversion or exchange of the qualifying property under this paragraph (b)(2)(i)(E)(4), then the foreign distributee corporation shall attach to its U.S. income tax return for the year of the acquisition such re-

placement property a schedule entitled "Amendment to Master Property Description Required by § 1.367(e)-2(b)(2)(i)" that lists the replacement property and the property being replaced.

(5) *Nontriggering transfers to qualified transferees.*—Gain (or loss) under this paragraph (b)(2)(i)(E) will not be triggered if qualifying property described in paragraph (b)(2)(i)(B) of this section is transferred to another person (qualified transferee) in a transaction qualifying for nonrecognition under the Internal Revenue Code (other than transactions described in paragraphs (b)(2)(i)(E)(4)(*i*) and (c)(1) of this section), if—

(*i*) The qualified transferee (and all other subsequent qualified transferees), immediately thereafter and for the ten-year period beginning on the date of the initial distribution of such qualifying property from the domestic liquidating corporation to the foreign distributee corporation, uses the property in the conduct of a trade or business in the United States;

(*ii*) The foreign distributee corporation (or its successor in interest) prepares and attaches to its U.S. income tax return for the year of transfer a statement entitled "Required Statement under § 1.367(e)-2(b)(2)(i)(E)(5) for Property Transferred to a Qualified Transferee" that is signed under penalties of perjury by an authorized officer of the foreign distributee corporation and by a person similarly authorized by the qualified transferee;

(*iii*) The statement described in paragraph (b)(2)(i)(E)(5)(*ii*) of this section shall contain a description of all qualifying property transferred by the foreign distributee corporation (or qualified transferee) to the qualified transferee (or subsequent qualified transferee);

(*iv*) The statement described in paragraph (b)(2)(i)(E)(5)(*ii*) of this section shall also contain an identification of the qualified transferee (or subsequent qualified transferee), including its name and address, taxpayer identification number, residence, and place of incorporation (if applicable);

(*v*) The statement described in paragraph (b)(2)(i)(E)(5)(*ii*) of this section shall also contain a declaration by the qualifying transferee (or subsequent qualifying transferee) that it irrevocably waives any right under any treaty (whether or not currently in force at the time of the liquidation) to sell or exchange any item of such property without U.S. income taxation or at a reduced rate of taxation, or to derive income from the use of any item of such qualifying property without U.S. income taxation or at a reduced rate of taxation; and

(*vi*) A declaration that the transfer to the qualifying transferee (or subsequent qualifying transferee) is one to which the rules of this paragraph (b)(2)(i)(E)(5) apply and a certification that the foreign distributee corporation (or its successor in interest) and the qualifying transferee (or subsequent qualifying transferee) agree to all of the terms and conditions set forth in paragraph (b)(2)(i)(E)(*1*) of this section, replacing "foreign distributee corporation" with "qualifying transferee" and replacing references to "section 882(a)" with "section 871(b)" (as the case may be).

(ii) *Distribution of certain U.S. real property interests.*—A domestic liquidating corporation shall not recognize gain (or loss) under paragraph (b)(1) of this section on the distribution of a U.S. real property interest (other than stock in a former U.S. real property holding corporation that is treated as a U.S. real property interest for five years under section 897(c)(1)(A)(ii)). If property distributed by the domestic liquidating corporation is a U.S. real property interest that qualifies for nonrecognition under this paragraph (b)(2)(ii) in addition to nonrecognition provided by paragraph (b)(2)(i) of this section, then the domestic liquidating corporation shall secure nonrecognition pursuant to this paragraph (b)(2)(ii) and not pursuant to the provisions of paragraph (b)(2)(i) of this section.

(iii) *Distribution of stock of domestic subsidiary corporations.*—(A) *Conditions for nonrecognition.*—A domestic liquidating corporation shall not recognize gain or loss under paragraph (b)(1) of this section on a distribution of stock of an 80 percent domestic subsidiary corporation, if the domestic liquidating corporation attaches a statement described in paragraph (b)(2)(iii)(D) of this section to its U.S. income tax return for the year of the distribution of such stock. For purposes of this paragraph (b)(2)(iii), a corporation is an 80 percent domestic subsidiary corporation, if—

(*1*) The subsidiary corporation is a domestic corporation (but not a foreign corporation that has made an election under section 897(i) to be treated as a U.S. corporation for purposes of section 897);

(*2*) The domestic liquidating corporation owns (directly and without regard to paragraph (b)(1)(iii) of this section) at least 80 percent of the total voting power of the stock of such corporation; and

(*3*) The domestic liquidating corporation owns (directly and without regard to paragraph (b)(1)(iii) of this section) at least 80 percent of the total value of all stock of such corporation.

Reg. § 1.367(e)-2(b)(2)(iii)(A)(3)

(B) *Exceptions when the liquidating corporation is a U.S. real property holding corporation.*—If the domestic liquidating corporation is a U.S. real property holding corporation (as defined in section 897(c)(2)) at the time of liquidation (or is a former U.S. real property holding corporation the stock of which is treated as a U.S. real property interest for five years under section 897(c)(1)(A)(ii)), then the exception in paragraph (b)(2)(iii)(A) of this section shall apply only to the distribution of stock of an 80 percent domestic subsidiary corporation that is a U.S. real property holding corporation (as defined in section 897(c)(2)) at the time of the liquidation and immediately thereafter.

(C) *Anti-abuse rule.*—*(1)* The exception in paragraph (b)(2)(iii)(A) of this section shall not apply, if a principal purpose of the distribution of the 80 percent domestic subsidiary corporation's stock is the avoidance of U.S. tax that would have been imposed on the domestic liquidating corporation's disposition of such stock (directly or indirectly) to an unrelated party. A distribution may have a principal purpose of tax avoidance even though the tax avoidance purpose is outweighed by other purposes when taken together.

(2) For purposes of paragraph (b)(2)(iii)(C)(*1*) of this section, a distribution of stock of the 80 percent domestic subsidiary corporation will be deemed to have been made pursuant to a plan, one of the principal purposes of which was the avoidance of U.S. tax, if the foreign distributee corporation disposes of (whether in a recognition or nonrecognition transaction) any such stock within two years of such distribution. The rule in this paragraph (b)(2)(iii)(C)(*2*) will not apply if the foreign distributee corporation can demonstrate to the satisfaction of the Commissioner that the avoidance of U.S. tax was not a principal purpose of the liquidation.

(D) *Required statement.*—The statement required by paragraph (b)(2)(iii)(A) of this section shall be entitled "Required Statement under § 1.367(e)-2(b)(2)(iii) for Stock of 80 Percent Domestic Subsidiary Corporations" and shall be prepared by the domestic liquidating corporation and shall be signed under penalties of perjury by an authorized officer of the domestic liquidating corporation and by an authorized officer of the foreign distributee corporation. The required statement shall contain a certification that states that if the foreign distributee corporation disposes of any stock subject to paragraph (b)(2)(iii)(A) of this section in a transaction described in paragraph (b)(2)(iii)(C) of this section, then the domestic liquidating corporation shall recognize all realized gain attributable to the distributed stock at the time of distribution, and the domestic liquidating corporation (or the foreign distributee corporation on behalf of the domestic liquidating corporation) shall file a U.S. income tax return (or amended U.S. income tax return, as the case may be) for the year of distribution reporting the gain attributable to such stock.

(3) *Other consequences.*—(i) *Distributee basis in property.*—The foreign distributee corporation's basis in property subject to this paragraph (b) shall be the same as the domestic liquidating corporation's basis in such property immediately before the liquidation, increased by any gain, or reduced by any loss recognized by the domestic liquidating corporation on such property pursuant to paragraph (b)(1) of this section.

(ii) *Reporting under section 6038B.*—Section 6038B and the regulations thereunder apply to a domestic liquidating corporation's transfer of property to a foreign distributee corporation under section 367(e)(2).

(iii) *Other rules.*—For other rules that may be applicable, see sections 1248, 897, and 381.

(c) *Distribution by a foreign corporation.*—(1) *General rule—gain and loss not recognized.*—If a foreign corporation (foreign liquidating) makes a distribution of property in complete liquidation under section 332 to a foreign corporation (foreign distributee) that meets the stock ownership requirements of section 332(b) with respect to stock in the foreign liquidating corporation, then, except as provided in paragraph (c)(2) of this section, section 337(a) and (b)(1) shall apply and the foreign liquidating corporation shall not recognize gain (or loss) on the distribution under section 367(e)(2). If a foreign liquidating corporation distributes a partnership interest (whether foreign or domestic), then such corporation shall be treated as having distributed a proportionate share of partnership property in accordance with the principles of paragraph (b)(1)(iii) of this section.

(2) *Exceptions.*—(i) *Property used in a U.S. trade or business.*—(A) *General rule.*—A foreign liquidating corporation (including a corporation that has made an effective election under section 897(i)) that makes a distribution described in paragraph (c)(1) of this section shall recognize gain (or loss in accordance with principles contained in paragraph (b)(1)(ii) of this section) on the distribution of qualified property, as described in paragraph (b)(2)(i)(B) of this section (other than U.S. real property interests), that is used by the foreign liquidating corporation in the conduct of a

trade or business within the United States at the time of distribution.

(B) *Ten-year active U.S. business exception.*—A foreign liquidating corporation shall not recognize gain under paragraph (c)(2)(i)(A) of this section, if—

(1) The foreign distributee corporation, immediately thereafter and for the ten-year period beginning on the date of the distribution of such property, uses the property in the conduct of a trade or business in the United States;

(2) The foreign distributee corporation is not entitled to benefits under a comprehensive income tax treaty (this requirement shall apply only if the foreign liquidating corporation (or predecessor corporation) was not entitled to benefits under a comprehensive income tax treaty); and

(3) The foreign liquidating corporation and foreign distributee corporation attach the statement described in paragraph (c)(2)(i)(C) of this section to their U.S. income tax returns for their taxable years that include the distribution.

(C) *Required statement.*—The statement required by paragraph (c)(2)(i)(B)(3) of this section shall be entitled "Required Statement under § 1.367(e)-2(c)(2)(i)," shall be prepared by foreign liquidating corporation, shall be signed under penalties of perjury by an authorized officer of the foreign liquidating corporation and by an authorized officer of the foreign distributee corporation, and shall be identical to the statement described in paragraph (b)(2)(i)(C) of this section, except that "§ 1.367(e)-2(c)(2)(i)(B)" shall be substituted for references to "§ 1.367(e)-2(b)(2)(i)" and "foreign liquidating corporation" shall be substituted for "domestic liquidating corporation" each time it appears. References in the rules of paragraph (b)(2)(i)(C) of this section to various rules in paragraph (b) of this section shall be applied as if such references were to this paragraph (c). However, the statement described in this paragraph (c)(2)(i)(C) shall be modified as follows:

(1) The foreign distributee corporation shall not be required to waive its income tax treaty benefits as required by § 1.367(e)-2(b)(2)(i)(C)(4), unless—

(i) The foreign liquidating corporation was required to waive its treaty benefits under paragraph (b)(2)(i)(C)(4) of this section in connection with the distribution of such property in a prior liquidation distribution subject to the provisions of this section; or

(ii) The foreign distributee corporation is entitled benefits under a treaty to which the foreign liquidating corporation was not entitled.

(2) If the foreign distributee is required to waive treaty benefits because of paragraph (c)(2)(i)(C)(1)(ii) of this section, then the foreign distributee shall only be required to waive benefits that were not available to the foreign liquidating corporation (or a predecessor corporation) prior to liquidation.

(3) The property description described in paragraph (b)(2)(i)(C)(2) of this section shall include only the qualified U.S. trade or business property described in paragraph (c)(2)(i) of this section.

(D) *Operating rules.*—By the foreign liquidating corporation's claiming nonrecognition under paragraph (c)(2)(i)(B) of this section and filing a statement described in paragraph (c)(2)(i)(C) of this section, the foreign liquidating corporation and the foreign distributee corporation agree to be subject to the rules of paragraph (c)(2)(i) of this section, as well as the rules of paragraphs (b)(2)(i)(D) and (E) of this section. In applying the rules of paragraphs (b)(2)(i)(D) and (E) of this section, "foreign liquidating corporation" shall be used instead of "domestic liquidating corporation" each time it appears. References in the rules of paragraphs (b)(2)(i)(D) and (E) of this section to various rules in paragraph (b) of this section shall be applied as if such references were to this paragraph (c).

(ii) *Property formerly used in a United States trade or business.*—A foreign liquidating corporation that makes a distribution described in paragraph (c)(1) of this section shall recognize gain (but not loss) on the distribution of property (other than U.S. real property interests) that had ceased to be used by the foreign liquidating corporation in the conduct of a U.S. trade or business within the ten-year period ending on the date of distribution and that would have been subject to section 864(c)(7) had it been disposed. Section 864(c)(7) shall govern the treatment of any gain recognized on the distribution of assets described in this paragraph as income effectively connected with the conduct of a trade or business within the United States.

(3) *Other consequences.*—(i) *Distributee basis in property.*—The foreign distributee corporation's basis in property subject to this paragraph (c) shall be the same as the foreign liquidating corporation's basis in such property immediately before the liquidation, increased by any gain, or reduced by any loss recognized by the foreign liquidating corporation on such property, pursuant to paragraph (c)(2) of this section.

(ii) *Other rules.*—For other rules that may apply, see sections 367(b) and 381.

(d) *Anti-abuse rule.*—The Commissioner may require a domestic liquidating corporation to recognize gain on a distribution in liquidation described in paragraph (b) of this section (or treat the liquidating corporation as if it had recognized loss on a distribution in liquidation), if a principal purpose of the liquidation is the avoidance of U.S. tax (including, but not limited to, the distribution of a liquidating corporation's earnings and profits with a principal purpose of avoiding U.S. tax). A liquidation may have a principal purpose of tax avoidance even though the tax avoidance purpose is outweighed by other purposes when taken together.

(e) *Effective date.*—This section shall be applicable to distributions occurring on or after September 7, 1999 or, if taxpayer so elects, to distributions in taxable years ending after August 8, 1999. [Reg. § 1.367(e)-2.]

☐ [*T.D.* 8834, 8-6-99 (*corrected* 3-2-2000). *Amended by T.D.* 9066, 7-1-2003.]

Section 482 Adjustments

§ 1.482-1. Allocation of income and deductions among taxpayers.—(a) *In general.*—(1) *Purpose and scope.*—The purpose of section 482 is to ensure that taxpayers clearly reflect income attributable to controlled transactions, and to prevent the avoidance of taxes with respect to such transactions. Section 482 places a controlled taxpayer on a tax parity with an uncontrolled taxpayer by determining the true taxable income of the controlled taxpayer. This § 1.482-1 sets forth general principles and guidelines to be followed under section 482. Section 1.482-2 provides rules for the determination of the true taxable income of controlled taxpayers in specific situations, including controlled transactions involving loans or advances, services, and property. Sections 1.482-3 through 1.482-6 elaborate on the rules that apply to controlled transactions involving property. Section 1.482-7T sets forth the cost sharing provisions applicable to taxable years beginning on or after October 6, 1994, and before January 1, 1996. Section 1.482-7 sets forth the cost sharing provisions applicable to taxable years beginning on or after January 1, 1996. Finally, § 1.482-8 provides examples illustrating the application of the best method rule.

(2) *Authority to make allocations.*—The district director may make allocations between or among the members of a controlled group if a controlled taxpayer has not reported its true taxable income. In such case, the district director may allocate income, deductions, credits, allowances, basis, or any other item or element affecting taxable income (referred to as allocations). The appropriate allocation may take the form of an increase or decrease in any relevant amount.

(3) *Taxpayer's use of section 482.*—If necessary to reflect an arm's length result, a controlled taxpayer may report on a timely filed U.S. income tax return (including extensions) the results of its controlled transactions based upon prices different from those actually charged. Except as provided in this paragraph, section 482 grants no other right to a controlled taxpayer to apply the provisions of section 482 at will or to compel the district director to apply such provisions. Therefore, no untimely or amended returns will be permitted to decrease taxable income based on allocations or other adjustments with respect to controlled transactions. See § 1.6662-6T(a)(2) or successor regulations.

(b) *Arm's length standard.*—(1) *In general.*—In determining the true taxable income of a controlled taxpayer, the standard to be applied in every case is that of a taxpayer dealing at arm's length with an uncontrolled taxpayer. A controlled transaction meets the arm's length standard if the results of the transaction are consistent with the results that would have been realized if uncontrolled taxpayers had engaged in the same transaction under the same circumstances (arm's length result). However, because identical transactions can rarely be located, whether a transaction produces an arm's length result generally will be determined by reference to the results of comparable transactions under comparable circumstances. See § 1.482-1(d)(2) (Standard of comparability). Evaluation of whether a controlled transaction produces an arm's length result is made pursuant to a method selected under the best method rule described in § 1.482-1(c).

(2) *Arm's length methods.*—(i) *Methods.*—Sections 1.482-2 through 1.482-6 provide specific methods to be used to evaluate whether transactions between or among members of the controlled group satisfy the arm's length standard, and if they do not, to determine the arm's length result. Section 1.482-7 provides the specific method to be used to evaluate whether a qualified cost sharing arrangement produces results consistent with an arm's length result.

(ii) *Selection of category of method applicable to transaction.*—The methods listed in § 1.482-2 apply to different types of transactions, such as transfers of property, services, loans or advances, and rentals. Accordingly, the method or methods most appropriate to the calculation of arm's length results for controlled transactions must be selected, and different methods may be applied to interrelated transactions if such transactions are most reliably evaluated on a separate basis. For example, if services are provided in connection with the transfer of property, it may be appropriate to separately apply the methods applicable to services and property in order to determine an arm's length result. But see § 1.482-1(f)(2)(i) (Aggregation of transactions). In addition, other applicable provisions of the Code may affect the characterization of a transaction, and therefore affect the methods applicable under section 482. See for example section 467.

(c) *Best method rule.*—(1) *In general.*—The arm's length result of a controlled transaction must be determined under the method that, under the facts and circumstances, provides the most reliable measure of an arm's length result. Thus, there is no strict priority of methods, and no method will invariably be considered to be more reliable than others. An arm's length result may be determined under any method without establishing the inapplicability of another method, but if another method subsequently is shown to produce a more reliable measure of an arm's length result, such other method must be used. Similarly, if two or more applications of a single method provide inconsistent results, the arm's length result must be determined under the application that, under the facts and circumstances, provides the most reliable measure of an arm's length result. See § 1.482-8 for examples of the application of the best method rule. See § 1.482-7 for the applicable method in the case of a qualified cost sharing arrangement.

(2) *Determining the best method.*—Data based on the results of transactions between unrelated parties provides the most objective basis for determining whether the results of a controlled transaction are arm's length. Thus, in determining which of two or more available methods (or applications of a single method) provides the most reliable measure of an arm's length result, the two primary factors to take into account are the degree of comparability between the controlled transaction (or taxpayer) and any uncontrolled comparables, and the quality of the data and assumptions used in the analysis. In addition, in certain circumstances, it also may be relevant to consider whether the results of an analysis are consistent with the results of an analysis under another method. These factors are explained in paragraphs (c)(2)(i), (ii), and (iii) of this section.

(i) *Comparability.*—The relative reliability of a method based on the results of transactions between unrelated parties depends on the degree of comparability between the controlled transaction or taxpayers and the uncontrolled comparables, taking into account the factors described in § 1.482-1(d)(3) (Factors for determining comparability), and after making adjustments for differences, as described in § 1.482-1(d)(2) (Standard of comparability). As the degree of comparability increases, the number and extent of potential differences that could render the analysis inaccurate is reduced. In addition, if adjustments are made to increase the degree of comparability, the number, magnitude, and reliability of those adjustments will affect the reliability of the results of the analysis. Thus, an analysis under the comparable uncontrolled price method will generally be more reliable than analyses obtained under other methods if the analysis is based on closely comparable uncontrolled transactions, because such an analysis can be expected to achieve a higher degree of comparability and be susceptible to fewer differences than analyses under other methods. See § 1.482-3(b)(2)(ii)(A). An analysis will be relatively less reliable, however, as the uncontrolled transactions become less comparable to the controlled transaction.

(ii) *Data and assumptions.*—Whether a method provides the most reliable measure of an arm's length result also depends upon the completeness and accuracy of the underlying data, the reliability of the assumptions, and the sensitivity of the results to possible deficiencies in the data and assumptions. Such factors are particularly relevant in evaluating the degree of comparability between the controlled and uncontrolled transactions. These factors are discussed in paragraphs (c)(2)(ii)(A), (B), and (C) of this section.

(A) *Completeness and accuracy of data.*—The completeness and accuracy of the data affects the ability to identify and quantify those factors that would affect the result under any particular method. For example, the completeness and accuracy of data will determine the extent to which it is possible to identify differences between the controlled and uncontrolled transactions, and the reliability of adjustments that are made to account for such differences. An analysis will be relatively more reliable as the completeness and accuracy of the data increases.

(B) *Reliability of assumptions.*—All methods rely on certain assumptions. The reliability of the results derived from a method depends on the soundness of such assumptions. Some assumptions are relatively reliable.

For example, adjustments for differences in payment terms between controlled and uncontrolled transactions may be based on the assumption that at arm's length such differences would lead to price differences that reflect the time value of money. Although selection of the appropriate interest rate to use in making such adjustments involves some judgement, the economic analysis on which the assumption is based is relatively sound. Other assumptions may be less reliable. For example, the residual profit split method may be based on the assumption that capitalized intangible development expenses reflect the relative value of the intangible property contributed by each party. Because the costs of developing an intangible may not be related to its market value, the soundness of this assumption will affect the reliability of the results derived from this method.

(C) *Sensitivity of results to deficiencies in data and assumptions.*—Deficiencies in the data used or assumptions made may have a greater effect on some methods than others. In particular, the reliability of some methods is heavily dependent on the similarity of property or services involved in the controlled and uncontrolled transaction. For certain other methods, such as the resale price method, the analysis of the extent to which controlled and uncontrolled taxpayers undertake the same or similar functions, employ similar resources, and bear similar risks is particularly important. Finally, under other methods, such as the profit split method, defining the relevant business activity and appropriate allocation of costs, income, and assets may be of particular importance. Therefore, a difference between the controlled and uncontrolled transactions for which an accurate adjustment cannot be made may have a greater effect on the reliability of the results derived under one method than the results derived under another method. For example, differences in management efficiency may have a greater effect on a comparable profits method analysis than on a comparable uncontrolled price method analysis, while differences in product characteristics will ordinarily have a greater effect on a comparable uncontrolled price method analysis than on a comparable profits method analysis.

(iii) *Confirmation of results by another method.*—If two or more methods produce inconsistent results, the best method rule will be applied to select the method that provides the most reliable measure of an arm's length result. If the best method rule does not clearly indicate which method should be selected, an additional factor that may be taken into account in selecting a method is whether any of the competing methods produce results that are consistent with the results obtained from the appropriate application of another method. Further, in evaluating different applications of the same method, the fact that a second method (or another application of the first method) produces results that are consistent with one of the competing applications may be taken into account.

(d) *Comparability.*—(1) *In general.*—Whether a controlled transaction produces an arm's length result is generally evaluated by comparing the results of that transaction to results realized by uncontrolled taxpayers engaged in comparable transactions under comparable circumstances. For this purpose, the comparability of transactions and circumstances must be evaluated considering all factors that could affect prices or profits in arm's length dealings (comparability factors). While a specific comparability factor may be of particular importance in applying a method, each method requires analysis of all of the factors that affect comparability under that method. Such factors include the following—

(i) Functions;

(ii) Contractual terms;

(iii) Risks;

(iv) Economic conditions; and

(v) Property or services.

(2) *Standard of comparability.*—In order to be considered comparable to a controlled transaction, an uncontrolled transaction need not be identical to the controlled transaction, but must be sufficiently similar that it provides a reliable measure of an arm's length result. If there are material differences between the controlled and uncontrolled transactions, adjustments must be made if the effect of such differences on prices or profits can be ascertained with sufficient accuracy to improve the reliability of the results. For purposes of this section, a material difference is one that would materially affect the measure of an arm's length result under the method being applied. If adjustments for material differences cannot be made, the uncontrolled transaction may be used as a measure of an arm's length result, but the reliability of the analysis will be reduced. Generally, such adjustments must be made to the results of the uncontrolled comparable and must be based on commercial practices, economic principles, or statistical analyses. The extent and reliability of any adjustments will affect the relative reliability of the analysis. See § 1.482-1(c)(1) (Best method rule). In any event, unadjusted industry average returns themselves cannot establish arm's length results.

(3) *Factors for determining comparability.*—The comparability factors listed in § 1.482-1(d)(1) are discussed in this section. Each of these factors must be considered in determining the degree of comparability between transactions or taxpayers and the extent to which comparability adjustments may be necessary. In addition, in certain cases involving special circumstances, the rules under paragraph (d)(4) of this section must be considered.

(i) *Functional analysis.*—Determining the degree of comparability between controlled and uncontrolled transactions requires a comparison of the functions performed, and associated resources employed, by the taxpayers in each transaction. This comparison is based on a functional analysis that identifies and compares the economically significant activities undertaken, or to be undertaken, by the taxpayers in both controlled and uncontrolled transactions. A functional analysis should also include consideration of the resources that are employed, or to be employed, in conjunction with the activities undertaken, including consideration of the type of assets used, such as plant and equipment, or the use of valuable intangibles. A functional analysis is not a pricing method and does not itself determine the arm's length result for the controlled transaction under review. Functions that may need to be accounted for in determining the comparability of two transactions include—

(A) Research and development;

(B) Product design and engineering;

(C) Manufacturing, production and process engineering;

(D) Product fabrication, extraction, and assembly;

(E) Purchasing and materials management;

(F) Marketing and distribution functions, including inventory management, warranty administration, and advertising activities;

(G) Transportation and warehousing; and

(H) Managerial, legal, accounting and finance, credit and collection, training, and personnel management services.

(ii) *Contractual terms.*—(A) *In general.*—Determining the degree of comparability between the controlled and uncontrolled transactions requires a comparison of the significant contractual terms that could affect the results of the two transactions. These terms include—

(1) The form of consideration charged or paid;

(2) Sales or purchase volume;

(3) The scope and terms of warranties provided;

(4) Rights to updates, revisions or modifications;

(5) The duration of relevant license, contract or other agreements, and termination or renegotiation rights;

(6) Collateral transactions or ongoing business relationships between the buyer and the seller, including arrangements for the provision of ancillary or subsidiary services; and

(7) Extension of credit and payment terms. Thus, for example, if the time for payment of the amount charged in a controlled transaction differs from the time for payment of the amount charged in an uncontrolled transaction, an adjustment to reflect the difference in payment terms should be made if such difference would have a material effect on price. Such comparability adjustment is required even if no interest would be allocated or imputed under § 1.482-2(a) or other applicable provisions of the Internal Revenue Code or regulations.

(B) *Identifying contractual terms.*—(1) *Written agreement.*—The contractual terms, including the consequent allocation of risks, that are agreed to in writing before the transactions are entered into will be respected if such terms are consistent with the economic substance of the underlying transactions. In evaluating economic substance, greatest weight will be given to the actual conduct of the parties, and the respective legal rights of the parties (see, for example, § 1.482-4(f)(3) (Ownership of intangible property)). If the contractual terms are inconsistent with the economic substance of the underlying transaction, the district director may disregard such terms and impute terms that are consistent with the economic substance of the transaction.

(2) *No written agreement.*—In the absence of a written agreement, the district director may impute a contractual agreement between the controlled taxpayers consistent with the economic substance of the transaction. In determining the economic substance of the transaction, greatest weight will be given to the actual conduct of the parties and their respective legal rights (see, for example, § 1.482-4(f)(3) (Ownership of intangible property)). For example, if, without a written agreement, a controlled taxpayer operates at full capacity and regularly sells all of its output to another member of its controlled group, the district director may impute a purchasing contract from the course of conduct of the controlled taxpayers, and determine that the producer bears little risk that the buyer will fail

Reg. § 1.482-1(d)(3)(ii)(B)(2)

to purchase its full output. Further, if an established industry convention or usage of trade assigns a risk or resolves an issue, that convention or usage will be followed if the conduct of the taxpayers is consistent with it. See UCC § 1-205. For example, unless otherwise agreed, payment generally is due at the time and place at which the buyer is to receive goods. See UCC § 2-310.

(C) *Examples.*—The following examples illustrate this paragraph (d)(3)(ii).

Example 1—Differences in volume. USP, a United States agricultural exporter, regularly buys transportation services from FSub, its foreign subsidiary, to ship its products from the United States to overseas markets. Although FSub occasionally provides transportation services to URA, an unrelated domestic corporation, URA accounts for only 10% of the gross revenues of FSub, and the remaining 90% of FSub's gross revenues are attributable to FSub's transactions with USP. In determining the degree of comparability between FSub's uncontrolled transaction with URA and its controlled transaction with USP, the difference in volumes involved in the two transactions and the regularity with which these services are provided must be taken into account if such difference would have a material effect on the price charged. Inability to make reliable adjustments for these differences would affect the reliability of the results derived from the uncontrolled transaction as a measure of the arm's length result.

Example 2—Reliability of adjustment for differences in volume. (i) FS manufactures product XX and sells that product to its parent corporation, P. FS also sells product XX to uncontrolled taxpayers at a price of $100 per unit. Except for the volume of each transaction, the sales to P and to uncontrolled taxpayers take place under substantially the same economic conditions and contractual terms. In uncontrolled transactions, FS offers a 2% discount for quantities of 20 per order, and a 5% discount for quantities of 100 per order. If P purchases product XX in quantities of 60 per order, in the absence of other reliable information, it may reasonably be concluded that the arm's length price to P would be $100, less a discount of 3.5%.

(ii) If P purchases product XX in quantities of 1,000 per order, a reliable estimate of the appropriate volume discount must be based on proper economic or statistical analysis, not necessarily a linear extrapolation from the 2% and 5% catalog discounts applicable to sales of 20 and 100 units, respectively.

Example 3—Contractual term imputed from economic substance. (i) USD, a United States corporation, is the exclusive distributor of products manufactured by FP, its foreign parent. The FP products are sold under a tradename that is not known in the United States. USD does not have an agreement with FP for the use of FP's tradename. For Years 1 through 6, USD bears marketing expenses promoting FP's tradename in the United States that are substantially above the level of such expenses incurred by comparable distributors in uncontrolled transactions. FP does not directly or indirectly reimburse USD for its marketing expenses. By Year 7, the FP tradename has become very well known in the market and commands a price premium. At this time, USD becomes a commission agent for FP.

(ii) In determining USD's arm's length result for Year 7, the district director considers the economic substance of the arrangements between USD and FP throughout the course of their relationship. It is unlikely that at arm's length, USD would incur these above-normal expenses without some assurance it could derive a benefit from these expenses. In this case, these expenditures indicate a course of conduct that is consistent with an agreement under which USD received a long-term right to use the FP tradename in the United States. Such conduct is inconsistent with the contractual arrangements between FP and USD under which USD was merely a distributor, and later a commission agent, for FP. Therefore, the district director may impute an agreement between USD and FP under which USD will retain an appropriate portion of the price premium attributable to the FP tradename.

(iii) *Risk.*—(A) *Comparability.*—Determining the degree of comparability between controlled and uncontrolled transactions requires a comparison of the significant risks that could affect the prices that would be charged or paid, or the profit that would be earned, in the two transactions. Relevant risks to consider include—

(1) Market risks, including fluctuations in cost, demand, pricing, and inventory levels;

(2) Risks associated with the success or failure of research and development activities;

(3) Financial risks, including fluctuations in foreign currency rates of exchange and interest rates;

(4) Credit and collection risks;

(5) Product liability risks; and

(6) General business risks related to the ownership of property, plant, and equipment.

(B) *Identification of taxpayer that bears risk.*—In general, the determination of which controlled taxpayer bears a particular risk will be made in accordance with the provisions of § 1.482-1(d)(3)(ii)(B) (Identifying contractual terms). Thus, the allocation of risks specified or implied by the taxpayer's contractual terms will generally be respected if it is consistent with the economic substance of the transaction. An allocation of risk between controlled taxpayers after the outcome of such risk is known or reasonably knowable lacks economic substance. In considering the economic substance of the transaction, the following facts are relevant—

(1) Whether the pattern of the controlled taxpayer's conduct over time is consistent with the purported allocation of risk between the controlled taxpayers; or where the pattern is changed, whether the relevant contractual arrangements have been modified accordingly;

(2) Whether a controlled taxpayer has the financial capacity to fund losses that might be expected to occur as the result of the assumption of a risk, or whether, at arm's length, another party to the controlled transaction would ultimately suffer the consequences of such losses; and

(3) The extent to which each controlled taxpayer exercises managerial or operational control over the business activities that directly influence the amount of income or loss realized. In arm's length dealings, parties ordinarily bear a greater share of those risks over which they have relatively more control.

(C) *Examples.*—The following examples illustrate this paragraph (d)(3)(iii).

Example 1. FD, the wholly-owned foreign distributor of USM, a U.S. manufacturer, buys widgets from USM under a written contract. Widgets are a generic electronic appliance. Under the terms of the contract, FD must buy and take title to 20,000 widgets for each of the five years of the contract at a price of $10 per widget. The widgets will be sold under FD's label, and FD must finance any marketing strategies to promote sales in the foreign market. There are no rebate or buy back provisions. FD has adequate financial capacity to fund its obligations under the contract under any circumstances that could reasonably be expected to arise. In Years 1, 2 and 3, FD sold only 10,000 widgets at a price of $11 per unit. In Year 4, FD sold its entire inventory of widgets at a price of $25 per unit. Since the contractual terms allocating market risk were agreed to before the outcome of such risk was known or reasonably knowable, FD had the financial capacity to bear the market risk that it would be unable to sell all of the widgets it purchased currently, and its conduct was consistent over time, FD will be deemed to bear the risk.

Example 2. The facts are the same as in *Example 1*, except that in Year 1 FD had only $100,000 in total capital, including loans. In subsequent years USM makes no additional contributions to the capital of FD, and FD is unable to obtain any capital through loans from an unrelated party. Nonetheless, USM continues to sell 20,000 widgets annually to FD under the terms of the contract, and USM extends credit to FD to enable it to finance the purchase. FD does not have the financial capacity in Years 1, 2 and 3 to finance the purchase of the widgets given that it could not sell most of the widgets it purchased during those years. Thus, notwithstanding the terms of the contract, USM and not FD assumed the market risk that a substantial portion of the widgets could not be sold, since in that event FD would not be able to pay USM for all of the widgets it purchased.

Example 3. S, a Country X corporation, manufactures small motors that it sells to P, its U.S. parent. P incorporates the motors into various products and sells those products to uncontrolled customers in the United States. The contract price for the motors is expressed in U.S. dollars, effectively allocating the currency risk for these transactions to S for any currency fluctuations between the time the contract is signed and payment is made. As long as S has adequate financial capacity to bear this currency risk (including by hedging all or part of the risk) and the conduct of S and P is consistent with the terms of the contract (i.e., the contract price is not adjusted to reflect exchange rate movements), the agreement of the parties to allocate the exchange risk to S will be respected.

Example 4. USSub is the wholly-owned U.S. subsidiary of FP, a foreign manufacturer. USSub acts as a distributor of goods manufactured by FP. FP and USSub execute an agreement providing that FP will bear any ordinary product liability costs arising from defects in the goods manufactured by FP. In practice, however, when ordinary product liability claims are sustained against USSub and FP, USSub pays the resulting damages. Therefore, the district director disregards the contractual arrangement regarding product liability costs between FP and USSub, and treats the risk as having been assumed by USSub.

(iv) *Economic conditions.*—Determining the degree of comparability between controlled and uncontrolled transactions requires a comparison of the significant economic conditions that could affect the prices that would be charged or paid, or the profit that would be earned in each of the transactions. These factors include—

(A) The similarity of geographic markets;

(B) The relative size of each market, and the extent of the overall economic development in each market;

(C) The level of the market (e.g., wholesale, retail, etc.);

(D) The relevant market shares for the products, properties, or services transferred or provided;

(E) The location-specific costs of the factors of production and distribution;

(F) The extent of competition in each market with regard to the property or services under review;

(G) The economic condition of the particular industry, including whether the market is in contraction or expansion; and

(H) The alternatives realistically available to the buyer and seller.

(v) *Property or services.*—Evaluating the degree of comparability between controlled and uncontrolled transactions requires a comparison of the property or services transferred in the transactions. This comparison may include any intangibles that are embedded in tangible property or services being transferred. The comparability of the embedded intangibles will be analyzed using the factors listed in § 1.482-4(c)(2)(iii)(B)(*1*) (Comparable intangible property). The relevance of product comparability in evaluating the relative reliability of the results will depend on the method applied. For guidance concerning the specific comparability considerations applicable to transfers of tangible and intangible property, see §§ 1.482-3 through 1.482-6; see also § 1.482-3(f), dealing with the coordination of the intangible and tangible property rules.

(4) *Special circumstances.*—(i) *Market share strategy.*—In certain circumstances, taxpayers may adopt strategies to enter new markets or to increase a product's share of an existing market (market share strategy). Such a strategy would be reflected by temporarily increased market development expenses or resale prices that are temporarily lower than the prices charged for comparable products in the same market. Whether or not the strategy is reflected in the transfer price depends on which party to the controlled transaction bears the costs of the pricing strategy. In any case, the effect of a market share strategy on a controlled transaction will be taken into account only if it can be shown that an uncontrolled taxpayer engaged in a comparable strategy under comparable circumstances for a comparable period of time, and the taxpayer provides documentation that substantiates the following—

(A) The costs incurred to implement the market share strategy are borne by the controlled taxpayer that would obtain the future profits that result from the strategy, and there is a reasonable likelihood that the strategy will result in future profits that reflect an appropriate return in relation to the costs incurred to implement it;

(B) The market share strategy is pursued only for a period of time that is reasonable, taking into consideration the industry and product in question; and

(C) The market share strategy, the related costs and expected returns, and any agreement between the controlled taxpayers to share the related costs, were established before the strategy was implemented.

(ii) *Different geographic markets.*—(A) *In general.*—Uncontrolled comparables ordinarily should be derived from the geographic market in which the controlled taxpayer operates, because there may be significant differences in economic conditions in different markets. If information from the same market is not available, an uncontrolled comparable derived from a different geographic market may be considered if adjustments are made to account for differences between the two markets. If information permitting adjustments for such differences is not available, then information derived from uncontrolled comparables in the most similar market for which reliable data is available may be used, but the extent of such differences may affect the reliability of the method for purposes of the best method rule. For this purpose, a geographic market is any geographic area in which the economic conditions for the relevant product or service are substantially the same, and may include multiple countries, depending on the economic conditions.

(B) *Example.*—The following example illustrates this paragraph (d)(4)(ii).

Example. Manuco, a wholly-owned foreign subsidiary of P, a U.S. corporation, manufactures products in Country Z for sale to P. No uncontrolled transactions are located that would provide a reliable measure of the arm's length result under the comparable uncontrolled price method. The district director considers applying the cost plus method or the comparable profits method. Information on uncontrolled taxpayers performing comparable functions under comparable circumstances in the same geographic market is not available. Therefore, adjusted data from uncontrolled manufacturers in other markets may be considered in order to apply the cost plus method. In this case, comparable uncontrolled manufacturers are found in the United States. Accordingly, data from the comparable U.S. uncontrolled manufacturers, as adjusted to account for differences between the United States and Country Z's geographic market, is used to test the arm's length price paid by P to Manuco. However, the use of such data may affect the reliability of the results for purposes of the best method rule. See § 1.482-1(c).

(C) *Location savings.*—If an uncontrolled taxpayer operates in a different geographic market than the controlled taxpayer, adjustments may be necessary to account for significant differences in costs attributable to the geographic markets. These adjustments must be based on the effect such differences would have on the consideration charged or paid in the controlled transaction given the relative competitive positions of buyers and sellers in each market. Thus, for example, the fact that the total costs of operating in a controlled manufacturer's geographic market are less than the total costs of operating in other markets ordinarily justifies higher profits to the manufacturer only if the cost differences would increase the profits of comparable uncontrolled manufacturers operating at arm's length, given the competitive positions of buyers and sellers in that market.

(D) *Example.*—The following example illustrates the principles of this paragraph (d)(4)(ii)(C).

Example. Couture, a U.S. apparel design corporation, contracts with Sewco, its wholly owned Country Y subsidiary, to manufacture its clothes. Costs of operating in Country Y are significantly lower than the operating costs in the United States. Although clothes with the Couture label sell for a premium price, the actual production of the clothes does not require significant specialized knowledge that could not be acquired by actual or potential competitors to Sewco at reasonable cost. Thus, Sewco's functions could be performed by several actual or potential competitors to Sewco in geographic markets that are similar to Country Y. Thus, the fact that production is less costly in Country Y will not, in and of itself, justify additional profits derived from lower operating costs in Country Y inuring to Sewco, because the competitive positions of the other actual or potential producers in similar geographic markets capable of performing the same functions at the same low costs indicate that at arm's length such profits would not be retained by Sewco.

(iii) *Transactions ordinarily not accepted as comparables.*—(A) *In general.*—Transactions ordinarily will not constitute reliable measures of an arm's length result for purposes of this section if—

(1) They are not made in the ordinary course of business; or

(2) One of the principal purposes of the uncontrolled transaction was to establish an arm's length result with respect to the controlled transaction.

(B) *Examples.*—The following examples illustrate the principle of this paragraph (d)(4)(iii).

Example 1—Not in the ordinary course of business. USP, a United States manufacturer of computer software, sells its products to FSub, its foreign distributor in country X. Compco, a United States competitor of USP, also sells its products in X through unrelated distributors. However, in the year under review, Compco is forced into bankruptcy, and Compco liquidates its inventory by selling all of its products to unrelated distributors in X for a liquidation price. Because the sale of its entire inventory was not a sale in the ordinary course of business, Compco's sale cannot be used as an uncontrolled comparable to determine USP's arm's length result from its controlled transaction.

Example 2—Principal purpose of establishing an arm's length result. USP, a United States manufacturer of farm machinery, sells its products to FSub, its wholly-owned distributor in Country Y. USP, operating at nearly full capacity, sells 95% of its inventory to FSub. To make use of its excess capacity, and also to establish a comparable uncontrolled price for its transfer price to FSub, USP increases its production to full capacity. USP sells its excess inventory to Compco, an unrelated foreign distributor in Country X. Country X has approximately the same economic conditions as that of Country Y. Because one of the principal purposes of selling to Compco was to establish an arm's length price for its controlled transactions with FSub, USP's sale to Compco cannot be used as an uncontrolled comparable to determine USP's arm's length result from its controlled transaction.

(e) *Arm's length range.*—(1) *In general.*—In some cases, application of a pricing method will produce a single result that is the most reliable measure of an arm's length result. In other cases, application of a method may produce a number of results from which a range of reliable results may be derived. A taxpayer will not be subject to adjustment if its results fall within such range (arm's length range).

(2) *Determination of arm's length range.*—(i) *Single method.*—The arm's length range is ordinarily determined by applying a single pricing method selected under the best method rule to two or more uncontrolled transactions of similar comparability and reliability. Use of

more than one method may be appropriate for the purposes described in paragraph (c)(2)(iii) of this section (Best method rule).

(ii) *Selection of comparables.*—Uncontrolled comparables must be selected based upon the comparability criteria relevant to the method applied and must be sufficiently similar to the controlled transaction that they provide a reliable measure of an arm's length result. If material differences exist between the controlled and uncontrolled transactions, adjustments must be made to the results of the uncontrolled transaction if the effect of such differences on price or profits can be ascertained with sufficient accuracy to improve the reliability of the results. See § 1.482-1(d)(2) (Standard of comparability). The arm's length range will be derived only from those uncontrolled comparables that have, or through adjustments can be brought to, a similar level of comparability and reliability, and uncontrolled comparables that have a significantly lower level of comparability and reliability will not be used in establishing the arm's length range.

(iii) *Comparables included in arm's length range.*—(A) *In general.*—The arm's length range will consist of the results of all of the uncontrolled comparables that meet the following conditions: the information on the controlled transaction and the uncontrolled comparables is sufficiently complete that it is likely that all material differences have been identified, each such difference has a definite and reasonably ascertainable effect on price or profit, and an adjustment is made to eliminate the effect of each such difference.

(B) *Adjustment of range to increase reliability.*—If there are no uncontrolled comparables described in paragraph (e)(2)(iii)(A) of this section, the arm's length range is derived from the results of all the uncontrolled comparables, selected pursuant to paragraph (e)(2)(ii) of this section, that achieve a similar level of comparability and reliability. In such cases the reliability of the analysis must be increased, where it is possible to do so, by adjusting the range through application of a valid statistical method to the results of all of the uncontrolled comparables so selected. The reliability of the analysis is increased when statistical methods are used to establish a range of results in which the limits of the range will be determined such that there is a 75 percent probability of a result falling above the lower end of the range and a 75 percent probability of a result falling below the upper end of the range. The interquartile range ordinarily provides an acceptable measure of this range; however a different statistical method may be applied if it provides a more reliable measure.

(C) *Interquartile range.*—For purposes of this section, the interquartile range is the range from the 25th to the 75th percentile of the results derived from the uncontrolled comparables. For this purpose, the 25th percentile is the lowest result derived from an uncontrolled comparable such that at least 25 percent of the results are at or below the value of that result. However, if exactly 25 percent of the results are at or below a result, then the 25th percentile is equal to the average of that result and the next higher result derived from the uncontrolled comparables. The 75th percentile is determined analogously.

(3) *Adjustment if taxpayer's results are outside arm's length range.*—If the results of a controlled transaction fall outside the arm's length range, the district director may make allocations that adjust the controlled taxpayer's result to any point within the arm's length range. If the interquartile range is used to determine the arm's length range, such adjustment will ordinarily be to the median of all the results. The median is the 50th percentile of the results, which is determined in a manner analogous to that described in paragraph (e)(2)(iii)(C) of this section (Interquartile range). In other cases, an adjustment normally will be made to the arithmetic mean of all the results. See § 1.482-1(f)(2)(iii)(D) for determination of an adjustment when a controlled taxpayer's result for a multiple year period falls outside an arm's length range consisting of the average results of uncontrolled comparables over the same period.

(4) *Arm's length range not prerequisite to allocation.*—The rules of this paragraph (e) do not require that the district director establish an arm's length range prior to making an allocation under section 482. Thus, for example, the district director may properly propose an allocation on the basis of a single comparable uncontrolled price if the comparable uncontrolled price method, as described in § 1.482-3(b), has been properly applied. However, if the taxpayer subsequently demonstrates that the results claimed on its income tax return are within the range established by additional equally reliable comparable uncontrolled prices in a manner consistent with the requirements set forth in § 1.482-1(e)(2)(iii), then no allocation will be made.

(5) *Examples.*—The following examples illustrate the principles of this paragraph (e).

Example 1—Selection of comparables. (i) To evaluate the arm's length result of a controlled transaction between USSub, the United

States taxpayer under review, and FP, its foreign parent, the district director considers applying the resale price method. The district director identifies ten potential uncontrolled transactions. The distributors in all ten uncontrolled transactions purchase and resell similar products and perform similar functions to those of USSub.

(ii) Data with respect to three of the uncontrolled transactions is very limited, and although some material differences can be identified and adjusted for, the level of comparability of these three uncontrolled comparables is significantly lower than that of the other seven. Further, of those seven, adjustments for the identified material differences can be reliably made for only four of the uncontrolled transactions. Therefore, pursuant to § 1.482-1(e)(2)(ii) only these four uncontrolled comparables may be used to establish an arm's length range.

Example 2—Arm's length range consists of all the results. (i) The facts are the same as in *Example 1*. Applying the resale price method to the four uncontrolled comparables, and making adjustments to the uncontrolled comparables pursuant to § 1.482-1(d)(2), the district director derives the following results:

Comparable	Result ($ price)
1	44.00
2	45.00
3	45.00
4	45.50

(ii) The district director determines that data regarding the four uncontrolled transactions is sufficiently complete and accurate so that it is likely that all material differences between the controlled and uncontrolled transactions have been identified, such differences have a definite and reasonably ascertainable effect, and appropriate adjustments were made for such differences. Accordingly, if the resale price method is determined to be the best method pursuant to § 1.482-1(c), the arm's length range for the controlled transaction will consist of the results of all of the uncontrolled comparables, pursuant to paragraph (e)(2)(iii)(A) of this section. Thus, the arm's length range in this case would be the range from $44 to $45.50.

Example 3—Arm's length range limited to interquartile range. (i) The facts are the same as in *Example 2*, except in this case there are some product and functional differences between the four uncontrolled comparables and USSub. However, the data is insufficiently complete to determine the effect of the differences. Applying the resale price method to the four uncontrolled comparables, and making adjustments to the uncontrolled comparables pursuant to § 1.482-1(d)(2), the district director derives the following results:

Uncontrolled Comparable	Result ($ price)
1	42.00
2	44.00
3	45.00
4	47.50

(ii) It cannot be established in this case that all material differences are likely to have been identified and reliable adjustments made for those differences. Accordingly, if the resale price method is determined to be the best method pursuant to § 1.482-1(c), the arm's length range for the controlled transaction must be established pursuant to paragraph (e)(2)(iii)(B) of this section. In this case, the district director uses the interquartile range to determine the arm's length range, which is the range from $43 to $46.25. If USSub's price falls outside this range, the district director may make an allocation. In this case that allocation would be to the median of the results, or $44.50.

Example 4—Arm's length range limited to interquartile range. (i) To evaluate the arm's length result of controlled transactions between USP, a United States manufacturing company, and FSub, its foreign subsidiary, the district director considers applying the comparable profits method. The district director identifies 50 uncontrolled taxpayers within the same industry that potentially could be used to apply the method.

(ii) Further review indicates that only 20 of the uncontrolled manufacturers engage in activities requiring similar capital investments and technical know-how. Data with respect to five of the uncontrolled manufacturers is very limited, and although some material differences can be identified and adjusted for, the level of comparability of these five uncontrolled comparables is significantly lower than that of the other 15. In addition, for those five uncontrolled comparables it is not possible to accurately allocate costs between the business activity associated with the relevant transactions and other business activities. Therefore, pursuant to § 1.482-1(e)(2)(ii) only the other fifteen uncontrolled comparables may be used to establish an arm's length range.

(iii) Although the data for the fifteen remaining uncontrolled comparables is relatively complete and accurate, there is a significant possibility that some material differences may remain. The district director has determined, for example, that it is likely that there are material differences in the level of technical expertise or in management efficiency. Accordingly, if the comparable profits method is determined to be the best method pursuant to § 1.482-1(c), the arm's length range for the controlled transaction may be established only pursuant to paragraph (e)(2)(iii)(B) of this section.

(f) *Scope of review.*—(1) *In general.*—The authority to determine true taxable income extends to any case in which either by inadvertence or design the taxable income, in whole or in part, of a controlled taxpayer is other than it would have been had the taxpayer, in the conduct of its affairs, been dealing at arm's length with an uncontrolled taxpayer.

(i) *Intent to evade or avoid tax not a prerequisite.*—In making allocations under section 482, the district director is not restricted to the case of improper accounting, to the case of a fraudulent, colorable, or sham transaction, or to the case of a device designed to reduce or avoid tax by shifting or distorting income, deductions, credits, or allowances.

(ii) *Realization of income not a prerequisite.*—(A) *In general.*—The district director may make an allocation under section 482 even if the income ultimately anticipated from a series of transactions has not been or is never realized. For example, if a controlled taxpayer sells a product at less than an arm's length price to a related taxpayer in one taxable year and the second controlled taxpayer resells the product to an unrelated party in the next taxable year, the district director may make an appropriate allocation to reflect an arm's length price for the sale of the product in the first taxable year, even though the second controlled taxpayer had not realized any gross income from the resale of the product in the first year. Similarly, if a controlled taxpayer lends money to a related taxpayer in a taxable year, the district director may make an appropriate allocation to reflect an arm's length charge for interest during such taxable year even if the second controlled taxpayer does not realize income during such year. Finally, even if two controlled taxpayers realize an overall loss that is attributable to a particular controlled transaction, an allocation under section 482 is not precluded.

(B) *Example.*—The following example illustrates this paragraph (f)(1)(ii).

Example. USSub is a U.S. subsidiary of FP, a foreign corporation. Parent manufactures product X and sells it to USSub. USSub functions as a distributor of product X to unrelated customers in the United States. The fact that FP may incur a loss on the manufacture and sale of product X does not by itself establish that USSub, dealing with FP at arm's length, also would incur a loss. An independent distributor acting at arm's length with its supplier would in many circumstances be expected to earn a profit without regard to the level of profit earned by the supplier.

(iii) *Nonrecognition provisions may not bar allocation.*—(A) *In general.*—If necessary to prevent the avoidance of taxes or to clearly reflect income, the district director may make an allocation under section 482 with respect to transactions that otherwise qualify for nonrecognition of gain or loss under applicable provisions of the Internal Revenue Code (such as section 351 or 1031).

(B) *Example.*—The following example illustrates this paragraph (f)(1)(iii).

Example. (i) In Year 1 USP, a United States corporation, bought 100 shares of UR, an unrelated corporation, for $100,000. In Year 2, when the value of the UR stock had decreased to $40,000, USP contributed all 100 shares of UR stock to its wholly-owned subsidiary in exchange for subsidiary's capital stock. In Year 3, the subsidiary sold all of the UR stock for $40,000 to an unrelated buyer, and on its U.S. income tax return, claimed a loss of $60,000 attributable to the sale of the UR stock. USP and its subsidiary do not file a consolidated return.

(ii) In determining the true taxable income of the subsidiary, the district director may disallow the loss of $60,000 on the ground that the loss was incurred by USP. *National Securities Corp. v. Commissioner,* 137 F.2d 600 (3rd Cir. 1943), cert. denied, 320 U.S. 794 (1943).

(iv) *Consolidated returns.*—Section 482 and the regulations thereunder apply to all controlled taxpayers, whether the controlled taxpayer files a separate or consolidated U.S. income tax return. If a controlled taxpayer files a separate return, its true separate taxable income will be determined. If a controlled taxpayer is a party to a consolidated return, the true consolidated taxable income of the affiliated group and the true separate taxable income of the controlled taxpayer must be determined consistently with the principles of a consolidated return.

(2) *Rules relating to determination of true taxable income.*—The following rules must be taken into account in determining the true taxable income of a controlled taxpayer.

(i) *Aggregation of transactions.*—(A) *In general.*—The combined effect of two or more separate transactions (whether before, during, or after the taxable year under review) may be considered, if such transactions, taken as a whole, are so interrelated that consideration of multiple transactions is the most reliable means of determining the arm's length consideration for the controlled transactions. Generally, transactions will be aggregated only when they involve related products or services, as defined in § 1.6038A-3(c)(7)(vii).

(B) *Examples.*—The following examples illustrate this paragraph (f)(2)(i).

Example 1. P enters into a license agreement with S1, its subsidiary, that permits S1 to use a proprietary manufacturing process and to sell the output from this process throughout a specified region. S1 uses the manufacturing process and sells its output to S2, another subsidiary of P, which in turn resells the output to uncontrolled parties in the specified region. In evaluating the arm's length character of the royalty paid by S1 to P, it may be appropriate to consider the arm's length character of the transfer prices charged by S1 to S2 and the aggregate profits earned by S1 and S2 from the use of the manufacturing process and the sale to uncontrolled parties of the products produced by S1.

Example 2. S1, S2, and S3 are Country Z subsidiaries of U.S. manufacturer P. S1 is the exclusive Country Z distributor of computers manufactured by P. S2 provides marketing services in connection with sales of P computers in Country Z, and in this regard uses significant marketing intangibles provided by P. S3 administers the warranty program with respect to P computers in Country Z, including maintenance and repair services. In evaluating the arm's length character of the transfer price paid by S1 to P, of the fees paid by S2 to P for the use of P marketing intangibles, and of the service fees earned by S2 and S3, it may be appropriate to consider the combined effects of these separate transactions because they are so interrelated that they are most reliably analyzed on an aggregated basis.

Example 3. The facts are the same as in *Example 2.* In addition, U1, U2, and U3 are uncontrolled taxpayers that carry out functions comparable to those of S1, S2, and S3, respectively, with respect to computers produced by unrelated manufacturers. R1, R2, and R3 are a controlled group of taxpayers (unrelated to the P controlled group) that also carry out functions comparable to those of S1, S2, and S3 with respect to computers produced by their common parent. Prices charged to uncontrolled customers of the R group differ from the prices charged to customers of U1, U2, and U3. In determining whether the transactions of U1, U2, and U3, or the transactions of R1, R2, and R3 would provide a more reliable measure of the arm's length result, it is determined that the interrelated R group transactions are more reliable than the wholly independent transactions of U1, U2, and U3, given the interrelationship of the P group transactions.

Example 4. P enters into a license agreement with S1 that permits S1 to use a propriety process for manufacturing product X and to sell product X to uncontrolled parties throughout a specified region. P also sells to S1 product Y which is manufactured by P in the United States, and which is unrelated to product X. Product Y is resold by S1 to uncontrolled parties in the specified region. In evaluating the arm's length character of the royalty paid by S1 to P for the use of the manufacturing process for product X, and the transfer prices charged for unrelated product Y, it would not be appropriate to consider the combined effects of these separate and unrelated transactions.

(ii) *Allocation based on taxpayer's actual transactions.*—(A) *In general.*—The district director will evaluate the results of a transaction as actually structured by the taxpayer unless its structure lacks economic substance. However, the district director may consider the alternatives available to the taxpayer in determining whether the terms of the controlled transaction would be acceptable to an uncontrolled taxpayer faced with the same alternatives and operating under comparable circumstances. In such cases the district director may adjust the consideration charged in the controlled transaction based on the cost or profit of an alternative as adjusted to account for material differences between the alternative and the controlled transaction, but will not restructure the transaction as if the alternative had been adopted by the taxpayer. See § 1.482-1(d)(3) (Factors for determining comparability, Contractual terms and Risk); § § 1.482-3(e) and 1.482-4(d) (Unspecified methods).

(B) *Example.*—The following example illustrates this paragraph (f)(2)(ii).

Example. P and S are controlled taxpayers. P enters into a license agreement with S that permits S to use a proprietary process for manufacturing product X. Using its sales and marketing employees, S sells product X to related and unrelated customers outside the United States. If the license agreement between P and S has economic substance, the district director ordinarily will not restructure the taxpayer's transaction to treat P as if it had elected to exploit directly the manufacturing process. However, the fact that P could have manufactured product X may be taken into account under § 1.482-4(d) in determining the arm's length consideration for the controlled transaction. For an example of such an analysis, see *Example* in § 1.482-4(d)(2).

(iii) *Multiple year data.*—(A) *In general.*—The results of a controlled transaction ordinarily will be compared with the results of uncontrolled comparables occurring in the taxable year under review. It may be appropriate, however, to consider data relating to the uncontrolled comparables or the controlled taxpayer for one or more years before or after the year under review. If data relating to uncontrolled comparables from multiple years is used, data relating to the controlled taxpayer for the same years ordinarily must be considered. However, if such data is not available, reliable data from other years, as adjusted under paragraph (d)(2) (Standard of comparability) of this section may be used.

(B) *Circumstances warranting consideration of multiple year data.*—The extent to which it is appropriate to consider multiple-year data depends on the method being applied and the issue being addressed. Circumstances that may warrant consideration of data from multiple years include the extent to which complete and accurate data is available for the taxable year under review, the effect of business cycles in the controlled taxpayer's industry, or the effects of life cycles of the product or intangible being examined. Data from one or more years before or after the taxable year under review must ordinarily be considered for purposes of applying the provisions of §1.482-1(d)(3)(iii) (Risk), §1.482-1(d)(4)(i) (Market share strategy), §1.482-4(f)(2) (Periodic adjustments), and §1.482-5 (Comparable profits method). On the other hand, multiple-year data ordinarily will not be considered for purposes of applying the comparable uncontrolled price method (except to the extent that risk or market share strategy issues are present).

(C) *Comparable effect over comparable period.*—Data from multiple years may be considered to determine whether the same economic conditions that caused the controlled taxpayer's results had a comparable effect over a comparable period of time on the uncontrolled comparables that establish the arm's length range. For example, given that uncontrolled taxpayers enter into transactions with the ultimate expectation of earning a profit, persistent losses among controlled taxpayers may be an indication of non-arm's length dealings. Thus, if a controlled taxpayer that realizes a loss with respect to a controlled transaction seeks to demonstrate that the loss is within the arm's length range, the district director may take into account data from taxable years other than the taxable year of the transaction to determine whether the loss was attributable to arm's length dealings. The rule of this paragraph (f)(2)(iii)(C) is illustrated by *Example 3* of paragraph (f)(2)(iii)(E) of this section.

(D) *Applications of methods using multiple year averages.*—If a comparison of a controlled taxpayer's average result over a multiple year period with the average results of uncontrolled comparables over the same period would reduce the effect of short-term variations that may be unrelated to transfer pricing, it may be appropriate to establish a range derived from the average results of uncontrolled comparables over a multiple year period to determine if an adjustment should be made. In such a case the district director may make an adjustment if the controlled taxpayer's average result for the multiple year period is not within such range. Such a range must be determined in accordance with §1.482-1(e) (Arm's length range). An adjustment in such a case ordinarily will be equal to the difference, if any, between the controlled taxpayer's result for the taxable year and the mid-point of the uncontrolled comparables' results for that year. If the interquartile range is used to determine the range of average results for the multiple year period, such adjustment will ordinarily be made to the median of all the results of the uncontrolled comparables for the taxable year. See *Example 2* of §1.482-5(e). In other cases, the adjustment normally will be made to the arithmetic mean of all the results of the uncontrolled comparables for the taxable year. However, an adjustment will be made only to the extent that it would move the controlled taxpayer's multiple year average closer to the arm's length range for the multiple year period or to any point within such range. In determining a controlled taxpayer's average result for a multiple year period, adjustments made under this section for prior years will be taken into account only if such adjustments have been finally determined, as described in §1.482-1(g)(2)(iii). See *Example 3* of §1.482-5(e).

(E) *Examples.*—The following examples, in which S and P are controlled taxpayers, illustrate this paragraph (f)(2)(iii). *Examples 1* and *4* also illustrate the principle of the arm's length range of paragraph (e) of this section.

Example 1. P sold product Z to S for $60 per unit in 1995. Applying the resale price method to data from uncontrolled comparables for the same year establishes an arm's length range of prices for the controlled transaction from $52 to $59 per unit. Since the price charged in the controlled transaction falls outside the range, the district director would ordinarily make an allocation under section 482. However, in this case there are cyclical factors that affect the results of the uncontrolled comparables (and that of the controlled transaction) that cannot be adequately accounted for by specific adjustments to the data for 1995. Therefore, the district director considers results over multiple years to account for these factors. Under these circumstances, it is appropriate to average the results of the uncontrolled comparables over the years 1993, 1994, and 1995 to determine an arm's length range. The averaged results establish an arm's length range of $56 to $58 per unit. For consistency, the results of the controlled taxpayers must also be averaged over the same years. The average price in the controlled transaction over the three years is $57. Because the controlled transfer price of product Z falls within the arm's length range, the district director makes no allocation.

Example 2. (i) FP, a Country X corporation, designs and manufactures machinery in Country X. FP's costs are incurred in Country X currency. USSub is the exclusive distributor of FP's machinery in the United States. The price of the machinery sold by FP to USSub is expressed in Country X currency. Thus, USSub bears all of the currency risk associated with fluctuations in the exchange rate between the time the contract is signed and the payment is made. The prices charged by FP to USSub for 1995 are under examination. In that year, the value of the dollar depreciated against the currency of Country X, and as a result, USSub's gross margin was only 8%.

(ii) UD is an uncontrolled distributor of similar machinery that performs distribution functions substantially the same as those performed by USSub, except that UD purchases and resells machinery in transactions where both the purchase and resale prices are denominated in U.S. dollars. Thus, UD had no currency exchange risk. UD's gross margin in 1995 was 10%. UD's average gross margin for the period 1990 to 1998 has been 12%.

(iii) In determining whether the price charged by FP to USSub in 1995 was arm's length, the district director may consider USSub's average gross margin for an appropriate period before and after 1995 to determine whether USSub's average gross margin during the period was sufficiently greater than UD's average gross margin during the same period such that USSub was sufficiently compensated for the currency risk it bore throughout the period. See § 1.482-1(d)(3)(iii) (Risk).

Example 3. FP manufactures product X in Country M and sells it to USSub, which distributes X in the United States. USSub realizes losses with respect to the controlled transactions in each of five consecutive taxable years. In each of the five consecutive years a different uncontrolled comparable realized a loss with respect to comparable transactions equal to or greater than USSub's loss. Pursuant to paragraph (f)(3)(iii)(C) of this section, the district director examines whether the uncontrolled comparables realized similar losses over a comparable period of time, and finds that each of the five comparables realized losses in only one of the five years, and their average result over the five-year period was a profit. Based on this data, the district director may conclude that the controlled taxpayer's results are not within the arm's length range over the five year period, since the economic conditions that resulted in the controlled taxpayer's loss did not have a comparable effect over a comparable period of time on the uncontrolled comparables.

Example 4. (i) USP, a U.S. corporation, manufactures product Y in the United States and sells it to FSub, which acts as USP's exclusive distributor of product Y in Country N. The resale price method described in § 1.482-3(c) is used to evaluate whether the transfer price charged by USP to FSub for the 1994 taxable year for product Y was arm's length. For the period 1992 through 1994, FSub had a gross profit margin for each year of 13%. A, B, C and D are uncontrolled distributors of products that compete directly with product Y in country N. After making appropriate adjustments in accordance with §§ 1.482-1(d)(2) and 1.482-3(c), the gross profit margins for A, B, C, and D are as follows:

	1992	1993	1994	Average
A...	13	3	8	8.00
B...	11	13	2	8.67
C...	4	7	13	8.00
D...	7	9	6	7.33

(ii) Applying the provisions of § 1.482-1(e), the district director determines that the arm's length range of the average gross profit margins is between 7.33 and 8.67. The district director concludes that FSub's average gross margin of 13% is not within the arm's length range, despite the fact that C's gross profit margin for 1994 was also 13%, since the economic conditions that caused S's result did not have a comparable effect over a comparable period of time on the results of C or the other uncontrolled comparables. In this case, the district director makes an allocation equivalent to adjusting FSub's gross profit margin for 1994 from 13% to the mean of the uncontrolled comparables' results for 1994 (7.25%).

(iv) *Product lines and statistical techniques.*—The methods described in §§ 1.482-2 through 1.482-6 are generally stated in terms of individual transactions. However, because a taxpayer may have controlled transactions involving many different products, or many separate transactions involving the same product, it may be impractical to analyze every individual transaction to determine its arm's length price. In such cases, it is permissible to evaluate the arm's length results by applying the appropriate methods to the overall results for product lines or other groupings. In addition, the arm's length results of all related party transactions entered into by a controlled taxpayer may be evaluated by employing sampling and other valid statistical techniques.

(v) *Allocations apply to results, not methods.*—(A) *In general.*—In evaluating whether the result of a controlled transaction is arm's length, it is not necessary for the district director to determine whether the method or procedure that a controlled taxpayer employs to set the terms for its controlled transactions corresponds to the method or procedure that might have been used by a taxpayer dealing at arm's length with an uncontrolled taxpayer. Rather, the district director will evaluate the result achieved rather than the method the taxpayer used to determine its prices.

(B) *Example.*—The following example illustrates this paragraph (f)(2)(v).

Example. (i) FS is a foreign subsidiary of P, a U.S. corporation. P manufactures and sells household appliances. FS operates as P's exclusive distributor in Europe. P annually establishes the price for each of its appliances sold to FS as part of its annual budgeting, production allocation and scheduling, and performance evaluation processes. FS's aggregate gross margin earned in its distribution business is 18%.

(ii) ED is an uncontrolled European distributor of competing household appliances. After adjusting for minor differences in the level of inventory, volume of sales, and warranty programs conducted by FS and ED, ED's aggregate gross margin is also 18%. Thus, the district director may conclude that the aggregate prices charged by P for its appliances sold to FS are arm's length, without determining whether the budgeting, production, and performance evaluation processes of P are similar to such processes used by ED.

(g) *Collateral adjustments with respect to allocations under section 482.*—(1) *In general.*—The district director will take into account appropriate collateral adjustments with respect to allocations under section 482. Appropriate collateral adjustments may include correlative allocations, conforming adjustments, and setoffs, as described in this paragraph (g).

(2) *Correlative allocations.*—(i) *In general.*—When the district director makes an allocation under section 482 (referred to in this paragraph (g)(2) as the primary allocation), appropriate correlative allocations will also be made with respect to any other member of the group affected by the allocation. Thus, if the district director makes an allocation of income, the district director will not only increase the income of one member of the group, but correspondingly decrease the income of the other member. In addition, where appropriate, the district director may make such further correlative allocations as may be required by the initial correlative allocation.

(ii) *Manner of carrying out correlative allocation.*—The district director will furnish to the taxpayer with respect to which the primary allocation is made a written statement of the amount and nature of the correlative allocation. The correlative allocation must be reflected in the documentation of the other member of the group that is maintained for U.S. tax purposes, without regard to whether it affects the U.S. income tax liability of the other member for any open year. In some circumstances the allocation will have an immediate U.S. tax effect, by changing the taxable income computation of the other member (or the taxable income computation of a shareholder of the other member, for example, under the provisions of subpart F of the Internal Revenue Code). Alternatively, the correlative allocation may not be reflected on any U.S. tax return until a later year, for example when a dividend is paid.

(iii) *Events triggering correlative allocation.*—For purposes of this paragraph (g)(2), a primary allocation will not be considered to have been made (and therefore, correlative allocations are not required to be made) until the date of a final determination with respect to the allocation under section 482. For this purpose, a final determination includes—

(A) Assessment of tax following execution by the taxpayer of a Form 870 (Waiver of Restrictions on Assessment and Collection of Deficiency in Tax and Acceptance of Overassessment) with respect to such allocation;

(B) Acceptance of a Form 870-AD (Offer of Waiver of Restriction on Assessment and Collection of Deficiency in Tax and Acceptance of Overassessment);

(C) Payment of the deficiency;

(D) Stipulation in the Tax Court of the United States; or

(E) Final determination of tax liability by offer-in-compromise, closing agreement, or final resolution (determined under the principles of section 7481) of a judicial proceeding.

(iv) *Examples.*—The following examples illustrate this paragraph (g)(2). In each example, X and Y are members of the same group of controlled taxpayers and each regularly computes its income on a calendar year basis.

Example 1. (i) In 1996, Y, a U.S. corporation, rents a building owned by X, also a U.S. corporation. In 1998 the district director determines that Y did not pay an arm's length rental charge. The district director proposes to increase X's income to reflect an arm's length rental charge. X consents to the assessment reflecting such adjustment by executing Form 870, a Waiver of Restrictions on Assessment and Collection of Deficiency in Tax and Acceptance of Overassessment. The assessment of the tax with respect to the adjustment is made in 1998. Thus, the primary allocation, as defined in paragraph (g)(2)(i) of this section, is considered to have been made in 1998.

(ii) The adjustment made to X's income under section 482 requires a correlative allocation with respect to Y's income. The district director notifies X in writing of the amount and nature of the adjustment made with respect to Y. Y had net operating losses in 1993, 1994, 1995, 1996, and 1997. Although a correlative adjustment will not have an effect on Y's U.S. income tax liability for 1996, an adjustment increasing Y's net operating loss for 1996 will be made for purposes of determining Y's U.S. income tax liability for 1998 or a later taxable year to which the increased net operating loss may be carried.

Example 2. (i) In 1995, X, a U.S. construction company, provided engineering services to Y, a U.S. corporation, in the construction of Y's factory. In 1997, the district director determines that the fees paid by Y to X for its services were not arm's length and proposes to make an adjustment to the income of X. X consents to an assessment reflecting such adjustment by executing Form 870. An assessment of the tax with respect to such adjustment is made in 1997. The district director notifies X in writing of the amount and nature of the adjustment to be made with respect to Y.

(ii) The fees paid by Y for X's engineering services properly constitute a capital expenditure. Y does not place the factory into service until 1998. Therefore, a correlative adjustment increasing Y's basis in the factory does not affect Y's U.S. income tax liability for 1997. However, the correlative adjustment must be made in the books and records maintained by Y for its U.S. income tax purposes and such adjustment will be taken into account in computing Y's allowable depreciation or gain or loss on a subsequent disposition of the factory.

Example 3. In 1995, X, a U.S. corporation, makes a loan to Y, its foreign subsidiary not engaged in a U.S. trade or business. In 1997, the district director, upon determining that the interest charged on the loan was not arm's length, proposes to adjust X's income to reflect an arm's length interest rate. X consents to an assessment reflecting such allocation by executing Form 870, and an assessment of the tax with respect to the section 482 allocation is made in 1997. The district director notifies X in writing of the amount and nature of the correlative allocation to be made with respect to Y. Although the correlative adjustment does not have an effect on Y's U.S. income tax liability, the adjustment must be reflected in the documentation of Y that is maintained for U.S. tax purposes. Thus, the adjustment must be reflected in the determination of the amount of Y's earnings and profits for 1995 and subsequent years, and the adjustment must be made to the extent it has an effect on any person's U.S. income tax liability for any taxable year.

(3) *Adjustments to conform accounts to reflect section 482 allocations.*—(i) *In general.*—Appropriate adjustments must be made to conform a taxpayer's accounts to reflect allocations made under section 482. Such adjustments may include the treatment of an allocated amount as a dividend or a capital contribution (as appropriate), or, in appropriate cases, pursuant to such applicable revenue procedures as may be provided by the Commissioner (see § 601.601(d)(2) of this chapter), repayment of the allocated amount without further income tax consequences.

(ii) *Example.*—The following example illustrates the principles of this paragraph (g)(3).

Example—Conforming cash accounts. (i) USD, a United States corporation, buys Product from its foreign parent, FP. In reviewing USD's income tax return, the district director determines that the arm's length price would have increased USD's taxable income by $5 million. The district director accordingly adjusts USD's income to reflect its true taxable income.

(ii) To conform its cash accounts to reflect the section 482 allocation made by the district director, USD applies for relief under Rev. Proc. 65-17, 1965-1 C.B. 833 (see § 601.601(d)(2)(ii)(*b*) of this chapter), to treat the $5 million adjustment as an account receivable from FP, due as of the last day of the year of the transaction, with interest accruing therefrom.

(4) *Setoffs.*—(i) *In general.*—If an allocation is made under section 482 with respect to a transaction between controlled taxpayers, the district director will also take into account the effect of any other non-arm's length transaction between the same controlled taxpayers in the same taxable year which will result in a setoff against the original section 482 allocation. Such setoff, however, will be taken into account only if the requirements of § 1.482-1(g)(4)(ii) are satisfied. If the effect of the setoff is to change the characterization or source of the income or deductions, or otherwise distort taxable income, in such a manner as to affect the U.S. tax liability of any member, adjustments will be made to reflect the correct amount of each

Reg. § 1.482-1(g)(4)(i)

category of income or deductions. For purposes of this setoff provision, the term arm's length refers to the amount defined in paragraph (b) (Arm's length standard) of this section, without regard to the rules in § 1.482-2 under which certain charges are deemed to be equal to arm's length.

(ii) *Requirements.*—The district director will take a setoff into account only if the taxpayer—

(A) Establishes that the transaction that is the basis of the setoff was not at arm's length and the amount of the appropriate arm's length charge;

(B) Documents, pursuant to paragraph (g)(2) of this section, all correlative adjustments resulting from the proposed setoff; and

(C) Notifies the district director of the basis of any claimed setoff within 30 days after the earlier of the date of a letter by which the district director transmits an examination report notifying the taxpayer of proposed adjustments or the date of the issuance of the notice of deficiency.

(iii) *Examples.*—The following examples illustrate this paragraph (g)(4).

Example 1. P, a U.S. corporation, renders services to S, its foreign subsidiary in Country Y, in connection with the construction of S's factory. An arm's length charge for such services determined under § 1.482-2(b) would be $100,000. During the same taxable year P makes available to S the use of a machine to be used in the construction of the factory, and the arm's length rental value of the machine is $25,000. P bills S $125,000 for the services, but does not charge S for the use of the machine. No allocation will be made with respect to the undercharge for the machine if P notifies the district director of the basis of the claimed setoff within 30 days after the date of the letter from the district director transmitting the examination report notifying P of the proposed adjustment, establishes that the excess amount charged for services was equal to an arm's length charge for the use of the machine and that the taxable income and income tax liabilities of P are not distorted, and documents the correlative allocations resulting from the proposed setoff.

Example 2. The facts are the same as in *Example 1*, except that, if P had reported $25,000 as rental income and $25,000 less as service income, it would have been subject to the tax on personal holding companies. Allocations will be made to reflect the correct amounts of rental income and service income.

(h) *Special rules.*—(1) *Small taxpayer safe harbor.*—[Reserved]

(2) *Effect of foreign legal restrictions.*—(i) *In general.*—The district director will take into account the effect of a foreign legal restriction to the extent that such restriction affects the results of transactions at arm's length. Thus, a foreign legal restriction will be taken into account only to the extent that it is shown that the restriction affected an uncontrolled taxpayer under comparable circumstances for a comparable period of time. In the absence of evidence indicating the effect of the foreign legal restriction on uncontrolled taxpayers, the restriction will be taken into account only to the extent provided in paragraphs (h)(2)(iii) and (iv) of this section (Deferred income method of accounting).

(ii) *Applicable legal restrictions.*—Foreign legal restrictions (whether temporary or permanent) will be taken into account for purposes of this paragraph (h)(2) only if, and so long as, the conditions set forth in paragraphs (h)(2)(ii)(A) through (D) of this section are met.

(A) The restrictions are publicly promulgated, generally applicable to all similarly situated persons (both controlled and uncontrolled), and not imposed as part of a commercial transaction between the taxpayer and the foreign sovereign;

(B) The taxpayer (or other member of the controlled group with respect to which the restrictions apply) has exhausted all remedies prescribed by foreign law or practice for obtaining a waiver of such restrictions (other than remedies that would have a negligible prospect of success if pursued);

(C) The restrictions expressly prevented the payment or receipt, in any form, of part or all of the arm's length amount that would otherwise be required under section 482 (for example, a restriction that applies only to the deductibility of an expense for tax purposes is not a restriction on payment or receipt for this purpose); and

(D) The related parties subject to the restriction did not engage in any arrangement with controlled or uncontrolled parties that had the effect of circumventing the restriction, and have not otherwise violated the restriction in any material respect.

(iii) *Requirement for electing the deferred income method of accounting.*—If a foreign legal restriction prevents the payment or receipt of part or all of the arm's length amount that is due with respect to a controlled transaction, the restricted amount may be treated as deferrable if the following requirements are met—

(A) The controlled taxpayer establishes to the satisfaction of the district director that the payment or receipt of the arm's length amount was prevented because of a foreign legal restriction and circumstances described in paragraph (h)(2)(ii) of this section; and

(B) The controlled taxpayer whose U.S. tax liability may be affected by the foreign legal restriction elects the deferred income method of accounting, as described in paragraph (h)(2)(iv) of this section, on a written statement attached to a timely U.S. income tax return (or an amended return) filed before the IRS first contacts any member of the controlled group concerning an examination of the return for the taxable year to which the foreign legal restriction applies. A written statement furnished by a taxpayer subject to the Coordinated Examination Program will be considered an amended return for purposes of this paragraph (h)(2)(iii)(B) if it satisfies the requirements of a qualified amended return for purposes of §1.6664-2(c)(3) as set forth in those regulations or as the Commissioner may prescribe by applicable revenue procedures. The election statement must identify the affected transactions, the parties to the transactions, and the applicable foreign legal restrictions.

(iv) *Deferred income method of accounting.*—If the requirements of paragraph (h)(2)(ii) of this section are satisfied, any portion of the arm's length amount, the payment or receipt of which is prevented because of applicable foreign legal restrictions, will be treated as deferrable until payment or receipt of the relevant item ceases to be prevented by the foreign legal restriction. For purposes of the deferred income method of accounting under this paragraph (h)(2)(iv), deductions (including the cost or other basis of inventory and other assets sold or exchanged) and credits properly chargeable against any amount so deferred, are subject to deferral under the provisions of §1.461-1(a)(4). In addition, income is deferrable under this deferred income method of accounting only to the extent that it exceeds the related deductions already claimed in open taxable years to which the foreign legal restriction applied.

(v) *Examples.*—The following examples, in which Sub is a Country FC subsidiary of U.S. corporation, Parent, illustrate this paragraph (h)(2).

Example 1. Parent licenses an intangible to Sub. FC law generally prohibits payments by any person within FC to recipients outside the country. The FC law meets the requirements of paragraph (h)(2)(ii) of this section. There is no evidence of unrelated parties entering into transactions under comparable circumstances for a comparable period of time, and the foreign legal restrictions will not be taken into account in determining the arm's length amount. The arm's length royalty rate for the use of the intangible property in the absence of the foreign restriction is 10% of Sub's sales in country FC. However, because the requirements of paragraph (h)(2)(ii) of this section are satisfied, Parent can elect the deferred income method of accounting by attaching to its timely filed U.S. income tax return a written statement that satisfies the requirements of paragraph (h)(2)(iii)(B) of this section.

Example 2. (i) The facts are the same as in *Example 1*, except that Sub, although it makes no royalty payment to Parent, arranges with an unrelated intermediary to make payments equal to an arm's length amount on its behalf to Parent.

(ii) The district director makes an allocation of royalty income to Parent, based on the arm's length royalty rate of 10%. Further, the district director determines that because the arrangement with the third party had the effect of circumventing the FC law, the requirements of paragraph (h)(2)(ii)(D) of this section are not satisfied. Thus, Parent could not validly elect the deferred income method of accounting, and the allocation of royalty income cannot be treated as deferrable. In appropriate circumstances, the district director may permit the amount of the distribution to be treated as payment by Sub of the royalty allocated to Parent, under the provisions of §1.482-1(g) (Collateral adjustments).

Example 3. The facts are the same as in *Example 1*, except that the laws of FC do not prevent distributions from corporations to their shareholders. Sub distributes an amount equal to 8% of its sales in country FC. Because the laws of FC did not expressly prevent all forms of payment from Sub to Parent, Parent cannot validly elect the deferred income method of accounting with respect to any of the arm's length royalty amount. In appropriate circumstances, the district director may permit the 8% that was distributed to be treated as payment by Sub of the royalty allocated to Parent, under the provisions of §1.482-1(g) (Collateral adjustments).

Example 4. The facts are the same as in *Example 1*, except that Country FC law permits the payment of a royalty, but limits the amount to 5% of sales, and Sub pays the 5% royalty to Parent. Parent demonstrates the existence of a comparable uncontrolled transaction for purposes of the comparable uncontrolled transaction method in which an uncontrolled party accepted a royalty rate of 5%. Given the evidence of the comparable uncontrolled transaction, the 5% royalty rate is determined to be the arm's length royalty rate.

(3) *Coordination with section 936.*—(i) *Cost sharing under section 936.*—If a possessions corporation makes an election under section 936(h)(5)(C)(i)(I), the corporation must make a section 936 cost sharing payment that is at least equal to the payment that would be required under section 482 if the electing corporation were a foreign corporation. In determining the payment that would be required under section 482 for this purpose, the provisions of §§ 1.482-1 and 1.482-4 will be applied, and to the extent relevant to the valuation of intangibles, §§ 1.482-5 and 1.482-6 will be applied. The provisions of section 936(h)(5)(C)(i)(II) (Effect of Election—electing corporation treated as owner of intangible property) do not apply until the payment that would be required under section 482 has been determined.

(ii) *Use of terms.*—A cost sharing payment, for the purposes of section 936(h)(5)(C)(i)(I), is calculated using the provisions of section 936 and the regulations thereunder and the provisions of this paragraph (h)(3). The provisions relating to cost sharing under section 482 do not apply to payments made pursuant to an election under section 936(h)(5)(C)(i)(I). Similarly, a profit split payment, for the purposes of section 936(h)(5)(C)(ii)(I), is calculated using the provisions of section 936 and the regulations thereunder, not section 482 and the regulations thereunder.

(i) *Definitions.*—The definitions set forth in paragraphs (i)(1) through (10) of this section apply to §§ 1.482-1 through 1.482-8.

(1) *Organization* includes an organization of any kind, whether a sole proprietorship, a partnership, a trust, an estate, an association, or a corporation (as each is defined or understood in the Internal Revenue Code or the regulations thereunder), irrespective of the place of organization, operation, or conduct of the trade or business, and regardless of whether it is a domestic or foreign organization, whether it is an exempt organization, or whether it is a member of an affiliated group that files a consolidated U.S. income tax return, or a member of an affiliated group that does not file a consolidated U.S. income tax return.

(2) *Trade* or *business* includes a trade or business activity of any kind, regardless of whether or where organized, whether owned individually or otherwise, and regardless of the place of operation. Employment for compensation will constitute a separate trade or business from the employing trade or business.

(3) *Taxpayer* means any person, organization, trade or business, whether or not subject to any internal revenue tax.

(4) *Controlled* includes any kind of control, direct or indirect, whether legally enforceable or not, and however exercisable or exercised, including control resulting from the actions of two or more taxpayers acting in concert or with a common goal or purpose. It is the reality of the control that is decisive, not its form or the mode of its exercise. A presumption of control arises if income or deductions have been arbitrarily shifted.

(5) *Controlled taxpayer* means any one of two or more taxpayers owned or controlled directly or indirectly by the same interests, and includes the taxpayer that owns or controls the other taxpayers. *Uncontrolled taxpayer* means any one of two or more taxpayers not owned or controlled directly or indirectly by the same interests.

(6) *Group*, *controlled group*, and *group of controlled taxpayers* mean the taxpayers owned or controlled directly or indirectly by the same interests.

(7) *Transaction* means any sale, assignment, lease, license, loan, advance, contribution, or any other transfer of any interest in or a right to use any property (whether tangible or intangible, real or personal) or money, however such transaction is effected, and whether or not the terms of such transaction are formally documented. A transaction also includes the performance of any services for the benefit of, or on behalf of, another taxpayer.

(8) *Controlled transaction* or *controlled transfer* means any transaction or transfer between two or more members of the same group of controlled taxpayers. The term *uncontrolled transaction* means any transaction between two or more taxpayers that are not members of the same group of controlled taxpayers.

(9) *True taxable income* means, in the case of a controlled taxpayer, the taxable income that would have resulted had it dealt with the other member or members of the group at arm's length. It does not mean the taxable income resulting to the controlled taxpayer by reason of the particular contract, transaction, or arrangement the controlled taxpayer chose to make (even though such contract, transaction, or arrangement is legally binding upon the parties thereto).

(10) *Uncontrolled comparable* means the uncontrolled transaction or uncontrolled taxpayer that is compared with a controlled transaction or taxpayer under any applicable pricing methodology. Thus, for example, under the comparable profits method, an uncontrolled comparable is any uncontrolled taxpayer from

which data is used to establish a comparable operating profit.

(j) *Effective dates.*—(1) These regulations are generally effective for taxable years beginning after October 6, 1994.

(2) Taxpayers may elect to apply retroactively all of the provisions of these regulations for any open taxable year. Such election will be effective for the year of the election and all subsequent taxable years.

(3) Although these regulations are generally effective for taxable years as stated, the final sentence of section 482 (requiring that the income with respect to transfers or licenses of intangible property be commensurate with the income attributable to the intangible) is generally effective for taxable years beginning after December 31, 1986. For the period prior to the effective date of these regulations, the final sentence of section 482 must be applied using any reasonable method not inconsistent with the statute. The IRS considers a method that applies these regulations or their general principles to be a reasonable method.

(4) These regulations will not apply with respect to transfers made or licenses granted to foreign persons before November 17, 1985, or before August 17, 1986, for transfers or licenses to others. Nevertheless, they will apply with respect to transfers or licenses before such dates if, with respect to property transferred pursuant to an earlier and continuing transfer agreement, such property was not in existence or owned by the taxpayer on such date.

(5) The last sentences of paragraphs (b)(2)(i) and (c)(1) of this section and of paragraph (c)(2)(iv) of §1.482-5 apply for taxable years beginning on or after August 26, 2003. [Reg. § 1.482-1.]

☐ [*T.D.* 8552, 7-1-94. *Amended by T.D.* 9088, 8-25-2003.]

Proposed Amendments to Regulation

☐ Section 1.482-1 is amended by: **1.** Revising paragraphs (a)(1), (b)(2)(i), (d)(3)(ii)(C) *Example 3*, (f)(2)(iii)(B), (g)(4)(i), the first two sentences in paragraph (g)(4)(iii) *Example 1*, and paragraph (i) introductory text. **2.** Adding paragraph (d)(3)(ii)(C), *Example 4* and *Example 5*. **3.** Adding a sentence at the end of paragraph (d)(3)(v). The additions and revisions read as follows:

§ 1.482-1. Allocation of income and deductions among taxpayers.—(a) *In general.*—(1) *Purpose and scope.*—The purpose of section 482 is to ensure that taxpayers clearly reflect income attributable to controlled transactions, and to prevent the avoidance of taxes with respect to such transactions. Section 482 places a controlled taxpayer on a tax parity with an uncontrolled taxpayer by determining the true taxable income of the controlled taxpayer. This section sets forth general principles and guidelines to be followed under section 482. Section 1.482-2 provides rules for the determination of the true taxable income of controlled taxpayers in specific situations, including controlled transactions involving loans or advances or the use of tangible property. Sections 1.482-3 through 1.482-6 provide rules for the determination of the true taxable income of controlled taxpayers in cases involving the transfer of property. Section 1.482-7T sets forth the cost sharing provisions applicable to taxable years beginning on or after October 6, 1994, and before January 1, 1996. Section 1.482-7 sets forth the cost sharing provisions applicable to taxable years beginning on or after January 1, 1996. Section 1.482-8 provides examples illustrating the application of the best method rule. Finally, § 1.482-9 provides rules for the determination of the true taxable income of controlled taxpayers in cases involving the performance of services.

* * *

(b) * * *

(2) *Arm's length methods.*—(i) *Methods.*—Sections 1.482-2 through 1.482-6 and § 1.482-9 provide specific methods to be used to evaluate whether transactions between or among members of the controlled group satisfy the arm's length standard and if they do not to determine the arm's length result. Section 1.482-7 provides the specific method to be used to evaluate whether a qualified cost sharing arrangement produces results consistent with an arm's length result.

* * *

(d) * * *

(3) * * *

(ii) * * *

(C) * * *

Example 3. Contractual terms imputed from economic substance. (i) FP, a foreign producer of wristwatches, is the registered holder of the YY trademark in the United States and in other countries worldwide. In Year 1, FP enters the U.S. market by selling YY wristwatches to its newly organized U.S. subsidiary, USSub, for distribution in the U.S. market. USSub pays FP a fixed price per wristwatch, and USSub and FP undertake without separate compensation marketing activities to establish the YY trademark in the U.S. market. Unrelated foreign producers of trademarked wristwatches and U.S. distributors respectively undertake similar marketing activities in independent arrangements involving distribution of trademarked wristwatches in the U.S. market. In Years 1 through 6, USSub markets and sells YY wristwatches in the United States. Further, in Years 1 through 6, USSub undertakes incremental marketing activities in addition to the activities similar to those observed in the independent distribution transactions in the U.S. market. FP does not directly or indirectly compensate USSub for performing these incremental activities during Years 1 through 6. Assume that, aside from these incremental activities, and after any adjustments are made to improve the reliability of the comparison, the price paid per wristwatch by the independent distributors for wristwatches would provide the most reliable measure of the arm's length price paid per YY wristwatch by USSub.

(ii) By Year 7, the wristwatches with the YY trademark generate a premium return in the U.S. market, as compared to wristwatches marketed by the independent distributors. In Year 7, substantially all the premium return from the YY trademark in the U.S. market is attributed to FP, for example through an increase in the price paid per watch by USSub, or by some other means.

(iii) In determining whether an allocation of income is appropriate in Year 7, the Commissioner may consider the economic substance of the arrangements between USSub and FP, and the parties' course of conduct throughout their relationship. Based on this analysis, the Commissioner determines that it is unlikely that, *ex ante*, an uncontrolled taxpayer operating at arm's length would engage in marketing activities to develop or enhance an intangible owned by another party unless it received contemporaneous compensation or otherwise had a reasonable anticipation of receiving a future benefit from those activities. In this case, USSub's undertaking the incremental marketing activities in Years 1 through 6 is a course of conduct that is inconsistent with the parties' attribution to FP in Year 7 of substantially all the premium return from the enhanced YY trademark in the United States market. Therefore, the Commissioner may impute one or more agreements between USSub and FP, consistent with the economic substance of their course of conduct, which would afford USSub an appropriate portion of the premium return from the YY trademark wristwatches. For example, the Commissioner may impute a separate services agreement that affords USSub contingent-payment compensation for its incremental marketing activities in Years 1 through 6, which benefited FP by contributing to the value of the trademark owned by FP. In the alternative, the Commissioner may impute a long-term exclusive U.S. distribution agreement to exploit the YY trademark that allows USSub to benefit from the incremental marketing activities it performed. As another alternative, the Commissioner may require FP to compensate USSub for terminating USSub's imputed long-term distribution agreement, an agreement that USSub made more valuable at its own expense and risk. The taxpayer may present additional facts that could indicate which of these or other alternative agreements best reflects the economic substance of the underlying transactions, consistent with the parties' course of conduct in the particular case.

Example 4. Contractual terms imputed from economic substance. (i) FP, a foreign producer of athletic gear, is the registered holder of the AA trademark in the United States and in other countries worldwide. In Year 1, FP licenses to its newly organized U.S. subsidiary, USSub, exclusive rights to certain manufacturing and marketing intangibles (including the AA trademark) for purposes of manufacturing and marketing athletic gear in the United States under the AA trademark. The contractual terms obligate USSub to pay FP a royalty based on sales, and obligate both FP and USSub to undertake without separate compensation specified types and levels of marketing activities. Unrelated foreign businesses license independent U.S. businesses to manufacture and market athletic gear in the United States, using trademarks owned by the unrelated foreign businesses. The contractual terms of these uncontrolled transactions require the licensees to pay royalties based on sales of the merchandise, and obligate the licensors and licensees to undertake without separate compensation specified types and levels of marketing activities. In Years 1 through 6, USSub manufactures and sells athletic gear under the AA trademark in the United States. Assume that, after adjustments are made to improve the reliability of the comparison for any material differences relating to marketing activities, manufacturing or marketing intangibles, and other comparability factors, the royalties paid by independent licensees would provide the most reliable measure of the arm's length royalty owed by USSub to FP, apart from the additional facts.

(ii) In Years 1 through 6, USSub performs incremental marketing activities with respect to the AA trademark athletic gear, in addition to the activities required under the terms of the license agreement. FP does not directly or indirectly compensate USSub for performing these incremental activities during Years 1 through 6. By Year 7, AA trademark athletic gear generates a premium return in the United States, as compared to similar athletic gear marketed by independent licensees. In Year 7, USSub and FP enter into a separate services agreement under which FP agrees to compensate USSub on a cost basis for the incremental marketing activities that USSub performed during Years 1 through 6, and to compensate USSub on a cost basis for any incremental marketing activities it may perform in Year 7 and thereafter. In addition, the parties revise the license agreement executed in Year 1, and increase the royalty to a level that attributes to FP substantially all the premium return from sales of the AA trademark athletic gear in the United States.

(iii) In determining whether an allocation of income is appropriate in Year 7, the Commissioner may consider the economic substance of the arrangements between USSub and FP and the parties' course of conduct throughout their relationship. Based on this analysis, the Commissioner determines that it is unlikely that, *ex ante*, an uncontrolled taxpayer operating at arm's length would engage in incremental marketing activities to develop or enhance an intangible owned by another party unless it received contemporaneous compensation or otherwise had a reasonable anticipation of a future benefit. In this case, USSub's undertaking the incremental marketing activities in Years 1 through 6 is a course of conduct that is inconsistent with the parties' adoption in Year 7 of contractual terms whereby FP compensates USSub on a cost basis for the incremental marketing activities that it performed. Therefore, the Commissioner may impute one or more agreements between USSub and FP, consistent with the economic substance of their course of conduct, which would afford USSub an appropriate portion of the premium return from the AA trademark athletic gear. For example, the Commissioner may impute a separate services agreement that affords USSub contingent-payment compensation for the incremental activities it performed during Years 1 through 6, which benefited FP by contributing to the value of the trademark owned by FP. In the alternative, the Commissioner may impute a long-term exclusive U.S. license agreement that allows USSub to benefit from the incremental activities. As another alternative, the Commissioner may require FP to compensate USSub for terminating USSub's imputed long-term U.S. license agreement, a license that USSub made more valuable at its own expense and risk. The taxpayer may present additional facts that could indicate which of these or other alternative agreements best reflects the economic substance of the underlying transactions, consistent with the parties' course of conduct in this particular case.

Example 5. Contractual terms imputed from economic substance. (i) Company X is a member of a controlled group that has been in operation in the pharmaceutical sector for many years. In Years 1 through 4, Company X undertakes research and development activities. As a result of those activities, a compound is developed that may be more effective than existing medications in the treatment of certain conditions.

(ii) Company Y is acquired in Year 4 by the controlled group that includes Company X. Once Company Y is acquired, patent rights with respect to the compound in several jurisdictions are registered by Company Y, making Company Y the legal owner of such patents.

(iii) In determining whether an allocation is appropriate in Year 4, the Commissioner may consider the economic substance of the arrangements between Company X and Company Y, and the parties' course of conduct throughout their relationship. Based on this analysis, the Commissioner determines that it is unlikely that, *ex ante*, an uncontrolled taxpayer operating at arm's length would engage in research and development activities to develop a patentable compound to be registered by another party unless it received contemporaneous compensation or otherwise had a reasonable anticipation of receiving a future benefit from those activities. In this case, Company X's undertaking the research and development activities is inconsistent with the registration of the patent by Company Y. Therefore, the Commissioner may impute one or more agreements between Company X and Company Y consistent with the economic substance of their course of conduct, which would afford Company X an appropriate portion of the premium return from the patent rights. For example, the Commissioner may impute a separate services agreement that affords Company X contingent-payment compensation for its research and development activities in Years 1 through 4, which benefited Company Y by creating and further contributing to the value of the patent rights ultimately registered by Company Y. In the alternative, the Commissioner may impute a transfer of patentable intangible rights from Company X to Company Y immediately preceding the registration of patent rights by Company Y. The taxpayer may present additional facts that could indicate which of these or other alternative agreements best reflects the economic substance of the underlying transactions, consistent with the parties' course of conduct in the particular case.

* * *

(v) * * * See § 1.482-9(m).

* * *

(f) * * *

(2) * * *

(iii) * * *

(B) *Circumstances warranting consideration of multiple year data.*—The extent to which it is appropriate to consider multiple year data depends on the method being applied and the issue being addressed. Circumstances that may warrant consideration of data from multiple years include the extent to which complete and accurate data is available for the taxable year under review, the effect of business cycles in the controlled taxpayer's industry, or the effects of life cycles of the product or intangible being examined. Data from one or more years before or after the taxable year under review must ordinarily be considered for purposes of applying the provisions of paragraph (d)(3)(iii) of this section (Risk), paragraph (d)(4)(i) of this section (Market share strategy), § 1.482-4(f)(2) (Periodic adjustments), § 1.482-5 (Comparable profits method), § 1.482-9(e) (Comparable profits method for services), § 1.482-9(f) (Simplified cost-based method for services), and § 1.482-9(i) (Contingent-payment contractual terms for services). On the other hand, multiple year data ordinarily will not be considered for purposes of applying the comparable uncontrolled price method of § 1.482-3(b) or the comparable uncontrolled services price method of § 1.482-9(b) (except to the extent that risk or market share strategy issues are present).

* * *

(g) * * *

(4) *Setoffs.*—(i) *In general.*—If an allocation is made under section 482 with respect to a transaction between controlled taxpayers, the Commissioner will take into account the effect of any other non-arm's length transaction between the same controlled taxpayers in the same taxable year which will result in a setoff against the original section 482 allocation. Such setoff, however, will be taken into account only if the requirements of paragraph (g)(4)(ii) of this section are satisfied. If the effect of the setoff is to change the characterization or source of the income or deductions, or otherwise distort taxable income, in such a manner as to affect the U.S. tax liability of any member, adjustments will be made to reflect the correct amount of each category of income or deductions. For purposes of this setoff provision, the term arm's length refers to the amount defined in paragraph (b) of this section (Arm's length standard), without regard to the rules in § 1.482-2(a) that treat certain interest rates as arm's length rates of interest.

* * *

(iii) *Examples.*—* * *

Example 1. P, a U.S. corporation, renders construction services to S, its foreign subsidiary in Country Y, in connection with the construction of S's factory. An arm's length charge for such services determined under § 1.482-9 would be $100,000. * * *

* * *

(i) *Definitions.*—The definitions set forth in paragraphs (i)(1) through (i)(10) of this section apply to this §§ 1.482-1 through 1.482-9.

* * *

[Prop. Reg. § 1.482-1.]
[Proposed 9-10-2003.]

§ 1.482-2. Determination of taxable income in specific situations.—(a) *Loans or advances.*—(1) *Interest on bona fide indebtedness.*—(i) *In general.*—Where one member of a group of controlled entities makes a loan or advance directly or indirectly to, or otherwise becomes a creditor of, another member of such group and either charges no interest, or charges interest at a rate which is not equal to an arm's length rate of interest (as defined in paragraph (a)(2) of this section) with respect to such loan or advance, the district director may make appropriate allocations to reflect an arm's length rate of interest for the use of such loan or advance.

(ii) *Application of paragraph (a) of this section.*—(A) *Interest on bona fide indebtedness.*—Paragraph (a) of this section applies only to determine the appropriateness of the rate of interest charged on the principal amount of a bona fide indebtedness between members of a group of controlled entities, including—

(1) Loans or advances of money or other consideration (whether or not evidenced by a written instrument); and

(2) Indebtedness arising in the ordinary course of business from sales, leases, or the rendition of services by or between members of the group, or any other similar extension of credit.

(B) *Alleged indebtedness.*—This paragraph (a) does not apply to so much of an alleged indebtedness which is not in fact a bona fide indebtedness, even if the stated rate of interest thereon would be within the safe haven rates prescribed in paragraph (a)(2)(iii) of this section. For example, paragraph (a) of this section does not apply to payments with respect to all or a portion of such alleged indebtedness where in fact all or a portion of an alleged indebtedness is a contribution to the capital of a corporation or a distribution by a corporation with respect to its shares. Similarly, this paragraph (a) does not apply to payments with respect to an alleged purchase-money debt instrument given in consideration for an alleged sale of property between two controlled entities where in fact the transaction constitutes a lease of the property. Payments made with respect to alleged indebtedness (including alleged stated interest thereon) shall be treated according to their substance. See § 1.482-2(a)(3)(i).

(iii) *Period for which interest shall be charged.*—(A) *General rule.*—This paragraph (a)(1)(iii) is effective for indebtedness arising after June 30, 1988. See § 1.482-2(a)(3) (26 CFR Part 1 edition revised as of April 1, 1988) for indebtedness arising before July 1, 1988. Except as otherwise provided in paragraphs (a)(1)(iii)(B) through (E) of this section, the period for which interest shall be charged with respect to a bona fide indebtedness between controlled entities begins on the day after the day the indebtedness arises and ends on the day the indebtedness is satisfied (whether by payment, offset, cancellation, or otherwise). Paragraphs (a)(1)(iii)(B) through (E) of this section provide certain alternative periods during which interest is not required to be charged on certain indebtedness. These exceptions apply only to indebtedness described in paragraph (a)(1)(ii)(A)(2) of this section (relating to indebtedness incurred in the ordinary course of business from sales, services, etc., between members of the group) and not evidenced by a written instrument requiring the payment of interest. Such amounts are hereinafter referred to as intercompany trade receivables. The period for which interest is not required to be charged on intercompany trade receivables under this paragraph (a)(1)(iii) is called the interest-free period. In general, an intercompany trade receivable arises at the time economic performance occurs (within the meaning of section 461(h) and the regulations thereunder) with respect to the underlying transaction between controlled entities. For purposes of this paragraph (a)(1)(iii), the term United States includes any possession of the United States, and the term foreign country excludes any possession of the United States.

(B) *Exception for certain intercompany transactions in the ordinary course of business.*—Interest is not required to be charged on an intercompany trade receivable until the first day of the third calendar month following the month in which the intercompany trade receivable arises.

(C) *Exception for trade or business of debtor member located outside the United States.*—In the case of an intercompany trade receivable arising from a transaction in the ordinary course of a trade or business which is actively conducted outside the United States by the debtor member, interest is not required to be charged until the first day of the fourth calendar month following the month in which such intercompany trade receivable arises.

(D) *Exception for regular trade practice of creditor member or others in creditor's industry.*—If the creditor member or unrelated persons in the creditor member's industry, as a regular trade practice, allow unrelated parties a longer period without charging interest than that described in paragraph (a)(1)(iii)(B) or (C) of this section (whichever is applicable) with respect to transactions which are similar to transactions that give rise to intercompany trade receivables, such longer interest-free period shall be allowed with respect to a comparable amount of intercompany trade receivables.

(E) *Exception for property purchased for resale in a foreign country.*—(1) *General rule.*—If in the ordinary course of business one member of the group (related purchaser) purchases property from another member of the group (related seller) for resale to unrelated persons located in a particular foreign country, the related purchaser and the related seller may use as the interest-free period for the intercompany trade receivables arising during the related seller's taxable year from the purchase of such property within the same product group an interest-free period equal the sum of—

(i) The number of days in the related purchaser's average collection period (as determined under paragraph (a)(1)(iii)(E)(2) of this section) for sales of property within the same product group sold in the ordinary course of business to unrelated persons located in the same foreign country; plus

(ii) Ten (10) calendar days.

(2) *Interest-free period.*—The interest-free period under this paragraph (a)(1)(iii)(E), however, shall in no event exceed 183 days. The related purchaser does not have to conduct business outside the United States in order to be eligible to use the interest-free period of this paragraph (a)(1)(iii)(E). The interest-free period under this paragraph (a)(1)(iii)(E) shall not apply to intercompany trade receivables attributable to property which is manufactured, produced, or constructed (within the meaning of § 1.954-3(a)(4)) by the related purchaser. For purposes of this paragraph (a)(1)(iii)(E) a product group includes all products within the same three-digit Standard Industrial Classification (SIC) Code (as prepared by the Statistical Policy Division of the Office of Management and Budget, Executive Office of the President.)

(3) *Average collection period.*—An average collection period for purposes of this paragraph (a)(1)(iii)(E) is determined as follows—

Reg. § 1.482-2(a)(1)(iii)(E)(3)

(i) Step 1.—Determine total sales (less returns and allowances) by the related purchaser in the product group to unrelated persons located in the same foreign country during the related purchaser's last taxable year ending on or before the first day of the related seller's taxable year in which the intercompany trade receivable arises.

(ii) Step 2.—Determine the related purchaser's average month-end accounts receivable balance with respect to sales described in paragraph (a)(1)(iii)(E)(2)(i) of this section for the related purchaser's last taxable year ending on or before the first day of the related seller's taxable year in which the intercompany trade receivable arises.

(iii) Step 3.—Compute a receivables turnover rate by dividing the total sales amount described in paragraph (a)(1)(iii)(E)(2)(i) of this section by the average receivables balance described in paragraph (a)(1)(iii)(E)(2)(ii) of this section.

(iv) Step 4.—Divide the receivables turnover rate determined under paragraph (a)(1)(iii)(E)(2)(iii) of this section into 365, and round the result to the nearest whole number to determine the number of days in the average collection period.

(v) Other considerations.—If the related purchaser makes sales in more than one foreign country, or sells property in more than one product group in any foreign country, separate computations of an average collection period, by product group within each country, are required. If the related purchaser resells fungible property in more than one foreign country and the intercompany trade receivables arising from the related party purchase of such fungible property cannot reasonably be identified with resales in particular foreign countries, then solely for the purpose of assigning an interest-free period to such intercompany trade receivables under this paragraph (a)(1)(iii)(E), an amount of each such intercompany trade receivable shall be treated as allocable to a particular foreign country in the same proportion that the related purchaser's sales of such fungible property in such foreign country during the period described in paragraph (a)(1)(iii)(E)(2)(i) of this section bears to the related purchaser's sales of all such fungible property in all such foreign countries during such period. An interest-free period under this paragraph (a)(1)(iii)(E) shall not apply to any intercompany trade receivables arising in a taxable year of the related seller if the related purchaser made no sales described in paragraph (a)(1)(iii)(E)(2)(i) of this section from which the appropriate interest-free period may be determined.

(4) Illustration.—The interest-free period provided under paragraph (a)(1)(iii)(E) of this section may be illustrated by the following example:

Example—(i) *Facts.* X and Y use the calendar year as the taxable year and are members of the same group of controlled entities within the meaning of section 482. For Y's 1988 calendar taxable year X and Y intend to use the interest-free period determined under this paragraph (a)(1)(iii)(E) for intercompany trade receivables attributable to X's purchases of certain products from Y for resale by X in the ordinary course of business to unrelated persons in country Z. For its 1987 calendar taxable year all of X's sales in country Z were of products within a single product group based upon a three-digit SIC code, were not manufactured, produced, or constructed (within the meaning of § 1.954-3(a)(4)) by X, and were sold in the ordinary course of X's trade or business to unrelated persons located only in country Z. These sales and the month-end accounts receivable balances (for such sales and for such sales uncollected from prior months) are as follows:

Month	Sales	Accounts Receivable
January 1987	$500,000	$2,835,850
February	600,000	2,840,300
March	450,000	2,850,670
April	550,000	2,825,700
May	650,000	2,809,360
June	525,000	2,803,200
July	400,000	2,825,850
August	425,000	2,796,240
September	475,000	2,839,390
October	525,000	2,650,550
November	450,000	2,775,450
December 1987	650,000	2,812,600
TOTALS	$6,200,000	$33,665,160

Reg. § 1.482-2(a)(1)(iii)(E)(3)(i)

(ii) *Average collection period.* X's total sales within the same product group to unrelated persons within country Z for the period are $6,200,000. The average receivables balance for the period is $2,805,430 ($33,665,160/12). The average collection period in whole days is determined as follows:

$$\text{Receivables Turnover Rate} = \frac{\$6,200,000}{\$2,805,430} = 2.21$$

$$\text{Average Collection Period days.} = \frac{365}{2.21} = 165.16 \text{ days, rounded to the nearest whole day} = 165$$

(iii) *Interest-free period.* Accordingly, for intercompany trade receivables incurred by X during Y's 1988 calendar taxable year attributable to the purchase of property from Y for resale to unrelated persons located in country Z and included in the product group, X may use an interest-free period of 175 days (165 days in the average collection period plus 10 days, but not in excess of a maximum of 183 days). All other intercompany trade receivables incurred by X are subject to the interest-free periods described in paragraphs (a)(1)(iii)(B), (C), or (D), whichever are applicable. If X makes sales in other foreign countries in addition to country Z or makes sales of property in more than one product group in any foreign country, separate computations of X's average collection period, by product group within each country, are required in order for X and Y to determine an interest-free period for such product groups in such foreign countries under this paragraph (a)(1)(iii)(E).

(iv) *Payment; book entries*—(A) Except as otherwise provided in this paragraph (a)(1)(iv), in determining the period of time for which an amount owed by one member of the group to another member is outstanding, payments or other credits to an account are considered to be applied against the earliest amount outstanding, that is, payments or credits are applied against amounts in a first-in, first-out (FIFO) order. Thus, tracing payments to individual intercompany trade receivables is generally not required in order to determine whether a particular intercompany trade receivable has been paid within the applicable interest-free period determined under paragraph (a)(1)(iii) of this section. The application of this paragraph (a)(1)(iv)(A) may be illustrated by the following example:

Example—(i) *Facts.* X and Y are members of a group of controlled entities within the meaning of section 482. Assume that the balance of intercompany trade receivables owed by X to Y on June 1 is $100, and that all of the $100 balance represents amounts incurred by X to Y during the month of May. During the month of June X incurs an additional $200 of intercompany trade receivables to Y. Assume that on July 15, $60 is properly credited against X's intercompany account to Y, and that $240 is properly credited against the intercompany account on August 31. Assume that under paragraph (a)(1)(iii)(B) of this section interest must be charged on X's intercompany trade receivables to Y beginning with the first day of the third calendar month following the month the intercompany trade receivables arise, and that no alternative interest-free period applies. Thus, the interest-free period for intercompany trade receivables incurred during the month of May ends on July 31, and the interest-free period for intercompany trade receivables incurred during the month of June ends on August 31.

(ii) *Application of payments.* Using a FIFO payment order, the aggregate payments of $300 are applied first to the opening June balance, and then to the additional amounts incurred during the month of June. With respect to X's June opening balance of $100, no interest is required to be accrued on $60 of such balance paid by X on July 15, because such portion was paid within its interest-free period. Interest for 31 days, from August 1 to August 31 inclusive, is required to be accrued on the $40 portion of the opening balance not paid until August 31. No interest is required to be accrued on the $200 of intercompany trade receivables X incurred to Y during June because the $240 credited on August 31, after eliminating the $40 of indebtedness remaining from periods before June, also eliminated the $200 incurred by X during June prior to the end of the interest-free period for that amount. The amount of interest incurred by X to Y on the $40 amount during August creates bona fide indebtedness between controlled entities and is subject to the provisions of paragraph (a)(1)(iii)(A) of this section without regard to any of the exceptions contained in paragraphs (a)(1)(iii)(B) through (E).

(B) Notwithstanding the first-in, first-out payment application rule described in paragraph (a)(1)(iv)(A) of this section, the taxpayer may apply payments or credits against amounts owed in some other order on its books in accordance with an agreement or understanding of the related parties if the taxpayer can demonstrate that either it or others in its industry, as a regular trade practice, enter into such agreements or understandings in the case of similar balances with unrelated parties.

Reg. §1.482-2(a)(1)(iii)(E)(4)

(2) *Arm's length interest rate.*—(i) *In general.*—For purposes of section 482 and paragraph (a) of this section, an arm's length rate of interest shall be a rate of interest which was charged, or would have been charged, at the time the indebtedness arose, in independent transactions with or between unrelated parties under similar circumstances. All relevant factors shall be considered, including the principal amount and duration of the loan, the security involved, the credit standing of the borrower, and the interest rate prevailing at the situs of the lender or creditor for comparable loans between unrelated parties.

(ii) *Funds obtained at situs of borrower.*—Notwithstanding the other provisions of paragraph (a)(2) of this section, if the loan or advance represents the proceeds of a loan obtained by the lender at the situs of the borrower, the arm's length rate for any taxable year shall be equal to the rate actually paid by the lender increased by an amount which reflects the costs or deductions incurred by the lender in borrowing such amounts and making such loans, unless the taxpayer establishes a more appropriate rate under the standards set forth in paragraph (a)(2)(i) of this section.

(iii) *Safe haven interest rates for certain loans and advances made after May 8, 1986.*—(A) *Applicability.*—(1) *General rule.*—Except as otherwise provided in paragraph (a)(2) of this section, paragraph (a)(2)(iii)(B) applies with respect to the rate of interest charged and to the amount of interest paid or accrued in any taxable year—

(i) Under a term loan or advance between members of a group of controlled entities where (except as provided in paragraph (a)(2)(iii)(A)(2)(ii) of this section) the loan or advance is entered into after May 8, 1986; and

(ii) After May 8, 1986 under a demand loan or advance between such controlled entities.

(2) *Grandfather rule for existing loans.*—The safe haven rates prescribed in paragraph (a)(2)(iii)(B) of this section shall not apply, and the safe haven rates prescribed in § 1.482-2(a)(2)(iii) (26 CFR part 1 edition revised as of April 1, 1985), shall apply to—

(i) Term loans or advances made before May 9, 1986; and

(ii) Term loans or advances made before August 7, 1986, pursuant to a binding written contract entered into before May 9, 1986.

(B) *Safe haven interest rate based on applicable Federal rate.*—Except as otherwise provided in this paragraph (a)(2), in the case of a loan or advance between members of a group of controlled entities, an arm's length rate of interest referred to in paragraph (a)(2)(i) of this section shall be for purposes of chapter 1 of the Internal Revenue Code—

(1) The rate of interest actually charged if that rate is—

(i) Not less than 100 percent of the applicable Federal rate (lower limit); and

(ii) Not greater than 130 percent of the applicable Federal rate (upper limit); or

(2) If either no interest is charged or if the rate of interest charged is less than the lower limit, then an arm's length rate of interest shall be equal to the lower limit, compounded semiannually; or

(3) If the rate of interest charged is greater than the upper limit, then an arm's length rate of interest shall be equal to the upper limit, compounded semiannually, unless the taxpayer establishes a more appropriate compound rate of interest under paragraph (a)(2)(i) of this section. However, if the compound rate of interest actually charged is greater than the upper limit and less than the rate determined under paragraph (a)(2)(i) of this section, or if the compound rate actually charged is less than the lower limit and greater than the rate determined under paragraph (a)(2)(i) of this section, then the compound rate actually charged shall be deemed to be an arm's length rate under paragraph (a)(2)(i). In the case of any sale-leaseback described in section 1274(e), the lower limit shall be 110 percent of the applicable Federal rate, compounded semiannually.

(C) *Applicable Federal rate.*—For purposes of paragraph (a)(2)(iii)(B) of this section, the term applicable Federal rate means, in the case of a loan or advance to which this section applies and having a term of—

(1) Not over 3 years, the Federal short-term rate;

(2) Over 3 years but not over 9 years, the Federal mid-term rate; or

(3) Over 9 years, the Federal long-term rate,

as determined under section 1274(d) in effect on the date such loan or advance is made. In the case of any sale or exchange between controlled entities, the lower limit shall be the lowest of the applicable Federal rates in effect for any month in the 3-calendar-month period ending with the first calendar month in which there is a binding written contract in effect for such sale or exchange (lowest 3-month rate, as defined in section 1274(d)(2)). In the case of a demand loan or advance to which this section applies, the applicable Federal rate means the Federal short-term rate determined under section 1274(d) (determined without regard to the lowest 3-month short term rate determined under section 1274(d)(2)) in effect for each day on which any amount of such loan or advance (including unpaid accrued interest determined under paragraph (a)(2) of this section) is outstanding.

(D) *Lender in business of making loans.*—If the lender in a loan or advance transaction to which paragraph (a)(2) of this section applies is regularly engaged in the trade or business of making loans or advances to unrelated parties, the safe haven rates prescribed in paragraph (a)(2)(iii)(B) of this section shall not apply, and the arm's length interest rate to be used shall be determined under the standards described in paragraph (a)(2)(i) of this section, including reference to the interest rates charged in such trade or business by the lender on loans or advances of a similar type made to unrelated parties at and about the time the loan or advance to which paragraph (a)(2) of this section applies was made.

(E) *Foreign currency loans.*—The safe haven interest rates prescribed in paragraph (a)(2)(iii)(B) of this section do not apply to any loan or advance the principal or interest of which is expressed in a currency other than U.S. dollars.

(3) *Coordination with interest adjustments required under certain other Code sections.*—If the stated rate of interest on the stated principal amount of a loan or advance between controlled entities is subject to adjustment under section 482 and is also subject to adjustment under any other section of the Internal Revenue Code (for example, section 467, 483, 1274 or 7872), section 482 and paragraph (a) of this section may be applied to such loan or advance in addition to such other Internal Revenue Code section. After the enactment of the Tax Reform Act of 1964, Pub. L. 98-369, and the enactment of Pub. L. 99-121, such other Internal Revenue Code sections include sections 467, 483, 1274 and 7872. The order in which the different provisions shall be applied is as follows—

(i) First, the substance of the transaction shall be determined; for this purpose, all the relevant facts and circumstances shall be considered and any law or rule of law (assignment of income, step transaction, etc.) may apply. Only the rate of interest with respect to the stated principal amount of the bona fide indebtedness (within the meaning of paragraph (a)(1) of this section), if any, shall be subject to adjustment under section 482, paragraph (a) of this section, and any other Internal Revenue Code section.

(ii) Second, the other Internal Revenue Code section shall be applied to the loan or advance to determine whether any amount other than stated interest is to be treated as interest, and if so, to determine such amount according to the provisions of such other Internal Revenue Code section.

(iii) Third, whether or not the other Internal Revenue Code section applies to adjust the amounts treated as interest under such loan or advance, section 482 and paragraph (a) of this section may then be applied by the district director to determine whether the rate of interest charged on the loan or advance, as adjusted by any other Code section, is greater or less than an arm's length rate of interest, and if so, to make appropriate allocations to reflect an arm's length rate of interest.

(iv) Fourth, section 482 and paragraphs (b) through (d) of this section and §§ 1.482-3 through 1.482-7, if applicable, may be applied by the district director to make any appropriate allocations, other than an interest rate adjustment, to reflect an arm's length transaction based upon the principal amount of the loan or advance and the interest rate as adjusted under paragraph (a)(3)(i), (ii) or (iii) of this section. For example, assume that two commonly controlled taxpayers enter into a deferred payment sale of tangible property and no interest is provided, and assume also that section 483 is applied to treat a portion of the stated sales price as interest, thereby reducing the stated sales price. If after this recharacterization of a portion of the stated sales price as interest, the recomputed sales price does not reflect an arm's length sales price under the principles of § 1.482-3, the district director may make other appropriate allocations (other than an interest rate adjustment) to reflect an arm's length sales price.

(4) *Examples.*—The principles of paragraph (a)(3) of this section may be illustrated by the following examples:

Example 1. An individual, A, transfers $20,000 to a corporation controlled by A in exchange for the corporation's note which bears adequate stated interest. The district director recharacterizes the transaction as a contribution to the capital of the corporation in exchange for preferred stock. Under paragraph (a)(3)(i) of this section, section 1.482-2(a) does not apply to the transaction because there is no bona fide indebtedness.

Example 2. B, an individual, is an employee of Z corporation, and is also the controlling shareholder of Z. Z makes a term loan of $15,000 to B at a rate of interest that is less than the applicable Federal rate. In this instance the other operative Code section is section 7872. Under section 7872(b), the difference between the amount loaned and the present value of all payments due under the loan using a discount rate equal to 100 percent of the applicable Federal rate is treated as an amount of cash transferred from the corporation to B and the loan is treated as having original issue discount equal to such amount. Under paragraph (a)(3)(iii) of this section, section 482 and paragraph (a) of this section may also be applied by the district director to determine if the rate of interest charged on this $15,000 loan (100 percent of the AFR, compounded semiannually, as adjusted by section 7872) is an arm's length rate of interest. Because the rate of interest on the loan, as adjusted by section 7872, is within the safe haven range of 100-130 percent of the AFR, compounded semiannually, no further interest rate adjustments under section 482 and paragraph (a) of this section will be made to this loan.

Example 3. The facts are the same as in *Example 2* except that the amount lent by Z to B is $9,000, and that amount is the aggregate outstanding amount of loans between Z and B. Under the $10,000 de minimis exception of section 7872(c)(3), no adjustment for interest will be made to this $9,000 loan under section 7872. Under paragraph (a)(3)(iii) of this section, the district director may apply section 482 and paragraph (a) of this section to this $9,000 loan to determine whether the rate of interest charged is less than an arm's length rate of interest, and if so, to make appropriate allocations to reflect an arm's length rate of interest.

Example 4. X and Y are commonly controlled taxpayers. At a time when the applicable Federal rate is 12 percent, compounded semiannually, X sells property to Y in exchange for a note with a stated rate of interest of 18 percent, compounded semiannually. Assume that the other applicable Code section to the transaction is section 483. Section 483 does not apply to this transaction because, under section 483(d), there is no total unstated interest under the contract using the test rate of interest equal to 100 percent of the applicable Federal rate. Under paragraph (a)(3)(iii) of this section, section 482 and paragraph (a) of this section may be applied by the district director to determine whether the rate of interest under the note is excessive, that is, to determine whether the 18 percent stated interest rate under the note exceeds an arm's length rate of interest.

Example 5. Assume that A and B are commonly controlled taxpayers and that the applicable Federal rate is 10 percent, compounded semiannually. On June 30, 1986, A sells property to B and receives in exchange B's purchase-money note in the amount of $2,000,000. The stated interest rate on the note is 9%, compounded semiannually, and the stated redemption price at maturity on the note is $2,000,000. Assume that the other applicable Code section to this transaction is section 1274. As provided in section 1274A(a) and (b), the discount rate for purposes of section 1274 will be nine percent, compounded semiannually, because the stated principal amount of B's note does not exceed $2,800,000. Section 1274 does not apply to this transaction because there is adequate stated interest on the debt instrument using a discount rate equal to 9%, compounded semiannually, and the stated redemption price at maturity does not exceed the stated principal amount. Under paragraph (a)(3)(iii) of this section, the district director may apply section 482 and paragraph (a) of this section to this $2,000,000 note to determine whether the 9% rate of interest charged is less than an arm's length rate of interest, and if so, to make appropriate allocations to reflect an arm's length rate of interest.

(b) *Performance of services for another.*—(1) *General rule.*—Where one member of a group of controlled entities performs marketing, managerial, administrative, technical, or other services for the benefit of, or on behalf of another member of the group without charge, or at a charge which is not equal to an arm's length charge as defined in paragraph (b)(3) of this section, the district director may make appropriate allocations to reflect an arm's length charge for such services.

(2) *Benefit test.*—(i) Allocations may be made to reflect arm's length charges with respect to services undertaken for the joint benefit of the members of a group of controlled entities, as well as with respect to services performed by one member of the group exclusively for the benefit of another member of the group. Any allocations made shall be consistent with the relative benefits intended from the services, based upon the facts known at the time the services were rendered, and shall be made even if the potential benefits anticipated are not realized. No allocations shall be made if the probable benefits to the other members were so indirect or remote that unrelated parties would not have charged for such services. In general, allocations may be made if the service, at the time it was performed, related to the carrying on of an activity by another member or was intended to benefit another member, either in the member's overall operations or in its day-to-day activities. The principles of this paragraph (b)(2)(i) may be illustrated by the following examples in each of which it is assumed that X and Y are corporate members of the same group of controlled entities:

Example 1. X's International Division engages in a wide range of sales promotion activities. Although most of these activities are undertaken exclusively for the benefit of X's international operations, some are intended to jointly benefit both X and Y and others are undertaken exclusively for the benefit of Y. The district director may make an allocation to reflect an arm's length charge with respect to the activities undertaken for the joint benefit of X and Y consistent with the relative benefits intended as well as with respect to the services performed exclusively for the benefit of Y.

Example 2. X operates an international airline, and Y owns and operates hotels in several cities which are serviced by X. X, in conjunction with its advertising of the airline, often pictures Y's hotels and mentions Y's name. Although such advertising was primarily intended to benefit X's airline operations, it was reasonable to anticipate that there would be substantial benefits to Y resulting from patronage by travelers who responded to X's advertising. Since an unrelated hotel operator would have been charged for such advertising, the district director may make an appropriate allocation to reflect an arm's length charge consistent with the relative benefits intended.

Example 3. Assume the same facts as in *Example 2* except that X's advertising neither mentions nor pictures Y's hotels. Although it is reasonable to anticipate that increased air travel attributable to X's advertising will result in some benefit to Y due to increased patronage by air travelers, the district director will not make an allocation with respect to such advertising since the probable benefit to Y was so indirect and remote that an unrelated hotel operator would not have been charged for such advertising.

(ii) Allocations will generally not be made if the service is merely a duplication of a service which the related party has independently performed or is performing for itself. In this connection, the ability to independently perform the service (in terms of qualification and availability of personnel) shall be taken into account. The principles of this paragraph (b)(2)(ii) may be illustrated by the following examples, in each of which it is assumed that X and Y are corporate members of the same group of controlled entities:

Example 1. At the request of Y, the financial staff of X makes an analysis to determine the amount and source of the borrowing needs of Y. Y does not have personnel qualified to make the analysis, and it does not undertake the same analysis. The district director may make an appropriate allocation to reflect an arm's length charge for such analysis.

Example 2. Y, which has a qualified financial staff, makes an analysis to determine the amount and source of its borrowing needs. Its report, recommending a loan from a bank, is submitted to X. X's financial staff reviews the analysis to determine whether X should advise Y to reconsider its plan. No allocation should be made with respect to X's review.

(3) *Arm's length charge.*—For the purpose of this paragraph an arm's length charge for services rendered shall be the amount which was charged or would have been charged for the same or similar services in independent transactions with or between unrelated parties under similar circumstances considering all relevant facts. However, except in the case of services which are an integral part of the business activity of either the member rendering the services or the member receiving the benefit of the services (as described in paragraph (b)(7) of this section) the arm's length charge shall be deemed equal to the costs or deductions incurred with respect to such services by the member or members rendering such services unless the taxpayer establishes a more appropriate charge under the standards set forth in the first sentence of this subparagraph. Where costs or deductions are a factor in applying the provisions of this paragraph adequate books and records must be maintained by taxpayers to permit verification of such costs or deductions by the Internal Revenue Service.

(4) *Costs or deductions to be taken into account.*—(i) Where the amount of an arm's length charge for services is determined with reference to the costs or deductions incurred with respect to such services, it is necessary to take into account on some reasonable basis all the costs or deductions which are directly or indirectly related to the service performed.

(ii) Direct costs or deductions are those identified specifically with a particular service. These include, but are not limited to, costs or deductions for compensation, bonuses, and travel expenses attributable to employees directly engaged in performing such services, for material and supplies directly consumed in rendering such services, and for other costs such as the cost of overseas cables in connection with such services.

(iii) Indirect costs or deductions are those which are not specifically identified with a particular activity or service but which relate to the direct costs referred to in paragraph (b)(4)(ii) of this section. Indirect costs or deductions generally include costs or deductions with respect to utilities, occupancy, supervisory and clerical compensation, and other overhead burden of the department incurring the direct costs or deductions referred to in paragraph (b)(4)(ii) of this section. Indirect costs or deductions also generally include an appropriate share of the costs or deductions relating to supporting departments and other applicable general and administrative expenses to the extent reasonably allocable to a particular service or activity. Thus, for example, if a domestic corporation's advertising department performs services for the direct benefit of a foreign subsidiary, in addition to direct costs of such department, such as salaries of employees and fees paid to advertising agencies or consultants, which are attributable to such foreign advertising, indirect costs must be taken into account on some reasonable basis in determining the amount of costs or deductions with respect to which the arm's length charge to the foreign subsidiary is to be determined. These generally include depreciation, rent, property taxes, other costs of occupancy, and other overhead costs of the advertising department itself, and allocations of costs from other departments which service the advertising department, such as the personnel, accounting, payroll, and maintenance departments, and other applicable general and administrative expenses including compensation of top management.

(5) *Costs and deductions not to be taken into account.*—Costs or deductions of the member rendering the services which are not to be taken into account in determining the amount of an arm's length charge for services include—

(i) Interest expense on indebtedness not incurred specifically for the benefit of another member of the group;

(ii) Expenses associated with the issuance of stock and maintenance of shareholder relations; and

(iii) Expenses of compliance with regulations or policies imposed upon the member rendering the services by its government which are not directly related to the service in question.

(6) *Methods.*—(i) Where an arm's length charge for services rendered is determined with reference to costs or deductions, and a member has allocated and apportioned costs or deductions to reflect arm's length charges by employing in a consistent manner a method of allocation and apportionment which is reasonable and in keeping with sound accounting practice, such method will not be disturbed. If the member has not employed a method of allocation and apportionment which is reasonable and in keeping with sound accounting practice, the method of allocating and apportioning costs or deductions for the purpose of determining the amount of arm's length charges shall be based on the particular circumstances involved.

(ii) The methods of allocation and apportionment referred to in this paragraph (b)(6) are applicable both in allocating and apportioning indirect costs to a particular activity or service (see paragraph (b)(4)(iii) of this section) and in allocating and apportioning the total costs (direct and indirect) of a particular activity or service where such activity or service is undertaken for the joint benefit of two or more members of a group (see paragraph (b)(2)(i) of this section). While the use of one or more bases may be appropriate under the circumstances, in establishing the method of allocation and apportionment, appropriate consideration should be given to all bases and factors, including, for example, total expenses, asset size, sales, manufacturing expenses, payroll, space utilized, and time spent. The costs incurred by supporting departments may be apportioned to other departments on the basis of reasonable overall estimates, or such costs may be reflected in the other departments' costs by means of application of reasonable departmental overhead rates. Allocations and apportionments of costs or deductions must be made on the basis of the full cost as opposed to the incremental cost. Thus, if an electronic data processing machine, which is rented by the taxpayer, is used for the joint benefit of itself and other members of a controlled group, the determination of the arm's length charge to each member must be made with reference to the full rent and cost of operating the machine by each member, even if the additional use of the machine for the benefit of the other members did not increase the cost to the taxpayer.

(iii) Practices actually employed to apportion costs or expenses in connection with the preparation of statements and analyses for the use of management, creditors, minority shareholders, joint venturers, clients, customers, potential investors, or other parties or agencies in interest shall be considered by the district director. Similarly, in determining the extent to which allocations are to be made to or from foreign members of a controlled group, practices employed by the domestic members of a controlled group in apportioning costs between themselves shall also be considered if the relationships with the foreign members of the group are comparable to the relationships between the domestic members of the group. For example, if, for purposes of reporting to public stockholders or to a governmental agency, a corporation apportions the costs attributable to its executive officers among the domestic members of a controlled group on a reasonable and consistent basis, and such officers exercise comparable control over foreign members of such group, such domestic apportionment practice will be taken into consideration in determining the amount of allocations to be made to the foreign members.

(7) *Certain services.*—An arm's length charge shall not be deemed equal to costs or deductions with respect to services which are an integral part of the business activity of either the member rendering the services (referred to in this paragraph (b) as the renderer) or the member receiving the benefit of the services

(referred to in this paragraph (b) as the recipient). Paragraphs (b)(7)(i) through (b)(7)(iv) of this section describe those situations in which services shall be considered an integral part of the business activity of a member of a group of controlled entities.

(i) Services are an integral part of the business activity of a member of a controlled group where either the renderer or the recipient is engaged in the trade or business of rendering similar services to one or more unrelated parties.

(ii)(A) Services are an integral part of the business activity of a member of a controlled group where the renderer renders services to one or more related parties as one of its principal activities. Except in the case of services which constitute a manufacturing, production, extraction, or construction activity, it will be presumed that the renderer does not render services to related parties as one of its principal activities if the cost of services of the renderer attributable to the rendition of services for the taxable year to related parties do not exceed 25 percent of the total costs or deductions of the renderer for the taxable year. Where the cost of services rendered to related parties is in excess of 25 percent of the total costs or deductions of the renderer for the taxable year or where the 25-percent test does not apply, the determination of whether the rendition of such services is one of the principal activities of the renderer will be based on the facts and circumstances of each particular case. Such facts and circumstances may include the time devoted to the rendition of the services, the relative cost of the services, the regularity with which the services are rendered, the amount of capital investment, the risk of loss involved, and whether the services are in the nature of supporting services or independent of the other activities of the renderer.

(B) For purposes of the 25-percent test provided in this paragraph (b)(7)(ii), the cost of services rendered to related parties shall include all costs or deductions directly or indirectly related to the rendition of such services including the cost of services which constitute a manufacturing, production, extraction, or construction activity; and the total costs or deductions of the renderer for the taxable year shall exclude amounts properly reflected in the cost of goods sold of the renderer. Where any of the costs or deductions of the renderer do not reflect arm's length consideration and no adjustment is made under any provision of the Internal Revenue Code to reflect arm's length consideration, the 25-percent test will not apply if, had an arm's length charge been made, the costs or deductions attributable to the renderer's rendition of services to related entities would exceed 25 percent of the total costs or deductions of the renderer for the taxable year.

(C) For purposes of the 25-percent test in this paragraph (b)(7)(ii), a consolidated group (as defined in this paragraph (b)(7)(ii)(C)) may, at the option of the taxpayer, be considered as the renderer where one or more members of the consolidated group render services for the benefit of or on behalf of a related party which is not a member of the consolidated group. In such case, the cost of services rendered by members of the consolidated group to any related parties not members of the consolidated group, as well as the total costs or deductions of the members of the consolidated group, shall be considered in the aggregate to determine if such services constitute a principal activity of the renderer. Where a consolidated group is considered the renderer in accordance with this paragraph (b)(7)(ii)(C), the costs or deductions referred to in this paragraph (b)(7)(ii) shall not include costs or deductions paid or accrued to any member of the consolidated group. In addition to the preceding provisions of this paragraph (b)(7)(ii)(C), if part or all of the services rendered by a member of a consolidated group to any related party not a member of the consolidated group are similar to services rendered by any other member of the consolidated group to unrelated parties as part of a trade or business, the 25-percent test in this paragraph (b)(7)(ii) shall be applied with respect to such similar services without regard to this paragraph (b)(7)(ii)(C). For purposes of this paragraph (b)(7)(ii)(C), the term consolidated group means all members of a group of controlled entities created or organized within a single country and subjected to an income tax by such country on the basis of their combined income.

(iii) Services are an integral part of the business activity of a member of a controlled group where the renderer is peculiarly capable of rendering the services and such services are a principal element in the operations of the recipient. The renderer is peculiarly capable of rendering the services where the renderer, in connection with the rendition of such services, makes use of a particularly advantageous situation or circumstance such as by utilization of special skills and reputation, utilization of an influential relationship with customers, or utilization of its intangible property (as defined in § 1.482-4(b)). However, the renderer will not be considered peculiarly capable of rendering services unless the value of the services is substantially in excess of the costs or deductions of the renderer attributable to such services.

(iv) Services are an integral part of the business activity of a member of a controlled group where the recipient has received the benefit of a substantial amount of services from one or more related parties during its taxable year. For purposes of this paragraph (b)(7)(iv), services rendered by one or more related parties shall be considered substantial in amount if the total costs or deductions of the related party or parties rendering services to the recipient during its taxable year which are directly or indirectly related to such services exceed an amount equal to 25 percent of the total costs or deductions of the recipient during its taxable year. For purposes of the preceding sentence, the total costs or deductions of the recipient shall include the renderers' costs or deductions directly or indirectly related to the rendition of such services and shall exclude any amounts paid or accrued to the renderers by the recipient for such services and shall also exclude any amounts paid or accrued for materials the cost of which is properly reflected in the cost of goods sold of the recipient. At the option of the taxpayer, where the taxpayer establishes that the amount of the total costs or deductions of a recipient for the recipient's taxable year are abnormally low due to the commencement or cessation of an operation by the recipient, or other unusual circumstances of a nonrecurring nature, the costs or deductions referred to in the preceding two sentences shall be the total of such amount for the 3-year period immediately preceding the close of the taxable year of the recipient (or for the first 3 years of operation of the recipient if the recipient had been in operation for less than 3 years as of the close of the taxable year in which the services in issue were rendered).

(v) The principles of paragraphs (b)(7)(i) through (iv) of this section may be illustrated by the following examples:

Example 1. Y is engaged in the business of selling merchandise and X, an entity related to Y, is a printing company regularly engaged in printing and mailing advertising literature for unrelated parties. X also prints circulars advertising Y's products, mails the circulars to potential customers of Y, and in addition, performs the art work involved in the preparation of the circulars. Since the printing, mailing, and art work services rendered by X to Y are similar to the printing and mailing services rendered by X as X's trade or business, the services rendered to Y are an integral part of the business activity of X as described in paragraph (b)(7)(i) of this section.

Example 2. V, W, X, and Y are members of the same group of controlled entities. Each member of the group files a separate income tax return. X renders wrecking services to V, W, and Y, and, in addition, sells building materials to unrelated parties. The total costs or deductions incurred by X for the taxable year (exclusive of amounts properly reflected in the cost of goods sold of X) are $4 million. The total costs or deductions of X for the taxable year which are directly or indirectly related to the services rendered to V, W, and Y are $650,000. Since $650,000 is less than 25 percent of the total costs or deductions of X (exclusive of amounts properly reflected in the cost of goods sold of X) for the taxable year ($4,000,000 * 25% = $1,000,000), the services rendered by X to V, W, and Y will not be considered one of X's principal activities within the meaning of paragraph (b)(7)(ii) of this section.

Example 3. Assume the same facts as in *Example 2,* except that the total costs or deductions of X for the taxable year which are directly or indirectly related to the services rendered to V, W, and Y are $1,800,000. Assume in addition, that there is a high risk of loss involved in the rendition of the wrecking services by X, that X has a large investment in the wrecking equipment, and that a substantial amount of X's time is devoted to the rendition of wrecking services to V, W, and Y. Since $1,800,000 is greater than 25 percent of the total costs or deductions of X for the taxable year (exclusive of amounts properly reflected in the cost of goods sold of X), i.e., $1 million, the services rendered by X to V, W, and Y will not be automatically excluded from classification as one of the principal activities of X as in *Example 2,* and consideration must be given to the facts and circumstances of the particular case. Based on the facts and circumstances in this case, X would be considered to render wrecking services to related parties as one of its principal activities. Thus, the wrecking services are an integral part of the business activity of X as described in paragraph (b)(7)(ii) of this section.

Example 4. Z is a domestic corporation and has several foreign subsidiaries. Z and X, a domestic subsidiary of Z, have exercised the privilege granted under section 1501 to file a consolidated return and, therefore, constitute a *consolidated group* within the meaning of paragraph (b)(7)(ii)(C) of this section. Pursuant to paragraph (b)(7)(ii)(C) of this section, the taxpayer treats X and Z as the renderer. The sole function of X is to provide accounting, billing, communication, and travel services to the foreign subsidiaries of Z. Z also provides some other services for the benefit of its foreign subsidiaries. The total costs or deductions of X and Z related to the services rendered for the benefit of the foreign subsidiaries is $750,000. Of that amount, $710,000 represents the costs of X, which are X's total operating costs. The total costs or deductions of X and Z for the taxable year with respect to their operations (exclusive of amounts properly reflected in the cost of goods sold of X and Z) is $6,500,000. Since the total costs or deductions related to the services rendered to the foreign subsidiaries ($750,000) is less than 25 percent of the total costs or deductions of X and Z (exclusive of amounts properly reflected in the costs of goods sold of X or Z) in the aggregate ($6,500,000 * 25% = $1,625,000), the services rendered by X and Z to the foreign subsidiaries will not be considered one of the principal activities of X and Z within the meaning of paragraph (b)(7)(ii) of this section.

Example 5. Assume the same facts as in *Example 4,* except that all the communication services rendered for the benefit of the foreign subsidiaries are rendered by X and that Z renders communication services to unrelated parties as part of its trade or business. X is regularly engaged in rendering communication services to foreign subsidiaries and devotes a substantial amount of its time to this activity. The costs or deductions of X related to the rendition of the communication services to the foreign subsidiaries are $355,000. By application of the paragraph (b)(7)(ii)(C) of this section, the services provided by X and Z to related entities other than the communication services will not be considered one of the principal activities of X and Z. However, since Z renders communication services to unrelated parties as a part of its trade or business, the communication services rendered by X to the foreign subsidiaries will be subject to the provisions of paragraph (b)(7)(ii) of this section without regard to paragraph (b)(7)(ii)(C) of this section. Since the costs or deductions of X related to the rendition of the communication services ($355,000) are in excess of 25 percent of the total costs or deductions of X (exclusive of amounts properly reflected in the cost of goods sold of X) for the taxable year ($710,000 × 25% = $177,500), the determination of whether X renders the communication services as one of its principal activities will depend on the particular facts and circumstances. The given facts and circumstances indicate that X renders the communication services as one of its principal activities.

Example 6. X and Y are members of the same group of controlled entities. Y produces and sells product D. As a part of the production process, Y sends materials to X who converts the materials into component parts. This conversion activity constitutes only a portion of X's operations. X then ships the component parts back to Y who assembles them (along with other components) into the finished product for sale to unrelated parties. Since the services rendered by X to Y constitute a manufacturing activity, the 25-percent test in paragraph (b)(7)(ii) of this section does not apply.

Example 7. X and Y are members of the same group of controlled entities. X manufactures product D for distribution and sale in the United States, Canada, and Mexico. Y manufactures product D for distribution and sale in South and Central America. Due to a breakdown of machinery, Y is forced to cease its manufacturing operations for a 1-month period. In order to meet demand for product D during the shutdown period, Y sends partially finished goods to X. X, for that period, completes the manufacture of product D for Y and ships the finished product back to Y. The costs or deductions of X related to the manufacturing services rendered to Y are $750,000. The total costs or deductions of X are $24,000,000. Since the services in issue constitute a manufacturing activity, the 25-percent test in paragraph (b)(7)(ii) of this section does not apply. However, under these facts and circumstances, i.e., the insubstantiality of the services rendered to Y in relation to X's total operations, the lack of regularity with which the services are rendered, and the short duration for which the services are rendered, X's rendition of manufacturing services to Y is not considered one of X's principal activities within the meaning of paragraph (b)(7)(ii) of this section.

Example 8. Assume the same facts as in *Example 7,* except that, instead of temporarily ceasing operations, Y requests assistance from X in correcting the defects in the manufacturing equipment. In response, X sends a team of engineers to discover and correct the defects without the necessity of a shutdown. Although the services performed by the engineers were related to a manufacturing activity, the services are essentially supporting in nature and, therefore, do not constitute a manufacturing, production, extraction, or construction activity. Thus, the 25-percent test in paragraph (b)(7)(ii) of this section applies.

Example 9. X is a domestic manufacturing corporation. Y, a foreign subsidiary of X, has decided to construct a plant in Country A. In connection with the construction of Y's plant, X draws up the architectural plans for the plant, arranges the financing of the construction, negotiates with various Government authorities in Country A, invites bids from unrelated parties for several phases of construction, and negotiates, on Y's behalf, the contracts with unrelated parties who are retained to carry out certain phases of the construction. Although the unrelated parties retained by X for Y perform the physical construction, the aggregate services performed by X for Y are such that they, in themselves, constitute a construction activity. Thus, the 25-percent test in paragraph (b)(7)(ii) of this section does not apply with respect to such services.

Example 10. X and Y are members of the same group of controlled entities. X is a finance company engaged in financing automobile loans. In connection with such loans it requires the borrower to have life insurance in the amount of the loan. Although X's borrowers are not required to take out life insurance from any particular insurance company, at the same time that the loan agreement is being finalized, X's employees suggest that the borrower take out life insurance from Y, which is an agency for life insurance companies. Since there would be a delay in the processing of the loan if some other company were selected by the borrower, almost all of X's borrowers take out life insurance through Y. Because of this utilization of its influential relationship with its borrowers, X is peculiarly capable of rendering selling services to Y and, since a substantial amount of Y's business is derived from X's borrowers, such selling services are a principal element in the operation of Y's insurance business. In addition, the value of the services is substantially in excess of the costs incurred by X. Thus, the selling services rendered by X to Y are an integral part of the business activity of a member of the controlled group as described in paragraph (b)(7)(iii) of this section.

Example 11. X and Y are members of the same group of controlled entities. Y is a manufacturer of product E. In past years product E has not always operated properly because of imperfections present in the finished product. X owns an exclusive patented process by which such imperfections can be detected and removed prior to sale of the product, thereby greatly increasing the marketability of the product. In connection with its manufacturing operations Y sends its products to X for inspection which involves utilization of the patented process. The inspection of Y's products by X is not one of the principal activities of X. However, X is peculiarly capable of rendering the inspection services to Y because of its utilization of the patented process. Since this inspection greatly increases the marketability of product E it is extremely valuable. Such value is substantially in excess of the cost incurred by X in rendition of such services. Because of the impact of the inspection on sales, such services are a principal element in the operations of Y. Thus, the inspection services rendered by X to Y are an integral part of the business activity of a member of the controlled group as described in paragraph (b)(7)(iii) of this section.

Example 12. Assume the same facts as in *Example 11* except that Y owns the patented process for detecting the imperfections. Y, however, does not have the facilities to implement the inspection process. Therefore, Y sends its products to X for inspection which involves utilization of the patented process owned by Y. Since Y owns the patent, X is not peculiarly capable of rendering the inspection services to Y within the meaning of paragraph (b)(7)(iii) of this section.

Example 13. Assume the same facts as in *Example 12* except that X and Y both own interests in the patented process as a result of having developed the process pursuant to a bona fide cost sharing plan (within the meaning of § 1.482-7T. Since Y owns the requisite interest in the patent, X is not peculiarly capable of rendering the inspection services to Y within the meaning of paragraph (b)(7)(iii) of this section.

Example 14. X and Y are members of the same group of controlled entities. X is a large manufacturing concern. X's accounting department has, for many years, maintained the financial records of Y, a distributor of X's products. Although X is able to render these accounting services more efficiently than others due to its thorough familiarity with the operations of Y, X is not peculiarly capable of rendering the accounting services to Y because such familiarity does not, in and of itself, constitute a particularly advantageous situation or circumstance within the meaning of paragraph (b)(7)(iii) of this section. Furthermore, under these circumstances, the accounting services are supporting in nature and, therefore, do not constitute a principal element in the operations of Y. Thus, the accounting services rendered by X to Y are not an integral part of the business activity of either X or Y within the meaning of paragraph (b)(7)(iii) of this section.

Example 15. (i) Corporations X, Y, and Z are members of the same group of controlled entities. X is a manufacturer, and Y and Z are distributors of X's products. X provides a variety of services to Y including billing, shipping, accounting, and other general and administrative services. During Y's taxable year, on several occasions, Z renders selling and other promotional services to Y. None of the services rendered to Y constitute one of the principal activities of any of the renderers within the meaning of paragraph (b)(7)(ii) of this section. Y's total costs and deductions for Y's taxable year (exclusive of amounts paid to X and Z for services rendered and amounts paid for goods purchased for resale) are $1,600,000. The total direct and indirect costs of X and Z for services rendered to Y during Y's taxable year are as follows:

Services provided by X:
Billing	$50,000
Shipping	250,000
Accounting	150,000

Other	200,000
Services provided by Z:	
Selling	500,000
Total Costs	$1,150,000

(ii) Since the total costs or deductions of X and Z related to the rendition of services to Y exceed the amount equal to 25 percent of the total costs or deductions of Y (exclusive of amounts paid to X and Z for the services rendered and amounts paid for goods purchased for resale) plus the total costs or deductions of X and Z related to the rendition of services to Y ($1,150,000 ÷ [$1,600,000 + $1,150,000] = 41.8%), the services rendered by X and Z to Y are substantial within the meaning of paragraph (b)(7)(iv) of this section. Thus, the services rendered by X and Z to Y are an integral part of the business activity of Y as described in paragraph (b)(7)(iv) of this section.

Example 16. Assume the same facts as in *Example 15,* except that the taxpayer establishes that, due to a major change in the operations of Y, Y's total costs or deductions for Y's taxable year were abnormally low. Y has always used the calendar year as its taxable year. Y's total costs and deductions for the 2 years immediately preceding the taxable year in issue (exclusive of amounts paid to X and Z for services rendered and amounts paid for goods purchased for resale) were $6 million and $6,200,000 respectively. The total direct and indirect costs of X and Z for services rendered to Y were $1,150,000 for each of the 3 years. Applying the same formula to the costs or deductions for the 3 years immediately preceding the close of the taxable year in issue, the costs or deductions of X and Z related to the rendition of services to Y (3 × $1,150,000 = $3,450,000) amount to 20 percent of the sum of the total costs or deductions of Y (exclusive of amounts paid to X and Z for the services rendered and amounts paid for goods purchased for resale) plus the total costs or deductions of X and Z related to the rendition of services to Y ($3,450,000 ÷ [$1,600,000 + $6,000,000 + $6,200,000 + $3,450,000] = 20%). If the taxpayer chooses to use the 3-year period, the services rendered by X and Z to Y are not substantial within the meaning of paragraph (b)(7)(iv) of this section. Thus, the services will not be an integral part of the business activity of a member of the controlled group as described in paragraph (b)(7)(iv) of this section.

(8) *Services rendered in connection with the transfer of property.*—Where tangible or intangible property is transferred, sold, assigned, loaned, leased, or otherwise made available in any manner by one member of a group to another member of the group and services are rendered by the transferor to the transferee in connection with the transfer, the amount of any allocation that may be appropriate with respect to such transfer shall be determined in accordance with the rules of paragraph (c) of this section, or §§ 1.482-3 or 1.482-4, whichever is appropriate and a separate allocation with respect to such services under this paragraph shall not be made. Services are rendered in connection with the transfer of property where such services are merely ancillary and subsidiary to the transfer of the property or to the commencement of effective use of the property by the transferee. Whether or not services are merely ancillary and subsidiary to a property transfer is a question of fact. Ancillary and subsidiary services could be performed, for example, in promoting the transaction by demonstrating and explaining the use of the property, or by assisting in the effective starting-up of the property transferred, or by performing under a guarantee relating to such effective starting-up. Thus, where an employee of one member of a group, acting under the instructions of his employer, reveals a valuable secret process owned by his employer to a related entity, and at the same time supervises the integration of such process into the manufacturing operation of the related entity, such services could be considered to be rendered in connection with the transfer, and, if so considered, shall not be the basis for a separate allocation. However, if the employee continues to render services to the related entity by supervising the manufacturing operation after the secret process has been effectively integrated into such operation, a separate allocation with respect to such additional services may be made in accordance with the rules of this paragraph.

(c) *Use of tangible property.*—(1) *General rule.*—Where possession, use, or occupancy of tangible property owned or leased by one member of a group of controlled entities (referred to in this paragraph as the owner) is transferred by lease or other arrangement to another member of such group (referred to in this paragraph as the user) without charge or at a charge which is not equal to an arm's length rental charge (as defined in paragraph (c)(2)(i) of this section) the district director may make appropriate allocations to properly reflect such arm's length charge. Where possession, use, or occupancy of only a portion of such property is transferred, the determination of the arm's length charge and the allocation shall be made with reference to the portion transferred.

(2) *Arm's length charge.*—(i) *In general.*—For purposes of paragraph (c) of this section,

an arm's length rental charge shall be the amount of rent which was charged, or would have been charged for the use of the same or similar property, during the time it was in use, in independent transactions with or between unrelated parties under similar circumstances considering the period and location of the use, the owner's investment in the property or rent paid for the property, expenses of maintaining the property, the type of property involved, its condition, and all other relevant facts.

(ii) *Safe haven rental charge.*—See § 1.482-2(c)(2)(ii) (26 CFR Part 1 revised as of April 1, 1985), for the determination of safe haven rental charges in the case of certain leases entered into before May 9, 1986, and for leases entered into before August 7, 1986, pursuant to a binding written contract entered into before May 9, 1986.

(iii) *Subleases.*—(A) Except as provided in paragraph (c)(2)(iii)(B) of this section, where possession, use, or occupancy of tangible property, which is leased by the owner (lessee) from an unrelated party is transferred by sublease or other arrangement to the user, an arm's length rental charge shall be considered to be equal to all the deductions claimed by the owner (lessee) which are attributable to the property for the period such property is used by the user. Where only a portion of such property was transferred, any allocations shall be made with reference to the portion transferred. The deductions to be considered include the rent paid or accrued by the owner (lessee) during the period of use and all other deductions directly and indirectly connected with the property paid or accrued by the owner (lessee) during such period. Such deductions include deductions for maintenance and repair, utilities, management and other similar deductions.

(B) The provisions of paragraph (c)(2)(iii)(A) of this section shall not apply if either—

(1) The taxpayer establishes a more appropriate rental charge under the general rule set forth in paragraph (c)(2)(i) of this section; or

(2) During the taxable year, the owner (lessee) or the user was regularly engaged in the trade or business of renting property of the same general type as the property in question to unrelated persons.

(d) *Transfer of property.*—For rules governing allocations under section 482 to reflect an arm's length consideration for controlled transactions involving the transfer of property, see §§ 1.482-3 through 1.482-6. [Reg. § 1.482-2.]

□ [*T.D.* 8552, 7-1-94.]

Proposed Amendments to Regulation

§ 1.482-2. Determination of taxable income in specific situations.

* * *

(b) *Rendering of services.*—For rules governing allocations under section 482 to reflect an arm's length charge for controlled transactions involving the rendering of services, see § 1.482-9.

* * *

[Prop. Reg. § 1.482-2.]

[Proposed 9-10-2003.]

§ 1.482-3. Methods to determine taxable income in connection with a transfer of tangible property.—(a) *In general.*—The arm's length amount charged in a controlled transfer of tangible property must be determined under one of the six methods listed in this paragraph (a). Each of the methods must be applied in accordance with all of the provisions of § 1.482-1, including the best method rule of § 1.482-1(c), the comparability analysis of § 1.482-1(d), and the arm's length range of § 1.482-1(e). The methods are—

(1) The comparable uncontrolled price method, described in paragraph (b) of this section;

(2) The resale price method, described in paragraph (c) of this section;

(3) The cost plus method, described in paragraph (d) of this section;

(4) The comparable profits method, described in § 1.482-5;

(5) The profit split method, described in § 1.482-6; and

(6) Unspecified methods, described in paragraph (e) of this section.

(b) *Comparable uncontrolled price method.*—(1) *In general.*—The comparable uncontrolled price method evaluates whether the amount charged in a controlled transaction is arm's length by reference to the amount charged in a comparable uncontrolled transaction.

(2) *Comparability and reliability considerations.*—(i) *In general.*—Whether results derived from applications of this method are the most reliable measure of the arm's length result must be determined using the factors described under the best method rule in § 1.482-1(c). The application of these factors under the comparable uncontrolled price method is discussed in paragraph (b)(2)(ii) and (iii) of this section.

(ii) *Comparability.*—(A) *In general.*— The degree of comparability between controlled and uncontrolled transactions is determined by applying the provisions of

§ 1.482-1(d). Although all of the factors described in § 1.482-1(d)(3) must be considered, similarity of products generally will have the greatest effect on comparability under this method. In addition, because even minor differences in contractual terms or economic conditions could materially affect the amount charged in an uncontrolled transaction, comparability under this method depends on close similarity with respect to these factors, or adjustments to account for any differences. The results derived from applying the comparable uncontrolled price method generally will be the most direct and reliable measure of an arm's length price for the controlled transaction if an uncontrolled transaction has no differences with the controlled transaction that would affect the price, or if there are only minor differences that have a definite and reasonably ascertainable effect on price and for which appropriate adjustments are made. If such adjustments cannot be made, or if there are more than minor differences between the controlled and uncontrolled transactions, the comparable uncontrolled price method may be used, but the reliability of the results as a measure of the arm's length price will be reduced. Further, if there are material product differences for which reliable adjustments cannot be made, this method ordinarily will not provide a reliable measure of an arm's length result.

(B) *Adjustments for differences between controlled and uncontrolled transactions.*—If there are differences between the controlled and uncontrolled transactions that would affect price, adjustments should be made to the price of the uncontrolled transaction according to the comparability provisions of § 1.482-1(d)(2). Specific examples of the factors that may be particularly relevant to this method include—

(1) Quality of the product;

(2) Contractual terms, (e.g., scope and terms of warranties provided, sales or purchase volume, credit terms, transport terms);

(3) Level of the market (i.e., wholesale, retail, etc.);

(4) Geographic market in which the transaction takes place;

(5) Date of the transaction;

(6) Intangible property associated with the sale;

(7) Foreign currency risks; and

(8) Alternatives realistically available to the buyer and seller.

(iii) *Data and assumptions.*—The reliability of the results derived from the comparable uncontrolled price method is affected by the completeness and accuracy of the data used and the reliability of the assumptions made to apply the method. See § 1.482-1(c) (Best method rule).

(3) *Arm's length range.*—See § 1.482-1(e)(2) for the determination of an arm's length range.

(4) *Examples.*—The principles of this paragraph (b) are illustrated by the following examples.

Example 1—Comparable Sales of Same Product. USM, a U.S. manufacturer, sells the same product to both controlled and uncontrolled distributors. The circumstances surrounding the controlled and uncontrolled transactions are substantially the same, except that the controlled sales price is a delivered price and the uncontrolled sales are made f.o.b. USM's factory. Differences in the contractual terms of transportation and insurance generally have a definite and reasonably ascertainable effect on price, and adjustments are made to the results of the uncontrolled transaction to account for such differences. No other material difference has been identified between the controlled and uncontrolled transactions. Because USM sells in both the controlled and uncontrolled transactions, it is likely that all material differences between the two transactions have been identified. In addition, because the comparable uncontrolled price method is applied to an uncontrolled comparable with no product differences, and there are only minor contractual differences that have a definite and reasonably ascertainable effect on price, the results of this application of the comparable uncontrolled price method will provide the most direct and reliable measure of an arm's length result. See § 1.482-3(b)(2)(ii)(A).

Example 2—Effect of Trademark. The facts are the same as in *Example 1*, except that USM affixes its valuable trademark to the property sold in the controlled transactions, but does not affix its trademark to the property sold in the uncontrolled transactions. Under the facts of this case, the effect on price of the trademark is material and cannot be reliably estimated. Because there are material product differences for which reliable adjustments cannot be made, the comparable uncontrolled price method is unlikely to provide a reliable measure of the arm's length result. See § 1.482-3(b)(2)(ii)(A).

Example 3—Minor Product Differences. The facts are the same as in *Example 1*, except that USM, which manufactures business machines, makes minor modifications to the physical properties of the machines to satisfy specific requirements of a customer in controlled sales, but does not make these modifications in uncontrolled sales. If the minor physical differences in the product have a material affect on prices, adjustments to account for these differences must be made to the results of the uncontrolled transactions according to the provisions of § 1.482-1(d)(2), and such adjusted results may be used as a measure of the arm's length result.

Example 4—Effect of Geographic Differences. FM, a foreign specialty radio manufacturer, sells its radios to a controlled U.S. distributor, AM, that serves the West Coast of the United States. FM sells its radios to uncontrolled distributors to serve other regions in the United States. The product in the controlled and uncontrolled transactions is the same, and all other circumstances surrounding the controlled and uncontrolled transactions are substantially the same, other than the geographic differences. If the geographic differences are unlikely to have a material effect on price, or they have definite and reasonably ascertainable effects for which adjustments are made, then the adjusted results of the uncontrolled sales may be used under the comparable uncontrolled price method to establish an arm's length range pursuant to § 1.482-1(e)(2)(iii)(A). If the effects of the geographic differences would be material but cannot be reliably ascertained, then the reliability of the results will be diminished. However, the comparable uncontrolled price method may still provide the most reliable measure of an arm's length result, pursuant to the best method rule of § 1.482-1(c), and, if so, an arm's length range may be established pursuant to § 1.482-1(e)(2)(iii)(B).

(5) *Indirect evidence of comparable uncontrolled transactions.*—(i) *In general.*—A comparable uncontrolled price may be derived from data from public exchanges or quotation media, but only if the following requirements are met—

(A) The data is widely and routinely used in the ordinary course of business in the industry to negotiate prices for uncontrolled sales;

(B) The data derived from public exchanges or quotation media is used to set prices in the controlled transaction in the same way it is used by uncontrolled taxpayers in the industry; and

(C) The amount charged in the controlled transaction is adjusted to reflect differences in product quality and quantity, contractual terms, transportation costs, market conditions, risks borne, and other factors that affect the price that would be agreed to by uncontrolled taxpayers.

(ii) *Limitation.*—Use of data from public exchanges or quotation media may not be appropriate under extraordinary market conditions.

(iii) *Examples.*—The following examples illustrate this paragraph (b)(5).

Example 1—Use of Quotation Medium. (i) On June 1, USOil, a United States corporation, enters into a contract to purchase crude oil from its foreign subsidiary, FS, in Country Z. USOil and FS agree to base their sales price on the average of the prices published for that crude in a quotation medium in the five days before August 1, the date set for delivery. USOil and FS agree to adjust the price for the particular circumstances of their transactions, including the quantity of the crude sold, contractual terms, transportation costs, risks borne, and other factors that affect the price.

(ii) The quotation medium used by USOil and FS is widely and routinely used in the ordinary course of business in the industry to establish prices for uncontrolled sales. Because USOil and FS use the data to set their sales price in the same way that unrelated parties use the data from the quotation medium to set their sales prices, and appropriate adjustments were made to account for differences, the price derived from the quotation medium used by USOil and FS to set their transfer prices will be considered evidence of a comparable uncontrolled price.

Example 2—Extraordinary Market Conditions. The facts are the same as in *Example 1*, except that before USOil and FS enter into their contract, war breaks out in Countries X and Y, major oil producing countries, causing significant instability in world petroleum markets. As a result, given the significant instability in the price of oil, the prices listed on the quotation medium may not reflect a reliable measure of an arm's length result. See § 1.482-3(b)(5)(ii).

(c) *Resale price method.*—(1) *In general.*—The resale price method evaluates whether the amount charged in a controlled transaction is arm's length by reference to the gross profit margin realized in comparable uncontrolled transactions. The resale price method measures the value of functions performed, and is ordinarily used in cases involving the purchase and resale of tangible property in which the reseller has not added substantial value to the tangible goods by physically altering the goods before resale. For this purpose, packaging, repackaging, labelling, or minor assembly do not ordinarily constitute physical alteration. Further the resale price method is not ordinarily used in cases where the controlled taxpayer uses its intangible property to add substantial value to the tangible goods.

(2) *Determination of arm's length price.*—
(i) *In general.*—The resale price method measures an arm's length price by subtracting the appropriate gross profit from the applicable resale price for the property involved in the controlled transaction under review.

(ii) *Applicable resale price.*—The applicable resale price is equal to either the resale price of the particular item of property involved or the price at which contemporaneous resales of the same property are made. If the property purchased in the controlled sale is resold to one or more related parties in a series of controlled sales before being resold in an uncontrolled sale, the applicable resale price is the price at which the property is resold to an uncontrolled party, or the price at which contemporaneous resales of the same property are made. In such case, the determination of the appropriate gross profit will take into account the functions of all members of the group participating in the series of controlled sales and final uncontrolled resales, as well as any other relevant factors described in § 1.482-1(d)(3).

(iii) *Appropriate gross profit.*—The appropriate gross profit is computed by multiplying the applicable resale price by the gross profit margin (expressed as a percentage of total revenue derived from sales) earned in comparable uncontrolled transactions.

(iv) *Arm's length range.*—See § 1.482-1(e)(2) for determination of the arm's length range.

(3) *Comparability and reliability considerations.*—(i) *In general.*—Whether results derived from applications of this method are the most reliable measure of the arm's length result must be determined using the factors described under the best method rule in § 1.482-1(c). The application of these factors under the resale price method is discussed in paragraphs (c)(3)(ii) and (iii) of this section.

(ii) *Comparability.*—(A) *Functional comparability.*—The degree of comparability between an uncontrolled transaction and a controlled transaction is determined by applying the comparability provisions of § 1.482-1(d). A reseller's gross profit provides compensation for the performance of resale functions related to the product or products under review, including an operating profit in return for the reseller's investment of capital and the assumption of risks. Therefore, although all of the factors described in § 1.482-1(d)(3) must be considered, comparability under this method is particularly dependent on similarity of functions performed, risks borne, and contractual terms, or adjustments to account for the effects of any such differences. If possible, appropriate gross profit margins should be derived from comparable uncontrolled purchases and resales of the reseller involved in the controlled sale, because similar characteristics are more likely to be found among different resales of property made by the same reseller than among sales made by other resellers. In the absence of comparable uncontrolled transactions involving the same reseller, an appropriate gross profit margin may be derived from comparable uncontrolled transactions of other resellers.

(B) *Other comparability factors.*—Comparability under this method is less dependent on close physical similarity between the products transferred than under the comparable uncontrolled price method. For example, distributors of a wide variety of consumer durables might perform comparable distribution functions without regard to the specific durable goods distributed. Substantial differences in the products may, however, indicate significant functional differences between the controlled and uncontrolled taxpayers. Thus, it ordinarily would be expected that the controlled and uncontrolled transactions would involve the distribution of products of the same general type (e.g., consumer electronics). Furthermore, significant differences in the value of the distributed goods due, for example, to the value of a trademark, may also affect the reliability of the comparison. Finally, the reliability of profit measures based on gross profit may be adversely affected by factors that have less effect on prices. For example, gross profit may be affected by a variety of other factors, including cost structures (as reflected, for example, in the age of plant and equipment), business experience (such as whether the business is in a start-up phase or is mature), or management efficiency (as indicated, for example, by expanding or contracting sales or executive compensation over time). Accordingly, if material differences in these factors are identified based on objective evidence, the reliability of the analysis may be affected.

(C) *Adjustments for differences between controlled and uncontrolled transactions.*—If there are material differences between the controlled and uncontrolled transactions that would affect the gross profit margin, adjustments should be made to the gross profit margin earned with respect to the uncontrolled transaction according to the comparability provisions of § 1.482-1(d)(2). For this purpose, consideration of operating expenses associated with functions performed and risks assumed may be necessary, because differences in functions performed are often reflected in operating expenses. If there are differences in functions performed, however,

Reg. § 1.482-3(c)(3)(ii)(C)

the effect on gross profit of such differences is not necessarily equal to the differences in the amount of related operating expenses. Specific examples of the factors that may be particularly relevant to this method include—

(1) Inventory levels and turnover rates, and corresponding risks, including any price protection programs offered by the manufacturer;

(2) Contractual terms (e.g., scope and terms of warranties provided, sales or purchase volume, credit terms, transport terms);

(3) Sales, marketing, advertising programs and services, (including promotional programs, rebates, and co-op advertising);

(4) The level of the market (e.g., wholesale, retail, etc.); and

(5) Foreign currency risks.

(D) *Sales agent.*—If the controlled taxpayer is comparable to a sales agent that does not take title to goods or otherwise assume risks with respect to ownership of such goods, the commission earned by such sales agent, expressed as a percentage of the uncontrolled sales price of the goods involved, may be used as the comparable gross profit margin.

(iii) *Data and assumptions.*—(A) *In general.*—The reliability of the results derived from the resale price method is affected by the completeness and accuracy of the data used and the reliability of the assumptions made to apply this method. See § 1.482-1(c) (Best method rule).

(B) *Consistency in accounting.*—The degree of consistency in accounting practices between the controlled transaction and the uncontrolled comparables that materially affect the gross profit margin affects the reliability of the result. Thus, for example, if differences in inventory and other cost accounting practices would materially affect the gross profit margin, the ability to make reliable adjustments for such differences would affect the reliability of the results. Further, the controlled transaction and the uncontrolled comparable should be consistent in the reporting of items (such as discounts, returns and allowances, rebates, transportation costs, insurance, and packaging) between cost of goods sold and operating expenses.

(4) *Examples.*—The following examples illustrate the principles of this paragraph (c).

Example 1. A controlled taxpayer sells property to another member of its controlled group that resells the property in uncontrolled sales. There are no changes in the beginning and ending inventory for the year under review. Information regarding an uncontrolled comparable is sufficiently complete to conclude that it is likely that all material differences between the controlled and uncontrolled transactions have been identified and adjusted for. If the applicable resale price of the property involved in the controlled sale is $100 and the appropriate gross profit margin is 20%, then an arm's length result of the controlled sale is a price of $80 ($100 minus (20% × $100)).

Example 2. (i) S, a U.S. corporation, is the exclusive distributor for FP, its foreign parent. There are no changes in the beginning and ending inventory for the year under review. S's total reported cost of goods sold is $800, consisting of $600 for property purchased from FP and $200 of other costs of goods sold incurred to unrelated parties. S's applicable resale price and reported gross profit are as follows:

Applicable resale price	$1000
Cost of goods sold	
Cost of purchases from FP	600
Costs incurred to unrelated parties	200
Reported gross profit	$200

(ii) The district director determines that the appropriate gross profit margin is 25%. Therefore, S's appropriate gross profit is $250 (i.e., 25% of the applicable resale price of $1000). Because S is incurring costs of sales to unrelated parties, an arm's length price for property purchased from FP must be determined under a two-step process. First, the appropriate gross profit ($250) is subtracted from the applicable resale price ($1000). The resulting amount ($750) is then reduced by the costs of sales incurred to unrelated parties ($200). Therefore, an arm's length price for S's cost of sales of FP's product in this case equals $550 (i.e., $750 minus $200).

Example 3. FP, a foreign manufacturer, sells Product to USSub, its U.S. subsidiary, which in turn sells Product to its domestic affiliate Sister. Sister sells Product to unrelated buyers. In this case, the applicable resale price is the price at which Sister sells Product in uncontrolled transactions. The determination of the appropriate gross profit margin for the sale from FP to USSub will take into account the functions performed by USSub and Sister, as well as other relevant factors described in § 1.482-1(d)(3).

Example 4. USSub, a U.S. corporation, is the exclusive distributor of widgets for its foreign parent. To determine whether the gross profit margin of 25% earned by USSub is an arm's length result, the district director considers applying the resale price method. There are several uncontrolled distributors that perform similar functions under similar circumstances in uncontrolled transactions. However, the uncontrolled distributors treat certain costs such as discounts and insurance as cost of goods sold, while USSub treats such costs as operating expenses. In such cases, accounting reclassifications, pursuant to § 1.482-3(c)(3)(iii)(B), must be made to ensure consistent treatment of such material items. Inability to make such accounting reclassifications will decrease the reliability of the results of the uncontrolled transactions.

Example 5. (i) USP, a U.S. corporation, manufactures Product X, an unbranded widget, and sells it to FSub, its wholly owned foreign subsidiary. FSub acts as a distributor of Product X in country M, and sells it to uncontrolled parties in that country. Uncontrolled distributors A, B, C, D, and E distribute competing products of approximately similar value in country M. All such products are unbranded.

(ii) Relatively complete data is available regarding the functions performed and risks borne by the uncontrolled distributors and the contractual terms under which they operate in the uncontrolled transactions. In addition, data is available to ensure accounting consistency between all of the uncontrolled distributors and FSub. Because the available data is sufficiently complete and accurate to conclude that it is likely that all material differences between the controlled and uncontrolled transactions have been identified, such differences have a definite and reasonably ascertainable effect, and reliable adjustments are made to account for such differences, the results of each of the uncontrolled distributors may be used to establish an arm's length range pursuant to § 1.482-1(e)(2)(iii)(A).

Example 6. The facts are the same as *Example 5,* except that sufficient data is not available to determine whether any of the uncontrolled distributors provide warranties or to determine the payment terms of the contracts. Because differences in these contractual terms could materially affect price or profits, the inability to determine whether these differences exist between the controlled and uncontrolled transactions diminishes the reliability of the results of the uncontrolled comparables. However, the reliability of the results may be enhanced by the application of a statistical method when establishing an arm's length range pursuant to § 1.4821(e)(2)(iii)(B).

Example 7. The facts are the same as in *Example 5,* except that Product X is branded with a valuable trademark that is owned by P. A, B, and C distribute unbranded competing products, while D and E distribute products branded with other trademarks. D and E do not own any rights in the trademarks under which their products are sold. The value of the products that A, B, and C sold are not similar to the value of the products sold by S. The value of products sold by D and E, however, is similar to that of Product X. Although close product similarity is not as important for a reliable application of the resale price method as for the comparable uncontrolled price method, significant differences in the value of the products involved in the controlled and uncontrolled transactions may affect the reliability of the results. In addition, because in this case it is difficult to determine the effect the trademark will have on price or profits, reliable adjustments for the differences cannot be made. Because D and E have a higher level of comparability than A, B, and C with respect to S, pursuant to § 1.482-1(e)(2)(ii), only D and E may be included in an arm's length range.

(d) *Cost plus method.*—(1) *In general.*—The cost plus method evaluates whether the amount charged in a controlled transaction is arm's length by reference to the gross profit markup realized in comparable uncontrolled transactions. The cost plus method is ordinarily used in cases involving the manufacture, assembly, or other production of goods that are sold to related parties.

(2) *Determination of arm's length price.*—(i) *In general.*—The cost plus method measures an arm's length price by adding the appropriate gross profit to the controlled taxpayer's costs of producing the property involved in the controlled transaction.

(ii) *Appropriate gross profit.*—The appropriate gross profit is computed by multiplying the controlled taxpayer's cost of producing the transferred property by the gross profit markup, expressed as a percentage of cost, earned in comparable uncontrolled transactions.

(iii) *Arm's length range.*—See § 1.482-1(e)(2) for determination of an arm's length range.

(3) *Comparability and reliability considerations.*—(i) *In general.*—Whether results derived from the application of this method are the most reliable measure of the arm's length result must be determined using the factors described under the best method rule in § 1.482-1(c).

(ii) *Comparability.*—(A) *Functional comparability.*—The degree of comparability between controlled and uncontrolled transactions is determined by applying the comparability provisions of § 1.482-1(d). A producer's gross profit provides compensation for the performance of the production functions related to the product or products under review, including an operating profit for the producer's investment of capital and assumption of risks. Therefore, although all of the factors described in § 1.482-1(d)(3) must be considered, comparability under this method is particularly dependent on similarity of functions performed, risks borne, and contractual terms, or adjustments to account for the effects of any such differences. If possible, the appropriate gross profit markup should be derived from comparable uncontrolled transactions of the taxpayer involved in the controlled sale, because similar characteristics are more likely to be found among sales of property by the same producer than among sales by other producers. In the absence of such sales, an appropriate gross profit markup may be derived from comparable uncontrolled sales of other producers whether or not such producers are members of the same controlled group.

(B) *Other comparability factors.*—Comparability under this method is less dependent on close physical similarity between the products transferred than under the comparable uncontrolled price method. Substantial differences in the products may, however, indicate significant functional differences between the controlled and uncontrolled taxpayers. Thus, it ordinarily would be expected that the controlled and uncontrolled transactions involve the production of goods within the same product categories. Furthermore, significant differences in the value of the products due, for example, to the value of a trademark, may also affect the reliability of the comparison. Finally, the reliability of profit measures based on gross profit may be adversely affected by factors that have less effect on prices. For example, gross profit may be affected by a variety of other factors, including cost structures (as reflected, for example, in the age of plant and equipment), business experience (such as whether the business is in a start-up phase or is mature), or management efficiency (as indicated, for example, by expanding or contracting sales or executive compensation over time). Accordingly, if material differences in these factors are identified based on objective evidence, the reliability of the analysis may be affected.

(C) *Adjustments for differences between controlled and uncontrolled transactions.*—If there are material differences between the controlled and uncontrolled transactions that would affect the gross profit markup, adjustments should be made to the gross profit markup earned in the comparable uncontrolled transaction according to the provisions of § 1.482-1(d)(2). For this purpose, consideration of the operating expenses associated with the functions performed and risks assumed may be necessary, because differences in functions performed are often reflected in operating expenses. If there are differences in functions performed, however, the effect on gross profit of such differences is not necessarily equal to the differences in the amount of related operating expenses. Specific examples of the factors that may be particularly relevant to this method include—

(1) The complexity of manufacturing or assembly;

(2) Manufacturing, production, and process engineering;

(3) Procurement, purchasing, and inventory control activities;

(4) Testing functions;

(5) Selling, general, and administrative expenses;

(6) Foreign currency risks; and

(7) Contractual terms (e.g., scope and terms of warranties provided, sales or purchase volume, credit terms, transport terms).

(D) *Purchasing agent.*—If a controlled taxpayer is comparable to a purchasing agent that does not take title to property or otherwise assume risks with respect to ownership of such goods, the commission earned by such purchasing agent, expressed as a percentage of the purchase price of the goods, may be used as the appropriate gross profit markup.

(iii) *Data and assumptions.*—(A) *In general.*—The reliability of the results derived from the cost plus method is affected by the completeness and accuracy of the data used and the reliability of the assumptions made to apply this method. See § 1.482-1(c) (Best method rule).

(B) *Consistency in accounting.*—The degree of consistency in accounting practices between the controlled transaction and the uncontrolled comparables that materially affect the gross profit markup affects the reliability of the result. Thus, for example, if differences in inventory and other cost accounting practices would materially affect the gross profit markup, the ability to make reliable adjustments for such differences would affect the reliability of the results. Further, the controlled transaction and the comparable uncontrolled transaction should be consistent in the reporting of costs between cost of goods sold and operating expenses. The term *cost of producing* includes the cost of acquiring property that is held for resale.

Reg. § 1.482-3(d)(3)(ii)(B)

(4) *Examples.*—The following examples illustrate the principles of this paragraph (d).

Example 1. (i) USP, a domestic manufacturer of computer components, sells its products to FS, its foreign distributor. UT1, UT2, and UT3 are domestic computer component manufacturers that sell to uncontrolled foreign purchasers.

(ii) Relatively complete data is available regarding the functions performed and risks borne by UT1, UT2, and UT3, and the contractual terms in the uncontrolled transactions. In addition, data is available to ensure accounting consistency between all of the uncontrolled manufacturers and USP. Because the available data is sufficiently complete to conclude that it is likely that all material differences between the controlled and uncontrolled transactions have been identified, the effect of the differences are definite and reasonably ascertainable, and reliable adjustments are made to account for the differences, an arm's length range can be established pursuant to § 1.482-1(e)(2)(iii)(A).

Example 2. The facts are the same as in *Example 1*, except that USP accounts for supervisory, general, and administrative costs as operating expenses, which are not allocated to its sales to FS. The gross profit markups of UT1, UT2, and UT3, however, reflect supervisory, general, and administrative expenses because they are accounted for as costs of goods sold. Accordingly, the gross profit markups of UT1, UT2, and UT3 must be adjusted as provided in paragraph (d)(3)(iii)(B) of this section to provide accounting consistency. If data is not sufficient to determine whether such accounting differences exist between the controlled and uncontrolled transactions, the reliability of the results will be decreased.

Example 3. The facts are the same as in *Example 1*, except that under its contract with FS, USP uses materials consigned by FS. UT1, UT2, and UT3, on the other hand, purchase their own materials, and their gross profit markups are determined by including the costs of materials. The fact that USP does not carry an inventory risk by purchasing its own materials while the uncontrolled producers carry inventory is a significant difference that may require an adjustment if the difference has a material effect on the gross profit markups of the uncontrolled producers. Inability to reasonably ascertain the effect of the difference on the gross profit markups will affect the reliability of the results of UT1, UT2, and UT3.

Example 4. (i) FS, a foreign corporation, produces apparel for USP, its U.S. parent corporation. FS purchases its materials from unrelated suppliers and produces the apparel according to designs provided by USP. The district director identifies 10 uncontrolled foreign apparel producers that operate in the same geographic market and are similar in many respect to FS.

(ii) Relatively complete data is available regarding the functions performed and risks borne by the uncontrolled producers. In addition, data is sufficiently detailed to permit adjustments for differences in accounting practices. However, sufficient data is not available to determine whether it is likely that all material differences in contractual terms have been identified. For example, it is not possible to determine which parties in the uncontrolled transactions bear currency risks. Because differences in these contractual terms could materially affect price or profits, the inability to determine whether differences exist between the controlled and uncontrolled transactions will diminish the reliability of these results. Therefore, the reliability of the results of the uncontrolled transactions must be enhanced by the application of a statistical method in establishing an arm's length range pursuant to § 1.482-1(e)(2)(iii)(B).

(e) *Unspecified methods.*—(1) *In general.*—Methods not specified in paragraphs (a)(1), (2), (3), (4), and (5) of this section may be used to evaluate whether the amount charged in a controlled transaction is arm's length. Any method used under this paragraph (e) must be applied in accordance with the provisions of § 1.482-1. Consistent with the specified methods, an unspecified method should take into account the general principle that uncontrolled taxpayers evaluate the terms of a transaction by considering the realistic alternatives to that transaction, and only enter into a particular transaction if none of the alternatives is preferable to it. For example, the comparable uncontrolled price method compares a controlled transaction to similar uncontrolled transactions to provide a direct estimate of the price to which the parties would have agreed had they resorted directly to a market alternative to the controlled transaction. Therefore, in establishing whether a controlled transaction achieved an arm's length result, an unspecified method should provide information on the prices or profits that the controlled taxpayer could have realized by choosing a realistic alternative to the controlled transaction. As with any method, an unspecified method will not be applied unless it provides the most reliable measure of an arm's length result under the principles of the best method rule. See § 1.482-1(c). Therefore, in accordance with § 1.482-1(d) (Comparability), to the extent that a method relies on internal data rather than uncontrolled comparables, its reliability will be reduced. Similarly, the reliability of a method will be affected by the relia-

Reg. § 1.482-3(e)(1)

bility of the data and assumptions used to apply the method, including any projections used.

(2) *Example.*—The following example illustrates an application of the principle of this paragraph (e).

Example. Amcan, a U.S. company, produces unique vessels for storing and transporting toxic waste, toxicans, at its U.S. production facility. Amcan agrees by contract to supply its Canadian subsidiary, Cancan, with 4000 toxicans per year to serve the Canadian market for toxicans. Prior to entering into the contract with Cancan, Amcan had received a bona fide offer from an independent Canadian waste disposal company, Cando, to serve as the Canadian distributor for toxicans and to purchase a similar number of toxicans at a price of $5,000 each. If the circumstances and terms of the Cancan supply contract are sufficiently similar to those of the Cando offer, or sufficiently reliable adjustments can be made for differences between them, then the Cando offer price of $5,000 may provide reliable information indicating that an arm's length consideration under the Cancan contract will not be less than $5,000 per toxican.

(f) *Coordination with intangible property rules.*—The value of an item of tangible property may be affected by the value of intangible property, such as a trademark affixed to the tangible property (embedded intangible). Ordinarily, the transfer of tangible property with an embedded intangible will not be considered a transfer of such intangible if the controlled purchaser does not acquire any rights to exploit the intangible property other than rights relating to the resale of the tangible property under normal commercial practices. Pursuant to § 1.482-1(d)(3)(v), however, the embedded intangible must be accounted for in evaluating the comparability of the controlled transaction and uncontrolled comparables. For example, because product comparability has the greatest effect on an application of the comparable uncontrolled price method, trademarked tangible property may be insufficiently comparable to unbranded tangible property to permit a reliable application of the comparable uncontrolled price method. The effect of embedded intangibles on comparability will be determined under the principles of § 1.482-4. If the transfer of tangible property conveys to the recipient a right to exploit an embedded intangible (other than in connection with the resale of that item of tangible property), it may be necessary to determine the arm's length consideration for such intangible separately from the tangible property, applying methods appropriate to determining the arm's length result for a transfer of intangible property under § 1.482-4. For example, if the transfer of a machine conveys the right to exploit a manufacturing process incorporated in the machine, then the arm's length consideration for the transfer of that right must be determined separately under § 1.482-4. [Reg. § 1.482-3.]

□ [*T.D.* 8552, 7-1-94.]

§ 1.482-4. Methods to determine taxable income in connection with a transfer of intangible property.—(a) *In general.*—The arm's length amount charged in a controlled transfer of intangible property must be determined under one of the four methods listed in this paragraph (a). Each of the methods must be applied in accordance with all of the provisions of § 1.482-1, including the best method rule of § 1.482-1(c), the comparability analysis of § 1.482-1(d), and the arm's length range of § 1.482-1(e). The arm's length consideration for the transfer of an intangible determined under this section must be commensurate with the income attributable to the intangible. See § 1.482-4(f)(2) (Periodic adjustments). The available methods are—

(1) The comparable uncontrolled transaction method, described in paragraph (c) of this section;

(2) The comparable profits method, described in § 1.482-5;

(3) The profit split method, described in § 1.482-6; and

(4) Unspecified methods described in paragraph (d) of this section.

(b) *Definition of intangible.*—For purposes of section 482, an intangible is an asset that comprises any of the following items and has substantial value independent of the services of any individual—

(1) Patents, inventions, formulae, processes, designs, patterns, or know-how;

(2) Copyrights and literary, musical, or artistic compositions;

(3) Trademarks, trade names, or brand names;

(4) Franchises, licenses, or contracts;

(5) Methods, programs, systems, procedures, campaigns, surveys, studies, forecasts, estimates, customer lists, or technical data; and

(6) Other similar items. For purposes of section 482, an item is considered similar to those listed in paragraph (b)(1) through (5) of this section if it derives its value not from its physical attributes but from its intellectual content or other intangible properties.

(c) *Comparable uncontrolled transaction method.*—(1) *In general.*—The comparable uncontrolled transaction method evaluates whether the amount charged for a controlled transfer of intangible property was arm's length by reference to the amount charged in a comparable uncontrolled transaction. The amount determined under this method may be adjusted as required by paragraph (f)(2) of this section (Periodic adjustments).

(2) *Comparability and reliability considerations.*—(i) *In general.*—Whether results derived from applications of this method are the most reliable measure of an arm's length result is determined using the factors described under the best method rule in § 1.482-1(c). The application of these factors under the comparable uncontrolled transaction method is discussed in paragraphs (c)(2)(ii), (iii), and (iv) of this section.

(ii) *Reliability.*—If an uncontrolled transaction involves the transfer of the same intangible under the same, or substantially the same, circumstances as the controlled transaction, the results derived from applying the comparable uncontrolled transaction method will generally be the most direct and reliable measure of the arm's length result for the controlled transfer of an intangible. Circumstances between the controlled and uncontrolled transactions will be considered substantially the same if there are at most only minor differences that have a definite and reasonably ascertainable effect on the amount charged and for which appropriate adjustments are made. If such uncontrolled transactions cannot be identified, uncontrolled transactions that involve the transfer of comparable intangibles under comparable circumstances may be used to apply this method, but the reliability of the analysis will be reduced.

(iii) *Comparability.*—(A) *In general.*— The degree of comparability between controlled and uncontrolled transactions is determined by applying the comparability provisions of § 1.482-1(d). Although all of the factors described in § 1.482-1(d)(3) must be considered, specific factors may be particularly relevant to this method. In particular, the application of this method requires that the controlled and uncontrolled transactions involve either the same intangible property or comparable intangible property, as defined in paragraph (c)(2)(iii)(B)(*1*) of this section. In addition, because differences in contractual terms, or the economic conditions in which transactions take place, could materially affect the amount charged, comparability under this method also depends on similarity with respect to these factors, or adjustments to account for material differences in such circumstances.

(B) *Factors to be considered in determining comparability.*—(*1*) *Comparable intangible property.*—In order for the intangible property involved in an uncontrolled transaction to be considered comparable to the intangible property involved in the controlled transaction, both intangibles must—

(*i*) Be used in connection with similar products or processes within the same general industry or market; and

(*ii*) Have similar profit potential. The profit potential of an intangible is most reliably measured by directly calculating the net present value of the benefits to be realized (based on prospective profits to be realized or costs to be saved) through the use or subsequent transfer of the intangible, considering the capital investment and start-up expenses required, the risks to be assumed, and other relevant considerations. The need to reliably measure profit potential increases in relation to both the total amount of potential profits and the potential rate of return on investment necessary to exploit the intangible. If the information necessary to directly calculate net present value of the benefits to be realized is unavailable, and the need to reliably measure profit potential is reduced because the potential profits are relatively small in terms of total amount and rate of return, comparison of profit potential may be based upon the factors referred to in paragraph (c)(2)(iii)(B)(*2*) of this section. See *Example 3* of § 1.482-4(c)(4). Finally, the reliability of a measure of profit potential is affected by the extent to which the profit attributable to the intangible can be isolated from the profit attributable to other factors, such as functions performed and other resources employed.

(*2*) *Comparable circumstances.*—In evaluating the comparability of the circumstances of the controlled and uncontrolled transactions, although all of the factors described in § 1.482-1(d)(3) must be considered, specific factors that may be particularly relevant to this method include the following—

(*i*) The terms of the transfer, including the exploitation rights granted in the intangible, the exclusive or nonexclusive character of any rights granted, any restrictions on use, or any limitations on the geographic area in which the rights may be exploited;

(*ii*) The stage of development of the intangible (including, where appropriate, necessary governmental approvals, authorizations, or licenses) in the market in which the intangible is to be used;

(*iii*) Rights to receive updates, revisions, or modifications of the intangible;

(*iv*) The uniqueness of the property and the period for which it remains unique, including the degree and duration of protection afforded to the property under the laws of the relevant countries;

Reg. § 1.482-4(c)(2)(iii)(B)(2)(iv)

(v) The duration of the license, contract, or other agreement, and any termination or renegotiation rights;

(vi) Any economic and product liability risks to be assumed by the transferee;

(vii) The existence and extent of any collateral transactions or ongoing business relationships between the transferee and transferor; and

(viii) The functions to be performed by the transferor and transferee, including any ancillary or subsidiary services.

(iv) *Data and assumptions.*—The reliability of the results derived from the comparable uncontrolled transaction method is affected by the completeness and accuracy of the data used and the reliability of the assumptions made to apply this method. See § 1.482-1(c) (Best method rule).

(3) *Arm's length range.*—See § 1.482-1(e)(2) for the determination of an arm's length range.

(4) *Examples.*—The following examples illustrate the principles of this paragraph (c).

Example 1. (i) USpharm, a U.S. pharmaceutical company, develops a new drug Z that is a safe and effective treatment for the disease zeezee. USpharm has obtained patents covering drug Z in the United States and in various foreign countries. USpharm has also obtained the regulatory authorizations necessary to market drug Z in the United States and in foreign countries.

(ii) USpharm licenses its subsidiary in country X, Xpharm, to produce and sell drug Z in country X. At the same time, it licenses an unrelated company, Ydrug, to produce and sell drug Z in country Y, a neighboring country. Prior to licensing the drug, USpharm had obtained patent protection and regulatory approvals in both countries and both countries provide similar protection for intellectual property rights. Country X and country Y are similar countries in terms of population, per capita income and the incidence of disease zeezee. Consequently, drug Z is expected to sell in similar quantities and at similar prices in both countries. In addition, costs of producing and marketing drug Z in each country are expected to be approximately the same.

(iii) USpharm and Xpharm establish terms for the license of drug Z that are identical in every material respect, including royalty rate, to the terms established between USpharm and Ydrug. In this case the district director determines that the royalty rate established in the Ydrug license agreement is a reliable measure of the arm's length royalty rate for the Xpharm license agreement.

Example 2. The facts are the same as in *Example 1,* except that the incidence of the disease zeezee in Country Y is much higher than in Country X. In this case, the profit potential from exploitation of the right to make and sell drug Z is likely to be much higher in country Y than it is in Country X. Consequently, the Ydrug license agreement is unlikely to provide a reliable measure of the arm's length royalty rate for the Xpharm license.

Example 3. (i) FP is a foreign company that designs, manufactures and sells industrial equipment. FP has developed proprietary components that are incorporated in its products. These components are important in the operation of FP's equipment and some of them have distinctive features, but other companies produce similar components and none of these components by itself accounts for a substantial part of the value of FP's products.

(ii) FP licenses its U.S. subsidiary, USSub, exclusive North American rights to use the patented technology for producing component X, a heat exchanger used for cooling operating mechanisms in industrial equipment. Component X incorporates proven technology that makes it somewhat more efficient than the heat exchangers commonly used in industrial equipment. FP also agrees to provide technical support to help adapt component X to USSub's products and to assist with initial production. Under the terms of the license agreement USSub pays FP a royalty equal to 3 percent of sales of USSub equipment incorporating component X.

(iii) FP does not license unrelated parties to use component X, but many similar components are transferred between uncontrolled taxpayers. Consequently, the district director decides to apply the comparable uncontrolled transaction method to evaluate whether the 3 percent royalty for component X is an arm's length royalty.

(iv) The district director uses a database of company documents filed with the Securities and Exchange Commission (SEC) to identify potentially comparable license agreements between uncontrolled taxpayers that are on file with the SEC. The district director identifies 40 license agreements that were entered into in the same year as the controlled transfer or in the prior or following year, and that relate to transfers of technology associated with industrial equipment that has similar applications to USSub's products. Further review of these uncontrolled agreements indicates that 25 of them involved components that have a similar level of technical sophistication as component X and could be expected to play a similar role in contributing to the total value of the final product.

(v) The district director makes a detailed review of the terms of each of the 25 uncontrolled agreements and finds that 15 of them are similar to the controlled agreement in that they all involve—

(A) The transfer of exclusive rights for the North American market;

(B) Products for which the market could be expected to be of a similar size to the market for the products into which USSub incorporates component X;

(C) The transfer of patented technology;

(D) Continuing technical support;

(E) Access to technical improvements;

(F) Technology of a similar age; and

(G) A similar duration of the agreement.

(vi) Based on these factors and the fact that none of the components to which these license agreements relate accounts for a substantial part of the value of the final products, the district director concludes that these fifteen intangibles have similar profit potential to the component X technology.

(vii) The 15 uncontrolled comparables produce the following royalty rates:

License	Royalty rate (percent)
1	1.0
2	1.0
3	1.25
4	1.25
5	1.5
6	1.5
7	1.75
8	2.0
9	2.0
10	2.0
11	2.25
12	2.5
13	2.5
14	2.75
15	3.0

(viii) Although the uncontrolled comparables are clearly similar to the controlled transaction, it is likely that unidentified material differences exist between the uncontrolled comparables and the controlled transaction. Therefore, an appropriate statistical technique must be used to establish the arm's length range. In this case the district director uses the interquartile range to determine the arm's length range. Therefore, the arm's length range covers royalty rates from 1.25 to 2.5 percent, and an adjustment is warranted to the 3 percent royalty charged in the controlled transfer. The district director determines that the appropriate adjustment corresponds to a reduction in the royalty rate to 2.0 percent, which is the median of the uncontrolled comparables.

Example 4. (i) USdrug, a U.S. pharmaceutical company, has developed a new drug, Nosplit, that is useful in treating migraine headaches and produces no significant side effects. Nosplit replaces another drug, Lessplit, that USdrug had previously produced and marketed as a treatment for migraine headaches. A number of other drugs for treating migraine headaches are already on the market, but Nosplit can be expected rapidly to dominate the worldwide market for such treatments and to command a premium price since all other treatments produce side effects. Thus, USdrug projects that extraordinary profits will be derived from Nosplit in the U.S. market and other markets.

(ii) USdrug licenses its newly established European subsidiary, Eurodrug, the rights to produce and market Nosplit in the European market. In setting the royalty rate for this license, USdrug considers the royalty that it established previously when it licensed the right to produce and market Lessplit in the European market to an unrelated European pharmaceutical company. In many respects the two license agreements are closely comparable. The drugs were licensed at the same stage in their development and the agreements conveyed identical rights to the licensees. Moreover, there appear to have been no significant changes in the European market for migraine headache treatments since Lessplit was licensed. However, at the time that Lessplit was licensed there were several other similar drugs already on the market to which Lessplit was not in all cases superior. Consequently, the projected and actual Lessplit profits were substantially less than the projected Nosplit profits. Thus, USdrug concludes that the profit potential of Lessplit is not similar to the profit potential of Nosplit, and the Lessplit license agreement consequently is not a comparable uncontrolled transaction for purposes of this paragraph (c) in spite of the other indicia of comparability between the two intangibles.

(d) *Unspecified methods.*—(1) *In general.*—Methods not specified in paragraphs (a)(1), (2), and (3) of this section may be used to evaluate whether the amount charged in a controlled transaction is arm's length. Any method used under this paragraph (d) must be applied in accordance with the provisions of § 1.482-1. Consistent with the specified methods, an unspecified method should take into account the general principle that uncontrolled taxpayers evaluate the terms of a transaction by considering the realistic alternatives to that transaction, and only enter into a particular transaction if none of the alternatives is preferable to it. For example, the comparable uncontrolled transaction method compares a controlled transaction to similar uncontrolled transactions to provide a direct estimate of the price the parties would have agreed to had they resorted directly to a market alternative to the controlled transaction. Therefore, in establishing whether a controlled transaction achieved an arm's length result, an unspecified method should provide information on the prices or profits that the controlled taxpayer could have realized by choosing a realistic alternative to the controlled transaction. As with any method, an unspecified method will not be applied unless it provides the most reliable measure of an arm's length result under the principles of the best method rule. See § 1.482-1(c). Therefore, in accordance with § 1.482-1(d) (Comparability), to the extent that a method relies on internal data rather than uncontrolled comparables, its reliability will be reduced. Similarly, the reliability of a method will be affected by the reliability of the data and assumptions used to apply the method, including any projections used.

(2) *Example.*—The following example illustrates an application of the principle of this paragraph (d).

Example. (i) USbond is a U.S. company that licenses to its foreign subsidiary, Eurobond, a proprietary process that permits the manufacture of Longbond, a long-lasting industrial adhesive, at a substantially lower cost than otherwise would be possible. Using the proprietary process, Eurobond manufactures Longbond and sells it to related and unrelated parties for the market price of $550 per ton. Under the terms of the license agreement, Eurobond pays USbond a royalty of $100 per ton of Longbond sold. USbond also manufactures and markets Longbond in the United States.

(ii) In evaluating whether the consideration paid for the transfer of the proprietary process to Eurobond was arm's length, the district director may consider, subject to the best method rule of § 1.482-1(c), USbond's alternative of producing and selling Longbond itself. Reasonably reliable estimates indicate that if USbond directly supplied Longbond to the European market, a selling price of $300 per ton would cover its costs and provide a reasonable profit for its functions, risks and investment of capital associated with the production of Longbond for the European market. Given that the market price of Longbond was $550 per ton, by licensing the proprietary process to Eurobond, USbond forgoes $250 per ton of profit over the profit that would be necessary to compensate it for the functions, risks and investment involved in supplying Longbond to the European market itself. Based on these facts, the district director concludes that a royalty of $100 for the proprietary process is not arm's length.

(e) *Coordination with tangible property rules.*—See § 1.482-3(f) for the provisions regarding the coordination between the tangible property and intangible property rules.

(f) *Special rules for transfers of intangible property.*—(1) *Form of consideration.*—If a transferee of an intangible pays nominal or no consideration and the transferor has retained a substantial interest in the property, the arm's length consideration shall be in the form of a royalty, unless a different form is demonstrably more appropriate.

(2) *Periodic adjustments.*—(i) *General rule.*—If an intangible is transferred under an arrangement that covers more than one year, the consideration charged in each taxable year may be adjusted to ensure that it is commensurate with the income attributable to the intangible. Adjustments made pursuant to this paragraph (f)(2) shall be consistent with the arm's length standard and the provisions of § 1.482-1. In determining whether to make such adjustments in the taxable year under examination, the district director may consider all relevant facts and circumstances throughout the period the intangible is used. The determination in an earlier year that the amount charged for an intangible was an arm's length amount will not preclude the district director in a subsequent taxable year from making an adjustment to the amount charged for the intangible in the subsequent year. A periodic adjustment under the commensurate with income requirement of section 482 may be made in a subsequent taxable year without regard to whether the taxable year of the original transfer remains open for statute of limitation purposes. For exceptions to this rule see paragraph (f)(2)(ii) of this section.

(ii) *Exceptions.*—(A) *Transactions involving the same intangible.*—If the same intangible was transferred to an uncontrolled taxpayer under substantially the same circumstances as those of the controlled transaction; this transaction serves as the basis for the application of the comparable uncontrolled transaction method in the first taxable year in which substantial periodic consideration was required to be paid; and the amount paid in that year was an arm's length amount, then no allocation in a subsequent year will be made under paragraph (f)(2)(i) of this paragraph for a controlled transfer of intangible property.

(B) *Transactions involving comparable intangible.*—If the arm's length result is derived from the application of the comparable uncontrolled transaction method based on the transfer of a comparable intangible under comparable circumstances to those of the controlled transaction, no allocation will be made under paragraph (f)(2)(i) of this section if each of the following facts is established—

(1) The controlled taxpayers entered into a written agreement (controlled agreement) that provided for an amount of consideration with respect to each taxable year subject to such agreement, such consideration was an arm's length amount for the first taxable year in which substantial periodic consideration was required to be paid under the agreement, and such agreement remained in effect for the taxable year under review;

(2) There is a written agreement setting forth the terms of the comparable uncontrolled transaction relied upon to establish the arm's length consideration (uncontrolled agreement), which contains no provisions that would permit any change to the amount of consideration, a renegotiation, or a termination of the agreement, in circumstances comparable to those of the controlled transaction in the taxable year under review (or that contains provisions permitting only specified, non-contingent, periodic changes to the amount of consideration);

(3) The controlled agreement is substantially similar to the uncontrolled agreement, with respect to the time period for which it is effective and the provisions described in paragraph (f)(2)(ii)(B)(2) of this section;

(4) The controlled agreement limits use of the intangible to a specified field or purpose in a manner that is consistent with industry practice and any such limitation in the uncontrolled agreement;

(5) There were no substantial changes in the functions performed by the controlled transferee after the controlled agreement was executed, except changes required by events that were not foreseeable; and

(6) The aggregate profits actually earned or the aggregate cost savings actually realized by the controlled taxpayer from the exploitation of the intangible in the year under examination, and all past years, are not less than 80% nor more than 120% of the prospective profits or cost savings that were foreseeable when the comparability of the uncontrolled agreement was established under paragraph (c)(2) of this section.

(C) *Methods other than comparable uncontrolled transaction.*—If the arm's length amount was determined under any method other than the comparable uncontrolled transaction method, no allocation will be made under paragraph (f)(2)(i) of this section if each of the following facts is established—

(1) The controlled taxpayers entered into a written agreement (controlled agreement) that provided for an amount of consideration with respect to each taxable year subject to such agreement, and such agreement remained in effect for the taxable year under review;

(2) The consideration called for in the controlled agreement was an arm's length amount for the first taxable year in which substantial periodic consideration was required to be paid, and relevant supporting documentation was prepared contemporaneously with the execution of the controlled agreement;

(3) There have been no substantial changes in the functions performed by the transferee since the controlled agreement was executed, except changes required by events that were not foreseeable; and

(4) The total profits actually earned or the total cost savings realized by the controlled transferee from the exploitation of the intangible in the year under examination, and all past years, are not less than 80% nor more than 120% of the prospective profits or cost savings that were foreseeable when the controlled agreement was entered into.

(D) *Extraordinary events.*—No allocation will be made under paragraph (f)(2)(i) of this section if the following requirements are met—

(1) Due to extraordinary events that were beyond the control of the controlled taxpayers and that could not reasonably have been anticipated at the time the controlled agreement was entered into, the aggregate actual profits or aggregate cost savings realized by the taxpayer are less than 80% or more than 120% of the prospective profits or cost savings; and

(2) All of the requirements of paragraph (f)(2)(ii)(B) or (C) of this section are otherwise satisfied.

(E) *Five-year period.*—If the requirements of §1.482-4(f)(2)(ii)(B) or (f)(2)(ii)(C)

Reg. §1.482-4(f)(2)(ii)(E)

are met for each year of the five-year period beginning with the first year in which substantial periodic consideration was required to be paid, then no periodic adjustment will be made under paragraph (f)(2)(i) of this section in any subsequent year.

(iii) *Examples.*—The following examples illustrate this paragraph (f)(2).

Example 1. (i) USdrug, a U.S. pharmaceutical company, has developed a new drug, Nosplit, that is useful in treating migraine headaches and produces no significant side effects. A number of other drugs for treating migraine headaches are already on the market, but Nosplit can be expected rapidly to dominate the worldwide market for such treatments and to command a premium price since all other treatments produce side effects. Thus, USdrug projects that extraordinary profits will be derived from Nosplit in the U.S. and European markets.

(ii) USdrug licenses its newly established European subsidiary, Eurodrug, the rights to produce and market Nosplit for the European market for 5 years. In setting the royalty rate for this license, USdrug makes projections of the annual sales revenue and the annual profits to be derived from the exploitation of Nosplit by Eurodrug. Based on the projections, a royalty rate of 3.9% is established for the term of the license.

(iii) In Year 1, USdrug evaluates the royalty rate it received from Eurodrug. Given the high profit potential of Nosplit, USdrug is unable to locate any uncontrolled transactions dealing with licenses of comparable intangible property. USdrug therefore determines that the comparable uncontrolled transaction method will not provide a reliable measure of an arm's length royalty. However, applying the comparable profits method to Eurodrug, USdrug determines that a royalty rate of 3.9% will result in Eurodrug earning an arm's length return for its manufacturing and marketing functions.

(iv) In Year 5, the U.S. income tax return for USdrug is examined, and the district director must determine whether the royalty rate between USdrug and Eurodrug is commensurate with the income attributable to Nosplit. In making this determination, the district director considers whether any of the exceptions in § 1.482-4(f)(2)(ii) are applicable. In particular, the district director compares the profit projections attributable to Nosplit made by USdrug against the actual profits realized by Eurodrug. The projected and actual profits are as follows:

	Profit projections	Actual profits
Year 1	200	250
Year 2	250	300
Year 3	500	600
Year 4	350	200
Year 5	100	100
Total	1400	1450

(v) The total profits earned through Year 5 were not less than 80% nor more than 120% of the profits that were projected when the license was entered into. If the district director determines that the other requirements of § 1.482-4(f)(2)(ii)(C) were met, no adjustment will be made to the royalty rate between USdrug and Eurodrug for the license of Nosplit.

Example 2. (i) The facts are the same as in *Example 1*, except that Eurodrug's actual profits earned were much higher than the projected profits, as follows:

	Profit projections	Actual profits
Year 1	200	250
Year 2	250	500
Year 3	500	800
Year 4	350	700
Year 5	100	600
Total	1400	2850

(ii) In examining USdrug's tax return for Year 5, the district director considers the actual profits realized by Eurodrug in Year 5, and all past years. Accordingly, although Years 1 through 4 may be closed under the statute of limitations, for purposes of determining whether an adjustment should be made with respect to the royalty rate in Year 5 with respect to Nosplit, the district director aggregates the actual profits from those years with the profits of Year 5. However, the district director will make an adjustment, if any, only with respect to Year 5.

Example 3. (i) FP, a foreign corporation, licenses to USS, its U.S. subsidiary, a new air-filtering process that permits manufacturing plants to meet new environmental standards. The license runs for a 10-year period, and the profit derived from the new process is projected to be $15 million per year, for an aggregate profit of $150 million.

(ii) The royalty rate for the license is based on a comparable uncontrolled transaction involving a comparable intangible under comparable circumstances. The requirements of paragraphs (f)(2)(ii)(B)(*1*) through (*5*) of this section have been met. Specifically, FP and USS have entered into a written agreement that provides for a royalty in each year of the license, the royalty rate is considered arm's length for the first taxable year in which a substantial royalty was required to be paid, the license limited the use of the process to a specified field, consistent with industry practice, and there are no substantial changes in the functions performed by USS after the license was entered into.

(iii) In examining Year 4 of the license, the district director determines that the aggregate actual profits earned by USS through Year 4 are $30 million, less than 80% of the projected profits of $60 million. However, USS establishes to the satisfaction of the district director that the aggregate actual profits from the process are less than 80% of the projected profits in Year 3 because an earthquake severely damaged USS's manufacturing plant. Because the difference between the projected profits and actual profits was due to an extraordinary event that was beyond the control of USS, and could not reasonably have been anticipated at the time the license was entered into, the requirement under § 1.482-4(f)(2)(ii)(D) has been met, and no adjustment under this section is made.

(3) *Ownership of intangible property.*— (i) *In general.*—If the owner of the rights to exploit an intangible transfers such rights to a controlled taxpayer, the owner must receive an amount of consideration with respect to such transfer that is determined in accordance with the provisions of this section. If another controlled taxpayer provides assistance to the owner in connection with the development or enhancement of an intangible, such person may be entitled to receive consideration with respect to such assistance. See § 1.482-4(f)(3)(iii) (Allocations with respect to assistance provided to the owner). Because the right to exploit an intangible can be subdivided in various ways, a single intangible may have multiple owners for purposes of this paragraph (3)(i). Thus, for example, the owner of a trademark may license to another person the exclusive right to use that trademark in a specified geographic area for a specified period of time (while otherwise retaining the right to use the intangible). In such a case, both the licensee and the licensor will be considered owners for purposes of this paragraph (f)(3)(i), with respect to their respective exploitation rights.

(ii) *Identification of owner.*—(A) *Legally protected intangible property.*—The legal owner of a right to exploit an intangible ordinarily will be considered the owner for purposes of this section. Legal ownership may be acquired by operation of law or by contract under which the legal owner transfers all or part of its rights to another. Further, the district director may impute an agreement to convey legal ownership if the conduct of the controlled taxpayers indicates the existence in substance of such an agreement. See § 1.482-1(d)(3)(ii)(B) (Identifying contractual terms).

(B) *Intangible property that is not legally protected.*—In the case of intangible property that is not legally protected, the developer of the intangible will be considered the owner. Except as provided in § 1.482-7T, if two or more controlled taxpayers jointly develop an intangible, for purposes of section 482, only one of the controlled taxpayers will be regarded as the developer and owner of the intangible, and the other participating members will be regarded as assisters. Ordinarily, the developer is the controlled taxpayer that bore the largest portion of the direct and indirect costs of developing the intangible, including the provision, without adequate compensation, of property or services likely to contribute substantially to developing the intangible. A controlled taxpayer will be presumed not to have borne the costs of development if, pursuant to an agreement entered into before the success of the project is known, another person is obligated to reimburse the controlled taxpayer for its costs. If it cannot be determined which controlled taxpayer bore the largest portion of the costs of development, all other facts and circumstances will be taken into consideration, including the location of the development activities, the capability of each controlled taxpayer to carry on the project independently, the extent to which each controlled taxpayer controls the project, and the conduct of the controlled taxpayers.

(iii) *Allocations with respect to assistance provided to the owner.*—Allocations may be made to reflect an arm's length consideration for assistance provided to the owner of an intangible in connection with the development or enhancement of the intangible. Such assistance may include loans, services, or the use of tangible or intangible property. Assistance does not, however, include expenditures of a routine nature that an unrelated party dealing at arm's length would be expected to incur under circumstances similar to those of the controlled taxpayer. The amount of any allocation required with respect to that assistance must be determined in accordance with the applicable rules under section 482.

(iv) *Examples.*—The principles of this paragraph are illustrated by the following examples.

Example 1. A, a member of a controlled group, allows B, another member of the controlled group and the owner of an intangible, to use tangible property, such as laboratory equipment, in connection with the development of the intangible. Any allocations with respect to the owner's use of the property will be determined under § 1.482-2(c).

Example 2. FP, a foreign producer of cheese, markets the cheese in countries other than the United States under the tradename Fromage Frere. FP owns all the worldwide rights to this name. The name is widely known and is valuable outside the United States but is not known within the United States. In 1995, FP decides to enter the United States market and incorporates U.S. subsidiary, USSub, to be its U.S. distributor and to supervise the advertising and other marketing efforts that will be required to develop the name Fromage Frere in the United States. USSub incurs expenses that are not reimbursed by FP for developing the U.S. market for Fromage Frere. These expenses are comparable to the levels of expense incurred by independent distributors in the U.S. cheese industry when introducing a product in the U.S. market under a brand name owned by a foreign manufacturer. Since USSub would have been expected to incur these expenses if it were unrelated to FP, no allocation to USSub is made with respect to the market development activities performed by USSub.

Example 3. The facts are the same as in *Example 2*, except that the expenses incurred by USSub are significantly larger than the expenses incurred by independent distributors under similar circumstances. FP does not reimburse USSub for its expenses. The district director concludes based on this evidence that an unrelated party dealing at arm's length under similar circumstances would not have engaged in the same level of activity relating to the development of FP's marketing intangibles. The expenditures in excess of the level incurred by the independent distributors therefore are considered to be a service provided to FP that adds to the value of FP's trademark for Fromage Frere. Accordingly, the district director makes an allocation under section 482 for the fair market value of the services that USSub is considered to have performed for FP.

Example 4. The facts are the same as in *Example 3*, except that FP and USSub conclude a long term agreement under which USSub receives the exclusive right to distribute cheese in the United States under FP's trademark. USSub purchases cheese from FP at an arm's length price. Since USSub is the owner of the trademark under paragraph (f)(3)(ii)(A) of this section, and its conduct is consistent with that status, its activities related to the development of the trademark are not considered to be a service performed for the benefit of FP, and no allocation is made with respect to such activities.

(4) *Consideration not artificially limited.*—The arm's length consideration for the controlled transfer of an intangible is not limited by the consideration paid in any uncontrolled transactions that do not meet the requirements of the comparable uncontrolled transaction method described in paragraph (c) of this section. Similarly, the arm's length consideration for an intangible is not limited by the prevailing rates of consideration paid for the use or transfer of intangibles within the same or similar industry.

(5) *Lump sum payments.*—(i) *In general.*—If an intangible is transferred in a controlled transaction for a lump sum, that amount must be commensurate with the income attributable to the intangible. A lump sum is commensurate with income in a taxable year if the equivalent royalty amount for that taxable year is equal to an arm's length royalty. The equivalent royalty amount for a taxable year is the amount determined by treating the lump sum as an advance payment of a stream of royalties over the useful life of the intangible (or the period covered by an agreement, if shorter), taking into account the projected sales of the licensee as of the date of the transfer. Thus, determining the equivalent royalty amount requires a present value calculation based on the lump sum, an appropriate discount rate, and the projected sales over the relevant period. The equivalent royalty amount is subject to periodic adjustments under § 1.482-4(f)(2)(i) to the same extent as an actual royalty payment pursuant to a license agreement.

(ii) *Exceptions.*—No periodic adjustment will be made under paragraph (f)(2)(i) of this section if any of the exceptions to periodic adjustments provided in paragraph (f)(2)(ii) of this section apply.

(iii) *Example.*—The following example illustrates the principle of this paragraph (f)(5).

Example. Calculation of the equivalent royalty amount. (i) FSub is the foreign subsidiary of USP, a U.S. company. USP licenses FSub the right to produce and sell the whopperchopper, a patented new kitchen appliance, for the foreign market. The license is for a period of five years, and payment takes the form of a single lump-sum charge of $500,000 that is paid at the beginning of the period.

(ii) The equivalent royalty amount for this license is determined by deriving an equivalent royalty rate equal to the lump-sum payment divided by the present discounted value of FSub's projected sales of whopperchoppers over the life of the license. Based on the riskiness of the whopperchopper business, an appropriate discount rate is determined to be 10 percent. Projected sales of whopperchoppers for each year of the license are as follows:

Year	Projected Sales ($)
1	2,500,000
2	2,600,000
3	2,700,000
4	2,700,000
5	2,750,000

(iii) Based on this information, the present discounted value of the projected whopperchopper sales is approximately $10 million, yielding an equivalent royalty rate of approximately 5%. Thus, the equivalent royalty amounts for each year are as follows:

Year	Projected Sales ($)	Equivalent royalty amount ($)
1	2,500,000	125,000
2	2,600,000	130,000
3	2,700,000	135,000
4	2,700,000	135,000
5	2,750,000	137,500

(iv) If in any of the five taxable years the equivalent royalty amount is determined not to be an arm's length amount, a periodic adjustment may be made pursuant to § 1.482-4(f)(2)(i). The adjustment in such case would be equal to the difference between the equivalent royalty amount and the arm's length royalty in that taxable year. [Reg. § 1.482-4.]

☐ [*T.D.* 8552, 7-1-94.]

Proposed Amendments to Regulation

☐ Section 1.482-4 is amended by:

1. Redesignating paragraphs (f)(4) and (f)(5) as paragraphs (f)(5) and (f)(6), respectively.

2. Revising paragraph (f)(3) and adding new paragraph (f)(4).

The revisions and additions read as follows:

§ 1.482-4. Methods to determine taxable income in connection with a transfer of intangible property.

* * *

(f) * * *

(3) *Ownership of intangible property.*—(i) *Identification of owner.*—(A) *In general.*—The legal owner of an intangible pursuant to the intellectual property law of the relevant jurisdiction, or the holder of rights constituting an intangible pursuant to contractual terms (such as the terms of a license) or other legal provision, will be considered the sole owner of the respective intangible for purposes of this section unless such ownership is inconsistent with the economic substance of the underlying transactions. See § 1.482-1(d)(3)(ii)(B) (Identifying contractual terms). If no owner of the respective intangible is identified under the intellectual property law of the relevant jurisdiction, or pursuant to contractual terms (including terms imputed pursuant to § 1.482-1(d)(3)(ii)(B)) or other legal provision, then the controlled taxpayer who has control of the intangible, based on all the facts and circumstances, will be considered the sole owner of the intangible for purposes of this section.

(B) *Cost sharing arrangements.*—The rule in paragraph (f)(3)(i)(A) of this section shall apply to interests in covered intangibles, as defined in § 1.482-7(b)(4)(iv), only as provided in § 1.482-7 (Sharing of costs).

(ii) *Examples.*—The principles of this paragraph (f)(3) are illustrated by the following examples:

Example 1. FP, a foreign corporation, is the registered holder of the AA trademark in the United States. FP licenses to a U.S. subsidiary, USSub, the exclusive rights to manufacture and market products in the United States under the AA trademark. FP is the owner of the trademark pursuant to intellectual property law. USSub is the owner of the license pursuant to the contractual terms of the license, but is not the owner of the trademark. See paragraphs (b)(3) and (4) of this section (defining an intangible as, among other things, a trademark or a license).

Example 2. The facts are the same as in *Example 1.* As a result of its sales and marketing activities, USSub develops a list of several hundred creditworthy customers that regularly purchase AA trademarked products. Neither the terms of the contract between FP and USSub nor the relevant intellectual property law specify which party owns the customer list. Because USSub has knowledge of the contents of the list, and has practical control over its use and dissemination, USSub is considered the sole owner of the customer list for purposes of this paragraph (f)(3).

(4) *Contribution to the value of an intangible owned by another.*—(i) *In general.*—The arm's length consideration for a contribution by one controlled taxpayer that develops or enhances the value, or may be reasonably anticipated to develop or enhance the value, of an intangible owned by another controlled taxpayer shall be determined in accordance with the applicable rules under section 482. If the consideration for such a contribution is embed-

ded within the contractual terms for a controlled transaction that involves such intangible, then ordinarily no separate allocation will be made with respect to such contribution. In such cases, pursuant to § 1.482-1(d)(3), the contribution must be accounted for in evaluating the comparability of the controlled transaction to uncontrolled comparables, and accordingly in determining the arm's length consideration in the controlled transaction.

(ii) *Examples.*—The principles of this paragraph (f)(4) are illustrated by the following examples:

Example 1. A, a member of a controlled group, allows B, another member of the controlled group, to use tangible property, such as laboratory equipment, in connection with B's development of an intangible that B owns. By furnishing tangible property, A makes a contribution to the development of an intangible owned by another controlled taxpayer, B. Pursuant to paragraph (f)(4)(i) of this section, the arm's length charge for A's furnishing of tangible property will be determined under the rules for use of tangible property in § 1.482-2(c).

Example 2. (i) *Facts.* FP, a foreign producer of wristwatches, is the registered holder of the YY trademark in the United States and in other countries worldwide. FP enters into a five-year, renewable distribution agreement with its newly organized U.S. subsidiary, USSub. The contractual terms of the agreement grant USSub the right to sell trademark YY wristwatches in the United States, obligate USSub to pay a fixed price per wristwatch throughout the entire term of the contract, and obligate both FP and USSub to undertake without separate compensation specified types and levels of marketing activities.

(ii) The consideration for FP's and USSub's marketing activities, as well as the consideration for the license to sell YY trademarked merchandise, are embedded in the transfer price paid for the wristwatches. Accordingly, pursuant to paragraph (f)(4)(i) of this section, ordinarily no separate allocation would be appropriate with respect to these embedded contributions.

(iii) Whether an allocation is warranted with respect to the transfer price for the wristwatches is determined under § 1.482-1 and §§ 1.482-3 through 1.482-6. The comparability analysis would include consideration of all relevant factors, including the nature of the intangible embedded in the wristwatches and the nature of the marketing activities required under the contract. This analysis would also take into account that the compensation for the activities performed by USSub and FP, as well as the consideration for USSub's use of the YY trademark, is embedded in the transfer price for the wristwatches, rather than provided for in separate agreements. See §§ 1.482-3(f) and 1.482-9(m)(4). If it is not possible to identify uncontrolled transactions that incorporate a similar range of interrelated elements and there are nonroutine contributions by each of FP and USSub, then the most reliable measure of the arm's length price for the wristwatches may be the residual profit split method. The analysis would take into account routine and nonroutine contributions by USSub and FP in order to determine an appropriate allocation of the combined operating profits from the sale of the wristwatches and related activities.

Example 3. (i) *Facts.* FP, a foreign producer of athletic gear, is the registered holder of the AA trademark in the United States and in other countries. In Year 1, FP licenses to a newly organized U.S. subsidiary, USSub, the exclusive rights to use certain manufacturing and marketing intangibles to manufacture and market athletic gear in the United States under the AA trademark. The license agreement obligates USSub to pay a royalty based on sales of trademarked merchandise. The license agreement also obligates FP and USSub to perform without separate compensation specified types and levels of marketing activities. In Year 1, USSub manufactures and sells athletic gear under the AA trademark in the United States.

(ii) The consideration for FP's and USSub's respective marketing activities is embedded in the contractual terms of the license for the AA trademark. Accordingly, pursuant to paragraph (f)(4)(i) of this section, ordinarily no separate allocation would be appropriate with respect to the embedded contributions in Year 1. See § 1.482-9(m)(4).

(iii) Whether an allocation is warranted with respect to the royalty under the license agreement would be analyzed under § 1.482-1 and this section through § 1.482-6. The comparability analysis would include consideration of all relevant factors, such as the term and geographical exclusivity of the license, the nature of the intangibles subject to the license, and the nature of the marketing activities required to be undertaken pursuant to the license. Pursuant to paragraph (f)(4)(i) of this section, the analysis would also take into account the fact that the compensation for the marketing services is embedded in the royalty for the AA trademark, rather than provided for in a separate services agreement. If it is not possible to identify uncontrolled transactions that incorporate a similar range of interrelated elements and there are nonroutine contributions by each of FP and USSub, then the most reliable measure of the arm's length royalty for the AA trademark may be the residual profit split method. The analysis would take into account routine and nonroutine contributions by USSub and FP in order to determine an appropriate allocation of the combined operating profits from the sale of the AA trademarked merchandise and related activities.

Example 4. (i) *Facts.* The Year 1 facts are the same as in *Example 3*, with the following exceptions. In Year 2, USSub undertakes certain incremental marketing activities, in addition to those required by the contractual terms of the license for the AA trademark. The parties do not execute a separate agreement with respect to the incremental marketing activities performed by USSub. The license agreement executed in Year 1 is of sufficient duration that it is reasonable to anticipate that USSub will obtain the benefit of its incremental activities, in the form of increased sales or revenues of trademarked products in the U.S. market.

(ii) To the extent that it was reasonable to anticipate that USSub's incremental marketing activities would increase the value only of USSub's intangible (that is, USSub's license to use the AA trademark for a specified term), and not the value of the AA trademark owned by FP, USSub's incremental activities do not constitute a contribution for which an allocation is warranted under paragraph (f)(4)(i) of this section.

Example 5. (i) *Facts.* The Year 1 facts are the same as in *Example 3*. In Year 2, FP and USSub enter into a separate services agreement that obligates USSub to perform certain incremental marketing activities to promote AA trademark athletic gear in the United States, beyond the activities specified in license agreement. In Year 2, USSub begins to perform these incremental activities, pursuant to the separate services agreement with FP.

(ii) Whether an allocation is warranted with respect to USSub's incremental marketing activities covered by the separate services agreement would be evaluated under §§ 1.482-1 and 1.482-9, including a comparison of the compensation provided for the services with the results obtained under a method pursuant to § 1.482-9, selected and applied in accordance with the best method rule of § 1.482-1(c).

(iii) Whether an allocation is warranted with respect to the royalty under the license agreement is determined under § 1.482-1 and this section through § 1.482-6. The comparability analysis would include consideration of all relevant factors, such as the term and geographical exclusivity of the license, the nature of the intangibles subject to the license, and the nature of the marketing activities required to be undertaken pursuant to the license. The comparability analysis would take into account that the compensation for the incremental activities by USSub is provided for in the separate services agreement, rather than embedded in the royalty for the AA trademark. If it is not possible to identify uncontrolled transactions that incorporate a similar range of interrelated elements and there are nonroutine contributions by each of FP and USSub, then the most reliable measure of the arm's length royalty for the AA trademark may be the residual profit split method. The analysis would take into account routine and nonroutine contributions by USSub and FP in order to determine an appropriate allocation of the combined operating profits from the sale of the AA trademarked merchandise and related activities.

Example 6. (i) *Facts.* The Year 1 facts are the same as in *Example 3*. In Year 2, FP and USSub enter into a separate services agreement that obligates FP to perform incremental marketing activities by advertising AA trademarked athletic gear in selected international sporting events, such as the Olympics and the soccer World Cup. FP's corporate advertising department develops and coordinates these special promotions. The separate services agreement obligates USSub to pay an amount to FP for the benefit to USSub that may reasonably be anticipated as the result of FP's incremental activities. The separate services agreement is not a qualified cost sharing arrangement under § 1.482-7. FP begins to perform the incremental activities in Year 2 pursuant to the separate services agreement.

(ii) Whether an allocation is warranted with respect to the incremental marketing activities performed by FP under the separate services agreement would be evaluated under § 1.482-9. Under the circumstances, it is reasonable to anticipate that FP's activities would increase the value of USSub's license as well as the value of FP's trademark. Accordingly, the incremental activities by FP may constitute in part a controlled services transaction for which USSub must compensate FP. The analysis of whether an allocation is warranted would include a comparison of the compensation provided for the services with the results obtained under a method pursuant to § 1.482-9, selected and applied in accordance with the best method rule of § 1.482-1(c).

(iii) Whether an allocation is appropriate with respect to the royalty under the license agreement would be evaluated under § 1.482-1 and this section through § 1.482-6. The comparability analysis would include consideration of all relevant factors, such as the term and geographical exclusivity of USSub's license, the nature of the intangibles subject to the license, and the marketing activities required to be undertaken by both FP and USSub pursuant to the license. This comparability analysis would take into account that the compensation for the incremental activities performed by FP was provided for in the separate services agreement, rather than embedded in the royalty for the AA trademark. If it is not possible to identify uncontrolled transactions that incorporate a similar range of interrelated elements and there are nonroutine contributions by each of FP and USSub, then the most reliable measure of the arm's length royalty for the AA trademark may be the residual profit split method. The analysis would take into account routine and nonroutine contributions by USSub and FP in order to determine an appropriate allocation of the combined operating profits from the sale of the AA trademarked merchandise and related activities.

* * *

[Prop. Reg. § 1.482-4.]

[Proposed 9-10-2003.]

§ 1.482-5. Comparable profits method.—(a) *In general.*—The comparable profits method evaluates whether the amount charged in a controlled transaction is arm's length based on objective measures of profitability (profit level indicators) derived from uncontrolled taxpayers that engage in similar business activities under similar circumstances.

(b) *Determination of arm's length result.*—(1) *In general.*—Under the comparable profits method, the determination of an arm's length result is based on the amount of operating profit that the tested party would have earned on related party transactions if its profit level indicator were equal to that of an uncontrolled comparable (comparable operating profit). Comparable operating profit is calculated by determining a profit level indicator for an uncontrolled comparable, and applying the profit level indicator to the financial data related to the tested party's most narrowly identifiable business activity for which data incorporating the controlled transaction is available (relevant business activity). To the extent possible, profit level indicators should be applied solely to the tested party's financial data that is related to controlled transactions. The tested party's reported operating profit is compared to the comparable operating profits derived from the profit level indicators of uncontrolled comparables to determine whether the reported operating profit represents an arm's length result.

(2) *Tested party.*—(i) *In general.*—For purposes of this section, the tested party will be the participant in the controlled transaction whose operating profit attributable to the controlled transactions can be verified using the most reliable data and requiring the fewest and most reliable adjustments, and for which reliable data regarding uncontrolled comparables can be located. Consequently, in most cases the tested party will be the least complex of the controlled taxpayers and will not own valuable intangible property or unique assets that distinguish it from potential uncontrolled comparables.

(ii) *Adjustments for tested party.*—The tested party's operating profit must first be adjusted to reflect all other allocations under section 482, other than adjustments pursuant to this section.

(3) *Arm's length range.*—See § 1.482-1(e)(2) for the determination of the arm's length range. For purposes of the comparable profits method, the arm's length range will be established using comparable operating profits derived from a single profit level indicator.

(4) *Profit level indicators.*—Profit level indicators are ratios that measure relationships between profits and costs incurred or resources employed. A variety of profit level indicators can be calculated in any given case. Whether use of a particular profit level indicator is appropriate depends upon a number of factors, including the nature of the activities of the tested party, the reliability of the available data with respect to uncontrolled comparables, and the extent to which the profit level indicator is likely to produce a reliable measure of the income that the tested party would have earned had it dealt with controlled taxpayers at arm's length, taking into account all of the facts and circumstances. The profit level indicators should be derived from a sufficient number of years of data to reasonably measure returns that accrue to uncontrolled comparables. Generally, such a period should encompass at least the taxable year under review and the preceding two taxable years. This analysis must be applied in accordance with § 1.482-1(f)(2)(iii)(D). Profit level indicators that may provide a reliable basis for comparing operating profits of the tested party and uncontrolled comparables include the following—

(i) *Rate of return on capital employed.*—The rate of return on capital employed is the ratio of operating profit to operating assets. The reliability of this profit level indicator increases as operating assets play a greater role in generating operating profits for both the tested party and the uncontrolled comparable. In addition, reliability under this profit level indicator depends on the extent to which the composition of the tested party's assets is similar to that of the uncontrolled comparable. Finally, difficulties in properly valuing operating assets will diminish the reliability of this profit level indicator.

(ii) *Financial ratios.*—Financial ratios measure relationships between profit and costs or sales revenue. Since functional differences generally have a greater effect on the relationship between profit and costs or sales revenue than the relationship between profit and operating assets, financial ratios are more sensitive to functional differences than the rate of return on capital employed. Therefore, closer functional comparability normally is required under a financial ratio than under the rate of return on capital employed to achieve a similarly reliable measure of an arm's length result. Financial ratios that may be appropriate include the following—

(A) Ratio of operating profit to sales; and

(B) Ratio of gross profit to operating expenses.

Reliability under this profit level indicator also depends on the extent to which the composition of the tested party's operating expenses is similar to that of the uncontrolled comparables.

(iii) *Other profit level indicators.*—Other profit level indicators not described in this paragraph (b)(4) may be used if they provide reliable measures of the income that the tested party would have earned had it dealt with controlled taxpayers at arm's length. However, profit level indicators based solely on internal data may not be used under this paragraph (b)(4) because they are not objective measures of profitability derived from operations of uncontrolled taxpayers engaged in similar business activities under similar circumstances.

(c) *Comparability and reliability considerations.*—(1) *In general.*—Whether results derived from application of this method are the most reliable measure of the arm's length result must be determined using the factors described under the best method rule in § 1.482-1(c).

(2) *Comparability.*—(i) *In general.*—The degree of comparability between an uncontrolled taxpayer and the tested party is determined by applying the provisions of § 1.482-1(d)(2). The comparable profits method compares the profitability of the tested party, measured by a profit level indicator (generally based on operating profit), to the profitability of uncontrolled taxpayers in similar circumstances. As with all methods that rely on external market benchmarks, the greater the degree of comparability between the tested party and the uncontrolled taxpayer, the more reliable will be the results derived from the application of this method. The determination of the degree of comparability between the tested party and the uncontrolled taxpayer depends upon all the relevant facts and circumstances, including the relevant lines of business, the product or service markets involved, the asset composition employed (including the nature and quantity of tangible assets, intangible assets and working capital), the size and scope of operations, and the stage in a business or product cycle.

(ii) *Functional, risk and resource comparability.*—An operating profit represents a return for the investment of resources and assumption of risks. Therefore, although all of the factors described in § 1.482-1(d)(3) must be considered, comparability under this method is particularly dependent on resources employed and risks assumed. Moreover, because resources and risks usually are directly related to functions performed, it is also important to consider functions performed in determining the degree of comparability between the tested party and an uncontrolled taxpayer. The degree of functional comparability required to obtain a reliable result under the comparable profits method, however, is generally less than that required under the resale price or cost plus methods. For example, because differences in functions performed often are reflected in operating expenses, taxpayers performing different functions may have very different gross profit margins but earn similar levels of operating profit.

(iii) *Other comparability factors.*—Other factors listed in § 1.482-1(d)(3) also may be particularly relevant under the comparable profits method. Because operating profit usually is less sensitive than gross profit to product differences, reliability under the comparable profits method is not as dependent on product similarity as the resale price or cost plus method. However, the reliability of profitability measures based on operating profit may be adversely affected by factors that have less effect on results under the comparable uncontrolled price, resale price, and cost plus methods. For example, operating profit may be affected by varying cost structures (as reflected, for example, in the age of plant and equipment), differences in business experience (such as whether the business is in a start-up phase or is mature), or differences in management efficiency (as indicated, for example, by objective evidence such as expanding or contracting sales or executive compensation over time). Accordingly, if material differences in these factors are identified based on objective evidence, the reliability of the analysis may be affected.

(iv) *Adjustments for the differences between the tested party and the uncontrolled taxpayers.*—If there are differences between the tested party and an uncontrolled comparable

Reg. § 1.482-5(c)(2)(iv)

that would materially affect the profits determined under the relevant profit level indicator, adjustments should be made according to the comparability provisions of § 1.482-1(d)(2). In some cases, the assets of an uncontrolled comparable may need to be adjusted to achieve greater comparability between the tested party and the uncontrolled comparable. In such cases, the uncontrolled comparable's operating income attributable to those assets must also be adjusted before computing a profit level indicator in order to reflect the income and expense attributable to the adjusted assets. In certain cases it may also be appropriate to adjust the operating profit of the tested party and comparable parties. For example, where there are material differences in accounts payable among the comparable parties and the tested party, it will generally be appropriate to adjust the operating profit of each party by increasing it to reflect an imputed interest charge on each party's accounts payable. As another example, it may be appropriate to adjust the operating profit of a party to account for material differences in the utilization of or accounting for stock-based compensation (as defined by § 1.482-7(d)(2)(i)) among the tested party and comparable parties.

(3) *Data and assumptions.*—(i) *In general.*—The reliability of the results derived from the comparable profits method is affected by the quality of the data and assumptions used to apply this method.

(ii) *Consistency in accounting.*—The degree of consistency in accounting practices between the controlled transaction and the uncontrolled comparables that materially affect operating profit affects the reliability of the result. Thus, for example, if differences in inventory and other cost accounting practices would materially affect operating profit, the ability to make reliable adjustments for such differences would affect the reliability of the results.

(iii) *Allocations between the relevant business activity and other activities.*—The reliability of the allocation of costs, income, and assets between the relevant business activity and other activities of the tested party or an uncontrolled comparable will affect the reliability of the determination of operating profit and profit level indicators. If it is not possible to allocate costs, income, and assets directly based on factual relationships, a reasonable allocation formula may be used. To the extent direct allocations are not made, the reliability of the results derived from the application of this method is reduced relative to the results of a method that requires fewer allocations of costs, income, and assets. Similarly, the reliability of the results derived from the application of this method is affected by the extent to which it is possible to apply the profit level indicator to the tested party's financial data that is related solely to the controlled transactions. For example, if the relevant business activity is the assembly of components purchased from both controlled and uncontrolled suppliers, it may not be possible to apply the profit level indicator solely to financial data related to the controlled transactions. In such a case, the reliability of the results derived from the application of this method will be reduced.

(d) *Definitions.*—The definitions set forth in paragraphs (d)(1) through (6) of this section apply for purposes of this section.

(1) *Sales revenue* means the amount of the total receipts from sale of goods and provision of services, less returns and allowances. Accounting principles and conventions that are generally accepted in the trade or industry of the controlled taxpayer under review must be used.

(2) *Gross profit* means sales revenue less cost of goods sold.

(3) *Operating expenses* includes all expenses not included in cost of goods sold except for interest expense, foreign income taxes (as defined in § 1.901-2(a)), domestic income taxes, and any other expenses not related to the operation of the relevant business activity. Operating expenses ordinarily include expenses associated with advertising, promotion, sales, marketing, warehousing and distribution, administration, and a reasonable allowance for depreciation and amortization.

(4) *Operating profit* means gross profit less operating expenses. Operating profit includes all income derived from the business activity being evaluated by the comparable profits method, but does not include interest and dividends, income derived from activities not being tested by this method, or extraordinary gains and losses that do not relate to the continuing operations of the tested party.

(5) *Reported operating profit* means the operating profit of the tested party reflected on a timely filed U.S. income tax return. If the tested party files a U.S. income tax return, its operating profit is considered reflected on a U.S. income tax return if the calculation of taxable income on its return for the taxable year takes into account the income attributable to the controlled transaction under review. If the tested party does not file a U.S. income tax return, its operating profit is considered reflected on a U.S. income tax return in any taxable year for which income attributable to the controlled transaction under review affects the calculation of the U.S. taxable income of any other member of the same controlled group. If the comparable operating profit of the tested party is

determined from profit level indicators derived from financial statements or other accounting records and reports of comparable parties, adjustments may be made to the reported operating profit of the tested party in order to account for material differences between the tested party's operating profit reported for U.S. income tax purposes and the tested party's operating profit for financial statement purposes. In addition, in accordance with § 1.482-1(f)(2)(iii)(D), adjustments under section 482 that are finally determined may be taken into account in determining reported operating profit.

(6) *Operating assets.*—The term operating assets means the value of all assets used in the relevant business activity of the tested party, including fixed assets and current assets (such as cash, cash equivalents, accounts receivable, and inventories). The term does not include investments in subsidiaries, excess cash, and portfolio investments. Operating assets may be measured by their net book value or by their fair market value, provided that the same method is consistently applied to the tested party and the comparable parties, and consistently applied from year to year. In addition, it may be necessary to take into account recent acquisitions, leased assets, intangibles, currency fluctuations, and other items that may not be explicitly recorded in the financial statements of the tested party or uncontrolled comparable. Finally, operating assets must be measured by the average of the values for the beginning of the year and the end of the year, unless substantial fluctuations in the value of operating assets during the year make this an inaccurate measure of the average value over the year. In such a case, a more accurate measure of the average value of operating assets must be applied.

(e) *Examples.*—The following examples illustrate the application of this section.

Example 1—Transfer of tangible property resulting in no adjustment. (i) FP is a publicly traded foreign corporation with a U.S. subsidiary, USSub, that is under audit for its 1996 taxable year. FP manufactures a consumer product for worldwide distribution. USSub imports the assembled product and distributes it within the United States at the wholesale level under the FP name.

(ii) FP does not allow uncontrolled taxpayers to distribute the product. Similar products are produced by other companies but none of them is sold to uncontrolled taxpayers or to uncontrolled distributors.

(iii) Based on all the facts and circumstances, the district director determines that the comparable profits method will provide the most reliable measure of an arm's length result. USSub is selected as the tested party because it engages in activities that are less complex than those undertaken by FP. There is data from a number of independent operators of wholesale distribution businesses. These potential comparables are further narrowed to select companies in the same industry segment that perform similar functions and bear similar risks to USSub. An analysis of the information available on these taxpayers shows that the ratio of operating profit to sales is the most appropriate profit level indicator, and this ratio is relatively stable where at least three years are included in the average. For the taxable years 1994 through 1996, USSub shows the following results:

	1994	1995	1996	Average
Sales	500,000	560,000	500,000	520,000
Cost of Goods Sold	393,000	412,400	400,000	401,800
Operating Expenses	80,000	110,000	104,600	98,200
Operating Profit	27,000	37,600	(4,600)	20,000

(iv) After adjustments have been made to account for identified material differences between USSub and the uncontrolled distributors, the average ratio of operating profit to sales is calculated for each of the uncontrolled distributors. Applying each ratio to USSub would lead to the following comparable operating profit (COP) for USSub:

Uncontrolled Distributor	OP/S	USSub COP
A	1.7%	$8,840
B	3.1%	16,120
C	3.8%	19,760
D	4.5%	23,400
E	4.7%	24,440
F	4.8%	24,960
G	4.9%	25,480
H	6.7%	34,840
I	9.9%	51,480
J	10.5%	54,600

(v) The data is not sufficiently complete to conclude that it is likely that all material differences between USSub and the uncontrolled distributors have been identified. Therefore, an

Reg. § 1.482-5(e)

arm's length range can be established only pursuant to § 1.482-1(e)(2)(iii)(B). The district director measures the arm's length range by the interquartile range of results, which consists of the results ranging from $19,760 to $34,840. Although USSub's operating income for 1996 shows a loss of $4,600, the district director determines that no allocation should be made, because USSub's average reported operating profit of $20,000 is within this range.

	1994
Sales	500,000
Cost of Goods Sold	370,000
Operating Expenses	110,000
Operating Profit	20,000

(ii) The interquartile range of comparable operating profits remains the same as derived in *Example 1*: $19,760 to $34,840. USSub's average operating profit for the years 1994 through 1996 ($0) falls outside this range. Therefore, the district director determines that an allocation may be appropriate.

Uncontrolled Distributor
C
D
E
A
F
B
J
I
H
G

(iv) Based on these results, the median of the comparable operating profits for 1996 is $14,250. Therefore, USSub's income for 1996 is increased by $24,250, the difference between USSub's reported operating profit for 1996 and the median of the comparable operating profits for 1996.

	1995
Sales	560,000
Cost of Goods Sold	460,000
Operating Expenses	110,000
Operating Profit	(10,000)

(ii) The interquartile range of comparable operating profits, based on average results from the uncontrolled comparables and average sales for USSub for the years 1995 through 1997, ranges from $15,500 to $30,000. In determining whether an allocation for the 1997 taxable year may be made, the district director compares USSub's average reported operating profit for the years 1995 through 1997 to the interquartile range of average comparable operating profits over this period. USSub's average reported operating profit is determined without regard to the adjustment made with respect to the 1996 taxable year. See § 1.482-1(f)(2)(iii)(D). Therefore, USSub's average reported operating profit for the years 1995

Example 2—Transfer of tangible property resulting in adjustment. (i) The facts are the same as in *Example 1* except that USSub reported the following income and expenses:

	1995	1996	Average
	560,000	500,000	520,000
	460,000	400,000	410,000
	110,000	110,000	110,000
	(10,000)	(10,000)	0

(iii) To determine the amount, if any, of the allocation, the district director compares USSub's reported operating profit for 1996 to comparable operating profits derived from the uncontrolled distributors' results for 1996. The ratio of operating profit to sales in 1996 is calculated for each of the uncontrolled comparables and applied to USSub's 1996 sales to derive the following results:

OP/S	USSub COP
0.5%	$ 2,500
1.5%	7,500
2.0%	10,000
1.6%	13,000
2.8%	14,000
2.9%	14,500
3.0%	15,000
4.4%	22,000
6.9%	34,500
7.4%	37,000

Example 3—Multiple year analysis. (i) The facts are the same as in *Example 2*. In addition, the district director examines the taxpayer's results for the 1997 taxable year. As in *Example 2*, the district director increases USSub's income for the 1996 taxable year by $24,250. The results for the 1997 taxable year, together with the 1995 and 1996 taxable years, are as follows:

1996	1997	Average
500,000	530,000	530,000
400,000	430,000	430,000
110,000	110,000	110,000
(10,000)	(10,000)	(10,000)

through 1997 is ($10,000). Because this amount of income falls outside the interquartile range, the district director determines that an allocation may be appropriate.

(iii) To determine the amount, if any, of the allocation for the 1997 taxable year, the district director compares USSub's reported operating profit for 1997 to the median of the comparable operating profits derived from the uncontrolled distributors' results for 1997. The median of the comparable operating profits derived from the uncontrolled comparables results for the 1997 taxable year is $12,000. Based on this comparison, the district director increases USSub's 1997 taxable income by $22,000, the difference between the median of the comparable operating profits for the 1997 taxable year and US-Sub's reported operating profit of ($10,000) for the 1997 taxable year.

Example 4—Transfer of intangible to offshore manufacturer. (i) DevCo is a U.S. developer, producer and marketer of widgets. DevCo develops a new "high tech widget" (htw) that is manufactured by its foreign subsidiary ManuCo located in Country H. ManuCo sells the htw to MarkCo (a U.S. subsidiary of DevCo) for distribution and marketing in the United States. The taxable year 1996 is under audit, and the district director examines whether the royalty rate of 5 percent paid by ManuCo to DevCo is an arm's length consideration for the htw technology.

(ii) Based on all the facts and circumstances, the district director determines that the comparable profits method will provide the most reliable measure of an arm's length result. ManuCo is selected as the tested party because it engages in relatively routine manufacturing activities, while DevCo engages in a variety of complex activities using unique and valuable intangibles. Finally, because ManuCo engages in manufacturing activities, it is determined that the ratio of operating profit to operating assets is an appropriate profit level indicator.

(iii) Uncontrolled taxpayers performing similar functions cannot be found in country H. It is determined that data available in countries M and N provides the best match of companies in a similar market performing similar functions and bearing similar risks. Such data is sufficiently complete to identify many of the material differences between ManuCo and the uncontrolled comparables, and to make adjustments to account for such differences. However, data is not sufficiently complete so that it is likely that no material differences remain. In particular, the differences in geographic markets might have materially affected the results of the various companies.

(iv) In a separate analysis, it is determined that the price that ManuCo charged to MarkCo for the htw's is an arm's length price under § 1.482-3(b). Therefore, ManuCo's financial data derived from its sales to MarkCo are reliable. ManuCo's financial data from 1994-1996 is as follows:

	1994	1995	1996	Average
Assets	$24,000	$25,000	$26,000	$25,000
Sales to MarkCo	25,000	30,000	35,000	30,000
Cost of Goods Sold	6,250	7,500	8,750	7,500
Royalty to DevCo (5%)	1,250	1,500	1,750	1,500
Other	5,000	6,000	7,000	6,000
Operating Expenses	1,000	1,000	1,000	1,000
Operating Profit	17,750	21,500	25,250	21,500

(v) Applying the ratios of average operating profit to operating assets for the 1994 through 1996 taxable years derived from a group of similar uncontrolled comparables located in country M and N to Manuco's average operating assets for the same period provides a set of comparable operating profits. The interquartile range for these average comparable operating profits is $3,000 to $4,500. ManuCo's average reported operating profit for the years 1994 through 1996 ($21,500) falls outside this range. Therefore, the district director determines that an allocation may be appropriate for the 1996 taxable year.

(vi) To determine the amount, if any, of the allocation for the 1996 taxable year, the district director compares ManuCo's reported operating profit for 1996 to the median of the comparable operating profits derived from the uncontrolled distributors' results for 1996. The median result for the uncontrolled comparables for 1996 is $3,750. Based on this comparison, the district director increases royalties that ManuCo paid by $21,500 (the difference between $25,250 and the median of the comparable operating profits, $3,750).

Example 5—Adjusting operating assets and operating profit for differences in accounts receivable. (i) USM is a U.S. company that manufactures parts for industrial equipment and sells them to its foreign parent corporation. For purposes of applying the comparable profits method, 15 uncontrolled manufacturers that are similar to USM have been identified.

(ii) USM has a significantly lower level of accounts receivable than the uncontrolled manufacturers. Since the rate of return on capital employed is to be used as the profit level indicator, both operating assets and operating profits must be adjusted to account for this difference. Each uncontrolled comparable's operating assets is reduced by the amount (relative to sales) by which they exceed USM's accounts receivable. Each uncontrolled comparable's operating profit is adjusted by deducting imputed interest income on the excess accounts receivable. This imputed interest income is calculated by multiplying the uncontrolled comparable's excess accounts receivable by an interest rate appropriate for short-term debt.

Example 6—Adjusting operating profit for differences in accounts payable. (i) USD is the U.S. subsidiary of a foreign corporation. USD purchases goods from its foreign parent and sells them in the U.S. market. For purposes of applying the comparable profits method, 10 uncontrolled distributors that are similar to USD have been identified.

(ii) There are significant differences in the level of accounts payable among the uncontrolled distributors and USD. To adjust for these differences, the district director increases the operating profit of the uncontrolled distributors and USD to reflect interest expense imputed to the accounts payable. The imputed interest expense for each company is calculated by multiplying the company's accounts payable by an interest rate appropriate for its short-term debt. [Reg. § 1.482-5.]

☐ [*T.D.* 8552, 7-1-94. *Amended by T.D.* 9088, 8-25-2003.]

§ 1.482-6. Profit split method.—(a) *In general.*—The profit split method evaluates whether the allocation of the combined operating profit or loss attributable to one or more controlled transactions is arm's length by reference to the relative value of each controlled taxpayer's contribution to that combined operating profit or loss. The combined operating profit or loss must be derived from the most narrowly identifiable business activity of the controlled taxpayers for which data is available that includes the controlled transactions (relevant business activity).

(b) *Appropriate share of profits and losses.*—The relative value of each controlled taxpayer's contribution to the success of the relevant business activity must be determined in a manner that reflects the functions performed, risks assumed, and resources employed by each participant in the relevant business activity, consistent with the comparability provisions of § 1.482-1(d)(3). Such an allocation is intended to correspond to the division of profit or loss that would result from an arrangement between uncontrolled taxpayers, each performing functions similar to those of the various controlled taxpayers engaged in the relevant business activity. The profit allocated to any particular member of a controlled group is not necessarily limited to the total operating profit of the group from the relevant business activity. For example, in a given year, one member of the group may earn a profit while another member incurs a loss. In addition, it may not be assumed that the combined operating profit or loss from the relevant business activity should be shared equally, or in any other arbitrary proportion. The specific method of allocation must be determined under paragraph (c) of this section.

(c) *Application.*—(1) *In general.*—The allocation of profit or loss under the profit split method must be made in accordance with one of the following allocation methods—

(i) The comparable profit split, described in paragraph (c)(2) of this section; or

(ii) The residual profit split, described in paragraph (c)(3) of this section.

(2) *Comparable profit split.*—(i) *In general.*—A comparable profit split is derived from the combined operating profit of uncontrolled taxpayers whose transactions and activities are similar to those of the controlled taxpayers in the relevant business activity. Under this method, each uncontrolled taxpayer's percentage of the combined operating profit or loss is used to allocate the combined operating profit or loss of the relevant business activity.

(ii) *Comparability and reliability considerations.*—(A) *In general.*—Whether results derived from application of this method are the most reliable measure of the arm's length result is determined using the factors described under the best method rule in § 1.482-1(c).

(B) *Comparability.*—(1) *In general.*—The degree of comparability between the controlled and uncontrolled taxpayers is determined by applying the comparability provisions of § 1.482-1(d). The comparable profit split compares the division of operating profits among the controlled taxpayers to the division of operating profits among uncontrolled taxpayers engaged in similar activities under similar circumstances. Although all of the factors described in § 1.482-1(d)(3) must be considered, comparability under this method is particularly dependent on the considerations described under the comparable profits method in § 1.482-5(c)(2), because this method is based on a comparison of the operating profit of the controlled and uncontrolled taxpayers. In addition, because the contractual terms of the relationship among the participants in the relevant business activity will be a principal determinant of the allocation of functions and risks among them, comparability under this method also depends particularly on the degree of similarity of the contractual terms of the controlled and uncontrolled taxpayers. Finally, the comparable profit split may not be used if the combined operating profit (as a percentage of the combined assets) of the uncontrolled comparables varies significantly from that earned by the controlled taxpayers.

(2) *Adjustments for differences between the controlled and uncontrolled taxpayers.*—If there are differences between the controlled and uncontrolled taxpayers that would materially affect the division of operating profit, adjustments must be made according to the provisions of § 1.482-1(d)(2).

(C) *Data and assumptions.*—The reliability of the results derived from the comparable profit split is affected by the quality of the data and assumptions used to apply this method. In particular, the following factors must be considered—

(1) The reliability of the allocation of costs, income, and assets between the relevant business activity and the participants' other activities will affect the accuracy of the determination of combined operating profit and its allocation among the participants. If it is not possible to allocate costs, income, and assets directly based on factual relationships, a reasonable allocation formula may be used. To the extent direct allocations are not made, the reliability of the results derived from the application of this method is reduced relative to the results of a method that requires fewer allocations of costs, income, and assets. Similarly, the reliability of the results derived from the application of this method is affected by the extent to which it is possible to apply the method to the parties' financial data that is related solely to the controlled transactions. For example, if the relevant business activity is the assembly of components purchased from both controlled and uncontrolled suppliers, it may not be possible to apply the method solely to financial data related to the controlled transactions. In such a case, the reliability of the results derived from the application of this method will be reduced.

(2) The degree of consistency between the controlled and uncontrolled taxpayers in accounting practices that materially affect the items that determine the amount and allocation of operating profit affects the reliability of the result. Thus, for example, if differences in inventory and other cost accounting practices would materially affect operating profit, the ability to make reliable adjustments for such differences would affect the reliability of the results. Further, accounting consistency among the participants in the controlled transaction is required to ensure that the items determining the amount and allocation of operating profit are measured on a consistent basis.

(D) *Other factors affecting reliability.*—Like the methods described in §§ 1.482-3, 1.482-4, and 1.482-5, the comparable profit split relies exclusively on external market benchmarks. As indicated in § 1.482-1(c)(2)(i), as the degree of comparability between the controlled and uncontrolled transactions increases, the relative weight accorded the analysis under this method will increase. In addition, the reliability of the analysis under this method may be enhanced by the fact that all parties to the controlled transaction are evaluated under the comparable profit split. However, the reliability of the results of an analysis based on information from all parties to a transaction is affected by the reliability of the data and the assumptions pertaining to each party to the controlled transaction. Thus, if the data and assumptions are significantly more reliable with respect to one of the parties than with respect to the others, a different method, focusing solely on the results of that party, may yield more reliable results.

(3) *Residual profit split.*—(i) *In general.*—Under this method, the combined operating profit or loss from the relevant business activity is allocated between the controlled taxpayers following the two-step process set forth in paragraphs (c)(3)(i)(A) and (B) of this section.

(A) *Allocate income to routine contributions.*—The first step allocates operating income to each party to the controlled transactions to provide a market return for its routine contributions to the relevant business activity. Routine contributions are contributions of the same or a similar kind to those made by uncontrolled taxpayers involved in similar business activities for which it is possible to identify market returns. Routine contributions ordinarily include contributions of tangible property, services and intangibles that are generally owned by uncontrolled taxpayers engaged in similar activities. A functional analysis is required to identify these contributions according to the functions performed, risks assumed, and resources employed by each of the controlled taxpayers. Market returns for the routine contributions should be determined by reference to the returns achieved by uncontrolled taxpayers engaged in similar activities, consistent with the methods described in §§ 1.482-3, 1.482-4 and 1.482-5.

(B) *Allocate residual profit.*—The allocation of income to the controlled taxpayers' routine contributions will not reflect profits attributable to the controlled group's valuable intangible property where similar property is not owned by the uncontrolled taxpayers from which the market returns are derived. Thus, in cases where such intangibles are present there normally will be an unallocated residual profit after the allocation of income described in paragraph (c)(3)(i)(A) of this section. Under this second step, the residual profit generally should be divided among the controlled taxpayers based upon the relative value of their contributions of intangible property to the relevant business activity that was not accounted for as a routine contribution. The relative value of the intangible property contributed by each taxpayer may be measured by external market benchmarks that reflect the fair market value of such intangible property. Alternatively, the relative value of intangible contributions may be estimated by the capitalized cost of develop-

Reg. § 1.482-6(c)(3)(i)(B)

ing the intangibles and all related improvements and updates, less an appropriate amount of amortization based on the useful life of each intangible. Finally, if the intangible development expenditures of the parties are relatively constant over time and the useful life of the intangible property of all parties is approximately the same, the amount of actual expenditures in recent years may be used to estimate the relative value of intangible contributions. If the intangible property contributed by one of the controlled taxpayers is also used in other business activities (such as transactions with other controlled taxpayers), an appropriate allocation of the value of the intangibles must be made among all the business activities in which it is used.

(ii) *Comparability and reliability considerations.*—(A) *In general.*—Whether results derived from this method are the most reliable measure of the arm's length result is determined using the factors described under the best method rule in § 1.482-1(c). Thus, comparability and the quality of data and assumptions must be considered in determining whether this method provides the most reliable measure of an arm's length result. The application of these factors to the residual profit split is discussed in paragraph (c)(3)(ii)(B), (C), and (D) of this section.

(B) *Comparability.*—The first step of the residual profit split relies on market benchmarks of profitability. Thus, the comparability considerations that are relevant for the first step of the residual profit split are those that are relevant for the methods that are used to determine market returns for the routine contributions. The second step of the residual profit split, however, may not rely so directly on market benchmarks. Thus, the reliability of the results under this method is reduced to the extent that the allocation of profits in the second step does not rely on market benchmarks.

(C) *Data and assumptions.*—The reliability of the results derived from the residual profit split is affected by the quality of the data and assumptions used to apply this method. In particular, the following factors must be considered—

(*1*) The reliability of the allocation of costs, income, and assets as described in paragraph (c)(2)(ii)(C)(*1*) of this section;

(*2*) Accounting consistency as described in paragraph (c)(2)(ii)(C)(*2*) of this section;

(*3*) The reliability of the data used and the assumptions made in valuing the intangible property contributed by the participants. In particular, if capitalized costs of development are used to estimate the value of intangible property, the reliability of the results is reduced relative to the reliability of other methods that do not require such an estimate, for the following reasons. First, in any given case, the costs of developing the intangible may not be related to its market value. Second, the calculation of the capitalized costs of development may require the allocation of indirect costs between the relevant business activity and the controlled taxpayer's other activities, which may affect the reliability of the analysis. Finally, the calculation of costs may require assumptions regarding the useful life of the intangible property.

(D) *Other factors affecting reliability.*—Like the methods described in §§ 1.482-3, 1.482-4, and 1.482-5, the first step of the residual profit split relies exclusively on external market benchmarks. As indicated in § 1.482-1(c)(2)(i), as the degree of comparability between the controlled and uncontrolled transactions increases, the relative weight accorded the analysis under this method will increase. In addition, to the extent the allocation of profits in the second step is not based on external market benchmarks, the reliability of the analysis will be decreased in relation to an analysis under a method that relies on market benchmarks. Finally, the reliability of the analysis under this method may be enhanced by the fact that all parties to the controlled transaction are evaluated under the residual profit split. However, the reliability of the results of an analysis based on information from all parties to a transaction is affected by the reliability of the data and the assumptions pertaining to each party to the controlled transaction. Thus, if the data and assumptions are significantly more reliable with respect to one of the parties than with respect to the others, a different method, focusing solely on the results of that party, may yield more reliable results.

(iii) *Example.*—The provisions of this paragraph (c)(3) are illustrated by the following example.

Example—Application of Residual Profit Split. (i) XYZ is a U.S. corporation that develops, manufactures and markets a line of products for police use in the United States. XYZ's research unit developed a bulletproof material for use in protective clothing and headgear (Nulon). XYZ obtains patent protection for the chemical formula for Nulon. Since its introduction in the U.S., Nulon has captured a substantial share of the U.S. market for bulletproof material.

(ii) XYZ licensed its European subsidiary, XYZ-Europe, to manufacture and market Nulon in Europe. XYZ-Europe is a well-established company that manufactures and markets

XYZ products in Europe. XYZ-Europe has a research unit that adapts XYZ products for the defense market, as well as a well-developed marketing network that employs brand names that it developed.

(iii) XYZ-Europe's research unit alters Nulon to adapt it to military specifications and develops a high-intensity marketing campaign directed at the defense industry in several European countries. Beginning with the 1995 taxable year, XYZ-Europe manufactures and sells Nulon in Europe through its marketing network under one of its brand names.

(iv) For the 1995 taxable year, XYZ has no direct expenses associated with the license of Nulon to XYZ-Europe and incurs no expenses related to the marketing of Nulon in Europe. For the 1995 taxable year, XYZ-Europe's Nulon sales and pre-royalty expenses are $500 million and $300 million, respectively, resulting in net pre-royalty profit of $200 million related to the Nulon business. The operating assets employed in XYZ-Europe's Nulon business are $200 million. Given the facts and circumstances, the district director determines under the best method rule that a residual profit split will provide the most reliable measure of an arm's length result. Based on an examination of a sample of European companies performing functions similar to those of XYZ-Europe, the district director determines that an average market return on XYZ-Europe's operating assets in the Nulon business is 10 percent, resulting in a market return of $20 million (10% × $200 million) for XYZ-Europe's Nulon business, and a residual profit of $180 million.

(v) Since the first stage of the residual profit split allocated profits to XYZ-Europe's contributions other than those attributable to highly valuable intangible property, it is assumed that the residual profit of $180 million is attributable to the valuable intangibles related to Nulon, i.e., the European brand name for Nulon and the Nulon formula (including XYZ-Europe's modifications). To estimate the relative values of these intangibles, the district director compares the ratios of the capitalized value of expenditures as of 1995 on Nulon-related research and development and marketing over the 1995 sales related to such expenditures.

(vi) Because XYZ's protective product research and development expenses support the worldwide protective product sales of the XYZ group, it is necessary to allocate such expenses among the worldwide business activities to which they relate. The district director determines that it is reasonable to allocate the value of these expenses based on worldwide protective product sales. Using information on the average useful life of its investments in protective product research and development, the district director capitalizes and amortizes XYZ's protective product research and development expenses. This analysis indicates that the capitalized research and development expenditures have a value of $0.20 per dollar of global protective product sales in 1995.

(vii) XYZ-Europe's expenditures on Nulon research and development and marketing support only its sales in Europe. Using information on the average useful life of XYZ-Europe's investments in marketing and research and development, the district director capitalizes and amortizes XYZ-Europe's expenditures and determines that they have a value in 1995 of $0.40 per dollar of XYZ-Europe's Nulon sales.

(viii) Thus, XYZ and XYZ-Europe together contributed $0.60 in capitalized intangible development expenses for each dollar of XYZ-Europe's protective product sales for 1995, of which XYZ contributed one-third (or $0.20 per dollar of sales). Accordingly, the district director determines that an arm's length royalty for the Nulon license for the 1995 taxable year is $60 million, i.e., one-third of XYZ-Europe's $180 million in residual Nulon profit. [Reg. § 1.482-6.]

☐ [*T.D.* 8552, 7-1-94.]

Proposed Amendments to Regulation

☐ Section 1.482-6 is amended by:

1. Revising the third sentence in paragraph (c)(2)(ii)(B)(*1*), the first sentence in paragraph (c)(2)(ii)(D), the last sentence in paragraph (c)(3)(i)(A) and the first sentence in paragraph (c)(3)(ii)(D).

2. Revising paragraph (c)(3)(i)(B).

The revisions read as follows:

§ 1.482-6. Profit split method.

* * *

(c) * * *

  (2) * * *

    (ii) * * *

      (B) * * * (*1*) * * * Although all of the factors described in § 1.482-1(d)(3) must be considered, comparability under this method is particularly dependent on the considerations described under the comparable profits method in § 1.482-5(c)(2) or § 1.482-9(e)(2)(iii), because this method is based on a comparison of the operating profit of the controlled and uncontrolled taxpayers. * * *

* * *

      (D) *Other factors affecting reliability.*—Like the methods described in §§ 1.482-3, 1.482-4, 1.482-5 and 1.482-9, the comparable profit split relies exclusively on external market benchmarks. * * *

* * *

Prop. Reg. § 1.482-6(c)(2)(ii)(D)

(3) *** (i) ***

(A) *** Market returns for the routine contributions should be determined by reference to the returns achieved by uncontrolled taxpayers engaged in similar activities, consistent with the methods described in §§ 1.482-3, 1.482-4, 1.482-5 and 1.482-9.

(B) *Allocate residual profit.*—(1) *Nonroutine contributions generally.*—The allocation of income to the controlled taxpayer's routine contributions will not reflect profits attributable to each controlled taxpayer's contributions to the relevant business activity that are not routine (nonroutine contributions). A nonroutine contribution is a contribution that cannot be fully accounted for by reference to market returns, or that is so interrelated with other transactions that it cannot be reliably evaluated on a separate basis. Thus, in cases where such nonroutine contributions are present there normally will be an unallocated residual profit after the allocation of income described in paragraph (c)(3)(i)(A) of this section. Under this second step, the residual profit generally should be divided among the controlled taxpayers based upon the relative value of their nonroutine contributions to the relevant business activity. The relative value of the nonroutine contributions of each taxpayer should be measured in a manner that most reliably reflects each nonroutine contribution made to the controlled transaction and each controlled taxpayer's role in the nonroutine contributions. If the nonroutine contribution by one of the controlled taxpayers is also used in other business activities (such as transactions with other controlled taxpayers), an appropriate allocation of the value of the nonroutine contribution must be made among all the business activities in which it is used.

(2) *Nonroutine contributions of intangible property.*—In many cases, nonroutine contributions of a taxpayer to the relevant business activity may be contributions of intangible property. For purposes of paragraph (c)(3)(i)(B)(*1*) of this section, the relative value of nonroutine intangible property contributed by taxpayers may be measured by external market benchmarks that reflect the fair market value of such intangible property. Alternatively, the relative value of nonroutine intangible property contributions may be estimated by the capitalized cost of developing the intangible property and all related improvements and updates, less an appropriate amount of amortization based on the useful life of each intangible. Finally, if the intangible development expenditures of the parties are relatively constant over time and the useful life of the intangible property contributed by all parties is approximately the same, the amount of actual expenditures in recent years may be used to estimate the relative value of nonroutine intangible property contributions.

(ii) ***

***

(D) *Other factors affecting reliability.*—Like the methods described in §§ 1.482-3, 1.482-4, 1.482-5 and 1.482-9, the first step of the residual profit split relies exclusively on external market benchmarks. ***

***

[Prop. Reg. § 1.482-6.]

[Proposed 9-10-2003.]

§ 1.482-7. Sharing of costs.—(a) *In general.*—(1) *Scope and application of the rules in this section.*—A cost sharing arrangement is an agreement under which the parties agree to share the costs of development of one or more intangibles in proportion to their shares of reasonably anticipated benefits from their individual exploitation of the interests in the intangibles assigned to them under the arrangement. A taxpayer may claim that a cost sharing arrangement is a qualified cost sharing arrangement only if the agreement meets the requirements of paragraph (b) of this section. Consistent with the rules of § 1.482-1(d)(3)(ii)(B) (Identifying contractual terms), the district director may apply the rules of this section to any arrangement that in substance constitutes a cost sharing arrangement, notwithstanding a failure to comply with any requirement of this section. A qualified cost sharing arrangement, or an arrangement to which the district director applies the rules of this section, will not be treated as a partnership to which the rules of subchapter K apply. See § 301.7701-3(e) of this chapter. Furthermore, a participant that is a foreign corporation or nonresident alien individual will not be treated as engaged in trade or business within the United States solely by reason of its participation in such an arrangement. See generally § 1.864-2(a).

(2) *Limitation on allocations.*—The district director shall not make allocations with respect to a qualified cost sharing arrangement except to the extent necessary to make each controlled participant's share of the costs (as determined under paragraph (d) of this section) of intangible development under the qualified cost sharing arrangement equal to its share of reasonably anticipated benefits attributable to such development, under the rules of this section. If a controlled taxpayer acquires an interest in intangible property from another controlled taxpayer (other than in considera-

tion for bearing a share of the costs of the intangible's development), then the district director may make appropriate allocations to reflect an arm's length consideration for the acquisition of the interest in such intangible under the rules of §§ 1.482-1 and 1.482-4 through 1.482-6. See paragraph (g) of this section. An interest in an intangible includes any commercially transferable interest, the benefits of which are susceptible of valuation. See § 1.482-4(b) for the definition of an intangible.

(3) *Coordination with § 1.482-1.*—A qualified cost sharing arrangement produces results that are consistent with an arm's length result within the meaning of § 1.482-1(b)(1) if, and only if, each controlled participant's share of the costs (as determined under paragraph (d) of this section) of intangible development under the qualified cost sharing arrangement equals its share of reasonably anticipated benefits attributable to such development (as required by paragraph (a)(2) of this section) and all other requirements of this section are satisfied.

(4) *Cross references.*—Paragraph (c) of this section defines participant. Paragraph (d) of this section defines the costs of intangible development. Paragraph (e) of this section defines the anticipated benefits of intangible development. Paragraph (f) of this section provides rules governing cost allocations. Paragraph (g) of this section provides rules governing transfers of intangibles other than in consideration for bearing a share of the costs of the intangible's development. Rules governing the character of payments made pursuant to a qualified cost sharing arrangement are provided in paragraph (h) of this section. Paragraph (i) of this section provides accounting requirements. Paragraph (j) of this section provides administrative requirements. Paragraph (k) of this section provides an effective date. Paragraph (l) provides a transition rule.

(b) *Qualified cost sharing arrangement.*—A qualified cost sharing arrangement must—

(1) Include two or more participants;

(2) Provide a method to calculate each controlled participant's share of intangible development costs, based on factors that can reasonably be expected to reflect that participant's share of anticipated benefits;

(3) Provide for adjustment to the controlled participants' shares of intangible development costs to account for changes in economic conditions, the business operations and practices of the participants, and the ongoing development of intangibles under the arrangement; and

(4) Be recorded in a document that is contemporaneous with the formation (and any revision) of the cost sharing arrangement and that includes—

(i) A list of the arrangement's participants, and any other member of the controlled group that will benefit from the use of intangibles developed under the cost sharing arrangement;

(ii) The information described in paragraphs (b)(2) and (b)(3) of this section;

(iii) A description of the scope of the research and development to be undertaken, including the intangible or class of intangibles intended to be developed;

(iv) A description of each participant's interest in any covered intangibles. A covered intangible is any intangible property that is developed as a result of the research and development undertaken under the cost sharing arrangement (intangible development area);

(v) The duration of the arrangement; and

(vi) The conditions under which the arrangement may be modified or terminated and the consequences of such modification or termination, such as the interest that each participant will receive in any covered intangibles.

(c) *Participant.*—(1) *In general.*—For purposes of this section, a participant is a controlled taxpayer that meets the requirements of this paragraph (c)(1) (controlled participant) or an uncontrolled taxpayer that is a party to the cost sharing arrangement (uncontrolled participant). See § 1.482-1(i)(5) for the definitions of controlled and uncontrolled taxpayers. A controlled taxpayer may be a controlled participant only if it—

(i) Reasonably anticipates that it will derive benefits from the use of covered intangibles;

(ii) Substantially complies with the accounting requirements described in paragraph (i) of this section; and

(iii) Substantially complies with the administrative requirements described in paragraph (j) of this section.

(iv) The following example illustrates paragraph (c)(1)(i) of this section:

Example. Foreign Parent (FP) is a foreign corporation engaged in the extraction of a natural resource. FP has a U.S. subsidiary (USS) to which FP sells supplies of this resource for sale in the United States. FP enters into a cost sharing arrangement with USS to develop a new machine to extract the natural resource. The machine uses a new extraction process that will be patented in the United States and in other countries. The cost sharing arrangement provides that USS will receive the rights to use the machine in the extraction of the natural resource in the United States, and

FP will receive the rights in the rest of the world. This resource does not, however, exist in the United States. Despite the fact that USS has received the right to use this process in the United States, USS is not a qualified participant because it will not derive a benefit from the use of the intangible developed under the cost sharing arrangement.

(2) *Treatment of a controlled taxpayer that is not a controlled participant.*—(i) *In general.*—If a controlled taxpayer that is not a controlled participant (within the meaning of this paragraph (c)) provides assistance in relation to the research and development undertaken in the intangible development area, it must receive consideration from the controlled participants under the rules of § 1.482-4(f)(3)(iii) (Allocations with respect to assistance provided to the owner). For purposes of paragraph (d) of this section, such consideration is treated as an operating expense and each controlled participant must be treated as incurring a share of such consideration equal to its share of reasonably anticipated benefits (as defined in paragraph (f)(3) of this section).

(ii) *Example.*—The following example illustrates this paragraph (c)(2):

Example. (i) U.S. Parent (USP), one foreign subsidiary (FS), and a second foreign subsidiary constituting the group's research arm (R+D) enter into a cost sharing agreement to develop manufacturing intangibles for a new product line A. USP and FS are assigned the exclusive rights to exploit the intangibles respectively in the United States and the rest of the world, where each presently manufactures and sells various existing product lines. R+D is not assigned any rights to exploit the intangibles. R+D's activity consists solely in carrying out research for the group. It is reliably projected that the shares of reasonably anticipated benefits of USP and FS will be 66$\frac{2}{3}$% and 33$\frac{1}{3}$%, respectively, and the parties' agreement provides that USP and FS will reimburse 66$\frac{2}{3}$% and 33$\frac{1}{3}$%, respectively, of the intangible development costs incurred by R+D with respect to the new intangible.

(ii) R+D does not qualify as a controlled participant within the meaning of paragraph (c) of this section, because it will not derive any benefits from the use of covered intangibles. Therefore, R+D is treated as a service provider for purposes of this section and must receive arm's length consideration for the assistance it is deemed to provide to USP and FS, under the rules of § 1.482-4(f)(3)(iii). Such consideration must be treated as intangible development costs incurred by USP and FS in proportion to their shares of reasonably anticipated benefits (i.e., 66$\frac{2}{3}$% and 33$\frac{1}{3}$%, respectively). R+D will not be considered to bear any share of the intangible development costs under the arrangement.

(iii) The Asian rights nominally assigned to R+D under the agreement must be treated as being held by USP and FS in accordance with their shares of the intangible development costs (i.e., 66$\frac{2}{3}$% and 33$\frac{1}{3}$%, respectively). See paragraph (g)(6) of this section. Thus, since under the cost sharing agreement the Asian rights are owned by R+D, the district director may make allocations to reflect an arm's length consideration owed by R+D to USP and FS for these rights under the rules of §§ 1.482-1 and 1.482-4 through 1.482-6.

(3) *Treatment of consolidated group.*—For purposes of this section, all members of the same affiliated group (within the meaning of section 1504(a)) that join in the filing of a consolidated return for the taxable year under section 1501 shall be treated as one taxpayer.

(d) *Costs.*—(1) *Intangible development costs.*—For purposes of this section, a controlled participant's costs of developing intangibles for a taxable year mean all of the costs incurred by that participant related to the intangible development area, plus all of the cost sharing payments it makes to other controlled and uncontrolled participants, minus all of the cost sharing payments it receives from other controlled and uncontrolled participants. Costs incurred related to the intangible development area consist of the following items: operating expenses as defined in § 1.482-5(d)(3), other than depreciation or amortization expense, plus (to the extent not included in such operating expenses, as defined in § 1.482-5(d)(3)) the charge for the use of any tangible property made available to the qualified cost sharing arrangement. If tangible property is made available to the qualified cost sharing arrangement by a controlled participant, the determination of the appropriate charge will be governed by the rules of § 1.482-2(c) (Use of tangible property). Intangible development costs do not include the consideration for the use of any intangible property made available to the qualified cost sharing arrangement. See paragraph (g)(2) of this section. If a particular cost contributes to the intangible development area and other areas or other business activities, the cost must be allocated between the intangible development area and the other areas or business activities on a reasonable basis. In such a case, it is necessary to estimate the total benefits attributable to the cost incurred. The share of such cost allocated to the intangible development area must correspond to covered intangibles' share of the total benefits. Costs that do not contribute to the intangible development area are not taken into account.

(2) *Stock-based compensation.*—(i) *In general.*—For purposes of this section, a controlled participant's operating expenses include all costs attributable to compensation, including stock-based compensation. As used in this section, the term *stock-based compensation* means any compensation provided by a controlled participant to an employee or independent contractor in the form of equity instruments, options to acquire stock (stock options), or rights with respect to (or determined by reference to) equity instruments or stock options, including but not limited to property to which section 83 applies and stock options to which section 421 applies, regardless of whether ultimately settled in the form of cash, stock, or other property.

(ii) *Identification of stock-based compensation related to intangible development.*—The determination of whether stock-based compensation is related to the intangible development area within the meaning of paragraph (d)(1) of this section is made as of the date that the stock-based compensation is granted. Accordingly, all stock-based compensation that is granted during the term of the qualified cost sharing arrangement and is related at date of grant to the development of intangibles covered by the arrangement is included as an intangible development cost under paragraph (d)(1) of this section. In the case of a repricing or other modification of a stock option, the determination of whether the repricing or other modification constitutes the grant of a new stock option for purposes of this paragraph (d)(2)(ii) will be made in accordance with the rules of section 424(h) and related regulations.

(iii) *Measurement and timing of stock-based compensation expense.*—(A) *In general.*—Except as otherwise provided in this paragraph (d)(2)(iii), the operating expense attributable to stock-based compensation is equal to the amount allowable to the controlled participant as a deduction for Federal income tax purposes with respect to that stock-based compensation (for example, under section 83(h)) and is taken into account as an operating expense under this section for the taxable year for which the deduction is allowable.

(1) *Transfers to which section 421 applies.*—Solely for purposes of this paragraph (d)(2)(iii)(A), section 421 does not apply to the transfer of stock pursuant to the exercise of an option that meets the requirements of section 422(a) or 423(a).

(2) *Deductions of foreign controlled participants.*—Solely for purposes of this paragraph (d)(2)(iii)(A), an amount is treated as an allowable deduction of a controlled participant to the extent that a deduction would be allowable to a United States taxpayer.

(3) *Modification of stock option.*—Solely for purposes of this paragraph (d)(2)(iii)(A), if the repricing or other modification of a stock option is determined, under paragraph (d)(2)(ii) of this section, to constitute the grant of a new stock option not related to the development of intangibles, the stock option that is repriced or otherwise modified will be treated as being exercised immediately before the modification, provided that the stock option is then exercisable and the fair market value of the underlying stock then exceeds the price at which the stock option is exercisable. Accordingly, the amount of the deduction that would be allowable (or treated as allowable under this paragraph (d)(2)(iii)(A)) to the controlled participant upon exercise of the stock option immediately before the modification must be taken into account as an operating expense as of the date of the modification.

(4) *Expiration or termination of qualified cost sharing arrangement.*—Solely for purposes of this paragraph (d)(2)(iii)(A), if an item of stock-based compensation related to the development of intangibles is not exercised during the term of a qualified cost sharing arrangement, that item of stock-based compensation will be treated as being exercised immediately before the expiration or termination of the qualified cost sharing arrangement, provided that the stock-based compensation is then exercisable and the fair market value of the underlying stock then exceeds the price at which the stock-based compensation is exercisable. Accordingly, the amount of the deduction that would be allowable (or treated as allowable under this paragraph (d)(2)(iii)(A)) to the controlled participant upon exercise of the stock-based compensation must be taken into account as an operating expense as of the date of the expiration or termination of the qualified cost sharing arrangement.

(B) *Election with respect to options on publicly traded stock.*—(1) *In general.*—With respect to stock-based compensation in the form of options on publicly traded stock, the controlled participants in a qualified cost sharing arrangement may elect to take into account all operating expenses attributable to those stock options in the same amount, and as of the same time, as the fair value of the stock options reflected as a charge against income in audited financial statements or disclosed in footnotes to such financial statements, provided that such statements are prepared in accordance with United States generally accepted accounting principles by or on behalf of the company issuing the publicly traded stock.

(2) Publicly traded stock.—As used in this paragraph (d)(2)(iii)(B), the term *publicly traded stock* means stock that is regularly traded on an established United States securities market and is issued by a company whose financial statements are prepared in accordance with United States generally accepted accounting principles for the taxable year.

(3) Generally accepted accounting principles.—For purposes of this paragraph (d)(2)(iii)(B), a financial statement prepared in accordance with a comprehensive body of generally accepted accounting principles other than United States generally accepted accounting principles is considered to be prepared in accordance with United States generally accepted accounting principles provided that either—

(i) The fair value of the stock options under consideration is reflected in the reconciliation between such other accounting principles and United States generally accepted accounting principles required to be incorporated into the financial statement by the securities laws governing companies whose stock is regularly traded on United States securities markets; or

(ii) In the absence of a reconciliation between such other accounting principles and United States generally accepted accounting principles that reflects the fair value of the stock options under consideration, such other accounting principles require that the fair value of the stock options under consideration be reflected as a charge against income in audited financial statements or disclosed in footnotes to such statements.

(4) Time and manner of making the election.—The election described in this paragraph (d)(2)(iii)(B) is made by an explicit reference to the election in the written cost sharing agreement required by paragraph (b)(4) of this section or in a written amendment to the cost sharing agreement entered into with the consent of the Commissioner pursuant to paragraph (d)(2)(iii)(C) of this section. In the case of a qualified cost sharing arrangement in existence on August 26, 2003, the election must be made by written amendment to the cost sharing agreement not later than the latest due date (with regard to extensions) of a federal income tax return of any controlled participant for the first taxable year beginning after August 26, 2003, and the consent of the Commissioner is not required.

(C) *Consistency.*—Generally, all controlled participants in a qualified cost sharing arrangement taking options on publicly traded stock into account under paragraph (d)(2)(iii)(A) or (B) of this section must use that same method of measurement and timing for all options on publicly traded stock with respect to that qualified cost sharing arrangement. Controlled participants may change their method only with the consent of the Commissioner and only with respect to stock options granted during taxable years subsequent to the taxable year in which the Commissioner's consent is obtained. All controlled participants in the qualified cost sharing arrangement must join in requests for the Commissioner's consent under this paragraph. Thus, for example, if the controlled participants make the election described in paragraph (d)(2)(iii)(B) of this section upon the formation of the qualified cost sharing arrangement, the election may be revoked only with the consent of the Commissioner, and the consent will apply only to stock options granted in taxable years subsequent to the taxable year in which consent is obtained. Similarly, if controlled participants already have granted stock options that have been or will be taken into account under the general rule of paragraph (d)(2)(iii)(A) of this section, then except in cases specified in the last sentence of paragraph (d)(2)(iii)(B)(*4*) of this section, the controlled participants may make the election described in paragraph (d)(2)(iii)(B) of this section only with the consent of the Commissioner, and the consent will apply only to stock options granted in taxable years subsequent to the taxable year in which consent is obtained.

(3) *Examples.*—The following examples illustrate this paragraph (d):

Example 1. Foreign Parent (FP) and U.S. Subsidiary (USS) enter into a qualified cost sharing arrangement to develop a better mousetrap. USS and FP share the costs of FP's research and development facility that will be exclusively dedicated to this research, the salaries of the researchers, and reasonable overhead costs attributable to the project. They also share the cost of a conference facility that is at the disposal of the senior executive management of each company but does not contribute to the research and development activities in any measurable way. In this case, the cost of the conference facility must be excluded from the amount of intangible development costs.

Example 2. U.S. Parent (USP) and Foreign Subsidiary (FS) enter into a qualified cost sharing arrangement to develop a new device. USP and FS share the costs of a research and development facility, the salaries of researchers, and reasonable overhead costs attributable to the project. USP also incurs costs related to field testing of the device, but does not include them in the amount of intangible development costs of the cost sharing arrangement. The district director may determine that the field testing costs are intangible development costs that must be shared.

(e) *Anticipated benefits.*—(1) *Benefits.*—Benefits are additional income generated or costs saved by the use of covered intangibles.

(2) *Reasonably anticipated benefits.*—For purposes of this section, a controlled participant's reasonably anticipated benefits are the aggregate benefits that it reasonably anticipates that it will derive from covered intangibles.

(f) *Cost allocations.*—(1) *In general.*—For purposes of determining whether a cost allocation authorized by paragraph (a)(2) of this section is appropriate for a taxable year, a controlled participant's share of intangible development costs for the taxable year under a qualified cost sharing arrangement must be compared to its share of reasonably anticipated benefits under the arrangement. A controlled participant's share of intangible development costs is determined under paragraph (f)(2) of this section. A controlled participant's share of reasonably anticipated benefits under the arrangement is determined under paragraph (f)(3) of this section. In determining whether benefits were reasonably anticipated, it may be appropriate to compare actual benefits to anticipated benefits, as described in paragraph (f)(3)(iv) of this section.

(2) *Share of intangible development costs.*—(i) *In general.*—A controlled participant's share of intangible development costs for a taxable year is equal to its intangible development costs for the taxable year (as defined in paragraph (d) of this section), divided by the sum of the intangible development costs for the taxable year (as defined in paragraph (d) of this section) of all the controlled participants.

(ii) *Example.*—The following example illustrates this paragraph (f)(2):

Example. (i) U.S. Parent (USP), Foreign Subsidiary (FS), and Unrelated Third Party (UTP) enter into a cost sharing arrangement to develop new audio technology. In the first year of the arrangement, the controlled participants incur $2,250,000 in the intangible development area, all of which is incurred directly by USP. In the first year, UTP makes a $250,000 cost sharing payment to USP, and FS makes a $800,000 cost sharing payment to USP, under the terms of the arrangement. For that year, the intangible development costs borne by USP are $1,200,000 (its $2,250,000 intangible development costs directly incurred, minus the cost sharing payments it receives of $250,000 from UTP and $800,000 from FS); the intangible development costs borne by FS are $800,000 (its cost sharing payment); and the intangible development costs borne by all of the controlled participants are $2,000,000 (the sum of the intangible development costs borne by USP and FS of $1,200,000 and $800,000, respectively). Thus, for the first year, USP's share of intangible development costs is 60% ($1,200,000 divided by $2,000,000), and FS's share of intangible development costs is 40% ($800,000 divided by $2,000,000).

(ii) For purposes of determining whether a cost allocation authorized by paragraph § 1.482-7(a)(2) is appropriate for the first year, the district director must compare USP's and FS's shares of intangible development costs for that year to their shares of reasonably anticipated benefits. See paragraph (f)(3) of this section.

(3) *Share of reasonably anticipated benefits.*—(i) *In general.*—A controlled participant's share of reasonably anticipated benefits under a qualified cost sharing arrangement is equal to its reasonably anticipated benefits (as defined in paragraph (e)(2) of this section), divided by the sum of the reasonably anticipated benefits (as defined in paragraph (e)(2) of this section) of all the controlled participants. The anticipated benefits of an uncontrolled participant will not be included for purposes of determining each controlled participant's share of anticipated benefits. A controlled participant's share of reasonably anticipated benefits will be determined using the most reliable estimate of reasonably anticipated benefits. In determining which of two or more available estimates is most reliable, the quality of the data and assumptions used in the analysis must be taken into account, consistent with § 1.482-1(c)(2)(ii) (Data and assumptions). Thus, the reliability of an estimate will depend largely on the completeness and accuracy of the data, the soundness of the assumptions, and the relative effects of particular deficiencies in data or assumptions on different estimates. If two estimates are equally reliable, no adjustment should be made based on differences in the results. The following factors will be particularly relevant in determining the reliability of an estimate of anticipated benefits—

(A) The reliability of the basis used for measuring benefits, as described in paragraph (f)(3)(ii) of this section; and

(B) The reliability of the projections used to estimate benefits, as described in paragraph (f)(3)(iv) of this section.

(ii) *Measure of benefits.*—In order to estimate a controlled participant's share of anticipated benefits from covered intangibles, the amount of benefits that each of the controlled participants is reasonably anticipated to derive from covered intangibles must be measured on a basis that is consistent for all such participants. See paragraph (f)(3)(iii)(E), *Example 8*, of this section. If a controlled participant transfers covered intangibles to another controlled taxpayer, such participant's benefits from the transferred intangibles must be measured by reference to the transferee's benefits, disregarding any consideration paid by the transferee to the controlled participant (such as a royalty pursuant to a license agreement). Anticipated benefits are measured either on a direct basis, by reference to estimated additional income to be generated or costs to be saved by the use of covered intangibles, or on an indirect basis, by reference to certain measurements that reasonably can be assumed to be related to income generated or costs saved. Such indirect bases of measurement of anticipated benefits are described in paragraph (f)(3)(iii) of this section. A controlled participant's anticipated benefits must be measured on the most reliable basis, whether direct or indirect. In determining which of two bases of measurement of reasonably anticipated benefits is most reliable, the factors set forth in §1.482-1(c)(2)(ii) (Data and assumptions) must be taken into account. It normally will be expected that the basis that provided the most reliable estimate for a particular year will continue to provide the most reliable estimate in subsequent years, absent a material change in the factors that affect the reliability of the estimate. Regardless of whether a direct or indirect basis of measurement is used, adjustments may be required to account for material differences in the activities that controlled participants undertake to exploit their interests in covered intangibles. See *Example 6* of paragraph (f)(3)(iii)(E) of this section.

(iii) *Indirect bases for measuring anticipated benefits.*—Indirect bases for measuring anticipated benefits from participation in a qualified cost sharing arrangement include the following:

(A) *Units used, produced or sold.*—Units of items used, produced or sold by each controlled participant in the business activities in which covered intangibles are exploited may be used as an indirect basis for measuring its anticipated benefits. This basis of measurement will be more reliable to the extent that each controlled participant is expected to have a similar increase in net profit or decrease in net loss attributable to the covered intangibles per unit of the item or items used, produced or sold. This circumstance is most likely to arise when the covered intangibles are exploited by the controlled participants in the use, production or sale of substantially uniform items under similar economic conditions.

(B) *Sales.*—Sales by each controlled participant in the business activities in which covered intangibles are exploited may be used as an indirect basis for measuring its anticipated benefits. This basis of measurement will be more reliable to the extent that each controlled participant is expected to have a similar increase in net profit or decrease in net loss attributable to covered intangibles per dollar of sales. This circumstance is most likely to arise if the costs of exploiting covered intangibles are not substantial relative to the revenues generated, or if the principal effect of using covered intangibles is to increase the controlled participants' revenues (e.g., through a price premium on the products they sell) without affecting their costs substantially. Sales by each controlled participant are unlikely to provide a reliable basis for measuring benefits unless each controlled participant operates at the same market level (e.g., manufacturing, distribution, etc.).

(C) *Operating profit.*—Operating profit of each controlled participant from the activities in which covered intangibles are exploited may be used as an indirect basis for measuring its anticipated benefits. This basis of measurement will be more reliable to the extent that such profit is largely attributable to the use of covered intangibles, or if the share of profits attributable to the use of covered intangibles is expected to be similar for each controlled participant. This circumstance is most likely to arise when covered intangibles are integral to the activity that generates the profit and the activity could not be carried on or would generate little profit without use of those intangibles.

(D) *Other bases for measuring anticipated benefits.*—Other bases for measuring anticipated benefits may, in some circumstances, be appropriate, but only to the extent that there is expected to be a reasonably identifiable relationship between the basis of measurement used and additional income generated or costs saved by the use of covered intangibles. For example, a division of costs based on employee compensation would be considered unreliable unless there were a relationship between the amount of compensation and the expected income of the controlled participants from the use of covered intangibles.

(E) *Examples.*—The following examples illustrate this paragraph (f)(3)(iii):

Example 1. Foreign Parent (FP) and U.S. Subsidiary (USS) both produce a feedstock for the manufacture of various high-performance plastic products. Producing the feedstock requires large amounts of electricity, which accounts for a significant portion of its production cost. FP and USS enter into a cost sharing arrangement to develop a new process that will reduce the amount of electricity required to produce a unit of the feedstock. FP and USS currently both incur an electricity cost of X% of its other production costs and rates for each are expected to remain similar in the future. How much the new process, if it is successful, will reduce the amount of electricity required to produce a unit of the feedstock is uncertain, but it will be about the same amount for both companies. Therefore, the cost savings each company is expected to achieve after implementing the new process are similar relative to the total amount of the feedstock produced. Under the cost sharing arrangement FP and USS divide the costs of developing the new process based on the units of the feedstock each is anticipated to produce in the future. In this case, units produced is the most reliable basis for measuring benefits and dividing the intangible development costs because each participant is expected to have a similar decrease in costs per unit of the feedstock produced.

Example 2. The facts are the same as in *Example 1*, except that USS pays X% of its other production costs for electricity while FP pays 2X% of its other production costs. In this case, units produced is not the most reliable basis for measuring benefits and dividing the intangible development costs because the participants do not expect to have a similar decrease in costs per unit of the feedstock produced. The district director determines that the most reliable measure of benefit shares may be based on units of the feedstock produced if FP's units are weighted relative to USS' units by a factor of 2. This reflects the fact that FP pays twice as much as USS as a percentage of its other production costs for electricity and, therefore, FP's savings per unit of the feedstock would be twice USS's savings from any new process eventually developed.

Example 3. The facts are the same as in *Example 2*, except that to supply the particular needs of the U.S. market USS manufactures the feedstock with somewhat different properties than FP's feedstock. This requires USS to employ a somewhat different production process than does FP. Because of this difference, it will be more costly for USS to adopt any new process that may be developed under the cost sharing agreement. In this case, units produced is not the most reliable basis for measuring benefit shares. In order to reliably determine benefit shares, the district director offsets the reasonably anticipated costs of adopting the new process against the reasonably anticipated total savings in electricity costs.

Example 4. U.S. Parent (USP) and Foreign Subsidiary (FS) enter into a cost sharing arrangement to develop new anesthetic drugs. USP obtains the right to use any resulting patent in the U.S. market, and FS obtains the right to use the patent in the European market. USP and FS divide costs on the basis of anticipated operating profit from each patent under development. USP anticipates that it will receive a much higher profit than FS per unit sold because drug prices are uncontrolled in the U.S., whereas drug prices are regulated in many European countries. In this case, the controlled taxpayers' basis for measuring benefits is the most reliable.

Example 5. (i) Foreign Parent (FP) and U.S. Subsidiary (USS) both manufacture and sell fertilizers. They enter into a cost sharing arrangement to develop a new pellet form of a common agricultural fertilizer that is currently available only in powder form. Under the cost sharing arrangement, USS obtains the rights to produce and sell the new form of fertilizer for the U.S. market while FP obtains the rights to produce and sell the fertilizer for the rest of the world. The costs of developing the new form of fertilizer are divided on the basis of the anticipated sales of fertilizer in the participants' respective markets.

(ii) If the research and development is successful the pellet form will deliver the fertilizer more efficiently to crops and less fertilizer will be required to achieve the same effect on crop growth. The pellet form of fertilizer can be expected to sell at a price premium over the powder form of fertilizer based on the savings in the amount of fertilizer that needs to be used. If the research and development is successful, the costs of producing pellet fertilizer are expected to be approximately the same as the costs of producing powder fertilizer and the same for both FP and USS. Both FP and USS operate at approximately the same market levels, selling their fertilizers largely to independent distributors.

(iii) In this case, the controlled taxpayers' basis for measuring benefits is the most reliable.

Example 6. The facts are the same as in *Example 5*, except that FP distributes its fertilizers directly while USS sells to independent distributors. In this case, sales of USS and FP are not the most reliable basis for measuring benefits unless adjustments are made to account for the difference in market levels at which the sales occur.

Example 7. Foreign Parent (FP) and U.S. Subsidiary (USS) enter into a cost sharing arrangement to develop materials that will be used to train all new entry-level employees. FP and USS determine that the new materials will

Reg. § 1.482-7(f)(3)(iii)(E)

save approximately ten hours of training time per employee. Because their entry-level employees are paid on differing wage scales, FP and USS decide that they should not divide costs based on the number of entry-level employees hired by each. Rather, they divide costs based on compensation paid to the entry-level employees hired by each. In this case, the basis used for measuring benefits is the most reliable because there is a direct relationship between compensation paid to new entry-level employees and costs saved by FP and USS from the use of the new training materials.

Example 8. U.S. Parent (USP), Foreign Subsidiary 1 (FS1) and Foreign Subsidiary 2 (FS2) enter into a cost sharing arrangement to develop computer software that each will market and install on customers' computer systems. The participants divide costs on the basis of projected sales by USP, FS1, and FS2 of the software in their respective geographic areas. However, FS1 plans not only to sell but also to license the software to unrelated customers, and FS1's licensing income (which is a percentage of the licensees' sales) is not counted in the projected benefits. In this case, the basis used for measuring the benefits of each participant is not the most reliable because all of the benefits received by participants are not taken into account. In order to reliably determine benefit shares, FS1's projected benefits from licensing must be included in the measurement on a basis that is the same as that used to measure its own and the other participants' projected benefits from sales (e.g., all participants might measure their benefits on the basis of operating profit).

(iv) *Projections used to estimate anticipated benefits.*—(A) *In general.*—The reliability of an estimate of anticipated benefits also depends upon the reliability of projections used in making the estimate. Projections required for this purpose generally include a determination of the time period between the inception of the research and development and the receipt of benefits, a projection of the time over which benefits will be received, and a projection of the benefits anticipated for each year in which it is anticipated that the intangible will generate benefits. A projection of the relevant basis for measuring anticipated benefits may require a projection of the factors that underlie it. For example, a projection of operating profits may require a projection of sales, cost of sales, operating expenses, and other factors that affect operating profits. If it is anticipated that there will be significant variation among controlled participants in the timing of their receipt of benefits, and consequently benefit shares are expected to vary significantly over the years in which benefits will be received, it may be necessary to use the present discounted value of the projected benefits to reliably determine each controlled participant's share of those benefits. If it is not anticipated that benefit shares will significantly change over time, current annual benefit shares may provide a reliable projection of anticipated benefit shares. This circumstance is most likely to occur when the cost sharing arrangement is a long-term arrangement, the arrangement covers a wide variety of intangibles, the composition of the covered intangibles is unlikely to change, the covered intangibles are unlikely to generate unusual profits, and each controlled participant's share of the market is stable.

(B) *Unreliable projections.*—A significant divergence between projected benefit shares and actual benefit shares may indicate that the projections were not reliable. In such a case, the district director may use actual benefits as the most reliable measure of anticipated benefits. If benefits are projected over a period of years, and the projections for initial years of the period prove to be unreliable, this may indicate that the projections for the remaining years of the period are also unreliable and thus should be adjusted. Projections will not be considered unreliable based on a divergence between a controlled participant's projected benefit share and actual benefit share if the amount of such divergence for every controlled participant is less than or equal to 20% of the participant's projected benefit share. Further, the district director will not make an allocation based on such divergence if the difference is due to an extraordinary event, beyond the control of the participants, that could not reasonably have been anticipated at the time that costs were shared. For purposes of this paragraph, all controlled participants that are not U.S. persons will be treated as a single controlled participant. Therefore, an adjustment based on an unreliable projection will be made to the cost shares of foreign controlled participants only if there is a matching adjustment to the cost shares of controlled participants that are U.S. persons. Nothing in this paragraph (f)(3)(iv)(B) will prevent the district director from making an allocation if the taxpayer did not use the most reliable basis for measuring anticipated benefits. For example, if the taxpayer measures anticipated benefits based on units sold, and the district director determines that another basis is more reliable for measuring anticipated benefits, then the fact that actual units sold were within 20% of the projected unit sales will not preclude an allocation under this section.

(C) *Foreign-to-foreign adjustments.*—Notwithstanding the limitations on adjustments provided in paragraph (f)(3)(iv)(B) of this section, adjustments to cost shares based on an unreliable projection also may be made solely among foreign controlled participants if the variation between actual and projected benefits has the effect of substantially reducing U.S. tax.

(D) *Examples.*—The following examples illustrate this paragraph (f)(3)(iv):

Example 1. (i) Foreign Parent (FP) and U.S. Subsidiary (USS) enter into a cost sharing arrangement to develop a new car model. The participants plan to spend four years developing the new model and four years producing and selling the new model. USS and FP project total sales of $4 billion and $2 billion, respectively, over the planned four years of exploitation of the new model. Cost shares are divided for each year based on projected total sales. Therefore, USS bears 66 2/3% of each year's intangible development costs and FP bears 33 1/3% of such costs.

(ii) USS typically begins producing and selling new car models a year after FP begins producing and selling new car models. The district director determines that in order to reflect USS' one-year lag in introducing new car models, a more reliable projection of each participant's share of benefits would be based on a projection of all four years of sales for each participant, discounted to present value.

Example 2. U.S. Parent (USP) and Foreign Subsidiary (FS) enter into a cost sharing arrangement to develop new and improved household cleaning products. Both participants have sold household cleaning products for many years and have stable market shares. The products under development are unlikely to produce unusual profits for either participant. The participants divide costs on the basis of each participant's current sales of household cleaning products. In this case, the participants' future benefit shares are reliably projected by current sales of cleaning products.

Example 3. The facts are the same as in *Example 2*, except that FS's market share is rapidly expanding because of the business failure of a competitor in its geographic area. The district director determines that the participants' future benefit shares are not reliably projected by current sales of cleaning products and that FS's benefit projections should take into account its growth in sales.

Example 4. Foreign Parent (FP) and U.S. Subsidiary (USS) enter into a cost sharing arrangement to develop synthetic fertilizers and insecticides. FP and USS share costs on the basis of each participant's current sales of fertilizers and insecticides. The market shares of the participants have been stable for fertilizers, but FP's market share for insecticides has been expanding. The district director determines that the participants' projections of benefit shares are reliable with regard to fertilizers, but not reliable with regard to insecticides; a more reliable projection of benefit shares would take into account the expanding market share for insecticides.

Example 5. U.S. Parent (USP) and Foreign Subsidiary (FS) enter into a cost sharing arrangement to develop new food products, dividing costs on the basis of projected sales two years in the future. In year 1, USP and FS project that their sales in year 3 will be equal, and they divide costs accordingly. In year 3, the district director examines the participants' method for dividing costs. USP and FS actually accounted for 42% and 58% of total sales, respectively. The district director agrees that sales two years in the future provide a reliable basis for estimating benefit shares. Because the differences between USP's and FS's actual and projected benefit shares are less than 20% of their projected benefit shares, the projection of future benefits for year 3 is reliable.

Example 6. The facts are the same as in *Example 5*, except that the in year 3 USP and FS actually accounted for 35% and 65% of total sales, respectively. The divergence between USP's projected and actual benefit shares is greater than 20% of USP's projected benefit share and is not due to an extraordinary event beyond the control of the participants. The district director concludes that the projection of anticipated benefit shares was unreliable, and uses actual benefits as the basis for an adjustment to the cost shares borne by USP and FS.

Example 7. U.S. Parent (USP), a U.S. corporation, and its foreign subsidiary (FS) enter a cost sharing arrangement in year 1. They project that they will begin to receive benefits from covered intangibles in years 4 through 6, and that USP will receive 60% of total benefits and FS 40% of total benefits. In years 4 through 6, USP and FS actually receive 50% each of the total benefits. In evaluating the reliability of the participants' projections, the district director compares these actual benefit shares to the projected benefit shares. Although USP's actual benefit share (50%) is within 20% of its projected benefit share (60%), FS's actual benefit share (50%) is not within 20% of its projected benefit share (40%). Based on this discrepancy, the district director may conclude that the participants' projections were not reliable and may use actual benefit shares as the basis for an adjustment to the cost shares borne by USP and FS.

Example 8. Three controlled taxpayers, USP, FS1 and FS2 enter into a cost sharing arrangement. FS1 and FS2 are foreign. USP is a United States corporation that controls all the stock of FS1 and FS2. The participants project that they will share the total benefits of the covered intangibles in the following percentages: USP 50%; FS1 30%; and FS2 20%. Actual benefit shares are as follows: USP 45%; FS1 25%; and FS2 30%. In evaluating the reliability of the participants' projections, the district director compares these actual benefit shares to the projected benefit shares. For this purpose, FS1 and FS2 are treated as a single participant. The actual benefit share received by USP (45%) is within 20% of its projected benefit share (50%). In addition, the non-US participants' actual benefit share (55%) is also within 20% of their projected benefit share (50%). Therefore, the district director concludes that the participants' projections of future benefits were reliable, despite the fact that FS2's actual benefit share (30%) is not within 20% of its projected benefit share (20%).

Example 9. The facts are the same as in *Example 8.* In addition, the district director determines that FS2 has significant operating losses and has no earnings and profits, and that FS1 is profitable and has earnings and profits. Based on all the evidence, the district director concludes that the participants arranged that FS1 would bear a larger cost share than appropriate in order to reduce FS1's earnings and profits and thereby reduce inclusions USP otherwise would be deemed to have on account of FS1 under subpart F. Pursuant to § 1.482-7(f)(3)(iv)(C), the district director may make an adjustment solely to the cost shares borne by FS1 and FS2 because FS2's projection of future benefits was unreliable and the variation between actual and projected benefits had the effect of substantially reducing USP's U.S. income tax liability (on account of FS1 subpart F income).

Example 10. (i) (A) Foreign Parent (FP) and U.S. Subsidiary (USS) enter into a cost sharing arrangement in 1996 to develop a new treatment for baldness. USS's interest in any treatment developed is the right to produce and sell the treatment in the U.S. market while FP retains rights to produce and sell the treatment in the rest of the world. USS and FP measure their anticipated benefits from the cost sharing arrangement based on their respective projected future sales of the baldness treatment. The following sales projections are used:

Sales ($ millions)

Year	USS	FP
1997	5	10
1998	20	20
1999	30	30
2000	40	40
2001	40	40
2002	40	40
2003	40	40
2004	20	20
2005	10	10
2006	5	5

(B) In 1997, the first year of sales, USS is projected to have lower sales than FP due to lags in U.S. regulatory approval for the baldness treatment. In each subsequent year USS and FP are projected to have equal sales. Sales are projected to build over the first three years of the period, level off for several years, and then decline over the final years of the period as new and improved baldness treatments reach the market.

(ii) To account for USS's lag in sales in the first year, the present discounted value of sales over the period is used as the basis for measuring benefits. Based on the risk associated with this venture, a discount rate of 10 percent is selected. The present discounted value of projected sales is determined to be approximately $154.4 million for USS and $158.9 million for FP. On this basis USS and FP are projected to obtain approximately 49.3% and 50.7% of the benefit, respectively, and the costs of developing the baldness treatment are shared accordingly.

(iii) (A) In the year 2002 the district director examines the cost sharing arrangement. USS and FP have obtained the following sales results through the year 2001:

Sales ($ millions)

Year	USS	FP
1997	0	17
1998	17	35
1999	25	41
2000	38	41
2001	39	41

(B) USS's sales initially grew more slowly than projected while FP's sales grew more quickly. In each of the first three years of the period the share of total sales of at least one of the parties diverged by over 20% from its projected share of sales. However, by the year 2001 both parties' sales had leveled off at approximately their projected values. Taking into account this leveling off of sales and all the facts and circumstances, the district director determines that it is appropriate to use the original projections for the remaining years of sales. Combining the actual results through the year 2001 with the projections for subsequent years, and using a discount rate of 10%, the present discounted value of sales is approximately $141.6 million for USS and $187.3 million for FP. This result implies that USS and FP obtain approximately 43.1% and 56.9%, respectively, of the anticipated benefits from the baldness treatment. Because these benefit shares are within 20% of the benefit shares calculated based on the original sales projections, the district director determines that, based on the difference between actual and projected benefit shares, the original projections were not unreliable. No adjustment is made based on the difference between actual and projected benefit shares.

Example 11. (i) The facts are the same as in *Example 10*, except that the actual sales results through the year 2001 are as follows:

Sales ($ millions)

Year	USS	FP
1997	0	17
1998	17	35
1999	25	44
2000	34	54
2001	36	55

(ii) Based on the discrepancy between the projections and the actual results and on consideration of all the facts, the district director determines that for the remaining years the following sales projections are more reliable than the original projections:

Sales ($ millions)

Year	USS	FP
2002	36	55
2003	36	55
2004	18	28
2005	9	14
2006	4.5	7

(iii) Combining the actual results through the year 2001 with the projections for subsequent years, and using a discount rate of 10%, the present discounted value of sales is approximately $131.2 million for USS and $229.4 million for FP. This result implies that USS and FP obtain approximately 35.4% and 63.6%, respectively, of the anticipated benefits from the baldness treatment. These benefit shares diverge by greater than 20% from the benefit shares calculated based on the original sales projections, and the district director determines that, based on the difference between actual and projected benefit shares, the original projections were unreliable. The district director adjusts costs shares for each of the taxable years under examination to conform them to the recalculated shares of anticipated benefits.

(4) *Timing of allocations.*—If the district director reallocates costs under the provisions of this paragraph (f), the allocation must be reflected for tax purposes in the year in which the costs were incurred. When a cost sharing payment is owed by one member of a qualified cost sharing arrangement to another member, the district director may make appropriate allocations to reflect an arm's length rate of interest for the time value of money, consistent with the provisions of §1.482-2(a) (Loans or advances).

(g) *Allocations of income, deductions or other tax items to reflect transfers of intangibles (buy-in).*—(1) *In general.*—A controlled participant that makes intangible property available to a qualified cost sharing arrangement will be treated as having transferred interests in such property to the other controlled participants, and such other controlled participants must make buy-in payments to it, as provided in paragraph (g)(2) of this section. If the other controlled participants fail to make such payments, the district director may make appropriate allocations, under the provisions of §§1.482-1 and 1.482-4 through 1.482-6, to reflect an arm's length consideration for the transferred intangible property. Further, if a group of controlled taxpayers participates in a qualified cost sharing arrangement, any change in the controlled participants' interests in covered intangibles, whether by reason of entry of a new participant or otherwise by reason of transfers (including deemed transfers) of interests among existing participants, is a transfer of intangible property, and the district director may make appropriate allocations, under the provisions of §§1.482-1 and 1.482-4 through 1.482-6, to reflect an arm's length consideration for the transfer. See paragraphs (g)(3), (4), and (5) of this section. Paragraph (g)(6) of this section provides rules for assigning unassigned interests under a qualified cost sharing arrangement.

(2) *Pre-existing intangibles.*—If a controlled participant makes pre-existing intangible property in which it owns an interest available to other controlled participants for purposes of research in the intangible development area under a qualified cost sharing arrangement, then each such other controlled participant must make a buy-in payment to the owner. The buy-in payment by each such other controlled participant is the arm's length charge for the use of the intangible under the rules of §§ 1.482-1 and 1.482-4 through 1.482-6, multiplied by the controlled participant's share of reasonably anticipated benefits (as defined in paragraph (f)(3) of this section). A controlled participant's payment required under this paragraph (g)(2) is deemed to be reduced to the extent of any payments owed to it under this paragraph (g)(2) from other controlled participants. Each payment received by a payee will be treated as coming pro rata out of payments made by all payors. See paragraph (g)(8), *Example 4*, of this section. Such payments will be treated as consideration for a transfer of an interest in the intangible property made available to the qualified cost sharing arrangement by the payee. Any payment to or from an uncontrolled participant in consideration for intangible property made available to the qualified cost sharing arrangement will be shared by the controlled participants in accordance with their shares of reasonably anticipated benefits (as defined in paragraph (f)(3) of this section). A controlled participant's payment required under this paragraph (g)(2) is deemed to be reduced by such a share of payments owed from an uncontrolled participant to the same extent as by any payments owed from other controlled participants under this paragraph (g)(2). See paragraph (g)(8), *Example 5*, of this section.

(3) *New controlled participant.*—If a new controlled participant enters a qualified cost sharing arrangement and acquires any interest in the covered intangibles, then the new participant must pay an arm's length consideration, under the provisions of §§ 1.482-1 and 1.482-4 through 1.482-6, for such interest to each controlled participant from whom such interest was acquired.

(4) *Controlled participant relinquishes interests.*—A controlled participant in a qualified cost sharing arrangement may be deemed to have acquired an interest in one or more covered intangibles if another controlled participant transfers, abandons, or otherwise relinquishes an interest under the arrangement, to the benefit of the first participant. If such a relinquishment occurs, the participant relinquishing the interest must receive an arm's length consideration, under the provisions of §§ 1.482-1 and 1.482-4 through 1.482-6, for its interest. If the controlled participant that has relinquished its interest subsequently uses that interest, then that participant must pay an arm's length consideration, under the provisions of §§ 1.482-1 and 1.482-4 through 1.482-6, to the controlled participant that acquired the interest.

(5) *Conduct inconsistent with the terms of a cost sharing arrangement.*—If, after any cost allocations authorized by paragraph (a)(2) of this section, a controlled participant bears costs of intangible development that over a period of years are consistently and materially greater or lesser than its share of reasonably anticipated benefits, then the district director may conclude that the economic substance of the arrangement between the controlled participants is inconsistent with the terms of the cost sharing arrangement. In such a case, the district director may disregard such terms and impute an agreement consistent with the controlled participants' course of conduct, under which a controlled participant that bore a disproportionately greater share of costs received additional interests in covered intangibles. See § 1.482-1(d)(3)(ii)(B) (Identifying contractual terms) and § 1.482-4(f)(3)(ii) (Identification of owner). Accordingly, that participant must receive an arm's length payment from any controlled participant whose share of the intangible development costs is less than its share of reasonably anticipated benefits over time, under the provisions of §§ 1.482-1 and 1.482-4 through 1.482-6.

(6) *Failure to assign interests under a qualified cost sharing arrangement.*—If a qualified cost sharing arrangement fails to assign an interest in a covered intangible, then each controlled participant will be deemed to hold a share in such interest equal to its share of the costs of developing such intangible. For this purpose, if cost shares have varied materially over the period during which such intangible was developed, then the costs of developing the intangible must be measured by their present discounted value as of the date when the first such costs were incurred.

(7) *Form of consideration.*—The consideration for an acquisition described in this paragraph (g) may take any of the following forms:

(i) *Lump sum payments.*—For the treatment of lump sum payments, see § 1.482-4(f)(5) (Lump sum payments);

(ii) *Installment payments.*—Installment payments spread over the period of use of the intangible by the transferee, with interest calculated in accordance with § 1.482-2(a) (Loans or advances); and

(iii) *Royalties.*—Royalties or other payments contingent on the use of the intangible by the transferee.

(8) *Examples.*—The following examples illustrate allocations described in this paragraph (g):

Example 1. In year one, four members of a controlled group enter into a cost sharing arrangement to develop a commercially feasible process for capturing energy from nuclear fusion. Based on a reliable projection of their future benefits, each cost sharing participant bears an equal share of the costs. The cost of developing intangibles for each participant with respect to the project is approximately $1 million per year. In year ten, a fifth member of the controlled group joins the cost sharing group and agrees to bear one-fifth of the future costs in exchange for part of the fourth member's territory reasonably anticipated to yield benefits amounting to one-fifth of the total benefits. The fair market value of intangible property within the arrangement at the time the fifth company joins the arrangement is $45 million. The new member must pay one-fifth of that amount (that is, $9 million total) to the fourth member from whom it acquired its interest in covered intangibles.

Example 2. U.S. Subsidiary (USS), Foreign Subsidiary (FS) and Foreign Parent (FP) enter into a cost sharing arrangement to develop new products within the Group X product line. USS manufactures and sells Group X products in North America, FS manufactures and sells Group X products in South America, and FP manufactures and sells Group X products in the rest of the world. USS, FS and FP project that each will manufacture and sell a third of the Group X products under development, and they share costs on the basis of projected sales of manufactured products. When the new Group X products are developed, however, USS ceases to manufacture Group X products, and FP sells its Group X products to USS for resale in the North American market. USS earns a return on its resale activity that is appropriate given its function as a distributor, but does not earn a return attributable to exploiting covered intangibles. The district director determines that USS' share of the costs (one-third) was greater than its share of reasonably anticipated benefits (zero) and that it has transferred an interest in the intangibles for which it should receive a payment from FP, whose share of the intangible development costs (one-third) was less than its share of reasonably anticipated benefits over time (two-thirds). An allocation is made under §§ 1.482-1 and 1.482-4 through 1.482-6 from FP to USS to recognize USS' one-third interest in the intangibles. No allocation is made from FS to USS because FS did not exploit USS' interest in covered intangibles.

Example 3. U.S. Parent (USP), Foreign Subsidiary 1 (FS1), and Foreign Subsidiary 2 (FS2) enter into a cost sharing arrangement to develop a cure for the common cold. Costs are shared USP-50%, FS1-40% and FS2-10% on the basis of projected units of cold medicine to be produced by each. After ten years of research and development, FS1 withdraws from the arrangement, transferring its interests in the intangibles under development to USP in exchange for a lump sum payment of $10 million. The district director may review this lump sum payment, under the provisions of § 1.482-4(f)(5), to ensure that the amount is commensurate with the income attributable to the intangibles.

Example 4. (i) Four members A, B, C, and D of a controlled group form a cost sharing arrangement to develop the next generation technology for their business. Based on a reliable projection of their future benefits, the participants agree to bear shares of the costs incurred during the term of the agreement in the following percentages: A 40%; B 15%; C 25%; and D 20%. The arm's length charges, under the rules of §§ 1.482-1 and 1.482-4 through 1.482-6, for the use of the existing intangible property they respectively make available to the cost sharing arrangement are in the following amounts for the taxable year: A 80X; B 40X; C 30X; and D 30X. The provisional (before offsets) and final buy-in payments/receipts among A, B, C, and D are shown in the table as follows:

(All amounts stated in X's)

	A	B	C	D
Payments	< 40 >	< 21 >	< 37.5 >	< 30 >
Receipts	48	34	22.5	24
Final	8	13	< 15 >	< 6 >

(ii) The first row/first column shows A's provisional buy-in payment equal to the product of 100X (sum of 40X, 30X, and 30X) and A's share of anticipated benefits of 40%. The second row/first column shows A's provisional buy-in receipts equal to the sum of the products of 80X and B's, C's, and D's anticipated benefits shares (15%, 25%, and 20%, respectively). The other entries in the first two rows of the table are similarly computed. The last row shows the final buy-in receipts/payments after offsets. Thus, for the taxable year, A and B are treated as receiving the 8X and 13X, respectively, pro rata out of payments by C and D of 15X and 6X, respectively.

Example 5. A and B, two members of a controlled group form a cost sharing arrangement with an unrelated third party C to develop a new technology useable in their respective businesses. Based on a reliable projection of their future benefits, A and B agree to bear shares of 60% and 40%, respectively, of the costs incurred during the term of the agreement. A also makes available its existing technology for purposes of the research to be undertaken. The arm's length charge, under the rules of §§ 1.482-1 and 1.482-4 through 1.482-6, for the use of the existing technology is 100X for the taxable year. Under its agreement with A and B, C must make a specified cost sharing payment as well as a payment of 50X for the taxable year on account of the pre-existing intangible property made available to the cost sharing arrangement. B's provisional buy-in payment (before offsets) to A for the taxable year is 40X (the product of 100X and B's anticipated benefits share of 40%). C's payment of 50X is shared provisionally between A and B in accordance with their shares of reasonably anticipated benefits, 30X (50X times 60%) to A and 20X (50X times 40%) to B. B's final buy-in payment (after offsets) is 20X (40X less 20X). A is treated as receiving the 70X total provisional payments (40X plus 30X) pro rata out of the final payments by B and C of 20X and 50X, respectively.

(h) *Character of payments made pursuant to a qualified cost sharing arrangement.*—(1) *In general.*—Payments made pursuant to a qualified cost sharing arrangement (other than payments described in paragraph (g) of this section) generally will be considered costs of developing intangibles of the payor and reimbursements of the same kind of costs of developing intangibles of the payee. For purposes of this paragraph (h), a controlled participant's payment required under a qualified cost sharing arrangement is deemed to be reduced to the extent of any payments owed to it under the arrangement from other controlled or uncontrolled participants. Each payment received by a payee will be treated as coming pro rata out of payments made by all payors. Such payments will be applied pro rata against deductions for the taxable year that the payee is allowed in connection with the qualified cost sharing arrangement. Payments received in excess of such deductions will be treated as in consideration for use of the tangible property made available to the qualified cost sharing arrangement by the payee. For purposes of the research credit determined under section 41, cost sharing payments among controlled participants will be treated as provided for intragroup transactions in § 1.41-6(e). Any payment made or received by a taxpayer pursuant to an arrangement that the district director determines not to be a qualified cost sharing arrangement, or a payment made or received pursuant to paragraph (g) of this section, will be subject to the provisions of §§ 1.482-1 and 1.482-4 through 1.482-6. Any payment that in substance constitutes a cost sharing payment will be treated as such for purposes of this section, regardless of its characterization under foreign law.

(2) *Examples.*—The following examples illustrate this paragraph (h):

Example 1. U.S. Parent (USP) and its wholly owned Foreign Subsidiary (FS) form a cost sharing arrangement to develop a miniature widget, the Small R. Based on a reliable projection of their future benefits, USP agrees to bear 40% and FS to bear 60% of the costs incurred during the term of the agreement. The principal costs in the intangible development area are operating expenses incurred by FS in Country Z of 100X annually, and operating expenses incurred by USP in the United States also of 100X annually. Of the total costs of 200X, USP's share is 80X and FS's share is 120X, so that FS must make a payment to USP of 20X. This payment will be treated as a reimbursement of 20X of USP's operating expenses in the United States. Accordingly, USP's Form 1120 will reflect an 80X deduction on account of activities performed in the United States for purposes of allocation and apportionment of the deduction to source. The Form 5471 for FS will reflect a 100X deduction on account of activities performed in Country Z, and a 20X deduction on account of activities performed in the United States.

Example 2. The facts are the same as in *Example 1,* except that the 100X of costs borne by USP consist of 5X of operating expenses incurred by USP in the United States and 95X of fair market value rental cost for a facility in the United States. The depreciation deduction attributable to the U.S. facility is 7X. The 20X net payment by FS to USP will first be applied in reduction pro rata of the 5X deduction for operating expenses and the 7X depreciation deduction attributable to the U.S. facility. The 8X remainder will be treated as rent for the U.S. facility.

(i) *Accounting requirements.*—The accounting requirements of this paragraph are that the controlled participants in a qualified cost sharing arrangement must use a consistent method of accounting to measure costs and benefits, and must translate foreign currencies on a consistent basis.

(j) *Administrative requirements.*—(1) *In general.*—The administrative requirements of this paragraph consist of the documentation requirements of paragraph (j)(2) of this section and the reporting requirements of paragraph (j)(3) of this section.

(2) *Documentation.*—(i) *Requirements.*—A controlled participant must maintain sufficient documentation to establish that the requirements of paragraphs (b)(4) and (c)(1) of this section have been met, as well as the additional documentation specified in this paragraph (j)(2)(i), and must provide any such documentation to the Internal Revenue Service within 30 days of a request (unless an extension is granted by the district director). Documents necessary to establish the following must also be maintained—

(A) The total amount of costs incurred pursuant to the arrangement;

(B) The costs borne by each controlled participant;

(C) A description of the method used to determine each controlled participant's share of the intangible development costs, including the projections used to estimate benefits, and an explanation of why that method was selected;

(D) The accounting method used to determine the costs and benefits of the intangible development (including the method used to translate foreign currencies), and, to the extent that the method materially differs from U.S. generally accepted accounting principles, an explanation of such material differences;

(E) Prior research, if any, undertaken in the intangible development area, any tangible or intangible property made available for use in the arrangement, by each controlled participant, and any information used to establish the value of pre-existing and covered intangibles; and

(F) The amount taken into account as operating expenses attributable to stockbased compensation, including the method of measurement and timing used with respect to that amount as well as the data, as of date of grant, used to identify stock-based compensation related to the development of covered intangibles.

(ii) *Coordination with penalty regulation.*—The documents described in paragraph (j)(2)(i) of this section will satisfy the principal documents requirement under § 1.6662-6(d)(2)(iii)(B) with respect to a qualified cost sharing arrangement.

(3) *Reporting requirements.*—A controlled participant must attach to its U.S. income tax return a statement indicating that it is a participant in a qualified cost sharing arrangement, and listing the other controlled participants in the arrangement. A controlled participant that is not required to file a U.S. income tax return must ensure that such a statement is attached to Schedule M of any Form 5471 or to any Form 5472 filed with respect to that participant.

(k) *Effective date.*—This section applies for taxable years beginning on or after January 1, 1996. However, paragraphs (a)(3), (d)(2) and (j)(2)(i)(F) of this section apply for stock-based compensation granted in taxable years beginning on or after August 26, 2003.

(l) *Transition rule.*—A cost sharing arrangement will be considered a qualified cost sharing arrangement, within the meaning of this section, if, prior to January 1, 1996, the arrangement was a bona fide cost sharing arrangement under the provisions of § 1.482-7T (as contained in the 26 CFR part 1 edition revised as of April 1, 1995), but only if the arrangement is amended, if necessary, to conform with the provisions of this section by December 31, 1996. [Reg. § 1.482-7.]

☐ [*T.D.* 8632, 12-19-95. *Amended by T.D.* 8670, 5-9-96; *T.D.* 8930, 12-27-2000 *and T.D.* 9088, 8-25-2003 (*corrected* 3-22-2004).]

§ 1.482-8. Examples of the best method rule.—In accordance with the best method rule of § 1.482-1(c), a method may be applied in a particular case only if the comparability, quality of data, and reliability of assumptions under that method make it more reliable than any other available measure of the arm's length result. The following examples illustrate the comparative analysis required to apply this rule. As with all of the examples in these regulations, these examples are based on simplified facts, are provided solely for purposes of illustrating the type of analysis required under the relevant rule, and do not provide rules of general application. Thus, conclusions reached in these examples as to the relative reliability of methods are based on the assumed facts of the examples, and are not general conclusions concerning the relative reliability of any method.

Example 1—Preference for comparable uncontrolled price method. Company A is the U.S. distribution subsidiary of Company B, a foreign manufacturer of consumer electrical appliances. Company A purchases toaster ovens from Company B for resale in the U.S. market. To exploit other outlets for its toaster ovens, Company B also sells its toaster ovens to Company C, an unrelated U.S. distributor of toaster ovens. The products sold to Company A and Company C are identical in every respect and there are no material differences between the transactions. In this case application of the CUP method, using the sales of toaster ovens to Company C, generally will provide a more reliable measure of an arm's length result for the controlled sale of toaster ovens to Company A than the application of any other method. See §§ 1.482-1(c)(2)(i) and -3(b)(2)(ii)(A).

Example 2—Resale price method preferred to comparable uncontrolled price method. The facts are the same as in *Example 1*, except that the toaster ovens sold to Company A are of substantially higher quality than those sold to Company C and the effect on price of such quality differences cannot be accurately determined. In addition, in order to round out its line of consumer appliances Company A purchases blenders from unrelated parties for resale in the United States. The blenders are resold to substantially the same customers as the toaster ovens, have a similar resale value to the toaster ovens, and are purchased under similar terms and in similar volumes. The distribution functions performed by Company A appear to be similar for toaster ovens and blenders. Given the product differences between the toaster ovens, application of the resale price method using the purchases and resales of blenders as the uncontrolled comparables is likely to provide a more reliable measure of an arm's length result than application of the comparable uncontrolled price method using Company B's sales of toaster ovens to Company C.

Example 3—Resale price method preferred to comparable profits method. (i) The facts are the same as in *Example 2* except that Company A purchases all its products from Company B and Company B makes no uncontrolled sales into the United States. However, six uncontrolled U.S. distributors are identified that purchase a similar line of products from unrelated parties. The uncontrolled distributors purchase toaster ovens from unrelated parties, but there are significant differences in the characteristics of the toaster ovens, including the brandnames under which they are sold.

(ii) Under the facts of this case, reliable adjustments for the effect of the different brandnames cannot be made. Except for some differences in payment terms and inventory levels, the purchases and resales of toaster ovens by the three uncontrolled distributors are closely similar to the controlled purchases in terms of the markets in which they occur, the volume of the transactions, the marketing activities undertaken by the distributor, inventory levels, warranties, allocation of currency risk, and other relevant functions and risks. Reliable adjustments can be made for the differences in payment terms and inventory levels. In addition, sufficiently detailed accounting information is available to permit adjustments to be made for differences in accounting methods or in reporting of costs between cost of goods sold and operating expenses. There are no other material differences between the controlled and uncontrolled transactions.

(iii) Because reliable adjustments for the differences between the toaster ovens, including the trademarks under which they are sold, cannot be made, these uncontrolled transactions will not serve as reliable measures of an arm's length result under the comparable uncontrolled price method. There is, however, close functional similarity between the controlled and uncontrolled transactions and reliable adjustments have been made for material differences that would be likely to affect gross profit. Under these circumstances, the gross profit margins derived under the resale price method are less likely to be susceptible to any unidentified differences than the operating profit measures used under the comparable profits method. Therefore, given the close functional comparability between the controlled and uncontrolled transactions, and the high quality of the data, the resale price method achieves a higher degree of comparability and will provide a more reliable measure of an arm's length result. See § 1.482-1(c) (Best method rule).

Example 4—Comparable profits method preferred to resale price method. The facts are the same as in *Example 3*, except that the accounting information available for the uncontrolled comparables is not sufficiently detailed to ensure consistent reporting between cost of goods sold and operating expenses of material items such as discounts, insurance, warranty costs, and supervisory, general and administrative expenses. These expenses are significant in amount. Therefore, whether these expenses are treated as costs of goods sold or operating expenses would have a significant effect on gross margins. Because in this case reliable adjustments can not be made for such accounting differences, the reliability of the resale price method is significantly reduced. There is, however, close functional similarity between the controlled and uncontrolled transactions and reliable adjustments have been made for all material differences other than the potential accounting differences. Because the comparable profits method is not adversely affected by the potential accounting differences, under these circumstances the comparable profits method is likely to produce a more reliable measure of an arm's length result than the resale price method. See § 1.482-1(c) (Best method rule).

Example 5—Cost plus method preferred to comparable profits method. (i) USS is a U.S. company that manufactures machine tool parts and sells them to its foreign parent corporation, FP. Four U.S. companies are identified that also manufacture various types of machine tool parts but sell them to uncontrolled purchasers.

Reg. § 1.482-8

(ii) Except for some differences in payment terms, the manufacture and sales of machine tool parts by the four uncontrolled companies are closely similar to the controlled transactions in terms of the functions performed and risks assumed. Reliable adjustments can be made for the differences in payment terms. In addition, sufficiently detailed accounting information is available to permit adjustments to be made for differences between the controlled transaction and the uncontrolled comparables in accounting methods and in the reporting of costs between cost of goods sold and operating expenses.

(iii) There is close functional similarity between the controlled and uncontrolled transactions and reliable adjustments can be made for material differences that would be likely to affect gross profit. Under these circumstances, the gross profit markups derived under the cost plus method are less likely to be susceptible to any unidentified differences than the operating profit measures used under the comparable profits method. Therefore, given the close functional comparability between the controlled and uncontrolled transactions, and the high quality of the data, the cost plus method achieves a higher degree of comparability and will provide a more reliable measure of an arm's length result. See § 1.482-1(c) (Best method rule).

Example 6—Comparable profits method preferred to cost plus method. The facts are the same as in *Example 5*, except that there are significant differences between the controlled and uncontrolled transactions in terms of the types of parts and components manufactured and the complexity of the manufacturing process. The resulting functional differences are likely to materially affect gross profit margins, but it is not possible to identify the specific differences and reliably adjust for their effect on gross profit. Because these functional differences would be reflected in differences in operating expenses, the operating profit measures used under the comparable profits method implicitly reflect to some extent these functional differences. Therefore, because in this case the comparable profits method is less sensitive than the cost plus method to the potentially significant functional differences between the controlled and uncontrolled transactions, the comparable profits method is likely to produce a more reliable measure of an arm's length result than the cost plus method. See § 1.482-1(c) (Best method rule).

Example 7—Preference for comparable uncontrolled transaction method. (i) USpharm, a U.S. pharmaceutical company, develops a new drug Z that is a safe and effective treatment for the disease zeezee. USpharm has obtained patents covering drug Z in the United States and in various foreign countries. USpharm has also obtained the regulatory authorizations necessary to market drug Z in the United States and in foreign countries.

(ii) USpharm licenses its subsidiary in country X, Xpharm, to produce and sell drug Z in country X. At the same time, it licenses an unrelated company, Ydrug, to produce and sell drug Z in country Y, a neighboring country. Prior to licensing the drug, USpharm had obtained patent protection and regulatory approvals in both countries and both countries provide similar protection for intellectual property rights. Country X and country Y are similar countries in terms of population, per capita income and the incidence of disease zeezee. Consequently, drug Z is expected to sell in similar quantities and at similar prices in both countries. In addition, costs of producing drug Z in each country are expected to be approximately the same.

(iii) USpharm and Xpharm establish terms for the license of drug Z that are identical in every material respect, including royalty rate, to the terms established between USpharm and Ydrug. In this case the district director determines that the royalty rate established in the Ydrug license agreement is a reliable measure of the arm's length royalty rate for the Xpharm license agreement. Given that the same property is transferred in the controlled and uncontrolled transactions, and that the circumstances under which the transactions occurred are substantially the same, in this case the comparable uncontrolled transaction method is likely to provide a more reliable measure of an arm's length result than any other method. See § 1.482-4(c)(2)(ii).

Example 8—Residual profit split method preferred to other methods. (i) USC is a U.S. company that develops, manufactures and sells communications equipment. EC is the European subsidiary of USC. EC is an established company that carries out extensive research and development activities and develops, manufactures and sells communications equipment in Europe. There are extensive transactions between USC and EC. USC licenses valuable technology it has developed to EC for use in the European market but EC also licenses valuable technology it has developed to USC. Each company uses components manufactured by the other in some of its products and purchases products from the other for resale in its own market.

(ii) Detailed accounting information is available for both USC and EC and adjustments can be made to achieve a high degree of consistency in accounting practices between them. Relatively reliable allocations of costs, income and assets can be made between the business activities that are related to the controlled transactions and those that are not. Relevant marketing and research and development expenditures can be identified and reasonable estimates of the useful life of the related intangibles are available so that the capitalized value of the intangible development expenses of USC and EC can be calculated. In this case there is no reason to believe that the relative value of these capitalized expenses is substantially different from the relative value of the intangible property of USC and EC. Furthermore, comparables are identified that could be used to estimate a market return for the routine contributions of USC and EC. Based on these facts, the residual profit split could provide a reliable measure of an arm's length result.

(iii) There are no uncontrolled transactions involving property that is sufficiently comparable to much of the tangible and intangible property transferred between USC and EC to permit use of the comparable uncontrolled price method or the comparable uncontrolled transaction method. Uncontrolled companies are identified in Europe and the United States that perform somewhat similar activities to USC and EC; however, the activities of none of these companies are as complex as those of USC and EC and they do not use similar levels of highly valuable intangible property that they have developed themselves. Under these circumstances, the uncontrolled companies may be useful in determining a market return for the routine contributions of USC and EC, but that return would not reflect the value of the intangible property employed by USC and EC. Thus, none of the uncontrolled companies is sufficiently similar so that reliable results would be obtained using the resale price, cost plus, or comparable profits methods. Moreover, no uncontrolled companies can be identified that engaged in sufficiently similar activities and transactions with each other to employ the comparable profit split method.

(iv) Given the difficulties in applying the other methods, the reliability of the internal data on USC and EC, and the fact that acceptable comparables are available for deriving a market return for the routine contributions of USC and EC, the residual profit split method is likely to provide the most reliable measure of an arm's length result in this case.

Example 9—Comparable profits method preferred to profit split. (i) Company X is a large, complex U.S. company that carries out extensive research and development activities and manufactures and markets a variety of products. Company X has developed a new process by which compact disks can be fabricated at a fraction of the cost previously required. The process is expected to prove highly profitable, since there is a large market for compact disks. Company X establishes a new foreign subsidiary, Company Y, and licenses it the rights to use the process to fabricate compact disks for the foreign market as well as continuing technical support and improvements to the process. Company Y uses the process to fabricate compact disks which it supplies to related and unrelated parties.

(ii) The process licensed to Company Y is unique and highly valuable and no uncontrolled transfers of intangible property can be found that are sufficiently comparable to permit reliable application of the comparable uncontrolled transaction method. Company X is a large, complex company engaged in a variety of activities that owns unique and highly valuable intangible property. Consequently, no uncontrolled companies can be found that are similar to Company X. Furthermore, application of the profit split method in this case would involve the difficult and problematic tasks of allocating Company X's costs and assets between the relevant business activity and other activities and assigning a value to Company X's intangible contributions. On the other hand, Company Y performs relatively routine manufacturing and marketing activities and there are a number of similar uncontrolled companies. Thus, application of the comparable profits method using Company Y as the tested party is likely to produce a more reliable measure of an arm's length result than a profit split in this case. [Reg. § 1.482-8.]

☐ [*T.D.* 8552, 7-1-94.]

Proposed Regulation

Section 1.482-8 is redesignated as § 1.482-9 and a new § 1.482-8 is added to read as follows:

§ 1.482-8. Allocation of income earned in a global securities dealing operation.—

(a) *General requirements and definitions.—*
(1) *In general.—*Where two or more controlled taxpayers are participants in a global dealing operation, the allocation of income, gains, losses, deductions, credits and allowances (referred to herein as income and deductions) from the global dealing operation is determined under this section. The arm's length allocation of income and deductions related to a global dealing operation must be determined under one of the methods listed in paragraphs (b) through (f) of this section. Each of the methods must be applied in accordance with all of the provisions of § 1.482-1, including the best method rule of § 1.482-1(c), the comparability analysis of § 1.482-1(d), and the arm's length range of § 1.482-1(e), as those sections are supplemented or modified in paragraphs (a)(3) and (a)(4) of this section. The available methods are—

(i) The comparable uncontrolled financial transaction method, described in paragraph (b) of this section;

(ii) The gross margin method, described in paragraph (c) of this section;

(iii) The gross markup method, described in paragraph (d) of this section;

(iv) The profit split method, described in paragraph (e) of this section; and

(v) Unspecified methods, described in paragraph (f) of this section.

(2) *Definitions.*—(i) *Global dealing operation.*—A global dealing operation consists of the execution of customer transactions, including marketing, sales, pricing and risk management activities, in a particular financial product or line of financial products, in multiple tax jurisdictions and/or through multiple participants, as defined in paragraph (a)(2)(ii) of this section. The taking of proprietary positions is not included within the definition of a global dealing operation unless the proprietary positions are entered into by a regular dealer in securities in its capacity as such a dealer under paragraph (a)(2)(iii) of this section. Lending activities are not included within the definition of a global dealing operation. Therefore, income earned from such lending activities or from securities held for investment is not income from a global dealing operation and is not governed by this section. A global dealing operation may consist of several different business activities engaged in by participants. Whether a separate business activity is a global dealing operation shall be determined with respect to each type of financial product entered on the taxpayer's books and records.

(ii) *Participant.*—(A) A participant is a controlled taxpayer, as defined in § 1.482-1(i)(5), that is—

(1) A regular dealer in securities as defined in paragraph (a)(2)(iii) of this section; or

(2) A member of a group of controlled taxpayers which includes a regular dealer in securities, but only if that member conducts one or more activities related to the activities of such dealer.

(B) For purposes of paragraph (a)(2)(ii)(A)(*2*) of this section, such related activities are marketing, sales, pricing, risk management or brokering activities. Such related activities do not include credit analysis, accounting services, back office services, general supervision and control over the policies of the controlled taxpayer, or the provision of a guarantee of one or more transactions entered into by a regular dealer in securities or other participant.

(iii) *Regular dealer in securities.*—For purposes of this section, a regular dealer in securities is a taxpayer that—

(A) Regularly and actively offers to, and in fact does, purchase securities from and sell securities to customers who are not controlled taxpayers in the ordinary course of a trade or business; or

(B) Regularly and actively offers to, and in fact does, enter into, assume, offset, assign or otherwise terminate positions in securities with customers who are not controlled entities in the ordinary course of a trade or business.

(iv) *Security.*—For purposes of this section, a security is a security as defined in section 475(c)(2) or foreign currency.

(3) *Factors for determining comparability for a global dealing operation.*—The comparability factors set out in this paragraph (a)(3) must be applied in place of the comparability factors described in § 1.482-1(d)(3) for purposes of evaluating a global dealing operation.

(i) *Functional analysis.*—In lieu of the list set forth in § 1.482-1(d)(3)(i)(A) through (H), functions that may need to be accounted for in determining the comparability of two transactions are—

(A) Product research and development;

(B) Marketing;

(C) Pricing;

(D) Brokering; and

(E) Risk management.

(ii) *Contractual terms.*—In addition to the terms set forth in § 1.482-1(d)(3)(ii)(A), and subject to § 1.482-1(d)(3)(ii)(B), significant contractual terms for financial products transactions include—

(A) Sales or purchase volume;

(B) Rights to modify or transfer the contract;

(C) Contingencies to which the contract is subject or that are embedded in the contract;

(D) Length of the contract;

(E) Settlement date;

(F) Place of settlement (or delivery);

(G) Notional principal amount;

(H) Specified indices;

(I) The currency or currencies in which the contract is denominated;

(J) Choice of law and jurisdiction governing the contract to the extent chosen by the parties; and

(K) Dispute resolution, including binding arbitration.

Prop. Reg. § 1.482-8(a)(3)(ii)(K)

(iii) *Risk.*—In lieu of the list set forth in §1.482-1(d)(3), significant risks that could affect the prices or profitability include—

(A) Market risks, including the volatility of the price of the underlying property;

(B) Liquidity risks, including the fact that the property (or the hedges of the property) trades in a thinly traded market;

(C) Hedging risks;

(D) Creditworthiness of the counterparty; and

(E) Country and transfer risk.

(iv) *Economic conditions.*—. In lieu of the list set forth in §1.482-1(d)(3)(iv)(A) through (H), significant economic conditions that could affect the prices or profitability include—

(A) The similarity of geographic markets;

(B) The relative size and sophistication of the markets;

(C) The alternatives reasonably available to the buyer and seller;

(D) The volatility of the market; and

(E) The time the particular transaction is entered into.

(4) *Arm's length range.*—(i) *General rule.*—Except as modified in this paragraph (a)(4), §1.482-1(e) will apply to determine the arm's length range of transactions entered into by a global dealing operation as defined in paragraph (a)(2)(i) of this section. In determining the arm's length range, whether the participant is a buyer or seller is a relevant factor.

(ii) *Reliability.*—In determining the reliability of an arm's length range, it is necessary to consider the fact that the market for financial products is highly volatile and participants in a global dealing operation frequently earn only thin profit margins. The reliability of using a statistical range in establishing a comparable price of a financial product in a global dealing operation is based on facts and circumstances. In a global dealing operation, close proximity in time between a controlled transaction and an uncontrolled transaction may be a relevant factor in determining the reliability of the uncontrolled transaction as a measure of the arm's length price. The relevant time period will depend on the price volatility of the particular product.

(iii) *Authority to make adjustments.*—The district director may, notwithstanding §1.482-1(e)(1), adjust a taxpayer's results under a method applied on a transaction by transaction basis if a valid statistical analysis demonstrates that the taxpayer's controlled prices, when analyzed on an aggregate basis, provide results that are not arm's length. See §1.482-1(f)(2)(iv). This may occur, for example, when there is a pattern of prices in controlled transactions that are higher or lower than the prices of comparable uncontrolled transactions.

(5) *Examples.*—The following examples illustrate the principles of this paragraph (a).

Example 1. Identification of participants. (i) B is a foreign bank that acts as a market maker in foreign currency in country X, the country of which it is a resident. C, a country Y resident corporation, D, a country Z resident corporation, and USFX, a U.S. resident corporation are all members of a controlled group of taxpayers with B, and each acts as a market maker in foreign currency. In addition to market-making activities conducted in their respective countries, C, D, and USFX each employ marketers and traders, who also perform risk management with respect to their foreign currency operations. In a typical business day, B, C, D, and USFX each enter into several hundred spot and forward contracts to purchase and sell Deutsche marks (DM) with unrelated third parties on the interbank market. In the ordinary course of business, B, C, D, and USFX also enter into contracts to purchase and sell DM with each other.

(ii) Under §1.482-8(a)(2)(iii), B, C, D, and USFX are each regular dealers in securities because they each regularly and actively offer to, and in fact do, purchase and sell currencies to customers who are not controlled taxpayers, in the ordinary course of their trade or business. Consequently, each controlled taxpayer is also a participant. Together, B, C, D, and USFX conduct a global dealing operation within the meaning of §1.482-8(a)(2)(i) because they execute customer transactions in multiple tax jurisdictions. Accordingly, the controlled transactions between B, C, D, and USFX are evaluated under the rules of §1.482-8.

Example 2. Identification of participants. (i) The facts are the same as in Example 1, except that USFX is the only member of the group of controlled taxpayers that buys from and sells foreign currency to customers. C performs marketing and pricing activities with respect to the controlled group's foreign currency operation. D performs accounting and back office services for B, C, and USFX, but does not perform any marketing, sales, pricing, risk management or brokering activities with respect to the controlled group's foreign currency operation. B provides guarantees for all transactions entered into by USFX.

(ii) Under §1.482-8(a)(2)(iii), USFX is a regular dealer in securities and therefore is a participant. C also is a participant because it performs activities related to USFX's foreign currency dealing activities. USFX's and C's controlled transactions relating to their DM activities are evaluated under § 1.482-8. D is not a participant in a global dealing operation because its accounting and back office services are not related activities within the meaning of § 1.482-8(a)(2)(ii)(B). B also is not a participant in a global dealing operation because its guarantee function is not a related activity within the meaning of § 1.482-8(a)(2)(ii)(B). Accordingly, the determination of whether transactions between B and D and other members of the controlled group are at arm's length is not determined under § 1.482-8.

Example 3. Scope of a global dealing operation. (i) C, a U.S. resident commercial bank, conducts a banking business in the United States and in countries X and Y through foreign branches. C regularly and actively offers to, and in fact does, purchase from and sell foreign currency to customers who are not controlled taxpayers in the ordinary course of its trade or business in the United States and countries X and Y. In all the same jurisdictions, C also regularly and actively offers to, and in fact does, enter into, issume, offset, assign, or otherwise terminate positions in interest rate and cross-currency swaps with customers who are not controlled taxpayers. In addition, C regularly makes loans to customers through its U.S. and foreign branches. C regularly sells these loans to a financial institution that repackages the loans into securities.

(ii) C is a regular dealer in securities within the meaning of § 1.482-8(a)(2)(ii) because it purchases and sells foreign currency and enters into interest rate and cross-currency swaps with customers. Because C conducts these activities through U.S. and foreign branches, these activities constitute a global dealing operation within the meaning of § 1.482-8(a)(2)(i). The income, expense, gain or loss from C's global dealing operation is sourced under §§ 1.863-3(h) and 1.988-4(h). Under § 1.482-8(a)(2)(i), C's lending activities are not, however, part of a global dealing operation.

Example 4. Dissimilar products. The facts are the same as in Example 1, but B, C, D, and USFX also act as a market maker in Malaysian ringgit-U.S. dollar cross-currency options in the United States and countries X, Y, and Z. The ringgit is not widely traded throughout the world and is considered a thinly traded currency. The functional analysis required by § 1.482-8(a)(3)(i) shows that the development, marketing, pricing, and risk management of ringgit-U.S. dollar cross-currency option contracts are different than that of other foreign currency contracts, including option contracts. Moreover, the contractual terms, risks, and economic conditions of ringgit-U.S. dollar cross-currency option contracts differ considerably from that of other foreign currency contracts, including option contracts. See § 1.482-8(a)(3)(ii) through (iv). Accordingly, the ringgit-U.S. dollar cross-currency option contracts are not comparable to contracts in other foreign currencies.

Example 5. Relevant time period. (i) USFX is a U.S. resident corporation that is a regular dealer in securities acting as a market maker in foreign currency by buying from and selling currencies to customers. C performs marketing and pricing activities with respect to USFX's foreign currency operation. Trading in Deutsche marks (DM) is conducted between 10:00 a.m. and 10:30 a.m. and between 10:45 a.m. and 11:00 a.m. under the following circumstances.

10:00 a.m.	1.827DM: $1	Uncontrolled Transaction
10:04 a.m.	1.827DM: $1	Controlled Transaction
10:06 a.m.	1.826DM: $1	Uncontrolled Transaction
10:08 a.m.	1.825DM: $1	Uncontrolled Transaction
10:10 a.m.	1.827DM: $1	Controlled Transaction
10:12 a.m.	1.824DM: $1	Uncontrolled Transaction
10:15 a.m.	1.825DM: $1	Uncontrolled Transaction
10:18 a.m.	1.826DM: $1	Controlled Transaction
10:20 a.m.	1.824DM: $1	Uncontrolled Transaction
10:23 a.m.	1.825DM: $1	Uncontrolled Transaction
10:25 a.m.	1.825DM: $1	Uncontrolled Transaction
10:27 a.m.	1.827DM: $1	Controlled Transaction
10:30 a.m.	1.824DM: $1	Uncontrolled Transaction
10:45 a.m.	1.822DM: $1	Uncontrolled Transaction
10:50 a.m.	1.821DM: $1	Uncontrolled Transaction
10:55 a.m.	1.822DM: $1	Uncontrolled Transaction
11:00 a.m.	1.819DM: $1	Uncontrolled Transaction

(ii) USFX and C are participants in a global dealing operation under § 1.482-8(a)(2)(i). Therefore, USFX determines its arm's length price for its controlled DM contracts under § 1.482-8(a)(4). Under § 1.482-8(a)(4), the relevant arm's length range for setting the prices of USFX's controlled DM transactions occurs between 10:00 a.m. and 10:30 a.m. Because USFX has no controlled transactions between 10:45 a.m. and 11:00 a.m., and the price movement during this later time period continued to decrease, the 10:45 a.m. to 11:00 a.m. time period is not part of the relevant arm's length range for pricing USFX's controlled transactions.

(b) *Comparable uncontrolled financial transaction method.*—(1) *General rule.*—The comparable uncontrolled financial transaction (CUFT) method evaluates whether the amount charged in a controlled financial transaction is arm's length by reference to the amount charged in a comparable uncontrolled financial transaction.

(2) *Comparability and reliability.*—(i) *In general.*—The provisions of § 1.482-1(d), as modified by paragraph (a)(3) of this section, apply in determining whether a controlled financial transaction is comparable to a particular uncontrolled financial transaction. All of the relevant factors in paragraph (a)(3) of this section must be considered in determining the comparability of the two financial transactions. Comparability under this method depends on close similarity with respect to these factors, or adjustments to account for any differences. Accordingly, unless the controlled taxpayer can demonstrate that the relevant aspects of the controlled and uncontrolled financial transactions are comparable, the reliability of the results as a measure of an arm's length price is substantially reduced.

(ii) Adjustments for differences between controlled and *uncontrolled transactions.* If there are differences between controlled and uncontrolled transactions that would affect price, adjustments should be made to the price of the uncontrolled transaction according to the comparability provisions of § 1.482-1(d)(2) and paragraph (a)(3) of this section.

(iii) *Data and assumptions.*—The reliability of the results derived from the CUFT method is affected by the completeness and accuracy of the data used and the reliability of the assumptions mace to apply the method. See § 1.482-1(c)(2)(ii). In the case of a global dealing operation in which the CUFT is set through the use of indirect evidence, participants generally must establish data from a public exchange or quotation media contemporaneously to the time of the transaction, retain records of such data, and upon request furnish to the district director any pricing model used to establish indirect evidence of a CUFT, in order for this method to be a reliable means of evaluating the arm's length nature of the controlled transactions.

(3) *Indirect evidence of the price of a comparable uncontrolled financial transaction.*—(i) *In general.*—The price of a CUFT may be derived from data from public exchanges or quotation media if the following requirements are met—

(A) The data is widely and routinely used in the ordinary course of business in the industry to negotiate prices for uncontrolled sales;

(B) The data derived from public exchanges or quotation media is used to set prices in the controlled transaction in the same way it is used for uncontrolled transactions of the taxpayer, or the same way it is used by uncontrolled taxpayers; and

(C) The amount charged in the controlled transaction is adjusted to reflect differences in quantity, contractual terms, counterparties, and other factors that affect the price to which uncontrolled taxpayers would agree.

(ii) *Public exchanges or quotation media.*—For purposes of paragraph (b)(3)(i) of this section, an established financial market, as defined in § 1.1092(d)-1(b), qualifies as a public exchange or a quotation media.

(iii) *Limitation on use of data from public exchanges or quotation media.*—Use of data from public exchanges or quotation media is not appropriate under extraordinary market conditions. For example, under circumstances where the trading or transfer of a particular country's currency has been suspended or blocked by another country, causing significant instability in the prices of foreign currency contracts in the suspended or blocked currency, the prices listed on a quotation medium may not reflect a reliable measure of an arm's length result.

(4) *Arm's length range.*—See § 1.482-1(e)(2) and paragraph (a)(4) of this section for the determination of an arm's length range.

(5) *Examples.*—The following examples illustrate the principles of this paragraph (b).

Example 1. Comparable uncontrolled financial transactions. (i) B is a foreign bank resident in country X that acts as a market maker in foreign currency in country X. C, a country Y resident corporation, D, a country Z resident corporation, and USFX, a U.S. resident corporation are all members of a controlled group of taxpayers with B, and each acts as a market maker in foreign currency. In addition to market marking activities conducted in their respective countries, C, D, and USFX each employ marketers and traders, who also perform risk management with respect to their foreign currency operations. In a typical business day, B, C, D, and USFX each enter into several hundred spot and forward contracts to purchase and sell Deutsche marks (DM) with unrelated third parties on the interbank market. In the ordinary course of business, B, C, D, and USFX also each enter into contracts to purchase and sell DM with each other. On a typical day, no more than 10% of USFX's DM trades are with controlled taxpayers. USFX's DM-denominated spot and forward contracts do not vary in their terms, except as to the volume of DM purchased or sold. The differences in volume of DM purchased and sold by USFX do not affect the pricing of the DM. USFX maintains contemporaneous records of its trades, accounted for by type of trade and counterparty. The daily volume of USFX's DM-denominated spot and forward contracts consistently provides USFX with third party transactions that are contemporaneous with the transactions between controlled taxpayers.

(ii) Under § 1.482-8(a)(2)(iii), B, C, D, and USFX each are regular dealers in securities because they each regularly and actively offer to, and in fact do, purchase and sell currencies to customers who are not controlled taxpayers, in the ordinary course of their trade or business. Consequently, each controlled taxpayer is also a participant. Together, B, C, D, and USFX conduct a global dealing operation within the meaning of § 1.482-8(a)(2)(i) because they execute customer transactions in multiple tax jurisdictions. To determine the comparability of USFX's controlled and uncontrolled DM-denominated spot and forward transactions, the factors in § 1.482-8(a)(3) must be considered. USFX performs the same functions with respect to controlled and uncontrolled DM-denominated spot and forward transactions. See § 1.482-8(a)(3)(i). In evaluating the contractual terms under § 1.482-8(a)(3)(ii), it is determined that the volume of DM transactions varies, but these variances do not affect the pricing of USFX's uncontrolled DM transactions. Taking into account the risk factors of § 1.482-8(a)(3)(iii), USFX's risk associated with both the controlled and uncontrolled DM transactions does not vary in any material respect. In applying the significant factors for evaluating the economic conditions under § 1.482-8(a)(3)(iv), USFX has sufficient third party DM transactions to establish comparable economic conditions for evaluating an arm's length price. Accordingly, USFX's uncontrolled transactions are comparable to its controlled transactions in DM spot and forward contracts.

Example 2. Lack of comparable uncontrolled financial transactions. The facts are the same as in Example 1, except that USFX trades Italian lira (lira) instead of DM. USFX enters into few uncontrolled and controlled lira-denominated forward contracts each day. The daily volume of USFX's lira forward purchases and sales does not provide USFX with sufficient third party transactions to establish that uncontrolled transactions are sufficiently contemporaneous with controlled transactions to be comparable within the meaning of § 1.482-8(a)(3). In applying the comparability factors of § 1.482-8(a)(3), and of paragraph (a)(3)(iv) of this section in particular, USFX's controlled and uncontrolled lira forward purchases and sales are not entered into under comparable economic conditions. Accordingly, USFX's uncontrolled transactions in lira forward contracts are not comparable to its controlled lira forward transactions.

Example 3. Indirect evidence of the price of a comparable uncontrolled financial transaction. (i) The facts are the same as in Example 2, except that USFX uses a computer quotation system (CQS) that is an interdealer market, as described in § 1.1092(d)-1(b)(2), to set its price on lira forward contracts with controlled and uncontrolled taxpayers. Other financial institutions also use CQS to set their prices on lira forward contracts. CQS is an established financial market within the meaning of § 1.1092(d)-1(b).

(ii) Because CQS is an established financial market, it is a public exchange or quotation media within the meaning of § 1.482-8(b)(3)(i). Because other financial institutions use prices from CQS in the same manner as USFX, prices derived from CQS are deemed to be widely and routinely used in the ordinary course of business in the industry to negotiate prices for uncontrolled sales. See § 1.482-8(b)(3)(i)(A) and (B). If USFX adjusts the price quoted by CQS under the criteria specified in § 1.482-8(b)(2)(ii)(A)(3), the controlled price derived by USFX from CQS qualifies as indirect evidence of the price of a comparable uncontrolled financial transaction.

Example 4. Indirect evidence of the price of a comparable uncontrolled financial transaction—internal pricing models. (i) T is a U.S. resident corporation that acts as a market maker in U.S. dollar-denominated notional principal contracts. T's marketers and traders work together to sell notional principal contracts (NPCs), primarily to T's North and South American customers. T typically earns 4 basis points at the inception of each standard 3 year U.S. dollar-denominated interest rate swap that is entered into with an unrelated, financially sophisticated, creditworthy counterparty. TS, T's wholly owned U.K. subsidiary, also acts as a market maker in U.S. dollar-denominated NPCs, employing several traders and marketers who initiate contracts primarily with European customers. On occasion, for various business reasons, TS enters into a U.S. dollar-denominated NPC with T. The U.S. dollar-denominated NPCs that T enters into with unrelated parties are comparable in all material respects to the transactions that T enters into

Prop. Reg. § 1.482-8(b)(5)

with TS. TS prices all transactions with T using the same pricing models that TS uses to price transactions with third parties. The pricing models analyze relevant data, such as interest rates and volatilities, derived from public exchanges. TS records the data that were used to determine the price of each transaction at the time the transaction was entered into. Because the price produced by the pricing models is a mid-market price, TS adjusts the price so that it receives the same 4 basis point spread on its transaction with T that it would earn on comparable transactions with comparable counterparties during the same relevant time period.

(ii) Under §1.482-8(a)(2), T and TS are participants in a global dealing operation that deals in U.S. dollar-denominated NPCs. Because the prices produced by TS's pricing model are derived from information on public exchanges and TS uses the same pricing model to set prices for controlled and uncontrolled transactions, the requirements of §1.482-8(b)(3)(i)(A) and (B) are met. Because the U.S. dollar-denominated NPCs that T enters into with customers (uncontrolled transactions) are comparable to the transactions between T and TS within the meaning of §1.482-8(a)(3) and TS earns 4 basis points at inception of its uncontrolled transactions that are comparable to its controlled transactions, TS has also satisfied the requirements of §1.482-8(b)(3)(i)(C). Accordingly, the price produced by TS's pricing model constitutes indirect evidence of the price of a comparable uncontrolled financial transaction.

(c) *Gross margin method.*—(1) *General rule.*—The gross margin method evaluates whether the amount allocated to a participant in a global dealing operation is arm's length by reference to the gross profit margin realized on the sale of financial products in comparable uncontrolled transactions. The gross margin method may be used to establish an arm's length price for a transaction where a participant resells a financial product to an unrelated party that the participant purchased from a related party. The gross margin method may apply to transactions involving the purchase and resale of debt and equity instruments. The method may also be used to evaluate whether a participant has received an arm's length commission for its activities in a global dealing operation when the participant has not taken title to a security or has not become a party to a derivative financial product. To meet the arm's length standard, the gross profit margin on controlled transactions should be similar to that of comparable uncontrolled transactions.

(2) *Determination of an arm's length price.*—(i) *In general.*—The gross margin method measures an arm's length price by subtracting the appropriate gross profit from the applicable resale price for the financial product involved in the controlled transaction under review.

(ii) *Applicable resale price.*—The applicable resale price is equal to either the price at which the financial product involved is sold in an uncontrolled sale or the price at which contemporaneous resales of the same product are made. If the product purchased in the controlled sale is resold to one or more related parties in a series of controlled sales before being resold in an uncontrolled sale, the applicable resale price is the price at which the product is resold to an uncontrolled party, or the price at which contemporaneous resales of the same product are made. In such case, the determination of the appropriate gross profit will take into account the functions of all members of the controlled group participating in the series of controlled sales and final uncontrolled resales, as well as any other relevant factors described in paragraph (a)(3) of this section.

(iii) *Appropriate gross profit.*—The appropriate gross profit is computed by multiplying the applicable resale price by the gross profit margin, expressed as a percentage of total revenue derived from sales, earned in comparable uncontrolled transactions.

(3) *Comparability and reliability.*—(i) *In general.*—The provisions of §1.482-1(d), as modified by paragraph (a)(3) of this section, apply in determining whether a controlled transaction is comparable to a particular uncontrolled transaction. All of the factors described in paragraph (a)(3) of this section must be considered in determining the comparability of two financial products transactions, including the functions performed. The gross margin method considers whether a participant has earned a sufficient gross profit margin on the resale of a financial product (or line of products) given the functions performed by the participant. A reseller's gross profit margin provides compensation for performing resale functions related to the product or products under review, including an operating profit in return for the reseller's investment of capital and the assumption of risks. Accordingly, where a participant does not take title, or does not become a party to a financial product, the reseller's return to capital and assumption of risk are additional factors that must be considered in determining an appropriate gross profit margin. An appropriate gross profit margin primarily should be derived from comparable uncontrolled purchases and resales of the reseller involved in the controlled sale. This is because similar characteristics are more likely to be found among different resales of a financial

product or products made by the same reseller than among sales made by other resellers. In the absence of comparable uncontrolled transactions involving the same reseller, an appropriate gross profit margin may be derived from comparable uncontrolled transactions of other resellers.

(ii) *Adjustments for differences between controlled and uncontrolled transactions.*—If there are material differences between controlled and uncontrolled transactions that would affect the gross profit margin, adjustments should be made to the gross profit margin earned in the uncontrolled transaction according to the comparability provisions of § 1.482-1(d)(2) and paragraph (a)(3) of this section. For this purpose, consideration of operating expenses associated with functions performed and risks assumed may be necessary because differences in functions performed are often reflected in operating expenses. The effect of a difference in functions performed on gross profit, however, is not necessarily equal to the difference in the amount of related operating expenses.

(iii) *Reliability.*—In order for the gross margin method to be considered a reliable measure of an arm's length price, the gross profit should ordinarily represent an amount that would allow the participant who resells the product to recover its expenses (whether directly related to selling the product or more generally related to maintaining its operations) and to earn a profit commensurate with the functions it performed. The gross margin method may be a reliable means of establishing an arm's length price where there is a purchase and resale of a financial product and the participant who resells the property does not substantially participate in developing a product or in tailoring the product to the unique requirements of a customer prior to the resale.

(iv) *Data and assumptions.*—(A) *In general.*—The reliability of the results derived from the gross margin method is affected by the completeness and accuracy of the data used and the reliability of the assumptions made to apply the method. See § 1.482-1(c)(2)(ii). A participant may establish the gross margin by comparing the bid and offer prices on a public exchange or quotation media. In such case, the prices must be contemporaneous to the controlled transaction, and the participant must retain records of such data.

(B) *Consistency in accounting.*—The degree of consistency in accounting practices between the controlled transaction and the uncontrolled transactions may affect the reliability of the gross margin method. For example, differences as between controlled and uncontrolled transactions in the method used to value similar financial products (including methods of accounting, methods of estimation, and the timing for changes of such methods) could affect the gross profit. The ability to make reliable adjustments for such differences could affect the reliability of the results.

(4) *Arm's length range.*—See § 1.482-1(e)(2) and paragraph (a)(4) of this section for the determination of an arm's length range.

(5) *Example.*—The following example illustrates the principles of this paragraph (c).

Example 1. Gross margin method. (i) T is a U.S. resident financial institution that acts as a market maker in debt and equity instruments issued by U.S. corporations. Most of T's sales are to U.S.-based customers. TS, T's U.K. subsidiary, acts as a market maker in debt and equity instruments issued by European corporations and conducts most of its business with European-based customers. On occasion, however, a customer of TS wishes to purchase a security that is either held by or more readily accessible to T. To facilitate this transaction, T sells the security it owns or acquires to TS, who then promptly sells it to the customer. T and TS generally derive the majority of their profit on the difference between the price at which they purchase and the price at which they sell securities (the bid/offer spread). On average, TS's gross profit margin on its purchases and sales of securities from unrelated persons is 2%. Applying the comparability factors specified in § 1.482-8(a)(3), T's purchases and sales with unrelated persons are comparable to the purchases and sales between T and TS.

(ii) Under § 1.482-8(a)(2), T and TS are participants in a global dealing operation that deals in debt and equity securities. Since T's related purchases and sales are comparable to its unrelated purchases and sales, if TS's gross profit margin on purchases and sales of comparable securities from unrelated persons is 2%, TS should also typically earn a 2% gross profit on the securities it purchases from T. Thus, when TS resells for $100 a security that it purchased from T, the arm's length price at which TS would have purchased the security from T would normally be $98 ($100 sales price minus (2% gross profit margin x $100)).

(d) *Gross markup method.*—(1) *General rule.*—The gross markup method evaluates whether the amount allocated to a participant in a global dealing operation is arm's length by reference to the gross profit markup realized in comparable uncontrolled transactions. The gross markup method may be used to establish an arm's length price for a transaction where a participant purchases a financial product from an unrelated party that the participant sells to a related party. This method may apply to transactions involving the purchase and resale of debt and equity instruments. The method may also be used to evaluate whether a participant has received an arm's length commission for its role in a global dealing operation when the participant has not taken title to a security or has not become a party to a derivative financial product. To meet the arm's length standard, the gross profit markup on controlled transactions should be similar to that of comparable uncontrolled transactions.

(2) *Determination of an arm's length price.*—(i) *In general.*—The gross markup method measures an arm's length price by adding the appropriate gross profit to the participant's cost or anticipated cost, of purchasing, holding, or structuring the financial product involved in the controlled transaction under review (or in the case of a derivative financial product, the initial net present value, measured by the anticipated cost of purchasing, holding, or structuring the product).

(ii) *Appropriate gross profit.*—The appropriate gross profit is computed by multiplying the participant's cost or anticipated cost of purchasing, holding, or structuring a transaction by the gross profit markup, expressed as a percentage of cost, earned in comparable uncontrolled transactions.

(3) *Comparability and reliability.*—(i) *In general.*—The provisions of § 1.482-1(d), as modified by paragraph (a)(3) of this section, apply in determining whether a controlled transaction is comparable to a particular uncontrolled transaction. All of the factors described in paragraph (a)(3) of this section must be considered in determining the comparability of two financial products transactions, including the functions performed. The gross markup method considers whether a participant has earned a sufficient gross markup on the sale of a financial product, or line of products, given the functions it has performed. A participant's gross profit markup provides compensation for purchasing, hedging, and transactional structuring functions related to the transaction under review, including an operating profit in return for the investment of capital and the assumption of risks. Accordingly, where a participant does not take title, or does not become a party to a financial product, the reseller's return to capital and assumption of risk are additional factors that must be considered in determining the gross profit markup. An appropriate gross profit markup primarily should be derived from comparable uncontrolled purchases and sales of the participant involved in the controlled sale. This is because similar characteristics are more likely to be found among different sales of property made by the same participant than among sales made by other resellers. In the absence of comparable uncontrolled transactions involving the same participant, an appropriate gross profit markup may be derived from comparable uncontrolled transactions of other parties whether or not such parties are members of the same controlled group.

(ii) *Adjustments for differences between controlled and uncontrolled transactions.*—If there are material differences between controlled and uncontrolled transactions that would affect the gross profit markup, adjustments should be made to the gross profit markup earned in the uncontrolled transaction according to the comparability provisions of § 1.482-1(d)(2) and paragraph (a)(3) of this section. For this purpose, consideration of operating expenses associated with the functions performed and risks assumed may be necessary, because differences in functions performed are often reflected in operating expenses. The effect of a difference in functions on gross profit, however, is not necessarily equal to the difference in the amount of related operating expenses.

(iii) *Reliability.*—In order for the gross markup method to be considered a reliable measure of an arm's length price, the gross profit should ordinarily represent an amount that would allow the participant who purchases the product to recover its expenses (whether directly related to selling the product or more generally related to maintaining its operations) and to earn a profit commensurate with the functions it performed. As with the gross margin method, the gross markup method may be a reliable means of establishing an arm's length price where there is a purchase and resale of a financial product and the participant who resells the property does not substantially participate in developing a product or in tailoring the product to the unique requirements of a customer prior to the resale.

(iv) *Data and assumptions.*—(A) *In general.*—The reliability of the results derived from the gross markup method is affected by the completeness and accuracy of the data used and the reliability of the assumptions made to apply the method. See § 1.482-1(c)(2)(ii). A participant may establish the gross markup by comparing the bid and offer prices on a public exchange or quotation media. In such case, the prices must be contemporaneous with the controlled transaction, and the participant must retain records of such data.

(B) *Consistency in accounting.*—The degree of consistency in accounting practices between the controlled transaction and the uncontrolled transactions may affect the reliability of the gross markup method. For example, differences as between controlled and uncontrolled transactions in the method used to value similar financial products (including methods in accounting, methods of estimation, and the timing for changes of such methods) could affect the gross profit. The ability to make reliable adjustments for such differences could affect the reliability of the results.

(4) *Arm's length range.*—See § 1.482-1(e)(2) and paragraph (a)(4) of this section for the determination of an arm's length range.

(e) *Profit split method.*—(1) *General rule.*—The profit split method evaluates whether the allocation of the combined operating profit or loss of a global dealing operation to one or more participants is at arm's length by reference to the relative value of each participant's contribution to that combined operating profit or loss. The combined operating profit or loss must be derived from the most narrowly identifiable business activity of the participants for which data is available that includes the controlled transactions (relevant business activity).

(2) *Appropriate share of profit and loss.*—(i) *In general.*—The relative value of each participant's contribution to the global dealing activity must be determined in a manner that reflects the functions performed, risks assumed, and resources employed by each participant in the activity, consistent with the comparability provisions of § 1.482-1(d), as modified by paragraph (a)(3) of this section. Such an allocation is intended to correspond to the division of profit or loss that would result from an arrangement between uncontrolled taxpayers, each performing functions similar to those of the various controlled taxpayers engaged in the relevant business activity. The relative value of the contributions of each participant in the global dealing operation should be measured in a manner that most reliably reflects each contribution made to the global dealing operation and each participant's role in that contribution. In appropriate cases, the participants may find that a multi-factor formula most reliably measures the relative value of the contributions to the profitability of the global dealing operation. The profit allocated to any particular participant using a profit split method is not necessarily limited to the total operating profit from the global dealing operation. For example, in a given year, one participant may earn a profit while another participant incurs a loss, so long as the arrangement is comparable to an arrangement to which two uncontrolled parties would agree. In addition, it may not be assumed that the combined operating profit or loss from the relevant business activity should be shared equally or in any other arbitrary proportion. The specific method must be determined under paragraph (e)(4) of this section.

(ii) *Adjustment of factors to measure contribution clearly.*—In order to reliably measure the value of a participant's contribution, the factors, for example, those used in a multifactor formula, must be expressed in units of measure that reliably quantify the relative contribution of the participant. If the data or information is influenced by factors other than the value of the contribution, adjustments must be made for such differences so that the factors used in the formula only measure the relative value of each participant's contribution. For example, if trader compensation is used as a factor to measure the value added by the participants' trading expertise, adjustments must be made for variances in compensation paid to traders due solely to differences in the cost of living.

(3) *Definitions.*—The definitions in this paragraph (e)(3) apply for purposes of applying the profit split methods in this paragraph (e).

Gross profit is gross income earned by the global dealing operation.

Operating expenses includes all expenses not included in the computation of gross profit, except for interest, foreign income taxes as defined in § 1.901-2(a), domestic income taxes, and any expenses not related to the global dealing activity that is evaluated under the profit split method. With respect to interest expense, see section 864(e) and the regulations thereunder and § 1.882-5.

Operating profit or loss is gross profit less operating expenses, and includes all income, expense, gain, loss, credits or allowances attributable to each global dealing activity that is evaluated under the profit split method. It does not include income, expense, gain, loss, credits or allowances from activities that are not evaluated under the profit split method, nor does it include extraordinary gains or losses that do not relate to the continuing global dealing activities of the participant.

(4) *Application.*—Profit or loss shall be allocated under the profit split method using either the total profit split, described in paragraph (e)(5) of this section, or the residual profit split, described in paragraph (e)(6) of this section.

Prop. Reg. § 1.482-8(e)(4)

(5) *Total profit split.*—(i) *In general.*—The total profit split derives the percentage of the combined operating profit of the participants in a global dealing operation allocable to a participant in the global dealing operation by evaluating whether uncontrolled taxpayers who perform similar functions, assume similar risks, and employ similar resources would allocate their combined operating profits in the same manner.

(ii) *Comparability.*—The total profit split evaluates the manner by which comparable uncontrolled taxpayers divide the combined operating profit of a particular global dealing activity. The degree of comparability between the controlled and uncontrolled taxpayers is determined by applying the comparability standards of § 1.482-1(d), as modified by paragraph (a)(3) of this section. In particular, the functional analysis required by § 1.482-1(d)(3)(i) and paragraph (a)(3)(i) of this section is essential to determine whether two situations are comparable. Nevertheless, in certain cases, no comparable ventures between uncontrolled taxpayers may exist. In this situation, it is necessary to analyze the remaining factors set forth in paragraph (a)(3) of this section that could affect the division of operating profits between parties. If there are differences between the controlled and uncontrolled taxpayers that would materially affect the division of operating profit, adjustments must be made according to the provisions of § 1.482-1(d)(2) and paragraph (a)(3) of this section.

(iii) *Reliability.*—As indicated in § 1.482-1(c)(2)(i), as the degree of comparability between the controlled and uncontrolled transactions increases, the reliability of a total profit split also increases. In a global dealing operation, however, the absence of external market benchmarks (for example, joint ventures between uncontrolled taxpayers) on which to base the allocation of operating profits does not preclude use of this method if the allocation of the operating profit takes into account the relative contribution of each participant. The reliability of this method is increased to the extent that the allocation has economic significance for purposes other than tax (for example, satisfying regulatory standards and reporting, or determining bonuses paid to management or traders). The reliability of the analysis under this method may also be enhanced by the fact that all parties to the controlled transaction are evaluated under this method. The reliability of the results, however, of an analysis based on information from all parties to a transaction is affected by the reliability of the data and assumptions pertaining to each party to the controlled transaction. Thus, if the data and assumptions are significantly more reliable with respect to one of the parties than with respect to the others, a different method, focusing solely on the results of that party, may yield more reliable results.

(iv) *Data and assumptions.*—(A) *In general.*—The reliability of the results derived from the total profit split method is affected by the quality of the data used and the assumptions used to apply the method. See § 1.482-1(c)(2)(ii). The reliability of the allocation of income, expense, or other attributes between the participants' relevant business activities and the participants' other activities will affect the reliability of the determination of the combined operating profit and its allocation among the participants. If it is not possible to allocate income, expense, or other attributes directly based on factual relationships, a reasonable allocation formula may be used. To the extent direct allocations are not made, the reliability of the results derived from application of this method is reduced relative to the results of a method that requires fewer allocations of income, expense, and other attributes. Similarly, the reliability of the results derived from application of this method is affected by the extent to which it is possible to apply the method to the participants' financial data that is related solely to the controlled transactions. For example, if the relevant business activity is entering into interest rate swaps with both controlled and uncontrolled taxpayers, it may not be possible to apply the method solely to financial data related to the controlled transactions. In such case, the reliability of the results derived from application of this method will be reduced.

(B) *Consistency in accounting.*—The degree of consistency between the controlled and uncontrolled taxpayers in accounting practices that materially affect the items that determine the amount and allocation of operating profit affects the reliability of the result. Thus, for example, if differences in financial product valuation or in cost allocation practices would materially affect operating profit, the ability to make reliable adjustments for such differences would affect the reliability of the results.

(6) *Residual profit split.*—(i) *In general.*—The residual profit split allocates the combined operating profit or loss between participants following the two-step process set forth in paragraphs (e)(6)(ii) and (iii) of this section.

(ii) *Allocate income to routine contributions.*—The first step allocates operating income to each participant to provide an arm's length return for its routine contributions to the global dealing operation. Routine contributions are contributions of the same or similar kind as those made by uncontrolled taxpayers involved in similar business activities for which it is possible to identify market returns. Routine contributions ordinarily include contributions of tangible property, services, and intangibles that are generally owned or performed by uncontrolled taxpayers engaged in similar activities. For example, transactions processing and credit analysis are typically routine contributions. In addition, a participant that guarantees obligations of or otherwise provides credit support to another controlled taxpayer in a global dealing operation is regarded as making a routine contribution. A functional analysis is required to identify the routine contributions according to the functions performed, risks assumed, and resources employed by each of the participants. Market returns for the routine contributions should be determined by reference to the returns achieved by uncontrolled taxpayers engaged in similar activities, consistent with the methods described in §§ 1.482-2 through 1.482-4 and this § 1.482-8.

(iii) *Allocate residual profit.*—The allocation of income to the participant's routine contributions will not reflect profits attributable to each participant's valuable nonroutine contributions to the global dealing operation. Thus, in cases where valuable nonroutine contributions are present, there normally will be an unallocated residual profit after the allocation of income described in paragraph (e)(6)(ii) of this section. Under this second step, the residual profit generally should be divided among the participants based upon the relative value of each of their nonroutine contributions. Nonroutine contributions are contributions so integral to the global dealing operation that it is impossible to segregate them from the operation and find a separate market return for the contribution. Pricing and risk managing financial products almost invariably involve nonroutine contributions. Similarly, product development and information technology are generally nonroutine contributions. Marketing may be a nonroutine contribution if the marketer substantially participates in developing a product or in tailoring the product to the unique requirements of a customer. The relative value of the nonroutine contributions of each participant in the global dealing operation should be measured in a manner that most reliably reflects each nonroutine contribution made to the global dealing operation and each participant's role in the nonroutine contributions.

(iv) *Comparability.*—The first step of the residual profit split relies on external market benchmarks of profitability. Thus, the comparability considerations that are relevant for the first step of the residual profit split are those that are relevant for the methods that are used to determine market returns for routine contributions. In the second step of the residual profit split, however, it may not be possible to rely as heavily on external market benchmarks. Nevertheless, in order to divide the residual profits of a global dealing operation in accordance with each participant's nonroutine contributions, it is necessary to apply the comparability standards of § 1.482-1(d), as modified by paragraph (a)(3) of this section. In particular, the functional analysis required by § 1.482-1(d)(3)(i) and paragraph (a)(3)(i) of this section is essential to determine whether two situations are comparable. Nevertheless, in certain cases, no comparable ventures between uncontrolled taxpayers may exist. In this situation, it is necessary to analyze the remaining factors set forth in paragraph (a)(3) of this section that could affect the division of operating profits between parties. If there are differences between the controlled and uncontrolled taxpayers that would materially affect the division of operating profit, adjustments must be made according to the provisions of § 1.482-1(d)(2) and paragraph (a)(3) of this section.

(v) *Reliability.*—As indicated in § 1.482-1(c)(2)(i), as the degree of comparability between the controlled and uncontrolled transactions increases, the reliability of a residual profit split also increases. In a global dealing operation, however, the absence of external market benchmarks (for example, joint ventures between uncontrolled taxpayers) on which to base the allocation of operating profits does not preclude use of this method if the allocation of the residual profit takes into account the relative contribution of each participant. The reliability of this method is increased to the extent that the allocation has economic significance for purposes other than tax (for example, satisfying regulatory standards and reporting, or determining bonuses paid to management or traders). The reliability of the analysis under this method may also be enhanced by the fact that all parties to the controlled transaction are evaluated under this method. The reliability of the results, however, of an analysis based on information from all parties to a transaction is affected by the reliability of the data and assumptions pertaining to each party to the controlled transaction. Thus, if the data and assumptions are significantly more reliable with respect to one of the parties than with respect to the others, a different method, focusing solely on the results of that party, may yield more reliable results.

(vi) *Data and assumptions.*—(A) *General rule.*—The reliability of the results derived from the residual profit split is mea-

Prop. Reg. § 1.482-8(e)(6)(vi)(A)

sured under the standards set forth in paragraph (e)(5)(iv)(A) of this section.

(B) *Consistency in accounting.*—The degree of accounting consistency between controlled and uncontrolled taxpayers is measured under the standards set forth in paragraph (e)(5)(iv)(B) of this section.

(7) *Arm's length range.*—See § 1.482-1(e)(2) and paragraph (a)(4) of this section for the determination of an arm's length range.

(8) *Examples.*—The following examples illustrate the principles of this paragraph (e).

Example 1. Total profit split. (i) P, a U.S. corporation, establishes a separate U.S. subsidiary (USsub) to conduct a global dealing operation in over-the-counter derivatives. USsub in turn establishes subsidiaries incorporated and doing business in the U.K. (UKsub) and Japan (Jsub). Ussub, Uksub, and Jsub each employ marketers and traders who work closely together to design and sell derivative products to meet the particular needs of customers. Each also employs personnel who process and confirm trades, reconcile trade tickets and provide ongoing administrative support (back office services) for the global dealing operation. The global dealing operation maintains a single common book for each type of risk, and the book is maintained where the head trader for that type of risk is located. Thus, notional principal contracts denominated in North and South American currencies are booked in USsub, notional principal contracts denominated in European currencies are booked in UKsub, and notional principal contracts denominated in Japanese yen are booked in Jsub. However, each of the affiliates has authorized a trader located in each of the other affiliates to risk manage its books during periods when the booking location is closed. This grant of authority is necessary because marketers, regardless of their location, are expected to sell all of the group's products, and need to receive pricing information with respect to products during their clients' business hours, even if the booking location is closed. Moreover, P is known for making a substantial amount of its profits from trading activities, and frequently does not hedge the positions arising from its customer transactions in an attempt to profit from market changes. As a result, the traders in "off-hours" locations must have a substantial amount of trading authority in order to react to market changes.

(ii) Under § 1.482-8(a)(2), USsub, UKsub and Jsub are participants in a global dealing operation in over-the-counter derivatives. P determines that the total profit split method is the best method to allocate an arm's length amount of income to each participant. P allocates the operating profit from the global dealing operation between USsub, UKsub and Jsub on the basis of the relative compensation paid to marketers and traders in each location. In making the allocation, P adjusts the compensation amounts to account for factors unrelated to job performance, such as the higher cost of living in certain jurisdictions. Because the traders receive significantly greater compensation than marketers in order to account for their greater contribution to the profits of the global dealing operation, P need not make additional adjustments or weight the compensation of the traders more heavily in allocating the operating profit between the affiliates. For rules concerning the source of income allocated to Ussub, Uksub and Jsub (and any U.S. trade or business of the participants), see § 1.863-3(h).

Example 2. Total profit split. The facts are the same as in Example 1, except that the labor market in Japan is such that traders paid by Jsub are paid the same as marketers paid by Jsub at the same seniority level, even though the traders contribute substantially more to the profitability of the global dealing operation. As a result, the allocation method used by P is unlikely to compensate the functions provided by each affiliate so as to be a reliable measure of an arm's length result under §§ 1.482-8(e)(2) and 1.482-1(c)(1), unless P weights the compensation of traders more heavily than the compensation of marketers or develops another method of measuring the contribution of traders to the profitability of the global dealing operation.

Example 3. Total profit split. The facts are the same as in Example 2, except that, in P's annual report to shareholders, P divides its operating profit from customer business into "dealing profit" and "trading profit." Because both marketers and traders are involved in the dealing function, P divides the "dealing profit" between the affiliates on the basis of the relative compensation of marketers and traders. However, because only the traders contribute to the trading profit, P divides the trading profit between the affiliates on the basis of the relative compensation only of the traders. In making that allocation, P must adjust the compensation of traders in Jsub in order to account for factors not related to job performance.

Example 4. Total profit split. The facts are the same as in Example 1, except that P is required by its regulators to hedge its customer positions as much as possible and therefore does not earn any "trading profit." As a result, the marketing intangibles, such as customer relationships, are relatively more important than the intangibles used by traders. Accordingly, P must weight the compensation of marketers more heavily than the compensation of traders in order to take into account accurately the contribution each function makes to the profitability of the business.

Example 5. Residual profit split. (i) P is a U.S. corporation that engages in a global dealing operation in foreign currency options directly and through controlled taxpayers that are incorporated and operate in the United Kingdom (UKsub) and Japan (Jsub). Each controlled taxpayer is a participant in a global dealing operation. Each participant employs marketers and traders who work closely together to design and sell foreign currency options that meet the particular needs of customers. Each participant also employs salespeople who sell foreign currency options with standardized terms and conditions, as well as other financial products offered by the controlled group. The traders in each location risk manage a common book of transactions during the relevant business hours of each location. P has a AAA credit rating and is the legal counterparty to all third party transactions. The traders in each location have discretion to execute contracts in the name of P. UKsub employs personnel who process and confirm trades, reconcile trade tickets, and provide ongoing administrative support (back office services) for all the participants in the global dealing operation. The global dealing operation has generated $192 of operating profit for the period.

(ii) After analyzing the foreign currency options business, P has determined that the residual profit split method is the best method to allocate the operating profit of the global dealing operation and to determine an arm's length amount of compensation allocable to each participant in the global dealing operation.

(iii) The first step of the residual profit split method (§ 1.482-8(e)(6)(ii)) requires P to identify the routine contributions performed by each participant. P determines that the functions performed by the salespeople are routine. P determines that the arm's length compensation for salespeople is $3, $4, and $5 in the United States, the United Kingdom, and Japan, respectively. Thus, P allocates $3, $4, and $5 to P, UKsub, and Jsub, respectively.

(iv) Although the back office function would not give rise to participant status, in the context of a residual profit split allocation, the back office function is relevant for purposes of receiving remuneration for routine contributions to a global dealing operation. P determines that an arm's length compensation for the back office is $20. Since the back office services constitute routine contributions, $20 of income is allocated to UKsub under step 1 of the residual profit split method. In addition, P determines that the comparable arm's length compensation for the risk to which P is subject as counterparty is $40. Accordingly, $40 is allocated to P as compensation for acting as counterparty to the transactions entered into in P's name by Jsub and UKsub.

(v) The second step of the residual profit split method (§ 1.482-8(e)(6)(iii)) requires that the residual profit be allocated to participants according to the relative value of their nonroutine contributions. Under P's transfer pricing method, P allocates the residual profit of $120 ($192 gross income minus $12 salesperson commissions minus $20 payment for back office services minus $40 compensation for the routine contribution of acting as counterparty) using a multi-factor formula that reflects the relative value of the nonroutine contributions. Applying the comparability factors set out in § 1.482-8(a)(3), P allocates 40% of the residual profit to UKsub, 35% of the residual profit to P, and the remaining 25% of residual profit to Jsub. Accordingly, under step 2, $48 is allocated to UKsub, $42 is allocated to P, and $30 is allocated to Jsub. See § 1.863-3(h) for the source of income allocated to P with respect to its counterparty function.

(f) *Unspecified methods.*—Methods not specified in paragraphs (b), (c), (d), or (e) of this section may be used to evaluate whether the amount charged in a controlled transaction is at arm's length. Any method used under this paragraph (f) must be applied in accordance with the provisions of § 1.482-1 as modified by paragraph (a)(3) of this section.

(g) *Source rule for qualified business units.*—See § 1.863-3(h) for application of the rules of this section for purposes of determining the source of income, gain or loss from a global dealing operation among qualified business units (as defined in section 989(c) and §§ 1.863-3(h)(3)(iv) and 1.989(a)-1). [Prop. Reg. § 1.482-8.]

[Proposed 3-6-98.]

Corporations Improperly Accumulating Surplus

§ 1.532-1. Corporations subject to accumulated earnings tax.—

* * *

(c) *Foreign corporations.*—Section 531 is applicable to any foreign corporation, whether resident or nonresident, with respect to any income derived from sources within the United States, if any of its shareholders are subject to income tax on the distributions of the corporation by reason of being (1) citizens or residents of the United States, or (2) nonresident alien individuals to whom section 871 is applicable, or (3) foreign corporations if a beneficial interest therein is owned directly or indirectly by any shareholder specified in subparagraph (1) or (2) of this paragraph. [Reg. § 1.532-1.]

☐ [T.D. 6377, 5-12-59.]

§ 1.535-1. Definition.—

* * *

(b) In the case of a foreign corporation, whether resident or nonresident, which files or causes to be filed a return, the accumulated taxable income shall be the taxable income from sources within the United States with the adjustments prescribed by section 535(b) and § 1.535-2 minus the sum of the dividends paid deduction and the accumulated earnings credit. In the case of a foreign corporation which files no return, the accumulated taxable income shall be the gross income from sources within the United States without allowance of any deductions (including the accumulated earnings credit). [Reg. § 1.535-1.]

☐ [T.D. 6377, 5-12-59. Amended by T.D. 7244, 12-29-72.]

§ 1.535-2. Adjustments to taxable income.—(a) *Taxes.*—

* * *

(2) *Taxes of foreign countries and United States possessions.*—In determining accumulated taxable income for any taxable year, if the taxpayer chooses the benefits of section 901 for such taxable year, a deduction shall be allowed for—

(i) The income, war profits, and excess profits taxes imposed by foreign countries or possessions of the United States and accrued during such taxable year, and

(ii) In the case of a domestic corporation, the foreign income taxes deemed to be paid for such taxable year under section 902(a) in accordance with §§ 1.902-1 and 1.902-2 or section 960(a)(1) in accordance with § 1.960-7. In no event shall the amount under subdivision (ii) of this subparagraph exceed the amount includible in gross income with respect to such taxes under section 78 and § 1.78-1. The credit for such taxes provided by section 901 shall not be allowed against the accumulated earnings tax imposed by section 531. See section 901(a).

* * *

[Reg. § 1.535-2.]

☐ [T.D. 6377, 5-12-59. *Amended by T.D.* 6805, 3-8-65; T.D. 6841, 7-26-65; T.D. 7301, 1-3-74 *and* T.D. 7649, 10-17-79.]

Estates, Trusts, and Beneficiaries

§ 1.679-1. U.S. transferor treated as owner of foreign trust.—(a) *In general.*—A U.S. transferor who transfers property to a foreign trust is treated as the owner of the portion of the trust attributable to the property transferred if there is a U.S. beneficiary of any portion of the trust, unless an exception in § 1.679-4 applies to the transfer.

(b) *Interaction with sections 673 through 678.*—The rules of this section apply without regard to whether the U.S. transferor retains any power or interest described in sections 673 through 677. If a U.S. transferor would be treated as the owner of a portion of a foreign trust pursuant to the rules of this section and another person would be treated as the owner of the same portion of the trust pursuant to section 678, then the U.S. transferor is treated as the owner and the other person is not treated as the owner.

(c) *Definitions.*—The following definitions apply for purposes of this section and §§ 1.679-2 through 1.679-7:

(1) *U.S. transferor.*—The term *U.S. transferor* means any U.S. person who makes a transfer (as defined in § 1.679-3) of property to a foreign trust.

(2) *U.S. person.*—The term *U.S. person* means a United States person as defined in section 7701(a)(30), a nonresident alien individual who elects under section 6013(g) to be treated as resident of the United States, and an individual who is a dual resident taxpayer within the meaning of § 301.7701(b)-7(a) of this chapter.

(3) *Foreign trust.*—Section 7701(a)(31)(B) defines the term *foreign trust*. See also § 301.7701-7 of this chapter.

(4) *Property.*—The term *property* means any property including cash.

(5) *Related person.*—A person is a *related person* if, without regard to the transfer at issue, the person is—

(i) A grantor of any portion of the trust (within the meaning of § 1.671-2(e)(1));

(ii) An owner of any portion of the trust under sections 671 through 679;

(iii) A beneficiary of the trust; or

(iv) A person who is related (within the meaning of section 643(i)(2)(B)) to any grantor, owner or beneficiary of the trust.

(6) *Obligation.*—The term *obligation* means any bond, note, debenture, certificate, bill receivable, account receivable, note receiva-

ble, open account, or other evidence of indebtedness, and, to the extent not previously described, any annuity contract.

(d) *Examples.*—The following examples illustrate the rules of paragraph (a) of this section. In these examples, A is a resident alien, B is A's son, who is a resident alien, C is A's father, who is a resident alien, D is A's uncle, who is a nonresident alien, and FT is a foreign trust. The examples are as follows:

Example 1. Interaction with section 678. A creates and funds FT. FT may provide for the education of B by paying for books, tuition, room and board. In addition, C has the power to vest the trust corpus or income in himself within the meaning of section 678(a)(1). Under paragraph (b) of this section, A is treated as the owner of the portion of FT attributable to the property transferred to FT by A and C is not treated as the owner thereof.

Example 2. U.S. person treated as owner of a portion of FT. D creates and funds FT for the benefit of B. D retains a power described in section 676 and § 1.672(f)-3(a)(1). A transfers property to FT. Under sections 676 and 672(f), D is treated as the owner of the portion of FT attributable to the property transferred by D. Under paragraph (a) of this section, A is treated as the owner of the portion of FT attributable to the property transferred by A.

[Reg. § 1.679-1.]

☐ [T.D. 8955, 7-19-2001.]

§ 1.679-2. Trusts treated as having a U.S. beneficiary.—(a) *Existence of U.S. beneficiary.*—(1) *In general.*—The determination of whether a foreign trust has a U.S. beneficiary is made on an annual basis. A foreign trust is treated as having a U.S. beneficiary unless during the taxable year of the U.S. transferor—

(i) No part of the income or corpus of the trust may be paid or accumulated to or for the benefit of, directly or indirectly, a U.S. person; and

(ii) If the trust is terminated at any time during the taxable year, no part of the income or corpus of the trust could be paid to or for the benefit of, directly or indirectly, a U.S. person.

(2) *Benefit to a U.S. person.*—(i) *In general.*—For purposes of paragraph (a)(1) of this section, income or corpus may be paid or accumulated to or for the benefit of a U.S. person during a taxable year of the U.S. transferor if during that year, directly or indirectly, income may be distributed to, or accumulated for the benefit of, a U.S. person, or corpus may be distributed to, or held for the future benefit of, a U.S. person. This determination is made without regard to whether income or corpus is actually distributed to a U.S. person during that year, and without regard to whether a U.S. person's interest in the trust income or corpus is contingent on a future event.

(ii) *Certain unexpected beneficiaries.*—Notwithstanding paragraph (a)(2)(i) of this section, for purposes of paragraph (a)(1) of this section, a person who is not named as a beneficiary and is not a member of a class of beneficiaries as defined under the trust instrument is not taken into consideration if the U.S. transferor demonstrates to the satisfaction of the Commissioner that the person's contingent interest in the trust is so remote as to be negligible. The preceding sentence does not apply with respect to persons to whom distributions could be made pursuant to a grant of discretion to the trustee or any other person. A class of beneficiaries generally does not include heirs who will benefit from the trust under the laws of intestate succession in the event that the named beneficiaries (or members of the named class) have all deceased (whether or not stated as a named class in the trust instrument).

(iii) *Examples.*—The following examples illustrate the rules of paragraphs (a)(1) and (2) of this section. In these examples, A is a resident alien, B is A's son, who is a resident alien, C is A's daughter, who is a nonresident alien, and FT is a foreign trust. The examples are as follows:

Example 1. Distribution of income to U.S. person. A transfers property to FT. The trust instrument provides that all trust income is to be distributed currently to B. Under paragraph (a)(1) of this section, FT is treated as having a U.S. beneficiary.

Example 2. Income accumulation for the benefit of a U.S. person. In 2001, A transfers property to FT. The trust instrument provides that from 2001 through 2010, the trustee of FT may distribute trust income to C or may accumulate the trust income. The trust instrument further provides that in 2011, the trust will terminate and the trustee may distribute the trust assets to either or both of B and C, in the trustee's discretion. If the trust terminates unexpectedly prior to 2011, all trust assets must be distributed to C. Because it is possible that income may be accumulated in each year, and that the accumulated income ultimately may be distributed to B, a U.S. person, under paragraph (a)(1) of this section FT is treated as having a U.S. beneficiary during each of A's tax years from 2001 through 2011. This result applies even though no U.S. person may receive distributions from the trust during the tax years 2001 through 2010.

Example 3. Corpus held for the benefit of a U.S. person. The facts are the same as in *Example 2*, except that from 2001 through 2011, all trust income must be distributed to *C*. In 2011, the trust will terminate and the trustee may distribute the trust corpus to either or both of *B* and *C*, in the trustee's discretion. If the trust terminates unexpectedly prior to 2011, all trust corpus must be distributed to *C*. Because during each of *A*'s tax years from 2001 through 2011 trust corpus is held for possible future distribution to *B*, a U.S. person, under paragraph (a)(1) of this section *FT* is treated as having a U.S. beneficiary during each of those years. This result applies even though no U.S. person may receive distributions from the trust during the tax years 2001 through 2010.

Example 4. Distribution upon U.S. transferor's death. *A* transfers property to *FT*. The trust instrument provides that all trust income must be distributed currently to *C* and, upon *A*'s death, the trust will terminate and the trustee may distribute the trust corpus to either or both of *B* and *C*. Because *B* may receive a distribution of corpus upon the termination of *FT*, and *FT* could terminate in any year, *FT* is treated as having a U.S. beneficiary in the year of the transfer and in subsequent years.

Example 5. Distribution after U.S. transferor's death. The facts are the same as in *Example 4*, except the trust instrument provides that the trust will not terminate until the year following *A*'s death. Upon termination, the trustee may distribute the trust assets to either or both of *B* and *C*, in the trustee's discretion. All trust assets are invested in the stock of *X*, a foreign corporation, and *X* makes no distributions to *FT*. Although no U.S. person may receive a distribution until the year after *A*'s death, and *FT* has no realized income during any year of its existence, during each year in which *A* is living corpus may be held for future distribution to *B*, a U.S. person. Thus, under paragraph (a)(1) of this section *FT* is treated as having a U.S. beneficiary during each of *A*'s tax years from 2001 through the year of *A*'s death.

Example 6. Constructive benefit to U.S. person. *A* transfers property to *FT*. The trust instrument provides that no income or corpus may be paid directly to a U.S. person. However, the trust instrument provides that trust corpus may be used to satisfy *B*'s legal obligations to a third party by making a payment directly to the third party. Under paragraphs (a)(1) and (2) of this section, *FT* is treated as having a U.S. beneficiary.

Example 7. U.S. person with negligible contingent interest. *A* transfers property to *FT*. The trust instrument provides that all income is to be distributed currently to *C*, and upon *C*'s death, all corpus is to be distributed to whomever of *C*'s three children is then living. All of *C*'s children are nonresident aliens. Under the laws of intestate succession that would apply to *FT*, if all of *C*'s children are deceased at the time of *C*'s death, the corpus would be distributed to *A*'s heirs. *A*'s living relatives at the time of the transfer consist solely of two brothers and two nieces, all of whom are nonresident aliens, and two first cousins, one of whom, *E*, is a U.S. citizen. Although it is possible under certain circumstances that *E* could receive a corpus distribution under the applicable laws of intestate succession, for each year the trust is in existence *A* is able to demonstrate to the satisfaction of the Commissioner under paragraph (a)(2)(ii) of this section that *E*'s contingent interest in *FT* is so remote as to be negligible. Provided that paragraph (a)(4) of this section does not require a different result, *FT* is not treated as having a U.S. beneficiary.

Example 8. U.S. person with non-negligible contingent interest. *A* transfers property to *FT*. The trust instrument provides that all income is to be distributed currently to *D*, *A*'s uncle, who is a nonresident alien, and upon *A*'s death, the corpus is to be distributed to D if he is then living. Under the laws of intestate succession that would apply to *FT*, *B* and *C* would share equally in the trust corpus if *D* is not living at the time of *A*'s death. *A* is unable to demonstrate to the satisfaction of the Commissioner that *B*'s contingent interest in the trust is so remote as to be negligible. Under paragraph (a)(2)(ii) of this section, *FT* is treated as having a U.S. beneficiary as of the year of the transfer.

Example 9. U.S. person as member of class of beneficiaries. *A* transfers property to *FT*. The trust instrument provides that all income is to be distributed currently to *D*, *A*'s uncle, who is a nonresident alien, and upon *A*'s death, the corpus is to be distributed to *D* if he is then living. If *D* is not then living, the corpus is to be distributed to *D*'s descendants. *D*'s grandson, *E*, is a resident alien. Under paragraph (a)(2)(ii) of this section, *FT* is treated as having a U.S. beneficiary as of the year of the transfer.

Example 10. Trustee's discretion in choosing beneficiaries. *A* transfers property to *FT*. The trust instrument provides that the trustee may distribute income and corpus to, or accumulate income for the benefit of, any person who is pursuing the academic study of ancient Greek, in the trustee's discretion. Because it is possible that a U.S. person will receive distributions of income or corpus, or will have income accumulated for his benefit, *FT* is treated as having a U.S. beneficiary. This result applies even if, during a tax year, no distributions or accumulations are actually made to or for the benefit of a U.S. person. *A* may not invoke paragraph (a)(2)(ii) of this section because a U.S. person could benefit pursuant to a grant of discretion in the trust instrument.

Example 11. Appointment of remainder beneficiary. *A* transfers property to *FT*. The trust instrument provides that the trustee may distribute current income to C, or may accumulate income, and, upon termination of the trust, trust assets are to be distributed to C. However, the trust instrument further provides that D, A's uncle, may appoint a different remainder beneficiary. Because it is possible that a U.S. person could be named as the remainder beneficiary, and because corpus could be held in each year for the future benefit of that U.S. person, FT is treated as having a U.S. beneficiary for each year.

Example 12. Trust not treated as having a U.S. beneficiary. A transfers property to FT. The trust instrument provides that the trustee may distribute income and corpus to, or accumulate income for the benefit of C. Upon termination of the trust, all income and corpus must be distributed to C. Assume that paragraph (a)(4) of this section is not applicable under the facts and circumstances and that A establishes to the satisfaction of the Commissioner under paragraph (a)(2)(ii) of this section that no U.S. persons are reasonably expected to benefit from the trust. Because no part of the income or corpus of the trust may be paid or accumulated to or for the benefit of, either directly or indirectly, a U.S. person, and if the trust is terminated no part of the income or corpus of the trust could be paid to or for the benefit of, either directly or indirectly, a U.S. person, FT is not treated as having a U.S. beneficiary.

Example 13. U.S. beneficiary becomes non-U.S. person. In 2001, A transfers property to FT. The trust instrument provides that, as long as B remains a U.S. resident, no distributions of income or corpus may be made from the trust to B. The trust instrument further provides that if B becomes a nonresident alien, distributions of income (including previously accumulated income) and corpus may be made to him. If B remains a U.S. resident at the time of FT's termination, all accumulated income and corpus is to be distributed to C. In 2007, B becomes a nonresident alien and remains so thereafter. Because income may be accumulated during the years 2001 through 2007 for the benefit of a person who is a U.S. person during those years, FT is treated as having a U.S. beneficiary under paragraph (a)(1) of this section during each of those years. This result applies even though B cannot receive distributions from FT during the years he is a resident alien and even though B might remain a resident alien who is not entitled to any distribution from FT. Provided that paragraph (a)(4) of this section does not require a different result and that A establishes to the satisfaction of the Commissioner under paragraph (a)(2)(ii) of this section that no other U.S. persons are reasonably expected to benefit from the trust, FT is not treated as having a U.S. beneficiary under paragraph (a)(1) of this section during tax years after 2007.

(3) *Changes in beneficiary's status.*—(i) *In general.*—For purposes of paragraph (a)(1) of this section, the possibility that a person that is not a U.S. person could become a U.S. person will not cause that person to be treated as a U.S. person for purposes of paragraph (a)(1) of this section until the tax year of the U.S. transferor in which that individual actually becomes a U.S. person. However, if a person who is not a U.S. person becomes a U.S. person for the first time more than 5 years after the date of a transfer to the foreign trust by a U.S. transferor, that person is not treated as a U.S. person for purposes of applying paragraph (a)(1) of this section with respect to that transfer.

(ii) *Examples.*—The following examples illustrate the rules of paragraph (a)(3) of this section. In these examples, A is a resident alien, B is A's son, who is a resident alien, C is A's daughter, who is a nonresident alien, and FT is a foreign trust. The examples are as follows:

Example 1. Non-U.S. beneficiary becomes U.S. person. In 2001, A transfers property to FT. The trust instrument provides that all income is to be distributed currently to C and that, upon the termination of FT, all corpus is to be distributed to C. Assume that paragraph (a)(4) of this section is not applicable under the facts and circumstances and that A establishes to the satisfaction of the Commissioner under paragraph (a)(2)(ii) of this section that no U.S. persons are reasonably expected to benefit from the trust. Under paragraph (a)(3)(i) of this section, FT is not treated as having a U.S. beneficiary during the tax years of A in which C remains a nonresident alien. If C first becomes a resident alien in 2004, FT is treated as having a U.S. beneficiary commencing in that year under paragraph (a)(3) of this section. See paragraph (c) of this section regarding the treatment of A upon FT's acquisition of a U.S. beneficiary.

Example 2. Non-U.S. beneficiary becomes U.S. person more than 5 years after transfer. The facts are the same as in *Example 1*, except C first becomes a resident alien in 2007. FT is treated as not having a U.S. beneficiary under paragraph (a)(3)(i) of this section with respect to the property transfer by A. However, if C had previously been a U.S. person during any prior period, the 5-year exception in paragraph (a)(3)(i) of this section would not apply in 2007 because it would not have been the first time C became a U.S. person.

(4) *General rules.*—(i) *Records and documents.*—Even if, based on the terms of the trust instrument, a foreign trust is not treated as

Reg. § 1.679-2(a)(4)(i)

having a U.S. beneficiary within the meaning of paragraph (a)(1) of this section, the trust may nevertheless be treated as having a U.S. beneficiary pursuant to paragraph (a)(1) of this section based on the following—

(A) All written and oral agreements and understandings relating to the trust;

(B) Memoranda or letters of wishes;

(C) All records that relate to the actual distribution of income and corpus; and

(D) All other documents that relate to the trust, whether or not of any purported legal effect.

(ii) *Additional factors.*—For purposes of determining whether a foreign trust is treated as having a U.S. beneficiary within the meaning of paragraph (a)(1) of this section, the following additional factors are taken into account—

(A) If the terms of the trust instrument allow the trust to be amended to benefit a U.S. person, all potential benefits that could be provided to a U.S. person pursuant to an amendment must be taken into account;

(B) If the terms of the trust instrument do not allow the trust to be amended to benefit a U.S. person, but the law applicable to a foreign trust may require payments or accumulations of income or corpus to or for the benefit of a U.S. person (by judicial reformation or otherwise), all potential benefits that could be provided to a U.S. person pursuant to the law must be taken into account, unless the U.S. transferor demonstrates to the satisfaction of the Commissioner that the law is not reasonably expected to be applied or invoked under the facts and circumstances; and

(C) If the parties to the trust ignore the terms of the trust instrument, or if it is reasonably expected that they will do so, all benefits that have been, or are reasonably expected to be, provided to a U.S. person must be taken into account.

(iii) *Examples.*—The following examples illustrate the rules of paragraph (a)(4) of this section. In these examples, *A* is a resident alien, *B* is *A*'s son, who is a resident alien, *C* is *A*'s daughter, who is a nonresident alien, and *FT* is a foreign trust. The examples are as follows:

Example 1. Amendment pursuant to local law. *A* creates and funds *FT* for the benefit of *C*. The terms of *FT* (which, according to the trust instrument, cannot be amended) provide that no part of the income or corpus of *FT* may be paid or accumulated during the taxable year to or for the benefit of any U.S. person, either during the existence of *FT* or at the time of its termination. However, pursuant to the applicable foreign law, *FT* can be amended to provide for additional beneficiaries, and there is an oral understanding between *A* and the trustee that *B* can be added as a beneficiary. Under paragraphs (a)(1) and (a)(4)(ii)(B) of this section, *FT* is treated as having a U.S. beneficiary.

Example 2. Actions in violation of the terms of the trust. *A* transfers property to *FT*. The trust instrument provides that no U.S. person can receive income or corpus from *FT* during the term of the trust or at the termination of *FT*. Notwithstanding the terms of the trust instrument, a letter of wishes directs the trustee of *FT* to provide for the educational needs of *B*, who is about to begin college. The letter of wishes contains a disclaimer to the effect that its contents are only suggestions and recommendations and that the trustee is at all times bound by the terms of the trust as set forth in the trust instrument. Under paragraphs (a)(1) and (a)(4)(ii)(C) of this section, *FT* is treated as having a U.S. beneficiary.

(b) *Indirect U.S. beneficiaries.*—(1) *Certain foreign entities.*—For purposes of paragraph (a)(1) of this section, an amount is treated as paid or accumulated to or for the benefit of a U.S. person if the amount is paid to or accumulated for the benefit of—

(i) A controlled foreign corporation, as defined in section 957(a);

(ii) A foreign partnership, if a U.S. person is a partner of such partnership; or

(iii) A foreign trust or estate, if such trust or estate has a U.S. beneficiary (within the meaning of paragraph (a)(1) of this section).

(2) *Other indirect beneficiaries.*—For purposes of paragraph (a)(1) of this section, an amount is treated as paid or accumulated to or for the benefit of a U.S. person if the amount is paid to or accumulated for the benefit of a U.S. person through an intermediary, such as an agent or nominee, or by any other means where a U.S. person may obtain an actual or constructive benefit.

(3) *Examples.*—The following examples illustrate the rules of this paragraph (b). Unless otherwise noted, *A* is a resident alien. *B* is *A*'s son and is a resident alien. *FT* is a foreign trust. The examples are as follows:

Example 1. Trust benefitting foreign corporation. *A* transfers property to *FT*. The beneficiary of *FT* is *FC*, a foreign corporation. *FC* has outstanding solely 100 shares of common stock. *B* owns 49 shares of the *FC* stock and *FC2*, also a foreign corporation, owns the remaining 51 shares. *FC2* has outstanding solely 100 shares of common stock. *B* owns 49 shares of *FC2* and nonresident alien individuals own the remaining 51 *FC2* shares. *FC* is a controlled foreign corporation (as defined in section 957(a), after the application of section

958(a)(2)). Under paragraphs (a)(1) and (b)(1)(i) of this section, *FT* is treated as having a U.S. beneficiary.

Example 2. Trust benefitting another trust. A transfers property to *FT*. The terms of *FT* permit current distributions of income to *B*. A transfers property to another foreign trust, *FT2*. The terms of *FT2* provide that no U.S. person can benefit either as to income or corpus, but permit current distributions of income to *FT*. Under paragraph (a)(1) of this section, *FT* is treated as having a U.S. beneficiary and, under paragraphs (a)(1) and (b)(1)(iii) of this section, *FT2* is treated as having a U.S. beneficiary.

Example 3. Trust benefitting another trust after transferor's death. A transfers property to *FT*. The terms of *FT* require that all income from *FT* be accumulate during *A*'s lifetime. In the year following *A*'s death, a share of *FT* is to be distributed to *FT2*, another foreign trust, for the benefit of *B*. Under paragraphs (a)(1) and (b)(1)(iii) of this section, *FT* is treated as having a U.S. beneficiary beginning with the year of *A*'s transfer of property to *FT*.

Example 4. Indirect benefit through use of debit card. A transfers property to *FT*. The trust instrument provides that no U.S. person can benefit either as to income or corpus. However, *FT* maintains an account with *FB*, a foreign bank, and *FB* issues a debit card to *B* against the account maintained by *FT* and *B* is allowed to make withdrawals. Under paragraphs (a)(1) and (b)(2) of this section, *FT* is treated as having a U.S. beneficiary.

Example 5. Other indirect benefit. A transfers property to *FT*. *FT* is administered by *FTC*, a foreign trust company. *FTC* forms *IBC*, an international business corporation formed under the laws of a foreign jurisdiction. *IBC* is the beneficiary of *FT*. *IBC* maintains an account with *FB*, a foreign bank. *FB* issues a debit card to *B* against the account maintained by *IBC* and *B* is allowed to make withdrawals. Under paragraphs (a)(1) and (b)(2) of this section, *FT* is treated as having a U.S. beneficiary.

(c) *Treatment of U.S. transferor upon foreign trust's acquisition or loss of U.S. beneficiary.*—(1) *Trusts acquiring a U.S. beneficiary.*—If a foreign trust to which a U.S. transferor has transferred property is not treated as having a U.S. beneficiary (within the meaning of paragraph (a) of this section) for any taxable year of the U.S. transferor, but the trust is treated as having a U.S. beneficiary (within the meaning of paragraph (a) of this section) in any subsequent taxable year, the U.S. transferor is treated as having additional income in the first such taxable year of the U.S. transferor in which the trust is treated as having a U.S. beneficiary. The amount of the additional income is equal to the trust's undistributed net income, as defined in section 665(a), at the end of the U.S. transferor's immediately preceding taxable year and is subject to the rules of section 668, providing for an interest charge on accumulation distributions from foreign trusts.

(2) *Trusts ceasing to have a U.S. beneficiary.*—If, for any taxable year of a U.S. transferor, a foreign trust that has received a transfer of property from the U.S. transferor ceases to be treated as having a U.S. beneficiary, the U.S. transferor ceases to be treated as the owner of the portion of the trust attributable to the transfer beginning in the first taxable year following the last taxable year of the U.S. transferor during which the trust was treated as having a U.S. beneficiary (unless the U.S. transferor is treated as an owner thereof pursuant to sections 673 through 677). The U.S. transferor is treated as making a transfer of property to the foreign trust on the first day of the first taxable year following the last taxable year of the U.S. transferor during which the trust was treated as having a U.S. beneficiary. The amount of the property deemed to be transferred to the trust is the portion of the trust attributable to the prior transfer to which paragraph (a)(1) of this section applied. For rules regarding the recognition of gain on transfers to foreign trusts, see section 684.

(3) *Examples.*—The rules of this paragraph (c) are illustrated by the following examples. *A* is a resident alien, *B* is *A*'s son, and *FT* is a foreign trust. The examples are as follows:

Example 1. Trust acquiring U.S. beneficiary. (i) In 2001, *A* transfers stock with a fair market value of $100,000 to *FT*. The stock has an adjusted basis of $50,000 at the time of the transfer. The trust instrument provides that income may be paid currently to, or accumulated for the benefit of, *B* and that, upon the termination of the trust, all income and corpus is to be distributed to *B*. At the time of the transfer, *B* is a nonresident alien. *A* is not treated as the owner of any portion of *FT* under sections 673 through 677. *FT* accumulates a total of $30,000 of income during the taxable years 2001 through 2003. In 2004, *B* moves to the United States and becomes a resident alien. Assume paragraph (a)(4) of this section is not applicable under the facts and circumstances.

(ii) Under paragraph (c)(1) of this section, *A* is treated as receiving an accumulation distribution in the amount of $30,000 in 2004 and immediately transferring that amount back to the trust. The accumulation distribution is subject to the rules of section 668, providing for an interest charge on accumulation distributions.

(iii) Under paragraphs (a)(1) and (3) of this section, beginning in 2005, *A* is treated as the owner of the portion of *FT* attributable to the stock transferred by *A* to *FT* in 2001 (which includes the portion attributable to the accumulated income deemed to be retransferred in 2004).

Example 2. Trust ceasing to have U.S. beneficiary. (i) The facts are the same as in *Example 1.* In 2008, *B* becomes a nonresident alien. On the date *B* becomes a nonresident alien, the stock transferred by *A* to *FT* in 2001 has a fair market value of $125,000 and an adjusted basis of $50,000.

(ii) Under paragraph (c)(2) of this section, beginning in 2009, *FT* is not treated as having a U.S. beneficiary, and *A* is not treated as the owner of the portion of the trust attributable to the prior transfer of stock. For rules regarding the recognition of gain on the termination of ownership status, see section 684.

[Reg. § 1.679-2.]

□ [T.D. 8955, 7-19-2001.]

§ 1.679-3. Transfers.—(a) *In general.*—A transfer means a direct, indirect, or constructive transfer.

(b) *Transfers by certain trusts.*—(1) *In general.*—If any portion of a trust is treated as owned by a U.S. person, a transfer of property from that portion of the trust to a foreign trust is treated as a transfer from the owner of that portion to the foreign trust.

(2) *Example.*—The following example illustrates this paragraph (b):

Example. In 2001, *A*, a U.S. citizen, creates and funds *DT*, a domestic trust. *A* has the power to revest absolutely in himself the title to the property in *DT* and is treated as the owner of *DT* pursuant to section 676. In 2004, *DT* transfers property to *FT*, a foreign trust. *A* is treated as having transferred the property to *FT* in 2004 for purposes of this section.

(c) *Indirect transfers.*—(1) *Principal purpose of tax avoidance.*—A transfer to a foreign trust by any person (intermediary) to whom a U.S. person transfers property is treated as an indirect transfer by a U.S. person to the foreign trust if such transfer is made pursuant to a plan one of the principal purposes of which is the avoidance of United States tax.

(2) *Principal purpose of tax avoidance deemed to exist.*—For purposes of paragraph (c)(1) of this section, a transfer is deemed to have been made pursuant to a plan one of the principal purposes of which was the avoidance of United States tax if—

(i) The U.S. person is related (within the meaning of paragraph (c)(4) of this section) to a beneficiary of the foreign trust, or has another relationship with a beneficiary of the foreign trust that establishes a reasonable basis for concluding that the U.S. transferor would make a transfer to the foreign trust; and

(ii) The U.S. person cannot demonstrate to the satisfaction of the Commissioner that—

(A) The intermediary has a relationship with a beneficiary of the foreign trust that establishes a reasonable basis for concluding that the intermediary would make a transfer to the foreign trust;

(B) The intermediary acted independently of the U.S. person;

(C) The intermediary is not an agent of the U.S. person under generally applicable United States agency principles; and

(D) The intermediary timely complied with the reporting requirements of section 6048, if applicable.

(3) *Effect of disregarding intermediary.*—(i) *In general.*—Except as provided in paragraph (c)(3)(ii) of this section, if a transfer is treated as an indirect transfer pursuant to paragraph (c)(1) of this section, then the intermediary is treated as an agent of the U.S. person, and the property is treated as transferred to the foreign trust by the U.S. person in the year the property is transferred, or made available, by the intermediary to the foreign trust. The fair market value of the property transferred is determined as of the date of the transfer by the intermediary to the foreign trust.

(ii) *Special rule.*—If the Commissioner determines, or if the taxpayer can demonstrate to the satisfaction of the Commissioner, that the intermediary is an agent of the foreign trust under generally applicable United states agency principles, the property will be treated as transferred to the foreign trust in the year the U.S. person transfers the property to the intermediary. The fair market value of the property transferred will be determined as of the date of the transfer by the U.S. person to the intermediary.

(iii) *Effect on intermediary.*—If a transfer of property is treated as an indirect transfer under paragraph (c)(1) of this section, the intermediary is not treated as having transferred the property to the foreign trust.

(4) *Related parties.*—For purposes of this paragraph (c), a U.S. transferor is treated as related to a U.S. beneficiary of a foreign trust if the U.S. transferor and the beneficiary are related for purposes of section 643(i)(2)(B), with the following modifications—

(i) For purposes of applying section 267 (other than section 267(f)) and section

707(b)(1), "at least 10 percent" is used instead of "more than 50 percent" each place it appears; and

(ii) The principles of section 267(b)(10), using "at least 10 percent" instead of "more than 50 percent," apply to determine whether two corporations are related.

(5) *Examples.*—The rules of this paragraph (c) are illustrated by the following examples:

Example 1. Principal purpose of tax avoidance. A, a U.S. citizen, creates and funds FT, a foreign trust, for the benefit of A's children, who are U.S. citizens. In 2004, A decides to transfer an additional 1000X to the foreign trust. Pursuant to a plan with a principal purpose of avoiding the application of section 679, A transfers 1000X to I, a foreign person. I subsequently transfers 1000X to FT. Under paragraph (c)(1) of this section, A is treated as having made a transfer of 1000X to FT.

Example 2. U.S. person unable to demonstrate that intermediary acted independently. A, a U.S. citizen, creates and funds FT, a foreign trust, for the benefit of A's children, who are U.S. citizens. On July 1, 2004, A transfers XYZ stock to D, A's uncle, who is a nonresident alien. D immediately sells the XYZ stock and uses the proceeds to purchase ABC stock. On January 1, 2007, D transfers the ABC stock to FT. A is unable to demonstrate to the satisfaction of the Commissioner, pursuant to paragraph (c)(2) of this section, that D acted independently of A in making the transfer to FT. Under paragraph (c)(1) of this section, A is treated as having transferred the ABC stock to FT. Under paragraph (c)(3) of this section, D is treated as an agent of A, and the transfer is deemed to have been made on January 1, 2007.

Example 3. Indirect loan to foreign trust. A, a U.S. citizen, previously created and funded FT, a foreign trust, for the benefit of A's children, who are U.S. citizens. On July 1, 2004, A deposits 500X with FB, a foreign bank. On January 1, 2005, FB loans 450X to FT. A is unable to demonstrate to the satisfaction of the Commissioner, pursuant to paragraph (c)(2) of this section, that FB has a relationship with FT that establishes a reasonable basis for concluding that FB would make a loan to FT or that FB acted independently of A in making the loan. Under paragraph (c)(1) of this section, A is deemed to have transferred 450X directly to FT on January 1, 2005. Under paragraph (c)(3) of this section, FB is treated as an agent of A. For possible exceptions with respect to qualified obligations of the trust, and the treatment of principal repayments with respect to obligations of the trust that are not qualified obligations, see § 1.679-4.

Example 4. Loan to foreign trust prior to deposit of funds in foreign bank. The facts are the same as in *Example 3*, except that A makes the 500X deposit with FB on January 2, 2005, the day after FB makes the loan to FT. The result is the same as in *Example 3*.

(d) *Constructive transfers.*—(1) *In general.*—For purposes of paragraph (a) of this section, a constructive transfer includes any assumption or satisfaction of a foreign trust's obligation to a third party.

(2) *Examples.*—The rules of this paragraph (d) are illustrated by the following examples. In each example, A is a U.S. citizen and FT is a foreign trust. The examples are as follows:

Example 1. Payment of debt of foreign trust. FT owes 1000X to Y, an unrelated foreign corporation, for the performance of services by Y for FT. In satisfaction of FT's liability to Y, A transfers to Y property with a fair market value of 1000X. Under paragraph (d)(1) of this section, A is treated as having made a constructive transfer of the property to FT.

Example 2. Assumption of liability of foreign trust. FT owes 1000X to Y, an unrelated foreign corporation, for the performance of services by Y for FT. A assumes FT's liability to pay Y. Under paragraph (d)(1) of this section, A is treated as having made a constructive transfer of property with a fair market value of 1000X to FT.

(e) *Guarantee of trust obligations.*—(1) *In general.*—If a foreign trust borrows money or other property from any person who is not a related person (within the meaning of § 1.679-1(c)(5)) with respect to the trust (lender) and a U.S. person (U.S. guarantor) that is a related person with respect to the trust guarantees (within the meaning of paragraph (e)(4) of this section) the foreign trust's obligation, the U.S. guarantor is treated for purposes of this section as a U.S. transferor that has made a transfer to the trust on the date of the guarantee in an amount determined under paragraph (e)(2) of this section. To the extent this paragraph causes the U.S. guarantor to be treated as having made a transfer to the trust, a lender that is a U.S. person shall not be treated as having transferred that amount to the foreign trust.

(2) *Amount transferred.*—The amount deemed transferred by a U.S. guarantor described in paragraph (e)(1) of this section is the guaranteed portion of the adjusted issue price of the obligation (within the meaning of § 1.1275-1(b)) plus any accrued but unpaid qualified stated interest (within the meaning of § 1.1273-1(c)).

(3) *Principal repayments.*—If a U.S. person is treated under this paragraph (e) having made a transfer by reason of the guarantee of an obligation, payments of principal to the lender by the foreign trust with respect to the obligation are taken into account on and after the date of the payment in determining the portion of the trust attributable to the property deemed transferred by the U.S. guarantor.

(4) *Guarantee.*—For purposes of this section, the term guarantee—

(i) Includes any arrangement under which a person, directly or indirectly, assures, on a conditional or unconditional basis, the payment of another's obligation;

(ii) Encompasses any form of credit support, and includes a commitment to make a capital contribution to the debtor or otherwise maintain its financial viability; and

(iii) Includes an arrangement reflected in a comfort letter, regardless of whether the arrangement gives rise to a legally enforceable obligation. If an arrangement is contingent upon the occurrence of an event, in determining whether the arrangement is a guarantee, it is assumed that the event has occurred.

(5) *Examples.*—The rules of this paragraph (e) are illustrated by the following examples. In all of the examples, A is a U.S. resident and FT is a foreign trust. The examples are as follows:

Example 1. Foreign lender. X, a foreign corporation, loans 1000X of cash to FT in exchange for FT's obligation to repay the loan. A guarantees the repayment of 600X of FT's obligation. Under paragraph (e)(2) of this section, A is treated as having transferred 600X to FT.

Example 2. Unrelated U.S. lender. The facts are the same as in *Example 1*, except X is a U.S. person that is not a related person within the meaning of § 1.679-1(c)(5). The result is the same as in *Example 1*.

(f) *Transfers to entities owned by a foreign trust.*—(1) *General rule.*—If a U.S. person is a related person (as defined in § 1.679-1(c)(5)) with respect to a foreign trust, any transfer of property by the U.S. person to an entity in which the foreign trust holds an ownership interest is treated as a transfer of such property by the U.S. person to the foreign trust followed by a transfer of the property from the foreign trust to the entity owned by the foreign trust, unless the U.S. person demonstrates to the satisfaction of the Commissioner that the transfer to the entity is properly attributable to the U.S. person's ownership interest in the entity.

(2) *Examples.*—The rules of this paragraph (f) are illustrated by the following examples. In all of the examples, A is a U.S. citizen, FT is a foreign trust, and FC is a foreign corporation. The examples are as follows:

Example 1. Transfer treated as transfer to trust. A creates and funds FT, which is treated as having a U.S. beneficiary under § 1.679-2. FT owns all of the outstanding stock of FC. A transfers property directly to FC. Because FT is the sole shareholder of FC, A is unable to demonstrate to the satisfaction of the Commissioner that the transfer is properly attributable to A's ownership interest in FC. Accordingly, under this paragraph (f), A is treated as having transferred the property to FT, followed by a transfer of such property by FT to FC. Under § 1.679-1(a), A is treated as the owner of the portion of FT attributable to the property treated as transferred directly to FT. Under § 1.367(a)-1T(c)(4)(ii), the transfer of property by FT to FC is treated as a transfer of the property by A to FC.

Example 2. Transfer treated as transfer to trust. The facts are the same as in *Example 1*, except that FT is not treated as having a U.S. beneficiary under § 1.679-2. Under this paragraph (f), A is treated as having transferred the property to FT, followed by a transfer of such property by FT to FC. A is not treated as the owner of FT for purposes of § 1.679-1(a). For rules regarding the recognition of gain on the transfer, see section 684.

Example 3. Transfer not treated as transfer to trust. A creates and funds FT. FC has outstanding solely 100 shares of common stock. FT owns 50 shares of FC stock, and A owns the remaining 50 shares. On July 1, 2001, FT and A each transfer 1000X to FC. A is able to demonstrate to the satisfaction of the Commissioner that A's transfer to FC is properly attributable to A's ownership interest in FC. Accordingly, under this paragraph (f), A's transfer to FC is not treated as a transfer to FT.

[Reg. § 1.679-3.]

☐ [*T.D.* 8955, 7-19-2001.]

§ 1.679-4. Exceptions to general rule.—(a) *In general.*—Section 1.679-1 does not apply to—

(1) Any transfer of property to a foreign trust by reason of the death of the transferor;

(2) Any transfer of property to a foreign trust described in sections 402(b), 404(a)(4), or 404A;

(3) Any transfer of property to a foreign trust described in section 501(c)(3) (without regard to the requirements of section 508(a)); and

(4) Any transfer of property to a foreign trust to the extent the transfer is for fair market value.

(b) *Transfers for fair market value.*—(1) *In general.*—For purposes of this section, a transfer is for fair market value only to the extent of the value of property received from the trust, services rendered by the trust, or the right to use property of the trust. For example, rents, royalties, interest, and compensation paid to a trust are transfers for fair market value only to the extent that the payments reflect an arm's length price for the use of the property of, or for the services rendered by, the trust. For purposes of this determination, an interest in the trust is not property received from the trust. For purposes of this section, a distribution to a trust with respect to an interest held by such trust in an entity other than a trust or an interest in certain investment trusts described in § 301.7701-4(c) of this chapter, liquidating trusts described in § 301.7701-4(d) of this chapter, or environmental remediation trusts described in § 301.7701-4(e) of this chapter is considered to be a transfer for fair market value.

(2) *Special rule.*—(i) *Transfers for partial consideration.*—For purposes of this section, if a person transfers property to a foreign trust in exchange for property having a fair market value that is less than the fair market value of the property transferred, the exception in paragraph (a)(4) of this section applies only to the extent of the fair market value of the property received.

(ii) *Example.*—This paragraph (b) is illustrated by the following example:

Example. A, a U.S. citizen, transfers property that has a fair market value of 1000X to FT, a foreign trust, in exchange for 600X of cash. Under this paragraph (b), § 1.679-1 applies with respect to the transfer of 400X (1000X less 600X) to FT.

(c) *Certain obligations not taken into account.*—Solely for purposes of this section, in determining whether a transfer by a U.S. transferor that is a related person (as defined in § 1.679-1(c)(5)) with respect to the foreign trust is for fair market value, any obligation (as defined in § 1.679-1(c)(6)) of the trust or a related person (as defined in § 1.679-1(c)(5)) that is not a qualified obligation within the meaning of paragraph (d)(1) of this section shall not be taken into account.

(d) *Qualified obligations.*—(1) *In general.*— For purposes of this section, an obligation is treated as a qualified obligation only if—

(i) The obligation is reduced to writing by an express written agreement;

(ii) The term of the obligation does not exceed five years (for purposes of determining the term of an obligation, the obligation's maturity date is the last possible date that the obligation can be outstanding under the terms of the obligation);

(iii) All payments on the obligation are denominated in U.S. dollars;

(iv) The yield to maturity is not less than 100 percent of the applicable Federal rate and not greater that 130 percent of the applicable Federal rate (the applicable Federal rate for an obligation is the applicable Federal rate in effect under section 1274(d) for the day on which the obligation is issued, as published in the Internal Revenue Bulletin (see § 601.601(d)(2) of this chapter));

(v) The U.S. transferor extends the period for assessment of any income or transfer tax attributable to the transfer and any consequential income tax changes for each year that the obligation is outstanding, to a date not earlier than three years after the maturity date of the obligation (this extension is not necessary if the maturity date of the obligation does not extend beyond the end of the U.S. transferor's taxable year for the year of the transfer and is paid within such period); when properly executed and filed, such an agreement is deemed to be consented to for purposes of § 301.6501(c)-1(d) of this chapter; and

(vi) The U.S. transferor reports the status of the loan, including principal and interest payments, on Form 3520 for every year that the loan is outstanding.

(2) *Additional loans.*—If, while the original obligation is outstanding, the U.S. transferor or a person related to the trust (within the meaning of § 1.679-1(c)(5)) directly or indirectly obtains another obligation issued by the trust, or if the U.S. transferor directly or indirectly obtains another obligation issued by a person related to the trust, the original obligation is deemed to have the maturity date of any such subsequent obligation in determining whether the term of the original obligation exceeds the specified 5-year term. In addition, a series of obligations issued and repaid by the trust (or a person related to the trust) is treated as a single obligation if the transactions giving rise to the obligations are structured with a principal purpose to avoid the application of this provision.

(3) *Obligations that cease to be qualified.*— If an obligation treated as a qualified obligation subsequently fails to be a qualified obligation (e.g., renegotiation of the terms of the obligation causes the term of the obligation to exceed five years), the U.S. transferor is treated as making a transfer to the trust in an amount equal to the original obligation's adjusted issue price (within the meaning of § 1.1275-1(b)) plus any accrued but unpaid qualified stated interest (within the meaning of § 1.1273-1(c)) as of the

date of the subsequent event that causes the obligation to no longer be a qualified obligation. If the maturity date is extended beyond five years by reason of the issuance of a subsequent obligation by the trust (or person related to the trust), the amount of the transfer will not exceed the issue price of the subsequent obligation. The subsequent obligation is separately tested to determine if it is a qualified obligation.

(4) *Transfers resulting from failed qualified obligations.*—In general, a transfer resulting from a failed qualified obligation is deemed to occur on the date of the subsequent event that causes the obligation to no longer be a qualified obligation. However, based on all of the facts and circumstances, the Commissioner may deem a transfer to have occurred on any date on or after the issue date of the original obligation. For example, if at the time the original obligation was issued, the transferor knew or had reason to know that the obligation would not be repaid, the Commissioner could deem the transfer to have occurred on the issue date of the original obligation.

(5) *Renegotiated loans.*—Any loan that is renegotiated, extended, or revised is treated as a new loan, and any transfer of funds to a foreign trust after such renegotiation, extension, or revision under a pre-existing loan agreement is treated as a transfer subject to this section.

(6) *Principal repayments.*—The payment of principal with respect to any obligation that is not treated as a qualified obligation under this paragraph is taken into account on and after the date of the payment in determining the portion of the trust attributable to the property transferred.

(7) *Examples.*—The rules of this paragraph (d) are illustrated by the following examples. In the examples, A and B are U.S. residents and FT is a foreign trust. The examples are as follows:

Example 1. Demand loan. A transfers 500X to FT in exchange for a demand note that permits A to require repayment by FT at any time. A is a related person (as defined in § 1.679-1(c)(5)) with respect to FT. Because FT's obligation to A could remain outstanding for more than five years, the obligation is not a qualified obligation within the meaning of paragraph (d) of this section and, pursuant to paragraph (c) of this section, it is not taken into account for purposes of determining whether A's transfer is eligible for the fair market value exception of paragraph (a)(4) of this section. Accordingly, § 1.679-1 applies with respect to the full 500X transfer to FT.

Example 2. Private annuity. A transfers 4000X to FT in exchange for an annuity from the foreign trust that will pay A 100X per year for the rest of A's life. A is a related person (as defined in § 1.679-1(c)(5)) with respect to FT. Because FT's obligation to A could remain outstanding for more than five years, the obligation is not a qualified obligation within the meaning of paragraph (d)(1) of this section and, pursuant to paragraph (c) of this section, it is not taken into account for purposes of determining whether A's transfer is eligible for the fair market value exception of paragraph (a)(4) of this section. Accordingly, § 1.679-1 applies with respect to the full 4000X transfer to FT.

Example 3. Loan to unrelated foreign trust. B transfers 1000X to FT in exchange for an obligation of the trust. The term of the obligation is fifteen years. B is not a related person (as defined in § 1.679-1(c)(5)) with respect to FT. Because B is not a related person, the fair market value of the obligation received by B is taken into account for purposes of determining whether B's transfer is eligible for the fair market value exception of paragraph (a)(4) of this section, even though the obligation is not a qualified obligation within the meaning of paragraph (d)(1) of this section.

Example 4. Transfer for an obligation with term in excess of 5 years. A transfers property that has a fair market value of 5000X to FT in exchange for an obligation of the trust. The term of the obligation is ten years. A is a related person (as defined in § 1.679-1(c)(5)) with respect to FT. Because the term of the obligation is greater than five years, the obligation is not a qualified obligation within the meaning of paragraph (d)(1) of this section and, pursuant to paragraph (c) of this section, it is not taken into account for purposes of determining whether A's transfer is eligible for the fair market value exception of paragraph (a)(4) of this section. Accordingly, § 1.679-1 applies with respect to the full 5000X transfer to FT.

Example 5. Transfer for a qualified obligation. The facts are the same as in *Example 4*, except that the term of the obligation is 3 years. Assuming the other requirements of paragraph (d)(1) of this section are satisfied, the obligation is a qualified obligation and its adjusted issue price is taken into account for purposes of determining whether A's transfer is eligible for the fair market value exception of paragraph (a)(4) of this section.

Example 6. Effect of subsequent obligation on original obligation. A transfers property that has a fair market value of 1000X to FT in exchange for an obligation that satisfies the requirements of paragraph (d)(1) of this section. A is a related person (as defined in § 1.679-1(c)(5)) with respect to FT. Two years later, A transfers an additional 2000X to FT and receives another obligation from *FT* that has a maturity date four years from the date that the second obligation was issued. Under paragraph (d)(2) of this section, the original obligation is deemed to have the maturity date of the second obligation. Under paragraph (a) of this section, *A* is treated as having made a transfer in an amount equal to the original obligation's adjusted issue price (within the meaning of § 1.1275-1(b)) plus any accrued but unpaid qualified stated interest (within the meaning of § 1.1273-1(c)) as of the date of issuance of the second obligation. The second obligation is tested separately to determine whether it is a qualified obligation for purposes of applying paragraph (a) of this section to the second transfer.

[Reg. § 1.679-4.]

☐ [T.D. 8955, 7-19-2001.]

§ 1.679-5. Pre-immigration trusts.— (a) *In general.*—If a nonresident alien individual becomes a U.S. person and the individual has a residency starting date (as determined under section 7701(b)(2)(A)) within 5 years after directly or indirectly transferring property to a foreign trust (the original transfer), the individual is treated as having transferred to the trust on the residency starting date an amount equal to the portion of the trust attributable to the property transferred by the individual in the original transfer.

(b) *Special rules.*—(1) *Change in grantor trust status.*—For purposes of paragraph (a) of this section, if a nonresident alien individual who is treated as owning any portion of a trust under the provisions of subpart E of part I of subchapter J, chapter 1 of the Internal Revenue Code, subsequently ceases to be so treated, the individual is treated as having made the original transfer to the foreign trust immediately before the trust ceases to be treated as owned by the individual.

(2) *Treatment of undistributed income.*—For purposes of paragraph (a) of this section, the property deemed transferred to the foreign trust on the residency starting date includes undistributed net income, as defined in section 665(a), attributable to the property deemed transferred. Undistributed net income for periods before the individual's residency starting date is taken into account only for purposes of determining the amount of the property deemed transferred.

(c) *Examples.*—The rules of this section are illustrated by the following examples:

Example 1. Nonresident alien becomes resident alien. On January 1, 2002, *A*, a nonresident alien individual, transfers property to a foreign trust, *FT*. On January 1, 2006, *A* becomes a resident of the United States within the meaning of section 7701(b)(1)(A) and has a residency starting date of January 1, 2006, within the meaning of section 7701(b)(2)(A). Under paragraph (a) of this section, *A* is treated as a U.S. transferor and is deemed to transfer the property to *FT* on January 1, 2006. Under paragraph (b)(2) of this section, the property deemed transferred to *FT* on January 1, 2006, includes the undistributed net income of the trust, as defined in section 665(a), attributable to the property originally transferred.

Example 2. Nonresident alien loses power to revest property. On January 1, 2002, *A*, a nonresident alien individual, transfers property to a foreign trust, *FT*. *A* has the power to revest absolutely in himself the title to such property transferred and is treated as the owner of the trust pursuant to sections 676 and 672(f). On January 1, 2008, the terms of *FT* are amended to remove *A*'s power to revest in himself title to the property transferred, and *A* ceases to be treated as the owner of *FT*. On January 1, 2010, *A* becomes a resident of the United States. Under paragraph (b)(1) of this section, for purposes of paragraph (a) of this section *A* is treated as having originally transferred the property to *FT* on January 1, 2008. Because this date is within five years of *A*'s residency starting date, *A* is deemed to have made a transfer to the foreign trust on January 1, 2010, his residency starting date. Under paragraph (b)(2) of this section, the property deemed transferred to the foreign trust on January 1, 2010, includes the undistributed net income of the trust, as defined in section 665(a), attributable to the property deemed transferred.

[Reg. § 1.679-5.]

☐ [T.D. 8955, 7-19-2001.]

§ 1.679-6. Outbound migrations of domestic trusts.— (a) *In general.*—Subject to the provisions of paragraph (b) of this section, if an individual who is a U.S. person transfers property to a trust that is not a foreign trust, and such trust becomes a foreign trust while the U.S. person is alive, the U.S. individual is treated as a U.S. transferor and is deemed to transfer the property to a foreign trust on the date the domestic trust becomes a foreign trust.

(b) *Amount deemed transferred.*—For purposes of paragraph (a) of this section, the property deemed transferred to the trust when it becomes a foreign trust includes undistributed net income, as defined in section 665(a), attributable to the property previously transferred. Undistributed net income for periods prior to the migration is taken into account only for purposes of determining the portion of the trust that is attributable to the property transferred by the U.S. person.

(c) *Example.*—The following example illustrates the rules of this section. For purposes of the example, A is a resident alien, B is A's son, who is a resident alien, and DT is a domestic trust. The example is as follows:

Example. Outbound migration of domestic trust. On January 1, 2002, A transfers property to DT, for the benefit of B. On January 1, 2003, DT acquires a foreign trustee who has the power to determine whether and when distributions will be made to B. Under section 7701(a)(30)(E) and §301.7701-7(d)(ii)(A) of this chapter, DT becomes a foreign trust on January 1, 2003. Under paragraph (a) of this section, A is treated as transferring property to a foreign trust on January 1, 2003. Under paragraph (b) of this section, the property deemed transferred to the trust when it becomes a foreign trust includes undistributed net income, as defined in section 665(a), attributable to the property deemed transferred.

[Reg. § 1.679-6.]

☐ [T.D. 8955, 7-19-2001.]

§ 1.684-1. Recognition of gain on transfers to certain foreign trusts and estates.—

(a) *Immediate recognition of gain.*—(1) *In general.*—Any U.S. person who transfers property to a foreign trust or foreign estate shall be required to recognize gain at the time of the transfer equal to the excess of the fair market value of the property transferred over the adjusted basis (for purposes of determining gain) of such property in the hands of the U.S. transferor unless an exception applies under the provisions of § 1.684-3. The amount of gain recognized is determined on an asset-by-asset basis.

(2) *No recognition of loss.*—Under this section a U.S. person may not recognize loss on the transfer of an asset to a foreign trust or foreign estate. A U.S. person may not offset gain realized on the transfer of an appreciated asset to a foreign trust or foreign estate by a loss realized on the transfer of a depreciated asset to the foreign trust or foreign estate.

(b) *Definitions.*—The following definitions apply for purposes of this section:

(1) *U.S. person.*—The term *U.S. person* means a United States person as defined in section 7701(a)(30), and includes a nonresident alien individual who elects under section 6013(g) to be treated as a resident of the United States.

(2) *U.S. transferor.*—The term *U.S. transferor* means any U.S. person who makes a transfer (as defined in § 1.684-2) of property to a foreign trust or foreign estate.

(3) *Foreign trust.*—Section 7701(a)(31)(B) defines foreign trust. See also § 301.7701-7 of this chapter.

(4) *Foreign estate.*—Section 7701(a)(31)(A) defines foreign estate.

(c) *Reporting requirements.*—A U.S. person who transfers property to a foreign trust or foreign estate must comply with the reporting requirements under section 6048.

(d) *Examples.*—The following examples illustrate the rules of this section. In all examples, A is a U.S. person and FT is a foreign trust. The examples are as follows:

Example 1. Transfer to foreign trust. A transfers property that has a fair market value of 1000X to FT. A's adjusted basis in the property is 400X. FT has no U.S. beneficiary within the meaning of § 1.679-2, and no person is treated as owning any portion of FT. Under paragraph (a)(1) of this section, A recognizes gain at the time of the transfer equal to 600X.

Example 2. Transfer of multiple properties. A transfers property Q, with a fair market value of 1000X, and property R, with a fair market value of 2000X, to FT. At the time of the transfer, A's adjusted basis in property Q is 700X, and A's adjusted basis in property R is 2200X. FT has no U.S. beneficiary within the meaning of § 1.679-2, and no person is treated as owning any portion of FT. Under paragraph (a)(1) of this section, A recognizes the 300X of gain attributable to property Q. Under paragraph (a)(2) of this section, A does not recognize the 200X of loss attributable to property R, and may not offset that loss against the gain attributable to property Q.

Example 3. Transfer for less than fair market value. A transfers property that has a fair market value of 1000X to FT in exchange for 400X of cash. A's adjusted basis in the property is 200X. FT has no U.S. beneficiary within the meaning of § 1.679-2, and no person is treated as owning any portion of FT. Under paragraph (a)(1) of this section, A recognizes gain at the time of the transfer equal to 800X.

Example 4. Exchange of property for private annuity. A transfers property that has a fair market value of 1000X to FT in exchange for FT's obligation to pay A 50X per year for the rest of A's life. A's adjusted basis in the property is 100X. FT has no U.S. beneficiary within the meaning of § 1.679-2, and no person is treated as owning any portion of FT. A is required to recognize gain equal to 900X immediately upon transfer of the property to the trust. This result applies even though A might otherwise have been allowed to defer recognition of gain under another provision of the Internal Revenue Code.

Example 5. Transfer of property to related foreign trust in exchange for qualified obligation. A transfers property that has a fair market value of 1000X to *FT* in exchange for *FT*'s obligation to make payments to *A* during the next four years. *FT* is related to *A* as defined in § 1.679-1(c)(5). The obligation is treated as a qualified obligation within the meaning of § 1.679-4(d), and no person is treated as owning any portion of *FT*. *A*'s adjusted basis in the property is 100X. *A* is required to recognize gain equal to 900X immediately upon transfer of the property to the trust. This result applies even though *A* might otherwise have been allowed to defer recognition of gain under another provision of the Internal Revenue Code. Section 1.684-3(d) provides rules relating to transfers for fair market value to unrelated foreign trusts.

[Reg. § 1.684-1.]

☐ [T.D. 8956, 7-19-2001.]

§ 1.684-2. Transfers.—(a) *In general.*—A transfer means a direct, indirect, or constructive transfer.

(b) *Indirect transfers.*—(1) *In general.*—Section 1.679-3(c) shall apply to determine if a transfer to a foreign trust or foreign estate, by any person, is treated as an indirect transfer by a U.S. person to the foreign trust or foreign estate.

(2) *Examples.*—The following examples illustrate the rules of this paragraph (b). In all examples, *A* is a U.S. citizen, *FT* is a foreign trust, and *I* is *A*'s uncle, who is a nonresident alien. The examples are as follows:

Example 1. Principal purpose of tax avoidance. A creates and funds *FT* for the benefit of *A*'s cousin, who is a nonresident alien. *FT* has no U.S. beneficiary within the meaning of § 1.679-2, and no person is treated as owning any portion of *FT*. In 2004, *A* decides to transfer additional property with a fair market value of 1000X and an adjusted basis of 600X to *FT*. Pursuant to a plan with a principal purpose of avoiding the application of section 684, *A* transfers the property to *I*. *I* subsequently transfers the property to *FT*. Under paragraph (b) of this section and § 1.679-3(c), *A* is treated as having transferred the property to *FT*.

Example 2. U.S. person unable to demonstrate that intermediary acted independently. A creates and funds *FT* for the benefit of *A*'s cousin, who is a nonresident alien. *FT* has no U.S. beneficiary within the meaning of § 1.679-2, and no person is treated as owning any portion of *FT*. On July 1, 2004, *A* transfers property with a fair market value of 1000X and an adjusted basis of 300X to *I*, a foreign person. On January 1, 2007, at a time when the fair market value of the property is 1100X, *I* transfers the property to *FT*. *A* is unable to demonstrate to the satisfaction of the Commissioner, under § 1.679-3(c)(2)(ii), that *I* acted independently of *A* in making the transfer to *FT*. Under paragraph (b) of this section and § 1.679-3(c), *A* is treated as having transferred the property to *FT*. Under paragraph (b) of this section and § 1.679-3(c)(3), *I* is treated as an agent of *A*, and the transfer is deemed to have been made on January 1, 2007. Under § 1.684-1(a), *A* recognizes gain equal to 800X on that date.

(c) *Constructive transfers.*—Section 1.679-3(d) shall apply to determine if a transfer to a foreign trust or foreign estate is treated as a constructive transfer by a U.S. person to the foreign trust or foreign estate.

(d) *Transfers by certain trusts.*—(1) *In general.*—If any portion of a trust is treated as owned by a U.S. person, a transfer of property from that portion of the trust to a foreign trust is treated as a transfer from the owner of that portion to the foreign trust.

(2) *Examples.*—The following examples illustrate the rules of this paragraph (d). In all examples, *A* is a U.S. person, *DT* is a domestic trust, and *FT* is a foreign trust. The examples are as follows:

Example 1. Transfer by a domestic trust. On January 1, 2001, *A* transfers property which has a fair market value of 1000X and an adjusted basis of 200X to *DT*. *A* retains the power to revoke *DT*. On January 1, 2003, *DT* transfers property which has a fair market value of 500X and an adjusted basis of 100X to *FT*. At the time of the transfer, *FT* has no U.S. beneficiary as defined in § 1.679-2 and no person is treated as owning any portion of *FT*. *A* is treated as having transferred the property to *FT* and is required to recognize gain of 400X, under § 1.684-1, at the time of the transfer by *DT* to *FT*.

Example 2. Transfer by a foreign trust. On January 1, 2001, *A* transfers property which has a fair market value of 1000X and an adjusted basis of 200X to *FT1*. At the time of the transfer, *FT1* has a U.S. beneficiary as defined in § 1.679-2 and *A* is treated as the owner of *FT1* under section 679. On January 1, 2003, *FT1* transfers property which has a fair market value of 500X and an adjusted basis of 100X to *FT2*. At the time of the transfer, *FT2* has no U.S. beneficiary as defined in § 1.679-2 and no person is treated as owning any portion of *FT2*. *A* is treated as having transferred the property to *FT2* and is required to recognize gain of 400X, under § 1.684-1, at the time of the transfer by *FT1* to *FT2*.

(e) *Deemed transfers when foreign trust no longer treated as owned by a U.S. person.*—(1) *In general.*—If any portion of a foreign trust is treated as owned by a U.S. person under subpart E of part I of subchapter J, chapter 1 of the Internal Revenue Code, and such portion ceases to be treated as owned by that person under such subpart (other than by reason of an actual transfer of property from the trust to which § 1.684-2(d) applies), the U.S. person shall be treated as having transferred, immediately before (but on the same date that) the trust is no longer treated as owned by that U.S. person, the assets of such portion to a foreign trust.

(2) *Examples.*—The following examples illustrate the rules of this paragraph (e). In all examples, *A* is a U.S. citizen and *FT* is a foreign trust. The examples are as follows:

Example 1. Loss of U.S. beneficiary. (i) On January 1, 2001, *A* transfers property, which has a fair market value of 1000X and an adjusted basis of 400X, to *FT*. At the time of the transfer, *FT* has a U.S. beneficiary within the meaning of § 1.679-2, and *A* is treated as owning *FT* under section 679. Under § 1.684-3(a), § 1.684-1 does not cause *A* to recognize gain at the time of the transfer.

(ii) On July 1, 2003, *FT* ceases to have a U.S. beneficiary as defined in § 1.679-2(c) and as of that date neither *A* nor any other person is treated as owning any portion of *FT*. Pursuant to § 1.679-2(c)(2), if *FT* ceases to be treated as having a U.S. beneficiary, *A* will cease to be treated as owner of *FT* beginning on the first day of the first taxable year following the last taxable year in which there was a U.S. beneficiary. Thus, on January 1, 2004, *A* ceases to be treated as owner of *FT*. On that date, the fair market value of the property is 1200X and the adjusted basis is 350X. Under paragraph (e)(1) of this section, *A* is treated as having transferred the property to *FT* on January 1, 2004, and must recognize 850X of gain at that time under § 1.684-1.

Example 2. Death of grantor. (i) The initial facts are the same as in paragraph (i) of *Example 1.*

(ii) On July 1, 2003, *A* dies, and as of that date no other person is treated as the owner of *FT*. On that date, the fair market value of the property is 1200X, and its adjusted basis equals 350X. Under paragraph (e)(1) of this section, *A* is treated as having transferred the property to *FT* immediately before his death, and generally is required to recognize 850X of gain at that time under § 1.684-1. However, an exception may apply under § 1.684-3(c).

Example 3. Release of a power. (i) On January 1, 2001, *A* transfers property that has a fair market value of 500X and an adjusted basis of 200X to *FT*. At the time of the transfer, FT does not have a U.S. beneficiary within the meaning of § 1.679-2. However, *A* retains the power to revoke the trust. *A* is treated as the owner of the trust under section 676 and, therefore, under § 1.684-3(a), *A* is not required to recognize gain under § 1.684-1 at the time of the transfer.

(ii) On January 1, 2007, *A* releases the power to revoke the trust and, as of that date, neither *A* nor any other person is treated as owning any portion of FT. On that date, the fair market value of the property is 900X, and its adjusted basis is 200X. Under paragraph (e)(1) of this section, *A* is treated as having transferred the property to *FT* on January 1, 2007, and must recognize 700X of gain at that time.

(f) *Transfers to entities owned by a foreign trust.*—Section 1.679-3(f) provides rules that apply with respect to transfers of property by a U.S. person to an entity in which a foreign trust holds an ownership interest. [Reg. § 1.684-2.]

☐ [*T.D.* 8956, 7-19-2001.]

§ 1.684-3. Exceptions to general rule of gain recognition.—(a) *Transfers to grantor trusts.*—The general rule of gain recognition under § 1.684-1 shall not apply to any transfer of property by a U.S. person to a foreign trust to the extent that any person is treated as the owner of the trust under section 671. Section 1.684-2(e) provides rules regarding a subsequent change in the status of the trust.

(b) *Transfers to charitable trusts.*—The general rule of gain recognition under § 1.684-1 shall not apply to any transfer of property to a foreign trust that is described in section 501(c)(3) (without regard to the requirements of section 508(a)).

(c) *Certain transfers at death.*—The general rule of gain recognition under § 1.684-1 shall not apply to any transfer of property by reason of death of the U.S. transferor if the basis of the property in the hands of the foreign trust is determined under section 1014(a).

(d) *Transfers for fair market value to unrelated trusts.*—The general rule of gain recognition under § 1.684-1 shall not apply to any transfer of property for fair market value to a foreign trust that is not a related foreign trust as defined in § 1.679-1(c)(5). Section 1.671-2(e)(2)(ii) defines fair market value.

(e) *Transfers to which section 1032 applies.*—The general rule of gain recognition under § 1.684-1 shall not apply to any transfer of stock (including treasury stock) by a domestic corporation to a foreign trust if the domestic corporation is not required to recognize gain on the transfer under section 1032.

(f) *Certain distributions to trusts.*—For purposes of this section, a transfer does not include a distribution to a trust with respect to an interest held by such trust in an entity other than a trust or an interest in certain investment trusts described in § 301.7701-4(c) of this chapter, liquidating trusts described in § 301.7701-4(d) of this chapter, or environmental remediation trusts described in § 301.7701-4(e) of this chapter.

(g) *Examples.*—The following examples illustrate the rules of this section. In all examples, *A* is a U.S. citizen and *FT* is a foreign trust. The examples are as follows:

Example 1. Transfer to owner trust. In 2001, *A* transfers property which has a fair market value of 1000X and an adjusted basis equal to 400X to *FT*. At the time of the transfer, *FT* has a U.S. beneficiary within the meaning of § 1.679-2, and *A* is treated as owning *FT* under section 679. Under paragraph (a) of this section, § 1.684-1 does not cause *A* to recognize gain at the time of the transfer. See § 1.684-2(e) for rules that may require *A* to recognize gain if the trust is no longer owned by *A*.

Example 2. Transfer of property at death: Basis determined under section 1014(a). (i) The initial facts are the same as *Example 1*.

(ii) *A* dies on July 1, 2004. The fair market value at *A*'s death of all property transferred to *FT* by *A* is 1500X. The basis in the property is 400X. *A* retained the power to revoke *FT*, thus, the value of all property owned by *FT* at *A*'s death is includible in *A*'s gross estate for U.S. estate tax purposes. Pursuant to paragraph (c) of this section, *A* is not required to recognize gain under § 1.684-1 because the basis of the property in the hands of the foreign trust is determined under section 1014(a).

Example 3. Transfer of property at death: Basis not determined under section 1014(a). (i) The initial facts are the same as *Example 1*.

(ii) *A* dies on July 1, 2004. The fair market value at *A*'s death of all property transferred to *FT* by *A* is 1500X. The basis in the property is 400X. *A* retains no power over *FT*, and *FT*'s basis in the property transferred is not determined under section 1014(a). Under § 1.684-2(e)(1), *A* is treated as having transferred the property to *FT* immediately before his death, and must recognize 1100X of gain at that time under § 1.684-1.

Example 4. Transfer of property for fair market value to an unrelated foreign trust. *A* sells a house with a fair market value of 1000X to *FT* in exchange for a 30-year note issued by *FT*. *A* is not related to *FT* as defined in § 1.679-1(c)(5). *FT* is not treated as owned by any person. Pursuant to paragraph (d) of this section, *A* is not required to recognize gain under § 1.684-1.

[Reg. § 1.684-3.]

☐ [*T.D.* 8956, 7-19-2001.]

§ 1.684-4. Outbound migrations of domestic trusts.—(a) *In general.*—If a U.S. person transfers property to a domestic trust, and such trust becomes a foreign trust, and neither trust is treated as owned by any person under subpart E of part I of subchapter J, chapter 1 of the Internal Revenue Code, the trust shall be treated for purposes of this section as having transferred all of its assets to a foreign trust and the trust is required to recognize gain on the transfer under § 1.684-1(a). The trust must also comply with the rules of section 6048.

(b) *Date of transfer.*—The transfer described in this section shall be deemed to occur immediately before, but on the same date that, the trust meets the definition of a foreign trust set forth in section 7701(a)(31)(B).

(c) *Inadvertent migrations.*—In the event of an inadvertent migration, as defined in § 301.7701-7(d)(2) of this chapter, a trust may avoid the application of this section by complying with the procedures set forth in § 301.7701-7(d)(2) of this chapter.

(d) *Examples.*—The following examples illustrate the rules of this section. In all examples, *A* is a U.S. citizen, *B* is a U.S. citizen, *C* is a nonresident alien, and *T* is a trust. The examples are as follows:

Example 1. Migration of domestic trust with U.S. beneficiaries. *A* transfers property which has a fair market value of 1000X and an adjusted basis equal to 400X to *T*, a domestic trust, for the benefit of *A*'s children who are also U.S. citizens. *B* is the trustee of *T*. On January 1, 2001, while *A* is still alive, *B* resigns as trustee and *C* becomes successor trustee under the terms of the trust. Pursuant to § 301.7701-7(d) of this chapter, *T* becomes a foreign trust. *T* has U.S. beneficiaries within the meaning of § 1.679-2 and *A* is, therefore, treated as owning *FT* under section 679. Pursuant to § 1.684-3(a), neither *A* nor *T* is required to recognize gain at the time of the migration. Section 1.684-2(e) provides rules that may require *A* to recognize gain upon a subsequent change in the status of the trust.

Example 2. Migration of domestic trust with no U.S. beneficiaries. *A* transfers property which has a fair market value of 1000X and an adjusted basis equal to 400X to *T*, a domestic trust for the benefit of *A*'s mother who is not a citizen or resident of the United States. *T* is not treated as owned by another person. *B* is the trustee of *T*. On January 1, 2001, while *A* is still alive, B resigns as trustee and *C* becomes successor trustee under the terms of the trust. Pursuant to § 301.7701-7(d) of this chapter, *T* becomes a foreign trust, *FT. FT* has no U.S. beneficiaries within the meaning of § 1.679-2 and no person is treated as owning any portion of *FT. T* is required to recognize gain of 600X on January 1, 2001. Paragraph (c) of this section provides rules with respect to an inadvertent migration of a domestic trust.

[Reg. § 1.684-4.]

☐ [T.D. 8956, 7-19-2001.]

Partnerships

§ 1.701-2. Anti-abuse rule.—(a) *Intent of subchapter K.*—Subchapter K is intended to permit taxpayers to conduct joint business (including investment) activities through a flexible economic arrangement without incurring an entity-level tax. Implicit in the intent of subchapter K are the following requirements—

(1) The partnership must be bona fide and each partnership transaction or series of related transactions (individually or collectively, the transaction) must be entered into for a substantial business purpose.

(2) The form of each partnership transaction must be respected under substance over form principles.

(3) Except as otherwise provided in this paragraph (a)(3), the tax consequences under subchapter K to each partner of partnership operations and of transactions between the partner and the partnership must accurately reflect the partners' economic agreement and clearly reflect the partner's income (collectively, *proper reflection of income*). However, certain provisions of subchapter K and the regulations thereunder were adopted to promote administrative convenience and other policy objectives, with the recognition that the application of those provisions to a transaction could, in some circumstances, produce tax results that do not properly reflect income. Thus, the proper reflection of income requirement of this paragraph (a)(3) is treated as satisfied with respect to a transaction that satisfies paragraphs (a)(1) and (2) of this section to the extent that the application of such a provision to the transaction and the ultimate tax results, taking into account all the relevant facts and circumstances, are clearly contemplated by that provision. See, for example, paragraph (d) *Example 6* of this section (relating to the value-equals-basis rule in § 1.704-1(b)(2)(iii)(*c*)), paragraph (d) *Example 9* of this section (relating to the election under section 754 to adjust basis in partnership property), and paragraph (d) *Examples 10 and 11* of this section (relating to the basis in property distributed by a partnership under section 732). See also, for example, §§ 1.704-3(e)(1) and 1.752-2(e)(4) (providing certain de minimis exceptions).

(b) *Application of subchapter K rules.*—The provisions of subchapter K and the regulations thereunder must be applied in a manner that is consistent with the intent of subchapter K as set forth in paragraph (a) of this section (*intent of subchapter K*). Accordingly, if a partnership is formed or availed of in connection with a transaction a principal purpose of which is to reduce substantially the present value of the partners' aggregate federal tax liability in a manner that is inconsistent with the intent of subchapter K, the Commissioner can recast the transaction for federal tax purposes, as appropriate to achieve tax results that are consistent with the intent of subchapter K, in light of the applicable statutory and regulatory provisions and the pertinent facts and circumstances. Thus, even though the transaction may fall within the literal words of a particular statutory or regulatory provision, the Commissioner can determine, based on the particular facts and circumstances, that to achieve tax results that are consistent with the intent of subchapter K—

(1) The purported partnership should be disregarded in whole or in part, and the partnership's assets and activities should be considered, in whole or in part, to be owned and conducted, respectively, by one or more of its purported partners;

(2) One or more of the purported partners of the partnership should not be treated as a partner;

(3) The methods of accounting used by the partnership or a partner should be adjusted to reflect clearly the partnership's or the partner's income;

(4) The partnership's items of income, gain, loss, deduction, or credit should be reallocated; or

(5) The claimed tax treatment should otherwise be adjusted or modified.

(c) *Facts and circumstances analysis; factors.*—Whether a partnership was formed or availed of with a principal purpose to reduce substantially the present value of the partners' aggregate federal tax liability in a manner inconsistent with the intent of subchapter K is determined based on all of the facts and circumstances, including a comparison of the purported business purpose for a transaction and the claimed tax benefits resulting from the transaction. The factors set forth below may be indicative, but do not necessarily establish, that a partnership was used in such a manner. These factors are illustrative only, and therefore may not be the only factors taken into account in making the determination under this section. Moreover, the weight given to any factor (whether specified in this paragraph or otherwise) depends on all the facts and circumstances. The presence or absence of any factor described in this paragraph does not create a presumption that a partnership was (or was not) used in such a manner. Factors include:

(1) The present value of the partners' aggregate federal tax liability is substantially less than had the partners owned the partnership's assets and conducted the partnership's activities directly;

(2) The present value of the partners' aggregate federal tax liability is substantially less than would be the case if purportedly separate transactions that are designed to achieve a particular end result are integrated and treated as steps in a single transaction. For example, this analysis may indicate that it was contemplated that a partner who was necessary to achieve the intended tax results and whose interest in the partnership was liquidated or disposed of (in whole or in part) would be a partner only temporarily in order to provide the claimed tax benefits to the remaining partners;

(3) One or more partners who are necessary to achieve the claimed tax results either have a nominal interest in the partnership, are substantially protected from any risk of loss from the partnership's activities (through distribution preferences, indemnity or loss guaranty agreements, or other arrangements), or have little or no participation in the profits from the partnership's activities other than a preferred return that is in the nature of a payment for the use of capital;

(4) Substantially all of the partners (measured by number or interests in the partnership) are related (directly or indirectly) to one another;

(5) Partnership items are allocated in compliance with the literal language of §§ 1.704-1 and 1.704-2 but with results that are inconsistent with the purpose of section 704(b) and those regulations. In this regard, particular scrutiny will be paid to partnerships in which income or gain is specially allocated to one or more partners that may be legally or effectively exempt from federal taxation (for example, a foreign person, an exempt organization, an insolvent taxpayer, or a taxpayer with unused federal tax attributes such as net operating losses, capital losses, or foreign tax credits);

(6) The benefits and burdens of ownership of property nominally contributed to the partnership are in substantial part retained (directly or indirectly) by the contributing partner (or a related party); or

(7) The benefits and burdens of ownership of partnership property are in substantial part shifted (directly or indirectly) to the distributee partner before or after the property is actually distributed to the distributee partner (or a related party).

(d) *Examples.*—The following examples illustrate the principles of paragraphs (a), (b), and (c) of this section. The examples set forth below do not delineate the boundaries of either permissible or impermissible types of transactions. Further, the addition of any facts or circumstances that are not specifically set forth in an example (or the deletion of any facts or circumstances) may alter the outcome of the transaction described in the example. Unless otherwise indicated, parties to the transactions are not related to one another.

* * *

Example 3. Choice of entity; avoidance of more restrictive foreign tax credit limitation; use of partnership consistent with the intent of subchapter K. (i) X, a domestic corporation, and Y, a foreign corporation, form partnership PRS under the laws of foreign Country A to conduct a bona fide joint business. X and Y each owns a 50% interest in PRS. PRS is properly classified as a partnership under §§ 301.7701-2 and 301.7701-3. PRS pays income taxes to Country A. X and Y chose partnership form to enable X to qualify for a direct foreign tax credit under section 901, with look-through treatment under § 1.904-5(h)(1). Conversely, if PRS were a foreign corporation for U.S. tax purposes, X would be entitled only to indirect foreign tax credits under section 902 with respect to dividend distributions from PRS. The look-through rules, however, would not apply, and pursuant to section 904(d)(1)(E) and § 1.904-4(g), the dividends and associated taxes would be subject to a separate foreign tax credit limitation for dividends from PRS, a noncontrolled section 902 corporation.

(ii) Subchapter K is intended to permit taxpayers to conduct joint business activity through a flexible economic arrangement without incurring an entity-level tax. See paragraph (a) of this section. The decision to organize and conduct business through PRS in order to take advantage of the look-through rules for foreign tax credit purposes, thereby maximizing X's use of its proper share of foreign taxes paid by PRS, is consistent with this intent. In addition, on these facts, the requirements of paragraphs (a)(1), (2), and (3) of this section have been satisfied. The Commissioner therefore cannot invoke paragraph (b) of this section to recast the transaction.

* * *

(e) *Abuse of entity treatment.*—(1) *General rule.*—The Commissioner can treat a partnership as an aggregate of its partners in whole or in part as appropriate to carry out the purpose of any provision of the Internal Revenue Code or the regulations promulgated thereunder.

(2) *Clearly contemplated entity treatment.*—Paragraph (e)(1) of this section does not apply to the extent that—

(i) A provision of the Internal Revenue Code or the regulations promulgated thereunder prescribes the treatment of a partnership as an entity, in whole or in part, and

(ii) That treatment and the ultimate tax results, taking into account all the relevant facts and circumstances, are clearly contemplated by that provision.

(f) *Examples.*—The following examples illustrate the principles of paragraph (e) of this section. The examples set forth below do not delineate the boundaries of either permissible or impermissible types of transactions. Further, the addition of any facts or circumstances that are not specifically set forth in an example (or the deletion of any facts or circumstances) may alter the outcome of the transaction described in the example. Unless otherwise indicated, parties to the transactions are not related to one another.

* * *

Example 3. Prescribed entity treatment of partnership; determination of CFC status clearly contemplated. (i) X, a domestic corporation, and Y, a foreign corporation, intend to conduct a joint venture in foreign Country A. They form PRS, a bona fide domestic general partnership in which X owns a 40% interest and Y owns a 60% interest. PRS is properly classified as a partnership under §§ 301.7701-2 and 301.7701-3. PRS holds 100% of the voting stock of Z, a Country A entity that is classified as an association taxable as a corporation for federal tax purposes under § 301.7701-2. Z conducts its business operations in Country A. By investing in Z through a domestic partnership, X seeks to obtain the benefit of the look-through rules of section 904(d)(3) and, as a result, maximize its ability to claim credits for its proper share of Country A taxes expected to be incurred by Z.

(ii) Pursuant to sections 957(c) and 7701(a)(30), PRS is a United States person. Therefore, because it owns 10% or more of the voting stock of Z, PRS satisfies the definition of a U.S. shareholder under section 951(b). Under section 957(a), Z is a controlled foreign corporation (CFC) because more than 50% of the voting power or value of its stock is owned by PRS. Consequently, under section 904(d)(3), X qualifies for look-through treatment in computing its credit for foreign taxes paid or accrued by Z. In contrast, if X and Y owned their interests in Z directly, Z would not be a CFC because only 40% of its stock would be owned by U.S. shareholders. X's credit for foreign taxes paid or accrued by Z in that case would be subject to a separate foreign tax credit limitation for dividends from Z, a noncontrolled section 902 corporation. See section 904(d)(1)(E) and § 1.904-4(g).

(iii) Sections 957(c) and 7701(a)(30) prescribe the treatment of a domestic partnership as an entity for purposes of defining a U.S. shareholder, and thus, for purposes of determining whether a foreign corporation is a CFC. The CFC rules prevent the deferral by U.S. shareholders of U.S. taxation of certain earnings of the CFC and reduce disparities that otherwise might occur between the amount of income subject to a particular foreign tax credit limitation when a taxpayer earns income abroad directly rather than indirectly through a CFC. The application of the look-through rules for foreign tax credit purposes is appropriately tied to CFC status. See sections 904(d)(2)(E) and 904(d)(3). This analysis confirms that Congress clearly contemplated that taxpayers could use a bona fide domestic partnership to subject themselves to the CFC regime, and the resulting application of the look-through rules of section 904(d)(3). Accordingly, under paragraph (e) of this section, the Commissioner cannot treat PRS as an aggregate of its partners for purposes of determining X's foreign tax credit limitation.

* * *

(i) *Application of nonstatutory principles and other statutory authorities.*—The Commissioner can continue to assert and to rely upon applicable nonstatutory principles and other statutory and regulatory authorities to challenge transactions. This section does not limit the applicability of those principles and authorities. [Reg. § 1.701-2.]

☐ [*T.D.* 8588, 12-29-94. *Amended by T.D.* 8592, 4-12-95.]

§ 1.702-1. Income and credits of partner.—(a) *General rule.*—Each partner is required to take into account separately in his return his distributive share, whether or not distributed, of each class or item of partnership income, gain, loss, deduction, or credit described in subparagraphs (1) through (9) of this paragraph. (For the taxable year in which a partner includes his distributive share of partnership taxable income, see section 706(a) and § 1.706-1(a). Such distributive share shall be determined as provided in section 704 and § 1.704-1.) Accordingly, in determining his income tax:

(1) Each partner shall take into account, as part of his gains and losses from sales or exchanges of capital assets held for not more than 1 year (6 months for taxable years begin-

ning before 1977; 9 months for taxable years beginning in 1977), his distributive share of the combined net amount of such gains and losses of the partnership.

(2) Each partner shall take into account, as part of his gains and losses from sales or exchanges of capital assets held for more than 1 year (6 months for taxable years beginning before 1977; 9 months for taxable years beginning in 1977), his distributive share of the combined net amount of such gains and losses of the partnership.

(3) Each partner shall take into account, as part of his gains and losses from sales or exchanges of property described in section 1231 (relating to property used in the trade or business and involuntary conversions), his distributive share of the combined net amount of such gains and losses of the partnership. The partnership shall not combine such items with items set forth in subparagraph (1) or (2) of this paragraph.

(4) Each partner shall take into account, as part of the charitable contributions paid by him, his distributive share of each class of charitable contributions paid by the partnership within the partnership's taxable year. Section 170 determines the extent to which such amount may be allowed as a deduction to the partner. For the definition of the term "charitable contribution", see section 170(c).

(5) Each partner shall take into account, as part of the dividends received by him from domestic corporations, his distributive share of dividends received by the partnership, with respect to which the partner is entitled to a credit under section 34 (for dividends received on or before December 31, 1964), an exclusion under section 116, or a deduction under part VIII, subchapter B, chapter 1 of the Code.

(6) Each partner shall take into account, as part of his taxes described in section 901 which have been paid or accrued to foreign countries or to possessions of the United States, his distributive share of such taxes which have been paid or accrued by the partnership, according to its method of treating such taxes. A partner may elect to treat his total amount of such taxes, including his distributive share of such taxes of the partnership, as a deduction under section 164 or as a credit under section 901, the subject to the provisions of sections 901 through 905.

(7) Each partner shall take into account, as part of the partially tax-exempt interest received by him on obligations of the United States or on obligations of instrumentalities of the United States, as described in section 35 or section 242, his distributive share of such partially tax-exempt interest received by the partnership. However, if the partnership elects to amortize premiums on bonds as provided in section 171, the amount received on such obligations by the partnership shall be reduced by the amortizable bond premium applicable to such obligations as provided in section 171(a)(3).

(8)(i) Each partner shall take into account separately, as part of any class of income, gain, loss, deduction, or credit, his distributive share of the following items: recoveries of bad debts, prior taxes, and delinquency amounts (section 111); gains and losses from wagering transactions (section 165(d)); soil and water conservation expenditures (section 175); nonbusiness expenses as described in section 212; medical, dental, etc., expenses (section 213); expenses for care of certain dependents (section 214); alimony, etc., payments (section 215); amounts representing taxes and interest paid to cooperative housing corporations (section 216); intangible drilling and developments costs (section 263(c)); pre-1970 exploration expenditures (section 615); certain mining exploration expenditures (section 617); income, gain, or loss to the partnership under section 751(b); and any items of income, gain, loss, deduction, or credit subject to a special allocation under the partnership agreement which differs from the allocation of partnership taxable income or loss generally.

(ii) Each partner must also take into account separately the partner's distributive share of any partnership item which, if separately taken into account by any partner, would result in an income tax liability for that partner, or for any other person, different from that which would result if that partner did not take the item into account separately. Thus, if any partner is a controlled foreign corporation, as defined in section 957, items of income that would be gross subpart F income if separately taken into account by the controlled foreign corporation must be separately stated for all partners. Under section 911(a), if any partner is a bona fide resident of a foreign country who may exclude from gross income the part of the partner's distributive share which qualifies as earned income, as defined in section 911(b), the earned income of the partnership for all partners must be separately stated. Similarly, all relevant items of income or deduction of the partnership must be separately stated for all partners in determining the applicability of section 183 (relating to activities not engaged in for profit) and the recomputation of tax thereunder for any partner. This paragraph (a)(8)(ii) applies to taxable years beginning on or after July 23, 2002.

(iii) Each partner shall aggregate the amount of his separate deductions or exclusions and his distributive share of partnership deductions or exclusions separately stated in determining the amount allowable to him of any deduction or exclusion under subtitle A of the Code as to which a limitation is imposed. For example, partner A has individual domestic exploration expenditures of $300,000. He is also a member of the AB partnership which in 1971, in its first year of operation has foreign exploration expenditures of $400,000. A's distributable share of this item is $200,000. However, the total amount of his distributable share that A can deduct as exploration expenditures under section 617(a) is limited to $100,000 in view of the limitation provided in section 617(h). Therefore, the excess of $100,000 ($200,000 minus $100,000) is not deductible by A.

(9) Each partner shall also take into account separately his distributive share of the taxable income or loss of the partnership, exclusive of items requiring separate computations under subparagraphs (1) through (8) of this paragraph. For limitation on allowance of a partner's distributive share of partnership losses, see section 704(d) and paragraph (d) of § 1.704-1.

(b) *Character of items constituting distributive share.*—The character in the hands of a partner of any item of income, gain, loss, deduction, or credit described in section 702(a)(1) through (8) shall be determined as if such item were realized directly from the source from which realized by the partnership or incurred in the same manner as incurred by the partnership. For example, a partner's distributive share of gain from the sale of depreciable property used in the trade or business of the partnership shall be considered as gain from the sale of such depreciable property in the hands of the partner. Similarly, a partner's distributive share of partnership "hobby losses" (section 270) or his distributive share of partnership charitable contributions to organizations qualifying under section 170(b)(1)(A) retains such character in the hands of the partner.

(c) *Gross income of a partner.*—(1) Where it is necessary to determine the amount or character of the gross income of a partner, his gross income shall include the partner's distributive share of the gross income of the partnership, that is, the amount of gross income of the partnership from which was derived the partner's distributive share of partnership taxable income or loss (including items described in section 702(a)(1) through (8)). For example, a partner is required to include his distributive share of partnership gross income:

(i) In computing his gross income for the purpose of determining the necessity of filing a return (section 6012(a));

(ii) In determining the application of the provisions permitting the spreading of income for services rendered over a 36-month period (section 1301, as in effect for taxable years beginning before January 1, 1964);

(iii) In computing the amount of gross income received from sources within possessions of the United States (section 937);

(iv) In determining a partner's "gross income from farming" (sections 175 and 6073); and

(v) In determining whether the de minimis or full inclusion rules of section 954(b)(3) apply.

(2) In determining the applicability of the 6-year period of limitation on assessment and collection provided in section 6501(e) (relating to omission of more than 25 percent of gross income), a partner's gross income includes his distributive share of partnership gross income (as described in section 6501(e)(1)(A)(i)). In this respect, the amount of partnership gross income from which was derived the partner's distributive share of any item of partnership income, gain, loss, deduction, or credit (as included or disclosed in the partner's return) is considered as an amount of gross income stated in the partner's return for the purposes of section 6501(e). For example, A, who is entitled to one-fourth of the profits of the ABCD partnership, which has $10,000 gross income and $2,000 taxable income, reports only $300 as his distributive share of partnership profits. A should have shown $500 as his distributive share of profits, which amount was derived from $2,500 of partnership gross income. However, since A included only $300 on his return without explaining in the return the difference of $200, he is regarded as having stated in his return only $1,500 ($300/$500 of $2,500) as gross income from the partnership.

* * *

[Reg. § 1.702-1.]

☐ [*T.D.* 6175, 5-23-56. *Amended by T.D.* 6605, 8-14-62; *T.D.* 6777, 12-15-64; *T.D.* 6885, 6-1-66; *T.D.* 7192, 6-29-72; *T.D.* 7564, 9-11-78; *T.D.* 7728, 10-31-80; *T.D.* 8247, 4-5-89; *T.D.* 8348, 5-10-91; *T.D.* 9008, 7-22-2002 *and T.D.* 9194, 4-6-2005.]

§ 1.704-1. Partner's distributive share.—(a) *Effect of partnership agreement.*—A partner's distributive share of any item or class of items of income, gain, loss, deduction, or credit of the partnership shall be determined by the partnership agreement, unless otherwise provided by section 704 and paragraphs (b) through (e) of this section. For definition of partnership agreement see section 761(c).

(b) *Determination of partner's distributive share.*— * * *

(1) *In general.*—(i) *Basic principles.*—Under section 704(b) if a partnership agreement does not provide for the allocation of income, gain, loss, deduction, or credit (or item thereof) to a partner, or if the partnership agreement provides for the allocation of income, gain, loss, deduction, or credit (or item thereof) to a partner but such allocation does not have substantial economic effect, then the partner's distributive share of such income, gain, loss, deduction, or credit (or item thereof) shall be determined in accordance with such partner's interest in the partnership (taking into account all facts and circumstances). If the partnership agreement provides for the allocation of income, gain, loss, deduction, or credit (or item thereof) to a partner, there are three ways in which such allocation will be respected under section 704(b) and this paragraph. First, the allocation can have substantial economic effect in accordance with paragraph (b)(2) of this section. Second, taking into account all facts and circumstances, the allocation can be in accordance with the partner's interest in the partnership. See paragraph (b)(3) of this section. Third, the allocation can be deemed to be in accordance with the partner's interest in the partnership pursuant to one of the special rules contained in paragraph (b)(4) of this section and § 1.704-2. To the extent an allocation under the partnership agreement of income, gain, loss, deduction, or credit (or item thereof) to a partner does not have substantial economic effect, is not in accordance with the partner's interest in the partnership, and is not deemed to be in accordance with the partner's interest in the partnership, such income, gain, loss, deduction, or credit (or item thereof) will be reallocated in accordance with the partner's interest in the partnership (determined under paragraph (b)(3) of this section).

* * *

(2) *Substantial economic effect.*—(i) *Two-part analysis.*—The determination of whether an allocation of income, gain, loss, or deduction (or item thereof) to a partner has substantial economic effect involves a two-part analysis that is made as of the end of the partnership taxable year to which the allocation relates. First, the allocation must have economic effect (within the meaning of paragraph (b)(2)(ii) of this section). Second, the economic efect of the allocation must be substantial (within the meaning of paragraph (b)(2)(iii) of this section).

(ii) *Economic effect.*—(*a*) *Fundamental principles.*—In order for an allocation to have economic effect, it must be consistent with the underlying economic arrangement of the partners. This means that in the event there is an economic benefit or economic burden that corresponds to an allocation, the partner to whom the allocation is made must receive such economic benefit or bear such economic burden.

(*b*) *Three requirements.*—Based on the principles contained in paragraph (b)(2)(ii)(*a*) of this section, and except as otherwise provided in this paragraph, an allocation of income, gain, loss, or deduction (or item thereof) to a partner will have economic effect if, and only if, throughout the full term of the partnership, the partnership agreement provides—

(*1*) For the determination and maintenance of the partners' capital accounts in accordance with the rules of paragraph (b)(2)(iv) of this section,

(*2*) Upon liquidation of the partnership (or any partner's interest in the partnership), liquidating distributions are required in all cases to be made in accordance with the positive capital account balances of the partners, as determined after taking into account all capital account adjustments for the partnership taxable year during which such liquidation occurs (other than those made pursuant to this requirement (*2*) and requirement (*3*) of this paragraph (b)(2)(ii)(*b*)), by the end of such taxable year (or, if later, within 90 days after the date of such liquidation), and

(*3*) If such partner has a deficit balance in his capital account following the liquidation of his interest in the partnership, as determined after taking into account all capital account adjustments for the partnership taxable year during which such liquidation occurs (other than those made pursuant to this requirement (*3*)), he is unconditionally obligated to restore the amount of such deficit balance to the partnership by the end of such taxable year (or, if later, within 90 days after the date of such liquidation), which amount shall, upon liquidation of the partnership, be paid to creditors of the partnership or distributed to other partners in accordance with their positive capital account balances (in accordance with requirement (*2*) of this paragraph (b)(2)(ii)(*b*)).

Requirements (*2*) and (*3*) of this paragraph (b)(2)(ii)(*b*) are not violated if all or part of the partnership interest of one or more partners is purchased (other than in connection with the liquidation of the partnership) by the partnership or by one or more partners (or one or more persons related, within the meaning of section 267(b) (without modification by section 267(e)(1)) or section 707(b)(1), to a partner) pursuant to an agreement negotiated at arm's length by persons who at the time such agreement is entered into have materially adverse interests and if a principal purpose of such purchase and sale is not to avoid the principles of the second sentence of paragraph (b)(2)(ii)(a) of this section. In addition, requirement (2) of this paragraph (b)(2)(ii)(b) is not violated if, upon the liquidation of the partnership, the capital accounts of the partners are increased or decreased pursuant to paragraph (b)(2)(iv)(f) of this section as of the date of such liquidation and the partnership makes liquidating distributions within the time set out in that requirement (2) in the ratios of the partners' positive capital accounts, except that it does not distribute (A) reserves reasonably required to provide for liabilities (contingent or otherwise) of the partnership and (B) installment obligations owed to the partnership, so long as such withheld amounts are distributed as soon as practicable and in the ratios of the partners' positive capital account balances. For purposes of the preceding sentence, a partnership taxable year shall be determined without regard to section 706(c)(2)(A). See examples (1)(i) and (ii), (4)(i), (8)(i), and (16)(i) of paragraph (b)(5) of this section.

(c) *Obligation to restore deficit.*—If a partner is not expressly obligated to restore the deficit balance in his capital account, such partner nevertheless will be treated as obligated to restore the deficit balance in his capital account (in accordance with requirement (3) of paragraph (b)(2)(ii)(b) of this section) to the extent of—

(1) The outstanding principal balance of any promissory note (of which such partner is the maker) contributed to the partnership by such partner (other than a promissory note that is readily tradable on an established securities market), and

(2) The amount of any unconditional obligation of such partner (whether imposed by the partnership agreement or by State or local law) to make subsequent contributions to the partnership (other than pursuant to a promissory note of which such partner is the maker),

provided that such note or obligation is required to be satisfied at a time no later than the end of the partnership taxable year in which such partner's interest is liquidated (or, if later, within 90 days after the date of such liquidation). If a promissory note referred to in the previous sentence is negotiable, a partner will be considered required to satisfy such note within the time period specified in such sentence if the partnership agreement provides that, in lieu of actual satisfaction, the partnership will retain such note and such partner will contribute to the partnership the excess, if any, of the outstanding principal balance of such note over its fair market value at the time of liquidation. See paragraph (b)(2)(iv)(d)(2) of this section. See examples (1)(ix) and (x) of

paragraph (b)(5) of this section. A partner in no event will be considered obligated to restore the deficit balance in his capital account to the partnership (in accordance with requirement (3) of paragraph (b)(2)(ii)(b) of this section) to the extent such partner's obligation is not legally enforceable, or the facts and circumstances otherwise indicate a plan to avoid or circumvent such obligation. See paragraphs (b)(2)(ii)(f), (b)(2)(ii)(h), and (b)(4)(vi) of this section for other rules regarding such obligation. For purposes of this paragraph (b)(2), if a partner contributes a promissory note to the partnership during a partnership taxable year beginning after December 29, 1988, and the maker of such note is a person related to such partner (within the meaning of §1.752-1T(h), but without regard to subdivision (4) of that section), then such promissory note shall be treated as a promissory note of which such partner is the maker.

(d) *Alternate test for economic effect.*—If—

(1) Requirements (1) and (2) of paragraph (b)(2)(ii)(b) of this section are satisfied, and

(2) The partner to whom an allocation is made is not obligated to restore the deficit balance in his capital account to the partnership (in accordance with requirement (3) of paragraph (b)(2)(ii)(b) of this section), or is obligated to restore only a limited dollar amount of such deficit balance, and

(3) The partnership agreement contains a "qualified income offset,"

such allocation will be considered to have economic effect under this paragraph (b)(2)(ii)(d) to the extent such allocation does not cause or increase a deficit balance in such partner's capital account (in excess of any limited dollar amount of such deficit balance that such partner is obligated to restore) as of the end of the partnership taxable year to which such allocation relates. In determining the extent to which the previous sentence is satisfied, such partner's capital account also shall be reduced for—

(4) Adjustments that, as of the end of such year, reasonably are expected to be made to such partner's capital account under paragraph (b)(2)(iv)(k) of this section for depletion allowances with respect to oil and gas properties of the partnership, and

(5) Allocations of loss and deduction that, as of the end of such year, reasonably are expected to be made to such partner pursuant to section 704(e)(2), section 706(d), and paragraph (b)(2)(ii) of §1.751-1, and

(6) Distributions that, as of the end of such year, reasonably are expected to be made to such partner to the extent they exceed

offsetting increases to such partner's capital account that reasonably are expected to occur during (or prior to) the partnership taxable years in which such distributions reasonably are expected to be made (other than increases pursuant to a minimum gain chargeback under paragraph (b)(4)(iv)(*e*) of this section or under § 1.704-2(f); however, increases to a partner's capital account pursuant to a minimum gain chargeback requirement are taken into account as an offset to distributions of nonrecourse liability proceeds that are reasonably expected to be made and that are allocable to an increase in partnership minimum gain).

For purposes of determining the amount of expected distributions and expected capital account increases described in (6) above, the rule set out in paragraph (b)(2)(iii)(*c*) of this section concerning the presumed value of partnership property shall apply. The partnership agreement contains a "qualified income offset" if, and only if, it provides that a partner who unexpectedly receives an adjustment, allocation, or distribution described in (*4*), (*5*), or (*6*) above, will be allocated items of income and gain (consisting of a pro rata portion of each item of partnership income, including gross income, and gain for such year) in an amount and manner sufficient to eliminate such deficit balance as quickly as possible. Allocations of items of income and gain made pursuant to the immediately preceding sentence shall be deemed to be made in accordance with the partners' interests in the partnership if requirements (*1*) and (*2*) of paragraph (b)(2)(ii)(*b*) of this section are satisfied. See examples (1)(iii), (iv), (v), (vi), (viii), (ix), and (x), (15), and (16)(ii) of paragraph (b)(5) of this section.

(*e*) *Partial economic effect.*—If only a portion of an allocation made to a partner with respect to a partnership taxable year has economic effect, both the portion that has economic effect and the portion that is reallocated shall consist of a proportionate share of all items that made up the allocation to such partner for such year. See examples (15)(ii) and (iii) of paragraph (b)(5) of this section.

(*f*) *Reduction of obligation to restore.*—If requirements (*1*) and (*2*) of paragraph (b)(2)(ii)(*b*) of this section are satisfied, a partner's obligation to restore the deficit balance in his capital account (or any limited dollar amount thereof) to the partnership may be eliminated or reduced as of the end of a partnership taxable year without affecting the validity of prior allocations (see paragraph (b)(4)(vi) of this section) to the extent the deficit balance (if any) in such partner's capital account, after reduction for the items described in (*4*), (*5*), and (*6*) of paragraph (b)(2)(ii)(*d*) of this section, will not exceed the partner's remaining obligation (if any) to restore the deficit balance in his capital account. See example (l)(viii) of paragraph (b)(5) of this section.

(*g*) *Liquidation defined.*—For purposes of this paragraph, a liquidation of a partner's interest in the partnership occurs upon the earlier of (*1*) the date upon which there is a liquidation of the partnership, or (*2*) the date upon which there is a liquidation of the partner's interest in the partnership under paragraph (d) of § 1.761-1. For purposes of this paragraph, the liquidation of a partnership occurs upon the earlier of (*3*) the date upon which the partnership is terminated under section 708(b)(1), or (*4*) the date upon which the partnership ceases to be a going concern (even though it may continue in existence for the purpose of winding up its affairs, paying its debts, and distributing any remaining balance to its partners). Requirements (*2*) and (*3*) of paragraph (b)(2)(ii)(*b*) of this section will be considered unsatisfied if the liquidation of a partner's interest in the partnership is delayed after its primary business activities have been terminated (for example, by continuing to engage in a relatively minor amount of business activity, if such actions themselves do not cause the partnership to terminate pursuant to section 708(b)(1)) for a principal purpose of deferring any distribution pursuant to requirement (*2*) of paragraph (b)(2)(ii)(*b*) of this section or deferring any partner's obligation under requirement (*3*) of paragraph (b)(2)(ii)(*b*) of this section.

(*h*) *Partnership agreement defined.*— For purposes of this paragraph, the partnership agreement includes all agreements among the partners, or between one or more partners and the partnership, concerning affairs of the partnership and responsibilities of partners, whether oral or written, and whether or not embodied in a document referred to by the partners as the partnership agreement. Thus, in determining whether distributions are required in all cases to be made in accordance with the partners' positive capital account balances (requirement (*2*) of paragraph (b)(2)(ii)(*b*) of this section), and in determining the extent to which a partner is obligated to restore a deficit balance in his capital account (requirement (*3*) of paragraph (b)(2)(ii)(*b*) of this section), all arrangements among partners, or between one or more partners and the partnership relating to the partnership, direct and indirect, including puts, options, and other buy-sell agreements, and any other "stop-loss" arrangement, are considered to be part of the partnership agreement. (Thus, for example, if one partner who assumes a liability of the partnership is indemnified by another partner for a portion of such liability, the indemnifying partner (depending upon the particular facts) may be viewed as in effect having a partial deficit makeup obligation as a result of such indemnity agreement.) In addition, the partnership agreement includes provisions of Federal, State, or local law that govern the affairs of the partnership or are considered under such law to be a part of the partnership agreement (see the last sentence of paragraph (c) of § 1.761-1). For purposes of this paragraph (b)(2)(ii)(h), an agreement with a partner or a partnership shall include an agreement with a person related, within the meaning of section 267(b) (without modification by section 267(e)(1)) or section 707(b)(1), to such partner or partnership. For purposes of the preceding sentence, sections 267(b) and 707(b)(1) shall be applied for partnership taxable years beginning after December 29, 1988, by (*1*) substituting "80 percent or more" for "more than 50 percent" each place it appears in such sections, (*2*) excluding brothers and sisters from the members of a person's family, and (*3*) disregarding section 267(f)(1)(A).

(i) *Economic effect equivalence.*—Allocations made to a partner that do not otherwise have economic effect under this paragraph (b)(2)(ii) shall nevertheless be deemed to have economic effect, provided that as of the end of each partnership taxable year a liquidation of the partnership at the end of such year or at the end of any future year would produce the same economic results to the partners as would occur if requirements (*1*), (*2*), and (*3*) of paragraph (b)(2)(ii)(b) of this section had been satisfied, regardless of the economic performance of the partnership. See examples (4)(ii) and (iii) of paragraph (b)(5) of this section.

(iii) *Substantiality.*—*(a) General rules.*—Except as otherwise provided in this paragraph (b)(2)(iii), the economic effect of an allocation (or allocations) is substantial if there is a reasonable possibility that the allocation (or allocations) will affect substantially the dollar amounts to be received by the partners from the partnership, independent of tax consequences. Notwithstanding the preceding sentence, the economic effect of an allocation (or allocations) is not substantial if, at the time the allocation becomes part of the partnership agreement, (*1*) the after-tax economic consequences of at least one partner may, in present value terms, be enhanced compared to such consequences if the allocation (or allocations) were not contained in the partnership agreement, and (*2*) there is a strong likelihood that the after-tax economic consequences of no partner will, in present value terms, be substantially diminished compared to such consequences if the allocation (or allocations) were not contained in the partnership agreement. In determining the after-tax economic benefit or detriment to a partner, tax consequences that result from the interaction of the allocation with such partner's tax attributes that are unrelated to the partnership will be taken into account. See examples (5) and (9) of paragraph (b)(5) of this section. The economic effect of an allocation is not substantial in the two situations described in paragraphs (b)(2)(iii)(b) and (c) of this section. However, even if an allocation is not described therein, its economic effect may be insubstantial under the general rules stated in this paragraph (b)(2)(iii)(a). References in this paragraph (b)(2)(iii) to allocations includes capital account adjustments made pursuant to paragraph (b)(2)(iv)(k) of this section.

(b) *Shifting tax consequences.*—The economic effect of an allocation (or allocations) in a partnership taxable year is not substantial if, at the time the allocation (or allocations) becomes part of the partnership agreement, there is a strong likelihood that—

(*1*) The net increases and decreases that will be recorded in the partners' respective capital accounts for such taxable year will not differ substantially from the net increases and decreases that would be recorded in such partners' respective capital accounts for such year if the allocations were not contained in the partnership agreement, and

(*2*) The total tax liability of the partners (for their respective taxable years in which the allocations will be taken into account) will be less than if the allocations were not contained in the partnership agreement (taking into account tax consequences that result from the interaction of the allocation (or allocations) with partner tax attributes that are unrelated to the partnership).

If, at the end of a partnership taxable year to which an allocation (or allocations) relates, the net increases and decreases that are recorded in the partners' respective capital accounts do not differ substantially from the net increases and decreases that would have been recorded in such partners' respective capital accounts had the allocation (or allocations) not been contained in the partnership agreement, and the total tax liability of the partners is (as described in (*2*) above) less than it would have been had the allocation (or allocations) not been contained in the partnership agreement, it will be presumed that, at the time the allocation (or allocations) became part of such partnership agreement, there was a strong likelihood that these results would occur. This presumption may be overcome by a showing of facts and circumstances that prove otherwise. See examples (6), (7)(ii) and (iii), and (10)(ii) of paragraph (b)(5) of this section.

(c) Transitory allocations.—If a partnership agreement provides for the possibility that one or more allocations (the "original allocation(s)") will be largely offset by one or more other allocations (the "offsetting allocations(s)"), and, at the time the allocations become part of the partnership agreement, there is a strong likelihood that—

(1) The net increases and decreases that will be recorded in the partners' respective capital accounts for the taxable years to which the allocations relate will not differ substantially from the net increases and decreases that would be recorded in such partners' respective capital accounts for such years if the original allocation(s) and offsetting allocation(s) were not contained in the partnership agreement, and

(2) The total tax liability of the partners (for their respective taxable years in which the allocations will be taken into account) will be less than if the allocations were not contained in the partnership agreement (taking into account tax consequences that result from the interaction of the allocation (or allocations) with partner tax attributes that are unrelated to the partnership)

the economic effect of the original allocation(s) and offsetting allocation(s) will not be substantial. If, at the end of a partnership taxable year to which an offsetting allocation(s) relates, the net increases and decreases recorded in the partners' respective capital accounts do not differ substantially from the net increases and decreases that would have been recorded in such partners' respective capital accounts had the original allocation(s) and the offsetting allocation(s) not been contained in the partnership agreement, and the total tax liability of the partners is (as described in *(2)* above) less than it would have been had such allocations not been contained in the partnership agreement, it will be presumed that, at the time the allocations became part of the partnership agreement, there was a strong likelihood that these results would occur. This presumption may be overcome by a showing of facts and circumstances that prove otherwise. See examples (1)(xi), (2), (3), (7), (8)(ii), and (17) of paragraph (b)(5) of this section. Notwithstanding the foregoing, the original allocation(s) and the offsetting allocation(s) will not be insubstantial (under this paragraph (b)(2)(iii)(*c*)) and, for purposes of paragraph (b)(2)(iii)(*a*), it will be presumed that there is a reasonable possibility that the allocations will affect substantially the dollar amounts to be received by the partners from the partnership if, at the time the allocations become part of the partnership agreement, there is a strong likelihood that the offsetting allocation(s) will not, in large part, be made within five years after the original allocation(s) is made (determined on a first-in, first-out basis). See example (2) of paragraph (b)(5) of this section. For purposes of applying the provisions of this paragraph (b)(2)(iii) (and paragraphs (b)(2)(ii)(*d*)(*6*) and (b)(3)(iii) of this section), the adjusted tax basis of partnership property (or, if partnership property is properly reflected on the books of the partnership at a book value that differs from its adjusted tax basis, the book value of such property) will be presumed to be the fair market value of such property, and adjustments to the adjusted tax basis (or book value) of such property will be presumed to be matched by corresponding changes in such property's fair market value. Thus, there cannot be a strong likelihood that the economic effect of an allocation (or allocations) will be largely offset by an allocation (or allocations) of gain or loss from the disposition of partnership property. See examples (1)(vi) and (xi) of paragraph (b)(5) of this section.

* * *

(3) Partner's interest in the partnership.—(i) *In general.*—References in section 704(b) and this paragraph to a partner's interest in the partnership, or to the partners' interests in the partnership, signify the manner in which the partners have agreed to share the economic benefit or burden (if any) corresponding to the income, gain, loss, deduction, or credit (or item thereof) that is allocated.

Except with respect to partnership items that cannot have economic effect (such as nonrecourse deductions of the partnership), this sharing arrangement may or may not correspond to the overall economic arrangement of the partners. (For example, in the case of an unexpected downward adjustment to the capital account of a partner who does not have a deficit makeup obligation that causes such partner to have a negative capital account, it may be necessary to allocate a disproportionate amount of gross income of the partnership to such partner for such year so as to bring that partner's capital account back up to zero.) Thus, a partner who has a 50 percent overall interest in the partnership may have a 90 percent interest in a particular item of income or deduction. The determination of a partner's interest in a partnership shall be made by taking into account all facts and circumstances relating to the economic arrangement of the partners. All partners' interests in the partnership are presumed to be equal (determined on a per capita basis). However, this presumption may be rebutted by the taxpayer or the Internal Revenue Service by establishing facts and circumstances that show that the partners' interests in the partnership are otherwise.

(ii) *Factors considered.*—In determining a partner's interest in the partnership, the following factors are among those that will be considered:

(a) The partners' relative contributions to the partnership,

(b) The interests of the partners in economic profits and losses (if different than that in taxable income or loss),

(c) The interests of the partners in cash flow and other non-liquidating distributions, and

(d) The rights of the partners to distributions of capital upon liquidation.

The provisions of this subparagraph (b)(3) are illustrated by examples (1)(i) and (ii), (4)(i), (5)(i) and (ii), (6), (7)(i), (ii), and (iv), (8), (10)(ii), (16)(i), and (19)(iii) of paragraph (b)(5) of this section. See paragraph (b)(4)(i) of this section concerning rules for determining the partners' interests in the partnership with respect to certain tax items.

(iii) *Certain determinations.*—If—

(a) Requirements (*1*) and (*2*) of paragraph (b)(2)(ii)(*b*) of this section are satisfied, and

(b) All or a portion of an allocation of income, gain, loss, or deduction made to a partner for a partnership taxable year does not have economic effect under paragraph (b)(2)(ii) of this section,

the partners' interests in the partnership with respect to the portion of the allocation that lacks economic effect will be determined by comparing the manner in which distributions (and contributions) would be made if all partnership property were sold at book value and the partnership were liquidated immediately following the end of the taxable year to which the allocation relates with the manner in which distributions (and contributions) would be made if all partnership property were sold at book value and the partnership were liquidated immediately following the end of the prior taxable year, and adjusting the result for the items described in (*4*), (*5*), and (*6*) of paragraph (b)(2)(ii)(*d*) of this section. A determination made under this paragraph (b)(3)(iii) will have no force if the economic effect of valid allocations made in the same manner is insubstantial under paragraph (b)(2)(iii) of this section. See examples (1)(iv), (v), and (vi), and (15)(ii) and (iii) of paragraph (b)(5) of this section.

* * *

[Reg. § 1.704-1.]

☐ [*T.D.* 6175, 5-23-56. *Amended by T.D.* 6771, 11-19-64; *T.D.* 8065, 12-24-85; *T.D.* 8099, 9-8-86; *T.D.* 8237, 12-29-88; *T.D.* 8385, 12-26-91; *T.D.* 8500, 12-21-93; *T.D.* 8585, 12-27-94; *T.D.* 8717, 5-8-97; *T.D.* 9121, 4-20-2004; *T.D.* 9126, 5-5-2004 and *T.D.* 9207, 5-23-2005.]

§ 1.704-1T. Partner's distributive share (temporary).—(a) through (b)(1)(ii)(*a*) [Reserved]. For further guidance, see § 1.704-1(a) through (b)(1)(ii)(*a*).

(b)(1)(ii)(*b*) *Rules relating to foreign tax expenditures.*—(*1*) *In general.*—The provisions of paragraphs (b)(4)(xi) (regarding the allocation of foreign tax expenditures) apply for partnership taxable years beginning on or after April 21, 2004.

(*2*) *Transition rule.*—If a partnership agreement was entered into before April 21, 2004, then the partnership may apply the provisions of this paragraph (b) as if the amendments made by this temporary regulation had not occurred, until any subsequent material modification to the partnership agreement, which includes any change in ownership, occurs. This transition rule does not apply if, as of April 20, 2004, persons that are related to each other (within the meaning of section 267(b) and 707(b)) collectively have the power to amend the partnership agreement without the consent of any unrelated party.

(b)(1)(iii) through (b)(4)(vii) [Reserved]. For further guidance, see § 1.704-1(b)(1)(iii) through (b)(4)(vii).

(b)(4)(viii) through (b)(4)(x) [Reserved].

(b)(4)(xi) *Allocations of creditable foreign taxes.*—(*a*) *In general.*—Allocations of creditable foreign taxes cannot have substantial economic effect and, accordingly, such expenditures must be allocated in accordance with the partners' interests in the partnership. An allocation of a creditable foreign tax will be deemed to be in accordance with the partners' interests in the partnership if—

(*1*) The requirements of either paragraph (b)(2)(ii)(*b*) or (b)(2)(ii)(*d*) of this section are satisfied (i.e., capital accounts are maintained in accordance with paragraph (b)(2)(iv) of this section, liquidating distributions are required to be made in accordance with positive capital account balances, and each partner either has an unconditional deficit restoration obligation or agrees to a qualified income offset); and

(*2*) The partnership agreement provides for the allocation of the creditable foreign tax in proportion to the partners' distributive shares of income (including income allocated pursuant to section 704(c)) to which the creditable foreign tax relates.

(*b*) *Creditable foreign taxes.*—A creditable foreign tax is a foreign tax paid or accrued for U.S. tax purposes by a partnership and that is eligible for a credit under section 901(a). A foreign tax is a creditable foreign tax for these purposes without regard to whether a partner receiving an allocation of such foreign tax elects to claim a credit for such amount.

(c) *Income related to foreign taxes.*—A foreign tax is related to income if the income is included in the base upon which the taxes are imposed, which determination must be made in accordance with the principles of § 1.904-6. See *Examples (25)* through *(28)* of paragraph (b)(5) of this section.

(b)(5) * * *

Examples 1 through *19* [Reserved]. For further guidance, see § 1.704-1(b)(5), *Examples 1* through *19*.

Examples 20 through *24* [Reserved].

Example 25. (i) A and B form AB, an eligible entity (as defined in § 301.7701-3(a) of this chapter), treated as a partnership for U.S. tax purposes. AB's partnership agreement (within the meaning of paragraph (b)(2)(ii)(j) of this section) provides that the partners' capital accounts will be determined and maintained in accordance with paragraph (b)(2)(iv) of this section, that liquidation proceeds will be distributed in accordance with the partners' positive capital account balances, and that any partner with a deficit balance in his capital account following the liquidation of his interest must restore that deficit to the partnership. AB operates business M and earns income from passive investments in country X. Assume that country X imposes a 40 percent tax on business M income, which tax is a creditable foreign tax, but exempts from tax income from passive investments. In year 1, AB earns $100 of income from business M and $30 from passive investments and pays or accrues $40 of country X taxes. For purposes of section 904(d), the income from business M is general limitation income and the income from the passive investments is passive income. Pursuant to the partnership agreement, all partnership items, including creditable foreign taxes, from business M are allocated 60 percent to A and 40 percent to B, and all partnership items, including creditable foreign taxes, from passive investments are allocated 80 percent to A and 20 percent to B. Accordingly, A is allocated 60 percent of the business M income ($60) and 60 percent of the country X taxes ($24), and B is allocated 40 percent of the business M income ($40) and 40 percent of the country X taxes ($16).

(ii) Under paragraph (b)(4)(xi) of this section, the $40 of taxes is related to the $100 of general limitation income and no portion of the taxes is related to the passive income. Because AB's partnership agreement allocates the general limitation income 60/40 and the country X taxes 60/40, the allocations of the country X taxes are in proportion to the allocation of the income to which the foreign tax relates. Because AB satisfies the requirement of paragraph (b)(4)(xi) of this section, the allocations of the country X taxes are deemed to be in accordance with the partners' interests in the partnership.

Example 26. (i) A and B form AB, an eligible entity (as defined in § 301.7701-3(a) of this chapter), treated as a partnership for U.S. tax purposes. AB's partnership agreement (within the meaning paragraph (b)(2)(ii)(*i*) of this section) provides that the partners' capital accounts will be determined and maintained in accordance with paragraph (b)(2)(iv) of this section, that liquidation proceeds will be distributed in accordance with the partners' positive capital account balances, and that any partner with a deficit balance in his capital account following the liquidation of his interest must restore that deficit to the partnership. AB operates business M in country X and business N in country Y. Assume that country X imposes a 40 percent tax on business M income, country Y imposes a 20 percent tax on business N income, and the country X and country Y taxes are creditable foreign taxes. In year 1, AB has $100 of income from business M and $50 of income from business N. Country X imposes $40 of tax on the income from business M and country Y imposes $10 of tax on the income of business N. Pursuant to the partnership agreement, all partnership items, including creditable foreign taxes, from business M are allocated 75 percent to A and 25 percent to B, and all partnership items, including creditable foreign taxes, from business N are split evenly between A and B (50/50). Accordingly, A is allocated 75 percent of the income from business M ($75), 75 percent of the country X taxes ($30), 50 percent of the income from business N ($25), and 50 percent of the country Y taxes ($5). B is allocated 25 percent of the income from business M ($25), 25 percent of the country X taxes ($10), 50 percent of the income from business N ($25), and 50 percent of the country Y taxes ($5).

(ii) Because the income from business M and business N is general limitation income and the partnership agreement provides for different allocations with respect to such income, it is necessary to determine which foreign taxes are related to the business M income and which foreign taxes are related to the business N income. Under paragraph (b)(4)(xi) of this section, the $40 of country X taxes is related to business M and the $10 of country Y taxes is related to business N. Because AB's partnership agreement allocates the $40 of country X taxes in the same proportion as the general limitation income from business M, and the $10 of country Y taxes in the same proportion as the general limitation income from business N, the allocations of the country X taxes and the country Y taxes are in proportion to the allocation of the income to which the foreign taxes relate. Because AB satisfies the requirements of paragraph (b)(4)(xi), the allocations of the country X and country Y taxes are deemed to be in accordance with the partners' interests in the partnership.

Example 27. (i) The facts are the same as in *Example 26*, except that AB does not actually receive the $50 accrued with respect to business N until year 2. Also assume that A, B and AB each report taxable income on an accrual basis for U.S. tax purposes and AB reports taxable income on a cash basis for country X and country Y purposes. In year 1, AB pays country X taxes of $40. In year 2, AB pays country Y taxes of $10. Pursuant to the partnership agreement, in year 1, A is allocated 75 percent of business M income ($75) and country X taxes ($30) and 50 percent of business N income ($25). B is allocated 25 percent of business M income ($25) and country X taxes ($10) and 50 percent of business N income ($25). In year 2, A and B will each be allocated 50 percent of the country Y taxes ($5).

(ii) Because the income from business M and business N is general limitation income and the partnership agreement provides for different allocations with respect to such income, it is necessary to determine which foreign taxes are related to business M income and which foreign taxes are related to business N income. Under paragraph (b)(4)(xi) of this section, $40 of country X taxes is related to the $100 of general limitation income from business M. Under paragraph (b)(4)(xi), the country Y tax imposed in year 2 is allocable to the $50 of business N income AB recognizes in year 2 under country Y law and is treated as paid in year 2 on the $50 of business N income recognized for U.S. tax purposes in year 1. See § 1.904-6(a)(1)(iv) and (c), *Example 5*. Accordingly, the $10 of country Y taxes is related to the $50 of general limitation income from business N. Because AB's partnership agreement allocates the $40 of country X taxes in proportion to the general limitation income from business M, and the $10 of country X taxes from business N in proportion to the year 1 general limitation income from business N, the allocations of the country X and country Y taxes are in proportion to the allocation of the income to which the foreign taxes relate. Therefore, AB's partnership agreement satisfies the requirement of paragraph (b)(4)(xi)(*a*)(*2*) of this section. Because AB also satisfies the requirements of paragraph (b)(4)(xi)(*a*)(*1*) of this section, the allocations of the country X and Y taxes are deemed to be in accordance with the partners' interests in the partnership under paragraph (b)(4)(xi) of this section.

Example 28. (i) A and B form AB, an eligible entity (as defined in § 301.7701-3(a) of this chapter), treated as a partnership for U.S. tax purposes. AB's partnership agreement provides that the partners' capital accounts will be determined and maintained in accordance with paragraph (b)(2)(iv) of this section, that liquidation proceeds will be distributed in accordance with the partners' positive capital account balances, and that any partner with a deficit balance in his capital account following the liquidation of his interest must restore that deficit to the partnership. AB operates business M in country X. Assume that country X imposes a 20 percent tax on the net income from business M, which tax is a creditable foreign tax. In year 1, AB earns $300 of gross income, has deductible expenses, exclusive of creditable foreign taxes, of $100, and pays or accrues $40 of country X tax. For purposes of section 904(d), all income from business M is general limitation income. Pursuant to the partnership agreement, the first $100 of gross income each year is allocated to A as a return on excess capital contributed by A. All remaining partnership items, including creditable foreign taxes, are split evenly (50/50) between A and B. Assume that the gross income allocation is not deductible for country X purposes.

(ii) Under paragraph (b)(4)(xi) of this section, the $40 of taxes is related to the $200 of general limitation net income. In year 1, AB's partnership agreement allocates $150 or 75 percent of the general limitation income to A ($100 attributable to the gross income allocation plus $50 of the remaining $100 of net income) and $50 or 25 percent of the net income to B. AB's partnership agreement allocates the country X taxes in accordance with the partners' shares of partnership items remaining after the $100 gross income allocation. Therefore, AB allocates the country X taxes 50 percent to A ($20) and 50 percent to B ($20). Under paragraph (b)(4)(xi) of this section, the allocation of country X taxes cannot have substantial economic effect and must be allocated in accordance with the partners' interests in the partnership. AB's allocations of country X taxes are not deemed to be in accordance with the partners' interests in the partnership under paragraph (b)(4)(xi) of this section, because they are not in proportion to the allocation of the income to which the country X taxes relates.

(c) through (e)(4)(ii)(*b*) [Reserved]. For further guidance, see § 1.704-1(c) through (e)(4)(ii)(*b*). [Temporary Reg. § 1.704-1T.]

☐ [*T.D.* 9121, 4-20-2004.]

§ 1.706-1. Taxable years of partner and partnership.

* * *

(b) * * *

(6) *Certain foreign partners disregarded.*—(i) *Interests of disregarded foreign partners not taken into account.*—In determining the taxable year (the current taxable year) of a partnership under section 706(b) and the regulations thereunder, any interest held by a disregarded foreign partner is not taken into account. A foreign partner is a disregarded foreign partner unless such partner is allocated any gross income of the partnership that was effectively connected (or treated as effectively connected) with the conduct of a trade or business within the United States during the partnership's taxable year immediately preceding the current taxable year (or, if such partner was not a partner during the partnership's immediately preceding taxable year, the partnership reasonably believes that the partner will be allocated any such income during the current taxable year) and taxation of that income is not otherwise precluded under any U.S. income tax treaty.

(ii) *Definition of foreign partner.*—For purposes of this paragraph (b)(6), a foreign partner is any partner that is not a U.S. person (as defined in section 7701(a)(30)), except that a partner that is a controlled foreign corporation (as defined in section 957(a)) or a foreign personal holding company (as defined in section 552) shall not be treated as a foreign partner.

(iii) *Minority interest rule.*—If each partner that is not a disregarded foreign partner under paragraph (b)(6)(i) of this section (regarded partner) holds less than a 10-percent interest, and the regarded partners, in the aggregate, hold less than a 20-percent interest in the capital or profits of the partnership, then paragraph (b)(6)(i) of this section does not apply. In determining ownership in a partnership for purposes of this paragraph (b)(6)(iii), each regarded partner is treated as owning any interest in the partnership owned by a related partner. For this purpose, partners are treated as related if they are related within the meaning of sections 267(b) or 707(b) (using the language "10 percent" instead of "50 percent" each place it appears). However, for purposes of determining if partners hold less than a 20-percent interest in the aggregate, the same interests will not be considered as being owned by more than one regarded partner.

(iv) *Example.*—The provisions of paragraph (b)(6) of this section may be illustrated by the following example:

Example. Partnership B is owned by two partners, F, a foreign corporation that owns a 95-percent interest in the capital and profits of partnership B, and D, a domestic corporation that owns the remaining 5-percent interest in the capital and profits of partnership B. Partnership B is not engaged in the conduct of a trade or business within the United States, and, accordingly, partnership B does not earn any income that is effectively connected with a U.S. trade or business. F uses a March 31 fiscal year, and causes partnership B to maintain its books and records on a March 31 fiscal year as well. D is a calendar year taxpayer. Under paragraph (b)(6)(i) of this section, F would be disregarded and partnership B's taxable year would be determined by reference to D. However, because D owns less than a 10-percent interest in the capital and profits of partnership B, the minority interest rule of paragraph (b)(6)(iii) of this section applies, and partnership B must adopt the March 31 fiscal year for Federal tax purposes.

(v) *Effective date.*—(A) *Generally.*—The provisions of this paragraph (b)(6) are applicable for the first taxable year of a partnership other than an existing partnership that begins on or after July 23, 2002. For this purpose, an existing partnership is a partnership that was formed prior to September 23, 2002.

(B) *Voluntary change in taxable year.*—An existing partnership may change its taxable year to a year determined in accordance with this section. An existing partnership that makes such a change will cease to be exempted from the requirements of paragraph (b)(6) of this section.

(C) *Subsequent sale or exchange of interests.*—If an existing partnership terminates under section 708(b)(1)(B), the resulting partnership is not an existing partnership for purposes of paragraph (b)(6)(v)(A) of this section.

(D) *Transition rule.*—If, in the first taxable year beginning on or after July 23, 2002, an existing partnership voluntarily changes its taxable year to a year determined in accordance with this paragraph (b)(6), then the partners of that partnership may apply the provisions of § 1.702-3T to take into account all items of income, gain, loss, deduction, and credit attributable to the partnership year of change ratably over a four-year period.

* * *

[Reg. § 1.706-1.]

□ [*T.D.* 6175, 5-23-56. Amended by *T.D.* 7286, 9-26-73; *T.D.* 8123, 2-4-87; *T.D.* 8996, 5-16-2002 and *T.D.* 9009, 7-22-2002.]

Determination of Sources of Income

§ 1.861-1. Income from sources within the United States.—(a) *Categories of income.*—Part 1 (section 861 and following), subchapter N, chapter 1 of the Code, and the regulations thereunder determine the sources of income for purposes of the income tax. These sections explicitly allocate certain important sources of income to the United States or to areas outside the United States, as the case may be; and, with respect to the remaining income (particularly that derived partly from sources within and partly from sources without the United States), authorize the Secretary or his delegate to determine the income derived from sources within the United States, either by rules of separate allocation or by processes or formulas of general apportionment. The statute provides for the following three categories of income:

(1) *Within the United States.*—The gross income from sources within the United States, consisting of the items of gross income specified in section 861(a) plus the items of gross income allocated or apportioned to such sources in accordance with section 863(a). See §§ 1.861-2 to 1.861-7, inclusive, and § 1.863-1. The taxable income from sources within the United States, in the case of such income, shall be determined by deducting therefrom, in accordance with sections 861(b) and 863(a), the expenses, losses, and other deductions properly apportioned or allocated thereto and a ratable part of any other expenses, losses, or deductions which cannot definitely be allocated to some item or class of gross income. See §§ 1.861-8 and 1.863-1.

(2) *Without the United States.*—The gross income from sources without the United States, consisting of the items of gross income specified in section 862(a) plus the items of gross income allocated or apportioned to such sources in accordance with section 863(a). See §§ 1.862-1 and 1.863-1. The taxable income from sources without the United States, in the case of such income, shall be determined by deducting therefrom, in accordance with sections 862(b) and 863(a), the expenses, losses, and other deductions properly apportioned or allocated thereto and a ratable part of any other expenses, losses, or deductions which cannot definitely be allocated to some item or class of gross income. See §§ 1.862-1 and 1.863-1.

(3) *Partly within and partly without the United States.*—The gross income derived from sources partly within and partly without the United States, consisting of the items specified in section 863(b)(1), (2), and (3). The taxable income allocated or apportioned to sources within the United States, in the case of such income, shall be determined in accordance with section 863(a) or (b). See §§ 1.863-2 to 1.863-5, inclusive.

(4) *Exceptions.*—An owner of certain aircraft or vessels first leased on or before December 28, 1980, may elect to treat income in respect of these aircraft or vessels as income from sources within the United States for purposes of sections 861(a) and 862(a). See § 1.861-9. An owner of certain aircraft, vessels, or spacecraft first leased after December 28, 1980, must treat income in respect of these craft as income from sources within the United States for purposes of sections 861(a) and 862(a). See § 1.861-9A.

(b) *Taxable income from sources within the United States.*—The taxable income from sources within the United States shall consist of the taxable income described in paragraph (a)(1) of this section plus the taxable income allocated or apportioned to such sources, as indicated in paragraph (a)(3) of this section.

(c) *Computation of income.*—If a taxpayer has gross income from sources within or without the United States, together with gross income derived partly from sources within and partly from sources without the United States, the amounts thereof, together with the expenses and investment applicable thereto, shall be segregated; and the taxable income from sources within the United States shall be separately computed therefrom. [Reg. § 1.861-1.]

☐ [*T.D. 6258, 10-23-57. Amended by T.D. 7635, 8-7-79 and T.D. 7928, 12-15-83.*]

§ 1.861-2. Interest.—(a) *In general.*—(1) Gross income consisting of interest from the United States or any agency or instrumentality thereof (other than a possession of the United States or an agency or instrumentality of a possession), a State or any political subdivision thereof, or the District of Columbia, and interest from a resident of the United States on a bond, note, or other interest-bearing obligation issued or assumed or incurred by such person shall be treated as income from sources within the United States. Thus, for example, income from sources within the United States includes interest received on any refund of income tax imposed by the United States, a State or any political subdivision thereof, or the District of Columbia. Interest other than that described in this paragraph is not to be treated as income from sources within the United States. See paragraph (a)(7) of this section for special rules concerning substitute interest paid or accrued pursuant to a securities lending transaction.

(2) The term "resident of the United States", as used in this paragraph, includes (i) an individual who at the time of payment of the interest is a resident of the United States, (ii) a domestic corporation, (iii) a domestic partnership which at any time during its taxable year is engaged in trade or business in the United States, or (iv) a foreign corporation or a foreign partnership, which at any time during its taxable year is engaged in trade or business in the United States.

(3) The method by which, or the place where, payment of the interest is made is immaterial in determining whether interest is derived from sources within the United States.

(4) For purposes of this section, the term "interest" includes all amounts treated as interest under section 483, and the regulations thereunder. It also includes original issue discount, as defined in section 1232(b)(1), whether or not the underlying bond, debenture, note, certificate, or other evidence of indebtedness is a capital asset in the hands of the taxpayer within the meaning of section 1221.

(5) If interest is paid on an obligation of a resident of the United States by a nonresident of the United States acting in the nonresident's capacity as a guarantor of the obligation of the resident, the interest will be treated as income from sources within the United States.

(6) In the case of interest received by a nonresident alien individual or foreign corporation this paragraph (a) applies whether or not the interest is effectively connected for the taxable year with the conduct of a trade or business in the United States by such individual or corporation.

(7) A substitute interest payment is a payment, made to the transferor of a security in a securities lending transaction or a sale-repurchase transaction, of an amount equivalent to an interest payment which the owner of the transferred security is entitled to receive during the term of the transaction. A securities lending transaction is a transfer of one or more securities that is described in section 1058(a) or a substantially similar transaction. A sale-repurchase transaction is an agreement under which a person transfers a security in exchange for cash and simultaneously agrees to receive substantially identical securities from the transferee in the future in exchange for cash. A substitute interest payment shall be sourced in the same manner as the interest accruing on the transferred security for purposes of this section and §1.862-1. See also §§1.864-5(b)(2)(iii), 1.871-7(b)(2), 1.881-2(b)(2) and for the character of such payments and §1.894-1(c) for the application tax treaties to these transactions.

(b) *Interest not derived from U.S. sources.*—Notwithstanding paragraph (a) of this section, interest shall be treated as income from sources without the United States to the extent provided by subparagraphs (A) through (H), of section 861(a)(1) and by the following subparagraphs of this paragraph.

(1) *Interest on bank deposits and on similar amounts.*—(i) Interest paid or credited before January 1, 1977, to a nonresident alien individual or foreign corporation on—

(a) Deposits with persons, including citizens of the United States or alien individuals and foreign or domestic partnerships or corporations, carrying on the banking business in the United States,

(b) Deposits or withdrawable accounts with savings institutions chartered and supervised as savings and loan or similar associations under Federal or State law, or

(c) Amounts held by an insurance company under an agreement to pay interest thereon,

shall be treated as income from sources without the United States if such interest is not effectively connected for the taxable year with the conduct of a trade or business in the United States by such nonresident alien individual or foreign corporation. If such interest is effectively connected for the taxable year with the conduct of a trade or business in the United States by such nonresident alien individual or foreign corporation, it shall be treated as income from sources within the United States under paragraph (a) of this section unless it is treated as income from sources without the United States under another subparagraph of this paragraph. For a special rule for determining whether such interest is effectively connected for the taxable year with the conduct of a trade or business in the United States, see paragraph (c)(1)(ii) or §1.864-4.

(ii) Subdivision (i)(b) of this subparagraph applies to interest on deposits or withdrawable accounts described therein only to the extent that the interest paid or credited by the savings institution described therein is deductible under section 591 in determining the taxable income of such institution; and, for this purpose, whether an amount is deductible under section 591 shall be determined without regard to section 265, relating to deductions allocable to tax-exempt income. Thus, for example, such subdivision does not apply to amounts paid by a savings and loan or similar association on or with respect to its nonwithdrawable capital stock or on or with respect to funds held in restricted accounts which represent a proprietary interest in such association. Subdivision (i)(b) of this subparagraph also applies to so-called dividends paid or credited on deposits or withdrawable accounts if such dividends are deductible under section 591 without reference to section 265.

(iii) For purposes of subdivision (i)(c) of this subparagraph, amounts held by an insurance company under an agreement to pay interest thereon include policyholder dividends left with the company to accumulate, prepaid insurance premiums, proceeds of policies left on deposit with the company, and overcharges of premiums. Such subdivision does not apply to (a) the so-called "interest element" in the case of annuity or installment payments under life insurance or endowment contracts or (b) interest paid by an insurance company to its creditors on notes, bonds, or similar evidences of indebtedness, if the debtor-creditor relationship does not arise by virtue of a contract of insurance with the insurance company.

(iv) For purposes of subdivision (i) of this subparagraph, interest received by a partnership shall be treated as received by each partner of such partnership to the extent of his distributive share of such item.

(2) *Interest from a resident alien individual or domestic corporation deriving substantial income from sources without the United States.*—Interest received from a resident alien individual or a domestic corporation shall be treated as income from sources without the United States when it is shown to the satisfaction of the district director (or, if applicable, the Director of International Operations) that less than 20 percent of the gross income from all sources of such individual or corporation has been derived from sources within the United States, as determined under the provisions of sections 861 to 863, inclusive, and the regulations thereunder, for the 3-year period ending with the close of the taxable year of such individual or corporation preceding its taxable year in which such interest is paid or credited, or for such part of such period as may be applicable. If 20 percent or more of the gross income from all sources of such individual or corporation has been derived from sources within the United States, as so determined, for such 3-year period (or part thereof), the entire amount of the interest from such individual or corporation shall be treated as income from sources within the United States.

(3) *Interest from a foreign corporation not deriving major portion of its income from a U.S. business.*—(i) Interest from a foreign corporation which, at any time during the taxable year, is engaged in trade or business in the United States shall be treated as income from sources without the United States when it is shown to the satisfaction of the district director (or, if applicable, the Director of International Operations) that (a) less than 50 percent of the gross income from all sources of such foreign corporation for the 3-year period ending with the close of its taxable year preceding its taxable year in which such interest is paid or credited (or for such part of such period as the corporation has been in existence) was effectively connected with the conduct by such corporation of a trade or business in the United States, as determined under section 864(c) and § 1.864-3, or (b) such foreign corporation had gross income for such 3-year period (or part thereof) but none was effectively connected with the conduct of a trade or business in the United States.

(ii) If 50 percent or more of the gross income from all sources of such foreign corporation for such 3-year period (or part thereof) was effectively connected with the conduct by such corporation of a trade or business in the United States, see section 861(a)(1)(D) and paragraph (c)(1) of this section for determining the portion of interest from such corporation which is treated as income from sources within the United States.

(iii) For purposes of this subparagraph the gross income which is effectively connected with the conduct of a trade or business in the United States includes the gross income which, pursuant to section 882(d) or (e) and the regulations thereunder, is treated as income which is effectively connected with the conduct of a trade or business in the United States.

(iv) This subparagraph does not apply to interest paid or credited after December 31, 1969, by a branch in the United States of a foreign corporation if, at the time of payment or crediting, such branch is engaged in the commercial banking business in the United States; furthermore, such interest is treated under paragraph (a) of this section as income from sources within the United States unless it is treated as income from sources without the United States under subparagraph (1) or (4) of this paragraph.

(4) *Bankers' acceptances.*—Interest derived by a foreign central bank of issue from bankers' acceptances shall be treated as income from sources without the United States. For this purpose, a foreign central bank of issue is a bank which is by law or government sanction the principal authority, other than the government itself, issuing instruments intended to circulate as currency. Such a bank is generally the custodian of the banking reserves of the country under whose law it is organized.

(5) *Foreign banking branch of a domestic corporation or partnership.*—Interest paid or credited on deposits with a branch outside the United States (as defined in section 7701(a)(9)) of a domestic corporation or of a domestic partnership shall be treated as income from sources without the United States if, at the time of payment or crediting, such branch is engaged in the commercial banking business. For purposes of applying this subparagraph, it is immaterial (i) whether the domestic corporation or domestic partnership is carrying on a banking business in the United States, (ii) whether the recipient of the interest is a citizen or resident of the United States, a foreign corporation, or a foreign partnership, (iii) whether the interest is effectively connected with the conduct of a trade or business in the United States by the recipient, or (iv) whether the deposits with the branch located outside the United States are payable in the currency of a foreign country. Notwithstanding the provisions of § 1.863-6, interest to which this subparagraph applies shall be treated as income from sources within the foreign country, possession of the United States, or other territory in which the branch is located.

(6) *Section 4912(c) debt obligations.*—(i) *In general.*—Under section 861(a)(1)(G), interest on a debt obligation shall not be treated as income from sources within the United States if—

(a) The debt obligation was part of an issue of debt obligations with respect to which an election has been made under section 4912(c) (relating to the treatment of such debt obligations as debt obligations of a foreign obligor for purposes of the interest equalization tax),

(b) The debt obligation had a maturity not exceeding 15 years (within the meaning of subdivision (ii) of this subparagraph) on the date it is originally issued or on the date it is treated under section 4912(c)(2) as issued by reason of being assumed by a certain domestic corporation,

(c) The debt obligation, when originally issued, was purchased by one or more underwriters (within the meaning of subdivision (iii) of this subparagraph) with a view to distribution through resale (within the meaning of subdivision (iv) of this subparagraph), and

(d) The interest on the debt obligation is attributable to periods after the effective date of an election under section 4912(c) to treat such debt obligations as debt obligations of a foreign obligor for purposes of the interest equalization tax.

(ii) *Maturity not exceeding 15 years.*—The date the debt obligation is issued or treated as issued is not included in the 15 year computation, but the date of maturity of the debt obligation is included in such computation.

(iii) *Purchased by one or more underwriters.*—For purposes of this subparagraph, the debt obligation when originally issued will not be treated as purchased by one or more underwriters unless the underwriter purchases the debt obligation for his own account and bears the risk of gain or loss on resale. Thus, for example, a debt obligation, when originally issued, will not be treated as purchased by one or more underwriters if the underwriter acts only in the capacity of an agent of the issuer. Neither will a debt obligation, when originally issued, be treated as purchased by one or more underwriters if the agreement between the underwriter and issuer is merely for a "best efforts" underwriting, for the purchase by the underwriter of all or a portion of the debt obligations remaining unsold at the expiration of a fixed period of time, or for any other arrangement under the terms of which the debt obligations are not purchased by the underwriter with a view to distribution through resale. The fact that an underwriter is related to the issuer will not prevent the underwriter from meeting the requirements of this subparagraph. In determining whether a related underwriter meets the requirement of this subparagraph consideration shall be given to whether the purchase by the underwriter of the debt obligation from the issuer for resale was effected by a transaction subject to conditions similar to those which would have been imposed between independent persons.

(iv) *With a view to distribution through resale.*—(a) An underwriter who purchased a debt obligation shall be deemed to have purchased it with a view to distribution through resale if the requirements of (b) or (c) of this subdivision (iv) are met.

(b) The requirement of this subdivision (b) is that—

(1) The debt obligation is registered, approved, or listed for trading on one or more foreign securities exchanges or foreign established securities markets within 4 months after the date on which the underwriter purchases the debt obligation, or by the date of the first interest payment on the debt obligation, whichever is later, or

(2) The debt obligation, or any substantial portion of the issue of which the debt obligation is a part, is actually traded on one or more foreign securities markets on or

within 15 calendar days after the date on which the underwriter purchases the debt obligation. For purposes of this subdivison (iv), a foreign established securities market includes any foreign over-the-counter market as reflected by the existence of an inter-dealer quotation system for regularly disseminating to brokers and dealers quotations of obligations by identified brokers or dealers, other than quotations prepared and distributed by a broker or dealer in the regular course of his business and containing only quotations of such broker or dealer.

(c) The requirements of this subdivision (c) are that, except as provided in (d) of this subdivision, the underwriter is under no written or implied restriction imposed by the issuer with respect to whom he may resell the debt obligation and either—

(1) Within 30 calendar days after he purchased the debt obligation the underwriter or underwriters either (i) sold it or (ii) sold at least 95 percent of the face amount of the issue of which the debt obligation is a part, or

(2)(i) The debt obligation is evidenced by an instrument which, under the laws of the jurisdiction in which it is issued, is either negotiable or transferable by assignment (whether or not it is registered for trading), and (ii) it appears from all the relevant facts and circumstances, including any written statements or assurances made by the purchasing underwriter or underwriters, that such debt obligation was purchased with a view to distribution through resale.

(d) The requirements of (c) of this subdivision may be met whether or not the underwriter is restricted from reselling the debt obligations—

(1) To a United States person (as defined in section 7701(a)(30)) or

(2) To any particular person or persons pursuant to a restriction imposed by, or required to be met in order to comply with, United States or foreign securities or other law.

(v) *Statement with return.*—Any taxpayer who is required to file a tax return and who excludes from gross income interest of the type specified in this subparagraph must comply with the requirements of paragraph (d) of this section.

(vi) *Effect of termination of IET.*—If the interest equalization tax expires, the provisions of section 861(a)(1)(G) and this subparagraph shall apply to interest paid on debt obligations only with respect to which a section 4912(c) election was made.

(vii) *Definition of term underwriter.*—For purposes of section 861(a)(1)(G) and this subparagraph, the term "underwriter" shall mean any underwriter as defined in section 4919(c)(1).

(c) *Special rules.*—(1) *Proration of interest from a foreign corporation deriving major portion of its income from U.S. business.*—If, after applying the first sentence of paragraph (b)(3) of this section to interest to which that paragraph applies, it is determined that the interest may not be treated as income from sources without the United States, the amount of the interest from the foreign corporation which at some time during the taxable year is engaged in trade or business in the United States which is to be treated as income from sources within the United States shall be the amount that bears the same ratio to such interest as the gross income of such foreign corporation for the 3-year period ending with the close of its taxable year preceding its taxable year in which such interest is paid or credited (or for such part of such period as the corporation has been in existence) which was effectively connected with the conduct by such corporation of a trade or business in the United States bears to its gross income from all sources for such period.

(2) *Payors having no gross income for period preceding taxable year of payment.*—If the resident alien individual, domestic corporation, or foreign corporation, as the case may be, paying interest has no gross income from any source for the 3-year period (or part thereof) specified in subparagraph (2) or (3) of paragraph (b) of this section, or subparagraph (1) of this paragraph, the 20-percent test or the 50-percent test, or the apportionment formula, as the case may be, described in such subparagraph shall be applied solely with respect to the taxable year of the payor in which the interest is paid or credited. This subparagraph applies whether the lack of gross income for the 3-year period (or part thereof) stems from the business inactivity of the payor, from the fact that the payor is a corporation which is newly created or organized, or from any other cause.

(3) *Transitional rule.*—For purposes of applying paragraph (b)(3) of this section, and subparagraph (1) of this paragraph, the gross income of the foreign corporation for any period before the first taxable year beginning after December 31, 1966, which is from sources within the United States (determined as provided by sections 861 through 863, and the regulations thereunder, as in effect immediately before amendment by section 102 of the Foreign Investors Tax Act of 1966 (Pub. L. 89-809, 80 Stat. 1541)) shall be treated as gross income for such period which is effectively connected with the conduct of a trade or business

in the United States by such foreign corporation.

(4) *Gross income determinations.*—In making determinations under subparagraph (2) or (3) of paragraph (b) of this section, or subparagraph (1) or (3) of this paragraph—

(i) The gross income of a domestic corporation or a resident alien individual is to be determined by excluding any items specifically excluded from gross income under chapter 1 of the Code, and

(ii) The gross income of a foreign corporation which is effectively connected with the conduct of a trade or business in the United States is to be determined under section 882(b)(2) and by excluding any items specifically excluded from gross income under chapter 1 of the Code, and

(iii) The gross income from all sources of a foreign corporation is to be determined without regard to section 882(b) and without excluding any items otherwise specifically excluded from gross income under chapter 1 of the Code.

(d) *Statement with return.*—Any taxpayer who is required to file a return and applies any provision of this section to exclude an amount of interest from his gross income must file with his return a statement setting forth the amount so excluded, the date of its receipt, the name and address of the obligor of the interest, and, if known, the location of the records which substantiate the amount of the exclusion. A statement from the obligor setting forth such information and indicating the amount of interest to be treated as income from sources without the United States may be used for this purpose. See §§ 1.6012-1(b)(1)(i) and 1.6012-2(g)(1)(i).

(e) *Effective dates.*—Except as otherwise provided, this section applies with respect to taxable years beginning after December 31, 1966. For corresponding rules applicable to taxable years beginning before January 1, 1967, (see 26 CFR part 1 revised April 1, 1971). Paragraph (a)(7) of this section is applicable to payments made after November 13, 1997. [Reg. § 1.861-2.]

☐ [*T.D.* 6258, 10-23-57. *Amended by T.D.* 6873, 1-24-66; *T.D.* 7314, 5-22-74; *T.D.* 7378, 9-29-75; *T.D.* 8257, 8-1-89 *and T.D.* 8735, 10-6-97.]

§ 1.861-3. Dividends.—(a) [*In*] *General.*—(1) *Dividends included in gross income.*—Gross income from sources within the United States includes a dividend described in subparagraph (2), (3), (4), or (5) of this paragraph. For purposes of subparagraphs (2), (3), and (4) of this paragraph, the term "dividend" shall have the same meaning as set forth in section 316 and the regulations thereunder. See subparagraph (5) of this paragraph for special rules with respect to certain dividends from a DISC or former DISC. See also paragraph (a)(6) of this section for special rules concerning substitute dividend payments received pursuant to a securities lending transaction.

(2) [Reserved]. For further guidance, see § 1.861-3T(a)(2).

(3) *Dividend from a foreign corporation.*—(i) *In general.*—(a) A dividend described in this subparagraph is a dividend from a foreign corporation (other than a dividend to which subparagraph (4) of this paragraph applies) unless less than 50 percent of the gross income from all sources of such foreign corporation for the 3-year period ending with the close of its taxable year preceding the taxable year in which occurs the declaration of such dividend (or for such part of such period as the corporation has been in existence) was effectively connected with the conduct by such corporation of a trade or business in the United States, as determined under section 864(c) and § 1.864-3. Thus, no portion of a dividend from a foreign corporation shall be treated as income from sources within the United States under section 861(a)(2)(B) if less than 50 percent of the gross income of such foreign corporation from all sources for such 3-year period (or part thereof) was effectively connected with the conduct of a trade or business in the United States or if such foreign corporation had gross income for such 3-year period (or part thereof) but none was effectively connected with the conduct by such corporation of a trade or business in the United States.

(b) If 50 percent or more of the gross income from all sources of such foreign corporation for such 3-year period (or part thereof) was effectively connected with the conduct by such corporation of a trade or business in the United States, the amount of the dividend which is to be treated as income from sources within the United States under section 861(a)(2)(B) shall be the amount that bears the same ratio to such dividend as the gross income of such foreign corporation for such 3-year period (or part thereof) which was effectively connected with the conduct by such corporation of a trade or business in the United States bears to its gross income from all sources for such period.

(c) For purposes of this subdivision (i), the gross income which is effectively connected with the conduct of a trade or business in the United States includes the gross income which, pursuant to section 882(d) or (e), is treated as income which is effectively connected with the conduct of a trade or business in the United States.

(ii) *Rule applicable in applying limitation on amount of foreign tax credit.*—For purposes of determining under section 904 the limitation upon the amount of the foreign tax credit—

(a) So much of a dividend from a foreign corporation as exceeds (and only to the extent it so exceeds) the amount which is 100/85ths of the amount of the deduction allowable under section 245(a) in respect of such dividend, plus

(b) An amount which bears the same proportion to any section 78 dividend to which the dividend from the foreign corporation gives rise as the amount of the excess determined under (a) of this subdivision bears to the total amount of the dividend from the foreign corporation,

shall, notwithstanding subdivision (i) of this subparagraph, be treated as income from sources without the United States. This subdivision applies to a dividend for which no dividends-received deduction is allowed under section 245 or for which the 85 percent dividends-received deduction is allowed under section 245(a) but does not apply to a dividend for which a deduction is allowable under section 245(b). All of a dividend for which the 100 percent dividends-received deduction is allowed under section 245(b) shall be treated as income from sources within the United States for purposes of determining under section 904 the limitation upon the amount of the foreign tax credit. If the amount of a distribution of property other than money (constituting a dividend under section 316) is determined by applying section 301(b)(1)(C), such amount must be used as the dividend for purposes of applying (a) of this subdivision even though the amount used for purposes of section 245(a) is determined by applying section 301(b)(1)(D). In making determinations under this subdivision, a dividend (other than a section 78 dividend referred to in (b) of this subdivision) shall be determined without regard to section 78.

(iii) *Illustrations.*—The application of this subparagraph may be illustrated by the following examples:

Example (1). D, a domestic corporation, owns 80 percent of the outstanding stock of M, a foreign manufacturing corporation. M, which makes its returns on the basis of the calendar year, has earnings and profits of $200,000 for 1971 and 60 percent of its gross income for that year is effectively connected for 1971 with the conduct of a trade or business in the United States. For an uninterrupted period of 36 months ending on December 31, 1970, M has been engaged in trade or business in the United States and has received gross income effectively connected with the conduct of a trade or business in the United States amounting to 60 percent of its gross income from all sources for such period. The only distribution by M to D for 1971 is a cash dividend of $100,000; of this amount, $60,000 ($100,000 × 60%) is treated under subdivision (i) of this subparagraph as income from sources within the United States, and $40,000 ($100,000 − $60,000) is treated under § 1.862-1(a)(2) as income from sources without the United States. Accordingly, under section 245(a), D is entitled to a dividends-received deduction of $51,000 ($60,000 × 85%), and under subdivision (ii) of this subparagraph $40,000 ($100,000 − [$51,000 × 100/85]) is treated as income from sources without the United States for purposes of determining under section 904(a)(1) or (2) the limitation upon the amount of the foreign tax credit.

Example (2). (a) The facts are the same as in example (1) except that the distribution for 1971 consists of property which has a fair market value of $100,000 and an adjusted basis of $30,000 in M's hands immediately before the distribution. The amount of the dividend under section 316 is $58,000, determined by applying section 301(b)(1)(C) as follows:

Portion of adjusted basis of property attributable to gross income of M effectively connected for 1971 with conduct of trade or business in United States ($30,000 × 60%)	$18,000
Portion of fair market value of property attributable to gross income of M not effectively connected for 1971 with conduct of trade or business in United States ($100,000 × 40%)	40,000
Total dividend	$58,000

(b) Of the total dividend, $34,800 ($58,000 × 60% (percentage applicable to 3-year period)) is treated under subdivision (i) of this subparagraph as income from sources within the United States, and $23,200 ($58,000 × 40%) is treated under § 1.862-1(a)(2) as income from sources without the United States. However, by reason of section 245(c) the adjusted basis of the property ($30,000) is used under section 245(a) in determining the dividends-received deduction. Thus, under section 245(a), D is entitled to a dividends-received deduction of $15,300 ($30,000 × 60% × 85%).

(c) Under subdivision (ii) of this subparagraph, the amount of the dividend for purposes of applying (a) of that subdivision is the amount ($58,000) determined by applying section 301(b)(1)(C) rather than the amount ($30,000) determined by applying section 301(b)(1)(B). Accordingly, under subdivision

(ii) of this subparagraph $40,000 ($58,000 − [$15,300 × 100/85]) is treated as income from sources without the United States for purposes of determining under section 904(a) (1) or (2) the limitation upon the amount of the foreign tax credit.

Example (3). (a) D, a domestic corporation which makes its returns on the basis of the calendar year, owns 100 percent of the outstanding stock of N, a foreign corporation which is not a less developed country corporation under section 902(d). N, which makes its returns on the basis of the calendar year, has total gross income for 1971 of $100,000, of which $80,000 (including $60,000 from sources within foreign country X) is effectively connected for that year with the conduct of a trade or business in the United States. For 1971 N is assumed to have paid $27,000 of income taxes to Country X and to have accumulated profits of $81,000 for purposes of section 902(c)(1)(A). N's accumulated profits in excess of foreign income taxes amount to $54,000. For 1971 D receives a cash dividend of $42,000 from N, which is D's only income for that year.

(b) For 1971 D chooses the benefits of the foreign tax credit under section 901, and as a result is required under section 78 to include in gross income an amount equal to the foreign income taxes of $21,000 ($27,000 × $42,000/$54,000) it is deemed to have paid under section 902(a)(1). Thus, assuming no other deductions for the taxable year, D has gross income of $63,000 ($42,000 + $21,000) for 1971 less a dividends-received deduction under section 245(a) of $28,560 ([$42,000 × $80,000/$100,000] × 85%), or taxable income for 1971 of $34,440.

(c) Under subdivision (ii) of this subparagraph, for purposes of determining under section 904(a) (1) or (2) the limitation upon the amount of the foreign tax credit, $12,600 is treated as income from sources without the United States, determined as follows:

Excess of dividend from N over amount which is 100/85ths of amount of sec. 245(a) deduction ($42,000 − [$28,560 × 100/85])	$8,400
Proportionate part of sec. 78 dividend ($21,000 × $8,400/$42,000)	4,200
Taxable income from sources without the United States	$12,600

Example (4). A, an individual citizen of the United States who makes his return on the basis of the calendar year, receives in 1971 a cash dividend of $10,000 from M, a foreign corporation, which makes its return on the basis of the calendar year. For the 3-year period ending with 1970 M has been engaged in trade or business in the United States and has received gross income effectively connected with the conduct of a trade or business in the United States amounting to 80 percent of its gross income from all sources for such period. Of the total dividend, $8,000 ($10,000 × 80%) is treated under subdivision (i) of this subparagraph as income from sources within the United States and $2,000 ($10,000 − $8,000) is treated under § 1.862-1(a)(2) as income from sources without the United States. Since under section 245 no dividends-received deduction is allowable to an individual, A is entitled under subdivision (ii) of this subparagraph to treat the entire dividend of $10,000 ($10,000 − [$0 × 100/85]) as income from sources without the United States for purposes of determining under section 904(a) (1) or (2) the limitation upon the amount of the foreign tax credit.

(4) *Dividend from a foreign corporation succeeding to earnings of a domestic corporation.*—A dividend described in this subparagraph is a dividend from a foreign corporation, if such dividend is received by a corporation after December 31, 1959, but only to the extent that such dividend is treated by such recipient corporation under the provisions of § 1.243-3 as a dividend from a domestic corporation subject to taxation under chapter 1 of the Code. To the extent that this subparagraph applies to a dividend received from a foreign corporation, subparagraph (3) of this paragraph shall not apply to such dividend.

(5) *Certain dividends from a DISC or former DISC.*—(i) *General rule.*—A dividend described in this subparagraph is a dividend from a corporation that is a DISC or former DISC (as defined in section 992(a)) other than a dividend that—

(a) Is deemed paid by a DISC, for taxable years beginning before January 1, 1976, under section 995(b)(1)(D) as in effect for taxable years beginning before January 1, 1976, and for taxable years beginning after December 31, 1975, under section 995(b)(1)(D), (E), and (F) to the extent provided in subdivision (iii) of this subparagraph or

(b) Reduces under § 1.996-3(b)(3) accumulated DISC income (as defined in subdivision (ii)(*b*) of this subparagraph) to the extent provided in subdivision (iv) of this subparagraph.

Thus, a dividend deemed paid under section 995(b)(1)(A), (B), or (C) (relating to certain deemed distributions in qualified years) will be treated in full as gross income from sources within the United States. To the extent that a dividend from a DISC or former DISC is paid out of other earnings and profits (as defined in § 1.996-3(d)), subparagraph (2) of this paragraph shall apply. To the extent that a dividend from a DISC or former DISC is paid out of

Reg. § 1.861-3(a)(5)(i)(b)

previously taxed income (as defined in § 1.996-3(c)), see section 996(a)(3) (relating to the exclusion from gross income of amounts distributed out of previously taxed income). In determining the source of income of certain dividends from a DISC or former DISC, the source of income from any transaction which gives rise to gross receipts (as defined in § 1.993-6), in the hands of the DISC or former DISC, is immaterial.

(ii) *Definitions.*—For purposes of this subparagraph, the term—

(a) "Dividend from" means any amount actually distributed which is a dividend within the meaning of section 316 (including distributions to meet qualification requirements under section 992(c)) and any amount treated as a distribution taxable as a dividend pursuant to section 995(b) (relating to deemed distributions in qualified years or upon disqualification) or included in gross income as a dividend pursuant to section 995(c) (relating to gain on certain dispositions of stock in a DISC or former DISC), and

(b) "Accumulated DISC income" means the amount of accumulated DISC income as of the close of the taxable year immediately preceding the taxable year in which the dividend was made increased by the amount of DISC income for the taxable year in which the dividend was made (as determined under § 1.996-3(b)(2)).

(c) "Nonqualified export taxable income" means the taxable income of a DISC from any transaction which gives rise to gross receipts (as defined in § 1.993-6) which are not qualified export receipts (as defined in § 1.993-1) other than a transaction giving rise to gain described in section 995(b)(1)(B) or (C).

For purposes of subdivisions (i) *(b)* and (iv) of this subparagraph, if by reason of section 995(c), gain is included in the shareholder's gross income as a dividend, accumulated DISC income shall be treated as if it were reduced under § 1.996-3(b)(3).

(iii) *Determination of source of income for deemed distributions, for taxable years beginning before January 1, 1976, under section 995(b)(1)(D) as in effect for taxable years beginning before January 1, 1976, and for taxable years beginning after December 31, 1975, under section 995(b)(1)(D), (E), and (F).*—*(a)* If for its taxable year a DISC does not have any nonqualified export taxable income, then for such year the entire amount treated, for taxable years beginning before January 1, 1976, under section 995(b)(1)(D) as in effect for taxable years beginning before January 1, 1976, and for taxable years beginning after December 31, 1975, under section 995(b)(1)(D), (E), and (F) as a deemed distribution taxable as a dividend will be treated as gross income from sources without the United States.

(b) If for its taxable year a DISC has any nonqualified export taxable income, then for such year the portion of the amount treated, for taxable years beginning before January 1, 1976, under section 995(b)(1)(D) as in effect for taxable years beginning before January 1, 1976, and for taxable years beginning after December 31, 1975, under section 995(b)(1)(D), (E), and (F) as a deemed distribution taxable as a dividend that will be treated as income from sources within the United States shall be equal to the amount of such nonqualified export taxable income multiplied by the following fraction. The numerator of the fraction is the sum of the amounts treated, for taxable years beginning before January 1, 1976, under section 995(b)(1)(D) as in effect for taxable years beginning before January 1, 1976, and for taxable years beginning after December 31, 1975, under section 995(b)(1)(D), (E), and (F) as deemed distributions taxable as dividends. The denominator of the fraction is the taxable income of the DISC for the taxable year, reduced by the amounts treated under section 995(b)(1)(A), (B), and (C) as deemed distributions taxable as dividends. However, in no event shall the numerator exceed the denominator. The remainder of such dividend will be treated as gross income from sources without the United States.

(iv) *Determination of source of income for dividends that reduce accumulated DISC income.*—*(a)* If no portion of the accumulated DISC income of a DISC or former DISC is attributable to nonqualified export taxable income from any transaction during a year for which it is (or is treated as) a DISC, then the entire amount of any dividend that reduces under § 1.996-3(b)(3) accumulated DISC income will be treated as income from sources without the United States.

(b) If any portion of the accumulated DISC income of a DISC or former DISC is attributable to nonqualified export taxable income from any transaction during a year for which it is (or is treated as) a DISC, then the portion of any dividend during its taxable year that reduces under § 1.996-3(b)(3) accumulated DISC income that will be treated as income from sources within the United States shall be equal to the amount of such dividend multiplied by a fraction (determined as of the close of such year) the numerator of which is the amount of accumulated DISC income attributable to nonqualified export taxable income, and the denominator of which is the total amount of accumulated DISC income. The remainder of

such dividend will be treated as gross income from sources without the United States.

(v) *Special rules.*—For purposes of subdivisions (iii) and (iv) of this subparagraph—

(a) Taxable income shall be determined under § 1.992-3(b)(2)(i) (relating to the computation of deficiency distribution), and

(b) The portion of any deemed distribution taxable as a dividend, for taxable years beginning before January 1, 1976, under section 995(b)(1)(D) as in effect for taxable years beginning before January 1, 1976, and for taxable years beginning after December 31, 1975, under section 995(b)(1)(D), (E), and (F) or amount under § 1.996-3(b)(3)(i) through (iv) that is treated as gross income from sources within the United States during the taxable year shall be considered to reduce the amount of nonqualified export taxable income as of the close of such year.

(vi) *Illustrations.*—This subparagraph may be illustrated by the following examples:

Example (1). (a) Y is a corporation which uses the calendar year as its taxable year and which elects to be treated as a DISC beginning with 1972. X is its sole shareholder. In 1973, Y has $18,000 of taxable income from qualified export receipts (none of which are interest and gains described in section 995(b)(1)(A), (B), and (C)) and $1,000 of nonqualified export taxable income. Under these facts, X is deemed to have received a distribution under section 995(b)(1)(D) as in effect for taxable years beginning before January 1, 1976, of $9,500, *i.e.,* $19,000 × ½. X is treated under subdivision (iii) (b) of this subparagraph as having $500, *i.e.,* $1,000 × $9,500/$19,000, from sources within the United States and $9,000 from sources without the United States.

(b) For 1972, assume that Y did not have any nonqualified export taxable income. Pursuant to subdivision (v)(b) of this subparagraph, at the beginning of 1974, $500 of Y's accumulated DISC income is attributable to nonqualified export taxable income, i.e., $1,000 – $500.

Example (2). The facts are the same as in example (1) except that in 1973, in addition to the taxable income described in such example, Y has $450 of taxable income from gross interest from producer's loans described in section 995(b)(1)(A). Under these facts, the deemed distribution of $450 under section 995(b)(1)(A) is treated in full under subdivision (i) of this subparagraph as gross income from sources within the United States. The deemed distribution under section 995(b)(1)(D) as in effect for taxable years beginning before January 1, 1976, of $9,500 will be treated in the same manner as in example (1), *i.e.,* $1,000 × $9,500/($19,450 – $450).

Example (3). (a) The facts are the same as in example (1) except that in 1973, in addition to the distribution described in such example, Y makes a deemed distribution taxable as a dividend of $100 under section 995(b)(1)(G) (relating to foreign investment attributable to producer's loans) and actual distributions of all of its previously taxed income and of $2,000 taxable as a dividend which reduces accumulated DISC income (as defined in subdivision (ii)(b) of this subparagraph). Undre § 1.996-3(b)(3), accumulated DISC income is first reduced by the deemed distribution of $100 and then by the actual distribution taxable as a dividend of $2,000. As indicated in example (1), for 1972 Y did not have any nonqualified export taxable income. Assume that Y had accumulated DISC income of $12,000 at the end of 1973, $500 of which under example (1) is attributable to nonqualified export taxable income.

(b) The distribution from previously taxed income is excluded from gross income pursuant to section 996(a)(3).

(c) Of the deemed distribution of $100, X is treated under subdivision (iv)(b) as having $4.17, i.e., $100 × 500/12,000, from sources within the United States and $95.83, i.e., $100 – $4.17, from sources without the United States.

(d) Of the actual distribution taxable as a dividend of $2,000, X is treated under subdivision (iv)(b) as having $83.33, i.e., $2000 × 500/12,000, from sources within the United States and $1,916.67, i.e., $2,000 – $83.33, from sources without the United States.

(e) The sum of the amounts deemed and actually distributed as dividends for 1973 that are treated as gross income from sources within the United States is as follows:

	Total dividend	Amount of dividend from sources within the United States
Deemed distribution under sec. 995(b)(1)(D) as in effect for taxable years beginning before Jan. 1, 1976	$9,500	$500.00
Deemed distribution under sec. 995(b)(1)(G)	100	4.17
Actual distribution that reduces accumulated DISC income	2,000	83.33
Totals	$11,600	$587.50

Reg. § 1.861-3(a)(5)(vi)

Thus, pursuant to subdivision (v)(b) of this subparagraph, at the beginning of 1974 Y has $412.50, i.e., $1,000 − $587.50, of nonqualified export taxable income.

(f) The result would be the same if Y made an actual distribution taxable as a dividend of $1,500 on March 30, 1973, and another distribution of $500 on December 31, 1973.

Example (4). (a) Z is a corporation which uses the calendar year as its taxable year and which elects to be treated as a DISC beginning with 1972. W is its sole shareholder. At the end of 1976 Z has previously taxed income of $12,000 and accumulated DISC income of $4,000, $900 of which is attributable to nonqualified export taxable income. In 1977, Z has $20,050 of taxable income from qualified export receipts, of which $550 is from gross income from producer's loans described in section 995(b)(1)(A); Z has $950 of taxable income giving rise to gross receipts which are not qualified export receipts, of which $450 is gain described in section 995(b)(1)(B). Of its total taxable income of $21,000 (which is equal to its earnings and profits for 1977), $1,000 is attributable to sales of military property. Z has an international boycott factor (determined under section 999) of .10, and made an illegal bribe (within the meaning of section 162(c)) of $1,265. The proportion which the amount of Z's adjusted base period export receipts bears to Z's export gross receipts for 1977 is .40 (see section 995(e)(1)). Z makes a deemed distribution taxable as a dividend of $1,000 under section 995(b)(1)(G) (relating to foreign investment attributable to producer's loans) and actual distributions of $32,000.

(b) The deemed distributions of $550 under section 995(b)(1)(A) and $450 under section 995(b)(1)(B) are treated in full under subdivision (i) of this subparagraph as gross income from sources within the United States.

(c) Under these facts, Z has also made the following deemed distributions taxable as dividends to W under the following subdivisions of section 995(b)(1):

(D)	$ 500, *i.e.,* ½ × $1,000.
(E)	7,800, *i.e.,* 40 × [$21,000 − $(550 + 450 + 500)].
(F)(i)	5,850, *i.e.,* ½ × [$21,000 − $(550 + 450 + 500 + 7,800)].
(F)(ii)	585, *i.e.,* $5,850 × .10.
(F)(iii)	1,265
Total	$16,000

(d) The portion of the total amount of these deemed distributions ($16,000) that is treated under subdivision (iii)(b) as gross income from sources within the United States is computed as follows:

(1) The amount of nonqualified export taxable income is $500, *i.e.,* taxable income giving rise to gross receipts which are not qualified export receipts ($950) minus gain described in section 995(b)(1)(B) or (C) ($450).

(2) $500 × {$16,000/$[21,000 − (550 + 450)]} = $400. The remainder of these distributions, $15,600 ($16,000 minus $400), is treated under subdivision (iii)(b) of this subparagraph as gross income from sources without the United States.

(e) The earnings and profits accounts of Z at the end of 1977 are computed as follows:

		Total earnings and profits	Previously taxed income	Accumulated DISC income attributable to taxable income from transactions which give rise to gross receipts which	
				are qualified export receipts	are not qualified export receipts
(1)	Balance—January 1, 1977	$16,000	$12,000	$3,100	$900
(2)	Earnings and profits for 1977, before actual and section 995(b)(1)(G) distributions	21,000	17,000	3,900	100 [1]
(3)	Balance—December 31, 1977	$37,000	$29,000	$7,000	$1,000
(4)	Distribution under section 995(b)(1)(G) .	.....	1,000	(875)	(125) [2]

		Total earnings and profits	Previously taxed income	Accumulated DISC income attributable to taxable income from transactions which give rise to gross receipts which	
				are qualified export receipts	are not qualified export receipts
(5)	Balance..................	$37,000	$30,000	$6,125	$ 875
(6)	Actual distribution.............	(32,000)	(30,000)	(1,750)	(250)[3]
(7)	Balance—January 1, 1978...........	$ 5,000	.....	$4,375	$ 625

[1] The total of nonqualified export taxable income ($500) minus the portion of such income, under subdivision (iii)(b) of this subparagraph, deemed distributed pursuant to section 995(b)(1)(D), (E), and (F) ($400), as computed under (d)(2) of this example.

[2] Under subdivision (iv)(b) of this subparagraph,

$$\frac{\$1,000}{\$8,000} \times \$1,000.$$

[3] Under subdivision (iv)(b) of this subparagraph,

$$\frac{\$1,000}{\$8,000} \times \$2,000 \text{ (amount of actual distribution that reduces accumulated DISC income)}.$$

(6) *Substitute dividend payments.*—A substitute dividend payment is a payment, made to the transferor of a security in a securities lending transaction or a sale-repurchase transaction, of an amount equivalent to a dividend distribution which the owner of the transferred security is entitled to receive during the term of the transaction. A securities lending transaction is a transfer of one or more securities that is described in section 1058(a) or a substantially similar transaction. A sale-repurchase transaction is an agreement under which a person transfers a security in exchange for cash and simultaneously agrees to receive substantially identical securities from the transferee in the future in exchange for cash. A substitute dividend payment shall be sourced in the same manner as the distributions with respect to the transferred security for purposes of this section and § 1.862-1. See also §§ 1.864-5(b)(2)(iii), 1.871-7(b)(2) and 1.881-2(b)(2) for the character of such payments and § 1.894-1(c) for the application of tax treaties to these transactions.

(b) *Special rules.*—(1) *Foreign corporation having no gross income for period preceding declaration of dividend.*—If the foreign corporation has no gross income from any source for the 3-year period (or part thereof) specified in paragraph (a)(3)(i) of this section, the 50-percent test, or the apportionment formula, as the case may be, described in such paragraph shall be applied solely with respect to the taxable year of such corporation in which the declaration of the dividend occurs. This subparagraph applies whether the lack of gross income for the 3-year period (or part thereof) stems from the business inactivity of the foreign corporation, from the fact that such corporation is newly created or organized, or from any other cause.

(2) *Transitional rule.*—For purposes of applying paragraph (a)(3)(i) of this section, the gross income of the foreign corporation for any period before the first taxable year beginning after December 31, 1966, which is from sources within the United States (determined as provided by sections 861 through 863, and the regulations thereunder, as in effect immediately before amendment by section 102 of the Foreign Investors Tax Act of 1966 (Pub. L. 89-809, 80 Stat. 1541)) shall be treated as gross income for such period which is effectively connected with the conduct of a trade or business within the United States by such foreign corporation.

(3) *Gross income determinations.*—In making determinations under subparagraph (2) or (3) of paragraph (a) of this section, or subparagraph (2) of this paragraph—

(i) The gross income of a domestic corporation is to be determined by excluding any items specifically excluded from gross income under chapter 1 of the Code,

(ii) The gross income of a foreign corporation which is effectively connected with the conduct of a trade or business in the United States is to be determined under section 882(b)(2) and by excluding any items specifically excluded from gross income under chapter 1 of the Code, and

Reg. § 1.861-3(b)(3)(ii)

(iii) The gross income from all sources of a foreign corporation is to be determined without regard to section 882(b) and without excluding any items otherwise specifically excluded from gross income under chapter 1 of the Code.

(c) *Statement with return.*—Any taxpayer who is required to file a return and applies any provision of this section to exclude any dividend from his gross income must file with his return a statement setting forth the amount so excluded, the date of its receipt, the name and address of the corporation paying the dividend, and, if known, the location of the records which substantiate the amount of the exclusion. A statement from the paying corporation setting forth such information and indicating the amount of the dividend to be treated as income from sources within the United States may be used for this purpose. See §§ 1.6012-1(b)(1)(i) and 1.6012-2(g)(1)(i).

(d) *Effective date.*—Except as otherwise provided in this paragraph this section applies with respect to dividends received or accrued after December 31, 1966. Paragraph (a)(5) of this section applies to certain dividends from a DISC or former DISC in taxable years ending after December 31, 1971. Paragraph (a)(6) of this section is applicable to payments made after November 13, 1997. For purposes of paragraph (a)(5) of this section, any reference to a distribution taxable as a dividend under section 995(b)(1)(F)(ii) and (iii) for taxable years beginning after December 31, 1975, shall also constitute a reference to any distribution taxable as a dividend under section 995(b)(1)(F)(ii) and (iii) for taxable years beginning after November 30, 1975, but before January 1, 1976. For corresponding rules applicable with respect to dividends received or accrued before January 1, 1967, see 26 CFR 1.861-3 (Rev. as of Jan. 1, 1972). [Reg. § 1.861-3.]

☐ [T.D. 6258, 10-23-57. Amended by T.D. 6830, 6-22-65, T.D. 7378, 9-29-75, T.D. 7472, 2-28-77, T.D. 7591, 1-19-79; T.D. 7854, 11-15-82; T.D. 8735, 10-6-97 and T.D. 9194, 4-6-2005.]

§ 1.861-4. Compensation for labor or personal services.—(a) *In general.*—(1) Gross income from sources within the United States includes compensation for labor or personal services performed in the United States irrespective of the residence of the payer, the place in which the contract for service was made, or the place or time of payment; except that such compensation shall be deemed not to be income from sources within the United States, if—

(i) The labor or services are performed by a nonresident alien individual temporarily present in the United States for a period or periods not exceeding a total of 90 days during his taxable year,

(ii) The compensation for such labor or services does not exceed in the aggregate a gross amount of $3,000, and

(iii) The compensation is for labor or services performed as an employee of, or under any form of contract with—

(a) A nonresident alien individual, foreign partnership, or foreign corporation, not engaged in trade or business within the United States, or

(b) An individual who is a citizen or resident of the United States, a domestic partnership, or a domestic corporation, if such labor or services are performed for an office or place of business maintained in a foreign country or in a possession of the United States by such individual, partnership, or corporation.

(2) As a general rule, the term "day," as used in subparagraph (1)(i) of this paragraph, means a calendar day during any portion of which the nonresident alien individual is physically present in the United States.

(3) Solely for purposes of applying this paragraph, the nonresident alien individual, foreign partnership, or foreign corporation for which the nonresident alien individual is performing personal services in the United States shall not be considered to be engaged in trade or business in the United States by reason of the performance of such services by such individual.

(4) In determining for purposes of subparagraph (1)(ii) of this paragraph whether compensation received by the nonresident alien individual exceeds in the aggregate a gross amount of $3,000, any amounts received by the individual from an employer as advances or reimbursements for travel expenses incurred on behalf of the employer shall be omitted from the compensation received by the individual, to the extent of expenses incurred, where he was required to account and did account to his employer for such expenses and has met the tests for such accounting provided in § 1.162-17 and paragraph (e)(4) of § 1.274-5. If advances or reimbursements exceed such expenses, the amount of the excess shall be included as compensation for personal services for purposes of such subparagraph. Pensions and retirement pay attributable to labor or personal services performed in the United States are not to be taken into account for purposes of subparagraph (1)(ii) of this paragraph.

(5) For definition of the term "United States," when used in a geographical sense, see sections 638 and 7701(a)(9).

(b) *Amount includible in gross income.*—(1) *Taxable years beginning after December 31,*

1975.—(i) If a specific amount is paid for labor or personal services performed in the United States, that amount (if income from sources within the United States) shall be included in the gross income. If no accurate allocation or segregation of compensation for labor or personal services performed in the United States can be made, or when such labor or service is performed partly within and partly without the United States, the amount to be included in the gross income shall be determined on the basis that most correctly reflects the proper source of income under the facts and circumstances of the particular case. In many cases the facts and circumstances will be such that an apportionment on the time basis will be acceptable, that is, the amount to be included in gross income will be that amount which bears the same relation to the total compensation as the number of days of performance of the labor or services within the United States bears to the total number of days of performance of labor or services for which the payment is made. In other cases, the facts and circumstances will be such that another method of apportionment will be acceptable.

(ii) The application of this subparagraph may be illustrated by the following examples:

Example (1). B, a nonresident alien individual, was employed by M from March 1, 1976, to June 12, 1976, a total of 104 days, for which he received compensation in the amount of $12,240. During that period B was present in the United States 59 days. Under his contract B was subject to call at all times by his employer and was in a payment status on a 7-day week basis. There was no specific agreement as to the amount of pay for services performed within the United States; moreover, he received his stipulated salary payments regardless of the number of days per week he actually performed services. Under these circumstances the amount of compensation to be included in gross income as income from sources within the United States will be $6,943.85 ($12,240 × 59/104).

Example (2). C, a citizen of the United States, was a resident of a foreign country during his entire taxable year. He is employed by N, a domestic corporation, and paid a salary of $17,600 per annum. Under his contract C is required to work only on a 5-day week basis, Monday through Friday. During 1976 he was in the United States for 6 weeks, performing services therein for N for 30 work days. During the year he worked 240 days for N for which payment was made, determined by eliminating his vacation period for which no payment was made. Under these circumstances the amount of compensation for personal services performed in the United States is $2,200 ($17,600 × 30/240).

(2) *Taxable years beginning before January 1, 1976.*—If a specific amount is paid for labor or personal services performed in the United States, that amount (if income from sources within the United States) shall be included in the gross income. If no accurate allocation or segregation of compensation for labor or personal services performed in the United States can be made, or when such labor or service is performed partly within and partly without the United States, the amount to be included in the gross income shall be determined by an apportionment on the time basis; that is, there shall be included in the gross income an amount which bears the same relation to the total compensation as the number of days of performance of the labor or services within the United States bears to the total number of days of performance of labor or services for which the payment is made.

(c) *Coastwise travel.*—Except as to income excluded by paragraph (a) of this section, wages received for services rendered inside the territorial limits of the United States and wages of an alien seaman earned on a coastwise vessel are to be regarded as from sources within the United States.

(d) *Effective date.*—This section applies with respect to taxable years beginning after December 31, 1966. For corresponding rules applicable to taxable years beginning before January 1, 1967, see 26 CFR 1.861-4 (Rev. as of Jan. 1, 1972). [Reg. § 1.861-4.]

☐ [*T.D.* 6258, 10-23-57. *Amended by T.D.* 7378, 9-29-75.]

Proposed Amendments to Regulation

§ 1.861-4. Compensation for labor or personal services.—(a) *Compensation for labor or personal services performed wholly within the United States.*—(1) Generally, compensation for labor or personal services, including fees, commissions, fringe benefits, and similar items, performed wholly within the United States is gross income from sources within the United States. * * *

(b) *Compensation for labor or personal services performed partly within and partly without the United States.*—(1) *Compensation for labor or personal services performed by persons other than individuals.*—(i) *In general.*—In the case of compensation for labor or personal services performed partly within and partly without the United States by a person other than an individual, the part of that compensation that is attributable to the labor or personal services performed within the United States, and that is therefore included in gross income as income from sources within the United States, is determined on the basis that most correctly reflects the proper source of the income under the facts and circumstances of the particular case. In many cases, the facts and circumstances will be such that an apportionment on the time basis, as defined in paragraph (b)(2)(ii)(E) of this section, will be acceptable.

(ii) *Example.*—Corp X, a domestic corporation, receives compensation of $150,000 under a contract for services to be performed concurrently in the United States and in several foreign countries by numerous Corp X employees. Each Corp X employee performing services under this contract performs his or her services exclusively in one jurisdiction. Although the number of employees (and hours spent by employees) performing services under the contract within the United States equals the number of employees (and hours spent by employees) performing services under the contract without the United States, the compensation paid to employees performing services under the contract within the United States is higher because of the more sophisticated nature of the services performed by the employees within the United States. Accordingly, the payroll cost for employees performing services under the contract within the United States is $20,000 out of a total contract payroll cost of $30,000. Under these facts and circumstances, a determination based upon relative payroll costs would be the basis that most correctly reflects the proper source of the income received under the contract. Thus, of the $150,000 of compensation included in Corp X's gross income, $100,000 ($150,000 × $20,000/$30,000) is attributable to the labor or personal services performed within the United States and $50,000 ($150,000 × $10,000/$30,000) is attributable to the labor or personal services performed without the United States.

(2) *Compensation for labor or personal services performed by an individual.*—(i) *In general.*—Except as provided in paragraph (b)(2)(ii) of this section, in the case of compensation for labor or personal services performed partly within and partly without the United States by an individual, the part of such compensation that is attributable to the labor or personal services performed within the United States, and that is therefore included in gross income as income from sources within the United States, is determined on the basis that most correctly reflects the proper source of that income under the facts and circumstances of the particular case. In many cases, the facts and circumstances will be such that an apportionment on a time basis, as defined in paragraph (b)(2)(ii)(E) of this section, will be acceptable.

(ii) *Employee compensation.*—(A) *In general.*—Except as provided in paragraph (b)(2)(ii)(B) or (C) of this section, in the case of compensation for labor or personal services performed partly within and partly without the United States by an individual as an employee, the part of such compensation that is attributable to the labor or personal services performed within the United States, and that is therefore included in gross income as income from sources within the United States, is determined on a time basis, as defined in paragraph (b)(2)(ii)(E) of this section.

(B) *Certain fringe benefits sourced on a geographical basis.*—Except as provided in paragraph (b)(2)(ii)(C) of this section, items of compensation of an individual as an employee for labor or personal services performed partly within and partly without the United States that are described in paragraph (b)(2)(ii)(D)(*1*) through (*6*) of this section are sourced on a geographical basis in accordance with those paragraphs.

(C) *Exceptions and special rules.*—(*1*) *Alternative basis.*—(*i*) *Individual as an employee generally.*—An individual may determine the source of his or her compensation as an employee for labor or personal services performed partly within and partly without the United States under an alternative basis if the individual establishes to the satisfaction of the Commissioner that, under the facts and circumstances of the particular case, the alternative basis more properly determines the source of the compensation than a basis described in paragraph (b)(2)(ii)(A) or (B), whichever is applicable, of this section. An individual that uses an alternative basis must retain in his or her records documentation setting forth why the alternative basis more properly determines the source of the compensation. In addition, the individual must comply with the requirements set forth in any applicable administrative pronouncement issued by the Commissioner.

(*ii*) *Determination by Commissioner.*—The Commissioner may, under the facts and dircumstances of the particular case, determine the source of compensation that is received by an individual as an employee for labor or personal services performed partly within and partly without the United States under an alternative basis other than a basis described in paragraph (b)(2)(ii)(A) or (B) of this section if such compensation either is not for a specific time period or constitutes in substance a fringe benefit described in paragraph (b)(2)(ii)(D) of this section notwithstanding a failure to meet any requirement of paragraph (b)(2)(ii)(D) of this section. The Commissioner may make this determination only if such alternative basis determines the source of compensation in a more reasonable manner than the basis used by the individual pursuant to paragraph (b)(2)(i)(A) or (B) of this section.

(2) Ruling or other administrative pronouncement with respect to groups of taxpayers.—The Commissioner may, by ruling or other administrative pronouncement applying to similarly situated taxpayers generally, permit individuals to determine the source of their compensation as an employee for labor or personal services performed partly within and partly without the United States under an alternative basis. Any such individual shall be treated as having met the requirement to establish such alternative basis to the satisfaction of the Commissioner under the facts and circumstances of the particular case, provided that the individual meets the other requirements of paragraph (b)(2)(ii)(C)(*1*)(*i*) of this section. The Commissioner also may, by ruling or other administrative pronouncement, indicate the circumstances in which he will require individuals to determine the source of certain compensation as an employee for labor or personal services performed partly within and partly without the United States under an alternative basis pursuant to the authority under paragraph (b)(2)(ii)(C)(*1*)(*ii*) of this section.

(3) Artists and athletes.— [RESERVED.]

(D) *Fringe benefits sourced on a geographical basis.*—Except as provided in paragraph (b)(2)(ii)(C) of this section, compensation of an individual as an employee for labor or personal services performed partly within and partly without the United States in the form of the following fringe benefits is sourced on a geographical basis as indicated in this paragraph (b)(2)(ii)(D). The amount of the compensation in the form of the fringe benefit must be reasonable, and the individual must substantiate such amounts by adequate records or by sufficient evidence under rules similar to those set forth in § 1.274-5T(c) or (h) or § 1.132-5. For purposes of this paragraph (b)(2)(ii)(D), the term *principal place of work* has the same meaning that it has for purposes of section 217 and § 1.217-2(c)(3).

(1) Housing fringe benefit.—The source of compensation in the form of a housing fringe benefit is determined based on the location of the individual's principal place of work. For purposes of this paragraph (b)(2)(ii)(D)(*1*), a housing fringe benefit includes payments to or on behalf of an individual (and the individual's family if the family resides with the individual) only for rent, utilities (other than telephone charges), real and personal property insurance, occupancy taxes not deductible under section 164 or 216(a), nonrefundable fees paid for securing a leasehold, rental of furniture and accessories, household repairs, residential parking, and the fair rental value of housing provided in kind by the individual's employer. A housing fringe benefit does not include payments for expenses or items set forth in § 1.911-4(b)(2).

(2) Education fringe benefit.—The source of compensation in the form of an education fringe benefit for the education expenses of the individual's dependents is determined based on the location of the individual's principal place of work. For purposes of this paragraph (b)(2)(ii)(D)(*2*), an education fringe benefit includes payments only for qualified tuition and related expenses of the type described in section 530(b)(4)(A)(i) and expenditures for room and board and uniforms as described in section 530(b)(4)(A)(ii) with respect to education at an elementary or secondary educational institution.

(3) Local transportation fringe benefit.—The source of compensation in the form of a local transportation fringe benefit is determined based on the location of the individual's principal place of work. For purposes of this paragraph (b)(2)(ii)(D)(*3*), an individual's local transportation fringe benefit is the amount that the individual receives as compensation for local transportation of the individual or the individual's spouse or dependents at the location of the individual's principal place of work. The amount treated as a local transportation fringe benefit is limited to the actual expenses incurred for local transportation and the fair rental value of any vehicle provided by the employer and used predominantly by the individual or the individual's spouse or dependents for local transportation. For this purpose, actual expenses incurred for local transportation do not include the cost (including interest) of the purchase by the individual, or on behalf of the individual, of an automobile or other vehicle.

(4) Tax reimbursement fringe benefit.—The source of compensation in the form of a foreign tax reimbursement fringe benefit is determined based on the location of the jurisdiction that imposed the tax for which the individual is reimbursed.

(5) Hazardous or hardship duty pay fringe benefit.—The source of compensation in the form of a hazardous or hardship duty pay fringe benefit is determined based on the location of the hazardous or hardship duty zone for

which the hazardous or hardship duty pay fringe benefit is paid. For purposes of this paragraph (b)(2)(ii)(D)(5), a hazardous or hardship duty zone is any place in a foreign country which is either designated by the Secretary of State as a place where living conditions are extraordinarily difficult, notably unhealthy, or where excessive physical hardships exist, and for which a post differential of 15 percent or more would be provided under section 5925(b) of Title 5 of the U.S. Code to any officer or employee of the U.S. Government present at that place, or where a civil insurrection, civil war, terrorism, or wartime conditions threatens physical harm or imminent danger to the health and well-being of the individual. Compensation provided an employee during the period that the employee performs labor or personal services in a hazardous or hardship duty zone may be treated as a hazardous or hardship duty pay fringe benefit only if the employer provides the hazardous or hardship duty pay fringe benefit only to employees performing labor or personal services in a hazardous or hardship duty zone. The amount of compensation treated as a hazardous or hardship duty pay fringe benefit may not exceed the maximum amount that the U.S. government would allow its officers or employees present at that location.

(6) Moving expense reimbursement fringe benefit.—Except as otherwise provided in this paragraph (b)(2)(ii)(D)(6), the source of compensation in the form of a moving expense reimbursement is determined based on the location of the employee's new principal place of work. The source of such compensation is determined based on the location of the employee's former principal place of work, however, if the individual provides sufficient evidence that such determination of source is more appropriate under the facts and circumstances of the particular case. For purposes of this paragraph (b)(2)(ii)(D)(6), sufficient evidence generally requires an agreement, between the employer and the employee, or a written statement of company policy, which is reduced to writing before the move and which is entered into or established to induce the employee or employees to move to another country. The writing must state that the employer will reimburse the employee for moving expenses that the employee incurs to return to the employee's former principal place of work regardless of whether he or she continues to work for the employer after returning to that location. The writing may contain certain conditions upon which the right to reimbursement is determined as long as those conditions set forth standards that are definitely ascertainable and can only be fulfilled prior to, or through completion of, the employee's return move to the employee's former principal place of work.

(E) *Time basis.*—The amount of compensation for labor or personal services performed within the United States determined on a time basis is the amount that bears the same relation to the individual's total compensation as the number of days of performance of the labor or personal services by the individual within the United States bears to his or her total number of days of performance of labor or personal services. A unit of time less than a day may be appropriate for purposes of this calculation. The time period for which the compensation for labor or personal services is made is presumed to be the calendar year in which the labor or personal services are performed, unless the taxpayer establishes to the satisfaction of the Commissioner, or the Commissioner determines, that another distinct, separate, and continuous period of time is more appropriate. For example, a transfer during a year from a position in the United States to a foreign posting that lasted through the end of that year would generally establish two separate time periods within that taxable year. The first of these time periods would be the portion of the year preceding the start of the foreign posting, and the second of these time periods would be the portion of the year following the start of the foreign posting. However, in the case of a foreign posting that requires short-term returns to the United States to perform services for the employer, such short-term returns would not be sufficient to establish distinct, separate, and continuous time periods within the foreign posting time period but would be relevant to the allocation of compensation relating to the overall time period. In each case, the source of the compensation on a time basis is based upon the number of days (or unit of time less than a day, if appropriate) in that separate time period.

(F) *Multi-year compensation arrangements.*—The source of multi-year compensation is determined generally on a time basis, as defined in paragraph (b)(2)(ii)(E) of this section, over the period to which such compensation is attributable. For purposes of this paragraph (b)(2)(ii)(F), *multi-year compensation* means compensation that is included in the income of an individual in one taxable year but that is attributable to a period that includes two or more taxable years. The determination of the period to which such compensation is attributable, for purposes of determining its source, is based upon the facts and circumstances of the particular case. For example, an amount of compensation that specifically relates to a period of time that includes several calendar years is attributable to the entirety of that multi-year period. The amount of such compensation that is treated as from sources within the United States is the amount that bears the same relationship to the total multi-year compensation as the number of days (or unit of time less than a day, if appropriate) that labor or personal services were performed within the United States in connection with the project bears to the total number of days (or unit of time less than a day, if appropriate) that labor or personal services were performed in connection with the project. In the case of stock options, the facts and circumstances generally will be such that the applicable period to which the compensation is attributable is the period between the grant of an option and the date on which all employment-related conditions for its exercise have been satisfied (the vesting of the option).

(G) *Examples.*—The following examples illustrate the application of this paragraph (b)(2)(ii):

Example 1. B, a nonresident alien individual, was employed by Corp M, a domestic corporation, from March 1 to December 25 of the taxable year, a total of 300 days, for which B received compensation in the amount of $80,000. Under B's employment contract with Corp M, B was subject to call at all times by Corp M and was in a payment status on a 7-day week basis. Pursuant to that contract, B performed services (or was available to perform services) within the United States for 180 days and performed services (or was available to perform services) without the United States for 120 days. None of B's $80,000 compensation was for fringe benefits as identified in paragraph (b)(2)(ii)(D) of this section. B determined the amount of compensation that is attributable to his labor or personal services performed within the United States on a time basis under paragraph (b)(2)(ii)(A) and (E) of this section. B did not assert, pursuant to paragraph (b)(2)(ii)(C)(*1*)(*i*) of this section, that, under the particular facts and circumstances, an alternative basis more properly determines the source of that compensation than the time basis. Therefore, B must include in income from sources within the United States $48,000 ($80,000 × 180/300) of his compensation from Corporation M.

Example 2. (i) Same facts as in *Example 1* except that Corp M had a company-wide arrangement with its employees, including B, that they would receive an education fringe benefit, as described in paragraph (b)(2)(ii)(D)(*2*) of this section, while working in the United States. During the taxable year, B incurred education expenses for his dependent daughter that qualified for the education fringe benefit in the amount of $10,000, for which B received a reimbursement from Corp M. B did not maintain adequate records or sufficient evidence of this fringe benefit as required by paragraph (b)(2)(ii)(D) of this section. When B filed his Federal income tax return for the taxable year, B did not apply paragraphs (b)(2)(ii)(B) and (D)(*2*) of this section to treat the compensation in the form of the education fringe benefit as income from sources within the United States, the location of his principal place of work during the 300-day period. Rather, B combined the $10,000 reimbursement with his base compensation of $80,000 and applied the time basis of paragraph (b)(2)(ii)(A) of this section to determine the source of his gross income.

(ii) On audit, B argues that because he failed to substantiate the education fringe benefit in accordance with paragraph (b)(2)(ii)(D) of this section, his entire employment compensation from Corp M is sourced on a time basis pursuant to paragraph (b)(2)(ii)(A) of this section. The Commissioner, after reviewing Corp M's fringe benefit arrangement, determines, pursuant to paragraph (b)(2)(ii)(C)(*1*)(*ii*) of this section, that the $10,000 educational expense reimbursement constitutes in substance a fringe benefit described in paragraph (b)(2)(ii)(D)(*2*) of this section, notwithstanding a failure to meet all of the requirements of paragraph (b)(2)(ii)(D) of this section, and that an alternative geographic source basis, under the facts and circumstances of this particular case, is a more reasonable manner to determine the source of the compensation than the time basis used by B.

Example 3. (i) A, a United States citizen, is employed by Corp N, a domestic corporation. A's principal place of work is in the United States. A earns an annual salary of $100,000. During the first quarter of the calendar year (which is also A's taxable year), A performed services entirely within the United States. At the beginning of the second quarter of the calendar year, A was transferred to Country X for the remainder of the year and received, in addition to her annual salary, $30,000 in fringe benefits that are attributable to her new principal place of work in Country X. Corp N paid these fringe benefits separately from A's annual salary. Corp N supplied A with a statement detailing that $25,000 of the fringe benefit was paid for housing, as defined in paragraph (b)(2)(ii)(D)(*1*) of this section, and $5,000 of the fringe benefit was paid for local transportation, as defined in paragraph (b)(2)(ii)(D)(*3*) of this section. None of the local transportation fringe benefit is excluded from the employee's gross income as a qualified transportation fringe benefit under section 132(a)(5). Under A's employment contract, A was required to work on a 5-day week basis, Monday through Friday. During the last three quarters of the year, A performed services 30 days in the United States and 150 days in Country X and other foreign countries.

(ii) A determined the source of all of her compensation from Corp N pursuant to paragraph (b)(2)(ii)(A), (B), and (D)(*1*) and (*3*) of this section. A did not assert, pursuant to paragraph (b)(2)(ii)(C)(*1*)(*i*) of this section, that, under the particular facts and circumstances, an alternative basis more properly determines the source of that compensation than the bases set forth in paragraphs (b)(2)(ii)(A), (B), and (D)(*1*) and (*3*) of this section. However, in applying the time basis set forth in paragraph (b)(2)(ii)(E) of this section, A establishes to the satisfaction of the Commissioner that the first quarter of the calendar year and the last three quarters of the calendar year are two separate, distinct, and continuous periods of time. Accordingly, $25,000 of A's annual salary is attributable to the first quarter of the year (25 percent of $100,000). This amount is entirely compensation that was attributable to the labor or personal services performed within the United States and is, therefore, included in gross income as income from sources within the United States. The balance of A's compensation as an employee of Corp N, $105,000 (which includes the $30,000 in fringe benefits that are attributable to the location of A's principal place of work in Country X), is compensation attributable to the final three quarters of her taxable year. During those three quarters, A's periodic performance of services in the United States does not result in distinct, separate, and continuous periods of time. Of the $75,000 paid for annual salary, $12,500 (30/180 × $75,000) is compensation that was attributable to the labor or personal services performed within the United States and $62,500 (150/180 × $75,000) is compensation that was attributable to the labor or personal services performed outside the United States. Pursuant to paragraphs (b)(2)(ii)(B) and (D)(*1*) and (*3*) of this section, A sourced the $25,000 received for the housing fringe benefit and the $5,000 received for the local transportation fringe benefit based on the location of her principal place of work, Country X. Accordingly, A included the $30,000 in fringe benefits in her gross income as income from sources without the United States.

Example 4. Same facts as in *Example 3.* Of the 150 days during which A performed services in Country X and in other foreign countries (during the final three quarters of A's taxable year), she performed 30 days of those services in Country Y. Country Y is a country designated by the Secretary of State as a place where living conditions are extremely difficult, notably unhealthy, or where excessive physical hardships exist and for which a post differential of 15 percent or more would be provided under section 5925(b) of Title 5 of the U.S. Code to any officer or employee of the U.S. government present at that place. Corp N has a policy of paying its employees a $65 premium per day for each day worked in countries so designated. The $65 premium per day does not exceed the maximum amount that the U.S. government would pay its officers or employees stationed in Country Y. Because A performed services in Country Y for 30 days, she earned additional compensation of $1,950. The $1,950 is considered a hazardous duty or hardship pay fringe benefit and is sourced under paragraphs (b)(2)(ii)(B) and (D)(*5*) of this section based on the location of the hazardous or hardship duty zone, Country Y. Accordingly, A included the amount of the hazardous duty or hardship pay fringe benefit ($1,950) in her gross income as income from sources without the United States.

Example 5. (i) During 2006 and 2007, Corp P, a domestic corporation, employed four United States citizens, E, F, G, and H to work in its manufacturing plant in Country V. As part of his or her compensation package, each employee arranged for local transportation unrelated to Corp P's business needs. None of the local transportation fringe benefit is excluded from the employee's gross income as a qualified transportation fringe benefit under section 132(a)(5) and (f).

(ii) Under the terms of the compensation package that E negotiated with Corp P, Corp P permitted E to use an automobile owned by Corp P. In addition, Corp P agreed to reimburse E for all expenses incurred by E in maintaining and operating the automobile, including gas and parking. Provided that the local transportation fringe benefit meets the requirements of paragraph (b)(2)(ii)(D)(*3*) of this section, E's compensation with respect to the fair rental value of the automobile and reimbursement for the expenses E incurred is sourced under paragraphs (b)(2)(ii)(B) and (D)(*3*) of this section based on E's principal place of work in Country V. Thus, the local transportation fringe benefit will be included in E's gross income as income from sources without the United States.

(iii) Under the terms of the compensation package that F negotiated with Corp P, Corp P let F use an automobile owned by Corp P. However, Corp P did not agree to reimburse F for any expenses incurred by F in maintaining and operating the automobile. Provided that the local transportation fringe benefit meets the requirements of paragraph (b)(2)(ii)(D)(*3*) of this section, F's compensation with respect to the fair rental value of the automobile is sourced under paragraphs (b)(2)(ii)(B) and (D)(*3*) of this section based on F's principal place of work in Country V. Thus, the local transportation fringe benefit will be included in F's gross income as income from sources without the United States.

(iv) Under the terms of the compensation package that G negotiated with Corp P, Corp P agreed to reimburse G for the purchase price of an automobile that G purchased in Country V. Corp P did not agree to reimburse G for any expenses incurred by G in maintaining and operating the automobile. Because the cost to purchase an automobile is not a local transportation fringe benefit as defined in paragraph (b)(2)(ii)(D)(3) of this section, the source of the compensation to G will be determined pursuant to paragraph (b)(2)(ii)(A) or (C) of this section.

(v) Under the terms of the compensation package that H negotiated with Corp P, Corp P agreed to reimburse H for the expenses that H incurred in maintaining and operating an automobile, including gas and parking, which H purchased in Country V. Provided that the local transportation fringe benefit meets the requirements of paragraph (b)(2)(ii)(D)(3) of this section, H's compensation with respect to the reimbursement for the expenses H incurred is sourced under paragraphs (b)(2)(ii)(B) and (D)(3) of this section based on H's principal place of work in Country V. Thus, the local transportation fringe benefit will be included in H's gross income as income from sourdes without the United States.

Example 6. (i) On January 1, 2006, Company Q compensates employee J with a grant of options to which section 421 does not apply that do not have a readily ascertainable fair market value when granted. The stock options permit J to purchase 100 shares of Company Q stock for $5 per share. The stock options do not become exerdisable unless and until J performs services for Company Q (or a related company) for 5 years. J works for Company Q for the 5 years required by the stock option grant. In years 2006-08, J performs all of his services for Company Q within the United States. In 2009, J performs ½ of his services for Company Q within the United States and ½ of his services for Company Q without the United States. In year 2010, J performs his services entirely without the United States. On December 31, 2012, J exercises the options when the stock is worth $10 per share. J recognizes $500 in taxable compensation (($10 − $5) × 100) in 2012.

(ii) Under the facts and circumstances, the applicable period is the 5-year period between the date of grant (January 1, 2006) and the date the stock options become exercisable (December 31, 2010). On the date the stock options become exercisable, J performs all services necessary to obtain the compensation from Company Q. Accordingly, the services performed after the date the stock options become exercisable are not taken into account in sourcing the compensation from the stock options. Therefore, pursuant to paragraph (b)(2)(ii)(A), since J performs 3½ years of services for Company Q within the United States and 1½ years of services for Company Q without the United States during the 5-year period, 7/10 of the $500 of compensation (or $350) recognized in 2012 is income from sources within the United States and the remaining 3/10 of the compensation (or $150) is income from sources without the United States.

* * *

(d) *Effective date.*—* * * The first sentence of § 1.861-4(a)(1) and § 1.861-4(b) apply to taxable years beginning on or after publication of the Treasury Decision adopting these rules as final regulations in the Federal Register.

[Prop. Reg. § 1.861-4.]

[Proposed 8-6-2004 (corrected 8-17-2004).]

§ 1.861-5. Rentals and royalties.—Gross income from sources within the United States includes rentals or royalties from property located in the United States or from any interest in such property, including rentals or royalties for the use of, or for the privilege of using, in the United States, patents, copyrights, secret processes and formulas, good will, trademarks, trade brands, franchises, and other like property. The income arising from the rental of property, whether tangible or intangible, located within the United States, or from the use of property, whether tangible or intangible, within the United States, is from sources within the United States. For taxable years beginning after December 31, 1966, gains described in section 871(a)(1)(D) and section 881(a)(4) from the sale or exchange after October 4, 1966, of patents, copyrights, and other like property shall be treated, as provided in section 871(e)(2), as rentals or royalties for the use of, or privilege of using, property or an interest in property. See paragraph (e) of § 1.871-11. [Reg. § 1.861-5.]

☐ [*T.D.* 6258, 10-23-57. *Amended by T.D.* 7378, 9-29-75.]

§ 1.861-6. Sale of real property.—Gross income from sources within the United States includes gain, computed under the provisions of section 1001 and the regulations thereunder, derived from the sale or other disposition of real property located in the United States. For the treatment of capital gains and losses, see subchapter P (section 1201 and following) chapter 1 of the Code, and the regulations thereunder. [Reg. § 1.861-6.]

☐ [*T.D.* 6258, 10-23-57.]

§ 1.861-7. Sale of personal property.—(a) *General.*—Gains, profits, and income derived from the purchase and sale of personal property shall be treated as derived entirely from the country in which the property is sold. Thus, gross income from sources within the United States includes gains, profits, and income derived from the purchase of personal property without the United States and its sale within the United States.

(b) *Purchase within a possession.*—Notwithstanding paragraph (a) of this section, income derived from the purchase of personal property within a possession of the United States and its sale within the United States shall be treated as derived partly from sources within and partly from sources without the United States. See section 863(b)(3) and § 1.863-2.

(c) *Country in which sold.*—For the purposes of part I (section 861 and following), subchapter N, chapter 1 of the Code, and the regulations thereunder, a sale of personal property is consummated at the time when, and the place where, the rights, title, and interest of the seller in the property are transferred to the buyer. Where bare legal title is retained by the seller, the sale shall be deemed to have occurred at the time and place of passage to the buyer of beneficial ownership and the risk of loss. However, in any case in which the sales transaction is arranged in a particular manner for the primary purpose of tax avoidance, the foregoing rules will not be applied. In such cases, all factors of the transaction, such as negotiations, the execution of the agreement, the location of the property, and the place of payment, will be considered, and the sale will be treated as having been consummated at the place where the substance of the sale occurred.

(d) *Production and sale.*—For provisions respecting the source of income derived from the sale of personal property produced by the taxpayer, see section 863(b)(2) and paragraphs (b) of §§ 1.863-1 and 1.863-2.

(e) *Section 306 stock.*—For determining the source of gain on the disposition of section 306 stock, see section 306(f) and the regulations thereunder. [Reg. § 1.861-7.]

☐ [T.D. 6258, 10-23-57.]

§ 1.861-8. Computation of taxable income from sources within the United States and from other sources and activities.—(a) *In general.*—(1) *Scope.*—Sections 861(b) and 863(a) state in general terms how to determine taxable income of a taxpayer from sources within the United States after gross income from sources within the United States has been determined. Sections 862(b) and 863(a) state in general terms how to determine taxable income of a taxpayer from sources without the United States after gross income from sources without the United States has been determined. This section provides specific guidance for applying the cited Code sections by prescribing rules for the allocation and apportionment of expenses, losses, and other deductions (referred to collectively in this section as "deductions") of the taxpayer. The rules contained in this section apply in determining taxable income of the taxpayer from specific sources and activities under other sections of the Code, referred to in this section as operative sections. See paragraph (f)(1) of this section for a list and description of operative sections. The operative sections include, among others, sections 871(b) and 882 (relating to taxable income of a nonresident alien individual or a foreign corporation which is effectively connected with the conduct of a trade or business in the United States), section 904(a)(1) (as in effect before enactment of the Tax Reform Act of 1976, relating to taxable income from sources within specific foreign countries), and section 904(a)(2) (as in effect before enactment of the Tax Reform Act of 1976, or section 904(a) after such enactment, relating to taxable income from all sources without the United States).

(2) *Allocation and apportionment of deductions in general.*—A taxpayer to which this section applies is required to allocate deductions to a class of gross income and, then, if necessary to make the determination required by the operative section of the Code, to apportion deductions within the class of gross income between the statutory grouping of gross income (or among the statutory groupings) and the residual grouping of gross income. Except for deductions, if any, which are not definitely related to gross income (see paragraphs (c)(3) and (e)(9) of this section) and which, therefore, are ratably apportioned to all gross income, all deductions of the taxpayer (except the deductions for personal exemptions enumerated in paragraph (e)(11) of this section) must be so allocated and apportioned. As further detailed below, allocations and apportionments are made on the basis of the factual relationship of deductions to gross income.

(3) *Class of gross income.*—For purposes of this section, the gross income to which a specific deduction is definitely related is referred to as a "class of gross income" and may consist of one or more items (or subdivisions of these items) of gross income enumerated in section 61, namely:

(i) Compensation for services, including fees, commissions, and similar items;

(ii) Gross income derived from business;

(iii) Gains derived from dealings in property;

(iv) Interest;

(v) Rents;

(vi) Royalties;

(vii) Dividends;

(viii) Alimony and separate maintenance payments;

(ix) Annuities;

(x) Income from life insurance and endowment contracts;

(xi) Pensions;

(xii) Income from discharge of indebtedness;

(xiii) Distributive share of partnership gross income;

(xiv) Income in respect of a decedent;

(xv) Income from an interest in an estate or trust.

(4) *Statutory grouping of gross income and residual grouping of gross income.*—For purposes of this section, the term "statutory grouping of gross income" or "statutory grouping" means the gross income from a specific source or activity which must first be determined in order to arrive at taxable income" from such specific source or activity under an operative section. (See paragraph (f)(1) of this section.) Gross income from other sources or activities is referred to as the "residual grouping of gross income" or "residual grouping". For example, for purposes of determining taxable income from sources within specific foreign countries and possessions of the United States, in order to apply the per-country limitation to the foreign tax credit (as in effect before enactment of the Tax Reform Act of 1976), the statutory groupings are the separate gross incomes from sources within each country and possession. Moreover, if the taxpayer has income subject to section 904(d) (as in effect after enactment of the Tax Reform Act of 1976), such income constitutes one or more separate statutory groupings. In the case of the per-country limitation, the residual grouping is the aggregate of gross income from sources within the United States. In some instances, where the operative section so requires, the statutory grouping or the residual grouping may include, or consist entirely of, excluded income. See paragraph (d)(2) of this section with respect to the allocation and apportionment of deductions to excluded income.

(5) *Effective date.*—(i) *Taxable years beginning after December 31 1976.*—The provisions of this section apply to taxable years beginning after December 31, 1976. Paragraph (g) *Example 18* (i)(B) applies to charitable contributions made on or after July 28, 2004.

(ii) *Taxable years beginning before January 1, 1977.*—For taxable years beginning before January 1, 1977, §1.861-8 applies as in effect on October 23, 1957 (T.D. 6258), as amended on August 22, 1966 (T.D. 6892) and on September 29, 1975 (T.D. 7378). The specific rules for allocation and apportionment of deductions set forth in this section may, at the option of the taxpayer, apply to those taxable years on a deduction-by-deduction basis if the rules are applied consistently to all taxable years with respect to which action by the Internal Revenue Service is not barred by any statute of limitations. Thus, for example, a calendar year taxpayer may choose to have the rules of paragraph (e)(2) of this section apply for the allocation and apportionment of all interest expenses for the two taxable years ending December 31, 1975 and 1976, which are open years under examination, and may justify the allocation and apportionment of all research and development expenses for those years on a basis supportable under §1.861-8 as in effect for 1975 and 1976 without regard to the rules of paragraph (e)(3) of this section.

(b) *Allocation.*—(1) *In general.*—For purposes of this section, the gross income to which a specific deduction is definitely related is referred to as a "class of gross income" and may consist of one or more items of gross income. The rules emphasize the factual relationship between the deduction and a class of gross income. See paragraph (d)(1) of this section which provides that in a taxable year there may be no item of gross income in a class or less gross income than deductions allocated to the class, and paragraph (d)(2) of this section which provides that a class of gross income may include excluded income. Allocation is accomplished by determining, with respect to each deduction, the class of gross income to which the deduction is definitely related and then allocating the deduction to such class of gross income (without regard to the taxable year in which such gross income is received or accrued or is expected to be received or accrued). The classes of gross income are not predetermined but must be determined on the basis of the deductions to be allocated. Although most deductions will be definitely related to some class of a taxpayer's total gross income, some deductions are related to all gross income. In addition, some deductions are treated as not definitely related to any gross income and are ratably apportioned to all gross income. (See paragraph (e)(9) of this section.) In allocating deductions it is not necessary to differentiate between deductions related to one item of gross income and deductions related to another item of gross income where both items of gross income are exclusively within the same statutory grouping or exclusively within the residual grouping.

(2) *Relationship to activity or property.*—A deduction shall be considered definitely related to a class of gross income and therefore allocable to such class if it is incurred as a result of, or incident to, an activity or in connection with property from which such class of gross income is derived. Where a deduction is incurred as a result of, or incident to, an activity or in connection with property, which activity or property generates, has generated, or could reasonably have been expected to generate gross income, such deduction shall be considered definitely related to such gross income as a class whether or not there is any item of gross income in such class which is received or accrued during the taxable year and whether or not the amount of deductions exceeds the amount of the gross income in such class. See paragraph (d)(1) of this section and example (17) of paragraph (g) of this section with respect to cases in which there is an excess of deductions. In some cases, it will be found that this subparagraph can most readily be applied by determining, with respect to a deduction, the categories of gross income to which it is not related and concluding that it is definitely related to a class consisting of all other gross income.

(3) *Supportive functions.*—[Reserved] For guidance, see § 1.861-8T(b)(3).

(4) *Deductions related to a class of gross income.*—See paragraph (e) of this section for rules relating to the allocation and apportionment of certain specific deductions definitely related to a class of gross income. See paragraph (c)(1) of this section for rules relating to the apportionment of deductions.

(5) *Deductions related to all gross income.*—If a deduction does not bear a definite relationship to a class of gross income constituting less than all of gross income, it shall ordinarily be treated as definitely related and allocable to all of the taxpayer's gross income except where provided to the contrary under paragraph (e) of this section. Paragraph (e)(9) of this section lists various deductions which generally are not definitely related to any gross income and are ratably apportioned to all gross income.

(c) *Apportionment of deductions.*—(1) *Deductions definitely related to a class of gross income.*—[Reserved] For guidance, see § 1.861-8T(c)(1).

(2) *Apportionment based on assets.*—[Reserved] For guidance, see § 1.861-8T(c)(2).

(3) *Deductions not definitely related to any gross income.*—If a deduction is not definitely related to any gross income (see paragraph (e)(9) of this section), the deduction must be apportioned ratably between the statutory grouping (or among the statutory groupings) of gross income and the residual grouping. Thus, the amount apportioned to each statutory grouping shall be equal to the same proportion of the deduction which the amount of gross income in the statutory grouping bears to the total amount of gross income. The amount apportioned to the residual grouping shall be equal to the same proportion of the deduction which the amount of the gross income in the residual grouping bears to the total amount of gross income.

(d) *Excess of deductions and excluded and eliminated income.*—(1) *Excess of deductions.*—Each deduction which bears a definite relationship to a class of gross income shall be allocated to that class in accordance with paragraph (b)(1) of this section even though, for the taxable year, no gross income in such class is received or accrued or the amount of the deduction exceeds the amount of such class of gross income. In apportioning deductions, it may be that, for the taxable year, there is no gross income in the statutory grouping (or residual grouping), or that deductions exceed the amount of gross income in the statutory grouping (or residual grouping). If there is no gross income in a statutory grouping or the amount of deductions allocated and apportioned to a statutory grouping exceeds the amount of gross income in the statutory grouping, the effects are determined under the operative section. If the taxpayer is a member of a group filing a consolidated return, such excess of deductions allocated or apportioned to a statutory grouping of income of such member is taken into account in determining the consolidated taxable income from such statutory grouping, and such excess of deductions allocated or apportioned to the residual grouping of income is taken into account in determining the consolidated taxable income from the residual grouping. See § 1.1502-4(d)(1) and the last sentence of § 1.1502-12. For an illustration of the principles of this paragraph (d)(1), see example (17) of paragraph (g) of this section.

(2) *Allocation and apportionment to exempt, excluded, or eliminated income.*—[Reserved] For guidance, see § 1.861-8T(d)(2).

(e) *Allocation and apportionment of certain deductions.*—(1) *In general.*—Paragraphs (e)(2) and (e)(3) of this section contain rules with respect to the allocation and apportionment of interest expense and research and development expenditures, respectively. Paragraphs (e)(4) through (e)(8) of this section contain rules with respect to the allocation of certain other deductions. Paragraph (e)(9) of this section lists those deductions which are ordinarily considered as not being definitely related to any class of gross income. Paragraph (e)(10) of this section lists special deductions of corporations which must be allocated and apportioned. Paragraph (e)(11) of this section lists personal exemptions which are neither allocated nor apportioned. Paragraph (e)(12) of this section contains rules with respect to the allocation and apportionment of deductions for charitable contributions. Examples of allocation and apportionment are contained in paragraph (g) of this section.

(2) *Interest.*—[Reserved] For guidance, see § 1.861-8T(e)(2).

(3) *Research and experimental expenditures.*—For rules regarding the allocation and apportionment of research and experimental expenditures, see § 1.861-17.

(4) *Stewardship expenses attributable to dividends received.*—If a corporation renders services for the benefit of a related corporation and the corporation charges the related corporation for such services (see section 482 and the regulations thereunder which provide for an allocation where the charge is not on an arm's length basis as determined therein), the deductions for expenses of the corporation attributable to the rendering of such services are considered definitely related to the amounts so charged and are to be allocated to such amounts. However, the regulations under section 482 (§ 1.482-2(b)(2)(ii)) recognize a type of activity which is not considered to be for the benefit of a related corporation but is considered to constitute "stewardship" or "overseeing" functions undertaken for the corporation's own benefit as an investor in the related corporation, and therefore, a charge to the related corporation for such stewardship or overseeing functions is not provided for. Services undertaken by a corporation of a stewardship or overseeing character generally represent a duplication of services which the related corporation has independently performed for itself. For example, assume that a related corporation, which has a qualified financial staff, makes an analysis to determine the amount and source of its borrowing needs and submits a report of its findings and a plan of borrowing to the parent corporation, and the parent corporation's financial staff reviews the findings and plans to determine whether to advise the related corporation to reconsider its plan. The services of review performed by the parent corporation for its own benefit are of a stewardship or overseeing character. The deductions resulting from stewardship or overseeing functions are incurred as a result of, or incident to, the ownership of the related corporation and, thus, shall be considered definitely related and allocable to dividends received or to be received from the related corporation. If a corporation has a foreign or international department which exercises stewardship or overseeing functions with respect to related foreign corporations and, in addition, the department has other functions which are attributable to other foreign-source income (such as fees for services rendered outside of the United States for the benefit of foreign related corporations, foreign royalties, and gross income of foreign branches) to which its deductions are also to be allocated, some part of the deductions with respect to that department are considered definitely related to the other foreign-source income. In some instances, the operations of a foreign or international department will also be attributable to United States source income (such as fees for services performed in the United States) to which its deductions are to be allocated. Methods of apportionment which could possibly be utilized with respect to stewardship expenses include comparisons of time spent by employees weighted to take into account differences in compensation, or comparisons of each related corporation's gross receipts, gross income, or unit sales volume, assuming that stewardship activities are not substantially disproportionate to such factors. See paragraph (f)(5) of this section for the type of verification that may be required in this respect. See examples (17) and (18) of paragraph (g) of this section for the allocation and apportionment of stewardship expenses. See paragraph (b)(3) of this section for the allocation and apportionment of deductions attributable to supportive functions other than stewardship activities.

(5) *Legal and accounting fees and expenses.*—Fees and other expenses for legal and accounting services are ordinarily definitely related and allocable to specific classes of gross income or to all the taxpayer's gross income, depending on the nature of the services rendered (and are apportioned as provided in paragraph (c)(1) of this section). For example, accounting fees for the preparation of a study of the costs involved in manufacturing a specific product will ordinarily be definitely related to the class of gross income derived from (or which could reasonably have been expected to be derived from) that specific product. The taxpayer is not relieved from his responsibility to make a proper allocation and apportionment

of fees on the grounds that the statement of services rendered does not identify the services performed beyond a generalized designation such as "professional," or does not provide any type of allocation, or does not properly allocate the fees involved.

(6) *Income taxes.*—(i) *In general.*—The deduction for state, local, and foreign income, war profits and excess profits taxes ("state income taxes") allowed by section 164 shall be considered definitely related and allocable to the gross income with respect to which such state income taxes are imposed. For example, if a domestic corporation is subject to state income taxation and the state income tax is imposed in part on an amount of foreign source income, then that part of the taxpayer's deduction for state income tax that is attributable to foreign source income is definitely related and allocable to foreign source income. In allocating and apportioning the deduction for state income tax for purposes including (but not limited to) the computation of the foreign tax credit limitation under section 904 of the Code and the consolidated foreign tax credit under § 1.1502-4 of the regulations, the income upon which the state income tax is imposed is determined by reference to the law of the jurisdiction imposing the tax. Thus, if a state attributes taxable income to a corporate taxpayer by applying an apportionment formula that takes into consideration the income and factors of one or more corporations related by ownership to the corporate taxpayer and engaging in activities related to the business of the corporate taxpayer, then the income so attributed is the income upon which the state income tax is imposed. If the income so attributed to the corporate taxpayer includes foreign source income, then, in computing the taxpayer's foreign tax credit limitation under section 904, for example, the taxpayer's deduction for state income tax will be considered definitely related and allocable to a class of gross income that includes the statutory grouping of foreign source income. When the law of the state includes dividends that are treated under section 862(a)(2) as income from sources without the United States in taxable income apportionable to the state, but does not include factors of the corporation paying such dividends in the apportionment formula used to determine state taxable income, an appropriate portion of the deduction for state income tax will be considered definitely related and allocable to a class of gross income consisting solely of foreign source dividend income. A deduction for state income tax will not be considered definitely related to a hypothetical amount of income calculated under federal tax principles when the jurisdiction imposing the tax computes taxable income under different principles. A corporate taxpayer's deduction for a state franchise tax that is computed on the basis of income attributable to business activities conducted within the state must be allocated and apportioned in the same manner as the deduction for state income taxes. In determining, for example, both the foreign tax credit under section 904 of the Code and the consolidated foreign tax credit limitation under § 1.1502-4 of the regulations, the deduction for state income tax may be allocable and apportionable to foreign source income in a statutory grouping described in section 904(d) in a taxable year in which the taxpayer has no foreign source income in such statutory grouping. Alternatively, such an allocation or apportionment may be appropriate if a taxpayer corporation has no foreign source income in a statutory grouping, but its deduction is attributable to foreign source income in such grouping that is attributed to the taxpayer corporation under the law of a state which attributes taxable income to a corporation by applying an apportionment formula that takes into consideration the income and factors of one or more corporations related by ownership to the taxpayer corporation and engaging in activities related to the business of the taxpayer corporation. *Example 30* of paragraph (g) of this section illustrates the application of this last rule.

(ii) *Methods of allocation and apportionment.*—(A) *In general.*—A taxpayer's deduction for a state income tax is to be allocated (and then apportioned, if necessary, subject to the rules of § 1.861-8(d)) by reference to the taxable income that the law of the taxing jurisdiction attributes to the taxpayer ("state taxable income").

(B) *Effect of subsequent recomputations of state income tax.*—[Reserved]

(C) *Illustrations.*—(1) *In general.*— *Examples 25* through *32* of paragraph (g) of § 1.861-8 illustrate, in the given factual situations, the application of this paragraph (e)(6) and the general rule of paragraph (b)(1) of this section that a deduction must be allocated to the class of gross income to which the deduction is factually related. In general, these examples employ a presumption that state income taxes are allocable to a class of gross income that includes the statutory grouping of income from sources without the United States when the total amount of taxable income determined under state law exceeds the amount of taxable income determined under the Code (without taking into account the deduction for state income taxes) in the residual grouping of income from sources within the United States. A taxpayer that allocates and apportions the deduction for state income tax in accordance with the methodology of *Example 25* of paragraph (g) of this section must also apply the modifications illustrated in *Examples 26* and *27* of paragraph (g) of this section, when applicable. The modification illustrated in *Example 26* is applicable when the deduction for state income tax is attributable in part to taxes imposed by a state which factually excludes foreign source income (as determined for federal income tax purposes) from state taxable income. The modification illustrated in *Example 27* is applicable when the taxpayer has income-producing activities in a state which does not impose a corporate income tax. The specific allocation of state income tax illustrated in *Example 28* follows the rule in paragraph (e)(6)(i) of this section, and must be applied whenever a taxpayer's state taxable income includes dividends apportioned to the state under a formula that does not take into account the factors of the corporations paying those dividends, regardless of whether the taxpayer uses the methodology of *Example 25* with respect to the remainder of the deduction for state income taxes.

(2) Modifications.—Before applying a method of allocation and apportionment illustrated in the examples, the computation of state taxable income under state law may be modified, subject to the approval of the District Director, to reflect more accurately the income with respect to which the state income tax is imposed. Any modification to the state law computation of state taxable income must yield an allocation and apportionment of the deduction for state income taxes that is consistent with the rules contained in this paragraph (e)(6), and that accurately reflects the factual relationship between the state income tax and the income on which that tax is imposed. For example, a modification to the computation of taxable income under state law might be appropriate to compensate for differences between the state law definition of taxable income and the federal definition of taxable income, due to a difference in the rate of allowable depreciation or the amount of another deduction that is allowable under both systems. This rule is illustrated in *Example 31* of paragraph (g) of this section. However, a modification to the computation of taxable income under state law will not be appropriate, and will not more accurately reflect the factual relationship between the state tax and the income on which the tax is imposed, to the extent such modification reflects the fact that the state does not follow federal tax principles in attributing income to the taxpayer's activities in the state. This rule is illustrated in *Example 32* of paragraph (g) of this section. A taxpayer may not modify the methods illustrated in the examples, or use an alternative method of allocation and apportionment of the deduction for state income taxes, if the modification or alternative method would be inconsistent with the rules of paragraph (e)(6)(i) of this section. A taxpayer that uses a method of allocation and apportionment other than one illustrated in *Example 25* (as modified by *Examples 26* and *27*), or *29* with respect to a factual situation similar to those of the examples, must describe the alternative method on an attachment to its federal income tax return and establish to the satisfaction of the District Director, upon examination, that the result of the alternative method more accurately reflects the factual relationship between the state income tax and the income on which the tax is imposed.

(D) *Elective safe harbor methods.*— *(1) In general.*—In lieu of applying the rules set forth in paragraphs (e)(6)(ii)(A) through (C) of this section, a taxpayer may elect to allocate and apportion the deduction for state income tax in accordance with one of the two safe harbor methods described in paragraph (e)(6)(ii)(D)(2) and (3) of this section. A taxpayer shall make this election for a taxable year by filing a timely tax return for that year that reflects an allocation and apportionment of the deduction for state income tax under one of the safe harbor methods and attaching to such return a statement that the taxpayer has elected to use the safe harbor method provided in either paragraph (e)(6)(ii)(D)(2) or (3) of this section, as appropriate. Once made, this election is effective for the taxable year for which made and all subsequent taxable years, and may be revoked only with the consent of the Commissioner. *Example 33* of paragraph (g) of this section illustrates the application of these safe harbor methods.

(2) Method One.—(i) Step One— Specific allocation to foreign source portfolio dividends and other income.—If any portion of the deduction for state income tax is attributable to tax imposed by a state which includes in a corporate taxpayer's taxable income apportionable to the state, portfolio dividends (as defined in paragraph (i) of *Example 28* of paragraph (g) of this section) that are treated under section 862(a)(2) as income from sources without the United States, but does not include factors of the corporations paying the portfolio dividends in the apportionment formula used to determine state taxable income, the taxpayer shall allocate an appropriate portion of the deduction to a class of gross income consisting solely of foreign source portfolio dividends. The portion of the deduction so allocated, and the amount of foreign source portfolio dividends included in such class, shall be determined in accordance with the methodology illustrated in para-

graph (ii) of *Example 28* of paragraph (g). If a state income tax is determined based upon formulary apportionment of the total taxable income attributable to the taxpayer's unitary business, the taxpayer must also apply the methodology illustrated in paragraph (ii)(C) through (G) of *Example 29* of paragraph (g) of this section to make specific allocations of appropriate portions of the deduction for state income tax on the basis of income that, under separate accounting, would have been attributed to other members of the unitary group. The taxpayer shall reduce its aggregate state taxable income by the amount of foreign source portfolio dividends and other income to which a specific allocation is made (the reduced amount being referred to hereinafter as "adjusted state taxable income").

(ii) Step Two—Adjustment of U.S. source federal taxable income.—If the taxpayer has significant income producing activities in a state which does not impose a corporate income tax or other state tax measured by income derived from business activities in the state, the taxpayer shall reduce its U.S. source federal taxable income (solely for purposes of this safe harbor method) by the amount of federal taxable income attributable to its activities in such state. This amount shall be determined in accordance with the methodology illustrated in paragraph (ii) of *Example 27* of paragraph (g) of this section, provided that the taxpayer shall be required to use the rules of the Uniform Division of Income for Tax Purposes Act to attribute income to the relevant state. The taxpayer's U.S. source federal taxable income, as so reduced, is referred to hereinafter as "adjusted U.S. source federal taxable income."

(iii) Step Three—Allocation.—The taxpayer shall allocate the remainder of the deduction for state income tax (after reduction by the portion allocated to foreign source portfolio dividends and other income under Step One) in accordance with the methodology illustrated in paragraph (ii) of *Example 25* of paragraph (g) of this section. However, the taxpayer shall substitute for the comparison of aggregate state taxable income to U.S. source federal taxable income, illustrated in paragraph (ii) of *Example 25* of paragraph (g), a comparison of its adjusted state taxable income to an amount equal to 110% of its adjusted U.S. source federal taxable income.

(iv) Step Four—Apportionment.—In the event that apportionment of the remainder of the deduction for state income tax is required, the taxpayer shall apportion that remaining deduction to U.S. source income in accordance with the methodology illustrated in paragraph (iii) of *Example 25* of paragraph (g) of this section, substituting for domestic source income in that paragraph an amount equal to 110% of the taxpayer's adjusted U.S. source federal taxable income. The remaining portion of the deduction shall be apportioned to the statutory groupings of foreign source income described in section 904(d) of the Code in accordance with the proportion of the income in each statutory grouping of foreign source income described in section 904(d) to the taxpayer's total foreign source federal taxable income (after reduction by the amount of foreign source portfolio dividends to which tax has been specifically allocated under Step One, above).

(3) Method Two.—*(i) Step One—Specific allocation to foreign source portfolio dividends and other income.*—Step One of this method is the same as Step One of Method One (as described in paragraph (e)(6)(ii)(D)(*2*)(*i*) of this section).

(ii) Step Two—Adjustment of U.S. source federal taxable income.—Step Two of this method is the same as Step Two of Method One (as described in paragraph (e)(6)(ii)(D)(*2*)(*ii*) of this section).

(iii) Step Three—Allocation.—The taxpayer shall allocate the remainder of the deduction for state income tax (after reduction by the portion allocated to foreign source portfolio dividends and other income under Step One) in accordance with the methodology illustrated in paragraph (ii) of *Example 25* of paragraph (g) of this section. However, the taxpayer shall substitute for the comparison of aggregate state taxable income to U.S. source federal taxable income, illustrated in paragraph (ii) of *Example 25* of paragraph (g) of this section, a comparison of its adjusted state taxable income to its adjusted U.S. source federal taxable income.

(iv) Step Four—Apportionment.—In the event that apportionment of the deduction is required, the taxpayer shall apportion to U.S. source income that portion of the deduction that is attributable to state income taxes imposed upon an amount of state taxable income equal to adjusted U.S. source federal taxable income. The taxpayer shall apportion the remaining amount of the deduction to U.S. and foreign source income in the same proportions that the taxpayer's adjusted U.S. source federal taxable income and foreign source federal taxable income (after reduction by the amount of foreign source portfolio dividends to which tax has been specifically allocated under Step One, above) bear to its total federal taxable income (taking into account the adjustment

of U.S. source federal taxable income under Step Two and after reduction by the amount of foreign source portfolio dividends to which tax has been specifically allocated under Step One). The portion of the deduction apportioned to foreign source income shall be apportioned among the statutory groupings described in section 904(d) of the Code in accordance with the proportions of the taxpayer's total foreign source federal taxable income (after reduction by the amount of foreign source portfolio dividends to which tax has been specifically allocated under Step One, above) in each grouping.

(iii) *Effective dates.*—The rules of § 1.861-8(e)(6)(i) and the language preceding the examples in § 1.861-8(g) are effective for taxable years beginning after December 31, 1976. The rules of § 1.861-8(e)(6)(ii) (other than § 1.861-8(e)(6)(ii)(D)) and *Examples 25 through 32* of § 1.861-8(g) are effective for taxable years beginning on or after January 1, 1988. The rules of § 1.861-8(e)(6)(ii)(D) and *Example 33* of § 1.861-8(g) are effective for taxable years ending after [date of publication of this regulation in the Federal Register]. At the option of the taxpayer, however, the rules of § 1.861-8(e)(6)(ii) (other than § 1.861-8(e)(6)(ii)(D)) and *Examples 25 through 32* of § 1.861-8(g) may be applied with respect to deductions for state taxes incurred in taxable years beginning before January 1, 1988.

(7) *Losses on the sale, exchange, or other disposition of property.*—(i) *Allocation.*—The deduction allowed for loss recognized on the sale, exchange, or other disposition of a capital asset or property described in section 1231(b) shall be considered a deduction which is definitely related and allocable to the class of gross income to which such asset or property ordinarily gives rise in the hands of the taxpayer. Where the nature of gross income generated from the asset or property has varied significantly over several taxable years of the taxpayer, such class of gross income shall generally be determined by reference to gross income generated from the asset or property during the taxable year or years immediately preceding the sale, exchange, or other disposition of such asset or property. Thus, for example, where an asset generates primarily sales income from domestic sources in the early years of its operation and then is leased by the taxpayer to a foreign subsidiary in later years, the class of gross income to which the asset gives rise will be considered to be the rental income derived from the lease and will not include sales income from domestic sources.

(ii) *Apportionment of losses.*—Where in the unusual circumstances that an apportionment of a deduction for losses on the sale, exchange, or other disposition of a capital asset or property described in section 1231(b) is necessary, the amount of such deduction shall be apportioned between the statutory grouping (or among the statutory groupings) of gross income (within the class of gross income) and the residual grouping (within the class of gross income) in the same proportion that the amount of gross income within such statutory grouping (or statutory groupings) and such residual grouping bear, respectively, to the total amount of gross income within the class of gross income. Apportionment will be necessary where, for example, the class of gross income to which the deduction is allocated consists of gross income (such as royalties) attributable to an intangible asset used both within and without the United States, or gross income (such as from sales or services) attributable to a tangible asset used both within and without the United States.

(iii) *Allocation of loss recognized in taxable years after 1986.*—See §§ 1.865-1 and 1.865-2 for rules regarding the allocation of certain loss recognized in taxable years beginning after December 31, 1986.

* * *

(9) *Deductions which are not definitely related.*—Deductions which shall generally be considered as not definitely related to any gross income, and therefore are ratably apportioned as provided in paragraph (c)(3) of this section, are—

(i) The deduction allowed by section 163 for interest described in subparagraph (2)(iii) of this paragraph (e);

(ii) The deduction allowed by section 164 for real estate taxes on a personal residence or for sales tax on the purchase of items for personal use;

(iii) The deduction for medical expenses allowed by section 213; and

(iv) The deduction for alimony payments allowed by section 215.

(10) *Special deductions.*—The special deductions allowed in the case of a corporation by section 241 (relating to the deductions for partially tax exempt interest, dividends received, etc.), section 922 (relating to Western Hemisphere trade corporations), and section 941 (relating to China Trade Act corporations) shall be allocated and apportioned consistent with the principles of this section.

(11) *Personal exemptions.*—The deductions for the personal exemptions allowed by section 151, 642(b), or 873(b)(3) shall not be

taken into account for purposes of allocation and apportionment under this section.

(12) [Reserved]. For further guidance, see § 1.861-8T(e)(12).

(f) *Miscellaneous matters.*—(1) *Operative sections.*—The operative sections of the Code which require the determination of taxable income of the taxpayer from specific sources or activities and which give rise to statutory groupings to which this section is applicable include the sections described below.

(i) *Overall limitation to the foreign tax credit.*—Under the overall limitation to the foreign tax credit, as provided in section 904(a)(2) (as in effect before enactment of the Tax Reform Act of 1976, or section 904(a) after such enactment) the amount of the foreign tax credit may not exceed the tentative U.S. tax (i.e., the U.S. tax before application of the foreign tax credit) multiplied by a fraction, the numerator of which is the taxable income from sources without the United States and the denominator of which is the entire taxable income. Accordingly, in this case, the statutory grouping is foreign source income (including, for example, interest received from a domestic corporation which meets the tests of section 861(a)(1)(B), dividends received from a domestic corporation which has an election in effect under section 936, and other types of income specified in section 862). Pursuant to sections 862(b) and 863(a) and §§ 1.862-1 and 1.863-1, this section provides rules for identifying the deductions to be taken into account in determining taxable income from sources without the United States. See section 904(d) (as in effect after enactment of the Tax Reform Act of 1976) and the regulations thereunder which require separate treatment of certain types of income. See example (3) of paragraph (g) of this section for one example of the application of this section to the overall limitation.

(ii) [Reserved].

(iii) *DISC and FSC taxable income.*—Sections 925 and 994 provide rules for determining the taxable income of a FSC and DISC, respectively, with respect to qualified sales and leases of export property and qualified services. The combined taxable income method available for determining a DISC's taxable income provides, without consideration of export promotion expenses, that the taxable income of the DISC shall be 50 percent of the combined taxable income of the DISC and the related supplier derived from sales and leases of export property and from services. In the FSC context, the taxable income of the FSC equals 23 percent of the combined taxable income of the FSC and the related supplier. Pursuant to regulations under sections 925 and 994, this section provides rules for determining the deductions to be taken into account in determining combined taxable income, except to the extent modified by the marginal costing rules set forth in the regulations under sections 925(b)(2) and 994(b)(2) if used by the taxpayer. See *Examples* (22) and (23) of paragraph (g) of this section. In addition, the computation of combined taxable income is necessary to determine the applicability of the section 925(d) limitation and the "no loss" rules of the regulations under sections 925 and 994.

(iv) *Effectively connected taxable income.*—Nonresident alien individuals and foreign corporations engaged in trade or business within the United States are taxed, as provided under sections 871(b)(1) and 882(a)(1), on taxable income which is effectively connected with the conduct of a trade or business within the United States. Such taxable income is determined in most instances by initially determining, under section 864(c), the amount of gross income which is effectively connected with the conduct of a trade or business within the United States. Pursuant to sections 873 and 882(c), this section is applicable for purposes of determining the deductions from such gross income (other than the deduction for interest expense allowed to foreign corporations (see § 1.882-5)) which are to be taken into account in determining taxable income. See example (21) of paragraph (g) of this section.

(v) *Foreign base company income.*—Section 954 defines the term "foreign base company income" with respect to controlled foreign corporations. Section 954(b)(5) provides that in determining foreign base company income the gross income shall be reduced by the deductions of the controlled foreign corporation "properly allocable to such income". This section provides rules for identifying which deductions are properly allocable to foreign base company income.

(vi) *Other operative sections.*—The rules provided in this section also apply in determining—

(A) The amount of foreign source items of tax preference under section 58(g) determined for purposes of the minimum tax;

(B) The amount of foreign mineral income under section 901(e);

(C) [Reserved];

(D) The amount of foreign oil and gas extraction income and the amount of foreign oil related income under section 907;

(E) [Reserved];

(F) [Reserved];

(G) The limitation under section 934 on the maximum reduction in income tax liability incurred to the Virgin Islands;

(H) [Reserved];

(I) The special deduction granted to China Trade Act corporations under section 941;

(J) The amount of certain U.S. source income excluded from the subpart F income of a controlled foreign corporation under section 952(b);

(K) The amount of income from the insurance of U.S. risks under section 953(b)(5);

(L) The international boycott factor and the specifically attributable taxes and income under section 999; and

(M) The taxable income attributable to the operation of an agreement vessel under section 607 of the Merchant Marine Act of 1936, as amended, and the Capital Construction Fund Regulations thereunder (26 CFR, pt. 3). See 26 CFR 3.2(b)(3).

(2) *Application to more than one operative section.*—(i) Where more than one operative section applies, it may be necessary for the taxpayer to apply this section separately for each applicable operative section. In such a case, the taxpayer is required to use the same method of allocation and the same principles of apportionment for all operative sections.

(ii) When expenses, losses, and other deductions that have been properly allocated and apportioned between combined gross income of a related supplier and a DISC or former DISC and residual gross income, regardless of which of the administrative pricing methods of section 994 has been applied, such deductions are not also allocated and apportioned to gross income consisting of distributions from the DISC or former DISC attributable to income of the DISC or former DISC as determined under the administrative pricing methods with respect to DISC or former DISC taxable years beginning after December 31, 1986. Accordingly, *Example* (22) of paragraph (g) of this section does not apply to distributions from a DISC or former DISC with respect to DISC or former DISC taxable years beginning after December 31, 1986. This rule does not apply to the extent that the taxable income of the DISC or former DISC is determined under the section 994(a)(3) transfer pricing method. In addition, for taxable years beginning after December 31, 1986, in the case of expenses, losses, and other deductions that have been properly allocated and apportioned between combined gross income of a related supplier and a FSC and residual gross income, regardless of which of the administrative pricing methods of section 925 has been applied, such deductions are not also allocated and apportioned to gross income consisting of distributions from the FSC or former FSC which are attributable to the foreign trade income of the FSC or former FSC as determined under the administrative pricing methods. This rule does not apply to the extent that the foreign trade income of the FSC or former FSC is determined under the section 925(a)(3) transfer pricing method. See *Example* (23) of paragraph (g) of this section.

(3) *Special rules of section 863(b).*—(i) *In general.*—Special rules under section 863(b) provide for the application of rules of general apportionment provided in §§ 1.863-3 to 1.863-5, to worldwide taxable income in order to attribute part of such worldwide taxable income to U.S. sources and the remainder of such worldwide taxable income to foreign sources. The activities specified in section 863(b) are—

(A) Transportation or other services rendered partly within and partly without the United States,

(B) Sales of personal property produced by the taxpayer within and sold without the United States, or produced by the taxpayer without and sold within the United States, and

(C) Sales within the United States of personal property purchased within a possession of the United States.

In the instances provided in §§ 1.863-3 and 1.863-4 with respect to the activities described in (A), (B), and (C) of this subsection, this section is applicable only in determining worldwide taxable income attributable to these activities.

(ii) *Relationship of sections 861, 862, 863(a), and 863(b).*—Sections 861, 862, 863(a), and 863(b) are the four provisions applicable in determining taxable income from specific sources. Each of these four provisions applies independently. Where a deduction has been allocated and apportioned to income under one of these four provisions, the deduction shall not again be allocated and apportioned to gross income under any of the other three provisions. However, two or more of these provisions may have to be applied at the same time to determine the proper allocation and apportionment of a deduction. The special rules under section 863(b) take precedence over the general rules of Code sections 861, 862 and 863(a). For example, where a deduction is allocable in whole or in part to gross income to which section 863(b) applies, such deduction or part thereof shall not otherwise be allocated under section 861, 862, or 863(a). However, where the gross income to which the deduction is allocable includes both gross income to which section 863(b) applies and gross income to which section 861, 862, or 863(a) applies, more than one section must be applied at the same time in order to determine the proper allocation and apportionment of the deduction.

(4) *Adjustments made under other provisions of the Code.*—(i) *In general.*—If an adjustment which affects the taxpayer is made under section 482 or any other provision of the Code, it may be necessary to recompute the allocations and apportionments required by this section in order to reflect changes resulting from the adjustment. The recomputation made by the District Director shall be made using the same method of allocation and apportionment as was originally used by the taxpayer, provided such method as originally used conformed with paragraph (a)(5) of this section and, in light of the adjustment, such method does not result in a material distortion. In addition to adjustments which would be made aside from this section, adjustments to the taxpayer's income and deductions which would not otherwise be made may be required before applying this section in order to prevent a distortion in determining taxable income from a particular source of activity. For example, if an item included as a part of the cost of goods sold has been improperly attributed to specific sales, and, as a result, gross income under one of the operative sections referred to in paragraph (f)(1) of this section is improperly determined, it may be necessary for the District Director to make an adjustment to the cost of goods sold, consistent with the principles of this section, before applying this section. Similarly, if a domestic corporation transfers the stock in its foreign subsidiaries to a domestic subsidiary and the parent continues to incur expenses in connection with the supervision of the foreign subsidiaries (see paragraph (e)(4) of this section), it may be necessary for the District Director to make an allocation under section 482 with respect to such expenses before making allocations and apportionments required by this section, even though the section 482 allocation might not otherwise be made.

(ii) *Example.*—X, a domestic corporation, purchases and sells consumer items in the United States and foreign markets. Its sales in foreign markets are made to related foreign subsidiaries. X reported $1,500,000 as sales during the taxable year of which $1,000,000 was domestic sales and $500,000 was foreign sales. X took a deduction for expenses incurred by its marketing department during the taxable year in the amount of $150,000. These expenses were determined to be allocable to both domestic and foreign sales and are apportionable between such sales. Thus, X allocated and apportioned the marketing department deduction as follows:

To gross income from domestic sales:

$$\$150{,}000 \times \frac{\$1{,}000{,}000}{1{,}500{,}000} \quad \ldots\ldots\ldots\ldots\ldots\ldots\ldots\ldots\ldots\ldots \quad \$100{,}000$$

To gross income from foreign sales:

$$\$150{,}000 \times \frac{\$500{,}000}{1{,}500{,}000} \quad \ldots\ldots\ldots\ldots\ldots\ldots\ldots\ldots\ldots\ldots \quad 50{,}000$$

Total 150,000

On audit of X's return for the taxable year, the District Director adjusted, under section 482, X's sales to related foreign subsidiaries by increasing the sales price by a total of $100,000, thereby increasing X's foreign sales and total sales by the same amount. As a result of the section 482 adjustment, the apportionment of the deduction for the marketing department expenses is redetermined as follows:

To gross income from domestic sales:

$$\$150{,}000 \times \frac{\$1{,}000{,}000}{1{,}600{,}000} \quad \ldots\ldots\ldots\ldots\ldots\ldots\ldots\ldots\ldots\ldots \quad \$93{,}750$$

To gross income from foreign sales:

$$\$150{,}000 \times \frac{\$600{,}000}{1{,}600{,}000} \quad \ldots\ldots\ldots\ldots\ldots\ldots\ldots\ldots\ldots\ldots \quad \$56{,}250$$

Total 150,000

(5) *Verification of allocations and apportionments.*—Since, under this section, allocations and apportionments are made on the basis of the factual relationship between deductions and gross income, the taxpayer is required to furnish, at the request of the District Director, information from which such factual relationships can be determined. In reviewing the overall limitation to the foreign tax credit of a domestic corporation, for example, the Dis-

trict Director should consider information which would enable him to determine the extent to which deductions attributable to functions performed in the United States are related to earning foreign source income, United States source income, or income from both sources. In addition to functions with a specific international purpose, consideration should be given to the functions of management, the direction and results of an acquisition program, the functions of operating units and personnel located at the head office, the functions of support units (including but not limited to engineering, legal, budget, accounting, and industrial relations), the functions of selling and advertising units and personnel, the direction and uses of research and development, and the direction and uses of services furnished by independent contractors. Thus, for example when requested by the District Director, the taxpayer shall make available any of its organization charts, manuals, and other writings which relate to the manner in which its gross income arises and to the functions of organizational units, employees, and assets of the taxpayer and arrange for the interview of such of its employees as the District Director deems desirable in order to determine the gross income to which deductions relate. See section 7602 and the regulations thereunder which generally provide for the examination of books and witnesses. See also section 905(b) and the regulations thereunder which require proof of foreign tax credits to the satisfaction of the Secretary or his delegate.

(g) *General examples.*—The following examples illustrate the principles of this section. In each example, unless otherwise specified, the operative section which is applied and gives rise to the statutory grouping of gross income is the overall limitation to the foreign tax credit under section 904(a). In addition, in each example, where a method of allocation or apportionment is illustrated as an acceptable method, it is assumed that such method is used by the taxpayer on a consistent basis from year to year (except in the case of the optional method for apportioning research and development expense under paragraph (e)(3)(iii) of § 1.861-8). Further, it is assumed that each party named in each example operates on a calendar year accounting basis and, where the party is a U.S. taxpayer, files returns on a calendar year basis.

Example (1)—[Reserved]
Example (2)—[Reserved]
Example (3)—[Reserved]
Example (4)—[Reserved]
Example (5)—[Reserved]
Example (6)—[Reserved]
Example (7)—[Reserved]
Example (8)—[Reserved]
Example (9)—[Reserved]
Example (10)—[Reserved]
Example (11)—[Reserved]
Example (12)—[Reserved]
Example (13)—[Reserved]
Example (14)—[Reserved]
Example (15)—[Reserved]
Example (16)—[Reserved]

Example (17)—Stewardship Expenses (Consolidation)—(i) *Facts.* X, a domestic corporation, wholly owns M, N, and O, also domestic corporations. X, M, N, and O file a consolidated income tax return. All the income of X and O is from sources within the United States, all of M's income is from sources within South America, and all of N's income is from sources within Africa. X receives no dividends from M, N, or O. During the taxable year, the consolidated group of corporations earned consolidated gross income of $550,000 and incurred total deductions of $370,000 as follows:

	Gross income	Deductions
Corporations:		
X	$100,000	$50,000
M	250,000	100,000
N	150,000	200,000
O	50,000	20,000
Total	$550,000	$370,000

Of the $50,000 of deductions incurred by X, $15,000 relates to X's ownership of M; $10,000 relates to X's ownership of N; $5,000 relates to X's ownership of O; and the entire $30,000 constitute stewardship expenses. The remainder of X's deductions ($20,000) relates to production of income from its plant in the United States.

(ii) *Allocation.* In accordance with § 1.1502-4, each corporation must first compute its separate taxable income for purposes of computing the limitation on the foreign tax credit. X's deductions of $50,000 are definitely related and thus allocable to the types of gross income to which they give rise, namely $25,000 wholly to income from sources outside the United States ($15,000 for stewardship of M and $10,000 for stewardship of N) and the remainder ($25,000) wholly to gross income from sources within the United States. Expenses incurred by M and N are entirely related and thus wholly allocable to income earned from sources without the United States and expenses incurred by O are entirely related and thus wholly allocable to income earned within the United States. Hence, no apportionment of expenses of X, M, N, or O is necessary. For purposes of applying the overall limitation, the statutory grouping is gross income from sources without the United States and the residual grouping is gross in-

Reg. § 1.861-8(g)

come from sources within the United States. As a result of the allocation of deductions, X, M, and N have separate taxable income (losses) from sources without the United States in the amounts of ($25,000), $150,000 and ($50,000), respectively, computed as follows:

	X	M	N
Foreign gross income		$250,000	$150,000
Less: Deductions allocable to foreign gross income	$25,000	100,000	200,000
Total, taxable income (loss)	($25,000)	$150,000	($50,000)

Thus, in the combined computation of the overall limitation, the numerator of the limiting fraction (taxable income from sources outside the United States) is $75,000 ($150,000 or separate taxable income of M less $50,000 of losses of N and less $25,000 of losses of X).

Example (18)—Stewardship and Supportive Expenses—(i)(A) *Facts.* X, a domestic corporation, manufactures and sells pharmaceuticals in the United States. X's domestic subsidiary S, and X's foreign subsidiaries T, U, and V perform similar functions in the United States and foreign countries T, U, and V, respectively. Each corporation derives substantial net income during the taxable year. X's gross income for the taxable year consists of:

Domestic sales income	$32,000,000
Dividends from S (before dividends received deduction)	3,000,000
Dividends from T	2,000,000
Dividends from U	1,000,000
Dividends from V	0
Royalties from T and U	1,000,000
Fees from U for services performed in the United States	1,000,000
Total gross income	$40,000,000

(i)(B) In addition, X incurs expenses of its supervision department of $1,600,000.

(i)(C) X's Supervision Department (the Department) is responsible for the supervision of its four subsidiaries and for rendering certain services to the subsidiaries, and this Department provides all the supportive functions necessary for X's foreign activities. The Department performs three principal types of activities. The first type consists of services for the direct benefit of U for which a fee is paid by U to X. The cost of the services for U is $1,000,000. The second type consists of stewardship activities which are in the nature of a management review and generally duplicate functions performed by the subsidiaries' own employees (and are, therefore, of a type described in § 1.482-2(b)(2)(ii) which would not be subject to an allocation under section 482). For example, a team of auditors from X's accounting department periodically audits the subsidiaries' books and prepares internal reports for use by X's management. Similarly, X's treasurer periodically reviews for the board of directors of X the subsidiaries' financial policies. The cost of the duplicative services and related supportive expenses is $540,000. The third type of activity consists of providing services which are ancillary to the license agreements which X maintains with subsidiaries T and U. The cost of the ancillary services is $60,000.

(ii) *Allocation.* The Department's outlay of $1,000,000 is the basis for the charge to U for services rendered, and therefore $1,000,000 is allocated to the fees paid by U. The remaining $600,000 in the Department's deductions are definitely related to the types of gross income to which they give rise, namely dividends from subsidiaries S, T, U and V and royalties from T and U. However, $60,000 of the $600,000 in deductions are found to be attributable to the ancillary services and are definitely related (and therefore allocable) solely to royalties received from T and U, while the remaining $540,000 in deductions are definitely related (and therefore allocable) to dividends received from all the subsidiaries.

(iii) *Apportionment.* For purposes of applying the overall limitation, the statutory grouping is gross income from sources outside the United States and the residual grouping is gross income from sources within the United States. X's deduction of $540,000 for the Supervision Department expenses and related supportive expenses which is allocable to dividends received from the subsidiaries must be apportioned between the statutory and residual groupings before the overall limitation may be applied. In determining an appropriate method for apportioning the $540,000, a basis other than X's gross income must be used since the dividend payment policies of the subsidiaries bear no relationship either to the activities of the Department or to the amount of income earned by each subsidiary. This is evidenced by the fact that V paid no dividends during the year, whereas S, T, and U paid dividends of $1 million or more each. In the absence of facts that would indicate a material distortion resulting from the use of such method, the stewardship expenses ($540,000) may be apportioned on the basis of the gross receipts of each subsidiary.

The gross receipts of the subsidiaries were as follows:

S	$4,000,000
T	3,000,000
U	500,000
V	1,500,000
Total	$9,000,000

$$\$540,000 \times \frac{(\$3,000,000 + \$500,000 + \$1,500,000)}{\$9,000,000} \dots \dots \$300,000$$

Apportionment of supervisory expenses to the residual grouping of gross income:

$$\$540,000 \times \frac{\$4,000,000}{9,000,000} \dots \dots 240,000$$

Total: Apportioned stewardship expense $540,000

Example (19)—Supportive Expense—(i) *Facts.* X, a domestic corporation, purchases and sells products both in the United States and in foreign countries. X has no foreign subsidiary and no international department. During the taxable year, X incurs the following expenses with respect to its worldwide activities:

Personnel department expenses	$50,000
Training department expenses	35,000
General and administrative expenses	55,000
President's salary	40,000
Sales manager's salary	20,000
Total	$200,000

X has domestic gross receipts from sales of $750,000 and foreign gross receipts from sales of $500,000 and has gross income from such sales in the same ratio, namely $300,000 from domestic sources and $200,000 from foreign sources.

(ii) *Allocation.* The above expenses are definitely related and allocable to all of X's gross income derived from both domestic and foreign markets.

$$\$200,000 \times \frac{\$500,000}{(\$500,000 + \$750,000)}$$

Apportionment of the $200,000 expense to the residual grouping of gross income:

$$\$200,000 \times \frac{\$750,000}{(\$500,000 + \$750,000)} \dots \dots 120,000$$

Total apportioned supportive expense $200,000

Example (20)—Supportive Expense—(i) *Facts.* Assume the same facts as above except that X's president devotes only 5 percent of his time to the foreign operations and 95 percent of his time to the domestic operations and that X's sales manager devotes approximately 10 percent of his time to foreign sales and 90 percent of his time to domestic sales.

Thus, the expenses of the Department are apportioned for purposes of the overall limitation as follows:

Apportionment of stewardship expenses to the statutory grouping of gross income:

(iii) *Apportionment.* For purposes of applying the overall limitation, the statutory grouping is gross income from sources outside the United States and the residual grouping is gross income from sources within the United States. X's deductions for its worldwide sales activities must be apportioned between these groupings. Company X in this example (unlike Company X in example (18)) does not have a separate international division which performs essentially all of the functions required to manage and oversee its foreign activities. The president and sales manager do not maintain time records. The division of their time between domestic and foreign activities varies from day to day and cannot be estimated on an annual basis with any reasonable degree of accuracy. Similarly, there are no facts which would justify a method of apportionment of their salaries or of one of the other listed deductions based on more specific factors than gross receipts or gross income. An acceptable method of apportionment would be on the basis of gross receipts. The apportionment of the $200,000 deduction is as follows:

Apportionment of the $200,000 expense to the statutory grouping of gross income:

. . . . $80,000

(ii) *Allocation.* The expenses incurred by X with respect to its worldwide activities are definitely related, and therefore allocable to X's gross income from both its foreign and domestic markets.

(iii) *Apportionment.* On the basis of the additional facts it is not acceptable to apportion the salaries of the president and the sales manager on the basis of gross receipts. It is acceptable to apportion such salaries between the statutory grouping (gross income from sources without the United States) and residual grouping (gross income from sources within the United States) on the basis of time devoted to each sales activity. Remaining expenses may still be apportioned on the basis of gross receipts. The apportionment is as follows:

Apportionment of the $200,000 expense to the statutory grouping of gross income:

President's salary: $40,000 × 5%	$ 2,000
Sales manager's salary: $20,000 × 10%	2,000
$140,000 × $\dfrac{\$500,000}{(\$500,000 + \$750,000)}$	$56,000
Subtotal: Apportionment of expense to statutory grouping	60,000

Apportionment of the $200,000 expense to the residual grouping of gross income:

President's salary: $40,000 × 95%	38,000
Sales manager's salary: $20,000 × 90%	18,000
$140,000 × $\dfrac{\$750,000}{(\$500,000 + \$750,000)}$	84,000
Subtotal: Apportionment of expense to residual grouping	$140,000
Total: Apportioned general and administrative expense	$200,000

Example (21)—Supportive Expense—(i) *Facts.* X, a foreign corporation doing business in the United States, is a manufacturer of metal stamping machines. X has no United States subsidiaries and no separate division to manage and oversee its business in the United States. X manufactures and sells these machines in the United States and in foreign countries A and B and has a separate manufacturing facility in each country. Sales of these machines are X's only source of income. In 1977, X incurs general and administrative expenses related to both its U.S. and foreign operations of $100,000. It has machine sales of $500,000, $1,000,000 and $1,000,000 on which it earns gross income of $200,000, $400,000 and $400,000 in the United States, country A, and country B, respectively. The income from the manufacture and sale of the machines in countries A and B is not effectively connected with X's business in the United States.

(ii) *Allocation.* The $100,000 of general and administrative expense is definitely related to the income to which it gives rise, namely a part of the gross income from sales of machines in the United States, in country A, and in country B. The expenses are allocable to this class of income, even though X's gross income from sources outside the United States is excluded income since it is not effectively connected with a U.S. trade or business.

(iii) *Apportionment.* Since X is a foreign corporation, the statutory grouping is gross income effectively connected with X's trade or business in the United States, namely gross income from sources within the United States, and the residual grouping is gross income not effectively connected with a trade or business in the United States, namely gross income from countries A and B. Since there are no facts which would require a method of apportionment other than on the basis of sales or gross income, the amount may be apportioned between the two groupings on the basis of amounts of gross income as follows:

Apportionment of general and administrative expense to the statutory grouping, gross income from sources within the United States:

$100,000 × $\dfrac{\$200,000}{(\$200,000 + \$400,000 + \$400,000)}$	$20,000

Apportionment of general and administrative expense to the residual grouping, gross income from sources within the United States:

$100,000 × $\dfrac{(\$400,000 + \$400,000)}{(\$200,000 + \$400,000 + \$400,000)}$	80,000
Total apportioned general and administrative expense	$100,000

Example (22)—Domestic International Sales Corporations—(i) *Facts.* X, a domestic corporation, manufactures a line of kitchenware and sells it to retailers in the United States, France, and the United Kingdom. After the Domestic International Sales Corporation (DISC) legislation was passed in 1971, X established, as of January 1, 1972, a DISC and thereafter did all of its foreign marketing through sales by the DISC. In 1977 the DISC has total sales of $7,700,000 for which X's cost of goods sold is $6,000,000. Thus, the gross income attributable to exports through the DISC is $1,700,000 ($7,700,000 − $6,000,000). Moreover, X has U.S. domestic sales of kitchenware of $12,000,000 on which it earned gross income of $900,000, and X receives royalty income from the foreign license of its kitchenware technology in the amount of $800,000. The DISC's expenses attributable to the resale of export property are $400,000 of which $300,000 qualify as export promotion expenses. X also incurs $125,000 of general and administrative expenses in connection with its domestic and foreign sales activities, and its foreign licensing activities. X and the DISC determine transfer prices charged on the basis of a single product grouping and the "50-50" combined taxable income method (without marginal costing) which permits the DISC to have a taxable income equal to 50 percent of the combined taxable income attributable to the production and sales of the export property, plus 10 percent of the DISC's export promotion expenses.

(ii) *Allocation.* For purposes of determining combined taxable income of X and the DISC from export sales, general and administrative expenses of $125,000 must be allocated to and apportioned between gross income resulting from the production and sale of kitchenware for export, and from the production and sale of kitchenware for the domestic market. The deduction of $400,000 for expenses attributable to the resale of export property is allocated solely to gross income from the production and sale of kitchenware in foreign markets.

(iii) *Apportionment.* Apportionment of expense takes place in two stages. In the first stage, for computing combined taxable income from the production and sale of export property, the general and administrative expense should be apportioned between the statutory grouping of gross income from the export of kitchenware and the residual grouping of gross income from domestic sales and foreign licenses. In the second stage, since the limitation on the foreign tax credit requires the use of a separate limitation with respect to dividends from a DISC (section 904(d)), the general and administrative expense should be apportioned between two statutory groupings, DISC dividends and foreign royalty income (for which the overall limitation is used), and the residual grouping of gross income from sales within the United States. In the first stage, in the absence of more specific or contrary information, the general and administrative expense may be apportioned on the basis of gross income in the respective groupings, as follows:

Apportionment of general and administrative expense to the statutory grouping, gross income from exports of kitchenware:

$$\$125,000 \times \frac{\$1,700,000}{(\$1,700,000 + \$900,000 + \$800,000)} \dots\dots\dots\dots \$62,500$$

Apportionment of general and administrative expense to the residual grouping, gross income from domestic sales of kitchenware and foreign royalty income from licensing kitchenware technology:

$$\$125,000 \times \frac{(\$900,000 + \$800,000)}{(\$1,700,000 + \$900,000 + \$800,000)} \dots\dots\dots\dots 62,500$$

Total apportionment of general and administrative expense $125,000

On the basis of this apportionment, the combined taxable income, and the DISC portion of taxable income may be calculated as follows:

Gross income from exports		$1,700,000
Less:		
DISC expense for resale of export property	$400,000	
Apportioned general and administrative expense	62,500	
		462,500
Combined taxable income from production and export of kitchenware		$1,237,500
DISC income:		
50 pct. of combined taxable income		618,750
10 pct. of export promotion expense of $300,000		30,000
Total DISC income		$648,750
DISC income as a percentage of combined taxable income		52.4

Reg. §1.861-8(g)

In the second stage, in the absence of more specific or contrary information, the general and administrative expense may also be apportioned on the basis of gross income in the respective groupings. Since DISC taxable income is 52.4 percent of combined taxable income, DISC gross income is treated as 52.4 percent of the gross income from exports, $1,700,000. The apportionment follows:

Apportionment of general and administrative expense to the statutory grouping, DISC dividends:

$$\$125,000 \times \frac{(0.524 \times \$1,700,00)}{(\$1,700,000 + \$900,000 + \$800,000)} \quad \ldots\ldots\ldots\ldots\ldots\ldots \quad \$32,750$$

Apportionment of general and administrative expense to the statutory grouping, foreign royalty income:

$$\$125,000 \times \frac{\$800,000}{(\$1,700,000 + \$900,000 + \$800,000)} \quad \ldots\ldots\ldots\ldots\ldots\ldots \quad \$29,412$$

Apportionment of general and administrative expense to the residual grouping, gross income from sources within the United States:

$$\$125,000 \times \frac{(\$900,000 + (0.476 \times \$1,700,000))}{(\$1,700,000 + \$900,000 + \$800,000)} \quad \ldots\ldots\ldots\ldots\ldots\ldots \quad 62,838$$

Total apportioned general and administrative expense $125,000

(iv) This *Example (22)* applies only to DISC taxable years ending before January 1, 1987, and to distributions from a DISC or former DISC with respect to DISC or former DISC taxable years ending before January 1, 1987.

Example (23)—[Reserved]

Example (24)—[Reserved] For guidance, see § 1.861-8T(g) *Example (24)*.

Example 25—Income Taxes—(i) *Facts.* X, a domestic corporation, is a manufacturer and distributor of electronic equipment with operations in states A, B, and C. X also has a branch in country Y which manufactures and distributes the same type of electronic equipment. In 1988, X has taxable income from these activities, as determined under the Code (without taking into account the deduction for state income taxes), of $1,000,000, of which $200,000 is foreign source general limitation income subject to a separate limitation under section 904(d)(1)(I) ("general limitation income") and $800,000 is domestic source income. States A, B, and C each determine X's income subject to tax within their state by making adjustments to X's taxable income as determined under the Code, and then apportioning the adjusted taxable income on the basis of the relative amounts of X's payroll, property, and sales within each state as compared to X's worldwide payroll, property, and sales. The adjustments made by states A, B, and C all involve adding and subtracting enumerated items from taxable income as determined under the Code. However, in making these adjustments to taxable income, none of the states specifically exempts foreign source income as determined under the Code. On this basis, it is determined that X has taxable income of $550,000, $200,000, and $200,000 in states A, B, and C, respectively. The corporate tax rates in states A, B, and C are 10 percent, 5 percent, and 2 percent, respectively, and X has total state income tax liabilities of $69,000 ($55,000 + $10,000 + $4,000), which it deducts as an expense for federal income tax purposes.

(ii) *Allocation.* X's deduction of $69,000 for state income taxes is definitely related and thus allocable to the gross income with respect to which the taxes are imposed. Since the statutes of states A, B, and C do not specifically exempt foreign source income (as determined under the Code) from taxation and since, in the aggregate, states A, B, and C tax $950,000 of X's income while only $800,000 is domestic source income under the Code, it is presumed that state income taxes are imposed on $150,000 of foreign source income. The deduction for state income taxes is therefore related and allocable to both X's foreign source and domestic source income.

(iii) *Apportionment.* For purposes of computing the foreign tax credit limitation, X's income is comprised of one statutory grouping, foreign source general limitation gross income, and one residual grouping, gross income from sources within the United States. The state income tax deduction of $69,000 must be apportioned between these two groupings. Corporation X calculates the apportionment on the basis of the relative amounts of foreign source general limitation taxable income and U.S. source taxable income subject to state taxation. In this case, state income taxes are presumed to be imposed on $800,000 of domestic source income and $150,000 of foreign source general limitation income.

State income tax deduction apportioned to foreign source general limitation income (statutory grouping):
$69,000 × ($150,000/$950,000) $10,895
State income tax deduction apportioned to income from sources within the United States (residual grouping):
$69,000 × ($800,000/$950,000) $58,105
Total apportioned state income tax deduction $69,000

Example 26—Income Taxes—(i) *Facts.* Assume the same facts as in *Example 25* except that the language of state A's statute and the statute's operation exempt from taxation all foreign source income, as determined under the Code, so that foreign source income is not included in adjusted taxable income subject to apportionment in state A (and factors relating to X's country Y branch are not taken into account in computing the state A apportionment fraction).

(ii) *Allocation.* X's deduction of $69,000 for state income taxes is definitely related and thus allocable to the gross income with respect to which the taxes are imposed. Since state A exempts all foreign source income by statute, state A is presumed to impose tax on $550,000 of X's $800,000 of domestic source income. X's state A tax of $55,000 is allocable, therefore, solely to domestic source income. Since the statutes of states B and C do not specifically exclude all foreign source income as determined under the Code, and since states B and C impose tax on $400,000 ($200,000 + $200,000) of X's income of which only $250,000 ($800,000 − $550,000) is presumed to be domestic source, the deduction for the $14,000 of income taxes imposed by states B and C is related and allocable to both foreign source and domestic source income.

(iii) *Apportionment.* (A) For purposes of computing the foreign tax credit limitation, X's income is comprised of one statutory grouping, foreign source general limitation gross income, and one residual grouping, gross income from sources within the United States. The deduction of $14,000 for income taxes of states B and C must be apportioned between these two groupings.

(B) Corporation X calculates the apportionment on the basis of the relative amounts of foreign source general limitation income and U.S. source income subject to state taxation.

States B and C income tax deduction apportioned to foreign source general limitation income (statutory grouping):
$14,000 × ($150,000/$400,000) $5,250
States B and C income tax deduction apportioned to income from sources within the United States (residual grouping):
$14,000 × ($250,000/$400,000) $8,750
Total apportioned state income tax deduction $14,000

(C) Of X's total income taxes of $69,000, the amount allocated and apportioned to foreign source general limitation income equals $5,250. The total amount of state income taxes allocated and apportioned to U.S. source income equals $63,750 ($55,000 + $8,750).

Example 27—Income Tax—(i) *Facts.* Assume the same facts as in *Example 25* except that state A, in which X has significant income-producing activities, does not impose a corporate income tax or other state tax computed on the basis of income derived from business activities conducted in state A. X therefore has a total state income tax liability in 1988 of $14,000 ($10,000 paid to state B plus $4,000 paid to state C), all of which is subject to allocation and apportionment under paragraph (b) of this section.

(ii) *Allocation.* (A) X's deduction of $14,000 for state income taxes is definitely related and allocable to the gross income with respect to which the taxes are imposed. However, in these facts, an adjustment is necessary before the aggregate state taxable incomes can be compared with U.S. source income on the federal income tax return in the manner described in *Examples 25* and *26.* Unlike the facts in *Examples 25* and *26,* state A imposes no income tax and does not define taxable income attributable to activities in state A. The total amount of X's income subject to state taxation is, therefore, $400,000 ($200,000 in state B and $200,000 in state C). This total presumptively does not include any income attributable to activities performed in state A and therefore can not properly be compared to total U.S. source taxable income reported by X for federal income tax purposes, which does include income attributable to state A activities.

(B)(1) Accordingly, before applying the method used in *Examples 25* and *26* to the facts of this example, it is necessary first to estimate the amount of taxable income that state A could reasonably attribute to X's activities in state A, and then to reduce federal taxable income by that amount.

(2) Any reasonable method may be used to attribute taxable income to X's activities in state A. For example, the rules of the Uniform Division of Income for Tax Purposes Act

Reg. §1.861-8(g)

("UDITPA") attribute income to a state on the basis of the average of three ratios that are based upon the taxpayer's facts—property within the state over total property, payroll within the state over total payroll, and sales within the state over total sales—and, with adjustments, provide a reasonable method for this purpose. When applying the rules of UDITPA to estimate U.S. source income derived from state A activities, the taxpayer's UDITPA factors must be adjusted to eliminate both taxable income and factors attributable to a foreign branch. Therefore, in this example all taxable income as well as UDITPA apportionment factors (property, payroll, and sales) attributable to X's country Y branch must be eliminated.

(C)(1) Since it is presumed that, if state A had had an income tax, state A would not attempt to tax the income derived by X's country Y branch, any reasonable estimate of the income that would be taxed by state A must exclude any foreign source income.

(2) When using the rules of UDITPA to estimate the income that would have been taxable by state A in these facts, foreign source income is excluded by starting with federally defined taxable income (before deduction for state income taxes) and subtracting any income derived by X's country Y branch. The hypothetical state A taxable income is then determined by multiplying the resulting difference by the average of X's state A property, payroll, and sales ratios, determined using the principles of UDITPA (after adjustment by eliminating the country Y branch factors). The resulting product is presumed to be exclusively U.S. source income, and the allocation and apportionment method described in *Example 26* must then be applied.

(3) If, for example, state A taxable income were determined to equal $550,000, then $550,000 of U.S. source income for federal income tax purposes would be presumed to constitute state A taxable income. Under *Example 26*, the remaining $250,000 ($800,000 - $550,000) of U.S. source income for federal income tax purposes would be presumed to be subject to tax in states B and C. Since states B and C impose tax on $400,000, the application of *Example 25* would result in a presumption that $150,000 is foreign source income and $250,000 is domestic source income. The deduction for the $14,000 of income taxes of states B and C would therefore be related and allocable to both foreign source and domestic source income and would be subject to apportionment.

(iii) *Apportionment.* The deduction of $14,000 for income taxes of states B and C is apportioned in the same manner as in *Example 26*. As a result, $5,250 of the $14,000 of state B and state C income taxes is apportioned to foreign source general limitation income ($14,000× $150,000/$400,000), and $8,750 ($14,000× $250,000/$400,000) of the $14,000 of state B and state C income taxes is apportioned to U.S. source income.

Example 28—Income Tax—(i) *Facts.* (A) Assume the same facts as in *Example 25* (X has $1,000,000 of taxable income for federal income tax purposes, $800,000 of which is U.S. source income and $200,000 of which is foreign source general limitation income), except that $100,000 of X's $200,000 of foreign source general limitation income consists of dividends from first-tier controlled foreign corporations ("CFCs") (as defined in section 957(a) of the Code) which derive exclusively foreign source general limitation income. X owns stock representing 10 to 50 percent of the vote and value in such CFCs.

(B) State A taxable income is computed by first making adjustments to X's federal taxable income. These adjustments result in X having a total of $1,100,000 of apportionable taxable income for state A tax purposes. None of the $100,000 of adjustments made by state A relate to the dividends paid by the CFCs. As in *Example 25*, the amount of apportionable taxable income attributable to business activities conducted in state A is determined by multiplying apportionable taxable income by a fraction (the "state apportionment fraction") that compares the relative amounts of X's payroll, property, and sales within state A with X's worldwide payroll, property and sales. An analysis of state A law indicates that state A law includes in its definition of the taxable business income of X which is apportionable to X's state A activities, dividends paid to X by its subsidiaries that are in the same business as X, but are less than 50 percent owned by X ("portfolio dividends"). The dividends received by X from the 10 to 50 percent owned first-tier CFCs, therefore, are considered to be portfolio dividends includable in apportionable business income for state A tax purposes. However, the factors of these CFCs are not included in the state A apportionment fraction for purposes of apportioning income to X's activities in the state. The comparison of X's state A factors with X's worldwide factors results in a state apportionment fraction of 50 percent. Applying this fraction to apportionable taxable income of $1,100,000, as determined under state law, results in attributing 50 percent of apportionable taxable income to state A, and produces total state A taxable income of $550,000. State A imposes an income tax at a rate of 10 percent on the amount of income that is attributed to state A, which results in $55,000 of tax imposed by state A.

(ii) *Allocation.* (A) States A, B, and C impose income taxes of $69,000 which must be allocated to the classes of gross income upon which the taxes are imposed. A portion of X's federal income tax deduction of $55,000 for state A income tax is definitely related and thus allocable to the class of gross income consisting of foreign source portfolio dividends. A definite relationship exists between a deduction for state income tax and portfolio dividends when a state includes portfolio dividends in state taxable income apportionable to the state, but determines state taxable income by applying an apportionment fraction that excludes the factors of the corporations paying those dividends. By applying a state apportionment fraction that excludes factors of the corporations paying portfolio dividends to apportionable taxable income that includes the $100,000 of foreign source portfolio dividends, $50,000 (50 percent of the $100,000) of the portfolio dividends is attributed to X's activities in state A and subjected to state A income tax. Applying the state A income tax rate of 10 percent to the $50,000 of foreign source portfolio dividends subjected to state A income tax, $5,000 of X's $55,000 total state A income tax liability is definitely related and allocable to a class of gross income consisting of the foreign source portfolio dividends. Since under the look-through rules of section 904(d)(3) the foreign source portfolio dividends from the first-tier CFCs are included within the general limitation described in section 904(d)(1)(I), the $5,000 of state A tax on foreign source portfolio dividends is allocated entirely to foreign source general limitation income and, therefore, is not apportioned. (If the total amount of state A tax imposed on foreign source portfolio dividends were to exceed the actual amount of X's state A income tax liability (for example, due to net operating losses), the actual amount of state A tax would be allocated entirely to those foreign source portfolio dividends.) After allocation of a portion of the state A tax to portfolio dividends, $50,000 ($55,000 - $5,000) of state A tax remains to be allocated.

(B) A total of $64,000 (the aggregate of the $50,000 remaining state A tax, and the $10,000 and $4,000 of taxes imposed by states B and C, respectively) is to be allocated (as provided in *Example 25*) by comparing U.S. source taxable income (as determined under the Code) with the aggregate of the state taxable incomes determined by states A, B, and C (after reducing state apportionable taxable incomes by the amount of any portfolio dividends included in apportionable taxable income to which tax has been specifically allocated). X's state A taxable income, after reduction by the $50,000 of portfolio dividends taxed by state A, equals $500,000. X also has taxable income of $200,000 and $200,000 in states B and C, respectively. In the aggregate, therefore, states A, B, and C tax $900,000 of X's income, after excluding state taxable income attributable to portfolio dividends. Since X has only $800,000 of U.S. source taxable income for federal income tax purposes, it is presumed that state income taxes are imposed on $100,000 of foreign source income. The remaining deduction of $64,000 for state income taxes is therefore related and allocable to both foreign source and domestic source income and is subject to apportionment.

(iii) *Apportionment*. For purposes of computing the foreign tax credit limitation, X's income is comprised of one statutory grouping, foreign source general limitation income, and one residual grouping, gross income from sources within the United States. The remaining state income tax deduction of $64,000 must be apportioned between these two groupings on the basis of relative amounts of foreign source general limitation taxable income and U.S. source taxable income subject to state taxation. In this case, the $64,000 of state income taxes is considered to be imposed on $800,000 of domestic source income and $100,000 of foreign source general limitation income and is apportioned as follows:

State income tax deduction apportioned to foreign source general limitation income (statutory grouping):	
$64,000 × ($100,000/$900,000)	$7,111
State income tax deduction apportioned to income from sources within the United States (residual grouping):	
$64,000 × ($800,000/$900,000)	$56,889
Total apportioned state income tax deduction	$64,000

Of the total state income taxes of $69,000, the amount allocated and apportioned to foreign source general limitation income equals $12,111 ($5,000+$7,111). The total amount of state income taxes allocated and apportioned to U.S. source income equals $56,889.

Example 29—Income Taxes—(i) *Facts*. (A) P, a domestic corporation, is a manufacturer and distributor of electronic equipment with operations in states F, G, and H. P also has a branch in country Y which manufactures and distributes the same type of electronic equipment. In addition, P has three wholly owned subsidiaries, US1, US2, and FS, the latter a controlled foreign corporation ("CFC") as defined in section 957(a) of the Code. P also owns stock representing 10 to 50 percent of the vote and value of various other first-tier CFCs that derive exclusively foreign source general limitation income.

(B) In 1988, P derives $1,000,000 of federal taxable income (without taking into account the deduction for state income taxes), which consists of $250,000 of foreign source general limitation income and $750,000 of U.S. source income. The foreign source general limitation income consists of a $25,000 subpart F inclusion with respect to FS, $150,000 of dividends

Reg. §1.861-8(g)

from the other first-tier CFCs deriving exclusively foreign source general limitation income, in which P owns stock representing 10 to 50 percent of the vote and value, and $75,000 of manufacturing and sales income derived by P's U.S. operations and country Y branch. The $750,000 of U.S. source income consists of manufacturing and sales income derived by P's U.S. operations.

(C) For federal income tax purposes, US1 derives $75,000 of taxable income, before deduction for state income taxes, which consists entirely of U.S. source income. US2, a so-called "80/20" corporation described in section 861(c)(1), derives $250,000 of federal taxable income before deduction for state or foreign income taxes, all of which is derived from foreign operations and consists entirely of foreign source general limitation income. FS is not engaged in a U.S. trade or business and derives $550,000 of foreign source general limitation income before deduction for foreign income taxes.

(D) State F imposes a corporate income tax of 10 percent on P's state F taxable income, which is determined by formulary apportionment of the total taxable income attributable to P's worldwide unitary business. State F determines P's taxable income for state F tax purposes by first making adjustments to the taxable income, as determined for federal income tax purposes, of the members of the unitary business group to determine the total taxable income of the group. State F then computes P's state taxable income by attributing a portion of that unitary business taxable income to activities of P that are conducted in state F. State F does this by multiplying the unitary business taxable income (federal taxable income with state adjustments) by a fraction (the "state apportionment fraction") that compares the relative amounts of the unitary business group's payroll, property, and sales (the "factors") in state F with the payroll, property, and sales of the unitary business group. P is the only member of its unitary business group that has state F factors and that is thereby subject to state F income tax and filing requirements. State F defines the unitary business group to include any corporation more than 50 percent of which is directly or indirectly owned by a state F taxpayer and is engaged in the same unitary business. P's unitary business group, therefore, includes P, US1, US2, and FS, but does not include the 10 to 50 percent owned CFCs. The income of the unitary business group excludes intercompany dividends between members of the unitary business group and subpart F inclusions with respect to a member of the unitary business group. Dividends paid from nonmembers of the unitary group (the 10 to 50 percent owned CFCs) for state F tax purposes are referred to as "portfolio dividends" and are included in taxable income of the unitary business. None of the factors (in state F or worldwide) of the corporations paying portfolio dividends are included in the state F apportionment fraction for purposes of apportioning total taxable income of the unitary business to P's state F activities.

(E) After state adjustments to the taxable income of the unitary business group, as determined under federal tax principles, the total taxable income of P's unitary business group equals $2,000,000, consisting of $1,050,000 of P's income ($100,000 of foreign source manufacturing and sales income, $150,000 of foreign source portfolio dividends, and $800,000 of U.S. source manufacturing and sales income, but excluding the $25,000 subpart F inclusion attributable to FS since FS is a member of the unitary business group), $100,000 of US1's income (from sales made in the United States), $275,000 of US2's income (from an active business outside the United States), and $575,000 of FS's income. The differences between taxable income under federal tax principles and state F apportionable taxable income for P, US1, US2, and FS represent adjustments to taxable income under federal tax principles that are made pursuant to the tax laws of state F.

(F) The taxable income for each member of the unitary business group under federal tax principles and state law principles is summarized in the following table. (The items of income listed in the "Federal" column of the table refer to taxable income before deduction for state income tax.)

		Federal	State F
P			
	U.S. source income	$750,000	$800,000
	Foreign source general limitation income:		
	Portfolio dividends	150,000	150,000
	Subpart F income	25,000	0
	Manufacturing and sales income	75,000	100,000
	Total taxable income	$1,000,000	$1,050,000
US1			
	U.S. source income	$75,000	100,000
US2			
	Foreign source general limitation income	$250,000	275,000
FS			
	Foreign source general limitation income	$550,000	575,000
	Taxable income of the unitary business group		$2,000,000

Reg. § 1.861-8(g)

(G) State F deems P to have state F taxable income of $500,000, which is determined by multiplying the total taxable income of the unitary business group ($2,000,000) by the group's state F apportionment fraction, which is assumed to be 25 percent in these facts. P's state F taxable income is then multiplied by the state F tax rate of 10 percent, resulting in a state F tax liability of $50,000. State G and state H, unlike state F, do not tax portfolio dividends. Although state G and state H apportion taxable income, respectively, on the basis of an apportionment fraction that compares state factors to total factors, state G and state H, unlike state F, do not apply a unitary business theory and consider only P's taxable income and factors in computing P's taxable income. P's taxable income under state G law equals $300,000, which is subject to a 5 percent tax rate resulting in a state G tax liability of $15,000. P's taxable income under state H law is $300,000, which is subject to a tax rate of 2 percent resulting in a state H tax liability of $6,000. P has a total federal income tax deduction for state income taxes of $71,000 ($50,000 + 15,000 + 6,000).

(ii) *Allocation.* (A) P's deduction of $71,000 for state income taxes is definitely related and allocable to the gross income with respect to which the taxes are imposed. Adjustments may be necessary, however, before aggregate state taxable incomes can be compared with U.S. source taxable income on the federal income tax return in the manner described in *Examples 25* and *26*. In allocating P's deduction for state income taxes, it is necessary first to determine the portion, if any, of the deduction that is definitely related and allocable to a particular class of gross income. A definite relationship exists between a deduction for state income tax and dividend income when a state includes portfolio dividends in state taxable income apportionable to the taxpayer's activities in the state, but determines state taxable income by applying an apportionment formula that excludes the factors of the corporations paying portfolio dividends.

(B) In this case, $150,000 of foreign source portfolio dividends are subject to a state F apportionment fraction of 25 percent, which results in a total of $37,500 of state F taxable income attributable to such dividends. As illustrated in *Example 28*, $3,750 ($150,000 × 25 percent state F apportionment percentage × 10 percent state F tax rate) of P's state F income tax is definitely related and allocable to a class of gross income consisting entirely of the foreign source portfolio dividends. Since under the look-through rules of section 904(d)(3) the foreign source portfolio dividends paid by first-tier CFCs are included within the general limitation described in section 904(d)(1)(I), the $3,750 of state F tax on foreign source portfolio dividends is allocated entirely to foreign source general limitation income and, therefore, is not apportioned.

(C) After reducing state F taxable income of the unitary business group by the taxable income attributable to portfolio dividends, P's remaining state F taxable income equals $462,500 ($500,000 − $37,500), the portion of the taxable income of the unitary business that state F attributes to P's activities in state F. Accordingly, in order to allocate and apportion the remaining $46,250 of state F tax ($50,000 of state F tax minus the $3,750 of state F tax allocated to foreign source portfolio dividends), it is necessary first to determine if state F is taxing only P's non-unitary taxable income (as defined below) or is imposing its tax partly on other unitary business income that is attributed under state F law to P's activities in state F. P's state F non-unitary taxable income is computed by applying the state F apportionment formula, solely on the basis of P's income (excluding portfolio dividends) and state F apportionment factors. If the state F taxable income (after reduction by the portfolio dividends attributed to state F) attributed to P under state F law exceeds P's non-unitary taxable income, a portion of the state F tax must be allocated and apportioned on the basis of the other unitary business income that is attributed to and taxable to P under state F law. If P's non-unitary taxable income equals or exceeds the $462,500 of remaining state F taxable income, it is presumed that state F is only taxing P's non-unitary taxable income, so that the entire amount of the remaining state F tax should be allocated and apportioned in the manner described in *Example 25*.

(D) If P's non-unitary taxable income is less than the $462,500 of remaining state F taxable income (after reduction for the $37,500 of state F taxable income attributable to portfolio dividends), it is presumed that state F is attributing to P, and taxing P upon, other unitary business income. In such a case, it is necessary to determine if state F is attributing to P, and imposing its income tax on, a part of the foreign source income that would be generally presumed under separate accounting to be the income of foreign affiliates and 80/20 companies included in the unitary group, or whether state F is limiting the income it attributes to P, and its taxation of P, to the U.S. source income that would be generally presumed under separate accounting to be the income of domestic members of the unitary group.

(E) Assume for purposes of this example that the non-unitary taxable income attributable to P equals $396,000, computed by multiplying P's state F taxable income of $900,000 (P's state F taxable income (before state F apportionment) of $1,050,000 less the $150,000 of foreign source portfolio dividends) by P's non-unitary state F apportionment fraction, which is assumed to be 44 percent. Because P's non-unitary taxable income of $396,000 is less than the $462,500 of remaining state F taxable income, state F is presumed to be attributing to P and taxing the income that would have been generally attributed under separate accounting to P's affiliates in the unitary group. To determine if state F tax is being imposed on members of the unitary group (other than P) that produce foreign source income, it is necessary to compute a hypothetical state F taxable income for all companies in the unitary group with significant U.S. operations. (For this purpose, the hypothetical group of companies with significant domestic operations is referred to as the "water's edge group.") State F is presumed to be attributing to P and taxing income that would have been generally attributable under separate accounting to foreign corporations and 80/20 companies to the extent that the remaining state F taxable income ($462,500) of P exceeds the hypothetical state F taxable income that would have been attributed under state F law to P if state F had defined the unitary group to be the water's edge group.

(F) The members of the water's edge group would have been P and US1. The unitary business income of this water's edge group is $1,000,000, the sum of $900,000 (P's state F taxable income (before state F apportionment) of $1,050,000 less the $150,000 of foreign source portfolio dividends) and $100,000 (US1's state F taxable income). For purposes of this example, the state F apportionment fraction determined on a unitary basis for this water's edge group is assumed to equal 40 percent, the average of P and US1's state F payroll, property, and sales factor ratios (the water's edge group's state F factors over its worldwide factors). Applying this apportionment fraction to the $1,000,000 of unitary business income of the water's edge group yields state F water's edge taxable income of $400,000. The excess of the remaining $462,500 of P's state F taxable income over the $400,000 of P's state F water's edge taxable income equals $62,500, and is attributable to the inclusion of US2 and FS in the unitary group. The state F tax attributable to the $62,500 of taxable income attributed to P under state F law, and that would have generally been attributed to US2 and FS under non-unitary accounting, equals $6,250 and is allocated entirely to a class of gross income consisting of foreign source general limitation income, because the income of FS and US2 consists entirely of such income. After the $6,250 of state F tax attributable to US2 and FS is subtracted from the remaining $46,250 of net state F tax, P has $40,000 of state F tax remaining to be allocated and apportioned.

(G) To the extent that the remainder of P's state F taxable income ($400,000) exceeds P's non-unitary state F taxable income ($396,000), it is presumed that state F is attributing to and imposing on P a tax on U.S. source income that would have been attributed under separate accounting to members of the water's edge group other than P. In these facts, the $4,000 difference in P's state F taxable income results from the inclusion of US1 in the unitary group. The $400 of P's state F tax attributable to this $4,000 is allocated entirely to P's U.S. source income. P's remaining $39,600 of state F tax ($40,000 of P's state F tax resulting from the attribution to P of income that would have been attributed under non-unitary accounting to other members of the water's edge group, minus $400 of state F tax attributable to US1 and allocated to P's U.S. source income) is the state F tax attributable to P's non-unitary state F taxable income that is to be allocated and apportioned together with P's state G tax of $15,000 and state H tax of $6,000 as illustrated in *Example 25*.

(H) In allocating the $60,600 of state tax liabilities ($39,600 state F tax attributable to P's non-unitary state F income + $15,000 state G tax + $6,000 state H tax) under *Example 25*, P's state taxable income in state G and state H ($300,000 + $300,000) must be added to P's non-unitary state F taxable income ($396,000). The resulting $996,000 of combined state taxable incomes is compared with $750,000 of U.S. source income on P's federal income tax return. Because P's combined state taxable incomes exceed P's federal U.S. source taxable income, it is presumed that the remaining $60,600 of P's total state income taxes is imposed in part on foreign source income. Accordingly, P's remaining deduction of $60,600 ($39,600 + $15,000 + $6,000) for state income taxes is related and allocable to both P's foreign source and domestic source income and is subject to apportionment.

(iii) *Apportionment*. The $60,600 of state taxes (the remaining $39,600 of state F tax + $15,000 of state G tax + $6,000 of state H tax) must be apportioned between foreign source general limitation income and U.S. source income for federal income tax purposes. This apportionment is based upon the relative amounts of foreign source general limitation taxable income and U.S. source taxable income comprising the $996,000 of income subject to tax by the states, after reducing the total amount of income subject to tax by the portfolio dividends and the income attributed to P under state F law that would have been attributed under arm's length principles to other members of P's state F unitary business group. The deduction for the $60,600 of state income taxes is apportioned as follows:

State income tax deduction apportioned to foreign source general limitation income (statutory grouping):	
$60,600 × ($246,000/$996,000)	$14,967
State income tax deduction apportioned to income from sources within the United States (residual grouping):	
$60,600 × ($750,000/$996,000)	$45,633
Total apportioned state income tax deduction	$60,600

Of the total state income taxes of $71,000, the amount allocated and apportioned to foreign source general limitation income is $24,967—the sum of $14,967 of state F, state G, and state H taxes apportioned to foreign source general limitation income, $3,750 of state F tax allocated to foreign source apportionable dividend income, and the $6,250 of state F tax allocated to foreign source general limitation income as the result of state F's worldwide unitary business theory of taxation. The total amount of state income taxes allocated and apportioned to U.S. source income equals $46,033—the sum of the $400 of state F tax attributable to the inclusion of US1 in the state F unitary business group and $45,633 of combined state F, G, and H tax apportioned under the method provided in *Example 25*.

Example 30—Income Taxes—(i) *Facts.* (A) As in *Example 17* of § 1.861-8(g), X is a domestic corporation that wholly owns M, N, and O, also domestic corporations. X, M, N, and O file a consolidated income tax return. All the income of X and O is from sources within the United States, all of M's income is from sources within South America, and all of N's income is from sources within Africa. X receives no dividends from M, N, or O. During the taxable year, the consolidated group of corporations earned consolidated gross income of $550,000 and incurred total deductions of $370,000. X has gross income of $100,000 and deductions of $50,000, without regard to its deduction for state income tax. Of the $50,000 of deductions incurred by X, $15,000 relates to X's ownership of M; $10,000 relates to X's ownership of N; $5,000 relates to X's ownership of O; and the entire $30,000 constitutes stewardship expenses. The remainder of X's $20,000 of deductions (which is assumed not to include state income tax) relates to production of income from its plant in the United States. M has gross income of $250,000 and deductions of $100,000, which yield foreign source taxable income of $150,000. N has gross income of $150,000 and deductions of $200,000, which yield a foreign source loss of $50,000. O has gross income of $50,000 and deductions of $20,000, which yield U.S. source taxable income of $30,000.

(B) Unlike *Example 17* of § 1.861-8(g), however, X also has a deduction of $1,800 for state A income taxes. X's state A taxable income is computed by first making adjustments to the federal taxable income of X to derive apportionable taxable income for state A tax purposes. An analysis of state A law indicates that state A law also includes in its definition of the taxable business income of X which is apportionable to X's state A activities, the taxable income of M, N, and O, which is related to X's business. As in *Example 25*, the amount of apportionable taxable income attributable to business activities conducted in state A is determined by multiplying apportionable taxable income by a fraction (the "state apportionment fraction") that compares the relative amounts of payroll, property, and sales within state A with worldwide payroll, property and sales. Assuming that X's apportionable taxable income equals $180,000, $100,000 of which is from sources without the United States, and $80,000 is from sources within the United States, and that the state apportionment fraction is equal to 10 percent, X has state A taxable income of $18,000. The state A income tax of $1,800 is then derived by applying the state A income tax rate of 10 percent to the $18,000 of state A taxable income.

(ii) *Allocation and apportionment.* In accordance with § 1.1502-4, each corporation must first compute its separate taxable income for purposes of computing the consolidated limitation on the foreign tax credit. Assume that under *Example 29*, it is determined that X's deduction for state A income tax is definitely related to a class of gross income consisting of income from sources both within and without the United States, and that the state A tax is apportioned $1,000 to sources without the United States, and $800 to sources within the United States. Under *Example 17*, without regard to the deduction for X's state A income tax, X has a separate loss of ($25,000) from sources without the United States. After taking into account the deduction for state A income tax, X's separate loss from sources without the United States is increased by the $1,000 state A tax apportioned to sources without the United States, and equals a loss of ($26,000), for purposes of computing the numerator of the consolidated foreign tax credit limitation.

Example 31—Income Taxes—(i) *Facts.* Assume that the facts are the same as in *Example*

29, except that state G requires P to adjust its federal taxable income by depreciating an asset at a different rate than is allowed P under the Internal Revenue Code for the same asset. Before using the methodology of *Example 25* to determine whether a portion of its deduction for state income taxes is allocable to a class of gross income that includes foreign source income, P recomputes its taxable income under state G law by using the rate of depreciation that it is entitled to use under the Code, and uses this recomputed amount in applying the methodology of *Example 25*.

(ii) *Allocation.* P's modification of its state G taxable income is permissible. Under the methodology of *Example 25*, this modification of state G taxable income will produce a reasonable determination of the portion (if any) of P's state income taxes that is allocable to a class of gross income that includes foreign source income.

Example 32—Income Taxes—(i) *Facts.* Assume the facts are the same as *Example 29*, except that P's state F taxable income differs from the amount of its U.S. source income under federal income tax principles solely because state F determines P's state taxable income under a worldwide unitary business theory instead of the arm's length principles applied in the Code. Before using the methodology of *Example 25* to determine whether a portion of its deduction for state income taxes is allocable to a class of gross income that includes foreign source income, P recomputes state F taxable income under the arm's length principles applied in the Code. P substitutes that recomputed amount for the amount of taxable income actually determined under state F law in applying the methodology of *Example 25*.

(ii) *Allocation.* P's modification of state F taxable income does not accurately reflect the factual relationship between the deduction for state F income tax and the income on which the tax is imposed, because there is no factual relationship between the state F income tax and the state F taxable income as recomputed under Code principles. State F does not impose its income tax upon P's income as it might have been defined under the Internal Revenue Code. Consequently, P's modification of state F taxable income is impermissible because it will not produce a reasonable determination of the portion (if any) of P's state income taxes that is allocable to a class of gross income that includes foreign source income.

Example 33—Income Taxes—(i) *Facts.* Assume the same facts as in *Example 29*, except that state G does not impose an income tax on corporations and P's non-unitary state F taxable income equals $462,500. Thus only $56,000 of state income taxes ($50,000 of state F income tax and $6,000 of state H income tax) are deductible and required to be allocated and (if necessary) apportioned. As in *Example 29*, P has $800,000 of aggregate state taxable income ($500,000 of state F taxable income and $300,000 of state H taxable income).

(ii) *Method One.* Assume that P has elected to allocate and apportion its deduction for state income tax under the safe harbor method provided in § 1.861-8(e)(6)(ii)(D)(2) ("Method One").

(A) *Step One—Specific allocation to foreign source portfolio dividends.* P applies the methodology of paragraph (ii) of *Example 28* to determine the portion of the deduction that must be allocated to a class of gross income consisting solely of foreign source portfolio dividends. As illustrated in paragraphs (ii) (A) and (B) of *Example 29*, $3,750 of the deduction for state F income tax is attributable to the $37,500 of foreign source portfolio dividends attributed under state F law to P's activities in state F. Thus $3,750 of P's deduction for state income tax must be specifically allocated to a class of gross income consisting solely of $37,500 of foreign source portfolio dividends. No apportionment of the $3,750 is necessary. P's adjusted state taxable income is $762,500 (aggregate state taxable income of $800,000 reduced by $37,500 of foreign source portfolio dividends). Because the remaining amount of state F taxable income ($462,500) equals P's non-unitary state F taxable income, no further specific allocation of state tax is required.

(B) *Step Two—Adjustment of U.S. source federal taxable income.* P applies the methodology illustrated in paragraph (ii) of *Example 27* (including the rules of UDITPA described therein) to determine the amount of its federal taxable income attributable to its activities in state G. Assume that P determines under this methodology that $300,000 of its federal taxable income is attributable to activities in state G. P's adjusted U.S. source federal taxable income equals $450,000 ($750,000 minus the $300,000 attributed to P's activities in state G).

(C) *Step Three—Allocation.* The portion of P's deduction for state income tax remaining to be allocated equals $52,250 ($56,000 minus the $3,750 specifically allocated to foreign source portfolio dividends). P allocates this portion by applying the methodology illustrated in paragraph (ii) of *Example 25*, as modified by paragraph (e)(6)(ii)(D)(2)(*iii*) of this section. Thus, P compares its adjusted state taxable income (as determined under Step One in paragraph (A) above) with an amount equal to 110% of its adjusted U.S. source federal taxable income (as determined under Step Two in paragraph (B) above). Because P's adjusted state taxable income ($762,500) exceeds 110% of P's adjusted U.S. source federal taxable income

($495,000, or 110% of $450,000), the remaining portion of P's deduction for state income tax ($52,500) must be allocated to a class of gross income that includes both U.S. and foreign source income.

(D) *Step Four—Apportionment.* P must apportion to U.S. source income the portion of the deduction that is attributable to state income tax imposed upon state taxable income in an amount equal to 110% of P's adjusted U.S. source federal taxable income. The remainder of the deduction must be apportioned to foreign source general limitation income and reduced by the amount of foreign source portfolio dividends to which the tax has been specifically allocated.

Amount of deduction to be apportioned
.... $52,250.00
Less
Portion of deduction to be apportioned to income from sources within the United States (residual grouping):
($52,250 × ($495,000/$762,500)) . $33,919.67
Equals
Portion of deduction to be apportioned to foreign source general limitation income (statutory grouping): $18,330.33

(iii) *Method Two.* Assume that P has elected to allocate and apportion its deduction for state income tax under the safe harbor method provided in § 1.861-8(e)(6)(ii)(D)(*3*) ("Method Two").

(A) *Step One—Specific allocation.* Step One of Method Two is the same as Step One of Method One. Therefore, as described in paragraph (A) of paragraph (ii) above, $3,750 of P's deduction for state income tax must be specifically allocated to a class of gross income consisting solely of $37,500 of foreign source portfolio dividends. No apportionment of the $3,750 is necessary. P's adjusted state taxable income is $762,500 (aggregate state taxable income of $800,000 reduced by $37,500 of foreign source portfolio dividends).

(B) *Step Two—Adjustment of U.S. source federal taxable income.* Step Two of Method Two is the same as Step Two of Method One. Therefore, as described in paragraph (B) of paragraph (ii) above, assume that P determines that $300,000 of its federal taxable income is attributable to activities in state G. P's adjusted U.S. source federal taxable income equals $450,000 ($750,000 minus the $300,000 attributed to P's activities in state G).

(C) *Step Three—Allocation.* The portion of P's deduction for state income tax remaining to be allocated equals $52,250 ($56,000 minus the $3,750 of state F income tax specifically allocated to foreign source portfolio dividends). P allocates this portion by applying the methodology illustrated in paragraph (ii) of *Example 25*, as modified by paragraph (e)(6)(ii)(D)(*3*)(*iii*) of this section. Thus, P compares its adjusted state taxable income (as determined under Step One in paragraph (A) above) with its adjusted U.S. source federal taxable income (as determined under Step Two in paragraph (B) above). Because P's adjusted state taxable income ($762,500) exceeds P's adjusted U.S. source federal taxable income ($450,000), the remaining portion of P's deduction for state income tax ($52,500) must be allocated to a class of gross income that includes both U.S. and foreign source income.

(D) *Step Four—Apportionment.* P must apportion to U.S. source income the portion of the deduction that is attributable to state income tax imposed upon state taxable income in an amount equal to P's adjusted U.S. source federal taxable income.

Amount of deduction to be apportioned
.... $52,250.00
Less
Portion of deduction initially apportioned to income from sources within the United States (residual grouping):
$52,250 × ($450,000/$762,500) . . $30,836.07
Remainder requiring further apportionment:
$52,250 × ($312,500/$762,500) . . $21,413.93

The remainder of $21,413.93 must be further apportioned between foreign source general limitation income and U.S. source federal taxable income in the same proportions that P's adjusted U.S. source federal taxable income and foreign source general limitation income bear to P's total federal taxable income (taking into account the adjustment of U.S. source federal taxable income).

Portion of remainder apportioned to foreign source general limitation income (statutory grouping):
$21,413.93 × ($212,500/$662,500) . $6,868.62
Remaining state income tax deduction to be apportioned to income from sources within the United States (residual grouping):
$21,413.93 × ($450,000/$662,500) . $14,545.31

Of P's total deduction of $56,000 for state income tax, the portion allocated and apportioned to foreign source general limitation income equals $10,618.62—the sum of $6,868.62 apportioned under Step Four and the $3,750.00 specifically allocated to foreign source portfolio dividend income under Step One. The portion of the deduction allocated and apportioned to U.S. source income equals $45,381.38—the sum of the $30,836.07 and the $14,545.31 apportioned under Step Four. [Reg. § 1.861-8.]

Reg. § 1.861-8(g)

☐ [*T.D.* 6258, 10-23-57. *Amended by T.D.* 6892, 8-22-66; *T.D.* 7378, 9-29-75; *T.D.* 7456, 1-3-77; *T.D.* 7749, 12-30-80; *T.D.* 7939, 2-2-84; *T.D.* 8228, 9-9-88; *T.D.* 8236, 12-7-88; *T.D.* 8286, 1-29-90; *T.D.* 8337, 3-11-91; *T.D.* 8646, 12-21-95; *T.D.* 8805, 1-8-99; *T.D.* 8973, 12-27-2001; *T.D.* 9143, 7-27-2004 *and T.D.* 9194, 4-6-2005.]

Proposed Amendments to Regulation

§ 1.861-8. Computation of taxable income from sources within the United States and from other sources and activities.

* * *

(e) * * *

(1) * * *

(e)(12)(i) and (ii) [The text of the proposed addition of § 1.861-8(e)(12)(i) and (ii) is the same as § 1.861-8T(e)(12)(i) and (ii) as added by T.D. 9143.]

(e)(12)(iii) *Treaty provisions.*—(A) *In general.*—If a deduction for charitable contributions not otherwise permitted by sections 170, 873(b)(2) and 882(c)(1)(B) is allowed under a U.S. income tax treaty, and such treaty limits the amount of the deduction based on a percentage of income arising from sources within the treaty partner, the deduction is definitely related and allocable to all of the taxpayer's gross income. The deduction allocated under this paragraph (e)(12)(iii) shall be apportioned between the statutory grouping (or among the statutory groupings) of gross income and the residual grouping on the basis of the relative amounts of gross income from sources within the treaty partner within each grouping.

(B) The rules of this paragraph (e)(12)(iii) are applicable for charitable contributions made on or after the date of publication of this document as a final regulation in the Federal Register.

(e)(12)(iv)(A) [The text of the proposed addition of § 1.861-8(e)(12)(iv)(A) is the same as § 1.861-8T(e)(12)(iv)(A) as added by T.D. 9143.]

(e)(12)(iv)(B) [Reserved.]

[Prop. Reg. § 1.861-8.]

[Proposed 7-28-2004.]

§ 1.861-8T. Computation of taxable income from sources within the United States and from other sources and activities (Temporary).—(a) *In general.*

(1) [Reserved]

(2) *Allocation and apportionment of deductions in general.*—If an affiliated group of corporations joins in filing a consolidated return under section 1501, the provisions of this section are to be applied separately to each member in that affiliated group for purposes of determining such member's taxable income, except to the extent that expenses, losses, and other deductions are allocated and apportioned as if all domestic members of an affiliated group were a single corporation under section 864(e) and the regulations thereunder. See § 1.861-9T through § 1.861-11T for rules regarding the affiliated group allocation and apportionment of interest expense, and § 1.861-14T for rules regarding the affiliated group allocation and apportionment of expenses other than interest.

(3) through (5) [Reserved]

(b) *Allocation.*

(1) and (2) [Reserved]

(3) *Supportive functions.*—Deductions which are supportive in nature (such as overhead, general and administrative, and supervisory expenses) may relate to other deductions which can more readily be allocated to gross income. In such instance, such supportive deductions may be allocated and apportioned along with the deductions to which they relate. On the other hand, it would be equally acceptable to attribute supportive deductions on some reasonable basis directly to activities or property which generate, have generated, or could be reasonably expected to generate gross income. This would ordinarily be accomplished by allocating the supportive expenses to all gross income or to another broad class of gross income and apportioning the expenses in accordance with paragraph (c)(1) of this section. For this purpose, reasonable departmental overhead rates may be utilized. For examples of the application of the principles of this paragraph (b)(3) other than to expenses attributable to stewardship activities, see examples (19) through (21) of paragraph (g) of this section. See paragraph (e)(4) of this section for the allocation and apportionment of deductions attributable to stewardship activities. However, supportive deductions that are described in § 1.861-14T(e)(3) shall be allocated and apportioned in accordance with the rules of § 1.861-14T and shall not be allocated and apportioned by reference only to the gross income of a single member of an affiliated group of corporations as defined in § 1.861-14T(d).

(4) and (5) [Reserved]

(c) *Apportionment of deductions.*—(1) *Deductions definitely related to a class of gross income.*—Where a deduction has been allocated in accordance with paragraph (b) of this section to a class of gross income which is included in one statutory grouping and the residual grouping, the deduction must be apportioned between the statutory grouping and the residual grouping. Where a deduction has been allocated to a class of gross income which is included in more than one statutory grouping, such deduction must be apportioned among the statutory groupings and, where necessary, the residual grouping. Thus, in determining the separate limitations on the foreign tax credit imposed by section 904(d)(1) or by section 907, the income within a separate limitation category constitutes a statutory grouping of income and all other income not within that separate limitation category (whether domestic or within a different separate limitation category) constitutes the residual grouping. In this regard, the same method of apportionment must be used in apportioning a deduction to each separate limitation category. Also, see paragraph (f)(1)(iii) of this section with respect to the apportionment of deductions among the statutory groupings designated in section 904(d)(1). If the class of gross income to which a deduction has been allocated consists entirely of a single statutory grouping or the residual grouping, there is no need to apportion that deduction. If a deduction is not definitely related to any gross income, it must be apportioned ratably as provided in paragraph (c)(3) of this section. A deduction is apportioned by attributing the deduction to gross income (within the class to which the deduction has been allocated) which is in one or more statutory groupings and to gross income (within the class) which is in the residual grouping. Such attribution must be accomplished in a manner which reflects to a reasonably close extent the factual relationship between the deduction and the grouping of gross income. In apportioning deductions, it may be that for the taxable year there is no gross income in the statutory grouping or that deductions will exceed the amount of gross income in the statutory grouping. See paragraph (d)(1) of this section with respect to cases in which deductions exceed gross income. In determining the method of apportionment for a specific deduction, examples of bases and factors which should be considered include, but are not limited to—

    (i) Comparison of units sold,

    (ii) Comparison of the amount of gross sales or receipts,

    (iii) Comparison of costs of goods sold,

    (iv) Comparison of profit contribution,

    (v) Comparison of expenses incurred, assets used, salaries paid, space utilized, and time spent which are attributable to the activities or properties giving rise to the class of gross income, and

    (vi) Comparison of the amount of gross income.

Paragraph (e)(2) through (8) of this section provides the applicable rules for allocation and apportionment of deductions for interest, research and development expenses, and certain other deductions. The effects on tax liability of the apportionment of deductions and the burden of maintaining records not otherwise maintained and making computations not otherwise made shall be taken into consideration in determining whether a method of apportionment and its application are sufficiently precise. A method of apportionment described in this paragraph (c)(1) may not be used when it does not reflect, to a reasonably close extent, the factual relationship between the deduction and the groupings of income. Furthermore, certain methods of apportionment described in this paragraph (c)(1) may not be used in connection with any deduction for which another method is prescribed. The principles set forth above are applicable in apportioning both deductions definitely related to a class which constitutes less than all of the taxpayer's gross income and to deductions related to all of the taxpayer's gross income. If a deduction is not related to any class of gross income, it must be apportioned ratably as provided in paragraph (c)(3) of this section.

    (2) *Apportionment based on assets.*—Certain taxpayers are required by paragraph (e)(2) of this section and § 1.861-9T to apportion interest expense on the basis of assets. A taxpayer may apportion other deductions based on the comparative value of assets that generate income within each grouping, provided that such method reflects the factual relationship between the deduction and the groupings of income and is applied in accordance with the rules of § 1.861-9T(g). In general, such apportionments must be made either on the basis of the tax book value of those assets or on their fair market value. However, once the taxpayer uses fair market value, the taxpayer and all related persons must continue to use such method unless expressly authorized by the Commissioner to change methods. For purposes of this paragraph (c)(2) the term "related persons" means two or more persons in a relationship described in section 267(b). In determining whether two or more corporations are members of same controlled group under section 267(b)(3), a person is considered to own stock owned directly by such person, stock owned with the application of section 1563(e)(1), and stock owned by the application of section 267(c). In determining whether a corporation is related to a partnership under section 267(b)(10), a person is considered to own the partnership interest owned directly by such person and the partnership interest owned with the application of section 267(e)(3). In the case of any corporate taxpayer that—

Reg. § 1.861-8T(c)(2)

(i) Uses tax book value, and

(ii) Owns directly or indirectly (within the meaning of § 1.861-11T(b)(2)(ii)) 10 percent or more of the total combined voting power of all classes of stock entitled to vote in any other corporation (domestic or foreign) that is not a member of the affiliated group (as defined in section 864(e)(5)), such taxpayer shall adjust its basis in that stock in the manner described in § 1.861-11T(b).

(3) [Reserved]

(d) *Excess of deductions and excluded and eliminated items of income.*

(1) [Reserved]

(2) *Allocation and apportionment to exempt, excluded or eliminated income.*—(i) *In general.*—In the case of taxable years beginning after December 31, 1986, except to the extent otherwise permitted by § 1.861-13T, the following rules shall apply to take account of income that is exempt or excluded, or assets generating such income, with respect to allocation and apportionment of deductions.

(A) *Allocation of deductions.*—In allocating deductions that are definitely related to one or more classes of gross income, exempt income (as defined in paragraph (d)(2)(ii) of this section) shall be taken into account.

(B) *Apportionment of deductions.*—In apportioning deductions that are definitely related either to a class of gross income consisting of multiple groupings of income (whether statutory or residual) or to all gross income, exempt income and exempt assets (as defined in paragraph (d)(2)(ii) of this section) shall not be taken into account.

For purposes of apportioning deductions which are not taken into account under § 1.1502-13 in determining gain or loss from intercompany transactions, as defined in § 1.1502-13, income from such transactions shall be taken into account in the year such income is ultimately included in gross income.

(ii) *Exempt income and exempt assets defined.*—(A) *In general.*—For purposes of this section, the term "exempt income" means any income that is, in whole or in part, exempt, excluded, or eliminated for federal income tax purposes. The term "exempt asset" means any asset the income from which is, in whole or in part, exempt, excluded, or eliminated for federal tax purposes.

(B) *Certain stock and dividends.*—The term "exempt income" includes the portion of the dividends that are deductible under—

(1) Section 243(a)(1) or (2) (relating to the dividends received deduction),

(2) Section 245(a) (relating to the dividends received deduction for dividends from certain foreign corporations).

Thus, for purposes of apportioning deductions using a gross income method, gross income would not include a dividend to the extent that it gives rise to a dividends received deduction under either section 243(a)(1), section 243(a)(2), or section 245(a). In the case of a life insurance company taxable under section 801, the amount of such stock that is treated as tax exempt shall not be reduced because a portion of the dividends received deduction is disallowed as attributable to the policyholder's share of such dividends. See § 1.861-14T(h) for a special rule concerning the allocation of reserve expenses of a life insurance company. In addition, for purposes of apportioning deductions using an asset method, assets would not include that portion of stock equal to the portion of dividends paid thereon that would be deductible under either section 243(a)(1), section 243(a)(2), or section 245(a). In the case of stock which generates, has generated, or can reasonably be expected to generate qualifying dividends deductible under section 243(a)(3), such stock shall not constitute a tax exempt asset. Such stock and the dividends thereon will, however, be eliminated from consideration in the apportionment of interest expense under the consolidation rule set forth in § 1.861-10T(c), and in the apportionment of other expenses under the consolidation rules set forth in § 1.861-14T.

(iii) *Income that is not considered tax exempt.*—The following items are not considered to be exempt, eliminated, or excluded income and, thus, may have expenses, losses, or other deductions allocated and apportioned to them:

(A) In the case of a foreign taxpayer (including a foreign sales corporation (FSC)) computing its effectively connected income, gross income (whether domestic or foreign source) which is not effectively connected to the conduct of a United States trade or business;

(B) In computing the combined taxable income of a DISC or FSC and its related supplier, the gross income of a DISC or a FSC;

(C) For all purposes under subchapter N of the Code, including the computation of combined taxable income of a possessions corporation and its affiliates under section 936(h), the gross income of a possessions corporation for which a credit is allowed under section 936(a); and

(D) Foreign earned income as defined in section 911 and the regulations thereunder (however, the rules of § 1.911-6 do not require the allocation and apportionment of certain deductions, including home mortgage

Reg. § 1.861-8T(c)(2)(i)

interest, to foreign earned income for purposes of determining the deductions disallowed under section 911(d)(6)).

(iv) *Prior years.*—For expense allocation and apportionment rules applicable to taxable years beginning before January 1, 1987, and for later years to the extent permitted by § 1.861-13T, see § 1.861-8(d)(2) (Revised as of April 1, 1986).

(e) *Allocation and apportionment of certain deductions.*

(1) [Reserved].—For further guidance, see § 1.861-8(e)(1).

(2) *Interest.*—The rules concerning the allocation and apportionment of interest expense and certain interest equivalents are set forth in §§ 1.861-9T through 1.861-13T.

(3) through (11) [Reserved]. For further guidance, see § 1.861-8(e)(3) through (e)(11).

(12) *Deductions for certain charitable contributions.*—(i) *In general.*—The deduction for charitable contributions that is allowed under sections 170, 873(b)(2), and 882(c)(1)(B) is definitely related and allocable to all of the taxpayer's gross income. The deduction allocated under this paragraph (e)(12)(i) shall be apportioned between the statutory grouping (or among the statutory groupings) of gross income and the residual grouping on the basis of the relative amounts of gross income from sources in the United States in each grouping.

(ii) *Coordination with § 1.861-14T.*—A deduction for a charitable contribution by a member of an affiliated group shall be allocated and apportioned under the rules of this section and § 1.861-14T(c)(1).

(iii) *Treaty provisions.*—[Reserved]

(iv) *Effective date.*—(A) The rules of paragraphs (e)(12)(i) and (ii) shall apply to charitable contributions made on or after July 28, 2004. Taxpayers may apply the provisions of paragraphs (e)(12)(i) and (ii) to charitable contributions made before July 28, 2004 but during the taxable year ending on or after July 28, 2004.

(B) The applicability of this section expires on or before July 27, 2007.

(f) *Miscellaneous matters.*—(1) *Operative sections.*

(1) through (1)(ii) [Reserved]

(ii) *Separate limitations to the foreign tax credit.*—Section 904(d)(1) requires that the foreign tax credit limitation be determined separately in the case of the types of income specified therein. Accordingly, the income within each separate limitation category constitutes a statutory grouping of income and all other income not within that separate limitation category (whether domestic or within a different separate limitation category) constitutes the residual grouping.

(f)(1)(iv) through (5) [Reserved]

(g) *General examples.*

Examples (1) through (23). [Reserved]

Example (24)—Exempt, excluded, or eliminated income—(i) *Income method*—(A) *Facts.* X, a domestic corporation organized on January 1, 1987, is engaged in a number of businesses worldwide. X owns a 25-percent voting interest in each of five corporations engaged in the business A, two of which are domestic and three of which are foreign. X incurs stewardship expenses in connection with these five stock investments in the amount of $100. X apportions its stewardship expenses using a gross income method. Each of the five companies pays a dividend in the amount of $100. X is entitled to claim the 80-percent dividends received deduction on dividends paid by the two domestic companies. Because tax exempt income is considered in the allocation of deductions, X's $100 stewardship expense is allocated to the class of income consisting of dividends from business A companies. However, because tax exempt income is not considered in the apportionment of deductions within a class of gross income, the gross income of the two domestic companies must be reduced to reflect the availability of the dividends received deduction. Thus, for purposes of apportionment, the gross income paid by the three foreign companies is considered to be $100 each, while the gross income paid by the domestic companies is considered to be $20 each. Accordingly, X has total gross income from business A companies, for purposes of apportionment, of $340. As a result, $29.41 of X's stewardship expense is apportioned to each of the foreign companies and $5.88 of X's stewardship expense is apportioned to each of the domestic companies.

(ii) *Asset method*—(A) *Facts.* X, a domestic corporation organized on January 1, 1987, carries on a trade or business in the United States. X has deductible interest expense incurred in 1987 of $60,000. X owns all the stock of Y, a foreign corporation. X also owns 49 percent of the voting stock of Z, a domestic corporation. Neither Y nor Z has retained earnings and profits at the end of 1987. X apportions its interest expense on the basis of the fair market value of its assets. X has assets worth $1,500,000 that generate domestic source income, among which are tax exempt municipal bonds worth $100,000, and the stock of Z, which has a value of $500,000. The Y stock owned by X has a fair market value of

$2,000,000 and generates solely foreign source general limitation income.

(B) *Allocation.* No portion of X's interest expense is directly allocable solely to identified property within the meaning of § 1.861-10T. Thus, X's deduction for interest is definitely related to all its gross income as a class.

(C) *Apportionment.* For purposes of apportioning expenses, assets that generate exempt, eliminated, or excluded income are not taken into account. Because X's municipal bonds are tax exempt, they are not taken into account in apportioning interest expense. Since X is entitled to claim under section 243 the 80-percent dividends received deduction with respect to the dividend it received from Z, 80 percent of the value of that stock is not taken into account as an asset for purposes of apportionment under the asset method. X apportions its interest deduction between the statutory grouping of foreign source general limitation income and the residual grouping of domestic source income as follows:

To foreign source general limitation income:

$$\text{Interest expense} \times \frac{\text{General limitation assets that are not tax exempt}}{\text{Worldwide assets that are not tax exempt}}$$

$$\$60,000 \times \frac{\$2,000,000}{(\$100,000 + \$900,000 + \$2,000,000)} = \$40,000$$

$$\frac{\text{nonexempt foreign assets}}{\text{20 percent of Z stock value} + \text{nonexempt domestic assets} + \text{nonexempt foreign assets}}$$

To domestic source income:

$$\text{Interest expense} \times \frac{\text{Domestic assets that are not tax exempt}}{\text{Worldwide assets that are not tax exempt}}$$

$$\$60,000 \times \frac{\$100,000 + \$900,000}{(\$100,000 + \$900,000 + \$2,000,000)} = \$20,000$$

$$\frac{\text{20 percent of Z stock value} + \text{nonexempt domestic assets}}{\text{20 percent of Z stock value} + \text{nonexempt domestic assets} + \text{nonexempt foreign assets}}$$

(h) *Effective dates.*—In general, the rules of this section, as well as the rules of §§ 1.861-9T, 1.861-10T, 1.861-11T, 1.861-12T, and 1.861-14T shall apply for taxable years beginning after December 31, 1986. However, see paragraph (e)(12)(iv) of this section and § 1.861-14T(e)(6)(ii) for rules concerning the allocation and apportionment of deductions for charitable contributions. In the case of corporate taxpayers, transition rules set forth in § 1.861-13T provide for the gradual phase-in of certain [of] the provisions of this and the foregoing sections. However, the following rules are effective for taxable years commencing after December 31, 1988:

(1) Section 1.861-9T(b)(2) (concerning the treatment of certain foreign currency borrowings),

(2) Section 1.861-9T(d)(2) (concerning the treatment of interest incurred by nonresident aliens),

(3) Section 1.861-10T(b)(3)(ii) (providing an operating costs test for purposes of the nonrecourse indebtedness exception), and

(4) Section 1.861-10T(b)(6) (concerning excess collateralization of nonrecourse borrowings).

In addition, 1.861-10T(e) (concerning the treatment of related controlled foreign corporation indebtedness) is effective for taxable years commencing after December 31, 1987. For rules for taxable years beginning before January 1, 1987, and for later years to the extent permitted by § 1.861-13T, see § 1.861-8 (Revised as of April 1, 1986). [Temporary Reg. § 1.861-8T.]

☐ [T.D. 8228, 9-9-88. Amended by T.D. 8236, 12-7-88; T.D. 8286, 1-29-90; T.D. 8337, 3-11-91; T.D. 8597, 7-12-95; T.D. 8805, 1-8-99; T.D. 8973, 12-27-2001 and T.D. 9143, 7-27-2004.]

§ 1.861-9. Allocation and apportionment of interest expense.—(a) through (g)(1)(i) [Reserved]. For further guidance, see § 1.861-9T(a) through (g)(1)(i).

(g)(1)(ii) [Reserved]. For further guidance, see the second sentence in § 1.861-9T(g)(1)(ii).

(g)(1)(iii) through (h)(4) [Reserved]. For further guidance, see § 1.861-9T(g)(1)(iii) through (h)(4).

(h)(5) *Characterizing stock in related persons.*—(i) *General rule.*—Stock in a related person held by the taxpayer or by another related person shall be characterized on the basis of the fair market value of the taxpayer's pro rata share of assets held by the related person attributed to each statutory grouping and the residual grouping under the stock characterization rules of § 1.861-12T(c)(3)(ii), except that the portion of the value of intangible assets of the taxpayer and related persons that is apportioned to the related person under § 1.861-9T(h)(2) shall be characterized on the basis of the net income before interest expense of the related person within each statutory grouping or residual grouping (excluding income that is passive under § 1.904-4(b)).

(ii) *Special rule for section 936 corporations regarding alternative minimum tax.*—For purposes of characterizing stock in a related section 936 corporation in determining foreign source alternative minimum taxable income within each separate category and the alternative minimum tax foreign tax credit pursuant to section 59(a), the rules of § 1.861-9T(g)(3) shall apply and § 1.861-9(h)(5)(i) shall not apply. Thus, for taxable years beginning after December 31, 1989, and before January 1, 1994, stock in a related section 936 corporation is characterized for alternative minimum tax purposes as a foreign source passive asset because the stock produces foreign source passive dividend income under sections 861(a)(2)(A), 862(a)(2), and 904(d)(2)(A) and the regulations under those sections. For taxable years beginning after December 31, 1993, stock in a related section 936 corporation would be characterized for alternative minimum tax purposes as an asset subject to the separate limitation for section 936 corporation dividends because the stock produces foreign source dividend income that, for alternative minimum tax purposes, is subject to a separate foreign tax credit limitation under section 56(g)(4)(C)(iii)(IV). However, stock in a section 936 corporation is characterized as a U.S. source asset to the extent required by section 904(g). For the definition of the term *section 936 corporation* see § 1.861-11(d)(2)(ii).

(iii) *Effective date.*—This paragraph (h)(5) applies to taxable years beginning after December 31, 1989.

(h)(6) through (j) [Reserved]. For further guidance, see § 1.861-9T(h)(6) through (j). [Reg. § 1.861-9.]

☐ [T.D. 8916, 12-29-2000. Amended by T.D. 9120, 3-25-2004.]

§ 1.861-9T. Allocation and apportionment of interest expense (temporary).—(a) *In general.*—Any expense that is deductible under section 163 (including original issue discount) constitutes interest expense for purposes of this section, as well as for purposes of §§ 1.861-10T, 1.861-11T, 1.861-12T, and 1.861-13T. The term interest refers to the gross amount of interest expense incurred by a taxpayer in a given tax year. The method of allocation and apportionment for interest set forth in this section is based on the approach that, in general, money is fungible and that interest expense is attributable to all activities and property regardless of any specific purpose for incurring an obligation on which interest is paid. Exceptions to the fungibility rule are set forth in § 1.861-10T. The fungibility approach recognizes that all activities and property require funds and that management has a great deal of flexibility as to the source and use of funds. When borrowing will generally free other funds for other purposes, and it is reasonable under this approach to attribute part of the cost of borrowing to such other purposes. Consistent with the principles of fungibility, except as otherwise provided, the aggregate of deductions for interest in all cases shall be considered related to all income producing activities and assets of the taxpayer and, thus, allocable to all the gross income which the assets of the taxpayer generate, have generated, or could reasonably have been expected to generate. In the case of the interest expense of members of an affiliated group, interest expense shall be considered to be allocable to all the gross income of the members of the group under § 1.861-11T.

That section requires the members of an affiliated group to allocate and apportion the interest expense of each member of the group as if all members of such group were a single corporation. For the method of determining the interest deduction allowed to foreign corporations under section 882(c), see § 1.882-5.

(b) *Interest equivalents.*—(1) *Certain expenses and losses.*—(i) *General rule.*—Any expense or loss (to the extent deductible) incurred in a transaction or series of integrated or related transactions in which the taxpayer secures the use of funds for a period of time shall be subject to allocation and apportionment under the rules of this section if such expense or loss is substantially incurred in consideration of the time value of money. However, the allocation and apportionment of a loss under this paragraph (b) shall not affect the characterization of such loss as capital or ordinary for other purposes of the Code and the regulations thereunder.

(ii) *Examples.*—The rule of this paragraph (b)(1) may be illustrated by the following example.

Example (1). W, a domestic corporation, borrows from X two ounces of gold at a time when the spot price for gold is $500 per ounce. W agrees to return the two ounces of gold in six months. W sells the two ounces of gold to Y for $1000. W then enters into a contract with Z to purchase two ounces of gold six months in the future for $1,050. In exchange for the use of $1,000 in cash, W has sustained a loss of $50 on related transactions. This loss is subject to allocation and apportionment under the rules of this section in the same manner as interest expense.

Example (2). X, a domestic corporation with a dollar functional currency, borrows 100 pounds on January 1, 1987 for a three-year term at an interest rate greater than the applicable federal rate for dollar loans. At this time, the interest rate on the pound was approximately equal to the interest rate on dollar borrowings and the forward price on the pound, vis-a-vis the dollar, was approximately equal to the spot price. On January 1, 1987, X converted 100 pounds into dollars and entered into a currency swap that substantially hedged X's foreign currency exposure on the pound borrowing, both with respect to interest and principal. The borrowing, coupled with the swap, represents a series of related transactions in which the taxpayer secures the use of funds in its functional currency. Any net foreign currency loss on this series of transactions constitutes a loss incurred substantially in consideration of the time value of money and shall be apportioned in the same manner as interest expense. Thus, if the pound depreciates against the dollar, such that when the first payment on the pound borrowing is due the taxpayer has a currency loss on the swap payment hedging its first interest payment, such loss shall, even if the transaction is not integrated under section 988(d), be allocated and apportioned in the same manner as interest expense under the authority of this paragraph (b)(1).

Example (3). On January 1, 1987, X, a domestic corporation with a dollar functional currency, enters into a dollar interest rate swap contract with Y, a domestic counterparty. Under the terms of this agreement, X agrees to pay Y floating rate interest with respect to a notional principal amount of $100 for five years. In return, Y agrees to pay X fixed rate interest at 10 percent with respect to a notional principal amount of $100 for five years. On the same day, Y prepays the fixed leg of the swap by making a lump sum payment of $37 to X. This lump sum payment represents the present value of five $10 swap payments. Because X secures the use of $37 in this transaction, any net swap expense arising from the transaction represents an expense incurred substantially in consideration of the time value of money. Assuming this lump sum payment is not otherwise characterized as a loan from Y to X, and that X must amortize the $37 lump sum payment under the principles of Notice 89-21, any net swap expense incurred by X with respect to this transaction (*i.e.,* the excess, if any, of X's annual swap payment to Y over the annual amortization of the $37 lump sum payment that is taken into income by X) represents an expense equivalent to interest expense. The result would be the same if X sold the fixed leg to a third party for $37. While this example presents the case of a lump sum payment, the rules of paragraph (b)(1) would also apply to any transaction in which the swap payments are not substantially contemporaneous if the pricing of the transaction is materially affected by the time value of money. Thus, expenses and losses will be subject to apportionment under the rules of this section to the extent that such expenses or losses were incurred in consideration of the time value of money.

(2) *Certain foreign currency borrowings.*—(i) *Rule.*—If a taxpayer borrows in a nonfunctional currency at a rate of interest that is less than the applicable federal rate (or its equivalent in functional currency if the functional currency is not the dollar), any swap, forward, future, option, or similar financial arrangement (or any combination thereof) entered into by the taxpayer or by a related person (as defined in § 1.861-8T(c)(2)) that exists during the term of the borrowing and that

substantially diminishes currency risk with respect to the borrowing or interest expense thereon will be presumed to constitute a hedge of such borrowing, unless the taxpayer can demonstrate on the basis of facts and circumstances that the two transactions are in fact unrelated. Under this presumption, the currency loss incurred on the borrowing during taxable years beginning after December 31, 1988, in connection with hedged nonfunctional currency borrowings, reduced or increased by the gain or loss on the hedge, will be apportioned in the same manner as interest expense. This presumption can be rebutted by a showing that the financial arrangement was entered into in connection with hedging currency exposure arising in the ordinary course of a trade or business (other than with respect to the borrowing).

(ii) *Examples.*—The principles of this paragraph (b)(2) may be illustrated by the following examples.

Example (1). Taxpayer has a dollar functional currency and does not have any qualified business units with a functional currency other than the dollar. On January 1, 1989, when the unit of foreign currency is worth $1, taxpayer borrows 100 units of foreign currency for a three-year period bearing interest at the annual rate of 3 percent and immediately converts the proceeds of the borrowing into dollars for use in its business. In the ordinary course of its business, taxpayer has no foreign currency exposure in this currency. In March 1989, taxpayer enters into a three-year swap agreement that covers most, but not all, of the payment of interest and principal. Because the swap substantially diminishes currency risk with respect to the borrowing, it is presumed to hedge the loan. Since taxpayer cannot demonstrate that it was hedging currency exposure arising in the ordinary course of its business (other than currency exposure with respect to the borrowing), the net currency loss on the borrowing adjusted for any gain or loss on the swap must be apportioned in the same manner as interest expense.

Example (2). Assume the same facts as in Example 1, except that the taxpayer borrows in two separate foreign currencies on terms described in Example 1 and enters into a swap agreement in a single currency that substantially diminishes the taxpayer's aggregate foreign currency risk. The net currency loss on the borrowings adjusted for any gain or loss on the swap must be apportioned in the same manner as interest expense.

(3) *Losses on sale of certain receivables.*—
(i) *General rule.*—Any loss on the sale of a trade receivable (as defined in § 1.954-2(h)) shall be allocated and apportioned, solely for purposes of this section and §§ 1.861-10T, 1.861-11T, 1.861-12T, and 1.861-13T, in the same manner as interest expense, unless at the time of sale of the receivable, it bears interest at a rate which is at least 120 percent of the short term applicable federal rate (as determined under section 1274(d) of the Code), or its equivalent in foreign currency in the case of receivables denominated in foreign currency, determined at the time the receivable arises. This treatment shall not affect the characterization of such expense as interest for other purposes of the Internal Revenue Code.

(ii) *Exceptions.*—To the extent that a loss on the sale of a trade receivable exceeds the discount on the receivable that would be computed applying to the amount received on the sale of the receivable 120 percent of the applicable federal rate (or its equivalent in foreign currency in the case of receivables denominated in foreign currency) for the period commencing with the date on which the receivable is sold and ending with the earlier of the date on which the receivable begins to bear interest at such rate or the anticipated payment date of the receivable, such excess shall not be allocated and apportioned in the same manner as interest expense but rather shall be allocated and apportioned to the gross income generated by the receivable. In cases of transfers of receivables to a domestic international sales corporation described in § 1.994-1(c)(6)(v), the rule of this paragraph (b)(3) shall not apply for purposes of computing combined taxable income. In computing the combined taxable income of a foreign sales corporation and its related supplier, loss on the sale of receivables to a third party incurred either by the foreign sales corporation or its related supplier shall offset combined taxable income, notwithstanding the provisions of this paragraph (b)(3). See § 1.924(a)-1T(g)(7).

Example. On October 1, X sells a widget to Y for $100 payable in 30 days, after which the receivable will bear stated interest at 13 percent. On October 4, X sells Y's obligation to Z for $98. Assume that the applicable federal rate for the month of October is 10 percent. Applying 120 percent of the applicable federal rate to the $98 received on the sale of the receivable, the obligation is discounted at a 12 percent rate for a period of 27 days. At this discount rate, the obligation would have sold for $99.22. Thus, 88 cents of the $2 loss on the sale is apportioned in the same manner as interest expense, and $1.22 of the $2 loss on the sale is directly allocated to the income generated on the widget sale.

(4) *Rent in certain leasing transactions.*—[Reserved.]

Reg. § 1.861-9T(b)(4)

(5) *Treatment of bond premium.*—(i) *Treatment by the issuer.*—If a bond or other debt obligation is issued at a premium, an amount of interest expense incurred by the issuer on that bond or other debt obligation equal to the amortized portion of that premium that is included in gross income for the year shall be allocated and apportioned solely to the amortized portion of premium derived by the issuer for the year.

(ii) *Treatment by the holder.*—If a bond or debt obligation is purchased at a premium, the portion of that premium amortized during the year by the holder under section 171 and the regulations thereunder shall be allocated and apportioned solely to interest income derived from the bond by the holder for the year.

(6) *Financial products that alter effective cost of borrowing.*—(i) *In general.*—Various derivative financial products can be part of transactions or series of transactions described in paragraph (b)(1) of this section. Such derivative financial products, including interest rate swaps, options, forwards, caps, and collars, potentially alter a taxpayer's effective cost of borrowing with respect to an actual liability of the taxpayer. For example, a taxpayer that is obligated to pay interest at a fixed rate may, in effect, pay interest at a floating rate by entering into an interest rate swap. Similarly, a taxpayer that is obligated to pay interest at a floating rate may, in effect, limit its exposure to rising interest rates by purchasing a cap. Such a taxpayer may have gains or losses associated with such derivative financial products. This paragraph (b)(6) provides rules for the treatment of gains and losses from such derivative financial products ("financial products") that are part of transactions described in paragraph (b)(1) of this section and that are used by the taxpayer to alter its effective cost of borrowing with respect to an actual liability. This paragraph (b)(6) shall only apply where the hedge and the borrowing are in the same currency and shall not apply to the extent otherwise provided in section 988 and the regulations thereunder. The allocation and apportionment of a loss under this paragraph (b) shall not affect the characterization of such loss as capital or ordinary for other purposes of the Code and the regulations thereunder.

(ii) *Definition of gain and loss.*—For purposes of this paragraph (b)(6), the term "gain" refers to the excess of the amounts properly taken into income under a financial product that alters the effective cost of borrowing over the amounts properly allowed as a deduction thereunder within a given taxable year. *See, e.g.,* Notice 89-21. The term "loss" refers to the excess of the amounts properly allowed as a deduction under such a financial product over the amounts properly taken into income thereunder within a given taxable year.

(iii) *Treatment of gain or loss on the disposition of a financial product.*—[Reserved.]

(iv) *Entities that are not financial services entities.*—An entity that does not constitute a financial services entity within the meaning of § 1.904-4(e)(3) shall treat gains and losses on financial products described in paragraph (b)(6)(i) of this section as follows.

(A) *Losses.*—Losses on any financial product described in paragraph (b)(6)(i) of this section shall be apportioned in the same manner as interest expense whether or not such financial product is identified by the taxpayer under paragraph (b)(6)(iv)(C) of this section as a liability hedge.

(B) *Gains.*—Gains on any financial product described in paragraph (b)(6)(i) of this section shall reduce the taxpayer's total interest expense that is subject to apportionment, but only if such financial product is identified by the taxpayer under paragraph (b)(6)(iv)(C) of this section as a liability hedge. Such reduction is accomplished by directly allocating interest expense to the income derived from such a financial product.

(C) *Identification of financial products.*—A taxpayer can identify a financial product described in paragraph (b)(6)(i) of this section as hedging a particular interest-bearing liability (or any group of such liabilities) by clearly identifying on its books and records on the same day that it becomes a party to such arrangement that such arrangement hedges a given liability (or group of liabilities). In the case of a partial hedge, such identification shall apply to only that part of the liability that is hedged. If the taxpayer clearly identifies on its books and records a financial product as a hedge of an interest-bearing asset (or any group of such assets), it will create a rebuttable presumption that such financial product is not described in paragraph (b)(6)(i) of this section. A taxpayer may identify a hedge as relating to an anticipated liability, provided that such liability is in fact incurred within 120 days following the date of such identification. Gains and losses on such anticipatory arrangement accruing prior to the time at which the liability is incurred shall constitute an adjustment to interest expense.

(v) *Financial services entities.*—[Reserved.]

(vi) *Dealers.*—The rule of paragraph (b)(6)(iv) of this section shall not apply to a person acting in its capacity as a regular dealer in the financial products described in paragraph (b)(6)(i) of this section. Instead, losses sustained by a regular dealer in connection with such financial products shall be allocated to the class of gross income from such arrangements. Gains of a regular dealer in notional principal contracts are governed by the rules of § 1.863-7T(b). Amounts received or accrued by any person from any financial product that is integrated as specified in Notice 89-90 with an asset shall not be treated as amounts received or accrued by a person acting in its capacity as a regular dealer in financial products.

(vii) *Examples.*—The principles of this paragraph (b)(6) may be illustrated by the following examples.

Example (1). X is not a financial services entity or regular dealer in the financial products described in paragraph (b)(6)(i) of this section and has a dollar functional currency. In 1990, X incurred a total of $200 of interest expense. On January 1, 1990, X entered into an interest rate swap agreement with Y, in order to hedge its interest rate exposure with respect to a pre-existing floating rate liability. On the same day, X properly identified the agreement as a hedge of such liability. Under the agreement, X is required to pay Y an amount equal to a fixed rate of 10 percent on a notional principal amount of $1,000. Y is required to pay X an amount equal to a floating rate of interest on the same notional principal amount. Under the agreement, X received from Y during 1990 a net payment of $25. Because X identified the swap agreement as a liability hedge under the rules of paragraph (b)(6)(iv)(C), X may effectively reduce its total allocable interest expense for 1990 to $175 by directly allocating $25 of interest expense to the swap income. Had X not properly identified the swap as a liability hedge, this swap payment would have been treated as domestic source income in accordance with the rule of § 1.863-7T(b).

Example (2). Assume the same facts as Example (1), except that X did not properly identify the agreement as a liability hedge on January 1, 1990. In 1990, X made a net payment of $25 to Y under the swap agreement. This swap payment is allocated and apportioned in the same manner as interest expense under the rules of paragraph (b)(6)(iv)(A).

(viii) *Effective dates.*—(A) *Losses.*—The rules of this paragraph (b)(6) shall apply to losses on any transaction described in paragraph (b)(6)(i) of this section that was entered into after September 14, 1988.

(B) *Gains.*—Except as provided in paragraph (b)(6)(viii)(C) of this section, the rules of this paragraph (b)(6) shall apply to any gain that was realized on any transaction described in paragraph (b)(6)(i) of this section that was entered into after August 11, 1989.

(C) *Exception for interim gains.*—Taxpayers shall be permitted to apply the rules of this paragraph (b)(6) to any gain that was realized on any transaction described in paragraph (b)(6)(i) of this section that was entered into after September 14, 1988 and on or before August 11, 1989 if the taxpayer can demonstrate to the satisfaction of the Commissioner that substantially all of the arrangements described in paragraph (b)(6)(i) of this section to which the taxpayer became a party during that interim period were identified on the taxpayer's books and records with the liabilities of the taxpayer in a substantially contemporaneous manner and that all losses and expenses that are subject to the rules of this paragraph (b)(6) were treated in the same manner as interest expense. For this purpose, arrangements that were identified in a substantially contemporaneous manner with the taxpayer's assets shall be ignored.

(7) *Foreign currency gain or loss.*—In addition to the rules of paragraph (b)(1), (b)(2), and (b)(6) of this section, any foreign currency loss that is treated as an adjustment to interest expense under regulations issued under section 988 shall be allocated and apportioned in the same manner as interest expense. Any foreign currency gain that is treated as an adjustment to interest expense under regulations issued under section 988 shall offset apportionable interest expense.

(c) *Allowable deductions.*—In order for an interest expense to be allocated and apportioned, it must first be determined that the interest expense is currently deductible. A number of provisions in the Code disallow or suspend deductions of interest expense or require the capitalization thereof.

(1) *Disallowed deductions.*—A taxpayer does not allocate and apportion interest expense under this section that is permanently disallowed as a deduction by operation of section 163(h), section 265, or any other provision or rule that permanently disallows the deduction of interest expense.

(2) *Section 263A.*—Section 263A requires the capitalization of interest expense that is allocable to designated types of property. Any interest expense that is capitalized under section 263A does not constitute deductible interest expense for purposes of this section. Furthermore, interest expense capitalized in inventory or depreciable property is not separately allocated and apportioned when the inventory is sold or depreciation is allowed.

Capitalized interest expense is effectively allocated and apportioned as part of, and in the same manner as, the cost of goods sold, amortization, or depreciation deduction.

(3) *Section 163(d).*—Section 163(d) suspends the deduction for interest expense to the extent that it exceeds net investment income. In the year that suspended investment interest expense becomes allowable under the rules of section 163(d), that interest expense is apportioned under rules set forth in paragraph (d)(1) of this section as though it were incurred in the taxable year in which the expense is deducted.

(4) *Section 469.*—(i) *General rule.*—Section 469 suspends the deduction of passive activity losses to the extent that they exceed passive activity income for the year. Passive activity losses may consist in part of interest expense properly allocable to passive activity. In the year that suspended interest expense becomes allowable as a deduction under the rules of section 469, that interest expense is apportioned under rules set forth in paragraph (d)(1) of this section as though it were incurred in the taxable year in which the expense is deducted.

(ii) *Identification of the interest component of a suspended passive loss.*—A suspended passive loss may consist of a variety of items of expense other than interest expense. Suspended interest expense for any taxable year is computed by multiplying the total suspended passive loss for the year by a fraction, the numerator of which is passive interest expense for the year (determined under regulations issued under section 163) and the denominator of which is total passive expenses for the year. The amount of the suspended interest expense that is considered to be deductible in a subsequent taxable year is computed by multiplying the amount of any cumulative suspended interest expense (reduced by suspended interest expense allowed as a deduction in prior taxable years) times a fraction, the numerator of which is the portion of cumulative suspended passive losses that become deductible in the taxable year and the denominator of which is the cumulative suspended passive losses for prior taxable years (reduced by suspended passive losses allowed as deductions in prior taxable years).

(iii) *Example.*—The rules of this paragraph (c)(4) may be illustrated by the following example.

Example. On January 1, 1987, A, a United States citizen, invested in a passive activity. In 1987, the passive activity generated no passive income and $100 in passive losses, all of which were suspended by operation of section 469. The suspended loss included $10 of suspended interest expense. In 1988, the passive activity generated $50 in passive income and $150 in passive expenses which included $30 of interest expense. The entire $100 passive loss was suspended in 1988 and included $20 of interest expense ($100 suspended passive loss × $30 passive interest expense / $150 total passive expenses). Thus, at the end of 1988, A had total suspended passive losses of $200, including $30 of suspended interest expense. In 1989, the passive activity generated $100 in passive income and no passive expenses. Thus, $100 of A's cumulative suspended passive loss was therefore allowed in 1989. The $100 of deductible passive loss includes $15 of suspended interest expense ($30 cumulative suspended interest expense × $100 of cumulative suspended passive losses allowable in 1989 / $200 of total cumulative suspended passive losses). The $15 of interest expense is apportioned under the rules of paragraph (d) of this section as though it were incurred in 1989.

(d) *Apportionment rules for individuals, estates, and certain trusts.*—(1) *United States individuals.*—In the case of taxable years beginning after December 31, 1986, individuals generally shall apportion interest expense under different rules according to the type of interest expense incurred. The interest expense of individuals shall be characterized under the regulations issued under section 163. However, in the case of an individual whose foreign source income (including income that is excluded under section 911) does not exceed a gross amount of $5,000, the apportionment of interest expense under this section is not required. Such an individual's interest expense may be allocated entirely to domestic source income.

(i) *Interest incurred in the conduct of a trade or business.*—An individual who incurs business interest described in section 163(h)(2)(A) shall apportion such interest expense using an asset method by reference to the individual's business assets.

(ii) *Investment interest.*—An individual who incurs investment interest described in section 163(h)(2)(B) shall apportion that interest expense on the basis of the individual's investment assets.

(iii) *Interest incurred in a passive activity.*—An individual who incurs passive activity interest described in section 163(h)(2)(C) shall apportion that interest expense on the basis of the individual's passive activity assets. Individuals who receive a distributive share of interest expense incurred in a partnership are subject to special rules set forth in paragraph (e) of this section.

(iv) *Qualified residence and deductible personal interest.*—Individuals who incur qualified residence interest described in section 163(h)(2)(D) shall apportion that interest expense under a gross income method, taking into account all income (including business, passive activity, and investment income) but excluding income that is exempt under section 911. For purposes of this section, any qualified residence that is rented shall be considered to be a business asset for the period in which it is rented, with the result that the interest on such a residence is not apportioned under this subdivision (iv) but instead under subdivisions (i) or (iii) of this paragraph (d)(1). To the extent that personal interest described in section 163(h)(2) remains deductible under transitional rules, individuals shall apportion such interest expense in the same manner as qualified residence interest.

(v) *Example.*—The following example illustrates the principles of this section.

Example—(i) *Facts.* A is a resident individual taxpayer engaged in the active conduct of a trade or business, which A operates as a sole proprietor. A's business generates only domestic source income. A's investment portfolio consists of several less than 10 percent stock investments. Certain stocks in which A's adjusted basis is $40,000 generate domestic source income and other stocks in which A's adjusted basis is $60,000 generate foreign source passive income. In addition, A owns his personal residence, which is subject to a mortgage in the amount of $100,000. All interest expense incurred with respect to A's mortgage is qualified residence interest for purposes of section 163(h)(2)(D). A's other indebtedness consists of a bank loan in the amount of $40,000. Under the regulations issued under section 163(h), it is determined that the proceeds of the $40,000 loan were divided equally between A's business and his investment portfolio. In 1987, the gross income of A's business, before the apportionment of interest expense, was $50,000. A's investment portfolio generated $4,000 in domestic source income and $6,000 in foreign source passive income. All of A's debt obligations bear interest at the annual rate of 10 percent.

(ii) *Analysis of business interest.* Under section 163(h) of the Code, $2,000 of A's interest expense is attributable to his business. Under the rules of paragraph (d)(1)(i), such interest must be apportioned on the basis of the business assets. Applying the asset method described in paragraph (g) of this section, it is determined that all of A's business assets generate domestic income and, therefore, constitute domestic assets. Thus, the $2,000 in interest expense on the business loan is allocable to domestic source income.

(iii) *Analysis of investment interest.* Under section 163(h) of the Code, $2,000 of A's interest expense is investment interest. Under the rules of paragraph (d)(1)(ii) of this section, such interest must be apportioned on the basis of investment assets. Applying the asset method, A's investment assets consist of stock generating domestic source income with an adjusted basis of $40,000 and stock generating foreign source passive income with an adjusted basis of $60,000. Thus, 40 percent ($800) of A's investment interest is apportioned to domestic source income and 60 percent ($1,200) of A's investment interest is apportioned to foreign source passive income for purposes of section 904.

(iv) *Analysis of qualified residence interest.* The $10,000 of qualified residence interest expense is apportioned under the rules of paragraph (d)(1)(iv) of this section on the basis of all of A's gross income. A's gross income consists of $60,000, $54,000 of which is domestic source and $6,000 of which is foreign source passive income. Thus, $9,000 of A's qualified residence interest is apportioned to domestic source income and $1,000 of A's qualified residence interest is apportioned to foreign source passive income.

(2) *Nonresident aliens.*—(i) *General rule.*—For taxable years beginning on or after January 1, 1988, interest expense incurred by a nonresident alien shall be considered to be connected with income effectively connected with a United States trade or business only to the extent that interest expense is incurred with respect to liabilities that—

(A) Are entered on the books and records of the United States trade or business when incurred, or

(B) Are secured by assets that generate such effectively connected income.

(ii) *Limitations.*—(A) *Maximum debt capitalization.*—Interest expense incurred by a nonresident alien is not considered to be connected with effectively connected income to the extent that it is incurred with respect to liabilities that exceed 80 percent of the gross assets of the United States trade or business.

(B) *Collateralization by other assets.*—Interest expense on indebtedness that is secured by specific assets (not including the general credit of the nonresident alien) other than the assets of the United States trade or business shall not be considered to be connected with effectively connected income.

(3) *Estates and trusts.*—Estates shall be treated in the same manner as individuals. In the case of a trust that is beneficially owned by individuals and is a complex trust, the trust shall be treated in the same manner as individuals under the rules of paragraph (d) of this section, except that no de minimis amount shall apply. In the case of a trust that is beneficially owned by one or more corporations, the trust shall be treated either as a partnership or as a corporation depending on how the trust is characterized under the rules of section 7701 and the regulations thereunder.

(e) *Partnerships.*—(1) *In general—aggregate rule.*—A partner's distributive share of the interest expense of a partnership that is directly allocable under § 1.861-10T to income from specific partnership property shall be treated as directly allocable to the income generated by such partnership property. Subject to the exceptions set forth in paragraph (e)(4), a partner's distributive share of the interest expense of a partnership that is not directly allocable under § 1.861-10T generally is considered related to all income producing activities and assets of the partner and shall be subject to apportionment under the rules described in this paragraph. For purposes of this section, a partner's percentage interest in a partnership shall be determined by reference to the partner's interest in partnership income for the year. Similarly, a partner's pro rata share of partnership assets shall be determined by reference to the partner's interest in partnership income for the year.

(2) *Corporate partners whose interest in the partnership is 10 percent or more.*—A corporate partner shall apportion its distributive share of partnership interest expense by reference to the partner's assets, including the partner's pro rata share of partnership assets, under the rules of paragraph (f) of this section if the corporate partner's direct and indirect interest in the partnership (as determined under the attribution rules of section 318) is 10 percent or more. A corporation using the tax book value method of apportionment shall use the partnership's inside basis in its assets, adjusted to the extent required under § 1.861-10T(d)(2). A corporation using the fair market value method of apportionment shall use the fair market value of the partnership's assets, adjusted to the extent required under § 1.861-10T(d)(2).

(3) *Individual partners who are general partners or who are limited partners with an interest in the partnership of 10 percent or more.*—An individual partner is subject to the rules of this paragraph (e)(3) if either the individual is a general partner or the individual's direct and indirect interest (as determined under the attribution rules of section 318) in the partnership is 10 percent or more. The individual shall first classify his or her distributive share of partnership interest expense as interest incurred in the active conduct of a trade or business, as passive activity interest, or as investment interest under regulations issued under sections 163 and 469. The individual must then apportion his or her interest expense (including the partner's distributive share of partnership interest expense) under the rules of paragraph (d) of this section. Each such individual partner shall take into account his or her distributive share of partnership gross income or pro rata share of the partnership assets in applying such rules. An individual using the tax book value method of apportionment shall use the partnership's inside basis in its assets, adjusted to the extent required under § 1.861-10T(d)(2). An individual using the fair market value method of apportionment shall use the fair market value of the partnership's assets, adjusted to the extent required under § 1.861-10T(d)(2).

(4) *Less than 10 percent limited partners and less than 10 percent corporate general partners—entity rule.*—(i) *Partnership interest expense.*—A limited partner (whether individual or corporate) or corporate general partner whose direct and indirect interest (as determined under the attribution rules of section 318) in the partnership is less than 10 percent shall directly allocate its distributive share of partnership interest expense to its distributive share of partnership gross income. Under § 1.904-7(i)(2) of the regulations, such a partner's distributive share of foreign source income of the partnership is treated as passive income (subject to the high taxed income exception of section 904(d)(2)(F)), except in the case of high withholding tax interest or income from a partnership interest held in the ordinary course of the partner's active trade or business, as defined in § 1.904-7(i)(2). A partner's distributive share of partnership interest expense (other than partnership interest expense that is directly allocated to identified property under § 1.861-10T) shall be apportioned in accordance with the partner's relative distributive share of gross foreign source income in each limitation category and of domestic source income from the partnership. To the extent that partnership interest expense is directly allocated under § 1.861-10T, a comparable portion of the income to which such interest expense is allocated shall be disregarded in determining the partner's relative distributive share of gross foreign source income in each limitation category and domestic source income. The partner's distributive share of the interest expense of the partnership that is directly allocable under

§ 1.861-10T shall be allocated according to the treatment, after application of § 1.904-7(i)(2), of the partner's distributive share of the income to which the expense is allocated.

(ii) *Other interest expense of the partner.*—For purposes of apportioning other interest expense of the partner on an asset basis, the partner's interest in the partnership, and not the partner's pro rata share of partnership assets, is considered to be the relevant asset. The value of this asset for apportionment purposes is either the tax book value or fair market value of the partner's partnership interest, depending on the method of apportionment used by the taxpayer. This amount of a partner's interest in the partnership is allocated among various limitation categories in the same manner as partnership interest expense (that is not directly allocable under § 1.861-10T) is apportioned in subdivision (i) of this paragraph (e)(4). If the partner uses the tax book value method of apportionment, the partner's interest in the partnership must be reduced, for this purpose, to the extent that the partner's basis consists of liabilities that are taken into account under section 752. Under either the tax book value or fair market value method of apportionment, for purposes of this section only, the value of the partner's interest in the partnership must be reduced by the principal amount of any indebtedness of the partner the interest on which is directly allocated to its partnership interest under § 1.861-10T.

(5) *Tiered partnerships.*—If a partnership is a partner in another partnership, the distributive share of interest expense of a lower-tier partnership that is subject to the rules of paragraph (e)(4) shall not be reapportioned in the hands of any higher-tier partner. However, the distributive share of interest expense of lower-tier partnership that is subject to the rules of paragraph (e)(2) or (3) shall be apportioned by the partner of the higher-tier partnership or by any higher-tier partnership to which the rules of paragraph (e)(4) apply, taking into account the partner's indirect pro rata share of the lower-tier partnership's income or assets.

(6) *Example.*—(i) *Facts.*—A, B, and C are partners in a limited partnership. A is a corporate general partner, owns a 5 percent interest in the partnership, and has an adjusted basis in its partnership interest, determined without regard to section 752 of the Code, of $5. A's investment in the partnership is not held in the ordinary course of the taxpayer's active trade or business, as defined in § 1.904-7(i)(2). B, a corporate limited partner, owns a 70 percent interest in the partnership, and has an adjusted basis in its partnership interest, determined without regard to section 752 of the Code, of $70. C is an individual limited partner, owns a 25 percent interest in the partnership, and has an adjusted basis in the partnership interest, determined without regard to section 752 of the Code, of $25. The partners' interests in the profits and losses of the partnership conform to their respective interests. None of the interest expense incurred directly by any of the partners is directly allocable to their partnership interest under § 1.861-10T. The ABC partnership's sole assets are two apartment buildings, one domestic and the other foreign. The domestic building has an adjusted inside basis of $600 and the foreign building has an adjusted inside basis of $500. Each of the buildings is subject to a nonrecourse liability in the amount of $500. The ABC partnership's total interest expense for the taxable year is $120, both nonrecourse liabilities bearing interest at the rate of 12 percent. The indebtedness on the domestic building qualifies for direct allocation under the rules of § 1.861-10T. The indebtedness on the foreign building does not so qualify. The partnership incurred no foreign taxes. The partnership's gross income for the taxable year is $360, consisting of $100 in foreign source income and $260 in domestic source income. Under § 1.752-1(e), the nonrecourse liabilities of the partnership are allocated among the partners according to their share of the partnership profits. Accordingly, the adjusted basis of A, B, and C in their respective partnership interests (for other than apportionment purposes) is, respectively, $55, $770, and $275.

(ii) *Determination of the amount of partnership interest expense that is subject to allocation and apportionment.*—Interest on the nonrecourse loan on the domestic building is, under § 1.861-10T, directly allocable to income from that investment. The interest expense is therefore directly allocable to domestic income. Interest on the nonrecourse loan on the foreign building is not directly allocable. The interest expense is therefore subject to allocation and apportionment. Thus, $60 of interest expense is directly allocable to domestic income and $60 of interest expense is subject to allocation and apportionment.

(iii) *Analysis for Partner A.*—A's distributive share of the partnership's gross income is $18, which consists of $5 in foreign source income and $13 in domestic source income. A's distributive share of the ABC interest expense is $6, $3 of which is directly allocable to domestic income and $3 of which is subject to apportionment. After direct allocation of qualifying interest expense, A's distributive share of the partnership's gross income consists of $5 in foreign source income and $10 in domestic source income. Because A is a less than 10 percent corporate partner, A's distributive share of any foreign source partnership income is considered to be passive income. Accordingly, in apportioning the $3 of partnership interest expense that is subject to apportionment on a gross income method, one-third ($1) is apportioned to foreign source passive income and two-thirds ($2) is apportioned to domestic source income. In apportioning its other interest expense, A uses the tax book value method. A's adjusted basis in A's partnership interest ($55) includes A's share of the partnership's liabilities ($50), which are included in basis under section 752. For purposes of apportioning other interest expense, A's adjusted basis in the partnership must be reduced to the extent of such liabilities. Thus, A's adjusted basis in the partnership, for purposes of apportionment, is $5. For the purpose of apportioning A's other interest expense, this $5 in basis is characterized one-third as a foreign passive asset and two-thirds as a domestic asset, which is the ratio determined in paragraph (e)(4)(i).

(iv) *Analysis for Partner B.*—B's distributive share of the ABC interest expense is $84, $42 of which is directly allocable to domestic income and $42 of which is subject to apportionment. As a corporate limited partner whose interest in the partnership is 10 percent or more, B is subject to the rules of paragraph (e)(2) and paragraph (f) of this section. These rules require that a corporate partner apportion its distributive share of partnership interest expense at the partner level on the asset method described in paragraph (g) of this section by reference to its corporate assets, which include, for this purpose, 70 percent of the partnership's assets, adjusted in the manner described in § 1.861-10T(e) to reflect directly allocable interest expense.

(v) *Analysis for Partner C.*—C's distributive share of the ABC interest expense is $30, $15 of which is directly allocable to domestic income and $15 of which is subject to apportionment. As an individual limited partner whose interest in the partnership is 10 percent or more, C is subject to the rules of paragraph (e)(3) of this section. These rules require that an individual's share of partnership interest expense be classified under regulations issued under section 163(h) and then apportioned under the rules applicable to individuals, which are set forth in paragraph (d) of this section.

(7) *Foreign partners.*—The distributive share of partnership interest expense of a nonresident alien who is a partner in a partnership shall be considered to be connected with effectively connected income based on the percentage of the assets of the partnership that generate effectively connected income. No interest expense directly incurred by the partner may be allocated and apportioned to effectively connected income derived by the partnership.

(f) *Corporations.*—(1) *Domestic corporations.*—Domestic corporations shall apportion interest expense using the asset method described in paragraph (g) of this section and the applicable rules of §§ 1.861-10T through 1.861-13T.

(2) *Foreign branches of domestic corporations.*—In the application of the asset method described in paragraph (g) of this section, a domestic corporation shall—

(i) Take into account the assets of any foreign branch, translated according to the rules set forth in paragraph (g) of this section, and

(ii) Combine with its own interest expense any deductible interest expense incurred by a branch, translated according to the rules of section 987 and the regulations thereunder.

For purposes of computing currency gain or loss on any remittance from a branch or other qualified business unit (as defined in § 1.989(a)-1T) under section 987, the rules of this paragraph (f) shall not apply. The branch shall compute its currency gain or loss on remittances by taking into account only its separate expenses and its separate income.

Example—(i) *Facts.* X is a domestic corporation which operates B, a branch doing business in a foreign country. In 1988, without regard to branch B, X has gross domestic source income of $1,000 and gross foreign source general limitation income of $500 and incurs $200 of interest expense. Using the tax book value method of apportionment, X, without regard to branch B, determines the value of its assets that generate domestic source income to be $6,000 and the value of its assets that generate foreign source general limitation income to be $1,000. B constitutes a qualified business unit within the meaning of section 989 with a functional currency other than the U.S. dollar and uses the profit and loss method prescribed by section 987. Applying the translation rules of section 987, B earned $500 of gross foreign general limitation income and incurred $100 of interest expense. B incurred no other expenses. For 1988, the average functional currency book value of B's assets that generate foreign general limitation income translated at the year-end rate for 1988 is $3,000.

(ii) *Computation of net income.* The combined assets of X and B for 1988 (averaged under the rules of § 1.861-9T(g)(3)) consist 60 percent of assets generating domestic source income and 40 percent of assets generating foreign source general limitation income. The combined interest expense of both X and B is

$300. Thus, $180 of the combined interest expense is apportioned to domestic source income and $120 is apportioned to the foreign source income, yielding net domestic source income of $820 and net foreign source general limitation income of $880.

(iii) *Computation of currency gain or loss.* For purposes of computing currency gain or loss on branch remittances, B takes into account only its gross income and its separate expenses. In 1988, B therefore has a net amount of income in foreign currency units equal in value to $400. Gain or loss on remittances shall be computed by reference to this amount.

(3) *Controlled foreign corporations.*—(i) *In general.*—For purposes of computing subpart F income and computing earnings and profits for all other federal tax purposes, the interest expense of a controlled foreign corporation may be apportioned either using the asset method described in paragraph (g) of this section or using the modified gross income method described in paragraph (j) of this section, subject to the rules of subdivisions (ii) and (iii) of this paragraph (f)(2). However, the gross income method described in paragraph (j) of this section is not available to any controlled foreign corporation if a United States shareholder and the members of its affiliated group (as defined in § 1.861-11T(d)) constitute controlling shareholders of such controlled foreign corporation and such affiliated group elects the fair market value method of apportionment under paragraph (g) of this section.

(ii) *Manner of election.*—The election to use the asset method described in paragraph (g) of this section or the modified gross income method described in paragraph (j) of this section may be made either by the controlled foreign corporation or by the controlling United States shareholders on behalf of the controlled foreign corporation. The term "controlling United States shareholders" means those United States shareholders (as defined in section 951(b)) who, in aggregate, own (within the meaning of section 958(a)) greater than 50 percent of the total combined voting power of all classes of stock of the foreign corporation entitled to vote. In the case of a controlled foreign corporation in which the United States shareholders own stock representing more than 50 percent of the value of the stock in such corporation, but less than 50 percent of the combined voting power of all classes of stock in such corporation, the term "controlling United States shareholders" means all the United States shareholders (as defined in section 951(b)) who own (within the meaning of section 958(a)) stock of the controlled foreign corporation. All United States shareholders are bound by the election of either the controlled foreign corporation or the controlling United States shareholders. The election shall be made by filing a written statement described in § 1.964-1(c)(3)(ii) at the time and in the manner described therein and providing a written notice described in § 1.964-1(c)(3)(iii), except that no such written statement or notice is required to be filed or sent before March 13, 1989.

(iii) *Consistency requirement.*—The same method of apportionment must be employed by all controlled foreign corporations in which a United States taxpayer and the members of its affiliated group (as defined in § 1.861-11T(d)) constitute controlling United States shareholders. A controlled foreign corporation that is required by this paragraph (f)(3)(iii) to utilize a particular method of apportionment must do so with respect to all United States shareholders.

(iv) *Stock characterization.*—Pursuant to § 1.861-12T(c)(2), the stock of a controlled foreign corporation shall be characterized in the hands of any United States shareholder using the same method that the controlled foreign corporation uses to apportion its interest expense.

(4) *Other relevant provisions.*—Affiliated groups of corporations are subject to special rules set forth in § 1.861-11T. Section 1.861-12T sets forth rules relating to basis adjustments for stock in nonaffiliated 10 percent owned corporations, special rules relating to the consideration and characterization of certain assets in the apportionment of interest expense, and to other special rules pertaining to the apportionment of interest expense. Section 1.861-13T contains transition rules limiting the application of the rules of §§ 1.861-8T through 1.861-12T, which are otherwise applicable to taxable years beginning after 1986. In the case of an affiliated group of corporations as defined in § 1.861-11T(d), any reference in §§ 1.861-8T through 1.861-13T to the "taxpayer" with respect to the allocation and apportionment of interest expense generally denotes the entire affiliated group of corporations and not the separate members thereof, unless the context otherwise requires.

(g) *Asset method.*—(1) *In general.*—(i) Under the asset method, the taxpayer apportions interest expense to the various statutory groupings based on the average total value of assets within each such grouping for the taxable year, as determined under the asset valuation rules of this paragraph (g)(1) and paragraph (g)(2) of this section and the asset characterization rules of paragraph (g)(3) of this section and § 1.861-12T. Except to the extent otherwise provided (*see, e.g.,* paragraph (d)(1)(iv) of this section), taxpayers must apportion interest expense only on the basis of asset values and may not apportion any interest deduction on the basis of gross income.

(ii) A taxpayer may elect to determine the value of its assets on the basis of either the tax book value or the fair market value of its assets. For rules concerning the application of an alternative method of valuing assets for purposes of the tax book value method, see paragraph (i) of this section. For rules concerning the application of the fair market value method, see paragraph (h) of this section. In the case of an affiliated group—

(A) The parent of which used the fair market value method prior to 1987, or

(B) A substantial portion of which used the fair market value method prior to 1987, such a taxpayer may use either the fair market value method or the tax book value method for its tax year commencing in 1987 and may use either such method in its tax year commencing in 1988 without regard to which method was used in its tax year commencing in 1987 and without securing the Commissioner's consent. The use of the fair market value method in 1988, however, shall operate as a binding election as described in §1.861-8T(c)(2). For rules requiring consistency in the use of the tax book value or fair market value method, see §1.861-8T(c)(2).

(iii) A taxpayer electing to apportion its interest expense on the basis of the fair market value of its assets must establish the fair market value to the satisfaction of the Commissioner. If a taxpayer fails to establish the fair market value of an asset to the satisfaction of the Commissioner, the Commissioner may determine the appropriate asset value. If a taxpayer fails to establish the value of a substantial portion of its assets to the satisfaction of the Commissioner, the Commissioner may require the taxpayer to use the tax book value method of apportionment.

(iv) For rules relating to earnings and profits adjustments by taxpayers using the tax book value method for the stock in certain nonaffiliated 10 percent owned corporations, see §1.861-12T(b).

(v) The provisions of this paragraph (g)(1) may be illustrated by the following examples.

Example (1)—(i) *Facts.* X, a domestic corporation organized on January 1, 1987, has deductible interest expense in 1987 in the amount of $150,000. X apportions its expenses according to the tax book value method. The adjusted basis of X's assets is $3,600,000, $3,000,000 of which generate domestic source income and $600,000 of which generate foreign source general limitation income.

(ii) *Allocation.* No portion of the $150,000 deduction is directly allocable solely to identified property within the meaning of §1.861-10T. Thus, X's deduction for interest is related to all its activities and assets.

(iii) *Apportionment.* X apportions its interest expense as follows:

To foreign source general limitation income:

$$\$150,000 \times \frac{\$600,000}{\$3,600,000} = \$25,000$$

To domestic source income:

$$\$150,000 \times \frac{\$3,000,000}{\$3,600,000} = \$125,000$$

Example (2)—(i) *Facts.* Assume the same facts as in Example (1), except that X apportions its interest expense on the basis of the fair market value of its assets. X's total assets have a fair market value of $4,000,000, $3,200,000 of which generate domestic source income and $800,000 of which generate foreign source general limitation income.

(ii) *Allocation.* No portion of the $150,000 deduction is directly allocable solely to identified property within the meaning of §1.861-10T. Thus, X's deduction for interest is related to all its activities and properties.

(iii) *Apportionment.* If it establishes the fair market value of its assets to the satisfaction of the Commissioner, X may apportion its interest expense as follows:

To foreign source general limitation income:

$$\$150,000 \times \frac{\$800,000}{\$4,000,000} = \$30,000$$

To domestic source income:

$$\$150,000 \times \frac{\$3,200,000}{\$4,000,000} = \$120,000$$

(2) *Asset values.*—(i) *General rule.*—For purposes of determining the value of assets under this section, an average of values (book or market) within each statutory grouping and the residual grouping shall be computed for the year on the basis of values of assets at the beginning and end of the year. For the first taxable year beginning after 1986, a taxpayer may choose to determine asset values solely by reference to the year-end value of its assets, provided that all the members of an affiliated group as defined in §1.861-11T(d) make the same choice. Thus, no averaging is required for the first taxable year beginning after 1986. Where a substantial distortion of asset values would result from averaging beginning-of-year and year-end values, as might be the case in

the event of a major corporate acquisition or disposition, the taxpayer must use a different method of asset valuation that more clearly reflects the average value of assets weighted to reflect the time such assets are held by the taxpayer during the taxable year.

(ii) *Special rule for qualified business units of domestic corporations with functional currency other than the U.S. dollar.*—(A) *Tax book value method.*—In the case of taxpayers using the tax book value method of apportionment, the following rules shall apply to determine the value of the assets of a qualified business unit (as defined in section 989(a)) of a domestic corporation with a functional currency other than the dollar.

(1) *Profit and loss branch.*—In the case of a branch for which an election is not effective under § 1.985-2T to use the dollar approximate separate transactions method of computing currency gain or loss, the tax book value shall be determined by applying the rules of paragraph (g)(2)(i) and (3) of this section with respect to beginning-of-year and end-of-year tax book value in units of functional currency that are translated into dollars at the end-of-year exchange rate between the functional currency and the U.S. dollar.

Example. At the end of 1987, a profit and loss branch has assets that generate foreign source general limitation income with a tax book value in units of functional currency of 100. At the end of 1987, the unit is worth $1. At the end of 1988, the branch has assets that generate foreign source general limitation income with a tax book value in units of functional currency of 80. At the end of 1988, the unit is worth $2. The average value of foreign source general limitation assets for 1988 is 90 units, which is worth $180.

(2) *Approximate separate transactions method.*—In the case of a branch for which an election is effective under § 1.985-2T to use the dollar approximate separate transactions method to compute currency gain or loss, the beginning-of-year dollar amount of the assets shall be determined by reference to the end-of-year balance sheet of the branch for the immediately preceding taxable year, adjusted for United States generally accepted accounting principles and United States tax accounting principles, and translated into U.S. dollars as provided in § 1.985-3T. The year-end dollar amount of the assets of the branch shall be determined in the same manner by reference to the end-of-year balance sheet for the current taxable year. The beginning-of-year and end-of-year dollar tax book value of assets, as so determined, within each grouping must then be averaged as provided in paragraph (g)(2)(i) of this section.

(B) *Fair market value method.*—In the case of taxpayers using the fair market value method of apportionment, the beginning-of-year and end-of-year fair market values of branch assets within each grouping shall be computed in dollars and averaged as provided in this paragraph (g)(2).

(iii) *Adjustment for directly allocated interest.*—Prior to averaging, the year-end value of any asset to which interest expense is directly allocated during the current taxable year under the rules of § 1.861-10T(b) or (c) shall be reduced (but not below zero) by the percentage of the principal amount of indebtedness outstanding at year-end equal to the percentage of all interest on the debt for the taxable year that is directly allocated.

(iv) *Assets in intercompany transactions.*—In the application of the asset method described in this paragraph (g), the tax book value of assets transferred between affiliated corporations in intercompany transactions shall be determined without regard to the gain or loss that is deferred under the regulations issued under section 1502.

(v) *Example.*—X is a domestic corporation that uses the fair market value method of apportionment. X is a calendar year taxpayer. X owns 25 percent of the stock of A, a noncontrolled section 902 corporation. At the end of 1987, the fair market value of X's assets by income grouping are as follows:

Domestic	$1,000,000
Foreign general limitation	500,000
Foreign passive	500,000
Noncontrolled section 902 corporation	50,000

For its 1987 tax year, X apportions its interest expense by reference to the 1987 year-end values. In July of 1988, X sells a portion of its investment in A and in an asset acquisition purchases a shipping business, the assets of which generate exclusively foreign shipping income. At the end of 1988, the fair market values of X's assets by income grouping are as follows:

Domestic	$800,000
Foreign general limitation	900,000
Foreign passive	300,000
Noncontrolled section 902 corporation	40,000
Foreign shipping	100,000

For its 1988 tax year, X shall apportion its interest expense by reference to the average of the 1988 beginning-of-year values (the 1987 year-end values) and the 1988 year-end values, assuming that the averaging of beginning-of-year and end-of-year values does not cause a substantial distortion of asset values. These averages are as follows:

Domestic	$900,000
Foreign general limitation	700,000
Foreign passive	400,000
Foreign shipping	50,000
Noncontrolled section 902 corporation	45,000

(3) *Characterization of assets.*—Assets are characterized for purposes of this section according to the source and type of the income that they generate, have generated, or may reasonably be expected to generate. The physical location of assets is not relevant to this determination. Subject to the special rules of paragraph (h) concerning the application of the fair market value method of apportionment, the value of assets within each statutory grouping and the residual grouping at the beginning and end of each year shall be determined by dividing the taxpayer's assets into three types—

(i) *Single category assets.*—Assets that generate income that is exclusively within a single statutory grouping or the residual grouping;

(ii) *Multiple category assets.*—Assets that generate income within more than one grouping of income (statutory or residual); and

(iii) *Assets without directly identifiable yield.*—Assets that produce no directly identifiable income yield or that contribute equally to the generation of all the income of the taxpayer (such as assets used in general and administrative functions).

Single category assets are directly attributable to the relevant statutory or residual grouping of income. In order to attribute multiple category assets to the relevant groupings of income, the income yield of each such asset for the taxable year must be analyzed to determine the proportion of gross income generated by it within each relevant grouping. The value of each asset is then prorated among the relevant groupings of income according to their respective proportions of gross income. The value of each asset without directly identifiable income yield must be identified. However, because prorating the value of such assets cannot alter the ratio of assets within the various groupings of income (as determined by reference to the single and multiple category assets), they are not taken into account in determining that ratio. Special asset characterization rules that are set forth in § 1.861-12T. An example demonstrating the application of the asset method is set forth in § 1.861-12T(d).

(h) *The fair market value method.*—An affiliated group (as defined in § 1.861-11T(d)) or other taxpayer (the "taxpayer") that elects to use the fair market value method of apportionment shall value its assets according to the following methodology.

(1) *Determination of values.*—
(i) *Valuation of group assets.*—The taxpayer shall first determine the aggregate value of the assets of the taxpayer on the last day of its taxable year without excluding the value of stock in foreign subsidiaries or any other asset. In the case of a publicly traded corporation, this determination shall be equal to the aggregate trading value of the taxpayer's stock traded on established securities markets at year-end increased by the taxpayer's year-end liabilities to unrelated persons and its pro rata share of year-end liabilities of all related persons owed to unrelated persons. In determining whether persons are related, § 1.861-8T(c)(2) shall apply. In the case of a corporation that is not publicly traded, this determination shall be made by reference to the capitalization of corporate earnings, in accordance with the rules of Rev. Rul. 68-609. In either case, control premium shall not be taken into account.

(ii) *Valuation of tangible assets.*—The taxpayer shall determine the value of all assets held by the taxpayer and its pro rata share of assets held by other related persons on the last day of its taxable year, excluding stock or indebtedness in such persons, any intangible property as defined in section 936(h)(3)(B), or goodwill or going concern value intangibles. Such valuations shall be made using generally accepted valuation techniques. For this purpose, assets may be combined into reasonable groupings. Statistical methods of valuation may only be used in connection with fungible property, such as commodities. The value of stock in any corporation that is not a related person shall be determined under the rules of paragraph (h)(1)(i) of this section, except that no liabilities shall be taken into account.

(iii) *Computation of intangible asset value.*—The value of the intangible assets of the taxpayer and of intangible assets of all related persons attributable to the taxpayer's ownership in related persons is equal to the amount obtained by subtracting the amount determined under paragraph (h)(1)(ii) of this section from the amount determined under paragraph (h)(1)(i) of this section.

(2) *Apportionment of intangible asset value.*—The value of the intangible assets determined under paragraph (h)(1)(iii) of this section is apportioned among the taxpayer and all related persons in proportion to the net income before interest expense of the taxpayer and the taxpayer's pro rata share of the net income before interest expense of each related person held by the taxpayer, excluding income that is passive under § 1.904-4(b). For this purpose, net income is determined before reduction for income taxes. Net income of the

taxpayer and of related persons shall be computed without regard to dividends or interest received from any person that is related to the taxpayer.

(3) *Characterization of affiliated group's portion of intangible asset value.*—The portion of the value of intangible assets of the taxpayer and related persons that is apportioned to the taxpayer under paragraph (h)(2) of this section is characterized on the basis of net income before interest expense, as determined under paragraph (h)(2) of this section, of the taxpayer within each statutory or residual grouping of income.

(4) *Valuing stock in related persons held by the taxpayer.*—The value of stock in a related person held by the taxpayer or by another person related to the taxpayer equals the sum of the following amounts reduced by the taxpayer's pro rata share of liabilities of such related person:

(i) The portion of the value of intangible assets of the taxpayer and related persons that is apportioned to such related person under paragraph (h)(2) of this section;

(ii) The taxpayer's pro rata share of tangible assets held by the related person (as determined under paragraph (h)(1)(ii) of this section); and

(iii) The total value of stock in all related person held by the related person as determined under this paragraph (h)(4).

(5) [Reserved].—For further guidance, see § 1.861-9(h)(5).

(6) *Adjustments for apportioning related person expenses.*—For purposes of apportioning expenses of a related person, the value of stock in a second related person as otherwise determined under paragraph (h)(4) of this section (which is determined on the basis of the taxpayer's percentage ownership interest in the second related person) shall be increased to reflect the first related person's percentage ownership interest in the second related person to the extent it is larger.

Example. Assume that a taxpayer owns 80 percent of CFC1, which owns 100 percent of CFC2. The value of CFC1 is determined generally under paragraph (h)(4) on the basis of the taxpayer's 80 percent indirect interest in CFC2. For purposes of apportioning expenses of CFC1, 100 percent of the stock of CFC1 must be taken into account. Therefore, the value of CFC2 stock in the hands of CFC1 shall equal the value of CFC2 stock in the hands of CFC1 as determined under paragraph (h)(4) of this section, increased by 25 percent of such amount to reflect the fact that CFC1 owns 100 percent and not 80 percent of CFC2.

(i) *Alternative tax book value method.*—(1) *Alternative value for certain tangible property.*—A taxpayer may elect to determine the tax book value of its tangible property that is depreciated under section 168 (section 168 property) using the rules provided in this paragraph (the alternative tax book value method). The alternative tax book value method applies solely for purposes of apportioning expenses (including the calculation of the alternative minimum tax foreign tax credit pursuant to section 59(a)) under the asset method described in paragraph (g) of this section.

(i) The tax book value of section 168 property placed in service during or after the first taxable year to which the election to use the alternative tax book value method applies shall be determined as though such property were subject to the alternative depreciation system under section 168(g) for the entire period that such property has been in service.

(ii) In the case of section 168 property placed in service prior to the first taxable year to which the election to use the alternative tax book value method applies, the tax book value of such property shall be determined under the depreciation method, convention, and recovery period provided for under section 168(g) for the first taxable year to which the election applies.

(iii) If a taxpayer revokes an election to use the alternative tax book value method ("the prior election") and later makes another election to use the alternative tax book value method (the "subsequent election") that is effective for a taxable year that begins within 3 years of the end of the last taxable year to which the prior election applied, the taxpayer shall determine the tax book value of its section 168 property as though the prior election has remained in effect.

(iv) The tax book value of section 168 property shall be determined without regard to the election to expense certain depreciable assets under section 179.

(v) *Examples.*—The provisions of this paragraph (i)(1) are illustrated in the following examples:

Example 1. In 2000, a taxpayer purchases and places in service section 168 property used solely in the United States. In 2005, the taxpayer elects to use the alternative tax book value method, effective for the current taxable year. For purposes of determining the tax book value of its section 168 property, the taxpayer's depreciation deduction is determined by applying the method, convention, and recovery period rules of the alternative depreciation system under section 168(g)(2) as in effect in 2005 to the taxpayer's original cost basis in such property. In 2006, the taxpayer acquires

Reg. § 1.861-9T(i)(1)(v)

and places in service in the United States new section 168 property. The tax book value of this section 168 property is determined under the rules of section 168(g)(2) applicable to property placed in service in 2006.

Example 2. Assume the same facts as in *Example 1*, except that the taxpayer revokes the alternative tax book value method election effective for taxable year 2010. Additionally, in 2011, the taxpayer acquires new section 168 property and places it in service in the United States. If the taxpayer elects to use the alternative tax book value method effective for taxable year 2012, the taxpayer must determine the tax book value of its section 168 property as though the prior election still applied. Thus, the tax book value of property placed in service prior to 2005 would be determined by applying the method, convention, and recovery period rules of the alternative depreciation system under section 168(g)(2) applicable to property placed in service in 2005. The tax book value of section 168 property placed in service during any taxable year after 2004 would be determined by applying the method, convention, and recovery period rules of the alternative depreciation system under section 168(g)(2) applicable to property placed in service in such taxable year.

(2) *Timing and scope of election.*—(i) Except as provided in this paragraph (i)(2), a taxpayer may elect to use the alternative tax book value method with respect to any taxable year beginning on or after March 26, 2004. However, pursuant to § 1.861-8T(c)(2), a taxpayer that has elected the fair market value method must obtain the consent of the Commissioner prior to electing the alternative tax book value method. Any election made pursuant to this paragraph (i)(2) shall apply to all members of an affiliated group of corporations as defined in §§ 1.861-11(d) and 1.861-11T(d). Any election made pursuant to this paragraph (i)(2) shall apply to all subsequent taxable years of the taxpayer unless revoked by the taxpayer. Revocation of such an election, other than in conjunction with an election to use the fair market value method, for a taxable year prior to the sixth taxable year for which the election applies requires the consent of the Commissioner.

(ii) *Example.*—The provisions of this paragraph (i)(2) are illustrated in the following example:

Example. Corporation X, a calendar year taxpayer, elects on its original, timely filed tax return for the taxable year ending December 31, 2007, to use the alternative tax book value method for its 2007 year. The alternative tax book value method applies to X's 2007 year and all subsequent taxable years. X may not, without the consent of the Commissioner, revoke its election and determine tax book value using a method other than the alternative tax book value method with respect to any taxable year beginning before January 1, 2012. However, X may automatically elect to change from the alternative tax book value method to the fair market value method for any open year.

(3) *Effective date.*—(i) Paragraph (i) of this section applies to taxable years beginning on or after March 26, 2004.

(ii) The applicability of this paragraph (i) expires on or before March 26, 2007.

(j) *Modified gross income method.*—Subject to rules set forth in paragraph (f)(3) of this section, the interest expense of a controlled foreign corporation may be allocated according to the following rules.

(1) *Single-tier controlled foreign corporation.*—In the case of a controlled foreign corporation that does not hold stock in any lower-tier controlled foreign corporation, the interest expense of the controlled foreign corporation shall be apportioned based on its gross income.

(2) *Multiple vertically owned controlled foreign corporations.*—In the case of a controlled foreign corporation that holds stock in any lower-tier controlled foreign corporation, the interest expense of that controlled foreign corporation and each upper-tier controlled foreign corporation shall be apportioned based on the following methodology:

(i) *Step 1.*—Commencing with the lowest-tier controlled foreign corporation in the chain, allocate and apportion its interest expense based on its gross income as provided in paragraph (j)(1) of this section, yielding gross income in each grouping net of interest expense.

(ii) *Step 2.*—Moving to the next higher-tier controlled foreign corporation, combine the gross income of such corporation within each grouping with its pro rata share of the gross income net of interest expense of all lower-tier controlled foreign corporations held by such higher-tier corporation within the same grouping adjusted as follows:

(A) Exclude from the gross income of the upper-tier corporation any dividends or other payments received from the lower-tier corporation other than interest subject to look-through under section 904(d)(3); and

(B) Exclude from the gross income net of interest expense of any lower-tier corporation any subpart F income (net of interest expense apportioned to such income).

Then apportion the interest expense of the higher-tier controlled foreign corporation based on the adjusted combined gross income amounts. Repeat this step 2 for each next higher-tier controlled foreign corporation in the chain. For purposes of this paragraph (j)(2)(ii), pro rata share shall be determined under principles similar to section 951(a)(2). [Temporary Reg. § 1.861-9T.]

☐ [T.D. 8228, 9-9-88. Amended by T.D. 8257, 8-1-89; T.D. 8597, 7-12-95; T.D. 8658, 3-5-96; T.D. 8916, 12-29-2000 and T.D. 9120, 3-25-2004.]

Proposed Amendments to Regulation

☐ Section 1.861-9T is amended by redesignating the text of paragraph (g)(2)(iii) as paragraph (g)(2)(iii)(A) and adding a heading to new paragraph (g)(2)(iii)(A), and adding paragraph (g)(2)(iii)(B):

§ 1.861-9T. Allocation and apportionment of interest expense (temporary regulation).

* * *

(g) * * *
  (2) * * *

  (iii) *Adjustment for directly allocated interest.*—(A) *Nonrecourse indebtedness and integrated financial transactions.*—* * *

  (B) *FASIT interest expense.*—The rules of paragraph (g)(2)(iii)(A) of this section shall also apply to all assets to which FASIT interest expense is directly allocated during the current taxable year under the rules of § 1.861-10T(f). This paragraph (g)(2)(iii)(B) applies on the date final regulations are filed with the FEDERAL REGISTER.

[Prop. Reg. § 1.861-9T.]
[Proposed 2-7-2000.]

§ 1.861-10. Special allocations of interest ex-pense.—

* * *

(e) *Treatment of certain related group indebtedness.*—(1) *In general.*—If, for any taxable year beginning after December 31, 1991, a U.S. shareholder (as defined in paragraph (e)(5)(i) of this section) has both—

  (i) Excess related group indebtedness (as determined under Step One in paragraph (e)(2) of this section) and

  (ii) Excess U.S. shareholder indebtedness (as determined under Step Two in paragraph (e)(3) of this section),

the U.S. shareholder shall allocate, to its gross income in the various separate limitation categories described in section 904(d)(1), a portion of its interest expense paid or accrued to any obligee who is not a member of the affiliated group (as defined in § 1.861-11T(d)) of the U.S. shareholder ("third party interest expense"), excluding amounts allocated under paragraphs (b) and (c) of § 1.861-10T. The amount of third party interest expense so allocated shall equal the total amount of interest income derived by the U.S. shareholder during the year from related group indebtedness, multiplied by the ratio of the lesser of the foregoing two amounts of excess indebtedness for the year to related group indebtedness for the year. This amount of third party interest expense is allocated as described in Step Three in paragraph (e)(4) of this section.

(2) *Step One: Excess related group indebtedness.*—(i) The excess related group indebtedness of a U.S. shareholder for the year equals the amount by which its related group indebtedness for the year exceeds its allowable related group indebtedness for the year.

  (ii) The "related group indebtedness" of the U.S. shareholder is the average of the aggregate amounts at the beginning and end of the year of indebtedness owed to the U.S. shareholder by each controlled foreign corporation which is a related person (as defined in paragraph (e)(5)(ii) of this section) with respect to the U.S. shareholder.

  (iii) The "allowable related group indebtedness" of a U.S. shareholder for the year equals—

    (A) The average of the aggregate values at the beginning and end of the year of the assets (including stock holdings in and obligations of related persons, other than related controlled foreign corporations) of each related controlled foreign corporation, multiplied by

    (B) The foreign base period ratio of the U.S. shareholder for the year.

  (iv) The "foreign base period ratio" of the U.S. shareholder for the year is the average of the related group debt-to-asset ratios of the U.S. shareholder for each taxable year comprising the foreign base period for the current year (each a "base year"). For this purpose, however, the related group debt-to-asset ratio of the U.S. shareholder for any base year may not exceed 110 percent of the foreign base period ratio for that base year. This limitation shall not apply with respect to any of the five taxable years chosen as initial base years by the U.S. shareholder under paragraph (e)(2)(v) of this section or with respect to any base year for which the related group debt-to-asset ratio does not exceed 0.10.

    (v)(A) The foreign base period for any current taxable year (except as described in paragraphs (e)(2)(v)(B) and (C) of this section) shall consist of the five taxable years immediately preceding the current year.

(B) The U.S. shareholder may choose as foreign base periods for all of its first five taxable years for which this paragraph (e) is effective the following alternative base periods:

(1) For the first effective taxable year, the 1982, 1983, 1984, 1985 and 1986 taxable years;

(2) For the second effective taxable year, the 1983, 1984, 1985 and 1986 taxable years and the first effective taxable year;

(3) For the third effective taxable year, the 1984, 1985 and 1986 taxable years and the first and second effective taxable years;

(4) For the fourth effective taxable year, the 1985 and 1986 taxable years and the first, second and third effective taxable years; and

(5) For the fifth effective taxable year, the 1986 taxable year and the first, second, third and fourth effective taxable years.

(C) If, however, the U.S. shareholder does not choose, under paragraph (e)(10)(ii) of this section, to apply this paragraph (e) to one or more taxable years beginning before January 1, 1992, the U.S. shareholder may not include within any foreign base period the taxable year immediately preceding the first effective taxable year. Thus, for example, a U.S. shareholder for which the first effective taxable year is the taxable year beginning on October 1, 1992, may not include the taxable year beginning on October 1, 1991, in any foreign base period. Assuming that the U.S. shareholder does not elect the alternative base periods described in paragraph (e)(2)(v)(B) of this section, the initial foreign base period for the U.S. shareholder will consist of the taxable years beginning on October 1 of 1986, 1987, 1988, 1989, and 1990. The foreign base period for the U.S. shareholder for the following taxable year, beginning on October 1, 1993, will consist of the taxable years beginning on October 1 of 1987, 1988, 1989, 1990, and 1992.

(D) If the U.S. shareholder chooses the base periods described in paragraph (e)(2)(v)(B) of this section as foreign base periods, it must make a similar election under paragraph (e)(3)(v)(B) of this section with respect to its U.S. base periods.

(vi) The "related group debt-to-asset ratio" of a U.S. shareholder for a year is the ratio between—

(A) The related group indebtedness of the U.S. shareholder for the year (as determined under paragraph (e)(2)(ii) of this section); and

(B) The average of the aggregate values at the beginning and end of the year of the assets (including stock holdings in and obligations of related persons, other than related controlled foreign corporations) of each related controlled foreign corporation.

(vii) Notwithstanding paragraph (e)(2)(i) of this section, a U.S. shareholder is considered to have no excess related group indebtedness for the year if—

(A) Its related group indebtedness for the year does not exceed its allowable related group indebtedness for the immediately preceding year (as determined under paragraph (e)(2)(iii) of this section); or

(B) Its related group debt-to-asset ratio (as determined under paragraph (e)(2)(vi) of this section) for the year does not exceed 0.10.

(3) *Step Two: Excess U.S. shareholder indebtedness.*—(i) The excess indebtedness of a U.S. shareholder for the year equals the amount by which its unaffiliated indebtedness for the year exceeds its allowable indebtedness for the year.

(ii) The "unaffiliated indebtedness" of the U.S. shareholder is the average of the aggregate amounts at the beginning and end of the year of indebtedness owed by the U.S. shareholder to any obligee, other than a member of the affiliated group (as defined in § 1.861-11T(d)) of the U.S. shareholder.

(iii) The "allowable indebtedness" of a U.S. shareholder for the year equals—

(A) The average of the aggregate values at the beginning and end of the year of the assets of the U.S. shareholder (including stock holdings in and obligations of related controlled foreign corporations, but excluding stock holdings in and obligations of members of the affiliated group (as defined in § 1.861-11T(d)) of the U.S. shareholder), reduced by the amount of the excess related group indebtedness of the U.S. shareholder for the year (as determined under Step One in paragraph (e)(2) of this section), multiplied by

(B) The U.S. base period ratio of the U.S. shareholder for the year.

(iv) The "U.S. base period ratio" of the U.S. shareholder for the year is the average of the debt-to-asset ratios of the U.S. shareholder for each taxable year comprising the U.S. base period for the current year (each a "base year"). For this purpose, however, the debt-to-asset ratio of the U.S. shareholder for any base year may not exceed 110 percent of the U.S. base period ratio for that base year. This limitation shall not apply with respect to any of the five taxable years chosen as initial base years by the U.S. shareholder under paragraph (e)(3)(v) of this section or with respect to any base year for which the debt-to-asset ratio does not exceed 0.10.

(v)(A) The U.S. base period for any current taxable year (except as described in paragraphs (e)(3)(v)(B) and (C) of this section) shall consist of the five taxable years immediately preceding the current year.

(B) The U.S. shareholder may choose as U.S. base periods for all of its first five taxable years for which this paragraph (e) is effective the following alternative base periods:

(1) For the first effective taxable year, the 1982, 1983, 1984, 1985 and 1986 taxable years;

(2) For the second effective taxable year, the 1983, 1984, 1985 and 1986 taxable years and the first effective taxable year;

(3) For the third effective taxable year, the 1984, 1985 and 1986 taxable years and the first and second effective taxable years;

(4) For the fourth effective taxable year, the 1985 and 1986 taxable years and the first, second and third effective taxable years; and

(5) For the fifth effective taxable year, the 1986 taxable year and the first, second, third and fourth effective taxable years.

(C) If, however, the U.S. shareholder does not choose, under paragraph (e)(10)(ii) of this section, to apply this paragraph (e) to one or more taxable years beginning before January 1, 1992, the U.S. shareholder may not include within any U.S. base period the taxable year immediately preceding the first effective taxable year. Thus, for example, a U.S. shareholder for which the first effective taxable year is the taxable year beginning on October 1, 1992, may not include the taxable year beginning on October 1, 1991, in any U.S. base period. Assuming that the U.S. shareholder does not elect the alternative base periods described in paragraph (e)(3)(v)(B) of this section, the initial U.S. base period for the U.S. shareholder will consist of the taxable years beginning on October 1 of 1986, 1987, 1988, 1989, and 1990. The U.S. base period for the U.S. shareholder for the following taxable year, beginning on October 1, 1993, will consist of the taxable years beginning on October 1, 1987, 1988, 1989, 1990, and 1992.

(D) If the U.S. shareholder chooses the base periods described in paragraph (e)(3)(v)(B) of this section as U.S. base periods, it must make a similar election under paragraph (e)(2)(v)(B) of this section with respect to its foreign base periods.

(vi) The "debt-to-asset ratio" of a U.S. shareholder for a year is the ratio between—

(A) The unaffiliated indebtedness of the U.S. shareholder for the year (as determined under paragraph (e)(3)(ii) of this section); and

(B) The average of the aggregate values at the beginning and end of the year of the assets of the U.S. shareholder. For this purpose, the assets of the U.S. shareholder include stock holdings in and obligations of related controlled foreign corporations but do not include stock holdings in and obligations of members of the affiliated group (as defined in § 1.861-11T(d)).

(vii) A U.S. shareholder is considered to have no excess indebtedness for the year if its debt-to-asset ratio (as determined under paragraph (e)(3)(vi) of this section) for the year does not exceed 0.10.

(4) *Step Three: Allocation of third party interest expense.*—(i) A U.S. shareholder shall allocate to its gross income in the various separate limitation categories described in section 904(d)(1) a portion of its third party interest expense incurred during the year equal in amount to the interest income derived by the U.S. shareholder during the year from allocable related group indebtedness.

(ii) The "allocable related group indebtedness" of a U.S. shareholder for any year is an amount of related group indebtedness equal to the lesser of—

(A) The excess related group indebtedness of the U.S. shareholder for the year (determined under Step One in paragraph (e)(2) of this section); or

(B) The excess U.S. shareholder indebtedness for the year (determined under Step Two in paragraph (e)(3) of this section).

(iii) The amount of interest income derived by a U.S. shareholder from allocable related group indebtedness during the year equals the total amount of interest income derived by the U.S. shareholder during the year with respect to related group indebtedness, multiplied by the ratio of allocable related group indebtedness for the year to the aggregate amount of related group indebtedness for the year.

(iv) The portion of third party interest expense described in paragraph (e)(4)(i) of this section shall be allocated in proportion to the relative average amounts of related group indebtedness held by the U.S. shareholder in each separate limitation category during the year. The remaining portion of third party interest expense of the U.S. shareholder for the year shall be apportioned as provided in §§ 1.861-8T through 1.861-13T, excluding paragraph (e) of § 1.861-10T and this paragraph (e).

(v) The average amount of related group indebtedness held by the U.S. shareholder in each separate limitation category during the year equals the average of the aggregate amounts of such indebtedness in each separate limitation category at the beginning and end of the year. Solely for purposes of this paragraph (e)(4), each debt obligation of a related controlled foreign corporation held by the U.S. shareholder at the beginning or end of the year is attributed to separate limitation categories in the same manner as the stock of the obligor would be attributed under the rules of § 1.861-12T(c)(3), whether or not such stock is held directly by the U.S. shareholder.

(vi) The amount of third party interest expense of a U.S. shareholder allocated pursuant to this paragraph (e)(4) shall not exceed the total amount of the third party interest expense of the U.S. shareholder for the year (excluding any third party interest expense allocated under paragraphs (b) and (c) of § 1.861-10T).

(5) *Definitions.*—For purposes of this paragraph (e), the following terms shall have the following meanings.

(i) *U.S. shareholder.*—The term "U.S. shareholder" has the same meaning as the term "United States shareholder" when used in section 957, except that, in the case of a United States shareholder that is a member of an affiliated group (as defined in § 1.861-11T(d)), the entire affiliated group is considered to constitute a single U.S. shareholder.

(ii) *Related person.*—For the definition of the term "related person", see § 1.861-8T(c)(2). A controlled foreign corporation is considered "related" to a U.S. shareholder if it is a related person with respect to the U.S. shareholder.

(6) *Determination of asset values.*—A U.S. shareholder shall determine the values of the assets of each related controlled foreign corporation (for purposes of Step One in paragraph (e)(2) of this section) and the assets of the U.S. shareholder (for purposes of Step Two in paragraph (e)(3) of this section) for any year in accordance with the valuation method (tax book value or fair market value) elected for that year pursuant to § 1.861-9T(g). However, solely for purposes of this paragraph (e), a U.S. shareholder may instead choose to determine the values of the assets of all related controlled foreign corporations by reference to their values as reflected on Forms 5471 (the annual information return with respect to each related controlled foreign corporation), subject to the translation rules of paragraph (e)(8)(i) of this section. This method of valuation may be used only if the taxable years of each of the related controlled foreign corporations begin with, or no more than one month earlier than, the taxable year of the U.S. shareholder. Once chosen for a taxable year, this method of valuation must be used in each subsequent taxable year and may be changed only with the consent of the Commissioner.

(7) *Adjustments to asset value.*—For purposes of apportioning remaining interest expense under § 1.861-9T, a U.S. shareholder shall reduce (but not below zero) the value of its assets for the year (as determined under § 1.861-9T(g)(3) or (h)) by an amount equal to the allocable related group indebtedness of the U.S. shareholder for the year (as determined under Step Three in paragraph (e)(4)(ii) of this section). This reduction is allocated among assets in each separate limitation category in proportion to the average amount of related group indebtedness held by the U.S. shareholder in each separate limitation category during the year (as determined under Step Three in paragraph (e)(4)(v) of this section).

(8) *Special rules.*—(i) *Exchange rates.*—All indebtedness amounts and asset values (including current year and base year amounts and values) denominated in a foreign currency shall be translated into U.S. dollars at the exchange rate for the current year. The exchange rate for the current year may be determined under any reasonable method (*e.g.,* average of month-end exchange rates for each month in the current year) if it is consistently applied to the current year and all base years. Once chosen for a taxable year, a method for determining an exchange rate must be used in each subsequent taxable year and will be treated as a method of accounting for purposes of section 446. A taxpayer may apply a different translation rule only with the prior consent of the Commissioner. In this regard, the Commissioner will be guided by the extent to which a different rule would reduce the comparability of dollar amounts of indebtedness and dollar asset values for the base years and the current year.

(ii) *Exempt assets.*—Solely for purposes of this paragraph (e), any exempt assets otherwise excluded under section 864(e)(3) and § 1.861-8T(d) shall be included as assets of the U.S. shareholder or related controlled foreign corporation.

(iii) *Exclusion of certain directly allocated indebtedness and assets.*—Qualified nonrecourse indebtedness (as defined in § 1.861-10T(b)(2)) and indebtedness incurred in connection with an integrated financial transaction (as defined in § 1.861-10T(c)(2)) shall be excluded from U.S. shareholder indebtedness and related group indebtedness. In addition, assets which are the subject of qualified nonrecourse indebtedness or integrated financial transactions shall be excluded from the assets of the U.S. shareholder and each related controlled foreign corporation.

(iv) *Exclusion of certain receivables.*—Receivables between related controlled foreign corporations (or between members of the affiliated group constituting the U.S. shareholder) shall be excluded from the assets of the related controlled foreign corporation (or affiliated group member) holding such receivables. See also § 1.861-11T(e)(1).

(v) *Classification of certain loans as related group indebtedness.*—If—

(A) A U.S. shareholder owns stock in a related controlled foreign corporation which is a resident of a country that—

(1) Does not impose a withholding tax of 5 percent or more upon payments of dividends to a U.S. shareholder; and

(2) Does not, for the taxable year of the controlled foreign corporation, subject the income of the controlled foreign corporation to an income tax which is greater than that percentage specified under § 1.954-1T (d)(1)(i) of the maximum rate of tax specified under section 11 of the Code, and

(B) The controlled foreign corporation has outstanding a loan or loans to one or more other related controlled foreign corporations, or the controlled foreign corporation has made a direct or indirect capital contribution to one or more other related controlled foreign corporations which have outstanding a loan or loans to one or more other related controlled foreign corporations,

then, to the extent of the aggregate amount of its capital contributions in taxable years beginning after December 31, 1986, to the related controlled foreign corporation that made such loans or additional contributions, the U.S. shareholder itself shall be treated as having made the loans described in paragraph (e)(8)(v)(B) of this section and, thus, such loan amounts shall be considered related group indebtedness. However, for purposes of paragraph (e)(4) of this section, interest income derived by the U.S. shareholder during the year from related group indebtedness shall not include any income derived with respect to the U.S. shareholder's ownership of stock in the related controlled foreign corporation that made such loans or additional contributions.

(vi) *Classification of certain stock as related person indebtedness.*—In determining the amount of its related group indebtedness for any taxable year, a U.S. shareholder must treat as related group indebtedness its holding of stock in a related controlled foreign corporation if, during such taxable year, such related controlled foreign corporation claims a deduction for interest under foreign law for distributions on such stock. However, for purposes of paragraph (e)(4) of this section, interest income derived by the U.S. shareholder during the year from related group indebtedness shall not include any income derived with respect to the U.S. shareholder's ownership of stock in the related controlled foreign corporation.

(9) *Corporate events.*—(i) *Initial acquisition of a controlled foreign corporation.*—If the foreign base period of the U.S. shareholder for any year includes a base year in which the U.S. shareholder did not hold stock in any related controlled foreign corporation, then, in computing the foreign base period ratio, the related group debt-to-asset ratio of the U.S. shareholder for any such base year shall be deemed to be 0.10.

(ii) *Incorporation of U.S. shareholder.*—(A) *Nonapplication.*—This paragraph (e) does not apply to the first taxable year of the U.S. shareholder. However, this paragraph (e) does apply to all following years, including years in which later members of the affiliated group may be incorporated.

(B) *Foreign and U.S. base period ratios.*—In computing the foreign and U.S. base period ratios, the foreign and U.S. base periods of the U.S. shareholder shall be considered to be only the period prior to the current year that the U.S. shareholder was in existence if this prior period is less than five taxable years.

(iii) *Acquisition of additional corporations.*—(A) If a U.S. shareholder acquires (directly or indirectly) stock of a foreign or domestic corporation which, by reason of the acquisition, then becomes a related controlled foreign corporation or a member of the affiliated group, then in determining excess related group indebtedness or excess U.S. shareholder indebtedness, the indebtedness and assets of the acquired corporation shall be taken into account only at the end of the acquisition year and in following years. Thus, amounts of indebtedness and assets and the various debt-to-asset ratios of the U.S. shareholder existing at the beginning of the acquisition year or relating to preceding years are not recalculated to take account of indebtedness and assets of the acquired corporation existing as of dates before the end of the year. If, however, a major acquisition is made within the last three months of the year and a substantial distortion of values for the year would otherwise result, the taxpayer must take into account the average values of the acquired indebtedness and assets weighted to reflect the time such indebtedness is owed and such assets are held by the taxpayer during the year.

Reg. § 1.861-10(e)(9)(iii)(A)

(B) In the case of a reverse acquisition subject to this paragraph (e)(9), the rules of § 1.1502-75(d)(3) apply in determining which corporations are the acquiring and acquired corporations. For this purpose, whether corporations are affiliated is determined under § 1.861-11T(d).

(C) If the stock of a U.S. shareholder is acquired by (and, by reason of such acquisition, the U.S. shareholder becomes affiliated with) a corporation described below, then such U.S. shareholder shall be considered to have acquired such corporation for purposes of the application of the rules of this paragraph (e). A corporation to which this paragraph (e)(9)(iii)(C) applies is—

(1) A corporation which is not affiliated with any other corporation (other than another similarly described corporation); and

(2) Substantially all of the assets of which consist of cash, securities and stock.

(iv) *Election to compute base period ratios by including acquired corporations.*—A U.S. shareholder may choose, solely for purposes of paragraph (e)(9)(i) and (iii) of this section, to compute its foreign and U.S. base period ratios for the acquisition year and all subsequent years by taking into account the indebtedness and asset values of the acquired corporation or corporations (including related group indebtedness owed to a former U.S. shareholder) at the beginning of the acquisition year and in each of the five base years preceding the acquisition year. This election, if made for an acquisition, must be made for all other acquisitions occurring during the same taxable year or initiated in that year and concluded in the following year.

(v) *Dispositions.*—If a U.S. shareholder disposes of stock of a foreign or domestic corporation which, by reason of the disposition, then ceases to be a related controlled foreign corporation or a member of the affiliated group (unless liquidated or merged into a related corporation), in determining excess related group indebtedness or excess U.S. shareholder indebtedness, the indebtedness and assets of the divested corporation shall be taken into account only at the beginning of the disposition year and for the relevant preceding years. Thus, amounts of indebtedness and assets and the various debt-to-asset ratios of the U.S. shareholder existing at the end of the year or relating to following years are not affected by indebtedness and assets of the divested corporation existing as of dates after the beginning of the year. If, however, a major disposition is made within the first three months of the year and a substantial distortion of values for the year would otherwise result, the taxpayer must take into account the average values of the divested indebtedness and assets weighted to reflect the time such indebtedness is owed and such assets are held by the taxpayer during the year.

(vi) *Election to compute base period ratios by excluding divested corporations.*—A U.S. shareholder may choose, solely for purposes of paragraph (e)(9)(v) and (vii) of this section, to compute its foreign and U.S. base period ratios for the disposition year and all subsequent years without taking into account the indebtedness and asset values of the divested corporation or corporations at the beginning of the disposition year and in each of the five base years preceding the disposition year. This election, if made for a disposition, must be made for all other dispositions occurring during the same taxable year or initiated in that year and concluded in the following year.

(vii) *Section 355 transactions.*—A U.S. corporation which becomes a separate U.S. shareholder as a result of a distribution of its stock to which section 355 applies shall be considered—

(A) As disposed of by the U.S. shareholder of the affiliated group of which the distributing corporation is a member, with this disposition subject to the rules of paragraphs (e)(9)(v) and (vi) of this section; and

(B) As having the same related group debt-to-asset ratio and debt-to-asset ratio as the distributing U.S. shareholder in each year preceding the year of distribution for purposes of applying this paragraph (e) to the year of distribution and subsequent years of the distributed corporation.

(10) *Effective date.*—(i) *Taxable years beginning after December 31, 1991.*—The provisions of this paragraph (e) apply to all taxable years beginning after December 31, 1991.

(ii) *Taxable years beginning after December 31, 1987 and before January 1, 1992.*—The provisions of § 1.861-10T(e) apply to taxable years beginning after December 31, 1987, and before January 1, 1992. The taxpayer may elect to apply the provisions of this paragraph (e) (in lieu of the provisions of § 1.861-10T(e)) for any taxable year beginning after December 31, 1987, but this paragraph (e) must then be applied to all subsequent taxable years.

(11) The following example illustrates the provisions of this paragraph (e):

Example. (i) *Facts.* X, a domestic corporation, elects to apply this paragraph (e) to its 1990 tax year. X has a calendar taxable year and apportions its interest expense on the basis of the tax book value of its assets. In 1990, X incurred deductible third-party interest ex-

Determination of Sources of Income

pense of $24,960 on an average amount of indebtedness (determined on the basis of beginning-of-year and end-of-year amounts) of $249,600. X manufactures widgets, all of which are sold in the United States. X owns all of the stock of Y, a controlled foreign corporation that also has a calendar taxable year and is also engaged in the manufacture and sale of widgets. Y has no earnings and profits or deficit of earnings and profits attributable to taxable years prior to 1987. X's total assets and their average tax book values (determined on the basis of beginning-of-year and end-of-year tax book values) for 1990 are:

Asset	Average Tax Book Value
Plant and equipment	$315,000
Corporate headquarters	60,000
Y stock	75,000
Y note	50,000
	$500,000

(1) X's "foreign base period ratio" for 1990, an average of its ratios of related group indebtedness to related group assets for 1985 through 1989, is:

$$(.11 + .12 + .12 + .12 + .13)/5 = .12$$

(2) X's "allowable related group indebtedness" for 1990 is:

$$\$250{,}000 \times .12 = \$30{,}000$$

(3) X's "excess related group indebtedness" for 1990 is:

$$\$50{,}000 - \$30{,}000 = \$20{,}000$$

Y had $25,000 of income before the deduction of any interest expense. Of this total, $5,000 is high withholding tax interest income. The remaining $20,000 is derived from widget sales, and constitutes foreign source general limitation income. Assume that Y has no deductions from gross income other than interest expense. During 1990, Y paid $5,000 of interest expense to X on the Y note and $10,000 of interest expense to third parties, giving Y total interest expense of $15,000. X elects pursuant to § 1.861-9T to apportion Y's interest expense under the gross income method prescribed in section 1.861-9T(j).

(ii) *Step 1:* Using a beginning and end of year average, X (the U.S. shareholder) held the following average amounts of indebtedness of Y and Y had the following average asset values:

	1985	1986-88	1989	1990
(A) Related group indebtedness	$11,000	24,000	26,000	50,000
(B) Average Value of Assets of Related CFC	$100,000	200,000	200,000	250,000
(C) Related Group Debt-to-Asset Ratio	.11	.12	.13	.20

X's related group indebtedness of $50,000 for 1990 is greater than its allowable related group indebtedness of $24,000 for 1989 (assuming a foreign base period ratio in 1989 of .12), and X's related group debt-to-asset ratio for 1990 is .20, which is greater than the ratio of .10 described in paragraph (e)(2)(vii)(B) of this section. Therefore, X's excess related group indebtedness for 1990 remains at $20,000.

(iii) *Step 2:* Using a beginning and end of year average, X has the following average amounts of U.S. and foreign indebtedness and average asset values:

	1985	1986	1987	1988	1989	1990
(1)	$231,400	225,000	225,000	225,000	220,800	249,600
(2)	$445,000	450,000	450,000	450,000	460,000	480,000 (a)
(3)	.52	.50	.50	.50	.48	.52

(1) U.S. and foreign indebtedness
(2) Average value of assets of U.S. shareholder
(3) Debt-to-Asset ratio of U.S. shareholder
(a) [500,000 – 20,000 (excess related group indebtedness determined in Step 1)]

X's "U.S. base period ratio" for 1990 is:
$$(.52 + .50 + .50 + .50 + .48)/5 = .50$$

X's "allowable indebtedness" for 1990 is:
$$\$480{,}000 \times .50 = \$240{,}000$$

X's "excess U.S. shareholder indebtedness" for 1990 is:
$$\$249{,}600 - \$240{,}000 = \$9{,}600$$

X's debt-to-asset ratio for 1990 is .52, which is greater than the ratio of .10 described in paragraph (e)(3)(vii) of this section. Therefore, X's excess U.S. shareholder indebtedness for 1990 remains at $9,600.

Reg. §1.861-10(e)(11)

(iv) *Step 3:* (a) Since X's excess U.S. shareholder indebtedness of $9,600 is less than its excess related group indebtedness of $20,000, X's allocable related group indebtedness for 1990 is $9,600. The amount of interest received by X during 1990 on allocable related group indebtedness is:

$$\$5,000 \times \frac{\$9,600}{\$50,000} = \$960$$

(b) Therefore, $960 of X's third party interest expense ($24,960) shall be allocated among various separate limitation categories in proportion to the relative average amounts of Y obligations held by X in each such category. The amount of Y obligations in each limitation category is determined in the same manner as the stock of Y would be attributed under the rules of § 1.861-12T(c)(3). Since Y's interest expense is apportioned under the gross income method prescribed in § 1.861-9T(j), the Y stock must be characterized under the gross income method described in § 1.861-12T(c)(3)(iii). Y's gross income net of interest expense is determined as follows:

Foreign source high withholding tax interest income = $5,000 − [($15,000) multiplied by ($5,000)/($5,000 + $20,000)]
= $2,000

and

Foreign source general limitation income = $20,000 − [($15,000) multiplied by ($20,000)/($5,000 + $20,000)]
= $8,000

(c) Therefore, $192 [($960 × $2,000/($2,000+$8,000)] of X's third party interest expense is allocated to foreign source high withholding tax interest income and $768 [$960 × $8,000/($2,000+$8,000)] is allocated to foreign source general limitation income.

(v) As a result of these direct allocations, for purposes of apportioning X's remaining interest expense under § 1.861-9T, the value of X's assets generating foreign source general limitation income is reduced by the principal amount of indebtedness the interest on which is directly allocated to foreign source general limitation income ($7,680), and the value of X's assets generating foreign source high withholding tax interest income is reduced by the principal amount of indebtedness the interest on which is directly allocated to foreign source high withholding tax interest income ($1,920), determined as follows:

Reduction of X's assets generating foreign source general limitation income:

$$\text{X's allocable related group indebtedness} \times \frac{\text{Y's Foreign source general limitation income}}{\text{Y's Foreign source income}}$$

$$\$9,600 \times \$8,000/(\$8,000 + \$2,000) = \$7,680$$

Reduction of X's assets generating foreign source high withholding tax interest income:

$$\text{X's allocable related group indebtedness} \times \frac{\text{Y's Foreign source high withholding tax interest income}}{\text{Y's Foreign source income}}$$

$$\$9,600 \times \$2,000/(\$8,000 + \$2,000) = \$1,920$$

[Reg. § 1.861-10.]

☐ [T.D. 8410, 4-14-92.]

§ 1.861-10T. Special allocations of interest expense (Temporary).

(a) *In general.*—This section applies to all taxpayers and provides three exceptions to the rules of § 1.861-9T that require the allocation and apportionment of interest expense on the basis of all assets of all members of the affiliated group. Paragraph (b) of this section describes the direct allocation of interest expense to the income generated by certain assets that are subject to qualified nonrecourse indebtedness. Paragraph (c) of this section describes the direct allocation of interest expense to income generated by certain assets that are acquired in integrated financial transactions. Paragraph (d) of this section provides special rules that are applicable to all transactions described in paragraphs (b) and (c) of this section. Paragraph (e) of this section requires the direct allocation of third party interest of an affiliated group to such group's investment in related controlled foreign corporations in cases involving excess related person indebtedness (as defined therein). See also § 1.861-9T(b)(5), which requires direct allocation of amortizable bond premium.

(b) *Qualified nonrecourse indebtedness.*—(1) *In general.*—In the case of qualified nonrecourse indebtedness (as defined in paragraph (b)(2) of this section), the deduction for interest shall be considered directly allocable solely to the gross income which the property acquired, constructed, or improved with the proceeds of the indebtedness generates, has generated, or could reasonably be expected to generate.

(2) *Qualified nonrecourse indebtedness defined.*—The term "qualified nonrecourse indebtedness" means any borrowing that is not excluded by paragraph (b)(4) of this section if:

(i) The borrowing is specifically incurred for the purpose of purchasing, constructing, or improving identified property that is either depreciable tangible personal property or real property with a useful life of more than one year or for the purpose of purchasing amortizable intangible personal property with a useful life of more than one year;

(ii) The proceeds are actually applied to purchase, construct, or improve the identified property;

(iii) Except as provided in paragraph (b)(7)(ii) (relating to certain third party guarantees in leveraged lease transactions), the creditor can look only to the identified property (or any lease or other interest therein) as security for payment of the principal and interest on the loan and, thus, cannot look to any other property, the borrower, or any third party with respect to repayment of principal or interest on the loan;

(iv) The cash flow from the property, as defined in paragraph (b)(3) of this section, is reasonably expected to be sufficient in the first year of ownership as well as in each subsequent year of ownership to fulfill the terms and conditions of the loan agreement with respect to the amount and timing of payments of interest and original issue discount and periodic payments of principal in each such year; and

(v) There are restrictions in the loan agreement on the disposal or use of the property consistent with the assumptions described in subdivisions (iii) and (iv) of this paragraph (b)(2).

(3) *Cash flow defined.*—(i) *In general.*—The term "cash flow from the property" as used in paragraph (b)(2)(iv) of this section means a stream of revenue (as computed under paragraph (b)(3)(ii) of this section) substantially all of which derives directly from the property. The phrase "cash flow from the property" does not include revenue if a significant portion thereof is derived from activities such as sales, labor, services, or the use of other property. Thus, revenue derived from the sale or lease of inventory or of similar property does not constitute cash flow from the property, including plant or equipment used in the manufacture and sale or lease, or purchase and sale or lease, of such inventory or similar property. In addition, revenue derived in part from the performance of services that are not ancillary and subsidiary to the use of property does not constitute cash flow from the property.

(ii) *Self-constructed assets.*—The activities associated with self-construction of assets shall be considered to constitute labor or services for purposes of paragraph (b)(3)(i) only if the self-constructed asset—

(A) Is constructed for the purposes of resale, or

(B) Without regard to purpose, is sold to an unrelated person within one year from the date that the property is placed in service for purposes of section 167.

(iii) *Computation of cash flow.*—Cash flow is computed by subtracting cash disbursements excluding debt service from cash receipts.

(iv) *Analysis of operating costs.*—[Reserved]

(iv) *Examples.*—The principles of this paragraph may be demonstrated by the following examples.

Example (1). In 1987, X borrows $100,000 in order to purchase an apartment building, which X then purchases. The loan is secured only by the building and the leases thereon. Annual debt service on the loan is $12,000. Annual gross rents from the building are $20,000. Annual taxes on the building are $2,000. Other expenses deductible under section 162 are $2,000. Rents are reasonably expected to remain stable or increase in subsequent years, and taxes and expenses are reasonably expected to remain proportional to gross rents in subsequent years. X provides security, maintenance, and utilities to the tenants of the building. Based on facts and circumstances, it is determined that, although services are provided to tenants, these services are ancillary and subsidiary to the occupancy of the apartments. Accordingly, the cash flow of $16,000 is considered to constitute a return from the property. Furthermore, such cash flow is sufficient to fulfill the terms and conditions of the loan agreement as required by paragraph (b)(2)(iii).

Example (2). In 1987, X borrows funds in order to purchase a hotel, which X then purchases and operates. The loan is secured only by the hotel. Based on facts and circumstances, it is determined that the operation of the hotel involves services the value of which is significant in relation to amounts paid to occupy the rooms. Thus, a significant portion of the cash flow is derived from the performance of services incidental to the occupancy of hotel rooms. Accordingly, the cash flow from the hotel is considered not to constitute a return on or from the property.

Example (3). In 1987, X borrows funds in order to build a factory, which X then builds and operates. The loan is secured only by the factory and the equipment therein. Based on the facts and circumstances, it is determined that the operation of the factory involves significant expenditures for labor and raw materials. Thus, a significant portion of the cash flow is derived from labor and the processing of raw materials. Accordingly, the cash flow from the factory is considered not to constitute a return on or from the property.

(4) *Exclusions.*—The term "qualified nonrecourse indebtedness" shall not include any transaction that—

(i) Lacks economic significance within the meaning of paragraph (b)(5) of this section;

(ii) Involves cross collateralization within the meaning of paragraph (b)(6) of this section;

(iii) Except in the case of a leveraged lease described in paragraph (b)(7)(ii) of this section, involves credit enhancement within the meaning of paragraph (b)(7) of this section or, with respect to loans made on or after October 14, 1988, does not, under the terms of the loan documents, prohibit the acquisition by the holder of bond insurance or similar forms of credit enhancement;

(iv) Involves the purchase of inventory;

(v) Involves the purchase of any financial asset, including stock in a corporation, an interest in a partnership or a trust, or the debt obligation of any obligor (although interest incurred in order to purchase certain financial instruments may qualify for direct allocation under paragraph (c) of this section);

(vi) Involves interest expense that constitutes qualified residence interest as defined in section 163(h)(3); or

(vii) [Reserved].

(5) *Economic significance.*—Indebtedness that otherwise qualifies under paragraph (b)(2) shall nonetheless be subject to apportionment under § 1.861-9T if, taking into account all the facts and circumstances, the transaction (including the security arrangement) lacks economic significance.

(6) *Cross collateralization.*—The term "cross collateralization" refers to the pledge as security for a loan of—

(i) Any asset of the borrower other than the identified property described in paragraph (b)(2) of this section, or

(ii) Any asset belonging to any related person, as defined in § 1.861-8T(c)(2).

(7) *Credit enhancement.*—(i) *In general.*—Except as provided in paragraph (b)(7)(ii) of this section, the term "credit enhancement" refers to any device, including a contract, letter of credit, or guaranty, that expands the creditor's rights, directly or indirectly, beyond the identified property purchased, constructed, or improved with the funds advanced and, thus, effectively provides as security for a loan the assets of any person other than the borrower. The acquisition of bond insurance or any other contract of suretyship by an initial or subsequent holder of an obligation shall constitute credit enhancement.

(ii) *Special rule for leveraged leases.*—For purposes of this paragraph (b), the term "credit enhancement" shall not include any device under which any person that is not a related person within the meaning of § 1.861-8T(c)(2) agrees to guarantee, without recourse to the lessor or any person related to the lessor, a lessor's payment of principal and interest on indebtedness that was incurred in order to purchase or improve an asset that is depreciable tangible personal property or depreciable tangible real property (and the land on which such real property is situated) that is leased to a lessee that is not a related person in a transaction that constitutes a lease for federal income tax purposes.

(iii) *Syndication of credit risk and sale of loan participations.*—The term "syndication of credit risk" refers to an arrangement in which one primary lender secures the promise of a secondary lender to bear a portion of the primary lender's credit risk on a loan. The term "sale of loan participations" refers to an arrangement in which one primary lender divides a loan into several portions, sells and assigns all rights with respect to one or more portions to participating secondary lenders, and does not remain at risk in any manner with respect to the portion assigned. For purposes of this paragraph (b), the syndication of credit risk shall constitute credit enhancement because the primary lender can look to secondary lenders for payment of the loan, notwithstanding limitations on the amount of the secondary lender's liability. Conversely, the sale of loan participations does not constitute credit enhancement, because the holder of each portion of the loan can look solely to the asset securing the loan and not to the credit or other assets of any person.

(8) *Other arrangements that do not constitute cross collateralization or credit enhancement.*—For purposes of paragraphs (b)(6) and (7) of this section, the following arrangements do not constitute cross collateralization or credit enhancement:

(i) *Integrated projects.*—A taxpayer's pledge of multiple assets of an integrated project, provided that the integrated project. An integrated project consists of functionally related and geographically contiguous assets that, as to the taxpayer, are used in the same trade or business.

(ii) *Insurance.*—A taxpayer's purchase of third-party casualty and liability insurance on the collateral or, by contract, bearing the risk of loss associated with destruction of the collateral or with respect to the attachment of third party liability claims.

(iii) *After-acquired property.*—Extension of a creditor's security interest to improvements made to the collateral, provided that the extension does not constitute excess collateralization under paragraph (b)(6), determined by taking into account the value of improvements at the time the improvements are made and the value of the original property at the time the loan was made.

(iv) *Warranties of completion and maintenance.*—A taxpayer's warranty to a creditor that it will complete construction or manufacture of the collateral or that it will maintain the collateral in good condition.

(v) *Substitution of collateral.*—A taxpayer's right to substitute collateral under any loan contract. However, after the right is exercised, the loan shall no longer constitute qualified nonrecourse indebtedness.

(9) *Refinancings.*—If a taxpayer refinances qualified nonrecourse indebtedness (as defined in paragraph (b)(2) of this section) with new indebtedness, such new indebtedness shall continue to qualify only if—

(i) The principal amount of the new indebtedness does not exceed by more than five percent the remaining principal amount of the original indebtedness,

(ii) The term of the new indebtedness does not exceed by more than six months the remaining term of the original indebtedness, and

(iii) The requirements of this paragraph (other than those of paragraph (b)(2)(i) and (ii) of this section) are satisfied at the time of the refinancing, and the exclusions contained in this paragraph (b)(4) do not apply.

(10) *Post-construction permanent financing.*—Financing that is obtained after the completion of constructed property will be deemed to satisfy the requirements of paragraph (b)(2)(i) and (ii) of this section if—

(i) The financing is obtained within one year after the constructed property or substantially all of a constructed integrated project (as defined in paragraph (b)(9)(i) of this section) is placed in service for purposes of section 167; and

(ii) The financing does not exceed the cost of construction (including construction period interest).

(11) *Assumptions of pre-existing qualified nonrecourse indebtedness.*—If a transferee of property that is subject to qualified nonrecourse indebtedness assumes such indebtedness, the indebtedness shall continue to constitute qualified nonrecourse indebtedness, provided that the assumption in no way alters the qualified status of the debt.

(12) *Excess collateralization.*—[Reserved]

(c) *Direct allocations in the case of certain integrated financial transactions.*—(1) *General rule.*—Interest expense incurred on funds borrowed in connection with an integrated financial transaction (as defined in paragraph (c)(2) of this section) shall be directly allocated to the income generated by the investment funded with the borrowed amounts.

(2) *Definition.*—The term "integrated financial transaction" refers to any transaction in which—

(i) The taxpayer—

(A) Incurs indebtedness for the purpose of making an identified term investment,

(B) Identifies the indebtedness as incurred for such purpose at the time the indebtedness is incurred, and

(C) Makes the identified term investment within ten business days after incurring the indebtedness;

(ii) The return on the investment is reasonably expected to be sufficient throughout the term of the investment to fulfill the terms and conditions of the loan agreement with respect to the amount and timing of payments of principal and interest or original issue discount;

(iii) The income constitutes interest or original issue discount or would constitute income equivalent to interest if earned by a controlled foreign corporation (as described in § 1.954-2T(h));

(iv) The debt incurred and the investment mature within ten business days of each other;

(v) The investment does not relate in any way to the operation of, and is not made in the normal course of, the trade or business of the taxpayer or any related person, including the financing of the sale of goods or the performance of services by the taxpayer or any related person, or the compensation of the taxpayer's employees (including any contribution or loan to an employee stock ownership plan (as defined in section 4975(e)(7)) or other plan that is qualified under section 401(a)); and

(vi) The borrower does not constitute a financial services entity (as defined in section 904 and the regulations thereunder).

(3) *Roll-overs.*—In the event that a taxpayer sells or otherwise liquidates an investment described in paragraph (c)(2) of this section, the interest expense incurred on the borrowing shall, subsequent to that liquidation, no longer qualify for direct allocation under this paragraph (c).

(4) *Examples.*—The principles of this paragraph (c) may be demonstrated by the following examples.

Example (1). X is a manufacturer and does not constitute a financial services entity as defined in the regulations under section 904. On January 1, 1988, X borrows $100 for 6 months at an annual interest rate of 10 percent. X identifies on its books and records by the close of that day that the indebtedness is being incurred for the purpose of making an investment that is intended to qualify as an integrated financial transaction. On January 5, 1988, X uses the proceeds to purchase a portfolio of stock that approximates the composition of the Standard & Poor's 500 Index. On that day, X also enters into a forward sale contract that requires X to sell the stock on June 1, 1988 for $110. X identifies on its books and records by the close of January 5, 1988, that the portfolio stock purchases and the forward sale contract constitute part of the integrated financial transaction with respect to which the identified borrowing was incurred. Under § 1.954-2T(h), the income derived from the transaction would constitute income equivalent to interest. Assuming that the return on the investment to be derived on June 1, 1988, will be sufficient to pay the interest due on June 1, 1988, the interest on the borrowing is directly allocated to the gain from the investment.

Example (2). X does not constitute a financial services entity as defined in the regulations under section 904. X is in the business of, among other things, issuing credit cards to consumers and purchasing from merchants who accept the X card the receivables of consumers who make purchases with the X card. X borrows from Y in order to purchase X credit card receivables from Z, a merchant. Assuming that the Y borrowing satisfies the other requirements of paragraph (c)(2) of this section, the transaction nonetheless cannot constitute an integrated financial transaction because the purchase relates to the operation of X's trade or business.

Example (3). Assume the same facts as in Example 2, except that X borrows in order to purchase the receivables of A, a merchant who does not accept the X card and is not otherwise engaged directly or indirectly in any business transaction with X. Because the borrowing is not related to the operation of X's trade or business, the borrowing may qualify as an integrated financial transaction if the other requirements of paragraph (c)(2) of this section are satisfied.

(d) *Special rules.*—In applying paragraphs (b) and (c) of this section, the following special rules shall apply.

(1) *Related person transactions.*—The rules of this section shall not apply to the extent that any transaction—

(i) Involves either indebtedness between related persons (as defined in section § 1.861-8T(c)(2)) or indebtedness incurred from unrelated persons for the purpose of purchasing property from a related person; or

(ii) Involves the purchase of property that is leased to a related person (as defined in section § 1.861-8T(c)(2)) in a transaction described in paragraph (b) of this section. If a taxpayer purchases property and leases such property in whole or in part to a related person, a portion of the interest incurred in connection with such an acquisition, based on the ratio that the value of the property leased to the related person bears to the total value of the property, shall not qualify for direct allocation under this section.

(2) *Consideration of assets or income to which interest is directly allocated in apportioning other interest expense.*—In apportioning interest expense under § 1.861-9T, the year-end value of any asset to which interest expense is directly allocated under this section during the current taxable year shall be reduced to the extent provided in § 1.861-9T(g)(2)(iii) to reflect the portion of the principal amount of the indebtedness outstanding at year-end relating to the interest which is directly allocated. A similar adjustment shall be made to the end-of-year value of assets for the prior year for purposes of determining the beginning-of-year value of assets for the current year. These adjustments shall be made prior to averaging be-

ginning-of-year and end-of-year values pursuant to § 1.861-9T(g)(2). In apportioning interest expense under the modified gross income method, gross income shall be reduced by the amount of income to which interest expense is directly allocated under this section.

* * *

[Temporary Reg. § 1.861-10T.]

☐ [*T.D.* 8228, 9-9-88.]

§ 1.861-11. Special rules for allocating and apportioning interest expense of an affiliated group of corporations.—(a) through (c) [Reserved]. For further guidance, see § 1.861-11T(a) through (c).

(d) *Definition of affiliated group.*—(1) *General rule.*—For purposes of this section, in general, the term *affiliated group* has the same meaning as is given that term by section 1504, except that section 936 corporations are also included within the affiliated group to the extent provided in paragraph (d)(2) of this section. Section 1504(a) defines an affiliated group as one or more chains of includible corporations connected through 80-percent stock ownership with a common parent corporation which is an includible corporation (as defined in section 1504(b)). In the case of a corporation that either becomes or ceases to be a member of the group during the course of the corporation's taxable year, only the interest expense incurred by the group member during the period of membership shall be allocated and apportioned as if all members of the group were a single corporation. In this regard, assets held during the period of membership shall be taken into account. Other interest expense incurred by the group member during its taxable year but not during the period of membership shall be allocated and apportioned without regard to the other members of the group.

(2) *Inclusion of section 936 corporations.*—(i) *Rule.*—(A) *In general.*—Except as otherwise provided in paragraph (d)(2)(i)(B) of this section, the exclusion of section 936 corporations from the affiliated group under section 1504(b)(4) does not apply for purposes of this section. Thus, a section 936 corporation that meets the ownership requirements of section 1504(a) is a member of the affiliated group.

(B) *Exception for purposes of alternative minimum tax.*—The exclusion from the affiliated group of section 936 corporations under section 1504(b)(4) shall be operative for purposes of the application of this section solely in determining the amount of foreign source alternative minimum taxable income within each separate category and the alternative minimum tax foreign tax credit pursuant to section 59(a). Thus, a section 936 corporation that meets the ownership requirements of section 1504(a) is not a member of the affiliated group for purposes of determining the amount of foreign source alternative minimum taxable income within each separate category and the alternative minimum tax foreign tax credit pursuant to section 59(a).

(ii) *Section 936 corporation defined.*—For purposes of this section, § 1.861-9, and § 1.861-14, the term *section 936 corporation* means, for any taxable year, a corporation with an election in effect to be eligible for the credit provided under section 936(a)(1) or section 30A for the taxable year.

(iii) *Example.*—This example illustrates the provisions of paragraph (d)(2)(i) of this section:

Example—(A) *Facts.* X owns all of the stock of Y. XY constitutes an affiliated group of corporations within the meaning of section 1504(a) and uses the tax book value method of apportionment. In 2000, Y owns all of the stock of Z, a section 936 corporation. Z manufactures widgets in Puerto Rico. Y purchases these widgets and markets them exclusively in the United States. Of the three corporations, only Z has foreign source income, which includes both qualified possessions source investment income and general limitation income. For purposes of section 904, Z's qualified possessions source investment income constitutes foreign source passive income. In computing the section 30A benefit, Y and Z have elected the cost sharing method. Of the three corporations, only X has debt and, thus, only X incurs interest expense.

(B) *Analysis for regular tax.* Assume first that X has no alternative minimum tax liability. Under paragraph (d)(2) of this section, Z is treated as a member of the XY affiliated group for purposes of allocating and apportioning interest expense for regular tax purposes. As provided in § 1.861-11T(b)(2), section 864(e)(1) and (5) do not apply in computing the combined taxable income of Y and Z under section 936, but these rules do apply in computing the foreign source taxable income of the XY affiliated group. The effect of including Z in the affiliated group is that X, the only debtor corporation in the group, must, under the asset method described in § 1.861-9T(g), apportion a part of its interest expense to foreign source passive income and foreign source general limitation income. This is because the assets of Z that generate qualified possessions source investment income and general limitation income are included in computing the group apportionment fractions. The result is that, under section 904(f), X has an overall foreign loss in both the passive and general limitation categories, which currently offsets domestic income and must be recaptured against any subsequent years' foreign passive income and general limitation income, respectively, under the rules of that section.

(C) *Analysis for alternative minimum tax.* Assume, alternatively, that X is liable to pay the alternative minimum tax. Pursuant to section 59(a), X must compute its alternative minimum tax foreign tax credit as if section 904 were applied on the basis of alternative minimum taxable income instead of taxable income. Under paragraph (d)(2)(i)(B) of this section, for purposes of the apportionment of interest expense in determining alternative minimum taxable income within each limitation category, Z is not considered a member of the XY affiliated group. Thus, the stock (and not the assets) of Z are included in computing the group apportionment fractions. Pursuant to sections 59(g)(4)(C)(iii)(IV), 861(a)(2)(A), and 862(a)(2), dividends paid by a section 936 corporation are foreign source income subject to a separate foreign tax credit limitation for alternative minimum tax purposes. Thus, under §1.861-9T(g)(3), the stock of Z must be considered attributable solely to the statutory grouping consisting of foreign source dividends from Z. The effect of excluding Z from the affiliated group is that X must apportion a part of its interest expense to the separate category for foreign source dividends from Z in computing alternative minimum taxable income within each separate category. If, as a result, under section 904(f), X has a separate limitation loss or an overall foreign loss in the category for dividends from Z for alternative minimum tax purposes, then that loss must be allocated against X's other income (separate limitation or United States source, as the case may be). The loss must be recaptured in subsequent years under the rules of section 904(f) for purposes of the alternative minimum tax foreign tax credit.

(iv) *Effective date.*—This paragraph (d)(2) applies to taxable years beginning after December 31, 1989.

(d)(3) through (6) [Reserved]. For further guidance see §1.861-11T(d)(3) through (6).

(7) *Special rules for the application of §1.861-11T(d)(6).*—The attribution rules of section 1563(e) and the regulations under that section shall apply in determining indirect ownership under §1.861-11T(d)(6). The Commissioner shall have the authority to disregard trusts, partnerships, and pass-through entities that break affiliated status. Corporations described in §1.861-11T(d)(6) shall be considered to constitute members of an affiliated group that does not file a consolidated return and shall therefore be subject to the limitations imposed under §1.861-11T(g). The affiliated group filing a consolidated return shall be considered to constitute a single corporation for purposes of applying the rules of §1.861-11T(g). For taxable years beginning after December 31, 1989, §1.861-11T(d)(6)(i) shall not apply in determining foreign source alternative minimum taxable income within each separate category and the alternative minimum tax foreign tax credit pursuant to section 59(a) to the extent that such application would result in the inclusion of a section 936 corporation within the affiliated group. This paragraph (d)(7) applies to taxable years beginning after December 31, 1986.

(e) through (g) [Reserved]. For further guidance, see §1.861-11T(e) through (g). [Reg. §1.861-11.]

☐ [T.D. 8916, 12-29-2000.]

§1.861-11T. Special rules for allocating and apportioning interest expense of an affiliated group of corporations (Temporary regulations).—(a) *In general.*—Sections 1.861-9T, 1.861-10T, 1.861-12T, and 1.861-13T provide rules that are generally applicable in apportioning interest expense. The rules of this section relate to affiliated groups of corporations and implement section 864(e)(1) and (5), which requires affiliated group allocation and apportionment of interest expense. The rules of this section apply to taxable years beginning after December 31, 1986, except as otherwise provided in §1.861-13T. Paragraph (b) of this section describes the scope of the application of the rule for the allocation and apportionment of interest expense of affiliated groups of corporations, which is contained in paragraph (c) of this section. Paragraph (d) of this section sets forth the definition of the term "affiliated group" for purposes of this section. Paragraph (e) describes the treatment of loans between members of an affiliated group. Paragraph (f) of this section provides rules concerning the affiliated group allocation and apportionment of interest expense in computing the combined taxable income of a FSC or DISC and its related supplier. Paragraph (g) of this section describes the treatment of losses caused by apportionment of interest expense in the case of an affiliated group that does not file a consolidated return.

(b) *Scope of application.*—(1) *Application of section 864(e)(1) and (5) (concerning the definition and treatment of affiliated groups).*—Section 864(e)(1) and (5) and the portions of this section implementing section 864(e)(1) and (5) apply to the computation of foreign source taxable income for purposes of section 904 (relating to various limitations on the foreign tax credit).

Section 904 imposes separate foreign tax credit limitations on passive income, high withholding interest income, financial services income, shipping income, income consisting of dividends from each noncontrolled section 902 corporation, income consisting of dividends from a DISC or former DISC, taxable income attributable to foreign trade income within the meaning of section 923(b), distributions from an FSC or former FSC, and all other forms of foreign source income not enumerated above ("general limitation income"). Section 864(e)(1) and (5) and the portions of this section implementing section 864(e)(1) and (5) also apply in connection with section 907 to determine reductions in the amount allowed as a foreign tax credit under section 901. Section 864(e)(1) and (5) and the portions of this section implementing section 864(e)(1) and (5) also apply to the computation of the combined taxable income of the related supplier and a foreign sales corporation (FSC) (under sections 921 through 927) as well as the combined taxable income of the related supplier and a domestic international sales corporation (DISC) (under sections 991 through 997).

(2) *Nonapplication of section 864(e)(1) and (5) (concerning the definition and treatment of affiliated groups).*—Section 864(e)(1) and (5) and the portions of this section implementing section 864(e)(1) and (5) do not apply to the computation of subpart F income of controlled foreign corporations (under sections 951 through 964), the computation of combined taxable income of a possessions corporation and its affiliates (under section 936), or the computation of effectively connected taxable income of foreign corporations. For the rules with respect to the allocation and apportionment of interest expenses of foreign corporations other than controlled foreign corporations, see §§ 1.882-4 and 1.882-5.

(c) *General rule for affiliated corporations.*— Except as otherwise provided in this section, the taxable income of each member of an affiliated group within each statutory grouping shall be determined by allocating and apportioning the interest expense of each member according to apportionment fractions which are computed as if all members of such group were a single corporation. For purposes of determining these apportionment fractions, stock in corporations within the affiliated group (as defined in section 864(e)(5) and the rules of this section) shall not be taken into account. In the case of an affiliated group of corporations that files a consolidated return, consolidated foreign tax credit limitations are computed for the group in accordance with the rules of § 1.1502-4. Except as otherwise provided, all the interest expense of all members of the group will be treated as definitely related and therefore allocable to all the gross income of the members of the group and all the assets of all the members of the group shall be taken into account in apportioning this interest expense. For purposes of this section, the term "taxpayer" refers to the affiliated group (regardless of whether the group files a consolidated return), rather than to the separate members thereof.

(d)(1) and (2) [Reserved]. For further guidance, see § 1.861-11(d)(1) and (2).

(3) *Treatment of life insurance companies subject to taxation under section 801.*— (i) *General rule.*—A life insurance company that is subject to taxation under section 801 shall be considered to constitute a member of the affiliated group composed of companies not taxable under section 801 only if a parent corporation so elects under section 1504(c)(2)(A) of the Code. If a parent does not so elect, no adjustments shall be required with respect to such an insurance company under paragraph (g) of this section.

(ii) *Treatment of stock.*—Stock of a life insurance company that is subject to taxation under section 801 that is not included in an affiliated group shall be disregarded in the allocation and apportionment of the interest expense of such affiliated group.

(4) *Treatment of certain financial corporations.*—(i) *In general.*—In the case of an affiliated group (as defined in paragraph (d)(1) of this section), any members that constitute financial corporations as defined in paragraph (d)(4)(ii) of this section shall be treated as a separate affiliated group consisting of financial corporations (the "financial group"). The members of the group that do not constitute financial corporations shall be treated as members of a separate affiliated group consisting of nonfinancial corporations ("the nonfinancial group").

(ii) *Financial corporation defined.*—The term "financial corporation" means any corporation which meets all of the following conditions:

(A) It is described in section 581 (relating to the definition of a bank) or section 591 (relating to the deduction for dividends paid on deposits by mutual savings banks, cooperative banks, domestic building and loan associations, and other savings institutions chartered and supervised as savings and loan or similar associations);

(B) Its business is predominantly with persons other than related persons (within the meaning of section 864(d)(4) and the regulations thereunder) or their customers; and

Reg. § 1.861-11T(d)(4)(ii)(B)

(C) It is required by state or Federal law to be operated separately from any other entity which is not such an institution.

(iii) *Treatment of bank holding companies.*—The total aggregate interest expense of any member of an affiliated group that constitutes a bank holding company subject to regulation under the Bank Holding Company Act of 1956 shall be prorated between the financial group and the nonfinancial group on the basis of the assets in the financial and nonfinancial groups. For purposes of making this proration, the assets of each member of each group, and not the stock basis in each member, shall be taken into account. Any direct or indirect subsidiary of a bank holding company that is predominantly engaged in the active conduct of a banking, financing, or similar business shall be considered to be a financial corporation for purposes of this paragraph (d)(4). The interest expense of the bank holding company must be further apportioned in accordance with § 1.861-9T(f) to the various section 904(d) categories of income contained in both the financial group and the nonfinancial group on the basis of the assets owned by each group. For purposes of computing the apportionment fractions for each group, the assets owned directly by a bank holding company within each limitation category described in section 904(d)(1) (other than stock in affiliates or assets described in § 1.861-9T(f)) shall be treated as owned pro rata by the nonfinancial group and the financial group based on the relative amounts of investment of the bank holding company in the nonfinancial group and financial group.

(iv) *Consideration of stock of the members of one group held by members of the other group.*—In apportioning interest expense, the nonfinancial group shall not take into account the stock of any lower-tier corporation that is treated as a member of the financial group under paragraph (d)(4)(i) of this section. Conversely, in apportioning interest expense, the financial group shall not take into account the stock of any lower-tier corporation that is treated as a member of the nonfinancial group under paragraph (d)(4)(i) of this section. For the treatment of loans between members of the financial group and members of the nonfinancial group, see paragraph (e)(1) of this section.

(5) *Example.*—(i) *Facts.*—X, a domestic corporation which is not a bank holding company, is the parent of domestic corporations Y and Z. Z owns 100 percent of the stock Z1, which is also a domestic corporation. X, Y, Z, and Z1 were organized after January 1, 1987, and constitute an affiliated group within the meaning of paragraph (d)(1) of this section. Y and Z are financial corporations described in paragraph (d)(4) of this section. X also owns 25 percent of the stock of A, a domestic corporation. Y owns 25 percent of the voting stock of B, a foreign corporation that is not a controlled foreign corporation. Z owns less than 10 percent of the voting stock of C, another foreign corporation. The foreign source income generated by Y's or Z's direct assets is exclusively financial services income. The foreign source income generated by X's or Z1's direct assets is exclusively general limitation income. X and Z1 are not financial corporations described in paragraph (d)(4)(ii) of this section. Y and Z, therefore, constitute a separate affiliated group apart from X and Z1 for purposes of section 864(e). The combined interest expense of Y and Z of $100,000 ($50,000 each) is apportioned separately on the basis of their assets. The combined interest expense of X and Z1 of $50,000 ($25,000 each) is allocated on the basis of the assets of the XZ1 group.

Analysis of the YZ group assets

Adjusted basis of assets of the YZ group that generate foreign source financial services income (excluding stock of foreign subsidiaries not included in the YZ affiliated group)	$200,000
Z's basis in the C stock (not adjusted by the allocable amount of C's earnings and profits because Z owns less than 10 percent of the stock) which would be considered to generate passive income in the hands of a nonfinancial services entity but is considered to generate financial services income when in the hands of Z, a financial services entity	$100,000
Y's basis in the B stock (adjusted by the allocable amount of B's earnings and profits) which generates dividends subject to a separate limitation for B dividends	$100,000
Adjusted basis of assets of the YZ group that generate U.S. source income	$600,000
Total assets	$1,000,000

Analysis of the XZ1 group assets

Adjusted basis of assets of the XZ1 group that generate foreign source general limitation income	$500,000
Adjusted basis of assets of the XZ1 group other than A stock that generate domestic source income	$1,900,000
X's basis in the A stock adjusted by the allocable amount of A's earnings and profits	$100,000
Total domestic assets	$2,000,000
Total assets	$2,500,000

(ii) *Allocation.*—No portion of the $50,000 deduction of the YZ group is definitely related solely to specific property within the meaning of § 1.861-10T. Thus, the YZ group's deduction for interest is related to all its activities and properties. Similarly, no portion of the $50,000 deduction of the XZ1 group is definitely related solely to specific property within the meaning of § 1.861-10T. Thus, the XZ1 group's deduction for interest is related to all its activities and properties.

(iii) *Apportionment.*—The YZ group would apportion its interest expense as follows:

To gross financial services income from sources outside the United States:
$$\$50{,}000 \times \frac{\$300{,}000}{\$1{,}000{,}000} \dots \dots \$15{,}000$$

To gross income subject to a separate limitation for dividends from B:
$$\$50{,}000 \times \frac{\$100{,}000}{\$1{,}000{,}000} \dots \dots \$5{,}000$$

To gross income from sources inside the United States:
$$\$50{,}000 \times \frac{\$600{,}000}{\$1{,}000{,}000} \dots \dots \$30{,}000$$

The XZ1 group would apportion its interest expense as follows:
To gross general limitation income from sources outside the United States:
$$\$50{,}000 \times \frac{\$500{,}000}{\$2{,}500{,}000} \dots \dots \$10{,}000$$

To gross income from sources inside the United States:
$$\$50{,}000 \times \frac{\$2{,}000{,}000}{\$2{,}500{,}000} \dots \dots \$40{,}000$$

(6) *Certain unaffiliated corporations.*—Certain corporations that are not described in paragraph (d)(1) of this section will nonetheless be considered to constitute affiliated corporations for purposes of §§ 1.861-9T through 1.861-13T. These corporations include:

(i) Any includible corporation (as defined in section 1504(b) without regard to section 1504(b)(4)) if 80 percent of either the vote or value of all outstanding stock of such corporation is owned directly or indirectly by an includible corporation or by members of an affiliated group, and

(ii) Any foreign corporation if 80 percent of the either the vote or value of all outstanding stock of such corporation is owned directly or indirectly by members of an affiliated group, and if more than 50 percent of the gross income of such corporation for the taxable year is effectively connected with the conduct of a United States trade or business. If 80 percent or more of the gross income of such corporation is effectively connected income, then all the assets of such corporation and all of its interest expense shall be taken into account. If between 50 and 80 percent of the gross income of such corporation is effectively connected income, then only the assets of such corporation that generate effectively connected income and a percentage of its interest expense equal to the percentage of its assets that generate effectively connected income shall be taken into account.

(7) *Special rules for the application of § 1.861-11T(d)(6).*—[Reserved]. For special rules for the application of § 1.861-11T(d)(6), see § 1.861-11(d)(7).

(e) *Loans between members of an affiliated group.*—(1) *General rule.*—In the case of loans (including any receivable) between members of an affiliated group, as defined in paragraph (d) of this section, for purposes of apportioning interest expense, the indebtedness of the member borrower shall not be considered as asset of the member lender. However, in the case of members of separate financial and nonfinancial groups under paragraph (d)(4) of this section, the indebtedness of the member borrower shall be considered an asset of the member lender and such asset shall be characterized by reference to the member lender's income from the asset as determined under paragraph (e)(2)(ii) of this section. For purposes of this paragraph (e), the terms "related person interest income" and "related person interest payment" refer to interest paid and received by members of the same affiliated group as defined in paragraph (d) of this section.

(2) *Treatment of interest expense within the affiliated group.*—(i) *General rule.*—A member borrower shall deduct related person interest payments in the same manner as unrelated

person interest expense using group apportionment fractions computed under § 1.861-9T(f). A member lender shall include related person interest income in the same class of gross income as the class of gross income from which the member borrower deducts the related person interest payment.

(ii) *Special rule for loans between financial and nonfinancial affiliated corporations.*—In the case of a loan between two affiliated corporations only one of which constitutes a financial corporation under paragraph (d)(4) of this section, the member borrower shall allocate and apportion related person interest payments in the same manner as unrelated person interest expense using group apportionment fractions computed under § 1.861-9T(f). The source of the related person interest income to the member lender shall be determined under section 861(a)(1).

(iii) *Special rule for high withholding tax interest.*—In the case of an affiliated corporation that pays interest that is high withholding tax interest under § 1.904-5(f)(1) to another affiliated corporation, the interest expense of the payor shall be allocated to high withholding tax interest.

(3) *Back-to-back loans.*—If a member of the affiliated group makes a loan to a nonmember who makes a loan to a member borrower, the rule of paragraph (e)(1) and (2) of this section shall apply, in the Commissioner's discretion, as if the member lender made the loan directly to the member borrower, provided that the loans constitute a back-to-back loan transaction. Such loans will constitute a back-to-back loan for purposes of this paragraph (e) if the loan by the nonmember would not have been made or maintained on substantially the same terms irrespective of the loan of funds by the lending member to the nonmember or other intermediary party.

(4) *Examples.*—The rules of this paragraph (e) may be illustrated by the following examples.

Example (1). X, a domestic corporation, is the parent of Y, a domestic corporation. X and Y were organized after January 1, 1987, and constitute an affiliated group within the meaning of paragraph (d)(1) of this section. Among X's assets is the note of Y for the amount of $100,000. Because X and Y are members of an affiliated group, Y's note does not constitute an asset for purposes of apportionment. The apportionment fractions for the relevant tax year of the XY group are 50 percent domestic, 40 percent foreign general, and 10 percent foreign passive. Y deducts its related person interest payment using those apportionment fractions. Of the $10,000 in related person interest income received by X, $5,000 consists of domestic source income, $4,000 consists of foreign general limitation income, and $1,000 consists of foreign passive income.

Example (2). X is a domestic corporation organized after January 1, 1987. X owns all the stock of Y, a domestic corporation. On June 1, 1987, X loans $100,000 to Z, an unrelated person. On June 2, 1987, Z makes a loan to Y with terms substantially similar to those of the loan from X to Z. Based on the facts and circumstances of the transaction, it is determined that Z would not have made the loan to Y on the same terms if X had not made the loan to Z. Because the transaction constitutes a back-to-back loan, as defined in paragraph (e)(3) of this section, the Commissioner may require, in his discretion, that neither the note of Y nor the note of Z may be considered an asset of X for purposes of this section.

(f) *Computations of combined taxable income.*—In the computation of the combined taxable income of any FSC or DISC and its related supplier which is a member of an affiliated group under the pricing rules of sections 925 or 994, the combined taxable income of such FSC or DISC and its related supplier shall be reduced by the portion of the total interest expense of the affiliated group that is incurred in connection with those assets of the group used in connection with export sales involving that FSC or DISC. This amount shall be computed by multiplying the total interest expense of the affiliated group and interest expense of the FSC or DISC by a fraction the numerator of which is the assets of the affiliated group and of the FSC or DISC generating foreign trade income or gross income attributable to qualified export receipts, as the case may be, and the denominator of which is the total assets of the affiliated group and the FSC or DISC. Under this rule, interest of other group members may be attributed to the combined taxable income of a FSC or DISC and its related supplier without affecting the amount of interest otherwise deductible by the FSC or DISC, the related supplier or other member of the affiliated group. The FSC or DISC is entitled to only the statutory portion of the combined taxable income, net of any deemed interest expense, which determines the commission paid to the FSC or DISC or the transfer price of qualifying export property sold to the FSC or DISC.

(g) *Losses created through apportionment.*—(1) *General rules.*—In the case of an affiliated group that is eligible to file, but does not file, a consolidated return and in the case of any corporation described in paragraph (d)(6) of this section, the foreign tax credits in any separate limitation category are limited to the credits computed under the rules of this paragraph (g). As a consequence of the affiliated group allocation and apportionment of interest expense required by section 864(e)(1) and this section, interest expense of a group member may be apportioned for section 904 purposes to a limitation category in which that member has no gross income, resulting in a loss in that limitation category. The same is true in connection with any expense other than interest that is subject to apportionment under the rules of section 864(e)(6) of the Code. Any reference to "interest expense" in this paragraph (g) shall be treated as including such expenses. For purposes of this paragraph, the term "limitation category" includes domestic source income, as well as the types of income described in section 904(d)(1)(A) through (I). A loss of one affiliate in a limitation category will reduce the income of another member in the same limitation category if a consolidated return is filed. (See § 1.1502-4.) If a consolidated return is not filed, this netting does not occur. Accordingly, in such a case, the following adjustments among members are required in order to give effect to the group allocation of interest expense:

(i) Losses created through group apportionment of interest expense in one or more limitation categories within a given member must be eliminated; and

(ii) A corresponding amount of income of other members in the same limitation category must be recharacterized.

Such adjustments shall be accomplished, in accordance with paragraph (g)(2) of this section, without changing the total taxable income of any member and before the application of section 904(f). Section 904(f) (including section 904(f)(5)) does not apply to a loss created through the apportionment of interest expense to the extent that the loss is eliminated pursuant to paragraph (g)(2)(ii) of this section. For purposes of this section, the terms "limitation adjustment" and "recharacterization" mean the recharacterization of income in one limitation category as income in another limitation category.

(2) *Mechanics of computation.*—(i) *Step 1: Computation of consolidated taxable income.*—The members of an affiliated group must first allocate and apportion all other deductible expenses other than interest. The members must then deduct from their respective gross incomes within each limitation category interest expense apportioned under the rules of § 1.861-9T(f). The taxable income of the entire affiliated group within each limitation category is then totalled.

(ii) *Step 2: Loss offset adjustments.*—If, after step 1, a member has losses in a given limitation category or limitation categories created through apportionment of interest expense, any such loss (*i.e.,* the portion of such loss equal to interest expense) shall be eliminated by offsetting that loss against taxable income in other limitation categories of that member to the extent of the taxable income of other members within the same limitation category as the loss. If the member has taxable income in more than one limitation category, then the loss shall offset taxable income in all such limitation categories on a pro rata basis. If there is insufficient domestic income of the member to offset the net losses in all foreign limitation categories caused by the apportionment of interest expense, the losses in each limitation category shall be recharacterized as domestic losses to the extent of the taxable income of other members in the same respective limitation categories. After these adjustments are made, the income of the entire affiliated group within each limitation category is totalled again.

(iii) *Step 3: Determination of amount subject to recharacterization.*—In order to determine the amount of income to be recharacterized in step 4, the income totals computed under step 1 in each limitation category shall be subtracted from the income totals computed under step 2 in each limitation category.

(iv) *Step 4: Recharacterization.*—Because any differences determined under step 3 represent deviations from the consolidated totals computed under step 1, such differences (in any limitation category) must be eliminated.

(A) *Limitation categories to be reduced.*—In the case of any limitation category in which there is a positive change, the income of group members with income in that limitation category must be reduced on a pro rata basis (by reference to net income figures as determined under Step 2) to the extent of such positive change ("limitation reductions"). Each member shall separately compute the sum of the limitation reductions.

(B) *Limitation categories to be increased.*—In any case in which only one limitation category has a negative change in Step 3, the sum of the limitation reductions within each member is added to that limitation category. In the case in which multiple limitation categories have negative changes in Step 3, the sum of the limitation reductions within each member is prorated among the negative change limitation categories based on the ratio that the negative change for the entire group in each limitation category bears to the total of all negative changes for the entire group in all limitation categories.

(3) *Examples.*—The following examples illustrate the principles of this paragraph.

Example (1)—(i) *Facts.* X, a domestic corporation, is the parent of domestic corporations Y and Z. X, Y, and Z were organized after January 1, 1987, constitute an affiliated group within the meaning of paragraph (d)(1) of this section, but do not file a consolidated return. The XYZ group apportions its interest expense on the basis of the fair market value of its assets. X, Y, and Z have the following assets, interest expense, and taxable income before apportioning interest expense:

Assets	X	Y	Z	Total
Domestic	2,000.00	0.00	1,000.00	3,000.00
Foreign Passive	0.00	50.00	50.00	100.00
Foreign General	0.00	700.00	200.00	900.00
Interest expense	48.00	12.00	80.00	140.00
Taxable Income (pre-interest)				
Domestic	100.00	0.00	63.00	163.00
Foreign Passive	0.00	5.00	5.00	10.00
Foreign General	0.00	60.00	35.00	95.00

(ii) *Step 1: Computation of consolidated taxable income.* Each member of the XYZ group apportions its interest expense according to group apportionment ratios determined under the asset method described in § 1.861-9T(f), yielding the following results:

Apportioned interest expense	X	Y	Z	Total
Domestic	36.00	9.00	60.00	105.00
Foreign Passive	1.20	0.30	2.00	3.50
Foreign General	10.80	2.70	18.00	31.50
Total	48.00	12.00	80.00	140.00

The members of the group then compute taxable income within each category by deducting the apportioned interest expense from the amounts of pre-interest taxable income specified in the facts in paragraph (i), yielding the following results:

Taxable Income	X	Y	Z	Total
Domestic	64.00	-9.00	3.00	58.00
Foreign Passive	-1.20	4.70	3.00	6.50
Foreign General	-10.80	57.30	17.00	63.50
Total	52.00	53.00	23.00	128.00

(iii) *Step 2: Loss offset adjustments.* Because X and Y have losses created through apportionment, these losses must be eliminated by reducing taxable income of the member in other limitation categories. Because X has a total of $12 in apportionment losses and because it has only one limitation category with income (*i.e.,* domestic), domestic income must be reduced by $12, thus eliminating its apportionment losses. Because Y has a total of $9 in apportionment losses and because it has two limitation categories with income (*i.e.,* foreign passive and foreign general limitation), the income in these two limitation categories must be reduced on a pro rata basis in order to eliminate its apportionment losses. In summary, the following adjustments are required:

Loss Offset Adjustments	X	Y	Z	Total
Domestic	-12.00	+9.00	0	-3.00
Foreign Passive	+1.20	-0.68	0	+0.52
Foreign General	+10.80	-8.32	0	+2.48

These adjustments yield the following adjusted taxable income figures:

Adjusted Taxable Income	X	Y	Z	Total
Domestic	52.00	0.00	3.00	55.00
Foreign Passive	0.00	4.02	3.00	7.02
Foreign General	0.00	48.98	17.00	65.98
Total	52.00	53.00	23.00	128.00

(iv) *Step 3: Determination of amount subject to recharacterization.* The adjustments performed under Step 2 led to a change in the group's taxable income within each limitation category. The total loss offset adjustments column shown in paragraph (iii) above shows the net deviations between Steps 1 and 2.

Reg. § 1.861-11T(g)(3)

(v) *Step 4: Recharacterization.* The loss offset adjustments yield a positive change in the foreign passive and the foreign general limitation categories. Y and Z both have income in these limitation categories. Accordingly, the income of Y and Z in each of these limitation categories must be reduced on a pro rata basis (by reference to the adjusted taxable income figures) to the extent of the positive change in each limitation category. The total positive change in the foreign passive limitation category is $0.52. The adjusted taxable income of Y in the foreign passive limitation category is $4.02 and the adjusted taxable income of Z in the foreign passive limitation category is $3. Therefore, $0.30 is drawn from Y and $0.22 is drawn from Z. The total positive change in the foreign general limitation category is $2.48. The adjusted taxable income of Y in the foreign general limitation category is $48.98, and the adjusted taxable income of Z in the foreign general limitation category is $17. Therefore, $1.84 is drawn from Y and $.64 is drawn from Z.

The members must then separately compute the sum of the limitation reductions. Y has limitation reductions of $0.30 in the foreign passive limitation category and $1.84 in the foreign general limitation category, yielding total limitation reduction of $2.14. Under these facts, domestic income is the only limitation category requiring a positive adjustment. Accordingly, Y's domestic income is increased by $2.14. Z has limitation reductions of $0.22 in the foreign passive limitation category and $0.64 in the foreign general limitation category, yielding total limitation reductions of $0.86. Under these facts, domestic income is the only limitation category of Z requiring a positive adjustment. Accordingly, Z's domestic income is increased by $0.86.

Recharacterization Adjustments	X	Y	Z	Total
Domestic	0	+2.14	+0.86	+3.00
Foreign Passive	0	−0.30	−0.22	−0.52
Foreign General	0	−1.84	−0.64	−2.48

These recharacterization adjustments yield the following final taxable income figures:

Final Taxable Income	X	Y	Z	Total
Domestic	52.00	2.14	3.86	58.00
Foreign Passive	0.00	3.72	2.78	6.50
Foreign General	0.00	47.14	16.36	63.50
Total	52.00	53.00	23.00	128.00

Example (2)—(i) *Facts.* X, a domestic corporation, is the parent of domestic corporations Y and Z. X, Y, and Z were organized after January 1, 1987, constitute an affiliated group within the meaning of paragraph (d)(1) of this section, but do not file a consolidated return. Moreover, X has served as the sole borrower in the group and, as a result, has sustained an overall loss. The XYZ group apportions its interest expense on the basis of the fair market value of its assets. X, Y, and Z have the following assets, interest expense, and taxable income before interest expense:

Assets	X	Y	Z	Total
Domestic	2,000.00	0.00	1,000.00	3,000.00
Foreign Passive	0.00	50.00	50.00	100.00
Foreign General	0.00	700.00	200.00	900.00
Interest Expense	140.00	0.00	0.00	140.00
Taxable Income (pre-interest)				
Domestic	100.00	0.00	100.00	200.00
Foreign Passive	0.00	5.00	5.00	10.00
Foreign General	0.00	70.00	35.00	105.00

(ii) *Step 1: Computation of consolidated taxable income.* Each member of the XYZ group apportions its interest expense according to group apportionment ratios determined under the asset method described in § 1.861-9T(g), yielding the following results:

Apportioned Interest Expense	X	Y	Z	Total
Domestic	105.00	0	0	105.00
Foreign Passive	3.50	0	0	3.50
Foreign General	31.50	0	0	31.50
Total	140.00	0	0	140.00

The members of the group then compute taxable income within each category by deducting the apportioned interest expense from the amounts of pre-interest taxable income speci-

Reg. § 1.861-11T(g)(3)

fied in the facts in paragraph (i), yielding the following results:

Taxable Income	X	Y	Z	Total
Domestic	−5.00	0.00	100.00	95.00
Foreign Passive	−3.50	5.00	5.00	6.50
Foreign General	−31.50	70.00	35.00	73.50
Total	−40.00	75.00	140.00	175.00

(iii) *Step 2: Loss offset adjustment.* Because X has insufficient domestic income to offset the sum of the losses in the foreign limitation categories caused by apportionment, the amount of apportionment losses in each limitation category shall be recharacterized as domestic losses to the extent of taxable income of other members in the same limitation category. This is accomplished by adding to each foreign limitation categories an amount equal to the loss therein and by subtracting the sum of such foreign losses from domestic income, as follows:

Loss Offset Adjustments	X	Y	Z	Total
Domestic	−35.00	0	0	−35.00
Foreign Passive	+3.50	0	0	+3.50
Foreign General	+31.50	0	0	+31.50

These adjustments yield the following adjusted taxable income figures:

Adjusted Taxable Income	X	Y	Z	Total
Domestic	−40.00	0.00	100.00	60.00
Foreign Passive	0.00	5.00	5.00	10.00
Foreign General	0.00	70.00	35.00	105.00
Total	−40.00	75.00	140.00	175.00

(iv) *Step 3: Determination of amount subject to recharacterization.* The adjustments performed under Step 2 led to a change in the group's taxable income within each limitation category. The total loss offset adjustments column shown in paragraph (iii) above shows the net deviations between Steps 1 and 2.

(v) *Step 4: Recharacterization.* The loss offset adjustments yield a positive change in the foreign passive and the foreign general limitation categories. Y and Z both have income in these limitation categories. Accordingly, the income of Y and Z in each of these limitation categories must be reduced on a pro rata basis (by reference to the adjusted taxable income figures) to the extent of the positive change in each limitation category. The total positive change in the foreign passive limitation category is $3.50. The adjusted taxable income of Y in the foreign passive limitation category is $5, and the adjusted taxable income of Z in the foreign passive limitation category is $5. Therefore, $1.75 is drawn from Y and $1.75 is drawn from Z. The total positive change in the foreign general limitation category is $31.50. The adjusted taxable income of Y in the foreign general limitation category is $70, and the adjusted taxable income of Z in the foreign general limitation category is $35. Therefore, $21 is drawn from Y and $10.50 is drawn from Z.

The members must then separately compute the sum of the limitation reductions. Y has limitation reductions of $1.75 in the foreign passive limitation category and $21 in the foreign general limitation category, yielding total limitation reductions of $22.75. Under these facts, domestic income is the only limitation category requiring a positive adjustment. Accordingly, Y's domestic income is increased by $22.75. Z has limitation reductions of $1.75 in the foreign passive limitation category and $10.50 in the foreign general limitation category, yielding total limitation reductions of $12.25. Under these facts, domestic income is the only limitation category requiring a positive adjustment. Accordingly, Z's domestic income is increased by $12.25.

Recharacterization Adjustments	X	Y	Z	Total
Domestic	0	+22.75	+12.25	+35.00
Foreign Passive	0	−1.75	−1.75	−3.50
Foreign General	0	−21.00	−10.50	−31.50

These recharacterization adjustments yield the following final taxable income figures:

Reg. §1.861-11T(g)(3)

Final Taxable Income	X	Y	Z	Total
Domestic	−40.00	22.75	112.25	95.00
Foreign Passive	0.00	3.25	3.25	6.50
Foreign General	0.00	49.00	24.50	73.50
Total	−40.00	75.00	140.00	175.00

[Temporary Reg. § 1.861-11T.]

☐ [T.D. 8228, 9-9-88. Amended by T.D. 8916, 12-29-2000.]

§ 1.861-12T. Characterization rules and adjustments for certain assets (Temporary regulations.).—(a) *In general.*—These rules are applicable to taxpayers in apportioning expenses under an asset method to income in various separate limitation categories under section 904(d), and supplement other rules provided in §§ 1.861-9T, 1.861-10T, and 1.861-11T. The rules of this section apply to taxable years beginning after December 31, 1986, except as otherwise provided in § 1.861-13T. Paragraph (b) of this section describes the treatment of inventories. Paragraph (c)(1) of this section concerns the treatment of various stock assets. Paragraph (c)(2) of this section describes a basis adjustment for stock in nonaffiliated 10 percent owned corporations. Paragraph (c)(3) of this section sets forth rules for characterizing the stock in controlled foreign corporations. Paragraph (c)(4) of this section describes the treatment of stock of noncontrolled section 902 corporations. Paragraph (d)(1) of this section concerns the treatment of notes. Paragraph (d)(2) of this section concerns the treatment of the notes of controlled foreign corporations. Paragraph (e) of this section describes the treatment of certain portfolio securities that constitute inventory or generate income primarily in the form of gains. Paragraph (f) of this section describes the treatment of assets that are subject to the capitalization rules of section 263A. Paragraph (g) of this section concerns the treatment of FSC stock and of assets of the related supplier generating foreign trade income. Paragraph (h) of this section concerns the treatment of DISC stock and of assets of the related supplier generating qualified export receipts. Paragraph (i) of this section is reserved. Paragraph (j) of this section sets forth an example illustrating the rules of this section, as well as the rules of § 1.861-9T(g).

(b) *Inventories.*—Inventory must be characterized by reference to the source and character of sales income, or sales receipts in the case of LIFO inventory, from that inventory during the taxable year. If a taxpayer maintains separate inventories for any federal tax purpose, including the rules for establishing pools of inventory items under sections 472 and 474 of the Code, each separate inventory shall be separately characterized in accordance with the previous sentence.

(c) *Treatment of stock.*—(1) *In general.*—Subject to the adjustment and special rules of this paragraphs 160 (c) and (e) of this section, stock in a corporation is taken into account in the application of the asset method described in § 1.861-9T(g). However, an affiliated group (as defined in § 1.861-11T(d)) does not take into account the stock of any member in the application of the asset method.

(2) *Basis adjustment for stock in nonaffiliated 10 percent owned corporations.*—(i) *Taxpayers using the tax book value method.*—For purposes of apportioning expenses on the basis of the tax book value of assets, the adjusted basis of any stock in a 10 percent owned corporation owned directly by the taxpayer shall be—

(A) Increased by the amount of the earnings and profits of such corporation (and of lower-tier 10 percent owned corporations) attributable to such stock and accumulated during the period the taxpayer or other members of its affiliated group held 10 percent or more of such stock, or

(B) Reduced (but not below zero) by any deficit in earnings and profits of such corporation (and of lower-tier 10 percent owned corporations) attributable to such stock for such period.

Solely for purposes of this section, a taxpayer's basis in the stock of a controlled foreign corporation shall not include any amount included in basis under section 961 or 1293(d) of the Code. For purposes of this paragraph (c)(2), earnings and profits and deficits are computed under the rules of section 312 and, in the case of a foreign corporation, section 902 and the regulations thereunder for taxable years of the 10 percent owned corporation ending on or before the close of the taxable year of the taxpayer. The rules of section 1248 and the regulations thereunder shall apply to determine the amount of earnings and profits that is attributable to stock without regard to whether earned and profits (or deficits) were derived (or incurred) during taxable years beginning before or after December 31, 1962. This adjustment is to be made annually and is noncumulative. Thus, the adjusted basis of the stock (determined without prior years' adjustments under this section) is to be adjusted annually by the amount of accumulated earnings and profits (or any deficit) attributable to such stock as of the end of each year. Earnings and profits or deficits of a qualified business unit that has a functional currency other than the dollar must be computed under this paragraph (c)(2) in functional currency and translated into dollars using the exchange rate at the end of the taxpayer's current taxable year with respect to which interest is being allocated (and not the exchange rates for the years in which the earnings and profits or deficits were derived or incurred).

(ii) *10 percent owned corporation defined.*—(A) *In general.*—The term "10 percent owned corporation" means any corporation (domestic or foreign)—

(*1*) Which is not included within the taxpayer's affiliated group as defined in § 1.861-11T(d)(1) or (6),

(*2*) In which the members of the taxpayer's affiliated group own directly or indirectly 10 percent or more of the total combined voting power of all classes of the stock entitled to vote, and

(*3*) Which is taken into account for purposes of apportionment.

(B) *Rule of attribution.*—Stock that is owned by a corporation, partnership, or trust shall be treated as being indirectly owned proportionately by its shareholders, partners, or beneficiaries. For this purpose, a partner's interest in stock held by a partnership shall be determined by reference to the partner's distributive share of partnership income.

(iii) *Earnings and profits of lower-tier corporations taken into account.*—For purposes of the adjustment to the basis of the stock of the 10 percent owned corporation owned by the taxpayer under paragraph (c)(2)(i) of this section, the earnings and profits of that corporation shall include its pro rata share of the earnings and profits (or any deficit therein) of each succeeding lower-tier 10 percent owned corporation. Thus, a first-tier 10 percent owned corporation shall combine with its own earnings and profits its pro rata share of the earnings and profits of all such lower-tier corporations. The affiliated group shall then adjust its basis in the stock of the first-tier corporation by its pro rata share of the total combined earnings and profits of the first-tier and the lower-tier corporations. In the case of a 10 percent owned corporation whose tax year does not conform to that of the taxpayer, the taxpayer shall include the annual earnings and profits of such 10 percent owned corporation for the tax year ending within the tax year of the taxpayer, whether or not such 10 percent owned corporation is owned directly by the taxpayer.

(iv) *Special rules for foreign corporations in pre-effective date tax years.*—Solely for purposes of determining the adjustment required under paragraph (c)(2)(i) of this section, for tax years beginning after 1912 and before 1987, financial earnings (or losses) of a foreign corporation computed using United States generally accepted accounting principles may be substituted for earnings and profits in making the adjustment required by paragraph (c)(2)(i) of this section. A taxpayer is not required to isolate the financial earnings of a foreign corporation derived or incurred during its period of 10 percent ownership or during the post-1912 taxable years and determine earnings and profits (or deficits) attributable under section 1248 principles to the taxpayer's stock in a 10 percent owned corporation. Instead, the taxpayer may include all historic financial earnings for purposes of this adjustment. If the affiliated group elects to use financial earnings with respect to any foreign corporation, financial earnings must be used by that group with respect to all foreign corporations, except that earnings and profits may in any event be used for controlled foreign corporations for taxable years beginning after 1962 and before 1987. However, if the affiliated group elects to use earnings and profits with respect to any single controlled foreign corporation for the 1963 through 1986 period, such election shall apply with respect to all its controlled foreign corporations.

(v) *Taxpayers using the fair market value method.*—Because the fair market value of any asset which is stock will reflect retained earnings and profits, taxpayers who use the fair market value method shall not adjust stock basis by the amount of retained earnings and profits, as otherwise required by paragraph (c)(2)(i) of this section.

(vi) *Examples.*—Certain of the rules of this paragraph (c)(2) may be illustrated by the following examples.

Example (1). X, an affiliated group that uses the tax book value method of apportionment, owns 20 percent of the stock of Y, which owns 50 percent of the stock of Z. X's basis in the Y stock is $1000. X, Y, and Z have calendar taxable years. The undistributed earnings and profits of Y and Z at year-end attributable to X's period of ownership are $80 and $40, respectively. Because Y owns half of the Z stock, X's pro rata share of Z's earnings and profits attributable to X's Y stock is $4. X's pro rata share of Y's earnings attributable to X's Y stock is $16. For purposes of apportionment, the tax book value of the Y stock is, therefore, considered to be $1,020.

Example (2). X, an unaffiliated domestic corporation that was organized on January 1, 1987, has owned all the stock of Y, a foreign corporation with a functional currency other than the U.S. dollar, since January 1, 1987. Both X and Y have calendar taxable years. All of Y's assets generate general limitation income. X has a deductible interest expense incurred in 1987 of $160,000. X apportions its interest expense using the tax book value method. The adjusted basis of its assets that generate domestic income is $7,500,000. The adjusted basis of its assets that generate foreign source general limitation income (other than the stock of Y) is $400,000. X's adjusted basis in the Y stock is $2,000,000. Y has undistributed earnings and profits for 1987 of $100,000, translated into dollars from Y's functional currency at the exchange rate on the last day of X's taxable year. Because X is required under paragraph (b)(1) of this § 1.861-10T to increase its basis in the Y stock by the computed amount of earnings and profits, X's adjusted basis in the Y stock is considered to be $2,100,000, and its adjusted basis of assets that generates foreign source general limitation income is, thus, considered to be $2,500,000. X would apportion its interest expense as follows:

To foreign source general limitation income:

$$\text{Interest expense} \times \frac{\text{Adjusted basis of foreign general limitation assets}}{\text{Adjusted basis of foreign general limitation assets} + \text{Adjusted basis of domestic assets}}$$

$$\$160,000 \times \frac{\$2,500,000}{\$2,500,000 + \$7,500,000} = \$40,000$$

To domestic source income:

$$\text{Interest expense} \times \frac{\text{Adjusted basis of domestic assets}}{\text{Adjusted basis of foreign general limitation assets} + \text{Adjusted basis of domestic assets}}$$

$$\$160,000 \times \frac{\$7,500,000}{\$2,500,000 + \$7,500,000} = \$120,000$$

(3) *Characterization of stock of controlled foreign corporations.*—(i) *In general.*—Stock in a controlled foreign corporation (as defined in section 957) shall be characterized as an asset in the various separate limitation categories either on the basis of:

(A) The asset method described in paragraph (c)(3)(ii) of this section, or

(B) The modified gross income method described in paragraph (c)(3)(iii) of this section.

Stock in a controlled foreign corporation whose interest expense is apportioned on the basis of assets shall be characterized in the hands of its United States shareholders under the asset method described in paragraph (c)(3)(ii). Stock in a controlled foreign corporation whose interest expense is apportioned on the basis of gross income shall be characterized in the hands of its United States shareholders under the gross income method described in paragraph (c)(3)(iii).

(ii) *Asset method.*—Under the asset method, the taxpayer characterizes the tax book value or fair market value of the stock of a controlled foreign corporation based on an analysis of the assets owned by the controlled foreign corporation during the foreign corporation's taxable year that ends with or within the taxpayer's taxable year. This process is based on the application of § 1.861-9T(g) at the level of the controlled foreign corporation. In the case of a controlled foreign corporation that owns stock in one or more lower-tier controlled foreign corporations in which the United States taxpayer is a United States shareholder, the characterization of the tax book value or the fair market value of the stock of the first-tier controlled foreign corporation to the various separate limitation categories of the affiliated group must take into account the stock in lower-tier corporations. For this purpose, the stock of each such lower-tier corporation shall be characterized by reference to the assets owned during the lower-tier corporation's taxable year that ends during the taxpayer's taxable year. The analysis of assets within a chain of controlled foreign corporations must begin at the lowest-tier controlled foreign corporation and proceed up the chain to the first-tier controlled foreign corporation. For purposes of this paragraph (c), the value of any passive asset to which related person interest is allocated under § 1.904-5(c)(2)(ii) must be reduced by the principal amount of indebtedness on which such interest is incurred. Furthermore, the value of any asset to which interest expense is directly allocated under § 1.861-10T must be reduced as provided in § 1.861-9T(g)(2)(iii). See § 1.861-9T(h)(5) for further guidance concerning characterization of stock in a related person under the fair market value method.

(iii) *Modified gross income method.*—Under the gross income method, the taxpayer characterizes the tax book value of the stock of the first-tier controlled foreign corporation based on the gross income net of interest expense of the controlled foreign corporation (as computed under § 1.861-9T(j)) within each relevant category for the taxable year of the controlled foreign corporation ending with or within the taxable year of the taxpayer. For this purpose, however, the gross income of the first-tier controlled foreign corporation shall include the total amount of net subpart F income of any lower-tier controlled foreign corporation that was excluded under the rules of § 1.861-9T(j)(2)(ii)(B).

(4) *Stock of noncontrolled section 902 corporations.*—(i) *General rule.*—Because each noncontrolled section 902 corporation constitutes a separate limitation category, the value of such stock, increased to the extent required under paragraph (c)(2) of this section, is attributable solely to each such category.

(ii) *Special rule for separate limitation losses.*—(A) *Election.*—If, as a result of the allocation and apportionment of interest expense using the asset method described in § 1.861-9T(g), the taxpayer has a loss in the separate limitation category for a given noncontrolled section 902 corporation, the taxpayer may elect to reallocate interest expense equal to such loss to any other separate limitation category that is in excess credit (without regard to carryovers from other years), to the extent that the reallocation of such interest to such other category does not create a loss in that category. For this purpose, the term "category in excess credit" means any category of income with respect to which the foreign income taxes paid or accrued for the current taxable year exceed the limitation computed under section 904 with respect to such category. The election to reallocate interest expense under this paragraph shall be made in the manner prescribed in § 1.861-9T(f)(3) (relating to the election to use a gross income method for controlled foreign corporations). Furthermore, such election is irrevocable and, thus, cannot be amended by an amended return.

(B) *Example.*—X, a domestic corporation organized on January 1, 1987, incurred deductible interest expense in 1987 in the amount of $1,000,000. X uses the tax book value method of apportionment. X owns 25 percent of the stock of A, a noncontrolled section 902 corporation. At the end of 1987, the tax book value of X's assets by income grouping are as follows:

Domestic	$3,500,000
Foreign general limitation	1,000,000
Noncontrolling section 902 corporation	500,000

In 1987, A paid no dividends. X received $100,000 of foreign general limitation income, on which it incurred $50,000 of tax to foreign governments.

The stock of A constitutes ten percent of X's assets. Therefore, ten percent of X's interest expense ($100,000) is allocated and apportioned to the separate limitation category for dividends on the A stock. Since A paid no dividends, this amount would constitute a separate limitation loss under the rules of section 904(f)(5).

Because X incurred more tax to foreign governments on its foreign general limitation income than it can credit against its U.S. tax liability, for the current tax year, and because the reallocation of interest expense allocated and apportioned to dividends from A to foreign general limitation income would not create a loss in that category, X may elect to reallocate such interest expense to the foreign general limitation category to the extent of the loss in the separate limitation category for dividends received from A.

(d) *Treatment of notes.*—(1) *General rule.*—Subject to the adjustments and special rules of this paragraph (d) and paragraph (e) of this section, all notes held by a taxpayer are taken into account in the application of the asset method described in § 1.861-9T(g). However, the notes of an affiliated corporation are subject to special rules set forth in § 1.861-11T(e). For purposes of this section, the term notes means all interest bearing debt, including debt bearing original issue discount.

(2) *Characterization of related controlled foreign corporation notes.*—The debt of a controlled foreign corporation shall be characterized according to the taxpayer's treatment of the interest income derived from that debt obligation after application of the look-through rule of section 904(d)(3)(C). Thus, a United States shareholder includes interest income from a controlled foreign corporation in the same category of income as the category of income from which the controlled foreign corporation deducts the interest expense. See section 954(b)(5) and § 1.904-5(c)(2) for rules concern-

ing the allocation of related person interest payments to the foreign personal holding company income of a controlled foreign corporation.

(e) *Portfolio securities that constitute inventory or generate primarily gains.*—Because gain on the sale of securities is sourced by reference to the residence of the seller, a resident of the United States will generally receive domestic source income (and a foreign resident will generally receive foreign source income) upon sale or disposition of securities that otherwise generate foreign source dividends and interest (or domestic source dividends and interest in the case of a foreign resident). Although under paragraphs (c) and (d) of this section securities are characterized by reference to the source and character of dividends and interest, the source and character of income on gain or disposition must also be taken into account for purposes of characterizing portfolio securities if:

(1) The securities constitute inventory in the hands of the holder, or

(2) 80 percent or more of the gross income generated by a taxpayer's entire portfolio of such securities during a taxable year consists of gains.

For this purpose, a portfolio security is a security in any entity other than a controlled foreign corporation with respect to which the taxpayer is a United States shareholder under section 957, a noncontrolled section 902 corporation with respect to the taxpayer, or a 10 percent owned corporation as defined in § 1.861-12(c)(2)(ii). In taking gains into account, a taxpayer must treat all portfolio securities generating foreign source dividends and interest as a single asset and all portfolio securities generating domestic source dividends as a single asset and shall characterize the total value of that asset based on the source of all income and gain generated by those securities in the taxable year.

(f) *Assets funded by disallowed interest.*—(1) *Rule.*—In the case of any asset in connection with which interest expense accruing at the end of the taxable year is capitalized, deferred, or disallowed under any provision of the Code, the adjusted basis or fair market value (depending on the taxpayer's choice of apportionment methods) of such an asset shall be reduced by the principal amount of indebtedness the interest on which is so capitalized, deferred, or disallowed.

(2) *Example.*—The rules of this paragraph (f) may be illustrated by the following example.

Example. X is a domestic corporation which uses the tax book value method of apportionment. X has $1000 of indebtedness and $100 of interest expense. X constructs an asset with an adjusted basis of $800 before interest capitalization and is required under the rules of section 263A to capitalize $80 in interest expense. Because interest on $800 of debt is capitalized and because the production period is in progress at the end of X's taxable year, $800 of the principal amount of X's debt is allocable to the building. The $800 of debt allocable to the building reduces its adjusted basis for purposes of apportioning the balance of X's interest expense ($20).

(g) *Special rules for FSCs.*—(1) *Treatment of FSC stock.*—No interest expense shall be allocated or apportioned to stock of a foreign sales corporation ("FSC") to the extent that the FSC stock is attributable to the separate limitation for certain FSC distributions described in section 904(d)(1)(H). FSC stock is considered to be attributable solely to the separate limitation category described in section 904(d)(1)(H) unless the taxpayer can demonstrate that more than 20 percent of the FSC's gross income for the taxable year consists of income other than foreign trading income.

(2) *Treatment of assets that generate foreign trade income.*—Assets of the related supplier that generate foreign trade income must be prorated between assets attributable to foreign source general limitation income and assets attributable to domestic source income in proportion to foreign source general limitation income and domestic source income derived from transactions generating foreign trade income.

(i) *Value of assets attributable to foreign source income.*—The value of assets attributable to foreign source general limitation income is computed by multiplying the value of assets for the taxable year generating foreign trading gross receipts by a fraction:

(A) The numerator of which is foreign source general limitation income for the taxable year derived from transactions giving rise to foreign trading gross receipts, after the application of the limitation provided in section 927(e)(1), and

(B) The denominator of which is total income for the taxable year derived from the transactions giving rise to foreign trading gross receipts.

(ii) *Value of assets attributable to domestic source income.*—The value of assets attributable to domestic source income is computed by subtracting from the total value of assets for the taxable year generating foreign trading gross receipts the value of assets attributable to foreign source general limitation income as computed under paragraph (g)(2)(i) of this section.

(h) *Special rules for DISCs.*—(1) *Treatment of DISC stock.*—No interest shall be allocated or apportioned to stock in a DISC (or stock in a former DISC to the extent that the stock in the former DISC is attributable to the separate limitation category described in section 904(d)(1)(F)).

(2) *Treatment of assets that generate qualified export receipts.*—Assets of the related supplier that generate qualified export receipts must be prorated between assets attributable to foreign source general limitation income and assets attributable to domestic source income in proportion to foreign source general limitation income and domestic source income derived from transactions during the taxable year from transactions generating qualified export receipts.

(i) [Reserved.]

(j) *Examples.*—Certain of the rules in this section and §§ 1.861-9T(g) and 1.861-10(e) are illustrated by the following example.

Example (1):

(1) *Facts.* X, a domestic corporation organized on January 1, 1987, has a calendar taxable year and apportions its interest expense on the basis of the tax book value of its assets. In 1987, X incurred a deductible third-party interest expense of $100,000 on an average month-end debt amount of $1 million. The total tax book value of X's assets (adjusted as required under paragraph (b) of this section for retained earnings and profits) is $2 million. X manufactures widgets. One-half of the widgets are sold in the United States and one-half are exported and sold through a foreign branch with title passing outside the United States.

X owns all the stock of Y, a controlled foreign corporation that also has a calendar taxable year and is also engaged in the manufacture and sale of widgets. Y has no earnings and profits or deficits in earnings and profits prior to 1987. For 1987, Y has taxable income and earnings and profits of $50,000 before the deduction for related person interest expense. Half of the $50,000 is foreign source personal holding company income and the other half is derived from widget sales and constitutes foreign source general limitation income. Assume that Y has no deductions from gross income other than interest expense. Y's foreign personal holding company taxable income is included in X's gross income under section 951. Y paid no dividends in 1987. Prior to 1987, Y did not borrow any funds from X. The average month-end level of borrowings by Y from X in 1987 is $100,000, on which Y paid a total of $10,000 in interest. The total tax book value of Y's assets in 1987 is $500,000. Y has no liabilities to third parties. X elects pursuant to § 1.861-9T for Y to apportion Y's interest expense under the gross income method prescribed in § 1.861-9T(g).

In addition to its stock in Y, X owns 20 percent of the stock of Z, a noncontrolled section 902 corporation.

X's total assets and their tax book values are:

Asset	Tax Book Value
Plant & equipment	$1,000,000
Corporate headquarters	500,000
Inventory	200,000
Automobiles	20,000
Patents	50,000
Trademarks	10,000
Y stock (including paragraph (c)(2) adjustment)	80,000
Y note	100,000
Z stock	40,000

(2) *Categorization of Assets*

Single Category Assets

1. Automobiles: X's automobiles are used exclusively by its domestic sales force in the generation of United States source income. Thus, these assets are attributable solely to the grouping of domestic income.

2. Y Note: Under paragraph (d)(2) of this section, the Y note in the hands of X is characterized according to X's treatment of the interest income received on the Y note. In determining the source and character of the interest income on the Y note, the look-through rules of sections 904(d)(3)(C) and 904(g) apply. Under section 954(b)(5) and § 1.904-5(c)(2)(ii), Y's $10,000 interest payment to X is allocated directly to, and thus reduces, Y's foreign personal holding company income of $25,000 (yielding foreign personal holding company taxable income of $15,000). Therefore, the Y note is attributable solely to the statutory grouping of foreign source passive income.

3. Z stock: Because Z is a noncontrolled section 902 corporation, the dividends paid by Z are subject to a separate limitation under section 904(d)(1)(E). Thus, this asset is attributable solely to the statutory grouping consisting of Z dividends.

Multiple Category Assets

1. Plant & equipment, inventory, patents, and trademarks: In 1987, X sold half its widgets in the United States and exported half outside the United States. A portion of the taxable income from export sales will be foreign source income, since the export sales were accomplished through a foreign branch and title passed outside the United States. Thus, these assets are attributable both to the statutory grouping of foreign general limitation and the grouping of domestic income.

2. Y Stock: Since Y's interest expense is apportioned under the gross income method prescribed in §1.861-9T(j), the Y stock must be characterized under the gross income method described in paragraph (c)(3)(iii) of this section.

Assets without Directly Identifiable Yield

1. Corporate headquarters: This asset generates no directly identifiable income yield. The value of the asset is disregarded.

(3) *Analysis of Income Yield for Multiple Category Assets*

1. Plant & equipment, inventory, patents, and trademarks: As noted above, X's 1987 widget sales were half domestic and half foreign. Assume that Example 2 of §1.863-3(b)(2) applies in sourcing the export income from the export sales. Under Example 2, the income generated by the export sales is sourced half domestic and half foreign. The income generated by the domestic sales is entirely domestic source. Accordingly, three-quarters of the income generated on all sales is domestic source and one-quarter of the income is foreign source. Thus, three-quarters of the fair market value of these assets are attributed to the grouping of domestic source income and one-quarter of the fair market value of these assets is attributed to the statutory grouping of foreign source general limitation income.

2. Y Stock: Under the gross income method described in paragraph (c)(3)(iii) of this section, Y's gross income net of interest expense in each limitation category must be determined—$25,000 foreign source general limitation income and $15,000 of foreign source passive income. Of X's adjusted basis of $80,000 in Y stock, $50,000 is attributable to foreign source general limitation income and $30,000 is attributable to foreign source passive income.

(4) *Application of the Special Allocation Rule of §1.861-10T(e).* Assume that the taxable year in question is 1990 and that the applicable percentage prescribed by §1.861-10T(e)(1)(iv)(A) is 80 percent. Assume that X has elected to use the quadratic formula provided in §1.861-10T(e)(1)(iv)(B).

Step 1. X's average month-end level of debt owning to unrelated persons is $1 million. The tax book value of X's assets is $2 million. Thus, X's debt-to-asset ratio computed under §1.861-10T(e)(1)(i) is 1 to 2.

Step 2. The tax book value of Y's assets is $500,000. Because Y has no debt to persons other than X, Y's debt-to-asset ratio computed under §1.861-10T(e)(1)(ii) is $0 to $500,000.

Step 3. Y's average month-end liabilities to X, as computed under §1.861-10T(e)(1)(iii) for 1987 are $100,000.

Step 4. Adding the $100,000 of Y's liabilities owed to X as computed under Step 3 to Y's third party liabilities ($0) would be insufficient to make Y's debt-to-asset ratio computed in Step 2 ($100,000-to-$500,000, or 1:5) equal to at least 80 percent of X's debt-to-asset ratio computed under Step 1, as adjusted to reflect a reduction in X's debt and assets by the $100,000 of excess related person indebtedness (.80 × $900,000/$1,900,000 or 1:2.6). Therefore, the entire amount of Y's liabilities to X ($100,000) constitute excess related person indebtedness under §1.861-10T(e)(1)(ii). Thus, the entire $10,000 of interest received by X from Y during 1987 constitutes interest received on excess related person indebtedness.

Step 5. The Y note held by X has a tax book value of $100,000. Solely for purposes of §1.861-10(e)(1)(v), the Y note is attributed to separate limitation categories in the same manner as the Y stock. Under paragraph (c)(3)(iii) of this section, of the $80,000 of Y stock held by X, $50,000 is attributable to foreign source general limitation income, and $30,000 is attributable to foreign source passive income. Thus, for purposes of §1.861-10T(e)(1)(v), $62,500 of the $100,000 Y note is considered to be a foreign source general limitation asset and $37,500 of the $100,000 Y note is considered to be a foreign source passive asset.

Step 6. Since $8,000 of the $10,000 in related person interest income received by Y constitutes interest received on excess related person indebtedness, $10,000 of X's third party interest expense is allocated to X's debt investment in Y. Under §1.861-10T(e)(1)(vi), 62.5 percent of the $10,000 of X's third party interest expense ($6,250) is allocated to foreign source general limitation income and 37.5 percent of the $10,000 of X's third party interest expense ($3,750) is allocated to foreign source passive income. As a result of this direct allocation, the value of X's assets generating foreign source general limitation income shall be reduced by the principal amount of indebtedness the interest on which is directly allocated to foreign source general limitation income ($62,500), and X's assets generating foreign general limitation income shall be reduced by the principal amount of indebtedness the interest on which is directly allocated to foreign passive income ($37,500).

(5) *Totals*

Having allocated $10,000 of its third party interest expense to its debt investment in Y, X would apportion the $90,000 balance of its interest according to the following apportionment fractions:

Asset	Domestic Source	Foreign General	Foreign Passive	Noncontrolled Section 902
Plant & equipment	$750,000	$250,000		
Inventory	150,000	50,000		
Automobiles	20,000			
Patents	37,500	12,500		
Trademarks	7,500	2,500		
Y stock		50,000	30,000	
Y note			100,000	
Z stock				$40,000
TOTALS:	965,000	365,000	130,000	40,000
Adjustments for directly allocable interest		(62,250)	(37,750)	
ADJUSTED TOTALS:	965,000	302,750	92,250	40,000
Percentage	69%	22%	6%	3%

Example 2: Assume the same facts as in Example 1, except that Y has $100,000 of third party indebtedness. Further, assume for purposes of the application of the special allocation rule of § 1.861-10T(e) that the taxable year is 1990 and that the applicable percentage prescribed by § 1.861-10T(e)(1)(iv)(A) is 80 percent. The application of the § 1.861-10(e) would be modified as follows.

Step 1. X's debt-to-asset ratio computed under § 1.861-10T(e)(1)(i) remains 1 to 2 (or 0.5).

Step 2. The tax book value of Y's assets is $500,000. Y has $100,000 of indebtedness to third parties. Y's debt-to-asset ratio computed under § 1.861-10T(e)(1)(ii) is $100,000 to $500,000 (1:5 or 0.2).

Step 3. Y's average month-end liabilities to X, as computed under § 1.861-10T(e)(1)(iii) remain $100,000.

Step 4. X's debt-to-asset ratio is 0.5 and 80 percent of 0.5 is 0.4. Because Y's debt-to-asset ratio is 0.2, there is excess related person indebtedness, the amount of which can be computed based on the following formula:

$$\frac{\text{Aggregate Third Party Debt of Related US Shareholder} - X}{\text{US Shareholder} - X \text{ Assets}} \times \text{Applicable Percentage For Year } (0.8) = \frac{\text{Aggregate Third Party Debt of Related CFCs} + X}{\text{Related CFC Assets}}$$

Supplying the facts as given, this equation is as follows:

$$\frac{1{,}000{,}000 - X}{2{,}000{,}000 - X} \times .8 = \frac{100{,}000 + X}{500{,}000}$$

Multiply both sides by 500,000 and (2,000,000 − X), yielding:
$4 \times 10^{11} - 400{,}000X = 2 \times 10^{11} + 2{,}000{,}000X - 100{,}000X - X^2$

Since there is an X^2 in this equation, a quadratic formula must be utilized to solve for X. Group the components in this equation, segregating the X and the X^2:
$X^2 + (-2{,}300{,}000)X + (2 \times 10^{11}) = 0$
Apply the quadratic formula:

$$X = \frac{-b \pm \sqrt{b^2 - 4(a)(c)}}{2(a)}$$

a = 1 (coefficient of X^2)
b = −2,300,000 (coefficient of X)
c = 2×10^{11} (remaining element of equation)

Therefore, X equals either 90,519 or (2.21×10^{11}). For purposes of computing excess related person indebtedness, X is the lowest positive amount derived from this equation, which is 90,519.

Steps 5 and 6 are unchanged from *Example 1*, except that the total amount of interest on excess related party indebtedness is $9,051.

[Temporary Reg. § 1.861-12T.]

☐ [*T.D.* 8228, 9-9-88.]

§ 1.861-13T. Transition rules for interest expenses (Temporary.).—(a) *In general.*—(1) *Optional application.*—The rules of this section may be applied at the choice of a

corporate taxpayer. In the case of an affiliated group, however, the choice must be made on a consistent basis for all members. Therefore, a corporate taxpayer (or affiliated group) may allocate and apportion its interest expense entirely on the basis of the rules contained in §§ 1.861-8T through 1.861-12T and without regard to the rules of this section. The choice is made on an annual basis and, thus, is not binding with respect to subsequent tax years.

(2) *Transition relief.*—This section contains transitional rules that limit the application of the rules for allocating and apportioning interest expense of corporate taxpayers contained in §§ 1.861-8T through 1.861-12T, which are applicable in allocating and apportioning the interest expense of corporate taxpayers generally for taxable years beginning after 1986. Sections 1.861-9(d) (relating to individuals, estates, and certain trusts) and 1.861-9(e) (relating to partnerships) are effective for taxable years beginning after 1986. Thus, the taxpayers to whom those sections apply do not qualify for transition relief under this section. To the extent that the rules of §§ 1.861-8T through 1.861-12T do not apply by reason of these transition rules, interest expense shall be allocated and apportioned under the rules of § 1.861-8 as in effect for taxable years beginning before 1987.

(3) *Indebtedness defined.*—For purposes of this section, the term "indebtedness" means any obligation or other evidence of indebtedness that generates an expense that constitutes interest expense within the meaning of § 1.861-9T(a). In the case of an obligation that does not bear interest initially, but becomes interest bearing with the lapse of time or upon the occurrence of an event, such obligation shall only be considered to constitute indebtedness when it first bears interest. Obligations that are outstanding as of November 16, 1985 shall only qualify for transition relief under this section if they bear interest-bearing as of that date. For this purpose, any obligation that has original issue discount within the meaning of section 1273(a)(1) of the Code shall be considered to be interest-bearing.

(4) *Exceptions.*—The term "indebtedness" shall not include any obligation existing between affiliated corporations, as defined in § 1.861-11T(d). Moreover, the term "indebtedness" shall not include any obligation the interest on which is directly allocable under §§ 1.861-10T(b) and 1.861-10T(c). Under § 1.861-9T(b)(6)(iv)(B), certain interest expense is directly allocated to the gain derived from an appropriately identified financial product. When interest expense on a liability is reduced by such gain, the principal amount of such liability shall be reduced pro rata by the relative amount of interest expense that is directly allocated.

(b) *General phase-in.*—(1) *In general.*—In the case of each of the first three taxable years of the taxpayer beginning after December 31, 1986, the rules of §§ 1.861-8T through 1.861-12T shall not apply to interest expenses paid or accrued by the taxpayer during the taxable year with respect to an aggregate amount of indebtedness which does not exceed the general phase-in amount, as defined in paragraph (b)(2) of this section.

(2) *General phase-in amount defined.*—Subject to the limitation imposed by paragraph (b)(3) of this section, the general phase-in amount means the amount which is the applicable percentage (determined under the following table) of the aggregate amount of indebtedness of the taxpayer outstanding on November 16, 1985:

Taxable year
beginning after
December 31, 1986 *Percentage*
  First 75
  Second 50
  Third 25

(3) *Reductions in indebtedness.*—The general phase-in amount shall not exceed the taxpayer's historic lowest month-end debt level taking into account all months after October 1985. However, for the taxable year in which a taxpayer attains a new historic lowest month-end debt level (but not for subsequent taxable years), the general phase-in amount shall not exceed the average of month-end debt levels within that taxable year (without taking into account any increase in month-end debt levels occurring in such taxable year after the new historic lowest month-end debt level is attained).

Example. X is a calendar year taxpayer that had $100 of indebtedness outstanding on November 16, 1985. X's month-end debt level remained $100 for all subsequent months until July 1987, when X's month-end debt level fell to $50. In computing transition relief for 1987, X's general phase-in amount cannot exceed $75 (900 divided by 12), which is the average of month-end debt levels in 1987. Assuming that X's month-end debt level for any subsequent month does not fall below $50, the limitation on its general phase-in amount for all taxable years after 1987 will be $50, its historic lowest month-end debt level after October 1985.

(c) *Nonapplication of the consolidation rule.*—(1) *General rule.*—In the case of each of the first five taxable years of the taxpayer beginning after December 31, 1986, the consolidation rule contained in § 1.861-11T(c) shall not apply to interest expenses paid or accrued by the taxpayer during the taxable year with respect to an aggregate amount of indebtedness which does not exceed the special phase-in amount, as defined in paragraph (c)(2) of this section.

(2) *Special phase-in amount.*—The special phase-in amount is the sum of—

   (i) The general phase-in amount,
   (ii) The five-year phase-in amount, and
   (iii) The four-year phase-in amount.

(3) *Five-year phase-in amount.*—The five-year phase-in amount is the lesser of—

   (i) The applicable percentage (the "unreduced percentage" in the following table) of the five-year debt amount, or

   (ii) The applicable percentage (the "reduced percentage" in the following table) of the five-year debt amount reduced by paydowns (if any):

Transition Year	Unreduced Percentage	Reduced Percentage
Year 1	8⅓	10
Year 2	16⅔	25
Year 3	25	50
Year 4	33⅓	100
Year 5	16⅔	100

(4) *Four-year phase-in amount.*—The four-year phase-in amount is the lesser of—

   (i) The applicable percentage (the "unreduced percentage" in the following table) of the four-year debt amount, or

   (ii) The applicable percentage (the "reduced percentage" in the following table) of the four-year debt amount reduced by paydowns (if any) to the extent that such paydowns exceed the five-year debt amount:

Transition Year	Unreduced Percentage	Reduced Percentage
Year 1	5	6¼
Year 2	10	16⅔
Year 3	15	37½
Year 4	20	100

(5) *Five-year debt amount.*—The "five-year debt amount" means the excess (if any) of—

   (i) The amount of the outstanding indebtedness of the taxpayer on May 29, 1985, over

   (ii) The amount of the outstanding indebtedness of the taxpayer on December 31, 1983.

The five-year debt amount shall not exceed the aggregate amount of indebtedness of the taxpayer outstanding on November 16, 1985.

(6) *Four-year debt amount.*—The "four-year debt amount" means the excess (if any) of—

   (i) The amount of the outstanding indebtedness of the taxpayer on December 31, 1983, over

   (ii) The amount of the outstanding indebtedness of the taxpayer on December 31, 1982.

The four-year debt amount shall not exceed the aggregate amount of indebtedness of the taxpayer outstanding on November 16, 1985, reduced by the five-year debt amount.

(7) *Paydowns.*—The term "paydowns" means the excess (if any) of—

   (i) The aggregate amount of indebtedness of the taxpayer outstanding on November 16, 1985, over

   (ii) The limitation on the general phase-in amount described in paragraph (b)(3) of this section.

Paydowns are first applied to the five-year debt amount to the extent thereof and then to the four-year debt amount for purposes of computing the five-year and the four-year phase-in amounts.

(d) *Treatment of affiliated group.*—For purposes of this section, all members of the same affiliated group of corporations (as defined in § 1.861-11(d)) shall be treated as one taxpayer whether or not such members filed a consolidated return. Interaffiliate debt is not taken into account in computing transition relief. Moreover, any reduction in the amount of interaffiliate debt is not taken into account in determining the amount of paydowns.

(e) *Mechanics of computation.*—(1) *Step 1: Determination of the amounts within the various categories of debt.*—Each separate member of an affiliated group must determine each of its following amounts:

   (i) *November 16, 1985 amount.*—The amount of its debt outstanding on November 16, 1985 (after the elimination of interaffiliate indebtedness),

   (ii) *Unreduced five-year debt.*—The amount of any net increase in the amount of its indebtedness on May 29, 1985 (after elimination of inter-affiliate indebtedness) over the amount of its indebtedness on December 31, 1983 (after elimination of interaffiliate indebtedness),

(iii) *Unreduced four-year debt.*—The amount of any net increase in the amount of its indebtedness on December 31, 1983 (after elimination of interaffiliate indebtedness) over the amount of its indebtedness on December 31, 1982 (after elimination of interaffiliate indebtedness), and

(iv) *Month-end debt.*—The amount of its month-end debt level for all months after October 1985 (after elimination of interaffiliate indebtedness).

(2) *Step 2: Aggregation of the separate company amounts.*—Each of the designated amounts for the separate companies identified in Step 1 must be aggregated in order to compute consolidated transition relief. Paragraph (e)(10)(iv) of this section (Step 10) requires the use of the taxpayer's current year average debt level for the purpose of computing the percentages of debt that are subject to the three sets of rules that are identified in Step 10. For use in that computation, the taxpayer should compute the current year average debt level by aggregating separate company month-end debt levels and then by averaging those aggregate amounts.

(3) *Step 3: Calculation of the lowest historic month-end debt level of the taxpayer.*—In order to calculate the lowest historic month-end debt level of the taxpayer, determine the month-end debt level of each separate company for each month ending after October 1985 and aggregate these amounts on a month-by-month basis. On such aggregate basis, in any taxable year in which the taxpayer attains an aggregate new lowest historic month-end debt level, add together all the aggregate month-end debt levels within the taxable year (without taking into account any increase in aggregate debt level subsequent to the attainment of such lowest historic month-end debt level) and divide by the number of months in that taxable year, yielding the average of month-end debt levels for such year. Such average shall constitute the taxpayer's lowest historic month-end debt level for that taxable year in which the aggregate new lowest historic month-end debt level was attained. Unless otherwise specified, all subsequent references to any amount refer to the aggregate amount for all members of the same affiliated group of corporations.

(4) *Step 4: Computation of paydowns.*—Paydowns equal the amount by which the November 16, 1985 amount exceeds the taxpayer's lowest historic month-end debt level, determined under Step 3.

(5) *Step 5: Computation of limitations on unreduced five-year debt and unreduced four-year debt.*—(i) The unreduced five-year debt cannot exceed the November 16, 1985 amount.

(ii) The unreduced four-year debt cannot exceed the November 16, 1985 amount less the unreduced five-year debt.

(6) *Step 6: Computation of reduced five-year and reduced four-year debt.*—(i) *Reduced five-year debt.*—Compute the amount of reduced five-year debt by subtracting from the unreduced five-year debt (see Step 5) the amount of paydowns (see Step 4).

(ii) *Reduced four-year debt.*—To the extent that the amount of paydowns (see step 4) exceeds the amount of unreduced five-year debt (see Step 5), compute the amount of reduced four-year debt by subtracting such excess from the unreduced four-year debt (see Step 1).

(iii) To the extent that paydowns do not offset either the unreduced five-year amount or the unreduced four-year amount, the reduced and the unreduced amounts are the same.

(7) *Step 7: Computation of the general phase-in amount.*—The general phase-in amount is the lesser of—

(i) The percentage of the November 16, 1985 amount designated for the relevant transition year in the table below, or

(ii) The lowest group month-end debt level (see Step 3).

General Phase-in Table

Transition Year	Percentage
Year 1	75
Year 2	50
Year 3	25

(8) *Step 8: Computation of Five-year Phase-in Amount.*—The five-year phase-in amount is the lesser of—

(i) The percentage of the unreduced five-year debt designated for the relevant transition year in the table below, or

(ii) The percentage of the reduced five-year debt designated for the relevant transition year in the table below.

Reg. § 1.861-13T(e)(8)(ii)

Five-year Phase-in Table

Transition Year	Unreduced Percentage	Reduced Percentage
Year 1	8⅓	10
Year 2	16⅔	25
Year 3	25	50
Year 4	33⅓	100
Year 5	16⅔	100

(9) *Step 9: Computation of Four-year Phase-in Amount.*—The four-year phase-in amount is the lesser of—

(i) The percentage of the unreduced four-year debt designated for the relevant transition year in the table below, or

(ii) The percentage of the reduced four-year debt designated for the relevant transition year in the table below.

Four-year Phase-in Table

Transition Year	Unreduced Percentage	Reduced Percentage
Year 1	5	6¼
Year 2	10	16⅔
Year 3	15	37½
Year 4	20	100

(10) *Step 10: Determination of group debt ratio and application of transition relief to separate company interest expense.*—(i) The general phase-in amount consists of the amount computed under Step 7. Interest expense on this amount is subject to pre-1987 rules of allocation and apportionment.

(ii) The post-1986 separate company amount consists of the sum of the amounts determined under Steps 8 and 9. Interest expense on this amount is subject to post-1986 rules of allocation and apportionment as applied on a separate company basis. Thus, § 1.861-11T(c) does not apply with respect to this amount of indebtedness. Because the consolidation rule does not apply, stock in affiliated corporations shall be taken into account in computing the apportionment fractions for each separate company in the same manner as under pre-1987 rules.

(iii) The post-1986 one-taxpayer amount consists of any indebtedness that does not qualify for transition relief under Steps 7, 8, and 9. Interest expense on this amount is subject to post-1986 rules as applied on a consolidated basis.

(iv) To determine the extent to which the interest expense of each separate company is subject to any of these sets of allocation and apportionment rules, each company shall prorate its own interest expense using two fractions. The general phase-in fraction is the general phase-in amount over the current year average debt level of the affiliated group (see Step 2). The post-1986 separate company fraction is the post-1986 separate company amount over the current year average debt level of the affiliated group. The balance of each separate company's interest expense is subject to post-1986 one-taxpayer rules.

(f) *Example.*—XYZ form an affiliated group.

(1) *Step 1:* Determination of the amounts within the various debt categories

Company X	Historic 3rd party Debt		Increase
November 16, 1985	$100,000		
May 29, 1985	90,000	5-year	$10,000
December 31, 1983	80,000	4-year	10,000
December 31, 1982	70,000		
Current Interest Expense	10,000		

Company Y	Historic 3rd party Debt		Increase
November 16, 1985	$200,000		
May 29, 1985	170,000	5-year	$120,000
December 31, 1983	50,000	4-year	10,000
December 31, 1982	40,000		
Current Interest Expense	30,000		

Company Z	Historic 3rd party Debt		Increase
November 16, 1985	$300,000		
May 29, 1985	300,000	5-year	$50,000
December 31, 1983	250,000	4-year	100,000
December 31, 1982	150,000		
Current Interest Expense	30,000		

(2) *Step 2:* Aggregation of the separate company amounts.

Aggregate November 16, 1985	$600,000
Aggregate 5-year debt	180,000
Aggregate 4-year debt	120,000
Current year average debt level	700,000

(3) *Step 3:* Calculation of lowest historic month-end debt level.

An analysis of historic month-end debt levels indicates that in 1986, XYZ's aggregate month-end debt level fell to $500,000, which represents the lowest sum for all years under consideration. Because this historic low occurred in a prior tax year, there is no averaging of month-end debt levels in the current taxable year.

Aggregate November 16, 1985 amount	$600,000
Aggregate unreduced 5-year debt	180,000
Aggregate unreduced 4-year debt	120,000

Because the November 16, 1985 amount exceeds the unreduced 4- and 5-year debt, the full amount of the 4- and 5-year debt qualify for transition relief. In cases where the November 16, 1985 amount is less than the 4- or 5-year debt (or the sum of both), the latter amounts are limited to the November 16, 1985 amount. See the limitations on the 4-year and 5-year debt amounts in paragraphs (c)(6) and (c)(5), respectively, of this section.

(6) *Step 6:* Computation of reduced five-year and four-year debt.

The paydowns computed under Step 4 are deemed to first offset the aggregate unreduced five-year debt. Accordingly, the reduced amount of five-year debt is $80,000. Since the paydowns are less than the aggregate unreduced five-year debt, there is no paydown in connection with aggregate unreduced four-year debt. Accordingly, the unreduced four-year debt and the reduced four-year debt are both considered to be $120,000.

(7) *Step 7:* Computation of the general phase-in amount.

In transition year 1, the general transition amount is the lesser of:

(i) 75 percent of the aggregate November 16, 1985 amount (75% of $600,000 = $450,000); or

(ii) the lowest month-end debt level since November 16, 1985 ($500,000).

Therefore, the general transition amount is $450,000.

(8) *Step 8:* Computation of the five-year phase-in amount.

In transition year 1, the five-year phase-in amount is the lesser of:

(4) *Step 4:* Computation of paydowns.

The aggregate November 16, 1985 amount ($600,000), less the lowest historic month-end debt level ($500,000), yields a total paydown in the amount of $100,000.

(5) *Step 5:* Computation of limitations on aggregate unreduced five-year debt and aggregate unreduced four-year debt.

(i) 8⅓ percent of the unreduced five-year amount (8⅓% of $180,000 = $15,000); or

(ii) 10 percent of the reduced five-year amount (10% of $80,000 = $8,000).

Therefore, the five-year phase-in amount is $8,000.

(9) *Step 9:* Computation of the four-year phase-in amount.

In transition year 1, the four-year phase-in amount is the lesser of:

(i) 5 percent of the unreduced four-year amount (5% of $120,000 = $6,000); or

(ii) 6¼ percent of the reduced four-year amount (6¼% of $120,000 = $7,500).

Therefore, the four-year phase-in amount is $6,000.

(10) *Step 10:* Determination of group debt ratio and application of relief to separate company interest expense.

(i) As determined under Step 7, interest expense on a total of $450,000 of the XYZ debt in the first transition year is computed under pre-1987 rules of allocation and apportionment.

(ii) The sum of Steps 8 ($8,000) and 9 ($6,000) is $14,000. Interest expense on a total of $14,000 of XYZ debt is computed under post-1986 rules of allocation and apportionment as applied on a separate company basis.

(iii) The balance of XYZ's current year interest expense is computed under post-1986 rules of allocation and apportionment as applied on a consolidated basis. X, Y, and Z, respectively, have current interest expense of $10,000, $30,000, and $30,000. Thus, 64.3 percent (450,000/700,000) of the interest expense of each separate company is subject to pre-1987 rules. Two percent (14,000/700,000) of the interest expense of each separate company is subject to post-1986 rules applied on a separate company basis. Finally, the balance of each separate company's current year interest expense (33.7 percent) is subject to post-1986 rules applied on a consolidated basis.

(g) *Corporate transfers.*—(1) *Effect on transferee.*—(i) *General rule.*—Except as provided in paragraph (g)(1)(ii) of this section, if a domestic corporation or an affiliated group acquires stock in a domestic corporation that was not a member of the transferee's affiliated group before the acquisition, but becomes a member of the transferee's affiliated group after the acquisition, the transferee group shall take into account the following transition attributes of the acquired corporation in computing its transition relief:

(A) November 16, 1985 amount,

(B) Unreduced five-year amount,

(C) Unreduced four-year amount, and

(D) The amount of any transferor paydowns attributed to the acquired corporation under the rules of paragraph (h)(1) of this section.

(ii) *Special rule for year of acquisition.*—To compute the amount of the transition attributes described in paragraph (g)(1)(i) of this section that a transferee takes into account in the transferee's taxable year of the acquisition, such transition attributes shall be multiplied by a fraction, the numerator of which is the number of months within the taxable year that the transferee held the acquired corporation and the denominator of which is the number of months in such taxable year. In order for the transferee to assert ownership of a subsidiary for a given month, the transferee and the acquired corporation must be affiliated corporations as of the last day of the month. In addition, the transferor and the transferee shall take account of the month-end debt level of the transferred corporation only for those months at the end of which the transferred corporation was a member of the transferor's or the transferee's respective affiliated group.

(iii) *Aggregation of transition attributes.*—The transition attributes of the acquired corporation shall be aggregated with the respective amounts of the transferee group.

(iv) *Conveyance of transferor paydowns.*—The total paydowns of the transferee group shall include the amount of any paydown of the transferor group that was attributed to the acquired corporation under the rules of paragraph (h)(1) of this section.

(v) *Effect of certain elections.*—If an election—

(A) Is made under section 338(g) (whether or not an election under 338(h)(10) is made),

(B) Is deemed to be made under section 338(e) (other than (e)(2)), or section 338(f), or,

(C) Is made under section 336(e), no indebtedness of the acquired corporation shall qualify for transition relief for the year such election first becomes effective and for subsequent taxable years, and no other transition attributes of the acquired corporation shall be taken into account by the transferee group.

(2) *Effect on transferor.*—(i) *General rule.*—Except as provided in paragraph (g)(2)(ii) of this section, in the case of an acquisition of a member of an affiliated group by a nonmember of the group, the transferor shall not take into account the transition attributes of the acquired corporation in computing the transition relief of the transferor group in subsequent taxable years. Thus, the November 16, 1985 amount, the unreduced five-year and four-year debt amounts, and the end-of-month debt levels of the transferor group shall be computed without regard to the acquired corporation's respective amounts for purposes of computing transition relief of the transferor group for years thereafter.

(ii) *Special rule for the year of disposition.*—To compute the amount of the transition attributes described in paragraph (g)(2)(i) of this section that a transferor shall take into account in the transferor's taxable year of the disposition, such transition attributes shall be multiplied by a fraction, the numerator of which is the number of months within the taxable year that the transferor held the acquired corporation and the denominator of which is the number of months in such taxable year. In order for the transferor to assert ownership of a subsidiary for a given month, the transferor and the acquired corporation must be affiliated corporations as of the last day of the month.

(iii) *Effect of prior paydowns.*—Any paydowns of the acquired corporation that are considered to reduce the debt of other members of the transferor group under the rules of paragraph (h)(1) of this section (whether incurred in a prior taxable year or in that portion of a year of disposition that is taken into account by the transferor) shall continue to be taken into account by the transferor group after the disposition.

(3) *Special rule for assumptions of indebtedness.*—In connection with the transfer of a corporation, if the indebtedness of an acquired

Reg. § 1.861-13T(g)(1)

corporation is assumed by any party other than the transferee or another member of the transferee's affiliated group, the transition attributes of the acquired corporation shall not be taken into account in computing the transition relief of the transferee group. See paragraph (g)(2) of this section concerning the treatment of the transferor group. Also in connection with the transfer of a corporation, if the transferee or another member of the transferee's affiliated group assumes the indebtedness of an acquired corporation, such assumed indebtedness shall only qualify for transition relief during the period in which the acquired corporation remains a member of the transferee group. Further, if the transferee group subsequently disposes of the acquired corporation, the indebtedness of the acquired corporation will continue to qualify for transition relief only if the indebtedness is assumed by the new purchaser as of the time such corporation is acquired.

(4) *Effect of asset sales.*—If substantially all of the assets of a corporation are sold, the indebtedness of such corporation shall cease to be qualified for transition relief. Thus, the transition attributes of such corporation shall not be taken into account in computing transition relief.

(h) *Rules for attributing paydowns among separate companies.*—(1) *General rule.*—In the case of a corporate transfer under paragraph (g) of this section, it is necessary to determine the amount of paydowns attributable to the acquired corporation. Under paragraph (c)(7) of this section, paydowns are deemed to reduce first the five-year phase-in amount, then the four-year phase-in amount, and then the general phase-in amount. Thus, for example, a reduction in indebtedness of the group caused by a reduction in the debt of a group member that has no five-year debt will nevertheless be deemed under this ordering rule to reduce the indebtedness of those group members that do have five-year debt. In order to preserve the effect of paydowns caused by a reduction, each member must determine on a separate company basis at the time of any transfer of any member of the affiliated group the impact of paydowns (including those paydowns occurring in the year of transfer prior to the time of the transfer) on the various categories of indebtedness.

(2) *Mechanics of computation.*—Separate company accounts of paydowns are determined by prorating any paydown among all group members with five-year debt to the extent thereof on the basis of the relative amounts of five-year debt. Paydowns in excess of five-year debt are prorated on a similar basis among all group members with four-year debt to the extent thereof on the basis of the relative amounts of four-year debt. Paydowns in excess of four-year and five-year debt are prorated among all group members with general phase-in debt to the extent thereof on the basis of the relative amounts of general phase-in debt. After an initial paydown has been prorated among the members of an affiliated group, any further reduction in the amount of aggregate month-end debt level as compared to the November 16, 1985 amount is prorated among all members of the affiliated group based on the remaining net amounts of four-year and five-year debt.

(3) *Examples.*—The rules of paragraphs (g) and (h) of this section may be illustrated by the following examples.

Example (1): Computing separate company accounts of reductions—(i) *Facts.* XYZ constitutes an affiliated group of corporations that has a calendar taxable year and the following transition attributes:

Company X		Historic 3rd party Debt		Increase
November	16, 1985	$100,000		
May	29, 1985	80,000	5-year	$0
December	31, 1983	80,000	4-year	10,000
December	31, 1982	70,000		

Company Y		Historic 3rd party Debt		Increase
November	16, 1985	$200,000		
May	29, 1985	170,000	5-year	$120,000
December	31, 1983	50,000	4-year	10,000
December	31, 1982	40,000		

Company Z		Historic 3rd party Debt		Increase
November	16, 1985	$300,000		
May	29, 1985	290,000	5-year	$40,000
December	31, 1983	250,000	4-year	100,000
December	31, 1982	150,000		

Reg. §1.861-13T(h)(3)

In 1986, the XYZ group attained its lowest historic month-end debt level of $500,000. Because the November 16, 1985 amount is $600,000, the XYZ group therefore has a paydown in the amount of $100,000. This paydown partially offsets the $160,000 of five-year debt in the XYZ group.

(ii) *Analysis.* Applying the rule of paragraph (h)(1) of this section, separate company accounts of paydowns are computed by prorating the $100,000 paydown among those members of the group that have five-year debt. Accordingly, the paydown is prorated between Y and Z as follows:

$$\text{To Y:} \quad \$100,000 \times \frac{\$120,000}{\$160,000} = \$75,000.$$

$$\text{To Z:} \quad \$100,000 \times \frac{\$40,000}{\$160,000} = \$25,000.$$

Example (2): Corporate acquisitions—(i) *Facts.* The facts are the same as in example (1). On July 15, 1987, the XYZ group sells all the stock of Y to A. Having held the stock of Y for six months in 1987, the XZ group computes its transition relief for that year taking into account half of the transition attributes of Y. AY constitutes an affiliated group of corporations after the acquisition. Having held the stock of Y for six months in 1987, the AY group computes its transition relief for that year taking into account half of the transition attributes of Y. In 1987, the AY group attained a new lowest month-end debt level that yields an average lowest month-end debt level for 1987 of $150,000.

(ii) *Transferee group.* The following analysis applies in determining transition relief for purposes of apportioning the interest expense of the transferee group for 1987. The AY group has the following transition attributes for 1987:

Company A	Historic 3rd party Debt		Increase
November 16, 1985	$100,000		
May 29, 1985	250,000	5-year	$5,000
December 31, 1983	245,000	4-year	10,000
December 31, 1982	235,000		

Company Y (half-year amounts)	Historic 3rd party Debt		Increase
November 16, 1985	$100,000		
May 29, 1985	85,000	5-year	$60,000
December 31, 1983	25,000	4-year	5,000
December 31, 1982	20,000		
Pre-acquisition year paydown by another member of the transferor group that reduced Y's five-year debt	37,500 (one half of $75,000)		

Because the November 16, 1985 amount of the AY group in 1987 is $200,000 and because the 1987 average of historic month-end debt levels was $150,000, the AY group has a paydown in the amount of $50,000. In addition, the 1986 paydown by the XYZ group that was deemed to reduce Y debt is added to the paydown computed above, yielding a total paydown of $87,500. This amount is prorated between members, eliminating the four and five year debt of the AY group. Note that Y is only a member of the AY group for half of the 1987 taxable year. In 1988, Y's entire transition indebtedness and a $75,000 paydown must be taken into account in computing the amount of interest expense eligible for transition relief.

(iii) *Transferor group.* The following analysis applies in determining transition relief for purposes of apportioning the interest expense of the transferor group for 1987. The XZ group has the transition attributes stated below for 1987. In 1987, the XZ group attained a new lowest month-end debt level that yields an average lowest month-end debt level for 1987 of $250,000.

Company X:	Historic 3rd party debt	Increase
Nov. 16, 1985	$100,000	.....
May 29, 1985 (5-year)	80,000	$0
Dec. 31, 1983 (4-year)	80,000	10,000
Dec. 31, 1982	70,000	.....
Pre-disposition paydown that reduced X's debt	0	.....

	Historic 3rd party debt	Increase
Company Y (half-year amounts):		
Nov. 16, 1985	100,000	.....
May 29, 1985 (5-year)	85,000	60,000
Dec. 31, 1983 (4-year)	25,000	5,000
Dec. 31, 1982	20,000	.....
Pre-disposition paydown that reduced Y's debt	37,500	.....
Company Z:		
Nov. 16, 1985	300,000	.....
May 29, 1985 (5-year)	290,000	40,000
Dec. 31, 1983 (4-year)	250,000	100,000
Dec. 31, 1982	150,000	.....
Pre-disposition paydown that reduced Z's debt	25,000	.....

Because the revised November 16, 1985 amount of the XZ group is $500,000 and because the 1987 average of lowest historic month-end debt levels of the XZ group was $250,000, the XZ group has a paydown in the amount of $250,000. This paydown offsets the total five and four year debt of the XZ group. Had the 1987 paydown of the XZ group been an amount less than the five-year amount, the paydown would have been prorated based on Y's adjusted 5-year amount of $22,500 and Z's adjusted 5-year amount of $15,000. [Temporary Reg. § 1.861-13T.]

☐ [*T.D.* 8257, 8-1-89.]

§ 1.861-14. Special rules for allocating and apportioning certain expenses (other than interest expense) of an affiliated group of corporations.—(a) through (c) [Reserved]. For further guidance, see § 1.861-14T(a) through (c).

(d) *Definition of affiliated group.*—(1) *General rule.*—For purposes of this section, the term *affiliated group* has the same meaning as is given that term by section 1504, except that section 936 corporations (as defined in § 1.861-11(d)(2)(ii)) are also included within the affiliated group to the extent provided in paragraph (d)(2) of this section. Section 1504(a) defines an affiliated group as one or more chains of includible corporations connected through 80% stock ownership with a common parent corporation which is an includible corporation (as defined in section 1504(b)). In the case of a corporation that either becomes or ceases to be a member of the group during the course of the corporation's taxable year, only the expenses incurred by the group member during the period of membership shall be allocated and apportioned as if all members of the group were a single corporation. In this regard, the apportionment factor chosen shall relate only to the period of membership. For example, if apportionment on the basis of assets is chosen, the average amount of assets (tax book value or fair market value) for the taxable year shall be multiplied by a fraction, the numerator of which is the number of months of the corporation's taxable year during which the corporation was a member of the affiliated group, and the denominator of which is the number of months within the corporation's taxable year. If apportionment on the basis of gross income is chosen, only gross income generated during the period of membership shall be taken into account. If apportionment on the basis of units sold or sales receipts is chosen, only units sold or sales receipts during the period of membership shall be taken into account. Expenses incurred by the group member during its taxable year, but not during the period of membership, shall be allocated and apportioned without regard to other members of the group. This paragraph (d)(1) applies to taxable years beginning after December 31, 1989.

(2) *Inclusion of section 936 corporations.*—(i) *General rule.*—Except as otherwise provided in paragraph (d)(2)(ii) of this section, the exclusion from the affiliated group of section 936 corporations under section 1504(b)(4) does not apply for purposes of this section. Thus, a section 936 corporation that meets the ownership requirements of section 1504(a) is a member of the affiliated group.

(ii) *Exception for purposes of alternative minimum tax.*—The exclusion from the affiliated group of section 936 corporations under section 1504(b)(4) shall be operative for purposes of the application of this section solely in determining the amount of foreign source alternative minimum taxable income within each separate category and the alternative minimum tax foreign tax credit pursuant to section 59(a). Thus, a section 936 corporation that meets the ownership requirements of section 1504(a) is not a member of the affiliated group for purposes of determining the amount of foreign source alternative minimum taxable income within each separate category and the alternative minimum tax foreign tax credit pursuant to section 59(a).

(iii) *Effective date.*—This paragraph (d)(2) applies to taxable years beginning after December 31, 1989.

(d)(3) through (j) [Reserved]. For further guidance see § 1.861-14T(d)(3) through (j). [Reg. § 1.861-14.]

☐ [T.D. 8916, 12-29-2000.]

§ 1.861-14T. Special rules for allocating and apportioning certain expenses (other than interest expense) of an affiliated group of corporations (temporary).—(a) *In general.*—Section 1.861-11T provides special rules for allocating and apportioning interest expense of an affiliated group of corporations. The rules of this § 1.861-14T also relate to affiliated groups of corporations and implement section 864(e)(6), which requires affiliated group allocation and apportionment of expenses other than interest which are not directly allocable and apportionable to any specific income producing activity or property. In general, the rules of this section apply to taxable years beginning after December 31, 1986. Paragraph (b) of this section describes the scope of the application of the rule for the allocation and apportionment of such expenses of affiliated groups of corporations. Such rule is then set forth in paragraph (c) of this section. Paragraph (d) of this section contains the definition of the term "affiliated group" for purposes of this section. Paragraph (e) of this section describes the expenses subject to allocation and apportionment under the rules of this section. Paragraph (f) of this section provides rules concerning the affiliated group allocation and apportionment of such expenses in computing the combined taxable income of a FSC or DISC and its related supplier. Paragraph (g) of this section describes the treatment of losses caused by apportionment of such expenses in the case of an affiliated group that does not file a consolidated return. Paragraph (h) of this section provides rules concerning the treatment of the reserve expenses of a life insurance company. Paragraph (j) of this section provides examples illustrating the application of this section.

(b) *Scope.*—(1) *Application of section 864(e)(6).*—Section 864(e)(6) and this section apply to the computation of taxable income for purposes of computing separate limitations on the foreign tax credit under section 904. Section 864(e)(6) and this section also apply in connection with section 907 to determine reductions in the amount allowed as a foreign tax credit under section 901. Section 864(e)(6) and this section also apply to the computation of the combined taxable income of the related supplier and a foreign sales corporation (FSC) (under sections 921 through 927) as well as the combined taxable income of the related supplier and a domestic international sales corporation (DISC) (under sections 991 through 997).

(2) *Nonapplication of section 864(e)(6).*—Section 864(e)(6) and this section do not apply to the computation of subpart F income of controlled foreign corporations (under sections 951 through 964) or the computation of effectively connected taxable income of foreign corporations.

(3) *Application of section 864(e)(6) to the computation of combined taxable income of a possessions corporation and its affiliates.*—[Reserved.]

(c) *General rule for affiliated corporations.*—(1) *General rule.*—(i) Except as otherwise provided in paragraph (c)(2) of this section, the taxable income of each member of an affiliated group within each statutory grouping shall be determined by allocating and apportioning the expenses described in paragraph (e) of this section of each member according to apportionment fractions which are computed as if all members of such group were a single corporation. For purposes of determining these apportionment fractions, any interaffiliate transactions or property that are duplicative with respect to the measure of apportionment chosen shall be eliminated. For example, in the application of an asset method of apportionment, stock in affiliated corporations shall not be taken into account, and loans between members of an affiliated group shall be treated in accordance with the rules of § 1.861-11T(e). Similarly, in the application of a gross income method of apportionment, interaffiliate dividends and interest, gross income from sales or services, and other interaffiliate gross income shall be eliminated. Likewise, in the application of a method of apportionment based on units sold or sales receipts, interaffiliate sales shall be eliminated.

(ii) Except as otherwise provided in this section, the rules of § 1.861-8T apply to the allocation and apportionment of the expenses described in paragraph (e) of this section. Thus, allocation under this paragraph (c) is accomplished by determining, with respect to each expense described in paragraph (e), the class of gross income to which the expense is definitely related and then allocating the deduction to such class of gross income. For this purpose, the gross income of all members of the affiliated group must be taken in account. Then, the expense is apportioned by attributing the expense to gross income (within the class to which the expense has been allocated) which is in the statutory grouping and to gross income (within the class) which is in the residual grouping. Section 1.861-8T(c)(1) identifies a number of factors upon which apportionment may be based, such as comparison of units sold, gross sales or receipts, assets used, or gross income. The apportionment method chosen must be applied consistently by each member of the affiliated group in apportioning the expense when more than one member incurred the expense or when members incurred separate portions of the expense. The apportionment fraction must take into account the apportionment factors contributed by all members of the affiliated group. In the case of an affiliated group of corporations that files a consolidated return, consolidated foreign tax credit limitations are computed for the group in accordance with the rules of § 1.1502-4. For purposes of this section the term "taxpayer" refers to the affiliated group (regardless of whether the group files a consolidated return), rather than to the separate members thereof.

(2) *Expenses relating to fewer than all members.*—An expense relates to fewer than all members of an affiliated group if the expense is allocable under paragraph (e)(1) of this section to gross income of at least one member other than the member that incurred the expense but fewer than all members of the affiliated group. The taxable income of the member that incurred the expense shall be determined by apportioning that expense under the rules of paragraph (c)(1) of this section as if the members of the affiliated group that derive gross income to which such expense is allocable under paragraph (e)(1) were treated as a single corporation.

(3) *Prior application of section 482.*—The rules of this section do not supersede the application of section 482 and the regulations thereunder. Section 482 may be applied effectively to deny a deduction for an expense to one member of an affiliated group and to allow a deduction for that expense to another member of the affiliated group. In cases to which section 482 is applied, expenses shall be reallocated and reapportioned under section 864(e)(6) and this section after taking into account the application of section 482.

(d)(1) and (2) [Reserved]. For further guidance, see § 1.861-14(d)(1) and (2).

(3) *Inclusion of financial corporations.*—For purposes of this section, in the case of an affiliated group (as defined in paragraph (d)(1) of this section), any members that constitute financial corporations as defined in § 1.861-11T(d)(4)(ii) shall be treated as members of the affiliated group. The rule of § 1.861-11T(d)(4)(i), which treats such financial corporations as a separate affiliated group, applies only for purposes of allocation and apportionment of interest expense and does not apply to the allocation and apportionment of other expenses under this section.

(4) *Treatment of life insurance companies subject to taxation under section 801.*—A life insurance company that is subject to taxation under section 801 shall be considered to constitute a member of the affiliated group composed of companies not taxable under section 801 only if a parent corporation so elects under section 1504(c)(2)(A) of the Code.

(e) *Expenses to be allocated and apportioned under this section.*—(1) *Expenses not directly traceable to specific income producing activities or property.*—(i) The expenses that are required to be allocated and apportioned under the rules of this section are expenses related to certain supportive functions, research and experimental expenses, stewardship expenses, and legal and accounting expenses, to the extent that such expenses are not directly allocable to specific income producing activities or property solely of the member of the affiliated group that incurred the expense. Interest expense of members of an affiliated group of corporations is allocated and apportioned under § 1.861-11T and not under the rules of this section. Expenses that are included in inventory costs or that are capitalized are not subject to allocation and apportionment under the rules of this section.

(ii) An item of expense is not considered to be directly allocable to specific income producing activities or property solely of the member incurring the expense if, were all members of the affiliated group treated as a single corporation, the expense would not be considered definitely related, within the meaning of § 1.861-8T(b)(2), only to a class of gross income derived solely by the member which actually incurred the expense. Furthermore, the expense is presumed not to be definitely related only to a class of gross income derived solely by the member incurring the expense (and is, therefore, presumed not to be directly allocable to specific income producing activities or property of that member) unless the taxpayer is able affirmatively to establish otherwise. As provided in paragraph (c)(1) of this section, expenses described in this paragraph (e)(1) generally shall be apportioned by the member incurring the expense according to apportionment fractions computed as if all members of the affiliated group were a single corporation. Under paragraph (c)(2) of this section, however, an expense shall be apportioned according to apportionment fractions computed as if only some (but fewer than all) members of the affiliated group were a single corporation, if the expense is considered allocable to gross income of at least one member other than the member incurring the expense but fewer than all members of the affiliated group. An item of expense shall be considered to be allocable to gross income of fewer than all members of the group if, were all members of the affiliated group treated as a single corporation, the expense would not be considered definitely related within the meaning of § 1.861-8T(b)(2) to gross income derived by all members of the group. In such case, the expense shall be considered allocable, for purposes of paragraph (c)(2) of this section, to gross income of those members of the group that generated (or could reasonably be expected to generate) the gross income to which the expense would be considered definitely related if the group were treated as a single corporation.

(2) *Research and experimental expenses.*—(i) *In general.*—The allocation and apportionment of research and experimental expenses is governed by the rules of § 1.861-8T(e)(3). In the case of research and experimental expenses incurred by a member of an affiliated group, the rules of § 1.861-8T(e)(3) shall be applied as if all members of the affiliated group were a single taxpayer. Thus, research and experimental expenses shall be allocated to all income of all members of the affiliated group reasonably connected with the relevant broad product category to which such expenses are definitely related under § 1.861-8T(e)(3)(i). If fewer than all members of the affiliated group derive gross income reasonably connected with that relevant broad product category, then such expenses shall be apportioned under the rules of this paragraph (c)(2) only among those members, as if those members were a single corporation. See *Example* (1) of paragraph (j) of this section. Such expenses shall then be apportioned, if the sales method is used, in accordance with the rules of § 1.861-8T(e)(3)(ii) between the statutory grouping (within the class of gross income) and the residual grouping (within the class of gross income) taking into account the amount of sales of all members of the affiliated group from the product category which resulted in such gross income. Section 1.861-8T(e)(3)(ii)(D), relating to sales of controlled parties, shall be applied as if all members of the affiliated group were the "taxpayer" referred to therein. If either of the optional gross income methods of apportionment is used, gross income of all members of the affiliated group that generate, have generated, or could reasonably have been expected to generate gross income within the relevant class of gross income must be taken into account.

(ii) *Expenses subject to the statutory moratorium.*—The rules of this section do not apply to research and experimental expenses allocated under section 126 of P.L. 98-369.

(3) *Expenses related to supportive functions.*—Expenses which are supportive in nature (such as overhead, general and administrative, supervisory expenses, advertising, marketing, and other sales expenses) are to be allocated and apportioned in accordance with the rules of § 1.861-8T(b)(3). To the extent that such expenses are not directly allocable under paragraph (e)(1)(ii) of this section to specific income producing activities or property of the member of the affiliated group that incurred the expense, such expenses must be allocated and apportioned as if all members of the affiliated group were a single corporation in accordance with the rules of paragraph (c) of this section. Specifically, such expenses must be allocated to a class of gross income that takes into account gross income that is generated, has been generated, or could reasonably have been expected to have been generated by the members of the affiliated group. If the expenses relate to the gross income of fewer than all members of the affiliated group as determined under paragraph (c)(2) of this section, then those expenses must be apportioned under the rules of paragraph (c)(2) of this section, as if those fewer members were a single corporation. See *Example* (3) of paragraph (j) of this section. Such expenses must be apportioned between statutory and residual groupings of income within the appropriate class of gross income by reference to the apportionment factors contributed by the members of the affiliated group that are treated as a single corporation.

(4) *Stewardship expenses.*—Stewardship expenses are to be allocated and apportioned in accordance with the rules of § 1.861-8T(e)(4). In general, stewardship expenses are considered definitely related and allocable to dividends received or to be received from a related corporation. If members of the affiliated group, other than the member that incurred the stewardship expense, receive or may receive dividends from the related corporation, such expense must be allocated and apportioned in accordance with the rules of paragraph (c) of this section as if all such members of the affiliated group that receive or may receive dividends were a single corporation. See *Example* (4) of paragraph (j) of this section. Such expenses must be apportioned between statutory and residual groupings of income within the appropriate class of gross income by reference to the apportionment factors contributed by the members of the affiliated group treated as a single corporation.

(5) *Legal and accounting fees and expenses.*—Legal and accounting fees and expenses are to be allocated and apportioned under the rules of § 1.861-8T(e)(5). To the extent that such expenses are not directly allocable under paragraph (e)(1)(ii) of this section to specific income producing activities or property of the member of the affiliated group that incurred the expense, such expenses must be allocated and apportioned as if all members of the affiliated group were a single corporation. Specifically, such expenses must be allocated to a class of gross income that takes into account the gross income which is generated, has been generated, or could reasonably have been expected to have been generated by the other members of the affiliated group. If the expenses relate to the gross income of fewer than all members of the affiliated group as determined under paragraph (c)(2) of this section, then those expenses must be apportioned under the rules of paragraph (c)(2) of this section, as if those fewer members were a single corporation. See *Example* (5) of paragraph (j) of this section. Such expenses must be apportioned taking into account the apportionment factors contributed by the members of the group that are treated as a single corporation.

(6) *Charitable contribution expenses.*—
(i) *In general.*—A deduction for a charitable contribution by a member of an affiliated group shall be allocated and apportioned under the rules of § 1.861-8T(e)(12) and paragraph (c)(1) of this section.

(ii) *Effective date.*—(A) The rules of this paragraph shall apply to charitable contributions made on or after July 28, 2004 and, for taxpayers applying the second sentence of § 1.861-8T(e)(12)(iv)(A), to charitable contributions made during the taxable year ending on or after July 28, 2004.

(B) The applicability of this section expires on or before July 27, 2007.

(f) *Computation of FSC or DISC combined taxable income.*—In the computation under the pricing rules of sections 925 and 994 of the combined taxable income of any FSC or DISC and its related supplier which are members of an affiliated group, the combined taxable income of such FSC or DISC and its related supplier shall be reduced by the portion of the expenses of the affiliated group described in paragraph (e) of this section that is incurred in connection with export sales involving that FSC or DISC. In order to determine the portion of the expenses of the affiliated group that is incurred in connection with export sales by or through a FSC or DISC, the portion of the total of the apportionment factor chosen that relates to the generation of that export income must be determined. Thus, if gross income is the apportionment factor chosen, the portion of total gross income of the affiliated group that consists of combined gross income derived from transactions involving the FSC or DISC and related supplier must be determined. Similarly, if units sold or sales receipts is the apportionment factor chosen, the portion of total units sold or sales receipts that generated export income of the FSC or DISC and related supplier must be determined. The amount of the expense shall then be multiplied by a fraction, the numerator of which is the export related apportionment factor as determined above, and the denominator of which is the total apportionment factor. Thus, if gross income is the apportionment factor chosen, apportionment is based on a fraction, the numerator of which is export related combined gross income of the FSC or DISC and related supplier and the denominator of which is the total gross income of the affiliated group. Similarly, if units sold or sales receipts is the apportionment factor chosen, the fraction is the units sold or sales receipts that generated export income of the FSC or DISC and related supplier over the total units sold or sales receipts of the affiliated group. Under this rule, expenses of other group members may be attributed to the combined gross income of a FSC or DISC and its related supplier without affecting the amount of expenses (other than any commission payable by the related supplier to the FSC or DISC) otherwise deductible by the FSC or DISC, the related supplier, or other members of the affiliated group. The FSC or DISC must calculate combined taxable income, taking into account any reduction by expenses attributed from other members of the affiliated group to determine the commission derived by the FSC or DISC or the transfer price of qualifying export property sold to the FSC or DISC.

(g) *Losses created through apportionment.*—In the case of an affiliated group that does not file a consolidated return, the taxable income in any separate limitation category must be adjusted under this paragraph (g) for purposes of computing the separate foreign tax credit limitations under section 904(d). As a consequence of the affiliated group allocation and apportionment of expenses required by section 864(e)(6) and this section, expenses of a group member may be apportioned for section 904 purposes to a limitation category with a consequent loss in that limitation category. For purposes of this paragraph, the term "limitation category" includes domestic source income, as well as the types of income described in section 904(d)(1)(A) through (I). A loss of one affiliate in a limitation category will reduce the income of another member in the same limitation category if a consolidated return is filed. (*See* § 1.1502-4.) If a consolidated return is not filed, this netting does not occur. Accordingly, in such a case, the following adjustments among members are required, in order to give effect to the group allocation of expense:

(1) Losses created through group apportionment of expense in one or more limitation categories within a given member must be eliminated; and

(2) A corresponding amount of income of other members in the same limitation category must be recharacterized.

Such adjustments shall be accomplished in accordance with the rules of § 1.861-11T(g).

(h) *Special rule for the allocation of reserve expenses of a life insurance company.*—An amount of reserve expenses of a life insurance company equal to the dividends received deduction that is disallowed because it is attributable to the policyholders' share of dividends received shall be treated as definitely related to such dividends. The remaining reserve expenses of such company shall be allocated and apportioned under the rules of § 1.861-8 and this section.

(i) [Reserved.]

(j) *Examples.*—The rules of this section may be illustrated by the following examples. All of these examples assume that section 482 has not been applied by the Commissioner.

Example (1)—(i) *Facts.* P owns all of the stock of X and all of the stock of Y. P, X and Y are domestic corporations. P is a holding company for the stock of X and Y. Both X and Y manufacture and sell a product which is included in a broad product category listed in § 1.861-8(e)(3)(i). During 1988, X incurred $100,000 on research connected with that product. All of the research was performed in the United States. In 1988, the domestic sales by X of the product totalled $400,000 and the foreign sales of the product totalled $200,000; Y's domestic sales of the product totalled $200,000 and Y's foreign sales of the product totalled $200,000. In 1988, X's gross income is $300,000, of which $200,000 is from domestic sales and $100,000 is from foreign sales; Y's gross income is $200,000 of which $100,000 is from domestic sales and $100,000 is from foreign sales.

(ii) P, X and Y are affiliated corporations within the meaning of section 864(e)(5) and this section. The research expenses incurred by X are allocable to all income connected with the relevant broad category listed in § 1.861-8T(e)(3)(i). Both X and Y have gross income includible within the class of gross income related to that product category. Accordingly, the research and experimental expenses incurred by X are to be allocated and apportioned as if X and Y were a single corporation. The apportionment for 1988 is as follows:

Tentative Apportionment on the Basis of Sales

Research expenses to be apportioned	$100,000
Exclusive apportionment to United States source gross income	$ 30,000
Research expense to be apportioned on the basis of sales	$ 70,000

Apportionment of research expense to foreign source general limitation income:

$$70{,}000 \times \frac{200{,}000 + 200{,}000}{600{,}000 + 400{,}000} \;\ldots\ldots\; 28{,}000$$

Apportionment of research expense to United States source gross income:

$$70{,}000 \times \frac{400{,}000 + 200{,}000}{600{,}000 + 400{,}000} \;\ldots\ldots\; 42{,}000$$

Total apportioned deduction for research	$100,000
Of which—	
Apportioned to foreign source gross income	$28,000
Apportioned to U.S. source gross income ($30,000 + $42,000)	$72,000

Tentative Apportionment on the Basis of Gross Income

Research expense apportioned to foreign source gross income:

$$100{,}000 \times \frac{100{,}000 + 100{,}000}{300{,}000 + 200{,}000} \;\ldots\ldots\; 40{,}000$$

Research expense apportioned to United States income:

$$100{,}000 \times \frac{200{,}000 + 100{,}000}{300{,}000 + 200{,}000} \;\ldots\ldots\; 60{,}000$$

Reg. § 1.861-14T(g)(1)

Example (2)—(i) *Facts.* P owns all of the stock of X, which owns all of the stock of Y. P, X and Y are all domestic corporations. P has incurred general training program expenses of $100,000 in 1987. Employees of P, X and Y participate in the training program. In 1987, P had United States source gross income of $200,000 and foreign source general limitation income of $200,000; X had U.S. source gross income of $100,000 and foreign source general limitation income of $100,000; and Y had U.S. source gross income of $300,000 and foreign source general limitation income of $100,000.

(ii) *Analysis.* P, X and Y are an affiliated group of corporations within the meaning of section 864(e)(5). The training expenses incurred by P are not definitely related solely to specific income producing activities or property of P. The employees of X and Y also participate in the training program. Thus, this expense relates to gross income generated by P, X and Y. This expense is definitely related and allocable to all of the gross income from foreign and domestic sources of P, X and Y. It is assumed that apportionment on the basis of gross income is reasonable. The apportionment of the expense is as follows:

Apportionment of $100,000 expense to foreign source general limitation income:

$$\$100{,}000 \times \frac{\$200{,}000 + \$100{,}000 + \$100{,}000}{\$400{,}000 + \$200{,}000 + \$400{,}000} \quad \ldots\ldots \quad \$40{,}000$$

Apportionment of $100,000 expense to United States source gross income:

$$\$100{,}000 \times \frac{\$200{,}000 + \$100{,}000 + \$300{,}000}{\$400{,}000 + \$200{,}000 + \$400{,}000} \quad \ldots\ldots \quad \$60{,}000$$

Total apportioned expense $100,000

Example (3)—(i) *Facts.* The facts are the same as in *Example* (2) above, except that only employees of P and X participate in the training program.

(ii) *Analysis.* Because only the employees of P and X participate in the training program and they perform no services for Y, the expense relates only to gross income generated by P and X. Accordingly, the $100,000 expense must be allocated and apportioned as if P and X were a single corporation. The apportionment of the $100,000 expense is as follows:

Apportionment of $100,000 expense to foreign source general limitation income:

$$\$100{,}000 \times \frac{\$200{,}000 + \$100{,}000}{\$400{,}000 + \$200{,}000} \quad \ldots\ldots \quad \$50{,}000$$

Apportionment of $100,000 expense to United States source gross income:

$$\$100{,}000 \times \frac{\$200{,}000 + \$100{,}000}{\$400{,}000 + \$200{,}000} \quad \ldots\ldots \quad \$50{,}000$$

Example (4)—(i) *Facts.* P owns all of the stock of X which owns all of the stock of Y. P and X are domestic corporations; Y is a foreign corporation. In 1987 P incurred $10,000 of stewardship expenses relating to an audit of Y.

(ii) *Analysis.* The stewardship expenses incurred by P are not directly allocable to specific income producing activities or property of P. The expense is definitely related and allocable to dividends received or to be received by X. Accordingly, the expense of P is allocated and apportioned as if P and X were a single corporation. The expense is definitely related to dividends received or to be received by X from Y, a foreign corporation. Such dividends are foreign source general limitation income. Thus, the entire amount of the expense must be allocated to foreign source dividend income.

Example (5)—(i) *Facts.* P owns all of the stock of X which owns all of the stock of Y. P, X and Y are all domestic corporations. In 1987, P incurred $10,000 legal expense relating to the testimony of certain employees of P in connection with litigation to which Y is a party. This expense is not allocable to specific income of Y. In 1987, Y had $100,000 foreign source general limitation income and $300,000 U.S. source gross income.

(ii) *Analysis.* The legal expenses incurred by P are not definitely related solely to specific income producing activities or property of P. The expense is definitely related and allocable to the class of gross income which includes only gross income generated by Y. Accordingly, the expense of P is allocated and appor-

Reg. §1.861-14T(j)

tioned as if Y were the only member of the affiliated group, as follows:

$$10{,}000 \times \frac{\$100{,}000}{\$400{,}000}$$

Apportionment of legal expenses to U.S. source gross income:

$$10{,}000 \times \frac{\$300{,}000}{\$400{,}000}$$

Apportionment of legal expenses to foreign source general limitation income:
...... $2,500

...... $7,500

Example (6)—(i) *Facts.* P owns all of the stock of R, which owns all of the stock of F. P and R are domestic corporations, and F is a foreign sales corporation under section 922 of the Code. R and F have entered into an agreement whereby F is paid a commission with respect to sales of product A. In 1987, P had gross receipts of $1,000,000 from domestic sales of product A, and gross receipts of $1,000,000 from foreign sales of product A. R had gross receipts of $1,000,000 from domestic sales of product A, and $1,000,000 from export sales of product A. R's cost of goods sold attributable to export sales is $500,000. R has deductible expenses of $100,000 directly related to its export sales, and F has such deductible expenses of $100,000. During 1987, P incurred an expense of $100,000 for marketing studies involving the worldwide market for product A.

(ii) *Analysis.* P and R are an affiliated group of corporations within the meaning of section 864(e)(5) and this section. The expense incurred by P for marketing studies regarding the worldwide market for product A is an expense that is not directly related solely to the activities of P, but also to the activities of R. This expense must be allocated and apportioned under the rules of paragraph (c)(1) of this section, as if P and R were a single corporation. The expense is allocable to the class of gross income that includes all gross income generated by sales of product A. Apportionment on the basis of gross receipts is reasonable under these facts. F, a foreign corporation, is not a member of the affiliated group. However, for purposes of determining F's commission on its sales, the combined gross income of F and R must be reduced by the portion of the marketing studies expense of P that is incurred in connection with export sales involving F under the rules of paragraph (f) of this section. The computation of the combined taxable income of R and F is as follows:

Combined Taxable Income of R and F

R's gross receipts from export sales	$1,000,000
R's cost of goods sold	$500,000
Combined Gross Income	$500,000
Less:	
R's other deductible expenses	$100,000
F's other deductible expenses	$100,000
Apportionment of P's expense:	
$100{,}000 \times \dfrac{\$1{,}000{,}000}{\$2{,}000{,}000 + \$2{,}000{,}000}$	$25,000
Total	$225,000
Combined Taxable Income	$275,000

[Temporary Reg. § 1.861-14T.]

☐ [*T.D. 8228, 9-9-88. Amended by T.D. 8916, 12-29-2000 and T.D. 9143, 7-27-2004.*]

§ 1.861-17. Allocation and apportionment of research and experimental expenditures.—(a) *Allocation.*—(1) *In general.*—The methods of allocation and apportionment of research and experimental expenditures set forth in this section recognize that research and experimentation is an inherently speculative activity, that findings may contribute unexpected benefits, and that the gross income derived from successful research and experimentation must bear the cost of unsuccessful research and experimentation. Expenditures for research and experimentation that a taxpayer deducts under section 174 ordinarily shall be considered deductions that are definitely related to all income reasonably connected with the relevant broad product category (or categories) of the taxpayer and therefore allocable to all items of gross income as a class (including income from sales, royalties, and dividends) related to such product category (or categories). For purposes of this allocation, the product category (or categories) that a taxpayer may be considered to have shall be determined in accordance with the provisions of paragraph (a)(2) of this section.

(2) *Product categories.*—(i) *Allocation based on product categories.*—Ordinarily, a taxpayer's research and experimental expenditures may be divided between the relevant product categories. Where research and experimentation is conducted with respect to more than one product category, the taxpayer may aggregate the categories for purposes of allocation and apportionment; however, the taxpayer may not subdivide the categories. Where research and experimentation is not clearly identified with any product category (or categories), it will be considered conducted with respect to all the taxpayer's product categories.

(ii) *Use of three digit standard industrial classification codes.*—A taxpayer shall determine the relevant product categories by reference to the three digit classification of the Standard Industrial Classification Manual (SIC code). A copy may be purchased from the Superintendent of Documents, United States Government Printing Office, Washington, DC 20402. The individual products included within each category are enumerated in Executive Office of the President, Office of Management and Budget, Standard Industrial Classification Manual, 1987 (or later edition, as available).

(iii) *Consistency.*—Once a taxpayer selects a product category for the first taxable year for which this section is effective with respect to the taxpayer, it must continue to use that product category in following years, unless the taxpayer establishes to the satisfaction of the Commissioner that, due to changes in the relevant facts, a change in the product category is appropriate. For this purpose, a change in the taxpayer's selection of a product category shall include a change from a three digit SIC code category to a two digit SIC code category, a change from a two digit SIC code category to a three digit SIC code category, or any other aggregation, disaggregation or change of a previously selected SIC code category.

(iv) *Wholesale trade category.*—The two digit SIC code category "Wholesale trade" is not applicable with respect to sales by the taxpayer of goods and services from any other of the taxpayer's product categories and is not applicable with respect to a domestic international sales corporation (DISC) or foreign sales corporation (FSC) for which the taxpayer is a related supplier of goods and services from any of the taxpayer's product categories.

(v) *Retail trade category.*—The two digit SIC code category "Retail trade" is not applicable with respect to sales by the taxpayer of goods and services from any other of the taxpayer's product categories, except wholesale trade, and is not applicable with respect to a DISC or FSC for which the taxpayer is a related supplier of goods and services from any other of the taxpayer's product categories, except wholesale trade.

(3) *Affiliated groups.*—(i) In general.—Except as provided in paragraph (a)(3)(ii) of this section, the allocation and apportionment required by this section shall be determined as if all members of the affiliated group (as defined in § 1.861-14T(d)) were a single corporation. See § 1.861-14T.

(ii) *Possessions corporations.*—(A) For purposes of the allocation and apportionment required by this section, sales and gross income from products produced in whole or in part in a possession by an electing corporation (within the meaning of section 936(h)(5)(E)), and dividends from an electing corporation, shall not be taken into account, except that this paragraph (a)(3)(ii) shall not apply to sales of (and gross income and dividends attributable to sales of) products with respect to which an election under section 936(h)(5)(F) is not in effect.

(B) The research and experimental expenditures taken into account for purposes of this section shall be reduced by the amount of such expenditures included in computing the cost-sharing amount (determined under section 936(h)(5)(C)(i)).

(4) *Legally mandated research and experimentation.*—Where research and experimentation is undertaken solely to meet legal requirements imposed by a political entity with respect to improvement or marketing of specific products or processes, and the results cannot reasonably be expected to generate amounts of gross income (beyond de minimis amounts) outside a single geographic source, the deduction for such research and experimentation shall be considered definitely related and therefore allocable only to the grouping (or groupings) of gross income within that geographic source as a class (and apportioned, if necessary, between such groupings as set forth in paragraphs (c) and (d) of this section). For example, where a taxpayer performs tests on a product in response to a requirement imposed by the U.S. Food and Drug Administration, and the test results cannot reasonably be expected to generate amounts of gross income (beyond de minimis amounts) outside the United States, the costs of testing shall be allocated solely to gross income from sources within the United States.

(b) *Exclusive apportionment.*—(1) *In general.*—An exclusive apportionment shall be made under this paragraph (b), where an apportionment based upon geographic sources of income of a deduction for research and experimentation is necessary (after applying the exception in paragraph (a)(4) of this section).

(i) *Exclusive apportionment under the sales method.*—If the taxpayer apportions on the sales method under paragraph (c) of this section, an amount equal to fifty percent of such deduction for research and experimentation shall be apportioned exclusively to the statutory grouping of gross income or the residual grouping of gross income, as the case may be, arising from the geographic source where the research and experimental activities which account for more than fifty percent of the amount of such deduction were performed.

(ii) *Exclusive apportionment under the optional gross income methods.*—If the taxpayer apportions on the optional gross income methods under paragraph (d) of this section, an amount equal to twenty-five percent of such deduction for research and experimentation shall be apportioned exclusively to the statutory grouping or the residual grouping of gross income, as the case may be, arising from the geographic source where the research and experimental activities which account for more than fifty percent of the amount of such deduction were performed.

(iii) *Exception.*—If the applicable fifty percent geographic source test of the preceding paragraph (b)(1)(i) or (ii) is not met, then no part of the deduction shall be apportioned under this paragraph (b)(1).

(2) *Facts and circumstances supporting an increased exclusive apportionment.*—(i) *In general.*—The exclusive apportionment provided for in paragraph (b)(1) of this section reflects the view that research and experimentation is often most valuable in the country where it is performed, for two reasons. First, research and experimentation often benefits a broad product category, consisting of many individual products, all of which may be sold in the nearest market but only some of which may be sold in foreign markets. Second, research and experimentation often is utilized in the nearest market before it is used in other markets, and in such cases, has a lower value per unit of sales when used in foreign markets. The taxpayer may establish to the satisfaction of the Commissioner that, in its case, one or both of the conditions mentioned in the preceding sentences warrant a significantly greater exclusive allocation percentage than allowed by paragraph (b)(1) of this section because the research and experimentation is reasonably expected to have very limited or long delayed application outside the geographic source where it was performed. Past experience with research and experimentation may be considered in determining reasonable expectations.

(ii) *Not all products sold in foreign markets.*—For purposes of establishing that only some products within the product category (or categories) are sold in foreign markets, the taxpayer shall compare the commercial production of individual products in domestic and foreign markets made by itself, by uncontrolled parties (as defined under paragraph (c)(2)(i) of this section) of products involving intangible property which was licensed or sold by the taxpayer, and by those controlled corporations (as defined under paragraph (c)(3)(ii) of this section) that can reasonably be expected to benefit directly or indirectly from any of the taxpayer's research expense connected with the product category (or categories). The individual products compared for this purpose shall be limited, for nonmanufactured categories, solely to those enumerated in Executive Office of the President, Office of Management and Budget Standard Industrial Classification Manual, 1987 (or later edition, as available), and, for manufactured categories, solely to those enumerated at a 7-digit level in the U.S. Bureau of the Census, Census of Manufacturers: 1992, Numerical List of Manufactured Products, 1993, (or later edition, as available). Copies of both of these documents may be purchased from the Superintendent of Documents, United States Government Printing Office, Washington, DC 20402.

(iii) *Delayed application of research findings abroad.*—For purposes of establishing the delayed application of research findings abroad, the taxpayer shall compare the commercial introduction of its own particular products and processes (not limited by those listed in the Standard Industrial Classification Manual or the Numerical List of Manufactured Products) in the United States and foreign markets, made by itself, by uncontrolled parties (as defined under paragraph (c)(2)(i) of this section) of products involving intangible property that was licensed or sold by the taxpayer, and by those controlled corporations (as defined under paragraph (c)(3)(i) of this section) that can reasonably be expected to benefit, directly or indirectly, from the taxpayer's research expense. For purposes of evaluating the delay in the application of research findings in foreign markets, the taxpayer shall use a safe haven discount rate of 10 percent per year of delay unless he is able to establish to the satisfaction of the Commissioner, by reference to the cost of money and the number of years during which economic benefit can be directly attributable to the results of the taxpayer's research, that another discount rate is more appropriate.

(c) *Sales method.*—(1) *In general.*—The amount equal to the remaining portion of such deduction for research and experimentation, not apportioned under paragraph (a)(4) or (b)(1)(i) of this section, shall be apportioned between the statutory grouping (or among the statutory groupings) within the class of gross income and the residual grouping within such class in the same proportions that the amount of sales from the product category (or categories) that resulted in such gross income within the statutory grouping (or statutory groupings) and in the residual grouping bear, respectively, to the total amount of sales from the product category (or categories).

(i) *Apportionment in excess of gross income.*—Amounts apportioned under this section may exceed the amount of gross income related to the product category within the statutory grouping. In such case, the excess shall be applied against other gross income within the statutory grouping. See § 1.861-8(d)(1) for instances where the apportionment leads to an excess of deductions over gross income within the statutory grouping.

(ii) *Leased property.*—For purposes of this paragraph (c), amounts received from the lease of equipment during a taxable year shall be regarded as sales receipts for such taxable year.

(2) *Sales of uncontrolled parties.*—For purposes of the apportionment under paragraph (c)(1) of this section, the sales from the product category (or categories) by each party uncontrolled by the taxpayer, of particular products involving intangible property that was licensed or sold by the taxpayer to such uncontrolled party shall be taken fully into account both for determining the taxpayer's apportionment and for determining the apportionment of any other member of a controlled group of corporations to which the taxpayer belongs if the uncontrolled party can reasonably be expected to benefit directly or indirectly (through any member of the controlled group of corporations to which the taxpayer belongs) from the research expense connected with the product category (or categories) of such other member. An uncontrolled party can reasonably be expected to benefit from the research expense of a member of a controlled group of corporations to which the taxpayer belongs if such member can reasonably be expected to license, sell, or transfer intangible property to that uncontrolled party or transfer secret processes to that uncontrolled party, directly or indirectly through a member of the controlled group of corporations to which the taxpayer belongs. Past experience with research and experimentation shall be considered in determining reasonable expectations.

(i) *Definition of uncontrolled party.*—For purposes of this paragraph (c)(2) the term *uncontrolled party* means a party that is not a person with a relationship to the taxpayer specified in section 267(b), or is not a member of a controlled group of corporations to which the taxpayer belongs (within the meaning of section 993(a)(3) or 927(d)(4)).

(ii) *Licensed products.*—In the case of licensed products, if the amount of sales of such products is unknown (for example, where the licensed product is a component of a large machine), a reasonable estimate based on the principles of section 482 should be made.

(iii) *Sales of intangible property.*—In the case of sales of intangible property, regardless of whether the consideration received in exchange for the intangible is a fixed amount or is contingent on the productivity, use, or disposition of the intangible, if the amount of sales of products utilizing the intangible property is unknown, a reasonable estimate of sales shall be made annually. If necessary, appropriate economic analyses shall be used to estimate sales.

(3) *Sales of controlled parties.*—For purposes of the apportionment under paragraph (c)(1) of this section, the sales from the product category (or categories) of the taxpayer shall be taken fully into account and the sales from the product category (or categories) of a corporation controlled by the taxpayer shall be taken into account to the extent provided in this paragraph (c)(3) for determining the taxpayer's apportionment, if such corporation can reasonably be expected to benefit directly or indirectly (through another member of the controlled group of corporations to which the taxpayer belongs) from the taxpayer's research expense connected with the product category (or categories). A corporation controlled by the taxpayer can reasonably be expected to benefit from the taxpayer's research expense if the taxpayer can be expected to license, sell, or transfer intangible property to that corporation or transfer secret processes to that corporation, either directly or indirectly through a member of the controlled group of corporations to which the taxpayer belongs. Past experience with research and experimentation shall be considered in determining reasonable expectations.

(i) *Definition of a corporation controlled by the taxpayer.*—For purposes of this paragraph (c)(3), the term *a corporation controlled by the taxpayer* means any corporation that has a relationship to the taxpayer specified in section 267(b) or is a member of a controlled group of corporations to which the taxpayer belongs (within the meaning of section 993(a)(3) or 927(d)(4)).

(ii) *Sales to be taken into account.*—The sales from the product category (or categories) of a corporation controlled by the taxpayer taken into account shall be equal to the amount of sales that bear the same proportion to the total sales of the controlled corporation as the total value of all classes of the stock of such corporation owned directly or indirectly by the taxpayer, within the meaning of section 1563, bears to the total value of all classes of stock of such corporation.

(iii) *Sales not to be taken into account more than once.*—Sales from the product category (or categories) between or among such controlled corporations or the taxpayer shall not be taken into account more than once; in such a situation, the amount sold by the selling corporation to the buying corporation shall be subtracted from the sales of the buying corporation.

(iv) *Effect of cost-sharing arrangements.*—If the corporation controlled by the taxpayer has entered into a bona fide cost-sharing arrangement, in accordance with the provisions of § 1.482-7, with the taxpayer for the purpose of developing intangible property, then that corporation shall not reasonably be expected to benefit from the taxpayer's share of the research expense.

(d) *Gross income methods.*—(1)(i) *In general.*—In lieu of applying the sales method of paragraph (c) of this section, the remaining amount of the deduction for research and experimentation, not apportioned under paragraph (a)(4) or (b)(1)(ii) of this section, shall be apportioned as prescribed in paragraphs (d)(2) and (3) of this section, between the statutory grouping (or among the statutory groupings) of gross income and the residual grouping of gross income.

(ii) *Optional methods to be applied to all research and experimental expenditures.*—These optional methods must be applied to the taxpayer's entire deduction for research and experimental expense remaining after applying the exception in paragraph (a)(4) of this section, and may not be applied on a product category basis. Thus, after the allocation of the taxpayer's entire deduction for research and experimental expense under paragraph (a)(2) of this section (by attribution to SIC code categories), the taxpayer must then apportion as necessary the entire deduction as allocated by separate amounts to various product categories, using only the sales method under paragraph (c) of this section or only the optional gross income methods under this paragraph (d). The taxpayer may not use the sales method for a portion of the deduction and optional gross income methods for the remainder of the deduction separately allocated.

(2) *Option one.*—The taxpayer may apportion its research and experimental expenditures ratably on the basis of gross income between the statutory grouping (or among the statutory groupings) of gross income and the residual grouping of gross income in the same proportions that the amount of gross income in the statutory grouping (or groupings) and the amount of gross income in the residual grouping bear, respectively, to the total amount of gross income, if the conditions described in paragraph (d)(2)(i) and (ii) of this section are both met.

(i) The amount of research and experimental expense ratably apportioned to the statutory grouping (or groupings in the aggregate) is not less than fifty percent of the amount that would have been so apportioned if the taxpayer had used the method described in paragraph (c) of this section; and

(ii) The amount of research and experimental expense ratably apportioned to the residual grouping is not less than fifty percent of the amount that would have been so apportioned if the taxpayer had used the method described in paragraph (c) of this section.

(3) *Option two.*—If, when the amount of research and experimental expense is apportioned ratably on the basis of gross income, either of the conditions described in paragraph (d)(2)(i) or (ii) of this section is not met, the taxpayer may either—

(i) Where the condition of paragraph (d)(2)(i) of this section is not met, apportion fifty percent of the amount of research and experimental expense that would have been apportioned to the statutory grouping (or groupings in the aggregate) under paragraph (c) of this section to such statutory grouping (or to such statutory groupings in the aggregate and then among such groupings on the basis of gross income within each grouping), and apportion the balance of the amount of research and experimental expenses to the residual grouping; or

(ii) Where the condition of paragraph (d)(2)(ii) of this section is not met, apportion fifty percent of the amount of research and experimental expense that would have been apportioned to the residual grouping under paragraph (c) of this section to such residual grouping, and apportion the balance of the amount of research and experimental expenses to the statutory grouping (or to the statutory groupings in the aggregate and then among such groupings ratably on the basis of gross income within each grouping).

(e) *Binding election.*—(1) *In general.*—A taxpayer may choose to use either the sales method under paragraph (c) of this section or the optional gross income methods under paragraph (d) of this section for its original return for its first taxable year to which this section applies. The taxpayer's use of either the sales method or the optional gross income methods for its return filed for its first taxable year to which this section applies shall constitute a binding election to use the method chosen for that year and for four taxable years thereafter.

(2) *Change of method.*—The taxpayer's election of a method may not be revoked during the period referred to in paragraph (e)(1) of this section without the prior consent of the Commissioner. After the expiration of that period, the taxpayer may change methods without the prior consent of the Commissioner. However, the taxpayer's use of the new method shall constitute a binding election to use the new method for its return filed for the first year for which the taxpayer uses the new method and for four taxable years thereafter. The taxpayer's election of the new method may not be revoked during that period without the prior consent of the Commissioner.

(i) *Short taxable years.*—For purposes of this paragraph (e), the term taxable year includes a taxable year of less than twelve months.

(ii) *Affiliated groups.*—In the case of an affiliated group, the period referred to in paragraph (e)(1) of this section shall commence as of the latest taxable year in which any member of the group has changed methods.

(f) *Special rules for partnerships.*—(1) *Research and experimental expenditures.*—For purposes of applying this section, if research and experimental expenditures are incurred by a partnership in which the taxpayer is a partner, the taxpayer's research and experimental expenditures shall include the taxpayer's distributive share of the partnership's research and experimental expenditures.

(2) *Purpose and location of expenditures.*— In applying the exception for expenditures undertaken to meet legal requirements under paragraph (a)(4) of this section and the exclusive apportionment for the sales method and the optional gross income methods under paragraph (b) of this section, a partner's distributive share of research and experimental expenditures incurred by a partnership shall be treated as incurred by the partner for the same purpose and in the same location as incurred by the partnership.

(3) *Apportionment under the sales method.*—In applying the remaining apportionment for the sales method under paragraph (c) of this section, a taxpayer's sales from a product category shall include the taxpayer's share of any sales from the product category of any partnership in which the taxpayer is a partner. For purposes of the preceding sentence, a taxpayer's share of sales shall be proportionate to the taxpayer's distributive share of the partnership's gross income in the product category.

(g) *Effective date.*—This section applies to taxable years beginning after December 31, 1995. However, a taxpayer may at its option, apply this section in its entirety to all taxable years beginning after August 1, 1994.

(h) *Examples.*—The following examples illustrate the application of this section:

Example 1—(i) *Facts.* X, a domestic corporation, is a manufacturer and distributor of small gasoline engines for lawn mowers. Gasoline engines are a product within the category, Engines and Turbines (SIC Industry Group 351). Y, a wholly owned foreign subsidiary of X, also manufactures and sells these engines abroad. During 1996, X incurred expenditures of $60,000 on research and experimentation, which it deducts as a current expense, to invent and patent a new and improved gasoline engine. All of the research and experimentation was performed in the United States. In 1996, the domestic sales by X of the new engine total $500,000 and foreign sales by Y total $300,000. X provides technology for the manufacture of engines to Y via a license that requires the payment of an arm's length royalty. In 1996, X's gross income is $160,000, of which $140,000 is U.S. source income from domestic sales of gasoline engines and $10,000 is foreign source royalties from Y, and $10,000 is U.S. source interest income.

(ii) *Allocation.* The research and experimental expenditures were incurred in connection with small gasoline engines and they are definitely related to the items of gross income to which the research gives rise, namely gross income from the sale of small gasoline engines in the United States and royalties received from subsidiary Y, a foreign manufacturer of gasoline engines. Accordingly, the expenses are allocable to this class of gross income. The U.S. source interest income is not within this class of gross income and, therefore, is not taken into account.

(iii) *Apportionment.* (A) For purposes of applying the foreign tax credit limitation, the statutory grouping is general limitation gross income from sources without the United States and the residual grouping is gross income from sources within the United States. Since the related class of gross income derived from the use of engine technology consists of both gross income from sources without the United States (royalties from Y) and gross income from sources within the United States (gross income from engine sales), X's deduction of $60,000 for its research and experimental expenditure must be apportioned between the statutory and residual grouping before the foreign tax credit limitation may be determined. Because more than 50 percent of X's research and experimental activity was performed in the United States, 50 percent of that deduction can be apportioned exclusively to the residual grouping of gross income, gross income from sources within the United States. The remaining 50 percent of the deduction can then be apportioned between the residual and statutory groupings on the basis of sales of small gasoline engines by X and Y. Alternatively, X's deduction for research and experimentation can be apportioned under the optional gross income method. The apportionment for 1996 is as follows:

(1) *Tentative Apportionment on the Basis of Sales.*

(i) Research and experimental expense to be apportioned between residual and statutory groupings of gross income: $60,000

(ii) Less: Exclusive apportionment of research and experimental expense to the residual grouping of gross income ($60,000 × 50 percent): $30,000

(iii) Research and experimental expense to be apportioned between residual and statutory groupings of gross income on the basis of sales: $30,000

(iv) Apportionment of research and experimental expense to the residual grouping of gross income ($30,000 × $500,000/($500,000 + $300,000)): $18,750

(v) Apportionment of research and experimental expense to the statutory grouping of gross income ($30,000 × $300,000/($500,000 + $300,000)): $11,250

(vi) Total apportioned deduction for research and experimentation: $60,000

(vii) Amount apportioned to the residual grouping ($30,000 + $18,750): $48,750

(viii) Amount apportioned to the statutory grouping: $11,250

(2) *Tentative Apportionment on the Basis of Gross Income.*

(i) Exclusive apportionment of research and experimental expense to the residual grouping of gross income ($60,000 × 25 percent): $15,000

(ii) Research and experimental expense apportioned to sources within the United States (residual grouping) ($45,000 × $140,000/($140,000 + $10,000)): $42,000

(iii) Research and experimental expense apportioned to sources within country Y (statutory grouping) ($45,000 × $10,000/($140,000 + $10,000)): $3,000

(iv) Amount apportioned to the residual grouping: $57,000

(v) Amount apportioned to the statutory grouping: $3,000

(B) The total research and experimental expense apportioned to the statutory grouping ($3,000) under the gross income method is approximately 26 percent of the amount apportioned to the statutory grouping under the sales method. Thus, X may use option two of the gross income method (paragraph (d)(3) of this section) and apportion to the statutory grouping fifty percent (50%) of the $11,250 apportioned to that grouping under the sales method. Thus, X apportions $5,625 of research and experimental expense to the statutory grouping. X's use of the optional gross income methods will constitute a binding election to use the optional gross income methods for 1996 and four taxable years thereafter.

Example 2—(i) *Facts.* Assume the same facts as in *Example 1* except that X also spends $30,000 in 1996 for research on steam turbines, all of which is performed in the United States, and X has steam turbine sales in the United States of $400,000. X's foreign subsidiary Y neither manufactures nor sells steam turbines. The steam turbine research is in addition to the $60,000 in research which X does on gasoline engines for lawnmowers. X thus has a deduction of $90,000 for its research activity. X's gross income is $200,000, of which $140,000 is U.S. source income from domestic sales of gasoline engines, $50,000 is U.S. source income from domestic sales of steam turbines, and $10,000 is foreign source royalties from Y.

(ii) *Allocation.* X's research expenses generate income from sales of small gasoline engines and steam turbines. Both of these products are in the same three digit SIC code category, Engines and Turbines (SIC Industry Group 351). Therefore, the deduction is definitely related to this product category and allocable to all items of income attributable to it. These items of X's income are gross income from the sale of small gasoline engines and steam turbines in the United States and royalties from foreign subsidiary Y, a foreign manufacturer and seller of small gasoline engines.

(iii) *Apportionment.* (A) For purposes of applying the foreign tax credit limitation, the statutory grouping is general limitation gross income from sources outside the United States and the residual grouping is gross income from sources within the United States. X's deduction of $90,000 must be apportioned between the statutory and residual groupings. Because more than 50 percent of X's research and experimental activity was performed in the United States, 50 percent of that deduction can be apportioned exclusively to the residual grouping, gross income from sources within the United States. The remaining 50 percent of the deduction can then be apportioned between the residual and statutory groupings on the basis of total sales of small gasoline engines and steam turbines by X and Y. Alternatively, X's deduction for research and experimentation can be apportioned under the optional gross income methods. The apportionment for 1996 is as follows:

(*1*) *Tentative Apportionment on the Basis of Sales.*

(*i*) Research and experimental expense to be apportioned between residual and statutory groupings of gross income: $90,000

(*ii*) Less: Exclusive apportionment of the research and experimental expense to the residual grouping of gross income ($90,000 × 50 percent): $45,000

(*iii*) Research and experimental expense to be apportioned between the residual and statutory groupings of gross income on the basis of sales: $45,000

(*iv*) Apportionment of research and experimental expense to the residual grouping of gross income ($45,000 × ($500,000 + $400,000)/($500,000 + $400,000 + $300,000)): $33,750

(*v*) Apportionment of research and experimental expense to the statutory grouping of gross income ($45,000 × $300,000/($500,000 + $400,000 + $300,000)): $11,250

(*vi*) Total apportioned deduction for research and experimentation: $90,000

(*vii*) Amount apportioned to the residual grouping ($45,000 + $33,750): $78,750

(*viii*) Amount apportioned to the statutory grouping: $11,250

(*2*) *Tentative Apportionment on the Basis of Gross Income.*

(*i*) Exclusive apportionment of research and experimental expense to the residual grouping of gross income ($90,000 × 25 percent): $22,500

(*ii*) Research and experimental expense apportioned to sources within the United States (residual grouping) ($67,500 × $190,000/($140,000 + $50,000 + $10,000)): $64,125

(*iii*) Research and experimental expense apportioned to sources within country Y (statutory grouping) ($67,500 × $10,000/($140,000 + $50,000 + $10,000)): $3,375

(*iv*) Amount apportioned to the residual grouping: $86,625

(*v*) Amount apportioned to the statutory grouping: $3,375

(B) The total research and experimental expense apportioned to the statutory grouping ($3,375) under the gross income method is 30 percent of the amount apportioned to the statutory grouping under the sales method. Thus, X may use option two of the gross income method (paragraph (d)(3) of this section) and apportion to the statutory grouping fifty percent (50%) of the $11,250 apportioned to that grouping under the sales method. Thus, X apportions $5,625 of research and experimental expense to the statutory grouping. X's use of the optional gross income methods will constitute a binding election to use the optional gross income methods for 1996 and four taxable years thereafter.

Example 3—(i) *Facts.* Assume the same facts as in *Example 1* except that in 1997 X continues its sales of the new engines, with sales of $600,000 in the United States and $400,000 abroad by subsidiary Y. X also acquires a 60 percent (by value) ownership interest in foreign corporation Z and a 100 percent ownership interest in foreign corporation C. X transfers its engine technology to Z for a royalty equal to 5 percent of sales, and X enters into an arm's length cost-sharing arrangement with C to share the funding of all of X's research activity. In 1997, corporation Z has sales in country Z equal to $1,000,000. X incurs expense of $80,000 on research and experimentation in 1997, and in addition, X performs $15,000 of research on gasoline engines which was funded by the cost-sharing arrangement with C. All of Z's sales are from the product category, Engines and Turbines (SIC Industry Group 351). X performs all of its research in the United States and $20,000 of its expenditure of $80,000 is made solely to meet pollution standards mandated by law. X establishes, to the satisfaction of the Commissioner, that the expenditure in response to pollution standards is not expected to generate gross income (beyond *de minimis* amounts) outside the United States.

(ii) *Allocation.* The $20,000 of research expense which X incurred in connection with pollution standards is definitely related and thus allocable to the residual grouping, gross income from sources within the United States. The remaining $60,000 in research and experimental expenditure incurred by X is definitely related to all gasoline engines and is therefore allocable to the class of gross income to which the engines give rise, gross income from sales of gasoline engines in the United States, royalties from country Y, and royalties from country Z. No part of the $60,000 research expense is

Reg. §1.861-17(h)

allocable to dividends from country C, because corporation C has already paid, through its cost-sharing arrangement, for research activity performed by X which may benefit C.

(iii) *Apportionment.* For purposes of applying the foreign tax credit limitation, the statutory grouping is general limitation gross income from sources without the United States, and the residual grouping is gross income from sources within the United States. X's deduction of $60,000 for its research and experimental expenditure must be apportioned between these groupings. Because more than 50 percent of the research and experimentation was performed in the United States, 50 percent of the $60,000 deduction can be apportioned exclusively to the residual grouping. The remaining 50 percent of the deduction can then be apportioned between the residual and the statutory grouping on the basis of sales of gasoline engines by X, Y, and Z. (If X utilized the optional gross income methods in 1996, then its use of such methods constituted a binding election to use the optional gross income methods in 1996 and for four taxable years thereafter. If X utilized the sales method in 1996, then its use of such method constituted a binding election to use the sales method in 1996 and for four taxable years thereafter.) The optional gross income methods are not illustrated in this *Example 3* (see instead *Examples 1* and *2*). Since X has only a 60 percent ownership interest in corporation Z, only 60 percent of Z's sales (60% of $1,000,000, or $600,000) are included for purposes of apportionment. The allocation and apportionment for 1997 is as follows:

(A) X's total research expense: $80,000

(B) Less: Legally mandated research directly allocated to the residual grouping of gross income: $20,000

(C) Tentative apportionment on the basis of sales.

(*1*) Research and experimental expense to be apportioned between residual and statutory groupings of gross income: $60,000

(*2*) Less: Exclusive apportionment of research and experimental expense to the residual grouping of gross income ($60,000 × 50 percent): $30,000

(*3*) Research and experimental expense to be apportioned between the residual and the statutory groupings on the basis of sales: $30,000

(*4*) Apportionment of research and experimental expense to gross income from sources within the United States (residual grouping) ($30,000 × $600,000 / ($600,000 + $400,000 + $600,000)): $11,250

(*5*) Apportionment of research and experimental expense to general limitation gross income from countries Y and Z (statutory grouping) ($30,000 × $400,000 + $600,000/($600,000 + $400,000 +$600,000)): $18,750

(*6*) Total apportioned deduction for research and experimentation ($30,000 + $30,000): $60,000

(*7*) Amount apportioned to the residual grouping ($30,000 + $11,250): $41,250

(*8*) Amount apportioned to the statutory grouping of gross income from sources within countries Y and Z: $18,750

Example 4—Research and Experimentation— (i) *Facts.* X, a domestic corporation, manufactures and sells forklift trucks and other types of materials handling equipment in the United States. The manufacture and sale of forklift trucks and other materials handling equipment belongs to the product category, Construction, Mining, and Materials Handling Machinery and Equipment (SIC Industry Group 353). X also sells its forklift trucks to a wholesaling subsidiary located in foreign country Y (but title passes in the United States), and X manufactures forklift trucks in foreign country Z. The wholesaling of forklift trucks to country Y also belongs to X's product category Transportation equipment and, therefore, may not belong to the product category, Wholesale trade (SIC Major Group 50 and 51). In 1997, X sold $7,000,000 of forklift trucks to purchasers in the United States, $3,000,000 of forklift trucks to the wholesaling subsidiary in Y, and transferred forklift truck components with an FOB export value of $2,000,000 to its branch in Z. The branch's sales of finished forklift trucks were $5,000,000. In response to legally mandated emission control requirements, X's United States research department has been engaged in a research project to improve the performance and quality of engine exhaust systems used on its products in the United States. It incurs expenses of $100,000 for this purpose in 1997. In the past, X has customarily adapted the product improvements developed originally for the domestic market to its forklift trucks manufactured abroad. During the taxable year 1997, development of an improved engine exhaust system is completed and X begins installing the new system during the latter part of the taxable year in products manufactured and sold in the United States. X continues to manufacture and sell forklift trucks in foreign countries without the improved engine exhaust systems.

(ii) *Allocation.* X's deduction for its research expense is definitely related to the income to which it gives rise, namely income from the manufacture and sale of forklift trucks within the United States and in country Z. Although the research is undertaken in response to a legal mandate, it can reasonably be expected to generate gross income from the manufacture and sale of trucks by the branch in Z. Therefore, the deduction is not allocable solely to income from X's domestic sales of forklift trucks. It is allocable to income from such sales and income from the sales of X's branch in Z.

(iii) *Apportionment.* For the method of apportionment on the basis of either sales or gross income, see *Example 3.* However, in determining the amount of research apportioned to income from foreign and domestic sources, the net sales of the branch in Z are $3,000,000 ($5,000,000 less $2,000,000) and the sales within the United States are $12,000,000 ($7,000,000 plus $3,000,000 plus $2,000,000). See § 1.861-17(c)(3)(iii).

Example 5—(i) *Facts.* X, a domestic corporation, is a drug company that manufactures a wide variety of pharmaceutical products for sale in the United States. Pharmaceutical products belong to the product category, Drugs (SIC Industry Group 283). X exports its pharmaceutical products through a foreign sales corporation (FSC). X's wholly owned foreign subsidiary Y also manufactures pharmaceutical products. In 1997, X has domestic sales of pharmaceutical products of $10,000,000, the FSC has sales of pharmaceutical products of $3,000,000, and Y has sales of pharmaceutical products of $5,000,000. In that same year, 1997, X incurs expense of $200,000 on research to test a product in response to requirements imposed by the United States Food and Drug Administration (FDA). X is able to show that, even though country Y imposes certain testing requirements on pharmaceutical products, the research performed in the United States is not accepted by country Y for purposes of its own licensing requirements, and the research has minimal use abroad. X is further able to show that FSC sells goods to countries that do not accept or do not require research performed in the United States for purposes of their own licensing standards.

(ii) *Allocation.* Since X's research expense of $200,000 is undertaken to meet the requirements of the United States Food and Drug Administration, and since it is reasonable to expect that the expenditure will not generate gross income (beyond *de minimis* amounts) outside the United States, the deduction is definitely related and thus allocable to the residual grouping.

(iii) *Apportionment.* No apportionment is necessary since the entire expense is allocated to the residual grouping, gross income from sales within the United States.

Example 6—(i) *Facts.* X, a domestic corporation, is engaged in continuous research and experimentation to improve the quality of the products that it manufactures and sells, which are floodlights, flashlights, fuse boxes, and solderless connectors. X incurs and deducts $100,000 of expenditure for research and experimentation in 1997 that was performed exclusively in the United States. As a result of this research activity, X acquires patents that it uses in its own manufacturing activity. X licenses its floodlight patent to Y and Z, uncontrolled foreign corporations, for use in their own territories, countries Y and Z, respectively. Corporation Y pays X an arm's length royalty of $3,000 plus $0.20 for each floodlight sold. Sales of floodlights by Y for the taxable year are $135,000 (at $4.50 per unit) or 30,000 units, and the royalty is $9,000 ($3,000 + $0.20 × 30,000). Y has sales of other products of $500,000. Z pays X an arm's length royalty of $3,000 plus $0.30 for each unit sold. Z manufactures 30,000 floodlights in the taxable year, and the royalty is $12,000 ($3,000 + $0.30 × 30,000). The dollar value of Z's floodlight sales is not known and cannot be reasonably estimated because, in this case, the floodlights are not sold separately by Z but are instead used as a component in Z's manufacture of lighting equipment for theaters. The sales of all Z's products, including the lighting equipment for theaters, are $1,000,000. Y and Z each sell the floodlights exclusively within their respective countries. X's sales of floodlights for the taxable year are $500,000 and its sales of its other products, flashlights, fuse boxes, and solderless connectors, are $400,000. X has gross income of $500,000, consisting of gross income from domestic sources from sales of floodlights, flashlights, fuse boxes, and solderless connectors of $479,000, and royalty income of $9,000 and $12,000 from foreign corporations Y and Z respectively. X utilized the optional gross income methods of apportionment for its return filed for its first taxable year to which this section applies.

(ii) *Allocation.* X's research and experimental expenses are definitely related to all of the products that it produces, which are floodlights, flashlights, fuse boxes, and solderless connectors. All of these products are in the same three digit SIC Code category, Electric Lighting and Wiring Equipment (SIC Industry Group 364). Thus, X's research and experimental expenses are allocable to all items of income attributable to this product category, domestic sales income and royalty income from the foreign countries in which corporations Y and Z operate.

(iii) *Apportionment.* (A) The statutory grouping of gross income is general limitation income from sources without the United States. The residual grouping is gross income from sources within the United States. X's deduction of $100,000 for its research expenditures must be apportioned between the groupings. For apportionment on the basis of sales in accordance with paragraph (c) of this section, X is entitled to an exclusive apportionment of 50 percent of its research and experimental expense to the residual grouping, gross income from sources within the United States, since more than 50 percent of the research activity was performed in the United States. The remaining 50 percent of the deduction can then be apportioned between the residual and statutory groupings on the basis of sales. Since Y and Z are unrelated licensees of X, only their sales of the licensed product, floodlights, are included for purposes of apportionment. Floodlight sales of Z are unknown, but are estimated at ten times royalties from Z, or $120,000. All of X's sales from the entire product category are included for purposes of apportionment on the basis of sales. Alternatively, X may apportion its deduction on the basis of gross income, in accordance with paragraph (d) of this section. The apportionment is as follows:

(*1*) *Tentative Apportionment on the basis of sales.*

(*i*) Research and experimental expense to be apportioned between statutory and residual groupings of gross income: $100,000

(*ii*) Less: Exclusive apportionment of research and experimental expense to the residual groupings of gross income ($100,000 × 50 percent): $50,000

(*iii*) Research and experimental expense to be apportioned between the statutory and residual groupings of gross income on the basis of sales: $50,000

(*iv*) Apportionment of research and experimental expense to the residual groupings of gross income ($50,000 × $900,000/($900,000 + $135,000 + $120,000)): $38,961

(*v*) Apportionment of research and experimental expense to the statutory grouping, royalty income from countries Y and Z ($50,000 × $135,000 + $120,000/($900,000 + $135,000 + $120,000)): $11,039

(*vi*) Total apportioned deduction for research and experimentation: $100,000

(*vii*) Amount apportioned to the residual grouping ($50,000 + $38,961): $88,961

(*viii*) Amount apportioned to the statutory grouping of sources within countries Y and Z: $11,039

(*2*) *Tentative apportionment on gross income basis.*

(*i*) Exclusive apportionment of research and experimental expense to the residual grouping of gross income ($100,000 × 25 percent): $25,000

(*ii*) Apportionment of research and experimental expense to the residual grouping of gross income ($75,000 × $479,000/$500,000): $71,850

(*iii*) Apportionment of research and experimental expense to the statutory grouping of gross income ($75,000 × $9,000 + $12,000/$500,000): $3,150

(*iv*) Amount apportioned to the residual grouping: $96,850

(*v*) Amount apportioned to the statutory grouping of general limitation income from sources without the United States: $3,150

(B) Since X has elected to use the optional gross income methods of apportionment and its apportionment on the basis of gross income to the statutory grouping, $3,150, is less than 50 percent of its apportionment on the basis of sales to the statutory grouping, $11,039, it must use Option two of paragraph (d)(3) of this section and apportion $5,520 (50 percent of $11,039) to the statutory grouping. [Reg. § 1.861-17.]

☐ [T.D. 8646, 12-21-95.]

§ 1.861-18. Classification of transactions involving computer programs.—(a) *General.*—(1) *Scope.*—This section provides rules for classifying transactions relating to computer programs for purposes of subchapter N of chapter 1 of the Internal Revenue Code, sections 367, 404A, 482, 551, 679, 1059A, chapter 3, chapter 5, sections 842 and 845 (to the extent involving a foreign person), and transfers to foreign trusts not covered by section 679.

(2) *Categories of transactions.*—This section generally requires that such transactions be treated as being solely within one of four categories (described in paragraph (b)(1) of this section) and provides certain rules for categorizing such transactions. In the case of a transfer of a copyright right, this section provides rules for determining whether the transaction should be classified as either a sale or exchange, or a license generating royalty income. In the case of a transfer of a copyrighted article, this section provides rules for determining whether the transaction should be classified as either a sale or exchange, or a lease generating rental income.

(3) *Computer program.*—For purposes of this section, a computer program is a set of statements or instructions to be used directly or indirectly in a computer in order to bring about a certain result. For purposes of this paragraph (a)(3), a computer program includes any media, user manuals, documentation, data base or similar item if the media, user manuals, documentation, data base or similar item is incidental to the operation of the computer program.

(b) *Categories of transactions.*—(1) *General.*—Except as provided in paragraph (b)(2) of this section, a transaction involving the transfer of a computer program, or the provision of services or of know-how with respect to a computer program (collectively, a transfer of a computer program) is treated as being solely one of the following—

(i) A transfer of a copyright right in the computer program;

(ii) A transfer of a copy of the computer program (a copyrighted article);

(iii) The provision of services for the development or modification of the computer program; or

(iv) The provision of know-how relating to computer programming techniques.

(2) *Transactions consisting of more than one category.*—Any transaction involving computer programs which consists of more than one of the transactions described in paragraph (b)(1) of this section shall be treated as separate transactions, with the appropriate provisions of this section being applied to each such transaction. However, any transaction that is de minimis, taking into account the overall transaction and the surrounding facts and circumstances, shall not be treated as a separate transaction, but as part of another transaction.

(c) *Transfers involving copyright rights and copyrighted articles.*—(1) *Classification.*—(i) *Transfers treated as transfers of copyright rights.*—A transfer of a computer program is classified as a transfer of a copyright right if, as a result of the transaction, a person acquires any one or more of the rights described in paragraphs (c)(2)(i) through (iv) of this section. Whether the transaction is treated as being solely the transfer of a copyright right or is treated as separate transactions is determined pursuant to paragraph (b)(1) and (b)(2) of this section. For example, if a person receives a disk containing a copy of a computer program which enables it to exercise, in relation to that program, a non-de minimis right described in paragraphs (c)(2)(i) through (iv) of this section (and the transaction does not involve, or involves only a de minimis provision of services as described in paragraph (d) of this section or of know-how as described in paragraph (e) of this section), then, under paragraph (b)(2) of this section, the transfer is classified solely as a transfer of a copyright right.

(ii) *Transfers treated solely as transfers of copyrighted articles.*—If a person acquires a copy of a computer program but does not acquire any of the rights described in paragraphs (c)(2)(i) through (iv) of this section (or only acquires a de minimis grant of such rights), and the transaction does not involve, or involves only a de minimis, provision of services as described in paragraph (d) of this section or of know-how as described in paragraph (e) of this section, the transfer of the copy of the computer program is classified solely as a transfer of a copyrighted article.

(2) *Copyright rights.*—The copyright rights referred to in paragraph (c)(1) of this section are as follows—

(i) The right to make copies of the computer program for purposes of distribution to the public by sale or other transfer of ownership, or by rental, lease or lending;

(ii) The right to prepare derivative computer programs based upon the copyrighted computer program;

(iii) The right to make a public performance of the computer program; or

(iv) The right to publicly display the computer program.

(3) *Copyrighted article.*—A copyrighted article includes a copy of a computer program from which the work can be perceived, reproduced, or otherwise communicated, either directly or with the aid of a machine or device. The copy of the program may be fixed in the magnetic medium of a floppy disk, or in the main memory or hard drive of a computer, or in any other medium.

(d) *Provision of services.*—The determination of whether a transaction involving a newly developed or modified computer program is treated as either the provision of services or another transaction described in paragraph (b)(1) of this section is based on all the facts and circumstances of the transaction, including, as appropriate, the intent of the parties (as evidenced by their agreement and conduct) as to which party is to own the copyright rights in the computer program and how the risks of loss are allocated between the parties.

(e) *Provision of know-how.*—The provision of information with respect to a computer program will be treated as the provision of know-how for purposes of this section only if the information is—

(1) Information relating to computer programming techniques;

(2) Furnished under conditions preventing unauthorized disclosure, specifically contracted for between the parties; and

(3) Considered property subject to trade secret protection.

(f) *Further classification of transfers involving copyright rights and copyrighted articles.*—(1) *Transfers of copyright rights.*—The determination of whether a transfer of a copyright right is a sale or exchange of property is made on the basis of whether, taking into account all facts and circumstances, there has been a transfer of all substantial rights in the copyright. A transaction that does not constitute a sale or exchange because not all substantial rights have been transferred will be classified as a license generating royalty income. For this purpose, the principles of sections 1222 and 1235 may be applied. Income derived from the sale or exchange of a copyright right will be sourced under section 865(a), (c), (d), (e), or (h), as appropriate. Income derived from the licensing of a copyright right will be sourced under section 861(a)(4) or 862(a)(4), as appropriate.

(2) *Transfers of copyrighted articles.*—The determination of whether a transfer of a copyrighted article is a sale or exchange is made on the basis of whether, taking into account all facts and circumstances, the benefits and burdens of ownership have been transferred. A transaction that does not constitute a sale or exchange because insufficient benefits and burdens of ownership of the copyrighted article have been transferred, such that a person other than the transferee is properly treated as the owner of the copyrighted article, will be classified as a lease generating rental income. Income from transactions that are classified as sales or exchanges of copyrighted articles will be sourced under sections 861(a)(6), 862(a)(6), 863, 865(a), (b), (c), or (e), as appropriate. Income derived from the leasing of a copyrighted article will be sourced under section 861(a)(4) or section 862(a)(4), as appropriate.

(3) *Special circumstances of computer programs.*—In connection with determinations under this paragraph (f), consideration must be given as appropriate to the special characteristics of computer programs in transactions that take advantage of these characteristics (such as the ability to make perfect copies at minimal cost). For example, a transaction in which a person acquires a copy of a computer program on disk subject to a requirement that the disk be destroyed after a specified period is generally the equivalent of a transaction subject to a requirement that the disk be returned after such period. Similarly, a transaction in which the program deactivates itself after a specified period is generally the equivalent of returning the copy.

(g) *Rules of operation.*—(1) *Term applied to transaction by parties.*—Neither the form adopted by the parties to a transaction, nor the classification of the transaction under copyright law, shall be determinative. Therefore, for example, if there is a transfer of a computer program on a single disk for a one-time payment with restrictions on transfer and reverse engineering, which the parties characterize as a license (including, but not limited to, agreements commonly referred to as shrink-wrap licenses), application of the rules of paragraphs (c) and (f) of this section may nevertheless result in the transaction being classified as the sale of a copyrighted article.

(2) *Means of transfer not to be taken into account.*—The rules of this section shall be applied irrespective of the physical or electronic or other medium used to effectuate a transfer of a computer program.

(3) *To the public.*—(i) *In general.*—For purposes of paragraph (c)(2)(i) of this section, a transferee of a computer program shall not be considered to have the right to distribute copies of the program to the public if it is permitted to distribute copies of the software to only either a related person, or to identified persons who may be identified by either name or by legal relationship to the original transferee. For purposes of this subparagraph, a related person is a person who bears a relationship to the transferee specified in section 267(b)(3), (10), (11), or (12), or section 707(b)(1)(B). In applying section 267(b), 267(f), 707(b)(1)(B), or 1563(a), "10 percent" shall be substituted for "50 percent."

(ii) *Use by individuals.*—The number of employees of a transferee of a computer program who are permitted to use the program in connection with their employment is not relevant for purposes of this paragraph (g)(3). In addition, the number of individuals with a contractual agreement to provide services to the transferee of a computer program who are permitted to use the program in connection with the performance of those services is not relevant for purposes of this paragraph (g)(3).

(h) *Examples.*—The provisions of this section may be illustrated by the following examples:

Example 1. (i) *Facts.* Corp A, a U.S. corporation, owns the copyright in a computer program, Program X. It copies Program X onto disks. The disks are placed in boxes covered with a wrapper on which is printed what is generally referred to as a shrink-wrap license. The license is stated to be perpetual. Under the license no reverse engineering, decompilation, or disassembly of the computer program is permitted. The transferee receives, first, the right to use the program on two of its own computers (for example, a laptop and a desktop) provided that only one copy is in use at any one time, and, second, the right to make one copy of the program on each machine as an essential step in the utilization of the program. The transferee is permitted by the shrink-wrap license to sell the copy so long as it destroys any other copies it has made and imposes the same terms and conditions of the license on the purchaser of its copy. These disks are made available for sale to the general public in Country Z. In return for valuable consideration, P, a Country Z resident, receives one such disk.

(ii) *Analysis.* (A) Under paragraph (g)(1) of this section, the label license is not determinative. None of the copyright rights described in paragraph (c)(2) of this section have been transferred in this transaction. P has received a copy of the program, however, and, therefore, under paragraph (c)(1)(ii) of this section, P has acquired solely a copyrighted article.

(B) Taking into account all of the facts and circumstances, P is properly treated as the owner of a copyrighted article. Therefore, under paragraph (f)(2) of this section, there has been a sale of a copyrighted article rather than the grant of a lease.

Example 2. (i) *Facts.* The facts are the same as those in *Example 1*, except that instead of selling disks, Corp A, the U.S. corporation, decides to make Program X available, for a fee, on a World Wide Web home page on the Internet. P, the Country Z resident, in return for payment made to Corp A, downloads Program X (via modem) onto the hard drive of his computer. As part of the electronic communication, P signifies his assent to a license agreement with terms identical to those in *Example 1*, except that in this case P may make a back-up copy of the program on to a disk.

(ii) *Analysis.* (A) None of the copyright rights described in paragraph (c)(2) of this section have passed to P. Although P did not buy a physical copy of the disk with the program on it, paragraph (g)(2) of this section provides that the means of transferring the program is irrelevant. Therefore, P has acquired a copyrighted article.

(B) As in *Example 1*, P is properly treated as the owner of a copyrighted article. Therefore, under paragraph (f)(2) of this section, there has been a sale of a copyrighted article rather than the grant of a lease.

Example 3. (i) *Facts.* The facts are the same as those in *Example 1*, except that Corp A only allows P, the Country Z resident, to use Program X for one week. At the end of that week, P must return the disk with Program X on it to Corp A. P must also destroy any copies made of Program X. If P wishes to use Program X for a further period he must enter into a new agreement to use the program for an additional charge.

(ii) *Analysis.* (A) Under paragraph (c)(2) of this section, P has received no copyright rights. Because P has received a copy of the program under paragraph (c)(1)(ii) of this section, he has, therefore, received a copyrighted article.

(B) Taking into account all of the facts and circumstances, P is not properly treated as the owner of a copyrighted article. Therefore, under paragraph (f)(2) of this section, there has been a lease of a copyrighted article rather than a sale. Taking into account the special characteristics of computer programs as provided in paragraph (f)(3) of this section, the result would be the same if P were required to destroy the disk at the end of the one week period instead of returning it since Corp A can make additional copies of the program at minimal cost.

Example 4. (i) *Facts.* The facts are the same as those in *Example 2*, where P, the Country Z resident, receives Program X from Corp A's home page on the Internet, except that P may only use Program X for a period of one week at the end of which an electronic lock is activated and the program can no longer be accessed. Thereafter, if P wishes to use Program X, it must return to the home page and pay Corp A to send an electronic key to reactivate the program for another week.

(ii) *Analysis.* (A) As in *Example 3*, under paragraph (c)(2) of this section, P has not received any copyright rights. P has received a copy of the program, and under paragraph (g)(2) of this section, the means of transmission is irrelevant. P has, therefore, under paragraph (c)(1)(ii) of this section, received a copyrighted article.

(B) As in *Example 3*, P is not properly treated as the owner of a copyrighted article. Therefore, under paragraph (f)(2) of this section, there has been a lease of a copyrighted article rather than a sale. While P does retain Program X on its computer at the end of the one week period, as a legal matter P no longer has the right to use the program (without further payment) and, indeed, cannot use the program without the electronic key. Functionally, Program X is no longer on the hard drive of P=s computer. Instead, the hard drive contains only a series of numbers which no longer perform the function of Program X. Although in *Example 3*, P was required to physically return the disk, taking into account the special characteristics of computer programs as provided in paragraph (f)(3) of this section, the result in this *Example 4* is the same as in *Example 3*.

Example 5. (i) *Facts.* Corp A, a U.S. corporation, transfers a disk containing Program X to Corp B, a Country Z corporation, and grants Corp B an exclusive license for the remaining term of the copyright to copy and distribute an unlimited number of copies of Program X in the geographic area of Country Z, prepare derivative works based upon Program X, make public performances of Program X, and publicly display Program X. Corp B will pay Corp A a royalty of $y a year for three years, which is the expected period during which Program X will have commercially exploitable value.

(ii) *Analysis.* (A) Although Corp A has transferred a disk with a copy of Program X on it to Corp B, under paragraph (c)(1)(i) of this section because this transfer is accompanied by a copyright right identified in paragraph (c)(2)(i) of this section, this transaction is a transfer solely of copyright rights, not of copyrighted articles. For purposes of paragraph (b)(2) of this section, the disk containing a copy of Program X is a de minimis component of the transaction.

(B) Applying the all substantial rights test under paragraph (f)(1) of this section, Corp A will be treated as having sold copyright rights to Corp B. Corp B has acquired all of the copyright rights in Program X, has received the right to use them exclusively within Country Z, and has received the rights for the remaining life of the copyright in Program X. The fact the payments cease before the copyright term expires is not controlling. Under paragraph (g)(1) of this section, the fact that the agreement is labelled a license is not controlling (nor is the fact that Corp A receives a sum labelled a royalty). (The result in this case would be the same if the copy of Program X to be used for the purposes of reproduction were transmitted electronically to Corp B, as a result of the application of the rule of paragraph (g)(2) of this section.)

Example 6. (i) *Facts.* Corp A, a U.S. corporation, transfers a disk containing Program X to Corp B, a Country Z corporation, and grants Corp B the non exclusive right to reproduce (either directly or by contracting with either Corp A or another person to do so) and distribute for sale to the public an unlimited number of disks at its factory in Country Z in return for a payment related to the number of disks copied and sold. The term of the agreement is two years, which is less than the remaining life of the copyright.

(ii) *Analysis.* (A) As in *Example 5*, the transfer of the disk containing the copy of the program does not constitute the transfer of a copyrighted article under paragraph (c)(1) of this section because Corp B has also acquired a copyright right under paragraph (c)(2)(i) of this section, the right to reproduce and distribute to the public. For purposes of paragraph (b)(2) of this section, the disk containing Program X is a de minimis component of the transaction.

(B) Taking into account all of the facts and circumstances, there has been a license of Program X to Corp B, and the payments made by Corp B are royalties. Under paragraph (f)(1) of this section, there has not been a transfer of all substantial rights in the copyright to Program X because Corp A has the right to enter into other licenses with respect to the copyright of Program X, including licenses in Country Z (or even to sell that copyright, subject to Corp B's interest). Corp B has acquired no right itself to license the copyright rights in Program X. Finally, the term of the license is for less than the remaining life of the copyright in Program X.

Example 7. (i) *Facts.* Corp C, a distributor in Country Z, enters into an agreement with Corp A, a U.S. corporation, to purchase as many copies of Program X on disk as it may from time-to-time request. Corp C will then sell these disks to retailers. The disks are shipped in boxes covered by shrink-wrap licenses (identical to the license described in *Example 1*).

(ii) *Analysis.* (A) Corp C has not acquired any copyright rights under paragraph (c)(2) of this section with respect to Program X. It has acquired individual copies of Program X, which it may sell to others. The use of the term license is not dispositive under paragraph (g)(1) of this section. Under paragraph (c)(1)(ii) of this section, Corp C has acquired copyrighted articles.

(B) Taking into account all of the facts and circumstances, Corp C is properly treated as the owner of copyrighted articles. Therefore, under paragraph (f)(2) of this section, there has been a sale of copyrighted articles.

Example 8. (i) *Facts.* Corp A, a U.S. corporation, transfers a disk containing Program X to Corp D, a foreign corporation engaged in the manufacture and sale of personal computers in Country Z. Corp A grants Corp D the non-exclusive right to copy Program X onto the hard drive of an unlimited number of computers, which Corp D manufactures, and to distribute those copies (on the hard drive) to the public. The term of the agreement is two years, which is less than the remaining life of the copyright in Program X. Corp D pays Corp A an amount based on the number of copies of Program X it loads on to computers.

(ii) *Analysis.* The analysis is the same as in *Example 6*. Under paragraph (c)(2)(i) of this section, Corp D has acquired a copyright right enabling it to exploit Program X by copying it on to the hard drives of the computers that it manufactures and then sells. For purposes of paragraph (b)(2) of this section, the disk containing Program X is a de minimis component of the transaction. Taking into account all of the facts and circumstances, Corp D has not, however, acquired all substantial rights in the copyright to Program X (for example, the term of the agreement is less than the remaining life of the copyright). Under paragraph (f)(1) of this section, this transaction is, therefore, a license of Program X to Corp D rather than a sale and the payments made by Corp D are royalties. (The result would be the same if Corp D included with the computers it sells an archival copy of Program X on a floppy disk.)

Reg. §1.861-18(h)

Example 9. (i) *Facts.* The facts are the same as in *Example 8*, except that Corp D, the Country Z corporation, receives physical disks. The disks are shipped in boxes covered by shrink-wrap licenses (identical to the licenses described in *Example 1*). The terms of these licenses do not permit Corp D to make additional copies of Program X. Corp D uses each individual disk only once to load a single copy of Program X onto each separate computer. Corp D transfers the disk with the computer when it is sold.

(ii) *Analysis.* (A) As in *Example 7* (unlike *Example 8*) no copyright right identified in paragraph (c)(2) of this section has been transferred. Corp D acquires the disks without the right to reproduce and distribute publicly further copies of Program X. This is therefore the transfer of copyrighted articles under paragraph (c)(1)(ii) of this section.

(B) Taking into account all of the facts and circumstances, Corp D is properly treated as the owner of copyrighted articles. Therefore, under paragraph (f)(2) of this section, the transaction is classified as the sale of a copyrighted article. (The result would be the same if Corp D used a single physical disk to copy Program X onto each computer, and transferred an unopened box containing Program X with each computer, if Corp D were not permitted to copy Program X onto more computers than the number of individual copies purchased.)

Example 10. (i) *Facts.* Corp A, a U.S. corporation, transfers a disk containing Program X to Corp E, a Country Z corporation, and grants Corp E the right to load Program X onto 50 individual workstations for use only by Corp E employees at one location in return for a one-time per-user fee (generally referred to as a site license or enterprise license). If additional workstations are subsequently introduced, Program X may be loaded onto those machines for additional one-time per-user fees. The license which grants the rights to operate Program X on 50 workstations also prohibits Corp E from selling the disk (or any of the 50 copies) or reverse engineering the program. The term of the license is stated to be perpetual.

(ii) *Analysis.* (A) The grant of a right to copy, unaccompanied by the right to distribute those copies to the public, is not the transfer of a copyright right under paragraph (c)(2) of this section. Therefore, under paragraph (c)(1)(ii) of this section, this transaction is a transfer of copyrighted articles (50 copies of Program X).

(B) Taking into account all of the facts and circumstances, P is properly treated as the owner of copyrighted articles. Therefore, under paragraph (f)(2) of this section, there has been a sale of copyrighted articles rather than the grant of a lease. Notwithstanding the restriction on sale, other factors such as, for example, the risk of loss and the right to use the copies in perpetuity outweigh, in this case, the restrictions placed on the right of alienation.

(C) The result would be the same if Corp E were permitted to copy Program X onto an unlimited number of workstations used by employees of either Corp E or corporations that had a relationship to Corp E specified in paragraph (g)(3) of this section.

Example 11. (i) *Facts.* The facts are the same as in *Example 10*, except that Corp E, the Country Z corporation, acquires the right to make Program X available to workstation users who are Corp E employees by way of a local area network (LAN). The number of users that can use Program X on the LAN at any one time is limited to 50. Corp E pays a one-time fee for the right to have up to 50 employees use the program at the same time.

(ii) *Analysis.* Under paragraph (g)(2) of this section the mode of utilization is irrelevant. Therefore, as in *Example 10*, under paragraph (c)(2) of this section, no copyright right has been transferred, and, thus, under paragraph (c)(1)(ii) of this section, this transaction will be classified as the transfer of a copyrighted article. Under the benefits and burdens test of paragraph (f)(2) of this section, this transaction is a sale of copyrighted articles. The result would be the same if an unlimited number of Corp E employees were permitted to use Program X on the LAN or if Corp E were permitted to copy Program X onto LANs maintained by corporations that had a relationship to Corp E specified in paragraph (g)(3) of this section.

Example 12. (i) *Facts.* The facts are the same as in *Example 11*, except that Corp E pays a monthly fee to Corp A, the U.S. corporation, calculated with reference to the permitted maximum number of users (which can be changed) and the computing power of Corp E's server. In return for this monthly fee, Corp E receives the right to receive upgrades of Program X when they become available. The agreement may be terminated by either party at the end of any month. When the disk containing the upgrade is received, Corp E must return the disk containing the earlier version of Program X to Corp A. If the contract is terminated, Corp E must delete (or otherwise destroy) all copies made of the current version of Program X. The agreement also requires Corp A to provide technical support to Corp E but the agreement does not allocate the monthly fee between the right to receive upgrades of Program X and the technical support services. The amount of technical support that Corp A will provide to Corp E is not foreseeable at the time the contract is entered into but is expected to be de minimis. The agreement specifically provides that Corp

E has not thereby been granted an option to purchase Program X.

(ii) *Analysis.* (A) Corp E has received no copyright rights under paragraph (c)(2) of this section. Corp A has not provided any services described in paragraph (d) of this section. Based on all the facts and circumstances of the transaction, Corp A has provided de minimis technical services to Corp E. Therefore, under paragraph (c)(1)(ii) of this section, the transaction is a transfer of a copyrighted article.

(B) Taking into account all facts and circumstances, under the benefits and burdens test Corp E is not properly treated as the owner of the copyrighted article. Corp E does not receive the right to use Program X in perpetuity, but only for so long as it continues to make payments. Corp E does not have the right to purchase Program X on advantageous (or, indeed, any) terms once a certain amount of money has been paid to Corp A or a certain period of time has elapsed (which might indicate a sale). Once the agreement is terminated, Corp E will no longer possess any copies of Program X, current or superseded. Therefore under paragraph (f)(2) of this section there has been a lease of a copyrighted article.

Example 13. (i) *Facts.* The facts are the same as in *Example 12*, except that, while Corp E must return copies of Program X as new upgrades are received, if the agreement terminates, Corp E may keep the latest version of Program X (although Corp E is still prohibited from selling or otherwise transferring any copy of Program X).

(ii) *Analysis.* For the reasons stated in *Example 10*, paragraph (ii)(B), the transfer of the program will be treated as a sale of a copyrighted article rather than as a lease.

Example 14. (i) *Facts.* Corp G, a Country Z corporation, enters into a contract with Corp A, a U.S. corporation, for Corp A to modify Program X so that it can be used at Corp G's facility in Country Z. Under the contract, Corp G is to acquire one copy of the program on a disk and the right to use the program on 5,000 workstations. The contract requires Corp A to rewrite elements of Program X so that it will conform to Country Z accounting standards and states that Corp A retains all copyright rights in the modified Program X. The agreement between Corp A and Corp G is otherwise identical as to rights and payment terms as the agreement described in *Example 10*.

(ii) *Analysis.* (A) As in *Example 10*, no copyright rights are being transferred under paragraph (c)(2) of this section. In addition, since no copyright rights are being transferred to Corp G, this transaction does not involve the provision of services by Corp A under paragraph (d) of this section. This transaction will be classified, therefore, as a transfer of copyrighted articles under paragraph (c)(1)(ii) of this section.

(B) Taking into account all facts and circumstances, Corp G is properly treated as the owner of copyrighted articles. Therefore, under paragraph (f)(2) of this section, there has been the sale of a copyrighted article rather than the grant of a lease.

Example 15. (i) *Facts.* Corp H, a Country Z corporation, enters into a license agreement for a new computer program. Program Q is to be written by Corp A, a U.S. corporation. Corp A and Corp H agree that Corp A is writing Program Q for Corp H and that, when Program Q is completed, the copyright in Program Q will belong to Corp H. Corp H gives instructions to Corp A programmers regarding program specifications. Corp H agrees to pay Corp A a fixed monthly sum during development of the program. If Corp H is dissatisfied with the development of the program, it may cancel the contract at the end of any month. In the event of termination, Corp A will retain all payments, while any procedures, techniques or copyrightable interests will be the property of Corp H. All of the payments are labelled royalties. There is no provision in the agreement for any continuing relationship between Corp A and Corp H, such as the furnishing of updates of the program, after completion of the modification work.

(ii) *Analysis.* Taking into account all of the facts and circumstances, Corp A is treated as providing services to Corp H. Under paragraph (d) of this section, Corp A is treated as providing services to Corp H because Corp H bears all of the risks of loss associated with the development of Program Q and is the owner of all copyright rights in Program Q. Under paragraph (g)(1) of this section, the fact that the agreement is labelled a license is not controlling (nor is the fact that Corp A receives a sum labelled a royalty).

Example 16. (i) *Facts.* Corp A, a U.S. corporation, and Corp I, a Country Z corporation, agree that a development engineer employed by Corp A will travel to Country Z to provide know-how relating to certain techniques not generally known to computer programmers, which will enable Corp I to more efficiently create computer programs. These techniques represent the product of experience gained by Corp A from working on many computer programming projects, and are furnished to Corp I under nondisclosure conditions. Such information is property subject to trade secret protection.

(ii) *Analysis.* This transaction contains the elements of know-how specified in paragraph (e) of this section. Therefore, this transaction will be treated as the provision of know-how.

Reg. § 1.861-18(h)

Example 17. (i) *Facts.* Corp A, a U.S. corporation, transfers a disk containing Program Y to Corp E, a Country Z corporation, in exchange for a single fixed payment. Program Y is a computer program development program, which is used to create other computer programs, consisting of several components, including libraries of reusable software components that serve as general building blocks in new software applications. No element of these libraries is a significant component of any overall new program. Because a computer program created with the use of Program Y will not operate unless the libraries are also present, the license agreement between Corp A and Corp E grants Corp E the right to distribute copies of the libraries with any program developed using Program Y. The license agreement is otherwise identical to the license agreement in *Example 1.*

(ii) *Analysis.* (A) No non-de minimis copyright rights described in paragraph (c)(2) of this section have passed to Corp E. For purposes of paragraph (b)(2) of this section, the right to distribute the libraries in conjunction with the programs created using Program Y is a de minimis component of the transaction. Because Corp E has received a copy of the program under paragraph (c)(1)(ii) of this section, it has received a copyrighted article.

(B) Taking into account all the facts and circumstances, Corp E is properly treated as the owner of a copyrighted article. Therefore, under paragraph (f)(2) of this section, there has been the sale of a copyrighted article rather than the grant of a lease.

Example 18. (i) *Facts.* (A) Corp A, a U.S. corporation, transfers a disk containing Program X to Corp E, a country Z Corporation. The disk contains both the object code and the source code to Program X and the license agreement grants Corp E the right to—

(*1*) Modify the source code in order to correct minor errors and make minor adaptations to Program X so it will function on Corp E=s computer; and

(*2*) Recompile the modified source code.

(B) The license does not grant Corp E the right to distribute the modified Program X to the public. The license is otherwise identical to the license agreement in *Example 1.*

(ii) *Analysis.* (A) No non-de minimis copyright rights described in paragraph (c)(2) of this section have passed to Corp E. For purposes of paragraph (b)(2) of this section, the right to modify the source code and recompile the source code in order to create new code to correct minor errors and make minor adaptations is a de minimis component of the transaction. Because Corp E has received a copy of the program under paragraph (c)(1)(ii) of this section, it has received a copyrighted article.

(B) Taking into account all the facts and circumstances, Corp E is properly treated as the owner of a copyrighted article. Therefore, under paragraph (f)(2) of this section, there has been the sale of a copyrighted article rather than the grant of a lease.

(i) *Effective date.*—(1) *General.*—This section applies to transactions occurring pursuant to contracts entered into on or after December 1, 1998.

(2) *Elective transition rules.*—(i) *Contracts entered into in taxable years ending on or after October 2, 1998.*—A taxpayer may elect to apply this section to transactions occurring pursuant to contracts entered into in taxable years ending on or after October 2, 1998. A taxpayer that makes an election under this paragraph (i)(2)(i) must apply this section to all contracts entered into in taxable years ending on or after October 2, 1998.

(ii) *Contracts entered into before October 2, 1998.*—A taxpayer may elect to apply this section to transactions occurring in taxable years ending on or after October 2, 1998, pursuant to contracts entered into before October 2, 1998, provided the taxpayer would not be required under this section to change its method of accounting as a result of such election, or the taxpayer would be required to change its method of accounting but the resulting section 481(a) adjustment would be zero. A taxpayer that makes an election under this paragraph (i)(2)(ii) must apply this section to all transactions occurring in taxable years ending on or after October 2, 1998, pursuant to contracts entered into before October 2, 1998.

(3) *Manner of making election.*—Taxpayers may elect, under paragraph (i)(2)(i) or (i)(2)(ii) of this section, to apply this section, by treating the transactions in accordance with these regulations on their original tax return.

(4) *Examples.*—The following examples illustrate application of the transition rule of paragraph (i)(2)(ii) of this section:

Example 1. Corp A develops computer programs for sale to third parties. Corp A uses an overall accrual method of accounting and files its tax return on a calendar-year basis. In year 1, Corp A enters into a contract to deliver a computer program in that year, and to provide updates for each of the following four years. Under the contract, the computer program and the updates are priced separately, and Corp A is entitled to receive payments for the computer program and each of the updates upon delivery. Assume Corp A properly accounts for the contract as a contract for the provision of services. Corp A properly includes the payments under the contract in gross income in the taxable year the payments are received and the computer program or updates are delivered. Corp A properly deducts the cost of developing the computer program and updates when the costs are incurred. Year 3 includes October 2, 1998. Assume under the rules of this section, the provision of updates would properly be accounted for as the transfer of copyrighted articles. If Corp A made an election under paragraph (i)(2)(ii) of this section, Corp A would not be required to change its method of accounting for income under the contract as a result of the election. Corp A would also not be required to change its method of accounting for the cost of developing the computer program and the updates under the contract as a result of the election. Therefore, under paragraph (i)(2)(ii) of this section, Corp A may elect to apply the provisions of this section to the updates provided in years 3, 4, and 5, because Corp A is not required to change from its method of accounting for the contract as a result of the election.

Example 2. Corp A develops computer programs for sale to third parties. Corp A uses an overall accrual method of accounting and files its tax return on a calendar-year basis. In year 1, Corp A enters into a contract to deliver a computer program and to provide one update the following year. Under the contract, the computer program and the update are priced separately, and Corp A is entitled to receive payment for the computer program and the update upon delivery of the computer program. Assume Corp A properly accounts for the contract as a contract for the provision of services. Corp A properly includes the portion of the payment relating to the computer program in gross income in year 1, the taxable year the payment is received and the program delivered. Corp A properly includes the portion of the payment relating to the update in gross income in year 2, the taxable year the update is provided, under Rev. Proc. 71-21, 1971-2 CB 549 (see § 601.601(d)(2) of this chapter). Corp A properly deducts the cost of developing the computer program and update when the costs are incurred. Year 2 includes October 2, 1998. Assume under the rules of this section, provision of the update would properly be accounted for as the transfer of a copyrighted article. If Corp A made an election under paragraph (i)(2)(ii) of this section, Corp A would be required to change its method of accounting for deferring income under its contract as a result of the election. However, the section 481(a) adjustment would be zero because the portion of the payment relating to the update would be includible in gross income in year 2, the taxable year the update is provided, under both Rev. Proc. 71-21 and § 1.451-5. Corp A would not be required to change its method of accounting for the cost of developing the computer program and the update under the contract as a result of the election. Therefore, under paragraph (i)(2)(ii) of this section, Corp A may elect to apply the provisions of this section to the update in year 2, because the section 481(a) adjustment resulting from the change in method of accounting for deferring advance payments under the contract is zero, and because Corp A is not required to change from its method of accounting for the cost of developing the computer program and updates under the contract as a result of the election.

Example 3. Assume the same facts as in *Example 1* except that Corp A is entitled to receive payments for the computer program and each of the updates 30 days after delivery. Corp A properly includes the amounts due under the contract in gross income in the taxable year the computer program or updates are provided. Assume that Corp A properly uses the nonaccrual-experience method described in section 448(d)(5) and § 1.448-2T to account for income on its contracts. If Corp A made an election under paragraph (i)(2)(ii) of this section, Corp A would be required to change from the nonaccrual-experience method for income as a result of the election, because the method is only available with respect to amounts to be received for the performance of services. Therefore, Corp A may not elect to apply the provisions of this section to the updates provided in years 3, 4, and 5, under paragraph (i)(2)(ii) of this section, because Corp A would be required to change from the nonaccrual-experience method of accounting for income on the contract as a result of the election.

(j) *Change in method of accounting required by this section.*—(1) *Consent.*—A taxpayer is granted consent to change its method of accounting for contracts involving computer programs, to conform with the classification prescribed in this section. The consent is granted for contracts entered into on or after December 1, 1998, or in the case of a taxpayer making an election under paragraph (i)(2)(i) of this section, the consent is granted for contracts entered into in taxable years ending on or after October 2, 1998. In addition, a taxpayer that makes an election under paragraph (i)(2)(ii) of this section is granted consent to change its method of accounting for any contract with transactions subject to the election, if the taxpayer is required to change its method of accounting as a result of the election.

(2) *Year of change.*—The year of change is the taxable year that includes December 1, 1998, or in the case of a taxpayer making an

election under paragraph (i)(2)(i) or (i)(2)(ii) of this section, the taxable year that includes October 2, 1998.

(k) *Time and manner of making change in method of accounting.*—(1) *General.*—A taxpayer changing its method of accounting in accordance with this section must file a Form 3115, Application for Change in Method of Accounting, in duplicate. The taxpayer must type or print the following statement at the top of page 1 of the Form 3115: "FILED UNDER TREASURY REGULATION § 1.861-18." The original Form 3115 must be attached to the taxpayers original return for the year of change. A copy of the Form 3115 must be filed with the National Office no later than when the original Form 3115 is filed for the year of change.

(2) *Copy of Form 3115.*—The copy required by this paragraph (k)(l) to be sent to the national office should be sent to the Commissioner of Internal Revenue, Attention: CC:DOM:IT&A, P.O. Box 7604, Benjamin Franklin Station, Washington DC 20044 (or in the case of a designated private delivery service: Commissioner of Internal Revenue, Attention: CC:DOM:IT&A, 1111 Constitution Avenue, NW., Washington, DC 20224).

(3) *Effect of consent and Internal Revenue Service review.*—A change in method of accounting granted under this section is subject to review by the district director and the national office and may be modified or revoked in accordance with the provisions of Rev. Proc. 97-37 (1997-33 IRB 18) (or its successors) (see § 601.601(d)(2) of this chapter). [Reg. § 1.861-18.]

☐ [*T.D.* 8785, 9-30-98 (*corrected* 11-24-98).]

§ 1.862-1. Income specifically from sources without the United States.—(a) *Gross income.*—(1) The following items of gross income shall be treated as income from sources without the United States:

(i) Interest other than that specified in section 861(a)(1) and § 1.861-2 as being derived from sources within the United States;

(ii) Dividends other than those derived from sources within the United States as provided in section 861(a)(2) and § 1.861-3;

(iii) Compensation for labor or personal services performed without the United States;

(iv) Rentals or royalties from property located without the United States or from any interest in such property, including rentals or royalties for the use of, or for the privilege of using, without the United States, patents, copyrights, secret processes and formulas, goodwill, trademarks, trade brands, franchises, and other like property;

(v) Gains, profits, and income from the sale of real property located without the United States; and

(vi) Gains, profits, and income derived from the purchase of personal property within the United States and its sale without the United States.

For rules treating certain interest as income from sources without the United States, see paragraph (b) of § 1.861-2. For the treatment of compensation for labor or personal services performed partly within the United States and partly without the United States, see paragraph (b) of § 1.861-4.

(2) In applying subparagraph (1)(iv) of this paragraph for taxable years beginning after December 31, 1966, gains described in section 871(a)(1)(D) and section 881(a)(4) from the sale or exchange after October 4, 1966, of patents, copyrights, and other like property shall be treated, as provided in section 871(e)(2), as rentals or royalties for the use of, or privilege of using, property or an interest in property. See paragraph (e) of § 1.871-11.

(3) For determining the time and place of sale of personal property for purposes of subparagraph (1)(vi) of this paragraph, see paragraph (c) of § 1.861-7.

(4) Income derived from the purchase of personal property within the United States and its sale within a possession of the United States shall be treated as derived entirely from within that possession.

(5) If interest is paid on an obligation of a nonresident of the United States by a resident of the United States acting in the resident's capacity as a guarantor of the obligation of the nonresident, the interest will be treated as income from sources without the United States.

(6) For rules treating certain interest as income from sources without the United States, see paragraph (b) of § 1.861-2.

(7) For the treatment of compensation for labor or personal services performed partly within the United States and partly without the United States, see paragraph (b) of § 1.861-4.

(b) *Taxable income.*—The taxable income from sources without the United States, in the case of the items of gross income specified in paragraph (a) of this section, shall be determined on the same basis as that used in § 1.861-8 for determining the taxable income from sources within the United States.

(c) *Income from certain property.*—For provisions permitting a taxpayer to elect to treat amounts of gross income attributable to certain aircraft or vessels first leased on or before December 28, 1980, as income from sources within the United States which would otherwise be treated as income from sources without the United States under paragraph (a) of this section, see § 1.861-9. For provisions requiring amounts of gross income attributable to certain aircraft, vessels, or spacecraft first leased by the taxpayer after December 28, 1980, to be treated as income from sources within the United States which would otherwise be treated as income from sources without the United States under paragraph (a) of this section, see § 1.861-9A. [Reg. § 1.862-1.]

☐ [*T.D. 6258, 10-23-57. Amended by T.D. 7378, 9-29-75; T.D. 7635, 8-7-79 and T.D. 7928, 12-15-83.*]

§ 1.863-1. Allocation of gross income under section 863(a).—(a) *In general.*—Items of gross income other than those specified in section 861(a) and section 862(a) will generally be separately allocated to sources within or without the United States. See § 1.863-2 for alternate methods to determine the income from sources within or without the United States in the case of items specified in § 1.863-2(a). See also sections 865(b) and (e)(2). In the case of sales of property involving partners and partnerships, the rules of § 1.863-3(g) apply.

(b) *Natural resources.*—(1) *In general.*—Notwithstanding any other provision, except to the extent provided in paragraph (b)(2) of this section, gross receipts from the sale outside the United States of products derived from the ownership or operation of any farm, mine, oil or gas well, other natural deposit, or timber within the United States, must be allocated between sources within and without the United States based on the fair market value of the product at the export terminal (as defined in paragraph (b)(3)(iii) of this section). Notwithstanding any other provision, except to the extent provided in paragraph (b)(2) of this section, gross receipts from the sale within the United States of products derived from the ownership or operation of any farm, mine, oil or gas well, other natural deposit, or timber outside the United States must be allocated between sources within and without the United States based on the fair market value of the product at the export terminal. For place of sale, see §§ 1.861-7(c) and 1.863-3(c)(2). The source of gross receipts equal to the fair market value of the product at the export terminal will be from sources where the farm, mine, well, deposit, or uncut timber is located. The source of gross receipts from the sale of the product in excess of its fair market value at the export terminal (excess gross receipts) will be determined as follows—

(i) If the taxpayer engages in additional production activities subsequent to shipment from the export terminal and outside the country of sale, the source of excess gross receipts must be determined under § 1.863-3. For purposes of applying § 1.863-3, only production assets used in additional production activity subsequent to the export terminal are taken into account.

(ii) In all other cases, excess gross receipts will be from sources within the country of sale. This paragraph (b)(1)(ii) applies to a taxpayer that engages in additional production activities in the country of sale, as well as to a taxpayer that does not engage in additional production activities at all.

(2) *Additional production prior to export terminal.*—Notwithstanding any other provision of this section, gross receipts from the sale of products derived by a taxpayer who performs additional production activities as defined in paragraph (b)(3)(ii) of this section before the relevant product is shipped from the export terminal are allocated between sources within and without the United States based on the fair market value of the product immediately prior to the additional production activities. The source of gross receipts equal to the fair market value of the product immediately prior to the additional production activities will be from sources where the farm, mine, well, deposit, or uncut timber is located. The source of gross receipts from the sale of the product in excess of the fair market value immediately prior to the additional production activities must be determined under § 1.863-3. For purposes of applying § 1.863-3, only production assets used in the additional production activities are taken into account.

(3) *Definitions.*—(i) *Production activity.*—For purposes of this section, production activity means an activity that creates, fabricates, manufactures, extracts, processes, cures, or ages inventory. See § 1.864-1. Except as otherwise provided in §§ 1.1502-13 or 1.863-3(g)(2), only production activities conducted directly by the taxpayer are taken into account.

(ii) *Additional production activities.*—For purposes of this section, additional production activities are substantial production activities performed directly by the taxpayer in addition to activities from the ownership or operation of any farm, mine, oil or gas well, other natural deposit, or timber. Whether a taxpayer's activities constitute additional production activities will be determined under the principles of § 1.954-3(a)(4). However, in no case will activities that prepare the natural resource itself for export, including those that are designed to facilitate the transportation of the natural resource to or from the export terminal, be considered additional production activities for purposes of this section.

(iii) *Export terminal.*—Where the farm, mine, well, deposit, or uncut timber is located without the United States, the export terminal will be the final point in a foreign from which goods are shipped to the United States. If there is no such final point in a foreign country (e.g., the property is extracted and produced on the high seas), the export terminal will be the place of production. Where the farm, mine, well, deposit, or uncut timber is located within the United States, the export terminal will be the final point in the United States from which goods are shipped from the United States to a foreign country. The location of the export terminal is determined without regard to any contractual terms agreed to by the taxpayer and without regard to whether there is an actual sale of the products at the export terminal.

(4) *Determination of fair market value.*—For purposes of this section, fair market value depends on all of the facts and circumstances as they exist relative to a party in any particular case. Where the products are sold to a related party in a transaction subject to section 482, the determination of fair market value under this section must be consistent with the arm's length price determined under section 482.

(5) *Determination of gross income.*—To determine the amount of a taxpayer's gross income from sources within or without the United States, the taxpayer's gross receipts from sources within or without the United States determined under this paragraph (b) must be reduced by the cost of goods sold properly attributable to gross receipts from sources within or without the United States.

(6) *Tax return disclosure.*—A taxpayer that determines the source of its income under this paragraph (b) shall attach a statement to its return explaining the methodology used to determine fair market value under paragraph (b)(4) of this section, and explaining any additional production activities (as defined in paragraph (b)(3)(ii) of this section) performed by the taxpayer. In addition, the taxpayer must provide such other information as is required by § 1.863-3.

(7) *Examples.*—The following examples illustrate the rules of this paragraph (b):

Example 1. No additional production. U.S. Mines, a U.S. corporation, operates a copper mine and mill in country X. U.S. Mines extracts copper-bearing rocks from the ground and transports the rocks to the mill where the rocks are ground and processed to produce copper-bearing concentrate. The concentrate is transported to a port where it is dried in preparation for export, stored and then shipped to purchasers in the United States. Because title to the property is passed in the United States and, under the facts and circumstances, none of U.S. Mine's activities constitutes additional production prior to the export terminal within the meaning of paragraph (b)(3)(ii) of this section, under paragraph (b)(1) and (b)(1)(ii) of this section, gross receipts equal to the fair market value of the concentrate at the export terminal will be from sources without the United States, and excess gross receipts will be from sources within the United States.

Example 2. No additional production. US Gas, a U.S. corporation, extracts natural gas within the United States, and transports the natural gas to a U.S. port where it is liquified in preparation for shipment. The liquified natural gas is then transported via freighter and sold without additional production activities in a foreign country. Liquefaction of natural gas is not an additional production activity because liquefaction prepares the natural gas for transportation from the export terminal. Therefore, under paragraph (b)(1) and (b)(1)(ii) of this section, gross receipts equal to the fair market value of the liquefied natural gas at the export terminal will be from sources within the United States, and excess gross receipts will be from sources without the United States.

Example 3. Sale in third country. US Gold, a U.S. corporation, mines gold in country X, produces gold jewelry in the United States, and sells the jewelry in country Y. Assume that the fair market value of the gold at the export terminal in country X is $40, and that US Gold ultimately sells the gold jewelry in country Y for $100. Under § 1.863-1(b), $40 of US Gold's gross receipts will be allocated to sources without the United States. Under paragraph (b)(1)(i) of this section, the source of the remaining $60 of gross receipts will be determined under § 1.863-3. If US Gold applies the 50/50 method described in § 1.863-3, $20 of cost of goods sold is properly attributable to activities subsequent to the export terminal, and all of US Gold's production assets subsequent to the export terminal are located in the United States, then $20 of gross income will be allocated to sources within the United States and $20 of gross income will be allocated to sources without the United States.

Example 4. Production in country of sale. US Oil, a U.S. corporation, extracts oil in country X, transports the oil via pipeline to the export terminal in country Y, refines the oil in the United States, and sells the refined product in the United States to unrelated persons. Assume that the fair market value of the oil at the export terminal in country Y is $80, and that US Oil ultimately sells the refined product for $100. Under paragraph (b)(1) of this section, $80 of US Oil's gross receipts will be allocated to sources without the United States, and under paragraph (b)(1)(ii) of this section the remaining $20 of gross receipts will be allocated to sources within the United States.

Example 5. Additional production prior to export. The facts are the same as in *Example 1*, except that U.S. Mines also operates a smelter in country X. The concentrate output from the mill is transported to the smelter where it is transformed into smelted copper. The smelted copper is exported to purchasers in the United States. Under the facts and circumstances, all of the processes applied to make copper concentrate are considered mining. Therefore, under paragraph (b)(2) of this section, gross receipts equal to the fair market value of the concentrate at the smelter will be from sources without the United States. Under the facts and circumstances, the conversion of the concentrate into smelted copper is an additional production activity in a foreign country within the meaning of paragraph (b)(3)(ii) of this section. Therefore, the source of U.S. Mine's excess gross receipts will be determined pursuant to paragraph (b)(2) of this section.

(c) *Determination of taxable income.*—The taxpayer's taxable income from sources within or without the United States will be determined under the rules of §§ 1.861-8 through 1.861-14T for determining taxable income from sources within the United States.

(d) *Scholarships, fellowship grants, grants, prizes and awards.*—(1) *In general.*—This paragraph (d) applies to scholarships, fellowship grants, grants, prizes and awards. The provisions of this paragraph (d) do not apply to amounts paid as salary or other compensation for services.

(2) *Source of income.*—The source of income from scholarships, fellowship grants, grants, prizes and awards is determined as follows:

(i) *United States source income.*—Except as provided in paragraph (d)(2)(iii) of this section, scholarships, fellowship grants, grants, prizes and awards made by a U.S. citizen or resident, a domestic partnership, a domestic corporation, an estate or trust (other than a foreign estate or trust within the meaning of section 7701(a)(31)), the United States (or an instrumentality or agency thereof), a State (or any political subdivision thereof), or the District of Columbia shall be treated as income from sources within the United States.

(ii) *Foreign source income.*—Scholarships, fellowship grants, grants, prizes and awards made by a foreign government (or an instrumentality, agency, or any political subdivision thereof), an international organization (as defined in section 7701(a)(18)), or a person other than a U.S. person (as defined in section 7701(a)(30)) shall be treated as income from sources without the United States.

(iii) *Certain activities conducted outside the United States.*—Scholarships, fellowship grants, targeted grants, and achievement awards received by a person other than a U.S. person (as defined in section 7701(a)(30)) with respect to activities previously conducted (in the case of achievement awards) or to be conducted (in the case of scholarships, fellowships grants, and targeted grants) outside the United States shall be treated as income from sources without the United States.

(3) *Definitions.*—The following definitions apply for purposes of this paragraph (d):

(i) *Scholarships* are defined in section 117 and the regulations thereunder.

(ii) *Fellowship grants* are defined in section 117 and the regulations thereunder.

(iii) *Prizes and awards* are defined in section 74 and the regulations thereunder.

(iv) *Grants* are amounts described in subparagraph (3) of section 4945(g) and the regulations thereunder, and are not amounts otherwise described in paragraphs (d)(3)(i), (ii), or (iii) of this section. For purposes of this paragraph (d), the reference to section 4945(g)(3) is applied without regard to the identity of the payor or recipient and without the application of the objective and nondiscriminatory basis test and the requirement of a procedure approved in advance.

(v) *Targeted grants* are grants—

(A) Issued by an organization described in section 501(c)(3), the United States (or an instrumentality or agency thereof), a State (or any political subdivision thereof), or the District of Columbia; and

(B) For an activity undertaken in the public interest and not primarily for the private financial benefit of a specific person or persons or organization.

(vi) *Achievement awards* are awards—

(A) Issued by an organization described in section 501(c)(3), the United States (or an instrumentality or agency thereof), a State (or political subdivision thereof), or the District of Columbia; and

(B) For a past activity undertaken in the public interest and not primarily for the private financial benefit of a specific person or persons or organization.

(4) *Effective dates.*—The following are the effective dates concerning this paragraph (d):

(i) *Scholarships and fellowship grants.*—This paragraph (d) is effective for scholarship and fellowship grant payments made after December 31, 1986. However, for scholarship and fellowship grant payments made after May 14, 1989, and before June 16, 1993, the residence of the payor rule of paragraph (d)(2)(i) and (ii) of this section may be applied without applying paragraph (d)(2)(iii) of this section.

(ii) *Grants, prizes and awards.*—This paragraph (d) is effective for payments made for grants, prizes and awards, targeted grants, and achievement awards after September 25, 1995. However, the taxpayer may elect to apply the provisions of this paragraph (d) to payments made for grants, prizes and awards, targeted grants, and achievement awards after December 31, 1986, and before September 26, 1995.

(e) *REMIC inducement fees.*—An inducement fee (as defined in § 1.446-6(b)(2)) shall be treated as income from sources within the United States.

(f) *Effective dates.*—The rules of paragraphs (a), (b), and (c) of this section apply to taxable years beginning after December 30, 1996. However, taxpayers may apply the rules of paragraphs (a), (b), and (c) of this section for taxable years beginning after July 11, 1995, and on or before December 30, 1996. For years beginning before December 30, 1996, see § 1.863-1 (as contained in 26 CFR part 1 revised as of April 1, 1996). See paragraph (d)(4) of this section for rules regarding the applicability date of paragraph (d) of this section. Paragraph (e) of this section is applicable for taxable years ending on or after May 11, 2004. [Reg. § 1.863-1.]

☐ [*T.D.* 6258, 10-23-57. *Amended by T.D.* 6348, 12-21-58; *T.D.* 8615, 8-24-95; *T.D.* 8687, 11-27-96 *and T.D.* 9128, 5-7-2004.]

§ 1.863-2. Allocation and apportionment of taxable income.—(a) *Determination of taxable income.*—Section 863(b) provides an alternate method for determining taxable income from sources within the United States in the case of gross income derived from sources partly within and partly without the United States. Under this method, taxable income is determined by deducting from such gross income the expenses, losses, or other deductions properly apportioned or allocated thereto and a ratable part of any other expenses, losses, or deductions that cannot definitely be allocated to some item or class of gross income. The income to which this section applies (and that is treated as derived partly from sources within and partly from sources without the United States) will consist of gains, profits, and income

(1) From certain transportation or other services rendered partly within and partly without the United States to the extent not within the scope of section 863(c) or other specific provisions of this title;

(2) From the sale of inventory property (within the meaning of section 865(i)) produced (in whole or in part) by the taxpayer in the United States and sold outside the United States or produced (in whole or in part) by the taxpayer outside the United States and sold in the United States; or

(3) Derived from the purchase of personal property within a possession of the United States and its sale within the United States, to the extent not excluded from the scope of these regulations under § 1.936-6(a)(5), Q&A 7.

(b) *Determination of source of taxable income.*—Income treated as derived from sources partly within and partly without the United States under paragraph (a) of this section may be allocated to sources within and without the United States pursuant to § 1.863-1 or apportioned to such sources in accordance with the methods described in other regulations under section 863. To determine the source of certain types of income described in paragraph (a)(1) of this section, see § 1.863-4. To determine the source of gross income described in paragraph (a)(2) of this section, see § 1.863-1 for natural resources and see § 1.863-3 for other inventory. Taxpayers, at their election, may apply the principles of § 1.863-3(b)(1) and (c) to determine the source of taxable income (rather than gross income) from sales of inventory property (other than natural resources). To determine the source of income partly from sources within a possession of the United States, including income described in paragraph (a)(3) of this section, see § 1.863-3(f).

(c) *Effective dates.*—This section will apply to taxable years beginning after December 30, 1996. However, taxpayers may apply the rules of this section for taxable years beginning after July 11, 1995, and on or before December 30, 1996. For years beginning before December 30, 1996, see § 1.863-2 (as contained in 26 CFR part 1 revised as of April 1, 1996). [Reg. § 1.863-2.]

☐ [*T.D.* 6258, 10-23-57. *Amended by T.D.* 8687, 11-27-96.]

§ 1.863-3. Allocation and apportionment of income from certain sales of inventory.—(a) *In general.*—(1) *Scope.*—Paragraphs (a) through (e) of this section apply to determine the source of income derived from the sale of inventory property (inventory), which a taxpayer produces (in whole or in part) within the United States and sells outside the United States, or which a taxpayer produces (in whole or in part) outside the United States and sells within the United States (Section 863 Sales). A taxpayer must divide gross income from Section 863 Sales between production activity and sales activity using one of the methods described in paragraph (b) of this section. The source of gross income from production activity and from sales activity must then be determined under paragraph (c) of this section. Taxable income from Section 863 Sales is determined under paragraph (d) of this section. Paragraph (e) of this section describes the rules for electing the methods described in paragraph (b) of this section and the information that a taxpayer must disclose on a tax return. Paragraph (f) of this section applies to determine the source of certain income derived from a possession of the United States. Paragraph (g) of this section provides special rules for partnerships for all sales subject to §§ 1.863-1 through 1.863-3. Paragraph (h) of this section provides effective dates for the rules in this section.

(2) *Rules of application for Section 863 Sales.*—Once a taxpayer has elected a method described in paragraph (b) of this section, the taxpayer must separately apply that method to Section 863 Sales in the United States and to Section 863 Sales outside the United States. In addition, the taxpayer must apply the rules of paragraphs (c) and (d) of this section by aggregating all Section 863 Sales to which a method described in paragraph (b) of this section applies, after separately applying that method to Section 863 Sales in the United States and to Section 863 Sales outside the United States. See section 865(i)(1) for the definition of inventory property. See also section 865(e)(2). See § 1.861-7(c) and paragraph (c)(2) of this section for the time and place of sale.

(b) *Methods to determine income attributable to production activity and sales activity.*— (1) *50/50 method.*—(i) *Determination of gross income.*—Generally, gross income from Section 863 Sales will be apportioned between production activity and sales activity under the 50/50 method as described in this paragraph (b)(1). Under the 50/50 method, one-half of the taxpayer's gross income will be considered income attributable to production activity and the source of that income will be determined under the rules of paragraph (c)(1) of this section. The remaining one-half of such gross income will be considered income attributable to sales activity and the source of that income will be determined under the rules of paragraph (c)(2) of this section. In lieu of the 50/50 method, the taxpayer may elect to determine the source of income from Section 863 Sales under the IFP method described in paragraph (b)(2) of this section or, with the consent of the District Director, the books and records method described in paragraph (b)(3) of this section.

(ii) *Example.*—The following example illustrates the rules of this paragraph (b)(1):

Example. 50/50 method. (i) P, a U.S. corporation, produces widgets in the United States. P sells the widgets for $100 to D, an unrelated foreign distributor, in another country. P's cost of goods sold is $40. Thus, P's gross income is $60.

(ii) Pursuant to the 50/50 method, one-half of P's gross income, or $30, is considered income attributable to production activity, and one-half of P's gross income, or $30, is considered income attributable to sales activity.

(2) *IFP method.*—(i) *Establishing an IFP.*—A taxpayer may elect to allocate gross income earned from production activity and sales activity using the independent factory price (IFP) method described in this paragraph (b)(2) if an IFP is fairly established. An IFP is fairly established based on a sale by the taxpayer only if the taxpayer regularly sells part of its output to wholly independent distributors or other selling concerns in such a way as to reasonably reflect the income earned from production activity. A sale will not be considered to fairly establish an IFP if sales activity by the taxpayer with respect to that sale is significant in relation to all of the activities with respect to that product.

(ii) *Applying the IFP method.*—If the taxpayer elects to use the IFP method, the amount of the gross sales price equal to the IFP will be treated as attributable to production activity, and the excess of the gross sales price over the IFP will be treated as attributable to sales activity. If a taxpayer elects to use the IFP method, the IFP must be applied to all Section 863 Sales of inventory that are substantially similar in physical characteristics and function, and are sold at a similar level of distribution as the inventory sold in the sale fairly establishing an IFP. The IFP will only be applied to sales that are reasonably contemporaneous with the sale fairly establishing the IFP. An IFP cannot be applied to sales in other geographic markets if the markets are substantially different. If the taxpayer elects the IFP method, the rules of this paragraph will also apply to determine the division of gross receipts between production activity and sales activity in a Section 863 Sale that itself fairly establishes an IFP. If the taxpayer elects to apply the IFP method, the IFP method must be applied to all sales for which an IFP may be fairly established and applied for that taxable year and each subsequent taxable year. The taxpayer will apply either the 50/50 method described in paragraph (b)(1) of this section or the books and records method described in paragraph (b)(3) of this section to any other Section 863 Sale for which an IFP cannot be established or applied for each taxable year.

(iii) *Determination of gross income.*—The amount of a taxpayer's gross income from production activity is determined by reducing the amount of gross receipts from production activity by the cost of goods sold properly attributable to production activity. The amount of a taxpayer's gross income from sales activity is determined by reducing the amount of gross receipts from sales activity by the cost of goods sold (if any) properly attributable to sales activity. The source of gross income from production activity is determined under the rules of paragraph (c)(1) of this section, and the source of gross income from sales activity will be determined under the rules of paragraph (c)(2) of this section.

(iv) *Examples.*—The following examples illustrate the rules of this paragraph (b)(2):

Example 1. IFP method. (i) P, a U.S. producer, purchases cotton and produces cloth in the United States. P sells cloth in country X to D, an unrelated foreign clothing manufacturer, for $100. Cost of goods sold for cloth is $80, entirely attributable to production activity. P does not engage in significant sales activity in relation to its other activities in the sales to D. Under these facts, the sale to D fairly establishes an IFP of $100. Assume that P elects to use the IFP method. Accordingly, $100 of the gross sales price is treated as attributable to production activity, and no amount of income from this sale is attributable to sales activity. After reducing the gross sales price by cost of goods sold, $20 of the gross income is treated as attributable to production activity ($100-$80).

(ii) P also sells cloth in country X to A, a unrelated foreign retail outlet, for $110. Because P elected the IFP method and the cloth is substantially similar to the cloth sold to D, the IFP fairly established in the sales to D must be used to determine the amount attributable to production activity in the sale to A. Accordingly, $100 of the gross sales price is treated as attributable to production activity and $10 ($110-$100) is attributable to sales activity. After reducing the gross sales price by cost of goods sold, $20 of the gross income is treated as attributable to production activity ($100-$80) and $10 is attributable to sales activity.

Example 2. Scope of IFP Method. (i) USCo manufactures three dissimilar products. USCo elects to apply the IFP method. In year 1, an IFP can be established for sales of product X, but not for products Y and Z. In year 2, an IFP cannot be established for any of USCo's products. In year 3, an IFP can be established for products X and Y, but not for product Z.

(ii) In year 1, USCo must apply the IFP method to sales of product X. In year 2, although USCo's IFP election remains in effect, USCo is not required to apply the IFP election to any products. In year 3, USCo is required to apply the IFP method to sales of products X and Y.

(3) *Books and records method.*—A taxpayer may elect to determine the amount of its gross income from Section 863 Sales that is attributable to production and sales activities for the taxable year based upon its books of account if it has received in advance the permission of the District Director having audit responsibility over its tax return. The taxpayer must establish to the satisfaction of the District Director that the taxpayer, in good faith and unaffected by considerations of tax liability, will regularly employ in its books of account a detailed allocation of receipts and expenditures which clearly reflects the amount of the taxpayer's income from production and sales activities. If a taxpayer receives permission to apply the books and records method, but does not comply with a material condition set forth by the District Director, the District Director may, in its discretion, revoke permission to use the books and records method. The source of gross income treated as attributable to production activity under this method may be determined under the rules of paragraph (c)(1) of this section, and the source of gross income attributable to sales activity will be determined under the rules of paragraph (c)(2) of this section.

(c) *Determination of the source of gross income from production activity and sales activity.*—(1) *Income attributable to production activity.*—(i) *Production only within the United States or only within foreign countries.*—(A) *Source of income.*—For purposes of this section, production activity means an activity that creates, fabricates, manufactures, extracts, processes, cures, or ages inventory. See § 1.864-1. Subject to the provisions in § 1.1502-13 or paragraph (g)(2)(ii) of this section, the only production activities that are taken into account for purposes of §§ 1.863-1, 1.863-2, and this section are those conducted directly by the taxpayer. Where the taxpayer's production assets are located only within the United States or only outside the United States, the income attributable to production activity is sourced where the taxpayer's production assets are located. For rules regarding the source of income when production assets are located both within the United States and without the United States, see paragraph (c)(1)(ii) of this section.

Reg. § 1.863-3(c)(1)(i)(A)

(B) *Definition of production assets.*—Subject to the provisions of § 1.1502-13 and paragraph (g)(2)(ii) of this section, production assets include only tangible and intangible assets owned directly by the taxpayer that are directly used by the taxpayer to produce inventory described in paragraph (a) of this section. Production assets do not include assets that are not directly used to produce inventory described in paragraph (a) of this section. Thus, production assets do not include such assets as accounts receivables, intangibles not related to production of inventory (e.g., marketing intangibles, including trademarks and customer lists), transportation assets, warehouses, the inventory itself, raw materials, or work-in-process. In addition, production assets do not include cash or other liquid assets (including working capital), investment assets, prepaid expenses, or stock of a subsidiary.

(C) *Location of production assets.*—For purposes of this section, a tangible production asset will be considered located where the asset is physically located. An intangible production asset will be considered located where the tangible production assets owned by the taxpayer to which it relates are located.

(ii) *Production both within the United States and within foreign countries.*—(A) *Source of income.*—Where the taxpayer's production assets are located both within and without the United States, income from sources without the United States will be determined by multiplying the income attributable to the taxpayer's production activity by a fraction, the numerator of which is the average adjusted basis of production assets that are located outside the United States and the denominator of which is the average adjusted basis of all production assets within and without the United States. The remaining income is treated as from sources within the United States.

(B) *Adjusted basis of production assets.*—For purposes of paragraph (c)(1)(ii)(A) of this section, the adjusted basis of an asset is determined under section 1011. The average adjusted basis is computed by averaging the adjusted basis of the asset at the beginning and end of the taxable year, unless by reason of material changes during the taxable year such average does not fairly represent the average for such year. In this event, the average adjusted basis will be determined upon a more appropriate basis. If production assets are used to produce inventory sold in Section 863 Sales and are also used to produce other property during the taxable year, the portion of its adjusted basis that is included in the fraction described in paragraph (c)(1)(ii)(A) of this section will be determined under any method that reasonably reflects the portion of the assets that produces inventory sold in Section 863 Sales. For example, the portion of such an asset that is included in the formula may be determined by multiplying the asset's average adjusted basis by a fraction, the numerator of which is the gross receipts from sales of inventory from Section 863 Sales produced by the asset, and the denominator of which is the gross receipts from all property produced by that asset.

(iii) *Anti-abuse rule.*—The purpose of this paragraph (c)(1) is to attribute the source of the taxpayer's production income to the location of the taxpayer's production activity. Therefore, if the taxpayer has entered into or structured one or more transactions with a principal purpose of reducing its U.S. tax liability by manipulating the formula described in paragraph (c)(1)(ii)(A) of this section in a manner inconsistent with the purpose of this paragraph (c)(1), the District Director may make appropriate adjustments so that the source of the taxpayer's income from production activity more clearly reflects the source of that income.

(iv) *Examples.*—The following examples illustrate the rules of this paragraph (c)(1):

Example 1. Source of production income. (i) A, a U.S. corporation, produces widgets that are sold both within the United States and within a foreign country. The initial manufacture of all widgets occurs in the United States. The second stage of production of widgets that are sold within a foreign country is completed within the country of sale. A's U.S. plant and machinery which is involved in the initial manufacture of the widgets has an average adjusted basis of $200. A also owns warehouses used to store work-in-process. A owns foreign equipment with an average adjusted basis of $25. A's gross receipts from all sales of widgets is $100, and its gross receipts from export sales of widgets is $25. Assume that apportioning average adjusted basis using gross receipts is reasonable. Assume A's cost of goods sold from the sale of widgets in the foreign countries is $13 and thus, its gross income from widgets sold in foreign countries is $12. A uses the 50/50 method to divide its gross income between production activity and sales activity.

(ii) A determines its production gross income from sources without the United States by multiplying one-half of A's $12 of gross income from sales of widgets in foreign countries, or $6, by a fraction, the numerator of which is all relevant foreign production assets, or $25, and the denominator of which is all relevant production assets, or $75 ($25 foreign assets + ($200 U.S. assets X $25 gross receipts from export sales/$100 gross receipts from all sales)). Therefore, A's gross production income from sources without the United States is $2 ($6 X ($25/$75).

Example 2. Location of intangible property. Assume the same facts as *Example 1*, except that A employs a patented process that applies only to the initial production of widgets. In computing the formula used to determine the source of income from production activity, A's patent, if it has an average adjusted basis, would be located in the United States.

Example 3. Anti-abuse rule. (i) Assume the same facts as *Example 1*. A sells its U.S. assets to B, an unrelated U.S. corporation, with a principal purpose of reducing its U.S. tax liability by manipulating the property fraction. A then leases these assets from B. After this transaction, under the general rule of paragraph (c)(1)(ii) of this section, all of A's production income would be considered from sources without the United States, because all of A's relevant production assets are located within a foreign country. Since the leased property is not owned by the taxpayer, it is not included in the fraction.

(ii) Because A has entered into a transaction with a principal purpose of reducing its U.S. tax liability by manipulating the formula described in paragraph (c)(1)(ii)(A) of this section, A's income must be adjusted to more clearly reflect the source of that income. In this case, the District Director may redetermine the source of A's production income by ignoring the sale-leaseback transactions.

(2) *Income attributable to sales activity.*—The source of the taxpayer's income that is attributable to sales activity will be determined under the provisions of § 1.861-7(c). However, notwithstanding any other provision, for purposes of section 863, the place of sale will be presumed to be the United States if personal property is wholly produced in the United States and the property is sold for use, consumption, or disposition in the United States. See § 1.864-6(b)(3)(ii) to determine the country of use, consumption, or disposition. Also, in applying this paragraph, property will be treated as wholly produced in the United States if it is subject to no more than packaging, repackaging, labeling, or other minor assembly operations outside the United States, within the meaning of § 1.954-3(a)(4)(iii) (property manufactured or produced by a controlled foreign corporation).

(d) *Determination of source of taxable income.*—Once the source of gross income has been determined under paragraph (c) of this section, the taxpayer must properly allocate and apportion separately under §§ 1.861-8 through 1.861-14T the amounts of its expenses, losses, and other deductions to its respective amounts of gross income from Section 863 Sales determined separately under each method described in paragraph (b) of this section. In addition, if the taxpayer deducts expenses for research and development under section 174 that may be attributed to its Section 863 Sales under § 1.861-8(e)(3), the taxpayer must separately allocate or apportion expenses, losses, and other deductions to its respective amounts of gross income from each relevant product category that the taxpayer uses in applying the rules of § 1.861-8(e)(3)(i)(A). In the case of gross income from Section 863 Sales determined under the IFP method or the books and records method, the rules of §§ 1.861-8 through 1.861-14T must apply to properly allocate or apportion amounts of expenses, losses and other deductions allocated and apportioned to such gross income between gross income from sources within and without the United States. In the case of gross income from Section 863 Sales determined under the 50/50 method, the amounts of expenses, losses, and other deductions allocated and apportioned to such gross income must be apportioned between sources within and without the United States pro rata based on the relative amounts of gross income from sources within and without the United States determined under the 50/50 method. Research and experimental expenditures qualifying under § 1.861-17 are allocated under that section, and are not allocated and apportioned pro rata under the 50/50 method.

(e) *Election and reporting rules.*—(1) *Elections under paragraph (b) of this section.*—If a taxpayer does not elect a method specified in paragraph (b)(2) or (3) of this section, the taxpayer must apply the method specified in paragraph (b)(1) of this section. The taxpayer may elect to apply the method specified in paragraph (b)(2) of this section by using the method on a timely filed original return (including extensions). A taxpayer may elect to apply the method specified in paragraph (b)(3) of this section by using the method on a timely filed original return (including extensions), but only if the taxpayer has received permission from the District Director to apply that method. Once a method under paragraph (b) of this section has been used, that method must be used in later taxable years unless the Commissioner consents to a change. However, if a taxpayer elects to change to or from the method specified in paragraph (b)(3) of this section, the taxpayer must obtain permission from the District Director instead of the Commissioner. Permission to change methods from one year to another year will not be withheld unless the change would result in a substantial

Reg. § 1.863-3(e)(1)

distortion of the source of the taxpayer's income.

(2) *Disclosure on tax return.*—A taxpayer who uses one of the methods described in paragraph (b) of this section must fully explain in a statement attached to the return the methodology used, the circumstances justifying use of that methodology, the extent that sales are aggregated, and the amount of income so allocated.

(f) *Income partly from sources within a possession of the United States.*—(1) *In general.*—This paragraph (f) relates to gains, profits, and income, which are treated as derived partly from sources within the United States and partly from sources within a possession of the United States (Section 863 Possession Sales). This paragraph (f) applies to determine the source of income derived from the sale of inventory produced (in whole or in part) by the taxpayer within the United States and sold within a possession, or produced (in whole or in part) by a taxpayer in a possession and sold within the United States (Possession Production Sales). It also applies to determine the source of income derived from the purchase of personal property within a possession of the United States and its sale within the United States (Possession Purchase Sales). A taxpayer subject to this paragraph (f) must divide gross income from Section 863 Possession Sales using one of the methods described in either paragraph (f)(2)(i) of this section (in the case of Possession Production Sales) or paragraph (f)(3)(i) of this section (in the case of Possession Purchase Sales). Once a taxpayer has elected a method, the taxpayer must separately apply that method to the applicable category of Section 863 Possession Sales in the United States and to those in a possession. The source of gross income from each type of activity must then be determined under either paragraph (f)(2)(ii) or (3)(ii) of this section, as appropriate. The source of taxable income from Section 863 Possession Sales is determined under paragraph (f)(4) of this section. The taxpayer must apply the rules for computing gross and taxable income by aggregating all Section 863 Possession Sales to which a method in this section applies after separately applying that method to Section 863 Possession Sales in the United States and to Section 863 Possession Sales in a possession. This section does not apply to determine the source of a taxpayer's gross income derived from a sale of inventory purchased from a corporation that has an election in effect under section 936, if the taxpayer's income from sales of that inventory is taken into account to determine benefits under section 936 for the section 936 corporation. For rules to be applied to determine the source of such income, see § 1.936-6(a)(5) Q&A 7a and 1.936-6(b)(1) Q&A 13.

(2) *Allocation or apportionment for Possession Production Sales.*—(i) *Methods for determining the source of gross income for Possession Production Sales.*—(A) *Possession 50/50 method.*—Under the possession 50/50 method, gross income from Possession Production Sales is allocated between production activity and business sales activity as described in this paragraph (f)(2)(i)(A). Under the possession 50/50 method, one-half of the taxpayer's gross income will be considered income attributable to production activity and the source of that income will be determined under the rules of paragraph (f)(2)(ii)(A) of this section. The remaining one-half of such gross income will be considered income attributable to business sales activity and the source of that income will be determined under the rules of paragraph (f)(2)(ii)(B) of this section.

(B) *IFP method.*—In lieu of the possession 50/50 method, a taxpayer may elect the independent factory price (IFP) method. Under the IFP method, gross income from Possession Production Sales is allocated to production activity or sales activity using the IFP method, as described in paragraph (b)(2) of this section, if an IFP is fairly established under the rules of paragraph (b)(2) of this section. See paragraphs (f)(2)(ii)(A) and (C) of this section for rules for determining the source of gross income attributable to production activity and sales activity.

(C) *Books and records method.*—A taxpayer may elect to allocate gross income using the books and records method described in paragraph (b)(3) of this section, if it has received in advance the permission of the District Director having audit responsibility over its return. See paragraph (f)(2)(ii) of this section for rules for determining the source of gross income.

(ii) *Determination of source of gross income from production, business sales, and sales activity.*—(A) *Gross income attributable to production activity.*—The source of gross income from production activity is determined under the rules of paragraph (c)(1) of this section, except that the term possession is substituted for foreign country wherever it appears.

(B) *Gross income attributable to business sales activity.*—(1) *Source of gross income.*—Gross income from the taxpayer's business sales activity is sourced in the possession in the same proportion that the amount of the taxpayer's business sales activity for the taxable year within the possession bears to the amount of the taxpayer's business sales activity for the taxable year both within the possession and outside the possession, with respect to Possession Production Sales. The remaining income is sourced in the United States.

(2) Business sales activity.—For purposes of this paragraph (f)(2)(ii)(B), the taxpayer's business sales activity is equal to the sum of—

(i) The amounts for the taxable period paid for wages, salaries, and other compensation of employees, and other expenses attributable to Possession Production Sales (other than amounts that are nondeductible under section 263A, interest, and research and development); and

(ii) Possession Production Sales for the taxable period.

(3) Location of business sales activity.—For purposes of determining the location of the taxpayer's business activity within a possession, the following rules apply:

(i) Sales.—Receipts from gross sales will be attributed to a possession under the provisions of paragraph (c)(2) of this section.

(ii) Expenses.—Expenses will be attributed to a possession under the rules of §§ 1.861-8 through 1.861-14T.

(C) *Gross income attributable to sales activity.*—The source of the taxpayer's income that is attributable to sales activity, as determined under the IFP method or the books and records method, will be determined under the provisions of paragraph (c)(2) of this section.

(3) *Allocation or apportionment for Possession Purchase Sales.*—(i) *Methods for determining the source of gross income for Possession Purchase Sales.*—(A) *Business activity method.*—Gross income from Possession Purchase Sales is allocated in its entirety to the taxpayer's business activity, and is then apportioned between U.S. and possession sources under paragraph (f)(3)(ii) of this section.

(B) *Books and records method.*—A taxpayer may elect to allocate gross income using the books and records method described in paragraph (b)(3) of this section, subject to the conditions set forth in paragraph (b)(3) of this section. See paragraph (f)(2)(ii) of this section for rules for determining the source of gross income.

(ii) *Determination of source of gross income from business activity.*—(A) *Source of gross income.*—Gross income from the taxpayer's business activity is sourced in the possession in the same proportion that the amount of the taxpayer's business activity for the taxable year within the possession bears to the amount of the taxpayer's business activity for the taxable year both within the possession and outside the possession, with respect to Possession Purchase Sales. The remaining income is sourced in the United States.

(B) *Business activity.*—For purposes of this paragraph (f)(3)(ii), the taxpayer's business activity is equal to the sum of—

(1) The amounts for the taxable period paid for wages, salaries, and other compensation of employees, and other expenses attributable to Possession Purchase Sales (other than amounts that are nondeductible under section 263A, interest, and research and development);

(2) Cost of goods sold attributable to Possession Purchase Sales during the taxable period; and

(3) Possession Purchase Sales for the taxable period.

(C) *Location of business activity.*—For purposes of determining the location of the taxpayer's business activity within a possession, the following rules apply:

(1) Sales.—Receipts from gross sales will be attributed to a possession under the provisions of paragraph (c)(2) of this section.

(2) Cost of goods sold.—Payments for cost of goods sold will be properly attributable to gross receipts from sources within the possession only to the extent that the property purchased was manufactured, produced, grown, or extracted in the possession (within the meaning of section 954(d)(1)(A)).

(3) Expenses.—Expenses will be attributed to a possession under the rules of §§ 1.861-8 through 1.861-14T.

(iii) *Examples.*—The following examples illustrate the rules of paragraph (f)(3)(ii) of this section relating to the determination of source of gross income from business activity:

Example 1. (i) U.S. Co. purchases in a possession product X for $80 from A. A manufactures X in the possession. Without further production, U.S. Co. sells X in the United States for $100. Assume U.S. Co. has sales and administrative expenses in the possession of $10.

(ii) To determine the source of U.S. Co.'s gross income, the $100 gross income from sales of X is allocated entirely to U.S. Co.'s business activity. Forty-seven dollars of U.S. Co.'s gross income is sourced in the possession. [Possession expenses ($10) plus possession purchases (i.e., cost of goods sold) ($80) plus possessions sales ($0), divided by total expenses ($10) plus total purchases ($80) plus total sales ($100).] The remaining $53 is sourced in the United States.

Example 2. (i) Assume the same facts as in *Example 1*, except that A manufactures X outside the possession.

(ii) To determine the source of U.S. Co.'s gross income, the $100 gross income is allocated entirely to U.S. Co.'s business activity. Five dollars of U.S. Co.'s gross income is sourced in the possession. [Possession expenses ($10) plus possession purchases ($0) plus possession sales ($0), divided by total expenses ($10) plus total purchases ($80) plus total sales ($100).] The $80 purchase is not included in the numerator used to determine U.S. Co.'s business activity in the possession, since product X was not manufactured in the possession. The remaining $95 is sourced in the United States.

(4) *Determination of source of taxable income.*—Once the source of gross income has been determined under paragraph (f)(2) or (3) of this section, the taxpayer must properly allocate and apportion separately under §§ 1.861-8 through 1.861-14T the amounts of its expenses, losses, and other deductions to its respective amounts of gross income from Section 863 Possession Sales determined separately under each method described in paragraph (f)(2) or (3) of this section. In addition, if the taxpayer deducts expenses for research and development under section 174 that may be attributed to its Section 863 Possession Sales under § 1.861-17, the taxpayer must separately allocate or apportion expenses, losses, and other deductions to its respective amounts of gross income from each relevant product category that the taxpayer uses in applying the rules of § 1.861-17. Thus, in the case of gross income from Section 863 Possession Sales determined under the IFP method or books and records method, a taxpayer must apply the rules of §§ 1.861-8 through 1.861-14T to properly allocate or apportion amounts of expenses, losses and other deductions, allocated and apportioned to such gross income, between gross income from sources within and without the United States. However, in the case of gross income from Possession Production Sales determined under the possessions 50/50 method or gross income from Possession Purchase Sales computed under the business activity method, the amounts of expenses, losses, and other deductions allocated and apportioned to such gross income must be apportioned between sources within and without the United States pro rata based on the relative amounts of gross income from sources within and without the United States determined under those methods, except that the rules regarding the allocation and apportionment of research and experimental expenditures in § 1.861-17 shall apply to such expenditures of taxpayers using the 50/50 method.

(5) *Special rules for partnerships.*—In applying the rules of this paragraph (f) to transactions involving partners and partnerships, the rules of paragraph (g) of this section apply.

(6) *Election and reporting rules.*—(i) *Elections under paragraph (f)(2) or (3) of this section.*—If a taxpayer does not elect one of the methods specified in paragraph (f)(2) or (3) of this section, the taxpayer must apply the possession 50/50 method in the case of Possession Production Sales or the business activity method in the case of Possession Purchase Sales. The taxpayer may elect to apply a method specified in either paragraph (f)(2) or (3) of this section by using the method on a timely filed original return (including extensions). Once a method has been used, that method must be used in later taxable years unless the Commissioner consents to a change. Permission to change methods from one year to another year will be granted unless the change would result in a substantial distortion of the source of the taxpayer's income.

(ii) *Disclosure on tax return.*—A taxpayer who uses one of the methods described in paragraph (f)(2) or (3) of this section must fully explain in a statement attached to the tax return the methodology used, the circumstances justifying use of that methodology, the extent that sales are aggregated, and the amount of income so allocated.

(g) *Special rules for partnerships.*—(1) *General rule.*—For purposes of § 1.863-1 and this section, a taxpayer's production or sales activity does not include production and sales activities conducted by a partnership of which the taxpayer is a partner either directly or through one or more partnerships, except as otherwise provided in paragraph (g)(2) of this section.

(2) *Exceptions.*—(i) *In general.*—For purposes of determining the source of the partner's distributive share of partnership income or determining the source of the partner's income from the sale of inventory property which the partnership distributes to the partner in kind, the partner's production or sales activity includes an activity conducted by the partnership. In addition, the production activity of a partnership includes the production activity of a taxpayer that is a partner either directly or through one or more partnerships, to the extent that the partner's production activity is related to inventory that the partner contrib-

utes to the partnership in a transaction described under section 721.

(ii) *Attribution of production assets to or from a partnership.*—A partner will be treated as owning its proportionate share of the partnership's production assets only to the extent that, under paragraph (g)(2)(i) of this section, the partner's activity includes production activity conducted through a partnership. A partner's share of partnership assets will be determined by reference to the partner's distributive share of partnership income for the year attributable to such production assets. Similarly, to the extent a partnership's activities include the production activities of a partner, the partnership will be treated as owning the partner's production assets related to the inventory that is contributed in kind to the partnership. See paragraph (c)(1)(ii)(B) of this section for rules apportioning the basis of assets to Section 863 Sales.

(iii) *Basis.*—For purposes of this section, in those cases where the partner is treated as owning its proportionate share of the partnership's production assets, the partner's basis in production assets held through a partnership shall be determined by reference to the partnership's adjusted basis in its assets (including a partner's special basis adjustment, if any, under section 743). Similarly, a partnership's basis in a partner's production assets is determined with reference to the partner's adjusted basis in its assets.

(iv) *Separate application of methods.*—If, under paragraph (g)(2) of this section, a partner is treated as conducting the activity of a partnership, and is treated as owning its proportionate share of a partnership's production assets, a partner must apply the method it has elected under paragraph (b) of this section separately to Section 863 Sales described in this paragraph (g) and all other Section 863 Sales.

(3) *Examples.*—The following examples illustrate the rules of this paragraph (g):

Example 1. Distributive share of partnership income. A, a U.S. corporation, forms a partnership in the United States with B, a country X corporation. A and B each have a 50 percent interest in the income, gains, losses, deductions and credits of the partnership. The partnership is engaged in the manufacture and sale of widgets. The widgets are manufactured in the partnership's plant located in the United States and are sold by the partnership outside the United States. The partnership owns the manufacturing facility and all other production assets used to produce the widgets. A's distributive share of partnership income includes 50 percent of the sales income from these sales. In applying the rules of section 863 to determine the source of its distributive share of partnership income from the export sales of widgets, A is treated as carrying on the activity of the partnership related to production of these widgets and as owning a proportionate share of the partnership's assets related to production of the widgets, based upon its distributive share of partnership income.

Example 2. Distribution in kind. Assume the same facts as in *Example 1* except that the partnership, instead of selling the widgets, distributes the widgets to A and B. A then further processes the widgets and then sells them outside the United States. In determining the source of the income earned by A on the sales outside the United States, A is treated as conducting the activities of the partnership related to production of the distributed widgets. Thus, the source of gross income on the sale of the widgets is determined under section 863 and these regulations. A applies the 50/50 method described in paragraph (b)(1) of this section to determine the source of income from the sales. In applying paragraph (c)(1) of this section, A is treated as owning its proportionate share of the partnership's production assets based upon its distributive share of partnership income.

(h) *Effective dates.*—The rules of this section apply to taxable years beginning after December 30, 1996. However, taxpayers may apply these regulations for taxable years beginning after July 11, 1995, and on or before December 30, 1996. For years beginning before December 30, 1996, see §§ 1.863-3A and 1.863-3AT. However, the rules of paragraph (f) of this section apply to taxable years beginning on or after November 13, 1998. [Reg. § 1.863-3.]

☐ [*T.D. 8687, 11-27-96. Amended by T.D. 8786, 10-13-98.*]

Proposed Amendments to Regulation

§ 1.863-3. Allocation and apportionment of income from certain sales of inventory.—(a)

* * *

(1) * * * To determine the source of income from sales of property produced by the taxpayer, when the property is either produced in whole or in part in space or on or under water not within the jurisdiction (as recognized by the United States) of a foreign country, possession of the United States, or the United States (in international water), or is sold in space or in international water, the rules of § 1.863-8 apply, and the rules of this section do not apply, except to the extent provided in § 1.863-8. * * *

* * *

(c) * * *

(1) * * *

(i) * * *

(A) * * * For rules regarding the source of income when production takes place, in whole or in part, in space or in international water, the rules of § 1.863-8 apply, and the rules of this section do not apply except to the extent provided in § 1.863-8.

* * *

(2) * * * Notwithstanding any other provision, for rules regarding the source of income when a sale takes place in space or in international water, the rules of § 1.863-8 apply, and the rules of this section do not apply except to the extent provided in § 1.863-8. * * * The place of sale will be presumed to be the United States under this rule when property is produced in the United States and the property is sold to a U.S. resident, who uses the property in space or in international water. In such cases, the property will be treated as sold for use, consumption, or disposition in the United States.

* * *

[Prop. Reg. § 1.863-3.]

[Proposed 1-17-2001.]

Proposed Amendments to Regulation

☐ Paragraph (h) is redesignated as paragraph (i) and a new paragraph (h) is added to read as follows:

§ 1.863-3. Allocation and apportionment of income from certain sales of inventory.

* * *

(h) *Income from a global dealing operation.*—(1) *Purpose and scope.*—This paragraph (h) provides rules for sourcing income, gain and loss from a global dealing operation that, under the rules of § 1.482-8, is earned by or allocated to a controlled taxpayer qualifying as a participant in a global dealing operation under § 1.482-8(a)(2)(ii). This paragraph (h) does not apply to income earned by or allocated to a controlled taxpayer qualifying as a participant in a global dealing operation that is specifically sourced under sections 861, 862 or 865, or to substitute payments earned by a participant in a global dealing operation that are sourced under § 1.861-2(a)(7) or § 1.861-3(a)(6).

(2) *In general.*—The source of any income, gain or loss to which this section applies shall be determined by reference to the residence of the participant. For purposes of this paragraph (h), the residence of a participant shall be determined under section 988(a)(3)(B).

(3) *Qualified business units as participants in global dealing operations.*—(i) *In general.*—Except as otherwise provided in this paragraph (h), where a single controlled taxpayer conducts a global dealing operation through one or more qualified business units (QBUs), as defined in section 989(a) and § 1.989(a)-1, the source of income, gain or loss generated by the global dealing operation and earned by or allocated to the controlled taxpayer shall be determined by applying the rules of § 1.482-8 as if each QBU that performs activities of a regular dealer in securities as defined in § 1.482-8(a)(2)(ii)(A) or the related activities described in § 1.482-8(a)(2)(ii)(B) were a separate controlled taxpayer qualifying as a participant in the global dealing operation within the meaning of § 1.482-8(a)(2)(ii). Accordingly, the amount of income sourced in the United States and outside of the United States shall be determined by treating the QBU as a participant in the global dealing operation, allocating income to each participant under § 1.482-8, as modified by paragraph (h)(3)(ii) of this section, and sourcing the income to the United States or outside of the United States under § 1.863-3(h)(2).

(ii) *Economic effects of a single legal entity.*—In applying the principles of § 1.482-8, the taxpayer shall take into account the economic effects of conducting a global dealing operation through a single entity instead of multiple legal entities. For example, since the entire capital of a corporation supports all of the entity's transactions, regardless of where those transactions may be booked, the payment of a guarantee fee within the entity is inappropriate and will be disregarded.

(iii) *Treatment of interbranch and interdesk amounts.*—An agreement among QBUs of the same taxpayer to allocate income, gain or loss from transactions with third parties is not a transaction because a taxpayer cannot enter into a contract with itself. For purposes of this paragraph (h)(3), however, such an agreement, including a risk transfer agreement (as defined in § 1.475(g)-2(b)) may be used to determine the source of global dealing income from transactions with third parties in the same manner and to the same extent that transactions between controlled taxpayers in a global dealing operation may be used to allocate income, gain or loss from the global dealing operation under the rules of § 1.482-8.

(iv) *Deemed QBU.*—For purposes of this paragraph (h)(3), a QBU shall include a U.S. trade or business that is deemed to exist because of the activities of a dependent agent in the United States, without regard to the books and records requirement of § 1.989(a)-1(b).

(v) *Examples.*—The following examples illustrate this paragraph (h)(3).

Example 1. Use of comparable uncontrolled financial transactions method to source global dealing income between branches. (i) F is a foreign bank that acts as a market maker in foreign currency through branch offices in London, New York, and Tokyo. In a typical business day, the foreign exchange desk in F's U.S. branch (USFX) enters into several hundred spot and forward contracts on the interbank market to purchase and sell Deutsche marks (DM) with unrelated third parties. Each of F's branches, including USFX, employs both marketers and traders for their foreign currency dealing. In addition, USFX occasionally transfers risk with respect to its third party DM contracts to F's London and Tokyo branches. These interbranch transfers are entered into in the same manner as trades with unrelated third parties. On a typical day, risk management responsibility for no more than 10% of USFX's DM trades are transferred interbranch. F records these transfers by making notations on the books of each branch that is a party to the transfers. The accounting procedures are nearly identical to those followed when a branch enters into an offsetting hedge with a third party. USFX maintains contemporaneous records of its interbranch transfers and third party transactions, separated according to type of trade and counterparty. Moreover, the volume of USFX's DM spot purchases and sales each day consistently provides USFX with third party transactions that are contemporaneous with the transfers between the branches.

(ii) As provided in paragraph (h)(3)(i) of this section, USFX and F's other branches that trade DM are participants in a global dealing operation. Accordingly, the principles of § 1.482-8 apply in determining the source of income earned by F's qualified business units that are participants in a global dealing operation. Applying the comparability factors in § 1.482-8(a)(3) shows that USFX's interbranch transfers and uncontrolled DM-denominated spot and forward contracts have no material differences. Because USFX sells DM in uncontrolled transactions and transfers risk management responsibility for DM-denominated contracts, and the uncontrolled transactions and interbranch transfers are consistently entered into contemporaneously, the interbranch transfers provide a reliable measure of an arm's length allocation of third party income from F's global dealing operation in DM-denominated contracts. This allocation of third party income is treated as U.S. source in accordance with §§ 1.863-3(h) and 1.988-4(h) and accordingly will be treated as income effectively connected with F's U.S. trade or business under § 1.864-4.

Example 2. Residual profit split between branches. (i) F is a bank organized in country X that has a AAA credit rating and engages in a global dealing operation in foreign currency options through branch offices in London, New York, and Tokyo. F has dedicated marketers and traders in each branch who work closely together to design and sell foreign currency options that meet the particular needs of customers. Each branch also employs general salespeople who sell standardized foreign currency options, as well as other financial products and foreign currency offered by F. F's traders work from a common book of transactions that is risk managed at each branch during local business hours. Accordingly, all three branches share the responsibility for risk managing the book of products. Personnel in the home office of F process and confirm trades, reconcile trade tickets, and provide ongoing administrative support (back office services) for the other branches. The global dealing operation has generated $223 of operating profit for the period.

(ii) Under § 1.863-3(h), F applies § 1.482-8 to allocate global dealing income among its branches, because F's London, New York, and Tokyo branches are treated as participants in a global dealing operation that deals in foreign currency options under § 1.482-8(a)(2). After analyzing the foreign currency options business, F has determined that the residual profit split method is the best method to determine an arm's length amount of compensation allocable to each participant in the global dealing operation.

(iii) Under the first step of the residual profit split method (§ 1.482-8(e)(6)(ii)), F identifies and compensates the routine contributions performed by each participant. F determines that an arm's length compensation for general salespeople is $3, $4, and $5 in New York, London, and Tokyo, respectively, and that the home office incurred $11 of expenses in providing the back office services. Since F's capital legally supports all of the obligations of the branches, no amount is allocated to the home office of F for the provision of capital.

(iv) The second step of the residual profit split method (§ 1.482-8(e)(6)(iii)) requires that the residual profit be allocated to participants according to their nonroutine contributions. F determines that a multi-factor formula best reflects these contributions. After a detailed functional analysis, and applying the comparability factors in § 1.482-8(a)(3), 40% of the residual profit is allocated to the London branch, 35% to the New York branch, and the remaining 25% to the Tokyo branch. Thus, the residual profit of $200 ($223 operating profit

Prop. Reg. § 1.863-3(h)(3)(v)

minus $12 general salesperson commissions minus $11 back office allocation) is allocated $80 to London (40% allocation × $200), $70 to New York (35% × $200) and $50 to Tokyo (25% × $200).

Example 3. Residual profit split—deemed branches. (i) P, a U.K. corporation, conducts a global dealing operation in notional principal contracts, directly and through a U.S. subsidiary (USsub) and a Japanese subsidiary (Jsub). P is the counterparty to all transactions entered into with third parties. P, USsub, and Jsub each employ marketers and traders who work closely together to design and sell derivative products to meet the particular needs of customers. USsub also employs personnel who process and confirm trades, reconcile trade tickets and provide ongoing administrative support (back office services) for the global dealing operation. The global dealing operation maintains a single common book for each type of risk, and the book is maintained where the head trader for that type of risk is located. However, P, USsub, and Jsub have authorized a trader located in each of the other affiliates to risk manage its books during periods when the primary trading location is closed. This grant of authority is necessary because marketers, regardless of their location, are expected to sell all of the group's products, and need to receive pricing information with respect to products during their clients' business hours, even if the booking location is closed. The global dealing operation has generated $180 of operating profit for the period.

(ii) Because employees of USsub have authority to enter into contracts in the name of P, P is treated as being engaged in a trade or business in the United States through a deemed QBU. § 1.863-3(h)(3)(iv). Similarly, under U.S. principles, P would be treated as being engaged in business in Japan through a QBU. Under § 1.482-8(a)(2), P, USsub, and Jsub are participants in the global dealing operation relating to notional principal contracts. Additionally, under § 1.863-3(h)(3), the U.S. and Japanese QBUs are treated as participants in a global dealing operation for purposes of sourcing the income from that operation. Under § 1.863-3(h), P applies the methods in § 1.482-8 to determine the source of income allocated to the U.S. and non-U.S. QBUs of P.

(iii) After analyzing the notional principal contract business, P has concluded that the residual profit split method is the best method to allocate income under § 1.482-8 and to source income under § 1.863-3(h).

(iv) Under the first step of the residual profit split method (§ 1.482-8(e)(6)(ii)), P identifies and compensates the routine contributions performed by each participant. Although the back office function does not give rise to participant status, in the context of a residual profit split allocation, the back office function is relevant for purposes of receiving remuneration for a routine contribution to a global dealing operation. P determines that an arm's length compensation for the back office is $20. Since the back office services constitute a routine contribution, $20 of income is allocated to USsub under step 1 of the residual profit split method. Similarly, as the arm's length compensation for the risk to which P is subject as counterparty is $40, $40 is allocated to P as compensation for acting as counterparty.

(v) The second step of the residual profit split method (§ 1.482-8(e)(6)(iii)) requires that the residual profit be allocated to participants according to the relative value of their nonroutine contributions. Under P's transfer pricing method, P allocates the residual profit of $120 ($180 gross income minus $20 for back office services minus $40 compensation for the routine contribution of acting as counterparty) using a multi-factor formula that reflects the relative value of the nonroutine contributions. Applying the comparability factors set out in § 1.482-8(a)(3), P allocates 40% of the residual profit to P, 35% of the residual profit to USsub, and the remaining 25% of residual profit to Jsub. Accordingly, under step 2, $48 is allocated to P, $42 is allocated to USsub, and $30 is allocated to Jsub. Under § 1.863-3(h), the amounts allocated under the residual profit split is sourced according to the residence of each participant to which it is allocated.

(vi) Because the $40 allocated to P consists of compensation for the use of capital, the allocation is sourced according to where the capital is employed. Accordingly, the $40 is sourced 35% to P's deemed QBU in the United States under § 1.863-3(h)(3)(iv) and 65% to non-U.S. sources.

* * *

[Prop. Reg. § 1.863-3.]

[Proposed 3-6-98.]

§ 1.863-4. Certain transportation services.—(a) *General.*—A taxpayer carrying on the business of transportation service (other than an activity giving rise to transportation income described in section 863(c) or to income subject to other specific provisions of this title) between points in the United States and points outside the United States derives income partly from sources within and partly from sources without the United States.

(b) *Gross income.*—The gross income from sources within the United States derived from such services shall be determined by taking such a portion of the total gross revenues therefrom as (1) the sum of the costs or expenses of such transportation business carried on by the taxpayer within the United States and a reasonable return upon the property used in its transportation business while within the United States bears to (2) the sum of the total costs or expenses of such transportation business carried on by the taxpayer and a reasonable return upon the total property used in such transportation business. Revenues from operations incidental to transportation services, such as the sale of money orders, shall be apportioned on the same basis as direct revenues from transportation services.

(c) *Allocation of costs or expenses.*—In allocating the total costs or expenses incurred in such transportation business, costs or expenses incurred in connection with that part of the services which was wholly rendered in the United States shall be assigned to the cost of transportation business within the United States. For example, expenses of loading and unloading in the United States, rentals, office expenses, salaries, and wages wholly incurred for services rendered to the taxpayer in the United States belong to this class. Costs and expenses incurred in connection with services rendered partly within and partly without the United States may be prorated on a reasonable basis between such services. For example, ship wages, charter money, insurance, and supplies chargeable to voyage expenses shall ordinarily be prorated for each voyage on the basis of the proportion which the number of days the ship was within the territorial limits of the United States bears to the total number of days on the voyage; and fuel consumed on each voyage may be prorated on the basis of the proportion which the number of miles sailed within the territorial limits of the United States bears to the total number of miles sailed on the voyage. For other expenses entering into the cost of services, only such expenses as are allowable deductions under the internal revenue laws shall be taken into account.

(d) *Items not included as costs or expenses.*—(1) *Taxes and interest.*—Income, war profits, and excess profits taxes shall not be regarded as costs or expenses for the purpose of determining the proportion of gross income from sources within the United States; and, for such purpose, interest and other expenses for the use of borrowed capital shall not be taken into the cost of services rendered, for the reason that the return upon the property used measures the extent to which such borrowed capital is the source of the income. See paragraph (f)(2) of this section.

(2) *Other business activity and general expenses.*—If a taxpayer subject to this section is also engaged in a business other than that of providing transportation service between points in the United States and points outside the United States, the costs and expenses, including taxes, properly apportioned or allocated to such other business shall be excluded both from the deductions and from the apportionment process prescribed in paragraph (c) of this section; but, for the purpose of determining taxable income, a ratable part of any general expenses, losses, or deductions, which cannot definitely be allocated to some item or class of gross income, may be deducted from the gross income from sources within the United States after the amount of such gross income has been determined. Such ratable part shall ordinarily be based upon the ratio of gross income from sources within the United States to the total gross income. See paragraph (f)(3) of this section.

(3) *Personal exemptions and special deductions.*—The deductions for the personal exemptions, and the special deductions described in paragraph (c) of §1.861-8, shall not be taken into account for purposes of paragraph (c) of this section.

(e) *Property used while within the United States.*—(1) *General.*—The value of the property used shall be determined upon the basis of cost less depreciation. Eight percent may ordinarily be taken as a reasonable rate of return to apply to such property. The property taken shall be the average property employed in the transportation service between points in the United States and points outside the United States during the taxable year.

(2) *Average property.*—For ships, the average shall be determined upon a daily basis for each ship, and the amount to be apportioned for each ship as assets employed within the United States shall be computed upon the proportion which the number of days the ship was within the territorial limits of the United States bears to the total number of days the ship was in service during the taxable period. For other assets employed in the transportation business, the average of the assets at the beginning and end of the taxable period ordinarily may be taken, but if the average so obtained does not, by reason of material changes during the taxable year, fairly represent the average for such year either for the assets employed in the transportation business in the United States or in total, the average must be determined upon a monthly or daily basis.

(3) *Current assets.*—Current assets shall be decreased by current liabilities and allocated to services between the United States and foreign countries and to other services. The part allocated to services between the United States

and foreign countries shall be based on the proportion which the gross receipts from such services bear to the gross receipts from all services. The amount so allocated to services between the United States and foreign countries shall be further allocated to services rendered within the United States and to services rendered without the United States. The portion allocable to services rendered within the United States shall be based on the proportion which the expenses incurred within the territorial limits of the United States bear to the total expenses incurred in services between the United States and foreign countries.

(f) *Taxable income.*—(1) *General.*—In computing taxable income from sources within the United States there shall be allowed as deductions from the gross income from such sources, determined in accordance with paragraph (b) of this section, (i) the expenses of the transportation business carried on within the United States (as determined under paragraphs (c) and (d) of this section) and (ii) the expenses and deductions determined in accordance with this paragraph.

(2) *Interest and taxes.*—Interest and income, war-profits, and excess profits taxes shall be excluded from the apportionment process, as indicated in paragraph (d) of this section; but, for the purpose of computing taxable income, there may be deducted from the gross income from sources within the United States, after the amount of such gross income has been determined, a ratable part of all interest deductible under section 163 and of all income, war-profits, and excess profits taxes deductible under section 164, paid or accrued in respect of the business of transportation service between points in the United States and points outside the United States. The ratable part shall ordinarily be based upon the ratio of gross income from sources within the United States to the total gross income, from such transportation service.

(3) *General expenses.*—General expenses, losses, or deductions shall be deducted under this paragraph to the extent indicated in paragraph (d)(2) of this section.

(4) *Personal exemptions.*—The deductions for the personal exemptions shall be allowed under this paragraph to the same extent as provided by paragraph (b) of § 1.861-8.

(5) *Special deductions.*—The special deductions allowed in the case of a corporation by sections 241, 922, and 941 shall be allowed under this paragraph to the same extent as provided by paragraph (c) of § 1.861-8.

(g) *Allocation based on books of account.*—Application for permission to base the return upon the taxpayer's books of account will be considered by the district director (or, if applicable, the Director of International Operations) in the case of any taxpayer subject to this section, who, in good faith and unaffected by considerations of tax liability, regularly employs in his books of account a detailed allocation of receipts and expenditures which more clearly reflects the income derived from sources within the United States than does the process prescribed by paragraphs (b) to (f), inclusive, of this section. [Reg. § 1.863-4.]

☐ [T.D. 6258, 10-23-57. Amended by T.D. 8687, 11-27-96.]

§ 1.863-7. Allocation of income attributable to certain notional principal contracts under section 863(a).—(a) *Scope.*—(1) *Introduction.*—This section provides rules relating to the source and, in certain cases, the character of notional principal contract income. However, this section does not apply to income from a section 988 transaction within the meaning of section 988 and the regulations thereunder, relating to the treatment of certain nonfunctional currency transactions. Notional principal contract income is income attributable to a notional principal contract. A notional principal contract is a financial instrument that provides for the payment of amounts by one party to another at specified intervals calculated by reference to a specified index upon a notional principal amount in exchange for specified consideration or a promise to pay similar amounts. An agreement between a taxpayer and a qualified business unit (as defined in section 989(a)) of the taxpayer, or among qualified business units of the same taxpayer, is not a notional principal contract, because a taxpayer cannot enter into a contract with itself.

(2) *Effective date.*—This section applies to notional principal contract income includible in income on or after February 13, 1991. However, any taxpayer desiring to apply paragraph (b)(2)(iv) of this section to notional principal contract income includible in income prior to February 13, 1991 in lieu of temporary Income Tax Regulations § 1.863-7T(b)(2)(iv) may (on a consistent basis) so choose. See paragraph (c) of this section for an election to apply the rules of this section to notional principal contract income includible in income before December 24, 1986.

(b) *Source of notional principal contract income.*—(1) *General rule.*—Unless paragraph (b)(2) or (3) of this section applies, the source of notional principal contract income shall be determined by reference to the residence of the taxpayer as determined under section 988(a)(3)(B)(i).

(2) *Qualified business unit exception.*—The source of notional principal contract income shall be determined by reference to the residence of a qualified business unit of a taxpayer if—

(i) The taxpayer's residence, determined under section 988(a)(3)(B)(i), is the United States;

(ii) The qualified business unit's residence, determined under section 988(a)(3)(B)(ii), is outside the United States;

(iii) The qualified business unit is engaged in the conduct of a trade or business where it is a resident as determined under section 988(a)(3)(B)(ii); and

(iv) The notional principal contract is properly reflected on the books of the qualified business unit. Whether a notional principal contract is properly reflected on the books of such qualified business unit is a question of fact. The degree of participation in the negotiation and acquisition of a notional principal contract shall be considered in this determination. Participation in connection with the negotiation or acquisition of a notional principal contract may be disregarded if the district director determines that a purpose for such participation was to affect the source of notional principal contract income.

(3) *Effectively connected notional principal contract income.*—Notional principal contract income that under principles similar to those set forth in §1.864-4(c) arises from the conduct of a United States trade or business shall be sourced in the United States and such income shall be treated as effectively connected to the conduct of a United States trade or business for purposes of sections 871(b) and 882(a)(1).

(c) *Election.*—(1) *Eligibility and effect.*—A taxpayer described in paragraph (b)(2)(i) of this section may make an election to apply the rules of this section to all, but not part, of the taxpayer's income attributable to notional principal contracts for all taxable years (or portion thereof) beginning before December 24, 1986, for which the period of limitations for filing a claim for refund under section 6511(a) has not expired. A taxpayer not described in paragraph (b)(2)(i) of this section that is engaged in trade or business within the United States may make an election to apply the rules of this section to all, but not part, of the taxpayer's income described in paragraph (b)(3) of this section for all taxable years (or portion thereof) beginning before December 24, 1986, for which the period of limitations for filing a claim for refund under section 6511(a) has not expired. If a taxpayer makes an election pursuant to this paragraph (c)(1) in the time and manner provided in paragraph (c)(2) and (3) of this section, then, with respect to such taxable years (or portion thereof), no tax shall be deducted or withheld under sections 1441 and 1442 with respect to payments made by the taxpayer pursuant to a notional principal contract the income attributable to which is subject to such election. The election may be revoked only with the consent of the Commissioner.

(2) *Time for making election.*—The election specified in paragraph (c)(1) of this section shall be made by May 15, 1991.

(3) *Manner of making election.*—The election described in paragraph (c)(1) of this section shall be made by attaching a statement to the tax return or an amended tax return for each taxable year beginning before December 24, 1986, in which the taxpayer accrued or received notional principal contract income. The statement shall—

(i) Contain the name, address, and taxpayer identifying number of the electing taxpayer;

(ii) Identify the election as a "Notional Principal Contract Election under §1.863-7"; and

(iii) Specify each taxable year described in paragraph (c)(1) of this section in which payments were made.

(d) *Example.*—The operation of this section is illustrated by the following example:

(1) On January 1, 1990, X, a calendar year domestic corporation, entered into an interest rate swap contract with FZ, an unrelated foreign corporation. X does not have a qualified business unit outside the United States. Under the contract, X is required to pay FZ fixed rate dollar amounts, and FZ is required to pay X floating rate dollar amounts, each determined solely by reference to a notional dollar denominated principal amount specified under the contract. The contract is a notional principal contract under §1.863-7(a) because the contract provides for the payment of amounts at specified intervals calculated by reference to a specified index upon a notional principal amount in exchange for a promise to pay similar amounts.

(2) Assume that during 1990 X had notional principal contract income of $100 in connection with the notional principal contract described in (1) above. Also assume that the contract provides that payments more than 30 days late give rise to a $5 fee, and that X receives such a fee in 1990. Under paragraph (b)(1) of this section, the source of X's $100 of income attributable to the swap agreement is domestic. The $5 fee is not notional principal contract income.

(e) *Cross references.*—See § 1.861-9T(b) for the allocation of expense to certain notional principal contracts. For rules relating to the source of income from nonfunctional currency notional principal contracts, see § 1.988-4T. For rules relating to the taxable amount of notional principal contract income allocable under this section to sources inside or outside the United States, see § 1.863-1(c). [Reg. § 1.863-7.]

☐ [*T.D.* 8330, 1-11-91.]

Proposed Amendments to Regulation

§ 1.863-7. Allocation of income attributable to certain notional principal contracts under section 863(a).—(a) *Scope.*—(1) *Introduction.*—* * * This section does not apply to income from a section 988 transaction (as defined in section 988(c) and § 1.988-1(a)), or to income from a global dealing operation (as defined in § 1.482-8(a)(2)(i)) that is sourced under the rules of § 1.863-3(h). * * *

* * *

[Prop. Reg. § 1.863-7.]

[Proposed 3-6-98.]

Proposed Regulation

§ 1.863-8. Source of income from space and ocean activity under section 863(d).—(a) *In general.*—Income of a U.S. or a foreign person derived from space or ocean activity (space or ocean income) is sourced under the rules of this section, notwithstanding any other provision, including sections 861, 862, 863, and 865. A taxpayer will not be considered to derive income from space or ocean activity, as defined in paragraph (d) of this section, if such activity is performed by another person, subject to the rules for the treatment of consolidated groups in section § 1.1502-13.

(b) *Source of gross income from space or ocean activity.*—(1) *In general.*—Income derived by a U.S. person from space or ocean activity is income from sources within the United States, except as otherwise provided in this paragraph (b). Income derived by a person other than a United States person from space or ocean activity is income from sources without the United States, except as otherwise provided in this paragraph (b).

(2) *Income derived by certain foreign corporations.*—If a U.S. person or U.S. persons own 50 percent or more of the vote or value of the stock of a foreign corporation (directly, indirectly or constructively) that is not a controlled foreign corporation within the meaning of section 957, all income derived by that foreign corporation from space or ocean activity is U.S. source income.

(3) *Income derived by foreign persons engaged in a U.S. trade or business.*—If a foreign person, other than a controlled foreign corporation within the meaning of section 957 or a foreign person described in paragraph (b)(2) of this section, is engaged in a U.S. trade or business, all income derived by that person from space or ocean activity is presumed to be U.S. source income. However, if the foreign person can allocate income between sources within the United States, or space, or international water, and sources outside the United States and space and international water, to the satisfaction of the Commissioner, based on the facts and circumstances, which may include functions performed, resources employed, risks assumed, or other contributions to value, then space or ocean income allocated to sources outside the United States and space and international water shall be treated as from sources outside the United States.

(4) *Source rules for income from certain sales of property.*—(i) *Sales of purchased property.*—When a taxpayer sells property in space or in international water, the source of gross income shall be determined under paragraph (b)(1), (2), or (3) of this section as applicable. However, if inventory, within the meaning of section 1221(1), is sold on international water, the source of income shall be determined under § 1.863-3(c)(2).

(ii) *Sales of property produced by the taxpayer.*—(A) *General.*—If the taxpayer both produces property and also sells such property, the taxpayer must divide gross income from such sales between production activity and sales activity under the 50/50 method as described in this paragraph (b)(4)(ii)(A). Under the 50/50 method, one-half of the taxpayer's gross income will be considered income attributable to production activity, and the source of that income will be determined under paragraphs (b)(4)(ii)(B) or (C) of this section. The remaining one-half of such gross income will be considered income attributable to sales activity and the source of that income will be determined under paragraph (b)(4)(i) of this section. However, if the taxpayer sells such property outside space and outside international water, the source of gross income attributable to sales activity will be determined under § 1.863-3(c)(2).

(B) *Production only in space or in international water, or only outside space and international water.*—When production occurs only in space or in international water, income attributable to production activity is sourced under paragraph (b)(1), (2), or (3) of this section as space or ocean income. When production occurs only outside space and international water, income attributable to production activity is sourced under § 1.863-3(c)(1).

(C) *Production both in space or in international water and outside space and international water.*—When property is produced in space or in international water and outside space and international water, gross income must be allocated to production occurring in space or in international water and production occurring outside space and international water, to the satisfaction of the Commissioner, based on all the facts and circumstances, which may include functions performed, resources employed, risks assumed, and any other contributions to value. The source of gross income allocated to space or international water is determined under paragraph (b)(1), (2), or (3) of this section. The source of gross income allocated outside space and international water is determined under § 1.863-3(c)(1).

(5) *Special rule for determining the source of gross income from services.*—If a transaction characterized as the performance of services constitutes a space or ocean activity by reason of the performance of part of the service in space or in international water, as determined under paragraph (d)(2)(ii)(A) of this section, the source of all gross income derived from such transaction of which such performance is a part is determined under paragraph (b)(1), (2), or (3) of this section. However, if the taxpayer can allocate gross income between performance occurring outside space and international water, and performance occurring in space or international water, to the satisfaction of the Commissioner, based on the facts and circumstances, including functions performed, resources employed, risks assumed, or other contributions to value, then the source of income allocated to performance occurring outside space and international water shall be determined under sections 861, 862, 863, and 865.

(6) *Special rule for determining source of income from communications activity (other than income from international communications activity).*—Space and ocean activity, as defined in paragraphs (d)(1) and (2) of this section, includes activity occurring in space or in international water that is characterized as a communications activity as defined in § 1.863-9(d). The source of gross income from space or ocean activity that is also a communications activity as defined in § 1.863-9(d) is determined under the rules of § 1.863-9(b), rather than under paragraph (b) of this section.

(c) *Taxable income.*—When a taxpayer allocates gross income under paragraph (b)(3), (b)(4)(ii)(C), or (b)(5) of this section, to the satisfaction of the Commissioner, based on all the facts and circumstances, the taxpayer must allocate or apportion expenses, losses, and other deductions as prescribed in §§ 1.861-8 through 1.861-14T to the class of gross income, which must include the total income so allocated in each case. A taxpayer must then apply the rules of §§ 1.861-8 through 1.861-14T to properly allocate or apportion amounts of expenses, losses, and other deductions allocated or apportioned to such gross income between gross income from sources within the United States and without the United States.

(d) *Space and ocean activity.*—(1) *Definition.*—(i) *Space activity.*—In general, space activity is any activity conducted in space. Space activity includes performance and provision of services in space, as defined in paragraph (d)(2)(ii)(A) of this section, leasing of equipment located in space, including spacecraft (e.g., satellites) or transponders located in space, licensing of technology or other intangibles for use in space, and the production, processing, or creation of property in space, as defined in paragraph (d)(2)(i) of this section. Space activity includes activity occurring in space that is characterized as communications activity (other than international communications activity) under § 1.863-9(d). Space activity also includes underwriting income from the insurance of risks on activities that produce space income. Space activity includes the sale in space of property, as defined in paragraph (d)(2)(iii) of this section. For purposes of this section, space means any area not within the jurisdiction (as recognized by the United States) of a foreign country, possession of the United States, or the United States, and not in international water. For purposes of determining space activity, the Commissioner may separate parts of a single transaction into separate transactions or combine separate transactions as parts of a single transaction. Paragraph (d)(3) of this section lists exceptions to the general rule.

(ii) *Ocean activity.*—In general, ocean activity is any activity conducted on or under water not within the jurisdiction (as recognized by the United States) of a foreign country, possession of the United States, or the United States (collectively, in international water). Ocean activity includes performance and provision of services in international water, as defined in paragraph (d)(2)(ii)(A) of this section, leasing of equipment located in international water, including underwater cables, licensing of technology or other intangibles for use in international water, and the production, processing, or creation of property in international water, as defined in paragraph (d)(2)(i) of this section. Ocean activity includes sales of

Prop. Reg. § 1.863-8(d)(1)(ii)

property in international water, as defined in paragraph (d)(2)(iii) of this section, but ocean activity does not include the selling of inventory as defined in section 1221(1) on international water. Ocean activity includes activity occurring in international water that is characterized as communications activity (other than international communications activity) under § 1.863-9(d). Ocean activity also includes underwriting income from the insurance of risks on activities that produce ocean income. Ocean activity also includes any activity performed in Antarctica. Ocean activity further includes the leasing of a vessel if such vessel does not transport cargo or persons for hire between ports-of-call. Thus, for example, the leasing of a vessel that is to engage only in research activities in international water is an ocean activity. Except as provided in paragraph (d)(3)(ii) of this section, ocean activity also includes the leasing of drilling rigs, extraction of minerals, and performance and provision of services related thereto. For purposes of determining ocean activity, the Commissioner may separate parts of a single transaction into separate transactions or combine separate transactions as parts of a single transaction. Paragraph (d)(3) of this section lists exceptions to the general rule.

(2) *Determining a space or ocean activity.*—(i) *Production of property in space or in international water.*—For purposes of this section', production activity means an activity that creates, fabricates, manufactures, extracts, processes, cures, or ages property within the meaning of sections 864(a) and § 1.864-1.

(ii) *Special rule for performance of services.*—(A) *General.*—If a transaction is characterized as the performance of a service, then such service will be treated as a space or ocean activity when a part of the service, even if de minimis, is performed in space or in international water. Services are performed in space or in international water if functions are performed, resources employed, risks assumed, or other contributions to value occur in space or in international water, regardless of whether performed by personnel, or equipment, or otherwise.

(B) *Exception to the general rule—facilitating the taxpayer's own communications.*— If a taxpayer's only activity in space or in international water is to facilitate the taxpayer's own communications as part of the provision or delivery of a service provided by the taxpayer, and that service would not otherwise be in whole or in part a space or ocean activity, such service will not be treated as either space or ocean activity because of such facilitation.

(iii) *Sale in space or in international water.*—In applying § 1.861-7(c) to determine where a sale takes place, property will be sold in space or in international water if the property is located in space or in international water when rights, title and interest pass to the buyer (or when bare legal title is retained, at the time and place of passage of beneficial ownership and risk of loss), or if property is sold for use in space or in international water.

(3) *Exceptions to space or ocean activity.*— Space or ocean activity does not include the following types of activities—

(i) Any activity giving rise to transportation income as defined in section 863(c); or

(ii) Any activity with respect to mines, oil and gas wells, or other natural deposits to the extent the mines or wells are located within the jurisdiction (as recognized by the United States) of any country, including the United States and its possessions; or

(iii) Any activity giving rise to international communications income as defined in § 1.863-9(d)(3)(ii).

(e) *Treatment of partnerships.*—In the case of a U.S. partnership, this section will be applied at the partnership level. In the case of a foreign partnership, this section will be applied at the partner level.

(f) *Examples.*—The following examples illustrate the rules of this section:

Example 1. Space activity—activity occurring on land and in space. (i) *Facts.* S owns satellites, and leases one of its satellites to A. S, as lessor, will not operate the satellite. Part of S's performance as lessor in this transaction occurs on land.

(ii) *Analysis.* The combination of S's activities is characterized as the lease of equipment. Since the equipment is located in space, the transaction is defined as space activity under paragraph (d)(1)(i) of this section. Income derived from the lease will be sourced in its entirety under paragraph (b) of this section.

Example 2. Space activity. (i) *Facts.* X is an Internet service provider, offering a service to personal computer users accessing the Internet. This service permits a customer, C, to make a call, initiated by a modem, routed to a control center, for connection to the World Wide Web. X transmits the requested information over its satellite capacity leased from S to C's personal computer. X charges its customers a flat monthly fee. Assume neither X nor S derive international communications income within the meaning of § 1.863-9(d)(3)(ii).

(ii) *Analysis.* In this case, X performs a service, and X's activity in space is not simply facilitation within the meaning of paragraph (d)(2)(ii)(B) of this section, because X's activity is not simply the facilitation of X's own communications and because X's activity is not just part of another service provided by X. Thus, X's activity constitutes space activity in its entirety under paragraph (d)(2)(ii)(A) of this section, and the source of X's income is determined under paragraph (b) of this section. To the extent X derives income from communications activity, within the meaning of § 1.863-9(d), the source of X's income is determined under § 1.863-9(b), as provided in paragraph (b)(6) of this section. S derives communications income within the meaning of § 1.863-9(d), and therefore the source of S's income is determined under § 1.863-9(b), as provided in paragraph (b)(6) of this section.

Example 3. Services as space activity—facilitation of communications. (i) *Facts.* R owns a retail outlet in the United States. R employs S to provide a security system for R's premises. S operates its security system by transmitting images from R's premises to a satellite, and from there to a group of S employees located in Country B, who then monitor the premises by viewing the transmitted images. O provides S with transponder capacity on O's satellite, which S uses to transmit those images.

(ii) *Analysis.* S derives income for providing monitoring services. Because, in this case, S uses O's satellite transponder to transmit images to facilitate S's own communications in space as part of its provision of a security service, S's activity in space is limited to facilitating communications as described in paragraph (d)(2)(ii)(B) of this section. Thus, S is not engaged in a space activity, and none of S's income is space income. Assuming O's provision of capacity is viewed as the provision of a service, O's activity in space is not simply the facilitation of communications as provided in paragraph (d)(2)(ii)(B) of this section, because O is not just facilitating its own communications. Thus, O's activity is characterized as space activity in its entirety under paragraph (d)(2)(ii)(A) of this section (unless O's activity in space qualifies as international communications activity). To the extent O derives income from communications activity, within the meaning of § 1.863-9(d), the source of O's income is determined under § 1.863-9(b), as provided in paragraph (b)(6) of this section. On these facts, R does not derive any income from space activity.

Example 4. Space activity. (i) *Facts.* L, a U.S. company, offers programming and also certain services to customers located both in the United States and in foreign countries. Assume L's provision of programming and services in this case was viewed as the provision of a service, with no part of that service occurring in space. L uses satellite capacity acquired from S to deliver the service directly to customers' television sets, so that the delivery of the service occurs in space. Assume the delivery in this case is not considered de minimis. L also acquires programming from H, and L pays H a royalty for use of copyrighted material in the United States and in foreign countries. Customer, C, pays L for delivery of the service to C's residence in the United States. Assume S's provision of capacity in this case was viewed as the provision of a service, and also that S does not derive international communications income within the meaning of § 1.863-9(d)(3)(ii).

(ii) *Analysis.* On these facts, S's activity in space is not just the facilitation of its own communications within the meaning of paragraph (d)(2)(ii)(B) of this section, because S is facilitating the communications of others. To the extent S derives income from a space activity that is also a communications activity under § 1.863-9(d), the source of S's income is determined under § 1.863-9(b), as provided in paragraph (b)(6) of this section. On these facts, L is treated as providing a service and is paid to deliver that service to its customers, and each transaction, i.e., the provision of the service and the delivery of the service, constitutes a separate transaction. L's income derived from provision of the service is not income derived from space activity. L's income derived from delivery of the service is space activity. L's delivery of the service is not just the facilitation of L's own communications within the meaning of paragraph (d)(2)(ii)(B) of this section, because it is not just a part of the provision of a service, but instead the entire service. Since L derives communications income within the meaning of § 1.863-9(d), the source of L's income is determined under § 1.863-9(b), as provided in paragraph (b)(6) of this section. If on other facts, L provides a service and delivers that service, and L treats the provision of the service and the delivery of the service as one separate transaction, then L performs services in space under paragraph (d)(2)(ii)(A) of this section, because the delivery of the service occurs in space. However, L's activity in space would be limited to facilitating its own communications within the meaning of paragraph (d)(2)(ii)(B) of this section, because it is part of another service that would not otherwise be a space activity. As a result, L's provision of the service would not be a space activity under paragraph (d)(2)(ii)(A) of this section.

Example 5. Space activity—treatment of land activity. (i) *Facts.* S, a U.S. person, offers remote imaging products and services to its customers. In year 1, S uses its satellite's remote sensors to gather data on certain geographical terrain. In year 3, C, a construction development company, contracts with S to obtain a satellite image of an area for site development

Prop. Reg. § 1.863-8(f)

work. S pulls data from its archives and transfers to C the images gathered in year 1, in a transaction that is characterized as a sale of the data. Title to the data passes to C in the United States. Before transferring the images to C, S uses computer software to enhance the images so that the images can be used.

(ii) *Analysis.* The collection of data and creation of images in space is characterized as the creation of property in space. S's income is derived from production of property in part in Space, and is, therefore, derived in part from space activity. The source of S's income from production and sale of property is, therefore, determined under paragraph (b)(4) of this section. Since production activity occurs both in space and on land, the source of S's production income is determined under paragraphs (b)(4)(ii)(A) and (C) of this section. The source of S's income attributable to sales activity is determined under paragraph (b)(4)(ii)(A) of this section and §1.863-3(c)(2) as U.S. source income.

Example 6. Use of intangible property in space. (i) *Facts.* X acquires a license to use a particular satellite slot or orbit, which X sublicenses to C. C pays X a royalty.

(ii) *Analysis.* Since the royalty is paid for the right to use intangible property in space, the source of X's royalty is determined under paragraph (b) of this section.

Example 7. Performance of services. (i) *Facts.* E, a U.S. company, operates satellites with sensing equipment that can determine how much heat and light particular plants emit and reflect. Based on the data, E will provide F, a U.S. farmer, a report analyzing the data, which F will use in growing crops. E analyzes the data from U.S. offices.

(ii) *Analysis.* Assume E's combined activities are characterized as the performance of services. Because part of the service is performed in space, all income E derives from the transaction will be treated as derived from space activity under paragraph (d)(2)(ii)(A) of this section. The source of such income will be determined under paragraph (b)(5) of this section. If, however, E can allocate gross income, to the satisfaction of the Commissioner, as prescribed in paragraph (b)(5) of this section, then the source of gross income attributable to services performed outside space may be determined as provided in paragraph (b)(5) of this section.

Example 8. Separate transactions. (i) *Facts.* The same facts as *Example 7*, except that E provides the raw data to F in a transaction characterized as a sale of a copyrighted article, and in addition also provides an analysis in the form of a report to F, a U.S. farmer who uses the information in growing crops. The price F pays E for the raw data is separately stated.

(ii) *Analysis.* To the extent the provision of raw data and the analysis of the data are each treated as separate transactions, the source of income from the production and sale of data is determined under paragraph (b)(4) of this section. The provision of services would be analyzed in the same manner as in *Example 7*.

Example 9. Sale of property under international water. (i) *Facts.* T owns transatlantic cable lying under the ocean, which it purchased. T sells the cable to B.

(ii) *Analysis.* Because the property is sold under international water as provided in paragraph (d)(2)(iii) of this section, the transaction is ocean activity under paragraph (d)(1)(ii) of this section, and the source of income is determined under paragraph (b)(4)(i) of this section, by reference to paragraph (b)(1), (2), or (3) of this section.

Example 10. Sales of property in space. (i) *Facts.* S manufactures a satellite in the United States and sells it to a U.S. customer, with the rights, title, and interest passing to the customer when the satellite is located in space.

(ii) *Analysis.* The source of income derived from the sale of the satellite in space is determined under paragraph (b)(4) of this section, with the source of income attributable to production activity determined under paragraphs (b)(4)(ii)(A) and (B) of this section, and the source of income attributable to sales activity determined under paragraphs (b)(4)(ii)(A) and (b)(4)(i) of this section, by reference to paragraph (b)(1), (2), or (3) of this section.

Example 11. Sale of property located in space. (i) *Facts.* S has a right to operate from a particular position in space. S sells the right to operate from that satellite slot or orbit to P.

(ii) *Analysis.* Because the sale takes place in space, as provided in paragraph (d)(2)(iii) of this section, gain on the sale of the satellite slot or orbit is income derived from space activity under paragraph (d)(1)(i) of this section, and income from the sale is sourced under paragraph (b)(4)(i) of this section, by reference to paragraph (b)(1), (2), or (3) of this section.

Example 12. Source of income of a foreign person. (i) *Facts.* FP, a foreign company, not a controlled foreign corporation within the meaning of section 957, derives income from the operation of satellites. FP operates a ground station in the United States and in foreign country, FC.

(ii) *Analysis.* In this case, FP is engaged in a U.S. trade or business of operating the ground station. Thus, under paragraph (b)(3) of this section, all FP's income derived from space activity is presumed to be U.S. source income. However, if FP can allocate space income to contributions occurring outside the United States, space, and international water, as provided in paragraph (b)(3) of this section, for example, to the ground station located in FC, then such space income so allocated will be from sources outside the United States.

Example 13. Source of income of a foreign person. (i) *Facts.* FP, a foreign company, not a controlled foreign corporation within the meaning of Section 957, operates remote sensing satellites, collecting data and images in space for its customers. FP uses an independent agent, A, in the United States who provides marketing, order taking, and other customer service functions.

(ii) *Analysis.* In this case, FP is engaged in a U.S. trade or business on the basis of A's activities on its behalf in the United States. Therefore, under paragraph (b)(3) of this section, all of FP's income derived from space activity is presumed to be space income. However, if FP can allocate income to contributions occurring outside the United States, space, and international water, as provided in paragraph (b)(3) of this section, then such income so allocated will be from sources outside the United States.

(g) *Reporting and documentation requirements.*—When a taxpayer allocates gross income, to the satisfaction of the Commissioner, under paragraph (b)(3), (b)(4)(ii)(C), or (b)(5) of this section, it does so by making the allocation on a timely filed original return (including extensions). An amended return does not qualify for this purpose, nor shall the provisions of §301.9100-1 of this chapter and any guidance promulgated thereunder apply. In all cases, a taxpayer must maintain contemporaneous documentation in existence when such return is filed regarding the allocation of gross income and allocation or apportionment of expenses, losses and other deductions, the methodology used, and the circumstances justifying use of that methodology. The taxpayer must produce such documentation within 30 days upon request.

(h) *Effective date.*—This section applies to taxable years beginning on or after the date that is 30 days after the date of publication of final regulations in the Federal Register. [Prop. Reg. § 1.863-8.]

[Proposed 1-17-2001.]

Proposed Regulation

§ 1.863-9. Source of income derived from communications activity under sections 863(a), (d), and (e).—(a) *In general.*—Income of a U.S. or foreign person derived from communications activity is sourced under the rules of this section, notwithstanding any other provision including sections 861, 862, 863, and 865.

(b) *Source of gross income derived from communications activity.*—(1) *In general.*—The source of gross income derived from each type of communications activity, as defined in paragraph (d)(3) of this section, is determined under this paragraph (b). If a communications activity would qualify as space or ocean activity under section 863(d) and the regulations thereunder, the source of income derived from such communications activity is determined under this section, and not under section 863(d) and the regulations thereunder. See § 1.863-8(b)(6).

(2) *Source of international communications income.*—(i) *Income derived by a U.S. person.*—Under the 50/50 method of this paragraph (b)(2)(i), income derived by a U.S. person from international communications activity is one-half from sources within the United States and one-half from sources without the United States.

(ii) *Income derived by foreign persons.*—(A) *General rule.*—Income derived by a person other than a U.S. person from international communications activity is, except as otherwise provided in this paragraph (b), wholly from sources without the United States.

(B) *Income derived by certain foreign corporations.*—If a foreign corporation, including a controlled foreign corporation within the meaning of section 957, is 50 percent or more owned by vote or value (directly, indirectly, or constructively) by U.S. persons, all income derived by that corporation from international communications activity is from sources within the United States.

(C) *Income derived by foreign persons with a U.S. fixed place of business.*—If a foreign person (other than a foreign person described in paragraph (b)(2)(ii)(B) of this section) maintains an office or other fixed place of business in the United States, the foreign person's international communications income, as determined to the satisfaction of the Commissioner, attributable to the office or other fixed place of business is from sources within the United States. The principles of section 864(c)(5) apply in determining whether a foreign person has an office or fixed place of business in the United States. See § 1.864-6 and -7. This paragraph does not apply if the foreign person is engaged in a U.S. trade or business.

(D) *Income derived by foreign persons engaged in a U.S. trade or business.*—If a foreign person (other than a foreign person described in paragraph (b)(2)(ii)(B) of this section) is engaged in a U.S. trade or business, all of the foreign person's international communications income is presumed to be from sources within the United States. However, if the foreign person can allocate income between sources within the United States, or space, or international water and sources outside the United States and space and international water, to the satisfaction of the Commissioner, based on the facts and circumstances, which may include functions performed, resources employed, risks assumed, or other contributions to value, then the income allocated to sources outside the United States and space and international water shall be treated as from sources without the United States.

(3) *Source of U.S. communications income.*—The source of income derived by U.S. or a foreign person from U.S. communications activity is from sources within the United States.

(4) *Source of foreign communications income.*—The source of income derived by a U.S. or a foreign person from foreign communications activity is from sources without the United States.

(5) *Source of space/ocean communications income.*—The source of income derived by a U.S. or a foreign person from space/ocean communications activity is determined under section 863(d) and the regulations thereunder, without regard to § 1.863-8(b)(6).

(6) *Source of communications income when taxpayer cannot establish the two points between which the taxpayer is paid to transmit the communication.*—The income derived by a U.S. person or foreign person from communications activity, when the taxpayer cannot establish the two points between which the taxpayer is paid to transmit the communication as required in paragraph (d)(3)(i) of this section, is from sources within the United States.

(c) *Taxable income.*—When a taxpayer allocates gross income under paragraph (b)(2)(ii)(D) or (d)(1)(ii) of this section, to the satisfaction of the Commissioner, based on all the facts and circumstances, the taxpayer must allocate or apportion expenses, losses, and other deductions as prescribed in §§ 1.861-8 through 1.861-14T to the class of gross income, which must include the total income so allocated in each case. A taxpayer must then apply the rules of §§ 1.861-8 through 1.861-14T to properly allocate or apportion amounts of expenses, losses, and other deductions allocated or apportioned to such gross income between gross income from sources within the United States and without the United States. For amounts of expenses, losses, and other deductions allocated or apportioned to gross income derived from international communications activity, when the source of income is determined under the 50/50 method of paragraph (b)(2)(i) of this section, taxpayers must apportion expenses, losses, and other deductions between sources within and sources without pro rata based on the relative amounts of gross income from sources within the United States and without the United States. Research and experimental expenditures qualifying under § 1.861-17 are allocated under that section, and are not allocated and apportioned pro rata under the method of paragraph (b)(2)(i) of this section.

(d) *Communications activity and income derived from communications activity.*—(1) *Communications activity.*—(i) *General rule.*—For purposes of this part, communications activity consists solely of the delivery by transmission of communications or data (communications). Delivery of communications other than by transmission, for example, by delivery of physical packages and letters, is not communications activity within the meaning of this section. Communications activity also includes the provision of capacity to transmit communications. Provision of content or any other additional service provided along with, or in connection with, a non-de minimis communications activity must be treated as a separate non-communications activity unless de minimis.

(ii) *Separate transaction.*—To the extent a taxpayer's transaction consists in part of non-de minimis communications activity and in part of non-de minimis non-communications activity, such parts of the transaction must be treated as separate transactions. Gross income must be allocated to each such transaction involving the communications activity and the non-communications activity to the satisfaction of the Commissioner, based on all relevant facts and circumstances, which may include functions performed, resources employed, risks assumed, and any other contributions to the value of the respective transactions. For purposes of determining whether income is derived from communications activity, the Commissioner may treat communications activity and non-communications activity, treated as a single transaction, as separate transactions, or combine separate communications activity and non-communications activity transactions into a single transaction.

(2) *Income derived from communications activity.*—Income derived from communications activity (communications income) is income derived from the delivery by transmission of communications, including income derived from the provision of capacity to transmit communications. Income may be considered derived from a communications activity

even if the taxpayer itself does not perform the transmission function, but in all cases, the taxpayer derives communications income only if the taxpayer is paid to transmit, and bears the risk of transmitting, the communications.

(3) *Determining the type of communications activity.*—(i) *In general.*—Whether income is derived from international communications activity, U.S. communications activity, foreign communications activity, or space/ocean communications activity is determined by identifying the two points between which the taxpayer is paid to transmit the communication. The taxpayer must establish to the satisfaction of the Commissioner the two points between which the taxpayer is paid to transmit, and bears the risk of transmitting, the communication. Whether the taxpayer contracts out part or all of the transmission function is not relevant.

(ii) *Income derived from international communications activity.*—Income derived by a taxpayer from international communications activity (international communications income) is income derived from communications activity, as defined in paragraph (d)(1) of this section, when the taxpayer is paid to transmit between a point in the United States and a point in a foreign country (or a possession of the United States).

(iii) *Income derived from U.S. communications activity.*—Income derived by a taxpayer from U.S. communications activity (U.S. communications income) is income derived from communications activity, as defined in paragraph (d)(1) of this section, when the taxpayer is paid to transmit—

(A) Between two points in the United States; or

(B) Between the United States and a point in space or in international water.

(iv) *Income derived from foreign communications activity.*—Income derived by a taxpayer from foreign communications activity (foreign communications income) is income derived from communications activity, as defined in paragraph (d)(1) of this section, when the taxpayer is paid to transmit—

(A) Between two points in a foreign country or countries (or possession or possessions of the United States); or

(B) Between a foreign country (or a possession of the United States) and a point in space or in international water.

(v) *Income derived from space/ocean communications activity.*—Income derived by a taxpayer from space/ocean communications activity (space/ocean communications income) is income derived from a communications activity, as defined in paragraph (d)(1) of this section, when the taxpayer is paid to transmit between a point in space or in international water and another point in space or in international water.

(e) *Treatment of partnerships.*—(1) *General.*—In the case of a U.S. partnership, this section will be applied at the partnership level. In the case of a foreign partnership, this section will be applied at the partner level.

(2) *Exception.*—In the case of a U.S. partnership in which 50 percent or more of the partnership interests are owned by foreign persons, this section will be applied at the partner level.

(f) *Examples.*—The following examples illustrate the rules of this section:

Example 1. Income derived from communications activity. (i) *Facts.* D provides its customers in various foreign countries with access to its data base. A customer, C, places a toll call to D's telephone number, and can then access D's data base to obtain certain information, such as C's customers' health care coverage.

(ii) *Analysis.* D is not paid to transmit communications and does not derive income solely from transmission of communications within the meaning of paragraph (d) of this section. D instead derives income from provision of content or provision of services to its customers.

Example 2. Income derived from U.S. communications activity. (i) *Facts.* Local telephone company (TC) receives access fees from an international carder for picking up calls from a local telephone customer and delivering the call to a U.S. point of presence (POP) of the international carrier. The international carrier picks up the call from its U.S. POP and delivers the call to a foreign country.

(ii) *Analysis.* TC is not paid to carry the transmission between the United States and a foreign country. It is paid to transmit communications between two points in the United States. TC derives income from U.S. communications activity as defined in paragraph (d)(3)(iii) of this section, which is sourced under paragraph (b)(3) of this section as U.S. source income.

Example 3. Income derived from international communications activity. (i) *Facts.* TC, a U.S. company, owns an underwater fiber optic cable. Pursuant to three year contracts, TC makes capacity to transmit communications via the cable available to its customers. Such customers then solicit telephone customers and arrange for transmitting their calls. The cable runs in part through U.S. waters, through international waters, and in part through foreign country waters.

(ii) *Analysis.* TC derives income from communications activity under paragraph (d)(2) of this section. The income is derived from international communications activity as provided in paragraph (d)(3)(ii) of this section, since TC is paid to make available capacity to transmit between the United States and a foreign country, and vice versa. Since TC is a U.S. person, TC's international communications income is sourced under paragraph (b)(2)(i) of this section as one-half from sources within the United States and one-half from sources without the United States.

Example 4. Character of communications activity: the paid-to-do rule. (i) *Facts.* TC is paid to transmit communications from Toronto, Canada, to Paris, France. TC transmits the communication to New York. TC pays another communications company, IC, to transmit the communications from New York to Paris.

(ii) *Analysis.* Under the paid-to-do rule of paragraph (d)(3)(i) of this section, TC derives income from foreign communications activity under paragraph (d)(3)(iv) of this section, since it is paid to transmit communications between two foreign points, Toronto and Paris. Under paragraph (d)(3)(i) of this section, the character of TC's activity is determined without regard to the fact that TC pays IC to transmit the communication for some portion of the delivery path. IC has international communications income under paragraph (d)(3)(ii) of this section, because it is paid to transmit the communication between a point in the United States and a point in a foreign country.

Example 5. Income derived from international communications activity. (i) *Facts.* S, a U.S. satellite operator, owns satellites and the uplink facilities in Country X, a foreign country. B, a resident of Country X, pays S to deliver its programming from Country X to its downlink facility in the United States, owned by C, a customer of B.

(ii) *Analysis.* S derives communications income under paragraph (d) of this section. S's income is characterized as international communications income under paragraph (d)(3)(ii) of this section, because S is paid to transmit the communication between the beginning point in a foreign country to an end point in the United States. The source of S's international communications income is determined under paragraph (b)(2)(i) of this section as one-half from sources within the United States and one-half from sources without the United States.

Example 6. Character of income derived from communications activity: the paid-to-do rule. (i) *Facts.* TC is paid to take a call from North Carolina to Iowa, two points in the United States, but routes the call through Canada.

(ii) *Analysis.* Under paragraph (d)(3)(i) of this section, the character of the income derived from communications activity is determined by the two points between which the taxpayer is paid to transmit, and bears the risk of transmitting, the communications, without regard to the path of the transmission between those two points. Thus, under paragraph (d)(3)(iii) of this section, TC derives income from U.S. communications activity because it is paid to transmit between two U.S. points.

Example 7. Source of income derived from communications activity. (i) *Facts.* A, a U.S. company, is an Internet access provider. A charges C a lump sum, paid monthly, for Internet access. A transmits a call made by C in France to a recipient in England, over the public Internet. A does not maintain records as to the beginning and end points of the transmission.

(ii) *Analysis.* Although A derives income from communications activity as defined in paragraph (d)(1) of this section, the source of income is determined under paragraph (b)(6) of this section as income from sources within the United States, because A cannot establish the two points between which it is paid to transmit the communications.

Example 8. Income derived from communications and non-communications activity. (i) *Facts.* A, a U.S. company, offers customers local and long distance phone service, video, and Internet services. Customers pay one monthly fee, and in addition 10 cents a minute for all long-distance calls, including international calls.

(ii) *Analysis.* To the extent A derives income from communications activity, A must allocate income to its communications activity as provided in paragraph (d)(1)(ii) of this section. To the extent A can establish that it derives international communications income as defined in paragraph (d)(3)(ii) of this section, A would determine the source of such income under paragraph (b)(2)(i) of this section. If A cannot establish the points between which it is paid to transmit communications, as required in paragraph (d)(3)(i) of this section, the source of A's income must be determined under paragraph (b)(6) of this section as from within the United States.

Example 9. Income derived from communications activity. (i) *Facts.* T purchases capacity from TC to transmit telephone calls. T sells prepaid telephone calling cards, giving customers access to TC's lines, for a certain number of minutes.

(ii) *Analysis.* T derives income from communications activity, under paragraph (d)(2) of this section, because T makes capacity to transmit available to its customers. In this case, T cannot establish the points between which communications are transmitted. Therefore, the source of its income must be determined under paragraph (b)(6) of this section as U.S. source income.

Example 10. Income derived from communications and non-communications activity. (i) *Facts.* B, a U.S. company, transmits television programs using its satellite transponder, from the United States to downlink facilities in foreign country Y, owned by D, a cable system operator in Country Y. D receives the transmission, unscrambles the signals, and distributes the broadcast to customers in Country Y.

(ii) *Analysis.* B derives income both from communications activity as defined under paragraph (d)(1)(i) of this section, and from non-communications activity. Gross income must be allocated to the communications activity as required in paragraph (d)(1)(ii) of this section. Income derived by B for transmission to D is international communications income within paragraph (d)(3)(ii) of this section, because B is paid to transmit communications from the United States to a foreign country.

Example 11. Income derived from communications activity. (i) *Facts.* TC is paid for Internet access. TC replicates frequently requested sites on its servers, solely to speed up response time.

(ii) *Analysis.* On these facts, the replication service would be treated as de minimis under paragraph (d)(1)(i) of this section, so that TC derives income from communications activity. The type and source of TC's communications income depends on demonstrating the points between which TC is paid by its customer to transmit the communications, under paragraph (d)(3)(i) of this section.

Example 12. Income derived from foreign communications activity. (i) *Facts.* S leases capacity to B, a broadcaster located in Australia. B beams programming to the satellite, and S's satellite picks the communications up in space, and beams the programming over Southeast Asia.

(ii) *Analysis.* S derives income from communications activity under paragraph (d)(2) of this section. S's income is characterized as income derived from foreign communications activity under paragraph (d)(3)(iv) of this section, because S picks up the communication in space, and beams it to a footprint entirely covering a foreign area. The source of S's income is determined under paragraph (b)(4) of this section as from sources without the United States. If S were beaming the programming over a satellite footprint that covered area both in the United States and outside the United States, S would be required to allocate the income derived from the different types of communications activity.

(g) *Reporting rules and disclosure on tax return.*—When a taxpayer allocates gross income to the satisfaction of the Commissioner under paragraph (b)(2)(ii)(D) or (d)(1)(ii) of this section, it does so by making the allocation on a timely filed original return (including extensions). An amended return does not qualify for this purpose, nor shall the provisions of § 301.9100-1 of this chapter and any guidance promulgated thereunder apply. In all cases, a taxpayer must maintain contemporaneous documentation in existence when such return is filed regarding the allocation of gross income, and allocation and apportionment of expenses, losses, and other deductions, the methodology used, and the circumstances justifying use of that methodology. The taxpayer must produce such documentation within 30 days of a request.

(h) *Effective date.*—This section applies to taxable years beginning on or after the date that is 30 days after the date of publication of final regulations in the Federal Register. [Prop. Reg. § 1.863-9.]

[Proposed 1-17-2001.]

§ 1.864-1. Meaning of sale, etc.—For purposes of § § 1.861 through 1.864-7, the word "sale" includes "exchange"; the word "sold" includes "exchanged"; and the word "produced" includes "created", "fabricated", "manufactured", "extracted", "processed", "cured", and "aged". [Reg. § 1.864-1.]

☐ [*T.D.* 6948, 3-27-68.]

§ 1.864-2. Trade or business within the United States.—(a) *In general.*—As used in part I (section 861 and following) and part II (section 871 and following), subchapter N, chapter 1 of the Code, and chapter 3 (section 1441 and following) of the Code, and the regulations thereunder, the term "engaged in trade or business within the United States" does not include the activities described in paragraphs (c) and (d) of this section, but includes the performance of personal services within the United States at any time within the taxable year except to the extent otherwise provided in this section.

(b) *Performance of personal services for foreign employer.*—(1) *Excepted services.*—For purposes of paragraph (a) of this section, the term "engaged in trade or business within the United States" does not include the performance of personal services—

(i) For a nonresident alien individual, foreign partnership, or foreign corporation, not engaged in trade or business within the United States at any time during the taxable year, or

(ii) For an office or place of business maintained in a foreign country or in a possession of the United States by an individual who is a citizen or resident of the United States or by a domestic partnership or a domestic corporation,

by a nonresident alien individual who is temporarily present in the United States for a period or periods not exceeding a total of 90 days during the taxable year and whose compensation for such services does not exceed in the aggregate a gross amount of $3,000.

(2) *Rules of application.*—(i) As a general rule, the term "day", as used in subparagraph (1) of this paragraph, means a calendar day during any portion of which the nonresident alien individual is physically present in the United States.

(ii) Solely for purposes of applying this paragraph, the nonresident alien individual, foreign partnership, or foreign corporation for which the nonresident alien individual is performing personal services in the United States shall not be considered to be engaged in trade or business in the United States by reason of the performance of such services by such individual.

(iii) In applying subparagraph (1) of this paragraph it is immaterial whether the services performed by the nonresident alien individual are performed as an employee for his employer or under any form of contract with the person for whom the services are performed.

(iv) In determining for purposes of subparagraph (1) of this paragraph whether compensation received by the nonresident alien individual exceeds in the aggregate a gross amount of $3,000, any amounts received by the individual from an employer as advances or reimbursements for travel expenses incurred on behalf of the employer shall be omitted from the compensation received by the individual, to the extent of expenses incurred, where he was required to account and did account to his employer for such expenses and has met the tests for such accounting provided in § 1.162-17 and paragraph (e)(4) of § 1.274-5. If advances or reimbursements exceed such expenses, the amount of the excess shall be included as compensation for personal services for purposes of such subparagraph. Pensions and retirement pay attributable to personal services performed in the United States are not to be taken into account for purposes of subparagraph (1) of this paragraph.

(v) See section 7701(a)(5) and § 301.7701-5 of this chapter (Procedure and Administration Regulations) for the meaning of "foreign" when applied to a corporation or partnership.

(vi) As to the source of compensation for personal services, see §§ 1.861-4 and 1.862-1.

(3) *Illustrations.*—The application of this paragraph may be illustrated by the following examples:

Example (1). During 1967, A, a nonresident alien individual, is employed by the London office of a domestic partnership. A, who uses the calendar year as his taxable year, is temporarily present in the United States during 1967 for 60 days performing personal service in the United States for the London office of the partnership and is paid by that office a total gross salary of $2,600 for such services. During 1967, A is not engaged in trade or business in the United States solely by reason of his performing such personal services for the London office of the domestic partnership.

Example (2). The facts are the same as in example (1), except that A's total gross salary for the services performed in the United States during 1967 amounts to $3,500, of which $2,625 is received in 1967 and $875 is received in 1968. During 1967, A is engaged in trade or business in the United States by reason of his performance of personal services in the United States.

(c) *Trading in stocks or securities.*—For purposes of paragraph (a) of this section—

(1) *In general.*—The term "engaged in trade or business within the United States" does not include the effecting of transactions in the United States in stocks or securities through a resident broker, commission agent, custodian, or other independent agent. This subparagraph shall apply to any taxpayer, including a broker or dealer in stocks or securities, except that it shall not apply if at any time during the taxable year the taxpayer has an office or other fixed place of business in the United States through which, or by the direction of which, the transactions in stocks or securities are effected. The volume of stock or security transactions effected during the taxable year shall not be taken into account in determining under this subparagraph whether the taxpayer is engaged in trade or business within the United States.

(2) *Trading for taxpayer's own account.*—(i) *In general.*—The term "engaged in trade or business within the United States" does not include the effecting of transactions in the United States in stocks or securities for the taxpayer's own account, irrespective of whether such transactions are effected by or through—

(a) The taxpayer himself while present in the United States,

(b) Employees of the taxpayer, whether or not such employees are present in the United States while effecting the transactions, or

(c) A broker, commission agent, custodian, or other agent of the taxpayer, whether or not such agent while effecting the transactions is *(1)* dependent or independent, or *(2)* resident, nonresident, or present, in the United States,

and irrespective of whether any such employee or agent has discretionary authority to make decisions in effecting such transactions. For purposes of this paragraph, the term "securities" means any note, bond, debenture, or other evidence of indebtedness, or any evidence of an interest in or right to subscribe to or purchase any of the foregoing; and the effecting of transactions in stocks or securities includes buying, selling (whether or not by entering into short sales), or trading in stocks, securities, or contracts or options to buy or sell stocks or securities, on margin or otherwise, for the account and risk of the taxpayer, and any other activity closely related thereto (such as obtaining credit for the purpose of effectuating such buying, selling, or trading). The volume of stock or security transactions effected during the taxable year shall not be taken into account in determining under this subparagraph whether the taxpayer is engaged in trade or business within the United States. The application of this subdivision may be illustrated by the following example:

Example. A, a nonresident alien individual who is not a dealer in stocks or securities, authorizes B, an individual resident of the United States, as his agent to effect transactions in the United States in stocks and securities for the account of A. B is empowered with complete authority to trade in stocks and securities for the account of A and to use his own discretion as to when to buy or sell for A's account. This grant of discretionary authority from A to B is also communicated in writing by A to various domestic brokerage firms through which A ordinarily effects transactions in the United States in stocks or securities. Under the agency arrangement B has the authority to place orders with the brokers, and all confirmations are to be made by the brokers to B, subject to his approval. The brokers are authorized by A to make payments to B and to charge such payments to the account of A. In addition, B is authorized to obtain and advance the necessary funds, if any, to maintain credits with the brokerage firms. Pursuant to his authority B carries on extensive trading transactions in the United States during the taxable year through the various brokerage firms for the account of A. During the taxable year A makes several visits to the United States in order to discuss with B various aspects of his trading activities and to make necessary changes in his trading policy. A is not engaged in trade or business within the United States during the taxable year solely because of the effecting by B of transactions in the United States in stocks or securities during such year for the account of A.

(ii) *Partnerships.*—A nonresident alien individual, foreign partnership, foreign estate, foreign trust, or foreign corporation shall not be considered to be engaged in trade or business within the United States solely because such person is a member of a partnership (whether domestic or foreign) which, pursuant to discretionary authority granted to such partnership by such person, effects transactions in the United States in stock or securities for the partnership's own account or solely because an employee of such partnership, or a broker, commission agent, custodian, or other agent, pursuant to discretionary authority granted by such partnership, effects transactions in the United States in stocks or securities for the account of such partnership. This subdivision shall not apply, however, to any member of *(a)* a partnership which is a dealer in stocks or securities or *(b)* a partnership (other than a partnership in which, at any time during the last half of its taxable year, more than 50 percent of either the capital interest or the profits interest is owned, directly or indirectly, by five or fewer partners who are individuals) the principal business of which is trading in stocks or securities for its own account, if the principal office of such partnership is in the United States at any time during the taxable year. The principles of subdivision (iii) of this subparagraph for determining whether a foreign corporation has its principal office in the United States shall apply in determining under this subdivision whether a partnership has its principal office in the United States. See section 707(b)(3) and paragraph (b)(3) of §1.707-1 for rules for determining the extent of the ownership by a partner of a capital interest or profits interest in a partnership. The application of this subdivision may be illustrated by the following examples:

Example (1). B, a nonresident alien individual, is a member of partnership X, the members of which are U.S. citizens, nonresident alien individuals, and foreign corporations. The principal business of partnership X is trading in stocks or securities for its own account. Pursuant to discretionary authority granted by B, partnership X effects transactions in the United States in stock or securities for its own account. Partnership X is not a dealer in stocks or securities, and more than 50 percent of either the capital interest or the profits interest in partnership X is owned throughout its taxable year by five or fewer partners who are individuals. B is not engaged in trade or business within the United States solely by reason of such effecting of transactions in the United States in stocks or securities by partnership X for its own account.

Example (2). The facts are the same as in example (1), except that not more than 50 percent of either the capital interest or the profits interest in partnership X is owned throughout the taxable year by five or fewer partners who are individuals. However, partnership X does not maintain its principal office in the United States at any time during the taxable year. B is not engaged in trade or business within the United States solely by reason of the trading in stocks or securities by partnership X for its own account.

Example (3). The facts are the same as in example (1), except that, pursuant to discretionary authority granted by partnership X, domestic broker D effects transactions in the United States in stocks or securities for the account of partnership X. B is not engaged in trade or business in the United States solely by reason of such trading in stocks or securities for the account of partnership X.

(iii) *Dealers in stocks or securities and certain foreign corporations.*—This subparagraph shall not apply to the effecting of transactions in the United States for the account of *(a)* a dealer in stocks or securities or *(b)* a foreign corporation (other than a corporation which is, or but for section 542(c)(7) or 543(b)(1)(C) would be, a personal holding company) the principal business of which is trading in stocks or securities for its own account, if the principal office of such corporation is in the United States at any time during the taxable year. Whether a foreign corporation's principal office is in the United States for this purpose is to be determined by comparing the activities (other than trading in stocks or securities) which the corporation conducts from its office or other fixed place of business located in the United States with the activities it conducts from its offices or other fixed places of business located outside the United States. For purposes of this subdivision, a foreign corporation is considered to have only one principal office, and an office of such corporation will not be considered to be its principal office merely because it is a statutory office of such corporation. For example, a foreign corporation which carries on most or all of its investment activities in the United States but maintains a general business office or offices outside the United States in which its management is located will not be considered as having its principal office in the United States if all or a substantial portion of the following functions is carried on at or from an office or offices located outside the United States:

(1) Communicating with its shareholders (including the furnishing of financial reports),

(2) Communicating with the general public,

(3) Soliciting sales of its own stock,

(4) Accepting the subscriptions of new stockholders,

(5) Maintaining its principal corporate records and books of account,

(6) Auditing its books of account,

(7) Disbursing payments of dividends, legal fees, accounting fees, and officers' and directors' salaries,

(8) Publishing or furnishing the offering and redemption price of the shares of stock issued by it,

(9) Conducting meetings of its shareholders and board of directors, and

(10) Making redemptions of its own stock.

The application of this subdivision may be illustrated by the following examples:

Example (1). (a) Foreign corporation X (not a corporation which is, or but for section 542(c)(7) or 543(b)(1)(C) would be, a personal holding company) was organized to sell its shares to nonresident alien individuals and foreign corporations and to invest the proceeds from the sale of such shares in stocks or securities in the United States. Foreign corporation X is engaged primarily in the business of investing, reinvesting, and trading in stocks or securities for its own account.

(b) For a period of three years, foreign corporation X irrevocably authorizes domestic corporation Y to exercise its discretion in effecting transactions in the United States in stocks or securities for the account and risk of foreign corporation X. Foreign corporation X issues a prospectus in which it is stated that its funds will be invested pursuant to an investment advisory contract with domestic corporation Y and otherwise advertises its services. Shares of foreign corporation X are sold to nonresident aliens and foreign corporations who are customers of United States brokerage firms unrelated to domestic corporation Y or foreign corporation X. The principal functions performed for foreign corporation X by domestic corporation Y are the rendering of investment advice and the effecting of transactions in the United States in stocks or securities for the account of foreign corporation X. Moreover, domestic corporation Y occasionally communicates with prospective foreign investors in foreign corporation X (through speaking engagements abroad by management of domestic corporation Y, and otherwise) for the purpose of explaining the investment techniques and policies used by domestic corporation Y in investing the funds of foreign corporation X. However, domestic corporation Y does not participate in the day-to-day conduct of other business activities of foreign corporation X.

(c) Foreign corporation X maintains a general business office or offices outside the United States in which its management is permanently located and from which it carries on, except to the extent noted heretofore, the functions enumerated in *(b)(1)* through *(10)* of this subdivision. The management of foreign corporation X at all times retains the independent power to cancel the investment advisory contract with domestic corporation Y subject to the contractual limitations contained therein and is in all other respects independent of the management of domestic corporation Y. The managing personnel of foreign corporation X communicate on a regular basis with domestic corporation Y, and periodically visit the offices of domestic corporation Y, in connection with the business activities of foreign corporation X.

(d) The principal office of foreign corporation X will not be considered to be in the United States; and, therefore, foreign corporation X is not engaged in trade or business within the United States solely by reason of its relationship with domestic corporation Y.

Example (2). The facts are the same as in example (1) except that, in lieu of having the investment advisory contract with domestic corporation Y, foreign corporation X has an office in the United States in which its employees perform the same functions as are performed by domestic corporation Y in example (1). Foreign corporation X is not engaged in trade or business within the United States during the taxable year solely because the employees located in its United States office effect transactions in the United States in stocks or securities for the account of that corporation.

(iv) *Definition of dealer in stocks or securities.*—*(a) In general.*—For purposes of this subparagraph, a dealer in stocks or securities is a merchant of stocks or securities, with an established place of business, regularly engaged as a merchant in purchasing stocks or securities and selling them to customers with a view to the gains and profits that may be derived therefrom. Persons who buy and sell, or hold, stocks or securities for investment or speculation, irrespective of whether such buying or selling constitutes the carrying on of a trade or business, and offices of corporations, members of partnerships, or fiduciaries, who in their individual capacities buy and sell, or hold, stocks or securities for investment or speculation are not dealers in stocks or securities within the meaning of this subdivision whether a person is a dealer in stocks or securities such person's transactions in stocks or securities effected both in and outside the United States shall be taken into account.

(b) Underwriting syndicates and dealers trading for others.—A foreign person who otherwise may be considered a dealer in stocks or securities under *(a)* of this subdivision shall not be considered a dealer in stocks or securities for purposes of this subparagraph—

(1) Solely because he acts as an underwriter, or as a selling group member, for the purpose of making a distribution of stocks or securities of a domestic issuer to foreign purchasers of such stocks or securities, irrespective of whether other members of the selling group distribute the stocks or securities of the domestic issuer to domestic purchasers, or

(2) Solely because of transactions effected in the United States in stocks or securities pursuant to his grant of discretionary authority to make decisions in effecting those transactions, if he can demonstrate to the satisfaction of the Commissioner that the broker, commission agent, custodian, or other agent through whom the transactions were effected acted pursuant to his written representation that the funds in respect of which such discretion was granted were the funds of a customer who is neither a dealer in stocks or securities, a partnership described in subdivision (ii) *(b)* of this subparagraph, or a foreign corporation described in subdivision (iii) *(b)* of this subparagraph.

For purposes of this *(b)*, a foreign person includes a nonresident alien individual, a foreign corporation, or a partnership any member of which is a nonresident alien individual or a foreign corporation. This *(b)* shall apply only if the foreign person at no time during the taxable year has an office or other fixed place of business in the United States through which, or by the direction of which, the transaction in stocks or securities are effected.

(c) Illustrations.—The application of this subdivision may be illustrated by the following examples:

Example (1). Foreign corporation X is a member of an underwriting syndicate organized to distribute stock issued by domestic corporation Y. Foreign corporation X distributes the stock of domestic corporation Y to foreign purchasers only. Domestic corporation M is syndicate manager of the underwriting syndicate and, pursuant to the terms of the underwriting agreement, reserves the right to sell certain quantities of the underwritten stock on behalf of all the members of the syndicate so as to engage in stabilizing transactions and to take

Reg. § 1.864-2(c)(2)(iv)(c)

certain other actions which may result in the realization of profit by all members of the underwriting syndicate. Foreign corporation X is not engaged in trade or business within the United States solely by reason of its participation as a member of such underwriting syndicate for the purpose of distributing the stock of domestic corporation Y to foreign purchasers or by reason of the exercise by M corporation of its discretionary authority as manager of such syndicate.

Example (2). Foreign corporation Y, a calendar year taxpayer, is a bank which trades in stocks or securities both for its own account and for the account of others. During 1967 foreign corporation Y authorizes domestic corporation M, a broker, to exercise its discretion in effecting transactions in the United States in stocks or securities for the account of B, a nonresident alien individual who has a trading account with foreign corporation Y. Foreign corporation Y furnishes a written representation to domestic corporation M to the effect that the funds in respect of which foreign corporation Y has authorized domestic corporation M to use its discretion in trading in the United States in stocks or securities are not funds in respect of which foreign corporation Y is trading for its own account but are the funds of one of its customers who is neither a dealer in stocks or securities, a partnership described in subdivision (ii)*(b)* of this subparagraph, or a foreign corporation described in subdivision (iii)*(b)* of this subparagraph. Pursuant to the discretionary authority so granted, domestic corporation M effects transactions in the United States during 1967 in stocks or securities for the account of the customer of foreign corporation Y. At no time during 1967 does foreign corporation Y have an office or other fixed place of business in the United States through which, or by the direction of which, such transactions in stocks or securities are effected by domestic corportion M. During 1967 foreign corporation Y is not engaged in trade or business within the United States solely by reason of such trading in stocks or securities during such year by domestic corporation M for the account of the customer of foreign corporation Y. Copies of the written representations furnished to domestic corporation M should be retained by foreign corporation Y for inspection by the Commissioner, if inspection is requested.

(d) *Trading in commodities.*—For purposes of paragraph (a) of this section—

(1) *In general.*—The term "engaged in trade or business within the United States" does not include the effecting of transactions in the United States in commodities (including hedging transactions) through a resident broker, commission agent, custodian, or other independent agent if (i) the commodities are of a kind customarily dealt in on an organized commodity exchange, such as a grain futures or a cotton futures market, (ii) the transaction is of a kind customarily consummated at such place, and (iii) the taxpayer at no time during the taxable year has an office or other fixed place of business in the United States through which, or by the direction of which, the transactions in commodities are effected. The volume of commodity transactions effected during the taxable year shall not be taken into account in determining under this subparagraph whether the taxpayer is engaged in trade or business in the United States.

(2) *Trading for taxpayer's own account.*—(i) *In general.*—The term "engaged in trade or business within the United States" does not include the effecting of transactions in the United States in commodities (including hedging transactions) for the taxpayer's own account if the commodities are of a kind customarily dealt in on an organized commodity exchange and if the transaction is of a kind customarily consummated at such place. This rule shall apply irrespective of whether such transactions are effected by or through—

(a) The taxpayer himself while present in the United States,

(b) Employees of the taxpayer, whether or not such employees are present in the United States while effecting the transactions, or

(c) A broker, commission agent, custodian, or other agent of the taxpayer, whether or not such agent while effecting the transactions is *(1)* dependent or independent, or *(2)* resident, nonresident, or present, in the United States,

and irrespective of whether any such employee or agent has discretionary authority to make decisions in effecting such transactions. The volume of commodity transactions effected during the taxable year shall not be taken into account in determining under this subparagraph whether the taxpayer is engaged in trade or business within the United States. This subparagraph shall not apply to the effecting of transactions in the United States for the account of a dealer in commodities.

(ii) *Partnerships.*—A nonresident alien individual, foreign partnership, foreign estate, foreign trust, or foreign corporation shall not be considered to be engaged in trade or business within the United States solely because such person is a member of a partnership (whether domestic or foreign) which, pursuant to discretionary authority granted to such partnership by such person, effects transactions in the United States in commodities for the partnership's account or solely because an employee of such partnership, or a broker, commission agent, custodian, or other agent, pursuant to discretionary authority granted by such partnership, effects transactions in the United States in commodities for the account of such partnership. This subdivision shall not apply to any member of a partnership which is a dealer in commodities.

(iii) *Illustration.*—The application of this subparagraph may be illustrated by the following example:

Example. Foreign corporation X, a calendar year taxpayer, is engaged as a merchant in the business of purchasing grain in South America and selling such cash grain outside the United States under long-term contracts for delivery in foreign countries. Foreign corporation X consummates a sale of 100,000 bushels of cash grain in February 1967 for July delivery to Sweden. Because foreign corporation X does not actually own such grain at the time of the sales transaction, such corporation buys as a hedge a July "futures contract" for delivery of 100,000 bushels of grain, in order to protect itself from loss by reason of a possible rise in the price of grain between February and July. The "futures contract" is ordered through domestic corporation Y, a futures commission merchant registered under the Commodity Exchange Act. Foreign corporation X is not engaged in trade or business within the United States during 1967 solely by reason of its effecting of such futures contract for its own account through domestic corporation Y.

(3) *Definition of commodity.*—For purposes of section 864(b)(2)(B) and this paragraph the term "commodities" does not include goods or merchandise in the ordinary channels of commerce.

(e) *Other rules.*—The fact that a person is not determined by reason of this section to be not engaged in trade or business with the United States is not to be considered a determination that such person is engaged in trade or business within the United States. Whether or not such person is engaged in trade or business within the United States shall be determined on the basis of the facts and circumstances in each case. For other rules relating to the determination of whether a taxpayer is engaged in trade or business in the United States see section 875 and the regulations thereunder.

(f) *Effective date.*—The provisions of this section shall apply only in the case of taxable years beginning after December 31, 1966. [Reg. § 1.864-2.]

☐ [*T.D.* 6948, 3-27-68. *Amended by T.D.* 7378, 9-29-75.]

§ 1.864-3. Rules for determining income effectively connected with U.S. business of nonresident aliens or foreign corporations.—(a) *In general.*—For purposes of the Income Revenue Code, in the case of a nonresident alien individual or a foreign corporation that is engaged in a trade or business in the United States at any time during the taxable year, the rules set forth in §§ 1.864-4 through 1.864-7 and this section shall apply in determining whether income, gain, or loss shall be treated as effectively connected for a taxable year beginning after December 31, 1966, with the conduct of a trade or business in the United States. Except as provided in sections 871(c) and (d) and 882(d) and (e), and the regulations thereunder, in the case of a nonresident alien individual or a foreign corporation that is at no time during the taxable year engaged in a trade or business in the United States, no income, gain, or loss shall be treated as effectively connected for the taxable year with the conduct of a trade or business in the United States. The general rule prescribed by the preceding sentence shall apply even though the income, gain, or loss would have been treated as effectively connected with the conduct of a trade or business in the United States if such income or gain had been received or accrued, or such loss had been sustained, in an earlier taxable year when the taxpayer was engaged in a trade or business in the United States. In applying §§ 1.864-4 through 1.864-7 and this section, the determination whether an item of income, gain, or loss is effectively connected with the conduct of a trade or business in the United States shall not be controlled by any administrative, judicial, or other interpretation made under the laws of any foreign country.

(b) *Illustrations.*—The application of this section may be illustrated by the following examples:

Example (1). During 1967 foreign corporation N, which uses the calendar year as the taxable year, is engaged in the business of purchasing and selling household equipment on the installment plan. During 1967 N is engaged in business in the United States by reason of the sales activities it carries on in the United States for the purpose of selling therein some of the equipment which it has purchased. During 1967 N receives installment payments of $800,000 on sales it makes that year in the United States, and the income from sources within the United States for 1967 attributable to such payments is $200,000. By reason of section 864(c)(3) and paragraph (b) of § 1.864-4 this income of $200,000 is effectively connected for 1967 with the conduct of a trade or business in the United States by N. In December of 1967, N discontinues its efforts to make any further sales of household equipment in the United States, and at no time during 1968 is N engaged in a trade or business in the United States. During 1968 N receives installment payments of $500,000 on the sales it made in the United States during 1967, and the income from sources within the United States for 1968 attributable to such payments is $125,000. By reason of section 864(c)(1)(B) and this section, this income of $125,000 is not effectively connected for 1968 with the conduct of a trade or business in the United States by N, even though such amount, if it had been received by N during 1967, would have been effectively connected for 1967 with the conduct of a trade or business in the United States by that corporation.

Example (2). R, a foreign holding company, owns all of the voting stock in five corporations, two of which are domestic corporations. All of the subsidiary corporations are engaged in the active conduct of a trade or business. R has an office in the United States where its chief executive officer, who is also the chief executive officer of one of the domestic corporations, spends a substantial portion of the taxable year supervising R's investment in its operating subsidiaries and performing his function as chief executive officer of the domestic operating subsidiary. R is not considered to be engaged in a trade or business in the United States during the taxable year by reason of the activities carried on in the United States by its chief executive officer in the supervision of its investment in its operating subsidiary corporations. Accordingly, the dividends from sources within the United States received by R during the taxable year from its domestic subsidiary corporations are not effectively connected for that year with the conduct of a trade or business in the United States by R.

Example (3). During the months of June through December 1971, B, a nonresident alien individual who uses the calendar year as the taxable year and the cash receipts and disbursements method of accounting, is employed in the United States by domestic corporation M for a salary of $2,000 per month, payable semimonthly. During 1971, B receives from M salary payments totaling $13,000, all of which income by reason of section 864(c)(2) and paragraph (c)(6)(ii) of § 1.864-4, is effectively connected for 1971 with the conduct of a trade or business in the United States by B. On December 31, 1971, B terminates his employment with M and departs from the United States. At no time during 1972 is B engaged in a trade or business in the United States. In January of 1972, B receives from M salary of $1,000 for the last half of December 1971, and a bonus of $1,000 in consideration of the services B performed in the United States during 1971 for that corporation. By reason of section 864(c)(1)(B) and this section, the $2,000 received by B during 1972 from sources within the United States is not effectively connected for that year with the conduct of a trade or business in the United States, even though such amount, if it had been received by B during 1971, would have been effectively connected for 1971 with the conduct of a trade or business in the United States by B. [Reg. § 1.864-3.]

☐ [*T.D.* 7216, 11-2-72.]

§ 1.864-4. U.S. source income effectively connected with U.S. business.— (a) *In general.*—This section applies only to a nonresident alien individual or a foreign corporation that is engaged in a trade or business in the United States at some time during a taxable year beginning after December 31, 1966, and to the income, gain, or loss of such person from sources within the United States. If the income, gain, or loss of such person for the taxable year from sources within the United States consists of (1) gain or loss from the sale or exchange of capital assets or (2) fixed or determinable annual or periodical gains, profits, and income or certain other gains described in section 871(a)(1) or 881(a), certain factors must be taken into account, as prescribed by section 864(c)(2) and paragraph (c) of this section, in order to determine whether the income, gain, or loss is effectively connected for the taxable year with the conduct of a trade or business in the United States by that person. All other income, gain, or loss of such person for the taxable year from sources within the United States shall be treated as effectively connected for the taxable year with the conduct of a trade or business in the United States by that person, as prescribed by section 864(c)(3) and paragraph (b) of this section.

(b) *Income other than fixed or determinable income and capital gains.*—All income, gain, or loss for the taxable year derived by a nonresident alien individual or foreign corporation engaged in a trade or business in the United States from sources within the United States which does not consist of income, gain, or loss described in section 871(a)(1) or 881(a), or of gain or loss from the sale or exchange of capital assets, shall, for purposes of paragraph (a) of this section, be treated as effectively connected for the taxable year with the conduct of a trade or business in the United States. This income, gain, or loss shall be treated as effectively connected for the taxable year with the conduct of a trade or business in the United States, whether or not the income, gain, or loss is derived from the trade or business being carried on in the United States during the taxable year. The application of this paragraph may be illustrated by the following examples:

Example (1). M, a foreign corporation which uses the calendar year as the taxable year, is engaged in the business of manufacturing machine tools in a foreign country. It establishes a branch office in the United States during 1968 which solicits orders from customers in the United States for the machine tools manufactured by that corporation. All negotiations with respect to such sales are carried on in the United States. By reason of its activity in the United States M is engaged in business in the United States during 1968. The income or loss from sources within the United States from such sales during 1968 is treated as effectively connected for that year with the conduct of a business in the United States by M. Occasionally, during 1968 the customers in the United States write directly to the home office of M, and the home office makes sales directly to such customers without routing the transactions through its branch office in the United States. The income or loss from sources within the United States for 1968 from these occasional direct sales by the home office is also treated as effectively connected for that year with the conduct of a business in the United States by M.

Example (2). The facts are the same as in example (1) except that during 1967 M was also engaged in the business of purchasing and selling office machines and that it used the installment method of accounting for the sales made in this separate business. During 1967 M was engaged in business in the United States by reason of the sales activities it carried on in the United States for the purpose of selling therein a number of the office machines which it had purchased. Although M discontinued this business activity in the United States in December of 1967, it received in 1968 some installment payments on the sales which it had made in the United States during 1967. The income of M for 1968 from sources within the United States which is attributable to such installment payments is effectively connected for 1968 with the conduct of a business in the United States, even though such income is not connected with the business carried on in the United States during 1968 through its sales office located in the United States for the solicitation of orders for the machine tools it manufactures.

Example (3). Foreign corporation S, which uses the calendar year as the taxable year, is engaged in the business of purchasing and selling electronic equipment. The home office of such corporation is also engaged in the business of purchasing and selling vintage wines. During 1968, S establishes a branch office in the United States to sell electronic equipment to customers, some of whom are located in the United States and the balance, in foreign countries. This branch office is not equipped to sell, and does not participate in sale of, wine purchased by the home office. Negotiations for the sales of the electronic equipment take place in the United States. By reason of the activity of its branch office in the United States, S is engaged in business in the United States during 1968. As a result of advertisements which the home office of S places in periodicals sold in the United States, customers in the United States frequently place orders for the purchase of wines with the home office in the foreign country, and the home office makes sales of wine in 1968 directly to such customers without routing the transactions through its branch office in the United States. The income or loss from sources within the United States for 1968 from sales of electronic equipment by the branch office, together with the income or loss from sources within the United States for that year from sales of wine by the home office, is treated as effectively connected for that year with the conduct of a business in the United States by S.

(c) *Fixed or determinable income and capital gains.*—(1) *Principal factors to be taken into account.*—(i) *In general.*—In determining for purposes of paragraph (a) of this section whether any income for the taxable year from sources within the United States which is described in section 871(a)(1) or 881(a), relating to fixed or determinable annual or periodical gains, profits, and income and certain other gains, or whether gain or loss from sources within the United States for the taxable year from the sale or exchange of capital assets, is effectively connected for the taxable year with the conduct of a trade or business in the United States, the principal tests to be applied are *(a)* the asset-use test, that is, whether the income, gain, or loss is derived from assets used in, or held for use in, the conduct of the trade or business in the United States, and *(b)* the business-activities test, that is, whether the activities of the trade or business conducted in the United States were a material factor in the realization of the income, gain, or loss.

(ii) *Special rule relating to interest on certain deposits.*—For purposes of determining under section 861(a)(1)(A) (relating to interest on deposits with banks, savings and loan associations, and insurance companies paid or credited before Jan. 1, 1976) whether the interest described therein is effectively connected for the taxable year with the conduct of a trade or business in the United States, such interest shall be treated as income from sources within the United States for purposes of applying this paragraph and §1.864-5. If by reason of the application of this paragraph such interest is determined to be income which is not effectively connected for the taxable year with the conduct of a trade or business in the United States, it shall then be treated as interest from sources without the United States which is not subject to the application of §1.864-5.

(2) *Application of the asset-use test.*—(i) *In general.*—For purposes of subparagraph (1) of this paragraph, the asset-use test ordinarily shall apply in making a determination with respect to income, gain, or loss of a passive type where the trade or business activities as such do not give rise directly to the realization of the income, gain, or loss. However, even in the case of such income, gain, or loss, any activities of the trade or business which materially contribute to the realization of such income, gain, or loss shall also be taken into account as a factor in determining whether the income, gain, or loss is effectively connected with the conduct of a trade or business in the United States. The asset-use test is of primary significance where, for example, interest income is derived from sources within the United States by a nonresident alien individual or foreign corporation that is engaged in the business of manufacturing or selling goods in the United States. See also subparagraph (5) of this paragraph for rules applicable to taxpayers conducting a banking, financing, or similar business in the United States.

(ii) *Cases where applicable.*—Ordinarily, an asset shall be treated as used in, or held for use in, the conduct of a trade or business in the United States if the asset is—

(a) Held for the principal purpose of promoting the present conduct of the trade or business in the United States; or

(b) Acquired and held in the ordinary course of the trade or business conducted in the United States, as, for example, in the case of an account or note receivable arising from that trade or business; or

(c) Otherwise held in a direct relationship to the trade or business conducted in the United States, as determined under paragraph (c)(2)(iv) of this section.

(iii) *Application of asset-use test to stock.*—(a) *In general.*—Except as provided in paragraph (c)(2)(iii)(b) of this section, stock of a corporation (whether domestic or foreign) shall not be treated as an asset used in, or held for use in, the conduct of a trade or business in the United States.

(b) *Stock held by foreign insurance companies.*—[Reserved]

(iv) *Direct relationship between holding of asset and trade or business.*—(a) *In general.*—In determining whether an asset is held in a direct relationship to the trade or business conducted in the United States, principal consideration shall be given to whether the asset is needed in that trade or business. An asset shall be considered needed in a trade or business, for this purpose, only if the asset is held to meet the present needs of that trade or business and not its anticipated future needs. An asset shall be considered as needed in the trade or business conducted in the United States if, for example, the asset is held to meet the operating expenses of that trade or business. Conversely, an asset shall be considered as not needed in the trade or business conducted in the United States if, for example, the asset is held for the purpose of providing for *(1)* future diversification into a new trade or business, *(2)* expansion of trade or business activities conducted outside of the United States, *(3)* future plant replacement, or *(4)* future business contingencies.

(b) *Presumption of direct relationship.*—Generally, an asset will be treated as held in a direct relationship to the trade or business if *(1)* the asset was acquired with funds generated by that trade or business, *(2)* the income from the asset is retained or reinvested in that trade or business, and *(3)* personnel who are present in the United States and actively involved in the conduct of that trade or business exercise significant management and control over the investment of such asset.

(v) *Illustration.*—The application of paragraph (iv) may be illustrated by the following examples:

Example (1). M, a foreign corporation which uses the calendar year as the taxable year, is engaged in industrial manufacturing in a foreign country. M maintains a branch in the United States which acts as importer and distributor of the merchandise it manufactures abroad; by reason of these branch activities, M is engaged in business in the United States during 1968. The branch in the United States is required to hold a large current cash balance for business purposes, but the amount of the cash balance so required varies because of the fluctuating seasonal nature of the branch's business. During 1968 at a time when large cash balances are not required the branch invests the surplus amount in U.S. Treasury bills. Since these Treasury bills are held to meet the present needs of the business conducted in the United States they are held in a direct relationship to that business, and the interest for 1968 on these bills is effectively connected for that year with the conduct of the business in the United States by M.

Example (2). Foreign corporation M, which uses the calendar year as the taxable year, has a branch office in the United States where it sells to customers located in the United States various products which are manufactured by that corporation in a foreign country. By reason of this activity M is engaged in business in the United States during 1997. The U.S. branch establishes in 1997 a fund to which are periodically credited various amounts which are derived from the business carried on at such branch. The amounts in this fund are invested in various securities issued by domestic corporations by the managing officers of the U.S. branch, who have the responsibility for maintaining proper investment diversification and investment of the fund. During 1997, the branch office derives from sources within the United States interest on these securities, and gains and losses resulting from the sale or exchange of such securities. Since the securities were acquired with amounts generated by the business conducted in the United States, the interest is retained in that business, and the portfolio is managed by personnel actively involved in the conduct of that business, the securities are presumed under paragraph (c)(2)(iv)(b) of this section to be held in a direct relationship to that business. However, M is able to rebut this presumption by demonstrating that the fund was established to carry out a program of future expansion and not to meet the present needs of the business conducted in the United States. Consequently, the income, gains, and losses from the securities for 1997 are not effectively connected for that year with the conduct of a trade or business in the United States by M.

(3) *Application of the business-activities test.*—(i) *In general.*—For purposes of subparagraph (1) of this paragraph, the business-activities test shall ordinarily apply in making a determination with respect to income, gain, or loss which, even though generally of the passive type, arises directly from the active conduct of the taxpayer's trade or business in the United States. The business-activities test is of primary significance, for example, where *(a)* dividends or interest are derived by a dealer in stocks or securities, *(b)* gain or loss is derived from the sale or exchange of capital assets in the active conduct of a trade or business by an investment company, *(c)* royalties are derived in the active conduct of a business consisting of the licensing of patents or similar intangible property, or *(d)* service fees are derived in the active conduct of a servicing business. In applying the business-activities test, activities relating to the management of investment portfolios shall not be treated as activities of the trade or business conducted in the United States unless the maintenance of the investments constitutes the principal activity of that trade or business. See also subparagraph (5) of this paragraph for rules applicable to taxpayers conducting a banking, financing, or similar business in the United States.

(ii) *Illustrations.*—The application of this subparagraph may be illustrated by the following examples:

Example (1). Foreign corporation S is a foreign investment company organized for the purpose of investing in stocks and securities. S is not a personal holding company or a corporation which would be a personal holding company but for section 542(c)(7) or 543(b)(1)(C). Its investment portfolios consist of common stocks issued by both foreign and domestic corporations and a substantial amount of high grade bonds. The business activity of S consists of the management of its portfolios for the purpose of investing, reinvesting, or trading in stocks and securities. During the taxable year 1968, S has its principal office in the United States within the meaning of paragraph (c)(2)(iii) of § 1.864-2 and, by reason of its trading in the United States in stocks and securities, is engaged in business in the United States. The dividends and interest derived by S during 1968 from sources within the United States, and the gains and losses from sources within the United States for such year from the sale of stocks and securities from its investment portfolios, are effectively connected for 1968 with the conduct of the business in the United States by that corporation, since its activities in connection with the management of its investment portfolios are activities of that business and such activities are a material factor in the realization of such income, gains, and losses.

Example (2). N, a foreign corporation which uses the calendar year as the taxable year, has a branch in the United States which acts as an importer and distributor of merchandise: by reason of the activities of that branch, N is engaged in business in the United States during 1968. N also carries on a business in which it licenses patents to unrelated persons in the United States for use in the United States. The businesses of the licensees in which these patents are used have no direct relationship to the business carried on in N's branch in the United States, although the merchandise marketed by the branch is similar in type to that manufactured under the patents. The negotiations and other activities leading up to the consummation of these licenses are conducted by employees of N who are not connected with the U.S. branch of that corporation,

Reg. § 1.864-4(c)(3)(ii)

and the U.S. branch does not otherwise participate in arranging for the licenses. Royalties received by N during 1968 from these licenses are not effectively connected for that year with the conduct of its business in the United States because the activities of that business are not a material factor in the realization of such income.

(4) *Method of accounting as a factor.*—In applying the asset-use test or the business-activities test described in subparagraph (1) of this paragraph, due regard shall be given to whether or not the asset, or the income, gain, or loss, is accounted for through the trade or business conducted in the United States, that is, whether or not the asset, or the income, gain, or loss, is carried on books of account separately kept for that trade or business, but this accounting test shall not by itself be controlling. In applying this subparagraph, consideration shall be given to whether the accounting treatment of an item reflects the consistent application of generally accepted accounting principles in a particular trade or business in accordance with accepted conditions or practices in that trade or business and whether there is a consistent accounting treatment of that item from year to year by the taxpayer.

(5) *Special rules relating to banking, financing, or similar business activity.*—(i) *Definition of banking, financing or similar business.*—A nonresident alien individual or a foreign corporation shall be considered for purposes of this section and paragraph (b)(2) of § 1.864-5 to be engaged in the active conduct of a banking, financing, or similar business in the United States if at some time during the taxable year the taxpayer is engaged in business in the United States and the activities of such business consist of any one or more of the following activities carried on, in whole or in part, in the United States in transactions with persons situated within or without the United States:

(a) Receiving deposits of funds from the public,

(b) Making personal, mortgage, industrial, or other loans to the public,

(c) Purchasing, selling, discounting, or negotiating for the public on a regular basis, notes, drafts, checks, bills of exchange, acceptances, or other evidences of indebtedness,

(d) Issuing letters of credit to the public and negotiating drafts drawn thereunder,

(e) Providing trust services for the public, or

(f) Financing foreign exchange transactions for the public.

Although the fact that the taxpayer is subjected to the banking and credit laws of a foreign country shall be taken into account in determining whether he is engaged in the active conduct of a banking, financing, or similar business, the character of the business actually carried on during the taxable year in the United States shall determine whether the taxpayer is actively conducting a banking, financing, or similar business in the United States. A foreign corporation which acts merely as a financing vehicle for borrowing funds for its parent corporation or any other person who would be a related person within the meaning of section 954(d)(3) if such foreign corporation were a controlled foreign corporation shall not be considered to be engaged in the active conduct of a banking, financing, or similar business in the United States.

(ii) *Effective connection of income from stocks or securities with active conduct of a banking, financing, or similar business.*—Notwithstanding the rules in subparagraphs (2) and (3) of this paragraph with respect to the asset-use test and the business-activities test, any dividends or interest from stocks or securities, or any gain or loss from the sale or exchange of stocks or securities which are capital assets, which is from sources within the United States and derived by a nonresident alien individual or a foreign corporation in the active conduct during the taxable year of a banking, financing, or similar business in the United States shall be treated as effectively connected for such year with the conduct of that business only if the stocks or securities giving rise to such income, gain, or loss are attributable to the U.S. office through which such business is carried on and—

(a) Were acquired—

(1) As a result of, or in the course of making loans to the public,

(2) In the course of distributing such stocks or securities to the public, or

(3) For the purpose of being used to satisfy the reserve requirements, or other requirements similar to reserve requirements, established by a duly constituted banking authority in the United States, or

(b) Consist of securities (as defined in subdivision (v) of this subparagraph) which are—

(1) Payable on demand or at a fixed maturity date not exceeding 1 year from the date of acquisition,

(2) Issued by the United States, or any agency or instrumentality thereof, or

(3) Not described in (a) or in (1) or (2) of this (b).

However, the amount of interest from securities described in (b)(3) of this subdivision (ii) which shall be treated as effectively connected for the taxable year with the active conduct of a banking, financing, or similar business in the United States shall be an amount (but not in excess of the entire interest for the taxable year from sources within the United States from such securities) determined by multiplying the entire interest for the taxable year from sources within the United States from such securities by a fraction the numerator of which is 10 percent and the denominator of which is the same percentage, determined on the basis of a monthly average for the taxable year, as the book value of the total of such securities held by the U.S. office through which such business is carried on bears to the book value of the total assets of such office. The amount of gain or loss, if any, for the taxable year from the sale or exchange of such securities which shall be treated as effectively connected for the taxable year with the active conduct of a banking, financing, or similar business in the United States shall be an amount (but not in excess of the entire gain or loss for the taxable year from sources within the United States from the sale or exchange of such securities) determined by multiplying the entire gain or loss for the taxable year from sources within the United States from the sale or exchange of such securities by the fraction described in the immediately preceding sentence. The percentage of the denominator of the limiting fraction for such purposes shall be the percentage obtained by separately adding the book value of such securities and such total assets held at the close of each month in the taxable year, dividing each such sum by 12, and then dividing the amount of securities so obtained by the amount of assets so obtained. This subdivision does not apply to dividends from stock owned by a foreign corporation in a domestic corporation of which more than 50 percent of the total combined voting power of all classes of stock entitled to vote is owned by such foreign corporation and which is engaged in the active conduct of a banking business in the United States. The application of this subdivision may be illustrated by the following example:

Example. Foreign corporation M, created under the laws of foreign country Y, has in the United States a branch, B, which during the taxable year is engaged in the active conduct of the banking business in the United States within the meaning of subdivision (i) of this subparagraph. During the taxable year M derives from sources within the United States through the activities carried on through B, $7,500,000 interest from securities described in subdivision *(b)(3)* of this subdivision (ii) and $7,500,000 gain from the sale or exchange of such securities. The monthly average, determined as of the last day of each month in the taxable year, of such securities held by B divided by the monthly average, as so determined, of the total assets held by B equals 15 percent. Under this subdivision, the amount of interest income from such securities that shall be treated as effectively connected for the taxable year with the active conduct by M of a banking business in the United States is $5 million ($7,500,000 interest × 10%/15%), and the amount of gain from the sale or exchange of such securities that shall be treated as effectively connected for such year with the active conduct of such business is $5 million ($7,500,000 gain × 10%/15%).

(iii) *Stocks or securities attributable to U.S. office.*—*(a) In general.*—For purposes of paragraph (c)(5)(ii) of this section, a stock or security shall be deemed to be attributable to a U.S. office only if such office actively and materially participated in soliciting, negotiating, or performing other activities required to arrange the acquisition of the stock or security. The U.S. office need not have been the only active participant in arranging the acquisition of the stock or security.

(b) Exceptions.—A stock or security shall not be deemed to be attributable to a U.S. office merely because such office conducts one or more of the following activities:

(1) Collects or accounts for the dividends, interest, gain, or loss from such stock or security,

(2) Exercises general supervision over the activities of the persons directly responsible for carrying on the activities described in paragraph (c)(5)(iii)*(a)* of this section,

(3) Performs merely clerical functions incident to the acquisition of such stock or security,

(4) Exercises final approval over the execution of the acquisition of such stock or security, or

(5) Holds such stock or security in the United States or records such stock or security on its books or records as having been acquired by such office or for its account.

(c) Effective date.—This paragraph (c)(5)(iii) shall be effective for income includible in taxable years beginning on or after June 18, 1984, except that 26 CFR § 1.864-4(c)(5)(iii) as it appeared in the Code of Federal Regulations revised as of April 1, 1983, shall apply to income received or accrued under a loan made by the taxpayer on or before May 18, 1984 or pursuant to a written binding commitment entered into on or before May 18, 1984.

(iv) *Acquisitions in course of making loans to the public.*—For purposes of subdivision (ii) of this subparagraph—

Reg. § 1.864-4(c)(5)(iv)

(a) A stock or security shall be considered to have been acquired in the course of making a loan to the public where, for example, such stock or security was acquired as additional consideration for the making of the loan,

(b) A stock or security shall be considered to have been acquired as a result of making a loan to the public if, for example, such stock or security was acquired by foreclosure upon a bona fide default of the loan and is held as an ordinary and necessary incident to the active conduct of the banking, financing, or similar business in the United States, and

(c) A stock or security acquired on a stock exchange or organized over-the-counter market shall be considered not to have been acquired as a result of, or in the course of, making loans to the public.

(v) *Security defined.*—For purposes of this subparagraph, a security is any bill, note, bond, debenture, or other evidence of indebtedness, or any evidence of an interest in, or right to subscribe to or purchase, any of the foregoing items.

(vi) *Limitations on application of subparagraph.*—*(a) Other business activity.*—This subparagraph provides rules for determining when certain income from stocks or securities is effectively connected with the active conduct of a banking, financing, or similar business in the United States. Any dividends, interest, gain, or loss from sources within the United States which by reason of the application of subdivision (ii) of this subparagraph is not effectively connected with the active conduct by a nonresident alien individual or a foreign corporation of a banking, financing, or similar business in the United States may be effectively connected for the taxable year, under subparagraph (2) or (3) of this paragraph with the conduct by such taxpayer of another trade or business in the United States, such as, for example, the business of selling or manufacturing goods or merchandise or of trading in stocks or securities for the taxpayer's own account.

(b) Other income.—For rules relating to income, gain, or loss from sources within the United States (other than dividends or interest from, or gain or loss from the sale or exchange of, stocks or securities referred to in subdivision (ii) of this subparagraph) derived in the active conduct of a banking, financing, or similar business in the United States, see subparagraphs (2) and (3) of this paragraph and paragraph (b) of this section.

(vii) *Illustrations.*—The application of this subparagraph may be illustrated by the following examples:

Example (1). Foreign Corporation F, which is created under the laws of foreign country X and engaged in the active conduct of the banking business in country X and a number of other foreign countries, has in the United States a branch, B, which during the taxable year is engaged in the active conduct of the banking business in the United States within the meaning of subdivision (i) of this subparagraph. In the course of its banking business in foreign countries, F receives at its branches located in country X and other foreign countries substantial deposits in U.S. dollars which are transferred to the accounts of B in the United States. During the taxable year, B actively participates in negotiating loans to residents of the United States, such as call loans to U.S. brokers, which are financed from the U.S. dollar deposits transferred to B by F. In addition, B actively participates in purchasing on the New York Stock Exchange and over-the-counter markets long-term bonds and notes issued by the U.S. Government, U.S. Treasury bills, and long-term interest-bearing bonds issued by domestic corporations and having a maturity date of less than 1 year from the date of acquisition, all of which are purchased from the deposits transferred to B by F. All of the securities so acquired are held by B and recorded on its books in the United States. Pursuant to subdivision (ii) of this subparagraph, the interest received by F during the taxable year on these loans, bonds, notes, and bills is effectively connected for such year with the active conduct by F of a banking business in the United States.

Example (2). The facts are the same as in example (1) except that B also actively participates in using part of the U.S. dollar deposits, which are transferred to it by F, to purchase on the New York Stock Exchange shares of common stock issued by various domestic corporations. All of the shares so purchased are considered to be capital assets within the meaning of section 1221 and are recorded on B's books in the United States. None of the shares so purchased were acquired for the purpose of meeting reserve or other similar requirements. During the taxable year some of the shares are sold by B on the stock exchange. Pursuant to subdivision (ii) of this subparagraph, the dividends and gains received by F during the taxable year on these shares of stock are not effectively connected with the active conduct by F of a banking, financing, or similar business in the United States.

Example (3). The facts are the same as in example (1) except that B also uses part of the U.S. dollar deposits, which are transferred to it by F, to make a loan to domestic corporation M. As part of the consideration for the loan, M gives to B a number of shares of common stock issued by M. All of these shares of stock are considered to be capital assets within the meaning of section 1221 and are recorded on B's books in the United States. During the taxable year one-half of these shares of stock is sold by B on the New York Stock Exchange. Pursuant to subdivision (ii) of this subparagraph, the dividends and gains received by F during the taxable year on these shares of stock are effectively connected for such year with the active conduct by F of a banking business in the United States.

Example (4). The facts are the same as in example (1) except that during the taxable year the home office of F in country X actively participates in negotiating loans to residents of the United States, such as call loans to U.S. brokers, which are financed by the U.S. dollar deposits received at the home office and are recorded on the books of the home office. B does not participate in negotiating these loans. Pursuant to subdivision (ii) of this subparagraph the interest received by F during the taxable year on these loans made by the home office in country X is not effectively connected with the active conduct by F of a banking, financing, or similar business in the United States.

Example (5). Foreign corporation Y, which is created under the laws of foreign country X and is engaged in the active conduct of a banking business in country X and other foreign countries, has a branch, C, in the United States that is engaged in the active conduct of a banking business in the United States, within the meaning of paragraph (c)(5)(i) of this section, during the taxable year. C handles the negotiation and acquisition of securities involved in loans made by Y to U.S. persons. C also presents interest coupons with respect to such securities for payment, presents all such securities for payment at maturity, and maintains complete photocopy files with respect to such securities. The activities of the office of Y in country X with respect to these securities consist of giving pro forma approval of the loans, storing the original securities, and recording the securities on the books of the country X office. Pursuant to paragraphs (c)(5)(ii) and (c)(5)(iii) of this section, the U.S. source interest income received by Y during the taxable year on these securities is effectively connected for such year with the active conduct by Y of a banking business in the United States.

(6) *Income related to personal services of an individual.*—(i) *Income, gain, or loss from assets.*—Income or gains from sources within the United States described in section 871(a)(1) and derived from an asset, and gain or loss from sources within the United States from the sale or exchange of capital assets realized by a nonresident alien individual engaged in a trade or business in the United States during the taxable year solely by reason of his performing personal services in the United States shall not be treated as income, gain, or loss which is effectively connected for the taxable year with the conduct of a trade or business in the United States, unless there is a direct economic relationship between his holding of the asset from which the income, gain, or loss results and his trade or business of performing the personal services.

(ii) *Wages, salaries, and pensions.*—Wages, salaries, fees, compensations, emoluments, or other remunerations, including bonuses, received by a nonresident alien individual for performing personal services in the United States which, under paragraph (a) of § 1.864-2, constitute engaging in a trade or business in the United States, and pensions and retirement pay attributable to such personal services, constitute income which is effectively connected for the taxable year with the conduct of a trade or business in the United States by that individual if he is engaged in a trade or business in the United States at some time during the taxable year in which such income is received.

(7) *Effective date.*—Paragraphs (c)(2) and (c)(6)(i) of this section are effective for taxable years beginning on or after June 6, 1996. [Reg. § 1.864-4.]

☐ [*T.D.* 7216, 11-2-72. *Amended by T.D.* 7332, 12-30-74; *T.D.* 7958, 5-17-84 *and T.D.* 8657, 3-5-96.]

Proposed Amendments to Regulation

§ 1.864-4. U.S. source income effectively connected with U.S. business.

* * *

(c) * * *

(2) * * *

(iv) *Special rule relating to a global dealing operation.*—An asset used in a global dealing operation, as defined in § 1.482-8(a)(2)(i), will be treated as an asset used in a U.S. trade or business only if and to the extent that the U.S. trade or business is a participant in the global dealing operation under § 1.863-3(h)(3), and income, gain or loss produced by the asset is U.S. source under § 1.863-3(h) or would be treated as U.S. source if § 1.863-3(h) were to apply to such amounts.

* * *

(3) * * *

(ii) *Special rule relating to a global dealing operation.*—A U.S. trade or business shall be treated as a material factor in the realization of income, gain or loss derived in a global dealing operation, as defined in § 1.482-8(a)(2)(i), only if and to the extent that the U.S. trade or business is a participant in the global dealing operation under § 1.863-3(h)(3), and income, gain or loss realized by the U.S. trade or business is U.S. source under § 1.863-3(h) or would be treated as U.S. source if § 1.863-3(h) were to apply to such amounts.

* * *

(5) * * *
(vi) * * *

(a) Certain income earned by a global dealing operation.—Notwithstanding paragraph (c)(5)(ii) of this section, U.S. source interest, including substitute interest as defined in § 1.861-2(a)(7), and dividend income, including substitute dividends as defined in § 1.861-3(a)(6), derived by a participant in a global dealing operation, as defined in § 1.482-8(a)(2)(i), shall be treated as attributable to the foreign corporation's U.S. trade or business, only if and to the extent that the income would be treated as U.S. source if § 1.863-3(h) were to apply to such amounts.

[Prop. Reg. § 1.864-4.]

[Proposed 3-6-98.]

Proposed Amendments to Regulation

§ 1.864-4. U.S. source income effectively connected with U.S. business.

* * *

(c) * * *
(2) * * *
(iii) * * *

(b) Paragraph (c)(2)(iii) of this section shall not apply to stock of a corporation (whether domestic or foreign) held by a foreign insurance company unless the foreign insurance company owns 10 percent or more of the total voting power or value of all classes of stock of such corporation. For purposes of this section, section 318(a) shall be applied in determining ownership, except that in applying section 318(a)(2)(C), the phrase "10 percent" is used instead of the phrase "50 percent."

* * *

[Prop. Reg. § 1.864-4.]

[Proposed 6-25-2004.]

§ 1.864-5. Foreign source income effectively connected with U.S. business.—(a) *In general.*—This section applies only to a nonresident alien individual or a foreign corporation that is engaged in a trade or business in the United States at some time during a taxable year beginning after December 31, 1966, and to the income, gain, or loss of such person from sources without the United States. The income, gain, or loss of such person for the taxable year from sources without the United States which is specified in paragraph (b) of this section shall be treated as effectively connected for the taxable year with the conduct of a trade or business in the United States, only if he also has in the United States at some time during the taxable year, but not necessarily at the time the income, gain, or loss is realized, an office or other fixed place of business, as defined in § 1.864-7, to which such income, gain, or loss is attributable in accordance with § 1.864-6. The income of such person for the taxable year from sources without the United States which is specified in paragraph (c) of this section shall be treated as effectively connected for the taxable year with the conduct of a trade or business in the United States when derived by a foreign corporation carrying on a life insurance business in the United States. Except as provided in paragraphs (b) and (c) of this section, no income, gain, or loss of a nonresident alien individual or a foreign corporation for the taxable year from sources without the United States shall be treated as effectively connected for the taxable year with the conduct of a trade or business in the United States by that person. Any income, gain, or loss described in paragraph (b) or (c) of this section which, if it were derived by the taxpayer from sources within the United States for the taxable year, would not be treated under § 1.864-4 as effectively connected for the taxable year with the conduct of a trade or business in the United States shall not be treated under this section as effectively connected for the taxable year with the conduct of a trade or business in the United States.

(b) *Income other than income attributable to U.S. life insurance business.*—Income, gain, or loss from sources without the United States other than income described in paragraph (c) of this section shall be taken into account pursuant to paragraph (a) of this section in applying §§ 1.864-6 and 1.864-7 only if it consists of—

(1) *Rents, royalties, or gains on sales of intangible property.*—(i) Rents or royalties for the use of, or for the privilege of using, intangible personal property located outside the United States or from any interest in such property, including rents or royalties for the use, or for the privilege of using, outside the United States, patents, copyrights, secret processes and formulas, good will, trademarks, trade brands, franchises, and other like properties, if such rents or royalties are derived in the active conduct of the trade or business in the United States.

(ii) Gains or losses on the sale or exchange of intangible personal property located outside the United States or from any interest in such property, including gains or losses on the sale or exchange of the privilege of using, outside the United States, patents, copyrights, secret processes and formulas, good will, trademarks, trade brands, franchises, and other like properties, if such gains or losses are derived in the active conduct of the trade or business in the United States.

(iii) Whether or not such an item of income, gain, or loss is derived in the active conduct of a trade or business in the United States shall be determined from the facts and circumstances of each case. The frequency with which a nonresident alien individual or a foreign corporation enters into transactions of the type from which the income, gain, or loss is derived shall not of itself determine that the income, gain, or loss is derived in the active conduct of a trade or business.

(iv) This subparagraph shall not apply to rents or royalties for the use of, or for the privilege of using, real property or tangible personal property, or to gain or loss from the sale or exchange of such property.

(2) *Dividends or interest, or gains or loss from sales of stocks or securities.*—(i) *In general.*—Dividends or interest from any transaction, or gains or losses on the sale or exchange of stocks or securities, realized by *(a)* a nonresident alien individual or a foreign corporation in the active conduct of a banking, financing, or similar business in the United States or *(b)* a foreign corporation engaged in business in the United States whose principal business is trading in stocks or securities for its own account. Whether the taxpayer is engaged in the active conduct of a banking, financing, or similar business in the United States for purposes of this subparagraph shall be determined in accordance with the principles of paragraph (c)(5)(i) of § 1.864-4.

(ii) *Substitute payments.*—For purposes of this paragraph (b)(2), a substitute interest payment (as defined in § 1.861-2(a)(7)) received by a foreign person subject to tax under this paragraph (b) pursuant to a securities lending transaction or a sale-repurchase transaction (as defined in § 1.861-2(a)(7)) with respect to a security (as defined in § 1.864-6(b)(2)(ii)(c)) shall have the same character as interest income paid or accrued with respect to the terms of the transferred security. Similarly, for purposes of this paragraph (b)(2), a substitute dividend payment (as defined in § 1.861-3(a)(6)) received by a foreign person pursuant to a securities lending transaction or a sale-repurchase transaction (as defined in § 1.861-3(a)(6)) with respect to a stock shall have the same character as a distribution received with respect to the transferred security. This paragraph (b)(2)(ii) is applicable to payments made after November 13, 1997.

(iii) *Incidental investment activity.*—This subparagraph shall not apply to income, gain, or loss realized by a nonresident alien individual or foreign corporation on stocks or securities held, sold, or exchanged in connection with incidental investment activities carried on by that person. Thus, a foreign corporation which is primarily a holding company owning significant percentages of the stocks or securities issued by other corporations shall not be treated under this subparagraph as a corporation the principal business of which is trading in stocks or securities for its own account, solely because it engages in sporadic purchases or sales of stocks or securities to adjust its portfolio. The application of this subdivision may be illustrated by the following example:

Example. F, a foreign corporation, owns voting stock in foreign corporations M, N, and P, its holdings in such corporations constituting 15, 20, and 100 percent, respectively, of all classes of their outstanding voting stock. Each of such stock holdings by F represents approximately 20 percent of its total assets. The remaining 40 percent of F's assets consist of other investments, 20 percent being invested in securities issued by foreign governments and in stocks and bonds issued by other corporations in which F does not own a significant percentage of their outstanding voting stock, and 20 percent being invested in bonds issued by N. None of the assets of F are held primarily for sale; but, if the officers of that corporation were to decide that other investments would be preferable to its holding of such assets, F would sell the stocks and securities and reinvest the proceeds therefrom in other holdings. Any income, gain, or loss which F may derive from this investment activity is not considered to be realized by a foreign corporation described in subdivision (i) of this subparagraph.

(3) *Sale of goods or merchandise through U.S. office.*—(i) Income, gain, or loss from the sale of inventory items or of property held primarily for sale to customers in the ordinary course of business, as described in section 1221(1), where the sale is outside the United States but through the office or other fixed place of business which the nonresident alien or foreign corporation has in the United States, irrespective of the destination to which such property is sent for use, consumption, or disposition.

(ii) This subparagraph shall not apply to income, gain, or loss resulting from a sales contract entered into on or before February 24, 1966. See section 102(e)(1) of the Foreign Investors Tax Act of 1966 (80 Stat. 1547). Thus, for example, the sales office in the United States of a foreign corporation enters into negotiations for the sale of 500,000 industrial bearings which the corporation produces in a foreign country for consumption in the Western Hemisphere. These negotiations culminate in a binding agreement entered into on January 1, 1966. By its terms delivery under the contract is to be made over a period of 3 years beginning in March of 1966. Payment is due upon delivery. The income from sources without the United States resulting from this sale negotiated by the U.S. sales office of the foreign corporation shall not be taken into account under this subparagraph for any taxable year.

(iii) This subparagraph shall not apply to gains or losses on the sale or exchange of intangible personal property to which subparagraph (1) of this paragraph applies or of stocks or securities to which subparagraph (2) of this paragraph applies.

(c) *Income attributable to U.S. life insurance business.*—(1) All of the income for the taxable year of a foreign corporation described in subparagraph (2) of this paragraph from sources without the United States, which is attributable to its U.S. life insurance business, shall be treated as effectively connected for the taxable year with the conduct of a trade or business in the United States by that corporation. Thus, in determining its life insurance company taxable income from its U.S. business for purposes of section 802, the foreign corporation shall include all of its items of income from sources without the United States which would appropriately be taken into account in determining the life insurance company taxable income of a domestic corporation. The income to which this subparagraph applies shall be taken into account for purposes of paragraph (a) of this section without reference to §§ 1.864-6 and 1.864-7.

(2) A foreign corporation to which subparagraph (1) of this paragraph applies is a foreign corporation carrying on an insurance business in the United States during the taxable year which—

(i) Without taking into account its income not effectively connected for that year with the conduct of any trade or business in the United States, would qualify as a life insurance company under part I (section 801 and following) of subchapter L, chapter 1 of the Code, if it were a domestic corporation, and

(ii) By reason of section 842 is taxable under that part on its income which is effectively connected for that year with its conduct of any trade or business in the United States.

(d) *Excluded foreign source income.*—Notwithstanding paragraphs (b) and (c) of this section, no income from sources without the United States shall be treated as effectively connected for any taxable year with the conduct of a trade or business in the United States by a nonresident alien individual or a foreign corporation if the income consists of—

(1) *Dividends, interest, or royalties paid by a related foreign corporation.*—Dividends, interest, or royalties paid by a foreign corporation in which the nonresident alien individual or the foreign corporation described in paragraph (a) of this section owns, within the meaning of section 958(a), or is considered as owning, by applying the ownership rules of section 958(b), at the time such items are paid more than 50 percent of the total combined voting power of all classes of stock entitled to vote.

(2) *Subpart F income of a controlled foreign corporation.*—Any income of the foreign corporation described in paragraph (a) of this section which is subpart F income for the taxable year, as determined under section 952(a), even though part of the income is attributable to amounts which, if distributed by the foreign corporation, would be distributed with respect to its stock which is owned by shareholders who are not U.S. shareholders within the meaning of section 951(b). This subparagraph shall not apply to any income of the foreign corporation which is excluded in determining its subpart F income for the taxable year for purposes of section 952(a). Thus, for example, this subparagraph shall not apply to—

(i) Foreign base company shipping income which is excluded under section 954(b)(2),

(ii) Foreign base company income amounting to less than 10 percent (30 percent in the case of taxable years of foreign corporations ending before January 1, 1976) of gross income which by reason of section 954(b)(3)(A) does not become subpart F income for the taxable year,

(iii) Any income excluded from foreign base company income under section 954(b)(4), relating to exception for foreign corporations not availed of to reduce taxes,

(iv) Any income derived in the active conduct of a trade or business which is excluded under section 954(c)(3), or

(v) Any income received from related persons which is excluded under section 954(c)(4).

This subparagraph shall apply to the foreign corporation's entire subpart F income for the taxable year determined under section 952(a), even though no amount is included in the gross income of a U.S. shareholder under section

951(a) with respect to that subpart F income because of the minimum distribution provisions of section 963(a) or because of the reduction under section 970(a) with respect to an export trade corporation. This subparagraph shall apply only to a foreign corporation which is a controlled foreign corporation within the meaning of section 957 and the regulations thereunder. The application of this subparagraph may be illustrated by the following examples:

Example (1). Controlled foreign corporation M, incorporated under the laws of foreign country X, is engaged in the business of purchasing and selling merchandise manufactured in foreign country Y by an unrelated person. M negotiates sales, through its sales office in the United States, of its merchandise for use outside of country X. These sales are made outside the United States, and the merchandise is sold for use outside the United States. No office maintained by M outside the United States participates materially in the sales made through its U.S. sales office. These activities constitute the only activities of M. During the taxable year M derives $100,000 income from these sales made through its U.S. sales office, and all of such income is foreign base company sales income by reason of section 954(d)(2) and paragraph (b) of § 1.954-3. The entire $100,000 is also subpart F income, determined under section 952(a). In addition, all of this income would, without reference to section 864(c)(4)(D)(ii) and this subparagraph, be treated as effectively connected for the taxable year with the conduct of a trade or business in the United States by M. Through its entire taxable year 60 percent of the one class of stock of M is owned within the meaning of section 958(a) by U.S. shareholders, as defined in section 951(b), and 40 percent of its one class of stock is owned within the meaning of section 958(a) by persons who are not U.S. shareholders, as defined in section 951(b). Although only $60,000 of the subpart F income of M for the taxable year is includible in the income of the U.S. shareholders under section 951(a), the entire subpart F income of $100,000 constitutes income which, by reason of section 864(c)(4)(D)(ii) and this subparagraph, is not effectively connected for the taxable year with the conduct of a trade or business in the United States by M.

Example (2). The facts are the same as in example (1) except that the foreign base company sales income amounts to $150,000 determined in accordance with paragraph (d)(3)(i) of § 1.954-1, and that M also has gross income from sources without the United States of $50,000 from sales, through its sales office in the United States, of merchandise for use in country X. These sales are made outside the United States. All of this income would, without reference to section 864(c)(4)(D)(ii) and this subparagraph, be treated as effectively connected for the taxable year with the conduct of a trade or business in the United States by M. Since the foreign base company income of $150,000 amounts to 75 percent of the entire gross income of $200,000, determined as provided in paragraph (d)(3)(ii) of § 1.954-1, the entire $200,000 constitutes foreign base company income under section 954(b)(3)(B). Assuming that M has no amounts to be taken into account under paragraphs (1), (2), (4), and (5) of section 954(b), the $200,000 is also subpart F income, determined under section 952(a). This subpart F income of $200,000 constitutes income which, by reason of section 864(c)(4)(D)(ii) and this subparagraph, is not effectively connected for the taxable year with the conduct of a trade or business in the United States by M.

(3) *Interest on certain deposits.*—Interest which, by reason of section 861(a)(1)(A) (relating to interest on deposits with banks, savings and loan associations, and insurance companies paid or credited before January 1, 1976) and paragraph (c) of § 1.864-4, is determined to be income from sources without the United States because it is not effectively connected for the taxable year with the conduct of a trade or business in the United States by the nonresident alien individual or foreign corporation. [Reg. § 1.864-5.]

☐ [*T.D.* 7216, 11-2-72. *Amended by T.D.* 7893, 5-11-83 *and T.D.* 8735, 10-6-97.]

§ 1.864-6. Income, gain, or loss attributable to an office or other fixed place of business in the United States.—(a) *In general.*—Income, gain, or loss from sources without the United States which is specified in paragraph (b) of § 1.864-5 and received by a nonresident alien individual or a foreign corporation engaged in a trade or business in the United States at some time during a taxable year beginning after December 31, 1966, shall be treated as effectively connected for the taxable year with the conduct of a trade or business in the United States only if the income, gain, or loss is attributable under paragraphs (b) and (c) of this section to an office or other fixed place of business, as defined in § 1.864-7, which the taxpayer has in the United States at some time during the taxable year.

(b) *Material factor test.*—(1) *In general.*—For purposes of paragraph (a) of this section, income, gain, or loss is attributable to an office or other fixed place of business which a nonresident alien individual or a foreign corporation has in the United States only if such office or other fixed place of business is a material factor in the realization of the income, gain, or loss, and if the income, gain, or loss is realized in the ordinary course of the trade or business carried on through that office or other fixed place of business. For this purpose, the activities of the office or other fixed place of business shall not be considered to be a material factor in the realization of the income, gain, or loss unless they provide a significant contribution to, by being an essential economic element in, the realization of the income, gain, or loss. Thus, for example, meetings in the United States of the board of directors of a foreign corporation do not of themselves constitute a material factor in the realization of income, gain, or loss. It is not necessary that the activities of the office or other fixed place of business in the United States be a major factor in the realization of income, gain, or loss. An office or other fixed place of business located in the United States at some time during a taxable year may be a material factor in the realization of an item of income, gain, or loss for that year even though the office or other fixed place of business is not present in the United States when the income, gain, or loss is realized.

(2) *Application of material factor test to specific classes of income.*—For purposes of paragraph (a) of this section, an office or other fixed place of business which a nonresident alien individual or a foreign corporation, engaged in a trade or business in the United States at some time during the taxable year, had in the United States, shall be considered a material factor in the realization of income, gain, or loss consisting of—

(i) *Rents, royalties, or gains on sales of intangible property.*—Rents, royalties, or gains or losses, from intangible personal property specified in paragraph (b)(1) of § 1.864-5, if the office or other fixed place of business either actively participates in soliciting, negotiating, or performing other activities required to arrange, the lease, license, sale, or exchange from which such income, gain, or loss is derived or performs significant services incident to such lease, license, sale, or exchange. An office or other fixed place of business in the United States shall not be considered to be a material factor in the realization of income, gain, or loss for purposes of this subdivision merely because the office or other fixed place of business conducts one or more of the following activities: (*a*) develops, creates, produces, or acquires and adds substantial value to, the property which is leased, licensed, or sold, or exchanged, (*b*) collects or accounts for the rents, royalties, gains, or losses, (*c*) exercises general supervision over the activities of the persons directly responsible for carrying on the activities or services described in the immediately preceding sentence, (*d*) performs merely clerical functions incident to the lease, license, sale or exchange or (*e*) exercises final approval over the execution of the lease, license, sale, or exchange. The application of this subdivision may be illustrated by the following examples:

Example (1). F, a foreign corporation, is engaged in the active conduct of the business of licensing patents which it has either purchased or developed in the United States. F has a business office in the United States. Licenses for the use of such patents outside the United States are negotiated by offices of F located outside the United States, subject to approval by an officer of such corporation located in the U.S. office. All services which are rendered to F's foreign licensees are performed by employees of F's offices located outside the United States. None of the income, gain, or loss resulting from the foreign licenses so negotiated by F is attributable to its business office in the United States.

Example (2). N, a foreign corporation, is engaged in the active conduct of the business of distributing motion picture films and television programs. N does not distribute such films or programs in the United States. The foreign distribution rights to these films and programs are acquired by N's U.S. business office from the U.S. owners of these films and programs. Employees of N's offices located in various foreign countries carry on in such countries all the solicitations and negotiations for the licensing of these films and programs to licensees located in such countries and provide the necessary incidental services to the licensees. N's U.S. office collects the rentals from the foreign licensees and maintains the necessary records of income and expense. Officers of N located in the United States also maintain general supervision over the employees of the foreign offices, but the foreign employees conduct the day to day business of N outside the United States of soliciting, negotiating, or performing other activities required to arrange the foreign licenses. None of the income, gain, or loss resulting from the foreign licenses so negotiated by N is attributable to N's U.S. office.

(ii) *Dividends or interest, or gains or losses from sales of stock or securities.*—(*a*) *In general.*—Dividends or interest from any transaction, or gains or losses on the sale or exchange of stocks or securities, specified in paragraph (b)(2) of § 1.864-5, if the office or other fixed place of business either actively participates in soliciting, negotiating, or performing other activities required to arrange, the issue, acquisition, sale, or exchange, of the asset from which such income, gain, or loss is derived or performs significant services incident to such issue, acquisition, sale, or ex-

Reg. § 1.864-6(b)(2)

change. An office or other fixed place of business in the United States shall not be considered to be a material factor in the realization of income, gain, or loss for purposes of this subdivision merely because the office or other fixed place of business conducts one or more of the following activities: (*1*) collects or accounts for the dividends, interest, gains, or losses, (*2*) exercises general supervision over the activities of the persons directly responsible for carrying on the activities or services described in the immediately preceding sentence, (*3*) performs merely clerical functions incident to the issue, acquisition, sale, or exchange, or (*4*) exercises final approval over the execution of the issue, acquisition, sale, or exchange.

(*b*) *Effective connection of income from stocks or securities with active conduct of a banking, financing, or similar business.*—Notwithstanding (*a*) of this subdivision (ii), the determination as to whether any dividends or interest from stocks or securities, or gain or loss from the sale or exchange of stocks or securities which are capital assets, which is from sources without the United States and derived by a nonresident alien individual or a foreign corporation in the active conduct during the taxable year of a banking, financing, or similar business in the United States, shall be treated as effectively connected for such year with the active conduct of that business shall be made by applying the principles of paragraph (c)(5)(ii) of § 1.864-4 for determining whether income, gain, or loss of such type from sources within the United States is effectively connected for such year with the active conduct of that business.

(*c*) *Security defined.*—For purposes of this subdivision (ii), a security is any bill, note, bond, debenture, or other evidence of indebtedness, or any evidence of an interest in, or right to subscribe to or purchase, any of the foregoing items.

(*d*) *Limitations on application of rules on banking, financing, or similar business.*—(*1*) *Trading for taxpayer's own account.*—The provisions of (*b*) of this subdivision (ii) apply for purposes of determining when certain income, gain, or loss from stocks or securities is effectively connected with the active conduct of a banking, financing, or similar business in the United States. Any dividends, interest, gain, or loss from sources without the United States which by reason of the application of (*b*) of this subdivision (ii) is not effectively connected with the active conduct by a foreign corporation of a banking, financing, or similar business in the United States may be effectively connected for the taxable year, under (*a*) of this subdivision (ii), with the conduct by such taxpayer of a trade or business in the United States which consists of trading in stocks or securities for the taxpayer's own account.

(*2*) *Other income.*—For rules relating to dividends or interest from sources without the United States (other than dividends or interest from, or gain or loss from the sale or exchange of, stocks or securities referred to in (*b*) of this subdivision (ii)) derived in the active conduct of a banking, financing, or similar business in the United States, see (*a*) of this subdivision (ii).

(iii) *Sale of goods or merchandise through U.S. office.*—Income, gain, or loss from sales of goods or merchandise specified in paragraph (b)(3) of § 1.864-5, if the office or other fixed place of business actively participates in soliciting the order, negotiating the contract of sale, or performing other significant services necessary for the consummation of the sale which are not the subject of a separate agreement between the seller and the buyer. The office or other fixed place of business in the United States shall be considered a material factor in the realization of income, gain, or loss from a sale made as a result of a sales order received in such office or other fixed place of business except where the sales order is received unsolicited and that office or other fixed place of business is not held out to potential customers as the place to which such sales orders should be sent. The income, gain, or loss must be realized in the ordinary course of the trade or business carried on through the office or other fixed place of business in the United States. Thus, if a foreign corporation is engaged solely in a manufacturing business in the United States, the income derived by its office in the United States as a result of an occasional sale outside the United States is not attributable to the U.S. office if the sales office of the manufacturing business is located outside the United States. On the other hand, if a foreign corporation establishes a sales office in the United States to sell for consumption in the Western Hemisphere merchandise which the corporation produces in Africa, the income derived by the sales office in the United States as a result of an occasional sale made by it in Europe shall be attributable to the U.S. sales office. An office or other fixed place of business in the United States shall not be considered to be a material factor in the realization of income, gain, or loss for purposes of this subdivision merely because of one or more of the following activities: (*a*) the sale is made subject to the final approval of such office or other fixed place of business, (*b*) the property sold is held in, and distributed from, such office or other fixed place of business, (*c*) samples of the property sold are displayed (but not otherwise promoted or sold) in

Reg. § 1.864-6(b)(2)(iii)

such office or other fixed place of business, or (d) such office or other fixed place of business performs merely clerical functions incident to the sale. Activities carried on by employees of an office or other fixed place of business constitute activities of that office or other fixed place of business.

(3) *Limitation where foreign office is a material factor in realization of income.*—(i) *Goods or merchandise destined for foreign use, consumption, or disposition.*—Notwithstanding subparagraphs (1) and (2) of this paragraph, an office or other fixed place of business which a nonresident alien individual or a foreign corporation has in the United States shall not be considered, for purposes of paragraph (a) of this section, to be a material factor in the realization of income, gain or loss from sales of goods or merchandise specified in paragraph (b)(3) of § 1.864-5 if the property is sold for use, consumption, or disposition outside the United States and an office or other fixed place of business, as defined in § 1.864-7, which such nonresident alien individual or foreign corporation has outside the United States participates materially in the sale. For this purpose an office or other fixed place of business which the taxpayer has outside the United States shall be considered to have participated materially in a sale made through the office or other fixed place of business in the United States if the office or other fixed place of business outside the United States actively participates in soliciting the order resulting in the sale, negotiating the contract of sale, or performing other significant services necessary for the consummation of the sale which are not the subject of a separate agreement between the seller and buyer. An office or other fixed place of business which the taxpayer has outside the United States shall not be considered to have participated materially in a sale merely because of one or more of the following activities: (a) The sale is made subject to the final approval of such office or other fixed place of business, (b) the property sold is held in, and distributed from, such office or other fixed place of business, (c) samples of the property sold are displayed (but not otherwise promoted or sold) in such office or other fixed place of business, (d) such office or other fixed place of business is used for purposes of having title to the property pass outside the United States, or (e) such office or other fixed place of business performs merely clerical functions incident to the sale.

(ii) *Rules for determining country of use, consumption, or disposition.*—(a) *In general.*— As a general rule, personal property which is sold to an unrelated person shall be presumed for purposes of this subparagraph to have been sold for use, consumption, or disposition in the country of destination of the property sold; for such purpose, the occurrence in a country of a temporary interruption in shipment of property shall not cause that country to be considered the country of destination. However, if at the time of a sale of personal property to an unrelated person the taxpayer knew, or should have known from the facts and circumstances surrounding the transaction, that the property probably would not be used, consumed, or disposed of in the country of destination, the taxpayer must determine the country of ultimate use, consumption, or disposition of the property or the property shall be presumed to have been sold for use, consumption, or disposition in the United States. A taxpayer who sells personal property to a related person shall be presumed to have sold the property for use, consumption, or disposition in the United States unless the taxpayer establishes the use made of the property by the related person; once he has established that the related person has disposed of the property, the rules in the two immediately preceding sentences relating to sales to an unrelated person shall apply at the first stage in the chain of distribution at which a sale is made by a related person to an unrelated person. Notwithstanding the preceding provisions of this subdivision (a), a taxpayer who sells personal property to any person whose principal business consists of selling from inventory to retail customers at retail outlets outside the United States may assume at the time of the sale to that person that the property will be used, consumed, or disposed of outside the United States. For purposes of this (a), a person is related to another person if either person owns or controls directly or indirectly the other, or if any third person or persons own or control directly or indirectly both. For this purpose, the term "control" includes any kind of control, whether or not legally enforceable, and however exercised or exercisable. For illustrations of the principles of this subdivision, see paragraph (a)(3)(iv) of § 1.954-3.

(b) *Fungible goods.*—For purposes of this subparagraph, a taxpayer who sells to a purchaser personal property which because of its fungible nature cannot reasonably be specifically traced to other purchasers and to the countries of ultimate use, consumption, or disposition shall, unless the taxpayer establishes a different disposition as being proper, treat that property as being sold, for ultimate use, consumption, or disposition in those countries, and to those other purchasers, in the same proportions in which property from the fungible mass of the first purchaser is sold in the ordinary course of business by such first purchaser. No apportionment is required to be made, however, on the basis of sporadic sales by the first purchaser. This (*b*) shall apply only in a case where the taxpayer knew, or should have known from the facts and circumstances surrounding the transaction, the manner in which the first purchaser disposes of property from the fungible mass.

(iii) *Illustration.*—The application of this subparagraph may be illustrated by the following example:

Example. Foreign corporation M has a sales office in the United States during the taxable year through which it sells outside the United States for use in foreign countries industrial electrical generators which such corporation manufactures in a foreign country. M is not a controlled foreign corporation within the meaning of section 957 and the regulations thereunder, and, by reason of its activities in the United States, is engaged in business in the United States during the taxable year. The generators require specialized installation and continuous adjustment and maintenance services. M has an office in foreign country X which is the only organization qualified to perform these installation, adjustment, and maintenance services. During the taxable year M sells several generators through its U.S. office for use in foreign country Y under sales contracts which also provide for installation, adjustment, and maintenance by its office in country X. The generators are installed in country Y by employees of M's office in country X, who also are responsible for the servicing of the equipment. Since the office of M in country X performs significant services incident to these sales which are necessary for their consummation and are not subject of a separate agreement between M and the purchaser, the U.S. office of M is not considered to be a material factor in the realization of the income from the sales and, for purposes of paragraph (a) of this section, such income is not attributable to the U.S. office of that corporation.

(c) *Amount of income, gain, or loss allocable to U.S. office.*—(1) *In general.*—If, in accordance with paragraph (b) of this section, an office or other fixed place of business which a nonresident alien individual or a foreign corporation has in the United States at some time during the taxable year is a material factor in the realization for that year of an item of income, gain, or loss specified in paragraph (b) of §1.864-5, such item of income, gain, or loss shall be considered to be allocable in its entirety to that office or other fixed place of business. In no case may any income, gain, or loss for the taxable year from sources within the United States, or part thereof, be allocable under this paragraph to an office or other fixed place of business which a nonresident alien individual or a foreign corporation has in the United States if the taxpayer is at no time during the taxable year engaged in a trade or business in the United States.

(2) *Special limitation in case of sales of goods or merchandise through U.S. office.*—Notwithstanding subparagraph (1) of this paragraph, in the case of a sale of goods or merchandise specified in paragraph (b)(3) of §1.864-5, which is not a sale to which paragraph (b)(3)(i) of this section applies, the amount of income which shall be considered to be allocable to the office or other fixed place of business which the nonresident alien individual or foreign corporation has in the United States shall not exceed the amount which would be treated as income from sources within the United States if the taxpayer had sold the goods or merchandise in the United States. See, for example, section 863(b)(2) and paragraph (b) of §1.863-3, which prescribes, as available method for determining the income from sources within the United States, the independent factory or production price method, the gross sales and property apportionment method, and any other method regularly employed by the taxpayer which more clearly reflects taxable income from such sources than those specifically authorized.

(3) *Illustrations.*—The application of this paragraph may be illustrated by the following examples:

Example (1). Foreign corporation M, which is not a controlled foreign corporation within the meaning of section 957 and the regulations thereunder, manufactures machinery in a foreign country and sells the machinery outside the United States through its sales office in the United States for use in foreign countries. Title to the property which is sold is transferred to the foreign purchaser outside the United States, but no office or other fixed place of business of M in a foreign country participates materially in the sale made through its U.S. office. During the taxable year M derives a total taxable income (determined as though M were a domestic corporation) of $250,000 from these sales. If the sales made through the U.S. office for the taxable year had been made in the United States and the property had been sold for use in the United States, the taxable income from sources within the United States from such sales would have been $100,000, determined as provided in section 863 and 882(c) and the regulations thereunder. The taxable income which is allocable to M's U.S. sales office pursuant to this paragraph and which is effectively connected for the taxable year with the conduct of a trade or business within the United States by that corporation is $100,000.

Reg. §1.864-6(c)(3)

Example (2). Foreign corporation N, which is not a controlled foreign corporation within the meaning of section 957 and the regulations thereunder, has an office in a foreign country which purchases merchandise and sells it through its sales office in the United States for use in various foreign countries, such sales being made outside the United States and title to the property passing outside the United States. No other office of N participates materially in these sales made through its U.S. office. By reason of its sales activities in the United States, N is engaged in business in the United States during the taxable year. During the taxable year N derives taxable income (determined as though N were a domestic corporation) of $300,000 from these sales made through its U.S. sales office. If the sales made through the U.S. office for the taxable year had been made in the United States and the property had been sold for use in the United States, the taxable income from sources within the United States from such sales would also have been $300,000, determined as provided in sections 861 and 882(c) and the regulations thereunder. The taxable income which is allocable to N's U.S. sales office pursuant to this paragraph and which is effectively connected for the taxable year with the conduct of a trade or business in the United States by that corporation is $300,000.

Example (3). The facts are the same as in example (2), except that N has an office in a foreign country which participates materially in the sales which are made through its U.S. office. The taxable income which is allocable to N's U.S. sales office is not effectively connected for the taxable year with the conduct of a trade or business in the United States by that corporation. [Reg. § 1.864-6.]

☐ [*T.D.* 7216, 11-2-72.]

§ 1.864-7. Definition of office or other fixed place of business.—(a) *In general.*—(1) This section applies for purposes of determining whether a nonresident alien individual or a foreign corporation that is engaged in a trade or business in the United States at some time during a taxable year beginning after December 31, 1966, has an office or other fixed place of business in the United States for purposes of applying section 864(c)(4)(B) and § 1.864-6 to income, gain, or loss specified in paragraph (b) of § 1.864-5 from sources without the United States or has an office or other fixed place of business outside the United States for purposes of applying section 864(c)(4)(B)(iii) and paragraph (b)(3)(i) of § 1.864-6 to sales of goods or merchandise for use, consumption, or disposition outside the United States.

(2) In making a determination under this section due regard shall be given to the facts and circumstances of each case, particularly to the nature of the taxpayer's trade or business and the physical facilities actually required by the taxpayer in the ordinary course of the conduct of his trade or business.

(3) The law of a foreign country shall not be controlling in determining whether a nonresident alien individual or a foreign corporation has an office or other fixed place of business.

(b) *Fixed facilities.*—(1) *In general.*—As a general rule, an office or other fixed place of business is a fixed facility, that is, a place, site, structure, or other similar facility, through which a nonresident alien individual or a foreign corporation engages in a trade or business. For this purpose an office or other fixed place of business shall include, but shall not be limited to, a factory; a store or other sales outlet; a workshop; or a mine, quarry, or other place of extraction of natural resources. A fixed facility may be considered an office or other fixed place of business whether or not the facility is continuously used by a nonresident alien individual or foreign corporation.

(2) *Use of another person's office or other fixed place of business.*—A nonresident alien individual or a foreign corporation shall not be considered to have an office or other fixed place of business merely because such alien individual or foreign corporation uses another person's office or other fixed place of business, whether or not the office or place of business of a related person, through which to transact a trade or business, if the trade or business activities of the alien individual or foreign corporation in that office or other fixed place of business are relatively sporadic or infrequent, taking into account the overall needs and conduct of that trade or business.

(c) *Management activity.*—A foreign corporation shall not be considered to have an office or other fixed place of business merely because a person controlling that corporation has an office or other fixed place of business from which general supervision and control over the policies of the foreign corporation are exercised. The fact that top management decisions affecting the foreign corporation are made in a country shall not of itself mean that the foreign corporation has an office or other fixed place of business in that country. For example, a foreign sales corporation which is a wholly owned subsidiary of a domestic corporation shall not be considered to have an office or other fixed place of business in the United States merely because of the presence in the United States of officers of the domestic parent corporation who are generally responsible only for the policy decisions affecting the foreign sales corporation, provided that the foreign corporation has a chief executive officer, whether or not he is also an officer of the domestic parent corporation, who conducts the day-to-day trade or business of the foreign corporation from a foreign office. The result in this example would be the same even if the executive officer should (1) regularly confer with the officers of the domestic parent corporation, (2) occasionally visit the U.S. office of the domestic parent corporation, and (3) during such visits to the United States temporarily conduct the business of the foreign subsidiary corporation out of the domestic parent corporation's office in the United States.

(d) *Agent activity.*—(1) *Dependent agents.*—(i) *In general.*—In determining whether a nonresident alien individual or a foreign corporation has an office or other fixed place of business, the office or other fixed place of business of an agent who is not an independent agent, as defined in subparagraph (3) of this paragraph, shall be disregarded unless such agent (*a*) has the authority to negotiate and conclude contracts in the name of the nonresident alien individual or foreign corporation, and regularly exercises that authority, or (*b*) has a stock of merchandise belonging to the nonresident alien individual or foreign corporation from which orders are regularly filed on behalf of such alien individual or foreign corporation. A person who purchases goods from a nonresident alien individual or a foreign corporation shall not be considered to be an agent for such alien individual or foreign corporation for purposes of this paragraph where such person is carrying on such purchasing activities in the ordinary course of its own business, even though such person is related in some manner to the nonresident alien individual or foreign corporation. For example, a wholly owned domestic subsidiary corporation of a foreign corporation shall not be treated as an agent of the foreign parent corporation merely because the subsidiary corporation purchases goods from the foreign parent corporation and resells them in its own name. However, if the domestic subsidiary corporation regularly negotiates and concludes contracts in the name of its foreign parent corporation or maintains a stock of merchandise from which it regularly fills orders on behalf of the foreign parent corporation, the office or other fixed place of business of the domestic subsidiary corporation shall be treated as the office or other fixed place of business of the foreign parent corporation unless the domestic subsidiary corporation is an independent agent within the meaning of subparagraph (3) of this paragraph.

(ii) *Authority to conclude contracts or fill orders.*—For purposes of subdivision (i) of this subparagraph, an agent shall be considered regularly to exercise authority to negotiate and conclude contracts or regularly to fill orders on behalf of his foreign principal only if the authority is exercised, or the orders are filled, with some frequency over a continuous period of time. This determination shall be made on the basis of the facts and circumstances in each case, taking into account the nature of the business of the principal; but, in all cases, the frequency and continuity tests are to be applied conjunctively. Regularity shall not be evidenced by occasional or incidental activity. An agent shall not be considered regularly to negotiate and conclude contracts on behalf of his foreign principal if the agent's authority to negotiate and conclude contracts is limited only to unusual cases or such authority must be separately secured by the agent from his principal with respect to each transaction effected.

(2) *Independent agents.*—The office or other fixed place of business of an independent agent, as defined in subparagraph (3) of this paragraph, shall not be treated as the office or other fixed place of business of his principal who is a nonresident alien individual or a foreign corporation, irrespective of whether such agent has authority to negotiate and conclude contracts in the name of his principal, and regularly exercises that authority, or maintains a stock of goods from which he regularly fills orders on behalf of his principal.

(3) *Definition of independent agent.*—(i) *In general.*—For purposes of this paragraph, the term "independent agent" means a general commission agent, broker, or other agent of an independent status acting in the ordinary course of his business in that capacity. Thus, for example, an agent who, in pursuance of his usual trade or business, and for compensation, sell goods or merchandise consigned or entrusted to his possession, management, and control for that purpose by or for the owner of such goods or merchandise is an independent agent.

(ii) *Related persons.*—The determination of whether an agent is an independent agent for purposes of this paragraph shall be made without regard to facts indicating that either the agent or the principal owns or controls directly or indirectly the other or that a third person or persons own or control directly or indirectly both. For example, a wholly owned domestic subsidiary corporation of a foreign corporation which acts as an agent for the foreign parent corporation may be treated as acting in the capacity of independent agent for the foreign parent corporation. The facts and circumstances of a specific case shall determine whether the agent, while acting for his principal, is acting in pursuance of his usual trade or business and in such manner as to constitute him an independent agent in his relations with the nonresident alien individual or foreign corporation.

(iii) *Exclusive agents.*—Where an agent who is otherwise an independent agent within the meaning of subdivision (i) of this subparagraph acts in such capacity exclusively, or almost exclusively, for one principal who is a nonresident alien individual or a foreign corporation, the facts and circumstances of a particular case shall be taken into account in determining whether the agent, while acting in that capacity, may be classified as an independent agent.

(e) *Employee activity.*—Ordinarily, an employee of a nonresident alien individual or a foreign corporation shall be treated as a dependent agent to whom the rules of paragraph (d)(1) of this section apply if such employer does not in and of itself have a fixed facility (as defined in paragraph (b) of this section) in the United States or outside the United States, as the case may be. However, where the employee, in the ordinary course of his duties, carries on the trade or business of his employer in or through a fixed facility of such employer which is regularly used by the employee in the course of carrying out such duties, such fixed facility shall be considered the office or other fixed place of business of the employer, irrespective of the rules of paragraph (d)(1) of this section. The application of this paragraph may be illustrated by the following example:

Example. M, a foreign corporation, opens a showroom office in the United States for the purpose of promoting its sales of merchandise which it purchases in foreign country X. The employees of the U.S. office, consisting of salesmen and general clerks, are empowered only to run the office, to arrange for the appointment of distributing agents for the merchandise offered by M, and to solicit orders generally. These employees do not have the authority to negotiate and conclude contracts in the name of M, nor do they have a stock of merchandise from which to fill orders on behalf of M. Any negotiations entered into by these employees are under M's instructions and subject to its approval as to any decision reached. The only independent authority which the employees have is in the appointment of distributors to whom M is to sell merchandise, but even this authority is subject to the right of M to approve or disapprove these buyers on receipt of information as to their business standing. Under the circumstances, this office used by a group of salesmen for sales promotion is a fixed place of business which M has in the United States.

(f) *Office or other fixed place of business of a related person.*—The fact that a nonresident alien individual or a foreign corporation is related in some manner to another person who has an office or other fixed place of business shall not of itself mean that such office or other fixed place of business of the other person is the office or other fixed place of business of the nonresident alien individual or foreign corporation. Thus, for example, the U.S. office of foreign corporation M, a wholly owned subsidiary corporation of foreign corporation N, shall not be considered the office or other fixed place of business of N unless the facts and circumstances show that N is engaged in trade or business in the United States through that office or other fixed place of business. However, see paragraph (b)(2) of this section.

(g) *Illustrations.*—The application of this section may be illustrated by the following examples:

Example (1). S, a foreign corporation, is engaged in the business of buying and selling tangible personal property. S is a wholly owned subsidiary of P, a domestic corporation engaged in the business of buying and selling similar property, which has an office in the United States. Officers of P are generally responsible for the policies followed by S and are directors of S, but S has an independent group of officers, none of whom are regularly employed in the United States. In addition to this group of officers, S has a chief executive officer, D, who is also an officer of P but who is permanently stationed outside the United States. The day-to-day conduct of S's business is handled by D and the other officers of such corporation, but they regularly confer with the officers of P and on occasion temporarily visit P's offices in the United States, at which time they continue to conduct the business of S. S does not have an office or other fixed place of business in the United States for purposes of this section.

Example (2). The facts are the same as in example (1) except that, on rare occasions, an employee of P receives an order which he, after consultation with officials of S and because P cannot fill the order, accepts on behalf of S rather than on behalf of P. P does not hold itself out as a person which those wishing to do business with S should contact. Assuming that orders for S are seldom handled in this manner and that they do not constitute a significant part of that corporation's business, S shall not be considered to have an office or other fixed place of business in the United States because of these activities of an employee of P.

Example (3). The facts are the same as in example (1) except that all orders received by S are subject to review by an officer of P before acceptance. S has a business office in the United States.

Example (4). S, a foreign corporation organized under the laws of Puerto Rico, is engaged in the business of manufacturing dresses in Puerto Rico and is entitled to an income tax exemption under the Puerto Rico Industrial Incentive Act of 1963. S is a wholly owned subsidiary of P, a domestic corporation engaged in the business of buying and selling dresses to customers in the United States. S sells most of the dresses it produces to P, the assumption being made that the income from these sales is derived from sources without the United States. P in turn sells these dresses in the United States in its name and through the efforts of its own employees and of distributors appointed by it. S does not have a fixed facility in the United States, and none of its employees are stationed in the United States. On occasion, employees of S visit the office of P in the United States, and executives of P visit the office of S in Puerto Rico, to discuss with one another matters of mutual business interest involving both corporations, including the strategy for marketing the dresses produced by S. These matters are also regularly discussed by such persons by telephone calls between the United States and Puerto Rico. S's employees do not otherwise participate in P's marketing activities. Officers of P are generally responsible for the policies followed by S and are directors of S, but S has a chief executive officer in Puerto Rico who, from its office therein, handles the day-to-day conduct of S's business. Based upon the facts presented, and assuming there are no other facts which would lead to a different determination, S shall not be considered to have an office or other fixed place of business in the United States for purposes of this section.

Example (5). The facts are the same as in example (4) except that the dresses are manufactured by S in styles and designs furnished by P and out of goods and raw materials purchased by P and sold to S. Based upon the facts presented, and assuming there are no other facts which would lead to a different determination, S shall not be considered to have an office or other fixed place of business in the United States for purposes of this section.

Example (6). The facts are the same as in example (5) except that pursuant to the instructions of P, the dresses sold by P are shipped by S directly to P's customers in the United States. Based upon the facts presented, and assuming there are no other facts which would lead to a different determination, S shall not be considered to have an office or other fixed place of business in the United States for purposes of this section. [Reg. § 1.864-7.]

☐ [*T.D.* 7216, 11-2-72.]

§ 1.864-8T. Treatment of related person factoring income (temporary).—
(a) *Applicability.*—(1) *General rule.*—This section applies for purposes of determining the treatment of income derived by a person from a trade or service receivable acquired from a related person. Except as provided in paragraph (d) of this section, if a person acquires (directly or indirectly) a trade or service receivable from a related person, any income (including any stated interest, discount or service fee) derived from the trade or service receivable shall be treated as if it were interest received on a loan to the obligor under the receivable. The characterization of income as interest pursuant to this section shall apply only for purposes of sections 551-558 (relating to foreign personal holding companies), sections 951-964 (relating to controlled foreign corporations), and section 904 (relating to the limitation on the foreign tax credit) of the Code and the regulations thereunder. The principles of sections 861 through 863 and the regulations thereunder shall be applied to determine the source of such interest income for purposes of section 904.

(2) *Override.*—With respect to income characterized as interest under this section, the special rules of section 864(d) and this section override any conflicting provisions of the Code and regulations relating to foreign personal holding companies, controlled foreign corporations, and the foreign tax credit limitation. Thus, for example, pursuant to section 864(d)(5) and paragraph (e) of this section, stated interest derived from a factored trade or service receivable is not eligible for the subpart F de minimis rule of section 954(b)(3), the same country exception of section 954(c)(3)(A)(i), or the special rules for export financing interest of sections 904(d)(2) and 954(c)(2)(B), even if in the absence of this section the treatment of such stated interest would be governed by those sections.

(3) *Limitation.*—Section 864(d) and this section apply only with respect to the tax treatment of income derived from a trade or service receivable acquired from a related person. Therefore, neither section 864(d) nor this section affects the characterization of an expense or loss of either the seller of a receivable or the obligor under a receivable. Accordingly, the obligor under a trade or service receivable shall not be allowed to treat any part of the purchase price of property or services as interest (other than amounts treated as interest under provisions other than section 864(d)).

(b) *Definitions.*—The following definitions apply for purposes of this section and § 1.956-3T.

(1) *Trade or service receivable.*—The term "trade or service receivable" means any account receivable or evidence of indebtedness, whether or not issued at a discount and whether or not bearing stated interest, arising out of the disposition by a related person of property described in section 1221(l) (hereinafter referred to as "inventory property") or the performance of services by a related person.

(2) *Related person.*—A "related person" is:

(i) A person who is a related person within the meaning of section 267(b) and the regulations thereunder;

(ii) A United States shareholder (as defined in section 951(b)); or

(iii) A person who is related (within the meaning of section 267(b) and the regulations thereunder) to a United States shareholder.

(c) *Acquisition of a trade or service receivable.*—(1) *General rule.*—A trade or service receivable is considered to be acquired by a person at the time when that person is entitled to receive all or a portion of the income from the trade or service receivable. A person who acquires a trade or service receivable (hereinafter referred to as the "factor") is considered to have acquired a trade or service receivable regardless of whether:

(i) The acquisition is characterized for federal income tax purposes as a sale, a pledge of collateral for a loan, an assignment, a capital contribution, or otherwise;

(ii) The factor takes title to or obtains physical possession of the trade or service receivable;

(iii) The related person assigns the trade or service receivable with or without recourse;

(iv) The factor or some other person is obligated to collect the payments due under the trade or service receivable;

(v) The factor is liable for all property, excise, sales, or similar taxes due upon collection of the receivable;

(vi) The factor advances the entire face amount of the trade or service receivable transferred;

(vii) All trade or service receivables assigned by the related person are assigned to one factor; and

(viii) The obligor under the trade or service receivable is notified of the assignment.

(2) *Example.*—The following example illustrates the application of paragraphs (a), (b), and (c)(1) of this section.

Example. P, a domestic corporation, owns all of the outstanding stock of FS, a controlled foreign corporation. P manufactures and sells paper products to customers, including X, an unrelated domestic corporation. As part of a sales transaction, P takes back a trade receivable from X and sells the receivable to FS. Because FS has acquired a trade or service receivable from a related person, the income derived by FS from P's receivable is interest income described in paragraph (a)(1) of this section.

(3) *Indirect acquisitions.*—(i) *Acquisition through unrelated person.*—A trade or service receivable will be considered to be acquired from a related person if it is acquired from an unrelated person who acquired (directly or indirectly) such receivable from a person who is a related person to the factor. The following example illustrates the application of this paragraph (c)(3)(i).

Example. A, a United States citizen, owns all of the outstanding stock of FPHC, a foreign personal holding company. A performs engineering services within and without the United States for customers, including X, an unrelated corporation. A performs engineering services for X and takes back a service receivable. A sells the receivable to Y, an unrelated corporation engaged in the factoring business. Y resells the receivable to FPHC. Because FPHC has indirectly acquired a service receivable from a related person, the income derived by FPHC from A's receivable is interest income described in paragraph (a)(1) of this section.

(ii) *Acquisition by nominee or pass-through entity.*—A factor will be considered to have acquired a trade or service receivable held on its behalf by a nominee or by a partnership, simple trust, S corporation or other pass-through entity to the extent the factor owns (directly or indirectly) a beneficial interest in such partnership or other pass-through entity. The rule of this paragraph (c)(3)(ii) does not limit the application of paragraph (c)(3)(iii) of this section regarding the characterization of trade or service receivables of unrelated persons acquired pursuant to certain swap or pooling arrangements. The following example illustrates the application of this paragraph (c)(3)(ii).

Example. FS1, a controlled foreign corporation, acquires a 20 percent limited partnership interest in PS, a partnership. PS purchases trade or service receivables resulting from the sale of inventory property by FS1's domestic parent, P. PS does not purchase receivables of any person who is related to any other partner in PS. FS1 is considered to have acquired a 20 percent interest in the receivables acquired by PS. Thus, FS1's distributive share of the income derived by PS from the receivables of P is considered to be interest income described in paragraph (a)(1) of this section.

(iii) *Swap or pooling arrangements.*—A trade or service receivable of a person unrelated to the factor will be considered to be a trade or service receivable acquired from a related person and subject to the rules of this section if it is acquired in accordance with an arrangement that involves two or more groups of related persons that are unrelated to each other and the effect of the arrangement is that one or more related persons in each group acquire (directly or indirectly) trade or service receivables of one or more unrelated persons who are also parties to the arrangement, in exchange for reciprocal purchases of the first group's receivables. The following example illustrates the application of this paragraph (c)(3)(iii).

Example. Controlled foreign corporations A, B, C, and D are wholly-owned subsidiaries of domestic corporations M, N, O, and P, respectively. M, N, O, and P are not related persons. According to a prearranged plan, A, B, C, and D each acquire trade or service receivables of M, N, O, and/or P, except that neither A, B, C nor D acquires receivables of its own parent corporation. Because the effect of this arrangement is that the unrelated groups acquire each other's trade or service receivables pursuant to the arrangement, income derived by A, B, C, and D from the receivables acquired from M, N, O, and P is interest income described in paragraph (a)(1) of this section.

(iv) *Financing arrangements.*—If a controlled foreign corporation (as defined in section 957(a)) participates (directly or indirectly) in a lending transaction that results in a loan to the purchaser of inventory property, services, or trade or service receivables of a related person (or a loan to a person who is related to the purchaser), and if the loan would not have been made or maintained on the same terms but for the corresponding purchase, then the controlled foreign corporation shall be considered to have indirectly acquired a trade or service receivable, and income derived by the controlled foreign corporation from such a loan shall be considered to be income described in paragraph (a)(1) of this section. For purposes of this paragraph (c)(3)(iv), it is immaterial that the sums lent are not, in fact, the sums used to finance the purchase of a related person's inventory property, services, or trade or service receivables. The amount of income derived by the controlled foreign corporation to be taken into account shall be the total amount of income derived from a lending transaction described in this paragraph (c)(3)(iv), if the amount lent is less than or equal to the purchase price of the inventory property, services, or trade or service receivables. If the amount lent is greater than the purchase price of the inventory property, services or receivables, the amount to be taken into account shall be the proportion of the interest charge (including original issue discount) that the purchase price bears to the total amount lent pursuant to the lending transaction. The following examples illustrate the application of this paragraph (c)(3)(iv).

Example (1). P, a domestic corporation, owns all of the outstanding stock of FS1, a controlled foreign corporation engaged in the financing business in Country X. P manufactures and sells toys, including sales to C, an unrelated corporation. Prior to P's sale of toys to C for $2,000, D, a wholly-owned Country X subsidiary of C, borrows $3,000 from FS1. The loan from FS1 to D would not have been made or maintained on the same terms but for C's purchase of toys from P. Two-thirds of the income derived by FS1 from the loan to D is interest income described in paragraph (a)(1) of this section.

Example (2). P, a domestic corporation, owns all of the outstanding stock of FS1, a controlled foreign corporation organized under the laws of Country X. FS1 has accumulated cash reserves. P has uncollected trade and service receivables of foreign obligors. FS1 makes a $1,000 loan to U, a foreign corporation that is unrelated to P or FS1. U purchases P's trade and service receivables for $2,000. The loan would not have been made or maintained on the same terms but for U's purchase of P's receivables. The income derived by U from the receivables is not interest income within the meaning of paragraph (a) of this section. However, the interest paid by U to FS1 is interest income described in paragraph (a)(1) of this section.

Example (3). The facts are the same as in Example (2), except that U is a wholly-owned Country Y subsidiary of FS1. Because U is related to P within the meaning of paragraph (b)(2) of this section, under paragraph (c)(1) of this section, income derived by U from P's receivables is interest income described in paragraph (a)(1) of this section. In addition, the income derived by FS1 from the loan to U is interest income described in paragraph (a)(1) of this section.

(d) *Same country exception.*—(1) *Income from trade or service receivables.*—Income derived from a trade or service receivable acquired from a related person shall not be treated as interest income described in paragraph (a)(1) of this section if:

(i) The person acquiring the trade or service receivable and the related person are created or organized under the laws of the same foreign country;

Reg. §1.864-8T(d)(1)(i)

(ii) The related person has a substantial part of its assets used in its trade or business located in such foreign country; and

(iii) The related person would not have derived foreign base company income, as defined in section 954(a) and the regulations thereunder, or income effectively connected with a United States trade or business from such receivable if the related person had collected the receivable.

For purposes of paragraph (d)(1)(ii) of this section, the standards contained in § 1.954-2(e) shall apply in determining the location of a substantial part of the assets of a related person. For purposes of paragraph (d)(1)(iii) of this section, a determination of whether the related person would have derived foreign base company income shall be made without regard to the de minimis test described in section 954(b)(3)(A). The following examples illustrate the application of this paragraph (d)(1).

Example (1). FS1, a controlled foreign corporation incorporated under the laws of Country X, owns all of the outstanding stock of FS2, which is also incorporated under the laws of Country X. FS1 has a substantial part of its assets used in its business in Country X. FS1 manufactures and sells toys for use in Country Y. The toys sold are considered to be manufactured in Country X under § 1.954-3(a)(2). FS1 is not considered to have a branch or similar establishment in Country Y that is treated as a separate corporation under section 954(d)(2) and § 1.954-3(b). Thus, gross income derived by FS1 from the toy sales is not foreign base company sales income. FS1 takes back receivables without stated interest from its customers. FS1 assigns those receivables to FS2. The income derived by FS2 from the receivables of FS1 is not interest income described in paragraph (a)(1) of this section, because it satisfies the same country exception under paragraph (d)(1) of this section.

Example (2). The facts are the same as in Example (1), except that the toys sold by FS1 are purchased from FS1's U.S. parent and are sold for use outside of Country X. Thus, any income derived by FS1 from the sale of the toys would be foreign base company sales income. Therefore, income derived by FS2 from the receivables of FS1 is interest income described in paragraph (a)(1) of this section. FS2 is considered to derive interest income from the receivable even if, solely by reason of the de minimis rule of section 954(b)(3)(A), FS1 would not have derived foreign base company income if FS1 had collected the receivable.

(2) *Income from financing arrangements.*—Income derived by a controlled foreign corporation from a loan to a person that purchases inventory property or services of a person that is related to the controlled foreign corporation, or from other loans described in paragraph (c)(3)(iv) of this section, shall not be treated as interest income described in paragraph (a)(1) of this section if:

(i) The person providing the financing and the related person are created or organized under the laws of the same foreign country;

(ii) The related person has a substantial part of its assets used in its trade or business located in such foreign country; and

(iii) The related person would not have derived foreign base company income or income effectively connected with a United States trade or business:

(A) From the sale of inventory property or services to the borrower or from financing the borrower's purchase of inventory property or services, in the case of a loan to the purchaser of inventory property or services of a related person; or

(B) From collecting amounts due under the receivable or from financing the purchase of the receivable, in the case of a loan to the purchaser of a trade or service receivable of a related person.

For purposes of paragraph (d)(2)(ii) of this section, the standards contained in § 1.954-2(e) shall apply in determining the location of a substantial part of the assets of a related person. For purposes of paragraph (d)(2)(iii) of this section, a determination of whether the related person would have derived foreign base company income shall be made without regard to the de minimis test described in section 954(b)(3)(A). The following examples illustrate the application of this paragraph (d)(2).

Example (1). FS1, a controlled foreign corporation incorporated under the laws of Country X, owns all of the outstanding stock of FS2, which is also incorporated under the laws of Country X. FS1, which has a substantial part of its assets used in its business located in Country X, manufactures and sells toys for use in Country Y. The toys sold are considered to be manufactured in Country X under § 1.954-3(a)(2). FS1 is not considered to have a branch or similar establishment in Country Y that is treated as a separate corporation under section 954(d)(2) and § 1.954-3(b). Thus, the gross income derived by FS1 from the toy sales is not foreign base company sales income. FS2 makes a loan to FS3, a wholly-owned subsidiary of FS1 which is also incorporated under the laws of Country X, in connection with FS3's purchase of toys from FS1. FS3 does not earn any subpart F gross income. Thus, FS1 would not have derived foreign personal holding company interest income if FS1 had made the loan to FS3, because the interest would be covered by the same country exception of section

954(c)(3). Therefore, the income derived by FS2 from its loan to FS3 is not treated as interest income described in paragraph (a)(1) of this section, because it satisfies the same country exception under paragraph (d)(2) of this section. Such income is also not treated as foreign personal holding company income described in section 954(c)(1)(A) because the same country exception of section 954(c)(3) also applies to the interest actually derived by FS2 from its loan to FS3.

Example (2). FS1, a controlled foreign corporation incorporated under the laws of Country X, owns all of the outstanding stock of FS2, which is also incorporated under the laws of Country X. FS1 purchases toys from its U.S. parent and resells them for use outside of Country X. As part of a sales transaction, FS1 takes back trade receivables. FS2 makes a loan to U, an unrelated corporation, to finance U's purchase of FS1's trade receivables. Because FS1 would have derived foreign base company income if FS1 had collected the receivables or made the loan itself, the same country exception of paragraph (d)(2) of this section does not apply. Accordingly, under paragraph (c)(3)(iv) of this section, the income derived by FS2 from its loan to U is treated as interest income described in paragraph (a)(1) of this section.

(e) *Special rules.*—(1) *Foreign personal holding companies and controlled foreign corporations.*—For purposes of sections 551-558 (relating to foreign personal holding companies), the exclusion provided by section 552(c) for interest described in section 954(c)(3)(A) shall not apply to income described in paragraph (a)(1) of this section. For purposes of the sections 951-964 (relating to controlled foreign corporations), income described in paragraph (a)(1) of this section shall be included in a United States shareholder's pro rata share of a controlled foreign corporation's subpart F income without regard to the de minimis rule under section 954(b)(3)(A). However, income described in paragraph (a)(1) of this section shall be included in the computation of a controlled foreign corporation's foreign base company income for purposes of applying the de minimis rule under section 954(b)(3)(A) and the more than 70 percent of gross income test under section 954(b)(3)(B). In addition, income described in paragraph (a)(1) of this section shall be considered to be subpart F income without regard to the exclusions from foreign base company income provided by section 954(c)(2)(B) (relating to export financing interest derived in the conduct of a banking business) and section 954(c)(3)(A)(i) (relating to certain interest income received from related persons).

(2) *Foreign tax credit.*—Income described in paragraph (a)(1) of this section shall be considered to be interest income for purposes of the section 904 foreign tax credit limitation and is not eligible for the exceptions for export financing interest provided in section 904(d)(2)(A)(iii)(II), (B)(ii), and (C)(iii). In addition, such income will be subject to the look-through rule for subpart F income set forth in section 904(d)(3) without regard to the de minimis exception provided in section 904(d)(3)(E).

(3) *Possessions corporations.*—(i) *Limitation on credit.*—Income described in paragraph (a)(1) of this section shall not be treated as income described in section 936(a)(1)(A) or (B) unless the income is considered under the principles of § 1.863-6 to be derived from sources within the possessions. Thus, the credit provided by section 936 is not available for income described in paragraph (a)(1) of this section unless the obligor under the receivable is a resident of a possession. In the case of a loan described in section 864(d)(6), the credit provided by section 936 is not available for income described in paragraph (a)(1) of this section unless the purchaser of the inventory property or services is a resident of a possession.

(ii) *Eligibility determination.*—Notwithstanding the limitation on the availability of the section 936 credit for income described in paragraph (a)(1) of this section, if income treated as interest income under paragraph (a)(1) of this section is derived from sources within a possession (determined without regard to this section), such income shall be eligible for inclusion in a corporation's gross income for purposes of section 936(a)(2)(A). If such income is derived from the active conduct of a trade or business within a possession (determined without regard to this section), such income shall be eligible for inclusion in a corporation's gross income for purposes of section 936(a)(2)(B). (These rules apply for purposes of determining whether a corporation is eligible to elect the credit provided under section 936(a)).

(iii) *Example.*—The following example illustrates the application of paragraph (e)(3) of this section.

Example. Corporation X is operating in a possession as a possessions corporation. In 1985, X earned $50,000 from the active conduct of a business in the possession, including $5,000 from trade or service receivables acquired from a related party. Obligors under the receivables acquired by X are not residents of the possession. Corporation X also earned $20,000 from activities other than its active conduct of business in the possession. The $5,000

Reg. § 1.864-8T(e)(3)(iii)

derived by X from the receivables is not eligible for the section 936 credit. However, the $5,000 may be used by X to meet the percentage tests under section 936(a)(2) to the extent that such income is considered to be derived from sources within the possession (for purposes of section 936(a)(2)(A)) or is considered to be derived from the active conduct of a trade or business in the possession (for purposes of section 936(a)(2)(B)), in either case determined without regard to the characterization of such income under this section.

(f) *Effective date.*—The provisions of this section shall apply with respect to accounts receivable and evidences of indebtedness transferred after March 1, 1984 and are effective June 14, 1988. [Temporary Reg. § 1.864-8T.]

☐ [T.D. 8209, 6-13-88.]

§ 1.865-1. Loss with respect to personal property other than stock.—(a) *General rules for allocation of loss.*—(1) *Allocation against gain.*—Except as otherwise provided in § 1.865-2 and paragraph (c) of this section, loss recognized with respect to personal property shall be allocated to the class of gross income and, if necessary, apportioned between the statutory grouping of gross income (or among the statutory groupings) and the residual grouping of gross income, with respect to which gain from a sale of such property would give rise in the hands of the seller. For purposes of this section, loss includes bad debt deductions under section 166 and loss on property that is marked-to-market (such as under section 475) and subject to the rules of this section. Thus, for example, loss recognized by a United States resident on the sale or worthlessness of a bond generally is allocated to reduce United States source income.

(2) *Loss attributable to foreign office.*—Except as otherwise provided in § 1.865-2 and paragraph (c) of this section, and except with respect to loss subject to paragraph (b) of this section, in the case of loss recognized by a United States resident with respect to property that is attributable to an office or other fixed place of business in a foreign country within the meaning of section 865(e)(3), the loss shall be allocated to reduce foreign source income if a gain on the sale of the property would have been taxable by the foreign country and the highest marginal rate of tax imposed on such gains in the foreign country is at least 10 percent. However, paragraph (a)(1) of this section and not this paragraph (a)(2) will apply if gain on the sale of such property would be sourced under section 865(c), (d)(1)(B), or (d)(3).

(3) *Loss recognized by United States citizen or resident alien with foreign tax home.*—Except as otherwise provided in § 1.865-2 and paragraph (c) of this section, and except with respect to loss subject to paragraph (b) of this section, in the case of loss with respect to property recognized by a United States citizen or resident alien that has a tax home (as defined in section 911(d)(3)) in a foreign country, the loss shall be allocated to reduce foreign source income if a gain on the sale of such property would have been taxable by a foreign country and the highest marginal rate of tax imposed on such gains in the foreign country is at least 10 percent.

(4) *Allocation for purposes of section 904.*—For purposes of section 904, loss recognized with respect to property that is allocated to foreign source income under this paragraph (a) shall be allocated to the separate category under section 904(d) to which gain on the sale of the property would have been assigned (without regard to section 904(d)(2)(A)(iii)(III)). For purposes of § 1.904-4(c)(2)(ii)(A), any such loss allocated to passive income shall be allocated (prior to the application of § 1.904-4(c)(2)(ii)(B)) to the group of passive income to which gain on a sale of the property would have been assigned had a sale of the property resulted in the recognition of a gain under the law of the relevant foreign jurisdiction or jurisdictions.

(5) *Loss recognized by partnership.*—A partner's distributive share of loss recognized by a partnership with respect to personal property shall be allocated and apportioned in accordance with this section as if the partner had recognized the loss. If loss is attributable to an office or other fixed place of business of the partnership within the meaning of section 865(e)(3), such office or fixed place of business shall be considered to be an office of the partner for purposes of this section.

(b) *Special rules of application.*—(1) *Depreciable property.*—In the case of a loss recognized with respect to depreciable personal property, the gain referred to in paragraph (a)(1) of this section is the gain that would be sourced under section 865(c)(1) (depreciation recapture).

(2) *Contingent payment debt instrument.*—Loss described in the last sentence of § 1.1275-4(b)(9)(iv)(A) that is recognized with respect to a contingent payment debt instrument to which § 1.1275-4(b) applies (instruments issued for money or publicly traded property) shall be allocated to the class of gross income and, if necessary, apportioned between the statutory grouping of gross income (or among the statutory groupings) and the residual grouping of gross income, with

respect to which interest income from the instrument (in the amount of the loss subject to this paragraph (b)(2)) would give rise.

(c) *Exceptions.*—(1) *Foreign currency and certain financial instruments.*—This section does not apply to loss governed by section 988 and loss recognized with respect to options contracts or derivative financial instruments, including futures contracts, forward contracts, notional principal contracts, or evidence of an interest in any of the foregoing.

(2) *Inventory.*—This section does not apply to loss recognized with respect to property described in section 1221(a)(1).

(3) *Interest equivalents and trade receivables.*—Loss subject to § 1.861-9T(b) (loss equivalent to interest expense and loss on trade receivables) shall be allocated and apportioned under the rules of § 1.861-9T and not under the rules of this section.

(4) *Unamortized bond premium.*—If a taxpayer recognizing loss with respect to a bond (within the meaning of § 1.171-1(b)) did not amortize bond premium to the full extent permitted by section 171 and the regulations thereunder, then, to the extent of the amount of bond premium that could have been, but was not, amortized by the taxpayer, loss recognized with respect to the bond shall be allocated to the class of gross income and, if necessary, apportioned between the statutory grouping of gross income (or among the statutory groupings) and the residual grouping of gross income, with respect to which interest income from the bond was assigned.

(5) *Accrued interest.*—Loss attributable to accrued but unpaid interest on a debt obligation shall be allocated to the class of gross income and, if necessary, apportioned between the statutory grouping of gross income (or among the statutory groupings) and the residual grouping of gross income, with respect to which interest income from the obligation was assigned. For purposes of this section, whether loss is attributable to accrued but unpaid interest (rather than to principal) shall be determined under the principles of §§ 1.61-7(d) and 1.446-2(e).

(6) *Anti-abuse rules.*—(i) *Transactions involving built-in losses.*—If one of the principal purposes of a transaction is to change the allocation of a built-in loss with respect to personal property by transferring the property to another person, qualified business unit, office or other fixed place of business, or branch that subsequently recognizes the loss, the loss shall be allocated by the transferee as if it were recognized by the transferor immediately prior to the transaction. If one of the principal purposes of a change of residence is to change the allocation of a built-in loss with respect to personal property, the loss shall be allocated as if the change of residence had not occurred. If one of the principal purposes of a transaction is to change the allocation of a built-in loss on the disposition of personal property by converting the original property into other property and subsequently recognizing loss with respect to such other property, the loss shall be allocated as if it were recognized with respect to the original property immediately prior to the transaction. Transactions subject to this paragraph shall include, without limitation, reorganizations within the meaning of section 368(a), liquidations under section 332, transfers to a corporation under section 351, transfers to a partnership under section 721, transfers to a trust, distributions by a partnership, distributions by a trust, transfers to or from a qualified business unit, office or other fixed place of business, or branch, or exchanges under section 1031. A person may have a principal purpose of affecting loss allocation even though this purpose is outweighed by other purposes (taken together or separately).

(ii) *Offsetting positions.*—If a taxpayer recognizes loss with respect to personal property and the taxpayer (or any person described in section 267(b) (after application of section 267(c)), 267(e), 318 or 482 with respect to the taxpayer) holds (or held) offsetting positions with respect to such property with a principal purpose of recognizing foreign source income and United States source loss, the loss shall be allocated and apportioned against such foreign source income. For purposes of this paragraph (c)(6)(ii), positions are offsetting if the risk of loss of holding one or more positions is substantially diminished by holding one or more other positions.

(iii) *Matching rule.*—If a taxpayer (or a person described in section 1059(c)(3)(C) with respect to the taxpayer) engages in a transaction or series of transactions with a principal purpose of recognizing foreign source income that results in the creation of a corresponding loss with respect to personal property (as a consequence of the rules regarding the timing of recognition of income, for example), the loss shall be allocated and apportioned against such income to the extent of the recognized foreign source income. For an example illustrating a similar rule with respect to stock loss, see § 1.865-2(b)(4)(iv) *Example 3*.

(d) *Definitions.*—(1) *Contingent payment debt instrument.*—A contingent payment debt instrument is any debt instrument that is subject to § 1.1275-4.

(2) *Depreciable personal property.*—Depreciable personal property is any property described in section 865(c)(4)(A).

(3) *Terms defined in § 1.861-8.*—See § 1.861-8 for the meaning of *class of gross income, statutory grouping of gross income,* and *residual grouping of gross income.*

(e) *Examples.*—The application of this section may be illustrated by the following examples:

Example 1. On January 1, 2000, *A*, a domestic corporation, purchases for $1,000 a machine that produces widgets, which *A* sells in the United States and throughout the world. Throughout *A*'s holding period, the machine is located and used in Country *X*. During *A*'s holding period, *A* incurs depreciation deductions of $400 with respect to the machine. Under § 1.861-8, *A* allocates and apportions depreciation deductions of $250 against foreign source general limitation income and $150 against U.S. source income. On December 12, 2002, *A* sells the machine for $100 and recognizes a loss of $500. Because the machine was used predominantly outside the United States, under sections 865(c)(1)(B) and 865(c)(3)(B)(ii) gain on the disposition of the machine would be foreign source general limitation income to the extent of the depreciation adjustments. Therefore, under paragraph (b)(1) of this section, the entire $500 loss is allocated against foreign source general limitation income.

Example 2. On January 1, 2002, *A*, a domestic corporation, loans $2,000 to *N*, its wholly-owned controlled foreign corporation, in exchange for a contingent payment debt instrument subject to § 1.1275-4(b). During 2002 through 2004, *A* accrues and receives interest income of $630, $150 of which is foreign source general limitation income and $480 of which is foreign source passive income under section 904(d)(3). Assume there are no positive or negative adjustments pursuant to § 1.1275-4(b)(6) in 2002 through 2004. On January 1, 2005, *A* disposes of the debt instrument and recognizes a $770 loss. Under § 1.1275-4(b)(8)(ii), $630 of the loss is treated as ordinary loss and $140 is treated as capital loss. Assume that $140 of interest income earned in 2005 with respect to the debt instrument would be foreign source passive income under section 904(d)(3). Under § 1.1275-4(b)(9)(iv), $150 of the ordinary loss is allocated against foreign source general limitation income and $480 of the ordinary loss is allocated against foreign source passive income. Under paragraph (b)(2) of this section, the $140 capital loss is allocated against foreign source passive income.

Example 3. (i) On January 1, 2003, *A*, a domestic corporation, purchases for $1,200 a taxable bond maturing on December 31, 2008, with a stated principal amount of $1,000, payable at maturity. The bond provides for unconditional payments of interest of $100, payable December 31 of each year. The issuer of the bond is a foreign corporation and interest on the bond is thus foreign source. Interest payments for 2003 and 2004 are timely made. *A* does not elect to amortize its bond premium under section 171 and the regulations thereunder, which would have permitted *A* to offset the $100 of interest income by $28.72 of bond premium in 2003, and by $30.42 in 2004. On January 1, 2005, *A* sells the bond and recognizes a $100 loss. Under paragraph (c)(4) of this section, $59.14 of the loss is allocated against foreign source income. Under paragraph (a)(1) of this section, the remaining $40.86 of the loss is allocated against U.S. source income.

(ii) The facts are the same as in paragraph (i) of this *Example 3*, except that *A* made the election to amortize its bond premium effective for taxable year 2004 (see § 1.171-4(c)). Under paragraph (c)(4) of this section, $28.72 of the loss is allocated against foreign source income. Under paragraph (a)(1) of this section, the remaining $71.28 of the loss is allocated against U.S. source income.

Example 4. On January 1, 2002, *A*, a domestic corporation, purchases for $1,000 a bond maturing December 31, 2014, with a stated principal amount of $1,000, payable at maturity. The bond provides for unconditional payments of interest of $100, payable December 31 of each year. The issuer of the bond is a foreign corporation and interest on the bond is thus foreign source. Between 2002 and 2006, *A* accrues and receives foreign source interest income of $500 with respect to the bond. On January 1, 2007, *A* sells the bond and recognizes a $500 loss. Under paragraph (a)(1) of this section, the $500 loss is allocated against U.S. source income.

Example 5. On January 1, 2002, *A*, a domestic corporation on the accrual method of accounting, purchases for $1,000 a bond maturing December 31, 2012, with a stated principal amount of $1,000, payable at maturity. The bond provides for unconditional payments of interest of $100, payable December 31 of each year. The issuer of the bond is a foreign corporation and interest on the bond is thus foreign source. On June 10, 2002, after *A* has accrued $44 of interest income, but before any interest has been paid, the issuer suddenly becomes insolvent and declares bankruptcy. *A* sells the bond (including the accrued interest) for $20. Assuming that *A* properly accrued $44 of interest income, *A* treats the $20 proceeds from the sale of the bond as payment of interest previously accrued and recognizes a $1,000 loss with respect to the bond principal and a $24 loss with respect to the accrued interest. See § 1.61-7(d). Under paragraph (a)(1) of this section, the $1,000 loss with respect to the principal is allocated against U.S. source income. Under paragraph (c)(5) of this section, the $24 loss with respect to accrued but unpaid interest is allocated against foreign source interest income.

(f) *Effective date.*—(1) *In general.*—Except as provided in paragraph (f)(2) of this section, this section is applicable to loss recognized on or after January 8, 2002. For purposes of this paragraph (f), loss that is recognized but deferred (for example, under section 267 or 1092) shall be treated as recognized at the time the loss is taken into account.

(2) *Application to prior periods.*—A taxpayer may apply the rules of this section to losses recognized in any taxable year beginning on or after January 1, 1987, and all subsequent years, provided that—

(i) The taxpayer's tax liability as shown on an original or amended tax return is consistent with the rules of this section for each such year for which the statute of limitations does not preclude the filing of an amended return on June 30, 2002; and

(ii) The taxpayer makes appropriate adjustments to eliminate any double benefit arising from the application of this section to years that are not open for assessment.

(3) *Examples.*—See § 1.865-2(e)(3) for examples illustrating an applicability date provision similar to the applicability date provided in this paragraph (f). [Reg. § 1.865-1.]

☐ [T.D. 8973, 12-27-2001.]

§ 1.865-2. Loss with respect to stock.—(a) *General rules for allocation of loss with respect to stock.*—(1) *Allocation against gain.*—Except as otherwise provided in paragraph (b) of this section, loss recognized with respect to stock shall be allocated to the class of gross income and, if necessary, apportioned between the statutory grouping of gross income (or among the statutory groupings) and the residual grouping of gross income, with respect to which gain (other than gain treated as a dividend under section 964(e)(1) or 1248) from a sale of such stock would give rise in the hands of the seller (without regard to section 865(f)). For purposes of this section, loss includes loss on property that is marked-to-market (such as under section 475) and subject to the rules of this section. Thus, for example, loss recognized by a United States resident on the sale of stock generally is allocated to reduce United States source income.

(2) *Stock attributable to foreign office.*—Except as otherwise provided in paragraph (b) of this section, in the case of loss recognized by a United States resident with respect to stock that is attributable to an office or other fixed place of business in a foreign country within the meaning of section 865(e)(3), the loss shall be allocated to reduce foreign source income if a gain on the sale of the stock would have been taxable by the foreign country and the highest marginal rate of tax imposed on such gains in the foreign country is at least 10 percent.

(3) *Loss recognized by United States citizen or resident alien with foreign tax home.*—(i) *In general.*—Except as otherwise provided in paragraph (b) of this section, in the case of loss with respect to stock that is recognized by a United States citizen or resident alien that has a tax home (as defined in section 911(d)(3)) in a foreign country, the loss shall be allocated to reduce foreign source income if a gain on the sale of the stock would have been taxable by a foreign country and the highest marginal rate of tax imposed on such gains in the foreign country is at least 10 percent.

(ii) *Bona fide residents of Puerto Rico.*—Except as otherwise provided in paragraph (b) of this section, in the case of loss with respect to stock in a corporation described in section 865(g)(3) recognized by a United States citizen or resident alien that is a bona fide resident of Puerto Rico during the entire taxable year, the loss shall be allocated to reduce foreign source income. If gain from a sale of such stock would give rise to income exempt from tax under section 933, the loss with respect to such stock shall be allocated to amounts that are excluded from gross income under section 933(1) and therefore shall not be allowed as a deduction from gross income. See section 933(1) and § 1.933-1(c).

(4) *Stock constituting a United States real property interest.*—Loss recognized by a nonresident alien individual or a foreign corporation with respect to stock that constitutes a United States real property interest shall be allocated to reduce United States source income. For additional rules governing the treatment of such loss, see section 897 and the regulations thereunder.

(5) *Allocation for purposes of section 904.*—For purposes of section 904, loss recognized with respect to stock that is allocated to foreign source income under this paragraph (a) shall be allocated to the separate category under section 904(d) to which gain on a sale of the stock would have been assigned (without regard to section 904(d)(2)(A)(iii)(III)). For purposes of § 1.904-4(c)(2)(ii)(A), any such loss

allocated to passive income shall be allocated (prior to the application of § 1.904–4(c)(2)(ii)(B)) to the group of passive income to which gain on a sale of the stock would have been assigned had a sale of the stock resulted in the recognition of a gain under the law of the relevant foreign jurisdiction or jurisdictions.

(b) *Exceptions.*—(1) *Dividend recapture exception.*—(i) *In general.*—If a taxpayer recognizes a loss with respect to shares of stock, and the taxpayer (or a person described in section 1059(c)(3)(C) with respect to such shares) included in income a dividend recapture amount (or amounts) with respect to such shares at any time during the recapture period, then, to the extent of the dividend recapture amount (or amounts), the loss shall be allocated and apportioned on a proportionate basis to the class or classes of gross income or the statutory or residual grouping or groupings of gross income to which the dividend recapture amount was assigned.

(ii) *Exception for de minimis amounts.*—Paragraph (b)(1)(i) of this section shall not apply to a loss recognized by a taxpayer on the disposition of stock if the sum of all dividend recapture amounts (other than dividend recapture amounts eligible for the exception described in paragraph (b)(1)(iii) of this section (passive limitation dividends)) included in income by the taxpayer (or a person described in section 1059(c)(3)(C)) with respect to such stock during the recapture period is less than 10 percent of the recognized loss.

(iii) *Exception for passive limitation dividends.*—Paragraph (b)(1)(i) of this section shall not apply to the extent of a dividend recapture amount that is treated as income in the separate category for passive income described in section 904(d)(2)(A) (without regard to section 904(d)(2)(A)(iii)(III)). The exception provided for in this paragraph (b)(1)(iii) shall not apply to any dividend recapture amount that is treated as income in the separate category for financial services income described in section 904(d)(2)(C).

(iv) *Examples.*—The application of this paragraph (b)(1) may be illustrated by the following examples:

Example 1. (i) *P*, a domestic corporation, is a United States shareholder of *N*, a controlled foreign corporation. *N* has never had any subpart F income and all of its earnings and profits are described in section 959(c)(3). On May 5, 1998, *N* distributes a dividend to *P* in the amount of $100. The dividend gives rise to a $5 foreign withholding tax, and *P* is deemed to have paid an additional $45 of foreign income tax with respect to the dividend under section 902. Under the look-through rules of section 904(d)(3) the dividend is general limitation income described in section 904(d)(1)(I).

(ii) On February 6, 2000, *P* sells its shares of *N* and recognizes a $110 loss. In 2000, *P* has the following taxable income, excluding the loss on the sale of *N*:

(A) $1,000 of foreign source income that is general limitation income described in section 904(d)(1)(I);

(B) $1,000 of foreign source capital gain from the sale of stock in a foreign affiliate that is sourced under section 865(f) and is passive income described in section 904(d)(1)(A); and

(C) $1,000 of U.S. source income.

(iii) The $100 dividend paid in 1998 is a dividend recapture amount that was included in *P*'s income within the recapture period preceding the disposition of the *N* stock. The de minimis exception of paragraph (b)(1)(ii) of this section does not apply because the $100 dividend recapture amount exceeds 10 percent of the $110 loss. Therefore, to the extent of the $100 dividend recapture amount, the loss must be allocated under paragraph (b)(1)(i) of this section to the separate limitation category to which the dividend was assigned (general limitation income).

(iv) *P*'s remaining $10 loss on the disposition of the *N* stock is allocated to U.S. source income under paragraph (a)(1) of this section.

(v) After allocation of the stock loss, *P*'s foreign source taxable income in 2000 consists of $900 of foreign source general limitation income and $1,000 of foreign source passive income.

Example 2. (i) *P*, a domestic corporation, owns all of the stock of *N1*, which owns all of the stock of *N2*, which owns all of the stock of *N3*. *N1*, *N2*, and *N3* are controlled foreign corporations. All of the corporations use the calendar year as their taxable year. On February 5, 1997, *N3* distributes a dividend to *N2*. The dividend is foreign personal holding company income of *N2* under section 954(c)(1)(A) that results in an inclusion of $100 in *P*'s income under section 951(a)(1)(A)(i) as of December 31, 1997. Under section 904(d)(3)(B) the inclusion is general limitation income described in section 904(d)(1)(I). The income inclusion to *P* results in a corresponding increase in *P*'s basis in the stock of *N1* under section 961(a).

(ii) On March 5, 1999, *P* sells its shares of *N1* and recognizes a $110 loss. The $100 1997 subpart F inclusion is a dividend recapture amount that was included in *P*'s income within the recapture period preceding the disposition of the *N1* stock. The de minimis exception of paragraph (b)(1)(ii) of this section does not apply because the $100 dividend recapture amount exceeds 10 percent of the $110 loss. Therefore, to the extent of the $100 dividend recapture amount, the loss must be allocated under paragraph (b)(1)(i) of this section to the separate limitation category to which the dividend recapture amount was assigned (general limitation income). The remaining $10 loss is allocated to U.S. source income under paragraph (a)(1) of this section.

Example 3. (i) P, a domestic corporation, owns all of the stock of N1, which owns all of the stock of N2. N1 and N2 are controlled foreign corporations. All the corporations use the calendar year as their taxable year and the U.S. dollar as their functional currency. On May 5, 1998, N2 pays a dividend of $100 to N1 out of general limitation earnings and profits.

(ii) On February 5, 2000, N1 sells its N2 stock to an unrelated purchaser. The sale results in a loss to N1 of $110 for U.S. tax purposes. In 2000, N1 has the following current earnings and profits, excluding the loss on the sale of N2:

(A) $1,000 of non-subpart F foreign source general limitation earnings and profits described in section 904(d)(1)(I);

(B) $1,000 of foreign source gain from the sale of stock that is taken into account in determining foreign personal holding company income under section 954(c)(1)(B)(i) and which is passive limitation earnings and profits described in section 904(d)(1)(A);

(C) $1,000 of foreign source interest income received from an unrelated person that is foreign personal holding company income under section 954(c)(1)(A) and which is passive limitation earnings and profits described in section 904(d)(1)(A).

(iii) The $100 dividend paid in 1998 is a dividend recapture amount that was included in N1's income within the recapture period preceding the disposition of the N2 stock. The de minimis exception of paragraph (b)(1)(ii) of this section does not apply because the $100 dividend recapture amount exceeds 10 percent of the $110 loss. Therefore, to the extent of the $100 dividend recapture amount, the loss must be allocated under paragraph (b)(1)(i) of this section to the separate limitation category to which the dividend was assigned (general limitation earnings and profits).

(iv) N1's remaining $10 loss on the disposition of the N2 stock is allocated to foreign source passive limitation earnings and profits under paragraph (a)(1) of this section.

(v) After allocation of the stock loss, N1's current earnings and profits for 1998 consist of $900 of foreign source general limitation earnings and profits and $1,990 of foreign source passive limitation earnings and profits.

(vi) After allocation of the stock loss, N1's subpart F income for 2000 consists of $1,000 of foreign source interest income that is foreign personal holding company income under section 954(c)(1)(A) and $890 of foreign source net gain that is foreign personal holding company income under section 954(c)(1)(B)(i). P includes $1,890 in income under section 951(a)(1)(A)(i) as passive income under sections 904(d)(1)(A) and 904(d)(3)(B).

Example 4. P, a foreign corporation, has two wholly-owned subsidiaries, S, a domestic corporation, and B, a foreign corporation. On January 1, 2000, S purchases a one-percent interest in N, a foreign corporation, for $100. On January 2, 2000, N distributes a $20 dividend to S. The $20 dividend is foreign source financial services income. On January 3, 2000, S sells its N stock to B for $80 and recognizes a $20 loss that is deferred under section 267(f). On June 10, 2008, B sells its N stock to an unrelated person for $55. Under section 267(f) and § 1.267(f)-1(c)(1), S's $20 loss is deferred until 2008. Under this paragraph (b)(1), the $20 loss is allocated to reduce foreign source financial services income in 2008 because the loss was recognized (albeit deferred) within the 24-month recapture period following the receipt of the dividend. See §§ 1.267(f)-1(a)(2)(i)(B) and 1.267(f)-1(c)(2).

Example 5. The facts are the same as in *Example 4*, except P, S, and B are domestic corporations and members of the P consolidated group. Under the matching rule of § 1.1502-13(c)(1), the separate entity attributes of S's intercompany items and B's corresponding items are redetermined to the extent necessary to produce the same effect on consolidated taxable income as if S and B were divisions of a single corporation and the intercompany transaction was a transaction between divisions. If S and B were divisions of a single corporation, the transfer of N stock on January 3, 2000 would be ignored for tax purposes, and the corporation would be treated as selling that stock only in 2008. Thus, the corporation's entire $45 loss would have been allocated against U.S. source income under paragraph (a)(1) of this section because a dividend recapture amount was not received during the corporation's recapture period. Accordingly, S's $20 loss and B's $25 loss are allocated to reduce U.S. source income.

Example 6. (i) On January 1, 1998, P, a domestic corporation, purchases N, a foreign corporation, for $1,000. On March 1, 1998, P causes N to sell its operating assets, distribute a $400 general limitation dividend to P, and invest its remaining $600 in short-term government securities. P converted the N assets into low-risk investments with a principal purpose of

Reg. § 1.865-2(b)(1)(iv)

holding the N stock without significant risk of loss until the recapture period expired. N earns interest income from the securities. The income constitutes subpart F income that is included in P's income under section 951, increasing P's basis in the N stock under section 961(a). On March 1, 2002, P sells N and recognizes a $400 loss.

(ii) Pursuant to paragraph (d)(3) of this section, the recapture period is increased by the period in which N's assets were held as low-risk investments because P caused N's assets to be converted into and held as low-risk investments with a principal purpose of enabling P to hold the N stock without significant risk of loss. Accordingly, under paragraph (b)(1)(i) of this section the $400 loss is allocated against foreign source general limitation income.

(2) *Exception for inventory.*—This section does not apply to loss recognized with respect to stock described in section 1221(1).

(3) *Exception for stock in an S corporation.*—This section does not apply to loss recognized with respect to stock in an S corporation (as defined in section 1361).

(4) *Anti-abuse rules.*—(i) *Transactions involving built-in losses.*—If one of the principal purposes of a transaction is to change the allocation of a built-in loss with respect to stock by transferring the stock to another person, qualified business unit (within the meaning of section 989(a)), office or other fixed place of business, or branch that subsequently recognizes the loss, the loss shall be allocated by the transferee as if it were recognized with respect to the stock by the transferor immediately prior to the transaction. If one of the principal purposes of a change of residence is to change the allocation of a built-in loss with respect to stock, the loss shall be allocated as if the change of residence had not occurred. If one of the principal purposes of a transaction is to change the allocation of a built-in loss with respect to stock (or other personal property) by converting the original property into other property and subsequently recognizing loss with respect to such other property, the loss shall be allocated as if it were recognized with respect to the original property immediately prior to the transaction. Transactions subject to this paragraph shall include, without limitation, reorganizations within the meaning of section 368(a), liquidations under section 332, transfers to a corporation under section 351, transfers to a partnership under section 721, transfers to a trust, distributions by a partnership, distributions by a trust, or transfers to or from a qualified business unit, office or other fixed place of business. A person may have a principal purpose of affecting loss allocation even though this purpose is outweighed by other purposes (taken together or separately).

(ii) *Offsetting positions.*—If a taxpayer recognizes loss with respect to stock and the taxpayer (or any person described in section 267(b) (after application of section 267(c)), 267(e), 318 or 482 with respect to the taxpayer) holds (or held) offsetting positions with respect to such stock with a principal purpose of recognizing foreign source income and United States source loss, the loss will be allocated and apportioned against such foreign source income. For purposes of this paragraph (b)(4)(ii), positions are offsetting if the risk of loss of holding one or more positions is substantially diminished by holding one or more other positions.

(iii) *Matching rule.*—If a taxpayer (or a person described in section 1059(c)(3)(C) with respect to the taxpayer) engages in a transaction or series of transactions with a principal purpose of recognizing foreign source income that results in the creation of a corresponding loss with respect to stock (as a consequence of the rules regarding the timing of recognition of income, for example), the loss shall be allocated and apportioned against such income to the extent of the recognized foreign source income. This paragraph (b)(4)(iii) applies to any portion of a loss that is not allocated under paragraph (b)(1)(i) of this section (dividend recapture rule), including a loss in excess of the dividend recapture amount and a loss that is related to a dividend recapture amount described in paragraph (b)(1)(ii) (de minimis exception) or (b)(1)(iii) (passive dividend exception) of this section.

(iv) *Examples.*—The application of this paragraph (b)(4) may be illustrated by the following examples. No inference is intended regarding the application of any other Internal Revenue Code section or judicial doctrine that may apply to disallow or defer the recognition of loss. The examples are as follows:

Example 1. (i) *Facts.* On January 1, 2000, P, a domestic corporation, owns all of the stock of N1, a controlled foreign corporation, which owns all of the stock of N2, a controlled foreign corporation. N1's basis in the stock of N2 exceeds its fair market value, and any loss recognized by N1 on the sale of N2 would be allocated under paragraph (a)(1) of this section to reduce foreign source passive limitation earnings and profits of N1. In contemplation of the sale of N2 to an unrelated purchaser, P causes N1 to liquidate with principal purposes of recognizing the loss on the N2 stock and allocating the loss against U.S. source income. P sells the N2 stock and P recognizes a loss.

(ii) *Loss allocation.* Because one of the principal purposes of the liquidation was to transfer the stock to P in order to change the allocation of the built-in loss on the N2 stock, under paragraph (b)(4)(i) of this section the loss is allocated against P's foreign source passive limitation income.

Example 2. (i) *Facts.* On January 1, 2000, P, a domestic corporation, forms N and F, foreign corporations, and contributes $1,000 to the capital of each. N and F enter into offsetting positions in financial instruments that produce financial services income. Holding the N stock substantially diminishes P's risk of loss with respect to the F stock (and vice versa). P holds N and F with a principal purpose of recognizing foreign source income and U.S. source loss. On March 31, 2000, when the financial instrument held by N is worth $1,200 and the financial instrument held by F is worth $800, P sells its F stock and recognizes a $200 loss.

(ii) *Loss allocation.* Because P held an offsetting position with respect to the F stock with a principal purpose of recognizing foreign source income and U.S. source loss, the $200 loss is allocated against foreign source financial services income under paragraph (b)(4)(ii) of this section.

Example 3. (i) *Facts.* On January 1, 2002, P and Q, domestic corporations, form R, a domestic partnership. The corporations and partnership use the calendar year as their taxable year. P contributes $900 to R in exchange for a 90-percent partnership interest and Q contributes $100 to R in exchange for a 10-percent partnership interest. R purchases a dance studio in Country X for $1,000. On January 2, 2002, R enters into contracts to provide dance lessons in Country x for a 5-year period beginning January 1, 2003. These contracts are prepaid by the dance studio customers on December 31, 2002, and R recognizes foreign source taxable income of $500 from the prepayments (R's only income in 2002). P takes into income its $450 distributive share of partnership taxable income. On January 1, 2003, P's basis in its partnership interest is $1,350 ($900 from its contribution under section 722, increased by its $450 distributive share of partnership income under section 705). On September 22, 2003, P contributes its R partnership interest to S, a newly-formed domestic corporation, in exchange for all the stock of S. Under section 358, P's basis in S is $1,350. On December 1, 2003, P sells S to an unrelated party for $1050 and recognizes a $300 loss.

(ii) *Loss allocation.* P recognized foreign source income for tax purposes before the income had economically accrued, and the accelerated recognition of income increased P's basis in R without increasing its value by a corresponding amount, which resulted in the creation of a built-in loss with respect to the S stock. Under paragraph (b)(4)(iii) of this section the $300 loss is allocated against foreign source income if P had a principal purpose of recognizing foreign source income and corresponding loss.

(c) *Loss recognized by partnership.*—A partner's distributive share of loss recognized by a partnership shall be allocated and apportioned in accordance with this section as if the partner had recognized the loss. If loss is attributable to an office or other fixed place of business of the partnership within the meaning of section 865(e)(3), such office or fixed place of business shall be considered to be an office of the partner for purposes of this section.

(d) *Definitions.*—(1) *Terms defined in § 1.861-8.*—See § 1.861-8 for the meaning of *class of gross income, statutory grouping of gross income,* and *residual grouping of gross income.*

(2) *Dividend recapture amount.*—A dividend recapture amount is a dividend (except for an amount treated as a dividend under section 78), an inclusion described in section 951(a)(1)(A)(i) (but only to the extent attributable to a dividend (including a dividend under section 964(e)(1)) included in the earnings of a controlled foreign corporation (held directly or indirectly by the person recognizing the loss) that is included in foreign personal holding company income under section 954(c)(1)(A)) and an inclusion described in section 951(a)(1)(B).

(3) *Recapture period.*—A recapture period is the 24-month period ending on the date on which a taxpayer recognized a loss with respect to stock. For example, if a taxpayer recognizes a loss on March 15, 2002, the recapture period begins on and includes March 16, 2000, and ends on and includes March 15, 2002. A recapture period is increased by any period of time in which the taxpayer has diminished its risk of loss in a manner described in section 246(c)(4) and the regulations thereunder and by any period in which the assets of the corporation are hedged against risk of loss (or are converted into and held as low-risk investments) with a principal purpose of enabling the taxpayer to hold the stock without significant risk of loss until the recapture period has expired. In the case of a loss recognized after a dividend is declared but before such dividend is paid, the recapture period is extended through the date on which the dividend is paid.

(4) *United States resident.*—See section 865(g) and the regulations thereunder for the definition of United States resident.

Reg. § 1.865-2(d)(4)

(e) *Effective date.*—(1) *In general.*—This section is applicable to loss recognized on or after January 11, 1999, except that paragraphs (a)(3)(ii), (b)(1)(iv) *Example 6*, (b)(4)(iii), (b)(4)(iv) *Example 3*, and (d)(3) of this section are applicable to loss recognized on or after January 8, 2002. For purposes of this paragraph (e), loss that is recognized but deferred (for example, under section 267 or 1092) shall be treated as recognized at the time the loss is taken into account.

(2) *Application to prior periods.*—A taxpayer may apply the rules of this section to losses recognized in any taxable year beginning on or after January 1, 1987, and all subsequent years, provided that—

(i) The taxpayer's tax liability as shown on an original or amended tax return is consistent with the rules of this section for each such year for which the statute of limitations does not preclude the filing of an amended return on June 30, 2002; and

(ii) The taxpayer makes appropriate adjustments to eliminate any double benefit arising from the application of this section to years that are not open for assessment.

(3) *Examples.*—The rules of this paragraph (e) may be illustrated by the following examples:

Example 1. (i) *P*, a domestic corporation, has a calendar taxable year. On March 10, 1985, *P* recognizes a $100 capital loss on the sale of *N*, a foreign corporation. Pursuant to sections 1211(a) and 1212(a), the loss is not allowed in 1985 and is carried over to the 1990 taxable year. The loss is allocated against foreign source income under §1.861-8(e)(7). In 1999, *P* chooses to apply this section to all losses recognized in its 1987 taxable year and in all subsequent years.

(ii) Allocation of the loss on the sale of *N* is not affected by the rules of this section because the loss was recognized in a taxable year that did not begin after December 31, 1986.

Example 2. (i) *P*, a domestic corporation, has a calendar taxable year. On March 10, 1988, *P* recognizes a $100 capital loss on the sale of *N*, a foreign corporation. Pursuant to sections 1211(a) and 1212(a), the loss is not allowed in 1988 and is carried back to the 1985 taxable year. The loss is allocated against foreign source income under §1.861-8(e)(7) on *P*'s federal income tax return for 1985 and increases an overall foreign loss account under §1.904(f)-1.

(ii) In 1999, *P* chooses to apply this section to all losses recognized in its 1987 taxable year and in all subsequent years. Consequently, the loss on the sale of *N* is allocated against U.S. source income under paragraph (a)(1) of this section. Allocation of the loss against U.S. source income reduces *P*'s overall foreign loss account and increases *P*'s tax liability in 2 years: 1990, a year that will not be open for assessment on June 30, 1999, and 1997, a year that will be open for assessment on June 30, 1999. Pursuant to paragraph (e)(2)(i) of this section, *P* must file an amended federal income tax return that reflects the rules of this section for 1997, but not for 1990.

Example 3. (i) *P*, a domestic corporation, has a calendar taxable year. On March 10, 1989, *P* recognizes a $100 capital loss on the sale of *N*, a foreign corporation. The loss is allocated against foreign source income under §1.861-8(e)(7) on *P*'s federal income tax return for 1989 and results in excess foreign tax credits for that year. The excess credit is carried back to 1988, pursuant to section 904(c). In 1999, *P* chooses to apply this section to all losses recognized in its 1989 taxable year and in all subsequent years. On June 30, 1999, *P*'s 1988 taxable year is closed for assessment, but *P*'s 1989 taxable year is open with respect to claims for refund.

(ii) Because *P* chooses to apply this section to its 1989 taxable year, the loss on the sale of *N* is allocated against U.S. source income under paragraph (a)(1) of this section. Allocation of the loss against U.S. source income would have permitted the foreign tax credit to be used in 1989, reducing *P*'s tax liability in 1989. Nevertheless, under paragraph (e)(2)(ii) of this section, because the credit was carried back to 1988, *P* may not claim the foreign tax credit in 1989.

[Reg. §1.865-2.]

☐ [*T.D.* 8805, 1-8-99. *Amended by T.D.* 8973, 12-27-2001.]

Nonresident Aliens and Foreign Corporations

§1.871-1. Classification and manner of taxing alien individuals.—(a) *Classes of aliens.*—For purposes of the income tax, alien individuals are divided generally into two classes, namely, resident aliens and nonresident aliens. Resident alien individuals are, in general, taxable the same as citizens of the United States; that is, a resident alien is taxable on income derived from all sources, including sources without the United States. See §1.1-1(b). Nonresident alien individuals are taxable only on certain income from sources within the United States and on the income described in section 864(c)(4) from sources without the United States which is effectively connected for the taxable year with the conduct of a trade or business in the United States. However, nonresident alien individuals may elect, under section 6013(g) or (h), to be treated as U.S. residents for purposes of determining their income tax liability under chapters 1, 5, and 24 of the Code. Accordingly, any reference in §§ 1.1-1 through 1.1388-1 and §§ 1.1491-1 through 1.1494-1 of this part to nonresident alien individuals does not include those with respect to whom an election under section 6013(g) or (h) is in effect, unless otherwise specifically provided. Similarly, any reference to resident aliens or U.S. residents includes those with respect to whom an election is in effect, unless otherwise specifically provided.

(b) *Classes of nonresident aliens.*—(1) *In general.*—For purposes of the income tax, nonresident alien individuals are divided into the following three classes:

(i) Nonresident alien individuals who at no time during the taxable year are engaged in a trade or business in the United States,

(ii) Nonresident alien individuals who at any time during the taxable year are, or are deemed under § 1.871-9 to be, engaged in a trade or business in the United States, and

(iii) Nonresident alien individuals who are bona fide residents of Puerto Rico during the entire taxable year.

An individual described in subdivision (i) or (ii) of this subparagraph is subject to tax pursuant to the provisions of subpart A (section 871 and following), part II, subchapter N, chapter 1 of the Code, and the regulations thereunder. See §§ 1.871-7 and 1.871-8. The provisions of subpart A do not apply to individuals described in subdivision (iii) of this subparagraph, but such individuals, except as provided in section 933 with respect to Puerto Rican source income, are subject to the tax imposed by section 1 or section 1201(b). See § 1.876-1.

(2) *Treaty income.*—If the gross income of a nonresident alien individual described in subparagraph (1)(i) or (ii) of this paragraph includes income on which the tax is limited by tax convention, see § 1.871-12.

(3) *Exclusions from gross income.*—For rules relating to the exclusion of certain items from the gross income of a nonresident alien individual, including annuities excluded under section 871(f), see §§ 1.872-2 and 1.894-1.

(4) *Expatriation to avoid tax.*—For special rules applicable in determining the tax of a nonresident alien individual who has lost United States citizenship with a principal purpose of avoiding certain taxes, see section 877.

(5) *Adjustment of tax of certain nonresident aliens.*—For the application of pre-1967 income tax provisions to residents of a foreign country which imposes a more burdensome income tax than the United States, and for the adjustment of the income tax of a national or resident of a foreign country which imposes a discriminatory income tax on the income of citizens of the United States or domestic corporations, see section 896.

(6) *Conduit financing arrangements.*—For rules regarding conduit financing arrangements, see §§ 881-3 and 1.881-4.

(c) Reserved.

(d) *Effective date.*—This section shall apply for taxable years beginning after December 31, 1966. For corresponding rules applicable to taxable years beginning before January 1, 1967, see 26 CFR 1.871-1 and 1.871-7(a) (Rev. as of Jan. 1, 1971). [Reg. § 1.871-1.]

☐ [*T.D.* 6258, 10-23-57. *Amended by T.D.* 7332, 12-20-74; *T.D.* 7670, 1-30-80; *T.D.* 8611, 8-10-95 *and T.D.* 9194, 4-6-2005.]

§ 1.871-2. Determining residence of alien individuals.—(a) *General.*—The term "nonresident alien individual" means an individual whose residence is not within the United States, and who is not a citizen of the United States. The term includes a nonresident alien fiduciary. For such purpose the term "fiduciary" shall have the meaning assigned to it by section 7701(a)(6) and the regulations in Part 301 of this chapter (Regulations on Procedure and Administration). For presumption as to an alien's nonresidence, see paragraph (b) of § 1.871-4.

(b) *Residence defined.*—An alien actually present in the United States who is not a mere transient or sojourner is a resident of the United States for purposes of the income tax. Whether he is a transient is determined by his intentions with regard to the length and nature of his stay. A mere floating intention, indefinite as to time, to return to another country is not sufficient to constitute him a transient. If he lives in the United States and has no definite intention as to his stay, he is a resident. One who comes to the United States for a definite purpose which in its nature may be promptly accomplished is a transient; but, if his purpose is of such a nature that an extended stay may be necessary for its accomplishment, and to that end the alien makes his home temporarily in the United States, he becomes a resident, though it may be his intention at all times to return to his domicile abroad when the purpose for which he came has been consummated or abandoned. An alien whose stay in the United States is limited to a definite period by the immigration laws is not a resident of the United States within the meaning of this section, in the absence of exceptional circumstances.

(c) *Application and effective dates.*—Unless the context indicates otherwise, §§ 1.871-2 through 1.871-5 apply to determine the residence of aliens for taxable years beginning before January 1, 1985. To determine the residence of aliens for taxable years beginning after December 31, 1984, see section 7701(b) and §§ 301.7701(b)-1 through 301.7701(b)-9 of this chapter. However, for purposes of determining whether an individual is a qualified individual under section 911(d)(1)(A), the rules of §§ 1.871-2 and 1.871-5 shall continue to apply for taxable years beginning after December 31, 1984. For purposes of determining whether an individual is a resident of the United States for estate and gift tax purposes, see § 20.0-1(b)(1) and (2) and § 25.2501-1(b) of this chapter, respectively. [Reg. § 1.871-2.]

☐ [*T.D.* 6258, 10-23-57. *Amended by T.D.* 8411, 4-24-92.]

§ 1.871-3. Residence of alien seamen.—In order to determine whether an alien seaman is a resident of the United States for purposes of the income tax, it is necessary to decide whether the presumption of nonresidence (as prescribed by paragraph (b) of § 1.871-4) is overcome by facts showing that he has established a residence in the United States. Residence may be established on a vessel regularly engaged in coastwise trade, but the mere fact that a sailor makes his home on a vessel which is flying the United States flag and is engaged in foreign trade is not sufficient to establish residence in the United States, even though the vessel, while carrying on foreign trade, touches at American ports. An alien seaman may acquire an actual residence in the United States within the rules laid down in § 1.871-4, although the nature of his calling requires him to be absent for a long period from the place where his residence is established. An alien seaman may acquire such a residence at a sailors' boarding house or hotel, but such a claim should be carefully scrutinized in order to make sure that such residence is bona fide. The filing of Form 1078 or taking out first citizenship papers is proof of residence in the United States from the time the form is filed or the papers taken out, unless rebutted by other evidence showing an intention to be a transient. [Reg. § 1.871-3.]

☐ [*T.D.* 6258, 10-23-57.]

§ 1.871-4. Proof of residence of aliens.—(a) *Rules of evidence.*—The following rules of evidence shall govern in determining whether or not an alien within the United States has acquired residence therein for purposes of the income tax.

(b) *Nonresidence presumed.*—An alien, by reason of his alienage, is presumed to be a nonresident alien.

(c) *Presumption rebutted.*—(1) *Departing alien.*—In the case of an alien who presents himself for determination of tax liability before departure from the United States, the presumption as to the alien's nonresidence may be overcome by proof—

(i) That the alien, at least six months before the date he so presents himself, has filed a declaration of his intention to become a citizen of the United States under the naturalization laws; or

(ii) That the alien, at least six months before the date he so presents himself, has filed Form 1078 or its equivalent; or

(iii) Of acts and statements of the alien showing a definite intention to acquire residence in the United States or showing that his stay in the United States has been of such an extended nature as to constitute him a resident.

(2) *Other aliens.*—In the case of other aliens, the presumption as to the alien's nonresidence may be overcome by proof—

(i) That the alien has filed a declaration of his intention to become a citizen of the United States under the naturalization laws; or

(ii) That the alien has filed Form 1078 or its equivalent; or

(iii) Of acts and statements of the alien showing definite intention to acquire residence in the United States or showing that his stay in the United States has been of such an extended nature as to constitute him a resident.

(d) *Certificate.*—If, in the application of paragraphs (c)(1)(iii) or (2)(iii) of this section, the internal revenue officer or employee who examines the alien is in doubt as to the facts, such officer or employee may, to assist him in determining the facts, require a certificate or certificates setting forth the facts relied upon by the alien seeking to overcome the presumption. Each such certificate, which shall contain, or be verified by, a written declaration that it is made under the penalties of perjury, shall be executed by some credible person or persons, other than the alien and members of his family, who have known the alien at least six months before the date of execution of the certificate or certificates. [Reg. § 1.871-4.]

☐ [*T.D.* 6258, 10-23-57.]

§ 1.871-5. Loss of residence by an alien.—An alien who has acquired residence in the United States retains his status as a resident until he abandons the same and actually departs from the United States. An intention to change his residence does not change his status as a resident alien to that of a nonresident alien. Thus, an alien who has acquired a residence in the United States is taxable as a resident for the remainder of his stay in the United States. [Reg. § 1.871-5.]

☐ [T.D. 6258, 10-23-57.]

§ 1.871-6. Duty of withholding agent to determine status of alien payees.—For the obligation of a withholding agent to withhold the tax imposed by this section, see chapter 3 of the Internal Revenue Code and the regulations thereunder. [Reg. § 1.871-6.]

☐ [T.D. 6258, 10-23-57. *Amended by T.D.* 7332, 12-20-74; *T.D.* 7977, 9-19-84 *and T.D.* 8734, 10-6-97 (T.D. 8804 extended the effective date of T.D. 8734 from January 1, 1999, to January 1, 2000; T.D. 8856 further delayed the effective date of T.D. 8734 until January 1, 2001).]

§ 1.871-7. Taxation of nonresident alien individuals not engaged in U.S. business.—(a) *Imposition of tax.*—(1) This section applies for purposes of determining the tax of a nonresident alien individual who at no time during the taxable year is engaged in trade or business in the United States. However, see also § 1.871-8 where such individual is a student or trainee deemed to be engaged in trade or business in the United States or where he has an election in effect for the taxable year in respect to real property income. Except as otherwise provided in § 1.871-12, a nonresident alien individual to whom this section applies is not subject to the tax imposed by section 1 or section 1201(b) but, pursuant to the provisions of section 871(a), is liable to a flat tax of 30 percent upon the aggregate of the amounts determined under paragraphs (b), (c), and (d) of this section which are received during the taxable year from sources within the United States. Except as specifically provided in such paragraphs, such amounts do not include gains from the sale or exchange of property. To determine the source of such amounts, see sections 861 through 863, and the regulations thereunder.

(2) The tax of 30 percent is imposed by section 871(a) upon an amount only to the extent the amount constitutes gross income. Thus, for example, the amount of an annuity which is subject to such tax shall be determined in accordance with section 72.

(3) Deductions shall not be allowed in determining the amount subject to tax under this section except that losses from sales or exchanges of capital assets shall be allowed to the extent provided in section 871(a)(2) and paragraph (d) of this section.

(4) Except as provided in §§ 1.871-9 and 1.871-10, a nonresident alien individual not engaged in trade or business in the United States during the taxable year has no income, gain, or loss for the taxable year which is effectively connected for the taxable year with the conduct of a trade or business in the United States. See section 864(c)(1)(B) and § 1.864-3.

(5) Gains and losses which, by reason of section 871(d) and § 1.871-10, are treated as gains or losses which are effectively connected for the taxable year with the conduct of a trade or business in the United States by the nonresident alien individual shall not be taken into account in determining the tax under this section. See, for example, paragraph (c)(2) of § 1.871-10.

(6) For special rules applicable in determining the tax of certain nonresident alien individuals, see paragraph (b) of § 1.871-1.

(b) *Fixed or determinable annual or periodical income.*—(1) *General rule.*—The tax of 30 percent imposed by section 871(a)(1) applies to the gross amount received from sources within the United States as fixed or determinable annual or periodical gains, profits, or income. Specific items of fixed or determinable annual or periodical income are enumerated in section 871(a)(1)(A) as interest, dividends, rents, salaries, wages, premiums, annuities, compensations, remunerations, and emoluments, but other items of fixed or determinable annual or periodical gains, profits, or income are also subject to the tax, as, for instance, royalties, including royalties for the use of patents, copyrights, secret processes and formulas, and other like property. As to the determination of fixed or determinable annual or periodical income, see § 1.1441-2(b). For special rules treating gain on the disposition of section 306 stock as fixed or determinable annual or periodical income for purposes of section 871(a), see section 306(f) and paragraph (h) of § 1.306-3.

(2) *Substitute payments.*—For purposes of this section, a substitute interest payment (as defined in § 1.861-2(a)(7)) received by a foreign person pursuant to a securities lending transaction or a sale-repurchase transaction (as defined in § 1.861-2(a)(7)) shall have the same character as interest income paid or accrued with respect to the terms of the transferred security. Similarly, for purposes of this section, a substitute dividend payment (as defined in § 1.861-3(a)(6)) received by a foreign person pursuant to a securities lending transaction or a sale-repurchase transaction (as defined in § 1.861-3(a)(6)) shall have the same character as a distribution received with respect to the transferred security. Where, pursuant to a securities lending transaction or a sale-repur-

chase transaction, a foreign person transfers to another person a security the interest on which would qualify as portfolio interest under section 871(h) in the hands of the lender, substitute interest payments made with respect to the transferred security will be treated as portfolio interest, provided that in the case of interest on an obligation in registered form (as defined in § 1.871-14(c)(1)(i)), the transferor complies with the documentation requirement described in § 1.871-14(c)(1)(ii)(C) with respect to the payment of the substitute interest and none of the exceptions to the portfolio interest exemption in sections 871(h)(3) and (4) apply. See also §§ 1.861-2(b)(2) and 1.894-1(c).

(c) *Other income and gains.*—(1) *Items subject to tax.*—The tax of 30 percent imposed by section 871(a)(1) also applies to the following gains received during the taxable year from sources within the United States:

(i) Gains described in section 402(a)(2), relating to the treatment of total distributions from certain employees' trusts; section 403(a)(2), relating to treatment of certain payments under certain employee annuity plans; and section 631(b) or (c), relating to treatment of gain on the disposal of timber, coal, or iron ore with a retained economic interest;

(ii) [Reserved]

(iii) Gains on transfers described in section 1235, relating to certain transfers of patent rights, made on or before October 4, 1966; and

(iv) Gains from the sale or exchange after October 4, 1966, of patents, copyrights, secret processes and formulas, good will, trademarks, trade brands, franchises, or other like property, or of any interest in any such property, to the extent the gains are from payments (whether in a lump sum or in installments) which are contingent on the productivity, use, or disposition of the property or interest sold or exchanged, or from payments which are treated under section 871(e) and § 1.871-11 as being so contingent.

(2) *Nonapplication of 183-day rule.*—The provisions of section 871(a)(2), relating to gains from the sale or exchange of capital assets, and paragraph (d)(2) of this section do not apply to the gains described in this paragraph; as a consequence, the taxpayer receiving gains described in subparagraph (1) of this paragraph during a taxable year is subject to the tax of 30 percent thereon without regard to the 183-day rule contained in such provisions.

(3) *Determination of amount of gain.*—The tax of 30 percent imposed upon the gains described in subparagraph (1) of this paragraph applies to the full amount of the gains and is determined (i) without regard to the alternative tax imposed by section 1201(b) upon the excess of the net long-term capital gain over the net short-term capital loss; (ii) without regard to the deduction allowed by section 1202 in respect of capital gains; (iii) without regard to section 1231, relating to property used in the trade or business and involuntary conversions; and (iv), except in the case of gains described in subparagraph (1)(ii) of this paragraph, whether or not the gains are considered to be gains from the sale or exchange of property which is a capital asset.

(d) *Gains from sale or exchange of capital assets.*—(1) *Gains subject to tax.*—The tax of 30 percent imposed by section 871(a)(2) applies to the excess of gains derived from sources within the United States over losses allocable to sources within the United States, which are derived from the sale or exchange of capital assets, determined in accordance with the provisions of subparagraphs (2) through (4) of this paragraph.

(2) *Presence in the United States 183 days or more.*—(i) If the nonresident alien individual has been present in the United States for a period or periods aggregating 183 days or more during the taxable year, he is liable to a tax of 30 percent upon the amount by which his gains, derived from sources within the United States, from sales or exchanges of capital assets effected at any time during the year exceed his losses, allocable to sources within the United States, from sales or exchanges of capital assets effected at any time during that year. Gains and losses from sales or exchanges effected at any time during such taxable year are to be taken into account for this purpose even though the nonresident alien individual is not present in the United States at the time the sales or exchanges are effected. In addition, if the nonresident alien individual has been present in the United States for a period or periods aggregating 183 days or more during the taxable year, gains and losses for such taxable year from sales or exchanges of capital assets effected during a previous taxable year beginning after December 31, 1966, are to be taken into account, but only if he was also present in the United States during such previous taxable year for a period or periods aggregating 183 days or more.

(ii) If the nonresident alien individual has not been present in the United States during the taxable year, or if he has been present in the United States for a period or periods aggregating less than 183 days during the taxable year, gains and losses from sales or exchanges of capital assets effected during the year are not to be taken into account, except as required by paragraph (c) of this section, in determining the tax of such individual even though the sales or exchanges are effected during his presence in the United States. Moreover, gains and losses for such taxable year from sales or exchanges of capital assets effected during a previous taxable year beginning after December 31, 1966, are not to be taken into account, even though the nonresident alien individual was present in the United States during such previous year for a period or periods aggregating 183 days or more.

(iii) For purposes of this subparagraph, a nonresident alien individual is not considered to be present in the United States by reason of the presence in the United States of a person who is an agent or partner of such individual or who is a fiduciary of an estate or trust of which such individual is a beneficiary or a grantor-owner to whom section 671 applies.

(iv) The application of this subparagraph may be illustrated by the following examples:

Example (1). B, a nonresident alien individual not engaged in trade or business in the United States and using the calendar year as the taxable year, is present in the United States from May 1, 1971, to November 15, 1971, a period of more than 182 days. While present in the United States, B effects for his own account on various dates a number of transactions in stocks and securities on the stock exchange, as a result of which he has recognized capital gains of $10,000. During the period from January 1, 1971, to April 30, 1971, he carries out similar transactions through an agent in the United States, as a result of which B has recognized capital gains of $5,000. On December 15, 1971, through an agent in the United States B sells a capital asset on the installment plan, no payments being made by the purchaser in 1971. During 1972, B receives installment payments of $50,000 on the installment sale made in 1971, and the capital gain from sources within the United States for 1972 attributable to such payments is $12,500. In addition, during the period from January 1, 1972, to May 31, 1972, B effects for his own account, through an agent in the United States, a number of transactions in stocks and securities on the stock exchange, as a result of which B has recognized capital gains of $20,000. At no time during 1972 is B present in the United States or engaged in trade or business in the United States. Accordingly, for 1971, B is subject to tax under section 871(a)(2) on his capital gains of $15,000 from the transactions in that year on the stock exchange. For 1972, B is not subject to tax on the capital gain of $12,500 from the installment sale in 1971 or on the capital gains of $20,000 from the transactions in 1972 on the stock exchange.

Example (2). The facts are the same as in example (1) except that B is present in the United States from June 15, 1972, to December 31, 1972, a period of more than 182 days. Accordingly, B is subject to tax under section 871(a)(2) for 1971 on his capital gains of $15,000 from the transactions in that year on the stock exchange. He is also subject to tax under section 871(a)(2) for 1972 on his capital gains of $32,500 ($12,500 from the installment sale in 1971 plus $20,000 from the transactions in 1972 on the stock exchange).

Example (3). D, a nonresident alien individual not engaged in trade or business in the United States and using the calendar year as the taxable year, is present in the United States from April 1, 1971, to August 31, 1971, a period of less than 183 days. While present in the United States, D effects for his own account on various dates a number of transactions in stocks and securities on the stock exchange, as a result of which he has recognized capital gains of $15,000. During the period from January 1, 1971, to March 31, 1971, he carries out similar transactions through an agent in the United States, as a result of which D has recognized capital gains of $8,000. On December 20, 1971, through an agent in the United States, D sells a capital asset on the installment plan, no payments being made by the purchaser in 1971. During 1972, D receives installment payments of $200,000 on the installment sale made in 1971, and the capital gain from sources within the United States for 1972 attributable to such payments is $50,000. In addition, during the period from February 1, 1972, to August 15, 1972, a period of more than 182 days, D effects for his own account, through an agent in the United States, a number of transactions in stocks and securities on the stock exchange, as a result of which D has recognized capital gains of $25,000. At no time during 1972 is D present in the United States or engaged in trade or business in the United States. Accordingly, D is not subject to tax for 1971 or 1972 on any of his recognized capital gains.

Example (4). The facts are the same as in example (3) except that D is present in the United States from February 1, 1972, to August 15, 1972, a period of more than 182 days. Accordingly, D is not subject to tax for 1971 on his capital gains of $23,000 from the transactions in that year on the stock exchange. For 1972 he is subject to tax under section 871(a)(2) on his capital gains of $25,000 from the transactions in that year on the stock exchange, but he is not subject to the tax on the capital gain of $50,000 from the installment sale in 1971.

(3) *Determination of 183-day period.*—
(i) *In general.*—In determining the total period of presence in the United States for a taxable year for purposes of subparagraph (2) of this paragraph, all separate periods of presence in the United States during the taxable year are to

be aggregated. If the nonresident alien individual has not previously established a taxable year, as defined in section 441(b), he shall be treated as having a taxable year which is the calendar year, as defined in section 441(d). Subsequent adoption by such individual of a fiscal year as the taxable year will be treated as a change in the taxpayer's annual accounting period to which section 442 applies, and the change must be authorized under this part (Income Tax Regulations) or prior approval must be obtained by filing an application on Form 1128 in accordance with paragraph (b) of § 1.442-1. If in the course of his taxable year the nonresident alien individual changes his status from that of a citizen or resident of the United States to that of a nonresident alien individual, or vice versa, the determination of whether the individual has been present in the United States for 183 days or more during the taxable year shall be made by taking into account the entire taxable year, and not just that part of the taxable year during which he has the status of a nonresident alien individual.

(ii) *Definition of "day".*—The term "day", as used in subparagraph (2) of this paragraph, means a calendar day during any portion of which the nonresident alien individual is physically present in the United States (within the meaning of sections 7701(a)(9) and 638) except that, in the case of an individual who is a resident of Canada or Mexico and, in the normal course of his employment in transportation service touching points within both Canada or Mexico and the United States, performs personal services in both the foreign country and the United States, the following rules shall apply:

(a) The performance of labor or personal services during eight hours or more in any one day within the United States shall be considered as one day in the United States, except that if a period of more or less than eight hours is considered a full work day in the transportation job involved, such period shall be considered as one day within the United States.

(b) The performance of labor or personal services during less than eight hours in any day in the United States shall, except as provided in *(a),* be considered as a fractional part of a day in the United States. The total number of hours during which such services are performed in the United States during the taxable year, when divided by eight, shall be the number of days during which such individual shall be considered present in the United States during the taxable year.

(c) The aggregate number of days determined under *(a)* and *(b)* shall be considered the total number of days during which such individual is present in the United States during the taxable year.

(4) *Determination of amount of excess gains.*—(i) *In general.*—For the purpose of determining the excess of gains over losses subject to tax under this paragraph, gains and losses shall be taken into account only if, and to the extent that, they would be recognized and taken into account if the nonresident alien individual were engaged in trade or business in the United States during the taxable year and such gains and losses were effectively connected for such year with the conduct of a trade or business in the United States by such individual. However, in determining such excess of gains over losses no deduction may be taken under section 1202, relating to the deduction for capital gains, or section 1212, relating to the capital loss carryover. Thus, for example, in determining such excess gains all amounts considered under chapter 1 of the Code as gains or losses from the sale or exchange of capital assets shall be taken into account, except those gains which are described in section 871(a)(1)(B) or (D) and taken into account under paragraph (c) of this section and are considered to be gains from the sale or exchange of capital assets. Also, for example, a loss described in section 631(b) or (c) which is considered to be a loss from the sale of a capital asset shall be taken into account in determining the excess gains which are subject to tax under this paragraph. In further illustration, in determining such excess gains no deduction shall be allowed, pursuant to the provisions of section 267, for losses from sales or exchanges of property between related taxpayers. Any gains which are taken into account under section 871(a)(1) and paragraph (c) of this section shall not be taken into account in applying section 1231 for purposes of this paragraph. Gains and losses are to be taken into account under this paragraph whether they are short-term or long-term capital gains or losses within the meaning of section 1222.

(ii) *Gains not included.*—The provisions of this paragraph do not apply to any gains described in section 871(a)(1)(B) or (D), and in subdivision (i), (iii), or (iv) of paragraph (c)(1) of this section, which are considered to be gains from the sale or exchange of capital assets.

(iii) *Allowance of losses.*—In determining the excess of gains over losses subject to tax under this paragraph losses shall be allowed only to the extent provided by section 165(c). Losses from sales or exchanges of capital assets in excess of gains from sales or exchanges of capital assets shall not be taken into account.

Reg. § 1.871-7(d)(3)(ii)

(e) *Credits against tax.*—The credits allowed by section 31 (relating to tax withheld on wages), by section 32 (relating to tax withheld at source on nonresident aliens), by section 39 (relating to certain uses of gasoline and lubricating oil), and by section 6402 (relating to overpayments of tax) shall be allowed against the tax of a nonresident alien individual determined in accordance with this section.

(f) *Effective date.*—Except as otherwise provided in this paragraph, this section shall apply for taxable years beginning after December 31, 1966. Paragraph (b)(2) of this section is applicable to payments made after November 13, 1997. For corresponding rules applicable to taxable years beginning before January 1, 1967, see 26 CFR 1.871-7(b) and (c) (Rev. as of Jan. 1, 1971). [Reg. § 1.871-7.]

☐ [*T.D.* 6258, 10-23-57. *Amended by T.D.* 6464, 5-11-60; *T.D.* 6782, 12-23-64; *T.D.* 6823, 5-5-65; *T.D.* 6841, 7-26-65; *T.D.* 7332, 12-20-74; *T.D.* 8734, 10-6-97 (T.D. 8804 extended the effective date of T.D. 8734 from January 1, 1999, to January 1, 2000; T.D. 8856 further delayed the effective date of T.D. 8734 until January 1, 2001) *and T.D.* 8735, 10-6-97.]

§ 1.871-8. Taxation of nonresident alien individuals engaged in U.S. business or treated as having effectively connected income.—(a) *Segregation of income.*—This section applies for purposes of determining the tax of a nonresident alien individual who at any time during the taxable year is engaged in trade or business in the United States. It also applies for purposes of determining the tax of a nonresident alien student or trainee who is deemed under section 871(c) and § 1.871-9 to be engaged in trade or business in the United States or of a nonresident alien individual who at no time during the taxable year is engaged in trade or business in the United States but has an election in effect for the taxable year under section 871(d) and § 1.871-10 in respect to real property income. A nonresident alien individual to whom this section applies must segregate his gross income for the taxable year into two categories, namely, (1) the income which is effectively connected for the taxable year with the conduct of a trade or business in the United States by that individual and (2) the income which is not effectively connected for the taxable year with the conduct of a trade or business in the United States by that individual. A separate tax shall then be determined upon each such category of income, as provided in paragraph (b) of this section. The determination of whether income or gain is or is not effectively connected for the taxable year with the conduct of a trade or business in the United States by the nonresident alien individual shall be made in accordance with section 864(c) and §§ 1.864-3 through 1.864-7. For purposes of this section income which is effectively connected for the taxable year with the conduct of a trade or business in the United States includes all income which is treated under section 871(c) or (d) and § 1.871-9 or § 1.871-10 as income which is effectively connected for such year with the conduct of a trade or business in the United States by the nonresident alien individual.

(b) *Imposition of tax.*—(1) *Income not effectively connected with the conduct of a trade or business in the United States.*—If a nonresident alien individual who is engaged in trade or business in the United States at any time during the taxable year derives during such year from sources within the United States income or gains described in section 871(a)(1) and paragraph (b) or (c) of § 1.871-7 or gains from the sale or exchange of capital assets determined as provided in section 871(a)(2) and paragraph (d) of § 1.871-7, which are not effectively connected for the taxable year with the conduct of a trade or business in the United States by that individual, such income or gains shall be subject to a flat tax of 30 percent of the aggregate amount of such items. This tax shall be determined in the manner, and subject to the same conditions, set forth in § 1.871-7 as though the income or gains were derived by a nonresident alien individual not engaged in trade or business in the United States during the taxable year, except that (i) the rule in paragraph (d)(3) of such section for treating the calendar year as the taxable year shall not apply and (ii) in applying paragraph (c) and (d)(4) of such section, there shall not be taken into account any gains or losses which are taken into account in determining the tax under section 871(b) and subparagraph (2) of this paragraph. A nonresident alien individual who has an election in effect for the taxable year under section 871(d) and § 1.871-10 and who at no time during the taxable year is engaged in trade or business in the United States must determine his tax under § 1.871-7 on his income which is not treated as effectively connected with the conduct of a trade or business in the United States, subject to the exception contained in subdivision (ii) of this subparagraph.

(2) *Income effectively connected with the conduct of a trade or business in the United States.*—(i) *In general.*—If a nonresident alien to whom this section applies derives income or gains which are effectively connected for the taxable year with the conduct of a trade or business in the United States by that individual, the taxable income or gains shall, except as provided in § 1.871-12, be taxed in accordance with section 1 or, in the alternative, section

1201(b). See section 871(b)(1). Any income of the nonresident alien individual which is not effectively connected for the taxable year with the conduct of a trade or business in the United States by that individual shall not be taken into account in determining either the rate or amount of such tax. See paragraph (b) of § 1.872-1.

(ii) *Determination of taxable income.*—The taxable income for any taxable year for purposes of this subparagraph consists only of the nonresident alien individual's taxable income which is effectively connected for the taxable year with the conduct of a trade or business in the United States by that individual; and, for this purpose, it is immaterial that the trade or business with which that income is effectively connected is not the same as the trade or business carried on in the United States by that individual during the taxable year. See example (2) in § 1.864-4(b). In determining such taxable income all amounts constituting, or considered to be, gains or losses for the taxable year from the sale or exchange of capital assets shall be taken into account if such gains or losses are effectively connected for the taxable year with the conduct of a trade or business in the United States by that individual, and, for such purpose, the 183-day rule set forth in section 871(a)(2) and paragraph (d)(2) of § 1.871-7 shall not apply. Losses which are not effectively connected for the taxable year with the conduct of a trade or business in the United States by that individual shall not be taken into account in determining taxable income under this subdivision, except as provided in section 873(b)(1).

(iii) *Cross references.*—For rules for determining the gross income and deductions for the taxable year, see sections 872 and 873, and the regulations thereunder.

(c) *Change in trade or business status.*—(1) *In general.*—The determination as to whether a nonresident alien individual is engaged in trade or business within the United States during the taxable year is to be made for each taxable year. If at any time during the taxable year he is engaged in a trade or business in the United States, he is considered to be engaged in trade or business within the United States during the taxable year for purposes of sections 864(c)(1) and 871(b), and the regulations thereunder. Income, gain, or loss of a nonresident alien individual is not treated as being effectively connected for the taxable year with the conduct of a trade or business in the United States if he is not engaged in trade or business within the United States during such year, even though such income, gain, or loss may have been effectively connected for a previous taxable year with the conduct of a trade or business in the United States. See § 1.864-3. However, income, gain, or loss which is treated as effectively connected for the taxable year with the conduct of a trade or business in the United States by a nonresident alien individual will generally be treated as effectively connected for a subsequent taxable year if he is engaged in a trade or business in the United States during such subsequent year, even though such income, gain, or loss is not effectively connected with the conduct of the trade or business carried on in the United States during such subsequent year. This subparagraph does not apply to income described in section 871(c) or (d). It may not apply to a nonresident alien individual who for the taxable year uses an accrual method of accounting or to income which is constructively received in the taxable year within the meaning of § 1.451-2.

(2) *Illustrations.*—The application of this paragraph may be illustrated by the following examples:

Example (1). B, a nonresident alien individual using the calendar year as the taxable year and the cash receipts and disbursements method of accounting, is engaged in business (business R) in the United States from January 1, 1971, to August 31, 1971. During the period of September 1, 1971, to December 31, 1971, B receives installment payments of $30,000 on sales made in the United States by business R during that year, and the income from sources within the United States for that year attributable to such payments is $7,500. On September 15, 1971, another business (business S) which is carried on by B only in a foreign country sells to U.S. customers on the installment plan several pieces of equipment from inventory. During the period of September 16, 1971, to December 31, 1971, B receives installment payments of $50,000 on these sales by business S, and the income from sources within the United States for that year attributable to such payments is $10,000. Under section 864(c)(3) and paragraph (b) of § 1.864-4 the entire income of $17,500 is effectively connected for 1971 with the conduct of a business in the United States by B. Accordingly, such income is taxable to B under paragraph (b)(2) of this section.

Example (2). Assume the same facts as in Example (1), except that during 1972 B receives installment payments of $20,000 from the sales made during 1971 in the United States by business R, and of $80,000 from the sales made in 1971 to U.S. customers by business S, the total income from sources within the United States for 1972 attributable to such payments being $13,000. At no time during 1972 is B engaged in a trade or business in the

United States. Under section 864(c)(1)(B) the income of $13,000 for 1972 is not effectively connected with the conduct of a trade or business in the United States by B. Moreover, such income is not fixed or determinable annual or periodical income. Accordingly, no amount of such income is taxable to B under section 871.

Example (3). Assume the same facts as in Example (2), except that during 1972 B is engaged in a new business (business T) in the United States from July 1, 1972, to December 31, 1972. Under section 864(c)(3) and paragraph (b) of § 1.864-4, the income of $13,000 is effectively connected for 1972 with the conduct of a business in the United States by B. Accordingly, such income is taxable to B under paragraph (b)(2) of this section.

Example (4). Assume the same facts as in Example (2), except that the installment payments of $20,000 from the sales made during 1971 in the United States by business R and not received by B until 1972 could have been received by B in 1971 if he had so desired. Under § 1.451-2, B is deemed to have constructively received the payments of $20,000 in 1971. Accordingly, the income attributable to such payments is effectively connected for 1971 with the conduct of a business in the United States by B and is taxable to B in 1971 under paragraph (b)(2) of this section.

(d) *Credits against tax.*—The credits allowed by section 31 (relating to tax withheld on wages), section 32 (relating to tax withheld at source on nonresident aliens), section 33 (relating to the foreign tax credit), section 35 (relating to partially tax-exempt interest), section 38 (relating to investment in certain depreciable property), section 39 (relating to certain uses of gasoline and lubricating oil), section 40 (relating to expenses of work incentive programs), and section 6402 (relating to overpayments of tax) shall be allowed against the tax determined in accordance with this section. However, the credits allowed by sections 33, 38 and 40 shall not be allowed against the flat tax of 30 percent imposed by section 871(a) and paragraph (b)(1) of this section. Moreover, no credit shall be allowed under section 35 to a nonresident alien individual with respect to whom a tax is imposed for the taxable year under section 871(a) and paragraph (b)(1) of this section, even though such individual has income for such year upon which tax is imposed under section 871(b) and paragraph (b)(2) of this section. For special rules applicable in determining the foreign tax credit, see section 906(b) and the regulations thereunder. For the disallowance of certain credits where a return is not filed for the taxable year, see section 874 and § 1.874-1.

(e) *Effective date.*—This section shall apply for taxable years beginning after December 31, 1966. For corresponding rules applicable to taxable years beginning before January 1, 1967, see 26 CFR 1.871-7(d) (Rev. as of Jan. 1, 1971). [Reg. § 1.871-8.]

☐ [T.D. 6258, 10-23-57. Amended by T.D. 6782, 12-23-64 and T.D. 7332, 12-20-74.]

§ 1.871-9. Nonresident alien students or trainees deemed to be engaged in U.S. business.—(a) *Participants in certain exchange or training programs.*—For purposes of §§ 1.871-7 and 1.871-8 a nonresident alien individual who is temporarily present in the United States during the taxable year as a nonimmigrant under subparagraph (F) (relating to the admission of students into the United States) or subparagraph (J) (relating to the admission of teachers, trainees, specialists, etc., into the United States) of section 101(a)(15) of the Immigration and Nationality Act (8 U.S.C. 1101(a)(15)(F) or (J)), and who without regard to this paragraph is not engaged in trade or business in the United States during such year, shall be deemed to be engaged in trade or business in the United States during the taxable year. For purposes of determining whether an alien who is present in the United States on an F visa or a J visa is a resident of the United States, see §§ 301.7701(b)-1 through 301.7701(b)-9 of this chapter.

(b) *Income treated as effectively connected with U.S. business.*—Any income described in paragraph (1) (relating to the nonexcluded portion of certain scholarship or fellowship grants) or paragraph (2) (relating to certain nonexcluded expenses incident to such grants) of section 1441(b) which is received during the taxable year from sources within the United States by a nonresident alien individual described in paragraph (a) of this section is to be treated for purposes of §§ 1.871-7, 1.871-8, 1.872-1, and 1.873-1 as income which is effectively connected for the taxable year with the conduct of a trade or business in the United States by that individual. However, such income is not to be treated as effectively connected for the taxable year with the conduct of a trade or business in the United States for purposes of section 1441(c)(1) and paragraph (a) of § 1.1441-4. For exclusion relating to compensation paid to such individual by a foreign employer, see paragraph (b) of § 1.872-2.

(c) *Exchange visitors.*—For purposes of paragraph (a) of this section a nonresident alien individual who is temporarily present in the United States during the taxable year as a nonimmigrant under subparagraph (J) of section 101(a)(15) of the Immigration and Nationality Act includes a nonresident alien individual admitted to the United States as an "exchange visitor" under section 201 of the United States Information and Educational Exchange Act of 1948 (22 U.S.C. 1446), which section was repealed by section 111 of the Mutual Educational and Cultural Exchange Act of 1961 (75 Stat. 538).

(d) *Mandatory application of rule.*—The application of this section is mandatory and not subject to an election by the taxpayer.

(e) *Effective date.*—This section shall apply for taxable years beginning after December 31, 1966. For corresponding rules applicable to taxable years beginning before January 1, 1967, see 26 CFR 1.871-7(a)(3) (Rev. as of Jan. 1, 1971). [Reg. § 1.871-9.]

☐ [*T.D.* 7332, 12-20-74. *Amended by T.D.* 8411, 4-24-92.]

§ 1.871-10. Election to treat real property income as effectively connected with U.S. business.—(a) *When election may be made.*—A nonresident alien individual or foreign corporation which during the taxable year derives any income from real property which is located in the United States and, in the case of a nonresident alien individual, held for the production of income, or derives income from any interest in any such property, may elect, pursuant to section 871(d) or 882(d) and this section, to treat all such income as income which is effectively connected for the taxable year with the conduct of a trade or business in the United States by that taxpayer. The election may be made whether or not the taxpayer is engaged in trade or business in the United States during the taxable year for which the election is made or whether or not the taxpayer has income from real property for the taxable year is effectively connected with the conduct of a trade or business in the United States, but it may be made only with respect to that income from sources within the United States which, without regard to this section, is not effectively connected for the taxable year with the conduct of a trade or business in the United States by the taxpayer. If for the taxable year the taxpayer has no income from real property located in the United States, or from any interest in such property, which is subject to the tax imposed by section 871(a) or 881(a), the election may not be made. But if an election has been properly made under this section for a taxable year, the election remains in effect, unless properly revoked, for subsequent taxable years even though during any such subsequent taxable year there is no income from the real property, or interest therein, in respect of which the election applies.

(b) *Income to which the election applies.*—(1) *Included income.*—An election under this section shall apply to all income from real property which is located in the United States and, in the case of a nonresident alien individual, held for the production of income, and to all income derived from any interest in such property, including (i) gains from the sale or exchange of such property or an interest therein, (ii) rents or royalties from mines, oil or gas wells, or other natural resources, and (iii) gains described in section 631(b) or (c), relating to treatment of gain on the disposal of timber, coal, or iron ore with a retained economic interest. The election may not be made with respect to only one class of such income. For purposes of the election, income from real property, or from any interest in real property, includes any amount included under section 652 or 662 in the gross income of a nonresident alien individual or foreign corporation that is the beneficiary of an estate or trust if, by reason of the application of section 652(b) or 662(b), and the regulations thereunder, such amount has the character in the hands of that beneficiary of income from real property, or from any interest in real property. It is immaterial that no tax would be imposed on the income by section 871(a) and paragraph (a) of § 1.871-7, or by section 881(a) and paragraph (a) of § 1.881-2, if the election were not in effect. Thus, for example, if an election under this section has been made by a nonresident alien individual not engaged in trade or business in the United States during the taxable year, the tax imposed by section 871(b)(1) and paragraph (b)(2) of § 1.871-8 applies to his gains derived from the sale of real property located in the United States and held for the production of income, even though such income would not be subject to tax under section 871(a) if the election had not been made. In further illustration, assume that a nonresident alien individual not engaged in trade or business, or present, in the United States during the taxable year has income from sources within the United States consisting of oil royalties, rentals from a former personal residence, and capital gain from the sale of another residence held for the production of income. If he makes an election under this section, it will apply with respect to his royalties, rentals, and capital gain, even though such capital gain would not be subject to tax under section 871(a) if the election had not been made.

(2) *Income not included.*—For purposes of subparagraph (1) of this paragraph, income from real property, or from any interest in real property, does not include (i) interest on a debt obligation secured by a mortgage of real property, (ii) any portion of a dividend, within the

meaning of section 316, which is paid by a corporation or a trust, such as a real estate investment trust described in section 857, which derives income from real property, (iii) in the case of a nonresident alien individual, income from real property, such as a personal residence, which is not held for the production of income or from any transaction in such property which was not entered into for profit, (iv) rentals from personal property, or royalties from intangible personal property, within the meaning of subparagraph (3) of this paragraph, or (v) income which, without regard to section 871(d) or 882(d) and this section, is treated as income which is effectively connected for the taxable year with the conduct of a trade or business in the United States.

(3) *Rules applicable to personal property.—* For purposes of subparagraph (2) of this paragraph, in the case of a sales agreement, or rental or royalty agreement, affecting both real and personal property, the income from the transaction is to be allocated between the real property and the personal property in proportion to their respective fair market values unless the agreement specifically provides otherwise. In the case of such a rental or royalty agreement, the respective fair market values are to be determined as of the time the agreement is signed. In making determinations under this subparagraph, the principles of paragraph (c) of § 1.48-1, relating to the definition of "section 38 property", apply for purposes of determining whether property is tangible or intangible personal property and of paragraph (a)(5) of § 1.1245-1 apply for purposes of making the allocation of income between real and personal property.

(c) *Effect of the election.—*(1) *Determination of tax.—*The income to which, in accordance with paragraph (b) of this section, an election under this section applies shall be subject to tax in the manner, and subject to the same conditions, provided by section 871(b)(1) and paragraph (b)(2) of § 1.871-8, or by section 882(a)(1) and paragraph (b)(2) of § 1.882-1. For purposes of determining such tax for the taxable year, income to which the election applies shall be aggregated with all other income of the nonresident alien individual or foreign corporation which is effectively connected for the taxable year with the conduct of a trade or business in the United States by that taxpayer. To the extent that deductions are connected with income from real property to which the election applies, they shall be treated for purposes of section 873(a) or section 882(c)(1) as connected with income which is effectively connected for the taxable year with the conduct of a trade or business in the United States by the nonresident alien individual or foreign corporation. An election under this section does not cause a nonresident alien individual or foreign corporation, which is not engaged in trade or business in the United States during the taxable year, to be treated as though such taxpayer were engaged in trade or business in the United States during the taxable year. Thus, for example, the compensation received during the taxable year for services performed in the United States in a previous taxable year by a nonresident alien individual, who has an election in effect for the taxable year under this section but is engaged in trade or business in the United States at no time during the taxable year, is not effectively connected for the taxable year with the conduct of a trade or business in the United States. In further illustration, gain for the taxable year from the casual sale of personal property described in section 1221(1) derived by a nonresident alien individual who is not engaged in trade or business in the United States during the taxable year but has an election in effect for such year under this section is not effectively connected with the conduct of a trade or business in the United States. See § 1.864-3. If an election under this section is in effect for the taxable year, the income to which the election applies shall be treated, for purposes of section 871(b)(1) or section 882(a)(1), section 1441(c)(1), and paragraph (a) of § 1.441-4, as income which is effectively connected for the taxable year with the conduct of a trade or business in the United States by the taxpayer.

(2) *Treatment of property to which election applies.—*Any real property, or interest in real property, with respect to which an election under this section applies shall be treated as a capital asset which, if depreciable, is subject to the allowance for depreciation provided in section 167 and the regulations thereunder. Such property, or interest in property, shall be treated as property not used in a trade or business for purposes of applying any provisions of the Code, such as section 172(d)(4)(A), relating to gain or loss attributable to a trade or business for purposes of determining a net operating loss; section 1221(2), relating to property not constituting a capital asset; or section 1231(b), relating to special rules for treatment of gains and losses. For example, if a nonresident alien individual makes the election under this section and, while the election is in effect, sells unimproved land which is located in the United States and held for investment purposes, any gain or loss from the sale shall be considered gain or loss from the sale of a capital asset and shall be treated, for purposes of determining the tax under section 871(b)(1) and paragraph (b)(2) of § 1.871-8, as a gain or loss which is effectively connected for the taxa-

Reg. § 1.871-10(c)(2)

ble year with the conduct of a trade or business in the United States.

(d) *Manner of making or revoking an election.*—(1) *Election, or revocation, without consent of Commissioner.*—(i) *In general.*—A nonresident alien individual or foreign corporation may, for the first taxable year for which the election under this section is to apply, make the initial election at any time before the expiration of the period prescribed by section 6511(a), or by section 6511(c) if the period for assessment is extended by agreement, for filing a claim for credit or refund of the tax imposed by chapter 1 of the Code for such taxable year. This election may be made without the consent of the Commissioner. Having made the initial election, the taxpayer may, within the time prescribed for making the election for such taxable year, revoke the election without the consent of the Commissioner. If the revocation is timely and properly made, the taxpayer may make his initial election under this section for a later taxable year without the consent of the Commissioner. If the taxpayer revokes the initial election without the consent of the Commissioner, he must file amended income tax returns, or claims for credit or refund, where applicable, for the taxable years to which the revocation applies.

(ii) *Statement to be filed with return.*—An election made under this section without the consent of the Commissioner shall be made for a taxable year by filing with the income tax return required under section 6012 and the regulations thereunder for such taxable year a statement to the effect that the election is being made. This statement shall include (*a*) a complete schedule of all real property, or any interest in real property, of which the taxpayer is titular or beneficial owner, which is located in the United States, (*b*) an indication of the extent to which the taxpayer has direct or beneficial ownership in each such item of real property, or interest in real property, (*c*) the location of the real property or interest therein, (*d*) a description of any substantial improvements on any such property, and (*e*) an identification of any taxable year or years in respect of which a revocation or new election under this section has previously occurred. This statement may not be filed with any return under section 6851 and the regulations thereunder.

(iii) *Exemption from withholding of tax.*—For statement to be filed with a withholding agent at the beginning of a taxable year in respect of which an election under this section is to be made, see paragraph (a) of § 1.1441-4.

(2) *Revocation, or election, with consent of Commissioner.*—(i) *In general.*—If the nonresident alien individual or foreign corporation makes the initial election under this section for any taxable year and the period prescribed by subparagraph (1)(i) of this paragraph for making the election for such taxable year has expired, the election shall remain in effect for all subsequent taxable years, including taxable years for which the taxpayer realizes no income from real property, or from any interest therein, or for which he is not required under section 6012 and the regulations thereunder to file an income tax return. However, the election may be revoked in accordance with subdivision (iii) of this subparagraph for any subsequent taxable year with the consent of the Commissioner. If the election for any such taxable year is revoked with the consent of the Commissioner, the taxpayer may not make a new election before his fifth taxable year which begins after the first taxable year for which the revocation is effective unless consent is given to such new election by the Commissioner in accordance with subdivision (iii) of this subparagraph.

(ii) *Effect of new election.*—A new election made for the fifth taxable year, or taxable year thereafter, without the consent of the Commissioner, and a new election made with the consent of the Commissioner, shall be treated as an initial election to which subparagraph (1) of this paragraph applies.

(iii) *Written request required.*—A request to revoke an election made under this section when such revocation requires the consent of the Commissioner, or to make a new election when such election requires the consent of the Commissioner, shall be made in writing and shall be addressesd to the Director of International Operations, Internal Revenue Service, Washington, D.C. 20225. The request shall include the name and address of the taxpayer and shall be signed by the taxpayer or his duly authorized representative. It must specify the taxable year for which the revocation or new election is to be effective and shall be filed within 75 days after the close of the first taxable year for which it is desired to make the change. The request must specify the grounds which are considered to justify the revocation or new election. The Director of International Operations may require such other information as may be necessary in order to determine whether the proposed change will be permitted. A copy of the consent by the Director of International Operations shall be attached to the taxpayer's return required under section 6012 and the regulations thereunder for the taxable year for which the revocation or new election is effective. A copy of such consent may not be filed with any return under section 6851 and the regulations thereunder.

(3) *Election by partnership.*—If a nonresident alien individual or foreign corporation is a member of a partnership which has income described in paragraph (b)(1) of this section from real property, any election to be made under this section in respect of such income shall be made by the partners and not by the partnership. A nonresident alien or foreign corporation that makes an election generally must provide the partnership a Form W-8ECI, "Certificate of Foreign Person's Claim for Exemption from Withholding on Income Effectively Connected with the Conduct of a Trade or Business in the United States," and attach to such form a copy of the election (or a statement that indicates that the nonresident alien or foreign corporation will make the election). However, if the nonresident alien or foreign corporation has already submitted a valid form to the partnership that establishes such partner's foreign status, the partner shall furnish the partnership a copy of the election (or a statement that indicates that the nonresident alien or foreign corporation will make the election). To the extent the partnership has income to which the election pertains, the partnership shall treat such income as effectively connected income subject to withholding under section 1446. See also § 1.1446-2.

(e) *Effective date.*—This section shall apply for taxable years beginning after December 31, 1966, except the last four sentences of paragraph (d)(3) of this section shall apply to partnership taxable years beginning after May 18, 2005, or such earlier time as the regulations under §§ 1.1446-1 through 1.1446-5 apply by reason of an election under § 1.1446-7. There are no corresponding rules in this part for taxable years beginning before January 1, 1967. [Reg. § 1.871-10.]

☐ [*T.D.* 7332, 12-20-74. *Amended by T.D.* 9200, 5-13-2005.]

§ 1.871-11. Gains from sale or exchange of patents, copyrights, or similar property.—(a) *Contingent payment defined.*—For purposes of section 871(a)(1)(D), section 881(a)(4), § 1.871-7(c)(1)(iv), § 1.881-2(c)(1)(iii), and this section, payments which are contingent on the productivity, use, or disposition of property or of an interest therein include continuing payments measured by a percentage of the selling price of the products marketed, or based on the number of units manufactured or sold, or based in a similar manner upon production, sale or use, or disposition of the property or interest transferred. A payment which is certain as to the amount to be received, but contingent as to the time of payment, or an installment payment of a principal sum agreed upon in a transfer agreement, shall not be treated as a contingent payment for purposes of this paragraph. For the inapplication of section 1253 to certain amounts described in this paragraph, see paragraph (a) of § 1.1253-1.

(b) *Payments treated as contingent on use.*—Pursuant to section 871(e), if more than 50 percent of the gain of a nonresident alien individual or foreign corporation for any taxable year from the sale or exchange after October 4, 1966, of any patent, copyright, secret process or formula, goodwill, trademark, trade brand, franchise, or other like property, or of any interest in any such property, is from payments which are contingent on the productivity, use, or disposition of such property or interest, all of the gain of such individual or corporation for the taxable year from the sale or exchange of such property or interest are, for purposes of section 871(a)(1)(D), section 881(a)(4), section 1441(b), or section 1442(a), and the regulations thereunder, to be treated as being from payments which are contingent on the productivity, use, or disposition of such property or interest. This paragraph does not apply for purposes of determining under section 871(b)(1) or 882(a)(1) the tax of a nonresident alien individual or foreign corporation on income which is effectively connected for the taxable year with the conduct of a trade or business in the United States.

(c) *Sale or exchange.*—A sale or exchange for purposes of this section includes, but is not limited to, a transfer by an individual which by reason of section 1235, relating to the sale or exchange of patents, is considered the sale or exchange of a capital asset. The provisions of section 1253, relating to transfers of franchises, trademarks, and trade names, do not apply in determining whether a transfer is a sale or exchange for purposes of this section.

(d) *Recovery of adjusted basis.*—For purposes of determining for any taxable year the amount of gains which are subject to tax under section 871(a)(1)(D) or 881(a)(4), payments received by the nonresident alien individual or foreign corporation during such year must be reduced by amounts representing recovery of the taxpayer's adjusted basis of the property or interest which is sold or exchanged. Where the taxpayer receives in the same taxable year payments which, without reference to section 871(e) and this section, are not contingent on the productivity, use, or disposition of the property or interest which is sold or exchanged and payments which are contingent on the productivity, use, or disposition of the property or interest which is sold or exchanged, the taxpayer's unrecovered adjusted basis in the property or interest which is sold or exchanged must be allocated for the taxable year between such payments on the basis of the gross amount of each such type of payments. Where the taxpayer receives in the taxable year only payments which are not so contingent or only payments which are so contingent, the taxpayer's unrecovered basis must be allocated in its entirety to such payments for the taxable year.

(e) *Source rule.*—In determining whether gains described in section 871(a)(1)(D) or 881(a)(4) and paragraph (b) of this section are received from sources within the United States, such gains shall be treated, for purposes of section 871(a)(1)(D), section 881(a)(4), section 1441(b), and section 1442(a), as rentals or royalties for the use of, or privilege of using, property or an interest in property. See section 861(a)(4), § 1.861-5, and paragraph (a) of § 1.862-1.

(f) *Illustrations.*—The application of this section may be illustrated by the following examples:

Example (1). (a) A, a nonresident alien individual who uses the cash receipts and disbursements method of accounting and the calendar year as the taxable year, holds a United States patent which he developed through his own effort. On December 15, 1967, A enters into an agreement of sale with M Corporation, a domestic corporation, whereby A assigns to M Corporation all of his United States rights in the patent. In consideration of the sale, M Corporation is obligated to pay a fixed sum of $60,000, $20,000 being payable on execution of the contract and the balance payable in four annual installments of $10,000 each. As additional consideration, M Corporation agrees to pay to A a royalty in the amount of 2 percent of the gross sales of the products manufactured by M Corporation under the patent. A is not engaged in trade or business in the United States at any time during 1967 and 1968. His adjusted basis in the patent at the time of sale is $28,800.

(b) In 1967, A receives only the $20,000 paid by M Corporation on the execution of the contract of sale. No gain is realized by A upon receipt of this amount, and his unrecovered adjusted basis in the patent is reduced to $8,800 ($28,800 less $20,000).

(c) In 1968, M Corporation has gross sales of $600,000 from products manufactured under the patent. Consequently, for 1968, M Corporation pays $22,000 to A, $10,000 being the annual installment on the fixed payment and $12,000 being payments under the terms of the royalty provision. A's recognized gain for 1968 is $13,200 ($22,000 reduced by the unrecovered adjusted basis of $8,800). Of the total gain of $13,200, gain in the amount of $6,000 ($10,000 − [$8,800 × $10,000/$22,000]) is considered to be from the fixed installment payment and of $7,200 ($12,000 − [$8,800 × $12,000/$22,000]) is considered to be from the royalty payment. Since 54.5 percent ($7,200/$13,200) of the gain recognized in 1968 from the sale of the patent is from payments which are contingent on the productivity, use, or disposition of the patent, all of the $13,200 gain recognized in 1968 is treated, for purposes of section 871(a)(1)(D) and section 1441(b), as being from payments which are contingent on the productivity, use, or disposition of the patent.

Example (2). (a) F, a foreign corporation using the calendar year as the taxable year and not engaged in trade or business in the United States, holds a U.S. patent on certain property which it developed through its own efforts. Corporation F uses the cash receipts and disbursements method of accounting. On December 1, 1966, F Corporation enters into an agreement of sale with D Corporation, a domestic corporation, whereby D Corporation purchases the exclusive right and license, and the right to sublicense to others, to manufacture, use, and/or sell certain devices under the patent in the United States during the term of the patent. The agreement grants D Corporation the right to dispose, anywhere in the world, of machinery manufactured in the United States and equipped with such devices. Corporation D is granted the right, at its own expense, to prosecute infringers in its own name or in the name of F Corporation, or both, and to retain any damages recovered.

(b) Corporation D agrees to pay to F Corporation annually $5 for each device manufactured under the patent during the year but in no case less than $5,000 per year. In 1967, D Corporation manufactures 2,500 devices under the patent; and, in 1968, 1,500 devices. Under the terms of the contract D Corporation pays to F Corporation in 1967 $12,500 with respect to production in that year and $7,500 in 1968 with respect to production in that year. F Corporation's basis in the patent at the time of the sale is $17,000.

(c) With respect to the payments received by F Corporation in 1967, no gain is realized by that corporation and its unrecovered adjusted basis in the patent is reduced to $4,500 ($17,000 less $12,500).

(d) With respect to the payments received by F Corporation in 1968, such corporation has recognized gain of $3,000 ($7,500 reduced by unrecovered adjusted basis of $4,500). Of the total gain of $3,000, gain in the amount of $2,000 ($5,000 − [$4,500 × $5,000/$7,500]) is considered to be from the fixed installment payment and of $1,000 ($2,500 − [$4,500 × $2,500/$7,500]) is considered to be from payments which are contingent on the productivity, use, or disposition of the patent. Since 33.3 percent ($1,000/$3,000) of the gain recognized in 1968 from the sale of the patent is from payments which are contingent on the productivity, use, or disposition of the patent, only $1,000 of the $3,000 gain for that year constitutes gains which, for purposes of section 881(a)(4) and section 1442(a), are from payments which are contingent on the productivity, use, or disposition of the patent. The balance of $2,000 is gain from the sale of property and is not subject to tax under section 881(a).

(g) *Effective date.*—This section shall apply for taxable years beginning after December 31, 1966, but only in respect of gains from sales or exchanges occurring after October 4, 1966. There are no corresponding rules in this part for taxable years beginning before January 1, 1967. [Reg. § 1.871-11.]

☐ [T.D. 7332, 12-20-74.]

§ 1.871-12. Determination of tax on treaty income.—(a) *In general.*—This section applies for purposes of determining under § 1.871-7 or § 1.871-8 the tax on a nonresident alien individual, or under § 1.881-2 or § 1.882-1 the tax of a foreign corporation, which for the taxable year has income described in section 872(a) or 882(b) upon which the tax is limited by an income tax convention to which the United States is a party. Income for such purposes does not include income of any kind which is exempt from tax under the provisions of an income tax convention to which the United States is a party. See §§ 1.872-2(c) and 1.883-1(b). This section shall not apply to a nonresident alien individual who is a bona fide resident of Puerto Rico during the entire taxable year.

(b) *Definition of treaty and nontreaty income.*—(1) *In general.*—(i) For purposes of this section the term "treaty income" shall be construed to mean the gross income of a nonresident alien individual or foreign corporation, as the case may be, the tax on which is limited by a tax convention. The term "nontreaty income" shall be construed, for such purposes, to mean the gross income of the nonresident alien individual or foreign corporation other than the treaty income. Neither term includes income of any kind which is exempt from the tax imposed by chapter 1 of the Code.

(ii) In determining either the treaty or nontreaty income the gross income shall be determined in accordance with §§ 1.872-1 and 1.872-2, or with §§ 1.882-3 and 1.883-1, except that in determining the treaty income the exclusion granted by section 116(a) for dividends shall not be taken into account. Thus, for example, treaty income includes the total amount of dividends paid by a domestic corporation not disqualified by section 116(b) and received from sources within the United States if, in accordance with a tax convention, the dividends are subject to the income tax at a rate not to exceed 15 percent but does not include interest which, in accordance with a tax convention, is exempt from the income tax. In further illustration, neither the treaty nor the nontreaty income includes interest on certain governmental obligations which by reason of section 103 is excluded from gross income, or interest which by reason of a tax convention is exempt from the tax imposed by chapter 1 of the Code.

(iii) For purposes of applying any income tax convention to which the United States is a party, original issue discount which is subject to tax under section 871(a)(1)(C) or 881(a)(3) is to be treated as interest, and gains which are subject to tax under section 871(a)(1)(D) or 881(a)(4) are to be treated as royalty income. This subdivision shall not apply, however, where its application would be contrary to any treaty obligation of the United States.

(2) *Application of permanent establishment rule of treaties.*—In applying this section with respect to income which is not effectively connected for the taxable year with the conduct of a trade or business in the United States by a nonresident alien individual or foreign corporation, see section 894(b), which provides that with respect to such income the nonresident alien individual or foreign corporation shall be deemed not to have a permanent establishment in the United States at any time during the taxable year for purposes of applying any exemption from, or reduction in rate of, tax provided by any tax convention.

(c) *Determination of tax.*—(1) *In general.*—If the gross income of a nonresident alien individual or foreign corporation, as the case may be, consists of both treaty and nontreaty income, the tax liability for the taxable year shall be the sum of the amounts determined in accordance with subparagraphs (2) and (3) of this paragraph. In no case, however, may the tax liability so determined exceed the tax liability (tax reduced by allowable credits) with respect to the taxpayer's entire income, determined in accordance with § 1.871-7 or § 1.871-8, or with § 1.881-2 or § 1.882-1, as though the tax convention had not come into effect and without reference to the provisions of this section. Determinations under this paragraph shall be made without taking into account any credits allowed by sections 31, 32, 39, and 6402, but such credits shall be allowed against the tax liability determined in accordance with this subparagraph.

Reg. § 1.871-12(c)(1)

(2) *Tax on nontreaty income.*—For purposes of subparagraph (1) of this paragraph, compute a partial tax (determined without the allowance of any credit) upon only the nontreaty income in accordance with § 1.871-7 or § 1.871-8, or with § 1.881-2 or § 1.882-1, whichever applies, as though the tax convention had not come into effect. To the extent allowed by paragraph (d) of § 1.871-8, or paragraph (c) of § 1.882-1, the credits allowed by sections 33, 35, 38, and 40 shall then be allowed, without taking into account any item included in the treaty income, against the tax determined under this subparagraph.

(3) *Tax on treaty income.*—For purposes of subparagraph (1) of this paragraph, compute a tax upon the gross amount, determined without the allowance of any deduction, of each separate item of treaty income at the reduced rate applicable to that item under the tax convention. No credits shall be allowed against the tax determined under this subparagraph.

(d) *Illustration.*—The application of this section may be illustrated by the following example:

Example. (a) A nonresident alien individual who is a resident of a foreign country with which the United States has entered into a tax convention receives during the taxable year 1967 from sources within the United States total gross income of $22,000, consisting of the following items:

Compensation for personal services the tax on which is not limited by the tax convention (effectively connected income under § 1.864-4(c)(6)(ii)) . .	$20,000
Oil royalties the tax on which is limited by the tax convention to 15 percent of the gross amount thereof (effectively connected income by reason of election under § 1.871-10)	2,000
Total gross income	$22,000

(b) The taxpayer is engaged in business in the United States during the taxable year but does not have a permanent establishment therein. There are no allowable deductions, other than the deductions allowed by sections 613 and 873(b)(3).

(c) The tax liability for the taxable year is $6,100, determined as follows:

Nontreaty gross income		$20,000
Less: Deduction for personal exemption		600
Nontreaty taxable income . . .		$19,400
Tax under section 1 of the Code on nontreaty taxable income ($5,170 plus 45% of $1,400)		$ 5,800
Plus: Tax on treaty income (Gross oil royalties) ($2,000 × 15%)		300
Total tax (determined as provided in paragraph (c)(2) and (3) of this section) . .		$6,100

(d) If the tax had been determined under paragraph (b)(2) of § 1.871-8 as though the tax convention had not come into effect, the tax liability would have been $6,478, determined as follows and by taking into account the election under § 1.871-10:

Total gross income		$22,000
Less: Deduction under section 613 for percentage depletion ($2,000 × 27½%)	$550	
Deduction for personal exemption	600	1,150
Taxable income		$20,850
Tax under section 1 of the Code on taxable income ($6,070 plus 48% of $850)		$ 6,478

(e) *Effective date.*—This section shall apply for taxable years beginning after December 31, 1966. For corresponding rules applicable to taxable years beginning before January 1, 1967, see 26 CFR 1.871-7(e) (Rev. as of Jan. 1, 1971). [Reg. § 1.871-12.]

☐ [T.D. 7332, 12-20-74. Amended by T.D. 8657, 3-5-96.]

§ 1.871-13. Taxation of individuals for taxable year of change of U.S. citizenship or residence.

(a) *In general.*—(1) An individual who is a citizen or resident of the United States at the beginning of the taxable year but a nonresident alien at the end of the taxable year, or a nonresident alien at the beginning of the taxable year but a citizen or resident of the United States at the end of the taxable year, is taxable for such year as though his taxable year were comprised of two separate periods, one consisting of the time during which he is a citizen or resident of the United States and the other consisting of the time during which he is not a citizen or resident of the United States. Thus, for example, the income tax liability of an alien individual under chapter 1 of the Code for the taxable year in which he changes his residence will be computed under two different sets of rules, one relating to resident aliens for the period of residence and the other relating to nonresident aliens for the period of nonresidence. However, in determining the taxable income for such year which is subject to the graduated rate of tax imposed by section 1 or 1201 of the Code, all income for the period of U.S. citizenship or residence must be aggregated with the income for the period of nonresidence which is effectively connected for such year with the conduct of a trade or business in the United States. This section does not apply to alien individuals treated as residents for the entire taxable year under section 6013(g) or (h). These individuals are taxed under the rules in § 1.1-1(b).

(2) For purposes of this section, an individual is deemed to be a citizen or resident of the United States for the day on which he becomes a citizen or resident of the United States, a nonresident of the United States for the day on which he abandons his U.S. residence, and an alien for the day on which he gives up his U.S. citizenship.

(b) *Acquisition of U.S. citizenship or residence.*—Income from sources without the United States which is not effectively connected with the conduct by the taxpayer of a trade or business in the United States is not taxable if received by an alien individual while he is not a resident of the United States even though he becomes a citizen or resident of the United States after its receipt and before the close of the taxable year. However, income from sources without the United States which is not effectively connected with the conduct by the taxpayer of a trade or business in the United States is taxable if received by an individual while he is a citizen or resident of the United States, even though he earns the income earlier in the taxable year while he is neither a citizen nor resident of the United States.

(c) *Abandonment of U.S. citizenship or residence.*—Income from sources without the United States which is not effectively connected with the conduct by the taxpayer of a trade or business in the United States is not taxable if received by an alien individual while he is not a resident of the United States, even though he earns the income earlier in the taxable year while he is a citizen or resident of the United States. However, income from sources without the United States which is not effectively connected with the conduct by the taxpayer of a trade or business in the United States is taxable if received by an individual while he is a citizen or resident of the United States, even though he abandons his U.S. citizenship or residence after its receipt and before the close of the taxable year.

(d) *Special rules.*—(1) *Method of accounting.*—Paragraphs (b) and (c) of this section may not apply to an individual who for the taxable year uses an accrual method of accounting.

(2) *Deductions for personal exemptions.*—An alien individual to whom this section applies is entitled to deduct one personal exemption for the taxable year under section 151. In addition, he is entitled to such additional exemptions as are allowed as a deduction under section 151 but only to the extent the amount of such additional exemptions do not exceed his taxable income (determined without regard to any deduction for personal exemptions) for the period in the taxable year during which he is a citizen or resident of the United States. This subparagraph does not apply to the extent it is inconsistent with section 873, and the regulations thereunder, or with the provisions of an income tax convention to which the United States is a party.

(3) *Exclusion of dividends received.*—In determining the $100 exclusion for the taxable year provided by section 116 in respect of certain dividends, only those dividends for the period during which the individual is neither a citizen nor resident of the United States may be taken into account as are effectively connected for the taxable year with the conduct of a trade or business in the United States. See § 1.116-1(e)(1).

(e) *Illustrations.*—The application of this section may be illustrated by the following examples:

Example (1). A, a married alien individual who uses the calendar year as the taxable year and the cash receipts and disbursements method of accounting, becomes a resident of the United States on June 1, 1971. During the period of nonresidence from January 1, 1971, to May 31, 1971, inclusive, A receives $15,000 income from sources without the United States which is not effectively connected with the conduct of a trade or business in the United States. During the period of residence from June 1, 1971, to December 31, 1971, A receives wages of $10,000, dividends of $200 from a foreign corporation, and dividends of $75 from a domestic corporation qualifying under section 116(a). Of the amount of wages so received, $2,000 is for services performed by A outside the United States during the period of nonresidence. Total allowable deductions (other than for personal exemptions) amount to $700, none of which are deductible under section 62 in computing adjusted gross income. For 1971 A's spouse has no gross income and is not the dependent of another taxpayer. For 1971, A's taxable income is $8,200, all of which is subject to tax under section 1, as follows:

Wages		$10,000
Dividends from foreign corporation		200
Dividends from domestic corporation ($75 less $75 exclusion)		0
Adjusted gross income		$10,200
Less deductions:		
Personal exemptions (2 × $650)	$1,300	
Other allowable deductions	700	2,000
Taxable income		$ 8,200

Example (2). The facts are the same as in example (1) except that during the period of nonresidence from January 1, 1971, to May 31, 1971, A receives from sources within the United States income of $1,850 which is effectively connected with the conduct by A of a business in the United States and $350 in dividends from domestic corporations qualifying under section 116(a). Only $50 of these dividends are effectively connected with the conduct by A of a business in the United States. The assumption is made that there are no allowable deductions connected with such effectively connected income. For 1971, A has taxable income of $10,075 subject to tax under section 1 and $300 income subject to tax under section 871(a)(1)(A), as follows:

Wages		$10,000
Business income		1,850
Dividends from foreign corporation		200
Dividends from domestic corporation ($125 less $100 exclusion)		25
Adjusted gross income		$12,075
Less deductions:		
Personal exemptions (2 × $650)	$1,300	
Other allowable deductions	700	2,000
Taxable income subject to tax under section 1		$10,075
Income subject to tax under section 871(a)(1)(A)		$ 300

Example (3). A, a married alien individual with three children, uses the calendar year as the taxable year and the cash receipts and disbursements method of accounting. On October 1, 1971, A and his family become residents of the United States. During the period of nonresidence from January 1, 1971, to September 30, 1971, A receives income of $18,000 from sources without the United States which is not effectively connected with the conduct of a trade or business in the United States and of $2,500 from sources within the United States which is effectively connected with the conduct of a business in the United States. It is assumed there are no allowable deductions connected with such effectively connected income. During the period of residence from October 1, 1971, to December 31, 1971, A receives wages of $2,000, of which $400 is for services performed outside the United States during the period of nonresidence. Total allowable deductions (other than for personal exemptions) amount to $250, none of which are deductible under section 62 in computing adjusted gross income. Neither the spouse nor any of the children has any gross income for 1971, and the spouse is not the dependent of another taxpayer for such year. For 1971, A's taxable income is $1,850, all of which is subject to tax under section 1, as follows:

Wages (residence period)	$2,000	
Less: Allowable deductions	250	
Taxable income (without deduction for personal exemptions) (residence period)		$1,750
Business income (nonresidence period)		2,500
Total taxable income (without deduction for personal exemptions)		$4,250
Less deduction for personal exemptions:		
Taxpayer	$ 650	
Wife and 3 children (4 × $650, but not to exceed $1,750)	1,750	2,400
Taxable income		$1,850

(f) *Effective date.*—This section shall apply for taxable years beginning after December 31, 1966. There are no corresponding rules in this part for taxable years beginning before January 1, 1967. [Reg. § 1.871-13.]

☐ [T.D. 7332, 12-20-74. Amended by T.D. 7670, 1-30-80.]

§ 1.871-14. Rules relating to repeal of tax on interest of nonresident alien individuals and foreign corporations received from certain portfolio debt investments.— (a) *General rule.*—No tax shall be imposed under section 871(a)(1)(A), 871(a)(1)(C), 881(a)(1) or 881(a)(3) on any portfolio interest as defined in sections 871(h)(2) and 881(c)(2) received by a foreign person. But see section 871(b) or 882(a) if such interest is effectively connected with the conduct of a trade or business within the United States.

(b) *Rules concerning obligations in bearer form.*—(1) *In general.*—Interest (including original issue discount) with respect to an obligation in bearer form is portfolio interest within the meaning of section 871(h)(2)(A) or 881(c)(2)(A) only if it is paid with respect to an obligation issued after July 18, 1984, that is described in section 163(f)(2)(B) and the regulations under that section and an exception under section 871(h) or 881(c) does not apply. Any obligation that is not in registered form as defined in paragraph (c)(1)(i) of this section is an obligation in bearer form.

(2) *Coordination with withholding and reporting rules.*—For an exemption from withholding under section 1441 with respect to obligations described in this paragraph (b), see § 1.1441-1(b)(4)(i). For rules relating to an exemption from Form 1099 reporting and backup withholding under section 3406, see section 6049 and § 1.6049-5(b)(8) for the payment of interest and § 1.6045-1(g)(1)(ii) for the redemp-

tion, retirement, or sale of an obligation in bearer form.

(c) *Rules concerning obligations in registered form.*—(1) *In general.*—(i) *Obligation in registered form.*—For purposes of this section, an obligation is in registered form only as provided in this paragraph (c)(1)(i). The conditions for an obligation to be considered in registered form are identical to the conditions described in § 5f.103-1 of this chapter. Therefore, an obligation that would be an obligation in registered form except for the fact that it can be converted at any time in the future into an obligation that is not in registered form shall not be an obligation in registered form. An obligation that is not in registered form by reason of the preceding sentence may nevertheless be in registered form, but only after the possibility of conversion is terminated. An obligation that is not in registered form and can be converted into an obligation that would meet the requirements of this paragraph (c)(1)(i) for being in registered form shall be considered in registered form only after the conversion is effected. For purposes of this section, an obligation is convertible if the obligation can be transferred by any means not described in § 5f.103-1(c) of this chapter. An obligation is treated as an obligation in registered form if—

(A) The obligation is registered as to both principal and any stated interest with the issuer (or its agent) and transfer of the obligation may be effected only by surrender of the old instrument, and either the reissuance by the issuer of the old instrument to the new holder or the issuance by the issuer of a new instrument to the new holder;

(B) The right to the principal of, and stated interest on, the obligation may be transferred only through a book entry system maintained by the issuer (or its agent) described in this paragraph (c)(1)(i)(B). An obligation shall be considered transferable through a book entry system if the ownership of an interest in the obligation, is required to be reflected in a book entry, whether or not physical securities are issued. A book entry is a record of ownership that identifies the owner of an interest in the obligation; or

(C) It is registered as to both principal and any stated interest with the issuer (or its agent) and may be transferred by way of either of the methods described in paragraph (c)(1)(i)(A) or (B) of this section.

(ii) *Requirements for portfolio interest qualification in the case of an obligation in registered form.*—Interest (including original issue discount) received on an obligation that is in registered form qualifies as portfolio interest only if—

(A) The interest is paid on an obligation issued after July 18, 1984;

(B) The interest would be subject to tax under section 871(a)(1)(A), 871(a)(1)(C), 881(a)(1) or 881(a)(3) but for section 871(h) or 881(c);

(C) A United States (U.S.) person otherwise required to deduct and withhold tax under chapter 3 of the Internal Revenue Code (Code) receives a statement that meets the requirements of section 871(h)(5) that the beneficial owner of the obligation is not a U.S. person; and

(D) An exception under section 871(h) or 881(c) does not apply.

(2) *Required statement.*—For purposes of paragraph (c)(1)(ii)(C) of this section, a U.S. person will be considered to have received a statement that meets the requirements of section 871(h)(5) if either it complies with one of the procedures described in this paragraph (c)(2) and does not have actual knowledge or reason to know that the beneficial owner is a U.S. person or it complies with the procedures described in paragraph (d) or (e) of this section.

(i) The U.S. person (or its authorized foreign agent described in § 1.1441-7(c)(2)) can reliably associate the payment with documentation upon which it can rely to treat the payment as made to a foreign beneficial owner in accordance with § 1.1441-1(e)(1)(ii). See § 1.1441-1(b)(2)(vii) for rules regarding reliable association with documentation.

(ii) The U.S. person (or its authorized foreign agent described in § 1.1441-7(c)(2)) can reliably associate the payment with a withholding certificate described in § 1.1441-5(c)(2)(iv) from a person claiming to be withholding foreign partnership and the foreign partnership can reliably associate the payment with documentation upon which it can rely to treat the payment as made to a foreign beneficial owner in accordance with § 1.1441-1(e)(1)(ii).

(iii) The U.S. person (or its authorized foreign agent described in § 1.1441-7(c)(2)) can reliably associate the payment with a withholding certificate described in § 1.1441-1(e)(3)(ii) from a person representing to be a qualified intermediary that has assumed primary withholding responsibility in accordance with § 1.1441-1(e)(5)(iv) and the qualified intermediary can reliably associate the payment with documentation upon which it can rely to treat the payment as made to a foreign beneficial owner in accordance with its agreement with the Internal Revenue Service (IRS).

(iv) The U.S. person (or its authorized foreign agent described in § 1.1441-7(c)(2)) can reliably associate the payment with a withholding certificate described in § 1.1441-1(e)(3)(v) from a person claiming to be a U.S. branch of a foreign bank or of a foreign insurance company that is described in § 1.1441-1(b)(2)(iv)(A) or a U.S. branch designated in accordance with § 1.1441-1(b)(2)(iv)(E) and the U.S. branch can reliably associate the payment with documentation upon which it can rely to treat the payment as made to a foreign beneficial owner in accordance with § 1.1441-1(e)(1)(ii).

(v) The U.S. person receives a statement from a securities clearing organization, a bank, or another financial institution that holds customers' securities in the ordinary course of its trade or business. In such case the statement must be signed under penalties of perjury by an authorized representative of the financial institution and must state that the institution has received from the beneficial owner a withholding certificate described in § 1.1441-1(e)(2)(i) (a Form W-8 or an acceptable substitute form as defined § 1.1441-1(e)(4)(vi)) or that it has received from another financial institution a similar statement that it, or another financial institution acting on behalf of the beneficial owner, has received the Form W-8 from the beneficial owner. In the case of multiple financial institutions between the beneficial owner and the U.S. person, this statement must be given by each financial institution to the one above it in the chain. No particular form is required for the statement provided by the financial institutions. However, the statement must provide the name and address of the beneficial owner, and a copy of the Form W-8 provided by the beneficial owner must be attached. The statement is subject to the same rules described in § 1.1441-1(e)(4) that apply to intermediary Forms W-8 described in § 1.1441-1(e)(3)(iii). If the information on the Form W-8 changes, the beneficial owner must so notify the financial institution acting on its behalf within 30 days of such changes, and the financial institution must promptly so inform the U.S. person. This notice also must be given if the financial institution has actual knowledge that the information has changed but has not been so informed by the beneficial owner. In the case of multiple financial institutions between the beneficial owner and the U.S. person, this notice must be given by each financial institution to the institution above it in the chain.

(vi) The U.S. person complies with procedures that the U.S. competent authority may agree to with the competent authority of a country with which the United States has an income tax treaty in effect.

(3) *Time for providing certificate or documentary evidence.*—(i) *General rule.*—Interest on a registered obligation shall qualify as portfolio interest if the withholding certificate or documentary evidence that must be provided is furnished before expiration of the beneficial owner's period of limitation for claiming a refund of tax with respect to such interest. See, however, § 1.1441-1(b)(7) for consequences to a withholding agent that makes a payment without withholding even though it cannot reliably associate the payment with the documentation prior to the payment. If a withholding agent withholds an amount under chapter 3 of the Code because it cannot reliably associate the payment with the documentation for the beneficial owner on the date of payment, the beneficial owner may nevertheless claim the benefit of an exemption from tax under this section by claiming a refund or credit for the amount withheld based upon the procedures described in §§ 1.1464-1 and 301.6402-3(e) of this chapter. For this purpose, the taxpayer must attach a withholding certificate described in § 1.1441-1(e)(2)(i) to the income tax filed for claiming a refund of tax. In the alternative, adjustments to any amount of overwithheld tax may be made under the procedures described in § 1.1461-2(a) (for example, if the beneficial owner furnishes documentation to the withholding agent before the due date for filing the return required under § 1.1461-1(b) with respect to that payment).

(ii) *Example.*—The following example illustrates the rules of this paragraph (c)(3) and their coordination with § 1.1441-1(b)(7):

Example. A is a withholding agent who, on October 12, 2001, pays interest on a registered obligation to B, a foreign corporation. B is a calendar year taxpayer, engaged in the conduct of a trade or business in the United States, and is, therefore, required to file an annual income tax return on Form 1120F. The interest, however, is not effectively connected with B's U.S. trade or business. On the date of payment, B has not furnished, and A cannot associate the payment with documentation for B. However, A does not withhold under section 1442, even though, under § 1.1441-1(b)(3)(iii)(A), A should presume that B is a foreign person, because A's communications with B are mailed to an address in a foreign country. Assuming that B files a return for its taxable year ending December 31, 2001, and that its statute of limitations period with regard to that year expires on June 15, 2005, the interest paid on October 12, 2001, may qualify as portfolio interest only if B provides appropriate documentation to A on or before June 15, 2005. If B does not provide the documentation on or before June 15, 2005, and does not pay the tax, A is liable for the tax under section 1463, even if B provides the documentation to A after June 15, 2005. Therefore, the provisions in § 1.1441-1(b)(7), regarding late-received documentation would not help A avoid liability for tax under section 1463 even if the documentation is furnished within the statute of limitations period of A. This is because, in a case involving interest, the documentation received within the limitations period of the beneficial owner serves as a condition for the interest to qualify as portfolio interest. When documentation is received after the expiration of the beneficial owner's limitations period, the interest can no longer qualify as portfolio interest. On the other hand, A could rely on documentation that it receives after the expiration of B's limitations period to establish B's right to a reduced rate of withholding under an applicable income tax treaty (since, in such a case, a claim of treaty benefits is not conditioned upon providing documentation prior to the expiration of the beneficial owner's limitations period).

(4) *Coordination with withholding and reporting rules.*—For an exemption from withholding under section 1441 with respect to obligations described in this paragraph (c), see § 1.1441-1(b)(4)(i). For rules applicable to withholding certificates, see § 1.1441-1(e)(4). For rules regarding documentary evidence, see § 1.6049-5(c)(1). For application of presumptions when the U.S. person cannot reliably associate the payment with documentation, see § 1.1441-1(b)(3). For standards of knowledge applicable to withholding agents, see § 1.1441-7(b). For rules relating to an exemption from Form 1099 reporting and backup withholding under section 3406, see section 6049 and § 1.6049-5(b)(8) for the payment of interest and § 1.6045-1(g)(1)(i) for the redemption, retirement, or sale of an obligation in registered form. For rules relating to reporting on Forms 1042 and 1042-S, see § 1.1461-1(b) and (c).

(d) *Application of repeal of 30-percent withholding to pass-through certificates.*—(1) *In general.*—Interest received on a pass-through certificate qualifies as portfolio interest under section 871(h)(2) or 881(c)(2) if the interest satisfies the conditions described in paragraph (b)(1), (c)(1), or (e) of this section without regard to whether any obligation held by the fund or trust to which the pass-through certificate relates is described in paragraph (b)(1), (c)(1)(ii), or (e) of this section. This paragraph (d)(1) applies only to payments made to the holder of the pass-through certificate from the trustee of the pass-through trust and does not apply to payments made to the trustee of the pass-through trust. For example, a mortgage pass-through certificate in bearer form must meet the requirements set forth in paragraph (b)(1) of this section, but the obligations held by the fund or trust to which the mortgage pass-through certificate relates need not meet the requirements set forth in paragraph (b)(1), (c)(1)(ii), or (e) of this section. However, for purposes of paragraphs (b)(1), (c)(1)(ii), and (e) of this section and section 127 of the Tax Reform Act of 1984, a pass-through certificate will be considered as issued after July 18, 1984, only to the extent that the obligations held by the fund or trust to which the pass-through certificate relates are issued after July 18, 1984.

(2) *Interest in REMICs.*—Interest received on a regular or residual interest in a REMIC qualifies as portfolio interest under section 871(h)(2) or 881(c)(2) if the interest satisfies the conditions described in paragraph (b)(1), (c)(1)(ii), or (e) of this section. For purposes of paragraph (b)(1), (c)(1)(ii), or (e) of this section, interest on a regular interest in a REMIC is not considered interest on any mortgage obligations held by the REMIC. The foregoing rule, however, applies only to payments made to the holder of the regular interest from the REMIC and does not apply to payments made to the REMIC. For purposes of paragraph (b)(1), (c)(1)(ii), or (e) of this section, interest on a residual interest in a REMIC is considered to be interest on or with respect to the obligations held by the REMIC, and not on or with respect to the residual interest. For purposes of paragraphs (b)(1), (c)(1)(ii), and (e) of this section and section 127 of the Tax Reform Act of 1984, a residual interest in a REMIC will be considered as issued after July 18, 1984, only to the extent that the obligations held by the REMIC are issued after July 18, 1984, but a regular interest in a REMIC will be considered as issued after July 18, 1984, if the regular interest was issued after July 18, 1984, without regard to the date on which the mortgage obligations held by the REMIC were issued.

(3) *Date of issuance.*—In general, a mortgage pass-through certificate will be considered to have been issued after July 18, 1984, if all of the mortgages held by the fund or trust were issued after July 18, 1984. If some of the mortgages held by the fund or trust were issued before July 19, 1984, then the portion of any interest payment which represents interest on those mortgages shall not be considered to be portfolio interest. The preceding sentence shall not apply, however, if all of the following conditions are satisfied:

(i) The mortgage pass-through certificate is issued after December 31, 1986;

(ii) Payment of the mortgage pass-through certificate is guaranteed by, and a guarantee commitment has been issued by, an entity that is independent from the issuer of the underlying obligation;

(iii) The guarantee commitment with respect to the mortgage pass-through certificate cannot have been issued more than 14 months prior to the date on which the mortgage pass-through certificate is issued; and

(iv) The fund or trust to which the mortgage pass-through certificate relates cannot contain mortgage obligations on which the first scheduled monthly payment of principal and interest was made more than twelve months before the date on which the guarantee commitment was made.

(e) *Foreign-targeted registered obligations.*—(1) *General rule.*—The statement described in paragraph (c)(1)(ii)(C) of this section is not required with respect to interest paid on a registered obligation that is targeted to foreign markets in accordance with the provisions of paragraph (e)(2) of this section if the interest is paid by a U.S. person, a withholding foreign partnership, or a U.S. branch described in §1.1441-1(b)(2)(iv)(A) or (E) to a registered owner at an address outside the United States, provided that the registered owner is a financial institution described in section 871(h)(5)(B). In that case, the U.S. person otherwise required to deduct and withhold tax may treat the interest as portfolio interest if it does not have actual knowledge that the beneficial owner is a United States person and if it receives the certificate described in paragraph (e)(3)(i) of this section from a financial institution or member of a clearing organization, which member is the beneficial owner of the obligation, or the documentary evidence or statement described in paragraph (e)(3)(ii) of this section from the beneficial owner, in accordance with the procedures described in paragraph (e)(4) of this section.

(2) *Definition of a foreign-targeted registered obligation.*—An obligation is considered to be targeted to foreign markets for purposes of paragraph (e)(1) of this section if it is sold (or resold in connection with its original issuance) only to foreign persons (or to foreign branches of United States financial institutions described in section 871(h)(5)(B)) in accordance with procedures similar to those prescribed in §1.163-5(c)(2)(i)(A), (B), or (D). However, the provisions of that section that require an obligation to be offered for sale or resale in connection with its original issuance only outside the United States do not apply with respect to registered obligations offered for sale through a public auction. Similarly, the provisions of that section that require delivery to be made outside the United States do not apply to registered obligations offered for sale through a public auction if the obligations are considered to be in registered form by virtue of the fact that they may be transferred only through a book entry system. The obligation, if evidenced by a physical document other than a confirmation receipt, must contain on its face a legend indicating that it has been sold (or resold in connection with its original issuance) in accordance with those procedures.

(3) *Documentation.*—A certificate described in paragraph (e)(3)(i) of this section is required if the United States person otherwise required to deduct and withhold tax (the withholding agent) pays interest to a financial institution described in section 871(h)(5)(B) or to a member of a clearing organization, which member is the beneficial owner of the obligation. The documentation described in paragraph (e)(3)(ii) of this section is required if a withholding agent pays interest to a beneficial owner that is neither a financial institution described in section 871(h)(5)(B) nor a member of a clearing organization.

(i) *Interest paid to a financial institution or a member of a clearing organization.*—(A) *Requirement of a certificate.*—(1) If the withholding agent pays interest to a financial institution described in section 871(h)(5)(B) or to a member of a clearing organization, which member is the beneficial owner of the obligation, the withholding agent must receive a certificate which states that, beginning at the time the last preceding certificate under this paragraph (e)(3)(i) was provided and while the financial institution or clearing organization member has held the obligation, with respect to each foreign-targeted registered obligation which has been held by the person providing the certificate at any time since the provision of such last preceding certificate, either—

(i) The beneficial owner of the obligation has not been a United States person on each interest payment date; or

(ii) If the person providing the certificate is a financial institution which is holding or has held an obligation on behalf of the beneficial owner, the beneficial owner of the obligation has been a United States person on one or more interest payment dates (identifying such date or dates), and the person making the certification has forwarded or will forward the appropriate United States beneficial ownership notification to the withholding agent in accordance with the provisions of paragraph (e)(4) of this section.

(2) The person providing the certificate need not state the foregoing where no previous certificate has been required to be provided by the payee to the withholding agent under this paragraph (e)(3)(i).

(B) *Additional representations.*—Whether or not a previous certificate has been required to be provided with respect to the obligation, each certificate furnished pursuant to the provisions in this paragraph (e)(3)(i) must further state that, for each foreign-targeted registered obligation held and every other such obligation to be acquired and held by the person providing the certificate during the period beginning on the date of the certificate and ending on the date the next certificate is required to be provided, the beneficial owner of the obligation will not be a United States person on each interest payment date while the financial institution or clearing organization member holds the obligation and that, if the person providing the certificate is a financial institution which is holding or will be holding the obligation on behalf of a beneficial owner, such person will provide a United States beneficial ownership notification to the withholding agent (and a clearing organization that is not a withholding agent where a member organization is required by this paragraph (e)(3) to furnish the clearing organization with a statement) in accordance with paragraph (e)(4) of this section in the event such certificate (or statement in the case of a statement provided by a member organization to a clearing organization that is not a withholding agent) is or becomes untrue with respect to any obligation. A clearing organization is an entity which is in the business of holding obligations for member organizations and transferring obligations among such members by credit or debit to the account of a member without the necessity of physical delivery of the obligation.

(C) *Obligation must be identified.*—The certificate described in paragraph (e)(3)(ii)(A) of this section must identify the obligation or obligations with respect to which it is given, except where the certification is given with respect to an obligation that has not been acquired at the time the certification is made. An obligation is identified if it or the larger issuance of which it is a part is described on a list (e.g., $5 million principal amount of 12% debentures of ABC Savings and Loan Association due February 25, 1995, $3 million principal amount of 10% U.S. Treasury notes due May 28, 1990) of all registered obligations targeted to foreign markets held by or on behalf of the person providing the certificate and the list is attached to, and incorporated by reference into, the certificate. The certificate must identify and provide the address of the person furnishing the certificate.

(D) *Payment to a depository of a clearing organization.*—If the withholding agent pays interest to a depository of a clearing organization, then the clearing organization must provide the certificate described in this paragraph (e)(3)(i) to the withholding agent. Any certificate that is provided by a clearing organization must state that the clearing organization has received a statement from each member which complies with the provisions of this paragraph (e)(3)(i) and of paragraph (e)(4) of this section (as if the clearing organization were the withholding agent and regardless of whether the member is a financial institution described in section 871(h)(5)(B)).

(E) *Statement in lieu of Form W-8.*—Subject to the requirements set out in paragraph (e)(4) of this section, a certificate or statement in the form described in this paragraph (e)(3)(i), in conjunction with the next annual certificate or statement, will serve as the certificate that may be provided in lieu of a Form W-8 with respect to interest on all foreign-targeted registered obligations held by the person making the certification or statement and which is paid to such person within the period beginning on the date of the certificate and ending on the date the next certificate is required to be provided.

(F) *Electronic transmission.*—The certificate described in this paragraph (e)(3)(i) may be provided electronically under the terms and conditions of § 1.163-5(c)(2)(i)(D)(3)(*ii*).

(ii) *Payment to a person other than a financial institution or member of a clearing organization.*—If the withholding agent pays interest to the beneficial owner of an obligation that is neither a financial institution described in section 871(h)(5)(B) nor a member of a clearing organization, then such owner must provide the withholding agent a statement described in paragraph (c)(1)(ii)(C) of this section.

(4) *Applicable procedures regarding documentation.*—(i) *Procedures applicable to certificates required under paragraph (e)(3)(i) of this section.*—(A) *Time for providing certificate.*—Where no previous certificate for foreign-targeted registered obligations has been provided to the withholding agent by the person providing the certificate under paragraph (e)(3)(i) of this section, such certificate must be provided within the period beginning 90 days prior to the first interest payment date on which the person holds a foreign-targeted registered obligation. The withholding agent may, in its discretion, withhold under section 1441(a), 1442(a), or 1443 if the certificate is not received by the date 30 days prior to the interest payment. Thereafter the certificate must be filed within the period beginning on January 15 and ending January 31 of each year. If a certificate provided pursuant to the first sentence of this paragraph (e)(4)(i)(A) is provided during the period beginning on January 15 and ending on January 31 of any year, then no other certificate need be provided during such period in such year.

Reg. §1.871-14(e)(4)(i)(A)

(B) *Change of status notification on Form W-9.*—If, on any interest payment date after the obligation was acquired by the person making the certification, the beneficial owner of the obligation is a U.S. person, then the person to whom the withholding agent pays interest must furnish the withholding agent with a U.S. beneficial ownership notification within 30 days after such interest payment date. A U.S. beneficial ownership notification must include a statement that the beneficial owner of the obligation has been a U.S. person on an interest payment date (identifying such date), that such owner has provided to the person providing the notification a Form W-9 (or a substitute form that is substantially similar to Form W-9 and completed under penalties of perjury), and that the person providing the notification has been and will be complying with the information reporting requirements of section 6049, if applicable.

(C) *Alternative notification statement.*—Where the person providing the notification described in paragraph (e)(4)(i)(B) of this section is neither a controlled foreign corporation within the meaning of section 957(a), nor a foreign corporation 50-percent or more of the gross income of which from all sources for the three-year period ending with the close of the taxable year preceding the date of the statement was effectively connected with the conduct of trade or business in the United States, such person must attach to the notification a copy of the Form W-9 (or substitute form that is substantially similar to Form W-9 and completed under penalties of perjury) provided by the beneficial owner. When a person that provides the U.S. beneficial ownership notification does not attach to it a copy of such Form W-9 (or substitute form that is substantially similar to Form W-9 and completed under penalties of perjury), such person must state that it is either a controlled foreign corporation within the meaning of section 957(a), or a foreign corporation 50-percent or more of the gross income of which from all sources for the three-year period ending with the close of its taxable year preceding the date of the statement was effectively connected with the conduct of a trade or business in the United States. A withholding agent that receives a Form W-9 (or a substitute form that is substantially similar to Form W-9 and completed under penalties of perjury) must send a copy of such form to the IRS, at such address as the IRS shall indicate, within 30 days after receiving it and must attach a statement that the Form W-9 or substitute form was provided pursuant to this paragraph (e)(4) with respect to a U.S. person that has owned a foreign-targeted registered obligation on one or more interest payment dates.

(D) *Failure to provide notification.*—If either a Form W-9 (or a substitute form that is substantially similar to a Form W-9 and completed under penalties of perjury) or the statement described in paragraph (e)(4)(i)(C) of this section is not attached to the U.S. beneficial ownership notification provided pursuant to paragraph (e)(4)(i)(B) of this section, the withholding agent is required to withhold under section 1441, 1442, or 1443 on a payment of interest made after the withholding agent has received the notification unless such form or statement (or a statement that the beneficial owner of the obligation is no longer a U.S. person) is received before the interest payment date from the person who provided the notification (or transferee). If, during the period beginning on the next January 15 and ending on the next January 31, such person certifies as set out in paragraph (e)(3)(i) of this section (subject to paragraph (e)(3)(i)(A)(2) of this section) then the withholding agent is not required to withhold during the year following such certification (unless such person again provides a U.S. beneficial ownership notification without attaching a Form W-9 or substitute form that is substantially similar to Form W-9 and completed under penalties of perjury or the statement described in paragraph (e)(4)(i)(C) of this section).

(E) *Procedures for clearing organizations.*—Within the period beginning 10 days before the end of the calendar quarter and ending on the last day of each calendar quarter, any clearing organization (including a clearing organization that is a withholding agent) relying on annual certificates or statements from its member organizations, as set forth in paragraph (e)(3)(i) of this section, must send each member organization having submitted such certificate or statement a reminder that the member organization must give the clearing organization a U.S. beneficial ownership notification in the circumstances described in paragraph (e)(4)(i)(B) of this section.

(F) *Retention of certificates.*—The certificate described in paragraph (e)(3)(i) of this section must be retained in the records of the withholding agent for four years from the end of the calendar year in which it was received. The statement described in paragraph (e)(3)(i) of this section that is received by a clearing organization from a member organization must be retained in the records of the clearing organization for four years from the end of the calendar year in which it was received.

(G) *No reporting requirement.*—The withholding agent who receives the certificate described in paragraph (e)(3)(i) of this section is not required to file Form 1042S to report payments under § 1.1461-1(b) or (c) of interest that are made with respect to foreign-targeted registered obligations held by the person providing the certificate and are made within the period beginning with the certificate date and ending on the last date for filing the next certificate.

(ii) *Procedures regarding certificates required under paragraph (e)(3)(ii) of this section.*—(A) *Time for providing certificate.*—The statement described in paragraph (e)(3)(ii) of this section must be provided to the withholding agent within the period beginning 90 days prior to and ending on the first interest payment date on which the withholding agent pays interest to the beneficial owner. The withholding agent may, in its discretion, withhold under section 1441(a), 1442(a), or 1443 if the statement is not received by the date 30 days prior to the interest payment. The beneficial owner must confirm to the withholding agent the continuing validity of the documentary evidence within the period beginning 90 days prior to the first day of the third calendar year following the provision of such evidence and during the same period every three years thereafter while the owner still owns the obligation. The withholding agent who receives the statement described in paragraph (e)(3)(ii) of this section is not required to report payments of interest under § 1.1461-1(b) or (c) if the payments are made with respect to foreign-targeted registered obligations held by the person who provides the statement and are made within the period beginning with the date on which the statement is provided and ending on the last date for confirming the validity of the statement. The statement received for purposes of paragraph (e)(3)(ii) of this section is subject to the applicable procedures set forth in § 1.1441-1(e)(4).

(B) *Change of status notification on Form W-9.*—If on any interest payment date after the obligation was acquired by the person providing the statement described in paragraph (e)(3)(ii) of this section, the beneficial owner of the obligation is a U.S. person, then the beneficial owner must so inform the withholding agent within 30 days after such interest payment date and must provide a Form W-9 (or substitute form that is substantially similar completed under penalties of perjury) to the withholding agent. However, the beneficial owner is not required to provide another Form W-9 (or substitute form that is substantially similar and completed under penalties of perjury) if such person has already provided it to the withholding agent within the same calendar year.

(iii) *Disqualification of documentation.*—In accordance with the provisions of section 871(h)(4), the Secretary may make a determination in appropriate cases that a certificate or statement by any person, or class of persons, does not satisfy the requirements of that section. Should that determination be made, all payments of interest that otherwise qualify as portfolio interest to that person would become subject to 30-percent withholding under section 1441(a), 1442(a), or 1443.

(iv) *Special effective date.*—Notwithstanding the foregoing requirements of this section—

(A) Any certificate that is required to be filed with the withholding agent during the period beginning on January 15 and ending on January 31, 1986, is not required to state that the beneficial owner of an obligation, prior to the date of the certificate, either was not a United States person or was a United States person if the obligation was acquired by the person providing the certificate on or before September 19, 1985; and

(B) All of the requirements of this paragraph (e), as in effect prior to the effective date of these amendments, shall remain effective with respect to each interest payment prior to the filing of the certificate described in paragraph (e)(4)(iv)(A) of this section, except that the provisions of paragraph (e)(3) of this section relating to which persons are required to receive certificates or statements and paragraph (e)(3)(ii) or (4)(ii) of this section shall become effective with respect to each interest payment after September 20, 1985.

(5) *Information reporting.*—See § 1.6049-5(b)(7) for special information reporting rules applicable to interest on foreign-targeted registered obligations. See § 1.6045-1(g)(1)(ii) for information reporting rules applicable to the redemption, retirement, or sale of foreign-targeted registered obligations.

(f) *Securities lending transactions.*—For applicable rules regarding substitute interest payments received pursuant to a securities lending transaction or a sale-repurchase transaction, see §§ 1.871-7(b)(2) and 1.881-2(b)(2).

(g) *Definitions.*—For purposes of this section, the terms *U.S. person* and *foreign person* have the meaning set forth in § 1.1441-1(c)(2), the term *beneficial owner* has the meaning set forth in § 1.1441-1(c)(6), the term *withholding agent* has the meaning set forth in § 1.1441-7(a); the term *payee* has the meaning set forth in § 1.1441-1(b)(2); and the term *payment* has the meaning set forth in § 1.1441-2(e).

Reg. § 1.871-14(g)

(h) *Effective date.*—(1) *In general.*—This section shall apply to payments of interest made after December 31, 2000.

(2) *Transition rule.*—For purposes of this section, the validity of a Form W-8 that was valid on January 1, 1998, under the regulations in effect prior to January 1, 2001 (see 26 CFR parts 1 and 35a, revised April 1, 1999) and expired, or will expire, at any time during 1998, is extended until December 31, 1998. The validity of a Form W-8 that is valid on or after January 1, 1999 remains valid until its validity expires under the regualtions in effect prior to January 1, 2001 (see 26 CFR parts 1 and 35a, revised April 1, 1999) but in no event will such a form remain valid after December 31, 2000. The rule in this paragraph (h)(2), however, does not apply to extend the validity period of a Form W-8 that expired solely by reason of changes in the circumstances of the person whose name is on the certificate. Notwithstanding the first three sentences of this paragraph (h)(2), a withholding agent or payor may choose to not take advantage of the transition rule in this paragraph (h)(2) with respect to one or more withholding certificates valid under the regulations in effect prior to January 1, 2001 (see 26 CFR parts 1 and 35a, revised April 1, 1999) and, therefore, may choose to obtain withholding certificates conforming to the requirements described in this section (new withholding certificates). For purposes of this section, a new withholding certificate is deemed to satisfy the documentation requirement under the regulations in effect prior to January 1, 2001 (see 26 CFR parts 1 and 35a, revised April 1, 1999). Further, a new withholding certificate remains valid for the period specified in § 1.1441-1(e)(4)(ii), regardless of when the certificate is obtained. [Reg. § 1.871-14.]

☐ [*T.D.* 8734, 10-6-97. *Amended by T.D.* 8804, 12-30-98 *and T.D.* 8856, 12-29-99.]

§ 1.872-1. Gross income of nonresident alien individuals.—(a) *In general.*—(1) *Inclusions.*—The gross income of a nonresident alien individual for any taxable year includes only (i) the gross income which is derived from sources within the United States and which is not effectively connected for the taxable year with the conduct of a trade or business in the United States by that individual and (ii) the gross income, irrespective of whether such income is derived from sources within or without the United States, which is effectively connected for the taxable year with the conduct of a trade or business in the United States by that individual. For the determination of the sources of income, see sections 861 through 863 and the regulations thereunder. For the determination of whether income from sources within or without the United States is effectively connected for the taxable year with the conduct of a trade or business in the United States, see sections 864(c) and 871(c) and (d), §§ 1.864-3 through 1.864-7, and §§ 1.871-9 and 1.871-10. For special rules for determining the income of an alien individual who changes his residence during the taxable year, see § 1.871-13.

(2) *Exchange transactions.*—Even though a nonresident alien individual who effects certain transactions in the United States in stocks, securities, or commodities during the taxable year may not, by reason of section 864(b)(2) and paragraph (c) or (d) of § 1.864-2, be engaged in trade or business in the United States during the taxable year through the effecting of such transactions, nevertheless he shall be required to include in gross income for the taxable year the gains and profits from those transactions to the extent required by § 1.871-7 or § 1.871-8.

(3) *Exclusions.*—For exclusions from gross income, see § 1.872-2.

(b) *Individuals not engaged in U.S. business.*—In the case of a nonresident alien individual who at no time during the taxable year is engaged in trade or business in the United States, the gross income shall include only (1) the gross income from sources within the United States which is described in section 871(a) and paragraphs (b), (c), and (d) of § 1.871-7 and (2) the gross income from sources within the United States which, by reason of section 871(c) or (d) and § 1.871-9 or § 1.871-10, is treated as effectively connected for the taxable year with the conduct of a trade or business in the United States by that individual.

(c) *Individuals engaged in U.S. business.*—In the case of a nonresident alien individual who is engaged in trade or business in the United States at any time during the taxable year, the gross income shall include (1) the gross income from sources within and without the United States which is effectively connected for the taxable year with the conduct of a trade or business in the United States by that individual, (2) the gross income from sources within the United States which, by reason of the election provided in section 871(d) and § 1.871-10, is treated as effectively connected for the taxable year with the conduct of a trade or business in the United States by that individual, and (3) the gross income from sources within the United States which is described in section 871(a) and paragraphs (b), (c), and (d) of § 1.871-7 and is not effectively connected for the taxable year with the conduct of a trade or business in the United States by the individual.

(d) *Special rules applicable to certain expatriates.*—For special rules for determining the gross income of a nonresident alien individual who has lost United States citizenship with a principal purpose of avoiding certain taxes, see section 877(b)(1).

(e) *Alien resident of Puerto Rico.*—This section shall not apply in the case of a nonresident alien individual who is a bona fide resident of Puerto Rico during the entire taxable year. See section 876 and § 1.876-1.

(f) *Effective date.*—This section shall apply for taxable years beginning after December 31, 1966. For corresponding rules applicable to taxable years beginning before January 1, 1967, see 26 CFR 1.872-1 (Rev. as of Jan. 1, 1971). [Reg. § 1.872-1.]

☐ [T.D. 6528, 10-23-57. *Amended by* T.D. 7332, 12-20-74.]

§ 1.872-2. Exclusions from gross income of nonresident alien individuals.—

(a) *Earnings of foreign ships or aircraft.*—(1) *Basic rule.*—So much of the income from sources within the United States of a nonresident alien individual as consists of earnings derived from the operation of a ship or ships documented, or of aircraft registered, under the laws of a foreign country which grants an equivalent exemption to citizens of the United States nonresident in that foreign country and to corporations organized in the United States shall not be included in gross income.

(2) *Equivalent exemption.*—(i) *Ships.*—A foreign country which either imposes no income tax, or, in imposing an income tax, exempts from taxation so much of the income of a citizen of the United States nonresident in that foreign country and of a corporation organized in the United States as consists of earnings derived from the operation of a ship or ships documented under the laws of the United States is considered as granting an equivalent exemption for purposes of the exclusion from gross income of the earnings of a foreign ship or ships.

(ii) *Aircraft.*—A foreign country which either imposes no income tax, or, in imposing an income tax, exempts from taxation so much of the income of a citizen of the United States nonresident in that foreign country and of a corporation organized in the United States as consists of earnings derived from the operation of aircraft registered under the laws of the United States is considered as granting an equivalent exemption for purposes of the exclusion from gross income of the earnings of foreign aircraft.

(3) *Definition of earnings.*—For purposes of subparagraphs (1) and (2) of this paragraph, compensation for personal services performed by an individual aboard a ship or aircraft does not constitute earnings derived by such individual from the operation of ships or aircraft.

(b) *Compensation paid by foreign employer to participants in certain exchange or training programs.*—(1) *Exclusion from income.*—Compensation paid to a nonresident alien individual for the period that the nonresident alien individual is temporarily present in the United States as a nonimmigrant under subparagraph (F) (relating to the admission of students into the United States) or subparagraph (J) (relating to the admission of teachers, trainees, specialists, etc., into the United States) of section 101(a)(15) of the Immigration and Nationality Act (8 U.S.C. 1101(a)(15)(F) or (J)) shall be excluded from gross income if the compensation is paid to such alien by his foreign employer. Compensation paid to a nonresident alien individual by the United States office of a domestic bank which is acting as paymaster on behalf of a foreign employer constitutes compensation paid by a foreign employer for purposes of this paragraph if the domestic bank is reimbursed by the foreign employer for such payment. A nonresident alien individual who is temporarily present in the United States as a nonimmigrant under such subparagraph (J) includes a nonresident alien individual admitted to the United States as an "exchange visitor" under section 201 of the United States Information and Educational Exchange Act of 1948 (22 U.S.C. 1446), which section was repealed by section 111 of the Mutual Education and Cultural Exchange Act of 1961 (75 Stat. 538).

(2) *Definition of foreign employer.*—For purposes of this paragraph, the term "foreign employer" means a nonresident alien individual, a foreign partnership, a foreign corporation, or an office or place of business maintained in a foreign country or in a possession of the United States by a domestic corporation, a domestic partnership, or an individual who is a citizen or resident of the United States. The term does not include a foreign government. However, see section 893 and § 1.893-1. Thus, if a French citizen employed in the Paris branch of a banking company incorporated in the State of New York were admitted to the United States under section 101(a)(15)(J) of the Immigration and Nationality Act to study monetary theory and continued to receive a salary from such foreign branch while studying in the United States, such salary would not be includible in his gross income.

(c) *Tax convention.*—Income of any kind which is exempt from tax under the provisions of a tax convention or treaty to which the United States is a party shall not be included in the gross income of a nonresident alien individual. Income on which tax is limited by tax convention shall be included in the gross income of a nonresident alien individual if it is not otherwise excluded from gross income. See §§ 1.871-12 and 1.894-1.

(d) *Certain bond income of residents of the Ryukyu Islands or the Trust Territory of the Pacific Islands.*—Income derived by a nonresident alien individual from a series E or series H United States savings bond shall not be included in gross income if such individual acquired the bond while he was a resident of the Ryukyu Islands or the Trust Territory of the Pacific Islands. It is not necessary that the individual continue to be a resident of such Islands or Trust Territory for the period when, without regard to section 872(b)(4) and this paragraph, the income from the bond would otherwise be includible in his gross income under the provisions of section 446 or 454.

(e) *Certain annuities received under qualified plans.*—Pursuant to section 871(f), income received by a nonresident alien individual as an annuity under a qualified annuity plan described in section 403(a)(1) (relating to taxation of employee annuities), or from a qualified trust described in section 401(a) (relating to qualified pension, profit-sharing, and stock bonus plans) which is exempt from tax under section 501(a) (relating to exemption from tax on corporations, certain trusts, etc.), shall not be included in gross income, and shall be exempt from tax, for purposes of section 871 and §§ 1.871-7 and 1.871-8, if—

(1) All of the personal services by reason of which the annuity is payable were either—

(i) Personal services performed outside the United States by an individual (whether or not the annuitant) who, at the time of performance of the services, was a nonresident alien individual, or

(ii) Personal services performed in the United States by a nonresident alien individual (whether or not the annuitant) which, by reason of section 864(b)(1) (or corresponding provision of any prior law), were not personal services causing such individual to be engaged in trade or business in the United States during the taxable year, and

(2) At the time the first amount is paid (even though paid in a taxable year beginning before January 1, 1967) as such annuity under such annuity plan, or by such trust, to (i) the individual described in subparagraph (1) of this paragraph, or (ii) his nonresident alien beneficiary if such beneficiary is entitled to receive such first amount, 90 percent or more of the employees or annuitants for whom contributions or benefits are provided under the annuity plan, or under the plan or plans of which the trust is a part, are citizens or residents of the United States.

This paragraph shall apply whether or not the taxpayer is engaged in trade or business in the United States at any time during the taxable year in which the annuity is received. This paragraph shall not apply to distributions by an employees' trust or from an annuity plan which give rise to gains described in section 402(a)(2) or 403(a)(2), whichever applies. See section 871(a)(1)(B) and paragraph (c)(1)(i) of § 1.871-7. For exemption from withholding of tax at source on an annuity which is exempt from tax under section 871(f) and this paragraph, see paragraph (g) of § 1.1441-4.

(f) *Other exclusions.*—Income which is from sources without the United States, as determined under the provisions of sections 861 through 863, and the regulations thereunder, is not included in the gross income of a nonresident alien individual unless such income is effectively connected for the taxable year with the conduct of a trade or business in the United States by that individual. To determine specific exclusions in the case of other items which are from sources within the United States, see the applicable sections of the Code. For special rules under a tax convention for determining the sources of income and for excluding, from gross income, income from sources without the United States which is effectively connected with the conduct of a trade or business in the United States, see the applicable tax convention. For determining which income from sources without the United States is effectively connected with the conduct of a trade or business in the United States, see section 864(c)(4) and § 1.864-5.

(g) *Effective date.*—This section shall apply for taxable years beginning after December 31, 1966. For corresponding rules applicable to taxable years beginning before January 1, 1967, see 26 CFR 1.872-2 (Rev. as of Jan. 1, 1971). [Reg. § 1.872-2.]

☐ [T.D. 6258, 10-23-57. *Amended by T.D. 6782, 12-12-64 and T.D. 7332, 12-20-74.*]

§ 1.873-1. Deductions allowed nonresident alien individuals.—(a) *General provisions.*—(1) *Allocation of deductions.*—In computing the taxable income of a nonresident alien individual the deductions otherwise allowable shall be allowed only if, and to the extent that, they are connected with income from sources within the United States. No deduction shall be allowed in respect of any item, or portion thereof, which is not connected with income from such sources. For this purpose, the proper apportionment and allocation of the deductions with respect to sources of income within and without the United States shall be determined as provided in Part I (section 861 and following), subchapter N, chapter 1 of the Code, and the regulations thereunder, except as may otherwise be provided by tax convention. Thus, from the items of gross income specifically from sources within the United States and from the items allocated thereto under the provisions of section 863(a), there shall be deducted (i) the expenses, losses, and other deductions which are connected with those items of income and are properly apportioned or allocated thereto, and (ii) a ratable part of any other expenses, losses, or deductions which are connected with those items of income but cannot definitely be allocated to some item or class of gross income. The ratable part shall be based upon the ratio of gross income from sources within the United States to the total gross income. See §§ 1.861-8 and 1.863-1. In the case of income partly from within and partly from without the United States the expenses, losses, and other deductions connected with income from sources within the United States shall also be deducted in the manner prescribed by §§ 1.863-2 through 1.863-5 in order to ascertain under section 863 the portion of the taxable income attributable to sources within the United States.

(2) *Personal exemptions.*—The deductions for the personal exemptions allowed by section 151 or 642(b) shall not be taken into account for purposes of subparagraph (1) of this paragraph but shall be allowed to the extent provided by paragraphs (b) and (c) of this section.

(3) *Adjusted gross income.*—The adjusted gross income of a nonresident alien individual shall be the gross income from sources within the United States, determined in accordance with § 1.871-7, minus the deductions prescribed by section 62 to the extent such deductions are allowed under this section in computing taxable income.

(4) *Standard deduction.*—The standard deduction shall not be allowed in computing the taxable income of a nonresident alien individual. See section 142(b)(1) and the regulations thereunder.

(5) *Exempt income.*—No deduction shall be allowed under this section for the amount of any item or part thereof allocable to a class or classes of exempt income, including income exempt by tax convention. See section 265 and the regulations thereunder.

(b) *No United States business.*—(1) *Income of not more than $15,400.*—(i) *Deduction for losses only.*—A nonresident alien individual within class 1 shall not be allowed any deductions other than the deduction for losses from sales or exchanges of capital assets determined in the manner prescribed by paragraph (b)(4)(vii) of § 1.871-7. Thus, an individual within this class shall not be allowed any deductions for the personal exemptions otherwise allowed by section 151 or 642(b).

(ii) *Source of losses.*—Notwithstanding the provisions of section 873(b)(1), losses from sales or exchanges of capital assets shall be allowed under this subparagraph only if allocable to sources within the United States. See paragraph (b)(4)(i) of § 1.871-7.

(2) *Aggregate more than $15,400.*—(i) *Deductions allowed.*—In computing the income subject to tax under section 1 or section 1201(b), a nonresident alien individual within class 2 shall be allowed deductions to the extent prescribed by paragraph (c)(3) of § 1.871-7, but subject to the limitations of this section. For this purpose, the deduction for the personal exemptions shall be allowed in accordance with subdivision (iii) of this subparagraph.

(ii) *Deductions disallowed.*—In computing the minimum tax prescribed by section 871(b)(3), that individual shall not be allowed any deductions other than the deduction for losses from sales or exchanges of capital assets determined in the manner prescribed by paragraph (b)(4)(vii) of § 1.871-7. For this purpose, the deductions for the personal exemptions shall not be allowed. See paragraph (c)(4) of § 1.871-7.

(iii) *Personal exemptions.*—When the deductions for personal exemptions are allowed under this subparagraph, only one exemption under section 151 shall be allowed in the case of an individual who is not a resident of Canada or Mexico. A resident of either of those countries shall be allowed all the exemptions granted by section 151 to the extent prescribed therein. An estate or trust, whether or not a resident of Canada or Mexico, shall determine its deduction for the personal exemption in accordance with section 642(b) and the regulations thereunder.

(iv) *Source of losses.*—Notwithstanding the provisions of section 873(b), losses from sales or exchanges of capital assets shall be allowed under this subparagraph only if allocable to sources within the United States. See paragraph (c)(3)(i) of § 1.871-7.

(3) *Election to be taxed on a net basis.*—Notwithstanding the other provisions of this paragraph, a nonresident alien individual within class 1 or 2 shall be allowed the deductions

allowed by paragraph (c) of this section, if pursuant to a tax convention he is entitled, and does elect, to be subject to United States tax on a net basis as though he were engaged in trade or business within the United States through a permanent establishment situated therein.

(c) *United States business.*—(1) *Deductions in general.*—For purposes of computing the income subject to tax, a nonresident alien individual within class 3 shall be allowed deductions to the extent prescribed by paragraph (d) of § 1.871-7, but subject to the limitations of this section. For this purpose, the deductions for the personal exemptions shall be allowed in accordance with subparagraph (3) of this paragraph.

(2) *Special deductions.*—Notwithstanding the rule of source prescribed in paragraph (a) of this section, an individual within class 3 shall be allowed the following deductions whether or not they are connected with income from sources within the United States:

(i) *Losses on transactions for profit.*—Any loss sustained during the taxable year and not compensated for by insurance or otherwise, if incurred in any transaction entered into for profit, though not connected with a trade or business, shall be allowed to the extent allowed by section 165(c)(2), but only if and to the extent that the profit, if the transaction had resulted in a profit, would be taxable to such individual. Losses allowed under this subdivision shall be deducted in full, as provided in §§ 1.861-8 and 1.863-1, when the profit from the transaction, if it had resulted in a profit, would, under the provisions of section 861(a) or 863(a), have been taxable in full as income from sources within the United States; but shall be deducted under the provisions of § 1.863-3 when the profit from the transaction, if it had resulted in profit, would have been taxable only in part.

(ii) *Casualty losses.*—Any loss of property not connected with a trade or business, sustained during the taxable year and not compensated for by insurance or otherwise, if the loss arises from fire, storm, shipwreck, or other casualty, or from theft, shall be allowed to the extent allowed by section 165(c)(3), but only if the loss is of property within the United States. Losses allowed under this subdivision shall be deducted in full, as provided in §§ 1.861-8 and 1.863-1, from the items of gross income specified under sections 861(a) and 863(a) as being derived in full from sources within the United States; but, if greater than the sum of those items, the unabsorbed loss shall be deducted from the income apportioned under the provisions of § 1.863-3 to sources within the United States.

(iii) *Charitable contributions.*—The deduction for charitable contributions and gifts, to the extent allowed by section 170, shall be allowed under this subparagraph, but only as to contributions or gifts made to domestic corporations, or to community chests, funds, or foundations, created in the United States.

(3) *Personal exemptions.*—Only one exemption under section 151 shall be allowed in the case of an individual who is not a resident of Canada or Mexico. A resident of either of those countries shall be allowed all the exemptions granted by section 151 to the extent prescribed therein. An estate or trust, whether or not a resident of Canada or Mexico, shall determine its deduction for the personal exemption in accordance with section 642(b) and the regulations thereunder. [Reg. § 1.873-1.]

☐ [T.D. 6258, 10-23-57.]

§ 1.874-1. Allowance of deductions and credits to nonresident alien individuals.—(a) *Return required.*—A nonresident alien individual shall receive the benefit of the deductions and credits otherwise allowable with respect to the income tax, only if the nonresident alien individual timely files or causes to be filed with the Philadelphia Service Center, in the manner prescribed in subtitle F, a true and accurate return of the income which is effectively connected, or treated as effectively connected, with the conduct of a trade or business within the United States by the nonresident alien individual. No provision of this section (other than paragraph (c)(2)) shall be construed, however, to deny the credits provided by sections 31, 32, 33, 34 and 852(b)(3)(D)(ii). In addition, notwithstanding the requirement that a nonresident alien must file a timely return in order to receive the benefit of the deductions and credits otherwise allowable with respect to the income tax, the nonresident alien individual may, for purposes of determining the amount of tax to be withheld under section 1441 from remuneration paid for labor or personal services performed within the United States, receive the benefit of the deduction for personal exemptions provided in section 151, to the extent allowable under section 873(b)(3) and paragraph (c)(3) of § 1.873-1, or any applicable tax convention, by filing a claim therefor with the withholding agent. The amount of the deduction for the personal exemptions and the amount of the tax to be withheld under those circumstances shall be determined in accordance with paragraph (e)(2) of § 1.1441-3. The deductions and credits allowed such a nonresident alien individual electing under a tax convention to be subject to tax on a net basis may be obtained by filing a return of income in the manner prescribed in the regulations (if any) under the tax convention or under any other guidance issued by the Commissioner.

(b) *Filing deadline for return.*—(1) *General rule.*—As provided in paragraph (a) of this section, for purposes of computing the nonresident alien individual's taxable income for any taxable year, otherwise allowable deductions and credits will be allowed only if a true and accurate return for that taxable year is filed by the nonresident alien individual on a timely basis. For taxable years of a nonresident alien individual ending after July 31, 1990, whether a return for the current taxable year has been filed on a timely basis is dependent upon whether the nonresident alien individual filed a return for the taxable year immediately preceding the current taxable year. If a return was filed for that immediately preceding taxable year, or if the current taxable year is the first taxable year of the nonresident alien individual for which a return is required to be filed, the required return for the current taxable year must be filed within 16 months of the due date, as set forth in section 6072 and the regulations under that section, for filing the return for the current taxable year. If no return for the taxable year immediately preceding the current taxable year has been filed, the required return for the current taxable year (other than the first taxable year of the nonresident alien individual for which a return is required to be filed) must have been filed no later than the earlier of the date which is 16 months after the due date, as set forth in section 6072, for filing the return for the current taxable year or the date the Internal Revenue Service mails a notice to the nonresident alien individual advising the nonresident alien individual that the current year tax return has not been filed and that no deductions or credits (other than those provided in sections 31, 32, 33, 34 and 852(b)(3)(D)(ii)) may be claimed by the nonresident alien individual.

(2) *Waiver.*—The filing deadlines set forth in paragraph (b)(1) of this section may be waived if the nonresident alien individual establishes to the satisfaction of the Commissioner or his or her delegate that the individual, based on the facts and circumstances, acted reasonably and in good faith in failing to file a U.S. income tax return (including a protective return (as described in paragraph (b)(6) of this section)). For this purpose, a nonresident alien individual shall not be considered to have acted reasonably and in good faith if the individual knew that he or she was required to file the return and chose not to do so. In addition, a nonresident alien individual shall not be granted a waiver unless the individual cooperates in determining his or her U.S. income tax liability for the taxable year for which the return was not filed. The Commissioner or his or her delegate shall consider the following factors in determining whether the nonresident alien individual, based on the facts and circumstances, acted reasonably and in good faith in failing to file a U.S. income tax return—

(i) Whether the individual voluntarily identifies himself or herself to the Internal Revenue Service as having failed to file a U.S. income tax return before the Internal Revenue Service discovers the failure to file;

(ii) Whether the individual did not become aware of his or her ability to file a protective return (as described in paragraph (b)(6) of this section) by the deadline for filing the protective return;

(iii) Whether the individual had not previously filed a U.S. income tax return;

(iv) Whether the individual failed to file a U.S. income tax return because, after exercising reasonable diligence (taking into account his or her relevant experience and level of sophistication), the individual was unaware of the necessity for filing the return;

(v) Whether the individual failed to file a U.S. income tax return because of intervening events beyond the individual's control; and

(vi) Whether other mitigating or exacerbating factors existed.

(3) *Examples.*—The following examples illustrate the provisions of paragraph (b). In all examples, A is a nonresident alien individual and uses the calendar year as A's taxable year. The examples are as follows:

Example 1. Nonresident alien individual discloses own failure to file. In Year 1, A became a limited partner with a passive investment in a U.S. limited partnership that was engaged in a U.S. trade or business. During Year 1 through Year 4, A incurred losses with respect to A's U.S. partnership interest. A's foreign tax advisor incorrectly concluded that because A was a limited partner and had only losses from A's partnership interest, A was not required to file a U.S. income tax return. A was aware neither of A's obligation to file a U.S. income tax return for those years nor of A's ability to file a protective return for those years. A had never filed a U.S. income tax return before. In Year 5, A began realizing a profit rather than a loss with respect to the partnership interest and, for this reason, engaged a U.S. tax advisor to handle A's responsibility to file U.S. income tax returns. In preparing A's U.S. income tax return for Year 5, A's U.S. tax advisor discovered that returns were not filed for Year 1 through Year 4. Therefore, with respect to those years for which applicable filing deadlines in paragraph (b)(1) of this section were not met, A would be barred by paragraph (a) of this section from claiming any deductions that otherwise would have given rise to net operating losses on returns for these years, and that would have been available as loss carryforwards in subsequent years. At A's direction, A's U.S. tax advisor promptly contacted the appropriate examining personnel and cooperated with the Internal Revenue Service in determining A's income tax liability, for example, by preparing and filing the appropriate income tax returns for Year 1 through Year 4 and by making A's books and records available to an Internal Revenue Service examiner. A has met the standard described in paragraph (b)(2) of this section for waiver of any applicable filing deadlines in paragraph (b)(1) of this section.

Example 2. Nonresident alien individual refuses to cooperate. Same facts as in *Example 1*, except that while A's U.S. tax advisor contacted the appropriate examining personnel and filed the appropriate income tax returns for Year 1 through Year 4, A refused all requests by the Internal Revenue Service to provide supporting information (for example, books and records) with respect to those returns. Because A did not cooperate in determining A's U.S. tax liability for the taxable years for which an income tax return was not timely filed, A is not granted a waiver as described in paragraph (b)(2) of this section of any applicable filing deadlines in paragraph (b)(1) of this section.

Example 3. Nonresident alien individual fails to file a protective return. Same facts as in *Example 1*, except that in Year 1 through Year 4, A also consulted a U.S. tax advisor, who advised A that it was uncertain whether U.S. income tax returns were necessary for those years and that A could protect A's right subsequently to claim the loss carryforwards by filing protective returns under paragraph (b)(6) of this section. A did not file U.S. income tax returns or protective returns for those years. A did not present evidence that intervening events beyond A's control prevented A from filing an income tax return, and there were no other mitigating factors. A has not met the standard described in paragraph (b)(2) of this section for waiver of any applicable filing deadlines in paragraph (b)(1) of this section.

Example 4. Nonresident alien with effectively connected income. In Year 1, A, a computer programmer, opened an office in the United States to market and sell a software program that A had developed outside the United States. A had minimal business or tax experience internationally, and no such experience in the United States. Through A's personal efforts, U.S. sales of the software produced income effectively connected with a U.S. trade or business. A, however, did not file U.S. income tax returns for Year 1 or Year 2. A was aware neither of A's obligation to file a U.S. income tax return for those years, nor of A's ability to file a protective return for those years. A had never filed a U.S. income tax return before. In November of Year 3, A engaged U.S. counsel in connection with licensing software to an unrelated U.S. company. U.S. counsel reviewed A's U.S. activities and advised A that A should have filed U.S. income tax returns for Year 1 and Year 2. A immediately engaged a U.S. tax advisor who, at A's direction, promptly contacted the appropriate examining personnel and cooperated with the Internal Revenue Service in determining A's income tax liability, for example, by preparing and filing the appropriate income tax returns for Year 1 and Year 2 and by making A's books and records available to an Internal Revenue Service examiner. A has met the standard described in paragraph (b)(2) of this section for waiver of any applicable filing deadlines in paragraph (b)(1) of this section.

Example 5. IRS discovers nonresident alien's failure to file. In Year 1, A, a computer programmer, opened an office in the United States to market and sell a software program that A had developed outside the United States. Through A's personal efforts, U.S. sales of the software produced income effectively connected with a U.S. trade or business. A had extensive experience conducting similar business activities in other countries, including making the appropriate tax filings. A, however, was aware neither of A's obligation to file a U.S. income tax return for those years, nor of A's ability to file a protective return for those years. A had never filed a U.S. income tax return before. Despite A's extensive experience conducting similar business activities in other countries, A made no effort to seek advice in connection with A's U.S. tax obligations. A failed to file either U.S. income tax returns or protective returns for Year 1 and Year 2. In November of Year 3, an Internal Revenue Service examiner asked A for an explanation of A's failure to file U.S. income tax returns. A immediately engaged a U.S. tax advisor, and cooperated with the Internal Revenue Service in determining A's income tax liability, for example, by preparing and filing the appropriate income tax returns for Year 1 and Year 2 and by making A's books and records available to the examiner. A did not present evidence that intervening events beyond A's control prevented A from filing a return, and there were no other mitigating factors. A has not met the standard described in paragraph (b)(2) of this section for waiver of any applicable filing deadlines in paragraph (b)(1) of this section.

Example 6. Nonresident alien with prior filing history. A began a U.S. trade or business in Year 1 as a sole proprietorship. A's tax advisor filed the appropriate U.S. income tax returns for Year 1 through Year 6, reporting income effectively connected with A's U.S.

trade or business. In Year 7, A replaced this tax advisor with a tax advisor unfamiliar with U.S. tax law. A did not file a U.S. income tax return for any year from Year 7 through Year 10, although A had effectively connected income for those years. A was aware of A's ability to file a protective return for those years. In Year 11, an Internal Revenue Service examiner contacted A and asked for an explanation of A's failure to file income tax returns after Year 6. A immediately engaged a U.S. tax advisor and cooperated with the Internal Revenue Service in determining A's income tax liability, for example, by preparing and filing the appropriate income tax returns for Year 7 through Year 10 and by making A's books and records available to the examiner. A did not present evidence that intervening events beyond A's control prevented A from filing a return, and there were no other mitigating factors. A has not met the standard described in paragraph (b)(2) of this section for waiver of any applicable filing deadlines in paragraph (b)(1) of this section.

(4) *Effective date.*—Paragraphs (b)(2) and (3) of this section are applicable to open years for which a request for a waiver is filed on or after January 29, 2002.

(5) *Income tax treaties.*—A nonresident alien individual who has a permanent establishment or fixed base, as defined in an income tax treaty between the United States and the country of residence of the nonresident alien individual, in the United States is subject to the filing deadlines as set forth in paragraph (b)(1) of this section.

(6) *Protective return.*—If a nonresident alien individual conducts limited activities in the United States in a taxable year which the nonresident alien individual determines does not give rise to gross income which is effectively connected with the conduct of a trade or business within the United States as defined in sections 871(b) and 864(b) and (c) and the regulations under those sections, the nonresident alien individual may nonetheless file a return for that taxable year on a timely basis under paragraph (b)(1) of this section and thereby protect the right to receive the benefit of the deductions and credits attributable to that gross income if it is later determined, after the return was filed, that the original determination was incorrect. On that timely filed return, the nonresident alien individual is not required to report any gross income as effectively connected with a United States trade or business or any deductions or credits but should attach a statement indicating that the return is being filed for the reason set forth in this paragraph (b)(4). If the nonresident alien individual determines that part of the activities which he or she conducts in the United States in a taxable year gives rise to gross income which is effectively connected with the conduct of a trade or business and part does not, the nonresident alien individual must timely file a return for that taxable year to report the gross income determined to be effectively connected, or treated as effectively connected, with the conduct of that trade or business within the United States and the deductions and credits attributable to the gross income. In addition, the nonresident alien individual should attach to that return the statement described in this paragraph (b)(4) with regard to the other activities. The nonresident alien individual may follow the same procedure if the nonresident alien individual determines initially that he or she has no United States tax liability under the provisions of an applicable income tax treaty. In the event the nonresident alien individual relies on the provisions of an income tax treaty to reduce or eliminate the income subject to taxation, or to reduce the rate of tax to which that income is subject, disclosure may be required pursuant to section 6114.

(c) *Allowed deductions and credits.*—(1) *In general.*—Except for losses of property located within the United States, charitable contributions and personal exemptions (see section 873(b)), deductions are allowed to a nonresident alien individual only to the extent they are connected with gross income which is effectively connected, or treated as effectively connected, with the conduct of the nonresident alien individual's trade or business in the United States. Other than credits allowed by sections 31, 32, 33, 34 and 852(b)(3)(D)(ii), the nonresident alien individual is entitled to credits only if they are attributable to effectively connected income. See paragraph (a) of this section for the requirement that a return be timely filed. Except as provided by section 906, a nonresident alien individual shall not be allowed the credit against the tax for taxes of foreign countries and possessions of the United States allowed by section 901.

(2) *Verification.*—At the request of the Internal Revenue Service, a nonresident alien individual claiming deductions from gross income which is effectively connected or treated as effectively connected with the conduct of a trade or business in the United States and credits attributable to that income must furnish at the place designated pursuant to § 301.7605-1(a) information sufficient to establish that the nonresident alien individual is entitled to the deductions and credits in the amounts claimed. All information must be furnished in a form suitable to permit verification of the claimed deductions and credits. The Internal Revenue Service may require, as appro-

priate, that an English translation be provided with any information in a foreign language. If a nonresident alien individual fails to furnish sufficient information, the Internal Revenue Service may in its discretion disallow any claimed deductions and credits in full or in part.

(d) *Return by Internal Revenue Service.*—If a nonresident alien individual has various sources of income within the United States, so that from any one source, or from all sources combined, the amount of income shall call for the assessment of a tax greater than that withheld at the source in the case of that individual, and a return of income has not been filed in the manner prescribed by subtitle F, including the filing deadlines set forth in paragraph (b)(1) of this section, the Internal Revenue Service shall:

(1) Cause a return of income to be made,

(2) Include on the return the income described in § 1.871-7 or § 1.871-8 of that individual from all sources concerning which it has information, and

(3) *Assess the tax.*—If the nonresident alien individual is not engaged in, or does not receive income that is treated as being effectively connected with, a United States trade or business and § 1.871-7 is applicable, the tax shall be assessed on the basis of gross income without allowance for deductions or credits (other than the credits provided by sections 31, 32, 33, 34 and 852(b)(3)(D)(ii)) and collected from one or more sources of income within the United States. If the nonresident alien individual is engaged in a United States trade or business or is treated as having effectively connected income and § 1.871-8 applies, the tax on the income of the nonresident alien individual that is not effectively connected, or treated as effectively connected with the conduct of a United States trade or business shall be assessed on the basis of gross income, determined in accordance with the rules of § 1.871-7, without allowance for deductions or credits (other than the credits provided by sections 31, 32, 33, 34 and 852(b)(3)(D)(ii)) and collected from one or more of the sources of income within the United States. Tax on income that is effectively connected, or treated as effectively connected, with the conduct of a United States trade or business shall be assessed in accordance with either section 1, 55 or 402(e)(1) without allowance for deductions or credits (other than the credits provided by sections 31, 32, 33, 34 and 852(b)(3)(D)(ii)) and collected from one or more of the sources of income within the United States.

(e) *Alien resident of Puerto Rico, Guam, American Samoa, or the Commonwealth of the Northern Mariana Islands.*—This section shall not apply to a nonresident alien individual who is a bona fide resident of Puerto Rico, Guam, American Samoa, or the Commonwealth of the Northern Mariana Islands during the entire taxable year. *See* section 876 and § 1.876-1. [Reg. § 1.874-1.]

☐ [*T.D.* 6258, 10-23-57. Amended by *T.D.* 6462, 5-5-60; *T.D.* 6669, 8-26-63; *T.D.* 8322, 12-10-90; *T.D.* 8981, 1-28-2002 *and T.D.* 9043, 3-7-2003.]

§ 1.881-1. Manner of taxing foreign corporations.—(a) *Classes of foreign corporations.*—For purposes of the income tax, foreign corporations are divided into two classes, namely, foreign corporations which at no time during the taxable year are engaged in trade or business in the United States and foreign corporations which, at any time during the taxable year, are engaged in trade or business in the United States.

(b) *Manner of taxing.*—(1) *Foreign corporations not engaged in U.S. business.*—A foreign corporation which at no time during the taxable year is engaged in trade or business in the United States is taxable, as provided in § 1.881-2, on all income received from sources within the United States which is fixed or determinable annual or periodical income and on other items of income enumerated under section 881(a). Such a foreign corporation is also taxable on certain income from sources within the United States which, pursuant to § 1.882-2, is treated as effectively connected for the taxable year with the conduct of a trade or business in the United States.

(2) *Foreign corporations engaged in U.S. business.*—A foreign corporation which at any time during the taxable year is engaged in trade or business in the United States is taxable, as provided in § 1.882-1, on all income from whatever source derived, whether or not fixed or determinable annual or periodical income, which is effectively connected for the taxable year with the conduct of a trade or business in the United States. Such a foreign corporation is also taxable, as provided in § 1.882-1, on income received from sources within the United States which is not effectively connected for the taxable year with the conduct of a trade or business in the United States and consists of (i) fixed or determinable annual or periodical income, or (ii) other items of income enumerated in section 881(a). A foreign corporation which at any time during the taxable year is engaged in trade or business in the United States is also taxable on certain income from sources within the United States which, pursuant to § 1.882-2, is treated as effectively connected for the taxable year with the conduct of a trade or business in the United States.

(c) *Meaning of terms.*—For the meaning of the term "engaged in trade or business within the United States," as used in section 881 and this section, see section 864(b) and the regulations thereunder. For determining when income, gain, or loss of a foreign corporation for a taxable year is effectively connected for that year with the conduct of a trade or business in the United States, see section 864(c), the regulations thereunder, and § 1.882-2. The term *foreign corporation* has the meaning assigned to it by section 7701(a)(3) and (5) and the regulations thereunder. However, for special rules relating to possessions of the United States, see § 1.881-5T.

(d) *Rules applicable to foreign insurance companies.*—(1) *Corporations qualifying under subchapter L.*—A foreign corporation carrying on an insurance business in the United States at any time during the taxable year, which, without taking into account its income not effectively connected for the taxable year with the conduct of a trade or business in the United States, would qualify for the taxable year under part I, II, or III of subchapter L if it were a domestic corporation, shall be taxable for such year under that part on its entire taxable income (whether derived from sources within or without the United States) which is, or which pursuant to section 882(d) or (e) and § 1.882-2 is treated as, effectively connected for the taxable year with the conduct of a trade or business (whether or not its insurance business) in the United States. Any income derived by that foreign corporation from sources within the United States which is not effectively connected for the taxable year with the conduct of a trade or business in the United States is taxable as provided in section 881(a) an § 1.882-1. See sections 842 and 861 through 864, and the regulations thereunder.

(2) *Corporations not qualifying under subchapter L.*—A foreign corporation which carries on an insurance business in the United States at any time during the taxable year, and which, without taking into account its income not effectively connected for the taxable year with the conduct of a trade or business in the United States, would not qualify for the taxable year under part I, II, or III of subchapter L if it were a domestic corporation, and a foreign insurance company which does not carry on an insurance business in the United States at any time during the taxable year, shall be taxable—

(i) Under section 881(a) and § 1.881-2 or § 1.882-1 on its income from sources within the United States which is not effectively connected for the taxable year with the conduct of a trade or business in the United States,

(ii) Under section 882(a)(1) and § 1.882-1 on its income (whether derived from sources within or without the United States) which is effectively connected for the taxable year with the conduct of a trade or business in the United States, and

(iii) Under section 882(a)(1) and § 1.882-1 on its income from sources within the United States which pursuant to section 882(d) or (e) and § 1.882-2, is treated as effectively connected for the taxable year with the conduct of a trade or business in the United States.

(e) *Other provisions applicable to foreign corporations.*—(1) *Accumulated earnings tax.*—For the imposition of the accumulated earnings tax upon the accumulated taxable income of a foreign corporation formed or availed of for tax avoidance purposes, whether or not such corporation is engaged in trade or business in the United States, see section 532 and the regulations thereunder.

(2) *Personal holding company tax.*—For the imposition of the personal holding company tax upon the undistributed personal holding company income of a foreign corporation which is a personal holding company, whether or not such corporation is engaged in trade or business in the United States, see sections 541 through 547, and the regulations thereunder. Except in the case of a foreign corporation having personal service contract income to which section 543(a)(7) applies, a foreign corporation is not a personal holding company if all of its stock outstanding during the last half of the taxable year is owned by nonresident alien individuals, whether directly or indirectly through foreign estates, foreign trusts, foreign partnerships, or other foreign corporations. See section 542(c)(7).

(3) *Foreign personal holding companies.*—For the mandatory inclusion in the gross income of the United States shareholders of the undistributed foreign personal holding company income of a foreign personal holding company, see section 551 and the regulations thereunder.

(4) *Controlled foreign corporations.*—(i) *Subpart F income and increase of earnings invested in U.S. property.*—For the mandatory inclusion in the gross income of the U.S. shareholders of the subpart F income, of the previously excluded subpart F income withdrawn from investment in less developed countries, of the previously excluded subpart F income withdrawn from investment in foreign base company shipping operations, and of the increase in earnings invested in U.S. property, of a controlled foreign corporation, see sections 951 through 964, and the regulations thereunder.

Reg. § 1.881-1(e)(4)(i)

(ii) *Certain accumulations of earnings and profits.*—For the inclusion in the gross income of U.S. persons as a dividend of the gain recognized on certain sales or exchanges of stock in a foreign corporation, to the extent of certain earnings and profits attributable to the stock which were accumulated while the corporation was a controlled foreign corporation, see section 1248 and the regulations thereunder.

(5) *Changes in tax rate.*—For provisions respecting the effect of any change in rate of tax during the taxable year on the income of a foreign corporation, see section 21 and the regulations thereunder.

(6) *Consolidated returns.*—Except in the case of certain corporations organized under the laws of Canada or Mexico and maintained solely for the purpose of complying with the laws of that country as to title and operation of property, a foreign corporation is not an includible corporation for purposes of the privilege of making a consolidated return by an affiliated group of corporations. See section 1504 and the regulations thereunder.

(7) *Adjustment of tax of certain foreign corporations.*—For the application of pre-1967 income tax provisions to corporations of a foreign country which imposes a more burdensome income tax than the United States, and for the adjustment of the income tax of a corporation of a foreign country which imposes a discriminatory income tax on the income of citizens of the United States or domestic corporations, see section 896.

(f) *Effective date.*—This section applies for taxable years beginning after December 31, 1966. For corresponding rules applicable to taxable years beginning before January 1, 1967, see 26 CFR 1.881-1 (Rev. as of Jan. 1, 1971). [Reg. § 1.881-1.]

☐ [*T.D.* 6258, 10-23-57. *Amended by T.D.* 7293, 11-27-73, *T.D.* 7385, 10-28-75; *T.D.* 7893, 5-11-83 *and T.D.* 9194, 4-6-2005.]

§ 1.881-2. Taxation of foreign corporations not engaged in U.S. business.—(a) *Imposition of tax.*—(1) This section applies for purposes of determining the tax of a foreign corporation which at no time during the taxable year is engaged in trade or business in the United States. However, see also § 1.882-2 where such corporation has an election in effect for the taxable year in respect to real property income or receives interest on obligations of the United States. Except as otherwise provided in § 1.871-12, a foreign corporation to which this section applies is not subject to the tax imposed by section 11 or section 1201(a) but, pursuant to the provisions of section 881(a), is liable to a flat tax of 30 percent upon the aggregate of the amounts determined under paragraphs (b) and (c) of this section which are received during the taxable year from sources within the United States. Except as specifically provided in such paragraphs, such amounts do not include gains from the sale or exchange of property. To determine the source of such amounts, see sections 861 through 863, and the regulations thereunder.

(2) The tax of 30 percent is imposed by section 881(a) upon an amount only to the extent the amount constitutes gross income.

(3) Deductions shall not be allowed in determining the amount subject to tax under this section.

(4) Except as provided in § 1.882-2, a foreign corporation which at no time during the taxable year is engaged in trade or business in the United States has no income, gain, or loss for the taxable year which is effectively connected for the taxable year with the conduct of a trade or business in the United States. See section 864(c)(1)(B) and § 1.864-3.

(5) Gains and losses which, by reason of section 882(d) and § 1.882-2, are treated as gains or losses which are effectively connected for the taxable year with the conduct of a trade or business in the United States by such a foreign corporation shall not be taken into account in determining the tax under this section. See, for example, paragraph (c)(2) of § 1.871-10.

(b) *Fixed or determinable annual or periodical income.*—(1) *General rule.*—The tax of 30 percent imposed by section 881(a) applies to the gross amount received from sources within the United States as fixed or determinable annual or periodical gains, profits, or income. Specific items of fixed or determinable annual or periodical income are enumerated in section 881(a)(1) as interest, dividends, rents, salaries, wages, premiums, annuities, compensations, remunerations, and emoluments, but other items of fixed or determinable annual or periodical gains, profits, or income are also subject to the tax as, for instance, royalties, including royalties for the use of patents, copyrights, secret processes and formulas, and other like property. As to the determination of fixed or determinable annual or periodical income, see paragraph (a) of § 1.441-2. For special rules treating gain on the disposition of section 306 stock as fixed or determinable annual or periodical income for purposes of section 881(a), see section 306(f) and paragraph (h) of § 1.306-3.

(2) *Substitute payments.*—For purposes of this section, a substitute interest payment (as defined in § 1.861-2(a)(7)) received by a foreign person pursuant to a securities lending transac-

tion or a sale-repurchase transaction (as defined in § 1.861-2(a)(7)) shall have the same character as interest income received pursuant to the terms of the transferred security. Similarly, for purposes of this section, a substitute dividend payment (as defined in § 1.861-3(a)(6)) received by a foreign person pursuant to a securities lending transaction or a sale-repurchase transaction (as defined in § 1.861-2(a)(7)) shall have the same character as a distribution received with respect to the transferred security. Where, pursuant to a securities lending transaction or a sale-repurchase transaction, a foreign person transfers to another person a security the interest on which would qualify as portfolio interest under section 881(c) in the hands of the lender, substitute interest payments made with respect to the transferred security will be treated as portfolio interest, provided that in the case of interest on an obligation in registered form (as defined in § 1.871-14(c)(1)(i)), the transferor complies with the documentation requirement described in § 1.871-14(c)(1)(ii)(C) with respect to the payment of substitute interest and none of the exceptions to the portfolio interest exemption in sections 881(c)(3) and (4) apply. See also §§ 1.871-7(b)(2) and 1.894-1(c).

(c) *Other income and gains.*—(1) *Items subject to tax.*—The tax of 30 percent imposed by section 881(a) also applies to the following gains received during the taxable year from sources within the United States:

(i) Gains described in section 631(b) or (c), relating to the treatment of gain on the disposal of timber, coal, or iron ore with a retained economic interest;

(ii) [Reserved]

(iii) Gains from the sale or exchange after October 4, 1966, of patents, copyrights, secret processes and formulas, goodwill, trademarks, trade brands, franchises, or other like property, or of any interest in any such property, to the extent the gains are from payments (whether in a lump sum or in installments) which are contingent on the productivity, use, or disposition of the property or interest sold or exchanged, or from payments which are treated under section 871(e) and § 1.871-11 as being so contingent.

(2) *Determination of amount of gain.*—The tax of 30 percent imposed upon the gains described in subparagraph (1) of this paragraph applies to the full amount of the gains and is determined (i) without regard to the alternative tax imposed by section 1201(a) upon the excess of net long-term capital gain over the net short-term capital loss; (ii) without regard to section 1231, relating to property used in the trade or business and involuntary conversions; and (iii) except in the case of gains described in subparagraph (1)(ii) of this paragraph, whether or not the gains are considered to be gains from the sale or exchange of property which is a capital asset.

(d) *Credits against tax.*—The credits allowed by section 32 (relating to tax withheld at source on foreign corporations), by section 39 (relating to certain uses of gasoline and lubricating oil), and by section 6402 (relating to overpayments of tax) shall be allowed against the tax of a foreign corporation determined in accordance with this section.

(e) *Effective date.*—Except as otherwise provide[d] in this paragraph, this section applies for taxable years beginning after December 31, 1966. Paragraph (b)(2) of this section is applicable to payments made after November 13, 1997. For corresponding rules applicable to taxable years beginning before January 1, 1967, see 26 CFR 1.881-2 (Rev. as of Jan. 1, 1971). [Reg. § 1.881-2.]

☐ [*T.D.* 6258, 10-23-57. *Amended by T.D.* 6841, 7-26-65; *T.D.* 7293, 11-27-73 *and T.D.* 8735, 10-6-97.]

§ 1.881-3. Conduit financing arrangements.—(a) *General rules and definitions.*—(1) *Purpose and scope.*—Pursuant to the authority of section 7701(l), this section provides rules that permit the district director to disregard, for purposes of section 881, the participation of one or more intermediate entities in a financing arrangement where such entities are acting as conduit entities. For purposes of this section, any reference to tax imposed under section 881 includes, except as otherwise provided and as the context may require, a reference to tax imposed under sections 871 or 884(f)(1)(A) or required to be withheld under section 1441 or 1442. See § 1.881-4 for recordkeeping requirements concerning financing arrangements. See §§ 1.1441-3(j) and 1.1441-7(d) for withholding rules applicable to conduit financing arrangements.

(2) *Definitions.*—The following definitions apply for purposes of this section and §§ 1.881-4, 1.1441-3(j) and 1.1441-7(d).

(i) *Financing arrangement.*—(A) *In general.*—Financing arrangement means a series of transactions by which one person (the financing entity) advances money or other property, or grants rights to use property, and another person (the financed entity) receives money or other property, or rights to use property, if the advance and receipt are effected through one or more other persons (intermediate entities) and, except in cases to which paragraph (a)(2)(i)(B) of this section applies, there are financing transactions linking the financing entity, each of the intermediate entities, and the financed entity. A transfer of money or other property in satisfaction of a repayment obligation is not an advance of money or other property. A financing arrangement exists regardless of the order in which the transactions are entered into, but only for the period during which all of the financing transactions coexist. See *Examples 1, 2,* and *3* of paragraph (e) of this section for illustrations of the term financing arrangement.

(B) *Special rule for related parties.*—If two (or more) financing transactions involving two (or more) related persons would form part of a financing arrangement but for the absence of a financing transaction between the related persons, the district director may treat the related persons as a single intermediate entity if he determines that one of the principal purposes for the structure of the financing transactions is to prevent the characterization of such arrangement as a financing arrangement. This determination shall be based upon all of the facts and circumstances, including, without limitation, the factors set forth in paragraph (b)(2) of this section. See *Examples 4* and *5* of paragraph (e) of this section for illustrations of this paragraph (a)(2)(i)(B).

(ii) *Financing transaction.*—(A) *In general.*—Financing transaction means—

(1) Debt;

(2) Stock in a corporation (or a similar interest in a partnership or trust) that meets the requirements of paragraph (a)(2)(ii)(B) of this section;

(3) Any lease or license; or

(4) Any other transaction (including an interest in a trust described in sections 671 through 679) pursuant to which a person makes an advance of money or other property or grants rights to use property to a transferee who is obligated to repay or return a substantial portion of the money or other property advanced, or the equivalent in value. This paragraph (a)(2)(ii)(A)(4) shall not apply to the posting of collateral unless the collateral consists of cash or the person holding the collateral is permitted to reduce the collateral to cash (through a transfer, grant of a security interest or similar transaction) prior to default on the financing transaction secured by the collateral.

(B) *Limitation on inclusion of stock or similar interests.*—(1) *In general.*—Stock in a corporation (or a similar interest in a partnership or trust) will constitute a financing transaction only if one of the following conditions is satisfied—

(i) The issuer is required to redeem the stock or similar interest at a specified time or the holder has the right to require the issuer to redeem the stock or similar interest or to make any other payment with respect to the stock or similar interest;

(ii) The issuer has the right to redeem the stock or similar interest, but only if, based on all of the facts and circumstances as of the issue date, redemption pursuant to that right is more likely than not to occur; or

(iii) The owner of the stock or similar interest has the right to require a person related to the issuer (or any other person who is acting pursuant to a plan or arrangement with the issuer) to acquire the stock or similar interest or make a payment with respect to the stock or similar interest.

(2) *Rules of special application.*—(i) *Existence of a right.*—For purposes of this paragraph (a)(2)(ii)(B), a person will be considered to have a right to cause a redemption or payment if the person has the right (other than rights arising, in the ordinary course, between the date that a payment is declared and the date that a payment is made) to enforce the payment through a legal proceeding or to cause the issuer to be liquidated if it fails to redeem the interest or to make a payment. A person will not be considered to have a right to force a redemption or a payment if the right is derived solely from ownership of a controlling interest in the issuer in cases where the control does not arise from a default or similar contingency under the instrument. The person is considered to have such a right if the person has the right as of the issue date or, as of the issue date, it is more likely than not that the person will receive such a right, whether through the occurrence of a contingency or otherwise.

(ii) *Restrictions on payment.*—The fact that the issuer does not have the legally available funds to redeem the stock or similar interest, or that the payments are to be made in a blocked currency, will not affect the determinations made pursuant to this paragraph (a)(2)(ii)(B).

(iii) Conduit entity means an intermediate entity whose participation in the financing arrangement may be disregarded in whole or in part pursuant to this section, whether or not the district director has made a determination that the intermediate entity should be disregarded under paragraph (a)(3)(i) of this section.

(iv) Conduit financing arrangement means a financing arrangement that is effected through one or more conduit entities.

(v) Related means related within the meaning of sections 267(b) or 707(b)(1), or

Reg. § 1.881-3(a)(2)(i)(B)

controlled within the meaning of section 482, and the regulations under those sections. For purposes of determining whether a person is related to another person, the constructive ownership rules of section 318 shall apply, and the attribution rules of section 267(c) also shall apply to the extent they attribute ownership to persons to whom section 318 does not attribute ownership.

(3) *Disregard of participation of conduit entity.*—(i) *Authority of district director.*—The district director may determine that the participation of a conduit entity in a conduit financing arrangement should be disregarded for purposes of section 881. For this purpose, an intermediate entity will constitute a conduit entity if it meets the standards of paragraph (a)(4) of this section. The district director has discretion to determine the manner in which the standards of paragraph (a)(4) of this section apply, including the financing transactions and parties composing the financing arrangement.

(ii) *Effect of disregarding conduit entity.*—(A) *In general.*—If the district director determines that the participation of a conduit entity in a financing arrangement should be disregarded, the financing arrangement is recharacterized as a transaction directly between the remaining parties to the financing arrangement (in most cases, the financed entity and the financing entity) for purposes of section 881. To the extent that a disregarded conduit entity actually receives or makes payments pursuant to a conduit financing arrangement, it is treated as an agent of the financing entity. Except as otherwise provided, the recharacterization of the conduit financing arrangement also applies for purposes of sections 871, 884(f)(1)(A), 1441, and 1442 and other procedural provisions relating to those sections. This recharacterization will not otherwise affect a taxpayer's Federal income tax liability under any substantive provisions of the Internal Revenue Code. Thus, for example, the recharacterization generally applies for purposes of section 1461, in order to impose liability on a withholding agent who fails to withhold as required under § 1.1441-3(j), but not for purposes of § 1.882-5.

(B) *Character of payments made by the financed entity.*—If the participation of a conduit financing arrangement is disregarded under this paragraph (a)(3), payments made by the financed entity generally shall be characterized by reference to the character (e.g., interest or rent) of the payments made to the financing entity. However, if the financing transaction to which the financing entity is a party is a transaction described in paragraph (a)(2)(ii)(A)(2) or (4) of this section that gives rise to payments that would not be deductible if paid by the financed entity, the character of the payments made by the financed entity will not be affected by the disregard of the participation of a conduit entity. The characterization provided by this paragraph (a)(3)(ii)(B) does not, however, extend to qualification of a payment for any exemption from withholding tax under the Internal Revenue Code or a provision of any applicable tax treaty if such qualification depends on the terms of, or other similar facts or circumstances relating to, the financing transaction to which the financing entity is a party that do not apply to the financing transaction to which the financed entity is a party. Thus, for example, payments made by a financed entity that is not a bank cannot qualify for the exemption provided by section 881(i) of the Code even if the loan between the financed entity and the conduit entity is a bank deposit.

(C) *Effect of income tax treaties.*—Where the participation of a conduit entity in a conduit financing arrangement is disregarded pursuant to this section, it is disregarded for all purposes of section 881, including for purposes of applying any relevant income tax treaties. Accordingly, the conduit entity may not claim the benefits of a tax treaty between its country of residence and the United States to reduce the amount of tax due under section 881 with respect to payments made pursuant to the conduit financing arrangement. The financing entity may, however, claim the benefits of any income tax treaty under which it is entitled to benefits in order to reduce the rate of tax on payments made pursuant to the conduit financing arrangement that are recharacterized in accordance with paragraph (a)(3)(ii)(B) of this section.

(D) *Effect on withholding tax.*—For the effect of recharacterization on withholding obligations, see §§ 1.1441-3(j) and 1.1441-7(d).

(E) *Special rule for a financing entity that is unrelated to both intermediate entity and financed entity.*—(1) *Liability of financing entity.*—Notwithstanding the fact that a financing arrangement is a conduit financing arrangement, a financing entity that is unrelated to the financed entity and the conduit entity (or entities) shall not itself be liable for tax under section 881 unless the financing entity knows or has reason to know that the financing arrangement is a conduit financing arrangement. But see § 1.1441-3(j) for the withholding agent's withholding obligations.

(2) *Financing entity's knowledge.*—(i) *In general.*—A financing entity knows or has reason to know that the financing arrange-

ment is a conduit financing arrangement only if the financing entity knows or has reason to know of facts sufficient to establish that the financing arrangement is a conduit financing arrangement, including facts sufficient to establish that the participation of the intermediate entity in the financing arrangement is pursuant to a tax avoidance plan. A person that knows only of the financing transactions that comprise the financing arrangement will not be considered to know or have reason to know of facts sufficient to establish that the financing arrangement is a conduit financing arrangement.

(ii) *Presumption regarding financing entity's knowledge.*—It shall be presumed that the financing entity does not know or have reason to know that the financing arrangement is a conduit financing arrangement if the financing entity is unrelated to all other parties to the financing arrangement and the financing entity establishes that the intermediate entity who is a party to the financing transaction with the financing entity is actively engaged in a substantial trade or business. An intermediate entity will not be considered to be engaged in a trade or business if its business is making or managing investments, unless the intermediate entity is actively engaged in a banking, insurance, financing or similar trade or business and such business consists predominantly of transactions with customers who are not related persons. An intermediate entity's trade or business is substantial if it is reasonable for the financing entity to expect that the intermediate entity will be able to make payments under the financing transaction out of the cash flow of that trade or business. This presumption may be rebutted if the district director establishes that the financing entity knew or had reason to know that the financing arrangement is a conduit financing arrangement. See *Example 6* of paragraph (e) of this section for an illustration of the rules of this paragraph (a)(3)(ii)(E).

(iii) *Limitation on taxpayer's use of this section.*—A taxpayer may not apply this section to reduce the amount of its Federal income tax liability by disregarding the form of its financing transactions for Federal income tax purposes or by compelling the district director to do so. See, however, paragraph (b)(2)(i) of this section for rules regarding the taxpayer's ability to show that the participation of one or more intermediate entities results in no significant reduction in tax.

(4) *Standard for treatment as a conduit entity.*—(i) *In general.*—An intermediate entity is a conduit entity with respect to a financing arrangement if—

(A) The participation of the intermediate entity (or entities) in the financing arrangement reduces the tax imposed by section 881 (determined by comparing the aggregate tax imposed under section 881 on payments made on financing transactions making up the financing arrangement with the tax that would have been imposed under paragraph (d) of this section);

(B) The participation of the intermediate entity in the financing arrangement is pursuant to a tax avoidance plan; and

(C) Either—

(1) The intermediate entity is related to the financing entity or the financed entity; or

(2) The intermediate entity would not have participated in the financing arrangement on substantially the same terms but for the fact that the financing entity engaged in the financing transaction with the intermediate entity.

(ii) *Multiple intermediate entities.*—(A) *In general.*—If a financing arrangement involves multiple intermediate entities, the district director will determine whether each of the intermediate entities is a conduit entity. The district director will make the determination by applying the special rules for multiple intermediate entities provided in this section or, if no special rules are provided, applying principles consistent with those of paragraph (a)(4)(i) of this section to each of the intermediate entities in the financing arrangement.

(B) *Special rule for related persons.*—The district director may treat related intermediate entities as a single intermediate entity if he determines that one of the principal purposes for the involvement of multiple intermediate entities in the financing arrangement is to prevent the characterization of an intermediate entity as a conduit entity, to reduce the portion of a payment that is subject to withholding tax or otherwise to circumvent the provisions of this section. This determination shall be based upon all of the facts and circumstances, including, but not limited to, the factors set forth in paragraph (b)(2) of this section. If a district director determines that related persons are to be treated as a single intermediate entity, financing transactions between such related parties that are part of the conduit financing arrangement shall be disregarded for purposes of applying this section. See *Examples 7* and *8* of paragraph (e) of this section for illustrations of the rules of this paragraph (a)(4)(ii).

(b) *Determination of whether participation of intermediate entity is pursuant to a tax avoidance plan.*—(1) *In general.*—A tax avoidance plan is a plan one of the principal purposes of which is the avoidance of tax imposed by section 881. Avoidance of the tax imposed by section 881 may be one of the principal purposes for such a plan even though it is outweighed by other purposes (taken together or separately). In this regard, the only relevant purposes are those pertaining to the participation of the intermediate entity in the financing arrangement and not those pertaining to the existence of a financing arrangement as a whole. The plan may be formal or informal, written or oral, and may involve any one or more of the parties to the financing arrangement. The plan must be in existence no later than the last date that any of the financing transactions comprising the financing arrangement is entered into. The district director may infer the existence of a tax avoidance plan from the facts and circumstances. In determining whether there is a tax avoidance plan, the district director will weigh all relevant evidence regarding the purposes for the intermediate entity's participation in the financing arrangement. See *Examples 11* and *12* of paragraph (e) of this section for illustrations of the rule of this paragraph (b)(1).

(2) *Factors taken into account in determining the presence or absence of a tax avoidance purpose.*—The factors described in paragraphs (b)(2)(i) through (iv) of this section are among the facts and circumstances taken into account in determining whether the participation of an intermediate entity in a financing arrangement has as one of its principal purposes the avoidance of tax imposed by section 881.

(i) *Significant reduction in tax.*—The district director will consider whether the participation of the intermediate entity (or entities) in the financing arrangement significantly reduces the tax that otherwise would have been imposed under section 881. The fact that an intermediate entity is a resident of a country that has an income tax treaty with the United States that significantly reduces the tax that otherwise would have been imposed under section 881 is not sufficient, by itself, to establish the existence of a tax avoidance plan. The determination of whether the participation of an intermediate entity significantly reduces the tax generally is made by comparing the aggregate tax imposed under section 881 on payments made on financing transactions making up the financing arrangement with the tax that would be imposed under paragraph (d) of this section. However, the taxpayer is not barred from presenting evidence that the financing entity, as determined by the district director, was itself an intermediate entity and another entity should be treated as the financing entity for purposes of applying this test. A reduction in the absolute amount of tax may be significant even if the reduction in rate is not. A reduction in the amount of tax may be significant if the reduction is large in absolute terms or in relative terms. See *Examples 13, 14* and *15* of paragraph (e) of this section for illustrations of this factor.

(ii) *Ability to make the advance.*—The district director will consider whether the intermediate entity had sufficient available money or other property of its own to have made the advance to the financed entity without the advance of money or other property to it by the financing entity (or in the case of multiple intermediate entities, whether each of the intermediate entities had sufficient available money or other property of its own to have made the advance to either the financed entity or another intermediate entity without the advance of money or other property to it by either the financing entity or another intermediate entity).

(iii) *Time period between financing transactions.*—The district director will consider the length of the period of time that separates the advances of money or other property, or the grants of rights to use property, by the financing entity to the intermediate entity (in the case of multiple intermediate entities, from one intermediate entity to another), and ultimately by the intermediate entity to the financed entity. A short period of time is evidence of the existence of a tax avoidance plan while a long period of time is evidence that there is not a tax avoidance plan. See *Example 16* of paragraph (e) of this section for an illustration of this factor.

(iv) *Financing transactions in the ordinary course of business.*—If the parties to the financing transaction are related, the district director will consider whether the financing transaction occurs in the ordinary course of the active conduct of complementary or integrated trades or businesses engaged in by these entities. The fact that a financing transaction is described in this paragraph (b)(2)(iv) is evidence that the participation of the parties to that transaction in the financing arrangement is not pursuant to a tax avoidance plan. A loan will not be considered to occur in the ordinary course of the active conduct of complementary or integrated trades or businesses unless the loan is a trade receivable or the parties to the transaction are actively engaged in a banking, insurance, financing or similar trade or business and such business consists predominantly of transactions with customers who are not related persons. See *Example 17* of paragraph (e) of this section for an illustration of this factor.

(3) *Presumption if significant financing activities performed by a related intermediate en-*

tity.—(i) *General rule.*—It shall be presumed that the participation of an intermediate entity (or entities) in a financing arrangement is not pursuant to a tax avoidance plan if the intermediate entity is related to either or both the financing entity or the financed entity and the intermediate entity performs significant financing activities with respect to the financing transactions forming part of the financing arrangement to which it is a party. This presumption may be rebutted if the district director establishes that the participation of the intermediate entity in the financing arrangement is pursuant to a tax avoidance plan. See *Examples 21, 22* and *23* of paragraph (e) of this section for illustrations of this presumption.

(ii) *Significant financing activities.*—For purposes of this paragraph (b)(3), an intermediate entity performs significant financing activities with respect to such financing transactions only if the financing transactions satisfy the requirements of either paragraph (b)(3)(ii)(A) or (B) of this section.

(A) *Active rents or royalties.*—An intermediate entity performs significant financing activities with respect to leases or licenses if rents or royalties earned with respect to such leases or licenses are derived in the active conduct of a trade or business within the meaning of section 954(c)(2)(A), to be applied by substituting the term *intermediate entity* for the term *controlled foreign corporation.*

(B) *Active risk management.*—(*1*) *In general.*—An intermediate entity is considered to perform significant financing activities with respect to financing transactions only if officers and employees of the intermediate entity participate actively and materially in arranging the intermediate entity's participation in such financing transactions (other than financing transactions described in paragraph (b)(3)(ii)(B)(*3*) of this section) and perform the business activity and risk management activities described in paragraph (b)(3)(ii)(B)(*2*) of this section with respect to such financing transactions, and the participation of the intermediate entity in the financing transactions produces (or reasonably can be expected to produce) efficiency savings by reducing transaction costs and overhead and other fixed costs.

(*2*) *Business activity and risk management requirements.*—An intermediate entity will be considered to perform significant financing activities only if, within the country in which the intermediate entity is organized (or, if different, within the country with respect to which the intermediate entity is claiming the benefits of a tax treaty), its officers and employees—

(*i*) Exercise management over, and actively conduct, the day-to-day operations of the intermediate entity. Such operations must consist of a substantial trade or business or the supervision, administration and financing for a substantial group of related persons; and

(*ii*) Actively manage, on an ongoing basis, material market risks arising from such financing transactions as an integral part of the management of the intermediate entity's financial and capital requirements (including management of risks of currency and interest rate fluctuations) and management of the intermediate entity's short-term investments of working capital by entering into transactions with unrelated persons.

(*3*) *Special rule for trade receivables and payables entered into in the ordinary course of business.*—If the activities of the intermediate entity consist in whole or in part of cash management for a controlled group of which the intermediate entity is a member, then employees of the intermediate entity need not have participated in arranging any such financing transactions that arise in the ordinary course of a substantial trade or business of either the financed entity or the financing entity. Officers or employees of the financing entity or financed entity, however, must have participated actively and materially in arranging the transaction that gave rise to the trade receivable or trade payable. Cash management includes the operation of a sweep account whereby the intermediate entity nets intercompany trade payables and receivables arising from transactions among the other members of the controlled group and between members of the controlled group and unrelated persons.

(*4*) *Activities of officers and employees of related persons.*—Except as provided in paragraph (b)(3)(ii)(B)(*3*) of this section, in applying this paragraph (b)(3)(ii)(B), the activities of an officer or employee of an intermediate entity will not constitute significant financing activities if any officer or employee of a related person participated materially in any of the activities described in this paragraph, other than to approve any guarantee of a financing transaction or to exercise general supervision and control over the policies of the intermediate entity.

(c) *Determination of whether an unrelated intermediate entity would not have participated in financing arrangement on substantially the same terms.*—(1) *In general.*—The determination of whether an intermediate entity would not have participated in a financing arrangement on substantially the same terms but for the financing transaction between the financing entity and the intermediate entity shall be based upon all of the facts and circumstances.

(2) *Effect of guarantee.*—(i) *In general.*— The district director may presume that the intermediate entity would not have participated in the financing arrangement on substantially the same terms if there is a guarantee of the financed entity's liability to the intermediate entity (or in the case of multiple intermediate entities, a guarantee of the intermediate entity's liability to the intermediate entity that advanced money or property, or granted rights to use other property). However, a guarantee that was neither in existence nor contemplated on the last date that any of the financing transactions comprising the financing arrangement is entered into does not give rise to this presumption. A taxpayer may rebut this presumption by producing clear and convincing evidence that the intermediate entity would have participated in the financing transaction with the financed entity on substantially the same terms even if the financing entity had not entered into a financing transaction with the intermediate entity.

(ii) *Definition of guarantee.*—For the purposes of this paragraph (c)(2), a guarantee is any arrangement under which a person, directly or indirectly, assures, on a conditional or unconditional basis, the payment of another person's obligation with respect to a financing transaction. The term shall be interpreted in accordance with the definition of the term in section 163(j)(6)(D)(iii).

(d) *Determination of amount of tax liability.*—(1) *Amount of payment subject to recharacterization.*—(i) *In general.*—If a financing arrangement is a conduit financing arrangement, a portion of each payment made by the financed entity with respect to the financing transactions that comprise the conduit financing arrangement shall be recharacterized as a transaction directly between the financed entity and the financing entity. If the aggregate principal amount of the financing transaction(s) to which the financed entity is a party is less than or equal to the aggregate principal amount of the financing transaction(s) linking any of the parties to the financing arrangement, the entire amount of the payment shall be so recharacterized. If the aggregate principal amount of the financing transaction(s) to which the financed entity is a party is greater than the aggregate principal amount of the financing transaction(s) linking any of the parties to the financing arrangement, then the recharacterized portion shall be determined by multiplying the payment by a fraction the numerator of which is equal to the lowest aggregate principal amount of the financing transaction(s) linking any of the parties to the financing arrangement (other than financing transactions that are disregarded pursuant to paragraphs (a)(2)(i)(B) and (a)(4)(ii)(B) of this section) and the denominator of which is the aggregate principal amount of the financing transaction(s) to which the financed entity is a party. In the case of financing transactions the principal amount of which is subject to adjustment, the fraction shall be determined using the average outstanding principal amounts for the period to which the payment relates. The average principal amount may be computed using any method applied consistently that reflects with reasonable accuracy the amount outstanding for the period. See *Example 24* of paragraph (e) of this section for an illustration of the calculation of the amount of tax liability.

(ii) *Determination of principal amount.*—(A) *In general.*—Unless otherwise provided in this paragraph (d)(1)(ii), the principal amount equals the amount of money advanced, or the fair market value of other property advanced or subject to a lease or license, in the financing transaction. In general, fair market value is calculated in U.S. dollars as of the close of business on the day on which the financing transaction is entered into. However, if the property advanced, or the right to use property granted, by the financing entity is the same as the property or rights received by the financed entity, the fair market value of the property or right shall be determined as of the close of business on the last date that any of the financing transactions comprising the financing arrangement is entered into. In the case of fungible property, property of the same type shall be considered to be the same property. See *Example 25* of paragraph (e) for an illustration of the calculation of the principal amount in the case of financing transactions involving fungible property. The principal amount of a financing transaction shall be subject to adjustments, as set forth in this paragraph (d)(1)(ii).

(B) *Debt instruments and certain stock.*—In the case of a debt instrument or of stock that is subject to the current inclusion rules of sections 305(c)(3) or (e), the principal amount generally will be equal to the issue price. However, if the fair market value on the issue date differs materially from the issue price, the fair market value of the debt instrument shall be used in lieu of the instrument's issue price. Appropriate adjustments will be made for accruals of original issue discount and repayments of principal (including accrued original issue discount).

Reg. § 1.881-3(d)(1)(ii)(B)

(C) *Partnership and trust interests.*—In the case of a partnership interest or an interest in a trust, the principal amount is equal to the fair market value of the money or property contributed to the partnership or trust in return for that partnership or trust interest.

(D) *Leases or licenses.*—In the case of a lease or license, the principal amount is equal to the fair market value of the property subject to the lease or license on the date on which the lease or license is entered into. The principal amount shall be adjusted for depreciation or amortization, calculated on a basis that accurately reflects the anticipated decline in the value of the property over its life.

(2) *Rate of tax.*—The rate at which tax is imposed under section 881 on the portion of the payment that is recharacterized pursuant to paragraph (d)(1) of this section is determined by reference to the nature of the recharacterized transaction, as determined under paragraphs (a)(3)(ii)(B) and (C) of this section.

(e) *Examples.*—The following examples illustrate this section. For purposes of these examples, unless otherwise indicated, it is assumed that FP, a corporation organized in country N, owns all of the stock of FS, a corporation organized in country T, and DS, a corporation organized in the United States. Country T, but not country N, has an income tax treaty with the United States. The treaty exempts interest, rents and royalties paid by a resident of one state (the source state) to a resident of the other state from tax in the source state.

Example 1. Financing arrangement. (i) On January 1, 1996, BK, a bank organized in country T, lends $1,000,000 to DS in exchange for a note issued by DS. FP guarantees to BK that DS will satisfy its repayment obligation on the loan. There are no other transactions between FP and BK.

(ii) BK's loan to DS is a financing transaction within the meaning of paragraph (a)(4)(ii)(A)(*1*) of this section. FP's guarantee of DS's repayment obligation is not a financing transaction as described in paragraphs (a)(2)(ii)(A)(*1*) through (*4*) of this section. Therefore, these transactions do not constitute a financing arrangement as defined in paragraph (a)(2)(i) of this section.

Example 2. Financing arrangement. (i) On January 1, 1996, FP lends $1,000,000 to DS in exchange for a note issued by DS. On January 1, 1997, FP assigns the DS note to FS in exchange for a note issued by FS. After receiving notice of the assignment, DS remits payments due under its note to FS.

(ii) The DS note held by FS and the FS note held by FP are financing transactions within the meaning of paragraph (a)(2)(ii)(A)(*1*) of this section, and together constitute a financing arrangement within the meaning of paragraph (a)(2)(i) of this section.

Example 3. Financing arrangement. (i) On December 1, 1994 FP creates a special purposes subsidiary, FS. On that date FP capitalizes FS with $1,000,000 in cash and $10,000,000 in debt from BK, a Country N bank. On January 1, 1995, C, a U.S. person, purchases an automobile from DS in return for an installment note. On August 1, 1995, DS sells a number of installment notes, including C's, to FS in exchange for $10,000,000. DS continues to service the installment notes for FS.

(ii) The C installment note now held by FS (as well as all of the other installment notes now held by FS) and the FS note held by BK are financing transactions within the meaning of paragraph (a)(2)(ii)(A)(*1*) of this section, and together constitute a financing arrangement within the meaning of paragraph (a)(2)(i) of this section.

Example 4. Related persons treated as a single intermediate entity. (i) On January 1, 1996, FP deposits $1,000,000 with BK, a bank that is organized in country N and is unrelated to FP and its subsidiaries. M, a corporation also organized in country N, is wholly-owned by the sole shareholder of BK but is not a bank within the meaning of section 881(c)(3)(A). On July 1, 1996, M lends $1,000,000 to DS in exchange for a note maturing on July 1, 2006. The note is in registered form within the meaning of section 881(c)(2)(B)(i) and DS has received from M the statement required by section 881(c)(2)(B)(ii). One of the principal purposes for the absence of a financing transaction between BK and M is the avoidance of the application of this section.

(ii) The transactions described above would form a financing arrangement but for the absence of a financing transaction between BK and M. However, because one of the principal purposes for the structuring of these financing transactions is to prevent characterization of such arrangement as a financing arrangement, the district director may treat the financing transactions between FP and BK, and between M and DS as a financing arrangement under paragraphs (a)(2)(i)(B) of this section. In such a case, BK and M would be considered a single intermediate entity for purposes of this section. See also paragraph (a)(4)(ii)(B) of this section for the authority to treat BK and M as a single intermediate entity.

Example 5. Related persons treated as a single intermediate entity. (i) On January 1, 1995, FP lends $10,000,000 to FS in exchange for a 10-year note that pays interest annually at a rate of 8 percent per annum. On January 2, 1995, FS contributes $10,000,000 to FS2, a wholly-owned subsidiary of FS organized in country T, in exchange for common stock of FS2. On January 1, 1996, FS2 lends $10,000,000 to DS in exchange for an 8-year note that pays interest annually at a rate of 10 percent per annum. FS is a holding company whose most significant asset is the stock of FS2. Throughout the period that the FP-FS loan is outstanding, FS causes FS2 to make distributions to FS, most of which are used to make interest and principal payments on the FP-FS loan. Without the distributions from FS2, FS would not have had the funds with which to make payments on the FP-FS loan. One of the principal purposes for the absence of a financing transaction between FS and FS2 is the avoidance of the application of this section.

(ii) The conditions of paragraph (a)(4)(i)(A) of this section would be satisfied with respect to the financing transactions between FP, FS, FS2 and DS but for the absence of a financing transaction between FS and FS2. However, because one of the principal purposes for the structuring of these financing transactions is to prevent characterization of an entity as a conduit, the district director may treat the financing transactions between FP and FS, and between FS2 and DS as a financing arrangement. See paragraph (a)(4)(ii)(B) of this section. In such a case, FS and FS2 would be considered a single intermediate entity for purposes of this section. See also paragraph (a)(2)(i)(B) of this section for the authority to treat FS and FS2 as a single intermediate entity.

Example 6. Presumption with respect to unrelated financing entity. (i) FP is a corporation organized in country T that is actively engaged in a substantial manufacturing business. FP has a revolving credit facility with a syndicate of banks, none of which is related to FP and FP's subsidiaries, which provides that FP may borrow up to a maximum of $100,000,000 at a time. The revolving credit facility provides that DS and certain other subsidiaries of FP may borrow directly from the syndicate at the same interest rates as FP, but each subsidiary is required to indemnify the syndicate banks for any withholding taxes imposed on interest payments by the country in which the subsidiary is organized. BK, a bank that is organized in country N, is the agent for the syndicate. Some of the syndicate banks are organized in country N, but others are residents of country O, a country that has an income tax treaty with the United States which allows the United States to impose a tax on interest at a maximum rate of 10 percent. It is reasonable for BK and the syndicate banks to have determined that FP will be able to meet its payment obligations on a maximum principal amount of $100,000,000 out of the cash flow of its manufacturing business. At various times throughout 1995, FP borrows under the revolving credit facility until the outstanding principal amount reaches the maximum amount of $100,000,000. On December 31, 1995, FP receives $100,000,000 from a public offering of its equity. On January 1, 1996, FP pays BK $90,000,000 to reduce the outstanding principal amount under the revolving credit facility and lends $10,000,000 to DS. FP would have repaid the entire principal amount, and DS would have borrowed directly from the syndicate, but for the fact that DS did not want to incur the U.S. withholding tax that would have applied to payments made directly by DS to the syndicate banks.

(ii) Pursuant to paragraph (a)(3)(ii)(E)(*1*) of this section, even though the financing arrangement is a conduit financing arrangement (because the financing arrangement meets the standards for recharacterization in paragraph (a)(4)(i)), BK and the other syndicate banks have no section 881 liability unless they know or have reason to know that the financing arrangement is a conduit financing arrangement. Moreover, pursuant to paragraph (a)(3)(ii)(E)(*2*)(*ii*) of this section, BK and the syndicate banks are presumed not to know that the financing arrangement is a conduit financing arrangement. The syndicate banks are unrelated to both FP and DS, and FP is actively engaged in a substantial trade or business—that is, the cash flow from FP's manufacturing business is sufficient for the banks to expect that FP will be able to make the payments required under the financing transaction. See § 1.1441-3(j) for the withholding obligations of the withholding agents.

Example 7. Multiple intermediate entities—special rule for related persons. (i) On January 1, 1995, FP lends $10,000,000 to FS in exchange for a 10-year note that pays interest annually at a rate of 8 percent per annum. On January 2, 1995, FS contributes $9,900,000 to FS2, a wholly-owned subsidiary of FS organized in country T, in exchange for common stock and lends $100,000 to FS2. On January 1, 1996, FS2 lends $10,000,000 to DS in exchange for an 8-year note that pays interest annually at a rate of 10 percent per annum. FS is a holding company that has no significant assets other than the stock of FS2. Throughout the period that the FP-FS loan is outstanding, FS causes FS2 to make distributions to FS, most of which are used to make interest and principal payments on the FP-FS loan. Without the distributions from FS2, FS would not have had the funds with which to make payments on the FP-FS loan. One of the principal purposes for structuring the transactions between FS and FS2 as primarily a contribution of capital is to the amount of the payment that would be recharacterized under paragraph (d) of this section.

(ii) Pursuant to paragraph (a)(4)(ii)(B) of this section, the district director may treat FS and FS2 as a single intermediate entity for purposes of this section since one of the principal purposes for the participation of multiple intermediate entities is to reduce the amount of the tax liability on any recharacterized payment by inserting a financing transaction with a low principal amount.

Example 8. Multiple intermediate entities. (i) On January 1, 1995, FP deposits $1,000,000 with BK, a bank that is organized in country T and is unrelated to FP and its subsidiaries, FS and DS. On January 1, 1996, at a time when the FP-BK deposit is still outstanding, BK lends $500,000 to BK2, a bank that is wholly-owned by BK and is organized in country T. On the same date, BK2 lends $500,000 to FS. On July 1, 1996, FS lends $500,000 to DS. FP pledges its deposit with BK to BK2 in support of FS' obligation to repay the BK2 loan. FS', BK's and BK2's participation in the financing arrangement is pursuant to a tax avoidance plan.

(ii) The conditions of paragraphs (a)(4)(i)(A) and (B) of this section are satisfied because the participation of BK, BK2 and FS in the financing arrangement reduces the tax imposed by section 881, and FS', BK's and BK2's participation in the financing arrangement is pursuant to a tax avoidance plan. However, since BK and BK2 are unrelated to FP and DS, under paragraph (a)(4)(i)(C)(2) of this section, BK and BK2 will be treated as conduit entities only if BK and BK2 would not have participated in the financing arrangement on substantially the same terms but for the financing transaction between FP and BK.

(iii) It is presumed that BK2 would not have participated in the financing arrangement on substantially the same terms but for the BK-BK2 financing transaction because FP's pledge of an asset in support of FS' obligation to repay the BK2 loan is a guarantee within the meaning of paragraph (c)(2)(ii) of this section. If the taxpayer does not rebut this presumption by clear and convincing evidence, then BK2 will be a conduit entity.

(iv) Because BK and BK2 are related intermediate entities, the district director must determine whether one of the principal purposes for the involvement of multiple intermediate entities was to prevent characterization of an entity as a conduit entity. In making this determination, the district director may consider the fact that the involvement of two related intermediate entities prevents the presumption regarding guarantees from applying to BK. In the absence of evidence showing a business purpose for the involvement of both BK and BK2, the district director may treat BK and BK2 as a single intermediate entity for purposes of determining whether they would have participated in the financing arrangement on substantially the same terms but for the financing transaction between FP and BK. The presumption that applies to BK2 therefore will apply to BK. If the taxpayer does not rebut this presumption by clear and convincing evidence, then BK will be a conduit entity.

Example 9. Reduction of tax. (i) On February 1, 1995, FP issues debt to the public that would satisfy the requirements of section 871(h)(2)(A) (relating to obligations that are not in registered form) if issued by a U.S. person. FP lends the proceeds of the debt offering to DS in exchange for a note.

(ii) The debt issued by FP and the DS note are financing transactions within the meaning of paragraph (a)(2)(ii)(A)(1) of this section and together constitute a financing arrangement within the meaning of paragraph (a)(2)(i) of this section. The holders of the FP debt are the financing entities, FP is the intermediate entity and DS is the financed entity. Because interest payments on the debt issued by FP would not have been subject to withholding tax if the debt had been issued by DS, there is no reduction in tax under paragraph (a)(4)(i)(A) of this section. Accordingly, FP is not a conduit entity.

Example 10. Reduction of tax. (i) On January 1, 1995, FP licenses to FS the rights to use a patent in the United States to manufacture product A. FS agrees to pay FP a fixed amount in royalties each year under the license. On January 1, 1996, FS sublicenses to DS the rights to use the patent in the United States. Under the sublicense, DS agrees to pay FS royalties based upon the units of product A manufactured by DS each year. Although the formula for computing the amount of royalties paid by DS to FS differs from the formula for computing the amount of royalties paid by FS to FP, each represents an arm's length rate.

(ii) Although the royalties paid by DS to FS are exempt from U.S. withholding tax, the royalty payments between FS and FP are income from U.S. sources under section 861(a)(4) subject to the 30 percent gross tax imposed by § 1.881-2(b) and subject to withholding under § 1.1441-2(a). Because the rate of tax imposed on royalties paid by FS to FP is the same as the rate that would have been imposed on royalties paid by DS to FP, the participation of FS in the FP-FS-DS financing arrangement does not reduce the tax imposed by section 881 within the meaning of paragraph (a)(4)(i)(A) of this section. Accordingly, FP is not a conduit entity.

Example 11. A principal purpose. (i) On January 1, 1995, FS lends $10,000,000 to DS in exchange for a 10-year note that pays interest annually at a rate of 8 percent per annum. As was intended at the time of the loan from FS to DS, on July 1, 1995, FP makes an interest-free demand loan of $10,000,000 to FS. A principal purpose for FS' participation in the FP-FS-DS financing arrangement is that FS generally coordinates the financing for all of FP's subsidiaries (although FS does not engage in significant financing activities with respect to such financing transactions). However, another principal purpose for FS' participation is to allow the parties to benefit from the lower withholding tax rate provided under the income tax treaty between country T and the United States.

(ii) The financing arrangement satisfies the tax avoidance purpose requirement of paragraph (a)(4)(i)(B) of this section because FS participated in the financing arrangement pursuant to a plan one of the principal purposes of which is to allow the parties to benefit from the country T-U.S. treaty.

Example 12. A principal purpose. (i) DX is a U.S. corporation that intends to purchase property to use in its manufacturing business. FX is a partnership organized in country N that is owned in equal parts by LC1 and LC2, leasing companies that are unrelated to DX. BK, a bank organized in country N and unrelated to DX, LC1 and LC2, lends $100,000,000 to FX to enable FX to purchase the property. On the same day, FX purchases the property and engages in a transaction with DX which is treated as a lease of the property for country N tax purposes but a loan for U.S. tax purposes. Accordingly, DX is treated as the owner of the property for U.S. tax purposes. The parties comply with the requirements of section 881(c) with respect to the debt obligation of DX to FX. FX and DX structured these transactions in this manner so that LC1 and LC2 would be entitled to accelerated depreciation deductions with respect to the property in country N and DX would be entitled to accelerated depreciation deductions in the United States. None of the parties would have participated in the transaction if the payments made by DX were subject to U.S. withholding tax.

(ii) The loan[s] from BK to FX and from FX to DX are financing transactions and, together constitute a financing arrangement. The participation of FX in the financing arrangement reduces the tax imposed by section 881 because payments made to FX, but not BK, qualify for the portfolio interest exemption of section 881(c) because BK is a bank making an extension of credit in the ordinary course of its trade or business within the meaning of section 881(c)(3)(A). Moreover, because DX borrowed the money from FX instead of borrowing the money directly from BK to avoid the tax imposed by section 881, one of the principal purposes of the participation of FX was to avoid that tax (even though another principal purpose of the participation of FX was to allow LC1 and LC2 to take advantage of accelerated depreciation deductions in country N). Assuming that FX would not have participated in the financing arrangement on substantially the same terms but for the fact that BK loaned it $100,000,000, FX is a conduit entity and the financing arrangement is a conduit financing arrangement.

Example 13. Significant reduction of tax. (i) FS owns all of the stock of FS1, which also is a resident of country T. FS1 owns all of the stock of DS. On January 1, 1995, FP contributes $10,000,000 to the capital of FS in return for perpetual preferred stock. On July 1, 1995, FS lends $10,000,000 to FS1. On January 1, 1996, FS1 lends $10,000,000 to DS. Under the terms of the country T-U.S. income tax treaty, a country T resident is not entitled to the reduced withholding rate on interest income provided by the treaty if the resident is entitled to specified tax benefits under country T law. Although FS1 may deduct interest paid on the loan from FS, these deductions are not pursuant to any special tax benefits provided by country T law. However, FS qualifies for one of the enumerated tax benefits pursuant to which it may deduct dividends paid with respect to the stock held by FP. Therefore, if FS had made a loan directly to DS, FS would not have been entitled to the benefits of the country T-U.S. tax treaty with respect to payments it received from DS, and such payments would have been subject to tax under section 881 at a 30 percent rate.

(ii) The FS-FS1 loan and the FS1-DS loan are financing transactions within the meaning of paragraph (a)(2)(ii)(A)(*1*) of this section and together constitute a financing arrangement within the meaning of paragraph (a)(2)(i) of this section. Pursuant to paragraph (b)(2)(i) of this section, the significant reduction in tax resulting from the participation of FS1 in the financing arrangement is evidence that the participation of FS1 in the financing arrangement is pursuant to a tax avoidance plan. However, other facts relevant to the presence of such a plan must also be taken into account.

Example 14. Significant reduction of tax. (i) FP owns 90 percent of the voting stock of FX, an unlimited liability company organized in country T. The other 10 percent of the common stock of FX is owned by FP1, a subsidiary of FP that is organized in country N. Although FX is a partnership for U.S. tax purposes, FX is entitled to the benefits of the U.S.-country T income tax treaty because FX is subject to tax in country T as a resident corporation. On January 1, 1996, FP contributes $10,000,000 to FX in exchange for an instrument denominated as preferred stock that pays a dividend of 7 percent and that must be redeemed by FX in seven years. For U.S. tax purposes, the preferred stock is a partnership interest. On July 1, 1996, FX makes a loan of $10,000,000 to DS in exchange for a 7-year note paying interest at 6 percent.

(ii) Because FX is required to redeem the partnership interest at a specified time, the partnership interest constitutes a financing transaction within the meaning of paragraph (a)(2)(ii)(A)(2) of this section. Moreover, because the FX-DS note is a financing transaction within the meaning of paragraph (a)(2)(ii)(A)(1) of this section, together the transactions constitute a financing arrangement within the meaning of (a)(2)(i) of this section. Payments of interest made directly by DS to FP and FP1 would not be eligible for the portfolio interest exemption and would not be entitled to a reduction in withholding tax pursuant to a tax treaty. Therefore, there is a significant reduction in tax resulting from the participation of FX in the financing arrangement, which is evidence that the participation of FX in the financing arrangement is pursuant to a tax avoidance plan. However, other facts relevant to the existence of such a plan must also be taken into account.

Example 15. Significant reduction of tax. (i) FP owns a 10 percent interest in the profits and capital of FX, a partnership organized in country N. The other 90 percent interest in FX is owned by G, an unrelated corporation that is organized in country T. FX is not engaged in business in the United States. On January 1, 1996, FP contributes $10,000,000 to FX in exchange for an instrument documented as perpetual subordinated debt that provides for quarterly interest payments at 9 percent per annum. Under the terms of the instrument, payments on the perpetual subordinated debt do not otherwise affect the allocation of income between the partners. FP has the right to require the liquidation of FX if FX fails to make an interest payment. For U.S. tax purposes, the perpetual subordinated debt is treated as a partnership interest in FX and the payments on the perpetual subordinated debt constitute guaranteed payments within the meaning of section 707(c). On July 1, 1996, FX makes a loan of $10,000,000 to DS in exchange for a 7-year note paying interest at 8 percent per annum.

(ii) Because FP has the effective right to force payment of the "interest" on the perpetual subordinated debt, the instrument constitutes a financing transaction within the meaning of paragraph (a)(2)(ii)(A)(2) of this section. Moreover, because the note between FX and DS is a financing transaction within the meaning of paragraph (a)(2)(ii)(A)(1) of this section, together the transactions are a financing arrangement within the meaning of (a)(2)(i) of this section. Without regard to this section, 90 percent of each interest payment received by FX would be treated as exempt from U.S. withholding tax because it is beneficially owned by G, while 10 percent would be subject to a 30 percent withholding tax because beneficially owned by FP. If FP held directly the note issued by DS, 100 percent of the interest payments on the note would have been subject to the 30 percent withholding tax. The significant reduction in the tax imposed by section 881 resulting from the participation of FX in the financing arrangement is evidence that the participation of FX in the financing arrangement is pursuant to a tax avoidance plan. However, other facts relevant to the presence of such a plan must also be taken into account.

Example 16. Time period between transactions. (i) On January 1, 1995, FP lends $10,000,000 to FS in exchange for a 10-year note that pays no interest annually. When the note matures, FS is obligated to pay $24,000,000 to FP. On January 1, 1996, FS lends $10,000,000 to DS in exchange for a 10-year note that pays interest annually at a rate of 10 percent per annum.

(ii) The FS note held by FP and the DS note held by FS are financing transactions within the meaning of paragraph (a)(2)(ii)(A)(1) of this section and together constitute a financing arrangement within the meaning of (a)(2)(i) of this section. Pursuant to paragraph (b)(2)(iii) of this section, the short period of time (twelve months) between the loan by FP to FS and the loan by FS to DS is evidence that the participation of FS in the financing arrangement is pursuant to a tax avoidance plan. However, other facts relevant to the presence of such a plan must also be taken into account.

Example 17. Financing transactions in the ordinary course of business. (i) FP is a holding company. FS is actively engaged in country T in the business of manufacturing and selling product A. DS manufactures product B, a principal component in which is product A. FS' business activity is substantial. On January 1, 1995, FP lends $100,000,000 to FS to finance FS' business operations. On January 1, 1996, FS ships $30,000,000 of product A to DS. In return, FS creates an interest-bearing account receivable on its books. FS' shipment is in the ordinary course of the active conduct of its trade or business (which is complementary to DS' trade or business.)

(ii) The loan from FP to FS and the accounts receivable opened by FS for a payment owed by DS are financing transactions within the meaning of paragraph (a)(2)(ii)(A)(1) of this section and together constitute a financing arrangement within the meaning of paragraph (a)(2)(i) of this section. Pursuant to paragraph (b)(2)(iv) of this section, the fact that DS' liability to FS is created in the ordinary course of the active conduct of DS' trade or business that is complementary to a business actively engaged in by DS is evidence that the participation of FS in the financing arrangement is not pursuant to a tax avoidance plan. However, other facts relevant to the presence of such a plan must also be taken into account.

Example 18. Tax avoidance plan—other factors. (i) On February 1, 1995, FP issues debt in Country N that is in registered form within the meaning of section 881(c)(3)(A). The FP debt would satisfy the requirements of section 881(c) if the debt were issued by a U.S. person and the withholding agent received the certification required by section 871(h)(2)(B)(ii). The purchasers of the debt are financial institutions and there is no reason to believe that they would not furnish Forms W-8. On March 1, 1995, FP lends a portion of the proceeds of the offering to DS.

(ii) The FP debt and the loan to DS are financing transactions within the meaning of paragraph (a)(2)(ii)(A)(*1*) of this section and together constitute a financing arrangement within the meaning of paragraph (a)(2)(i) of this section. The owners of the FP debt are the financing entities, FP is the intermediate entity and DS is the financed entity. Interest payments on the debt issued by FP would be subject to withholding tax if the debt were issued by DS, unless DS received all necessary Forms W-8. Therefore, the participation of FP in the financing arrangement potentially reduces the tax imposed by section 881(a). However, because it is reasonable to assume that the purchasers of the FP debt would have provided certifications in order to avoid the withholding tax imposed by section 881, there is not a tax avoidance plan. Accordingly, FP is not a conduit entity.

Example 19. Tax avoidance plan—other factors. (i) Over a period of years, FP has maintained a deposit with BK, a bank organized in the United States, that is unrelated to FP and its subsidiaries. FP often sells goods and purchases raw materials in the United States. FP opened the bank account with BK in order to facilitate this business and the amounts it maintains in the account are reasonably related to its dollar-denominated working capital needs. On January 1, 1995, BK lends $5,000,000 to DS. After the loan is made, the balance in FP's bank account remains within a range appropriate to meet FP's working capital needs.

(ii) FP's deposit with BK and BK's loan to DS are financing transactions within the meaning of paragraph (a)(2)(ii)(A)(*1*) of this section and together constitute a financing arrangement within the meaning of paragraph (a)(2)(i) of this section. Pursuant to section 881(i), interest paid by BK to FP with respect to the bank deposit is exempt from withholding tax. Interest paid directly by DS to FP would not be exempt from withholding tax under section 881(i) and therefore would be subject to a 30% withholding tax. Accordingly, there is a significant reduction in the tax imposed by section 881, which is evidence of the existence of a tax avoidance plan. See paragraph (b)(2)(i) of this section. However, the district director also will consider the fact that FP historically has maintained an account with BK to meet its working capital needs and that, prior to and after BK's loan to DS, the balance within the account remains within a range appropriate to meet those business needs as evidence that the participation of BK in the FP-BK-DS financing arrangement is not pursuant to a tax avoidance plan. In determining the presence or absence of a tax avoidance plan, all relevant facts will be taken into account.

Example 20. Tax avoidance plan—other factors. (i) Assume the same facts as in *Example 19,* except that on January 1, 2000, FP's deposit with BK substantially exceeds FP's expected working capital needs and on January 2, 2000, BK lends additional funds to DS. Assume also that BK's loan to DS provides BK with a right of offset against FP's deposit. Finally, assume that FP would have lent the funds to DS directly but for the imposition of the withholding tax on payments made directly to FP by DS.

(ii) As in *Example 19,* the transactions in paragraph (i) of this *Example 20* are a financing arrangement within the meaning of paragraph (a)(2)(i) and the participation of the BK reduces the section 881 tax. In this case, the presence of funds substantially in excess of FP's working capital needs and the fact that FP would have been willing to lend funds directly to DS if not for the withholding tax are evidence that the participation of BK in the FP-BK-FS financing arrangement is pursuant to a tax avoidance plan. However, other facts relevant to the presence of such a plan must also be taken into account. Even if the district director determines that the participation of BK in the financing arrangement is pursuant to a tax avoidance plan, BK may not be treated as a conduit entity unless BK would not have participated in the financing arrangement on substantially the same terms in the absence of FP's deposit with BK. BK's right of offset against FP's deposit (a form of guarantee of BK's loan to DS) creates a presumption that BK would not have made the loan to DS on substantially the same terms in the absence of FP's deposit with BK. If the taxpayer overcomes the presumption by clear and convincing evidence, BK will not be a conduit entity.

Example 21. Significant financing activities. (i) FS is responsible for coordinating the financing of all of the subsidiaries of FP, which

Reg. §1.881-3(e)

are engaged in substantial trades or businesses and are located in country T, country N, and the United States. FS maintains a centralized cash management accounting system for FP and its subsidiaries in which it records all intercompany payables and receivables; these payables and receivables ultimately are reduced to a single balance either due from or owing to FS and each of FP's subsidiaries. FS is responsible for disbursing or receiving any cash payments required by transactions between its affiliates and unrelated parties. FS must borrow any cash necessary to meet those external obligations and invests any excess cash for the benefit of the FP group. FS enters into interest rate and foreign exchange contracts as necessary to manage the risks arising from mismatches in incoming and outgoing cash flows. The activities of FS are intended (and reasonably can be expected) to reduce transaction costs and overhead and other fixed costs. FS has 50 employees, including clerical and other back office personnel, located in country T. At the request of DS, on January 1, 1995, FS pays a supplier $1,000,000 for materials delivered to DS and charges DS an open account receivable for this amount. On February 3, 1995, FS reverses the account receivable from DS to FS when DS delivers to FP goods with a value of $1,000,000.

(ii) The accounts payable from DS to FS and from FS to other subsidiaries of FP constitute financing transactions within the meaning of paragraph (a)(2)(ii)(A)(*1*) of this section, and the transactions together constitute a financing arrangement within the meaning of paragraph (a)(2)(i) of this section. FS's activities constitute significant financing activities with respect to the financing transactions even though FS did not actively and materially participate in arranging the financing transactions because the financing transactions consisted of trade receivables and trade payables that were ordinary and necessary to carry on the trades or businesses of DS and the other subsidiaries of FP. Accordingly, pursuant to paragraph (b)(3)(i) of this section, FS' participation in the financing arrangement is presumed not to be pursuant to a tax avoidance plan.

Example 22. Significant financing activities—active risk management. (i) The facts are the same as in *Example 21,* except that, in addition to its short-term funding needs, DS needs long-term financing to fund an acquisition of another U.S. company; the acquisition is scheduled to close on January 15, 1995. FS has a revolving credit agreement with a syndicate of banks located in Country N. On January 14, 1995, FS borrows ¥10 billion for 10 years under the revolving credit agreement, paying yen LIBOR plus 50 basis points on a quarterly basis. FS enters into a currency swap with BK, an unrelated bank that is not a member of the syndicate, under which FS will pay BK ¥10 billion and will receive $100 million on January 15, 1995; these payments will be reversed on January 15, 2004. FS will pay BK U.S. dollar LIBOR plus 50 basis points on a notional principal amount of $100 million semi-annually and will receive yen LIBOR plus 50 basis points on a notional principal amount of ¥10 billion quarterly. Upon the closing of the acquisition on January 15, 1995, DS borrows $100 million from FS for 10 years, paying U.S. dollar LIBOR plus 50 basis points semiannually.

(ii) Although FS performs significant financing activities with respect to certain financing transactions to which it is a party, FS does not perform significant financing activities with respect to the financing transactions between FS and the syndicate of banks and between FS and DS because FS has eliminated all material market risks arising from those financing transactions through its currency swap with BK. Accordingly, the financing arrangement does not benefit from the presumption of paragraph (b)(3)(i) of this section and the district director must determine whether the participation of FS in the financing arrangement is pursuant to a tax avoidance plan on the basis of all the facts and circumstances. However, if additional facts indicated that FS reviews its currency swaps daily to determine whether they are the most cost efficient way of managing their currency risk and, as a result, frequently terminates swaps in favor of entering into more cost efficient hedging arrangements with unrelated parties, FS would be considered to perform significant financing activities and FS' participation in the financing arrangements would not be pursuant to a tax avoidance plan.

Example 23. Significant financing activities— presumption rebutted. (i) The facts are the same as in *Example 21,* except that, on January 1, 1995, FP lends to FS DM 15,000,000 (worth $10,000,000) in exchange for a 10 year note that pays interest annually at a rate of 5 percent per annum. Also, on March 15, 1995, FS lends $10,000,000 to DS in exchange for a 10-year note that pays interest annually at a rate of 8 percent per annum. FS would not have had sufficient funds to make the loan to DS without the loan from FP. FS does not enter into any long-term hedging transaction with respect to these financing transactions, but manages the interest rate and currency risk arising from the transactions on a daily, weekly or quarterly basis by entering into forward currency contracts.

(ii) Because FS performs significant financing activities with respect to the financing transactions between FS, DS and FP, the participation of FS in the financing arrangement is presumed not to be pursuant to a tax avoidance plan. The district director may rebut this presumption by establishing that the participation of FS is pursuant to a tax avoidance plan, based on all the facts and circumstances. The mere fact that FS is a resident of country T is not sufficient to establish the existence of a tax avoidance plan. However, the existence of a plan can be inferred from other factors in addition to the fact that FS is a resident of country T. For example, the loans are made within a short time period and FS would not have been able to make the loan to DS without the loan from FP.

Example 24. Determination of amount of tax liability. (i) On January 1, 1996, FP makes two three-year installment loans of $250,000 each to FS that pay interest at a rate of 9 percent per annum. The loans are self-amortizing with payments on each loan of $7,950 per month. On the same date, FS lends $1,000,000 to DS in exchange for a two-year note that pays interest semi-annually at a rate of 10 percent per annum, beginning on June 30, 1996. The FS-DS loan is not self-amortizing. Assume that for the period of January 1, 1996 through June 30, 1996, the average principal amount of the financing transactions between FP and FS that comprise the financing arrangement is $469,319. Further, assume that for the period of July 1, 1996 through December 31, 1996, the average principal amount of the financing transactions between FP and FS is $393,632. The average principal amount of the financing transaction between FS and DS for the same periods is $1,000,000. The district director determines that the financing transactions between FP and FS, and FS and DS, are a conduit financing arrangement.

(ii) Pursuant to paragraph (d)(1)(i) of this section, the portion of the $50,000 interest payment made by DS to FS on June 30, 1996, that is recharacterized as a payment to FP is $23,450 computed as follows: ($50,000 × $469,319/$1,000,000) = $23,450. The portion of the interest payment made on December 31, 1996 that is recharacterized as a payment to FP is $19,650, computed as follows: ($50,000 × $393,632/$1,000,000) = $19,650. Furthermore, under § 1.1441-3(j), DS is liable for withholding tax at a 30 percent rate on the portion of the $50,000 payment to FS that is recharacterized as a payment to FP, i.e., $7,035 with respect to the June 30, 1996 payment and $5,895 with respect to the December 31, 1996 payment.

Example 25. Determination of principal amount. (i) FP lends DM 5,000,000 to FS in exchange for a ten year note that pays interest semi-annually at a rate of 8 percent per annum. Six months later, pursuant to a tax avoidance plan, FS lends DM 10,000,000 to DS in exchange for a 10 year note that pays interest semi-annually at a rate of 10 percent per annum. At the time FP make its loan to FS, the exchange rate is DM 1.5/$1. At the time FS makes its loan to DS the exchange rate is DM 1.4/$1.

(ii) FP's loan to FS and FS' loan to DS are financing transactions and together constitute a financing arrangement. Furthermore, because the participation of FS reduces the tax imposed under section 881 and FS' participation is pursuant to a tax avoidance plan, the financing arrangement is a conduit financing arrangement.

(iii) Pursuant to paragraph (d)(1)(i) of this section, the amount subject to recharacterization is a fraction the numerator of which is the lowest aggregate principal amount advanced and the denominator of which is the principal amount advanced from FS to DS. Because the property advanced in these financing transactions is the same type of fungible property, under paragraph (d)(1)(ii)(A) of this section, both are valued on the date of the last financing transaction. Accordingly, the portion of the payments of interest that is recharacterized is ((DM 5,000,000 × DM 1.4/$1)/(DM 10,000,000 × DM 1.4/$1) or 0.5.

(f) *Effective date.*—This section is effective for payments made by financed entities on or after September 11, 1995. This section shall not apply to interest payments covered by section 127(g)(3) of the Tax Reform Act of 1984, and to interest payments with respect to other debt obligations issued prior to October 15, 1984 (whether or not such debt was issued by a Netherlands Antilles corporation). [Reg. § 1.881-3.]

☐ [*T.D.* 8611, 8-10-95.]

§ 1.881-4. Recordkeeping requirements concerning conduit financing arrangements.—(a) *Scope.*—This section provides rules for the maintenance of records concerning certain financing arrangements to which the provisions of § 1.881-3 apply.

(b) *Recordkeeping requirements.*—(1) *In general.*—Any person subject to the general recordkeeping requirements of section 6001 must keep the permanent books of account or records, as required by section 6001, that may be relevant to determining whether that person is a party to a financing arrangement and whether that financing arrangement is a conduit financing arrangement.

(2) *Application of Sections 6038 and 6038A.*—A financed entity that is a reporting corporation within the meaning of section 6038A(a) and the regulations under that section, and any other person that is subject to the recordkeeping requirements of § 1.6038A-3, must comply with those recordkeeping require-

ments with respect to records that may be relevant to determining whether the financed entity is a party to a financing arrangement and whether that financing arrangement is a conduit financing arrangement. Such records, including records that a person is required to maintain pursuant to paragraph (c) of this section, shall be considered records that are required to be maintained pursuant to section 6038 or 6038A. Accordingly, the provisions of sections 6038 and 6038A (including, without limitation, the penalty provisions thereof), and the regulations under those sections, shall apply to any records required to be maintained pursuant to this section.

(c) *Records to be maintained.*—(1) *In general.*—An entity described in paragraph (b) of this section shall be required to retain any records containing the following information concerning each financing transaction that the entity knows or has reason to know comprises the financing arrangement—

(i) The nature (e.g., loan, stock, lease, license) of each financing transaction;

(ii) The name, address, taxpayer identification number (if any) and country of residence of—

(A) Each person that advanced money or other property, or granted rights to use property;

(B) Each person that was the recipient of the advance or rights; and

(C) Each person to whom a payment was made pursuant to the financing transaction (to the extent that person is a different person than the person who made the advance or granted the rights);

(iii) The date and amount of—

(A) Each advance of money or other property or grant of rights; and

(B) Each payment made in return for the advance or grant of rights;

(iv) The terms of any guarantee provided in conjunction with a financing transaction, including the name of the guarantor; and

(v) In cases where one or both of the parties to a financing transaction are related to each other or another entity in the financing arrangement, the manner in which these persons are related.

(2) *Additional documents.*—An entity described in paragraph (b) of this section must also retain all records relating to the circumstances surrounding its participation in the financing transactions and financing arrangements. Such documents may include, but are not limited to—

(i) Minutes of board of directors meetings;

(ii) Board resolutions or other authorizations for the financing transactions;

(iii) Private letter rulings;

(iv) Financial reports (audited or unaudited);

(v) Notes to financial statements;

(vi) Bank statements;

(vii) Copies of wire transfers;

(viii) Offering documents;

(ix) Materials from investment advisors, bankers and tax advisors; and

(x) Evidences of indebtedness.

(3) *Effect of record maintenance requirement.*—Record maintenance in accordance with paragraph (b) of this section generally does not require the original creation of records that are ordinarily not created by affected entities. If, however, a document that is actually created is described in this paragraph (c), it is to be retained even if the document is not of a type ordinarily created by the affected entity.

(d) *Effective date.*—This section is effective September 11, 1995. This section shall not apply to interest payments covered by section 127(g)(3) of the Tax Reform Act of 1984, and to interest payments with respect to other debt obligations issued prior to October 15, 1984 (whether or not such debt was issued by a Netherlands Antilles corporation). [Reg. § 1.881-4.]

☐ [*T.D.* 8611, 8-10-95].

§ 1.882-1. Taxation of foreign corporations engaged in U.S. business or of foreign corporations treated as having effectively connected income.—(a) *Segregation of income.*—This section applies for purposes of determining the tax of a foreign corporation which at any time during the taxable year is engaged in trade or business in the United States. It also applies for purposes of determining the tax of a foreign corporation which at no time during the taxable year is engaged in trade or business in the United States but has for the taxable year real property income or interest on obligations of the United States which, by reason of section 882(d) or (e) and § 1.882-2, is treated as effectively connected for the taxable year with the conduct of a trade or business in the United States by that corporation. A foreign corporation to which this section applies must segregate its gross income for the taxable year into two categories, namely, the income which is effectively connected for the taxable year with the conduct of a trade or business in the United States by that corporation and the income which is not effectively connected for the taxable year with the conduct of a trade or business in the United

States by that corporation. A separate tax shall then be determined upon each such category of income, as provided in paragraph (b) of this section. The determination of whether income or gain is or is not effectively connected for the taxable year with the conduct of a trade or business in the United States by the foreign corporation shall be made in accordance with section 864(c) and §§ 1.864-3 through 1.864-7. For purposes of this section income which is effectively connected for the taxable year with the conduct of a trade or business in the United States includes all income which is treated under section 882(d) or (e) and § 1.882-2 as income which is effectively connected for the taxable year with the conduct of a trade or business in the United States by the foreign corporation.

(b) *Imposition of tax.*—(1) *Income not effectively connected with the conduct of a trade or business in the United States.*—If a foreign corporation to which this section applies derives during the taxable year from sources within the United States income or gains described in section 881(a) and paragraph (b) or (c) of § 1.881-2 which are not effectively connected for the taxable year with the conduct of a trade or business in the United States by that corporation, such income or gains shall be subject to a flat tax of 30 percent of the aggregate amount of such items. This tax shall be determined in the manner, and subject to the same conditions, set forth in § 1.881-2 as though the income or gains were derived by a foreign corporation not engaged in trade or business in the United States during the taxable year, except that in applying paragraph (c) of such section there shall not be taken into account any gains which are taken into account in determining the tax under section 882(a)(1) and subparagraph (2) of this paragraph.

(2) *Income effectively connected with the conduct of a trade or business in the United States.*—(i) *In general.*—If a foreign corporation to which this section applies derives income or gains which are effectively connected for the taxable year with the conduct of a trade or business in the United States by that corporation, the taxable income or gains shall, except as provided in § 1.871-12, be taxed in accordance with section 11 or, in the alternative, section 1201(a). See sections 11(f) and 882(a)(1). Any income of the foreign corporation which is not effectively connected for the taxable year with the conduct of a trade or business in the United States by that corporation shall not be taken into account in determining either the rate or amount of such tax.

(ii) *Determination of taxable income.*—The taxable income for any taxable year for purposes of this subparagraph consists only of the foreign corporation's taxable income which is effectively connected for the taxable year with the conduct of a trade or business in the United States by that corporation; and, for this purpose, it is immaterial that the trade or business with which that income is effectively connected is not the same as the trade or business carried on in the United States by that corporation during the taxable year. See example (2) in § 1.864-4(b). In determining such taxable income all amounts constituting, or considered to be, gains or losses for the taxable year from the sale or exchange of capital assets shall be taken into account if such gains or losses are effectively connected for the taxable year with the conduct of a trade or business in the United States by that corporation.

(iii) *Cross references.*—For rules for determining the gross income and deductions for the taxable year, see section 882(b) and (c)(1) and the regulations thereunder.

(c) *Change in trade or business status.*—The principles of paragraph (c) of § 1.871-8 shall apply to cases where there has been a change in the trade or business status of a foreign corporation.

(d) *Credits against tax.*—The credits allowed by section 32 (relating to tax withheld at source on foreign corporations), section 33 (relating to the foreign tax credit), section 38 (relating to investment in certain depreciable property), section 39 (relating to certain uses of gasoline and lubricating oil), section 40 (relating to expenses of work incentive programs), and section 6042 (relating to overpayments of a tax) shall be allowed against the tax determined in accordance with this section. However, the credits allowed by sections 33, 38, and 40 shall not be allowed against the flat tax of 30 percent imposed by section 881(a) and paragraph (b)(1) of this section. For special rules applicable in determining the foreign tax credit, see section 906(b) and the regulations thereunder. For the disallowance of certain credits where a return is not filed for the taxable year see section 882(c)(2) and the regulations thereunder.

(e) *Payment of estimated tax.*—Every foreign corporation which for the taxable year is subject to tax under section 11 or 1201(a) and this section must make payment of its estimated tax in accordance with section 6154 and the regulations thereunder. In determining the amount of the estimated tax the foreign corporation must treat the tax imposed by section 881(a) and paragraph (b)(1) of this section as though it were a tax imposed by section 11.

Reg. § 1.882-1(e)

(f) *Effective date.*—This section applies for taxable years beginning after December 31, 1966. For corresponding rules applicable to taxable years beginning before January 1, 1967, see 26 CFR 1.882-1 (Rev. as of Jan. 1, 1971). [Reg. § 1.882-1.]

☐ [*T.D.* 6258, 10-23-57. *Amended by T.D.* 7244, 12-29-72 *and T.D.* 7293, 11-27-73.]

§ 1.882-2. Income of foreign corporation treated as effectively connected with U.S. business.—(a) *Election as to real property income.*—A foreign corporation which during the taxable year derives any income from real property which is located in the United States, or derives income from any interest in any such real property, may elect, pursuant to section 882(d) and § 1.871-10, to treat all such income as income which is effectively connected for the taxable year with the conduct of a trade or business in the United States by that corporation. The election may be made whether or not the foreign corporation is engaged in trade or business in the United States during the taxable year for which the election is made or whether or not the corporation has income from real property which for the taxable year is effectively connected with the conduct of a trade or business in the United States, but it may be made only with respect to income from sources within the United States which, without regard to section 882(d) and § 1.871-10, is not effectively connected for the taxable year with the conduct of a trade or business in the United States by that corporation. The income to which the election applies shall be determined as provided in paragraph (b) of § 1.871-10 and shall be subject to tax in the manner, and subject to the same conditions, provided by section 882(a)(1) and paragraph (b)(2) of § 1.882-1. Section 871(d)(2) and (3) and the provisions of § 1.871-10 thereunder shall apply in respect of an election under section 882(d) in the same manner and to the same extent as they apply in respect of elections under section 871(d).

(b) *Interest on U.S. obligations received by banks organized in possessions.*—Interest received from sources within the United States during the taxable year on obligations of the United States by a foreign corporation created or organized in, or under the law of, a possession of the United States and carrying on the banking business in a possession of the United States during the taxable year shall be treated, pursuant to section 882(e) and this paragraph, as income which is effectively connected for the taxable year with the conduct of a trade or business in the United States by that corporation. This paragraph applies whether or not the foreign corporation is engaged in trade or business in the United States at any time during the taxable year but only with respect to income which, without regard to this paragraph, is not effectively connected for the taxable year with the conduct of a trade or business in the United States by that corporation. Any interest to which this paragraph applies shall be subject to tax in the manner, and subject to the same conditions, provided by section 882(a)(1) and paragraph (b)(2) of § 1.882-1. To the extent that deductions are connected with interest to which this paragraph applies, they shall be treated for purposes of section 882(c)(1) and the regulations thereunder as connected with income which is effectively connected for the taxable year with the conduct of a trade or business in the United States by the foreign corporation. An election by the taxpayer is not required in respect of the income to which this paragraph applies. For purposes of this paragraph the term "possession of the United States" includes Guam, the Midway Islands, the Panama Canal Zone, the Commonwealth of Puerto Rico, American Samoa, the Virgin Islands, and Wake Island.

(c) *Treatment of income.*—Any income in respect of which an election described in paragraph (a) of this section is in effect, and any interest to which paragraph (b) of this section applies, shall be treated, for purposes of paragraph (b)(2) of § 1.882-1 and paragraph (a) of § 1.441-4, as income which is effectively connected for the taxable year with the conduct of a trade or business in the United States by the foreign corporation. A foreign corporation shall not be treated as being engaged in trade or business in the United States merely by reason of having such income for the taxable year.

(d) *Effective date.*—This section applies for taxable years beginning after December 31, 1966. There are no corresponding rules in this part for taxable years beginning before January 1, 1967. [Reg. § 1.882-2.]

☐ [*T.D.* 6258, 10-23-57. *Amended by T.D.* 7293, 11-27-73.]

§ 1.882-3. Gross income of a foreign corporation.—(a) *In general.*—(1) *Inclusions.*—The gross income of a foreign corporation for any taxable year includes only (i) the gross income which is derived from sources within the United States and which is not effectively connected for the taxable year with the conduct of a trade or business in the United States by that corporation, and (ii) the gross income, irrespective of whether such income is derived from sources within or without the United States, which is effectively connected for the taxable year with the conduct of a trade or business in the United States by that corporation. For the determination of the sources of income, see sections 861 through 863, and the regulations thereunder. For the determination of whether income from sources within or without the United States is effectively connected for the taxable year with the conduct of a trade or business in the United States, see sections 864(c) and 882(d) and (e), §§ 1.864-3 through 1.864-7, and § 1.882-2.

(2) *Exchange transactions.*—Even though a foreign corporation which effects certain transactions in the United States in stocks, securities, or commodities during the taxable year may not, by reason of section 864(b)(2) and paragraph (c) or (d) of § 1.864-2, be engaged in trade or business in the United States during the taxable year through the effecting of such transactions, nevertheless it shall be required to include in gross income for the taxable year the gains and profits from those transactions to the extent required by paragraph (c) of § 1.881-2 or by paragraph (a) of § 1.882-1.

(3) *Exclusions.*—For exclusions from gross income of a foreign corporation, see § 1.883-1.

(b) *Foreign corporations not engaged in U.S. business.*—In the case of a foreign corporation which at no time during the taxable year is engaged in trade or business in the United States the gross income shall include only (1) the gross income from sources within the United States which is described in section 881(a) and paragraphs (b) and (c) of § 1.881-2, and (2) the gross income from sources within the United States which, by reason of section 882(d) or (e) and § 1.882-2, is treated as effectively connected for the taxable year with the conduct of a trade or business in the United States by that corporation.

(c) *Foreign corporations engaged in U.S. business.*—In the case of a foreign corporation which is engaged in trade or business in the United States at any time during the taxable year, the gross income shall include (1) the gross income from sources within and without the United States which is effectively connected for the taxable year with the conduct of a trade or business in the United States by that corporation, (2) the gross income from sources within the United States which, by reason of section 882(d) or (e) and § 1.882-2, is treated as effectively connected for the taxable year with the conduct of a trade or business in the United States by that corporation, and (3) the gross income from sources within the United States which is described in section 881(a) and paragraphs (b) and (c) of § 1.881-2 and is not effectively connected for the taxable year with the conduct of a trade or business in the United States by that corporation.

(d) *Effective date.*—This section applies for taxable years beginning after December 31, 1966. For corresponding rules applicable to taxable years beginning before January 1, 1967, see 26 CFR 1.882-2 (Rev. as of Jan. 1, 1971). [Reg. § 1.882-3.]

☐ [*T.D.* 6258, 10-23-57. *Amended by T.D.* 7293, 11-27-73.]

§ 1.882-4. Allowance of deductions and credits to foreign corporations.—(a) *Foreign corporations.*—(1) *In general.*—A foreign corporation that is engaged in, or receives income treated as effectively connected with, a trade or business within the United States is allowed the deductions which are properly allocated and apportioned to the foreign corporation's gross income which is effectively connected, or treated as effectively connected, with its conduct of a trade or business within the United States. The foreign corporation is entitled to credits which are attributable to that effectively connected income. No provision of this section (other than paragraph (b)(2)) shall be construed to deny the credits provided by sections 33, 34 and 852(b)(3)(D)(ii) or the deduction allowed by section 170.

(2) *Return necessary.*—A foreign corporation shall receive the benefit of the deductions and credits otherwise allowed to it with respect to the income tax, only if it timely files or causes to be filed with the Philadelphia Service Center, in the manner prescribed in subtitle F, a true and accurate return of its taxable income which is effectively connected, or treated as effectively connected, for the taxable year with the conduct of a trade or business in the United States by that corporation. The deductions and credits allowed such a corporation electing under a tax convention to be subject to tax on a net basis may be obtained by filing a return of income in the manner prescribed in the regulations (if any) under the tax convention or under any other guidance issued by the Commissioner.

(3) *Filing deadline for return.*—(i) As provided in paragraph (a)(2) of this section, for purposes of computing the foreign corporation's taxable income for any taxable year, otherwise allowable deductions (other than that allowed by section 170) and credits (other than those allowed by sections 33, 34 and 852(b)(3)(D)(ii)) will be allowed only if a return for that taxable year is filed by the foreign corporation on a timely basis. For taxable years of a foreign corporation ending after July 31, 1990, whether a return for the current taxable year has been filed on a timely basis is dependent upon whether the foreign corporation filed a return for the taxable year immediately pre-

ceding the current taxable year. If a return was filed for that immediately preceding taxable year, or if the current taxable year is the first taxable year of the foreign corporation for which a return is required to be filed, the required return for the current taxable year must be filed within 18 months of the due date as set forth in section 6072 and the regulations under that section, for filing the return for the current taxable year. If no return for the taxable year immediately preceding the current taxable year has been filed, the required return for the current taxable year (other than the first taxable year of the foreign corporation for which a return is required to be filed) must have been filed no later than the earlier of the date which is 18 months after the due date, as set forth in section 6072, for filing the return for the current taxable year or the date the Internal Revenue Service mails a notice to the foreign corporation advising the corporation that the current year tax return has not been filed and that no deductions (other than that allowed under section 170) or credits (other than those allowed under sections 33, 34 and 852(b)(3)(D)(ii)) may be claimed by the taxpayer.

(ii) The filing deadlines set forth in paragraph (a)(3)(i) of this section may be waived if the foreign corporation establishes to the satisfaction of the Commissioner or his or her delegate that the corporation, based on the facts and circumstances, acted reasonably and in good faith in failing to file a U.S. income tax return (including a protective return (as described in paragraph (a)(3)(vi) of this section)). For this purpose, a foreign corporation shall not be considered to have acted reasonably and in good faith if it knew that it was required to file the return and chose not to do so. In addition, a foreign corporation shall not be granted a waiver unless it cooperates in the process of determining its income tax liability for the taxable year for which the return was not filed. The Commissioner or his or her delegate shall consider the following factors in determining whether the foreign corporation, based on the facts and circumstances, acted reasonably and in good faith in failing to file a U.S. income tax return—

(A) Whether the corporation voluntarily identifies itself to the Internal Revenue Service as having failed to file a U.S. income tax return before the Internal Revenue Service discovers the failure to file;

(B) Whether the corporation did not become aware of its ability to file a protective return (as described in paragraph (a)(3)(vi) of this section) by the deadline for filing a protective return;

(C) Whether the corporation had not previously filed a U.S. income tax return;

(D) Whether the corporation failed to file a U.S. income tax return because, after exercising reasonable diligence (taking into account its relevant experience and level of sophistication), the corporation was unaware of the necessity for filing the return;

(E) Whether the corporation failed to file a U.S. income tax return because of intervening events beyond its control; and

(F) Whether other mitigating or exacerbating factors existed.

(iii) The following examples illustrate the provisions of this section. In all examples, FC is a foreign corporation and uses the calendar year as its taxable year. The examples are as follows:

Example 1. Foreign corporation discloses own failure to file. In Year 1, FC became a limited partner with a passive investment in a U.S. limited partnership that was engaged in a U.S. trade or business. During Year 1 through Year 4, FC incurred losses with respect to its U.S. partnership interest. FC's foreign tax director incorrectly concluded that because it was a limited partner and had only losses from its partnership interest, FC was not required to file a U.S. income tax return. FC's management was aware neither of FC's obligation to file a U.S. income tax return for those years, nor of its ability to file a protective return for those years. FC had never filed a U.S. income tax return before. In Year 5, FC began realizing a profit rather than a loss with respect to its partnership interest and, for this reason, engaged a U.S. tax advisor to handle its responsibility to file U.S. income tax returns. In preparing FC's income tax return for Year 5, FC's U.S. tax advisor discovered that returns were not filed for Year 1 through Year 4. Therefore, with respect to those years for which applicable filing deadlines in paragraph (a)(3)(i) of this section were not met, FC would be barred by paragraph (a)(2) of this section from claiming any deductions that otherwise would have given rise to net operating losses on returns for those years, and that would have been available as loss carryforwards in subsequent years. At FC's direction, its U.S. tax advisor promptly contacted the appropriate examining personnel and cooperated with the Internal Revenue Service in determining FC's income tax liability, for example, by preparing and filing the appropriate income tax returns for Year 1 through Year 4 and by making FC's books and records available to an Internal Revenue Service examiner. FC has met the standard described in paragraph (a)(3)(ii) of this section for waiver of any applicable filing deadlines in paragraph (a)(3)(i) of this section.

Example 2. Foreign corporation refuses to cooperate. Same facts as in *Example 1*, except that while FC's U.S. tax advisor contacted the appropriate examining personnel and filed the appropriate income tax returns for Year 1 through Year 4, FC refused all requests by the Internal Revenue Service to provide supporting information (for example, books and records) with respect to those returns. Because FC did not cooperate in determining its U.S. tax liability for the taxable years for which an income tax return was not timely filed, FC is not granted a waiver as described in paragraph (a)(3)(ii) of this section of any applicable filing deadlines in paragraph (a)(3)(i) of this section.

Example 3. Foreign corporation fails to file a protective return. Same facts as in *Example 1*, except that in Year 1 through Year 4, FC's tax director also consulted a U.S. tax advisor, who advised FC's tax director that it was uncertain whether U.S. income tax returns were necessary for those years and that FC could protect its right subsequently to claim the loss carryforwards by filing protective returns under paragraph (a)(3)(vi) of this section. FC did not file U.S. income tax returns or protective returns for those years. FC did not present evidence that intervening events beyond FC's control prevented it from filing an income tax return, and there were no other mitigating factors. FC has not met the standard described in paragraph (a)(3)(ii) of this section for waiver of any applicable filing deadlines in paragraph (a)(3)(i) of this section.

Example 4. Foreign corporation with effectively connected income. In Year 1, FC, a technology company, opened an office in the United States to market and sell a software program that FC had developed outside the United States. FC had minimal business or tax experience internationally, and no such experience in the United States. Through FC's direct efforts, U.S. sales of the software produced income effectively connected with a U.S. trade or business. FC, however, did not file U.S. income tax returns for Year 1 or Year 2. FC's management was aware neither of FC's obligation to file a U.S. income tax return for those years, nor of its ability to file a protective return for those years. FC had never filed a U.S. income tax return before. In January of Year 4, FC engaged U.S. counsel in connection with licensing software to an unrelated U.S. company. U.S. counsel reviewed FC's U.S. activities and advised FC that it should have filed U.S. income tax returns for Year 1 and Year 2. FC immediately engaged a U.S. tax advisor who, at FC's direction, promptly contacted the appropriate examining personnel and cooperated with the Internal Revenue Service in determining FC's income tax liability, for example, by preparing and filing the appropriate income tax returns for Year 1 and Year 2 and by making FC's books and records available to an Internal Revenue Service examiner. FC has met the standard described in paragraph (a)(3)(ii) of this section for waiver of any applicable filing deadlines in paragraph (a)(3)(i) of this section.

Example 5. IRS discovers foreign corporation's failure to file. In Year 1, FC, a technology company, opened an office in the United States to market and sell a software program that FC had developed outside the United States. Through FC's direct efforts, U.S. sales of the software produced income effectively connected with a U.S. trade or business. FC had extensive experience conducting similar business activities in other countries, including making the appropriate tax filings. However, FC's management was aware neither of FC's obligation to file a U.S. income tax return for those years, nor of its ability to file a protective return for those years. FC had never filed a U.S. income tax return before. Despite FC's extensive experience conducting similar business activities in other countries, it made no effort to seek advice in connection with its U.S. tax obligations. FC failed to file either U.S. income tax returns or protective returns for Year 1 and Year 2. In January of Year 4, an Internal Revenue Service examiner asked FC for an explanation of FC's failure to file U.S. income tax returns. FC immediately engaged a U.S. tax advisor, and cooperated with the Internal Revenue Service in determining FC's income tax liability, for example, by preparing and filing the appropriate income tax returns for Year 1 and Year 2 and by making FC's books and records available to the examiner. FC did not present evidence that intervening events beyond its control prevented it from filing a return, and there were no other mitigating factors. FC has not met the standard described in paragraph (a)(3)(ii) of this section for waiver of any applicable filing deadlines in paragraph (a)(3)(i) of this section.

Example 6. Foreign corporation with prior filing history. FC began a U.S. trade or business in Year 1. FC's tax advisor filed the appropriate U.S. income tax returns for Year 1 through Year 6, reporting income effectively connected with FC's U.S. trade or business. In Year 7, FC replaced its tax advisor with a tax advisor unfamiliar with U.S. tax law. FC did not file a U.S. income tax return for any year from Year 7 through Year 10, although it had effectively connected income for those years. FC's management was aware of FC's ability to file a protective return for those years. In Year 11, an Internal Revenue Service examiner contacted FC and asked its chief financial officer for an explanation of FC's failure to file U.S. income tax returns after Year 6. FC immediately engaged a U.S. tax advisor and cooperated with the Internal Revenue Service in determining FC's income tax liability, for example, by preparing and filing the appropriate income tax returns for Year 7 through Year 10 and by making FC's books and records available to the examiner. FC did not present evidence that intervening events beyond its control prevented it from filing a return, and there were no other mitigating factors. FC has not met the standard described in paragraph (a)(3)(ii) of this section for waiver of any applicable filing deadlines in paragraph (a)(3)(i) of this section.

(iv) Paragraphs (a)(3)(ii) and (iii) of this section are applicable to open years for which a request for a waiver is filed on or after January 29, 2002.

(v) A foreign corporation which has a permanent establishment, as defined in an income tax treaty between the United States and the foreign corporation's country of residence, in the United States is subject to the filing deadlines set forth in paragraph (a)(3)(i) of this section.

(vi) If a foreign corporation conducts limited activities in the United States in a taxable year which the foreign corporation determines does not give rise to gross income which is effectively connected with the conduct of a trade or business within the United States as defined in sections 882(b) and 864(b) and (c) and the regulations under those sections, the foreign corporation may nonetheless file a return for that taxable year on a timely basis under paragraph (a)(3)(i) of this section and thereby protect the right to receive the benefit of the deductions and credits attributable to that gross income if it is later determined, after the return was filed, that the original determination was incorrect. On that timely filed return, the foreign corporation is not required to report any gross income as effectively connected with a United States trade or business or any deductions or credits but should attach a statement indicating that the return is being filed for the reason set forth in this paragraph (a)(3). If the foreign corporation determines that part of the activities which it conducts in the United States in a taxable year gives rise to gross income which is effectively connected with the conduct of a trade or business and part does not, the foreign corporation must timely file a return for that taxable year to report the gross income determined to be effectively connected, or treated as effectively connected, with the conduct of the trade or business within the United States and the deductions and credits attributable to the gross income. In addition, the foreign corporation should attach to that return the statement described in this paragraph (b)(3) with regard to the other activities. The foreign corporation may follow the same procedure if it determines initially that it has no United States tax liability under the provisions of an applicable income tax treaty. In the event the foreign corporation relies on the provisions of an income tax treaty to reduce or eliminate the income subject to taxation, or to reduce the rate of tax, disclosure may be required pursuant to section 6114.

(vii) In order to be eligible for any deductions and credits for purposes of computing the accumulated earnings tax of section 531, a foreign corporation must file a true and accurate return; on a timely basis, in the manner as set forth in paragraph (a)(2) and (3) of this section.

(4) *Return by Internal Revenue Service.*—If a foreign corporation has various sources of income within the United States and a return of income has not been filed, in the manner prescribed by subtitle F, including the filing deadlines set forth in paragraph (a)(3) of this section, the Internal Revenue Service shall:

(i) Cause a return of income to be made,

(ii) Include on the return the income described in § 1.882-1 of that corporation from all sources concerning which it has information, and

(iii) Assess the tax and collect it from one or more of those sources of income within the United States, without allowance for any deductions (other than that allowed by section 170) or credits (other than those allowed by sections 33, 34 and 852(b)(3)(D)(ii)).

If the income of the corporation is not effectively connected with, or if the corporation did not receive income that is treated as being effectively connected with, the conduct of a United States trade or business, the tax will be assessed under § 1.882-1(b)(1) on a gross basis, without allowance for any deduction (other than that allowed by section 170) or credit (other than the credits allowed by sections 33, 34 and 852(b)(3)(d)(ii)). If the income is effectively connected, or treated as effectively connected, with the conduct of a United States trade or business, tax will be assessed in accordance with either section 11, 55 or 1201(a) without allowance for any deduction (other than that allowed by section 170) or credit (other than the credits allowed by sections 33, 34 and 852(b)(3)(D)(ii)).

(b) *Allowed deductions and credits.*—(1) *In general.*—Except for the deduction allowed under section 170 for charitable contributions and gifts (see section 882(c)(1)(B)), deductions are allowed to a foreign corporation only to the extent they are connected with gross income which is effectively connected, or treated as effectively connected, with the conduct of a trade or business in the United States. Deductible expenses (other than interest expense) are properly allocated and apportioned to effectively connected gross income in accordance with the rules of § 1.861-8. For the method of determining the interest deduction allowed to a foreign corporation, see § 1.882-5. Other than the credits allowed by sections 33, 34 and 852(b)(3)(D)(ii), the foreign corporation is entitled to credits only if they are attributable to effectively connected income. See paragraph (a)(2) of this section for the requirement that a return be filed. Except as provided by section 906, a foreign corporation shall not be allowed the credit against the tax for taxes of foreign countries and possessions of the United States allowed by section 901.

(2) *Verification.*—At the request of the Internal Revenue Service, a foreign corporation claiming deductions from gross income which is effectively connected, or treated as effectively connected, with the conduct of a trade or business in the United States or credits which are attributable to that income must furnish at the place designated pursuant to § 301.7605-1(a) information sufficient to establish that the corporation is entitled to the deductions and credits in the amounts claimed. All information must be furnished in a form suitable to permit verification of claimed deductions and credits. The Internal Revenue Service may require, as appropriate, that an English translation be provided with any information in a foreign language. If a foreign corporation fails to furnish sufficient information, the Internal Revenue Service may in its discretion disallow any claimed deductions and credits in full or in part. For additional filing requirements and for penalties for failure to provide information, see also section 6038A. [Reg. § 1.882-4.]

☐ [T.D. 6258, 10-23-57. Amended by T.D. 7749, 12-30-80; T.D. 8322, 12-10-90; T.D. 8981, 1-28-2002 and T.D. 9043, 3-7-2003.]

§ 1.882-5. Determination of interest deduction.—(a) *Rules of general application.*—(1) *Overview.*—(i) *In general.*—The amount of interest expense of a foreign corporation that is allocable under section 882(c) to income which is (or is treated as) effectively connected with the conduct of a trade or business within the United States (ECI) is the sum of the interest paid or accrued by the foreign corporation on its liabilities booked in the United States, as adjusted under the three-step process set forth in paragraphs (b), (c) and (d) of this section and the specially allocated interest expense determined under section (a)(1)(ii) of this section. The provisions of this section provide the exclusive rules for allocating interest expense to the ECI of a foreign corporation. Under the three-step process, the total value of the U.S. assets of a foreign corporation is first determined under paragraph (b) of this section (Step 1). Next, the amount of U.S.-connected liabilities is determined under paragraph (c) of this section (Step 2). Finally, the amount of interest paid or accrued on liabilities booked in the United States, as determined under paragraph (d)(2) of this section, is adjusted for interest expense attributable to the difference between U.S.-connected liabilities and U.S. booked liabilities (Step 3). Alternatively, a foreign corporation may elect to determine its interest rate on U.S.-connected liabilities by reference to its U.S. assets, using the separate currency pools method described in paragraph (e) of this section.

(ii) *Direct allocations.*—(A) *In general.*—A foreign corporation that has a U.S. asset and indebtedness that meet the requirements of § 1.861-10T(b) and (c), as limited by § 1.861-10T(d)(1), may directly allocate interest expense from such indebtedness to income from such asset in the manner and to the extent provided in § 1.861-10T. For purposes of paragraphs (b)(1) or (c)(2) of this section, a foreign corporation that allocates its interest expense under the direct allocation rule of this paragraph (a)(1)(ii)(A) shall reduce the basis of the asset that meets the requirements of § 1.861-10T(b) and (c) by the principal amount of the indebtedness that meets the requirements of § 1.861-10T(b) and (c). The foreign corporation shall also disregard any indebtedness that meets the requirements of § 1.861-10T(b) and (c) in determining the amount of the foreign corporation's liabilities under paragraphs (c)(2) and (d)(2) of this section, and shall not take into account any interest expense paid or accrued with respect to such a liability for purposes of paragraphs (d) or (e) of this section.

(B) *Partnership interest.*—A foreign corporation that is a partner in a partnership that has a U.S. asset and indebtedness that meet the requirements of § 1.861-10T(b) and (c), as limited by § 1.861-10T(d)(1), may directly allocate its distributive share of interest expense from that indebtedness to its distributive share of income from that asset in the manner and to the extent provided in § 1.861-10T. A foreign corporation that allocates its distributive share of interest expense under the direct allocation rule of this paragraph (a)(1)(ii)(B) shall disregard any partnership indebtedness that meets the requirements of § 1.861-10T(b) and (c) in determining the amount of its distributive share of partnership liabilities for purposes of paragraphs (b)(1), (c)(2)(vi), and (d)(2)(vii) or (e)(1)(ii) of this section, and shall not take into account any partnership interest expense paid or accrued with respect to such a liability for purposes of paragraph (d) or (e) of this section. For purposes of paragraph (b)(1) of this section, a foreign corporation that directly allocates its distributive share of interest expense under this paragraph (a)(1)(ii)(B) shall—

(1) Reduce the partnership's basis in such asset by the amount of such indebtedness in allocating its basis in the partnership under § 1.884-1(d)(3)(ii); or

(2) Reduce the partnership's income from such asset by the partnership's interest expense from such indebtedness under § 1.884-1(d)(3)(iii).

(2) *Coordination with tax treaties.*—The provisions of this section provide the exclusive rules for determining the interest expense attributable to the business profits of a permanent establishment under a U.S. income tax treaty.

(3) *Limitation on interest expense.*—In no event may the amount of interest expense computed under this section exceed the amount of interest on indebtedness paid or accrued by the taxpayer within the taxable year (translated into U.S. dollars at the weighted average exchange rate for each currency prescribed by § 1.989(b)-1 for the taxable year).

(4) *Translation convention for foreign currency.*—For each computation required by this section, the taxpayer shall translate values and amounts into the relevant currency at a spot rate or a weighted average exchange rate consistent with the method such taxpayer uses for financial reporting purposes, provided such method is applied consistently from year to year. Interest expense paid or accrued, however, shall be translated under the rules of § 1.988-2. The district director or the Assistant Commissioner (International) may require that any or all computations required by this section be made in U.S. dollars if the functional currency of the taxpayer's home office is a hyperinflationary currency, as defined in § 1.985-1, and the computation in U.S. dollars is necessary to prevent distortions.

(5) *Coordination with other sections.*—Any provision that disallows, defers, or capitalizes interest expense applies after determining the amount of interest expense allocated to ECI under this section. For example, in determining the amount of interest expense that is disallowed as a deduction under section 265 or 163(j), deferred under section 163(e)(3) or 267(a)(3), or capitalized under section 263A with respect to a United States trade or business, a taxpayer takes into account only the amount of interest expense allocable to ECI under this section.

(6) *Special rule for foreign governments.*—The amount of interest expense of a foreign government, as defined in § 1.892-2T(a), that is allocable to ECI is the total amount of interest paid or accrued within the taxable year by the United States trade or business on U.S. booked liabilities (as defined in paragraph (d)(2) of this section). Interest expense of a foreign government, however, is not allocable to ECI to the extent that it is incurred with respect to U.S. booked liabilities that exceed 80 percent of the total value of U.S. assets for the taxable year (determined under paragraph (b) of this section). This paragraph (a)(6) does not apply to controlled commercial entities within the meaning of § 1.892-5T.

(7) *Elections under § 1.882-5.*—(i) *In general.*—A corporation must make each election provided in this section on the corporation's federal income tax return for the first taxable year beginning on or after the effective date of this section. An amended return does not qualify for this purpose, nor shall the provisions of § 301.9100-1 of this chapter and any guidance promulgated thereunder apply. Each election under this section, whether an election for the first taxable year or a subsequent change of election, shall be made by the corporation calculating its interest expense deduction in accordance with the methods elected. An elected method must be used for a minimum period of five years before the taxpayer may elect a different method. To change an election before the end of the requisite five-year period, a taxpayer must obtain the consent of the Commissioner or her delegate. The Commissioner or her delegate will generally consent to a taxpayer's request to change its election only in rare and unusual circumstances.

(ii) *Failure to make the proper election.*—If a taxpayer, for any reason, fails to make an election provided in this section in a timely fashion, the district director or the Assistant Commissioner (International) may make any or all of the elections provided in this section on behalf of the taxpayer, and such elections shall be binding as if made by the taxpayer.

(8) *Examples.*—The following examples illustrate the application of paragraph (a) of this section:

Example 1. Direct allocations—(i) *Facts*: *FC* is a foreign corporation that conducts business through a branch, *B*, in the United States. Among *B*'s U.S. assets is an interest in a partnership, *P*, that is engaged in airplane leasing solely in the U.S. *FC* contributes 200x to *P* in exchange for its partnership interest. *P* incurs qualified nonrecourse indebtedness within the meaning of § 1.861-10T to purchase an airplane. *FC*'s share of the liability of *P*, as determined under section 752, is 800x.

(ii) *Analysis*: Pursuant to paragraph (a)(1)(ii)(B) of this section, *FC* is permitted to directly allocate its distributive share of the interest incurred with respect to the qualified nonrecourse indebtedness to *FC*'s distributive share of the rental income generated by the airplane. A liability the interest on which is allocated directly to the income from a particular asset under paragraph (a)(1)(ii)(B) of this section is disregarded for purposes of paragraphs (b)(1), (c)(2)(vi), and (d)(2)(vii) or (e)(1)(ii) of this section. Consequently, for purposes of determining the value of *FC*'s assets under paragraphs (b)(1) and (c)(2)(vi) of this section, *FC*'s basis in *P* is reduced by the 800x liability as determined under section 752, but is not increased by the 800x liability that is directly allocated under paragraph (a)(1)(ii)(B) of this section. Similarly, pursuant to paragraph (a)(1)(ii)(B) of this section, the 800x liability is disregarded for purposes of determining *FC*'s liabilities under paragraphs (c)(2)(vi) and (d)(2)(vii) of this section.

Example 2. Limitation on interest expense—(i) *FC* is a foreign corporation that conducts a real estate business in the United States. In its 1997 tax year, *FC* has no outstanding indebtedness, and therefore incurs no interest expense. *FC* elects to use the 50% fixed ratio under paragraph (c)(4) of this section.

(ii) Under paragraph (a)(3) of this section, *FC* is not allowed to deduct any interest expense that exceeds the amount of interest on indebtedness paid or accrued in that taxable year. Since *FC* incurred no interest expense in taxable year 1997, *FC* will not be entitled to any interest deduction for that year under § 1.882-5, notwithstanding the fact that *FC* has elected to use the 50% fixed ratio.

Example 3. Coordination with other sections—(i) *FC* is a foreign corporation that is a bank under section 585(a)(2) and a financial institution under section 265(b)(5). *FC* is a calendar year taxpayer, and operates a U.S. branch, *B*. Throughout its taxable year 1997, *B* holds only two assets that are U.S. assets within the meaning of paragraph (b)(1) of this section. *FC* does not make a fair-market value election under paragraph (b)(2)(ii) of this section, and, therefore, values its U.S. assets according to their bases under paragraph (b)(2)(i) of this section. The first asset is a taxable security with an adjusted basis of $100. The second asset is an obligation the interest on which is exempt from federal taxation under section 103, with an adjusted basis of $50. The tax-exempt obligation is not a qualified tax-exempt obligation as defined by section 265(b)(3)(B).

(ii) *FC* calculates its interest expense under § 1.882-5 to be $12. Under paragraph (a)(5) of this section, however, a portion of the interest expense that is allocated to *FC*'s effectively connected income under § 1.882-5 is disallowed in accordance with the provisions of section 265(b). Using the methodology prescribed under section 265, the amount of disallowed interest expense is $4, calculated as follows:

$$\$12 \times \frac{\$50 \text{ Tax-exempt U.S. assets}}{\$150 \text{ Total U.S. assets}} = \$4$$

(iii) Therefore, *FC* deducts a total of $8 ($12 − $4) of interest expense attributable to its effectively connected income in 1997.

Example 4. Treaty exempt asset—(i) *FC* is a foreign corporation, resident in Country X, that is actively engaged in the banking business in the United States through a permanent establishment, *B*. The income tax treaty in effect between Country X and the United States provides that *FC* is not taxable on foreign source income earned by its U.S. permanent establishment. In its 1997 tax year, *B* earns $90 of U.S. source income from U.S. assets with an adjusted tax basis of $900, and $12 of foreign source interest income from U.S. assets with an adjusted tax basis of $100. *FC*'s U.S. interest expense deduction, computed in accordance with § 1.882-5, is $500.

(ii) Under paragraph (a)(5) of this section, *FC* is required to apply any provision that disallows, defers, or capitalizes interest expense after determining the interest expense allocated to ECI under § 1.882-5. Section 265(a)(2) disallows interest expense that is allocable to one or more classes of income that are wholly exempt from taxation under subtitle A of the Internal Revenue Code. Section 1.265-1(b) provides that income wholly exempt from taxes includes both income excluded from tax under any provision of subtitle A and income wholly exempt from taxes under any other law. Section 894 specifies that the provisions of subtitle A are applied with due regard to any relevant treaty obligation of the United States. Because the treaty between the United States and Country X exempts foreign source income earned by *B* from U.S. tax, *FC* has assets that produce income wholly exempt from taxes under subtitle A, and must therefore allocate a portion of its § 1.882-5 interest expense to its exempt income. Using the methodology prescribed under section 265, the amount of disallowed interest expense is $50, calculated as follows:

$$\$500 \times \frac{\$100 \text{ Treaty-exempt U.S. assets}}{\$1000 \text{ Total U.S. assets}} = \$50$$

(iii) Therefore, *FC* deducts a total of $450 ($500 $50) of interest expense attributable to its effectively connected income in 1997.

(b) *Step 1: Determination of total value of U.S. assets for the taxable year.*—(1) *Classification of an asset as a U.S. asset.*—(i) *General rule.*—Except as otherwise provided in this paragraph (b)(1), an asset is a U.S. asset for purposes of this section to the extent that it is a U.S. asset under § 1.884-1(d). For purposes of this section, the term *determination date,* as used in § 1.884-1(d), means each day for which the total value of U.S. assets is computed under paragraph (b)(3) of this section.

(ii) *Items excluded from the definition of U.S. asset.*—For purposes of this section, the term *U.S. asset* excludes an asset to the extent it produces income or gain described in sections 883(a)(3) and (b).

(iii) *Items included in the definition of U.S. asset.*—For purposes of this section, the term *U.S. asset* includes—

(A) U.S. real property held in a wholly-owned domestic subsidiary of a foreign corporation that qualifies as a bank under section 585(a)(2)(B) (without regard to the second sentence thereof), provided that the real property would qualify as used in the foreign corporation's trade or business within the meaning of § 1.864-4(c)(2) or (3) if held directly by the foreign corporation and either was initially acquired through foreclosure or similar proceedings or is U.S. real property occupied by the foreign corporation (the value of which shall be adjusted by the amount of any indebtedness that is reflected in the value of the property);

(B) An asset that produces income treated as ECI under section 921(d) or 926(b) (relating to certain income of a FSC and certain dividends paid by a FSC to a foreign corporation);

(C) An asset that produces income treated as ECI under section 953(c)(3)(C) (relating to certain income of a captive insurance company that a corporation elects to treat as ECI) that is not otherwise ECI; and

(D) An asset that produces income treated as ECI under section 882(e) (relating to certain interest income of possessions banks).

(iv) *Interbranch transactions.*—A transaction of any type between separate offices or branches of the same taxpayer does not create a U.S. asset.

(v) *Assets acquired to increase U.S. assets artificially.*—An asset shall not be treated as a U.S. asset if one of the principal purposes for acquiring or using that asset is to increase artificially the U.S. assets of a foreign corporation on the determination date. Whether an asset is acquired or used for such purpose will depend upon all the facts and circumstances of each case. Factors to be considered in determining whether one of the principal purposes in acquiring or using an asset is to increase artificially the U.S. assets of a foreign corporation include the length of time during which the asset was used in a U.S. trade or business, whether the asset was acquired from a related person, and whether the aggregate value of the U.S. assets of the foreign corporation increased temporarily on or around the determination date. A purpose may be a principal purpose even though it is outweighed by other purposes (taken together or separately).

(2) *Determination of the value of a U.S. asset.*—(i) *General rule.*—The value of a U.S. asset is the adjusted basis of the asset for determining gain or loss from the sale or other disposition of that item, further adjusted as provided in paragraph (b)(2)(iii) of this section.

(ii) *Fair-market value election.*—(A) *In general.*—A taxpayer may elect to value all of its U.S. assets on the basis of fair market value, subject to the requirements of § 1.861-9T(g)(1)(iii), and provided the taxpayer uses the methodology prescribed in § 1.861-9T(h). Once elected, the fair market value must be used by the taxpayer for both Step 1 and Step 2 described in paragraphs (b) and (c) of this section, and must be used in all subsequent taxable years unless the Commissioner or her delegate consents to a change.

(B) *Adjustment to partnership basis.*—If a partner makes a fair market value election under paragraph (b)(2)(ii) of this section, the value of the partner's interest in a partnership that is treated as an asset shall be the fair market value of his partnership interest, increased by the fair market value of the partner's share of the liabilities determined under paragraph (c)(2)(vi) of this section. See § 1.884-1(d)(3).

(iii) *Reduction of total value of U.S. assets by amount of bad debt reserves under section 585.*—(A) *In general.*—The total value of loans that qualify as U.S. assets shall be reduced by the amount of any reserve for bad debts additions to which are allowed as deductions under section 585.

(B) *Example.*—The following example illustrates the provisions of paragraph (b)(2)(iii)(A) of this section:

Example. Foreign banks; bad debt reserves. FC is a foreign corporation that qualifies as a bank under section 585(a)(2)(B) (without regard to the second sentence thereof), but is not a large bank as defined in section 585(c)(2). *FC* conducts business through a branch, *B,* in the United States. Among *B*'s U.S. assets are a portfolio of loans with an adjusted basis of $500. *FC* accounts for its bad debts for U.S. federal income tax purposes under the reserve method, and *B* maintains a deductible reserve for bad debts of $50. Under paragraph (b)(2)(iii) of this section, the total value of *FC*'s portfolio of loans is $450 ($500 $50).

(iv) *Adjustment to basis of financial instruments.*—[Reserved]

(3) *Computation of total value of U.S. assets.*—The total value of U.S. assets for the taxable year is the average of the sums of the values (determined under paragraph (b)(2) of this section) of U.S. assets. For each U.S. asset, value shall be computed at the most frequent, regular intervals for which data are reasonably available. In no event shall the value of any U.S. asset be computed less frequently than monthly (beginning of taxable year and monthly thereafter) by a large bank (as defined in section 585(c)(2)) and semi-annually (beginning, middle and end of taxable year) by any other taxpayer.

(c) *Step 2: Determination of total amount of U.S.-connected liabilities for the taxable year.*— (1) *General rule.*—The amount of U.S.-connected liabilities for the taxable year equals the total value of U.S. assets for the taxable year (as determined under paragraph (b)(3) of this section) multiplied by the actual ratio for the taxable year (as determined under paragraph (c)(2) of this section) or, if the taxpayer has made an election in accordance with paragraph (c)(4) of this section, by the fixed ratio.

(2) *Computation of the actual ratio.*— (i) *In general.*—A taxpayer's actual ratio for the taxable year is the total amount of its worldwide liabilities for the taxable year divided by the total value of its worldwide assets for the taxable year. The total amount of worldwide liabilities and the total value of worldwide assets for the taxable year is the average of the sums of the amounts of the taxpayer's worldwide liabilities and the values of its worldwide assets (determined under paragraphs (c)(2)(iii) and (iv) of this section). In each case, the sums must be computed semi-annually (beginning, middle and end of taxable year) by a large bank (as defined in section 585(c)(2)) and annually (beginning and end of taxable year) by any other taxpayer.

(ii) *Classification of items.*—The classification of an item as a liability or an asset must be consistent from year to year and in accordance with U.S. tax principles.

(iii) *Determination of amount of worldwide liabilities.*—The amount of a liability must be determined consistently from year to year and must be substantially in accordance with U.S. tax principles. To be substantially in accordance with U.S. tax principles, the principles used to determine the amount of a liability must not differ from U.S. tax principles to a degree that will materially affect the value of taxpayer's worldwide liabilities or the taxpayer's actual ratio.

(iv) *Determination of value of worldwide assets.*—The value of an asset must be determined consistently from year to year and must be substantially in accordance with U.S. tax principles. To be substantially in accordance with U.S. tax principles, the principles used to determine the value of an asset must not differ from U.S. tax principles to a degree that will materially affect the value of the taxpayer's worldwide assets or the taxpayer's actual ratio. The value of an asset is the adjusted basis of that asset for determining the gain or loss from the sale or other disposition of that asset, adjusted in the same manner as the basis of U.S. assets are adjusted under paragraphs (b)(2)(ii) through (iv) of this section.

(v) *Hedging transactions.*—[Reserved]

(vi) *Treatment of partnership interests and liabilities.*—For purposes of computing the actual ratio, the value of a partner's interest in a partnership that will be treated as an asset is the partner's adjusted basis in its partnership interest, reduced by the partner's share of liabilities of the partnership as determined under section 752 and increased by the partner's share of liabilities determined under this paragraph (c)(2)(vi). If the partner has made a fair market value election under paragraph (b)(2)(ii) of this section, the value of its interest in the partnership shall be increased by the fair market value of the partner's share of the liabilities determined under this paragraph (c)(2)(vi). For purposes of this section a partner shares in any liability of a partnership in the same proportion that it shares, for income tax purposes, in the expense attributable to that liability for the taxable year. A partner's adjusted basis in a partnership interest cannot be less than zero.

(vii) *Computation of actual ratio of insurance companies.*—[Reserved]

(viii) *Interbranch transactions.*—A transaction of any type between separate offices or branches of the same taxpayer does not create an asset or a liability.

(ix) *Amounts must be expressed in a single currency.*—The actual ratio must be computed in either U.S. dollars or the functional currency of the home office of the taxpayer, and that currency must be used consistently from year to year. For example, a taxpayer that determines the actual ratio annually using British pounds converted at the spot rate for financial reporting purposes must translate the U.S. dollar values of assets and amounts of liabilities of the U.S. trade or business into pounds using the spot rate on the last day of its taxable year. The district director or the Assistant Commissioner (International) may require that the actual ratio be computed in dollars if the functional currency of the taxpayer's home office is a hyperinflationary currency, as defined in § 1.985-1, that materially distorts the actual ratio.

(3) *Adjustments.*—The district director or the Assistant Commissioner (International) may make appropriate adjustments to prevent a foreign corporation from intentionally and artificially increasing its actual ratio. For example, the district director or the Assistant Commissioner (International) may offset a loan made from or to one person with a loan made to or from another person if any of the parties to the loans are related persons, within the meaning of section 267(b) or 707(b)(1), and one of the principal purposes for entering into the loans was to increase artificially the actual ratio of a foreign corporation. A purpose may be a principal purpose even though it is outweighed by other purposes (taken together or separately).

(4) *Elective fixed ratio method of determining U.S. liabilities.*—A taxpayer that is a bank as defined in section 585(a)(2)(B) (without regard to the second sentence thereof) may elect to use a fixed ratio of 93 percent in lieu of the actual ratio. A taxpayer that is neither a bank nor an insurance company may elect to use a fixed ratio of 50 percent in lieu of the actual ratio.

(5) *Examples.*—The following examples illustrate the application of paragraph (c) of this section:

Example 1. Classification of item not in accordance with U.S. tax principles. Bank Z, a resident of country X, has a branch in the United States through which it conducts its banking business. In preparing its financial statements in country X, Z treats an instrument documented as perpetual subordinated debt as a liability. Under U.S. tax principles, however, this instrument is treated as equity. Consequently, the classification of this instrument as a liability for purposes of paragraph (c)(2)(iii) of this section is not in accordance with U.S. tax principles.

Example 2. Valuation of item not substantially in accordance with U.S. tax principles. Bank Z, a resident of country X, has a branch in the United States through which it conducts its banking business. Bank Z is a large bank as defined in section 585(c)(2). The tax rules of country X allow Bank Z to take deductions for additions to certain reserves. Bank Z decreases the value of the assets on its financial statements by the amounts of the reserves. The additions to the reserves under country X tax rules cause the value of Bank Z's assets to differ from the value of those assets determined under U.S. tax principles to a degree that materially affects the value of taxpayer's worldwide assets. Consequently, the valuation of Bank Z's worldwide assets under country X tax principles is not substantially in accordance with U.S. tax principles. Bank Z must increase the value of its worldwide assets under paragraph (c)(2)(iii) of this section by the amount of its country X reserves.

Example 3. Valuation of item substantially in accordance with U.S. tax principles. Bank Z, a resident of country X, has a branch in the United States through which it conducts its banking business. In determining the value of its worldwide assets, Bank Z computes the adjusted basis of certain non-U.S. assets according to the depreciation methodology provided under country X tax laws, which is different than the depreciation methodology provided under U.S. tax law. If the depreciation methodology provided under country X tax laws does not differ from U.S. tax principles to a degree that materially affects the value of Bank Z's worldwide assets or Bank Z's actual ratio as computed under paragraph (c)(2) of this section, then the valuation of Bank Z's worldwide assets under paragraph (c)(2)(iv) of this section is substantially in accordance with U.S. tax principles.

Example 4. [Reserved]

Example 5. Adjustments. FC is a foreign corporation engaged in the active conduct of a banking business through a branch, B, in the United States. P, an unrelated foreign corporation, deposits $100,000 in the home office of FC. Shortly thereafter, in a transaction arranged by the home office of FC, B lends $80,000 bearing interest at an arm's length rate to S, a wholly owned U.S. subsidiary of P. The district director or the Assistant Commissioner (International) determines that one of the principal purposes for making and incurring such loans is to increase FC's actual ratio. For purposes of this section, therefore, P is treated as having directly lent $80,000 to S. Thus, for purposes of paragraph (c) of this section (Step 2), the district director or the Assistant Commissioner (International) may offset FC's liability and asset arising from this transaction, resulting in a net liability of $20,000 that is not a booked liability of B. Because the loan to S from B was initiated and arranged by the home office of FC, with no material participation by B, the loan to S will not be treated as a U.S. asset.

(d) *Step 3: Determination of amount of interest expense allocable to ECI under the adjusted U.S. booked liabilities method.*—(1) *General rule.*—The adjustment to the amount of interest expense paid or accrued on U.S. booked liabilities is determined by comparing the amount of U.S.-connected liabilities for the taxable year, as determined under paragraph (c) of this section, with the average total amount of U.S. booked liabilities, as determined under paragraphs (d)(2) and (3) of this section. If the average total amount of U.S. booked liabilities equals or exceeds the amount of U.S.-connected liabilities, the adjustment to the interest expense on U.S. booked liabilities is determined under paragraph (d)(4) of this section. If the amount of U.S.-connected liabilities exceeds the average total amount of U.S. booked liabilities, the adjustment to the amount of interest expense paid or accrued on U.S. booked liabilities is determined under paragraph (d)(5) of this section.

(2) *U.S. booked liabilities.*—(i) *In general.*—A liability is a *U.S. booked liability* if it is properly reflected on the books of the U.S. trade or business, within the meaning of paragraph (d)(2)(ii) or (iii) of this section.

(ii) *Properly reflected on the books of the U.S. trade or business of a foreign corporation that is not a bank.*—(A) *In general.*—A liability, whether interest bearing or non-interest bearing, is properly reflected on the books of the U.S. trade or business of a foreign corporation that is not a bank as described in section 585(a)(2)(B) (without regard to the second sentence thereof) if—

(1) The liability is secured predominantly by a U.S. asset of the foreign corporation;

(2) The foreign corporation enters the liability on a set of books relating to an activity that produces ECI at a time reasonably contemporaneous with the time at which the liability is incurred; or

(3) The foreign corporation maintains a set of books and records relating to an activity that produces ECI and the District Director or Assistant Commissioner (International) determines that there is a direct connection or relationship between the liability and that activity. Whether there is a direct connection between the liability and an activity that produces ECI depends on the facts and circumstances of each case.

(B) *Identified liabilities not properly reflected.*—A liability is not properly reflected on the books of the U.S. trade or business merely because a foreign corporation identifies the liability pursuant to § 1.884-4(b)(1)(ii) and (b)(3).

(iii) *Properly reflected on the books of the U.S. trade or business of a foreign corporation that is a bank.*—(A) *In general.*—A liability, whether interest bearing or non-interest bearing, is properly reflected on the books of the U.S. trade or business of a foreign corporation that is a bank as described in section 585(a)(2)(B) (without regard to the second sentence thereof) if—

(1) The bank enters the liability on a set of books relating to an activity that produces ECI before the close of the day on which the liability is incurred; and

(2) There is a direct connection or relationship between the liability and that activity. Whether there is a direct connection between the liability and an activity that produces ECI depends on the facts and circumstances of each case.

(B) *Inadvertent error.*—If a bank fails to enter a liability in the books of the activity that produces ECI before the close of the day on which the liability was incurred, the liability may be treated as a U.S. booked liability only if, under the facts and circumstances, the taxpayer demonstrates a direct connection or relationship between the liability and the activity that produces ECI and the failure to enter the liability in those books was due to inadvertent error.

(iv) *Liabilities of insurance companies.*—[Reserved]

(v) *Liabilities used to increase artificially interest expense on U.S. booked liabilities.*—U.S. booked liabilities shall not include a liability if one of the principal purposes for incurring or holding the liability is to increase artificially the interest expense on the U.S. booked liabilities of a foreign corporation. Whether a liability is incurred or held for the purpose of artificially increasing interest expense will depend upon all the facts and circumstances of each case. Factors to be considered in determining whether one of the principal purposes for incurring or holding a liability is to increase artificially the interest expense on U.S. booked liabilities of a foreign corporation include whether the interest expense on the liability is excessive when compared to other liabilities of the foreign corporation denominated in the same currency and whether the currency denomination of the liabilities of the U.S. branch substantially matches the currency denomination of the U.S. branch's assets. A purpose may be a principal purpose even though it is outweighed by other purposes (taken together or separately).

(vi) *Hedging transactions.*—[Reserved]

Reg. § 1.882-5(d)(2)(vi)

(vii) *Amount of U.S. booked liabilities of a partner.*—A partner's share of liabilities of a partnership is considered a booked liability of the partner provided that it is properly reflected on the books (within the meaning of paragraph (d)(2)(ii) of this section) of the U.S. trade or business of the partnership.

(viii) *Interbranch transactions.*—A transaction of any type between separate offices or branches of the same taxpayer does not result in the creation of a liability.

(3) *Average total amount of U.S. booked liabilities.*—The *average total amount* of U.S. booked liabilities for the taxable year is the average of the sums of the amounts (determined under paragraph (d)(2) of this section) of U.S. booked liabilities. The amount of U.S. booked liabilities shall be computed at the most frequent, regular intervals for which data are reasonably available. In no event shall the amount of U.S. booked liabilities be computed less frequently than monthly by a large bank (as defined in section 585(c)(2)) and semi-annually by any other taxpayer.

(4) *Interest expense where U.S. booked liabilities equal or exceed U.S. liabilities.*—(i) *In general.*—If the average total amount of U.S. booked liabilities (as determined in paragraphs (d)(2) and (3) of this section) exceeds the amount of U.S.-connected liabilities (as determined under paragraph (c) of this section (Step 2)), the interest expense allocable to ECI is the product of the total amount of interest paid or accrued within the taxable year by the U.S. trade or business on U.S. booked liabilities and the scaling ratio set out in paragraph (d)(4)(ii) of this section. For purposes of this section, the reduction resulting from the application of the scaling ratio is applied pro-rata to all interest expense paid or accrued by the foreign corporation. A similar reduction in income, expense, gain, or loss from a hedging transaction (as described in paragraph (d)(2)(vi) of this section) must also be determined by multiplying such income, expense, gain, or loss by the scaling ratio. If the average total amount of U.S. booked liabilities (as determined in paragraph (d)(3) of this section) equals the amount of U.S.-connected liabilities (as determined under *Step 2*), the interest expense allocable to ECI is the total amount of interest paid or accrued within the taxable year by the U.S. trade or business on U.S. booked liabilities.

(ii) *Scaling ratio.*—For purposes of this section, the scaling ratio is a fraction the numerator of which is the amount of U.S.-connected liabilities and the denominator of which is the average total amount of U.S. booked liabilities.

(iii) *Special rules for insurance companies.*—[Reserved]

(5) *U.S.-connected interest rate where U.S. booked liabilities are less than U.S.-connected liabilities.*—(i) *In general.*—If the amount of U.S.-connected liabilities (as determined under paragraph (c) of this section (Step 2)) exceeds the average total amount of U.S. booked liabilities, the interest expense allocable to ECI is the total amount of interest paid or accrued within the taxable year by the U.S. trade or business on U.S. booked liabilities, plus the excess of the amount of U.S.-connected liabilities over the average total amount of U.S. booked liabilities multiplied by the interest rate determined under paragraph (d)(5)(ii) of this section.

(ii) *Interest rate on excess U.S.-connected liabilities.*—The applicable interest rate on excess U.S.-connected liabilities is determined by dividing the total interest expense paid or accrued for the taxable year on U.S.-dollar liabilities shown on the books of the offices or branches of the foreign corporation outside the United States by the average U.S.-dollar denominated liabilities (whether interest-bearing or not) shown on the books of the offices or branches of the foreign corporation outside the United States for the taxable year.

(6) *Examples.*—The following examples illustrate the rules of this section:

Example 1. Computation of interest expense; actual ratio—(i) *Facts.* (A) *FC* is a foreign corporation that is not a bank and that actively conducts a real estate business through a branch, *B*, in the United States. For the taxable year, *FC*'s balance sheet and income statement is as follows (assume amounts are in U.S. dollars and computed in accordance with paragraphs (b)(2) and (b)(3) of this section):

	Value	
Asset 1	$2,000	
Asset 2	$2,500	
Asset 3	$5,500	
	Amount	Interest Expense
Liability 1	$800	56
Liability 2	$3,200	256
Capital	$6,000	0

(B) Asset 1 is the stock of *FC*'s wholly-owned domestic subsidiary that is also actively engaged in the real estate business. Asset 2 is a building in the United States producing rental income that is entirely ECI to *FC*. Asset 3 is a building in the home country of *FC* that produces rental income. Liabilities 1 and 2 are loans that bear interest at the rates of 7% and 8%, respectively. Liability 1 is a booked liability of *B*, and Liability 2 is booked in *FC*'s home country. Assume that *FC* has not elected to use the fixed ratio in Step 2.

Reg. §1.882-5(d)(2)(vii)

(ii) *Step 1.* Under paragraph (b)(1) of this section, Assets 1 and 3 are not U.S. assets, while Asset 2 qualifies as a U.S. asset. Thus, under paragraph (b)(3) of this section, the total value of U.S. assets for the taxable year is $2,500, the value of Asset 2.

(iii) *Step 2.* Under paragraph (c)(1) of this section, the amount of *FC*'s U.S.-connected liabilities for the taxable year is determined by multiplying $2,500 (the value of U.S. assets determined under Step 1) by the actual ratio for the taxable year. The actual ratio is the average amount of *FC*'s worldwide liabilities divided by the average value of *FC*'s worldwide assets. The amount of Liability 1 is $800, and the amount of Liability 2 is $3,200. Thus, the numerator of the actual ratio is $4,000. The average value of worldwide assets is $10,000 (Asset 1 + Asset 2 + Asset 3). The actual ratio, therefore, is 40% ($4,000/$10,000), and the amount of U.S.-connected liabilities for the taxable year is $1,000 ($2,500 U.S. assets × 40%).

(iv) *Step 3.* Because the amount of *FC*'s U.S.-connected liabilities ($1,000) exceeds the average total amount of U.S. booked liabilities of *B* ($800), *FC* determines its interest expense in accordance with paragraph (d)(5) of this section by adding the interest paid or accrued on U.S. booked liabilities, and the interest expense associated with the excess of its U.S.-connected liabilities over its average total amount of U.S. booked liabilities. Under paragraph (d)(5)(ii) of this section, *FC* determines the interest rate attributable to its excess U.S.-connected liabilities by dividing the interest expense paid or accrued by the average amount of U.S.-dollar denominated liabilities, which produces an interest rate of 8% ($256/$3200). Therefore, *FC*'s allocable interest expense is $72 ($56 of interest expense from U.S. booked liabilities plus $16 ($200 × 8%) of interest expense attributable to its excess U.S.-connected liabilities).

Example 2. Computation of interest expense; fixed ratio—(i) The facts are the same as in *Example 1*, except that *FC* makes a fixed ratio election under paragraph (c)(4) of this section. The conclusions under Step 1 are the same as in *Example 1*.

(ii) *Step 2.* Under paragraph (c)(1) of this section, the amount of U.S.-connected liabilities for the taxable year is determined by multiplying $2,500 (the value of U.S. assets determined under Step 1) by the fixed ratio for the taxable year, which, under paragraph (c)(4) of this section is 50 percent. Thus, the amount of U.S.-connected liabilities for the taxable year is $1,250 ($2,500 U.S. assets × 50%).

(iii) *Step 3.* As in *Example 1*, the amount of *FC*'s U.S.-connected liabilities exceed the average total amount of U.S. booked liabilities of *B*, requiring *FC* to determine its interest expense under paragraph (d)(5) of this section. In this case, however, *FC* has excess U.S.-connected liabilities of $450 ($1,250 U.S.-connected liabilities – $800 U.S. booked liabilities). *FC* therefore has allocable interest expense of $92 ($56 of interest expense from U.S. booked liabilities plus $36 ($450 × 8%) of interest expense attributable to its excess U.S.-connected liabilities).

Example 3. Scaling ratio.—(i) *Facts.* Bank *Z*, a resident of country *X*, has a branch in the United States through which it conducts its banking business. For the taxable year, *Z* has U.S.-connected liabilities, determined under paragraph (c) of this section, equal to $300. *Z*, however, has U.S. booked liabilities of $300 and *U* 500. Therefore, assuming an exchange rate of the *U* to the U.S. dollar of 5:1, *Z* has U.S. booked liabilities of $400 ($300 + (*U* 500 ÷5)).

(ii) *U.S.-connected liabilities.* Because *Z*'s U.S. booked liabilities of $400 exceed its U.S.-connected liabilities by $100, all of *Z*'s interest expense allocable to its U.S. trade or business must be scaled back pro-rata. To determine the scaling ratio, *Z* divides its U.S.-connected liabilities by its U.S. booked liabilities, as required by paragraph (d)(4) of this section. *Z*'s interest expense is scaled back pro rata by the resulting ratio of 3/4 ($300 ÷ $400). *Z*'s income, expense, gain or loss from hedging transactions described in paragraph (d)(2)(vi) of this section must be similarly reduced.

Example 4. [Reserved]

(e) *Separate currency pools method.*—(1) *General rule.*—If a foreign corporation elects to use the method in this paragraph, its total interest expense allocable to ECI is the sum of the separate interest deductions for each of the currencies in which the foreign corporation has U.S. assets. The separate interest deductions are determined under the following three-step process.

(i) *Determine the value of U.S. assets in each currency pool.*—First, the foreign corporation must determine the amount of its U.S. assets, using the methodology in paragraph (b) of this section, in each currency pool. The foreign corporation may convert into U.S. dollars any currency pool in which the foreign corporation holds less than 3% of its U.S. assets. A transaction (or transactions) that hedges a U.S. asset shall be taken into account for purposes of determining the currency denomination and the value of the U.S. asset.

(ii) *Determine the U.S.-connected liabilities in each currency pool.*—Second, the foreign corporation must determine the amount of its U.S.-connected liabilities in each currency pool by multiplying the amount of U.S. assets (as determined under paragraph (b)(3) of this section) in the currency pool by the foreign corporation's actual ratio (as determined under paragraph (c)(2) of this section) for the taxable year or, if the taxpayer has made an election in accordance with paragraph (c)(4) of this section, by the fixed ratio.

(iii) *Determine the interest expense attributable to each currency pool.*—Third, the foreign corporation must determine the interest expense attributable to each currency pool by multiplying the U.S.-connected liabilities in each currency pool by the prescribed interest rate as defined in paragraph (e)(2) of this section.

(2) *Prescribed interest rate.*—For each currency pool, the prescribed interest rate is determined by dividing the total interest expense that is paid or accrued for the taxable year with respect to the foreign corporation's worldwide liabilities denominated in that currency, by the foreign corporation's average worldwide liabilities (whether interest bearing or not) denominated in that currency. The interest expense and liabilities are to be stated in that currency.

(3) *Hedging transactions.*—[Reserved]

(4) *Election not available if excessive hyperinflationary assets.*—The election to use the separate currency pools method of this paragraph (e) is not available if the value of the foreign corporation's U.S. assets denominated in a hyperinflationary currency, as defined in §1.985-1, exceeds ten percent of the value of the foreign corporation's total U.S. assets. If a foreign corporation made a valid election to use the separate currency pools method in a prior year but no longer qualifies to use such method pursuant to this paragraph (e)(4), the taxpayer must use the method provided by paragraphs (b) through (d) of this section.

(5) *Examples.*—The separate currency pools method of this paragraph (e) is illustrated by the following examples:

Example 1. Separate currency pools method—(i) *Facts.* (A) Bank Z, a resident of country X, has a branch in the United States through which it conducts its banking business. For its 1997 taxable year, Z has U.S. assets, as defined in paragraph (b) of this section, that are denominated in U.S. dollars and in U, the country X currency. Accordingly, Z's U.S. assets are as follows:

	Average Value
U.S. Dollar Assets	$20,000
U Assets	U 5,000

(B) Z's worldwide liabilities are also denominated in U.S. Dollars and in U. The average interest rates on Z's worldwide liabilities, including those in the United States, are 6% on its U.S. dollar liabilities, and 12% on its liabilities denominated in U. Assume that Z has properly elected to use its actual ratio of 95% to determine its U.S.-connected liabilities in Step 2, and has also properly elected to use the separate currency pools method provided in paragraph (e) of this section.

(ii) *Determination of interest expense.* Z determines the interest expense attributable to its U.S.-connected liabilities according to the steps described below.

(A) First, Z separates its U.S. assets into two currency pools, one denominated in U.S. dollars ($20,000) and the other denominated in U (U 5,000).

(B) Second, Z multiplies each pool of assets by the applicable ratio of worldwide liabilities to assets, which in this case is 95%. Thus, Z has U.S.-connected liabilities of $19,000 ($20,000 × 95%), and U 4750 (U 5000 × 95%).

(C) Third, Z calculates its interest expense by multiplying each pool of its U.S.-connected liabilities by the relevant interest rates. Accordingly, Z's allocable interest expense for the year is $1140 ($19,000 × 6%), the sum of the expense associated with its U.S. dollar liabilities, plus U 570 (U 4750 × 12%), the interest expense associated with its liabilities denominated in U. Z must translate its interest expense denominated in U in accordance with the rules provided in section 988, and then must determine whether it is subject to any other provision of the Code that would disallow or defer any portion of its interest expense so determined.

Example 2. [Reserved]

(f) *Effective date.*—(1) *General rule.*—This section is effective for taxable years beginning on or after June 6, 1996.

(2) *Special rules for financial products.*—[Reserved] [Reg. § 1.882-5.]

☐ [T.D. 7749, 12-30-80. Amended by T.D. 7939, 2-2-84 and T.D. 8658, 3-5-96.]

Proposed Amendments to Regulation

§ 1.882-5. Determination of interest deduction.

* * *

(b) * * *
(2) * * *

(iv) *Adjustment to basis of financial instruments.*—The basis of a security or contract that is marked to market pursuant to section 475 or section 1256 will be determined as if each determination date were the last business day of the taxpayer's taxable year. A financial instrument with a fair market value of less than zero is a liability, not an asset, for purposes of this section.

* * *

(c) * * *

(2) * * *

(v) *Hedging transactions.*—A transaction (or transactions) that hedges an asset or liability, or a pool of assets or a pool of liabilities, will be taken into account in determining the value, amount and currency denomination of the asset or liability that it hedges. A transaction will be considered to hedge an asset or liability only if the transaction meets the requirements of § 1.1221-2.

* * *

(5) * * *

Example 4. Partnership liabilities. X and Y are each foreign corporations engaged in the active conduct of a trade or business within the United States through a partnership, P. Under the partnership agreement, X and Y each have a 50% interest in the capital and profits of P, and X is also entitled to a return of 6% per annum on its capital account that is a guaranteed payment under section 707(c). In addition, P has incurred a liability of $100x to an unrelated bank, B. Under paragraph (c)(2)(vi) of this section, X and Y each share equally in P's liability to B. In accordance with U.S. tax principles, P's obligation to make guaranteed payments to X does not constitute a liability of P, and therefore neither X nor Y take into account that obligation of the partnership in computing their actual ratio.

* * *

Example 6. Securities in ratio as assets. FC is a foreign corporation engaged in a trade or business in the United States through a U.S. branch. FC is a dealer in securities within the meaning of section 475(c)(1)(B) because it regularly offers to enter into positions in currency spot and forward contracts with customers in the ordinary course of its trade or business. FC has not elected to use the fixed ratio. On December 31, 1996, the end of FC's taxable year, the mark-to-market value of the spot and forward contracts entered into by FC worldwide is 1000x, which includes a mark-to-market gain of 500x with respect to the spot and forward contracts that are shown on the books of its U.S. branch and that produce effectively connected income. On its December 31, 1996, determination date, FC includes 500x in its U.S. assets, and 1000x in its worldwide assets.

Example 7. Securities in ratio as assets and liabilities. The facts are the same as in *Example 4*, except that on December 31, 1996, the mark-to-market value of the spot and forward contracts entered into by FC worldwide is 1000x, and FC has a mark-to-market loss of 500x with respect to the spot and forward contracts that are shown on the books of its U.S. branch and that would produce effectively connected income. On its December 31, 1996, determination date, FC includes the 1000x in its worldwide assets for purposes of determining its ratio of worldwide liabilities to worldwide assets. For purposes of Step 3, however, FC has U.S-booked liabilities in the United States equal to the 500x U.S. loss position.

(d) * * *

(2) * * *

(vi) *Hedging transactions.*—A transaction (or transactions) that hedges a U.S. booked liability, or a pool of U.S. booked liabilities, will be taken into account in determining the currency denomination, amount of, and interest rate associated with, that liability. A transaction will be considered to hedge a U.S. booked liability only if the transaction meets the requirements of § 1.1221-2(a), (b), and (c), and is identified in accordance with the requirements of § 1.1221-2(e).

* * *

(6) * * *

Example 4. Liability hedge—(i) *Facts.* FC is a foreign corporation that meets the definition of a bank, as defined in section 585(a)(2)(B) (without regard to the second sentence thereof), and that is engaged in a banking business in the United States through its branch, B. FC's corporate policy is to match the currency denomination of its assets and liabilities, thereby minimizing potential gains and losses from currency fluctuations. Thus, at the close of each business day, FC enters into one or more hedging transactions as needed to maintain a balanced currency position, and instructs each branch to do the same. At the close of business on December 31, 1998, B has 100x of U.S. dollar assets, and U.S. booked liabilities of 90x U.S. dollars and 1000x Japanese yen (exchange rate: $1 = 100). To eliminate the currency mismatch in this situation, B enters into a forward contract with an unrelated third party that requires FC to pay 10x dollars in return for 1000x yen. Through this hedging transaction, FC has effectively converted its 1000x Japanese yen liability into a U.S. dollar liability. FC uses its actual ratio of 90% in 1998 for Step 2, the adjusted U.S. booked liabilities method for purposes of Step 3, and is a calendar year taxpayer.

(ii) *Analysis.* Under paragraph 1.882-5(d)(2)(vi), FC is required to take into account hedges of U.S. booked liabilities in determining the currency denomination, amount, and interest rate associated with those liabilities. Accordingly, FC must treat the Japanese yen liabilities booked in the United States on December 31, 1998, as U.S. dollar liabilities to determine both the amount of the liabilities and the interest paid or accrued on U.S. booked liabilities for purposes of this section.

Prop. Reg. § 1.882-5(d)(6)

Moreover, in applying the scaling ratio prescribed in paragraph (d)(4)(i) of this section, *FC* must scale back both the U.S. booked liabilities and the hedge(s) of those liabilities. Assuming that *FC*'s average U.S. booked liabilities for the year ending December 31, 1998, exceed its U.S.-connected liabilities determined under paragraphs (a)(1) through (c)(5) of this section by 10%, *FC* must scale back by 10% both its interest expense associated with U.S. booked liabilities, and any income or loss from the forward contract to purchase Japanese yen that hedges its U.S. booked liabilities.

(e) * * *

(3) *Hedging transactions.*—A transaction (or transactions) that hedges a liability, or a pool of liabilities, will be taken into account in determining the amount of, or interest rate associated with, that liability. A transaction will be considered to hedge a liability only if the transaction meets the requirements of § 1.1221-2(a),(b), and (c).

* * *

(5) * * *

Example 2. Asset hedge—(i) *Facts. FC* is a foreign corporation that meets the definition of a bank, as defined in section 585(a)(2)(B) (without regard to the second sentence thereof), and that is engaged in the banking business in the United States through its branch, *B. FC*'s corporate policy is to match the currency denomination of its assets and liabilities, thereby minimizing potential gains and losses from currency fluctuations. Thus, at the close of each business day, *FC* enters into one or more hedging transactions as needed to maintain a balanced currency position, and instructs each branch to do the same. At the close of business on December 31, 1998, *B* has two U.S. assets, a loan of 90x U.S. dollars and a loan of 1000x Japanese yen (exchange rate: $1 = ¥100). *B* has U.S. booked liabilities, however, of 100x U.S. dollars. To eliminate the currency mismatch, *B* enters into a forward contract with an unrelated third party that requires *FC* to pay 1000x yen in return for 10x dollars. Through this hedging transaction, *FC* has effectively converted its 1000x Japanese yen asset into a U.S. dollar asset. *FC* uses its actual ratio of 90% in 1998 for Step 2, has elected the separate currency pools method in paragraph (e) of this section, and is a calendar year taxpayer.

(ii) *Analysis*. Under paragraph (e)(1)(i) of this section, *FC* must take into account any transaction that hedges a U.S. asset in determining the currency denomination and value of that asset. *FC*'s Japanese yen asset will therefore be treated as a U.S. dollar asset in determining its U.S. assets in each currency. Accordingly, *FC* will be treated as having only U.S. dollar assets in making its separate currency pools computation.

(f) * * *

(2) *Special rules for financial products.*—Paragraphs (b)(2)(iv), (c)(2)(v), (d)(2)(vi), and (e)(3) of this section will be effective for taxable years beginning on or after the date these regulations are published as final regulations in the Federal Register.

[Prop. Reg. § 1.882-5.]

[Proposed 3-8-96.]

§ 1.883-1. Exclusion of income from the international operation of ships or aircraft.—(a) *General rule.*—Qualified income derived by a qualified foreign corporation from its international operation of ships or aircraft is excluded from gross income and exempt from United States Federal income tax. Paragraph (b) of this section defines the term *qualified income*. Paragraph (c) of this section defines the term *qualified foreign corporation*. Paragraph (f) of this section defines the term *international operation of ships or aircraft*.

(b) *Qualified income.*—Qualified income is income derived from the international operation of ships or aircraft that—

(1) Is properly includible in any of the income categories described in paragraph (h)(2) of this section; and

(2) Is the subject of an equivalent exemption, as defined in paragraph (h) of this section, granted by the qualified foreign country, as defined in paragraph (d) of this section, in which the foreign corporation seeking qualified foreign corporation status is organized.

(c) *Qualified foreign corporation.*—(1) *General rule.*—A qualified foreign corporation is a corporation that is organized in a qualified foreign country and considered engaged in the international operation of ships or aircraft. The term *corporation* is defined in section 7701(a)(3) and the regulations thereunder. Paragraph (d) of this section defines the term *qualified foreign country*. Paragraph (e) of this section defines the term *operation of ships or aircraft*, and paragraph (f) of this section defines the term *international operation of ships or aircraft*. To be a qualified foreign corporation, the corporation must satisfy the stock ownership test of paragraph (c)(2) of this section and satisfy the substantiation and reporting requirements described in paragraph (c)(3) of this section. A corporation may be a qualified foreign corporation with respect to one category of qualified income but not with respect to another such category. See paragraph (h)(2) of this section for a discussion of the categories of qualified income.

(2) *Stock ownership test.*—To be a qualified foreign corporation, a foreign corporation must satisfy the publicly-traded test of § 1.883-2(a), the CFC stock ownership test of § 1.883-3(a), or the qualified shareholder stock ownership test of § 1.883-4(a).

(3) *Substantiation and reporting requirements.*—(i) *General rule.*—To be a qualified foreign corporation, a foreign corporation must include the following information in its Form 1120-F, "U.S. Income Tax Return of a Foreign Corporation," in the manner prescribed by such form and its accompanying instructions—

(A) The corporation's name and address (including mailing code);

(B) The corporation's U.S. taxpayer identification number;

(C) The foreign country in which the corporation is organized;

(D) The applicable authority for an equivalent exemption, for example, citation of a statute in the country where the corporation is organized, a diplomatic note between the United States and such country, (for further guidance, see Rev. Rul. 2001-48 (2001-2 C.B. 324) (see § 601.601(d)(2) of this chapter)), or, in the case of a corporation described in paragraph (h)(3)(ii) of this section, an income tax convention between the United States and such country;

(E) The category or categories of qualified income for which an exemption is being claimed;

(F) A reasonable estimate of the gross amount of income in each category of qualified income for which the exemption is claimed, to the extent such amounts are readily determinable;

(G) Any other information required under § 1.883-2(f), 1.883-3(d), or 1.883-4(e), as applicable; and

(H) Any other relevant information specified by the Form 1120-F and its accompanying instructions.

(ii) *Further documentation.*—If the Commissioner requests in writing that the foreign corporation document or substantiate representations made under paragraph (c)(3)(i) of this section, or under § 1.883-2(f), 1.883-3(d) or 1.883-4(c), the foreign corporation must provide the documentation or substantiation within 60 days following the written request. If the foreign corporation does not provide the documentation and substantiation requested within the 60-day period, but demonstrates that the failure was due to reasonable cause and not willful neglect, the Commissioner may grant the foreign corporation a 30-day extension to provide the documentation or substantiation.

Whether a failure to obtain the documentation or substantiation in a timely manner was due to reasonable cause and not willful neglect shall be determined by the Commissioner after considering all the facts and circumstances.

(4) *Commissioner's discretion to cure defects in documentation.*—The Commissioner retains the discretion to cure any defects in the documentation where the Commissioner is satisfied that the foreign corporation would otherwise be a qualified foreign corporation.

(d) *Qualified foreign country.*—A qualified foreign country is a foreign country that grants to corporations organized in the United States an equivalent exemption, as described in paragraph (h) of this section, for the category of qualified income, as described in paragraph (h)(2) of this section, derived by the foreign corporation seeking qualified foreign corporation status. A foreign country may be a qualified foreign country with respect to one category of qualified income but not with respect to another such category.

(e) *Operation of ships or aircraft.*—(1) *General rule.*—Except as provided in paragraph (e)(2) of this section, a foreign corporation is considered engaged in the operation of ships or aircraft only during the time it is an owner or lessee of one or more entire ships or aircraft and uses such ships or aircraft in one or more of the following activities—

(i) Carriage of passengers or cargo for hire;

(ii) In the case of a ship, the leasing out of the ship under a time or voyage charter (full charter), space or slot charter, or bareboat charter, as those terms are defined in paragraph (e)(5) of this section, provided the ship is used to carry passengers or cargo for hire; and

(iii) In the case of aircraft, the leasing out of the aircraft under a wet lease (full charter), space, slot, or block-seat charter, or dry lease, as those terms are defined in paragraph (e)(5) of this section, provided the aircraft is used to carry passengers or cargo for hire.

(2) *Pool, partnership, strategic alliance, joint operating agreement, code-sharing arrangement or other joint venture.*—A foreign corporation is considered engaged in the operation of ships or aircraft within the meaning of paragraph (e)(1) of this section with respect to its participation in a pool, partnership, strategic alliance, joint operating agreement, code-sharing arrangement or other joint venture if it directly, or indirectly through one or more fiscally transparent entities under the income tax laws of the United States, as defined in paragraph (e)(5)(v) of this section—

(i) Owns an interest in a partnership, disregarded entity, or other fiscally transparent entity under the income tax laws of the United States that itself would be considered engaged in the operation of ships or aircraft under paragraph (e)(1) of this section if it were a foreign corporation; or

(ii) Participates in a pool, strategic alliance, joint operating agreement, code-sharing arrangement, or other joint venture that is not an entity, as defined in paragraph (e)(5)(iv) of this section, involving one or more activities described in paragraphs (e)(1)(i) through (iii) of this section, but only if—

(A) In the case of a direct interest, the foreign corporation is otherwise engaged in the operation of ships or aircraft under paragraph (e)(1) of this section; or

(B) In the case of an indirect interest, either the foreign corporation is otherwise engaged, or one of the fiscally transparent entities would be considered engaged if it were a foreign corporation, in the operation of ships or aircraft under paragraph (e)(1) of this section.

(3) *Activities not considered operation of ships or aircraft.*—Activities that do not constitute operation of ships or aircraft include, but are not limited to—

(i) The activities of a nonvessel operating common carrier, as defined in paragraph (e)(5)(vii) of this section;

(ii) Ship or aircraft management;

(iii) Obtaining crews for ships or aircraft operated by another party;

(iv) Acting as a ship's agent;

(v) Ship or aircraft brokering;

(vi) Freight forwarding;

(vii) The activities of travel agents and tour operators;

(viii) Rental by a container leasing company of containers and related equipment; and

(ix) The activities of a concessionaire.

(4) *Examples.*—The rules of paragraphs (e)(1) through (3) of this section are illustrated by the following examples:

Example 1. Three tiers of charters—(i) *Facts.* A, B, and C are foreign corporations. A purchases a ship. A and B enter into a bareboat charter of the ship for a term of 20 years, and B, in turn, enters into a time charter of the ship with C for a term of 5 years. Under the time charter, B is responsible for the complete operation of the ship, including providing the crew and maintenance. C uses the ship during the term of the time charter to carry its customers' freight between U.S. and foreign ports. C owns no ships.

(ii) *Analysis.* Because A is the owner of the entire ship and leases out the ship under a bareboat charter to B, and because the sublessor, C, uses the ship to carry cargo for hire, A is considered engaged in the operation of a ship under paragraph (e)(1) of this section during the term of the time charter. B leases in the entire ship from A and leases out the ship under a time charter to C, who uses the ship to carry cargo for hire. Therefore, B is considered engaged in the operation of a ship under paragraph (e)(1) of this section during the term of the time charter. C time charters the entire ship from B and uses the ship to carry its customers' freight during the term of the charter. Therefore, C is also engaged in the operation of a ship under paragraph (e)(1) of this section during the term of the time charter.

Example 2. Partnership with contributed shipping assets—(i) *Facts.* X, Y, and Z, each a foreign corporation, enter into a partnership, P. P is a fiscally transparent entity under the income tax laws of the United States, as defined in paragraph (e)(5)(v) of this section. Under the terms of the partnership agreement, each partner contributes all of the ships in its fleet to P in exchange for interests in the partnership and shares in the P profits from the international carriage of cargo. The partners share in the overall management of P, but each partner, acting in its capacity as partner, continues to crew and manage all ships previously in its fleet.

(ii) *Analysis.* P owns the ships contributed by the partners and uses these ships to carry cargo for hire. Therefore, if P were a foreign corporation, it would be considered engaged in the operation of ships within the meaning of paragraph (e)(1) of this section. Accordingly, because P is a fiscally transparent entity under the income tax laws of the United States, as defined in paragraph (e)(5)(v) of this section, X, Y, and Z are each considered engaged in the operation of ships through P, within the meaning of paragraph (e)(2)(i) of this section, with respect to their distributive share of income from P's international carriage of cargo.

Example 3. Joint venture with chartered in ships—(i) *Facts.* Foreign corporation A owns a number of foreign subsidiaries involved in various aspects of the shipping business, including S1, S2, S3, and S4. S4 is a foreign corporation that provides cruises but does not own any ships. S1, S2, and S3 are foreign corporations that own cruise ships. S1, S2, S3, and S4 form joint venture JV, in which they are all interest holders, to conduct cruises. JV is a fiscally transparent entity under the income tax laws of the United States, as defined in paragraph (e)(5)(v) of this section. Under the terms of the joint venture, S1, S2, and S3 each enter into time charter agreements with JV, pursuant to which S1, S2, and S3 retain control of the navigation and management of the individual ships, and JV will use the ships to carry passengers for hire. The overall management of the cruise line will be provided by S4.

(ii) *Analysis.* S1, S2, and S3 each owns ships and time charters those ships to JV, which uses the ships to carry passengers for hire. Accordingly, S1, S2, and S3 are each considered engaged in the operation of ships under paragraph (e)(1) of this section. JV leases in entire ships by means of the time charters, and JV uses those ships to carry passengers on cruises. Thus, JV would be engaged in the operation of ships within the meaning of paragraph (e)(1) of this section if it were a foreign corporation. Therefore, although S4 does not directly own or lease in a ship, S4 also is engaged in the operation of ships, within the meaning of paragraph (e)(2)(i) of this section, with respect to its participation in JV.

Example 4. Tiered partnerships—(i) *Facts.* Foreign corporations A, B, and C enter into a partnership, P1. P1 is one of several shareholders of Poolco, a foreign limited liability company that makes an election pursuant to § 301.7701-3 of this chapter to be treated as a partnership for U.S. tax purposes. P1 acquires several ships and time charters them out to Poolco. Poolco slot or voyage charters such ships out to third parties for use in the carriage of cargo for hire. P1 and Poolco are fiscally transparent entities under the income tax laws of the United States, as defined in paragraph (e)(5)(v) of this section.

(ii) *Analysis.* A, B, and C are considered engaged in the operation of ships under paragraph (e)(2)(i) of this section with respect to their direct interest in P1 and with respect to their indirect interest in Poolco because both P1 and Poolco are fiscally transparent entities under the income tax laws of the United States and would be considered engaged in the operation of ships under paragraph (e)(1) of this section if they were foreign corporations. The result would be the same if Poolco were a single-member disregarded entity owned solely by P1.

(5) *Definitions.*—(i) *Bareboat charter.*—A bareboat charter is a contract for the use of a ship or aircraft whereby the lessee is in complete possession, control, and command of the ship or aircraft. For example, in a bareboat charter, the lessee is responsible for the navigation and management of the ship or aircraft, the crew, supplies, repairs and maintenance, fees, insurance, charges, commissions and other expenses connected with the use of the ship or aircraft. The lessor of the ship bears none of the expense or responsibility of operation of the ship or aircraft.

(ii) *Code-sharing arrangement.*—A code-sharing arrangement is an arrangement in which one air carrier puts its identification code on the flight of another carrier. This arrangement allows the first carrier to hold itself out as providing service in markets where it does not otherwise operate or where it operates infrequently. Code-sharing arrangements can range from a very limited agreement between two carriers involving only one market to agreements involving multiple markets and alliances between or among international carriers which also include joint marketing, baggage handling, one-stop check-in service, sharing of frequent flyer awards, and other services. For rules involving the sale of code-sharing tickets, see paragraph (g)(1)(vi) of this section.

(iii) *Dry lease.*—A dry lease is the bareboat charter of an aircraft.

(iv) *Entity.*—For purposes of this paragraph (e), an entity is any person that is treated by the United States as other than an individual for U.S. Federal income tax purposes. The term includes disregarded entities.

(v) *Fiscally transparent entity under the income tax laws of the United States.*—For purposes of this paragraph (e), an entity is fiscally transparent under the income tax laws of the United States if the entity would be considered fiscally transparent under the income tax laws of the United States under the principles of § 1.894-1(d)(3).

(vi) *Full charter.*—Full charter (or full rental) means a time charter or a voyage charter of a ship or a wet lease of an aircraft but during which the full crew and management are provided by the lessor.

(vii) *Nonvessel operating common carrier.*—A nonvessel operating common carrier is an entity that does not exercise control over any part of a vessel, but holds itself out to the public as providing transportation for hire, issues bills of lading, assumes responsibility or is liable by law as a common carrier for safe transportation of shipments, and arranges in its own name with other common carriers, including those engaged in the operation of ships, for the performance of such transportation.

(viii) *Space or slot charter.*—A space or slot charter is a contract for use of a certain amount of space (but less than all of the space) on a ship or aircraft, and may be on a time or voyage basis. When used in connection with passenger aircraft this sort of charter may be referred to as the sale of block seats.

(ix) *Time charter.*—A time charter is a contract for the use of a ship or aircraft for a specific period of time, during which the lessor of the ship or aircraft retains control of the navigation and management of the ship or aircraft (i.e., the lessor continues to be responsible for the crew, supplies, repairs and maintenance, fees and insurance, charges, commissions and other expenses connected with the use of the ship or aircraft).

(x) *Voyage charter.*—A voyage charter is a contract similar to a time charter except that the ship or aircraft is chartered for a specific voyage or flight rather than for a specific period of time.

(xi) *Wet lease.*—A wet lease is the time or voyage charter of an aircraft.

(f) *International operation of ships or aircraft.*—(1) *General rule.*—The term *international operation of ships or aircraft* means the operation of ships or aircraft, as defined in paragraph (e) of this section, with respect to the carriage of passengers or cargo on voyages or flights that begin or end in the United States, as determined under paragraph (f)(2) of this section. The term does not include the carriage of passengers or cargo on a voyage or flight that begins and ends in the United States, even if the voyage or flight contains a segment extending beyond the territorial limits of the United States, unless the passenger disembarks or the cargo is unloaded outside the United States. Operation of ships or aircraft beyond the territorial limits of the United States does not constitute in itself international operation of ships or aircraft.

(2) *Determining whether income is derived from international operation of ships or aircraft.*—Whether income is derived from international operation of ships or aircraft is determined on a passenger by passenger basis (as provided in paragraph (f)(2)(i) of this section) and on an item-of-cargo by item-of-cargo basis (as provided in paragraph (f)(2)(ii) of this section). In the case of the bareboat charter of a ship or the dry lease of an aircraft, whether the charter income for a particular period is derived from international operation of ships or aircraft is determined by reference to how the ship or aircraft is used by the lowest-tier lessee in the chain of lessees (as provided in paragraph (f)(2)(iii) of this section).

(i) *International carriage of passengers.*—(A) *General rule.*—Except in the case of a round trip described in paragraph (f)(2)(i)(B) of this section, income derived from the carriage of a passenger will be income from international operation of ships or aircraft if the passenger is carried between a beginning point in the United States and an ending point outside the United States, or vice versa. Carriage of a passenger will be treated as ending at the passenger's final destination even if, en route to the passenger's final destination, a stop is made at an intermediate point for refueling, maintenance, or other business reasons, provided the passenger does not change ships or aircraft at the intermediate point. Similarly, carriage of a passenger will be treated as beginning at the passenger's point of origin even if, en route to the passenger's final destination, a stop is made at an intermediate point, provided the passenger does not change ships or aircraft at the intermediate point. Carriage of a passenger will be treated as beginning or ending at a U.S. or foreign intermediate point if the passenger changes ships or aircraft at that intermediate point. Income derived from the sale of a ticket for international carriage of a passenger will be treated as income derived from international operation of ships or aircraft even if the passenger does not begin or complete an international journey because of unanticipated circumstances.

(B) *Round trip travel on ships.*—In the case of income from the carriage of a passenger on a ship that begins its voyage in the United States, calls on one or more foreign intermediate ports, and returns to the same or another U.S. port, such income from carriage of a passenger on the entire voyage will be treated as income derived from international operation of ships or aircraft under paragraph (f)(2)(i)(A) of this section. This result obtains even if such carriage includes one or more intermediate stops at a U.S. port or ports and even if the passenger does not disembark at the foreign intermediate point.

(ii) *International carriage of cargo.*—Income from the carriage of cargo will be income derived from international operation of ships or aircraft if the cargo is carried between a beginning point in the United States and an ending point outside the United States, or vice versa. Carriage of cargo will be treated as ending at the final destination of the cargo even if, en route to that final destination, a stop is made at a U.S. intermediate point, provided the cargo is transported to its ultimate destination on the same ship or aircraft. If the cargo is transferred to another ship or aircraft, the carriage of the cargo may nevertheless be treated as ending at its final destination, if the same taxpayer transports the cargo to and from the U.S. intermediate point and the cargo does not pass through customs at the U.S. intermediate point. Similarly, carriage of cargo will be treated as beginning at the cargo's point of origin, even if en route to its final destination a stop is made at a U.S. intermediate point, provided the cargo is transported to its ultimate destination on the same ship or aircraft. If the cargo is transferred to another ship or aircraft at the U.S. intermediate point, the carriage of the cargo may nevertheless be treated as beginning at the point of origin, if the same taxpayer transports the cargo to and from the U.S. intermediate point and the cargo does not pass through customs at the U.S. intermediate point. Repackaging, recontainerization, or any other activity involving the unloading of the cargo at the U.S. intermediate point does not change these results, provided the same taxpayer transports the cargo to and from the U.S. intermediate point and the cargo does not pass through customs at the U.S. intermediate point. A lighter vessel that carries cargo to, or picks up cargo from, a vessel located beyond the territorial limits of the United States and correspondingly loads or unloads that cargo at a U.S. port, carries cargo between a point in the United States and a point outside the United States. However, a lighter vessel that carries cargo to, or picks up cargo from, a vessel located within the territorial limits of the United States, and correspondingly loads or unloads that cargo at a U.S. port, is not engaged in international operation of ships or aircraft. Income from the carriage of military cargo on a voyage that begins in the United States, stops at a foreign intermediate port or a military prepositioning location, and returns to the same or another U.S. port without unloading its cargo at the foreign intermediate point, will nevertheless be treated as derived from international operation of ships or aircraft.

(iii) *Bareboat charter of ships or dry lease of aircraft used in international operation of ships or aircraft.*—If a qualified foreign corporation bareboat charters a ship or dry leases an aircraft to a lessee, and the lowest tier lessee in the chain of ownership uses such ship or aircraft for the international carriage of passengers or cargo for hire, as described in paragraphs (f)(2)(i) and (ii) of this section, then the amount of charter income attributable to the period the ship or aircraft is used by the lowest tier lessee is income from international operation of ships or aircraft. The foreign corporation generally must determine the amount of the charter income that is attributable to such international operation of ships or aircraft by multiplying the amount of charter income by a fraction, the numerator of which is the total number of days of uninterrupted travel on voyages or flights of such ship or aircraft between the United States and the farthest point or points where cargo or passengers are loaded en route to, or discharged en route from, the United States during the smaller of the taxable year or the particular charter period, and the denominator of which is the total number of days in the smaller of the taxable year or the particular charter period. For this purpose, the number of days during which the ship or aircraft is not generating transportation income, within the meaning of section 863(c)(2), are not included in the numerator or denominator of the fraction. However, the foreign corporation may adopt an alternative method for determining the amount of the charter income that is attributable to the international operation of ships or aircraft if it can establish that the alternative method more accurately reflects the amount of such income.

(iv) *Charter of ships or aircraft for hire.*—For purposes of this section, if a foreign corporation time, voyage, or bareboat charters out a ship or aircraft, and the lowest-tier lessee uses the ship or aircraft to carry passengers or cargo on a fee basis, the ship or aircraft is considered used to carry passengers or cargo for hire, regardless of whether the ship or aircraft may be empty during a portion of the charter period due to a backhaul voyage or flight or for purposes of repositioning. If a foreign corporation time, voyage, or bareboat charters out a ship or aircraft, and the lowest-tier lessee uses the ship or aircraft for the carriage of proprietary goods, including an empty backhaul voyage or flight or repositioning related to such carriage of proprietary goods, the ship or aircraft similarly will be treated as used to carry cargo for hire.

(g) *Activities incidental to the international operation of ships or aircraft.*—(1) *General rule.*—Certain activities of a foreign corporation engaged in the international operation of ships or aircraft are so closely related to the international operation of ships or aircraft that they are considered incidental to such operation, and income derived by the foreign corporation from its performance of these incidental activities is deemed to be income derived from the international operation of ships or aircraft. Examples of such activities include—

(i) Temporary investment of working capital funds to be used in the international operation of ships or aircraft by the foreign corporation;

(ii) Sale of tickets by the foreign corporation engaged in the international operation of ships for the international carriage of passengers by ship on behalf of another corporation engaged in the international operation of ships;

(iii) Sale of tickets by the foreign corporation engaged in the international operation of aircraft for the international carriage of passengers by air on behalf of another corporation engaged in the international operation of aircraft;

(iv) Contracting with concessionaires for performance of services onboard during the

Reg. § 1.883-1(g)(1)(iv)

international operation of the foreign corporation's ships or aircraft;

(v) Providing (either by subcontracting or otherwise) for the carriage of cargo preceding or following the international carriage of cargo under a through bill of lading, airway bill or similar document through a related corporation or through an unrelated person (and the rules of section 267(b) shall apply for purposes of determining whether a corporation or other person is related to the foreign corporation);

(vi) To the extent not described in paragraph (g)(1)(iii) of this section, the sale or issuance by the foreign corporation engaged in the international operation of aircraft of intraline, interline, or code-sharing tickets for the carriage of persons by air between a U.S. gateway and another U.S. city preceding or following international carriage of passengers, provided that all such flight segments are provided pursuant to the passenger's original invoice, ticket or itinerary and in the case of intraline tickets are a part of uninterrupted international air transportation (within the meaning of section 4262(c)(3));

(vii) Arranging for port city hotel accommodations within the United States for a passenger for the one night before or after the international carriage of that passenger by the foreign corporation engaged in the international operation of ships;

(viii) Bareboat charter of ships or dry lease of aircraft normally used by the foreign corporation in international operation of ships or aircraft but currently not needed, if the ship or aircraft is used by the lessee for international carriage of cargo or passengers;

(ix) Arranging by means of a space or slot charter for the carriage of cargo listed on a bill of lading or airway bill or similar document issued by the foreign corporation on the ship or aircraft of another corporation engaged in the international operation of ships or aircraft; and

(x) The provision of containers or other related equipment by the foreign corporation in connection with the international carriage of cargo for use by its customers, including short-term use within the United States immediately preceding or following the international carriage of cargo (and for this purpose, a period of five days or less shall be presumed to be short-term).

(2) *Activities not considered incidental to the international operation of ships or aircraft.*—Examples of activities that are not considered incidental to the international operation of ships or aircraft include—

(i) The sale of or arranging for train travel, bus transfers, single day shore excursions, or land tour packages;

(ii) Arranging for hotel accommodations within the United States other than as provided in paragraph (g)(1)(vii) of this section;

(iii) The sale of airline tickets or cruise tickets other than as provided in paragraph (g)(1)(ii), (iii), or (vi) of this section;

(iv) The sale or rental of real property;

(v) Treasury activities involving the investment of excess funds or funds awaiting repatriation, even if derived from the international operation of ships or aircraft;

(vi) The carriage of passengers or cargo on ships or aircraft on domestic legs of transportation not treated as either international operation of ships or aircraft under paragraph (f) of this section or as an activity that is incidental to such operation under paragraph (g)(1) of this section;

(vii) The carriage of cargo by bus, truck or rail by a foreign corporation between a U.S. inland point and a U.S. gateway port or airport preceding or following the international carriage of such cargo by the foreign corporation; and

(viii) The provision of containers or other related equipment by the foreign corporation within the United States other than as provided in paragraph (g)(1)(x) of this section, including warehousing.

(3) *Services.*—(i) *Ground services, maintenance and catering.*—[Reserved]

(ii) *Other services.*—[Reserved]

(4) *Activities involved in a pool, partnership, strategic alliance, joint operating agreement, code-sharing arrangement or other joint venture.*—Notwithstanding paragraph (g)(1) of this section, an activity is considered incidental to the international operation of ships or aircraft by a foreign corporation, and income derived by the foreign corporation with respect to such activity is deemed to be income derived from the international operation of ships or aircraft, if the activity is performed by or pursuant to a pool, partnership, strategic alliance, joint operating agreement, code-sharing arrangement or other joint venture in which such foreign corporation participates directly, or indirectly through a fiscally transparent entity under the income tax laws of the United States, provided that—

(i) Such activity is incidental to the international operation of ships or aircraft by the pool, partnership, strategic alliance, joint operating agreement, code-sharing arrangement or other joint venture, and provided that it is described in paragraph (e)(2)(i) of this section; or

(ii) Such activity would be incidental to the international operation of ships or aircraft by the foreign corporation, or fiscally transparent entity if it performed such activity itself, and provided the foreign corporation is engaged or the fiscally transparent entity would be considered engaged if it were a foreign corporation in the operation of ships or aircraft under paragraph (e)(1) of this section.

(h) *Equivalent exemption.*—(1) *General rule.*—A foreign country grants an equivalent exemption when it exempts from taxation income from the international operation of ships or aircraft derived by corporations organized in the United States. Whether a foreign country provides an equivalent exemption must be determined separately with respect to each category of income, as provided in paragraph (h)(2) of this section. An equivalent exemption may be available for income derived from the international operation of ships even though income derived from the international operation of aircraft may not be exempt, and vice versa. For rules regarding foreign corporations organized in countries that provide exemptions only through an income tax convention, see paragraph (h)(3) of this section. An equivalent exemption may exist where the foreign country—

(i) Generally imposes no tax on income, including income from the international operation of ships or aircraft;

(ii) Specifically provides a domestic law tax exemption for income derived from the international operation of ships or aircraft, either by statute, decree, or otherwise; or

(iii) Exchanges diplomatic notes with the United States, or enters into an agreement with the United States, that provides for a reciprocal exemption for purposes of section 883.

(2) *Determining equivalent exemptions for each category of income.*—Whether a foreign country grants an equivalent exemption must be determined separately with respect to income from the international operation of ships and income from the international operation of aircraft for each category of income listed in paragraphs (h)(2)(i) through (v), (vii), and (viii) of this section. If an exemption is unavailable in the foreign country for a particular category of income, the foreign country is not considered to grant an equivalent exemption with respect to that category of income. Income in that category is not considered to be the subject of an equivalent exemption and, thus, is not eligible for exemption from income tax in the United States, even though the foreign country may grant an equivalent exemption for other categories of income. With respect to paragraph (h)(2)(vi) of this section, a foreign country may be considered to grant an equivalent exemption for one or more types of income described in paragraph (g)(1) of this section. The following categories of income derived from the international operation of ships or aircraft may be exempt from United States income tax if an equivalent exemption is available—

(i) Income from the carriage of passengers and cargo;

(ii) Time or voyage (full) charter income of a ship or wet lease income of an aircraft;

(iii) Bareboat charter income of a ship or dry charter income of an aircraft;

(iv) Incidental bareboat charter income or incidental dry lease income;

(v) Incidental container-related income;

(vi) Income incidental to the international operation of ships or aircraft other than incidental income described in paragraphs (h)(2)(iv) and (v) of this section;

(vii) Capital gains derived by a qualified foreign corporation engaged in the international operation of ships or aircraft from the sale, exchange or other disposition of a ship, aircraft, container or related equipment or other moveable property used by that qualified foreign corporation in the international operation of ships or aircraft; and

(viii) Income from participation in a pool, partnership, strategic alliance, joint operating agreement, code-sharing arrangement, international operating agency, or other joint venture described in paragraph (e)(2) of this section.

(3) *Special rules with respect to income tax conventions.*—(i) *General rule.*—Except as provided in paragraph (h)(3)(ii) of this section, if a corporation is organized in a foreign country that provides an exemption only through an income tax convention with the United States, the foreign corporation is not organized in a foreign country that grants an equivalent exemption. Rather, the foreign corporation must satisfy the terms of that convention to receive a benefit under the convention, and the foreign corporation may not claim an exemption under section 883. If the corporation is organized in a foreign country that offers an exemption under an income tax convention and also by some other means, such as by diplomatic note or domestic statutory law, the foreign corporation may choose annually whether to claim an exemption under section 883 based upon the equivalent exemption provided by such other means or under the income tax convention. However, if a corporation chooses to claim an exemption under an income tax convention under the preceding sentence, it may simultaneously claim an exemption under section 883 with respect to any category of income listed in

Reg. §1.883-1(h)(3)(i)

paragraphs (h)(2)(i) through (v), (vii), and (viii) of this section and to any type of income described in paragraph (h)(2)(vi) of this section, but only to the extent that such income also is exempt under the income tax convention. Any such choice will apply with respect to all qualified income of the corporation from the international operation of ships or aircraft and cannot be made separately with respect to different categories of such income. If a foreign corporation bases its claim for an exemption on section 883, the foreign corporation must satisfy all of the requirements of this section to qualify for an exemption from U.S. income tax. See § 1.883-4(b)(3) for rules regarding satisfying the ownership test of paragraph (c)(2) of this section using shareholders resident in a foreign country that offers an exemption under an income tax convention.

(ii) *Participation in certain joint ventures.*—Notwithstanding paragraph (h)(3)(i) of this section, if a corporation is organized in a foreign country that provides an exemption only through an income tax convention with the United States, the foreign corporation will be treated as organized in a foreign country that grants an equivalent exemption under section 883 with respect to a category of income derived through participation, directly or indirectly, in a pool, partnership, strategic alliance, joint operating agreement, code-sharing arrangement or other joint venture described in paragraph (e)(2) of this section, but only where treaty benefits would be available under the treaty but for the treatment of the pool, partnership, strategic alliance, joint operating agreement, code-sharing arrangement or other joint venture as not fiscally transparent with respect to that category of income under the income tax laws of the foreign country in which the foreign corporate interest holder is organized for purposes of § 1.894-1(d)(3)(iii)(A).

(iii) *Independent interpretation of income tax conventions.*—Nothing in this section and §§ 1.883-2 through 1.883-5 affects the rights or obligations under any income tax convention. The definitions provided in this section and §§ 1.883-2 through 1.883-5 shall neither give meaning to similar terms used in income tax conventions nor provide guidance regarding the scope of any exemption provided by such conventions, unless an income tax convention that entered into force after August 26, 2003 or its legislative history explicitly refers to section 883 and guidance thereunder for its meaning.

(4) *Exemptions not qualifying as equivalent exemptions.*—(i) *General rule.*—Certain types of exemptions provided to corporations organized in the United States by foreign countries do not satisfy the equivalent exemption requirements of this section. Paragraphs (h)(4)(ii) through (vii) of this section provide descriptions of some of the types of exemptions that do not qualify as equivalent exemptions for purposes of this section.

(ii) *Reduced tax rate or time limited exemption.*—The exemption granted by the foreign country's law or income tax convention must be a complete exemption. The exemption may not constitute merely a reduction to a nonzero rate of tax levied against the income of corporations organized in the United States derived from the international operation of ships or aircraft or a temporary reduction to a zero rate of tax, such as in the case of a tax holiday.

(iii) *Inbound or outbound freight tax.*—With respect to the carriage of cargo, the foreign country must provide an exemption from tax for income from transporting freight both inbound and outbound. For example, a foreign country that imposes tax only on outbound freight will not be treated as granting an equivalent exemption for income from transporting freight inbound into that country.

(iv) *Exemptions for limited types of cargo.*—A foreign country must provide an exemption from tax for income from transporting all types of cargo. For example, if a foreign country were generally to impose tax on income from the international carriage of cargo but were to provide a statutory exemption for income from transporting agricultural products, the foreign country would not be considered to grant an equivalent exemption with respect to income from the international carriage of cargo, including agricultural products.

(v) *Territorial tax systems.*—A foreign country with a territorial tax system will be treated as granting an equivalent exemption if it treats all income derived from the international operation of ships or aircraft derived by a U.S. corporation as entirely foreign source and therefore not subject to tax, including income derived from a voyage or flight that begins or ends in that foreign country.

(vi) *Countries that tax on a residence basis.*—A foreign country that provides an equivalent exemption to corporations organized in the United States but also imposes a residencebased tax on certain corporations organized in the United States may nevertheless be considered to grant an equivalent exemption if the residence-based tax is imposed only on a corporation organized in the United States that maintains its center of management and control or other comparable attributes in that foreign country. If the residence-based tax is imposed on corporations organized in the United States and engaged in the international operation of ships or aircraft that are not managed and controlled in that foreign country, the foreign country shall not be treated as a qualified foreign country and shall not be considered to grant an equivalent exemption for purposes of this section.

(vii) *Exemptions within categories of income.*—With respect to paragraphs (h)(2)(i) through (v), (vii), and (viii) of this section, a foreign country must provide an exemption from tax for all income in a category of income, as defined in paragraph (h)(2) of this section. For example, a country that exempts income from the bareboat charter of passenger aircraft but not the bareboat charter of cargo aircraft does not provide an equivalent exemption. However, an equivalent exemption may be available for income derived from the international operation of ships even though income derived from the international operation of aircraft may not be exempt, and vice versa. With respect to paragraph (h)(2)(vi) of this section, a foreign country may be considered to grant an equivalent exemption for one or more types of income described in paragraph (g)(1) of this section.

(i) *Treatment of possessions.*—For purposes of this section, a possession of the United States will be treated as a foreign country. A possession of the United States will be considered to grant an equivalent exemption and will be treated as a qualified foreign country if it applies a mirror system of taxation. If a possession does not apply a mirror system of taxation, the possession may nevertheless be a qualified foreign country if, for example, it provides for an equivalent exemption through its internal law. A possession applies the mirror system of taxation if the U.S. Internal Revenue Code of 1986, as amended, applies in the possession with the name of the possession used instead of "United States" where appropriate.

(j) *Expenses related to qualified income.*—If a qualified foreign corporation derives qualified income from the international operation of ships or aircraft as well as income that is not qualified income, and the nonqualified income is effectively connected with the conduct of a trade or business within the United States, the foreign corporation may not deduct from such nonqualified income any amount otherwise allowable as a deduction from qualified income, if that qualified income is excluded under this section. See section 265(a)(1). [Reg. § 1.883-1.]

☐ [T.D. 6258, 10-23-57. Amended by T.D. 7293, 11-27-73 and T.D. 9087, 8-25-2003.]

§ 1.883-2. Treatment of publicly-traded corporations.—(a) *General rule.*—A foreign corporation satisfies the stock ownership test of § 1.883-1(c)(2) if it is considered a publicly-traded corporation and satisfies the substantiation and reporting requirements of paragraphs (e) and (f) of this section. To be considered a publicly-traded corporation, the stock of the foreign corporation must be primarily traded and regularly traded, as defined in paragraphs (c) and (d) of this section, respectively, on one or more established securities markets, as defined in paragraph (b) of this section, in either the United States or any qualified foreign country.

(b) *Established securities market.*—(1) *General rule.*—For purposes of this section, the term *established securities market* means, for any taxable year—

(i) A foreign securities exchange that is officially recognized, sanctioned, or supervised by a governmental authority of the qualified foreign country in which the market is located, and has an annual value of shares traded on the exchange exceeding $1 billion during each of the three calendar years immediately preceding the beginning of the taxable year;

(ii) A national securities exchange that is registered under section 6 of the Securities Act of 1934 (15 U.S.C. 78f);

(iii) A United States over-the-counter market, as defined in paragraph (b)(4) of this section;

(iv) Any exchange designated under a Limitation on Benefits article in a United States income tax convention; and

(v) Any other exchange that the Secretary may designate by regulation or otherwise.

(2) *Exchanges with multiple tiers.*—If an exchange in a foreign country has more than one tier or market level on which stock may be separately listed or traded, each such tier shall be treated as a separate exchange.

(3) *Computation of dollar value of stock traded.*—For purposes of paragraph (b)(1)(i) of this section, the value in U.S. dollars of shares traded during a calendar year shall be determined on the basis of the dollar value of such shares traded as reported by the International Federation of Stock Exchanges located in Paris, or, if not so reported, then by converting into U.S. dollars the aggregate value in local currency of the shares traded using an exchange rate equal to the average of the spot rates on the last day of each month of the calendar year.

(4) *Over-the-counter market.*—An over-the-counter market is any market reflected by the existence of an interdealer quotation system. An interdealer quotation system is any system of general circulation to brokers and dealers that regularly disseminates quotations of

stocks and securities by identified brokers or dealers, other than by quotation sheets that are prepared and distributed by a broker or dealer in the regular course of business and that contain only quotations of such broker or dealer.

(5) *Discretion to determine that an exchange does not qualify as an established securities market.*—The Commissioner may determine that a securities exchange that otherwise meets the requirements of paragraph (b) of this section does not qualify as an established securities market, if—

(i) The exchange does not have adequate listing, financial disclosure, or trading requirements (or does not adequately enforce such requirements); or

(ii) There is not clear and convincing evidence that the exchange ensures the active trading of listed stocks.

(c) *Primarily traded.*—For purposes of this section, stock of a corporation is primarily traded in a country on one or more established securities markets, as defined in paragraph (b) of this section, if, with respect to each class of stock described in paragraph (d)(1)(i) of this section (relating to classes of stock relied on to meet the regularly traded test)—

(1) The number of shares in each such class that are traded during the taxable year on all established securities markets in that country exceeds

(2) The number of shares in each such class that are traded during that year on established securities markets in any other single country.

(d) *Regularly traded.*—(1) *General rule.*—For purposes of this section, stock of a corporation is regularly traded on one or more established securities markets, as defined in paragraph (b) of this section, if—

(i) One or more classes of stock of the corporation that, in the aggregate, represent more than 50 percent of the total combined voting power of all classes of stock of such corporation entitled to vote and of the total value of the stock of such corporation are listed on such market or markets during the taxable year; and

(ii) With respect to each class relied on to meet the more than 50 percent requirement of paragraph (d)(1)(i) of this section—

(A) Trades in each such class are effected, other than in de minimis quantities, on such market or markets on at least 60 days during the taxable year (or $\frac{1}{6}$ of the number of days in a short taxable year); and

(B) The aggregate number of shares in each such class that are traded on such market or markets during the taxable year are at least 10 percent of the average number of shares outstanding in that class during the taxable year (or, in the case of a short taxable year, a percentage that equals at least 10 percent of the average number of shares outstanding in that class during the taxable year multiplied by the number of days in the short taxable year, divided by 365).

(2) *Classes of stock traded on a domestic established securities market treated as meeting trading requirements.*—A class of stock that is traded during the taxable year on an established securities market located in the United States shall be considered to meet the trading requirements of paragraph (d)(1)(ii) of this section if the stock is regularly quoted by dealers making a market in the stock. A dealer makes a market in a stock only if the dealer regularly and actively offers to, and in fact does, purchase the stock from, and sell the stock to, customers who are not related persons (as defined in section 954(d)(3)) with respect to the dealer in the ordinary course of a trade or business.

(3) *Closely-held classes of stock not treated as meeting trading requirements.*—(i) *General rule.*—Except as provided in paragraph (d)(3)(ii) of this section, a class of stock of a foreign corporation that otherwise meets the requirements of paragraph (d)(1) or (2) of this section shall not be treated as meeting such requirements for a taxable year if, for more than half the number of days during the taxable year, one or more persons who own at least 5 percent of the vote and value of the outstanding shares of the class of stock, as determined under paragraph (d)(3)(iii) of this section (each a 5-percent shareholder), own, in the aggregate, 50 percent or more of the vote and value of the outstanding shares of the class of stock. If one or more 5-percent shareholders own, in the aggregate, 50 percent or more of the vote and value of the outstanding shares of the class of stock, such shares held by the 5-percent shareholders will constitute a closely-held block of stock.

(ii) *Exception.*—Paragraph (d)(3)(i) of this section shall not apply to a class of stock if the foreign corporation can establish that qualified shareholders, as defined in §1.883-4(b), applying the attribution rules of §1.883-4(c), own sufficient shares in the closely-held block of stock to preclude nonqualified shareholders in the closely- held block of stock from owning 50 percent or more of the total value of the class of stock of which the closely-held block is a part for more than half the number of days during the taxable year. Any shares that are owned, after application of the attribution rules in §1.883-4(c), by a qualified shareholder shall not also be treated as owned by a nonqualified shareholder in the chain of ownership for purposes of the preceding sentence. A foreign corporation must obtain the documentation described in § 1.883-4(d) from the qualified shareholders relied upon to satisfy this exception. However, no person shall be treated for purposes of this paragraph (d)(3) as a qualified shareholder if such person holds an interest in the class of stock directly or indirectly through bearer shares.

(iii) *Five-percent shareholders.*—(A) *Related persons.*—Solely for purposes of determining whether a person is a 5-percent shareholder, persons related within the meaning of section 267(b) shall be treated as one person. In determining whether two or more corporations are members of the same controlled group under section 267(b)(3), a person is considered to own stock owned directly by such person, stock owned through the application of section 1563(e)(1), and stock owned through the application of section 267(c). In determining whether a corporation is related to a partnership under section 267(b)(10), a person is considered to own the partnership interest owned directly by such person and the partnership interest owned through the application of section 267(e)(3).

(B) *Investment companies.*—For purposes of this paragraph (d)(3), an investment company registered under the Investment Company Act of 1940, as amended (54 Stat. 789), shall not be treated as a 5-percent shareholder.

(4) *Anti-abuse rule.*—Trades between or among related persons described in section 267(b), as modified by paragraph (d)(3)(iii) of this section, and trades conducted in order to meet the requirements of paragraph (d)(1) of this section shall be disregarded. A class of stock shall not be treated as meeting the trading requirements of paragraph (d)(1) of this section if there is a pattern of trades conducted to meet the requirements of that paragraph. For example, trades between two persons that occur several times during the taxable year may be treated as an arrangement or a pattern of trades conducted to meet the trading requirements of paragraph (d)(1)(ii) of this section.

(5) *Example.*—The closely-held test in paragraph (d)(3) of this section is illustrated by the following example:

Example. Closely-held exception—(i) *Facts.* X is a foreign corporation organized in a qualified foreign country and engaged in the international operation of ships. X has one class of stock, which is primarily traded on an established securities market in the qualified foreign country. The stock of X meets the regularly traded requirements of paragraph (d)(1)(ii) of this section without regard to paragraph (d)(3)(i) of this section. A, B, C and D are four members of the corporation's founding family who each own, during the entire taxable year, 25 percent of the stock of Hold Co, a company that issues registered shares. Hold Co, in turn, owns 60 percent of the stock of X during the entire taxable year. The remaining 40 percent of the stock of X is not owned by any 5-percent shareholder, as determined under paragraph (d)(3)(iii) of this section. A, B, and C are not residents of a qualified foreign country, but D is a resident of a qualified foreign country.

(ii) *Analysis.* Because Hold Co owns 60 percent of the stock of X for more than half the number of days during the taxable year, Hold Co is a 5-percent shareholder that owns 50 percent or more of the value of the stock of X. Thus, the shares owned by Hold Co constitute a closely-held block of stock. Under paragraph (d)(3)(i) of this section, the stock of X will not be regularly traded within the meaning of paragraph (d)(1) of this section unless X can establish, under paragraph (d)(3)(ii) of this section, that qualified shareholders within the closely-held block of stock own sufficient shares in the closely-held block of stock to preclude nonqualified shareholders in the closely-held block of stock from owning 50 percent or more of the value of the outstanding shares in the class of stock for more than half the number of days during the taxable year. A, B, and C are not qualified shareholders within the meaning of § 1.883-4(b) because they are not residents of a qualified foreign country, but D is a resident of a qualified foreign country and therefore is a qualified shareholder. D owns 15 percent of the outstanding shares of X through Hold Co (25 percent × 60 percent = 15 percent) while A, B, and C in the aggregate own 45 percent of the outstanding shares of X through Hold Co. D, therefore, owns sufficient shares in the closely-held block of stock to preclude the nonqualified shareholders in the closely-held block of stock, A, B and C, from owning 50 percent or more of the value of the class of stock (60 percent − 15 percent = 45 percent) of which the closely-held block is a part. Provided that X obtains from D the documentation described in § 1.883-4(d), X's sole class of stock meets the exception in paragraph (d)(3)(ii) of this section and will not be disqualified from the regularly traded test by virtue of paragraph (d)(3)(i) of this section.

(e) *Substantiation that a foreign corporation is publicly traded.*—(1) *General rule.*—A foreign corporation that relies on the publicly traded test of this section to meet the stock ownership test of § 1.883-1(c)(2) must substantiate that the stock of the foreign corporation is primarily and regularly traded on one or more established securities markets, as that term is defined in paragraph (b) of this section. If one of the classes of stock on which the foreign corporation relies to meet this test is closely-held within the meaning of paragraph (d)(3)(i) of this section, the foreign corporation must obtain an ownership statement described in § 1.883-4(d) from each qualified shareholder and intermediary that it relies upon to satisfy the exception to the closely-held test, but only to the extent such statement would be required if the foreign corporation were relying on the qualified shareholder stock ownership test of § 1.883-4 with respect to those shares of stock. The foreign corporation must also maintain and provide to the Commissioner upon request a list of its shareholders of record and any other relevant information known to the foreign corporation supporting its entitlement to an exemption under this section.

(2) *Availability and retention of documents for inspection.*—The documentation described in paragraph (e)(1) of this section must be retained by the corporation seeking qualified foreign corporation status until the expiration of the statute of limitations for the taxable year of the foreign corporation to which the documentation relates. Such documentation must be made available for inspection by the Commissioner at such time and such place as the Commissioner may request in writing.

(f) *Reporting requirements.*—A foreign corporation relying on this section to satisfy the stock ownership test of § 1.883-1(c)(2) must provide the following information in addition to the information required in § 1.883-1(c)(3) to be included in its Form 1120-F, "U.S. Income Tax Return of a Foreign Corporation," for the taxable year. The information must be current as of the end of the corporation's taxable year and must include the following—

(1) The name of the country in which the stock is primarily traded;

(2) The name of the established securities market or markets on which the stock is listed;

(3) A description of each class of stock relied upon to meet the requirements of paragraph (d) of this section, including the number of shares issued and outstanding as of the close of the taxable year;

(4) For each class of stock relied upon to meet the requirements of paragraph (d) of this section, if one or more 5-percent shareholders, as defined in paragraph (d)(3)(i) of this section, own in the aggregate 50 percent or more of the vote and value of the outstanding shares of that class of stock for more than half the number of days during the taxable year—

(i) The days during the taxable year of the corporation in which the stock was closely-held without regard to the exception in paragraph (d)(3)(ii) of this section and the percentage of the vote and value of the class of stock that is owned by 5-percent shareholders during such days;

(ii) For each qualified shareholder who owns or is treated as owning stock in the closely-held block upon whom the corporation intends to rely to satisfy the exception to the closely-held test of paragraph (d)(3)(ii) of this section—

(A) The name of each such shareholder;

(B) The percentage of the total value of the class of stock held by each such shareholder and the days during which the stock was held;

(C) The address of record of each such shareholder; and

(D) The country of residence of each such shareholder, determined under § 1.883-4(b)(2) (residence of individual shareholders) or § 1.883-4(d)(3) (special rules for residence of certain shareholders); and

(5) Any other relevant information specified by Form 1120-F and its accompanying instructions. [Reg. § 1.883-2.]

☐ [T.D. 9087, 8-25-2003.]

§ 1.883-3. Treatment of controlled foreign corporations.—(a) *General rule.*—A foreign corporation satisfies the stock ownership test of § 1.883-1(c)(2) if it is a controlled foreign corporation (CFC), as defined in section 957(a), and satisfies the income inclusion test in paragraph (b) of this section and the substantiation and reporting requirements of paragraphs (c) and (d) of this section, respectively. A CFC that fails the income inclusion test of paragraph (b) of this section will not be a qualified foreign corporation unless it meets either the publicly traded test of § 1.883-2(a) or the qualified shareholder stock ownership test of § 1.883-4(a).

(b) *Income inclusion test.*—(1) *General rule.*—A CFC shall not be considered to satisfy the requirements of paragraph (a) of this section unless more than 50 percent of the CFC's adjusted net foreign base company income (as defined in § 1.954-1(d) and as increased or decreased by section 952(c)) derived from the international operation of ships or aircraft is includible in the gross income of one or more United States citizens, individual residents of the United States or domestic corporations, pursuant to section 951(a)(1)(A) or another provision of the Internal Revenue Code, for the taxable years of such persons in which the taxable year of the CFC ends.

(2) *Examples.*—The income inclusion test of paragraph (b)(1) of this section is illustrated in the following examples:

Example 1. Ship Co is a CFC organized in a qualified foreign country. All of Ship Co's income is foreign base company shipping income that is derived from the international operation of ships. All of its shares are owned by a domestic partnership that is a United States shareholder for purposes of section 951(b). All of the partners in the domestic partnership are citizens and residents of foreign countries. Ship Co fails the income inclusion test of paragraph (b)(1) of this section because no amount of Ship Co's subpart F income that is adjusted net foreign base company income derived from the international operation of ships is includible under any provision of the Internal Revenue Code in the gross income of one or more United States citizens, individual residents of the United States or domestic corporations. Therefore, Ship Co must satisfy the qualified shareholder stock ownership test of § 1.883-4(a), in order to satisfy the stock ownership test of § 1.883-1(c)(2) and to be considered a qualified foreign corporation.

Example 2. Ship Co is a CFC organized in a qualified foreign country. All of Ship Co's income is foreign base company shipping income that is derived from the international operation of ships. Corp A, a domestic corporation, owns 50 percent of the value of the stock of Ship Co. X, a domestic partnership, owns the remaining 50 percent of the value of the stock of Ship Co. A United States citizen is a partner owning a 10 percent income interest in X. Individual partners owning 90 percent of X are citizens and residents of foreign countries. There are no special allocations of partnership income. Ship Co satisfies the income inclusion test of paragraph (b)(1) of this section because 55 percent (50 percent + (10 percent × 50 percent)) of the subpart F income that is adjusted net foreign base company income derived from the international operation of ships would be includible in the gross income of U.S. citizens, individual residents of the United States or domestic corporations. If Ship Co satisfies the substantiation and reporting requirements of paragraphs (c) and (d) of this section, it will meet the stock ownership test of § 1.883-1(c)(2).

(c) *Substantiation of CFC stock ownership.*—(1) *General rule.*—A foreign corporation that relies on this section to satisfy the stock ownership test of § 1.883-1(c)(2) must substantiate all the facts necessary to satisfy the Commissioner that it qualifies under the income inclusion test of paragraph (b)(1) of this section. For purposes of the income inclusion test, if the CFC has one or more United States shareholders, as defined in section 951(b), that are domestic partnerships, estates, or trusts, the pro rata share of the subpart F income includible in the gross income of such shareholders will only be treated as includible in the income of any partner, beneficiary or other interest owner of such United States shareholder that is a United States citizen, resident of the United States or a domestic corporation if the CFC obtains the documentation described in paragraph (c)(2) of this section.

(2) *Documentation from certain United States shareholders.*—(i) *General rule.*—A CFC only meets the documentation requirements of paragraph (c)(1) of this section if the CFC obtains the following documentation with respect to each United States shareholder, as defined in section 951(b), that is a partnership, estate or trust, for the taxable year of the shareholder which ends with or within the taxable year of the CFC—

(A) A copy of the Form 5471, "Information Return of U.S. Persons with Respect to Certain Foreign Corporations," filed with the controlling United States shareholder's return;

(B) A written statement, signed under penalties of perjury by a person authorized to sign the U.S. Federal tax return of each such United States shareholder, providing the following information with respect to each United States citizen, individual resident of the United States or domestic corporation that is a partner, beneficiary or other interest owner of each such United States shareholder and upon whom the CFC intends to rely to satisfy the income inclusion test of paragraph (b)(1) of this section—

(1) The name, address from the CFC's corporate records (that is a specific street address and not a nonresidential address, such as a post office box or in care of a financial intermediary or stock transfer agent), and taxpayer identification number of the interest owner;

(2) The interest owner's proportionate interest in the United States shareholder that reflects that owner's share of subpart F income required to be included in income on such interest owner's U.S. Federal income tax return;

(3) The percentage of the value of shares of the CFC owned by each such interest owner pursuant to the attribution rules in § 1.883-4(c); and

(C) Any other information as specified in guidance published by the Internal Revenue Service (see § 601.601(d)(2) of this chapter).

(ii) *Availability and retention of documents for inspection.*—The documentation described in paragraph (c)(2)(i) of this section must be retained by the corporation seeking qualified foreign corporation status (the CFC) until the expiration of the statute of limitations for the taxable year of the CFC to which the documentation relates. Such documentation must be made available for inspection by the Commissioner at such place as the Commissioner may request in writing.

(d) *Reporting requirements.*—A foreign corporation that relies on the CFC test of this section to satisfy the stock ownership test of § 1.883-1(c)(2) must provide the following information in addition to the information required in § 1.883-1(c)(3) to be included in its Form 1120-F, "U.S. Income Tax Return of a Foreign Corporation," for the taxable year. The information must be current as of the end of the corporation's taxable year and must include the following—

(1) The name, address from the CFC's corporate records (that is a specific street address and not a nonresidential address, such as a post office box or in care of a financial intermediary or stock transfer agent), and taxpayer identification number of each United States shareholder, as defined in section 951(b), of the CFC;

(2) The percentage of the vote and value of the shares of the CFC that is owned by each United States shareholder, as defined in section 951(b);

(3) If one or more of the United States shareholders is a domestic partnership, estate or trust, the name, address, taxpayer identification number and the percentage of the value of shares of the CFC owned (as determined under § 1.883-4(c)) by each interest owner of each such United States shareholder that is a United States citizen, individual resident of the United States or a domestic corporation; and

(4) Any other relevant information specified by Form 1120-F and its accompanying instructions. [Reg. § 1.883-3.]

☐ [*T.D.* 9087, 8-25-2003.]

§ 1.883-4. Qualified shareholder stock ownership test.—(a) *General rule.*—A foreign corporation satisfies the stock ownership test of § 1.883-1(c)(2) if more than 50 percent of the value of its outstanding shares is owned, or treated as owned by applying the attribution rules of paragraph (c) of this section, for at least half of the number of days in the foreign corporation's taxable year by one or more qualified shareholders, as defined in paragraph (b) of this section. A shareholder may be a qualified shareholder with respect to one category of income while not being a qualified shareholder with respect to another. A foreign corporation will not be considered to satisfy the stock ownership test of § 1.883-1(c)(2) pursuant to this section unless the foreign corporation meets the substantiation and reporting requirements of paragraphs (d) and (e) of this section.

(b) *Qualified shareholder.*—(1) *General rule.*—A shareholder is a qualified shareholder only if the shareholder—

(i) With respect to the category of income for which the foreign corporation is seeking an exemption, is—

(A) An individual who is a resident, as described in paragraph (b)(2) of this section, of a qualified foreign country;

(B) The government of a qualified foreign country (or a political subdivision or local authority of such country);

(C) A foreign corporation that is organized in a qualified foreign country and meets the publicly traded test of § 1.883-2(a);

(D) A not-for-profit organization described in paragraph (b)(4) of this section that is not a pension fund as defined in paragraph (b)(5) of this section and that is organized in a qualified foreign country;

(E) An individual beneficiary of a pension fund (as defined in paragraph (b)(5)(iv) of this section) that is administered in or by a qualified foreign country, who is treated as a resident under paragraph (d)(3)(iii) of this section, of a qualified foreign country; or

(F) A shareholder of a foreign corporation that is an airline covered by a bilateral Air Services Agreement in force between the United States and the qualified foreign country in which the airline is organized, provided the United States has not waived the ownership requirement in the Air Services Agreement, or that the ownership requirement has not otherwise been made ineffective;

(ii) Does not own its interest in the foreign corporation through bearer shares, either directly or by applying the attribution rules of paragraph (c) of this section; and

(iii) Provides to the foreign corporation the documentation required in paragraph (d) of this section and the foreign corporation meets the reporting requirements of paragraph (e) of this section with respect to such shareholder.

(2) *Residence of individual shareholders.*—(i) *General rule.*—An individual described in paragraph (b)(1)(i)(A) of this section is a resident of a qualified foreign country only if the individual is fully liable to tax as a resident in such country (e.g., an individual who is liable to tax on a remittance basis in a foreign country will not be treated as a resident of that country

unless all residents of that country are taxed on a remittance basis only) and, in addition—

(A) The individual has a tax home, within the meaning of paragraph (b)(2)(ii) of this section, in that qualified foreign country for 183 days or more of the taxable year; or

(B) The individual is treated as a resident of a qualified foreign country based on special rules pursuant to paragraph (d)(3) of this section.

(ii) *Tax home.*—For purposes of this section, an individual's tax home is considered to be located at the individual's regular or principal (if more than one regular) place of business. If the individual has no regular or principal place of business because of the nature of his business (or lack of a business), then the individual's tax home is located at his regular place of abode in a real and substantial sense. If an individual has no regular or principal place of business and no regular place of abode in a real and substantial sense in a qualified foreign country for 183 days or more of the taxable year, that individual does not have a tax home for purposes of this section. A foreign estate or trust, as defined in section 7701(a)(31), does not have a tax home for purposes of this section. See paragraph (c)(3) of this section for alternative rules in the case of trusts or estates.

(3) *Certain income tax convention restrictions applied to shareholders.*—For purposes of paragraph (b)(1) of this section, a shareholder described in paragraph (b)(1) of this section may be considered a resident of, or organized in, a qualified foreign country if that foreign country provides an exemption by means of an income tax convention with the United States, but only if the shareholder demonstrates that it is treated as a resident of that country under the convention and qualifies for benefits under any Limitation on Benefits article, and that the convention provides an exemption for the relevant category of income. If the convention has a requirement in the shipping and air transport article other than residence, such as place of registration or documentation of the ship or aircraft, the shareholder is not required to demonstrate that the corporation seeking qualified foreign corporation status could satisfy any such additional requirement.

(4) *Not-for-profit organizations.*—The term *not-for-profit organization* means an organization that meets the following requirements—

(i) It is a corporation, association taxable as a corporation, trust, fund, foundation, league or other entity operated exclusively for religious, charitable, educational, or recreational purposes, and not organized for profit;

(ii) It is generally exempt from tax in its country of organization by virtue of its not-for-profit status; and

(iii) Either—

(A) More than 50 percent of its annual support is expended on behalf of individuals described in paragraph (b)(1)(i)(A) of this section (see paragraph (d)(3)(v) of this section for special rules to substantiate the residence of individual beneficiaries of not-for-profit organizations) and on behalf of U.S. exempt organizations that have received determination letters under section 501(c)(3); or

(B) More than 50 percent of its annual support is derived from individuals described in paragraph (b)(1)(i)(A) of this section (see paragraph (d)(3)(v) of this section for special rules to substantiate the residence of individual supporters of not-for-profit organizations).

(5) *Pension funds.*—(i) *Pension fund defined.*—The term *pension fund* shall mean a government pension fund or a nongovernment pension fund, as those terms are defined, respectively, in paragraphs (b)(5)(ii) and (iii) of this section, that is a trust, fund, foundation, or other entity that is established exclusively for the benefit of employees or former employees of one or more employers, the principal purpose of which is to provide retirement, disability, and death benefits to beneficiaries of such entity and persons designated by such beneficiaries in consideration for prior services rendered.

(ii) *Government pension funds.*—A government pension fund is a pension fund that is a controlled entity of a foreign sovereign within the principles of §1.892-2T(c)(1) (relating to pension funds established for the benefit of employees or former employees of a foreign government).

(iii) *Nongovernment pension funds.*—A nongovernment pension fund is a pension fund that—

(A) Is administered in a foreign country and is subject to supervision or regulation by a governmental authority (or other authority delegated to perform such supervision or regulation by a governmental authority) in such country;

(B) Is generally exempt from income taxation in its country of administration;

(C) Has 100 or more beneficiaries; and

(D) The trustees, directors or other administrators of which pension fund provide the documentation required in paragraph (d) of this section.

(iv) *Beneficiary of a pension fund.*—The term *beneficiary of a pension fund* shall mean any person who has made contributions to a pension fund, as that term is defined in paragraph (b)(5)(i) of this section, or on whose behalf contributions have been made, and who is currently receiving retirement, disability, or death benefits from the pension fund or can reasonably be expected to receive such benefits in the future, whether or not the person's right to receive benefits from the fund has vested. See paragraph (c)(7) of this section for rules regarding the computation of stock ownership through nongovernment pension funds.

(c) *Rules for determining constructive ownership.*—(1) *General rules for attribution.*—For purposes of applying paragraph (a) of this section and the exception to the closely-held test in § 1.883-2(d)(3)(ii), stock owned by or for a corporation, partnership, trust, estate, or mutual insurance company or similar entity shall be treated as owned proportionately by its shareholders, partners, beneficiaries, grantors, or other interest holders, as provided in paragraphs (c)(2) through (7) of this section. The proportionate interest rules of this paragraph (c) shall apply successively upward through a chain of ownership, and a person's proportionate interest shall be computed for the relevant days or period taken into account in determining whether a foreign corporation satisfies the requirements of paragraph (a) of this section. Stock treated as owned by a person by reason of this paragraph (c) shall be treated as actually owned by such person for purposes of this section. An owner of an interest in an association taxable as a corporation shall be treated as a shareholder of such association for purposes of this paragraph (c). No attribution will apply to an interest held directly or indirectly through bearer shares.

(2) *Partnerships.*—(i) *General rule.*—A partner shall be treated as having an interest in stock of a foreign corporation owned by a partnership in proportion to the least of—

(A) The partner's percentage distributive share of the partnership's dividend income from the stock;

(B) The partner's percentage distributive share of gain from disposition of the stock by the partnership; or

(C) The partner's percentage distributive share of the stock (or proceeds from the disposition of the stock) upon liquidation of the partnership.

(ii) *Partners resident in the same country.*—For purposes of this paragraph, all qualified shareholders that are partners in a partnership and that are residents of, or organized in, the same qualified foreign country shall be treated as one partner. Thus, the percentage distributive shares of dividend income, gain and liquidation rights of all qualified shareholders that are partners in a partnership and that are residents of, or organized in, the same qualified foreign country are aggregated prior to determining the least of the three percentages set out in paragraph (c)(2)(i) of this section. For the meaning of the term *resident*, see paragraph (b)(2) of this section.

(iii) *Examples.*—The rules of paragraph (c)(2)(ii) of this section are illustrated by the following examples:

Example 1. Stock held solely by qualified shareholders through a partnership. Country X grants an equivalent exemption. A and B are individual residents of Country X and are qualified shareholders within the meaning of paragraph (b)(1) of this section. A and B are the sole partners of Partnership P. P's only asset is the stock of Corporation Z, a Country X corporation seeking a reciprocal exemption under this section. A's distributive share of P's income and gain on the disposition of P's assets is 80 percent, but A's distributive share of P's assets (or the proceeds therefrom) on P's liquidation is 20 percent. B's distributive share of P's income and gain is 20 percent and B is entitled to 80 percent of the assets (or proceeds therefrom) on P's liquidation. Under the attribution rules of paragraph (c)(2)(ii) of this section, A and B will be treated as a single partner owning in the aggregate 100 percent of the stock of Z owned by P.

Example 2. Stock held by both qualified and nonqualified shareholders through a partnership. Assume the same facts as in *Example 1* except that C, an individual who is not a resident of a qualified foreign country, is also a partner in P and that C's distributive share of P's income is 60 percent. The distributive shares of A and B are the same as in *Example 1*, except that A's distributive share of income is 20 percent. Under the attribution rules of paragraph (c)(2)(ii) of this section, qualified shareholders A and B will be treated as a single partner owning in the aggregate 40 percent of the stock of Z owned by P (i.e., the lowest aggregate percentage of A and B's distributive shares of dividend income (40 percent), gain (100 percent), and liquidation rights (100 percent) with respect to the Z stock). Thus, only 40 percent of the Z stock is treated as owned by qualified shareholders.

Example 3. Stock held through tiered partnerships. Country X grants an equivalent exemption. A and B are individual residents of Country X and are qualified shareholders within the meaning of paragraph (b)(1) of this section. A and B are the sole partners of Partnership P. P is a partner in Partnership P1, which owns the stock of Corporation Z, a Country X corporation seeking a reciprocal exemption under this section. Assume that P's distributive share of the dividend income, gain and liquidation rights with respect to the Z stock held by P1 is 40 percent. Assume that of the remaining partners of P1 only D is a qualified shareholder. D's distributive share of P1's dividend income and gain is 15 percent; D's distributive share of P1's assets on liquidation is 25 percent. Under the attribution rules of paragraph (c)(2)(ii) of this section, A and B, treated as a single partner, will own 40 percent of the Z stock owned by P1 (100 percent × 40 percent) and D will be treated as owning 15 percent of the Z stock owned by P1 (the least of D's dividend income (15 percent), gain (15 percent), and liquidation rights (25 percent) with respect to the Z stock). Thus, 55 percent of the Z stock owned by P1 is treated as owned by qualified shareholders.

(3) *Trusts and estates.*—
(i) *Beneficiaries.*—In general, an individual shall be treated as having an interest in stock of a foreign corporation owned by a trust or estate in proportion to the individual's actuarial interest in the trust or estate, as provided in section 318(a)(2)(B)(i), except that an income beneficiary's actuarial interest in the trust will be determined as if the trust's only asset were the stock. The interest of a remainder beneficiary in stock will be equal to 100 percent minus the sum of the percentages of any interest in the stock held by income beneficiaries. The ownership of an interest in stock owned by a trust shall not be attributed to any beneficiary whose interest cannot be determined under the preceding sentence, and any such interest, to the extent not attributed by reason of this paragraph (c)(3)(i), shall not be considered owned by a beneficiary unless all potential beneficiaries with respect to the stock are qualified shareholders. In addition, a beneficiary's actuarial interest will be treated as zero to the extent that someone other than the beneficiary is treated as owning the stock under paragraph (c)(3)(ii) of this section. A substantially separate and independent share of a trust, within the meaning of section 663(c), shall be treated as a separate trust for purposes of this paragraph (c)(3)(i), provided that payment of income, accumulated income or corpus of a share of one beneficiary (or group of beneficiaries) cannot affect the proportionate share of income, accumulated income or corpus of another beneficiary (or group of beneficiaries).

(ii) *Grantor trusts.*—A person is treated as the owner of stock of a foreign corporation owned by a trust to the extent that the stock is included in the portion of the trust that is treated as owned by the person under sections 671 through 679 (relating to grantors and others treated as substantial owners).

(4) *Corporations that issue stock.*—A shareholder of a corporation that issues stock shall be treated as owning stock of a foreign corporation that is owned by such corporation on any day in a proportion that equals the value of the stock owned by such shareholder to the value of all stock of such corporation. If, however, there is an agreement, express or implied, that a shareholder of a corporation will not receive distributions from the earnings of stock owned by the corporation, the shareholder will not be treated as owning that stock owned by the corporation.

(5) *Taxable nonstock corporations.*—A taxable nonstock corporation that is entitled in its country of organization to deduct from its taxable income amounts distributed for charitable purposes may deem a recipient of such charitable distributions to be a shareholder of such taxable nonstock corporation in the same proportion as the amount that such beneficiary receives in the taxable year bears to the total income of such taxable nonstock corporation in the taxable year. Whether each such recipient is a qualified shareholder may then be determined under paragraph (b) of this section or under the special rules of paragraph (d)(3)(vii) of this section.

(6) *Mutual insurance companies and similar entities.*—Stock held by a mutual insurance company, mutual savings bank, or similar entity (including an association taxable as a corporation that does not issue stock interests) shall be considered owned proportionately by the policyholders, depositors, or other owners in the same proportion that such persons share in the surplus of such entity upon liquidation or dissolution.

(7) *Computation of beneficial interests in nongovernment pension funds.*—Stock held by a pension fund shall be considered owned by the beneficiaries of the fund equally on a pro-rata basis if—

(i) The pension fund meets the requirements of paragraph (b)(5)(iii) of this section;

(ii) The trustees, directors or other administrators of the pension fund have no knowledge, and no reason to know, that a pro-rata allocation of interests of the fund to all beneficiaries would differ significantly from an actuarial allocation of interests in the fund (or, if the beneficiaries' actuarial interest in the stock held directly or indirectly by the pension fund differs from the beneficiaries' actuarial interest in the pension fund, the actuarial interests computed by reference to the beneficiaries' actuarial interest in the stock);

(iii) Either—

(A) Any overfunding of the pension fund would be payable, pursuant to the governing instrument or the laws of the foreign country in which the pension fund is administered, only to, or for the benefit of, one or more corporations that are organized in the country in which the pension fund is administered, individual beneficiaries of the pension fund or their designated beneficiaries, or social or charitable causes (the reduction of the obligation of the sponsoring company or companies to make future contributions to the pension fund by reason of overfunding shall not itself result in such overfunding being deemed to be payable to or for the benefit of such company or companies); or

(B) The foreign country in which the pension fund is administered has laws that are designed to prevent overfunding of a pension fund and the funding of the pension fund is within the guidelines of such laws; or

(C) The pension fund is maintained to provide benefits to employees in a particular industry, profession, or group of industries or professions and employees of at least 10 companies (other than companies that are owned or controlled, directly or indirectly, by the same interests) contribute to the pension fund or receive benefits from the pension fund; and

(iv) The trustees, directors or other administrators provide the relevant documentation as required in paragraph (d) of this section.

(d) *Substantiation of stock ownership.*—(1) *General rule.*—A foreign corporation that relies on this section to satisfy the stock ownership test of §1.883-1(c)(2), must establish all the facts necessary to satisfy the Commissioner that more than 50 percent of the value of its shares is owned, or treated as owned applying paragraph (c) of this section, by qualified shareholders. A foreign corporation cannot meet this requirement with respect to any stock that is issued in bearer form. A shareholder that holds shares in the foreign corporation either directly or indirectly in bearer form cannot be a qualified shareholder.

(2) *Application of general rule.*—(i) *Ownership statements.*—Except as provided in paragraph (d)(3) of this section, a person shall only be treated as a qualified shareholder of a foreign corporation if—

(A) For the relevant period, the person completes an ownership statement described in paragraph (d)(4) of this section or has a valid ownership statement in effect under paragraph (d)(2)(ii) of this section;

(B) In the case of a person owning stock in the foreign corporation indirectly through one or more intermediaries (including mere legal owners or recordholders acting as nominees), each intermediary in the chain of ownership between that person and the foreign corporation seeking qualified foreign corporation status completes an intermediary ownership statement described in paragraph (d)(4)(v) of this section or has a valid intermediary ownership statement in effect under paragraph (d)(2)(ii) of this section; and

(C) The foreign corporation seeking qualified foreign corporation status obtains the statements described in paragraphs (d)(2)(i)(A) and (B) of this section.

(ii) *Three-year period of validity.*—The ownership statements required in paragraph (d)(2)(i) of this section shall remain valid until the earlier of the last day of the third calendar year following the year in which the ownership statement is signed, or the day that a change of circumstance occurs that makes any information on the ownership statement incorrect. For example, an ownership statement signed on September 30, 2000, remains valid through December 31, 2003, unless a change of circumstance occurs that makes any information on the ownership statement incorrect.

(3) *Special rules.*—(i) *Substantiating residence of certain shareholders.*—A foreign corporation seeking qualified foreign corporation status or an intermediary that is a direct or indirect shareholder of such foreign corporation may substantiate the residence of certain shareholders, for purposes of paragraph (b)(2)(i)(B) of this section, under one of the following special rules in paragraphs (d)(3)(ii) through (viii) of this section, in lieu of obtaining the ownership statements required in paragraph (d)(2)(i) of this section from such shareholders.

(ii) *Special rule for registered shareholders owning less than one percent of widely-held corporations.*—A foreign corporation with at least 250 registered shareholders, that is not a publicly-traded corporation, as described in §1.883-2 (a widely-held corporation), is not required to obtain an ownership statement from an individual shareholder owning less than one percent of the widely-held corporation at all times during the taxable year if the requirements of paragraphs (d)(3)(ii)(A) and (B) of this section are satisfied. If the widely-held foreign corporation is the foreign corporation seeking qualified foreign corporation status, or an intermediary that meets the documentation requirements of paragraphs (d)(4)(v)(A) and (B) of this section, the widely-held foreign corporation may treat the address of record in its ownership records as the residence of any less than one percent individual shareholder if—

(A) The individual's address of record is a specific street address and not a nonresidential address, such as a post office box or in care of a financial intermediary or stock transfer agent; and

(B) The officers and directors of the widely-held corporation neither know nor have reason to know that the individual does not reside at that address.

(iii) *Special rule for beneficiaries of pension funds.*—(A) *Government pension fund.*—An individual who is a beneficiary of a government pension fund, as defined in paragraph (b)(5)(ii) of this section, may be treated as a resident of the country in which the pension fund is administered if the pension fund satisfies the documentation requirements of paragraphs (d)(4)(v)(A) and (C)(*1*) of this section.

(B) *Nongovernment pension fund.*—An individual who is a beneficiary of a nongovernment pension fund, as described in paragraph (b)(5)(iii) of this section, may be treated as a resident of the country of the beneficiary's address as it appears on the records of the fund, provided it is not a nonresidential address, such as a post office box or an address in care of a financial intermediary, and provided none of the trustees, directors or other administrators of the pension fund know, or have reason to know, that the beneficiary is not an individual resident of such foreign country. The rules of this paragraph (d)(3)(iii)(B) shall apply only if the nongovernment pension fund satisfies the documentation requirements of paragraphs (d)(4)(v)(A) and (C)(*2*) of this section.

(iv) *Special rule for stock owned by publicly-traded corporations.*—Any stock in a foreign corporation seeking qualified foreign corporation status that is owned by a publicly-traded corporation will be treated as owned by an individual resident in the country where the publicly-traded corporation is organized if the foreign corporation receives the statement described in paragraph (d)(4)(iii) of this section from the publicly-traded corporation and copies of any relevant ownership statements from shareholders of the publicly-traded corporation relied on to satisfy the exception to the closely-held test of §1.883-2(d)(3)(ii), as required in paragraph (d)(2)(i) of this section.

(v) *Special rule for not-for-profit organizations.*—For purposes of meeting the ownership requirements of paragraph (a) of this section, a not-for-profit organization may rely on the addresses of record of its individual beneficiaries and supporters to determine the residence of an individual beneficiary or supporter, within the meaning of paragraph (b)(2)(i)(B) of this section, to the extent required under paragraph (b)(4) of this section, provided that—

(A) The addresses of record are not nonresidential addresses such as a post office box or in care of a financial intermediary;

(B) The officers, directors or administrators of the organization do not know or have reason to know that the individual beneficiaries or supporters do not reside at that address; and

(C) The foreign corporation seeking qualified foreign corporation status receives the statement required in paragraph (d)(4)(iv) of this section from the not-for-profit organization.

(vi) *Special rule for a foreign airline covered by an air services agreement.*—A foreign airline that is covered by a bilateral Air Services Agreement in force between the United States and the qualified foreign country in which the airline is organized may rely exclusively on the Air Services Agreement currently in effect and will not have to otherwise substantiate its ownership under this section, provided that the United States has not waived the ownership requirements in the agreement or that the ownership requirements have not otherwise been made ineffective. Such an airline will be treated as owned by qualified shareholders resident in the country where the foreign airline is organized.

(vii) *Special rule for taxable nonstock corporations.*—Any stock in a foreign corporation seeking qualified foreign corporation status that is owned by a taxable nonstock corporation will be treated as owned, in any taxable year, by the recipients of distributions made during that taxable year, as set out in paragraph (c)(5) of this section. The taxable nonstock corporation may treat the address of record in its distribution records as the residence of any recipient if—

(A) An individual recipient's address is in a qualified foreign country and is a specific street address and not a nonresidential address, such as a post office box or in care of a financial intermediary or stock transfer agent;

(B) The address of a nonindividual recipient's principal place of business is in a qualified foreign country;

(C) The officers and directors of the taxable nonstock corporation neither know nor have reason to know that the recipients do not reside or have their principal place of business at such addresses; and

(D) The foreign corporation receives the statement described in paragraph (d)(4)(v)(D) of this section from the taxable nonstock corporation intermediary.

(viii) *Special rule for closely-held corporations traded in the United States.*—To demonstrate that a class of stock is not closely-held for purposes of § 1.883-2(d)(3)(i), a foreign corporation whose stock is traded on an established securities market in the United States may rely on current Schedule 13D and Schedule 13G filings with the Securities and Exchange Commission to identify its 5-percent shareholders in each class of stock relied upon to meet the regularly traded test, without having to make any independent investigation to determine the identity of the 5-percent shareholder. However, if any class of stock is determined to be closely-held within the meaning of § 1.883-2(d)(3)(i), the publicly traded corporation cannot satisfy the requirements of § 1.883-2(e) unless it obtains sufficient documentation described in this paragraph (d) to demonstrate that the requirements of § 1.883-2(d)(3)(ii) are met with respect to the 5-percent shareholders.

(4) *Ownership statements from shareholders.*—(i) *Ownership statements from individuals.*—An ownership statement from an individual is a written statement signed by the individual under penalties of perjury stating—

(A) The individual's name, permanent address, and country where the individual is fully liable to tax as a resident, if any;

(B) If the individual was not a resident of the country for the entire taxable year of the foreign corporation seeking qualified foreign corporation status, each of the foreign countries in which the individual resided and the dates of such residence during the taxable year of such foreign corporation;

(C) If the individual directly owns stock in the corporation seeking qualified foreign corporation status, the name of the corporation, the number of shares in each class of stock of the corporation that are so owned, and the period of time during the taxable year of the foreign corporation during which the individual owned the stock;

(D) If the individual directly owns an interest in a corporation, partnership, trust, estate or other intermediary that directly or indirectly owns stock in the corporation seeking qualified foreign corporation status, the name of the intermediary, the number and class of shares or amount and nature of the interest of the individual in such intermediary, and the period of time during the taxable year of the corporation seeking qualified foreign corporation status during which the individual held such interest;

(E) To the extent known by the individual, a description of the chain of ownership through which the individual owns stock in the corporation seeking qualified foreign corporation status, including the name and address of each intermediary standing between the intermediary described in paragraph (d)(4)(i)(D) of this section and the foreign corporation and whether this interest is owned either directly or indirectly through bearer shares; and

(F) Any other information as specified in guidance published by the Internal Revenue Service (see § 601.601(d)(2) of this chapter).

(ii) *Ownership statements from foreign governments.*—An ownership statement from a foreign government that is a qualified shareholder is a written statement—

(A) Signed by any one of the following—

(1) An official of the governmental authority, agency or office who has supervisory authority with respect to the government's ownership interest and who is authorized to sign such a statement on behalf of the authority, agency or office; or

(2) The competent authority of the foreign country (as defined in the income tax convention between the United States and the foreign country); or

(3) An income tax return preparer that, for purposes of this paragraph (d)(4)(ii) only, shall mean a firm of licensed or certified public accountants, a law firm whose principals or members are admitted to practice in one or more states, territories or possessions of the United States or the country of such government, or a bank or other financial institution licensed to do business in such foreign country and having assets at least equivalent to 50 million U.S. dollars and who is authorized to represent the government or governmental authority; and

(B) That provides—

(1) The title of the official or other person signing the statement;

(2) The name and address of the government authority, agency or office that has supervisory authority and, if applicable, the income tax preparer which has prepared such ownership statement;

(3) The information described in paragraphs (d)(4)(i)(C) through (E) of this section (as if the language applied "government" instead of "individual") with respect to the government's direct or indirect ownership of stock in the corporation seeking qualified resident status;

(4) In the case of an ownership statement prepared by an income tax return

preparer, a statement under penalties of perjury identifying the documentation relied upon in the conduct of due diligence for the taxable year to determine the aggregate government investment in the stock of the shipping or aircraft company in preparation of such ownership statement attached to a valid power of attorney to represent the taxpayer for the taxable year; and

(5) Any other information as specified in guidance published by the Internal Revenue Service (see § 601.601(d)(2) of this chapter).

(iii) *Ownership statements from publicly-traded corporate shareholders.*—An ownership statement from a publicly-traded corporation that is a direct or indirect owner of the corporation seeking qualified foreign corporation status is a written statement, signed under penalties of perjury by a person that would be authorized to sign a tax return on behalf of the shareholder corporation containing the following information—

(A) The name of the country in which the stock is primarily traded;

(B) The name of the established securities market or markets on which the stock is listed;

(C) A description of each class of stock relied upon to meet the requirements of § 1.883-2(d)(1), including the number of shares issued and outstanding as of the close of the taxable year;

(D) For each class of stock relied upon to meet the requirements of § 1.883-2(d)(1), if one or more 5-percent shareholders, as defined in § 1.883-2(d)(3)(i), own in the aggregate 50 percent or more of the vote and value of the outstanding shares of that class of stock for more than half the number of days during the taxable year—

(1) The days during the taxable year of the corporation in which the stock was closely-held without regard to the exception in paragraph (d)(3)(ii) of this section and the percentage of the vote and value of the class of stock that is owned by 5-percent shareholders during such days;

(2) For each qualified shareholder who owns or is treated as owning stock in the closely-held block upon whom the corporation intends to rely to satisfy the exception to the closely-held test of § 1.883-2(d)(3)(ii)—

(i) The name of each such shareholder;

(ii) The percentage of the total value of the class of stock held by each such shareholder and the days during which the stock was held;

(iii) The address of record of each such shareholder; and

(iv) The country of residence of each such shareholder, determined under paragraph (b)(2) or (d)(3) of this section;

(E) The information described in paragraphs (d)(4)(i)(C) through (E) of this section (as if the language applied "publicly-traded corporation" instead of "individual") with respect to the publicly-traded corporation's direct or indirect ownership of stock in the corporation seeking qualified resident status; and

(F) Any other information as specified in guidance published by the Internal Revenue Service (see § 601.601(d)(2) of this chapter).

(iv) *Ownership statements from not-for-profit organizations.*—An ownership statement from a not-for-profit organization (other than a pension fund as defined in paragraph (b)(5) of this section) is a written statement signed by a person authorized to sign a tax return on behalf of the organization under penalties of perjury stating—

(A) The name, permanent address, and principal location of the activities of the organization (if different from its permanent address);

(B) The information described in paragraphs (d)(4)(i)(C) through (E) of this section (as if the language applied "not-for-profit organization" instead of "individual");

(C) A representation that the not-for-profit organization satisfies the requirements of paragraph (b)(4) of this section; and

(D) Any other information as specified in guidance published by the Internal Revenue Service (see § 601.601(d)(2) of this chapter).

(v) *Ownership statements from intermediaries.*—(A) *General rule.*—The foreign corporation seeking qualified foreign corporation status under the shareholder stock ownership test must obtain an intermediary ownership statement from each intermediary standing in the chain of ownership between it and the qualified shareholders on whom it relies to meet this test. An intermediary ownership statement is a written statement signed under penalties of perjury by the intermediary (if the intermediary is an individual) or a person who would be authorized to sign a tax return on behalf of the intermediary (if the intermediary is not an individual) containing the following information—

(1) The name, address, country of residence, and principal place of business (in the case of a corporation or partnership) of the intermediary, and, if the intermediary is a trust

or estate, the name and permanent address of all trustees or executors (or equivalent under foreign law), or if the intermediary is a pension fund, the name and permanent address of place of administration of the intermediary;

(2) The information described in paragraphs (d)(4)(i)(C) through (E) of this section (as if the language applied "intermediary" instead of "individual");

(3) If the intermediary is a nominee for a shareholder or another intermediary, the name and permanent address of the shareholder, or the name and principal place of business of such other intermediary;

(4) If the intermediary is not a nominee for a shareholder or another intermediary, the name and country of residence (within the meaning of paragraph (b)(2) of this section) and the proportionate interest in the intermediary of each direct shareholder, partner, beneficiary, grantor, or other interest holder (or if the direct holder is a nominee, of its beneficial shareholder, partner, beneficiary, grantor, or other interest holder), on which the foreign corporation seeking qualified foreign corporation status intends to rely to satisfy the requirements of paragraph (a) of this section. In addition, such intermediary must obtain from all such persons an ownership statement that includes the period of time during the taxable year for which the interest in the intermediary was owned by the shareholder, partner, beneficiary, grantor or other interest holder. For purposes of this paragraph (d)(4)(v)(A), the proportionate interest of a person in an intermediary is the percentage interest (by value) held by such person, determined using the principles for attributing ownership in paragraph (c) of this section;

(5) If the intermediary is a widely-held corporation with registered shareholders owning less than one percent of the stock of such widely-held corporation, the statement set out in paragraph (d)(4)(v)(B) of this section, relating to ownership statements from widely-held intermediaries with registered shareholders owning less than one percent of such widely-held intermediaries;

(6) If the intermediary is a pension fund, within the meaning of paragraph (b)(5) of this section, the statement set out in paragraph (d)(4)(v)(C) of this section, relating to ownership statements from pension funds;

(7) If the intermediary is a taxable nonstock corporation, within the meaning of paragraph (c)(5) of this section, the statement set out in paragraph (d)(4)(v)(D) of this section, relating to ownership statements from intermediaries that are taxable nonstock corporations; and

(8) Any other information as specified in guidance published by the Internal Revenue Service (see § 601.601(d)(2) of this chapter).

(B) *Ownership statements from widely-held intermediaries with registered shareholders owning less than one percent of such widely-held intermediary.*—An ownership statement from an intermediary that is a corporation with at least 250 registered shareholders, but that is not a publicly-traded corporation within the meaning of § 1.883-2, and that relies on paragraph (d)(3)(ii) of this section, relating to the special rule for registered shareholders owning less than one percent of widely-held corporations, must provide the following information in addition to the information required in paragraph (d)(4)(v)(A) of this section—

(1) The aggregate proportionate interest by country of residence in the widely-held corporation of such registered shareholders or other interest holders whose address of record is a specific street address and not a nonresidential address, such as a post office box or in care of a financial intermediary or stock transfer agent; and

(2) A representation that the officers and directors of the widely-held intermediary neither know nor have reason to know that the individual shareholder does not reside at his or her address of record in the corporate records; and

(3) Any other information as specified in guidance published by the Internal Revenue Service (see § 601.601(d)(2) of this chapter).

(C) *Ownership statements from pension funds.*—*(1) Ownership statements from government pension funds.*—A government pension fund (as defined in paragraph (b)(5)(ii) of this section) that relies on paragraph (d)(3)(iii) of this section (relating to the special rules for pension funds) generally must provide the documentation required in paragraph (d)(4)(v)(A) of this section, and, in addition, the government pension fund must also provide the following information—

(i) The name of the country in which the plan is administered;

(ii) A representation that the fund is established exclusively for the benefit of employees or former employees of a foreign government, or employees or former employees of a foreign government and nongovernmental employees or former employees that perform or performed governmental or social services;

(iii) A representation that the funds that comprise the trust are managed by

trustees who are employees of, or persons appointed by, the foreign government;

(iv) A representation that the trust forming part of the pension plan provides for retirement, disability, or death benefits in consideration for prior services rendered;

(v) A representation that the income of the trust satisfies the obligations of the foreign government to the participants under the plan, rather than inuring to the benefit of a private person; and

(vi) Any other information as specified in guidance published by the Internal Revenue Service (see § 601.601(d)(2) of this chapter).

(2) Ownership statements from nongovernment pension funds.—The trustees, directors, or other administrators of the nongovernment pension fund, as defined in paragraph (b)(5)(iii) of this section, that rely on paragraph (d)(3)(iii) of this section, relating to the special rules for pension funds, generally must provide the pension fund's intermediary ownership statement described in paragraph (d)(4)(v)(A) of this section. In addition, the nongovernment pension fund must also provide the following information—

(i) The name of the country in which the pension fund is administered;

(ii) A representation that the pension fund is subject to supervision or regulation by a governmental authority (or other authority delegated to perform such supervision or regulation by a governmental authority) in such country, and, if so, the name of the governmental authority (or other authority delegated to perform such supervision or regulation);

(iii) A representation that the pension fund is generally exempt from income taxation in its country of administration;

(iv) The number of beneficiaries in the pension plan;

(v) The aggregate percentage interest of beneficiaries by country of residence based on addresses shown on the books and records of the fund, provided the addresses are not nonresidential addresses, such as a post office box or an address in care of a financial intermediary, and provided none of the trustees, directors or other administrators of the pension fund know, or have reason to know, that the beneficiary is not a resident of such foreign country;

(vi) A representation that the pension fund meets the requirements of paragraph (b)(5)(iii) of this section;

(vii) A representation that the trustees, directors or other administrators of the pension fund have no knowledge, and no reason to know, that a pro-rata allocation of interests of the fund to all beneficiaries would differ significantly from an actuarial allocation of interests in the fund (or, if the beneficiaries' actuarial interest in the stock held directly or indirectly by the pension fund differs from the beneficiaries' actuarial interest in the pension fund, the actuarial interests computed by reference to the beneficiaries' actuarial interest in the stock);

(viii) A representation that any overfunding of the pension fund would be payable, pursuant to the governing instrument or the laws of the foreign country in which the pension fund is administered, only to, or for the benefit of, one or more corporations that are organized in the country in which the pension fund is administered, individual beneficiaries of the pension fund or their designated beneficiaries, or social or charitable causes (the reduction of the obligation of the sponsoring company or companies to make future contributions to the pension fund by reason of overfunding shall not itself result in such overfunding being deemed to be payable to or for the benefit of such company or companies); or that the foreign country in which the pension fund is administered has laws that are designed to prevent overfunding of a pension fund and the funding of the pension fund is within the guidelines of such laws; or that the pension fund is maintained to provide benefits to employees in a particular industry, profession, or group of industries or professions, and that employees of at least 10 companies (other than companies that are owned or controlled, directly or indirectly, by the same interests) contribute to the pension fund or receive benefits from the pension fund; and

(ix) Any other information as specified in guidance published by the Internal Revenue Service (see § 601.601(d)(2) of this chapter).

(3) Time for making determinations.—The determinations required to be made under this paragraph (d)(4)(v)(C) shall be made using information shown on the records of the pension fund for a date during the foreign corporation's taxable year to which the determination is relevant.

(D) *Ownership statements from taxable nonstock corporations.*—An ownership statement from an intermediary that is a taxable nonstock corporation must provide the following information in addition to the information required in paragraph (d)(4)(v)(A) of this section—

(1) With respect to paragraph (d)(4)(v)(A)(7) of this section, for each beneficiary that is treated as a qualified shareholder,

the name, address of residence (in the case of an individual beneficiary, the address must be a specific street address and not a nonresidential address, such as a post office box or in care of a financial intermediary; in the case of a nonindividual beneficiary, the address of the principal place of business) and percentage that is the same proportion as the amount that the beneficiary receives in the tax year bears to the total net income of the taxable nonstock corporation in the tax year;

(2) A representation that the officers and directors of the taxable nonstock corporation neither know nor have reason to know that the individual beneficiaries do not reside at the address listed in paragraph (d)(4)(v)(D)(1) of this section or that any other nonindividual beneficiary does not conduct its primary activities at such address or in such country of residence; and

(3) Any other information as specified in guidance published by the Internal Revenue Service (see § 601.601(d)(2) of this chapter).

(5) *Availability and retention of documents for inspection.*—The documentation described in paragraphs (d)(3) and (4) of this section must be retained by the corporation seeking qualified foreign corporation status (the foreign corporation) until the expiration of the statute of limitations for the taxable year of the foreign corporation to which the documentation relates. Such documentation must be made available for inspection by the Commissioner at such time and place as the Commissioner may request in writing.

(e) *Reporting requirements.*—A foreign corporation relying on the qualified shareholder stock ownership test of this section to meet the stock ownership test of § 1.883-1(c)(2) must provide the following information in addition to the information required in § 1.883-1(c)(3) to be included in its Form 1120-F, "U.S. Income Tax Return of a Foreign Corporation," for each taxable year. The information should be current as of the end of the corporation's taxable year. The information must include the following—

(1) A representation that more than 50 percent of the value of the outstanding shares of the corporation is owned (or treated as owned by reason of paragraph (c) of this section) by qualified shareholders for each category of income for which the exemption is claimed;

(2) With respect to each individual qualified shareholder owning 5 percent or more of the foreign corporation, applying the attribution rules of paragraph (c) of this section, and relied upon to meet the 50 percent ownership test of paragraph (a) of this section, the name and street address, as represented on each such individual's ownership statement;

(3) With respect to all qualified shareholders relied upon to satisfy the 50 percent ownership test of paragraph (a) of this section, the total percentage of the value of the outstanding shares owned, applying the attribution rules of paragraph (c) of this section, by all qualified shareholders resident in a qualified foreign country, by country; and

(4) Any other relevant information specified by the Form 1120-F and its accompanying instructions. [Reg. § 1.883-4.]

☐ [*T.D.* 9087, 8-25-2003.]

§ 1.883-5. Effective dates.—(a) *General rule.*—Sections 1.883-1 through 1.883-4 apply to taxable years of a foreign corporation seeking qualified foreign corporation status beginning 30 days or more after August 26, 2003.

(b) *Election for retroactive application.*—Taxpayers may elect to apply §§ 1.883-1 through 1.883-4 for any open taxable year of the foreign corporation beginning after December 31, 1986, except that the substantiation and reporting requirements of § 1.883-1(c)(3) (relating to the substantiation and reporting required to be treated as a qualified foreign corporation) or §§ 1.883-2(f), 1.883-3(d) and 1.883-4(e) (relating to additional information to be included in the return to demonstrate whether the foreign corporation satisfies the stock ownership test) will not apply to any year beginning before September 25, 2003. Such election shall apply to the taxable year of the election and to all subsequent taxable years beginning before September 25, 2003.

(c) *Transitional information reporting rule.*—For taxable years of the foreign corporation beginning 30 days or more after August 26, 2003, and until such time as the Form 1120-F, "U.S. Income Tax Return of a Foreign Corporation," or its instructions are revised to provide otherwise, the information required in § 1.883-1(c)(3) and § 1.883-2(f), § 1.883-3(d) or § 1.883-4(e), as applicable, must be included on a written statement attached to the Form 1120-F and filed with the return. [Reg. § 1.883-5.]

☐ [*T.D.* 9087, 8-25-2003.]

§ 1.884-0. Overview of regulation provisions for section 884.—(a) *Introduction.*—Section 884 consists of three main parts: a branch profits tax on certain earnings of a foreign corporation's U.S. trade or business; a branch-level interest tax on interest paid, or deemed paid, by a foreign corporation's U.S. trade or business; and an anti-treaty shopping rule. A foreign corporation is subject to section

884 by virtue of owning an interest in a partnership, trust, or estate that is engaged in a U.S. trade or business or has income treated as effectively connected with the conduct of a trade or business in the United States. An international organization (as defined in section 7701(a)(18)) is not subject to the branch profits tax by reason of section 884(e)(5). A foreign government treated as a corporate resident of its country of residence under section 892(a)(3) shall be treated as a corporation for purposes of section 884. The preceding sentence shall be effective for taxable years ending on or after September 11, 1992, except that, for the first taxable year ending on or after that date, the branch profits tax shall not apply to effectively connected earnings and profits of the foreign government earned prior to that date nor to decreases in the U.S. net equity of a foreign government occurring after the close of the preceding taxable year and before that date. Similarly, § 1.884-4 shall apply, in the case of branch interest, only with respect to amounts of interest accrued and paid by a foreign government on or after that date, or, in the case of excess interest, only with respect to amounts attributable to interest accrued by a foreign government on or after that date and apportioned to ECI, as defined in § 1.884-1(d)(1)(iii). Except as otherwise provided, for purposes of the regulations under section 884, the term "U.S. trade or business" includes all the U.S. trades or businesses of a foreign corporation.

(1) *The branch profits tax.*—Section 1.884-1 provides rules for computing the branch profits tax and defines various terms that affect the computation of the tax. In general, section 884(a) imposes a 30-percent branch profits tax on the after-tax earnings of a foreign corporation's U.S. trade or business that are not reinvested in a U.S. trade or business by the close of the taxable year, or are disinvested in a later taxable year. Changes in the value of the equity of the foreign corporation's U.S. trade or business are used as the measure of whether earnings have been reinvested in, or disinvested from, a U.S. trade or business. An increase in the equity during the taxable year is generally treated as a reinvestment of the earnings for the current taxable year; a decrease in the equity during the taxable year is generally treated as a disinvestment of prior years' earnings that have not previously been subject to the branch profits tax. The amount subject to the branch profits tax for the taxable year is the dividend equivalent amount. Section 1.884-2T contains special rules relating to the effect on the branch profits tax of the termination or incorporation of a U.S. trade or business or the liquidation or reorganization of a foreign corporation or its domestic subsidiary.

(2) *The branch-level interest tax.*—Section 1.884-4 provides rules for computing the branch-level interest tax. In general, interest paid by a U.S. trade or business of a foreign corporation ("branch interest", as defined in § 1.884-4(b)) is treated as if it were paid by a domestic corporation and may be subject to tax under section 871(a) or 881, and to withholding under section 1441 or 1442. In addition, if the interest apportioned to ECI exceeds branch interest, the excess is treated as interest paid to the foreign corporation by a wholly-owned domestic corporation and is subject to tax under section 881(a).

(3) *Qualified resident.*—Section 1.884-5 provides rules for determining whether a foreign corporation is a qualified resident of a foreign country. In general, a foreign corporation must be a qualified resident of a foreign country with which the United States has an income tax treaty in order to claim an exemption or rate reduction with respect to the branch profits tax, the branch-level interest tax, and the tax on dividends paid by the foreign corporation.

* * *

[Reg. § 1.884-0.]

☐ [T.D. 8432, 9-10-92. *Amended by T.D.* 8657, 3-5-96 *and T.D.* 9194, 4-6-2005.]

§ 1.884-1. Branch profits tax.— (a) *General rule.*—A foreign corporation shall be liable for a branch profits tax in an amount equal to 30 percent of the foreign corporation's dividend equivalent amount for the taxable year. The branch profits tax shall be in addition to the tax imposed by section 882 and shall be reported on a foreign corporation's income tax return for the taxable year. The tax shall be due and payable as provided in section 6151 and such other provisions of Subtitle F of the Internal Revenue Code as apply to the income tax liability of corporations. However, no estimated tax payments shall be due with respect to a foreign corporation's liability for the branch profits tax. See paragraph (g) of this section for the application of the branch profits tax to corporations that are residents of countries with which the United States has an income tax treaty, and § 1.884-2T for the effect on the branch profits tax of the termination or incorporation of a U.S. trade or business, or the liquidation or reorganization of a foreign corporation or its domestic subsidiary.

(b) *Dividend equivalent amount.*—(1) *Definition.*—The term "dividend equivalent amount" means a foreign corporation's effectively connected earnings and profits ("ECEP", as defined in paragraph (f)(1) of this section) for the taxable year, adjusted pursuant to paragraph (b)(2) or (3) of this section, as applicable. The dividend equivalent amount cannot be less than zero.

(2) *Adjustment for increase in U.S. net equity.*—If a foreign corporation's U.S. net equity (as defined in paragraph (c) of this section) as of the close of the taxable year exceeds the foreign corporation's U.S. net equity as of the close of the preceding taxable year, then, for purposes of computing the foreign corporation's dividend equivalent amount for the taxable year, the foreign corporation's ECEP for the taxable year shall be reduced (but not below zero) by the amount of such excess.

(3) *Adjustment for decrease in U.S. net equity.*—(i) *In general.*—Except as provided in paragraph (b)(3)(ii) of this section, if a foreign corporation's U.S. net equity as of the close of the taxable year is less than the foreign corporation's U.S. net equity as of the close of the preceding taxable year, then, for purposes of computing the foreign corporation's dividend equivalent amount for the taxable year, the foreign corporation's ECEP for the taxable year shall be increased by the amount of such difference.

(ii) *Limitation based on accumulated ECEP.*—The increase of a foreign corporation's ECEP under paragraph (b)(3)(i) of this section shall not exceed the accumulated ECEP of the foreign corporation as of the beginning of the taxable year. The term "accumulated ECEP" means the aggregate amount of ECEP of a foreign corporation for preceding taxable years beginning after December 31, 1986, minus the aggregate dividend equivalent amounts for such preceding taxable years. Accumulated ECEP may be less than zero.

(4) *Examples.*—The principles of paragraph (b)(2) and (3) of this section are illustrated by the following examples.

Example 1. Reinvestment of all ECEP. Foreign corporation A, a calendar year taxpayer, had $1,000 U.S. net equity as of the close of 1986 and $100 of ECEP for 1987. A acquires $100 of additional U.S. assets during 1987 and its U.S. net equity as of the close of 1987 is $1,100. In computing A's dividend equivalent amount for 1987, A's ECEP of $100 is reduced under paragraph (b)(2) of this section by the $100 increase in U.S. net equity between the close of 1986 and the close of 1987. A has no dividend equivalent amount for 1987.

Example 2. Partial reinvestment of ECEP. Assume the same facts as in *Example 1* except that A acquires $40 (rather than $100) of U.S. assets during 1987 and its U.S. net equity as of the close of 1987 is $1,040. In computing A's dividend equivalent amount for 1987, A's ECEP of $100 is reduced under paragraph (b)(2) of this section by the $40 increase in U.S. net equity between the close of 1986 and the close of 1987. A has a dividend equivalent amount of $60 for 1987.

Example 3. Disinvestment of prior year's ECEP. Assume the same facts as in *Example 1* for 1987. A has no ECEP for 1988. A's U.S. net equity decreases by $40 (to $1,060) as of the close of 1988. A has a dividend equivalent amount of $40 for 1988, even though it has no ECEP for 1988. A's ECEP of $0 for 1988 is increased under paragraph (b)(3)(i) of this section by the $40 reduction in U.S. net equity (subject to the limitation in paragraph (b)(3)(ii) of this section of $100 of accumulated ECEP).

Example 4. Accumulated ECEP limitation. Assume the same facts as in *Example 2* for 1987. For 1988, A has $125 of ECEP and its U.S. net equity decreases by $50. A's U.S. net equity as of the close of 1988 is $990 ($1,040-$50). In computing A's dividend equivalent amount for 1988, the $125 of ECEP for 1988 is not increased under paragraph (b)(3)(i) of this section by the full amount of the $50 decrease in U.S. net equity during 1988. Rather, the increase in ECEP resulting from the decrease in U.S. net equity is limited to A's accumulated ECEP as of the beginning of 1988. A had $100 of ECEP for 1987 and a dividend equivalent amount of $60 for that year, so A had $40 of accumulated ECEP as of the beginning of 1988. The increase in ECEP resulting from a decrease in U.S. net equity is thus limited to $40, and the dividend equivalent amount for 1988 is $165 ($125 ECEP + $40 decrease in U.S. net equity).

Example 5. Effect of deficits in ECEP. Foreign corporation A, a calendar year taxpayer, has $150 of accumulated ECEP as of the beginning of 1991 ($200 aggregate ECEP less $50 aggregate dividend equivalent amounts for years preceding 1991). A has U.S. net equity of $450 as of the close of 1990, U.S. net equity of $350 as of the close of 1991 (*i.e.,* a $100 decrease in U.S. net equity) and a $90 deficit in ECEP for 1991. A's dividend equivalent amount is $10 for 1991, *i.e.,* A's deficit of $90 in ECEP for 1991 increased by $100, the decrease in A's U.S. net equity during 1991. A portion of the reduction in U.S. net equity in 1991 ($90) is attributable to A's deficit in ECEP for that year. The reduction in U.S. net equity in 1991 ($100) triggers a dividend equivalent amount only to the extent it exceeds the $90 current year deficit in ECEP for 1991. As of the beginning of 1992, A has $50 of accumulated ECEP (*i.e.,* $110 aggregate ECEP less $60 aggregate dividend equivalent amounts for years preceding 1992).

Example 6. Nimble dividend equivalent amount. Foreign corporation A, a calendar year taxpayer, had a deficit in ECEP of $100 for 1987 and $100 for 1988, and has $90 of ECEP for 1989. A had $2,000 U.S. net equity as of the close of 1988 and has $2,000 U.S. net equity as of the close of 1989. A has a dividend equivalent amount of $90 for 1989, its ECEP for the year, even though it has a net deficit of $110 in ECEP for the period 1987-1989.

(c) *U.S. net equity.*—(1) *Definition.*—The term "U.S. net equity" means the aggregate amount of the U.S. assets (as defined in paragraphs (c)(2) and (d)(1) of this section) of a foreign corporation as of the determination date (as defined in paragraph (c)(3) of this section), reduced (including below zero) by the U.S. liabilities (as defined in paragraph (e) of this section) of the foreign corporation as of the determination date.

(2) *Definition of the amount of a U.S. asset.*—(i) *In general.*—For purposes of this section, the term "amount of a U.S. asset" means the U.S. asset's adjusted basis for purposes of computing earnings and profits ("E&P basis") multiplied by the proportion of the asset that is treated as a U.S. asset under paragraphs (d)(1) through (4) of this section. The amount of a U.S. asset that is money shall be its face value. See paragraph (d)(6) of this section for rules concerning the computation of the E&P basis of a U.S. asset.

(ii) *Bad debt reserves.*—A bank described in section 585(a)(2)(B) (without regard to the second sentence thereof) that uses the reserve method of accounting for bad debts for U.S. federal income tax purposes shall decrease the amount of loans that qualify as U.S. assets by any reserve that is permitted under section 585.

(3) *Definition of determination date.*—For purposes of this section, the term "determination date" means the close of the day on which the amount of U.S. net equity is required to be determined. Unless otherwise provided, the U.S. net equity of a foreign corporation is required to be determined as of the close of the foreign corporation's taxable year.

(d) *U.S. assets.*—(1) *Definition of a U.S. asset.*—(i) *General rule.*—Except as provided in paragraph (d)(5) of this section, the term "U.S. asset" means an asset of a foreign corporation (other than an interest in a partnership, trust, or estate) that is held by the corporation as of the determination date if—

(A) All income produced by the asset on the determination date is ECI (as defined in paragraph (d)(1)(iii) of this section) (or would be ECI if the asset produced income on that date); and

(B) All gain from the disposition of the asset would be ECI if the asset were disposed of on that date and the disposition produced gain.

For purposes of determining whether income or gain from an asset would be ECI under this paragraph (d)(1)(i), it is immaterial whether the asset is of a type that is unlikely to, or cannot, produce income or gain. For example, money may be a U.S. asset although it does not produce income or gain. In the case of an asset that does not produce income, however, the determination of whether income from the asset would be ECI shall be made under the principles of section 864 and the regulations thereunder, but without regard to § 1.864-4(c)(2)(iii)(*b*). For purposes of determining whether an asset is a U.S. asset under this paragraph (d)(1), a foreign corporation may presume, unless it has reason to know otherwise, that gain from the sale of personal property (including inventory property) would be U.S. source if gain from the sale of that type of property would ordinarily be attributable to an office or other fixed place of business of the foreign corporation within the United States (within the meaning of section 865(e)(2)).

(ii) *Special rules for assets not described in paragraph (d)(1)(i) of this section.*—An asset of a foreign corporation that is held by the corporation as of the determination date and is not described in paragraph (d)(1)(i) of this section shall be treated as a U.S. asset to the extent provided in paragraph (d)(2) of this section (relating to special rules for certain assets, including assets that produce income or gain at least a portion of which is ECI), and in paragraphs (d)(3) and (4) of this section (relating to special rules for interests in a partnership, trust, and estate).

(iii) *Definition of ECI.*—For purposes of the regulations under section 884, the term "ECI" means income that is effectively connected with the conduct of a trade or business in the United States and income that is treated as effectively connected with the conduct of a trade or business in the United States under any provision of the Code. The term "ECI" also includes all income that is or is treated as effectively connected with the conduct of a U.S. trade or business whether or not the income is included in gross income (for example, interest income earned with respect to tax-exempt bonds).

(2) *Special rules for certain assets.*—(i) *Depreciable and amortizable property.*—An item of depreciable personal property or an item of amortizable intangible property shall be

treated as a U.S. asset of a foreign corporation in the same proportion that the amount of the depreciation or amortization with respect to the item of property that is allowable as a deduction, or is includible in cost of goods sold, for the taxable year in computing the effectively connected taxable income of the foreign corporation bears to the total amount of depreciation or amortization computed for the taxable year with respect to the item of property.

(ii) *Inventory.*—An item or pool of inventory property (as defined in section 865(i)(1)) shall be treated as a U.S. asset in the same proportion as the amount of gross receipts from the sale or exchange of such property for the three preceding taxable years (or for such part of the three-year period as the corporation has been in existence) that is effectively connected with the conduct of a U.S. trade or business bears to the total amount of gross receipts from the sale or exchange of such property during such period (or part thereof). If a foreign corporation has not sold or exchanged such property during such three-year period (or part thereof), then the property shall be treated as a U.S. asset in the same proportion that the anticipated amount of gross receipts from the sale or exchange of the property that is reasonably anticipated to be ECI bears to the anticipated total amount of gross receipts from the sale or exchange of the property.

(iii) *Installment obligations.*—An installment obligation received in connection with an installment sale (as defined in section 453(b)) for which an election under section 453(d) has not been made shall be treated as a U.S. asset to the extent that it is received in connection with the sale of a U.S. asset. If an obligation is received in connection with the sale of an asset that is wholly a U.S. asset, it shall be treated as a U.S. asset in its entirety. If a single obligation is received in connection with the sale of an asset that is in part a U.S. asset under the rules of paragraphs (d)(2) through (4) of this section, or in connection with the sale of several assets including one or more non-U.S. assets, the obligation shall be treated as U.S. asset in the same proportion as—

(A) The sum of the amount of gain from the installment sale that would be ECI if the obligation were satisfied in full on the determination date and the adjusted basis of the obligation on such date (as determined under section 453B) attributable to the amount of gain that would be ECI bears to

(B) The sum of the total amount of gain from the sale if the obligation were satisfied in full and the adjusted basis of the obligation on such date (as determined under section 453B).

However, the obligation will only be treated as a U.S. asset if the interest income or original issue discount with respect to the obligation is ECI or the foreign corporation elects to treat the interest or original issue discount as ECI in the same proportion that the obligation is treated as a U.S. asset. A foreign corporation may elect to treat interest income or original issue discount as ECI by reporting such interest income or original issue discount as ECI on its income tax return or an amended return for the taxable year. See paragraph (d)(6)(ii) of this section to determine the E&P basis of an installment obligation for purposes of this paragraph (d)(2)(iii).

(iv) *Receivables.*—(A) *Receivables arising from the sale or exchange of inventory property.*—An account or note receivable (whether or not bearing stated interest) with a maturity not exceeding six months that arises from the sale or exchange of inventory property (as defined in section 865(i)(1)) shall be treated as a U.S. asset in the proportion determined under paragraph (d)(2)(iii) of this section as if the receivable were an installment obligation.

(B) *Receivables arising from the performance of services or leasing of property.*—An account or note receivable (whether or not bearing stated interest) with a maturity not exceeding six months that arises from the performance of services or the leasing of property in the ordinary course of a foreign corporation's trade or business shall be treated as a U.S. asset in the same proportion that the amount of gross income represented by the receivable that is ECI bears to the total amount of gross income represented by the receivable. For purposes of this paragraph (d)(2)(iv)(B), the amount of income represented by a receivable shall not include interest income or original issue discount.

(v) *Bank and other deposits.*—A deposit or credit balance with a person described in section 871(i)(3) or a Federal Reserve Bank that is interest-bearing shall be treated as a U.S. asset if all income derived by the foreign corporation with respect to the deposit or credit balance during the taxable year is ECI. Any other deposit or credit balance shall only be treated as a U.S. asset if the deposit or credit balance is needed in a U.S. trade or business within the meaning of § 1.864-4(c)(2)(iii)(*a*).

(vi) *Debt instruments.*—A debt instrument, as defined in section 1275(a)(1) (other than an asset treated as a U.S. asset under any other subdivision of this paragraph (d)) shall be treated as a U.S. asset, notwithstanding the fact that gain from the sale or exchange of the obligation on the determination date would not be ECI, if—

(A) All income derived by the foreign corporation from such obligation during the taxable year is ECI; and

(B) The yield for the period that the instrument was held during the taxable year equals or exceeds the Applicable Federal Rate for instruments of similar type and maturity.

Shares in a regulated investment company that purchases solely instruments that, under this paragraph (d)(2)(vi), would be U.S. assets if held directly by the foreign corporation shall also be treated as a U.S. asset.

(vii) *Securities held by a foreign corporation engaged in a banking, financing or similar business.*—Securities described in § 1.864-4(c)(5)(ii)(*b*)(*3*) held by a foreign corporation engaged in the active conduct of a banking, financing, or similar business in the United States during the taxable year shall be treated as U.S. assets in the same proportion that income, gain, or loss from such securities is ECI for the taxable year under § 1.864-4(c)(5)(ii).

(viii) *Federal income taxes.*—An overpayment of Federal income taxes shall be treated as a U.S. asset to the extent that the tax would reduce a foreign corporation's ECEP for the taxable year but for the fact that the tax does not accrue during the taxable year.

(ix) *Losses involving U.S. assets.*—A foreign corporation that sustains, with respect to a U.S. asset, a loss for which a deduction is not allowed under section 165 (in whole or in part) because there exists a reasonable prospect of recovering compensation for the loss shall be treated as having a U.S. asset ("loss property") from the date of the loss in the same proportion that the asset was treated as a U.S. asset immediately before the loss. See paragraph (d)(6)(iv) of this section to determine the E&P basis of the loss property.

(x) *Ruling for involuntary conversion.*—If property that is a U.S. asset of a foreign corporation is compulsorily or involuntarily converted into property not similar or related in service or use (within the meaning of section 1033), the foreign corporation may apply to the Commissioner for a ruling to determine its U.S. assets for the taxable year of the involuntary conversion.

(xi) *Examples.*—The principles of paragraphs (c) and (d)(1) and (2) of this section are illustrated by the following examples.

Example 1. Depreciable property. Foreign corporation A, a calendar year taxpayer, is engaged in a trade or business in the United States. A owns equipment that is used in its manufacturing business in country X and in the United States. Under § 1.861-8, A's depreciation deduction with respect to the equipment is allocated to sales income and is apportioned 70 percent to ECI and 30 percent to income that is not ECI. Under paragraph (d)(2)(ii) of this section, the equipment is 70 percent a U.S. asset. The equipment has an E&P basis of $100 at the beginning of 1993. A's depreciation deduction (for purposes of computing earnings and profits) with respect to the equipment is $10 for 1993. To determine the amount of A's U.S. asset at the close of 1993, the equipment's $90 E&P basis at the close of 1993 is multiplied by 70 percent (the proportion of the asset that is a U.S. asset). The amount of the U.S. asset as of the close of 1993 is $63.

Example 2. U.S. real property interest connected to a U.S. business. FC is a foreign corporation that is a bank, within the meaning of section 585(a)(2)(B) (without regard to the second sentence thereof), and is engaged in the business of taking deposits and making loans through its branch in the United States. In 1996, FC makes a loan in the ordinary course of its lending business in the United States, securing the loan with a mortgage on the U.S. real property being financed by the borrower. In 1997, after the borrower has defaulted on the loan, FC takes title to the real property that secures the loan. On December 31, 1997, FC continues to hold the property, classifying it on its financial statement as *Other Real Estate Owned.* Because all income and gain from the property would be ECI to FC under the principles of section 864(c)(2), the U.S. real property constitutes a U.S. asset within the meaning of paragraph (d) of this section.

Example 3. U.S. real property interest not connected to a U.S. business. Foreign corporation A owns a condominium apartment in the United States. Assume that holding the apartment does not constitute a U.S. trade or business and the foreign corporation has not made an election under section 882(d) to treat income with respect to the property as ECI. The condominium apartment is not a U.S. asset of A because the income, if any, from the asset would not be ECI. However, the disposition by A of the condominium apartment at a gain will give rise to ECEP.

Example 4. Stock in a domestically-controlled REIT. As an investment, foreign corporation A owns stock in a domestically-controlled REIT, within the meaning of section 897(h)(4)(B). Under section 897(h)(2), gain on disposition of stock in the REIT is not treated as ECI. For this reason the stock does not qualify as a U.S. asset under paragraph (d)(1) of this section even if dividend distributions from the REIT are treated as ECI. Thus, A will have a dividend equivalent amount based on the ECEP attributable to a distribution of ECI from the REIT, even if A invests the proceeds from the dividend in additional stock of the REIT. (Stock in a REIT that is not a domestically-controlled REIT is also not a U.S. asset. See § 1.884-1(d)(5)).

Example 5. Section 864(c)(7) property. Foreign corporation A is engaged in the equipment leasing business in the United States and Canada. A transfers the equipment leased by its U.S. trade or business to its Canadian business after the equipment is fully depreciated in the United States. The Canadian business sells the equipment two years later. Section 864(c)(7) would treat the gain on the disposition of the equipment by A as taxable under section 882 as if the sale occurred immediately before the equipment was transferred to the Canadian business. The equipment would not be treated as a U.S. asset even if the gain was ECI because the income from the equipment in the year of the sale in Canada would not be ECI.

(3) *Interest in a partnership.*—(i) *In general.*—A foreign corporation that is a partner in a partnership must take into account its interest in the partnership (and not the partnership assets) in determining its U.S. assets. For purposes of determining the proportion of the partnership interest that is a U.S. asset, a foreign corporation may elect to use either the asset method described in paragraph (d)(3)(ii) of this section or the income method described in paragraph (d)(3)(iii) of this section.

(ii) *Asset method.*—(A) *In general.*—A partner's interest in a partnership shall be treated as a U.S. asset in the same proportion that the sum of the partner's proportionate share of the adjusted bases of all partnership assets as of the determination date, to the extent that the assets would be treated as U.S. assets if the partnership were a foreign corporation, bears to the sum of the partner's proportionate share of the adjusted bases of all partnership assets as of the determination date. Generally a partner's proportionate share of a partnership asset is the same as its proportionate share of all items of income, gain, loss, and deduction that may be generated by the asset.

(B) *Non-uniform proportionate shares.*—If a partner's proportionate share of all items of income, gain, loss, and deduction that may be generated by a single asset of the partnership throughout the period that includes the taxable year of the partner is not uniform, then, for purposes of determining the partner's proportionate share of the adjusted basis of that asset, a partner must take into account the portion of the adjusted basis of the asset that reflects the partner's economic interest in that asset. A partner's economic interest in an asset of the partnership must be determined by applying the following presumptions. These presumptions may, however, be rebutted if the partner or the Internal Revenue Service shows that the presumption is inconsistent with the partner's true economic interest in the asset during the corporation's taxable year.

(1) If a partnership asset ordinarily generates directly identifiable income, a partner's economic interest in the asset is determined by reference to its proportionate share of income that may be generated by the asset for the partnership's taxable year ending with or within the partner's taxable year.

(2) If a partnership asset ordinarily generates current deductions and ordinarily generates no directly identifiable income, for example because the asset contributes equally to the generation of all the income of the partnership (such as an asset used in general and administrative functions), a partner's economic interest in the asset is determined by reference to its proportionate share of the total deductions that may be generated by the asset for the partnership's taxable year ending with or within the partner's taxable year.

(3) For other partnership assets not described in paragraph (d)(3)(ii)(B)(1) or (2) of this section, a partner's economic interest in the asset is determined by reference to its proportionate share of the total gain or loss to which it would be entitled if the asset were sold at a gain or loss in the partnership's taxable year ending with or within the partner's taxable year.

(C) *Partnership election under section 754.*—If a partnership files an election in accordance with section 754, then for purposes of this paragraph (d)(3)(ii), the basis of partnership property shall reflect adjustments made pursuant to sections 734 (relating to distributions of property to a partner) and 743 (relating to the transfer of an interest in a partnership). However, adjustments made pursuant to section 743 may be made with respect to a transferee partner only.

(iii) *Income method.*—Under the income method, a partner's interest in a partnership shall be treated as a U.S. asset in the same proportion that its distributive share of partnership ECI for the partnership's taxable year that ends with or within the partner's taxable year bears to its distributive share of all partnership income for that taxable year.

(iv) *Manner of election.*—(A) *In general.*—In determining the proportion of a foreign corporation's interest in a partnership that is a U.S. asset, a foreign corporation must elect one of the methods described in paragraph (d)(3) of this section on a timely filed return for the first taxable year beginning on or after the effective date of this section. An amended return does not qualify for this purpose, nor shall the provisions of §301.9100-1 of this chapter and any guidance promulgated thereunder apply. An election shall be made by the foreign corporation calculating its U.S. assets in accordance with the method elected. An elected method must be used for a minimum period of five years before the foreign corporation may elect a different method. To change an election before the end of the requisite five-year period, a foreign corporation must obtain the consent of the Commissioner or her delegate. The Commissioner or her delegate will generally consent to a foreign corporation's request to change its election only in rare and unusual circumstances. A foreign corporation that is a partner in more than one partnership is not required to elect to use the same method for each partnership interest.

(B) *Elections with tiered partnerships.*—If a foreign corporation elects to use the asset method with respect to an interest in a partnership, and that partnership is a partner in a lower-tier partnership, the foreign corporation may apply either the asset method or the income method to determine the proportion of the upper-tier partnership's interest in the lower-tier partnership that is a U.S. asset.

(v) *Failure to make proper election.*—If a foreign corporation, for any reason, fails to make an election to use one of the methods required by paragraph (d)(3) of this section in a timely fashion, the district director or the Assistant Commissioner (International) may make the election on behalf of the foreign corporation and such election shall be binding as if made by that corporation.

(vi) *Special rule for determining a partner's adjusted basis in a partnership interest.*—For purposes of paragraphs (d)(3) and (6) of this section, a partner's adjusted basis in a partnership interest shall be the partner's basis in such interest (determined under section 705) reduced by the partner's share of the liabilities of the partnership determined under section 752 and increased by a proportionate share of each liability of the partnership equal to the partner's proportionate share of the expense, for income tax purposes, attributable to such liability for the taxable year. A partner's adjusted basis in a partnership interest cannot be less than zero.

(vii) *E&P basis of a partnership interest.*—See paragraph (d)(6)(iii) of this section for special rules governing the calculation of a foreign corporation's E&P basis in a partnership interest.

(viii) The application of this paragraph (d)(3) is illustrated by the following examples:

Example 1. General rule—(i) *Facts.* Foreign corporation, FC, is a partner in partnership ABC, which is engaged in a trade or business within the United States. FC and ABC are both calendar year taxpayers. ABC owns and manages two office buildings located in the United States, each with an adjusted basis of $50. ABC also owns a non-U.S. asset with an adjusted basis of $100. ABC has no liabilities. Under the partnership agreement, FC has a 50 percent interest in the capital of ABC and a 50 percent interest in all items of income, gain, loss, and deduction that may be generated by the partnership's assets. FC's adjusted basis in ABC is $100. In determining the proportion of its interest in ABC that is a U.S. asset, FC elects to use the asset method described in paragraph (d)(3)(ii) of this section.

(ii) *Analysis.* FC's interest in ABC is treated as a U.S. asset in the same proportion that the sum of FC's proportionate share of the adjusted bases of all ABC's U.S. assets (50% of $100), bears to the sum of FC's proportionate share of the adjusted bases of all of ABC's assets (50% of $200). Under the asset method, the amount of FC's interest in ABC that is a U.S. asset is $50 ($100 × $50/$100).

Example 2. Special allocation of gain with respect to real property—(i) *Facts.* The facts are the same as in *Example 1*, except that under the partnership agreement, FC is allocated 20 percent of the income from the partnership property but 80 percent of the gain on disposition of the partnership property.

(ii) *Analysis.* Assuming that the buildings ordinarily generate directly identifiable income, there is a rebuttable presumption under paragraph (d)(3)(ii)(B)(*1*) of this section that FC's proportionate share of the adjusted basis of the buildings is FC's proportionate share of the income generated by the buildings (20%) rather than the total gain that it would be entitled to under the partnership agreement (80%) if the buildings were sold at a gain on the determination date. Thus, the sum of FC's proportionate share of the adjusted bases in ABC's U.S. assets (the buildings) is presumed to be $20 [(20% of $50) + (20% of $50)]. Assuming that the non-U.S. asset is not income-producing and does not generate current deductions, there is a rebuttable presumption under paragraph (d)(3)(ii)(B)(*3*) of this section that FC's proportionate share of the adjusted basis of that asset is FC's interest in the gain on the

Reg. §1.884-1(d)(3)(viii)

disposition of the asset (80%) rather than its proportionate share of the income that may be generated by the asset (20%). Thus, FC's proportionate share of the adjusted basis of ABC's non-U.S. asset is presumed to be $80 (80% of $100). FC's proportionate share of the adjusted bases of all of the assets of ABC is $100 ($20 + $80). The amount of FC's interest in ABC that is a U.S. asset is $20 ($100 × $20/$100).

Example 3. Tiered partnerships (asset method)—(i) *Facts.* The facts are the same as in *Example 1*, except that FC's adjusted basis in ABC is $175 and ABC also has a 50 percent interest in the capital of partnership DEF. DEF owns and operates a commercial shopping center in the United States with an adjusted basis of $200 and also owns non-U.S. assets with an adjusted basis of $100. DEF has no liabilities. ABC's adjusted basis in its interest in DEF is $150 and ABC has a 50 percent interest in all the items of income, gain, loss and deduction that may be generated by the assets of DEF.

(ii) *Analysis.* Because FC has elected to use the asset method described in paragraph (d)(3)(ii) of this section, it must determine what proportion of ABC's partnership interest in DEF is a U.S. asset. As permitted by paragraph (d)(3)(iv)(B) of this section, FC also elects to use the asset method with respect to ABC's interest in DEF. ABC's interest in DEF is treated as a U.S. asset in the same proportion that the sum of ABC's proportionate share of the adjusted bases of all DEF's U.S. assets (50% of $200), bears to the sum of ABC's proportionate share of the adjusted bases of all of DEF's assets (50% of $300). Thus, the amount of ABC's interest in DEF that is a U.S. asset is $100 ($150 × $100/$150). FC must then apply the rules of paragraph (d)(3)(ii) of this section to all the assets of ABC, including ABC's interest in DEF that is treated in part as a U.S. asset ($100) and in part as a non-U.S. asset ($50). FC's interest in ABC is treated as a U.S. asset in the same proportion that the sum of FC's proportionate share of the adjusted bases of the U.S. assets of ABC (including ABC's interest in DEF), bears to the sum of FC's proportionate share of the adjusted bases of all ABC's assets (including ABC's interest in DEF). Thus, the amount of FC's interest in ABC that is a U.S. asset is $100 (FC's adjusted basis in ABC ($175) multiplied by FC's proportionate share of the sum of the adjusted bases of ABC's U.S. assets ($100)) over FC's proportionate share of the sum of the adjusted bases of ABC's assets ($175)).

Example 4. Tiered partnerships (income method)—(i) *Facts.* The facts are the same as in *Example 3*, except that FC has elected to use the income method described in paragraph (d)(3)(iii) of this section to determine the proportion of its interest in ABC that is a U.S. asset. The two office buildings located in the United States generate $60 of income that is ECI for the taxable year. The non-U.S. asset is not-income producing. In addition ABC's distributive share of income from DEF consists of $40 of income that is ECI and $140 of income that is not ECI.

(ii) *Analysis.* Because FC has elected to use the income method it does need to determine what proportion of ABC's partnership interest in DEF is a U.S. asset. FC's interest in ABC is treated as a U.S. asset in the same proportion that its distributive share of ABC's income for the taxable year that is ECI ($50) ($30 earned directly by ABC + $20 distributive share from DEF) bears to its distributive share of all ABC's income for the taxable year ($55) ($30 earned directly by ABC + $25 distributive share from DEF). Thus, FC's interest in ABC that is a U.S. asset is $159 ($175 × $50/$55).

(4) *Interest in a trust or estate.*—(i) *Estates and non-grantor trusts.*—A foreign corporation that is a beneficiary of a trust or estate shall not be treated as having a U.S. asset by virtue of its interest in the trust or estate.

(ii) *Grantor trusts.*—If, under sections 671 through 678, a foreign corporation is treated as owning a portion of a trust that includes all the income and gain that may be generated by a trust asset (or pro rata portion of a trust asset), the foreign corporation will be treated as owning the trust asset (or pro rata portion thereof) for purposes of determining its U.S. assets under this section.

(5) *Property that is not a U.S. asset.*—(i) *Property that does not give rise to ECEP.*—Property described in paragraphs (d)(1) through (4) of this section shall not be treated as a U.S. asset of a foreign corporation if, on the determination date, income from the use of the property, or gain or loss from the disposition of the property, would be described in paragraph (f)(2) of this section (relating to certain income that does not produce ECEP).

(ii) *Assets acquired to increase U.S. net equity artificially.*—U.S. assets shall not include assets acquired or used by a foreign corporation if one of the principal purposes of such acquisition or use is to increase artificially the U.S. assets of a foreign corporation on the determination date. Whether assets are acquired or used for such purpose will depend upon all the facts and circumstances of each case. Factors to be considered in determining whether one of the principal purposes in acquiring or using an asset is to increase artificially the U.S. assets of a foreign corporation include the length of time during which the asset was used in a U.S. trade or business, whether the asset was acquired from, or disposed of to, a related person, and whether the aggregate value of the U.S. assets of the foreign corporation increased temporarily on the determination date. For purposes of this paragraph (d)(5)(ii), to be one of the principal purposes, a purpose must be important, but it is not necessary that it be the primary purpose.

(iii) *Interbranch transactions.*—A transaction of any type between separate offices or branches of the same taxpayer does not create a U.S. asset.

(6) *E&P basis of a U.S. asset.*—(i) *General rule.*—The E&P basis of a U.S. asset for purposes of this section is its adjusted basis for purposes of computing the foreign corporation's earnings and profits. In determining the E&P basis of a U.S. asset, the adjusted basis of the asset (for purposes of computing taxable income) must be increased or decreased to take into account inclusions of income or gain, and deductions or similar charges, that affect the basis of the asset where such items are taken into account in a different manner for purposes of computing earnings and profits than for purposes of computing taxable income. For example, if section 312(k) requires that depreciation with respect to a U.S. asset be determined using the straight line method for purposes of computing earnings and profits, but depreciation with respect to the asset is determined using a different method for purposes of computing taxable income, the E&P basis of the property for purposes of this section must be computed using the straight line method of depreciation.

(ii) *Installment obligations.*—(A) *Sales in taxable year beginning on or after January 1, 1987.*—For purposes of this section, the E&P basis of an installment obligation described in paragraph (d)(2)(iii) of this section that arises in connection with an installment sale occurring in a taxable year beginning on or after January 1, 1987, shall equal the sum of the total amount of gain from the sale if the obligation were satisfied in full and the adjusted basis of the property sold as of the date of sale, reduced by payments received with respect to the obligation that are not interest or original issue discount. See paragraph (j)(2)(ii) of this section, however, for a special E&P basis rule for an installment obligation arising in connection with a sale of a U.S. asset by a foreign corporation described in section 312(k)(4), where such sale occurs in a taxable year beginning in 1987.

(B) *Sales in taxable year prior to January 1, 1987.*—For purposes of this section, the E&P basis of an installment obligation described in paragraph (d)(2)(iii) of this section that arises in connection with an installment sale occurring in a taxable year beginning before January 1, 1987, shall equal zero.

(iii) *Computation of E&P basis in a partnership.*—For purposes of this section, a foreign corporation's E&P basis in a partnership interest shall be the foreign corporation's adjusted basis in such interest (as determined under paragraph (d)(3)(vi) of this section), further adjusted to take into account any differences between the foreign corporation's distributive share of items of partnership income, gain, loss, and deduction for purposes of computing the taxable income of the foreign corporation and the foreign corporation's distributive share of items of partnership income, gain, loss, and deduction for purposes of computing the earnings and profits of the foreign corporation.

(iv) *Computation of E&P basis of a loss property.*—The E&P basis of a loss property (as defined in paragraph (d)(2)(ix) of this section) shall equal the E&P basis, immediately before the loss, of the U.S. asset with respect to which the loss was sustained, reduced (but not below zero) by—

(A) The amount of any deduction claimed under section 165 by the foreign corporation with respect to the loss for earnings and profits purposes; and

(B) Any compensation received with respect to the loss.

(v) *Computation of E&P basis of financial instruments.*—[Reserved]

(vi) *Example.*—The application of paragraph (d)(6)(ii) of this section is illustrated by the following example.

Example. Sale in taxable year beginning on or after January 1, 1987. Foreign corporation A, a calendar year taxpayer, sells a U.S. asset on the installment method in 1993. Under the terms of the sale, A is to receive $100, payable in ten annual installments of $10 beginning in 1994, plus an arm's-length rate of interest on the unpaid balance of the sales price. A's adjusted basis in the property sold is $70. The obligation received in connection with the installment sale is treated as a U.S. asset with an E&P basis of $100 ($30 (the amount of gain from the sale if the obligation were satisfied in full) + $70 (the adjusted basis of the property sold)). If A receives a payment of $10 (not including interest) in 1994 with respect to the obligation, the obligation is treated as a U.S. asset with an E&P basis of $90 ($100 − $10) as of the close of 1994.

Reg. § 1.884-1(d)(6)(vi)

(e) *U.S. liabilities.*—The term "U.S. liabilities" means the amount of liabilities determined under paragraph (e)(1) of this section decreased by the amount of liabilities determined under paragraph (e)(3) of this section, and increased by the amount of liabilities determined under paragraph (e)(2) of this section.

(1) *Liabilities based on § 1.882-5.*—The amount of liabilities determined under this paragraph (e)(1) is the amount of U.S.-connected liabilities of a foreign corporation under § 1.882-5 if the U.S.-connected liabilities were computed using the assets and liabilities of the foreign corporation as of the determination date (rather than the average of such assets and liabilities for the taxable year) and without regard to paragraph (e)(3) of this section.

(2) *Additional liabilities—Insurance reserves.*—(i) The amount of liabilities determined under this paragraph (e)(2)(i) is the amount (as of the determination date) of the total insurance liabilities on United States business (within the meaning of section 842 (b)(2)(B)) of a foreign corporation described in section 842(a) (relating to foreign corporations carrying on an insurance business in the United States) to the extent that such liabilities are not otherwise treated as U.S. liabilities by reason of paragraph (e)(1) of this section.

(ii) *Liabilities described in § 1.882-5(a)(1)(ii).*—The amount of liabilities determined under this paragraph (e)(2)(ii) is the amount (as of the determination date) of liabilities described in § 1.882-5(a)(1)(ii) (relating to liabilities giving rise to interest expense that is directly allocated to income from a U.S. asset).

(3) *Election to reduce liabilities.*—(i) *General rule.*—The amount of liabilities determined under this paragraph (e)(3) is the amount by which a foreign corporation elects to reduce its liabilities under paragraph (e)(1) of this section.

(ii) *Limitation.*—For any taxable year, a foreign corporation may elect to reduce the amount of its liabilities determined under paragraph (e)(1) of this section by an amount that does not exceed the excess, if any, of the amount of liabilities in paragraph (e)(1) of this section over the amount, as of the determination date, of U.S. booked liabilities (determined under § 1.882-5(d)(2)) and liabilities described in paragraph (e)(2) of this section.

(iii) *Effect of election on interest deduction and branch-level interest tax.*—A foreign corporation that elects to reduce its liabilities under this paragraph (e)(3) must, for purposes of computing the amount of its interest apportioned to ECI under § 1.882-5, reduce its U.S.-connected liabilities for the taxable year of the election by the amount of the reduction in liabilities under this paragraph (e)(3). The reduction of its U.S.-connected liabilities will also require a corresponding decrease in the amount of its interest apportioned to ECI under § 1.882-5 for purposes of § 1.884-4(a) and for all other Code sections for which the amount of interest apportioned under § 1.882-5 is relevant.

(iv) *Method of election.*—A foreign corporation that elects the benefits of this paragraph (e)(3) for a taxable year shall state on its return for the taxable year (or on a statement attached to the return) that it has elected to reduce its liabilities for the taxable year under this paragraph (e)(3) and that it has reduced the amount of its U.S.-connected liabilities as provided in paragraph (e)(3)(iii) of this section, and shall indicate the amount of such reductions on the return or attachment. An election under this paragraph (e)(3) must be made before the due date (including extensions) for the foreign corporation's income tax return for the taxable year.

(v) *Effect of election on complete termination.*—If a foreign corporation completely terminates its U.S. trade or business (within the meaning of § 1.884-2T (a)(2)), notwithstanding § 1.884-2T(a), the foreign corporation will be subject to tax on a dividend equivalent amount that equals the lesser of—

(A) The foreign corporation's accumulated ECEP that is attributable to an election to reduce liabilities; or

(B) The amount by which the corporation elected to reduce liabilities at the end of the taxable year preceding the year of complete termination.

For purposes of the preceding sentence, accumulated ECEP is attributable to an election to reduce liabilities to the extent that the ECEP was accumulated because of such an election rather than because of an increase in U.S. assets. For example, if a foreign corporation did not have positive ECEP in any year for which an election was made, it would not be required to include an amount as a dividend equivalent amount under this paragraph (e)(3)(v) because any accumulated ECEP that it may have is not attributable to an election to reduce liabilities.

(4) *Artificial decrease in U.S. liabilities.*—If a foreign corporation repays or otherwise decreases its U.S. liabilities and one of the principal purposes of such decrease is to decrease artificially its U.S. liabilities on the determination date, then such decrease shall not be taken into account for purposes of computing the foreign corporation's U.S. net equity. Whether the U.S. liabilities of a foreign corpo-

ration are artificially decreased will depend on all the facts and circumstances of each case. Factors to be considered in determining whether one of the principal purposes for the repayment or decrease of the liabilities is to decrease artificially the U.S. liabilities of a foreign corporation shall include whether the aggregate liabilities are temporarily decreased on or before the determination date by, for example, the repayment of liabilities, or U.S. liabilities are temporarily decreased on or before the determination date by the acquisition with contributed funds of passive-type assets that are not U.S. assets. For purposes of this paragraph (e)(4), to be one of the principal purposes, a purpose must be important, but it is not necessary that it be the primary purpose.

(5) *Examples.*—The application of this paragraph (e) is illustrated by the following examples.

Example 1. General rule for computation of U.S. liabilities. As of the close of 1997, foreign corporation A, a calendar year taxpayer computes its U.S.-connected liabilities under § 1.882-5(c) using its actual ratio of liabilities to assets. For purposes of computing its U.S. connected liabilities under § 1.882-5(c), A must determine the average total value of its assets that are U.S. assets. Assume that the average value of such assets is $100, while the amount of such assets as of the close of 1997 is $125. For purposes of § 1.882-5(c)(2), A must determine the ratio of the average of its worldwide liabilities for the year to the average total value of worldwide assets for the taxable year. Assume that A's average liabilities-to-assets ratio under § 1.882-5(c)(2) is 55 percent, while its liabilities-to-assets ratio at the close of 1997 is only 50 percent. Thus, assuming no further adjustments under paragraph (e)(3) of this section, A's U.S.-connected liabilities for purposes of § 1.882-5 are $55 ($100 × 55%). However, A's U.S. liabilities are $62.50 for purposes of this section, the value of its assets determined under § 1.882-5(b)(2) as of the close of December ($125) multiplied by the liabilities-to-assets ratio (50%) as of such date.

Example 2. Election made to reduce liabilities. (i) As of the close of 1997, foreign corporation A, a real estate company, owns U.S. assets with an E&P basis of $1000. A has $800 of liabilities under paragraph (e)(1) of this section and $300 of liabilities properly reflected on the books of its U.S. trade or business under § 1.882-5(d)(2). A has accumulated ECEP of $500 and in 1998, A has $60 of ECEP that it intends to retain for future expansion of its U.S. trade or business. A elects under paragraph (e)(3) of this section to reduce its liabilities by $60 from $800 to $740. As a result of the election, assuming A's U.S. assets and U.S. liabilities would otherwise have remained constant, A's U.S. net equity as of the close of 1998 will increase by the amount of the decrease in liabilities ($60) from $200 to $260 and its ECEP will be reduced to zero. Under paragraph (e)(3)(iii) of this section, A's interest expense for the taxable year is reduced by the amount of interest attributable to $60 of liabilities and A's excess interest is reduced by the same amount. A's taxable income and ECEP are increased by the amount of the reduction in interest expense attributable to the liabilities, and A may make an election under paragraph (e)(3) of this section to further reduce its liabilities, thus increasing its U.S. net equity and reducing the amount of additional ECEP created by the election.

(ii) In 1999, assuming A again has $60 of ECEP, A may again make the election under paragraph (e)(3) to reduce its liabilities. However, assuming A's U.S. assets and liabilities under paragraph (e)(1) of this section remain constant, A will need to make an election to reduce its liabilities by $120 to reduce to zero its ECEP in 1999 and to continue to retain for expansion (without the payment of the branch profits tax) the $60 of ECEP earned in 1998. Without an election to reduce liabilities, A's dividend equivalent amount for 1999 would be $120 ($60 of ECEP plus the $60 reduction in U.S. net equity from $260 to $200). If A makes the election to reduce liabilities by $120 (from $800 to $680), A's U.S. net equity will increase by $60 (from $260 at the end of the previous year to $320), the amount necessary to reduce its ECEP to $0. However, the reduction of liabilities will itself create additional ECEP subject to section 884 because of the reduction in interest expense attributable to the $120 of liabilities. A can make the election to reduce liabilities by $120 without exceeding the limitation on the election provided in paragraph (e)(3)(ii) of this section because $120 does not exceed the excess of $800 (the amount of A's liabilities under paragraph (e)(1) of this section) over $300 (the amount of liabilities on A's books).

(iii) If A terminates its U.S. trade or business in 1999 in accordance with the rules in § 1.884-2T(a), A would not be subject to the branch profits tax on the $60 of ECEP earned in that year. Under paragraph (e)(3)(v) of this section, however, it would be subject to the branch profits tax on the portion of the $60 of ECEP that it earned in 1998 that became accumulated ECEP because of an election to reduce liabilities.

(f) *Effectively connected earnings and profits.*—(1) *In general.*—Except as provided in paragraph (f)(2) of this section and as modified by § 1.884-2T (relating to the incorporation or complete termination of a U.S. trade or business or the reorganization or liquidation of a foreign corporation or its domestic subsidiary), the term "effectively connected earnings and profits" ("ECEP") means the earnings and profits (or deficits therein) determined under section 312 and this paragraph (f) that are attributable to ECI (within the meaning of paragraph (d)(1)(iii) of this section). Because the term "ECI" includes income treated as effectively connected, income that is ECI under section 842(b) (relating to minimum net investment income of an insurance business) or 864(c)(7) (relating to gain from property formerly held for use in a U.S. trade or business) gives rise to ECEP. ECEP also includes earnings and profits attributable to ECI of a foreign corporation earned through a partnership, and through a trust or estate. For purposes of section 884, gain on the sale of a U.S. real property interest by a foreign corporation that has made an election to be treated as a domestic corporation under section 897(i) will also give rise to ECEP. ECEP is not reduced by distributions made by the foreign corporation during any taxable year or by the amount of branch profits tax or tax on excess interest (as defined in § 1.884-4(a)(2)) paid by the foreign corporation. Earnings and profits are treated as attributable to ECI even if the earnings and profits are taken into account under section 312 in an earlier or later taxable year than the taxable year in which the ECI is taken into account.

(2) *Income that does not produce ECEP.*— The term "ECEP" does not include any earnings and profits attributable to—

(i) Income excluded from gross income under section 883(a)(1) or 883(a)(2) (relating to certain income derived from the operation of ships or aircraft);

(ii) Income that is ECI by reason of section 921(d) or 926(b) (relating to certain income of a FSC and certain dividends paid by a FSC to a foreign corporation or nonresident alien) that is not otherwise ECI;

(iii) Gain on the disposition of a U.S. real property interest described in section 897(c)(1)(A)(ii) (relating to certain interests in a domestic corporation);

(iv) Income that is ECI by reason of section 953(c)(3)(C) (relating to certain income of a captive insurance company that a corporation elects to treat as ECI) that is not otherwise ECI;

(v) Income that is exempt from tax under section 892 (relating to certain income of foreign governments); and

(vi) Income that is ECI by reason of section 882(e) (relating to certain interest income of banks organized under the laws of a possession of the United States) that is not otherwise ECI.

(3) *Allocation of deductions attributable to income that does not produce ECEP.*—In determining the amount of a foreign corporation's ECEP for the taxable year, deductions and other adjustments shall be allocated and apportioned under the principles of § 1.861-8 between ECI that gives rise to ECEP and income described in paragraph (f)(2) of this section (relating to income that is ECI but does not give rise to ECEP).

(4) *Examples.*—The principles of paragraph (f) of this section are illustrated by the following examples.

Example 1. Tax-exempt income. Foreign corporation A owns a tax-exempt municipal bond that is a U.S. asset as of the close of its 1989 taxable year. The municipal bond gives rise in 1989 to ECI (even though the income is excluded from gross income under section 103(a) and is not gross income of a foreign corporation by reason of section 882(b)), and therefore gives rise to ECEP in 1989.

Example 2. Income exempt under a treaty. Foreign corporation A derives ECI that constitutes business profits that are not attributable to a permanent establishment maintained by A in the United States. The ECI is exempt from taxation under section 882(a) by reason of an income tax treaty and section 894(a). The income nevertheless gives rise to ECEP under this paragraph (f). However, a dividend equivalent amount attributable to such ECEP may be exempt from the branch profits tax by reason of paragraph (g) of this section (relating to the application of the branch profits tax to corporations that are residents of countries with which the United States has an income tax treaty).

(g) *Corporations resident in countries with which the United States has an income tax treaty.*—(1) *General rule.*—Except as provided in paragraph (g)(2) of this section, a foreign corporation that is a resident of a country with which the United States has an income tax treaty in effect for a taxable year in which it has a dividend equivalent amount and that meets the requirements, if any, of the limitation on benefits provisions of such treaty with respect to the dividend equivalent amount shall not be subject to the branch profits tax on such amount (or will qualify for a reduction in the amount of tax with respect to such amount) only if—

(i) The foreign corporation is a qualified resident of such country for the taxable year, within the meaning of § 1.884-5(a); or

(ii) The limitation on benefits provision, or an amendment to that provision, entered into force after December 31, 1986.

If, after application of § 1.884-5(e)(4)(iv), a foreign corporation is a qualified resident under § 1.884-5(e) (relating to the active trade or business test) only with respect to one of its trades or businesses in the United States, *i.e.*, the trade or business that is an integral part of its business conducted in its country of residence, and not with respect to another, the rules of this paragraph shall apply only to that portion of its dividend equivalent amount attributable to the trade or business for which the foreign corporation is a qualified resident.

(2) *Special rules for foreign corporations that are qualified residents on the basis of their ownership.*—(i) *General rule.*—A foreign corporation that, in any taxable year, is a qualified resident of a country with which the United States has an income tax treaty in effect solely by reason of meeting the requirements of § 1.884-5(b) and (c) (relating, respectively, to stock ownership and base erosion) shall be exempt from the branch profits tax or subject to a reduced rate of branch profits tax under paragraph (g)(1) of this section with respect to the portion of its dividend equivalent amount for the taxable year attributable to accumulated ECEP only if the foreign corporation is a qualified resident of such country within the meaning of § 1.884-5(a) for the taxable years includible, in whole or in part, in a consecutive 36-month period that includes the taxable year of the dividend equivalent amount. A foreign corporation that fails the 36-month test described in the preceding sentence shall be exempt from the branch profits tax or subject to the branch profits tax at a reduced rate under paragraph (g)(1) of this section with respect to accumulated ECEP (determined on a last-in-first-out basis) accumulated only during prior years in which the foreign corporation was a qualified resident of such country within the meaning of § 1.884-5(a).

(ii) *Rules of application.*—A foreign corporation that has not satisfied the 36-month test as of the close of the taxable year of the dividend equivalent amount but satisfies the test with respect to such dividend equivalent amount by meeting the 36-month test by the close of the second taxable year succeeding the taxable year of the dividend equivalent amount shall be subject to the branch profits tax for the year of the dividend equivalent amount without regard to paragraph (g)(1) of this section on the portion of the dividend equivalent amount attributable to accumulated ECEP derived in a taxable year in which the foreign corporation was not a qualified resident within the meaning of § 1.884-5(a). Upon meeting the 36-month test, the foreign corporation shall be entitled to claim by amended return a refund of the tax paid with respect to the dividend equivalent amount in excess of the branch profits tax calculated by taking into account paragraph (g)(2)(i) of this section, provided the foreign corporation establishes in the amended return for the taxable year that it has met the requirements of such paragraph. For purposes of section 6611 (dealing with interest on overpayments), any overpayment of branch profits tax by reason of this paragraph (g)(2)(ii) shall be deemed not to have been made before the filing date for the taxable year in which the foreign corporation establishes that it has met the 36-month test.

(iii) *Example.*—The application of this paragraph (g)(2) is illustrated by the following example.

Example. (i) Foreign corporation A, a calendar year taxpayer, is a resident of the United Kingdom. A has a dividend equivalent amount for its taxable year 1991 of $300, of which $100 is attributable to 1991 ECEP and $200 to accumulated ECEP. A is a qualified resident for its taxable year 1991 because for that year it meets the requirements of § 1.884-5(b) and (c), relating, respectively, to stock ownership and base erosion. For 1991 A does not meet the requirements of § 1.884-5(d), (e), or (f) for qualified residence. A is not a qualified resident of the United Kingdom for any taxable year prior to 1990 but is a qualified resident for its taxable years 1990 and 1992.

(ii) Because A is a qualified resident for the 3-year period (1990, 1991, and 1992) that includes the taxable year of the dividend equivalent amount (1991), A satisfies the 36-month test of this paragraph (g)(2) and no branch profits tax is imposed on the total $300 dividend equivalent amount. However, since A was not a qualified resident for any taxable year prior to 1990 and therefore cannot establish that it has satisfied the 36-month test until the taxable year following the year of the dividend equivalent amount, A must pay the branch profits tax for its taxable year 1991 with respect to the portion of the dividend equivalent amount attributable to accumulated ECEP relating to years prior to 1990 without regard to paragraph (g)(1) of this section. A may file for a refund of the branch profits tax paid with respect to its 1991 taxable year at any time after it establishes that it is a qualified resident for its 1992 taxable year.

(3) *Exemptions for foreign corporations resident in certain countries with income tax treaties in effect on January 1, 1987.*—The branch profits tax shall not be imposed on the portion of the dividend equivalent amount with respect

to which a foreign corporation satisfies the requirements of paragraphs (g)(1) and (2) of this section for a country listed below, so long as the income tax treaty between the United States and that country, as in effect on January 1, 1987, remains in effect, except to the extent the treaty is modified on or after January 1, 1987, to expressly provide for the imposition of the branch profits tax:

Aruba	Greece	Morocco
Austria	Hungary	Netherlands
Belgium	Iceland	Netherlands Antilles
People's Republic of China	Ireland	Norway
	Italy	Pakistan
Cyprus	Jamaica	Philippines
Denmark	Japan	Sweden
Egypt	Korea	Switzerland
Finland	Luxembourg	United Kingdom
Germany	Malta	

(4) *Modifications with respect to other income tax treaties.*—(i) *Limitation on rate of tax.*—(A) *General rule.*—If, under paragraphs (g)(1) and (2) of this section, a corporation qualifies for a reduction in the amount of the branch profits tax and paragraph (g)(3) of this section does not apply, the rate of tax shall be the rate of tax on branch profits specified in the treaty between the United States and the corporation's country of residence or, if no rate of tax on branch profits is specified, the rate of tax that would apply under such treaty to dividends paid to the foreign corporation by a wholly-owned domestic corporation.

(B) *Certain treaties in effect on January 1, 1987.*—The branch profits tax shall generally be imposed at the following rates on the portion of the dividend equivalent amount with respect to which a foreign corporation satisfies the requirements of paragraphs (g)(1) and (2) of this section for a country listed below, for as long as the relevant provisions of those income tax treaties remain in effect and are not modified or superseded by subsequent agreement:

Australia (15%)	France (5%)	Romania (10%)
Barbados (5%)	New Zealand (5%)	South Africa (30%)
Canada (10%)	Poland (5%)	Trinidad & Tobago (10%)
		U.S.S.R. (30%)

However, for special rates imposed on corporations resident in France and Trinidad & Tobago that have certain amounts of dividend and interest income, see the dividend articles of the income tax treaties with those countries.

(ii) *Limitations other than rate of tax.*—If, under paragraphs (g)(1) and (2) of this section, a foreign corporation qualifies for a reduction in the amount of branch profits tax and paragraph (g)(3) of this section does not apply, then—

(A) The foreign corporation shall be entitled to the benefit of any limitations on imposition of a tax on branch profits (in addition to any limitations on the rate of tax) contained in the treaty; and

(B) No branch profits tax shall be imposed with respect to a dividend equivalent amount out of ECEP or accumulated ECEP of the foreign corporation unless the ECEP or accumulated ECEP is attributable to a permanent establishment in the United States or, if not otherwise prohibited under the treaty, to gain from the disposition of a U.S. real property interest described in section 897(c)(1)(A)(i), except to the extent the treaty specifically permits the imposition of the branch profits tax on such earnings and profits.

No article in such treaty shall be construed to provide any limitations on imposition of the branch profits tax other than as provided in this paragraph (g)(4).

(iii) *Computation of the dividend equivalent amount if a foreign corporation has both ECEP attributable to a permanent establishment and not attributable to a permanent establishment.*—To determine the dividend equivalent amount of a foreign corporation out of ECEP that is attributable to a permanent establishment, the foreign corporation may only take into account its U.S. assets, U.S. liabilities, U.S. net equity and ECEP attributable to its permanent establishment. Thus, a foreign corporation may not reduce the amount of its ECEP attributable to its permanent establishment by reinvesting all or a portion of that amount in U.S. assets not attributable to the permanent establishment.

(iv) *Limitations under the Canadian treaty.*—The limitations on the imposition of the branch profits tax under the Canadian treaty include, but are not limited to, those described in paragraphs (g)(4)(iv)(A) and (B).

(A) *Effect of deficits in earnings and profits.*—In the case of a foreign corporation that is a qualified resident of Canada, the dividend equivalent amount for any taxable year shall not exceed the foreign corporation's accumulated ECEP as of the beginning of the taxable year plus the corporation's ECEP for the taxable year. Thus, for example, if a foreign corporation that is a qualified resident of Canada has a deficit in accumulated ECEP of $200 as of the beginning of the taxable year and ECEP of $100 for the taxable year, it will have no dividend equivalent amount for the taxable year because it would have a cumulative deficit in ECEP of $100 as of the close of the taxable year. For purposes of this paragraph (g)(4)(iii)(A), any net deficit in accumulated earnings and profits attributable to taxable years beginning before January 1, 1987, shall be includible in determining accumulated ECEP.

(B) *One-time exemption of Canadian $500,000.—(1) General rule.*—In the case of a foreign corporation that is a qualified resident of Canada, the branch profits tax shall be imposed only with respect to that portion of the dividend equivalent amount for the taxable year that, when translated into Canadian dollars and added to the dividend equivalent amounts for preceding taxable years translated into Canadian dollars, exceeds Canadian $500,000. The value of the dividend equivalent amount in Canadian currency shall be determined by translating the ECEP for each taxable year that is includible in the dividend equivalent amount (as determined in U.S. dollars under the currency translation method used in determining the foreign corporation's taxable income for U.S. tax purposes) by the weighted average exchange rate for the taxable year (determined under the rules of section 989(b)(3)) during which the earnings and profits were derived.

(2) *Reduction in amount of exemption in the case of related corporations.*—The amount of a foreign corporation's exemption under this paragraph (g)(4)(iii)(B) shall be reduced by the amount of any exemption that reduced the dividend equivalent amount of an associated foreign corporation with respect to the same or a similar business. For purposes of this paragraph (g)(4)(iii)(B), a foreign corporation is an associated foreign corporation if it is related to the foreign corporation for purposes of section 267(b) or it and the foreign corporation are stapled entities (within the meaning of section 269B(c)(2)) or are effectively stapled entities. A business is the same as or similar to another business if it involves the sale, lease, or manufacture of the same or a similar type of property or the provision of the same or a similar type of services. A U.S. real property interest described in section 897(c)(1)(A)(i) shall be treated as a business and all such U.S. real property interests shall be treated as businesses that are the same or similar.

(3) *Coordination with second-tier withholding tax.*—The value of the dividend equivalent amount that is exempt from the branch profits tax by reason of paragraph (g)(4)(iii)(B)(1) of this section shall not be subject to tax under section 871(a) or 881, or to withholding under section 1441 or 1442, when distributed by the foreign corporation.

(5) *Benefits under treaties other than income tax treaties.*—A treaty that is not an income tax treaty does not exempt a foreign corporation from the branch profits tax or reduce the amount of the tax.

(h) *Stapled entities.*—Any foreign corporation that is treated as a domestic corporation by reason of section 269B (relating to stapled entities) shall continue to be treated as a foreign corporation for purposes of section 884 and the regulations thereunder, notwithstanding section 269B or the regulations thereunder. Dividends paid by such foreign corporation shall be treated as paid by a domestic corporation and shall be subject to the tax imposed by section 871(a) or 881(a), and to withholding under section 1441 or 1442, as applicable, to the extent paid out of earnings and profits that are not subject to tax under section 884(a). Dividends paid by such foreign corporation out of earnings and profits subject to tax under section 884(a) shall be exempt from the tax imposed by sections 871(a) and 881(a) and shall not be subject to withholding under section 1441 or 1442. Whether dividends are paid out of earnings and profits that are subject to tax under section 884(a) shall be determined under section 884(e)(3)(A) and the regulations thereunder. The limitation on the application of treaty benefits in section 884(e)(3)(B) (relating to qualified residents) shall apply to a foreign corporation described in this paragraph (h).

(i) *Effective date.*—(1) *General rule.*—This section is effective for taxable years beginning on or after [*the date that is 30 days after these regulations are published in the Federal Register*]. With respect to a taxable year beginning before [*the date that is 30 days after these regulations are published in the Federal Register*] and after December 31, 1986, a foreign corporation may elect to apply this section in lieu of §1.884-1T of the temporary regulations (as contained in the CFR edition revised as of April 1, 1992), but only if the foreign corporation also makes an election under §1.884-4(e) to apply §1.884-4 in lieu of §1.884-4T (as contained in the CFR edition revised as of April 1, 1992) for that taxable year, and the statute of limitations for assessment of a deficiency has not expired for that taxable year. Once an election has been made, an election under this section shall apply to all subsequent taxable years. However, paragraph (f)(2)(vi) of this section (relating to certain interest income of Possessions banks) shall not apply for taxable years beginning before January 1, 1990.

(2) *Election to reduce liabilities.*—A foreign corporation may make an election to reduce its liabilities under paragraph (e)(3) of this section with respect to a taxable year for which an election under paragraph (i)(1) of this section is in effect by filing an amended return for the taxable year and recomputing its interest deduction and any other item affected by the election on an amended Form 1120F to take into account the reduction in liabilities for such year.

(3) *Separate election for installment obligations.*—A foreign corporation may make a separate election to apply paragraphs (d)(2)(iii) and (d)(6)(ii) of this section (relating to installment obligations treated as U.S. assets) to any prior taxable year without making an election under paragraph (i)(1) of this section, provided the statute of limitations for assessment of a deficiency has not expired for that taxable year and each succeeding taxable year. Once an election under this paragraph (i)(3) has been made, it shall apply to all subsequent taxable years.

(4) *Special rules for certain U.S. assets and liabilities.*—Paragraphs (c)(2)(i) and (ii), (d)(3), (d)(4), (d)(5)(iii), (d)(6)(iii), (d)(6)(vi), (e)(2), and (e)(3)(ii), of this section are effective for taxable years beginning on or after June 6, 1996.

(j) *Transition rules.*—(1) *General rule.*—Except as provided in paragraph (j)(2) of this section, in order to compute its dividend equivalent amount in the first taxable year to which this section applies (whether or not such year begins before [*the date that is 30 days after these regulations are published in the Federal Register*]), a foreign corporation must recompute its U.S. net equity as of close of the preceding taxable year using the rules of this section and use such recomputed amount, rather than the amount computed under §1.884-1T (as contained in the CFR edition revised as of April 1, 1992), to determine the amount of any increase or decrease in the U.S. net equity as of the close of that taxable year.

(2) *Installment obligations.*—(i) *Interest election.*—In recomputing its U.S. net equity as of the close of the preceding taxable year, a foreign corporation that holds an installment obligation treated as a U.S. asset under §1.884-1T(d)(7) (as contained in the CFR edition revised as of April 1, 1992) as of such date may apply the rules of paragraph (d)(2)(iii) of this section without regard to the rule in that paragraph that requires interest or original issue discount on the obligation to be treated as ECI in order for such obligation to be treated as a U.S. asset.

(ii) *1987 sales by certain foreign corporations.*—The E&P basis of an installment obligation arising in connection with a sale of property by a foreign corporation described in section 312(k)(4), where such sale occurs in a taxable year beginning in 1987, shall equal the E&P basis of the property sold as of the determination date reduced by payments received with respect to the obligation that do not represent gain for earnings and profits purposes, interest or original issue discount. [Reg. §1.884-1.]

☐ [*T.D. 8432, 9-10-92. Amended by T.D. 8657, 3-5-96.*]

§1.884-2. Special rules for termination or incorporation of a U.S. trade or business or liquidation or reorganization of a foreign corporation or its domestic subsidiary.—(a) through (a)(2)(i) [Reserved]. For further information, see §1.884-2T(a) through (a)(2)(ii).

(a)(2)(ii) *Waiver of period of limitations.*—The waiver referred to in §1.884-2T(a)(2)(i)(D) shall be executed on Form 8848, or substitute form, and shall extend the period for assessment of the branch profits tax for the year of complete termination to a date not earlier than the close of the sixth taxable year following that taxable year. This form shall include such information as is required by the form and accompanying instructions. The waiver must be signed by the person authorized to sign the income tax returns for the foreign corporation (including an agent authorized to do so under a general or specific power of attorney). The waiver must be filed on or before the date (including extensions) prescribed for filing the foreign corporation's income tax return for the year of complete termination. With respect to a complete termination occurring in a taxable year ending prior to June 6, 1996, a foreign corporation may also satisfy the requirements of this paragraph (a)(2)(ii) by applying §1.884-2T(a)(2)(ii) of the temporary regulations (as contained in the CFR edition revised as of April 1, 1995). A properly executed Form 8848, substitute form, or other form of waiver authorized by this paragraph (a)(2)(ii) shall be deemed to be consented to and signed by a Service Center Director or the Assistant Commissioner (International) for purposes of §301.6501(c)-1(d) of this chapter.

(a)(3) through (a)(4) [Reserved]. For further information, see § 1.884-2T(a)(3) through (a)(4).

(a)(5) *Special rule if a foreign corporation terminates an interest in a trust.*—A foreign corporation whose beneficial interest in a trust terminates (by disposition or otherwise) in any taxable year shall be subject to the branch profits tax on ECEP attributable to amounts (including distributions of accumulated income or gain) treated as ECI to such beneficiary in such taxable year notwithstanding any other provision of § 1.884-2T(a).

(b) through (c)(2)(ii) [Reserved]. For further information, see § 1.884-2T(b) through (c)(2)(ii).

(c)(2)(iii) *Waiver of period of limitations and transferee agreement.*—In the case of a transferee that is a domestic corporation, the provisions of § 1.884-2T(c)(2)(i) shall not apply unless, as part of the section 381(a) transaction, the transferee executes a Form 2045 (Transferee Agreement) and a waiver of period of limitations as described in this paragraph (c)(2)(iii), and files both documents with its timely filed (including extensions) income tax return for the taxable year in which the section 381(a) transaction occurs. The waiver shall be executed on Form 8848, or substitute form, and shall extend the period for assessment of any additional branch profits tax for the taxable year in which the section 381(a) transaction occurs to a date not earlier than the close of the sixth taxable year following the taxable year in which such transaction occurs. This form shall include such information as is required by the form and accompanying instructions. The waiver must be signed by the person authorized to sign Form 2045. With respect to a complete termination occurring in a taxable year ending prior to June 6, 1996, a foreign corporation may also satisfy the requirements of this paragraph (c)(2)(iii) by applying § 1.884-2T(c)(2)(iii) of the temporary regulations (as contained in the CFR edition revised as of April 1, 1995). A properly executed Form 8848, substitute form, or other form of waiver authorized by this paragraph (c)(2)(iii) shall be deemed to be consented to and signed by a Service Center Director or the Assistant Commissioner (International) for purposes of § 301.6501(c)-1(d) of this chapter.

(c)(3) through (f) [Reserved]. For further information, see § 1.884-2T(c)(3) through (f).

(g) *Effective dates.*—Paragraphs (a)(2)(ii) and (c)(2)(iii) of this section are effective for taxable years beginning after December 31, 1986. Paragraph (a)(5) of this section is effective for taxable years beginning on or after June 6, 1996. [Reg. § 1.884-2.]

□ [T.D. 8657, 3-5-96.]

§ 1.884-2T. Special rules for termination or incorporation of a U.S. trade or business or liquidation or reorganization of a foreign corporation or its domestic subsidiary (Temporary).—(a) *Complete termination of a U.S. trade or business.*—(1) *General rule.*—A foreign corporation shall not be subject to the branch profits tax for the taxable year in which it completely terminates all of its U.S. trade or business within the meaning of paragraph (a)(2) of this section. A foreign corporation's non-previously taxed accumulated effectively connected earnings and profits as of the close of the taxable year of complete termination shall be extinguished for purposes of section 884 and the regulations thereunder, but not for other purposes (for example, sections 312, 316 and 381).

(2) *Operating rules.*—(i) *Definition of complete termination.*—A foreign corporation shall have completely terminated all of its U.S. trade or business for any taxable year ("the year of complete termination") only if—

(A) As of the close of that taxable year, the foreign corporation either has no U.S. assets, or its shareholders have adopted an irrevocable resolution in that taxable year to completely liquidate and dissolve the corporation and, before the close of the immediately succeeding taxable year (also a "year of complete termination" for purposes of applying this paragraph (a)(2)), all of its U.S. assets are either distributed, used to pay off liabilities, or cease to be U.S. assets;

(B) Neither the foreign corporation nor a related corporation uses, directly or indirectly, any of the U.S. assets or the terminated U.S. trade or business, or property attributable thereto or to effectively connected earnings and profits earned by the foreign corporation in the year of complete termination, in the conduct of a trade or business in the United States at any time during a period of three years from the close of the year of complete termination;

(C) The foreign corporation has no income that is, or is treated as, effectively connected with the conduct of a trade or business in the United States (other than solely by reason of section 864(c)(6) or (c)(7)) during the period of three years from the close of the year of complete termination; and

(D) The foreign corporation attaches to its income tax return for each year of complete termination a waiver of the period of limitations, as described in paragraph (a)(2)(ii) of this section.

If a foreign corporation fails to completely terminate all of its U.S. trade or business because of the failure to meet any of the requirements of this paragraph (a)(2), then its branch profits tax liability for the taxable year and all subsequent taxable years shall be determined under the provisions of §1.884-1, without regard to any provisions in this paragraph (a), taking into account any reduction in U.S. net equity that results from a U.S. trade or business of the foreign corporation ceasing to have U.S. assets. Any additional branch profits tax liability that may result, together with interest thereon (charged at the underpayment rates determined under section 6621(a)(2) with respect to the period between the date that was prescribed for filing the foreign corporation's income tax return for the taxable year with respect to which the branch profits tax liability arises and the date on which the additional tax for that year is paid), and applicable penalties, if any, shall be the liability of the foreign corporation (or of any person who is a transferee of the foreign corporation within the meaning of section 6901).

(ii) *Waiver of period of limitations.*—[Reserved] See §1.884-2(a)(2)(ii) for rules relating to this paragraph.

(iii) *Property subject to reinvestment prohibition rule.*—For purposes of paragraph (a)(2)(i)(B) of this section—

(A) The term "U.S. assets of the terminated U.S. trade or business" shall mean all the money and other property that qualified as U.S. assets of the foreign corporation as of the close of the taxable year immediately preceding the year of complete termination; and

(B) Property attributable to U.S. assets or to effectively connected earnings and profits earned by the foreign corporation in the year of complete termination shall mean money or other property into which any part or all of such assets or effectively connected earnings and profits are converted at any time before the expiration of the three-year period specified in paragraph (a)(2)(i)(B) of this section by way of sale, exchange, or other disposition, as well as any money or other property attributable to the sale by a shareholder of the foreign corporation of its interest in the foreign corporation (or a successor corporation) at any time after a date which is 12 months before the close of the year of complete termination (24 months in the case of a foreign corporation that makes an election under paragraph (b) of this section).

(iv) *Related corporation.*—For purposes of paragraph (a)(2)(i)(B) of this section, a corporation shall be related to a foreign corporation if either corporation is a 10-percent shareholder of the other corporation or, where the foreign corporation completely liquidates, if either corporation would have been a 10-percent shareholder of the other corporation had the foreign corporation remained in existence. For this purpose, the term "10-percent shareholder" means any person described in section 871(h)(3)(B) as well as any person who owns 10 percent or more of the total value of the stock of the corporation, and stock ownership shall be determined on the basis of the attribution rules described in section 871(h)(3)(C).

(v) *Direct or indirect use of U.S. assets.*—The use of any part or all of the property referred to in paragraph (a)(2)(i)(B) of this section shall include the loan thereof to a related corporation or the use thereof as security (as a pledge, mortgage, or otherwise) for any indebtedness of a related corporation.

(3) *Complete termination in the case of a section 338 election.*—A foreign corporation whose stock is acquired by another corporation that makes (or is deemed to make) an election under section 338 with respect to the stock of the foreign corporation shall be treated as having completely liquidated as of the close of the acquisition date (as defined in section 338(h)(2)) and to have completely terminated all of its U.S. trade or business with respect to the taxable year ending on such acquisition date provided the foreign corporation that exists prior to the section 338 transactions complies with the requirements of paragraph (a)(2)(i)(B) and (D) of this section. For purposes of the preceding sentence, any of the money or other property paid as consideration for the acquisition of the stock in the foreign corporation (and for any debt claim against the foreign corporation) shall be treated as property attributable to the U.S. assets of the terminated U.S. trade or business and to the effectively connected earnings and profits of the foreign corporation earned in the year of complete termination.

(4) *Complete termination in the case of a foreign corporation with income under section 864(c)(6) or 864(c)(7).*—No branch profits tax shall be imposed on effectively connected earnings and profits attributable to income that is treated as effectively connected with the conduct of a trade or business in the United States solely by reason of section 864(c)(6) or 864(c)(7) if—

(i) No income of the foreign corporation for the taxable year is, or is treated as, effectively connected with the conduct of a trade or business in the United States, without regard to section 864(c)(6) or 864(c)(7),

(ii) The foreign corporation has no U.S. assets as of the close of the taxable year, and

(iii) Such effectively connected earnings and profits would not have been subject to branch profits tax pursuant to the complete termination provisions of paragraph (a)(1) of this section if income or gain subject to section 864(c)(6) had not been deferred or if property subject to section 864(c)(7) had been sold immediately prior to the date the property ceased to have been used in the conduct of a trade or business in the United States.

(5) *Special rule if a foreign corporation terminates an interest in a trust.*—[Reserved] See § 1.884-2(a)(5) for rules relating to this paragraph.

(6) *Coordination with second-level withholding tax.*—Effectively connected earnings and profits and non-previously taxed accumulated effectively connected earnings and profits of a foreign corporation that are exempt from branch profits tax by reason of the provisions of paragraph (a)(1) of this section shall not be subject to tax under section 871(a), 881(a), 1441 or 1442 when paid as a dividend by such foreign corporation (or a successor-in-interest).

(b) *Election to remain engaged in a U.S. trade or business.*—(1) *General rule.*—A foreign corporation that would be considered to have completely terminated all of its U.S. trade or business for the taxable year under the provisions of paragraph (a)(2)(i) of this section, but for the provisions of paragraph (a)(2)(i)(B) of this section that prohibit reinvestment within a three-year period, may make an election under this paragraph (b) for the taxable year in which it completely terminates all its U.S. trade or business (as determined without regard to paragraph (a)(2)(i)(B) of this section) and, if it so chooses, for the following taxable year (but not for any succeeding taxable year). The election under this paragraph (b) is an election by the foreign corporation to designate an amount of marketable securities as U.S. assets for purposes of § 1.884-1. The marketable securities identified pursuant to the election under paragraph (b)(3) of this section shall be treated as being U.S. assets in an amount equal, in the aggregate, to the lesser of the adjusted basis of the U.S. assets that ceased to be U.S. assets during the taxable year in which the election is made (determined on the date or dates the U.S. assets ceased to be U.S. assets) or the adjusted basis of the marketable securities as of the end of the taxable year. The securities must be held from the date that they are identified until the end of the taxable year for which the election is made, or if disposed of during the taxable year, must be replaced on the date of disposition with other marketable securities that are acquired on or before that date and that have a fair market value as of the date of substitution not less than their adjusted basis.

(2) *Marketable security.*—For purposes of this paragraph (b), the term "marketable security" means a security (including stock) that is part of an issue any portion of which is regularly traded on an established securities market (within the meaning of § 1.884-5(d)(2) and (4)) and a deposit described in section 871(i)(3)(A) or (B).

(3) *Identification requirements.*—In order to qualify for this election—

(i) The marketable securities must be identified on the books and records of the U.S. trade or business within 30 days of the date an equivalent amount of U.S. assets ceases to be U.S. assets; and

(ii) On the date a marketable security is identified, its adjusted basis must not exceed its fair market value.

(4) *Treatment of income from deemed U.S. assets.*—The income or gain from the marketable securities (or replacement securities) subject to an election under this paragraph (b) that arises in a taxable year for which an election is made shall be treated as ECI (other than for purposes of section 864(c)(7)), and losses from the disposition of such marketable securities shall be allocated entirely to income that is ECI. In addition, all such securities shall be treated as if they had been sold for their fair market value on the earlier of the last business day of a taxable year for which an election is in effect or the day immediately prior to the date of substitution by the foreign corporation of a U.S. asset for the marketable security, and any gain (but not loss) and accrued interest on the securities shall also be treated as ECI. The adjusted basis of such property shall be increased by the amount of any gain recognized by reason of this paragraph (b).

(5) *Method of election.*—A foreign corporation may make an election under this paragraph (b) by attaching to its income tax return for the taxable year a statement—

(i) Identifying the marketable securities treated as U.S. assets under this paragraph (b);

(ii) Setting forth the E&P bases of such securities; and

(iii) Agreeing to treat any income, gain or loss as provided in paragraph (b)(4) of this section.

Such statement must be filed on or before the due date (including extensions) of the foreign corporation's income tax return for the taxable year. A foreign corporation shall not be permitted to make an election under this paragraph (b) more than once.

(6) *Effective date.*—This paragraph (b) is effective for taxable years beginning on or after October 13, 1992. However, if a foreign corporation has made a valid election under § 1.884-1(i) to apply that section with respect to a taxa-

ble year beginning before October 13, 1992, and after December 31, 1986, this paragraph (b) shall be effective beginning with such taxable year.

(c) *Liquidation, reorganization, etc., of a foreign corporation.*—The following rules apply to the transfer by a foreign corporation engaged (or deemed engaged) in the conduct of a U.S. trade or business (the "transferor") of its U.S. assets to another corporation (the "transferee") in a complete liquidation or reorganization described in section 381(a) (a "section 381(a) transaction") if the transferor is engaged (or deemed engaged) in the conduct of a U.S. trade or business immediately prior to the section 381(a) transaction. For purposes of this paragraph (c), a section 381(a) transaction is considered to occur in the taxable year that ends on the date of distribution or transfer (as defined in § 1.381(b)-1(b)) pursuant to the section 381(a) transaction.

(1) *Inapplicability of paragraph (a)(1) of this section to section 381(a) transactions.*—Paragraph (a)(1) of this section (relating to the complete termination of a U.S. trade or business of a foreign corporation) does not apply to exempt the transferor from branch profits tax liability for the taxable year in which the section 381(a) transaction occurs or in any succeeding taxable year.

(2) *Transferor's dividend equivalent amount for the taxable year in which a section 381(a) transaction occurs.*—The dividend equivalent amount for the taxable year, including a short taxable year, in which a section 381(a) transaction occurs shall be determined under the provisions of § 1.884-1, as modified under the provisions of this paragraph (c)(2).

(i) *U.S. net equity.*—The transferor's U.S. net equity as of the close of the taxable year shall be determined without regard to any transfer in that taxable year of U.S. assets to or from the transferee pursuant to a section 381(a) transaction, and without regard to any U.S. liabilities assumed or acquired by the transferee from the transferor in that taxable year pursuant to a section 381(a) transaction. The transferor's adjusted basis (for earnings and profits purposes) in U.S. assets transferred to the transferee pursuant to a section 381(a) transaction shall be the adjusted basis of those assets (for earnings and profits purposes) immediately prior to the section 381(a) transaction, adjusted as provided under section 362(b), treating the transferor, for that purpose, as though it were the transferee and treating the gain taken into account for earnings and profits purposes as gain recognized.

(ii) *Effectively connected earnings and profits.*—The transferor's effectively connected earnings and profits for the taxable year in which the section 381(a) transaction occurs and its non-previously taxed accumulated effectively connected earnings and profits shall be determined without regard to the carryover to the transferee of the transferor's earnings and profits under section 381(a) and (c)(2) of paragraph (c)(4) of this section. Effectively connected earnings and profits for the taxable year in which a section 381(a) transaction occurs shall be adjusted by the amount of any gain recognized to the transferor in that year pursuant to the section 381(a) transaction (to the extent taken into account for earnings and profits purposes).

(iii) *Waiver of period of limitations and transferee agreement.*—[Reserved] See § 1.884-2(c)(2)(iii) for rules relating to this paragraph.

(3) *Transferor's dividend equivalent amount for any taxable year succeeding the taxable year in which the section 381(a) transaction occurs.*—Any decrease in U.S. net equity in any taxable year succeeding the taxable year in which the section 381(a) transaction occurs shall increase the transferor's dividend equivalent amount for those years without regard to the limitation in § 1.884-1(b)(3)(ii), to the extent such decrease in U.S. net equity does not exceed the balance of effectively connected earnings and profits and non-previously taxed accumulated effectively connected earnings and profits carried over to the transferee pursuant to section 381(a) and (c)(2), as determined under paragraph (c)(4) of this section.

(4) *Earnings and profits of the transferor carried over to the transferee pursuant to the section 381(a) transaction.*—(i) *Amount.*—The amount of effectively connected earnings and profits and non-previously taxed accumulated effectively connected earnings and profits of the transferor that carry over to the transferee under section 381(a) and (c)(2) shall be the effectively connected earnings and profits and the non-previously taxed accumulated effectively connected earnings and profits of the transferor immediately before the close of the taxable year in which the section 381(a) transaction occurs. For this purpose, the provisions in § 1.381(c)(2)-1 shall generally apply with proper adjustments to reflect the fact that effectively connected earnings and profits and non-previously taxed accumulated effectively connected earnings and profits are not affected by distributions to shareholders but, rather, by dividend equivalent amounts. Therefore, the amounts of effectively connected earnings and profits and non-previously taxed accumulated

effectively connected earnings and profits that carry over to the transferee pursuant to those provisions are reduced by the transferor's dividend equivalent amount for the taxable year in which the section 381(a) transaction occurs. Such amounts are also reduced to the extent of any dividend equivalent amount determined for any succeeding taxable year solely as a result of the provisions of paragraph (c)(3) of this section. For purposes of this paragraph (c)(4)(i), if the transferor accumulates non-previously taxed effectively connected earnings and profits, or incurs a deficit in effectively connected earnings and profits, attributable to a period that is after the close of the taxable year in which the section 381(a) transaction occurs and before the liquidation of the transferor, then such effectively connected earnings and profits, or deficits therein, shall be deemed to have been accumulated or incurred on or before the close of the taxable year in which the section 381(a) transaction occurs.

(ii) *Retention of character.*—All of the transferor's effectively connected earnings and profits and non-previously taxed accumulated effectively connected earnings and profits that carry over to the transferee shall constitute non-previously taxed accumulated effectively connected earnings and profits of the transferee. In the case of a domestic transferee, such non-previously taxed accumulated effectively connected earnings and profits shall also constitute accumulated earnings and profits of the transferee for purposes of section 316(a)(2).

(iii) *Treatment of distributions by a domestic transferee out of non-previously taxed accumulated effectively connected earnings and profits.*—In the event the transferee is a domestic corporation, distributions out of the transferee's non-previously taxed accumulated effectively connected earnings and profits that are received by a foreign distributee shall qualify for benefits under an applicable income tax treaty only (A) if the distributee qualifies for the benefits under such treaty and (B) to the extent that the transferor foreign corporation would have qualified under the principles of § 1.884-1(g)(1) and (2)(i) for an exemption or reduction in rate with respect to the branch profits tax if the non-previously taxed accumulated effectively connected earnings and profits had been reflected in a dividend equivalent amount for the taxable year in which the section 381(a) transaction occurs. (The tax rate on dividends specified in the treaty between the distributee's country of residence and the United States shall apply to any dividends received by a distributee who qualifies for a treaty benefit under the preceding sentence.) In addition, distributions out of such non-previously taxed accumulated effectively connected earnings and profits shall retain their character in the hands of any domestic distributee up a chain of corporate shareholders for purposes of applying this paragraph (c)(4)(iii) to distributions made by any such person to a foreign distributee. If a domestic transferee has non-previously taxed accumulated effectively connected earnings and profits carried over from the transferor as well as accumulated earnings and profits, then each category of earnings and profits shall be accounted for in two separate pools, and any distribution of earnings and profits shall be treated as a distribution out of each pool in proportion to the respective amount of undistributed earnings and profits in each pool. Section 871(i) (relating, in part, to dividends paid by a domestic corporation meeting the 80-percent foreign business requirements of section 861(c)(1)) shall not apply to any dividends paid by a domestic transferee out of its non-previously taxed accumulated effectively connected earnings and profits.

(5) *Determination of U.S. net equity of a transferee that is a foreign corporation.*—In the event the transferee is a foreign corporation, then for purposes of determining the transferee's increase or decrease in U.S. net equity under § 1.884-1 for its taxable year during which the section 381(a) transaction occurs, its U.S. net equity as of the close of its immediately preceding taxable year shall be increased by the amount of U.S. net equity acquired by the transferee from the transferor pursuant to the section 381(a) transaction, taking into account the adjustments to the basis (for earnings and profits purposes) of U.S. assets under the principles of section 362(b).

(6) *Special rules in the case of the disposition of stock or securities in a domestic transferee or in the transferor.*—(i) *General rule.*—This paragraph (c)(6)(i) shall apply where the transferee is a domestic corporation, subdivision (A), (B), or (C) of this paragraph applies and subdivision (D) of this paragraph applies.

(A) Shareholders of the transferor sell, exchange or otherwise dispose of stock in the transferor at any time during a 12-month period before the date of distribution or transfer (as defined in § 1.381(b)-1(b)) and the aggregate amount of such stock sold, exchanged or otherwise disposed of exceeds 25 percent of the value of the stock of the transferor, determined on a date that is 12 months before the date of distribution or transfer.

(B) Shareholders of the transferee (or of the transferee's parent in the case of a reorganization described in the parenthetical clause in section 368(a)(1)(C)) who in the aggregate owned more than 25 percent of the value of the stock of the transferor at any time within the 12-month period preceding the close of the year in which the section 381(a) transaction occurs sell, exchange or otherwise dispose of their stock or securities in the transferee at any time during a period of three years from the close of the taxable year in which the section 381(a) transaction occurs.

(C) In the case of a reorganization described in the parenthetical clause in section 368(a)(1)(C), the transferee's parent sells, exchanges or otherwise disposes of its stock or securities in the transferee at any time during a period of three years from the close of the taxable year in which the section 381(a) transaction occurs.

(D) A corporation related to any such shareholder or the shareholder itself if it is a corporation (subsequent to an event described in subdivision (A) or (B) of this paragraph (c)(6)(i)), or the transferee's parent (subsequent to an event described in subdivision (C) of this paragraph (c)(6)(i)), uses, directly or indirectly, the proceeds or property received in such sale, exchange or disposition, or property attributable thereto, in the conduct of a trade or business in the United States at any time during a period of three years from the date of sale in the case of a disposition of stock in the transferor, or from the close of the taxable year in which the section 381(a) transaction occurs in the case of a disposition of the stock or securities in the transferee (or the transferee's parent in the case of a reorganization described in the parenthetical clause in section 368(a)(1)(C)). Where this paragraph (c)(6)(i) applies, the transferor's branch profits tax liability for the taxable year in which the section 381(a) transaction occurs shall be determined under § 1.884-1, taking into account all the adjustments in U.S. net equity that result from the transfer of U.S. assets and liabilities to the transferee pursuant to the section 381(a) transaction, without regard to any provisions in this paragraph (c). If an event described in paragraph (c)(6)(i)(A), (B), or (C) of this section occurs after the close of the taxable year in which the section 381(a) transaction occurs, and if additional branch profits tax is required to be paid by reason of the application of this paragraph (c)(6)(i), then interest must be paid on that amount at the underpayment rates determined under section 6621(a)(2), with respect to the period between the date that was prescribed for filing the transferor's income tax return for the year in which the section 381(a) transaction occurs and the date on which the additional tax for that year is paid. Any such additional tax liability together with interest thereon shall be the liability of the transferee within the meaning of section 6901 pursuant to section 6901 and the regulations thereunder.

(ii) *Operating rule.*—For purposes of paragraph (c)(6)(i) of this section paragraph (a)(2)(iii)(B), (iv) and (v) of this section shall apply for purposes of making the determinations under paragraph (c)(6)(i)(D) of this section.

(d) *Incorporation under section 351.*—(1) *In general.*—The following rules apply to the transfer by a foreign corporation engaged (or deemed engaged) in the conduct of a U.S. trade or business (the "transferor") of part or all of its U.S. assets to a U.S. corporation (the "transferee") in exchange for stock or securities in the transferee in a transaction that qualifies under section 351(a) (a "section 351 transaction"), provided that immediately after the transaction, the transferor is in control (as defined in section 368(c)) of the transferee, without regard to other transferors.

(2) *Inapplicability of paragraph (a)(1) of this section to section 351 transactions.*—Paragraph (a)(1) of this section does not apply to exempt the transferor from branch profits tax liability for the taxable year in which a section 351 transaction described in paragraph (d)(1) of this section occurs and shall not apply for any subsequent taxable year of the transferor in which it, or a successor-in-interest, owns stock or securities of a transferee as of the close of the transferor's taxable year.

(3) *Transferor's dividend equivalent amount for the taxable year in which a section 351 transaction occurs.*—The dividend equivalent amount of the transferor for the taxable year in which a section 351 transaction described in paragraph (d)(1) of this section occurs shall be determined under the provisions of § 1.884-1, as modified by the provisions of this paragraph (d)(3) provided that the transferee elects under paragraph (d)(4) of this section to be allocated a proportionate amount of the transferor's effectively connected earnings and profits and non-previously taxed accumulated effectively connected earnings and profits and the foreign corporation files a statement as provided in paragraph (d)(5)(i) of this section and complies with the agreement included in such statement with respect to a subsequent disposition of the transferee's stock.

(i) *U.S. net equity.*—The transferor's U.S. net equity as of the close of the taxable year shall be determined without regard to any transfer in that taxable year of U.S. assets to or from the transferee pursuant to a section 351 transaction, and without regard to any U.S. liabilities assumed or acquired by the transferee from the transferor in that taxable year pursuant to a section 351 transaction. The transferor's adjusted basis for earnings and profits purposes in U.S. assets transferred to the transferee pursuant to a section 351 transaction shall be the adjusted basis of those assets for earnings and profits purposes immediately prior to the section 351 transaction, increased by the amount of any gain recognized by the transferor on the transfer of such assets in the section 351 transaction to the extent taken into account for earnings and profits purposes.

(ii) *Effectively connected earnings and profits.*—Subject to the limitation in paragraph (d)(3)(iii) of this section, the calculation of the transferor's dividend equivalent amount shall take into account the transferor's effectively connected earnings and profits for the taxable year in which a section 351 transaction occurs (including any amount of gain recognized to the transferor pursuant to the section 351 transaction to the extent the gain is taken into account for earnings and profits purposes) and, for purposes of applying the limitation of § 1.884-1(b)(3)(ii), its non-previously taxed accumulated effectively connected earnings and profits, determined without regard to the allocation to the transferee of the transferor's effectively connected earnings and profits and non-previously taxed accumulated effectively connected earnings and profits pursuant to the election under paragraph (d)(4)(i) of this section.

(iii) *Limitation on dividend equivalent amount.*—The dividend equivalent amount determined under this paragraph (d)(3) shall not exceed the sum of the transferor's effectively connected earnings and profits and non-previously taxed accumulated effectively connected earnings and profits determined after taking into account the allocation to the transferee of the transferor's earnings pursuant to an election under paragraph (d)(4)(i) of this section.

(4) *Election to increase earnings and profits.*—(i) *General rule.*—The election referred to in paragraph (d)(3) of this section is an election by the transferee to increase its earnings and profits by the amount determined under paragraph (d)(4)(ii) of this section. An election under this paragraph (d)(4)(i) shall be effective only if the transferee attaches a statement to its timely filed (including extensions) income tax return for the taxable year in which the section 351 transaction occurs, in which—

(A) It agrees to be subject to the rules of paragraph (c)(4)(ii) and (iii) of this section with respect to the transferor's effectively connected earnings and profits and non-previously taxed accumulated effectively connected earnings and profits allocated to the transferee pursuant to the election under this paragraph (d)(4)(i) in the same manner as if such earnings and profits had been carried over to the transferee pursuant to section 381(a) and (c)(2), and

(B) It identifies the amount of effectively connected earnings and profits and non-previously taxed accumulated effectively connected earnings and profits that are allocated from the transferor.

An election with respect to a taxable year ending on or before December 1, 1988, may be made by filing an amended Form 1120F on or before January 3, 1989, to which the statement described in this paragraph (d)(4)(i) shall be attached.

(ii) *Amount of the transferor's effectively connected earnings and profits and non-previously taxed accumulated effectively connected earnings and profits allocated to the transferee.*—The amount referred to in paragraph (d)(4)(i) of this section is equal to the same proportion of the transferor's effectively connected earnings and profits and non-previously taxed accumulated effectively connected earnings and profits (determined immediately prior to the section 351 transaction and without regard to this paragraph (d)(4) or any dividend equivalent amount for the taxable year) that the adjusted bases for purposes of computing earnings and profits in all the U.S. assets transferred to the transferee by the transferor pursuant to the section 351 transaction bear to the adjusted bases for purposes of computing earnings and profits in all the U.S. assets of the transferor, determined immediately prior to the section 351 transaction.

(iii) *Effect of election on transferor.*—For purposes of computing the transferor's dividend equivalent amount for the taxable year succeeding the taxable year in which a section 351 transaction occurs, the transferor's effectively connected earnings and profits and non-previously taxed accumulated effectively connected earnings and profits as of the close of the taxable year in which the section 351 transaction occurs shall be reduced by the amount of its effectively connected earnings and profits and non-previously taxed accumulated effectively connected earnings and profits allocated to the transferee pursuant to the election under paragraph (d)(4)(i) of this section (and by its dividend equivalent amount for the taxable year in which the section 351 transaction occurs).

(5) *Dispositions of stock or securities of the transferee by the transferor.*—(i) *General rule.*—The statement referred to in paragraph (d)(3) of this section is a statement executed by the transferor stating the transferor's agreement that, upon the disposition of part or all of the stock or securities it owns in the transferee (or

a successor-in-interest), it shall treat as a dividend equivalent amount for the taxable year in which the disposition occurs an amount equal to the lesser of (A) the amount realized upon such disposition or (B) the total amount of effectively connected earnings and profits and non-previously taxed accumulated effectively connected earnings and profits that was allocated from the transferor to that transferee pursuant to an election under paragraph (d)(4)(i) of this section, which amount shall be reduced to the extent previously taken into account by the transferor as dividends or dividend equivalent amounts for tax or branch profits tax purposes. The extent and manner in which such dividend equivalent amount may be subject to the branch profits tax in the taxable year of disposition shall be determined under the provisions of section 884 and the regulations thereunder, including the provisions of paragraph (a) of this section (relating to complete terminations), as limited under paragraph (d)(2) of this section. Except as otherwise provided in paragraph (d)(5)(ii) of this section, the term "disposition" means any transfer that would constitute a disposition by the transferor for any purpose of the Internal Revenue Code and the regulations thereunder. This paragraph (d)(5)(i) shall apply regardless of whether the stock or securities of the transferee are U.S. assets in the hands of the transferor at the time of sale, exchange or disposition.

(ii) *Exception for certain tax-free dispositions.*—For purposes of paragraph (d)(5)(i) of this section, a disposition does not include a transfer of stock or securities of the transferee by the transferor in a transaction that qualifies as a transfer pursuant to a complete liquidation described in section 332(b) or a transfer pursuant to a reorganization described in section 368(a)(1)(F). Any other transfer that qualifies for non-recognition of gain or loss shall be treated as a disposition for purposes of paragraph (d)(5)(i) of this section, unless the Commissioner has, by published guidance or by prior ruling issued to the taxpayer upon its request, determined such transfer not to be a disposition for purposes of paragraph (d)(5)(i) of this section.

(iii) *Distributions governed by section 355.*—In the case of a distribution or exchange of stock or securities of a transferee to which section 355 applies (or so much of section 356 as relates to section 355) and that is not in pursuance of a plan meeting the requirements of a reorganization as defined in section 368(a)(1)(D), §1.312-10(b) (relating to the allocation of earnings and profits in certain corporate separations), shall not apply to reduce the transferor's effectively connected earnings and profits or non-previously taxed accumulated effectively connected earnings and profits.

(iv) *Filing of statement.*—The statement referred to in paragraph (d)(5)(i) of this section shall be attached to a timely filed (including extensions) income tax return of the transferor for the taxable year in which the section 351 transaction occurs. An election with respect to a taxable year ending on or before December 1, 1988, may be made by filing an amended Form 1120F on or before January 3, 1989, to which the statement described in this paragraph (d)(5)(iv) shall be attached.

(6) *Example.*—The provisions of this paragraph (d) are illustrated by the following example.

Example. Foreign corporation X has a calendar taxable year. X's only assets are U.S. assets and X computes its interest deduction using the actual ratio of liabilities to assets under §1.882-5(b)(2)(ii). X's U.S. net equity as of the close of its 1988 taxable year is $2,000, resulting from the following amounts of U.S. assets and liabilities:

U.S. assets		U.S. liabilities	
U.S. building A	$1,000	Mortgage A	$800
U.S. building B	$2,500	Mortgage B	$1,500
Other U.S. assets	$800		
Total	$4,300		$2,300

Assume that X's adjusted basis in its assets is equal to X's adjusted basis in its assets for earnings and profits purposes. On September 30, 1989, X transfers building A, which has a fair market value of $1,800, to a newly created U.S. corporation Y under section 351 in exchange for 100% of the stock of Y with a fair market value of $800, other property with a fair market value of $200, and the assumption of Mortgage A. Assume that under sections 11 and 351(b), tax of $30 is imposed with respect to the $200 of other property received by X. X's non-previously taxed accumulated effectively connected earnings and profits as of the close of its 1988 taxable year are $200 and its effectively connected earnings and profits for its 1989 taxable year are $330, including $170 of gain recognized to X on the transfer as adjusted for earnings and profits purposes (*i.e.,* $200 of gain recognized minus $30 of tax paid with respect to the gain). Y takes a $1,200 basis in the building transferred from X, equal to the basis in the hands of X ($1,000) increased by the amount of gain recognized to X in the section 351 transaction ($200). Y makes an election in the manner described in paragraph (d)(4)(i) of this section to increase its earnings and profits by the amount described in paragraph (d)(4)(ii) of this section and X files a statement as provided in paragraph (d)(5)(i) of this section. The branch profits tax consequences to X and Y in the taxable year in which the section 351 transaction occurs and in subsequent taxable years are as follows:

(i) *X's dividend equivalent amount for 1989.* The determination of X's dividend equivalent amount for 1989 is a three-step process: determining X's U.S. net equity as of the close of its 1989 taxable year under paragraph (d)(3)(i) of this section; determining the amount of X's effectively connected earnings

U.S. assets	
Building A	$1,170
Building B	$2,500
Other U.S. assets	$500
Total	$4,170

Thus, X's U.S. net equity as of the close of its 1989 taxable year has decreased by $130 relative to its U.S. net equity as of the close of its 1988 taxable year.

Step two: Pursuant to paragraph (d)(3)(ii) of this section, X's effectively connected earnings and profits and non-previously taxed accumulated effectively connected earnings and profits for the taxable year are determined without taking into account the allocation to Y of X's effectively connected earnings and profits and non-previously taxed accumulated effectively connected earnings and profits pursuant to the election under paragraph (d)(4)(i) of this section. Thus, X's effectively connected earnings and profits for its 1989 taxable year are $330 and X's non-previously taxed accumulated effectively connected earnings and profits are $200. Thus, but for the limitation in paragraph (d)(3)(iii) of this section, X's dividend equivalent amount for the taxable year would be $460, equal to X's effectively connected earnings and profits for the taxable year ($330), increased by the decrease in X's U.S. net equity ($130).

Step three: Pursuant to paragraph (d)(3)(iii) of this section, X's dividend equivalent amount for its 1989 taxable year may not exceed the sum of the transferor's effectively connected earnings and profits and non-previously taxed accumulated effectively connected earnings and profits, determined as of the close of its 1989 taxable year, after taking into account the allocation of the transferor's earnings and profits pursuant to the election under paragraph (d)(4)(i) of this section. Based upon subdivision (ii) of this example, X's dividend equivalent amount for 1989 cannot exceed $423, which is equal to the total amount of X's effectively connected earnings and profits and non-previously taxed accumulated effectively connected earnings and profits for its 1989 taxable year under paragraph (d)(3)(ii) of this section; and applying the limitation in paragraph (d)(3)(iii) of this section.

Step one: Pursuant to paragraph (d)(3)(i) of this section, X's U.S. net equity as of the close of its 1989 taxable year is calculated without regard to the section 351 transaction except that X's basis in its U.S. assets is increased by the $170 amount of gain it has recognized for earnings and profits in connection with the section 351 transaction. Thus, X's U.S. net equity as of the close of its 1989 taxable year is $1,870, consisting of the following U.S. assets and liabilities, taking into account the fact that X's other U.S. assets have decreased to $500:

U.S. liabilities	
Mortgage A	$800
Mortgage B	$1,500
	$2,300

effectively connected earnings and profits and non-previously taxed accumulated effectively connected earnings and profits, determined as of the close of its 1989 taxable year without regard to the allocation of earnings and profits to Y pursuant to Y's election under paragraph (d)(4)(i) of this section ($530), reduced by the amount of X's effectively connected earnings and profits and non-previously taxed accumulated effectively connected earnings and profits allocated to Y pursuant to Y's election under paragraph (d)(4)(i) of this section ($107). Thus, X's dividend equivalent amount for its 1989 taxable year is limited to $423.

(ii) *Amount of X's effectively connected earnings and profits and non-previously taxed accumulated effectively connected earnings and profits transferred to Y.* Pursuant to Y's election under paragraph (d)(4)(i) of this section, Y increases its earnings and profits by the amount prescribed in paragraph (d)(4)(ii) of this section. This amount is equal to the sum of X's effectively connected earnings and profits and non-previously taxed accumulated effectively connected earnings and profits determined immediately before the section 351 transaction, without regard to X's dividend equivalent amount for the year, allocated in the same proportion that X's basis in the U.S. assets transferred to Y bears to the bases of all of X's U.S. assets, which bases are determined immediately prior to the section 351(a) transaction. The amount of X's effectively connected earnings and profits immediately before the section 351 transaction is assumed to be $260. The total amount of effectively connected earnings and profits ($260) and non-previously taxed accumulated effectively connected earnings and profits ($200) determined immediately before

Reg. §1.884-2T(d)(6)

the section 351 transaction is, therefore, $460. The portion of $460 that is allocated to Y pursuant to Y's election under paragraph (d)(4)(i) of this section is $107, calculated as $460 multiplied by a fraction, the numerator of which is the basis of the U.S. assets transferred to Y pursuant to the section 351 transaction ($1,000), and the denominator of which is the bases of X's U.S. assets determined immediately before the section 351 transaction ($4,300). Pursuant to paragraph (d)(4)(i) of this section, the amount of $107 of X's effectively connected earnings and profits and non-previously taxed accumulated effectively connected earnings and profits allocated to Y pursuant to paragraph (d)(4)(i) of this section constitutes non-previously taxed accumulated effectively connected earnings and profits of Y.

(iii) *X's non-previously taxed accumulated effectively connected earnings and profits for 1990.* Pursuant to paragraph (d)(4)(iii) of this section, X's non-previously taxed accumulated effectively connected earnings and profits as of the close of its 1989 taxable year for purposes of computing its dividend equivalent amount for its taxable year 1990 are zero, *i.e.,* $530 of effectively connected earnings and profits and non-previously taxed accumulated effectively connected earnings and profits reduced by $107 of effectively connected earnings and profits and non-previously taxed accumulated effectively connected earnings and profits allocated to Y, and further reduced by X's $423 dividend equivalent amount for its 1989 taxable year.

(iv) *X's U.S. net equity for purposes of determining the dividend equivalent amount for succeeding taxable years.* For 1990, X must determine its U.S. net equity as of December 31, 1989, in order to determine whether there has been an increase or decrease in its U.S. net equity as of December 31, 1990. For this purpose, X's U.S. net equity as of December 31, 1989 is determined under the provisions of § 1.884-1 without regard to the special rules in paragraph (d)(3)(i) of this section. Thus, X's U.S. net equity as of December 31, 1989 is $1,500, consisting of the following U.S. assets and liabilities:

U.S. assets	
Building B	$2,500
Other U.S. assets	500
	$3,000

U.S. liabilities	
Mortgage B	$1,500
	$1,500

(e) *Certain transactions with respect to a domestic subsidiary.*—In the case of a section 381(a) transaction in which a domestic subsidiary of a foreign corporation transfers assets to that foreign corporation or to another foreign corporation with respect to which the first foreign corporation owns stock (directly or indirectly) meeting the requirements of section 1504(a)(2), the transferee's non-previously taxed accumulated effectively connected earnings and profits for the taxable year in which the section 381(a) transaction occurs shall be increased by all of the domestic subsidiary's current earnings and profits and earnings and profits accumulated after December 31, 1986, that carry over to the transferee under sections 381(a) and (c)(1) (including non-previously taxed accumulated effectively connected earnings and profits, if any, transferred to the domestic subsidiary under paragraphs (c)(4) and (d)(4) of this section and treated as earnings and profits under paragraphs (c)(4)(ii) and (d)(4)(ii) of this section). For purposes of determining the transferee's dividend equivalent amount for the taxable year in which the section 381(a) transaction occurs, the transferee's U.S. net equity as of the close of its taxable year immediately preceding the taxable year during which the section 381(a) transaction occurs shall be increased by the greater of (1) the amount by which the transferee's U.S. net equity computed immediately prior to the transfer would have increased due to the transfer of the subsidiary's assets and liabilities if U.S. net equity were computed immediately prior to the transfer and immediately after the transfer (taking into account in the earnings and profits basis of the assets transferred any gain recognized on the transfer to the extent reflected in earnings and profits), or (2) the total amount of U.S. net equity transferred (directly or indirectly) by the foreign parent to the domestic subsidiary in one or more prior section 351 or 381(a) transactions.

(f) *Effective date.*—This section is effective for taxable years beginning after December 31, 1986. [Temporary Reg. § 1.884-2T.]

☐ [T.D. 8223, 8-29-88. Amended by T.D. 8432, 9-10-92 and T.D. 8657, 3-5-96.]

§ 1.884-4. Branch-level interest tax.— (a) *General rule.*—(1) *Tax on branch interest.*—In the case of a foreign corporation that, during the taxable year, is engaged in trade or business in the United States or has gross income that is ECI (as defined in § 1.884-1(d)(1)(iii)), any interest paid by such trade or business (hereinafter "branch interest," as defined in paragraph (b) of this section) shall, for purposes of subtitle A (Income Taxes), be treated as if it were paid by a domestic corporation (other than a corporation described in section 861(c)(1), relating to a domestic corporation that meets the 80 percent foreign business requirement). Thus, for example, whether such interest is treated as income from sources within the United States by the person who receives the interest shall be determined in the same manner as if such interest were paid by a domestic corporation (other than a corporation described in section 861(c)(1)). Such interest shall be subject to tax under section 871(a) or 881, and to withholding under section 1441 or 1442, in the same manner as interest paid by a domestic corporation (other than a corporation described in section 861(c)(1)) if received by a foreign person and not effectively connected with the conduct by the foreign person of a trade or business in the United States, unless the interest, if paid by a domestic corporation, would be exempt under section 871(h) or 881(c) (relating to exemption for certain portfolio interest received by a foreign person), section 871(i) or 881(d) (relating, in part, to exemption for certain bank deposit interest received by a foreign person), or another provision of the Code. Such interest shall also be treated as interest paid by a domestic corporation (other than a corporation described in section 861(c)(1)) for purposes of sections 864(c), 871(b) and 882(a) (relating to income that is effectively connected with the conduct of a trade or business within the United States) and section 904 (relating to the limitation on the foreign tax credit). For purposes of this section, a foreign corporation also shall be treated as engaged in trade or business in the United States if, at any time during the taxable year, it owns an asset taken into account under § 1.882-5(a)(1)(ii) or (b)(1) for purposes of determining the amount of the foreign corporation's interest expense allocated or apportioned to ECI. See paragraph (b)(8) of this section for the effect of income tax treaties on branch interest.

(2) *Tax on excess interest.*—(i) *Definition of excess interest.*—For purposes of this section, the term "excess interest" means—

(A) The amount of interest allocated or apportioned to ECI of the foreign corporation under § 1.882-5 for the taxable year, after application of § 1.884-1(e)(3); minus

(B) The foreign corporation's branch interest (as defined in paragraph (b) of this section) for the taxable year, but not including interest accruing in a taxable year beginning before January 1, 1987; minus

(C) The amount of interest determined under paragraph (c)(2) of this section (relating to interest paid by a partnership).

(ii) *Imposition of tax.*—A foreign corporation shall be liable for tax on excess interest under section 881(a) in the same manner as if such excess interest were interest paid to the foreign corporation by a wholly-owned domestic corporation (other than a corporation described in section 861(c)(1)) on the last day of the foreign corporation's taxable year. Excess interest shall be exempt from tax under section 881(a) only as provided in paragraph (a)(2)(iii) of this section (relating to treatment of certain excess interest of banks as interest on deposits) or paragraph (c)(3) of this section (relating to income tax treaties).

(iii) *Treatment of a portion of the excess interest of banks as interest on deposits.*—A portion of the excess interest of a foreign corporation that is a bank (as defined in section 585(a)(2)(B) without regard to the second sentence thereof) provided that a substantial part of its business in the United States, as well as all other countries in which it operates, consists of receiving deposits and making loans and discounts, shall be treated as interest on deposits (as described in section 871(i)(3)), and shall be exempt from the tax imposed by section 881(a) as provided in such section. The portion of the excess interest of the foreign corporation that is treated as interest on deposits shall equal the product of the foreign corporation's excess interest and the greater of—

(A) The ratio of the amount of interest bearing deposits, within the meaning of section 871(i)(3)(A), of the foreign corporation as of the close of the taxable year to the amount of all interest bearing liabilities of the foreign corporation on such date; or

(B) 85 percent.

(iv) *Reporting and payment of tax on excess interest.*—The amount of tax due under section 884(f) and this section with respect to excess interest of a foreign corporation shall be reported on the foreign corporation's income tax return for the taxable year in which the excess interest is treated as paid to the foreign corporation under section 884(f)(1)(B) and paragraph (a)(2) of this section, and shall not be subject to withholding under section 1441 or 1442. The tax shall be due and payable as provided in section 6151 and such other sections of Subtitle F of the Internal Revenue Code as apply, and estimated tax payments shall be due with respect to a foreign corporation's liability for the tax on excess interest as provided in section 6655.

(3) *Original issue discount.*—For purposes of this section, the term "interest" includes original issue discount, as defined in section 1273(a)(1).

(4) *Examples.*—The application of this paragraph (a) is illustrated by the following examples.

Example 1. Taxation of branch interest and excess interest. Foreign corporation A, a calendar year taxpayer that is not a corporation described in paragraph (a)(2)(iii) of this section (relating to banks), has $120 of interest allocated or apportioned to ECI under § 1.882-5 for 1997. A's branch interest (as defined in paragraph (b) of this section) for 1997 is as follows: $55 of portfolio interest (as defined in section 871(h)(2)) to B, a nonresident alien; $25 of interest to foreign corporation C, which owns 15 percent of the combined voting power of A's stock, with respect to bonds issued by A; and $20 to D, a domestic corporation. B and C are not engaged in the conduct of a trade or business in the United States. A, B and C are residents of countries with which the United States does not have an income tax treaty. The interest payments made to B and D are not subject to tax under section 871(a) or 881 and are not subject to withholding under section 1441 or 1442. The payment to C, which does not qualify as portfolio interest because C owns at least 10 percent of the combined voting power of A's stock, is subject to withholding of $7.50 ($25 × 30%). In addition, because A's interest allocated or apportioned to ECI under § 1.882-5 ($120) exceeds its branch interest ($100), A has excess interest of $20, which is subject to a tax of $6 ($20 × 30%) under section 881. The tax on A's excess interest must be reported on A's income tax return for 1997.

Example 2. Taxation of excess interest of a bank. Foreign corporation A, a calendar year taxpayer, is a corporation described in paragraph (a)(2)(iii) of this section (relating to banks) and is a resident of a country with which the United States does not have an income tax treaty. A has excess interest of $100 for 1997. At the close of 1997, A has $10,000 of interest-bearing liabilities (including liabilities that give rise to branch interest), of which $8,700 are interest-bearing deposits. For purposes of computing the tax on A's excess interest, $87 of the excess interest ($100 excess interest × ($8,700 interest-bearing deposits/$10,000 interest-bearing liabilities)) is treated as interest on deposits. Thus, $87 of A's excess interest is exempt from tax under section 881(a) and the remaining $13 of excess interest is subject to a tax of $3.90 ($13 × 30%) under section 881(a).

(b) *Branch interest.*—(1) *Definition of branch interest.*—For purposes of this section, the term "branch interest" means interest that is—

(i) Paid by a foreign corporation with respect to a liability that is—

(A) A U.S. booked liability within the meaning of § 1.882-5(d)(2) (other than a U.S. booked liability of a partner within the meaning of § 1.882-5(d)(2)(vii)); or

(B) Described in § 1.884-1(e)(2) (relating to insurance liabilities on U.S. business and liabilities giving rise to interest expense that is directly allocated to income from a U.S. asset); or

(ii) In the case of a foreign corporation other than a corporation described in paragraph (a)(2)(iii) of this section, a liability specifically identified (as provided in paragraph (b)(3)(i) of this section) as a liability of a U.S. trade or business of the foreign corporation on or before the earlier of the date on which the first payment of interest is made with respect to the liability or the due date (including extensions) of the foreign corporation's income tax return for the taxable year, provided that—

(A) The amount of such interest does not exceed 85 percent of the amount of interest of the foreign corporation that would be excess interest before taking into account interest treated as branch interest by reason of this paragraph (b)(1)(ii);

(B) The requirements of paragraph (b)(3)(ii) of this section (relating to notification of recipient of interest) are satisfied; and

(C) The liability is not described in paragraph (b)(3)(iii) of this section (relating to liabilities incurred in the ordinary course of a foreign business or secured by foreign assets) or paragraph (b)(1)(i) of this section.

(2) [Reserved]

(3) *Requirements relating to specifically identified liabilities.*—(i) *Method of identification.*—A liability described in paragraph (b)(1)(ii) of this section is identified as a liability of a U.S. trade or business only if the liability is shown on the records of the U.S. trade or business, or is identified as a liability of the U.S. trade or business on other records of the foreign corporation or on a schedule established for the purpose of identifying the liabilities of the U.S. trade or business. Each such liability must be identified with sufficient specificity so that the amount of branch interest attributable to the liability, and the name and address of the recipient, can be readily identified from such records or schedule. However, with respect to liabilities that give rise to portfolio interest (as defined in sections 871(h) and 881(c)) or that are payable 183 days or less from the date of original issue, and form part of a larger debt issue, such liabilities may be identified by reference to the issue and maturity date, principal amount and interest payable with respect to the entire debt issue. Records or schedules described in this paragraph that identify liabilities that give rise to branch interest must be maintained in the United States by the foreign corporation or an agent of the foreign corporation for the entire period commencing with the due date (including extensions) of the income tax return for the taxable year to which the records or schedules

relate and ending with the expiration of the period of limitations for assessment of tax for such taxable year. A foreign corporation that is subject to this section may identify a liability under paragraph (b)(1)(ii) of this section whether or not it is actually engaged in the conduct of a trade or business in the United States.

(ii) *Notification to recipient.*—Interest with respect to a liability described in paragraph (b)(1)(ii) of this section shall not be treated as branch interest unless the foreign corporation paying the interest either—

(A) Makes a return, pursuant to section 6049, with respect to the interest payment; or

(B) Sends a notice to the person who receives such interest in a confirmation of the transaction, a statement of account, or a separate notice, within two months of the end of the calendar year in which the interest was paid, stating that the interest paid with respect to the liability is from sources within the United States.

(iii) *Liabilities that do not give rise to branch interest under paragraph (b)(1)(ii) of this section.*—A liability is described in this paragraph (b)(3)(iii) (and interest with respect to the liability may not be treated as branch interest of a foreign corporation by reason of paragraph (b)(1)(ii) of this section) if—

(A) The liability is directly incurred in the ordinary course of the profit-making activities of a trade or business of the foreign corporation conducted outside the United States, as, for example, an account or note payable arising from the purchase of inventory or receipt of services by such trade or business; or

(B) The liability is secured (during more than half the days during the portion of the taxable year in which the interest accrues) predominantly by property that is not a U.S. asset (as defined in §1.884-1(d)) unless such liability is secured by substantially all the property of the foreign corporation.

(4) [Reserved]

(5) *Increase in branch interest where U.S. assets constitute 80 percent or more of a foreign corporation's assets.*—(i) *General rule.*—If a foreign corporation would have excess interest before application of this paragraph (b)(5) and the amount of the foreign corporation's U.S. assets as of the close of the taxable year equals or exceeds 80 percent of all money and the aggregate E&P basis of all property of the foreign corporation on such date, then all interest paid and accrued by the foreign corporation during the taxable year that was not treated as branch interest before application of this paragraph (b)(5) and that is not paid with respect to a liability described in paragraph (b)(3)(iii) of this section (relating to liabilities incurred in the ordinary course of a foreign business or secured by non-U.S. assets) shall be treated as branch interest. However, if application of the preceding sentence would cause the amount of the foreign corporation's branch interest to exceed the amount permitted by paragraph (b)(6)(i) of this section (relating to branch interest in excess of a foreign corporation's interest allocated or apportioned to ECI under §1.882-5) the amount of branch interest arising by reason of this paragraph shall be reduced as provided in paragraphs (b)(6)(ii) and (iii) of this section, as applicable.

(ii) *Example.*—The application of this paragraph (b)(5) is illustrated by the following example.

Example. Application of 80 percent test. Foreign corporation A, a calendar year taxpayer, has $90 of interest allocated or apportioned to ECI under §1.882-5 for 1993. Before application of this paragraph (b)(5), A has $40 of branch interest in 1993. A pays $60 of other interest during 1993, none of which is attributable to a liability described in paragraph (b)(3)(iii) of this section (relating to liabilities incurred in the ordinary course of a foreign business and liabilities predominantly secured by foreign assets). As of the close of 1993, A has an amount of U.S. assets that exceeds 80 percent of the money and E&P bases of all A's property. Before application of this paragraph (b)(5), A would have $50 of excess interest (*i.e.*, the $90 interest allocated or apportioned to its ECI under §1.882-5 less $40 of branch interest). Under this paragraph (b)(5), the $60 of additional interest paid by A is also treated as branch interest. However, to the extent that treating the $60 of additional interest as branch interest would create an amount of branch interest that would exceed the amount of branch interest permitted under paragraph (b)(6) of this section (relating to branch interest that exceeds a foreign corporation's interest allocated or apportioned to ECI under §1.882-5) the amount of the additional branch interest is reduced under paragraph (b)(6)(iii) of this section, which generally allows a foreign corporation to specify certain liabilities that do not give rise to branch interest or paragraph (b)(6)(ii) of this section, which generally specifies liabilities that do not give rise to branch interest beginning with the most-recently incurred liability.

(6) *Special rule where branch interest exceeds interest allocated or apportioned to ECI of a foreign corporation.*—(i) *General rule.*—If the amount of branch interest that is both paid and

accrued by a foreign corporation during the taxable year (including interest that the foreign corporation elects under paragraph (c)(1) of this section to treat as paid during the taxable year) exceeds the amount of interest allocated or apportioned to ECI of a foreign corporation under § 1.882-5 for the taxable year, then the amount of the foreign corporation's branch interest shall be reduced by the amount of such excess as provided in paragraphs (b)(6)(ii) and (iii) of this section, as applicable. The rules of paragraphs (b)(6)(ii) and (iii) of this section shall also apply where the amount of branch interest with respect to liabilities identified under paragraph (b)(1)(ii) of this section exceeds the maximum amount that may be treated as branch interest under that paragraph. This paragraph (b)(6) shall apply whether or not a reduction in the amount of branch interest occurs as a result of adjustments made during the examination of the foreign corporation's income tax return, such as a reduction in the amount of interest allocated or apportioned to ECI of the foreign corporation under § 1.882-5.

(ii) *Reduction of branch interest beginning with most-recently incurred liability.*—Except as provided in paragraph (b)(6)(iii) of this section (relating to an election to specify liabilities that do not give rise to branch interest), the amount of the excess in paragraph (b)(6)(i) of this section shall first reduce branch interest attributable to liabilities described in paragraph (b)(1)(ii) of this section (relating to liabilities identified as giving rise to branch interest) and then, if such excess has not been reduced to zero, branch interest attributable to the group of liabilities described in paragraph (b)(1)(i) of this section. The reduction of branch interest attributable to each group of liabilities (*i.e.*, liabilities described in paragraph (b)(1)(ii) of this section and liabilities described in paragraph (b)(1)(i) of this section) shall be made beginning with interest attributable to the latest-incurred liability and continuing, in reverse chronological order, with branch interest attributable to the next-latest incurred liability. The branch interest attributable to a liability must be reduced to zero before a reduction is made with respect to branch interest attributable to the next-latest incurred liability. Where only a portion of the branch interest attributable to a liability is reduced by reason of this paragraph (b)(6)(ii), the reduction shall be made beginning with the last interest payment made with respect to the liability during the taxable year and continuing, in reverse chronological order, with the next-latest payment until the amount of branch interest has been reduced by the amount specified in paragraph (b)(6)(i) of this section. The amount of interest that is not treated as branch interest by reason of this paragraph (b)(6)(ii) shall not be treated as paid by a domestic corporation and thus shall not be subject to tax under section 871(a) or 881(a).

(iii) *Election to specify liabilities that do not give rise to branch interest.*—For purposes of reducing the amount of branch interest under paragraph (b)(6)(i) of this section, a foreign corporation may, instead of using the method described in paragraph (b)(6)(ii) of this section, elect for any taxable year to specify which liabilities will not be treated as giving rise to branch interest or will be treated as giving rise only in part to branch interest. Branch interest paid during the taxable year with respect to a liability specified under this paragraph (b)(6)(iii) must be reduced to zero before a reduction is made with respect to branch interest attributable to the next-specified liability. If all interest payments with respect to a specified liability, when added to all interest payments with respect to other liabilities specified under this paragraph (b)(6)(iii), would exceed the amount of the reduction under paragraph (b)(6)(i) of this section, then only a portion of the branch interest attributable to that specified liability shall be reduced under this paragraph (b)(6)(iii), and the reduction shall be made beginning with the last interest payment made with respect to the liability during the taxable year and continuing, in reverse chronological order, with the next-latest payment until the amount of branch interest has been reduced by the amount of the reduction under paragraph (b)(6)(i) of this section. A foreign corporation that elects to have this paragraph (b)(6)(iii) apply shall note on its books and records maintained in the United States that the liability is not to be treated as giving rise to branch interest, or is to be treated as giving rise to branch interest only in part. Such notation must be made after the close of the taxable year in which the foreign corporation pays the interest and prior to the due date (with extensions) of the foreign corporation's income tax return for the taxable year. However, if the excess interest in paragraph (b)(6)(i) of this section occurs as a result of adjustments made during the examination of the foreign corporation's income tax return, the election and notation may be made at the time of examination. The amount of interest that is not treated as branch interest by reason of this paragraph (b)(6)(iii) shall not be treated as paid by a domestic corporation and thus shall not be subject to tax under section 871(a) or 881(a).

(iv) *Examples.*—The application of this paragraph (b)(6) is illustrated by the following examples.

Example 1. Branch interest exceeds interest apportioned to ECI with no election in effect.

Foreign corporation A, a calendar year, accrual method taxpayer, has interest expense apportioned to ECI under § 1.882-5 of $230 for 1997. A's branch interest for 1997 is as follows:

(i) $130 paid to B, a domestic corporation, with respect to a note issued on March 10, 1997, and secured by real property located in the United States;

(ii) $60 paid to C, an individual resident of country X who is entitled to a 10 percent rate of withholding on interest payments under the income tax treaty between the United States and X, with respect to a note issued on October 15, 1996, which gives rise to interest subject to tax under section 871(a);

(iii) $80 paid to D, an individual resident of country Y who is entitled to a 15 percent rate of withholding on interest payments under the income tax treaty between the United States and Y, with respect to a note issued on February 15, 1997, which gives rise to interest subject to tax under section 871(a); and

(iv) $70 of portfolio interest (as defined in section 871(h)(2)) paid to E, a nonresident alien, with respect to a bond issued on March 1, 1997.

A's branch interest accrues during 1997 for purposes of calculating the amount of A's interest apportioned to ECI under § 1.882-5. A has identified under paragraph (b)(1)(ii) of this section the liabilities described in paragraphs (ii), (iii) and (iv) of this example. A has not made an election under paragraph (b)(6)(iii) of this section to specify liabilities that do not give rise to branch interest. The amount of A's branch interest in 1997 is limited under paragraph (b)(6)(i) of this section to $230, the amount of the interest apportioned to A's ECI for 1997. The amount of A's branch interest must thus be reduced by $110 ($340 – $230) under paragraph (b)(6)(ii) of this section. The reduction is first made with respect to interest attributable to liabilities described in paragraph (b)(1)(ii) of this section (*i.e.*, liabilities identified as giving rise to branch interest) and, within the group of liabilities described in paragraph (b)(1)(ii) of this section, is first made with respect to the latest-incurred liability. Thus, the $70 of interest paid to E with respect to the bond issued on March 1, 1997, and $40 of the $80 of interest paid to D with respect to the note issued on February 15, 1997, are not treated as branch interest. The interest paid to D is no longer subject to tax under section 871(a), and D may claim a refund of amounts withheld with respect to the interest payments. There is no change in the tax consequences to E because the interest received by E was portfolio interest and was not subject to tax when it was treated as branch interest.

Example 2. Effect of election to specify liabilities. Assume the same facts as in *Example 1* except that A makes an election under paragraph (b)(6)(iii) of this section to specify which liabilities are not to be treated as giving rise to branch interest. A specifies the liability to D, who would be taxable at a rate of 15 percent on interest paid with respect to the liability, as a liability that does not give rise to branch interest, and D is therefore not subject to tax under section 871(a) and is entitled to a refund of amounts withheld with respect to the interest payments. A also specifies the liability to C as a liability that gives rise to branch interest only in part. As a result, $30 of the $60 of interest paid to C is not treated as branch interest, and C is entitled to a refund with respect to the $30 of interest that is not treated as branch interest.

(7) *Effect of election under paragraph (c)(1) of this section to treat interest as if paid in year of accrual.*—If a foreign corporation accrues an interest expense in a taxable year earlier than the taxable year of payment and elects under paragraph (c)(1) of this section to compute its excess interest as if the interest expense were branch interest paid in the year of accrual, the interest expense shall be treated as branch interest that is paid at the close of such year (and not in the actual year of payment) for all purposes of this section. Such interest shall thus be subject to tax under section 871(a) or 881(a) and withholding under section 1441 or section 1442, as if paid on the last day of the taxable year of accrual. Interest that is treated under paragraph (c)(1) of this section as paid in a later year for purposes of computing excess interest shall be treated as paid only in the actual year of payment for all purposes of this section other than paragraphs (a)(2) and (c)(1) of this section (relating to excess interest).

(8) *Effect of treaties.*—(i) *Payor's treaty.*— In the case of a foreign corporation's branch interest, relief shall be available under an article of an income tax treaty between the United States and the foreign corporation's country of residence relating to interest paid by the foreign corporation only if, for the taxable year in which the branch interest is paid (or if the branch interest is treated as paid in an earlier taxable year under paragraph (b)(7) of this section, for the earlier taxable year)—

(A) The foreign corporation meets the requirements of the limitation on benefits provision, if any, in the treaty, and either—

(1) The corporation is a qualified resident (as defined in § 1.884-5(a)) of that foreign country in such year; or

Reg. § 1.884-4(b)(8)(i)(A)(1)

(2) The corporation meets the requirements of paragraph (b)(8)(iii) of this section in such year; or

(B) The limitation on benefits provision, or an amendment to that provision, entered into force after December 31, 1986.

(ii) *Recipient's treaty.*—A foreign person (other than a foreign corporation) that derives branch interest is entitled to claim benefits under provisions of an income tax treaty between the United States and its country of residence relating to interest derived by the foreign person. A foreign corporation may claim such benefits if it meets, with respect to the branch interest, the requirements of the limitation on benefits provision, if any, in the treaty and—

(A) The foreign corporation meets the requirements of paragraphs (b)(8)(i)(A) or (B) of this section; and

(B) In the case of interest paid in a taxable year beginning after December 31, 1988, with respect to an obligation with a maturity not exceeding one year, each foreign corporation that beneficially owned the obligation prior to maturity was a qualified resident (for the period specified in paragraph (b)(8)(i) of this section) of a foreign country with which the United States has an income tax treaty or met the requirements of the limitation on benefits provision in a treaty with respect to the interest payment and such provision entered into force after December 31, 1986.

(iii) *Presumption that a foreign corporation continues to be a qualified resident.*—For purposes of this paragraph (b)(8), a foreign corporation that was a qualified resident for the prior taxable year because it fulfills the requirements of § 1.884-5 shall be considered a qualified resident with respect to branch interest that is paid or received during the current taxable year if—

(A) In the case of a foreign corporation that met the stock ownership and base erosion tests in § 1.884-5(b) and (c) for the preceding taxable year, the foreign corporation does not know, or have reason to know, that either 50 percent of its stock (by value) is not beneficially owned (or treated as beneficially owned by reason of § 1.884-5(b)(2)) by qualifying shareholders at any time during the portion of the taxable year that ends with the date on which the interest is paid, or that the base erosion test is not met during the portion of the taxable year that ends with the date on which the interest is paid;

(B) In the case of a foreign corporation that met the requirements of § 1.884-5(d) (relating to publicly-traded corporations) for the preceding taxable year, the foreign corporation is listed on an established securities exchange in the United States or its country of residence at all times during the portion of the taxable year that ends with the date on which the interest is paid and does not fail the requirements of § 1.884-5(d)(4)(iii) (relating to certain closely-held corporations) at any time during such period; or

(C) In the case of a foreign corporation that met the requirements of § 1.884-5(e) (relating to the active trade or business test) for the preceding taxable year, the foreign corporation continues to operate (other than in a nominal degree), at all times during the portion of the taxable year that ends with the date on which the interest is paid, the same business in the U.S. and its country of residence that caused it to meet such requirements for the preceding taxable year.

(iv) *Treaties other than income tax treaties.*—A treaty that is not an income tax treaty does not provide any benefits with respect to branch interest.

(v) *Effect of income tax treaties on interest paid by a partnership.*—If a foreign corporation is a partner (directly or indirectly) in a partnership that is engaged in a trade or business in the United States and owns an interest of 10 percent or more (as determined under the attribution rules of section 318) in the capital, profits, or losses of the partnership at any time during the partner's taxable year, the relief that may be claimed under an income tax treaty with respect to the foreign corporation's distributive share of interest paid or treated as paid by the partnership shall not exceed the relief that would be available under paragraphs (b)(8)(i) and (ii) of this section if such interest were branch interest of the foreign corporation. See paragraph (c)(2) of this section for the effect on a foreign corporation's excess interest of interest paid by a partnership of which the foreign corporation is a partner.

(vi) *Examples.*—The following examples illustrate the application of this paragraph (b)(8).

Example 1. Payor's treaty. The income tax treaty between the United States and country X provides that the United States may not impose a tax on interest paid by a corporation that is a resident of that country (and that is not a domestic corporation) if the recipient of the interest is a nonresident alien or a foreign corporation. Corp A is a qualified resident of country X and meets the limitation on benefits provision in the treaty. A's branch interest is not subject to tax under section 871(a) or 881(a) regardless of whether the recipient is entitled to benefits under an income tax treaty.

Example 2. Recipient's treaty and interest received from a partnership. A, a foreign corporation, and B, a nonresident alien, are partners in a partnership that owns and operates U.S. real estate and each has a distributive share of partnership interest deductions equal to 50 percent of the interest deductions of the partnership. There is no income tax treaty between the United States and the countries of residence of A and B. The partnership pays $1,000 of interest to a bank that is a resident of a foreign country, Y, and that qualifies under an income tax treaty in effect with the United States for a 5 percent rate of tax on U.S. source interest paid to a resident of country Y. However, the bank is not a qualified resident of country Y and the limitation on benefits provision of the treaty has not been amended since December 31, 1986. The partnership is required to withhold at a rate of 30 percent on $500 of the interest paid to the bank (*i.e.*, A's 50 percent distributive share of interest paid by the partnership) because the bank cannot, under paragraph (b)(8)(iv) of this section, claim greater treaty benefits by lending money to the partnership than it could claim if it lent money to A directly and the $500 were branch interest of A.

(c) *Rules relating to excess interest.*—(1) *Election to compute excess interest by treating branch interest that is paid and accrued in different years as if paid in year of accrual.*—(i) *General rule.*—If branch interest is paid in one or more taxable years before or after the year in which the interest accrues, a foreign corporation may elect to compute its excess interest as if such branch interest were paid on the last day of the taxable year in which it accrues, and not in the taxable year in which it is actually paid. The interest expense will thus reduce the amount of the foreign corporation's excess interest in the year of accrual rather than in the year of actual payment. Except as provided in paragraph (c)(1)(ii) of this section, if an election is made for a taxable year, this paragraph (c)(1)(i) shall apply to all branch interest that is paid or accrued during that year. See paragraph (b)(7) of this section for the effect of an election under this paragraph (c)(1) on branch interest that accrues in a taxable year after the year of payment.

(ii) *Election not to apply in certain cases.*—An election under this paragraph (c)(1) shall not apply to an interest expense that accrued in a taxable year beginning before January 1, 1987, and shall not apply to an interest expense that was paid in a taxable year beginning before such date unless the interest was income from sources within the United States. An election under this paragraph (c)(1) shall not apply to branch interest that accrues during the taxable year and is paid in an earlier taxable year if the branch interest reduced excess interest in such earlier year. However, a foreign corporation may amend its income tax return for such earlier taxable year so that the branch interest does not reduce excess interest in such year.

(iii) *Requirements for election.*—A foreign corporation that elects to apply this paragraph (c)(1) shall attach to its income tax return (or to an amended income tax return) a statement that it elects to have the provisions of this paragraph (c)(1) apply, or shall provide written notice to the Commissioner during an examination that it elects to apply this paragraph (c)(1). The election shall be effective for the taxable year to which the return relates and for all subsequent taxable years unless the Commissioner consents to revocation of the election.

(iv) *Examples.*—The following examples illustrate the application of this paragraph (c)(1).

Example 1. Interest accrued before paid. Foreign corporation A, a calendar year, accrual method taxpayer, has $100 of interest allocated or apportioned to ECI under § 1.882-5 for 1997. A has $60 of branch interest in 1997 before application of this paragraph (c)(1). A has an interest expense of $20 that properly accrues for tax purposes in 1997 but is not paid until 1998. When the interest is paid in 1998 it will meet the requirements for branch interest under paragraph (b)(1) of this section. A makes a timely election under this paragraph (c)(1) to treat the accrued interest as if it were paid in 1997. A will be treated as having branch interest of $80 for 1997 and excess interest of $20 in 1997. The $20 of interest treated as branch interest of A in 1997 will not again be treated as branch interest in 1998.

Example 2. Interest paid before accrued. Foreign corporation A, a calendar year, accrual method taxpayer, has $60 of branch interest in 1997. The interest expense does not accrue until 1998 and the amount of interest allocated or apportioned to A's ECI under § 1.882-5 is zero for 1997 and $60 for 1998. A makes an election under this paragraph (c)(1) with respect to 1997. As a result of the election, A's $60 of branch interest in 1997 reduces the amount of A's excess interest for 1998 rather than in 1997.

(2) *Interest paid by a partnership.*—(i) *General rule.*—Except as otherwise provided in paragraphs (c)(2)(i) and (ii) of this section, if a foreign corporation is a partner in a partnership that is engaged in trade or business in the United States, the amount of the foreign corporation's distributive share of interest paid or accrued by the partnership shall

reduce (but not below zero) the amount of the foreign corporation's excess interest for the year to the extent such interest is taken into account by the foreign corporation in that year for purposes of calculating the interest allocated or apportioned to the ECI of the foreign corporation under § 1.882-5. A foreign corporation's excess interest shall not be reduced by its distributive share of partnership interest that is attributable to a liability described in paragraph (b)(3)(iii) of this section (relating to interest on liabilities incurred in the ordinary course of a foreign business or secured predominantly by assets that are not U.S. assets) or would be described in paragraph (b)(3)(iii) of this section if entered on the partner's books. See paragraph (b)(8)(v) of this section for the effect of income tax treaties on interest paid by a partnership.

(ii) *Special rule for interest that is paid and accrued in different years.*—Paragraph (c)(2)(i) of this section shall not apply to any portion of a foreign corporation's distributive share of partnership interest that is paid and accrued in different taxable years unless the foreign corporation has an election in effect under paragraph (c)(1) of this section that is effective with respect to such interest and any tax due under section 871(a) or 881(a) with respect to such interest has been deducted and withheld at source in the earlier of the taxable year of payment or accrual.

(3) *Effect of treaties.*—(i) *General rule.*—The rate of tax imposed on the excess interest of a foreign corporation that is a resident of a country with which the United States has an income tax treaty shall not exceed the rate provided under such treaty that would apply with respect to interest paid by a domestic corporation to that foreign corporation if the foreign corporation meets, with respect to the excess interest, the requirements of the limitation on benefits provision, if any, in the treaty and either—

(A) The corporation is a qualified resident (as defined in § 1.884-5(a)) of that foreign country for the taxable year in which the excess interest is subject to tax; or

(B) The limitation on benefits provision, or an amendment to that provision, entered into force after December 31, 1986.

(ii) *Provisions relating to interest paid by a foreign corporation.*—Any provision in an income tax treaty that exempts or reduces the rate of tax on interest paid by a foreign corporation does not prevent imposition of the tax on excess interest or reduce the rate of such tax.

(4) *Example.*—The application of paragraphs (c)(2) and (3) of this section is illustrated by the following example.

Example. Interest paid by a partnership. Foreign corporation A, a calendar year taxpayer, is not a resident of a foreign country with which the United States has an income tax treaty. A is engaged in the conduct of a trade or business both in the United States and in foreign countries, and owns a 50 percent interest in X, a calendar year partnership engaged in the conduct of a trade or business in the United States. For 1997, all of X's liabilities are of a type described in paragraph (b)(1) of this section (relating to liabilities on U.S. books) and none are described in paragraph (b)(3)(iii) of this section (relating to liabilities that may not give rise to branch interest). A's distributive share of interest paid by X in 1997 is $20. For 1997, A has $150 of interest allocated or apportioned to its ECI under § 1.882-5, $120 of which is attributable to branch interest. Thus, the amount of A's excess interest for 1997, before application of paragraph (c)(2)(i) of this section, is $30. Under paragraph (c)(2)(i) of this section, A's $30 of excess interest is reduced by $20, representing A's share of interest paid by X. Thus, the amount of A's excess interest for 1997 is reduced to $10. A is subject to a tax of 30 percent on its $10 of excess interest.

(d) *Stapled entities.*—A foreign corporation that is treated as a domestic corporation by reason of section 269B (relating to stapled entities) shall continue to be treated as a foreign corporation for purposes of section 884(f) and this section, notwithstanding section 269B and the regulations thereunder. Interest paid by such foreign corporation shall be treated as paid by a domestic corporation and shall be subject to the tax imposed by section 871(a) or 881(a), and to withholding under sections 1441 and 1442, as applicable, to the extent such interest is not subject to tax by reason of section 884(f) and this section.

(e) *Effective dates.*—(1) *General rule.*—Except as provided in paragraph (e)(2) of this section, this section is effective for taxable years beginning October 13, 1992, and for payments of interest described in section 884(f)(1)(A) made (or treated as made under paragraph (b)(7) of this section) during taxable years of the payor beginning after such date. With respect to taxable years beginning before October 13, 1992 and after December 31, 1986, a foreign corporation may elect to apply this section in lieu of § 1.884-4T of the temporary regulations (as contained in the CFR edition revised as of April 1, 1992) as they applied to the foreign corporation after issuance of Notice 89-80, 1989-2 C.B. 394, but only if the foreign corporation has made an election under

§ 1.884-1(i) to apply § 1.884-1 in lieu of § 1.884-1T (as contained in the CFR edition revised as of April 1, 1992) for that year, and the statute of limitations for assessment of a deficiency has not expired for that taxable year. Once an election has been made, an election under this section shall apply to all subsequent taxable years.

(2) *Special rule.*—Paragraphs (a)(1), (a)(2)(i)(A), (a)(2)(iii), (b)(1), (b)(3), (b)(5)(i), (b)(6)(i), (b)(6)(ii), and (c)(2)(i) of this section are effective for taxable years beginning on or after June 6, 1996.

(f) *Transition rules.*—(1) *Election under paragraph (c)(1) of this section.*—If a foreign corporation has made an election described in § 1.884-4T(b)(7) (as contained in the CFR edition revised as of April 1, 1992) with respect to interest that has accrued and been paid in different taxable years, such election shall be effective for purposes of paragraph (c)(1) of this section as if the corporation had made the election under paragraph (c)(1) of this section of these regulations.

(2) *Waiver of notification requirement for non-banks under Notice 89-80.*—If a foreign corporation that is not a bank has made an election under Notice 89-80 to apply the rules in Part 2 of Section I of the Notice in lieu of the rules in § 1.884-4T(b) (as contained in the CFR edition revised as of April 1, 1992) to determine the amount of its interest paid and excess interest in taxable years beginning prior to 1990, the requirement that the foreign corporation satisfy the notification requirements described in paragraph (b)(3)(ii) of this section is waived with respect to interest paid in taxable years ending on or before the date the Notice was issued.

(3) *Waiver of legending requirement for certain debt issued prior to January 3, 1989.*—For purposes of sections 871(h), 881(c), and this section, branch interest of a foreign corporation that would be treated as portfolio interest under section 871(h) or 881(c) but for the fact that it fails to meet the requirements of section 163 (f)(2)(B)(ii)(II) (relating to the legend requirement), shall nevertheless be treated as portfolio interest provided the interest arises with respect to a liability incurred by the foreign corporation before January 3, 1989, and interest with respect to the liability was treated as branch interest in a taxable year beginning before January 1, 1990. [Reg. § 1.884-4.]

☐ [*T.D.* 8432, 9-10-92. *Amended by T.D.* 8657, 3-5-96.]

§ 1.884-5. Qualified resident.—(a) *Definition of qualified resident.*—A foreign corporation is a qualified resident of a foreign country with which the United States has an income tax treaty in effect if, for the taxable year, the foreign corporation is a resident of that country (within the meaning of such treaty) and either—

(1) Meets the requirements of paragraphs (b) and (c) of this section (relating to stock ownership and base erosion);

(2) Meets the requirements of paragraph (d) of this section (relating to publicly-traded corporations);

(3) Meets the requirements of paragraph (e) of this section (relating to the conduct of an active trade or business); or

(4) Obtains a ruling as provided in paragraph (f) of this section that it shall be treated as a qualified resident of its country of residence.

(b) *Stock ownership requirement.*—(1) *General rule.*—(i) *Ownership by qualifying shareholders.*—A foreign corporation satisfies the stock ownership requirement of this paragraph (b) for the taxable year if more than 50 percent of its stock (by value) is beneficially owned (or is treated as beneficially owned by reason of paragraph (b)(2) of this section) during at least half of the number of days in the foreign corporation's taxable year by one or more qualifying shareholders. A person shall be treated as a qualifying shareholder only if such person meets the requirements of paragraph (b)(3) of this section and is either—

(A) An individual who is either a resident of the foreign country of which the foreign corporation is a resident or a citizen or resident of the United States;

(B) The government of the country of which the foreign corporation is a resident (or a political subdivision or local authority of such country), or the United States, a State, the District of Columbia, or a political subdivision or local authority of a State;

(C) A corporation that is a resident of the foreign country of which the foreign corporation is a resident and whose stock is primarily and regularly traded on an established securities market (within the meaning of paragraph (d) of this section) in that country or the United States or a domestic corporation whose stock is primarily and regularly traded on an established securities market (within the meaning of paragraph (d) of this section) in the United States;

(D) A not-for-profit organization described in paragraph (b)(1)(iv) of this section that is not a pension fund as defined in paragraph (b)(8)(i)(A) of this section and that is organized under the laws of the foreign country of which the foreign corporation is a resident or the United States; or

(E) A beneficiary of certain pension funds (as defined in paragraph (b)(8)(i)(A) of this section) administered in or by the country in which the foreign corporation is a resident to the extent provided in paragraph (b)(8) of this section.

Beneficial owners of an association taxable as a corporation shall be treated as shareholders of such association for purposes of this paragraph (b)(1). If stock of a foreign corporation is owned by a corporation that is treated as a qualifying shareholder under paragraph (b)(1)(i)(C) of this section, such stock shall not also be treated as owned, directly or indirectly, by any qualifying shareholders of such corporation for purposes of this paragraph (b). Notwithstanding the above, a foreign corporation will not be treated as a qualified resident unless it obtains the documentation described in paragraph (b)(3) of this section to show that the requirements of this paragraph (b)(1)(i) have been met and maintains the documentation as provided in paragraph (b)(9) of this section. See also paragraph (b)(1)(iii) of this section, which treats certain publicly-traded classes of stock as owned by qualifying shareholders.

(ii) *Special rules relating to qualifying shareholders.*—For purposes of applying paragraph (b)(1)(i) of this section—

(A) Stock owned on any day shall be taken into account only if the beneficial owner is a qualifying shareholder on that day or, in the case of a corporation or not-for-profit organization that is a qualifying shareholder under paragraph (b)(1)(i)(C) or (D) of this section, for a one-year period that includes such day; and

(B) An individual, corporation or not-for-profit organization is a resident of a foreign country if it is a resident of that country for purposes of the income tax treaty between the United States and that country.

(iii) *Publicly-traded class of stock treated as owned by qualifying shareholders.*—A class of stock of a foreign corporation shall be treated as owned by qualifying shareholders if—

(A) The class of stock is listed on an established securities market in the United States or in the country of residence of the foreign corporation seeking qualified resident status; and

(B) The class of stock is primarily and regularly traded on such market (within the meaning of paragraphs (d)(3) and (4) of this section, applied as if the class of stock were the sole class of stock relied on to meet the requirements of paragraph (d)(4)(i)(A)).

For purposes of this paragraph (b), stock in such class shall not also be treated as owned by any qualifying shareholders who own such stock, either directly or indirectly.

(iv) *Special rule for not-for-profit organizations.*—A not-for-profit organization is described in paragraph (b)(1)(iv) of this section if it meets the following requirements—

(A) It is a corporation, association taxable as a corporation, trust, fund, foundation, league or other entity operated exclusively for religious, charitable, educational, or recreational purposes, and it is not organized for profit;

(B) It is generally exempt from tax in its country of organization by virtue of its not-for-profit status; and

(C) Either—

(1) More than 50 percent of its annual support is expended on behalf of persons described in paragraphs (b)(1)(i)(A) through (E) of this section or on qualified residents of the country in which the organization is organized; or

(2) More than 50 percent of its annual support is derived from persons described in paragraphs (b)(1)(i)(A) through (E) of this section or from persons who are qualified residents of the country in which the organization is organized.

For purposes of meeting the requirements of paragraph (b)(1)(iv)(C) of this section, a not-for-profit organization may rely on the addresses of record of its individual beneficiaries and supporters to determine if such persons are resident in the country in which the not-for-profit organization is organized, provided that the addresses of record are not nonresidential addresses such as a post office box or in care of a financial intermediary, and the officers, directors or administrators of the organization do not know or have reason to know that the individual beneficiaries or supporters do not reside at that address.

(2) *Rules for determining constructive ownership.*—(i) *General rules for attribution.*—For purposes of this section, stock owned by a corporation, partnership, trust, estate, or mutual insurance company or similar entity shall be treated as owned proportionately by its shareholders, partners, beneficiaries, grantors or other interest holders as provided in paragraph (b)(2)(ii) through (v) of this section. The proportionate interest rules of this paragraph (b)(2) shall apply successively upward through a chain of ownership, and a person's proportionate interest shall be computed for the relevant days or period that is taken into account in determining whether a foreign corporation is a qualified resident. Except as otherwise provided, stock treated as owned by a person by reason of this paragraph (b)(2) shall, for pur-

poses of applying this paragraph (b)(2), be treated as actually owned by such person.

(ii) *Partnerships.*—A partner shall be treated as having an interest in stock of a foreign corporation owned by a partnership in proportion to the least of—

(A) The partner's percentage distributive share of the partnership's dividend income from the stock;

(B) The partner's percentage distributive share of gain from disposition of the stock by the partnership;

(C) The partner's percentage distributive share of the stock (or proceeds from the disposition of the stock) upon liquidation of the partnership.

For purposes of this paragraph (b)(2)(ii), however, all qualifying shareholders that are partners of a partnership shall be treated as one partner. Thus, the percentage distributive shares of dividend income, gain and liquidation rights of all qualifying shareholders that are partners in a partnership are aggregated prior to determining the least of the three percentages.

(iii) *Trusts and estates.*—(A) *Beneficiaries.*—In general, a person shall be treated as having an interest in stock of a foreign corporation owned by a trust or estate in proportion to the person's actuarial interest in the trust or estate, as provided in section 318(a)(2)(B)(i), except that an income beneficiary's actuarial interest in the trust will be determined as if the trust's only asset were the stock. The interest of a remainder beneficiary in stock will be equal to 100 percent minus the sum of the percentages of any interest in the stock held by income beneficiaries. The ownership of an interest in stock owned by a trust shall not be attributed to any beneficiary whose interest cannot be determined under the preceding sentence, and any such interest, to the extent not attributed by reason of this paragraph (b)(2)(iii)(A), shall not be considered owned by a beneficiary unless all potential beneficiaries with respect to the stock are qualifying shareholders. In addition, a beneficiary's actuarial interest will be treated as zero to the extent that a grantor is treated as owning the stock under paragraph (b)(2)(iii)(B) of this section. A substantially separate and independent share of a trust, within the meaning of section 663(c), shall be treated as a separate trust for purposes of this paragraph (b)(2)(iii)(A), provided that payment of income, accumulated income or corpus of a share of one beneficiary (or group of beneficiaries) cannot affect the proportionate share of income, accumulated income or corpus of another beneficiary (or group of beneficiaries).

(B) *Grantor trusts.*—A person is treated as the owner of stock of a foreign corporation owned by a trust to the extent that the stock is included in the portion of the trust that is treated as owned by the person under sections 671 to 679 (relating to grantors and others treated as substantial owners).

(iv) *Corporations that issue stock.*—A shareholder of a corporation that issues stock shall be treated as owning stock of a foreign corporation that is owned by such corporation on any day in a proportion that equals the value of the stock owned by such shareholder to the value of all stock of such corporation. If there is an agreement, express or implied, that a shareholder of a corporation will not receive distributions from the earnings of stock owned by the corporation, the shareholder will not be treated as owning that stock owned by the corporation.

(v) *Mutual insurance companies and similar entities.*—Stock held by a mutual insurance company, mutual savings bank, or similar entity (including an association taxable as a corporation that does not issue stock interests) shall be considered owned proportionately by the policy holders, depositors, or other owners in the same proportion that such persons share in the surplus of such entity upon liquidation or dissolution.

(vi) *Pension funds.*—See paragraphs (b)(8)(ii) and (iii) of this section for the attribution of stock owned by a pension fund (as defined in paragraph (b)(8)(i)(A)) to beneficiaries of the fund.

(vii) *Examples.*—The rules of paragraph (b)(2)(ii) of this section are illustrated by the following examples.

Example 1. Stock held solely by qualifying shareholders through a partnership. A and B, residents of country X, are qualifying shareholders, within the meaning of paragraphs (b)(1)(i)(A) through (E) of this section, and the sole partners of partnership P. P's only asset is the stock of foreign corporation Z, a country X corporation seeking qualified resident status under this section. A's distributive share of P's income and gain on the disposition of P's assets is 80 percent, but A's distributive share of P's assets (or the proceeds therefrom) on P's liquidation is 20 percent. B's distributive share of P's income and gain is 20 percent and S is entitled to 80 percent of the assets (or proceeds therefrom) on P's liquidation. Under the attribution rules of paragraph (b)(2)(ii) of this section, A and B will be treated as a single partner owning in the aggregate 100 percent of the stock of Z owned by P.

*Example 2. Stock held by both qualifying and nonqualifying shareholders through a partnership. Assume the same facts as in *Example 1* except that C, an individual who is not a qualifying shareholder, is also a partner in P and that C's distributive share of P's income is 60 percent. The distributive shares of A and B are the same as in *Example 1* except that A's distributive share of income is 20 percent. Under the attribution rules of paragraph (b)(2)(ii) of this section, A and B will be treated as a single partner owning in the aggregate 40 percent of the stock of Z owned by P (*i.e.*, the least of A and B's aggregate distributive shares of dividend income (40 percent), gain (100 percent), and liquidation rights (100 percent) with respect to the Z stock).

Example 3. Stock held through tiered partnerships. Assume the same facts as in *Example 1,* except that P does not own the stock of Z directly, but rather is a partner in partnership Pl, which owns the stock of Z. Assume that P's distributive share of the dividend income, gain and liquidation rights with respect to the Z stock held by Pl is 40 percent. Assume that of the remaining partners of Pl only D is a qualifying shareholder. D's distributive share of Pl's dividend income and gain is 15 percent; D's distributive share of Pl's assets on liquidation is 25 percent. Under the attribution rules of paragraph (b)(2)(ii) of this section, A and B, treated as a single partner, will own 40 percent of the Z stock owned by Pl (100 percent × 40 percent) and D will be treated as owning 15 percent of the Z stock owned by Pl (the least of D's dividend income (15 percent), gain (15 percent), and liquidation rights (25 percent) with respect to the Z stock). Thus, 55 percent of the Z stock owned by Pl is treated as owned by qualifying shareholders under paragraph (b)(2)(ii) of this section.

(3) *Required documentation.*—(i) *Ownership statements, certificates of residency and intermediary ownership statements.*—Except as provided in paragraphs (b)(3)(ii), (iii) and (iv) and paragraph (b)(8) of this section, a person shall only be treated as a qualifying shareholder of a foreign corporation if—

(A) For the relevant period, the person completes an ownership statement described in paragraph (b)(4) of this section and, in the case of an individual who is not a U.S. citizen or resident, also obtains a certificate of residency described in paragraph (b)(5) of this section;

(B) In the case of a person owning stock in the foreign corporation indirectly through one or more intermediaries (including mere legal owners or recordholders acting as nominees), each intermediary completes an intermediary ownership statement described in paragraph (b)(6) of this section; and

(C) Such ownership statements and certificates of residency are received by the foreign corporation on or before the earlier of the date it files its income tax return for the taxable year to which the statements relate or the due date (including extensions) for filing such return or, in the case of a foreign corporation claiming treaty benefits under §1.884-4(b)(8)(i) or (ii) (relating to branch interest) on or before the date on which such interest is paid.

(ii) *Substitution of intermediary verification statement for ownership statements and certificates of residency.*—If a qualifying shareholder owns stock through an intermediary that is either a domestic corporation, a resident of the United States, or a resident (for treaty purposes) of a country with which the United States has an income tax treaty in effect, the intermediary may provide an intermediary verification statement (as described in paragraph (b)(7) of this section) in place of any relevant ownership statements and certificates of residency from qualifying shareholders, and in place of intermediary ownership statements (or, where applicable, intermediary verification statements) from all intermediaries standing in the chain of ownership between the qualifying shareholders and the intermediary issuing the intermediary verification statement. An intermediary verification statement generally certifies that the verifying intermediary holds the documentation described in the preceding sentence and agrees to make it available to the District Director on request. Such intermediary verification statements, along with an intermediary ownership statement from the verifying intermediary, must be received by the foreign corporation on or before the earlier of the date it files its income tax return for the taxable year to which the statements relate or the due date (including extensions) for filing such return. An indirect owner of a foreign corporation is thus treated as a qualifying shareholder of a foreign corporation if the foreign corporation receives, on or before the time specified above, an intermediary verification statement and an intermediary ownership statement from the verifying intermediary and an intermediary ownership statement from all intermediaries standing in the chain of the verifying intermediary's ownership of its interest in the foreign corporation.

(iii) *Special rule for registered shareholders of widely-held corporations.*—An ownership statement and a certificate of residency shall not be required in the case of an individual who is a shareholder of record of a corporation that has at least 250 shareholders if—

(A) The individual owns less than one percent of the stock (by value) (applying the attribution rules of section 318) of the corporation at all times during the taxable year;

(B) The individual's address of record is in the corporation's country of residence and is not a nonresidential address such as a post office box or in care of a financial intermediary or stock transfer agent; and

(C) The officers and directors of the corporation do not know or have reason to know that the individual does not reside at that address.

The rule in this paragraph (b)(3)(iii) may also be applied with respect to individual owners of mutual insurance companies, mutual savings banks or similar entities, provided that the same conditions set forth in this paragraph (b)(3)(iii) are met with respect to such individuals.

(iv) *Special rule for pension funds.*—See paragraphs (b)(8)(ii) through (v) of this section for special documentation rules applicable to pension funds (as defined in paragraph (b)(8)(i)(A) of this section).

(v) *Reasonable cause exception.*—If a foreign corporation does not obtain the documentation described in this paragraph (b)(3) or (b)(8) of this section in a timely manner but is able to show prior to notification of an examination of the return for the taxable year that the failure was due to reasonable cause and not willful neglect, the foreign corporation may perfect the documentation after the deadlines specified in this paragraph (b)(3) or (b)(8) of this section. It may make such a showing by providing a written statement to the District Director having jurisdiction over the taxpayer's return or the Office of the Assistant Commissioner (International), as applicable, setting forth the reasons for the failure to obtain the documentation in a timely manner and describing the documentation that was received after the deadline had passed. Whether a failure to obtain the documentation in a timely manner was due to reasonable cause shall be determined by the District Director or the Office of the Assistant Commissioner (International), as applicable, under all the facts and circumstances.

(4) *Ownership statements from qualifying shareholders.*—(i) *Ownership statements from individuals.*—An ownership statement from an individual is a written statement signed by the individual under penalties of perjury stating—

(A) The name, permanent address, and country of residence of the individual and, if the individual was not a resident of the country for the entire taxable year of the foreign corporation seeking qualified resident status, the period during which it was a resident of the foreign corporation's country of residence;

(B) If the individual is a direct beneficial owner of stock in the foreign corporation, the name of the corporation, the number of shares in each class of stock of the corporation that are so owned, and the period of time during the taxable year of the foreign corporation during which the individual owned the stock (or, in the case of an association taxable as a corporation, the amount and nature of the owner's interest in such association);

(C) If the individual directly owns an interest in a corporation, partnership, trust, estate or other intermediary that owns (directly or indirectly) stock in the foreign corporation, the name of the intermediary, the number and class of shares or amount and nature of the interest of the individual in such intermediary (that is relevant for purposes of attributing ownership in paragraph (b)(2) of this section), and the period of time during the taxable year of the foreign corporation during which the individual held such interest; and

(D) To the extent known by the individual, a description of the chain of ownership through which the individual owns stock in the foreign corporation, including the name and address of each intermediary standing between the intermediary described in paragraph (b)(4)(i)(C) of this section and the foreign corporation.

(ii) *Ownership statements from governments.*—An ownership statement from a government that is a qualifying shareholder is a written statement signed by either—

(A) An official of the governmental authority, agency or office that has supervisory authority with respect to the government's ownership interest who is authorized to sign such a statement on behalf of the authority, agency or office; or

(B) The competent authority of the foreign country (as defined in the income tax treaty between the United States and the foreign country).

Such statement shall provide the title of the official signing the statement and the name and address of the government agency, and shall provide the information described in paragraphs (b)(4)(i)(B) through (D) of this section (substituting "government" for "individual") with respect to the government's direct or indirect ownership of stock in the foreign corporation seeking qualified resident status.

(iii) *Ownership statements from publicly-traded corporations.*—An ownership statement from a corporation that is a qualifying shareholder under paragraph (b)(1)(i)(C) of this section is a written statement signed by a person authorized to sign a tax return on behalf of the corporation under penalties of perjury stating—

(A) The name, permanent address, and principal place of business of the corporation (if different from its permanent address);

(B) The information described in paragraphs (b)(4)(i)(B) through (D) of this section (substituting "corporation" for "individual"); and

(C) That the corporation's stock is primarily and regularly traded on an established securities exchange (within the meaning of paragraph (d) of this section) in the United States or its country of residence.

(iv) *Ownership statements from not-for-profit organizations.*—An ownership statement from a not-for-profit organization (other than a pension fund as defined in paragraph (b)(8)(i)(A) of this section) is a written statement signed by a person authorized to sign a tax return on behalf of the organization under penalties of perjury stating—

(A) The name, permanent address, and principal location of the activities of the organization (if different from its permanent address);

(B) The information described in paragraphs (b)(4)(i)(B) through (D) of this section (substituting "not-for-profit organization" for "individual") with respect to the not-for-profit organization's direct or indirect ownership of stock in the foreign corporation seeking qualified resident status; and

(C) That the not-for-profit organization satisfies the requirements of paragraph (b)(1)(iv) of this section.

(v) *Ownership through a nominee.*—For purposes of this paragraph (b)(4) and paragraph (b)(6) of this section, a person who owns either stock in a foreign corporation seeking qualified resident status or an interest in an intermediary described in paragraph (b)(4)(i)(C) of this section through a nominee shall be treated as owning such stock or interest directly and must, therefore, provide the information described in paragraphs (b)(4)(i) through (iv) of this section, as applicable. Such person must also provide the name and address of the nominee.

(5) *Certificate of residency.*—A certificate of residency must be signed by the relevant authorities (as described below) of the country of residence of the individual shareholder and must state that the individual is a resident of that country for purposes of its income tax laws or, if the authorities do not customarily make such a determination, that the individual has filed a tax return claiming resident status and subjecting the individual's income to tax on a resident basis for the taxable year or period that ends with or within the taxable year for which the corporation is seeking qualified resident status. In the case of an individual who is not legally required to file a tax return in his or her country of residence or in any other country, a certificate of residency of a parent or guardian residing at such individual's address shall be considered sufficient to meet that individual's obligation under this paragraph (b)(5). The relevant authorities shall be the competent authority of the foreign country of which the foreign corporation is a resident, as defined in the income tax treaty between the foreign country and the United States, or such other governmental office of the foreign country (or political subdivision thereof) that customarily provides statements of residence. Notwithstanding the foregoing, the Commissioner may consult with the competent authority of a country regarding the procedures set forth in this paragraph (b)(5) and if necessary agree on additional or alternative procedures under which these certificates may be issued.

(6) *Intermediary ownership statement.*—An intermediary ownership statement is a written statement signed under penalties of perjury by the intermediary (if the intermediary is an individual) or a person that would be authorized to sign a tax return on behalf of the intermediary (if the intermediary is not an individual) containing the following information:

(i) The name, address, country of residence, and principal place of business (in the case of a corporation or partnership) of the intermediary and, if the intermediary is a trust or estate, the name and permanent address of all trustees or executors (or equivalent under foreign law);

(ii) The information described in paragraphs (b)(4)(i)(B) through (D) (substituting "intermediary making the ownership statement" for "individual") with respect to the intermediary's direct or indirect ownership in the stock in the foreign corporation seeking qualified resident status;

(iii) If the intermediary is a nominee for a qualifying shareholder or another intermediary, the name and permanent address of the qualifying shareholder, or the name and principal place of business of such other intermediary;

(iv) If the intermediary is not a nominee for a qualifying shareholder or another intermediary, the proportionate interest in the intermediary of each direct shareholder, partner, beneficiary, grantor, or other interest holder (or if the direct holder is a nominee, of its beneficial shareholder, partner, beneficiary, grantor, or other interest holder) from which the intermediary received an ownership statement and the period of time during the taxable year for which the interest in the intermediary was owned by such shareholder, partner, beneficiary, grantor or other interest holder. For purposes of this paragraph (b)(6)(iv), the proportionate interest of a person in an intermediary is the percentage interest (by value) held by such person, determined using the principles for attributing ownership in paragraph (b)(2) of this section. If an intermediary is not required to receive an ownership statement from its individual registered shareholders or other interest holders by reason of paragraph (b)(3)(iii) of this section, then it must provide a list of the names and addresses of such registered shareholders or other interest holders and the aggregate proportionate interest in the intermediary of such registered shareholders or other interest holders.

(7) *Intermediary verification statement.*—An intermediary verification statement that may be substituted for certain documentation under paragraph (b)(3)(ii) of this section is a written statement signed under penalties of perjury by the intermediary (if the intermediary is an individual) or by a person that would be authorized to sign a tax return on behalf of the intermediary (if the verifying intermediary is not an individual) containing the following information—

(i) The name, principal place of business, and country of residence of the verifying intermediary;

(ii) A statement that the verifying intermediary has obtained either—

(A) An ownership statement and, if applicable, a certificate of residency from a qualifying shareholder with respect to the foreign corporation seeking qualified resident status, and an intermediary ownership statement from each intermediary standing in the chain of ownership between the verifying intermediary and the qualifying shareholder; or

(B) An intermediary verification statement substituting for the documentation described in paragraph (b)(7)(ii)(A) and an intermediary ownership statement from such intermediary and each intermediary standing in the chain of ownership between such intermediary and the verifying intermediary;

(iii) The proportionate interest (as computed using the documentation described in paragraph (b)(7)(ii) of this section) in the intermediary owned directly or indirectly by qualifying shareholders;

(iv) An agreement to make available to the Commissioner at such time and place as the Commissioner may request the underlying documentation described in paragraph (b)(7)(ii) of this section; and

(v) A specific and valid waiver of any right to bank secrecy or other secrecy under the laws of the country in which the verifying intermediary is located, with respect to any qualifying shareholder ownership statements, certificates of residency, intermediary ownership statements or intermediary verification statements that the verifying intermediary has obtained pursuant to paragraph (b)(7)(ii) of this section.

A foreign corporation may combine, in a single statement, the information in an intermediary ownership statement and the information in an intermediary verification statement.

(8) *Special rules for pension funds.*—(i) *Definitions.*—(A) *Pension fund.*—For purposes of this section, the term "pension fund" shall mean a trust, fund, foundation, or other entity that is established exclusively for the benefit of employees or former employees of one or more employers, the principal purpose of which is to provide retirement, disability, and death benefits to beneficiaries of such entity and persons designated by such beneficiaries in consideration for prior services rendered.

(B) *Beneficiary.*—For purposes of this section, the term "beneficiary" of a pension fund shall mean any person who has made contributions to the pension fund, or on whose behalf contributions have been made, and who is currently receiving retirement, disability, or death benefits from the pension fund or can reasonably be expected to receive such benefits in the future, whether or not the person's right to receive benefits from the fund has vested.

(ii) *Government pension funds.*—An individual who is a beneficiary of a pension fund that would be a controlled entity of a foreign sovereign within the principles of § 1.892-2T(c)(1) of the regulations (relating to pension funds established for the benefit of employees or former employees of a foreign government) shall be treated as a qualifying shareholder of a foreign corporation in which the pension fund owns a direct or indirect interest without having to meet the documentation requirements under paragraph (b)(3)(i)(A) of this section, if the foreign corporation is resident in the country of the foreign sovereign and the trustees, directors, or other administrators of the pension fund provide, with the pension fund's intermediary ownership statement described in paragraph (b)(6) of this section, a written statement that the fund is a controlled entity described in this paragraph (b)(8)(ii). See paragraph (b)(4)(ii) of this section regarding an ownership statement from a pension fund that is an integral part of a foreign government.

(iii) *Non-government pension funds.*—For purposes of this section, an individual who is a beneficiary of a pension fund not described in paragraph (b)(8)(ii) of this section shall be treated as a qualifying shareholder of a foreign corporation owned directly or indirectly by such pension fund without having to meet the documentation requirements under paragraph (b)(3)(i)(A) of this section, if—

(A) The pension fund is administered in the foreign corporation's country of residence and is subject to supervision or regulation by a governmental authority (or other authority delegated to perform such supervision or regulation by a governmental authority) in such country;

(B) The pension fund is generally exempt from income taxation in its country of administration;

(C) The pension fund has 100 or more beneficiaries;

(D) The beneficiary's address, as it appears on the records of the fund, is in the foreign corporation's country of residence or the United States and is not a nonresidential address, such as a post office box or in care of a financial intermediary, and none of the trustees, directors or other administrators of the pension fund know, or have reason to know, that the beneficiary is not an individual resident of such foreign country or the United States;

(E) In the case of a pension fund that has fewer than 500 beneficiaries, the beneficiary's employer provides (if the beneficiary is currently contributing to the fund) to the trustees, directors or other administrators a written statement that the beneficiary is currently employed in the country in which the fund is administered or is usually employed in such country but is temporarily employed by the company outside of the country; and

(F) The trustees, directors or other administrators of the pension fund provide, with the pension fund's intermediary ownership statement described in paragraph (b)(6) of this section, a written statement signed under penalties of perjury declaring that the pension fund meets the requirements in paragraphs (b)(8)(iii)(A), (B) and (C) of this section and giving the number of beneficiaries who meet the requirements of paragraph (b)(8)(iii)(D) of this section, and, if applicable, paragraph (b)(8)(iii)(E) of this section.

(iv) *Computation of beneficial interests in nongovernment pension funds.*—The number of shares in a foreign corporation that are held indirectly by beneficiaries of a pension fund who are qualifying shareholders may be computed based on the ratio of the number of such beneficiaries to all beneficiaries of the pension fund (rather than on the basis of the rules in paragraph (b)(2) of this section) if—

(A) The pension fund meets the requirements of paragraphs (b)(8)(iii)(A), (B) and (C) of this section;

(B) The trustees, directors or other administrators of the pension fund have no knowledge, and no reason to know, that the ratio of the pension fund's beneficiaries who are residents of either the country in which the pension fund is administered or of the United States to all beneficiaries of the pension fund would differ significantly from the ratio of the sum of the actuarial interests of such residents in the pension fund to the actuarial interests of all beneficiaries in the pension fund (or, if the beneficiaries' actuarial interest in the stock held directly or indirectly by the pension fund differs from the beneficiaries's actuarial interest in the pension fund, the ratio of actuarial interests computed by reference to the beneficiaries' actuarial interest in the stock);

(C) Either—

(1) Any overfunding of the pension fund would be payable, pursuant to the governing instrument or the laws of the foreign country in which the pension fund is administered, only to, or for the benefit of, one or more corporations that are qualified residents of the country in which the pension fund is administered, individual beneficiaries of the pension fund or their designated beneficiaries, or social or charitable causes (the reduction of the obligation of the sponsoring company or companies to make future contributions to the pension fund by reason of overfunding shall not itself result in such overfunding being deemed to be payable to or for the benefit of such company or companies); or

(2) The foreign country in which the pension fund is administered has laws that are designed to prevent overfunding of a pension fund and the funding of the pension fund is within the guidelines of such laws; or

(3) The pension fund is maintained to provide benefits to employees in a particular industry, profession, or group of industries or professions and employees of at least 10 companies (other than companies that are owned or controlled, directly or indirectly, by the same interests) contribute to the pension fund or receive benefits from the pension fund; and

(D) The trustees, directors or other administrators provide, with the pension fund's intermediary ownership statement described in paragraph (b)(6) of this section, a written statement signed under penalties of perjury certifying that the requirements in paragraphs (b)(8)(iv)(A), (B), and either (C)(*1*), (C)(*2*) or (C)(*3*) of this section have been met.

The statement described in paragraph (b)(8)(iv)(D) of this section may be combined, in a single statement, with the information required in paragraph (b)(8)(iii)(F) of this section.

(v) *Time for making determinations.*—The determinations required to be made under this paragraph (b)(8) shall be made using information shown on the records of the pension fund for a date on or after the beginning of the foreign corporation's taxable year to which the determination is relevant.

(9) *Availability of documents for inspection.*—(i) *Retention of documents by the foreign corporation.*—The documentation described in paragraphs (b)(3) and (b)(8) of this section must be retained by the foreign corporation until expiration of the period of limitations for the taxable year to which the documentation relates and must be made available for inspection by the District Director at such time and place as the District Director may request.

(ii) *Retention of documents by an intermediary issuing an intermediary verification statement.*—The documentation upon which an intermediary relies to issue an intermediary verification statement under paragraph (b)(7) of this section must be retained by the intermediary for a period of six years from the date of issuance of the intermediary verification statement and must be made available for inspection by the District Director at such time and place as the District Director may request.

(10) *Examples.*—The application of this paragraph (b) is illustrated by the following examples.

Example 1. Foreign corporation A is a resident of country L, which has an income tax treaty in effect with the United States. Foreign corporation A has one class of stock issued and outstanding consisting of 1,000 shares, which are beneficially owned by the following alien individuals, directly or by application of paragraph (b)(2) of this section:

Individual	Shares owned, directly or indirectly by application of paragraph (b) (2) of this section	Percentage
T—resident of the U.S.	200	20%
U—resident of country L	400	40%
V—resident of country M	100	10%
W—resident of country L	210	21%
X—resident of country N	90	9%
Total	1,000	100%

(i) T owns his 200 shares directly and is a beneficial owner.

(ii) U and V own, respectively, an 80 percent and a 20 percent actuarial interest in foreign trust FT, (which interest does not differ from their respective interests in the stock owned by FT), which beneficially owns 100 percent of the stock of a foreign corporation B with bearer shares, which beneficially owns 500 shares of foreign corporation A. Foreign corporation B is incorporated in a country that does not have an income tax treaty with the United States. The foreign trust has deposited the bearer shares it owns in B with a bank in a foreign country that has an income tax treaty with the United States.

(iii) W beneficially owns all the shares of foreign corporation C, which are registered in the name of individual Z, a nominee, who resides in country L; foreign corporation C beneficially owns a 70 percent interest in foreign corporation D, which beneficially owns 300 shares of A. D's shares are bearer shares that C (not a resident of a country with which the United States has an income tax treaty) has deposited with a bank in a foreign country that has an income tax treaty with the United States.

(iv) X beneficially owns a 30 percent interest in foreign corporation D.

(v) A is a qualified resident of country L if it obtains the applicable documentation described in paragraph (b)(3) of this section either with respect to ownership by individuals U and W or with respect to ownership by individuals T and U, since either combination of qualifying shareholders of foreign corporation A will exceed 50 percent.

Example 2. Assume the same facts as in *Example 1* and assume that foreign corporation A chooses to obtain documentation with respect to individuals T and U.

(i) A must obtain, pursuant to paragraph (b)(3)(i) of this section, an ownership statement (as described in paragraph (b)(4)(i) of this section) signed by T. T is not required to furnish a certificate of residency because T is a U.S. resident.

Reg. § 1.884-5(b)(10)

(ii) U must provide foreign trust FT with an ownership statement and certificate of residency, as described in paragraphs (b)(4) and (b)(5) of this section. The trustees of FT must provide the depository bank holding foreign corporation B's bearer shares with an intermediary ownership statement concerning its beneficial ownership of B's shares and must attach to it the documentation provided by U. The depository bank must provide B with an intermediary ownership statement regarding its holding of B shares on behalf of FT and has the choice of attaching—

(A) The documentation from U and the intermediary ownership statement from FT; or

(B) An intermediary verification statement described in paragraph (b)(7) of this section, in which case foreign corporation B would not be provided with U's individual documentation or FT's intermediary ownership statement, both of which are retained by the depository bank.

(iii) In either case, B must then provide foreign corporation A with an intermediary ownership statement regarding its direct beneficial ownership of shares in A and, as the case may be, either—

(A) U's documentation and the intermediary ownership statements by FT and the depository bank; or

(B) The depository bank's intermediary ownership and verification statements.

(iv) Thus, with respect to U, A must obtain under paragraph (b)(3)(i) of this section the individual documentation regarding U and an intermediary ownership statement from each intermediary standing in the chain of U's indirect beneficial ownership of shares in A, *i.e.*, from FT, the depository bank and B. In the alternative, A must obtain under paragraph (b)(3)(ii) of this section an intermediary verification statement issued by the depository bank and an intermediary ownership statement from the bank and from B, which, in this example, are the only intermediaries standing in the chain of ownership of the verifying intermediary (*i.e.*, the depository bank).

Example 3. Assume the same facts as in *Example 1.* In addition, assume that foreign corporation A chooses to obtain documentation with respect to individuals U and W. With respect to U, A must obtain the same documentation that is described in *Example 2.* With respect to W, A must obtain, under paragraph (b)(3)(i) of this section, individual documentation regarding W and an intermediary ownership statement from each intermediary standing in the chain of W's indirect beneficial ownership of shares in A, *i.e.*, from individual Z, foreign corporation C, the depository bank in the foreign treaty country, and foreign corporation D. In the alternative, A must obtain, under paragraph (b)(3)(ii) of this section, either—

(i) An intermediary verification statement by the depository bank in the foreign treaty country and an intermediary ownership statement from the bank and from D; or

(ii) An intermediary verification statement from Z and an intermediary ownership statement from Z and from each intermediary standing in the chain of ownership of shares in foreign corporation A, *i.e.*, from C, the depository bank in the foreign treaty country and D. C may not issue an intermediary verification statement because it is not a resident of a country with which the United States has an income tax treaty.

(c) *Base erosion.*—A foreign corporation satisfies the requirement relating to base erosion for a taxable year if it establishes that less than 50 percent of its income for the taxable year is used (directly or indirectly) to make deductible payments in the current taxable year to persons who are not residents (or, in the case of foreign corporations, qualified residents) of the foreign country of which the foreign corporation is a resident and who are not citizens or residents (or, in the case of domestic corporations, qualified residents) of the United States. Whether a domestic corporation is a qualified resident of the United States shall be determined under the principles of this section. For purposes of this paragraph (c), the term "deductible payments" includes payments that would be ordinarily deductible under U.S. income tax principles without regard to other provisions of the Code that may require the capitalization of the expense, or disallow or defer the deduction. Such payments include, for example, interest, rents, royalties and reinsurance premiums. For purposes of this paragraph (c), the income of a foreign corporation means the corporation's gross income for the taxable year (or, if the foreign corporation has no gross income for the taxable year, the average of its gross income for the three previous taxable years) under U.S. tax principles, but not excluding items of income otherwise excluded from gross income under U.S. tax principles.

(d) *Publicly-traded corporations.*—(1) *General rule.*—A foreign corporation that is a resident of a foreign country shall be treated as a qualified resident of that country for any taxable year in which—

(i) Its stock is primarily and regularly traded (as defined in paragraphs (d)(3) and (4) of this section) on one or more established securities markets (as defined in paragraph (d)(2) of this section) in that country, or in the United States, or both; or

(ii) At least 90 percent of the total combined voting power of all classes of stock of such foreign corporation entitled to vote and at least 90 percent of the total value of the stock of such foreign corporation is owned, directly or by application of paragraph (b)(2) of this section, by a foreign corporation that is a resident of the same foreign country or a domestic corporation and the stock of such parent corporation is primarily and regularly traded on an established securities market in that foreign country or in the United States, or both.

(2) *Established securities market.*—(i) *General rule.*—For purposes of section 884, the term "established securities market" means, for any taxable year—

(A) A foreign securities exchange that is officially recognized, sanctioned, or supervised by a governmental authority of the country in which the market is located, is the principal exchange in that country, and has an annual value of shares traded on the exchange exceeding $1 billion during each of the three calendar years immediately preceding the beginning of the taxable year;

(B) A national securities exchange that is registered under section 6 of the Securities Act of 1934 (15 U.S.C. 78f); and

(C) A domestic over-the-counter market (as defined in paragraph (d)(2)(iv) of this section).

(ii) *Exchanges with multiple tiers.*—If a principal exchange in a foreign country has more than one tier or market level on which stock may be separately listed or traded, each such tier shall be treated as a separate exchange.

(iii) *Computation of dollar value of stock traded.*—For purposes of paragraph (d)(2)(i)(A) of this section, the value in U.S. dollars of shares traded during a calendar year shall be determined on the basis of the dollar value of such shares traded as reported by the International Federation of Stock Exchanges, located in Paris, or, if not so reported, then by converting into U.S. dollars the aggregate value in local currency of the shares traded using an exchange rate equal to the average of the spot rates on the last day of each month of the calendar year.

(iv) *Definition of over-the-counter market.*—An over-the-counter market is any market reflected by the existence of an interdealer quotation system. An interdealer quotation system is any system of general circulation to brokers and dealers that regularly disseminates quotations of stocks and securities by identified brokers or dealers, other than by quotation sheets that are prepared and distributed by a broker or dealer in the regular course of business and that contain only quotations of such broker or dealer.

(v) *Discretion to determine that an exchange qualifies as an established securities market.*—The Commissioner may, in his sole discretion, determine in a published document that a securities exchange that does not meet the requirements of paragraph (d)(2)(i)(A) of this section qualifies as an established securities market. Such a determination will be made only if it is established that—

(A) The exchange, in substance, has the attributes of an established securities market (including adequate trading volume, and comparable listing and financial disclosure requirements);

(B) The rules of the exchange ensure active trading of listed stocks; and

(C) The exchange is a member of the International Federation of Stock Exchanges.

(vi) *Discretion to determine that an exchange does not qualify as an established securities market.*—The Commissioner may, in his sole discretion, determine in a published document that a securities exchange that meets the requirements of paragraph (d)(2)(i) of this section does not qualify as an established securities market. Such determination shall be made if, in the view of the Commissioner—

(A) The exchange does not have adequate listing, financial disclosure, or trading requirements (or does not adequately enforce such requirements); or

(B) There is not clear and convincing evidence that the exchange ensures the active trading of listed stocks.

(3) *Primarily traded.*—For purposes of this section, stock of a corporation is "primarily traded" on one or more established securities markets in the corporation's country of residence or in the United States in any taxable year if, with respect to each class described in paragraph (d)(4)(i)(A) of this section (relating to classes of stock relied on to meet the regularly traded test)—

(i) The number of shares in each such class that are traded during the taxable year on all established securities markets in the corporation's country of residence or in the United States during the taxable year exceeds

(ii) The number of shares in each such class that are traded during that year on established securities markets in any other single foreign country.

(4) *Regularly traded.*—(i) *General rule.*—For purposes of this section, stock of a corporation is "regularly traded" on one or more established securities markets in the foreign

Reg. §1.884-5(d)(4)(i)

corporation's country of residence or in the United States for the taxable year if—

(A) One or more classes of stock of the corporation that, in the aggregate, represent 80 percent or more of the total combined voting power of all classes of stock of such corporation entitled to vote and of the total value of the stock of such corporation are listed on such market or markets during the taxable year;

(B) With respect to each class relied on to meet the 80 percent requirement of paragraph (d)(4)(i)(A) of this section—

(1) Trades in each such class are effected, other than in *de minimis* quantities, on such market or markets on at least 60 days during the taxable year (or 1/6 of the number of days in a short taxable year); and

(2) The aggregate number of shares in each such class that is traded on such market or markets during the taxable year is at least 10 percent of the average number of shares outstanding in that class during the taxable year (or, in the case of a short taxable year, a percentage that equals at least 10 percent of the number of days in the short taxable year divided by 365).

If stock of a foreign corporation fails the 80 percent requirement of paragraph (d)(4)(i)(A) of this section, but a class of such stock meets the trading requirements of paragraph (d)(4)(i)(B) of this section, such class of stock may be taken into account under paragraph (b)(1)(iii) of this section as owned by qualifying shareholders for purposes of meeting the ownership test of paragraph (b)(1) of this section.

(ii) *Classes of stock traded on a domestic established securities market treated as meeting trading requirements.*—A class of stock that is traded during the taxable year on an established securities market located in the United States shall be treated as meeting the trading requirements of paragraph (d)(4)(i)(B) of this section if the stock is regularly quoted by brokers or dealers making a market in the stock. A broker or dealer makes a market in a stock only if the broker or dealer holds himself out to buy or sell the stock at the quoted price.

(iii) *Closely-held classes of stock not treated as meeting trading requirement.*—(A) *General rule.*—A class of stock shall not be treated as meeting the trading requirements of paragraph (d)(4)(i)(B) of this section (or the requirements of paragraph (d)(4)(ii) of this section) for a taxable year if, at any time during the taxable year, one or more persons who are not qualifying shareholders (as defined in paragraph (b)(1) of this section) and who each beneficially own 5 percent or more of the value of the outstanding shares of the class of stock own, in the aggregate, 50 percent or more of the outstanding shares of the class of stock for more than 30 days during the taxable year. For purposes of the preceding sentence, shares shall not be treated as owned by a qualifying shareholder unless such shareholder provides to the foreign corporation, by the time prescribed in paragraph (b)(3) of this section, the documentation described in paragraph (b)(3) of this section necessary to establish that it is a qualifying shareholder. For purposes of this paragraph (d)(4)(iii)(A), shares of stock owned by a pension fund, as defined in paragraph (b)(8)(i)(A) of this section, shall be treated as beneficially owned by the beneficiaries of such fund, as defined in paragraph (b)(8)(i)(B) of this section.

(B) *Treatment of related persons.*—Persons related within the meaning of section 267(b) shall be treated as one person for purposes of this paragraph (d)(4)(iii). In determining whether two or more corporations are members of the same controlled group under section 267(b)(3), a person is considered to own stock owned directly by such person, stock owned with the application of section 1563(e)(1), and stock owned with the application of section 267(c). Further, in determining whether a corporation is related to a partnership under section 267(b)(10), a person is considered to own the partnership interest owned directly by such person and the partnership interest owned with the application of section 267(e)(3).

(iv) *Anti-abuse rule.*—Trades between persons described in section 267(b) (as modified in paragraph (d)(4)(iii)(B) of this section) and trades conducted in order to meet the requirements of paragraph (d)(4)(i)(B) of this section shall be disregarded. A class of stock shall not be treated as meeting the trading requirements of paragraph (d)(4)(i)(B) of this section if there is a pattern of trades conducted to meet the requirements of that paragraph. For example, trades between two persons that occur several times during the taxable year may be treated as an arrangement or a pattern of trades conducted to meet the trading requirements of paragraph (d)(4)(i)(B) of this section.

(5) *Burden of proof for publicly-traded corporations.*—A foreign corporation that relies on this paragraph (d) to establish that it is a qualified resident of a country with which the United States has an income tax treaty shall have the burden of proving all the facts necessary for the corporation to be treated as a qualified resident, except that with respect to paragraphs (d)(4)(iii) and (iv) of this section, a

foreign corporation, with either registered or bearer shares, will meet the burden of proof if it has no reason to know and no actual knowledge of facts that would cause the corporation's stock not to be treated as regularly traded under such paragraphs. A foreign corporation that has shareholders of record must also maintain a list of such shareholders and, on request, make available to the District Director such list and any other relevant information known to the foreign corporation.

(e) *Active trade or business.*—(1) *General rule.*—A foreign corporation that is a resident of a foreign country shall be treated as a qualified resident of that country with respect to any U.S. trade or business if, during the taxable year—

(i) It is engaged in the active conduct of a trade or business (as defined in paragraph (e)(2) of this section) in its country of residence;

(ii) It has a substantial presence (within the meaning of paragraph (e)(3) of this section) in its country of residence; and

(iii) Either—

(A) Such U.S. trade or business is an integral part (as defined in paragraph (e)(4) of this section) of an active trade or business conducted by the foreign corporation in its country of residence; or

(B) In the case of interest received by the foreign corporation for which a treaty exemption or rate reduction is claimed pursuant to § 1.884-4(b)(8)(ii), the interest is derived in connection with, or is incidental to, a trade or business described in paragraph (e)(1)(i) of this section.

A foreign corporation may determine whether it is a qualified resident under this paragraph (e) by applying the rules of this paragraph (e) to the entire affiliated group (as defined in section 1504(a) without regard to section 1504(b)(2) or (3)) of which the foreign corporation is a member rather than to the foreign corporation separately. If a foreign corporation chooses to apply the rules of this paragraph (e) to its entire affiliated group as provided in the preceding sentence, then it must apply such rules consistently to all of its U.S. trades or businesses conducted during the taxable year.

(2) *Active conduct of a trade or business.*—A foreign corporation is engaged in the active conduct of a trade or business only if either—

(i) It is engaged in the active conduct of a trade or business within the meaning of section 367(a)(3) and the regulations thereunder; or

(ii) It qualifies as a banking or financing institution under the laws of the foreign country of which it is a resident, it is licensed to do business with residents of its country of residence, and it is engaged in the active conduct of a banking, financing, or similar business within the meaning of § 1.864-4(c)(5)(i) in its country of residence.

A foreign corporation that is an insurance company within the meaning of § 1.801-3(a) or (b) is engaged in the active conduct of a trade or business only if it is predominantly engaged in the active conduct of an insurance business within the meaning of section 952(c)(1)(B)(v) and the regulations thereunder.

(3) *Substantial presence test.*—(i) *General rule.*—Except as provided in paragraph (e)(3)(ii) of this section, a foreign corporation that is engaged in the active conduct of a trade or business in its country of residence has a substantial presence in that country if, for the taxable year, the average of the following three ratios exceeds 25 percent and each ratio is at least equal to 20 percent—

(A) The ratio of the value of the assets of the foreign corporation used or held for use in the active conduct of a trade or business in its country of residence at the close of the taxable year to the value of all assets of the foreign corporation at the close of the taxable year;

(B) The ratio of gross income from the active conduct of the foreign corporation's trade or business in its country of residence that is derived from sources within such country for the taxable year to the worldwide gross income of the foreign corporation for the taxable year; and

(C) The ratio of the payroll expenses in the foreign corporation's country of residence for the taxable year to the foreign corporation's worldwide payroll expenses for the taxable year.

(ii) *Special rules.*—(A) *Asset ratio.*—For purposes of paragraph (e)(3)(i)(A) of this section, the value of an asset shall be determined using the method used by the taxpayer in keeping its books for purposes of financial reporting in its country of residence. An asset shall be treated as used or held for use in a foreign corporation's trade or business if it meets the requirements of § 1.367(a)-2T(b)(5). Stock held by a foreign corporation shall not be treated as an asset of the foreign corporation for purposes of paragraph (e)(3)(i)(A) of this section if the foreign corporation owns 10 percent or more of the total combined voting power of all classes of stock of such corporation entitled to vote. The rules of § 1.954-2T(b)(3) (other than § 1.954-2T(b)(3)(x)) shall apply to determine the location of assets used or held for use in a trade or business. Loans originated or acquired in the course of the normal customer loan activities of a banking, financing or similar institution, and securities and derivative financial instruments held by dealers, traders and insurance companies for use in a trade or business shall be treated as located in the country in which an office or other fixed place of business is primarily responsible for the acquisition of the asset and the realization of income, gain or loss with respect to the asset.

(B) *Gross income ratio.*—*(1) General rule.*—For purposes of paragraph (e)(3)(i)(B) of this section, the term "gross income" means the gross income of a foreign corporation for purposes of financial reporting in its country of residence. Gross income shall not include, however, dividends, interest, rents, or royalties unless such corporation derives such dividends, interest, rents, or royalties in the active conduct of its trade or business. Gross income shall also not include gain from the disposition of stock if the foreign corporation owns 10 percent or more of the total combined voting power of all classes of stock of such corporation entitled to vote. Except as provided in this paragraph (e)(3)(ii)(B), the principles of sections 861 through 865 shall apply to determine the amount of gross income of a foreign corporation derived within its country of residence.

(2) Banks, dealers and traders.—Dividend income and gain from the sale of securities, or from entering into or disposing of derivative financial instruments by dealers and traders in such securities or derivative financial instruments shall be treated as derived within the country where the assets are located under paragraph (e)(3)(ii)(A) of this section. Other income, including interest and fees, earned in the active conduct of a banking, financing or similar business shall be treated as derived within the country where the payor of such interest or other income resides. For purposes of the preceding sentence, if a branch or similar establishment outside the country in which the payor resides makes a payment of interest or other income, such amounts shall be treated as derived within the country in which the branch or similar establishment is located.

(3) Insurance companies.—The gross income of a foreign insurance company shall include only gross premiums received by the company.

(4) Other corporations.—Gross income from the performance of services, including transportation services, shall be treated as derived within the country of residence of the person for whom the services are performed. Gross income from the sale of property by a foreign corporation shall be treated as derived within the country in which the purchaser resides.

(5) Anti-abuse rule.—The Commissioner may disregard the source of income from a transaction determined under this paragraph (e)(3)(ii)(B) if it is determined that one of the principal purposes of the transaction was to increase the source of income derived within the country of residence of the foreign corporation for purposes of this section.

(C) *Payroll ratio.*—For purposes of paragraph (e)(3)(i)(C) of this section, the payroll expenses of a foreign corporation shall include expenses for "leased employees" (within the meaning of section 414(n)(2) but without regard to subdivision (B) of that section) and commission expenses paid to employees and agents for services performed for or on behalf of the corporation. Payroll expense for an employee, agent or a "leased employee" shall be treated as incurred where the employee, agent or "leased employee" performs services on behalf of the corporation.

(iii) *Exception to gross income test for foreign corporations engaged in certain trades or businesses.*—In determining whether a foreign corporation engaged primarily in selling tangible property or in manufacturing, producing, growing, or extracting tangible property has a substantial presence in its country of residence for purposes of paragraph (e)(3)(i) of this section, the foreign corporation may apply the ratio provided in this paragraph (e)(3)(iii) instead of the ratio described in paragraph (e)(3)(i)(B) of this section (relating to the ratio of gross income derived from its country of residence). This ratio shall be the ratio of the direct material costs of the foreign corporation with respect to tangible property manufactured, produced, grown, or extracted in the foreign corporation's country of residence to the total direct material costs of the foreign corporation.

(4) *Integral part of an active trade or business in a foreign corporation's country of residence.*—(i) *In general.*—A U.S. trade or business of a foreign corporation is an integral part of an active trade or business conducted by a foreign corporation in its country of residence if the active trade or business conducted by the foreign corporation in both its country of residence and in the United States comprise, in principal part, complementary and mutually interdependent steps in the United States and its country of residence in the production and sale or lease of goods or in the provision of services. Subject to the presumption and de minimis rule in paragraphs (e)(4)(iii) and (iv) of this section, if a U.S. trade or business of a foreign corporation sells goods that are not, in principal part,

manufactured, produced, grown, or extracted by the foreign corporation in its country of residence, such business shall not be treated as an integral part of an active trade or business conducted in the foreign corporation's country of residence unless the foreign corporation takes physical possession of the goods in a warehouse or other storage facility that is located in its country of residence and in which goods of such type are normally stored prior to sale to customers in such country.

(ii) *Presumption for banks.*—A U.S. trade or business of a foreign corporation that is described in § 1.884-4(a)(2)(iii) shall be presumed to be an integral part of an active banking business conducted by the foreign corporation in its country of residence provided that a substantial part of the business of the foreign corporation in both its country of residence and the United States consists of receiving deposits and making loans and discounts. This paragraph shall be effective for taxable years beginning on or after June 6, 1996.

(iii) *Presumption if business principally conducted in country of residence.*—A U.S. trade or business of a foreign corporation shall be treated as an integral part of an active trade or business of a foreign corporation in its country of residence with respect to the sale or lease of property (or the performance of services) if at least 50 percent of the foreign corporation's worldwide gross income from the sale or lease of property of the type sold in the United States (or from the performance of services of the type performed in the United States) is derived from the sale or lease of such property for consumption, use, or disposition in the foreign corporation's country of residence (or from the performance of such services in the foreign corporation's country of residence). In determining whether property or services are of the same type, a foreign corporation shall follow recognized industry or trade usage or the three-digit major groups (or any narrower classification) of the Standard Industrial Classification as prepared by the Statistical Policy Division of the Office of Management and Budget, Executive Office of the President. The determination of whether income is of the same kind must be made in a consistent manner from year to year.

(iv) *De minimis rule.*—If a foreign corporation is engaged in more than one U.S. trade or business and if at least 80 percent of the sum of the ECEP from the current year and the preceding two years is attributable to one or more trades or businesses that meet the integral part test of this paragraph (e)(4), all of the U.S. trades or businesses of the foreign corporation shall be treated as an integral part of an active trade or business conducted by the foreign corporation. If a foreign corporation has more than one U.S. trade or business and does not meet the requirements of the preceding sentence but otherwise meets the requirements of this paragraph (e)(4) with regard to one or more trade or business, see § 1.884-1(g)(1) to determine the extent to which treaty benefits apply to such corporation.

(f) *Qualified resident ruling.*—(1) *Basis for ruling.*—In his or her sole discretion, the Commissioner may rule that a foreign corporation is a qualified resident of its country of residence if the Commissioner determines that individuals who are not residents of the foreign country of which the foreign corporation is a resident do not use the treaty between that country and the United States in a manner inconsistent with the purposes of section 884. The purposes of section 884 include, but are not limited to, the prevention of treaty shopping by an individual with respect to any article of an income tax treaty between the country of residence of the foreign corporation and the United States.

(2) *Factors.*—In order to make this determination, the Commissioner may take into account the following factors, including, but not limited to:

(i) The business reasons for establishing and maintaining the foreign corporation in its country of residence;

(ii) The date of incorporation of the foreign corporation in relation to the date that an income tax treaty between the United States and the foreign corporation's country of residence entered into force;

(iii) The continuity of the historical business and ownership of the foreign corporation;

(iv) The extent to which the foreign corporation meets the requirements of one or more of the tests described in paragraphs (b) through (e) of this section;

(v) The extent to which the U.S. trade or business is dependent on capital, assets, or personnel of the foreign trade or business;

(vi) The extent to which the foreign corporation receives special tax benefits in its country of residence;

(vii) Whether the foreign corporation is a member of an affiliated group (as defined in section 1504(a) without regard to section 1504(b)(2) or (3)), that has no members resident outside the country of residence of the foreign corporation; and

(viii) The extent to which the foreign corporation would be entitled to comparable treaty benefits with respect to all articles of an income tax treaty that would apply to that corporation if it had been incorporated in the country or countries of residence of the majority of

Reg. § 1.884-5(f)(2)(viii)

its shareholders. For purposes of the preceding sentence, shareholders taken into account shall generally be limited to persons described in paragraph (b)(1)(i) of this section but for the fact that they are not residents of the foreign corporation's country of residence.

(3) *Procedural requirements.*—A request for a ruling under this paragraph (f) must be submitted on or before the due date (including extensions) of the foreign corporation's income tax return for the taxable year for which the ruling is requested. A foreign corporation receiving a ruling will be treated as a qualified resident of its country of residence for the taxable year for which the ruling is requested and for the succeeding two taxable years. If there is a material change in any fact that formed the basis of the ruling, such as the ownership or the nature of the trade or business of the foreign corporation, the foreign corporation must notify the Secretary within 90 days of such change and submit a new private letter ruling request. The Commissioner will then rule whether the change affects the foreign corporation's status as a qualified resident, and such ruling will be valid for the taxable year in which the material change occurred and the two succeeding taxable years, subject to the requirement in the preceding sentence to notify the Commissioner of a material change.

(g) *Effective dates.*—Except as provided in paragraph (e)(4)(ii) of this section, this section is effective for taxable years beginning on or after October 13, 1992.

(h) *Transition rule.*—If a foreign corporation elects to apply this section in lieu of § 1.884-5T (as contained in the CFR edition revised as of April 1, 1992) as provided in paragraph (g) of this section, and the application of paragraph (b) of this section results in additional documentation requirements in order for the foreign corporation to be treated as a qualified resident, the foreign corporation must obtain the documentation required under that paragraph on or before March 11, 1993. [Reg. § 1.884-5.]

☐ [*T.D.* 8432, 9-10-92. *Amended by T.D.* 8657, 3-5-96.]

§ 1.892-1T. Purpose and scope of regulations (Temporary).

—(a) *In general.*—These regulations provide guidance with respect to the taxation of income derived by foreign governments and international organizations from sources within the United States. Under section 892, certain specific types of income received by foreign governments are excluded from gross income and are exempt, unless derived from the conduct of a commercial activity or received from or by a controlled commercial entity. This section sets forth the effective date of the regulations. Section 1.892-2T defines a foreign government. In particular it describes the extent to which either an integral part of a foreign sovereign or an entity which is not an integral part of a foreign sovereign will be treated as a foreign government for purposes of section 892. Section 1.892-3T describes the types of income that generally qualify for exemption and certain limitations on the exemption. Section 1.892-4T provides rules concerning the characterization of activities as commercial activities. Section 1.892-5T defines a controlled commercial entity. Section 1.892-6T sets forth the extent to which income of international organizations from sources within the United States is excluded from gross income and is exempt from taxation. Section 1.892-7T sets forth the relationship of section 892 to other Internal Revenue Code sections.

(b) *Effective date.*—The regulations set forth in §§ 1.892-1T through 1.892-7T apply to income received by a foreign government on or after July 1, 1986. No amount of income shall be required to be deducted and withheld, by reason of the amendment of section 892 by section 1247 of the Tax Reform Act of 1986 (Pub.L. 99-514, 100 Stat. 2085, 2583) from any payment made before October 22, 1986. [Temporary Reg. § 1.892-1T.]

☐ [*T.D.* 8211, 6-24-88.]

§ 1.892-2T. Foreign government defined (Temporary).

—(a) *Foreign government.*—(1) *Definition.*—The term "foreign government" means only the integral parts or controlled entities of a foreign sovereign.

(2) *Integral part.*—An "integral part" of a foreign sovereign is any person, body of persons, organization, agency, bureau, fund, instrumentality, or other body, however designated, that constitutes a governing authority of a foreign country. The net earnings of the governing authority must be credited to its own account or to other accounts of the foreign sovereign, with no portion inuring to the benefit of any private person. An integral part does not include any individual who is a sovereign, official, or administrator acting in a private or personal capacity. Consideration of all the facts and circumstances will determine whether an individual is acting in a private or personal capacity.

(3) *Controlled entity.*—The term "controlled entity" means an entity that is separate in form from a foreign sovereign or otherwise constitutes a separate juridical entity if it satisfies the following requirements:

(i) It is wholly owned and controlled by a foreign sovereign directly or indirectly through one or more controlled entities;

(ii) It is organized under the laws of the foreign sovereign by which owned;

(iii) Its net earnings are credited to its own account or to other accounts of the foreign sovereign, with no portion of its income inuring to the benefit of any private person; and

(iv) Its assets vest in the foreign sovereign upon dissolution.

A controlled entity does not include partnerships or any other entity owned and controlled by more than one foreign sovereign. Thus, a foreign financial organization organized and wholly owned and controlled by several foreign sovereigns to foster economic, financial, and technical cooperation between various foreign nations is not a controlled entity for purposes of this section.

(b) *Inurement to the benefit of private persons.*—For purposes of this section, income will be presumed not to inure to the benefit of private persons if such persons (within the meaning of section 7701(a)(1)) are the intended beneficiaries of a governmental program which is carried on by the foreign sovereign and the activities of which constitute governmental functions (within the meaning of § 1.892-4T(c)(4)). Income will be considered to inure to the benefit of private persons if such income benefits:

(1) Private persons through the use of a governmental entity as a conduit for personal investment; or

(2) Private persons who divert such income from its intended use by the exertion of influence or control through means explicitly or implicitly approved of by the foreign sovereign.

(c) *Pension trusts.*—(1) *In general.*—A controlled entity includes a separately organized pension trust if it meets the following requirements:

(i) The trust is established exclusively for the benefit of (A) employees or former employees of a foreign government or (B) employees or former employees of a foreign government and non-governmental employees or former employees that perform or performed governmental or social services;

(ii) The funds that comprise the trust are managed by trustees who are employees of, or persons appointed by, the foreign government;

(iii) The trust forming a part of the pension plan provides for retirement, disability, or death benefits in consideration for prior services rendered; and

(iv) Income of the trust satisfies the obligations of the foreign government to participants under the plan, rather than inuring to the benefit of a private person.

Income of a pension trust is subject to the rules of § 1.892-5T(b)(3) regarding the application of the rules for controlled commercial entities to pension trusts. Income of a superannuation or similar pension fund of an integral part or controlled entity (which is not a separate pension trust as defined in this paragraph (c)(1)) is subject to the rules that generally apply to a foreign sovereign. Such a pension fund may also benefit non-governmental employees or former employees that perform or performed governmental or social services.

(2) *Illustrations.*—The following examples illustrate the application of paragraph (c)(1).

Example (1). The Ministry of Welfare (MW), an integral part of foreign sovereign FC, instituted a retirement plan for FC's employees and former employees. Retirement benefits under the plan are based on a percentage of the final year's salary paid to an individual, times the number of years of government service. Pursuant to the plan, contributions are made by MW to a pension trust managed by persons appointed by MW to the extent actuarially necessary to fund accrued pension liabilities. The pension trust in turn invests such contributions partially in United States Treasury obligations. The income of the trust is credited to the trust's account and subsequently used to satisfy the pension plan's obligations to retired employees. Under these circumstances, the income of the trust is not deemed to inure to the benefit of private persons. Accordingly, the trust is considered a controlled entity of FC.

Example (2). The facts are the same as in *Example* (1), except that the retirement plan also benefits employees performing governmental or social services for the following non-government institutions: (i) a university in a local jurisdiction; (ii) a harbor commission; and (iii) a library system. The retirement benefits under the plan are based on the total amounts credited to an individual's account over the term of his or her employment. MW makes annual contributions to each covered employee's account equal to a percentage of annual compensation. In addition, the income derived from investment of the annual contributions is credited annually to individual accounts. The annual contributions do not exceed an amount that is determined to be actuarially necessary to provide the employee with reasonable retirement benefits. Notwithstanding that retirement benefits vary depending upon the investment experience of the trust, no portion of the income of the trust is deemed to inure to the benefit of private persons. Accordingly, the trust is considered a controlled entity of FC.

Example (3). The facts are the same as in *Example* (1), except that employees are allowed to make unlimited contributions to the trust, and such contributions are credited to the employee's account as well as interest accrued on such contributions. Retirement benefits will reflect the amounts credited to the individual accounts in addition to the usual annuity computation based on the final year's salary and years of service. A pension plan established under these rules is in part acting as an investment conduit. As a result, the income of the trust is deemed to inure to the benefit of private persons. Accordingly, the trust is not considered a controlled entity of FC.

Example (4). (a) The facts are the same as in *Example* (2), except that MW establishes a pension fund rather than a separate pension trust. A pension fund is merely assets of an integral part or controlled entity allocated to a separate account and held and invested for purposes of providing retirement benefits. Under these circumstances, the income of the pension fund is not deemed to inure to the benefit of private persons. Accordingly, income earned from the United States Treasury obligations by the pension fund is considered to be received by a foreign government and is exempt from taxation under section 892.

(b) The facts are the same as in *Example* (4)(a), except that MW is a controlled entity of foreign sovereign FC. The result is the same as in *Example* (4)(a). However, should MW engage in commercial activities (whether within or outside the United States), the income from the Treasury obligations earned by the pension fund will not be exempt from taxation under section 892 since MW will be considered a controlled commercial entity within the meaning of § 1.892-5T(a).

(d) *Political subdivision and transnational entity.*—The rules that apply to a foreign sovereign apply to political subdivisions of a foreign country and to transnational entities. A transnational entity is an organization created by more than one foreign sovereign that has broad powers over external and domestic affairs of all participating foreign countries stretching beyond economic subjects to those concerning legal relations and transcending state or political boundaries. [Temporary Reg. § 1.892-2T.]

☐ [*T.D.* 8211, 6-24-88.]

§ 1.892-3T. Income of foreign governments (Temporary).—(a) *Types of income exempt.*—(1) *In general.*—Subject to the exceptions contained in §§ 1.892-4T and 1.892-5T for income derived from the conduct of a commercial activity or received from or by a controlled commercial entity, the following types of income derived by a foreign government (as defined in § 1.892-2T) are not included in gross income and are exempt:

(i) Income from investments in the United States in stocks, bonds, or other securities;

(ii) Income from investments in the United States in financial instruments held in the execution of governmental financial or monetary policy; and

(iii) Interest on deposits in banks in the United States of moneys belonging to such foreign government.

Income derived from sources other than described in this paragraph (such as income earned from a U.S. real property interest described in section 897(c)(1)(A)(i)) is not exempt from taxation under section 892. Furthermore, any gain derived from the disposition of a U.S. real property interest defined in section 897(c)(1)(A)(i) shall in no event qualify for exemption under section 892.

(2) *Income from investments.*—For purposes of paragraph (a) of this section, income from investments in stocks, bonds or other securities includes gain from their disposition and income earned from engaging in section 1058 securities lending transactions. Gain on the disposition of an interest in a partnership or a trust is not exempt from taxation under section 892.

(3) *Securities.*—For purposes of paragraph (a) of this section, the term "other securities" includes any note or other evidence of indebtedness. Thus, an annuity contract, a mortgage, a banker's acceptance or a loan are securities for purposes of this section. However, the term "other securities" does not include partnership interests (with the exception of publicly traded partnerships within the meaning of section 7704) or trust interests. The term also does not include commodity forward or futures contracts and commodity options unless they constitute securities for purposes of section 864(b)(2)(A).

(4) *Financial instrument.*—For purposes of paragraph (a) of this section, the term "financial instrument" includes any forward, futures, options contract, swap agreement or similar instrument in a functional or nonfunctional currency (see section 985(b) for the definition of functional currency) or in precious metals when held by a foreign government or central bank of issue (as defined in § 1.895-1(b)). Nonfunctional currency or gold shall be considered a "financial instrument" also when physically held by a central bank of issue.

(5) *Execution of financial or monetary policy.*—(i) *Rule.*—A financial instrument shall be deemed held in the execution of governmental financial or monetary policy if the primary purpose for holding the instrument is to implement or effectuate such policy.

(ii) *Illustration.*—The following example illustrates the application of this paragraph (a)(5).

Example. In order to ensure sufficient currency reserves, the monetary authority of foreign country FC issues short-term government obligations. The amount received from the obligations is invested in U.S. financial instruments. Since the primary purpose for obtaining the U.S. financial instruments is to implement FC's monetary policy, the income received from the financial instruments is exempt from taxation under section 892.

(b) *Illustrations.*—The principles of paragraph (a) of this section may be illustrated by the following examples.

Example (1). X, a foreign corporation not engaged in commercial activity anywhere in the world, is a controlled entity of a foreign sovereign within the meaning of § 1.892-2T(a)(3). X is not a central bank of issue as defined in § 1.895-1(b). In 1987, X received the following items of income from investments in the United States: (i) dividends from a portfolio of publicly traded stocks in U.S. corporations in which X owns less than 50 percent of the stock; (ii) dividends from BTB Corporation, an automobile manufacturer, in which X owns 50 percent of the stock; (iii) interest from bonds issued by noncontrolled entities and from interest bearing bank deposits in noncontrolled entities; (iv) rents from a net lease on real property; (v) gains from silver futures contracts; (vi) gains from wheat futures contracts; (vii) gains from spot sales of nonfunctional foreign currency in X's possession; (viii) gains from the disposition of a publicly traded partnership interest, and (ix) gains from the disposition of the stock of Z Corporation, a United States real property holding company as defined in section 897, of which X owns 12 percent of the stock. Only income derived from sources described in paragraph (a)(1) of this section is treated as income of a foreign government eligible for exemption from taxation. Accordingly, only income received by X from items (i), (iii), (v) provided that the silver futures contracts are held in the execution of governmental financial or monetary policy, and (ix) is exempt from taxation under section 892.

Example (2). The facts are the same as in *Example (1),* except that X is also a central bank of issue within the meaning of section 895. Since physical possession of nonfunctional foreign currency when held by a central bank of issue is considered a financial instrument, the item (vii) gains from spot sales of nonfunctional foreign currency are exempt from taxation under paragraph (a)(1) of this section, if physical possession of the currency was an essential part of X's reserve policy in the execution of its governmental financial or monetary policy.

Example (3). State Concert Bureau, an integral part of a foreign sovereign within the meaning of § 1.892-2T(a)(2), entered into an agreement with a U.S. corporation engaged in the business of promoting international cultural programs. Under the agreement the State Concert Bureau agreed to send a ballet troupe on tour for 5 weeks in the United States. The Bureau received approximately $60,000 from the performances. Regardless of whether the performances themselves constitute commercial activities under § 1.892-4T, the income received by the Bureau is not exempt from taxation under section 892 since the income is from sources other than described in paragraph (a)(1) of this section. [Temporary Reg. § 1.892-3T.]

☐ [*T.D.* 8211, 6-24-88.]

§ 1.892-4T. Commercial activities (Temporary).—(a) *Purpose.*—The exemption generally applicable to a foreign government (as defined in § 1.892-2T) for income described in § 1.892-3T does not apply to income derived from the conduct of a commercial activity or income received by a controlled commercial entity or received (directly or indirectly) from a controlled commercial entity. This section provides rules for determining whether income is derived from the conduct of a commercial activity. These rules also apply in determining under § 1.892-5T whether an entity is a controlled commercial entity.

(b) *In general.*—Except as provided in paragraph (c) of this section, all activities (whether conducted within or outside the United States) which are ordinarily conducted by the taxpayer or by other persons with a view towards the current or future production of income or gain are commercial activities. An activity may be considered a commercial activity even if such activity does not constitute the conduct of a trade or business in the United States under section 864(b).

(c) *Activities that are not commercial.*—(1) *Investments.*—(i) *In general.*—Subject to the provisions of paragraphs (ii) and (iii) of this paragraph (c)(1), the following are not commercial activities: investments in stock, bonds, and other securities; loans; investments in financial instruments held in the execution of governmental financial or monetary policy; the holding of net leases on real property or land which is not producing income (other than on its sale or from an investment in net leases on real property); and the holding of bank deposits in banks. Transferring securities under a loan agreement which meets the requirements of section 1058 is an investment for purposes of this paragraph (c)(1)(i). An activity will not cease to be an investment solely because of the volume of transactions of that activity or because of other unrelated activities.

(ii) *Trading.*—Effecting transactions in stocks, securities, or commodities for a foreign government's own account does not constitute a commercial activity regardless of whether such activities constitute a trade or business for purposes of section 162 or a U.S. trade or business for purposes of section 864. Such transactions are not commercial activities regardless of whether they are effected by the foreign government through its employees or through a broker, commission agent, custodian, or other independent agent and regardless of whether or not any such employee or agent has discretionary authority to make decisions in effecting the transactions. An activity undertaken as a dealer, however as defined in § 1.864-2(c)(2)(iv)(*a*) will not be an investment for purposes of this paragraph (c)(1)(i). For purposes of this paragraph (c)(1)(ii), the term "commodities" means commodities of a kind customarily dealt in on an organized commodity exchange but only if the transaction is of a kind customarily consummated at such place.

(iii) *Banking, financing, etc.*—Investments (including loans) made by a banking, financing, or similar business constitute commercial activities, even if the income derived from such investments is not considered to be income effectively connected to the active conduct of a banking, financing, or similar business in the U.S. by reason of the application of § 1.864-4(c)(5).

(2) *Cultural events.*—Performances and exhibitions within or outside the United States of amateur athletic events and events devoted to the promotion of the arts by cultural organizations are not commercial activities.

(3) *Non-profit activities.*—Activities that are not customarily attributable to or carried on by private enterprise for profit are not commercial activities. The fact that in some instances Federal, State, or local governments of the United States also are engaged in the same or similar activity does not mean necessarily that it is a non-profit activity. For example, even though the United States Government may be engaged in the activity of operating a railroad, operating a railroad is not a non-profit activity.

(4) *Governmental functions.*—Governmental functions are not commercial activities. The term "governmental functions" shall be determined under U.S. standards. In general, activities performed for the general public with respect to the common welfare or which relate to the administration of some phase of government will be considered governmental functions. For example, the operation of libraries, toll bridges, or local transportation services and activities substantially equivalent to the Federal Aviation Authority, Interstate Commerce Commission, or United States Postal Service will all be considered governmental functions for purposes of this section.

(5) *Purchasing.*—The mere purchasing of goods for the use of a foreign government is not a commercial activity. [Temporary Reg. § 1.892-4T.]

☐ [*T.D.* 8211, 6-24-88.]

§ 1.892-5. Controlled commercial entity.—(a) through (a)(2) [Reserved]. For further information, see § 1.892-5T(a) through (a)(2).

(3) For purposes of section 892(a)(2)(B), the term *entity* means and includes a corporation, a partnership, a trust (including a pension trust described in § 1.892-2T(c)) and an estate.

(4) *Effective date.*—This section applies on or after January 14, 2002. See § 1.892-5T(a) for the rules that apply before January 14, 2002.

(b) through (d) [Reserved]. For further information, see § 1.892-5T(b) through (d). [Reg. § 1.892-5.]

☐ [*T.D.* 9012, 7-31-2002.]

§ 1.892-5T. Controlled commercial entity (Temporary).—(a) *In general.*—The exemption generally applicable to a foreign government (as defined in § 1.892-2T) for income described in § 1.892-3T does not apply to income received by a controlled commercial entity or received (directly or indirectly) from a controlled commercial entity. The term "controlled commercial entity" means any entity engaged in commercial activities as defined in § 1.892-4T (whether conducted within or outside the United States) if the government—

(1) holds (directly or indirectly) any interest in such entity which (by value or voting power) is 50 percent or more of the total of such interests in such entity, or

(2) holds (directly or indirectly) a sufficient interest (by value or voting power) or any other interest in such entity which provides the foreign government with effective practical control of such entity.

(3) [Reserved]. For further information, see § 1.892-5(a)(3).

(b) *Entities treated as engaged in commercial activity.*—(1) *U.S. real property holding corporations.*—A United States real property holding corporation, as defined in section 897(c)(2) or a foreign corporation that would be a United States real property holding corporation if it was a United States corporation, shall be treated as engaged in commercial activity and, therefore, is a controlled commercial entity if the requirements of paragraph (a)(1) or (a)(2) of this section are satisfied.

(2) *Central banks.*—Notwithstanding paragraph (a) of this section, a central bank of issue (as defined in § 1.895-1(b)) shall be treated as a controlled commercial entity only if it engages in commercial activities within the United States.

(3) *Pension trusts.*—A pension trust, described in § 1.892-2T(c), which engages in commercial activities within or outside the United States, shall be treated as a controlled commercial entity. Income derived by such a pension trust is not income of a foreign government for purposes of the exemption from taxation provided in section 892. A pension trust described in § 1.892-2T(c) shall not be treated as a controlled commercial entity if such trust solely earns income which would not be unrelated business taxable income (as defined in section 512(a)(1)) if the trust were a qualified trust described in section 401(a). However, only income derived by a pension trust that is described in § 1.892-3T and which is not from commercial activities as defined in § 1.892-4T is exempt from taxation under section 892.

(c) *Control.*—(1) *Attribution.*—(i) *Rule.*—In determining for purposes of paragraph (a) of this section the interest held by a foreign government, any interest in an entity (whether or not engaged in commercial activity) owned directly or indirectly by an integral part or controlled entity of a foreign sovereign shall be treated as actually owned by such foreign sovereign.

(ii) *Illustration.*—The following example illustrates the application of paragraph (c)(1)(i) above.

Example. FX, a controlled entity of foreign sovereign FC, owns 20 percent of the stock of Corp 1. Neither FX nor Corp 1 is engaged in commercial activity anywhere in the world. Corp 1 owns 60 percent of the stock of Corp 2, which is engaged in commercial activity. The remaining 40 percent of Corp 2's stock is owned by Bureau, an integral part of foreign sovereign FC. For purposes of determining whether Corp 2 is a controlled commercial entity of FC, Bureau will be treated as actually owning the 12 percent of Corp 2's stock indirectly owned by FX. Therefore, since Bureau directly and indirectly owns 52 percent of the stock of Corp 2, Corp 2 is a controlled commercial entity of FC within the meaning of paragraph (a) of this section. Accordingly, dividends or other income received, directly or indirectly, from Corp 2 by either Bureau or FX will not be exempt from taxation under section 892. Furthermore, dividends from Corp 1 to the extent attributable to dividends from Corp 2 will not be exempt from taxation. Thus, a distribution from Corp 1 to FX shall be exempt only to the extent such distribution exceeds Corp 1's earnings and profits attributable to the Corp 2 dividend amount received by Corp 1.

(2) *Effective practical control.*—An entity engaged in commercial activity may be treated as a controlled commercial entity if a foreign government holds sufficient interests in such entity to give it "effective practical control" over the entity. Effective practical control may be achieved through a minority interest which is sufficiently large to achieve effective control, or through creditor, contractual or regulatory relationships which, together with ownership interests held by the foreign government, achieve effective control. For example, an entity engaged in commercial activity may be treated as a controlled commercial entity if a foreign government, in addition to holding a small minority interest (by value or voting power), is also a substantial creditor of the entity or controls a strategic natural resource which such entity uses in the conduct of its trade or business, giving the foreign government effective practical control over the entity.

(d) *Related controlled entities.*—(1) *Brother/sister entities.*—Commercial activities of a controlled entity are not attributed to such entity's other brother/sister related entities. Thus, investment income described in § 1.892-2T that is derived by a controlled entity that is not itself engaged in commercial activity within or outside the United States is exempt from taxation notwithstanding the fact that such entity's brother/sister related entity is a controlled commercial entity.

(2) *Parent/subsidiary entities.*—(i) *Subsidiary to parent attribution.*—Commercial activities of a subsidiary controlled entity are not attributed to its parent. Thus, investment income described in § 1.892-3T that is derived by a parent controlled entity that is not itself engaged in commercial activity within or outside the United States is exempt from taxation notwithstanding the fact that its subsidiary is a controlled commercial entity. Dividends or other payments of income received by the parent controlled entity from the subsidiary are not exempt under section 892, because it con-

stitutes income received from a controlled commercial entity. Furthermore, dividends paid by the parent are not exempt to the extent attributable to the dividends received by the parent from the subsidiary. Thus, a distribution by the parent shall be exempt only to the extent such distribution exceeds earnings and profits attributable to the dividend received from its subsidiary.

(ii) *Parent to subsidiary attribution.*—Commercial activities of a parent controlled entity are attributed to its subsidiary. Thus, investment income described in § 1.892-3T that is derived by a subsidiary controlled entity (not engaged in commercial activity within or outside the United States) is not exempt from taxation under section 892 if its parent is a controlled commercial entity.

(3) *Partnerships.*—Except for partners of publicly traded partnerships, commercial activities of a partnership are attributable to its general and limited partners for purposes of section 892. For example, where a controlled entity is a general partner in a partnership engaged in commercial activities, the controlled entity's distributive share of partnership income (including income described in § 1.892-3T) will not be exempt from taxation under section 892.

(4) *Illustrations.*—The principles of this section may be illustrated by the following examples.

Example (1). (a) The Ministry of Industry and Development is an integral part of a foreign sovereign under § 1.892-2T(a)(2). The Ministry is engaged in commercial activity within the United States. In addition, the Ministry receives income from various publicly traded stocks and bonds, soybean futures contracts and net leases on U.S. real property. Since the Ministry is an integral part, and not a controlled entity, of a foreign sovereign, it is not a controlled commercial entity within the meaning of paragraph (a) of this section. Therefore, income described in § 1.892-3T is ineligible for exemption under section 892 only to the extent derived from the conduct of commercial activities. Accordingly, the Ministry's income from the stocks and bonds is exempt from U.S. tax.

(b) The facts are the same as in *Example* (1)(a), except that the Ministry also owns 75 percent of the stock of R, a U.S. holding company that owns all the stock of S, a U.S. operating company engaged in commercial activity. Ministry's dividend income from R is income received indirectly from a controlled commercial entity. The Ministry's income from the stocks and bonds, with the exception of dividend income from R, is exempt from U.S. tax.

(c) The facts are the same as in *Example* (1)(a), except that the Ministry is a controlled entity of a foreign sovereign. Since the Ministry is a controlled entity and is engaged in commercial activity, it is a controlled commercial entity within the meaning of paragraph (a) of this section, and none of its income is eligible for exemption.

Example (2). (a) Z, a controlled entity of a foreign sovereign, has established a pension trust as part of a pension plan for the benefit of its employees and former employees. The pension trust (T), which meets the requirements of § 1.892-2T(c), has investments in the U.S. in various stocks, bonds, annuity contracts, and a shopping center which is leased and managed by an independent real estate management firm. T also makes securities loans in transactions that qualify under section 1058. T's investment in the shopping center is not considered an unrelated trade or business within the meaning of section 513(b). Accordingly, T will not be treated as engaged in commercial activity. Since T is not a controlled commercial entity, its investment income described in § 1.892-3T, with the exception of income received from the operations of the shopping center, is exempt from taxation under section 892.

(b) The facts are the same as *Example* (2)(a), except that T has an interest in a limited partnership which owns the shopping center. The shopping center is leased and managed by the partnership rather than by an independent management firm. Managing a shopping center, directly or indirectly through a partnership of which a trust is a member, would be considered an unrelated trade or business within the meaning of section 513(b) giving rise to unrelated business taxable income. Since the commercial activities of a partnership are attributable to its partners, T will be treated as engaged in commercial activity and thus will be considered a controlled commercial entity. Accordingly, none of T's income will be exempt from taxation under section 892.

(c) The facts are the same as *Example* (2)(a), except that Z is a controlled commercial entity. The result is the same as in *Example* (2)(a).

Example (3). (a) The Department of Interior, an integral part of foreign sovereign FC, wholly owns corporations G and H. G, in turn, wholly owns S. G, H and S are each controlled entities. G, which is not engaged in commercial activity anywhere in the world, receives interest income from deposits in banks in the United States. Both H and S do not have any investments in the U.S. but are both engaged in commercial activities. However, only S is engaged in commercial activities within the United States. Because neither the commercial activities of H nor the commercial activities of S are attributable to the Department of Interior or G, G's interest income is exempt from taxation under section 892.

(b) The facts are the same as *Example (3)*(a), except that G rather than S is engaged in commercial activities and S rather than G receives the interest income from the United States. Since the commercial activities of G are attributable to S, S's interest income is not exempt from taxation.

Example (4). (a) K, a controlled entity of a foreign sovereign, is a general partner in the Daj partnership. The Daj partnership has investments in the U.S. in various stocks and bonds and also owns and manages an office building in New York. K will be deemed to be engaged in commercial activity by being a general partner in Daj even if K does not actually make management decisions with regard to the partnership's commercial activity, the operation of the office building. Accordingly, K's distributive share of partnership income (including income derived from stocks and bonds) will not be exempt from taxation under section 892.

(b) The facts are the same as in *Example (4)*(a), except that the Daj partnership has hired a real estate management firm to lease offices and manage the building. Notwithstanding the fact that an independent contractor is performing the activities, the partnership shall still be deemed to be engaged in commercial activity. Accordingly, K's distributive share of partnership income (including income derived from stocks and bonds) will not be exempt from taxation under section 892.

(c) The facts are the same as in *Example (4)*(a), except that K is a partner whose partnership interest is considered a publicly traded partnership interest within the meaning of section 7704. Under paragraph (d)(3) of this section, the partnership's commercial activity will not be attributed to K. Since K will not be deemed to be engaged in commercial activity, K's distributive share of partnership income derived from stocks and bonds will be exempt from taxation under section 892. [Temporary Reg. § 1.892-5T.]

☐ [*T.D.* 8211, 6-24-88. *Amended by T.D.* 9012, 7-31-2002.]

§ 1.892-6T. Income of international organizations (Temporary).—(a) *Exempt from tax.*—Subject to the provisions of section 1 of the International Organizations Immunities Act (22 U.S.C. 288) (the provisions of which are set forth in paragraph (b)(3) of § 1.893-1), the income of an international organization (as defined in section 7701(a)(18)) received from investments in the United States in stocks, bonds, or other domestic securities, owned by such international organization, or from interest on deposits in banks in the United States of moneys belonging to such international organization, or from any other source within the United States, is exempt from Federal income tax.

(b) *Income received prior to Presidential designation.*—An organization designated by the President through appropriate Executive order as entitled to enjoy the privileges, exemptions, and immunities provided in the International Organizations Immunities Act may enjoy the benefits of the exemption with respect to income of the prescribed character received by such organization prior to the date of the issuance of such Executive order, if (i) the Executive order does not provide otherwise and (ii) the organization is a public international organization in which the United States participates, pursuant to a treaty or under the authority of an act of Congress authorizing such participation or making an appropriation for such participation, at the time such income is received. [Temporary Reg. § 1.892-6T.]

☐ [*T.D.* 8211, 6-24-88.]

§ 1.892-7T. Relationship to other Internal Revenue Code sections (Temporary).—(a) *Section 893.*—The term "foreign government" referred to in section 893 (relating to the exemption for compensation of employees of foreign governments) has the same meaning as given such term in § 1.892-2T.

(b) *Section 895.*—A foreign central bank of issue (as defined in § 1.895-1(b)) that fails to qualify for the exemption from tax provided by this section (for example, it is not wholly owned by a foreign sovereign) may nevertheless be exempt from tax on the items of income described in section 895.

(c) *Section 883(b).*—Nothing in section 892 or these regulations shall limit the exemption provided under section 883(b) relating generally to the exemption of earnings derived by foreign participants from the ownership or operation of communications satellite systems.

(d) *Section 884.*—Earnings and profits attributable to income of a controlled entity of a foreign sovereign which is exempt from taxation under section 892 shall not be subject to the tax imposed by section 884(a).

(e) *Sections 1441 and 1442.*—No withholding is required under sections 1441 and 1442 in the case of income exempt from taxation under section 892. [Temporary Reg. § 1.892-7T.]

☐ [*T.D.* 8211, 6-24-88.]

§ 1.893-1. **Compensation of employees of foreign governments or international organizations.**—(a) *Employees of foreign governments.*—(1) *Exempt from tax.*—Except to the extent that the exemption is limited by the execution and filing of the waiver provided for in section 247(b) of the Immigration and Nationality Act (8 U.S.C. 1257(b)), all employees of a foreign government (including consular or other officers, or nondiplomatic representatives) who are not citizens of the United States, or are citizens of the Republic of the Philippines (whether or not citizens of the United States), are exempt from Federal income tax with respect to wages, fees, or salaries received by them as compensation for official services rendered to such foreign government, provided (i) the services are of a character similar to those performed by employees of the Government of the United States in that foreign country and (ii) the foreign government whose employees are claiming exemption grants an equivalent exemption to employees of the Government of the United States performing similar services in that foreign country.

(2) *Certificate by Secretary of State.*—Section 893(b) provides that the Secretary of State shall certify to the Secretary of the Treasury the names of the foreign countries which grant an equivalent exemption to the employees of the Government of the United States performing services in such foreign countries, and the character of the services performed by employees of the Government of the United States in foreign countries.

(3) *Items not exempt.*—The income received by employees of foreign governments from sources other than their salaries, fees, or wages, referred to in subparagraph (1) of this paragraph, is subject to Federal income tax.

(4) *Immigration and Nationality Act.*—Section 247(b) of the Immigration and Nationality Act provides as follows:

Sec. 247. Adjustment of status of certain resident aliens. * * *

(b) The adjustment of status required by subsection (a) [of section 247 of the Immigration and Nationality Act] shall not be applicable in the case of any alien who requests that he be permitted to retain his status as an immigrant and who, in such form as the Attorney General may require, executes and files with the Attorney General a written waiver of all rights, privileges, exemptions, and immunities under any law or any executive order which would otherwise accrue to him because of the acquisition of an occupational status entitling him to a nonimmigrant status under paragraph (15)(A), (15)(E), or (15)(G) of section 101(a).

(5) *Effect of waiver.*—An employee of a foreign government who executes and files with the Attorney General the waiver provided for in section 247(b) of the Immigration and Nationality Act thereby waives the exemption conferred by section 893 of the Code. As a consequence, that exemption does not apply to income received by that alien after the date of filing of the waiver.

(6) *Citizens of the United States.*—The compensation of citizens of the United States (other than those who are also citizens of the Republic of the Philippines) who are officers or employees of a foreign government is not exempt from income tax pursuant to this paragraph. But see section 911 and the regulations thereunder.

(b) *Employees of international organizations.*—(1) *Exempt from tax.*—Except to the extent that the exemption is limited by the execution and filing of the waiver provided for in section 247(b) of the Immigration and Nationality Act and subject to the provisions of sections 1, 8, and 9 of the International Organizations Immunities Act (22 U.S.C. 288, 288e, 288f), wages, fees, or salary of any officer or employee of an international organization (as defined in section 7701(a)(18)) received as compensation for official services to that international organization is exempt from Federal income tax, if that officer or employee (i) is not a citizen of the United States or (ii) is a citizen of the Republic of the Philippines (whether or not a citizen of the United States).

(2) *Income earned prior to executive action.*—An individual of the prescribed class who receives wages, fees, or salary as compensation for official services to an organization designated by the President through appropriate Executive order as entitled to enjoy the privileges, exemptions, and immunities provided in the International Organizations Immunities Act and who has been duly notified to, and accepted by, the Secretary of State as an officer or employee of that organization, or who has been designated by the Secretary of State, prior to formal notification and acceptance, as a prospective officer or employee of that organization, may enjoy the benefits of the exemption with respect to compensation of the prescribed character earned by that individual, either prior to the date of the issuance of the Executive order, or prior to the date of the acceptance or designation by the Secretary of State, for official services to that organization, if (i) the Executive order does not provide otherwise, (ii) the organization is a public international organization in which the United States participates, pursuant to a treaty or under the authority of an act of Congress authorizing such participation or making an appropriation for such partic-

ipation, at the time the compensation is earned, and (iii) the individual is an officer or employee of that organization at that time.

(3) *International Organizations Immunities Act.*—Sections 1, 8, and 9 of the International Organizations Immunities Act (22 U.S.C. 288, 288e, 288f) provide in part as follows:

Section 1. For the purposes of this title [International Organizations Immunities Act], the term "international organization" means a public international organization in which the United States participates pursuant to any treaty or under the authority of any Act of Congress authorizing such participation or making an appropriation for such participation, and which shall have been designated by the President through appropriate Executive order as being entitled to enjoy the privileges, exemptions, and immunities herein provided. The President shall be authorized, in the light of the functions performed by any such international organization, by appropriate Executive order to withhold or withdraw from any such organization or its officers or employees any of the privileges, exemptions, and immunities provided for in this title (including the amendments made by this title) or to condition or limit the enjoyment by any such organization or its officers or employees of any such privilege, exemption, or immunity. The President shall be authorized, if in his judgment such action should be justified by reason of the abuse by an international organization or its officers and employees of the privileges, exemptions, and immunities herein provided or for any other reason, at any time to revoke the designation of any international organization under this section, whereupon the international organization in question shall cease to be classed as an international organization for the purposes of this title.

* * *

Sec. 8. (a) No person shall be entitled to the benefits of this title [International Organizations Immunities Act] unless he (1) shall have been duly notified to and accepted by the Secretary of State as a * * * officer, or employee; or (2) shall have been designated by the Secretary of State, prior to formal notification and acceptance, as a prospective * * * officer, or employee; * * *

(b) Should the Secretary of State determine that the continued presence in the United States of any person entitled to the benefits of this title is not desirable, he shall so inform the * * * international organization concerned * * * and after such person shall have had a reasonable length of time, to be determined by the Secretary of State, to depart from the United States, he shall cease to be entitled to such benefits.

(c) No person shall, by reason of the provisions of this title, be considered as receiving diplomatic status or as receiving any of the privileges incident thereto other than such as are specifically set forth herein.

Sec. 9. The privileges, exemptions, and immunities of international organizations and of their officers and employees * * * provided for in this title [International Organizations Immunities Act], shall be granted notwithstanding the fact that the similar privileges, exemptions, and immunities granted to a foreign government, its officers, or employees, may be conditioned upon the existence of reciprocity by that foreign government: *Provided,* That nothing contained in this title shall be construed as precluding the Secretary of State from withdrawing the privileges, exemptions, and immunities herein provided from persons who are nationals of any foreign country on the ground that such country is failing to accord corresponding privileges, exemptions, and immunities to citizens of the United States.

(4) *Effect of waiver.*—An officer or employee of an international organization who executes and files with the Attorney General the waiver provided for in section 247(b) of the Immigration and Nationality Act (8 U.S.C. 1257(b)) thereby waives the exemption conferred by section 893 of the Code. As a consequence, that exemption does not apply to income received by that individual after the date of filing of the waiver.

(5) *Citizens of the United States.*—The compensation of citizens of the United States (other than those who are also citizens of the Republic of the Philippines) who are officers or employees of an international organization is not exempt from income tax pursuant to this paragraph. But see section 911 and the regulations thereunder.

(c) *Tax conventions, consular conventions, and international agreements.*—(1) *Exemption dependent upon internal revenue laws.*—A tax convention or consular convention between the United States and a foreign country, which provides that the United States may include in the tax base of its residents all income taxable under the internal revenue laws, and which makes no specific exception for the income of the employees of that foreign government, does not provide any exemption (with respect to residents of the United States) beyond that which is provided by the internal revenue laws. Accordingly, the effect of the execution and filing of a waiver under section 247(b) of the Immigration and Nationality Act by an employee of a foreign government which is a party to such a convention is to subject the employee to tax to the same extent as provided in paragraph (a)(5) of this section with respect to the waiver of exemption under section 893.

(2) *Exemption not dependent upon internal revenue laws.*—If a tax convention, consular convention, or international agreement provides that compensation paid by the foreign government or international organization to its employees is exempt from Federal income tax, and the application of this exemption is not dependent upon the provisions of the internal revenue laws, the exemption so conferred is not affected by the execution and filing of a waiver under section 247(b) of the Immigration and Nationality Act. For examples of exemptions which are not affected by the Immigration and Nationality Act, see article X of the income tax convention between the United States and the United Kingdom (60 Stat. 1383); article IX, section 9(b), of the Articles of Agreement of the International Monetary Fund (60 Stat. 1414); and article VII, section 9(b), of the Articles of Agreement of the International Bank for Reconstruction and Development (60 Stat. 1458). [Reg. § 1.893-1.]

☐ [*T.D.* 6258, 10-23-57.]

§ 1.894-1. Income affected by treaty.—(a) *Income exempt under treaty.*—Income of any kind is not included in gross income and is exempt from tax under subtitle A (relating to income taxes), to the extent required by any income tax convention to which the United States is a party. However, unless otherwise provided by an income tax convention, the exclusion from gross income under section 894(a) and this paragraph does not apply in determining the accumulated taxable income of a foreign corporation under section 535 and the regulations thereunder or the undistributed personal holding company income of a foreign corporation under section 545 and the regulations thereunder. Moreover, the distributable net income of a foreign trust is determined without regard to section 894 and this paragraph, to the extent provided by section 643(a)(6)(B). Further, the compensating tax adjustment required by section 819(a)(3) in the case of a foreign life insurance company is to be determined without regard to section 894 and this paragraph, to the extent required by section 819(a)(3)(A). See § 1.871-12 for the manner of determining the tax liability of a nonresident alien individual or foreign corporation whose gross income includes income on which the tax is reduced under a tax convention.

(b) *Taxpayer treated as having no permanent establishment in the United States.*—(1) *In general.*—A nonresident alien individual or a foreign corporation, that is engaged in trade or business in the United States through a permanent establishment located therein at any time during a taxable year beginning after December 31, 1966, shall be deemed not to have a permanent establishment in the United States at any time during that year for purposes of applying any exemption from, or reduction in the rate of, any tax under subtitle A of the Code which is provided by any income tax convention with respect to income which is not effectively connected for that year with the conduct of a trade or business in the United States by the taxpayer. This paragraph applies to all treaties or conventions entered into by the United States, whether entered into before, on, or after November 13, 1966, the date of enactment of the Foreign Investors Tax Act of 1966 (80 Stat. 1539). This paragraph is not considered to be contrary to any obligation of the United States under an income tax convention to which it is a party. The benefit granted under section 894(b) and this paragraph applies only to those items of income derived from sources within the United States which are subject to the tax imposed by section 871(a) or 881(a), and section 1441, 1442, or 1451, on the noneffectively connected income received from sources within the United States by a nonresident alien individual or a foreign corporation. The benefit does not apply to any income from real property in respect of which an election is in effect for the taxable year under § 1.871-10 or in determining under section 877(b) the tax of a nonresident alien individual who has lost United States citizenship at any time after March 8, 1965. The benefit granted by section 894(b) and this paragraph is not elective.

(2) *Illustrations.*—The application of this paragraph may be illustrated by the following examples:

Example (1). M, a corporation organized in foreign country X, uses the calendar year as the taxable year. The United States and country X are parties to an income tax convention which provides in part that dividends received from sources within the United States by a corporation of country X not having a permanent establishment in the United States are subject to tax under chapter 1 of the Code at a rate not to exceed 15 percent. During 1967, M is engaged in business in the United States through a permanent establishment located therein and receives $100,000 in dividends from domestic corporation B, which under section 861(a)(2)(A) constitute income from sources within the United States. Under section 864(c)(2) and § 1.864-4(c), the dividends received from B are not effectively connected for 1967 with the conduct of a trade or business in the United States by M. Although M has a permanent establishment in the United States during 1967, it is deemed, under section 894(b) and this paragraph, not to have a permanent establishment in the United States during that year with respect to the dividends. Accordingly, in accordance with paragraph (c)(3) of §1.871-12 the tax on the dividends is $15,000, that is, 15 percent of $100,000, determined without the allowance of any deductions.

Example (2). T, a corporation organized in foreign country X, uses the calendar year as the taxable year. The United States and country X are parties to an income tax convention which provides in part that an enterprise of country X is not subject to tax under chapter 1 of the Code in respect of its industrial or commercial profits unless it is engaged in trade or business in the United States during the taxable year through a permanent establishment located therein and that, if it is so engaged, the tax may be imposed upon the entire income of that enterprise from sources within the United States. The convention also provides that the tax imposed by chapter 1 of the Code on dividends received from sources within the United States by a corporation of X which is not engaged in trade or business in the United States through a permanent establishment located therein shall not exceed 15 percent of the dividend. During 1967, T is engaged in a business (business A) in the United States which is carried on through a permanent establishment in the United States; in addition, T is engaged in a business (business B) in the United States which is not carried on through a permanent establishment. During 1967, T receives from sources within the United States $60,000 in service fees through the operation of business A and $10,000 in dividends through the operation of business B, both of which amounts are, under section 864(c)(2)(B), and §1.864-4(c)(3), effectively connected for that year with the conduct of a trade or business in the United States by that corporation. The service fees are considered to be industrial or commercial profits under the tax convention with country X. Since T has no income for 1967 which is not effectively connected for that year with the conduct of a trade or business in the United States by that corporation, section 894(b), this paragraph, and §1.871-12 do not apply. Accordingly, for 1967 T's entire income of $70,000 from sources within the United States is subject to tax, after allowance of deductions, in accordance with section 882(a)(1) and paragraph (b)(2) of §1.882-1.

Example (3). S, a corporation organized in foreign country W, uses the calendar year as the taxable year. The United States and country W are parties to an income tax convention which provides in part that a corporation of country W is not subject to tax under chapter 1 of the Code in respect of its industrial or commercial profits unless it is engaged in trade or business in the United States during the taxable year through a permanent establishment located therein and that, if it is so engaged, the tax may be imposed upon the entire income of that corporation from sources within the United States. The convention also provides that the tax imposed by chapter 1 of the Code on dividends received from sources within the United States by a corporation of country W which is not engaged in trade or business in the United States through a permanent establishment located therein shall not exceed 15 percent of the dividend. During 1967, S is engaged in business in the United States through a permanent establishment located therein and derives from sources within the United States $100,000 in service fees which, under section 864(c)(2)(B) and §1.864-4(c)(3), are effectively connected for that year with the conduct of a trade or business in the United States by S and which are considered to be industrial or commercial profits under the tax convention with country W. During 1967, S also derives from sources within the United States, through another business it carries on in foreign country X, $10,000 in sales income which, under section 864(c)(3) and §1.864-4(b), is effectively connected for that year with the conduct of a trade or business in the United States by S and $5,000 in dividends which, under section 864(c)(2)(A) and §1.864-4(c)(2), are not effectively connected for that year with the conduct of a trade or business in the United States by S. The sales income is considered to be industrial or commercial profits under the tax convention with country W. Although S is engaged in a trade or business in the United States during 1967 through a permanent establishment located therein, it is deemed, under section 894(b) and this paragraph, not to have a permanent establishment therein with respect to the $5,000 in dividends. Accordingly, in accordance with paragraph (c) of §1.871-12, for 1967 S is subject to a tax of $750 on the dividends ($5,000 × .15) and a tax, determined under section 882(a) and §1.882-1, on its $110,000 industrial or commercial profits.

Example (4). (a) N, a corporation organized in foreign country Z, uses the calendar year as the taxable year. The United States and country Z are parties to an income tax convention which provides in part that the tax imposed by chapter 1 of the Code on dividends received from sources within the United States by a corporation of country Z shall not exceed 15 percent of the amount distributed if the recipient does not have a permanent establishment in the United States or, where the recipient does have a permanent establishment in the United States, if the shares giving rise to the dividends are not effectively connected with the permanent establishment. The tax convention also provides that if a corporation of country Z is engaged in industrial or commercial activity in the United States through a permanent establishment in the United States, income tax may be imposed by the United States on so much of the industrial or commercial profits of such corporation as are attributable to the permanent establishment in the United States.

(b) During 1967, N is engaged in a business (business A) in the United States which is not carried on through a permanent establishment in the United States. In addition, N has a permanent establishment in the United States through which it carries on another business (business B) in the United States. During 1967, N holds shares of stock in domestic corporation D which are not effectively connected with N's permanent establishment in the United States. During 1967, N receives $100,000 in dividends from D which, pursuant to section 864(c)(2)(A) and § 1.864-4(c)(2), are effectively connected for that year with the conduct of business A. Under section 861(a)(2)(A) these dividends are treated as income from sources within the United States. In addition, during 1967, N receives from sources within the United States $150,000 in sales income which, pursuant to section 864(c)(3) and § 1.864-4(b), is effectively connected with the conduct of a trade or business in the United States and which is considered to be industrial or commercial profits under the tax convention with country Z. Of these total profits, $70,000 is from business A and $80,000 is from business B. Only the $80,000 of industrial or commercial profits is attributable to N's permanent establishment in the United States.

(c) Since N has no income for 1967 which is not effectively connected for that year with the conduct of a trade or business in the United States by that corporation, section 894(b) and this paragraph do not apply. However, N is entitled to the reduced rate of tax under the tax convention with country Z with respect to the dividends because the shares of stock are not effectively connected with N's permanent establishment in the United States. Accordingly, assuming that there are no deductions connected with N's industrial or commercial profits, the tax for 1967, determined as provided in paragraph (c) of § 1.871-12, is $46,900 as follows:

Tax on nontreaty income:
$80,000 × .48 .... $38,400
Less $25,000 × .26 6,500
                                 31,900
Tax on treaty income:
$100,000 (gross dividends) × .15 ... 15,000
Total tax $46,900

Example (5). M, a corporation organized in foreign country Z, uses the calendar year as the taxable year. The United States and country Z are parties to an income tax convention which provides in part that a corporation of country Z is not subject to tax under chapter 1 of the Code in respect of its commercial and industrial profits except such profits as are allocable to its permanent establishment in the United States. The regulations in this chapter under the tax convention with country Z provide that a corporation of country Z having a permanent establishment in the United States is subject to U.S. tax upon its industrial and commercial profits from sources within the United States and that its industrial and commercial profits from such sources are deemed to be allocable to the permanent establishment in the United States. During 1967, M is engaged in a business (business A) in the United States, which is carried on through a permanent establishment in the United States; in addition, M is engaged in a business (business B) in foreign country X and none of such business is carried on in the United States. During 1967, M receives from sources within the United States $40,000 in sales income through the operation of business A and $10,000 in sales income through the operation of business B, both of which amounts are, under section 864(c)(3) and § 1.864-4(b), effectively connected for that year with the conduct of a trade or business in the United States by that corporation. The sales income is considered to be industrial and commercial profits under the tax convention with country Z. Since M has no income for 1967 which is not effectively connected for that year with the conduct of a trade or business in the United States by that corporation, section 894(b) and this paragraph do not apply. Accordingly, for 1967 M's entire income of $50,000 from sources within the United States is subject to tax, after allowance of deductions, in accordance with section 882(a)(1) and paragraph (b)(2) of § 1.882-1.

(c) *Substitute interest and dividend payments.*—The provisions of an income tax convention dealing with interest or dividends paid to or derived by a foreign person include substitute interest or dividend payments that have the same character as interest or dividends under § 1.864-5(b)(2)(ii), 1.871-7(b)(2) or 1.881-2(b)(2). The provisions of this paragraph (c) shall apply for purposes of securities lending transactions or sale-repurchase transactions as defined in § 1.861-2(a)(7) and § 1.861-3(a)(6).

(d) *Special rule for items of income received by entities.*—(1) *In general.*—The tax imposed by sections 871(a), 881(a), 1443, 1461, and 4948(a) on an item of income received by an entity, wherever organized, that is fiscally transparent under the laws of the United States and/or any other jurisdiction with respect to an item of income shall be eligible for reduction under the terms of an income tax treaty to which the United States is a party only if the item of income is derived by a resident of the applicable treaty jurisdiction. For this purpose, an item of income may be derived by either the entity receiving the item of income or by the interest holders in the entity or, in certain circumstances, both. An item of income paid to an entity shall be considered to be derived by the entity only if the entity is not fiscally transparent under the laws of the entity's jurisdiction, as defined in paragraph (d)(3)(ii) of this section, with respect to the item of income. An item of income paid to an entity shall be considered to be derived by the interest holder in the entity only if the interest holder is not fiscally transparent in its jurisdiction with respect to the item of income and if the entity is considered to be fiscally transparent under the laws of the interest holder's jurisdiction with respect to the item of income, as defined in paragraph (d)(3)(iii) of this section. Notwithstanding the preceding two sentences, an item of income paid directly to a type of entity specifically identified in a treaty as a resident of a treaty jurisdiction shall be treated as derived by a resident of that treaty jurisdiction.

(2) *Application to domestic reverse hybrid entities.*—(i) *In general.*—An income tax treaty may not apply to reduce the amount of federal income tax on U.S. source payments received by a domestic reverse hybrid entity. Further, notwithstanding paragraph (d)(1) of this section, the foreign interest holders of a domestic reverse hybrid entity are not entitled to the benefits of a reduction of U.S. income tax under an income tax treaty on items of income received from U.S. sources by such entity. A domestic reverse hybrid entity is a domestic entity that is treated as not fiscally transparent for U.S. tax purposes and as fiscally transparent under the laws of the interest holder's jurisdiction, with respect to the item of income received by the domestic entity.

(ii) *Payments by domestic reverse hybrid entities.*—(A) *General rule.*—Except as otherwise provided in paragraph (d)(2)(ii)(B) of this section, an item of income paid by a domestic reverse hybrid entity to an interest holder in such entity shall have the character of such item of income under U.S. law and shall be considered to be derived by the interest holder, provided the interest holder is not fiscally transparent in its jurisdiction, as defined in paragraph (d)(3)(iii) of this section, with respect to the item of income. In determining whether the interest holder is fiscally transparent with respect to the item of income under this paragraph (d)(2)(ii)(A), the determination under paragraph (d)(3)(ii) of this section shall be made based on the treatment that would have resulted had the item of income been paid by an entity that is not fiscally transparent under the laws of the interest holder's jurisdiction with respect to any item of income.

(B) *Payment made to related foreign interest holder.*—*(1) General rule.*—If—

(i) A domestic entity makes a payment to a related domestic reverse hybrid entity that is treated as a dividend under either the laws of the United States or the laws of the jurisdiction of a related foreign interest holder in the domestic reverse hybrid entity, and under the laws of the jurisdiction of the related foreign interest holder in the domestic reverse hybrid entity, the related foreign interest holder is treated as deriving its proportionate share of the payment under the principles of paragraph (d)(1) of this section; and

(ii) The domestic reverse hybrid entity makes a payment of a type that is deductible for U.S. tax purposes to the related foreign interest holder or to a person, wherever organized, the income and losses of which are available, under the laws of the jurisdiction of the related foreign interest holder, to offset the income and losses of the related foreign interest holder, and for which a reduction in U.S. withholding tax would be allowed under an applicable income tax treaty; then

(iii) To the extent the amount of the payment described in paragraph (d)(2)(ii)(B)(*1*)(*ii*) of this section does not exceed the sum of the portion of the payment described in paragraph (d)(2)(ii)(B)(*1*)(*i*) of this section treated as derived by the related foreign interest holder and the portion of any other prior payments described in paragraph (d)(2)(ii)(B)(*1*)(*i*) of this section treated as derived by the related foreign interest holder, the amount of the payment described in (d)(2)(ii)(B)(*1*)(*ii*) of this section will be treated for all purposes of the Internal Revenue Code and any applicable income tax treaty as a distribution within the meaning of section 301(a) of the Internal Revenue Code, and the tax to be withheld from the payment described in paragraph (d)(2)(ii)(B)(*1*)(*ii*) of this section (assuming the payment is a dividend under section 301(c)(1) of the Internal Revenue Code) shall be determined based on the appropriate rate of withholding that would be applicable to dividends paid from the domestic reverse hybrid entity to the related foreign interest holder in accordance with the principles of paragraph (d)(2)(ii)(A) of this section.

(2) Determining amount to be recharacterized under paragraph (d)(2)(ii)(B)(1)(iii).—For purposes of determining the amount to be recharacterized under paragraph (d)(2)(ii)(B)(*1*)(*iii*) of this section,

the portion of the payment described in paragraph (d)(2)(ii)(B)(*1*)(*i*) of this section treated as derived by the related foreign interest holder shall be increased by the portion of the payment derived by any other person described in paragraph (d)(2)(ii)(B)(*1*)(*ii*), and shall be reduced by the amount of any prior section 301(c) distributions made by the domestic reverse hybrid entity to the related foreign interest holder or any other person described in paragraph (d)(2)(ii)(B)(*1*)(*ii*) and by the amount of any payments from the domestic reverse hybrid entity previously recharacterized under paragraph (d)(2)(ii)(B)(*1*)(*iii*) of this section.

(*3*) *Tiered entities.*—The principles of this paragraph (d)(2)(ii)(B) also shall apply to payments referred to in this paragraph (d)(2)(ii)(B) made among related entities when there is more than one domestic reverse hybrid entity or other fiscally transparent entity involved.

(*4*) *Definition of related.*—For purposes of this section, a person shall be treated as related to a domestic reverse hybrid entity if it is related by reason of the ownership requirements of section 267(b) or 707(b)(1), except that the language "at least 80 percent" applies instead of "more than 50 percent," where applicable. For purposes of determining whether a person is related by reason of the ownership requirements of section 267(b) or 707(b)(1), the constructive ownership rules of section 318 shall apply, and the attribution rules of section 267(c) also shall apply to the extent they attribute ownership to persons to whom section 318 does not attribute ownership.

(C) *Payments to persons not described in paragraph (d)(2)(ii)(B)(1)(ii).*—(*1*) *Related persons.*—The Commissioner may treat a payment by a domestic reverse hybrid entity to a related person (who is neither the related foreign interest holder nor otherwise described in paragraph (d)(2)(ii)(B)(*1*)(*ii*) of this section), in whole or in part, as being made to a related foreign interest holder for purposes of applying paragraph (d)(2)(ii)(B) of this section, if—

(*i*) The payment to the related person is of a type that is deductible by the domestic reverse hybrid entity; and

(*ii*) The payment is made in connection with one or more transactions the effect of which is to avoid the application of paragraph (d)(2)(ii)(B) of this section.

(*2*) *Unrelated persons.*—The Commissioner may treat a payment by a domestic reverse hybrid entity to an unrelated person, in whole or in part, as being made to a related foreign interest holder for purposes of applying paragraph (d)(2)(ii)(B) of this section, if—

(*i*) The payment to the unrelated person is of a type that is deductible by the domestic reverse hybrid entity;

(*ii*) The unrelated person (or other person (whether related or not) which receives a payment in a series of transactions that includes a transaction involving such unrelated person) makes a payment to the related foreign interest holder (or other person described in paragraph (d)(2)(ii)(B)(*1*)(*ii*));

(*iii*) The foregoing payments are made in connection with a series of transactions which constitute a financing arrangement, as defined in § 1.881-3(a)(2)(i); and

(*iv*) The transactions have the effect of avoiding the application of paragraph (d)(2)(ii)(B) of this section.

(iii) *Examples.*—The rules of this paragraph (d)(2) are illustrated by the following examples:

Example 1. Dividend paid by unrelated entity to domestic reverse hybrid entity. (i) *Facts.* Entity A is a domestic reverse hybrid entity, as defined in paragraph (d)(2)(i) of this section, with respect to the U.S. source dividends it receives from B, a domestic corporation to which A is not related within the meaning of paragraph (d)(2)(ii)(B)(*4*) of this section. A's 85-percent shareholder, FC, is a corporation organized under the laws of Country X, which has an income tax treaty in effect with the United States. A's remaining 15-percent shareholder is an unrelated domestic corporation. Under Country X law, FC is not fiscally transparent with respect to the dividend, as defined in paragraph (d)(3)(ii) of this section. In year 1, A receives $100 of dividend income from B. Under Country X law, FC is treated as deriving $85 of the $100 dividend payment received by A. The applicable rate of tax on dividends under the U.S.-Country X income tax treaty is 5 percent with respect to a 10-percent or more corporate shareholder.

(ii) *Analysis.* Under paragraph (d)(2)(i) of this section, the U.S.-Country X income tax treaty does not apply to the dividend income received by A because the payment is made by B, a domestic corporation, to A, another domestic corporation. A remains fully taxable under the U.S. tax laws as a domestic corporation with regard to that item of income. Further, pursuant to paragraph (d)(2)(i) of this section, notwithstanding the fact that A is treated as fiscally transparent with respect to the dividend income under the laws of Country X, FC may not claim a reduced rate of taxation on its share of the U.S. source dividend income received by A.

Example 2. Interest paid by domestic reverse hybrid entity to related foreign interest holder where dividend is paid by unrelated entity. (i) *Facts.* The facts are the same as in *Example 1*. Both the United States and Country X characterize the payment by B in year 1 as a dividend. In addition, in year 2, A makes a payment of $25 to FC that is characterized under the Internal Revenue Code as interest on a loan from FC to A. Under the U.S.-Country X income tax treaty, the rate of tax on interest is zero. Under Country X laws, had the interest been paid by an entity that is not fiscally transparent under Country X's laws with respect to any item of income, FC would not be fiscally transparent as defined in paragraph (d)(2)(ii) of this section with respect to the interest.

(ii) *Analysis.* The analysis is the same as in *Example 1* with respect to the $100 payment from B to A. With respect to the $25 payment from A to FC, paragraph (d)(2)(ii)(B) of this section will not apply because, although FC is a related foreign interest holder in A, A is not related to B, the payor of the dividend income it received. Under paragraph (d)(2)(ii)(A) of this section, the $25 of interest paid by A to FC in year 2 is characterized under U.S. law as interest. Accordingly, in year 2, A is entitled to an interest deduction with respect to the $25 interest payment from A to FC, and FC is entitled to the reduced rate of withholding applicable to interest under the U.S.-Country X income tax treaty, assuming all other requirements for claiming treaty benefits are met.

Example 3. Interest paid by domestic reverse hybrid entity to related foreign interest holder where dividend is paid by a related entity. (i) *Facts.* The facts are the same as in *Example 2*, except the $100 dividend income received by A in year 1 is from A's wholly-owned subsidiary, S.

(ii) *Analysis.* The analysis is the same as in *Example 1* with respect to the $100 dividend payment from S to A. However, the $25 interest payment in year 2 by A to FC will be treated as a dividend for all purposes of the Internal Revenue Code and the U.S.-Country X income tax treaty because $25 does not exceed FC's share of the $100 dividend payment made by S to A ($85). Since FC is not fiscally transparent with respect to the payment as determined under paragraph (d)(2)(ii)(A) of this section, FC is entitled to the reduced rate applicable to dividends under the U.S.-Country X income tax treaty with respect to the $25 payment. Because the $25 payment in year 2 is recharacterized as a dividend for all purposes of the Internal Revenue Code and the U.S.-Country X income tax treaty, A is not entitled to an interest deduction with respect to that payment and FC is not entitled to claim the reduced rate of withholding applicable to interest.

Example 4. Definition of related foreign interest holder. (i) *Facts.* The facts are the same as in *Example 3*, except that A has two 50-percent shareholders, FC1 and FC2. In year 2, A makes an interest payment of $25 to both FC1 and FC2. FC1 is a corporation organized under the laws of Country X, which has an income tax treaty in effect with the United States. FC2 is a corporation organized under the laws of Country Y, which also has an income tax treaty in effect with the United States. FP owns 100-percent of both FC1 and FC2, and is organized under the laws of Country X. Under Country X law, FC1 is not fiscally transparent with respect to the dividend, as defined in paragraph (d)(3)(ii) of this section. Under Country X law, FC1 is treated as deriving $50 of the $100 dividend payment received by A because A is fiscally transparent under the laws of Country X, as determined under paragraph (d)(3)(iii) of this section. The applicable rate of tax on dividends under the U.S.-Country X income tax treaty is 5-percent with respect to a 10-percent or more corporate shareholder. Under Country Y law, FC2 is not treated as deriving any of the $100 dividend payment received by A because, under the laws of Country Y, A is not a fiscally transparent entity.

(ii) *Analysis.* The analysis is the same as in *Example 1* with respect to the $100 dividend payment from S to A. With respect to the $25 payment in year 2 by A to FC1, the payment will be treated as a dividend for all purposes of the Internal Revenue Code and the U.S.-Country X income tax treaty because FC1 is a related foreign interest holder as determined under paragraph (d)(2)(ii)(B)(4) of this section, and because $25 does not exceed FC1's share of the dividend payment made by S to A ($50). FC1 is a related foreign interest holder because FC1 is treated as owning the stock of A owned by FC2 under section 267(b)(3). Since FC1 is not fiscally transparent with respect to the payment as determined under paragraph (d)(2)(ii)(A) of this section, FC1 is entitled to the 5-percent reduced rate applicable to dividends under the U.S.-Country X income tax treaty with respect to the $25 payment. Because the $25 payment in year 2 is recharacterized as a dividend for all purposes of the Internal Revenue Code and the U.S.-Country X income tax treaty, A is not entitled to an interest deduction with respect to that payment. Even though FC2 is also a related foreign interest holder, the $25 interest payment by A to FC2 in year 2 is not recharacterized because A is not fiscally transparent under the laws of Country Y, and FC2 is not treated as deriving any of the $100 dividend payment received by A. Thus, the U.S.-Country Y income tax treaty is not implicated.

Example 5. Higher treaty withholding rate on dividends. (i) *Facts.* The facts are the same as in *Example 3*, except that under the U.S.-Country X income tax treaty, the rate of tax on interest is 10-percent and the rate of tax on dividends is 5-percent.

(ii) *Analysis.* The analysis is the same as in *Example 1* with respect to the $100 dividend payment from S to A. The analysis is the same as in *Example 3* with respect to the $25 interest payment in year 2 from A to FC.

Example 6. Foreign sister corporation the income and losses of which may offset the income and losses of related foreign interest holder. (i) *Facts.* The facts are the same as in *Example 3*, except that in year 2, A makes the interest payment of $25 to FS, a subsidiary of FC also organized in Country X. Under the laws of Country X, FS is not fiscally transparent with respect to the interest payment, and the income and losses of FS may be used to offset the income and losses of FC.

(ii) *Analysis.* The analysis is the same as in *Example 1* with respect to the $100 dividend payment from S to A. With respect to the $25 interest payment from A to FS in year 2, FS is a person described in paragraph (d)(2)(ii)(B)(*1*)(*ii*) of this section because the income and losses of FS may be used under the laws of Country X to offset the income and losses of FC, the related foreign interest holder that derived its proportionate share of the payment from S to A. Therefore, paragraph (d)(2)(ii)(B) of this section applies, and the $25 interest payment in year 2 by A to FS is treated as a dividend for all purposes of the Internal Revenue Code and the U.S.-Country X income tax treaty because the $25 payment does not exceed FC's share of the $100 dividend payment made by S to A ($85). Since FS is not fiscally transparent with respect to the payment as determined under paragraph (d)(2)(ii)(A) of this section, FS is entitled to obtain the rate applicable to dividends under the U.S.-Country X income tax treaty with respect to the $25 payment. Because the $25 payment in year 2 is recharacterized as a dividend for all purposes of the Internal Revenue Code and the U.S.-Country X income tax treaty, A is not entitled to an interest deduction with respect to the payment and FS is not entitled to claim the reduced rate of withholding applicable to interest under the U.S.-Country X income tax treaty.

Example 7. Interest paid by domestic reverse hybrid entity to unrelated foreign bank. (i) *Facts.* The facts are the same as in *Example 3*, except that in year 2, A makes the interest payment of $25 to FB, a Country Y unrelated foreign bank, on a loan from FB to A.

(ii) *Analysis.* The analysis is the same as in *Example 1* with respect to the $100 dividend payment from S to A. With respect to the payment from A to FB, paragraph (d)(2)(ii)(B) of this section will not apply because, although A is related to S, the payor of the dividend income it received, A is not related to FB under paragraph (d)(2)(ii)(B)(*4*) of this section. Under paragraph (d)(2)(ii)(A) of this section, the $25 interest payment made from A to FB in year 2 is characterized as interest under the Internal Revenue Code.

Example 8. Interest paid by domestic reverse hybrid to an unrelated entity pursuant to a financing arrangement. (i) *Facts.* The facts are the same as in *Example 7*, except that in year 3, FB makes an interest payment of $25 to FC on a deposit made by FC with FB.

(ii) *Analysis.* The analysis is the same as in *Example 1* with respect to the $100 dividend payment from S to A. With respect to the $25 payment from A to FB in year 2, because the payment is made in connection with a transaction that constitutes a financing arrangement within the meaning of paragraph (d)(2)(ii)(C)(*2*) of this section, the payment may be treated by the Commissioner as being made directly to FC. If the Commissioner disregards FB, then the analysis is the same as in *Example 3* with respect to the $25 interest payment in year 2 from A to FC.

Example 9. Royalty paid by related entity to domestic reverse hybrid entity. (i) *Facts.* The facts are the same as in *Example 3*, except the $100 income received by A from S in year 1 is a royalty payment under both the laws of the United States and the laws of Country X. The royalty rate under the treaty is 10 percent and the interest rate is 0 percent.

(ii) *Analysis.* The analysis as to the royalty payment from S to A is the same as in *Example 1* with respect to the $100 dividend payment from S to A. With respect to the $25 payment from A to FC, paragraph (d)(2)(ii)(B) of this section will not apply because the payment from S to A is not treated as a dividend under the Internal Revenue Code or the laws of Country X. Under paragraph (d)(2)(ii)(A) of this section, the $25 of interest paid by A to FC in year 2 is characterized as interest under the Internal Revenue Code. Accordingly, in year 2, FC may obtain the reduced rate of withholding applicable to interest under the U.S.-Country X income tax treaty, assuming all other requirements for claiming treaty benefits are met.

(3) *Definitions.*—(i) *Entity.*—For purposes of this paragraph (d), the term *entity* shall mean any person that is treated by the United States or the applicable treaty jurisdiction as other than an individual. The term *entity* includes disregarded entities, including single member disregarded entities with individual owners.

(ii) *Fiscally transparent under the law of the entity's jurisdiction.*—(A) *General rule.*—For purposes of this paragraph (d), an entity is fiscally transparent under the laws of the entity's jurisdiction with respect to an item of income to the extent that the laws of that jurisdiction require the interest holder in the entity, wherever resident, to separately take into account on a current basis the interest holder's respective share of the item of income paid to the entity, whether or not distributed to the interest holder, and the character and source of the item in the hands of the interest holder are determined as if such item were realized directly from the source from which realized by the entity. However, the entity will be fiscally transparent with respect to the item of income even if the item of income is not separately taken into account by the interest holder, provided the item of income, if separately taken into account by the interest holder, would not result in an income tax liability for that interest holder different from that which would result if the interest holder did not take the item into account separately, and provided the interest holder is required to take into account on a current basis the interest holder's share of all such nonseparately stated items of income paid to the entity, whether or not distributed to the interest holder. In determining whether an entity is fiscally transparent with respect to an item of income in the entity's jurisdiction, it is irrelevant that, under the laws of the entity's jurisdiction, the entity is permitted to exclude such item from gross income or that the entity is required to include such item in gross income but is entitled to a deduction for distributions to its interest holders.

(B) *Special definitions.*—For purposes of this paragraph (d)(3)(ii), an entity's jurisdiction is the jurisdiction where the entity is organized or incorporated or may otherwise be considered a resident under the laws of that jurisdiction. An interest holder will be treated as taking into account that person's share of income paid to an entity on a current basis even if such amount is taken into account by the interest holder in a taxable year other than the taxable year of the entity if the difference is due solely to differing taxable years.

(iii) *Fiscally transparent under the law of an interest holder's jurisdiction.*—(A) *General rule.*—For purposes of this paragraph (d), an entity is treated as fiscally transparent under the law of an interest holder's jurisdiction with respect to an item of income to the extent that the laws of the interest holder's jurisdiction require the interest holder resident in that jurisdiction to separately take into account on a current basis the interest holder's respective share of the item of income paid to the entity, whether or not distributed to the interest holder, and the character and source of the item in the hands of the interest holder are determined as if such item were realized directly from the source from which realized by the entity. However, an entity will be fiscally transparent with respect to the item of income even if the item of income is not separately taken into account by the interest holder, provided the item of income, if separately taken into account by the interest holder, would not result in an income tax liability for that interest holder different from that which would result if the interest holder did not take the item into account separately, and provided the interest holder is required to take into account on a current basis the interest holder's share of all such nonseparately stated items of income paid to the entity, whether or not distributed to the interest holder. An entity will not be treated as fiscally transparent with respect to an item of income under the laws of the interest holder's jurisdiction, however, if, under the laws of the interest holder's jurisdiction, the interest holder in the entity is required to include in gross income a share of all or a part of the entity's income on a current basis year under any type of anti-deferral or comparable mechanism. In determining whether an entity is fiscally transparent with respect to an item of income under the laws of an interest holder's jurisdiction, it is irrelevant how the entity is treated under the laws of the entity's jurisdiction.

(B) *Special definitions.*—For purposes of this paragraph (d)(3)(iii), an interest holder's jurisdiction is the jurisdiction where the interest holder is organized or incorporated or may otherwise be considered a resident under the laws of that jurisdiction. An interest holder will be treated as taking into account that person's share of income paid to an entity on a current basis even if such amount is taken into account by such person in a taxable year other than the taxable year of the entity if the difference is due solely to differing taxable years.

(iv) *Applicable treaty jurisdiction.*—The term *applicable treaty jurisdiction* means the jurisdiction whose income tax treaty with the United States is invoked for purposes of reducing the rate of tax imposed under sections 871(a), 881(a), 1461, and 4948(a).

(v) *Resident.*—The term *resident* shall have the meaning assigned to such term in the applicable income tax treaty.

(4) *Application to all income tax treaties.*—Unless otherwise explicitly agreed upon in the text of an income tax treaty, the rules contained

in this paragraph (d) shall apply in respect of all income tax treaties to which the United States is a party. Notwithstanding the foregoing sentence, the competent authorities may agree on a mutual basis to depart from the rules contained in this paragraph (d) in appropriate circumstances. However, a reduced rate under a tax treaty for an item of U.S. source income paid will not be available irrespective of the provisions in this paragraph (d) to the extent that the applicable treaty jurisdiction would not grant a reduced rate under the tax treaty to a U.S. resident in similar circumstances, as evidenced by a mutual agreement between the relevant competent authorities or by a public notice of the treaty jurisdiction. The Internal Revenue Service shall announce the terms of any such mutual agreement or public notice of the treaty jurisdiction. Any denial of tax treaty benefits as a consequence of such a mutual agreement or notice shall affect only payment of U.S. source items of income made after announcement of the terms of the agreement or of the notice.

(5) *Examples.*—This paragraph (d) is illustrated by the following examples:

Example 1. Treatment of entity treated as partnership by U.S. and country of organization. (i) *Facts.* Entity A is a business organization formed under the laws of Country X that has an income tax treaty in effect with the United States. A is treated as a partnership for U.S. federal income tax purposes. A is also treated as a partnership under the laws of Country X, and therefore Country X requires the interest holders in A to separately take into account on a current basis their respective shares of the items of income paid to A, whether or not distributed to the interest holders, and the character and source of the items in the hands of the interest holders are determined as if such items were realized directly from the source from which realized by A. A receives royalty income from U.S. sources that is not effectively connected with the conduct of a trade or business in the United States.

(ii) *Analysis.* A is fiscally transparent in its jurisdiction within the meaning of paragraph (d)(3)(ii) of this section with respect to the U.S. source royalty income in Country X and, thus, A does not derive such income for purposes of the U.S.-X income tax treaty.

Example 2. Treatment of interest holders in entity treated as partnership by U.S. and country of organization. (i) *Facts.* The facts are the same as under *Example 1.* A's partners are M, a corporation organized under the laws of Country Y that has an income tax treaty in effect with the United States, and T, a corporation organized under the laws of Country Z that has an income tax treaty in effect with the United States. M and T are not fiscally transparent under the laws of their respective countries of incorporation. Country Y requires M to separately take into account on a current basis M's respective share of the items of income paid to A, whether or not distributed to M, and the character and source of the items of income in M's hands are determined as if such items were realized directly from the source from which realized by A. Country Z treats A as a corporation and does not require T to take its share of A's income into account on a current basis whether or not distributed.

(ii) *Analysis.* M is treated as deriving its share of the U.S. source royalty income for purposes of the U.S.-Y income tax treaty because A is fiscally transparent under paragraph (d)(3)(iii) with respect to that income under the laws of Country Y. Under Country Z law, however, because T is not required to take into account its share of the U.S. source royalty income received by A on a current basis whether or not distributed, A is not treated as fiscally transparent. Accordingly, T is not treated as deriving its share of the U.S. source royalty income for purposes of the U.S.-Z income tax treaty.

Example 3. Dual benefits to entity and interest holder. (i) *Facts.* The facts are the same as under *Example 2,* except that A is taxable as a corporation under the laws of Country X. Article 12 of the U.S.-X income tax treaty provides for a source country reduced rate of taxation on royalties of 5-percent. Article 12 of the U.S.-Y income tax treaty provides that royalty income may only be taxed by the beneficial owner's country of residence.

(ii) *Analysis.* A is treated as deriving the U.S. source royalty income for purposes of the U.S.-X income tax treaty because it is not fiscally transparent with respect to the item of income within the meaning of paragraph (d)(3)(ii) of this section in Country X, its country of organization. M is also treated as deriving its share of the U.S. source royalty income for purposes of the U.S.-Y income tax treaty because A is fiscally transparent under paragraph (d)(3)(iii) of this section with respect to that income under the laws of Country Y. T is not treated as deriving the U.S. source royalty income for purposes of the U.S.-Z income tax treaty because under Country Z law A is not fiscally transparent. Assuming all other requirements for eligibility for treaty benefits have been satisfied, A is entitled to the 5-percent treaty reduced rate on royalties under the U.S.-X income tax treaty with respect to the entire royalty payment. Assuming all other requirements for treaty benefits have been satisfied, M is also entitled to a zero rate under the U.S.-Y income tax treaty with respect to its share of the royalty income.

Example 4. Treatment of grantor trust. (i) *Facts.* Entity A is a trust organized under the laws of Country X, which does not have an income tax treaty in effect with the United States. M, the grantor and owner of A for U.S. income tax purposes, is a resident of Country Y, which has an income tax treaty in effect with the United States. M is also treated as the grantor and owner of the trust under the laws of Country Y. Thus, Country Y requires M to take into account all items of A's income in the taxable year, whether or not distributed to M, and determines the character of each item in M's hands as if such item was realized directly from the source from which realized by A. Country X does not treat M as the owner of A and does not require M to account for A's income on a current basis whether or not distributed to M. A receives interest income from U.S. sources that is neither portfolio interest nor effectively connected with the conduct of a trade or business in the United States.

(ii) *Analysis.* A is not fiscally transparent under the laws of Country X within the meaning of paragraph (d)(3)(ii) of this section with respect to the U.S. source interest income, but A may not claim treaty benefits because there is no U.S.-X income tax treaty. M, however, does derive the income for purposes of the U.S.-Y income tax treaty because under the laws of Country Y, A is fiscally transparent.

Example 5. Treatment of complex trust. (i) *Facts.* The facts are the same as in *Example 4* except that M is treated as the owner of the trust only under U.S. tax law, after application of section 672(f), but not under the law of Country Y. Although the trust document governing A does not require that A distribute any of its income on a current basis, some distributions are made currently to M. There is no requirement under Country Y law that M take into account A's income on a current basis whether or not distributed to him in that year. Under the laws of Country Y, with respect to current distributions, the character of the item of income in the hands of the interest holder is determined as if such item were realized directly from the source from which realized by A. Accordingly, upon a current distribution of interest income to M, the interest income retains its source as U.S. source income.

(ii) *Analysis.* M does not derive the U.S. source interest income because A is not fiscally transparent under paragraph (d)(3)(ii) of this section with respect to the U.S. source interest income under the laws of Country Y. Although the character of the interest in the hands of M is determined as if realized directly from the source from which realized by A, under the laws of Country Y, M is not required to take into account his share of A's interest income on a current basis whether or not distributed. Accordingly, neither A nor M is entitled to claim treaty benefits, since A is a resident of a nontreaty jurisdiction and M does not derive the U.S. source interest income for purposes of the U.S.-Y income tax treaty.

Example 6. Treatment of interest holders required to include passive income under anti-deferral regime. (i) *Facts.* The facts are the same as under *Example 2*. However, Country Z does require T, who is treated as owning 60-percent of the stock of A, to take into account its respective share of the royalty income of A under an anti-deferral regime applicable to certain passive income of controlled foreign corporations.

(ii) *Analysis.* T is still not eligible to claim treaty benefits with respect to the royalty income. T is not treated as deriving the U.S. source royalty income for purposes of the U.S.-Z income tax treaty under paragraph (d)(3)(iii) of this section because T is only required to take into account its pro rata share of the U.S. source royalty income by reason of Country Z's anti-deferral regime.

Example 7. Treatment of contractual arrangements operating as collective investment vehicles. (i) *Facts.* A is a contractual arrangement without legal personality for all purposes under the laws of Country X providing for joint ownership of securities. Country X has an income tax treaty in effect with the United States. A is a collective investment fund which is of a type known as a Common Fund under Country X law. Because of the absence of legal personality in Country X of the arrangement, A is not liable to tax as a person at the entity level in Country X and is thus not a resident within the meaning of the Residence Article of the U.S.-X income tax treaty. A is treated as a partnership for U.S. income tax purposes and receives U.S. source dividend income. Under the laws of Country X, however, investors in A only take into account their respective share of A's income upon distribution from the Common Fund. Some of A's interest holders are residents of Country X and some of Country Y. Country Y has no income tax treaty in effect with the United States.

(ii) *Analysis.* A is not fiscally transparent under paragraph (d)(3)(ii) of this section with respect to the U.S. source dividend income because the interest holders in A are not required to take into account their respective shares of such income in the taxable year whether or not distributed. Because A is an arrangement without a legal personality that is not considered a person in Country X and thus not a resident of Country X under the Residence Article of the U.S.-X income tax treaty, however, A does not derive the income as a resident of Country X for purposes of the U.S.-X income tax treaty. Further, because A is not fiscally transparent under paragraph (d)(3)(iii)

Reg. §1.894-1(d)(5)

of this section with respect to the U.S. source dividend income, A's interest holders that are residents of Country X do not derive the income as residents of Country X for purposes of the U.S.-X income tax treaty.

Example 8. Treatment of person specifically listed as resident in applicable treaty. (i) *Facts.* The facts are the same as in *Example 7* except that A (the Common Fund) is organized in Country Z and the Residence Article of the U.S.-Z income tax treaty provides that "the term 'resident of a Contracting State' includes, in the case of Country Z, Common Funds . . . ."

(ii) *Analysis.* A is treated, for purposes of the U.S.-Z income tax treaty as deriving the dividend income as a resident of Country Z under paragraph (d)(1) of this section because the item of income is paid directly to A, A is a Common Fund under the laws of Country Z, and Common Funds are specifically identified as residents of Country Z in the U.S.-Z treaty. There is no need to determine whether A meets the definition of fiscally transparent under paragraph (d)(3)(ii) of this section.

Example 9. Treatment of investment company when entity receives distribution deductions, and all distributions sourced by residence of entity. (i) *Facts.* Entity A is a business organization formed under the laws of Country X, which has an income tax treaty in effect with the United States. A is treated as a partnership for U.S. income tax purposes. Under the laws of Country X, A is an investment company taxable at the entity level and a resident of Country X. It is also entitled to a distribution deduction for amounts distributed to its interest holders on a current basis. A distributes all its net income on a current basis to its interest holders and, thus, in fact, has no income tax liability to Country X. A receives U.S. source dividend income. Under Country X law, all amounts distributed to interest holders of this type of business entity are treated as dividends from sources within Country X and Country X imposes a withholding tax on all payments by A to foreign persons. Under Country X laws, the interest holders in A do not have to separately take into account their respective shares of A's income on a current basis if such income is not, in fact, distributed.

(ii) *Analysis.* A is not fiscally transparent under paragraph (d)(3)(ii) of this section with respect to the U.S. source dividends because the interest holders in A do not have to take into account their respective share of the U.S. source dividends on a current basis whether or not distributed. A is also not fiscally transparent under paragraph (d)(3)(ii) of this section because there is a change in source of the income received by A when A distributes the income to its interest holders and, thus, the character and source of the income in the hands of A's interest holder are not determined as if such income were realized directly from the source from which realized by A. Accordingly, A is treated as deriving the U.S. source dividends for purposes of the U.S.-Country X treaty.

Example 10. Item by item determination of fiscal transparency. (i) *Facts.* Entity A is a business organization formed under the laws of Country X, which has an income tax treaty in effect with the United States. A is treated as a partnership for U.S. income tax purposes. Under the laws of Country X, A is an investment company taxable at the entity level and a resident of Country X. It is also entitled to a distribution deduction for amounts distributed to its interest holders on a current basis. A receives both U.S. source dividend income and interest income from U.S. sources that is neither portfolio interest nor effectively connected with the conduct of a trade or business in the United States. Country X law sources all distributions attributable to dividend income based on the residence of the investment company. In contrast, Country X law sources all distributions attributable to interest income based on the residence of the payor of the interest. No withholding applies with respect to distributions attributable to U.S. source interest and the character of the distributions attributable to the interest income remains the same in the hands of A's interest holders as if such items were realized directly from the source from which realized by A. However, under Country X law the interest holders in A do not have to take into account their respective share of the interest income received by A on a current basis whether or not distributed.

(ii) *Analysis.* An item by item analysis is required under paragraph (d) of this section. The analysis is the same as *Example 9* with respect to the dividend income. A is also not fiscally transparent under paragraph (d)(3)(ii) of this section with respect to the interest income because, although the character of the distributions attributable to the interest income in the hands of A's interest holders is determined as if realized directly from the source from which realized by A, under Country X law the interest holders in A do not have to take into account their respective share of the interest income received by A on a current basis whether or not distributed. Accordingly, A derives the U.S. source interest income for purpose of the U.S.-X treaty.

Example 11. Treatment of charitable organizations. (i) *Facts.* Entity A is a corporation organized under the laws of Country X that has an income tax treaty in effect with the United States. Entity A is established and operated exclusively for religious, charitable, scientific, artistic, cultural, or educational purposes. Entity A receives U.S. source dividend income from U.S. sources. A provision of Country X law generally exempts Entity A's income from Country X tax due to the fact that Entity A is established and operated exclusively for religious, charitable, scientific, artistic, cultural, or educational purposes. But for such provision, Entity A's income would be taxed by Country X.

(ii) *Analysis.* Entity A is not fiscally transparent under paragraph (d)(3)(ii) of this section with respect to the U.S. source dividend income because, under Country X law, the dividend income is treated as an item of income of A and no other persons are required to take into account their respective share of the item of income on a current basis, whether or not distributed. Accordingly, Entity A is treated as deriving the U.S. source dividend income.

Example 12. Treatment of pension trusts. (i) *Facts.* Entity A is a trust established and operated in Country X exclusively to provide pension or other similar benefits to employees pursuant to a plan. Entity A receives U.S. source dividend income. A provision of Country X law generally exempts Entity A's income from Country X tax due to the fact that Entity A is established and operated exclusively to provide pension or other similar benefits to employees pursuant to a plan. Under the laws of Country X, the beneficiaries of the trust are not required to take into account their respective share of A's income on a current basis, whether or not distributed and the character and source of the income in the hands of A's interest holders are not determined as if realized directly from the source from which realized by A.

(ii) *Analysis.* A is not fiscally transparent under paragraph (d)(3)(ii) of this section with respect to the U.S. source dividend income because under the laws of Country X, the beneficiaries of A are not required to take into account their respective share of A's income on a current basis, whether or not distributed. A is also not fiscally transparent under paragraph (d)(3)(ii) of this section with respect to the U.S. source dividend income because under the laws of Country X, the character and source of the income in the hands of A's interest holders are not determined as if realized directly from the source from which realized by A. Accordingly, A derives the U.S. source dividend income for purposes of the U.S.-X income tax treaty.

(6) *Effective dates.*—This paragraph (d) applies to items of income paid on or after June 30, 2000, except paragraphs (d)(2)(ii) and (d)(2)(iii) of this section apply to items of income paid by a domestic reverse hybrid entity on or after June 12, 2002 with respect to amounts received by the domestic reverse hybrid entity on or after June 12, 2002.

(e) *Effective dates.*—Paragraphs (a) and (b) of this section apply for taxable years beginning after December 31, 1966. For corresponding rules applicable to taxable years beginning before January 1, 1967, (see 26 CFR part 1 revised April 1, 1971). Paragraph (c) of this section is applicable to payments made after November 13, 1997. See paragraph (d)(6) of this section for applicability dates for paragraph (d) of this section. [Reg. § 1.894-1.]

☐ [*T.D.* 6258, 10-23-57. *Amended by T.D.* 7293, 11-27-73; *T.D.* 8735, 10-6-97; *T.D.* 8889, 6-30-2000 (*corrected* 12-7-2000) *and T.D.* 8999, 6-11-2002.]

Proposed Amendments to Regulation

§ 1.894-1. Income affected by treaty.

* * *

(d) *Income from a global dealing operation.*—If a taxpayer that is engaged in a global dealing operation, as defined in § 1.482-8(a)(2)(i), has a permanent establishment in the United States under the principles of an applicable U.S. income tax treaty, the principles of § 1.863-3(h), § 1.864-4(c)(2)(iv), § 1.864-4(c)(3)(ii), § 1.864-4(c)(5)(vi)(a) or § 1.864-6(b)(2)(ii)(*d*)(3) shall apply for purposes of determining the income attributable to that U.S. permanent establishment.

* * *

[Prop. Reg. § 1.894-1.]
[Proposed 3-6-98.]

§ 1.897-1. Taxation of foreign investment in United States real property interests, definition of terms.—(a) *In general.*—(1) *Purpose and scope of regulations.*—These regulations provide guidance with respect to the taxation of foreign investment in U.S. real property interests and related matters. This section defines various terms for purposes of sections 897, 1445, and 6039C and the regulations thereunder. Section 1.897-2 provides rules regarding the definition of, and consequences of, U.S. real property holding corporation status. Section 1.897-3 sets forth rules pursuant to which certain foreign corporations may elect under section 897(i) to be treated as domestic corporations for purposes of sections 897 and 6039C. Finally, § 1.897-4 provides rules concerning the similar election under section 897(k) for certain foreign corporations in the process of liquidation.

(2) *Effective date.*—The regulations set forth in § § 1.897-1 through 1.897-4 are effective for transactions occurring after June 18, 1980. However, with respect to all transactions occurring after June 18, 1980, and before January 30, 1985, taxpayers may at their option choose to apply the Temporary Regulations under section

897 (in their entirety). The Temporary Regulations are located at 26 CFR §§ 6a. 897-1 through 6a. 897-4 (Revised as of April 1, 1983), and were originally published in the *Federal Register* for September 21, 1982 (47 FR 41532) and amended by T.D. 7890, published in the *Federal Register* on April 28, 1983 (48 FR 19163).

(b) *Real property.*—(1) *In general.*—The term "real property" includes the following three categories of property: Land and unsevered natural products of the land, improvements, and personal property associated with the use of real property. The three categories of real property are defined in subparagraphs (2), (3), and (4) of this paragraph (b). Local law definitions will not be controlling for purposes of determining the meaning of the term "real property" as it is used in sections 897, 1445, and 6039C and the regulations thereunder.

(2) *Land and unsevered natural products of the land.*—The term "real property" includes land, growing crops and timber, and mines, wells, and other natural deposits. Crops and timber cease to be real property at the time that they are severed from the land. Ores, minerals, and other natural deposits cease to be real property when they are extracted from the ground. The storage of severed or extracted crops, timber, or minerals in or upon real property will not cause such property to be recharacterized as real property.

(3) *Improvements.*—(i) *In general.*—The term "real property" includes improvements on land. An improvement is a building, any other inherently permanent structure, or the structural components of either, as defined in subdivisions (ii) through (iv) of this paragraph (b)(3).

(ii) *Building.*—The term "building" generally means any structure or edifice enclosing a space within its walls, and usually covered by a roof, the purpose of which is, for example, to provide shelter or housing or to provide working, office, parking, display, or sales space. The term includes, for example, structures such as apartment houses, factory and office buildings, warehouses, barns, garages, railway or bus stations, and stores. Any structure that is classified as a building for purposes of section 48(a)(1)(B) and § 1.48-1 shall be treated as such for purposes of this section.

(iii) *Inherently permanent structure.*—(A) *In general.*—The term "inherently permanent structure" means any property not otherwise described in this paragraph (b)(3) that is affixed to real property and that will ordinarily remain affixed for an indefinite period of time. Property that is not classified as a building for purposes of section 48(a)(1)(B) and § 1.48-1 may nevertheless constitute an inherently permanent structure. For purposes of this section, affixation to real property may be accomplished by weight alone.

(B) *Use of precedents under section 48.*—Any property not otherwise described in this paragraph (b)(3) that constitutes "other tangible property" under the principles of section 48(a)(1)(B) and § 1.48-1(c) and (d) shall be treated for purposes of this section as an inherently permanent structure. Thus, for example, the term includes swimming pools, paved parking areas and other pavements, special foundations for heavy equipment, wharves and docks, bridges, fences, inherently permanent advertising displays, inherently permanent outdoor lighting facilities, railroad tracks and signals, telephone poles, permanently installed telephone and television cables, broadcasting towers, oil derricks, oil and gas pipelines, oil and gas storage tanks, grain storage bins, and silos. However, property that is determined to be either property in the nature of machinery under § 1.48-1(c) or property which is essentially an item of machinery or equipment under § 1.48-1(e)(1)(i) shall not be treated as an inherently permanent structure.

(C) *Absence of precedents under section 48.*—Where precedents developed under the principles of section 48 fail to provide adequate guidance with respect to the classification of particular property, the determination of whether such property constitutes an inherently permanent structure shall be made in view of all the facts and circumstances. In particular, the following factors must be taken into account:

(1) The manner in which the property is affixed to real property;

(2) Whether the property was designed to be easily removable or to remain in place indefinitely;

(3) Whether the property has been moved since its initial installation;

(4) Any circumstances that suggest the expected period of affixation (e.g., a lease that requires removal of the property upon its expiration);

(5) The amount of damage that removal of the property would cause to the property itself or to the real property to which it is affixed; and

(6) The extent of the effort that would be required to remove the property, in terms of time and expense.

(iv) *Structural components of buildings and other inherently permanent structures.*—Structural components of buildings and other inherently permanent structures, as defined in § 1.48-1(e)(2), themselves constitute improvements. Structural components include walls, partitions, floors, ceilings, windows, doors, wiring, plumbing, central heating and central air conditioning systems, lighting fixtures, pipes, ducts, elevators, escalators, sprinkler systems, fire escapes, and other components relating to the operation or maintenance of a building. However, the term "structural components" does not include machinery the sole justification for the installation of which is the fact that such machinery is required to meet temperature or humidity requirements which are essential for the operation of other machinery or the processing of materials or foodstuffs. Machinery may meet the "sole justification" test provided by the preceding sentence even though it incidentally provides for the comfort of employees or serves to an insubstantial degree areas where such temperature or humidity requirements are not essential.

(4) *Personal property associated with the use of the real property.*—(i) *In general.*—The term "real property" includes movable walls, furnishings, and other personal property associated with the use of the real property. Personal property is associated with the use of real property only if it is described in one of the categories set forth in subdivisions (A) through (D) of this paragraph (b)(4)(i). "Personal property" for purposes of this section means any property that constitutes "tangible personal property" under the principles of § 1.48-1(c), without regard to whether such property qualifies as section 38 property. Such property will be associated with the use of the real property only where both the personal property and the United States real property interest with which it is associated are held by the same person or by related persons within the meaning of § 1.897-1(i). For purposes of this paragraph (b)(4)(i), property is used "predominantly" in a named activity if it is devoted to that activity during at least half of the time in which it is in use during a calendar year.

(A) *Property used in mining, farming, and forestry.*—Personal property is associated with the use of real property if it is predominantly used to exploit unsevered natural products in or upon the land. Such property includes mining equipment used to extract ores, minerals, and other natural deposits from the ground. It also includes any property used to cultivate the soil and harvest its products, such as farm machinery, draft animals, and equipment used in the growing and cutting of timber. However, personal property used to process or transport minerals, crops, or timber after they are severed from the land is not associated personal property.

(B) *Property used in the improvement of real property.*—Personal property is associated with the use of real property if it is predominantly used to construct or otherwise carry out improvements to real property. Such property includes equipment used to alter the natural contours of the land, equipment used to clear and prepare raw land for construction, and equipment used to carry out the construction of improvements.

(C) *Property used in the operation of a lodging facility.*—Personal property is associated with the use of real property if it is predominantly used in connection with the operation of a lodging facility. Property that is used in connection with the operation of a lodging facility includes property used in the living quarters of such facility, such as beds and other furniture, refrigerators, ranges and other equipment, as well as property used in the common areas of such facility, such as lobby furniture and laundry equipment. Such property constitutes personal property associated with the use of real property in the hands of the owner or operator of the facility, not of the tenant or guest. A lodging facility is an apartment house or apartment, hotel, motel, dormitory, residence, or any other facility (or part of a facility) predominantly used to provide, at a charge, living and/or sleeping accommodations, whether on a daily, weekly, monthly, annual, or other basis. The term "lodging facility" does not include a personal residence occupied solely by its owner, or a facility used primarily as a means of transportation (such as an aircraft, vessel, or a railroad car) or used primarily to provide medical or convalescent services, even though sleeping accommodations are provided. Nor does the term include temporary living quarters provided by an employer due to the unavailability of lodgings within a reasonable distance of a worksite (such as a mine or construction project). The term "lodging facility" does not include any portion of a facility that constitutes a nonlodging commercial facility and that is available to persons not using the lodging facility on the same basis that it is available to tenants of the lodging facility. Examples of nonlodging commercial facilities include restaurants, drug stores, and grocery stores located in a lodging facility.

(D) *Property used in the rental of furnished office and other work space.*—Personal property is associated with the use of real property if it is predominantly used by a lessor to provide furnished office or other work space to lessees. Property that is so used includes office furniture and equipment included in the rental of furnished space. Such property constitutes personal property associated with the use of

Reg. § 1.897-1(b)(4)(i)(D)

real property in the hands of the lessor, not of the lessee.

(ii) *Dispositions of associated personal property.*—(A) *In general.*—Personal property that has become associated with the use of a real property interest shall itself be treated as real property interest upon its disposition, unless either:

(*1*) The personal property is disposed of more than one year before the disposition of any present right to use or occupy the real property with which it was associated (and subject to the provisions of subdivision (B) of this paragraph (b)(4)(ii));

(*2*) The personal property is disposed of more than one year after the disposition of all present rights to use or occupy the real property with which it was associated (and subject to the provisions of subdivision (C) of this paragraph (b)(4)(ii); or

(*3*) The personal property and the real property with which it was associated are separately sold to persons that are related neither to the transferor nor to one another (and subject to the provisions of subdivision (D) of this paragraph (b)(4)(ii)).

(B) *Personalty disposed of one year before realty.*—A transferor of personal property associated with the use of real property need not treat such property as a real property interest upon disposition if on the date of disposition the transferor does not expect or intend to dispose of the real property until more than one year later. However, if the real property is in fact disposed of within the following year, the transferor must treat the personal property as having been a real property interest as of the date on which the personalty was disposed of. If the transferor had not previously filed an income tax return, a return must be filed and tax paid, together with any interest due thereon, by the later of the date on which a tax return or payment is actually due (with extensions), or the 60th day following the date of disposition. If the transferor had previously filed an income tax return, an amended return must be filed and tax paid, together with any interest due thereon, by the later of the dates specified above. Such a transferor may be liable to penalties for failure to file, for late payment of tax, or for understatement of liability, but only if the transferor knew or had reason to anticipate that the real property would be disposed of within one year of the disposition of the associated personal property.

(C) *Personalty disposed of one year after realty.*—A disposition of real property shall be disregarded for purposes of subdivision (A)(*2*) of this paragraph (b)(4)(ii) if any right to use or occupy the real property is reacquired within the one-year period referred to in that subdivision. However, the disposition shall not be disregarded if such reacquisition is made in foreclosure of a mortgage or other security interest, in the exercise of a contractual remedy, or in the enforcement of a judgment. If, however, the reacquisition of the property is made pursuant to a plan the principal purpose of which is the avoidance of the provisions of section 897, 1445, or 6039C and the regulations thereunder, then the initial disposition shall be disregarded for purposes of subdivision (A)(*2*) of this paragraph (b)(4)(ii).

(D) *Separate dispositions of personalty and realty.*—A transferor of personal property associated with the use of real property need not treat such property as a real property interest upon disposition if within 90 days before or after such disposition the transferor separately disposes of the real property interest to persons that are related neither to the transferor nor to the purchaser of the personal property. A transferor may rely upon this rule unless the transferor knows or has reason to know that the purchasers of the real property and the personal property—

(*1*) Are related persons; or

(*2*) Intend to reassociate the personal property with the use of the real property within one year of the date of disposition of the personal property.

(E) *Status of property in hands of transferee.*—Personal property that has been associated with the use of real property and that is sold to an unrelated party will be treated as real property in the hands of the transferee only if the personal property becomes associated with the use of real property held or acquired by the transferee, in the manner described in paragraph (b)(4)(i) of this section.

(iii) *Determination dates.*—The determination of whether personal property is personal property associated with the use of real property as defined in this paragraph (b)(4) is to be made on the date the personal property is disposed of and on each applicable determination date. See § 1.897-2(c).

(c) *United States real property interest.*—(1) *In general.*—The term "United States real property interest" means any interest, other than an interest solely as a creditor, in either:

(i) Real property located in the United States or the Virgin Islands, or

(ii) A domestic corporation unless it is established that the corporation was not a U.S. real property holding corporation within the period described in section 897(c)(1)(A)(ii).

In addition, for the limited purpose of determining whether any corporation is a U.S. real property holding corporation, the term "United States real property interest" means an interest, other than an interest solely as a creditor, in a foreign corporation unless it is established that the foreign corporation is not a U.S. real property holding corporation within the period prescribed in section 897(c)(1)(A)(ii). See § 1.897-2 for rules regarding the manner of establishing that a corporation is not a United States real property holding corporation.

(2) *Exceptions and special rules.*—(i) *Domestically-controlled REIT.*—An interest in a domestically-controlled real estate investment trust (REIT) is not a U.S. real property interest. A domestically-controlled REIT is one in which less than 50 percent of the fair market value of the outstanding stock was directly or indirectly held by foreign persons during the five-year period ending on the applicable determination date (or the period since June 18, 1980, if shorter). For purposes of this determination the actual owners of stock, as determined under § 1.857-8, must be taken into account.

(ii) *Corporation that has disposed of all U.S. real property interests.*—The term "United States real property interest" does not include an interest in a corporation which has disposed of all its U.S. real property interests in transactions in which the full amount of gain, if any, was recognized, as provided in section 897(c)(1)(B). See § 1.897-2(f) for rules regarding the requirements of section 897(c)(1)(B).

(iii) *Publicly-traded corporations.*—If, at any time during the calendar year, any class of stock of a domestic corporation is regularly traded on an established securities market, an interest in such corporation shall be treated as a U.S. real property interest only in the case of:

(A) A regularly traded interest owned by a person who beneficially owned more than 5 percent of the total fair market value of that class of interests at any time during the five-year period ending either on the date of disposition of such interest or other applicable determination date (or the period since June 18, 1980, if shorter), or

(B) [Reserved]

(iv) *Publicly traded partnerships and trusts.*—If any class of interests in a partnership or trust is, within the meaning of § 1.897-1(m) and (n), regularly traded on an established securities market, then for purposes of sections 897(g) and 1445 and § 1.897-2(d) and (e) an interest in the entity shall not be treated as an interest in a partnership or trust. Instead, such an interest shall be subject to the rules applicable to interests in publicly traded corporations pursuant to paragraph (c)(2)(iii) of this section. Such interests can be real property interests in the hands of a person that holds a greater than 5 percent interest. Therefore, solely for purposes of determining whether greater than 5 percent interests in such an entity constitutes U.S. real property interests the disposition of which is subject to tax, the entity is required to determine pursuant to the provisions of § 1.897-2 whether the assets it holds would cause it to be classified as a U.S. real property holding corporation if it were a corporation. The treatment of dispositions of U.S. real property interests by publicly traded partnerships and trusts is not affected by the rules of this paragraph (c)(2)(iv); by reason of the operation of section 897(a), foreign partners or beneficiaries are subject to tax upon their distributive share of any gain recognized upon such dispositions by the partnership or trust. The rules of this paragraph (c)(2)(iv) are illustrated by the following example.

Example. PTP is a partnership one class of interests in which is regularly traded on an established securities market. A is a nonresident alien individual who owns 1 percent of a class of limited partnership interests in PTP. B is a nonresident alien individual who owns 10 percent of the same class of limited partnership interests in PTP. On July 1, 1986, A and B sell their interests in PTP. Pursuant to the rules of this paragraph (c)(2)(iv), neither disposition is treated as the disposition of a partnership interest subject to the provisions of section 897(g). Instead, A and B are treated as having disposed of interests in a publicly traded corporation. Therefore, pursuant to the rule of paragraph (c)(2)(iii) of this section, A's disposition of a 1 percent interest has no consequences under section 897. However, B's disposition of a 10 percent interest will constitute the disposition of a U.S. real property interest subject to tax by reason of the operation of section 897 unless it is established pursuant to the rules of § 1.897-2 that the interest is not a U.S. real property interest.

(d) *Interest other than an interest solely as a creditor.*—(1) *In general.*—This paragraph defines an interest other than an interest solely as a creditor, with respect to real property, and with respect to corporations, partnerships, trusts, and estates. An interest solely as a creditor either in real property or in a domestic corporation does not constitute a United States real property interest. Similarly, where one corporation holds an interest solely as a creditor in a second corporation or in a partnership, trust, or estate, that interest will be disregarded for purposes of determining whether the first corporation is a U.S. real property holding corporation (except to the extent that such interest constitutes an asset used or held for use in a trade or business, in accordance with the rules of §1.897-1(f)). In addition, the disposition of an interest solely as a creditor in a partnership, trust, or estate is not subject to sections 897, 1445, and 6039C. Whether an interest is considered debt under any provisions of the Code is not determinative of whether it constitutes an interest solely as a creditor for purpose of sections 897, 1445, and 6039C and the regulations thereunder.

(2) *Interests in real property other than solely as creditor.*—(i) *In general.*—An interest in real property other than an interest solely as a creditor includes a fee ownership, co-ownership, or leasehold interest in real property, a time sharing interest in real property, and a life estate, remainder, or reversionary interest in such property. The term also includes any direct or indirect right to share in the appreciation in the value, or in the gross or net proceeds or profits generated by, the real property. A loan to an individual or entity under the terms of which a holder of the indebtedness has any direct or indirect right to share in the appreciation in value of, or the gross or net proceeds or profits generated by, an interest in real property of the debtor or of a related person is, in its entirety, an interest in real property other than solely as a creditor. An interest in production payments described in section 636 does not generally constitute an interest in real property other than solely as a creditor. However, a right to production payments shall constitute an interest in real property other than solely as a creditor if it conveys a right to share in the appreciation in value of the mineral property. A production payment that is limited to a quantum of mineral (including a percentage of recoverable reserves produced) or a period of time will be considered to convey a right to share in the appreciation in value of the mineral property. The rules of this paragraph (d)(2)(i) are illustrated by the following example.

Example. A, a U.S. citizen, purchases a condominium unit located in the United States for $500,000. A makes a $100,000 down payment and borrows $400,000 from B, a foreign person, to pay the balance of the purchase price. Under the terms of the loan, A is to pay B 13 percent annual interest each year for 10 years and 35 percent of the appreciation in the fair market value of the condominium at the end of the 10-year period. Because B has a right to share in the appreciation in value of the condominium, B has an interest other than solely as a creditor in the condominium. B's entire interest in the obligation from A, therefore, is a United States real property interest.

(ii) *Special rules.*—(A) *Installment obligations.*—A right to installment or other deferred payments from the disposition of an interest in real property will constitute an interest solely as a creditor if the transferor elects not to have the installment method of section 453(a) apply, any gain or loss is recognized in the year of disposition, and all tax due is timely paid. See section 1445 and regulations thereunder for further guidance concerning the availability of installment sale treatment under section 453. If an agreement for the payment of tax with respect to an installment sale is entered into with the Internal Revenue Service pursuant to section 1445, that agreement may specify whether or not the installment obligation will constitute an interest solely as a creditor. If an installment obligation constitutes an interest other than solely as a creditor then the receipt of each payment shall be treated as the disposition of an interest in real property that is subject to section 897(a) to the extent of any gain required to be taken into account pursuant to section 453. If the original holder of an installment obligation that constitutes an interest other than solely as a creditor subsequently disposes of the obligation to an unrelated party and recognizes gain or loss pursuant to section 453B, the obligation will constitute an interest in real property solely as a creditor in the hands of the subsequent holder. However, if the obligation is disposed of to a related person and the full amount of gain realized upon the disposition of the real property has not been recognized upon such disposition of the installment obligation, then the obligation shall continue to be an interest in real property other than solely as a creditor in the hands of the subsequent holder subject to the rules of this paragraph (d)(2)(ii)(A).

In addition, if the obligation is disposed of to any person for a principal purpose of avoiding the provisions of section 897, 1445, or 6039C, then the obligation shall continue to be an interest in real property other than solely as a creditor in the hands of the subsequent holder subject to the rules of this paragraph (d)(2)(ii)(A). However, rights to payments arising from dispositions that took place before June 19, 1980, shall in no event constitute interests in real property other than solely as a creditor, even if such payments are received after June 18, 1980. In addition, rights to payments arising from dispositions to unrelated parties that took place before January 1, 1985, and that were not subject to U.S. tax pursuant to the provisions of a U.S. income tax treaty, shall not constitute interests in real property other than solely as a creditor, even if such payments are received after December 31, 1984.

(B) *Options.*—An option, a contract, or a right of first refusal to acquire any interest in real property (other than an interest solely as a creditor) will itself constitute an interest in real property other than solely as a creditor.

(C) *Security interests.*—A right to repossess or foreclose on real property under a mortgage, security agreement, financing statement, or other collateral instrument securing a debt will not be considered a reversionary interest in, or a right to share in the appreciation in value of or gross or net proceeds or profits generated by, an interest in real property. Thus, no such right of repossession or foreclosure will of itself cause an interest in real property which is otherwise an interest solely as a creditor to become an interest other than solely as a creditor. In addition, a person acting as mortgagee in possession shall not be considered to hold an interest in real property other than solely as a creditor, if the mortgagee's interest in the property otherwise constitutes an interest solely as a creditor.

(D) *Indexed interest rates.*—An interest will not constitute a right to share in the appreciation in the value of, or gross or net proceeds or profits generated by, real property solely because it bears a rate of interest that is tied to an index of any kind that is intended to reflect general inflation or deflation of prices and interest rates (e.g., the Consumer Price Index). However, where an interest in real property bears a rate of interest that is tied to an index the principal purpose of which is to reflect changes in real property values, the real property interest will be considered an indirect right to share in the appreciation in value of, or gross or net proceeds or profits generated by, real property. Such an indirect right constitutes an interest in real property other than solely as a creditor.

(E) *Commissions.*—A right to payment of a commission, brokerage fee, or similar charge for professional services rendered in connection with the arrangement or financing of a purchase, sale, or lease of real property does not constitute a right to share in the appreciation in value of, or gross or net proceeds or profits of, real property solely because it is based upon a percentage of the purchase price or rent. Thus, a right to a commission earned by a real estate agent based on a percentage of the sales price does not constitute an interest in real property other than solely as a creditor. However, a right to a commission, brokerage fee, or similar charge will constitute an interest other than solely as a creditor if the total amount of the payment is contingent upon appreciation, proceeds, or profits of the real property occurring or arising after the date of the transaction with respect to which the professional services were rendered. For example, a commission earned in connection with the purchase of a real property interest that is contingent upon the amount of gain ultimately realized by the purchaser will constitute an interest in real property other than solely as a creditor.

(F) *Trustees' fees, etc.*—A right to payment of reasonable compensation for services rendered as a trustee, as an administrator of an estate, or in a similar capacity does not constitute a right to share in the appreciation in the value of, or gross or net proceeds or profits of, real property solely because the assets of the trust or estate include U.S. real property interests.

(3) *Interest in an entity other than solely as a creditor.*—(i) *In general.*—For purposes of sections 897, 1445, and 6039C, an interest in an entity other than an interest solely as a creditor is—

(A) Stock of a corporation;

(B) An interest in a partnership as a partner within the meaning of section 761(b) and the regulations thereunder;

(C) An interest in a trust or estate as a beneficiary within the meaning of section 643(c) and the regulations thereunder or an ownership interest in any portion of a trust as provided in section 671 through 679 and the regulations thereunder;

(D) An interest which is, in whole or in part, a direct or indirect right to share in the appreciation in value of an interest in an entity described in subdivision (A), (B), or (C) of this paragraph (d)(3)(i) or a direct or indirect right to share in the appreciation in value of assets of, or gross or net proceeds or profits derived by, the entity; or

(E) A right (whether or not presently exercisable) directly or indirectly to acquire, by purchase, conversion, exchange, or in any other manner, an interest described in subdivision (A), (B), (C), or (D) of this paragraph (d)(3)(i).

(ii) *Special rules.*—(A) *Installment obligations.*—A right to installment or other deferred payments from the disposition of an interest in an entity will constitute an interest solely as a creditor if the transferor elects not to have the installment method of section 453(a) apply, any gain or loss is recognized in the year of disposition, and tax due is timely paid. See section 1445 and regulations thereunder for further guidance concerning the availability of installment sale treatment under section 453. If an agreement for the payment of tax with respect to an installment sale is entered into with the Internal Revenue Service pursuant to section 1445, that agreement may specify whether or not the installment obligation will constitute an interest solely as a creditor. If an installment obligation constitutes an interest other than solely as a creditor then the receipt of each payment shall be treated as the disposition of such an interest and shall be subject to section 897(a) to the extent that: (*1*) It constitutes the disposition of a U.S. real property interest and (*2*) Gain or loss is required to be taken into account pursuant to section 453. Such treatment shall apply to payments arising from dispositions of interests in a corporation any class of the stock of which is regularly traded on an established securities market, but only in the case of a disposition of any portion of an interest described in paragraph (c)(2)(iii)(A) or (B) of this section. If the original holder of an installment obligation that constitutes an interest other than solely as a creditor subsequently disposes of the obligation to an unrelated party and recognizes gain or loss pursuant to section 453B, the obligation will constitute an interest in the entity solely as a creditor in the hands of the subsequent holder. However, if the obligation is disposed of to a related person and the full amount of gain realized upon the disposition of the interest in the entity has not been recognized upon such disposition of the installment obligation, then the obligation shall continue to be an interest in the entity other than solely as a creditor in the hands of the subsequent holder subject to the rules of this paragraph (d)(3)(ii)(A). In addition, if the obligation is disposed of to any person for a principal purpose of avoiding the provisions of section 897, 1445, or 6039C, then the obligation shall continue to be an interest in the entity other than solely as a creditor in the hands of the subsequent holder subject to the rules of this paragraph (d)(3)(ii)(A). However, rights to payments arising from dispositions that took place before June 19, 1980, shall in no event constitute interests in an entity other than solely as a creditor, even if such payments are received after June 18, 1980. In addition, such treatment shall not apply to payments arising from dispositions to unrelated parties that took place before January 1, 1985, and that were not subject to U.S. tax pursuant to the provisions of a U.S. income tax treaty, regardless of when such payments are received.

(B) *Contingent interests.*—The interests described in subdivision (D) of paragraph (d)(3)(i) of this section include any right to a payment from an entity the amount of which is contingent on the appreciation in value of an interest described in subdivision (A), (B), or (C) or paragraph (d)(3)(i) of this section or which is contingent on the appreciation in value of assets of, or the general gross or net proceeds or profits derived by, such entity. The right to such a payment is itself an interest in the entity other than solely as a creditor, regardless of whether the holder of such right actually holds an interest in the entity described in subdivision (A), (B), or (C) of paragraph (d)(3)(i) of this section. For example, a stock appreciation right constitutes an interest in a corporation other than solely as a creditor even if the holder of such right actually holds no stock in the corporation. However, the interests described in subdivision (D) of paragraph (d)(3)(i) of this section do not include any right to a payment that is (*1*) exclusively contingent upon and exclusively paid out of revenues from sales of personal property (whether tangible or intangible) or from services, or (*2*) exclusively contingent upon the resolution of a claim asserted against the entity by a person related neither to the entity nor to the holder of the interest.

(C) *Security interests.*—A right to repossess or foreclose on an interest in an entity under a mortgage, security agreement, financing statement, or other collateral instrument securing a debt will not of itself cause an interest in an entity which is otherwise an interest solely as a creditor to become an interest other than solely as a creditor.

(D) *Royalties.*—The interests described in subdivision (D) of paragraph (d)(3)(i) of this section do not include rights to payments representing royalties, license fees, or similar charges for the use of patents, inventions, formulas, copyrights, literary, musical or artistic compositions, trademarks, trade names, franchises, licenses, or similar intangible property.

(E) *Commissions.*—The interests described in subdivision (D) of paragraph (d)(3)(i) of this section do not include a right to a commission, brokerage fee or similar charge for professional services rendered in connection with the purchase or sale of an interest in an entity. However, a right to such a payment will constitute an interest other than solely as a creditor if the total amount of the payment is contingent upon appreciation in value of assets of, or proceeds or profits derived by, the entity after the date of the transaction with respect to which the payment was earned.

(F) *Trustee's fees.*—The interests described in subdivision (D) of paragraph (d)(3)(i) of this section do not include a right to payment representing reasonable compensation for services rendered as a trustee, as an administrator of an estate, or in a similar capacity.

(4) *Aggregation of interests.*—If a person holds both interests solely as a creditor and

interests other than solely as a creditor in real property or in an entity, those interests will generally be treated as separate and distinct interests. However, such interests shall be aggregated and treated as interests other than solely as a creditor in their entirety if the interest solely as a creditor has been separated from, or acquired separately from, the interest other than solely as a creditor, for a principal purpose of avoiding the provisions of section 897, 1445, or 6039C by causing one or more of such interests to be an interest solely as a creditor. The existence of such a purpose will be determined with reference to all the facts and circumstances. Where an interest solely as a creditor has arm's-length interest and repayment terms it shall in no event be aggregated with and treated as an interest other than solely as a creditor. For purposes of this paragraph (d)(4), an interest rate that does not exceed 120 percent of the applicable Federal rate (as defined in section 1274(d)) shall be presumed to be an arm's-length interest rate. For purposes of applying the rules of this paragraph (d)(4), a person shall be treated as holding any interests held by a related person within the meaning of § 1.897-1(i).

(5) *"Interest" means "interest other than solely as a creditor"*.—Unless otherwise stated, the term "interest" as used with regard to real property or with regard to an entity hereafter in the regulations under sections 897, 1445, and 6039C, means an interest in such real property or entity other than an interest solely as a creditor.

(e) *Proportionate share of assets held by an entity.*—(1) *In general.*—A person that holds an interest in an entity is for certain purposes treated as holding a proportionate or pro rata share of the assets held by the entity. Such proportionate share must be calculated, in accordance with the rules of this paragraph, for the following purposes.

(i) In determining whether a corporation is a U.S. real property holding corporation—

(A) A person holding an interest in a partnership, trust, or estate is treated as holding a proportionate share of the assets held by the partnership, trust, or estate (see § 1.897-2(e)(2)), and

(B) A corporation that holds a controlling interest in a second corporation is treated as holding a proportionate share of the assets held by the second corporation (see § 1.897-2(e)(3)).

(ii) In determining reporting obligations that may be imposed under section 6039C, the holder of an interest in a partnership, trust, or estate is treated as owning a proportionate share of the U.S. real property interests held by the partnership, trust, or estate.

(2) *Proportionate share of assets held by a corporation or partnership.*—(i) *In general.*—A person's proportionate or pro rata share of assets held by a corporation or partnership is determined by multiplying—

(A) The person's percentage ownership interest in the entity, by

(B) The fair market value of the assets held by the entity (or the book value of such assets, in the case of a determination pursuant to § 1.897-2(b)(2)).

(ii) *Percentage ownership interest.*—A person's percentage ownership interest in a corporation or partnership is the percentage equal to the ratio of (A) the sum of the liquidation values of all interests in the entity held by the person to (B) the sum of the liquidation values of all outstanding interests in the entity. The liquidation value of an interest in an entity is the amount of cash and the fair market value of any property that would be distributed with respect to such interest upon the liquidation of the entity after satisfaction of liabilities to persons having interests in the entity solely as creditors. With respect to an entity that has interests outstanding that grant a presently-exercisable option to acquire or right to convert into or otherwise acquire an interest in the entity other than solely as a creditor, the liquidation value of all interests in such entity shall be calculated as though such option or right had been exercised, giving effect both to the payment of any consideration required to exercise the option or right and to the issuance of the additional interest.

The fair market value of the assets of the entity, the amount of cash held by the entity, and the amount of liabilities to persons having interests solely as creditors is determined for this purpose on the date with respect to which the percentage ownership interest is determined.

(iii) *Examples.*—The rules of this paragraph (e)(2) are illustrated by the following examples.

Example (1). Corporation K's only assets are stock and securities with a fair market value as of the applicable determination date of $20,000,000. K's assets are subject to liabilities of $10,000,000. Among K's liabilities are a $1,000,000 loan from L, under the terms of which L is entitled, upon payment of the loan principal, to a profit share equal to 10 percent of the excess of the fair market value of K's assets over $18,000,000, but only if all other corporate liabilities have been paid. K has two classes of stock, common and preferred. PS1 and PS2 each own 100 of the 200 outstanding shares of preferred stock. CS1 and CS2 each own 500 of the 1,000 outstanding shares of common stock. Each preferred shareholder is entitled to $10,000 per share of preferred stock upon liquidation, subject to payment of all corporate liabilities and to any amount owed to L, but before any common shareholder is paid. The liquidation value of L's interest in K, which constitutes an interest other than an interest solely as a creditor, is $1,200,000 ($1,000,000 principal of the loan to K plus $200,000 (10 percent of the excess of $20,000,000 over $18,000,000). The liquidation value of each of PS1's and PS2's blocks of preferred stock is $1,000,000 ($10,000 times 100 shares each). The liquidation value of each of CS1's and CS2's blocks of common stock is $3,900,000 [$20,000,000 (the total fair market value of K's assets) − $9,000,000 (liabilities to creditors other than L) − $1,200,000 (L's liquidation value) − $2,000,000 (PS1's and PS2's liquidation value)) times 50 percent (the percentage of common stock owned by each)]. The sum of the liquidation values of all of the outstanding interests in K (i.e., interests other than solely as a creditor) is $11,000,000 [$1,200,000 (L's liquidation value) + $2,000,000 (PS1's and PS2's liquidation values) + $7,800,000 (CS1's and CS2's liquidation values)]. Each of CS1's and CS2's percentage ownership interests in K is 35.5 percent ($3,900,000 divided by $11,000,000). Each of PS1's and PS2's percentage ownership interests in K is 9 percent ($1,000,000 divided by $11,000,000). L's percentage ownership interest in K is 11 percent ($1,200,000 divided by $11,000,000).

Example (2). A, a U.S. person, and B, a foreign person are partners in a partnership the only asset of which is a parcel of undeveloped land located in the United States that was purchased by the partnership in 1980 for $300,000. The partnership has no liabilities, and its capital is $300,000. A's and B's interests in the capital of the partnership are 25 percent and 75 percent, respectively, and A and B each has a 50 percent profit interest in the partnership. The partnership agreement provides that upon liquidation any unrealized gain will be distributed in accordance with the partners' profit interests. In 1984 the partnership has no items of income or deduction, and the fair market value of its parcel of undeveloped land is $500,000. In 1984 the percentage ownership interest of A in the partnership is 35 percent [the ratio of $100,000 (the liquidation value of A's profit interest in 1984) plus $75,000 (the liquidation value of A's 25 percent interest in the partnership's $300,000 capital) to $500,000 (the sum of the liquidation values of all outstanding interests in the partnership)]. The percentage ownership interest of B in the partnership in 1984 is 65 percent [the ratio of $325,000 (B's $100,000 profit interest plus his $225,000 capital interest) to $500,000].

(3) *Proportionate share of assets held by trusts and estates.*—(i) *In general.*—A person's proportionate or pro rata share of assets held by a trust or estate is determined by multiplying—

(A) The person's percentage ownership interest in the trust or estate, by

(B) The fair market value of the assets held by the trust or estate (or the book value of such assets, in the case of a determination pursuant to § 1.897-2(b)(2)).

(ii) *Percentage ownership interest.*— (A) *General rule.*—A person's percentage ownership interest in a trust or an estate—is the percentage equal to the ratio of: (*1*) The sum of the actuarial values of such person's interests in the cash and other assets held by the trust or estate after satisfaction of the liabilities of the trust or estate to persons holding interests in the trust or estate solely as creditors, to (*2*) the entire amount of such cash and other assets after satisfaction of liabilities to persons holding interests in the trust or estate solely as creditors. For purposes of calculating this ratio, the fair market value of the trust's or estate's assets, the amount of cash held by the trust or estate, and the amount of the liabilities to persons having interests solely as creditors is determined on the date with respect to which the percentage ownership interest is determined. With respect to a trust or estate that has interests outstanding that grant a presently-exercisable option to acquire or right to convert into or otherwise acquire an interest in the trust or estate other than solely as a creditor, the liquidation value of all interests in such entity shall be calculated as though such option or right had been exercised, giving effect both to the payment of any consideration required to exercise the option or right and to the issuance of the additional interest. With respect to a trust or estate that has interests outstanding that entitle any person to a distribution of U.S. real property interests upon liquidation that is disproportionate to such person's interest in the total assets of the trust or estate, such disproportionate right shall be disregarded in the calculation of the interest-holders' proportionate share of the U.S. real property interests held by the entity. For purposes of determining his own percentage ownership interest in a trust, a grantor or other person will be treated as owning any portion of the trust's cash and other assets which such person is treated as owning under sections 671 through 679.

(B) *Discretionary trusts and estates.*— In determining percentage ownership interest in a trust or an estate, the sum of the definitely ascertainable actuarial values of interests in the cash and the other assets of the trust or estate held by persons in existence on the date with respect to which such determination is made must equal the amount in paragraph (e)(3)(ii)(A)(2) of this section. If the amount in paragraph (e)(3)(ii)(A)(2) of this section exceeds the sum of the definitely ascertainable actuarial values of the interests held by persons in existence on the determination date, the excess will be considered to be owned in total by each beneficiary who is in existence on such date, whose interest in the excess is not definitely ascertainable and who is potentially entitled to such excess. However, such excess shall not be considered to be owned in total by each beneficiary if the discretionary terms of the trust or estate were included for a principal purpose of avoiding the provisions of section 897, 1445, or 6039C by causing assets other than U.S. real property interests to be attributed in total to each beneficiary. The rules of this paragraph (e)(3) are illustrated by the following example.

Example. A, a U.S. person, established a trust on December 31, 1984, and contributed real property with a fair market value of $10,000 to the trust. The terms of that trust provided that the trustee, a bank that is unrelated to A, at its discretion may retain trust income or may distribute it to X, a foreign person, or to the head of state of any country other than the United States. The remainder upon the death of X is to go in equal shares to such of Y and Z, both foreign persons, as survive X. On December 31, 1984, the total value of the trust's assets is $10,000. On the same date, the actuarial values of the remainder interests of Y and Z in the corpus of the trust are definitely ascertainable. They are $1,000 and $500, respectively. Neither the income interest of X nor of the head of state of any country other than the United States has a definitely ascertainable actuarial value on December 31, 1984. The interests of Y and Z in the income portion of the trust similarly have no definitely ascertainable actuarial values on such date since the income may be distributed rather than retained by the trust. Since the sum of the actuarial values of definitely ascertainable interests of persons in existence ($1,500) is less than $10,000, the difference ($8,500) is treated as owned by each beneficiary who is in existence on December 31, 1984, and who is potentially entitled to such excess. Therefore, X, Y, Z, and the head of state of any country other than the United States are each considered as owning the entire $8,500 income interest in the trust. On December 31, 1984, the total actuarial value of X's interest is $8,500, and his percentage ownership interest is 85 percent. The total actuarial value of Y's interest in the trust is $9,500 ($1,000 plus $8,500), and his percentage ownership interest is 95 percent. The total actuarial value of Z's interest is $9,000 ($500 plus $8,500), and his percentage ownership interest is 90 percent. The actuarial value of the interest of the head of state of each country other than the United States is $8,500, and his percentage ownership interest is 85 percent.

(4) *Dates with respect to which percentage ownership interests are determined.*—The dates with respect to which percentage ownership interests are determined are the applicable determination dates outlined in §1.897-2 or in regulations under section 6039C.

(f) *Asset used or held for use in a trade or business.*—(1) *In general.*—The term "asset used or held for use in a trade or business" means—

(i) Property, other than a U.S. real property interest, that is—

(A) Stock in trade of an entity or other property of a kind which would properly be included in the inventory of the entity if on hand at the close of the taxable year, or property held by the entity primarily for sale to customers in the ordinary course of its trade or business, or

(B) Depreciable property used or held for use in the trade or business, as described in section 1231(b)(1) but without regard to the holding period limitations of section 1231(b), or

(C) Livestock, including poultry, used or held for use in a trade or business for draft, breeding, dairy, or sporting purposes, and

(ii) Goodwill and going concern value, patents, inventions, formulas, copyrights, literary, musical, or artistic compositions, trademarks, trade names, franchises, licenses, customer lists, and similar intangible property, but only to the extent that such property is used or held for use in the entity's trade or business and subject to the valuation rules of §1.897-1(o)(4), and

(iii) Cash, stock, securities, receivables of all kinds, options or contracts to acquire any of the foregoing, and options or contracts to acquire commodities, but only to the extent that such assets are used or held for use in the corporation's trade or business and do not constitute U.S. real property interests.

(2) *Used or held for use in a trade or business.*—An asset is used or held for use in an entity's trade or business if it is, under the principles of §1.864-4(c)(2)—

(i) Held for the principal purpose of promoting the present conduct of the trade or business,

(ii) Acquired and held in the ordinary course of the trade or business, as, for example, in the case of an account or note receivable arising from that trade or business (including the performance of services), or

(iii) Otherwise held in a direct relationship to the trade or business.

In determining whether an asset is held in a direct relationship to the trade or business, consideration shall be given to whether the asset is needed in that trade or business. An asset shall be considered to be needed in a trade or business only if the asset is held to meet the present needs of that trade or business and not its anticipated future needs. An asset shall be considered as needed in the trade or business if, for example, the asset is held to meet the operating expenses of that trade or business. Conversely, an asset shall be considered as not needed in the trade or business if, for example, the asset is held for the purpose of providing for future diversification into a new trade or business, future expansion of trade or business activities, future plant replacement, or future business contingencies. An asset that is held to meet reserve or capitalization requirements imposed by applicable law shall be presumed to be held in a direct relationship to the trade or business.

(3) *Special rules concerning liquid assets.*—(i) *Safe harbor amount.*—Assets described in paragraph (f)(1)(iii) of this section shall be presumed to be used or held for use in a trade or business, in an amount up to 5 percent of the fair market value of other assets used or held for use in the trade or business. However, the rule of this paragraph (f)(3)(i) shall not apply with respect to any assets described in paragraph (f)(1)(iii) of this section that are held or acquired for the principal purpose of avoiding the provisions of section 897 or 1445.

(ii) *Investment companies.*—Assets described in paragraph (f)(1)(iii) of this section shall be presumed to be used or held for use in an entity's trade or business if the principal business of the entity is trading or investing in such assets for its own account. An entity's principal business shall be presumed to be trading or investing in assets, described in paragraph (f)(1)(iii) of this section if the fair market value of such assets held by the entity equals or exceeds 90 percent of the sum of the fair market values of the entity's U.S. real property interests, interests in real property located outside the United States, assets otherwise used or held for use in a trade or business, and assets described in paragraph (f)(1)(iii) of this section.

(4) *Examples.*—The application of this paragraph (f) may be illustrated by the following examples:

Example (1). M, a domestic corporation engaged in industrial manufacturing, is required to hold a large current cash balance for the purposes of purchasing materials and meeting its payroll. The amount of the cash balance so required varies because of the fluctuating seasonal nature of the corporation's business. In months when large cash balances are not required, the corporation invests the surplus amount in U.S. Treasury bills. Since both the cash and the Treasury bills are held to meet the present needs of the business, they are held in a direct relationship to that business, and, therefore, constitute assets used or held for use in the trade or business.

Example (2). R, a domestic corporation engaged in the manufacture of goods, engages a stock brokerage firm to manage securities which were purchased with funds from R's general surplus reserves. The funds invested in these securities are intended to provide for the future expansion of R into a new trade or business. Thus, the funds are not necessary for the present needs of the business; they are accordingly not held in a direct relationship to the business and do not constitute assets used or held for use in the trade or business.

Example (3). B, a federally chartered and regulated bank, is required by law to hold substantial reserves of cash, stock, and securities. Pursuant to the rule of paragraph (f)(2) of this section, such assets are presumed to be held in a direct relationship to B's business, and thus constitute assets used or held for use in the trade or business. In addition, B holds substantial loan receivables which are acquired and held in the ordinary course of its banking business. Pursuant to the rule of paragraph (f)(1)(iii) of this section, such receivables constitute assets used or held for use in the trade or business.

(g) *Disposition:* For purposes of sections 897, 1445, and 6039C, the term "disposition" means any transfer that would constitute a disposition by the transferor for any purpose of the Internal Revenue Code and regulations thereunder. The severance of crops or timber and the extraction of minerals do not alone constitute the disposition of a U.S. real property interest.

(h) *Gain or loss,* the amount of gain or loss arising from the disposition of the U.S. real property interest shall be determined as provided in section 1001(a) and (b). Such gain or loss shall be subject to the provisions of section 897(a) and (b), unless a nonrecognition provision is applicable pursuant to section 897(d) or (e) and regulations thereunder. Amounts otherwise treated for Federal income tax purposes as principal and interest payments on debt obligations of all kinds (including obligations that are interests other than solely as a creditor) do not give rise to gain or loss that is subject to section 897(a). However, principal payments on installment obligations described in §§ 1.897-1(d)(2)(ii)(A) and 1.897-1(d)(3)(ii)(A) do give rise to gain or loss that is subject to section 897(a), to the extent such gain or loss is required to be recognized pursuant to section 453. The rules of paragraphs (g) and (h) are illustrated by the following examples.

Example (1). Foreign individual C has an undivided fee interest in a parcel of real property located in the United States. The fair market value of C's interest is $70,000, and C's basis in such interest is $50,000. The only liability to which the real property is subject is the liability of $65,000 secured by a mortgage in the same amount. C transfers his fee interest in the property subject to the mortgage by gift to D. C realizes $15,000 of gain upon such transfer. As a transfer by gift constitutes a disposition for purposes of the Code, and as gain is realized upon that transfer, the gift is a disposition for purposes of sections 897, 1445, and 6039C and is subject to section 897(a) to the extent of the gain realized. However, section 897(a) would not be applicable to the transfer if the mortgage on the U.S. real property were equal to or less than C's $50,000 basis, since the transfer then would not give rise to the realization of gain or loss under the Internal Revenue Code.

Example (2). Foreign corporation Y makes a loan of $1 million to domestic individual Z, secured by a mortgage on residential real property purchased with the loan proceeds. The loan agreement provides that Y is entitled to receive fixed monthly payments from Z, constituting repayment of principal plus interest at a fixed rate. In addition, the agreement provides that Y is entitled to receive a percentage of the appreciation in value of the real property as of the time that the loan is retired. The obligation in its entirety is considered debt for Federal income tax purposes. However, because of Y's right to share in the appreciation in value of the real property, the debt obligation gives Y an interest in the real property other than solely as a creditor. Nevertheless, as principal and interest payments do not constitute gain under section 1001 and paragraph (h) of this section, and both the monthly and final payments received by Y are considered to consist solely of principal and interest for Federal income tax purposes, section 897(a) shall not apply to Y's receipt of such payments. However, Y's sale of the debt obligation to foreign corporation A would give rise to gain that is subject to section 897(a).

(i) *Related person.*—For purposes of sections 897, 1445, and 6039C, persons are considered to be related if they are partners or partnerships described in section 707(b)(1) of the Code or if they are related within the meaning of section 267(b) and (c) of the Code (except that section 267(f) shall apply without regard to section 1563(b)(2)).

(j) *Domestic corporation.*—The term "domestic corporation" has the same meaning as set forth in section 7701(a)(3) and (4) and § 301.7701-5. For purposes of sections 897 and 6039C, it also includes a foreign corporation with respect to which an election under section 897(i) and § 1.897-3 or section 897(k) and § 1.897-4 to be treated as domestic corporation is in effect.

(k) *Foreign person.*—[Reserved]

(l) *Foreign corporation.*—The term "foreign corporation" has the meaning ascribed to such term in section 7701(a)(3) and (5) and § 301.7701-5. For purposes of sections 897 and 6039C, however, the term does not include a foreign corporation with respect to which there is in effect an election under section 897(i) and § 1.897-3 or section 897(k) and § 1.897-4 to be treated as a domestic corporation.

(m) *Established securities market.*—For purposes of sections 897, 1445, and 6039C, the term "established securities market" means—

(1) A national securities exchange which is registered under section 6 of the Securities Exchange Act of 1934 (15 U.S.C. 78f),

(2) A foreign national securities exchange which is officially recognized, sanctioned, or supervised by governmental authority, and

(3) Any over-the-counter market.

An over-the-counter market is any market reflected by the existence of an interdealer quotation system. An interdealer quotation system is any system of general circulation to brokers and dealers which regularly disseminates quotations of stocks and securities by identified brokers or dealers, other than by quotation sheets which are prepared and distributed by a broker or dealer in the regular course of business and which contain only quotations of such broker or dealer.

(n) *Regularly traded.*—[Reserved]

(o) *Fair market value.*—(1) *In general.*—For purposes of sections 897, 1445, and 6039C only, the term "fair market value" means the value of the property determined in accordance with the rules, contained in this paragraph (o). The definition of fair market value provided herein is not to be used in the calculation of gain or loss from the disposition of a U.S. real property interest pursuant to section 1001. An independent professional appraisal of the value of property must be submitted only if such an appraisal is specifically requested in connection with the negotiation of a security agreement pursuant to section 1445.

(2) *Method of calculating fair market value.*—(i) *In general.*—The fair market value of property is its gross value (as defined in paragraph (o)(2)(ii) of this section) reduced by the outstanding balance of any debts secured by the property which are described in paragraph (o)(2)(iii) of this section. See § 1.897-2(b) for the alternative use of book values in certain limited circumstances.

(ii) *Gross value.*—Gross value is the price at which the property would change hands between an unrelated willing buyer and willing seller, neither being under any compulsion to buy or sell and both having reasonable knowledge of all relevant facts. Generally, with respect to trade or business assets, going concern value should be used as it will provide the most accurate reflection of such a price. However, taxpayers may use other methods of valuation if they can establish that such method will provide a more accurate determination of gross value and if they consistently apply such method to all assets to be valued. See subdivisions (3) and (4) of this paragraph (o) for special rules with respect to the valuation of leases and of intangible assets.

(iii) *Debts secured by the property.*—The gross value of property shall be reduced by the outstanding balance of debts that are:

(A) Secured by a mortgage or other security interest in the property that is valid and enforceable under the law of the jurisdiction in which the property is located, and

(B) Either (*1*) incurred to acquire the property (including long-term financing obtained in replacement of construction loans or other short-term debt within one year of the acquisition or completion of the property), or (*2*) otherwise incurred in direct connection with the property, such as property tax liens upon real property or debts incurred to maintain or improve property.

In addition, if any debt described in this paragraph (o)(2)(iii) is refinanced for a valid business purpose (such as obtaining a more favorable rate of interest), the principal amount of the replacement debt does not exceed the outstanding balance of the original debt, and the replacement debt is secured by the property, then the gross value of the property shall be reduced by the replacement debt. Obligations to related persons shall not be taken into account for purposes of this paragraph (o)(2)(iii) unless such obligations constitute interests, solely as a creditor pursuant to the provisions of paragraph (d)(4) of this section and unless the related person has made similar loans to unrelated persons on similar terms and conditions.

(iv) *Anti-abuse rule.*—The gross value of real property located outside the United States and of assets used or held for use in a trade or business shall be reduced by the outstanding balance of any debt that was entered into for the principal purpose of avoiding the provisions of section 897, 1445, or 6039C by enabling the corporation to acquire such assets. The existence of such a purpose shall be determined with reference to all the facts and circumstances. Debts that a particular corporation routinely enters into the ordinary course of its acquisition of assets used or held for use in its trade or business will not be considered to be entered into for the principal purpose of avoiding the provisions of section 897, 1445, or 6039C.

(3) *Fair market value of leases and options.*—For purposes of sections 897, 1445, and 6039C, the fair market value of a leasehold interest in real property is the price at which the lease could be assigned or the property sublet, neither party to such transaction being under any compulsion to enter into the transaction and both having reasonable knowledge of all relevant facts. Thus, the value of a leasehold interest will generally consist of the present value, over the period of the lease remaining, of the difference between the rental provided for in the lease and the current rental value of the real property. A leasehold interest bearing restrictions on its assignment or sublease has a fair market value of zero, but only if those restrictions in practical effect preclude (rather than merely condition) the lessee's ability to transfer, at a gain, the benefits of a favorable lease. The normal commercial practice of lessors may be used to determine whether restrictions in a lease have the practical effect of precluding transfer at a gain. The fair market value of an option to purchase any property is, similarly, the price at which the option could be sold, consisting generally of the difference between the option price and the fair market value of the property, taking proper account of any restrictions upon the transfer of the option.

(4) *Fair market value of intangible assets.*—For purposes of determining whether a corporation is a U.S. real property holding corporation, the fair market value of intangible assets described in § 1.897-1(f)(1)(ii) may be determined in accordance with the following rules.

(i) *Purchase price.*—Intangible assets described in § 1.897-1(f)(1)(ii) that were acquired by purchase from a person not related to the purchaser within the meaning of § 1.897-1(i) may be valued at their purchase price. However, such purchase price must be adjusted to reflect any amortization required by generally accepted accounting principles applied in the United States. Intangible assets acquired by purchase shall include any amounts allocated to goodwill or going concern value pursuant to section 338(b)(3) and regulations thereunder. Intangible assets acquired by purchase shall not include assets that were acquired indirectly through an acquisition of stock to which section 338 does not apply. Such assets must be valued pursuant to a method described in subdivision (ii) or (iii) of this paragraph (o)(4).

(ii) *Book value.*—Intangible assets described in § 1.897-1(f)(1)(ii) (other than goodwill and going concern value) may be valued at the amount at which such assets are carried on the financial accounting records of the holder of such assets, provided that such amount is determined in accordance with generally accepted accounting principles applied in the United States. However, this method may not be used with respect to assets acquired by purchase from a related person within the meaning of § 1.897-1(i).

(iii) *Other methods.*—Intangible assets described in § 1.897-1(f)(1)(ii) may be valued pursuant to any other reasonable method at an amount reflecting the price at which the asset would change hands between an unrelated willing buyer and willing seller, neither being under any compulsion to buy or to sell and both having reasonable knowledge of all relevant facts. However, a corporation that uses a method of valuation other than the purchase price or book value methods may be required to comply with the special notification requirements of § 1.897-2(h)(1)(iii)(A).

(p) *Identifying number.*—The "identifying number" of an individual is the individual's United States social security number or the identification number assigned by the Internal Revenue Service (see § 301.6109-1 of this chapter). The "identifying number" of any other person is its United States employer identification number. [Reg. § 1.897-1.]

☐ [*T.D.* 7999, 12-26-84. *Amended by T.D.* 8113, 12-18-86; *T.D.* 8198, 5-4-88; *T.D.* 8657, 3-5-96 *and T.D.* 9082, 8-4-2003.]

§ 1.897-2. United States real property holding corporations.—(a) *Purpose and scope.*—This section provides rules regarding the definition and consequences of U.S. real property holding corporation status. U.S. real property holding corporation status is important for determining whether gain from the disposition by a foreign person of an interest in a domestic corporation is taxable. Such status is also important for purposes of the withholding and reporting requirements of sections 1445 and 6039C. For example, a person that buys stock of a U.S. real property holding corporation from a foreign person is required to withhold under section 1445. In addition, for purposes of determining whether another corporation is a U.S. real property holding corporation, an interest in a foreign corporation is a U.S. real property interest unless it is established that the foreign corporation is not a U.S. real property holding corporation. The general definition of a U.S. real property holding corporation is provided in paragraph (b) of this section. Paragraph (c) provides rules regarding the dates on which U.S. real property holding corporation status must be determined. The assets that must be included in making the determination of a corporation's status are set forth in paragraph (d), while paragraph (e) provides special rules regarding the treatment of interests held by a corporation in partnerships, trusts, estates, and other corporations. Rules regarding the termination of U.S. real property holding corporation status are set forth in paragraph (f). Paragraph (g) explains the manner in which an interest-holder can establish that a corporation is not a U.S. real property holding corporation, and paragraph (h) provides rules regarding certain notification requirements applicable to corporations.

(b) *U.S. real property holding corporation.*—(1) *In general.*—A corporation is a U.S. real property holding corporation if the fair market value of the U.S. real property interests held by the corporation on any applicable determination date equals or exceeds 50 percent of the sum of the fair market values of its—

(i) U.S. real property interests;

(ii) Interests in real property located outside the United States; and

(iii) Assets other than those described in subdivision (i) or (ii) of this paragraph (b)(1) that are used or held for use in its trade or business.

See paragraphs (d) and (e) of this section for rules regarding the directly and indirectly held assets that must be included in the determination of whether a corporation is a U.S. real property holding corporation. The term "interest in real property located outside the United States" means an interest other than solely as a creditor (as defined in § 1.897-1(d)) in real property (as defined in § 1.897-1(b)) that is located outside the United States or the Virgin Islands. If a corporation qualifies as a U.S. real property holding corporation on any applicable determination date after June 18, 1980, any interest in it shall be treated as a U.S. real property interest for a period of five years from that date, unless the provisions of paragraph (f)(2) of this section are applicable.

(2) *Alternative test.*—(i) *In general.*—The fair market value of a corporation's U.S. real property interests shall be presumed to be less than 50 percent of the fair market value of the aggregate of its assets described in paragraphs (d) and (e) of this section if on an applicable determination date the total book value of the U.S. real property interests held by the corporation is 25 percent or less of the book value of the aggregate of the corporation's assets described in paragraphs (d) and (e) of this section.

(ii) *Definition of book value.*—For purposes of this section and § 1.897-1(e) the term "book value" shall be defined as follows. In the case of assets that are held directly by the corporation, the term means the value at which an item is carried on the financial accounting records of the corporation, if such value is determined in accordance with generally accepted accounting principles applied in the United States. In the case of assets of which a corporation is treated as holding a pro rata share pursuant to paragraphs (e)(2) and (3) of this section and § 1.897-1(e), the term "book value" means the corporation's share of the value at which the asset is carried on the financial accounting records of the entity that directly holds the asset, if such value is determined in accordance with generally accepted accounting principles applied in the United States. For purposes of this paragraph (b)(2)(ii), an entity need not keep all of its books in accordance with U.S. accounting principles, so long as the value of the relevant assets is determined in accordance therewith.

(iii) *Denial of presumption.*—If the Internal Revenue Service determines, on the basis of information as to the fair market values of a corporation's assets, that the presumption allowed by this paragraph (b)(2) may not accurately reflect the status of the corporation, the Service will notify the corporation that it may not rely upon the presumption. The Service will provide a written notice to the corporation that sets forth the general grounds for the Service's conclusion that the presumption may be inaccurate. By the 90th day following the date on which the corporation receives the Service's notification, the corporation must determine whether on its most recent determination date it was a U.S. real property holding corporation pursuant to the general rule set forth in paragraph (b)(1) of this section and must notify the Service of its determination. If the corporation determines that it was not a U.S. real property holding corporation pursuant to the general rule, then the corporation may upon future determination dates rely upon the presumption allowed by this paragraph (b)(2), unless on the basis of additional information the Service again requests that the determination be made pursuant to the general rule. If the corporation determines that it was a U.S. real property holding corporation on its most recent determination date, then by the 180th day following the date on which the corporation received the Service's notification the corporation (if a domestic corporation) must notify each holder of an interest in it that contrary to any prior representations it was a U.S. real property holding corporation as of its most recent determination date.

(iv) *Applicability of penalties.*—A corporation that had previously relied upon the presumption allowed by this paragraph (b)(2) but that is determined to be a U.S. real property holding corporation shall not be subject to penalties for any incorrect notice previously given pursuant to the requirements of paragraph (h) of this section, if:

(A) The corporation in fact carried out the necessary calculations enabling it to rely upon the presumption allowed by this paragraph (b)(2); and

(B) The corporation complies with the provisions of paragraph (b)(2)(iii) of this section.

However, a corporation shall remain subject to any applicable penalties if at the time of its reliance on the presumption allowed by this paragraph (b)(2) the corporation knew that the book values of relevant assets was substantially higher or lower than the fair market value of those assets and therefore had reason to believe that under the general test of paragraph (b)(1) of this section the corporation would probably be a U.S. real property holding corporation. Information with respect to the fair market value of its assets is known by a corporation if such information is included on any books and records of the corporation or its agent, is known by its directors or officers, or is known by employees who in the course of their employment have reason to know such information. A corporation relying upon the presumption allowed by this paragraph (b)(2) has no affirmative duty to determine the fair market value of assets if such values are not otherwise known to it in accordance with the preceding sentence. The rules of this paragraph (b)(2)(iv) may be illustrated by the following examples.

Example 1. DC is a domestic corporation engaged in light manufacturing that knows that it has foreign shareholders. On its December 31, 1985 determination date DC held assets used in its trade or business, consisting largely of recently-purchased equipment, with a book value of $500,000. DC's only real property interest was a factory that it had occupied for over 50 years, which had a book value of $200,000. The factory was located in a deteriorated downtown area, and DC had no knowledge of any facts indicating that the fair market value of the property was substantially higher than its book value. Therefore, DC was entitled to rely upon the presumption allowed by § 1.897-2(b)(2) and any incorrect statement pursuant to § 1.897-2(h) that arose out of such reliance would not give rise to penalties.

Example 2. The facts are the same as in Example 1, except as follows. By the time of DC's December 31, 1989 determination date, the downtown area in which DC's factory was located had become the subject of an extensive urban renewal program. On December 1, 1989, the president of DC was offered $750,000 for the factory by a developer who planned to convert the property into condominiums. Because DC thus had knowledge of the fair market value of its assets which made it clear that the corporation would probably be a U.S. real property holding corporation under the general rule of § 1.897-2(b)(1), DC was not entitled to rely upon the presumption allowed by § 1.897-2(b)(2) after December 1, 1989, and any false statements arising out of such reliance thereafter would give rise to penalties.

(v) *Effect on interestholders and related persons.*—For the effect on interestholders and related persons of reliance on a statement issued by a corporation that made a determination as to whether it was a U.S. real property holding corporation under the provisions of § 1.897-2(b), see § 1.897-2(g)(1)(ii)(A) and 1.897-2(g)(2)(ii).

(c) *Determination dates for applying U.S. real property holding corporation test.*—(1) *In general.*—Whether a corporation is a U.S. real property holding corporation is to be determined as of the following dates:

(i) The last day of the corporation's taxable year;

(ii) The date on which the corporation acquires any U.S. real property interest;

(iii) The date on which the corporation disposes of an interest in real property located outside the United States or disposes of other assets used or held for use in a trade or business during the calendar year, subject to the provisions of paragraph (c)(2)(i) of this section; and

(iv) In the case of a corporation that is treated pursuant to paragraph (d)(4) or (5) of this section as owning a portion of the assets held by an entity in which the corporation directly or indirectly holds an interest, the date on which that entity either (A) acquires a U.S. real property interest, (B) disposes of an interest in real property located outside the United States or (C) disposes of other assets used or held for use in a trade or business during the calendar year, subject to the provisions of paragraph (c)(2)(ii) of this section. A determination that is triggered by a transaction described in subdivision (ii), (iii), or (iv) of this paragraph (c)(1) must take such transaction into account. However, the first determination of a corporation's status need not be made until the 120th day after the later of the date of incorporation or of the date on which the corporation first acquires a shareholder. In addition, no determination of a corporation's status need be made during the 12-month period beginning on the date on which a corporation adopts a plan of complete liquidation, provided that all the assets of the corporation (other than assets retained to meet claims) are distributed within such period.

(2) *Transactions not requiring a determination.*—(i) *Transactions by corporation.*—Notwithstanding the provisions of paragraph (c)(1) of this section, a determination of U.S. real property holding corporation status need not be made on the date of:

(A) A corporation's disposition of inventory or livestock (as described in § 1.897-1(f)(1)(i)(A) and (C));

(B) The satisfaction of accounts receivable arising from the disposition of inventory or livestock or from the performance of services;

(C) The disbursement of cash to meet the regular operating needs of the business (e.g., to acquire inventory or to pay wages and salaries);

(D) A corporation's disposition of assets used or held for use in a trade or business (other than inventory or livestock) not in excess of a limitation amount determined in accordance with the rules of subdivision (iii) of this paragraph (c)(2); or

(E) A corporation's acquisition of U.S. real property interests not in excess of a limitation amount determined in accordance with the rules of subdivision (iii) of this paragraph (c)(2).

(ii) *Transactions by entity other than corporation.*—Notwithstanding the provisions of paragraph (c)(1)(iv) or (c)(2)(v) of this section, in the case of a corporation that is treated as owning a portion of the assets held by an entity in which the corporation directly or indirectly holds an interest, a determination of U.S. real property holding corporation status need not be made on the date of:

(A) The entity's disposition of inventory or livestock (as described in § 1.897-1(f)(1)(i)(A) and (C));

(B) The satisfaction of accounts receivable arising from the entity's disposition of inventory or livestock or from the performance of personal services;

(C) The entity's disbursement of cash to meet the regular operating needs of its business (e.g. to acquire inventory or to pay wages and salaries);

(D) The entity's disposition of assets used or held for use in a trade or business (other than inventory or livestock) not in excess of a limitation amount determined in accordance with the rules of subdivision (iii) of this paragraph (c)(2); or

(E) The entity's acquisition of U.S. real property interests not in excess of a limitation amount determined in accordance with the rules of subdivision (iii) of this paragraph (c)(2).

(iii) *Calculation of limitation amount.*—The amount of assets used or held for use in a trade or business that may be disposed of, and the amount of U.S. real property interests that may be acquired, by a corporation or other entity without triggering a determination date shall be calculated in accordance with the following rules.

(A) If, in accordance with the provisions of paragraphs (d) and (e) of this section, a corporation on its most recent determination date was considered to hold U.S. real property interests having a fair market value that was less than 25 percent of the aggregate fair market value of all the assets it was considered to hold, then the applicable limitation amount shall be 10 percent of the fair market value of all trade or business assets or all U.S. real property interests (as applicable) held directly by the corporation or by another entity described in paragraph (c)(1)(iv) of this section on that determination date.

(B) If, in accordance with the provisions of paragraphs (d) and (e) of this section, a corporation on its most recent determination date was considered to hold U.S. real property interests having a fair market value that was equal to or greater than 25 and less than 35 percent of the aggregate fair market value of all the assets it was considered to hold, then the applicable limitation amount shall be 5 percent of the fair market value of all trade or business assets or all U.S. real property interests (as applicable) held directly by the corporation or by another entity described in paragraph (c)(1)(iv) of this section on that determination date.

(C) If, in accordance with the provisions of paragraphs (d) and (e) of this section, a corporation on its most recent determination date was considered to hold U.S. real property interests having a fair market value that was equal to or greater than 35 percent of the aggregate fair market value of all the assets it was considered to hold, then the applicable limitation amount shall be 2 percent of the fair market value of all trade or business assets or all U.S. real property interests (as applicable) held directly by the corporation or by another entity described in paragraph (c)(1)(iv) of this section on that determination date.

(D) If a corporation is not a U.S. real property holding corporation under the alternative test of paragraph (b)(2) of this section (relating to the book value of the corporation's assets), then the applicable limitation shall be 10 percent of the book value of all trade or business assets or all U.S. real property interests (as applicable) held directly by the corporation or by another entity described in paragraph (c)(1)(iv) of this section on the most recent determination date.

Dispositions or acquisitions by the corporation or other entity of assets having a value less than the applicable limitation amount must be cumulated by the corporation or entity making such dispositions or acquisitions, and a determination must be made on the date of a transaction that causes the total of either type to exceed the applicable limitation. Once a determination is triggered by a transaction that causes the applicable limitation to be exceeded, the computation of the amount of trade or business assets disposed of or real property interests acquired after that date shall begin again at zero.

The rules of this paragraph (c)(2) may be illustrated by the following examples.

Example (1). DC is a domestic corporation, no class of stock of which is regularly traded on an established securities market, that knows that it has several foreign shareholders. As of December 31, 1984, DC holds U.S. real property interests with a fair market value of $500,000, no real property interests located outside the U.S., and other assets used in its trade or business with a fair market value of $1,600,000. Thus, the fair market value of DC's U.S. real property interests ($500,000) is less than 25% ($525,000) of the total ($2,100,000) of DC's U.S. real property interests ($500,000), interests in real property located outside the United States (zero), and assets used or held for use in a trade or business ($1,600,000). DC is not a U.S. real property holding corporation, and under the rule of paragraph (c)(2)(i) of this section it may dispose of trade or business assets with a fair market value equal to 10 percent ($160,000) of the total fair market value ($1,600,000) of such assets held by it on its most recent determination date (December 31,

1984), without triggering a determination of its U.S. real property holding corporation status. Therefore, when DC disposes of $60,000 worth of trade or business assets (other than inventory or livestock) on March 1, 1985, and again on April 1, 1985, no determination of its status is required on either date. However, when DC disposes of a further $60,000 worth of such trade or business assets on May 1, its total disposition of such assets ($180,000) exceeds its applicable limitation amount, and DC is therefore required to determine its U.S. real property holding corporation status. On May 1, 1985, the fair market value of DC's U.S. real property interests ($500,000) is greater than 25 percent or ($480,000) and less than 35 percent ($672,000) of the total ($1,920,000) of DC's U.S. real property interests ($500,000), interests in real property located outside the United States (zero), and assets used or held for use in a trade or business ($1,420,000). DC is still not a U.S. real property holding corporation, but must now compute its applicable limitation amount as of the May 1 determination date. Under the rule of paragraph (c)(2)(iii)(B) of this section, DC could now dispose of trade or business assets other than inventory or livestock with a total fair market value equal to 5 percent of the fair market value of all trade or business assets held by DC on the May 1 determination date. Therefore, disposition of such trade or business assets with a fair market value of more than $71,000 (5 percent of $1,420,000) will trigger a further determination date for DC.

Example (2). DC is a domestic corporation, no class of stock of which is regularly traded on an established securities market, that knows that it has several foreign shareholders. As of December 31, 1986, DC's only assets are a U.S. real property interest with a fair market value of $300,000 other assets used or held for use in its trade or business with a fair market value of $600,000, and a 50 percent partnership interest in domestic partnership DP. DC's interest in DP constitutes a percentage ownership interest in the partnership of 50 percent, and pursuant to the rules of paragraph (e)(2) of this section DC is treated as owning a portion of the assets of DP determined by multiplying that percentage by the fair market value of DP's assets. As of December 31, 1986, DP's only assets are U.S. real property interests with a fair market value of $120,000 and other assets used in its trade or business with a fair market value of $380,000. As of its December 31, 1986, determination date, the fair market value ($360,000) of the U.S. real property interests DC holds ($300,000) and is treated as holding ($60,000 [The fair market value of DP's U.S. real property interest ($120,000) multiplied by DC's percentage ownership interest in DP (50 percent)]), is equal to 31 percent of the sum of the fair market values ($1,150,000) of the U.S. real property interests DC holds and is treated as holding ($360,000) DC's interest in real property located outside the United States (zero), and assets used or held for use in a trade or business that DC holds or is treated as holding ($790,000 [$600,000 (held directly) plus $190,000 (DC's 50 percent share of assets used or held for use in a trade or business by DP)]). Thus, under the rules of paragraph (c)(2)(i) and (iii)(B) of this section DC may dispose of assets used or held for use in its trade or business with a fair market value equal to 5 percent ($30,000) of the total fair market value ($600,000) of such assets held directly by it on its most recent determination date (December 31, 1986), without triggering a determination of its U.S. real property holding corporation status. In addition, under the rules of paragraph (c)(2)(ii) and (iii)(A) of this section, a determination date for DC would not be triggered by DP's disposition of trade or business assets (other than inventory or livestock) with a fair market value equal to 5 percent ($19,000) of the total fair market value ($380,000) of such assets held by it as of DC's most recent determination date (December 31, 1986). However, any disposition of such assets by DP exceeding that limitation would trigger a determination of DC's U.S. real property holding corporation status. In addition, under the rule of paragraph (c)(1)(iv) of this section, any disposition of a U.S. real property interest by DP would trigger a determination date for DC, while under the rule of paragraph (c)(2)(ii) of this section no disposition of inventory or livestock by DP would trigger a determination for DC.

(3) *Alternative monthly determination dates.*—(i) *In general.*—Notwithstanding the provisions of paragraph (c)(1) and (2) of this section, a corporation may choose to determine its U.S. real property holding corporation status in accordance with the rules of this paragraph (c)(3). In the case of a corporation that has determined that it is not a U.S. real property holding corporation pursuant to the alternative test of paragraph (b)(2) of this section (relating to the book value of the corporation's assets), the rules of this paragraph (c)(3) may be applied by using book values rather than fair market values in all relevant calculations.

(ii) *Monthly determinations.*—A corporation that determines its U.S. real property holding corporation status in accordance with the rules of this paragraph (c)(3) must make a determination at the end of each calendar month.

(iii) *Transactional determinations.*—A corporation that determines its U.S. real property holding corporation status in accordance with the rules of this paragraph (c)(3) must make a determination as of the date on which, pursuant to a single transaction (consisting of one or more transfers):

(A) U.S. real property interests are acquired, and/or

(B) Interests in real property located outside the U.S. and/or assets used or held for use in a trade or business are disposed of,

if the total fair market value of the assets acquired and/or disposed of exceeds 5 percent of the sum of the fair market values of the U.S. real property interests, interests in real property located outside the U.S., and assets used or held for use in a trade or business held by the corporation.

(iv) *Exceptions.*—Notwithstanding any other provision of this paragraph (c)(3), the first determination of a corporation's status need not be made until the 120th day after the later of the date of incorporation or the date on which the corporation first acquires a shareholder. In addition, no determination of a corporation's status need be made during the 12-month period beginning on the date on which a corporation adopts a plan of complete liquidation, if all the assets of the corporation (other than assets retained to meet claims) are distributed within such period.

(4) *Valuation date methods.*—(i) *In general.*—For purposes of determining whether a corporation is a U.S. real property holding corporation on any applicable determination date, the fair market value of the assets held by the corporation (in accordance with § 1.897-2(d)) as of that determination date must be used.

(ii) *Alternative valuation date method for determination dates other than the last day of the taxable year.*—For purposes of paragraph (c)(4)(i) of this section, if an applicable determination date under paragraph (c)(1), (2), or (3) of this section is other than the last day of the taxable year, property may be valued as of the later of the last day of the previous taxable year or the date such property was acquired. For purposes of the determination date that falls on the last day of the taxable year, fair market value as of that date must always be used.

(iii) *Consistent methods.*—The valuation date method selected under this paragraph (c)(4) for the first determination date in a taxable year must be used for all subsequent determination dates for such year. In addition, the valuation date method selected must be used for all property with respect to which the determination is made. The use of one method for one taxable year does not preclude the use of the other method for any other taxable year.

(5) *Illustrations.*—The rules of this paragraph (c) are illustrated by the following examples:

Example (1). Nonresident alien individual C purchased 100 shares of stock of domestic corporation K on July 26, 1985. Although K has additional shares of common stock outstanding, its stock has never been traded on an established securities market. At all times during calendar year 1985, K's only assets were a parcel of U.S. real estate (parcel A) and a parcel of country Z real estate (parcel B). On December 31, 1985, the fair market value of parcel A was $1,000,000 and the fair market value of parcel B was $2,000,000. For purposes of determining whether K was a U.S. real property holding corporation during 1985, the only applicable determination date was December 31, 1985, because K did not make any acquisitions or dispositions described in paragraph (c)(1) of this section during the year. The test of paragraph (b) of this section is applied using the fair market value of the property held on that date. K was not a U.S. real property holding corporation during 1985 because as of December 31, 1985, the fair market value ($1,000,000) of the U.S. real property interests held by K did not equal or exceed 50 percent ($1,500,000) of the sum ($3,000,000) of the fair market value of K's U.S. real property interest ($1,000,000), the interests in real property located outside the United States ($2,000,000), plus other assets used or held for use by K in a trade or business (zero).

Example (2). The facts are the same as in example (1), except that on April 7, 1986, K purchased another parcel of U.S. real estate for $2,000,000. K's purchase of real property on April 7 triggered a determination on that date. As provided in paragraph (c)(3)(ii) of this section, K chooses to use the value of parcels A and B as of the previous December 31, while newly acquired parcel C must be valued as of its acquisition on April 7, 1986. On that date, K qualifies as a U.S. real property holding corporation, since the fair market value of its U.S. real property interests ($3,000,000) exceeds 50 percent ($2,500,000) of the sum ($5,000,000) of the fair market value of K's U.S. real property interests ($3,000,000), its interests in real property located outside the U.S. ($2,000,000), and its other assets used or held for use in a trade or business (zero).

(d) *Assets held by a corporation.*—The assets that must be included in the determination of whether a corporation is a U.S. real property holding corporation are the following:

(1) U.S. real property interests that are held directly by the corporation (including directly-held interests in foreign corporations that are treated as U.S. real property interests pursuant to the rules of paragraph (e)(1) of this section);

(2) Interests in real property located outside the United States that are held directly by the corporation;

(3) Assets used or held for use in a trade or business that are held directly by the corporation;

(4) A proportionate share of assets held through a partnership, trust, or estate pursuant to the rules of paragraph (e)(2) of this section; and

(5) A proportionate share of assets held through a domestic or foreign corporation in which a corporation holds a controlling interest, pursuant to the rules of paragraph (e)(3) of this section.

(e) *Special rules regarding assets held by a corporation.*—(1) *Interests in foreign corporations.*—For purposes only of determining whether any corporation is a U.S. real property holding corporation, an interest in a foreign corporation shall be treated as a U.S. real property interest unless it is established that the interest was not a U.S. real property interest under the rules of this section on the applicable determination date. The rules of paragraph (g)(2) of this section must be complied with to establish that the interest is not a U.S. real property interest. However, regardless of whether an interest in a foreign corporation is treated as a U.S. real property interest for this purpose, gain or loss from the disposition of an interest in such corporation will not be treated as effectively connected with the conduct of a U.S. trade or business by reason of section 897(a). The rules of this paragraph (e)(1) are illustrated by the following examples. In each example, fair market value is determined as of the applicable determination dates under paragraph (c)(4)(i) of this section.

Example (1). Nonresident alien individual F holds all of the stock of domestic corporation DC. DC's only assets are 40 percent of the stock of foreign corporation FC, with a fair market value of $500,000, and a parcel of country W real estate, with a fair market value of $400,000. Foreign corporation FP, unrelated to DC, holds the other 60 percent of the stock of FC. FC's only asset is a parcel of U.S. real estate with a fair market value of $1,250,000. FC is a U.S. real property holding corporation because the fair market value of its U.S. real property interests ($1,250,000) exceeds 50 percent ($625,000) of the sum of the fair market values of its U.S. real property interests ($1,250,000), its interests in real property located outside the United States (zero), plus its other assets used or held for use in a trade or business (zero). Consequently DC's interest in FC is treated as a U.S. real property interest under the rules of this paragraph (e)(1). DC is a U.S. real property holding corporation because the fair market value ($500,000) of its U.S. real property interest (the stock of FC) exceeds 50 percent ($450,000) of the sum ($900,000) of the fair market value of its U.S. real property interests ($500,000), its interests in real property located outside the United States ($400,000), plus its other assets used or held for use in a trade or business (zero). If F disposes of her stock within 5 years of the current determination date, her gain or loss on the disposition of her stock in DC will be treated as effectively connected with a U.S. trade or business under section 897(a). However, FP's gain on the disposition of its FC stock would not be subject to the provisions of section 897(a) because the stock of FC is a U.S. real property interest only for purposes of determining whether DC is a U.S. real property holding corporation.

Example (2). Nonresident alien individual B holds all of the stock of domestic corporation US. US's only assets are 40 percent of the stock of foreign corporation FC1. Nonresident alien individual N, unrelated to US, holds the other 60 percent of FC1's stock. FC1's only assets are 40 percent of the stock of foreign corporation FC2. The remaining 60 percent of the stock of FC2 is owned by nonresident alien individual X, who is unrelated to FC1. FC2's only asset is a parcel of U.S. real estate with fair market value of $1,000,000. FC2, therefore, is a U.S. real property holding corporation, and the stock of FC2 held by FC1 is a U.S. real property interest for purposes of determining whether FC1 is a U.S. real property holding corporation (but not for purposes of treating FC1's gain from the disposition of FC2 stock as effectively connected with a U.S. trade or business under section 897(a)). As all of FC1's assets are U.S. real property interests, the stock of FC1 held by US is a U.S. real property interest for purposes of determining whether US is a U.S. real property holding corporation (but not for purposes of subjecting N's gain on the disposition of FC1 stock to the provisions of section 897(a)). As US is a domestic corporation and as all of its assets are U.S. real property interests, US is a U.S. real property holding corporation, and the stock of US held by B is a U.S. real property interest for purposes of section 897(a). Therefore, B's gain or loss upon the disposition of the stock of US within 5 years of the most recent determination date is subject to the provisions of section 897(a).

(2) *Proportionate ownership of assets held by partnerships, trusts, and estates.*—For purposes of determining whether a corporation is a U.S. real property holding corporation, a holder of an interest in a partnership, a trust, or an estate (whether domestic or foreign) shall be treated pursuant to section 897(c)(4)(B) as holding a proportionate share of the assets held by the entity. However, a holder of an interest shall not be treated as holding a proportionate share of assets that in the hands of the entity are subject to the rule of § 1.897-1(f)(3)(ii) (concerning the trade or business assets of investment companies). Such proportionate share is to be determined in accordance with the rules of § 1.897-1(e) on each applicable determination date. The interest in the entity shall itself be disregarded when a proportionate share of the entity's assets is attributed to the interest-holder pursuant to the rule of this paragraph (e)(2). Any asset treated as held by a holder of an interest by reason of this paragraph (e)(2) which is used or held for use in a trade or business by the partnership, trust, or estate shall be treated as so used or held for use by the holder of the interest. The proportionate ownership rule of this paragraph (e)(2) applies successively upward through a chain of ownership. The proportionate ownership rule of this paragraph (e)(2) is illustrated by the following examples. In each example fair market value is determined as of the applicable determination date under paragraph (c)(4)(i) of this section.

Example (1). Nonresident alien individual F holds all of the stock of domestic corporation DC. DC is a partner in foreign partnership FP, and DC's percentage ownership interest in FP is 50 percent. DC's other assets are a parcel of country F real estate with a fair market value of $500,000 and other assets which it uses in its business with a fair market value of $100,000. FP's assets are a parcel of country Z real estate with a fair market value of $300,000 and a parcel of U.S. real estate with a fair market value of $2,000,000. For purposes of determining whether DC is a U.S. real property holding corporation, DC is treated as holding its pro rata share of the assets held by FP. DC's pro rata share of the U.S. real estate held by FP is $1,000,000, determined by multiplying the fair market value ($2,000,000) of the U.S. real property interests held by FP by DC's percentage ownership interest in FP (50 percent). DC's pro rata share of the country Z real estate held by FP is $150,000, determined in the same manner. DC is a U.S. real property holding corporation because the fair market value ($1,000,000) of its U.S. real property interests (the U.S. real estate it is treated as holding proportionately) exceeds 50 percent ($875,000) of the sum ($1,750,000) of the fair market value of its U.S. real property interests ($1,000,000), its interests in real property located outside the United States [($650,000) (its country F real estate and its pro rata share of the country Z real estate)], plus its other assets which are used or held for use in a trade or business ($100,000). Because DC is a domestic U.S. real property holding corporation, the stock of DC is a U.S. real property interest and F's gain or loss on the disposition of his DC stock within 5 years of the current determination date will be treated as effectively connected with a U.S. trade or business under section 897(a).

Example (2). Nonresident alien individual B holds all of the stock of domestic corporation US. US is a beneficiary of foreign trust FT. US's percentage ownership interest in FT is 90 percent. US has no other assets. FT is a partner in domestic partnership DP. FT's percentage ownership interest in DP is 30 percent. FT has no other assets. DP's only asset is a parcel of U.S. real estate with a fair market value of $1,000,000. FT is treated as holding U.S. real estate with a fair market value of $300,000 (30 percent of the U.S. real estate held by DP with a fair market value of $1,000,000). For purposes of determining whether US is a U.S. real property holding corporation, the proportionate ownership rule is applied successively upward through the chain of ownership. Thus, US is treated as holding 90 percent of FT's $300,000 pro rata share of the U.S. real estate held by DP. US is a U.S. real property holding corporation because the fair market value ($270,000) of its U.S. real property interests (its pro rata share of the U.S. real estate held by DP) exceeds 50 percent ($135,000) of the sum of the fair market values of its U.S. real property interests ($270,000), its interests in real property located outside the United States (zero), plus its other assets used or held for use in a trade or business (zero). Because US is a domestic U.S. real property holding corporation, the stock of US is a U.S. real property interest, and B's gain or loss from the disposition of US stock within 5 years of the current determination date will be treated as effectively connected with a U.S. trade or business under section 897(a).

(3) *Controlling interests in corporations.*—For purposes only of determining whether a corporation is a U.S. real property holding corporation, if the corporation (the "first corporation") holds a controlling interest in a second corporation—

(i) The first corporation is treated as holding a proportionate share of each asset (i.e., U.S. real property interests, interests in real property located outside the United States, and assets used or held for use in a trade or business) held by the second corporation, determined in accordance with the rules of §1.897-1(e);

(ii) Any asset so treated as held proportionately by the first corporation which is used or held for use by the second corporation in a trade or business shall be treated as so used or held for use by the first corporation; and

(iii) Interests in the second corporation held by the first corporation are not themselves taken into account as U.S. real property interests (regardless of whether the second corporation is a U.S. real property holding corporation) or as trade or business assets.

However, the first corporation shall not be treated as holding a proportionate share of assets that in the hands of the second corporation are subject to the rule of §1.897-1(f)(3)(ii) (concerning the trade or business assets of investment companies). A determination of what portion of the assets of the second corporation are considered to be held by the first corporation shall be made as of the applicable dates for determining whether the first corporation is a U.S. real property holding corporation. A "controlling interest" means 50 percent or more of the fair market value of all classes of stock of the corporation, determined as of the applicable determination date. In determining whether a corporation holds a controlling interest in another corporation, section 318(a) shall apply (except that sections 318(a)(2)(C) and (3)(C) are applied by substituting the phrase "5 percent" for "50 percent"). However, a corporation that does not directly hold any interest in a second corporation shall not be treated as holding a controlling interest in the second corporation by reason of the application of section 318(a)(3)(C). The rules of this paragraph (e)(3) apply successively upward through a chain of ownership. For example, if the second corporation owns a controlling interest in a third corporation, the rules of this paragraph shall be applied first to determine the portion of the assets of the third corporation that is considered to be held by the second corporation and then to determine the portion of the assets held and considered to be held by the second corporation that is considered to be held by the first corporation. The controlling interest rules of this paragraph (e)(3) apply, regardless of whether a corporation is domestic or foreign, whenever it is necessary to determine whether a corporation is a U.S. real property holding corporation. The rules of this paragraph (e)(3) are illustrated by the following examples. In each example fair market value is determined as of the applicable determination date under paragraph (c)(4)(i) of this section and no corporation holds constructively any interest not specified in the example.

Example (1). Nonresident alien individual N owns all of the stock of domestic corporation DC. DC's only assets are 60 percent of the fair market value of all classes of stock of foreign corporation FS and 60 percent of the fair market value of all classes of stock of domestic corporation DS. The percentage ownership interest of DC in each of FS and DS is 60 percent. The balance of the stock in FS and DS is held by nonresident alien individual B, who is unrelated to DC. FS's only asset is a parcel of country F real estate with a fair market value of $1,000,000. DS's only asset is a parcel of U.S. real estate with a fair market value of $2,000,000. The value of DC stock in FS and DS is not taken into account for purposes of determining whether DC is a U.S. real property holding corporation. Rather, because DC holds a controlling interest (60 percent) in each of FS and DS, DC is treated as holding a portion of each asset held by FS and DS. DC's portion of the country F real estate held by FS is $600,000, determined by multiplying the fair market value ($1,000,000) of the country F real estate by DC's percentage ownership interest (60 percent). Similarly, DC's portion of the U.S. real estate held by DS is $1,200,000 (60 percent of $2,000,000). DC is a U.S. real property holding corporation, because the fair market value ($1,200,000) of its U.S. real property interests (its portion of the U.S. real estate) exceeds 50 percent ($900,000) of the sum ($1,800,000) of the fair market values of its U.S. real property interests ($1,200,000), its interests in real property located outside the United States (the $600,000 portion of country F real estate), plus its other assets used or held for use in a trade or business (zero). Because DC is a domestic U.S. real property holding corporation, the stock of DC is a U.S. real property interest, and N's gain or loss on the disposition of DC stock within 5 years of the current determination date would be treated as effectively connected with a U.S. trade or business under section 897(a).

Example (2). (i) Nonresident alien individual F owns all of the stock of domestic corporation US1. US1's only asset is 85 percent of the fair market value of all classes of stock of domestic corporation US2. US2's only assets are 60 percent of the fair market value of all classes of stock of domestic corporation US3, with a fair market value of $800,000, and a parcel of country D real estate with a fair market value of $800,000. US3's only asset is a parcel of U.S. real estate with a fair market value of $2,000,000. The percentage ownership interest of F in US1 is 100 percent. Although US1 owns 85 percent of the stock of US2, US1's percentage ownership interest in US2 is 75 percent, because US2 has other interests other than solely as a creditor outstanding. US2's percentage ownership interest in US3 is 60 percent.

Reg. §1.897-2(e)(3)(iii)

(ii) US2 holds a controlling interest in US3, since it holds more than 50 percent of the fair market value of all classes of stock of US3. Consequently, the value of US2's stock in US3 is not taken into account in determining whether US2 is a U.S. real property holding corporation, even though US3 is a U.S. real property holding corporation. Instead, US2 is treated as holding a portion of the U.S. real estate held by US3. US2's portion of the U.S. real estate is $1,200,000, determined by multiplying US2's percentage ownership interest (60 percent) by the fair market value ($2,000,000) of the U.S. real estate. US1 holds a controlling interest in US2 (75 percent). By reapplying the rules of paragraph (e)(3) of this section successively upward through the chain of ownership, US1's stock in US2 is not taken into account, and US1 is treated as holding a portion of the country D real estate held by US2 and the U.S. real estate which US2 is treated as holding proportionately. US1's portion of the country D real estate is $800,000, determined by multiplying US1's percentage ownership interest (75 percent) by the fair market value ($800,000) of the country D real estate. US1's portion of the U.S. real estate which US2 is treated as owning is $900,000, determined by multiplying US1's percentage ownership interest (75 percent) by the fair market value ($1,200,000) of US2's portion of U.S. real estate held by US3. US1 is a U.S. real property holding corporation, because the fair market value ($900,000) of its U.S. real property interests (its portion of US2's portion of U.S. real estate) is more than 50 percent ($750,000) of the sum ($1,500,000) of fair market values of its U.S. real property interests ($900,000), its interests in real property located outside the United States ($800,000), plus its other assets used or held for use in a trade or business (zero). Because US1 is a U.S. real property holding corporation and is a domestic corporation, the stock of US1 is a U.S. real property interest, and F's gain or loss on the disposition of US1 stock within 5 years of the current determination date will be treated as effectively connected with a U.S. trade or business under section 897(a).

Example (3). Nonresident alien individual B holds all of the stock of domestic corporation DC. DC's only assets are 40 percent of the fair market value of all classes of stock of foreign corporation FC and a parcel of country R real estate with a fair market value of $100,000. FC's only asset is one parcel of U.S. real estate with a fair market value of $1,000,000. The fair market value of the FC stock held by DC is $200,000. FC is a U.S. real property holding corporation. Since DC does not hold a controlling interest in FC, the controlling interest rules of paragraph (e)(3) of this section do not apply to treat DC as holding a portion of the U.S. real estate held by FC. However, because FC is a U.S. real property holding corporation, the stock of FC is a U.S. real property interest for purposes of determining whether DC is a U.S. real property holding corporation. DC is a U.S. real property holding corporation because the fair market value ($200,000) of its U.S. real property interest (the stock of FC) exceeds 50 percent ($150,000) of the sum ($300,000) of the fair market values of its U.S. real property interest ($200,000), its interests in real property located outside the United States ($100,000), plus its other assets used or held for use in a trade or business (zero). Because DC is a U.S. real property holding corporation and is a domestic corporation, its stock is a U.S. real property interest, and B's gain or loss on the disposition of DC stock within 5 years of the current determination date would be subject to the provisions of section 897(a).

Example (4). Nonresident alien individual C owns all of the stock of domestic corporation DC1. DC1's only assets are 25 percent of the fair market value of all classes of stock of domestic corporation DC2, and a parcel of U.S. real estate with a fair market value of $100,000. The stock of DC2 is not an asset used or held for use in DC1's trade or business. DC2's only assets are a building located in the U.S. with a fair market value of $100,000 and manufacturing equipment and inventory with a fair market value of $200,000. DC2 is not a U.S. real property holding corporation. Since DC1 does not hold a controlling interest in DC2, the rules of this paragraph (e)(3) do not apply to treat DC1 as holding a portion of the assets held by DC2. In addition, since DC2 is not a U.S. real property holding corporation, its stock does not constitute a U.S. real property interest. Therefore, for purposes of determining whether DC1 is a U.S. real property holding corporation, its interest in DC2 is not taken into account. Since DC1's only other asset is a parcel of U.S. real estate, DC1 is a U.S. real property holding corporation, and C's gain or loss on the disposition of DC1 stock within 5 years of the current determination date would be subject to the provisions of section 897(a).

(4) *Co-application of rules of this paragraph (e).*—The rules of this paragraph (e) apply in conjunction with one another for purposes of determining whether a corporation is a U.S. real property holding corporation. The rule of this paragraph (e)(4) is illustrated by the following example. In the example fair market value is determined as of the applicable determination date in accordance with paragraph (c)(4)(i) of this section.

Example. Nonresident alien individual B holds 100 percent of the stock of domestic corporation US. US's only asset is 10 percent of the stock of foreign corporation FC1. FC1's only asset is 100 percent of the stock of foreign corporation FC2. FC2's only asset is a 50 percent interest in domestic partnership DP. FC2's percentage ownership interest in DP is 50 percent. DP's only asset is a parcel of U.S. real estate with a fair market value of $10,000,000. In determining whether US is a U.S. real property holding corporation, the rules of this paragraph (e) apply in conjunction with one another. Consequently, under paragraph (e)(2) of this section FC2 is treated as holding U.S. real estate with a fair market value of $5,000,000 (50 percent of $10,000,000, its pro rata share of real estate held by DP). Under paragraph (e)(3) of this section, FC1 is treated as holding 100 percent of the assets of FC2 (U.S. real estate with a fair market value of $5,000,000). FC1, therefore, is a U.S. real property holding corporation. Under paragraph (e)(1) of this section, the stock of FC1 is treated as U.S. real property interest. US is a U.S. real property holding corporation because 100 percent of its assets (the stock of FC1) are U.S. real property interests. As US is a U.S. real property holding corporation and is a domestic corporation, the stock of US is a U.S. real property interest, and B's gain or loss from the disposition of stock of US within 5 years of the current determination date will be subject to the provisions of section 897(a).

(f) *Termination of U.S. real property holding corporation status.*—(1) *In general.*—A U.S. real property holding corporation may voluntarily determine its status as of the date of any acquisition or disposition of assets. If the fair market value of its U.S. real property interests on such date no longer equals or exceeds 50 percent of the fair market value of all assets described in paragraphs (d) and (e) of this section, such corporation shall cease to be U.S. real property holding corporation as of such date, and on the day that is five years after such date interests in such corporation shall cease to be treated as U.S. real property interests (unless subsequent transactions within the five-year period have caused the fair market value of the corporation's U.S. real property interests to equal or exceed 50 percent of the fair market value of assets described in paragraphs (d) and (e) of this section). A corporation that determines that interests in it have ceased to be U.S. real property interests pursuant to the rules of this paragraph (f) may so inform the Internal Revenue Service, as provided in paragraph (h) of this section.

(2) *Early termination.*—Interests in a U.S. real property holding corporation shall immediately cease to be U.S. real property interests as of the first date on which the following conditions are met—

(i) The corporation does not hold any U.S. real property interests, and

(ii) All of the U.S. real property interests directly or indirectly held by such corporation at any time during the previous five years (but disregarding any disposed of before June 19, 1980) either (A) were directly or indirectly disposed of in transactions in which the full amount of the gain (if any) was recognized or (B) ceased to be U.S. real property interests by reason of the application of this paragraph (f) to one or more other corporations.

For purposes of this paragraph (f)(2), a corporation that disposes of all U.S. real property interests other than a lease that has a fair market value of zero will be considered to have disposed of all of its U.S. real property interests, provided that the leased property is used in the conduct by the corporation of a trade or business in the United States. Such a lease may include an option to renew, but only if such option is for a renewal at fair market rental rates prevailing at the time of renewal.

(g) *Establishing that a corporation is not a U.S. real property holding corporation.*—(1) *Foreign persons disposing of interests.*—(i) *In general.*—A foreign person disposing of an interest in a domestic corporation (other than an interest solely as a creditor) must establish that the interest was not a U.S. real property interest as of the date of disposition, either by:

(A) Obtaining a statement from the corporation pursuant to the provisions of subdivision (ii) of this paragraph (g)(1), or

(B) Obtaining a determination by the Commissioner, Small Business/Self Employed Division (SB/SE) pursuant to the provisions of subdivision (iii) of this paragraph (g)(1).

If the foreign person does not establish by either method that the interest disposed of was not a U.S. real property interest then the interest shall be presumed to have been a U.S. real property interest the disposition of which is subject to section 897(a). See paragraph (g)(3) of this section for certain exceptions to this rule. It should be noted that the rules of this section relate solely to interests in a corporation that are interests other than solely as a creditor. Therefore, a statement by a corporation or a determination by the Commissioner (under paragraphs (g) and (h) of this section) that an interest is not a U.S. real property interest depends solely upon whether or not the corporation was a U.S. real property holding corporation during the period described in section 897(c)(1)(A)(ii) (subject to certain special rules). The determination of whether an interest is one solely as a creditor is made under the rules of § 1.897-1(d).

(ii) *Statement from corporation.*—(A) *In general.*—A foreign person disposing of an interest in a domestic corporation may establish that the interest was not a U.S. real property interest as of the date of the disposition by requesting and obtaining from the corporation a statement that the interest was not a U.S. real property interest as of that date. However, a corporation's statement shall not be valid for purposes of this rule, and thus may not be relied upon for purposes of establishing that an interest was not a U.S. real property interest, unless the corporation complies with the notice requirements of paragraph (h)(2) or (h)(4) of this section.

A foreign person that requests and obtains such a statement is not required to forward the statement to the Internal Revenue Service and is not required to take any further action to establish that the interest disposed of was not a U.S. real property interest. To qualify under this rule, the foreign person must obtain the corporation's statement no later than the date, including any extensions, on which a tax return would otherwise be due with respect to a disposition. A foreign person that relies in good faith upon a statement from the corporation is not thereby excused from filing a return and paying any taxes and interest due thereon if the corporation's statement is later found to have been incorrect. However, such reliance shall be taken into account in determining whether the foreign person shall be subject to any penalty for the previous failure to file. However, a foreign person that knew or had reason to know that a corporation's statement was incorrect is not entitled to rely upon such statement and shall remain liable for all applicable penalties.

(B) *Coordination with section 1445.*—Pursuant to section 1445 and regulations thereunder, withholding of tax is not required with respect to a foreign person's disposition of an interest in a domestic corporation, if the transferee is furnished with a statement by the corporation under paragraph (h) of this section that the interest is not a U.S. real property interest. A foreign person that obtains a corporation's statement for that purpose prior to the date of disposition may also rely upon the statement for purposes of this paragraph (g)(1)(ii), unless the corporation informs the foreign person (pursuant to paragraph (h)(1)(iv)(C) of this section) that it became a U.S. real property holding corporation after the date of the notice but prior to the actual date of disposition.

(iii) *Determination by Commissioner.*—(A) *In general.*—A foreign person disposing of an interest in a domestic corporation may establish that the interest was not a U.S. real property interest as of the date of disposition by requesting and obtaining a determination to that effect from the Commissioner. Such a determination may be requested pursuant to the provisions of subdivision (B) or (C) of this paragraph (g)(1)(iii). A request for a determination should be addressed to: Commissioner, Small Business/Self Employed Division (SB/SE); S C3-413 NCFB, 500 Ellin Road, Lanham, MD 20706. A foreign transferor who has requested a determination by the Commissioner pursuant to the rules of this paragraph (g)(1)(iii) is not thereby excused from filing a return and paying any tax due by the date, including any extensions, on which such return and payment would otherwise be due with respect to a disposition. If the Commissioner subsequently determines and notifies the foreign transferor that the interest was not a U.S. real property interest, the foreign transferor shall be entitled to a refund of any taxes, penalties, and interest paid by reason of the application of section 897(a) pursuant to the rules of paragraph (g)(1)(i) of this section, together with any interest otherwise due on such refund, if a claim for refund is made within the applicable time limits.

(B) *Determination based on Commissioner's information.*—A foreign person may request that the Commissioner make a determination based on information contained in the Commissioner's records, if:

(1) The foreign person made a request to the corporation for information as to the status of its interest no later than the 90th day before the date, including any extensions, on which a tax return would otherwise be due with respect to a disposition, and

(2) The corporation failed to respond to such request by the 30th day following the date the request was delivered to the corporation.

If the Commissioner is unable to make a determination based on information available to him, he shall inform the foreign person that the interest must be treated as a U.S. real property interest unless the person subsequently obtains either the necessary statement from the corporation or a determination pursuant to subdivision (C) of this paragraph (g)(1)(iii).

(C) *Determination based on information supplied by foreign person.*—A foreign person may request that the Commissioner make a determination based on information supplied by the foreign person. Such information may be drawn, for example, from annual reports, financial statements, or records of the corporation, and must establish to the satisfaction of the Commissioner that the foreign person's interest was not a U.S. real property interest as of the date of disposition.

(D) *Determination by Commissioner on his own motion.*—Notwithstanding any other provision of this section, a foreign person shall not treat the disposition of an interest in a domestic corporation as a disposition of a U.S. real property interest if such person is notified that the Commissioner has upon his own motion determined that the interest was not a U.S. real property interest as of the date of disposition.

(2) *Corporations determining U.S. real property holding corporation status.*—(i) *In general.*—A corporation that must determine whether it is a U.S. real property holding corporation, and that holds an interest in another corporation (other than a controlling interest as defined in paragraph (e)(3) of this section), must determine whether or not that interest was a U.S. real property interest as of its own determination date, by either:

(A) Obtaining a statement from the second corporation pursuant to the provisions of subdivision (ii) of this paragraph (g)(2);

(B) Obtaining a determination by the Commissioner pursuant to the provisions of subdivision (iii) of this paragraph (g)(2); or

(C) Making an independent determination pursuant to the provisions of subdivision (iv) of this paragraph (g)(2).

A corporation that is unable to determine by any of the above methods whether its interest in a second corporation is a U.S. real property interest must presume that such interest is a U.S. real property interest.

(ii) *Statement from corporation.*—A corporation may determine whether or not an interest in a second corporation was a U.S. real property interest as of its own determination date by obtaining from the second corporation a statement that the interest was not a U.S. real property interest as of that date. However, the second corporation's statement shall not be valid for purposes of this rule, and thus may not be relied upon for purposes of establishing that an interest was not a U.S. real property interest, unless such corporation complies with the notice requirements of paragraph (h)(2) or (h)(4) of this section.

A corporation that requests and obtains such a statement is not required to forward the statement to the Internal Revenue Service and is not required to take any further action to establish that the interest in the second corporation was not a U.S. real property interest. If the second corporation's statement is later found to have been incorrect, the first corporation shall not be subject to penalties arising out of past failures to comply with the requirements of section 897 or 1445, if such failures were attributable to reliance upon the second corporation's statement. By the 90th day following receipt of a notification from the Service or from the second corporation that a prior statement was incorrect, the first corporation must redetermine its status (as of its most recent determination date) and if appropriate notify the Internal Revenue Service that it is a U.S. real property holding corporation in accordance with paragraph (h)(1)(ii)(C) of this section. However, a corporation that knew or had reason to know that a second corporation's statement was incorrect is not entitled to rely upon such statement and shall remain liable for all applicable taxes, penalties, and interest arising out of the second corporation's status as a U.S. real property holding corporation.

(iii) *Determination by Commissioner.*—(A) *In general.*—A corporation may determine whether or not an interest in a second corporation was a U.S. real property interest as of its own determination date by requesting and obtaining a determination to that effect from the Commissioner. Such a determination may be requested pursuant to the provisions of subdivision (B) or (C) of this paragraph (g)(2)(iii). A request for a determination must be addressed to: Commissioner, Small Business/Self Employed Division (SB/SE); S C3-413 NCFB, 500 Ellin Road, Lanham, MD 20706. A corporation that has requested a determination by the Commissioner pursuant to the provisions of this paragraph is not thereby excused from taking any action required by section 897 or 1445 by the date on which such action would otherwise be due. However, the Commissioner may grant a reasonable extension of time for the satisfaction of any requirement if the Commissioner is satisfied that the corporation has not sought a determination pursuant to this paragraph (g)(2)(iii) for a principal purpose of delay.

(B) *Determination based on Commissioner's information.*—A corporation may request that the Commissioner make a determination based on information contained in the Commissioner's records, if:

(1) The corporation made a request to the second corporation for information as to the status of its interest no later than the fifth day following the first corporation's determination date, and

(2) The second corporation failed to respond to such request by the 30th day following the date the request was delivered to the second corporation.

Pending his resolution of such a request, the Commissioner will generally grant an extension with respect to the change-of-status notification that may otherwise be required pursuant to paragraph (h)(1)(ii) of this section. If the

Commissioner is unable to make a determination based on information available to him, he shall inform the corporation that the interest must be treated as a U.S. real property interest unless the corporation subsequently obtains either the necessary statement from the second corporation or a determination pursuant to paragraph (g)(2)(iii)(C) or (g)(2)(iv) of this section.

(C) *Determination based on information supplied by corporation.*—A corporation may request that the Commissioner make a determination based on information supplied by the corporation. Such information may be drawn, for example, from annual reports, financial statements, or records of the second corporation, and must establish to the satisfaction of the Commissioner that the interest in the second corporation was not a U.S. real property interest as of the first corporation's determination date.

(D) *Determination by Commissioner on his own motion.*—Notwithstanding any other provision of this section, a corporation shall not treat an interest in a second corporation as a U.S. real property interest if the corporation is notified that the Commissioner has upon his own motion determined that the interest in the second corporation is not a U.S. real property interest.

(iv) *Independent determination by corporation.*—A corporation may independently determine whether or not an interest in a second corporation was a U.S. real property interest as of the first corporation's own determination date. Such determination must be based upon the best evidence available, drawn from annual reports, financial statements, records of the second corporation, or from any other source, that demonstrates to a reasonable certainty that the interest in the second corporation was not a U.S. real property interest. A corporation that makes an independent determination pursuant to this paragraph (g)(2)(iv) shall be subject to the special notification rule of paragraph (h)(1)(iii)(D) of this section. If the Commissioner subsequently determines that the corporation's independent determination was incorrect, the corporation shall be subject to penalties for any past failure to comply with the requirements of section 897 or 1445 only if the corporation's determination was unreasonable in view of facts that the corporation knew or had reason to know.

(3) *Requirements not applicable.*—If at any time during the calendar year any class of stock of a corporation is regularly traded on an established securities market, the requirements of this paragraph (g) shall not apply with respect to any holder of an interest in such corporation other than a person who holds an interest described in § 1.897-1(c)(2)(iii)(A) or (B). For example, a corporation determining whether it is a U.S. real property holding corporation need not ascertain from a regularly traded corporation in which it neither holds, nor has held during the period described in section 897(c)(1)(A)(ii), more than a 5 percent interest whether that regularly traded corporation is itself a U.S. real property holding corporation. In addition, the requirements of this paragraph (g) do not apply to any holder of an interest in a domestically-controlled REIT, as defined in section 897(h)(4)(B).

(h) *Notice requirements applicable to corporations.*—(1) *Statement to foreign interest-holder.*—(i) *In general.*—A domestic corporation must, within a reasonable period after receipt of a request from a foreign person holding an interest in it, inform that person whether the interest constitutes a U.S. real property interest. No particular form is required for this statement, which need only indicate the corporation's determination. The statement must be dated and signed by a responsible corporate officer who must verify under penalties of perjury that the statement is correct to his knowledge and belief.

(ii) *Required determination.*—For purposes of the statement required by paragraph (h)(1)(i) of this section, an interest in a corporation is a U.S. real property interest if the corporation was a U.S. real property holding corporation on any determination date during the 5-year period ending on the date specified in the interest-holder's request, or on the date such request was received if no date is specified (or during such shorter period ending on the date that is applicable pursuant to section 897(c)(1)(A)(ii)). However, an interest in a corporation is not a U.S. real property interest if such interest is excluded under section 897(c)(1)(B).

(2) *Notice to the Internal Revenue Service.*—If a foreign interest holder requests that a domestic corporation provide a statement described in paragraph (h)(1) of this section, then such corporation must provide a notice to the Internal Revenue Service in accordance with this paragraph (h)(2). No particular form is required for such notice, but the following must be provided:

(i) A statement that the notice is provided pursuant to the requirements of § 1.897-2(h)(2);

(ii) The name, address, and identifying number of the corporation providing the notice;

(iii) The name, address, and identifying number (if any) of the foreign interest holder that requested the statement (this information may be omitted from the notice if fully set forth in the statement to the foreign interest holder attached to the notice);

(iv) Whether the interest in question is a U.S. real property interest;

(v) A statement signed by a responsible corporate officer verifying under penalties of perjury that the notice (including any attachments thereto) is correct to his knowledge and belief. A copy of any statement provided to the foreign interest holder must be attached to the notice. The notice must be mailed to the Director, Philadelphia Service Center, P.O. Box 21086, Drop Point 8731, FIRPTA Unit, Philadelphia, PA 19114-0586 on or before the 30th day after the statement referred to in § 1.897-2(h)(1) is mailed to the interest holder that requested it. Failure to mail such notice within the time period set forth in the preceding sentence will cause the statement provided pursuant to § 1.897-2(h)(1) to become an invalid statement.

(3) *Requirements not applicable.*—The requirements of this paragraph (h) do not apply to domestically-controlled REITS, as defined in section 897(h)(4)(B). These requirements also do not apply to a corporation any class of stock in which is regularly traded on an established securities market at any time during the calendar year. However, such a corporation may voluntarily choose to comply with the requirements of paragraph (h)(4) of this section.

(4) *Voluntary notice to Internal Revenue Service.*—(i) *In general.*—A domestic corporation which determines that it is not a U.S. real property holding corporation—

(A) on each of the applicable determination dates in a taxable year, or

(B) pursuant to section 897(c)(1)(B),

may attach to its income tax return for that year a statement informing the Internal Revenue Service of its determination. A corporation that has provided a voluntary notice described in this § 1.897-2(h)(4)(i) for the immediately preceding taxable year and that does not have an event described in § 1.897-2(c)(1)(ii), (iii) or (iv) prior to receiving a request from a foreign person under § 1.897-2(h)(1), is exempt from the notice requirement of § 1.897-2(h)(2).

(ii) *Early termination of real property holding corporation status.*—A corporation that determines during the course of its taxable year that interests in it have ceased to be U.S. real property interests pursuant to the rules of section 897(c)(1)(B) may, on the day of its determination or thereafter, provide a statement to the Director, Philadelphia Service Center, P.O. Box 21086, Drop Point 8731, FIRPTA Unit, Philadelphia, PA 19114-0586, informing the Service of its determination. No particular form is required but the statement must set forth the corporation's name, address, identification number, a brief statement regarding its determination and the date such determination was made. Such statement will enable foreign interest-holders to dispose of their interests without being subject to section 897(a), as provided in paragraph (g) of this section.

(5) *Supplemental statements.*—(i) *By corporations with substantial intangible assets.*—A corporation that is subject to the requirements of paragraph (h)(2) of this section (or that voluntarily complies with the requirements of paragraph (h)(4) of this section) must submit a supplemental statement to the Internal Revenue Service if—

(A) Such corporation values any of the intangible assets described in § 1.897-1(f)(1)(ii) (other than goodwill or going concern value) by a method other than the purchase price or book value methods described in § 1.897-1(o)(4); and

(B) The fair market value of such intangible assets equals or exceeds 25 percent of the total of the fair market values of the assets the corporation is considered to hold in accordance with the provisions of paragraphs (d) and (e) of this section.

The supplemental statement must inform the Internal Revenue Service that the corporation meets the criteria of subdivisions (A) and (B) of this paragraph (h)(5)(i), and must summarize the methods and calculations upon which the corporation's determination of the fair market value of its intangible assets is based. In addition, the supplemental statement must list any intangible assets that were purchased from any person that have been valued by the corporation at an amount other than their purchase price, and must provide a justification for such a departure from the purchase price. The supplemental statement must be attached to or incorporated in the statement provided under paragraph (h)(2) or (h)(4) of this section.

(ii) *Corporation not valuing goodwill or going concern value at purchase price.*—A corporation that is subject to the requirements of paragraph (h)(2) of this section (or that voluntarily complies with the requirements of paragraph (h)(4) of this section) must submit a supplemental statement to the Internal Revenue Service if such corporation values goodwill or going concern value pursuant to § 1.897-1(o)(4)(iii). The supplemental statement must set forth that it is made pursuant to this paragraph (h)(5)(ii), and must summarize the methods and calculations upon which the corporation's determination of the fair market value of such intangible assets is based. In addition, the supplemental statement must list any such assets that were purchased from any person that have been valued by the corporation at an amount other than their purchase price, and must provide a justification for such a departure from the purchase price. The supplemental statement must be attached to or incorporated in the statement provided under paragraph (h)(2) or (h)(4) of this section.

(iii) *Corporation using alternative U.S. real property holding corporation test.*—A corporation that is subject to the requirements of paragraph (h)(2) of this section (or that voluntarily complies with the requirements of paragraph (h)(4) of this section) must submit a supplemental statement to the Internal Revenue Service if—

(A) Such corporation utilizes the rule of paragraph (b)(2) of this section (regarding the book values of assets held by the corporation) to presume that it is not a U.S. real property holding corporation; and

(B) Such corporation is engaged in or is planning to engage in a trade or business of mining, farming, or forestry, or of buying and selling or developing real property, or of leasing real property to tenants.

The supplemental statement must inform the Internal Revenue Service that the corporation meets the criteria of subdivisions (A) and (B) of this paragraph (h)(5)(iii), and must be attached to or incorporated in the statement provided under paragraph (h)(2) or (h)(4) of this section.

(iv) *Corporation determining real property holding corporation status of second corporation.*—A corporation that is subject to the requirements of paragraph (h)(2) of this section (or that voluntarily complies with the requirements of paragraph (h)(4) of this section) must submit a supplemental statement to the Internal Revenue Service if such corporation independently determines whether or not an interest in a second corporation is a U.S. real property interest, pursuant to paragraph (g)(2)(iv) of this section. The supplemental statement must set forth that it is made pursuant to this paragraph (h)(5)(iv) and must briefly summarize the facts upon which the corporation's determination is based and the sources of the information relied upon by the corporation. The supplemental statement must be attached to or incorporated in the statement provided under paragraph (h)(2) or (h)(4) of this section.

(i) *Transition rules.*—(1) *General waiver of penalties for failure to file.*—If a foreign person disposed of an interest in a domestic corporation between June 18, 1980 and January 23, 1987, and such person establishes under the rules of paragraph (g) of this section at any time that the interest disposed of was not a U.S. real property interest, then such person shall not be subject to tax under section 897 and shall not be subject to penalties (or interest) for failure to file an income tax return with respect to such disposition.

(2) *Foreign persons that met the requirements of prior regulations.*—A foreign person that disposed of an interest in a domestic corporation between June 18, 1980 and January 23, 1987, shall be deemed to have satisfied the requirements of paragraph (g) of this section with respect to such disposition if such person established under prior temporary or prior final regulations issued under section 897 that the interest disposed of was not a U.S. real property interest. [Reg. § 1.897-2.]

☐ [*T.D.* 7999, 12-26-84. *Amended by T.D.* 8113, 12-18-86 *and T.D.* 9082, 8-4-2003.]

§ 1.897-3. Election by foreign corporation to be treated as a domestic corporation under section 897(i).—(a) *Purpose and scope.*—This section provides rules pursuant to which a foreign corporation may elect under section 897(i) to be treated as a domestic corporation for purposes of sections 897, 1445, and 6039C and the regulations thereunder. A foreign corporation with respect to which an election under section 897(i) is in effect is subject to all rules under sections 897 and 1445 that apply to domestic corporations. Thus, for example, if a foreign corporation that has made an election under section 897(i) is a U.S. real property holding corporation, interests in it are U.S. real property interests that are subject to withholding under section 1445, and any gain or loss from the disposition of such interests by a foreign person will be treated as effectively connected with a U.S. trade or business under section 897(a). Similarly, if a foreign corporation makes an election under section 897(i), its distribution of a U.S. real property interest pursuant to section 301 will be subject to the carryover basis rule of section 897(f). However, an interest in an electing corporation is not a U.S. real property interest if following the election the interest is described in section 897(c)(1)(B) or § 1.897-1(c)(2) (subject to the exceptions of subdivisions (i) and (ii) of that section). In addition, section 897(d) will not apply to any distribution of a U.S. real property interest by such corporation or to any sale or exchange of such interest pursuant to a plan of complete liquidation under section 337. A foreign corporation that makes an election under section 897(i) shall not be treated as a domestic corporation for purposes of any other provision of the Code or regulations, except to the extent that it is required to consent to such treatment as a condition to making the election. For further information concerning the effect of an election under section 897(i) upon the withholding requirements of section 1445, see § 1.1445-7. An election under section 897(i) is the exclusive remedy of any foreign person claiming discriminatory treatment under any treaty with respect to the application of sections 897, 1445, and 6039C to a foreign corporation. Therefore, if a corporation does not make an effective election, relief under a nondiscrimination article of any treaty shall not be otherwise available with respect to the application of sections 897, 1445, and 6039C to such corporation.

(b) *General conditions.*—A foreign corporation may make an election under section 897(i) only if it meets all three of the following conditions.

(1) *Holding a U.S. real property interest.*—The foreign corporation must hold a U.S. real property interest at the time of the election. This condition is satisfied when a U.S. real property interest is acquired simultaneously with the effective date of an election. For example, this condition is satisfied when real property is acquired in an exchange described in section 351 that is carried out simultaneously with the effective date of the election. This condition is also satisfied by a corporation that indirectly holds a U.S. real property interest through a partnership, trust, or estate.

(2) *Entitlement to nondiscriminatory treatment.*—The foreign corporation must be entitled to nondiscriminatory treatment with respect to its U.S. real property interest under any treaty to which the United States is a party. Where the corporation indirectly holds a U.S. real property interest through a partnership, trust, or estate, the corporation itself must be entitled to nondiscriminatory treatment with respect to such property interest.

(3) *Submission of election in proper form.*—The foreign corporation must comply with the requirements of paragraph (c) of this section respecting the manner and form in which an election must be submitted.

(c) *Manner and form of election.*—An election under section 897(i) is made by filing the documents described in subparagraphs (1) through (5) of this paragraph (c) with the Director, Philadelphia Service Center, P.O. Box 21086, Drop Point 8731, FIRPTA Unit, Philadelphia, PA 19114-0586. The required items may be incorporated in a single document.

(1) *General statement.*—The foreign corporation must supply a general statement indicating that an election under section 897(i) is being made. The general statement must be signed by a responsible corporate officer, who must verify under penalty of perjury that the statement and all other documents submitted pursuant to the requirements of this paragraph (c) are true and correct to his knowledge and belief. No particular form is required for the statement, which must contain all the following information—

(i) The name, address, identifying number, and place and date of incorporation of the foreign corporation;

(ii) The treaty and article under which the foreign corporation is seeking nondiscriminatory treatment;

(iii) A description of the U.S. real property interests held by the corporation, either directly or through a partnership, trust, or estate, including the dates such interests were acquired, the corporation's adjusted bases in such interests, and their fair market values as of the date of the election (or book values if the corporation is not a U.S. real property holding corporation under the alternative test of § 1.897-2(b)(2)); and

(iv) A list of all dispositions of any interests in the foreign corporation after December 31, 1979, and before June 19, 1980, between related persons (as defined in section 453(f)(1)), giving the type and the amount of any interest transferred, the name and address of the related person to whom the interest was transferred, the transferor's basis in the interest transferred, and the amount of any nontaxed gain as defined in section 1125(d) of Pub. L. 96-499.

(2) *Waiver of treaty benefits.*—The foreign corporation must submit a binding waiver of the benefits of any U.S. treaty with respect to any gain or loss from the disposition of a U.S. real property interest during the period in which the election is in effect.

(3) *Consent to be taxed.*—The foreign corporation must submit a binding agreement to treat as though it were a domestic corporation any gain or loss, that is recognized upon—

(i) The disposition of any U.S. real property interest during the period in which the election is in effect, and

(ii) The disposition of any property that it acquired in exchange for a U.S. real property interest in a nonrecognition transaction (as defined under section 897(e)) during the period in which the election is in effect.

(4) *Interest-holders' consent to election.*—(i) *In general.*—The foreign corporation must submit both a signed consent to the making of the election and a waiver of U.S. treaty benefits with respect to any gain or loss from the disposition of an interest in the corporation from

each person who holds an interest in the corporation on the date the election is made. In the case of a corporation any class of stock of which is regularly traded on an established securities market at any time during the calendar year, the signed consent and waiver need only be provided by a person who holds an interest described in § 1.897-1(c)(2)(iii)(A) or (B) (determined after application of the constructive ownership rules of section 897(c)(6)(C)). The foreign corporation must also include with the signed consents and waivers a list that identifies and describes the interest in the corporation held by each interest holder, including the type and amount of such interest and its fair market value as of the date of the election.

(ii) *Corporation's retention of interest-holders' consents.*—A corporation need not file the consents and waivers of its interest-holders as required by paragraph (c)(4)(i) of this section, if it instead complies with the requirements of subdivisions (A) through (D) of this paragraph (c)(4)(ii).

(A) The corporation must place a legend on each outstanding certificate for shares of its stock that reads substantially as follows: "[Name of corporation] has made an election under section 897(i) of the United States Internal Revenue Code to be treated as a U.S. corporation for certain tax purposes, and any purchaser of this interest may therefore be required to withhold tax at the time of the purchase." The corporation must certify that the foregoing requirement has been met and that it will place an equivalent legend on every stock certificate that is issued while the election under section 897(i) is in effect and the corporation retains the consents and waivers of its interest-holders under the rules of this paragraph (c)(4)(ii). However, with respect to any registered certificate issued prior to January 30, 1985, in lieu of placing a legend on the certificate the corporation may certify that it will provide the purchaser of the interest with a copy of the legend at the time the certificate is surrendered for issuance of a new certificate.

(B) The corporation must include with its election a statement that the corporation has received both a signed consent to the making of the election and a waiver of U.S. treaty benefits with respect to any gain or loss from the disposition of an interest in the corporation from each person who holds an interest in the corporation on the date the election is made. In the case of a corporation any class of stock of which is regularly traded on an established securities market at any time during the calendar year, the signed consent and waiver need only be provided by a person who holds or has held an interest described in § 1.897-1(c)(2)(iii)(A) or (B) (determined after application of the constructive ownership rules of section 897(c)(6)(C)).

(C) The corporation must include with its election a list that describes the interests in the corporation held by each interest-holder. The list need not identify the interest-holders by name, but must set forth the type, amount, and fair market value of the interests held by each.

(D) The corporation must include with its election an agreement that the corporation will retain all signed consents and waivers for a period of three years from the date of the election and supply such documents to the Director within 30 days of his request for production thereof. The Director's review of the signed consents and waivers pursuant to this provision shall not constitute an examination for purposes of section 7605(b).

(5) *Statement regarding prior dispositions.*—The foreign corporation must state that no interest in the corporation was disposed of during the shortest of (A) the period from June 19, 1980, through the date of the election, (B) the period from the date on which the corporation first holds a U.S. real property interest through the date of the election, or (C) the five-year period ending on the date of the election. If the corporation cannot state that no such dispositions have been made, it may make the section 897(i) election only if it states that it has complied with the requirements of paragraph (d)(2) of this section.

(d) *Time and duration of election.*—(1) *In general.*—A foreign corporation that meets the conditions of paragraph (b) of this section may make an election under section 897(i) at any time before the first disposition of an interest in the corporation which would be subject to section 897(a) if the election had been made before that disposition, except as otherwise provided in paragraph (d)(2) of this section. The period to which the election applies begins on the date on which the election is made, or such earlier date as is specified in the election, but not earlier than June 19, 1980. Unless revoked, an election applies for the duration of the time for which the corporation remains in existence. An election is made on the date that the statements described in paragraph (c) of this section are delivered to the Philadelphia Service Center. If the election is delivered by United States mail, the provisions of section 7502 and the regulations thereunder shall apply in determining the date of delivery.

(2) *Election after disposition of stock.*—An election under section 897(i) may be made after any disposition of an interest in the corporation which would have been subject to section

897(a) if the election had been made before that disposition, but only if the requirements of either subdivision (i) or (ii) of this paragraph (d)(2) are met with respect to all dispositions of interests during the period described in paragraph (c)(5) of this section.

(i) There is a payment of an amount equal to any taxes which would have been imposed by reason of the application of section 897 upon all persons who had disposed of interests in the corporation during the period described in paragraph (c)(5) of this section had the corporation made the election prior to such dispositions. Such payment must be made by the later of the date the election is made, or the date on which payment of such taxes would otherwise have been due, and must include any interest that would have accrued had tax actually been due with respect to the disposition. As an election made prior to any disposition of interests in the corporation would have been conditioned on a waiver of treaty benefits by the interest-holders, payment of an amount equal to tax and any interest with respect to such prior disposition is required as a condition to making a subsequent election under this subdivision (i) irrespective of the application of any treaty provision. For this purpose, it is not necessary that the payment be made by the person who would have owed the tax if the election under this section had been made prior to the disposition, and that person is under no obligation to supply any information to the present holders of interests in the electing corporation. The payment shall be made to the U.S. Treasury. Where the payment is made by a present holder of an interest, the basis of the person's interest in the corporation shall be increased to the extent of the amount paid.

(ii) Each person that acquired an interest in the electing corporation took a basis in the interest that was equal to the basis of the interest in the hands of the person from which the interest was acquired, increased by the sum of any gain recognized by the transferor of the interest and any tax paid under chapter 1 by the person that acquired the interest, if such interest was acquired after June 18, 1980.

(3) *Adequate proof of basis.*—For purposes of meeting the conditions of paragraph (d)(2)(i) or (ii) of this section, a corporation must establish the bases of and amount of gain realized by all persons who disposed of interests in the corporation during the period described in paragraph (c)(5) of this section. See paragraph (g)(3) of this section for an exception to this rule.

(4) *Acknowledgment of receipt.*—Within 60 days after its receipt of an election under section 897(i), the Internal Revenue Service will acknowledge receipt of the election. Such acknowledgment either will indicate that the information submitted with the election is complete or will specify any documents that remain to be submitted pursuant to the requirements of paragraph (c) of this section respecting the manner and form in which an election must be made.

(e) *Anti-abuse rule.*—(1) *In general.*—A corporation that is otherwise eligible to make an election under section 897(i) may do so only by complying with the requirements of subdivision (2) of this paragraph, if during the period described in paragraph (c)(5) of this section—

(i) Prior to receipt of a U.S. real property interest by the corporation seeking to make the election, stock in such corporation (or in any corporation controlled by such corporation) was acquired in a transaction in which the person acquiring such stock obtained an increase in basis in the stock over the adjusted basis of the stock in the hands of the person from whom it was acquired;

(ii) The full amount of gain realized by the person from whom the stock was acquired was not subject to U.S. tax; and

(iii) The corporation seeking to make the election received the U.S. real property interest in a transaction or series of transactions to which section 897(d)(1)(B) or (e)(1) applies to allow for nonrecognition of gain.

(2) *Recognition of gain.*—A corporation described in subparagraph (1) of this paragraph (e) may make an election under section 897(i) only if it pays an amount equal to the tax on the full amount of gain realized by the transferors of the stock of such corporation (or of any corporation controlled by it) in the transaction described in paragraph (e)(1)(i) of this section. However, such amount must be paid only if the stock of the corporation seeking to make the election (or the stock of a corporation controlled by it) would have constituted a U.S. real property interest had it (or a corporation controlled by it) made the election before that acquisition. Such amount must be paid by the later of the date of the election or the date on which such tax would otherwise be due, and must include any interest that would have accrued had tax actually been due with respect to the disposition.

(3) *Definition of control.*—For purposes of this paragraph, a corporation controls a second corporation if it holds 80 percent or more of the total combined voting power of all classes of stock entitled to vote, and 80 percent or more of the total number of shares of all other classes of stock of the second corporation. In a chain of corporations where each succeeding corporation is controlled within the meaning of

this subparagraph (3) by the corporation immediately above it in the chain, each corporation in the chain shall be considered to be controlled by all corporations that preceded it in the chain.

(4) *Examples.*—The rules of this paragraph (e) are illustrated by the following examples.

Example 1. Nonresident alien individual X owns 100 percent of the stock of foreign corporation L which was organized in 1981. L's only asset is a parcel of U.S. real property which it has held since 1981. The fair market value of the U.S. real property held by L on January 1, 1984, is $1,000,000. L's basis in the property is $200,000. X's basis in the L stock is $500,000. On June 1, 1984, M corporation, a foreign corporation owned by foreign persons who are unrelated to X, purchases the stock of L from X for $1,000,000 with title passing outside of the United States. Since the stock of L is not a U.S. real property interest, X's gain from the disposition of the L stock ($500,000) is not treated as effectively connected with a U.S. trade or business under section 897(a). In addition, since X was neither engaged in a U.S. trade or business nor present in the U.S. at any time during 1984, such gain is not subject to U.S. tax under section 871. On January 1, 1987, M liquidates L under a plan of liquidation adopted on that same date. Under section 332 of the Code M recognizes no gain on receipt of the parcel of U.S. real property distributed by L in liquidation. Under section 334(b)(1) M takes $200,000 as its basis in the U.S. real property received from L. Under section 897(d)(1)(B) no gain would be recognized to L under section 897(d)(1)(A) on the liquidating distribution. As a consequence, no gain is recognized to L under section 336 of the Code. After its receipt of the U.S. real property from L, M seeks to make an election to be treated as a domestic corporation. Thus, M acquired the L stock in a transaction in which it obtained a basis in such stock in excess of the adjusted basis of X in the stock, U.S. tax was not paid on the full amount of the gain realized by X, and M has received the property in a distribution in which section 897(d)(1)(B) applied to provide for nonrecognition of gain to L. Therefore, M may make the election only if it pays an amount equal to the tax on the full amount of X's gain, pursuant to the rule of subparagraph (e)(2) of this section.

Example 2. Nonresident alien individual X owns 100 percent of the stock of foreign corporation A which owns 100 percent of the stock of foreign corporation B. X's basis in the A stock is $500,000. A's basis in the B stock is $500,000. B owns U.S. real property with a fair market value of $1,000,000. B's basis in the U.S. real property is $500,000. On January 1, 1985, X sells the stock of A to Y, an unrelated individual, for $1,000,000 with title passing outside of the United States. In addition, X was neither engaged in a U.S. trade or business nor present in the U.S. at any time during 1985. Since the A stock is not a U.S. real property interest, X's gain on such disposition is not treated as effectively connected with a U.S. trade or business under section 897(a) and is therefore not subject to U.S. tax under section 871. On July 1, 1987, a plan of liquidation is adopted, and B is liquidated into A. Under sections 332, 334(b)(1), 336, and 897(d)(1)(B), there is no tax to A on receipt of U.S. real property from B and no tax to B on the distribution of the U.S. real property interest to A. After receipt of the property A seeks to make an election under section 897(i). Under the rules of paragraph (e) of this section, A may make the election only if it pays an amount equal to the tax on the full amount of X's gain. (Assuming that A is a U.S. real property holding corporation, the same result would be required by the rule of paragraph (d)(2) of this section.)

(f) *Revocation of election.*—(1) *In general.*—An election under section 897(i) may be revoked only with the consent of the Commissioner. A request for revocation shall be in writing and shall be addressed to the Director, Philadelphia Service Center, P.O. Box 21086, Drop Point 8731, FIRPTA Unit, Philadelphia, PA 19114-0586. The request shall include the name, address, and identifying number of the corporation seeking to revoke the election, and a description of all U.S. real property interests held by the corporation on the date of the request for revocation, including the dates such interests were acquired, the corporation's adjusted bases in such interests, and their fair market values as of the date of the request (or book value if the corporation is not a U.S. real property holding corporation under the alternative test of §1.897-2(b)(2)). The request shall be signed by a responsible officer of the corporation under penalty of perjury and shall contain a statement either that the corporation has made no distributions described in subparagraph (2) of this paragraph (f) or that the conditions of that subparagraph have been satisfied. A revocation will be effective as of the date the request is delivered to the Philadelphia Service Center (unless the Commissioner provides otherwise in his consent to the revocation. If the request is delivered by United States mail, the provisions of section 7502 and the regulations thereunder shall apply in determining the date of delivery. The Commissioner will generally consent to a revocation, provided either that there have been no distributions described in subparagraph (2) of this paragraph (f), or that the conditions of that subparagraph have been satisfied. Within 90 days after its receipt of a request to revoke an election under section 897(i), the Internal Revenue Service will acknowledge receipt of the request. Such acknowledgement either will indicate that the information submitted with the request is complete or will specify any information that remains to be submitted pursuant to the requirements of this paragraph (f).

(2) *Revocation after distribution.*—If there have been any distributions of U.S. real property interests by the corporation during the period to which an election made under section 897(i) applies, the Commissioner shall consent to the revocation of such election only if one of the following conditions is met.

(i) The full amount of gain realized by the corporation upon the distribution was subject to U.S. income tax.

(ii) There is a payment of an amount equal to the taxes that would have been imposed upon the corporation by reason of the application of section 897 if the election had not been in effect on the date of the distribution. Such payment must be made by the later of the date of the request for revocation or the date on which payment of such tax would otherwise have been due, and must include any interest that would have accrued had tax actually been due with respect to the distribution. If under the terms of any treaty to which the United States is a party such distribution would not have been subject to U.S. income tax notwithstanding the provisions of section 897, then this condition may be satisfied by providing a statement with the request for revocation setting forth the treaty and article which would have exempted the distribution from U.S. tax had the election under section 897(i) not been in effect on the date thereof.

(iii) At the time of the receipt of the distributed property, the distributee would be subject to taxation under chapter 1 of the Code on a subsequent disposition of the distributed property, and the basis of the distributed property in the hands of the distributee is no greater than the adjusted basis of such property before the distribution, increased by the amount of gain (if any) recognized by the distributing corporation. For purposes of this paragraph (f)(2)(i)(C), a distributee shall be considered to be subject to taxation upon a subsequent disposition of distributed property only if such distributee waives the benefits of any U.S. treaty that would otherwise render such disposition not taxable by the United States. Such waiver must be attached to the corporation's request for revocation.

(g) *Transitional rules.*—(1) *In general.*—An election under section 897(i) that was made at any time after June 18, 1980, must be amended to comply with the requirements of paragraphs (b), (c), and (d) of this section. Such amendment must be delivered in writing to the Director, Philadelphia Service Center by April 1, 1985. If the amendment is delivered by United States mail, the provisions of section 7502 and the regulations thereunder shall apply in determining the date of delivery. An election that is properly amended pursuant to the requirements of this section shall be effective as of the date of the original election.

(2) *Corporations previously entitled to make election.*—A foreign corporation that would have been entitled under the rules of this section to make a section 897(i) election at any time between June 19, 1980, and January 30, 1985, may retroactively make such an election pursuant to the requirements of this section. Such election must be delivered to the Director, Foreign Operations District, by March 1, 1985.

(3) *Interests in corporation disposed of prior to publication.*—Where interests in a corporation were disposed of before January 3, 1984, the requirement of paragraph (d)(2) of this section may be met, notwithstanding the requirement of paragraph (d)(3), by paying a tax that is based upon a reasonable estimate of the gain upon the prior dispositions. Such estimate must be based on all facts and circumstances known to, and ascertainable through the exercise of reasonable diligence by, the corporation seeking to make the election.

(h) *Effective date.*—The requirement in paragraph (c)(1)(i) of this section that the statement making the section 897(i) election contain the identifying number of the foreign corporation (in all cases) is applicable November 3, 2003. [Reg. § 1.897-3.]

☐ [*T.D.* 7999, 12-26-84. *Amended by T.D.* 8115, 12-16-86 *and T.D.* 9082, 8-4-2003.]

§ 1.897-5. Corporate distributions.—(a) through (d)(1)(iii)(E) [Reserved]. For further guidance, see § 1.897-5T(a) through (d)(1)(iii)(E).

(d)(1)(iii)(F) Identification by name and address of the distributee or transferee, including the distributee's or transferee's taxpayer identification number;

(d)(1)(iii)(G) through (d)(4) [Reserved]. For further guidance, see § 1.897-5T(d)(1)(iii)(G) through (d)(4).

(e) *Effective date.*—This section is applicable to transfers and distributions after November 3, 2003. [Reg. § 1.897-5.]

☐ [*T.D.* 9082, 8-4-2003.]

§ 1.897-5T. **Corporate distributions (Temporary).**—(a) *Purpose and scope.*—This section provides rules concerning the recognition of gain or loss and adjustments to basis required with respect to certain corporate distributions that are subject to section 897. Paragraph (b) of this section provides rules concerning such distributions by domestic corporations, including distributions under section 301, distributions in redemption of stock, and distributions in liquidation. Paragraph (c) sets forth rules concerning distributions by foreign corporations, including distributions under sections 301 and 355, distributions in redemption of stock, and distributions in liquidation. Finally, various rules generally applicable to distributions subject to this section, as well as to transfers subject to § 1.897-6T, are set forth in paragraph (d). The rules contained in this section are also subject to the tax avoidance rules of § 1.897-6T(c).

(b) *Distributions by domestic corporations.*—(1) *Limitation of basis upon dividend distribution of U.S. real property interest.*—Under section 897(f), if any domestic corporation (distributing corporation) distributes a U.S. real property interest to a shareholder that is a foreign person (distributee) in a distribution to which section 301 applies, then the basis of the distributed U.S. real property interest in the hands of the foreign distributee shall be determined in accordance with the provisions of section 301(d), and shall not exceed—

(i) The adjusted basis of the property before the distribution in the hands of the distributing corporation, increased by

(ii) The sum of—

(A) Any gain recognized by the distributing corporation on the distribution, and

(B) Any U.S. tax paid by or on behalf of the distributee with respect to the distribution.

(2) *Distributions by U.S. real property holding corporations which are taxable exchanges of stock under generally applicable rules.*—If a domestic corporation, stock in which is treated as a U.S. real property interest, distributes property with respect to such stock to a foreign shareholder, the distributee shall be treated as having disposed of a U.S. real property interest, and shall recognize gain or loss on the stock of such domestic corporation to the extent that, with respect to the distributees—

(i) Part or all of the distribution is treated pursuant to section 301(c)(3)(A) as a sale or exchange of stock;

(ii) Part or all of the distribution is treated pursuant to section 302(a) as made in part or full payment in exchange for stock; or

(iii) Part or all of the distribution is treated pursuant to section 331(a) as made in full payment in exchange for stock.

Stock in a domestic corporation shall not be considered a U.S. real property interest pursuant to the provisions of § 1.897-2(f)(2) if the corporation does not hold any U.S. real property interests and has disposed of all of its U.S. real property interests owned within the previous five years in transactions in which the full amount of gain was recognized under the rules of § 1.897-2(f)(2). If gain is recognized at the corporate level on either a distribution of a U.S. real property interest or a sale of a U.S. real property interest in a liquidation, such distribution or sale shall be considered a disposition for purposes of § 1.897-2(f)(2). With regard to the consequences of a distribution from a U.S. real property holding corporation under section 355(a), see § 1.897-6T(a)(1) and (4).

(3) *Section 332 liquidations of U.S. real property holding corporations.*—(i) *General rules.*—Exchanges that are subject to section 897(e) are normally covered by § 1.897-6T(a)(1), (2) and (3). This paragraph (b)(3) provides rules concerning the application of section 897(e) and the general principles of § 1.897-6T(a)(1), (2) and (3) to section 332 liquidations of U.S. real property holding corporations.

(ii) *Distribution to a foreign corporation under section 332 after June 18, 1980, and before the repeal of the General Utilities doctrine.*—Except for distributions under paragraph (b)(3)(iii) of this section (relating to section 332 and former section 334(b)(2)), the rules of this paragraph (b)(3)(ii) shall apply to section 332 distributions after June 18, 1980, and before January 1, 1990, pursuant to section 336(a) as in effect prior to the effective dates of the amendments made by section 631 of the Tax Reform Act of 1986. A foreign corporation that meets the stock ownership requirements of section 332(b) with respect to stock in a domestic corporation that is a U.S. real property interest shall not, after December 31, 1984, be subject to taxation by reason of section 367(a). The foreign corporation shall recognize gain pursuant to section 897(e)(1) on such stock upon the receipt of property in a section 332(a) liquidation from such domestic corporation, but only to the extent that the property received constitutes property other than a U.S. real property interest. The gain on the stock in the domestic corporation to be recognized by the foreign corporation pursuant to section 897(e)(1) shall be determined by multiplying the gain realized on the distribution by a fraction. The numerator of the fraction shall be the fair market value of the property other than U.S. real property interests received by the foreign corporation on the distribution, and the denominator shall be the fair market value of all property received by the foreign corporation on the distribution. The bases of the distributed U.S. real property interests in the hands of the foreign corporation shall be the same as the bases in the hands of the domestic corporation. The bases of the property other than U.S. real property interests in the hands of the foreign corporation shall be the same as the bases in the hands of the domestic corporation, plus any gain recognized by the foreign corporation on the distribution allocated among such assets in proportion to the potential gain inherent in each such asset at the time of distribution. However, the basis of each asset is limited to its fair market value. Property, other than a U.S. real property interest that is distributed by the domestic corporation, shall not be considered to be distributed by the domestic corporation pursuant to a section 332 liquidation (that is, the foreign corporation shall not be considered to be a corporation for purposes of section 332) if the requirements of section 367(a) are not satisfied. *See*, for example, sections 1245(b)(3) and 1250(d)(3) regarding the consequences to the distributing domestic corporation if the requirements of section 367(a) are not satisfied.

(iii) *Distribution to a foreign corporation under section 332 and former section 334(b)(2) after June 18, 1980.*—The rules of this paragraph (b)(2)(iii) shall apply to section 332 distributions after June 18, 1980 where the basis of the distributed property in the hands of the foreign corporation is determined under section 334(b)(2) as in effect prior to the Tax Equity and Fiscal Responsibility Act of 1982. A foreign corporation that meets the stock ownership requirements of section 332(b) with respect to stock in a domestic corporation that is a U.S. real property interest shall recognize gain on the receipt of property in a section 332(a) liquidation where section 334(b)(2) applies to the extent that the fair market value of the distributed assets that are not U.S. real property interests exceeds the basis of such assets determined under section 334(b)(2) (for example, if the liquidation does not occur immediately upon the purchase of stock in the domestic corporation). The gain recognized shall not exceed the excess of the fair market value of the stock of the domestic corporation in the hands of the foreign corporation at the time of the distribution over the shareholder's adjusted basis in such stock. The basis of the distributed U.S. real property interests in the hands of the foreign corporation shall be determined under section 334(b)(2), by reference to the adjusted basis of the stock with respect to which the distribution was made. The basis of such property other than U.S. real property interests shall be tentatively determined under section 334(b)(2), and then increased by any gain recognized by the foreign corporation on the distribution allocated among such assets in proportion to the potential gain inherent in each such asset at the time of distribution (computed using the tentative basis as determined under section 334(b)(2)). The basis of each asset is limited, however, to its fair market value.

(iv) *Distribution to a foreign corporation under section 332 after July 31, 1986 and after the repeal of the General Utilities doctrine.*—The rules of this subdivision (iv) shall apply to section 332 distributions after July 31, 1986, pursuant to section 337(a) as in effect after the effective dates of the amendments of section 631 of the Tax Reform Act of 1986.

(A) *Liquidation of domestic corporation.*—A foreign corporation that meets the stock ownership requirements of section 332(b) with respect to stock in a domestic corporation that is a U.S. real property interest (except a foreign corporation that has made an effective election under section 897(i) and the stock of which is treated as a U.S. real property interest) shall not recognize any gain under sections 367(a) or 897(e)(1) on the receipt of property in a section 332(a) liquidation. The domestic corporation shall not recognize gain under section 367(e)(2) on the distribution of U.S. real property interests (other than stock in a former U.S. real property holding corporation which is treated as a U.S. real property interest) to the foreign corporation. The domestic corporation shall recognize gain under section 367(e)(2) on the distribution of stock in a former U.S. real property holding corporation which is treated as a U.S. real property interest. With respect to the recognition of gain or loss by the domestic corporation under section 367(e)(2) on the distribution of property other than U.S. real property interests, see the regulations under section 367(e)(2). The basis of the distributed U.S. real property interests (other than stock in a former U.S. real property holding corporation) in the hands of the foreign corporation shall be the same as it was in the hands of the domestic corporation. The basis of any property (other than U.S. real property interests) and stock in a former U.S. real property holding corporation that is a U.S. real property interest in the hands of the foreign corporation shall be the same as it was in the hands of the domestic corporation increased by any gain recognized by the distributing corporation on the distribution that was subject to U.S. taxation.

(B) *Liquidation of certain foreign corporations making a section 897(i) election.*—A foreign corporation that meets the stock ownership requirements of section 332(b) with respect to stock in another foreign corporation, that has made an effective election under section 897(i) and the stock of which is treated as a U.S. real property interest, shall recognize gain pursuant to section 897(e)(1) on such stock upon the receipt from the distributing foreign corporation of property that is not a U.S. real property interest, and that is not used by the distributee foreign corporation in the conduct of a trade or business within the United States (if the distributee foreign corporation is not a resident of a country with which the United States maintains an income tax treaty) or in a permanent establishment within the United States (if the distributee foreign corporation is a resident of a country with which the United States maintains an income tax treaty). The gain on the stock in the foreign corporation (making an effective election under section 897(i)) to be recognized by the distributee foreign corporation pursuant to section 897(e)(1) shall be determined by multiplying the gain realized on the distribution by a fraction. The numerator of the fraction shall be the fair market value of the property received by the distributee foreign corporation upon which it must recognize gain, and the denominator of the fraction shall be the fair market value of all property received by the distributee foreign corporation on the distribution. The distributing foreign corporation shall not recognize gain under section 367(e)(2) on the distribution of U.S. real property interests to the distributee foreign corporation. With respect to the recognition of gain or loss under section 367(e)(2) on the distribution of property other than U.S. real property interests, see the regulations under section 367(e)(2). The basis of the distributed U.S. real property interests in the hands of the distributee foreign corporation shall be the same as it was in the hands of the distributing foreign corporation. The basis of the property upon which the distributee foreign corporation recognized gain in the hands of the distributee foreign corporation shall be the same as the basis in the hands of the distributing foreign corporation, plus any gain recognized by the distributee foreign corporation on the receipt of such property allocated among such property in proportion to the potential gain inherent in each such property at the time of the distribution. In regard to the basis of any other property received by the distributee foreign corporation in the liquidation, see the regulations under section 367(e)(2). However, the basis of each asset is limited to its fair market value.

(v) *Transfer of foreign corporation stock followed by a section 332 liquidation treated as a reorganization.*—If a nonresident alien or foreign corporation transfers the stock of a foreign corporation that owns a U.S. real property interest to a domestic corporation in exchange for stock of the domestic corporation (or its domestic or foreign parent corporation) in a reorganization under section 368(a)(1)(B) or in an exchange under section 351(a), and if the foreign corporation then distributes the U.S. real property interest to the domestic corporation in a liquidation described in section 332(a) within five years of the transfer of the stock of the foreign corporation to the domestic corporation, then the transfer of the foreign corporation stock and the liquidation shall be treated as a reorganization described in section 368(a)(1)(C) or (D). The rules of § 1.897-6T(a)(1) shall apply to the transfer of the U.S. real property interest to the domestic corporation in exchange for domestic corporation stock, and the rules of § 1.897-5T(c)(4) shall apply to the distribution of domestic corporation stock by the foreign corporation. However, the rules of this paragraph (b)(3)(v) shall not apply if the transfer of the foreign corporation stock and the liquidation under section 332(a) are separate and independent transactions justified by substantial and verifiable business purposes.

(4) *Section 897(i) companies.*—Except as otherwise provided herein for purposes of this section and § 1.897-6T, a foreign corporation that has made a valid election under section 897(i) shall be treated as a domestic corporation and not as a foreign corporation in determining the application of section 897. For rules concerning the making of a section 897(i) election, see §§ 1.897-3 and 1.897-8T. In regard to section 367(e)(2) and foreign corporations that have made an effective election under section 897(i), see paragraph (b)(3)(iv) of this section.

(5) *Examples.*—The following examples illustrate the rules of this paragraph (b). In each example there is no applicable income tax treaty to which the United States is a party.

Example (1). (i) A is a nonresident alien who owns 100 percent of the stock of DC, a U.S. real property holding corporation. DC's only asset is Parcel P, a U.S. real property interest, with a fair market value of $500,000 and an adjusted basis of $300,000. DC completely liquidates in 1987 and distributes Parcel P to A in exchange for the DC stock held by A.

(ii) Under section 336(a), DC must recognize gain to the extent of the excess of the fair market value ($500,000) over the adjusted basis ($300,000), or $200,000.

(iii) A does not recognize any gain under section 897(a) because the DC stock in the hands of A is no longer a U.S. real property interest under paragraph (b)(2) of this section and paragraph 2(f) of §1.897-2. A does recognize gain (if any) under section 331(a); however, the gain is not subject to taxation under section 871(a). A's adjusted basis in Parcel P is $500,000.

(iv) If DC did not recognize all of the gain on the disposition under a transitional rule to section 631 of the Tax Reform Act of 1986, then paragraph (b)(2) of this section and paragraph 2(f) of §1.897-2 would not apply to A. A would recognize gain (if any) under paragraph (b)(2) because the distribution is treated as in full payment in exchange for the DC stock under section 897(a).

Example (2). (i) FC, a Country F corporation, owns 100 percent of the stock of DC, a U.S. real property holding corporation. FC's basis in the stock of DC is $400,000, and the fair market value of the DC stock is $800,000. DC owns a U.S. real property interest with an adjusted basis of $350,000 and a fair market value of $600,000. DC also owns other assets that are not U.S. real property interests that have an adjusted basis of $125,000 and a fair market value of $200,000. DC completely liquidates in 1985 and distributes all of its property to FC in exchange for the DC stock held by FC.

(ii) Under paragraph (b)(3)(ii) of this section, FC recognizes $100,000 of gain under section 897(a) on the disposition of the DC stock. This is determined by multiplying FC's gain realized ($400,000) by a fraction. The numerator of the fraction is the fair market value of the property other than U.S. real property interests ($200,000), and the denominator of the fraction is the fair market value of all property received ($800,000). FC takes a carryover adjusted basis in the U.S. real property interest ($350,000). FC's adjusted basis in the assets that are not U.S. real property interests ($200,000) is the basis of those assets in the hands of DC ($125,000) plus the gain recognized by FC on the distribution ($100,000) not to exceed the fair market value ($200,000).

Example (3). (i) FC, a Country F corporation, owns 100 percent of the stock of DC, a U.S. real property holding corporation. FC's basis in the stock of DC is $300,000, and the fair market value of the DC stock is $500,000. DC owns Parcel P, a U.S. real property interest, with an adjusted basis of $250,000 and a fair market value of $400,000. DC also owns all of the stock of DX, a former U.S. real property holding corporation whose stock is a U.S. real property interest, with an adjusted basis of $50,000 and a fair market value of $100,000. DC completely liquidates in 1987 and distributes all of its property to FC in exchange for the DC stock held by FC.

(ii) Under paragraph (b)(3)(iv)(A) of this section, DC recognizes $50,000 of gain on the distribution to FC of the DX stock. DC does not recognize any gain for purposes of section 367(e)(2) on the distribution to FC of Parcel P.

(iii) Under paragraph (b)(3)(iv)(A) of this section, FC's disposition of its DC stock is not treated as a disposition of a U.S. real property interest. Under section 334(b)(1), FC takes a carryover adjusted basis of $250,000 in Parcel P. FC takes an increased basis of $100,000 in the DX stock which is equal to DC's basis ($50,000) increased by the gain recognized by DC ($50,000).

(iv) The result would be the same if FC had made an effective election under section 897(i).

(6) *Section 333 elections.*—(i) *General rule.*—A foreign shareholder that elects section 333 as in effect prior to its repeal by the Tax Reform Act of 1986 upon the distribution of property in a liquidation by a domestic corporation whose stock is treated as a U.S. real property interest shall recognize gain on such stock to the extent that—

(A) The property received by the foreign shareholder constitutes property other than U.S. real property interests subject to U.S. taxation upon its disposition as specified by paragraph (a)(1) of this section, or

(B) The basis of a U.S. real property interest subject to U.S. taxation upon its disposition in the hands of the recipient foreign shareholder exceeds the basis of the U.S. real property interest in the hands of the liquidating domestic corporation.

In determining the amount of gain recognized by the foreign shareholder, the foreign shareholder shall be considered to have exchanged the domestic corporation stock for all the property distributed on a proportionate fair market value basis. The gain recognized on a respective portion of domestic corporation stock shall not exceed the gain realized on that portion. Property other than U.S. real property interests subject to U.S. taxation upon disposition shall have a fair market value basis in the hands of the foreign shareholder. The basis of U.S. real property interests subject to U.S. taxation upon disposition shall be the basis of the proportionate part of the domestic corporation stock cancelled or redeemed in the liquidation, increased in the amount of gain recognized (other than gain recognized under this section) by the shareholder in respect to that proportionate part of the domestic corporation stock.

(ii) *Example.*—The rules of paragraph (b)(6)(i) of this section may be illustrated by the following example.

Example. (i) A is a citizen and resident of Country F with which the U.S. does not have an income tax treaty. A owns all of the stock of DC, a U.S. real property holding corporation. The DC stock has a fair market value of $1,000,000. A acquired the DC stock in two purchases. The basis of one lot of the DC stock is $150,000, and the basis of the other lot is $650,000.

(ii) DC owns Parcel P, a U.S. real property interest, with a fair market value of $750,000 and an adjusted basis of $400,000. DC's only other property is equipment with a fair market value of $250,000 and an adjusted basis of $100,000. DC does not have any earnings and profits.

(iii) DC completely liquidates in 1985 in accordance with section 333 by distributing Parcel P and the equipment to A. A elects section 333 treatment.

(iv) A is considered as having exchanged 75 percent (fair market value of Parcel P/fair market value of all property distributed) of the DC stock for Parcel P. A realized gain of $150,000 on that portion of the DC stock ($750,000 - $600,000). All of the gain of $150,000 is recognized under section 897(a) because A's basis in Parcel P under section 334(c) ($600,000) would exceed DC's basis in Parcel P ($400,000) by at least the amount of realized gain. A takes a basis of $750,000 in Parcel P.

(v) A is considered as having exchanged 25 percent (fair market value of equipment/fair market value of all property distributed) of the DC stock for the equipment. A realized gain of $50,000 on that portion of the DC stock ($250,000 - $200,000). All of the gain of $50,000 is recognized under section 897(a). A takes a basis of $250,000 in the equipment.

(c) *Distributions of U.S. real property interests by foreign corporations.*—(1) *Recognition of gain required.*—If a foreign corporation makes a distribution (including a distribution in liquidation or redemption) of a U.S. real property interest to a shareholder (whether foreign or domestic), then, except as provided in paragraph (c)(2), (3) or (4) of this section, the distributing corporation shall recognize gain (but not loss) on the distribution under section 897(d)(1). The gain recognized shall be equal to the excess of the fair market value of the U.S. real property interest (as of the time of the distribution) over its adjusted basis. Except as otherwise provided, the distributee's basis in the distributed U.S. real property interest shall be determined under the otherwise applicable sections of the Code. The distributee (whether domestic or foreign) of a foreign corporation in a liquidation under section 332 shall take the foreign corporation's basis in the distributed U.S. real property interest increased by any gain recognized (and subject to U.S. income taxation) by the foreign corporation on the distribution of such U.S. real property interest.

(2) *Recognition of gain not required.*—(i) *Statutory exception rule.*—Under section 897(d)(2)(A), gain shall not be recognized by a distributing foreign corporation if—

(A) At the time of the receipt of the distributed U.S. real property interest, the distributee would be subject to U.S. income taxation on a subsequent disposition of the U.S. real property interest, determined in accordance with the rules of paragraph (d)(1) of this section;

(B) The basis of the distributed U.S. real property interest in the hands of the distributee is no greater than the adjusted basis of such property before the distribution, increased by the amount of gain (if any) recognized by the distributing corporation upon the distribution and added to the adjusted basis under the otherwise applicable provisions; and

(C) The distributing corporation complies with the filing requirements of paragraph (d)(1)(iii) of this section.

(ii) *Section 332 liquidations.*—(A) *In general.*—A distributing foreign corporation that meets the requirements of paragraph (c)(2)(i) in a section 332(a) liquidation shall not recognize gain on the distribution of U.S. real property interests to a foreign corporation meeting the stock ownership requirements of section 332(b) if the distributing corporation complies with the procedural requirements of paragraph (d)(1)(iii). Whether a foreign corporation recognizes gain on the distribution of U.S. real property interests to a U.S. corporation meeting the stock ownership requirements of section 332(b) depends upon whether the U.S. corporation satisfies the subject to tax requirement provided in paragraph (d)(1)(i) (in addition to the procedural requirements of paragraph (d)(1)(iii)). With respect to section 332 distributions by a foreign corporation occurring after July 31, 1986, section 367(e)(2) shall not affect the application of section 337(a) (as in effect after the Tax Reform Act of 1986) and paragraph (c)(2)(i) of this section to the distribution of a U.S. real property interest.

(B) *Recognition of gain required in certain section 332 liquidations.*—Notwithstanding the other rules of this paragraph (c), a foreign corporation shall, pursuant to the authority conferred by section 897(e)(2), recognize gain on its distribution after May 5, 1988 of a U.S. real property interest to a domestic corporation meeting the stock ownership requirements of section 332(b) if—

(1) the foreign corporation has not made an election under section 897(i), and any gain on the stock in the foreign corporation would be subject to U.S. taxation if an election were made on the date of the liquidation; and

(2) The distribution of the U.S. real property interest by the foreign corporation to the domestic corporation pursuant to section 332(a) occurs less than five years after the date of the last gain from the disposition of stock of the foreign corporation that would be subject to payment of tax under section 1.897-3(d)(2)(i) if an election under section 897(i) were made by the foreign corporation on the date of its liquidation.

With regard to the treatment of certain foreign corporations as domestic corporations under section 897(i), however, see §§ 1.897-3 and 1.897-8T.

(iii) *Examples.*—The rules of this paragraph (c)(2) may be illustrated by the following examples.

Example (1). (i) DC, a domestic corporation, owns 100 percent of the stock of FC, a Country F corporation. FC's only asset is Parcel P, a U.S. real property interest, with a fair market value of $500x and an adjusted basis of $100x. In September 1987, FC liquidates under section 332(a) and transfers Parcel P to DC. The transitional rules contained in section 633 of the Tax Reform Act of 1986 concerning the repeal of the *General Utilities* doctrine would not be applicable to a subsequent distribution or disposition of assets by DC.

(ii) Assume that FC complies with the filing requirements of paragraph (d)(1)(iii). DC will be subject to U.S. income taxation on a subsequent disposition of Parcel P under the rules of paragraph (d)(1). The basis of Parcel P in the hands of DC will be $100x under section 334(b)(1), and thus no greater than the basis of Parcel P in the hands of FC. FC does not recognize any gain under the rules of paragraph (c)(1) of this section on the distribution because the exception of paragraph (d)(2)(i) applies.

Example (2). If in *Example (1)* the distribution by FC to DC occurred in September 1985, and DC sold or exchanged Parcel P under sections 336(a) or 337(a) as in effect prior to the Tax Reform Act of 1986, then FC must recognize gain of $400x on the distribution of Parcel P. The gain must be recognized because Parcel P in the hands of DC is not considered subject to U.S. income taxation on a subsequent disposition under the rules of paragraph (d)(1) of this section.

(3) *Limitation of gain recognized under paragraph (c)(1) of this section for certain section 355 distributions.*—(i) *In general.*—Under paragraph (c)(1) of this section, a foreign corporation that distributes stock in a domestic corporation that constitutes a U.S. real property interest in a distribution to which section 355 applies shall recognize gain on the distribution to the extent that the fair market value of the distributed stock exceeds its adjusted basis in the hands of the distributing foreign corporation. The gain recognized shall be limited under this paragraph (c)(3), however, to the amount by which the aggregate basis of the distributed stock in the hands of the distributees exceeds the aggregate adjusted basis of the distributed stock in the hands of the distributing corporation. The distributees' basis in the distributed U.S. real property interest shall be determined under the otherwise applicable provisions of section 358. (Thus, the distributees' basis in the distributed U.S. real property interest shall be determined without any increase for any gain recognized by the foreign corporation).

(ii) *Example.*—The rules of paragraph (c)(3)(i) of this section may be illustrated by the following example.

Example. (i) C is a citizen and resident of Country F. C owns all of the stock of FC, a Country F corporation. The fair market value of the FC stock is 1000x, and C has a basis of 600x in the FC stock. Country F does not have an income tax treaty with the United States.

(ii) In a transaction qualifying as a distribution of stock of a controlled corporation under section 355(a), FC distributes to C all of the stock of DC, a U.S. real property holding corporation. C does not surrender any of the FC stock. The DC stock has a fair market value of 600x, and FC has an adjusted basis of 200x in the DC stock. After the distribution, the FC stock has a fair market value of 400x.

(iii) Under paragraph (c)(3)(i) of this section, FC must recognize gain on the distribution of the DC stock to C equal to the difference between the fair market value of the DC stock (600x) and FC's adjusted basis in the DC stock (200x). This results in a potential gain of 400x. Under section 358, C takes a 360x adjusted basis in the DC stock. Provided that FC complies with the filing requirements of paragraph (d)(1)(iii) of this section, the gain recognized by FC is limited under paragraph (c)(3)(i) to 160x because (A) this is the amount by which the basis of the DC stock in the hands of C (360x) exceeds the adjusted basis of the DC stock in the hands of FC (200x), and (B) at the time of receipt of the DC stock, C would be subject to U.S. taxation on a subsequent disposition of the stock.

(iv) C's adjusted basis in the DC stock is not increased by the 160x recognized by FC.

(4) *Distribution by a foreign corporation in certain reorganizations.*—(i) *In general.*—Under paragraph (c)(1) of this section, a foreign corporation that transfers property to another corporation in an exchange under section 361(a) for stock of a domestic corporation which is a United States real property holding corporation immediately after the transfer in a reorganization under section 368(a)(1)(C), (D) or (F) shall recognize gain under section 897(d)(1) on the distribution (whether actual or deemed) of the stock of the domestic corporation received by the foreign corporation to its shareholders (whether domestic or foreign). See § 1.897-6T(a) of the regulations for the consequences to the foreign corporation of the exchange of its property for the domestic corporation stock.

(ii) *Statutory exception.*—Pursuant to the exception provided in section 897(d)(2)(A), no gain shall be recognized by the foreign corporation on its distribution of the domestic corporation stock if—

(A) At the time of the distribution, the distributee (*i.e.*, the exchanging shareholder in the section 354 exchange) would be subject to U.S. taxation on a subsequent disposition of the stock of the domestic corporation, determined in accordance with the rules of paragraph (d)(1) of this section;

(B) The distributee's adjusted basis in the stock of the foreign corporation immediately before the distribution was no greater than the foreign corporation's basis in the stock of the domestic corporation determined under section 358; and

(C) The distributing corporation complies with the filing requirements of paragraph (d)(1)(iii) of this section.

(iii) *Regulatory limitation on gain recognized.*—If the requirements of subdivisions (A) and (C) of paragraph (c)(4)(ii) are met, the amount of any gain recognized by the foreign corporation shall not exceed the excess of the distributee's adjusted basis in the stock of the foreign corporation immediately before the distribution over the foreign corporation's basis in the stock of the domestic corporation immediately before the distribution as determined under section 358.

(iv) *Examples.*—The rules of paragraph (c)(4) of this section may be illustrated by the following examples.

Example (1). (i) A, a nonresident alien, organized FC, a Country W corporation, in September 1980 to invest in U.S. real estate. In 1986, FC's only asset is Parcel P, a U.S. real property interest with a fair market value of $600,000 and an adjusted basis to FC of $200,000. Parcel P is subject to a mortgage with an outstanding balance of $100,000. The fair market value of the FC stock is $500,000, and A's adjusted basis in the stock is $100,000. FC does not have liabilities in excess of the adjusted basis in Parcel P. The United States does not have a treaty with Country W that entitles FC to nondiscriminatory treatment as described in section 1.897-3(b)(2) of the regulations.

(ii) Pursuant to a plan of reorganization under section 368(a)(1)(D), FC transfers Parcel P to DC, a newly formed domestic corporation, in exchange for DC stock. FC distributes the DC stock to A in exchange for A's FC stock.

(iii) FC's exchange of Parcel P for the DC stock is a disposition of a U.S. real property interest. Under § 1.897-6T(a)(1), there is an exchange of a U.S. real property interest (Parcel P) for another U.S. real property interest (DC stock) so that no gain is recognized on the exchange under section 897(e). DC takes FC's basis of $200,000 in Parcel P under section 362(b). Under section 358(a)(1), FC takes a $100,000 basis in the DC stock because FC's substituted basis of $200,000 in the DC stock is reduced by the $100,000 of liabilities to which Parcel P is subject.

(iv) Under section 897(d)(1) and paragraph (c)(4)(i) of this section, FC generally must recognize gain on the distribution of the DC stock received in exchange for FC's assets equal to the difference between the fair market value of the DC stock ($500,000) and FC's adjusted basis in the DC stock prior to the distribution ($100,000). This results in a potential gain of $400,000. Under section 358(a)(1), A takes a basis in the DC stock equal to the its basis in the FC stock of $100,000. Provided that FC complies with the filing requirements of paragraph (d)(1)(iii) of this section, no gain is recognized by FC on the distribution of the DC stock under the statutory exception to the general rule of section 897(d)(1) provided in section 897(d)(2)(A) and paragraph (c)(4)(ii) of this section because (*1*) A's basis in the DC stock ($100,000) does not exceed FC's adjusted basis in the DC stock ($100,000) immediately prior to the distribution and (*2*) A, at the time of receipt of the DC stock, would be subject to U.S. taxation on a subsequent disposition of the stock.

(v) The FC stock in the hands of A is not a U.S. real property interest because FC is a foreign corporation that has not elected to be treated as a domestic corporation under section 897(i). Accordingly, the exchange of the FC stock by A for DC stock is not a disposition of a

U.S. real property interest under section 897(a).

Example (2). The facts are the same as in *Example* (1), except that A purchased the FC stock in September 1983 for $100,000 from S, a nonresident alien, and that S had a basis of $40,000 in the FC stock at the time of the sale to A. The results are the same as in Example 1.

Example (3). (i) The facts are the same as in *Example* 1, except that A's adjusted basis in the FC stock prior to the reorganization is $300,000. Following the distribution, A takes its basis of $300,000 in the FC stock as its basis in the DC stock pursuant to section 358(a)(1).

(ii) FC does not qualify under the statutory exception of paragraph (c)(4)(ii) to the general recognition rule of section 897(d)(1) and paragraph (c)(4)(i) of this section because A's basis in the DC stock ($300,000) exceeds FC's adjusted basis in the DC stock ($100,000) immediately prior to the distribution. However, provided that FC complies with the filing requirements of paragraph (d)(1)(iii) of this section, the gain recognized by FC is limited to $200,000 under the regulatory limitation of gain provided by paragraph (c)(4)(iii). This is the excess of A's basis in the FC stock immediately before the distribution ($300,000) over A's adjusted basis in the DC stock immediately before the distribution ($100,000).

(iii) A takes a basis of $300,000 in the DC stock under section 358(a)(1). A's basis in the DC stock is not increased by the gain recognized by FC. DC takes a basis of $200,000 in Parcel P under section 362(b).

Example (4). (i) The facts are the same as in *Example* (3), except that the United States has an income tax treaty with Country W entitling FC to nondiscriminatory treatment under section 1.897-3(b)(2) of the regulations. A valid election under section 897(i) is made to treat FC as a U.S. corporation.

(ii) FC is treated as a domestic corporation for purposes of section 897 and is not required to recognize gain under section 897(d)(1) and paragraph (c)(4)(i) of this section on the distribution of the DC stock as described in *Example* 3. (If a valid section 897(i) election were not made, the result would be same as in *Example* (3).)

(iii) The FC stock in the hands of A is a U.S. real property interest because an election was made under section 897(i) to treat FC as a U.S. corporation. The exchange of the FC stock for DC stock by A is a disposition of a U.S. real property interest. Under section 897(e)(1) and paragraph (a) of §1.897-6T, A does not recognize gain on the exchange because there is an exchange of a U.S. real property interest (the FC stock) for another U.S. real property interest (the DC stock). Under section 358(a)(1), A takes as its basis in the DC stock A's basis in the FC stock ($300,000).

(5) *Sales of U.S. real property interests by foreign corporations under section 337.*—Section 337 as in effect prior to the Tax Reform Act of 1986 shall not apply to any sale or exchange (including a deemed section 337 sale pursuant to an election under section 338(a) to treat a stock purchase as an asset acquisition) of a U.S. real property interest by a foreign corporation.

(6) *Section 897(l) credit.*—If a foreign corporation adopts a plan of complete liquidation and if, solely by reason of section 897(d) and this section, section 337(a) (as in effect before the Tax Reform Act of 1986) does not apply to sales or exchanges of, or section 336 (as in effect before the Tax Reform Act of 1986) does not apply to distributions of, United States real property interests by the liquidating corporation, then—

(i) The amount realized by the shareholder on the distribution shall be increased by its proportionate share of the amount by which the tax imposed by chapter 1 of the Code, as modified by the provisions of any applicable U.S. income tax treaty, on the liquidating corporation would have been reduced if section 897(d) and this section had not been applicable, and

(ii) For purposes of the Code, the shareholder shall be deemed to have paid, on the last day prescribed by law for the payment of the tax imposed by subtitle A of the Code on the shareholder for the taxable year, an amount of tax equal to the amount of increase in the amount realized described in subdivision (i) of this paragraph (c).

The special rule provided by this paragraph (c)(5) applies only to shareholders who are United States citizens or residents, and who have held stock in the liquidating corporation continuously since June 18, 1980. This special rule also only applies for the first taxable year of any such shareholder in which the shareholder receives a distribution in complete liquidation from the foreign corporation.

(7) *Other applicable rules.*—For rules concerning exemption of gain pursuant to a U.S. income tax treaty, withholding of tax from distributions, and other applicable rules, see paragraph (d) of this section. For the treatment of liquidations described in section 334(b)(2)(A) of certain foreign corporations acquired before November 6, 1980, see §1.897-4.

(d) *Rules of general application.*—(1) *Interests subject to taxation upon later disposition.*—(i) *In general.*—Pursuant to the otherwise applicable rules of this section and §1.897-6T, nonrecognition of gain or loss may apply with respect to certain distributions or exchanges of U.S. real property interests if any gain from a subsequent disposition of the interests that are distributed or received by the transferor in the exchange would be included in the gross income of the distributee or transferor and be subject to U.S. taxation. Gain is considered subject to U.S. taxation if the gain is included on the income tax return of a U.S. tax paying entity even if there is no U.S. tax liability (for example, because of net operating losses or an investment tax credit). Gain is not considered subject to U.S. taxation if the gain is derived by a tax exempt entity. A real estate investment trust is considered to be a pass-through entity for purposes of the rule of taxability of this paragraph (d)(1)(i). Thus, for example, a tax exempt entity holding an interest in a real estate investment trust is not subject to tax. A domestic corporation (including a foreign corporation that makes an effective section 897(i) election after receipt of the U.S. real property interest) shall not be considered subject to U.S. taxation on a subsequent disposition of a U.S. real property interest if it received the U.S. real property interest prior to the effective date of the repeal of sections 336(a) or 337(a) as in effect prior to the Tax Reform Act of 1986, unless the U.S. real property interest has not been sold or exchanged by the domestic corporation prior to such effective date in a transaction to which either section 336(a) or section 337(a) (as in effect prior to such effective date) applied. In addition, an interest shall be considered to be subject to U.S. taxation upon its subsequent disposition only if the requirements set forth in subdivision (iii) of this paragraph (d)(1) are met.

(ii) *Effects of income tax treaties.*—(A) *Effect of treaty exemption from tax.*—Except as otherwise provided in subdivision (C) of this paragraph (d)(1)(ii), a U.S. real property interest shall not be considered to be subject to U.S. taxation upon a subsequent disposition if, at the time of its distribution or exchange, the recipient is entitled pursuant to the provisions of a U.S. income tax treaty to an exemption from U.S. taxation upon a disposition of the interest.

(B) *Effect of treaty reduction of tax.*—If, at the time of a distribution or exchange, a distributee of a U.S. real property interest in a distribution or a transferor who receives a U.S. real property interest in an exchange would be entitled pursuant to the provisions of a U.S. income tax treaty to reduced U.S. taxation upon the disposition of the interest, then a portion of the interest received shall be treated as an interest subject to U.S. taxation upon its disposition, and, therefore, that portion shall be entitled to nonrecognition treatment under the rules of this section or § 1.897-6T. The portion of the interest that is treated as subject to U.S. taxation is determined by multiplying the fair market value of the interest by a fraction. The numerator of the fraction is the amount of tax that would be due pursuant to the provisions of the applicable U.S. income tax treaty upon the recipient's disposition of the interest, determined as of the date of the distribution or transfer. The denominator of the fraction is the amount of tax that would be due upon such disposition but for the provisions of the treaty. However, nonrecognition treatment may be preserved in accordance with the provisions of subdivision (C) of this paragraph (d)(1)(ii). With regard to the provisions of this paragraph, see Article XIII (9) of the United States-Canada Income Tax Convention.

(C) *Waiver of treaty benefits to preserve nonrecognition.*—Notwithstanding the provisions of subdivisions (A) and (B) of this paragraph (d)(1)(ii), an interest shall be considered to be subject to U.S. taxation upon its subsequent disposition if, in accordance with paragraph (d)(1)(iii)(F) of this section, the recipient waives the benefits of a U.S. income tax treaty that would otherwise entitle the recipient to an exemption from (or reduction of) U.S. tax upon a disposition of the interest.

(iii) *Procedural requirements.*—If a U.S. real property interest is distributed or transferred after December 31, 1987, the transferor or distributor (that is a nonresident alien individual or a foreign corporation) shall file an income tax return for the taxable year of the distribution or transfer. Also, if a U.S. real property interest is distributed or transferred in a transaction before January 1, 1988, with respect to which nonrecognition treatment would not have been available under the express provisions of section 897(d) or (e) of the Code but is available under the provisions of this section or § 1.897-6T, then the person that would otherwise be subject to tax by reason of the operation of section 897 must file an income tax return for the taxable year of the distribution or transfer. This requirement is satisfied by filing a tax return or an amended tax return for the year of the distribution or transfer by May 5, 1989, or by the date that the filing of the return is otherwise required. The person filing the return must attach thereto a document setting forth the following:

(A) A statement that the distribution or transfer is one to which section 897 applies;

(B) A description of the U.S. real property interest distributed or transferred, including its location, its adjusted basis in the hands of the distributor or transferor immediately before the distribution or transfer, and the date of the distribution or transfer;

(C) A description of the U.S. real property interest received in an exchange;

(D) A declaration signed by an officer of the corporation that the distributing foreign corporation has substantiated the adjusted basis of the shareholder in its stock if the distributing corporation has nonrecognition or recognition limitation under paragraph (c)(3) or (4) of this section;

(E) The amount of any gain recognized and tax withheld by any person with respect to the distribution or transfer;

(F) [Reserved]. For further guidance, see § 1.897-5(d)(1)(iii)(F).

(G) The treaty and article (if any) under which the distributee or transferor would be exempt from U.S. taxation on a sale of the distributed U.S. real property interest or the U.S. real property interest received in the transfer; and

(H) A declaration, signed by the distributee or transferor or its authorized legal representative, that the distributee or transferor shall treat any subsequent sale, exchange, or other disposition of the U.S. real property interest as a disposition that is subject to U.S. taxation, notwithstanding the provisions of any U.S. income tax treaty or intervening change in circumstance.

A person who has provided or filed a notice described in § 1.1445-2(d)(2)(iii) or § 1.1445-5(b)(2)(ii) in connection with a transaction may satisfy the requirement of this paragraph (d)(1)(iii) by attaching to his return a copy of that notice together with any information or declaration required by this subdivision not contained in that notice.

(2) *Treaty exception to imposition of tax.*—If gain that would be currently recognized pursuant to the provisions of this section or § 1.897-6T is subject to an exemption from (or reduction of) U.S. tax pursuant to a U.S. income tax treaty, then gain shall be recognized only as provided by that treaty, for dispositions occurring before January 1, 1985. For dispositions occurring after December 31, 1984, all gain shall be recognized as provided in section 897 and the regulations thereunder, except as provided by Articles XIII (9) and XXX (5) of the United States-Canada Income Tax Convention or other income tax treaty entered into force after June 6, 1988. With regard to Article XXX (5) of the Income Tax Treaty with Canada, see, Rev. Rul. 85-76, 1985-1 C.B. 409. With regard to basis adjustments for certain related person transactions, see, § 1.897-6T (c)(3).

(3) *Withholding.*—Under sections 1441 and 1442, as modified by the provisions of any applicable U.S. income tax treaty, a corporation must withhold tax from a dividend distribution to which section 301 applies to a shareholder that is a foreign person, if the dividend is considered to be from sources inside the United States. For a description of dividends that are considered to be from sources inside the United States, see section 861(a)(2). Under section 1445, withholding is required with respect to certain dispositions and distributions of U.S. real property interests.

(4) *Effect on earnings and profits.*—With respect to adjustments to earnings and profits for gain recognized to a distributing corporation on a distribution, see section 312 and the regulations thereunder.

(e) *Effective date.*—Except as otherwise specifically provided in the text of these regulations, this section shall be effective for transfers, exchanges, distributions and other dispositions occurring after June 18, 1980. [Temporary Reg. § 1.897-5T.]

☐ [*T.D.* 8198, 5-4-88. *Amended by T.D.* 9082, 8-4-2003.]

§ 1.897-6T. Nonrecognition exchanges applicable to corporations, their shareholders, and other taxpayers, and certain transfers of property in corporate reorganizations (Temporary).—
(a) *Nonrecognition exchanges.*—(1) *In general.*—Except as otherwise provided in this section and in § 1.897-5T, for purposes of section 897(e) any nonrecognition provision shall apply to a transfer by a foreign person of a U.S. real property interest on which gain is realized only to the extent that the transferred U.S. real property interest is exchanged for a U.S. real property interest which, immediately following the exchange, would be subject to U.S. taxation upon its disposition, and the transferor complies with the filing requirements of paragraph (d)(1)(iii) of § 1.897-5T. No loss shall be recognized pursuant to section 897(e) or the rules of this section unless such loss is otherwise permitted to be recognized. In the case of an exchange of a U.S. real property interest for stock in a domestic corporation (that is otherwise treated as a U.S. real property interest), such stock shall not be considered a U.S. real property interest unless the domestic corporation is a U.S. real property holding corporation immediately after the exchange. Whether an interest would be subject to U.S. taxation in the hands of the transferor upon its disposition shall be determined in accordance with the rules of § 1.897-5T (d)(1).

(2) *Definition of "nonrecognition" provision.*—A "nonrecognition provision" is any provision of the Code which provides that gain or

loss shall not be recognized if the requirements of that provision are met. Nonrecognition provisions relevant to this section include, but are not limited to, sections 332, 351, 354, 355, 361, 721, 731, 1031, 1033 and 1036. For purposes of section 897(e), sections 121 and 453 are not nonrecognition provisions.

(3) *Consequence of nonapplication of nonrecognition provisions.*—If a nonrecognition provision does not apply to a transaction, then the U.S. real property interest transferred shall be considered exchanged pursuant to a transaction that is subject to U.S. taxation by reason of the operation of section 897. See, however, § 1.897-5T (d)(2) with respect to the treaty exceptions to the imposition of tax. If a U.S. real property interest is exchanged for an interest the disposition of which is only partially subject to taxation under chapter 1 of the Code (as modified by the provisions of any applicable U.S. income tax treaty), then any nonrecognition provision shall apply only to the extent that the interest received in the exchange would be subject to taxation under chapter 1 of the Code, as modified. For example, the exchange of a U.S. real property interest for an interest in a partnership will receive nonrecognition treatment pursuant to section 721 only to the extent that a disposition of the partnership interest will be subject to U.S. taxation by reason of the operation of section 897(g).

(4) *Section 355 distributions treated as exchanges.*—If a domestic corporation, stock in which is treated as a U.S. real property interest, distributes stock in a foreign corporation or stock in a domestic corporation that is not a U.S. real property holding corporation to a foreign person under section 355(a), then the foreign person shall be considered as having exchanged a proportionate part of the stock in the domestic corporation that is treated as a U.S. real property interest for stock that is not treated as a U.S. real property interest.

(5) [Reserved]

(6) *Determination of basis.*—If a nonrecognition provision applies to the transfer of a U.S. real property interest pursuant to the provisions of this section, then the basis of the property received in the exchange shall be determined in accordance with the rules generally applicable with respect to such nonrecognition provision. Similarly, the basis of the exchanged property in the hands of the transferee shall be determined in accordance with the rules that generally apply to such transfer.

(7) *Examples.*—The rules of paragraph (a)(1) through (6) of this section may be illustrated by the following examples. In each instance, the filing requirements of paragraph (d)(1)(iii) of § 1.897-5T have been satisfied.

Example (1). (i) A is a citizen and resident of Country F with which the U.S. does not have an income tax treaty. A owns Parcel P, a U.S. real property interest, with a fair market value of $500,000 and an adjusted basis of $300,000. A transfers Parcel P to DC, a newly formed U.S. real property holding corporation wholly owned by A, in exchange for DC stock.

(ii) Under paragraph (a)(1) of this section, A has exchanged a U.S. real property interest (Parcel P) for another U.S. real property interest (DC stock) which is subject to U.S. taxation upon its disposition. The nonrecognition provisions of section 351(a) apply to A's transfer of Parcel P.

(iii) Under paragraph (a)(6) of this section, the basis of the DC stock received by A is determined in accordance with the rules generally applicable to the transfer. A takes a $300,000 adjusted basis in the DC stock under the rules of section 358(a)(1).

Example (2). [Reserved]

Example (3). [Reserved]

Example (4). (i) B is a citizen and resident of Country F with which the U.S. does not have an income tax treaty. B owns stock in DC1, a U.S. real property holding corporation. In a reorganization qualifying for nonrecognition under section 368(a)(1)(B), B exchanges the DC1 stock under section 354(a) for stock in DC2, a U.S. real property holding corporation.

(ii) A does not recognize any gain under paragraph (a)(1) of this section on the exchange of the DC1 stock for DC2 stock because there is an exchange of a U.S. real property interest (the DC1 stock) for another U.S. real property interest (the DC2 stock) which is subject to U.S. taxation upon its disposition.

Example (5). (i) C is a citizen and resident of Country F with which the U.S. does not have an income tax treaty. C owns all of the stock of DC, a U.S. real property holding corporation. The fair market value of the DC stock is 500x, and C has a basis of 100x in the DC stock.

(ii) In a transaction qualifying as a distribution of stock of a controlled corporation under section 355(a), DC distributes to C all of the stock of FC, a foreign corporation that has not made a section 897(i) election. C does not surrender any of the DC stock. The FC stock has a fair market value of 200x. After the distribution, the DC stock has a fair market value of 300x.

(iii) Under the rules of paragraph (a)(4) of this section, C is considered to have exchanged DC stock with a fair market value of 200x and an adjusted basis of 40x for FC stock with a fair market value of 200x. Because the FC stock is not a U.S. real property interest, C must recognize gain of 160x under section 897(a) on the distribution. C takes a basis of 200x in the FC stock. C's basis in the DC stock is reduced to 60x pursuant to section 358(c).

Example (6). (i) A is an individual citizen and resident of Country F. F has an income tax treaty with the United States that exempts gain from the sale of stock, but not real property, by a resident of F from U.S. taxation. In 1981, A transferred Parcel P, an appreciated U.S. real property interest, to DC, a U.S. real property holding corporation, in exchange for DC stock. A owned all of the stock of DC.

(ii) Under the rules of paragraph (a)(1) of this section, A must recognize gain on the transfer of Parcel P. Even though there is an exchange of a U.S. real property interest for another U.S. real property interest, there is gain recognition because the U.S. real property interest received (the DC stock) would not have been subject to U.S. taxation upon a disposition immediately following the exchange. A may not convert a U.S. real property interest that was subject to taxation under section 897 into a U.S. real property interest that could be sold without taxation under section 897 due to a treaty exemption.

Example (7). (i) A, a nonresident alien, organized FC1, a Country W corporation in September 1980 to invest in U.S. real property. FC1's only asset is Parcel P, a U.S. real property interest with a fair market value of $500,000 and an adjusted basis of $200,000. The FC1 stock has a fair market value of $500,000 and A's basis in the FC1 stock is $100,000. The United States does not have a treaty with Country W.

(ii) A, organized FC2, a Country W corporation in July 1987. FC2 organized DC in August 1987. Pursuant to a plan of reorganization under section 368(a)(1)(C), FC1 transfers Parcel P to DC in exchange for FC2 voting stock. As a result of the transfer, DC is a U.S. real property holding corporation wholly owned by FC2. The FC2 stock used by DC in the acquisition had been transferred by FC2 to DC as part of the plan of reorganization. FC1 distributes the FC2 stock to A in exchange for A's FC1 stock.

(iii) FC1's exchange of Parcel P for the FC2 stock under section 361(a) is a disposition of a U.S. real property interest. FC1 must recognize gain of $300,000 under section 897(e) and paragraph (a)(1) of this section on the exchange because the FC2 stock received in exchange for Parcel P is not a U.S. real property interest.

(iv) Under section 362(b), DC takes a basis of $500,000 in Parcel P. FC2 takes a basis of $500,000 in the DC stock. A takes a basis of $100,000 in the FC2 stock under section 358(a)(1). Section 897(d) and paragraph (c)(1) of §1.897-5T do not apply to FC1's distribution of the FC2 stock because the FC2 stock is not a U.S. real property interest.

Example (8). The facts are the same as in *Example* 7, except that the United States has a treaty with Country W that entitles FC1 and FC2 to nondiscriminatory treatment as described in §1.897-3(b)(2). FC1, but not FC2, makes a valid section 897(i) election prior to the transaction.

(ii) FC1's transfer of Parcel P to DC in exchange for FC2 stock is not subject to section 897(e) and paragraph (a)(1) of this section because FC1 made an election under section 897(i). DC takes a basis of $200,000 in Parcel P under section 362(b).

(iii) FC1's distribution of the FC2 stock to A in exchange for the FC1 stock is not subject to the section 897(d) and paragraph (c)(1) of §1.897-5T because FC1 made an election under section 897(i).

(iv) A must recognize gain on the exchange under section 354(a) of the FC1 stock for the FC2 stock. A exchanged a U.S. real property interest (the FC1 stock) for an interest which is not a U.S. real property interest (the FC2 stock). A recognizes gain of $400,000. Under section 1012, A takes a $500,000 basis in the FC2 stock.

Example (9). (i) The facts are the same as in *Example* 7 except that the United States has a treaty with Country W that entitles FC1 and FC2 to nondiscriminatory treatment as described in §1.897-3(b)(2). FC2, but not FC1, makes a valid section 897(i) election prior to the transaction.

(ii) FC1's exchange of Parcel P for the FC2 stock under section 361(a) is a disposition of a U.S. real property interest. FC1 does not recognize any gain under section 897(e) and paragraph (a)(1) of this section because there is an exchange of a U.S. real property interest (Parcel P) for another U.S. real property interest (the FC2 stock). DC takes a basis of $200,000 in Parcel P under section 362(b). FC2 takes a basis of $200,000 in the DC stock.

(iii) FC1's distribution of the FC2 stock to A in exchange for the FC1 stock is subject to section 897(d) and paragraph (c)(1) of §1.897-5T. Because A takes a basis of $100,000 in the FC2 stock under section 358(a) (which is less than the $200,000 basis of the FC2 stock in the hands of FC1), and A would be subject to U.S. taxation under section 897(a) on a subsequent disposition of the FC2 stock, FC1 does not recognize any gain under paragraph (c)(1) of §1.897-5T due to the statutory exception of paragraph (c)(2)(i) of that section, provided that FC1 complies with the filing requirements of paragraph (d)(1)(C) of §1.897-5T.

(iv) Since the FC1 stock was not a U.S. real property interest, its disposition by A in the section 354(a) exchange for FC2 stock is not subject to section 897(e) and paragraph (a)(1) of this section.

Example (10). The facts are the same as in *Example 7*, except that the United States has a treaty with Country W that entitles FC1 and FC2 to nondiscriminatory treatment as described in §1.897-3(b)(2). FC1 and FC2 made valid section 897(i) elections prior to the transactions.

(ii) FC1's transfer of Parcel P to DC in exchange for FC2 stock is not subject to section 897(e) and paragraph (a)(1) of this section because FC1 made an election under section 897(i). DC takes a basis of $200,000 in Parcel P under section 362(a). FC2 takes a basis of $200,000 in the DC stock.

(iii) FC1's distribution of the FC2 stock to A in exchange for the FC1 stock is not subject to section 897(d) and paragraph (c)(1) of §1.897-5T because FC1 made an election under section 897(i).

(iv) A does not recognize any gain on the exchange of the FC1 stock for the FC2 stock under section 354(a). Under paragraph (a)(1) of this section, there is an exchange of a U.S. real property interest (FC1 stock) for another U.S. real property interest (FC2 stock). A takes a basis of $100,000 in the FC2 stock under section 358(a).

(8) *Treatment of nonqualifying property.*—(i) *In general.*—If, under paragraph (a)(1) of this section, a nonrecognition provision would apply to an exchange but for the fact that nonqualifying property (cash or property other than U.S. real property interests) is received in addition to property (U.S. real property interests) that is permitted to be received under paragraph (a)(1) of this section, then the transferor shall recognize gain under this section equal to the lesser of—

(A) The sum of the cash received plus the fair market value of the nonqualifying property received, or

(B) The gain realized with respect to the U.S. real property interest transferred.

However, no loss shall be recognized pursuant to this paragraph (a)(8) unless such loss is otherwise permitted to be recognized.

(ii) *Treatment of mixed exchanges.*—In a mixed exchange where both a U.S. real property interest and other property (including cash) is transferred in exchange both for property the receipt of which would qualify for nonrecognition treatment pursuant to paragraph (a)(1) of this section and for other property (including cash) which would not so qualify, the transferor will recognize gain in accordance with the rules set forth in subdivisions (A) through (C) of this paragraph (a)(8)(ii).

(A) *Allocation of nonqualifying property.*—The amount of nonqualifying property (including cash) considered to be received in exchange for U.S. real property interests shall be determined by multiplying the fair market value of the nonqualifying property received by a fraction ("real property fraction"). The numerator of the fraction is the fair market value of the U.S. real property interest transferred in the exchange. The denominator of the fraction is the fair market value of all property transferred in the exchange.

(B) *Recognition of gain.*—The amount of gain that must be recognized, and that shall be subject to U.S. taxation by reason of the operation of section 897, shall be equal to the lesser of:

(1) The amount determined under subdivision (A) of this paragraph (a)(8)(ii), or

(2) The gain or loss realized with respect to the U.S. real property interest exchanged.

(C) *Treatment of other amounts.*—The treatment of other amounts received in a mixed exchange shall be determined as follows:

(1) The amount of nonqualifying property (including cash) considered to be received in exchange for property (including cash) other than U.S. real property interests shall be treated in the manner provided in the relevant nonrecognition provision. Such amounts shall be determined by subtracting the amount determined under subdivision (A) of this paragraph (a)(8)(ii) from the total amount of nonqualifying property received in the exchange.

(2) The amount of qualifying property considered to be received in exchange for U.S. real property interests shall be treated in the manner provided in paragraph (a)(1) of this section. Such amount shall be determined by multiplying the total fair market value of qualifying property received in the exchange by the real property fraction described in subdivision (A) of this paragraph (a)(8)(ii).

(3) The amount of qualifying property considered to be received in exchange for property other than U.S. real property interests shall be treated in the manner provided in the relevant nonrecognition provision. Such amount shall be determined by subtracting the amount determined under subdivision *(2)* of this paragraph (a)(8)(ii)(C) from the total fair market value of qualifying property received in the exchange.

(iii) *Example.*—The rules of paragraph (a)(8)(ii) of this section may be illustrated by the following example.

Example. (i) A is an individual citizen and resident of country F. Country F does not have an income tax treaty with the United States. A is the sole proprietor of a business located in the United States, the assets of which consist of a U.S. real property interest with a fair market value of $1,000,000 and an adjusted basis of $700 000, and equipment used in the business with a fair market value of $500,000 and an adjusted basis of $250,000. A decides to incorporate the business, and on January 1, 1987, A transfers his assets to domestic corporation DC in exchange for 100 percent of the stock of DC, with a fair market value of $900,000. In addition, A receives a long term note (constituting a security) from DC for $600,000, bearing arm's length interest and repayment terms. DC has no assets other than those received in the exchange with A. Pursuant to section 897(c)(2) and § 1.897-2, DC is a U.S. real property holding corporation. Therefore, the stock of DC is a U.S. real property interest. Assume that the note from DC constitutes an interest in the corporation solely as a creditor as provided by § 1.897-1(d)(4) of the regulation. A complies with the filing requirements of paragraph (d)(1)(iii) of § 1.897-5T.

(ii) Because the note from DC would not be subject to U.S. taxation upon its disposition, it is nonqualifying property for purposes of determining whether A is entitled to receive nonrecognition treatment pursuant to section 351 with respect to his exchange of the U.S. real property interest. Thus, A must recognize gain in the manner provided in paragraph (a)(8)(ii) of this section. Pursuant to paragraph (a)(8)(ii)(A), the amount of nonqualifying property received in exchange for the real property interests is determined by multiplying the fair market value of such property ($600,000) by the real property fraction. The numerator of the fraction is $1,000,000, the fair market value of the real property transferred by A. The denominator is $1,500,000, the fair market value of all property transferred by A. Thus, A is considered to have received $400,000 of the note in exchange for the real property ($600,000 × $1,000,000/$1,500,000). Pursuant to paragraph (a)(8)(ii)(B), A must recognize the lesser of the amount initially determined or the gain realized with respect to the U.S. real property interest. Therefore, A must recognize the $300,000 gain realized with respect to the real property.

(iii) Pursuant to paragraph (a)(8)(ii)(C) of this section, A is considered to have received $200,000 of the note in exchange for equipment ($600,000 [total value of note received] minus $400,000 [portion of note received in exchange for real property]), $600,000 of the stock in exchange for real property ($900,000 [total value of stock received] times $1,000,000/1,500,000 [proportion of property exchanged consisting of real property]), and $300,000 of the stock in exchange for equipment ($900,000 [total value of stock received] minus $600,000 [portion of stock received in exchange for real property]). All three amounts are entitled to nonrecognition treatment pursuant to section 351.

(iv) Pursuant to paragraph (a)(2) of this section, A's basis in the stock and note received and DC's basis in the U.S. real property interest and equipment will be determined in accordance with the generally applicable rules. The $400,000 portion of the note received in exchange for the real property interest is other property. Pursuant to section 358(a)(2), A takes a fair market value ($400,000) basis for that portion of the note. Pursuant to section 358(a)(1), A's basis in the property received without the recognition of gain (the DC stock and the other portion of the note) will be equal to the basis of the property transferred ($950,000 [$700,000 basis of U.S. real property interest plus $250,000 basis of equipment]), decreased by the fair market value of the other property received ($400,000 portion of the note), and increased by the amount of gain recognized to A on the transaction ($300,000). Thus, A's basis in the stock and the nonrecognition portion of the note is $850,000 ($950,000 – $400,000 + $300,000). Under § 1.358-2(b)(2) of the regulations, the $850,000 is allocated between the stock and the nonrecognition portion of the note in proportion to their fair market values. A takes a basis of $697,000 in the DC stock ($850,000 × 900,000/1,100,000). A takes a basis of $153,000 in the nonrecognition portion of the note ($850,000 × 200,000/1,100,000). A's basis in the note is $553,000 ($400,000 + $153,000). DC's basis in the property received from A will be determined under section 362(a). DC takes a basis of $1,000,000 in the real property interest (A's basis of $700,000 increased by the $300,000 of gain recognized by A on it). DC takes a basis of $250,000 in the equipment (A's basis of $250,000).

(9) *Treaty exception to imposition of tax.*—If gain that would be currently recognized pursuant to the provisions of this section is subject to an exemption from, or reduction of, U.S. tax pursuant to a U.S. income tax treaty, then gain shall be recognized only as provided by that treaty for dispositions occurring before January 1, 1985. For dispositions occurring after December 31, 1984, all gain shall be recognized as provided in section 897 and the regulations thereunder, except as provided by Articles XII

(9) and XXX (5) of the United States-Canada Income Tax Convention or other income tax treaty entered into after June 6, 1988. In regard to Article XXX (5) the Income Tax Treaty with Canada, see, Rev. Rul. 85-76, 1985-1 C.B. 409.

(b) *Certain foreign to foreign exchanges.*—(1) *Exceptions to the general rule.*—Notwithstanding the provisions of paragraph (a)(1) of this section and pursuant to authority conferred by section 897(e)(2), a foreign person shall not recognize gain, in the instances described in paragraph (b)(2) of this section, on the transfer of a U.S. real property interest to a foreign corporation in exchange for stock in a foreign corporation, but only if the transferee's subsequent disposition of the transferred U.S. real property interest would be subject to U.S. taxation, as determined in accordance with the provisions of § 1.897-5T (d)(1), if the filing requirements of paragraph (d)(1)(iii) of § 1.897-5T have been satisfied, if one of the five conditions set forth in paragraph (b)(2) exists, and if one of the following three forms of exchange takes place.

(i) The exchange is made by a foreign corporation pursuant to section 361(a) in a reorganization described in section 368(a)(1)(D) or (F) and there is an exchange of the transferor corporation stock for the transferee corporation stock under section 354(a); or

(ii) The exchange is made by a foreign corporation pursuant to section 361(a) in a reorganization described in section 368(a)(1)(C); there is an exchange of the transferor corporation stock for the transferee corporation stock (or stock of the transferee corporation's parent in the case of a parenthetical C reorganization) under section 354(a); and the transferor corporation's shareholders own more than fifty percent of the voting stock of the transferee corporation (or stock of the transferee corporation's parent in the case of a parenthetical C reorganization) immediately after the reorganization; or

(iii) The U.S. real property interest exchanged is stock in a U.S. real property holding corporation; the exchange qualifies under section 351(a) or section 354(a) in a reorganization described in section 368(a)(1)(B); and immediately after the exchange, all of the outstanding stock of the transferee corporation (or stock of the transferee corporation's parent in the case of a parenthetical B reorganization) is owned in the same proportions by the same nonresident alien individuals and foreign corporations that, immediately before the exchange, owned the stock of the U.S. real property holding corporation.

If, however, a nonresident alien individual or foreign corporation which received stock in an exchange described in subdivision (iii) of this paragraph (b)(1) (or the transferee corporation's parent) disposes of any of such foreign stock within three years from the date of its receipt, then that individual or corporation shall recognize that portion of the gain realized with respect to the stock in the U.S. real property holding corporation for which foreign stock disposed of was received.

(2) *Applicability of exception.*—The exception to the provisions of paragraph (a)(1) provided by paragraph (b)(1) shall apply only if one of the following five conditions exists.

(i) Each of the interests exchanged or received in a transferor corporation or transferee corporation would not be a U.S. real property interest as defined in § 1.897-1(c)(1) if such corporations were domestic corporations; or

(ii) The transferee corporation (and the transferee corporation's parent in the case of a parenthetical B or C reorganization) is incorporated in a foreign country that maintains an income tax treaty with the United States that contains an information exchange provision; the transfer occurs after May 5, 1988; and the transferee corporation (and the transferee corporation's parent in the case of a parenthetical B or C reorganization) submit a binding waiver of all benefits of the respective income tax treaty (including the opportunity to make an election under section 897(i)), which must be attached to each of the transferor and transferee corporation's income tax returns for the year of the transfer; or

(iii) The transferee foreign corporation (and the transferee corporation's parent in the case of a parenthetical B or C reorganization) is a qualified resident as defined in section 884(e) and any regulations thereunder of the foreign country in which it is incorporated; or

(iv) The transferee foreign corporation (and the transferee corporation's parent in the case of a parenthetical B or C reorganization) is incorporated in the same foreign country as the transferor foreign corporation; and there is an income tax treaty in force between that foreign country and the United States at the time of the transfer that contains an exchange of information provision; or

(v) The transferee foreign corporation is incorporated in the same foreign country as the transferor foreign corporation; and the transfer is incident to a mere change in identity, form, or place of organization of one corporation under section 368(a)(1)(F).

For purposes of any election by a transferee foreign corporation (or the transferee corporation's parent in the case of a parenthetical C reorganization) to be treated as a domestic corporation under section 897(i) and § 1.897-3 where the exchange was described in subdivisions (i) or (ii) of paragraph (b)(1) of this section, any prior dispositions of the transferor foreign corporation stock will be subject to the requirements of § 1.897-3(d)(2) upon an election under section 897(i) by the transferee foreign corporation (or the transferee corporation's parent in the case of a parenthetical C reorganization).

(3) *No exceptions.*—No exception to recognition of gain under paragraph (a)(1) of this section is provided for the transfer of a U.S. real property interest by a foreign person to a foreign corporation in exchange for stock in a foreign corporation other than as provided in this paragraph (b). Thus, no exception is provided where—

(i) Such exchange is made pursuant to section 351 and the U.S. real property interest transferred is not stock in a U.S. real property holding corporation; or

(ii) Such exchange is made pursuant to section 361(a) in a reorganization described in section 368 (a)(1) that does not qualify for nonrecognition of gain under this paragraph (b). With regard to the treatment of certain foreign corporations as domestic corporations under section 897(i), see §§ 1.897-3 and 1.897-8T.

(4) *Examples.*—The rules of paragraph (b)(1) and (2) of this section may be illustrated by the following examples. In each instance, the filing requirements of paragraph (d)(1)(iii) of § 1.897-5T have been satisfied.

Example (1). (i) FC is a Country F corporation that has not made a section 897(i) election. FC owns Parcel P, a U.S. real property interest, with a fair market value of $450x and an adjusted basis of 100x.

(ii) FC transfers Parcel P to FS, its wholly owned Country F subsidiary, in exchange for FS stock under section 351(a). FS has not made a section 897(i) election. Under the rules of paragraph (a)(1) of this section, FC must recognize gain of 350x under section 897(a) because the FS stock received in the exchange is not a U.S. real property interest. No exception to the recognition rule of paragraph (a)(1) is provided under this paragraph (b) for a transfer under section 351(a) of a U.S. real property interest (that is not stock in a U.S. real property holding corporation) by a foreign corporation to another foreign corporation in exchange for stock of the transferee corporation.

Example (2). (i) FC is a Country F corporation that has not made a section 897(i) election. FC owns several U.S. real property interests that have appreciated in value since FC purchased the interests. FP, a Country F corporation, owns all of the outstanding stock of FC. Country F maintains an income tax treaty with the United States.

(ii) For valid business purposes, FC transferred substantially all of its assets including all of its U.S. real property interests to FS in 1989 under section 361(a) in a reorganization in exchange for FS stock. FS is a newly formed Country F corporation that is owned by FC. The transfer qualifies as a reorganization under section 368(a)(1)(D). FC immediately distributes the FS stock to FP in exchange for the FC stock and FC dissolves. FP has no gain or loss on the exchange of the FC stock for the FS stock under section 354(a).

(iii) Under the rules of paragraph (b)(1)(i) of this section, FC does not recognize any gain on the transfer of the U.S. real property interests to FS under section 361(a) in the reorganization under section 368(a)(1)(D) because FS would be subject to U.S. taxation on a subsequent disposition of the interests, as required by paragraph (b)(1) of this section; there is an exchange of stock under section 354(a), as required by paragraph (b)(1)(i); and FC and FS are incorporated in Country F which maintains an income tax treaty with the United States, as required by paragraph (b)(2)(iv).

(5) *Contributions of property.*—A foreign person that contributes a U.S. real property interest to a foreign corporation as paid in surplus or as a contribution to capital (including a contribution provided in section 304(a)) shall be treated, for purposes of section 897(j) and this section, as exchanging the U.S. real property interest for stock in the foreign corporation.

(c) *Denial of nonrecognition with respect to certain tax avoidance transfers.*—(1) *In general.*—The provisions of § 1.897-5T and paragraphs (a) and (b) of this section are subject to the rules of this paragraph (c).

(2) *Certain transfers to domestic corporations.*—(i) *General rule.*—If a foreign person transfers property, that is not a U.S. real property interest, to a domestic corporation in a nonrecognition exchange, where—

(A) The adjusted basis of such property transferred exceeded its fair market value on the date of the transfer to the domestic corporation;

(B) The property transferred will not immediately be used in, or held by the domestic corporation for use in, the conduct of a trade or business as defined in § 1.897-1(f); and

(C) Within two years of the transfer to the domestic corporation, the property transferred is sold at a loss;

then, it will be presumed, absent clear and convincing evidence to the contrary, that the

Reg. § 1.897-6T(c)(2)(i)(C)

purpose for transferring the loss property was the avoidance of taxation on the disposition of U.S. real property interests by the domestic corporation. Any loss recognized by the domestic corporation on the sale or exchange of such property shall not be used by the domestic corporation, either by direct offset or as part of a net operating loss or capital loss carryback or carryover, to offset any gain recognized from the sale or exchange of a U.S. real property interest by the domestic corporation.

(ii) *Example.*—The rules of paragraph (e)(2)(i) of this section may be illustrated by the following example.

Example. A is an individual citizen and resident of country F, which does not have an income tax treaty with the U.S. On January 1, 1987, A transfers a U.S. real property interest with a basis of $100,000 and a fair market value of $600,000 to domestic corporation DC in exchange for all of the stock of DC. On October 20, 1987, A transfers stock of a publicly traded domestic corporation with a basis in his hands of $900,000 and a fair market value of $500,000, in exchange for additional stock of DC. The stock of the publicly traded domestic corporation does not constitute an asset used or held for use in DC's trade or business. If DC sells the stock of the publicly traded domestic corporation before October 20, 1989 and recognizes a loss, the loss may not be used to offset any gain recognized on the sale of the U.S. real property interests by DC.

(3) *Basis adjustment for certain related person transactions.*—In the case of any disposition after December 31, 1979, of a U.S. real property interest to a related person (within the meaning of section 453(f)(1)), the basis of the interest in the hands of the person acquiring such interest shall be reduced by the amount of any gain which is not subject to taxation under section 871(b)(1) or 882(a)(1) because the disposition occurred before June 19, 1980 or because of any treaty obligation of the United States. If a foreign corporation makes an election under section 897 (i), and the stock of such corporation was transferred between related persons after December 31, 1979 and before June 19, 1980, then such stock shall be treated as a U.S. real property interest solely for purposes of this paragraph (c)(3).

(4) *Rearrangement of ownership to gain treaty benefit.*—A foreign person who directly or indirectly owns a U.S. real property interest may not directly or indirectly rearrange the incidents of ownership of the U.S. real property interest through the use of nonrecognition provisions in order to gain the benefit of a treaty exemption from taxation. Such nonrecognition will not apply to the foreign transferor. The transferor will recognize gain but not loss on the transfer under section 897(a).

(d) *Effective date.*—Except as specifically provided otherwise in the text of the regulations, paragraphs (a) through (c) shall be effective for transfers, exchanges and other dispositions occurring after June 18, 1980. Paragraph (a)(5)(ii) of this section shall be effective for exchanges and elections occurring after June 6, 1988. [Temporary Reg. § 1.897-6T.]

☐ [*T.D.* 8198, 5-4-88. *Amended by T.D.* 9082, 8-4-2003.]

§ 1.897-7T. Treatment of certain partnership interests as entirely U.S. real property interests under sections 897(g) and 1445(e) (Temporary).—(a) *Rule.*—Pursuant to section 897(g), an interest in a partnership in which, directly or indirectly, fifty percent or more of the value of the gross assets consist of U.S. real property interests, and ninety percent or more of the value of the gross assets consist of U.S. real property interests plus any cash or cash equivalents shall, for purposes of section 1445, be treated as entirely a U.S. real property interest. For purposes of section 897(g), such interest shall be treated as a U.S. real property interest only to the extent that the gain on the disposition is attributable to U.S. real property interests (and not cash, cash equivalents or other property). Consequently, a disposition of any portion of such partnership interest shall be subject to partial taxation under section 897(a) and full withholding under section 1445(a). For purposes of this paragraph, cash equivalent means any asset readily convertible into cash (whether or not denominated in U.S. dollars) including, but not limited to, bank accounts, certificates of deposit, money market accounts, commercial paper, U.S. and foreign treasury obligations and bonds, corporate obligations and bonds, precious metals or commodities, and publicly traded instruments.

* * *

[Temporary Reg. § 1.897-7T.]

☐ [*T.D.* 8198, 5-4-88.]

§ 1.897-9T. Treatment of certain interest in publicly traded corporations, definition of foreign person, and foreign governments and international organizations (Temporary).—(a) *Purpose and scope.*—This section provides a temporary regulation that, if and when adopted as a final regulation, will be added as new paragraphs (c)(2)(iii)(B), (k), (n) and (q) of § 1.897-1. Paragraph (b) of this section would then appear as paragraph (c)(2)(iii)(B) of § 1.897-1. Paragraph (c) of this section would then appear as paragraph (k) of § 1.897-1. Paragraph (d) of this section would then appear as paragraph (n) of § 1.897-1. Paragraph (e) of this section would then appear as paragraph (q) of § 1.897-1.

(b) Any other interest in the corporation (other than an interest solely as a creditor) if on the date such interest was acquired by its present holder it had a fair market value greater than the fair market value on that date of 5 percent of the regularly traded class of the corporation's stock with the lowest fair market value. However, if a non-regularly traded class of interests in the corporation is convertible into a regularly traded class of interests in the corporation, an interest in such non-regularly traded class shall be treated as a U.S. real property interest if on the date it was acquired by its present holder it had a fair market value greater than the fair market value on that date of 5 percent of the regularly traded class of the corporation's stock into which it is convertible. If a person holds interests in a corporation of a class that is not regularly traded, and subsequently acquires additional interests of the same class, then all such interests must be aggregated and valued as of the date of the subsequent acquisition. If the subsequent acquisition causes that person's interests to exceed the applicable limitation, then all such interests shall be treated as U.S. real property interests, regardless of when acquired. In addition, if a person holds interests in a corporation of separate classes that are not regularly traded, and if such interests were separately acquired for a principal purpose of avoiding the applicable 5 percent limitation of this paragraph, then such interests shall be aggregated for purposes of applying that limitation. This rule shall not apply to interests of separate classes acquired in transactions more than three years apart. For purposes of paragraph (c)(2)(iii) of § 1.897-1, section 318(a) shall apply (except that section 318(a)(2)(C) and (3)(C) shall each be applied by substituting "5 percent" for "50 percent").

(c) *Foreign person.*—The term "foreign person" means a nonresident alien individual (including an individual subject to the provisions of section 877), a foreign corporation as defined in paragraph (1) of this section, a foreign partnership, a foreign trust or a foreign estate, as such persons are defined respectively by § 1.871-2 and by 7701 and the regulations thereunder. A resident alien individual, including a nonresident alien with respect to whom there is in effect an election under section 6013(g) or (h) to be treated as United States resident, is not a foreign person. With respect to the status of foreign governments and international organizations, see paragraph (e) of this section.

(d) *Regularly traded.*—(1) *General rule.*—
(i) *Trading requirements.*—A class of interests that is traded on one or more established securities markets is considered to be regularly traded on such market or markets for any calendar quarter during which—

(A) Trades in such class are effected, other than in *de minimis* quantities, on at least 15 days during the calendar quarter;

(B) The aggregate number of the interests in such class traded is at least 7.5 percent or more of the average number of interests in such class outstanding during the calendar quarter; and

(C) The requirements of paragraph (d)(3) of this section are met.

(ii) *Exceptions.*—(A) In the case of the class of interests which is held by 2,500 or more record shareholders, the requirements of paragraph (d)(1)(i)(B) of this section shall be applied by substituting "2.5 percent" for "7.5 percent".

(B) If at any time during the calendar quarter 100 or fewer persons own 50 percent or more of the outstanding shares of a class of interests, such class shall not be considered to be regularly traded for purposes of sections 897, 1445 and 6039C. Related persons shall be treated as one person for purposes of this paragraph (d)(1)(ii)(B).

(iii) *Anti-abuse rule.*—Trades between related persons shall be disregarded. In addition, a class of interests shall not be treated as regularly traded if there is an arrangement or a pattern of trades designed to meet the requirements of this paragraph (d)(1). For example, trades between two persons that occur several times during the calendar quarter may be treated as an arrangement or a pattern of trades designed to meet the requirements of this paragraph (d)(1).

(2) *Interests traded on domestic established securities markets.*—For purposes of sections 897, 1445 and 6039C, a class of interests that is traded on an established securities market located in the United States is considered to be regularly traded for any calendar quarter during which it is regularly quoted by brokers or dealers making a market in such interests. A broker or dealer makes a market in a class of interests only if the broker or dealer holds himself out to buy or sell interests in such class at the quoted price. Stock of a corporation that is described in section 851(a)(1) and units of a unit investment trust registered under the Investment Company Act of 1940 (15 U.S.C. sections 80a-1 to 80a-2) shall be treated as regularly traded within the meaning of this paragraph.

(3) *Reporting requirement for interests traded on foreign securities markets.*—A class of interests in a domestic corporation that is

traded on one or more established securities markets located outside the United States shall not be considered to be regularly traded on such market or markets unless such class is traded in registered form, and—

(i) The corporation registers such class of interests pursuant to section 12 of the Securities Exchange Act of 1934, 15 U.S.C. sec. 78, or

(ii) The corporation attaches to its federal income tax return a statement providing the following:

(A) A caption which states "The following information concerning certain shareholders of this corporation is provided in accordance with the requirements of § 1.897-9T."

(B) The name under which the corporation is incorporated, the state in which such corporation is incorporated, the principal place of business of the corporation, and its employer identification number, if any;

(C) The identity of each person who, at any time during the corporation's taxable year, was the beneficial owner of more than 5 percent of any class of interests of the corporation to which this paragraph (d)(3) applies;

(D) The title, and the total number of shares issued, of any class of interests so owned; and

(E) With respect to each beneficial owner of more than 5 percent of any class of interests of the corporation, the number of shares owned, the percentage of the class represented thereby, and the nature of the beneficial ownership of each class of shares so owned.

Interests in a domestic corporation which has filed a report pursuant to this paragraph (d)(3)(ii) shall be considered to be regularly traded on an established securities market only for the taxable year of the corporation with respect to which such a report is filed.

(4) *Coordination with section 1445.*—For purposes of section 1445, a class of interests in a corporation shall be presumed to be regularly traded during a calendar quarter if such interests were regularly traded within the meaning of this paragraph during the previous calendar quarter.

(e) *Foreign governments and international organizations.*—A foreign government shall be treated as a foreign person with respect to U.S. real property interests, and shall be subject to sections 897, 1445, and 6039C on the disposition of a U.S. real property interest except to the extent specifically otherwise provided in the regulations issued under section 892. An international organization (as defined in section 7701(a)(18)) is not a foreign person with respect to U.S. real property interests, and is not subject to sections 897, 1445, and 6039C on the disposition of a U.S. real property interest. Buildings or parts of buildings and the land ancillary thereto (including the residence of the head of the diplomatic mission) used by the foreign government for a diplomatic mission shall not be a U.S. real property interest in the hands of the respective foreign government.

(f) *Effective date.*—Section 1.897-9T with the exception of paragraph (e) shall be effective for transfers, exchanges, distributions and other dispositions occurring on or after June 6, 1988. Paragraph (e) of this section shall be effective for transfers, exchanges, distributions and other dispositions occurring on or after July 1, 1986. [Temporary Reg. § 1.897-9T.]

☐ [T.D. 8198, 5-4-88.]

Foreign Tax Credits

§ 1.901-1. Allowance of credit for taxes.—(a) *In general.*—Citizens of the United States, domestic corporations, and certain aliens resident in the United States or Puerto Rico may choose to claim a credit, as provided in section 901, against the tax imposed by chapter 1 of the Code for taxes paid or accrued to foreign countries and possessions of the United States, subject to the conditions prescribed in the following subparagraphs:

(1) *Citizen of the United States.*—A citizen of the United States, whether resident or nonresident, may claim a credit for (i) the amount of any income, war profits, and excess profits taxes paid or accrued (or deemed paid or accrued under section 905(b)) during the taxable year to any foreign country or to any possession of the United States; and (ii) his share of any such taxes of a partnership of which he is a member, or of an estate or trust of which he is a beneficiary.

(2) *Domestic corporation.*—A domestic corporation may claim a credit for (i) the amount of any income, war profits, and excess profits taxes paid or accrued during the taxable year to any foreign country or to any possession of the United States; and (ii) the taxes deemed to have been paid or accrued under section 902, 905(b), or 960.

(3) *Alien resident of the United States or Puerto Rico.*—An alien resident of the United States, or an alien individual who is a bona fide resident of Puerto Rico during the entire taxable year, may claim a credit for—

(i) The amount of any income, war profits, and excess profits taxes paid or accrued during the taxable year to any possession of the United States;

(ii) The amount of any such taxes paid or accrued (or deemed paid or accrued under section 905(b)) during the taxable year to any foreign country, if the foreign country of which such alien resident is a citizen or subject, in imposing such taxes, allows a similar credit to citizens of the United States residing in such country; and

(iii) His share of any such taxes of a partnership of which he is a member, or of an estate or trust of which he is a beneficiary, paid or accrued (or deemed paid or accrued under section 905(b)) during the taxable year,

(a) To any foreign country, if the foreign country of which such alien resident is a citizen or subject, in imposing such taxes, allows a similar credit to citizens of the United States residing in such country, or

(b) To any possession of the United States, as the case may be.

(4) *Limitation.*—Section 907(a) limits the credit against the tax imposed by chapter 1 of the Code for certain foreign taxes paid or accrued with respect to foreign oil or gas extraction income. See § 1.907(a)-1.

(b) *Foreign countries which satisfy the similar credit requirement.*—(1) *Taxes of foreign country of which alien resident is citizen or subject.*—A foreign country of which an alien resident is a citizen or subject allows a similar credit, within the meaning of section 901(b)(3), to a United States citizen residing in such country either—

(i) If such country allows him a credit against its income taxes for the amount of income taxes paid or accrued to the United States; or

(ii) If, in imposing such taxes, such country exempts from taxation the income received by him from sources within the United States (as determined under part I (section 861 and following), subchapter N, chapter 1 of the Code).

(2) *Taxes of foreign country other than one of which alien resident is citizen or subject.*—An alien resident of the United States may claim a credit for income taxes paid or accrued by him to a foreign country other than the one of which he is a citizen or subject if the country of which he is a citizen or subject either—

(i) Allows a credit to a United States citizen residing therein for income taxes paid or accrued by him to such other foreign country; or

(ii) In imposing its income taxes, exempts from taxation the income of a United States citizen residing therein from sources within such other foreign country.

(c) *Deduction denied if credit claimed.*—If a taxpayer chooses with respect to any taxable year to claim a credit for taxes to any extent, such choice will be considered to apply to income, war profits, and excess profits taxes paid or accrued in such taxable year to all foreign countries and possessions of the United States, and no portion of any such taxes shall be allowed as a deduction from gross income in such taxable year or any succeeding taxable year. See section 275(a)(4).

(d) *Period during which election can be made or changed.*—The taxpayer may, for a particular taxable year, claim the benefits of section 901 (or claim a deduction in lieu of a foreign tax credit) at any time before the expiration of the period prescribed by section 6511(d)(3)(A) (or section 6511(c) if the period is extended by agreement).

(e) *Joint return.*—In the case of a husband and wife making a joint return, credit for taxes paid or accrued to any foreign country or to any possession of the United States shall be computed upon the basis of the total taxes so paid by or accrued against the spouses.

(f) *Taxes against which credit not allowed.*—The credit for taxes shall be allowed only against the tax imposed by chapter 1 of the Code, but it shall not be allowed against the following taxes imposed under that chapter:

(1) The minimum tax for tax preferences imposed by section 56;

(2) The 10 percent tax on premature distributions to owner-employees imposed by section 72(m)(5)(B);

(3) The tax on lump sum distributions imposed by section 402(e);

(4) The additional tax on income from certain retirement accounts imposed by section 408(f);

(5) The tax on accumulated earnings imposed by section 531;

(6) The personal holding company tax imposed by section 541;

(7) The additional tax relating to war loss recoveries imposed by section 1333; and

(8) The additional tax relating to recoveries of foreign expropriation losses imposed by section 1351.

(g) [Reserved]. For further guidance, see § 1.901-1T(g).

(h) *Taxpayers denied credit in a particular taxable year.*—Taxpayers who are denied the credit for taxes for particular taxable years are the following:

(1) An individual who elects to pay the optional tax imposed by section 3, or one who elects under section 144 to take the standard deduction (see section 36);

(2) A taxpayer who elects to deduct taxes paid or accrued to any foreign country or possession of the United States (see sections 164 and 275);

(3) A regulated investment company which has exercised the election under section 853.

(i) *Dividends from a DISC treated as foreign.*—For purposes of sections 901 through 906 and the regulations thereunder, any amount treated as a dividend from a corporation which is a DISC or former DISC (as defined in section 992(a)(1) or (3) as the case may be) will be treated as a dividend from a foreign corporation to the extent such dividend is treated under section 861(a)(2)(D) as income from sources without the United States. [Reg. § 1.901-1.]

☐ [T.D. 6275, 12-2-57. Amended by T.D. 6466, 5-12-60; T.D. 6780, 12-21-64; T.D. 6798, 12-30-64; T.D. 6795, 1-28-65; T.D. 7283, 8-2-73; T.D. 7564, 9-11-78; T.D. 7636, 8-9-79; T.D. 7961, 6-20-84; T.D. 8160, 9-8-87 *and* T.D. 9194, 4-6-2005.]

§ 1.901-1T. Allowance of credit for taxes (temporary).—(a) through (f) [Reserved]. For further guidance, see § 1.901-1(a) through (f).

(g) *Taxpayers to whom credit not allowed..*— Among those to whom the credit for taxes is not allowed are the following—

(1) Except as provided in section 906, a foreign corporation;

(2) Except as provided in section 906, a nonresident alien individual who is not described in section 876 (see sections 874(c) and 901(b)(4));

(3) A nonresident alien individual described in section 876 other than a bona fide resident (as defined in section 937(a) and the regulations thereunder) of Puerto Rico during the entire taxable year (see sections 901(b)(3) and (4)); and

(4) A U.S. citizen or resident alien individual who is a bona fide resident of a section 931 possession (as defined in § 1.931-1T(c)(1)), the U.S. Virgin Islands, or Puerto Rico, and who excludes certain income from U.S. gross income to the extent of taxes allocable to the income so excluded (see sections 931(b)(2), 933(1), and 932(c)(4)).

(h) [Reserved]. For further guidance, see § 1.901-1(h).

(i) [Reserved]. For further guidance, see § 1.901-1(i).

(j) *Effective date.*—This section shall apply for taxable years ending after October 22, 2004. [Temporary Reg. § 1.901-1T.]

☐ [T.D. 9194, 4-6-2005.]

§ 1.901-2. Income, war profits, or excess profits tax paid or accrued.—(a) *Definition of income, war profits, or excess profits tax.*—(1) *In general.*—Section 901 allows a credit for the amount of income, war profits or excess profits tax (referred to as "income tax" for purposes of this section and §§ 1.901-2A and 1.903-1) paid to any foreign country. Whether a foreign levy is an income tax is determined independently for each separate foreign levy. A foreign levy is an income tax if and only if—

(i) It is a tax; and

(ii) The predominant character of that tax is that of an income tax in the U.S. sense.

Except to the extent otherwise provided in paragraphs (a)(3)(ii) and (c) of this section, a tax either is or is not an income tax, in its entirety, for all persons subject to the tax. Paragraphs (a), (b) and (c) of this section define an income tax for purposes of section 901. Paragraph (d) of this section contains rules describing what constitutes a separate foreign levy. Paragraph (e) of this section contains rules for determining the amount of tax paid by a person. Paragraph (f) of this section contains rules for determining by whom foreign tax is paid. Paragraph (g) of this section contains definitions of the terms "paid by," "foreign country," and "foreign levy." Paragraph (h) of this section states the effective date of this section.

(2) *Tax.*—(i) *In general.*—A foreign levy is a tax if it requires a compulsory payment pursuant to the authority of a foreign country to levy taxes. A penalty, fine, interest, or similar obligation is not a tax, nor is a customs duty a tax. Whether a foreign levy requires a compulsory payment pursuant to a foreign country's authority to levy taxes is determined by principles of U.S. law and not by principles of law of the foreign country. Therefore, the assertion by a foreign country that a levy is pursuant to the foreign country's authority to levy taxes is not determinative that, under U.S. principles, it is pursuant thereto. Notwithstanding any assertion of a foreign country to the contrary, a foreign levy is not pursuant to a foreign country's authority to levy taxes, and thus is not a tax, to the extent a person subject to the levy receives (or will receive), directly or indirectly, a specific economic benefit (as defined in paragraph (a)(2)(ii)(B) of this section) from the foreign country in exchange for payment pursuant to the levy. Rather, to that extent, such levy requires a compulsory payment in ex-

change for such specific economic benefit. If, applying U.S. principles, a foreign levy requires a compulsory payment pursuant to the authority of a foreign country to levy taxes and also requires a compulsory payment in exchange for a specific economic benefit, the levy is considered to have two distinct elements: a tax and a requirement of compulsory payment in exchange for such specific economic benefit. In such a situation, these two distinct elements of the foreign levy (and the amount paid pursuant to each such element) must be separated. No credit is allowable for a payment pursuant to a foreign levy by a dual capacity taxpayer (as defined in paragraph (a)(2)(ii)(A) of this section) unless the person claiming such credit establishes the amount that is paid pursuant to the distinct element of the foreign levy that is a tax. See paragraph (a)(2)(ii) of this section and §1.901-2A.

(ii) *Dual capacity taxpayers.*—(A) *In general.*—For purposes of this section and §§1.901-2A and 1.903-1, a person who is subject to a levy of a foreign state or of a possession of the United States or of a political subdivision of such a state or possession and who also, directly or indirectly (within the meaning of paragraph (a)(2)(ii)(E) of this section) receives (or will receive) a specific economic benefit from the state or possession or from a political subdivision of such state or possession or from an agency or instrumentality of any of the foregoing is referred to as a "dual capacity taxpayer." Dual capacity taxpayers are subject to the special rules of §1.901-2A.

(B) *Specific economic benefit.*—For purposes of this section and §§1.901-2A and 1.903-1, the term "specific economic benefit" means an economic benefit that is not made available on substantially the same terms to substantially all persons who are subject to the income tax that is generally imposed by the foreign country, or, if there is no such generally imposed income tax, an economic benefit that is not made available on substantially the same terms to the population of the country in general. Thus, a concession to extract government-owned petroleum is a specific economic benefit, but the right to travel or to ship freight on a government-owned airline is not, because the latter, but not the former, is made generally available on substantially the same terms. An economic benefit includes property; a service; a fee or other payment; a right to use, acquire or extract resources, patents or other property that a foreign country owns or controls (within the meaning of paragraph (a)(2)(ii)(D) of this section); or a reduction or discharge of a contractual obligation. It does not include the right or privilege merely to engage in business generally or to engage in business in a particular form.

(C) *Pension, unemployment, and disability fund payments.*—A foreign levy imposed on individuals to finance retirement, old-age, death, survivor, unemployment, illness, or disability benefits, or for some substantially similar purpose, is not a requirement of compulsory payment in exchange for a specific economic benefit, as long as the amounts required to be paid by the individuals subject to the levy are not computed on a basis reflecting the respective ages, life expectancies or similar characteristics of such individuals.

(D) *Control of property.*—A foreign country controls property that it does not own if the country exhibits substantial indicia of ownership with respect to the property, for example, by both regulating the quantity of property that may be extracted and establishing the minimum price at which it may be disposed of.

(E) *Indirect receipt of a benefit.*—A person is considered to receive a specific economic benefit indirectly if another person receives a specific economic benefit and that other person—

(1) Owns or controls, directly or indirectly, the first person or is owned or controlled, directly or indirectly, by the first person or by the same persons that own or control, directly or indirectly, the first person; or

(2) Engages in a transaction with the first person under terms and conditions such that the first person receives, directly or indirectly, all or part of the value of the specific economic benefit.

(3) *Predominant character.*—The predominant character of a foreign tax is that of an income tax in the U.S. sense—

(i) If, within the meaning of paragraph (b)(1) of this section, the foreign tax is likely to reach net gain the normal circumstances in which it applies,

(ii) But only to the extent that liability for the tax is not dependent, within the meaning of paragraph (c) of this section, by its terms or otherwise, on the availability of a credit for the tax against income tax liability to another country.

(b) *Net gain.*—(1) *In general.*—A foreign tax is likely to reach net gain in the normal circumstances in which it applies if and only if the tax, judged on the basis of its predominant character, satisfies each of the realization, gross receipts, and net income requirements set forth in paragraphs (b)(2), (b)(3) and (b)(4), respectively, of this section.

Reg. §1.901-2(b)(1)

(2) *Realization.*—(i) *In general.*—A foreign tax satisfies the realization requirement if, judged on the basis of its predominant character, it is imposed—

(A) Upon or subsequent to the occurrence of events ("realization events") that would result in the realization of income under the income tax provisions of the Internal Revenue Code;

(B) Upon the occurrence of an event prior to a realization event (a "prerealization event") provided the consequence of such event is the recapture (in whole or part) of a tax deduction, tax credit or other tax allowance previously accorded to the taxpayer; or

(C) Upon the occurrence of a prerealization event, other than one described in paragraph (b)(2)(i)(B) of this section, but only if the foreign country does not, upon the occurrence of a later event (other than a distribution or a deemed distribution of the income), impose tax ("second tax") with respect to the income on which tax is imposed by reason of such prerealization event (or, if it does impose a second tax, a credit or other comparable relief is available against the liability for such a second tax for tax paid on the occurrence of the prerealization event) and—

(1) The imposition of the tax upon such prerealization event is based on the difference in the values of property at the beginning and end of a period; or

(2) The prerealization event is the physical transfer, processing, or export of readily marketable property (as defined in paragraph (b)(2)(iii) of this section).

A foreign tax that, judged on the basis of its predominant character, is imposed upon the occurrence of events described in this paragraph (b)(2)(i) satisfies the realization requirement even if it is also imposed in some situations upon the occurrence of events not described in this paragraph (b)(2)(i). For example, a foreign tax that, judged on the basis of its predominant character, is imposed upon the occurrence of events described in this paragraph (b)(2)(i) satisfies the realization requirement even though the base of that tax also includes imputed rental income from a personal residence used by the owner and receipt of stock dividends of a type described in section 305(a) of the Internal Revenue Code. As provided in paragraph (a)(1) of this section, a tax either is or is not an income tax, in its entirety, for all persons subject to the tax; therefore, a foreign tax described in the immediately preceding sentence satisfies the realization requirement even though some persons subject to the tax will on some occasions not be subject to the tax except with respect to such imputed rental income and such stock dividends. However, a foreign tax based only or predominantly on such imputed rental income or only or predominantly on receipt of such stock dividends does not satisfy the realization requirement.

(ii) *Certain deemed distributions.*—A foreign tax that does not satisfy the realization requirement under paragraph (b)(2)(i) of this section is nevertheless considered to meet the realization requirement if it is imposed with respect to a deemed distribution (*e.g.*, by a corporation to a shareholder) of amounts that meet the realization requirement in the hands of the person that, under foreign law, is deemed to distribute such amount, but only if the foreign country does not, upon the occurrence of a later event (*e.g.*, an actual distribution), impose tax ("second tax") with respect to the income on which tax was imposed by reason of such deemed distribution (or, if it does impose a second tax, a credit or other comparable relief is available against the liability for such a second tax for tax paid with respect to the deemed distribution).

(iii) *Readily marketable property.*—Property is readily marketable if—

(A) It is stock in trade or other property of a kind that properly would be included in inventory if on hand at the close of the taxable year or if it is held primarily for sale to customers in the ordinary course of business, and

(B) It can be sold on the open market without further processing or it is exported from the foreign country.

(iv) *Examples.*—The provisions of paragraph (b)(2) of this section may be illustrated by the following examples:

Example (1). Residents of country X are subject to a tax of 10 percent on the aggregate net appreciation in fair market value during the calendar year of all shares of stock held by them at the end of the year. In addition, all such residents are subject to a country X tax that qualifies as an income tax within the meaning of paragraph (a)(1) of this section. Included in the base of the income tax are gains and losses realized on the sale of stock, and the basis of stock for purposes of determining such gain or loss is its cost. The operation of the stock appreciation tax and the income tax as applied to sales of stock is exemplified as follows: A, a resident of country X, purchases stock in June, 1983 for 100u (units of country X currency) and sells it in May, 1985 for 160u. On December 31, 1983, the stock is worth 120u and on December 31, 1984, it is worth 155u. Pursuant to the stock appreciation tax, A pays 2u for 1983 (10 percent of (120u – 100u)), 3.5u for 1984 (10 percent of (155u – 120u)), and nothing in 1985 because no stock was held at the end of that year. For purposes of the income tax, A must include 60u (160u - 100u) in his income for 1985, the year of sale. Pursuant to paragraph (b)(2)(i)(C) of this section, the stock appreciation tax does not satisfy the realization requirement because country X imposes a second tax upon the occurrence of a later event (*i.e.*, the sale of stock) with respect to the income that was taxed by the stock appreciation tax and no credit or comparable relief is available against such second tax for the stock appreciation tax paid.

Example (2). The facts are the same as in example (1) except that if stock was held on December 31 last preceding the date of its sale, the basis of such stock for purposes of computing gain or loss under the income tax is the value of the stock on such December 31. Thus, in 1985, A includes only 5u (160u - 155u) as income from the sale for purposes of the income tax. Because the income tax imposed upon the occurrence of a later event (the sale) does not impose a tax with respect to the income that was taxed by the stock appreciation tax, the stock appreciation tax satisfies the realization requirement. The result would be the same if, instead of a basis adjustment to reflect taxation pursuant to the stock appreciation tax, the country X income tax allowed a credit (or other comparable relief) to take account of the stock appreciation tax. If a credit mechanism is used, see also paragraph (e)(4)(i) of this section.

Example (3). Country X imposes a tax on the realized net income of corporations that do business in country X. Country X also imposes a branch profits tax on corporations organized under the law of a country other than country X that do business in country X. The branch profits tax is imposed when realized net income is remitted or deemed to be remitted by branches in country X to home offices outside of country X. The branch profits tax is imposed subsequent to the occurrence of events that would result in realization of income (*i.e.*, by corporations subject to such tax) under the income tax provisions of the Internal Revenue Code; thus, in accordance with paragraph (b)(2)(i)(A) of this section, the branch profits tax satisfies the realization requirement.

Example (4). Country X imposes a tax on the realized net income of corporations that do business in country X (the "country X corporate tax"). Country X also imposes a separate tax on shareholders of such corporations (the "country X shareholder tax"). The country X shareholder tax is imposed on the sum of the actual distributions received during the taxable year by such a shareholder from the corporation's realized net income for that year (*i.e.*, income from past years is not taxed in a later year when it is actually distributed) plus the distributions deemed to be received by such a shareholder. Deemed distributions are defined as (A) a shareholder's pro rata share of the corporation's realized net income for the taxable year, less (B) such shareholder's pro rata share of the corporation's country X corporate tax for that year, less (C) actual distributions made by such corporation to such shareholder from such net income. A shareholder's receipt of actual distributions is a realization event within the meaning of paragraph (b)(2)(i)(A) of this section. The deemed distributions are not realization events, but they are described in paragraph (b)(2)(ii) of this section. Accordingly, the country X shareholder tax satisfies the realization requirement.

(3) *Gross receipts.*—(i) *In general.*—A foreign tax satisfies the gross receipts requirement if, judged on the basis of its predominant character, it is imposed on the basis of—

(A) Gross receipts; or

(B) Gross receipts computed under a method that is likely to produce an amount that is not greater than fair market value, in the case of—

(1) Transactions with respect to which it is reasonable to believe that gross receipts may not otherwise be clearly reflected, such as transactions between related parties; or

(2) Situations to which paragraph (b)(2)(i)(B) or, in the case of a deemed distribution, paragraph (b)(2)(ii) of this section applies.

A foreign tax that, judged on the basis of its predominant character, is imposed on the basis of amounts described in this paragraph (b)(3)(i) satisfies the gross receipts requirement even if it is also imposed on the basis of some amounts not described in this paragraph (b)(3)(i).

(ii) *Examples.*—The provisions of paragraph (b)(3)(i) of this section may be illustrated by the following examples:

Example (1). Country X imposes a "headquarters company tax" on country X corporations that serve as regional headquarters for affiliated nonresident corporations, and this tax is a separate tax within the meaning of paragraph (d) of this section. A headquarters company for purposes of this tax is a corporation that performs administrative, management or coordination functions solely for nonresident affiliated entities. Due to the difficulty of determining on a case-by-case basis the arm's length gross receipts that headquarters companies would charge affiliates for such services, gross receipts of a headquarters company are deemed, for purposes of this tax, to equal 110 percent of the business expenses incurred by the headquarters company. It is established that this formula is likely to produce an amount that is not greater than the fair market value of arm's length gross receipts from such transactions with affiliates. Pursuant to paragraph (b)(3)(i)(B) of this section, the headquarters company tax satisfies the gross receipts requirement.

Example (2). The facts are the same as in Example (1), with the added fact that in the case of a particular taxpayer, A, the formula actually produces an amount that is substantially greater than the fair market value of arm's length gross receipts from transactions with affiliates. As provided in paragraph (a)(1) of this section, the headquarters company tax either is or is not an income tax, in its entirety, for all persons subject to the tax. Accordingly, the result is the same as in example (1) for all persons subject to the headquarters company tax, including A.

Example (3). Country X imposes a separate tax (within the meaning of paragraph (d) of this section) on income from the extraction of petroleum. Under that tax, gross receipts from extraction income are deemed to equal 105 percent of the fair market value of petroleum extracted. This computation is designed to produce an amount that is greater than the fair market value of actual gross receipts; therefore, the tax on extraction income is not likely to produce an amount that is not greater than fair market value. Accordingly, the tax on extraction income does not satisfy the gross receipts requirement. However, if the tax satisfies the criteria of § 1.903-1(a), it is a tax in lieu of an income tax.

(4) *Net income.*—(i) *In general.*—A foreign tax satisfies the net income requirement if, judged on the basis of its predominant character, the base of the tax is computed by reducing gross receipts (including gross receipts as computed under paragraph (b)(3)(i)(B) of this section) to permit—

(A) Recovery of the significant costs and expenses (including significant capital expenditures) attributable, under reasonable principles, to such gross receipts; or

(B) Recovery of such significant costs and expenses computed under a method that is likely to produce an amount that approximates, or is greater than, recovery of such significant costs and expenses.

A foreign tax law permits recovery of significant costs and expenses even if such costs and expenses are recovered at a different time than they would be if the Internal Revenue Code applied, unless the time of recovery is such that under the circumstances there is effectively a denial of such recovery. For example, unless the time of recovery is such that under the circumstances there is effectively a denial of such recovery, the net income requirement is satisfied where items deductible under the Internal Revenue Code are capitalized under the foreign tax system and recovered either on a recurring basis over time or upon the occurrence of some future event or where the recovery of items capitalized under the Internal Revenue Code occurs less rapidly under the foreign tax system. A foreign tax law that does not permit recovery of one or more significant costs or expenses, but that provides allowances that effectively compensate for nonrecovery of such significant costs or expenses, is considered to permit recovery of such costs or expenses. Principles used in the foreign tax law to attribute costs and expenses to gross receipts may be reasonable even if they differ from principles that apply under the Internal Revenue Code (*e.g.,* principles that apply under section 265, 465, or 861(b) of the Internal Revenue Code). A foreign tax whose base, judged on the basis of its predominant character, is computed by reducing gross receipts by items described in paragraph (b)(4)(i)(A) or (B) of this section satisfies the net income requirement even if gross receipts are not reduced by some such items. A foreign tax whose base is gross receipts or gross income does not satisfy the net income requirement except in the rare situation where that tax is almost certain to reach some net gain in the normal circumstances in which it applies because costs and expenses will almost never be so high as to offset gross receipts or gross income, respectively, and the rate of the tax is such that after the tax is paid persons subject to the tax are almost certain to have net gain. Thus, a tax on the gross receipts or gross income of businesses can satisfy the net income requirement only if businesses subject to the tax are almost certain never to incur a loss (after payment of the tax). In determining whether a foreign tax satisfies the net income requirement, it is immaterial whether gross receipts are reduced, in the base of the tax, by another tax, provided that other tax satisfies the realization, gross receipts and net income requirements.

(ii) *Consolidation of profits and losses.*—In determining whether a foreign tax satisfies the net income requirement, one of the factors to be taken into account is whether, in computing the base of the tax, a loss incurred in one activity (*e.g.,* a contract area in the case of oil and gas exploration) in a trade or business is allowed to offset profit earned by the same person in another activity (*e.g.,* a separate contract area) in the same trade or business. If such an offset is allowed, it is immaterial whether the offset may be made in the taxable period in which the loss is incurred or only in a different taxable period, unless the period is such that under the circumstances there is effectively a denial of the ability to offset the loss against profit. In determining whether a foreign tax satisfies the net income requirement, it is immaterial that no such offset is allowed if a loss incurred in one such activity may be applied to offset profit earned in that activity in a different taxable period, unless the period is such that under the circumstances there is effectively a denial of the ability to offset such loss against profit. In determining whether a foreign tax satisfies the net income requirement, it is immaterial whether a person's profits and losses from one trade or business (*e.g.,* oil and gas extraction) are allowed to offset its profits and losses from another trade or business (*e.g.,* oil and gas refining and processing), or whether a person's business profits and losses and its passive investment profits and losses are allowed to offset each other in computing the base of the foreign tax. Moreover, it is immaterial whether foreign law permits or prohibits consolidation of profits and losses of related persons, unless foreign law requires separate entities to be used to carry on separate activities in the same trade or business. If foreign law requires that separate entities carry on such separate activities, the determination whether the net income requirement is satisfied is made by applying the same considerations as if such separate activities were carried on by a single entity.

(iii) *Carryovers.*—In determining whether a foreign tax satisfies the net income requirement, it is immaterial, except as otherwise provided in paragraph (b)(4)(ii) of this section, whether losses incurred during one taxable period may be carried over to offset profits incurred in different taxable periods.

(iv) *Examples.*—The provisions of this paragraph (b)(4) may be illustrated by the following examples:

Example (1). Country X imposes an income tax on corporations engaged in business in country X; however, that income tax is not applicable to banks. Country X also imposes a tax (the "bank tax") of 1 percent on the gross amount of interest income derived by banks from branches in country X; no deductions are allowed. Banks doing business in country X incur very substantial costs and expenses (*e.g.,* interest expense) attributable to their interest income. The bank tax neither provides for recovery of significant costs and expenses nor provides any allowance that significantly compensates for the lack of such recovery. Since such banks are not almost certain never to incur a loss on their interest income from branches in country X, the bank tax does not satisfy the net income requirement. However, if the tax on corporations is generally imposed, the bank tax satisfies the criteria of § 1.903-1(a) and therefore is a tax in lieu of an income tax.

Example (2). Country X law imposes an income tax on persons engaged in business in country X. The base of that tax is realized net income attributable under reasonable principles to such business. Under the tax law of country X, a bank is not considered to be engaged in business in country X unless it has a branch in country X and interest income earned by a bank from a loan to a resident of country X is not considered attributable to business conducted by the bank in country X unless a branch of the bank in country X performs certain significant enumerated activities, such as negotiating the loan. Country X also imposes a tax (the "bank tax") of 1 percent on the gross amount of interest income earned by banks from loans to residents of country X if such banks do not engage in business in country X or if such interest income is not considered attributable to business conducted in country X. For the same reasons as are set forth in example (1), the bank tax does not satisfy the net income requirement. However, if the tax on persons engaged in business in country X is generally imposed, the bank tax satisfies the criteria of § 1.903-1(a) and therefore is a tax in lieu of an income tax.

Example (3). A foreign tax is imposed at the rate of 40 percent on the amount of gross wages realized by an employee; no deductions are allowed. Thus, the tax law neither provides for recovery of costs and expenses nor provides any allowance that effectively compensates for the lack of such recovery. Because costs and expenses of employees attributable to wage income are almost always insignificant compared to the gross wages realized, such costs and expenses will almost always not be so high as to offset the gross wages and the rate of the tax is such that, under the circumstances, after the tax is paid, employees subject to the tax are almost certain to have net gain. Accordingly, the tax satisfies the net income requirement.

Example (4). Country X imposes a tax at the rate of 48 percent of the "taxable income" of nonresidents of country X who furnish specified types of services to customers who are residents of country X. "Taxable income" for purposes of the tax is defined as gross receipts received from residents of country X (regardless of whether the services to which the receipts relate are performed within or outside country X) less deductions that permit recovery of the significant costs and expenses (including significant capital expenditures) attributable under reasonable principles to such gross receipts. The country X tax satisfies the net income requirement.

Reg. § 1.901-2(b)(4)(iv)

Example (5). Each of country X and province Y (a political subdivision of country X) imposes a tax on corporations, called the "country X income tax" and the "province Y income tax," respectively. Each tax has an identical base, which is computed by reducing a corporation's gross receipts by deductions that, based on the predominant character of the tax, permit recovery of the significant costs and expenses (including significant capital expenditures) attributable under reasonable principles to such gross receipts. The country X income tax does not allow a deduction for the province Y income tax for which a taxpayer is liable, nor does the province Y income tax allow a deduction for the country X income tax for which a taxpayer is liable. As provided in paragraph (d)(1) of this section, each of the country X income tax and the province Y income tax is a separate levy. Both of these levies satisfy the net income requirement; the fact that neither levy's base allows a deduction for the other levy is immaterial in reaching that determination.

(c) *Soak-up taxes.*—(1) *In general.*—Pursuant to paragraph (a)(3)(ii) of this section, the predominant character of a foreign tax that satisfies the requirement of paragraph (a)(3)(i) of this section is that of an income tax in the U.S. sense only to the extent that liability for the foreign tax is not dependent (by its terms or otherwise) on the availability of a credit for the tax against income tax liability to another country. Liability for foreign tax is dependent on the availability of a credit for the foreign tax against income tax liability to another country only if and to the extent that the foreign tax would not be imposed on the taxpayer but for the availability of such a credit. See also § 1.903-1(b)(2).

(2) *Examples.*—The provisions of paragraph (c)(1) of this section may be illustrated by the following examples:

Example (1). Country X imposes a tax on the receipt of royalties from sources in country X by nonresidents of country X. The tax is 15 percent of the gross amount of such royalties unless the recipient is a resident of the United States or of country A, B, C or D, in which case the tax is 20 percent of the gross amount of such royalties. Like the United States, each of countries A, B, C and D allows its residents a credit against the income tax otherwise payable to it for income taxes paid to other countries. Because the 20 percent rate applies only to residents of countries which allow a credit for taxes paid to other countries and the 15 percent rate applies to residents of countries which do not allow such a credit, one-fourth of the country X tax would not be imposed on residents of the United States but for the availability of such a credit. Accordingly, one-fourth of the country X tax imposed on residents of the United States who receive royalties from sources in country X is dependent on the availability of a credit for the country X tax against income tax liability to another country.

Example (2). Country X imposes a tax on the realized net income derived by all nonresidents from carrying on a trade or business in country X. Although country X law does not prohibit other nonresidents from carrying on business in country X, United States persons are the only nonresidents of country X that carry on business in country X in 1984. The country X tax would be imposed in its entirety on a nonresident of country X irrespective of the availability of a credit for country X tax against income tax liability to another country. Accordingly, no portion of that tax is dependent on the availability of such a credit.

Example (3). Country X imposes tax on the realized net income of all corporations incorporated in country X. Country X allows a tax holiday to qualifying corporations incorporated in country X that are owned by nonresidents of country X, pursuant to which no country X tax is imposed on the net income of a qualifying corporation for the first ten years of its operations in country X. A corporation qualifies for the tax holiday if it meets certain minimum investment criteria and if the development office of country X certifies that in its opinion the operations of the corporation will be consistent with specified development goals of country X. The development office will not so certify to any corporation owned by persons resident in countries that allow a credit (such as that available under section 902 of the Internal Revenue Code) for country X tax paid by a corporation incorporated in country X. In practice, tax holidays are granted to a large number of corporations, but country X tax is imposed on a significant number of other corporations incorporated in country X (*e.g.*, those owned by country X persons and those which have had operations for more than 10 years) in addition to corporations denied a tax holiday because their shareholders qualify for a credit for the country X tax against income tax liability to another country. In the case of corporations denied a tax holiday because they have U.S. shareholders, no portion of the country X tax during the period of the denied 10-year tax holiday is dependent on the availability of a credit for the country X tax against income tax liability to another country.

Example (4). The facts are the same as in example (3), except that corporations owned by persons resident in countries that will allow a credit for country X tax at the time when dividends are distributed by the corporations are granted a provisional tax holiday. Under the provisional tax holiday, instead of relieving such a corporation from country X tax for 10 years, liability for such tax is deferred until the corporation distributes dividends. The result is the same as in example (3).

(d) *Separate levies.*—(1) *In general.*—For purposes of sections 901 and 903, whether a single levy or separate levies are imposed by a foreign country depends on U.S. principles and not on whether foreign law imposes the levy or levies in a single or separate statutes. A levy imposed by one taxing authority (*e.g.,* the national government of a foreign country) is always separate for purposes of sections 901 and 903 from a levy imposed by another taxing authority (*e.g.,* a political subdivision of that foreign country). Levies are not separate merely because different rates apply to different taxpayers. For example, a foreign levy identical to the tax imposed on U.S. citizens and resident alien individuals by section 1 of the Internal Revenue Code is a single levy notwithstanding the levy has graduated rates and applies different rate schedules to unmarried individuals, married individuals who file separate returns and married individuals who file joint returns. In general, levies are not separate merely because some provisions determining the base of the levy apply, by their terms or in practice, to some, but not all, persons subject to the levy. For example, a foreign levy identical to the tax imposed by section 11 of the Internal Revenue Code is a single levy even though some provisions apply by their terms to some but not all corporations subject to the section 11 tax (*e.g.,* section 465 is by its terms applicable to corporations described in sections 465(a)(1)(B) and 465(a)(1)(C), but not to other corporations), and even though some provisions apply in practice to some but not all corporations subject to the section 11 tax (*e.g.,* section 611 does not, in practice, apply to any corporation that does not have a qualifying interest in the type of property described in section 611(a)). However, where the base of a levy is different in kind, and not merely in degree, for different classes of persons subject to the levy, the levy is considered for purposes of sections 901 and 903 to impose separate levies for such classes of persons. For example, regardless of whether they are contained in a single or separate foreign statutes, a foreign levy indentical to the tax imposed by section 871(b) of the Internal Revenue Code is a separate levy from a foreign levy identical to the tax imposed by section 1 of the Internal Revenue Code as it applies to persons other than those described in section 871(b), and foreign levies identical to the taxes imposed by sections 11, 541, 881, 882, 1491 and 3111 of the Internal Revenue Code are each separate levies, because the base of each of those levies differs in kind, and not merely in degree, from the base of each of the others. Accordingly, each such levy must be analyzed separately to determine whether it is an income tax within the meaning of paragraph (a)(1) of this section and whether it is a tax in lieu of an income tax within the meaning of paragraph (a) of §1.903-1. Where foreign law imposes a levy that is the sum of two or more separately computed amounts, and each such amount is computed by reference to a separate base, separate levies are considered, for purposes of sections 901 and 903, to be imposed. A separate base may consist, for example, of a particular type of income or of an amount unrelated to income, *e.g.,* wages paid. Amounts are not separately computed if they are computed separately merely for purposes of a preliminary computation and are then combined as a single base. In the case of levies that apply to dual capacity taxpayers, see also §1.901-2A(a).

(2) *Contractual modifications.*—Notwithstanding paragraph (d)(1) of this section, if foreign law imposing a levy is modified for one or more persons subject to the levy by a contract entered into by such person or persons and the foreign country, then foreign law is considered for purposes of sections 901 and 903 to impose a separate levy for all persons to whom such contractual modification of the levy applies, as contrasted to the levy as applied to all persons to whom such contractual modification does not apply. In applying the provisions of paragraph (c) of this section to a tax as modified by such a contract, the provisions of §1.903-1(b)(2) shall apply.

(3) *Examples.*—The provisions of paragraph (d)(1) of this section may be illustrated by the following examples:

Example (1). A foreign statute imposes a levy on corporations equal to the sum of 15% of the corporation's realized net income plus 3% of its net worth. As the levy is the sum of two separately computed amounts, each of which is computed by reference to a separate base, each of the portion of the levy based on income and the portion of the levy based on net worth is considered, for purposes of sections 901 and 903, to be a separate levy.

Example (2). A foreign statute imposes a levy on nonresident alien individuals analogous to the taxes imposed by section 871 of the Internal Revenue Code. For the same reasons as set forth in example (1), each of the portion of the foreign levy analogous to the tax imposed by section 871(a) and the portion of the foreign levy analogous to the tax imposed by sections 871(b) and 1, is considered, for purposes of sections 901 and 903, to be a separate levy.

Example (3). A single foreign statute or separate foreign statutes impose a foreign levy that is the sum of the products of specified rates applied to specified bases, as follows:

base	rate
net income from mining	45%
net income from manufacturing	50%
net income from technical services	50%
net income from other services	45%
net income from investments	15%
all other net income	50%

In computing each such base, deductible expenditures are allocated to the type of income they generate. If allocated deductible expenditures exceed the gross amount of a specified type of in come, the excess may not be applied against income of a different specified type. Accordingly, the levy is the sum of several separately computed amounts, each of which is computed by reference to a separate base. Each of the levies on mining net income, manufacturing net income, technical services net income, other services net income, investment net income and other net income is, therefore, considered, for purposes of sections 901 and 903, to be a separate levy.

Example (4). The facts are the same as in example (3), except that excess deductible expenditures allocated to one type of income are applied against other types of income to which the same rate applies. The levies on mining net income and other services net income together are considered, for purposes of sections 901 and 903, to be a single levy since, despite a separate preliminary computation of the bases, by reason of the permitted application of excess allocated deductible expenditures, the bases are not separately computed. For the same reason, the levies on manufacturing net income, technical services net income and other net income together are considered, for purposes of sections 901 and 903, to be a single levy. The levy on investment net income is considered, for purposes of sections 901 and 903, to be a separate levy. These results are not dependent on whether the application of excess allocated deductible expenditures to a different type of income, as described above, is permitted in the same taxable period in which the expenditures are taken into account for purposes of the preliminary computation, or only in a different (*e.g.*, later) taxable period.

Example (5). The facts are the same as in example (3), except that excess deductible expenditures allocated to any type of income other than investment income are applied against the other types of income (including investment income) according to a specified set of priorities of application. Excess deductible expenditures allocated to investment income are not applied against any other type of income. For the reason expressed in example (4), all of the levies are together considered, for purposes of sections 901 and 903, to be a single levy.

(e) *Amount of income tax that is creditable.*—(1) *In general.*—Credit is allowed under section 901 for the amount of income tax (within the meaning of paragraph (a)(1) of this section) that is paid to a foreign country by the taxpayer. The amount of income tax paid by the taxpayer is determined separately for each taxpayer.

(2) *Refunds and credits.*—(i) *In general.*—An amount is not tax paid to a foreign country to the extent that it is reasonably certain that the amount will be refunded, credited, rebated, abated, or forgiven. It is not reasonably certain that an amount will be refunded, credited, rebated, abated, or forgiven if the amount is not greater than a reasonable approximation of final tax liability to the foreign country.

(ii) *Examples.*—The provisions of paragraph (e)(2)(i) of this section may be illustrated by the following examples:

Example (1). The internal law of country X imposes a 25 percent tax on the gross amount of interest from sources in country X that is received by a nonresident of country X. Country X law imposes the tax on the nonresident recipient and requires any resident of country X that pays such interest to a nonresident to withhold and pay over to country X 25 percent of such interest, which is applied to offset the recipient's liability for the 25 percent tax. A tax treaty between the United States and country X overrides internal law of country X and provides that country X may not tax interest received by a resident of the United States from a resident of country X at a rate in excess of 10 percent of the gross amount of such interest. A resident of the United States may claim the benefit of the treaty only by applying for a refund of the excess withheld amount (15 percent of the gross amount of interest income) after the end of the taxable year. *A*, a resident of the United States, receives a gross amount of 100u (units of country X currency) of interest income from a resident of country X from sources in country X in the taxable year 1984, from which 25u of country X tax is withheld. *A* files a timely claim for refund of the 15u excess withheld amount. 15u of the amount withheld (25u – 10u) is reasonably certain to be refunded; therefore, 15u is not considered an amount of tax paid to country X.

Example (2). *A*'s initial income tax liability under country X law is 100u (units of country X currency). However, under country X law *A*'s initial income tax liability is reduced in order to compute its final tax liability by an investment credit of 15u and a credit for charitable contributions of 5u. The amount of income tax paid by A is 80u.

Example (3). A computes his income tax liability in country X for the taxable year 1984 as 100u (units of country X currency), files a tax return on that basis, and pays 100u of tax. The day after A files that return, A files a claim for refund of 90u. The difference between the 100u of liability reflected in A's original return and the 10u of liability reflected in A's refund claim depends on whether a particular expenditure made by A is nondeductible or deductible, respectively. Based on an analysis of the country X tax law, A's country X tax advisors have advised A that it is not clear whether or not that expenditure is deductible. In view of the uncertainty as to the proper treatment of the item in question under country X tax law, no portion of the 100u paid by A is reasonably certain to be refunded. If A receives a refund, A must treat the refund as required by section 905(c) of the Internal Revenue Code.

Example (4). A levy of country X, which qualifies as an income tax within the meaning of paragraph (a)(1) of this section, provides that each person who makes payment to country X pursuant to the levy will receive a bond to be issued by country X with an amount payable at maturity equal to 10 percent of the amount paid pursuant to the levy. A pays 38,000u (units of country X currency) to country X and is entitled to receive a bond with an amount payable at maturity of 3800u. It is reasonably certain that a refund in the form of property (the bond) will be made. The amount of that refund is equal to the fair market value of the bond. Therefore, only the portion of the 38,000u payment in excess of the fair market value of the bond is an amount of tax paid.

(3) *Subsidies.*—(i) *General rule.*—An amount of foreign income tax is not an amount of income tax paid or accrued by a taxpayer to a foreign country to the extent that—

(A) The amount is used, directly or indirectly, by the foreign country imposing the tax to provide a subsidy by any means (including, but not limited to, a rebate, a refund, a credit, a deduction, a payment, a discharge of an obligation, or any other method) to the taxpayer, to a related person (within the meaning of section 482), to any party to the transaction, or to any party to a related transaction; and

(B) The subsidy is determined, directly or indirectly, by reference to the amount of the tax or by reference to the base used to compute the amount of the tax.

(ii) *Subsidy.*—The term "subsidy" includes any benefit conferred, directly or indirectly, by a foreign country to one of the parties enumerated in paragraph (e)(3)(i)(A) of this section. Substance and not form shall govern in determining whether a subsidy exists. The fact that the U.S. taxpayer may derive no demonstrable benefit from the subsidy is irrelevant in determining whether a subsidy exists.

(iii) *Official exchange rate.*—A subsidy described in paragraph (e)(3)(i)(B) of this section does not include the actual use of an official foreign government exchange rate converting foreign currency into dollars where a free exchange rate also exists if—

(A) The economic benefit represented by the use of the official exchange rate is not targeted to or tied to transactions that give rise to a claim for a foreign tax credit;

(B) The economic benefit of the official exchange rate applies to a broad range of international transactions, in all cases based on the total payment to be made without regard to whether the payment is a return of principal, gross income, or net income, and without regard to whether it is subject to tax; and

(C) Any reduction in the overall cost of the transaction is merely coincidental to the broad structure and operation of the official exchange rate.

In regard to foreign taxes paid or accrued in taxable years beginning before January 1, 1987, to which the Mexican Exchange Control Decree, effective as of December 20, 1982, applies, see Rev. Rul. 84-143, 1984-2 C.B. 127.

(iv) *Examples.*—The provisions of this paragraph (e)(3) may be illustrated by the following examples:

Example 1. (i) Country X imposes a 30 percent tax on nonresident lenders with respect to interest which the nonresident lenders receive from borrowers who are residents of Country X, and it is established that this tax is a tax in lieu of an income tax within the meaning of § 1.903-1(a). Country X provides the nonresident lenders with receipts upon their payment of the 30 percent tax. Country X remits to resident borrowers an incentive payment for engaging in foreign loans, which payment is an amount equal to 20 percent of the interest paid to nonresident lenders.

(ii) Because the incentive payment is based on the interest paid, it is determined by reference to the base used to compute the tax that is imposed on the nonresident lender. The incentive payment is considered a subsidy under this paragraph (e)(3) since it is provided to a party (the borrower) to the transaction and is based on the amount of tax that is imposed on the lender with respect to the transaction. Therefore, two-thirds (20 percent/30 percent) of the amount withheld by the resident borrower from interest payments to the nonresident lender is not an amount of income tax paid or accrued for purposes of section 901(b).

Example 2. (i) A U.S. bank lends money to a development bank in Country X. The development bank relends the money to companies resident in Country X. A withholding tax is imposed by Country X on the U.S. bank with respect to the interest that the development bank pays to the U.S. bank, and appropriate receipts are provided. On the date that the tax is withheld, fifty percent of the tax is credited by Country X to an account of the development bank. Country X requires the development bank to transfer the amount credited to the borrowing companies.

(ii) The amount successively credited to the account of the development bank and then to the account of the borrowing companies is determined by reference to the amount of the tax and the tax base. Since the amount credited to the borrowing companies is a subsidy provided to a party (the borrowing companies) to a related transaction and is based on the amount of tax and the tax base, it is not an amount paid or accrued as an income tax for purposes of section 901(b).

Example 3. (i) A U.S. bank lends dollars to a Country X borrower. Country X imposes a withholding tax on the lender with respect to the interest. The tax is to be paid in Country X currency, although the interest is payable in dollars. Country X has a dual exchange rate system, comprised of a controlled official exchange rate and a free exchange rate. Priority transactions such as exports of merchandise, imports of merchandise, and payments of principal and interest on foreign currency loans payable abroad to foreign lenders are governed by the official exchange rate which yields more dollars per unit of Country X currency than the free exchange rate. The Country X borrower remits the net amount of dollar interest due to the U.S. bank (interest due less withholding tax), pays the tax withheld in Country X currency to the Country X government, and provides to the U.S. bank a receipt for payment of the Country X taxes.

(ii) The use of the official exchange rate by the U.S. bank to determine foreign taxes with respect to interest is not a subsidy described in paragraph (e)(3)(i)(B) of this section. The official exchange rate is not targeted to or tied to transactions that give rise to a claim for a foreign tax credit. The use of the official exchange rate applies to the interest paid and to the principal paid. Any benefit derived by the U.S. bank through the use of the official exchange rate is merely coincidental to the broad structure and operation of the official exchange rate.

Example 4. (i) B, a U.S. corporation, is engaged in the production of oil and gas in Country X pursuant to a production sharing agreement between B, Country X, and the state petroleum authority of Country X. The agreement is approved and enacted into law by the Legislature of Country X. Both B and the petroleum authority are subject to the Country X income tax. Each entity files an annual income tax return and pays, to the tax authority of Country X, the amount of income tax due on its annual income. B is a dual capacity taxpayer as defined in § 1.901-2(a)(2)(ii)(A). Country X has agreed to return to the petroleum authority one-half of the income taxes paid by B by allowing it a credit in calculating its own tax liability to Country X.

(ii) The petroleum authority is a party to a transaction with B and the amount returned by Country X to the petroleum authority is determined by reference to the amount of the tax imposed on B. Therefore, the amount returned is a subsidy as described in this paragraph (e)(3) and one-half the tax imposed on B is not an amount of income tax paid or accrued.

Example 5. Assume the same facts as in *Example 4,* except that the state petroleum authority of Country X does not receive amounts from Country X related to tax paid by B. Instead, the authority of Country X receives a general appropriation from Country X which is not calculated with reference to the amount of tax paid by B. The general appropriation is therefore not a subsidy described in this paragraph (e)(3).

(v) *Effective Date.*—This paragraph (e)(3) shall apply to foreign taxes paid or accrued in taxable years beginning after December 31, 1986.

(4) *Multiple levies.*—(i) *In general.*—If, under foreign law, a taxpayer's tentative liability for one levy (the "first levy") is or can be reduced by the amount of the taxpayer's liability for a different levy (the "second levy"), then the amount considered paid by the taxpayer to the foreign country pursuant to the second levy is an amount equal to its entire liability for that levy, and the remainder of the amount paid is considered paid pursuant to the first levy. This rule applies regardless of whether it is or is not likely that liability for one such levy will always exceed liability for the other such levy. For an example of the application of this rule, see example (5) of § 1.903-1(b)(3). If, under foreign law, the amount of a taxpayer's liability is the greater or lesser of amounts computed pursuant to two levies, then the entire amount paid to the foreign country by the taxpayer is considered paid pursuant to the levy that imposes such greater or lesser amount, respectively,

and no amount is considered paid pursuant to such other levy.

(ii) *Integrated tax systems.*—[Reserved]

(5) *Noncompulsory amounts.*—(i) *In general.*—An amount paid is not a compulsory payment, and thus is not an amount of tax paid, to the extent that the amount paid exceeds the amount of liability under foreign law for tax. An amount paid does not exceed the amount of such liability if the amount paid is determined by the taxpayer in a manner that is consistent with a reasonable interpretation and application of the substantive and procedural provisions of foreign law (including applicable tax treaties) in such a way as to reduce, over time, the taxpayer's reasonably expected liability under foreign law for tax, and if the taxpayer exhausts all effective and practical remedies, including invocation of competent authority procedures available under applicable tax treaties, to reduce, over time, the taxpayer's liability for foreign tax (including liability pursuant to a foreign tax audit adjustment). Where foreign tax law includes options or elections whereby a taxpayer's tax liability may be shifted, in whole or part, to a different year or years, the taxpayer's use or failure to use such options or elections does not result in a payment in excess of the taxpayer's liability for foreign tax. An interpretation or application of foreign law is not reasonable if there is actual notice or constructive notice (*e.g.,* a published court decision) to the taxpayer that the interpretation or application is likely to be erroneous. In interpreting foreign tax law, a taxpayer may generally rely on advice obtained in good faith from competent foreign tax advisors to whom the taxpayer has disclosed the relevant facts. A remedy is effective and practical only if the cost thereof (including the risk of offsetting or additional tax liability) is reasonable in light of the amount at issue and the likelihood of success. A settlement by a taxpayer of two or more issues will be evaluated on an overall basis, not on an issue-by-issue basis, in determining whether an amount is a compulsory amount. A taxpayer is not required to alter its form of doing business, its business conduct, or the form of any business transaction in order to reduce its liability under foreign law for tax.

(ii) *Examples.*—The provisions of paragraph (e)(5)(i) of this section may be illustrated by the following examples:

Example (1). A, a corporation organized and doing business solely in the United States, owns all of the stock of B, a corporation organized in country X. In 1984 A buys merchandise from unrelated persons for $1,000,000, shortly thereafter resells that merchandise to B for $600,000, and B later in 1984 resells the merchandise to unrelated persons for $1,200,000. Under the country X income tax, which is an income tax within the meaning of paragraph (a)(1) of this section, all corporations organized in country X are subject to a tax equal to 3% of their net income. In computing its 1984 country X income tax liability B reports $600,000 ($1,200,000 − $600,000) of profit from the purchase and resale of the merchandise referred to above. The country X income tax law requires that transactions between related persons be reported at arm's length prices, and a reasonable interpretation of this requirement, as it has been applied in country X, would consider B's arm's length purchase price of the merchandise purchased from A to be $1,050,000. When it computes its country X tax liability B is aware that $600,000 is not an arm's length price (by country X standards). B's knowing use of a non-arm's length price (by country X standards) of $600,000, instead of a price of $1,050,000 (an arm's length price under country X's law), is not consistent with a reasonable interpretation and application of the law of country X, determined in such a way as to reduce over time B's reasonably expected liability for country X income tax. Accordingly, $13,500 (3% of $450,000 ($1,050,000 − $600,000)), the amount of country X income tax paid by B to country X that is attributable to the purchase of the merchandise from B's parent at less than an arm's length price, is in excess of the amount of B's liability for country X tax, and thus is not an amount of tax.

Example (2). A, a corporation organized and doing business solely in the United States, owns all of the stock of B, a corporation organized in country X. Country X has in force an income tax treaty with the United States. The treaty provides that the profits of related persons shall be determined as if the persons were not related. A and B deal extensively with each other. A and B, with respect to a series of transactions involving both of them, treat A as having $300,000 of income and B as having $700,000 of income for purposes of A's United States income tax and B's country X income tax, respectively. B has no actual or constructive notice that its treatment of these transactions under country X law is likely to be erroneous. Subsequently, the Internal Revenue Service reallocates $200,000 of this income from B to A under the authority of section 482 and the treaty. This reallocation constitutes actual notice to A and constructive notice to B that B's interpretation and application of country X's law and the tax treaty is likely to be erroneous. B does not exhaust all effective and practical remedies to obtain a refund of the amount of country X income tax paid by B to country X that is attributable to the reallocated $200,000 of income. This amount is in excess of the amount of *B*'s liability for country X tax and thus is not an amount of tax.

Example (3). The facts are the same as in example (2), except that *B* files a claim for refund (an administrative proceeding) of country X tax and *A* or *B* invokes the competent authority procedures of the treaty, the cost of which is reasonable in view of the amount at issue and the likelihood of success. Nevertheless, *B* does not obtain any refund of country X tax. The cost of pursuing any judicial remedy in country X would be unreasonable in light of the amount at issue and the likelihood of *B*'s success, and *B* does not pursue any such remedy. The entire amount paid by *B* to country X is a compulsory payment and thus is an amount of tax paid by *B*.

Example (4). The facts are the same as in example (2), except that, when the Internal Revenue Service makes the reallocation, the country X statute of limitations on refunds has expired; and neither the internal law of country X nor the treaty authorizes the country X tax authorities to pay a refund that is barred by the statute of limitations. *B* does not file a claim for refund, and neither *A* nor *B* invokes the competent authority procedures of the treaty. Because the country X tax authorities would be barred by the statute of limitations from paying a refund, *B* has no effective and practicable remedies. The entire amount paid by *B* to country X is a compulsory payment and thus is an amount of tax paid by *B*.

Example (5). *A* is a U.S. person doing business in country X. In computing its income tax liability to country X, *A* is permitted, at its election, to recover the cost of machinery used in its business either by deducting that cost in the year of acquisition or by depreciating that cost on the straight line method over a period of 2, 4, 6 or 10 years. *A* elects to depreciate machinery over 10 years. This election merely shifts *A*'s tax liability to different years (compared to the timing of *A*'s tax liability under a different depreciation period); it does not result in a payment in excess of the amount of *A*'s liability for country X income tax in any year since the amount of country X tax paid by *A* is consistent with a reasonable interpretation of country X law in such a way as to reduce over time *A*'s reasonably expected liability for country X tax. Because the standard of paragraph (e)(5)(i) of this section refers to *A*'s reasonably expected liability, not its actual liability, events actually occurring in subsequent years (*e.g.,* whether *A* has sufficient profit in such years so that such depreciation deductions actually reduce *A*'s country X tax liability or whether the country X tax rates change) are immaterial.

Example (6). The internal law of country X imposes a 25 percent tax on the gross amount of interest from sources in country X that is received by a nonresident of country X. Country X law imposes the tax on the nonresident recipient and requires any resident of country X that pays such interest to a nonresident to withhold and pay over to country X 25 percent of such interest, which is applied to offset the recipient's liability for the 25 percent tax. A tax treaty between the United States and country X overrides internal law of country X and provides that country X may not tax interest received by a resident of the United States from a resident of country X at a rate in excess of 10 percent of the gross amount of such interest. A resident of the United States may claim the benefit of the treaty only by applying for a refund of the excess withheld amount (15 percent of the gross amount of interest income) after the end of the taxable year. *A,* a resident of the United States, receives a gross amount of 100u (units of country X currency) of interest income from a resident of country X from sources in country X in the taxable year 1984, from which 25u of country X tax is withheld. *A* does not file a timely claim for refund. 15u of the amount withheld (25u–10u) is not a compulsory payment and hence is not an amount of tax.

(f) *Taxpayer.*—(1) *In general.*—The person by whom tax is considered paid for purposes of sections 901 and 903 is the person on whom foreign law imposes legal liability for such tax, even if another person (*e.g.,* a withholding agent) remits such tax. For purposes of this section, § 1.901-2A and § 1.903-1, the person on whom foreign law imposes such liability is referred to as the "taxpayer." A foreign tax of a type described in paragraph (a)(2)(ii)(C) of this section is considered to be imposed on the recipients of wages if such tax is deducted from such wages under provisions that are comparable to section 3102(a) and (b) of the Internal Revenue Code.

(2) *Party undertaking tax obligation as part of transaction.*—(i) *In general.*—Tax is considered paid by the taxpayer even if another party to a direct or indirect transaction with the taxpayer agrees, as a part of the transaction, to assume the taxpayer's foreign tax liability. The rules of the foregoing sentence apply notwithstanding anything to the contrary in paragraph (e)(3) of this section. See § 1.901-2A for additional rules regarding dual capacity taxpayers.

(ii) *Examples.*—The provisions of paragraphs f(1) and (f)(2)(i) of this section may be illustrated by the following examples:

Example (1). Under a loan agreement between *A,* a resident of country X, and *B,* a United States person, *A* agrees to pay *B* a certain amount of interest net of any tax that country X may impose on *B* with respect to its interest income. Country X imposes a 10 percent tax on the gross amount of interest income received by nonresidents of country X from sources in country X, and it is established that this tax is a tax in lieu of an income tax within the meaning of § 1.903-1(a). Under the law of country X this tax is imposed on the nonresident recipient, and any resident of country X that pays such interest to a nonresident is required to withhold and pay over to country X 10 percent of the amount of such interest, which is applied to offset the recipient's liability for the tax. Because legal liability for the tax is imposed on the recipient of such interest income, B is the taxpayer with respect to the country X tax imposed on B's interest income from B's loan to A. Accordingly, B's interest income for federal income tax purposes includes the amount of country X tax that is imposed on B with respect to such interest income and that is paid on B's behalf by A pursuant to the loan agreement, and, under paragraph (f)(2)(i) of this section, such tax is considered for purposes of section 903 to be paid by B.

Example (2). The facts are the same as in example (1), except that in collecting and receiving the interest B is acting as a nominee for, or agent of, C, who is a United States person. Because C (not B) is the beneficial owner of the interest, legal liability for the tax is imposed in C, not B (C's nominee or agent). Thus, C is the taxpayer with respect to the country X tax imposed on C's interest income from C's loan to A. Accordingly, C's interest income for federal income tax purposes includes the amount of country X tax that is imposed on C with respect to such interest income and that is paid on C's behalf by A pursuant to the loan agreement. Under paragraph (f)(2)(i) of this section, such tax is considered for purposes of section 903 to be paid by C. No such tax is considered paid by B.

Example (3). Country X imposes a tax called the "country X income tax." A, a United States person engaged in construction activities in country X, is subject to that tax. Country X has contracted with A for A to construct a naval base. A is a dual capacity taxpayer (as defined in paragraph (a)(2)(ii)(A) of this section) and, in accordance with paragraphs (a)(1) and (c)(1) of § 1.901-2A, A has established that the country X income tax as applied to dual capacity persons and the country X income tax as applied to persons other than dual capacity persons together constitute a single levy. A has also established that that levy is an income tax within the meaning of paragraph (a)(1) of this section. Pursuant to the terms of the contract, country X has agreed to assume any country X tax liability that A may incur with respect to A's income from the contract. For federal income tax purposes, A's income from the contract includes the amount of tax liability that is imposed by country X on A with respect to its income from the contract and that is assumed by country X; and for purposes of section 901 the amount of such tax liability assumed by country X is considered to be paid by A. By reason of paragraph (f)(2)(i) of this section, country X is not considered to provide a subsidy, within the meaning of paragraph (e)(3) of this section, to A.

(3) *Taxes paid on combined income.*—If foreign income tax is imposed on the combined income of two or more related persons (for example, a husband and wife or a corporation and one or more of its subsidiaries) and they are jointly and severally liable for the income tax under foreign law, foreign law is considered to impose legal liability on each such person for the amount of the foreign income tax that is attributable to its portion of the base of the tax, regardless of which person actually pays the tax.

(g) *Definitions.*—For purposes of this section and §§ 1.901-2A and 1.903-1, the following definitions apply:

(1) The term "paid" means "paid or accrued"; the term "payment" means "payment or accrual"; and the term "paid by" means "paid or accrued by or on behalf of."

(2) The term "foreign country" means any foreign state, any possession of the United States, and any political subdivision of any foreign state or of any possession of the United States. The term "possession of the United States" includes Puerto Rico, the Virgin Islands, Guam, the Northern Mariana Islands and American Samoa.

(3) The term "foreign levy" means a levy imposed by a foreign country.

(h) *Effective date.*—(1) *In general.*—This section, § 1.901-2A, and § 1.903-1 apply to taxable years beginning after November 14, 1983. In addition, a person may elect to apply the provisions of this section, § 1.901-2A, and § 1.903-1 to earlier years. See paragraph (h)(2) of this section.

(2) *Election to apply regulations to earlier years.*—(i) *Scope of election.*—An election to apply the provisions of this section, § 1.901-2A, and § 1.903-1 to taxable years beginning on or before November 14, 1983 is made with respect to one or more foreign states and possessions of the United States with respect to a taxable year of the person making the election beginning on or before November 14, 1983. Such election requires all of the provisions of this section, § 1.901-2A and § 1.903-1 to be applied to such taxable year and to all subsequent taxable

years of the person making the election ("elected years"). If an election applies to a foreign state or to a possession of the United States ("election country"), it applies to all taxes of the election country and to all taxes of all political subdivisions of the election country. An election does not apply to foreign taxes carried forward to any elected year from any taxable year to which the election does not apply. Such election does apply to foreign taxes carried back or forward from any elected year to any taxable year.

(ii) *Effect of election.*—An election to apply the regulations to earlier years has no effect on the limitations on assessment and collection or on the limitations on credit or refund (see Chapter 66 of the Internal Revenue Code).

(iii) *Manner of making election.*—An election to apply the regulations to one or more earlier taxable years is made by attaching a statement to a return, amended return, or claim for refund for the earliest taxable year to which the election relates. Such statement shall state that the election is made and, unless the election is to apply to all foreign countries, the statement shall designate the election countries. In the absence of such a designation of the election countries, all foreign countries shall be election countries.

(iv) *Time for making election.*—An election to apply the regulations to earlier taxable years must be made by October 12, 1984, except that if a person who has deducted (instead of credited) foreign taxes in its United States income tax return for such an earlier taxable year validly makes an election to credit (instead of deduct) such taxes in a timely filed amended return for such earlier taxable year and such amended return is filed after such date, an election to apply the regulations to such earlier taxable year must be made in such amended return.

(v) *Revocation of election.*—An election to apply the regulations to earlier taxable years may not be revoked.

(vi) *Affiliated groups.*—A member of an affiliated group that files a consolidated United States income tax return may apply the regulations to earlier years only if an election to so apply them has been made by the common parent of such affiliated group on behalf of all members of the group. [Reg. § 1.901-2.]

☐ [T.D. 7918, 10-6-83. Amended by T.D. 8372, 10-30-91.]

§ 1.901-2A. Dual capacity taxpayers.—
(a) *Application of separate levy rules as applied to dual capacity taxpayers.*—(1) *In general.*—If the application of a foreign levy (as defined in § 1.901-2(g)(3)) is different, either by the terms of the levy or in practice, for dual capacity taxpayers (as defined in § 1.901-2(a)(2)(ii)(A)) from its application to other persons, then, unless the only such difference is that a lower rate (but the same base) applies to dual capacity taxpayers, such difference is considered to be related to the fact that dual capacity taxpayers receive, directly or indirectly, a specific economic benefit (as defined in § 1.901-2(a)(2)(ii)(B)) from the foreign country and thus to be a difference in kind, and not merely of degree. In such a case, notwithstanding any contrary provision of § 1.901-2(d), the levy as applicable to such dual capacity taxpayers is a separate levy (within the meaning of § 1.901-2(d)) from the levy as applicable to such other persons, regardless of whether such difference is in the base of the levy, in the rate of the levy, or both. In such a case, each of the levy as applied to dual capacity taxpayers and the levy as applied to other persons must be analyzed separately to determine whether it is an income tax within the meaning of § 1.901-2(a)(1) and whether it is a tax in lieu of an income tax within the meaning of § 1.903-1(a). However, if the application of the levy is neither different by its terms nor different in practice for dual capacity taxpayers from its application to other persons, or if the only difference is that a lower rate (but the same base) applies to dual capacity taxpayers, then, in accordance with § 1.901-2(d), such foreign levy as applicable to dual capacity taxpayers and such levy as applicable to other persons together constitute a single levy. In such a case, no amount paid (as defined in § 1.901-2(g)(1)) pursuant to such levy by any such dual capacity taxpayer is considered to be paid in exchange for a specific economic benefit, and such levy, as applicable in the aggregate to such dual capacity taxpayers and to such other persons, is analyzed to determine whether it is an income tax within the meaning of § 1.901-2(a)(1) or a tax in lieu of an income tax within the meaning of § 1.903-1(a). Application of a foreign levy to dual capacity taxpayers will be considered to be different in practice from application of that levy to other persons, even if no such difference is apparent from the terms of the levy, unless it is established that application of that levy to dual capacity taxpayers does not differ in practice from its application to other persons.

(2) *Examples.*—The provisions of paragraph (a)(1) of this section may be illustrated by the following examples:

Example (1). Under a levy of country X called the country X income tax, every corporation that does business in country X is required to pay to country X 40% of its income from its business in country X. Income for purposes of the country X income tax is computed by subtracting specified deductions from the corporation's gross income derived from its business in country X. The specified deductions include the corporation's expenses attributable to such gross income and allowances for recovery of the cost of capital expenditures attributable to such gross income, except that under the terms of the country X income tax a corporation engaged in the exploitation of minerals K, L or M in country X is not permitted to recover, currently or in the future, expenditures it incurs in exploring for those minerals. In practice, the only corporations that engage in exploitation of the specified minerals in country X are dual capacity taxpayers. Thus, the application of the country X income tax to dual capacity taxpayers is different from its application to other corporations. The country X income tax as applied to corporations that engage in the exploitation of minerals K, L or M (dual capacity taxpayers) is, therefore, a separate levy from the country X income tax as applied to other corporations. Accordingly, each of (i) the country X income tax as applied to such dual capacity taxpayers and (ii) the country X income tax as applied to such other persons, must be analyzed separately to determine whether it is an income tax within the meaning of § 1.901-2(a)(1) and whether it is a tax in lieu of an income tax within the meaning of § 1.903-1(a).

Example (2). The facts are the same as in example (1), except that it is demonstrated that corporations that engage in exploitation of the specified minerals in country X and that are subject to the levy include both dual capacity taxpayers and other persons. The country X income tax as applied to all corporations is, therefore, a single levy. Accordingly, no amount paid pursuant to the country X income tax by a dual capacity taxpayer is considered to be paid in exchange for a specific economic benefit; and, if the country X income tax is an income tax within the meaning of § 1.901-2(a)(1) or a tax in lieu of an income tax within the meaning of § 1.903-1(a), it will be so considered in its entirety for all corporations subject to it.

Example (3). Under a levy of country Y called the country Y income tax, each corporation incorporated in country Y is required to pay to country Y a percentage of its worldwide income. The applicable percentage is greater for such corporations that earn more than a specified amount of income than for such corporations that earn less than that amount. Income for purposes of the levy is computed by deducting from gross income specified types of expenses and specified allowances for capital expenditures. The expenses for which deductions are permitted differ depending on the type of business in which the corporation subject to the levy is engaged, *e.g.,* a deduction for interest paid to a related party is not allowed for corporations engaged in enumerated types of activities. In addition, carryover of losses from one taxable period to another is permitted for corporations engaged in specified types of activities, but not for corporations engaged in other activities. By its terms, the foreign levy makes no distinction between dual capacity taxpayers and other persons. It is established that in practice the higher rate of the country Y income tax applies to both dual capacity taxpayers and other persons and that in practice the differences in the base of the country Y income tax (*e.g.,* the lack of a deduction for interest paid to related parties for some corporations subject to the levy and the lack of a carryover provision for some corporations subject to the levy) apply to both dual capacity taxpayers and other persons. The country Y income tax as applied to all corporations incorporated in country Y is therefore a single levy. Accordingly, no amount paid pursuant to the country Y income tax by a dual capacity taxpayer is considered to be paid in exchange for a specific economic benefit; and if the country Y income tax is an income tax within the meaning of § 1.901-2(a)(1) or a tax in lieu of an income tax within the meaning of § 1.903-1(a), it will be so considered in its entirety for all persons subject to it.

Example (4). The facts are the same as in example (3), except that it is not established that in practice the higher rate does not apply only to dual capacity taxpayers. By reason of such higher rate, application of the country Y income tax to dual capacity taxpayers is different in practice from application of the country Y income tax to other persons subject to it. The country Y income tax as applied to dual capacity taxpayers is therefore a separate levy from the country Y income tax as applied to other corporations incorporated in country Y. Accordingly, each of (i) the country Y income tax as applied to dual capacity taxpayers and (ii) the country Y income tax as applied to other corporations incorporated in country Y, must be analyzed separately to determine whether it is an income tax within the meaning of § 1.901-2(a)(1) and whether it is a tax in lieu of an income tax within the meaning of § 1.903-1(a).

Example (5). Under a levy of country X called the country X tax, all persons who do not engage in business in country X and who receive interest income from residents of country X are required to pay to country X 25 percent of the gross amount of such interest income. It is established that the country X tax applies by its terms and in practice to certain banks that are dual capacity taxpayers and to persons who are not dual capacity taxpayers and that application to such dual capacity taxpayers does not differ by its terms or in practice from application to such other persons. The country X tax as applied to all such persons (both the dual capacity taxpayers and the other persons) is, therefore, a single levy. Accordingly, no amount paid pursuant to the country X tax by such a dual capacity taxpayer is considered to be paid in exchange for a specific economic benefit; and, if the country X tax is a tax in lieu of an income tax within the meaning of § 1.903-1(a), it will be so considered in its entirety for all persons subject to it.

Example (6). Under a levy of country X called the country X tax, every corporation incorporated outside of country X ("foreign corporation") that maintains a branch in country X is required annually to pay to country X 52 percent of its net income attributable to that branch. It is established that the application of the country X tax is neither different by its terms nor different in practice for certain banks that are dual capacity taxpayers from its application to persons (which may, but do not necessarily, include other banks) that are not dual capacity taxpayers. The country X tax as applied to all foreign corporations with branches in country X (*i.e.,* both those banks that are dual capacity taxpayers and the foreign corporations that are not dual capacity taxpayers) is, therefore, a single levy. Accordingly, no amount paid pursuant to the country X tax by a bank that is a dual capacity taxpayer is considered to be paid in exchange for a specific economic benefit; and, if the country X tax is an income tax within the meaning of § 1.901-2(a)(1) or a tax in lieu of an income tax within the meaning of § 1.903-1(a), it will be so considered in its entirety for all persons subject to it.

Example (7). Under a levy of country H called the country H tax, all corporations that are organized outside country H and that do not engage in business in country H are required to pay to country H a percentage of the gross amount of interest income derived from residents of country H. The percentage is 30 percent, except that it is 15 percent for a specified category of corporations. All corporations in that category are dual capacity taxpayers. It is established that the country H tax applies by its terms and in practice to dual capacity taxpayers and to persons that are not dual capacity taxpayers and that the only difference in application between such dual capacity taxpayers and such other persons is that a lower rate (but the same base) applies to such dual capacity taxpayers. The country H tax as applied to all such persons (both the dual capacity taxpayers and the other persons) is, therefore, a single levy. Accordingly, no amount paid pursuant to the country H tax by such a dual capacity taxpayer is considered to be paid in exchange for a specific economic benefit, and if the country H tax is a tax in lieu of an income tax within the meaning of § 1.903-1(a), it will be so considered in its entirety for all persons subject to it.

(b) *Burden of proof for dual capacity taxpayers.*—(1) *In general.*—For credit to be allowable under section 901 or 903, the person claiming credit must establish that the foreign levy with respect to which credit is claimed is an income tax within the meaning of § 1.901-2(a)(1) or a tax in lieu of an income tax within the meaning of § 1.903-1(a), respectively. Thus, such person must establish, among other things, that such levy is a tax. See § 1.901-2(a)(2)(i) and § 1.903-1(a). Where a person claims credit under section 901 or 903 for an amount paid by a dual capacity taxpayer pursuant to a foreign levy, § 1.901-2(a)(2)(i) and § 1.903-1(a), respectively, require such person to establish the amount, if any, that is paid pursuant to the distinct element of the levy that is a tax. If, pursuant to paragraph (a)(1) of this section and § 1.901-2(d), such levy as applicable to dual capacity taxpayers and such levy as applicable to other persons together constitute a single levy, then no amount paid pursuant to that levy by any such dual capacity taxpayer is considered to be paid in exchange for a specific economic benefit. Accordingly, such levy has only one distinct element, and the levy either is or is not, in its entirety, a tax. If, however, such levy as applicable to dual capacity taxpayers is a separate levy from such levy as applicable to other persons, then a person claiming credit under section 901 or 903 for an amount paid by a dual capacity taxpayer pursuant to such separate levy may establish the amount, if any, that is paid pursuant to the distinct element of the levy that is a tax only by the facts and circumstances method or the safe harbor method described in paragraph (c) of this section. If such person fails to so establish such amount, no portion of the amount that is paid pursuant to the separate levy by the dual capacity taxpayer to such foreign country shall be treated as an amount of tax. Any amount that, either by reason of application of the methods of paragraph (c) of this section or by reason of the immediately preceding sentence, is not treated as an amount of tax shall (i) be considered to have been paid in exchange for a specific economic benefit; (ii) be characterized (*e.g.,* as royalty, purchase price, cost of sales, reduction of the proceeds of a sale, or reduction of interest income) according to the nature of the transaction and of the specific economic benefit received; and (iii) be treated according to such characterization for all purposes of Chapter 1 of the Internal Revenue Code, except that any determination that an amount is not tax for purposes of section 901 or 903 by reason of application of the safe harbor method shall not be taken into account in determining whether or not such an amount is to be characterized and treated as tax for purposes of computing an allowance for percentage depletion under sections 611 and 613.

(2) *Effect of certain treaties.*—If, irrespective of whether such credit would be allowable under section 901 or 903 in the absence of a treaty, the United States has in force a treaty with a foreign country that treats a foreign levy as an income tax for purposes of allowing credit for United States tax and if the person claiming credit is entitled to the benefit of such treaty, then, unless such person claims credit not under the treaty but under section 901 or 903, and except to the extent the treaty provides otherwise and subject to all terms, conditions and limitations provided in the treaty, no portion of an amount paid with respect to such levy by a dual capacity taxpayer shall be considered to be paid in exchange for a specific economic benefit. If, however, such person claims credit not under such treaty but rather under section 901 or 903 (*e.g.,* so as not to be subject to a limitation contained in such treaty), the provisions of this section apply to such levy.

(c) *Satisfaction of burden of proof.*—(1) *In general.*—This paragraph (c) sets out the methods by which a person who claims credit under section 901 or 903 for an amount paid by a dual capacity taxpayer pursuant to a foreign levy that satisfies all of the criteria of section 901 or 903 other than the determination of the distinct element of the levy that is a tax and of the amount that is paid pursuant to that distinct element (a "qualifying levy") may establish such distinct element and amount. Such person must establish the amount paid pursuant to a qualifying levy that is paid pursuant to the distinct element of the levy that is a tax (which amount therefore is an amount of income tax within the meaning of § 1.901-2(a)(1) or an amount of tax in lieu of income tax within the meaning of § 1.903-1(a) (a "qualifying amount")) only by the facts and circumstances method set forth in paragraph (c)(2) of this section or the safe harbor method set forth in paragraph (c)(3) of this section. A levy is not a qualifying levy, and neither the facts and circumstances method nor the safe harbor method applies to an amount paid by a dual capacity taxpayer pursuant to a foreign levy, if it has been established pursuant to § 1.901-2(d) and paragraph (a)(1) of this section that that levy as applied to that dual capacity taxpayer and that levy as applied to persons other than dual capacity taxpayers together constitute a single levy, or if it has been established in accordance with the first sentence of paragraph (b)(2) of this section that credit is allowable by reason of a treaty for an amount paid with respect to such levy.

(2) *Facts and circumstances method.*—(i) *In general.*—If the person claiming credit establishes, based on all of the relevant facts and circumstances, the amount, if any, paid by the dual capacity taxpayer pursuant to the qualifying levy that is not paid in exchange for a specific economic benefit, such amount is the qualifying amount with respect to such qualifying levy. In determining the qualifying amount with respect to a qualifying levy under the facts and circumstances method, neither the methodology nor the results that would have obtained if a person had elected to apply the safe harbor method to such qualifying levy is a relevant fact or circumstance. Accordingly, neither such methodology nor such results shall be taken into account in applying the facts and circumstances method.

(ii) *Examples.*—The application of the facts and circumstances method is illustrated by the following examples:

Example (1). Country A, which does not have a generally imposed income tax, imposes a levy, called the country A income tax, on corporations that carry on the banking business through a branch in country A. All such corporations lend money to the government of country A, and the consideration (interest) paid by the government of country A for the loans is not made available by the government on substantially the same terms to the population of country A in general. Thus, the country A income tax is imposed only on dual capacity taxpayers. L, a corporation that carries on the banking business through a branch in country A and that is a dual capacity taxpayer, establishes that all of the criteria of section 901 are satisfied by the country A income tax, except for the determination of the distinct element of the levy that is a tax and of *L*'s qualifying amount with respect thereto. The country A income tax is, therefore, a qualifying levy. *L* establishes that, although all persons subject to the country A income tax are dual capacity taxpayers, the country A income tax applies in the same manner to income from such persons' transactions with the government of country A as it does to income from their transactions with private persons; that there are significant transactions (either in volume or in amount) with private persons; and that the portion of such persons' income that is derived from transactions with the government of country A on the one hand or private persons on the other varies greatly among persons subject to the country A income tax. By making this showing, L has demonstrated that no portion of the amount paid by it to country A pursuant to the levy is paid in exchange for a specific economic benefit (the interest income). Accordingly, L has demonstrated under the facts and circumstances method that the entire amount it has paid pursuant to the country A income tax is a qualifying amount.

Example (2). A, a domestic corporation that is a dual capacity taxpayer subject to a qualifying levy of country X, pays 1000u (units of country X currency) to country X in 1986 pursuant to the qualifying levy. A does not elect to apply the safe harbor method to country X, but if it had so elected, 800u would have been A's qualifying amount with respect to the levy. Based on all of the relevant facts and circumstances (which do not include either the methodology of the safe harbor method or the qualifying amount that would have obtained under that method), A establishes that 628u of such 1000u is not paid in exchange for a specific economic benefit. A has demonstrated under the facts and circumstances method that 628u is a qualifying amount. Pursuant to paragraph (b)(1) of this section, 372u (1000u − 628u) is considered to have been paid by A in exchange for a specific economic benefit. That amount is characterized and treated as provided in paragraph (b)(1) of this section.

Example (3). The facts are the same as in example (2), except that under the safe harbor method 580u would have been A's qualifying amount with respect to the levy. That amount is not a relevant fact or circumstance and the result is the same as in example (2).

(3) *Safe harbor method.*—Under the safe harbor method, the person claiming credit makes an election as provided in paragraph (d) of this section and, pursuant to such election, applies the safe harbor formula described in paragraph (e) of this section to the qualifying levy or levies to which the election applies.

(d) *Election to use the safe harbor method.*— (1) *Scope of election.*—An election to use the safe harbor method is made with respect to one or more foreign states and possessions of the United States with respect to a taxable year of the person making the election (the "electing person"). Such election applies to such taxable year and to all subsequent taxable years of the electing person ("election years"), unless the election is revoked in accordance with paragraph (d)(4) of this section. If an election applies to a foreign state or possession of the United States ("elected country"), it applies to all qualifying levies of the elected country and to all qualifying levies of all political subdivisions of the elected country with respect to which the electing person claims credit for amounts paid (or deemed to be paid) by any dual capacity taxpayer. A member of an affiliated group that files a consolidated United States income tax return may use the safe harbor method for a foreign state or U.S. possession only if an election to use the safe harbor method for that state or possession has been made by the common parent of such affiliated group on behalf of all members of the group. Similarly, a member of an affiliated group that does not file a consolidated United States income tax return may elect to use the safe harbor method for a foreign state or U.S. possession only if an election to use the safe harbor method for that state or possession is made by each member of the affiliated group which claims credit for taxes paid to such state or possession or to any political subdivision thereof. An election to use the safe harbor method for an elected country does not apply to foreign taxes carried back or forward to any election year from any taxable year to which the election does not apply. Such election does apply to foreign taxes carried back or forward from any election year to any taxable year. A person who elects to use the safe harbor method for one or more foreign countries may, in a later taxable year, also elect to use that method for other foreign countries.

(2) *Effect of election.*—An election to use the safe harbor method described in paragraph (c)(3) of this section requires the electing person to apply the safe harbor formula of paragraph (e) of this section to all qualifying levies of all elected countries and their political subdivisions, and constitutes a specific waiver by such person of the right to use the facts and circumstances method described in paragraph (c)(2) of this section with respect to any levy of any elected country or any political subdivision thereof.

(3) *Time and manner of making election.*— (i) *In general.*—To elect to use the safe harbor method, an electing person must attach a statement to its United States income tax return for the taxable year for which the election is made and must file such return by the due date (including extensions) for the filing thereof. Such statement shall state that the electing person elects to use the safe harbor method for the foreign states and the possessions of the United States designated in the statement and their political subdivisions, and that the electing person waives the right, for any election year, to use the facts and circumstances method for any levy of the designated states, possessions and political subdivisions. Notwithstanding the foregoing, a person may, with the consent of the Commissioner, elect to use the safe harbor method for a taxable year for one or more foreign states or possessions of the

United States, at a date later than that specified in the first sentence of this paragraph (d)(3)(i), *e.g.,* upon audit of such person's United States income tax return for such taxable year. The Commissioner will normally consent to such a later election if such person demonstrates that it failed to make a timely election for such a foreign state or possession for such taxable year because such person reasonably believed either that it was not a dual capacity taxpayer with respect to such state or possession or that no levy that it paid to such state or possession or any political subdivision thereof was a qualifying levy (for example, because it reasonably, but incorrectly, believed that the levy it paid was not a separate levy from that applicable to persons other than dual capacity taxpayers). The Commissioner will not, however, consent to such a later election with respect to any state or possession for a taxable year if such person (or any other member of an affiliated group of which such person is a member) applied the facts and circumstances method to any levy of such state or possession or any political subdivision thereof for such taxable year.

(ii) *Certain retroactive elections.*—Notwithstanding the requirements of paragraph (d)(3)(i) of this section relating to the time and manner of making an election, an election may be made for a taxable year beginning on or before November 14, 1983, provided the electing person elects in accordance with § 1.901-2(h) to apply all of the provisions of this section, § 1.901-2 and § 1.903-1 to such taxable year and provided all of the requirements set forth in this paragraph (d)(3)(ii) are satisfied. Such an election shall be made by timely (including extensions) filing a federal income tax return or an amended federal income tax return for such taxable year; by attaching to such return a statement containing the statements and information set forth in paragraph (d)(3)(i) of this section; and by filing amended income tax returns for all subsequent election years for which income tax returns have previously been filed in which credit is claimed under section 901 or 903 and applying the safe harbor method in such amended returns. All amended returns referred to in the immediately preceding sentence must be filed on or before October 12, 1984 and at a time when neither assessment of a deficiency for any of such election years nor the filing of a claim for any refund claimed in any such amended return is barred.

(iii) *Election to credit taxes made in amended return.*—If a person has filed a United States income tax return for a taxable year to which this § 1.901-2A applies (including application by reason of the election provided in § 1.901-2(h)(2)) in which such person has deducted (instead of credited) qualifying foreign taxes and such person validly makes an election to credit (instead of deduct) such taxes in a timely filed amended return for such taxable year, an election to use the safe harbor method may be made in such amended return provided all of the requirements of paragraph (d)(3)(ii) of this section are satisfied other than the requirement that such amended return and the other amended returns referred to in that paragraph be filed on or before October 12, 1984.

(4) *Revocation of election.*—An election to use the safe harbor method described in paragraph (c)(3) of this section may not be revoked without the consent of the Commissioner. An application for consent to revoke such election with respect to one or more elected countries shall be made to the Commissioner of Internal Revenue, Washington, D.C. 20224. Such application shall be made not later than the 30th day before the due date (including extensions) for the filing of the income tax return for the first taxable year for which the revocation is sought to be effective, except in the case of an event described in (i), (ii), (iii) or (iv) below, in which case an application for revocation with retroactive effect may be made within a reasonable time after such event. The Commissioner may make his consent to any revocation conditioned upon adjustments being made in one or more taxable years so as to prevent the revocation from resulting in a distortion of the amount of any item relating to tax liability in any taxable year. The Commissioner will normally consent to a revocation (including, in the case of (i), (ii), (iii) or (iv) below, one with retroactive effect), if—

(i) An amendment to the Internal Revenue Code or the regulations thereunder is made which applies to the taxable year for which the revocation is to be effective and the amendment substantially affects the taxation of income from sources outside the United States under subchapter N of Chapter 1 of the Internal Revenue Code; or

(ii) After a safe harbor election is made with respect to a foreign state, a tax treaty between the United States and that state enters into force; that treaty covers a foreign tax to which the safe harbor election applies; and that treaty applies to the taxable year for which the revocation is to be effective; or

(iii) After a safe harbor election is made with respect to a foreign state or possession of the United States, a material change is made in the tax law of that state or possession or of a political subdivision of that state or possession; and the changed law applies to the taxable year for which the revocation is to be effective and has a material effect on the taxpayer; or

Reg. § 1.901-2A(d)(4)(iii)

(iv) With respect to a foreign country to which a safe harbor election applies, the Internal Revenue Service issues a letter ruling to the electing person and that letter ruling (A) relates to the availability or application of the safe harbor method to one or more levies of such foreign country; (B) does not relate to the facts and circumstances method described in paragraph (c)(2) of this section; and (C) fails to include a ruling requested by the electing person or includes a ruling contrary to one requested by such person (in either case, other than one relating to the facts and circumstances method) and such failure or inclusion has a material adverse effect on the amount of such electing person's credit for taxes paid to such foreign country for the taxable year for which the revocation is to be effective; or

(v) A corporation ("new member") becomes a member of an affiliated group; the new member and one or more pre-existing members of such group are dual capacity taxpayers with respect to the same foreign country; and, with respect to such country, either the new member or the pre-existing members (but not both) have made a safe harbor election; and the Commissioner in his discretion determines that obtaining the benefit of the right to revoke the safe harbor election with respect to such foreign country was not the principal purpose of the affiliation between such new member and such group; or

(vi) The election has been in effect with respect to at least three taxable years prior to the taxable year for which the revocation is to be effective.

The Commissioner may, in his discretion, consent to a revocation even if none of the foregoing subdivisions (i) through (vi) is applicable. If an election has been revoked with respect to an elected country, a subsequent election to apply the safe harbor method with respect to such elected country may be made only with the consent of the Commissioner and upon such terms and conditions as the Commissioner in his discretion may require.

(e) *Safe harbor formula.*—(1) *In general.*— The safe harbor formula applies to determine the distinct element of a qualifying levy that is a tax and the amount paid by a dual capacity taxpayer pursuant to such qualifying levy that is the qualifying amount with respect to such levy. Under the safe harbor formula the amount paid in a taxable year pursuant to a qualifying levy that is the qualifying amount with respect to such levy is an amount equal to:

$$(A - B - C) \times D/(1 - D)$$

where (except as otherwise provided in paragraph (e)(5) of this section):

A = the amount of gross receipts as determined under paragraph (e)(2) of this section

B = the amount of costs and expenses as determined under paragraph (e)(2) of this section

C = the total amount paid in the taxable year by the dual capacity taxpayer pursuant to the qualifying levy (the "actual payment amount")

D = the tax rate as determined under paragraph (e)(3) of this section

In no case, however, shall the qualifying amount exceed the actual payment amount; and the qualifying amount is zero if the safe harbor formula yields a qualifying amount less than zero. The safe harbor formula is intended to yield a qualifying amount that is approximately equal to the amount of generally imposed income tax within the meaning of paragraphs (a) and (b)(1) of §1.903-1 ("general tax") of the foreign country that would have been required to be paid in the taxable year by the dual capacity taxpayer if it had not been a dual capacity taxpayer and if the base of the general tax had allowed a deduction in such year for the amount ("specific economic benefit amount") by which the actual payment amount exceeds the qualifying amount. See, however, paragraph (e)(5) of this section if an elected country has no general tax. The specific economic benefit amount is considered to be the portion of the actual payment amount that is paid pursuant to the distinct portion of the qualifying levy that imposes an obligation in exchange for a specific economic benefit. The specific economic benefit amount is therefore considered to be an amount paid by the dual capacity taxpayer in exchange for such specific economic benefit, which amount must be treated for purposes of Chapter 1 of the Internal Revenue Code as provided in paragraph (b)(1) of this section.

(2) *Determination of gross receipts and costs and expenses.*—For purposes of the safe harbor formula, gross receipts and costs and expenses are, except as otherwise provided in this paragraph (e), the gross receipts and the deductions for costs and expenses, respectively, as determined under the foreign law applicable in computing the actual payment amount of the qualifying levy to which the safe harbor formula applies. However, except as otherwise provided in this paragraph (e), if provisions of the qualifying levy increase or decrease the liability imposed on dual capacity taxpayers compared to the general tax liability of persons other than dual capacity taxpayers by reason of the determination or treatment of gross receipts or of costs or expenses, the provisions generally applicable in computing

such other persons' tax base under the general tax shall apply to determine gross receipts and costs and expenses for purposes of computing the qualifying amount. If provisions of the qualifying levy relating to gross receipts meet the requirements of § 1.901-2(b)(3)(i), such provisions shall apply to determine gross receipts for purposes of computing the qualifying amount. If neither the general tax nor the qualifying levy permits recovery of one or more costs or expenses, and by reason of the failure to permit such recovery the qualifying levy does not satisfy the net income requirement of § 1.901-2(b)(4) (even though the general tax does satisfy that requirement), then such cost or expense shall be considered a cost or expense for purposes of computing the qualifying amount. If the qualifying levy does not permit recovery of one or more significant costs or expenses, but provides allowances that effectively compensate for nonrecovery of such significant costs or expenses, then, for purposes of computing the qualifying amount, costs and expenses shall not include the costs and expenses under the general tax whose nonrecovery under the qualifying levy is compensated for by such allowances but shall instead include such allowances. In determining costs and expenses for purposes of computing the qualifying amount with respect to a qualifying levy, the actual payment amount with respect to such levy shall not be considered a cost or expense. For purposes of this paragraph, the following differences in gross receipts and costs and expenses between the qualifying levy and the general tax shall not be considered to increase the liability imposed on dual capacity taxpayers compared to the general tax liability of persons other than dual capacity taxpayers, but only if the general tax would be an income tax within the meaning of § 1.901-2(a)(1) if such different treatment under the qualifying levy had also applied under the general tax:

(i) Differences in the time of realization or recognition of one or more items of income or in the time when recovery of one or more costs and expenses is allowed (unless the period of recovery of such costs and expenses pursuant to the qualifying levy is such that it effectively is a denial of recovery of such costs and expenses, as described in § 1.901-2(b)(4)(i)); and

(ii) Differences in consolidation or carryover provisions of the types described in paragraphs (b)(4)(ii) and (b)(4)(iii) of § 1.901-2.

(3) *Determination of tax rate.*—The tax rate for purposes of the safe harbor formula is the tax rate (expressed as a decimal) that is applicable in computing tax liability under the general tax. If the rate of the general tax varies according to the amount of the base of that tax, the rate to be applied in computing the qualifying amount is the rate that applies under the general tax to a person whose base is, using the terminology of paragraph (e)(1) of this section, "A" minus "B" minus the specific economic benefit amount paid by the dual capacity taxpayer pursuant to the qualifying levy, provided such rate applies in practice to persons other than dual capacity taxpayers, or, if such rate does not so apply in practice, the next lowest rate of the general tax that does so apply in practice.

(4) *Determination of applicable provisions of general tax.*—(i) *In general.*—If the general tax is a series of income taxes (*e.g.,* on different types of income), or if the application of the general tax differs by its terms for different classes of persons subject to the general tax (*e.g.,* for persons in different industries), then, except as otherwise provided in this paragraph (e), the qualifying amount shall be computed by reference to the income tax contained in such series of income taxes, or in the case of such different applications the application of the general tax, that by its terms and in practice imposes the highest tax burden on persons other than dual capacity taxpayers. Notwithstanding the preceding sentence, the general tax amount shall be computed by reference to the application of the general tax to entities of the same type (as determined under the general tax) as the dual capacity taxpayer and to persons of the same resident or nonresident status (as determined under the general tax) as the dual capacity taxpayer; and, if the general tax treats business income differently from non-business (*e.g.,* investment) income (as determined under the general tax), the dual capacity taxpayer's business and non-business income shall be treated as the general tax treats such income. If, for example, the dual capacity taxpayer would, under the general tax, be treated as a resident (*e.g.,* because the general tax treats an entity that is organized in the foreign country or managed or controlled there as a resident) and as a corporation (*i.e.,* because the rules of the general tax treat an entity like the dual capacity taxpayer as a corporation), and if some of the dual capacity taxpayer's income would, under the general tax, be treated as business income and some as non-business income, the dual capacity taxpayer and its income shall be so treated in computing the qualifying amount.

(ii) *Establishing that provisions apply in practice.*—For purposes of the safe harbor formula a provision (including tax rate) shall be considered a provision of the general tax only if it is reasonably likely that that provision applies by its terms and in practice to persons other than dual capacity taxpayers. In general, it will be assumed that a provision (including tax rate) that by its terms applies to persons other than dual capacity taxpayers is reasonably likely to apply in practice to such other persons, unless the person claiming credit knows or has reason to know otherwise. However, in cases of doubt, the person claiming credit may be required to demonstrate that such provision is reasonably likely so to apply in practice.

(5) *No general tax.*—If a foreign country does not impose a general tax (and thus a levy, in order to be a qualifying levy must satisfy all of the criteria of section 901 (because section 903 cannot apply, other than the determination of the distinct element of the levy that is a tax and of the amount that is paid pursuant to that distinct element), paragraphs (e)(2), (3) and (4) of this section to not apply to a qualifying levy of such country, and the terms of the safe harbor formula set forth in paragraph (e)(1) of this section are defined with respect to such levy as follows:

A = the amount of gross receipts as determined under the qualifying levy;
B = the amount of deductions for costs and expenses as determined under the qualifying levy;
C = the actual payment amount; and
D = the lower of the rate of the qualifying levy, or the rate of tax specified in section 11(b)(5) (or predecessor or successor section, as the case may be) of the Internal Revenue Code as applicable to the taxable year in which the actual payment amount is paid.

(6) *Certain taxes in lieu of an income tax.*—To the extent a tax in lieu of an income tax (within the meaning of § 1.903-1(a)) that applies in practice to persons other than dual capacity taxpayers would actually have been required to be paid in the taxable year by a dual capacity taxpayer if it had not been a dual capacity taxpayer (*e.g.,* in substitution for the general tax with respect to a type of income, such as interest income, dividend income, royalty income, insurance income), such tax in lieu of an income tax shall be treated as if it were an application of the general tax for purposes of applying the safe harbor formula of this paragraph (e) to such dual capacity taxpayer, and such formula shall be applied to yield a qualifying amount that is approximately equal to the general tax (so defined) that would have been required to be paid in the taxable year by such dual capacity taxpayer if the base of such general tax had allowed a deduction in such year for the specific economic benefit amount.

(7) *Multiple levies.*—If, in any election year of an electing person, with respect to any elected country and all of its political subdivisions,

(i) Amounts are paid by a dual capacity taxpayer pursuant to more than one qualifying levy or pursuant to one or more levies that are qualifying levies and one or more levies that are not qualifying levies by reason of the last sentence of paragraph (c)(1) of this section but with respect to which credit is allowable, or

(ii) More than one general tax (including a tax treated as if it were an application of the general tax under paragraph (e)(6)) would have been required to be paid by a dual capacity taxpayer (or taxpayers) if it (or they) had not been a dual capacity taxpayer (or taxpayers), or

(iii) Credit is claimed with respect to amounts paid by more than one dual capacity taxpayer,

the provisions of this paragraph (e) shall be applied such that the aggregate qualifying amount with respect to such qualifying levy or levies plus the aggregate amount paid with respect to levies referred to in (e)(7)(i) that are not qualifying levies shall be the aggregate amount that would have been required to be paid in the taxable year by such dual capacity taxpayer (or taxpayers) pursuant to such general tax or taxes if it (or they) had not been a dual capacity taxpayer (or taxpayers) and if the base of such general tax or taxes had allowed a deduction in such year for the aggregate specific economic benefit amount (except that, if paragraph (e)(5) applies to any levy of such elected country or any political subdivision thereof, the aggregate qualifying amount for qualifying levies of such elected country and all of its political subdivisions plus the aggregate amount paid with respect to levies referred to in paragraph (e)(7)(i) that are not qualifying levies shall not exceed the greater of the aggregate amount paid with respect to levies referred to in paragraph (e)(7)(i) that are not qualifying levies and the amount determined in accordance with paragraph (e)(5) where "D" is the rate of tax specified in section 11(b)(5) (or predecessor or successor section, as the case may be) of the Internal Revenue Code as applicable to the taxable year in which the actual payment amount is paid). However, in no event shall such aggregate amount exceed the aggregate actual payment amount plus the aggregate amount paid with respect to levies referred to in (e)(7)(i) that are not qualifying levies, nor be less than the aggregate amount paid with respect to levies referred to in (e)(7)(i) that are not qualifying levies. In applying (e)(7)(ii) a person who is not subject to a levy but who is considered to receive a specific economic benefit by reason of § 1.901-2(a)(2)(ii)(E) shall be treated as a dual capacity taxpayer. See example (12) in paragraph (e)(8) of this section.

(8) *Examples.*—The provisions of this paragraph (e) may be illustrated by the following examples:

Example (1). Under a levy of country X called the country X income tax, every corporation that does business in country X is required to pay to country X 40% of its income from its business in country X. Income for purposes of the country X income tax is computed by subtracting specified deductions from the corporation's gross income derived from its business in country X. The specified deductions include the corporation's expenses attributable to such gross income and allowances for recovery of the cost of capital expenditures attributable to such gross income, except that under the terms of the country X income tax a corporation engaged in the exploitation of minerals K, L or M in country X is not permitted to recover, currently or in the future, expenditures it incurs in exploring for those minerals. Under the terms of the country X income tax interest is not deductible to the extent it exceeds an arm's length amount (*e.g.,* if the loan to which the interest relates is not in accordance with normal commercial practice or to the extent the interest rate exceeds an arm's length rate). In practice, the only corporations that engage in exploitation of the specified minerals in country X are dual capacity taxpayers. Because no other persons subject to the levy engage in exploitation of minerals K, L or M in country X, the application of the country X income tax to dual capacity taxpayers is different from its application to other corporations. The country X income tax as applied to corporations that engage in the exploitation of minerals K, L or M (dual capacity taxpayers) is, therefore, a separate levy from the country X income tax as applied to other corporations.

A is a U.S. corporation that is engaged in country X in exploitation of mineral K. Natural deposits of mineral K in country X are owned by country X, and *A* has been allowed to extract mineral K in consideration of payment of a bonus and of royalties to an instrumentality of country X. Therefore, *A* is a dual capacity taxpayer. In 1984, *A* does business in country X within the meaning of the levy. *A* has validly elected the safe harbor method for country X for 1984. In 1984, as determined in accordance with the country X income tax as applied to *A*, *A* has gross receipts of 120u (units of country X currency), deducts 20u of costs and expenses, and pays 40u (40% of (120u − 20u)) to country X pursuant to the levy. *A* also incurs in 1984 10u of nondeductible expenditures for exploration for mineral K and 2u of nondeductible interest costs attributable to an advance of funds from a related party to finance an undertaking relating to the exploration for mineral K for which normal commercial financing was unavailable because of the substantial risk inherent in the undertaking. *A* establishes that the country X income tax as applied to persons other than dual capacity taxpayers is an income tax within the meaning of § 1.901-2(a)(1), that it is the generally imposed income tax of country X and hence the general tax, and that all of the criteria of section 903 are satisfied with respect to the country X income tax as applied to dual capacity taxpayers, except for the determination of the distinct element of the levy that is a tax and of *A*'s qualifying amount with respect thereto. (No conclusion is reached whether the country X income tax as applied to dual capacity taxpayers is an income tax within the meaning of § 1.901-2(a)(1). Such a determination would require, among other things, that the country X income tax as so applied, judged on the basis of its predominant character, meets the net income requirement of § 1.901-2(b)(4) notwithstanding its failure to permit recovery of exploration expenses.) *A* has therefore demonstrated that the country X income tax as applied to dual capacity taxpayers is a qualifying levy.

In applying the safe harbor formula, in accordance with paragraph (e)(2), the amount of *A*'s costs and expenses includes the 10u of nondeductible exploration expenses. The failure to permit recovery of interest in excess of arm's length amounts, a provision of both the general tax and the qualifying levy, does not cause the qualifying levy to fail to satisfy the net income requirement of § 1.901-2(b)(4); therefore, the amount of *A*'s cost and expenses does not include the 2u of nondeductible interest costs. Thus, under the safe harbor method, *A*'s qualifying amount with respect to the levy is 33.33u ((120u − 30u − 40u) × .40/(1 − .40)). *A*'s specific economic benefit amount is 6.67u (*A*'s actual payment amount (40u) less *A*'s qualifying amount (33.33u)). Under paragraph (a) of this section, this 6.67u is considered to be consideration paid by *A* for the right to extract mineral K. Pursuant to paragraph (b) of this section, this amount is characterized according to the nature of *A*'s transactions with country X and its instrumentality and of the specific economic benefit received (the right to extract mineral K), as an additional royalty or other business expense paid or accrued by *A* and is so treated for all purposes of Chapter 1 of the Internal Revenue Code, except that if an allowance for percentage depletion is allowable to *A* under sections 611 and 613 with respect to *A*'s interest in mineral K, the determination whether this 6.67u is tax or royalty for purposes of computing the amount of such allowance shall be made under sections 611 and 613 without regard to the determination that under the safe harbor formula such 6.67u is not tax for purposes of section 901 or 903.

Example (2). Under a levy of country Y called the country Y income tax, each corporation incorporated in country Y is required to pay to country Y a percentage of its worldwide income. The applicable percentage is 40 percent of the first 1,000u (units of country Y currency) of income and 50 percent of income in excess of 1,000u. Income for purposes of the levy is computed by deducting from gross income specified types of expenses and specified allowances for capital expenditures. The expenses for which deductions are permitted differ depending on the type of business in which the corporation subject to the levy is engaged, *e.g.,* a deduction for interest paid to a related party is not allowed for corporations engaged in enumerated types of activities. In addition, carryover of losses from one taxable period to another is permitted for corporations engaged in specified types of activities, but not for corporations engaged in other activities. By its terms, the foreign levy makes no distinction between dual capacity taxpayers and other persons. In practice the differences in the base of the country Y income tax (*e.g.,* the lack of a deduction for interest paid to related parties for some corporations subject to the levy and the lack of a carryover provision for some corporations subject to the levy) apply to both dual capacity taxpayers and other persons, but the 50 percent rate applies only to dual capacity taxpayers. By reason of such higher rate, application of the country Y income tax to dual capacity taxpayers is different in practice from application of the country Y income tax to other persons subject to it. The country Y income tax as applied to dual capacity taxpayers is therefore a separate levy from the country Y income tax as applied to other corporations incorporated in country Y.

B is a corporation incorporated in country Y that is engaged in construction activities in country Y. B has a contract with the government of country Y to build a hospital in country Y for a fee that is not made available on substantially the same terms to substantially all persons who are subject to the general tax of country X. Accordingly, B is a dual capacity taxpayer. B has validly elected the safe harbor method for country Y for 1985. In 1985, as determined in accordance with the country Y income tax as applied to B, B has gross receipts of 10,000u, deducts 6,000u of costs and expenses, and pays 1900u ((1,000u × 40%) + (3,000u × 50%)) to Country Y pursuant to the levy.

It is assumed that B has established that the country Y income tax as applied to persons other than dual capacity taxpayers is an income tax within the meaning of § 1.901-2(a)(1) and is the general tax. It is further assumed that B has demonstrated that all of the criteria of section 901 are satisfied with respect to the country Y income tax as applied to dual capacity taxpayers, except for the determination of the distinct element of such levy that is a tax and of B's qualifying amount with respect to that levy, and therefore that the country Y income tax as applied to dual capacity taxpayers is a qualifying levy.

In applying the safe harbor formula, in accordance with paragraph (e)(3), the 50 percent rate is not used because it does not apply in practice to persons other than dual capacity taxpayers. The next lowest rate of the general tax that does apply in practice to such persons, 40 percent, is used. Accordingly, under the safe harbor formula, B's qualifying amount with respect to the levy is 1400u ((10,000u − 6000u − 1900u) × .40/(1 − .40)). B's specific economic benefit amount is 500u (B's actual payment amount (1900u) less B's qualifying amount (1400u)). Pursuant to paragraph (b) of this section, B's specific economic benefit amount is characterized according to the nature of B's transactions with country Y and of the specific economic benefit received, as a reduction of B's proceeds of its contract with country Y; and this amount is so treated for all purposes of Chapter 1 of the Code, including the computation of B's accumulated profits for purposes of section 902.

Example (3). The facts are the same as in example (2), with the following additional facts: The contract between B and country Y is a cost plus contract. One of the costs of the contract which country Y is required to pay or for which it is required to reimburse B is any tax of country Y on B's income or receipts from the contract. Instead of reimbursing B therefor, country Y agrees with B to assume any such tax liability. Under country Y tax law, B is not considered to have additional income or receipts by reason of country Y's assumption of B's country Y tax liability. In 1985, B's gross receipts of 10,000u include 3000u from the contract, and its costs and expenses of 6000u include 2000u attributable to the contract. B's other gross receipts and expenses do not relate to any transaction in which B receives a specific economic benefit. In accordance with the contract, country Y, and not B, is required to bear the amount of B's country Y income tax liability on B's 1000u (3000u − 2000u) income from the contract. In accordance with the contract B computes its country Y income tax without taking this 1000u into account and therefore pays 1400u ((1000u × 40%) + (2000u × 50%)) to country Y pursuant to the levy.

In accordance with § 1.901-2(f)(2)(i), the country Y income tax which country Y is, under the contract, required to bear is considered to be paid by country Y on behalf of *B*. *B*'s proceeds of its contract, for all purposes of Chapter 1 of the Code (including the computation of *B*'s accumulated profits for purposes of section 902), therefore, are increased by the additional 500u (1900u computed as in example (2) less 1400u as computed above) of *B*'s liability under the country Y income tax that is assumed by country Y and such 500u is considered to be paid pursuant to the levy by country Y on behalf of *B*. In applying the safe harbor formula, therefore, the computation is exactly as in example (2) and the results are the same as in example (2).

Example (4). Country L issues a decree (the "April 11 decree"), in which it states it is exercising its tax authority to impose a tax on all corporations on their "net income" from country L. "Net income" is defined as actual gross receipts less all expenses attributable thereto, except that in the case of income from extraction of petroleum, gross receipts are defined as 105% of actual gross receipts, and no deduction is allowed for interest incurred on loans whose proceeds are used for exploration for petroleum. Under the April 11 decree, wages paid by corporations subject to the decree are deductible in the year of payment, except that corporations engaged in the extraction of petroleum may deduct such wages only by amortization over a 5-year period and, to the extent such wages are paid to officers, they may be deducted only by amortization over a period of 50 years. The April 11 decree permits related corporations subject to the decree to file consolidated returns in which net income and net losses of related corporations offset each other in computing net income for purposes of the April 11 decree, except that corporations engaged in petroleum exploration or extraction activities are not eligible for inclusion in such a consolidated return. The law of country L does not require separate entities to carry on separate activities in connection with exploring for or extracting petroleum. Net losses of a taxable year may be carried over for 10 years to offset income, except that no more than 25% of net income (before deducting the loss carryover) in any such future year may be offset by a carryover of net loss, and, in the case of any corporation engaged in exploration or extraction of petroleum, losses incurred prior to such a corporation's having net income from production may be carried forward for only 8 years and no more than 15% of net income in any such future year may be offset by such a net loss. The rate to be paid under the April 11 decree is 50% of net income (as defined in the levy), except that if net income exceeds 10,000u (units of country L currency), the rate is 75% of the corporation's net income (including the first 10,000u thereof). In practice, no corporations other than corporations engaged in extraction of petroleum have net income in excess of 10,000u. All petroleum resources of country L are owned by the government of country L, whose petroleum ministry licenses corporations to explore for and extract petroleum in consideration for payment of royalties as petroleum is produced.

J is a U.S. corporation that is engaged in country L in the exploration and extraction of petroleum and therefore is a dual capacity taxpayer. *J* has validly elected the safe harbor method for country L for the year of 1983, the year that *J* commenced activities in country L, and has not revoked such election. For the years 1983 through 1986, *J*'s gross receipts, deductions and net income before application of the carryover provisions, determined in accordance with the April 11 decree, are as follows:

Year A.	gross receipts (105% of actual gross receipts) B.	deductions other than wages C.	wages paid other than to officers (amortizable at 20%) D.	wages paid to officers (amortizable at 2%) E.	non-deductible exploration interest expense F.	net income (loss) (B-C-amortization of cumulative D-amortization of cumulative E) G.
1983	0	13,000u	100u	50u	1,000u	(13,021u)
1984	0	17,000u	100u	50u	2,800u	(17,042u)
1985	42,000u	15,000u	100u	50u	2,800u	26,937u
1986	105,000u	20,000u	100u	50u	2,800u	84,916u

After application of the carryover provisions, *J*'s net income and actual payment amounts pursuant to the April 11 levy are as follows:

Year H.	Net income (loss) I.	Actual payment amount $(I \times 75\%)$ J.
1983	(13,021u)	0
1984	(17,042u)	0
1985	22,896u	17,172u
1986	72,179u	54,134u

Pursuant to paragraph (a)(1) of this section, the April 11 decree as applied to corporations engaged in the exploration or extraction of petroleum in country L is a separate levy from the April 11 decree as applied to all other corporations. J establishes that the April 11 decree, as applied to such other corporations, is an income tax within the meaning of § 1.901-2(a)(1) and that the decree as so applied is the general tax.

The April 11 decree as applied to corporations engaged in the exploration or extraction of petroleum in country L does not meet the gross receipts requirement of § 1.901-2(b)(3); therefore, irrespective of whether it meets the other requirements of § 1.901-2(b)(1), it is not an income tax within the meaning of § 1.901-2(a)(1). However, the April 11 decree as applied to such corporations is a qualifying levy because J has demonstrated that all of the criteria of section 903 are satisfied with respect to the April 11 decree as applied to such corporations, except for the determination of the distinct element of such levy that imposes a tax and of J's qualifying amount with respect thereto.

In applying the safe harbor formula, in accordance with paragraph (e)(2), gross receipts are computed by reference to the general levy, and thus are 100%, not 105%, of actual gross receipts. Similarly, costs and expenses include exploration interest expense. In accordance with paragraph (e)(2)(i) of this section the difference between the general tax and the qualifying levy in the timing of the deduction for wages, other than wages of officers, is not considered to increase the liability of dual capacity taxpayers because the general tax would not have failed to be an income tax within the meaning of § 1.901-2(a)(1) if it had provided for 5-year amortization of such wages instead of for current deduction. See § 1.901-2(b)(4)(i). However, amortization of wages paid to officers over a 50-year period is such a deferred recovery of such wages that it effectively is a denial of the deduction of the excess of such wages paid in any year over the amortization of such cumulative wages permitted in such year. See § 1.901-2(b)(4)(i). The different treatment of wages paid to officers under the general tax and the qualifying levy is thus not merely a difference in timing within the meaning of paragraph (e)(2)(i) of this section. Accordingly, the difference between the amount of wages paid by J to officers in any year and J's deduction (in computing the actual payment amount) for amortization of such cumulative wages allowed in such year is, pursuant to paragraph (e)(2) of this section, treated as a cost and expense in computing J's qualifying amount for such year with respect to the April 11 decree. The differences in the consolidation and carryover provisions between the general tax and the qualifying levy are of the types described in paragraph (e)(2)(ii) of this section and, pursuant to paragraphs (b)(4)(ii) and (b)(4)(iii) of § 1.901-2, the general tax would not fail to be an income tax within the meaning of § 1.901-2(a)(i) even if it contained the consolidation and carryover provisions of the qualifying levy. Thus, such differences are not considered to increase the liability of dual capacity taxpayers pursuant to the qualifying levy as compared to the general tax liability of persons other than dual capacity taxpayers.

Accordingly, in applying the safe harbor formula to the qualifying levy for 1985 and 1986, gross receipts and costs and expenses are computed as follows:

Gross receipts
  1985: 42,000u × (100/105) = 40,000u
  1986: 105,000u × (100/105) = 100,000u

Costs and expenses

	Item	1985	1986
1.	Deductions other than wages (column C in the preceding chart)	15,000u	20,000u
2.	Amortization of cumulative wages paid in 1983 and thereafter other than to officers	60u	80u
3.	Deduction of wages to officers paid in current year, instead of amortization allowed in current year of such cumulative wages paid in 1983 and thereafter	50u	50u
4.	Deduction of exploration interest expense	2,800u	2,800u
5.	Costs and expenses before carryover of net loss (sum of lines 1 through 4)	17,910u	22,930u

Costs and expenses

Item		1985	1986
6.	Recalculation of loss carryover by recalculating 1983 and 1984 net income (loss) to reflect current deduction of wages to officers and exploration interest expense: 1983 adjusted net loss carryover: (13,021u) + (49u) + (1000u) = (14,070u) 1984 adjusted net loss carryover: (17,042u) + (48u) + (2800u) = (19,890u)		
7.	Recalculation of limitation on use of net loss carryover deduction:		

Item	1985	1986		
gross receipts	40,000u	100,000u		
less costs and expenses	(17,910u)	(22,930u)		
	22,090u	77,070u		
times 15% limitation			3,314u	11,561u
8. Costs and expenses including net loss carryover deduction (line 5 plus line 7)			21,224u	34,491u

In years after 1986, costs and expenses for purposes of determining the qualifying amount would reflect net loss carryforward deductions based on the recomputed losses carried forward from 1983 and 1984 (14,070u and 19,890u, respectively) less the amounts thereof that were utilized in determining costs and expenses for 1985 and 1986 (3,314u and 11,561u, respectively). The 1983 and 1984 loss carryforwards would be considered utilized in accordance with the order of priority in which such losses are utilized under the terms of the qualifying levy.

In applying the safe harbor formula, the tax rate to be used, in accordance with paragraph (e)(3) of this section, is .50.

Accordingly, under the safe harbor method, J's qualifying amounts with respect to the April 11 decree for 1985 and 1986 are computed as follows:

1985: (40,000u − 21,224u − 17,172u) × .50 / (1 − .50) = 1604u
1986: (100,000u − 34,491u − 54,134u) × .50 / (1 − .50) = 11,375u

Under the safe harbor method J's qualifying amounts with respect to the April 11 decree for 1985 and 1986 are thus 1604u and 11,375u, respectively; and its specific economic benefit amounts are 15,568u (17,172u − 1604u) and 42,759u (54,134u − 11,375u), respectively. Pursuant to paragraph (b) of this section, J's specific economic benefit amounts are characterized according to the nature of J's transactions with country L and of the specific economic benefit received by J as additional royalties paid to country L with respect to the petroleum extracted by J in country L in 1985 and 1986, and these amounts are so treated for all purposes of Chapter 1 of the Code.

Example (5). Country E, which has no generally imposed income tax, imposes a levy called the country E income tax only on corporations carrying on the banking business through a branch in Country E and on corporations engaged in the extraction of petroleum in country E. All of the petroleum resources of country E are owned by the government of country E, whose petroleum ministry licenses corporations to explore for and extract petroleum in consideration of payment of royalties as petroleum is extracted. The base of the country E income tax is a corporation's actual gross receipts from sources in country E less all expenses attributable, on reasonable principles, to such gross receipts; the rate of tax is 29%.

A is a U.S. corporation that carries on the banking business through a branch in country E. B is a U.S. corporation (unrelated to A) that is engaged in the extraction of petroleum in country E. In 1984 A receives interest on loans it has made to 160 borrowers in country E, seven of which are agencies and instrumentalities of the government of country E. The economic benefits received by A and B (*i.e.*, the interest received by A from the government and B's license to extract petroleum owned by the government) are not made available on substantially the same terms to the population of country E in general.

A and B are dual capacity taxpayers. Each of them has validly elected the safe harbor method for country E for 1984. A demonstrates that the country E income tax as applied to it (a dual capacity taxpayer) is not different by its terms or in practice from the country E income tax as applied to persons (in this case other banks) that are not dual capacity taxpayers. A has therefore established pursuant to paragraph (a)(1) of this section and § 1.901-2(d) that the country E income tax as applied to it and the country E income tax as applied to persons other than dual capacity taxpayers are together a single levy. A establishes that such levy is an income tax within the meaning of § 1.901-2(a)(1). In accordance with paragraph (a)(1) of this section, no portion of the amount paid by A pursuant to such levy is considered to be paid in exchange for a specific economic benefit. Thus, the entire amount paid by *A* pursuant to this levy is an amount of income tax paid.

B does not demonstrate that the country E income tax as applied to corporations engaged in the extraction of petroleum in country E (dual capacity taxpayers) is not different by its terms or in practice from the country E income tax as applied to persons other than dual capacity taxpayers (*i.e.,* banks that are not dual capacity taxpayers). Accordingly, pursuant to paragraph (a)(1) of this section and § 1.901-2(d), the country E income tax as applied to corporations engaged in the extraction of petroleum in country E is a separate levy from the country E income tax as applied to other persons.

B demonstrates that all of the criteria of section 901 are satisfied with respect to the country E income tax as applied to corporations engaged in the exploration of petroleum in country E, except for the determination of the distinct element of such levy that imposes a tax and of *B*'s qualifying amount with respect to the levy. Pursuant to paragraph (e)(5) of this section, in applying the safe harbor formula to *B*, "A" is the amount of *B*'s gross receipts as determined under the country E income tax as applied to *B*; "B" is the amount of *B*'s costs and expenses as determined thereunder; "C" is *B*'s actual payment amount; and "D" is .29, the lower of the rate (29 percent) of the qualifying levy (the country E income tax as applied to corporations engaged in the extraction of petroleum in country E) or the rate (46 percent) of tax specified for 1984 in section 11(b)(5) of the Internal Revenue Code. Thus, *B*'s qualifying amount is equal to its actual payment amount.

Example (6). The facts are the same as in example (5), except that the rate of the country E income tax is 55 percent. For the reasons stated in example (5), the results with respect to *A* are the same as in example (5). In applying the safe harbor formula to *B*, "A," "B," and "C" are the same as in example (5), but "D" is .46, as that rate is less than .55. Thus, *B*'s qualifying amount is less than *B*'s actual payment amount, and the difference is *B*'s specific economic benefit amount.

Example (7). Country E imposes a tax (called the country E income tax) on the realized net income derived by corporations from sources in country E, except that, with respect to interest income received from sources in country E and certain insurance income, nonresident corporations are instead subject to other levies. With respect to such interest income a levy (called the country E interest tax) requires nonresident corporations to pay to country E 20 percent of such gross interest income unless the nonresident corporation falls within a specified category of corporations ("special corporations"), all of which are dual capacity taxpayers, in which case the rate is instead 25 percent. With respect to such insurance income nonresident corporations are subject to a levy (called the country E insurance tax), which is not an income tax within the meaning of § 1.901-2(a)(1).

The country E interest tax applies at the 20 percent rate by its terms and in practice to persons other than dual capacity taxpayers. The country E interest tax as applied at the 25 percent rate to special corporations applies only to dual capacity taxpayers; therefore, the country E interest tax as applied to special corporations is a separate levy from the country E interest tax as applied at the 20 percent rate.

A is a U.S. corporation which is a special corporation subject to the 25 percent rate of the country E interest tax. *A* does not have insurance income that is subject to the country E insurance tax. *A,* a dual capacity taxpayer, has validly elected the safe harbor formula for 1984. In 1984 *A* receives 100u (units of country E currency) of gross interest income subject to the country E interest tax and pays 25u to country E.

A establishes that the country E income tax is the generally imposed income tax of country E; that all of the criteria of section 903 are satisfied with respect to the country E interest tax as applied to special corporations except for the determination of the distinct element of the levy that is a tax and of *A*'s qualifying amount with respect thereto. *A* has therefore demonstrated that the country E interest tax as applied to special corporations is a qualifying levy. *A* establishes that the country E interest tax at the 20 percent rate is a tax in lieu of an income tax within the meaning of § 1.903-1(a). Pursuant to paragraph (e)(6) of this section the country E interest tax at the 20 percent rate is treated as if it were an application of the general tax for purposes of the safe harbor formula of this paragraph (e), since that tax would actually have been required to have been paid by *A* with respect to its interest income had *A* not been a dual capacity taxpayer (special corporation) instead subject to the qualifying levy (the country E interest tax at the 25 percent rate).

Even if the country E insurance tax is a tax in lieu of an income tax within the meaning of § 1.903-1(a), that tax is not treated as if it were an application of the general tax for purposes of applying the safe harbor formula to *A* since *A* had no insurance income in 1984 and hence such tax would not actually have been required to be paid by *A* had *A* not been a dual capacity taxpayer.

Example (8). Under a levy of country S called the country S income tax, each corporation operating in country S is required to pay country S 50 percent of its income from operations in country S. Income for purposes of the country S income tax is computed by subtracting all attributable costs and expenses from a corporation's gross receipts derived from its business in country S. Among corporations on which the country S income tax is imposed are corporations engaged in the exploitation of mineral K in country S. Natural deposits of mineral K in country S are owned by country S, and all corporations engaged in the exploitation thereof do so under concession agreements with an instrumentality of country S. Such corporations, in addition to the 50 percent country S income tax, are also subject to a levy called a surtax, which is equal to 60 percent of posted price net income less the amount of the country S income tax. The surtax is not deductible in computing the country S income tax of corporations engaged in the exploitation of mineral K in country S.

A is a U.S. corporation engaged in country S in the exploitation of mineral K, and A has been allowed to extract mineral K under a concession agreement with an instrumentality of country S. Therefore, A is a dual capacity taxpayer. In accordance with a term of the concession agreement, certain of A's income (net of expenses attributable thereto) is exempted from the income tax and surtax.

The results for A in 1984 are as follows:

	Income Tax	Surtax
Gross Receipts		
Realized—Taxable	120u	—
Realized—Exempt	15u	—
Posted Price—Taxable	—	145u
Costs		
Attributable to Taxable Receipts	20u	20u
Attributable to Exempt Receipts	5u	—
Taxable Income	100u	125u
Tentative Surtax (60%)	—	75u
Petroleum Levy at 50%	50u	50u
Surtax	—	25u

Because of the difference (nondeductibility of the surtax) in the country S income tax as applied to dual capacity taxpayers from its application to other persons, the country S income tax as applied to dual capacity taxpayers and the country S income tax as applied to persons other than dual capacity taxpayers are separate levies. Moreover, because A's concession agreement provides for a modification (exemption of certain income) of the country S income tax and surtax as they otherwise apply to other persons engaged in the exploitation of mineral K in country S, those levies (contractual levies) as applied to A are separate levies from those levies as applied to other persons engaged in the exploitation of mineral K in country S.

A establishes that the country S income tax as applied to persons other than dual capacity taxpayers is an income tax within the meaning of § 1.901-2(a)(1) and is the general tax. A demonstrates that all the criteria of section 903 are satisfied with respect to the country S income tax as applied to A and with respect to the surtax as applied to A, except for the determination of the distinct elements of such levies that are taxes and of A's qualifying amounts with respect to such levies. Therefore, both the country S income tax as applied to A and the surtax as applied to A are qualifying levies.

In applying the safe harbor formula, in accordance with paragraph (e)(2), the amount of A's gross receipts includes the exempt realized income, and the amount of A's costs and expenses includes the costs attributable to such exempt income. In accordance with paragraph (e)(7)(i), the amount of the qualifying levy for purposes of the formula is the sum of A's liability for the country S income tax and A's liability for the surtax. Accordingly, under the safe harbor formula, A's qualifying amount with respect to the country S income tax and the surtax is 35u ((135u − 25u − 75u) × .50/(1 − .50)). A's specific economic benefit amount is 40u (A's actual payment amount (75u) less A's qualifying amount (35u)).

Example (9). Country T imposes a levy on corporations, called the country T income tax. The country T income tax is imposed at a rate of 50 percent on gross receipts less all costs and expenses, and affiliated corporations are allowed to consolidate their results in applying the country T income tax. Corporations engaged in the exploitation of mineral L in country T are subject to a levy that is identical to the country T income tax except that no consolidation among affiliated corporations is allowed. The levy allows unlimited loss carryforwards.

C and D are affiliated U.S. corporations engaged in country T in the exploitation of mineral L. Natural deposits of mineral L in country T are owned by country T, and C and D have been allowed to extract mineral L in consideration of certain payments to an instrumentality of country T. Therefore, C and D are dual capacity taxpayers.

The results for C and D in 1984 and 1985 are as follows:

	1984 C	1984 D	1985 C	1985 D
Gross Receipts	120u	0	120u	120u
Costs	20u	50u	20u	20u
Loss Carryforward	..	..	..	50u
Net Income (Loss)	100u	(50u)	100u	50u
Income Tax	50u	..	50u	25u

Reg. § 1.901-2A(e)(8)

C and D establish that the country T income tax as applied to persons other than dual capacity taxpayers is an income tax within the meaning of § 1.901-2(a)(1) and is the general tax. C and D demonstrate that all of the criteria of section 901 are satisfied with respect to the country T income tax as applied to dual capacity taxpayers, except for the determination of the distinct element of such levy that is a tax and of C and D's qualifying amounts with respect to that levy. Therefore, the country T income tax as applied to dual capacity taxpayers is a qualifying levy.

In applying the safe harbor formula, in accordance with paragraphs (e)(2)(ii) and (e)(7)(iii), the gross receipts, costs and expenses, and actual payment amounts of C and D are aggregated, except that in D's loss year (1984) its gross receipts and costs and expenses are disregarded. The results of any loss year are disregarded since the country T income tax as applied to dual capacity taxpayers does not allow consolidation, and, pursuant to paragraph (e)(2)(ii), differences in consolidation provisions between such levy and the country T income tax as applied to persons that are not dual capacity taxpayers are not considered. Accordingly, in 1984 the qualifying amount with respect to the country T income tax is 50u ((120u − 20u − 50u) × .50/(1 − .50)), all of which is considered paid by C. In 1985 the qualifying amount is 75u ((120u + 120u − 20u − 20u − 50u (loss carryforward) − 50u − 25u) × .50/(1 − .50)), of which 50u is considered to be paid by C and 25u by D.

Example (10). Country W imposes a levy called the country W income tax on corporations doing business in country W. The country W income tax is imposed at a 50 percent rate on gross receipts less all costs and expenses. Corporations engaged in the exploitation of mineral M in country W are subject to a levy that is identical in all respects to the country W income tax except that it is imposed at a rate of 80 percent (the "80 percent levy").

A is a U.S. corporation engaged in country W in exploitation of mineral M and is subject to the 80 percent levy. Natural deposits of mineral M in country W are owned by country W, and A has been allowed to extract mineral M in consideration of certain payments to an instrumentality of country W. Therefore, A is a dual capacity taxpayer. B, a U.S. corporation affiliated with A, also is engaged in business in country W, but has no transactions with country W. B is subject to the country W income tax. B is a dual capacity taxpayer within the meaning of § 1.901-2(a)(2)(ii)(A) by virtue of its affiliation with A.

The results for A and B in 1984 are as follows:

	A	B
Gross Receipts	120u	100u
Costs	20u	40u
Net Income	100u	60u
Tax Rate	.80	.50
Tax	80u	30u

A and B establish that the country W income tax as applied to persons other than dual capacity taxpayers is an income tax within the meaning of § 1.901-2(a)(1) and is the general tax. It is assumed that B has demonstrated that the country W income tax as applied to B does not differ by its terms or in practice from the country W income tax as applied to persons other than dual capacity taxpayers and hence that the country W income tax as applied to B, a dual capacity taxpayer, and the country W income tax as applied to such other persons is a single levy. Thus, with respect to B, the country W income tax is not a qualifying levy by reason of the last sentence of paragraph (c)(1) of this section. A demonstrates that all the criteria of section 901 are satisfied with respect to the 80 percent levy, except for the determination of the distinct element of such levy that is a tax and of A's qualifying amount with respect thereto. Accordingly, the 80 percent levy as applied to A is a qualifying levy.

In applying the safe harbor formula in accordance with paragraphs (e)(7)(i) and (e)(7)(iii) in the instant case, it is not necessary to incorporate B's results in the safe harbor formula because B's taxation in country W is identical to the taxation of persons other than dual capacity taxpayers and because neither A's and B's results nor their taxation in country W interact in any way to change A's taxation. All of the amount paid by B, 30u, is an amount of income tax paid by B within the meaning of § 1.901-2(a)(1). Accordingly, under the safe harbor formula, the qualifying amount for A with respect to the 80 percent levy is 20u ((120u − 20u − 80u) × .50/1(1 − .50)). The remaining 60u paid by A (80u − 20u) is A's specific economic benefit amount.

Example (11). The facts are the same as in example (10), except that it is assumed that B has not demonstrated that the country W income tax as applied to B does not differ by its terms or in practice from the country W income tax as applied to persons other than dual capacity taxpayers. In addition, A and B demonstrate that all the criteria of section 901 are satisfied with respect to each of the country W income tax and the 80 percent levy as applied to dual capacity taxpayers, except for the determination of the distinct elements of such levies that are taxes and of A and B's qualifying amounts with respect to such levies. Therefore, the country W income tax and 80 percent levy as applied to dual capacity taxpayers are qualifying levies.

In applying the safe harbor formula in accordance with paragraphs (e)(7)(i) and (e)(7)(iii), the results of A and B are aggregated. Accordingly, under the safe harbor formula, the aggregate qualifying amount for A and B with respect to the country W income tax and 80 percent levy is 50u ([(120u + 100u) − (20u + 40u) − (80u + 30u)] × .50/(1 − .50)).

Example (12). Country Y imposes a levy on corporations operating in country Y, called the country Y income tax. Income for purposes of the country Y income tax is computed by subtracting all costs and expenses from a corporation's gross receipts derived from its business in country Y. The rate of the country Y income tax is 50 percent. Country Y also imposes a 20 percent tax (the "withholding tax") on the gross amount of certain income, including dividends, received by persons who are not residents of country Y from persons who are residents of country Y and from corporations that operate there. Corporations engaged in the exploitation of mineral K in country Y are subject to a levy (the "75 percent levy") that is identical in all respects to the country Y income tax except that it is imposed at a rate of 75 percent. Dividends received from such corporations are not subject to the withholding tax.

C, a wholly-owned country Y subsidiary of D, a U.S. corporation, is engaged in country Y in the exploitation of mineral K. Natural deposits of mineral K in country Y are owned by country Y, and C has been allowed to extract mineral K in consideration of certain payments to an instrumentality of country Y. Therefore, C is a dual capacity taxpayer. D has elected the safe harbor method for country Y for 1984. In 1984, C's gross receipts are 120u (units of country Y currency), its costs and expenses are 20u, and its liability under the 75 percent levy is 75u. C distributes the amount that remains, 25u, as a dividend to D.

D establishes that the country Y income tax as applied to persons other than dual capacity taxpayers is an income tax within the meaning of § 1.901-2(a)(1) and the general tax, and that all the criteria of section 901 are satisfied with respect to the 75 percent levy, except for the determination of the distinct element of such levy that is tax and of C's qualifying amount with respect thereto. Accordingly, the 75 percent levy is a qualifying levy.

Pursuant to paragraph (e)(7), D (which is not subject to a levy of country Y but is considered to receive a specific economic benefit by reason of § 1.901-2(a)(2)(ii)(E)) is treated as a dual capacity taxpayer in applying paragraph (e)(7)(ii). D demonstrates that the withholding tax is a tax in lieu of an income tax within the meaning of § 1.903-1, which tax applies in practice to persons other than dual capacity taxpayers, and that such tax actually would have applied to D had D not been a dual capacity taxpayer (*i.e.,* had C not been a dual capacity taxpayer, in which case D also would not have been one). Accordingly, the withholding tax is treated for purposes of the safe harbor formula as if it were an application of the general tax.

In applying the safe harbor formula to this situation in accordance with paragraph (e)(7)(ii), the rates of the country Y income tax and the withholding tax are aggregated into a single effective general tax rate. In this case, that rate is .60 (.50 + [(1 − .50) × .20]). Accordingly, under the safe harbor forumla, C's qualifying amount with respect to the 75 percent levy is 37.5u [(120u − 20u − 75u) × .60/(1 − .60)], the aggregate amount that C and D would have paid if C had been subject to the country Y income tax and had distributed to D as a dividend subject to the withholding tax the entire amount that remained for the year after payment of the country Y income tax. Because C is in fact the only taxpayer, the entire qualifying amount is paid by C.

Example (13). The facts are the same as in example (12), except that dividends received from corporations engaged in the exploitation of mineral K in country Y are subject to the withholding tax. Thus, C's liability under the 75 percent levy is 75u, and D's liability under the withholding tax on the 25u distribution is 5u.

D, which is a dual capacity taxpayer, demonstrates that the withholding tax as applied to D does not differ by its terms or in practice from the withholding tax as applied to persons other than dual capacity taxpayers and hence that the withholding tax as applied to D and that levy as applied to such other persons is a single levy. D demonstrates that all of the criteria of section 903 are satisfied with respect to the withholding tax. The withholding tax is not a qualifying levy by reason of the last sentence of paragraph (c)(1) of this section.

Paragraphs (e)(7)(i), (e)(7)(ii) and (e)(7)(iii) all apply in this situation. As in example (10), it is not necessary to incorporate the withholding tax into the safe harbor formula. All of the amount paid by D, 5u, is an amount of tax paid by D in lieu of an income tax. In applying the safe harbor formula to C, therefore, with respect to the 75 percent levy, "A" is 120, "B" is "20", "C" is 75 and "D" is .50. Accordingly, C's qualifying amount with respect to the 75 percent levy is 25u; the remaining 50u that it paid is its specific economic benefit amount.

Example (14). The facts are the same as in example (12), except that dividends received from corporations engaged in the exploitation of mineral K in country Y are subject to a 10 percent withholding tax (the "10 percent withholding tax"). Thus, C's liability under the 75 percent levy is 75u, and D's liability under the 10 percent withholding tax on the 25u distribution is 2.5u.

The only difference between the withholding tax and the 10 percent withholding tax applicable only to dual capacity taxpayers (including D) is that a lower rate (but the same base) applies to dual capacity taxpayers. Although the withholding tax and the 10 percent withholding tax are together a single levy, this difference makes it necessary, when dealing with multiple levies, to incorporate the withholding tax and D's payment pursuant to the 10 percent withholding tax in the safe harbor formula. Accordingly, as in example (12), the safe harbor formula is applied by aggregation.

The aggregate effective rate of the general taxes for purposes of the safe harbor formula is .60 (.50 + [(1 − .50) × .20]). Pursuant to paragraph (e)(7), the aggregate actual payment amount of the qualifying levies for purposes of the formula is the sum of C and D's liability for the 75 percent levy and the 10 percent withholding tax. Accordingly, under the safe harbor formula, the aggregate qualifying amount with respect to the 75 percent levy on C and the 10 percent withholding tax on D is 33.75u ((120u − 20u − [75u + 2.5u]) × .60(1 − .60)), which is the aggregate amount of tax that C and D would have paid if C had been subject to the country Y income tax and had paid out its entire amount remaining after payment of that tax to D as a dividend subject to the withholding tax.

Example (15). The facts are the same as in example (5), except that the rate of the country E income tax is 45 percent and a political subdivision of country E also imposes a levy, called the "local tax," on all corporations subject to the country E income tax. The base of the local tax is the same as the base of the country E income tax; the rate is 10 percent.

The reasoning of example (5) with regard to the country E income tax as applied to A and B, respectively, applies equally with regard to the local tax as applied to A and B, respectively. Accordingly, the entire amount paid by A pursuant to each of the country E income tax and the local tax is an amount of income tax paid, and both the country E income tax as applied to B and the local tax as applied to B are qualifying levies.

Pursuant to paragraph (e)(7), in applying the safe harbor formula to B, "A" is the amount of B's gross receipts as determined under the (identical) country E income tax and local tax as applied to B; "B" is the amount of B's costs and expenses thereunder; and "C" is the sum of B's actual payment amounts with respect to the two levies. Pursuant to paragraph (e)(7), in applying the safe harbor formula to B, B's aggregate qualifying amount with respect to the two levies is limited to the amount determined in accordance with paragraph (e)(5) where "D" is the rate of tax specified in section 11(b)(5) of the Internal Revenue Code. Accordingly, "D" is .46, which is the lower of the aggregate rate (55 percent) of the qualifying levies or the section 11(b)(5) rate (46 percent). B's aggregate qualifying amount is, therefore, identical to B's qualifying amount in example (6), which is less than its aggregate actual payment amount, and the difference is B's specific economic benefit amount.

(f) *Effective date.*—The effective date of this section is as provided in § 1.901-2(h). [Reg. § 1.901-2A.]

☐ [T.D. 7918, 10-6-83.]

§ 1.902-1. Credit for domestic corporate shareholder of a foreign corporation for foreign income taxes paid by the foreign corporation.—(a) *Definitions and special effective date.*—For purposes of section 902, this section, and § 1.902-2, the definitions provided in paragraphs (a)(1) through (12) of this section and the special effective date of paragraph (a)(13) of this section apply.

(1) *Domestic shareholder.*—In the case of dividends received by a domestic corporation from a foreign corporation after December 31, 1986, the term domestic shareholder means a domestic corporation, other than an S corporation as defined in section 1361(a), that owns at least 10 percent of the voting stock of the foreign corporation at the time the domestic corporation receives a dividend from that foreign corporation.

(2) *First-tier corporation.*—In the case of dividends received by a domestic shareholder from a foreign corporation in a taxable year beginning after December 31, 1986, the term first-tier corporation means a foreign corporation, at least 10 percent of the voting stock of which is owned by a domestic shareholder at the time the domestic shareholder receives a dividend from that foreign corporation. The term first-tier corporation also includes a DISC or former DISC, but only with respect to dividends from the DISC or former DISC that are treated under sections 861(a)(2)(D) and 862(a)(2) as income from sources without the United States.

(3) *Second-tier corporation.*—In the case of dividends paid to a first-tier corporation by a foreign corporation in a taxable year beginning after December 31, 1986, the foreign corporation is a second-tier corporation if, at the time a first-tier corporation receives a dividend from that foreign corporation, the first-tier corporation owns at least 10 percent of the foreign

corporation's voting stock and the product of the following equals at least 5 percent—

(i) The percentage of voting stock owned by the domestic shareholder in the first-tier corporation; multiplied by

(ii) The percentage of voting stock owned by the first-tier corporation in the second-tier corporation.

(4) *Third-tier corporation.*—In the case of dividends paid to a second-tier corporation by a foreign corporation in a taxable year beginning after December 31, 1986, a foreign corporation is a third-tier corporation if, at the time a second-tier corporation receives a dividend from that foreign corporation, the second-tier corporation owns at least 10 percent of the foreign corporation's voting stock and the product of the following equals at least 5 percent—

(i) The percentage of voting stock owned by the domestic shareholder in the first-tier corporation; multiplied by

(ii) The percentage of voting stock owned by the first-tier corporation in the second-tier corporation; multiplied by

(iii) The percentage of voting stock owned by the second-tier corporation in the third-tier corporation.

(5) *Example.*—The following example illustrates the ownership requirements of paragraphs (a)(1) through (4) of this section:

Example. (i) Domestic corporation M owns 30 percent of the voting stock of foreign corporation A on January 1, 1991, and for all periods thereafter. Corporation A owns 40 percent of the voting stock of foreign corporation B on January 1, 1991, and continues to own that stock until June 1, 1991, when Corporation A sells its stock in Corporation B. Both Corporation A and Corporation B use the calendar year as the taxable year. Corporation B pays a dividend out of its post-1986 undistributed earnings to Corporation A, which Corporation A receives on February 16, 1991. Corporation A pays a dividend out of its post-1986 undistributed earnings to Corporation M, which Corporation M receives on January 20, 1992. Corporation M uses a fiscal year ending on June 30 as the taxable year.

(ii) On February 16, 1991, when Corporation B pays a dividend to Corporation A, Corporation M satisfies the 10-percent stock ownership requirement of paragraphs (a)(1) and (2) of this section with respect to Corporation A. Therefore, Corporation A is a first-tier corporation within the meaning of paragraph (a)(2) of this section and Corporation M is a domestic shareholder of Corporation A within the meaning of paragraph (a)(1) of this section. Also on February 16, 1991, Corporation B is a second-tier corporation within the meaning of paragraph (a)(3) of this section because Corporation A owns at least 10 percent of its voting stock, and the percentage of voting stock owned by Corporation M in Corporation A on February 16, 1991 (30 percent) multiplied by the percentage of voting stock owned by Corporation A in Corporation B on February 16, 1991 (40 percent) equals 12 percent. Corporation A shall be deemed to have paid foreign income taxes of Corporation B with respect to the dividend received from Corporation B on February 16, 1991.

(iii) On January 20, 1992, Corporation M satisfies the 10-percent stock ownership requirement of paragraphs (a)(1) and (2) of this section with respect to Corporation A. Therefore, Corporation A is a first-tier corporation within the meaning of paragraph (a)(2) of this section and Corporation M is a domestic shareholder within the meaning of paragraph (a)(1) of this section. Accordingly, for its taxable year ending on June 30, 1992, Corporation M is deemed to have paid a portion of the post-1986 foreign income taxes paid, accrued, or deemed to be paid, by Corporation A. Those taxes will include taxes paid by Corporation B that were deemed paid by Corporation A with respect to the dividend paid by Corporation B to Corporation A on February 16, 1991, even though Corporation B is no longer a second-tier corporation with respect to Corporations A and M on January 20, 1992, and has not been a second-tier corporation with respect to Corporations A and M at any time during the taxable years of Corporations A and M that include January 20, 1992.

(6) *Upper—and lower-tier corporations.*— In the case of a third-tier corporation, the term upper-tier corporation means a first—or second-tier corporation. In the case of a second-tier corporation, the term upper-tier corporation means a first-tier corporation. In the case of a first-tier corporation, the term lower-tier corporation means a second—or third-tier corporation. In the case of a second-tier corporation, the term lower-tier corporation means a third-tier corporation.

(7) *Foreign income taxes.*—The term foreign income taxes means income, war profits, and excess profits taxes as defined in §1.901-2(a), and taxes included in the term income, war profits, and excess profits taxes by reason of section 903, that are imposed by a foreign country or a possession of the United States, including any such taxes deemed paid by a foreign corporation under this section. Foreign income, war profits, and excess profits taxes shall not include amounts excluded from the definition of those taxes pursuant to section 901 and the regulations under that section. See also paragraphs (c)(4) and (5) of this section

(concerning foreign taxes paid with respect to foreign mineral income and in connection with the purchase or sale of oil and gas).

(8) *Post-1986 foreign income taxes.*—(i) *In general.*—Except as provided in paragraphs (a) (10) and (13) of this section, the term post-1986 foreign income taxes of a foreign corporation means the sum of the foreign income taxes paid, accrued, or deemed paid in the taxable year of the foreign corporation in which it distributes a dividend plus the foreign income taxes paid, accrued, or deemed paid in the foreign corporation's prior taxable years beginning after December 31, 1986, to the extent the foreign taxes were not paid or deemed paid by the foreign corporation on or with respect to earnings that in prior taxable years were distributed to, or otherwise included (e.g., under sections 304, 367(b), 551, 951(a), 1248 or 1293) in the income of, a foreign or domestic shareholder. Except as provided in paragraph (b)(4) of this section, foreign taxes paid or deemed paid by the foreign corporation on or with respect to earnings that weredistributed or otherwise removed from post-1986 undistributed earnings in prior post-1986 taxable years shall be removed from post-1986 foreign income taxes regardless of whether the shareholder is eligible to compute an amount of foreign taxes deemed paid under section 902, and regardless of whether the shareholder in fact chose to credit foreign income taxes under section 901 for the year of the distribution or inclusion. Thus, if an amount is distributed or deemed distributed by a foreign corporation to a United States person that is not a domestic shareholder within the meaning of paragraph (a)(1) of this section (e.g., an individual or a corporation that owns less than 10% of the foreign corporation's voting stock), or to a foreign person that does not meet the definition of a first- or second-tier corporation under paragraph (a)(2) or (3) of this section, then although no foreign income taxes shall be deemed paid under section 902, foreign income taxes attributable to the distribution or deemed distribution that would have been deemed paid had the shareholder met the ownership requirements of paragraphs (a) (1) through (4) of this section shall be removed from post-1986 foreign income taxes. Further, if a domestic shareholder chooses to deduct foreign taxes paid or accrued for the taxable year of the distribution or inclusion, it shall nonetheless be deemed to have paid a proportionate share of the foreign corporation's post-1986 foreign income taxes under section 902(a), and the foreign taxes deemed paid must be removed from post-1986 foreign income taxes. In the case of a foreign corporation the foreign income taxes of which are determined based on an accounting period of less than one year, the term year means that accounting period. See sections 441(b)(3) and 443.

(ii) *Distributions out of earnings and profits accumulated by a lower-tier corporation in its taxable years beginning before January 1, 1987, and included in the gross income of an upper-tier corporation in its taxable year beginning after December 31, 1986.*—Post-1986 foreign income taxes shall include foreign income taxes that are deemed paid by an upper-tier corporation with respect to distributions from a lower-tier corporation out of non-previously taxed pre-1987 accumulated profits, as defined in paragraph (a)(10) of this section, that are received by an upper-tier corporation in any taxable year of the upper-tier corporation beginning after December 31, 1986, provided the upper-tier corporation's earnings and profits in that year are included in its post-1986 undistributed earnings under paragraph (a)(9) of this section. Foreign income taxes deemed paid with respect to a distribution of pre-1987 accumulated profits shall be translated from the functional currency of the lower-tier corporation into dollars at the spot exchange rate in effect on the date of the distribution. To determine the character of the earnings and profits and associated taxes for foreign tax credit limitation purposes, see section 904 and § 1.904-7(a).

(iii) *Foreign income taxes paid or accrued with respect to high withholding tax interest.*—Post-1986 foreign income taxes shall not include foreign income taxes paid or accrued by a noncontrolled section 902 corporation (as defined in section 904(d)(2)(E)(i)) with respect to high withholding tax interest (as defined in section 904(d)(2)(B)) to the extent the foreign tax rate imposed on such interest exceeds 5 percent. See section 904(d)(2)(E)(ii) and § 1.904-4(g)(2)(iii). The reduction in foreign income taxes paid or accrued by the amount of tax in excess of 5 percent imposed on high withholding tax interest income must be computed in functional currency before foreign income taxes are translated into U.S. dollars and included in post-1986 foreign income taxes.

(9) *Post-1986 undistributed earnings.*—(i) *In general.*—Except as provided in paragraphs (a)(10) and (13) of this section, the term post-1986 undistributed earnings means the amount of the earnings and profits of a foreign corporation (computed in accordance with sections 964(a) and 986) accumulated in taxable years of the foreign corporation beginning after December 31, 1986, determined as of the close of the taxable year of the foreign corporation in which it distributes a dividend. Post-1986 undistributed earnings shall not be

reduced by reason of any earnings distributed or otherwise included in income, for example under section 304, 367(b), 551, 951(a), 1248 or 1293, during the taxable year. Post-1986 undistributed earnings shall be reduced to account for distributions or deemed distributions that reduced earnings and profits and inclusions that resulted in previously-taxed amounts described in section 959(c)(1) and (2) or section 1293(c) in prior taxable years beginning after December 31, 1986. Thus, post-1986 undistributed earnings shall not be reduced to the extent of the ratable share of a controlled foreign corporation's subpart F income, as defined in section 952, attributable to a shareholder that is not a United States shareholder within the meaning of section 951(b) or section 953(c)(1)(A), because that amount has not been included in a shareholder's gross income. Post-1986 undistributed earnings shall be reduced as provided herein regardless of whether any shareholder is deemed to have paid any foreign taxes, and regardless of whether any domestic shareholder chose to claim a foreign tax credit under section 901(a) for the year of the distribution. For rules on carrybacks and carryforwards of deficits and their effect on post-1986 undistributed earnings, see § 1.902-2. In the case of a foreign corporation the foreign income taxes of which are computed based on an accounting period of less than one year, the term year means that accounting period. See sections 441(b)(3) and 443.

(ii) *Distributions out of earnings and profits accumulated by a lower-tier corporation in its taxable years beginning before January 1, 1987, and included in the gross income of an upper-tier corporation in its taxable year beginning after December 31, 1986.*—Distributions by a lower-tier corporation out of non-previously taxed pre-1987 accumulated profits, as defined in paragraph (a)(10) of this section, that are received by an upper-tier corporation in any taxable year of the upper-tier corporation beginning after December 31, 1986, shall be treated as post-1986 undistributed earnings of the upper-tier corporation, provided the upper-tier corporation's earnings and profits for that year are included in its post-1986 undistributed earnings under paragraph (a)(9)(i) of this section. To determine the character of the earnings and profits and associated taxes for foreign tax credit limitation purposes, see section 904 and § 1.904-7(a).

(iii) *Reduction for foreign income taxes paid or accrued.*—In computing post-1986 undistributed earnings, earnings and profits shall be reduced by foreign income taxes paid or accrued regardless of whether the taxes are creditable. Thus, earnings and profits shall be reduced by foreign income taxes paid with respect to high withholding tax interest even though a portion of the taxes is not creditable pursuant to section 904(d)(2)(E)(ii) and is not included in post-1986 foreign income taxes under paragraph (a)(8)(iii) of this section. Earnings and profits of an upper-tier corporation, however, shall not be reduced by foreign income taxes paid by a lower-tier corporation and deemed to have been paid by the upper-tier corporation.

(iv) *Special allocations.*—The term post-1986 undistributed earnings means the total amount of the earnings of the corporation determined at the corporate level. Special allocations of earnings and taxes to particular shareholders, whether required or permitted by foreign law or a shareholder agreement, shall be disregarded. If, however, the Commissioner establishes that there is an agreement to pay dividends only out of earnings in the separate categories for passive or high withholding tax interest income, then only taxes imposed on passive or high withholding tax interest earnings shall be treated as related to the dividend. See § 1.904-6(a)(2).

(10) *Pre-1987 accumulated profits.*— (i) *Definition.*—The term pre-1987 accumulated profits means the amount of the earnings and profits of a foreign corporation computed in accordance with section 902 and attributable to its taxable years beginning before January 1, 1987. If the special effective date of paragraph (a)(13) of this section applies, pre-1987 accumulated profits also includes any earnings and profits (computed in accordance with sections 964(a) and 986) attributable to the foreign corporation's taxable years beginning after December 31, 1986, but before the first day of the first taxable year of the foreign corporation in which the ownership requirements of section 902(c)(3)(B) and paragraphs (a)(1) through (4) of this section are met with respect to that corporation.

(ii) *Computation of pre-1987 accumulated profits.*—Pre-1987 accumulated profits must be computed under United States principles governing the computation of earnings and profits. Pre-1987 accumulated profits are determined at the corporate level. Special allocations of accumulated profits and taxes to particular shareholders with respect to distributions of pre-1987 accumulated profits in taxable years beginning after December 31, 1986, whether required or permitted by foreign law or a shareholder agreement, shall be disregarded. Pre-1987 accumulated profits of a particular year shall be reduced by amounts distributed from those accumulated profits or otherwise included in income from those accumulated profits, for example under sections 304, 367(b), 551, 951(a), 1248 or 1293. If a deficit in post-1986 undistributed earnings is carried back to offset pre-1987 accumulated profits, pre-1987 accumulated profits of a particular taxable year shall be reduced by the amount of the deficit carried back to that year. See § 1.902-2. The amount of a distribution out of pre-1987 accumulated profits, and the amount of foreign income taxes deemed paid under section 902, shall be determined and translated into United States dollars by applying the law as in effect prior to the effective date of the Tax Reform Act of 1986. See §§ 1.902-3, 1.902-4 and 1.964-1.

(iii) *Foreign income taxes attributable to pre-1987 accumulated profits.*—The term pre-1987 foreign income taxes means any foreign income taxes paid, accrued, or deemed paid by a foreign corporation on or with respect to its pre-1987 accumulated profits. Pre-1987 foreign income taxes of a particular year shall be reduced by the amount of taxes paid or deemed paid by the foreign corporation on or with respect to amounts distributed or otherwise included in income from pre-1987 accumulated profits of that year. Thus, pre-1987 foreign income taxes shall be reduced by the amount of taxes deemed paid by a domestic shareholder (regardless of whether the shareholder chose to credit foreign income taxes under section 901 for the year of the distribution or inclusion) or a first-tier or second-tier corporation, and by the amount of taxes that would have been deemed paid had any other shareholder been eligible to compute an amount of foreign taxes deemed paid under section 902. Foreign income taxes deemed paid with respect to a distribution of pre-1987 accumulated profits shall be translated from the functional currency of the distributing corporation into United States dollars at the spot exchange rate in effect on the date of the distribution.

(11) *Dividend.*—For purposes of section 902, the definition of the term dividend in section 316 and the regulations under that section applies. Thus, for example, distributions and deemed distributions under sections 302, 304, 305(b) and 367(b) that are treated as dividends within the meaning of section 301(c)(1) also are dividends for purposes of section 902. In addition, the term dividend includes deemed dividends under sections 551 and 1248, but not deemed inclusions under sections 951(a) and 1293. For rules concerning excess distributions from section 1291 funds that are treated as dividends solely for foreign tax credit purposes, (see Regulation Project INTL-656-87 published in 1992-1 C.B. 1124; see § 601.601(d)(2)(ii)(*b*) of this chapter).

(12) *Dividend received.*—A dividend shall be considered received for purposes of section 902 when the cash or other property is unqualifiedly made subject to the demands of the distributee. See § 1.301-1(b). A dividend also is considered received for purposes of section 902 when it is deemed received under section 304, 367(b), 551, or 1248.

(13) *Special effective date.*—(i) *Rule.*—If the first day on which the ownership requirements of section 902(c)(3)(B) and paragraphs (a)(1) through (4) of this section are met with respect to a foreign corporation, without regard to whether a dividend is distributed, is in a taxable year of the foreign corporation beginning after December 31, 1986, then—

(A) The post-1986 undistributed earnings and post-1986 foreign income taxes of the foreign corporation shall be determined by taking into account only taxable years beginning on and after the first day of the first taxable year of the foreign corporation in which the ownership requirements are met, including subsequent taxable years in which the ownership requirements of section 902(c)(3)(B) and paragraphs (a)(1) through (4) of this section are not met; and

(B) Earnings and profits accumulated prior to the first day of the first taxable year of the foreign corporation in which the ownership requirements of section 902(c)(3)(13) and paragraphs (a) (1) through (4) of this section are met shall be considered pre-1987 accumulated profits.

(ii) *Example.*—The following example illustrates the special effective date rules of this paragraph (a)(13):

Example. As of December 31, 1991, and since its incorporation, foreign corporation A has owned 100 percent of the stock of foreign corporation B. Corporation B is not a controlled foreign corporation. Corporation B uses the calendar year as its taxable year, and its functional currency is the u. Assume 1u equals $1 at all relevant times. On April 1, 1992, Corporation B pays a 200u dividend to Corporation A and the ownership requirements of section 902(c)(3)(B) and paragraphs (a) (1) through (4) of this section are not met at that time. On July 1, 1992, domestic corporation M purchases 10 percent of the Corporation B stock from Corporation A and, for the first time, Corporation B meets the ownership requirements of section 902(c)(3)(B) and paragraph (a) (2) of this section. Corporation M uses the calendar year as its taxable year. Corporation B does not distribute any dividends to Corporation M during 1992. For its taxable year ending December 31, 1992, Corporation B has 500u of earnings and profits (after foreign taxes but before taking into account the 200u distribution to Corporation A) and pays 100u of foreign income taxes that is equal to $100. Pursuant to paragraph (a)(13)(i) of this section, Corporation B's post-1986 undistributed earnings and post-1986 foreign income taxes will include earnings and profits and foreign income taxes attributable to Corporation B's entire 1992 taxable year and all taxable years thereafter. Thus, the April 1, 1992, dividend to Corporation A will reduce post-1986 undistributed earnings to 300u (500u – 200u) under paragraph (a)(9)(i) of this section. The foreign income taxes attributable to the amount distributed as a dividend to Corporation A will not be creditable because Corporation A is not a domestic shareholder. Post-1986 foreign income taxes, however, will be reduced by the amount of foreign taxes attributable to the dividend. Thus, as of the beginning of 1993, Corporation B has $60 ($100–[$100 × 40% (200u/500u)]) of post-1986 foreign income taxes. See paragraphs (a)(8)(i) and (b)(1) of this section.

(b) *Computation of foreign income taxes deemed paid by a domestic shareholder, first-tier corporation, and second-tier corporation.*—(1) *General rule.*—If a foreign corporation pays a dividend in any taxable year out of post-1986 undistributed earnings to a shareholder that is a domestic shareholder or an upper-tier corporation at the time it receives the dividend, the recipient shall be deemed to have paid the same proportion of any post-1986 foreign income taxes paid, accrued or deemed paid by the distributing corporation on or with respect to post-1986 undistributed earnings which the amount of the dividend out of post-1986 undistributed earnings (determined without regard to the gross-up under section 78) bears to the amount of the distributing corporation's post-1986 undistributed earnings. An upper-tier corporation shall not be entitled to compute an amount of foreign taxes deemed paid on a dividend from a lower-tier corporation, however, unless the ownership requirements of paragraphs (a)(1) through (4) of this section are met at each tier at the time the upper-tier corporation receives the dividend. Foreign income taxes deemed paid by a domestic shareholder or an upper-tier corporation must be computed under the following formula:

$$\text{Foreign income taxes deemed paid by domestic shareholder (or upper-tier corporation)} = \text{Post-1986 foreign income taxes of first-tier corporation (or lower-tier corporation)} \times \frac{\text{Dividend paid to domestic shareholder (or upper-tier corporation) by first-tier corporation (or lower-tier corporation)}}{\text{Post-1986 undistributed earnings of first-tier corporation (or lower-tier corporation)}}$$

(2) *Allocation rule for dividends attributable to post-1986 undistributed earnings and pre-1987 accumulated profits.*—(i) *Portion of dividend out of post-1986 undistributed earnings.*—Dividends will be deemed to be paid first out of post-1986 undistributed earnings to the extent thereof. If dividends exceed post-1986 undistributed earnings and dividends are paid to more than one shareholder, then the dividend to each shareholder shall be deemed to be paid pro rata out of post-1986 undistributed earnings, computed as follows:

$$\text{Portion of Dividend to a Shareholder Attributable to Post-1986 Undistributed Earnings} = \text{Post-1986 Undistributed Earnings} \times \frac{\text{Dividend to Shareholder}}{\text{Total Dividends Paid To all Shareholders}}$$

(ii) *Portion of dividend out of pre-1987 accumulated profits.*—After the portion of the dividend attributable to post-1986 undistributed earnings is determined under paragraph (b)(2)(i) of this section, the remainder of the dividend received by a shareholder is attributable to pre-1987 accumulated profits to the extent thereof. That part of the dividend attributable to pre-1987 accumulated profits will be treated as paid first from the most recently accumulated earnings and profits. See § 1.902-3. If dividends paid out of pre-1987 accumulated profits are attributable to more than one pre-1987 taxable year and are paid to more than one shareholder, then the dividend to each shareholder attributable to earnings and profits accumulated in a particular pre-1987 taxable year shall be deemed to be paid pro rata out of accumulated profits of that taxable year, computed as follows:

$$\text{Portion of Dividend to a Shareholder Attributable to Accumulated Profits of a Particular Pre-1987 Taxable Year} = \text{Dividend Paid Out of Pre-1987 Accumulated Profits with Respect to the Particular Pre-1987 Taxable Year} \times \frac{\text{Dividend to Shareholder}}{\text{Total Dividends Paid to all Shareholders}}$$

(3) *Dividends paid out of pre-1987 accumulated profits.*—If dividends are paid by a first-tier corporation or a lower-tier corporation out of pre-1987 accumulated profits, the domestic shareholder or upper-tier corporation that receives the dividends shall be deemed to have

paid foreign income taxes to the extent provided under section 902 and the regulations thereunder as in effect prior to the effective date of the Tax Reform Act of 1986. See paragraphs (a)(10) and (13) of this section and §§ 1.902-3 and 1.902-4.

(4) *Deficits in accumulated earnings and profits.*—No foreign income taxes shall be deemed paid with respect to a distribution from a foreign corporation out of current earnings and profits that is treated as a dividend under section 316(a)(2), and post-1986 foreign income taxes shall not be reduced, if as of the end of the taxable year in which the dividend is paid or accrued, the corporation has zero or a deficit in post-1986 undistributed earnings and the sum of current plus accumulated earnings and profits is zero or less than zero. The dividend shall reduce post-1986 undistributed earnings and accumulated earnings and profits.

(5) *Examples.*—The following examples illustrate the rules of this paragraph (b):

Example 1. Domestic corporation M owns 100 percent of foreign corporation A. Both Corporation M and Corporation A use the calendar year as the taxable year, and Corporation A uses the u as its functional currency. Assume that 1u equals $1 at all relevant times. All of Corporation A's pre-1987 accumulated profits and post-1986 undistributed earnings are non-subpart F general limitation earnings and profits under section 904(d)(1)(I). As of December 31, 1992, Corporation A has 100u of post-1986 undistributed earnings and $40 of post-1986 foreign income taxes. For its 1986 taxable year, Corporation A has accumulated profits of 200u (net of foreign taxes) and paid 60u of foreign income taxes on those earnings. In 1992, Corporation A distributes 150u to Corporation M. Corporation A has 100u of post-1986 undistributed earnings and the dividend, therefore, is treated as paid out of post-1986 undistributed earnings to the extent of 100u. The first 100u distribution is from post-1986 undistributed earnings, and, because the distribution exhausts those earnings, Corporation M is deemed to have paid the entire amount of post-1986 foreign income taxes of Corporation A ($40). The remaining 50u dividend is treated as a dividend out of 1986 accumulated profits under paragraph (b)(2) of this section. Corporation M is deemed to have paid $15 (60u × 50u/200u, translated at the appropriate exchange rates) of Corporation A's foreign income taxes for 1986. As of January 1, 1993, Corporation A's post-1986 undistributed earnings and post-1986 foreign income taxes are 0. Corporation A has 150u of accumulated profits and 45u of foreign income taxes remaining in 1986.

Example 2. Domestic corporation M (incorporated on January 1, 1987) owns 100 percent of foreign corporation A (incorporated on January 1, 1987). Both Corporation M and Corporation A use the calendar year as the taxable year, and Corporation A uses the u as its functional currency. Assume that 1u equals $1 at all relevant times. Corporation A has no pre-1987 accumulated profits. All of Corporation A's post-1986 undistributed earnings are non-subpart F general limitation earnings and profits under section 904(d)(1)(I). On January 1, 1992, Corporation A has a deficit in accumulated earnings and profits and a deficit in post-1986 undistributed earnings of (200u). No foreign taxes have been paid with respect to post-1986 undistributed earnings. During 1992, Corporation A earns 100u (net of foreign taxes), pays $40 of foreign taxes on those earnings and distributes 50u to Corporation M. As of the end of 1992, Corporation A has a deficit of (100u) ((200u) post-1986 undistributed earnings + 100u current earnings and profits) in post-1986 undistributed earnings. Corporation A, however, has current earnings and profits of 100u. Therefore, the 50u distribution is treated as a dividend in its entirety under section 316(a)(2). Under paragraph (b)(4) of this section, Corporation M is not deemed to have paid any of the foreign taxes paid by Corporation A because post-1986 undistributed earnings and the sum of current plus accumulated earnings and profits are (100u). The dividend reduces both post-1986 undistributed earnings and accumulated earnings and profits. Therefore, as of January 1, 1993, Corporation A's post-1986 undistributed earnings are (150u) and its accumulated earnings and profits are (150u). Corporation A's post-1986 foreign income taxes at the start of 1993 are $40.

(c) *Special rules.*—(1) *Separate computations required for dividends from each first-tier and lower-tier corporation.*—(i) *Rule.*—If in a taxable year dividends are received by a domestic shareholder or an upper-tier corporation from two or more first-tier corporations or two or more lower-tier corporations, the foreign income taxes deemed paid by the domestic shareholder or the upper-tier corporation under sections 902(a) and (b) and paragraph (b) of this section shall be computed separately with respect to the dividends received from each first-tier corporation or lower-tier corporation. If a domestic shareholder receives dividend distributions from one or more first-tier corporations and in the same taxable year the first-tier corporation receives dividends from one or more lower-tier corporations, then the amount of foreign income taxes deemed paid shall be computed by starting with the lowest-tier corporation and working upward.

(ii) *Example.*—The following example illustrates the application of this paragraph (c)(1):

Example. P, a domestic corporation, owns 40 percent of the voting stock of foreign corporation S. S owns 30 percent of the voting stock of foreign corporation T, and 30 percent of the voting stock of foreign corporation U. Neither S, T, nor U is a controlled foreign corporation. P, S, T and U all use the calendar year as their taxable year. In 1993, T and U both pay dividends to S and S pays a dividend to P. To compute foreign taxes deemed paid, paragraph (c)(1) of this section requires P to start with the lowest tier corporations and to compute foreign taxes deemed paid separately for dividends from each first-tier and lower-tier corporation. Thus, S first will compute foreign taxes deemed paid separately on its dividends from T and U. The deemed paid taxes will be added to S's post-1986 foreign income taxes, and the dividends will be added to S's post-1986 undistributed earnings. Next, P will compute foreign taxes deemed paid with respect to the dividend from S. This computation will take into account the taxes paid by T and U and deemed paid by S.

(2) *Section 78 gross-up.*—(i) *Foreign income taxes deemed paid by a domestic shareholder.*—Except as provided in section 960(b) and the regulations under that section (relating to amounts excluded from gross income under section 959(b)), any foreign income taxes deemed paid by a domestic shareholder in any taxable year under section 902(a) and paragraph (b) of this section shall be included in the gross income of the domestic shareholder for the year as a dividend under section 78. Amounts included in gross income under section 78 shall, for purposes of section 904, be deemed to be derived from sources within the United States to the extent the earnings and profits on which the taxes were paid are treated under section 904(g) as United States source earnings and profits. Section 1.904-5(m)(6). Amounts included in gross income under section 78 shall be treated for purposes of section 904 as income in a separate category to the extent that the foreign income taxes were allocated and apportioned to income in that separate category. See section 904(d)(3)(G) and §1.904-6(b)(3).

(ii) *Foreign income taxes deemed paid by an upper-tier corporation.*—Foreign income taxes deemed paid by an upper-tier corporation on a distribution from a lower-tier corporation are not included in the earnings and profits of the upper-tier corporation. For purposes of section 904, foreign income taxes shall be allocated and apportioned to income in a separate category to the extent those taxes were allocated to the earnings and profits of the lower-tier corporation in that separate category. See section 904(d)(3)(G) and §1.904-6(b)(3). To the extent that section 904(g) treats the earnings of the lower-tier corporation on which those foreign income taxes were paid as United States source earnings and profits, the foreign income taxes deemed paid by the upper-tier corporation on the distribution from the lower-tier corporation shall be treated as attributable to United States source earnings and profits. See section 904(g) and §1.904-5(m)(6).

(iii) *Example.*—The following example illustrates the rules of this paragraph (c)(2):

Example. P, a domestic corporation, owns 100 percent of the voting stock of controlled foreign corporation S. Corporations P and S use the calendar year as their taxable year, and S uses the u as its functional currency. Assume that 1u equals $1 at all relevant times. As of January 1, 1992, S has -0- post-1986 undistributed earnings and -0- post-1986 foreign income taxes. In 1992, S earns 150u of non-subpart F general limitation income net of foreign taxes and pays 60u of foreign income taxes. As of the end of 1992, but before dividend payments, S has 150u of post-1986 undistributed earnings and $60 of post-1986 foreign income taxes. Assume that 50u of S's earnings for 1992 are from United States sources. S pays P a dividend of 75u which P receives in 1992. Under §1.904-5(m)(4), one-third of the dividend, or 25u (75u x 50u/150u), is United States source income to P. P computes foreign taxes deemed paid on the dividend under paragraph (b)(1) of this section of $30 ($60 x 50%[75u/150u]) and includes that amount in gross income under section 78 as a dividend. Because 25u of the 75u dividend is United States source income to P, $10 ($30 x 33.33%[25u/75u]) of the section 78 dividend will be treated as United States source income to P under this paragraph (c)(2).

(3) *Creditable foreign income taxes.*—The amount of creditable foreign income taxes under section 901 shall include, subject to the limitations and conditions of sections 902 and 904, foreign income taxes actually paid and deemed paid by a domestic shareholder that receives a dividend from a first-tier corporation. Foreign income taxes deemed paid by a domestic shareholder under paragraph (b) of this section shall be deemed paid by the domestic shareholder only for purposes of computing the foreign tax credit allowed under section 901.

(4) *Foreign mineral income.*—Certain foreign income, war profits and excess profits taxes paid or accrued with respect to foreign mineral income will not be considered foreign

income taxes for purposes of section 902. See section 901(e) and § 1.901-3.

(5) *Foreign taxes paid or accrued in connection with the purchase or sale of certain oil and gas.*—Certain income, war profits, or excess profits taxes paid or accrued to a foreign country in connection with the purchase and sale of oil or gas extracted in that country will not be considered foreign income taxes for purposes of section 902. See section 901(f).

(6) *Foreign oil and gas extraction income.*—For rules relating to reduction of the amount of foreign income taxes deemed paid with respect to foreign oil and gas extraction income, see section 907(a) and the regulations under that section.

(7) *United States shareholders of controlled foreign corporations.*—See paragraph (d) of this section and sections 960 and 962 and the regulations under those sections for special rules relating to the application of section 902 in computing foreign income taxes deemed paid by United States shareholders of controlled foreign corporations.

(8) *Credit for foreign taxes deemed paid in a section 304 transaction.*—[Reserved].

(9) *Effect of section 482 adjustments on post-1986 foreign income taxes and post-1986 undistributed earnings.*—[Reserved].

(d) *Dividends from controlled foreign corporations.*—(1) *General rule.*—Except as provided in paragraph (d) (3) of this section, if a dividend is received by a domestic shareholder that is a United States shareholder (as defined in section 951(b) or section 953(c) a (A)) from a first-tier corporation that is a controlled foreign corporation (as defined in section 957(a) or section 953(c)(1)(B)), or by an upper-tier corporation from a lower-tier corporation if the corporations are related look-through entities within the meaning of § 1.904-5(i), the following rule applies. If a dividend is paid out of post-1986 undistributed earnings or pre-1987 accumulated profits of the upper- or lower-tier controlled foreign corporation attributable to more than one separate category under section 904(d), the amount of foreign income taxes deemed paid by the domestic shareholder or the upper-tier corporation under section 902 and paragraph (b) of this section shall be computed separately with respect to the post-1986 undistributed earnings or pre1987 accumulated profits in each separate category out of which the dividend is paid. See § 1.904-5(c)(4) and paragraph (d)(2) of this section. The separately computed deemed paid taxes shall be added to other taxes paid by the U.S. shareholder or upper-tier corporation with respect to income in the appropriate separate category.

(2) *Look-through.*—(i) *Dividends.*—Except as otherwise provided in paragraph (d)(3) of this section, any dividend distribution out of post-1986 undistributed earnings of a look-through entity to a related look-through entity shall be deemed to be paid pro rata out of each separate category of income. See §§ 1.904-5(c)(4) and 1.904-7. The portion of the foreign income taxes attributable to a particular separate category that shall be deemed paid by the domestic shareholder or upper-tier corporation must be computed under the following formula:

| Foreign taxes deemed paid by domestic shareholder or upper-tier corporation with respect to a separate category under section 904(d) | = | Post-1986 foreign income taxes of first-tier or lower-tier corporation allocated and apportioned to a separate category under § 1.904-6 | × | Dividend amount attributable to a separate category / Post-1986 undistributed earnings of first-tier or lower-tier corporation attributable to the separate category |

(ii) *Coordination with section 960.*—For rules coordinating the computation of foreign taxes deemed paid with respect to amounts included in gross income under section 951(a) and dividends distributed by a controlled foreign corporation, see section 960 and the regulations under that section.

(3) *Dividends distributed out of earnings accumulated before a controlled foreign corporation became a controlled foreign corporation.*—(i) *General rule.*—Any dividend distributed by a controlled foreign corporation out of earnings accumulated before the controlled foreign corporation became a controlled foreign corporation shall be treated as a dividend from a noncontrolled section 902 corporation regardless of whether the earnings were accumulated in a taxable year beginning before January 1, 1987, or after December 31, 1986.

(ii) *Dividend distributions out of earnings and profits for a year during which a shareholder that is currently a more-than-90-percent United States shareholder of a controlled foreign corporation was not a United States shareholder of the controlled foreign corporation.*—[Reserved]. For rules regarding dividend distributions before August 6, 1997, to certain more-than-90-percent United States shareholders of a controlled foreign corporation, see § 1.904-4(g)(3)(ii).

(e) *Information to be furnished.*—If the credit for foreign income taxes claimed under section 901 includes foreign income taxes deemed paid under section 902 and paragraph (b) of this section, the domestic shareholder must furnish the same information with respect to the foreign income taxes deemed paid as it is required to furnish with respect to the foreign income taxes it directly paid or accrued and for which the credit is claimed. See § 1.905-2. For other information required to be furnished by the domestic shareholder for the annual accounting period of certain foreign corporations ending with or within the shareholder's taxable year, and for reduction in the amount of foreign income taxes paid, accrued, or deemed paid for failure to furnish the required information, see section 6038 and the regulations under that section.

(f) *Examples.*—The following examples illustrate the application of this section:

Example 1. Since 1987, domestic corporation M has owned 10 percent of the one class of stock of foreign corporation A. The remaining 90 percent of Corporation A's stock is owned by Z, a foreign corporation. Corporation A is not a controlled foreign corporation. Corporation A uses the u as its functional currency, and 1u equals $1 at all relevant times. Both Corporation A and Corporation M use the calendar year as the taxable year. In 1992, Corporation A pays a 30u dividend out of post-1986 undistributed earnings, 3u to Corporation M and 27u to Corporation Z. Corporation M is deemed, under paragraph (b) of this section, to have paid a portion of the post-1986 foreign income taxes paid by Corporation A and includes the amount of foreign taxes deemed paid in gross income under section 78 as a dividend. Both the foreign taxes deemed paid and the dividend would be subject to a separate limitation for dividends from Corporation A, a noncontrolled section 902 corporation. Under paragraph (a)(9)(i) of this section, Corporation A must reduce its post-1986 undistributed earnings as of January 1, 1993, by the total amount of dividends paid to Corporation M and Corporation Z in 1992. Under paragraph (a)(8)(i) of this section, Corporation A must reduce its post-1986 foreign income taxes as of January 1, 1993, by the amount of foreign income taxes that were deemed paid by Corporation M and by the amount of foreign income taxes that would have been deemed paid by Corporation Z had Corporation Z been eligible to compute an amount of foreign income taxes deemed paid with respect to the dividend received from Corporation A. Foreign income taxes deemed paid by Corporation M and Corporation A's opening balances in post-1986 undistributed earnings and post-1986 foreign income taxes for 1993 are computed as follows:

1.	Assumed post-1986 undistributed earnings of Corporation A at start of 1992	25u
2.	Assumed post-1986 foreign income taxes of Corporation A at start of 1992	$25
3.	Assumed pre-tax earnings and profits of Corporation A for 1992	50u
4.	Assumed foreign income taxes paid or accrued by Corporation A in 1992	15u
5.	Post-1986 undistributed earnings in Corporation A for 1992 (pre-dividend) (Line 1 plus Line 3 minus Line 4)	60u
6.	Post-1986 foreign income taxes in Corporation A for 1992 (pre-dividend) (Line 2 plus Line 4 translated at the appropriate exchange rates)	$40
7.	Dividends paid out of post-1986 undistributed earnings of Corporation A to Corporation M in 1992	3u
8.	Percentage of Corporation A's post-1986 undistributed earnings paid to Corporation M (Line 7 divided by Line 5)	5%
9.	Foreign income taxes of Corporation A deemed paid by Corporation M under section 902(a) (Line 6 multiplied by Line 8)	$2
10.	Total dividends paid out of post-1986 undistributed earnings of Corporation A to all shareholders in 1992	30u
11.	Percentage of Corporation A's post-1986 undistributed earnings paid to all shareholders in 1992 (Line 10 divided by Line 5)	50%
12.	Post-1986 foreign income taxes paid with respect to post-1986 undistributed earnings distributed to all shareholders in 1992 (Line 6 multiplied by Line 11)	$20

13.	Corporation A's post-1986 undistributed earnings at the start of 1993 (Line 5 minus Line 10)	30u
14.	Corporation A's post-1986 foreign income taxes at the start of 1993 (Line 6 minus Line 12)	$20

Example 2. (i) The facts are the same as in *Example 1*, except that Corporation M has also owned 10 percent of the one class of stock of foreign corporation B since 1987. Corporation B uses the calendar year as the taxable year. The remaining 90 percent of Corporation B's stock is owned by Corporation Z. Corporation B is not a controlled foreign corporation. Corporation B uses the u as its functional currency, and 1u equals $1 at all relevant times. In 1992, Corporation B has earnings and profits and pays foreign income taxes, a portion of which are attributable to high withholding tax interest, as defined in section 904(d)(2)(B)(i). Corporation B must reduce its pool of post-1986 foreign income taxes by the amount of tax imposed on high withholding tax interest in excess of 5 percent because that amount is not treated as a tax for purposes of section 902. See section 904(d)(2)(E)(ii) and paragraph (a)(8)(iii) of this section. Corporation B pays 50u in dividends in 1992, 5u to Corporation M and 45u to Corporation Z. Corporation M must compute its section 902(a) deemed paid taxes separately for the dividends it receives in 1992 from Corporation A (as computed in *Example 1*) and from Corporation B. Foreign income taxes of Corporation B deemed paid by Corporation M, and Corporation B's opening balances in post-1986 undistributed earnings and post-1986 foreign income taxes for 1993 are computed as follows:

1.	Assumed post-1986 undistributed earnings of Corporation B at start of 1992	(100u)
2.	Assumed post-1986 foreign income taxes of Corporation B at start of 1992	$0
3.	Assumed pre-tax earnings and profits of Corporation B for 1992 (including 50u of high withholding tax interest on which 5u of tax is withheld)	302.50u
4.	Assumed foreign income taxes paid or accrued by Corporation B in 1992	102.50u
5.	Post-1986 undistributed earnings in Corporation B for 1992 (pre-dividend) (Line 1 plus Line 3 minus Line 4)	100u
6.	Amount of foreign income tax of Corporation B imposed on high withholding tax interest in excess of 5% (5u withholding tax − [5% × 50u high withholding tax interest])	2.50u
7.	Post-1986 foreign income taxes in Corporation B for 1992 (pre-dividend) (Line 2 plus [Line 4 minus Line 6 translated at the appropriate exchange rate])	$100
8.	Dividends paid out of post-1986 undistributed earnings to Corporation M in 1992	5u
9.	Percentage of Corporation B's post-1986 undistributed earnings paid to Corporation M (Line 8 divided by Line 5)	5%
10.	Foreign income taxes of Corporation B deemed paid by Corporation M under section 902(a) (Line 7 multiplied by Line 9)	$5
11.	Total dividends paid out of post-1986 undistributed earnings of Corporation B to all shareholders in 1992	50u
12.	Percentage of Corporation B's post-1986 undistributed earnings paid to all shareholders in 1992 (Line 11 divided by Line 5)	50%
13.	Post-1986 foreign income taxes of Corporation B paid on or with respect to post-1986 undistributed earnings distributed to all shareholders in 1992 (Line 7 multiplied by Line 12)	$50
14.	Corporation B's post-1986 undistributed earnings at start of 1993 (Line 5 minus Line 11)	50u
15.	Corporation B's post-1986 foreign income taxes at start of 1993 (Line 7 minus Line 13)	$50

(ii) For 1992, as computed in *Example 1*, Corporation M is deemed to have paid $2 of the post-1986 foreign income taxes paid by Corporation A and includes $2 in gross income as a dividend under section 78. Both the income inclusion and the credit are subject to a separate limitation for dividends from Corporation A, a noncontrolled section 902 corporation.

Reg. §1.902-1(f)

Corporation M also is deemed to have paid $5 of the post-1986 foreign income taxes paid by Corporation B and includes $5 in gross income as a deemed dividend under section 78. Both the income inclusion and the foreign taxes deemed paid are subject to a separate limitation for dividends from Corporation B, a noncontrolled section 902 corporation.

Example 3. (i) Since 1987, domestic corporation M has owned 50 percent of the one class of stock of foreign corporation A. The remaining 50 percent of Corporation A is owned by foreign corporation Z. For the same time period, Corporation A has owned 40 percent of the one class of stock of foreign corporation B, and Corporation B has owned 30 percent of the one class of stock of foreign corporation C. The remaining 60 percent of Corporation B is owned by foreign corporation Y, and the remaining 70 percent of Corporation C is owned by foreign corporation X. Corporations A, B, and C are not controlled foreign corporations. Corporations A, B, and C use the u as their functional currency, and 1u equals $1 at all relevant times. Corporation B uses a fiscal year ending June 30 as its taxable year; all other corporations use the calendar year as the taxable year. On February 1, 1992, Corporation C pays a 500u dividend-out of post-1986 undistributed earnings, 150u to Corporation B and 350u to Corporation X. On February 15, 1992, Corporation B pays a 300u dividend out of post-1986 undistributed earnings computed as of the close of Corporation B's fiscal year ended June 30, 1992, 120u to Corporation A and 180u to Corporation Y. On August 15, 1992, Corporation A pays a 200u dividend out of post-1986 undistributed earnings, 100u to Corporation M and 100u to Corporation Z. In computing foreign taxes deemed paid by Corporations B and A, section 78 does not apply and Corporations B and A thus do not have to include the foreign taxes deemed paid in earnings and profits. See paragraph (c)(2)(ii) of this section. Foreign income taxes deemed paid by Corporations B, A and M, and the foreign corporations' opening balances in post-1986 undistributed earnings and post-1986 foreign income taxes for Corporation B's fiscal year beginning July 1, 1992, and Corporation C's and Corporation A's 1993 calendar years are computed as follows:

A. Corporation C (third-tier corporation):

1.	Assumed post-1986 undistributed earnings in Corporation C at start of 1992 . . .	1300u
2.	Assumed post-1986 foreign income taxes in Corporation C at start of 1992	$500
3.	Assumed pre-tax earnings and profits of Corporation C for 1992	500u
4.	Assumed foreign income taxes paid or accrued in 1992	300u
5.	Post-1986 undistributed earnings in Corporation C for 1992 (pre-dividend) (Line 1 plus Line 3 minus Line 4)	1500u
6.	Post-1986 foreign income taxes in Corporation C for 1992 (pre-dividend) (Line 2 plus Line 4 translated at the appropriate exchange rates)	$800
7.	Dividends paid out of post-1986 undistributed earnings of Corporation C to Corporation B in 1992.	150u
8.	Percentage of Corporation C's post-1986 undistributed earnings paid to Corporation B (Line 7 divided by Line 5)	10%
9.	Foreign income taxes of Corporation C deemed paid by Corporation B under section 902(b)(2) (Line 6 multiplied by Line 8)	$80
10.	Total dividends paid out of post-1986 undistributed earnings of Corporation C to all shareholders in 1992	500u
11.	Percentage of Corporation C's post-1986 undistributed earnings paid to all shareholders in 1992 (Line 10 divided by Line 5)	33.33%
12.	Post-1986 foreign income taxes paid with respect to post-1986 undistributed earnings distributed to all shareholders in 1992 (Line 6 multiplied by Line 11)	$266.66
13.	Post-1986 undistributed earnings in Corporation C at start of 1993 (Line 5 minus Line 10)	1000u
14.	Post-1986 foreign income taxes in Corporation C at start of 1993 (Line 6 minus Line 12)	$533.34

B.	Corporation B (second-tier corporation):	
1.	Assumed post-1986 undistributed earnings in Corporation B as of July 1, 1991	0
2.	Assumed post-1986 foreign income taxes in Corporation B as of July 1, 1991	0
3.	Assumed pre-tax earnings and profits of Corporation B for fiscal year ended June 30, 1992, (including 150u dividend from Corporation B)	1000u
4.	Assumed foreign income taxes paid or accrued by Corporation B in fiscal year ended June 30, 1992	200u
5.	Foreign income taxes of Corporation C deemed paid by Corporation B in its fiscal year ended June 30, 1992 (Part A, Line 9 of paragraph (i) of this *Example 3*)	$80
6.	Post-1986 undistributed earnings in Corporation B for fiscal year ended June 30, 1992 (pre-dividend) (Line 1 plus Line 3 minus Line 4)	800u
7.	Post-1986 foreign income taxes in Corporation B for fiscal year ended June 30, 1992 (pre-dividend) (Line 2 plus Line 4 translated at the appropriate exchange rates plus Line 5)	$280
8.	Dividends paid out of post-1986 undistributed earnings of Corporation B to Corporation A on February 15, 1992	120u
9.	Percentage of Corporation B's post-1986 undistributed earnings for fiscal year ended June 30, 1992, paid to Corporation A (Line 8 divided by Line 6)	15%
10.	Foreign income taxes paid and deemed paid by Corporation B as of June 30, 1992, deemed paid by Corporation A under section 902(b)(1) (Line 7 multiplied by Line 9)	$42
11.	Total dividends paid out of post-1986 undistributed earnings of Corporation B for fiscal year ended June 30, 1992	300u
12.	Percentage of Corporation B's post-1986 undistributed earnings for fiscal year ended June 30, 1992, paid to all shareholders (Line 11 divided by Line 6)	37.5%
13.	Post-1986 foreign income taxes paid and deemed paid with respect to post-1986 undistributed earnings distributed to all shareholders during Corporation B's fiscal year ended June 30, 1992 (Line 7 multiplied by Line 12)	$105
14.	Post-1986 undistributed earnings in Corporation B as of July 1, 1992 (Line 6 minus Line 11)	500u
15.	Post-1986 foreign income taxes in Corporation B as of July 1, 1992 (Line 7 minus Line 13)	$175
C.	Corporation A (first-tier corporation):	
1.	Assumed post-1986 undistributed earnings in Corporation A at start of 1992	250u
2.	Assumed post-1986 foreign income taxes in Corporation A at start of 1992	$100
3.	Assumed pre-tax earnings and profits of Corporation A for 1992 (including 120u dividend from Corporation B)	250u
4.	Assumed foreign income taxes paid or accrued by Corporation A in 1992	100u
5.	Foreign income taxes paid or deemed paid by Corporation B as of June 30, 1992, that are deemed paid by Corporation A in 1992 (Part B, Line 10 of paragraph (i) of this *Example 3*)	$42
6.	Post-1986 undistributed earnings in Corporation A for 1992 (pre-dividend) (Line 1 plus Line 3 minus Line 4)	400u
7.	Post-1986 foreign income taxes in Corporation A for 1992 (pre-dividend) (Line 2 plus Line 4 translated at the appropriate exchange rates plus Line 5)	$242
8.	Dividends paid out of post-1986 undistributed earnings of Corporation A to Corporation M on August 15, 1992	100u
9.	Percentage of Corporation A's post-1986 undistributed earnings paid to Corporation M in 1992 (Line 8 divided by Line 6)	25%

10.	Foreign income taxes paid and deemed paid by Corporation A in 1992 that are deemed paid by Corporation M under section 902(a) (Line 7 multiplied by Line 9)	$60.50
11.	Total dividends paid out of post-1986 undistributed earnings of Corporation A to all shareholders in 1992	200u
12.	Percentage of Corporation A's post-1986 undistributed earnings paid to all shareholders in 1992 (Line 11 divided by Line 6)	50%
13.	Post-1986 foreign income taxes paid and deemed paid by Corporation A with respect to post-1986 undistributed earnings distributed to all shareholders in 1992 (Line 7 multiplied by Line 12)	$121
14.	Post-1986 undistributed earnings in Corporation A at start of 1993 (Line 6 minus Line 11)	200u
15.	Post-1986 foreign income taxes in Corporation A at start of 1993 (Line 7 minus Line 13)	$121

(ii) Corporation M is deemed, under section 902(a) and paragraph (b) of this section, to have paid $60.50 of post-1986 foreign income taxes paid, or deemed paid, by Corporation A on or with respect to its post-1986 undistributed earnings (Part C, Line 10) and Corporation M includes that amount in gross income as a dividend under section 78. Both the income inclusion and the credit are subject to a separate limitation for dividends from Corporation A, a noncontrolled section 902 corporation.

Example 4. (i) Since 1987, domestic corporation M has owned 100 percent of the voting stock of controlled foreign corporation A, and Corporation A has owned 100 percent of the voting stock of controlled foreign corporation B. Corporations M, A and B use the calendar year as the taxable year. Corporations A and B are organized in the same foreign country and use the u as their functional currency. 1u equals $1 at all relevant times. Assume that all of the earnings of Corporations A and B are general limitation earnings and profits within the meaning of section 904(d)(2)(I), and that neither Corporation A nor Corporation B has any previously taxed income accounts. In 1992, Corporation B pays a dividend of 150u to Corporation A out of post-1986 undistributed earnings, and Corporation A computes an amount of foreign taxes deemed paid under section 902(b)(1). The dividend is not subpart F income to Corporation A because section 954(c)(3)(B)(i) (the same country dividend exception) applies. Pursuant to paragraph (c)(2)(ii) of this section, Corporation A is not required to include the deemed paid taxes in earnings and profits. Corporation A has no pre-1987 accumulated profits and a deficit in post-1986 undistributed earnings for 1992. In 1992, Corporation A pays a dividend of 100u to Corporation M out of its earnings and profits for 1992 (current earnings and profits). Under paragraph (b)(4) of this section, Corporation M is not deemed to have paid any of the foreign income taxes paid or deemed paid by Corporation A because Corporation A has a deficit in post-1986 undistributed earnings as of December 31, 1992, and the sum of its current plus accumulated profits is less than zero. Note that if instead of paying a dividend to Corporation A in 1992, Corporation B had made an additional investment of $150 in United States property under section 956, that amount would have been included in gross income by Corporation M under section 951(a)(1)(B) and Corporation M would have been deemed to have paid $50 of foreign income taxes paid by Corporation B. See sections 951(a)(1)(B) and 960. Foreign income taxes of Corporation B deemed paid by Corporation A and the opening balances in post-1986 undistributed earnings and post-1986 foreign income taxes for Corporation A and Corporation B for 1993 are computed as follows:

A. Corporation B (second-tier corporation):

1.	Assumed post-1986 undistributed earnings in Corporation B at start of 1992 ...	200u
2.	Assumed post-1986 foreign income taxes in Corporation B at start of 1992	$50
3.	Assumed pre-tax earnings and profits of Corporation B for 1992	150u
4.	Assumed foreign income taxes paid or accrued in 1992	50u
5.	Post-1986 undistributed earnings in Corporation B for 1992 (pre-dividend) (Line 1 plus Line 3 minus Line 4)	300u

6.	Post-1986 foreign income taxes in Corporation B for 1992 (pre-dividend) (Line 2 plus Line 4 translated at the appropriate exchange rates)	$100
7.	Dividends paid out of post-1986 undistributed earnings of Corporation B to Corporation A in 1992	150u
8.	Percentage of Corporation B's post-1986 undistributed earnings paid to Corporation A (Line 7 divided by Line 5)	50%
9.	Foreign income taxes of Corporation B deemed paid by Corporation A under section 902(b)(1) (Line 6 multiplied by Line 8)	$50
10.	Post-1986 undistributed earnings in Corporation B at start of 1993 (Line 5 minus Line 7)	150u
11.	Post-1986 foreign income taxes in Corporation B at start of 1993 (Line 6 minus Line 9)	$50

B. Corporation A (first-tier corporation):

1.	Assumed post-1986 undistributed earnings in Corporation A at start of 1992	(200u)
2.	Assumed post-1986 foreign income taxes in Corporation A at start of 1992	0
3.	Assumed pre-tax earnings and profits of Corporation A for 1992 (including 150u dividend from Corporation B)	200u
4.	Assumed foreign income taxes paid or accrued by Corporation A in 1992	40u
5.	Foreign income taxes paid by Corporation B in 1992 that are deemed paid by Corporation A (Part A, Line 9 of paragraph (i) of this *Example 4*)	$50
6.	Post-1986 undistributed earnings in Corporation A for 1992 (pre-dividend) (Line 1 plus Line 3 minus Line 4)	(40u)
7.	Post-1986 foreign income taxes in Corporation A for 1992 (pre-dividend) (Line 2 plus Line 4 translated at the appropriate exchange rates plus Line 5)	$90
8.	Dividends paid out of current earnings and profits of Corporation A for 1992	100u
9.	Percentage of post-1986 undistributed earnings of Corporation A paid to Corporation M in 1992 (Line 8 divided by the greater of Line 6 or zero)	0
10.	Foreign income taxes paid and deemed paid by Corporation A in 1992 that are deemed paid by Corporation M under section 902(a) (Line 7 multiplied by Line 9)	0
11.	Post-1986 undistributed earnings in Corporation A at start of 1993 (line 6 minus line 8)	(140u)
12.	Post-1986 foreign income taxes in Corporation A at start of 1993 (Line 7 minus Line 10)	$90

(ii) For 1993, Corporation A has 500u of earnings and profits on which it pays 160u of foreign income taxes. Corporation A receives no dividends from Corporation B, and pays a 100u dividend to Corporation M. The 100u dividend to Corporation M carries with it some of the foreign income taxes paid and deemed paid by Corporation A in 1992, which were not deemed paid by Corporation M in 1992 because Corporation A had no post-1986 undistributed earnings. Thus, for 1993, Corporation M is deemed to have paid $125 of post-1986 foreign income taxes paid and deemed paid by Corporation A and includes that amount in gross income as a dividend under section 78, determined as follows:

1.	Post-1986 undistributed earnings in Corporation A at start of 1993	(140u)
2.	Post-1986 foreign income taxes in Corporation A at start of 1993	$90
3.	Pre-tax earnings and profits of Corporation A for 1993	500u
4.	Foreign income taxes paid or accrued by Corporation A in 1993	160u
5.	Post-1986 undistributed earnings in Corporation A for 1993 (pre-dividend) (Line 1 plus Line 3 minus Line 4)	200u

6.	Post-1986 foreign income taxes in Corporation A for 1993 (pre-dividend) (Line 2 plus Line 4 translated at the appropriate exchange rates)	$250
7.	Dividends paid out of post-1986 undistributed earnings of Corporation A to Corporation M in 1993	100u
8.	Percentage of post-1986 undistributed earnings of Corporation A paid to Corporation M in 1993 (Line 7 divided by Line 5)	50%
9.	Foreign income taxes paid and deemed paid by Corporation A that are deemed paid by Corporation M in 1993 (Line 6 multiplied by Line 8)	$125
10.	Post-1986 undistributed earnings in Corporation A at start of 1994 (Line 5 minus Line 7)	100u
11.	Post-1986 foreign income taxes in Corporation A at start of 1994 (Line 6 minus Line 9)	$125

Example 5. (i) Since 1987, domestic corporation M has owned 100 percent of the voting stock of controlled foreign corporation A. Corporation M also conducts operations through a foreign branch. Both Corporation A and Corporation M use the calendar year as the taxable year. Corporation A uses the u as its functional currency and 1u equals $1 at all relevant times. Corporation A has no subpart F income, as defined in section 952, and no increase in earnings invested in United States property under section 956 for 1992. Corporation A also has no previously taxed income accounts. Corporation A has general limitation income and high withholding tax interest income that, by operation of section 954(b)(4), does not constitute foreign base company income under section 954(a). Because Corporation A is a controlled foreign corporation, it is not required to reduce post-1986 foreign income taxes by foreign taxes paid or accrued with respect to high withholding tax interest in excess of 5 percent. See § 1.902-1(a)(8)(iii). Corporation A pays a 60u dividend to Corporation M in 1992. For 1992, Corporation M is deemed, under paragraph (b) of this section, to have paid $24 of the post-1986 foreign income taxes paid by Corporation A and includes that amount in gross income under section 78 as a dividend, determined as follows:

1.	Assumed post-1986 undistributed earnings in Corporation A at start of 1992 attributable to:		
	(a)	Section 904(d)(1)(B) high withholding tax interest	20u
	(b)	Section 904(d)(1)(I) general limitation income	55u
2.	Assumed post-1986 foreign income taxes in Corporation A at start of 1992 attributable to:		
	(a)	Section 904(d)(1)(B) high withholding tax interest	$5
	(b)	Section 904(d)(1)(I) general limitation income	$20
3.	Assumed pre-tax earnings and profits of Corporation A for 1992 attributable to:		
	(a)	Section 904(d)(1)(B) high withholding tax interest	20u
	(b)	Section 904(d)(1)(I) general limitation income	20u
4.	Assumed foreign income taxes paid or accrued in 1992 on or with respect to:		
	(a)	Section 904(d)(1)(B) high withholding tax interest	10u
	(b)	Section 904(d)(1)(I) general limitation income	5u
5.	Post-1986 undistributed earnings in Corporation A for 1992 (pre-dividend) attributable to:		
	(a)	Section 904(d)(1)(B) high withholding tax interest (Line 1(a) + Line 3(a) minus Line 4(a))	30u
	(b)	Section 904(d)(1)(I) general limitation income (Line 1(b) + Line 3(b) minus Line 4(b))	70u
	(c)	Total	100u
6.	Post-1986 foreign income taxes in Corporation A for 1992 (pre-dividend) attributable to:		

(a) Section 904(d)(1)(B) high withholding tax interest (Line 2(a) + Line 4(a) translated at the appropriate exchange rates) $15

(b) Section 904(d)(1)(I) general limitation income (Line 2(b) + Line 4(b) translated at the appropriate exchange rates) $25

7. Dividends paid to Corporation M in 1992 .... 60u

8. Dividends paid to Corporation M in 1992 attributable to section 904(d) separate categories pursuant to § 1.904-5(d):

   (a) Dividends paid to Corporation M in 1992 attributable to section 904(d)(1)(B) high withholding tax interest (Line 7 multiplied by Line 5(a) divided by Line 5(c)) 18u

   (b) Dividends paid to Corporation M in 1992 attributable to section 904(d)(1)(I) general limitation income (Line 7 multiplied by Line 5(b) divided by Line 5(c)) 42u

9. Percentage of Corporation A's post-1986 undistributed earnings for 1992 paid to Corporation M attributable to:

   (a) Section 904(d)(1)(B) high withholding tax interest (Line 8(a) divided by Line 5(a)) 60%

   (b) Section 904(d)(1)(I) general limitation income (Line 8(b) divided by Line 5(b)) 60%

10. Foreign income taxes of Corporation A deemed paid by Corporation M under section 902(a) attributable to:

    (a) Foreign income taxes of Corporation A deemed paid by Corporation M under section 902(a) with respect to section 904(d)(1)(B) high withholding tax interest (Line 6(a) multiplied by Line 9(a)) $9

    (b) Foreign income taxes of Corporation A deemed paid by Corporation M under section 902(a) with respect to section 904(d)(1)(I) general limitation income (Line 6(b) multiplied by Line 9(b)) $15

11. Post-1986 undistributed earnings in Corporation A at start of 1993 attributable to:

    (a) Section 904(d)(1)(B) high withholding tax interest (Line 5(a) minus Line 8(a)) 12u

    (b) Section 904(d)(1)(I) general limitation income (Line 5(b) minus Line 8(b)) 28u

12. Post-1986 foreign income taxes in Corporation A at start of 1989 allocable to:

    (a) Section 904(d)(1)(B) high withholding tax interest (Line 6(a) minus Line 10(a)) $6

    (b) Section 904(d)(1)(I) general limitation income (Line 6(b) minus Line 10(b)) $10

(ii) For purposes of computing Corporation M's foreign tax credit limitation, the post-1986 foreign income taxes of Corporation A deemed paid by Corporation M with respect to income in separate categories will be added to the foreign income taxes paid or accrued by Corporation M associated with income derived from Corporation M's branch operation in the same separate categories. The dividend (and the section 78 inclusion with respect to the dividend) will be treated as income in separate categories and added to Corporation M's other income, if any, attributable to the same separate categories. See section 904(d) and § 1.904-6.

(g) *Effective date.*—This section applies to any distribution made in and after a foreign corporation's first taxable year beginning on or after January 1, 1987. [Reg. § 1.902-1.]

☐ [T.D. 8708, 1-6-97. Amended by T.D. 8916, 12-29-2000.]

§ 1.902-2. Treatment of deficits in post-1986 undistributed earnings and pre-1987 accumulated profits of a first-, second-, or third-tier corporation for purposes of computing an amount of foreign taxes deemed paid under § 1.902-1.—
(a) *Carryback of deficits in post-1986 undistributed earnings of a first-, second-, or third-tier corporation to pre-effective date taxable years.*—
(1) *Rule.*—For purposes of computing foreign income taxes deemed paid under § 1.902-1(b) with respect to dividends paid by a first-, second-, or third-tier corporation, when there is a deficit in the post-1986 undistributed earnings of that corporation and the corporation makes a distribution to shareholders that is a dividend or would be a dividend if there were current or

accumulated earnings and profits, then the post-1986 deficit shall be carried back to the most recent pre-effective date taxable year of the first-, second-, or third-tier corporation with positive accumulated profits computed under section 902. See § 1.902-3(e). For purposes of this § 1.902-2, a pre-effective date taxable year is a taxable year beginning before January 1, 1987, or a taxable year beginning after December 31, 1986, if the special effective date of § 1.902-1(a)(13) applies. The deficit shall reduce the section 902 accumulated profits in the most recent pre-effective date year to the extent thereof, and any remaining deficit shall be carried back to the next preceding year or years until the deficit is completely allocated. The amount carried back shall reduce the deficit in post-1986 undistributed earnings. Any foreign income taxes paid in a post-effective date year will not be carried back to pre-effective date taxable years or removed from post-1986 foreign income taxes. See section 960 and the regulations under that section for rules governing the carryback of deficits and the computation of foreign income taxes deemed paid with respect to deemed income inclusions from controlled foreign corporations.

(2) *Examples.*—The following examples illustrate the rules of this paragraph (a):

Example 1. (i) From 1985 through 1990, domestic corporation M owns 10 percent of the one class of stock of foreign corporation A. The remaining 90 percent of Corporation A's stock is owned by Z, a foreign corporation. Corporation A is not a controlled foreign corporation and uses the u as its functional currency. 1u equals $1 at all relevant times. Both Corporation A and Corporation M use the calendar year as the taxable year. Corporation A has pre-1987 accumulated profits and post-1986 undistributed earnings or deficits in post-1986 undistributed earnings, pays pre-1987 and post-1986 foreign income taxes, and pays dividends as summarized below:

Taxable year	1985	1986	1987	1988	1989	1990
Current E & P (Deficits) of Corp. A	150u	150u	(100u)	100u	-0-	-0-
Current Plus Accumulated E & P of Corp. A	150u	300u	200u	250u	250u	200u
Post-'86 Undistributed Earnings of Corp. A			(100u)	100u	100u	50u
Post-'86 Undistributed Earnings of Corp. A Reduced By Current Year Dividend Distributions (increased by deficit carryback)			-0-	100u	50u	50u
Foreign Income Taxes of Corp. A (Annual)	120u	120u	$10	$50	-0-	-0-
Post-'86 Foreign Income Taxes of Corp. A			$10	$60	$60	$30
12/31 Distributions to Corp. M	-0-	-0-	5u	-0-	5u	-0-
12/31 Distributions to Corp. Z	-0-	-0-	45u	-0-	45u	-0-

(ii) On December 31, 1987, Corporation A distributes a 5u dividend to Corporation M and a 45u dividend to Corporation Z. At that time Corporation A has a deficit of (100u) in post-1986 undistributed earnings and $10 of post-1986 foreign income taxes. The (100u) deficit (but not the post-1986 foreign income taxes) is carried back to offset the accumulated profits of 1986 and removed from post-1986 undistributed earnings. The accumulated profits for 1986 are reduced to 50u (150u − 100u). The dividend is paid out of the reduced 1986 accumulated profits. Foreign taxes deemed paid by Corporation M with respect to the 5u dividend are 12u (120u × (5u/50u)). See § 1.902-1(b)(3). Corporation M must include 12u in gross income (translated under the rule applicable to foreign income taxes paid on earnings accumulated in pre-effective date years) under section 78 as a dividend. Both the income inclusion and the foreign taxes deemed paid are subject to a separate limitation for dividends from Corporation A, a noncontrolled section 902 corporation. No accumulated profits remain in Corporation A with respect to 1986 after the carryback of the 1987 deficit and the December 31, 1987, dividend distributions to Corporations M and Z.

(iii) On December 31, 1989, Corporation A distributes a 5u dividend to Corporation M and a 45u dividend to Corporation Z. At that time Corporation A has 100u of post-1986 undistributed earnings and $60 of post-1986 foreign income taxes. Therefore, the dividend is considered paid out of Corporation A's post-1986 undistributed earnings. Foreign taxes deemed paid by Corporation M with respect to the 5u dividend are $3 ($60 × 5% [5u/100u]). Corporation M must include $3 in gross income under section 78 as a dividend. Both the income inclusion and the foreign taxes deemed paid are subject to a separate limitation for dividends from noncontrolled section 902 corporation A. Corporation A's post-1986 undistributed earnings as of January 1, 1990, are 50u (100u − 50u). Corporation A's post-1986 foreign income taxes must be reduced by the amount of foreign taxes that would have been deemed paid if both Corporations M and Z were eligible to compute an amount of deemed paid taxes. Section 1.902-1(a)(8)(i). The amount of foreign income taxes that would have been deemed paid if both Corporations M and Z were eligible to compute an amount of deemed paid taxes on the 50u dividend distributed by Corporation A is $30 ($60 × 50% [50u/100u]). Thus, post-1986 foreign income taxes as of January 1, 1990, are $30 ($60 $30).

Example 2. The facts are the same as in *Example 1*, except that Corporation A has a deficit in its post-1986 undistributed earnings of (150u) on December 31, 1987. The deficit is carried back to 1986 and reduces accumulated profits for that year to -0-. Thus, the foreign income taxes paid with respect to the 1986 accumulated profits will never be deemed paid. The 1987 dividend is deemed to be out of Corporation A's 1985 accumulated profits. Foreign taxes deemed paid by Corporation M under section 902 with respect to the 5u dividend paid on December 31, 1987, are 4u (120u × 5u/150u). See § 1.902-1(b)(3). As a result of the December 31, 1987, dividend distributions, 100u (150u − 50u) of accumulated profits and 80u (120u reduced by 40u[120u × 50u/150u] of foreign taxes that would have been deemed paid had all of Corporation A's shareholders been eligible to compute an amount of foreign taxes deemed paid with respect to the dividend paid out of 1985 accumulated profits) remain in Corporation A with respect to 1985.

Example 3. (i) From 1986 through 1991, domestic corporation M owns 10 percent of the one class of stock of foreign corporation A. The remaining 90 percent of Corporation A's stock is owned by Corporation Z, a foreign corporation. Corporation A is not a controlled foreign corporation and uses the u as its functional currency. 1u equals $1 at all relevant times. Both Corporation A and Corporation M use the calendar year as the taxable year. Corporation A has pre-1987 accumulated profits and post-1986 undistributed earnings or deficits in post-1986 undistributed earnings, pays pre-1987 and post-1986 foreign income taxes, and pays dividends as summarized below:

Taxable year	1986	1987	1988	1989	1990	1991
Current E & P (Deficits) of Corp. A	100u	(50u)	150u	75u	25u	-0-
Current Plus Accumulated E & P of Corp. A	100u	50u	200u	175u	200u	80u
Post-'86 Undistributed Earnings of Corp. A		(50u)	100u	75u	100u	-0-
Post-'86 Undistributed Earnings of Corp. A Reduced By Current Year Dividend Distributions (increased by deficit carryback)		(50u)	-0-	75u	-0-	-0-
Foreign Income Taxes (Annual) of Corp. A	80u	-0-	$120	$20	$20	-0-
Post-'86 Foreign Income Taxes of Corp. A		-0-	$120	$20	$40	-0-
12/31 Distributions to Corp. M	-0-	-0-	10u	-0-	12u	-0-
12/31 Distributions to Corp. Z	-0-	-0-	90u	-0-	108u	-0-

(ii) On December 31, 1988, Corporation A distributes a 10u dividend to Corporation M and a 90u dividend to Corporation Z. At that time Corporation A has 100u in its post-1986 undistributed earnings and $120 in its post-1986 foreign income taxes. Corporation M is deemed, under § 1.902-1(b)(1), to have paid $12 ($120 × 10% [10u/100u]) of the post-1986 foreign income taxes paid by Corporation A and includes that amount in gross income under section 78 as a dividend. Both the income inclusion and the foreign taxes deemed paid are subject to a separate limitation for dividends from noncontrolled section 902 corporation A. Corporation A's post-1986 undistributed earnings as of January 1, 1989, are -0- (100u − 100u). Its post-1986 foreign taxes as of January 1, 1989, also are -0-, $120 reduced by $120 of foreign income taxes paid that would have been deemed paid if both Corporations M and Z were eligible to compute an amount of foreign taxes deemed paid on the dividend from Corporation A ($120 × 100% [100u/100u]).

(iii) On December 31, 1990, Corporation A distributes a 12u dividend to Corporation M and a 108u dividend to Corporation Z. At that time Corporation A has 100u in its post-1986 undistributed earnings and $40 in its post-1986 foreign income taxes. The dividend is paid out of post-1986 undistributed earnings to the extent thereof (100u), and the remainder of 20u is paid out of 1986 accumulated profits. Under §1.902-1(b)(2), the 12u dividend to Corporation M is deemed to be paid out of post-1986 undistributed earnings to the extent of 10u (100u × 12u/120u) and the remaining 2u is deemed to be paid out of Corporation A's 1986 accumulated profits. Similarly, the 108u dividend to Corporation Z is deemed to be paid out of post-1986 undistributed earnings to the extent of 90u (100u × 108u/120u) and the remaining 18u is deemed to be paid out of Corporation A's 1986 accumulated profits. Foreign income taxes deemed paid by Corporation M under section 902 with respect to the portion of the dividend paid out of post-1986 undistributed earnings are $4 ($40 × 10% [10u/100u]), and foreign taxes deemed paid by Corporation M with respect to the portion of the dividend deemed paid out of 1986 accumulated profits are 1.6u (80u × 2u/100u). Corporation M must include $4 plus 1.6u translated under the rule applicable to foreign income taxes paid on earnings accumulated in taxable years prior to the effective date of the Tax Reform Act of 1986 in gross income as a dividend under section 78. The income inclusion and the foreign income taxes deemed paid are subject to a separate limitation for dividends from noncontrolled section 902 Corporation A. As of January 1, 1991, Corporation A's post-1986 undistributed earnings are -0- (100u − 100u). 80u (100u − 20u) of accumulated profits remain with respect to 1986. Post-1986 foreign income taxes as of January 1, 1991, are -0-, $40 reduced by $40 of foreign income taxes paid that would have been deemed paid if both Corporations M and Z were eligible to compute an amount of deemed paid taxes on the 100u dividend distributed by Corporation A out of post-1986 undistributed earnings ($40 × 100% [100u/100u]). Corporation A has 64u of foreign income taxes remaining with respect to 1986, 80u reduced by 16u [80u × 20u/100u] of foreign income taxes that would have been deemed paid if Corporations M and Z both were eligible to compute an amount of deemed paid taxes on the 20u dividend distributed by Corporation A out of 1986 accumulated profits.

(b) *Carryforward of deficits in pre-1987 accumulated profits of a first-, second-, or third-tier corporation to post-1986 undistributed earnings for purposes of section 902.*—(1) *General rule.*—For purposes of computing foreign income taxes deemed paid under §1.902-1(b) with respect to dividends paid by a first-, second-, or third-tier corporation out of post-1986 undistributed earnings, the amount of a deficit in accumulated profits of the foreign corporation determined under section 902 as of the end of its last pre-effective date taxable year is carried forward and reduces post-1986 undistributed earnings on the first day of the foreign corporation's first taxable year beginning after December 31, 1986, or on the first day of the first taxable year in which the ownership requirements of section 902(c)(3)(B) and §1.902-1(a)(1) through (4) are met if the special effective date of §1.902-1(a)(13) applies. Any foreign income taxes paid with respect to a pre-effective date year shall not be carried forward and included in post-1986 foreign income taxes. Post-1986 undistributed earnings may not be reduced by the amount of a pre-1987 deficit in earnings and profits computed under section 964(a). See section 960 and the regulations under that section for rules governing the carryforward of deficits and the computation of foreign income taxes deemed paid with respect to deemed income inclusions from controlled foreign corporations. For translation rules governing carryforwards of deficits in pre-1987 accumulated profits to post-1986 taxable years of a foreign corporation with a dollar functional currency, see §1.985-6(d)(2).

(2) *Effect of pre-effective date deficit.*—If a foreign corporation has a deficit in accumulated profits as of the end of its last pre-effective date taxable year, then the foreign corporation cannot pay a dividend out of pre-effective date years unless there is an adjustment made (for example, a refund of foreign taxes paid) that restores section 902 accumulated profits to a pre-effective date taxable year or years. Moreover, if a foreign corporation has a deficit in section 902 accumulated profits as of the end of its last pre-effective date taxable year, then no deficit in post-1986 undistributed earnings will be carried back under paragraph (a) of this section. For rules concerning carrybacks of eli-

Reg. §1.902-2(b)(2)

gible deficits from post-1986 undistributed earnings to reduce pre-1987 earnings and profits computed under section 964(a), see section 960 and the regulations under that section.

(3) *Examples.*—The following examples illustrate the rules of this paragraph (b):

Example 1. (i) From 1984 through 1988, domestic corporation M owns 10 percent of the one class of stock of foreign corporation A. The remaining 90 percent of Corporation A's stock is owned by Corporation Z, a foreign corporation. Corporation A is not a controlled foreign corporation and uses the u as its functional currency. 1u equals $1 at all relevant times. Both Corporation A and Corporation M use the calendar year as the taxable year. Corporation A has pre-1987 accumulated profits or deficits in accumulated profits and post-1986 undistributed earnings, pays pre-1987 and post-1986 foreign income taxes, and pays dividends as summarized below:

Taxable year	1984	1985	1986	1987	1988
Current E & P (Deficits) of Corp. A	25u	(100u)	(25u)	200u	100u
Current Plus Accumulated E & P (Deficits) of Corp. A	25u	(75u)	(100u)	100u	50u
Post-'86 Undistributed Earnings of Corp. A				100u	50u
Post-'86 Undistributed Earnings of Corp. A Reduced By Current Year Dividend Distributions (reduced by deficit carryforward)				(50u)	50u
Foreign Income Taxes (Annual) of Corp. A	20u	5u	-0-	$100	$50
Post-'86 Foreign Income Taxes of Corp. A				$100	$50
12/31 Distributions to Corp. M	-0-	-0-	-0-	15u	-0-
12/31 Distributions to Corp. Z	-0-	-0-	-0-	135u	-0-

(ii) On December 31, 1987, Corporation A distributes a 150u dividend, 15u to Corporation M and 135u to Corporation Z. Corporation A has 200u of current earnings and profits for 1987, but its post-1986 undistributed earnings are only 100u as a result of the reduction for pre-1987 accumulated deficits required under paragraph (b)(1) of this section. Corporation A has $100 of post-1986 foreign income taxes. Only 100u of the 150u distribution is a dividend out of post-1986 undistributed earnings. Foreign income taxes deemed paid by Corporation M in 1987 with respect to the 10u dividend attributable to post-1986 undistributed earnings, computed under §1.902-1(b), are $10 ($100 × 10% [10u/100u]). Corporation M includes this amount in gross income under section 78 as a dividend. Both the income inclusion and the foreign taxes deemed paid are subject to a separate limitation for dividends from noncontrolled section 902 corporation A. After the distribution, Corporation A has (50u) of post-1986 undistributed earnings (100u – 150u) and -0- post-1986 foreign income taxes, $100 reduced by $100 of foreign income taxes paid that would have been deemed paid if both Corporations M and Z were eligible to compute an amount of deemed paid taxes on the 100u dividend distributed by Corporation A out of post-1986 undistributed earnings ($100 × 100% [100u/100u]).

(iii) The remaining 50u of the 150u distribution cannot be deemed paid out of accumulated profits of a pre-1987 year because Corporation A has an accumulated deficit as of the end of 1986 that eliminated all pre-1987 accumulated profits. See paragraph (b)(2) of this section. The 50u is a dividend out of current earnings and profits under section 316(a)(2); but Corporation M is not deemed to have paid any additional foreign income taxes paid by Corporation A with respect to that 50u dividend out of current earnings and profits. See § 1.902-1(b)(4).

Example 2. (i) From 1986 through 1991, domestic corporation M owns 10 percent of the one class of stock of foreign corporation A. The remaining 90 percent of Corporation A's stock is owned by Corporation Z, a foreign corporation. Corporation A is not a controlled foreign corporation and uses the u as its functional currency. 1u equals $1 at all relevant times. Both Corporation A and Corporation M use the calendar year as the taxable year. Corporation A has pre-1987 accumulated profits or deficits in accumulated profits and post-1986 undistributed earnings, pays post-1986 foreign income taxes, and pays dividends as summarized below:

Taxable year	1986	1987	1988	1989	1990
Current E & P (Deficits) of Corp. A	(100u)	150u	(150u)	100u	250u
Current Plus Accumulated E & P (Deficits) of Corp. A	(100u)	50u	(200u)	(100u)	50u
Post-'86 Undistributed Earnings of Corp. A		50u	(200u)	(100u)	50u
Post-'86 Undistributed Earnings of Corp. A Reduced By Current Year Dividend Distributions (reduced by deficit carryforward)		(50u)	(200u)	(200u)	-0-
Foreign Income Taxes (Annual) of Corp. A	-0-	$120	-0-	$50	$100
Post-'86 Foreign Income Taxes of Corp. A		$120	-0-	$50	$150
12/31 Distributions to Corp. M	-0-	10u	-0-	10u	5u
12/31 Distributions to Corp. Z	-0-	90u	-0-	90u	45u

(ii) On December 31, 1987, Corporation A distributes a 10u dividend to Corporation M and a 90u dividend to Corporation Z. At the time of the distribution, Corporation A has 50u of post-1986 undistributed earnings and 150u of current earnings and profits. Thus, 50u of the dividend distribution (5u to Corporation M and 45u to Corporation Z) is a dividend out of post-1986 undistributed earnings. The remaining 50u is a dividend out of current earnings and profits under section 316(a)(2), but Corporation M is not deemed to have paid any additional foreign income taxes paid by Corporation A with respect to that 50u dividend out of current earnings and profits. See § 1.902-1(b)(4). Note that even if there were no current earnings and profits in Corporation A, the remaining 50u of the 100u distribution cannot be deemed paid out of accumulated profits of a pre-1987 year because Corporation A has an accumulated deficit as of the end of 1986 that eliminated all pre-1987 accumulated profits. See paragraph (b)(2) of this section. Corporation A has $120 of post-1986 foreign income taxes. Foreign taxes deemed paid by Corporation M under section 902 with respect to the 5u dividend out of post-1986 undistributed earnings are $12 ($120 × 10% [5u/50u]). Corporation M includes this amount in gross income as a dividend under section 78. Both the foreign taxes deemed paid and the deemed dividend are subject to a separate limitation for dividends from noncontrolled section 902 corporation A. As of January 1, 1988, Corporation A has (50u) in its post-1986 undistributed earnings (50u-100u) and -0- in its post-1986 foreign income taxes, $120 reduced by $120 of foreign taxes that would have been deemed paid if both Corporations M and Z were eligible to compute an amount of deemed paid taxes on the dividend distributed by Corporation A out of post-1986 undistributed earnings ($120 × 100% [50u/50u]).

(iii) On December 31, 1989, Corporation A distributes a 10u dividend to Corporation M and a 90u dividend to Corporation Z. Although the distribution is considered a dividend in its entirety out of 1989 earnings and profits pursuant to section 316(a)(2), post-1986 undistributed earnings are (100u). Accordingly, for purposes of section 902, Corporation M is deemed to have paid no post-1986 foreign income taxes. See § 1.902-1(b)(4). Corporation A's post-1986 undistributed earnings as of January 1, 1990, are (200u) ((100u)-100u). Corporation A's post-1986 foreign income taxes are not reduced because no taxes were deemed paid.

(iv) On December 31, 1990, Corporation A distributes a 5u dividend to Corporation M and a 45u dividend to Corporation Z. At that time Corporation A has 50u of post-1986 undistributed earnings, and $150 of post-1986 foreign income taxes. Foreign taxes deemed paid by Corporation M under section 902 with respect to the 5u dividend are $15 ($150 × 10% [5u/50u]). Post-1986 undistributed earnings as of January 1, 1991, are -0- (50u – 50u). Post-1986 foreign income taxes as of January 1, 1991, also are -0-, $150 reduced by $150 ($150 × 100% [50u/50u]) of foreign income taxes that would have been deemed paid if both Corporations M and Z were eligible to compute an amount of deemed paid taxes on the 50u dividend.

[Reg. § 1.902-2.]

☐ [*T.D.* 8708, 1-6-97.]

§ 1.902-3. Credit for domestic corporate shareholder of a foreign corporation for foreign income taxes paid with respect to accumulated profits of taxable years of the foreign corporation beginning before January 1, 1987.—(a) *Definitions.*—For purposes of section 902 and §§ 1.902-3 and 1.902-4:

(1) *Domestic shareholder.*—In the case of dividends received by a domestic corporation after December 31, 1964, from a foreign corporation, the term "domestic shareholder" means a domestic corporation which owns at least 10

percent of the voting stock of the foreign corporation at the time it receives a dividend from such foreign corporation.

(2) *First-tier corporation.*—In the case of dividends received by a domestic shareholder after December 31, 1964, from a foreign corporation, the term "first-tier corporation" means a foreign corporation at least 10 percent of the voting stock of which is owned by a domestic shareholder at the time it receives a dividend from such foreign corporation. The term "first-tier corporation" also means a DISC or former DISC, but only with respect to dividends from the DISC or former DISC to the extent they are treated under sections 861(a)(2)(D) and 862(a)(2) as income from sources without the United States.

(3) *Second-tier corporation.*—(i) In the case of dividends paid to a first-tier corporation by a foreign corporation after January 12, 1971 (*i.e.*, the date of enactment of Pub. L. 91-684, 84 Stat. 2068), but only for purposes of applying this section for a taxable year of a domestic shareholder ending after that date, the foreign corporation is a "second-tier corporation" if at least 10 percent of its voting stock is owned by the first-tier corporation at the time the first-tier corporation receives the dividend.

(ii) In the case of dividends paid to a first-tier corporation by a foreign corporation after January 12, 1971, but only for purposes of applying this section for a taxable year of a domestic shareholder ending before January 13, 1971, or in the case of any dividend paid to a first-tier corporation by a foreign corporation before January 13, 1971, the foreign corporation is a "second-tier corporation" if at least 50 percent of its voting stock is owned by the first-tier corporation at the time the first-tier corporation receives the dividend.

(4) *Third-tier corporation.*—In the case of dividends paid to a second-tier corporation (as defined in paragraph (a)(3)(i) or (ii) of this section) by a foreign corporation after January 12, 1971, but only for purposes of applying this section for a taxable year of a domestic shareholder ending after that date, the foreign corporation is a "third-tier corporation" if at least 10 percent of its voting stock is owned by the second-tier corporation at the time the second-tier corporation receives the dividend.

(5) *Foreign income taxes.*—The term "foreign income taxes" means income, war profits, and excess profits taxes, and taxes included in the term "income, war profits, and excess profits taxes" by reason of section 903, imposed by a foreign country or a possession of the United States.

(6) *Dividend.*—For the definition of the term "dividend" for purposes of applying section 902 and this section, see section 316 and the regulations thereunder.

(7) *Dividend received.*—A dividend shall be considered received for purposes of section 902 and this section when the cash or other property is unqualifiedly made subject to the demands of the distributee. See § 1.301-1(b).

(b) *Domestic shareholder owning stock in a first-tier corporation.*—(1) *In general.*—(i) If a domestic shareholder receives dividends in any taxable year from its first-tier corporation, the credit for foreign income taxes allowed by section 901 includes, subject to the conditions and limitations of this section, the foreign income taxes deemed, in accordance with paragraph (b)(2) of this section, to be paid by such domestic shareholder for such year.

(ii) If dividends are received by a domestic shareholder from more than one first-tier corporation, the taxes deemed to be paid by such shareholder under section 902(a) and this paragraph (b) shall be computed separately with respect to the dividends received from each of such first-tier corporations.

(iii) Any taxes deemed paid by a domestic shareholder for the taxable year pursuant to section 902(a) and paragraph (b)(2) of this section shall, except as provided in § 1.960-3(b), be included in the gross income of such shareholder for such year as a dividend pursuant to section 78 and § 1.78-1. For the source of such a section 78 dividend, see paragraph (h)(1) of this section.

(iv) Any taxes deemed, under paragraph (b)(2) of this section, to be paid by the domestic shareholder shall be deemed to be paid by such shareholder only for purposes of the foreign tax credit allowed under section 901. See section 904 for other limitations on the amount of the credit.

(v) For rules relating to reduction of the amount of foreign income taxes deemed paid or accrued with respect to foreign mineral income, see section 901(e) and § 1.901-3.

(vi) For the nonrecognition as a foreign income tax for purposes of this section of certain income, profits, or excess profits taxes paid or accrued to a foreign country in connection with the purchase and sale of oil or gas extracted in such country, see section 901(f) and the regulations thereunder.

(vii) For rules relating to reduction of the amount of foreign income taxes deemed paid with respect to foreign oil and gas extraction income, see section 907(a) and the regulations thereunder.

(viii) See the regulations under sections 960, 962, and 963 for special rules relating to the application of section 902 in computing the foreign tax credit of United States shareholders of controlled foreign corporations.

(2) *Amount of foreign taxes deemed paid by a domestic shareholder.*—To the extent dividends are paid by a first-tier corporation to its domestic shareholder out of accumulated profits, as defined in paragraph (e) of this section, for any taxable year, the domestic shareholder shall be deemed to have paid the same proportion of any foreign income taxes paid, accrued or deemed, in accordance with paragraph (c)(2) of this section, to be paid by such first-tier corporation on or with respect to such accumulated profits for such year which the amount of such dividends (determined without regard to the gross-up under section 78) bears to the amount by which such accumulated profits exceed the amount of such taxes (other than those deemed, under paragraph (c)(2) of this section, to be paid). For determining the amount of foreign income taxes paid or accrued by such first-tier corporation on or with respect to the accumulated profits for the taxable year of such first-tier corporation, see paragraph (f) of this section.

(c) *First-tier corporation owning stock in a second-tier corporation.*—(1) *In general.*—For purposes of applying section 902(a) and paragraph (b)(2) of this section, if a first-tier corporation receives dividends in any taxable year from its second-tier corporation, the foreign income taxes deemed to be paid by the first-tier corporation on or with respect to its own accumulated profits for such year shall be the amount determined in accordance with paragraph (c)(2) of this section. This paragraph (c) shall not apply unless the product of—

(i) The percentage of voting stock owned by the domestic shareholder in the first-tier corporation at the time that the domestic shareholder receives dividends from the first-tier corporation in respect of which foreign income taxes are deemed to be paid by the domestic shareholder under paragraph (b)(1) of this section, and

(ii) The percentage of voting stock owned by the first-tier corporation in the second-tier corporation equals at least 5 percent. The percentage under paragraph (c)(1)(ii) of this section of voting stock owned by the first-tier corporation in the second-tier corporation is determined as of the time that the dividend distributed by the second-tier corporation is received by the first-tier corporation and thus included in accumulated profits of the first-tier corporation out of which dividends referred to in paragraph (c)(1)(i) of this section are distributed by the first-tier corporation to the domestic shareholder.

Example. On February 10, 1976, foreign corporation B pays a dividend out of its accumulated profits for 1975 to foreign corporation A. On February 16, 1976, the date on which it receives the dividend, A Corporation owns 40 percent of the voting stock of B Corporation. Both corporations use the calendar year as the taxable year. On June 1, 1976, A Corporation sells its stock in B Corporation. On January 17, 1977, A Corporation pays a dividend out of its accumulated profits for 1976 to domestic corporation M. M Corporation owns 30 percent of the voting stock of A Corporation on January 20, 1977, the date on which it receives the dividend. M Corporation uses a fiscal year ending on April 30 as the taxable year. On February 16, 1976, A Corporation satisfies the 10-percent stock ownership requirement referred to in paragraph (a)(3) of this section with respect to B Corporation, and on January 20, 1977, M Corporation satisfies the 10-percent stock ownership requirement referred to in paragraph (a)(2) of this section with respect to A Corporation. The 5-percent requirement of this paragraph (c)(1) is also satisfied since 30 percent (the percentage of voting stock owned by M Corporation in A Corporation on January 20, 1977), when multiplied by 40 percent (the percentage of voting stock owned by A Corporation in B Corporation on February 16, 1976), equals 12 percent. Accordingly, for its taxable year ending on April 30, 1977, M Corporation is entitled to a credit for a portion of the foreign income taxes paid, accrued, or deemed to be paid, by A Corporation for 1976; and for 1976 A Corporation is deemed to have paid a portion of the foreign income taxes paid or accrued by B Corporation for 1975.

(2) *Amount of foreign taxes deemed paid by a first-tier corporation.*—A first-tier corporation which receives dividends in any taxable year from its second-tier corporation shall be deemed to have paid for such year the same proportion of any foreign income taxes paid, accrued, or deemed, in accordance with paragraph (d)(2) of this section, to be paid by its second-tier corporation on or with respect to the accumulated profits, as defined in paragraph (e) of this section, for the taxable year of the second-tier corporation from which such dividends are paid which the amount of such dividends bears to the amount by which such accumulated profits of the second-tier corporation exceed the taxes so paid or accrued. For determining the amount of the foreign income taxes paid or accrued by such second-tier corporation on or with respect to the accumulated profits for the taxable year of such second-tier corporation, see paragraph (f) of this section.

(d) *Second-tier corporation owning stock in a third-tier corporation.*—(1) *In general.*—For purposes of applying section 902(b)(1) and paragraph (c)(2) of this section, if a second-tier corporation receives dividends in any taxable year from its third-tier corporation, the foreign income taxes deemed to be paid by the second-tier corporation on or with respect to its own accumulated profits for such year shall be the amount determined in accordance with paragraph (d)(2) of this section. This paragraph (d) shall not apply unless the product of—

(i) The percentage of voting stock arrived at in applying the 5-percent requirement of paragraph (c)(1) of this section with respect to dividends received by the first-tier corporation from the second-tier corporation, and

(ii) The percentage of voting stock owned by the second-tier corporation in the third-tier corporation

equal at least 5 percent. The percentage under paragraph (d)(1)(ii) of this section of voting stock owned by the second-tier corporation in the third-tier corporation is determined as of the time that the dividend distributed by the third-tier corporation is received by the second-tier corporation and thus included in accumulated profits of the second-tier corporation out of which dividends referred to in paragraph (d)(1)(i) of this section are distributed by the second-tier corporation to the first-tier corporation.

Example. On February 27, 1975, foreign corporation C pays a dividend out of its accumulated profits for 1974 to foreign corporation B. On March 3, 1975, the date on which it receives the dividend, B Corporation owns 50 percent of the voting stock of C Corporation. On February 10, 1976, B Corporation pays a dividend out of its accumulated profits for 1975 to foreign corporation A. On February 16, 1976, the date on which it receives the dividend, A Corporation owns 40 percent of the voting stock of B Corporation. All three corporations use the calendar year as the taxable year. On January 17, 1977, A Corporation pays a dividend out of its accumulated profits for 1976 to domestic corporation M. M Corporation owns 30 percent of the voting stock of A Corporation on January 20, 1977, the date on which it receives the dividend. M Corporation uses a fiscal year ending on April 30 as the taxable year. On February 16, 1976, A Corporation satisfies the 10-percent stock ownership requirement referred to in paragraph (a)(3) of this section with respect to B Corporation, and on January 20, 1977, M Corporation satisfies the 10-percent stock ownership requirement referred to in paragraph (a)(2) of this section with respect to A Corporation. The 5-percent requirement of paragraph (c)(1) of this section is also satisfied since 30 percent (the percentage of voting stock owned by M Corporation in A Corporation on January 20, 1977), when multiplied by 40 percent (the percentage of voting stock owned by A Corporation in B Corporation on February 16, 1976), equals 12 percent. On March 3, 1975, B Corporation satisfies the 10-percent stock ownership requirement referred to in paragraph (a)(4) of this section with respect to C Corporation. The 5-percent requirement of this paragraph (d)(1) is also satisfied since 12 percent (the percentage of voting stock arrived at in applying the 5-percent requirement of paragraph (c)(1) of this section with respect to the dividends received by A Corporation from B Corporation on February 16, 1976), when multiplied by 50 percent (the percentage of voting stock owned by B Corporation in C Corporation on March 3, 1975), equals 6 percent. Accordingly, for its taxable year ending on April 30, 1977, M Corporation is entitled to a credit for a portion of the foreign income taxes paid, accrued, or deemed to be paid, by A Corporation for 1976; for 1976 A Corporation is deemed to have paid a portion of the foreign income taxes paid, accrued, or deemed to be paid, by B Corporation for 1975; and for 1975 B Corporation is deemed to have paid a portion of the foreign income taxes paid or accrued by C Corporation for 1974.

(2) *Amount of foreign taxes deemed paid by a second-tier corporation.*—For purposes of applying paragraph (c)(2) of this section to a first-tier corporation, a second-tier corporation which receives dividends in its taxable year from its third-tier corporation shall be deemed to have paid for such year the same proportion of any foreign income taxes paid or accrued by its third-tier corporation on or with respect to the accumulated profits, as defined in paragraph (e) of this section, for the taxable year of the third-tier corporation from which such dividends are paid which the amount of such dividends bears to the amount by which such accumulated profits of the third-tier corporation exceed the taxes so paid or accrued. For determining the amount of the foreign income taxes paid or accrued by such third-tier corporation on or with respect to the accumulated profits for the taxable year of such third-tier corporation, see paragraph (f) of this section.

(e) *Determination of accumulated profits of a foreign corporation.*—The accumulated profits for any taxable year of a first-tier corporation and the accumulated profits for any taxable year of a second-tier or third-tier corporation, which are taken into account in applying paragraph (c)(2) or (d)(2) of this section with respect to such first-tier corporation, shall be the sum of—

(1) The earnings and profits of such corporation for such year, and

(2) The foreign income taxes imposed on or with respect to the gains, profits, and income to which such earnings and profits are attributable.

(f) *Taxes paid on or with respect to accumulated profits of a foreign corporation.*—For purposes of this section, the amount of foreign income taxes paid or accrued on or with respect to the accumulated profits of a foreign corporation for any taxable year shall be the entire amount of the foreign income taxes paid or accrued for such year on or with respect to such gains, profits, and income. For purposes of this paragraph (f), the gains, profits, and income of a foreign corporation for any taxable year shall be determined after reduction by any income, war profits, or excess profits taxes imposed on or with respect to such gains, profits, and income by the United States.

(g) *Determination of earnings and profits of a foreign corporation.*—(1) *Taxable year to which section 963 does not apply.*—For purposes of this section, the earnings and profits of a foreign corporation for any taxable year beginning after December 31, 1962, other than a taxable year to which paragraph (g)(2) of this section applies, may, if the domestic shareholder chooses, be determined under the rules provided by § 1.964-1 exclusive of paragraphs (d) and (e) of such section. The translation of amounts so determined into United States dollars or other foreign currency shall be made at the proper exchange rate for the date of distribution with respect to which the determination is made.

(2) *Taxable year to which section 963 applies.*—For any taxable year of a foreign corporation with respect to which there applies under § 1.963-1(c)(1) an election by a corporate United States shareholder to exclude from its gross income for the taxable year the subpart F income of a controlled foreign corporation, the earnings and profits of such foreign corporation for such year with respect to such shareholder must be determined, for purposes of this section, under the rules provided by § 1.964-1, even though the amount of the minimum distribution required under § 1.963-2(a) to be received by such shareholder from such earnings and profits of such foreign corporation, or from the consolidated earnings and profits of the chain or group which includes such foreign corporation, is zero. Effective for taxable years of foreign corporations beginning after December 31, 1975, section 963 is repealed by section 602(a)(1) of the Tax Reduction Act of 1975 (89 Stat. 58); accordingly, this paragraph (g)(2) is inapplicable with respect to computing earnings and profits for such taxable years.

(3) *Time and manner of making choice.*—The controlling United States shareholders (as defined in § 1.964-1(c)(5)) of a foreign corporation shall make the choice referred to in paragraph (g)(1) of this section (including the elections permitted by § 1.964-1(b) and (c)) by filing a written statement to such effect with the Director of the Internal Revenue Service Center, 11601 Roosevelt Boulevard, Philadelphia, Pennsylvania 19155, within 180 days after the close of the first taxable year of the foreign corporation during which such shareholders receive a distribution of earnings and profits with respect to which the benefits of this section are claimed or on or before November 15, 1965, whichever is later. For purposes of this paragraph (g)(3), the 180-day period shall commence on the date of receipt of any distribution which is considered paid from the accumulated profits of a preceding year or years under paragraph (g)(4) of this section. See § 1.964-1(c)(3)(ii) and (iii) for procedures requiring notification of the Director of the Internal Revenue Service Center and noncontrolling shareholders of action taken.

(4) *Determination by district director.*—The district director in whose district is filed the income tax return of the domestic shareholder claiming a credit under section 901 for foreign income taxes deemed, under section 902 and this section, to be paid by such shareholder shall have the power to determine, with respect to a foreign corporation, from the accumulated profits of what taxable year or years the dividends were paid. In making such determination the district director shall, unless it is otherwise established to his satisfaction, treat any dividends which are paid in the first 60 days of any taxable year of such a corporation as having been paid from the accumulated profits of the preceding taxable year or years of such corporation and shall, in other respects, treat any dividends as having been paid from the most recently accumulated profits. For purposes of this paragraph (g)(4), in the case of a foreign corporation the foreign income taxes of which are determined on the basis of an accounting period of less than 1 year, the term "year" shall mean such accounting period. See sections 441(b)(3) and 443.

(h) *Source of income from first-tier corporation and country to which tax is deemed paid.*—(1) *Source of income.*—For purposes of section 904(a)(1) (relating to the per-country limitation), in the case of a dividend received by a domestic shareholder from a first-tier corporation there shall be deemed to be derived from sources within the foreign country or possession of the United States under the laws of which the first-tier corporation is created or organized the sum of the amounts which under

Reg. § 1.902-3(h)(1)

paragraph (a)(3)(ii) of §1.861-3 are treated, with respect to such dividend, as income from sources without the United States.

(2) *Country to which taxes deemed paid.*—For purposes of section 904, all foreign income taxes paid, or deemed under paragraph (c) of this section to be paid, by a first-tier corporation shall be deemed to be paid to the foreign country or possession of the United States under the laws of which such first-tier corporation is created or organized.

(i) *United Kingdom income taxes paid with respect to royalties.*—A taxpayer shall not be deemed under section 902 and this section to have paid any taxes with respect to which a credit is allowable to such taxpayer or any other taxpayer by virtue of section 905(b).

(j) *Information to be furnished.*—If the credit for foreign income taxes claimed under section 901 includes taxes deemed, under paragraph (b)(2) or (3) of this section, to be paid, the domestic shareholder must furnish the same information with respect to such taxes as it is required to furnish with respect to the taxes actually paid or accrued by it and for which credit is claimed. See §1.905-2. For other information required to be furnished by the domestic shareholder for the annual accounting period of certain foreign corporations ending with or within such shareholder's taxable year, and for reduction in the amount of foreign income taxes paid or deemed to be paid for failure to furnish such information, see section 6038 and the regulations thereunder.

(k) *Illustrations.*—The application of this section may be illustrated by the following examples:

Example (1). Throughout 1978, domestic corporation M owns all the one class of stock of foreign corporation A. Both corporations use the calendar year as the taxable year. Corporation A has accumulated profits, pays foreign income taxes, and pays dividends for 1978 as summarized below. For 1978, M Corporation is deemed, under paragraph (b)(2) of this section, to have paid $20 of the foreign income taxes paid by A Corporation for 1978 and includes such amount in gross income under section 78 as a dividend, determined as follows:

Gains, profits, and income of A Corp.	$100
Foreign income taxes imposed on or with respect to gains, profits, and income	40
Accumulated profits	100
Foreign income taxes paid on or with respect to accumulated profits (total foreign income taxes)	40
Accumulated profits in excess of foreign income taxes	60
Dividends paid to M Corp.	30
Foreign income taxes of A Corp. deemed paid by M Corp. under sec. 902(a) ($40 × $30/$60)	20

Example (2). The facts are the same as in example (1), except that M Corporation also owns all of the one class of stock of foreign corporation B which also uses the calendar year as the taxable year. Corporation B has accumulated profits, pays foreign income taxes, and pays dividends for 1978 as summarized below. For 1978, M Corporation is deemed under paragraph (b)(2) of this section, to have paid $20 of the foreign income taxes paid by A Corporation for 1978 and to have paid $50 of the foreign income taxes paid by B Corporation for 1978, and includes $70 in gross income as a dividend under section 78, determined as follows:

B Corporation

Gains, profits and income	$200
Foreign income taxes imposed on or with respect to gains, profits, and income	100
Accumulated profits	200
Foreign income taxes paid by B Corp. on or with respect to accumulated profits	100
Accumulated profits in excess of foreign income taxes	100
Dividends paid to M Corp.	50
Foreign income taxes of B Corporation deemed paid by M Corporation under section 902(a) ($100 × $50/100)	50

M Corporation

Foreign income taxes deemed paid under sec. 902(a):	
Taxes of A Corp. (from example (1))	$20
Taxes of B Corp. (as determined above)	50
Total	70
Foreign income taxes included in gross income under sec. 78 as a dividend:	
Taxes of A Corp. (from example (1))	20
Taxes of B Corp.	50
Total	70

Example (3). For 1978, domestic corporation M owns all the one class of stock of foreign corporation A, which in turn owns all the one class stock of foreign corporation B. All corporations use the calendar year as the taxable year. For 1978, M Corporation is deemed under paragraph (b)(2) of this section to have paid $50 of the foreign income taxes paid, or deemed under paragraph (c)(2) of this section to be paid, by A Corporation for such year and includes such amount in gross income as a dividend under section 78, determined as follows upon the basis of the facts assumed:

B Corp. (second-tier corporation):	
Gains, profits, and income	$300

Foreign income taxes imposed on or with respect to gains, profits, and income	120
Accumulated profits	300
Foreign income taxes paid by B Corp. on or with respect to its accumulated profits (total foreign income taxes)	120
Accumulated profits in excess of foreign income taxes	180
Dividends paid on Dec. 31, 1978 to A Corp.	90
Foreign income taxes of B Corp. deemed paid by A Corp. for 1978 under sec. 902(b)(1) ($120 × $90/$180)	60

A Corp. (first-tier corporation):

Gains, profits, and income:	
Business operations	200
Dividends from B Corp	90
Total	290
Foreign income taxes imposed on or with respect to gains, profits, and income	40
Accumulated profits	290
Foreign income taxes paid by A Corp. on or with respect to its accumulated profits (total foreign income taxes)	40
Accumulated profits in excess of foreign income taxes	250
Foreign income taxes paid, and deemed to be paid, by A Corp. for 1978 on or with respect to its accumulated profits for such year ($60 + $40)	100
Dividends paid on Dec. 31, 1978, to M Corp.	125

M Corp. (domestic shareholder):

Foreign income taxes of A Corp. deemed paid by M Corp. for 1978 under sec. 902(a) ($100 × $125/$250)	50
Foreign income taxes included in gross income of M Corp. under sec. 78 as a dividend received from A Corp.	$50

Example (4). Throughout 1978, domestic corporation M owns 50 percent of the voting stock of foreign corporation A. A Corporation has owned 40 percent of the voting stock of foreign corporation B since 1970; B Corporation has owned 30 percent of the voting stock of foreign corporation C since 1972. B Corporation uses a fiscal year ending on June 30 as its taxable year; all other corporations use the calendar year as the taxable year. On February 1, 1977, B Corporation receives a dividend from C Corporation out of C Corporation's accumulated profits for 1976. On February 15, 1977, A Corporation receives a dividend from B Corporation out of B Corporation's accumulated profits for its fiscal year ending in 1977. On February 15, 1978, M Corporation receives a dividend from A Corporation out of A Corporation's accumulated profits for 1977. For 1978, M Corporation is deemed under paragraph (b)(2) of this section to have paid $81.67 of the foreign income taxes paid, or deemed under paragraph (c)(2) of this section to be paid, by A Corporation on or with respect to its accumulated profits for 1977, and M Corporation includes that amount in gross income as a dividend under section 78, determined as follows upon the basis of the facts assumed:

C Corp. (third-tier corporation):

Gains, profits, and income for 1976	$2,000.00
Foreign income taxes imposed on or with respect to such gains, profits, and income	800.00
Accumulated profits	2,000.00
Foreign income taxes paid by C Corp. on or with respect to its accumulated profits (total foreign income taxes)	800.00
Accumulated profits in excess of foreign income taxes	1,200.00
Dividends paid on Feb. 1, 1977 to B Corp.	150.00
Foreign income taxes of C Corp. for 1976 deemed paid by B Corp. for its fiscal year ending in 1977 ($800 × $150/$1,200)	100.00

B Corp. (second-tier corporation):

Gains, profits, and income for fiscal year ending in 1977:	
Business operations	850.00
Dividends from C Corp.	150.00
Total	1,000.00
Foreign income taxes imposed on or with respect to gains, profits, and income	200.00
Accumulated profits	1,000.00
Foreign income taxes paid by B Corp. on or with respect to its accumulated profits (total foreign income taxes)	200.00
Accumulated profits in excess of foreign income taxes	800.00
Foreign income taxes paid, and deemed to be paid, by B Corp. for its fiscal year on or with respect to its accumulated profits for such year ($100 + $200)	300.00
Dividends paid on Feb. 15, 1977 to A Corp.	120.00
Foreign income taxes of B Corp. for its fiscal year deemed paid by A Corp. for 1977 ($300 × $120/$800)	45.00

A Corp. (first-tier corporation):

Gains, profits, and income for 1977:	
Business operations	380.00
Dividends from B Corp.	120.00
Total	500.00
Foreign income taxes imposed on or with respect to gains, profits, and income	200.00
Accumulated profits	500.00
Foreign income taxes paid by A Corp. on or with respect to its accumulated profits (total foreign income taxes)	200.00
Accumulated profits in excess of foreign taxes	300.00

Foreign income taxes paid, and deemed to be paid, by A Corp. for 1977 on or with respect to its accumulated profits for such year ($45 + $200) .	245.00
Dividends paid on Feb. 15, 1978 to M Corp.	100.00
M Corp. (domestic shareholder):	
Foreign income taxes of A Corp. for 1974 deemed paid by M Corp. for 1978 under sec. 902(a) ($245 × $100/$30)	81.67
Foreign income taxes included in gross income of M Corp. under sec. 78 as a dividend received from A Corp.	81.67

(l) *Effective date.*—Except as provided in § 1.902-4, this section applies to any distribution received from a first-tier corporation by its domestic shareholder after December 31, 1964, and before the beginning of the foreign corporation's first taxable year beginning after December 31, 1986. If, however, the first day on which the ownership requirements of section 902(c)(3)(B) and § 1.902-1(a)(1) through (4) are met with respect to the foreign corporation is in a taxable year of the foreign corporation beginning after December 31, 1986, then this section shall apply to all taxable years beginning after December 31, 1964, and before the year in which the ownership requirements are first met. See § 1.902-1(a)(13)(i). For corresponding rules applicable to distributions received by the domestic shareholder prior to January 1, 1965, see § 1.902-5 as contained in the 26 CFR part 1 edition revised April 1, 1976. [Reg. § 1.902-3.]

☐ [*T.D.* 7481, 4-15-77. *Amended by T.D.* 7490, 6-10-77; *T.D.* 7649, 10-17-79 *and T.D.* 8708, 1-6-97.]

§ 1.902-4. Rules for distributions attributable to accumulated profits for taxable years in which a first-tier corporation was a less developed country corporation.—
(a) *In general.*—If a domestic shareholder receives a distribution from a first-tier corporation before January 1, 1978, in a taxable year of the domestic shareholder beginning after December 31, 1964, which is attributable to accumulated profits of the first-tier corporation for a taxable year beginning before January 1, 1976, in which the first-tier corporation was a less developed country corporation (as defined in 26 CFR § 1.902-2 rev. as of April 1, 1978), then the amount of the credit deemed paid by the domestic shareholder with respect to such distribution shall be calculated under the rules relating to less developed country corporations contained in (26 CFR § 1.902-1 rev. as of April 1, 1978).

(b) *Combined distributions.*—If a domestic shareholder receives a distribution before January 1, 1978, from a first-tier corporation, a portion of which is described in paragraph (a) of this section, and a portion of which is attributable to accumulated profits of the first-tier corporation for a year in which the first-tier corporation was not a less developed country corporation, then the amount of taxes deemed paid by the domestic shareholder shall be computed separately on each portion of the dividend. The taxes deemed paid on that portion of the dividend described in paragraph (a) shall be computed as specified in paragraph (a). The taxes deemed paid on that portion of the dividend described in this paragraph (b), shall be computed as specified in § 1.902-3.

(c) *Distributions of a first-tier corporation attributable to certain distributions from second- or third-tier corporations.*—Paragraph (a) shall apply to a distribution received by a domestic shareholder before January 1, 1978, from a first-tier corporation out of accumulated profits for a taxable year beginning after December 31, 1975, if:

(1) The distribution is attributable to a distribution received by the first-tier corporation from a second- or third-tier corporation in a taxable year beginning after December 31, 1975.

(2) The distribution from the second- or third-tier corporation is made out of accumulated profits of the second- or third-tier corporation for a taxable year beginning before January 1, 1976, and

(3) The first-tier corporation would have qualified as a less developed country corporation under section 902(d) (as in effect on December 31, 1975), in the taxable year in which it received the distribution.

(d) *Illustrations.*—The application of this section may be illustrated by the following examples:

Example (1). M, a domestic corporation owns all of the one class of stock of foreign corporation A. Both corporations use the calendar year as the taxable year. A Corporation pays a dividend to M Corporation on January 1, 1977, partly out of its accumulated profits for calendar year 1976 and partly out of its accumulated profits for calendar year 1975. For 1975 A Corporation qualified as a less developed country corporation under the former section 902(d) (as in effect on December 31, 1975). M Corporation is deemed under paragraphs (a) and (b) of this section to have paid $63 of foreign income taxes paid by A Corporation on or with respect to its accumulated profits for 1976 and 1975 and M Corporation includes $36 of that amount in gross income as a dividend under section 78, determined as follows upon the basis of the facts assumed:

1976

Gains, profits, and income of A Corp. for 1976	$120.00
Foreign income taxes imposed on or with respect to such gains, profits, and income	36.00
Accumulated profits	120.00
Foreign income taxes paid by A Corp. on or with respect to its accumulated profits (total foreign income taxes) ...	36.00
Accumulated profits in excess of foreign income taxes	84.00
Dividend to M Corp. out of 1976 accumulated profits	84.00
Foreign income taxes of A for 1976 deemed paid by M Corp. ($84/$84 × $36) ...	36.00
Foreign income taxes included in gross income of M Corp. under sec. 78 as a dividend from A Corp.	36.00

1975

Gains, profits, and income of A Corp. for 1975	$257.14
Foreign income taxes imposed on or with respect to such gains, profits, and income	77.14
Accumulated profits (under sec. 902(c)(1)(B) as in effect prior to amendment by the Tax Reform Act of 1976) .	180.00
Foreign income taxes paid by A Corp. on or with respect to its accumulated profits ($77.14 × $180/$257.14) .	54.00
Dividends paid to M Corp. out of accumulated profits of A Corp. for 1975	90.00
Foreign income taxes of A Corp. for 1975 deemed paid by M Corp. (under sec. 902(a)(2) as in effect prior to amendment by the Tax Reform Act of 1976) ($54 × $90/$180)	27.00
Foreign income taxes included in gross income of M Corp. under sec. 78 as a dividend from A Corp.	0

Example (2). The facts are the same as in example (1), except that the distribution from A Corporation to M Corporation on January 1, 1977, was from accumulated profits of A Corporation for 1976. A Corporation's accumulated profits for 1976 were made up of income from its trade or business, and a dividend paid by B, a second-tier corporation in 1976. The dividend from B Corporation to A Corporation was from accumulated profits of B Corporation for 1975. A Corporation would have qualified as a less developed country corporation for 1976 under the former section 902(d) (as in effect on December 31, 1975), M Corporation is deemed under paragraphs (b) and (c) of this section to have paid $543 of the foreign taxes paid or deemed paid by A Corporation on or with respect to its accumulated profits for 1976, and M Corporation includes $360 of that amount in gross income as a dividend under section 78, determined as follows upon the basis of the facts assumed:

Total gains, profits, and income of A Corp. for 1976	$1,500
Gains and profits from business operations	1,200
Gains and profits from dividend A Corp. received in 1976 from B Corp. out of accumulated profits of B Corp. for 1975	300
Foreign taxes imposed on or with respect to such profits and income	450
Foreign taxes paid by A Corp. attributable to gains and profits from A Corp.'s business operations	360
Foreign taxes paid by A Corp. attributable to dividend from B Corp. in 1976	90
Dividends from A Corp. to M Corp. on Jan. 1, 1977	1,050
Portion of dividend attributable to gains and profits of A Corp. from business operations ($1,200/$1,500 × $1,050)	840
Portion of dividends attributable to gains on profits of A Corp. from dividend from B Corp. ($300/$1,500 × $1,050)	210

(a) *Amount of foreign taxes of A Corp. deemed paid by M Corp. on A Corp.'s gains and profits for 1976 from business operations.*

Gains, profits, and income of A Corp. from business operations	$1,200
Foreign income taxes imposed on or with respect to gains, profits, and income	360
Accumulated profits	1,200
Foreign income taxes paid A Corp. on or with respect to its accumulated profits (total foreign income taxes) .	360
Accumulated profits in excess of foreign income taxes	840
Dividend to M Corp	840
Foreign taxes of A Corp. deemed paid by M Corp. ($360 × $840/$840)	360
Foreign taxes included in gross income of M Corp. under sec. 78 as a dividend	360

(b) *Amount of foreign taxes of A Corp. deemed paid by M. Corp. on portion of the dividend attributable to B Corp.'s accumulated profits for 1975.*

Reg. §1.902-4(d)

B Corp. (second-tier corporation):
   Gains, profits, and income for calendar year 1975 .... $1,000
   Foreign income taxes imposed on or with respect to gains, profits, and income 400
   Accumulated profits (under sec. 902(c)(1)(B) as in effect prior to amendment by the Tax Reform Act of 1976) 600
   Foreign income taxes paid by B Corp. on or with respect to its accumulated profits ($400 × $600/$1,000) 240
   Dividend to A Corp. in 1976 300
   Foreign taxes of B Corp. for 1975 deemed paid by A Corp. (under sec. 902(b)(1)(B) as in effect prior to amendment by the Tax Reform Act of 1976) ($240 × $300/$600) 120

A Corp. (first-tier corporation):
   Gains, profits, and income for 1976 attributable to dividend from B Corp.'s accumulated profits for 1975 300
   Foreign income taxes imposed on or with respect to such gains, profits, and income 90
   Accumulated profits (under sec. 902(c)(1)(B) as in effect prior to amendment by the Tax Reform Act of 1976) 210
   Foreign taxes paid by A Corp. on or with respect to such accumulated profits ($90 × $210/$300) 63
   Foreign income taxes paid and deemed to be paid by A Corp. for 1976 on or with respect to such accumulated profits ($120 + $63) 183
   Dividend paid to M Corp. attributable to dividend from B Corp. out of accumulated profits for 1975 210
   Foreign taxes of A Corp. deemed paid by M Corp. (under sec. 902(a)(2) as in effect prior to amendment by the Tax Reform Act of 1976) ($183 × $210/$210) 183
   Amount included in gross income of M Corp. under sec. 78 0

[Reg. § 1.902-4.]

☐ [T.D. 6805, 3-8-65. *Amended by* T.D. 7283, 8-2-73; T.D. 7481, 4-15-77; T.D. 7649, 10-17-79 and T.D. 8708, 1-6-97.]

§ 1.903-1. Taxes in lieu of income taxes.

—(a) *In general.*—Section 903 provides that the term "income, war profits, and excess profits taxes" shall include a tax paid in lieu of a tax on income, war profits, or excess profits ("income tax") otherwise generally imposed by any foreign country. For purposes of this section and §§ 1.901-2 and 1.901-2A, such a tax is referred to as a "tax in lieu of an income tax"; and the terms "paid" and "foreign country" are defined in § 1.901-2(g). A foreign levy (within the meaning of § 1.901-2(g)(3)) is a tax in lieu of an income tax if and only if—

(1) It is a tax within the meaning of § 1.901-2(a)(2); and

(2) It meets the substitution requirement as set forth in paragraph (b) of this section.

The foreign country's purpose in imposing the foreign tax (*e.g.*, whether it imposes the foreign tax because of administrative difficulty in determining the base of the income tax otherwise generally imposed) is immaterial. It is also immaterial whether the base of the foreign tax bears any relation to realized net income. The base of the tax may, for example, be gross income, gross receipts or sales, or the number of units produced or exported. Determinations of the amount of a tax in lieu of an income tax that is paid by a person and determinations of the person by whom such tax is paid are made under § 1.901-2(e) and (f), respectively, substituting the phrase "tax in lieu of an income tax" for the phrase "income tax" wherever the latter appears in those sections. Section 1.901-2A contains additional rules applicable to dual capacity taxpayers (as defined in § 1.901-2(a)(2)(ii)(A)). The rules of this section are applied independently to each separate levy (within the meaning of §§ 1.901-2(d) and 1.901-2A(a)) imposed by the foreign country. Except as otherwise provided in paragraph (b)(2) of this section, a foreign tax either is or is not a tax in lieu of an income tax in its entirety for all persons subject to the tax.

(b) *Substitution.*—(1) *In general.*—A foreign tax satisfies the substitution requirement if the tax in fact operates as a tax imposed in substitution for, and not in addition to, an income tax or a series of income taxes otherwise generally imposed. However, not all income derived by persons subject to the foreign tax need be exempt from the income tax. If, for example, a taxpayer is subject to a generally imposed income tax except that, pursuant to an agreement with the foreign country, the taxpayer's income from insurance is subject to a gross receipts tax and not to the income tax, then the gross receipts tax meets the substitution requirement notwithstanding the fact that the taxpayer's income from other activities, such as the operation of a hotel, is subject to the generally imposed income tax. A comparison between the tax burden of this insurance gross receipts tax and the tax burden that would have obtained under the generally imposed income tax is irrelevant to this determination.

(2) *Soak-up taxes.*—A foreign tax satisfies the substitution requirement only to the extent that liability for the foreign tax is not dependent (by its terms or otherwise) on the availability of a credit for the foreign tax against income tax

liability to another country. If, without regard to this paragraph (b)(2), a foreign tax satisfies the requirement of paragraph (b)(1) of this section (including for this purpose any foreign tax that both satisfies such requirement and also is an income tax within the meaning of § 1.901-2(a)(1)), liability for the foreign tax is dependent on the availability of a credit for the foreign tax against income tax liability to another country only to the extent of the lesser of—

(i) The amount of foreign tax that would not be imposed on the taxpayer but for the availability of such a credit to the taxpayer (within the meaning of § 1.901-2(c)), or

(ii) The amount, if any, by which the foreign tax paid by the taxpayer exceeds the amount of foreign income tax that would have been paid by the taxpayer if it had instead been subject to the generally imposed income tax of the foreign country.

(3) *Examples.*—The provisions of this paragraph (b) may be illustrated by the following examples:

Example (1). Country X has a tax on realized net income that is generally imposed except that nonresidents are not subject to that tax. Nonresidents are subject to a gross income tax on income from country X that is not attributable to a trade or business carried on in country X. The gross income tax imposed on nonresidents satisfies the substitution requirement set forth in this paragraph (b). See also examples (1) and (2) of § 1.901-2(b)(4)(iv).

Example (2). The facts are the same as in example (1), with the additional fact that payors located in country X are required by country X law to withhold the gross income tax from payments they make to nonresidents, and to remit such withheld tax to the government of country X. The result is the same as in example (1).

Example (3). The facts are the same as in example (2), with the additional fact that the gross income tax on nonresidents applies to payments for technical services performed by them outside of country X. The result is the same as in example (2).

Example (4). Country X has a tax that is generally imposed on the realized net income of nonresident corporations that is attributable to a trade or business carried on in country X. The tax applies to all nonresident corporations that engage in business in country X except for such corporations that engage in contracting activities, each of which is instead subject to two different taxes. The taxes applicable to nonresident corporations that engage in contracting activities satisfy the substitution requirement set forth in this paragraph (b).

Example (5). Country X imposes both an excise tax and an income tax. The excise tax, which is payable independently of the income tax, is allowed as a credit against the income tax. For 1984 A has a tentative income tax liability of 100u (units of country X currency) but is allowed a credit for 30u of excise tax that it has paid. Pursuant to paragraph (e)(4)(i) of § 1.901-2, the amount of excise tax A has paid to country X is 30u and the amount of income tax A has paid to country X is 70u. The excise tax paid by A does not satisfy the substitution requirement set forth in this paragraph (b) because the excise tax is imposed on A in addition to, and not in substitution for, the generally imposed income tax.

Example (6). Pursuant to a contract with country X, A, a domestic corporation engaged in manufacturing activities in country X, must pay tax to country X equal to the greater of (i) 5u (units of country X currency) per item produced, or (ii) the maximum amount creditable by A against its U.S. income tax liability for that year with respect to income from its country X operations. Also pursuant to the contract, A is exempted from country X's otherwise generally imposed income tax. A produces 16 items in 1984 and the maximum amount creditable by A against its U.S. income tax liability for 1984 is 125u. If A had been subject to country X's otherwise generally imposed income tax it would have paid a tax of 150u. Pursuant to paragraph (b)(2) of this section, the amount of tax paid by A that is dependent on the availability of a credit against income tax of another country is 0 (lesser of (i) 45u, the amount that would not be imposed but for the availability of a credit (125u – 80u), or (ii) 0, the amount by which the contractual tax (125u) exceeds the generally imposed income tax (150u)).

Example (7). The facts are the same as in example (6) except that, of the 150u A would have paid if it had been subject to the otherwise generally imposed income tax, 60u is dependent on the availability of a credit against income tax of another country. The amount of tax actually paid by A (*i.e.,* 125u) that is dependent on the availability of a credit against income tax of another country is 35u (lesser of (i) 45u, computed as in example (6), or (ii) 35u, the amount by which the contractual tax (125u) exceeds the amount A would have paid as income tax if it had been subject to the otherwise generally imposed income tax (90u, *i.e.,* 150u – 60u)).

(c) *Effective date.*—The effective date of this section is as provided in § 1.901-2(h). [Reg. § 1.903-1.]

☐ [*T.D.* 7918, 10-6-83.]

§ 1.904-2. **Carryback and carryover of unused foreign tax.**—(a) *Credit for foreign tax carryback or carryover.*—A taxpayer who chooses to claim a credit under section 901 for a taxable year is allowed a credit under that section not only for taxes otherwise allowable as a credit but also for taxes deemed paid or accrued in that year as a result of a carryback or carryover of an unused foreign tax under section 904(d). However, the taxes so deemed paid or accrued shall not be allowed as a deduction under section 164(a). The following paragraphs of this section provide rules for the computation of carryovers and carrybacks under section 904(d). For special rules regarding the application of section 904(d) and this section in the case of taxes paid or accrued with respect to section 904(f) interest see section 904(f) and § 1.904-4. For special rules regarding the application of section 904(d) and this section in the case of taxes paid, accrued, or deemed to be paid with respect to section 904(f) dividends see section 904(f) and § 1.904-5. For special rules regarding these computations in the case of taxes paid, accrued, or deemed to be paid with respect to foreign oil and gas extraction income or foreign oil related income, see section 907(b), (e), and (f) and the regulations thereunder.

(b) *Years to which carried.*—(1) *General.*—If the taxpayer chooses the benefits of section 901 for a taxable year beginning after December 31, 1957, any unused foreign tax (as defined in subparagraph (2) of this paragraph) for such year shall, under section 904(d), be carried to the second preceding taxable year, the first preceding taxable year, and the first, second, third, fourth, and fifth succeeding taxable years, in that order and to the extent not absorbed as taxes deemed paid or accrued, under paragraph (c) of this section, in a prior taxable year. The entire unused foreign tax for any taxable year shall first be carried to the earliest of the taxable years to which, under the preceding sentence, such unused foreign tax may be carried. Any portion of such unused foreign tax not deemed paid or accrued under paragraph (c) of this section in such earliest taxable year shall then be carried to the next earliest taxable year to which such unused foreign tax may be carried, and any portion not absorbed in that year shall then be carried to the next earliest year, and so on.

(2) *Definitions.*—(i) When used with reference to a taxable year for which the per-country limitation provided in section 904(a)(1) applies, the term "unused foreign tax" means, with respect to a particular foreign country or possession of the United States, the excess of *(a)* the income, war profits, and excess profits taxes paid or accrued (or deemed paid or accrued other than by reason of section 904(d)) in such year to such foreign country or possession, over *(b)* the applicable per-country limitation under section 904(a)(1) for such year.

(ii) When used with reference to a taxable year for which the overall limitation provided in section 904(a)(2) applies, the term "unused foreign tax" means the excess of *(a)* the income, war profits, and excess profits taxes paid or accrued (or deemed paid or accrued other than by reason of section 904(d)) in such year to all foreign countries and possessions of the United States, over *(b)* the overall limitation under section 904(a)(2) for such year.

(iii) The term "unused foreign tax" does not include any amount by which the income, war profits, and excess profits taxes paid or accrued, or deemed to be paid, to any foreign country or possession of the United States with respect to foreign mineral income are reduced under section 901(e)(1) and § 1.901-3(b)(1).

(3) *Taxable years beginning before January 1, 1958.*—For purposes of this paragraph, the terms "second preceding taxable year" and "first preceding taxable year" do not include any taxable year beginning before January 1, 1958.

(c) *Tax deemed paid or accrued.*—(1) *Unused foreign tax for per-country limitation year.*—(i) The amount of an unused foreign tax with respect to a particular foreign country or possession of the United States, for a taxable year for which the per-country limitation under section 904(a)(1) applies, which shall be deemed paid or accrued in any taxable year to which such unused foreign tax may be carried under paragraph (b) of this section shall, except as provided in subdivision (iii) of this subparagraph, be equal to the smaller of—

(a) The portion of such unused foreign tax which, under paragraph (b) of this section, is carried to such taxable year, or

(b) Any excess limitation for such taxable year with respect to such unused foreign tax (as determined under subdivision (ii) of this subparagraph).

(ii) The excess limitation for any taxable year (hereinafter called the "excess limitation year") with respect to an unused foreign tax in respect of a particular foreign country or possession of the United States for another taxable year (hereinafter called the "year of origin") shall be the amount, if any, by which the limitation for the excess limitation year with respect to that foreign country or possession (computed under section 904(a)(1)) exceeds the sum of—

(a) The income, war profits, and excess profits taxes actually paid or accrued to

such foreign country or possession in the excess limitation year,

  (b) The income, war profits, and excess profits taxes deemed paid or accrued in such year to such foreign country or possession other than by reason of section 904(d), and

  (c) The portion of the unused foreign tax, with respect to such foreign country or possession for any taxable year earlier than the year of origin, which is absorbed as taxes deemed paid or accrued in the excess limitation year under subdivision (i) of this subparagraph.

 (iii) An unused foreign tax for a taxable year for which the per-country limitation provided in section 904(a)(1) applies shall not be deemed paid or accrued in a taxable year for which the overall limitation provided in section 904(a)(2) applies, notwithstanding that under paragraph (b) of this section such overall limitation year is counted as one of the years to which such unused foreign tax may be carried.

 (iv) Any portion of an unused foreign tax with respect to a particular foreign country or possession of the United States which is deemed paid or accrued under section 904(d) in the year to which it is carried shall be deemed paid or accrued to the same foreign country or possession to which such foreign tax was paid or accrued (or deemed paid or accrued other than by reason of section 904(d)) for the year in which it originated.

 (v) For determination of excess limitation for a year for which the taxpayer does not choose to claim a credit under section 901, see paragraph (d) of this section.

 (2) *Unused foreign tax for overall limitation year.*—(i) The amount of an unused foreign tax with respect to all foreign countries and possessions of the United States, for a taxable year for which the overall limitation provided in section 904(a)(2) applies, which shall be deemed paid or accrued in any taxable year to which such unused foreign tax may be carried under paragraph (b) of this section shall, except as provided in subdivision (iii) of this subparagraph, be equal to the smaller of—

  (a) The portion of such unused foreign tax which, under paragraph (b) of this section, is carried to such taxable year, or

  (b) Any excess limitation for such taxable year with respect to such unused foreign tax (as determined under subdivision (ii) of this subparagraph).

 (ii) The excess limitation for any taxable year (hereinafter called the "excess limitation year") with respect to an unused foreign tax in respect of all foreign countries and possessions of the United States for another taxable year (hereinafter called the "year of origin") shall be the amount, if any, by which the limitation for the excess limitation year with respect to all foreign countries and possessions of the United States (computed under section 904(a)(2)) exceeds the sum of—

  (a) The income, war profits, and excess profits taxes actually paid or accrued to all foreign countries and possessions in the excess limitation year,

  (b) The income, war profits, and excess profits taxes deemed paid or accrued in such year to all foreign countries and possessions other than by reason of section 904(d), and

  (c) The portion of the unused foreign tax, with respect to all foreign countries and possessions for any taxable year earlier than the year of origin, which is absorbed as taxes deemed paid or accrued in the excess limitation year under subdivision (i) of this subparagraph.

 (iii) An unused foreign tax for a taxable year for which the overall limitation provided in section 904(a)(2) applies shall not be deemed paid or accrued in a taxable year for which the per-country limitation provided in section 904(a)(1) applies, notwithstanding that under paragraph (b) of this section such per-country limitation year is counted as one of the years to which such unused foreign tax may be carried.

 (iv) For determination of excess limitation for a year for which the taxpayer does not choose to claim a credit under section 901, see paragraph (d) of this section.

 (3) *Unused foreign tax with respect to foreign mineral income.*—If any portion of an unused foreign tax for any taxable year beginning after December 31, 1969, consists of tax paid or accrued, or deemed to be paid, with respect to foreign mineral income, as defined in § 1.901-3(c), such portion shall not be deemed paid or accrued with respect to foreign mineral income in the taxable year to which it is carried under section 904(d).

 (d) *Determination of excess limitation for certain years.*—An excess limitation for a taxable year may exist, and may absorb all or some portion of an unused foreign tax, even though the taxpayer does not choose to claim a credit under section 901 for such year. In such case, the amount of the excess limitation, if any, for such year (hereinafter called the "deduction year") shall be determined in the same manner as though the taxpayer had chosen to claim a credit under section 901 for that year. For purposes of the preceding sentence—

 (1) If the taxpayer has not chosen the benefits of section 901 for any taxable year before the deduction year, the per-country limi-

tation under section 904(a)(1) shall be considered to be applicable for such year, and

(2) If the taxpayer has chosen the benefits of section 901 for any taxable year before the deduction year, the limitation (per-country or overall) applicable for the last taxable year (preceding such deduction year) for which a credit was claimed under section 901 shall be considered to be applicable for such deduction year.

(e) *Periods of less than 12 months.*—A fractional part of a year which is a taxable year under sections 441(b) and 7701(a)(23) is a preceding or a succeeding taxable year for the purpose of determining under section 904(d) the years to which the unused foreign tax may be carried, and any unused foreign tax or excess limitation for such fractional part of a year is the unused foreign tax or excess limitation for a taxable year.

(f) *Statement with tax return.*—Every taxpayer claiming the benefit of a carryback or carryover of the unused foreign tax to any taxable year for which he chooses to claim a credit under section 901 shall file with his return (or with his claim for refund, if appropriate) for that year as an attachment to his Form 1116 or 1118, as the case may be, a statement setting forth the unused foreign tax deemed paid or accrued under this section and all material and pertinent facts relative thereto, including a detailed schedule showing the computation of the unused foreign tax so carried back or over.

(g) *Illustration of carrybacks and carryovers.*—The application of this section may be illustrated by the following examples:

Example (1). (i) A, a calendar year taxpayer using the cash receipts and disbursements method of accounting, chooses to claim a credit under section 901 for each of the taxable years set forth below. Based upon the taxes actually paid to country X, and the section 904(a)(1) limitation applicable in respect of country X, in each of the taxable years, the unused foreign tax deemed paid under section 904(d) in each of the appropriate taxable years is as follows:

Taxable years	1958	1959	1960	1961	1962	1963	1964	1965	1966
Per-country limitation	$175	$150	$100	$100	$100	$300	$400	$200	$600
Taxes actually paid to country X in taxable year	75	60	830	170	150	100	200	140	400
Unused foreign tax to be carried back or over from year of origin	X	X	730	70	50	X	X	X	X
Excess limitation with respect to unused foreign tax for 1960	(100)	(90)	X	X	X	(200)	(200)	(60)	X
1961	X	X	X	X	X	X	X	X	(200)
1962	X	X	X	X	X	X	X	X	(130)
Unused foreign tax absorbed as taxes deemed paid under the carryback and carryover provisions as carried from—									
1960	$100	$90	X	X	X	$200	$200	$60	X
1961	X	X	X	X	X	X	X	X	$70
1962	X	X	X	X	X	X	X	X	50

(ii) The excess limitation for 1958, 1959, 1963, 1964 and 1965, respectively, which is available to absorb the unused foreign tax for 1960 is the amount by which the per-country limitation for each of those years exceeds the taxes actually paid to country X in each such year. The unused foreign tax for 1961 and 1962 are not taken into account, since neither of those years is a year earlier than 1960, the year of origin in respect of which the excess limitation is being determined. Thus, for example, the excess limitation for 1963 is $200, unreduced by the unused foreign tax for 1961 and 1962. There is no excess limitation for 1966 with respect to the unused foreign tax for 1960, since the unused foreign tax may be carried forward only 5 taxable years. The unused foreign tax ($730) for 1960 is thus absorbed as taxes deemed paid to the extent of the excess limitation for each of the taxable years 1958, 1959, 1963, 1964, and 1965, respectively, and in that order, leaving unused foreign tax in the amount of $80 which cannot be absorbed because it cannot be carried beyond 1965.

(iii) The amount of unused foreign tax for 1961 which is deemed paid in 1966 is $70, the smaller of *(a)* that portion of the unused foreign tax carried to 1966 ($70), or *(b)* the excess limitation for 1966 with respect to such unused foreign tax ($200). The unused foreign tax for

1962 ($50) is not taken into account for such purposes, since that year is not a year earlier than 1961, the year of origin in respect of which the excess limitation for 1966 is being determined.

(iv) The excess limitation for 1966 with respect to the unused foreign tax for 1962 is $130, the amount by which the limitation applicable under section 904(a)(1) for 1966 ($600) exceeds the sum of the taxes actually paid ($400) to country X in that year and the unused foreign tax ($70) for 1961 which is absorbed in 1966 as taxes deemed paid and which is carried from a taxable year earlier than 1962, the year of origin in respect of which the excess limitation for 1966 which is available to absorb the unused foreign unused foreign tax for 1960, a year earlier than 1962, is not taken into account in computing the excess limitation for 1966, since the unused foreign tax for 1960 may not be carried beyond 1965. The unused foreign tax ($50) for 1962 is thus absorbed in full in 1966 as taxes deemed paid, since the unused foreign tax does not exceed the excess limitation ($130) for that year.

Example (2). Assume the same facts as those in example (1) except that the taxpayer does not choose to have the benefits of section 901 for 1961. In that case there is no unused foreign tax for that year to carry back or over to be absorbed in other taxable years as taxes deemed paid. Moreover, the excess limitation is being determined. The unabsorbed part ($80) of the tax for 1962 is $200, instead of $130, that is, the amount by which the limitation applicable under section 904(a)(1) for 1966 ($600) exceeds the taxes actually paid ($400) to country X in that year. The amount of the unused foreign tax absorbed in each taxable year as taxes deemed paid is the same as in example (1) except for 1966. In that year only the unused foreign tax ($50) for 1962 is absorbed as taxes deemed paid.

Example (3). Assume the same facts as those in example (1) except that the taxpayer does not choose the benefits of section 901 for 1959. Since the excess limitation for a taxable year for which the taxpayer does not claim a credit under section 901 is determined in the same manner as though the taxpayer had chosen such credit, the excess limitation for 1959 is determined to be $90 just as in example (1). Moreover, even though such excess limitation absorbs a carryback of $90 from the unused tax for 1960, none of such $90 so deemed paid in 1959 is allowed as a deduction under section 164 or as a credit under section 901 for 1959 or for any other taxable year.

Example (4). (i) B, a calendar year taxpayer using the cash receipts and disbursements method of accounting, chooses the benefits of section 901 for each of the taxable years 1957, 1958, and 1959. Based upon the taxes actually paid to country Y and the per-country limitation applicable with respect to country Y, in each of the taxable years, the unused foreign tax deemed paid under section 904(d) for taxable year 1959 is as follows:

Taxable years	1957	1958	1959
Per-country limitation on credit for taxes paid to Y	$300	$200	$250
Taxes actually paid to Y in taxable year	200	300	150
Unused foreign tax to be carried back or over from year of origin	X	100	X
Excess limitation applicable to unused credit	X	X	(100)
Unused foreign tax absorbed as taxes deemed paid	X	X	100

(ii) Since a taxable year beginning before January 1, 1958, cannot constitute a preceding taxable year in which the unused foreign tax for 1958 may be absorbed as taxes deemed paid, the entire unused foreign tax ($100) is absorbed as taxes deemed paid in 1959.

Example (5). (i) C, a calendar year taxpayer using an accrual method of accounting, accrues foreign taxes for the first time in 1961. C chooses the benefits of section 901 for each of the taxable years set forth below and for 1962 elects the overall limitation provided by section 904(a)(2) which, with the Commissioner's consent, is revoked for 1966. Based upon the taxes actually accrued with respect to foreign countries X and Y for each of the taxable years, the unused foreign tax deemed accrued under section 904(d) in the appropriate taxable years is as follows:

Taxable year	Per country 1961	Overall 1962	Overall 1963	Overall 1964	Overall 1965	Per country 1966
Limitation:						
Country X	$175	X	X	X	X	$290
Country Y	125	X	X	X	X	95
Overall	X	$250	$800	$300	$400	X
Taxes actually accrued:						
Country X	$325	X	X	X	X	$200
Country Y	85	X	X	X	X	100
Aggregate	X	$350	$380	$425	$450	X

Reg. §1.904-2(g)

Taxable year	Per country 1961	Overall 1962	Overall 1963	Overall 1964	Overall 1965	Per country 1966
Unused foreign tax to be carried back or over from year of origin:						
Country X	150	X	X	X	X	X
Country Y	X	X	X	X	X	$5
Aggregate	X	100	X	125	50	X
Excess limitation:						
Country X	X	X	X	X	X	90
Country Y	40	X	X	X	X	X
Overall	X	X	420	X	X	X
Unused foreign tax absorbed as taxes deemed accrued under section 904(d) and carried from—						
1961 (Country X)	X	X	X	X	X	(90)
1962 (Overall)	X	X	(100)	X	X	X
1964 (Overall)	X	X	(125)	X	X	X
1965 (Overall)	X	X	(50)	X	X	X

(ii) Since the per-country limitation is applicable for 1961 and 1966 only, any unused foreign tax with respect to such years may not be deemed accrued in 1962, 1963, 1964, or 1965, years for which the overall limitation applies. However, the excess limitation for 1966 with respect to country X ($90) is available to absorb a part of the unused foreign tax for 1961 with respect to country X. The difference with respect to country X between the unused foreign tax for 1961 ($150) and the amount absorbed as taxes deemed accrued ($90) in 1966, or $60, may not be carried beyond 1966 since the unused foreign tax may be carried forward only 5 taxable years. There is no excess limitation with respect to country Y for 1961 in respect of the unused foreign tax of country Y for 1966, since the unused foreign tax may be carried back only 2 taxable years.

(iii) Since the overall limitation is applicable for 1962, 1963, 1964, and 1965, any unused foreign tax with respect to such years may not be absorbed as taxes deemed accrued in 1961 or 1966, years for which the per-country limitation applies. However, the excess limitation for 1963 ($420) computed on the basis of the overall limitation is available to absorb the unused foreign tax for 1962 ($100), the unused foreign tax for 1964 ($125), and the unused foreign tax for 1965 ($50), leaving an excess limitation above such absorption of $145 ($420 − $275). [Reg. § 1.904-2.]

☐ [*T.D.* 6789, 12-30-64. Amended by *T.D.* 7292, 11-30-73; *T.D.* 7294, 11-29-73; *T.D.* 7490, 6-10-77 and *T.D.* 7961, 6-27-84.]

§ 1.904-4. Separate application of section 904 with respect to certain categories of income.—(a) *In general.*—A taxpayer is required to compute a separate foreign tax credit limitation for income received or accrued in a taxable year that is described in section 904(d)(1)(A) (passive income), (B) (high withholding tax interest), (C) (financial services income), (D) (shipping income), (E) (dividends from each noncontrolled section 902 corporation), (F) (dividends from a DISC or former DISC), (G) (foreign trade income), (H) (distributions from a FSC or former FSC), or (I) (general limitation income), or in § 1.904-4(m) (additional separate categories).

(b) *Passive income.*—(1) *In general.*—(i) *Rule.*—The term "passive income" means any—

(A) Income received or accrued by any person that is of a kind that would be foreign personal holding company income (as defined in section 954(c)) if the taxpayer were a controlled foreign corporation, including any amount of gain on the sale or exchange of stock in excess of the amount treated as a dividend under section 1248; or

(B) Amount includible in gross income under section 551 or section 1293.

Passive income does not include any income that is also described in section 904(d)(1)(B) through (H), any export financing interest (as defined in section 904(d)(2)(G) and paragraph (h) of this section), any high taxed income (as defined in section 904(d)(2)(F) and paragraph (c) of this section, or, for taxable years beginning before January 1, 1993, any foreign oil and gas extraction income (as defined in section 907(c)). In addition, passive income does not include any income that would otherwise be passive but is characterized as income in another separate category under the look-through rules. In determining whether any income is of a kind that would be foreign personal holding company income, the rules of section 864(d)(5)(A)(i) and (6) (treating related person factoring income of a controlled foreign corporation as foreign personal holding company income that is not eligible for the export financing income exception to the separate limitation for passive income) shall apply only in the case of income of a controlled foreign corporation (as defined in section 957). Thus, income earned directly by a United States person that is related person factoring income may be eligible for the exception for export financing interest.

(ii) *Example.*—The following example illustrates the application of paragraph (b)(1)(i) of this section:

P is a domestic corporation with a branch in foreign country X. P does not have any financial services income. For 1988, P has a net foreign currency gain that would not constitute foreign personal holding company income if P were a controlled foreign corporation because the gain is directly related to the business needs of P. The currency gain is, therefore, general limitation income to P because it is not income of a kind that would be foreign personal holding company income.

(2) *Active rents or royalties.*—(i) *In general.*—For rents and royalties paid or accrued after September 20, 2004, passive income does not include any rents or royalties that are derived in the active conduct of a trade or business, regardless of whether such rents or royalties are received from a related or an unrelated person. Except as provided in paragraph (b)(2)(ii) of this section, the principles of section 954(c)(2)(A) and the regulations under that section shall apply in determining whether rents or royalties are derived in the active conduct of a trade or business. For this purpose, the term "taxpayer" shall be substituted for the term "controlled foreign corporation" if the recipient of the rents or royalties is not a controlled foreign corporation.

(ii) *Exception for certain rents and royalties.*—Rents and royalties are considered derived in the active conduct of a trade or business by a United States person or by a controlled foreign corporation (or other entity to which the look-through rules apply) for purposes of section 904 (but not for purposes of section 954) if the requirements of section 954(c)(2)(A) are satisfied by one or more corporations that are members of an affiliated group of corporations (within the meaning of section 1504(a), determined without regard to section 1504(b)(3)) of which the recipient is a member. For purposes of this paragraph (b)(2)(ii), an affiliated group includes only domestic corporations and foreign corporations that are controlled foreign corporations in which domestic members of the affiliated group own, directly or indirectly, at least 80 percent of the total voting power and value of the stock. For purposes of this paragraph (b)(2)(ii), indirect ownership shall be determined under section 318 and the regulations under that section.

(iii) *Example.*—The following example illustrates the application of paragraph (b)(2)(ii) of this section.

Example. Controlled foreign corporation S is a wholly-owned subsidiary of P, a domestic corporation. S is regularly engaged in the restaurant franchise business. P licenses trademarks, tradenames, certain know-how, related services, and certain restaurant designs for which S pays P an arm's length royalty. P is regularly engaged in the development and licensing of such property. The royalties received by P for the use of its property are allocable under the look-through rules of § 1.904-5 to the royalties S receives from the franchisees. Some of the franchisees are unrelated to S and P. Other franchisees are related to S or P and use the licensed property outside of S's country of incorporation. S does not satisfy, but P does satisfy, the active trade or business requirements of section 954(c)(2)(A) and the regulations thereunder. The royalty income earned by S with regard to both its related and unrelated franchisees is foreign personal holding company income because S does not satisfy the active trade or business requirements of section 954(c)(2)(A) and, in addition, the royalty income from the related franchisees does not qualify for the same country exception of section 954(c)(3). However, all of the royalty income earned by S is general limitation income to S under § 1.904-4(b)(2)(ii) because P, a member of S's affiliated group (as defined therein), satisfies the active trade or business test (which is applied without regard to whether the royalties are paid by a related person). S's royalty income that is taxable to P under subpart F and the royalties paid to P are general limitation income to P under the look-through rules of § 1.904-5(c)(1)(i) and (c)(3), respectively.

(c) *High-taxed income.*—(1) *In general.*—Income received or accrued by a United States person that would otherwise be passive income shall not be treated as passive income if the income is determined to be high-taxed income. Income shall be considered to be high-taxed income if, after allocating expenses, losses and other deductions of the United States person to that income under paragraph (c)(2)(ii) of this section, the sum of the foreign income taxes paid or accrued by the United States person with respect to such income and the foreign taxes deemed paid or accrued by the United States person with respect to such income under section 902 or section 960 exceeds the highest rate of tax specified in section 1 or 11, whichever applies (and with reference to section 15 if applicable), multiplied by the amount of such income (including the amount treated as a dividend under section 78). If, after application of this paragraph (c), income that would otherwise be passive income is determined to be high-taxed income, such income shall be treated as general limitation income, and any taxes imposed on that income shall be considered related to general limitation income under § 1.904-6. If, after application of this paragraph (c), passive income is zero or less than zero, any taxes imposed on the passive income shall be considered related to general limitation income. For additional rules regarding losses related to passive income, see paragraph (c)(2) of this section. Income and taxes shall be translated at the appropriate rates, as determined under sections 986, 987 and 989 and the regulations under those sections, before application of this paragraph (c). For purposes of allocating taxes to groups of income, United States source passive income is treated as any other passive income. In making the determination whether income is high-taxed, however, only foreign source income, as determined under United States tax principles, is relevant. See paragraph (c)(8) *Examples* 10 through 13 of this section for examples illustrating the application of this paragraph (c)(1) and paragraph (c)(2) of this section. This paragraph (c)(1) is applicable for taxable years beginning after March 12, 1999.

(2) *Grouping of items of income in order to determine whether passive income is high-taxed income.*—(i) *Effective dates.*—(A) *In general.*—For purposes of determining whether passive income is high-taxed income, the grouping rules of paragraphs (c)(3)(i) and (ii), (c)(4), and (c)(5) of this section apply to taxable years beginning after December 31, 1987. Except as provided in paragraph (c)(2)(i)(B) of this section, the rules of paragraph (c)(3)(iii) apply to taxable years beginning after December 31, 1987, and ending before December 31, 1998, and the rules of paragraph (c)(3)(iv) apply to taxable years ending on or after December 31, 1998. See Notice 87-6 (1987-1 C.B.417) for the grouping rules applicable to taxable years beginning after December 31, 1986 and before January 1, 1988. Paragraph (c)(2)(ii) of this section is applicable for taxable years beginning after March 12, 1999.

(B) *Application to prior periods.*—A taxpayer may apply the rules of paragraph (c)(3)(iv) to any taxable year beginning after December 31, 1991, and all subsequent years, provided that—

(1) The taxpayer's tax liability as shown on an original or amended tax return is consistent with the rules of this section for each such year for which the statute of limitations does not preclude the filing of an amended return on June 30, 1999; and

(2) The taxpayer makes appropriate adjustments to eliminate any double benefit arising from the application of this section to years that are not open for assessment.

(ii) *Grouping rules.*—(A) *Initial allocation and apportionment of deductions and taxes.*—For purposes of determining whether passive income is high-taxed, expenses, losses and other deductions shall be allocated and apportioned initially to each of the groups of passive income (described in paragraphs (c)(3), (4), and (5) of this section) under the rules of §§ 1.861-8 through 1.861-14T and 1.865-1 and 1.865-2. Taxpayers that allocate and apportion interest expense on an asset basis may nevertheless apportion passive interest expense among the groups of passive income on a gross income basis. Foreign taxes are allocated to groups under the rules of § 1.904-6(a)(iii). If a loss on a disposition of property gives rise to foreign tax (i.e., the transaction giving rise to the loss is treated under foreign law as having given rise to a gain), the foreign tax shall be allocated to the group of passive income to which gain on the sale would have been assigned under paragraph (c)(3) or (4) of this section. A determination of whether passive income is high-taxed shall be made only after application of paragraph (c)(2)(ii)(B) of this section (if applicable).

(B) *Reallocation of loss groups.*—If, after allocation and apportionment of expenses, losses and other deductions under paragraph (c)(2)(ii)(A) of this section, the sum of the allocable deductions exceeds the gross income in one or more groups, the excess deductions shall proportionately reduce income in the other groups (but not below zero).

(3) *Amounts received or accrued by United States persons.*—Except as provided in paragraph (c)(5) of this section, all passive income received by a United States person shall be subject to the rules of this paragraph (c)(3). However, subpart F inclusions that are passive income and income that is earned by a United States person through a foreign qualified business unit (foreign QBU) that is passive income shall be subject to the rules of this paragraph only to the extent provided in paragraph (c)(4)(ii) of this section. For purposes of this section, a foreign QBU is a QBU (as defined in section 989(a)) other than a controlled foreign corporation, that has its principal place of business outside the United States. These rules shall apply whether the income is received from a controlled foreign corporation of which the United States person is a United States shareholder or from any other person. For purposes of determining whether passive income is high-taxed income, the following rules apply:

(i) All passive income received during the taxable year that is subject to a withholding tax of fifteen percent or greater shall be treated as one item of income.

(ii) All passive income received during the taxable year that is subject to a withholding tax of less than fifteen percent (but greater than zero) shall be treated as one item of income.

(iii) For taxable years ending before December 31, 1998 (except as provided in paragraph (c)(2)(i)(B) of this section), all passive income received during the taxable year that is subject to no withholding tax shall be treated as one item of income.

(iv) For taxable years ending on or after December 31, 1998, all passive income received during the taxable year that is subject to no withholding tax or other foreign tax shall be treated as one item of income, and all passive income received during the taxable year that is subject to no withholding tax but is subject to a foreign tax other than a withholding tax shall be treated as one item of income.

(4) *Income of controlled foreign corporations and foreign QBUs.*—Except as provided in paragraph (c)(5) of this section, all amounts included in gross income of a United States shareholder under section 951(a)(1) for a particular year that (after application of the look-through rules of section 904(d)(3) and §1.904-5) are attributable to passive income received or accrued by a controlled foreign corporation and all amounts of passive income received or accrued by a United States person through a foreign QBU shall be subject to the rules of this paragraph (c)(4). This paragraph (c)(4) shall be applied separately to inclusions with respect to each controlled foreign corporation of which the taxpayer is a United States shareholder. This paragraph (c)(4) also shall be applied separately to income attributable to each QBU of a controlled foreign corporation or any other look-through entity as defined in §1.904-5(i), except that if the entity subject to the look-through rules is a United States person, then this paragraph (c)(4) shall be applied separately only to each foreign QBU of that United States person.

(i) *Income from sources within the QBU's country of operation.*—Passive income from sources within the QBU's country of operation shall be treated as one item of income.

(ii) *Income from sources without the QBU's country of operation.*—Passive income from sources without the QBU's country of operation shall be grouped on the basis of the tax imposed on that income as provided in paragraphs (c)(3)(i) through (iv) of this section.

(iii) *Determination of the source of income.*—For purposes of this paragraph (c)(4), income will be determined to be from sources within or without the QBU's country of operation under the laws of the foreign country of the payor of the income.

(5) *Special rules.*—(i) *Certain rents and royalties.*—All items of rent or royalty income to which an item of rent or royalty expense is directly allocable shall be treated as a single item of income and shall not be grouped with other amounts.

(ii) *Treatment of partnership income.*—A partner's distributive share of income from a foreign or United States partnership that is not subject to the look-through rules and that is treated as passive income under §1.904-5(h)(2)(i) (generally providing that a less than 10 percent partner's distributive share of partnership income is passive income) shall be treated as a single item of income and shall not be grouped with other amounts. A distributive share of income from a foreign partnership that is treated as passive income under the look-through rules shall be grouped according to the rules in paragraph (c)(4) of this section. A distributive share of income from a United States partnership that is treated as passive income under the look-through rules shall be grouped according to the rules in paragraph (c)(3) of this section, except that the portion, if any, of the distributive share of income attributable to income earned by a United States partnership through a foreign QBU shall be grouped under the rules of paragraph (c)(4) of this section.

(iii) *Currency gain or loss.*—(A) *Section 986(c).*—Any currency gain or loss with respect to a distribution received by a United States shareholder (other than a foreign QBU of that shareholder) of previously taxed earnings and profits that is recognized under section 986(c) and that is treated as an item of passive income shall be subject to the rules provided in paragraph (c)(3)(iii) of this section. If that item, however, is received or accrued by a foreign QBU of the United States shareholder, it shall be treated as an item of passive income from sources within the QBU's country of operation for purposes of paragraph (c)(4)(i) of this section. This paragraph (c)(5)(iii)(A) shall be applied separately for each foreign QBU of a United States shareholder.

(B) *Section 987(3).*—Any currency gain or loss with respect to remittances or transfers of property between QBUs of a United States shareholder that is recognized under section 987(3)(B) and that is treated as an item of passive income shall be subject to

Reg. §1.904-4(c)(5)(iii)(B)

the rules provided in paragraph (c)(3)(iii) of this section. If that item, however, is received or accrued by a foreign QBU of the United States shareholder, it shall be treated as an item of passive income from sources within the QBU's country of operation for purposes of paragraph (c)(4)(i) of this section. This paragraph (c)(5)(iii)(B) shall be applied separately for each foreign QBU of a United States shareholder.

(C) *Example.*—The following example illustrates the provisions of this paragraph (c)(5)(iii).

Example. P, a domestic corporation, owns all of the stock of S, a controlled foreign corporation that uses x as its functional currency. In 1993, S earns 100x of passive foreign personal holding company income. When included in P's income under subpart F, the exchange rate is 1x equals $1. Therefore, P's subpart F inclusion is $100. At the end of 1993, S has previously taxed earnings and profits of 100x and P's basis in those earnings is $100. In 1994, S has no earnings and distributes 100x to P. The value of the earnings when distributed is $150. Assume that under section 986(c), P must recognize $50 of passive income attributable to the appreciation of the previously taxed income. Country X does not recognize any gain or loss on the distribution. Therefore, the section 986(c) gain is not subject to any foreign withholding tax or other foreign tax. Thus, under paragraph (c)(3)(iii) of this section, the section 986(c) gain shall be grouped with other items of P's income that are subject to no withholding tax or other foreign tax.

(iv) *Certain passive dividends.*—A dividend from a controlled foreign corporation that is treated as passive income under the look-through rules shall be grouped according to the rules of paragraph (c)(4) of this section.

(v) *Coordination with section 954(b)(4).*—For rules relating to passive income of a controlled foreign corporation that is exempt from subpart F treatment because the income is subject to high foreign tax, see section 904(d)(3)(E), § 1.904-4(c)(7)(iii), and § 1.904-5(d)(2).

(6) *Application of this paragraph to additional taxes paid or deemed paid in the year of receipt of previously taxed income.*—
(i) *Determination made in year of inclusion.*—The determination of whether an amount included in gross income under section 951(a) is high-taxed income shall be made in the taxable year the income is included in the gross income of the United States shareholder under section 951(a) (hereinafter the "taxable year of inclusion"). Any increase in foreign taxes paid or accrued, or deemed paid or accrued, when the taxpayer receives an amount that is excluded from gross income under section 959(a) and that is attributable to a controlled foreign corporation's earnings and profits relating to the amount previously included in gross income will not be considered in determining whether the amount included in income in the taxable year of inclusion is high-taxed income.

(ii) *Exception.*—Paragraph (c)(6)(i) of this section shall not apply to an increase in tax in a case in which the taxpayer is required to adjust its foreign taxes in the year of inclusion under section 905(c).

(iii) *Allocation of foreign taxes imposed on distributions of previously taxed income.*—If an item of income is considered high-taxed income in the year of inclusion and paragraph (c)(6)(i) of this section applies, then any increase in foreign income taxes imposed with respect to that item shall be considered to be related to general limitation income. If an item of income is not considered to be high-taxed income in the taxable year of inclusion and paragraph (c)(6)(i) of this section applies, the following rules shall apply. The taxpayer shall treat an increase in taxes paid or accrued, or deemed paid or accrued, on any distribution of the earnings and profits attributable to the amount included in gross income in the taxable year of inclusion as taxes related to passive income to the extent of the excess of the product of (A) the highest rate of tax in section 11 (determined with regard to section 15 and determined as of the year of inclusion) and (B) the amount of the inclusion (after allocation of parent expenses) over (C) the taxes paid or accrued, or deemed paid or accrued, in the year of inclusion. The taxpayer shall treat any taxes paid or accrued, or deemed paid or accrued, on the distribution in excess of this amount as taxes related to general limitation income. If these additional taxes are not creditable in the year of distribution the carryover rules of section 904(c) apply. For purposes of this paragraph, the foreign tax on a subpart F inclusion shall be considered increased on distribution of the earnings and profits associated with that inclusion if the total of taxes paid and deemed paid on the inclusion and the distribution (taking into account any reductions in tax and any withholding taxes) is greater than the total taxes deemed paid in the year of inclusion. Any foreign currency loss associated with the earnings and profits that are distributed with respect to the inclusion is not to be considered as giving rise to an increase in tax.

(iv) *Increase in taxes paid by successors.*—(A) *General rule.*—Except as provided in paragraph (c)(6)(iv)(B) of this section, if passive earnings and profits previously included in income of a United States shareholder are distributed to a person that was not a United States shareholder of the distributing corporation in the year the earnings were included, any increase in foreign taxes paid or accrued, or deemed paid or accrued, on that distribution shall be treated as taxes related to general limitation income, regardless of whether the previously-taxed income was considered high-taxed income under section 904(d)(2)(F) in the year of inclusion.

(B) *Exception for U.S. shareholders not entitled to look-through.*—In the case of a United States shareholder that, by reason of paragraph (g)(3)(ii) of this section (relating to distributions prior to August 6, 1997, to new shareholders acquiring more than 90 percent of a controlled foreign corporation), is not entitled to look-through treatment with respect to pre-acquisition earnings and profits of the distributing corporation, the increase in foreign taxes described in paragraph (c)(6)(iv)(A) of this section shall be treated as taxes related to the noncontrolled section 902 corporation income of the distributing corporation.

(C) *Effective date.*—This paragraph (c)(6)(iv) applies to taxable years beginning after December 31, 1986. However, for taxable years beginning before January 1, 2001, taxpayers may rely on § 1.904-4(c)(6)(iv) of regulations project INTL-1-92, published at 1992-1 C.B. 1209. See § 601.601(d)(2) of this chapter.

(7) *Application of this paragraph to certain reductions of tax on distributions of income.*—(i) *In general.*—If the effective rate of tax imposed by a foreign country on income of a foreign corporation that is included in a taxpayer's gross income is reduced under foreign law on distribution of such income, the rules of this paragraph (c) apply at the time that the income is included in the taxpayer's gross income without regard to the possibility of subsequent reduction of foreign tax on the distribution. If the inclusion is considered to be high-taxed income, then the taxpayer shall treat the inclusion as general limitation income. When the foreign corporation distributes the earnings and profits to which the inclusion was attributable and the foreign tax on the inclusion is reduced, then the taxpayer shall redetermine whether the inclusion should be considered to be high-taxed income provided that a redetermination of United States tax liability is required under section 905(c). If, taking into account the reduction in foreign tax, the inclusion would not have been considered high-taxed income, then the taxpayer, in redetermining its United States tax liability for the year or years affected, shall treat the inclusion and the associated taxes (as reduced on the distribution) as passive income and taxes. See section 905(c) and the regulations thereunder regarding the method of adjustment. For this purpose, the foreign tax on a subpart F inclusion shall be considered reduced on distribution of the earnings and profits associated with the inclusion if the total of taxes paid and deemed paid on the inclusion and the distribution (taking into account any reductions in tax and any withholding taxes) is less than the total taxes deemed paid in the year of inclusion. Any foreign currency gain associated with the earnings and profits that are distributed with respect to the inclusion is not to be considered a reduction of tax.

(ii) *Allocation of reductions of foreign tax.*—For purposes of paragraph (c)(7)(i) of this section, reductions in foreign tax shall be allocated among the separate categories under the same principles as those of § 1.904-6 for allocating taxes among the separate categories. Thus, for purposes of determining to which year's taxes the reduction in taxes relates, foreign law shall apply. If, however, foreign law does not attribute a reduction in taxes to a particular year or years, then the reduction in taxes shall be attributable, on an annual last in-first out (LIFO) basis, to foreign taxes potentially subject to reduction that are associated with previously taxed income, then on a LIFO basis to foreign taxes associated with income that under paragraph (c)(7)(iii) of this section remains as passive income but that was excluded from subpart F income under section 954(b)(4), and finally on a LIFO basis to foreign taxes associated with other earnings and profits. Furthermore, in applying the ordering rules of section 959(c), distributions shall be considered made on a LIFO basis first out of earnings described in section 959(c)(1) and (2), then on a LIFO basis out of earnings and profits associated with income that remains passive income under paragraph (c)(7)(iii) of this section but that was excluded from subpart F under section 954(b)(4), and finally on a LIFO basis out of other earnings and profits. For purposes of this paragraph (c)(7)(ii), foreign law is not considered to attribute a reduction in tax to a particular year or years if foreign law attributes the tax reduction to a pool or group containing income from more than one taxable year and such pool or group is defined based on a characteristic of the income (for example, the rate of tax paid with respect to the income) rather than on the taxable year in which the income is derived.

(iii) *Interaction with section 954(b)(4).*—If the effective rate of tax imposed by a foreign country on income of a foreign corporation is reduced under foreign law on distribution of that income, the rules of section 954(b)(4) shall be applied without regard to the possibility of subsequent reduction of foreign tax. If a taxpayer excludes passive income from a controlled foreign corporation's foreign personal holding company income under these circumstances, then, notwithstanding the general rule of § 1.904-5(d)(2), the income shall be considered to be passive income until distribution of that income. At that time, the rules of this paragraph shall apply to determine whether the income is high-taxed income and, therefore, general limitation income. For purposes of determining whether a reduction in tax is attributable to taxes on income excluded under section 954(b)(4), the rules of paragraph (c)(7)(ii) of this section apply. The rules of paragraph (c)(7)(ii) of this section shall apply for purposes of ordering distributions to determine whether such distributions are out of earnings and profits associated with such excluded income. For an example illustrating the operation of this paragraph (c)(7)(iii), see paragraph (c)(8) *Example (7)* of this section.

(8) *Examples.*—The following examples illustrate the application of this paragraph (c).

Example (1). Controlled foreign corporation S is a wholly-owned subsidiary of domestic corporation P. S is a single qualified business unit (QBU) operating in foreign country X. In 1988, S earns $130 of gross passive royalty income from country X sources, and incurs $30 of expenses that do not include any payments to P. S's $100 of net passive royalty income is subject to $30 of foreign tax, and is included under section 951 in P's gross income for the taxable year. P allocates $50 of expenses to the $100 (consisting of the $70 section 951 inclusion and $30 section 78 amount), resulting in a net inclusion of $50. After application of the high-tax kick-out rules of paragraph (c)(1) of this section, the $50 inclusion is treated as general limitation income, and the $30 of taxes deemed paid are treated as taxes imposed on general limitation income, because the foreign taxes paid and deemed paid on the income exceed the highest United States tax rate multiplied by the $50 inclusion ($30>$17 (.34 × $50)).

Example (2). The facts are the same as in *Example (1)* except that instead of earning $130 of gross passive royalty income, S earns $65 of gross passive royalty income from country X sources and $65 of gross passive interest income from country Y sources. S incurs $15 of expenses and $5 of foreign tax with regard to the royalty income and incurs $15 of expenses and $10 of foreign tax with regard to the interest income. P allocates $50 of expenses pro rata to the $50 inclusion ($45 section 951 inclusion and $5 section 78 amount) attributable to the royalty income earned by S and the $50 inclusion ($40 section 951 inclusion and $10 section 78 amount) attributable to the interest income earned by S. Under paragraph (c)(4) of this section, the high-tax test is applied separately to the section 951 inclusion attributable to the income from X sources and the section 951 inclusion attributable to the income from Y sources. Therefore, after allocation of P's $50 of expenses, the resulting $25 inclusion attributable to the royalty income from X sources is still treated as passive income because the foreign taxes paid and deemed paid on the income do not exceed the highest United States tax rate multiplied by the $25 inclusion ($5<$8.50 (.34 × $25)). The $25 inclusion attributable to the interest income from Y sources is treated as general limitation income because the foreign taxes paid and deemed paid exceed the highest United States tax rate multiplied by the $25 inclusion ($10>$8.50 (.34 × $25)).

Example (3). Controlled foreign corporation S is a wholly-owned subsidiary of domestic corporation P. S is incorporated and operating in country Y and has a branch in country Z. S has two QBUs (QBU Y and QBU Z). In 1988, S earns $65 of gross passive royalty income in country Y through QBU Y and $65 of gross passive royalty income in country Z through QBU Z. S allocates $15 of expenses to the gross passive royalty income earned by each QBU, resulting in net income of $50 in each QBU. Country Y imposes $5 of foreign tax on the royalty income earned in Y, and country Z imposes $10 of tax on royalty income earned in Z. All of S's income constitutes subpart F foreign personal holding company income that is passive income and is included in P's gross income for the taxable year. P allocates $50 of expenses pro rata to the $100 subpart F inclusion attributable to the QBUs (consisting of the $45 section 951 inclusion derived through QBU Y, the $5 section 78 amount attributable to QBU Y, the $40 section 951 inclusion derived through QBU Z, and the $10 section 78 amount attributable to QBU Z), resulting in a net inclusion of $50. Pursuant to paragraph (c)(4) of this section, the high-tax kickout rules must be applied separately to the subpart F inclusion attributable to the income earned by QBU Y and the income earned by QBU Z. After application of the high-tax kickout rules, the $25 inclusion attributable to Y will still be treated as passive income because the foreign taxes paid and deemed paid on the income do not exceed the highest United States tax rate multiplied by the $25 inclusion ($5<$8.50 (.34 × $25)). The $25 inclusion attributable to Z will be treated as general limitation income because the foreign taxes paid and deemed paid on the income exceed the highest United States tax rate multiplied by the $25 inclusion ($10>$8.50 (.34 × $25)).

Example (4). Domestic corporation M operates in branch form in foreign countries X and Y. The branches are qualified business units (QBUs), within the meaning of section 989(a). In 1988, QBU X earns passive royalty income, interest income and rental income. All of the QBU X passive income is from Country Z sources. The royalty income is not subject to a withholding tax, and is not taxed by Country X, and the interest and the rental income are subject to a 4 percent and 10 percent withholding tax, respectively. QBU Y earns interest income in Country Y that is not subject to foreign tax. For purposes of determining whether M's foreign source passive income is high-taxed income, the rental income and the interest income earned in QBU X are treated as one item of income pursuant to paragraphs (c)(4)(ii) and (3)(ii) of this section. The interest income earned in QBU Y and the royalty income earned in QBU X are each treated as a separate item of income under paragraphs (c)(4)(i) (with respect to QBU Y's interest income) and (c)(4)(ii) and (3)(iii) (with respect to QBU X's royalty income) of this section.

Example (5). S, a controlled foreign corporation incorporated in foreign country R, is a wholly-owned subsidiary of P, a domestic corporation. For 1988, P is required under section 951(a) to include in gross income $80 (not including the section 78 amount) attributable to the earnings and profits of S for such year, all of which is foreign personal holding company income that is passive rent or royalty income. S does not make any distributions in 1988 or 1989. Foreign income taxes paid by S for 1988 that are deemed paid by P for such year under section 960(a) with respect to the section 951(a) inclusion equal $20. Twenty dollars ($20) of P's expenses are properly allocated to the section 951(a) inclusion. The foreign income tax paid with respect to the section 951(a) inclusion does not exceed the highest United States tax rate multiplied by the amount of income after allocation of parent expenses ($20<$27.20 (.34 × $80)). Thus, P's section 951(a) inclusion for 1988 is included in P's passive income and the $20 of taxes attributable to that inclusion are treated as taxes related to passive income. In 1990, S distributes $80 to P, and under section 959 that distribution is treated as attributable to the earnings and profits with respect to the amount included in income by P in 1988 and is excluded from P's gross income. Foreign country R imposes a withholding tax of $15 on the distribution in 1990. Under paragraph (c)(6)(i) of this section, the withholding tax in 1990 does not affect the characterization of the 1988 inclusion as passive income nor does it affect the characterization of the $20 of taxes paid in 1988 as taxes paid with respect to passive income. No further parent expenses are allocable to the receipt of that distribution. In 1990, the foreign taxes paid ($15) exceed the product of the highest United States tax rate and the amount of the inclusion reduced by taxes deemed paid in the year of inclusion ($15>((.34 × $80) − $20)). Thus, under paragraph (c)(6)(iii) of this section, $7.20 ((.34 × $80) − $20)) of the $15 withholding tax paid in 1990 is treated as taxes related to passive income and the remaining $7.80 ($15 − $7.20) of the withholding tax is treated as related to general limitation income.

Example (6). S, a controlled foreign corporation, is a wholly-owned subsidiary of P, a domestic corporation. P and S are calendar year taxpayers. In 1987, S's only earnings consist of $200 of passive income that is foreign personal holding company income that is earned in foreign country X. Under country X's tax system, the corporate tax on particular earnings is reduced on distribution of those earnings and no withholding tax is imposed. In 1987, S pays $100 of foreign tax. P does not elect to exclude this income from subpart F under section 954(b)(4) and includes $200 in gross income ($100 of net foreign personal holding company income and $100 of the section 78 amount). At the time of the inclusion, the income is considered to be high-taxed income under paragraphs (c)(1) and (c)(6)(i) of this section and is general limitation income to P. S does not distribute any of its earnings in 1987. In 1988, S has no earnings. On December 31, 1988, S distributes the $100 of earnings from 1987. At that time, S receives a $50 refund from X attributable to the reduction of the country X corporate tax imposed on those earnings. Under paragraph (c)(7)(i) of this section, P must redetermine whether the 1987 inclusion should be considered to be high-taxed income. By taking into account the reduction in foreign tax, the inclusion would not have been considered high-taxed income. Therefore, P must redetermine its foreign tax credit for 1987 and treat the inclusion and the taxes associated with the inclusion as passive income and taxes. P must follow the appropriate section 905(c) procedures.

Example (7). The facts are the same as in *Example (6)* except that P elects to apply section 954(b)(4) to S's passive income that is subpart F income. Although the income is not considered to be subpart F income, it remains passive income until distribution. In 1988, S distributes $150 to P. The distribution is a dividend to P because S has $150 of accumulated earnings and profits (the $100 of earnings in 1987 and the $50 refund in 1988). P has no expenses allocable to the dividend from S. In 1988, the income is subject to the high-tax kickout rules under paragraph (c)(7)(iii) of this section. The income is passive income to P because the foreign taxes paid and deemed paid by P with respect to the income do not exceed the highest United States tax rate on that income.

Example (8). The facts are the same as in *Example (6)* except that the distribution in 1988 is subject to a withholding tax of $25. Under paragraph (c)(7)(i) of this section, P must redetermine whether the 1987 inclusion should be considered to be high-taxed income because there is a net $25 reduction of foreign tax. By taking into account both the reduction in foreign corporate tax and the withholding tax, the inclusion would continue to be considered high-taxed income. P must follow the appropriate section 905(c) procedures. P must redetermine its foreign tax credit for 1987, but the inclusion and the $75 taxes ($50 of deemed paid tax and $25 withholding tax) will continue to be treated as general limitation income and taxes.

Example (9). (i) S, a controlled foreign corporation operating in country G, is a wholly-owned subsidiary of P, a domestic corporation. P and S are calendar year taxpayers. Country G imposes a tax of 50 percent on S's earnings. Under country G's system, the foreign corporate tax on particular earnings is reduced on distribution of those earnings to 30 percent and no withholding tax is imposed. Under country G's law, distributions are treated as made out of a pool of undistributed earnings subject to the 50% tax rate. For 1987, S's only earnings consist of passive income that is foreign personal holding company income that is earned in foreign country G. S has taxable income of $110 for United States purposes and $100 for country G purposes. Country G, therefore, imposes a tax of $50 on the 1987 earnings of S. P does not elect to exclude this income from subpart F under section 954(b)(4) and includes $110 in gross income ($60 of net foreign personal holding company income and $50 of the section 78 amount). At the time of the inclusion, the income is considered to be high-taxed income under paragraph (c) of this section and is general limitation income to P. S does not distribute any of its taxable income in 1987.

(ii) In 1988, S earns general limitation income that is not subpart F income. S again has $110 in taxable income for United States purposes and $100 in taxable income for country G purposes, and S pays $50 of tax to foreign country G. In 1989, S has no taxable income or earnings. On December 31, 1989, S distributes $60 of earnings and receives a refund of foreign tax of $24. Country G treats the distribution of earnings as out of the 50% tax rate pool of earnings accumulated in 1987 and 1988. However, under paragraph (c)(7)(ii) of this section, the distribution, and, therefore, the reduction of tax is treated as first attributable to the $60 of passive earnings attributable to income previously taxed in 1987. However, because, under foreign law, only 40 percent (the reduction in tax rates from 50 percent to 30 percent is a 40 percent reduction in tax) of the $50 of foreign taxes on the passive earnings can be refunded, $20 of the $24 foreign tax refund reduces foreign taxes on passive earnings. The other $4 of the tax refund reduces the general limitation taxes from $50 to $46 (even though for United States purposes the $60 distribution is entirely out of passive earnings).

(iii) Under paragraph (c)(7) of this section, P must redetermine whether the 1987 inclusion should be considered to be high-taxed income. By taking into account the reduction in foreign tax, the inclusion would not have been considered high-taxed income ($30 < .34 × $110). Therefore, P must redetermine its foreign tax credit for 1987 and treat the inclusion and the taxes associated with the inclusion as passive income and taxes. P must follow the appropriate section 905(c) procedures.

Example (10). P, a domestic corporation, earns $100 of passive royalty income from sources within the United States. Under the laws of Country X, however, that royalty is considered to be from sources within Country X and Country X imposes a 10 percent withholding tax on the payment of the royalty. P also earns $100 of passive foreign source dividend income subject to a 10 percent withholding tax to which $15 of expenses are allocated. In determining whether P's passive income is high-taxed, the $10 withholding tax on P's royalty income is allocated to passive income, and within the passive category to the group of income described in paragraph (c)(3)(ii) of this section (passive income subject to a withholding tax of less than 15 percent (but greater than zero)). For purposes of determining whether the income is high-taxed, however, only the foreign source dividend income is taken into account. The foreign source dividend income will still be treated as passive income because the foreign taxes paid on the passive income in the group ($20) do not exceed the highest United States tax rate multiplied by the $85 of net foreign source income in the group ($20 is less than $28.90 ($100 − $15) × .34).

Example (11). In 2001, P, a U.S. citizen with a tax home in Country X, earns the following items of gross income: $400 of foreign source, passive limitation interest income not subject to foreign withholding tax but subject to Country X income tax of $100, $200 of foreign source, passive limitation royalty income subject to a 5 percent foreign withholding tax (foreign tax paid is $10), $1,300 of foreign source, passive limitation rental income subject to a 25 percent foreign withholding tax (foreign tax paid is $325), $500 of foreign source, general limitation income that gives rise to a $250 foreign tax, and $2,000 of U.S. source capital gain that is not subject to any foreign tax. *P* has a $900 deduction allocable to its passive rental income. *P*'s only other deduction is a $700 capital loss on the sale of stock that is allocated to foreign source passive limitation income under § 1.865-2(a)(3)(i). The $700 capital loss is initially allocated to the group of passive income subject to no withholding tax but subject to foreign tax other than withholding tax. The $300 amount by which the capital loss exceeds the income in the group must be reapportioned to the other groups under paragraph (c)(2)(ii)(B) of this section. The royalty income is thus reduced by $100 to $100 ($200 − ($300 × (200/600))) and the rental income is thus reduced by $200 to $200 ($400 − ($300 × (400/600))). The $100 royalty income is not high-taxed and remains passive income because the foreign taxes do not exceed the highest United States rate of tax on that income. Under the high-tax kick-out, the $200 of rental income and the $325 of associated foreign tax are assigned to the general limitation category.

Example (12). The facts are the same as in *Example 11* except the amount of the capital loss that is allocated under § 1.865-2(a)(3)(i) and paragraph (c)(2) of this section to the group of foreign source passive income subject to no withholding tax but subject to foreign tax other than withholding tax is $1,200. Under paragraph (c)(2)(ii)(B) of this section, the excess deductions of $800 must be reapportioned to the $200 of net royalty income subject to a 5 percent withholding tax and the $400 of net rental income subject to a 15 percent or greater withholding tax. The income in each of these groups is reduced to zero, and the foreign taxes imposed on the rental and royalty income are considered related to general limitation income. The remaining loss of $200 constitutes a separate limitation loss with respect to passive income.

Example (13). In 2001, *P*, a domestic corporation, earns a $100 dividend that is foreign source passive limitation income subject to a 30-percent withholding tax. A foreign tax credit for the withholding tax on the dividend is disallowed under section 901(k). A deduction for the tax is allowed, however, under sections 164 and 901(k)(7). In determining whether *P*'s passive income is high-taxed, the $100 dividend and the $30 deduction are allocated to the first group of income described in paragraph (c)(3)(iv) of this section (passive income subject to no withholding tax or other foreign tax).

(d) *High withholding tax interest.*—The term "high withholding tax interest" means any interest if such interest is subject to a withholding tax of a foreign country or a possession of the United States and the rate of tax applicable to such interest is at least 5 percent. For purposes of the preceding sentence, a withholding tax is any tax imposed by a foreign country or possession of the United States that is determined on a gross basis. A withholding tax shall not be considered to be determined on a gross basis if the tax is not the final tax payable on the interest income, but is merely a prepayment or credit against a final foreign tax liability determined on a net basis on the interest alone or on interest and other income. High withholding tax interest does not include any interest described as export financing interest (as defined in section 904(d)(2)(G) and paragraph (h) of this section).

(e) *Financial services income.*—(1) *In general.*—The term "financial services income" means income derived by a financial services entity, as defined in paragraph (e)(3) of this section, that is:

(i) Income derived in the active conduct of a banking, insurance, financing, or similar business (active financing income as defined in paragraph (e)(2) of this section), except income described in paragraph (e)(2)(i)(W) of this section (high withholding tax interest);

(ii) Passive income as defined in section 904(d)(2)(A) and paragraph (b) of this section as determined before the application of the exception for high-taxed income;

(iii) Export financing interest as defined in section 904(d)(2)(G) and paragraph (h) of this section that, but for section 904(d)(2)(B)(ii), would also meet the definition of high withholding tax interest; or

(iv) Incidental income as defined in paragraph (e)(4) of this section.

(2) *Active financing income.*—(i) *Income included.*—For purposes of paragraph (e)(1) and (e)(3) of this section, income is active financing income only if it is described in any of the following subdivisions.

(A) Income that is of a kind that would be insurance income as defined in section 953(a) (including related party insurance income as defined in section 953(c)(2)) and determined without regard to those provisions of section 953(a)(1)(A) that limit insurance income to income from countries other than the country in which the corporation was created or organized.

(B) Income from the investment by an insurance company of its unearned premiums or reserves ordinary and necessary to the proper conduct of the insurance business, income from providing services as an insurance underwriter, income from insurance brokerage or agency services, and income from loss adjuster and surveyor services.

(C) Income from investing funds in circumstances in which the taxpayer holds itself out as providing a financial service by the acceptance or the investment of such funds, including income from investing deposits of money and income earned investing funds received for the purchase of traveller's checks or face amount certificates.

(D) Income from making personal, mortgage, industrial, or other loans.

(E) Income from purchasing, selling, discounting, or negotiating on a regular basis, notes, drafts, checks, bills of exchange, acceptances, or other evidences of indebtedness.

(F) Income from issuing letters of credit and negotiating drafts drawn thereunder.

(G) Income from providing trust services.

(H) Income from arranging foreign exchange transactions, or engaging in foreign exchange transactions.

(I) Income from purchasing stock, debt obligations, or other securities from an issuer or holder with a view to the public distribution thereof or offering or selling stock, debt obligations, or other securities for an issuer or holder in connection with the public distribution thereof, or participating in any such undertaking.

(J) Income earned by broker-dealers in the ordinary course of business (such as commissions) from the purchase or sale of stock, debt obligations, commodities futures, or other securities or financial instruments and dividend and interest income earned by broker dealers on stock, debt obligations, or other financial instruments that are held for sale.

(K) Service fee income from investment and correspondent banking.

(L) Income from interest rate and currency swaps.

(M) Income from providing fiduciary services.

(N) Income from services with respect to the management of funds.

(O) Bank-to-bank participation income.

(P) Income from providing charge and credit card services or for factoring receivables obtained in the course of providing such services.

(Q) Income from financing purchases from third parties.

(R) Income from gains on the disposition of tangible or intangible personal property or real property that was used in the active financing business (as defined in paragraph (e)(3)(i) of this section) but only to the extent that the property was held to generate or generated active financing income prior to its disposition.

(S) Income from hedging gain with respect to other active financing income.

(T) Income from providing traveller's check services.

(U) Income from servicing mortgages.

(V) Income from a finance lease. For this purpose, a finance lease is any lease that is a direct financing lease or a leveraged lease for accounting purposes and is also a lease for tax purposes.

(W) High withholding tax interest that would otherwise be described as active financing income.

(X) Income from providing investment advisory services, custodial services, agency paying services, collection agency services, and stock transfer agency services.

(Y) Any similar item of income that is disclosed in the manner provided in the instructions to the Form 1118 or 1116 or that is designated as a similar item of income in guidance published by the Internal Revenue Service.

(3) *Financial services entities.*—(i) *In general.*—The term "financial services entity" means an individual or entity that is predominantly engaged in the active conduct of a banking, insurance, financing, or similar business (active financing business) for any taxable year. Except as provided in paragraph (e)(3)(ii) of this section, a determination of whether an entity is a financial services entity shall be done on an entity-by-entity basis. An individual or entity is predominantly engaged in the active financing business for any year if for that year at least 80 percent of its gross income is income described in paragraph (e)(2)(i) of this section. For this purpose, gross income includes all income realized by an individual or entity, whether includible or excludible from gross income under other operative provisions of the Code, but excludes gain from the disposition of stock of a corporation that prior to the disposition of its stock is related to the transferor within the meaning of section 267(b). For this purpose, income received from a related person that is a financial services entity shall be excluded if such income is characterized under the look-through rules of section 904(d)(3) and §1.904-5. In addition, income received from a related person that is not a financial services entity but that is characterized as financial services income under the look-through rules shall be excluded. *See* paragraph (e)(3)(iv) *Example (5)* of this section. Any income received

from a related person that is characterized under the look-through rules and that is not otherwise excluded by this paragraph will retain its character either as active financing income or other income in the hands of the recipient for purposes of determining if the recipient is a financial services entity and if the income is financial services income to the recipient. For purposes of this paragraph, related person is defined in § 1.904-5(i)(1).

(ii) *Special rule for affiliated groups.*—In the case of any corporation that is not a financial services entity under paragraph (e)(3)(i) of this section, but is a member of an affiliated group, such corporation will be deemed to be a financial services entity if the affiliated group as a whole meets the requirements of paragraph (e)(3)(i) of this section. For purposes of this paragraph (e)(3)(ii), affiliated group means an affiliated group as defined in section 1504(a), determined without regard to section 1504(b)(3). In counting the income of the group for purposes of determining whether the group meets the requirements of paragraph (e)(3)(i) of this section, the following rules apply. Only the income of group members that are United States corporations or foreign corporations that are controlled foreign corporations in which United States members of the affiliated group own, directly or indirectly, at least 80 percent of the total voting power and value of the stock shall be included. For purposes of this paragraph (e)(3)(ii), indirect ownership shall be determined under section 318 and the regulations under that section. The income of the group will not include any income from transactions with other members of the group. Passive income will not be considered to be active financing income merely because that income is earned by a member of the group that is a financial services entity without regard to the rule of this paragraph (e)(3)(ii). This paragraph (e)(3)(ii) applies to taxable years beginning after December 31, 2000.

(iii) *Treatment of partnerships and other pass-through entities.*—For purposes of determining whether a partner (including a partnership that is a partner in a second partnership) is a financial services entity, all of the partner's income shall be taken into account, except that income that is excluded under paragraph (e)(3)(i) of this section shall not be taken into account. Thus, if a partnership is determined to be a financial services entity none of the income of the partner received from the partnership that is characterized under the look-through rules shall be included for purpose of determining if the partner is a financial services entity. If a partnership is determined not to be a financial services entity, then income of the partner from the partnership that is characterized under the look-through rules will be taken into account (unless such income is financial services income) and such income will retain its character either as active financing income or as other income in the hands of the partner for purposes of determining if the partner is a financial service entity and if the income is financial services income to the partner. If a partnership is a financial services entity and the partner's income from the partnership is characterized as financial services income under the look-through rules, then, for purposes of determining a partner's foreign tax credit limitation, the income from the partnership shall be considered to be financial services income to the partner regardless of whether the partner is itself a financial services entity. The rules of this paragraph (e)(3)(iii) will apply for purposes of determining whether an owner of an interest in any other pass-through entity the character of the income of which is preserved when such income is included in the income of the owner of the interest is a financial services entity.

(iv) *Examples.*—The principles of paragraph (e)(3) of this section are illustrated by the following examples.

Example (1). P is a domestic corporation that owns 100 percent of the stock of S, a controlled foreign corporation incorporated in Country X. For the 1990 taxable year, 60 percent of S's income is active financing income that consists of income that will be considered general limitation or passive income if S is not a financial services entity. The other 40 percent of S's income is passive non-active financing income. S is not a financial services entity and its active financing income thus retains its character as general limitation and passive income. S makes an interest payment to P in 1990 that is characterized under the look-through rules. Although the interest is not financial services income to S under the look-through rules, it retains its character as active financing income when paid to P and P must take that income into account in determining whether it is a financial services entity under paragraph (e)(3)(i) of this section. If P is determined to be a financial services entity, both the portion of the interest payment characterized as active financing income (whether general limitation or passive income in S's hands) and the portion characterized as passive non-active financing income received from S will be recharacterized as financial services income.

Example 2. Foreign corporation A, which is not a controlled foreign corporation, owns 100 percent of the stock of domestic corporation B, which owns 100 percent of the stock of domestic corporation C. A also owns

100 percent of the stock of foreign corporation D. D owns 100 percent of the stock of domestic corporation E, which owns 100 percent of the stock of controlled foreign corporation F. All of the corporations are members of an affiliated group within the meaning of section 1504(a) (determined without regard to section 1504(b)(3)). Pursuant to paragraph (e)(3)(ii) of this section, however, only the income of B, C, E, and F is counted in determining whether the group meets the requirements of paragraph (e)(3)(i) of this section. For the 2001 taxable year, B's income consists of $95 of active financing income and $5 of passive non-active financing income. C has $40 of active financing income and $20 of passive non-active financing income. E has $70 of active financing income and $15 of passive non-active financing income. F has $10 of passive income. B and E qualify as financial services entities under the entity test of paragraph (e)(3)(i) of this section. Therefore, B and E are financial services entities without regard to whether the group as a whole is a financial services entity and all of the income of B and E shall be treated as financial services income. C and F do not qualify as financial services entities under the entity test of paragraph (e)(3)(i) of this section. However, under the affiliated group test of paragraph (e)(3)(ii) of this section, C and F are financial services entities because at least 80 percent of the group's total income consists of active financing income ($205 of active financing income is 80.4 percent of $255 total income). B's and E's passive income is not treated as active financing income for purposes of the affiliated group test of paragraph (e)(3)(ii) of this section even though it is treated as financial services income without regard to whether the group satisfies the affiliated group test. Once C and F are determined to be financial services entities under the affiliated group test, however, all of the passive income of the group is treated as financial services income. Thus, 100 percent of the income of B, C, E, and F for 2001 is financial services income.

Example (3). PS is a domestic partnership operating in branch form in foreign country X. PS has two equal general partners, A and B. A and B are domestic corporations that each operate in branch form in foreign countries Y and Z. All of A's income, except that derived through PS, is manufacturing income. All of B's income, except that derived through PS, is active financing income. A and B's only income from PS are distributive shares of PS's income. PS is a financial services entity and all of its income is financial services income. The income from PS is excluded in determining if A or B are financial services entities. Thus, A is not a financial services entity because none of A's income is active financing income and B is a financial services entity because all of B's income is active financing income. However, both A and B's distributive shares of PS's taxable income consist of financial services income even though A is not a financial services entity.

Example (4). PS is a domestic partnership operating in foreign country X. A and B are domestic corporations that are equal general partners in PS and, therefore, the look-through rules apply for purposes of characterizing A's and B's distributive shares of PS's income. Fifty (50) percent of PS's gross income is active financing income that is not high withholding tax interest. The active financing income includes income that also meets the definition of passive income and income that meets the definition of general limitation income. The other 50 percent of PS's income is from manufacturing. PS is, therefore, not a financial services entity. A's and B's distributive shares of partnership taxable income consist of general limitation manufacturing income and active financing income. Under paragraph (c)(3)(i) of this section, the active financing income shall be financial services income to A or B if either A or B is determined to be a financial services entity. If A or B is not a financial services entity, the distributive shares of income from PS will not be financial services income to A or B and will consist of passive and general limitation income. All of the income from PS is included in determining if A or B are financial services entities.

Example (5). P is a United States corporation that is not a financial services entity. P owns 100 percent of the stock of S, a controlled foreign corporation that is not a financial services entity. S owns 100 percent of the stock of T, a controlled foreign corporation that is a financial services entity. In 1991, T pays a dividend to S. The dividend from T is characterized under the look-through rules of section 904(d)(3). Pursuant to paragraph (e)(3)(i) of this section, the dividend from T is excluded in determining whether S is a financial services entity. S is determined not to be a financial services entity but the dividend retains its character as financial services income in S's hands. Any subpart F inclusion or dividend to P out of earnings and profits attributable to the dividend from T will be excluded in determining whether P is a financial services entity but the inclusion or dividend will retain its character as financial services income.

(4) *Definition of incidental income.*—(i) *In general.*—(A) *Rule.*—Incidental income is income that is integrally related to active financing income of a financial services entity. Such income includes, for example, income from precious metals trading and commodity trading that is integrally related to futures income. If

securities, shares of stock, or other types of property are acquired by a financial services entity as an ordinary and necessary incident to the conduct of a active financing business, the income from such property will be considered to be financial services income but only so long as the retention of such property remains an ordinary or necessary incident to the conduct of such business. Thus property, including stock, acquired as the result of, or in order to prevent, a loss in an active financing business upon a loan held by the taxpayer in the ordinary course of such business will be considered ordinary and necessary to the conduct of such business, but income from such property will be considered financial services income only so long as the holding of such property remains an ordinary and necessary incident to the conduct of such business. If an entity holds such property for five years or less then the property is considered held incident to the financial services business. If an entity holds such property for more than five years, a presumption will be established that the entity is not holding such property incident to its financial services business. An entity will be able to rebut the presumption by demonstrating that under the facts and circumstances it is not holding the property as an investment. However, the fact that an entity holds the property for more than five years and is not able to rebut the presumption that it is not holding the property incident to its financial services business will not affect the characterization of any income received from the property during the first five years as financial services income.

(B) *Examples.*—The following examples illustrate the application of paragraph (e)(4)(i) of this section.

Example (1). X is a financial services entity within the meaning of paragraph (e)(3)(i) of this section. In 1987, X made a loan in the ordinary course of its business to an unrelated foreign corporation, Y. As security for that loan, Y pledged certain operating assets. Those assets generate income of a type that would be subject to the general limitation. In January 1989, Y defaulted on the loan and forfeited the collateral. During the period X held the assets, X earned operating income generated by those assets. This income was applied in partial satisfaction of Y's obligation. In 1993, X sold the forfeited assets. The sales proceeds were in excess of the remainder of Y's obligation. The operating income received in the period from 1989 to 1993 and the income on the sale of the assets in 1993 are financial services income of X.

Example (2). The facts are the same as in *Example (1),* except that instead of pledging its operating assets as collateral for the loan, Y pledged the stock of its operating subsidiary Z. In 1993, X sold the stock of Z in complete satisfaction of Y's obligation. X's income from the sale of Z stock in satisfaction of Y's obligation is financial services income.

Example (3). P, a domestic corporation, is a financial services entity within the meaning of paragraph (e)(3)(i) of this section. P holds a United States dollar denominated debt (the "obligation") of the Central Bank of foreign country X. The obligation evidences a loan of $100 made by P to the Central Bank. In 1988, pursuant to a program of country X, P delivers the obligation to the Central Bank which credits 70 units of country X currency to M, a country X corporation. M issues all of its only class of capital stock to P. M invests the 70 units of country X currency in the construction and operation of a new hotel in X. In 1994, M distributes 10 units of country X currency to P as a dividend. P is not able to rebut the presumption that it is not holding the stock of M incident to its financial services business. The dividend to P is, therefore, not financial services income.

(ii) *Income that is not incidental income.*—Income that is attributable to non-financial activity is not incidental income within the meaning of paragraph (e)(4)(i) and (ii) of this section solely because such income represents a relatively small proportion of the taxpayer's total income or that the taxpayer engages in non-financial activity on a sporadic basis. Thus, for example, income from data processing services provided to related or unrelated parties or income from the sale of goods or non-financial services (for example travel services) is not financial services income, even if the recipient is a financial services entity.

(5) *Exceptions.*—Financial services income does not include income that is:

(i) Export financing interest as defined in section 904(d)(2)(G) and paragraph (h) of this section unless that income would be high withholding tax interest as defined in section 904(d)(2)(B) but for paragraph (d)(2)(B)(ii) of that section;

(ii) High withholding tax interest as defined in section 904(d)(2)(B) unless that income also meets the definition of export financing interest; and

(iii) Dividends from noncontrolled section 902 corporations as defined in section 904(d)(2)(E) and paragraph (g) of this section.

(f) *Shipping income.*—The term "shipping income" means any income received or accrued by any person that is of a kind that would be foreign base company shipping income (as defined in section 954(f) and the regulations thereunder). Shipping income does not include

Reg. §1.904-4(f)

any dividends received or accrued from a noncontrolled section 902 corporation, any income that is financial services income, or any income described in section 904(d)(1)(G) (foreign trade income within the meaning of section 923(b)).

(g) *Noncontrolled section 902 corporation.*— (1) *Definition.*—Except as otherwise provided, the term "noncontrolled section 902 corporation" means any foreign corporation with respect to which the taxpayer meets the stock ownership requirements of section 902(a) or, for purposes of applying the look-through rules described in section 904(d)(3) and §1.904-5, the taxpayer meets the requirements of section 902(b). Except as provided in section 902 and the regulations under that section and paragraph (g)(3) of this section, a controlled foreign corporation shall not be treated as a noncontrolled section 902 corporation with respect to any distributions out of its earnings and profits for periods during which it was a controlled foreign corporation. In the case of a partnership owning a foreign corporation, the determination of whether a taxpayer meets the ownership requirements of section 902(a) or (b) will be made with respect to the partner's indirect ownership, and not the partnership's direct ownership, in the foreign corporation.

(2) *Treatment of dividends from each separate noncontrolled section 902 corporation.*— (i) *In general.*—Except as otherwise provided, a separate foreign tax credit limitation applies to dividends received or accrued by a corporation from each noncontrolled section 902 corporation. Any dividend distribution made by a noncontrolled section 902 corporation out of earnings and profits attributable to periods in which the shareholder did not meet the stock ownership requirements of section 902(a) or section 902(b) shall be treated as distributions made by a noncontrolled section 902 corporation.

(ii) *Special rule for dividends received by a controlled foreign corporation.*—If—

(A) Stock in a foreign corporation that is not a controlled foreign corporation is owned by a controlled foreign corporation, see paragraph (g)(4) *Example (1),*

(B) There are two or more shareholders of that controlled foreign corporation, and

(C) The ownership requirements of section 902(b) with respect to the foreign corporation are met by at least one of the United States shareholders of the controlled foreign corporation,

then any dividends received by the controlled foreign corporation from the foreign corporation shall be treated in their entirety to the controlled foreign corporation as dividends from a noncontrolled section 902 corporation, notwithstanding that all the United States shareholders of the controlled foreign corporation do not meet the requirements of section 902(b). Any income received or accrued by a United States shareholder of a controlled foreign corporation described in the preceding sentence that is attributable to a dividend paid by a foreign corporation shall be considered to be passive income if the shareholder's interest in that foreign corporation does not satisfy the requirements of section 902(b).

(iii) *Special rules for high withholding tax interest.*—If a taxpayer receives or accrues a dividend distribution from a noncontrolled section 902 corporation out of earnings and profits attributable to high withholding tax interest earned or accrued by the noncontrolled section 902 corporation, any gross basis foreign tax (as defined in paragraph (d) of this section) imposed on such interest, to the extent that the taxes are imposed at a rate in excess of 5 percent, shall not be treated as foreign taxes for purposes of determining the amount of foreign taxes deemed paid or accrued by the taxpayer under section 902. The preceding sentence shall have no effect upon the determination of the amount of earnings and profits of a noncontrolled section 902 corporation.

(iv) *Treatment of inclusions under section 1293.*—If a foreign corporation is a noncontrolled section 902 corporation with respect to a taxpayer, and inclusion in the taxpayer's gross income under section 1293 with respect to that corporation shall be treated as a dividend from a noncontrolled section 902 corporation and thus shall be subject to a separate limitation.

(v) *Examples.*—The following examples illustrate the application of this paragraph (g).

Example (1). A and B are domestic corporations. A owns 90 percent of the stock of C, a foreign corporation and B owns the remaining 10 percent of the C stock. C is a controlled foreign corporation. A and B are United States shareholders. C owns 20 percent of the stock of D, a foreign corporation, not a controlled foreign corporation, that is incorporated in a different country than C. D is a noncontrolled section 902 corporation with respect to C and A, but not with respect to B. In 1987, C has foreign personal holding company income of $1000, $100 of which is attributable to a dividend from D. The remainder of the foreign personal holding company income is passive income. Assume that gross income and net income are equal and that C pays no foreign taxes on its foreign personal holding company income. In 1987, A and B have section

951(a)(1)(A) inclusions of $900 and $100, respectively, attributable to the foreign personal holding company income. Under paragraph (g)(2)(ii) of this section, the $900 included by A consists of $810 passive income and $90 of income attributable to a dividend from a noncontrolled section 902 corporation. The $100 included by B in gross income is characterized as passive income in its entirety although $10 of the $100 is attributable to the dividend from D, and, as to C, that dividend is characterized as a dividend from a noncontrolled section 902 corporation. As to B, the $10 is characterized as passive income because B does not meet the ownership requirements of section 902(b) with regard to D.

Example (2). In 1987, A, a domestic corporation, owned 9 percent of the stock of B, a foreign corporation. In 1988, A acquired an additional 20 percent of the stock of B. Thus, in 1988, B is a noncontrolled section 902 corporation with regard to A. In 1989, A acquired an additional 25 percent of the stock of B. A acquired no additional stock in 1990. In 1989 and 1990, A owned 54 percent of the stock of B. For 1989 and 1990, B is a controlled foreign corporation in which A is a United States shareholder. B has no subpart F income in 1989 or 1990. In 1990, B pays a dividend of $3,000 to A. One thousand dollars ($1,000) of the dividend is attributable to earnings and profits from 1987, $1,000 is attributable to earnings and profits from 1988, and $1,000 is attributable to earnings and profits from 1989. Under paragraph (g)(1) of this section, the $1,000 attributable to the earnings and profits from 1989 is subject to the look through rules of section 904(d)(3) and § 1.904-5(c)(4) and is characterized in A's hands according to those rules. Under section 904(d)(2)(E)(i) and paragraph (g)(3) of this section, the $2,000 attributable to the 1987 and 1988 earnings and profits is treated as income subject to a separate limitation for dividends from a noncontrolled section 902 corporation (B corporation).

Example (3). M owns 40 percent of the voting stock of foreign corporation N. N is a noncontrolled section 902 corporation. In 1987, N earns $2,000 of gross interest income and incurs $1,700 of interest expense. N incurs no other expenses and earns no other income. One-thousand dollars ($1,000) of the interest income is subject to a 10 percent withholding tax and is, therefore, high withholding tax interest. N's earnings and profits are $200 ($2,000 gross interest income less $1,700 interest expense less $100 withholding tax). N pays the full $200 out as a dividend. M receives $80 (40 percent of the $200). Under paragraph (g)(2)(iii) of this section, $50 ($100 − 5% × $1,000) of the $100 withholding tax is not treated as a foreign tax for purposes of determining the amount of foreign taxes deemed paid by M under section 902. M's deemed paid credit with respect to the $80 dividend it receives is, therefore, reduced from $40 ($100 × $80/$200) to $20 ($50 × $80/$200).

(3) *Special rule for dividends paid by a controlled foreign corporation.*—(i) *Distributions out of earnings and profits accumulated when the distributing corporation was not a controlled foreign corporation.*—(A) *General rule.*—Distributions from a controlled foreign corporation shall be treated as dividends from a noncontrolled section 902 corporation, and therefore not subject to the look-through rules of § 1.904-5, to the extent that the distribution is out of earnings and profits accumulated during periods when the distributing corporation was not a controlled foreign corporation.

(B) *Ordering rule.*—The determination of the earnings to which a distribution from a controlled foreign corporation is attributable shall be made on a last-in first-out (LIFO) basis. Thus, a distribution shall be deemed made first from post-1986 undistributed earnings attributable to the period after the distributing corporation became a controlled foreign corporation (look-through pools), next from the non-look-through pool of post-1986 undistributed earnings, if any, and finally on a LIFO basis from pre-1987 accumulated profits.

(C) *Effect of intervening noncontrolled status.*—[Reserved]

(D) *Examples.*—The following examples illustrate the application of paragraph (g)(3)(i):

Example 1. S is a foreign corporation formed in 1980. Until 1992, S had no United States shareholders. In 1992, P, a domestic corporation, acquires 10 percent of the stock of S. Thus, for 1992 and subsequent years, S is a noncontrolled section 902 corporation. Because the 10-percent ownership requirement of section 902(a) was not satisfied until 1992, earnings accumulated by S before 1992 will be treated as pre-1987 accumulated profits for purposes of section 902, and the amount of foreign taxes deemed paid with respect to any distribution out of such pre-1987 accumulated profits will be computed on a year-by-year basis under the rules of section 902(c)(6)(A) and § 1.902-1(b)(3). In 2000, P acquires an additional 45% of the stock of S. Thus, for 2000 and subsequent years, S is a controlled foreign corporation. In 2000, S has no earnings and profits and pays a dividend out of prior years' earnings and profits. Pursuant to paragraph (g)(3)(i) of this section, because S was not a controlled foreign corporation before 2000, the dividend to P will be treated as a dividend from a noncontrolled section 902 corporation. The dividend is treated as paid first out of S's non-look-through pool of post-1986 undistributed earnings to the extent thereof, and then out of S's pre-1987 accumulated profits on a LIFO basis. The entire dividend will be subject to a single separate limitation for dividends from a noncontrolled section 902 corporation.

Examples 2 through 4. [Reserved]

(ii) *Pre-August 6, 1997, dividend distributions out of earnings and profits accumulated before a more-than-90-percent United States shareholder became a United States shareholder.*—(A) *General rule.*—Look-through principles do not apply to distributions made before August 6, 1997, to a more-than-90-percent United States shareholder in the distributing corporation, to the extent the distributions are made from earnings and profits accumulated before the taxpayer became a United States shareholder of the distributing corporation (pre-acquisition earnings). Therefore, in the case of a distribution made before August 6, 1997, a dividend shall be treated as a dividend from a noncontrolled section 902 corporation, and the look-through rules of section 904(d)(3) and § 1.904-5 shall not apply, if—

(*1*) The distribution is received by a United States shareholder, or by an upper-tier controlled foreign corporation of a United States shareholder, at a time when such United States shareholder is a more-than-90-percent United States shareholder of the distributing corporation; and

(*2*) The more-than-90-percent United States shareholder was not a United States shareholder at the time the distributed earnings and profits were accumulated by the distributing corporation.

(B) *Exception for certain intra-group acquisitions.*—Notwithstanding paragraph (g)(3)(ii)(A) of this section, a dividend recipient shall be entitled to look-through treatment on a distribution out of pre-acquisition earnings if—

(*1*) The dividend recipient is a United States shareholder of the distributing corporation;

(*2*) The immediately preceding owner or owners were entitled to look-through treatment on distributions from the distributing corporation (determined after the application of paragraphs (g)(3)(i) and (g)(3)(ii)(A) of this section); and

(*3*) Both at the time of such distribution and at the time that the dividend recipient acquired its interest from such immediately preceding owner or owners, such recipient and such preceding owner or owners are members of the same affiliated group (within the meaning of section 1504(a), determined without regard to section 1504(b)(3)).

(C) *Ordering rule.*—If, under paragraph (g)(3)(ii) of this section (or under paragraphs (g)(3)(i)(A) and (g)(3)(ii) of this section), a shareholder is not entitled to look-through treatment, the determination of whether a distribution from its controlled foreign corporation is attributable to pre-acquisition earnings shall be made on a last-in first-out (LIFO) basis. Thus, a distribution shall be deemed made first from the post-1986 undistributed earnings attributable to the period after the shareholder became a United States shareholder in the distributing corporation, and then from pre-acquisition earnings, in the order described in paragraph (g)(3)(i)(B) of this section.

(D) *Distributions after August 5, 1997.*—Look-through principles shall apply to distributions made after August 5, 1997, to a distribution from a controlled foreign corporation to a more-than-90-percent United States shareholder out of pre-acquisition earnings that were accumulated in years during which the corporation was a controlled foreign corporation. Post-1986 undistributed earnings attributable to the period after the shareholder became a United States shareholder in the distributing corporation and other post-1986 undistributed earnings accumulated while the distributing corporation was a controlled foreign corporation shall be combined into a single set of post-1986 undistributed earnings pools for each separate category described in § 1.904-5(a)(1) as of August 6, 1997.

(E) *Examples.*—The following examples illustrate the application of this paragraph (g)(3)(ii):

Example 1. (i) P, a domestic corporation, owns 100 percent of the stock of U, a controlled foreign corporation. In 1992, P sells 100 percent of the stock of U to T, an unrelated domestic corporation. In 1992, U has no earnings and pays a dividend to T out of earnings and profits attributable to prior years. T is not related to P and P's ownership of U will not be attributed to T. Because the dividend to T in 1992 is out of post-1986 undistributed earnings that are pre-acquisition earnings, the dividend will be treated as a dividend from a noncontrolled section 902 corporation. In 1993, U pays a dividend to T out of current earnings and profits. T is entitled to look-through treatment on the dividend.

(ii) In September 1997, U pays a dividend to T out of both post-acquisition earnings and pre-acquisition earnings accumulated while U was a controlled foreign corporation. Under paragraph (g)(3)(ii)(D) of this section, T is entitled to look-through treatment on the full amount of the dividend.

Example 2. (i) Domestic corporation P has owned 95 percent of the stock of S, a controlled foreign corporation, from the time of S's organization in 1990. Domestic corporation R owns the remaining 5 percent of the stock of S. On December 1, 1996, T, an unrelated domestic corporation, acquires P's 95 percent interest in S. On December 31, 1996, S pays a dividend out of current and prior years' earnings and profits. T is a more-than-90-percent United States shareholder of S at the time it receives the dividend, but was not a United States shareholder at the time the distributed earnings were accumulated. Under this paragraph (g)(3)(ii), the portion of the dividend to T attributable to pre-acquisition earnings will be treated as a dividend from a noncontrolled section 902 corporation. Under paragraph (g)(3)(iii) of this section, T will be entitled to look-through treatment on the portion of the dividend attributable to 1996 earnings and profits. Under paragraph (g)(3)(ii)(C) of this section, the dividend received by T will be treated as coming first from S's post-1986 undistributed earnings attributable to 1996, and then from pre-acquisition earnings.

(ii) On December 31, 1997, S pays a second dividend out of current and prior years' earnings and profits. Under paragraph (g)(3)(ii)(D) of this section, T will be entitled to look-through treatment on the full amount of the dividend because all of S's earnings and profits were accumulated in years during which S was a controlled foreign corporation. The dividends to R will be treated as passive income because R owns less than 10 percent of the stock of S and, therefore, is not entitled to look-through treatment.

Example 3. The facts are the same as in *Example 2* except that R, rather than T, acquires from P an 86 percent interest in S in 1996. Although R was a shareholder of S before the acquisition, it was not a United States shareholder because it did not own 10 percent of the voting stock of S. Thus, because R owns more than 90 percent of the stock of S, and received a distribution of earnings before August 7, 1997, that were accumulated before it became a United States shareholder of S, this paragraph (g)(3)(ii) applies and R is not entitled to look-through treatment on the 1996 dividend. R is entitled to look-through treatment on the 1997 dividend.

Example 4. Since its organization in 1980, S, a controlled foreign corporation, has been owned 60 percent by domestic corporation P and 40 percent by domestic corporation R. On November 15, 1996, domestic corporation T acquires R's 40 percent interest in the stock of S. S has no income in 1996 and pays a dividend on December 15, 1996, out of prior years' earnings and profits. This paragraph (g)(3)(ii) does not apply because T acquired less than 90 percent of the stock of S. Thus, T is entitled to look-through treatment on dividends distributed out of pre-acquisition earnings, because such earnings are attributable to periods in which S was a controlled foreign corporation.

(iii) *Treatment of earnings and profits accumulated in a transition year.*—Earnings and profits accumulated in the taxable year in which a corporation became a controlled foreign corporation or in which a more-than-90-percent United States shareholder became a United States shareholder shall be considered earnings and profits accumulated after the corporation became a controlled foreign corporation or the shareholder became a United States shareholder, respectively.

(iv) *Definitions.*—The following definitions apply for purposes of this paragraph (g)(3):

(A) *More-than-90-percent United States shareholder.*—The term *more-than-90-percent United States shareholder* means, with respect to any controlled foreign corporation, a United States shareholder that owns more than 90 percent of the total combined voting power of all classes of stock entitled to vote of the controlled foreign corporation. In determining ownership for purposes of this definition, the indirect stock ownership rules of sections 958 and 318 and the regulations under those sections shall apply.

(B) *Non-look-through pool.*—Except as otherwise provided, the term *non-look-through pool* means post-1986 undistributed earnings accumulated during periods in which the distributing corporation was a noncontrolled section 902 corporation that was not a controlled foreign corporation.

(C) *Post-1986 undistributed earnings.*—The term *post-1986 undistributed earnings* has the meaning set forth in § 1.902-1(a)(9).

(D) *Pre-1987 accumulated profits.*—The term *pre-1987 accumulated profits* has the meaning set forth in § 1.902-1(a)(10).

(E) *Upper tier controlled foreign corporation.*—The term *upper tier controlled foreign corporation* of a United States shareholder means a controlled foreign corporation in which the taxpayer is a United States shareholder and which is an upper-tier corporation as defined in § 1.902-1(a)(6) with respect to the distributing corporation.

(v) *Effective date.*—The provisions of this paragraph (g)(3) apply to taxable years beginning after December 31, 1986. However, for taxable years beginning before January 1, 2001, taxpayers may rely on § 1.904-4(g)(3)(ii), (iii) and (iv) of regulations project INTL-1-92, published at 1992-1 C.B. 1209. See § 601.601(d)(2) of this chapter.

(h) *Export financing interest.*—(1) *Definitions.*—(i) *Export financing interest.*—The term "export financing interest" means any interest derived from financing the sale (or other disposition) for use or consumption outside the United States of any property that is manufactured, produced, grown, or extracted in the United States by the taxpayer or a related person, and not more than 50 percent of the fair market value of which is attributable to products imported into the United States. For purposes of this paragraph, the term "United States" includes the fifty States, the District of Columbia, and the Commonwealth of Puerto Rico.

(ii) *Fair market value.*—For purposes of this paragraph, the fair market value of any property imported into the United States shall be its appraised value, as determined by the Secretary under section 402 of the Tariff Act of 1930 (19 U.S.C. 1401a) in connection with its importation. For purposes of determining the foreign content of an item of property imported into the United States, see section 927 and the regulations thereunder.

(iii) *Related person.*—For purposes of this paragraph, the term "related person" has the meaning given it by section 954(d)(3) except that such section shall be applied by substituting "the person with respect to whom the determination is being made" for "controlled foreign corporation" each place it applies.

(2) *Treatment of export financing interest.*—Except as provided in paragraph (h)(3) of this section, if a taxpayer (including a financial services entity) receives or accrues export financing interest from an unrelated person, then that interest shall be treated as general limitation income.

(3) *Exceptions.*—(i) *Export financing interest that is high withholding tax interest.*—If a financial services entity receives or accrues export financing interest that would also be high withholding tax interest but for section 904(d)(2)(B)(ii), that income shall be treated as financial services income.

(ii) *Export financing interest that is also related person factoring income.*—Export financing interest shall be treated as passive income if that income is also related person factoring income. For this purpose, related person factoring income is—

(A) Income received or accrued by a controlled foreign corporation that is income described in section 864(d)(6) (income of a controlled foreign corporation from a loan for the purpose of financing the purchase of inventory property of a related person); or

(B) Income received or accrued by any person that is income described in section 864(d)(1) (income from a trade receivable acquired from a related person).

(iii) *Export financing interest that is related person factoring income and is received or accrued by a financial services entity.*—If a financial services entity receives or accrues export financing interest that is also related person factoring income, then the income shall be treated as financial services income. See section 864(d)(5)(A)(i).

(iv) *Export financing interest that is related person factoring income and high withholding tax interest.*—If any taxpayer (including a financial services entity) receives or accrues export financing interest that is also related person factoring income and high withholding tax interest, then that income shall be treated as high withholding tax interest. See section 864(d)(5)(A)(i).

(4) *Examples.*—The following examples illustrate the operation of paragraph (h)(3) of this section:

Example (1). Controlled foreign corporation S is a wholly-owned subsidiary of domestic corporation P. S is not a financial services entity and has accumulated cash reserves. P has uncollected trade and service receivables of foreign obligors. P sells the receivables at a discount ("factors") to S. The income derived by S on the receivables is related person factoring income. The income is also export financing interest. Because the income is related person factoring income, the income is passive income to S.

Example (2). The facts are the same as in *Example (1)* except that S is a financial services entity and derives the income in an active financing business. The income derived by S on the receivables is related person factoring income and is also export financing interest. Therefore, pursuant to paragraph (h)(3)(iii) of this section, the income is financial services income to S.

Example (3). Domestic corporation S is a wholly-owned subsidiary of domestic corporation P. S is not a financial services entity and has uncollected trade and service receivables of foreign obligors. P factors the receivables to S. The income derived by S on the receivables is related person factoring income. The income is also export financing interest. The income will be passive income to S.

Example (4). The facts are the same as in *Example (3)* except that instead of factoring P's receivables, S finances the sales of P's goods by making loans to the purchasers of P's goods. The interest derived by S on these loans is export financing interest and is not related person factoring income. The income will be general limitation income to S.

(5) *Income eligible for section 864(d)(7) exception (same country exception) from related person factoring treatment.*—(i) *Income other than interest.*—If any foreign person that is not a financial services entity receives or accrues income that is described in section 864(d)(7) (income on a trade or service receivable acquired from a related person in the same foreign country as the recipient) and such income would also meet the definition of export financing interest if section 864(d)(1) applied to such income (income on a trade or service receivable acquired from a related person treated as interest), then the income shall be considered to be export financing interest and shall be treated as general limitation income. If a financial services entity receives or accrues that income, the income shall not be considered to be export financing interest and, therefore, shall be treated as financial services income.

(ii) *Interest income.*—If export financing interest is received or accrued by any foreign person and that income would otherwise be treated as related person factoring income under section 864(d)(6) if section 864(d)(7) did not apply, section 904(d)(2)(A)(iii)(II) shall apply, and the interest shall be treated as general limitation income unless the interest is received or accrued by a financial services entity. If that interest is received or accrued by a financial services entity, section 904(d)(2)(C)(iii)(III) shall apply and the interest shall be treated as general limitation income. If that interest also would be high withholding tax interest but for section 904(d)(2)(B)(ii), then the interest shall be treated as financial services income.

(iii) *Examples.*—The following examples illustrate the operation of this paragraph (h)(5):

Example (1). Controlled foreign corporation S is a wholly-owned subsidiary of domestic corporation P. Controlled foreign corporation T is a wholly-owned subsidiary of controlled foreign corporation S. S and T are incorporated in Country M. In 1987, P sells tractors to T, which T sells to X, an unrelated foreign corporation organized in country M. The tractors are to be used in country M. T uses a substantial part of its assets in its trade or business located in Country M. T has uncollected trade receivables from X that it factors to S. S derived more than 20 percent of its gross income for 1987 other than from an active financing business and the income derived by S from the receivables is not derived in an active financing business. Thus, pursuant to paragraph (e)(3)(i) of this section, S is not a financial services entity. The income is not related person factoring income because it is described in section 864(d)(7) (income eligible for the same country exception). If section 864(d)(1) applied, the income S derived from the receivables would meet the definition of export financing interest. The income, therefore, is considered to be export financing interest and is general limitation income to S.

Example (2). The facts are the same as in *Example (1)* except that S is a financial services entity and derives the income on the receivables from the conduct of an active financing business. The income S derives from the receivables is not related person factoring income because it is described in section 864(d)(7). If the income would be high withholding tax interest but for section 904(d)(2)(B)(ii), then the income will not be considered to be export financing interest and will be financial services income to S. Otherwise, the income will [be] considered to be export financing interest and will be general limitation income to S.

Example (3). Controlled foreign corporation S is a wholly-owned subsidiary of domestic corporation, P. Controlled foreign corporation T is a wholly-owned subsidiary of controlled foreign corporation S. S and T are incorporated in country M. S is not a financial services entity. In 1987, P sells tractors to T, which T sells to X, a foreign partnership that is organized in country M and is related to S and T. S makes a loan to X to finance the tractor sales. The interest earned by S from financing the sales is described in section 864(d)(7) and is export financing interest. Therefore, the income shall be general limitation income to S.

Example (4). The facts are the same as in *Example (3)* except that S is a financial services entity and derives the interest on the loan to X in an active financing business. The interest S earns is export financing interest that is not described in section 864(d)(1) because it is described in section 864(d)(7). Because the interest is described in section 864(d)(7) and is export financing interest, section 904(d)(2)(C)(iii)(III) shall apply and the income shall be general limitation income to S, unless it would also be high withholding tax interest but for section 904(d)(2)(B)(ii), in which case it will be financial services income to S.

(i) *Interaction of section 907(c) and income described in this section.*—If a person receives or accrues income that is income described in section 907(c) (relating to oil and gas income), the rules of section 907(c) and the regulations thereunder, as well as the rules of this section, shall apply to the income. Thus, for example, if a taxpayer receives or accrues a dividend distribution from two separate noncontrolled section 902 corporations out of earnings and profits attributable to income received or accrued by the noncontrolled section 902 corporations that is income described in section 907(c), the rules provided in section 907 shall apply separately to the dividends received from each noncontrolled section 902 corporation. The reduction in amount allowed as foreign tax provided by section 907(a) shall therefore be calculated separately for dividends received or accrued by the taxpayer from each separate noncontrolled section 902 corporation.

(j) *Special rule for DASTM gain or loss.*—Any DASTM gain or loss computed under § 1.985-3(d) must be allocated among the categories of income under the rules of § 1.985-3(e)(2)(iv) or (e)(3). The rules of § 1.985-3(e) apply before the rules of section 904(d)(2)(A)(iii)(III) (the exception from passive income for high-taxed income).

(k) *Special rule for alternative minimum tax foreign tax credit.*—For purposes of computing the alternative minimum tax foreign tax credit under section 59(a), items included in alternative minimum taxable income by reason of section 56(g) (adjustments based on adjusted current earnings) shall be characterized as income described in a separate category under section 904(d) and this section based on the character of the underlying items of income.

(l) *Priority rules.*—(1) *In general.*—In the case of income that meets the definitions of more than one category of separate limitation income, the following priority rules apply:

(i) Income that meets the definitions of passive income and of any other separate limitation income described in section 904(d)(1)(B) through (H) will be subject to the other separate limitation;

(ii) Income that meets the definitions of financial services income and of either shipping income or passive income will be subject to the separate limitation for financial services income;

(iii) Income that meets the definitions of financial services income and of any separate limitation income other than shipping or passive income will be subject to the other separate limitation;

(iv) Income that meets the definitions of dividends from a noncontrolled section 902 corporation and of any other separate limitation income will be subject to the separate limitation for dividends from a noncontrolled section 902 corporation unless that income is foreign oil and gas extraction income defined in section 907(c), in which case it will be treated as general limitation income pursuant to § 1.907(a)-1(f);

(v) Income that meets the definitions of high withholding tax interest and of any other separate limitation income will be high withholding tax interest;

(vi) Income that meets the definitions of shipping income and of foreign trade income will be subject to the separate limitation for foreign trade income; and

(vii) Income that meets the definitions of a separate category described in paragraph (m) of this section and of any other category of separate limitation income described in section 904(d)(1)(A) through (H) will be subject to the separate limitation described in paragraph (m) of this section and will not be treated as general limitation income described in section 904(d)(1)(I).

(2) *Examples.*—The provisions of this paragraph (1) are illustrated by the following examples:

Example (1). Controlled foreign corporation S is a wholly-owned subsidiary of domestic corporation P. S owns 20 percent of the voting stock of T, a foreign corporation that is not a controlled foreign corporation. In 1987, T pays S a dividend that qualifies as foreign base company shipping income to S under § 1.954-6(f)(1). The dividend from T is also a dividend from a noncontrolled section 902 corporation. Therefore, pursuant to section 904(d)(2)(D) and paragraph (l)(1)(iv) of this section, the dividend from T is treated as a dividend from a noncontrolled section 902 corporation.

Example (2). In 1987, domestic corporation P received a dividend from R, a foreign corporation that is not a controlled foreign corporation. P owns 30 percent of the voting stock of R. P is a financial services entity and the dividend from R qualifies as financial services income under paragraph (e)(4)(i)(A) of this section. The dividend from R is also a dividend from a noncontrolled section 902 corporation. Therefore, pursuant to section 904(d)(2)(C)(iii)(II) and paragraphs (l)(i)(iii) and (iv) of this section, the dividend from R is treated as a dividend from a noncontrolled section 902 corporation.

Example (3). P, a domestic corporation, owns 10 percent of foreign corporation S. S is a noncontrolled section 902 corporation. In 1990, S earns foreign oil and gas extraction income which is general limitation income. S pays a dividend to P out of its earnings and profits for 1990. The dividend from S is a dividend from a noncontrolled section 902 corporation that is also foreign oil and gas extraction income. Pursuant to section 907(c)(3)(A), § 1.907(a)-1(f) and paragraph (l)(1)(iv) of this section, P will include the dividend in income as general limitation income.

(m) *Income treated as allocable to an additional separate category.*—If section 904(a), (b), and (c) are applied separately to any category of income under the Internal Revenue Code (for example, under section 56(g)(4)(C)(iii)(IV), 245(a)(10), 865(h), 901(j), or 904(g)(10)), that category of income will be treated for all purposes of the Internal Revenue Code and regulations as if it were a separate category listed in section 904(d)(1) and (d)(3)(F)(i). [Reg. § 1.904-4.]

☐ [*T.D.* 8214, 7-15-88. *Amended by T.D.* 8412, 5-13-92; *T.D.* 8556, 7-22-94; *T.D.* 8805, 1-8-99 (*corrected* 6-16-99); *T.D.* 8916, 12-29-2000 (*corrected* 3-22-2001); *T.D.* 8973, 12-27-2001 *and* T.D. 9141, 7-19-2004.]

§ 1.904-5. Look-through rules as applied to controlled foreign corporations and other entities.—(a) *Definitions.*—For purposes of section 904(d)(3) and the regulations under section 904 the following definitions apply:

(1) The term *separate category* means, as the context requires, any category of income described in section 904(d)(1)(A), (B), (C), (D), (E), (F), (G), (H), or (I) and in § 1.904-4(b), (d), (e), (f), and (g), any category of income described in § 1.904-4(m), or any category of earnings and profits to which income described in such provisions is attributable.

(2) The term "controlled foreign corporation" has the meaning given such term by section 957 (taking into account the special rule for certain captive insurance companies contained in section 953 (c)).

(3) The term "United States shareholder" has the meaning given such term by section 951(b) (taking into account the special rule for certain captive insurance companies contained in section 953(c)), except that for purposes of this section, a United States shareholder shall include any member of the controlled group of the United States shareholder. For this purpose the controlled group is any member of the affiliated group within the meaning of section 1504(a)(1) except that "more than 50 percent" shall be substituted for "at least 80 percent" wherever it appears in section 1504(a)(2). For taxable years beginning before January 1, 2001, the preceding sentence shall be applied by substituting "50 percent" for "more than 50 percent".

(b) *In general.*—Except as otherwise provided in section 904(d)(2)(E) and (3) and this section, dividends, interest, rents, and royalties received or accrued by a taxpayer from a controlled foreign corporation in which the taxpayer is a United States shareholder shall be treated as general limitation income.

(c) *Rules for specific types of inclusions and payments.*—(1) *Subpart F inclusions.*—(i) *Rule.*—Any amount included in gross income under section 951(a)(1)(A) shall be treated as income in a separate category to the extent the amount so included is attributable to income received or accrued by the controlled foreign corporation that is described as income in such category. For purposes of this § 1.904-5, income shall be characterized under the rules of § 1.904-4 prior to the application of the rules of paragraph (c) of this section. For rules concerning inclusions under section 951(a)(1)(B), see paragraph (c)(4)(i) of this section.

(ii) *Examples.*—The following examples illustrate the application of this paragraph (c)(1):

Example (1). Controlled foreign corporation S is a wholly-owned subsidiary of P, a domestic corporation. S earns $200 of net income, $85 of which is foreign base company shipping income, $15 of which is foreign personal holding company income, and $100 of which is non-subpart F general limitation income. No foreign tax is imposed on the income. One hundred dollars ($100) of S's income is subpart F income taxed currently to P under section 951(a)(1)(A). Because $85 of the subpart F inclusion is attributable to shipping income of S, $85 of the subpart F inclusion is shipping income to P. Because $15 of the subpart F inclusion is attributable to passive income of S, $15 of the subpart F inclusion is passive income to P.

Example (2). Controlled foreign corporation S is a wholly-owned subsidiary of domestic corporation P. S is a financial services entity. P manufactures cars and is not a financial services entity. In 1987, S earns $200 of interest income unrelated to its banking business and $900 of interest income related to its banking business. Assume that S pays no foreign taxes and has no expenses. All of S's income is included in P's gross income as foreign personal holding company income. Because S is a financial services entity, income that would otherwise be passive income is considered to be financial services income. P, therefore, treats the entire subpart F inclusion as financial services income.

Example (3). Controlled foreign corporation S is a wholly-owned subsidiary of domestic corporation P. P is a financial services entity. S manufactures cars and is not a financial services entity. In 1987, S earns $200 of passive income that is subpart F income and $900 of general limitation non-subpart F income. Assume that S pays no foreign taxes on its passive earnings and has no expenses. P includes the $200 of subpart F income in gross income. Because P is a financial services entity, the inclusion will be financial services income to P.

Example (4). Controlled foreign corporation S is a wholly-owned subsidiary of domestic corporation P. Neither P nor S is a financial services entity. Controlled foreign corporation T is a wholly-owned subsidiary of controlled foreign corporation S. T is a financial services entity. In 1991, T pays a dividend to S. For purposes of determining whether S is a financial services entity under § 1.904-4(e)(3)(i), the dividend from T is ignored. For purposes of characterizing the dividend in S's hands under the look-through rules of paragraph (c)(4) of this section, however, the dividend retains its character as financial services income. Similarly, any subpart F inclusion or dividend to P out of the earnings and profits attributable to the dividend from S is excluded in determining whether P is a financial services entity under § 1.904-4(e)(3)(i), but retains its character in P's hands as financial services income under paragraph (c)(4) of this section.

Example (5). Controlled foreign corporation S is a wholly-owned subsidiary of domestic corporation P. S owns 40 percent of foreign corporation A, 45 percent of foreign corporation B, 30 percent of foreign corporation C and 20 percent of foreign corporation D. A, B, C, and D are noncontrolled section 902 corporations. In 1987, S's only income is a $100 dividend from each foreign corporation. Assume that S pays no foreign taxes and has no expenses. All $400 of the income is foreign personal holding company income and is included in P's gross income. P must include $100 in its separate limitation for dividends from A, $100 in its separate limitation for dividends from B, $100 in its separate limitation for dividends from C, and $100 in its separate limitation for dividends from D.

(2) *Interest.*—(i) *In general.*—For purposes of this paragraph, related person interest is any interest paid or accrued by a controlled foreign corporation to any United States shareholder in that corporation (or to any other related person) to which the look-through rules of section 904(d)(3) and this section apply. Unrelated person interest is all interest other than related person interest. Related person interest shall be treated as income in a separate category to the extent it is allocable to income of the controlled foreign corporation in that category. If related person interest is received or accrued from a controlled foreign corporation by two or more persons, the amount of interest received or accrued by each person that is allocable to any separate category of income shall be determined by multiplying the amount of related person interest allocable to that separate category of income by a fraction. The numerator of the fraction is the amount of related person interest received or accrued by that person and the denominator is the total amount of related person interest paid or accrued by the controlled foreign corporation.

(ii) *Allocating and apportioning expenses including interest paid to a related person.*—Related person interest and other expenses of a controlled foreign corporation shall be allocated and apportioned in the following manner:

(A) Gross income in each separate category shall be determined;

(B) Any expenses that are definitely related to less than all of gross income as a class, including unrelated person interest that is directly allocated to income from a specific property, shall be allocated and apportioned under the principles of §§ 1.861-8 or 1.861-10T, as applicable, to income in each separate category;

(C) Related person interest shall be allocated to and shall reduce (but not below zero) the amount of passive foreign personal holding company income as determined after the application of paragraph (c)(2)(ii)(B) of this section;

(D) To the extent that related person interest exceeds passive foreign personal holding company income as determined after the application of paragraphs (c)(2)(ii)(B) and (C) of this section, the related person interest shall be apportioned under the rules of this paragraph to separate categories other than passive income.

(1) If under § 1.861-9T, the modified gross income method of apportioning interest expense is elected, related person interest shall be apportioned as follows:

$$\left(\text{Related person interest} - \text{Related person interest allocated under paragraph (c)(2)(ii)(C) of this section}\right) \times \frac{\text{Gross income in a separate category (other than passive)}}{\text{Total gross income (other than passive)}}$$

(2) If under § 1.861-9T, the asset method of apportioning interest expense is elected, related person interest shall be apportioned according to the following formula:

$$\text{Related person interest} - \text{Related person interest allocated under paragraph (c)(2)(ii)(C) of this section} \times \frac{\text{Value of assets in a separate category (other than passive)}}{\text{Value of total assets (other than passive)}}$$

(E) Any other expenses (including unrelated person interest that is not directly allocated to income from a specific property) that are not definitely related expenses or that are definitely related to all of gross income as a class shall be apportioned under the rules of this paragraph to reduce income in each separate category.

(1) If under § 1.861-9T, the modified gross income method of apportioning interest expense is elected, the interest expense shall be apportioned as follows:

$$\text{Expense apportionable to a separate category} = \text{Expense} \times \frac{\text{Gross income in a separate category (minus related person interest allocated under paragraph (c)(2)(ii)(C) of this section if the category is passive)}}{\text{Total gross income minus related person interest allocated to passive income under paragraph (c)(2)(ii)(C) of this section}}$$

(2) If under § 1.861-9T, the asset method of apportioning interest expense is elected, then the expense shall be apportioned as follows:

$$\text{Expense apportionable to a separate category} = \text{Expense} \times \frac{\text{Value of assets in a separate category (minus related person debt allocated to passive assets if the category is passive)}}{\text{Value of total assets minus related person debt allocated to passive assets}}$$

(3) Expenses other than interest shall be apportioned in a similar manner depending on the apportionment method used. See § 1.861-8T(c)(1)(i)-(vi).

(iii) *Definitions.*—(A) *Value of assets and reduction in value of assets and gross income.*—For purposes of paragraph (c)(2)(ii)(D) and (E) of this section, the value of total assets is the value of assets in all categories (determined under the principles of § 1.861-9T(g)). See § 1.861-10T(d)(2) to determine the reduction in value of assets and gross income for purposes of apportioning additional third person interest expense that is not directly allocated when some interest expense has been directly allocated. For purposes of this paragraph and paragraph (c)(2)(ii)(E) of this section, any reduction in the value of assets for indebtedness that relates to interest allocated under paragraph (c)(2)(ii)(C) of this section is made before determining the average of asset values. For rules relating to the averaging of reduced asset values see § 1.861-9T(g)(2).

(B) *Related person debt allocated to passive assets.*—For purposes of paragraph (c)(2)(ii)(E) of this section, related person debt allocated to passive assets is determined as follows:

$$\text{Related person debt allocated to the passive category} = \text{Total related person debt} \times \frac{\text{Related person interest allocable to passive income under paragraph (c)(2)(ii)(C)}}{\text{All related person interest}}$$

For this purpose, the term "total related person debt" means the sum of the principal amounts of obligations of a controlled foreign corporation owed to any United States shareholder of such corporation or to any related entity (within the meaning of paragraph (g) of this section) determined at the end of the taxable year.

Reg. § 1.904-5(c)(2)(iii)(B)

(iv) *Examples.*—The following examples illustrate the operation of this paragraph (c)(2).

Example (1). (i) Controlled foreign corporation S is a wholly-owned subsidiary of P, a domestic corporation. In 1987, S earns $200 of foreign personal holding company income that is passive income. S also earns $100 of foreign base company sales income that is general limitation income. S has $2000 of passive assets and $2000 of general limitation assets. In 1987, S makes a $150 interest payment to P with respect to a $1500 loan from P. S also pays $100 of interest to an unrelated person on a $1000 loan from that person. S has no other expenses. S uses the asset method to apportion interest expense.

(ii) Under paragraph (c)(2)(ii)(C) of this section, the $150 related person interest payment is allocable to S's passive foreign personal holding company income. Therefore, the $150 interest payment is passive income to P. Because the entire related person interest payment is allocated to passive income under paragraph (c)(2)(ii)(C) of this section, none of the related person interest payment is apportioned to general limitation income under paragraph (c)(2)(ii)(D) of this section. Under paragraph (c)(2)(iii)(B) of this section, the entire amount of the related person debt is allocable to passive assets ($1500 = $1500 × $150/$150). Under paragraph (c)(2)(ii)(E) of this section, $20 of interest expense paid to an unrelated person is apportioned to passive income ($20 = $100 × ($2000 − $1500)/($4000 − $1500)). Eighty dollars ($80) of the interest expense paid to an unrelated person is apportioned to general limitation income ($80 = $100 × $2000/($4000 − $1500)).

Example (2). The facts are the same as in *Example* (1), except that S uses the gross income method to apportion interest expense. Under paragraph (c)(2)(ii)(E) of this section, the unrelated person interest expense would be apportioned on a gross income method. Therefore, $33 of interest expense paid to unrelated persons would be apportioned to passive income ($33 = $100 × ($200 − $150)/($300 − $150)) and $67 of interest expense paid to unrelated persons would be apportioned to general limitation income ($67 = $100 × $100/($300 − $150)).

Example (3). (i) The facts are the same as in *Example* (1), except that S has an additional $50 of third person interest expense that is directly allocated to income from a specific property that produces only passive income. The principal amount of indebtedness to which the interest relates is $500. S also has $50 of additional non-interest expenses that are not definitely related expenses and that are apportioned on an asset basis.

(ii) Under paragraph (c)(2)(ii)(B) of this section, the $50 of directly allocated third person interest is first allocated to reduce the passive income of S. Under paragraph (c)(2)(ii)(C) of this section, the $150 of related person interest is allocated to the remaining $150 of passive income. Under paragraph (c)(2)(iii)(B) of this section, all of the related person debt is allocated to passive assets. ($1500 = $1500 × $150/$150).

(iii) Under paragraph (c)(2)(ii)(E) of this section, the non-interest expenses that are not definitely related are apportioned on the basis of the asset values reduced by the allocated related person debt. Therefore, $10 of these expenses are apportioned to the passive category ($50 × ($2000 − $1500)/($4000 − $1500)) and $40 are apportioned to the general limitation category ($50 × $2000/($4000 − $1500)).

(iv) In order to apportion third person interest between the categories of assets, the value of assets in a separate category must also be reduced under the principles of § 1.861-8 by the indebtedness relating to the specifically allocated interest. Therefore, under paragraph (c)(2)(iii)(B) of this section, the value of assets in the passive category for purposes of apportioning the additional third person interest = 0 ($2000 minus $500 (the principal amount of the debt, the interest payment on which is directly allocated to specific interest producing properties) minus $1500 (the related person debt allocated to passive assets)). Under paragraph (c)(2)(ii)(E) of this section, all $100 of the non-definitely related third person interest is apportioned to the general limitation category ($100 = $100 × $2000/($4000 − $500 − $1500)).

Example (4). (i) Controlled foreign corporation S is a wholly-owned subsidiary of P, a domestic corporation. In 1987, S earns $100 of foreign personal holding company income that is passive income. S also earns $100 of foreign base company sales income that is general limitation income. S has $1000 of general limitation assets and $1000 of passive assets. In 1987, S makes a $150 interest payment to P on a $1500 loan from P and has $20 of general and administrative expenses (G & A) that under the principles of §§ 1.861-8 through 1.861-14T is treated as directly allocable to all of P's gross income. S also makes a $25 interest payment to an unrelated person on a $250 loan from the unrelated person. S has no other expenses. S uses the asset method to apportion interest expense. S uses the gross income method to apportion G & A.

(ii) Under paragraph (c)(2)(ii)(C) of this section, $100 of the interest payment to P is allocable to S's passive foreign personal holding company income. Under paragraph (c)(2)(ii)(D) of this section, the additional $50 of related person interest expense is apportioned to general limitation income ($50 = $50 × $1000/$1000). Under paragraph (c)(2)(iii)(B) of this section, related person debt allocated to passive assets equals $1000 ($1000 = $1500 × $100/$150).

(iii) Under paragraph (c)(2)(ii)(E) of this section, none of the $25 of interest expense paid to an unrelated person is apportioned to passive income ($0 = $25 × ($1000 − $1000)/($2000 − $1000)). Twenty-five dollars ($25) of the interest expense paid to an unrelated person is apportioned to general limitation income ($25 = $25 × $1000/($2000 − $1000)). Under paragraph (c)(2)(ii)(E) of this section, none of the G & A is apportioned to S's passive foreign personal holding company income ($0 = $20 × ($100 − $100)/($200 − $100)). All $20 of the G & A is apportioned to S's general limitation income ($20 = $20 × $100/($200 − $100)).

Example (5). The facts are the same as in *Example* (4), except that S uses the gross income method to apportion interest expense. As in *Example* (4), $100 of the interest payment to P is allocated to passive income under paragraph (c)(2)(ii)(C) of this section. Under paragraph (c)(2)(ii)(D) of this section, the additional $50 of related person interest expense is apportioned to general limitation income ($150 − 100 × $100/$100). Under paragraph (c)(2)(ii)(E) of this section, none of the unrelated person interest expense and none of the G & A is apportioned to passive income, because after the application of paragraph (c)(2)(ii)(C) of this section, no passive income remains in the passive income category.

Example (6). Controlled foreign corporation T is a wholly-owned subsidiary of S, a controlled foreign corporation. S is a wholly-owned subsidiary of P, a domestic corporation. S is not a financial services entity. S and T are incorporated in the same country. In 1987, P sells tractors to T, which T sells to X, a foreign corporation that is related to both S and T and is organized in the same country as S and T. S makes a loan to X to finance the tractor sales. Assume that the interest earned by S from financing the sales is export financing interest that is neither related person factoring income nor foreign personal holding company income. The export financing interest earned by S is, therefore, general limitation income. S earns no other income. S makes a $100 interest payment to P. The $100 of interest paid is allocable under the look-through rules of paragraph (c)(2)(ii) of this section to the general limitation income earned by S and is therefore general limitation income to P.

(3) *Rents and royalties.*—Any rents or royalties received or accrued from a controlled foreign corporation in which the taxpayer is a United States shareholder shall be treated as income in a separate category to the extent they are allocable to income of the controlled foreign corporation in that category under the principles of §§ 1.861-8 through 1.861-14T.

(4) *Dividends.*—(i) *Look-through rule.*—Any dividend paid or accrued out of the earnings and profits of any controlled foreign corporation, shall be treated as income in a separate category in proportion to the ratio of the portion of earnings and profits attributable to income in such category to the total amount of earnings and profits of the controlled foreign corporation. For purposes of this paragraph, the term "dividend" includes any amount included in gross income under section 951(a)(1)(B) as a pro rata share of a controlled foreign corporation's increase in earnings invested in United States property.

(ii) *Special rule for dividends attributable to certain loans.*—If a dividend is distributed to a taxpayer by a controlled foreign corporation, that controlled foreign corporation is the recipient of loan proceeds from a related look-through entity (within the meaning of § 1.904-5(i) of this section), and the purpose of such loan is to alter the characterization of the dividend for purposes of this section, then, to the extent of the principal amount of the loan, the dividend shall be characterized with respect to the earnings and profits of the related person lender rather than with respect to the earnings and profits of the dividend payor. A loan will not be considered made for the purpose of altering the characterization of a dividend if the loan would have been made or maintained on substantially the same terms irrespective of the dividend. The determination of whether a loan would have been made or maintained on substantially the same terms irrespective of the dividend will be made taking into account all the facts and circumstances of the relationship between the lender and the borrower. Thus, for example, a loan by a related party lender to a controlled foreign corporation that arises from the sale of inventory in the ordinary course of business will not be considered a loan made for the purpose of altering the character of any dividend paid by the borrower.

(iii) *Examples.*—The following examples illustrate the application of this paragraph (c)(4).

Example (1). Controlled foreign corporation S is a wholly-owned subsidiary of P, a domestic corporation. In 1987, S has earnings and profits of $1,000, $600 of which is attributable to general limitation income and $400 of which is attributable to dividends received by S from its wholly-owned subsidiary, T. T is a controlled foreign corporation and is incorporated and operates in the same country as S. All of T's income is financial services income. Neither S's general limitation income nor the dividend from T is subpart F income. In December 1987, S pays a dividend to P of $200, all of which is attributable to earnings and profits earned in 1987. Six-tenths of the dividend ($120) is treated as general limitation income because six-tenths of S's earnings and profits are attributable to general limitation income. Four-tenths of the dividend ($80) is treated as financial services income because four-tenths of S's earnings and profits are attributable to dividends from T, and all of T's earnings are financial services income.

Example (2). A, a United States person, has been the sole shareholder in controlled foreign corporation X since its organization on January 1, 1963. Both X and A are calendar year taxpayers. X's earnings and profits for 1963 through the end of 1987 totaled $3,000. A sells his stock in X at the end of 1987 and realizes a gain of $4,000. Of the total $4,000 gain, $3,000 (A's share of the post-1962 earnings and profits) is includible in A's gross income as a dividend and is subject to the look-through rules including the transition rule of §1.904-7(a) with respect to the portion of the distribution out of pre- 87 earnings and profits. The remaining $1,000 of the gain is includible as gain from the sale or exchange of the X stock and is passive income to A.

(d) *Effect of exclusions from subpart F income.*—(1) *De minimis amount of subpart F income.*—If the sum of a controlled foreign corporation's gross foreign base company income (determined under section 954(a) without regard to section 954(b)(5)) and gross insurance income (determined under section 953(a)) for the taxable year is less than the lesser of 5 percent of gross income of $1,000,000, then all of that income (other than income that would be financial services income without regard to this paragraph (d)(1)) shall be treated as general limitation income. In addition, if the test in the preceding sentence is satisfied, for purposes of paragraphs (c)(2)(ii)(D) and (E) of this section (apportionment of interest expense to passive income using the asset method), any passive limitation assets shall be treated as general limitation assets. The determination in the first sentence shall be made prior to the application of the exception for certain income subject to a high rate of foreign tax described in paragraph (d)(2) of this section.

(2) *Exception for certain income subject to high foreign tax.*—Except as provided in §1.904-4(c)(7)(iii) (relating to reductions in tax upon distribution), for purposes of the dividend look-through rule of paragraph (c)(4)(i) of this section, an item of net income that would otherwise be passive income (after application of the priority rules of §1.904-4(l)) and that is received or accrued by a controlled foreign corporation shall be treated as general limitation income, and the earnings and profits attributable to such income shall be treated as general limitation earnings and profits, if the taxpayer establishes to the satisfaction of the Secretary that such income was subject to an effective rate of income tax imposed by a foreign country greater than 90 percent of the maximum rate of tax specified in section 11 (with reference to section 15, if applicable). The preceding sentence has no effect on amounts (other than dividends) paid or accrued by a controlled foreign corporation to a United States shareholder of such controlled foreign corporation to the extent those amounts are allocable to passive income of the controlled foreign corporation.

(3) *Examples.*—The following examples illustrate the application of this paragraph.

Example (1). Controlled foreign corporation S is a wholly-owned subsidiary of P, a domestic corporation. In 1987, S earns $100 of gross income, $4 of which is interest that is subpart F foreign personal holding company income and $96 of which is gross manufacturing income that is not subpart F income. S has no other earnings for 1987. S has no expenses and pays no foreign taxes. S pays P a $100 dividend. Under the de minimis rule of section 954(b)(3), none of S's income is treated as foreign base company income. All of S's income, therefore, is treated as general limitation income. The entire $100 dividend is general limitation income to P.

Example (2). (i) Controlled foreign corporation S is a wholly-owned subsidiary of P, a domestic corporation. In 1987, S earns $50 of shipping income of a type that is foreign base company shipping income. S also earns $50 of dividends from T, a foreign corporation in which S owns 45 percent of the voting stock, and receives $50 of dividends from U, a foreign corporation in which S owns 5% of the voting stock. Foreign persons hold the remaining voting stock of both T and U. S, T, and U are all incorporated in different foreign countries. The dividends S receives from T and U are of a type that normally would be subpart F foreign personal holding company income that is passive income. Under §1.904-4(l)(1)(iv), however, the dividends from T are dividends from a noncontrolled section 902 corporation rather than passive income. S has no expenses. The earnings and profits of S are equal to the net income after taxes of S. The dividends and the shipping income are taxed abroad by S's country of incorporation at an effective rate of 40 percent. P establishes to the satisfaction of the Secretary that the effective rate of tax on both the dividends and the shipping income exceeds 90 percent of the maximum United States tax rate. Thus, under section 954(b)(4), neither the shipping income nor the dividends are taxed currently to P under subpart F. S's earnings attributable to shipping income and dividends from a noncontrolled section 902 corporation retain their character as such. Under paragraph (d)(2) of this section, S's earnings attributable to the dividends from U are treated as earnings attributable to general limitation income. See §§ 1.905-3T and 1.905-4T, however, for rules concerning adjustments to the pools of earnings and profits and foreign taxes and redeterminations of United States tax liability when foreign taxes are refunded in a later year.

(ii) In 1988, S has no earnings and pays a $150 dividend (including gross-up) to P. The dividend is paid out of S's post-1986 pool of earnings and profits. One-third of the dividend ($50) is attributable to S's shipping earnings, one-third ($50) is attributable to the dividend from T, and one-third ($50) is attributable to the dividend from U. Pursuant to section 904(d)(3)(E) and paragraph (c)(4) of this section, one-third of the dividend is shipping income, one-third is a dividend from a noncontrolled section 902 corporation, T, and one-third is general limitation income to P.

(e) *Treatment of subpart F income in excess of 70 percent of gross income.*—(1) *Rule.*—If the sum of a controlled foreign corporation's gross foreign base company income (determined without regard to section 954(b)(5)) and gross insurance income for the taxable year exceeds 70 percent of the gross income, then all of the controlled foreign corporation's gross income shall be treated as foreign base company income or gross insurance income (whichever is appropriate) and, thus, included in a United States shareholder's gross income. However, the inclusion in gross income of an amount that would not otherwise be subpart F income does not affect its character for purposes of determining whether the income is within a separate category. The determination of whether the controlled foreign corporation's gross foreign base company income and gross insurance income exceeds 70 percent of gross income is made before the exception for certain income subject to a high rate of foreign tax.

(2) *Example.*—The following example illustrates the application of this paragraph.

Example. Controlled foreign corporation S is a wholly-owned subsidiary of P, a domestic corporation. S earns $100, $75 of which is foreign personal holding company income and $25 of which is non-subpart F services income. S is not a financial services entity. S's gross and net income are equal. Under the 70 percent full inclusion rule of section 954(b)(3)(B), the entire $100 is foreign base company income currently taxable to P under section 951. Because $75 of the $100 section 951 inclusion is attributable to S's passive income, $75 of the inclusion is passive income to P. The remaining $25 of the inclusion is treated as general limitation income to P because $25 is attributable to S's general limitation income.

(f) *Modification of look-through rules for certain income.*—(1) *High withholding tax interest.*—If a taxpayer receives or accrues interest from a controlled foreign corporation that is a financial services entity, and the interest would be described as high withholding tax interest if section 904(d)(3) and paragraph (c)(2) of this section (the look-through rules for interest) did not apply, then the interest shall be treated as high withholding tax interest to the extent that the interest is allocable under section 904(d)(3) and paragraph (c)(2)(i) of this section to financial services income of the controlled foreign corporation. See section 904(d)(3)(H). The amount treated as high-withholding tax interest under this paragraph (f)(1) shall not exceed the interest, or equivalent income, of the payor that would be taken into account in determining the financial services income of the payor if the look-through rules applied.

(2) *Dividends from a noncontrolled section 902 corporation.*—(i) *Rule.*—If a United States shareholder that is a corporation receives or accrues income from a controlled foreign corporation that is attributable to dividends from a noncontrolled section 902 corporation, such income shall be subject to a separate limitation for such dividends except as provided in § 1.904-4(g)(2)(ii) (relating to dividends from a foreign corporation with respect to which the United States shareholder does not meet the stock ownership requirements of section 902).

(ii) *Example.*—The following example illustrates the provisions of this paragraph (f)(2).

Example. P, a domestic corporation, owns 40 percent of S, a controlled foreign corporation. U, an unrelated domestic corporation, owns the remaining 60 percent of S. S owns 10 percent of T, a noncontrolled section 902 corporation. In 1990, T pays S a dividend, which S includes in its gross income as a dividend from a noncontrolled section 902 corporation. S has no other income during 1990. P and U must include S's dividend income from T in their gross income under subpart F. Pursuant to § 1.904-4(g)(2)(ii)(C), the subpart F inclusion to U is characterized as a dividend from a noncontrolled section 902 corporation because U meets the 5 percent ownership requirement of section 902(b) (60% × 10% = 6%). The subpart F inclusion to P is characterized as passive income because P does not meet the 5 percent ownership requirement of section 902(b) (40% × 10% = 4%).

(3) *Distributions from a FSC.*—Income received or accrued by a taxpayer that, under the rules of paragraph (c)(4) of this section (look-through rules for dividends), would be treated as foreign trade income or as passive income that is interest and carrying charges (as defined in section 927(d)(1)), and that is also a distribution from a FSC (or a former FSC), shall be treated as a distribution from a FSC (or a former FSC).

(4) *Example.*—The following example illustrates the operation of paragraph (f)(1) of this section.

Example. Controlled foreign corporation S is a wholly-owned subsidiary of P, a domestic corporation. S is a financial services entity. In 1988, S earns $80 of interest that meets the definition of financial services income and $20 of high withholding tax interest. S makes a $100 interest payment to P. The interest payment to P is subject to a withholding tax of 15 percent. Twenty dollars ($20) of the interest payment to P is considered to be high withholding tax interest because, under section 904(d)(3), it is allocable to the high withholding tax interest earned by S. The remaining eighty dollars ($80) of the interest payment is also treated as high withholding tax interest to P because, under paragraph (f)(1) of this section, interest that is subject to a high withholding tax but would not be considered to be high withholding tax interest under the look-through rules of paragraph (c)(2) of this section, shall be treated as high withholding tax interest to the extent that the interest would have been treated as financial services interest income under the look-through rules of paragraph (c)(2)(i) of this section.

(g) *Application of look-through rules to certain domestic corporations.*—The principles of section 904(d)(3) and this section shall apply to any foreign source interest, rents and royalties paid by a United States corporation to a related corporation. For this purpose, a United States corporation and another corporation are considered to be related if one owns, directly or indirectly, stock possessing more than 50 percent of the total voting power of all classes of stock of the other corporation or more than 50 percent of the total value of the other corporation. In addition, a United States corporation and another corporation shall be considered to be related if the same United States shareholders own, directly or indirectly, stock possessing more than 50 percent of the total voting power of all classes of stock or more than 50 percent of the total value of each corporation. For purposes of this paragraph, the constructive stock ownership rules of section 318 and the regulations under that section apply. For taxable years beginning before January 1, 2001, this paragraph (g) shall be applied by substituting "50 percent or more" for "more than 50 percent" each place it appears.

(h) *Application of look-through rules to partnerships and other pass-through entities.*—(1) *General rule.*—Except as provided in paragraph (h)(2) of this section, a partner's distributive share of partnership income shall be characterized as income in a separate category to the extent that the distributive share is a share of income earned or accrued by the partnership in such category. Payments to a partner described in section 707 (*e.g.*, payments to a partner not acting in capacity as a partner) shall be characterized as income in a separate category to the extent that the payment is attributable under the principles of § 1.861-8 and this section to income earned or accrued by the partnership in such category, if the payments are interest, rents, or royalties that would be characterized under the look-through rules of this section if the partnership were foreign corporation, and the partner who receives the payment owns 10 percent or more of the value of the partnership. A payment by a partnership to a member of the controlled group (as defined in paragraph (a)(3) of this section) of the partner shall be characterized under the look-through rules of this section if the payment would be a section 707 payment entitled to look-through treatment if it were made to the partner.

(2) *Exception for certain partnership interests.*—(i) *Rule.*—Except as otherwise provided, if any limited partner or corporate general partner owns less than 10 percent of the value in a partnership, the partner's distributive share of partnership income from the partnership shall be passive income to the partner, and the partner's distributive share of partnership deductions from the partnership shall be allocated and apportioned under the principles of § 1.861-8 only to the partner's passive income from that partnership.

(ii) *Exceptions.*—To the extent a partner's distributive share of income from a partnership is a share of high withholding tax interest received or accrued by the partnership, that partner's distributive share of partnership income will be high withholding tax interest regardless of the partner's level of ownership in the partnership. If a partnership interest described in paragraph (h)(2)(i) of this section is held in the ordinary course of a partner's active trade or business, the rules of paragraph (h)(1) of this section shall apply for purposes of characterizing the partner's distributive share of the partnership income. A partnership interest will be considered to be held in the ordinary course of a partner's active trade or business if the partner (or a member of the partner's affiliated group of corporations (within the meaning of section 1504(a) and without regard to section 1504(b)(3))) engages (other than through a less than 10 percent interest in a partnership) in the same or related trade or business as the partnership.

(3) *Income from the sale of a partnership interest.*—To the extent a partner recognizes gain on the sale of a partnership interest, that income shall be treated as passive income to the partner, unless the income is considered to be high-taxed under section 904(d)(2)(A)(iii)(III) and § 1.904-4(c).

(4) *Value of a partnership interest.*—For purposes of paragraphs (i), (h)(1), and (h)(2) of this section, a partner will be considered as owning 10 percent of the value of a partnership for a particular year if the partner has 10 percent of the capital and profits interest of the partnership. Similarly, a partnership (first partnership) is considered as owning 50 percent of the value of another partnership (second partnership) if the first partnership owns fifty percent of the capital and profits interests of another partnership. For this purpose, value will be determined at the end of the partnership's taxable year. Similarly, a partnership (first partnership) is considered as owning more than 50 percent of the value of another partnership (second partnership) if the first partnership owns more than 50 percent of the capital and profits interests of the second partnership. For this purpose, value will be determined at the end of the partnership's taxable year. For taxable years beginning before January 1, 2001, the second preceding sentence shall be applied by substituting "50 percent" for "more than 50 percent".

(i) *Application of look-through rules to related entities.*—(1) *In general.*—Except as provided in paragraphs (i)(2) and (3) of this section, the principles of this section shall apply to distributions and payments that are subject to the look-through rules of section 904(d)(3) and this section from a controlled foreign corporation or other entity otherwise entitled to look-through treatment (a "look-through entity") under this section to a related look-through entity. Two look-through entities shall be considered to be related to each other if one owns, directly or indirectly, stock possessing more than 50 percent of the total voting power of all classes of voting stock of the other entity or more than 50 percent of the total value of such entity. In addition, two look-through entities are related if the same United States shareholders own, directly or indirectly, stock possessing more than 50 percent of the total voting power of all voting classes of stock (in the case of a corporation) or more than 50 percent of the total value of each look-through entity. In the case of a corporation, value shall be determined by taking into account all classes of stock. In the case of a partnership, value shall be determined under the rules in paragraph (h)(4) of this section. For purposes of this section, indirect ownership shall be determined under section 318 and the regulations thereunder. For taxable years beginning before January 1, 2001, the third sentence of this paragraph (i)(1) shall be applied by substituting "50 percent or more" for "more than 50 percent" each place it appears.

(2) *Exception for distributive shares of partnership income.*—In the case of tiered partnership arrangements, a distributive share of partnership income will be characterized under the look-through rules of section 904(d)(3) and this section if the partner meets the requirements of paragraph (h)(1) of this section with respect to the partnership (first partnership), whether or not the income is received through another partnership or partnerships (second partnership) and whether or not the first partnership and the second partnership are considered to be related under the rules of paragraph (i)(1) of this section.

(3) *Special rule for dividends.*—Solely for purposes of dividend payments between controlled foreign corporations in taxable years beginning after December 31, 2000, two controlled foreign corporations shall be considered related look-through entities if the same United States shareholder owns, directly or indirectly, at least 10 percent of the total voting power of all classes of stock of each foreign corporation. Taxpayers may choose to apply this paragraph (i)(3) in taxable years beginning after December 31, 1991, provided that appropriate adjustments are made to eliminate any double benefit arising from the application of this paragraph (i)(3) to taxable years that are not open for assessment.

(4) *Examples.*—The following examples illustrate the provisions of this paragraph (i):

Example (1). P, a domestic corporation, owns all of the stock of S, a controlled foreign corporation. S owns 40 percent of the stock of

T, a Country X corporation that is a controlled foreign corporation. The remaining 60 percent of the stock of T is owned by V, a domestic corporation. The percentages of value and voting power of T owned by S and V correspond to their percentages of stock ownership. T owns 40 percent (by vote and value) of the stock of U, a Country Z corporation that is a controlled foreign corporation. The remaining 60 percent of U is owned by unrelated U.S. persons. U earns exclusively general limitation non-subpart F income. In 2001, U makes an interest payment of $100 to T. Look-through principles do not apply because T and U are not related look-through entities under paragraph (i)(1) of this section (because T does not own more than 50 percent of the voting power or value of U). The interest is passive income to T, and is subpart F income to P and V. Under paragraph (c)(1) of this section, look-through principles determine P and V's characterization of the subpart F inclusion from T. P and V therefore must characterize the inclusion as passive income.

Example (2). The facts are the same as in *Example (1)* except that instead of a $100 interest payment, U pays a $50 dividend to T in 2001. P and V each own, directly or indirectly, more than 10 percent of the voting power of all classes of stock of both T and U. Pursuant to paragraph (i)(3) of this section, for purposes of applying this section to the dividend from U to T, U and T are treated as related look-through entities. Therefore, look-through principles apply to characterize the dividend income as general limitation income to T. The dividend is subpart F income of T that is taxable to P and V. The subpart F inclusions of P and V are also subject to look-through principles, under paragraph (c)(1) of this section, and are characterized as general limitation income to P and V because the income is general limitation income of T.

Example (3). The facts are the same as in *Example (1)*, except that U pays both a $100 interest payment and a $50 dividend to T, and T owns 80 percent (by vote and value) of U. Under paragraph (i)(1) of this section, T and U are related look-through entities, because T owns more than 50 percent (by vote and value) of U. Therefore, look-through principles apply to both the interest and dividend income paid or accrued by U to T, and T treats both types of income as general limitation income. Under paragraph (c)(1) of this section, P and V apply look-through principles to the resulting subpart F inclusions, which therefore are also general limitation income to P and V.

(j) *Look-through rules applied to passive foreign investment company inclusions.*—If a passive foreign investment company is a controlled foreign corporation and the taxpayer is a United States shareholder in that passive foreign investment company, any amount included in gross income under section 1293 shall be treated as income in a separate category to the extent the amount so included is attributable to income received or accrued by that controlled foreign corporation that is described as income in the separate category. For purposes of this paragraph (j), the priority rules of §1.904-4(l) shall apply prior to the application of the rules of this paragraph.

(k) *Ordering rules.*—(1) *In general.*—Income received or accrued by a related person to which the look-through rules apply is characterized before amounts included from, or paid or distributed by that person and received or accrued by a related person. For purposes of determining the character of income received or accrued by a person from a related person if the payor or another related person also receives or accrues income from the recipient and the look-through rules apply to the income in all cases, the rules of paragraph (k)(2) of this section apply.

(2) *Specific rules.*—For purposes of characterizing income under this paragraph, the following types of income are characterized in the order stated:

(i) Rents and royalties;

(ii) Interest;

(iii) Subpart F inclusions and distributive shares of partnership income;

(iv) Dividend distributions.

If an entity is both a recipient and a payor of income described in any one of the categories described in (i) through (iv) of this paragraph, the income received will be characterized before the income that is paid. In addition, the amount of interest paid or accrued, directly or indirectly, by a person to a related person shall be offset against and eliminate any interest received or accrued, directly or indirectly, by a person from that related person before application of the ordering rules of this paragraph. In a case in which a person pays or accrues interest to a related person, and also receives or accrues interest indirectly from the related person, the smallest interest payment is eliminated and the amount of all other interest payments are reduced by the amount of the smallest interest payment.

(l) *Examples.*—The following examples illustrate the application of paragraphs (g), (h), (i), and (k) of this section.

Example (1). S and T, controlled foreign corporations, are wholly-owned subsidiaries of P, a domestic corporation. S and T are incorporated in two different foreign countries and T is a financial services entity. In 1987, S earns $100 of income that is general limitation foreign base company sales income. After expenses, including a $50 interest payment to T, S's income is subject to foreign tax at an effective rate of 40 percent. P elects to exclude S's $50 of net income from subpart F under section 954(b)(4). T earns $350 of income that consists of $300 of subpart F financial services income and $50 of interest received from S. The $50 of interest is foreign personal holding company income in T's hands because section 954(c)(3)(A)(i) (same country exception for interest payments) does not apply. The $50 of interest is also general limitation income to T because S and T are related look-through entities within the meaning of paragraph (i)(1) of this section and, therefore, the look-through rules of paragraph (c)(2)(i) of this section apply to characterize the interest payment. Thus, with respect to T, P includes in its gross income $50 of general limitation foreign personal holding company income and $300 of financial services income.

Example (2). The facts are the same as in *Example (1)* except that instead of earning $100 of general limitation foreign base company sales income, S earns $100 of foreign personal holding company income that is passive income. Although the interest payment to T would otherwise be passive income, T is a financial services entity and, under § 1.904-4(e)(1), the income is treated as financial services income in T's hands. Thus, P's entire $350 section 951 inclusion consists of financial services income.

Example (3). P, a domestic corporation, wholly-owns S, a domestic corporation that is a 80/20 corporation. In 1987, S's earnings consist of $100 of foreign source shipping income and $100 of foreign source high withholding tax interest. S makes a $100 foreign source interest payment to P. The interest payment to P is subject to the look-through rules of paragraph (c)(2)(i) of this section, and is characterized as shipping income and high withholding tax interest to the extent that it is allocable to such income in S's hands.

Example (4). PS is a domestic partnership that is the sole shareholder of controlled foreign corporation S. PS has two general partners, A and B. A and B each have a greater than 10 percent interest in PS. PS also has two limited partners, C and D. C has a 50 percent interest in the partnership and D has a 9 percent interest. A, B, C and D are all United States persons. In 1987, S has $100 of general limitation non-subpart F income on which it pays no foreign tax. S pays a $100 dividend to PS. The dividend is the only income of PS. Under the look-through rule of paragraph (c)(4) of this section, the dividend to PS is general limitation income. Under paragraph (h)(1) of this section, A's, B's, and C's distributive shares of PS's income are general limitation income. Under paragraph (h)(2) of this section, because D is a limited partner with a less than 10 percent interest in PS, D's distributive share of PS's income is passive income.

Example (5). P has a 25 percent interest in partnership PS that he sells to X for $110. P's basis in his partnership interest is $35. P recognizes $75 of gain on the sale of its partnership interest and is subject to no foreign tax. Under paragraph (h)(3) of this section, the gain is treated as passive income.

Example (6). P, a domestic corporation, owns 100 percent of the stock of S, a controlled foreign corporation, and S owns 100 percent of the stock of T, a controlled foreign corporation. S has $100 of passive foreign personal holding company income from unrelated persons and $100 of general limitation income. S also has $50 of interest income from T. S pays T $100 of interest. Under paragraph (k)(2) of this section, the $100 interest payment from S to T is reduced for limitation purposes to the extent of the $50 interest payment from T to S before application of the rules in paragraph (c)(2)(ii) of this section. Therefore, the interest payment from T to S is disregarded. S is treated as if it paid $50 of interest to T, all of which is allocable to S's passive foreign personal holding company income. Therefore the $50 interest payment from S to T is passive income.

Example (7). P, a domestic corporation, owns 100 percent of the stock of S, a controlled foreign corporation. S owns 100 percent of the stock of T, a controlled foreign corporation and 100 percent of the stock of U, a controlled foreign corporation. In 1988, T pays S $5 of interest, S pays U $10 of interest and U pays T $20 of interest. Under paragraph (k)(2) of this section, the interest payments from S to U must be offset by the amount of interest that S is considered as receiving indirectly from U and the interest payment from U to T is offset by the amount of the interest payment that U is considered as receiving indirectly from T. The $10 payment by S to U is reduced by $5, the amount of the interest payment from T to S that is treated as being paid indirectly by U to S. Similarly, the $20 interest payment from U to T is reduced by $5, the amount of the interest payment from S to U that is treated as being paid indirectly by T to U. Therefore, under paragraph (k)(2) of this section, T is treated as having made no interest payment to S, S is treated as having paid $5 of interest to U, and U is treated as having paid $15 to T.

Example (8). (i) P, a domestic corporation, owns 100 percent of the stock of S, a controlled foreign corporation, and S owns 100 percent of the stock of T, a controlled foreign corporation.

In 1987, S earns $100 of passive foreign personal holding company income and $100 of general limitation non-subpart F sales income from unrelated persons and $100 of general limitation non-subpart F interest income from a related person, W. S pays $150 of interest to T. T earns $200 of general limitation sales income from unrelated persons and the $150 interest payment from S. T pays S $100 of interest.

(ii) Under paragraph (k)(2) of this section, the $100 interest payment from T to S reduces the $150 interest payment from S to T. S is treated as though it paid $50 of interest to T. T is treated as though it made no interest payment to S.

(iii) Under paragraph (k)(2)(ii) of this section, the remaining $50 interest payment from S to T is then characterized. The interest payment is first allocable under the rules of paragraph (c)(2)(ii)(C) of this section to S's passive income. Therefore, the $50 interest payment to T is passive income. The interest income is foreign personal holding company income in T's hands. T, therefore, has $50 of subpart F passive income and $200 of non-subpart F general limitation income.

(iv) Under paragraph (k)(2)(iii) of this section, subpart F inclusions are characterized next. P has a subpart F inclusion with respect to S of $50 that is attributable to passive income of S and is treated as passive income to P. P has a subpart F inclusion with respect to T of $50 that is attributable to passive income of T and is treated as passive income to P.

Example (9). (i) P, a domestic corporation, owns 100 percent of the stock of S, a controlled foreign corporation, and S owns 100 percent of the stock of T, a controlled foreign corporation. P also owns 100 percent of the stock of U, a controlled foreign corporation. In 1987, S earns $100 of passive foreign personal holding company income and $200 of non-subpart F general limitation income from unrelated persons. S also receives $150 of dividend income from T. S pays $100 of interest to T and $100 of interest to U. U earns $300 of non-subpart F general limitation income and the $100 of interest received from S. U pays a $100 royalty to T. T earns the $100 interest payment received from S and the $100 royalty received from U.

(ii) Under paragraph (k)(2)(i) of this section, the royalty paid by U to T is characterized first. Assume that the royalty is directly allocable to U's general limitation income. Also assume that the royalty is not subpart F income to T. With respect to T, the royalty is general limitation income.

(iii) Under paragraph (k)(2)(ii) of this section, the interest payments from S to T and U are characterized next. This characterization is done without regard to any dividend income received by S because, under paragraph (k)(2) of this section, dividends are characterized after interest payments from a related person. The interest payments are first allocable to S's passive income under paragraph (c)(2)(ii)(C) of this section. Therefore, $50 of the interest payment to T is passive and $50 of the interest payment to U is passive. The remaining $50 paid to T is general limitation income and the remaining $50 paid to U is general limitation income. All of the interest payments to T and U are subpart F foreign personal holding company income to both recipients.

(iv) Under paragraph (k)(2)(iii) of this section, P has a $100 subpart F inclusion with respect to T that is characterized next. Fifty dollars ($50) of the subpart F inclusion is passive income to P because it is attributable to the passive income portion of the interest income received by T from S, and $50 of the inclusion is treated as general limitation income to P because it is attributable to the general limitation portion of the interest income received by T from S. Under paragraph (k)(2)(iii) of this section, P also has a $100 subpart F inclusion with respect to U. Fifty dollars ($50) of the subpart F inclusion is passive income to P because it is attributable to the passive portion of the interest income received by U from S, and $50 of the inclusion is general limitation income to P because it is attributable to the general limitation portion of the interest income received by U from S.

(v) Under paragraph (k)(2)(iv) of this section, the $150 distribution from T to S is characterized next. One hundred dollars ($100) of the distribution is out of earnings and profits attributable to previously taxed income. Therefore, only $50 is a dividend that is subject to the look-through rules of paragraph (d) of this section. The $50 dividend is attributable to T's general limitation income and is general limitation income to S in its entirety.

Example (10). (i) P, a domestic corporation, owns 100 percent of the stock of S, a controlled foreign corporation, and S owns 100 percent of the stock of T, a controlled foreign corporation. P also owns 100 percent of the stock of U, a controlled foreign corporation. S, T and U are all incorporated in the same foreign country. In 1987, S earns $100 of passive foreign personal holding income and $200 of general limitation non-subpart F income from unrelated persons. S pays $100 of interest to T and $100 of interest to U. U earns $300 of general limitation non-subpart F income and the $100 of interest received from S. T's only income is the $100 interest payment received from S.

(ii) Under paragraph (k)(2)(ii) of this section, the interest payments from S to T and U are characterized first. The interest payments are first allocated under the rule of paragraph (c)(2)(ii)(C) of this section to S's passive income. Therefore, under that provision and paragraph (c)(2)(i) of this section, $50 of the interest payment to T is passive income to T and $50 of the interest payment to U is passive income to U. The remaining $50 paid to T is general limitation income and the remaining $50 paid to U is general limitation income.

(iii) Under paragraph (k)(2)(iii) of this section, any subpart F inclusion of P is determined and characterized next. Under paragraph (c)(1)(i) of this section, paragraphs (c)(2)(i) and (c)(2)(ii) apply not only for purposes of determining the separate category of income of S to which the interest payments from S to T and U are allocable but also for purposes of determining the subpart F income of T and U. Although the interest payments from S to T and U are "same country" interest payments that would otherwise be excludible from T's and U's subpart F income under section 954(c)(3)(A)(i), section 954(c)(3)(B) provides that the exception for same country payments between related persons shall not apply to the extent such payments have reduced the subpart F income of the payor. In this case, $50 of the $100 interest payment from S to T reduced S's subpart F income and $50 of the $100 interest payment from S to U reduced the remaining $50 of S's subpart F income. Therefore, T has $50 of subpart F income that is passive income and U has $50 of subpart F income that is passive income. P includes $100 of subpart F income in gross income that is passive income to P.

(iv) The remaining $50 of interest paid by S to T and the remaining $50 of interest paid by S to U is not subpart F income to T or U because it did not reduce S's subpart F income and is therefore eligible for the same country exception.

Example (11). P, a domestic corporation, owns 100 percent of the stock of S, a controlled foreign corporation, and S owns 100 percent of the stock of T, a controlled foreign corporation. P also owns 100 percent of the stock of U, a controlled foreign corporation. In 1991, T earns $100 of general limitation income that is not subpart F income and distributes the entire amount to S as a dividend. S earns $100 of passive foreign personal holding company income and the $100 dividend from T. S pays $100 of interest to U. U earns $200 of general limitation income that is foreign base company income and $100 of interest income from S. This transaction does not involve circular payments and, therefore, the ordering rules of paragraph (k)(2) of this section do not apply. Instead, pursuant to paragraph (k)(1) of this section, income received is characterized first. T's earnings and, thus, the dividend from T to S are characterized first. S includes the $100 dividend from T in gross income as general limitation income because all of T's earnings are general limitation income. S thus has $100 of passive foreign personal holding company income and $100 of general limitation income. The interest payment to U is then characterized as $100 passive income under paragraph (c)(2)(ii)(C) of this section (allocation of related person interest to passive foreign personal holding company income). For 1991, U thus has $200 of general limitation income that is subpart F income, and $100 of passive foreign personal holding company income. For 1991, P includes in its gross income $200 of general limitation subpart F income from U, $100 of passive subpart F income from U (relating to the interest payment from S to U), and $100 of general limitation subpart F income from S (relating to the dividend from T to S).

(m) *Application of section 904(g).*—(1) *In general.*—For purposes of determining the portion of an interest payment that is allocable to income earned or accrued by a controlled foreign corporation from sources within the United States under section 904(g)(3), the rules in paragraph (m)(2) of this section apply. For purposes of determining the portion of a dividend paid or accrued (or amount treated as a dividend, including amounts described in section 951(a)(1)(B)) by a controlled foreign corporation that is treated as from sources within the United States under section 904(g)(4), the rules in paragraph (m)(4) of this section apply. For purposes of determining the portion of an amount included in gross income under section 951(a)(1)(A) that is attributable to income of the controlled foreign corporation from sources within the United States under section 904(g)(2), the rules in paragraph (m)(5) of this section apply. In order to determine whether section 904(g) applies, section 904(g)(5) (exception if controlled foreign corporation has a de minimis amount of United States source income) shall be applied to the total amount of earnings and profits of a controlled foreign corporation for a taxable year without regard to the characterization of those earnings under section 904(d).

(2) *Treatment of interest payments.*—If interest is received or accrued by a United States shareholder or a person related to a United States shareholder (within the meaning of paragraph (c)(2)(ii) of this section) from a controlled foreign corporation, the interest shall be considered to be allocable to income of the controlled foreign corporation from sources within the United States for purposes of section 904(d) to the extent that the interest is allocable under paragraph (c)(2)(ii)(C) of this section to passive income that is from sources within the United States. If related person inter-

est is less than or equal to passive income, the related person interest will be allocable to United States source passive income based on the ratio of United States source passive income to total passive income. To the extent that related person interest exceeds passive income, and, therefore, is allocated under paragraph (c)(2)(ii)(D) of this section to income in a separate category other than passive, the following formulas apply in determining the portion of the interest payment that is from sources within the United States. If the taxpayer uses the gross income method to allocate interest, the portion of the interest payment from sources within the United States is determined as follows:

$$\text{The amount of the interest payment allocated to the separate category under paragraph (c)(2)(ii)(D) of this section} \times \frac{\text{Gross income from United States sources in that category}}{\text{Gross income from all sources in that category}}$$

If the taxpayer uses the asset method to allocate interest, then the portion of the interest payment from sources within the United States is determined as follows:

$$\text{The amount of the interest payment allocated to the separate category under paragraph (c)(2)(ii)(D) of this section} \times \frac{\text{Value of domestic assets in that category}}{\text{Value of total assets in that category}}$$

For purposes of this paragraph, the value of assets in a separate category is the value of assets as determined under the principles of § 1.861-9T(g). See § 1.861-10T(d)(2) for purposes of determining the value of assets and gross income in a separate category as reduced for indebtedness the interest on which is directly allocated.

(3) *Examples*.—The following examples illustrate the application of this paragraph.

Example (1). Controlled foreign corporation S is a wholly-owned subsidiary of P, a domestic corporation. In 1988, S pays P $300 of interest. S has no other expenses. In 1988, S has $3000 of assets that generate $650 of foreign source general limitation sales income and a $1000 loan to an unrelated foreign person that generates $20 of foreign source passive interest income. S also has a $4000 loan to an unrelated United States person that generates $70 of United States source passive income and $4000 of inventory that generates $100 of United States source general limitation income. S uses the asset method to allocate interest expense. The following chart summarizes S's assets and income:

Assets

	Foreign	U.S.	Totals
Passive	1000	4000	5000
General	3000	4000	7000
Total	4000	8000	12000

Income

	Foreign	U.S.	Totals
Passive	20	70	90
General	650	100	750
Total	670	170	840

Under paragraph (c)(2)(ii)(C) of this section, $90 of the related person interest payment is allocable to S's passive income. Under paragraph (m)(2) of this section, $70 is from sources within the United States and $20 is from foreign sources. Under paragraph (c)(2)(ii)(D) of this section, the remaining $210 of the related person interest payment is allocated to general limitation income. Under paragraph (m)(2) of this section, $120 of the remaining $210 is treated as income from sources within the United States ($120 = $210 × $4000/$7000) and $90 is treated as income from foreign sources ($90 = $210 × $3000/$7000).

Example (2). The facts are the same as in *Example (1)* except that S uses the gross income method to allocate interest expense. The first $90 of related person interest expense is allocated to passive income in the same manner as in Example (1). Under paragraph (c)(2)(ii)(D) of this section, the remaining $210 of the related person interest expense is allocated to general limitation income. Under paragraph (m)(2) of this section, $28 of the remaining $210 is treated as income from United States sources ($28 = $210 × $100/$750) and $182 is treated as income from foreign sources ($182 = $210 × $650/$750).

Example (3). Controlled foreign corporation S is a wholly-owned subsidiary of P, a domestic corporation. In 1988, S pays $300 of interest to P. S has no other expenses. S uses the asset method to allocate interest expense. In 1988, S has $4000 of assets that generate $650 of foreign source general limitation manufacturing income and a $1000 loan to an unrelated foreign person that generates $100 of foreign source passive interest income. S has $500 of shipping assets that generate $200 of foreign source shipping income and $500 of shipping assets that generate $200 of United

States source shipping income. S also has a $1000 loan to an unrelated United States person that generates $100 of United States source passive income. S's passive income is not also described as shipping income. The following chart summarizes S's assets and income:

Assets

	Foreign	U.S.	Totals
Passive	1000	1000	2000
Shipping	500	500	1000
General	4000	0	4000
Total	5500	1500	7000

Income

	Foreign	U.S.	Totals
Passive	100	100	200
Shipping	200	200	400
General	650	0	650
Total	950	300	1250

Under paragraph (c)(2)(ii)(C) of this section, $200 of the related person interest payment is allocable to S's passive income. Under paragraph (m)(2) of this section, $100 of this amount is from foreign sources and $100 is from sources within the United States.

Under paragraph (c)(2)(ii)(D) of this section, $80 of the remaining $100 of the related person interest payment is allocated to general limitation income ($80 = $100 × $4000/$5000) and $20 is allocated to shipping income ($20 = $100 × $1000/$5000).

Under paragraph (m)(2) of this section, none of $80 of the interest payment allocated to general limitation income is treated as income from United States sources ($0 = $80 × $0/$4000). Therefore, the entire $80 is treated as income from foreign sources.

Under paragraph (m)(2) of this section, $10 of the $20 of the interest payment allocated to the shipping income is treated as income from United States sources ($10 = $20 × $500/$1000) and $10 of the $20 is treated as income from foreign sources ($10 = $20 × $500/$1000).

Example (4). The facts are the same as in *Example (3)* except that S uses the gross income method to allocate interest expense. The interest allocated to passive income under paragraph (c)(2)(ii)(C) of this section is the same, $200, $100 from United States sources and $100 from foreign sources.

Under paragraph (c)(2)(ii)(D) of this section, the remaining $100 of related person interest is allocated between the shipping and general limitation categories based on the gross income in those categories. Therefore, $38 of the remaining $100 interest payment is allocated to shipping income ($38 = $100 × $400/($1250 − $200)) and $62 is treated as allocated to general limitation income ($62 = $100 × $650/($1250 − $200)).

Under paragraph (m)(2) of this section, $19 of the $38 allocable to shipping income is treated as income from United States sources ($19 = $38 × $200/$400) and $19 is treated as income from foreign sources ($19 = $38 × $200/$400).

Under paragraph (m)(2) of this section, all of the $62 allocated to general limitation income is treated as income from foreign sources ($62 = $62 × $650/$650).

(4) *Treatment of dividend payments.*—
(i) *Rule.*—Any dividend or distribution treated as a dividend under this section (including an amount included in gross income under section 951(a)(1)(B)) that is received or accrued by a United States shareholder from a controlled foreign corporation shall be treated as income in a separate category derived from sources within the United States in proportion to the ratio of the portion of the earnings and profits of the controlled foreign corporation in the corresponding separate category from United States sources to the total amount of earnings and profits of the controlled foreign corporation in that separate category.

(ii) *Determination of earnings and profits from United States sources.*—In order to determine the portions of earnings and profits from United States sources and from foreign sources within each separate category, related person interest shall be allocated to the United States source portion of income in a separate category by applying the rules of paragraph (m)(2) of this section. Other expenses shall be allocated by applying the rules of paragraph (c)(2)(ii) of this section separately to the United States source income and the foreign source income in each category. For example, unrelated person interest expense that is allocated among categories of income based upon the relative amounts of assets in a category must be allocated between United States and foreign source income within each category by applying the rules of paragraph (c)(2)(ii)(E) of this section separately to United States source and foreign source assets in the separate category.

(iii) *Example.*—The following example illustrates the application of this paragraph.

Example. Controlled foreign corporation, S, is a wholly owned subsidiary of P, a domestic corporation. S is a financial services entity. In 1987, S has $100 of non-subpart F general limitation earnings and profits and $100 of non-subpart F financial services income. None of the general limitation earnings and profits are from sources within the United States, and $50 of the financial services earnings and profits are from United States sources. In 1988, S earns $300 of non-subpart F general limitation earnings and profits and $500 of non-subpart F financial services earnings and profits. One hundred dollars ($100) of the general limitation earnings and profits are from sources within the United States. None of the financial services earnings and profits are from United States sources. In 1988, S pays P a $500 dividend. Under paragraph (c)(4) of this section, $200 of the dividend is attributable to general limitation earnings and profits ($200 = $500 × $400/$1000). Under this paragraph (m)(3), the portion of the dividend that is attributable to general limitation earnings and profits from sources within the United States is $50 ($200 × $100/$400). Under paragraph (c)(4) of this section, $300 of the dividend is attributable to financial services earnings and profits ($300 = $500 × $600/$1000). Under this paragraph (m)(3), the portion of the dividend that is attributable to financial services earnings and profits from sources within the United States is $25 ($300 × $50/$600).

(5) *Treatment of subpart F inclusions.*—(i) *Rule.*—Any amount included in the gross income of a United States shareholder of a controlled foreign corporation under section 951(a)(1)(A) shall be treated as income subject to a separate limitation that is derived from sources within the United States to the extent such amount is attributable to income of the controlled foreign corporation in the corresponding category of income from sources within the United States. In order to determine a controlled foreign corporation's taxable income and earnings and profits from sources within the United States in each separate category, the principles of paragraph (m)(4)(ii) of this section shall apply.

(ii) *Example.*—The following example illustrates the application of this paragraph (m)(5).

Example. Controlled foreign corporation S is a wholly-owned subsidiary of domestic corporation, P. In 1987, S earns $100 of subpart F foreign personal holding company income that is passive income. Of this amount, $40 is derived from sources within the United States. S also earns $50 of subpart F general limitation income. None of this income is from sources within the United States. Assume that S pays no foreign taxes and has no expenses. P is required to include $150 in gross income under section 951(a). Of this amount, $60 will be foreign source passive income to P and $40 will be United States source passive income to P. Fifty dollars ($50) will be foreign source general limitation income to P.

(6) *Treatment of section 78 amount.*—For purposes of treating taxes deemed paid by a taxpayer under section 902(a) and section 960(a)(1) as a dividend under section 78, taxes that are paid or accrued with respect to United States source income in a separate category shall be treated as United States source income in that separate category.

(7) *Coordination with treaties.*—(i) *Rule.*—If any amount of income derived from a United States-owned foreign corporation, as defined in section 904(g)(6), would be treated as derived from sources within the United States under section 904(g) and this paragraph (m) and, pursuant to an income tax convention with the United States, the taxpayer chooses to avail itself of benefits of the convention that treat that amount as arising from sources outside the United States under a rule explicitly treating the income as foreign source, then that amount will be treated as foreign source income. However, sections 904(a), (b), (c), (d) and (f), 902, 907, and 960 shall be applied separately to amounts described in the preceding sentence with respect to each treaty under which the taxpayer has claimed benefits and, within each treaty, to each separate category of income.

(ii) *Example.*—The following example illustrates the application of this paragraph (m)(7).

Example. Controlled foreign corporation S is incorporated in Country A and is a wholly-owned subsidiary of P, a domestic corporation. In 1990, S earns $80 of foreign base company sales income in Country A which is general limitation income and $40 of U.S. source interest income. S incurs $20 of expenses attributable to its sales business. S pays P $40 of interest that is allocated to U.S. source passive income under paragraphs (c)(2)(ii)(C) and (m)(2) of this section. Assume that earnings and profits equal net income. All of S's net income of $60 is includible in P's gross income under subpart F (section 951(a)(1)). For 1990, P also has $100 of passive income derived from investments in Country B. Pursuant to section 904(g)(3) and paragraph (m)(2) of this section, the $40 interest payment from S is United States source income to P because it is attributable to United States source interest income of S. The United States-Country A income tax treaty, however, treats all interest payments by residents of Country A as Country A sourced and P elects to apply the treaty. Pursuant to section 904(g)(10) and this paragraph (m)(7), the entire interest payment will be treated as foreign source income to P. P thus has $60 of foreign source general limitation income, $40 of foreign source passive income from S, and $100 of other foreign source passive income. In determining P's foreign tax credit limitation on passive income, the passive income from Country A shall be treated separately from any other passive income.

(n) *Order of application of sections 904(d), and (g).*—In order to apply the rules of this section, section 904(d)(1) shall first be applied to the controlled foreign corporation to determine the amount of income and earnings and profits derived by the controlled foreign corporation in each separate category. The income and earnings and profits in each separate category that is from United States sources shall then be determined. Sections 904(d)(3), 904(g), and this section shall then be applied for purposes of characterizing and sourcing income received, accrued, or included by a United States shareholder in the controlled foreign corporation that is attributable or allocable to income or earnings and profits of the controlled foreign corporation.

(o) *Effective date.*—Section 904(d)(3) and this section apply to distributions and section 951 inclusions of earnings and profits of a controlled foreign corporation (or other entity to which this section applies) derived during the first taxable year of the controlled foreign corporation (or other entity) beginning after December 31, 1986, and thereafter, and to payments made by a controlled foreign corporation (or other entity) during such taxable years, without regard to whether the corresponding taxable year of the recipient of the distribution or payment or of one or more of the United States shareholders of the controlled foreign corporation begins after December 31, 1986. [Reg. § 1.904-5.]

☐ [*T.D.* 8214, 7-15-88. *Amended by T.D.* 8412, 5-13-92; *T.D.* 8767, 3-23-98; *T.D.* 8827, 7-12-99 (*corrected* 10-29-99); *T.D.* 8916, 12-29-2000 *and T.D.* 9141, 7-19-2004.]

Proposed Amendments to Regulation

§ 1.904-5. Look-through rules as applied to controlled foreign corporations and other entities.—

* * *

(k) *Ordering rules.*—(1) *In general.*—Income received or accrued by a related person to which the look-through rules apply is characterized before amounts included from, or paid or distributed by, that person and received or accrued by a related person. For purposes of determining the character of income received or accrued by a person from a related person if the payor or another related person also receives or accrues income from the recipient and the look-through rules apply to the income in all cases, the rules of paragraph (k)(2) of this section apply. Notwithstanding any other provision of this section, the principles of § 1.954-1(c)(1)(i) will apply to any expense subject to § 1.954-1(c)(1)(i).

* * *

[Prop. Reg. § 1.904-5.]

[Proposed 7-13-99.]

§ 1.904-6. Allocation and apportionment of taxes.—(a) *Allocation and appointment of taxes to a separate category or categories of income.*—(1) *In general.*—(i) *Taxes related to a separate category of income.*—The amount of foreign taxes paid or accrued with respect to a separate category of income (including United States source income) shall include only those taxes that are related to income in that separate category. Taxes are related to income if the income is included in the base upon which the tax is imposed. If, for example, foreign law exempts certain types of income from foreign taxes, or certain types of income are exempt from foreign tax under an income tax convention, then no taxes are considered to be related to such income for purposes of this paragraph. As another example, if foreign law provides for a specific rate of tax with respect to certain types of income (*e.g.*, capital gains), or certain expenses, deductions, or credits are allowed under foreign law only with respect to a particular type of income, then such provisions shall be taken into account in determining the amount of foreign tax imposed on such income. A withholding tax (unless it is a withholding tax that is not the final tax payable on the income as described in § 1.904-4(d)) is related to the income from which it is withheld. A tax that is imposed on a base that includes more than one separate category of income is considered to be imposed on income in all such categories, and, thus, the taxes are related to all such categories included within the foreign country or possession's taxable income base.

(ii) *Apportionment of taxes related to more than one separate category.*—If a tax is related to more than one separate category, then, in order to determine the amount of the tax paid or accrued with respect to each separate category, the tax shall be apportioned on an annual basis among the separate categories on the basis of the following formula:

Reg. § 1.904-6(a)(1)(ii)

$$\text{Foreign tax related to more than one separate category} \times \frac{\text{Net income subject to that foreign tax included in a separate category}}{\text{Net income subject to that foreign tax}}$$

For purposes of apportioning foreign taxes among the separate categories, gross income is determined under the law of the foreign country or a possession of the United States to which the foreign income taxes have been paid or accrued. Gross income, as determined under foreign law, in the passive category shall first be reduced by any related person interest expense that is allocated to the income under the principles of section 954(b)(5) and § 1.904-5(c)(2)(ii)(C) (adjusted gross passive income). Gross income in all separate categories (including adjusted gross passive income) is next reduced by deducting any expenses, losses, or other amounts that are deductible under foreign law that are specifically allocable to the gross amount of such income under the laws of that foreign country or possession. If expenses are not specifically allocated under foreign law then the expenses will be apportioned under the principles of foreign law but only after taking into account the reduction of passive income by the application of section 954(b)(5). Thus, for example, if foreign law provides that expenses will be apportioned on a gross income basis, the gross income amounts will be those amounts determined under foreign law except that, in the case of passive income, the amount will be adjusted gross passive income. If foreign law does not provide for the direct allocation or apportionment of expenses, losses, or other deductions to a particular category of income, then the principles of §§ 1.861-8 through 1.861-14T and section 954(b)(5) shall apply in allocating and apportioning such expenses, losses, or other deductions to gross income as determined under foreign law after reduction of passive income by the amount of related person interest allocated to passive income under section 954(b)(5) and § 1.904-5(c)(2)(ii)(C). For example, the principles of §§ 1.861-8 through 1.861-14T apply to require definitely related expenses to be directly allocated to particular categories of gross income and provide the methods of apportioning expenses that are definitely related to more than one category of gross income or that are not definitely related to any particular category of gross income. For this purpose, the apportionment of expenses required to be made under §§ 1.861-8 through 1.861-14T need not be made on other than a separate company basis. The rules in this paragraph apply only for purposes of the apportionment of taxes among separate categories of income and do not affect the computation of a taxpayer's foreign tax credit limitation with respect to a specific category of income. If the taxpayer applies the principles of §§ 1.861-8 through 1.861-14T for purposes of allocating expenses at the level of the taxpayer (or at the level of the qualified business unit, foreign subsidiary, or other entity that paid or accrued the foreign taxes) under this paragraph (a)(1)(ii), such principles shall be applied (for such purposes) in the same manner as the taxpayer applies such principles in determining the income or earnings and profits for United States tax purposes of the taxpayer (or of the qualified business unit, foreign subsidiary, or other entity that paid or accrued the foreign taxes, as the case may be). For example, a taxpayer must use the modified gross income method under § 1.861-9T when applying the principles of that section for purposes of this paragraph (a)(1)(ii) to determine the amount of a controlled foreign corporation's income, in each separate category, that is taxed by a foreign country, if the taxpayer applies the modified gross income method under § 1.861-9T(f)(3) when applying § 1.861-9T to determine the income and earnings and profits of the controlled foreign corporation for United States tax purposes.

(iii) *Apportionment of taxes for purposes of applying the high-tax income test.*—If taxes have been allocated and apportioned to passive income under the rules of paragraph (a)(1)(i) or (ii) of this section, the taxes must further be apportioned to the groups of income described in § 1.904-4(c)(3), (4) and (5) for purposes of determining if the group is high-taxed income. Taxes will be related to income in a particular group under the same rules as those in paragraph (a)(1)(i) and (ii) of this section except that those rules shall be applied by substituting the term "group" for the term "category."

(iv) *Special rule for base and timing differences.*—If, under the law of a foreign country or possession of the United States, a tax is imposed on an item of income that does not constitute income under United States tax principles, that tax shall be treated as imposed with respect to general limitation income. If, under the law of a foreign country or possession of the United States, a tax is imposed on an item that would be income under United States tax principles in another year, that tax will be allocated to the appropriate separate category or categories as if the income were recognized under United States tax principles in the year in which the tax was imposed.

(2) *Treatment of certain dividends from noncontrolled section 902 corporations.*—If a taxpayer receives or accrues a dividend from a noncontrolled section 902 corporation, and if the Commissioner establishes that there is an agreement, express or implied, that such dividend is paid out of the passive earnings or high withholding tax interest income of the foreign corporation, then only the foreign taxes imposed on passive income or high withholding tax interest income of the noncontrolled section 902 corporation will be considered to be taxes related to the dividend. For an illustration of this rule, see paragraph (c) *Example (7)* of this section.

(b) *Application of paragraph (a) to sections 902 and 960.*—(1) *Determination of foreign taxes deemed paid.*—If, for the taxable year, there is included in the gross income of a domestic corporation under section 951 an amount attributable to the earnings and profits of a controlled foreign corporation for any taxable year and the amount included consists of income in more than one separate category of the controlled foreign corporation, then the domestic corporation shall be deemed to have paid only a portion of the taxes paid or accrued, or deemed paid or accrued, by the controlled foreign corporation that are allocated to each separate category to which the inclusion is attributable. The portion of the taxes allocated to a particular separate category that shall be deemed paid by the United States shareholder shall be equal to the taxes allocated to that separate category multiplied by the amount of the inclusion with respect to that category (as determined under § 1.904-5(c)(1)) and divided by the earnings and profits of the controlled foreign corporation with respect to that separate category (in accordance with § 1.904-5(c)(2)(ii)). The rules of this paragraph (b)(1) also apply for purposes of computing the foreign taxes deemed paid by United States shareholders of controlled foreign corporations under section 902.

(2) *Distributions received from foreign corporations that are excluded from gross income under section 959(b).*—The principles of this paragraph shall be applied to—

(i) Any portion of a distribution received from a first-tier corporation by a domestic corporation or individual that is excluded from the domestic corporation's or individual's income under section 959(a) and § 1.959-1; and

(ii) Any portion of a distribution received from an immediately lower-tier corporation by a second- or first-tier corporation that is excluded from such foreign corporation's gross income under section 959(b) and § 1.959-2, if such distribution is treated as a dividend pursuant to § 1.960-2(a).

(3) *Application of section 78.*—For purposes of treating taxes deemed paid by a taxpayer under section 902(a) and section 960(a)(1) as a dividend under section 78, taxes that were allocated to income in a separate category shall be treated as income in that same separate category.

(4) *Increase in limitation.*—The amount of the increase in the foreign tax credit limitation allowed by section 960(b) and § 1.960-4 shall be determined with regard to the applicable category of income under section 904(d).

(c) *Examples.*—The following examples illustrate the application of this section.

Example (1). M, a domestic corporation, conducts business in foreign country X. M earns $400 of shipping income, $200 of general limitation income and $200 of passive income as determined under foreign law. Under foreign law, none of M's expenses are directly allocated or apportioned to a particular category of income. Under the principles of §§ 1.861-8 through 1.861-14T, M allocates $75 of directly allocable expenses to shipping income, $10 of directly allocable expenses to general limitation income, and no such expenses to passive income. M also apportions expenses that are not directly allocable to a specific class of gross income—$40 to shipping income, $20 to general limitation income, and $20 to passive income. Therefore, for purposes of paragraph (a) of this section, M has $285 of net shipping income, $170 of net general limitation income, and $180 of net passive income. Country X imposes tax of $100 on a base that includes M's shipping income and general limitation income. Country X exempts passive income from tax. The tax paid by M is related to M's shipping and general limitation income. The $100 tax is apportioned between those limitations. Thus, M is considered to have paid $63 of X tax on its shipping income ($100 × $285/$455) and $37 of tax on its general limitation income ($100 × $170/$455). None of the X tax is allocated to M's passive income.

Example (2). The facts are the same as in example (1) except that X does not exempt all passive income from tax but only exempts interest income. M's passive income consists of $100 of gross dividend income, to which $10 of expenses that are not directly allocable are apportioned, and $100 of interest income, to which $10 of expenses that are not directly allocable are apportioned. The $90 of net dividend income is subject to X tax, and $90 of net interest income is exempt from X tax. M pays $130 of tax to X. The $130 of tax is related to

M's general, shipping, and passive income. The tax is apportioned among those limitations as follows: $68 to shipping income ($130 × $285/$545) $41 to general limitation income ($130 × $170/$545), and $21 to passive income ($130 × $90/$545).

Example (3). P, a domestic corporation, owns 100 percent of S, a controlled foreign corporation organized in country X. S owns 100 percent of T, a controlled foreign corporation that is also organized in country X. Country X grants group relief to S and T. In 1987, S earns $100 of income and T incurs an $80 loss. Under country X's group relief provisions, only $20 of S's income is subject to country X tax. Country X imposes a 30 percent tax on this income ($6). P includes $100 of S's income in gross income under section 951. Six dollars ($6) of foreign tax is related to that income for purposes of section 960.

Example (4). P, a domestic corporation, owns 100 percent of S, a controlled foreign corporation organized in country X and 100 percent of T, a controlled foreign corporation organized in country Y. T has $200 of gross manufacturing general limitation income and $50 of passive income. T also pays S $100 for shipping T's goods, a price that may be justified under section 482. T has no other expenses and S has no other income or expense. T's income and earnings and profits are the same. Foreign country X does not tax S on its shipping income. Foreign country Y taxes all of T's income at a rate of 20 percent. Under the law of foreign country Y, T is only allowed a $50 deduction for the payment to S. Therefore, for foreign law purposes, T has $150 of manufacturing income and earnings and profits and $50 of passive income and earnings and profits upon which it pays $40 of tax. Under the principles of foreign law, $30 of that tax is imposed on the general limitation manufacturing income and $10 of the tax is imposed on passive income. Therefore, the foreign effective rate on the general limitation income is 30 percent and the foreign effective rate on the passive income is 20 percent. T has $100 of general limitation income and $50 of passive income and pays $30 of general limitation taxes and $10 of passive taxes. S has $100 of shipping income and pays no foreign tax.

Example (5). R, a domestic corporation, owns 50 percent of T a foreign corporation that is not a controlled foreign corporation and that is organized in foreign country X. R licenses certain property to T. T then relicenses this property to a third person. In 1987, T paid R a royalty of $100 all of which is treated as passive income to R because it was not an active royalty as defined in § 1.904-4(b)(2). R has $10 of expenses associated with the royalty income and no foreign tax was imposed on the royalty so the high-tax kickout does not apply. In 1988, the Commissioner determined that the correct arm's length royalty was $150 and under the authority of section 482 reallocated an additional $50 of income to R for 1987. Under a closing agreement with the Commissioner, R elected the benefits of Rev. Proc. 65-17 in relation to the income reallocated from R and established an account receivable from T. In 1988, T paid R an additional $50 to reflect the section 482 adjustment and the account receivable that was established because of the adjustment. Foreign country X treats the $50 payment in 1988 as a dividend by T and imposes a $10 withholding tax on the payment. Under paragraph (a)(1) of this section, the $10 of withholding tax is treated as fully allocable to the $50 payment because under foreign law the tax is imposed only on that income. For U.S. purposes, the income is not characterized as a dividend but as a repayment of a bona fide debt and, therefore, the $50 of income is not required to be recognized by R in 1988. The $10 of tax is treated as a tax paid in 1988 on the $50 of passive income included by R in 1987 pursuant to the section 482 adjustment rather than as a tax associated with a dividend from a noncontrolled section 902 corporation. The $10 tax is a tax imposed on passive income under paragraph (a)(1)(iv) of this section.

Example (6). P, a domestic corporation owns all of the stock of S, a controlled foreign corporation that is incorporated in country X. In 1989, S has $100 of passive income, $200 of dividends from a non-controlled section 902 corporation and $200 of general limitation income. S also has $100 of related person interest expense and $100 of other expenses that under foreign law are directly allocable to the general limitation income of S. S has no other expenses. Country X imposes a tax of 25% on all of the net income of S and S, therefore, pays $75 in foreign tax. Under paragraph (a)(1)(ii) of this section, the passive income of S is first reduced by the amount of related person interest for purposes of determining the net amount for purposes of allocating the $75 of tax. Under paragraph (a)(1)(ii) of this section, the general limitation income of S is reduced by the $100 of other expenses. Therefore, $50 of the foreign tax is allocated to the dividends from a noncontrolled section 902 corporation ($50 = $75 × $200/$300), $25 is allocated to the general limitation income of S ($25 = $75 × $100/$300), and no taxes are allocated to S's passive income.

Example (7). R, a domestic corporation owns preferred stock in T, a foreign corporation that is not a controlled foreign corporation, incorporated in foreign country X. R's stock represents 15 percent of the value of T. Dividends on the preferred stock are paid only out of certain designated passive investments of T. Foreign country X does not tax the passive income of T. Under paragraph (a)(2) of this section, no taxes will be considered to be related to any dividend paid by T to R.

Example (8). Domestic corporation P owns all of the stock of controlled foreign corporation S, which owns all of the stock of controlled foreign corporation T. All such corporations use the calendar year as the taxable year. Assume that earnings and profits are equal to net income and that the income amounts are identical under United States and foreign law principles. In 1987, T earns (before foreign taxes) $187.50 of net passive income and $62.50 of net general limitation income and pays $50 of foreign taxes. S earns no income in 1987 and pays no foreign taxes. For 1987, P is required under section 951 to include in gross income $175 attributable to the earnings and profits of T for that year. One hundred and fifty dollars ($150) of the subpart F inclusion is attributable to passive income earned by T, and $25 of the subpart F inclusion is attributable to general limitation income earned by T. In 1988, T earns no income and pays no foreign taxes. T pays a $200 dividend to S, consisting of $175 from its earnings and profits attributable to amounts required to be included in P's gross income with respect to T and $25 from its other earnings and profits. Assume that no withholding tax is imposed with respect to the distribution from T to S. In 1988, S earns $100 of net general limitation income and receives a $200 dividend from T. S pays $30 in foreign taxes. For 1988, P is required under section 951 to include in gross income $22.50 attributable to the earnings and profits of S for such year. The entire subpart F inclusion is attributable to general limitation income earned by S. In 1988, S pays P a dividend of $247.50, consisting of $157.50 from its earnings and profits attributable to the amount required under section 951 to be included in P's gross income with respect to T, $22.50 from its earnings and profits attributable to the amount required under section 951 to be included in P's gross income with respect to S, and $67.50 from its other earnings and profits. Assume the de minimis rule of section 954(b)(3)(A) and the full inclusion rule of section 954(b)(3)(B) do not apply to the gross amounts of income earned by S and T. The foreign income taxes deemed paid by P for 1987 and 1988 under section 960(a)(1) and section 902(a) are determined as follows on the basis of the following facts and computations.

		T corporation (second-tier corporation):		
1.		Pre-tax earnings and profits:		
	(a)	Passive income (p.i.)	187.50	
		Plus:		
	(b)	General limitation income (g.l.i.)	62.50	
	(c)	Total	250.00	
		Less:		
	(d)	Foreign income taxes paid on or with respect to T's earnings and profits (20%)	50.00	
	(e)	Earnings and profits		200.00
2.		Allocation of taxes:		
	(a)	Foreign income taxes paid by T that are allocable to p.i. earned by T:		
		Line 1(d) taxes	50.00	
		Multiplied by: foreign law net p.i.	187.50	
		Divided by: foreign law total net income	250.00	
		Result		37.50
	(b)	Foreign income taxes paid by T that are allocable to g.l.i. earned by T:		
		Line 1(d) taxes	50.00	
		Multiplied by: foreign law net g.l.i.	62.50	
		Divided by: foreign law total net income	250.00	
		Result		12.50
3.		T's earnings and profits:		
	(a)	Earnings and profits attributable to T's p.i.:		
		Line (1)(a) e & p	187.50	
		Less: line 2(a) taxes	37.50	
		Result		150.00
	(b)	Earnings and profits attributable to T's g.l.i.:		
		Line (1)(b) e & p	62.50	
		Less: line 2(b) taxes	12.50	
		Result		50.00

Reg. § 1.904-6(c)

4.		Subpart F inclusion attributable to T:		
	(a)	Amount required to be included in P's gross income for 1987 under section 951 with respect to T that is attribuable to T's p.i.		150.00
	(b)	Amount required to be included in P's gross income for 1987 under section 951 with respect to T that is attributable to T's g.l.i. . .		25.00
5.		Foreign income taxes deemed paid by P under section 960(a)(1) with respect to T:		
	(a)	Taxes deemed paid that are attributable to T's subpart F inclusion that are attributable to T's p.i.:		
		Line 2(a) taxes	37.50	
		Multiplied by: line 4(a) sec. 951 incl.	150.00	
		Divided by: line 3(a) e & p	150.00	
		Result		37.50
	(b)	Taxes deemed paid that are attributable to T's subpart F inclusion that are attributable to T's g.l.i.		
		Line 2(b) taxes	12.50	
		Multiplied by: line 4(b) sec. 951 incl.	25.00	
		Divided by: line 3(b) e & p	50.00	
		Result		6.25
6.		Dividends paid to S:		
	(a)	Dividends attributable to T's previously taxed p.i.	150.00	
		Plus:		
	(b)	Dividends attributable to T's previously taxed g.l.i.	25.00	
		Plus:		
	(c)	Dividends from T's non-previously taxed earnings and profits attributable to p.i.	0.00	
		Plus:		
	(d)	Dividends from T's non-previously taxed earnings and profits attributable to g.l.i.	25.00	
	(e)	Total dividends paid to S		200.00
7.		Taxes deemed paid by S:		
	(a)	Taxes of T deemed paid by S for 1987 under section 902(b)(1) with regard to T's p.i.:		
		Line 2(a) taxes	37.50	
		Multiplied by: line 6(c) dividend	0.00	
		Divided by: line 3(a) e & p	150.00	
		Result		0.00
	(b)	Taxes of T deemed paid by S for 1987 under section 902(b)(1) with regard to T's g.l.i.:		
		Line 2(b) taxes	12.50	
		Multiplied by: line 6(d) dividend	25.00	
		Divided by: line 3(b) e & p	50.00	
		Result		6.25
		S corporation (first-tier corporation):		
8.		Pre-tax earnings and profits:		
	(a)	Dividends from T attributable to T's non-previously taxed p.i.	0.00	
		Plus:		
	(b)	Dividends from T attributable to T's non-previously taxed g.l.i.	25.00	
		Plus:		
	(c)	Dividends from T attributable to T's previously taxed p.i. .	150.00	
		Plus:		
	(d)	Dividends from T attributable to T's previously taxed g.l.i.	25.00	
		Plus:		
	(e)	Passive income other than dividend from T	0.00	
		Plus:		
	(f)	General limitation income other than dividend from T . . .	100.00	
	(g)	Total pre-tax earnings and profits	300.00	
	(h)	Foreign income taxes paid on or with respect to S's earnings and profits (10%)	30.00	
	(i)	Earnings and profits		270.00

Reg. § 1.904-6(c)

9. Allocation of taxes:
   (a) Foreign income taxes paid by S that are allocable to non-previously taxed p.i. earned by S:
Line 8(h) taxes	30.00
Multiplied by: foreign law line 8(a) & 8(e) p.i. amounts	0.00
Divided by: foreign law total net income	300.00
Result	0.00

   (b) Foreign income taxes paid by S that are allocable to S's previously taxed p.i. received from T:
Line 8(h) taxes	30.00
Multiplied by: foreign law line 8(c) p.i. amount	150.00
Divided by: foreign law total net income	300.00
Result	15.00

   (c) Foreign income taxes paid by S that are allocable to non-previously taxed g.l.i. earned by S:
Line 8(h) taxes	30.00
Multiplied by: foreign law line 8(b) & line 8(f) g.l.i. amounts	125.00
Divided by: foreign law total net income	300.00
Result	12.50

   (d) Foreign income taxes paid by S that are allocable to S's previously taxed g.l.i. received from T:
Line 8(h) taxes	30.00
Multiplied by: foreign law line 8(d) amount	25.00
Divided by: foreign law total net income	300.00
Result	2.50

10. (a) Non-previously taxed earnings and profits of S:
Lines 8(a), 8(b), 8(e), & 8(f) e & p	125.00
Less: lines 9(a) & 9(c) taxes	12.50
Result	112.50

    (b) Portion of result in 10(a) attributable to S's p.i. — 0.00
    (c) Portion of result in 10(a) attributable to S's g.l.i. — 112.50

11. (a) Previously taxed earnings and profits of S:
Lines 8(c) and 8(d) e & p	175.00
Less: lines 9(b) & 9(d) taxes	17.50
Result	157.50

    (b) Portion of result in 11(a) attributable to T's p.i.:
Line 8(c)	150.00
Less: line 9(b) taxes	15.00
Result	135.00

    (c) Portion of result in 11(a) attributable to T's g.l.i.:
Line 8(d)	25.00
Less: line 9(d) taxes	2.50
Result	22.50

12. Subpart F inclusion attributable to S:
    (a) Amount required to be included in P's gross income for 1988 under section 951 with respect to S that is attributable to S's p.i. — 0.00
    (b) Amount required to be included in P's gross income for 1988 under section 951 with respect to S that is attributable to S's g.l.i. — 22.50

13. Foreign income taxes deemed paid by P under section 960(a)(1) with respect to S:
    (a) Taxes deemed paid that are attributable to S's subpart F inclusion that are attributable to S's p.i.:
Line 9(a) taxes	0.00
Multiplied by: line 12(a) sec. 951 incl.	0.00
Divided by: line 10(b) e & p	0.00
Result	0.00

    (b) Taxes deemed paid that are attributable to S's subpart F inclusion that are attributable to S's g.l.i.:
Line 9(c) taxes	12.50
Multiplied by: line 12(b) sec. 951 incl	22.50
Divided by: line 10(c) e & p	112.50
Result	2.50

Reg. §1.904-6(c)

	(c)	Foreign income taxes deemed paid by S deemed paid by P that are allocable to S's p.i.:		
		Line 7(a) taxes deemed paid by S	0.00	
		Multiplied by: line 12(a) sec. 951 incl	0.00	
		Divided by: line 10(b) e & p	0.00	
		Result		0.00
	(d)	Foreign income taxes deemed paid by S deemed paid by P that are allowable to S's g.l.i.:		
		Line 7(b) taxes deemed paid by S	6.25	
		Multiplied by: line 12(b) sec. 951 incl	22.50	
		Divided by: line 10(c) e & p	112.50	
		Result		1.25
14.		Dividends paid to P:		
	(a)	Dividends from S attributable to S's previously taxed p.i. .... Plus:	0.00	
	(b)	Dividends from S attributable to S's previously taxed g.l.i. ...... Plus:	22.50	
	(c)	Dividends to which section 902(a) applies:		
		(i) Consisting of S's earnings and profits attributable to T's previously taxed p.i. .... 135.00 Plus:		
		(ii) Consisting of S's earnings and profits attributable to T's previously taxed g.l.i. .... 22.50 Plus:		
		(iii) Consisting of S's other p.i. earnings and profits ... 0.00 Plus:		
		(iv) Consisting of S's other g.l.i. earnings and profits .. 67.50		
		(v) Total section 902 dividend	225.00	
	(d)	Total dividends paid to P		247.50
15.		Foreign income taxes deemed paid by P under section 902 and section 960(a)(3) with respect to S:		
	(a)	Taxes paid by S deemed paid by P under section 902(a) with regard to S's p.i.:		
		Line 9(a) taxes	0.00	
		Multiplied by: line 14(c)(iii) div	0.00	
		Divided by: line 10(b) e & p	0.00	
		Result		0.00
	(b)	Taxes paid by S deemed paid by P under section 902(a) with regard to S's g.l.i.:		
		Line 9(c) taxes	12.50	
		Multiplied by: line 14(c)(iv) div.......................	67.50	
		Divided by: line 10(c) e & p	112.50	
		Result		7.50
	(c)	Taxes deemed paid by S deemed paid by P under section 902(a) with regard to S's p.i.:		
		Line 7(a) deemed paid taxes	0.00	
		Multiplied by: line 14(c)(iii) div	0.00	
		Divided by: line 10(b) e & p	0.00	
		Result		0.00
	(d)	Taxes deemed paid by S deemed paid by P under section 902(a) with regard to S's g.l.i.:		
		Line 7(b) deemed paid taxes	6.25	
		Multiplied by: line 14(c)(iv) div.......................	67.50	
		Divided by: line 10(c) e & p	112.50	
		Result		3.75
	(e)	Foreign income taxes paid by S under section 960(a)(3) deemed paid by P with regard to S's previously taxed p.i.:		
		Line 9(b) taxes	15.00	
		Multiplied by: line 14(c)(i) div	135.00	
		Divided by: line 11(b) e & p	135.00	
		Result		15.00

Reg. § 1.904-6(c)

(f) Foreign income taxes paid by S under section 960(a)(3) deemed paid by P with regard to S's previously taxed g.l.i.:

Line 9(d) taxes	2.50
Multiplied by: line 14(c)(ii) div	22.50
Divided by: line 11(c) e & p	22.50
Result	2.50

SUMMARY

Total taxes deemed paid by P under section 960(a)(1) with respect to—

Passive income of S and T included under section 951 in income of P:

Line 5(a)	37.50
Plus:	
Line 13(a)	0.00
Plus:	
Line 13(c)	0.00
Result	37.50

General limitation income of S and T included under section 951 in income of P:

Line 5(b)	6.25
Plus:	
Line 13(b)	2.50
Plus:	
Line 13(d)	1.25
Result	10.00
Total deemed paid taxes under section 960(a)(1)	47.50
Total taxes deemed paid by P under section 902 and section 960(a)(3) attributable to passive income of S and T (line 15(e))	15.00

Total taxes deemed paid by P under section 902 and section 960(a)(3) attributable to general limitation income of S and T:

Line 15(b)	7.50
Plus:	
Line 15(d)	3.75
Plus:	
Line 15(f)	2.50
Result	13.75

[Reg. § 1.904-6.]

☐ [*T.D. 8214, 7-15-88. Amended by T.D. 8412, 5-13-92 and T.D. 9141, 7-19-2004.*]

§ 1.904(b)-1. Special rules for capital gains and losses.—(a) *Capital gains and losses included in taxable income from sources outside the United States.*—(1) *Limitation on capital gain from sources outside the United States when the taxpayer has net capital losses from sources within the United States.*—(i) *In general.*—Except as otherwise provided in this section, for purposes of section 904 and this section, taxable income from sources outside the United States (in all of the taxpayer's separate categories in the aggregate) shall include capital gain net income from sources outside the United States (determined by considering all of the capital gain and loss items in all of the taxpayer's separate categories in the aggregate) only to the extent of capital gain net income from all sources. Thus, capital gain net income from sources outside the United States (determined by considering all of the capital gain and loss items in all of the taxpayer's separate categories in the aggregate) shall be reduced to the extent such amount exceeds capital gain net income from all sources.

(ii) *Allocation of reduction to separate categories or rate groups.*—(A) *In general.*—If capital gain net income from sources outside the United States exceeds capital gain net income from all sources, and the taxpayer has capital gain net income from sources outside the United States in only one separate category, such excess is allocated as a reduction to that separate category. If a taxpayer has capital gain net income from foreign sources in two or more separate categories, such excess must be apportioned on a pro rata basis as a reduction to each such separate category. For purposes of the preceding sentence, pro rata means based on the relative amounts of the capital gain net income from sources outside the United States in each separate category.

(B) *Taxpayer with capital gain rate differential.*—If a taxpayer with a capital gain rate differential for the year (within the meaning of paragraph (b) of this section) has capital gain net income from foreign sources in only one rate group within a separate category, any reduction to such separate category pursuant to paragraph (a)(1)(ii)(A) of this section must be allocated to such rate group. If a taxpayer with a capital gain rate differential for the year (within the meaning of paragraph (b) of this section) has capital gain net income from foreign sources in two or more rate groups within a separate category, any reduction to such separate category pursuant to paragraph (a)(1)(ii)(A) of this section must be apportioned on a pro rata basis among such rate groups. For purposes of the preceding sentence, pro rata means based on the relative amounts of the capital gain net income from sources outside the United States in each rate group within the applicable separate category.

(2) *Exclusivity of rules; no reduction by reason of net capital losses from sources outside the United States in a different separate category.*—Capital gains from sources outside the United States in any separate category shall be limited by reason of section 904(b)(2)(A) and the comparable limitation of section 904(b)(2)(B)(i) only to the extent provided in paragraph (a)(1) of this section (relating to limitation on capital gain from sources outside the United States when taxpayer has net capital losses from sources within the United States).

(3) *Capital losses from sources outside the United States in the same separate category.*—Except as otherwise provided in paragraph (d) of this section, taxable income from sources outside the United States in each separate category shall be reduced by any capital loss that is allocable or apportionable to income from sources outside the United States in such separate category to the extent such loss is allowable in determining taxable income for the taxable year.

(4) *Examples.*—The following examples illustrate the application of this paragraph (a) to taxpayers that do not have a capital gain rate differential for the taxable year. See paragraph (g) of this section for examples that illustrate the application of this paragraph (a) to taxpayers that have a capital gain rate differential for the year. The examples are as follows:

Example 1. Taxpayer A, a corporation, has a $3,000 capital loss from sources outside the United States in the general limitation category, a $6,000 capital gain from sources outside the United States in the passive category, and a $2000 capital loss from sources within the United States. A's capital gain net income from sources outside the United States in the aggregate, from all separate categories, is $3000 ($6,000 - $3,000). A's capital gain net income from all sources is $1000 ($6000 − $3000 − $2000). Thus, for purposes of section 904, A's taxable income from sources outside the United States in all of A's separate categories in the aggregate includes only $1000 of capital gain net income from sources outside the United States. See paragraph (a)(1)(i) of this section. Pursuant to paragraphs (a)(1)(i) and (a)(1)(ii)(A) of this section, A must reduce the $6000 of capital gain net income from sources outside the United States in the passive category by $2000 ($3000 of capital gain net income from sources outside the United States - $1000 of capital gain net income from all sources). After the adjustment, A has $4000 of capital gain from sources outside the United States in the passive category and $3000 of capital loss from sources outside the United States in the general limitation category.

Example 2. Taxpayer B, a corporation, has a $300 capital gain from sources outside the United States in the general limitation category and a $200 capital gain from sources outside the United States in the passive category. B's capital gain net income from sources outside the United States is $500 ($300 + $200). B also has a $150 capital loss from sources within the United States and a $50 capital gain from sources within the United States. Thus, B's capital gain net income from all sources is $400 ($300 + $200 − $150 + $50). Pursuant to paragraph (a)(1)(ii)(A) of this section, the $100 excess of capital gain net income from sources outside the United States over capital gain net income from all sources ($500 − $400) must be apportioned, as a reduction, three-fifths ($300/$500 of $100, or $60) to the general limitation category and two-fifths ($200/$500 of $100, or $40) to the passive category. Therefore, for purposes of section 904, the general limitation category includes $240 ($300 − $60) of capital gain net income from sources outside the United States and the passive category includes $160 ($200 − $40) of capital gain net income from sources outside the United States.

Example 3. Taxpayer C, a corporation, has a $10,000 capital loss from sources outside the United States in the general limitation category, a $4,000 capital gain from sources outside the United States in the passive category, and a $2,000 capital gain from sources within the United States. C's capital gain net income from sources outside the United States is zero, since losses exceed gains. C's capital gain net income from all sources is also zero. C's capital gain net income from sources outside the United States does not exceed its capital gain net income from all sources, and therefore paragraph (a)(1) of this section does not require any reduction of C's passive category capital gain. For purposes of section 904, C's passive category includes $4,000 of capital gain net income. C's general limitation category includes a capital loss of $6,000 because only $6,000 of capital loss is allowable as a deduction in the current year. The entire $4,000 of capital loss in excess of the $6,000 of capital loss that offsets capital gain in the taxable year is carried back or forward under section 1212(a), and none of such $4,000 is taken into account under section 904(a) or (b) for the current taxable year.

(b) *Capital gain rate differential.*—(1) *Application of adjustments only if capital gain rate differential exists.*—Section 904(b)(2)(B) and paragraphs (c) and (d) of this section apply only for taxable years in which the taxpayer has a capital gain rate differential.

(2) *Determination of whether capital gain rate differential exists.*—For purposes of section 904(b) and this section, a capital gain rate differential is considered to exist for the taxable year only if the taxpayer has taxable income (excluding net capital gain and qualified dividend income) for the taxable year, a net capital gain for the taxable year and—

(i) In the case of a taxpayer other than a corporation, tax is imposed on the net capital gain at a reduced rate under section 1(h) for the taxable year; or

(ii) In the case of a corporation, tax is imposed under section 1201(a) on the taxpayer at a rate less than any rate of tax imposed on the taxpayer by section 11, 511, or 831(a) or (b), whichever applies (determined without regard to the last sentence of section 11(b)(1)), for the taxable year.

(3) *Special rule for certain noncorporate taxpayers.*—A taxpayer that has a capital gain rate differential for the taxable year under paragraph (b)(2)(i) of this section and is not subject to alternative minimum tax under section 55 for the taxable year may elect not to apply the rate differential adjustments contained in section 904(b)(2)(B) and paragraphs (c) and (d) of this section if the highest rate of tax imposed on such taxpayer's taxable income (excluding net capital gain and any qualified dividend income) for the taxable year under section 1 does not exceed the highest rate of tax in effect under section 1(h) for the taxable year and the amount of the taxpayer's net capital gain from sources outside the United States, plus the amount of the taxpayer's qualified dividend income from sources outside the United States, is less than $20,000. A taxpayer that has a capital gain rate differential for the taxable year under paragraph (b)(2)(i) of this section and is subject to alternative minimum tax under section 55 for the taxable year may make such election if the rate of tax imposed on such taxpayer's alternative minimum taxable income (excluding net capital gain and any qualified dividend income) under section 55 does not exceed 26 percent, the highest rate of tax imposed on such taxpayer's taxable income (excluding net capital gain and any qualified dividend income) for the taxable year under section 1 does not exceed the highest rate of tax in effect under section 1(h) for the taxable year and the amount of the taxpayer's net capital gain from sources outside the United States, plus the amount of the taxpayer's qualified dividend income from sources outside the United States, is less than $20,000. A taxpayer who makes this election shall apply paragraph (a) of this section as if such taxpayer does not have a capital gain rate differential for the taxable year. An eligible taxpayer shall be presumed to have elected not to apply the rate differential adjustments, unless such taxpayer applies the rate differential adjustments contained in section 904(b)(2)(B) and paragraphs (c) and (d) of this section in determining its foreign tax credit limitation for the taxable year.

(c) *Rate differential adjustment of capital gains.*—(1) *Rate differential adjustment of capital gains in foreign source taxable income.*—(i) *In general.*—Subject to paragraph (c)(1)(ii) of this section, in determining taxable income from sources outside the United States for purposes of section 904 and this section, capital gain net income from sources outside the United States in each long-term rate group in each separate category (separate category long-term rate group), shall be reduced by the rate differential portion of such capital gain net income. For purposes of paragraph (c)(1) of this section, references to capital gain net income are references to capital gain net income remaining after any reduction to such income pursuant to paragraph (a)(1) of this section (i.e., paragraph (a)(1) of this section applies before paragraphs (c) and (d) of this section).

(ii) *Special rule for taxpayers with a net long-term capital loss from sources within the United States.*—If a taxpayer has a net long-term capital loss from sources within the United States (i.e., the taxpayer's long-term capital losses from sources within the United States exceed the taxpayer's long-term capital gains from sources within the United States) and also has any short-term capital gains from sources within or without the United States, then capital gain net income from sources outside the United States in each separate category long-term rate group shall be reduced by the rate differential portion of the applicable rate differential amount. The applicable rate differential amount is determined as follows:

(A) *Step 1: Determine the U.S. long-term capital loss adjustment amount.*—The U.S. long-term capital loss adjustment amount is the excess, if any, of the net long-term capital loss from sources within the United States over the amount, if any, by which the taxpayer reduced long-term capital gains from sources without the United States pursuant to paragraph (a)(1) of this section.

(B) *Step 2: Determine the applicable rate differential amount.*—If a taxpayer has capital gain net income from sources outside the United States in only one separate category long-term rate group, the applicable rate differential amount is the excess of such capital gain net income over the U.S. long-term capital loss adjustment amount. If a taxpayer has capital gain net income from sources outside the United States in more than one separate category long-term rate group, the U.S. long-term capital loss adjustment amount shall be apportioned on a pro rata basis to each separate category long-term rate group with capital gain net income. For purposes of the preceding sentence, pro rata means based on the relative amounts of capital gain net income from sources outside the United States in each separate category long-term rate group. The applicable rate differential amount for each separate category long-term rate group with capital gain net income is the excess of such capital gain net income over the portion of the U.S. long-term capital loss adjustment amount apportioned to the separate category long-term rate group pursuant to this Step 2.

(iii) *Examples.*—The following examples illustrate the provisions of paragraph (c)(1)(ii) of this section. The taxpayers in the examples are assumed to have taxable income (excluding net capital gain and qualified dividend income) subject to a rate of tax under section 1 greater than the highest rate of tax in effect under section 1(h) for the applicable taxable year. The examples are as follows:

Example 1. (i) M, an individual, has $300 of long-term capital gain from foreign sources in the passive category, $200 of which is subject to tax at a rate of 15 percent under section 1(h) and $100 of which is subject to tax at a rate of 28% under section 1(h). M has $150 of short-term capital gain from sources within the United States. M has a $100 long-term capital loss from sources within the United States.

(ii) M's capital gain net income from sources outside the United States ($300) does not exceed M's capital gain net income from all sources ($350). Therefore, paragraph (a)(1) of this section does not require any reduction of M's capital gain net income in the passive category.

(iii) Because M has a net long-term capital loss from sources within the United States ($100) and also has a short-term capital gain from U.S. sources ($150), M must apply the provisions of paragraph (c)(1)(ii) of this section to determine the amount of the $300 of capital gain net income in the passive category that is subject to a rate differential adjustment. Under *Step 1*, the U.S. long-term capital loss adjustment amount is $100 ($100 - $0). Under *Step 2*, M must apportion this amount to each rate group in the passive category pro rata based on the amount of capital gain net income in each rate group. Thus, $66.67 ($200/$300 of $100) is apportioned to the 15 percent rate group and $33.33 ($100/$300 of $100) is apportioned to the 28 percent rate group. The applicable rate differential amount for the 15 percent rate group is $133.33 ($200 - $66.67). Thus, $133.33 of the $200 of capital gain net income in the 15 percent rate group is subject to a rate differential adjustment pursuant to paragraph (c)(1) of this section. The remaining $66.67 is not subject to a rate differential adjustment. The applicable rate differential amount for the 28 percent rate group is $66.67 ($100 - $33.33). Thus, $66.67 of the $100 of capital gain net income in the 28 percent rate group is subject to a rate differential adjustment pursuant to paragraph (c)(1) of this section. The remaining $33.33 is not subject to a rate differential adjustment.

Example 2. (i) N, an individual, has $300 of long-term capital gain from foreign sources in the passive category, all of which is subject to tax at a rate of 15 percent under section 1(h). N has $50 of short-term capital gain from sources within the United States. N has a $100 long-term capital loss from sources within the United States.

(ii) N's capital gain net income from sources outside the United States ($300) exceeds N's capital gain net income from all sources ($250). Pursuant to paragraph (a)(1) of this section, N must reduce the $300 capital gain in the passive category by $50. N has $250 of capital gain remaining in the passive category.

(iii) Because N has a net long-term capital loss from sources within the United States ($100) and also has a short-term capital gain from U.S. sources ($50), N must apply the provisions of paragraph (c)(1)(ii) of this section to determine the amount of the $250 of capital gain in the passive category that is subject to a rate differential adjustment. Under *Step 1*, the U.S. long-term capital loss adjustment amount is $50 ($100 -$50). Under *Step 2*, the applicable rate differential amount is $200 ($250 - $50). Thus, $200 of the capital gain in the passive category is subject to a rate differential adjustment under paragraph (c)(1) of this section. The remaining $50 is not subject to a rate differential adjustment.

Example 3. (i) O, an individual, has a $100 short-term capital gain from foreign sources in the passive category. O has $300 of long-term capital gain from foreign sources in the passive category, all of which is subject to tax at a rate of 15 percent under section 1(h). O has a $100 long-term capital loss from sources within the United States.

(ii) O's capital gain net income from sources outside the United States ($400) exceeds O's capital gain net income from all sources ($300). Pursuant to paragraph (a)(1) of this section, O must reduce the $400 capital gain net income in the passive category by $100. Because C has capital gain net income in two or more rate groups in the passive category, O must apportion such amount, as a reduction, to each rate group on a pro rata basis pursuant to paragraph (a)(1)(ii)(B) of this section. Thus, $25 ($100/$400 of $100) is apportioned to the short-term capital gain and $75 ($300/$400 of $100) is apportioned to the long-term capital gain in the 15 percent rate group. After application of paragraph (a)(1) of this section, O has $75 of short-term capital gain in the passive category and $225 of long-term capital gain in the 15 percent rate group in the passive category.

(iii) Because O has a net long-term capital loss from sources within the United States ($100) and also has a short-term capital gain from foreign sources ($100), O must apply the provisions of paragraph (c)(1)(ii) of this section to determine the amount of the $225 of long-term capital gain in the 15 percent rate group that is subject to a rate differential adjustment. Under *Step 1*, the U.S. long-term capital loss adjustment amount is $25 ($100 – $75). Under *Step 2*, the applicable rate differential amount is $200 ($225 – $25). Thus, $200 of the long-term capital gain is subject to a rate differential adjustment under paragraph (c)(1) of this section. The remaining $25 of long-term capital gain is not subject to a rate differential adjustment.

(2) *Rate differential adjustment of capital gains in entire taxable income.*—For purposes of section 904 and this section, entire taxable income shall include gains from the sale or exchange of capital assets only to the extent of capital gain net income reduced by the sum of the rate differential portions of each rate group of net capital gain.

(d) *Rate differential adjustment of capital losses from sources outside the United States.*—(1) *In general.*—In determining taxable income from sources outside the United States for purposes of section 904 and this section, a taxpayer with a net capital loss in a separate category rate group shall reduce such net capital loss by the sum of the rate differential portions of the capital gain net income in each long-term rate group offset by such net capital loss. A net capital loss in a separate category rate group is the amount, if any, by which capital losses in a rate group from sources outside the United States included in a separate category exceed capital gains from sources outside the United States in the same rate group and the same separate category.

(2) *Determination of which capital gains are offset by net capital losses from sources outside the United States.*—For purposes of paragraph (d)(1) of this section, in order to determine the capital gain net income offset by net capital losses from sources outside the United States, the following rules shall apply in the following order:

(i) Net capital losses from sources outside the United States in each separate category rate group shall be netted against capital gain net income from sources outside the United States from the same rate group in other separate categories.

(ii) Capital losses from sources within the United States shall be netted against capital gains from sources within the United States in the same rate group.

(iii) Net capital losses from sources outside the United States in excess of the amounts netted against capital gains under paragraph (d)(2)(i) of this section shall be netted against the taxpayer's remaining capital gains from sources within and outside the United States in the following order, and without regard to any net capital losses, from any rate group, from sources within the United States—

(A) First against capital gain net income from sources within the United States in the same rate group;

(B) Next, against capital gain net income in other rate groups, in the order in which capital losses offset capital gains for purposes of determining the taxpayer's taxable income and without regard to whether such capital gain net income derives from sources within or outside the United States, as follows:

(1) A net capital loss in the short-term rate group is used first to offset any capital gain net income in the 28 percent rate group, then to offset capital gain net income in the 25 percent rate group, then to offset capital gain net income in the 15 percent rate group, and finally to offset capital gain net income in the 5 percent rate group.

(2) A net capital loss in the 28 percent rate group is used first to offset capital gain net income in the 25 percent rate group, then to offset capital gain net income in the 15 percent rate group, and finally to offset capital gain net income in the 5 percent rate group.

(3) A net capital loss in the 15 percent rate group is used first to offset capital gain net income in the 5 percent rate group, and then to offset capital gain net income in the 28 percent rate group, and finally to offset capital gain net income in the 25 percent rate group.

(iv) Net capital losses from sources outside the United States in any rate group, to the extent netted against capital gains in any other separate category under paragraph (d)(2)(i) of this section or against capital gains in the same or any other rate group under paragraph (d)(2)(iii) of this section, shall be treated as coming pro rata from each separate category that contains a net capital loss from sources outside the United States in that rate group. For example, assume that the taxpayer has $20 of net capital losses in the 15 percent rate group in the passive category and $40 of net capital losses in the 15 percent rate group in the general limitation category, both from sources outside the United States. Further assume that $50 of the total $60 net capital losses from sources outside the United States are netted against capital gain net income in the 28 percent rate group (from other separate categories or from sources within the United States). One-third of the $50 of such capital losses would be treated as coming from the passive category, and two-thirds of such $50 would be treated as coming from the general limitation category.

(v) In determining the capital gain net income offset by a net capital loss from sources outside the United States pursuant to this paragraph (d)(2), a taxpayer shall take into account any reduction to capital gain net income from sources outside the United States pursuant to paragraph (a) of this section and shall disregard any adjustments to such capital gain net income pursuant to paragraph (c)(1) of this section.

(vi) If at any time during a taxable year, tax is imposed under section 1(h) at a rate other than a rate of tax specified in this paragraph (d)(2), the principles of this paragraph (d)(2) shall apply to determine the capital gain net income offset by any net capital loss in a separate category rate group.

(vii) The determination of which capital gains are offset by capital losses from sources outside the United States under this paragraph (d)(2) is made solely in order to determine the appropriate rate-differential-based adjustments to such capital losses under this section and section 904(b), and does not change the source, allocation, or separate category of any such capital gain or loss for purposes of computing taxable income from sources within or outside the United States or for any other purpose.

(e) *Qualified dividend income.*—(1) *In general.*—A taxpayer that has taxable income (excluding net capital gain and qualified dividend income) for the taxable year and that qualifies for a reduced rate of tax under section 1(h) on its qualified dividend income (as defined in section 1(h)(11)) for the taxable year shall adjust the amount of such qualified dividend income in a manner consistent with the rules of paragraphs (c)(1)(i) (first sentence) and (c)(2) of this section irrespective of whether such taxpayer has a net capital gain for the taxable year. For purposes of making adjustments pursuant to this paragraph (e), the special rule in paragraph (c)(1)(ii) of this section for taxpayers with a net long-term capital loss from sources within the United States shall be disregarded.

(2) *Exception.*—A taxpayer that makes the election provided for in paragraph (b)(3) of this section shall not make adjustments pursuant to paragraph (e)(1) of this section. Additionally, a taxpayer other than a corporation that does not have a capital gain rate differential for the taxable year within the meaning of paragraph (b)(2) of this section may elect not to apply paragraph (e)(1) of this section if such taxpayer would have qualified for the election provided for in paragraph (b)(3) of this section had such taxpayer had a capital gain rate differential for the taxable year. Such a taxpayer shall be presumed to make the election provided for in the preceding sentence unless such taxpayer applies the rate differential adjustments provided for in paragraph (e)(1) of this section to the qualified dividend income in determining its foreign tax credit limitation for the taxable year.

(f) *Definitions.*—For purposes of section 904(b) and this section, the following definitions apply:

(1) *Alternative tax rate.*—The term *alternative tax rate* means, with respect to any rate group, the rate applicable to that rate group under section 1(h) (for taxpayers other than corporations) or section 1201(a) (for corporations). For example, the alternative tax rate for unrecaptured section 1250 gain is 25 percent.

(2) *Net capital gain.*—For purposes of this section, net capital gain shall not include any qualified dividend income (as defined in section 1(h)(11)). See paragraph (e) of this section for rules relating to qualified dividend income.

(3) *Rate differential portion.*—The term *rate differential portion* with respect to capital gain net income from sources outside the United States in a separate category long-term rate group (or the applicable portion of such amount), net capital gain in a rate group, or

capital gain net income in a long-term rate group, as the case may be, means the same proportion of such amount as—

(i) The excess of the highest applicable tax rate (as defined in section 904(b)(3)(E)(ii)) over the alternative tax rate; bears to

(ii) the highest applicable tax rate (as defined in section 904(b)(3)(E)(ii)).

(4) *Rate group.*—For purposes of this section, the term *rate group* means:

(i) *Short-term capital gains or losses.*—With respect to a short-term capital gain or loss, the rate group is the short-term rate group.

(ii) *Long-term capital gains.*—With respect to a long-term capital gain, the rate group is the particular rate of tax to which such gain is subject under section 1(h). Such a rate group is a long-term rate group. For example, the 28 percent rate group of capital gain net income from sources outside the United States consists of the capital gain net income from sources outside the United States that is subject to tax at a rate of 28 percent under section 1(h). Such 28 percent rate group is a long-term rate group. If a taxpayer has long-term capital gains that may be subject to tax at more than one rate under section 1(h) and the taxpayer's net capital gain attributable to such long-term capital gains and any qualified dividend income are taxed at one rate of tax under section 1(h), then all of such long-term capital gains shall be treated as long-term capital gains in that one rate group. If a taxpayer has long-term capital gains that may be subject to tax at more than one rate of tax under section 1(h) and the taxpayer's net capital gain attributable to such long-term capital gains and any qualified dividend income are taxed at more than one rate pursuant to section 1(h), the taxpayer shall determine the rate group for such long-term capital gains from sources within or outside the United States (and, to the extent from sources outside the United States, from each separate category) ratably based on the proportions of net capital gain and any qualified dividend income taxed at each applicable rate. For example, under the section 1(h) rates in effect for tax years beginning in 2004, a long-term capital gain (other than a long-term capital gain described in section 1(h)(4)(A) or (h)(6)) may be subject to tax at 5 percent or 15 percent.

(iii) *Long-term capital losses.*—With respect to a long-term capital loss, a loss described in section 1(h)(4)(B)(i) (collectibles loss) or (iii) (long-term capital loss carryover) is a loss in the 28 percent rate group. All other long-term capital losses shall be treated as losses in the highest rate group in effect under section 1(h) for the tax year with respect to long-term capital gains other than long-term capital gains described in section 1(h)(4)(A) or (h)(6). For example, under the section 1(h) rates in effect for tax years beginning in 2004, a long-term capital loss not described in section 1(h)(4)(B)(i) or (iii) shall be treated as a loss in the 15 percent rate group.

(5) *Terms used in sections 1(h), 904(b) or 1222.*—For purposes of this section, any term used in this section and also used in section 1(h), section 904(b) or section 1222 shall have the same meaning given such term by section 1(h), 904(b) or 1222, respectively, except as otherwise provided in this section.

(g) *Examples.*—The following examples illustrate the provisions of this section. In these examples, the rate differential adjustment is shown as a fraction, the numerator of which is the alternative tax rate percentage and the denominator of which is 35 percent (assumed to be the highest applicable tax rate for individuals under section 1). Finally, all dollar amounts in the examples are abbreviated from amounts in the thousands (for example, $50 represents $50,000). The examples are as follows:

Example 1. (i) AA, an individual, has items from sources outside the United States only in the passive category for the taxable year. AA has $1000 of long-term capital gains from sources outside the United States that are subject to tax at a rate of 15 percent under section 1(h). AA has $700 of long-term capital losses from sources outside the United States, which are not described in section 1(h)(4)(B)(i) or (iii). For the same taxable year, AA has $800 of long-term capital gains from sources within the United States that are taxed at a rate of 28 percent under section 1(h). AA also has $100 of long-term capital losses from sources within the United States, which are not described in section 1(h)(4)(B)(i) or (iii). AA also has $500 of ordinary income from sources within the United States. The highest tax rate in effect under section 1(h) for the taxable year with respect to long-term capital gains other than long-term capital gains described in section 1(h)(4)(A) or (h)(6) is 15 percent. Accordingly, AA's long-term capital losses are in the 15 percent rate group.

(ii) AA's items of ordinary income, capital gain and capital loss for the taxable year are summarized in the following table:

	U.S. source	foreign source: passive
15% rate group	($100)	$1,000 ($700)
28% rate group	$800	
Ordinary income	$500	

(iii) AA's capital gain net income from sources outside the United States ($300) does not exceed AA's capital gain net income from all sources ($1,000). Therefore, paragraph (a)(1) of this section does not require any reduction of AA's capital gain net income in the passive category.

(iv) In computing AA's taxable income from sources outside the United States in the numerator of the section 904(a) foreign tax credit limitation fraction for the passive category, AA's $300 of capital gain net income in the 15 rate group in the passive category must be adjusted as required under paragraph (c)(1) of this section. AA adjusts the $300 of capital gain net income using 15 percent as the alternative tax rate, as follows: $300(15%/35%).

(v) In computing AA's entire taxable income in the denominator of the section 904(a) foreign tax credit limitation fraction, AA combines the $300 of capital gain net income from sources outside the United States and the $100 net capital loss from sources within the United States in the same rate group (15 percent). AA must adjust the resulting $200 ($300 − $100) of net capital gain in the 15 percent rate group as required under paragraph (c)(2) of this section, using 15 percent as the alternative tax rate, as follows: $200(15%/35%). AA must also adjust the $800 of net capital gain in the 28 percent rate group, using 28 percent as the alternative tax rate, as follows: $800(28%/35%). AA must also include ordinary income from sources outside the United States in the numerator, and ordinary income from all sources in the denominator, of the foreign tax credit limitation fraction.

(vi) AA's passive category foreign tax credit limitation fraction is $128.58/$1225.72, computed as follows:

$$\frac{\$300(15\%/35\%)}{\$500 + \$200(15\%/35\%) + \$800(28\%/35\%)}$$

Example 2. (i) BB, an individual, has the following items of ordinary income, capital gain, and capital loss for the taxable year:

	U.S. source	foreign source: general	passive
15% rate group	$300	($500)	$100
25% rate group	$200		
28% rate group	$500	($300)	
Ordinary income	$1,000	$500	$500

(ii) BB's capital gain net income from sources outside the United States in the aggregate (zero, since losses exceed gains) does not exceed BB's capital gain net income from all sources ($300). Therefore, paragraph (a)(1) of this section does not require any reduction of BB's capital gain net income in the passive category.

(iii) In computing BB's taxable income from sources outside the United States in the numerators of the section 904(a) foreign tax credit limitation fractions for the passive and general limitation categories, BB must adjust capital gain net income from sources outside the United States in each separate category long-tem rate group and net capital losses from sources outside the United States in each separate category rate group as provided in paragraphs (c)(1) and (d) of this section.

(A) The $100 of capital gain net income in the 15 percent rate group in the passive category is adjusted under paragraph (c)(1) of this section as follows: $100(15%/35%).

(B) BB must adjust the net capital losses in the 15 percent and 28 percent rate groups in the general limitation category in accordance with the ordering rules contained in paragraph (d)(2) of this section. Under paragraph (d)(2)(i) of this section, BB's net capital loss in the 15 percent rate group is netted against capital gain net income from sources outside the United States in other separate categories in the same rate group. Thus, $100 of the $500 net capital loss in the 15 percent rate group in the general limitation category offsets $100 of capital gain net income in the 15 percent rate group in the passive category. Accordingly, $100 of the $500 net capital loss is adjusted under paragraph (d)(1) of this section as follows: $100(15%/35%).

(C) Next, under paragraph (d)(2)(iii)(A) of this section, BB's net capital losses from sources outside the United States in any separate category rate group are netted against capital gain net income in the same rate group from sources within the United States. Thus, $300 of the $500 net capital loss in the 15 percent rate group in the general limitation category offsets $300 of capital gain net income in the 15 percent rate group from sources within the United States. Accordingly, $300 of the $500 net capital loss is adjusted under paragraph (d)(1) of this section as follows: $300(15%/35%). Similarly, the $300 of net capital loss in the 28 percent rate group in the general limitation category offsets $300 of capital gain net income in the 28 percent rate group from sources within the United States. The $300 net capital loss is adjusted under paragraph (d)(1) of this section as follows: $300(28%/35%).

(D) Finally, under paragraph (d)(2)(iii)(B) of this section, the remaining net capital losses in a separate category rate group are netted against capital gain net income from other rate groups from sources within and outside the United States. Thus, the remaining $100 of the $500 net capital loss in the 15 percent rate group in the general limitation category offsets $100 of the remaining capital gain net income in the 28 percent rate group from sources within the United States. Accordingly, the remaining $100 of net capital loss is adjusted under paragraph (d)(1) of this section as follows: $100(28%/35%).

(iv) In computing BB's entire taxable income in the denominator of the section 904(a) foreign tax credit limitation fractions, BB must adjust net capital gain by netting all of BB's capital gains and losses, from sources within and outside the United States, and adjusting any remaining net capital gains, based on rate group, under paragraph (c)(2) of this section. BB must also include foreign source ordinary income in the numerators, and ordinary income from all sources in the denominator, of the foreign tax credit limitation fractions. The denominator of BB's foreign tax credit limitation fractions reflects $2,000 of ordinary income from all sources, $100 of net capital gain taxed at the 28% rate and adjusted as follows: $100(28%/35%), and $200 of net capital gain taxed at the 25% rate and adjusted as follows: $200(25%/35%).

(v) BB's foreign tax credit limitation fraction for the general limitation category is $8.56/$2222.86, computed as follows:

$$\frac{\$500 - \$100(15\%/35\%) - \$300(15\%/35\%) - \$300(28\%/35\%) - \$100(28\%/35\%)}{\$1,000 + \$500 + \$500 + \$100(28\%/35\%) + \$200(25\%/35\%)}$$

(vi) BB's foreign tax credit limitation fraction for the passive category is $542.86/$2222.86, computed as follows:

$$\frac{\$500 + \$100(15\%/35\%)}{\$1,000 + \$500 + \$500 + \$100(28\%/35\%) + \$200(25\%/35\%)}$$

Example 3. (i) CC, an individual, has the following items of ordinary income, capital gain, and capital loss for the taxable year:

	U.S. source	foreign source: general	foreign source: passive
15% rate group	$300	($720)	($80)
25% rate group	$200		
28% rate group	$500	($150)	$50
Ordinary income	$1,000	$1,000	$500

(ii) CC's capital gain net income from sources outside the United States (zero, since losses exceed gains) does not exceed CC's capital gain net income from all sources ($100). Therefore, paragraph (a)(1) of this section does not require any adjustment.

(iii) In computing CC's taxable income from sources outside the United States in the numerators of the section 904(a) foreign tax credit limitation fractions for the passive and general limitation categories, CC must adjust capital gain net income from sources outside the United States in each separate category long-tem rate group and net capital losses from sources outside the United States in each separate category rate group as provided in paragraphs (c)(1) and (d) of this section.

(A) CC must adjust the $50 of capital gain net income in the 28 percent rate group in the passive category pursuant to paragraph (c)(1) of this section as follows: $50(28%/35%).

(B) Under paragraph (d)(2)(i) of this section, $50 of CC's $150 net capital loss in the 28 percent rate group in the general limitation category offsets $50 of capital gain net income in the 28 percent rate group in the passive category. Thus, $50 of the $150 net capital loss is adjusted as follows: $50(28%/35%). Next, under paragraph (d)(2)(iii)(A) of this section, the remaining $100 of net capital loss in the 28 percent rate group in the general limitation category offsets $100 of capital gain net income in the 28 percent rate group from sources within the United States. Thus, the remaining $100 of net capital loss is adjusted as follows: $100(28%/35%).

(C) Under paragraphs (d)(2)(iii)(A) and (d)(2)(iv) of this section, the net capital losses in the 15 percent rate group in the passive and general limitation categories offset on a pro rata basis the $300 of capital gain net income in the 15 percent rate group from sources within the United States. The proportionate amount of the $720 net capital loss ($720/$800 of $300, or $270) is adjusted as follows: $270(15%/35%). The proportionate amount of the $80 net capital loss ($80/$800 of $300, or $30) is adjusted as follows $30(15%/35%).

(D) Of the remaining $500 of net capital loss in the 15 percent rate group in the general limitation and passive categories, $400 offsets the remaining $400 of capital gain net income in the 28 percent rate group from sources within the United States under paragraph (d)(2)(iii)(B)(3) of this section. The proportionate amount of the $720 net capital loss ($720/$800 of $400, or $360) is adjusted as follows: $360(28%/35%). The proportionate amount of the $80 net capital loss ($80/$800 of $400, or $40) is adjusted as follows: $40(28%/35%).

(E) Under paragraph (d)(2)(iii)(B)(3) of this section, the remaining $100 of net capital loss in the 15 percent rate group in the general limitation and passive limitation categories offsets $100 of capital gain net income in the 25 percent rate group from sources within the United States. The proportionate amount of the $720 net capital loss ($720/$800 of $100, or $90) is adjusted as follows: $90(25%/35%). The proportionate amount of the $80 net capital loss ($80/$800 of $100 of $10) is adjusted as follows: $10(25%/35%).

(iv) In computing CC's entire taxable income in the denominator of the section 904(a) foreign tax credit limitation fractions, CC must adjust capital gain net income by netting all of CC's capital gains and losses, from sources within and outside the United States, and adjusting any remaining net capital gains, based on rate group, under paragraph (c)(2) of this section. The denominator of CC's foreign tax credit limitation fractions reflects $2,500 of ordinary income from all sources and $100 of net capital gain taxed at the 25% rate and adjusted as follows: $100(25%/35%).

(v) CC's foreign tax credit limitation fraction for the general limitation category is $412/$2571.42, computed as follows:

$$\frac{\$1{,}000 - \$50\,(28\%/35\%) - \$100\,(28\%/35\%) - \$270\,(15\%/35\%) - \$360\,(28\%/35\%) - \$90\,(25\%/35\%)}{\$1{,}000 + \$1{,}000 + \$500 + \$100\,(25\%/35\%)}$$

(vi) CC's foreign tax credit limitation fraction for the passive category is $488.00/$2571.42, computed as follows:

$$\frac{\$500 + \$50\,(28\%/35\%) - \$30\,(15\%/35\%) - \$40\,(28\%/35\%) - \$10\,(25\%/35\%)}{\$1{,}000 + \$1{,}000 + \$500 + \$100\,(25\%/35\%)}$$

Example 4. (i) DD, an individual, has the following items of ordinary income, capital gain and capital loss for the taxable year:

	U.S. source	foreign source: general	passive
15% rate group	($80)	($100)	$300
Short-term		$500	$100
Ordinary income	$500		

(ii) DD's capital gain net income from outside the United States ($800) exceeds DD's capital gain net income from all sources ($720). Pursuant to paragraph (a)(1)(ii)(A) of this section, DD must apportion the $80 of excess of capital gain net income from sources outside the United States between the general limitation and passive categories based on the amount of capital gain net income in each separate category. Thus, one-half ($400/$800 of $100, or $40) is apportioned to the general limitation category and one-half ($400/$800 of $80, or $40) is apportioned to the passive category. The $40 apportioned to the general limitation category reduces DD's $500 short-term capital gain in the general limitation category to $460. Pursuant to paragraph (a)(1)(ii)(B) of this section, the $40 apportioned to the passive category must be apportioned further between the capital gain net income in the short-term rate group and the 15 percent rate group based on the relative amounts of capital gain net income in each rate group. Thus, one-fourth ($100/$400 of $40 or $10) is apportioned to the short-term rate group and three-fourths ($300/$400 of $40 or $30) is apportioned to the 15 percent rate group. DD's passive category includes $90 of short-term capital gain and $270 of capital gain net income in the 15% rate group.

(iii) Because DD has a net long-term capital loss from sources within the United States ($80) and also has short-term capital gains, DD must apply the provisions of paragraph (c)(1)(ii) of this section to determine the amount of DD's $270 of capital gain net income in the 15% rate group that is subject to a rate differential adjustment under paragraph (c)(1) of this section. Under *Step 1*, the U.S. long-term capital loss adjustment amount is $50 ($80 − $30). Under *Step 2*, the applicable rate differential amount is the excess of the remaining capital gain net income over the U.S. long-term adjustment amount. Thus, the applicable rate differential amount is $220 ($270 − $50). In computing DD's taxable income from sources outside the United States in the numerator of the section 904(a) foreign tax credit limitation fraction for the passive category, DD must adjust this amount as/follows: $220(15%/35). DD does not adjust the remaining $50 of capital gain net income in the 15% rate group.

(iv) The amount of capital gain net income in the 15% rate group in the passive category, taking into account the adjustment pursuant to paragraph (a)(1) of this section and disregarding the adjustment pursuant to paragraph (c)(1) of this section, is $270. Under paragraphs (d)(2)(i) and (d)(2)(v) of this section, DD's $100 net capital loss in the 15% rate group in the general limitation category offsets capital gain net income in the 15% rate group in the passive category. Accordingly, the $100 of net capital loss is adjusted as follows: $100(15%/35%).

(v) In computing DD's entire taxable income in the denominator of the section 904(a) foreign tax credit limitation fractions, DD must adjust capital gain net income by netting all of DD's capital gains and losses from sources within and outside the United States, and adjusting the remaining net capital gain in each rate group pursuant to paragraph (c)(2) of this section. The denominator of DD's foreign tax credit limitation fraction reflects $500 of ordinary income from all sources, $600 of short-term capital gain and $120 of net capital gain in the 15 percent rate group adjusted as follows: $120(15%/35%).

(vi) DD's foreign tax credit limitation fraction for the general limitation category is $417.14/$1151.43, computed as follows:

$$\frac{\$460 - \$100(15\%/35\%)}{\$500 + \$600 + \$120(15\%/35\%)}$$

(vii) DD's foreign tax credit limitation fraction for the passive category is $234.29/$1151.43, computed as follows:

$$\frac{\$90 + \$220(15\%/35\%) + \$50}{\$500 + \$600 + \$120(15\%/35\%)}$$

Example 5. (i) EE, an individual, has the following items of ordinary income, capital gain and capital loss for the taxable year:

	U.S. source	foreign source: passive
15% rate group	($150)	$300
28% rate group		$200
Short-term	$30	$100
Ordinary income		$500

(ii) EE's capital gain net income from sources outside the United States ($600) exceeds EE's capital gain net income from all sources ($480). Pursuant to paragraph (a)(1)(ii) of this section, the $120 of excess capital gain net income from sources outside the United States is allocated as a reduction to the passive category and must be apportioned pro rata to each rate group within the passive category with capital gain net income. Thus, $20 ($100/$600 of $120) is apportioned to the short-term rate group, $60 ($300/$600 of $120) is apportioned to the 15 percent rate group and $40($200/$600 of $120) is apportioned to the 28 percent rate group. After application of paragraph (a)(1) of this section, EE has $80 of capital gain net income in the short-term rate group, $240 of capital gain net income in the 15 percent rate group and $160 of capital gain net income in the 28 percent rate group.

(iii) Because EE has a net long-term capital loss from sources within the United States ($150) and also has short-term capital gains, EE must apply the provisions of paragraph (c)(1)(ii) of this section to determine the amount of EE's remaining $400 ($240 + $160) of capital gain net income in long-term rate groups in the passive category that is subject to a rate differential adjustment. Under *Step 1*, the U.S. long-term capital loss adjustment amount is $50 ($150 – $100). Under *Step 2*, EE must apportion this amount pro rata to each long-tem rate group within the passive category with capital gain net income. Thus, $30 ($240/$400 of $50) is apportioned to the 15 percent rate group and $20 ($160/$400 of $50) is apportioned to the 28 percent rate group. The applicable rate differential amount for the 15 percent rate group is $210 ($240 – $30). The applicable rate differential amount for the 28 percent rate group is $140 ($160 – $20).

(iv) Pursuant to paragraph (c)(1)(ii) of this section, EE must adjust $210 of the $240 capital gain in the 15 percent rate group as follows: $210 (15%/35%). EE does not adjust the remaining $30. Pursuant to paragraph (c)(1)(ii) of this section, EE must adjust $140 of the $160 capital gain in the 28 percent rate group as follows: $140 (28%/35%). EE does not adjust the remaining $20.

(v) In computing EE's entire taxable income in the denominator of the section 904(a) foreign tax credit limitation fractions, EE must adjust capital gain net income by netting all of EE's capital gains and losses from sources within and outside the United States, and adjusting the remaining net capital gain in each rate group pursuant to paragraph (c)(2) of this section. The denominator of EE's foreign tax credit limitation fraction reflects $500 of ordinary income from all sources, $130 of short-term capital gain, $150 of net capital gain in the 15 percent rate group adjusted as follows: $150(15%/35%), and $200 of net capital gain in the 28 percent rate group adjusted as follows: $200(28%/35%).

(vi) EE's foreign tax credit limitation fraction for the passive category is $332/$854.29, computed as follows:

$$\frac{\$80 + \$210(15\%/35\%) + \$30 + \$140(28\%/35\%) + \$20}{\$500 + \$130 + \$150(15\%/35\%) + \$200(28\%/35\%)}$$

(h) *Coordination with section 904(f).*—(1) *In general.*—Section 904(b) and this section shall apply before the provisions of section 904(f) as follows:

(i) The amount of a taxpayer's separate limitation income or loss in each separate category, the amount of overall foreign loss, and the amount of any additions to or recapture of separate limitation loss or overall foreign loss accounts pursuant to section 904(f) shall be determined after applying paragraphs (a), (c)(1), (d) and (e) of this section to adjust capital gains and losses and qualified dividend income from sources outside the United States in each separate category.

(ii) To the extent a capital loss from sources within the United States reduces a taxpayer's foreign source taxable income under paragraph (a)(1) of this section, such capital loss shall be disregarded in determining the amount of a taxpayer's taxable income from sources within the United States for purposes of computing the amount of any additions to the taxpayer's overall foreign loss accounts.

(iii) In determining the amount of a taxpayer's loss from sources in the United States under section 904(f)(5)(D) (section 904(f)(5)(D) amount), the taxpayer shall make appropriate adjustments to capital gains and losses from sources within the United States to reflect adjustments pursuant to section 904(b)(2) and this section. Therefore, for purposes of section 904, a taxpayer's section 904(f)(5)(D) amount shall be equal to the excess of the taxpayer's foreign source taxable income in all separate categories in the aggregate for the taxable year (taking into account any adjustments pursuant to paragraphs (a)(1), (c)(1), (d) and (e) of this section) over the taxpayer's entire taxable income for the taxable year (taking into account any adjustments pursuant to paragraphs (c)(2) and (e) of this section).

(2) *Examples.*—The following examples illustrate the application of paragraph (h) of this section:

Example 1. (i) W, an individual, has the following items of ordinary income, capital gain, and capital loss for the taxable year:

	U.S. source	foreign source: general	passive
15% rate group	$500	$100	($400)
Ordinary income	$900	$100	

(ii) In computing W's taxable income from sources outside the United States for purposes of section 904 and this section, W must adjust the capital gain net income and net capital loss in each separate category as provided in paragraphs (c)(1) and (d) of this section. Thus, W must adjust the $100 of capital gain net income in the general limitation category and the $400 of net capital loss in the passive category as follows: $100(15%/35%) and $400(15%/35%).

(iii) After the adjustment to W's net capital loss in the passive category, W has a $171.43 separate limitation loss in the passive category. After the adjustment to W's capital gain in the general limitation category, W has $142.86 of foreign source taxable income in the general limitation category. Thus, $142.86 of the separate limitation loss reduces foreign source taxable income in the general limitation category. See section 904(f)(5)(B). W adds $142.86 to the separate limitation loss account for the passive category. The remaining $28.57 of the separate limitation loss reduces income from sources within the United States. See section 904(f)(5)(A). Thus, W adds $28.57 to the overall foreign loss account for the passive category.

Example 2. (i) X, a corporation, has the following items of ordinary income, ordinary loss, capital gain and capital loss for the taxable year:

	U.S. source	foreign source: general
Capital gain	($500)	$700
Ordinary income	$1100	($1000)

(ii) X's capital gain net income from sources outside the United States ($700) exceeds X's capital gain net income from all sources ($200). Pursuant to paragraph (a)(1) of this section, X must reduce the $700 capital gain in the general limitation category by $500. After the adjustment, X has $200 of capital gain net income remaining in the general limitation category. Thus, X has an overall foreign loss attributable to the general limitation category of $800.

(iii) For purposes of computing the amount of the addition to X's overall foreign loss account for the general limitation category, the $500 capital loss from sources within the United States is disregarded and X's taxable income from sources within the United States is $1100. Accordingly, X must increase its overall foreign loss account for the general limitation category by $800.

Example 3. (i) Y, a corporation, has the following items of ordinary income, ordinary loss, capital gain and capital loss for the taxable year:

	U.S. source	foreign source: passive
Capital gain	($100)	$200
Ordinary income	($200)	$500

(ii) Y's capital gain net income from sources outside the United States ($200) exceeds Y's capital gain net income from all sources ($100). Pursuant to paragraph (a)(1) of this section, Y must reduce the $200 capital gain in the passive category by $100. Y has $100 of capital gain net income remaining in the passive category.

(iii) Y is not required to make adjustments pursuant to paragraph (c), (d) or (e) of this section. See paragraphs (b) and (e) of this section. Y's foreign source taxable income in the passive category after the adjustment pursuant to paragraph (a)(1) of this section is $600. Y's entire taxable income for the taxable year is $400.

(iv) Y's section 904(f)(5)(D) amount is the excess of Y's foreign source taxable income in all separate categories in the aggregate for the taxable year after taking into account the adjustment pursuant to paragraph (a)(1) of this section ($600) over Y's entire taxable income for the taxable year ($400). Therefore, Y's section 904(f)(5)(D) amount is $200 and Y's foreign source taxable income in the passive category is reduced to $400. See section 904(f)(5)(D).

Example 4. (i) Z, an individual, has the following items of ordinary income, ordinary loss and capital gain for the taxable year:

	U.S. source	foreign source: general	passive
15% rate group	$100		
Ordinary income	($200)	$300	$300

(ii) Z's foreign source taxable income in all of Z's separate categories in the aggregate for the taxable year is $600. (There are no adjustments to Z's foreign source taxable income pursuant to paragraph (a)(1), (c)(1), (d) or (e) of this section.)

(iii) In computing Z's entire taxable income in the denominator of the section 904(d) foreign tax credit limitation fractions, Z must adjust the $100 of net capital gain in the 15 percent rate group pursuant to paragraph (c)(2) of this section as follows: $100(15%/35%). Thus, Z's entire taxable income for the taxable year, taking into account the adjustment pursuant to paragraph (c)(2) of this section, is $442.86.

(iv) Z's section 904(f)(5)(D) amount is the excess of Z's foreign source taxable income in all separate categories in the aggregate for the taxable year ($600) over Z's entire taxable income for the taxable year after the adjustment pursuant to paragraph (c)(2) of this section ($442.86). Therefore, Z's section 904(f)(5)(D) amount is $157.32. This amount must be allocated pro rata to the passive and general limitation categories in accordance with section 904(f)(5)(D).

Example 5. (i) O, an individual, has the following items of ordinary income, ordinary loss and capital gain for the taxable year:

	U.S. source	foreign source: general	passive
15% rate group	$1100	($500)	
Ordinary income	($1000)	$1000	$500

(ii) In determining O's taxable income from sources outside the United States, O must reduce the $500 capital loss in the general limitation category to $214.29 ($500 × 15%/35%) pursuant to paragraph (d) of this section. Taking this adjustment into account, O's foreign source taxable income in all of O's separate categories in the aggregate is $1285.71 ($1000 − $214.29 + $500).

(iii) In computing O's entire taxable income in the denominator of the section 904(a) foreign tax credit limitation fraction, O must reduce the $600 of net capital gain for the year to $257.14 ($600 × 15%/35%) pursuant to paragraph (c)(2) of this section. Taking this adjustment into account, O's entire taxable income for the year is $757.14 ($500 + $257.14).

(iv) Therefore, O's section 904(f)(5)(D) amount is $528.57 ($1285.71 − $757.14). This amount must be allocated pro rata to O's $500 of income in the passive category and O's $785.71 of adjusted income in the general limitation category in accordance with section 904(f)(5)(D).

(i) *Effective date.*—This section shall apply to taxable years beginning after July 20, 2004. Taxpayers may choose to apply this section and §1.904(b)-2 to taxable years ending after July 20, 2004. [Reg. §1.904(b)-1.]

☐ [T.D. 7914, 9-28-83. Amended by T.D. 9141, 7-19-2004 (*corrected* 10-20-2004).]

§1.904(b)-2. Special rules for application of section 904(b) to alternative minimum tax foreign tax credit.—(a) *Application of section 904(b)(2)(B) adjustments.*—Section 904(b)(2)(B) shall apply for purposes of determining the alternative minimum tax foreign tax credit under section 59 (regardless of whether or not the taxpayer has made an election under section 59(a)(4)).

(b) *Use of alternative minimum tax rates.*—(1) *Taxpayers other than corporations.*—In the case of a taxpayer other than a corporation, for purposes of determining the alternative minimum tax foreign tax credit under section 59—

(i) Section 904(b)(3)(D)(i) shall be applied by using the language "section 55(b)(3)" instead of "subsection (h) of section 1";

(ii) Section 904(b)(3)(E)(ii)(I) shall be applied by using the language "section 55(b)(1)(A)(i)" instead of "subsection (a), (b), (c), (d), or (e) of section 1 (whichever applies)"; and

(iii) Section 904(b)(3)(E)(iii)(I) shall be applied by using the language "the alternative rate of tax determined under section 55(b)(3)" instead of "the alternative rate of tax determined under section 1(h)".

(2) *Corporate taxpayers.*—In the case of a corporation, for purposes of determining the alternative minimum tax foreign tax credit under section 59, section 904(b)(3)(E)(ii)(II) shall be applied by using the language "section 55(b)(1)(B)" instead of "section 11(b)".

(c) *Effective date.*—This section shall apply to taxable years beginning after July 20, 2004. See § 1.904(b)-1(i) for a rule permitting taxpayers to choose to apply § 1.904(b)-1 and this § 1.904(b)-2 to taxable years ending after July 20, 2004. [Reg. § 1.904(b)-2.]

☐ [*T.D.* 7914, 9-28-83. *Amended by T.D.* 9141, 7-19-2004 (*corrected* 10-20-2004).]

§ 1.904(f)-1. Overall foreign loss and the overall foreign loss account.—(a) *Overview of regulations.*—In general, section 904(f) and these regulations apply to any taxpayer that sustains an overall foreign loss (as defined in paragraph (c)(1) of this section) in a taxable year beginning after December 31, 1975. For taxable years ending after December 31, 1984, and beginning before January 1, 1987, there can be five types of overall foreign losses: a loss under each of the five separate limitations contained in former section 904(d)(1)(A) (passive interest limitation), (d)(1)(B) (DISC dividend limitation), (d)(1)(C) (foreign trade income limitation), (d)(1)(D) (foreign sales corporation (FSC) distributions limitation), and (d)(1)(E) (general limitation). For taxable years beginning after December 31, 1982, and ending before January 1, 1985, there can be three types of overall foreign losses under former section 904(d)(1)(A) (passive interest limitation), former section 904(d)(1)(B) (DISC dividend limitation) and former section 904(d)(1)(C) (general limitation). For taxpayers subject to section 907, the post-1982 general limitation overall foreign loss account may be further subdivided, as provided in § 1.904(f)-6. For taxable years beginning after December 31, 1975, and before January 1, 1983, taxpayers should have computed overall foreign losses separately under the passive interest limitation, the DISC dividend limitation, the general limitation, and the section 907(b) (FORI) limitation. However, for taxable years beginning after December 31, 1975, and before January 1, 1983, taxpayers may have computed only two types of overall foreign losses: a foreign oil related loss under the FORI limitation and an overall foreign loss computed on a combined basis for the passive interest limitation, the DISC dividend limitation, and the general limitation. A taxpayer that computed overall foreign losses for these years on a combined basis will not be required to amend its return to recompute such losses on a separate basis. If a taxpayer computed its overall foreign losses for these years separately under the passive interest limitation, the DISC dividend limitation, and the general limitation, on returns previously filed, a taxpayer may not amend those returns to compute such overall foreign losses on a combined basis. Section 1.904(f)-1 provides rules for determining a taxpayer's overall foreign losses, for establishing overall foreign loss accounts, and for making additions to and reductions of such accounts for purposes of section 904(f). Section 1.904(f)-2 provides rules for recapturing the balance in any overall foreign loss account under the general recapture rule of section 904(f)(1) and under the special recapture rule of section 904(f)(3) when the taxpayer disposes of property used predominantly outside the United States in a trade or business. Section 1.904(f)-3 provides rules for allocating overall foreign losses that are part of net operating losses or net capital losses to foreign source income in years to which such losses are carried. In addition, § 1.904(f)-3 provides transition rules for the treatment of net operating losses incurred in taxable years beginning after December 31, 1982, and carried back to taxable years beginning before January 1, 1983, and of net operating losses incurred in taxable years beginning before January 1, 1983, and carried forward to taxable years beginning after December 31, 1982. Section 1.904(f)-4 provides rules for recapture out of an accumulation distribution of a foreign trust. Section 1.904(f)-5 provides rules for recapture of overall foreign losses of domestic trusts. Section 1.904(f)-6 provides a transition rule for recapturing a taxpayer's pre-1983 overall foreign losses under the general limitation and the FORI limitation out of taxable income subject to the general limitation in taxable years beginning after December 31, 1982. Section § 1.1502-9 provides rules concerning the application of these regulations to corporations filing consolidated returns.

(b) *Overall foreign loss accounts.*—Any taxpayer that sustains an overall foreign loss under paragraph (c) of this section must establish an account for such loss. Separate types of overall foreign losses must be kept in separate accounts. For taxable years beginning prior to January 1, 1983, taxpayers that computed losses on a combined basis in accordance with § 1.904(f)-1(c)(1) will keep one overall foreign loss account for such overall foreign loss. The balance in each overall foreign loss account represents the amount of such overall foreign loss subject to recapture by the taxpayer in a given year. From year to year, amounts may be added to or subtracted from the balances in such accounts as provided in paragraphs (d) and (e) of this section. The taxpayer must report the balances (if any) in its overall foreign loss accounts annually on a Form 1116 or 1118. Such forms must be filed for each taxable year ending after September 24, 1987. The balance in each account does not have to be attributed to the year or years in which the loss was incurred.

(c) *Determination of a taxpayer's overall foreign loss.*—(1) *Overall foreign loss defined.*—For taxable years beginning after December 31, 1982, and before January 1, 1987, a taxpayer sustains an overall foreign loss in any taxable year in which its gross income from sources without the United States subject to a separate limitation (as defined in paragraph (c)(2) of this section) is exceeded by the sum of the deductions properly allocated and apportioned thereto. Such losses are to be determined separately in accordance with the principles of the separate limitations. Accordingly, income and deductions subject to a separate limitation are not to be netted with income and deductions subject to another separate limitation for purposes of determining the amount of an overall foreign loss. A taxpayer may, for example, have an overall foreign loss under the general limitation in the same taxable year in which it has taxable income under the DISC dividend limitation. The same principles of calculating overall foreign losses on a separate limitation basis apply for taxable years beginning before January 1, 1983, except that a taxpayer shall determine its overall foreign losses on a combined basis, except for income subject to the FORI limitation, if the taxpayer filed its pre-1983 returns on such basis. Thus, for taxable years beginning prior to January 1, 1983, a taxpayer can net income and losses among the passive interest limitation, the DISC dividend limitation, and the general limitation if the taxpayer calculated its overall foreign losses that way at the time. Taxpayers that computed overall foreign losses separately under each of the separate limitations on their returns filed for taxable years beginning prior to January 1, 1983, may not amend such returns to compute their overall foreign losses for pre-1983 years on a combined basis.

(2) *Separate limitation defined.*—For purposes of paragraph (c)(1) of this section and these regulations, the term separate limitation means any of the separate limitations under former section 904(d)(1)(A) (passive interest limitation), (B) (DISC dividend limitation), (C) (foreign trade income limitation), (D) (FSC distributions limitation), and (E) (general limitation) and the separate limitation under section 907(b) (FORI limitation) (for taxable years ending after December 31, 1975, and beginning before January 1, 1983).

(3) *Method of allocation and apportionment of deductions.*—In determining its overall foreign loss, a taxpayer shall allocate and apportion expenses, losses, and other deductions to the appropriate category of gross income in accordance with section 862(b) and § 1.861-8 of the regulations. However, the following deductions shall not be taken into account:

(i) The amount of any net operating loss deduction for such year under section 172(a); and

(ii) To the extent such losses are not compensated for by insurance or otherwise, the amount of any—

(A) Expropriation losses for such year (as defined in section 172(h)), or

(B) Losses for such year which arise from fire, storm, shipwreck, or other casualty, or from theft.

(d) *Additions to the overall foreign loss account.*—(1) *General rule.*—A taxpayer's overall foreign loss as determined under paragraph (c) of this section shall be added to the applicable overall foreign loss account at the end of its taxable year to the extent that the overall foreign loss has reduced United States source income during the taxable year or during a year to which the loss has been carried back. For rules with respect to carryovers see paragraph (d)(4) of this section and § 1.904(f)-3.

(2) *Overall foreign net capital loss.*—An overall foreign net capital loss shall be added to the applicable overall foreign loss account at the end of the taxable year to the extent that the foreign source capital loss has reduced United States source capital gain net income during the taxable year or during a year to which the loss has been carried back, subject to the adjustments in paragraph (d)(5) of this section. For rules with respect to carryovers, see paragraph (d)(4) of this section and § 1.904(f)-3. As provided under § 1211(b), to the extent that a foreign source net capital loss has reduced United States source income other than United States source capital gain net income, this additional amount would be added to the taxpayer's overall foreign loss account as if the United states source income had been offset by a foreign net operating loss that is not a capital loss.

(3) *Overall foreign losses of another taxpayer.*—If any portion of any overall foreign loss of another taxpayer is allocated to the taxpayer in accordance with § 1.904(f)-5 (relating to overall foreign losses of domestic trusts) or § 1.1502-9 (relating to consolidated overall foreign losses), the taxpayer shall add such amount to its applicable overall foreign loss account.

(4) *Additions to overall foreign loss account created by loss carryovers.*—Subject to the adjustments under § 1.904(f)-1(d)(5), the taxpayer shall add to each overall foreign loss account—

(i) All net operating loss carryovers to the current taxable year attributable to the same limitation to the extent that overall foreign losses included in the net operating loss carryovers reduced United States source income for the taxable year, and

(ii) All capital loss carryovers to the current taxable year attributable to the same limitation to the extent that foreign source capital loss carryovers reduced United States source capital gain net income for the taxable year.

(5) *Adjustments.*—The amount of overall foreign loss determined in paragraph (d)(1) of this section and the amount of overall foreign net capital loss determined in paragraph (d)(2) of this section which shall be added to a taxpayer's overall foreign loss account shall be adjusted as follows prior to being added to an account.

(i) *Adjustment due to reduction in foreign source income under section 904(b).*—A taxpayer's overall foreign loss acount shall not include any net capital loss from sources without the United States to the extent that the application of section 904(b) would result in a reduction of foreign source taxable income (but not below zero) for purposes of the numerator of the foreign tax credit limitation fraction.

(ii) *Adjustment to account for rate differential between ordinary income rate and capital gain rate.*—Subject to the provisions of paragraph (d)(5)(i) of this section, if an overall foreign loss for a taxable year includes an overall foreign net capital loss, such amount shall be reduced as follows, in accordance with the provisions of section 904(b), before being added to the overall foreign loss account:

(A) In the case of a corporate taxpayer, to the extent that the United States source capital gain net income reduced by the foreign source net capital loss consists of the United States source net capital gain, by an amount equal to the rate differential portion (as defined in section 904(b)(3)(D) of the Code and the regulations thereunder) of the United States source net capital gain; or

(B) In the case of a taxpayer other than a corporate taxpayer, for taxable years beginning prior to January 1, 1979, an amount equal to the taxpayer's United States source net capital gain that is offset by such foreign source net capital loss reduced by 50 percent of such gain, and for taxable years beginning after December 31, 1978, and before January 1, 1987, reduced by an amount equal to 60 percent of such gain.

(e) *Reductions of overall foreign loss accounts.*—The taxpayer shall subtract the following amounts from its overall foreign loss accounts at the end of its taxable year in the following order, if applicable:

(1) *Pre-recapture reduction for amounts allocated to other taxpayers.*—An overall foreign loss account is reduced by the amount of any overall foreign loss which is allocated to another taxpayer in accordance with § 1.904(f)-5 (relating to overall foreign losses of domestic trusts) or § 1.1502-9 (relating to consolidated overall foreign losses).

(2) *Reduction for amounts recaptured.*—An overall foreign loss account is reduced by the amount of any foreign source income that is subject to the same limitation as the loss that resulted in the account and that is recaptured in accordance with §§ 1.904(f)-2(c) (relating to recapture under section 904(f)(1)); 1.904(f)-2(d) (relating to recapture when the taxpayer disposes of certain properties under section 904(f)(3)); and 1.904(f)-4 (relating to recapture when the taxpayer receives an accumulation distribution from a foreign trust under section 904(f)(4)).

(f) *Illustrations.*—The rules of this section are illustrated by the following examples.

Example (1). X Corporation is a domestic corporation with foreign branch operations in country C. X's taxable income and losses for its taxable year 1983 are as follows:

U.S. source taxable income	$1,000
Foreign source taxable income (loss) subject to general limitation	($500)
Foreign source taxable income subject to the passive interest limitation	$200

X has a general limitation overall foreign loss of $500 for 1983 in accordance with paragraph (c)(1) of this section. Since the general limitation overall foreign loss is not considered to of set income under the separate limitation for passive interest income, it therefore offsets $500 of United States source taxable income. This amount is added to X's general limitation overall foreign loss account at the end of 1983 in accordance with paragraphs (c)(1) and (d)(1) of this section.

Example (2). Y Corporation is a domestic corporation with foreign branch operations in Country C. Y's taxable income and losses for its taxable year 1982 are as follows:

U.S. source taxable income	$1,000
Foreign source taxable income (loss) subject to general limitation	($500)
Foreign source taxable income subject to the passive interest limitation	$250

For its pre-1983 taxable years, Y filed its returns determining its overall foreign losses on a combined basis. In accordance with paragraphs (a) and (c)(1) of this section, Y may net the foreign source income and loss before offsetting the United States source income. Y therefore has a section 904(d)(1)(A-C) overall foreign loss account of $250 at the end of 1982.

Example (3). X Corporation is a domestic corporation with foreign branch operations in Country C. For its taxable year 1985, X has taxable income (loss) determined as follows:

U.S. source taxable income	$200
Foreign source taxable income (loss) subject to general limitation	($1,000)
Foreign source taxable income (loss) subject to the passive limitation	$1,800

X has a general limitation overall foreign loss of $1,000 in accordance with paragraph (c)(1) of this section. The overall foreign loss offsets $200 of United States source taxable income in 1985 and therefore, X has a $200 general limitation overall foreign loss account at the end of 1985. The remaining $800 general limitation loss is offset by the passive interest limitation income in 1985 so that X has no net operating loss carryover that is attributable to the general limitation loss and no additional amount attributable to that loss will be added to the overall foreign loss account in 1985 or in any other year.

Example (4). In 1986, V Corporation has $1,000 of general limitation foreign source taxable income and $500 of general limitation foreign source net capital loss which has reduced $500 of United States source capital gain net income ("short term gain") (none of which is net capital gain). Under section 904(b), the numerator of V's foreign tax credit limitation fraction for income subject to the general limitation is reduced by $500 (see § 1.904(b)-1(a)(3)). Under paragraph (d)(5)(i) of this section, none of that $500 goes into its general limitation overall foreign loss account.

Example (5). Z Corporation is a domestic corporation with foreign branch operations. For the taxable year 1984, Z's taxable income and (losses) are as follows:

U.S. source taxable ordinary income	$1,000
U.S. source net capital gain	$460
Foreign source taxable ordinary income subject to the general limitation	$200
Foreign source net capital loss subject to the general limitation	($800)

Z had no capital gain net income in any prior taxable year. Under paragraph (d)(2) and (5) of this section, the amount to be added to Z's general limitation overall foreign loss account is the excess of the amount which has reduced United States source capital gain net income for the taxable year ($460), adjusted for the rate differential because it has reduced United States source net capital gain ($460 × 28/46 = $280), over the amount which has reduced the numerator of Z's foreign tax credit limitation fraction under section 904(b)(2), which is $200. (The $200 amount is foreign source net capital loss that has reduced United States source net capital gain in the denominator of the fraction, but not exceeding the amount of foreign source income in the numerator before the section 904(b)(2) adjustment.) Thus, Z must add $80 (the excess of the $280 over $200) to its general limitation overall foreign loss account in 1984. [Reg. § 1.904(f)-1.]

☐ [*T.D.* 8153, 8-21-87.]

§ 1.904(f)-2. Recapture of overall foreign losses.—(a) *In general.*—A taxpayer shall be required to recapture an overall foreign loss as provided in this section. Recapture is accomplished by treating as United States source income a portion of the taxpayer's foreign source taxable income of the same limitation as the foreign source loss that resulted in an overall foreign loss account. As a result, if the taxpayer elects the benefits of section 901 or section 936, the taxpayer's foreign tax credit limitation with respect to such income is decreased. As provided in § 1.904(f)-1(e)(2), the balance in a taxpayer's overall foreign loss account is reduced by the amount of loss recaptured. Recapture continues until such time as the amount of foreign source taxable income recharacterized as United States source income equals the amount in the overall foreign loss account. As provided in § 1.904(f)-1(e)(2), the balance in an overall foreign loss account is reduced at the end of each taxable year by the amount of the loss recaptured during that taxable year. Regardless of whether recapture occurs in a year in which a taxpayer elects the benefits of section 901 or in a year in which a taxpayer deducts its foreign taxes under section 164, the overall foreign loss account is recaptured only to the extent of foreign source taxable income remaining after applying the appropriate section 904(b) adjustments, if any, as provided in paragraph (b) of this section.

(b) *Determination of taxable income from sources without the United States for purposes of recapture.*—(1) *In general.*—For purposes of determining the amount of an overall foreign loss subject to recapture, the taxpayer's taxable income from sources without the United States shall be computed with respect to each of the separate limitations described in § 1.904(f)-1(c)(2) in accordance with the rules set forth in § 1.904(f)-1(c)(1) and (3). This computation is made without taking into account foreign source taxable income (and deductions properly allocated and apportioned thereto) subject to other separate limitations. Before applying the recapture rules to foreign source taxable income, the following provisions shall be applied to such income in the following order:

(i) Former section 904(b)(3)(C) (prior to its removal by the Tax Reform Act of 1986) and the regulations thereunder shall be applied to treat certain foreign source gain as United States source gain; and

(ii) Section 904(b)(2) and the regulations thereunder shall be applied to make adjustments in the foreign tax credit limitation fraction for certain capital gains and losses.

(c) *Section 904(f)(1) recapture.*—(1) *In general.*—In a year in which a taxpayer elects the benefits of sections 901 or 936, the amount of any foreign source taxable income subject to recapture in a taxable year in which paragraph (a) of this section is applicable is the lesser of the balance in the applicable overall foreign loss account (after reduction of such account in accordance with §1.904(f)-1(e)) or fifty percent of the taxpayer's foreign source taxable income of the same limitation as the loss that resulted in the overall foreign loss account (as determined under paragraph (b) of this section). If, in any year, in accordance with sections 164(a) and section 275(a)(4)(A), a taxpayer deducts rather than credits its foreign taxes, recapture is applied to the extent of the lesser of (i) the balance in the applicable overall foreign loss account or (ii) foreign source taxable income of the same limitation type that resulted in the overall foreign loss minus foreign taxes imposed on such income.

(2) *Election to recapture more of the overall foreign loss than is required under paragraph (c)(1).*—In a year in which a taxpayer elects the benefits of sections 901 or 936, a taxpayer may make an annual revocable election to recapture a greater portion of the balance in an overall foreign loss account than is required to be recaptured under paragraph (c)(1) of this section. A taxpayer may make such an election or amend a prior election by attaching a statement to its annual Form 1116 or 1118. If an amendment is made to a prior year's election, an amended tax return should be filed. The statement attached to the Form 1116 or 1118 must indicate the percentage and dollar amount of the taxpayer's foreign source taxable income that is being recharacterized as United States source income and the percentage and dollar amount of the balance (both before and after recapture) in the overall foreign loss account that is being recaptured. Except for the special recapture rules for section 936 corporations and for recapture of pre-1983 overall foreign losses determined on a combined basis, the taxpayer that elects to credit its foreign taxes may not elect to recapture an amount in excess of the taxpayer's foreign source taxable income subject to the same limitation as the loss that resulted in the overall foreign loss account.

(3) *Special rule for recapture of losses incurred prior to section 936 election.*—If a corporation elects the application of section 936 and at the time of the election has a balance in any overall foreign loss account, such losses will be recaptured from the possessions source income of the electing section 936 corporation that qualifies for the section 936 credit, including qualified possession source investment income as defined in section 936(d)(2), even though the overall foreign loss to be recaptured may not be attributable to a loss in an income category of a type that would meet the definition of qualified possession source investment income. For purposes of recapturing an overall foreign loss incurred by a consolidated group including a corporation that subsequently elects to use section 936, the electing section 936 corporation's possession source income that qualifies for the section 936 credit, including qualified possession source investment income, shall be used to recapture the section 936 corporation's share of previously incurred overall foreign loss accounts. Rules for determining the section 936 corporation's share of the consolidated group's overall foreign loss accounts are provided in §1.1502-9(c).

(4) *Recapture of pre-1983 overall foreign losses determined on a combined basis.*—If a taxpayer computed its overall foreign losses on a combined basis in accordance with §1.904(f)-1(c)(1) for taxable years beginning before January 1, 1983, any losses recaptured in taxable years beginning after December 31, 1982, shall be recaptured from income subject to the general limitation, subject to the rules in §1.904(f)-6(a) and (b). Ordering rules for recapture of these losses are provided in §1.904(f)-6(c).

(5) *Illustrations.*—The rules of this paragraph (c) are illustrated by the following examples, all of which assume a United States corporate tax rate of 50 percent unless otherwise stated.

Example (1). X Corporation is a domestic corporation that does business in the United States and abroad. On December 31, 1983, the balance in X's general limitation overall foreign loss account is $600, all of which is attributable to a loss incurred in 1983. For 1984, X has United States source taxable income of $500 and foreign source taxable income subject to the general limitation of $500. For 1984, X pays $200 in foreign taxes and elects section 901. Under paragraph (c)(1) of this section, X is required to recapture $250 (the lesser of $600 or 50 percent of $500) of its overall foreign loss. As a consequence, X's foreign tax credit limitation under the general limitation is $250/$1,000 ×$500, or $125, instead of $500/$1,000 × $500, or $250. The balance in X's general limitation overall foreign loss account is reduced by $250 in accordance with §1.904(f)-1(e)(2).

Example (2). The facts are the same as in example (1) except that X makes an election to recapture its overall foreign loss to the extent of 80 percent of its foreign source taxable income subject to the general limitation (or $400) in accordance with paragraph (c)(2) of this section. As a result of recapture, X's 1984 foreign tax credit limitation for income subject to the general limitation is $100/$1,000 × $500, or $50, instead of $500/$1,000 × $500, or $250. X's general limitation overall foreign loss account is reduced by $400 in accordance with § 1.904(f)-1(e)(2).

Example (3). The facts are the same as in example (1) except that X does not elect the benefits of section 901 in 1984 and instead deducts its foreign taxes paid. In 1984, X recaptures $300 of its overall foreign loss, the difference between X's foreign source taxable income of $500 and $200 of foreign taxes paid. The balance in X's general limitation overall foreign loss account is reduced by $300 in accordance with § 1.904(f)-1(e)(2).

Example (4). The facts are the same as in example (1) except that in 1984, X also has $1,000 of foreign source DISC dividend income subject to the separate limitation for DISC dividends which carries a foreign tax of $50. Under paragraph (c)(1) of this section the amount of X's general limitation overall foreign loss subject to recapture is $250 (the lesser of the balance in the overall foreign loss account or 50 percent of the foreign source taxable income subject to the general limitation). There is no recapture with respect to the DISC dividend income. X's separate limitation for DISC dividend income is $1,000/$2,000 × $1,000, or $500. Its general limitation is $250/$2,000 × $1,000, or $125, instead of $500/$2,000 × $1,000, or $250. The balance in X's general limitation overall foreign loss account is reduced by $250 in accordance with § 1.904(f)-1(e)(2).

Example (5). On December 31, 1980, V, a domestic corporation that does business in the United States and abroad, has a balance in its section 904(d)(1)(A-C) overall foreign loss account of $600. V also has a balance in its FORI limitation overall foreign loss account of $900. For 1981, V has foreign source taxable income subject to the general limitation of $500 and $500 of United States source income. V also has foreign source taxable income subject to the FORI limitation of $800. V is required to recapture $250 of its section 904(d)(1)(A-C) overall foreign loss account (the lesser of $600 or 50% of $500) and its general limitation foreign tax credit limitation is $250/$1,800 × $900, or $125 instead of $500/$1,800 × $900, or $250. V is also required to recapture $400 of its FORI limitation overall foreign loss account (the lesser of $900 or 50% of $800). V's foreign tax credit limitation for FORI is $400/$1,800 × $900, or $200, instead of $800/$1,800 × $900, or $400. The balance in V's FORI limitation overall foreign loss account is reduced to $500 and the balance in V's section 904(d)(1)(A-C) account is reduced to $350, in accordance with § 1.904(f)-1(e)(2).

Example (6). This example assumes a United States corporate tax rate of 46 percent (under section 11(b)) and an alternative rate of tax under section 1201(a) of 28 percent. W is a domestic corporation that does business in the United States and abroad. On December 31, 1984, W has $350 in its general limitation overall foreign loss account. For 1985, W has $500 of United States source taxable income, and has foreign source income subject to the general limitation as follows:

Foreign source taxable income other than net capital gain	$720
Foreign source net capital gain	$460

Under paragraph (b)(2) of this section, foreign source taxable income for purposes of recapture includes foreign source capital gain net income, reduced, under section 904(b)(2), by the rate differential portion of foreign source net capital gain, which adjusts for the reduced tax rate for net capital gain under section 1201(a):

Foreign source capital gain net income	$460
Rate differential portion of foreign source net capital gain (18/46 of $460)	– 180
Foreign source capital gain included in foreign source taxable income	$280

The total foreign source taxable income of W for purposes of recapture in 1985 is $1,000 ($720 + $280). Under paragraph (c)(1) of this section, W is required to recapture $350 (the lesser of $350 or 50 percent of $1,000), and W's general limitation overall foreign loss account is reduced to zero. W's foreign tax credit limitation for income subject to the general limitation is $650/$1,500 × $690 ((.46) (500 + 720) + (.28)(460)), or $299, instead of $1,000/$1,500 × $690, or $460.

(d) *Recapture of overall foreign losses from dispositions under section 904(f)(3)*.—(1) *In general*.—If a taxpayer disposes of property used or held for use predominantly without the United States in a trade or business during a taxable year and that property generates foreign source taxable income subject to a separate limitation to which paragraph (a) of this section is applicable, (i) gain will be recognized on the disposition of such property, (ii) such gain will be treated as foreign source income subject to the same limitation as the income the property generated, and (iii) the applicable overall foreign loss account shall be recaptured as provided in paragraphs (d)(2), (d)(3), and (d)(4) of this section. See paragraph (d)(5) of this section for definitions.

(2) *Treatment of net capital gain.*—If the gain from a disposition of property to which this paragraph (d) applies is treated as net capital gain, all references to such gain in paragraphs (d)(3) and (d)(4) of this section shall mean such gain as adjusted under paragraph (b) of this section. The amount by which the overall foreign loss account shall be reduced shall be determined from such adjusted gain.

(3) *Dispositions where gain is recognized irrespective of section 904(f)(3).*—If a taxpayer recognizes foreign source gain subject to a separate limitation on the disposition of property described in paragraph (d)(1) of this section, and there is a balance in a taxpayer's overall foreign loss account that is attributable to a loss under such limitation after applying paragraph (c) of this section, an additional portion of such balance shall be recaptured in accordance with paragraphs (a) and (b) of this section. The amount recaptured shall be the lesser of such balance or 100 percent of the foreign source gain recognized on the disposition that was not previously recharacterized.

(4) *Dispositions in which gain would not otherwise be recognized.*—(i) *Recognition of gain to the extent of the overall foreign loss account.*—If a taxpayer makes a disposition of property described in paragraph (d)(1) of this section in which any amount of gain otherwise would not be recognized in the year of the disposition, and such property was used or held for use to generate foreign source taxable income subject to a separate limitation under which the taxpayer had a balance in its overall foreign loss account (including a balance that arose in the year of the disposition), the taxpayer shall recognize foreign source taxable income in an amount equal to the lesser of:

(A) The sum of the balance in the applicable overall foreign loss account (but only after such balance has been increased by amounts added to the account for the year of the disposition or has been reduced by amounts recaptured for the year of the disposition under paragraph (c) and paragraph (d)(3) of this section) plus the amount of any overall foreign loss that would be part of a net operating loss for the year of the disposition if gain from the disposition were not recognized under section 904(f)(3), plus the amount of any overall foreign loss that is part of a net operating loss carryover from a prior year, or

(B) The excess of the fair market value of such property over the taxpayer's adjusted basis in such property.

The excess of the fair market value of such property over its adjusted basis shall be determined on an asset by asset basis. Losses from the disposition of an asset shall not be recognized. Any foreign source taxable income deemed received and recognized under this paragraph (d)(4)(i) will have the same character as if the property had been sold or exchanged in a taxable transaction and will constitute gain for all purposes.

(ii) *Basis adjustment.*—The basis of the property received in an exchange to which this paragraph (d)(4) applies shall be increased by the amount of gain deemed recognized, in accordance with applicable sections of subchapters C (relating to corporate distributions and adjustments), K (relating to partners and partnerships), O (relating to gain or loss on the disposition of property), and P (relating to capital gains and losses). If the property to which this paragraph (d)(4) applies was transferred by gift, the basis of such property in the hands of the donor immediately preceding such gift shall be increased by the amount of the gain deemed recognized.

(iii) *Recapture of overall foreign loss to the extent of amount recognized.*—The provisions of paragraphs (a) and (b) of this section shall be applied to the extent of 100 percent of the foreign source taxable income which is recognized under paragraph (d)(4)(i) of this section. However, amounts of foreign source gain that would not be recognized except by application of section 904(f)(3) and paragraph (d)(4)(i) of this section, and which are treated as United States source gain by application of section 904(b)(3)(C) (prior to its removal by the Tax Reform Act of 1986) and paragraph (b)(1) of this section, shall reduce the overall foreign loss account (subject to the adjustments described in paragraph (d)(2) of this section) if such gain is net capital gain, notwithstanding the fact that such amounts would otherwise not be recaptured under the ordering rules in paragraph (b) of this section.

(iv) *Priorities among dispositions in which gain is deemed to be recognized.*—If, in a single taxable year, a taxpayer makes more than one disposition to which this paragraph (d)(4) is applicable, the rules of this paragraph (d)(4) shall be applied to each disposition in succession starting with the disposition which occurred earliest, until the balance in the applicable overall foreign loss account is reduced to zero. If the taxpayer simultaneously makes more than one disposition to which this paragraph (d)(4) is applicable, the rules of paragraph (d)(4) shall be applied so that the balance in the applicable overall foreign loss account to be recaptured will be allocated pro rata among the assets in proportion to the excess of the fair market value of each asset over the adjusted basis of each asset.

(5) *Definitions.*—(i) *Disposition.*—A disposition to which this paragraph (d) applies includes a sale; exchange; distribution; gift; transfer upon the foreclosure of a security interest (but not a mere transfer of title to a creditor upon creation of a security interest or to a debtor upon termination of a security interest); involuntary conversion; contribution to a partnership, trust, or corporation; transfer at death; or any other transfer of property whether or not gain or loss is recognized under other provisions of the Code. However, a disposition to which this paragraph (d) applies does not include:

(A) A distribution or transfer of property to a domestic corporation described in section 381(a) (provided that paragraph (d)(6) of this section applies);

(B) A disposition of property which is not a material factor in the realization of income by the taxpayer (as defined in paragraph (d)(5)(iv) of this section);

(C) A transaction in which gross income is not realized; or

(D) The entering into of a unitization or pooling agreement (as defined in §1.614-8(b)(6) of the regulations) containing a valid election under section 761(a)(2), and in which the source of the entire gain from any disposition of the interest created by the agreement would be determined to be foreign source under section 862(a)(5) if the disposition occurred presently.

(ii) *Property used in a trade or business.*—Property is used in a trade or business if it is held for the principal purpose of promoting the present or future conduct of the trade or business. This generally includes property acquired and held in the ordinary course of a trade or business or otherwise held in a direct relationship to a trade or business. In determining whether an asset is held in a direct relationship to a trade or business, principal consideration shall be given to whether the asset is used in the trade or business. Property will be treated as held in a direct relationship to a trade or business if the property was acquired with funds generated by that trade or business or if income generated from the asset is available for use in that trade or business. Property used in a trade or business may be tangible or intangible, real or personal property. It includes property, such as equipment, which is subject to an allowance for depreciation under section 167 or cost recovery under section 168. Property may be considered used in a trade or business even if it is a capital asset in the hands of the taxpayer. However, stock of another corporation shall not be considered property used in a trade or business if a substantial investment motive exists for acquiring and holding the stock. On the other hand, stock acquired or held to assure a source of supply for a trade or business shall be considered property used in that trade or business. Inventory is generally not considered property used in a trade or business. However, when disposed of in a manner not in the ordinary course of a trade or business, inventory will be considered property used in the trade or business. A partnership interest will be treated as property used in a trade or business if the underlying assets of the partnership would be property used in a trade or business. For purposes of section 904(f)(3) and §§1.904(f)-2(d)(1) and (5), a disposition of a partnership interest to which this section applies will be treated as a disposition of a proportionate share of each of the assets of the partnership. For purposes of allocating the purchase price of the interest and the seller's basis in the interest to those assets, the principles of §1.751-1(a) will apply.

(iii) *Property used predominantly outside the United States.*—Property will be considered used predominantly outside the United States if for a 3-year period ending on the date of the disposition (or, if shorter, the period during which the property has been used in the trade or business) such property was located outside the United States more than 50 percent of the time. An aircraft, railroad rolling stock, vessel, motor vehicle, container, or other property used for transportation purposes is deemed to be used predominantly outside the United States if, during the 3-year (or shorter) period, either such propery is located outside the United States more than 50 percent of the time or more than 50 percent of the miles traversed in the use of such property are traversed outside the United States.

(iv) *Property which is a material factor in the realization of income.*—For purposes of this section, property used in a trade or business will be considered a material factor in the realization of income unless the taxpayer establishes that it is not (or, if the taxpayer did not realize income from the trade or business in the taxable year, would not be expected to be) necessary to the realization of income by the taxpayer.

(6) *Carryover of overall foreign loss accounts in a corporate acquisition to which section 381(a) applies.*—In the case of a distribution or transfer described in section 381(a), an overall foreign loss account of the distributing or transferor corporation shall be treated as an overall foreign loss account of the acquiring or trans-

feree corporation as of the close of the date of the distribution or transfer. If the transferee corporation had an overall foreign loss account under the same separate limitation prior to the distribution or transfer, the balance in the transferor's account must be added to the transferee's account. If not, the transferee must adopt the transferor's overall foreign loss account. An overall foreign loss of the transferor will be treated as incurred by the transferee in the year prior to the year of the transfer.

(7) *Illustrations.*—The rules of this paragraph (d) are illustrated by the following examples which assume that the United States corporate tax rate is 50 percent (unless otherwise stated). For purposes of these examples, none of the foreign source gains are treated as net capital gains (unless so stated).

Example (1). X Corporation has a balance in its general limitation overall foreign loss account of $600 at the close of its taxable year ending December 31, 1984. In 1985, X sells assets used predominantly outside the United States in a trade or business and recognizes $1,000 of gain on the sale under section 1001. This gain is subject to the general limitation. This sale is a disposition within the meaning of paragraph (d)(5)(i) of this section, and to which this paragraph (d) applies. X has no other foreign source taxable income in 1985 and has $1,000 of United States source taxable income. Under paragraph (c), X is required to recapture $500 (the lesser of the balance in X's general limitation overall foreign loss account ($600) or 50 percent of $1,000) of its overall foreign loss account. The balance in X's general limitation overall foreign loss account is reduced to $100 in accordance with § 1.904(f)-1(e)(2). In addition, under paragraph (d)(3) of this section, X is required to recapture $100 (the lesser of the remaining balance in its general limitation overall foreign loss account ($100) or 100 percent of its foreign source taxable income recognized on such disposition that has not been previously recharacterized ($500)). The total amount recaptured is $600. X's foreign tax credit limitation for income subject to the general limitation in 1985 is $200 ($400/$2,000 × $1,000) instead of $500 ($1,000/$2,000 × $1,000). The balance in X's general limitation overall foreign loss account is reduced to zero in accordance with § 1.904(f)-1(e)(2).

Example (2). On December 31, 1984, Y Corporation has a balance in its general limitation overall foreign loss account of $1,500. In 1985, Y has $500 of United States source taxable income and $200 of foreign source taxable income subject to the general limitation. Y's foreign source taxable income is from the sale of property used predominantly outside of the United States in a trade or business. This sale is a disposition to which this paragraph (d) is applicable. In 1985, Y also transferred property used predominantly outside of the United States in a trade or business to another corporation. Under section 351, no gain was recognized on this transfer. Such property had been used to generate foreign source taxable income subject to the general limitation. The excess of the fair market value of the property transferred over Y's adjusted basis in such property was $2,000. In accordance with paragraph (c) of this section, Y is required to recapture $100 (the lesser of $1,500, the amount in Y's general limitation overall foreign loss account, or 50 percent of $200, the amount of general limitation foreign source taxable income for the current year) of its general limitation overall foreign loss. Y is then required to recapture an additional $100 of its general limitation overall foreign loss account under paragraph (d)(3) of this section out of the remaining gain recognized on the sale of assets, because 100 percent of such gain is subject to recapture. The balance in Y's general limitation overall foreign loss account is reduced to $1,300 in accordance with § 1.904(f)-1(e)(2). Y corporation is then required to recognize $1,300 of foreign source taxable income on its section 351 transfer under paragraph (d)(4) of this section. The remaining $700 of potential gain associated with the section 351 transfer is not recognized. Under paragraph (d)(4), 100 percent of the $1,300 is recharacterized as United States source taxable income, and Y's general limitation overall foreign loss account is reduced to zero. Y's entire taxable income for 1985 is:

U.S. source taxable income	$500
Foreign source taxable income subject to the general limitation that is recharacterized as U.S. source income by paragraphs (c) and (d)(3) of this section	$200
Gain recognized under section 904(f)(3) and paragraph (d)(4) of this section, and recharacterized as U.S. source income	$1,300
Total	$2,000

Y's foreign tax credit limitation for 1985 for income subject to the general limitation is $0 ($0/$2,000 × $1,000) instead of $100 ($200/$700 × $350).

Example (3). W Corporation is a calendar year domestic corporation with foreign branch operations in country C. As of December 31, 1984, W has no overall foreign loss accounts and has no net operating loss carryovers. W's entire taxable income in 1985 is:

U.S. source taxable income	$800
Foreign source taxable income (loss) subject to the general limitation	($1,000)

W cannot carry back its 1985 NOL to any earlier year. As of December 31, 1985, W therefore has $800 in its general limitation overall foreign loss account. In 1986, W earns $400 United States source taxable income and has an additional $1,000 loss from the operations of the foreign branch. Income in the loss category would be subject to the general limitation. Also in 1986, W disposes of property used predominantly outside the United States in a trade or business. Such property generated income subject to the general limitation. The excess of the property's fair market value over its adjusted basis is $3,000. The disposition is of a type described in § 1.904(f)-2(d)(4)(i). W has no other income in 1986. Under § 1.904(f)-2(d)(4)(i), W is required to recognize foreign source taxable income on the disposition in an amount equal to the lesser of $2,000 ($800 (the balance in the general limitation overall foreign loss account as of 1985) + $400 (the increase in the general limitation overall foreign loss account attributable to the disposition year) + $600 (the general limitation overall foreign loss that is part of the NOL from 1986) + $200 (the general limitation overall foreign loss that is part of the NOL from 1985)) or $3,000. The $2,000 foreign source income required to be recognized under section 904(f)(3) is reduced to $1,200 by the remaining $600 loss in 1986 and the $200 net operating loss carried forward from 1985. This $1,200 of income is subject to the general limitation. In computing the foreign tax credit limitation for general limitation income, the $1,200 of foreign source income is treated as United States source income and, therefore, W's foreign tax credit limitation for income subject to the general limitation is zero. W's overall foreign loss account is reduced to zero.

Example (4). Z Corporation has a balance in its FORI overall foreign loss account of $1,500 at the end of its taxable year 1980. In 1981, Z has $1,600 of foreign oil related income subject to the separate limitation for FORI income and no United States source income. In addition, in 1981, Z makes two dispositions of property used predominantly outside the United States in a trade or business on which no gain was recognized. Such property generated foreign oil related income. The excess of the fair market value of the property transferred in the first disposition over Z's adjusted basis in such property is $575. The excess of the fair market value of the property transferred in the second disposition over Z's adjusted basis in such property is $1,000. Under paragraph (c) of this section, Z is required to recapture $800 (the lesser of 50 percent of its foreign oil related income of $1,600 or the balance ($1,500) in its FORI overall foreign loss account) of its foreign oil related loss. In accordance with paragraphs (d)(4)(i) and (iv) of this section, Z is required to recognize foreign oil related income in the amount of $575 on the first disposition and, since the foreign oil related loss account is now reduced by $1,375 (the $800 and $575 amounts previously recaptured), Z is required to recognize foreign oil related income in the amount of $125 on the second disposition. In accordance with paragraph (d)(4)(iii) of this section, the entire amount recognized is treated as United States source income and the balance in the FORI overall foreign loss account is reduced to zero under § 1.904(f)-1(e)(2). Z's foreign tax credit limitation for FORI is $400 ($800/$2,300 × $1,150) instead of $800 ($1,600/$1,600 × $800).

Example (5). The facts are the same as in example (4), except that the gain from the two dispositions of property is treated as net capital gain and the United States corporate tax rate is assumed to be 46 percent. As in example (4), Z is required to recapture $800 of its foreign oil related loss from its 1981 ordinary foreign oil related income. In accordance with paragraph (d)(4)(i) and (iv) of this section, Z is first required to recognize foreign oil related income (which is net capital gain) on the first disposition in the amount of $575. Under paragraphs (b) and (d)(2) of this section, this net capital gain is adjusted by subtracting the rate differential portion of such gain from the total amount of such gain to determine the amount by which the foreign oil related loss account is reduced, which is $350 ($575 − ($575 × 18/46)). The balance remaining in Z's foreign oil related loss account after this step is $350. Therefore, this process will be repeated, in accordance with paragraph (d)(4)(iv) of this section, to recapture that remaining balance out of the gain deemed recognized on the second disposition, resulting in reduction of the foreign oil related loss account to zero and net capital gain required to be recognized from the second disposition in the amount of $575, which must also be adjusted by subtracting the rate differential portion to determine the amount by which the foreign oil related loss account is reduced (which is $350). The $575 of net capital gain from each disposition is recharacterized as United States source net capital gain. Z's section 907(b) foreign tax credit limitation is the same as in example (4), and Z has $1,150 ($575 + $575) of United States source net capital gain. [Reg. § 1.904(f)-2.]

☐ [*T.D.* 8153, 8-21-87.]

§ 1.904(i)-1. Limitation on use of deconsolidation to avoid foreign tax credit limitations.—(a) *General rule.*—If two or more includible corporations are affiliates, within the meaning of paragraph (b)(1) of this section, at any time during their taxable years, then, solely for purposes of applying the foreign tax credit provisions of section 59(a), sections 901 through 908, and section 960, the rules of this section will apply.

(1) *Determination of taxable income.*— (i) Each affiliate must compute its net taxable income or loss in each separate category (as defined in § 1.904-5(a)(1), and treating U.S. source income or loss as a separate category) without regard to sections 904(f) and 907(c)(4). Only affiliates that are members of the same consolidated group use the consolidated return regulations (other than those under sections 904(f) and 907(c)(4)) in computing such net taxable income or loss. To the extent otherwise applicable, other provisions of the Internal Revenue Code and regulations must be used in the determination of an affiliate's net taxable income or loss in a separate category.

(ii) The net taxable income amounts in each separate category determined under paragraph (a)(1)(i) of this section are combined for all affiliates to determine one amount for the group of affiliates in each separate category. However, a net loss of an affiliate (first affiliate) in a separate category determined under paragraph (a)(1)(i) of this section will be combined under this paragraph (a) with net income or loss amounts of other affiliates in the same category only if, and to the extent that, the net loss offsets taxable income, whether U.S. or foreign source, of the first affiliate. The consolidated return regulations that apply the principles of sections 904(f) and 907(c)(4) to consolidated groups will then be applied to the combined amounts in each separate category as if all affiliates were members of a single consolidated group.

(2) *Allocation.*—Any net taxable income in a separate category calculated under paragraph (a)(1)(ii) of this section for purposes of the foreign tax credit provisions must then be allocated among the affiliates under any consistently applied reasonable method, taking into account all of the facts and circumstances. A method is consistently applied if used by all affiliates from year to year. Once chosen, an allocation method may be changed only with the consent of the Commissioner. This allocation will only affect the source and foreign tax credit separate limitation character of the income for purposes of the foreign tax credit separate limitation of each affiliate, and will not otherwise affect an affiliate's total net income or loss. This section applies whether the federal income tax consequences of its application favor, or are adverse to, the taxpayer.

(b) *Definitions and special rules.*—For purposes of this section only, the following terms will have the meanings specified.

(1) *Affiliate.*—(i) *Generally.*—Affiliates are includible corporations—

(A) That are members of the same affiliated group, as defined in section 1504(a); or

(B) That would be members of the same affiliated group, as defined in section 1504(a) if—

(1) Any non-includible corporation meeting the ownership test of section 1504(a)(2) with respect to any such includible corporation was itself an includible corporation; or

(2) The constructive ownership rules of section 1563(e) were applied for purposes of section 1504(a).

(ii) *Rules for consolidated groups.*—Affiliates that are members of the same consolidated group are treated as a single affiliate for purposes of this section. The provisions of paragraph (a) of this section shall not apply if the only affiliates under this definition are already members of the same consolidated group without operation of this section.

(iii) *Exception for newly acquired affiliates.*—(A) With respect to acquisitions after December 7, 1995, an includible corporation acquired from unrelated third parties (First Corporation) will not be considered an affiliate of another includible corporation (Second Corporation) during the taxable year of the First Corporation beginning before the date on which the First Corporation originally becomes an affiliate with respect to the Second Corporation.

(B) With respect to acquisitions on or before December 7, 1995, an includible corporation acquired from unrelated third parties will not be considered an affiliate of another includible corporation during its taxable year beginning before the date on which the first includible corporation first becomes an affiliate with respect to that other includible corporation.

(C) This exception does not apply where the acquisition of an includible corporation is used to avoid the application of this section.

(2) *Includible corporation.*—The term *includible corporation* has the same meaning it has in section 1504(b).

(c) *Taxable years.*—If all of the affiliates use the same U.S. taxable year, then that taxable year must be used for purposes of applying this section. If, however, the affiliates use more than one U.S. taxable year, then an appropriate taxable year must be used for applying this section. The determination whether a taxable year is appropriate must take into account all of the relevant facts and circumstances, including the U.S. taxable years used by the affiliates for general U.S. income tax purposes. The taxable year chosen by the affiliates for purposes of applying this section must be used consistently from year to year. The taxable year may be changed only with the prior consent of the Commissioner. Those affiliates that do not use the year determined under this paragraph (c) as their U.S. taxable year for general U.S. income tax purposes must, for purposes of this section, use their U.S. taxable year or years ending within the taxable year determined under this paragraph (c). If, however, the stock of an affiliate is disposed of so that it ceases to be an affiliate, then the taxable year of that affiliate will be considered to end on the disposition date for purposes of this section.

(d) *Consistent treatment of foreign taxes paid.*—All affiliates must consistently either elect under section 901(a) to claim a credit for foreign income taxes paid or accrued, or deemed paid or accrued, or deduct foreign taxes paid or accrued under section 164. See also § 1.1502-4(a); § 1.905-1(a).

(e) *Effective date.*—Except as provided in paragraph (b)(1)(iii) of this section (relating to newly acquired affiliates), this section is effective for taxable years of affiliates beginning after December 31, 1993. [Reg. § 1.904(i)-1.]

☐ [*T.D.* 8627, 11-6-95.]

§ 1.904(j)-1. Certain individuals exempt from foreign tax credit limitation.—(a) *Election available only if all foreign taxes are creditable foreign taxes.*—A taxpayer may elect to apply section 904(j) for a taxable year only if all of the taxes for which a credit is allowable to the taxpayer under section 901 for the taxable year (without regard to carryovers) are creditable foreign taxes (as defined in section 904(j)(3)(B)).

(b) *Coordination with carryover rules.*—(1) *No carryovers to or from election year.*—If the taxpayer elects to apply section 904(j) for any taxable year, then no taxes paid or accrued by the taxpayer during such taxable year may be deemed paid or accrued under section 904(c) in any other taxable year, and no taxes paid or accrued in any other taxable year may be deemed paid or accrued under section 904(c) in such taxable year.

(2) *Carryovers to and from other years determined without regard to election years.*—The amount of the foreign taxes paid or accrued, and the amount of the foreign source taxable income, in any year for which the taxpayer elects to apply section 904(j) shall not be taken into account in determining the amount of any carryover to or from any other taxable year. However, an election to apply section 904(j) to any year does not extend the number of taxable years to which unused foreign taxes may be carried under section 904(c) and § 1.904-2(b). Therefore, in determining the number of such carryover years, the taxpayer must take into account years to which a section 904(j) election applies.

(3) *Determination of amount of creditable foreign taxes.*—Otherwise allowable carryovers of foreign tax credits from other taxable years shall not be taken into account in determining whether the amount of creditable foreign taxes paid or accrued by an individual during a taxable year exceeds $300 ($600 in the case of a joint return) for purposes of section 904(j)(2)(B).

(c) *Examples.*—The following examples illustrate the provisions of this section:

Example 1. In 2006, X, a single individual using the cash basis method of accounting for income and foreign tax credits, pays $100 of foreign taxes with respect to general limitation income that was earned and included in income for United States tax purposes in 2005. The foreign taxes would be creditable under section 901 but are not shown on a payee statement furnished to X. X's only income for 2006 from sources outside the United States is qualified passive income, with respect to which X pays $200 of creditable foreign taxes shown on a payee statement. X may not elect to apply section 904(j) for 2006 because some of X's foreign taxes are not creditable foreign taxes within the meaning of section 904(j)(3)(B).

Example 2. (i) In 2009, A, a single individual using the cash basis method of accounting for income and foreign tax credits, pays creditable foreign taxes of $250 attributable to passive income. Under section 904(c), A may also carry forward to 2009 $100 of unused foreign taxes paid in 2005 with respect to passive income, $300 of unused foreign taxes paid in 2005 with respect to general limitation income, $400 of unused foreign taxes paid in 2006 with respect to passive income, and $200 of unused foreign taxes paid in 2006 with respect to general limitation income. In 2009, A's only foreign source income is passive income described in section 904(j)(3)(A)(i), and this income is reported to A on a payee statement (within the meaning of section 6724(d)(2)). If A elects to apply section 904(j) for the 2009 taxable year, the unused foreign taxes paid in 2005 and 2006 are not deemed paid in 2009, and A therefore cannot claim a foreign tax credit for those taxes in 2009.

(ii) In 2010, A again is eligible for and elects the application of section 904(j). The carryforwards from 2005 expire in 2010. The carryforward period established under section 904(c) is not extended by A's election under section 904(j). In 2011, A does not elect the application of section 904(j). The $600 of unused foreign taxes paid in 2006 on passive and general limitation income are deemed paid in 2011, under section 904(c), without any adjustment for any portion of those taxes that might have been used as a foreign tax credit in 2009 or 2010 if A had not elected to apply section 904(j) to those years.

(d) *Effective date.*—Section 1.904(j)-1 applies to taxable years beginning after July 20, 2004. [Reg. § 1.904(j)-1.]

☐ [*T.D.* 9141, 7-19-2004.]

§ 1.905-1. When credit for taxes may be taken.—(a) *In general.*—The credit for taxes provided in subpart A (section 901 and following), part III, subchapter N, chapter 1 of the Code, may ordinarily be taken either in the return for the year in which the taxes accrued or in which the taxes were paid, dependent upon whether the accounts of the taxpayer are kept and his returns filed using an accrual method or using the cash receipts and disbursements method. Section 905(a) allows the taxpayer, at his option and irrespective of the method of accounting employed in keeping his books, to take such credit for taxes as may be allowable in the return for the year in which the taxes accrued. An election thus made under section 905(a) (or under the corresponding provisions of prior internal revenue laws) must be followed in returns for all subsequent years, and no portion of any such taxes accrued in a year in which a credit is claimed will be allowed as a deduction from gross income in any year. See also § 1.905-4.

(b) *Foreign income subject to exchange controls.*—If, however, under the provisions of the regulations under section 461, an amount otherwise constituting gross income for the taxable year from sources without the United States is, owing to monetary, exchange, or other restrictions imposed by a foreign country, not includible in gross income of the taxpayer for such year, the credit for income taxes imposed by such foreign country with respect to such amount shall be taken proportionately in any subsequent taxable year in which such amount or portion thereof is includible in gross income. [Reg. § 1.905-1.]

☐ [*T.D.* 6275, 12-2-57.]

§ 1.905-2. Conditions of allowance of credit.—(a) *Forms and information.*—(1) Whenever the taxpayer chooses, in accordance with paragraph (d) of § 1.901-1, to claim the benefits of the foreign tax credit, the claim for credit shall be accompanied by Form 1116 in the case of an individual or by Form 1118 in the case of a corporation.

(2) The form must be carefully filled in with all the information called for and with the calculations of credits indicated. Except where it is established to the satisfaction of the district director that it is impossible for the taxpayer to furnish such evidence, the taxpayer must provide upon request the receipt for each such tax payment if credit is sought for taxes already paid or the return on which each such accrued tax was based if credit is sought for taxes accrued. The receipt or return must be either the original, a duplicate original, or a duly certified or authenticated copy. The preceding two sentences are applicable for returns whose original due date falls on or after January 1, 1988. If the receipt or the return is in a foreign language, a certified translation thereof must be furnished by the taxpayer. Any additional information necessary for the determination under part I (section 861 and following), subchapter N, chapter 1 of the Code, of the amount of income derived from sources without the United States and from each foreign country shall, upon the request of the district director, be furnished by the taxpayer. If the taxpayer upon request fails without justification to furnish any such additional information which is significant, including any significant information which he is requested to furnish pursuant to § 1.861-8(f)(5) as proposed in the Federal Register for November 8, 1976, the District Director may disallow the claim of the taxpayer to the benefits of the foreign tax credit.

(b) *Secondary evidence.*—Where it has been established to the satisfaction of the district director that it is impossible to furnish a receipt for such foreign tax payment, the foreign tax return, or direct evidence of the amount of tax withheld at the source, the district director, may, in his discretion, accept secondary evidence thereof as follows:

(1) *Receipt for payment.*—In the absence of a receipt for payment of foreign taxes there shall be submitted a photostatic copy of the check, draft, or other medium of payment showing the amount and date thereof, with certification identifying it with the tax claimed to have been paid, together with evidence establishing that the tax was paid for taxpayer's account as his own tax on his own income. If credit is claimed on an accrual method, it must be shown that the tax accrued in the taxable year.

(2) *Foreign tax return.*—If the foreign tax return is not available, the foreign tax has not been paid, and credit is claimed on an accrual method, there shall be submitted—

(i) A certified statement of the amount claimed to have accrued,

(ii) Excerpts from the taxpayer's accounts showing amounts of foreign income and tax thereon accrued on its books,

(iii) A computation of the foreign tax based on income from the foreign country carried on the books and at current rates of tax to be established by data such as excerpts from the foreign law, assessment notices, or other documentary evidence thereof,

(iv) A bond, if deemed necessary by the district director, filed in the manner provided in cases where the foreign return is available, and

(v) In case a bond is not required, a specific agreement wherein the taxpayer shall recognize its liability to report the correct amount of tax when ascertained, as required by the provisions of section 905(c).

If at any time the foreign tax receipts or foreign tax returns become available to the taxpayer, they shall be promptly submitted to the district director.

(3) *Tax withheld at source.*—In the case of taxes withheld at the source from dividends, interest, royalties, compensation, or other form of income, where evidence of withholding and of the amount withheld cannot be secured from those who have made the payments, the district director may, in his discretion, accept secondary evidence of such withholding and of the amount of the tax so withheld, having due regard to the taxpayer's books of account and to the rates of taxation prevailing in the particular foreign country during the period involved.

(c) In the case of a credit sought for a tax accrued but not paid, the district director may, as a condition precedent to the allowance of a credit, require a bond from the taxpayer, in addition to Form 1116 or 1118. If such a bond is required, Form 1117 shall be used by an individual or by a corporation. It shall be in such sum as the Commissioner may prescribe, and shall be conditioned for the payment by the taxpayer of any amount of tax found due upon any redetermination of the tax made necessary by such credit proving incorrect, with such further conditions as the district director may require. This bond shall be executed by the taxpayer, or the agent or representative of the taxpayer, as principal, and by sureties satisfactory to and approved by the Commissioner. See also 6 U.S.C. 15. [Reg. § 1.905-2.]

☐ [*T.D.* 6275, 12-2-57. *Amended by T.D.* 6789, 12-30-64; *T.D.* 7292, 11-30-74; *T.D.* 7456, 1-3-77; *T.D.* 8210, 6-22-88; *T.D.* 8412, 5-13-92 *and T.D.* 8759, 1-26-98.]

§ 1.905-3T. Adjustments to the pools of foreign taxes and earnings and profits when the allowable foreign tax credit changes (Temporary).—(a) *Foreign tax redeterminations subject to sections 985 through 989 of the Internal Revenue Code.*—This section applies to a foreign tax redetermination that occurs in a taxpayer's taxable year beginning after December 31, 1986 with respect to—

(1) Tax that is paid or accrued by or on behalf of a taxpayer (including taxes paid or accrued prior to January 1, 1987), or

(2) Tax that is deemed paid or accrued by a taxpayer under section 902 or section 960 with respect to earnings and profits of a foreign corporation accumulated in taxable years of the foreign corporation beginning after December 31, 1986.

(b) *Currency translation rules.*—(1) *Accrual of foreign tax.*—Accrued and unpaid foreign tax liabilities denominated in foreign currency, as determined under foreign law, shall be translated into dollars at the exchange rate as of the last day of the taxable year of the taxpayer.

(2) *Payments of foreign tax.*—Foreign tax liabilities denominated in foreign currency shall be translated into dollars at the rate of exchange for the date of the payment of the foreign tax. Tax withheld in foreign currency shall be translated into dollars at the rate for the date on which the tax is withheld. Estimated tax paid in foreign currency shall be translated into dollars at the rate for the date on which the estimated tax payment is made.

(3) *Refunds of foreign tax.*—A refund of foreign tax shall be translated into dollars using the exchange rate for the date of the payment of the foreign taxes. If a refund of foreign tax relates to foreign taxes paid on more than one date, then the refund shall be deemed to be derived from, and shall reduce, the last payment of foreign taxes first, to the extent thereof. See § 1.905-3T(d)(3) relating to the method of adjustment of a foreign corporation's pools of earnings and profits and foreign taxes.

(4) *Allocation of refunds of foreign tax.*—Refunds of foreign tax shall be allocated to the same separate category as foreign taxes to which the refunded taxes relate. Refunds are related to foreign taxes of a separate category if the foreign tax that was refunded was imposed with respect to that separate category. See section 904(d) and § 1.904-6 concerning the allocation of taxes to separate categories of income. Earnings and profits of a foreign corporation in the separate category to which the refund re-

lates shall be increased to reflect the foreign tax refund.

(5) *Basis of foreign currency refunded.*—A recipient of a refund of foreign tax shall determine its basis in the currency refunded under the following rules.

(i) If the functional currency of the qualified business unit (as defined in section 989 and the regulations thereunder, hereinafter "QBU") that paid the tax and received the refund is the United States dollar or the person receiving the refund is not a QBU, then the recipient's basis in the foreign currency refunded shall be the dollar value of the refund determined, under paragraph (b)(2) of this section, on the date the foreign tax was paid.

(ii) If the functional currency of the QBU receiving the refund is not the United States dollar and is different from the currency in which the foreign tax was paid, then the recipient's basis in the foreign currency refunded shall be equal to the functional currency value of the non-functional refunded translated into functional currency at the exchange rate between the functional currency and the non-functional currency, determined under paragraph (b)(2) of this section, on the date the foreign tax was paid.

(iii) If the functional currency of the QBU receiving the refund is the currency in which the refund was made, then the recipient's basis in the currency received shall be the amount of the functional currency received.

For purposes of determining exchange gain or loss on the initial payment of foreign tax in a non-functional currency, see section 988. For purposes of determining subsequent exchange gain or loss on the disposition of non-functional currency the basis of which is determined under this rule, see section 988.

(c) *Foreign tax redetermination.*—For purposes of this section, the term "foreign tax redetermination" means a change in the foreign tax liability that may affect a United States taxpayer's foreign tax credit. A foreign tax redetermination includes—

(1) A refund of foreign taxes;

(2) A difference between the dollar value of the accrued foreign tax and the dollar value of the foreign tax actually paid attributable to differences in the units of foreign currency paid and the units of foreign currency accrued; or

(3) A difference between the dollar value of the accrued foreign tax and the dollar value of the foreign tax actually paid attributable to fluctuations in the value of the foreign currency relative to the dollar between the date of accrual and the date of payment.

(d) *Redetermination of United States tax liability.*—(1) *Foreign taxes paid directly by a United States person.*—If a foreign tax redetermination occurs with respect to foreign tax paid or accrued by or on behalf of a United States taxpayer, then a redetermination of United States tax liability is required for the taxable year for which the foreign tax was claimed as a credit. See § 1.905-4T(b) which requires notification to the Internal Revenue Service of a foreign tax redetermination in situations in which a redetermination of United States liability is required. However, a redetermination of United States tax liability is not required (and a taxpayer need not notify the Service) if the foreign tax redetermination is described in paragraph (c)(3) (that is, it is caused solely by a foreign currency fluctuation), and the amount of the foreign tax redetermination with respect to the foreign country is less than the lesser of ten thousand dollars or two percent of the total dollar amount of the foreign tax initially accrued with respect to that foreign country for the taxable year. In such case, an appropriate adjustment shall be made to the taxpayer's United States tax liability in the taxable year during which the foreign tax redetermination occurs.

⟫→ *Caution: Temporary Reg. § 1.905-3T(d)(2)(ii)(A) and so much of (C) as refers to (A) has been suspended by Notice 90-26.*

(2) *Foreign taxes deemed paid under sections 902 or 960.*—(i) *Redetermination of United States tax liability not required.*—Subject to the special rule of paragraph (d)(4), a redetermination of United States tax liability is not required to account for the effect of a redetermination of foreign tax paid or accrued by a foreign corporation on the foreign taxes deemed paid by a United States corporation under sections 902 or section 960. Instead, adjustments shall be made, and notification of such adjustments shall be filed, as required by paragraphs (d)(2) and (3) of this section.

(ii) *Adjustments to pools.*—In the case of a foreign tax redetermination that affects the amount of foreign taxes deemed paid by a United States corporation for a taxable year—

(A) If the foreign tax redetermination occurs more than 90 days before the due date (determined with extensions) of the United States taxpayer's United States income tax return for such taxable year and before the taxpayer actually files that return, then that United States taxpayer shall adjust the foreign tax credit to be claimed on that return for such taxable year to account for the effect of the foreign tax redetermination (including the impact of the foreign tax redetermination on the earnings and profits of the foreign corporation);

(B) If a foreign tax redetermination occurs after the filing of the United States tax return for such taxable year, then appropriate upward or downward adjustments shall be made at the time of the foreign tax redetermination to the pool of foreign taxes and the pool of earnings and profits of the foreign corporation as provided in paragraph (d)(3) to reflect the effect of the foreign tax redetermination in calculating foreign taxes deemed paid with respect to distributions and inclusions (and the amount of such distributions and inclusions) that are includible in taxable years subsequent to the taxable year for which such tax return is filed; and

(C) If the foreign tax redetermination occurs within 90 days of the due date (determined with extensions) of the United States tax return and before the taxpayer actually files its tax return, then the taxpayer may elect either to adjust the foreign tax credit to be claimed on that return in the manner described in subparagraph (A) of this paragraph (d)(2)(ii) or adjust the pools of foreign taxes and earnings and profits to reflect the effect of the foreign tax redetermination in the manner described in paragraph (d)(2)(ii)(B), provided that consistent elections are made by the taxpayer and all other members of the affiliated group, as defined in section 1504(a), of which the taxpayer is a member, with respect to all foreign tax redeterminations occurring on or before any date within the 90 day period.

(iii) *Reporting requirements.*—If an adjustment to the appropriate pool of foreign taxes and earnings and profits is required under paragraphs (d)(2)(ii)(B) or (C), the United States corporation shall attach a notice of such adjustment to its return for the year with or within which ends the foreign corporation's taxable year during which the foreign tax redetermination occurs. The United States corporation shall provide: its name and identifying number; the foreign corporation's name, address, and identifying number (if any); the amount of any refunds of foreign taxes and the exchange rate as of the time of the original payment of the refunded foreign taxes; the amounts of unrefunded foreign taxes when paid and when accrued in foreign currency, the exchange rates for the accrual and payment dates of unrefunded foreign taxes, and the dollar amounts of unrefunded foreign taxes paid and accrued; the current balances of the pools of earnings and profits and foreign taxes before and after the foreign tax redetermination; and such other information as the Service may require. If a taxpayer may be required to redetermine its United States tax liability under paragraph (d)(4)(ii) of §1.905-3T (relating to foreign tax adjustments of two percent or more), the notice shall specifically identify foreign tax adjustments described in such paragraph and shall include a complete factual description justifying the overaccrual of foreign tax. If the United States corporation fails to attach the required notice, to provide the necessary information, or to make the required adjustments, then it must provide notification of the foreign tax redetermination under §1.905-4T. The Service may, in its discretion, make a redetermination of United States tax liability, and subject the taxpayer to the interest provisions of section 6601 and the penalty provisions of section 6689 and the regulations thereunder.

(iv) *Examples.*—The following examples illustrate the application of paragraph (d)(2)(ii) and (iii) of this section. In each case, the exceptions of paragraph (d)(4) do not apply.

Example (1). Controlled foreign corporation S is a wholly-owned subsidiary of domestic corporation, P. P is a fiscal year taxpayer whose taxable year ends on June 30. P does not request an extension for filing its United States tax return for the taxable year ending June 30, 1988 and files its return on its September 15, 1988 due data. S is a calendar year taxpayer. In 1987, S earned 100u of Subpart F income and accrued foreign taxes with respect to that income of 20u. At the time of accrual, the exchange rate was $1:4u. S paid the 20u of accrued tax with respect to its income on June 15, 1988, when the exchange rate was $1:2u. P includes the 100u in gross income under section 951(a) and claims a credit under section 960. P must use the amount of taxes actually paid by S (20u = $10) in determining foreign taxes deemed paid by P. Pursuant to paragraph (d)(2)(ii)(A), P is required to compute foreign taxes deemed paid taking into account the foreign tax redetermination that occurred on June 15, which was more than 90 days before the due date of P's tax return (September 15, 1988) and before P actually filed its return.

Example (2). The facts are the same as in *Example (1),* except that S paid its tax liability on October 16, 1988. P filed its United States income tax return for 1987 on September 15, 1987, before the foreign tax redetermination. P properly computed its section 960 credit on its 1987 return with respect to its 100u Subpart F inclusion on the basis of the amount of accrued foreign tax. Subject to the special rule of paragraph (d)(3)(iv), P is required, pursuant to the provisions of paragraph (d)(2)(ii)(B), to make the appropriate adjustments to the relevant pool of foreign taxes and pool of earnings and profits for purposes of calculating foreign taxes deemed paid in subsequent taxable years.

Example (3). Controlled foreign corporation S is a wholly-owned subsidiary of domestic corporation, P. P is a fiscal year (June 30) taxpayer, and S is a calendar year taxpayer. In 1987, S earned 100u of general limitation manufacturing income that was not Subpart F income. S accrued 40u in foreign tax with respect to that income as of the end of its taxable year when the exchange rate was $1:4u. During 1987 and 1988, P received no distributions (and had no section 951(a)(1) inclusions) from S. S paid its taxes on March 15, 1988 when the exchange rate was $1:2u (40u = $20). S received a refund of foreign tax of 20u on July 1, 1988. No section 905(c) adjustment is required on these facts. As of the end of 1988, S's pool of general limitation accumulated earnings and profits equals 80u (100u - 20u), and its pool of foreign taxes imposed on general limitation income equals $10 (40u - 20u = 20u, translated as of the date of payment ($1:2u), equals $10).

(3) *Adjustments to the pools of earnings and profits and foreign taxes.*—(i) *In general.*—If a foreign corporation is required to adjust its earnings and profits and foreign taxes under § 1.905-3T(d)(2)(ii)(B) or (C), then that adjustment shall be made in accordance with the provisions of this section.

(ii) *Refunds of foreign taxes.*—A foreign corporation shall reduce its pool of foreign taxes in the appropriate separate category by the United States dollar amount of a foreign tax refund translated as provided in paragraph (b)(3). A foreign corporation shall increase its pool of earnings and profits in the appropriate separate category by the functional currency amount of the foreign tax refund. The allocation of the refund to the appropriate separate categories shall be made in accordance with §§ 1.905-3T(b)(4) and 1.904-6. If a foreign corporation receives a refund of foreign tax in a currency other than its functional currency, that refund shall be translated into its functional currency, for purposes of computing the increase to its pool of earnings and profits, at the exchange rate as of the date of the payment of the foreign tax.

(iii) *Additional assessments of foreign tax.*—A foreign corporation shall increase its pool of foreign taxes in the appropriate separate category by the United States dollar amount of the additional foreign tax paid or accrued translated as provided in paragraphs (b)(1) and (2). A foreign corporation shall decrease its earnings and profits in the appropriate separate category by the functional currency amount of the additional foreign tax paid or accrued. The allocation of the additional amount of foreign tax among separate categories shall be made in accordance with § 1.904-6.

(iv) *Refunds of foreign taxes of lower tier foreign corporations that cause deficits in foreign tax pools.*—If a lower tier foreign corporation receives a refund of foreign tax after making a distribution to an upper tier foreign corporation and the refund would have the effect of reducing below zero the lower tier corporation's pool of foreign taxes in any separate category, then both the lower tier and upper tier corporations shall adjust the appropriate pool of foreign taxes to reflect that refund. The upper tier foreign corporation shall adjust its pool of foreign taxes by the difference between the United States dollar amount of foreign tax deemed paid by the upper tier foreign corporation prior to the refund and the United States dollar amount of foreign tax recomputed as if the refund occurred prior to the distribution. The upper tier foreign corporation shall not make any adjustment to its earnings and profits because foreign taxes deemed paid by the upper tier corporation are not included in the upper tier corporation's earnings and profits. The lower tier foreign corporation shall adjust its pool of foreign taxes by the difference between the United States dollar amount of the refund and the United States dollar amount of the adjustment to the upper tier foreign corporation's pool of foreign taxes. The earnings and profits of the lower tier foreign corporation shall be adjusted to reflect the full amount of the refund. The provisions of this paragraph (d)(3)(iv) do not apply to distributions or inclusions to a United States person. See § 1.905-3T(d)(4)(iv) for rules relating to actual or deemed distributions made to a United States person.

(v) *Examples.*—The following examples illustrate the application of this paragraph (d)(3).

Example (1). Controlled foreign corporation (CFC) is a wholly-owned subsidiary of its domestic parent, P. Both CFC and P are calendar year taxpayers. CFC has a functional currency, the u, other than the dollar and maintains its pool of earnings and profits in that currency. At the end of year 1, CFC paid 100u in taxes with respect to non-Subpart F income when the exchange rate was $1:1u. In year 2, on a date that is after P filed its United States tax return, CFC receives a refund of 50u of its year 1 taxes. CFC made no distributions to P in year 1. In accordance with paragraph (d)(3)(ii) and subject to paragraph (d)(4), CFC shall reduce its pool of foreign taxes by $50 and increase its pool of earnings and profits by 50u.

Example (2). Controlled foreign corporation (CFC) is a wholly-owned subsidiary of its domestic parent, P. Both CFC and P are calendar year taxpayers. In year 1 CFC earned 400u of general limitation manufacturing income and 200u of shipping income. On date 1, CFC paid 200u of foreign tax, 100u with respect to general limitation manufacturing income, and 100u with respect to shipping income. On date 1, the exchange rate is $1:1u. On date 2, a date that is after the filing of P's United States tax return, CFC receives a refund of 75u, 25u of which is related to the manufacturing income and 50u of which is related to the shipping income. Subject to paragraph (d)(4), CFC shall reduce its pools of foreign taxes related to general limitation income and shipping income by $25 and $50, respectively (because the refund is translated at the rate of exchange prevailing on the date of payment of the foreign tax), and increase the respective pools of earnings and profits by 25u and 50u (because the earnings and profits are increased by the functional currency amount of the refund received). If the refund to CFC was not specifically related to any separate category of income, CFC, pursuant to §1.904-6, is required to allocate that refund in accordance with the provisions of that section.

Example (3). CFC1 is a foreign corporation that is wholly-owned by P, a domestic corporation. CFC2 is a foreign corporation that is wholly-owned by CFC1. Unless stated otherwise, the exchange rate is always $1:1u. In year 1, CFC2 has earnings and profits of 100u (net of foreign taxes) and paid 100u in foreign taxes with respect to those earnings. CFC2 has no income and pays no foreign taxes in years 2 and 3. CFC1 has no earnings and profits other than those resulting from distributions from CFC2 and pays no foreign taxes.

Situation (i). In year 2, CFC2 receives a refund of foreign taxes of 25u. In year 3, CFC2 makes a distribution to CFC1 of 50u. CFC1 is deemed to have paid $30 of foreign taxes with respect to that distribution (50u/125u × $75). At the end of year 3, the following reflects the pools of earnings and profits and foreign taxes of CFC1 and CFC2.

CFC2	Earnings and Profits (u)				Foreign Taxes			
Y1	100				$100			
Y2	100	+ 25	=	125	$100	− <$25>	=	$75
Y3	125	− <50>	=	75	$ 75	− <$30>	=	$45

CFC1	Earnings and Profits (u)	Foreign Taxes
Y3	50	30

Situation (ii). The facts are the same as situation (i), except that CFC2 makes a distribution of 50u in year 2 and receives a refund of 75u in year 3. In year 2 the amount of foreign taxes deemed paid by CFC1 would be $50 (50u/100u × $100). Both CFC1 and CFC2 must adjust their pools of foreign taxes in year 3 because the year 3 refund would have the effect of reducing below zero CFC2's pool of foreign taxes. CFC1 reduces its pool of foreign taxes by $42.86 determined as follows: $50 (foreign taxes deemed paid on the distribution from CFC2) - $7.14 (the foreign taxes that would have been deemed paid had the refund occurred prior to the distribution (50u/175u × $25)). CFC2 reduces its pool of foreign taxes by $32.14 (the difference between the dollar value of 75u refund determined as of the date of payment of the foreign tax and the $42.86 adjustment to CFC1's pool of foreign taxes). At the and of year 3, the following reflects the pools of foreign taxes and earnings and profits for CFC1 and CFC2.

CFC2	Earnings and Profits (u)				Foreign Taxes			
Y1	100				$100			
Y2	100	− <50>	=	50	$100	− <$50>	=	$50
Y3	50	+ 75	=	125	$ 50	− <$32.14>	=	$17.86

CFC1	Earnings and Profits (u)				Foreign Taxes			
Y2	50				$50			
Y3	50				$ 50	− <$42.86>	=	$ 7.14

(4) *Exceptions*.—The provisions of paragraph (d)(2) of this section shall not apply and a redetermination of United States tax liability is required to account for the effect of a redetermination of foreign tax on foreign taxes deemed paid by a United States corporation under section 902 or section 960 to the extent provided in this paragraph (d)(4).

(i) *Hyperinflationary currencies*.—A redetermination of United States tax liability is required if the foreign tax liability is in a hyperinflationary currency. The term "hyperinflationary currency" means the currency of a country in which there is cumulative inflation during the base period of at least 100% as determined by reference to the consumer price index of the country listed in the monthly issues of International Financial Statistics, or a successor publication, of the International Monetary Fund. "Base period" means, with respect to any taxable year, the thirty-six calendar months imme-

Reg. §1.905-3T(d)(4)(i)

diately preceding the last day of such taxable year (see § 1.985-2T(b)(2)).

(ii) *Foreign tax adjustment of two percent or more.*—If the foreign tax liability of a United States taxpayer is in a currency other than a hyperinflationary currency and the amount of foreign tax accrued for the taxable year to a foreign country, as measured in units of foreign currency, exceeds the amount of foreign tax paid to that foreign country for the taxable year (as measured in units of foreign currency) by at least two percent, then the Service, in its discretion, may require a redetermination of United States tax liability.

(iii) *Example.*—The provisions of paragraph (d)(4)(ii) are illustrated by the following example.

Example. Controlled foreign corporation is a wholly-owned subsidiary of its domestic parent, P. Both CFC and P are calendar year taxpayers. In year 1, CFC has general limitation income of 200u and, by year-end, had accrued foreign taxes with respect to that income of 100u when the exchange rate is $1:1u. In year 1, CFC makes a distribution to P of 50u, half of its earnings and profits of 100u. P is deemed to have paid $50 of foreign tax with respect to that distribution (50u/100u × $100). In year 2, after P has filed its United States tax return, CFC pays its actual foreign tax liability of 98.50 when the exchange rate is $1:1u. Subject to paragraph (d)(4), CFC must reduce its pool of foreign taxes by $1.50 and increase the corresponding pool of earnings and profits by 1.50u. (The refund is translated into dollars at the rate of exchange prevailing on the date of payment of the foreign tax, and the adjustment to earnings and profits is in "u" s.) In year 2, CFC earns 200u of general limitation income and accrues 120u of tax when the exchange rate is $1:1u. In year 2, CFC distributes 100u to P. P is deemed to have paid $128 of foreign tax (($48.50 + $120) × 100u/(51.50u + 80u)). In year 3, after P filed its year 2 United States tax return, CFC pays its actual year 2 tax liability of 100u when the exchange rate is $1:1u. The Service may require P to recompute its year 2 United States tax liability to account for the effect of the overaccrual of foreign tax pursuant to § 1.905-3T(d)(4)(ii).

(iv) *Deficit in foreign tax pool.*—A redetermination of United States tax liability is required if a foreign tax redetermination occurs with respect to foreign taxes deemed paid with respect to a Subpart F inclusion or an actual distribution which has the effect of reducing below zero the distributing foreign corporation's pool of foreign taxes in any separate category. Whether a foreign corporation's pool of foreign taxes is reduced below zero shall be determined at the close of the taxable year of the foreign corporation in which the foreign tax redetermination occurred. In no case shall taxes paid or accrued with respect to one separate category be applied to offset a negative balance in any other separate category.

(v) *Example.*—The provisions of paragraph (d)(4)(iv) are illustrated by the following example.

Example. Controlled foreign corporation (CFC) is a wholly-owned subsidiary of P, a domestic corporation. Both P and CFC are calendar year taxpayers. In year 1, CFC has 200u of general limitation income with respect to which 100 of taxes are paid when the exchange rate was $1:1u. In year 1, CFC distributes half (50u) of its earnings and profits (100u). Under section 902, P is deemed to have paid $50 of the foreign taxes paid by CFC with respect to that distribution (50u/100u × $100). In year 2, CFC receives a refund of all of its year 1 taxes (100u). In year 2, CFC earns an additional 290u of income—200u of shipping income with respect to which 100u of taxes are paid, and 90u of general limitation income with respect to which 45u of taxes are paid when the exchange rate was $1:1u. P is required to redetermine its year 1 United States tax liability to account for the foreign tax redetermination occurring in year 2 because, if an adjustment to CFC's pool of general limitation taxes were made, the pool would be <$5>. CFC is not permitted to carry a deficit in any pool of foreign taxes; therefore, P must redetermine its United States liability for year 1.

(e) *Foreign tax imposed on foreign refund.*—If the redetermination of foreign tax for a taxable year or years is occasioned by the refund to the taxpayer of taxes paid to a foreign country or possession of the United States and the foreign country or possession imposed tax on the refund, then the amount of the refund shall be considered to be reduced by the amount of any tax described in section 901 imposed by the foreign country or possession of the United States with respect to such refund. In such case, no other credit under section 901, and no deduction under section 164, shall be allowed for any taxable year with respect to such tax imposed on such refund.

(f) *Reduction of corporate level tax on distribution of earnings and profits.*—If a United States shareholder of a controlled foreign corporation receives a distribution out of previously taxed earnings and profits and a foreign country has imposed tax on the income of the controlled foreign corporation, which tax is reduced on distribution of the earnings and profits of the corporation, then the United States shareholder shall redetermine its United States tax liability for the year or years affected. [Temporary Reg. § 1.905-3T.]

☐ [T.D. 8210, 6-22-88.]

§ 1.905-4T. Notification and redetermination of United States tax liability (Temporary).—(a) *Application of this section.*—The rules of this section shall apply if, as a result of a foreign tax redetermination as defined in § 1.905-3T(c), a redetermination of United States tax liability is required under § 1.905-3T.

(b) *Notification.*—(1) *General rules.*—Any United States taxpayer for which a redetermination of United States tax liability is required shall notify the Secretary in the manner described in this paragraph (b), and the Service will redetermine the United States tax liability of the United States taxpayer. Notification shall be made by filing Form 1120X or 1040X, and Form 1118 or 1116, in the manner described in the instructions to Form 1118 with the Service Center where the taxpayer filed the tax return claiming the foreign tax credit to which the notice relates. Notification shall be filed within the time prescribed by and shall contain the information required by this paragraph (b). The amount of tax, if any, due upon a redetermination shall be paid by the taxpayer after notice and demand has been made by the Service. Subchapter B of chapter 63 of the Code (relating to deficiency procedures) shall not apply with respect to the assessment of the amount due upon such redetermination. In accordance with section 905(c) and section 6501(c)(5), the amount of additional tax due shall be assessed and collected without regard to the provisions of section 6401(a) (relating to limitations on assessment and collection). The amount of tax, if any, shown by a redetermination to have bean overpaid shall be credited or refunded to the taxpayer in accordance with the provisions of § 301.6511(d)-3.

(2) *Time for filing.*—If a redetermination of United States tax liability is necessitated by a foreign tax redetermination that reduced the amount of foreign taxes paid or deemed paid, then the United States taxpayer shall file the notification with respect to such foreign tax redetermination within 180 days after the date that the foreign tax redetermination occurs. If a redetermination of United States liability is necessitated by a foreign tax redetermination that increased the amount of foreign taxes paid or deemed paid, then the United States taxpayer claiming foreign tax credits for accrued foreign taxes must notify the Service within the period provided by section 6511(d)(3)(A). Filing of the appropriate notification within the prescribed time shall constitute a claim for refund of United States tax.

(3) *Notification contents.*—(i) *In general.*—The taxpayer shall provide the Service with information sufficient to redetermine the tax including, but not limited to, the following: the United States taxpayer's name, address, and identifying number; the taxable year or years of the taxpayer that are affected by the redetermination of United States tax liability; information required in paragraph (b)(ii) and (iii) below with respect to foreign tax redeterminations affecting the redetermination of United States tax liability, including information in a form that will enable the Service to verify and compare the original computations with respect to a claimed foreign tax credit, the revised computations resulting from the foreign tax redeterminations, and the net changes resulting therefrom.

(ii) *Direct foreign tax credit.*—In the case of foreign taxes paid by or on behalf of the taxpayer, if—

(A) The taxpayer receives a refund of foreign tax, the taxpayer's information shall include: the amount of foreign taxes paid in foreign currency; the date or dates the foreign taxes were paid; the rate of exchange on each date the foreign taxes were paid; the amount of the foreign taxes refunded in foreign currency;

(B) The foreign taxes when paid differ from the accrued amounts claimed as credits by the taxpayer because of fluctuation in the value of the foreign currency in which the foreign taxes were paid, the taxpayer's information shall include the following: the date on which foreign taxes were accrued and the dates on which the foreign taxes were paid; the rates of exchange for each such date; and the amount of foreign taxes accrued or paid in foreign currency on each such date;

(C) The foreign taxes when paid differ from accrued amounts claimed as credits by the taxpayer because the taxpayer is assessed additional or less foreign tax. The taxpayer's information shall include the following: the original amounts and information described in subdivision (B) of this paragraph (b)(3)(ii); the amount of additional or reduced foreign tax in foreign currency; and the revised amounts and information described in subdivision (B) of this paragraph (b)(3)(ii).

(iii) *Foreign taxes deemed paid.*—In the case of foreign taxes paid or accrued by a foreign corporation that are deemed paid or accrued under section 902 or section 960 and with respect to which the taxpayer is required to redetermine its United States tax liability, the United States taxpayer's information shall include the following: the foreign corporation's name and identifying number (if any); the dates and amounts of any dividend distributions or other inclusions made out of earnings and profits for the affected year or years; and the amount of earnings and profits from which such dividends were paid for the affected year or years; and information described in paragraph (b)(3)(ii) as applied to the foreign corporation. In the case of a failure to attach the required notification or to make the required adjustments described in § 1.905-3T(d)(2)(iii), the taxpayer's information shall also include a complete factual description justifying that failure.

(c) *Interest and penalty.*—(1) *General rules.*—If a foreign tax redetermination results in a redetermination of United States tax liability, then interest shall be computed on the deficiency or overpayment in accordance with sections 6601 and 6611 and the regulations thereunder. No interest shall be assessed or collected on any deficiency resulting from a refund of foreign tax for any period before the receipt of the refund, except to the extent interest was paid by the foreign country or possession of the United States on the refund for the period. In no case, however, shall interest assessed and collected pursuant to the preceding sentence for any period before receipt of the refund exceed the amount that otherwise would have been assessed and collected under section 6601 and the regulations thereunder for that period. Interest shall be assessed from the time the taxpayer (or the foreign corporation of which the taxpayer is a shareholder) receives a refund until the taxpayer pays the additional tax due the United States.

(2) *No interest on adjustments to pools of foreign taxes.*—A deficiency or overpayment of United States tax liability does not result from a redetermination of foreign tax unless a redetermination of United States liability is required. Consequently, no interest will be paid by or to a United States corporation as a result of adjustments by a foreign corporation to its pools of foreign taxes and earnings and profits under paragraph (d)(2) of § 1.905-3T.

(3) *Imposition of penalty.*—Failure to comply with the provisions of this section shall subject the taxpayer to the penalty provisions of section 6689 and the regulations thereunder.

(d) *Effective date.*—The provisions of this section apply to foreign tax redeterminations described in § 1.905-3T(a). Notwithstanding paragraph (b)(2) of this section (relating to time for filing the required notice), the taxpayer shall have 180 days after the publication of an Announcement in the Internal Revenue Bulletin notifying taxpayers of the availability of the Forms and instructions to comply with the provisions of this section. In no case, however, shall this paragraph (d) operate to extend the statute of limitations provided by section 6511(d)(3)(A). [Temporary Reg. § 1.905-4T.]

☐ [*T.D.* 8210, 6-22-88.]

Foreign Earned Income Exclusion

§ 1.911-1. Partial exclusion for earned income from sources within a foreign country and foreign housing costs.—(a) *In general.*—Section 911 provides that a qualified individual may elect to exclude the individual's foreign earned income and the housing cost amount from the individual's gross income for the taxable year. Foreign earned income is excludable to the extent of the applicable limitation for the taxable year. The housing cost amount for the taxable year is excludable to the extent attributable to employer provided amounts. If a portion of the housing cost amount for the taxable year is attributable to non-employer provided amounts, such amount may be deductible by the qualified individual subject to a limitation. The amounts excluded under section 911(a) and the amount deducted under section 911(c)(3)(A) for the taxable year shall not exceed the individual's foreign earned income for such taxable year. Foreign earned income must be earned during a period for which the individual qualifies to make an election under section 911(d)(1). A housing cost amount that would be deductible except for the application of this limitation may be carried over to the next taxable year and is deductible to the extent of the limitation for that year. Except as otherwise provided, §§ 1.911-1 through 1.911-7 apply to taxable years beginning after December 31, 1981. These sections do not apply to any item of income, expense, deduction, or credit arising before January 1, 1982, even if such item is attributable to services performed after December 31, 1981.

(b) *Scope.*—Section 1.911-2 provides rules for determining whether an individual qualifies to make an election under section 911. Section 1.911-3 provides rules for determining the amount of foreign earned income that is excludable under section 911(a)(1). Section 1.911-4 provides rules for determining the housing cost amount and the portions excludable under section 911(a)(2) or deductible under section 911(c)(3). Section 1.911-5 provides special rules applicable to married couples. Section 1.911-6 provides for the disallowance of deductions, exclusions, and credits attributable to amounts excluded under section 911. Section 1.911-7 provides procedural rules for making or revoking an election under section 911. Section 1.911-8 provides a reference to rules applicable to taxable years beginning before January 1, 1982. [Reg. § 1.911-1.]

☐ [*T.D.* 8006, 1-17-85. *Amended by T.D.* 8240, 1-19-89.]

§ 1.911-2. Qualified individuals.—(a) *In general.*—An individual is a qualified individual if:

(1) The individual's tax home is in a foreign country or countries throughout—

(i) The period of bona fide residence described in paragraph (a)(2)(i) of this section, or

(ii) The 330 full days of presence described in paragraph (a)(2)(ii) of this section; and

(2) The individual is either—

(i) A citizen of the United States who establishes to the satisfaction of the Commissioner or his delegate that the individual has been a bona fide resident of a foreign country or countries for an uninterrupted period which includes an entire taxable year, or

(ii) A citizen or resident of the United States who has been physically present in a foreign country or countries for at least 330 full days during any period of twelve consecutive months.

(b) *Tax home.*—For purposes of paragraph (a)(1) of this section, the term "tax home" has the same meaning which it has for purposes of section 162 (a)(2) (relating to travel expenses away from home). Thus, under section 911, an individual's tax home is considered to be located at his regular or principal (if more than one regular) place of business or, if the individual has no regular or principal place of business because of the nature of the business, then at his regular place of abode in a real and substantial sense. An individual shall not, however, be considered to have a tax home in a foreign country for any period for which the individual's abode is in the United States. Temporary presence of the individual in the United States does not necessarily mean that the individual's abode is in the United States during that time. Maintenance of a dwelling in the United States by an individual, whether or not that dwelling is used by the individual's spouse and dependents, does not necessarily mean that the individual's abode is in the United States.

(c) *Determination of bona fide residence.*—For purposes of paragraph (a)(2)(i) of this section, whether an individual is a bona fide resident of a foreign country shall be determined by applying, to the extent practical, the principles of section 871 and the regulations thereunder, relating to the determination of the residence of aliens. Bona fide residence in a foreign country or countries for an uninterrupted period may be established, even if temporary visits are made during the period to the United States or elsewhere on vacation or business. An individual with earned income from sources within a foreign country is not a bona fide resident of that country if:

(1) The individual claims to be a nonresident of that foreign country in a statement submitted to the authorities of that country, and

(2) The earned income of the individual is not subject, by reason of nonresidency in the foreign country, to the income tax of that country.

If an individual has submitted a statement of nonresidence to the authorities of a foreign country the accuracy of which has not been resolved as of any date when a determination of the individual's bona fide residence is being made, then the individual will not be considered a bona fide resident of the foreign country as of that date.

(d) *Determination of physical presence.*—For purposes of paragraph (a)(2)(ii) of this section, the following rules apply.

(1) *Twelve-month test.*—A period of twelve consecutive months may begin with any day but must end on the day before the corresponding day in the twelfth succeeding month. The twelve month period may begin before or after arrival in a foreign country and may end before or after departure.

(2) *330-day test.*—The 330 full days need not be consecutive but may be interrupted by periods during which the individual is not present in a foreign country. In computing the minimum 330 full days of presence in a foreign country or countries, all separate periods of such presence during the period of twelve consecutive months are aggregated. A full day is a continuous period of twenty-four hours beginning with midnight and ending with the following midnight. An individual who has been present in a foreign country and then travels over areas not within any foreign country for less than twenty-four hours shall not be deemed outside a foreign country during the period of travel. If an individual who is in transit between two points outside the United States is physically present in the United States for less than twenty-four hours, such individual shall not be treated as present in the United States during such transit but shall be treated as travelling over areas not within any foreign country. For purposes of this paragraph (d)(2), the term "transit between two points outside the United States" has the same meaning that it has when used in section 7701(b)(6)(C).

(3) *Illustrations of the physical presence requirement.*—The physical presence requirement of paragraph (a)(2)(ii) of this section is illustrated by the following examples:

Example (1). B, a U.S. citizen, arrives in Venezuela from New York at 12 noon on April 24, 1982. B remains in Venezuela until 2 p.m. on March 21, 1983, at which time B departs for the United States. Among other possible twelve month periods, B is present in a foreign country an aggregate of 330 full days during each of the following twelve month periods: March 21, 1982 through March 20, 1983; and April 25, 1982 through April 24, 1983.

Example (2). C, a U.S. citizen, travels extensively from the time C leaves the United States on March 5, 1982, until the time C departs the United Kingdom on January 1, 1984, to return to the United States permanently. The schedule of C's travel and the number of full days at each location are listed below:

Country	Time and date of arrival	Time and date of departure	Full days in foreign country
United States		10 p.m. (by air) Mar. 5, 1982	
United Kingdom	9 a.m. Mar. 6, 1982	10 p.m. (by ship) June 25, 1982	110
United States	11 a.m. June 30, 1982	1 p.m. (by ship) July 19, 1982	0
France	3 p.m. July 24, 1982	11 a.m. (by air) Aug. 22, 1983	393
United States	4 p.m. Aug. 22, 1983	9 a.m. (by air) Sept. 4, 1983	0
United Kingdom	9 a.m. Sept. 5, 1983	9 a.m. (by air) Jan. 1, 1984	117
United States	1 p.m. Jan. 1, 1984		

Among other possible twelve month periods, C is present in a foreign country or countries an aggregate of 330 full days during the following twelve month periods: March 2, 1982 through March 1, 1983; and January 21, 1983 through January 20, 1984. The computation of days with respect to each twelve month period may be illustrated as follows:

First twelve month period (March 2, 1982 through March 1, 1983):

	Full days in foreign country
Mar. 2, 1982 through Mar. 6, 1982	0
Mar. 7, 1982 through June 24, 1982	110
June 25, 1982 through July 24, 1982	0
July 25, 1982 through Mar. 1, 1983	220
Total full days	330

Second twelve month period (January 21, 1983 through January 20, 1984):

	Full days in foreign country
Jan. 21, 1983 through Aug. 21, 1983	213
Aug. 22, 1983 through Sept. 5, 1983	0
Sept. 6, 1983 through Dec. 31, 1983	117
Jan. 1, 1984 through Jan. 20, 1984	0
Total full days	330

(e) *Special rules.*—For purposes only of establishing that an individual is a qualified individual under paragraph (a) of this section, residence or presence in a foreign country while there employed by the U.S. government or any agency or instrumentality of the U.S. government counts towards satisfaction of the requirements of §1.911-2(a). (But see section 911(b)(1)(B)(ii) and §1.911-3(c)(3) for the rule excluding amounts paid by the U.S. government to an employee from the definition of foreign earned income.) Time spent in a foreign country prior to January 1, 1982, counts toward satisfaction of the bona fide residence and physical presence requirements, even though no exclusion or deduction may be allowed under section 911 for income attributable to services performed during that time. For purposes of paragraph (a)(2)(ii) of this section, the term "resident of the United States" includes an individual for whom a valid election is in effect under section 6013(g) or (h) for the taxable year or years during which the physical presence requirement is satisfied.

(f) *Waiver of period of stay in foreign country due to war or civil unrest.*—Notwithstanding the requirements of paragraph (a) of this section, an individual whose tax home is in a foreign country, and who is a bona fide resident of, or present in, a foreign country for any period, who leaves the foreign country after August 31, 1978, before meeting the requirements of paragraph (a) of this section, may, as provided in this paragraph, qualify to make an election under section 911(a) and §1.911-7(a). If the Secretary determines, after consultation with the Secretary of State or his delegate, that war, civil unrest, or similar adverse conditions existed in a foreign country, then the Secretary shall publish the name of the foreign country and the dates between which such conditions were deemed to exist. In order to qualify to make an election under this paragraph, the individual must establish to the satisfaction of the Secretary that the individual left a foreign country, the name of which has been published by the Secretary, during the period when adverse conditions existed and that the individual could reasonably have expected to meet the requirements of paragraph (a) of this section but for the adverse conditions. The individual shall attach to his return for the taxable year a statement that the individual expected to meet the requirements of paragraph (a) of this section but for the conditions in the foreign country which precluded the normal conduct of business by the individual. Such individual shall be treated as a qualified individual, but only for the actual period of residence or presence. Thus, in determining the number of the individual's qualifying days, only days within the period of actual residence or presence shall be counted.

(g) *United States.*—The term "United States" when used in a geographical sense includes any territory under the sovereignty of the United States. It includes the states, the District of Columbia, the possessions and territories of the United States, the territorial waters of the United States, the air space over the United States, and the seabed and subsoil of those submarine areas which are adjacent to the territorial waters of the United States and over which the United States has exclusive rights, in accordance with international law, with respect to the exploration and exploitation of natural resources.

(h) *Foreign country.*—The term "foreign country" when used in a geographical sense includes any territory under the sovereignty of a government other than that of the United States. It includes the territorial waters of the foreign country (determined in accordance with the laws of the United States), the air space over the foreign country, and the seabed and subsoil of those submarine areas which are adjacent to the territorial waters of the foreign country and over which the foreign country has exclusive rights, in accordance with international law, with respect to the exploration and exploitation of natural resources. [Reg. § 1.911-2.]

☐ [*T.D.* 8006, 1-17-85.]

§ 1.911-3. **Determination of amount of foreign earned income to be excluded.**—(a) *Definition of foreign earned income.*—For purposes of section 911 and the regulations thereunder, the term "foreign earned income" means earned income (as defined in paragraph (b) of this section) from sources within a foreign country (as defined in § 1.911-2(h)) that is earned during a period for which the individual qualifies under § 1.911-2(a) to make an election. Earned income is from sources within a foreign country if it is attributable to services performed by an individual in a foreign country or countries. The place of receipt of earned income is immaterial in determining whether earned income is attributable to services performed in a foreign country or countries.

(b) *Definition of earned income.*—(1) *In general.*—The term "earned income" means wages, salaries, professional fees, and other amounts received as compensation for personal services actually rendered including the fair market value of all remuneration paid in any medium other than cash. Earned income does not include any portion of an amount paid by a corporation which represents a distribution of earnings and profits rather than a reasonable allowance as compensation for personal services actually rendered to the corporation.

(2) *Earned income from business in which capital is material.*—In the case of an individual engaged in a trade or business (other than in corporate form) in which both personal services and capital are material income producing factors, a reasonable allowance as compensation for the personal services actually rendered by the individual shall be considered earned income, but the total amount which shall be treated as the earned income of the individual from such trade or business shall in no case exceed thirty percent of the individual's share of the net profits of such trade or business.

(3) *Professional fees.*—Earned income includes all fees received by an individual engaged in a professional occupation (such as doctor or lawyer) in the performance of professional activities. Professional fees constitute earned income even though the individual employs assistants to perform part or all of the services, provided the patients or clients are those of the individual and look to the individual as the person responsible for the services rendered.

(c) *Amounts not included in foreign earned income.*—Foreign earned income does not include an amount:

(1) Excluded from gross income under section 119;

(2) Received as a pension or annuity (including social security benefits);

(3) Paid to an employee by an employer which is the U.S. government or any U.S. government agency or instrumentality;

(4) Included in the individual's gross income by reason of section 402(b) (relating to the taxability of a beneficiary of a nonexempt trust) or section 403(c) (relating to the taxability of a beneficiary under a nonqualified annuity or under annuities purchased by exempt organizations);

(5) Included in gross income by reason of § 1.911-6(b)(4)(ii); or

(6) Received after the close of the first taxable year following the taxable year in which the services giving rise to the amounts were performed. For treatment of amounts received

after December 31, 1962, which are attributable to services performed on or before December 31, 1962, and with respect to which there existed on March 12, 1962, a right (whether forfeitable or nonforfeitable) to receive such amounts, see § 1.72-8.

(d) *Determination of the amount of foreign earned income that may be excluded under section 911(a)(1).*—(1) *In general.*—Foreign earned income described in this section may be excluded under section 911(a)(1) and this paragraph only to the extent of the limitation specified in paragraph (d)(2) of this section. Income is considered to be earned in the taxable year in which the services giving rise to the income are performed. The determination of the amount of excluded earned income in this manner does not affect the time for reporting any amounts included in gross income.

(2) *Limitation.*—(i) *In general.*—The term "section 911(a)(1) limitation" means the amount of foreign earned income for a taxable year which may be excluded under section 911(a)(1). The section 911(a)(1) limitation shall be equal to the lesser of the qualified individual's foreign earned income for the taxable year in excess of amounts that the individual elected to exclude from gross income under section 911(a)(2) or the product of the annual rate for the taxable year (as specified in paragraph (d)(2)(ii) of this section) multiplied by the following fraction:

$$\frac{\text{The number of qualifying days in the taxable year}}{\text{The number of days in the taxable year}}$$

(ii) *Annual rate for the taxable year.*—The annual rate for the taxable year is the rate set forth in section 911(b)(2)(A).

(3) *Number of qualifying days.*—For purposes of section 911 and the regulations thereunder, the number of qualifying days is the number of days in the taxable year within the period during which the individual met the tax home requirement and either the bona fide residence requirement or the physical presence requirement of § 1.911-2(a). Although the period of bona fide residence must include an entire taxable year, the entire uninterrupted period of residence may include fractional parts of a taxable year. For instance, if an individual who was a calendar year taxpayer established a tax home and a residence in a foreign country as of November 1, 1982, and maintained the tax home and the residence through March 31, 1984, then the uninterrupted period of bona fide residence includes fractional parts of the years 1982 and 1984, and all of 1983. The number of qualifying days in 1982 is sixty-one. The number of qualifying days in 1983 is 365. The number of qualifying days in 1984 is ninety-one. The period during which the physical presence requirement of § 1.911-2(a)(2)(ii) is met is any twelve consecutive month period during which the individual is physically present in one or more foreign countries for 330 days and the individual's tax home is in a foreign country during each day of such physical presence. Such period may include days when the individual is not physically present in a foreign country, and days when the individual does not maintain a tax home in a foreign country. Such period may include fractional parts of a taxable year. Thus, if an individual's period of physical presence is the twelve-month period beginning June 1, 1982, and ending May 31, 1983, the number of qualifying days in 1982 is 214 and the number of qualifying days in 1983 is 151.

(e) *Attribution rules.*—(1) *In general.*—Foreign earned income is considered to be earned in the taxable year in which the individual performed the services giving rise to the income. If income is earned in one taxable year and received in another taxable year, then, for purposes of determining the amount of foreign earned income that the individual may exclude under section 911(a), the individual must attribute the income to the taxable year in which the services giving rise to the income were performed. Thus, any reimbursement would be attributable to the taxable year in which the services giving rise to the obligation to pay the reimbursement were performed, not the taxable year in which the reimbursement was received. For example, tax equalization payments are normally received in the year after the year in which the services giving rise to the obligation to pay the tax equalization payment were performed. Therefore, such payments will almost always have to be attributed to the prior year. Foreign earned income attributable to services performed in a preceding taxable year shall be excludable from gross income in the year of receipt only to the extent such amount could have been excluded under paragraph (d)(1) in the preceding taxable year, had such amount been received in the preceding taxable year. The taxable year to which income is attributable will be determined on the basis of all the facts and circumstances.

(2) *Priority of use of the section 911(a)(1) limitation.*—Foreign earned income received in the year in which it is earned shall be applied to the section 911(a)(1) limitation for that year before applying income earned in that year that is received in any other year. Foreign earned income that is earned in one year and received in another year shall be applied to the section 911(a)(1) limitation for the year in which it was earned, on a year by year basis, in any order

that the individual chooses. (But see section 911(b)(1)(B)(iv).) An individual may not amend his return to change the treatment of income with respect to the section 911(a)(1) exclusion after the period provided by section 6511(a). The special period of limitation provided by section 6511(d)(3) does not apply for this purpose. For example, C, a qualified individual, receives an advance bonus of $10,000 in 1982, salary of $70,000 in 1983, and a performance bonus of $10,000 in 1984, all of which are foreign earned income for 1983. C has a section 911(a)(1) limitation for 1983 of $80,000, and has no housing cost amount exclusion. On his income tax return for 1983, C elects to exclude foreign earned income of $70,000 received in 1983. C may also exclude his $10,000 advance bonus received in 1982 (by filing an amended return for 1982), or he may exclude the $10,000 performance bonus received in 1984 on his 1984 income tax return. However, C may not exclude part of the 1982 bonus and part of the 1984 bonus.

(3) *Exception for year-end payroll period.*—Notwithstanding paragraph (e)(1) of this section, salary or wage payments of a cash basis taxpayer shall be attributed entirely to the year of receipt under the following circumstances:

(i) The period for which the payment is made is a normal payroll period of the employer which regularly applies to the employee;

(ii) The payroll period includes the last day of the employee's taxable year;

(iii) The payroll period does not exceed 16 days; and

(iv) The payment is part of a normal payroll of the employer that is distributed at the same time, in relation to the payroll period, that such payroll would normally be distributed, and is distributed before the end of the next succeeding payroll period.

(4) *Attribution of bonuses and substantially nonvested property to periods in which services were performed.*—(i) *In general.*—Bonuses and substantially nonvested property are attributable to all of the services giving rise to the income on the basis of all the facts and circumstances. If an individual receives a bonus or substantially nonvested property (as defined in §1.83-3(b)) and it is determined to be attributable to services performed in more than one taxable year, then, for purposes of determining the amount eligible for exclusion from gross income in the year the bonus is received or the property vests, a portion of such amount shall be treated as attributable to services performed in each taxable year (or portion thereof) during the period when services giving rise to the bonus or the substantially nonvested property were performed. Such portion shall be determined by dividing the amount of the bonus or the excess of the fair market value of the vested property over the amount paid, if any, for the vested property, by the number of months in the period when services giving rise to such amount were performed, and multiplying the quotient by the number of months in such period in the taxable year. For purposes of this section, the term "month" means a calendar month. A fraction of a calendar month shall be deemed a month if it includes fifteen or more days.

(ii) *Examples.*—The following examples illustrate the application of this paragraph (e)(4).

Example (1). A, an employee of M Corporation during all of 1983 and 1984, worked in the United States from January 1 through April 30, 1983, and received $12,000 of salary for that period. A worked in country F from May 1, 1983 through the end of 1984, and is a qualified individual under §1.911-2(a) for that period. For the period from May 1 through December 31, 1983, A received $32,000 of salary. M pays a bonus on December 20, 1983 to each of M's employees in an amount equal to 10 percent of the employee's regular wages or salary for the 1983 calendar year. The amount of A's bonus is $4,400 for 1983. The portion of A's bonus that is attributable to services performed in country F and is foreign earned income for 1983 is $3,200, or $32,000 × 10 percent. The remaining $1,200 of A's bonus is attributable to services performed in the United States, and is not foreign earned income.

Example (2). The facts are the same as in example (1), except that M determines bonuses separately for each country based on the productivity of the employees in that country. M pays a bonus to employees in country F, in the amount of 15 percent of each employee's wages or salary earned in country F. A's country F bonus is $4,800 for 1983 ($32,000 × 15 percent), and is foreign earned income for 1983. If A also receives a bonus (or if A's bonus is increased) for working in the United States during 1983, that amount is not foreign earned income.

Example (3). X corporation offers its employees a bonus of $40,000 if the employee accepts employment in a foreign country and remains in a foreign country for a period of at least four years. A, an employee of X, is a calendar year and cash basis taxpayer. A accepts employment with X in foreign country F. A begins work in F on July 1, 1983 and continues to work in F for X until June 30, 1987. In 1987 X pays A a $40,000 bonus. The bonus is attributable to services A performed from July 1, 1983 through June 30, 1987. The amount of the bonus attributable to 1987 is $5,000

(($40,000 ÷ 48) × 6). The amount of the bonus attributable to 1986 is $10,000 (($40,000 ÷ 48) × 12). A may exclude the $10,000 attributable to 1986 only to the extent that amount could have been excluded under section 911(a)(1) had A received it in 1986. The remaining $25,000 is attributable to services performed in taxable years before 1986. Such amounts may not be excluded under section 911 because they are received after the close of the taxable year following the taxable year in which the services giving rise to the income were performed.

(iii) *Special rule for elections under section 83(b).*—If an individual receives substantially nonvested property and makes an election under section 83(b) and § 1.83-2(a) to include in his gross income the amount determined under section 83(b)(1)(A) and (B) and § 1.83-2(a) for the taxable year in which the property is transferred (as defined in § 1.83-3(a)), then, for the purpose of determining the amount eligible for exclusion in the year of receipt, the individual may elect either of the following options:

(A) Substantially nonvested property may be treated as attributable entirely to services performed in the taxable year in which an election to include it in income is made. If so treated, then the amount otherwise included in gross income as determined under § 1.83-2(a) will be excludable under section 911(a) for such year subject to the limitation provided in § 1.911-3(d)(2) for such year.

(B) A portion of the substantially nonvested property may be treated as attributable to services performed or to be performed in each taxable year during which the substantial risk of forfeiture (as defined in section 83(c) and § 1.83-3(c)) exists. The portion treated as attributable to services performed or to be performed in each taxable year is determined by dividing the amount of the substantially nonvested property included in gross income as determined under § 1.83-2(a) by the number of months during the period when a substantial risk of forfeiture exists. The quotient is multiplied by the total number of months in the taxable year during which a substantial risk of forfeiture exists. The amount determined to be attributable to services performed in the year the election is made shall be excluded from gross income for such year as provided in paragraph (d)(2) of this section. Amounts treated as attributable to services performed in subsequent taxable years shall be excludable in the year of receipt only to the extent such amounts could be excluded under paragraph (d)(2) of this section in such subsequent year. An individual may obtain such additional exclusion by filing an amended return for the taxable year in which the property was transferred. The individual may only amend his or her return within the period provided by section 6511(a) and the regulations thereunder.

(5) *Moving expense reimbursements.*—(i) *Source of reimbursements.*—For the purpose of determining whether a moving expense reimbursement is attributable to services performed within a foreign country or within the United States, in the absence of evidence to the contrary, the reimbursement shall be attributable to future services to be performed at the new principal place of work. Thus, a reimbursement received by an employee from his employer for the expenses of a move to a foreign country will generally be attributable to services performed in the foreign country. A reimbursement received by an employee from his employer for the expenses of a move from a foreign country to the United States will generally be attributable to services performed in the United States. For purposes of this paragraph (e)(5), evidence to the contrary includes, but is not limited to, an agreement, between the employer and the employee, or a statement of company policy, which is reduced to writing before the move to the foreign country and which is entered into or established to induce the employee or employees to move to a foreign country. The writing must state that the employer will reimburse the employee for moving expenses incurred in returning to the United States regardless of whether the employee continues to work for the employer after the employee returns to the United States. The writing may contain conditions upon which the right to reimbursement is determined as long as the conditions set forth standards that are definitely ascertainable and the conditions can only be fulfilled prior to, or through completion of, the employee's return move to the United States that is the subject of the writing. In no case will an oral agreement or statement of company policy concerning moving expenses be considered evidence to the contrary. For the purpose of determining whether a storage expense reimbursement is attributable to services performed within a foreign country, in the case of storage expenses incurred after December 31, 1983, the reimbursement shall be attributable to services performed during the period of time for which the storage expenses are incurred.

(ii) *Attribution of foreign source reimbursements to taxable years in which services are performed.*—(A) *In general.*—If a reimbursement for moving expenses is determined to be from foreign sources under paragraph (e)(5)(i) of this section, then for the purpose of determining the amount eligible for exclusion in accordance with paragraphs (d)(2) and (e)(2) of this section, the reimbursement shall be considered attributable to services performed in the year of the move as long as the individual is a qualified individual for a period that includes 120 days in the year of the move. The period that is used in determining the number of qualifying days for purposes of the individual's section 911(a)(1) limitation (under paragraph (d)(2) of this section) must also be used in determining whether the individual is a qualified individual for a period that includes 120 days in the year of the move. If the individual is not a qualified individual for such period, then the individual shall treat a portion of the reimbursement as attributable to services performed in the year of the move, and a portion as attributable to services performed in the succeeding taxable year, if the move is from the United States to a foreign country, or to the prior taxable year, if the move is from a foreign country to the United States. The portion of the reimbursement treated as attributable to services performed in the year of the move shall be determined by multiplying the total reimbursement by the following fraction:

$$\frac{\text{The number of qualifying days (as defined in paragraph (d)(3) of this section) in the year of the move}}{\text{The number of days in the taxable year of the move.}}$$

The remaining portion of the reimbursement shall be treated as attributable to services performed in the year succeeding or preceding the year of the move. Amounts treated as attributable to services performed in a year succeeding or preceding the year of the move shall be excludable in the year of receipt only to the extent such amounts could be excluded under paragraph (d)(2) of this section in such succeeding or preceding year.

(B) *Moves beginning before January 1, 1984.*—Notwithstanding paragraph (e)(5)(ii)(A) of this section, this paragraph (e)(5)(ii)(B) shall apply for moves begun before January 1, 1984. If a reimbursement for moving expenses is determined to be from foreign sources under paragraph (e)(5)(i) of this section, then for the purpose of determining the amount eligible for exclusion in accordance with paragraphs (d)(2) and (e)(2) of this section, the reimbursement shall be considered attributable to services performed in the year of the move. However, if the individual does not qualify under section 911(d)(1) and § 1.911-2(a) for the entire taxable year of the move, then the individual shall treat a portion of the reimbursement as attributable to services performed in the succeeding taxable year, if the move is from the United States to a foreign country, or to the prior taxable year, if the move is from a foreign country to the United States. The portion of the reimbursement treated as attributable to services performed in the year succeeding or preceding the move shall be determined by multiplying the total reimbursement by the following fraction:

$$\frac{\text{The number of qualifying days (as defined in paragraph (d)(3) of this section) in the year of the move}}{\text{The number of days in the taxable year of the move.}}$$

and subtracting the product from the total reimbursement. Amounts treated as attributable to services performed in a year succeeding or preceding the year of the move shall be excludable in the year of receipt only to the extent such amounts could be excluded under paragraph (d)(2) of this section in such succeeding or preceding year.

(f) *Examples.*—The following examples illustrate the application of this section.

Example (1). A is a U.S. citizen and calendar year taxpayer. A's tax home was in foreign country F and A was physically present in F for 330 days during the period from July 4, 1982 through July 3, 1983. The number of A's qualifying days in 1982 as determined under paragraph (d)(2) of this section is 181. In 1982 A receives $40,000 attributable to services performed in foreign country F in 1982. Under paragraph (d)(2) of this section A's section 911(a)(1) limitation is $37,192, that is the lesser of $40,000 (foreign earned income) or

$$\$75,000 \text{ (annual rate)} \times \frac{181 \text{ (qualifying days)}}{365 \text{ (days in taxable year)}}.$$

Example (2). The facts are the same as in example (1) except that in 1982 A receives $30,000 attributable to services performed in foreign country F. A excludes this amount from gross income under paragraph (d) of this section. In addition, in 1983 A receives $10,000 attributable to services performed in F in 1982 and $35,000 attributable to services performed in F in 1983. On his return for 1983, A must report $45,000 of income. A's section 911(a)(1) limitation for 1983 is the lesser of $35,000 (foreign earned income) or $40,329, the annual rate for the taxable year multiplied by a fraction the numerator of which is A's qualifying days in the taxable year and the denominator of which is the number of days in the taxable year

($80,000 × 184/365). On his tax return for 1983 A may exclude $35,000 attributable to services performed in 1983. A may only exclude $7,192 of the $10,000 received in 1983 attributable to services performed in 1982 because such amount is only excludable in 1983 to the extent such amount could have been excluded in 1982 subject to the section 911(a)(1) limitation for 1982 which is $37,192 ($75,000 × 181/365). No portion of amounts attributable to services performed in 1982 may be used in calculating A's section 911(a)(1) limitation for 1983. Thus, even though A could have excluded an additional $6,329 in 1983 if A had had more foreign earned income attributable to 1983, A may not exclude the $2,808 of remaining foreign earned income attributable to 1982.

Example (3). C is a U.S. citizen and calendar year taxpayer. C establishes a bona fide residence and a tax home in foreign country J on March 1, 1982, and maintains a tax home and a residence in J until December 31, 1986. In March of 1982 C's employer, Y corporation, transfers stock in Y to C. The stock is subject to forfeiture if C returns to the U.S. before January 1, 1985. C elects under section 83(b) to include $15,000, the amount determined with respect to such stock under section 83(b)(1), in gross income in 1982. C's other foreign earned income in 1982 is $58,000. C elects under paragraph (e)(4)(iii)(B) of this section to treat the stock as if earned over the period of the substantial risk of forfeiture. The number of months in the period of the substantial risk of forfeiture is thirty-four. The number of months in the taxable year 1982 within the period of foreign employment is ten. For purposes of determining C's section 911(a)(1) limitation, $4,412 (($15,000/34) × 10) of the amount included in gross income under section 83(b) is treated as attributable to services performed in 1982, $5,294 is treated as attributable to services to be performed in 1983, and $5,294 is treated as attributable to services to be performed in 1984. In 1982, C excludes $62,412 under section 911(a)(1). That is the lesser of foreign earned income for 1982 ($56,000 + $4,412) or the annual rate for the taxable year multiplied by a fraction the numerator of which is C's qualifying days in the taxable year and the denominator of which is the number of days in the taxable year ($75,000 × 306/365). C continues to perform services in foreign country J throughout 1983 and 1984. C would be able to exclude the remaining $5,294 attributable to services performed in 1983 and $5,294 attributable to services performed in 1984 if those amounts would be excludable if they had been received in 1983 or 1984 respectively. If C is entitled to exclude the additional amounts, C must claim the exclusion by filing an amended return for 1982.

Example (4). D is a U.S. citizen and calendar year taxpayer. In September, 1984 D moves to foreign country K. D is physically present in K, and D's tax home is in K, from September 15, 1984 through December 31, 1985. D receives $6,000 in April, 1985 from his employer, as a reimbursement for expenses of moving to K, pursuant to a written agreement that such moving expenses would be reimbursed to D upon successful completion of 6 months employment in K. Under paragraph (e)(5)(i) of this section, the reimbursement is attributable to services performed in K. Under the physical presence test of § 1.911-2(a)(2)(ii), among other periods D is a qualified individual for the period of August 10, 1984 through August 9, 1985, which includes 144 days in 1984. Under paragraph (e)(5)(ii)(A) of this section, for the purpose of determining the amount eligible for exclusion, the reimbursement is considered attributable to services performed in 1984 (the year of the move) because D is a qualified individual under § 1.911-2(a) for a period that includes 120 days in 1984. The reimbursement may be excluded under paragraphs (d)(2) and (c)(2) of this section, to the extent that D's foreign earned income for 1984 that was earned and received in 1984 was less than the annual rate for the taxable year multiplied by the number of D's qualifying days in the taxable year over the number of days in D's taxable year ($80,000 × 144/366), or $31,475.

Example (5). The facts are the same as in example (4) except that D is not a qualified individual under the physical presence test, but is a qualified individual under the bona fide residence test for the period of September 15, 1984 through December 31, 1985. Under paragraph (e)(5)(ii)(A) of this section, for the purpose of determining the amount eligible for exclusion, the reimbursement is considered attributable to services performed in 1984 and 1985 because D is not a qualified individual for a period that includes 120 days in 1984 (the year of the move). The portion of the reimbursement treated as attributable to services performed in 1984 is $6,000 × 108/366, or $1,770, and may be excluded, subject to D's 1984 section 911(a)(1) limitation. The balance of the reimbursement, $4,230, is treated as attributable to services performed in 1985, and may be excluded to the extent provided in paragraphs (d)(2) and (e)(2) of this section.

Example (6). The facts are the same as in Example (4), with the following additions. Before D moved to K, D and his employer signed a written agreement that D would perform services for the employer for at least one year, primarily in country K, and, if D did not voluntarily cease to work for the employer primarily in country K before one year had elapsed, the employer would reimburse D for

Reg. § 1.911-3(f)

one-half of D's expenses, up to a maximum of $4,000, of moving back to the United States. The agreement also stated that, if D did not voluntarily leave the employment in K before two years had elapsed, the employer would reimburse D for all of D's reasonable expenses of moving back to the United States. The agreement further stated that D's right to reimbursement would not be conditioned upon the performance of services after D ceased to work in K. D worked in country K for all of 1985. On January 1, 1986, D left K and moved to the United States. In February, 1986 the employer paid D $3,500 as reimbursement for one-half of D's expenses of moving to the United States. Although D did not fulfill the condition in the agreement to receive full reimbursement, all of the conditions in the agreement set forth definitely ascertainable standards and no condition could be fulfilled after D moved back to the United States. The agreement fulfills the requirements of paragraph (e)(5)(i) of this section, and therefore is evidence that the reimbursement should not be attributable to future services to be performed at D's new principal place of work. Under the facts and circumstances, the reimbursement is attributable to services performed in K. Under paragraph (e)(5)(ii)(A) of this section, the entire reimbursement is attributable to services performed in 1985. The amount attributable in 1985 may be excluded to the extent provided in paragraphs (d)(2) and (e)(2) of this section. [Reg. § 1.911-3.]

☐ [*T.D.* 8006, 1-17-85.]

§ 1.911-4. Determination of housing cost amount eligible for exclusion or deduction.—(a) *Definition of housing cost amount.*—The term "housing cost amount" means an amount equal to the reasonable expenses paid or incurred (as defined in section 7701(a)(25)) during the taxable year by or on behalf of the individual attributable to housing in a foreign country for the individual and any spouse or dependents who reside with the individual (or live in a second foreign household described in paragraph (b)(5) of this section) less the base housing amount as defined in paragraph (c) of this section. The housing cost amount must be reduced by the amount of any military or section 912 allowance or similar allowance excludable from gross income that is intended to compensate the individual or the individual's spouse in whole or in part for the expenses of housing during the same period for which the individual claims a housing cost amount exclusion or deduction.

(b) *Housing expenses.*—(1) *Included expenses.*—For purposes of paragraph (a) of this section, housing expenses include rent, the fair rental value of housing provided in kind by the employer, utilities (other than telephone charges), real and personal property insurance, occupancy taxes not described in paragraph (b)(2)(v) of this section, nonrefundable fees paid for securing a leasehold, rental of furniture and accessories, household repairs, and residential parking.

(2) *Excluded expenses.*—Housing expenses do not include:

(i) The cost of house purchase, improvements, and other costs that are capital expenditures;

(ii) The cost of purchased furniture or accessories or domestic labor (maids, gardeners, etc.);

(iii) Amortized payments of principal with respect to an evidence of indebtedness secured by a mortgage on the taxpayers housing;

(iv) Depreciation of housing owned by the taxpayer, or amortization or depreciation of capital improvements made to housing leased by the taxpayer;

(v) Interest and taxes deductible under section 163 or 164 or other amounts deductible under section 216(a) (relating to deduction of interest and taxes by cooperative housing corporation tenant);

(vi) The expenses of more than one foreign household except as provided in paragraph (b)(5) of this section;

(vii) Expenses excluded from gross income under section 119;

(viii) Expenses claimed as deductible moving expenses under section 217; or

(ix) The cost of a pay television subscription.

(3) *Limitation.*—Housing expenses are taken into account for purposes of this section only to the extent attributable to housing for portions of the taxable year within the period during which the individual satisfies the requirements of § 1.911-2(a). Housing expenses are not taken into account for the period during which the value of the individual's housing is excluded from gross income under section 119, unless the individual maintains a second foreign household described in paragraph (b)(5) of this section. If an individual maintains two foreign households, only expenses incurred with respect to the abode which bears the closest relationship, not necessarily geographic, with respect to the individual's tax home shall be taken into account, unless one of the households is a second foreign household.

(4) *Reasonableness.*—An amount paid for housing shall not be treated as reasonable, for purposes of paragraph (a) of this section, to the

extent that the expense is lavish or extravagant under the circumstances.

(5) *Expenses of a second foreign household.*—(i) *In general.*—The term "second foreign household" means a separate abode maintained by an individual outside of the U.S. for his or her spouse or dependents (who, if minors, are in the individual's legal custody or the joint custody of the individual and the individual's spouse) at a place other than the tax home of the individual because of adverse living conditions at the individual's tax home. If an individual maintains a second foreign household the expenses of the second foreign household may be included in the individual's housing expenses under paragraph (b)(1) of this section. Under no circumstances shall an individual be considered to maintain more than one second foreign household at the same time.

(ii) *Adverse living conditions.*—Solely for purposes of paragraph (b)(5)(i) of this section, adverse living conditions are living conditions which are dangerous, unhealthful, or otherwise adverse. Adverse living conditions include a state of warfare or civil insurrection in the general area of the individual's tax home. Adverse living conditions exist if the individual resides on the business premises of the employer for the convenience of the employer and, because of the nature of the business (for example, a construction site or drilling rig), it is not feasible for the employer to provide housing for the individual's spouse or dependents. The criteria used by the Department of State in granting a separate maintenance allowance are relevant, but not determinative, for purposes of determining whether a separate household is provided because of adverse living conditions.

(c) *Base housing amount.*—(1) *In general.*—The base housing amount is equal to the product of 16 percent of the annual salary of an employee of the United States who is compensated at a rate equal to the annual salary rate paid for step 1 of grade GS-14, multiplied by the following fraction:

$$\frac{\text{The number of qualifying days}}{\text{The number of days in the taxable year}}$$

For purposes of the above fraction, the number of qualifying days is determined in accordance with § 1.911-3(d)(3).

(2) *Annual salary of step 1 of grade GS-14.*—The annual salary rate for a step 1 of grade GS-14 is determined on January first of the calendar year in which the individual's taxable year begins.

(d) *Housing costs amount exclusion.*—(1) *Limitation.*—A qualified individual who has elected to exclude his or her housing cost amount may only exclude the lesser of the full amount of either the individual's housing cost amount attributable to employer provided amounts or the individual's foreign earned income for the taxable year. A qualified individual who elects to exclude his or her housing cost amount may not claim less than the full amount of the housing cost exclusion determined under this paragraph.

(2) *Employer provided amounts.*—For purposes of this section, the term "employer provided amounts" means any amounts paid or incurred on behalf of the individual by the individual's employer which are foreign earned income included in the individual's gross income for the taxable year (without regard to section 911). Employer provided amounts include, but are not limited to, the following amounts: any salary paid by the employer to the employee; any reimbursement paid by the employer to the employee for housing expenses, educational expenses for the individual's dependents, or as part of a tax equalization plan; the fair market value of compensation provided in kind (including lodging, unless excluded under section 119, relating to meals and lodging furnished for the convenience of the employer); and any amount paid by the employer to any third party on behalf of the employee. An individual will only have earnings that are not employer provided amounts if the individual has earnings from self-employment.

(3) *Housing cost amount attributable to employer provided amounts.*—For the purpose of determining what portion of the housing cost amount is excludable and what portion is deductible the following rules apply. If the individual has no income from self-employment, then the entire housing cost amount is attributable to employer provided amounts and is, therefore, excludable to the extent of the limitation provided in paragraph (d)(1) of this section. If the individual only has income from self-employment, then the entire housing cost amount is attributable to non-employer provided amounts and is, therefore, deductible to the extent of the limitation provided in paragraph (e) of this section. In all other instances, the housing cost amount attributable to employer provided amounts shall be determined by multiplying the housing cost amount by the following fraction: employer provided amounts over foreign earned income for the taxable year. The housing cost amount attributable to non-employer provided amounts shall be determined by subtracting the portion of the housing cost amount attributable to employer

provided amounts from the total housing cost amount.

(e) *Housing cost amount deduction.*—(1) *In general.*—If a portion of the individual's housing cost amount is determined under paragraph (d)(3) of this section to be attributable to non-employer provided amounts, the individual may deduct that amount from gross income for the taxable year but only to the extent of the individual's foreign earned income (as defined in § 1.911-3) for the taxable year in excess of foreign earned income excluded and the housing cost amount excluded from gross income for the taxable year under § 1.911-3 and this section.

(2) *Carryover.*—If any portion of the individual's housing cost amount deduction is disallowed for the taxable year under paragraph (e)(1) of this section, such portion shall be carried over and treated as a deduction from gross income for the succeeding taxable year (but only for the succeeding taxable year) to the extent of the excess, if any, of:

(i) The amount of foreign earned income for the succeeding taxable year less the foreign earned income and the housing cost amount excluded from gross income under § 1.911-3 and this section for the succeeding taxable year over,

(ii) The portion, if any, of the housing cost amount that is deductible under paragraph (e)(1) of this section for the succeeding taxable year.

(f) *Examples.*—The following examples illustrate the application of this section. In all examples the annual rate for a step 1 of GS-14 as of January first of the calendar year in which the individual's taxable year begins is $39,689.

Example (1). B, a U.S. citizen, is a calendar year taxpayer who was a bona fide resident of and whose tax home was located in foreign country G for the entire taxable year 1982. B receives an $80,000 salary from B's employer for services performed in G. B incurs no business expenses. B receives housing provided by B's employer with a fair rental value of $15,000. The value of the housing furnished by B's employer is not excluded from gross income under section 119. B pays $10,000 for housing expenses. B's gross income and foreign earned income for 1982 is $95,000. B elects the foreign earned income exclusion of section 911(a)(1) and the housing cost amount exclusion of section 911(a)(2). B must first compute his housing cost amount exclusion. B's housing cost amount is $18,650 determined by reducing B's housing expenses, $25,000 ($15,000 fair rental value of housing and $10,000 of other expenses), by the base housing amount of $6,350 (($39,689 × .16) × 365/365). Because B has no income from self-employment, the entire amount is attributable to employer provided amounts and, therefore, is excludable. B's section 911(a)(1) limitation is over $75,000. That is the lesser of $75,000 × 365/365 or $95,000 - 18,650. B's total exclusion for 1982 under section 911(a)(1) and (2) is $93,650.

Example (2). The facts are the same as in example (1) except that B's salary for 1982 is $70,000. B's foreign earned income for 1982 is $85,000. B's housing cost amount is $18,650, all of which is attributable to employer provided amounts. B's housing cost amount is excludable to the extent of the lesser of B's housing cost amount attributable to employer provided amounts, $18,650, or the foreign earned income for the taxable year, $85,000. Thus, B excludes $18,650 under section 911(a)(2). B's section 911(a)(1) limitation for 1982 is $66,350 (the lesser of $75,000 × 365/365 or $85,000 - 18,650). B's total exclusion for 1982 under section 911(a)(1) and (2) is $85,000.

Example (3). The facts are the same as in example (2) except that in 1983, B receives $5,000 attributable to services performed in 1982. B may exclude the entire $5,000 in 1983 because such amount would have been excludable under § 1.911-3(d)(1) had it been received in 1982.

Example (4). C is a U.S. citizen, self-employed, and a calendar year and cash basis taxpayer. C arrived in foreign country H on October 3, 1982, and departed from H on March 8, 1984. C's tax home was located in H throughout that period. C was physically present for 330 full days during the twelve consecutive month period August 30, 1982 through August 29, 1983. The number of C's qualifying days in 1982 is 124. During 1982 C had $35,000 of foreign earned income, none of which was attributable to employer provided amounts, and $8,000 of reasonable housing expenses. C's housing cost amount is $5,843 ($8,000 - ((39,689 × .16) × 124/365)). C elects to exclude her foreign earned income under § 1.911-3(d)(1). C's section 911(a)(1) limitation for 1982 is $25,479 (the lesser of C's foreign earned income for the taxable year ($35,000) or the annual rate for the taxable year multiplied by the number of C's qualifying days over the number of days in the taxable year ($75,000 × 124/365 = $25,479)). C may not claim the housing cost amount exclusion under section 911(a)(2) because no portion of the housing cost amount is attributable to employer provided amounts. C may deduct the lesser of her housing cost amount ($5,843) or her foreign earned income in excess of amounts excluded under section 911(a) ($35,000 - 25,479 = $9,521). Thus, C's housing cost amount deduction is $5,843.

Reg. § 1.911-4(f)

Example (5). The facts are the same as in example (4) except that C had $30,000 of foreign earned income for 1982, none of which was attributable to employer provided amounts. C elects to exclude $25,479 under § 1.911-3(d)(1). C may only deduct $4,521 of her housing cost amount under paragraph (e)(1) of this section because her foreign earned income in excess of amounts excluded under section 911(a) is $4,521 ($30,000 − 25,479). The $1322 of unused housing cost amount deduction may be carried over to the subsequent taxable year.

Example (6). The facts are the same as in example (4) except that C had $15,000 of foreign earned income for 1982, none of which was attributable to employer provided amounts. C elects to exclude the entire $15,000 under § 1.911-3(d)(1). C is not entitled to a housing cost amount deduction for 1982 since she has no foreign earned income in excess of amounts excluded under section 911(a). C may carryover her entire housing cost amount deduction to 1983.

Example (7). The facts are the same as in example (6). In addition, during taxable year 1983 C had $115,000 of foreign earned income, none of which was attributable to employer provided amounts, and $40,000 of reasonable housing expenses. C elects to exclude her foreign earned income under § 1.911-3(d)(1). C's section 911(a)(1) limitation is the lesser of $115,000 or $80,000 ($80,000 × 365/365). C's housing cost amount for 1983 is $33,650 (40,000 − ($39,689 × .16) × 365/365). Since no portion of that amount is attributable to employer provided amounts, C may not claim a housing cost amount exclusion. C may deduct the lesser of her housing cost amount ($33,650) or her foreign earned income in excess of amounts excluded under section 911(a) ($115,000 − 80,000 = 35,000). Thus, C may deduct her $33,650 housing cost amount in 1983. In addition, C may deduct $1,350 of the housing cost amount deduction carried over from taxable year 1982 (($115,000 − 80,000) − 33,650 =$1,350). The remaining $4,493 ($5,843 − 1,350) of the housing cost amount deduction carried over from taxable year 1982 may not be deducted in 1983 or carried over to 1984.

Example (8). D is a U.S. citizen and a calendar year and cash basis taxpayer. D is a bona fide resident of and maintains his tax home in foreign country J for all of taxable year 1984. In 1984, D earns $80,000 of foreign earned income, $60,000 of which is an employer provided amount and $20,000 of which is a non-employer provided amount. D's total housing cost amount for 1984 is $25,000. D elects to exclude, under section 911(a)(2), the portion of his housing cost amount that is attributable to employer provided amounts. D's excludable housing cost amount is $18,750; that is the total housing cost amount ($25,000) multiplied by employer provided amounts for the taxable year ($60,000) over foreign earned income for the taxable year ($80,000). D also elects to exclude his foreign earned income under § 1.911-3(d)(1). D's section 911(a)(1) limitation for 1984 is $61,250 (the lesser of $80,000 − $18,750 or $80,000 × 366/366). D's total exclusion for 1984 under section 911(a)(1) and (2) is $80,000. D cannot claim a housing cost amount deduction in 1984 because D has no foreign earned income in excess of his foreign earned income and housing cost amount excluded from gross income for the taxable year under § 1.911-3 and this section. D may carry over his housing cost amount deduction of $6,250, the total housing cost amount less the portion attributable to employer provided amounts ($25,000 − 18,750), to taxable year 1985. [Reg. § 1.911-4.]

☐ [*T.D.* 8006, 1-17-85.]

§ 1.911-5. Special rules for married couples.—(a) *Married couples with two qualified individuals.*—(1) *In general.*—In the case in which a husband and wife both are qualified individuals under § 1.911-2(a), each individual may make one or more elections under § 1.911-7 and exclude from gross income foreign earned income and exclude or deduct housing cost amounts subject to the rules of paragraph (a)(2) and (3) of this section.

(2) *Computation of excluded foreign earned income.*—The amount of excludable foreign earned income is determined separately for each spouse under the rules of § 1.911-3 on the basis of the income attributable to the services of that spouse. If the spouses file separate returns each may exclude the amount of his or her foreign earned income attributable to his or her services subject to the limitations of § 1.911-3(d)(2). If the spouses file a joint return, the sum of these foreign earned income amounts so determined for each spouse may be excluded. For example, H and W both qualify under § 1.911-2(a)(2)(i) for the entire 1983 taxable year. During 1983 W earns $100,000 of foreign earned income and H earns $45,000 of foreign earned income. H and W file a joint return for 1983. On their joint return H and W may exclude from gross income a total of $125,000. That amount is determined by adding W's section 911(a)(1) limitation, $80,000 (the lesser of $80,000 × 365/365 or $100,000), and H's section 911(a)(1) limitation, $45,000 (the lesser of $80,000 × 365/365 or $45,000).

(3) *Computation of housing cost amount.*—(i) *Spouses residing together.*—If the spouses reside together, and file a joint return, they may compute their housing cost amount either

jointly or separately. If the spouses reside together and file separate returns, they must compute their housing cost amounts separately. If the spouses compute their housing cost amounts separately, they may allocate the housing expenses to either of them or between them for the purpose of calculating separate housing cost amounts, but each spouse claiming a housing cost amount exclusion or deduction must use his or her full base housing amount in such computation. If the spouses compute their housing cost amount jointly, then only one of the spouses may claim the housing cost amount exclusion or deduction. Either spouse may claim the housing cost amount exclusion or deduction; however, if the spouses have different periods of residence or presence and the spouse with the shorter period of residence or presence claims the exclusion or deduction, then only the expenses incurred in that shorter period may be claimed as housing expenses. The spouse claiming the exclusion or deduction may aggregate the couple's housing expenses, and subtract his or her base housing amount. For example, H and W reside together and file a joint return. H was a bona fide resident of and maintained his tax home in foreign country M from August 17, 1982 through December 31, 1983. W was a bona fide resident of and maintained her tax home in foreign country M from September 15, 1982 through December 31, 1983. During 1982, H and W earn and receive, respectively, $25,000 and $10,000 of foreign earned income. H paid $10,000 for qualified housing expenses in 1982, $7,500 of that was for qualified housing expenses incurred from September 15, 1982 through December 31, 1982. W paid $3,000 for qualified housing expenses in 1982 all of which were incurred during her period of residence. H and W may choose to compute their housing cost amount jointly. If they do so and H claims the housing cost amount exclusion his exclusion would be $10,617. H's housing expenses would be $13,000 ($10,000 + $3,000) and his base housing amount would be $2,383 (($39,689 × .16) × 137/365 = $2,383). If instead W claims the housing cost amount exclusion her exclusion would be $8,621. W's housing expenses would be $10,500 ($7,500 + 3,000) and her base housing amount would be $1,879 (($39,689 × .16) × 108/365 = $1,879). If H and W file jointly and both claim a housing cost amount exclusion, then H's and W's housing cost amounts would be, respectively, $7,617 ($10,000 − 2,383) and $1,121 ($3,000 − 1,879).

(ii) *Spouses residing apart.*—If the spouses reside apart, both spouses may exclude or deduct their housing cost amount if the spouses have different tax homes that are not within reasonable commuting distance (as defined in § 1.119-(d)(4)) of each other and neither spouse's residence is within a reasonable commuting distance of the other spouse's tax home. If the spouses' tax homes, or one spouse's residence and the other spouse's tax home, are within a reasonable commuting distance of each other, only one spouse may exclude or deduct his or her housing cost amount. Regardless of whether the spouses file joint or separate returns, the amount of the housing cost amount exclusion or deduction must be determined separately for each spouse under the rules of § 1.911-4. If both spouses claim a housing cost amount exclusion or deduction directly as qualified individuals, neither may claim any such exclusion or deduction under section 911(c)(2)(B)(ii), relating to a second foreign household maintained for the other spouse. If one spouse fails to claim a housing cost amount exclusion or deduction which that spouse could claim directly, the other spouse may claim such exclusion or deduction under section 911(c)(2)(B)(ii), relating to a second foreign household maintained for the first spouse, provided that all the requirements of that section are met. Spouses may not claim more than one second foreign household and the expenses of such household may only be claimed by one spouse. For example, if both H and W are qualified individuals and H's tax home is in London and W's tax home is in Paris, then both H and W may exclude or deduct their housing cost amounts; however, H and W must compute these amounts separately regardless of whether they file joint or separate returns. If instead of living in Paris, W lives in an area where there are adverse living conditions and W maintains H's home in London, then W may add those housing expenses to her housing expenses and compute one base housing amount. In that case H may not claim a housing cost amount exclusion or deduction.

(iii) *Housing cost amount attributable to employer provided amounts.*—Each spouse claiming a housing cost amount exclusion or deduction shall compute the portion of the housing cost amount that is attributable to employer provided amounts separately, based on his or her separate foreign earned income, in accordance with § 1.911-4(d)(3).

(b) *Married couples with community income.*—The amount of excludable foreign earned income of a husband and wife with community income is determined separately for each spouse in accordance with paragraph (a) of this section on the basis of income attributable to that spouse's services without regard to community property laws. See sections 879 and 6013(g) and (h) for special rules regarding treatment of community income of a nonresident alien individual married to a U.S. citizen or resident. [Reg. § 1.911-5.]

☐ [T.D. 8006, 1-17-85.]

§ 1.911-6. Disallowance of deductions, exclusions, and credits.—(a) *In general.*—No deduction or exclusion from gross income under Subtitle A of the Code or credit against the tax imposed by chapter 1 of the Code shall be allowed to the extent the deduction, exclusion, or credit is properly allocable to or chargeable against amounts excluded from gross income under section 911(a). For purposes of the preceding sentence, deductions, exclusions, and credits which are definitely related (as provided in § 1.861-8), in whole or in part, to earned income shall be allocated and apportioned to foreign earned income and U.S. source earned income in accordance with the rules contained in § 1.861-8. Deductions, exclusions, and credits which are definitely related to all gross income under § 1.861-8, including deductions for interest described in § 1.861-8(e)(2)(ii), are definitely related, in whole or in part, to earned income. In the case of interest expense allocable, in whole or in part, to foreign earned income under § 1.861-8(e)(2)(ii), the expense shall normally be apportioned under option one of the optional gross income methods of apportionment (§ 1.861-8(e)(2)(vi)(A)), but without regard to conditions *(1)* and *(2)* of subdivision (vi)(A) (the fifty percent conditions). Such interest expense shall not normally be apportioned under the asset method of § 1.861-8(e)(2)(v). This is because, where section 911 is the operative section, the expense normally relates more closely to gross income generated from activities than to the amount of capital utilized or invested in activities or property. Deductions that are allocated and apportioned to foreign earned income must then be allocated and apportioned to foreign earned income that is excluded under section 911(a). If an individual has foreign earned income from both self-employment and other employment, the amount excluded under section 911(a)(1) shall be deemed to include a pro rata amount of the self-employment income and the income from other employment; thus, a pro rata portion of deductible expenses attributable to self-employment income must be disallowed. For purposes of section 911(d)(6) and this section only, deductions, exclusions, or credits which are not definitely related to any class of gross income shall not be allocable or chargeable to excluded amounts and are, therefore, deductible to the extent allowed by chapter 1 of the Code. Examples of deductions that are not definitely related to a class of gross income are personal and family medical expenses, qualified retirement contributions (but see section 219(b)(1)), real estate taxes and mortgage interest on a personal residence, charitable contributions, alimony payments, and deductions for personal exemptions. In addition, for purposes of this section, amounts excludable or deductible under section 911 or 119 shall not be allocable or chargeable to other amounts excluded under section 911(a). Thus, an individual's housing cost amount which is excludable or deductible under § 1.911-4(d) for a taxable year is not apportioned in part to the individual's foreign earned income which is excluded for such year under § 1.911-3(d). Therefore, the entire amount of such exclusion or deduction is allowed to the extent provided in § 1.911-4. This section does not affect the time for claiming any deduction, exclusion, or credit that is not allocated or apportioned to excluded amounts.

(b) *Moving expenses.*—(1) *In general.*—No deduction shall be allowed for moving expenses under section 217 to the extent the deduction is properly allocable to or chargeable against amounts of foreign earned income excluded from gross income under section 911(a). If an individual's new principal place of work is in a foreign country, deductible moving expenses will be allocable to foreign earned income. If an individual treats a reimbursement from his employer for the expenses of a move from a foreign country to the United States as attributable to services performed in a foreign country under § 1.911-3(e)(5)(i), then deductible moving expenses attributable to that move will be allocable to foreign earned income. If the individual is a qualified individual who elects to exclude foreign earned income under section 911(a), then some or all of such moving expenses must be disallowed as a deduction.

(2) *Attribution of moving expense deduction to taxable years in which services are performed.*—If a moving expense deduction is properly allocable to foreign earned income, the deduction shall be considered attributable to services performed in the year of the move as long as the individual is a qualified individual under § 1.911-2(a) for a period that includes 120 days in the year of the move. If the individual is not a qualified individual for such period, then the individual shall treat the deduction as attributable to services performed in both the year of the move and the succeeding taxable year, if the move is from the United States to the foreign country, or the prior taxable year, if the move is from a foreign country to the United States. Notwithstanding the preceding two sentences, storage expenses incurred after December 31, 1983 shall be treated as attributable to services performed in the year in which the expenses are incurred.

(3) *Formula for disallowance of moving expense deduction.*—The portion of the moving expense deduction that is disallowed shall be determined by multiplying the moving expense deduction by a fraction the numerator of which is all amounts excluded under section 911(a) for the year or years to which the deduction is attributable (under paragraph (b)(2) of this section) and the denominator of which is foreign earned income (as defined in § 1.911-3(a)) for that year or years.

(4) *Effect of disallowance based on attribution of deduction to subsequent year's income.*—An individual may claim a moving expense deduction in the taxable year in which the amount of the expense is paid or incurred even if attributable, in part, to the succeeding year. However, at such time as the individual excludes income under section 911(a) for the year or years to which the deduction is attributable, the individual shall either—

(i) file an amended return for the year in which the deduction was claimed that does not claim the portion of the deduction that is disallowed because it is chargeable against excluded income, or

(ii) include in income for the year following the year in which the deduction was claimed an amount equal to the amount of the deduction that is disallowed.

Any amount included in income under paragraph (b)(4)(ii) of this section is not foreign earned income.

(5) *Moves beginning before January 1, 1984.*—Notwithstanding paragraph (b)(1) through (3) of this section, the rules of this paragraph (b)(5) shall apply for moves beginning before January 1, 1984.

(i) *Individual qualifies for the entire taxable year of the move.*—If the individual is a qualified individual for the entire taxable year of the move, then the amount of moving expenses disallowed shall be determined by multiplying the moving expense deduction otherwise allowable by a fraction the numerator of which is the foreign earned income excluded under section 911(a) for the taxable year of the move and the denominator of which is the foreign earned income for the same taxable year.

(ii) *Individual qualifies for less than the entire taxable year of the move.*—If the individual is a qualified individual for less than the entire taxable year of the move, then, for the purpose of determining the portion of the otherwise allowable moving expense deduction that is disallowed, the individual must attribute a portion of the otherwise allowable moving expense deduction either to the succeeding taxable year, if the move is from the United States to a foreign country, or to the prior taxable year, if the move is from a foreign country to the United States. The portion of the moving expense deduction treated as attributable to services performed in the year of the move shall be determined by multiplying the otherwise allowable moving expense deduction by the following fraction:

$$\frac{\text{The number of qualifying days (as defined in § 1.911-3(d)(3)) in the year of the move}}{\text{The number of days in the taxable year of the move.}}$$

The portion of the moving expense deduction treated as attributable to the year succeeding or preceding the move shall be determined by subtracting the portion of the moving expense deduction that is attributable to the year of the move from the total moving expense deduction. The allocation of a portion of the moving expense deduction to a succeeding or preceding taxable year does not affect the time for claiming the allowable moving expense deduction. The portion of the moving expense deduction that is disallowed shall be determined by multiplying the moving expense deduction attributable to the year of the move or the succeeding or preceding year, as the case may be, by a fraction the numerator of which is amounts excluded under section 911(a) for that year and the denominator of which is foreign earned income for that year.

(c) *Foreign taxes.*—(1) *Amount disallowed.*—No deduction or credit is allowed for foreign income, war profits, or excess profits taxes paid or accrued with respect to amounts excluded from gross income under section 911. To determine the amount of disallowed foreign taxes, multiply the foreign tax imposed on foreign earned income (as defined in § 1.911-3(a)) received or accrued during the taxable year by a fraction, the numerator of which is amounts excluded under section 911(a) in such taxable year less deductible expenses properly allocated to such amounts (see paragraphs (a) and (b) of this section), and the denominator of which is foreign earned income (as defined in § 1.911-3(a)) received or accrued during the taxable year less deductible expenses properly allocated or apportioned thereto. For the purpose of determining the extent to which foreign taxes are disallowed, the housing cost amount deduction is treated as definitely related to foreign earned income that is not excluded. If the foreign tax is imposed on foreign earned income and some other income (for example, earned income from sources within the United States or an amount not subject to tax in the

United States), and the taxes on the other amount cannot be segregated, then the denominator equals the total of the amounts subject to tax less deductible expenses allocable to all such amounts.

(2) *Definitions and special rules.*—(i) *Taxable year.*—For purposes of paragraph (c)(1) of this section, the term "taxable year" means the individual's taxable year for U.S. tax purposes. Such term includes the portion of any foreign taxable year within the individual's U.S. taxable year and excludes the portion of any foreign taxable year not within the individual's U.S. taxable year.

(ii) *Apportionment of foreign taxes.*—For purposes of this paragraph (c), foreign taxes imposed on foreign earned income shall be deemed to accrue, on a pro rata basis, to income as the income is received or accrued. The taxes so accrued shall be apportioned to the taxable year during which the income is received or accrued. This rule applies for all individuals, regardless of their method of accounting.

(iii) *Effect of disallowance.*—The disallowance of foreign taxes under this paragraph (c) shall not affect the time for claiming any deduction or credit for foreign taxes paid. Rather, the disallowance shall only affect the amount of taxes considered paid or accrued to any foreign country.

(iv) *Interest on foreign taxes.*—Any interest expense incurred on a liability for foreign taxes is allocated and apportioned not under this paragraph (c) but under paragraph (a) of this section to foreign earned income and then to excluded foreign earned income and to that extent disallowed as a deduction under paragraph (a). In that regard, see also § 1.861-8(e)(2) for the specific rules for allocation and apportionment of interest expense.

(d) *Examples.*—The following examples illustrate the application of this section.

Example (1). In 1982 A, an architect, operates his business as a sole proprietorship in which capital is not a material income producing factor. A receives $1,000,000 in gross receipts, all of which is foreign source earned income, and incurs $500,000 of otherwise deductible business expenses definitely related to the foreign earned income. A elects to exclude $75,000 under section 911(a)(1). The expenses must be apportioned to excluded earned income as follows: $500,000 × $75,000/1,000,000. Thus, $37,500 of the business expenses are not deductible.

Example (2). The facts are the same as in example (1), except that $100,000 of A's gross receipts is U.S. source earned income and $68,000 of A's business expenses are attributable to the U.S. source earned income. Thus, A has $900,000 of foreign earned income and $432,000 of deductions allocated to foreign earned income. The expenses apportioned to excluded earned income are $432,000 × $75,000/$900,000, or $36,000, which are not deductible.

Example (3). B is a U.S. citizen, calendar year and cash basis taxpayer. B moves to foreign country N and maintains a tax home and is physically present there from July 1, 1984 through May 26, 1985. Among other possible periods, B is a qualified individual for 219 days in the year of the move. B pays $6,000 of otherwise deductible moving expenses in 1984. For 1984, B's foreign earned income is $60,000 and B excludes $47,869 ($80,000 × 219/366) under section 911(a). Under paragraph (b)(2) of this section, B's moving expenses are attributable to services performed in 1984. Under paragraph (b)(3) of this section, $6,000 × $47,869/$60,000, or $4,789, of B's moving expense deduction is disallowed. B may deduct $1,211 of moving expenses on his 1984 return.

Example (4). The facts are the same as in example (3) except that B maintains a tax home and is physically present in foreign country N from October 9, 1984 through September 3, 1985. Among other possible periods, B is a qualified individual for no more than 119 days in 1984 and 281 days in 1985. B's foreign earned income for 1984 is $60,000. B's foreign earned income for 1985 is $150,000. Because B is a qualified individual for less than 120 days in the year of the move, under paragraph (b)(2) of this section, B's moving expenses are attributable to services performed in 1984 and 1985. At the close of 1984, B may either seek an extension of time to file under § 1.911-7(c) or may file an income tax return without claiming the exclusions or deduction under section 911. B does not seek an extension and files without excluding foreign earned income; thus B may deduct his moving expenses in full. B later amends his 1984 return and excludes foreign earned income for that year. B excludes foreign earned income for 1985. B must determine the portion of the moving expense deduction that is disallowed. The portion of the moving expense deduction that is disallowed is determined by multiplying the otherwise allowable moving expense deduction by a fraction. The numerator of the fraction is the sum of amounts excluded under section 911(a) for 1984 and 1985, that is, $26,082, or $80,000 × 119/365, plus $61,589, or $80,000 × 281/365, which totals $87,671. The denominator of the fraction is the sum of foreign earned income for 1984 and 1985, that is, $60,000 plus $150,000, or $210,000. B's allowable moving expense deduction is $3,495, or $6,000—($6,000 × $87,671/$210,000). If B does not file an amended 1984 return (and does not exclude foreign earned income for 1984), but excludes foreign earned income under section 911(a) for 1985, a portion of his moving expense deduction is disallowed, based on the same formula. The amount disallowed is $6,000 × $61,589/$210,000, or $1,760. This amount may be recaptured either by filing an amended return for 1984 or by including it in income for 1985 (in which case it is not foreign earned income).

Example (5). C is a U.S. citizen, a self-employed individual, and a cash basis and calendar year taxpayer. For the entire 1982 taxable year C maintained his tax home and his bona fide residence in foreign country P. During 1982 C earned and received $120,000 of foreign earned income, none of which was attributable to employer provided amounts. C paid $40,000 of business expenses. C elected to exclude foreign earned income under section 911(a)(1) and claimed a housing cost amount deduction of $15,000. C received $10,000 of foreign source interest income which was included with C's earned income in a single tax base and taxed at graduated rates. For 1982, C paid $30,000 in income tax to foreign country P. The amount of C's business expenses that is properly apportioned to excluded amounts (and therefore, not deductible) equals $25,000, which is determined by multiplying the otherwise allowable deductions by C's excluded amounts over C's foreign earned income ($40,000 × $75,000/$120,000). The amount of country P tax that is properly apportioned to excluded amounts (and therefore, not deductible or creditable) equals $20,000, which is determined by multiplying the tax of $30,000 by the following fraction:

$$\frac{\$50{,}000 \ (\$75{,}000 \text{ excluded amounts less } \$25{,}000 \text{ of deductible expenses allocable thereto})}{\$75{,}000 \ ((\$120{,}000 \text{ foreign earned income less } \$40{,}000 \text{ of deductible expenses allocable thereto}) \text{ less } \$15{,}000 \text{ (housing cost amount deduction allocable thereto) plus } \$10{,}000 \text{ other taxable income}).}$$

Example (6). D is a U.S. citizen and an accrual basis and calendar year taxpayer for U.S. tax purposes. For the entire period from January 1, 1982 through December 31, 1983, D maintains his tax home and his bona fide residence in foreign country R. For purposes of R's income tax, D is a cash basis taxpayer and uses a fiscal year that begins on April 1 and ends on the following March 31. During his entire period of residence in R, D receives foreign earned income of $10,000 each month, all of which is attributable to employer provided amounts. For his foreign taxable year ending March 31, 1982, D pays $10,000 of income tax to R. For his foreign taxable year ending March 31, 1983, D pays $54,000 of income tax to R. Under paragraph (c)(2)(ii) of this section, all of the $10,000 of tax paid for his foreign taxable year ending March 31, 1982 is imposed on foreign earned income received in 1982, as is $40,500 or 9/12 × $54,000, of tax paid for his foreign taxable year ending March 31, 1983. (D received $10,000 per month for the last 3 months of his foreign taxable year ending March 31, 1982, all of which are within his U.S. taxable year ending December 31, 1982 under paragraph (c)(2)(i) of this section, and $10,000 per month for each month of his foreign taxable year ending March 31, 1983, of which the first 9 months are within his U.S. taxable year ending December 31, 1982. Under paragraph (c)(2)(ii) of this section, foreign taxes are deemed to accrue on a pro rata basis to income as it is received or accrued. Thus, all of the $10,000 of foreign taxes imposed on the income received during D's foreign taxable year ending March 31, 1982 accrue to D's 1982 foreign earned income, as do 9/12 (or $90,000/$120,000) of foreign taxes imposed on income received during D's foreign taxable year ending March 31, 1983, for purposes of determining the amount of D's foreign taxes that is disallowed.) For 1982, D has no deductible expenses, and elects to exclude his housing cost amount of $21,000 under section 911(a)(2) and foreign earned income of $75,000 under section 911(a)(1). The amount of D's foreign taxes disallowed for deduction or credit purposes for 1982 is $8,000 (that is, $10,000 × $96,000/$120,000) of the taxes for his foreign taxable year ending March 31, 1982, plus $32,400 (that is, $40,500 × $96,000/$120,000) of the taxes for his foreign taxable year ending March 31, 1983, or $40,400. From 1982, D has $2,000 ($10,000 – $8,000) of deductible or creditable taxes accrued on March 31, 1982, and $8,100 ($40,500 – $32,400) of deductible or creditable taxes accrued on March 31, 1983, after the disallowance based on his 1982 excluded income.

Example (7). E is a United States citizen, calendar year and cash basis taxpayer. E is physically present in and establishes his tax home in foreign country S on May 1, 1981. For purposes of country S, E's taxable year begins on April 1 and ends the following March 31. E receives foreign earned income of $15,000 each month beginning May 1, 1981. At the end of his foreign taxable year ending on March 31, 1982, E pays $70,000 of income tax to S on $165,000 of foreign earned income. Under section 911, as in effect for taxable years beginning before January 1, 1982, E may not exclude any income that is earned or received during 1981. None of

Reg. §1.911-6(d)

E's taxes paid in 1982 that are attributable to income earned or received in 1981 are subject to disallowance because, under paragraph (c)(2)(ii) of this section, the only taxes disallowed are those deemed to accrue on income earned and received after December 31, 1981, and excluded from gross income. The amount of E's taxes paid in 1982 that are attributable to 1981 is $50,909, or $70,000 × $120,000/$165,000. E elects to exclude foreign earned income for 1982. The amount of E's taxes paid to S in 1982 that accrue to 1982 foreign earned income, and are therefore subject to disallowance based on excluded income, is $19,091, or $70,000 × $45,000/$165,000. [Reg. § 1.911-6.]

☐ [*T.D.* 8006, 1-17-85.]

§ 1.911-7. Procedural rules.— (a) *Elections of a qualified individual.*—(1) *In general.*—In order to receive either exclusion provided by section 911(a), a qualified individual must elect, separately with respect to each exclusion, to exclude foreign earned income under section 911(a)(1) and the housing cost amount under section 911(a)(2). Any such elections may be made on Form 2555 or on a comparable form. Each election must be filed either with the income tax return, or with an amended return, for the first taxable year of the individual for which the election is to be effective. An election once made remains in effect for that year and all subsequent years unless revoked under paragraph (b) of this section. Each election shall contain information sufficient to determine whether the individual is a qualified individual as provided in § 1.911-2. The statement shall include the following information:

(i) The individual's name, address, and social security number;

(ii) The name of the individual's employer;

(iii) Whether the individual claimed exclusions under section 911 for earlier years after 1981 and within the five preceding taxable years;

(iv) Whether the individual has revoked a previously made election and the taxable year for which such revocation was effective;

(v) The exclusion or exclusions the individual is electing;

(vi) The foreign country or countries in which the individual's tax home is located and the date when such tax home was established;

(vii) The status (either bona fide residence or physical presence) under which the individual claims the exclusion;

(viii) The individual's qualifying period of residence or presence;

(ix) The individual's foreign earned income for the taxable year including the fair market value of all noncash remuneration; and,

(x) If the individual elects to exclude the housing cost amount, the individual's housing expenses.

(2) *Requirement of a return.*—(i) *In general.*—In order to make a valid election under this paragraph (a), the election must be made:

(A) With an income tax return that is timely filed (including any extensions of time to file),

(B) With a later return filed within the period prescribed in section 6511(a) amending the foregoing timely filed income tax return,

(C) With an original income tax return that is filed within one year after the due date of the return (determined without regard to any extension of time to file); this one year period does not constitute an extension of time for any purpose—it is merely a period during which a valid election may be made on a late return, or

(D) With an income tax return filed after the period described in paragraphs (a)(2)(i)(A), (B), or (C) of this section provided—

(1) The taxpayer owes no federal income tax after taking into account the exclusion and files Form 1040 with Form 2555 or a comparable form attached either before or after the Internal Revenue Service discovers that the taxpayer failed to elect the exclusion; or

(2) The taxpayer owes federal income tax after taking into account the exclusion and files Form 1040 with Form 2555 or a comparable form attached before the Internal Revenue Service discovers that the taxpayer failed to elect the exclusion.

(3) A taxpayer filing an income tax return pursuant to paragraph (a)(2)(i)(D)(*1*) or (*2*) of this section must type or legibly print the following statement at the top of the first page of the Form 1040: "Filed Pursuant to Section 1.911-7(a)(2)(i)(D)."

(ii) *Election for 1982 and 1983 taxable years.*—Solely for purposes of paragraph (a)(2)(i)(A) of this section, an income tax return for any taxable year beginning before January 1, 1984 shall be considered timely filed if it is filed on or before July 23, 1985.

(3) *Housing cost amount deduction.*—An individual does not have to make an election in order to claim the housing cost amount deduction. However, such individual must provide the Commissioner with information sufficient to determine the individual's correct amount of tax. Such information shall include the follow-

ing: the individual's name, address, and social security number; the name of the individual's employer; the foreign country in which the individual's tax home was established; the status under which the individual claims the deduction; the individual's qualifying period of residence or presence; the individual's foreign earned income for the taxable year; and the individual's housing expenses.

(4) *Effect of immaterial error or omission.*—An inadvertent error or omission of information required to be provided to make an election under this paragraph (a) shall not render the election invalid if the error or omission is not material in determining whether the individual is a qualified individual or whether the individual intends to make the election.

(b) *Revocation of election.*—(1) *In general.*—An individual may revoke any election made under paragraph (a) of this section for any taxable year. A revocation must be made separately with respect to each election. The individual may revoke an election for any taxable year, including the first taxable year for which an election was effective, by filing a statement that the individual is revoking one or more of the previously made elections. The statement must be filed with the income tax return, or with an amended return, for the first taxable year of individual for which the revocation is to be effective. A revocation once made is effective for that year and all subsequent years. If an election is revoked for any taxable year, including the first taxable year for which the election was effective, the individual may not, without the consent of the Commissioner, again make the same election until the sixth taxable year following the taxable year for which the revocation was first effective. For example, a qualified individual makes an election to exclude foreign earned income under section 911(a)(1) and files it with his 1982 income tax return. The individual files 1983 and 1984 income tax returns on which he excludes his foreign earned income. Then, within 3 years after filing his 1982 income tax return, the individual files an amended 1982 income tax return with a statement revoking his election to exclude foreign earned income under section 911(a)(1). The revocation of the election is effective for taxable years 1982, 1983, and 1984. The individual may not elect to exclude income under section 911(a)(1) for any taxable year before 1988, unless he obtains consent to reelect under paragraph (b)(2) of this section.

(2) *Reelection before sixth taxable year after revocation.*—If an individual revoked an election under paragraph (b)(1) of this section and within five taxable years the individual wishes to reelect the same exclusion, then the individual may apply for consent to the reelection. The application for consent shall be made by requesting a ruling from the Associate Chief Counsel (Technical), National Office, Internal Revenue Service, 1111 Constitution Avenue NW., Washington, D.C. 20224. In determining whether to consent to a reelection the Associate Chief Counsel or his delegate shall consider any facts and circumstances that may be relevant to the determination. Relevant facts and circumstances may include the following: a period of United States residence, a move from one foreign country to another foreign country with differing tax rates, a substantial change in the tax laws of the foreign country of residence or physical presence, and a change of employer.

(c) *Returns and extensions.*—(1) *In general.*—Any return filed before completion of the period necessary to qualify an individual for any exclusion or deduction provided by section 911 shall be filed without regard to any exclusion or deduction provided by that section. A claim for a credit or refund of any overpayment of tax may be filed, however, if the taxpayer subsequently qualifies for any exclusion or deduction under section 911. See section 6012(c) and § 1.6012-1(a)(3), relating to returns to be filed and information to be furnished by individuals who qualify for any exclusion or deduction under section 911.

(2) *Extensions.*—An individual desiring an extension of time (in addition to the automatic extension of time granted by § 1.6081-2) for filing a return until after the completion of the qualifying period described in paragraph (c)(1) of this section for claiming any exclusion or deduction under section 911 may apply for an extension. An individual whose moving expense deduction is attributable to services performed in two years may apply for an extension of time for filing a return until after the end of the second year. The individual may make such application on Form 2350 or a comparable form. The application must be filed with the Director, Internal Revenue Service Center, Philadelphia, Pennsylvania 19255. The application must set forth the facts relied on to justify the extension of time requested and must include a statement as to the earliest date the individual expects to become entitled to any exclusion or deduction by reason of completion of the qualifying period.

(d) *Declaration of estimated tax.*—In estimating gross income for the purpose of determining whether a declaration of estimated tax must be made for any taxable year, an individual is not required to take into account income which the individual reasonably believes will be excluded from gross income under the provisions

Reg. § 1.911-7(d)

of section 911. In computing estimated tax, however, the individual must take into account, among other things, the denial of the foreign tax credit for foreign taxes allocable to the excluded income (see § 1.911-6(c)). [Reg. § 1.911-7.]

☐ [*T.D.* 8006, 1-17-85. *Amended by T.D.* 8480, 6-29-93.]

§ 1.911-8. Former deduction for certain expenses of living abroad.—For rules relating to the deduction for certain expenses of living abroad applicable to taxable years beginning before January 1, 1982, see 26 CFR §§ 1.913-1 through 1.913-13 as they appeared in the Code of Federal Regulations revised as of April 1, 1982. [Reg. § 1.911-8.]

☐ [*T.D.* 8006, 1-17-85.]

Controlled Foreign Corporations

§ 1.951-1. Amounts included in gross income of United States shareholders.—(a) *In general.*—If a foreign corporation is a controlled foreign corporation (within the meaning of section 957) for an uninterrupted period of 30 days or more (determined under paragraph (f) of this section) during any taxable year of such corporation beginning after December 31, 1962, every person—

(1) Who is a United States shareholder (as defined in section 951(b) and paragraph (g) of this section) of such corporation at any time during such taxable year, and

(2) Who owns (within the meaning of section 958(a)) stock in such corporation on the last day, in such year, on which such corporation is a controlled foreign corporation

shall include in his gross income for his taxable year in which or with which such taxable year of the corporation ends, the sum of—

(i) Except as provided in section 963, such shareholder's pro rata share (determined under paragraph (b) of this section) of the corporation's subpart F income (as defined in section 952) for such taxable year of the corporation,

(ii) Such shareholder's pro rata share (determined under paragraph (c)(1) of this section) of the corporation's previously excluded subpart F income withdrawn from investment in less developed countries for such taxable year of the corporation,

(iii) Such shareholder's pro rata share (determined under paragraph (c)(2) of this section) of the corporation's previously excluded subpart F income withdrawn from investment in foreign base company shipping operations for such taxable year of the corporation, and

(iv) Such shareholder's pro rata share (determined under paragraph (d) of this section) of the corporation's increase in earnings invested in United States property for such taxable year of the corporation (but only to the extent such pro rata share is not excluded from such shareholder's gross income for his taxable year under section 959(a)(2)).

For purposes of determining whether a United States shareholder which is a domestic corporation is a personal holding company under section 542 and § 1.542-1, the character of the amount includible in gross income of such domestic corporation under this paragraph shall be determined as if such amount were realized directly by such corporation from the source from which it is realized by the controlled foreign corporation. See paragraph (a) of § 1.957-2 for special limitation on the amount of subpart F income in the case of a controlled foreign corporation described in section 957(b). See section 970(a) and § 1.970-1 which provides for the reduction of subpart F income of export trade corporations.

(b) *Limitation on a United States shareholder's pro rata share of subpart F income.*— (1) *In general.*—For purposes of paragraph (a)(2)(i) of this section, a United States shareholder's pro rata share (determined in accordance with the rules of paragraph (e) of this section) of the foreign corporation's subpart F income for the taxable year of such corporation is—

(i) The amount which would have been distributed with respect to the stock which such shareholder owns (within the meaning of section 958(a)) in such corporation if on the last day, in such corporation's taxable year, on which such corporation is a controlled foreign corporation it had distributed pro rata to its shareholders an amount which bears the same ratio to its subpart F income for such taxable year as the part of such year during which such corporation is a controlled foreign corporation bears to the entire taxable year, reduced by—

(ii) The amount of distributions received by any other person during such taxable year as a dividend with respect to such stock, but only to the extent that such distributions do not exceed the dividend which would have been received by such other person if the distributions by such corporation to all its shareholders had been the amount which bears the same ratio to the subpart F income of such corporation for the taxable year as the part of such year during which such shareholder did not own (within the meaning of section 958(a)) such stock bears to the entire taxable year.

(2) *Illustrations.*—The application of this paragraph may be illustrated by the following examples:

Example (1). A, a United States shareholder, owns 100 percent of the only class of stock of M, a controlled foreign corporation throughout 1963. Both A and M Corporation use the calendar year as a taxable year. For 1963, M Corporation derives $100 of subpart F income, has $100 of earnings and profits, and makes no distributions. A must include $100 in his gross income for 1963 under section 951(a)(1)(A)(i).

Example (2). The facts are the same as in example (1), except that instead of holding 100 percent of the stock of M Corporation for the entire year, A sells 60 percent of such stock to B, a nonresident alien, on May 26, 1963. Thus, M Corporation is a controlled foreign corporation for the period January 1, 1963, through May 26, 1963. A must include $40 ($100 × 146/365) in his gross income for 1963 under section 951(a)(1)(A)(i).

Example (3). The facts are the same as in example (1), except that instead of holding 100 percent of the stock of M Corporation for the entire year, A holds 60 percent of such stock on December 31, 1963, having acquired such interest on May 26, 1963, from B, a nonresident alien, who owned such interest from January 1, 1963. Before A's acquisition of such stock, M Corporation had distributed a dividend of $15 to B in 1963 with respect to such stock. A must include $21 in his gross income for 1963 under section 951(a)(1)(A)(i), such amount being determined as follows:

Corporation M's subpart F income for 1963	$100
Less: Reduction under sec. 951(a)(2)(A) for period (1-1-63 through 5-26-63) during which M Corporation is not a controlled foreign corporation ($100 × 146/365)	40
Subpart F income for 1963 as limited by sec. 951(a)(2)(A)	60
A's pro rata share of subpart F income as determined under sec. 951(a)(2)(A) (60 percent of $60)	36
Less: Reduction under sec. 951(a)(2)(B) for dividends received by B during 1963 with respect to the stock acquired by A in M Corporation:	
(i) Dividend received by B $15	
(ii) B's pro rata share of the amount which bears the same ratio to M Corporation's subpart F income for 1963 ($100) as the period during which A did not own (within the meaning of section 958(a)) his stock (146 days) bears to the entire taxable year (365 days) (60 percent of ($100 × 146/365)) $24	
(iii) Amount of reduction (lesser of (i) or (ii))	$15
A's pro rata share of subpart F income as determined under sec. 951(a)(2)	21

Example (4). A, a United States shareholder, owns 100 percent of the only class of stock of P, a controlled foreign corporation throughout 1963, and P owns 100 percent of the only class of stock of R, a controlled foreign corporation throughout 1963. A and Corporations P and R each use the calendar year as a taxable year. For 1963, R Corporation derives $100 of subpart F income, has $100 of earnings and profits, and distributes a dividend of $20 to P Corporation. Corporation P has no income for 1963 other than the dividend received from R Corporation. A must include $100 in his gross income for 1963 under section 951(a)(1)(A)(i) as subpart F income of R Corporation for such year. Such subpart F income is not reduced under sec. 951(a)(2)(B) for the dividend of $20 paid to P Corporation because there was no part of the year 1963 during which A did not own (within the meaning of section 958(a)) the stock of R Corporation. By reason of the application of section 959(b), the $20 distribution from R Corporation to P Corporation is not again includible in the gross income of A under section 951(a).

Example (5). The facts are the same as in example (4), except that instead of holding the stock of R Corporation for the entire year, P Corporation acquires 60 percent of the only class of stock of R Corporation on March 14, 1963, from C, a nonresident alien, after R Corporation distributes in 1963 a dividend of $35 to C with respect to the stock so acquired by P Corporation. The stock interest so acquired by P Corporation was owned by C from January 1, 1963, until acquired by P Corporation. A must include $36 in his gross income for 1963 under section 951(a)(1)(A)(i), such amount being determined as follows:

Corporation R's subpart F income for 1963	$100
Less: Reduction under sec. 951(a)(2)(A) for period (1-1-63 through 3-14-63) during which R Corporation is not a controlled foreign corporation ($100 × 73/365)	20
Subpart F income for 1963 as limited by sec. 951(a)(2)(A)	80

Reg. §1.951-1(b)(2)

A's pro rata share of subpart F income as determined under sec. 951(a)(2)(A) (60 percent of $80)	48
Less: Reduction under sec. 951(a)(2)(B) for dividends received by C during 1963 with respect to the stock indirectly acquired by A in R Corporation:	
(i) Dividend received by C $35	
(ii) C's pro rata share of the amount which bears the same ratio to R Corporation's subpart F income for 1963 ($100) as the period during which A did not in indirectly own (within the meaning of section 958(a)(2)) his stock (73 days) bears to the entire taxable year (365 days) (60 percent of ($100 × 73/365)) $12	
(iii) Amount of reduction (lesser of (i) or (ii))	$12
A's pro rata share of subpart F income as determined under sec. 951(a)(2)	36

(c) *Limitation on a United States shareholder's pro rata share of previously excluded subpart F income withdrawn from investments.*—(1) *Investments in less developed countries.*—For purposes of paragraph (a)(2)(ii) of this section, a United States shareholder's pro rata share (determined in accordance with the rules of paragraph (e) of this section) of the foreign corporation's previously excluded subpart F income withdrawn from investment in less developed countries for the taxable year of such corporation shall not exceed an amount which bears the same ratio to such shareholder's pro rata share of such income withdrawn (as determined under section 955(a)(3), as in effect before the enactment of the Tax Reduction Act of 1975, and paragraph (c) of § 1.955-1) for such taxable year as the part of such year during which such corporation is a controlled foreign corporation bears to the entire taxable year. See paragraph (c)(2) of § 1.955-1 for a special rule applicable to exclusions and withdrawals occurring before the date on which the United States shareholder acquires his stock.

(2) *Investments in foreign base company shipping operations.*—For purposes of paragraph (a)(2)(iii) of this section, a United States shareholder's pro rata share (determined in accordance with the rules of paragraph (e) of this section) of the foreign corporation's previously excluded subpart F income withdrawn from investment in foreign base company shipping operations for the taxable year of such corporation shall not exceed an amount which bears the same ratio to such shareholder's pro rata share of such income withdrawn (as determined under section 955(a)(3) and paragraph (c) of § 1.955A-1) for such taxable year as the part of such year during which such corporation is a controlled foreign corporation bears to the entire taxable year. See paragraph (c)(2) of § 1.955A-1 for a special rule applicable to exclusions and withdrawals occurring before the date on which the United States shareholder acquires his stock.

(d) *Limitation on a United States shareholder's pro rata share of increase in investment in United States property.*—For purposes of paragraph (a)(2)(iv) of this section, a United States shareholder's pro rata share (determined in accordance with the rules of paragraph (e) of this section) of the foreign corporation's increase in earnings invested in United States property for the taxable year of such corporation shall not exceed an amount which bears the same ratio to such shareholder's pro rata share of such increase (as determined under section 956(a)(2) and paragraph (c) of § 1.956-1) for such taxable year as the part of such year during which such corporation is a controlled foreign corporation bears to the entire taxable year. The amount determined under the preceding sentence, however, shall be taken into account under paragraph (a)(2)(iv) of this section only to the extent such amount is not excluded from such shareholder's gross income for his taxable year under section 959(a)(2) and the regulations thereunder.

(e) *"Pro rata share" defined.*—(1) *In general.*—For purposes of paragraphs (b), (c), and (d) of this section, a United States shareholder's pro rata share of a controlled foreign corporation's subpart F income, previously excluded subpart F income withdrawn from investment in less developed countries, previously excluded subpart F income withdrawn from investment in foreign base company shipping operations, or increase in earnings invested in United States property, respectively, for any taxable year is his pro rata share determined under paragraph (a) of § 1.952-1, paragraph (c) of § 1.955-1, paragraph (c) of § 1.955A-1, or paragraph (c) of § 1.956-1, respectively.

(2) *More than one class of stock.*—If a controlled foreign corporation for a taxable year has more than one class of stock outstanding, the amount of such corporation's subpart F income, withdrawal, or increase in investment, for the taxable year which shall be taken into account with respect to any one class of such stock for purposes of subparagraph (1) of this paragraph shall be that amount which bears the same ratio to the total of such subpart F

income, withdrawal, or increase in investment for such year as the earnings and profits which would be distributed with respect to such class of stock if all earnings and profits of such corporation for such year were distributed on the last day of such corporation's taxable year on which such corporation is a controlled foreign corporation bear to the total earnings and profits of such corporation for such taxable year. For purposes of the preceding sentence, if an arrearage in dividends for prior taxable years exists with respect to a class of preferred stock of such corporation, the earnings and profits for the taxable year shall be attributed to such arrearage only to the extent such arrearage exceeds the earnings and profits of such corporation remaining from prior taxable years beginning after December 31, 1962.

(3) *Discretionary power to allocate earnings to different classes of stock.*—If the allocation of a foreign corporation's earnings and profits for the taxable year between two or more classes of stock depends upon the exercise of discretion by that body of persons which exercises with respect to such corporation the powers ordinarily exercised by the board of directors of a domestic corporation, the allocation of earnings and profits to such classes shall be made for purposes of this paragraph as if such classes constituted one class of stock in which each share has the same rights to dividends as any other share, unless a different method of allocation of earnings and profits is established as proper by the United States shareholder.

(4) *Illustrations.*—The application of this paragraph may be illustrated by the following examples:

Example (1). Throughout its taxable year 1964, controlled foreign corporation A has outstanding 40 shares of common stock and 60 shares of 6-percent, nonparticipating, nonvoting, preferred stock with a par value of $100 per share. D, a United States citizen who uses the calendar year as a taxable year, owns 30 shares of the common, and 15 shares of the preferred, stock during 1964: Corporation A for 1964 has earnings and profits of $1,000, and income of $500 with respect to which amounts are required to be included in gross income of United States shareholders under section 951(a). In such case, if the total $1,000 of earnings and profits were distributed on December 31, 1964, $360 (0.06 × $100 × 60) would be distributed with respect to A Corporation's preferred stock and $640 ($1,000 minus $360) would be distributed with respect to its common stock. Accordingly, of the $500 with respect to which amounts are required to be included in gross income of United States shareholders under section 951(a), $180 ($360/$1,000 × $500) is allocated to the outstanding preferred stock and $320 ($640/$1,000 × $500) is allocated to the outstanding common stock. D's pro rata share of such amounts for 1964 is $285 [($180 × 15/60) +($320 × 30/40)].

Example (2). The facts are the same as in example (1), except that the preferred stock is cumulative and there is an arrearage in dividends with respect to such stock of $900; on December 31, 1963, Corporation A has accumulated earnings and profits for 1963 of $700; therefore, for purposes of this paragraph, Corporation A's earnings and profits for 1964 attributable to such arrearage may not exceed $200 ($900 minus $700). In such case, for purposes of this paragraph, if the $1,000 earnings and profits for 1964 were distributed on December 31, 1964, $560 [(0.06 × $100 × 60) + $200] would be distributed with respect to A Corporation's preferred stock and $440 ($1,000 minus $560) would be distributed with respect to its common stock. Accordingly, of the $500 with respect to which amounts are required to be included in gross income of United States shareholders under section 951(a), $280 ($560/$1,000 × $500) is allocated to the outstanding preferred stock and $220 ($440/$1,000 × $500) is allocated to the outstanding common stock. D's pro rata share of such amounts for 1964 is $235 [($280 × 15/60) +($220 × 30/40)].

(f) *Determination of holding period.*—For purposes of sections 951 through 964, the holding period of an asset (including stock of a controlled foreign corporation) shall be determined by excluding the day on which such asset is acquired and including the day on which such asset is disposed of. The application of this paragraph may be illustrated by the following example:

Example. On June 30, 1963, United States person E acquires 70 of the 100 shares of the only class of stock of foreign corporation A from nonresident alien B, who until such time owns all such 100 shares. E sells 10 shares of stock of such corporation on November 30, 1963, and 60 shares on December 31, 1963, to nonresident alien F. Corporation A is a controlled foreign corporation for the period beginning with July 1, 1963, and extending through December 31, 1963. As to the 10 shares of stock sold on November 30, 1963, E is treated as not owning such shares at any time after November 30, 1963, nor before July 1, 1963. As to the remaining 60 shares of stock, E is treated as not owning them before July 1, 1963, or after December 31, 1963.

(g) *United States shareholder defined.*—
(1) *In general.*—For purposes of sections 951

through 964, the term "United States shareholder" means, with respect to a foreign corporation, a United States person (as defined in section 957(d)) who owns within the meaning of section 958(a), or is considered as owning by applying the rules of ownership of section 958(b), 10 percent or more of the total combined voting power of all classes of stock entitled to vote of such foreign corporation.

(2) *Percentage of total combined voting power owned by United States person.*—
(i) *Meaning of combined voting power.*—In determining for purposes of subparagraph (1) of this paragraph whether a United States person owns the requisite percentage of voting power of all classes of stock entitled to vote, consideration will be given to all the facts and circumstances in each case. In any case where—

(a) A foreign corporation has more than one class of stock outstanding, and

(b) One or more United States persons own (within the meaning of section 958) shares of any one class of stock which possesses the power to elect, appoint, or replace a person, or persons, who with respect to such corporation, exercise the powers ordinarily exercised by a member of the board of directors of a domestic corporation,

the percentage of the total combined voting power with respect to such corporation owned by any such United States person shall be his proportionate share of the percentage of the persons exercising the powers ordinarily exercised by members of the board of directors of a domestic corporation (described in (b) of this subdivision) which such class of stock (as a class) possesses the power to elect, appoint, or replace. In all cases, however, a United States person will be deemed to own 10 percent or more of the total combined voting power with respect to a foreign corporation if such person owns (within the meaning of section 958) 20 percent or more of the total number of shares of a class of stock of such corporation possessing one or more powers enumerated in paragraph (b)(1) of § 1.957-1. Whether a foreign corporation is a controlled foreign corporation for purposes of sections 951 through 964 shall be determined by applying the rules of section 957 and §§ 1.957-1 through 1.957-4.

(ii) *Illustration.*—The application of this paragraph may be illustrated by the following examples:

Example (1). Foreign corporation S has two classes of capital stock outstanding, consisting of 60 shares of class A stock and 40 shares of class B stock. Each class of the outstanding stock is entitled to participate on a share for share basis in any dividend distributions by S Corporation. The owners of a majority of the class A stock are entitled to elect 7 of the 10 corporate directors, and the owners of a majority of the class B stock are entitled to elect the other 3 of the 10 directors. Thus, the class A stock (as a class) possesses 70 percent of the total combined voting power of all classes of stock entitled to vote of S Corporation, and the class B stock (as a class) possesses 30 percent of such voting power. D, a United States person, owns 31 shares of the class A stock and thus owns 36.167 percent (31/60 × 70 percent) of the total combined voting power of all classes of stock entitled to vote of S Corporation. By reason of the ownership of such voting power, D is a United States shareholder of S Corporation under section 951(b). For purposes of section 957, S Corporation is a controlled foreign corporation by reason of D's ownership of a majority of the class A stock, as illustrated in example (2) of paragraph (c) of § 1.957-1. E, a United States person, owns eight shares of the class A stock and thus owns 9.333 percent (8/60 × 70 percent) of the total combined voting power of all classes of stock entitled to vote of S Corporation. Since E owns only 9.333 percent of such voting power and less than 20 percent of the number of shares of the class A stock, he is not a United States shareholder of S Corporation under section 951(b). F, a United States person, owns 14 shares of the class B stock and thus owns 10.5 percent (14/40 × 30 percent) of the total combined voting power of all classes of stock entitled to vote of S Corporation. By reason of the ownership of such voting power, F is a United States shareholder of S Corporation under section 951(b).

Example (2). Foreign corporation R has three classes of stock outstanding, consisting of 10 shares of class A stock, 20 shares of class B stock, and 300 shares of class C stock. Each class of the outstanding stock is entitled to participate on a share for share basis in any distribution by R Corporation. The owners of a majority of the class A stock are entitled to elect 6 of the 10 corporate directors, and the owners of a majority of the class B stock are entitled to elect the other 4 of the 10 directors. The class C stock is not entitled to vote. D, E, and F, United States persons, each own 2 shares of the class A stock and 100 shares of the class C stock. As owners of a majority of the class A stock, D, E, and F elect 6 members of the board of directors. D, E, and F are United States shareholders of R Corporation under section 951(b) since each owns 20 percent of the total number of shares of the class A stock which possesses the power to elect a majority of the board of directors of R Corporation. For purposes of section 957, R Corporation is a controlled foreign corporation by reason of the ownership by D, E, and F of a majority of the class A stock, as illustrated in example (2) of paragraph (c) of § 1.957-1. [Reg. § 1.951-1.]

☐ [*T.D.* 6795, 1-28-65. *Amended by T.D.* 7893, 5-11-83.]

Proposed Amendments to Regulation

Par. 2. Section 1.951-1 is amended by: 1. Removing the language "increase in earnings invested in United States property" in paragraph (e)(1) and adding "amount determined under section 956" in its place. 2. Revising paragraphs (e)(2) through (e)(4) and adding paragraphs (e)(5) through (e)(7).

§ 1.951-1. Amounts included in gross income of United States shareholders.

* * *

(e) * * *

(2) *One class of stock.*—If a controlled foreign corporation for a taxable year has only one class of stock outstanding, each United States shareholder's pro rata share of such corporation's subpart F income, withdrawal, or amount determined under section 956, for the taxable year under paragraph (e)(1) of this section shall be determined by allocating the controlled foreign corporation's earnings and profits on a per share basis.

(3) *More than one class of stock.*—(i) *In general.*—Subject to paragraphs (e)(3)(ii) and (e)(3)(iii) of this section, if a controlled foreign corporation for a taxable year has more than one class of stock outstanding, the amount of such corporation's subpart F income, withdrawal, or amount determined under section 956, for the taxable year taken into account with respect to any one class of stock for purposes of paragraph (e)(1) of this section shall be that amount which bears the same ratio to the total of such subpart F income, withdrawal, or amount determined under section 956 for such year as the earnings and profits which would be distributed with respect to such class of stock if all earnings and profits of such corporation for such year were distributed on the last day of such corporation's taxable year on which such corporation is a controlled foreign corporation (the hypothetical distribution date), bear to the total earnings and profits of such corporation for such taxable year.

(ii) *Discretionary power to allocate earnings to different classes of stock.*—(A) *In general.*—Subject to paragraph (e)(3)(iii) of this section, the rules of this paragraph apply for purposes of paragraph (e)(1) of this section if the allocation of a controlled foreign corporation's earnings and profits for the taxable year between two or more classes of stock depends upon the exercise of discretion by that body of persons which exercises with respect to such corporation the powers ordinarily exercised by the board of directors of a domestic corporation (discretionary distribution rights). First, the earnings and profits of the corporation are allocated under paragraph (e)(3)(i) of this section to any class or classes of stock with non-discretionary distribution rights (e.g., preferred stock entitled to a fixed return). Second, the amount of earnings and profits allocated to a class of stock with discretionary distribution rights shall be that amount which bears the same ratio to the remaining earnings and profits of such corporation for such taxable year as the value of all shares of such class of stock, determined on the hypothetical distribution date, bears to the total value of all shares of all classes of stock with discretionary distribution rights of such corporation, determined on the hypothetical distribution date. For purposes of the preceding sentence, in the case where the value of each share of two or more classes of stock with discretionary distribution rights is substantially the same on the hypothetical distribution date, the allocation of earnings and profits to such classes shall be made as if such classes constituted one class of stock in which each share has the same rights to dividends as any other share.

(B) *Special rule for redemption rights.*—For purposes of paragraph (e)(3)(ii)(A) of this section, discretionary distribution rights do not include rights to redeem shares of a class of stock (even if such redemption would be treated as a distribution of property to which section 301 applies pursuant to section 302(d)).

(iii) *Special allocation rule for stock with mixed distribution rights.*—For purposes of paragraphs (e)(3)(i) and (e)(3)(ii) of this section, in the case of a class of stock with both discretionary and non-discretionary distribution rights, earnings and profits shall be allocated to the non-discretionary distribution rights under paragraph (e)(3)(i) of this section and to the discretionary distribution rights under paragraph (e)(3)(ii) of this section. In such a case, paragraph (e)(3)(ii) of this section will be applied such that the value used in the ratio will be the value of such class of stock solely attributable to the discretionary distribution rights of such class of stock.

(iv) *Dividend arrearages.*—For purposes of paragraph (e)(3)(i) of this section, if an arrearage in dividends for prior taxable years exists with respect to a class of preferred stock of such corporation, the earnings and profits for the taxable year shall be attributed to such arrearage only to the extent such arrearage exceeds the earnings and profits of such corporation remaining from prior taxable years beginning after December 31, 1962.

(4) *Scope of deemed distribution.*—Notwithstanding the terms of any class of stock of the controlled foreign corporation or any agreement or arrangement with respect thereto, no amount shall be considered to be distributed with respect to a particular class of stock for purposes of paragraph (e)(3) of this section to the extent that such distribution would constitute a distribution in redemption of stock (even if such redemption would be treated as a distribution of property to which section 301 applies pursuant to section 302(d)), as a distribution in liquidation, or as a return of capital.

(5) *Restrictions or other limitations on distributions.*—(i) *In general.*—A restriction or other limitation on distributions of earnings and profits by a controlled foreign corporation will not be taken into account, for purposes of this section, in determining the amount of earnings and profits that shall be allocated to a class of stock of the controlled foreign corporation or the amount of the United States shareholder's pro rata share of the controlled foreign corporation's subpart F income, withdrawal, or amounts determined under section 956 for the taxable year.

(ii) *Definition.*—For purposes of this section, a *restriction or other limitation on distributions* includes any limitation that has the effect of limiting the allocation or distribution of earnings and profits by a controlled foreign corporation to a United States shareholder, other than currency or other restrictions or limitations imposed under the laws of any foreign country as provided in section 964(b).

(iii) *Exception for certain preferred distributions.*—The right to receive periodically a fixed amount (whether determined by a percentage of par value, a reference to a floating coupon rate, a stated return expressed in terms of a certain amount of dollars or foreign currency, or otherwise) with respect to a class of stock the distribution of which is a condition precedent to a further distribution of earnings and profits that year with respect to any class of stock (not including a distribution in partial or complete liquidation) is not a restriction or other limitation on the distribution of earnings and profits by a controlled foreign corporation under paragraph (e)(5) of this section.

(iv) *Illustrative list of restrictions and limitations.*—Except as provided in paragraph (e)(5)(iii) of this section, restrictions or other limitations on distributions include, but are not limited to—

(A) An arrangement that restricts the ability of the controlled foreign corporation to pay dividends on a class of shares of the corporation owned by United States shareholders until a condition or conditions are satisfied (e.g., until another class of stock is redeemed);

(B) A loan agreement entered into by a controlled foreign corporation that restricts or otherwise affects the ability to make distributions on its stock until certain requirements are satisfied; or

(C) An arrangement that conditions the ability of the controlled foreign corporation to pay dividends to its shareholders on the financial condition of the controlled foreign corporation.

(6) *Examples.*—The application of this section may be illustrated by the following examples:

Example 1. (i) *Facts.* FC1, a controlled foreign corporation within the meaning of section 957(a), has outstanding 100 shares of one class of stock. Corp E, a domestic corporation and a United States shareholder of FC1, within the meaning of section 951(b), owns 60 shares. Corp H, a domestic corporation and a United States shareholder of FC1, within the meaning of section 951(b), owns 40 shares. FC1, Corp E, and Corp H each use the calendar year as a taxable year. Corp E and Corp H are shareholders of FC1 for its entire 2004 taxable year. For 2004, FC1 has $100x of earnings and profits, and income of $100x with respect to which amounts are required to be included in gross income of United States shareholders under section 951(a). FC1 makes no distributions during that year.

(ii) *Analysis.* FC1 has one class of stock. Therefore, under paragraph (e)(2) of this section, FC1's earnings and profits are allocated on a per share basis. Accordingly, for the taxable year 2004, Corp E's pro rata share of FC1's subpart F income is $60x (60/100 × $100x) and Corp H's pro rata share of FC1's subpart F income is $40x (40/100 × $100x).

Example 2. (i) *Facts.* FC2, a controlled foreign corporation within the meaning of section 957(a), has outstanding 70 shares of common stock and 30 shares of 4-percent, nonparticipating, voting, preferred stock with a par value of $10x per share. The common shareholders are entitled to dividends when declared by the board of directors of FC2. Corp A, a domestic corporation and a United States shareholder of FC2, within the meaning of section 951(b), owns all of the common shares. Individual B, a foreign individual, owns all of the preferred shares. FC2 and Corp A each use the calendar year as a taxable year. Corp A and Individual B are shareholders of FC2 for its entire 2004 taxable year. For 2004, FC1 has $50x of earnings and profits, and income of $50x with respect to which amounts are required to be included in gross income of United States shareholders under section 951(a). In 2004, FC2 distributes as a dividend $12x to Individual B with respect to Individual B's preferred shares. FC2 makes no other distributions during that year.

(ii) *Analysis.* FC2 has two classes of stock, and there are no restrictions or other limitations on distributions within the meaning of paragraph (e)(5) of this section. If the total $50x of earnings were distributed on December 31, 2004, $12x would be distributed with respect to Individual B's preferred shares and the remainder, $38x, would be distributed with respect to Corp A's common shares. Accordingly, under paragraph (e)(3)(i) of this section, Corp A's pro rata share of FC1's subpart F income is $38x for taxable year 2004.

Example 3. (i) *Facts.* The facts are the same as in *Example 2*, except that the shares owned by Individual B are Class B common shares and the shares owned by Corp A are Class A common shares and the board of directors of FC2 may declare dividends with respect to one class of stock without declaring dividends with respect to the other class of stock. The value of the Class A common shares on the last day of FC2's 2004 taxable year is $680x and the value of the Class B common shares on that date is $300x. The board of directors of FC2 determines that FC2 will not make any distributions in 2004 with respect to the Class A and B common shares of FC2.

(ii) *Analysis.* The allocation of FC2's earnings and profits between its Class A and Class B common shares depends solely on the exercise of discretion by the board of directors of FC2. Therefore, under paragraph (e)(3)(ii)(A) of this section, the allocation of earnings and profits between the Class A and Class B common shares will depend on the value of each class of stock on the last day of the controlled foreign corporation's taxable year. On the last day of FC2's taxable year 2004, the Class A common shares had a value of $9.71x/share and the Class B common shares had a value of $10x/share. Because each share of the Class A and Class B common stock of FC2 has substantially the same value on the last day of FC2's taxable year, under paragraph (e)(3)(ii)(A) of this section, for purposes of allocating the earnings and profits of FC2, the Class A and Class B common shares will be treated as one class of stock. Accordingly, for FC2's taxable year 2004, the earnings and profits of FC2 are allocated $35x (70/100 × $50x) to the Class A common shares and $15x (30/100 × $50x) to the Class B common shares. For its taxable year 2004, Corp A's pro rata share of FC2's subpart F income will be $35x.

Example 4. (i) *Facts.* FC3, a controlled foreign corporation within the meaning of section 957(a), has outstanding 100 shares of Class A common stock, 100 shares of Class B common stock and 10 shares of 5-percent nonparticipating, voting preferred stock with a par value of $50x per share. The value of the Class A shares on the last day of FC3's 2004 taxable year is $800x. The value of the Class B shares on that date is $200x. The Class A and Class B shareholders each are entitled to dividends when declared by the board of directors of FC3, and the board of directors of FC3 may declare dividends with respect to one class of stock without declaring dividends with respect to the other class of stock. Corp D, a domestic corporation and a United States shareholder of FC3, within the meaning of section 951(b), owns all of the Class A shares. Corp N, a domestic corporation and a United States shareholder of FC3, within the meaning of section 951(b), owns all of the Class B shares. Corp S, a domestic corporation and a United States shareholder of FC3, within the meaning of section 951(b) owns all of the preferred shares. FC3, Corp D, Corp N, and Corp S each use the calendar year as a taxable year. Corp D, Corp N, and Corp S are shareholders of FC3 for all of 2004. For 2004, FC3 has $100x of earnings and profits, and income of $100x with respect to which amounts are required to be included in gross income of United States shareholders under section 951(a). In 2004, FC3 distributes as a dividend $25x to Corp S with respect to the preferred shares. The board of directors of FC3 determines that FC3 will make no other distributions during that year.

(ii) *Analysis.* The distribution rights of the preferred shares are not a restriction or other limitation within the meaning of paragraph (e)(5) of this section. Pursuant to paragraph (e)(3)(i) of this section, if the total $100x of earnings were distributed on December 31, 2004, $25x would be distributed with respect to Corp S's preferred shares and the remainder, $75x would be distributed with respect to Corp D's Class A shares and Corp N's Class B shares. The allocation of that $75x between its Class A and Class B shares depends solely on the exercise of discretion by the board of directors of FC3. The value of the Class A shares ($8x/share) and the value of the Class B shares ($2x/share) are not substantially the same on the last day of FC3's taxable year 2004. Therefore for FC3's taxable year 2004, under paragraph (e)(3)(ii)(A) of this section, the earnings and profits of FC3 are allocated $60x ($800/$1,000 × $75x) to the Class A shares and $15x ($200/$1,000 × $75x) to the Class B shares. For the 2004 taxable year, Corp D's pro rata share of FC3's subpart F income will be $60x, Corp N's pro rata share of FC3's subpart F income will be $15x and Corp S's pro rata share of FC3's subpart F income will be $25x.

Example 5. (i) *Facts.* FC4, a controlled foreign corporation within the meaning of section 957(a), has outstanding 40 shares of participating, voting, preferred stock and 200 shares of common stock. The owner of a share of preferred stock is entitled to an annual dividend equal to 0.5-percent of FC4's retained earnings for the taxable year and also is entitled to additional dividends when declared by the board of directors of FC4. The common shareholders are entitled to dividends when declared by the board of directors of FC4. The board of directors of FC4 has discretion to pay dividends to the participating portion of the preferred shares (after the payment of the preference) and the common shares. The value of the preferred shares on the last day of FC4's 2004 taxable year is $600x ($100x of this value is attributable to the discretionary distribution rights of these shares) and the value of the common shares on that date is $400x. Corp E, a domestic corporation and United States shareholder of FC4, within the meaning of section 951(b), owns all of the preferred shares. FC5, a foreign corporation that is not a controlled foreign corporation within the meaning of section 957(a), owns all of the common shares. FC 4 and Corp E each use the calendar year as a taxable year. Corp E and FC5 are shareholders of FC4 for all of 2004. For 2004, FC4 has $100x of earnings and profits, and income of $100x with respect to which amounts are required to be included in gross income of United States shareholders under section 951(a). In 2004, FC4's retained earnings are equal to its earnings and profits. FC4 distributes as a dividend $20x to Corp E that year with respect to Corp E's preferred shares. The board of directors of FC4 determines that FC4 will not make any other distributions during that year.

(ii) *Analysis.* The non-discretionary distribution rights of the preferred shares are not a restriction or other limitation within the meaning of paragraph (e)(5) of this section. The allocation of FC4's earnings and profits between its preferred shares and common shares depends, in part, on the exercise of discretion by the board of directors of FC4 because the preferred shares are shares with both discretionary distribution rights and non-discretionary distribution rights. Paragraph (e)(3)(i) of this section is applied first to determine the allocation of earnings and profits of FC4 to the non-discretionary distribution rights of the preferred shares. If the total $100x of earnings were distributed on December 31, 2004, $20x would be distributed with respect to the non-discretionary distribution rights of Corp E's preferred shares. Accordingly, $20x would be allocated to such shares under paragraphs (e)(3)(i) and (iii) of this section. The remainder, $80x, would be allocated under paragraph (e)(3)(ii)(A) and (e)(3)(iii) of this section between the preferred and common shareholders by reference to the value of the discretionary distribution rights of the preferred shares and the value of the common shares. Therefore, the remaining $80x of earnings and profits of FC4 are allocated $16x ($100x/$500x × $80x) to the preferred shares and $64x ($400x/$500x × $80) to the common shares. For its taxable year 2004, Corp E's pro rata share of FC4's subpart F income will be $36x ($20x + $16x).

Example 6. (i) *Facts.* FC6, a controlled foreign corporation within the meaning of section 957(a), has outstanding 10 shares of common stock and 400 shares of 2-percent nonparticipating, voting, preferred stock with a par value of $1x per share. The common shareholders are entitled to dividends when declared by the board of directors of FC6. Corp M, a domestic corporation and a United States shareholder of FC6, within the meaning of section 951(b), owns all of the common shares. FC7, a foreign corporation that is not a controlled foreign corporation within the meaning of section 957(a), owns all of the preferred shares. Corp M and FC7 cause the governing documents of FC6 to provide that no dividends may be paid to the common shareholders until FC6 cumulatively earns $100,000x of income. FC6 and Corp M each use the calendar year as a taxable year. Corp M and FC7 are shareholders of FC6 for all of 2004. For 2004, FC6 has $50x of earnings and profits, and income of $50x with respect to which amounts are required to be included in gross income of United States shareholders under section 951(a). In 2004, FC6 distributes as a dividend $8x to FC7 with respect to FC7's preferred shares. FC6 makes no other distributions during that year.

(ii) *Analysis.* The agreement restricting FC6's ability to pay dividends to common shareholders until FC6 cumulatively earns $100,000x of income is a restriction or other limitation, within the meaning of paragraph (e)(5) of this section, and will be disregarded for purposes of calculating Corp M's pro rata share of subpart F income. The non-discretionary distribution rights of the preferred shares are not a restriction or other limitation within the meaning of paragraph (e)(5) of this section. If the total $50x of earnings were distributed on December 31, 2004, $8x would be distributed with respect to FC7's preferred shares and the remainder, $42x, would be distributed with respect to Corp M's common shares. Accordingly, under paragraph (e)(3)(i) of this section, Corp M's pro rata share of FC6's subpart F income is $42x for taxable year 2004.

Example 7. (i) *Facts.* FC8, a controlled foreign corporation within the meaning of section

957(a), has outstanding 40 shares of common stock and 10 shares of 4-percent voting preferred stock with a par value of $50x per share. Pursuant to the terms of the preferred stock, FC8 has the right to redeem at any time, in whole or in part, the preferred stock. FP, a foreign corporation, owns all of the preferred shares. Corp G, a domestic corporation wholly owned by FP and a United States shareholder of FC8, within the meaning of section 951(b), owns all of the common shares. FC8 and Corp G each use the calendar year as a taxable year. FP and Corp G are shareholders of FC8 for all of 2004. For 2004, FC8 has $100x of earnings and profits, and income of $100x with respect to which amounts are required to be included in gross income of United States shareholder under section 951(a). In 2004, FC8 distributes as a dividend $20x to FP with respect to FP's preferred shares. FC8 makes no other distributions during that year.

(ii) *Analysis.* Pursuant to paragraph (e)(3)(ii)(B) of this section, the redemption rights of the preferred shares will not be treated as a discretionary distribution right under paragraph (e)(3)(ii)(A) of this section. Further, if FC8 were treated as having redeemed any preferred shares under paragraph (e)(3)(i) of this section, the redemption would be treated as a distribution to which section 301 applies under section 302(d) due to FP's constructive ownership of the common shares. However, pursuant to paragraph (e)(4) of this section, no amount of earnings and profits would be allocated to the preferred shareholders on the hypothetical distribution date, under paragraph (e)(3)(i) of this section, as a result of FC8's right to redeem, in whole or in part, the preferred shares. FC8's redemption rights with respect to the preferred shares cannot affect the allocation of earnings and profits between FC8's shareholders. Therefore, the redemption rights are not restrictions or other limitations within the meaning of paragraph (e)(5) of this section. Additionally, the non-discretionary distribution rights of the preferred shares are not restrictions or other limitations within the meaning of paragraph (e)(5) of this section. Therefore, if the total $100x of earnings were distributed on December 31, 2004, $20x would be distributed with respect to FP's preferred shares and the remainder, $80x, would be distributed with respect to Corp G's common shares. Accordingly, under paragraph (e)(3)(i) of this section, Corp G's pro rata share of FC8's subpart F income is $80 for taxable year 2004.

Example 8. (i) *Facts.* FC9, a controlled foreign corporation within the meaning of section 957(a), has outstanding 40 shares of common stock and 60 shares of 6-percent, nonparticipating, nonvoting, preferred stock with a par value of $100x per share. Individual J, a United States shareholder of FC9, within the meaning of section 951(b), who uses the calendar year as a taxable year, owns 30 shares of the common stock, and 15 shares of the preferred stock during tax year 2004. The remaining 10 common shares and 45 preferred shares of FC9 are owned by Foreign Individual N, a foreign individual. Individual J and Individual N are shareholders of FC9 for all of 2004. For taxable year 2004, FC9 has $1,000x of earnings and profits, and income of $500x with respect to which amounts are required to be included in gross income of United States shareholders under section 951(a).

(ii) *Analysis.* The non-discretionary distribution rights of the preferred shares are not a restriction or other limitation within the meaning of paragraph (e)(5) of this section. If the total $1,000x of earnings and profits were distributed on December 31, 2004, $360x (0.06 × $100x × 60) would be distributed with respect to FC9's preferred stock and $640x ($1,000x minus $360x) would be distributed with respect to its common stock. Accordingly, of the $500x with respect to which amounts are required to be included in gross income of United States shareholders under section 951(a), $180x ($360x/$1,000x × $500x) is allocated to the outstanding preferred stock and $320x ($640x/$1,000x × $500x) is allocated to the outstanding common stock. Therefore, under paragraph (e)(3)(i) of this section, Individual J's pro rata share of such amounts for 2004 is $285x [($180x × 15/60)+($320x × 30/40)].

(7) *Effective date.*—These regulations apply for taxable years of a controlled foreign corporation beginning on or after January 1, 2005.
[Prop. Reg. § 1.951-1.]
[Proposed 8-6-2004.]

§ 1.951-2. Coordination of subpart F with election of a foreign investment company to distribute income.—A United States shareholder who for his taxable year is a qualified shareholder (within the meaning of section 1247(c)) of a foreign investment company with respect to which an election under section 1247(a) and the regulations thereunder is in effect for the taxable year of such company which ends with or within such taxable year of such shareholder shall not be required to include any amount in his gross income for his taxable year under paragraph (a) of § 1.951-1 with respect to such company for that taxable year of such company. [Reg. § 1.951-2.]
☐ [*T.D.* 6795, 1-28-65.]

§ 1.951-3. Coordination of subpart F with foreign personal holding company provisions.—A United States shareholder (as defined in section 951(b)) who is required under section 551(b) to include in his gross income for his taxable year his share of the undistributed foreign personal holding company income for the taxable year of a foreign personal holding company (as defined in section 552) which for that taxable year is a controlled foreign corporation (as defined in section 957) shall not be required to include in his gross income for his taxable year under section 951(a) and paragraph (a) of §1.951-1 any amount attributable to the earnings and profits of such corporation for that taxable year of such corporation. If a foreign corporation is both a foreign personal holding company and a controlled foreign corporation for the same period which is only a part of its taxable year, then, for purposes of applying the immediately preceding sentence, such corporation shall be deemed to be, for such part of such year, a foreign personal holding company and not a controlled foreign corporation and the earnings and profits of such corporation for the taxable year shall be deemed to be that amount which bears the same ratio to its earnings and profits for the taxable year as such part of the taxable year bears to the entire taxable year. The application of this section may be illustrated by the following examples:

Example (1). A, a United States shareholder, owns 100 percent of the only class of stock of controlled foreign corporation M which, in turn, owns 100 percent of the only class of stock of controlled foreign corporation N. A and Corporations M and N use the calendar year as a taxable year. During 1963, N Corporation derives $40,000 of gross income all of which is foreign personal holding company income within the meaning of section 553; thus, N Corporation is a foreign personal holding company for such year within the meaning of section 552(a). For 1963, N Corporation has undistributed foreign personal holding company income (as defined in section 556(a)) of $30,000, derives $25,000 of subpart F income, and has earnings and profits of $32,000. During 1963, M Corporation derives $100,000 of gross income (including as a dividend under section 555(c)(2) the $30,000 of N Corporation's undistributed foreign personal holding company income), 65 percent of which is foreign personal holding company income within the meaning of section 553. Therefore, M Corporation is a foreign personal holding company for such year. For 1963, M Corporation has undistributed foreign personal holding company income (as defined in section 556(a)) of $90,000, determined by taking into account under section 552(c)(1) N Corporation's $30,000 of undistributed foreign personal holding company income for such year; in addition, M Corporation derives $50,000 of subpart F income and has earnings and profits of $92,000. Neither M Corporation nor N Corporation makes any actual distributions during 1963. A is required under section 551(b) to include in his gross income for 1963 as a dividend the $90,000 of M Corporation's undistributed foreign personal holding company income for such year. For 1963, A is not required to include in his gross income under section 951(a) any of the $50,000 subpart F income of M Corporation or of the $25,000 subpart F income of N Corporation.

Example (2). The facts are the same as in example (1), except that only 45 percent of M Corporation's gross income (determined by including under section 555(c)(2) the $30,000 of N Corporation's undistributed foreign personal holding company income) is foreign personal holding company income within the meaning of section 553; accordingly, M Corporation is not a foreign personal holding company for 1963. Since for such year M Corporation is not a foreign personal holding company, the undistributed foreign personal holding company income ($30,000) of N Corporation is not required under section 555(b) to be included in the gross income of M Corporation for 1963; as a result, such income is not required under section 551(b) to be included in the gross income of A for such year even though N Corporation is a foreign personal holding company for that year. For 1963, A is required to include $75,000 in his gross income under section 951(a)(1)(A)(i) and paragraph (a) of §1.951-1, consisting of the $50,000 subpart F income of M Corporation and the $25,000 subpart F income of N Corporation.

Example (3). The facts are the same as in example (1), except that in 1963 N Corporation actually distributes $30,000 to M Corporation and M Corporation, in turn, actually distributes $90,000 to A. Under section 556 the undistributed foreign personal holding company income of both M Corporation and N Corporation is thus reduced to zero; accordingly, no amount is included in the gross income of A under section 551(b) by reason of his interest in corporations M and N. A must include $75,000 in his gross income for 1963 under section 951(a)(1)(A)(i) and paragraph (a) of §1.951-1, consisting of the $50,000 subpart F income of M Corporation and the $25,000 subpart F income of N Corporation. Of the $90,000 distribution received by A from M Corporation, $75,000 is excludable from his gross income under section 959(a)(1) as previously taxed earnings and profits; the remaining $15,000 is includible in his gross income for 1963 as a dividend.

Example (4). (a) A, a United States shareholder, owns 100 percent of the only class of stock of controlled foreign corporation P, organized on January 1, 1963. Both A and P Corporation use the calendar year as a taxable year. During 1963, 1964, and 1965, P Corporation is not a foreign personal holding company as defined in section 552(a); in each of such years, P Corporation derives dividend income of $10,000 which constitutes foreign personal holding company income (within the meaning of § 1.954-2) but under 26 CFR § 1.954-1(b)(1) (Rev. as of Apr. 1, 1975) excludes such amounts from foreign base company income as dividends received from, and reinvested in, qualified investments in less developed countries. Corporation P's earnings and profits accumulated for 1963, 1964, and 1965 and determined under paragraph (b)(2) of § 1.955-1 are $40,000. For 1966, P Corporation is a foreign personal holding company, has predistribution earnings and profits of $10,000, derives $10,000 of income which is both foreign personal holding company income within the meaning of section 553 and subpart F income within the meaning of section 952, distributes $8,000 to A, and has undistributed foreign personal holding company income of $2,000 within the meaning of section 556. In addition, for 1966 P Corporation has a withdrawal (determined under section 955(a), as in effect before the enactment of the Tax Reduction Act of 1975, but without regard to its earnings and profits for such year) of $25,000 of previously excluded subpart F income from investment in less developed countries. A is required under section 551(b) to include in his gross income for 1966 as a dividend the $2,000 undistributed foreign personal holding company income. The $8,000 distribution is includible in A's gross income for 1966 under sections 61(a)(7) and 301 as a distribution to which section 316(a)(2) applies. Corporation P's $25,000 withdrawal of previously excluded subpart F income from investment in less developed countries is includible in A's gross income for 1966 under section 951(a)(1)(A)(ii) and paragraph (a)(2) of § 1.951-1.

(b) If P Corporation's earnings and profits accumulated for 1963, 1964, and 1965 were $15,000, instead of $40,000, the result would be the same as in paragraph (a) of this example, except that a withdrawal of only $15,000 of previously excluded subpart F income from investment in less developed countries would be includible in A's gross income for 1966 under section 951(a)(1)(A)(ii) and paragraph (a)(2) of § 1.951-1.

(c) The principles of this example also apply to withdrawals (determined under section 955(a), as in effect before the enactment of the Tax Reduction Act of 1975) of previously excluded subpart F income from investment in less developed countries effected after the effective date of such Act, and to withdrawals (determined under section 955(a), as amended by such Act) of previously excluded subpart F income from investment in foreign base company shipping operations.

Example (5). (a) The facts are the same as in paragraph (a) of example (4), except that, instead of having a $25,000 decrease in qualified investments in less developed countries for 1966, P Corporation invests $20,000 in tangible property (not described in section 956(b)(2)) located in the United States and such investment constitutes an increase (determined under section 956(a) but without regard to the earnings and profits of P Corporation for 1966) in earnings invested in United States property. Corporation P's earnings and profits accumulated for 1963, 1964, and 1965 and determined under paragraph (b)(1) of § 1.956-1 are $22,000. The result is the same as in paragraph (a) of example (4), except that instead of including the $25,000 withdrawal, A must include $20,000 in his gross income for 1966 under section 951(a)(1)(B) and paragraph (a)(2)(iv) of § 1.951-1 as an investment of earnings in United States property.

(b) If P Corporation's earnings and profits accumulated for 1963, 1964, and 1965 were $9,000 instead of $22,000, the result would be the same as in paragraph (a) of this example, except that only $9,000 would be includible in A's gross income for 1966 under section 951(a)(1)(B) and paragraph (a)(2)(iv) of § 1.951-1 as investment of earnings in United States property. [Reg. § 1.951-3.]

☐ [*T.D.* 6795, 1-28-65. *Amended by T.D.* 7893, 5-11-83.]

§ 1.952-1. Subpart F income defined.— (a) *In general.*—For purposes of sections 951 through 964, a controlled foreign corporation's subpart F income for any taxable year shall, except as provided in paragraph (b) of this section and subject to the limitations of paragraphs (c) and (d) of this section, consist of the sum of—

(1) The income derived by such corporation for such year from the insurance of United States risks (determined in accordance with the provisions of section 953 and §§ 1.953-1 through 1.953-6),

(2) The income derived by such corporation for such year which constitutes foreign base company income (determined in accordance with the provisions of section 954 and §§ 1.954-1 through 1.954-8),

(3)(i) An amount equal to the product of—

(A) The income of such corporation other than income which—

(1) Is attributable to earnings and profits of the foreign corporation included in the gross income of a United States person under section 951 (other than by reason of this

paragraph) (determined in accordance with the provisions of section 951 and § 1.951-1), or

(2) Is described in section 952(b), multiplied by

(B) The international boycott factor determined in accordance with the provisions of section 999(c)(1), or

(ii) In lieu of the amount determined under paragraph (a)(3)(i) of this section, the amount described under section 999(c)(2) of such international boycott income, and

(4) The sum of the amount of any illegal bribes, kickbacks, or other payments paid after November 3, 1976, by or on behalf of the corporation during the taxable year of the corporation directly or indirectly to an official, employee, or agent in fact of a government. An amount is paid by a controlled foreign corporation where it is paid by an officer, director, employee, shareholder or agent of such corporation for the benefit of such corporation. For purposes of this section, the principles of section 162(c) and the regulations thereunder shall apply. In the case of payments made after September 3, 1982, a payment is illegal if the payment would be unlawful under the Foreign Corrupt Practices Act of 1977 if the payor were a United States person. The fair market value of an illegal payment made in the form of property or services shall be considered the amount of such illegal payment.
Pursuant to section 951(a)(1)(A)(i) and § 1.951-1, a United States shareholder of such controlled foreign corporation must include his pro rata share of such subpart F income in his gross income for his taxable year in which or with which such taxable year of the foreign corporation ends. See section 952(a). However, see paragraph (a) of § 1.957-2 for special rule limiting the subpart F income to the income derived from the insurance of United States risks in the case of certain controlled foreign corporations described in section 957(b).

(b) *Exclusion of U.S. income.*—(1) *Taxable years beginning before January 1, 1967.*—For rules applicable to taxable years beginning before January 1, 1967, see 26 CFR § 1.952-1(b)(1) (Rev. as of April 1, 1975).

(2) *Taxable years beginning after December 31, 1966.*—Notwithstanding paragraph (a) of this section, a controlled foreign corporation's subpart F income for any taxable year beginning after December 31, 1966, shall not include any item of income from sources within the United States which is effectively connected for that year with the conduct by such corporation of a trade or business in the United States unless, pursuant to a treaty to which the United States is a party, such item of income either is exempt from the income tax imposed by chapter 1 (relating to normal taxes and surtaxes) of the Code or is subject to such tax at a reduced rate. Thus, for example, dividends received from sources within the United States by a foreign corporation engaged in business in the United States during the taxable year, which are not effectively connected for that year with the conduct of a trade or business in the United States by that corporation, shall not be excluded from subpart F income under section 952(b) and this subparagraph even though such dividends are subject to the tax of 30 percent imposed by section 881(a). Also, for example, if, by reason of an income tax convention to which the United States is a party, an amount of interest from sources within the United States which is effectively connected for the taxable year with the conduct of a business in the United States by a foreign corporation is subject to tax under chapter 1 at a flat rate of 15 percent, as provided in § 1.871-12, such interest is not excluded from subpart F income under section 952(b) and this subparagraph. The deductions attributable to items of income which are excluded from subpart F income under this subparagraph shall not be taken into account for purposes of section 952.

(3) *Rule applicable under section 956(b)(2).*—For purposes only of paragraph (b)(1)(viii) of § 1.956-2, an item of income derived by a controlled foreign corporation from sources within the United States with respect to which for the taxable year a tax is imposed in accordance with section 882(a) shall be considered described in section 952(b) whether or not such item of income would have constituted subpart F income for such year.

(c) *Limitation on a controlled foreign corporation's subpart F income.*—(1) *In general.*—A United States shareholder's pro rata share (determined in accordance with the rules of paragraph (e) of § 1.951-1) of a controlled foreign corporation's subpart F income for any taxable year shall not exceed his pro rata share of the earnings and profits (as defined in section 964(a) and § 1.964-1) of such corporation for such taxable year, computed as of the close of such taxable year without diminution by reason of any distributions made during such taxable year, minus the sum of—

(i) The amount, if any, by which such shareholder's pro rata share of—

(a) The sum of such corporation's deficits in earnings and profits for prior taxable years beginning after December 31, 1962, plus

(b) The sum of such corporation's deficits in earnings and profits for taxable years beginning after December 31, 1959, and before January 1, 1963 (reduced by the sum of the earnings and profits (as so defined) of such

corporation for any of such taxable years) exceeds

(c) The sum of such corporation's earnings and profits for prior taxable years beginning after December 31, 1962, which, with respect to such shareholder, are allocated to other earnings and profits under section 959(c)(3) and § 1.959-3; and

(ii) Such shareholder's pro rata share of any deficits in earnings and profits of other foreign corporations for a taxable year beginning after December 31, 1962, which are attributable to stock of such other foreign corporations owned by such shareholder within the meaning of section 958(a) and which, in accordance with section 952(d) and paragraph (d) of this section, are taken into account as a reduction in the controlled foreign corporation's earnings and profits for such taxable year.

For purposes of applying this subparagraph, the reduction (if any) provided by subdivision (i) of this subparagraph in a United States shareholder's pro rata share of the earnings and profits of a controlled foreign corporation shall be taken into account before the reduction provided by subdivision (ii) of this subparagraph. See section 952(c).

(2) *Special rules.*—For purposes only of determining the limitation under subparagraph (1) of this paragraph on a United States shareholder's pro rata share of a controlled foreign corporation's subpart F income for any taxable year—

(i) *Status of foreign corporation.*—The earnings and profits, or deficit in earnings and profits, of a foreign corporation for any taxable year shall be taken into account whether or not such foreign corporation is a controlled foreign corporation at the time such earnings and profits are derived or such deficit in earnings and profits is incurred.

(ii) *Deficits in earnings and profits taken into account only once.*—A controlled foreign corporation's deficit in earnings and profits for any taxable year preceding the taxable year shall be taken into account for the taxable year only to the extent such deficit has not been taken into account under this paragraph, paragraph (d) of this section, or paragraph (d)(2)(ii) of § 1.963-2 (applied as if section 963 had not been repealed by the Tax Reduction Act of 1975) in computing a minimum distribution, for any taxable year preceding the taxable year, to reduce earnings and profits of such preceding year of such controlled foreign corporation or of any other controlled foreign corporation. To the extent a controlled foreign corporation's (the "first corporation") excess foreign base company shipping deductions for any taxable year (determined under § 1.955A-3(c)(2)(i)) reduce the foreign base company shipping income of another member of a related group (as defined in § 1.955A-2(b)), such deductions shall not be taken into account in determining the earnings and profits or deficit in earnings and profits of such first corporation for such taxable year for purposes of this paragraph (c) and paragraph (d) of this section. The rule of the preceding sentence shall not apply to the extent the excess foreign base company shipping deductions of the first corporation reduce the foreign base company shipping income of another member of a related group below zero.

(iii) *Determination of pro rata share.*—A United States shareholder's pro rata share of a controlled foreign corporation's earnings and profits, or deficit in earnings and profits, for any taxable year shall be determined in accordance with the principles of paragraph (e) of § 1.951-1 and paragraph (d)(2)(ii) of § 1.963-2.

(3) *Illustrations.*—The application of this paragraph may be illustrated by the following examples:

Example (1). (a) A is a United States shareholder who owns 100 percent of the only class of stock of M Corporation, a controlled foreign corporation organized on January 1, 1963. Both A and M Corporation use the calendar year as a taxable year.

(b) During 1963, M Corporation derives $20,000 of subpart F income and has earnings and profits of $30,000. Corporation M makes no distributions to A during such year. The limitation under section 952(c) on M Corporation's subpart F income for 1963 is $30,000; and $20,000 is includible in A's gross income for such year under section 951(a)(1)(A)(i).

(c) On January 1, 1964, M Corporation acquires 100 percent of the only class of stock of N Corporation, a controlled foreign corporation which uses the calendar year as a taxable year. During 1964, N Corporation derives $6,000 of subpart F income, has $7,000 of earnings and profits, and distributes $5,000 to M Corporation. The limitation under section 952(c) on N Corporation's subpart F income for 1964 is $7,000; and $6,000 of subpart F income is includible in A's gross income for such year under section 951(a)(1)(A)(i).

(d) During 1964, M Corporation derives $8,000 of rents which constitute subpart F income, makes a $10,000 distribution to A, and has earnings and profits of $12,000 (including the $5,000 dividend received from N Corporation). The limitation under section 952(c) on M Corporation's subpart F income for 1964 is $7,000, determined as follows:

Corporation M's earnings and profits for 1964 (determined under section 964(a) and § 1.964-1 as of the close of such year without diminution for any distributions made during such year)	$12,000
Less: Corporation M's earnings and profits for 1964 described in section 959(b)	5,000
Limitation on M Corporation's subpart F income for 1964	$7,000

Thus, for 1964 with respect to A's interest in M Corporation, $7,000 of subpart F income is includible in his gross income under section 951(a)(1)(A)(i). The $10,000 dividend received from M Corporation is excludable from A's gross income for 1964 under section 959(a)(1) and paragraph (b) of § 1.959-1.

Example (2). A is a United States shareholder who owns 100 percent of the only class of stock of R Corporation which was organized on January 1, 1961. R Corporation is a controlled foreign corporation for the entire period after December 31, 1962, here involved. Both A and R Corporation use the calendar year as a taxable year. During 1963, R Corporation derives $25,000 of subpart F income and has $50,000 of earnings and profits. Corporation R has $15,000 of earnings and profits for 1961, and a deficit in earnings and profits of $45,000 for 1962. Thus, R Corporation has as of December 31, 1963, a net deficit in earnings and profits of $30,000 for the years 1961 and 1962. Corporation R makes no distributions to A during 1963. The limitation under section 952(c) on R Corporation's subpart F income for 1963 is $20,000 ($50,000 minus $30,000), and $20,000 of subpart F income is includible in A's gross income for 1963 under section 951(a)(1)(A)(i). During 1964, R Corporation derives $18,000 of subpart F income and has $30,000 of earnings and profits. Corporation R makes no distributions to A during 1964. The entire $18,000 of subpart F income is includible in A's gross income for 1964 under section 951(a)(1)(A)(i).

(d) *Treatment of deficits in earnings and profits attributable to stock of other foreign corporations indirectly owned by a United States shareholder.*—(1) *In general.*—For purposes of paragraph (c)(1)(ii) of this section, if—

(i) A United States shareholder owns (within the meaning of section 958(a)) stock in two or more foreign corporations in a chain of foreign corporations (as defined in subparagraph (2)(ii) of this paragraph), and

(ii) Any of the corporations in such chain has a deficit in earnings and profits for taxable year beginning after December 31, 1962,

then, with respect to such shareholder and only for purposes of determining the limitation on subpart F income under paragraph (c) of this section, the earnings and profits for the taxable year of each such foreign corporation which is a controlled foreign corporation shall, in accordance with the rules of subparagraph (2) of this paragraph, be reduced to take into account any deficit in earnings and profits referred to in subdivision (ii) of this subparagraph. See section 952(d).

(2) *Special rules.*—For purposes of this paragraph—

(i) *Applicable rules.*—The special rules set forth in paragraph (c)(2) of this section shall apply.

(ii) *"Chain" defined.*—A chain of foreign corporations shall, with respect to a United States shareholder, include—

(a) Any foreign corporation in which such shareholder owns (within the meaning of section 958(a)(1)(A)) stock, but only to the extent of the stock so owned, and

(b) All foreign corporations in which such shareholder owns (within the meaning of section 958(a)(2)) stock, but only to the extent of the stock so owned by reason of his ownership of the stock referred to in *(a)* of this subdivision.

(iii) *Allocation of deficit.*—If one or more foreign corporations (whether or not a controlled foreign corporation) includible in a chain of foreign corporations has a deficit in earnings and profits (determined under section 964(a) and § 1.964-1) for the taxable year, the amount of deficit taken into account under section 952(d) with respect to a United States shareholder in such chain as a reduction in earnings and profits for the taxable year of a controlled foreign corporation includible in such chain shall be an amount which bears the same ratio to such shareholder's pro rata share of the total deficits in earnings and profits for the taxable year of all includible foreign corporations as his pro rata share of the earnings and profits (determined under paragraph (c) of this section but without regard to the provisions of subparagraph (1)(ii) of such paragraph) for the taxable year of such includible controlled foreign corporation bears to his pro rata share of the total earnings and profits (as so determined under paragraph (c) of this section) for the taxable year of all includible controlled foreign corporations. The amount of deficit taken into account under this subdivision with respect to any controlled foreign corporation includible in a chain of foreign corporations shall not exceed the United States shareholder's pro rata share of the controlled foreign corporation's earnings and profits for the taxable year.

(iv) *Taxable year.*—The taxable year from which a deficit is allocated under this paragraph, and the taxable year to which such deficit is allocated to reduce earnings and profits, shall be the taxable year of the foreign corporation ending with or within the taxable year of the United States shareholder described in subparagraph (1)(i) of this paragraph.

(3) *Illustration.*—The application of this paragraph may be illustrated by the following examples:

Example (1). (a) Domestic corporation M owns 100 percent, 20 percent, and 100 percent, respectively, of the only class of stock of foreign corporations A, B, and F, respectively. Corporation A owns 80 percent of the only class of stock of each of foreign corporations B and C, respectively. Corporation F owns 20 percent of such stock of C Corporation. Corporation B owns 75 percent of the only class of stock of foreign corporation D, and 50 percent of the only class of stock of each of foreign corporations G and H, respectively. C Corporation owns 75 percent of the only class of stock of foreign corporation E. All the corporations use the calendar year as a taxable year, and all of the foreign corporations, except corporations G and H, are controlled foreign corporations throughout the period here involved.

(b) The subpart F income, and the earnings and profits (determined under paragraph (c) of this section but without regard to subparagraph (1)(ii) of such paragraph) or deficit in earnings and profits (determined under section 964(a) and §1.964-1), of each of the foreign corporations for 1963 are as follows, the deficits being set forth in parentheses:

	Subpart F income	Earnings and profits (deficits)
A Corporation	$6,000	$18,000
B Corporation	. .	(7,500)
C Corporation	. .	(2,500)
D Corporation	4,000	5,000
E Corporation	12,000	15,000
F Corporation	8,000	20,250
G Corporation	. .	(10,000)
H Corporation	. .	7,000

(c) The chains of foreign corporations (within the meaning of subparagraph (2)(ii) of this paragraph) for 1963 are the "A" chain, consisting of corporations A, B, C, D, E, G, and H, but only to the extent of M Corporation's stock interest in such corporations under section 958(a) by reason of its ownership of stock in A Corporation; the "B" chain, consisting of corporations B, D, G, and H, but only to the extent of M Corporation's stock interest in such corporations under section 958(a) by reason of its ownership of stock in B Corporation; and the "F" chain, consisting of corporations F, C, and E, but only to the extent of M Corporation's stock interest in such corporations under section 958(a) by reason of its ownership of stock in F Corporation.

(d) Corporation M's stock interest under section 958(a) in each of the chains of foreign corporations is as follows for 1963:

	A %	B %	C %	D %	E %	F %	G %	H %
A chain:								
Direct interest	100							
(100% × 80%)		80						
(100% × 80%)			80					
(80% × 75%)				60				
(80% × 75%)					60			
(80% × 50%)							40	
(80% × 50%)								40
B chain:								
Direct interest		20						
(20% × 75%)				15				
(20% × 50%)							10	
(20% × 50%)								10
F chain:								
Direct interest						100		
(100% × 20%)			20					
(20% × 75%)					15			
Total interests	100	100	100	75	75	100	50	50

(e) Corporation M's pro rata share of the earnings and profits (determined under paragraph (c) of this section but without regard to subparagraph (1)(ii) of such paragraph), or of the deficit, of each controlled foreign corporation or each foreign corporation, respectively, includible in the respective chains for 1963 is as follows:

Reg. §1.952-1(d)(3)

	Earnings and profits	Deficit
A chain:		
A Corporation (100%)	$18,000	....
B Corporation (80%)	....	($6,000)
C Corporation (80%)	....	(2,000)
D Corporation (60%)	3,000	....
E Corporation (60%)	9,000	....
G Corporation (40%)	....	(4,000)
H Corporation (40%)	*	....
Total	$30,000	($12,000)
B chain:		
B Corporation (20%)	....	($1,500)
D Corporation (15%)	$750	....
G Corporation (10%)	....	(1,000)
H Corporation (10%)	*	....
Total	$750	($2,500)
F chain:		
F Corporation (100%)	$20,250	....
C Corporation (20%)	....	($500)
E Corporation (15%)	2,250	....
Total	$22,500	($500)

*The earnings and profits of H Corporation are not included in the total earnings and profits for the chain because H Corporation is not a controlled foreign corporation.

(f) The amount by which M Corporation's pro rata share of the earnings and profits for 1963 of the controlled foreign corporations in each respective chain shall be reduced under section 952(d) by M Corporation's pro rata share of the deficits of corporations B, C, and G for 1963 is determined as follows:

		Amount of reduction
A chain:		
A Corporation ($12,000 × $18,000/$30,000)		$7,200
D Corporation ($12,000 × $3,000/$30,000)		1,200
E Corporation ($12,000 × $9,000/$30,000)		3,600
Total		$12,000
B chain:		
D Corporation ($2,500 × $750/$750)	$2,500	
Limitation: M Corporation's pro rata share of D Corporation's earnings and profits	750	
Allocation of used deficit ($750) to M Corporation's pro rata share of the deficits of corporations B and G:		
B Corporation ($750 × ($1,500/$2,500))	$450	
G Corporation ($750 × ($1,000/$2,500))	300	
Total	$750	$750
F chain:		
F Corporation ($500 × $20,250/$22,500)		$450
E Corporation ($500 × $2,250/$22,500)		50
Total		$500

(g) Corporation M's pro rata share of the earnings and profits (determined after reduction for deficits under section 952(d)) for 1963 of each controlled foreign corporation in the respective chains, determined on a chain-by-chain basis, is determined as follows:

	Earnings and profits before reduction	Reduction (sec. 952(d))	Reduced earnings and profits
A chain:			
A Corporation	$18,000	$7,200	$10,800
D Corporation	3,000	1,200	1,800
E Corporation	9,000	3,600	5,400
B chain:			
D Corporation	750	750	..
F chain:			
F Corporation	20,250	450	19,800
E Corporation	2,250	50	2,200

(h) Corporation M's pro rata share of each controlled foreign corporation's subpart F income, limited as provided by section 952(c) and paragraph (c) of this section, for 1963 which is includible in its gross income for such year under section 951(a)(1)(A)(i) and §1.951-1 is determined as follows:

	Subpart F income (before limitation)	Earnings and profits (sec. 952(c))	Amount includible in income
A Corporation (100%)	$6,000	$10,800	$6,000
D Corporation (75%)	3,000	1,800	1,800
E Corporation (75%)	9,000	7,600	7,600
F Corporation (100%)	8,000	19,800	8,000
Total includible under section 951(a)(1)(A)(i)			$23,400

Example (2). The facts are the same as in example (1) except that, in addition, for 1964, foreign corporations C, D, and E have no subpart F income and no earnings and profits and foreign corporations G and H have no earnings and profits. For 1964, B Corporation has subpart F income of $1,000 and earnings and profits (determined in accordance with section 964(a) and §1.964-1) of $1,500; A Corporation has subpart F income of $800 and earnings and profits of $1,000; and F Corporation has subpart F income of $500 and earnings and profits of $1,000. Such earnings and profits are determined without regard to distributions for 1964. Corporation B has an unused deficit in earnings and profits of $1,050 for 1963 ($1,500 minus $450) applicable to M Corporation's interest in such corporation (paragraph (f) of example (1)), and, under paragraph (c)(1)(i)(a) of this section, with respect to M Corporation, such deficit reduces B Corporation's earnings and profits for 1964 to $450. Inasmuch as G Corporation is not a controlled foreign corporation for 1964, such corporation's unused deficit in earnings and profits of $700 for 1963 ($1,000 minus $300) applicable to M Corporation's interest in such corporation (paragraph (f) of example (1)) may be used under paragraph (c)(1)(i)(a) of this section to reduce M Corporation's interest in G Corporation's earnings and profits in a later year or years for which G Corporation is a controlled foreign corporation. Corporation M's pro rata share of each controlled foreign corporation's subpart F income, limited as provided by section 952(c) and paragraph (c) of this section, for 1964 which is includible in its gross income for such year under section 951(a)(1)(A)(i) and §1.951-1 is determined as follows:

	Subpart F income (before limitation)	Earnings and profits (sec. 952(c))	Amount includible in income
A Corporation	$800	$1,000	$800
B Corporation	1,000	450	450
F Corporation	500	1,000	500

Example (3). The facts are the same as in example (2), except that for 1964 B Corporation has subpart F income of $550 and earnings and profits (determined in accordance with section 964(a) and §1.964-1) of $550; such earnings and profits are determined without regard to distributions for 1964. Under paragraph (c)(1)(i)(a) of this section, B Corporation's unused deficit of $1,050 for 1963 reduces its earnings and profits for 1964 with respect to M Corporation to zero. The remaining $500 of the unused deficit for 1963 applicable to M Corporation's interest in B Corporation may be used under paragraph (c)(1)(i)(a) of this section in later years to reduce M Corporation's interest in B Corporation's earnings and profits.

(e) *Application of current earnings and profits limitation.*—(1) *In general.*—If the subpart F income (as defined in section 952(a)) of a controlled foreign corporation exceeds the foreign corporation's earnings and profits for the taxable year, the subpart F income includible in the income of the corporation's United States shareholders is reduced under section 952(c)(1)(A) in accordance with the following rules. The excess of subpart F income over current year earnings and profits shall—

(i) First, proportionately reduce subpart F income in each separate category of the controlled foreign corporation, as defined in § 1.904-5(a)(1), in which current earnings and profits are zero or less than zero;

(ii) Second, proportionately reduce subpart F income in each separate category in which subpart F income exceeds current earnings and profits; and

(iii) Third, proportionately reduce subpart F income in other separate categories.

(2) *Allocation to a category of subpart F income.*—An excess amount that is allocated under paragraph (e)(1) of this section to a separate category must be further allocated to a category of subpart F income if the separate category contains more than one category of subpart F income described in section 952(a) or, in the case of foreign base company income, described in § 1.954-1(c)(1)(iii)(A)(*1*) or (*2*). In such case, the excess amount that is allocated to the separate category must be allocated to the various categories of subpart F income within that separate category on a proportionate basis.

(3) *Recapture of subpart F income reduced by operation of earnings and profits limitation.*—Any amount in a category of subpart F income described in section 952(a) or, in the case of foreign base company income, described in § 1.954-1(c)(1)(iii)(A)(*1*) or (*2*) that is reduced by operation of the current year earnings and profits limitation of section 952(c)(1)(A) and this paragraph (e) shall be subject to recapture in a subsequent year under the rules of section 952(c)(2) and paragraph (f) of this section.

(4) *Coordination with sections 953 and 954.*—The rules of this paragraph (e) shall be applied after the application of sections 953 and 954 and the regulations under those sections, except as provided in § 1.954-1(d)(4)(ii).

(5) *Earnings and deficits retain separate limitation character.*—The income reduction rules of paragraph (e)(1) of this section shall apply only for purposes of determining the amount of an inclusion under section 951(a)(1)(A) from each separate category as defined in § 1.904-5(a)(1) and the separate categories in which recapture accounts are established under section 952(c)(2) and paragraph (f) of this section. For rules applicable in computing post-1986 undistributed earnings, see generally section 902 and the regulations under that section. For rules relating to the allocation of deficits for purposes of computing foreign taxes deemed paid under section 960 with respect to an inclusion under section 951(a)(1)(A), see § 1.960-1(i).

(f) *Recapture of subpart F income in subsequent taxable year.*—(1) *In general.*—If a controlled foreign corporation's subpart F income for a taxable year is reduced under the current year earnings and profits limitation of section 952(c)(1)(A) and paragraph (e) of this section, recapture accounts will be established and subject to recharacterization in any subsequent taxable year to the extent the recapture accounts were not previously recharacterized or distributed, as provided in paragraphs (f)(2) and (3) of this section.

(2) *Rules of recapture.*—(i) *Recapture account.*—If a category of subpart F income described in section 952(a) or, in the case of foreign base company income, described in § 1.954-1(c)(1)(iii)(A)(*1*) or (*2*) is reduced under the current year earnings and profits limitation of section 952(c)(1)(A) and paragraph (e) of this section for a taxable year, the amount of such reduction shall constitute a recapture account.

(ii) *Recapture.*—Each recapture account of the controlled foreign corporation will be recharacterized, on a proportionate basis, as subpart F income in the same separate category (as defined in § 1.904-5(a)(1)) as the recapture account to the extent that current year earnings and profits exceed subpart F income in a taxable year. The United States shareholder must include his pro rata share (determined under the rules of § 1.951-1(e)) of each recharacterized amount in income as subpart F income in such separate category for the taxable year.

(iii) *Reduction of recapture account and corresponding earnings.*—Each recapture account, and post-1986 undistributed earnings in the separate category containing the recapture account, will be reduced in any taxable year by the amount which is recharacterized under paragraph (f)(2)(ii) of this section. In addition, each recapture account, and post-1986 undistributed earnings in the separate category containing the recapture account, will be reduced in the amount of any distribution out of that account (as determined under the ordering rules of section 959(c) and paragraph (f)(3)(ii) of this section).

(3) *Distribution ordering rules.*—(i) *Coordination of recapture and distribution rules.*—If a controlled foreign corporation distributes an amount out of earnings and profits described in section 959(c)(3) in a year in which current year earnings and profits exceed subpart F income and there is an amount in a recapture account for such year, the recapture rules will apply first.

(ii) *Distributions reduce recapture accounts first.*—Any distribution made by a controlled foreign corporation out of earnings and profits described in section 959(c)(3) shall be treated as made first on a proportionate basis out of the recapture accounts in each separate category to the extent thereof (even if the amount in the recapture account exceeds post-1986 undistributed earnings in the separate category containing the recapture account). Any remaining distribution shall be treated as made on a proportionate basis out of the remaining earnings and profits of the controlled foreign corporation in each separate category. See section 904(d)(3)(D).

(4) *Examples.*—The application of paragraphs (e) and (f) of this section may be illustrated by the following examples:

Example 1. (i) A, a U.S. person, is the sole shareholder of CFC, a controlled foreign corporation formed on January 1, 1998, whose functional currency is the u. In 1998, CFC earns 100u of foreign base company sales income that is general limitation income described in section 904(d)(1)(I) and incurs a (200u) loss attributable to activities that would have produced general limitation income that is not subpart F income. In 1998 CFC also earns 100u of foreign personal holding company income that is passive income described in section 904(d)(1)(A), and 100u of foreign personal holding company income that is dividend income subject to a separate limitation described in section 904(d)(1)(E) for dividends from a noncontrolled section 902 corporation. CFC's subpart F income for 1998, 300u, exceeds CFC's current earnings and profits, 100u, by 200u. Under section 952(c)(1)(A) and paragraph (e) of this section, subpart F income is limited to CFC's current earnings and profits of 100u, all of which is included in A's gross income under section 951(a)(1)(A). The 200u of CFC's 1998 subpart F income that is not included in A's income in 1998 by reason of section 952(c)(1)(A) is subject to recapture under section 952(c)(2) and paragraph (f) of this section.

(ii) For purposes of determining the amount and type of income included in A's gross income and the amount and type of income in CFC's recapture account, the rules of paragraphs (e)(1) and (2) of this section apply. Under paragraph (e)(1)(i) of this section, the amount by which CFC's subpart F income exceeds its earnings and profits for 1998, 200u, first reduces from 100u to 0 CFC's subpart F income in the general limitation category, which has a current year deficit of (100u) in earnings and profits. Next, under paragraph (e)(1)(iii) of this section, the remaining 100u by which CFC's 1998 subpart F income exceeds earnings and profits is applied proportionately to reduce CFC's subpart F income in the separate categories for passive income (100u) and dividends from the noncontrolled section 902 corporation (100u). Thus, A includes 50u of passive limitation/foreign personal holding company income and 50u of dividends from the noncontrolled section 902 corporation/foreign personal holding company income in gross income in 1998. CFC has 100u in its general limitation/foreign base company sales income recapture account attributable to the 100u of foreign base company sales income that is not included in A's income by reason of the earnings and profits limitation of section 952(c)(1)(A). CFC also has 50u in its passive limitation recapture account, all of which is attributable to foreign personal holding company income, and 50u in its recapture account for dividends from the noncontrolled section 902 corporation, all of which is attributable to foreign personal holding company income.

(iii) For purposes of computing post-1986 undistributed earnings, the rules of sections 902 and 960, including the rules of §1.960-1(i), apply. Under §1.960-1(i), the general limitation deficit of (100u) is allocated proportionately to reduce passive limitation earnings of 100u and noncontrolled section 902 dividend earnings of 100u. Thus, passive limitation earnings are reduced by 50u to 50u (100u passive limitation earnings/200u total earnings in positive separate categories × (100u) general limitation deficit = 50u reduction), and the noncontrolled section 902 corporation earnings are reduced by 50u to 50u (100u noncontrolled section 902 corporation earnings/200u total earnings in positive separate categories × (100u) general limitation deficit = 50u reduction). All of CFC's post-1986 foreign income taxes with respect to passive limitation income and dividends from the noncontrolled section 902 corporation are deemed paid by A under section 960 with respect to the subpart F inclusions (50u inclusion/50u earnings in each separate category). After the inclusion and deemed-paid taxes are computed, at the close of 1998 CFC has a (100u) deficit in general limitation earnings (100u subpart F earnings + (200u) nonsubpart F loss), 50u of passive limitation earnings (100u of earnings attributable to foreign personal holding company income – 50u inclusion) with a corresponding passive limitation/foreign personal holding company income recapture account of 50u, and 50u of earnings subject to a separate limitation for dividends from the noncontrolled section 902 corporation (100u earnings – 50u inclusion) with a corresponding noncontrolled section 902 corporation/foreign personal holding company income recapture account of 50u.

Example 2. (i) The facts are the same as in *Example 1* with the addition of the following facts. In 1999, CFC earns 100u of foreign base company sales income that is general limitation income and 100u of foreign personal holding company income that is passive limitation income. In addition, CFC incurs (10u) of expenses that are allocable to its separate limitation for dividends from the noncontrolled section 902 corporation. Thus, CFC's subpart F income for 1999, 200u, exceeds CFC's current earnings and profits, 190u, by 10u. Under section 952(c)(1)(A) and paragraph (e) of this section, subpart F income is limited to CFC's current earnings and profits of 190u, all of which is included in A's gross income under section 951(a)(1)(A).

(ii) For purposes of determining the amount and type of income included in A's gross income and the amount and type of income in CFC's recapture accounts, the rules of paragraphs (e)(1) and (2) of this section apply. While CFC's general limitation post-1986 undistributed earnings for 1999 are 0 ((100u) opening balance + 100u subpart F income), CFC's general limitation subpart F income (100u) does not exceed its general limitation current earnings and profits (100u) for 1999. Accordingly, under paragraph (e)(1)(iii) of this section, the amount by which CFC's subpart F income exceeds its earnings and profits for 1999, 10u, is applied proportionately to reduce CFC's subpart F income in the separate categories for general limitation income, 100u, and passive income, 100u. Thus, A includes 95u of general limitation foreign base company sales income and 95u of passive limitation foreign personal holding company income in gross income in 1999. At the close of 1999 CFC has 105u in its general limitation/foreign base company sales income recapture account (100u from 1998 + 5u from 1999), 55u in its passive limitation/foreign personal holding company income recapture account (50u from 1998 + 5u from 1999), and 50u in its dividends from the noncontrolled section 902 corporation/foreign personal holding company income recapture account (all from 1998).

(iii) For purposes of computing post-1986 undistributed earnings in each separate category, the rules of sections 902 and 960, including the rules of § 1.960-1(i), apply. Thus, post-1986 undistributed earnings (or an accumulated deficit) in each separate category are increased (or reduced) by current earnings and profits or current deficits in each separate category. The accumulated deficit in CFC's general limitation earnings and profits (100u) is reduced to 0 by the addition of 100u of 1999 earnings and profits. CFC's passive limitation earnings of 50u are increased by 100u to 150u, and CFC's noncontrolled section 902 corporation earnings of 50u are decreased by (10u) to 40u. After the addition of current year earnings and profits and deficits to the separate categories there are no deficits remaining in any separate category. Thus, the allocation rules of § 1.960-1(i)(4) do not apply in 1999. Accordingly, in determining the post-1986 foreign income taxes deemed paid by A, post-1986 undistributed earnings in each separate category are unaffected by earnings in the other categories. Foreign taxes deemed paid under section 960 for 1999 would be determined as follows for each separate category: with respect to the inclusion of 95u of foreign base company sales income out of general limitation earnings, the section 960 fraction is 95u inclusion/0 total earnings; with respect to the inclusion of 95u of passive limitation income the section 960 fraction is 95u inclusion/150u passive earnings. Thus, no general limitation taxes would be associated with the inclusion of the general limitation earnings because there are no accumulated earnings in the general limitation category. After the deemed-paid taxes are computed, at the close of 1999 CFC has a (95u) deficit in general limitation earnings and profits ((100u) opening balance + 100u current earnings − 95u inclusion), 55u of passive limitation earnings and profits (50u opening balance + 100u current foreign personal holding company income − 95u inclusion), and 40u of earnings and profits subject to the separate limitation for dividends from the noncontrolled section 902 corporation (50u opening balance + (10u) expense).

Example 3. (i) A, a U.S. person, is the sole shareholder of *CFC*, a controlled foreign corporation whose functional currency is the u. At the beginning of 1998, CFC has post-1986 undistributed earnings of 275u, all of which are general limitation earnings described in section 904(d)(1)(I). CFC has no previously-taxed earnings and profits described in section 959(c)(1) or (c)(2). In 1998, CFC has a (200u) loss in the shipping category described in section 904(d)(1)(D), 100u of foreign personal holding company income that is passive income described in section 904(d)(1)(A), and 125u of general limitation manufacturing earnings that are not subpart F income. CFC's subpart F income for 1998, 100u, exceeds CFC's current earnings and profits, 25u, by 75u. Under section 952(c)(1)(A) and paragraph (e) of this section, subpart F income is limited to CFC's current earnings and profits of 25u, all of which is included in A's gross income under section 951(a)(1)(A). The 75u of CFC's 1998 subpart F income that is not included in A's income in 1998 by reason of section 952(c)(1)(A) is subject to recapture under section 952(c)(2) and paragraph (f) of this section.

(ii) For purposes of determining the amount and type of income included in A's gross income and the amount and type of income in CFC's recapture account, the rules of paragraphs (e)(1) and (2) of this section apply. Under paragraph (e)(1) of this section, the amount of CFC's subpart F income in excess of earnings and profits for 1998, 75u, reduces the 100u of passive limitation foreign personal holding company income. Thus, A includes 25u of passive limitation foreign personal holding company income in gross income, and CFC has 75u in its passive limitation/foreign personal holding company income recapture account.

(iii) For purposes of computing post-1986 undistributed earnings in each separate category the rules of sections 902 and 960, including the rules of § 1.960-1(i), apply. Under § 1.960-1(i), the shipping limitation deficit of (200u) is allocated proportionately to reduce general limitation earnings of 400u and passive limitation earnings of 100u. Thus, general limitation earnings are reduced by 160u to 240u (400u general limitation earnings/500u total earnings in positive separate categories × (200u) shipping deficit = 160u reduction), and passive limitation earnings are reduced by 40u to 60u (100u passive earnings/500u total earnings in positive separate categories × (200u) shipping deficit = 40u reduction). Five-twelfths of CFC's post-1986 foreign income taxes with respect to passive limitation earnings are deemed paid by A under section 960 with respect to the subpart F inclusion (25u inclusion/60u passive earnings). After the inclusion and deemed-paid taxes are computed, at the close of 1998 CFC has 400u of general limitation earnings (275u opening balance + 125u current earnings), 75u of passive limitation earnings (100u of foreign personal holding company income – 25u inclusion), and a (200u) deficit in shipping limitation earnings.

Example 4. (i) The facts are the same as in *Example 3* with the addition of the following facts. In 1999, CFC earns 50u of general limitation earnings that are not subpart F income and 75u of passive limitation income that is foreign personal holding company income. Thus, CFC has 125u of current earnings and profits. CFC distributes 200u to A. Under paragraph (f)(3)(i) of this section, the recapture rules are applied first. Thus, the amount by which 1999 current earnings and profits exceed subpart F income, 50u, is recharacterized as passive limitation foreign personal holding company income. CFC's total subpart F income for 1999 is 125u of passive limitation foreign personal holding company income (75u current earnings plus 50u recapture account), and the passive limitation/foreign personal holding company income recapture account is reduced from 75u to 25u.

(ii) CFC has 150u of previously-taxed earnings and profits described in section 959(c)(2) (25u attributable to 1998 and 125u attributable to 1999), all of which is passive limitation earnings and profits. Under section 959(c), 150u of the 200u distribution is deemed to be made from earnings and profits described in section 959(c)(2). The remaining 50u is deemed to be made from earnings and profits described in section 959(c)(3). Under paragraph (f)(3)(ii) of this section, the dividend distribution is deemed to be made first out of the passive limitation recapture account to the extent thereof (25u). Under paragraph (f)(2)(iii) of this section, the passive limitation recapture account is reduced from 25u to 0. The remaining distribution of 25u is treated as made out of CFC's general limitation earnings and profits.

(iii) For purposes of computing post-1986 undistributed earnings, the rules of section 902 and 960, including the rules of § 1.960-1(i), apply. Thus, the shipping limitation accumulated deficit of (200u) reduces general limitation earnings and profits of 450u and passive limitation earnings and profits of 150u on a proportionate basis. Thus, 100% of CFC's post-1986 foreign income taxes with respect to passive limitation earnings are deemed paid by A under section 960 with respect to the 1999 subpart F inclusion of 125u (100u inclusion (numerator limited to denominator)/100u passive earnings). No post-1986 foreign income taxes remain to be deemed paid under section 902 in connection with the 25u distribution from the passive limitation/foreign personal holding company income recapture account. One-twelfth of CFC's post-1986 foreign income taxes with respect to general limitation earnings are deemed paid by A under section 902 with respect to the distribution of 25u general limitation earnings and profits described in section 959(c)(3) (25u inclusion/300u general limitation earnings). After the deemed-paid taxes are computed, at the close of 1999 CFC has 425u of general limitation earnings and profits (400u opening balance + 50u current earnings – 25u distribution), 0 of passive limitation earnings (75u recapture account + 75u current foreign personal holding company income – 125u inclusion – 25u distribution), and a (200u) deficit in shipping limitation earnings.

(5) *Effective date.*—Paragraph (e) of this section and this paragraph (f) apply to taxable years of a controlled foreign corporation beginning after March 3, 1997.

(g) *Treatment of distributive share of partnership income.*—(1) *In general.*—A controlled foreign corporation's distributive share of any item of income of a partnership is income that falls within a category of subpart F income described in section 952(a) to the extent the item of income would have been income in such category if received by the controlled foreign corporation directly. For specific rules regarding the treatment of a distributive share of partnership income under certain provisions of subpart F, see §§ 1.954-1(g), 1.954-2(a)(5), 1.954-3(a)(6), and 1.954-4(b)(2)(iii).

(2) *Example.*—The application of this paragraph (g) may be illustrated by the following example:

Example. CFC, a controlled foreign corporation, is an 80-percent partner in PRS, a foreign partnership. PRS earns $100 of interest income that is not export financing interest as defined in section 954(c)(2)(B), or qualified banking or financing income as defined in section 954(h)(3)(A), from a person unrelated to CFC. This interest income would have been foreign personal holding company income to CFC, under section 954(c), if it had received this income directly. Accordingly, CFC's distributive share of this interest income, $80, is foreign personal holding company income.

(3) *Effective date.*—This paragraph (g) applies to taxable years of a controlled foreign corporation beginning on or after July 23, 2002. [Reg. § 1.952-1.]

☐ [*T.D.* 6795, 1-28-65. *Amended by T.D.* 6892, 8-22-66; *T.D.* 7293, 11-27-73; *T.D.* 7545, 5-5-78; *T.D.* 7862, 12-16-82; *T.D.* 7893, 5-11-83; *T.D.* 7894, 5-11-83; *T.D.* 8331, 1-24-91; *T.D.* 8704, 12-31-96 *and T.D.* 9008, 7-22-2002.]

§ 1.952-2. Determination of gross income and taxable income of a foreign corporation.—(a) *Determination of gross income.*—(1) *In general.*—Except as provided in subparagraph (2) of this paragraph, the gross income of a foreign corporation for any taxable year shall, subject to the special rules of paragraph (c) of this section, be determined by treating such foreign corporation as a domestic corporation taxable under section 11 and by applying the principles of section 61 and the regulations thereunder.

(2) *Insurance gross income.*—(i) *Life insurance gross income.*—The gross income for any taxable year of a controlled foreign corporation which is engaged in the business of reinsuring or issuing insurance or annuity contracts and which, if it were a domestic corporation engaged only in such business, would be taxable as a life insurance company to which part I (sections 801 through 820) of subchapter L of chapter 1 of the Code applies, shall, subject to the special rules of paragraph (c) of this section, be the sum of—

(a) The gross investment income, as defined under section 804(b), except that interest which is excluded from gross income under section 103 shall not be taken into account;

(b) The sum of the items taken into account under section 809(c), except that advance premiums shall not be taken into account; and

(c) The amount by which the net long-term capital gain exceeds the net short-term capital loss.

(ii) *Mutual and other insurance gross income.*—The gross income for any taxable year of a controlled foreign corporation which is engaged in the business of reinsuring or issuing insurance or annuity contracts and which, if it were a domestic corporation engaged only in such business, would be taxable as a mutual insurance company to which part II (sections 821 through 826) of subchapter L of chapter 1 of the Code applies or as a mutual marine insurance or other insurance company to which part III (sections 831 and 832) of subchapter L of chapter 1 of the Code applies, shall, subject to the special rules of paragraph (c) of this section, be—

(a) The sum of—

(1) The gross income, as defined in section 832(b)(1);

(2) The amount of losses incurred, as defined in section 832(b)(5); and

(3) The amount of expenses incurred, as defined in section 832(b)(6); reduced by

(b) The amount of interest which under section 103 is excluded from gross income.

(b) *Determination of taxable income.*—(1) *In general.*—Except as provided in subparagraph (2) of this paragraph, the taxable income of a foreign corporation for any taxable year shall, subject to the special rules of paragraph (c) of this section, be determined by treating such foreign corporation as a domestic corporation taxable under section 11 and by applying the principles of section 63.

(2) *Insurance taxable income.*—The taxable income for any taxable year of a controlled foreign corporation which is engaged in the business of reinsuring or issuing insurance or annuity contracts and which, if it were a domestic corporation engaged only in such business, would be taxable as an insurance company to which subchapter L of chapter 1 of the Code applies shall, subject to the special rules of paragraph (c) of this section, be determined by treating such corporation as a domestic corporation taxable under subchapter L of chapter 1 of the Code and by applying the principles of §§ 1.953-4 and 1.953-5 for determining taxable income.

(c) *Special rules for purposes of this section.—* (1) *Nonapplication of certain provisions.—* Except where otherwise distinctly expressed, the provisions of subchapters F, G, H, L, M, N, S, and T of chapter 1 of the Internal Revenue Code shall not apply and, for taxable years of a controlled foreign corporation beginning after March 3, 1997, the provisions of section 103 of the Internal Revenue Code shall not apply.

(2) *Application of principles of § 1.964-1.—* The determinations with respect to a foreign corporation shall be made as follows:

(i) *Books of account.—* The books of account to be used shall be those regularly maintained by the corporation for the purpose of accounting to its shareholders.

(ii) *Accounting principles.—* Except as provided in subparagraphs (3) and (4) of this paragraph, the accounting principles to be employed are those described in paragraph (b) of § 1.964-1. Thus, in applying accounting principles generally accepted in the United States for purposes of reflecting in the financial statements of a domestic corporation the operations of foreign affiliates, no adjustment need be made unless such adjustment will have a material effect, within the meaning of paragraph (a) of § 1.964-1.

(iii) *Translation into United States dollars.—(a) In general.—* Except as provided in (*b*) of this subdivision, the amounts determined in accordance with subdivision (ii) of this subparagraph shall be translated into United States dollars in accordance with the principles of paragraph (d) of § 1.964-1.

(*b*) *Special rule.—* In any case in which the value of the foreign currency in relation to the United States dollar fluctuates more than 10 percent during any translation period (within the meaning of paragraph (d)(6) of § 1.964-1), the subpart F income and non-subpart F income shall be separately translated as if each constituted all the income of the controlled foreign corporation for the translation period.

(iv) *Tax accounting methods.—* The tax accounting methods to be employed as those established or adopted by or on behalf of the foreign corporation under paragraph (c) of § 1.964-1. Thus, such accounting methods must be consistent with the manner of treating inventories, depreciation, and elections referred to in subdivisions (ii), (iii), and (iv) of paragraph (c)(1) of § 1.964-1 and used for purposes of such paragraph; however, if, in accordance with paragraph (c)(6) of § 1.964-1, a foreign corporation receives foreign base company income before any elections are made or before an accounting method is adopted by or on behalf of such corporation under paragraph (c)(3) of § 1.964-1, the determinations of whether an exclusion set forth in section 954(b) applies shall be made as if no elections had been made and no accounting method had been adopted.

(v) *Exchange gain or loss.—* (*a*) Exchange gain or loss, determined in accordance with the principles of § 1.964-1(e), shall be taken into account for purposes of determining gross income and taxable income.

(*b*) Exchange gain or loss shall be treated as foreign base company shipping income (or as a deduction allocable thereto) to the extent that it is attributable to foreign base company shipping operations. The extent to which exchange gain or loss is attributable to foreign base company shipping operations may be determined under any reasonable method which is consistently applied from year to year. For example, the extent to which the exchange gain or loss is attributable to foreign base company shipping operations may be determined on the basis of the ratio which the foreign base company shipping income of the corporation for the taxable year bears to its total gross income for the taxable year, such ratio to be determined without regard to this subdivision (v).

(*c*) The remainder of the exchange gain or loss shall be allocated between subpart F income and non-subpart F income under any reasonable method which is consistently applied from year to year. For example, such remainder may be allocated to subpart F income in the same ratio that the gross subpart F income (exclusive of foreign base company shipping income) of the corporation for the taxable year bears to its total gross income (exclusive of foreign base company shipping income) for the taxable year, such ratio to be determined without regard to this subdivision (v).

(3) *Necessity for recognition of gain or loss.—* Gross income of a foreign corporation (including an insurance company) includes gain or loss only if such gain or loss would be recognized under the provisions of the Internal Revenue Code if the foreign corporation were a domestic corporation taxable under section 11 (subject to the modifications of subparagraph (1) of this paragraph). See section 1002. However, a foreign corporation shall not be treated as a domestic corporation for purposes of determining whether section 367 applies.

(4) *Gross income and gross receipts.—* The term "gross income" may not have the same meaning as the term "gross receipts". For example, in a manufacturing, merchandising, or

mining business, gross income means the total sales less the cost of goods sold, plus any income from investments and from incidental or outside operations or sources.

(5) *Treatment of capital loss and net operating loss.*—In determining taxable income of a foreign corporation for any taxable year—

(i) *Capital loss carryback and carryover.*—The capital loss carryback and carryover provided by section 1212(a) shall not be allowed.

(ii) *Net operating loss deduction.*—The net operating loss deduction under section 172(a) or the operations loss deduction under section 812 shall not be allowed.

(6) *Corporations which have insurance income.*—For purposes of paragraphs (a)(2) and (b)(2) of this section, in determining whether a controlled foreign corporation which is engaged in the business of reinsuring or issuing insurance or annuity contracts and which, if it were a domestic corporation engaged only in such business, would be taxable as an insurance company to which subchapter L of chapter 1 of the Code applies, it is immaterial that—

(i) The corporation would be exempt from taxation as an organization described in section 501(a),

(ii) The corporation would not be taxable as an insurance company to which subchapter L of the Code applies, or

(iii) The corporation would be subject to the alternative tax for small mutual insurance companies provided by section 821(c). [Reg. § 1.952-2.]

☐ [*T.D.* 6795, 1-28-65. *Amended by T.D.* 7893, 5-11-83; *T.D.* 7894, 5-11-83 *and T.D.* 8704, 12-31-96.]

§ 1.954-0. Introduction.—(a) *Effective dates.*—(1) *Final regulations.*—(i) *In general.*—Except as otherwise specifically provided, the provisions of §§ 1.954-1 and 1.954-2 apply to taxable years of a controlled foreign corporation beginning after November 6, 1995. If any of the rules described in §§ 1.954-1 and 1.954-2 are inconsistent with provisions of other regulations under subpart F, these final regulations are intended to apply instead of such other regulations.

(ii) *Election to apply final regulations retroactively.*—(A) *Scope of election.*—An election may be made to apply the final regulations retroactively with respect to any taxable year of the controlled foreign corporation beginning on or after January 1, 1987. If such an election is made, these final regulations must be applied in their entirety for such taxable year and all subsequent taxable years. All references to section 11 in the final regulations shall be deemed to include section 15, where applicable.

(B) *Manner of making election.*—An election under this paragraph (a)(1)(ii) is binding on all United States shareholders of the controlled foreign corporation and must be made—

(1) By the controlling United States shareholders, as defined in § 1.964-1(c)(5), by attaching a statement to such effect with their original or amended income tax returns for the taxable year of such United States shareholders in which or with which the taxable year of the CFC ends, and including any additional information required by applicable administrative pronouncements, or

(2) In such other manner as may be prescribed in applicable administrative pronouncements.

(C) *Time for making election.*—An election may be made under this paragraph (a)(1)(ii) with respect to a taxable year of the controlled foreign corporation beginning on or after January 1, 1987 only if the time for filing a return or claim for refund has not expired for the taxable year of any United States shareholder of the controlled foreign corporation in which or with which such taxable year of the controlled foreign corporation ends.

(D) *Revocation of election.*—An election made under this paragraph (a)(1)(ii) may not be revoked.

(2) *Temporary regulations.*—The provisions of §§ 4.954-1 and 4.954-2 of this chapter apply to taxable years of a controlled foreign corporation beginning after December 31, 1986 and on or before November 6, 1995. However, the provisions of § 4.954-2(b)(6) of this chapter continue to apply. For transactions entered into on or before October 9, 1995, taxpayers may rely on Notice 89-90, 1989-2 C.B. 407, in applying the temporary regulations.

* * *

[Reg. § 1.954-0.]

☐ [*T.D.* 8618, 9-6-95. *Amended by T.D.* 8767, 3-23-98 *and T.D.* 9039, 1-30-2003.]

§ 1.954-1. Foreign base company income.—(a) *In general.*—(1) *Purpose and scope.*—Section 954 and §§ 1.954-1 and 1.954-2 provide rules for computing the foreign base company income of a controlled foreign corporation. Foreign base company income is included in the subpart F income of a controlled foreign corporation under the rules of section 952. Subpart F income is included in the gross income of a United States shareholder of a controlled foreign corporation under the rules of section 951 and thus is subject to current taxation under section 1, 11 or 55 of the Internal Revenue Code. The determination of whether a foreign corporation is a controlled foreign corporation, the subpart F income of which is included currently in the gross income of its United States shareholders, is made under the rules of section 957.

(2) *Gross foreign base company income.*—The gross foreign base company income of a controlled foreign corporation consists of the following categories of gross income (determined after the application of section 952(b))—

  (i) Foreign personal holding company income, as defined in section 954(c);

  (ii) Foreign base company sales income, as defined in section 954(d);

  (iii) Foreign base company services income, as defined in section 954(e);

  (iv) Foreign base company shipping income, as defined in section 954(f); and

  (v) Foreign base company oil related income, as defined in section 954(g).

(3) *Adjusted gross foreign base company income.*—The term *adjusted gross foreign base company income* means the gross foreign base company income of a controlled foreign corporation as adjusted by the de minimis and full inclusion rules of paragraph (b) of this section.

(4) *Net foreign base company income.*—The term *net foreign base company income* means the adjusted gross foreign base company income of a controlled foreign corporation reduced so as to take account of deductions (including taxes) properly allocable or apportionable to such income under the rules of section 954(b)(5) and paragraph (c) of this section.

(5) *Adjusted net foreign base company income.*—The term *adjusted net foreign base company income* means the net foreign base company income of a controlled foreign corporation reduced, first, by any items of net foreign base company income excluded from subpart F income pursuant to section 952(c) and, second, by any items excluded from subpart F income pursuant to the high tax exception of section 954(b). See paragraph (d)(4)(ii) of this section. The term *foreign base company income* as used in the Internal Revenue Code and elsewhere in the Income Tax Regulations means adjusted net foreign base company income, unless otherwise provided.

(6) *Insurance income.*—The term *gross insurance income* includes all gross income taken into account in determining insurance income under section 953. The term *adjusted gross insurance income* means gross insurance income as adjusted by the de minimis and full inclusion rules of paragraph (b) of this section. The term *net insurance income* means adjusted gross insurance income reduced under section 953 so as to take into account deductions (including taxes) properly allocable or apportionable to such income. The term *adjusted net insurance income* means net insurance income reduced by any items of net insurance income that are excluded from subpart F income pursuant to section 952(b) or pursuant to the high tax exception of section 954(b). The term *insurance income* as used in subpart F of the Internal Revenue Code and in the regulations under that subpart means adjusted net insurance income, unless otherwise provided.

(7) *Additional items of adjusted net foreign base company income or adjusted net insurance income by reason of section 952(c).*—Earnings and profits of the controlled foreign corporation that are recharacterized as foreign base company income or insurance income under section 952(c) are items of adjusted net foreign base company income or adjusted net insurance income, respectively. Amounts subject to recharacterization under section 952(c) are determined after adjusted net foreign base company income and adjusted net insurance income are otherwise determined under subpart F and are not again subject to any exceptions or special rules that would affect the amount of subpart F income. Thus, for example, items of gross foreign base company income or gross insurance income that are excluded from adjusted gross foreign base company income or adjusted gross insurance income because the de minimis test is met are subject to recharacterization under section 952(c). Further, the de minimis and full inclusion tests of paragraph (b) of this section, and the high tax exception of paragraph (d) of this section, for example, do not apply to such amounts.

(b) *Computation of adjusted gross foreign base company income and adjusted gross insurance income.*—(1) *De minimis and full inclusion tests.*—(i) *De minimis test.*—(A) *In general.*—Except as provided in paragraph (b)(1)(i)(C) of this section, adjusted gross foreign base company income and adjusted gross insurance income are equal to zero if the sum of the gross foreign base company income and the gross insurance income of a controlled foreign corporation is less than the lesser of—

  (1) 5 percent of gross income; or
  (2) $1,000,000.

(B) *Currency translation.*—Controlled foreign corporations having a functional currency other than the United States dollar shall translate the $1,000,000 threshold using the exchange rate provided under section 989(b)(3) for amounts included in income under section 951(a).

(C) *Coordination with sections 864(d) and 881(c).*—Adjusted gross foreign base company income or adjusted gross insurance income of a controlled foreign corporation always includes income from trade or service receivables described in section 864(d)(1) or (6), and portfolio interest described in section 881(c), even if the de minimis test of this paragraph (b)(1)(i) is otherwise satisfied.

(ii) *Seventy percent full inclusion test.*—Except as provided in section 953, adjusted gross foreign base company income consists of all gross income of the controlled foreign corporation other than gross insurance income and amounts described in section 952(b), and adjusted gross insurance income consists of all gross insurance income other than amounts described in section 952(b), if the sum of the gross foreign base company income and the gross insurance income for the taxable year exceeds 70 percent of gross income. See paragraph (d)(6) of this section, under which certain items of full inclusion foreign base company income may nevertheless be excluded from subpart F income.

(2) *Character of gross income included in adjusted gross foreign base company income.*—The gross income included in the adjusted gross foreign base company income of a controlled foreign corporation generally retains its character as foreign personal holding company income, foreign base company sales income, foreign base company services income, foreign base company shipping income, or foreign base company oil related income. However, gross income included in adjusted gross foreign base company income because the full inclusion test of paragraph (b)(1)(ii) of this section is met is termed *full inclusion foreign base company income,* and constitutes a separate category of adjusted gross foreign base company income for purposes of allocating and apportioning deductions under paragraph (c) of this section.

(3) *Coordination with section 952(c).*—Income that is included in subpart F income because the full inclusion test of paragraph (b)(1)(ii) of this section is met does not reduce amounts that, under section 952(c), are subject to recharacterization.

(4) *Anti-abuse rule.*—(i) *In general.*—For purposes of applying the de minimis test of paragraph (b)(1)(i) of this section, the income of two or more controlled foreign corporations shall be aggregated and treated as the income of a single corporation if a principal purpose for separately organizing, acquiring, or maintaining such multiple corporations is to prevent income from being treated as foreign base company income or insurance income under the de minimis test. A purpose may be a principal purpose even though it is outweighed by other purposes (taken together or separately).

(ii) *Presumption.*—Two or more controlled foreign corporations are presumed to have been organized, acquired or maintained to prevent income from being treated as foreign base company income or insurance income under the de minimis test of paragraph (b)(1)(i) of this section if the corporations are related persons, as defined in paragraph (b)(4)(iii) of this section, and the corporations are described in paragraph (b)(4)(ii)(A), (B), or (C) of this section. This presumption may be rebutted by proof to the contrary.

(A) The activities carried on by the controlled foreign corporations, or the assets used in those activities, are substantially the same activities that were previously carried on, or assets that were previously held, by a single controlled foreign corporation. Further, the United States shareholders of the controlled foreign corporations or related persons (as determined under paragraph (b)(4)(iii) of this section) are substantially the same as the United States shareholders of the one controlled foreign corporation in a prior taxable year. A presumption made in connection with the requirements of this paragraph (b)(4)(ii)(A) may be rebutted by proof that the activities carried on by each controlled foreign corporation would constitute a separate branch under the principles of §1.367(a)-6T(g)(2) if carried on directly by a United States person.

(B) The controlled foreign corporations carry on a business, financial operation, or venture as partners directly or indirectly in a partnership (as defined in section 7701(a)(2) and §301.7701-3 of this chapter) that is a related person (as defined in paragraph (b)(4)(iii) of this section) with respect to each such controlled foreign corporation.

(C) The activities carried on by the controlled foreign corporations would constitute a single branch operation under §1.367(a)-6T(g)(2) if carried on directly by a United States person.

(iii) *Related persons.*—For purposes of this paragraph (b), two or more persons are related persons if they are in a relationship described in section 267(b). In determining for purposes of this paragraph (b) whether two or more corporations are members of the same controlled group under section 267(b)(3), a person is considered to own stock owned directly by such person, stock owned with the application of section 1563(e)(1), and stock owned with the application of section 267(c). In determining for purposes of this paragraph (b) whether a corporation is related to a partnership under section 267(b)(10), a person is considered to own the partnership interest owned directly by such person and the partnership interest owned with the application of section 267(e)(3).

(iv) *Example.*—The following example illustrates the application of this paragraph (b)(4).

Example. (i)(1) *USP* is the sole United States shareholder of three controlled foreign corporations: *CFC1, CFC2* and *CFC3.* The three controlled foreign corporations all have the same taxable year. The three controlled foreign corporations are partners in *FP,* a foreign entity classified as a partnership under section 7701(a)(2) and § 301.7701-3 of the regulations. For their current taxable years, each of the controlled foreign corporations derives all of its income other than foreign base company income from activities conducted through *FP,* and its foreign base company income from activities conducted both jointly through *FP* and separately without *FP.* Based on the facts in the table below, the foreign base company income derived by each controlled foreign corporation for its current taxable year, including income derived from *FP,* is less than five percent of the gross income of each controlled foreign corporation and is less than $1,000,000:

	CFC1	CFC2	CFC3
Gross income	$4,000,000	$8,000,000	$12,000,000
Five percent of gross income	200,000	400,000	600,000
Foreign base company income	199,000	398,000	597,000

(2) Thus, without the application of the anti-abuse rule of this paragraph (b)(4), each controlled foreign corporation would be treated as having no foreign base company income after the application of the de minimis test of section 954(b)(3)(A) and paragraph (b)(1)(i) of this section.

(ii) However, under these facts, the requirements of paragraph (b)(4)(i) of this section are met unless the presumption of paragraph (b)(4)(ii) of this section is successfully rebutted. The sum of the foreign base company income of the controlled foreign corporations is $1,194,000. Thus, the amount of gross foreign base company income of each controlled foreign corporation will not be reduced by reason of the de minimis rule of section 954(b)(3)(A) and this paragraph (b).

(c) *Computation of net foreign base company income.*—(1) *General rule.*—The net foreign base company income of a controlled foreign corporation (as defined in paragraph (a)(4) of this section) is computed under the rules of this paragraph (c)(1). The principles of § 1.904-5(k) shall apply where payments are made between controlled foreign corporations that are related persons (within the meaning of section 954(d)(3)). Consistent with these principles, only payments described in § 1.954-2(b)(4)(ii)(B)(*2*) may be offset as provided in § 1.904-5(k)(2).

(i) *Deductions against gross foreign base company income.*—The net foreign base company income of a controlled foreign corporation is computed first by taking into account deductions in the following manner:

(A) First, the gross amount of each item of income described in paragraph (c)(1)(iii) of this section is determined.

(B) Second, any expenses definitely related to less than all gross income as a class shall be allocated and apportioned under the principles of sections 861, 864 and 904(d) to the gross income described in paragraph (c)(1)(i)(A) of this section.

(C) Third, foreign personal holding company income that is passive within the meaning of section 904 (determined before the application of the high-taxed income rule of § 1.904-4(c)) is reduced by related person interest expense allocable to passive income under § 1.904-5(c)(2); such interest must be further allocated and apportioned to items described in paragraph (c)(1)(iii)(B) of this section.

(D) Fourth, the amount of each item of income described in paragraph (c)(1)(iii) of this section is reduced by other expenses allocable and apportionable to such income under the principles of sections 861, 864 and 904(d).

(ii) *Losses reduce subpart F income by operation of earnings and profits limitation.*—Except as otherwise provided in § 1.954-2(g)(4), if after applying the rules of paragraph (c)(1)(i) of this section, the amount remaining in any category of foreign base company income or foreign personal holding company income is less than zero, the loss in that category may not reduce any other category of foreign base company income or foreign personal holding company income except by operation of the earnings and profits limitation of section 952(c)(1).

(iii) *Items of income.*—(A) *Income other than passive foreign personal holding company income.*—A single item of income (other than foreign personal holding company income that is passive) is the aggregate amount from all transactions that falls within a single separate

Reg. § 1.954-1(c)(1)(iii)(A)

category (as defined in §1.904-5(a)(1)), and either—

(1) Falls within a single category of foreign personal holding company income as—

(i) Dividends, interest, rents, royalties and annuities;

(ii) Gain from certain property transactions;

(iii) Gain from commodities transactions;

(iv) Foreign currency gain; or

(v) Income equivalent to interest; or

(2) Falls within a single category of foreign base company income, other than foreign personal holding company income, as—

(i) Foreign base company sales income;

(ii) Foreign base company services income;

(iii) Foreign base company shipping income;

(iv) Foreign base company oil related income; or

(v) Full inclusion foreign base company income.

(B) *Passive foreign personal holding company income.*—A single item of foreign personal holding company income that is passive is an amount of income that falls within a single group of passive income under the grouping rules of §1.904-4(c)(3), (4) and (5) and a single category of foreign personal holding company income described in paragraphs (c)(1)(iii)(A)(*1*)(*i*) through (*v*).

(2) *Computation of net foreign base company income derived from same country insurance income.*—Deductions relating to foreign base company income attributable to the issuing (or reinsuring) of any insurance or annuity contract in connection with risks located in the country under the laws of which the controlled foreign corporation is created or organized shall be allocated and apportioned in accordance with the rules set forth in section 953.

(d) *Computation of adjusted net foreign base company income or adjusted net insurance income.*—(1) *Application of high tax exception.*—Adjusted net foreign base company income (or adjusted net insurance income) equals the net foreign base company income (or net insurance income) of a controlled foreign corporation, reduced by any net item of such income that qualifies for the high tax exception provided by section 954(b)(4) and this paragraph (d). Any item of income that is foreign base company oil related income, as defined in section 954(g), or portfolio interest, as described in section 881(c), does not qualify for the high tax exception. See paragraph (c)(1)(iii) of this section for the definition of the term *item of income*. For rules concerning the treatment for foreign tax credit purposes of amounts excluded from subpart F under section 954(b)(4), see §1.904-4(c). A net item of income qualifies for the high tax exception only if—

(i) An election is made under section 954(b)(4) and paragraph (d)(5) of this section to exclude the income from the computation of subpart F income; and

(ii) It is established that the net item of income was subject to foreign income taxes imposed by a foreign country or countries at an effective rate that is greater than 90 percent of the maximum rate of tax specified in section 11 for the taxable year of the controlled foreign corporation.

(2) *Effective rate at which taxes are imposed.*—The effective rate with respect to a net item of income shall be determined separately for each controlled foreign corporation in a chain of corporations through which a distribution is made. The effective rate at which taxes are imposed on a net item of income is—

(i) The United States dollar amount of foreign income taxes paid or accrued (or deemed paid or accrued) with respect to the net item of income, determined under paragraph (d)(3) of this section; divided by

(ii) The United States dollar amount of the net item of foreign base company income or insurance income, described in paragraph (c)(1)(iii) of this section, increased by the amount of foreign income taxes referred to in paragraph (d)(2)(i) of this section.

(3) *Taxes paid or accrued with respect to an item of income.*—(i) *Income other than passive foreign personal holding company income.*—The amount of foreign income taxes paid or accrued with respect to a net item of income (other than an item of foreign personal holding company income that is passive) for purposes of section 954(b)(4) and this paragraph (d) is the United States dollar amount of foreign income taxes that would be deemed paid under section 960 with respect to that item if that item were included in the gross income of a United States shareholder under section 951(a)(1)(A) (determined, in the case of a United States shareholder that is an individual, as if an election under section 962 has been made, whether or not such election is actually made). For this purpose, in accordance with the regulations under section 960, the amounts that would be deemed paid under section 960 shall be determined separately with respect to each controlled foreign corporation and without regard

to the limitation applicable under section 904(a). The amount of foreign income taxes paid or accrued with respect to a net item of income, determined in the manner provided in this paragraph (d), will not be affected by a subsequent reduction in foreign income taxes attributable to a distribution to shareholders of all or part of such income.

(ii) *Passive foreign personal holding company income.*—The amount of income taxes paid or accrued with respect to a net item of foreign personal holding company income that is passive for purposes of section 954(b)(4) and this paragraph (d) is the United States dollar amount of foreign income taxes that would be deemed paid under section 960 and that would be taken into account for purposes applying the provisions of §1.904-4(c) with respect to that net item of income.

(4) *Special rules.*—(i) *Consistency rule.*—An election to exclude income from the computation of subpart F income for a taxable year must be made consistently with respect to all items of passive foreign personal holding company income eligible to be excluded for the taxable year. Thus, high-taxed passive foreign personal holding company income of a controlled foreign corporation must either be excluded in its entirety, or remain subject to subpart F in its entirety.

(ii) *Coordination with earnings and profits limitation.*—If the amount of income included in subpart F income for the taxable year is reduced by the earnings and profits limitation of section 952(c)(1), the amount of income that is a net item of income, within the meaning of paragraph (c)(1)(iii) of this section, is determined after the application of the rules of section 952(c)(1).

(iii) *Example.*—The following example illustrates the provisions of paragraph (d)(4)(ii) of this section. All of the taxes referred to in the following example are foreign income taxes. For simplicity, this example assumes that the amount of taxes that are taken into account as a deduction under section 954(b)(5) and the amount of the gross-up required under sections 960 and 78 are equal. Therefore, this example does not separately illustrate the deduction for taxes and gross-up.

Example. During its 1995 taxable year, CFC, a controlled foreign corporation, earns royalty income, net of taxes, of $100 that is foreign personal holding company income. CFC has no expenses associated with this royalty income. CFC pays $50 of foreign income taxes with respect to the royalty income. For 1995, CFC has current earnings and profits of $50. CFC's subpart F income, as determined prior to the application of this paragraph (d), exceeds its current earnings and profits. Thus, under paragraph (d)(4)(ii) of this section, the amount of CFC's only net item of income, the royalty income, will be limited to $50. The remaining $50 will be subject to recharacterization in a subsequent taxable year under section 952(c)(2). Because the amount of foreign income taxes paid with respect to this net item of income is $50, the effective rate of tax on the item, for purposes of this paragraph (d), is 50 percent ($50 of taxes/$50 net item + $50 of taxes). Accordingly, an election under paragraph (d)(5) of this section may be made to exclude the item of income from the computation of subpart F income.

(5) *Procedure.*—An election made under the procedure provided by this paragraph (d)(5) is binding on all United States shareholders of the controlled foreign corporation and must be made—

(i) By the controlling United States shareholders, as defined in §1.964-1(c)(5), by attaching a statement to such effect with their original or amended income tax returns, and including any additional information required by applicable administrative pronouncements; or

(ii) In such other manner as may be prescribed in applicable administrative pronouncements.

(6) *Coordination of full inclusion and high tax exception rules.*—Notwithstanding paragraph (b)(1)(ii) of this section, full inclusion foreign base company income will be excluded from subpart F income if more than 90 percent of the adjusted gross foreign base company income and adjusted gross insurance company income of a controlled foreign corporation (determined without regard to the full inclusion test of paragraph (b)(1) of this section) is attributable to net amounts excluded from subpart F income pursuant to an election to have the high tax exception described in section 954(b)(4) and this paragraph (d) apply.

(7) *Examples.*—(i) The following examples illustrate the rules of this paragraph (d). All of the taxes referred to in the following examples are foreign income taxes. For simplicity, these examples assume that the amount of taxes that are taken into account as a deduction under section 954(b)(5) and the amount of the gross-up required under sections 960 and 78 are equal. Therefore, these examples do not separately illustrate the deduction for taxes and gross-up. Except as otherwise stated, these examples assume there are no earnings, deficits, or foreign income taxes in the post-1986 pools of earnings and profits or foreign income taxes.

Example 1. (i) *Items of income.* During its 1995 taxable year, controlled foreign corporation *CFC* earns from outside its country of operation portfolio dividend income of $100 and interest income, net of taxes, of $100 (consisting of a gross payment of $150 reduced by a third-country withholding tax of $50). For purposes of illustration, assume that *CFC* incurs no expenses. None of the income is taxed in *CFC*'s country of operation. The dividend income was not subject to third-country withholding taxes. Pursuant to the operation of section 904, the interest income is high withholding tax interest and the dividend income is passive income. Accordingly, pursuant to paragraph (c)(1)(iii) of this section, *CFC* has two net items of income—

(1) $100 of foreign personal holding company (FPHC)/passive income (the dividends); and

(2) $100 of FPHC/high withholding tax income (the interest).

(ii) *Effective rates of tax.* No foreign tax would be deemed paid under section 960 with respect to the net item of income described in paragraph (i)(1) of this *Example 1*. Therefore, the effective rate of foreign tax is 0, and the item may not be excluded from subpart F income under the rules of this paragraph (d). Foreign tax of $50 would be deemed paid under section 960 with respect to the net item of income described in paragraph (i)(2) of this *Example 1*. Therefore, the effective rate of foreign tax is 33 percent ($50 of creditable taxes paid, divided by $150, consisting of the net item of foreign base company income ($100) plus creditable taxes paid thereon ($50)). The highest rate of tax specified in section 11 for the 1995 taxable year is 35 percent. Accordingly, the net item of income described in paragraph (i)(2) of this *Example 1* may be excluded from subpart F income if an election under paragraph (d)(5) of this section is made, since it is subject to foreign tax at an effective rate that is greater than 31.5 percent (90 percent of 35 percent). However, for purposes of section 904(d), it remains high withholding tax interest.

Example 2. (i) The facts are the same as in *Example 1*, except that *CFC*'s country of operation imposes a tax of $50 with respect to *CFC*'s dividend income (and thus *CFC* earns portfolio dividend income, net of taxes, of only $50). The interest income is still high withholding tax interest. The dividend income is still passive income (without regard to the possible applicability of the high tax exception of section 904(d)(2)). Accordingly, *CFC* has two items of income for purposes of this paragraph (d)—

(1) $50 of FPHC/passive income (net of the $50 foreign tax); and

(2) $100 of FPHC/high withholding tax interest income.

(ii) Each item is taxed at an effective rate greater than 31.5 percent. The net item of income described in paragraph (i)(1) of this *Example 2*: foreign tax ($50) divided by sum ($100) of net item of income ($50) plus creditable tax thereon ($50) equals 50 percent. The net item of income described in paragraph (i)(2) of this *Example 2*: Foreign tax ($50) divided by sum ($150) of income item ($100) plus creditable tax thereon ($50) equals 33 percent. Accordingly, an election may be made under paragraph (d)(5) of this section to exclude either or both of the net items of income described in paragraphs (i)(1) and (2) of this *Example 2* from subpart F income. If no election is made the items would be included in the subpart F income of *CFC*.

Example 3. (i) The facts are the same as in *Example 1*, except that the $100 of portfolio dividend income is subject to a third-country withholding tax of $50, and the $150 of interest income is from sources within *CFC*'s country of operation, is subject to a $10 income tax therein, and is not subject to a withholding tax. Although the interest income and the dividend income are both passive income, under paragraph (c)(1)(iii)(B) of this section they constitute separate items of income pursuant to the application of the grouping rules of § 1.904-4(c). Accordingly, *CFC* has two net items of income for purposes of this paragraph (d)—

(1) $50 (net of $50 tax) of FPHC/non-country of operation/greater than 15 percent withholding tax income; and

(2) $140 (net of $10 tax) of FPHC/country of operation income.

(ii) The item described in paragraph (i)(1) of this *Example 3* is taxed at an effective rate greater than 31.5 percent, but Item 2 is not. The net item of income described in paragraph (i)(1) of this *Example 3*: foreign tax ($50) divided by sum ($100) of net item of income ($50) plus creditable tax thereon ($50) equals 50 percent. The net item of income described in paragraph (i)(2) of this *Example 3*: foreign tax ($10) divided by sum ($150) of net item of income ($140) plus creditable tax thereon ($10) equals 6.67 percent. Therefore, an election may be made under paragraph (d)(5) of this section to exclude the net item of income described in paragraph (i)(1) of this *Example 3* but not the net item of income described in paragraph (i)(2) of this *Example 3* from subpart F income.

Example 4. The facts are the same as in *Example 3*, except that the $150 of interest income is subject to an income tax of $50 in *CFC*'s country of operation. Accordingly, *CFC*'s items of income are the same as in *Example 3*, but both items are taxed at an effective rate greater than 31.5 percent. The net item of income described in paragraph (i)(1) of *Example 3:* Foreign tax ($50) divided by sum ($100) of net item of income ($50) plus creditable tax thereon ($50) equals 50 percent. The net item of income described in paragraph (i)(2) of *Example 3:* foreign tax ($50) divided by sum ($150) of net item of income ($100) plus creditable tax thereon ($50) equals 33 percent. Pursuant to the consistency rule of paragraph (d)(4)(i) of this section, an election made by *CFC*'s controlling United States shareholders must exclude from subpart F income both items of FPHC income under the high tax exception of section 954(b)(4) and this paragraph (d). The election may not be made only with respect to one item.

Example 5. The facts are the same as in *Example 1,* except that *CFC* earns $5 of portfolio dividend income and $150 of interest income. In addition, *CFC* earns $45 for performing consulting services within its country of operation for unrelated persons. *CFC*'s gross foreign base company income for 1995 of $155 ($150 of gross interest income and $5 of portfolio dividend income) is greater than 70 percent of its gross income of $200. Therefore, under the full inclusion test of paragraph (b)(1)(ii) of this section, *CFC*'s adjusted gross foreign base company income is $200, and under paragraph (b)(2) of this section, the $45 of consulting income is full inclusion foreign base company income. If *CFC* elects, under paragraph (d)(5) of this section, to exclude the interest income from subpart F income pursuant to the high tax exception, the $45 of full inclusion foreign base company income will be excluded from subpart F income under paragraph (d)(6) of this section because the $150 of gross interest income excluded under the high tax exception is more than 90 percent of *CFC*'s adjusted gross foreign base company income of $155.

(ii) The following examples generally illustrate the application of paragraph (c) of this section and this paragraph (d). *Example 1* illustrates the order of computations. *Example 2* illustrates the computations required by sections 952 and 954 and this § 1.954-1 if the full inclusion test of paragraph (b)(1)(ii) of this section is met and the income is not excluded from subpart F income under section 952(b). Computations in these examples involving the operation of section 952(c) are included for purposes of illustration only and do not provide substantive rules concerning the operation of that section. For simplicity, these examples assume that the amount of taxes that are taken into account as a deduction under section 954(b)(5) and the amount of the gross-up required under sections 960 and 78 are equal. Therefore, these examples do not separately illustrate the deduction for taxes and gross-up.

Example 1. (i) *Gross income. CFC,* a controlled foreign corporation, has gross income of $1000 for the current taxable year. Of that $1000 of income, $100 is interest income that is included in the definition of foreign personal holding company income under section 954(c)(1)(A) and § 1.954-2(b)(1)(ii), is not income from a trade or service receivable described in section 864(d)(1) or (6), or portfolio interest described in section 881(c), and is not excluded from foreign personal holding company income under any provision of section 952(b) or section 954(c). Another $50 is foreign base company sales income under section 954(d). The remaining $850 of gross income is not included in the definition of foreign base company income or insurance income under sections 954(c), (d), (e), (f) or (g) or 953, and is foreign source general limitation income described in section 904(d)(1)(I).

(ii) *Expenses.* For the current taxable year, *CFC* has expenses of $500. This amount includes $8 of interest paid to a related person that is allocable to foreign personal holding company income under section 904, and $2 of other expense that is directly related to foreign personal holding company income. Another $20 of expense is directly related to foreign base company sales. The remaining $470 of expenses is allocable to general limitation income that is not foreign base company income or insurance income.

(iii) *Earnings and losses. CFC* has earnings and profits for the current taxable year of $500. In the prior taxable year, *CFC* had losses with respect to income other than gross foreign base company income or gross insurance income. By reason of the limitation provided under section 952(c)(1)(A), those losses reduced the subpart F income (consisting entirely of foreign source general limitation income) of *CFC* by $600 for the prior taxable year.

(iv) *Taxes.* Foreign income tax of $30 is considered imposed on the interest income under the rules of section 954(b)(4), this paragraph (d), and § 1.904-6. Foreign income tax of $14 is considered imposed on the foreign base company sales income under the rules of section 954(b)(4), paragraph (d) of this section, and § 1.904-6. Foreign income tax of $177 is considered imposed on the remaining foreign source general limitation income under the rules of section 954(b)(4), this paragraph (d), and § 1.904-6. For the taxable year of *CFC,* the maximum United States rate of taxation under section 11 is 35 percent.

(v) *Conclusion.* Based on these facts, if *CFC* elects to exclude all items of income subject to a high foreign tax under section 954(b)(4) and this paragraph (d), it will have $500 of subpart F income as defined in section 952(a) (consisting entirely of foreign source general limitation income) determined as follows:

Step 1—Determine gross income:

(1) Gross income $1000

Step 2—Determine gross foreign base company income and gross insurance income:

(2) Interest income included in gross foreign personal holding company income under section 954(c) 100

(3) Gross foreign base company sales income under section 954(d) 50

(4) Total gross foreign base company income and gross insurance income as defined in sections 954(c), (d), (e), (f) and (g) and 953 (line (2) plus line (3)) 150

Step 3—Compute adjusted gross foreign base company income and adjusted gross insurance income:

(5) Five percent of gross income (.05 × line (1)) 50

(6) Seventy percent of gross income (.70 × line (1)) 700

(7) Adjusted gross foreign base company income and adjusted gross insurance income after the application of the de minimis test of paragraph (b) (line (4), or zero if line (4) is less than the lesser of line (5) or $1,000,000) (if the amount on this line 7 is zero, proceed to *Step 8*) 150

(8) Adjusted gross foreign base company income and adjusted gross insurance income after the application of the full inclusion test of paragraph (b) (line (4), or line (1) if line (4) is greater than line (6)) 150

Step 4—Compute net foreign base company income:

(9) Expenses directly related to adjusted gross foreign base company sales income 20

(10) Expenses (other than related person interest expense) directly related to adjusted gross foreign personal holding company income 2

(11) Related person interest expense allocable to adjusted gross foreign personal holding company income under section 904 8

(12) Net foreign personal holding company income after allocating deductions under section 954(b)(5) and paragraph (c) of this section (line (2) reduced by lines (10) and (11)) 90

(13) Net foreign base company sales income after allocating deductions under section 954(b)(5) and paragraph (c) of this section (line (3) reduced by line (9)) 30

(14) Total net foreign base company income after allocating deductions under section 954(b)(5) and paragraph (c) of this section (line (12) plus line (13)) 120

Step 5—Compute net insurance income:

(15) Net insurance income under section 953 0

Step 6—Compute adjusted net foreign base company income:

(16) Foreign income tax imposed on net foreign personal holding company income (as determined under section 954(b)(4) and this paragraph (d)) 30

(17) Foreign income tax imposed on net foreign base company sales income (as determined under section 954(b)(4) and this paragraph (d)) 14

(18) Ninety percent of the maximum United States corporate tax rate 31.5%

(19) Effective rate of foreign income tax imposed on net foreign personal holding company income ($90 of interest) under section 954(b)(4) and this paragraph (d) (line (16) divided by line (12)) 33%

(20) Effective rate of foreign income tax imposed on $30 of net foreign base company sales income under section 954(b)(4) and this paragraph (d) (line (17) divided by line (13)) 47%

(21) Net foreign personal holding company income subject to a high foreign tax under section 954(b)(4) and this paragraph (d) (zero, or line (12) if line (19) is greater than line (18)) 90

(22) Net foreign base company sales income subject to a high foreign tax under section 954(b)(4) and this paragraph (d) (zero, or line (13) if line (20) is greater than line (18)) 30

(23) Adjusted net foreign base company income after applying section 954(b)(4) and this paragraph (d) (line (14), reduced by the sum of line (21) and line (22)) 0

Step 7—Compute adjusted net insurance income:

(24) Adjusted net insurance income . 0

Step 8—Additions to or reduction of adjusted net foreign base company income by reason of section 952(c):

(25) Earnings and profits for the current year 500

(26) Amount subject to being recharacterized as subpart F income under section 952(c)(2) (excess of line (25) over the sum of lines (23) and (24)); if there is a deficit, then the limitation of section 952(c)(1) may apply for the current year 500

(27) Amount of reduction in subpart F income for prior taxable years by reason of the limitation of section 952(c)(1) 600

(28) Subpart F income as defined in section 952(a), assuming section 952(a)(3), (4), and (5) do not apply (the sum of line (23), line (24), and the lesser of line (26) or line (27)) 500

(29) Amount of prior year's deficit to be recharacterized as subpart F income in later years under section 952(c) (excess of line (27) over line (26)) 100

Example 2. (i) *Gross income. CFC,* a controlled foreign corporation, has gross income of $1000 for the current taxable year. Of that $1000 of income, $720 is interest income that is included in the definition of foreign personal holding company income under section 954(c)(1)(A) and §1.954-2(b)(1)(ii), is not income from trade or service receivables described in section 864(d)(1) or (6), or portfolio interest described in section 881(c), and is not excluded from foreign personal holding company income under any provision of section 954(c) and §1.954-2 or section 952(b). The remaining $280 is services income that is not included in the definition of foreign base company income or insurance income under sections 954(c), (d), (e), (f), or (g) or 953, and is foreign source general limitation income for purposes of section 904(d)(1)(I).

(ii) *Expenses.* For the current taxable year, *CFC* has expenses of $650. This amount includes $350 of interest paid to related persons that is allocable to foreign personal holding company income under section 904, and $50 of other expense that is directly related to foreign personal holding company income. The remaining $250 of expenses is allocable to services income other than foreign base company income or insurance income.

(iii) *Earnings and losses. CFC* has earnings and profits for the current taxable year of $350. In the prior taxable year, *CFC* had losses with respect to income other than foreign base company income or insurance income. By reason of the limitation provided under section 952(c)(1)(A), those losses reduced the subpart F income of *CFC* (consisting entirely of foreign source general limitation income) by $600 for the prior taxable year.

(iv) *Taxes.* Foreign income tax of $120 is considered imposed on the $720 of interest income under the rules of section 954(b)(4), paragraph (d) of this section, and §1.904-6. Foreign income tax of $2 is considered imposed on the services income under the rules of section 954(b)(4), paragraph (d) of this section, and §1.904-6. For the taxable year of *CFC,* the maximum United States rate of taxation under section 11 is 34 percent.

(v) *Conclusion.* Based on these facts, if *CFC* elects to exclude all items of income subject to a high foreign tax under section 954(b)(4) and this paragraph (d), it will have $350 of subpart F income as defined in section 952(a), determined as follows.

Step 1—Determine gross income:
(1) Gross income $1000

Step 2—Determine gross foreign base company income and gross insurance income:
(2) Gross foreign base company income and gross insurance income as defined in sections 954(c), (d), (e), (f) and (g) and 953 (interest income) 720

Step 3—Compute adjusted gross foreign base company income and adjusted gross insurance income:
(3) Seventy percent of gross income (.70 × line (1)) 700
(4) Adjusted gross foreign base company income and adjusted gross insurance income after the application of the full inclusion rule of this paragraph (b)(1) (line (2), or line (1) if line (2) is greater than line (3)) ... 1000
(5) Full inclusion foreign base company income under paragraph (b)(1)(ii) (line (4) minus line (2)) 280

Step 4—Compute net foreign base company income:
(6) Expenses (other than related person interest expense) directly related to adjusted gross foreign personal holding company income 50
(7) Related person interest expense allocable to adjusted gross foreign personal holding company income under section 904 ... 350
(8) Deductions allocable to full inclusion foreign base company income under section 954(b)(5) and paragraph (c) of this section 250
(9) Net foreign personal holding company income after allocating deductions under section 954(b)(5) and paragraph (c) of this section (line (2) reduced by line (6) and line (7)) 320
(10) Full inclusion foreign base company income after allocating deductions under section 954(b)(5) and paragraph (c) of this section (line (5) reduced by line (8)) 30
(11) Total net foreign base company income after allocating deductions under section 954(b)(5) and paragraph (c) of this section (line (9) plus line (10)) 350

Step 5—Compute net insurance income:
(12) Net insurance income under section 953 0

Step 6—Compute adjusted net foreign base company income:
(13) Foreign income tax imposed on net foreign personal holding company income (interest) 120

Reg. §1.954-1(d)(7)(ii)

(14) Foreign income tax imposed on net full inclusion foreign base company income 2

(15) Ninety percent of the maximum United States corporate tax rate 31.5%

(16) Effective rate of foreign income tax imposed on $320 of net foreign personal holding company income under section 954(b)(4) and this paragraph (d) (line (13) divided by line (9)) 38%

(17) Effective rate of foreign income tax imposed on $30 of net full inclusion foreign base company income under section 954(b)(4) and this paragraph (d) (line (14) divided by line (10)) 7%

(18) Net foreign personal holding company income subject to a high foreign tax under section 954(b)(4) and this paragraph (d) (zero, or line (9) if line (16) is greater than line (15)) 320

(19) Net full inclusion foreign base company income subject to a high foreign tax under section 954(b)(4) and this paragraph (d) (zero, or line (10) if line (17) is greater than line (15)) 0

(20) Adjusted net foreign base company income after applying section 954(b)(4) and this paragraph (d) (line (11) reduced by the sum of line (18) and line (19)) 30

Step 7—Compute adjusted net insurance income:

(21) Adjusted net insurance income . 0

Step 8—Reduction of adjusted net foreign base company income or adjusted net insurance income by reason of paragraph (d)(6) of this section:

(22) Adjusted gross foreign base company income and adjusted gross insurance income (determined without regard to the full inclusion test of paragraph (b)(1) of this section) (line (4) reduced by line (5)) 720

(23) Ninety percent of adjusted gross foreign base company income and adjusted gross insurance income (determined without regard to the full inclusion test of paragraph (b)(1)(ii) of this section) (90% of the amount on line (22)) 648

(24) Net foreign base company income and net insurance income excluded from subpart F income under section 954(b)(4), increased by the amount of expenses that reduced this income under section 954(b)(5) and paragraph (c) of this section (line (18) increased by the sum of line (6) and line (7)) 720

(25) Adjusted net full inclusion foreign base company income excluded from subpart F income under paragraph (d)(6) of this section (zero, or line (10) reduced by line (19) if line (24) is greater than line (23)) 30

(26) Adjusted net foreign base company income after application of paragraph (d)(6) of this section (line (20) reduced by line (25)) . 0

Step 9—Additions to or reduction of subpart F income by reason of section 952(c):

(27) Earnings and profits for the current year 350

(28) Amount subject to being recharacterized as subpart F income under section 952(c)(2) (excess of line (27) over the sum of line (21) and line (26)); if there is a deficit, then the limitation of 952(c)(1) may apply for the current year 350

(29) Amount of reduction in subpart F income for prior taxable years by reason of the limitation of section 952(c)(1) 600

(30) Subpart F income as defined in section 952(a), assuming section 952(a)(3), (4), and (5) do not apply (the sum of line (21) and line (26) plus the lesser of line (28) or line (29)) 350

(31) Amount of prior years' deficit remaining to be recharacterized as subpart F income in later years under section 952(c) (excess of line (29) over line (28)) 250

(e) *Character of income.*—(1) *Substance of the transaction.*—For purposes of section 954, income shall be characterized in accordance with the substance of the transaction, and not in accordance with the designation applied by the parties to the transaction. For example, an amount that is designated as rent by the taxpayer but actually constitutes income from the sale of property, royalties, or income from services shall not be characterized as rent but shall be characterized as income from the sale of property, royalties or income from services, as the case may be. Local law shall not be controlling in characterizing income.

(2) *Separable character.*—To the extent the definitional provisions of section 953 or 954 describe the income or gain derived from a transaction, or any portion or portions thereof, that income or gain, or portion or portions thereof, is so characterized for purposes of subpart F. Thus, a single transaction may give rise to income in more than one category of foreign base company income described in paragraph (a)(2) of this section. For example, if a controlled foreign corporation, in its business of purchasing personal property and selling it to related persons outside its country of incorporation, also performs services outside its country of incorporation with respect to the property it sells, the sales income will be treated as foreign base company sales income and the services income will be treated as foreign base company services income for purposes of these rules.

(3) *Predominant character.*—The portion of income or gain derived from a transaction that is included in the computation of foreign personal holding company income is always separately determinable and thus must always be segregated from other income and separately classified under paragraph (e)(2) of this section. However, the portion of income or gain derived from a transaction that would meet a particular definitional provision under section 954 or 953 (other than the definition of foreign personal holding company income) in unusual circumstances may not be separately determinable. If such portion is not separately determinable, it must be classified in accordance with the predominant character of the transaction. For example, if a controlled foreign corporation engineers, fabricates, and installs a fixed offshore drilling platform as part of an integrated transaction, and the portion of income that relates to services is not accounted for separately from the portion that relates to sales, and is otherwise not separately determinable, then the classification of income from the transaction shall be made in accordance with the predominant character of the arrangement.

(4) *Coordination of categories of gross foreign base company income or gross insurance income.*—(i) *In general.*—The computations of gross foreign base company income and gross insurance income are limited by the following rules:

(A) If income is foreign base company shipping income, pursuant to section 954(f), it shall not be considered insurance income or income in any other category of foreign base company income.

(B) If income is foreign base company oil related income, pursuant to section 954(g), it shall not be considered insurance income or income in any other category of foreign base company income, except as provided in paragraph (e)(4)(i)(A) of this section.

(C) If income is insurance income, pursuant to section 953, it shall not be considered income in any category of foreign base company income except as provided in paragraph (e)(4)(i)(A) or (B) of this section.

(D) If income is foreign personal holding company income, pursuant to section 954(c), it shall not be considered income in any other category of foreign base company income, other than as provided in paragraph (e)(4)(i)(A), (B) or (C) of this section.

(ii) *Income excluded from other categories of gross foreign base company income.*—Income shall not be excluded from a category of gross foreign base company income or gross insurance income under this paragraph (e)(4) by reason of being included in another category of gross foreign base company income or gross insurance income, if the income is excluded from that other category by a more specific provision of section 953 or 954. For example, income derived from a commodity transaction that is excluded from foreign personal holding company income under §1.954-2(f) as income from a qualified active sale may be included in gross foreign base company income if it also meets the definition of foreign base company sales income. See §1.954-2(a)(2) for the coordination of overlapping categories within the definition of foreign personal holding company income.

(f) *Definition of related person.*—(1) *Persons related to controlled foreign corporation.*—Unless otherwise provided, for purposes of section 954 and §§1.954-1 through 1.954-8 inclusive, the following persons are considered under section 954(d)(3) to be related persons with respect to a controlled foreign corporation:

(i) *Individuals.*—An individual, whether or not a citizen or resident of the United States, who controls the controlled foreign corporation.

(ii) *Other persons.*—A foreign or domestic corporation, partnership, trust or estate that controls or is controlled by the controlled foreign corporation, or is controlled by the same person or persons that control the controlled foreign corporation.

(2) *Control.*—(i) *Corporations.*—With respect to a corporation, control means the ownership, directly or indirectly, of stock possessing more than 50 percent of the total voting power of all classes of stock entitled to vote or of the total value of the stock of the corporation.

(ii) *Partnerships.*—With respect to a partnership, control means the ownership, directly or indirectly, of more than 50 percent (by value) of the capital or profits interest in the partnership.

(iii) *Trusts and estates.*—With respect to a trust or estate, control means the ownership, directly, or indirectly, of more than 50 percent (by value) of the beneficial interest in the trust or estate.

(iv) *Direct or indirect ownership.*—For purposes of this paragraph (f), to determine direct or indirect ownership, the principles of section 958 shall be applied without regard to whether a corporation, partnership, trust or estate is foreign or domestic or whether or not an individual is a citizen or resident of the United States.

Reg. §1.954-1(f)(2)(iv)

(g) *Distributive share of partnership income.*—(1) *Application of related person and country of organization tests.*—Unless otherwise provided, to determine the extent to which a controlled foreign corporation's distributive share of any item of gross income of a partnership would have been subpart F income if received by it directly, under §1.952-1(g), if a provision of subpart F requires a determination of whether an entity is a related person, within the meaning of section 954(d)(3), or whether an activity occurred within or outside the country under the laws of which the controlled foreign corporation is created or organized, this determination shall be made by reference to such controlled foreign corporation and not by reference to the partnership.

(2) *Application of related person test for sales and purchase transactions between a partnership and its controlled foreign corporation partner.*—For purposes of determining whether a controlled foreign corporation's distributive share of any item of gross income of a partnership is foreign base company sales income under section 954(d)(1) when the item of income is derived from the sale by the partnership of personal property purchased by the partnership from (or sold by the partnership on behalf of) the controlled foreign corporation; or the sale by the partnership of personal property to (or the purchase of personal property by the partnership on behalf of) the controlled foreign corporation (CFC-partnership transaction), the CFC-partnership transaction will be treated as a transaction with an entity that is a related person, within the meaning of section 954(d)(3), under paragraph (g)(1) of this section, if—

(i) The controlled foreign corporation purchased such personal property from (or sold it to the partnership on behalf of), or sells such personal property to (or purchases it from the partnership on behalf of), a related person with respect to the controlled foreign corporation (other than the partnership), within the meaning of section 954(d)(3); or

(ii) The branch rule of section 954(d)(2) applies to treat as foreign base company sales income the income of the controlled foreign corporation from selling to the partnership (or a third party) personal property that the controlled foreign corporation has manufactured, in the case where the partnership purchases personal property from (or sells personal property on behalf of) the controlled foreign corporation.

(3) *Examples.*—The application of this paragraph (g) is illustrated by the following examples:

Example 1. CFC, a controlled foreign corporation organized in Country A, is an 80-percent partner in Partnership, a partnership organized in Country A. All of the stock of CFC is owned by USP, a U.S. corporation. Partnership earns commission income from purchasing Product O on behalf of USP, from unrelated manufacturers in Country B, for sale in the United States. To determine whether CFC's distributive share of Partnership's commission income is foreign base company sales income under section 954(d), CFC is treated as if it purchased Product O on behalf of USP. Under section 954(d)(3), USP is a related person with respect to CFC. Thus, with respect to CFC, the sales income is deemed to be derived from the purchase of personal property on behalf of a related person. Because the property purchased is both manufactured and sold for use outside of Country A, CFC's country of organization, CFC's distributive share of the sales income is foreign base company sales income.

Example 2. (i) CFC 1, a controlled foreign corporation organized in Country A, is an 80-percent partner in Partnership, a partnership organized in Country B. CFC2, a controlled foreign corporation organized in Country B, owns the remaining 20 percent interest in Partnership. CFC1 and CFC2 are owned by a common U.S. parent, USP. CFC2 manufactures Product A in Country B. Partnership earns sales income from purchasing Product A from CFC2 and selling it to third parties located in Country B that are not related persons with respect to CFC1 or CFC2. To determine whether CFC1's distributive share of Partnership's sales income is foreign base company sales income under section 954(d), CFC1 is treated as if it purchased Product A from CFC2 and sold it to third parties in Country B. Under section 954(d)(3), CFC2 is a related person with respect to CFC1. Thus, with respect to CFC1, the sales income is deemed to be derived from the purchase of personal property from a related person. Because the property purchased is both manufactured and sold for use outside of Country A, CFC1's country of organization, CFC1's distributive share of the sales income is foreign base company sales income.

(ii) Because Product A is both manufactured and sold for use within CFC2's country of organization, CFC2's distributive share of Partnership's sales income is not foreign base company sales income.

Example 3. CFC, a controlled foreign corporation organized in Country A, is an 80 percent partner in MJK Partnership, a Country B partnership. CFC purchased goods from J Corp, a Country C corporation that is a related person with respect to CFC. CFC sold the goods to MJK Partnership. In turn, MJK Partnership sold the goods to P Corp, a Country D corporation that is unrelated to CFC. P Corp sold the goods to unrelated customers in Country D. The goods were manufactured in Country C by persons unrelated to J Corp. CFC's distributive share of the income of MJK Partnership from the sale of goods to P Corp will be treated as income from the sale of goods purchased from a related person for purposes of section 954(d)(1) because CFC purchased the goods from J Corp, a related person. Because the goods were both manufactured and sold for use outside of Country A, CFC's distributive share of the income attributable to the sale of the goods is foreign base company sales income. Further, CFC's income from the sale of the goods to MJK Partnership will also be foreign base company sales income.

Example 4. The facts of are the same as *Example 3*, except that MJK Partnership purchased the goods from P Corp and sold those goods to CFC. CFC sold the goods to J Corp. J Corp sold the goods to unrelated customers in Country C. CFC's distributive share of the income of MJK Partnership from the sale of the goods by the partnership to itself will be treated as income from the sale of goods to a related person, for purposes of section 954(d)(1). Because the goods were both manufactured and sold for use outside of Country A, CFC's distributive share of income attributable to the sale of the goods is foreign base company sales income. Further, CFC's income from the sale of the goods to J Corp is also foreign base company sales income.

(4) *Effective date.*—This paragraph (g) applies to taxable years of a controlled foreign corporation beginning on or after July 23, 2002. [Reg. § 1.954-1.]

☐ [*T.D.* 8618, 9-6-95. *Amended by T.D.* 8704, 12-31-96; *T.D.* 8767, 3-23-98; *T.D.* 8827, 7-12-99 and *T.D.* 9008, 7-22-2002.]

Proposed Amendment to Regulation

§ 1.954-1. Foreign base company income.

* * *

(c) * * *

(1) * * *

(i) *Deductions.*—(A) *Deductions against gross foreign base company income.*—

* * *

(B) *Special rule for deductible payments to certain non-fiscally transparent entities.*—Notwithstanding any other provision of this section, except as provided in paragraph (c)(1)(i)(C) of this section, an expense (including a distributive share of any expense) that would otherwise be allocable under section 954(b)(5) against the subpart F income of a controlled foreign corporation shall not be allocated against subpart F income of the controlled foreign corporation resulting from the payment giving rise to the expense if—

(1) Such expense arises from a payment between the controlled foreign corporation and a partnership in which the controlled foreign corporation is a partner and the partnership is not regarded as fiscally transparent, as defined in § 1.954-9(a)(7), by any country in which the controlled foreign corporation does business or has substantial assets; and

(2) The payment from which the expense arises would have reduced foreign tax, under § 1.954-9(a)(3), and would have fallen within the tax disparity rule of § 1.954-9(a)(5)(iv), if those provisions had been applicable to the payment.

(C) *Limitations.*—Paragraph (c)(1)(i)(B) of this section shall not apply to the extent that the controlled foreign corporation partner has no income against which to allocate the expense, other than its distributive share of a payment described in paragraph (c)(1)(i)(B) of this section. Similarly, to the extent an expense described in paragraph (c)(1)(i)(B) of this section exceeds the controlled foreign corporation partner's distributive share of the payment from which the expense arises, such excess amount of the expense may reduce subpart F income (other than such payment) to which it is properly allocable or apportionable under section 954(b)(5).

(D) *Example.*—The following example illustrates the application of paragraphs (c)(1)(i)(B) and (C) of this section:

Example. CFC, a controlled foreign corporation in Country A, is a 70 percent partner in partnership P, located in Country B. Country A's tax laws do not classify P as a fiscally transparent entity. The rate of tax in country B is 15 percent of the tax rate in country A. P loans $100 to CFC at a market rate of interest. In year 1, CFC pays P $10 of interest on the loan. The interest payment would have caused the recharacterization rules of § 1.954-9 to apply if the payment were made between the entities described in § 1.954-9(a)(2). CFC's distributive share of P's interest income is $7, which is foreign personal holding company income to CFC under section 954(c). Under paragraph (c)(1)(i)(B) of this section, $7 of the $10 interest expense may not be allocated against any of CFC's subpart F income. However, to the extent the remaining $3 of interest expense is properly allocable to subpart F income of CFC other than its distributive share of P's interest income, this expense may offset such other subpart F income.

(E) *Effective date.*—Paragraph (c)(1)(i)(B), (C) and (D) of this section shall be applicable for all payments made or accrued in taxable years commencing after [date that is 5 years after publication of the final regulations in the federal register], under hybrid arrangements, unless such payments are made pursuant to an arrangement that would qualify for permanent relief under § 1.954-9(c)(2) if made between a controlled foreign corporation and its hybrid branch, in which case the relief afforded under that section shall also be afforded under this section.

* * *

[Prop. Reg. § 1.954-1.]

[Proposed 7-13-99.]

§ 1.954-2. Foreign personal holding company income.—(a) *Computation of foreign personal holding company income.*—(1) *Categories of foreign personal holding company income.*—For purposes of subpart F and the regulations under that subpart, foreign personal holding company income consists of the following categories of income—

(i) Dividends, interest, rents, royalties, and annuities as described in paragraph (b) of this section;

(ii) Gain from certain property transactions as described in paragraph (e) of this section;

(iii) Gain from commodities transactions as described in paragraph (f) of this section;

(iv) Foreign currency gain as described in paragraph (g) of this section; and

(v) Income equivalent to interest as described in paragraph (h) of this section.

(2) *Coordination of overlapping categories under foreign personal holding company provisions.*—(i) *In general.*—If any portion of income, gain or loss from a transaction is described in more than one category of foreign personal holding company income (as described in paragraph (a)(2)(ii) of this section), that portion of income, gain or loss is treated solely as income, gain or loss from the category of foreign personal holding company income with the highest priority.

(ii) *Priority of categories.*—The categories of foreign personal holding company income, listed from highest priority (paragraph (a)(2)(ii)(A) of this section) to lowest priority (paragraph (a)(2)(ii)(E) of this section), are—

(A) Dividends, interest, rents, royalties, and annuities, as described in paragraph (b) of this section;

(B) Income equivalent to interest, as described in paragraph (h) of this section without regard to the exceptions in paragraph (h)(1)(ii)(A) of this section;

(C) Foreign currency gain or loss, as described in paragraph (g) of this section without regard to the exclusion in paragraph (g)(2)(ii) of this section;

(D) Gain or loss from commodities transactions, as described in paragraph (f) of this section without regard to the exclusion in paragraph (f)(1)(ii) of this section; and

(E) Gain or loss from certain property transactions, as described in paragraph (e) of this section without regard to the exceptions in paragraph (e)(1)(ii) of this section.

(3) *Changes in the use or purpose for which property is held.*—(i) *In general.*—Under paragraphs (e), (f), (g) and (h) of this section, transactions in certain property give rise to gain or loss included in the computation of foreign personal holding company income if the controlled foreign corporation holds that property for a particular use or purpose. The use or purpose for which property is held is that use or purpose for which it was held for more than one-half of the period during which the controlled foreign corporation held the property prior to the disposition.

(ii) *Special rules.*—(A) *Anti-abuse rule.*—If a principal purpose of a change in use or purpose of property was to avoid including gain or loss in the computation of foreign personal holding company income, all the gain or loss from the disposition of the property is treated as foreign personal holding company income. A purpose may be a principal purpose even though it is outweighed by other purposes (taken together or separately).

(B) *Hedging transactions.*—The provisions of paragraph (a)(3)(i) of this section shall not apply to bona fide hedging transactions, as defined in paragraph (a)(4)(ii) of this section. A transaction will be treated as a bona fide hedging transaction only so long as it satisfies the requirements of paragraph (a)(4)(ii) of this section.

(iii) *Example.*—The following example illustrates the application of this paragraph (a)(3).

Example. At the beginning of taxable year 1, *CFC*, a controlled foreign corporation, purchases a building for investment. During taxable years 1 and 2, *CFC* derives rents from the building that are included in the computation of foreign personal holding company income under paragraph (b)(1)(iii) of this section. At the beginning of taxable year 3, *CFC* changes the use of the building by terminating all leases and using it in an active trade or business. At the beginning of taxable year 4,

CFC sells the building at a gain. The building was not used in an active trade or business of *CFC* for more than one-half of the period during which it was held by *CFC*. Therefore, the building is considered to be property that gives rise to rents, as described in paragraph (e)(2) of this section, and gain from the sale is included in the computation of *CFC*'s foreign personal holding company income under paragraph (e) of this section.

(4) *Definitions and special rules.*—The following definitions and special rules apply for purposes of computing foreign personal holding company income under this section.

(i) *Interest.*—The term *interest* includes all amounts that are treated as interest income (including interest on a tax-exempt obligation) by reason of the Internal Revenue Code or Income Tax Regulations or any other provision of law. For example, interest includes stated interest, acquisition discount, original issue discount, de minimis original issue discount, market discount, de minimis market discount, and unstated interest, as adjusted by any amortizable bond premium or acquisition premium.

(ii) *Bona fide hedging transaction.*—(A) *Definition.*—The term *bona fide hedging transaction* means a transaction that meets the requirements of § 1.1221-2(a) through (d) and that is identified in accordance with the requirements of paragraph (a)(4)(ii)(B) of this section, except that in applying § 1.1221-2(b)(1), the risk being hedged may be with respect to ordinary property, section 1231 property, or a section 988 transaction. A transaction that hedges the liabilities, inventory or other assets of a related person (as defined in section 954(d)(3)), that is entered into to assume or reduce risks of a related person, or that is entered into by a person other than a person acting in its capacity as a regular dealer (as defined in paragraph (a)(4)(iv) of this section) to reduce risks assumed from a related person, will not be treated as a bona fide hedging transaction. For an illustration of how this rule applies with respect to foreign currency transactions, see paragraph (g)(2)(ii)(D) of this section.

(B) *Identification.*—The identification requirements of this section shall be satisfied if the taxpayer meets the identification and recordkeeping requirements of § 1.1221-2(f). However, for bona fide hedging transactions entered into prior to March 7, 1996, the identification and recordkeeping requirements of § 1.1221-2 shall not apply. Rather, for bona fide hedging transactions entered into on or after July 22, 1988 and prior to March 7, 1996, the identification and recordkeeping requirements shall be satisfied if such transactions are identified by the close of the fifth day after the day on which they are entered into. For bona fide hedging transactions entered into prior to July 22, 1988, the identification and recordkeeping requirements shall be satisfied if such transactions are identified reasonably contemporaneously with the date they are entered into, but no later than within the normal period prescribed under the method of accounting of the controlled foreign corporation used for financial reporting purposes.

(C) *Effect of identification and non-identification.*—(1) *Transactions identified.*—If a taxpayer identifies a transaction as a bona fide hedging transaction for purposes of this section, the identification is binding with respect to any loss arising from such transaction whether or not all of the requirements of paragraph (a)(4)(ii)(A) of this section are satisfied. Accordingly, such loss will be allocated against income that is not subpart F income (or, in the case of an election under paragraph (g)(3) of this section, against the category of subpart F income to which it relates) and apportioned among the categories of income described in section 904(d)(1). If the transaction is not in fact a bona fide hedging transaction described in paragraph (a)(4)(ii)(A) of this section, however, then any gain realized with respect to such transaction shall not be considered as gain from a bona fide hedging transaction. Accordingly, such gain shall be treated as gain from the appropriate category of foreign personal holding company income. Thus, the taxpayer's identification of the transaction as a hedging transaction does not itself operate to exclude gain from the appropriate category of foreign personal holding company income.

(2) *Inadvertent identification.*—Notwithstanding paragraph (a)(4)(ii)(C)(1) of this section, if the taxpayer identifies a transaction as a bona fide hedging transaction for purposes of this section, the characterization of the loss is determined as if the transaction had not been identified as a bona fide hedging transaction if—

(i) The transaction is not a bona fide hedging transaction (as defined in paragraph (a)(4)(ii)(A) of this section);

(ii) The identification of the transaction as a bona fide hedging transaction was due to inadvertent error; and

(iii) All of the taxpayer's transactions in all open years are being treated on either original or, if necessary, amended returns in a manner consistent with the principles of this section.

(3) *Transactions not identified.*—Except as provided in paragraphs

Reg. § 1.954-2(a)(4)(ii)(C)(3)

(a)(4)(ii)(C)(4) and (5) of this section, the absence of an identification that satisfies the requirements of paragraph (a)(4)(ii)(B) of this section is binding and establishes that a transaction is not a bona fide hedging transaction. Thus, subject to the exceptions, the characterization of gain or loss is determined without reference to whether the transaction is a bona fide hedging transaction.

(4) *Inadvertent error.*—If a taxpayer does not make an identification that satisfies the requirements of paragraph (a)(4)(ii)(B) of this section, the taxpayer may treat gain or loss from the transaction as gain or loss from a bona fide hedging transaction if—

(i) The transaction is a bona fide hedging transaction (as defined in paragraph (a)(4)(ii)(A) of this section);

(ii) The failure to identify the transaction was due to inadvertent error; and

(iii) All of the taxpayer's bona fide hedging transactions in all open years are being treated on either original or, if necessary, amended returns as bona fide hedging transactions in accordance with the rules of this section.

(5) *Anti-abuse rule.*—If a taxpayer does not make an identification that satisfies all the requirements of paragraph (a)(4)(ii)(B) of this section but the taxpayer has no reasonable grounds for treating the transaction as other than a bona fide hedging transaction, then loss from the transaction shall be treated as realized with respect to a bona fide hedging transaction. Thus, a taxpayer may not elect to exclude loss from its proper characterization as a bona fide hedging transaction. The reasonableness of the taxpayer's failure to identify a transaction is determined by taking into consideration not only the requirements of paragraph (a)(4)(ii)(A) of this section but also the taxpayer's treatment of the transaction for financial accounting or other purposes and the taxpayer's identification of similar transactions as hedging transactions.

(iii) *Inventory and similar property.*—(A) *Definition.*—The term *inventory and similar property* (or *inventory or similar property*) means property that is stock in trade of the controlled foreign corporation or other property of a kind that would properly be included in the inventory of the controlled foreign corporation if on hand at the close of the taxable year (if the controlled foreign corporation were a domestic corporation), or property held by the controlled foreign corporation primarily for sale to customers in the ordinary course of its trade or business.

(B) *Hedging transactions.*—A bona fide hedging transaction with respect to inventory or similar property (other than a transaction described in section 988(c)(1) without regard to section 988(c)(1)(D)(i)) shall be treated as a transaction in inventory or similar property.

(iv) *Regular dealer.*—The term *regular dealer* means a controlled foreign corporation that—

(A) Regularly and actively offers to, and in fact does, purchase property from and sell property to customers who are not related persons (as defined in section 954(d)(3)) with respect to the controlled foreign corporation in the ordinary course of a trade or business; or

(B) Regularly and actively offers to, and in fact does, enter into, assume, offset, assign or otherwise terminate positions in property with customers who are not related persons (as defined in section 954(d)(3)) with respect to the controlled foreign corporation in the ordinary course of a trade or business.

(v) *Dealer property.*—(A) *Definition.*—Property held by a controlled foreign corporation is *dealer property* if—

(1) The controlled foreign corporation is a regular dealer in property of such kind (determined under paragraph (a)(4)(iv) of this section); and

(2) The property is held by the controlled foreign corporation in its capacity as a dealer in property of such kind without regard to whether the property arises from a transaction with a related person (as defined in section 954(d)(3)) with respect to the controlled foreign corporation. The property is not held by the controlled foreign corporation in its capacity as a dealer if the property is held for investment or speculation on its own behalf or on behalf of a related person (as defined in section 954(d)(3)).

(B) *Securities dealers.*—If a controlled foreign corporation is a licensed securities dealer, only the securities that it has identified as held for investment in accordance with the provisions of section 475(b) or section 1236 will be considered to be property held for investment or speculation under this section. A licensed securities dealer is a controlled foreign corporation that is both a securities dealer, as defined in section 475, and a regular dealer, as defined in paragraph (a)(4)(iv) of this section, and that is either—

(1) registered as a securities dealer under section 15(a) of the Securities Exchange Act of 1934 or as a Government securities dealer under section 15C(a) of such Act; or

Reg. § 1.954-2(a)(4)(ii)(C)(4)

(2) licensed or authorized in the country in which it is chartered, incorporated, or organized to purchase and sell securities from or to customers who are residents of that country. The conduct of such securities activities must be subject to bona fide regulation, including appropriate reporting, monitoring, and prudential (including capital adequacy) requirements, by a securities regulatory authority in that country that regularly enforces compliance with such requirements and prudential standards.

(C) *Hedging transactions.*—A bona fide hedging transaction with respect to dealer property shall be treated as a transaction in dealer property.

(vi) *Examples.*—The following examples illustrate the application of paragraphs (a)(4)(ii), (iv) and (v) of this section.

Example 1. (i) *CFC1* and *CFC2* are related controlled foreign corporations (within the meaning of section 954(d)(3)) located in Countries F and G, respectively. *CFC1* and *CFC2* regularly purchase securities from and sell securities to customers who are not related persons with respect to *CFC1* or *CFC2* (within the meaning of section 954(d)(3)) in the ordinary course of their businesses and regularly and actively hold themselves out as being willing to, and in fact do, enter into either side of options, forward contracts, or other financial instruments. *CFC1* uses securities that are traded in securities markets in Country G to hedge positions that it enters into with customers located in Country F. *CFC1* is not a member of a securities exchange in Country G, so it purchases such securities from *CFC2* and unrelated persons that are registered as securities dealers in Country G and that are members of Country G securities exchanges. Such hedging transactions qualify as bona fide hedging transactions under paragraph (a)(4)(ii) of this section.

(ii) Transactions that *CFC1* and *CFC2* enter into with each other do not affect the determination of whether they are regular dealers. Because *CFC1* and *CFC2* regularly purchase securities from and sell securities to customers who are not related persons within the meaning of section 954(d)(3) in the ordinary course of their businesses and regularly and actively hold themselves out as being willing to, and in fact do, enter into either side of options, forward contracts, or other financial instruments, however, they qualify as regular dealers in such property within the meaning of paragraph (a)(4)(iv) of this section. Moreover, because *CFC1* purchases securities from *CFC2* as bona fide hedging transactions with respect to dealer property, the securities are dealer property under paragraph (a)(4)(v)(C) of this section. Similarly, because *CFC2* sells securities to *CFC1* in the ordinary course of its business as a dealer, the securities are dealer property under paragraph (a)(4)(v)(A) of this section.

Example 2. (i) *CFC* is a controlled foreign corporation located in Country B. *CFC* serves as the currency coordination center for the controlled group, aggregating currency risks incurred by the group and entering into hedging transactions that transfer those risks outside of the group. *CFC* regularly and actively holds itself out as being willing to, and in fact does, enter into either side of options, forward contracts, or other financial instruments with other members of the same controlled group. *CFC* hedges risks arising from such transactions by entering into transactions with persons who are not related persons (within the meaning of section 954(d)(3)) with respect to *CFC*. However, *CFC* does not regularly and actively hold itself out as being willing to, and does not, enter into either side of transactions with unrelated persons.

(ii) *CFC* is not a regular dealer in property under paragraph (a)(4)(iv) of this section and its options, forwards, and other financial instruments are not dealer property within the meaning of paragraph (a)(4)(v) of this section.

(vii) *Debt instrument.*—The term *debt instrument* includes bonds, debentures, notes, certificates, accounts receivable, and other evidences of indebtedness.

(5) *Special rules applicable to distributive share of partnership income.*—(i) [Reserved].

(ii) *Certain other exceptions applicable to foreign personal holding company income.*—To determine the extent to which a controlled foreign corporation's distributive share of an item of income of a partnership is foreign personal holding company income—

(A) The exceptions contained in section 954(c) that are based on whether the controlled foreign corporation is engaged in the active conduct of a trade or business, including section 954(c)(2) and paragraphs (b)(2) and (6), (e)(1)(ii) and (3)(ii), (iii) and (iv), (f)(1)(ii), (g)(2)(ii), and (h)(3)(ii) of this section, shall apply only if any such exception would have applied to exclude the income from foreign personal holding company income if the controlled foreign corporation had earned the income directly, determined by taking into account only the activities of, and property owned by, the partnership and not the separate activities or property of the controlled foreign corporation or any other person;

(B) A controlled foreign corporation's distributive share of partnership income will not be excluded from foreign personal holding company income under the exception contained in section 954(h) unless the controlled foreign corporation is an eligible controlled foreign corporation within the meaning of section 954(h)(2) (taking into account the income of the controlled foreign corporation and any partnerships or other qualified business units, within the meaning of section 989(a), of the controlled foreign corporation, including the controlled foreign corporation's distributive share of partnership income) and the partnership, of which the controlled foreign corporation is a partner, generates qualified banking or financing income within the meaning of section 954(h)(3) (taking into account only the income of the partnership);

(C) A controlled foreign corporation's distributive share of partnership income will not be excluded from foreign personal holding company income under the exception contained in section 954(i) unless the controlled foreign corporation partner is a qualifying insurance company, as defined in section 953(e)(3) (determined by examining premiums written by the controlled foreign corporation and any partnerships or other qualified business units, within the meaning of section 989(a), of the CFC partner), and the partnership, of which the controlled foreign corporation is a partner, generates qualified insurance income within the meaning of section 954(i)(2) (taking into account only the income of the partnership).

(iii) *Examples.*—The application of paragraph (a)(5)(ii) is demonstrated by the following examples:

Example 1. B Corp, a Country C corporation, is a controlled foreign corporation within the meaning of section 957(a). B Corp is an 80 percent partner of RKS Partnership, a Country D partnership whose principal office is located in Country D. RKS Partnership is a qualified business unit of B Corp, within the meaning of section 989(a). B Corp, including income earned through RKS Partnership, derives more than 70 percent of its gross income directly from the active and regular conduct of a lending or finance business, within the meaning of section 954(h)(4), from transactions in various countries with customers which are not related persons. Thus, B Corp is predominantly engaged in the active conduct of a banking, financing, or similar business within the meaning of section 954(h)(2)(A)(i). B Corp conducts substantial activity with respect to such business within the meaning of section 954(h)(2)(A)(ii). RKS Partnership derives more than 30 percent of its income from the active and regular conduct of a lending or finance business, within the meaning of section 954(h)(4), from transactions with customers which are not related persons and which are located solely within the home country of RKS Partnership, Country D. B Corp's distributive share of RKS Partnership's income from its lending or finance business will satisfy the special rule for income derived in the active conduct of banking, financing, or similar business of section 954(h). B Corp is an eligible controlled foreign corporation within the meaning of section 954(h)(2) and RKS Partnership generates qualified banking or financing income within the meaning of section 954(h)(3). B Corp does not have any foreign personal holding company income with respect to its distributive share of RKS Partnership income attributable to its lending or finance business income earned in Country D.

Example 2. D Corp, a Country F corporation, is a controlled foreign corporation within the meaning of section 957(a). D Corp satisfies the requirements of section 953(e)(3) and is a qualifying insurance company. D Corp is a 40 percent partner of DJ Partnership, a Country G partnership. DJ Partnership is a qualified business unit of D Corp, within the meaning of section 989(a), and is licensed by the applicable insurance regulatory body for Country G to sell insurance to persons other than related persons in its home country within the meaning of section 953(e)(4)(A). DJ Partnership receives income from persons who are not related persons, within the meaning of section 954(d)(3), from investments that satisfy the requirements of section 954(i)(2). D Corp's distributive share of DJ Partnership's income from investments that satisfy the requirements of section 954(i)(2) will not be treated as foreign personal holding company income because D Corp will satisfy the special rule of section 954(i) for income derived in the active conduct of insurance business. DJ Partnership is a qualifying insurance company branch within the meaning of section 953(e)(4) and its income is qualified insurance income within the meaning of section 954(i)(2). D Corp does not have any foreign personal holding company income as a result of its distributive share of DJ Partnership income that is attributable to the partnership's qualifying insurance income.

(iv) [Reserved].

(v) *Effective date.*—This paragraph (a)(5) applies to taxable years of a controlled foreign corporation beginning on or after July 23, 2002.

(b) *Dividends, interest, rents, royalties, and annuities.*—(1) *In general.*—Foreign personal holding company income includes—

(i) Dividends, except certain dividends from related persons as described in paragraph (b)(4) of this section and distributions of previously taxed income under section 959(b);

(ii) *Interest*, except export financing interest as defined in paragraph (b)(2) of this section and certain interest received from related persons as described in paragraph (b)(4) of this section;

(iii) *Rents and royalties*, except certain rents and royalties received from related persons as described in paragraph (b)(5) of this section and rents and royalties derived in the active conduct of a trade or business as defined in paragraph (b)(6) of this section; and

(iv) *Annuities*.

(2) *Exclusion of certain export financing interest.*—(i) *In general.*—Foreign personal holding company income does not include interest that is export financing interest. The term *export financing interest* means interest that is derived in the conduct of a banking business and is export financing interest as defined in section 904(d)(2)(G). Solely for purposes of determining whether interest is export financing interest, property is treated as manufactured, produced, grown, or extracted in the United States if it is so treated under § 1.927(a)-1T(c).

(ii) *Exceptions.*—Export financing interest does not include income from related party factoring that is treated as interest under section 864(d)(1) or (6) after the application of section 864(d)(7).

(iii) *Conduct of a banking business.*—For purposes of this section, export financing interest is considered derived in the conduct of a banking business if, in connection with the financing from which the interest is derived, the corporation, through its own officers or staff of employees, engages in all the activities in which banks customarily engage in issuing and servicing a loan.

(iv) *Examples.*—The following examples illustrate the application of this paragraph (b)(2).

Example 1. (i) *DS*, a domestic corporation, manufactures property in the United States. In addition to selling inventory (property described in section 1221(1)), *DS* occasionally sells depreciable equipment it manufactures for use in its trade or business, which is property described in section 1221(2). Less than 50 percent of the fair market value, determined in accordance with section 904(d)(2)(G), of each item of inventory or equipment sold by *DS* is attributable to products imported into the United States. *CFC*, a controlled foreign corporation with respect to which *DS* is a related person (within the meaning of section 954(d)(3)), provides loans described in section 864(d)(6) to unrelated persons for the purchase of property from *DS*. This property is purchased exclusively for use or consumption outside the United States and outside *CFC*'s country of incorporation.

(ii) If, in issuing and servicing loans made with respect to purchases from *DS* of depreciable equipment used in its trade or business, which is property described in section 1221(2) in the hands of *DS*, *CFC* engages in all the activities in which banks customarily engage in issuing and servicing loans, the interest accrued from these loans would be export financing interest meeting the requirements of this paragraph (b)(2) and, thus, not included in foreign personal holding company income. However, interest from the loans made with respect to purchases from *DS* of property that is inventory in the hands of *DS* cannot be export financing interest because it is treated as income from a trade or service receivable under section 864(d)(6) and the exception under section 864(d)(7) does not apply. Thus the interest from loans made with respect to this inventory is included in foreign personal holding company income under paragraph (b)(1)(ii) of this section.

Example 2. (i) DS, a domestic corporation, wholly owns two controlled foreign corporations organized in Country A, CFC1 and CFC2. CFC1 purchases from DS property that DS manufactures in the United States. CFC1 uses the purchased property as a component part of property that CFC1 manufactures in Country A within the meaning of § 1.954-3(a)(4). CFC2 provides loans described in section 864(d)(6) to unrelated persons in Country A for the purchase of the property that CFC1 manufactures in Country A.

(ii) The interest accrued from the loans by CFC2 is not export financing interest as defined in section 904(d)(2)(G) because the property sold by CFC1 is not manufactured in the United States under § 1.927(a)-1T(c). No portion of the interest is export financing interest as defined in this paragraph (b)(2). The full amount of the interest is, therefore, included in foreign personal holding company income under paragraph (b)(1)ii) of this section.

(3) *Treatment of tax exempt interest.*—For taxable years of a controlled foreign corporation beginning after March 3, 1997, foreign personal holding company income includes all interest income, including interest that is described in section 103 (see § 1.952-2(c)(1)).

(4) *Exclusion of dividends or interest from related persons.*—(i) *In general.*—(A) *Corporate payor.*—Foreign personal holding company income received by a controlled

foreign corporation does not include dividends or interest if the payor—

(1) Is a corporation that is a related person with respect to the controlled foreign corporation, as defined in section 954(d)(3);

(2) Is created or organized under the laws of the same foreign country (the *country of incorporation*) as is the controlled foreign corporation; and

(3) Uses a substantial part of its assets in a trade or business in its country of incorporation, as determined under this paragraph (b)(4).

(B) *Payment by a partnership.*—For purposes of this paragraph (b)(4), if a partnership with one or more corporate partners makes a payment of interest, a corporate partner will be treated as the payor of the interest—

(1) If the interest payment gives rise to a partnership item of deduction under the Internal Revenue Code or Income Tax Regulations, to the extent that the item of deduction is allocable to the corporate partner under section 704(b); or

(2) If the interest payment does not give rise to a partnership item of deduction under the Internal Revenue Code or Income Tax Regulations, to the extent that a partnership item reasonably related to the payment would be allocated to that partner under an existing allocation under the partnership agreement (made pursuant to section 704(b)).

(ii) *Exceptions.*—(A) *Dividends.*—Dividends are excluded from foreign personal holding company income under this paragraph (b)(4) only to the extent that they are paid out of earnings and profits that are earned or accumulated during a period in which—

(1) The stock on which dividends are paid with respect to which the exclusion is claimed was owned by the recipient controlled foreign corporation directly, or indirectly through a chain of one or more subsidiaries each of which meets the requirements of paragraph (b)(4)(i)(A) of this section; and

(2) Each of the requirements of paragraph (b)(4)(i)(A) of this section is satisfied or, to the extent earned or accumulated during a taxable year of the related foreign corporation ending on or before December 31, 1962, during a period in which the payor was a related corporation as to the controlled foreign corporation and the other requirements of paragraph (b)(4)(i)(A) of this section were substantially satisfied.

(3) This paragraph (b)(4)(ii)(A) is illustrated by the following example:

Example. A, a domestic corporation, owns all of the stock of B, a corporation created and organized under the laws of Country Y, and C, a corporation created and organized under the laws of Country X. The taxable year of each of the corporations is the calendar year. In Year 1, B earns $100 of income from the sale of products in Country Y that it manufactured in Country Y. C had no earnings and profits in Year 1. On January 1 of Year 2, A contributes all of the stock of B and C to Newco, a Country Y corporation, in exchange for all of the stock of Newco. Neither B nor C earns any income in Year 2, but at the end of Year 2 B distributes the $100 accumulated earnings and profits to Newco. Newco's income from the distribution, $100, is foreign personal holding company income because the earnings and profits distributed by B were not earned or accumulated during a period in which the stock of B was owned by Newco and in which each of the requirements of paragraph (b)(4)(i)(A) of this section was satisfied.

(B) *Interest paid out of adjusted foreign base company income or insurance income.*—(1) *In general.*—Interest may not be excluded from the foreign personal holding company income of the recipient under this paragraph (b)(4) to the extent that the deduction for the interest is allocated under § 1.954-1(a)(4) and (c) to the payor's adjusted gross foreign base company income (as defined in § 1.954-1(a)(3)), adjusted gross insurance income (as defined in § 1.954-1(a)(6)), or any other category of income included in the computation of subpart F income under section 952(a).

(2) *Rule for corporations that are both recipients and payors of interest.*—If a controlled foreign corporation is both a recipient and payor of interest, the interest that is received will be characterized before the interest that is paid. In addition, the amount of interest paid or accrued, directly or indirectly, by the controlled foreign corporation to a related person (as defined in section 954(d)(3)) shall be offset against and eliminate any interest received or accrued, directly or indirectly, by the controlled foreign corporation from that related person. In a case in which the controlled foreign corporation pays or accrues interest to a related person, as defined in section 954(d)(3), and also receives or accrues interest indirectly from the related person, the smallest interest payment is eliminated and the amounts of all other interest payments are reduced by the amount of the smallest interest payment.

(C) *Coordination with sections 864(d) and 881(c).*—Income of a controlled foreign corporation that is treated as interest under

Reg. § 1.954-2(b)(4)(i)(A)(1)

section 864(d)(1) or (6), or that is portfolio interest, as defined by section 881(c), is not excluded from foreign personal holding company income under section 954(c)(3)(A)(i) and this paragraph (b)(4).

(iii) *Trade or business requirement.*—Except as otherwise provided under this paragraph (b)(4), the principles of section 367(a) apply for purposes of determining whether the payor has a trade or business in its country of incorporation and whether its assets are used in that trade or business. Property purchased or produced for use in a trade or business is not considered used in a trade or business before it is placed in service or after it is retired from service as determined in accordance with the principles of sections 167 and 168.

(iv) *Substantial assets test.*—A substantial part of the assets of the payor will be considered to be used in a trade or business located in the payor's country of incorporation for a taxable year only if the average value of the payor's assets for such year that are used in the trade or business and are located in such country equals more than 50 percent of the average value of all the assets of the payor (including assets not used in a trade or business). The average value of assets for the taxable year is determined by averaging the values of assets at the close of each quarter of the taxable year. The value of assets is determined under paragraph (b)(4)(v) of this section, and the location of assets used in a trade or business of the payor is determined under paragraphs (b)(4)(vi) through (xi) of this section.

(v) *Valuation of assets.*—For purposes of determining whether a substantial part of the assets of the payor are used in a trade or business in its country of incorporation, the value of assets shall be their fair market value (not reduced by liabilities), which, in the absence of affirmative evidence to the contrary, shall be deemed to be their adjusted basis.

(vi) *Location of tangible property.*—(A) *In general.*—Tangible property (other than inventory and similar property as defined in paragraph (a)(4)(iii) of this section, and dealer property as defined in paragraph (a)(4)(v) of this section) used in a trade or business is considered located in the country in which it is physically located.

(B) *Exception.*—An item of tangible personal property that is used in the trade or business of a payor in the payor's country of incorporation is considered located within the payor's country of incorporation while it is temporarily located elsewhere for inspection or repair if the property is not placed in service in a country other than the payor's country of incorporation and is not to be so placed in service following the inspection or repair.

(vii) *Location of intangible property.*—(A) *In general.*—Intangible property (other than inventory and similar property as defined in paragraph (a)(4)(iii) of this section, dealer property as defined in paragraph (a)(4)(v) of this section, and debt instruments) is considered located entirely in the payor's country of incorporation for a quarter of the taxable year only if the payor conducts all of its activities in connection with the use or exploitation of the property in that country during that entire quarter. For this purpose, the country in which the activities connected to the use or exploitation of the property are conducted is the country in which the expenses associated with these activities are incurred. Expenses incurred in connection with the use or exploitation of an item of intangible property are included in the computation provided by this paragraph (b)(4) if they would be deductible under section 162 or includible in inventory costs or the cost of goods sold if the payor were a domestic corporation. If the payor conducts such activities through an agent or independent contractor, then the expenses incurred by the payor with respect to the agent or independent contractor shall be deemed to be incurred by the payor in the country in which the expenses of the agent or independent contractor were incurred by the agent or independent contractor.

(B) *Exception for property located in part in the payor's country of incorporation.*—If the payor conducts its activities in connection with the use or exploitation of an item of intangible property, including goodwill (other than inventory and similar property, dealer property and debt instruments) during a quarter of the taxable year both in its country of incorporation and elsewhere, then the value of the intangible considered located in the payor's country of incorporation during that quarter is a percentage of the value of the item as of the close of the quarter. That percentage equals the ratio that the expenses incurred by the payor (described in paragraph (b)(4)(vii)(A) of this section) during the entire quarter by reason of activities that are connected with the use or exploitation of the item of intangible property and are conducted in the payor's country of incorporation bear to all expenses incurred by the payor during the entire quarter by reason of all such activities worldwide.

(viii) *Location of inventory and dealer property.*—(A) *In general.*—Inventory and similar property, as defined in paragraph (a)(4)(iii) of this section, and dealer property, as defined in paragraph (a)(4)(v) of this section, are con-

Reg. § 1.954–2(b)(4)(viii)(A)

sidered located entirely in the payor's country of incorporation for a quarter of the taxable year only if the payor conducts all of its activities in connection with the production and sale, or purchase and resale, of such property in its country of incorporation during that entire quarter. If the payor conducts such activities through an agent or independent contractor, then the location of such activities is the place in which they are conducted by the agent or independent contractor.

(B) *Inventory and dealer property located in part in the payor's country of incorporation.*—If the payor conducts its activities in connection with the production and sale, or purchase and resale, of inventory or similar property or dealer property during a quarter of the taxable year both in its country of incorporation and elsewhere, then the value of the inventory or similar property or dealer property considered located in the payor's country of incorporation during each quarter is a percentage of the value of the inventory or similar property or dealer property as of the close of the quarter. That percentage equals the ratio that the costs and expenses incurred by the payor during the entire quarter by reason of activities connected with the production and sale, or purchase and resale, of inventory or similar property or dealer property that are conducted in the payor's country of incorporation bear to all costs or expenses incurred by the payor during the entire quarter by reason of all such activities worldwide. A cost incurred in connection with the production and sale or purchase and resale of inventory or similar property or dealer property is included in this computation if it—

(1) Would be included in inventory costs or otherwise capitalized with respect to inventory or similar property or dealer property under section 61, 263A, 471, or 472 if the payor were a domestic corporation; or

(2) Would be deductible under section 162 if the payor were a domestic corporation and is definitely related to gross income derived from such property (but not to all classes of gross income derived by the payor) under the principles of § 1.861-8.

(ix) *Location of debt instruments.*—For purposes of this paragraph (b)(4), debt instruments, other than debt instruments that are inventory or similar property (as defined in paragraph (a)(4)(iii) of this section) or dealer property (as defined in paragraph (a)(4)(v) of this section) are considered to be used in a trade or business only if they arise from the sale of inventory or similar property or dealer property by the payor or from the rendition of services by the payor in the ordinary course of a trade or business of the payor, and only until such time as interest is required to be charged under section 482. Debt instruments that arise from the sale of inventory or similar property or dealer property during a quarter are treated as having the same location, proportionately, as the inventory or similar property or dealer property held during that quarter. Debt instruments arising from the rendition of services in the ordinary course of a trade or business are considered located on a proportionate basis in the countries in which the services to which they relate are performed.

(x) *Treatment of certain stock interests.*—Stock in a controlled foreign corporation (lower-tier corporation) that is incorporated in the same country as the payor and that is more than 50-percent owned, directly or indirectly, by the payor within the meaning of section 958(a) shall be considered located in the payor's country of incorporation and, solely for purposes of section 954(c)(3), used in a trade or business of the payor in proportion to the value of the assets of the lower-tier corporation that are used in a trade or business in the country of incorporation. The location of assets used in a trade or business of the lower-tier corporation shall be determined under the rules of this paragraph (b)(4).

(xi) *Treatment of banks and insurance companies.*—[Reserved]

(5) *Exclusion of rents and royalties derived from related persons.*—(i) *In general.*—(A) *Corporate payor.*—Foreign personal holding company income received by a controlled foreign corporation does not include rents or royalties if—

(1) The payor is a corporation that is a related person with respect to the controlled foreign corporation, as defined in section 954(d)(3); and

(2) The rents or royalties are for the use of, or the privilege of using, property within the country under the laws of which the controlled foreign corporation receiving the payments is created or organized (the country of incorporation).

(B) *Payment by a partnership.*—For purposes of this paragraph (b)(5), if a partnership with one or more corporate partners makes a payment of rents or royalties, a corporate partner will be treated as the payor of the rents or royalties—

(1) If the rent or royalty payment gives rise to a partnership item of deduction under the Internal Revenue Code or Income Tax Regulations, to the extent the item of deduction is allocable to the corporate partner under section 704(b); or

(2) If the rent or royalty payment does not give rise to a partnership item of deduction under the Internal Revenue Code or Income Tax Regulations, to the extent that a partnership item reasonably related to the payment would be allocated to that partner under an existing allocation under the partnership agreement (made pursuant to section 704(b)).

(ii) *Exceptions.*—(A) *Rents or royalties paid out of adjusted foreign base company income or insurance income.*—Rents or royalties may not be excluded from the foreign personal holding company income of the recipient under this paragraph (b)(5) to the extent that deductions for the payments are allocated under section 954(b)(5) and § 1.954-1(a)(4) and (c) to the payor's adjusted gross foreign base company income (as defined in § 1.954-1(a)(3)), adjusted gross insurance income (as defined in § 1.954-1(a)(6)), or any other category of income included in the computation of subpart F income under section 952(a).

(B) *Property used in part in the controlled foreign corporation's country of incorporation.*—If the payor uses the property both in the controlled foreign corporation's country of incorporation and elsewhere, the part of the rent or royalty attributable (determined under the principles of section 482) to the use of, or the privilege of using, the property outside such country of incorporation is included in the computation of foreign personal holding company income under this paragraph (b).

(6) *Exclusion of rents and royalties derived in the active conduct of a trade or business.*—Foreign personal holding company income shall not include rents or royalties that are derived in the active conduct of a trade or business and received from a person that is not a related person (as defined in section 954(d)(3)) with respect to the controlled foreign corporation. For purposes of this section, rents or royalties are derived in the active conduct of a trade or business only if the provisions of paragraph (c) or (d) of this section are satisfied.

(c) *Excluded rents.*—(1) *Active conduct of a trade or business.*—Rents will be considered for purposes of paragraph (b)(6) of this section to be derived in the active conduct of a trade or business if such rents are derived by the controlled foreign corporation (the lessor) from leasing any of the following—

(i) Property that the lessor has manufactured or produced, or has acquired and added substantial value to, but only if the lessor is regularly engaged in the manufacture or production of, or in the acquisition and addition of substantial value to, property of such kind;

(ii) Real property with respect to which the lessor, through its own officers or staff of employees, regularly performs active and substantial management and operational functions while the property is leased;

(iii) Personal property ordinarily used by the lessor in the active conduct of a trade or business, leased temporarily during a period when the property would, but for such leasing, be idle; or

(iv) Property that is leased as a result of the performance of marketing functions by such lessor if the lessor, through its own officers or staff of employees located in a foreign country, maintains and operates an organization in such country that is regularly engaged in the business of marketing, or of marketing and servicing, the leased property and that is substantial in relation to the amount of rents derived from the leasing of such property.

(2) *Special rules.*—(i) *Adding substantial value.*—For purposes of paragraph (c)(1)(i) of this section, the performance of marketing functions will not be considered to add substantial value to property.

(ii) *Substantiality of foreign organization.*—For purposes of paragraph (c)(1)(iv) of this section, whether an organization in a foreign country is substantial in relation to the amount of rents is determined based on all of the facts and circumstances. However, such an organization will be considered substantial in relation to the amount of rents if active leasing expenses, as defined in paragraph (c)(2)(iii) of this section, equal or exceed 25 percent of the adjusted leasing profit, as defined in paragraph (c)(2)(iv) of this section.

(iii) *Active leasing expenses.*—The term *active leasing expenses* means the deductions incurred by an organization of the lessor in a foreign country that are properly allocable to rental income and that would be allowable under section 162 to the lessor if it were a domestic corporation, other than—

(A) Deductions for compensation for personal services rendered by shareholders of, or related persons (as defined in section 954(d)(3)) with respect to, the lessor;

(B) Deductions for rents paid or accrued;

(C) Deductions that, although generally allowable under section 162, would be specifically allowable to the lessor (if the lessor were a domestic corporation) under any section of the Internal Revenue Code other than section 162; and

(D) Deductions for payments made to agents or independent contractors with respect to the leased property other than payments for insurance, utilities and other expenses for like services, or for capitalized repairs.

(iv) *Adjusted leasing profit.*—The term *adjusted leasing profit* means the gross income of the lessor from rents, reduced by the sum of—

(A) The rents paid or incurred by the lessor with respect to such rental income;

(B) The amounts that would be allowable to such lessor (if the lessor were a domestic corporation) as deductions under sections 167 or 168 with respect to such rental income; and

(C) The amounts paid by the lessor to agents or independent contractors with respect to such rental income other than payments for insurance, utilities and other expenses for like services, or for capitalized repairs.

(3) *Examples.*—The application of this paragraph (c) is illustrated by the following examples.

Example 1. Controlled foreign corporation A is regularly engaged in the production of office machines which it sells or leases to others and services. Under paragraph (c)(1)(i) of this section, the rental income of Corporation A from these leases is derived in the active conduct of a trade or business for purposes of section 954(c)(2)(A).

Example 2. Controlled foreign corporation D purchases motor vehicles which it leases to others. In the conduct of its short-term leasing of such vehicles in foreign country X, Corporation D owns a large number of motor vehicles in country X which it services and repairs, leases motor vehicles to customers on an hourly, daily, or weekly basis, maintains offices and service facilities in country X from which to lease and service such vehicles, and maintains therein a sizable staff of its own administrative, sales, and service personnel. Corporation D also leases in country X on a long-term basis, generally for a term of one year, motor vehicles that it owns. Under the terms of the long-term leases, Corporation D is required to repair and service, during the term of the lease, the leased motor vehicles without cost to the lessee. By the maintenance in country X of office, sales, and service facilities and its complete staff of administrative, sales, and service personnel, Corporation D maintains and operates an organization therein that is regularly engaged in the business of marketing and servicing the motor vehicles that are leased. The deductions incurred by such organization satisfy the 25-percent test of paragraph (c)(2)(ii) of this section; thus, such organization is substantial in relation to the rents Corporation D receives from leasing the motor vehicles. Therefore, under paragraph (c)(1)(iv) of this section, such rents are derived in the active conduct of a trade or business for purposes of section 954(c)(2)(A).

Example 3. Controlled foreign corporation E owns a complex of apartment buildings that it has acquired by purchase. Corporation E engages a real estate management firm to lease the apartments, manage the buildings and pay over the net rents to Corporation E. The rental income of Corporation E from such leases is not derived in the active conduct of a trade or business for purposes of section 954(c)(2)(A).

Example 4. Controlled foreign corporation F acquired by purchase a twenty-story office building in a foreign country, three floors of which it occupies and the rest of which it leases. Corporation F acts as rental agent for the leasing of offices in the building and employs a substantial staff to perform other management and maintenance functions. Under paragraph (c)(1)(ii) of this section, the rents received by Corporation F from such leasing operations are derived in the active conduct of a trade or business for purposes of section 954(c)(2)(A).

Example 5. Controlled foreign corporation G owns equipment that it ordinarily uses to perform contracts in foreign countries to drill oil wells. For occasional brief and irregular periods it is unable to obtain contracts requiring immediate performance sufficient to employ all such equipment. During such a period it sometimes leases such idle equipment temporarily. After the expiration of such temporary leasing of the property, Corporation G continues the use of such equipment in the performance of its own drilling contracts. Under paragraph (c)(1)(iii) of this section, rents Corporation G receives from such leasing of idle equipment are derived in the active conduct of a trade or business for purposes of section 954(c)(2)(A).

(d) *Excluded royalties.*—(1) *Active conduct of a trade or business.*—Royalties will be considered for purposes of paragraph (b)(6) of this section to be derived in the active conduct of a trade or business if such royalties are derived by the controlled foreign corporation (the licensor) from licensing—

(i) Property that the licensor has developed, created, or produced, or has acquired and added substantial value to, but only so long as the licensor is regularly engaged in the development, creation or production of, or in the acquisition of and addition of substantial value to, property of such kind; or

(ii) Property that is licensed as a result of the performance of marketing functions by such licensor if the licensor, through its own officers or staff of employees located in a foreign country, maintains and operates an organization in such country that is regularly engaged in the business of marketing, or of marketing and servicing, the licensed property and that is substantial in relation to the amount of royalties derived from the licensing of such property.

(2) *Special rules.*—(i) *Adding substantial value.*—For purposes of paragraph (d)(1)(i) of this section, the performance of marketing functions will not be considered to add substantial value to property.

(ii) *Substantiality of foreign organization.*—For purposes of paragraph (d)(1)(ii) of this section, whether an organization in a foreign country is substantial in relation to the amount of royalties is determined based on all of the facts and circumstances. However, such an organization will be considered substantial in relation to the amount of royalties if active licensing expenses, as defined in paragraph (d)(2)(iii) of this section, equal or exceed 25 percent of the adjusted licensing profit, as defined in paragraph (d)(2)(iv) of this section.

(iii) *Active licensing expenses.*—The term *active licensing expenses* means the deductions incurred by an organization of the licensor in a foreign country that are properly allocable to royalty income and that would be allowable under section 162 to the licensor if it were a domestic corporation, other than—

(A) Deductions for compensation for personal services rendered by shareholders of, or related persons (as defined in section 954(d)(3)) with respect to, the licensor;

(B) Deductions for royalties paid or incurred;

(C) Deductions that, although generally allowable under section 162, would be specifically allowable to the licensor (if the controlled foreign corporation were a domestic corporation) under any section of the Internal Revenue Code other than section 162; and

(D) Deductions for payments made to agents or independent contractors with respect to the licensed property.

(iv) *Adjusted licensing profit.*—The term *adjusted licensing profit* means the gross income of the licensor from royalties, reduced by the sum of—

(A) The royalties paid or incurred by the licensor with respect to such royalty income;

(B) The amounts that would be allowable to such licensor as deductions under section 167 or 197 (if the licensor were a domestic corporation) with respect to such royalty income; and

(C) The amounts paid by the licensor to agents or independent contractors with respect to such royalty income.

(3) *Examples.*—The application of this paragraph (d) is illustrated by the following examples.

Example 1. Controlled foreign corporation A, through its own staff of employees, owns and operates a research facility in foreign country X. At the research facility, employees of Corporation A who are scientists, engineers, and technicians regularly perform experiments, tests, and other technical activities, that ultimately result in the issuance of patents that it sells or licenses. Under paragraph (d)(1)(i) of this section, royalties received by Corporation A for the privilege of using patented rights that it develops as a result of such research activity are derived in the active conduct of a trade or business for purposes of section 954(c)(2)(A), but only so long as the licensor is regularly engaged in the development, creation or production of, or in the acquisition of and addition of substantial value to, property of such kind.

Example 2. Assume that Corporation A in *Example 1*, in addition to receiving royalties for the use of patents that it develops, receives royalties for the use of patents that it acquires by purchase and licenses to others without adding any value thereto. Corporation A generally consummates royalty agreements on such purchased patents as the result of inquiries received by it from prospective licensees when the fact becomes known in the business community, as a result of the filing of a patent, advertisements in trade journals, announcements, and contacts by employees of Corporation A, that Corporation A has acquired rights under a patent and is interested in licensing its rights. Corporation A does not, however, maintain and operate an organization in a foreign country that is regularly engaged in the business of marketing the purchased patents. The royalties received by Corporation A for the use of the purchased patents are not derived in the active conduct of a trade or business for purposes of section 954(c)(2)(A).

Example 3. Controlled foreign corporation B receives royalties for the use of patents that it acquires by purchase. The primary business of Corporation B, operated on a regular basis, consists of licensing patents that it has purchased raw from inventors and, through the efforts of a substantial staff of employees consisting of scientists, engineers, and technicians, made susceptible to commercial application. For example, Corporation B, after purchasing patent rights covering a chemical process, designs specialized production equipment required for the commercial adaptation of the process and, by so doing, substantially in-

Reg. §1.954-2(d)(3)

creases the value of the patent. Under paragraph (d)(1)(i) of this section, royalties received by Corporation B from the use of such patent are derived in the active conduct of a trade or business for purposes of section 954(c)(2)(A).

Example 4. Controlled foreign corporation C receives royalties for the use of a patent that it developed through its own staff of employees at its facility in country X. Corporation C has developed no other patents. It does not regularly employ a staff of scientists, engineers or technicians to create new products to be patented. Further, it does not purchase and license patents developed by others to which it has added substantial value. The royalties received by Corporation C are not derived from the active conduct of a trade or business for purposes of section 954(c)(2)(A).

Example 5. Controlled foreign corporation D finances independent persons in the development of patented items in return for an ownership interest in such items from which it derives a percentage of royalty income, if any, subsequently derived from the use by others of the protected right. Corporation D also attempts to increase its royalty income from such patents by contacting prospective licensees and rendering to licensees advice that is intended to promote the use of the patented property. Corporation D does not, however, maintain and operate an organization in a foreign country that is regularly engaged in the business of marketing the patents. Royalties received by Corporation D for the use of such patents are not derived in the active conduct of a trade or business for purposes of section 954(c)(2)(A).

(e) *Certain property transactions.*—(1) *In general.*—(i) *Inclusions.*—Gain from certain property transactions described in section 954(c)(1)(B) includes the excess of gains over losses from the sale or exchange of—

(A) Property that gives rise to dividends, interest, rents, royalties or annuities, as described in paragraph (e)(2) of this section;

(B) Property that is an interest in a partnership, trust or REMIC; and

(C) Property that does not give rise to income, as described in paragraph (e)(3) of this section.

(ii) *Exceptions.*—Gain or loss from certain property transactions described in section 954(c)(1)(B) and paragraph (e)(1)(i) of this section does not include gain or loss from the sale or exchange of—

(A) Inventory or similar property, as defined in paragraph (a)(4)(iii) of this section;

(B) Dealer property, as defined in paragraph (a)(4)(v) of this section; or

(C) Property that gives rise to rents or royalties described in paragraph (b)(6) of this section that are derived in the active conduct of a trade or business from persons that are not related persons (as defined in section 954(d)(3)) with respect to the controlled foreign corporation.

(iii) *Treatment of losses.*—Section 1.954-1(c)(1)(ii) provides for the treatment of losses in excess of gains from the sale or exchange of property described in paragraph (e)(1)(i) of this section.

(iv) *Dual character property.*—Property may, in part, constitute property that gives rise to certain income as described in paragraph (e)(2) of this section or, in part, constitute property that does not give rise to any income as described in paragraph (e)(3) of this section. However, property that is described in paragraph (e)(1)(i)(B) of this section cannot be dual character property. Dual character property must be treated as two separate properties for purposes of paragraph (e)(2) or (3) of this section. Accordingly, the sale or exchange of such dual character property will give rise to gain or loss that in part must be included in the computation of foreign personal holding company income under paragraph (e)(2) or (3) of this section, and in part is excluded from such computation. Gain or loss from the disposition of dual character property must be bifurcated under this paragraph (e)(1)(iv) pursuant to the method that most reasonably reflects the relative uses of the property. Reasonable methods may include comparisons in terms of gross income generated or the physical division of the property. In the case of real property, the physical division of the property will in most cases be the most reasonable method available. For example, if a controlled foreign corporation owns an office building, uses 60 percent of the building in its trade or business, and rents out the other 40 percent, then 40 percent of the gain recognized on the disposition of the property would reasonably be treated as gain that is included in the computation of foreign personal holding company income under this paragraph (e)(1). This paragraph (e)(1)(iv) addresses the contemporaneous use of property for dual purposes. For rules concerning changes in the use of property affecting its classification for purposes of this paragraph (e), see paragraph (a)(3) of this section.

(2) *Property that gives rise to certain income.*—(i) *In general.*—Property the sale or exchange of which gives rise to foreign personal holding company income under this paragraph (e)(2) includes property that gives rise to dividends, interest, rents, royalties or annuities de-

scribed in paragraph (b) of this section, including—

(A) Property that gives rise to export financing interest described in paragraph (b)(2) of this section; and

(B) Property that gives rise to income from related persons described in paragraph (b)(4) or (5) of this section.

(ii) *Gain or loss from the disposition of a debt instrument.*—Gain or loss from the sale, exchange or retirement of a debt instrument is included in the computation of foreign personal holding company income under this paragraph (e) unless—

(A) In the case of gain—

(1) It is interest (as defined in paragraph (a)(4)(i) of this section); or

(2) It is income equivalent to interest (as described in paragraph (h) of this section); and

(B) In the case of loss—

(1) It is directly allocated to, or treated as an adjustment to, interest income (as described in paragraph (a)(4)(i) of this section) or income equivalent to interest (as defined in paragraph (h) of this section) under any provision of the Internal Revenue Code or Income Tax Regulations; or

(2) It is required to be apportioned in the same manner as interest expense under section 864(e) or any other provision of the Internal Revenue Code or Income Tax Regulations.

(3) *Property that does not give rise to income.*—Except as otherwise provided in this paragraph (e)(3), for purposes of this section, the term *property that does not give rise to income* includes all rights and interests in property (whether or not a capital asset) including, for example, forwards, futures and options. Property that does not give rise to income shall not include—

(i) Property that gives rise to dividends, interest, rents, royalties or annuities described in paragraph (e)(2) of this section;

(ii) Tangible property (other than real property) used or held for use in the controlled foreign corporation's trade or business that is of a character that would be subject to the allowance for depreciation under section 167 or 168 and the regulations under those sections (including tangible property described in § 1.167(a)-2);

(iii) Real property that does not give rise to rental or similar income, to the extent used or held for use in the controlled foreign corporation's trade or business;

(iv) Intangible property (as defined in section 936(h)(3)(B)), goodwill or going concern value, to the extent used or held for use in the controlled foreign corporation's trade or business;

(v) Notional principal contracts (but see paragraphs (f)(2), (g)(2) and (h)(3) of this section for rules that include income from certain notional principal contracts in gains from commodities transactions, foreign currency gains and income equivalent to interest, respectively); or

(vi) Other property that is excepted from the general rule of this paragraph (e)(3) by the Commissioner in published guidance. See § 601.601(d)(2) of this chapter.

(f) *Commodities transactions.*—(1) *In general.*—(i) *Inclusion in foreign personal holding company income.*—Foreign personal holding company income includes the excess of gains over losses from commodities transactions.

(ii) *Exception.*—Gains and losses from qualified active sales and qualified hedging transactions are excluded from the computation of foreign personal holding company income under this paragraph (f).

(iii) *Treatment of losses.*—Section 1.954-1(c)(1)(ii) provides for the treatment of losses in excess of gains from commodities transactions.

(2) *Definitions.*—(i) *Commodity.*—For purposes of this section, the term *commodity* includes tangible personal property of a kind that is actively traded or with respect to which contractual interests are actively traded.

(ii) *Commodities transaction.*—The term *commodities transaction* means the purchase or sale of a commodity for immediate (spot) delivery or deferred (forward) delivery, or the right to purchase, sell, receive, or transfer a commodity, or any other right or obligation with respect to a commodity accomplished through a cash or off-exchange market, an interbank market, an organized exchange or board of trade, or an over-the-counter market, or in a transaction effected between private parties outside of any market. Commodities transactions include, but are not limited to—

(A) A futures or forward contract in a commodity;

(B) A leverage contract in a commodity purchased from a leverage transaction merchant;

(C) An exchange of futures for physical transaction;

(D) A transaction, including a notional principal contract, in which the income or loss to the parties is measured by reference to the price of a commodity, a pool of commodities, or an index of commodities;

Reg. § 1.954-2(f)(2)(ii)(D)

(E) The purchase or sale of an option or other right to acquire or transfer a commodity, a futures contract in a commodity, or an index of commodities; and

(F) The delivery of one commodity in exchange for the delivery of another commodity, the same commodity at another time, cash, or nonfunctional currency.

(iii) *Qualified active sale.*—(A) *In general.*—The term *qualified active sale* means the sale of commodities in the active conduct of a commodities business as a producer, processor, merchant or handler of commodities if substantially all of the controlled foreign corporation's business is as an active producer, processor, merchant or handler of commodities. The sale of commodities held by a controlled foreign corporation other than in its capacity as an active producer, processor, merchant or handler of commodities is not a qualified active sale. For example, the sale by a controlled foreign corporation of commodities that were held for investment or speculation would not be a qualified active sale.

(B) *Active conduct of a commodities business.*—For purposes of this paragraph, a controlled foreign corporation is engaged in the active conduct of a commodities business as a producer, processor, merchant or handler of commodities only with respect to commodities for which each of the following conditions is satisfied—

(1) It holds the commodities directly, and not through an agent or independent contractor, as inventory or similar property (as defined in paragraph (a)(4)(iii) of this section) or as dealer property (as defined in paragraph (a)(4)(v) of this section); and

(2) With respect to such commodities, it incurs substantial expenses in the ordinary course of a commodities business from engaging in one or more of the following activities directly, and not through an independent contractor—

(i) Substantial activities in the production of the commodities, including planting, tending or harvesting crops, raising or slaughtering livestock, or extracting minerals;

(ii) Substantial processing activities prior to the sale of the commodities, including the blending and drying of agricultural commodities, or the concentrating, refining, mixing, crushing, aerating or milling of commodities; or

(iii) Significant activities as described in paragraph (f)(2)(iii)(B)(3) of this section.

(3) For purposes of paragraph (f)(2)(iii)(B)(2)(*iii*) of this section, the significant activities must relate to—

(i) The physical movement, handling and storage of the commodities, including preparation of contracts and invoices, arranging freight, insurance and credit, arranging for receipt, transfer or negotiation of shipping documents, arranging storage or warehousing, and dealing with quality claims;

(ii) Owning and operating facilities for storage or warehousing; or

(iii) Owning or chartering vessels or vehicles for the transportation of the commodities.

(C) *Substantially all.*—Substantially all of the controlled foreign corporation's business is as an active producer, processor, merchant or handler of commodities if the sum of its gross receipts from all of its qualified active sales (as defined in this paragraph (f)(2)(iii) without regard to the substantially all requirement) of commodities and its gross receipts from all of its qualified hedging transactions (as defined in paragraph (f)(2)(iv) of this section, applied without regard to the substantially all requirement of this paragraph (f)(2)(iii)(C)) equals or exceeds 85 percent of its total gross receipts for the taxable year (computed as though the corporation were a domestic corporation). In computing gross receipts, the District Director may disregard any sale or hedging transaction that has as a principal purpose manipulation of the 85 percent gross receipts test. A purpose may be a principal purpose even though it is outweighed by other purposes (taken together or separately).

(D) *Activities of employees of a related entity.*—For purposes of this paragraph (f), activities of employees of an entity related to the controlled foreign corporation, who are made available to and supervised on a day-to-day basis by, and whose salaries are paid by (or reimbursed to the related entity by), the controlled foreign corporation, are treated as activities engaged in directly by the controlled foreign corporation.

(iv) *Qualified hedging transaction entered into prior to January 31, 2003.*—(A) *In general.*—The term *qualified hedging transaction* means a bona fide hedging transaction, as defined in paragraph (a)(4)(ii) of this section, with respect to qualified active sales (other than transactions described in section 988(c)(1) without regard to section 988(c)(1)(D)(i)).

(B) *Exception.*—The term *qualified hedging transaction* does not include transactions that are not reasonably necessary to the conduct of business of the controlled foreign corporation as a producer, processor, merchant or handler of a commodity in the manner in which such business is customarily and usually conducted by others.

(C) *Effective date.*—This paragraph (f)(2)(iv) applies to gain or loss realized by a controlled foreign corporation with respect to a qualified hedging transaction entered into prior to January 31, 2003.

(v) *Qualified hedging transaction entered into on or after January 31, 2003.*—(A) *In general.*—The term *qualified hedging transaction* means a bona fide hedging transaction, as defined in paragraph (a)(4)(ii) of this section, with respect to one or more commodities transactions reasonably necessary to the conduct of any business by a producer, processor, merchant or handler of commodities in a manner in which such business is customarily and usually conducted by others. For purposes of this paragraph (f)(2)(v), a producer, processor, merchant or handler of commodities includes a controlled foreign corporation that regularly uses commodities in a manufacturing, construction, utilities, or transportation business.

(B) *Exception.*—The term *qualified hedging transaction* does not include a transaction described in section 988(c)(1) (without regard to section 988(c)(1)(D)(i)).

(C) *Examples.*—The following examples illustrate the provisions of this paragraph (f)(2)(v):

Example 1. CFC1 is a controlled foreign corporation located in country A. CFC1 manufactures and sells machinery in country B using aluminum and component parts purchased from third parties that contain significant amounts of aluminum. CFC1 conducts its manufacturing business in a manner in which such business is customarily and usually conducted by others. To protect itself against increases in the price of aluminum used in the machinery it manufactures, CFC1 enters into futures purchase contracts for the delivery of aluminum. These futures purchase contracts are bona fide hedging transactions. As CFC1 purchases aluminum and component parts containing significant amounts of aluminum in the spot market for use in its business, it closes out an equivalent amount of aluminum futures purchase contracts by entering into offsetting aluminum futures sales contracts. The aluminum futures purchase contracts are qualified hedging transactions as defined in paragraph (f)(2)(v)(A) of this section. Accordingly, any gain or loss on such aluminum futures purchase contracts is excluded from the computation of foreign personal holding company income.

Example 2. CFC2 is a controlled foreign corporation located in country B. CFC2 operates an airline business within country B in a manner in which such business is customarily and usually conducted by others. To protect itself against increases in the price of aviation fuel, CFC2 enters into forward contracts for the purchase of aviation fuel. These forward purchase contracts are bona fide hedging transactions. As CFC2 purchases aviation fuel in the spot market for use in its business, it closes out an equivalent amount of its forward purchase contracts for cash pursuant to a contractual provision that permits CFC2 to terminate the contract and make or receive a one-time payment representing the contract's fair market value. The aviation fuel forward purchase contracts are qualified hedging transactions as defined in paragraph (f)(2)(v)(A) of this section. Accordingly, any gain or loss on such aviation fuel forward purchase contracts is excluded from the computation of foreign personal holding company income.

(D) *Effective date.*—This paragraph (f)(2)(v) applies to gain or loss realized by a controlled foreign corporation with respect to a qualified hedging transaction entered into on or after January 31, 2003.

(vi) *Financial institutions not a producer, etc.*—For purposes of this paragraph (f), a corporation is not a producer, processor, merchant or handler of commodities if its business is primarily financial. For example, the business of a controlled foreign corporation is primarily financial if its principal business is making a market in notional principal contracts based on a commodities index.

(g) *Foreign currency gain or loss.*—(1) *Scope and purpose.*—This paragraph (g) provides rules for the treatment of foreign currency gains and losses. Paragraph (g)(2) of this section provides the general rule. Paragraph (g)(3) of this section provides an election to include foreign currency gains or losses that would otherwise be treated as foreign personal holding company income under this paragraph (g) in the computation of another category of subpart F income. Paragraph (g)(4) of this section provides an alternative election to treat any net foreign currency gain or loss as foreign personal holding company income. Paragraph (g)(5) of this section provides rules for certain gains and losses not subject to this paragraph (g).

(2) *In general.*—(i) *Inclusion.*—Except as otherwise provided in this paragraph (g), foreign personal holding company income includes the excess of foreign currency gains over foreign currency losses attributable to any section 988 transactions (foreign currency gain or loss). Section 1.954-1(c)(1)(ii) provides rules

for the treatment of foreign currency losses in excess of foreign currency gains. However, if an election is made under paragraph (g)(4) of this section, the excess of foreign currency losses over foreign currency gains to which the election would apply may be apportioned to, and offset, other categories of foreign personal holding company income.

(ii) *Exclusion for business needs.*—(A) *General rule.*—Foreign currency gain or loss directly related to the business needs of the controlled foreign corporation is excluded from foreign personal holding company income.

(B) *Business needs.*—Foreign currency gain or loss is directly related to the business needs of a controlled foreign corporation if—

(1) The foreign currency gain or loss—

(i) Arises from a transaction (other than a hedging transaction) entered into, or property used or held for use, in the normal course of the controlled foreign corporation's trade or business, other than the trade or business of trading foreign currency;

(ii) Arises from a transaction or property that does not itself (and could not reasonably be expected to) give rise to subpart F income other than foreign currency gain or loss;

(iii) Does not arise from a transaction described in section 988(c)(1)(B)(iii); and

(iv) Is clearly determinable from the records of the controlled foreign corporation as being derived from such transaction or property; or

(2) The foreign currency gain or loss arises from a bona fide hedging transaction, as defined in paragraph (a)(4)(ii) of this section, with respect to a transaction or property that satisfies the requirements of paragraphs (g)(2)(ii)(B)(*1*)(*i*) through (*iii*) of this section, provided that any gain or loss arising from such transaction or property that is attributable to changes in exchange rates is clearly determinable from the records of the CFC as being derived from such transaction or property. For purposes of this paragraph (g)(2)(ii)(B)(*2*), a hedging transaction will satisfy the aggregate hedging rules of § 1.1221-2(c)(3) only if all (or all but a de minimis amount) of the aggregate risk being hedged arises in connection with transactions or property that satisfy the requirements of paragraphs (g)(2)(ii)(B)(*1*)(*i*) through (*iii*) of this section, provided that any gain or loss arising from such transactions or property that is attributable to changes in exchange rates is clearly determinable from the records of the CFC as being derived from such transactions or property.

(C) *Regular dealers.*—(*1*) *General rule.*—Transactions in dealer property (as defined in paragraph (a)(4)(v) of this section) described in section 988(c)(1)(B) or (C) that are entered into by a controlled foreign corporation that is a regular dealer (as defined in paragraph (a)(4)(iv) of this section) in such property in its capacity as a dealer will be treated as directly related to the business needs of the controlled foreign corporation under paragraph (g)(2)(ii)(A) of this section.

(*2*) *Certain interest-bearing liabilities treated as dealer property.*—(*i*) *In general.*—For purposes of this paragraph (g)(2)(ii)(C), an interest-bearing liability incurred by a controlled foreign corporation that is denominated in (or determined by reference to) a non-functional currency shall be treated as dealer property of the type described in paragraph (g)(2)(ii)(C)(*1*) of this section if the liability, by being denominated in such currency, reduces the controlled foreign corporation's currency risk with respect to dealer property, and the liability is identified on the controlled foreign corporation's records as a liability treated as dealer property before the close of the day on which the liability is incurred.

(*ii*) *Failure to identify certain liabilities.*—If a controlled foreign corporation identifies certain interest-bearing liabilities as liabilities treated as dealer property under paragraph (g)(2)(ii)(C)(*2*)(*i*) of this section but fails to so identify other interest-bearing liabilities that manage its currency risk with respect to assets held that constitute dealer property, the Commissioner may treat such other liabilities as properly identified as dealer property under paragraph (g)(2)(ii)(C)(*2*)(*i*) of this section if the Commissioner determines that the failure to identify such other liabilities had as one of its principal purposes the avoidance of Federal income tax.

(*iii*) *Effective date.*—This paragraph (g)(2)(ii)(C)(*2*) applies only to gain or loss from an interest-bearing liability entered into by a controlled foreign corporation on or after January 31, 2003.

(D) *Example.*—The following example illustrates the provisions of this paragraph (g)(2).

Example. (i) *CFC1* and *CFC2* are controlled foreign corporations located in Country B, and are members of the same controlled group. *CFC1* is engaged in the active conduct of a trade or business that does not produce any subpart F income. *CFC2* serves as the currency coordination center for the controlled group, aggregating currency risks incurred by the group and entering into hedging transactions that transfer those risks outside of the group. Pursuant to this arrangement, and to hedge the currency risk on a non-interest bearing receivable incurred by *CFC1* in the normal course of its business, on Day 1 *CFC1* enters into a forward contract to sell Japanese Yen to *CFC2* in 30 days. Also on Day 1, *CFC2* enters into a forward contract to sell Yen to unrelated Bank X on Day 30. *CFC2* is not a regular dealer in Yen spot and forward contracts, and the Yen is not the functional currency for either *CFC1* or *CFC2*.

(ii) Because the forward contract entered into by *CFC1* to sell Yen hedges a transaction entered into in the normal course of *CFC1*'s business that does not give rise to subpart F income, it qualifies as a bona fide hedging transaction as defined in paragraph (a)(4)(ii) of this section. Therefore, *CFC1*'s foreign exchange gain or loss from that forward contract will not be treated as foreign personal holding company income or loss under this paragraph (g).

(iii) Because the forward contract to purchase Yen was entered into by *CFC2* in order to assume currency risks incurred by *CFC1* it does not qualify as a bona fide hedging transaction, as defined in paragraph (a)(4)(ii) of this section. Thus, foreign exchange gain or loss recognized by *CFC2* from that forward contract will be foreign personal holding company income. Because *CFC2* entered into the forward contract to sell Yen in order to hedge currency risks of *CFC1*, that forward contract also does not qualify as a bona fide hedging transaction. Thus, *CFC2*'s foreign currency gain or loss arising from that forward contract will be foreign personal holding company income.

(iii) *Special rule for foreign currency gain or loss from an interest-bearing liability.*—Except as provided in paragraph (g)(2)(ii)(C)(*2*) or (g)(5)(iv) of this section, foreign currency gain or loss arising from an interest-bearing liability is characterized as subpart F income and non-subpart F income in the same manner that interest expense associated with the liability would be allocated and apportioned between subpart F income and non-subpart F income under §§ 1.861-9T and 1.861-12T.

(3) *Election to characterize foreign currency gain or loss that arises from a specific category of subpart F income as gain or loss in that category.*—(i) *In general.*—For taxable years of a controlled foreign corporation beginning on or after November 6, 1995, elect, under this paragraph (g)(3), to exclude foreign currency gain or loss otherwise includible in the computation of foreign personal holding company income under this paragraph (g) from the computation of foreign personal holding company income under this paragraph (g) and include such foreign currency gain or loss in the category (or categories) of subpart F income (described in section 952(a), or, in the case of foreign base company income, described in § 1.954-1(c)(1)(iii)(A)(*1*) or (*2*)) to which such gain or loss relates. If an election is made under this paragraph (g)(3) with respect to a category (or categories) of subpart F income described in section 952(a), or, in the case of foreign base company income, described in § 1.954-1(c)(1)(iii)(A)(*1*) or (*2*), the election shall apply to all foreign currency gain or loss that arises from—

(A) A transaction (other than a hedging transaction) entered into, or property used or held for use, in the normal course of the controlled foreign corporation's trade or business that gives rise to income in that category (or categories) and that is clearly determinable from the records of the controlled foreign corporation as being derived from such transaction or property; and

(B) A bona fide hedging transaction, as defined in paragraph (a)(4)(ii) of this section, with respect to a transaction or property described in paragraph (g)(3)(i)(A) of this section. For purposes of this paragraph (g)(3)(i)(B), a hedging transaction will satisfy the aggregate hedging rules of § 1.1221-2(c)(3) only if all (or all but a de minimis amount) of the aggregate risk being hedged arises in connection with transactions or property that generate the same category of subpart F income described in section 952(a), or, in the case of foreign base company income, described in § 1.954-1(c)(1)(iii)(A)(*1*) or (*2*).

(ii) *Time and manner of election.*—The controlling United States shareholders, as defined in § 1.964-1(c)(5), make the election on behalf of the controlled foreign corporation by filing a statement with their original income tax returns for the taxable year of such United States shareholders ending with or within the taxable year of the controlled foreign corporation for which the election is made, clearly indicating that such election has been made. If the controlling United States shareholders elect to apply these regulations retroactively, under § 1.954-0(a)(1)(ii), the election under this paragraph (g)(3) may be made by the amended return filed pursuant to the election under § 1.954-0(a)(1)(ii). The controlling United States shareholders filing the election statement described in this paragraph (g)(3)(ii) must provide copies of the election statement to all other United States shareholders of the electing controlled foreign corporation. Failure to provide copies of such statement will not cause an election under this paragraph (g)(3) to be voidable by the controlled foreign corporation or the controlling United States shareholders. However, the District Director has discretion to void the election if it is determined that there was no reasonable cause for the failure to provide copies of such statement. The statement shall include the following information—

(A) The name, address, taxpayer identification number, and taxable year of each United States shareholder;

(B) The name, address, and taxable year of the controlled foreign corporation for which the election is effective; and

(C) Any additional information required by the Commissioner by administrative pronouncement.

(iii) *Revocation of election.*—This election is effective for the taxable year of the controlled foreign corporation for which it is made and all subsequent taxable years of such corporation unless revoked by or with the consent of the Commissioner.

(iv) *Example.*—The following example illustrates the provisions of this paragraph (g)(3).

Example. (i) *CFC*, a controlled foreign corporation, is a sales company that earns foreign base company sales income under section 954(d). *CFC* makes an election under this paragraph (g)(3) to treat foreign currency gains or losses that arise from a specific category (or categories) of subpart F income (as described in section 952(a), or, in the case of foreign base company income, as described in §1.954-1(c)(1)(iii)(A)(*1*) or (*2*)) as that type of income. *CFC* aggregates the currency risk on all of its transactions that generate foreign base company sales income and hedges this net currency exposure.

(ii) Assuming no more than a de minimis amount of risk in the pool of risks being hedged arises from transactions or property that generate income other than foreign base company sales income, pursuant to its election under (g)(3), *CFC*'s net foreign currency gain from the pool and the hedging transactions will be treated as foreign base company sales income under section 954(d), rather than as foreign personal holding company income under section 954(c)(1)(D). If the pool of risks and the hedging transactions generate a net foreign base company sales loss, however, *CFC* must apply the rules of §1.954-1(c)(1)(ii).

(4) *Election to treat all foreign currency gains or losses as foreign personal holding company income.*—(i) *In general.*—If the controlling United States shareholders make an election under this paragraph (g)(4), the controlled foreign corporation shall include in its computation of foreign personal holding company income the excess of foreign currency gains over losses or the excess of foreign currency losses over gains attributable to any section 988 transaction (except those described in paragraph (g)(5) of this section) and any section 1256 contract that would be a section 988 transaction but for section 988(c)(1)(D). Separate elections for section 1256 contracts and section 988 transactions are not permitted. An election under this paragraph (g)(4) supersedes an election under paragraph (g)(3) of this section.

(ii) *Time and manner of election.*—The controlling United States shareholders, as defined in §1.964-1(c)(5), make the election on behalf of the controlled foreign corporation in the same time and manner as provided in paragraph (g)(3)(ii) of this section.

(iii) *Revocation of election.*—This election is effective for the taxable year of the controlled foreign corporation for which it is made and all subsequent taxable years of such corporation unless revoked by or with the consent of the Commissioner.

(5) *Gains and losses not subject to this paragraph.*—(i) *Capital gains and losses.*—Gain or loss that is treated as capital gain or loss under section 988(a)(1)(B) is not foreign currency gain or loss for purposes of this paragraph (g). Such gain or loss is treated as gain or loss from the sale or exchange of property that is included in the computation of foreign personal holding company income under paragraph (e)(1) of this section. Paragraph (a)(2) of this section provides other rules concerning income described in more than one category of foreign personal holding company income.

(ii) *Income not subject to section 988.*—Gain or loss that is not treated as foreign currency gain or loss by reason of section 988(a)(2) or (d) is not foreign currency gain or loss for purposes of this paragraph (g). However, such gain or loss may be included in the computation of other categories of foreign personal holding company income in accordance with its characterization under section 988(a)(2) or (d) (for example, foreign currency gain that is treated as interest income under section 988(a)(2) will be included in the computation of foreign personal holding company income under paragraph (b)(ii) of this section).

Reg. §1.954-2(g)(3)(ii)(A)

(iii) *Qualified business units using the dollar approximate separate transactions method.*—This paragraph (g) does not apply to any DASTM gain or loss computed under § 1.985-3(d). Such gain or loss is allocated under the rules of § 1.985-3(e)(2)(iv) or (e)(3). However, the provisions of this paragraph (g) do apply to section 988 transactions denominated in a currency other than the United States dollar or the currency that would be the qualified business unit's functional currency were it not hyperinflationary.

(iv) *Gain or loss allocated under § 1.861-9.*—[Reserved]

(h) *Income equivalent to interest.*—(1) *In general.*—(i) *Inclusion in foreign personal holding company income.*—Except as provided in this paragraph (h), foreign personal holding company income includes income equivalent to interest as defined in paragraph (h)(2) of this section.

(ii) *Exceptions.*—(A) *Liability hedging transactions.*—Income, gain, deduction or loss that is allocated and apportioned in the same manner as interest expense under the provisions of § 1.861-9T is not income equivalent to interest for purposes of this paragraph (h).

(B) *Interest.*—Amounts treated as interest under section 954(c)(1)(A) and paragraph (b) of this section are not income equivalent to interest for purposes of this paragraph (h).

(2) *Definition of income equivalent to interest.*—(i) *In general.*—The term *income equivalent to interest* includes income that is derived from—

(A) A transaction or series of related transactions in which the payments, net payments, cash flows or return predominantly reflect the time value of money;

(B) Transactions in which the payments (or a predominant portion thereof) are, in substance, for the use or forbearance of money;

(C) Notional principal contracts, to the extent provided in paragraph (h)(3) of this section;

(D) Factoring, to the extent provided in paragraph (h)(4) of this section;

(E) Conversion transactions, but only to the extent that gain realized with respect to such a transaction is treated as ordinary income under section 1258;

(F) The performance of services, to the extent provided in paragraph (h)(5) of this section;

(G) The commitment by a lender to provide financing, if any portion of such financing is actually provided;

(H) Transfers of debt securities subject to section 1058; and

(I) Other transactions, as provided by the Commissioner in published guidance. See § 601.601(d)(2) of this chapter.

(ii) *Income from the sale of property.*—Income from the sale of property will not be treated as income equivalent to interest by reason of paragraph (h)(2)(i)(A) or (B) of this section. Income derived by a controlled foreign corporation will be treated as arising from the sale of property only if the corporation in substance carries out sales activities. Accordingly, an arrangement that is designed to lend the form of a sales transaction to a transaction that in substance constitutes an advance of funds will be disregarded. For example, if a controlled foreign corporation acquires property on 30-day payment terms from one person and sells that property to another person on 90-day payment terms and at prearranged prices and terms such that the foreign corporation bears no substantial economic risk with respect to the purchase and sale other than the risk of non-payment, the foreign corporation has not in substance derived income from the sale of property.

(3) *Notional principal contracts.*—(i) *In general.*—Income equivalent to interest includes income from notional principal contracts denominated in the functional currency of the taxpayer (or a qualified business unit of the taxpayer, as defined in section 989(a)), the value of which is determined solely by reference to interest rates or interest rate indices, to the extent that the income from such transactions accrues on or after August 14, 1989.

(ii) *Regular dealers.*—Income equivalent to interest does not include income earned by a regular dealer (as defined in paragraph (a)(4)(iv) of this section) from notional principal contracts that are dealer property (as defined in paragraph (a)(4)(v) of this section).

(4) *Income equivalent to interest from factoring.*—(i) *General rule.*—Income equivalent to interest includes factoring income. Except as provided in paragraph (h)(4)(ii) of this section, the term *factoring income* includes any income (including any discount income or service fee, but excluding any stated interest) derived from the acquisition and collection or disposition of a factored receivable. The amount of income equivalent to interest realized with respect to a factored receivable is the difference (if a positive number) between the amount paid for the receivable by the foreign corporation and the

amount that it collects on the receivable (or realizes upon its sale of the receivable). The rules of this paragraph (h)(4) apply only with respect to the tax treatment of factoring income derived from the acquisition and collection or disposition of a factored receivable and shall not affect the characterization of an expense or loss of either the person whose goods or services gave rise to a factored receivable or the obligor under a receivable.

(ii) *Exceptions.*—Factoring income shall not include—

(A) Income treated as interest under section 864(d)(1) or (6) (relating to income derived from trade or service receivables of related persons), even if such income is treated as not described in section 864(d)(1) by reason of the same-country exception of section 864(d)(7);

(B) Income derived from a factored receivable if payment for the acquisition of the receivable is made on or after the date on which stated interest begins to accrue, but only if the rate of stated interest equals or exceeds 120 percent of the Federal short-term rate (as defined under section 1274) (or the analogous rate for a currency other than the dollar) as of the date on which the receivable is acquired by the foreign corporation; or

(C) Income derived from a factored receivable if payment for the acquisition of the receivable by the foreign corporation is made only on or after the anticipated date of payment of all principal by the obligor (or the anticipated weighted average date of payment of a pool of purchased receivables).

(iii) *Factored receivable.*—For purposes of this paragraph (h)(4), the term *factored receivable* includes any account receivable or other evidence of indebtedness, whether or not issued at a discount and whether or not bearing stated interest, arising out of the disposition of property or the performance of services by any person, if such account receivable or evidence of indebtedness is acquired by a person other than the person who disposed of the property or provided the services that gave rise to the account receivable or evidence of indebtedness. For purposes of this paragraph (h)(4), it is immaterial whether the person providing the property or services agrees to transfer the receivable at the time of sale (as by accepting a third-party charge or credit card) or at a later time.

(iv) *Examples.*—The following examples illustrate the application of this paragraph (h)(4).

Example 1. DP, a domestic corporation, owns all of the outstanding stock of FS, a controlled foreign corporation. FS acquires accounts receivable arising from the sale of property by unrelated corporation X. The receivables have a face amount of $100, and after 30 days bear stated interest equal to at least 120 percent of the applicable Federal short-term rate (determined as of the date the receivables are acquired by FS). FS purchases the receivables from X for $95 on Day 1 and collects $100 plus stated interest from the obligor under the receivables on Day 40. Income (other than stated interest) derived by FS from the factored receivables is factoring income within the meaning of paragraph (h)(4)(i) of this section and, therefore, is income equivalent to interest.

Example 2. The facts are the same as in *Example 1*, except that, rather than collecting $100 plus stated interest from the obligor under the factored receivables on Day 40, FS sells the receivables to controlled foreign corporation Y on Day 15 for $97. Both the income derived by FS on the factored receivables and the income derived by Y (other than stated interest) on the receivables are factoring income within the meaning of paragraph (h)(4)(i) of this section, and therefore, constitute income equivalent to interest.

Example 3. The facts are the same as in *Example 1*, except that FS purchases the receivables from X for $98 on Day 30. Income derived by FS from the factored receivables is excluded from factoring income under paragraph (h)(4)(ii)(B) of this section and, therefore, does not give rise to income equivalent to interest.

Example 4. The facts are the same as in *Example 3*, except that it is anticipated that all principal will be paid by the obligor of the receivables by Day 30. Income derived by FS from this maturity factoring of the receivables is excluded from factoring income under paragraph (h)(4)(ii)(C) of this section and, therefore, does not give rise to income equivalent to interest.

Example 5. The facts are the same as in *Example 4*, except that FS sells the factored receivables to Y for $99 on day 45, at which time stated interest is accruing on the unpaid balance of $100. Because interest was accruing at the time Y acquired the receivables at a rate equal to at least 120 percent of the applicable Federal short-term rate, income derived by Y from the factored receivables is excluded from factoring income under paragraph (h)(4)(ii)(B) of this section and, therefore, does not give rise to income equivalent to interest.

Example 6. DP, a domestic corporation engaged in an integrated credit card business, owns all of the outstanding stock of FS, a controlled foreign corporation. On Day 1, individual A uses a credit card issued by DP to purchase shoes priced at $100 from X, a foreign corporation unrelated to *DP*, *FS*, or *A*. On Day 7, *X* transfers the receivable (which does not bear stated interest) arising from *A*'s purchase to *FS* in exchange for $95. *FS* collects $100 from *A* on Day 45. Income derived by *FS* on the factored receivable is factoring income within the meaning of paragraph (h)(4)(i) of this section and, therefore, is income equivalent to interest.

(5) *Receivables arising from performance of services.*—If payment for services performed by a controlled foreign corporation is not made until more than 120 days after the date on which such services are performed, then the income derived by the controlled foreign corporation constitutes income equivalent to interest to the extent that interest income would be imputed under the principles of section 483 or the original issue discount provisions (sections 1271 through 1275), if—

(i) Such provisions applied to contracts for the performance of services;

(ii) The time period referred to in sections 483(c)(1) and 1274(c)(1)(B) were 120 days rather than six months; and (iii) The time period referred to in section 483(c)(1)(A) were 120 days rather than one year.

(6) *Examples.*—The following examples illustrate the application of this paragraph (h).

Example 1. CFC, a controlled foreign corporation, promises that Corporation *A* may borrow up to $500 in principal for one year beginning at any time during the next three months at an interest rate of 10 percent. In exchange, Corporation *A* pays *CFC* a commitment fee of $2. Pursuant to this agreement, *CFC* lends $80 to Corporation *A*. As a result, the entire $2 fee is included in the computation of *CFC'S* foreign personal holding company income under paragraph (h)(2)(i)(G) of this section.

Example 2. (i) At the beginning of its current taxable year, *CFC*, a controlled foreign corporation, purchases at face value a one-year debt instrument issued by Corporation *A* having a $100 principal amount and bearing a floating rate of interest set at the LIBOR plus one percentage point. Contemporaneously, *CFC* borrows $100 from Corporation *B* for one year at a fixed interest rate of 10 percent, using the debt instrument as security.

(ii) During its current taxable year, *CFC* accrues $11 of interest from Corporation *A* on the bond. Because interest is excluded from the definition of income equivalent to interest under paragraph (h)(1)(ii)(B) of this section, the $11 is not income equivalent to interest.

(iii) During its current taxable year, *CFC* incurs $10 of interest expense with respect to the borrowing from Corporation *B*. That expense is allocated and apportioned to, and reduces, subpart F income to the extent provided in section 954(b)(5) and §§ 1.861-9T through 1.861-12T and 1.954-1(c).

Example 3. (i) On January 1, 1994, *CFC*, a controlled foreign corporation with the United States dollar as its functional currency, purchases at face value a 10-year debt instrument issued by Corporation *A* having a $100 principal amount and bearing a floating rate of interest set at the (LIBOR) plus one percentage point payable on December 31st of each year. *CFC* subsequently determines that it would prefer receiving a fixed rate of return. Accordingly, on January 1, 1995, *CFC* enters into a 9-year interest rate swap agreement with Corporation *B* whereby Corporation *B* promises to pay *CFC* on December 31st of each year an amount equal to 10 percent on a notional principal amount of $100. In exchange, *CFC* promises to pay Corporation *B* an amount equal to LIBOR plus one percentage point on the notional principal amount.

(ii) On December 31, 1995, *CFC* receives $9 of interest income from Corporation *A* with respect to the debt instrument. On the same day, *CFC* receives a total of $10 from Corporation *B* and pays $9 to Corporation *B* with respect to the interest rate swap.

(iii) The $9 of interest income is foreign personal holding income under section 954(c)(1). Pursuant to § 1.446-3(d), *CFC* recognizes $1 of swap income for its 1995 taxable year that is also foreign personal holding company income because it is income equivalent to interest under paragraph (h)(2)(i)(C) of this section.

Example 4. (i) *CFC*, a controlled foreign corporation, purchases commodity X on the spot market for $100 and, contemporaneously, enter into a 3 month forward contract to sell commodity X for $104, a price set by the forward market.

(ii) Assuming that substantially all of *CFC*'s expected return is attributable to the time value of the net investment, as described in section 1258(c)(1), the transaction is a conversion transaction under section 1258(c). Accordingly, any gain treated as ordinary income under section 1258(a) will be foreign personal holding company income because it is income equivalent to interest under paragraph (h)(2)(i)(E) of this section. [Reg. § 1.954-2.]

☐ [T.D. 8618, 9-6-95. *Amended by T.D.* 8704, 12-31-96; *T.D.* 8985, 3-15-2002; *T.D.* 9008, 7-22-2002; *T.D.* 9039, 1-30-2003 *and T.D.* 9141, 7-19-2004.]

Proposed Amendments to Regulation

§ 1.954-2. Foreign personal holding company income.—(a) * * *

(5) *Special rules applicable to distributive share of partnership income.*—(i) *Application of related person exceptions where payment reduces foreign tax of payor.*—If a partnership receives an item of income that reduced the foreign income tax of the payor (determined under the principles of § 1.954-9(a)(3)), to determine the extent to which a controlled foreign corporation's distributive share of such item of income is foreign personal holding company income, the exceptions contained in section 954(c)(3) shall apply only if—

(A) *(1)* Any such exception would have applied to exclude the income from foreign personal holding company income if the controlled foreign corporation had earned the income directly (determined by testing, with reference to such controlled foreign corporation, whether an entity is a related person, within the meaning of section 954(d)(3), or is organized under the laws of, or uses property in, the foreign country in which the controlled foreign corporation is created or organized); and

(2) The distributive share of such income is not in respect of a payment made by the controlled foreign corporation to the partnership; and

(B) *(1)* The partnership is created or organized, and uses a substantial part of its assets in a trade or business in the country under the laws of which the controlled foreign corporation is created or organized (determined under the principles of paragraph (b)(4) of this section);

(2) The partnership is regarded as fiscally transparent, as defined in § 1.954-9(a)(7), by all countries under the laws of which the controlled foreign corporation is created or organized or has substantial assets; or

(3) The income is taxed in the year when earned at an effective rate of tax (determined under the principles of § 1.954-1(d)(2)) that is not less than 90 percent of, and not more than five percentage points less than, the effective rate of tax that would have applied to such income under the laws of the country in which the controlled foreign corporation is created or organized if such income were earned directly by the controlled foreign corporation partner from local sources.

(ii) *Certain other exceptions applicable to foreign personal holding company income.*—[Reserved].

(iii) *Effective date.*—Paragraph (a)(5)(i) of this section shall apply to all amounts paid or accrued in taxable years commencing after [date that is 5 years after publication of the final regulations in the federal register], under hybrid arrangements, unless such payments are made pursuant to an arrangement which would qualify for permanent relief under § 1.954-9(c)(2) if made between a controlled foreign corporation and its hybrid branch, in which case the relief afforded under that section shall also be afforded under this section.

(6) *Special rules applicable to exceptions from foreign personal holding company income treatment in circumstances involving hybrid branches.*—(i) *In general.*—In the case of a payment between a controlled foreign corporation (or its hybrid branch, as defined in § 1.954-9(a)(6)) and the hybrid branch of a related controlled foreign corporation, the exceptions contained in section 954(c)(3) shall apply only if the payment would have qualified for the exception if the payor were a separate controlled foreign corporation created or organized in the jurisdiction where foreign tax is reduced and the payee were a separate controlled foreign corporation created or organized under the laws of the jurisdiction in which the payment is subject to tax (other than a withholding tax).

(ii) *Exception where no tax reduction or tax disparity.*—Paragraph (a)(6)(i) of this section shall not apply unless the payment would have reduced foreign tax, under § 1.954-9(a)(3), and fallen within the tax disparity rule of § 1.954-9(a)(5)(iv) if those provisions had been applicable to the payment.

(iii) *Effective date.*—The rules of this section shall apply to all amounts paid or accrued in taxable years commencing after [date that is 5 years after publication of the final regulations in the federal register], under hybrid arrangements, unless such payments are made pursuant to an arrangement which would qualify for permanent relief under § 1.954-9(c)(2) if made between a controlled foreign corporation and its hybrid branch, in which case the relief afforded under that section shall also be afforded under this section.

[Prop. Reg. § 1.954-2.]

[Proposed 7-13-99.]

§ 4.954-2. Foreign personal holding company income; taxable years beginning after December 31, 1986.—

* * *

(b) *Dividends, etc.—*

* * *

(6) *Treatment of tax exempt interest.*—Foreign personal holding company income includes all interest income, including interest

that is exempt from U.S. tax pursuant to section 103 ("tax-exempt interest"). However, the net foreign base company income of a controlled foreign corporation that is attributable to such tax-exempt interest shall be treated as tax-exempt interest in the hands of the U.S. shareholders of the foreign corporation. Accordingly, any net foreign base company income that is included in the subpart F income of a U.S. shareholder and that is attributable to such tax-exempt interest shall remain exempt from the regular income tax, but potentially subject to the alternative minimum tax, in the hands of the U.S. shareholder.

* * *

[Reg. § 4.954-2.]

☐ [T.D. 8216, 7-20-88. Amended by T.D. 8556, 7-22-94. Redesignated by T.D. 8618, 9-6-95.]

§ 1.954-3. Foreign base company sales income.—(a) *Income included.*—(1) *In general.*—(i) *General rules.*—Foreign base company sales income of a controlled foreign corporation shall, except as provided in subparagraphs (2), (3), and (4) of this paragraph, consist of gross income (whether in the form of profits, commissions, fees, or otherwise) derived in connection with (*a*) the purchase of personal property from a related person and its sale to any person, (*b*) the sale of personal property to any person on behalf of a related person, (*c*) the purchase of personal property from any person and its sale to a related person, or (*d*) the purchase of personal property from any person on behalf of a related person. See section 954(d)(1). This section shall apply to the purchase and/or sale of personal property, whether or not such property was purchased and/or sold in the ordinary course of trade or business, except that income derived in connection with the sale of tangible personal property will not be considered to be foreign base company sales income if such property is sold to an unrelated person, as defined in paragraph (e)(2) of § 1.954-1, after substantial use has been made of the property by the controlled foreign corporation in its trade or business. This section shall not apply to the excess of gains over losses from sales or exchanges of securities or from future transactions, to the extent such excess gains are includible in foreign personal holding company income of the controlled foreign corporation under § 1.954-2 or foreign base company shipping income under § 1.954-6; nor shall it apply to the sale of the controlled foreign corporation's property (other than its stock in trade or other property of a kind which would properly be included in its inventory if on hand at the close of the taxable year, or property held primarily for sale to customers in the ordinary course of its trade or business) if substantially all the property of such corporation is sold pursuant to the discontinuation of the trade or business previously carried on by such corporation. The term "any person" as used in this subparagraph includes a related person, as defined in paragraph (e)(1) of § 1.954-1.

(ii) *Special rule.*—(*a*) *In general.*—The term "personal property" as used in section 954(d) and this section shall not include agricultural commodities which are not grown in the United States (within the meaning of section 7701(a)(9)) in commercially marketable quantities. All of the agricultural commodities listed in Table I shall be considered grown in the United States in commercially marketable quantities. Bananas, black pepper, cocoa, coconut, coffee, crude rubber, and tea shall not be considered grown in the United States in commercially marketable quantities. All other agricultural commodities shall not be considered grown in the United States in commercially marketable quantities when, in consideration of all of the facts and circumstances of the individual case, such commodities are shown to be produced in the United States in insufficient quantity and quality to be marketed commercially. The term "agricultural commodities" includes, but is not limited to, livestock, poultry, fish produced in fish farms, fruit, furbearing animals as well as the products of truck farms, ranches, nurseries, ranges, and orchards. A fish farm is an area where fish are grown or raised (artificially protected and cared for), as opposed to merely caught or harvested. However, the term "agricultural commodities" shall not include timber (either standing or felled), or any commodity at least 50 percent of the fair market value of which is attributable to manufacturing or processing, determined in a manner consistent with the regulations under section 993(c) (relating to the definition of export property). For purposes of applying such regulations, the term "processing" shall be deemed not to include handling, packing, packaging, grading, storing, transporting, slaughtering, and harvesting. Subdivision (ii) shall apply in the computation of foreign base company sales income for taxable years of controlled foreign corporations beginning after December 31, 1975, and to taxable years of United States shareholders (within the meaning of section 951(b)) within which or with which such taxable years of such foreign corporations end.

(*b*) *Table.*

Table I—Agricultural Commodities Grown in the United States in Commercially Marketable Quantities

Livestock and Products

Beeswax	Horses
Cattle and calves	Milk
Chickens	Mink
Chicken eggs	Mohair
Ducks	Rabbits

Livestock and Products		
Geese		Sheep and lambs
Goats		Turkeys
Hogs		Wool
Honey		

Crops		
Alfalfa	Eggplant	Peanuts
Almonds	Escarole	Pears
Apples	Figs	Peas
Apricots	Filberts	Peppers
Artichokes	Flaxseed	Plums and prunes
Asparagus	Garlic	Potatoes
Avocadoes	Grapes	Potted plants
Barley	Grapefruit	Raspberries
Beans	Grass seed	Rice
Beets	Hay	Rhubarb
Blackberries	Honeydew melons	Rye
Blueberries	Hops	Sorghum grain
Brussel sprouts	Lemons	Soybeans
Broccoli	Lettuce	Spinach
Bulbs	Limes	Strawberries
Cabbage	Macadamia nuts	Sugar beets
Cantaloupes	Maple syrup and sugar	Sugarcane
Carrots	Mint	Sweet potatoes
Cauliflower	Mushrooms	Tangelos
Celery	Nectarines	Tangerines
Cherries	Oats	Tobacco
Corn	Olives	Tomatoes
Cotton	Onions	Walnuts
Cranberries	Oranges	Watermelons
Cucumbers	Papayas	Wheat
Cut flowers	Pecans	
Dates	Peaches	

(iii) *Examples.*—The application of this subparagraph may be illustrated by the following examples:

Example (1). Controlled foreign corporation A, incorporated under the laws of foreign country X, is a wholly owned subsidiary of domestic corporation M. Corporation A purchases from M Corporation, a related person, articles manufactured in the United States and sells the articles in the form in which purchased to P, not a related person, for delivery and use in foreign country Y. Gross income of A Corporation derived from the purchase and sale of the personal property is foreign base company sales income.

Example (2). Corporation A in example (1) also purchases from P, not a related person, articles manufactured in country Y and sells the articles in the form in which purchased to foreign corporation B, a related person, for use in foreign country Z. Gross income of A Corporation derived from the purchase and sale of the personal property is foreign base company sales income.

Example (3). Controlled foreign corporation C, incorporated under the laws of foreign country X, is a wholly owned subsidiary of domestic corporation N. By contract, N Corporation agrees to pay C Corporation, a related person, a commission equal to 6 percent of the gross selling price of all personal property shipped by N Corporation as the result of orders solicited by C Corporation in foreign countries Y and Z. In fulfillment of such orders, N Corporation ships products manufactured by it in the United States. Corporation C does not assume title to the property sold. Gross commissions received by C Corporation from N Corporation in connection with the sale of such property for use in countries Y and Z constitute foreign base company sales income.

Example (4). Controlled foreign corporation D, incorporated under the laws of foreign country Y, is a wholly owned subsidiary of domestic corporation R. In 1964, D Corporation acquires a United States manufactured lathe from R Corporation. In 1972, after having made a substantial use of the lathe in its manufacturing business, D Corporation sells the lathe to an unrelated person for use in foreign country Z. Gross income from the sale of the lathe is not foreign base company sales income since it is sold to an unrelated person after substantial use has been made of it by D Corporation in its business.

Example (5). Controlled foreign corporation E, incorporated under the laws of foreign country Y, is a wholly owned subsidiary of domestic corporation P. Corporation E purchases from P Corporation articles manufactured by P Corporation outside of country Y and sells the articles to F Corporation, an unrelated person, for use in foreign country Z. Corporation E finances the purchase of the articles by F Corporation by agreeing to accept payment over an extended period of time and receives not only the purchase price but also interest and service fees. All gross income of E Corporation derived in connection with the purchase and sale of the personal property, including interest and service fees derived from financing the sale to F Corporation, constitutes foreign base company sales income.

(2) *Property manufactured, produced, constructed, grown, or extracted within the country in which the controlled foreign corporation is created or organized.*—Foreign base company sales income does not include income derived in connection with the purchase and sale of personal property (or purchase or sale of personal property on behalf of a related person) in a transaction described in subparagraph (1) of this paragraph if the property is manufactured, produced, constructed, grown, or extracted in the country under the laws of which the controlled foreign corporation which purchases and sells the property (or acts on behalf of a related person) is created or organized. See section 954(d)(1)(A). The principles set forth in subparagraph (4) of this paragraph with respect to the manufacture, production, or con-

struction of personal property shall apply under this subparagraph in determining what constitutes manufacture, production, or construction of property. The application of this subparagraph may be illustrated by the following examples:

Example (1). Controlled foreign corporation A, incorporated under the laws of foreign country X, is a wholly owned subsidiary of domestic corporation M. Corporation A purchases coffee beans grown in country X from foreign corporation P, a related person, and sells the beans to M Corporation, a related person, for use in the United States. Income from the purchase and sale of the coffee beans by A Corporation is not foreign base company sales income since the beans were grown in country X.

Example (2). Controlled foreign corporation B, incorporated under the laws of foreign country X, is a wholly owned subsidiary of controlled foreign corporation C, also incorporated under the laws of country X. Corporation B purchases and imports into country X rough diamonds mined in foreign country Y; in country X it cuts, polishes, and shapes the diamonds in a process which constitutes manufacturing within the meaning of subparagraph (4) of this paragraph. Corporation B sells the finished diamonds to C Corporation, a related person, which in turn sells them for use in foreign country Z. Since for purposes of this subparagraph the finished diamonds are manufactured in country X, gross income derived by C Corporation from their sale is not foreign base company sales income.

(3) *Property sold for use, consumption, or disposition within the country in which the controlled foreign corporation is created or organized.*—(i) *In general.*—Foreign base company sales income does not include income derived in connection with the purchase and sale of personal property (or purchase or sale of personal property on behalf of a related person) in a transaction described in subparagraph (1) of this paragraph, (*a*) if the property is sold for use, consumption, or disposition in the country under the laws of which the controlled foreign corporation which purchases and sells the property (or sells on behalf of a related person) is created or organized or (*b*), where the property is purchased by the controlled foreign corporation on behalf of a related person, if such property is purchased for use, consumption, or disposition in the country under the laws of which such controlled foreign corporation is created or organized. See section 954(d)(1)(B).

(ii) *Rules for determining country of use, consumption, or disposition.*—As a general rule, personal property which is sold to an unrelated person will be presumed for purposes of this subparagraph to have been sold for use, consumption, or disposition in the country of destination of the property sold; for such purpose, the occurrence in a country of a temporary interruption in shipment of goods shall not constitute such country the country of destination. However, if at the time of a sale or personal property to an unrelated person the controlled foreign corporation knew, or should have known from the facts and circumstances surrounding the transaction, that the property probably would not be used, consumed, or disposed of in the country of destination, the controlled foreign corporation must determine the country of ultimate use, consumption, or disposition of the property or the property will be presumed to have been used, consumed, or disposed of outside the country under the laws of which the controlled foreign corporation is created or organized. A controlled foreign corporation which sells personal property to a related person is presumed to sell such property for use, consumption, or disposition outside the country under the laws of which the controlled foreign corporation is created or organized unless such corporation establishes the use made of the property by the related person; once it has established that the related person has disposed of the property, the rules in the two preceding sentences relating to sales by a controlled foreign corporation to an unrelated person will apply at the first stage in the chain of distribution at which a sale is made by a related person to an unrelated person. Notwithstanding the preceding provisions of this subdivision, a controlled foreign corporation which sells personal property to any person all of whose business except for an insubstantial part consists of selling from inventory to retail customers at retail outlets all within one country may assume at the time of such sale to such person that such property will be used, consumed, or disposed of within such country.

(iii) *Fungible goods.*—For purposes of this subparagraph, a controlled foreign corporation which sells to a purchaser personal property which because of its fungible nature cannot reasonably be specifically traced to other purchasers and to the countries of ultimate use, consumption, or disposition shall, unless such corporation establishes a different disposition as being proper, treat such property as being sold, for ultimate use, consumption, or disposition in those countries, and to those other purchasers, in the same proportions in which property from the fungible mass of the first purchaser is sold in the regular course of business by such first purchaser. No apportionment need be made, however, on the basis of sporadic sales by the first purchaser. This sub-

Reg. § 1.954-3(a)(3)(iii)

division shall apply only in a case where the controlled foreign corporation knew, or should have known from the facts and circumstances surrounding the transaction, the manner in which the first purchaser disposes of goods from the fungible mass.

(iv) *Illustrations.*—The application of this subparagraph may be illustrated by the following examples:

Example (1). Controlled foreign corporation A, incorporated under the laws of foreign country X, and controlled foreign corporation B, incorporated under the laws of foreign country Y, are related persons. Corporation A purchases from B Corporation electric transformers produced by B Corporation in country Y and sells the transformers to D Corporation, an unrelated person, for installation in a factory building being constructed in country X. Since the personal property purchased and sold by A Corporation is to be used within the country in which A Corporation is incorporated, income of A Corporation derived from the purchase and sale of the electric transformers is not foreign base company sales income.

Example (2). Controlled foreign corporation C, incorporated under the laws of foreign country X, is a wholly owned subsidiary of domestic corporation N. Corporation C purchases from N Corporation sewing machines manufactured in the United States by N Corporation and sells the sewing machines to retail department stores, unrelated persons, located in foreign country X. The entire activities of the department stores to which C Corporation sells the machines consist of selling goods from inventory to retail customers at retail outlets in country X. Under these circumstances, at the time of sale C Corporation may assume the sewing machines will be used, consumed, or disposed of in country X, and no attempt need be made by C Corporation to determine where the sewing machines will ultimately be used by the customers of the retail department stores. Gross income of C Corporation derived from the sales to the department stores located in country X is not foreign base company sales income.

Example (3). Controlled foreign corporation D, incorporated under the laws of foreign country Y, and controlled foreign corporation E, incorporated under the laws of foreign country X, are related persons. Corporation D purchases from E Corporation sulphur extracted by E Corporation from deposits located in country X. Corporation D sells the sulphur to F Corporation, an unrelated person, for delivery to F Corporation's storage facilities located in country Y. At the time of the sale of the sulphur from D Corporation to F Corporation, D Corporation knows that F Corporation is actively engaged in the business of selling a large amount of sulphur in country Y but also that F Corporation sells, in the normal course of its business, 25 percent of its sulphur for ultimate consumption in foreign country Z. However, D Corporation has no knowledge at the time of sale whether any portion of the particular shipment it sells to F Corporation will be resold by F Corporation for ultimate use, consumption, or disposition outside country Y. Moreover, delivery of the sulphur to F Corporation's storage facilities constitutes more than a temporary interruption in the shipment of the sulphur. Under such circumstances, D Corporation may, but is not required to, trace the ultimate disposition by F Corporation of the personal property sold to F Corporation; however, if D Corporation does not trace the ultimate disposition and if it does not establish a different disposition as being proper, 25 percent of the sulphur sold by D Corporation to F Corporation will be treated as being sold for consumption in country Z and 25 percent of the gross income from the sale of sulphur by D Corporation to F Corporation will be treated as foreign base company sales income.

Example (4). Controlled foreign corporation G, incorporated under the laws of foreign country X, is a wholly owned subsidiary of domestic corporation P. Corporation G purchases from P Corporation toys manufactured in the United States by P Corporation and sells the toys to R, an unrelated person, for delivery to a duty-free port in country X. Instructions for the assembly and operation of the toys are printed in a language which is not commonly used in country X. From the facts and circumstances surrounding the sales to R, G Corporation knows, or should know, that the toys will probably not be used, consumed, or disposed of within country X. Therefore, unless G Corporation determines the use to be made of the toys by R, such property will be presumed to have been sold by R for use, consumption, or disposition outside of country X, and the entire gross income of G Corporation derived from the sales will be considered foreign base company sales income.

(4) *Property manufactured or produced by the controlled foreign corporation.*—(i) *In general.*—Foreign base company sales income does not include income of a controlled foreign corporation derived in connection with the sale of personal property manufactured, produced, or constructed by such corporation in whole or in part from personal property which it has purchased. A foreign corporation will be considered, for purposes of this subparagraph, to have manufactured, produced, or constructed personal property which it sells if the property sold is in effect not the property which it pur-

chased. In the case of the manufacture, production, or construction of personal property, the property sold will be considered, for purposes of this subparagraph, as not being the property which is purchased if the provisions of subdivision (ii) or (iii) of this subparagraph are satisfied. For rules of apportionment in determining foreign base company sales income derived from the sale of personal property purchased and used as a component part of property which is not manufactured, produced, or constructed, see subparagraph (5) of this paragraph.

(ii) *Substantial transformation of property.*—If purchased personal property is substantially transformed prior to sale, the property sold will be treated as having been manufactured, produced, or constructed by the selling corporation. The application of this subdivision may be illustrated by the following examples:

Example (1). Controlled foreign corporation A, incorporated under the laws of foreign country X, operates a paper factory in foreign country Y. Corporation A purchases from a related person wood pulp grown in country Y. Corporation A, by a series of processes, converts the wood pulp to paper which it sells for use in foreign country Z. The transformation of wood pulp to paper constitutes the manufacture or production of property for purposes of this subparagraph.

Example (2). Controlled foreign corporation B, incorporated under the laws of foreign country X, purchases steel rods from a related person which produces the steel in foreign country Y. Corporation B operates a machining plant in country X in which it utilizes the purchased steel rods to make screws and bolts. The transformation of steel rods to screws and bolts constitutes the manufacture or production of property for purposes of this subparagraph.

Example (3). Controlled foreign corporation C, incorporated under the laws of foreign country X, purchases tuna fish from unrelated persons who own fishing boats which catch such fish on the high seas. Corporation C receives such fish in country X in the condition in which taken from the fishing boats and in such country processes, cans, and sells the fish to related person D, incorporated under the laws of foreign country Y, for consumption in foreign country Z. The transformation of such fish into canned fish constitutes the manufacture or production of property for purposes of this subparagraph.

(iii) *Manufacture of a product when purchased components constitute part of the property sold.*—If purchased property is used as a component part of personal property which is sold, the sale of the property will be treated as the sale of a manufactured product, rather than the sale of component parts, if the operations conducted by the selling corporation in connection with the property purchased and sold are substantial in nature and are generally considered to constitute the manufacture, production, or construction of property. Without limiting this substantive test, which is dependent on the facts and circumstances of each case, the operations of the selling corporation in connection with the use of the purchased property as a component part of the personal property which is sold will be considered to constitute the manufacture of a product if in connection with such property conversion costs (direct labor and factory burden) of such corporation account for 20 percent or more of the total cost of goods sold. In no event, however, will packaging, repackaging, labeling, or minor assembly operations constitute the manufacture, production, or construction of property for purposes of section 954(d)(1). The application of this subdivision may be illustrated by the following examples:

Example (1). Controlled foreign corporation A, incorporated under the laws of foreign country X, sells industrial engines for use, consumption, and disposition outside country X. Corporation A, in connection with the assembly of such engines, performs machining and assembly operations. In addition, A Corporation purchases, from related and unrelated persons, components manufactured in foreign country Y. On a per unit basis, A Corporation's selling price and costs of such engines are as follows:

Selling price		$400
Cost of goods sold:		
Material—		
Acquired from related persons	$100	
Acquired from others . .	40	
Total material	$140	
Conversion costs (direct labor and factory burden)	70	
Total cost of goods sold		$210
Gross profit		$190
Administrative and selling expenses		50
Taxable income		$140

The conversion costs incurred by A Corporation are more than 20 percent of total costs of goods sold ($70/$210 or 33 percent). Although the product sold, an engine, is not sufficiently distinguishable from the components to constitute a substantial transformation of the purchased parts within the meaning of subdivision (ii) of this subparagraph, A Corporation will be considered under this subdivision to have manufactured the product it sells.

Example (2). Controlled foreign corporation B, incorporated under the laws of foreign country X, operates an automobile assembly plant. In connection with such activity, B Corporation purchases from related persons assembled engines, transmissions, and certain other components, all of which are manufactured outside of country X; purchases additional components from unrelated persons; conducts stamping, machining, and subassembly operations; and has a substantial investment in tools, jigs, welding equipment, and other machinery and equipment used in the assembly of an automobile. On a per unit basis, B Corporation's selling price and costs of such automobiles are as follows:

Selling price		$2,500
Cost of goods sold:		
Material—		
Acquired from related persons	$1,200	
Acquired from others	275	
Total material	$1,475	
Conversion costs (direct labor and factory burden)	325	
Total cost of goods sold		$1,800
Gross profit		700
Administrative and selling expenses		300
Taxable income		$400

The product sold, an automobile, is not sufficiently distinguishable from the components purchased (the engine, transmission, etc.) to constitute a substantial transformation of purchased parts within the meaning of subdivision (ii) of this subparagraph. Although conversion costs of B Corporation are less than 20 percent of total cost of goods sold ($325/$1,800 or 18 percent), the operations conducted by B Corporation in connection with the property purchased and sold are substantial in nature and are generally considered to constitute the manufacture of a product. Corporation B will be considered under this subdivision to have manufactured the product it sells.

Example (3). Controlled foreign corporation C, incorporated under the laws of foreign country X, purchases from related persons radio parts manufactured in foreign country Y. Corporation C designs radio kits, packages component parts required for assembly of such kits, and sells the parts in a knocked-down condition to unrelated persons for use outside country X. These packaging operations of C Corporation do not constitute the manufacture, production, or construction of personal property for purposes of section 954(d)(1).

(5) *Rules for apportionment of income derived from the sale of purchased components used in property not manufactured, produced, or constructed.*—The foreign base company sales income derived by a controlled foreign corporation for the taxable year from sales of personal property purchased and used as a component part of property which is not manufactured, produced, or constructed by such corporation within the meaning of subparagraph (4) of this paragraph shall, unless the records of the controlled foreign corporation show that a different apportionment of income is proper or unless all the income from such sales is treated as foreign base company sales income, be determined by first making for such year the following separate classifications and subclassifications with respect to the property which is sold and then by apportioning the income for such year from such sales in accordance with the rules of this subparagraph:

(i) A classification of the cost of components used in the property which is sold into two classes consisting of the cost of components manufactured, produced, constructed, grown, or extracted—

(a) Within the country under the laws of which the controlled foreign corporation is created or organized, and

(b) Outside such country;

(ii) A subclassification of the class described in subdivision (i)(b) of this subparagraph into—

(a) The cost of such components purchased from unrelated persons, and

(b) The cost of such components purchased from related persons;

(iii) A classification of the income derived from such sales into two classes consisting of income derived from sales for use, consumption, or disposition—

(a) Within the country under the laws of which the controlled foreign corporation is created or organized, and

(b) Outside such country; and

(iv) A subclassification of the class described in subdivision (iii)(b) of this subparagraph into income from—

(a) Sales to unrelated persons, and

(b) Sales to related persons. The foreign base company sales income for the taxable year from purchases of the property from related persons and sales to unrelated persons shall be the amount which bears to the amount described in subdivision (iv)(a) of this subparagraph the same ratio that the amount described in subdivision (ii)(b) of this subparagraph bears to the total cost of components used in the product which is sold. The foreign base company sales income for the taxable year from purchases of the property from related persons and sales to related persons is the amount which bears to the amount described in subdivision (iv)(b) of this subparagraph the same ratio that the amount described in subdivision (ii)(b) of this subparagraph bears to the total cost of components used in the product which is sold. The foreign base company sales income for the taxble year from purchases of the property from unrelated persons and sales to related persons is the amount which bears to the amount described in subdivision (iv)(b) of this subparagraph the same ratio that the amount described in subdivision (ii)(a) of this subparagraph bears to the total cost of components used in the product which is sold. The application of this subparagraph may be illustrated by the following examples:

Example (1). Controlled foreign corporation C, which is incorporated under the laws of foreign country X, uses the calendar year as the taxable year. For 1964, C Corporation purchases radio parts of which some are manufactured in foreign country Y; and others, in country X. Some of the parts manufactured in country Y are purchased from related persons. Corporation C uses the purchased parts in radio kits which it designs and sells for assembly by its customers, unrelated persons, some of whom use the kits outside country X. Unless the records of C Corporation show that a different apportionment of income is proper, the foreign base company sales income for 1964 is determined in the following manner upon the basis of the following factual classifications for such year:

Cost of components purchased from all persons:	
Manufactured within country X	$ 20
Manufactured outside country X	40
Total cost	60
Cost of components manufactured outside country X:	
Purchased from unrelated persons	10
Purchased from related persons	30
Total cost	40
Gross income from sales:	
Gross receipts from sales	$120
Cost of goods sold:	
Components $60	
Direct labor and factory burden 10	70
Gross income	50
Gross income from sales:	
For use within country X	$ 26
For use outside country X	24
Gross income	50
Foreign base company sales income from purchases from related persons and sales to unrelated persons ($24 × $30/$60)	12

Example (2). The facts are the same as in example (1) except that none of the purchases are from related persons and some of the sales for use outside country X are to related persons. Unless the records of C Corporation show that a different apportionment of income is proper, the foreign base company sales income for 1964 is determined in the following manner upon the basis of the following additional factual classification for such year:

Gross income from sales for use outside country X—	
To unrelated persons	$ 8
To related persons	16
Total gross income	24
Foreign base company sales income from purchases from unrelated persons and sales to related persons ($16 × $40/$60)	$10.67

Example (3). The facts are the same as in example (1) except that some of the sales for use outside country X are to related persons as in example (2). Unless the records of C Corporation show that a different apportionment of income is proper, the foreign base company sales income for 1964 is determined in the following manner:

Foreign base company sales income from purchases from related persons and sales to unrelated persons ($8 × $30/$60)	$ 4.00
Foreign base company sales income from purchases from related persons and sales to related persons ($16 × $30/$60)	8.00
Foreign base company sales income from purchases from unrelated persons and sales to related persons ($16 × $10/$60)	2.67
Total foreign base company sales income	$14.67

(6) *Special rule applicable to distributive share of partnership income.*—(i) *In general.*—To determine the extent to which a controlled foreign corporation's distributive share of any item of gross income of a partnership would have been foreign base company sales income if received by it directly, under § 1.952-1(g), the property sold will be considered to be manufactured, produced or constructed by the controlled foreign corporation, within the meaning of paragraph (a)(4) of this section, only if the manufacturing exception of paragraph (a)(4) of this section would have applied to exclude the income from foreign base company sales income if the controlled foreign corporation had earned the income directly, determined by taking into account only the activities of, and property owned by, the partnership and not the separate activities or property of the controlled foreign corporation or any other person.

(ii) *Example.*—The application of paragraph (a)(6)(i) of this section is illustrated by the following example:

Example. CFC, a controlled foreign corporation organized under the laws of Country

Reg. § 1.954-3(a)(6)(ii)

A, is an 80 percent partner in Partnership X, a partnership organized under the laws of Country B. Partnership X performs activities in Country B that would constitute the manufacture of Product O, within the meaning of paragraph (a)(4) of this section, if performed directly by CFC. Partnership X, through its sales offices in Country B, then sells Product O to Corp D, a corporation that is a related person with respect to CFC, within the meaning of section 954(d)(3), for use within Country B. CFC's distributive share of Partnership X's sales income is not foreign base company sales income because the manufacturing exception of paragraph (a)(4) of this section would have applied to exclude the income from foreign base company sales income if CFC had earned the income directly.

(iii) *Effective date.*—This paragraph (a)(6) applies to taxable years of a controlled foreign corporation beginning on or after July 23, 2002.

(b) *Branches of controlled foreign corporation treated as separate corporations.*—(1) *General rules for determining when to apply separate treatment.*—(i) *Sales or purchase branch.*—(a) *In general.*—If a controlled foreign corporation carries on purchasing or selling activities by or through a branch or similar establishment located outside the country under the laws of which such corporation is created or organized and the use of the branch or similar establishment for such activities has substantially the same tax effect as if the branch or similar establishment were a wholly owned subsidiary corporation of such controlled foreign corporation, the branch or similar establishment and the remainder of the controlled foreign corporation will be treated as separate corporations for purposes of determining foreign base company sales income of such corporation. See section 954(d)(2).

(b) *Allocation of income and comparison of effective rates of tax.*—The determination as to whether such use of the branch or similar establishment has the same tax effect as if it were a wholly owned subsidiary corporation of the controlled foreign corporation shall be made by allocating to such branch or similar establishment only that income derived by the branch or establishment which, when the special rules of subparagraph (2)(i) of this paragraph are applied, is described in paragraph (a) of this section (but determined without applying subparagraphs (2), (3), and (4) of such paragraph). The use of the branch or similar establishment for such activities will be considered to have substantially the same tax effect as if it were a wholly owned subsidiary corporation of the controlled foreign corporation if the income allocated to the branch or similar establishment under the immediately preceding sentence is, by statute, treaty obligation, or otherwise, taxed in the year when earned at an effective rate of tax that is less than 90 percent of, and at least 5 percentage points less than, the effective rate of tax which would apply to such income under the laws of the country in which the controlled foreign corporation is created or organized, if, under the laws of such country, the entire income of the controlled foreign corporation were considered derived by the corporation from sources within such country from doing business through a permanent establishment therein, received in such country, and allocable to such permanent establishment, and the corporation were managed and controlled in such country.

(c) *Use of more than one branch.*—If a controlled foreign corporation carries on purchasing or selling activities by or through more than one branch or similar establishment located outside the country under the laws of which such corporation is created or organized, or by or through one or more such branches or similar establishments in a case where subdivision (ii) of this subparagraph also applies, then (b) of this subdivision shall be applied separately to the income derived by each such branch or similar establishment (by treating such purchasing or selling branch or similar establishment as if it were the only branch or similar establishment of the controlled foreign corporation and as if any such other branches or similar establishments were separate corporations) in determining whether the use of such branch or similar establishment has substantially the same tax effect as if such branch or similar establishment were a wholly owned subsidiary corporation of the controlled foreign corporation.

(ii) *Manufacturing branch.*—(a) *In general.*—If a controlled foreign corporation carries on manufacturing, producing, constructing, growing, or extracting activities by or through a branch or similar establishment located outside the country under the laws of which such corporation is created or organized and the use of the branch or similar establishment for such activities with respect to personal property purchased or sold by or through the remainder of the controlled foreign corporation has substantially the same tax effect as if the branch or similar establishment were a wholly owned subsidiary corporation of such controlled foreign corporation, the branch or similar establishment and the remainder of the controlled foreign corporation will be treated as separate corporations for purposes of determining foreign base company sales income of such corporation. See section 954(d)(2).

(b) Allocation of income and comparison of effective rates of tax.—The determination as to whether such use of the branch or similar establishment has substantially the same tax effect as if the branch or similar establishment were a wholly owned subsidiary corporation of the controlled foreign corporation shall be made by allocating to the remainder of such controlled foreign corporation only that income derived by the remainder of such corporation, which, when the special rules of subparagraph (2)(i) of this paragraph are applied, is described in paragraph (a) of this section (but determined without applying subparagraphs (2), (3), and (4) of such paragraph). The use of the branch or similar establishment for such activities will be considered to have substantially the same tax effect as if it were a wholly owned subsidiary corporation of the controlled foreign corporation if income allocated to the remainder of the controlled foreign corporation under the immediately preceding sentence is, by statute, treaty obligation, or otherwise, taxed in the year when earned at an effective rate of tax that is less than 90 percent of, and at least 5 percentage points less than, the effective rate of tax which would apply to such income under the laws of the country in which the branch or similar establishment is located, if, under the laws of such country, the entire income of the controlled foreign corporation were considered derived by such corporation from sources within such country from doing business through a permanent establishment therein, received in such country, and allocable to such permanent establishment, and the corporation were created or organized under the laws of, and managed and controlled in, such country.

(c) Use of one or more sales or purchase branches in addition to a manufacturing branch.—If, with respect to personal property manufactured, produced, constructed, grown, or extracted by or through a branch or similar establishment located outside the country under the laws of which the controlled foreign corporation is created or organized, purchasing or selling activities are carried on by or through more than one branch or similar establishment, or by or through one or more branches or similar establishments located outside such country, of such corporation, then (b) of this subdivision shall be applied separately to the income derived by each such purchasing or selling branch or similar establishment (by treating such purchasing or selling branch or similar establishment as though it alone were the remainder of the controlled foreign corporation) for purposes of determining whether the use of such manufacturing, producing, constructing, growing, or extracting branch or similar establishment has substantially the same tax effect as if such branch or similar establishment were a wholly owned subsidiary corporation of the controlled foreign corporation.

(2) *Special rules.*—(i) *Determination of treatment as a wholly owned subsidiary corporation.*—For purposes of determining under this paragraph whether the use of a branch or similar establishment which is treated as a separate corporation has substantially the same tax effect as if the branch or similar establishment were a wholly owned subsidiary corporation of a controlled foreign corporation—

(a) Treatment as separate corporations.—The branch or similar establishment will be treated as a wholly owned subsidiary corporation of the controlled foreign corporation, and such branch or similar establishment will be deemed to be incorporated in the country in which it is located.

(b) Activities treated as performed on behalf of remainder of corporation.—With respect to purchasing or selling activities performed by or through the branch or similar establishment, such purchasing or selling activities shall—

(1) With respect to personal property manufactured, produced, constructed, grown, or extracted by the controlled foreign corporation, or

(2) With respect to personal property (other than property described in *(1)* of this subdivision *(b)*) purchased or sold, or purchased and sold, by the controlled foreign corporation.

be treated as performed on behalf of the controlled foreign corporation.

(c) Activities treated as performed on behalf of branch.—With respect to manufacturing, producing, constructing, growing, or extracting activities performed by or through the branch or similar establishment, purchasing or selling activities performed by or through the remainder of the controlled foreign corporation with respect to the personal property manufactured, produced, constructed, grown, or extracted by or through the branch or similar establishment shall be treated as performed on behalf of the branch or similar establishment.

(d) Determination of hypothetical tax.—To the extent applicable, the principles of paragraph (b)(4)(ii) of §1.954-1 shall be used in determining, under subdivision (i) of subparagraph (1) of this paragraph, the effective rate of tax which would apply to the income of the

Reg. §1.954-3(b)(2)(i)(d)

branch or similar establishment under the laws of the country in which the controlled foreign corporation is created or organized, or in determining, under subdivision (ii) of such subparagraph, the effective rate of tax which would apply to the income of the branch or similar establishment under the laws of the country in which the manufacturing, producing, constructing, growing, or extracting branch or similar establishment is located.

(e) Tax laws to be taken into account.—Tax determinations shall be made by taking into account only the income, war profits, excess profits, or similar tax laws (or the absence of such laws) of the countries involved.

(ii) *Determination of foreign base company sales income.*—Once it has been determined under subparagraph (1) of this paragraph that a branch or similar establishment and the remainder of the controlled foreign corporation are to be treated as separate corporations, the determination of whether such branch or similar establishment, or the remainder of the controlled foreign corporation, as the case may be, has foreign base company sales income shall be made by applying the following rules:

(a) Treatment as separate corporations.—The branch or similar establishment will be treated as a wholly owned subsidiary corporation of the controlled foreign corporation, and such branch or similar establishment will be deemed to be incorporated in the country in which it is located.

(b) Activities treated as performed on behalf of remainder of corporation.—With respect to purchasing or selling activities performed by or through the branch or similar establishment, such purchasing or selling activities shall—

(1) With respect to personal property manufactured, produced, constructed, grown, or extracted by the controlled foreign corporation, or

(2) With respect to personal property (other than property described in *(1)* of this subdivision (*b*)) purchased or sold, or purchased and sold, by the controlled foreign corporation,

be treated as performed on behalf of the controlled foreign corporation.

(c) Activities treated as performed on behalf of branch.—With respect to manufacturing, producing, constructing, growing, or extracting activities performed by or through the branch or similar establishment, purchasing or selling activities performed by or through the remainder of the controlled foreign corporation with respect to the personal property manufactured, produced, constructed, grown, or extracted by or through the branch or similar establishment shall be treated as performed on behalf of the branch or similar establishment.

(d) Items not to be twice included in income.—Income which is classified as foreign base company sales income as a result of the application of subdivision (i) of subparagraph (1) of this paragraph shall not be again classified as foreign base company sales income as a result of the application of subdivision (ii) of such subparagraph.

(e) Comparison with ordinary treatment.—Income derived by the branch or similar establishment, or by the remainder of the controlled foreign corporation, shall not be considered foreign base company sales income if the income would not be so considered if it were derived by a separate controlled foreign corporation under like circumstances.

(f) Priority of application.—If income derived by the branch or similar establishment, or by the remainder of the controlled foreign corporation, from a transaction would be classified as foreign base company sales income of such controlled foreign corporation under section 954(d)(1) and paragraph (a) of this section, the income shall, notwithstanding this paragraph, be treated as foreign base company sales income under paragraph (a) of this section and the branch or similar establishment shall not be treated as a separate corporation with respect to such income.

(3) *Inclusion of amounts in gross income of United States shareholders.*—A branch or similar establishment of a controlled foreign corporation and the remainder of such corporation shall be treated as separate corporations under this paragraph solely for purposes of determining the foreign base company sales income of each such corporation and for purposes of including an amount in subpart F income of the controlled foreign corporation under section 952(a). See section 954(b)(3) and paragraph (d)(4) of § 1.954-1 for rules relating to the treatment of a branch or similar establishment of a controlled foreign corporation and the remainder of such corporation as separate corporations for purposes of independently determining if the foreign base company income of each such corporation is less than 10 percent, or more than 70 percent, of its gross income. For all other purposes, however, a branch or similar establishment of a controlled foreign corporation and the remainder of such corporation shall not be treated as separate corporations. For example, if the controlled for-

eign corporation has a deficit in earnings and profits to which section 952(c) applies, the limitation of such section on the amount includible in the subpart F income of such corporation will apply. Moreover, income, war profits, or excess profits taxes paid by a branch or similar establishment to a foreign country will be treated as having been paid by the controlled foreign corporation for purposes of section 960 (relating to special rules for foreign tax credit) and the regulations thereunder. Also, income of a branch or similar establishment, treated as a separate corporation under this paragraph, will not be treated as dividend income of the controlled foreign corporation of which it is a branch or similar establishment.

(4) *Illustrations.*—The application of this paragraph may be illustrated by the following examples:

Example (1). Controlled foreign corporation A, incorporated under the laws of foreign country X, is engaged in the manufacturing business in such country. Corporation A negotiates sales of its products for use outside of country X through a sales office, branch B, maintained in foreign country Y. These activities constitute the only activities of A Corporation. Country X levies an income tax at an effective rate of 50 percent on the income of A Corporation derived by the manufacturing plant in country X but does not tax the sales of income of A Corporation derived by branch B in country Y. Country Y levies an income tax at an effective rate of 10 percent on the sales income derived by branch B but does not tax the income of A Corporation derived by the manufacturing plant in country X. If the sales income derived by branch B were, under the laws of country X, derived from sources within country X by A Corporation, such income would be taxed by such country at an effective rate of 50 percent. In determining foreign base company sales income of A Corporation, branch B is treated as a separate wholly owned subsidiary corporation of A Corporation, the 10 percent rate of tax on branch B's income being less than 90 percent of, and at least 5 percentage points less than, the 50 percent rate. Income derived by branch B, treated as a separate corporation, from the sale by or through it for use, consumption, or disposition outside country Y of the personal property produced in country X is treated as income from the sale of personal property on behalf of A Corporation, a related person, and constitutes foreign base company sales income. The remainder of A Corporation, treated as a separate corporation, derives no foreign base company sales income since it produces the product which is sold.

Example (2). Controlled foreign corporation C is incorporated under the laws of foreign country X. Corporation C maintains branch B in foreign country Y. Branch B manufactures articles in country Y which are sold through the sales offices of C Corporation located in country X. These activities constitute the only activities of C Corporation. Country Y levies an income tax at an effective rate of 30 percent on the manufacturing profit of C Corporation derived by branch B but does not tax the sales income of C Corporation derived by the sales offices in country X. Country X does not impose an income, war profits, excess profits, or similar tax, and no tax is paid to any foreign country with respect to income of C Corporation which is not derived by branch B. If C Corporation were incorporated under the laws of country Y, the sales income of the sales offices in country X would be taxed by country Y at an effective rate of 30 percent. In determining foreign base company sales income of C Corporation, branch B is treated as a separate wholly owned subsidiary corporation of C Corporation, the zero rate of tax on the income derived by the remainder of C Corporation being less than 90 percent of, and at least 5 percentage points less than, the 30 percent rate. Branch B, treated as a separate corporation, derives no foreign base company sales income since it produces the product which is sold. Income derived by the remainder of C Corporation, treated as a separate corporation, from the sale by or through it for use, consumption, or disposition outside country X of the personal property produced in country Y is treated as income from the sale of personal property on behalf of branch B, a related person, and constitutes foreign base company sales income.

Example (3). Controlled foreign corporation E, incorporated under the laws of foreign country X, is a wholly owned subsidiary of controlled foreign corporation D, also incorporated under the laws of country X. Corporation E maintains branch B in foreign country Y. Both corporations use the calendar year as the taxable year. In 1964, E Corporation's sole activity, carried on through branch B, consists of the purchase of articles manufactured in country X by D Corporation, a related person, and the sale of the articles through branch B for use outside country X. The income of E Corporation derived by branch B from such transactions is taxed to E Corporation by country X only at the time E Corporation distributes such income to D Corporation and is then taxed on the basis of what the tax (a 40 percent effective rate) would have been if the income had been derived in 1964 by E Corporation from sources within country X from doing business through a permanent establishment therein. Country Y

Reg. §1.954-3(b)(4)

levies an income tax at an effective rate of 50 percent on income derived from sources within such country, but the income of branch B for 1964 is effectively taxed by country Y at a 5 percent rate since, under the laws of such country, only 10 percent of branch B's income is derived from sources within such country. Corporation E makes no distributions to D Corporation in 1964. In determining foreign base company sales income of E Corporation for 1964, branch B is treated as a separate wholly owned subsidiary corporation of E Corporation, the 5 percent rate of tax on branch B's income being less than 90 percent of, and at least 5 percentage points less than, the 40 percent rate. Income derived by branch B, treated as a separate corporation, from the sale by or through it for use, consumption, or disposition outside country Y of the personal property produced in country X is treated as income from the sale of personal property on behalf of E Corporation, a related person, and constitutes foreign base company sales income.

Example (4). Controlled foreign corporation F, incorporated under the laws of foreign country X, is a wholly owned subsidiary of domestic corporation M. Corporation F, through its branch B in foreign country Y, purchases from controlled foreign corporation G, a wholly owned subsidiary of M Corporation incorporated under the laws of foreign country Z, personal property which G Corporation manufactures in country Z. Corporation F sells such property for use in foreign country W. Since the income of F Corporation from such purchases and sales is classified as foreign base company sales income under section 954(d)(1) and paragraph (a) of this section, branch B will not be treated as a separate corporation with respect to such income even if the tax differential between countries X and Y would otherwise justify such treatment.

Example (5). Controlled foreign corporation A, incorporated under the laws of foreign country X, is engaged in manufacturing articles through its home office, located in country X, and selling such articles through branch B, located in foreign country Y, and through branch C, located in foreign country Z, for use outside country X. These activities constitute the only activities of A Corporation for its taxable year 1963. Each such country levies an income tax on only the income derived from sources within such country, and all income derived in 1963 by the home office, branch B, and branch C, respectively, is derived from sources within countries X, Y, and Z, respectively. The income and income taxes of A Corporation for 1963 are as follows:

	X Country	Y Country	Z Country
Income of:			
Home office	$200,000	....	....
Branch B	....	$100,000	....
Branch C	....	....	$100,000
Income tax	100,000	20,000	20,000
Effective rate of tax	50%	20%	20%

By applying subparagraph (1)(i) of this paragraph and by treating branch B as though it were the only branch of A Corporation, branch B is treated as a separate wholly owned subsidiary corporation of A Corporation in determining foreign base company sales income of A Corporation for 1963, the 20 percent rate of tax on the income of such branch being less than 90 percent of, and at least 5 percentage points less than, the 50 percent rate of tax which would apply to the income of branch B under the laws of country X if, under the laws of such country, all the income of A Corporation for 1963 derived through the home office and branch B were derived from sources within country X. Moreover, by applying subparagraph (1)(i) of this paragraph and by treating branch C as though it were the only branch of A Corporation, branch C is treated as a separate wholly owned subsidiary corporation of A Corporation, the 20 percent rate of tax on the income of such branch being less than 90 percent of, and at least 5 percentage points less than, the 50 percent rate of tax which would apply to the income of branch C under the laws of country X if, under the laws of such country, all the income of A Corporation for 1963 derived through the home office and branch C were derived from sources within country X. The income derived by branch B and branch C, respectively, each treated as a separate corporation, from the sale by or through each of them for use, consumption, or disposition outside country Y and country Z, respectively, is treated as income from the sale of personal property on behalf of A Corporation, a related person, and constitutes foreign base company sales income for 1963. The home office of A Corporation, treated as a separate corporation, derives no foreign base company sales income for 1963 since it produces the articles which are sold.

Example (6). Controlled foreign corporation A, incorporated under the laws of foreign country X, is engaged in manufacturing articles through branch B, located in foreign country Y, and selling such articles through branch C, located in foreign country Z, and through its home office, located in country X, for use outside country X. These activities constitute the only activities of A Corporation for its taxable year 1963. Each such country levies an income tax on only the income derived from sources within such country, and all income derived in 1963 by the home office, branch B, and branch C, respectively, is derived from sources within countries X, Y, and Z, respectively. The income and income taxes of A Corporation for 1963 are as follows:

	X Country	Y Country	Z Country
Income of:			
Home office	$100,000	....	.....
Branch B	....	$200,000	.....
Branch C	....	....	$100,000
Income tax	20,000	100,000	20,000
Effective rate of tax	20%	50%	20%

In determining foreign base company sales income of A Corporation for 1963 neither branch B nor branch C is treated, by applying subparagraph (1)(i) of this paragraph, as a separate wholly owned subsidiary corporation of A Corporation since branch B derives no income from the purchase or sale of personal property and since, in the case of branch C treated as though it were the only branch of A Corporation, the 20 percent rate of tax on the income of branch C is not less than 90 percent of, and not as much as 5 percentage points less than, the 20 percent rate of tax which would apply to the income of branch C under the laws of country X if, under the laws of such country, all the income of A Corporation for 1963 derived through the home office and branch C were derived from sources within country X. However, by applying subparagraph (1)(ii) of this paragraph and by treating the home office in country X as though it alone were the remainder of A Corporation, branch B is treated as a separate wholly owned subsidiary corporation of A Corporation, the 20 percent rate of tax on the income of the home office being less than 90 percent of, and at least 5 percentage points less than, the 50 percent rate of tax which would apply to the income of the home office under the laws of country Y if, under the laws of such country, all the income of A Corporation for 1963 derived through the home office and branch B were derived from sources within country Y. Moreover, by applying subparagraph (1)(ii) of this paragraph and by treating branch C as though it alone were the remainder of A Corporation, branch B and branch C are treated as separate wholly owned subsidiary corporations of A Corporation, the 20 percent rate of tax on the income of branch C being less than 90 percent of, and at least 5 percentage points less than, the 50 percent rate of tax which would apply to the income of branch C under the laws of country Y if, under the laws of such country, all the income of A Corporation for 1963 derived through branch B and branch C were derived from sources within country Y. The income derived by the home office and branch C, respectively, each treated as a separate corporation, from the sale by or through each of them for use, consumption, or disposition outside country X and country Z, respectively, is treated as income from the sale of personal property on behalf of branch B, a related person, and constitutes foreign base company sales income for 1963. Branch B, treated as a separate corporation, derives no foreign base company sales income since it produces the articles which are sold.

Example (7). Controlled foreign corporation A, incorporated under the laws of foreign country X, is engaged in manufacturing articles through branch B, located in foreign country Y, and selling such articles through the home office, located in country X, and through branch C, located in foreign country Z, for use outside country X. These activities constitute the only activities of A Corporation for its taxable year 1963. Each such country levies an income tax on only the income derived from sources within such country, and all income derived in 1963 by the home office, branch B, and branch C, respectively, is derived from sources within countries X, Y, and Z, respectively. The income and income taxes of A Corporation for 1963 are as follows:

	X Country	Y Country	Z Country
Income of:			
Home office	$100,000	....	.....
Branch B	....	$200,000	.....
Branch C	....	....	$100,000
Income tax	40,000	100,000	20,000
Effective rate of tax	40%	50%	20%

By applying subparagraph (1)(i) of this paragraph and by treating branch C as though it were the only branch of A Corporation, branch C is treated as a separate wholly owned subsidiary corporation of A Corporation in determining foreign base company sales income of A Corporation for 1963, the 20 percent rate of tax on the income of branch C being less than 90 percent of, and at least 5 percentage points less than, the 40 percent rate of tax which would apply to the income of branch C under the laws of country X if, under the laws of such country, all the income of A Corporation for 1963 derived through the home office and branch C were derived from sources within country X. In addition, by applying subparagraph (1)(ii) of this paragraph and by treating the home office in country X as though it alone were the remainder of A Corporation, branch B is treated as a separate wholly owned subsidiary corporation of A Corporation, the 40 percent rate of tax on the income of the home office being less than 90 percent of, and at least 5 percentage points less than, the 50 percent rate of tax which would apply to the income of the home office under the laws of country Y if, under the laws of such country, all the income of A Corporation for 1963 derived through the home office and branch B were derived from sources within country Y. Moreover, by applying subparagraph (1)(ii) of this paragraph and by treating branch C as though it alone were the remainder of A Corporation, branch B and branch C would again be treated as separate wholly owned subsidiary corporations of A Corporation, the 20 percent rate of tax on the income of branch C being less than 90 percent of, and at least 5 percentage points less than, the 50 percent rate of tax which would apply to the income of branch C under the laws of country Y if, under the laws of such country, all the income of A Corporation for 1963 derived through branch B and branch C were derived from sources within country Y; however, for purposes of determining foreign base company sales income of A Corporation for 1963, only the classification under subparagraph (1)(i) of this paragraph shall, by reason of the application of subparagraph (2)(ii)(d) of this paragraph, be applied with respect to the income derived by branch C. The income derived by the home office and branch C, respectively, each treated as a separate corporation, from the sale by or through each of them for use, consumption, or disposition outside country X and country Z, respectively, is treated as income from the sale of personal property on behalf of branch B, a related person, and constitutes foreign base company sales income for 1963. Branch B, treated as a separate corporation, derives no foreign base company sales income since it produces the articles which are sold.

(c) *Shipping income for taxable years beginning after December 31, 1975.*—For taxable years beginning after December 31, 1975, foreign base company shipping income (as determined under § 1.954-6) of a controlled foreign corporation shall not also be considered foreign base company sales income of that controlled foreign corporation. [Reg. § 1.954-3.]

☐ [*T.D.* 6734, 5-14-64. *Amended by T.D.* 7497, 7-6-77; *T.D.* 7555, 7-25-78; *T.D.* 7893, 5-11-83; *T.D.* 7894, 5-11-83 *and T.D.* 9008, 7-22-2002.]

§ 1.954-4. Foreign base company services income.—(a) *Items included.*—Except as provided in paragraph (d) of this section, foreign base company services income means income of a controlled foreign corporation, whether in the form of compensation, commissions, fees, or otherwise, derived in connection with the performance of technical, managerial, engineering, architectural, scientific, skilled, industrial, commercial, or like services which—

(1) Are performed for, or on behalf of, a related person, as defined in paragraph (e)(1) of § 1.954-1, and

(2) Are performed outside the country under the laws of which the controlled foreign corporation is created or organized.

(b) *Services performed for, or on behalf of, a related person.*—(1) *Specific cases.*—For purposes of paragraph (a)(1) of this section, "services which are performed for, or on behalf of, a related person" include (but are not limited to) services performed by a controlled foreign corporation in a case where—

(i) The controlled foreign corporation is paid or reimbursed by, is released from an obligation to, or otherwise receives substantial financial benefit from, a related person for performing such services;

(ii) The controlled foreign corporation performs services (whether or not with respect to property sold by a related person) which a related person is, or has been, obligated to perform;

(iii) The controlled foreign corporation performs services with respect to property sold by a related person and the performance of such services constitutes a condition or a material term of such sale; or

(iv) Substantial assistance contributing to the performance of such services has been furnished by a related person or persons.

(2) *Special rules.*—(i) *Guaranty of performance.*—Subparagraph (1)(ii) of this paragraph shall not apply with respect to services performed by a controlled foreign corporation pursuant to a contract the performance of which is guaranteed by a related person, if (*a*) the related person's sole obligation with respect to the contract is to guarantee performance of such services, (*b*) the controlled foreign corporation is fully obligated to perform the services under the contract, and (*c*) the related person (or any other person related to the controlled foreign corporation) does not in fact (*1*) pay for performance of, or perform, any of such services the performance of which is so guaranteed or (*2*) pay for performance of, or perform, any significant services related to such services. If the related person (or any other person related to the controlled foreign corporation) does in fact pay for performance of, or perform, any of such services or any significant services related to such services, subparagraph (1)(ii) of this paragraph shall apply with respect to the services performed by the controlled foreign corporation pursuant to the contract the performance of which is guaranteed by the related person, even though such payment or performance is not considered to be substantial assistance for purposes of subparagraph (1)(iv) of this paragraph. For purposes of this subdivision, a related person shall be considered to guarantee performance of the

services by the controlled foreign corporation whether it guarantees performance of such services by a separate contract of guaranty or enters into a service contract solely for purposes of guaranteeing performance of such services and immediately thereafter assigns the entire contract to the controlled foreign corporation for execution.

(ii) *Application of substantial assistance test.*—For purposes of subparagraph (1)(iv) of this paragraph—

(a) Assistance furnished by a related person or persons to the controlled foreign corporation shall include, but shall not be limited to, direction, supervision, services, know-how, financial assistance (other than contributions to capital), and equipment, material, or supplies.

(b) Assistance furnished by a related person or persons to a controlled foreign corporation in the form of direction, supervision, services, or know-how shall not be considered substantial unless either (1) the assistance so furnished provides the controlled foreign corporation with skills which are a principal element in producing the income from the performance of such services by such corporation or (2) the cost to the controlled foreign corporation of the assistance so furnished equals 50 percent or more of the total cost to the controlled foreign corporation of performing the services performed by such corporation. The term "cost," as used in this subdivision (b), shall be determined after taking into account adjustments, if any, made under section 482.

(c) Financial assistance (other than contributions to capital), equipment, material, or supplies furnished by a related person to a controlled foreign corporation shall be considered assistance only in that amount by which the consideration actually paid by the controlled foreign corporation for the purchase or use of such item is less than the arm's length charge for such purchase or use. The total of such amounts so considered to be assistance in the case of financial assistance, equipment, material, and supplies furnished by all related persons shall be compared with the profits derived by the controlled foreign corporation from the performance of the services to determine whether the financial assistance, equipment, material, and supplies furnished by a related person or persons are by themselves substantial assistance contributing to the performance of such services. For purposes of this subdivision (c), determinations shall be made after taking into account adjustments, if any, made under section 482 and the term "consideration actually paid" shall include any amount which is deemed paid by the controlled foreign corporation pursuant to such an adjustment.

(d) Even though assistance furnished by a related person or persons to a controlled foreign corporation in the form of direction, supervision, services, or know-how is not considered to be substantial under (b) of this subdivision and assistance furnished by a related person or persons in the form of financial assistance (other than contributions to capital), equipment, material, or supplies is not considered to be substantial under (c) of this subdivision, such assistance may nevertheless constitute substantial assistance when taken together or in combination with other assistance furnished by a related person or persons which in itself is not considered to be substantial.

(e) Assistance furnished by a related person or persons to a controlled foreign corporation in the form of direction, supervision, services, or know-how shall not be taken into account under (b) or (d) of this subdivision unless the assistance so furnished assists the controlled foreign corporation directly in the performance of the services performed by such corporation.

(iii) *Special rule applicable to distributive share of partnership income.*—A controlled foreign corporation's distributive share of a partnership's services income will be deemed to be derived from services performed for or on behalf of a related person, within the meaning of section 954(e)(1)(A), if the partnership is a related person with respect to the controlled foreign corporation, under section 954(d)(3), and, in connection with the services performed by the partnership, the controlled foreign corporation, or a person that is a related person with respect to the controlled foreign corporation, provided assistance that would have constituted substantial assistance contributing to the performance of such services, under paragraph (b)(2)(ii) of this section, if furnished to the controlled foreign corporation by a related person. This paragraph (b)(2)(iii) applies to taxable years of a controlled foreign corporation beginning on or after July 23, 2002.

(3) *Illustrations.*—The application of this paragraph may be illustrated by the following examples:

Example (1). Controlled foreign corporation A is paid by related corporation M for the installation and maintenance of industrial machines which M Corporation manufactures and sells to B Corporation. Such installation and maintenance services by A Corporation are performed for, or on behalf of, M Corporation for purposes of section 954(e).

Example (2). Controlled foreign corporation B enters into a contract with an unrelated person to drill an oil well in a foreign country. Domestic corporation M owns all the outstanding stock of B Corporation. Corporation B employs a relatively small clerical and administrative staff and owns the necessary well-drilling equipment. Most of the technical and supervisory personnel who oversee the drilling of the oil well by B Corporation are regular employees of M Corporation who are temporarily employed by B Corporation. In addition, B Corporation hires on the open market unskilled and semiskilled laborers to work on the drilling project. The services performed by B Corporation under the well-drilling contract are performed for, or on behalf of, a related person for purposes of section 954(e) because the services of the technical and supervisory personnel which are provided by M Corporation are of substantial assistance in the performance of such contract in that they assist B Corporation directly in the execution of the contract and provide B Corporation with skills which are a principal element in producing the income from the performance of such contract.

Example (3). Controlled foreign corporation F enters into a contract with an unrelated person to construct a dam in a foreign country. Domestic corporation M owns all the outstanding stock of F Corporation. Corporation F leases or buys from M Corporation, on an arm's length basis, the equipment and material necessary for the construction of the dam. The technical and supervisory personnel who design and oversee the construction of the dam are regular full-time employees of F Corporation who are not on loan from any related person. The principal clerical work, and the financial accounting, required in connection with the construction of the dam by F Corporation are performed, on a remunerated basis, by full-time employees of M Corporation. All other assistance F Corporation requires in completing the construction of the dam is paid for by that corporation and furnished by unrelated persons. The services performed by F Corporation under the contract for the construction of the dam are not performed for, or on behalf of, a related person for purposes of section 954(e) because the clerical and accounting services furnished by M Corporation do not assist F Corporation directly in the performance of the contract.

Example (4). Controlled foreign corporation D, a wholly owned subsidiary of domestic corporation M, procures and enters a contract with an unrelated person to construct a superhighway in a foreign country, but such person enters the contract only on the condition that M Corporation agrees to perform, or to pay for the performance by some person other than D Corporation of, the services called for by the contract if D Corporation should fail to complete their performance. Corporation D is capable of performing such contract. No related person as to D Corporation pays for, or performs, any services called for by the contract, or pays for, or performs, any significant services related to such services. The construction of the superhighway by D Corporation is not considered for purposes of section 954(e) to be the performance of services for, or on behalf of, M Corporation.

Example (5). Domestic corporation M is obligated under a contract with an unrelated person to construct a superhighway in a foreign country. At a later date M Corporation assigns the entire contract to its wholly owned subsidiary, controlled foreign corporation C, and the unrelated person releases M Corporation from any obligation under the contract. The construction of such highway by C Corporation is considered for purposes of section 954(e) to be the performance of services for, or on behalf of, M Corporation.

Example (6). Domestic corporation M enters a contract with an unrelated person to construct a superhighway in a foreign country. Corporation M immediately assigns the entire contract to its wholly owned subsidiary, controlled foreign corporation C. The unrelated person does not release M Corporation of its obligation under the contract, the sole purpose of these arrangements being to have M Corporation guarantee performance of the contract by C Corporation. Corporation C is capable of performing the construction contract. Neither M Corporation nor any other person related to C Corporation pays for, or performs, any services called for by the construction contract or at any time pays for, or performs, any significant services related to the services performed under such contract. The construction of the superhighway by C Corporation is not considered for purposes of section 954(e) to be the performance of services for, or on behalf of, M Corporation.

Example (7). The facts are the same as in example (6) except that M Corporation, preparatory to entering the construction contract, prepares plans and specifications which enable the submission of bids for the contract. Since M Corporation has performed significant services related to the services the performance of which it has guaranteed, the construction of such highway by C Corporation is considered for purposes of section 954(e) to be the performance of services for, or on behalf of, M Corporation.

Example (8). Domestic corporation M manufactures an industrial machine which requires specialized installation. Corporation M sells the machines for a basic price if the contract of sale contains no provision for installation. If, however, the customer agrees to employ controlled foreign corporation E, a wholly owned subsidiary of M Corporation, to install the machine and to pay E Corporation a specified installation charge, M Corporation sells the machine at a price which is less than the basic price. The installation services performed by E Corporation for customers of M Corporation purchasing the machine at the reduced price are considered for purposes of section 954(e) to be performed for, or on behalf of, M Corporation.

Example (9). Domestic corporation M manufactures and sells industrial machines with a warranty as to their performance conditional upon their installation and maintenance by a factory-authorized service agency. Controlled foreign corporation F, a wholly owned subsidiary of M Corporation, is the only authorized service agency. Any installation or maintenance services performed by F Corporation on such machines are considered for purposes of section 954(e) to be performed for, or on behalf of, M Corporation.

Example (10). Domestic corporation M manufactures electric office machines which it sells at a basic price without any provision for, or understanding as to, adjustment or maintenance of the machines. The machines require constant adjustment and maintenance services which M Corporation, certain wholly owned subsidiaries of M Corporation, and certain unrelated persons throughout the world are qualified to perform. From among the numerous persons qualified and available to perform adjustment and maintenance services with respect to such office machines, foreign corporation B, a customer of M Corporation, employs controlled foreign corporation G, a wholly owned subsidiary of M Corporation, to adjust and maintain the office machines which B Corporation purchases from M Corporation. The adjustment and maintenance services performed by G Corporation for B Corporation are not considered for purposes of section 954(e) to be performed for, or on behalf of, M Corporation.

(c) *Place where services are performed.*—The place where services will be considered to have been performed for purposes of paragraph (a)(2) of this section will depend on the facts and circumstances of each case. As a general rule, services will be considered performed where the persons performing services for the controlled foreign corporation which derives income in connection with the performance of technical, managerial, architectural, engineering, scientific, skilled, industrial, commercial, or like services are physically located when they perform their duties in the execution of the service activity resulting in such income. Therefore, in many cases, total gross income of a controlled foreign corporation derived in connection with each service contract or arrangement performed for or on behalf of a related person must be apportioned, between income which is not foreign base company services income and that which is foreign base company services income, on a basis of employee-time spent within the foreign country under the laws of which the controlled foreign corporation is created or organized and employee-time spent without the foreign country under the laws of which such corporation is created or organized. In allocating time spent within and without the foreign country under the laws of which the controlled foreign corporation is created or organized, relative weight must also be given to the value of the various functions performed by persons in fulfillment of the service contract or arrangement. For example, clerical work will ordinarily be assigned little value, while services performed by technical, highly skilled, and managerial personnel will be assigned greater values in relation to the type of function performed by each individual.

(d) *Items excluded.*—Foreign base company services income does not include—

(1) Income derived in connection with the performance of services by a controlled foreign corporation if—

(i) The services directly relate to the sale or exchange of personal property by the controlled foreign corporation,

(ii) The property sold or exchanged was manufactured, produced, grown, or extracted by such controlled foreign corporation, and

(iii) The services were performed before the sale or exchange of such property by the controlled foreign corporation;

(2) Income derived in connection with the performance of services by a controlled foreign corporation if the services directly relate to an offer or effort to sell or exchange personal property which was, or would have been, manufactured, produced, grown, or extracted by such controlled foreign corporation whether or not a sale or exchange of such property was in fact consummated; or

(3) For taxable years beginning after December 31, 1975, foreign base company shipping income (as determined under § 1.954-6). [Reg. § 1.954-4.]

☐ [*T.D.* 6734, 5-14-64. *Amended by T.D.* 6981, 11-12-68; *T.D.* 7894, 5-11-83 *and T.D.* 9008, 7-22-2002.]

§ 1.954-5. Increase in qualified investments in less developed countries; taxable years of controlled foreign corporations beginning before January 1, 1976.—For rules applicable to taxable years of controlled foreign corporations beginning before January 1, 1976, see section 954(b)(1) (as in effect before the enactment of the Tax Reduction Act of 1975) and 26 CFR § 1.954-5 (Rev. as of April 1, 1975). [Reg. § 1.954-5.]

☐ [*T.D. 6734, 5-14-64. Amended by T.D. 7893, 5-11-83.*]

Proposed Regulation

§ 1.954-9. Hybrid branches.— (a) *Subpart F income arising from certain payments involving hybrid branches.—*(1) *Payment causing foreign tax reduction gives rise to additional subpart F income.—*The non-subpart F income of a controlled foreign corporation will be recharacterized as subpart F income, to the extent provided in paragraph (a)(5) of this section, if—

(i) A hybrid branch payment, as defined in paragraph (a)(6) of this section, is made between the entities described in paragraph (a)(2) of this section;

(ii) The hybrid branch payment reduces foreign tax, as determined under paragraph (a)(3) of this section; and

(iii) The hybrid branch payment is treated as falling within a category of foreign personal holding company income under the rules of paragraph (a)(4) of this section.

(2) *Hybrid branch payment between certain entities.—*(i) *In general.—*Paragraph (a)(1) of this section shall apply to hybrid branch payments between—

(A) A controlled foreign corporation and its hybrid branch;

(B) Hybrid branches of a controlled foreign corporation;

(C) A partnership in which a controlled foreign corporation is a partner (either directly or through one or more branches or other partnerships) and a hybrid branch of the partnership; or

(D) Hybrid branches of a partnership in which a controlled foreign corporation is a partner (either directly or through one or more branches or other partnerships).

(ii) *Hybrid branch payment involving partnership.—*(A) *Fiscally transparent partnership.—*To the extent of the controlled foreign corporation's proportionate share of a hybrid branch payment, the rules of paragraphs (a)(3), (4) and (5) of this section shall be applied by treating the hybrid branch payment between the partnership and the hybrid branch as if it were made directly between the controlled foreign corporation and the hybrid branch, or as if the hybrid branches of the partnership were hybrid branches of the controlled foreign corporation, if the hybrid branch payment is made between—

(1) A fiscally transparent partnership in which a controlled foreign corporation is a partner (either directly or through one or more branches or other fiscally transparent partnerships) and the partnership's hybrid branch; or

(2) Hybrid branches of a fiscally transparent partnership in which a controlled foreign corporation is a partner (either directly or through one or more branches or other fiscally transparent partnerships).

(B) *Non-fiscally transparent partnership.—*To the extent of the controlled foreign corporation's proportionate share of a hybrid branch payment, the rules of paragraphs (a)(3) and (4) and (a)(5)(iv) of this section shall be applied to the non-fiscally transparent partnership as if it were the controlled foreign corporation, if the hybrid branch payment is made between—

(1) A non-fiscally transparent partnership in which a controlled foreign corporation is a partner (either directly or through one or more branches or other partnerships) and the partnership's hybrid branch; or

(2) Hybrid branches of a non-fiscally transparent partnership in which a controlled foreign corporation is a partner (either directly or through one or more branches or other partnerships).

(C) *Examples.—*The following examples illustrate the application of this paragraph (a)(2)(ii):

Example 1. CFC, a controlled foreign corporation in Country A, is a 90 percent partner in partnership P, which is treated as fiscally transparent under the laws of Country A. P has a hybrid branch, BR, in Country B. P makes an interest payment of $100 to BR. Under Country A law, CFC's 90 percent share of the payment reduces CFC's Country A income tax. Under paragraph (a)(2)(ii)(A) of this section, the recharacterization rules of this section are applied by treating the payment as if made by CFC to BR. Ninety dollars of CFC's non-subpart F income, to the extent available, and subject to the earnings and profits and tax rate limitations of paragraph (a)(5) of this section, is recharacterized as subpart F income.

Example 2. CFC, a controlled foreign corporation in country A, is a 90 percent partner in partnership P, which is treated as fiscally transparent under the laws of Country A. P has two branches in Country B, BR1 and BR2. BR1 is treated as fiscally transparent under the laws of Country A. BR2 is a hybrid branch. BR1 makes an interest payment of $100 to BR2. Under paragraph (a)(2)(ii)(A) of this section, the payment by BR1, the fiscally transparent branch, is treated as a payment by P, and the deemed payment by P, a fiscally transparent partnership, is treated as made by CFC. Under Country A law, CFC's 90 percent share of BR1's payment reduces CFC's Country A income tax. Ninety dollars of CFC's non-subpart F income, to the extent available, and subject to the earnings and profits and tax rate limitations of paragraph (a)(5) of this section, is recharacterized as subpart F income.

(3) *Application when payment reduces foreign tax.*—For purposes of paragraph (a)(1) of this section, a hybrid branch payment reduces foreign tax when the foreign tax imposed on the income of the payor, or any person that is a related person with respect to the payor (as determined under the principles of section 954(d)(3)), is less than the foreign tax that would have been imposed on such income had the hybrid branch payment not been made, or the hybrid branch payment creates or increases a loss or deficit or other tax attribute which may be carried back or forward to reduce the foreign income tax of the payor or any owner in another year (determined by taking into account any refund of such tax made to the payor, payee or any other person).

(4) *Hybrid branch payment that is included within a category of foreign personal holding company income.*—(i) *In general.*—For purposes of paragraph (a)(1) of this section, whether the hybrid branch payment is treated as income included within a category of foreign personal holding company income is determined by treating a hybrid branch that is either the payor or recipient of the hybrid branch payment as a separate wholly-owned subsidiary corporation of the controlled foreign corporation that is incorporated in the jurisdiction under the laws of which such hybrid branch is created, organized for foreign law purposes, or has substantial assets. Thus, the hybrid branch payment will be treated as included within a category of foreign personal holding company income if, taking into account any specific exceptions for that category, the payment would be included within a category of foreign personal holding company income if the branch or branches were treated as separately incorporated for U.S. tax purposes.

(ii) *Extent to which controlled foreign corporation and hybrid branches treated as separate entities.*—For purposes of this section, other than the determination under paragraph (a)(4)(i) of this section, a controlled foreign corporation and its hybrid branch, a partnership and its hybrid branch, or hybrid branches shall not be treated as separate entities. Thus, for example, if a controlled foreign corporation, including all of its hybrid branches, has an overall deficit in earnings and profits to which section 952(c) applies, the limitation of such section on the amount includible in the subpart F income of such corporation will apply. Similarly, for purposes of applying the de minimis and full inclusion rules of section 954(b)(3), a controlled foreign corporation and its hybrid branch, or hybrid branches shall not be treated as separate corporations. Further, a hybrid branch payment that would reduce foreign personal holding company income under section 954(b)(5) if made between two separate entities will not create an expense if made between a controlled foreign corporation and its hybrid branch, a partnership and its hybrid branch, or hybrid branches.

(5) *Recharacterization of income attributable to current earnings and profits as subpart F income.*—(i) *General rule.*—Non-subpart F income of a controlled foreign corporation in an amount equal to the excess of earnings and profits of the controlled foreign corporation for the taxable year over subpart F income, as defined in section 952(a), will be recharacterized as subpart F income under paragraph (a)(1) of this section only to the extent provided under paragraphs (a)(5)(ii) through (vi) of this section.

(ii) *Subpart F income.*—For purposes of determining the excess of current earnings and profits over subpart F income under paragraph (a)(1) of this section, the amount of subpart F income is determined before the application of the rules of this section but after the application of the rules of sections 952(c) and 954(b). Further, such amount is determined by treating the controlled foreign corporation and all of its hybrid branches as a single corporation.

(iii) *Recharacterization limited to gross amount of hybrid branch payment.*—(A) *In general.*—The amount recharacterized as subpart F income under paragraph (a)(1) of this section is limited to the amount of the hybrid branch payment.

(B) *Exception for duplicative payments.*—[Reserved].

(iv) *Tax disparity rule.*—(A) *In general.*—Paragraph (a)(1) of this section will apply only if the hybrid branch payment falls within the tax disparity rule. The hybrid branch payment falls within the tax disparity rule if it is taxed in the year when earned at an effective rate of tax that is less than 90 percent of, and at least 5 percentage points less than, the hypothetical effective rate of tax imposed on the hybrid branch payment, as determined under paragraph (a)(5)(iv)(B) of this section.

Prop. Reg. § 1.954-9(a)(5)(iv)(A)

(B) *Hypothetical effective rate of tax.*—(1) *In general.*—The hypothetical effective rate of tax imposed on the hybrid branch payment is—

(i) For the taxable year of the payor in which the hybrid branch payment is made, the amount of income taxes that would have been paid or accrued by the payor if the hybrid branch payment had not been made, less the amount of income taxes paid or accrued by the payor; divided by

(ii) The amount of the hybrid branch payment.

(2) *Hypothetical effective rate of tax when hybrid branch payment causes or increases loss or deficit.*—If the hybrid branch payment causes or increases a loss or deficit of the payor for foreign tax purposes, and such loss or deficit can be carried forward or back, the hypothetical effective rate of tax imposed on the hybrid branch payment is the effective rate of tax that would be imposed on the taxable income of the payor for the year in which the payment is made if the payor's taxable income were equal to the amount of the hybrid branch payment.

(C) *Examples.*—The application of this paragraph (a)(5)(iv) is illustrated by the following examples:

Example 1. In 2006, CFC organized in Country A had net income of $60 from manufacturing for Country A tax purposes. It also had a branch (BR) in Country B. BR is a hybrid entity under paragraph (a)(1) of this section. CFC made a payment of $40 to BR, which was a hybrid branch payment under paragraph (a)(6) of this section, and was treated by CFC as a deductible payment for Country A tax purposes. CFC paid $30 of Country A taxes in 2006. It would have paid $50 of Country A taxes without the deductible payment. Country A did not impose any withholding tax on the $40 payment to BR. Country B also did not impose a tax on the $40 received by BR. Therefore, the effective rate of tax on that payment is 0%. Furthermore, the hypothetical effective rate of tax on the $40 hybrid branch payment is 50% ($50 − $30/$40). The effective rate of tax (0%) is less than 90% of, and more than 5 percentage points less than, this hypothetical rate of tax of 50%. As a result, the $40 hybrid branch payment falls within the tax disparity rule of this paragraph (a)(5)(iv).

Example 2. Assume the same facts as in *Example 1*, except that CFC has a loss of $100 for the year for Country A tax purposes. Under Country A law, CFC can carry the loss forward for use in subsequent years. CFC paid no Country A taxes in 2006. The rate of tax in Country A is graduated from 20% to 50%. If the $40 hybrid branch payment were the only item of taxable income of CFC, Country A would have imposed tax at an effective rate of 30%. The effective rate of tax (0%) is less than 90% of, and more than 5 percentage points less than, the hypothetical effective rate of tax (30%) imposed on the hybrid branch payment. As a result, the $40 hybrid branch payment falls within the tax disparity rule of this paragraph (a)(5)(iv).

Example 3. Assume the same facts as in *Example 1*, except that Country B imposes tax on the $40 hybrid payment to BR at an effective rate of 50%. The effective rate of 50% is equal to the hypothetical effective rate of tax. As a result, the hybrid branch payment does not fall within the tax disparity rule of this paragraph (a)(5)(iv) and, thus, the recharacterization rules of paragraph (a)(1) of this section do not apply. See also the special high tax exception of paragraph (a)(5)(v) of this section.

(v) *Special high tax exception.*—(A) *In general.*—Paragraph (a)(1) of this section shall not apply if the non-subpart F income that would be recharacterized as subpart F income under this section was subject to foreign income taxes imposed by a foreign country or countries at an effective rate that is greater than 90 percent of the maximum rate of tax specified in section 11 for the taxable year of the controlled foreign corporation.

(B) *Effective rate of tax.*—The effective rate of tax imposed on the non-subpart F income that would be recharacterized as subpart F income under this section is determined under the principles of § 1.954-1(d)(2) and (3). See paragraph (b) of this section for the application of section 960 to amounts recharacterized as subpart F income under this section.

(vi) *No carryback or carryforward of amounts in excess of current year earnings and profits limitation.*—To the extent that some or all of the amount required to be recharacterized under this section is not recharacterized as subpart F income because the hybrid branch payment exceeds the amount that can be recharacterized, as determined under paragraph (a)(5)(i) of this section, this excess shall not be carried back or forward to another year.

(6) *Definitions for this section.*—For purposes of this section:

(i) *Arrangement* shall mean any agreement to pay interest, rents, royalties or similar amounts. It shall also include the declaration and payment of a dividend (but not an agreement or undertaking to pay future, unspecified dividends). An arrangement shall not, however, include the mere formation or acquisition (or similar event) of a hybrid branch that is intended to become a party to an arrangement.

(ii) *Entity* means any person that is treated by the United States or any jurisdiction as other than an individual.

(iii) *Hybrid branch* means an entity that—

(A) Is disregarded as an entity separate from its owner for federal tax purposes and is owned (including ownership through branches) by either a controlled foreign corporation or a partnership in which a controlled foreign corporation is a partner (either directly or indirectly through one or more branches or partnerships);

(B) Is treated as fiscally transparent by the United States; and

(C) Is treated as non-fiscally transparent by the country in which the payor entity, any owner of a fiscally-transparent payor entity, the controlled foreign corporation, or any intermediary partnership is created, organized or has substantial assets.

(iv) *Hybrid branch payment* means the gross amount of any payment (including any accrual) which, under the tax laws of any foreign jurisdiction to which the payor is subject, is regarded as a payment between two separate entities but which, under U.S. income tax principles, is not income to the recipient because it is between two parts of a single entity.

(7) *Fiscally transparent and non-fiscally transparent.*—For purposes of this section an entity shall be treated as fiscally transparent with respect to an interest holder of the entity, if such interest holder is required, under the laws of any jurisdiction to which it is subject, to take into account separately, on a current basis, such interest holder's share of all items which, if separately taken into account by such interest holder, would result in an income tax liability for the interest holder in such jurisdiction different from that which would result if the interest holder did not take the share of such items into account separately. A non-fiscally transparent entity is an entity that is not fiscally transparent under this paragraph (a)(7).

(b) *Application of section 960.*—For purposes of determining the amount of taxes deemed paid under section 960, the amount of non-subpart F income recharacterized as subpart F income under this section shall be treated as attributable to income in separate categories, as defined in § 1.904-5(a)(1), in proportion to the ratio of non-subpart F income in each such category to the total amount of non-subpart F income of the controlled foreign corporation for the taxable year.

(c) *Effective dates.*—(1) *In general.*—This section shall be applicable for all amounts paid or accrued in taxable years commencing after [date that is 5 years after publication of the final regulations in the federal register], under hybrid arrangements, except as otherwise provided.

(2) *Permanent relief.*—(i) *In general.*—This section shall not apply to any payments made under hybrid arrangements entered into before June 19, 1998. This exception shall be permanent so long as the arrangement is not substantially modified, within the meaning of paragraph (c)(2)(ii) of this section, on or after June 19, 1998.

(ii) *Substantial modification.*—(A) *In general.*—Substantial modification of a hybrid arrangement includes—

(1) The expansion of the hybrid arrangement (other than de minimis expansion);

(2) A more than 50% change in the U.S. ownership (direct or indirect) of any entity that is a party to the hybrid arrangement, other than—

(i) A transfer of ownership of such party within a controlled group determined under section 1563(a), without regard to section 1563(a)(4); or

(ii) A change in ownership of the entire controlled group (determined under section 1563(a), without regard to section 1563(a)(4)) of which such party is a member;

(3) Any measure taken by a party to the arrangement (or any related party) that materially increases the tax benefit of the hybrid arrangement, regardless of whether such measure alters the legal relationship between the parties to the arrangement. For example, in the case of a hybrid branch payment determined with reference to a percentage of sales, a growth in the amount of the hybrid branch payment (and, thus, the tax benefit) caused by a growth of sales will not, in general, be a substantial modification. However, in the case of a significant sales growth resulting from a transfer of assets by a related party, that transfer would be a measure which materially increased the benefit of the arrangement, and that arrangement would be deemed to have been substantially modified.

(B) *Transactions not treated as substantial modification.*—Substantial modification of a hybrid arrangement does not include—

(1) The daily reissuance of a demand loan by operation of law;

(2) The renewal of a loan, license or rental agreement on the same terms and conditions if—

(i) The renewal occurs pursuant to the terms of the agreement and without more than a de minimis amount of action of any party thereto;

(ii) As contemplated by the original agreement, the same parties agree to renew the agreement without modification; or

(iii) The renewal occurs solely by reason of a subsequent drawdown under a grandfathered master credit facility agreement;

(3) The renewal of a loan, license, or rental agreement by the same parties on terms which do not increase the tax benefit of the arrangement (other than a de minimis increase);

(4) The making of payments under a license agreement in respect of copyrights or patents (or know-how associated with such copyrights or patents), not in existence at the time the agreement was entered into, but only where the development of such property was anticipated by the agreement, and such property is substantially derived from (or otherwise incorporates substantial features of) copyrights and patents (or know-how associated with such copyrights or patents) in existence at the time of, and covered under, the original agreement;

(5) A final transfer pricing adjustment made by the taxation authorities of the jurisdiction in which the tax reduction occurs, so long as such adjustment would not have been a substantial valuation misstatement (as defined in section 6662(e)(1)(B)) if the adjustment had been made by the Internal Revenue Service; or

(6) A de minimis periodic adjustment by the parties to the arrangement made annually (or more frequently) to conform the payments to the requirements of section 482. [Prop. Reg. § 1.954-9.]

[Proposed 7-13-99.]

§ 1.956-1. Shareholder's pro rata share of a controlled foreign corporation's increase in earnings invested in United States property.—(a) *In general.*—Section 956(a)(1) and paragraph (b) of this section provide rules for determining the amount of a controlled foreign corporation's earnings invested in United States property at the close of any taxable year. Such amount is the aggregate amount invested in United States property to the extent such amount would have constituted a dividend if it had been distributed on such date. Subject to the provisions of section 951(a)(4) and the regulations thereunder, a United States shareholder of a controlled foreign corporation is required to include in his gross income his pro rata share, as determined in accordance with paragraph (c) of this section, of the controlled foreign corporation's increase for any taxable year in earnings invested in United States property but only to the extent such share is not excludable from his gross income under the provisions of section 959(a)(2) and the regulations thereunder.

(b) *Amount of a controlled foreign corporation's investment of earnings in United States property.*—(1) *Dividend limitation.*—The amount of a controlled foreign corporation's earnings invested at the close of its taxable year in United States property is the aggregate amount of such property held, directly or indirectly, by such corporation at the close of its taxable year to the extent such amount would have constituted a dividend under section 316 and §§ 1.316-1 and 1.316-2 (determined after the application of section 955(a)) if it had been distributed on such closing day. For purposes of this subparagraph, the determination of whether an amount would have constituted a dividend if distributed shall be made without regard to the provisions of section 959(d) and the regulations thereunder.

(2) *Aggregate amount of United States property.*—For purposes of determining an increase in earnings invested in United States property for any taxable year beginning after December 31, 1975, the aggregate amount of United States property held by a controlled foreign corporation at the close of—

(i) Any taxable year beginning after December 31, 1975, and

(ii) The last taxable year beginning before January 1, 1976

does not include stock or obligations of a domestic corporation described in section 956(b)(2)(F) or movable property described in section 956(b)(2)(G).

(3) *Treatment of earnings and profits.*—For purposes of making the determination under subparagraph (1) of this paragraph as to whether an amount of investment would have constituted a dividend if distributed at the close of any taxable year of a controlled foreign corporation, earnings and profits of the controlled foreign corporation shall be considered not to include any amounts which are attributable to—

(i) Amounts which have been included in the gross income of a United States shareholder of such controlled foreign corporation under section 951(a)(1)(B) (or which would have been so included but for section 959(a)(2)) and have not been distributed, or

(ii) *(a)* Amounts which are included in the gross income of a United States shareholder of such controlled foreign corporation under section 551(b) or would be so included under such section but for the fact that such amounts were distributed to such shareholder during the taxable year, or

(b) Amounts which, for any prior taxable year, have been included in the gross income of a United States shareholder of such controlled foreign corporation under section 551(b) and have not been distributed.

The rules of this subparagraph apply only in determining the limitation on a controlled foreign corporation's increase in earnings invested in United States property. See section 959 and the regulations thereunder for limitations on the exclusion from gross income of previously taxed earnings and profits.

(4) [Reserved.]

(c) *Shareholder's pro rata share of increase.*—(1) *General rule.*—A United States shareholder's pro rata share of a controlled foreign corporation's increase for any taxable year in earnings invested in United States property is the amount determined by subtracting the shareholder's pro rata share of—

(i) The controlled foreign corporation's earnings invested in United States property at the close of its preceding taxable year, as determined under paragraph (b) of this section, reduced by amounts paid by such corporation during such preceding taxable year to which section 959(c)(1) and the regulations thereunder apply, from his pro rata share of

(ii) The controlled foreign corporation's earnings invested in United States property at the close of its current taxable year, as determined under paragraph (b) of this section.

(2) *Illustration.*—The application of this paragraph may be illustrated by the following examples:

Example (1). A is a United States shareholder and direct owner of 60 percent of the only class of stock of R Corporation, a controlled foreign corporation during the entire period here involved. Both A and R Corporation use the calendar year as a taxable year. Corporation R's aggregate investment in United States property on December 31, 1964, which would constitute a dividend (as determined under paragraph (b) of this section) if distributed on such date is $150,000. During the taxable year 1964, R Corporation distributed $50,000 to which section 959(c)(1) applies. Corporation R's aggregate investment in United States property on December 31, 1965, is $250,000; and R Corporation's current and accumulated earnings and profits on such date (determined as provided in paragraph (b) of this section) are $225,000. A's pro rata share of R Corporation's increase for 1965 in earnings invested in United States property is $75,000, determined as follows:

(i) Aggregate investment in United States property on Dec. 31, 1965		$250,000
(ii) Current and accumulated earnings and profits on December 31, 1965		225,000
(iii) Amount of earnings invested in United States property on December 31, 1965, which would constitute a dividend if distributed on such date (lesser of item (i) or item (ii))		225,000
(iv) Aggregate investment in United States property on December 31, 1964, which would constitute a dividend if distributed on such date	$150,000	
Less: Amounts distributed during 1964 to which sec. 959(c)(1) applies	$ 50,000	$100,000
(v) R Corporation's increase for 1965 in earnings invested in United States property (item (iii) minus item (iv))		$125,000
(vi) A's pro rata share of R Corporation's increase for 1965 in earnings invested in United States property (item (v) times 60 percent)		75,000

Example (2). The facts are the same as in example (1), except that R Corporation's current and accumulated earnings and profits on December 31, 1965, are $100,000 instead of $225,000. Accordingly, even though R Corporation's aggregate investment in United States property on December 31, 1965, of $250,000 exceeds the net amount ($100,000) taken into account under subparagraph (1)(i) of this paragraph as of December 31, 1964, by $150,000, there is no increase for taxable year 1965 in earnings invested in United States property because of the dividend limitation of paragraph (b)(1) of this section. Corporation R's aggregate investment in United States property on December 31, 1966, is unchanged ($250,000). Corporation R's current and accumulated earnings and profits on December 31, 1966, are $175,000, and, as a consequence, its aggregate investment in United States property which would constitute a dividend if distributed on that date is $175,000. Corporation R pays no amount during 1965 to which section 959(c)(1) applies. Corporation R's increase for the taxable year 1966 in earnings invested in United States property is $75,000, and A's pro rata share of that amount is $45,000 ($75,000 times 60 percent).

(d) *Date and basis of determinations.*—The determinations made under paragraph (c)(1)(i) of this section with respect to the close of the preceding taxable year of a controlled foreign corporation and under paragraph (c)(1)(ii) with respect to the close of the current taxable year of such controlled foreign corporation, for purposes of determining the United States shareholder's pro rata share of such corporation's increased investment of earnings in United States property for the current taxable year, shall be made as of the last day of the current taxable year of such corporation but on the basis of stock owned, within the meaning of section 958(a) and the regulations thereunder, by such United States shareholder on the last day of the current taxable year of the foreign corporation on which such corporation is a controlled foreign corporation. See the last sentence of section 956(a)(2). The application of this paragraph may be illustrated from the following example:

Example. Domestic corporation M owns 60 percent of the only class of stock of A Corporation, a controlled foreign corporation during the entire period here involved. Both M Corporation and A Corporation use the calendar year as a taxable year. Corporation A's investment of earnings in United States property at the close of the taxable year 1963 is $100,000, as determined under paragraph (b) of this section, and M Corporation includes its pro rata share of such amount ($60,000) in gross income for its taxable year 1963. On June 1, 1964, M Corporation acquires an additional 25 percent of A Corporation's outstanding stock from a person who is not a United States person as defined in section 957(d). Corporation A's investment of earnings in United States property at the close of the taxable year 1964, as determined under paragraph (b) of this section, is unchanged ($100,000). Corporation A pays no amount during 1963 to which section 959(c)(1) applies. Corporation M is not required, by reason of the acquisition in 1964 of A Corporation's stock, to include an additional amount in its gross income with respect to A Corporation's investment of earnings in United States property even though the earnings invested in United States property by A Corporation attributable to the stock acquired by M Corporation were not previously taxed. The determination made under paragraph (c)(1)(i) of this section as well as the determination made under paragraph (c)(1)(ii) of this section with respect to A Corporation's investment for 1964 of earnings in United States property are made on the basis of stock owned by M Corporation (85 percent) at the close of 1964.

(e) *Amount attributable to property.*—(1) *General rule.*—Except as provided in subparagraph (2) of this paragraph, for purposes of paragraph (b)(1) of this section, the amount taken into account with respect to any United States property shall be its adjusted basis, as of the applicable determination date, reduced by any liability (other than a liability described in subparagraph (3) of this paragraph) to which such property is subject on such date. To be taken into account under this subparagraph, a liability must constitute a specific charge against the property involved. Thus, a liability evidenced by an open account or a liability secured only by the general credit of the controlled foreign corporation will not be taken into account. On the other hand, if a liability constitutes a specific charge against several items of property and cannot definitely be allocated to any single item of property, the liability shall be apportioned against each of such items of property in that ratio which the adjusted basis of such item on the applicable determination date bears to the adjusted basis of all such items at such time. A liability in excess of the adjusted basis of the property which is subject to such liability shall not be taken into account for the purpose of reducing the adjusted basis of other property which is not subject to such liability.

(2) *Rule for pledges and guarantees.*—For the purposes of this section the amount taken into account with respect to any pledge or guarantee described in paragraph (c)(1) of § 1.956-2 shall be the unpaid principal amount on the applicable determination date of the obligation with respect to which the controlled foreign corporation is a pledgor or guarantor.

(3) *Excluded charges.*—For purposes of subparagraph (1) of this paragraph, a specific charge created with respect to any item of property principally for the purpose of artificially increasing or decreasing the amount of a controlled foreign corporation's investment of earnings in United States property will not be recognized; whether a specific charge is created principally for such purpose will depend upon all the facts and circumstances of each case. One of the factors that will be considered in making such a determination with respect to a loan is whether the loan is from a related person, as defined in section 954(d)(3) and paragraph (e) of § 1.954-1.

(4) *Statement required.*—If for purposes of this section a United States shareholder of a controlled foreign corporation reduces the adjusted basis of property which constitutes United States property on the ground that such property is subject to a liability, he shall attach to his return a statement setting forth the adjusted basis of the property before the reduction and the amount and nature of the reduction. [Reg. § 1.956-1.]

☐ [*T.D.* 6704, 2-19-64. *Amended by T.D.* 6795, 1-28-65; *T.D.* 7712, 8-6-80 *and T.D.* 8209, 6-13-88.]

§ 1.956-1T. Shareholder's pro rata share of a controlled foreign corporation's increase in earnings invested in United States property (temporary).—
(a) (reserved).

(b) (1)—(3) (reserved).

(b) (4) *Treatment of certain investments of earnings in United States property.*—(i) *Special rule.*—For purposes of § 1.956-1(b)(1) of the regulations, a controlled foreign corporation will be considered to hold indirectly (A) the investments in United States property held on its behalf by a trustee or a nominee or (B) at the discretion of the District Director, investments in U.S. property acquired by any other foreign corporation that is controlled by the controlled foreign corporation, if one of the principal purposes for creating, organizing, or funding (through capital contributions or debt) such other foreign corporation is to avoid the application of section 956 with respect to the controlled foreign corporation. For purposes of this paragraph (b), a foreign corporation will be controlled by the controlled foreign corporation if the foreign corporation and the controlled foreign corporation are related parties under section 267(b). In determining for purposes of this paragraph (b) whether two or more corporations are members of the same controlled group under section 267(b)(3), a person is considered to own stock owned directly by such person, stock owned with the application of section 1563(e)(1), and stock owned with the application of section 267(c). The following examples illustrate the application of this paragraph.

Example (1). P, a domestic corporation, owns all of the outstanding stock of FS1, a controlled foreign corporation, and all of the outstanding stock of FS2, also a controlled foreign corporation. FS1 sells products to FS2 in exchange for trade receivables due in 60 days. FS2 has no earnings and profits. FS1 has substantial accumulated earnings and profits. FS2 loans to P an amount equal to the debt it owes FS1. FS2 pays the trade receivables according to the terms of the receivables. FS1 will not be considered to hold indirectly the investment in United States property under this paragraph (b)(4), because there was no transfer of funds to FS2.

Example (2). The facts are the same as in Example (1), except that FS2 does not pay the receivables. FS1 is considered to hold indirectly the investment in United States property under this paragraph (b)(4), because there was a transfer of funds to FS2, a principal purpose of which was to avoid the application of section 956 to FS1.

(ii) *Effective date.*—This section is effective June 14, 1988, with respect to investments made on or after June 14, 1988.

(c) (reserved).

(d) (reserved).

(e)(1)—(e)(4) (reserved).

(e)(5) *Excluded charges.*—(i) *Special rule.*—For purposes of § 1.956-1(e)(1) of the regulations, in the case of an investment in United States property consisting of an obligation of a related person, as defined in section 954(d)(3) and paragraph (e) of § 1.954-1, a liability will not be recognized as a specific charge if the liability representing the charge is with recourse with respect to the general credit or other assets of the investing controlled foreign corporation.

(ii) *Effective date.*—This section is effective June 14, 1988, with respect to investments made on or after June 14, 1988. [Temporary Reg. § 1.956-1T.]

☐ [*T.D.* 8209, 6-13-88.]

§ 1.956-2. Definition of United States property.—(a) *Included property.*—(1) *In general.*—For purposes of section 956(a) and § 1.956-1, United States property is (except as provided in paragraph (b) of this section) any property acquired (within the meaning of paragraph (d)(1) of this section) by a foreign corporation (whether or not a controlled foreign corporation at the time) during any taxable year of such foreign corporation beginning after December 31, 1962, which is—

(i) Tangible property (real or personal) located in the United States;

(ii) Stock of a domestic corporation;

(iii) An obligation (as defined in paragraph (d)(2) of this section) of a United States person (as defined in section 957(d)); or

(iv) Any right to the use in the United States of—

(a) A patent or copyright,

(b) An invention, model, or design (whether or not patented),

(c) A secret formula or process, or

(d) Any other similar property right,

which is acquired or developed by the foreign corporation for use in the United States by any person. Whether a right described in this subdivision has been acquired or developed for use in the United States by any person is to be determined from all the facts and circumstances of each case. As a general rule, a right actually used principally in the United States will be considered to have been acquired or developed for use in the United States in the absence of affirmative evidence showing that the right was not so acquired or developed for such use.

(2) *Illustrations.*—The application of the provisions of this paragraph may be illustrated by the following examples:

Example (1). Foreign corporation R uses as a taxable year a fiscal year ending on June 30. Corporation R acquires on June 1, 1963, and holds on June 30, 1963, $100,000 of tangible property (not described in section 956(b)(2)) located in the United States. Corporation R's aggregate investment in United States property at the close of its taxable year ending June 30, 1963, is zero since the property which is acquired on June 1, 1963, is not acquired during a taxable year of R Corporation beginning after December 31, 1962. Assuming no change in R Corporation's aggregate investment in United States property during its taxable year ending June 30, 1964, R Corporation's increase in earnings invested in United States property for such taxable year is zero.

Example (2). Foreign corporation S uses the calendar year as a taxable year and is a controlled foreign corporation for its entire taxable year 1965. Corporation S is not a controlled foreign corporation at any time during its taxable years 1963 and 1964. Corporation S owns on December 31, 1964, $100,000 of tangible property (not described in section 956(b)(2)) located in the United States which it acquires during taxable years beginning after December 31, 1962. Corporation S's aggregate investment in United States property on December 31, 1964, is $100,000. Corporation S's current and accumulated earnings and profits (determined as provided in paragraph (b) of § 1.956-1) as of December 31, 1964, are in excess of $100,000. Assuming no change in S Corporation's aggregate investment in United States property during its taxable year 1965, S Corporation's increase in earnings invested in United States property for such taxable year is zero.

Example (3). Foreign corporation T uses the calendar year as a taxable year and is a controlled foreign corporation for its entire taxable years 1963, 1964, and 1966. At December 31, 1964, T Corporation's investment in United States property is $100,000. Corporation T is not a controlled foreign corporation at any time during its taxable year 1965 in which it acquires $25,000 of tangible property (not described in section 956 (b)(2)) located in the United States. On December 31, 1965, T Corporation holds the United States property of $100,000 which it held on December 31, 1964, and, in addition, the United States property acquired in 1965. Corporation T's aggregate investment in United States property at December 31, 1965, is $125,000. Corporation T's current and accumulated earnings and profits (determined as provided in paragraph (b) of § 1.956-1) as of December 31, 1965, are in excess of $125,000, and T Corporation pays no amount during 1965 to which section 959(c)(1) applies. Assuming no change in T Corporation's aggregate investment in United States property during its taxable year 1966, T Corporation's increase in earnings invested in United States property for such taxable year is zero.

(3) *Property owned through partnership.*—For purposes of section 956, if a controlled foreign corporation is a partner in a partnership that owns property that would be United States property, within the meaning of paragraph (a)(1) of this section, if owned directly by the controlled foreign corporation, the controlled foreign corporation will be treated as holding an interest in the property equal to its interest in the partnership and such interest will be treated as an interest in United States property. This paragraph (a)(3) applies to taxable years of a controlled foreign corporation beginning on or after July 23, 2002.

(b) *Exceptions.*—(1) *Excluded property.*—For purposes of section 956(a) and paragraph (a) of this section, United States property does not include the following types of property held by a foreign corporation:

(i) Obligations of the United States.

(ii) Money.

(iii) Deposits with persons carrying on the banking business, unless the deposits serve directly or indirectly as a pledge or guarantee within the meaning of paragraph (c) of this section. See paragraph (e)(2) of § 1.956-1.

(iv) Property located in the United States which is purchased in the United States for export to, or use in, foreign countries. For purposes of this subdivision, property to be used outside the United States will be considered property to be used in a foreign country. Whether property is of a type described in this subdivision is to be determined from all the facts and circumstances in each case. Property which constitutes export trade assets within the meaning of section 971(c)(2) and paragraph (c)(3) of § 1.971-1, will be considered property of a type described in this subdivision.

(v) Any obligation (as defined in paragraph (d)(2) of this section) of a United States person (as defined in section 957(d)) arising in connection with the sale or processing of property if the amount of such obligation outstanding at any time during the taxable year of the foreign corporation does not exceed an amount which is ordinary and necessary to carry on trade or business of both the other party to the sale or processing transaction and the United States person, or, if the sale or processing transaction occurs between related persons, would be ordinary and necessary to carry on the trade or business of both the other party to the sale or processing transaction and the

United States person if such persons were unrelated persons. Whether the amount of an obligation described in this subdivision is ordinary and necessary is to be determined from all the facts and circumstances in each case.

(vi) Any aircraft, railroad rolling stock, vessel, motor vehicle, or container used in the transportation of persons or property in foreign commerce and used predominantly outside the United States. Whether transportation property described in this subdivision is used in foreign commerce and predominantly outside the United States is to be determined from all the facts and circumstances in each case. As a general rule, such transportation property will be considered to be used predominantly outside the United States if 70 percent or more of the miles traversed (during the taxable year at the close of which a determination is made under section 956(a)(2)) in the use of such property are traversed outside the United States or if such property is located outside the United States 70 percent of the time during such taxable year.

(vii) An amount of assets described in paragraph (a) of this section of an insurance company equivalent to the unearned premiums or reserves which are ordinary and necessary for the proper conduct of that part of its insurance business which is attributable to contracts other than those described in section 953(a)(1) and the regulations thereunder. For purposes of this subdivision, a reserve will be considered ordinary and necessary for the proper conduct of an insurance business if, under the principles of paragraph (c) of § 1.953-4, such reserve would qualify as a reserve required by law. See paragraph (d)(3) of § 1.954-2 for determining, for purposes of this subdivision, the meaning of insurance company and of unearned premiums.

(viii) For taxable years beginning after December 31, 1975, the voting or nonvoting stock or obligations of an unrelated domestic corporation. For purposes of this subdivision, an unrelated domestic corporation is a domestic corporation which is neither a United States shareholder (as defined in section 951(b)) of the controlled foreign corporation making the investment, nor a corporation 25 percent or more of whose total combined voting power of all classes of stock entitled to vote is owned or considered as owned (within the meaning of section 958(b)) by United States shareholders of the controlled foreign corporation making the investment. The determination of whether a domestic corporation is an unrelated corporation is made immediately after each acquisition of stock or obligations by the controlled foreign corporations.

(ix) For taxable years beginning after December 31, 1975, movable drilling rigs or barges and other movable exploration and exploitation equipment (other than a vessel or an aircraft) when used on the Continental Shelf (as defined in section 638) of the United States in the exploration for, development, removal, or transportation of natural resources from or under ocean waters. Property used on the Continental Shelf includes property located in the United States which is being constructed or is in storage or in transit within the United States for use on the Continental Shelf. In general, the type of property which qualifies for the exception under this subdivision includes any movable property which would be entitled to the investment credit if used outside the United States in certain geographical areas of the Western Hemisphere pursuant to section 48(a)(2)(B)(x) (without reference to sections 49 and 50).

(x) An amount of—

(a) A controlled foreign corporation's assets described in paragraph (a) of this section equivalent to its earnings and profits which are accumulated after December 31, 1962, and are attributable to items of income described in section 952(b) and the regulations thereunder, reduced by the amount of

(b) The earnings and profits of such corporation which are applied in a taxable year of such corporation beginning after December 31, 1962, to discharge a liability on property, but only if the liability was in existence at the close of such corporation's taxable year immediately preceding its first taxable year beginning after December 31, 1962, and the property would have been United States property if it had been acquired by such corporation immediately before such discharge.

For purposes of this subdivision, distributions made by such corporation for any taxable year shall be considered first made out of earnings and profits for such year other than earnings and profits referred to in *(a)* of this subdivision.

(2) *Statement required.*—If a United States shareholder of a controlled foreign corporation excludes any property from the United States property of such controlled foreign corporation on the ground that section 956(b)(2) applies to such excluded property, he shall attach to his return a statement setting forth, by categories described in paragraph (a)(1) of this section, the amount of United States property of the controlled foreign corporation and, by categories described in subparagraph (1) of this paragraph, the amount of such property which is excluded.

(c) *Treatment of pledges and guarantees.*— (1) *General rule.*—Except as provided in subparagraph (4) of this paragraph, any obligation (as defined in paragraph (d)(2) of this section) of a United States person (as defined in section 957(d)) with respect to which a controlled foreign corporation is a pledgor or guarantor shall be considered for purposes of section 956(a) and paragraph (a) of this section to be United States property held by such controlled foreign corporation.

(2) *Indirect pledge or guarantee.*—If the assets of a controlled foreign corporation serve at any time, even though indirectly, as security for the performance of an obligation of a United States person, then, for purposes of paragraph (c)(1) of this section, the controlled foreign corporation will be considered a pledgor or guarantor of that obligation. For this purpose the pledge of stock of a controlled foreign corporation will be considered as the indirect pledge of the assets of the corporation if at least 66⅔ percent of the total combined voting power of all classes of stock entitled to vote is pledged and if the pledge of stock is accompanied by one or more negative covenants or similar restrictions on the shareholder effectively limiting the corporation's discretion with respect to the disposition of assets and the incurrence of liabilities other than in the ordinary course of business. This paragraph (c)(2) applies only to pledges and guarantees which are made after September 8, 1980. For purposes of this paragraph (c)(2) a refinancing shall be considered as a new pledge or guarantee.

(3) *Illustrations.*—The following examples illustrate the application of this paragraph (c):

Example (1). A, a United States person, borrows $100,000 from a bank in foreign country X on December 31, 1964. On the same date controlled foreign corporation R pledges its assets as security for A's performance of A's obligation to repay such loan. The place at which or manner in which A uses the money is not material. For purposes of paragraph (b) of § 1.956-1, R Corporation will be considered to hold A's obligation to repay the bank $100,000, and, under the provisions of paragraph (e)(2) of § 1.956-1, the amount taken into account in computing R Corporation's aggregate investment in United States property on December 31, 1964, is the unpaid principal amount of the obligation on that date ($100,000).

Example (2). The facts are the same as in example (1), except that R Corporation participates in the transaction, not by pledging its assets as security for A's performance of A's obligation to repay the loan, but by agreeing to buy for $100,000 at maturity the note representing A's obligation if A does not repay the loan. Separate arrangements are made with respect to the payment of the interest on the loan. The agreement of R Corporation to buy the note constitutes a guarantee of A's obligation. For purposes of paragraph (b) of § 1.956-1, R Corporation will be considered to hold A's obligation to repay the bank $100,000, and, under the provisions of paragraph (e)(2) of § 1.956-1, the amount taken into account in computing R Corporation's aggregate investment in United States property on December 31, 1964, is the unpaid principal amount of the obligation on that date ($100,000).

Example (3). A, a United States person, borrows $100,000 from a bank on December 10, 1981, pledging 70 percent of the stock of X, a controlled foreign corporation, as collateral for the loan. A and X use the calendar year as their taxable year. In the loan agreement, among other things, A agrees not to cause or permit X Corporation to do any of the following without the consent of the bank:

(a) Borrow money or pledge assets, except as to borrowings in the ordinary course of business of X Corporation;

(b) Guarantee, assume, or become liable on the obligation of another, or invest in or lend funds to another;

(c) Merge or consolidate with any other corporation or transfer shares of any controlled subsidiary;

(d) Sell or lease (other than in the ordinary course of business) or otherwise dispose of any substantial part of its assets;

(e) Pay or secure any debt owing by X Corporation to A; and

(f) Pay any dividends, except in such amounts as may be required to make interest or principal payments on A's loan from the bank.

A retains the right to vote the stock unless a default occurs by A. Under paragraph (c)(2) of this section, the assets of X Corporation serve indirectly as security for A's performance of A's obligation to repay the loan and X Corporation will be considered a pledgor or guarantor with respect to that obligation. For purposes of paragraph (b) of § 1.956-1, X Corporation will be considered to hold A's obligation to repay the bank $100,000 and under paragraph (e)(2) of § 1.956-1, the amount taken into account in computing X Corporation's aggregate investment in United States property on December 31, 1981, is the unpaid principal amount of the obligation on that date.

(4) *Special rule for certain conduit financing arrangements.*—The rule contained in subparagraph (1) of this paragraph shall not apply to a pledge or a guarantee by a controlled foreign corporation to secure the obligation of a United States person if such United States person is a mere conduit in a financing arrangement. Whether the United States person is a mere conduit in a financing arrangement will depend upon all the facts and circumstances in each case. A United States person will be con-

sidered a mere conduit in a financing arrangement in a case in which a controlled foreign corporation pledges stock of its subsidiary corporation, which is also a controlled foreign corporation, to secure the obligation of such United States person, where the following conditions are satisfied:

(i) Such United States person is a domestic corporation which is not engaged in the active conduct of a trade or business and has no substantial assets other than those arising out of its relending of the funds borrowed by it on such obligation to the controlled foreign corporation whose stock is pledged; and

(ii) The assets of such United States person are at all times substantially offset by its obligation to the lender.

(d) *Definitions.*—(1) *Meaning of "acquired".*—(i) *Applicable rules.*—For purposes of this section—

(a) Property shall be considered acquired by a foreign corporation when such corporation acquires an adjusted basis in the property;

(b) Property which is an obligation of a United States person with respect to which a controlled foreign corporation is a pledgor or guarantor (within the meaning of paragraph (c) of this section) shall be considered acquired when the corporation becomes liable as a pledgor or guarantor or is otherwise considered a pledgor or guarantor (within the meaning of paragraph (c)(2) of this section); and

(c) Property shall not be considered acquired by a foreign corporation if—

(1) Such property is acquired in a transaction in which gain or loss would not be recognized under this chapter to such corporation if such corporation were a domestic corporation;

(2) The basis of the property acquired by the foreign corporation is the same as the basis of the property exchanged by such corporation; and

(3) The property exchanged by the foreign corporation was not United States property (as defined in paragraph (a)(1) of this section) but would have been such property if it had been acquired by such corporation immediately before such exchange.

(ii) *Illustrations.*—The application of the provisions of this subparagraph may be illustrated by the following examples:

Example (1). Foreign corporation R uses the calendar year as a taxable year and acquires before January 1, 1963, stock of domestic corporation M having as to R Corporation an adjusted basis of $10,000. The stock of M Corporation is not United States property of R Corporation on December 31, 1962, since it is not acquired in a taxable year of R Corporation beginning on or after January 1, 1963. On June 30, 1963, R Corporation sells the M Corporation stock for $15,000 in cash and expends such amount in acquiring stock of domestic corporation N which has as to R Corporation an adjusted basis of $15,000. For purposes of determining R Corporation's aggregate investment in United States property on December 31, 1963, R Corporation has, by virtue of acquiring the stock of N Corporation, acquired $15,000 of United States property.

Example (2). Foreign corporation S, a controlled foreign corporation for the entire period here involved, uses the calendar year as a taxable year and purchases for $100,000 on December 31, 1963, tangible property (not described in section 956(b)(2)) located in the United States and having a remaining estimated useful life of 10 years, subject to a mortgage of $80,000 payable in 5 annual installments. The property constitutes United States property as of December 31, 1963, and the amount taken into account for purposes of determining the aggregate amount of S Corporation's investment in United States property under paragraph (b) of §1.956-1 is $20,000. No depreciation is sustained with respect to the property during the taxable year 1963. During the taxable year 1964, S Corporation pays $16,000 on the mortgage and sustains $10,000 of depreciation with respect to the property. As of December 31, 1964, the amount taken into account with respect to the property for purposes of determining the aggregate amount of S Corporation's investment in United States property under paragraph (b) of §1.956-1 is $26,000, computed as follows:

Cost of property		$100,000
Less: Reserve for depreciation		10,000
Adjusted basis of property		90,000
Less: Liability to which property is subject:		
Gross amount of mortgage	$80,000	
Payment during 1964	16,000	$64,000
Amount taken into account (12/31/64)		$26,000

Example (3). Controlled foreign corporation T uses the calendar year as a taxable year and acquires on December 31, 1963, $10,000 of United States property not described in section 956(b)(2); no depreciation is sustained with respect to the property during 1963. Corporation T's current and accumulated earnings and profits (determined as provided in paragraph (b) of § 1.956-1) as of December 31, 1963, are in excess of $10,000, and T Corporation's United States shareholders include in their gross income under section 951(a)(1)(B) their pro rata share of T Corporation's increase ($10,000) for 1963 in earnings invested in United States property. On January 1, 1964, T Corporation acquires an additional $10,000 of United States property not described in section 956(b)(2). Each of the two items of property has an estimated useful life of 5 years, and T Corporation sustains $4,000 of depreciation with respect to such properties during its taxable year 1964. Corporation T's current and accumulated earnings and profits as of December 31, 1964, exceed $16,000, determined as provided in paragraph (b) of § 1.956-1. Corporation T pays no amounts during 1963 to which section 959(c)(1) applies. Corporation T's investment of earnings in United States property at December 31, 1964, is $16,000, and its increase for 1964 in earnings invested in United States property is $6,000.

Example (4). Foreign corporation U uses the calendar year as a taxable year and acquires before January 1, 1963, stock in domestic corporation M having as to U Corporation an adjusted basis of $10,000. On December 1, 1964, pursuant to a statutory merger described in section 368(a)(1), M Corporation merges into domestic corporation N, and U Corporation receives on such date one share of stock in N Corporation, the surviving corporation, for each share of stock it held in M Corporation. Pursuant to section 354 no gain or loss is recognized to U Corporation, and pursuant to section 358 the basis of the property received (stock of N Corporation) is the same as that of the property exchanged (stock of M Corporation). Corporation U is not considered for purposes of section 956 to have acquired United States property by reason of its receipt of the stock in N Corporation.

Example (5). The facts are the same as in example (4), except that U Corporation acquires the stock of M Corporation on February 1, 1963, rather than before January 1, 1963. For purposes of determining U Corporation's aggregate investment in United States property on December 31, 1963, U Corporation has, by virtue of acquiring the stock of M Corporation, acquired $10,000 of United States property. Corporation U pays no amount during 1963 to which section 959(c)(1) applies. The reorganization and resulting acquisition on December 1, 1964, by U Corporation of N Corporation's stock also represents an acquisition of United States property; however, assuming no other change in U Corporation's aggregate investment in United States property during 1964, U Corporation's increase for such year in earnings invested in United States property is zero.

(2) [Reserved.] [Reg. § 1.956-2.]

☐ [*T.D. 6704, 2-19-64. Amended by T.D. 7712, 8-6-80; T.D. 7797, 11-24-81; T.D. 8209, 6-13-88 and T.D. 9008, 7-22-2002.*]

§ 1.956-3T. Certain trade or service receivables acquired from United States persons (temporary).—(a) *In general.*—For purposes of section 956(a) and § 1.956-1, the term "United States property" also includes any trade or service receivable if the trade or service receivable is acquired (directly or indirectly) after March 1, 1984, from a related person who is a United States person (as defined in section 7701(a)(30)) (hereinafter referred to as a "related United States person") and the obligor under the receivable is a United States person. A trade or service receivable described in this paragraph shall be considered to be United States property notwithstanding the exceptions (other than subparagraph (H)) contained in section 956(b)(2). The terms "trade or service receivable" and "related person" have the respective meanings given to such terms by section 864(d) and the regulations thereunder. For purposes of this section, the exception contained in § 1.956-2T(d)(2)(i)(B) for short-term obligations shall not apply to service receivables described in this paragraph.

(b) *Acquisition of a trade or service receivable.*—(1) *General rule.*—The rules of § 1.864-8T(c)(1) shall be applied to determine whether a controlled foreign corporation has acquired a trade or service receivable.

(2) *Indirect acquisitions.*—(i) *Acquisition through unrelated person.*—A trade or service receivable will be considered to be acquired from a related person if it is acquired from an unrelated person who acquired (directly or indirectly) such receivable from a person who is a related person to the acquiring person.

(ii) *Acquisition by nominee or pass-through entity.*—A controlled foreign corporation will be considered to have acquired a trade or service receivable of a related United States person held on its behalf:

(A) By a nominee or by a partnership, simple trust, S corporation or other pass-through entity to the extent the controlled foreign corporation owns (directly or indirectly) a beneficial interest in such partnership or other pass-through entity; or

(B) By another foreign corporation that is controlled by the controlled foreign corporation, if one of the principal purposes for creating, organizing, or funding such other foreign corporation (through capital contributions or debt) is to avoid the application of section 956. See § 1.956-1T.

The rule of this paragraph (b)(2)(ii) does not limit the application of paragraph (b)(2)(iii) of this section regarding the characterization of trade or service receivables of unrelated persons acquired pursuant to certain swap or pooling arrangements. The following examples illustrate the application of this paragraph (b)(2)(ii).

Example (1). FS1, a controlled foreign corporation with substantial accumulated earnings and profits, contributes $2,000,000 to PS, a partnership, in exchange for a 20 percent limited partnership interest in PS. PS purchases trade or service receivables of FS1's domestic parent, P. The obligors under the receivables are United States persons. PS does not purchase receivables of any person who is related to any other partner in PS. Under paragraph (b)(2)(ii)(A) of this section, there is an investment of the earnings of FS1 in United States property equal to 20 percent of PS's basis in the receivables of P.

Example (2). FS1, a controlled foreign corporation, has accumulated more than $3,000,000 in earnings and profits. It organizes a wholly-owned foreign corporation, FS2, with a $2,000,000 equity contribution. FS2 has no earnings and profits. FS2 uses the funds to purchase trade or service receivables of FS1's domestic parent, P. The obligors under the receivables are United States persons. Under paragraph (b)(2)(ii)(B) of this section, there is an investment of the earnings of FS1 in United States property equal to $2,000,000.

(iii) *Swap or pooling arrangements.*—A trade or service receivable of an unrelated person will be considered to be a trade or service receivable acquired from a related United States person and subject to the rules of this section if it is acquired in accordance with an arrangement that involves two or more groups of related persons that are unrelated to each other and the effect of the arrangement is that one or more related persons in each group acquire (directly or indirectly) trade or service receivables of one or more unrelated United States persons who are also parties to the arrangement, in exchange for reciprocal purchases of receivables of United States persons in the first group. The following example illustrates the application of this paragraph (b)(2)(iii).

Example. Controlled foreign corporations A, B, C, and D are wholly-owned subsidiaries of domestic corporations M, N, O, and P, respectively. M, N, O, and P are not related persons. According to a prearranged plan, A, B, C, and D each acquire trade or service receivables of M, N, O, and/or P. The obligors under some or all of the receivables acquired by each of A, B, C, and D are United States persons. Because the effect of this arrangement is that the unrelated groups acquire each other's trade or service receivables of United States persons pursuant to the arrangement, there is an investment of the earnings of each of A, B, C, and D in United States property to the extent of the purchase price of those receivables under which the obligors are United States persons.

(iv) *Financing arrangements.*—If a controlled foreign corporation participates (directly or indirectly) in a lending transaction that results in a loan to a United States person who purchases property described in section 1221(1) (hereinafter referred to as "inventory property") or services of a related United States person, or to any person who purchases trade or service receivables of a related United States person under which the obligor is a United States person, or to a person who is related to any such purchaser, and if the loan would not have been made or maintained on the same terms but for the corresponding purchase, then the controlled foreign corporation shall be considered to have indirectly acquired a trade or service receivable described in paragraph (a) of this section. For purposes of this paragraph (b)(2)(iv), it is immaterial that the sums lent are not, in fact, the sums used to finance the purchase of the inventory property or services or trade or service receivables of a related United States person. The amount to be taken into account with respect to the controlled foreign corporation's investment in United States property (resulting from application of this paragraph (b)(2)(iv)) shall be the amount lent pursuant to a lending transaction described in this paragraph (b)(2)(iv), if the amount lent is equal to or less than the purchase price of the inventory property, services, or trade or service receivables. If the amount lent is greater than the purchase price of the inventory property, services or receivables, the amount to be taken into account shall be the purchase price. The following examples illustrate the application of this paragraph (b)(2)(iv).

Example (1). P, a domestic corporation, owns all of the outstanding stock of FS1, a controlled foreign corporation. P sells equipment for $2,000,000 to X, an unrelated United States person. FS1 makes a $1,000,000 short-term loan to X, which loan would not have been made or maintained on the same terms but for X's purchase of P's equipment. Because FS1 directly participates in a lending transaction described in this paragraph (b)(2)(iv), FS1 is considered to have acquired the receivable of a related United States person. Thus, there is an investment of FS1's earnings and profits in United States property in the amount of $1,000,000.

Example (2). The facts are the same as in Example (1), except that instead of loaning money to X directly, FS1 deposits $3,000,000 with an unrelated financial institution that loans $2,000,000 to X in order for X to purchase P's equipment. The loan would not have been made or maintained on the same terms but for the corresponding deposit. Accordingly, the deposit and the loan are treated as a direct loan from FS1 to X. See Rev. Rul. 87-89, 1987-37 I.R.B. 16. Because FS1 indirectly participates in a lending transaction described in this paragraph (b)(2)(iv), FS1 is considered to have acquired the receivable of a related United States person. Thus, there is an investment of FS1's earnings and profits in United States property in the amount of $2,000,000.

Example (3). P, a domestic corporation, owns all of the outstanding stock of FS1, a controlled foreign corporation. FS1 makes a $3,000,000 loan to U, an unrelated foreign corporation, in connection with U's purchase for $2,000,000 of receivables from the sale of inventory property by P to United States obligors. Because FS1 directly participates in a lending transaction described in this paragraph (b)(2)(iv), FS1 is considered to have acquired receivables of a related United States person. Thus, there is an investment of FS1's earnings and profits in United States property in the amount of $2,000,000.

(c) *Substitution of obligor.*—For purposes of this section, the substitution of another person for a United States obligor may be disregarded. Thus, if a purchaser who is a United States person arranges for a foreign person to pay a United States seller of inventory property or services and the seller transfers by sale or otherwise to its own controlled foreign corporation the foreign person's obligation for payment, then the acquisition of the foreign person's obligation shall constitute an investment in United States property by the seller's controlled foreign corporation, unless it can be demonstrated by the parties to the transaction that the primary purpose for the arrangement was not the avoidance of section 956. The following example illustrates the application of this paragraph.

Example. P, a domestic corporation, owns all of the outstanding stock of FS1, a controlled foreign corporation with substantial accumulated earnings and profits. P sells equipment to X, a domestic corporation unrelated to P. To pay for the equipment, X arranges for a foreign financing entity to issue a note to P. P then sells the note to FS1. FS1 has made an investment in United States property in the amount of the purchase price of the note. [Temporary Reg. § 1.956-3T.]

☐ [T.D. 8209, 6-13-88.]

§ 1.957-1. Definition of controlled foreign corporation.—(a) *In general.*—The term *controlled foreign corporation* means any foreign corporation of which more than 50 percent (or such lesser amount as is provided in section 957(b) or section 953(c)) of either—

(1) The total combined voting power of all classes of stock of the corporation entitled to vote; or

(2) The total value of the stock of the corporation, is owned within the meaning of section 958(a), or (except for purposes of section 953(c)) is considered as owned by applying the rules of section 958(b) and § 1.958-2, by United States shareholders on any day during the taxable year of such foreign corporation. For the definition of the term *United States shareholder*, see sections 951(b) and 953(c)(1)(A). For the definition of the term *foreign corporation*, see § 301.7701-5 of this chapter (Procedure and Administration Regulations). For the treatment of associations as corporations, see section 7701(a)(3) and §§ 301.7701-1 and 301.7701-2 of this chapter. For the definition of the term *stock*, see sections 958(a)(3) and 7701(a)(7). For the classification of a member in an association, joint stock company or insurance company as a shareholder, see section 7701(a)(8).

(b) *Percentage of total combined voting power owned by United States shareholders.*—(1) *Meaning of combined voting power.*—In determining for purposes of paragraph (a) of this section whether United States shareholders own the requisite percentage of total combined voting power of all classes of stock entitled to vote, consideration will be given to all the facts and circumstances of each case. In all cases, however, United States shareholders of a foreign corporation will be deemed to own the requisite percentage of total combined voting power with respect to such corporation—

(i) If they have the power to elect, appoint, or replace a majority of that body of persons exercising, with respect to such corporation, the powers ordinarily exercised by the board of directors of a domestic corporation;

(ii) If any person or persons elected or designated by such shareholders have the power, where such shareholders have the power to elect exactly one-half of the members of such governing body of such foreign corporation, either to cast a vote deciding an evenly divided vote of such body or, for the duration of any deadlock which may arise, to exercise the powers ordinarily exercised by such governing body; or

(iii) If the powers which would ordinarily be exercised by the board of directors of a domestic corporation are exercised with respect to such foreign corporation by a person whom such shareholders have the power to elect, appoint, or replace.

(2) *Shifting of formal voting power.*—Any arrangement to shift formal voting power away from United States shareholders of a foreign corporation will not be given effect if in reality voting power is retained. The mere ownership of stock entitled to vote does not by itself mean that the shareholder owning such stock has the voting power of such stock for purposes of section 957. For example, if there is any agreement, whether express or implied, that any shareholder will not vote his stock or will vote it only in a specified manner, or that sharehlders owning stock having not more than 50 percent of the total combined voting power will exercise voting power normally possessed by a majority of stockholders, then the nominal ownership of the voting power will be disregarded in determining which shareholders actually hold such voting power, and this determination will be made on the basis of such agreement. Moreover, where United States shareholders own shares of one or more classes of stock of a foreign corporation which has another class of stock outstanding, the voting power ostensibly provided such other class of stock will be deemed owned by any person or persons on whose behalf it is exercised or, if not exercised, will be disregarded if the percentage of voting power of such other class of stock is substantially greater than its proportionate share of the corporate earnings, if the facts indicate that the shareholders of such other class of stock do not exercise their voting rights independently or fail to exercise such voting rights, and if a principal purpose of the arrangement is to avoid the classification of such foreign corporation as a controlled foreign corporation under section 957.

(c) *Illustrations.*—The application of this section may be illustrated by the following examples:

Example (1). Foreign corporation R has two classes of capital stock outstanding, 60 shares of class A stock, and 40 shares of class B stock. Each share of each class of stock has one vote for all purposes. E, a United States person, owns 51 shares of class A stock. Corporation R is a controlled foreign corporation.

Example (2). Foreign corporation S has three classes of capital stock outstanding, consisting of 60 shares of class A stock, 40 shares of class B stock, and 200 shares of class C stock. The owners of a majority of class A stock are entitled to elect 6 of the 10 corporate directors, and the owners of a majority of the class B stock are entitled to elect the other 4 of the 10 directors. Class C stock has no voting rights. D, a United States person, owns all of the shares of the class C stock. He also owns 31 shares of class A stock and as such an owner can elect 6 members of the board of directors. None of the remaining shares of class A stock, or the 40 shares of class B stock, is owned, or considered as owned, within the meaning of section 958, by a United States person. Since, as owner of 31 shares of the class A stock, D has sufficient voting power to elect 6 directors, D has more than 50 percent of the total combined voting power of all classes of stock entitled to vote, and S Corporation is a controlled foreign corporation.

Example (3). M, a United States person, owns a 51-percent interest in R Company, a foreign company of which he is a member. The company, if it were domestic, would be taxable as a corporation. The remaining interest of 49 percent in the company is owned by seven other members none of whom is a United States person. The memorandum of association of R Company provides for only one manager, who with respect to the company exercises the powers ordinarily exercised by a board of directors of a domestic corporation. The manager is to be elected by unanimous agreement of all the members. Since M owns 51 percent of the company, he will be deemed to own more than 50 percent of the total combined voting power of all classes of stock of R Company entitled to vote, notwithstanding that he has power to elect a manager only with the agreement of the other members. Company R is a controlled foreign corporation.

Example (4). Domestic corporation M owns a 49-percent interest in S Company, a foreign company of which it is a member. The company, if it were domestic, would be taxable as a corporation. Company S is formed under the laws of foreign country Y. The remaining interest of 51 percent in S Company is owned by persons who are not United States persons. The organization contract of S Company provides for one manager, B, a citizen and resident of country Y who is an officer of M Corporation in charge of its foreign operations in such country, or any person M Corporation may at any time appoint to succeed B in such capacity. The manager has the sole authority with respect to S Company to exercise powers ordinarily exercised by a board of directors of a domestic corporation. Since M Corporation has the discretionary power to replace B and to appoint his successor as manager of S Company, the company is a controlled foreign corporation.

Example (5). N, a United States person, owns 50 percent of the outstanding shares of the only class of capital stock of foreign corporation R. An additional 48 percent of the outstanding shares is owned by foreign corporation S. The remaining 2 percent of shares is owned by P, a citizen and resident of foreign country T, who regularly acts as attorney for N in the conduct of N's business affairs in country T. All of the shares of the outstanding capital stock of R Corporation are bearer shares. At the time of the issuance of the shares to him, P places the certificates for such shares in a depository to which N has access. On several occasions N, with P's acquiescence, has taken such shares from the depository and, on one such occasion, used the shares as collateral in borrowing funds on a loan. Although dividends, when paid, are paid to P on his shares, his charges to N for legal fees are reduced by the amount of the dividends paid on such shares. Although P votes his shares at meetings of shareholders, the facts set forth above indicate an implied agreement between P and N that N is really to retain dominion over the stock. N is deemed to own the voting rights ostensibly attached to the stock owned by P, and R Corporation is a controlled foreign corporation.

Example (6). M, a domestic corporation which manufactures in the United States and distributes all of its production for foreign consumption through N, a person other than a related person or a United States person, forms foreign corporation S to purchase products from M Corporation and sell them to N. Corporations S and M have common directors. The outstanding capital stock of S Corporation consists of 10,000 shares of $100 par value class A stock, which has no voting rights except to vote for dissolution of the corporation on a share for share basis, and 500 shares of no par class B stock which has full voting rights. Each class of the outstanding stock is to participate on a share for share basis in any dividend. The class A stock has a preference as to assets on dissolution of the corporation to the extent of its par value as well as the right to participate with the class B stock in all other assets on a share for share basis. All of the shares of class A stock are issued to M Corporation in return for property having a value of $1 million. Of the class B stock, 300 of the shares are issued to N in return for $3,000 in cash and 200 shares are issued to M Corporation for $2,000 in cash. At stockholder meetings N never votes in opposition to M Corporation on important issues. Corporation S has average annual earnings of $200,000, all of which will be subpart F income if S Corporation is held to be a controlled foreign corporation. All such earnings are accumulated. Although N ostensibly has 60 percent of the voting power of S Corporation by virtue of his ownership of 300 shares of class B stock, he has the right to only approximately 3 percent of any dividends which may be paid by S Corporation; in addition, upon liquidation of S Corporation, N is entitled to share in the assets only after M Corporation has received the par value of its 10,000 shares of class A stock, or $1 million. Thus, the voting power owned by N is substantially greater than its proportionate share of the earnings of S Corporation. In addition, the facts set forth above indicate that N is not exercising his voting rights independently and that a principal purpose of the capitalization arrangement is to avoid classification of S Corporation as a controlled foreign corporation. For these reasons, the voting power ostensibly provided the class B stock will be deemed owned by M Corporation, and S Corporation is a controlled foreign corporation.

Example (7). Foreign corporation A, authorized to issue 100 shares of one class of capital stock, issues, for $1,000 per share, 45 shares to domestic corporation M, 45 shares to foreign corporation B, and 10 shares to foreign corporation C. Corporation C, a bank, lends $3 million to finance the operations of A Corporation. In the course of negotiating these financial arrangements, D, an officer of C Corporation, and E, an officer of M Corporation, orally agree that C Corporation will vote its stock as M Corporation directs. By virtue of such oral agreement M Corporation possesses the voting power ostensibly owned by C Corporation, and A Corporation is a controlled foreign corporation.

Example 8. For its prior taxable year, *JV*, a foreign corporation, had outstanding 1000 shares of class A stock, which is voting common, and 1000 shares of class B stock, which is nonvoting preferred. *DP*, a domestic corporation, and *FP*, a foreign corporation, each owned precisely 500 shares of both class A and class B stock, and each elected 5 of the 10 members of *JV*'s board of directors. The other facts and circumstances were such that *JV* was not a controlled foreign corporation on any day of the prior taxable year. On the first day of the current taxable year, *DP* purchased one share of class B stock from *FP*. *JV* was a controlled foreign corporation on the following day because over 50 percent of the total value in the corporation was held by a person that was a United States shareholder under section 951(b). See § 1.951-1(f).

Example 9. The facts are the same as in *Example 8* except that the stock of *FP* was publicly traded, *FP* had one class of stock, and on the first day of the current taxable year *DP* purchased one share of *FP* stock on the foreign stock exchange instead of purchasing one share of *JV* stock from *FP*. *JV* became a controlled foreign corporation on the following day because over 50 percent of the total value in the corporation was held by a person that was a

United States shareholder under section 951(b).

Example 10. X, a foreign corporation, is incorporated under the laws of country Y. Under the laws of country Y, X is considered a mutual insurance company. X issues insurance policies that provide the policyholder with the right to vote for directors of the corporation, the right to a share of the assets upon liquidation in proportion to premiums paid, and the right to receive policyholder dividends in proportion to premiums paid. Only policyholders are provided with the right to vote for directors, share in assets upon liquidation, and receive distributions. United States policyholders contribute 25 percent of the premiums and have 25 percent of the outstanding rights to vote for the board of directors. Based on these facts, the United States policyholders are United States shareholders owning the requisite combined voting power and value. Thus, X is a controlled foreign corporation for purposes of taking into account related person insurance income under section 953(c).

(d) *Effective date.*—Paragraphs (a) and (c) *Examples 8* through *10* of this section are effective for taxable years of a controlled foreign corporation beginning after March 7, 1996. [Reg. § 1.957-1.]

☐ [T.D. 6688, 10-30-63. *Amended by* T.D. 8216, 7-20-88; T.D. 8618, 9-6-95 *and* T.D. 8704, 12-31-96.]

§ 1.957-3T. United States person defined (temporary).—(a) *Basic rule.*—(1) *In general.*—The term *United States person* has the same meaning for purposes of sections 951 through 965 which it has under section 7701(a)(30) and the regulations thereunder, except as provided in paragraphs (b) and (c) of this section which provide, with respect to corporations organized in possessions of the United States, that certain residents of such possessions are not United States persons. The effect of determining that an individual is not a United States person for such purposes is to exclude such individual in determining whether a foreign corporation created or organized in, or under the laws of, a possession of the United States is a controlled foreign corporation. See § 1.957-1 for the definition of the term *controlled foreign corporation.*

(2) *Special provisions applicable to possessions of the United States.*—For purposes of this section—

(i) The term *possession of the United States* means the Commonwealth of Puerto Rico (Puerto Rico) or any section 931 possession.

(ii) The term *section 931 possession* has the same meaning which it has under § 1.931-1T(c)(1).

(iii) The rules of § 1.937-1T shall apply for determining whether an individual is a bona fide resident of a possession of the United States.

(iv) The rules of § 1.937-2T shall apply for determining whether income is from sources within a possession of the United States.

(v) The rules of § 1.937-3T shall apply for determining whether income is effectively connected with the conduct of a trade or business in a possession of the United States.

(b) *Puerto Rico corporation and resident.*—An individual (who, without regard to this paragraph (b), is a United States person) shall not be considered a United States person with respect to a foreign corporation created or organized in, or under the laws of, Puerto Rico for the taxable year of such corporation which ends with or within the taxable year of such individual if—

(1) Such individual is a bona fide resident of Puerto Rico during his entire taxable year in which or with which the taxable year of such foreign corporation ends; and

(2) A dividend received by such individual from such corporation during the taxable year of such corporation would, for purposes of section 933(1), be treated as income derived from sources within Puerto Rico.

(c) *Section 931 possession corporation and resident.*—An individual (who, without regard to this paragraph (c), is a United States person) shall not be considered a United States person with respect to a foreign corporation created or organized in, or under the laws of, a section 931 possession for the taxable year of such corporation which ends with or within the taxable year of such individual if—

(1) Such individual is a bona fide resident of such section 931 possession during his entire taxable year in which or with which the taxable year of such foreign corporation ends; and

(2) Such corporation satisfies the following conditions—

(i) 80 percent or more of its gross income for the 3-year period ending at the close of the taxable year (or for such part of such period as such corporation or any predecessor has been in existence) was derived from sources within section 931 possessions or was effectively connected with the conduct of a trade or business in section 931 possessions; and

(ii) 50 percent or more of its gross income for such period (or part) was derived from the active conduct of a trade or business within section 931 possessions.

(d) *Effective date.*—This section shall apply for taxable years ending after October 22, 2004. [Temporary Reg. § 1.957-3T.]

☐ [*T.D.* 9194, 4-6-2005.]

§ 1.958-1. Direct and indirect ownership of stock.—(a) *In general.*—Section 958(a) provides that, for purposes of sections 951 to 964 (other than sections 955(b)(1)(A) and (B) and 955(c)(2)(A)(ii) (as in effect before the enactment of the Tax Reduction Act of 1975), and 960(a)(1)), stock owned means—

(1) Stock owned directly; and

(2) Stock owned with the application of paragraph (b) of this section.

The rules of section 958(a) and this section provide a limited form of stock attribution primarily for use in determining the amount taxable to a United States shareholder under section 951(a). These rules also apply for purposes of other provisions of the Code and regulations which make express reference to section 958(a).

(b) *Stock ownership through foreign entities.*—For purposes of paragraph (a)(2) of this section, stock owned, directly or indirectly, by or for a foreign corporation, foreign partnership, foreign trust (within the meaning of section 7701(a)(31)) described in sections 671 through 679, or other foreign trust or foreign estate (within the meaning of section 7701(a)(31)) shall be considered as being owned proportionately by its shareholders, partners, grantors or other persons treated as owners under sections 671 through 679 of any portion of the trust that includes the stock, or beneficiaries, respectively. Stock considered to be owned by reason of the application of this paragraph shall, for purposes of reapplying this paragraph, be treated as actually owned by such person. Thus, this rule creates a chain of ownership; however, since the rule applies only to stock owned by a foreign entity, attribution under the rule stops with the first United States person in the chain of ownership running from the foreign entity. The application of this paragraph may be illustrated by the following example:

Example. Domestic corporation M owns 75 percent of the one class of stock in foreign corporation R, which in turn owns 80 percent of the one class of stock in foreign corporation S, which in turn owns 90 percent of the one class of stock in foreign corporation T. Under this paragraph, R Corporation is considered as owning 80 percent of the 90 percent of the stock which S Corporation owns in T Corporation, or 72 percent. Corporation M is considered as owning 75 percent of such 72 percent of the stock in T Corporation, or 54 percent. Since M Corporation is a domestic corporation, the attribution under this paragraph stops with M Corporation, even though, illustratively, such corporation is wholly owned by domestic corporation N.

(c) *Rules of application.*—(1) *Special rule for mutual insurance companies.*—For purposes of applying paragraph (a) of this section in the case of a foreign mutual insurance company, the term "stock" shall include any certificate entitling the holder to voting power in the corporation.

(2) *Amount of interest in foreign corporation, foreign partnership, foreign trust, or foreign estate.*—The determination of a person's proportionate interest in a foreign corporation, foreign partnership, foreign trust, or foreign estate will be made on the basis of all the facts and circumstances in each case. Generally, in determining a person's proportionate interest in a foreign corporation, the purpose for which the rules of section 958(a) and this section are being applied will be taken into account. Thus, if the rules of section 958(a) are being applied to determine the amount of stock owned for purposes of section 951(a), a person's proportionate interest in a foreign corporation will generally be determined with reference to such person's interest in the income of such corporation. If the rules of section 958(a) are being applied to determine the amount of voting power owned for purposes of section 951(b) or 957, a person's proportionate interest in a foreign corporation will generally be determined with reference to the amount of voting power in such corporation owned by such person. However, any arrangement which artificially decreases a United States person's proportionate interest will not be recognized. See §§ 1.951-1 and 1.957-1.

(d) *Illustration.*—The application of this section may be illustrated by the following examples:

Example (1). United States persons A and B own 25 percent and 50 percent, respectively, of the one class of stock in foreign corporation M. Corporation M owns 80 percent of the one class of stock in foreign corporation N, and N Corporation owns 60 percent of the one class of stock in foreign corporation P. Under paragraph (b) of this section, M Corporation is considered to own 48 percent (80% of 60%) of the stock in P Corporation; such 48 percent is treated as actually owned by M Corporation for the purpose of again applying paragraph (b) of this section. Thus, A and B are considered to own 12 percent (25% of 48%) and 24 percent

(50% of 48%), respectively, of the stock in P Corporation.

Example (2). United States person C is a 60-percent partner in foreign partnership X. Partnership X owns 40 percent of the one class of stock in foreign corporation Q. Corporation Q is a 50-percent partner in foreign partnership Y, and partnership Y owns 100 percent of the one class of stock in foreign corporation R. By the application of paragraph (b) of this section, C is considered to own 12 percent (60% of 40% of 50% of 100%) of the stock in R Corporation.

Example (3). Foreign trust Z was created for the benefit of United States persons D, E, and F. Under the terms of the trust instrument, the trust income is required to be divided into three equal shares. Each beneficiary's share of the income may either be accumulated for him or distributed to him in the discretion of the trustee. In 1970, the trust is to terminate and there is to be paid over to each beneficiary the accumulated income applicable to his share and one-third of the corpus. The corpus of trust Z is composed of 90 percent of the one class of stock in foreign corporation S. By the application of this section, each of D, E, and F is considered to own 30 percent (⅓ of 90 percent) of the stock in S Corporation.

Example (4). Among the assets of foreign estate W are Blackacre and a block of stock, consisting of 75 percent of the one class of stock of foreign corporation T. Under the terms of the will governing estate W, Blackacre is left to G, a nonresident alien, for life, remainder to H, a nonresident alien, and the block of stock is left to United States person K. By the application of this section, K is considered to own the 75 percent of the stock of T Corporation, and G and H are not considered to own any of such stock.

[Reg. § 1.958-1.]

☐ [T.D. 6889, 7-11-66. Amended by T.D. 7893, 5-11-83 and T.D. 8955, 7-19-2001.]

§ 1.958-2. Constructive ownership of stock.—(a) *In general.*—Section 958(b) provides that, for purposes of sections 951(b), 954(d)(3), 956(b)(2), and 957, the rules of section 318(a) as modified by section 958(b) and this section shall apply to the extent that the effect is to treat a United States person as a United States shareholder within the meaning of section 951(b), to treat a person as a related person within the meaning of section 954(d)(3), to treat the stock of a domestic corporation as owned by a United States shareholder of a controlled foreign corporation under section 956(b)(2), or to treat a foreign corporation as a controlled foreign corporation under section 957. The rules contained in this section also apply for purposes of other provisions of the Code and regulations which make express reference to section 958(b).

(b) *Members of family.*—(1) *In general.*—Except as provided in subparagraph (3) of this paragraph, an individual shall be considered as owning the stock owned, directly or indirectly, by or for—

(i) His spouse (other than a spouse who is legally separated from the individual under a decree of divorce or separate maintenance); and

(ii) His children, grandchildren, and parents.

(2) *Effect of adoption.*—For purposes of subparagraph (1)(ii) of this paragraph, a legally adopted child of an individual shall be treated as a child of such individual by blood.

(3) *Stock owned by nonresident alien individual.*—For purposes of this paragraph, stock owned by a nonresident alien individual (other than a foreign trust or foreign estate) shall not be considered as owned by a United States citizen or a resident alien individual. However, this limitation does not apply for purposes of determining whether the stock of a domestic corporation is owned or considered as owned by a United States shareholder under section 956(b)(2) and § 1.956-2(b)(1)(viii). See section 958(b)(1).

(c) *Attribution from partnerships, estates, trusts, and corporations.*—(1) *In general.*—Except as provided in subparagraph (2) of this paragraph—

(i) *From partnerships and estates.*—Stock owned, directly or indirectly, by or for a partnership or estate shall be considered as owned proportionately by its partners or beneficiaries.

(ii) *From trusts.*—(a) *To beneficiaries.*—Stock owned, directly or indirectly, by or for a trust (other than employees' trust described in section 401(a) which is exempt from tax under section 501(a)) shall be considered as owned by its beneficiaries in proportion to the actuarial interest of such beneficiaries in such trust.

(b) *To owner.*—Stock owned, directly or indirectly, by or for any portion of a trust of which a person is considered the owner under sections 671 to 679 (relating to grantors and others treated as substantial owners) shall be considered as owned by such person.

(iii) *From corporations.*—If 10 percent or more in value of the stock in a corporation is owned, directly or indirectly, by or for any person, such person shall be considered as owning the stock owned, directly or indirectly, by or for such corporation, in that proportion which the value of the stock which such person so owns bears to the value of all the stock in such corporation. See section 958(b)(3).

(2) *Rules of application.*—For purposes of subparagraph (1) of this paragraph, if a partnership, estate, trust, or corporation owns, directly or indirectly, more than 50 percent of the total combined voting power of all classes of stock entitled to vote in a corporation, it shall be considered as owning all the stock entitled to vote. See section 958(b)(2).

(d) *Attribution to partnerships, estates, trusts, and corporations.*—(1) *In general.*—Except as provided in subparagraph (2) of this paragraph—

(i) *To partnerships and estates.*—Stock owned, directly or indirectly, by or for a partner or a beneficiary of an estate shall be considered as owned by the partnership or estate.

(ii) *To trusts.*—(a) *From beneficiaries.*—Stock owned, directly or indirectly, by or for a beneficiary of a trust (other than an employees' trust described in section 401(a) which is exempt from tax under section 501(a)) shall be considered as owned by the trust, unless such beneficiary's interest in the trust is a remote contingent interest. For purposes of the preceding sentence, a contingent interest of a beneficiary in a trust shall be considered remote if, under the maximum exercise of discretion by the trustee in favor of such beneficiary, the value of such interest, computed actuarially, is 5 percent or less of the value of the trust property.

(b) *From owner.*—Stock owned, directly or indirectly, by or for a person who is considered the owner of any portion of a trust under sections 671 to 678 (relating to grantors and others treated as substantial owners) shall be considered as owned by the trust.

(iii) *To corporations.*—If 50 percent or more in value of the stock in a corporation is owned, directly or indirectly, by or for any person, such corporation shall be considered as owning the stock owned, directly or indirectly, by or for such person. This subdivision shall not be applied so as to consider a corporation as owning its own stock.

(2) *Limitation.*—Subparagraph (1) of this paragraph shall not be applied so as to consider a United States person as owning stock which is owned by a person who is not a United States person. This limitation does not apply for purposes of determining whether the stock of a domestic corporation is owned or considered as owned by a United States shareholder under section 956(b)(2) and § 1.956-2(b)(1)(viii). See section 958(b)(4).

(e) *Options.*—If any person has an option to acquire stock, such stock shall be considered as owned by such person. For purposes of the preceding sentence, an option to acquire such an option, and each one of a series of such options, shall be considered as an option to acquire such stock.

(f) *Rules of application.*—For purposes of this section—

(1) *Stock treated as actually owned.*—(i) *In general.*—Except as provided in subdivisions (ii) and (iii) of this subparagraph, stock constructively owned by a person by reason of the application of paragraphs (b), (c), (d), and (e) of this section shall, for purposes of applying such paragraphs, be considered as actually owned by such person.

(ii) *Members of family.*—Stock constructively owned by an individual by reason of the application of paragraph (b) of this section shall not be considered as owned by him for purposes of again applying such paragraph in order to make another the constructive owner of such stock.

(iii) *Partnerships, estates, trusts, and corporations.*—Stock constructively owned by a partnership, estate, trust, or corporation by reason of the application of paragraph (d) of this section shall not be considered as owned by it for purposes of applying paragraph (c) of this section in order to make another the constructive owner of such stock.

(iv) *Option rule in lieu of family rule.*—For purposes of this subparagraph, if stock may be considered as owned by an individual under paragraph (b) or (e) of this section, it shall be considered as owned by him under paragraph (e).

(2) *Coordination of different attribution rules.*—For purposes of any one determination, stock which may be owned under more than one of the rules of § 1.958-1 and this section, or by more than one person, shall be owned under that attribution rule which imputes to the person, or persons, concerned the largest total percentage of such stock. The application of this subparagraph may be illustrated by the following examples:

Example (1). (a) United States persons A and B, and domestic corporation M, own 9 percent, 32 percent, and 10 percent, respectively, of the one class of stock in foreign corporation R. A also owns 10 percent of the one class of stock in M Corporation. For purposes of determining whether A is a United States shareholder with respect to R Corporation, 10 percent of the 10-percent interest of M Corporation in R Corporation is considered as owned by A. See paragraph (c)(1)(iii) of this section. Thus, A owns 10 percent (9% plus 10% of 10%) of the stock in R Corporation and is a United States shareholder with respect to such corporation. Corporations M and B, by reason of owning 10 percent and 32 percent, respectively, of the stock in R Corporation are United States shareholders with respect to such corporation.

(b) For purposes of determining whether R Corporation is a controlled foreign corporation, the 1 percent of the stock in R Corporation directly owned by M Corporation and considered as owned by A cannot be counted twice. Therefore, the total amount of stock in R Corporation owned by United States shareholders is 51 percent, determined as follows:

Stock ownership in R Corporation	(percent)
A	9
B	32
M Corporation	10
Total	51

Example (2). United States person C owns 10 percent of the one class of stock in foreign corporation N, which owns 60 percent of the one class of stock in foreign corporation S. Under paragraph (a)(2) of § 1.958-1, C is considered as owning 6 percent (10% of 60%) of the stock in S Corporation. Under paragraph (c)(1)(iii) and (2) of this section, N Corporation is considered as owning 100 percent of the stock in S Corporation and C is considered as owning 10 percent of such 100 percent, or 10 percent of the stock in S Corporation. Thus, for purposes of determining whether C is a United States shareholder with respect to S Corporation, the attribution rules of paragraph (c)(1)(iii) and (2) of this section are used inasmuch as C owns a larger total percentage of the stock of S Corporation under such rules.

(g) *Illustration.*—The application of this section may be illustrated by the following examples:

Example (1). United States persons A and B own 5 percent and 25 percent, respectively, of the one class of stock in foreign corporation M. Corporation M owns 60 percent of the one class of stock in foreign corporation N. Under paragraph (a)(2) of § 1.958-1, A and B are considered as owning 3 percent (5% of 60%) and 15 percent (25% of 60%), respectively, of the stock in N Corporation. Under paragraph (c)(2) of this section, M Corporation is treated as owning all the stock in N Corporation, and, under paragraph (c)(1)(iii) of this section, B is considered as owning 25 percent of such 100 percent, or 25 percent of the stock in N Corporation. Inasmuch as A owns less than 10 percent of the stock in M Corporation, he is not considered as owning, under paragraph (c)(1)(iii) of this section, any of the stock in N Corporation owned by M Corporation. Thus, the attribution rules of paragraph (a)(2) of § 1.958-1 are used with respect to A inasmuch as he owns a larger total percentage of the stock of N Corporation under such rules; and the attribution rules of paragraph (c)(1)(iii) and (2) of this section are used with respect to B inasmuch as he owns a larger total percentage of the stock of N Corporation under such rules.

Example (2). United States person C owns 60 percent of the one class of stock in domestic corporation P; corporation P owns 60 percent of the one class of stock in foreign corporation Q; and corporation Q owns 60 percent of the one class of stock in foreign corporation R. Under paragraph (a)(2) of § 1.958-1, P Corporation is considered as owning 36 percent (60% of 60%) of the stock in R Corporation, and C is considered as owning none of the stock in R Corporation inasmuch as the chain of ownership stops at the first United States person and P Corporation is such a person. Under paragraph (c)(2) of this section, Q Corporation is treated as owning 100 percent of the stock in R Corporation, and under paragraph (c)(1)(iii) of this section, P Corporation is considered as owning 60 percent of such 100 percent, or 60 percent of the stock in R Corporation. For purposes of determining the amount of stock in R Corporation which C is considered as owning, P Corporation is treated under paragraph (c)(2) of this section as owning 100 percent of the stock in R Corporation; therefore, C is considered as owning 60 percent of the stock in R Corporation. Thus, the attribution rules of paragraph (c)(1)(iii) and (2) of this section are used with respect to C and P Corporation inasmuch as they each own a larger total percentage of the stock of R Corporation under such rules.

Example (3). United States person D owns 25 percent of the one class of stock in foreign corporation S. D is also a 40-percent partner in domestic partnership X, which owns 50 percent of the one class of stock in domestic corporation T. Under paragraph (d)(1)(i) of this section, the 25 percent of the stock in S Corporation owned by D is considered as being owned by partnership X; since such stock is treated as actually owned by partnership X under paragraph (f)(1)(i) of this section, such stock is in turn considered as being owned by T Corporation under paragraph (d)(1)(iii) of this section. Thus, under paragraphs (d)(1) and (f)(1)(i) of this section, T Corporation is considered as owning 25 percent of the stock in S Corporation.

Example (4). Foreign corporation U owns 100 percent of the one class of stock in domestic corporation V and also 100 percent of the one class of stock in foreign corporation W. By virtue of paragraph (d)(2) of this section, V Corporation may not be considered under paragraph (d)(1) of this section as owning the stock by its sole shareholder, U Corporation, in W Corporation.

Example (5). United States citizen E owns 15 percent of the one class of stock in foreign corporation Y, and United States citizen F, E's spouse, owns 5 percent of such stock. E and F's four nonresident alien grandchildren each own 20 percent of the stock in Y Corporation. Under paragraph (b)(1) of this section, E is considered as owning the stock owned by F in Y Corporation; however, by virtue of paragraph (b)(3) of this section, E may not be considered under paragraph (b)(1) of this section as owning any of the stock in Y Corporation owned by such grandchildren.

Example (6). United States person F owns 10 percent of the one class of stock in foreign corporation Z; corporation Z owns 10 percent of the one class of stock in foreign corporation K; and corporation K owns 100 percent of the one class of stock in foreign corporation L. United States person G, F's spouse, owns 9 percent of the stock in K Corporation. Under paragraph (c)(1)(iii) of this section or paragraph (a)(2) of § 1.958-1, F is considered as owning 1 percent (10% of 10% of 100%) of the stock in L Corporation by reason of his ownership of stock in Z Corporation, and, under paragraph (b)(1) of this section, G is considered as owning such 1 percent of the stock in L Corporation. Under paragraph (a)(2) of § 1.958-1, G is considered as owning 9 percent (9% of 100%) of the stock in L Corporation by reason of her ownership of stock in K Corporation, and, under paragraph (b)(1) of this section, F is considered as owning such 9 percent of the stock in L Corporation. Thus, for the purpose of determining whether F or G is a United States shareholder with respect to L Corporation, each of F and G is considered as owning a total of 10 percent of the stock in L Corporation by applying the rules of paragraph (a)(2) of § 1.958-1 and paragraphs (b)(1) and (c)(1)(iii) of this section. [Reg. § 1.958-2.]

☐ [*T.D.* 6889, 7-11-66. *Amended by T.D.* 7712, 8-6-80 *and T.D.* 8955, 7-19-2001.]

§ 1.959-1. Exclusion from gross income of United States persons of previously taxed earnings and profits.—(a) *In general.*—Sections 951 through 964 provide that certain types of income of controlled foreign corporations will be subject to United States income tax even though such amounts are not currently distributed to the United States shareholders of such corporations. The amounts so taxed to certain United States shareholders are described as subpart F income, previously excluded subpart F income withdrawn from investment in less developed countries, previously excluded subpart F income withdrawn from investment in foreign base company shipping operations, and increases in earnings invested in United States property. Section 959 provides that amounts taxed as subpart F income, as previously excluded subpart F income withdrawn from investment in less developed countries, or as previously excluded subpart F income withdrawn from investment in foreign base company shipping operations are not taxed again as increases in earnings invested in United States property. Section 959 also provides an exclusion whereby none of the amounts so taxed are taxed again when actually distributed directly, or indirectly through a chain of ownership described in section 958(a), to United States shareholders or to such shareholders' successors in interest. The exclusion also applies to amounts taxed to United States shareholders as income of one controlled foreign corporation and later distributed to another controlled foreign corporation in such a chain of ownership where such amounts would otherwise be again included in the income of such shareholders or their successors in interest as subpart F income of the controlled foreign corporation to which they are distributed. Section 959 also provides rules for the allocation of distributions to earnings and profits and for the non-dividend treatment of actual distributions which are excluded from gross income.

(b) *Actual distributions to United States persons.*—The earnings and profits for a taxable year of a foreign corporation attributable to amounts which are, or have been, included in the gross income of a United States shareholder of such corporation under section 951(a) shall not, when such amounts are distributed to such shareholder directly, or indirectly through a chain of ownership described in section 958(a), be again included in the gross income of such United States shareholder. See section 959(a)(1). Thus, earnings and profits attributable to amounts which are, or have been, included in the gross income of a United States shareholder of a foreign corporation under section 951(a)(1)(A)(i) as subpart F income, under section 951(a)(1)(A)(ii) as previously excluded subpart F income withdrawn from investment in less developed countries, under section 951(a)(1)(A)(iii) as previously excluded subpart F income withdrawn from investment in foreign base company shipping operations, or under section 951(a)(1)(B) as earnings invested in United States property, shall not be again included in the gross income of such shareholder when such amounts are actually distributed, directly or indirectly, to such shareholder. See paragraph (d) of this section for exclusion applicable to such shareholder's successor in interest. The application of this paragraph may be illustrated by the following example:

Example. (a) A, a United States shareholder, owns 100 percent of the only class of stock of R Corporation, a corporation organized on January 1, 1963, which is a controlled foreign corporation throughout the period here involved. Both A and R Corporation use the calendar year as a taxable year.

(b) During 1964, R Corporation derives $100 of subpart F income, and A includes such amount in his gross income under section 951(a)(1)(A)(i). Corporation R's current and accumulated earnings and profits (before taking into account distributions made during 1964) are $150. Also, during 1964, R Corporation distributes $50 to A. The $50 distribution is excludable from A's gross income for 1964 under this paragraph and § 1.959-3 because such distribution represents earnings and profits attributable to amounts which are included in A's gross income for such year under section 951(a).

(c) If instead of deriving the $100 of subpart F income in 1964, R Corporation derives such amount during 1963 and has earnings and profits for 1963 in excess of $100, A must include $100 in his gross income for 1963 under section 951(a)(1)(A)(i). However, the $50 distribution made by R Corporation to A during 1964 is excludable from A's gross income for such year under this paragraph and § 1.959-3 because such distribution represents earnings and profits attributable to amounts which have been included in A's gross income for 1963 under section 951(a).

(d) If, with respect to 1964—

(1) Instead of owning the stock of R Corporation directly, A owns such stock through a chain of ownership described in section 958(a), that is, A owns 100 percent of M Corporation which owns 100 percent of N Corporation which owns 100 percent of R Corporation,

(2) Both M and N Corporations use the calendar year as a taxable year and are controlled foreign corporations throughout the period here involved,

(3) Corporation R derives $100 of subpart F income and has earnings and profits in excess of $100,

(4) Neither M Corporation nor N Corporation has earnings and profits or a deficit in earnings and profits, and

(5) The $50 distribution is from R Corporation to N Corporation to M Corporation to A,

A must include $100 in his gross income for 1964 under section 951(a)(1)(A)(i) by reason of his indirect ownership of R Corporation. However, the $50 distribution is excludable from A's gross income for 1964 under this paragraph and § 1.959-3 because such distribution represents earnings and profits attributable to amounts which are included in A's gross income for such year under section 951(a) and are distributed indirectly to A through a chain of ownership described in section 958(a).

(c) *Excludable investment of earnings in United States property.*—The earnings and profits for a taxable year of a foreign corporation attributable to amounts which are, or have been, included in the gross income of a United States shareholder of such corporation under section 951(a)(1)(A) shall not, when such amounts would, but for section 959(a)(2) and this paragraph, be included under section 951(a)(1)(B) in the gross income of such shareholder directly, or indirectly through a chain of ownership described in section 958(a), be again included in the gross income of such United States shareholder. Thus, earnings and profits attributable to amounts which are, or have been, included in the gross income of a United States shareholder of a foreign corporation under section 951(a)(1)(A)(i) as subpart F income, under section 951(a)(1)(A)(ii) as previously excluded subpart F income withdrawn from investment in less developed countries, or under section 951(a)(1)(A)(iii) as previously excluded subpart F income withdrawn from investment in foreign base company shipping operations may be invested in United States property without being again included in such shareholder's income under section 951(a). Moreover, the first amounts deemed invested in United States property are amounts previously included in the gross income of a United States shareholder under section 951(a)(1)(A). See paragraph (d) of this section for exclusion applicable to such shareholder's successor in interest. The application of this paragraph may be illustrated by the following example:

Example. (a) A, a United States shareholder, owns 100 percent of the only class of stock of R Corporation, a corporation organized on January 1, 1963, which is a controlled foreign corporation throughout the period here involved. Both A and R Corporation use the calendar year as a taxable year.

(b) During 1964, R Corporation derives $35 of subpart F income, and A includes such amount in his gross income under section 951(a)(1)(A)(i). During 1964, R Corporation also invests $50 in tangible property (other than property described in section 956(b)(2)) located in the United States. Corporation R makes no distributions during the year, and its current earnings and profits are in excess of $50. Of the $50 investment of earnings in United States property, $35 is excludable from

A's gross income for 1964 under section 959(a)(2) because such amount represents earnings and profits which are attributable to amounts which are included in A's gross income for such year under section 951(a)(1)(A)(i) and therefore may be invested in United States property without again being included in A's gross income. The remaining $15 is includible in A's gross income for 1964 under section 951(a)(1)(B).

(c) If, instead of deriving $35 of subpart F income in 1964, R Corporation has no subpart F income for 1964 but derives the $35 of subpart F income during 1963 and has earnings and profits for such year in excess of $35, A must include $35 in his gross income for 1963 under section 951(a)(1)(A)(i). However, of the $50 investment of earnings in United States property made by R Corporation during 1964, $35 is excludable from A's gross income for 1964 under section 959(a)(2) because such amount represents earnings and profits attributable to amounts which have been included in A's gross income for 1963 under section 951(a)(1)(A)(i). The remaining $15 is includible in A's gross income for 1964 under section 951(a)(1)(B).

(d) *Application of exclusions to shareholder's successor in interest.*—If a United States person (as defined in § 1.957-4) acquires from any person any portion of the interest in the foreign corporation of a United States shareholder referred to in paragraph (b) or (c) of this section, the rules of such paragraph shall apply to such acquiring person but only to the extent that the acquiring person establishes to the satisfaction of the district director the right to the exclusion provided by such paragraph. The information to be furnished by the acquiring person to the district director with his return for the taxable year to support such exclusion shall include:

(1) The name, address, and taxable year of the foreign corporation from which the distribution is received and of all other corporations, partnerships, trusts, or estates in any applicable chain of ownership described in section 958(a);

(2) The name, address, and (in the case of information required to be furnished after June 20, 1983) taxpayer identification number of the person from whom the stock interest was acquired;

(3) A description of the stock interest acquired and its relation, if any, to a chain of ownership described in section 958(a);

(4) The amount for which an exclusion under section 959(a) is claimed; and

(5) Evidence showing that the earnings and profits for which an exclusion is claimed are attributable to amounts which were included in the gross income of a United States shareholder under section 951(a), that such amounts were not previously excluded from the gross income of a United States person, and the identity of the United States shareholder including such amounts.

The acquiring person shall also furnish to the district director such other information as may be required by the district director in support of the exclusion.

Example. (a) A, a United States shareholder, owns 100 percent of the only class of stock of R Corporation, a corporation organized on January 1, 1964, and a controlled foreign corporation throughout the period here involved. Both A and R Corporation use the calendar year as a taxable year.

(b) During 1964, R Corporation has $100 of subpart F income and earnings and profits in excess of $100. A includes $100 in his gross income for 1964 under section 951(a)(1)(A)(i). During 1965, A sells 40 percent of his stock in R Corporation to B, a United States person who uses the calendar year as a taxable year. In 1965, R Corporation has no earnings and profits and experiences no increase in earnings invested in United States property. Corporation R distributes $40 to B on December 1, 1965. If B establishes his right to the exclusion to the satisfaction of the district director, he may exclude $40 from his gross income for 1965 under section 959(a)(1).

(c) If, instead of selling his 40-percent interest directly to B, A sells on February 1, 1965, 40 percent of his stock in R Corporation to C, a nonresident alien, and on October 1, 1965, B acquires the 40-percent interest in R Corporation from C, the result is the same as in paragraph (b) of this example, if B establishes his right to the exclusion to the satisfaction of the district director.

(d) If, instead of acquiring 40 percent, B acquires only 5 percent of A's stock in R Corporation and R Corporation distributes $5 to B during 1965, B is not a United States shareholder (within the meaning of section 951(b)) with respect to R Corporation since he owns only 5 percent of the stock of R Corporation. Notwithstanding, B may exclude the $5 distribution from his gross income for 1965 under section 959(a)(1) if he establishes his right to the exclusion to the satisfaction of the district director.

(e) If the facts are assumed to be the same as in paragraphs (a) and (b) of this example except that—

(1) A owns the stock of R Corporation indirectly through a chain of ownership described in section 958(a), that is, A owns 100 percent of M corporation which owns 100 percent of N Corporation which owns 100 percent of R Corporation,

(2) B acquires from N Corporation 40 percent of the stock in R Corporation,

(3) Both M Corporation and N Corporation are controlled foreign corporations which use the calendar year as a taxable year,

(4) Neither M Corporation nor N Corporation has any amount in 1964 or 1965 which is includible in gross income of United States shareholders under section 951(a), and

(5) Neither M Corporation nor N Corporation has a deficit in earnings and profits for 1964,

the result is the same as in paragraph (b) of this example if B establishes his right to the exclusion to the satisfaction of the district director. [Reg. § 1.959-1.]

☐ [T.D. 6795, 1-28-65. Amended by T.D. 7893, 5-11-83.]

§ 1.959-2. Exclusion from gross income of controlled foreign corporations of previously taxed earnings and profits.—
(a) *Applicable rule.*—The earnings and profits for a taxable year of a controlled foreign corporation attributable to amounts which are, or have been, included in the gross income of a United States shareholder under section 951(a) shall not, when distributed through a chain of ownership described in section 958(a), be also included in the gross income of another controlled foreign corporation in such chain for purposes of the application of section 951(a) to such other controlled foreign corporation with respect to such United States shareholder. See section 959(b). The exclusion from the income of such other foreign corporation also applies with respect to any other United States shareholder who acquires from such United States shareholder or any other person any portion of the interest of such United States shareholder in the controlled foreign corporation, but only to the extent the acquiring shareholder establishes to the satisfaction of the district director the right to such exclusion. An acquiring shareholder claiming the exclusion under section 959(b) shall furnish to the district director with his return for the taxable year the information required under paragraph (d) of § 1.959-1 to support the exclusion under this paragraph.

(b) *Illustration.*—The application of this section may be illustrated by the following example:

Example. (a) A, a United States shareholder, owns 100 percent of the only class of stock of M Corporation which in turn owns 100 percent of the only class of stock of N Corporation. A and corporations M and N use the calendar year as a taxable year and corporations M and N are controlled foreign corporations throughout the period here involved.

(b) During 1963, N Corporation invests $100 in tangible property (other than property described in section 956(b)(2)) located in the United States and has earnings and profits in excess of $100. A is required to include $100 in his gross income for 1963 under section 951(a)(1)(B) by reason of his indirect ownership of the stock of N Corporation. During 1963, M Corporation has no income or investments other than the income derived from a distribution of $100 from N Corporation. Corporation M has earnings and profits of $100 for 1963. Under paragraph (a) of § 1.954-2, the $100 distribution received by M Corporation from N Corporation would otherwise constitute subpart F income of M Corporation; however, by reason of section 959(b) and this section, this amount does not constitute gross income of M Corporation for purposes of determining amounts includible in A's gross income under section 951(a)(1)(A)(i).

(c) During 1964, N Corporation derives $100 of subpart F income and distributes $100 to M Corporation which has no subpart F income for 1964 but which invests the $100 distribution in tangible property (other than property described in section 956(b)(2)) located in the United States. Corporation N's earnings and profits for 1964 are in excess of $100, and M Corporation's current and accumulated earnings and profits (before taking into account distributions made during 1964) are in excess of $100. A is required with respect to N Corporation to include $100 in his gross income for 1964 under section 951(a)(1)(A)(i) by reason of his indirect ownership of the stock of N Corporation. The investment by M Corporation in United States property would otherwise constitute an investment of earnings in United States property to which section 956 applies; however, by reason of section 959(b) and this section, such amount does not constitute gross income of M Corporation for purposes of determining amounts includible in A's gross income under section 951(a)(1)(B).

(d) If during 1965, N Corporation invests $100 in tangible property (other than property described in section 956(b)(2)) located in the United States and has earnings and profits in excess of $100, A will be required with respect to N Corporation to include $100 in his gross income for 1965 under section 951(a)(1)(B), because the $100 of earnings and profits for 1964 attributable to N Corporation's subpart F income which was taxed to A in 1964 was distributed to M Corporation in such year.

(e) If, with respect to 1966—

(1) Corporation N owns 100 percent of the only class of stock of R Corporation,

(2) Corporation R derives $100 of subpart F income, has earnings and profits in excess of $100, and makes no distributions to N Corporation,

(3) Corporation N invests $25 in tangible property (other than property described in section 956(b)(2)) located in the United States and has current and accumulated earnings and profits in excess of $25, and

(4) Corporation M has no income or investments and does not have a deficit in earnings and profits,

the $100 of subpart F income derived by R Corporation is includible in A's gross income for 1966 under section 951(a)(1)(A)(i) and the $25 investment of earnings in United States property by N Corporation is includible in A's gross income for 1966 under section 951(a)(1)(B).

(f) If, however, the facts are the same as in paragraph (e) of this example except that—

(1) During 1966, R Corporation distributes $20 to N Corporation, and

(2) Corporation N makes no distributions during such year to M Corporation,

of the $25 investment in United States property by N Corporation, $20 is not includible in A's gross income for 1966 because such amount represents earnings and profits which are attributable to amounts included in A's gross income for such year under section 951(a)(1)(A)(i) with respect to R Corporation and which have been distributed to N Corporation by R Corporation. By reason of section 959(b) and this section, such $20 distribution to N Corporation does not constitute gross income of N Corporation for purposes of determining amounts includible in A's gross income under section 951(a)(1)(B); however, the remaining $5 of investment of earnings in United States property by N Corporation in 1966 is includible in A's gross income for such year under section 951(a)(1)(B). [Reg. § 1.959-2.]

☐ [*T.D.* 6795, 1-28-65.]

§ 1.959-3. Allocation of distributions to earnings and profits of foreign corporations.—(a) *In general.*—For purposes of §§ 1.959-1 and 1.959-2, the source of the earnings and profits from which distributions are made by a foreign corporation as between earnings and profits attributable to increases in earnings invested in United States property, previously taxed subpart F income, previously excluded subpart F income withdrawn from investment in less developed countries, previously excluded subpart F income withdrawn from investment in foreign base company shipping operations, and other amounts shall be determined in accordance with section 959(c) and paragraphs (b) through (e) of this section.

(b) *Applicability of section 316(a).*—For purposes of this section, section 316(a) shall be applied, in determining the source of distributions from the earnings and profits of a foreign corporation, by first applying section 316(a)(2) and then by applying section 316(a)(1)—

(1) First, as provided by section 959(c)(1), to earnings and profits attributable to amounts included in gross income of a United States shareholder under section 951(a)(1)(B) (or which would have been so included but for section 959(a)(2) and paragraph (c) of § 1.959-1),

(2) Secondly, as provided by section 959(c)(2), to earnings and profits attributable to amounts included in gross income of a United States shareholder under section 951(a)(1)(A) (but reduced by amounts not included in such gross income under section 951(a)(1)(B) because of the exclusion provided by section 959(a)(2) and paragraph (c) of § 1.959-1), and

(3) Finally, as provided by section 959(c)(3), to other earnings and profits.

Thus, distributions shall be considered first attributable to amounts, if any, described in subparagraph (1) of this paragraph (first for the current taxable year and then for prior taxable years beginning with the most recent prior taxable year), secondly to amounts, if any, described in subparagraph (2) of this paragraph (first for the current taxable year and then for prior taxable years beginning with the most recent prior taxable year), and finally to the amounts, if any, described in subparagraph (3) of this paragraph (first for the current taxable year and then for prior taxable years beginning with the most recent prior taxable year). See, however, paragraph (e) of § 1.963-3 (applied as if section 963 had not been repealed by the Tax Reduction Act of 1975) for a special rule for determination of the source of distributions counting as minimum distributions. Earnings and profits are classified as to year and as to section 959(c) amount in the year in which such amounts are included in gross income of a United States shareholder under section 951(a) and are reclassified as to section 959(c) amount in the year in which such amounts would be so included but for the provisions of section 959(a)(2); any subsequent distribution of such amounts to a higher tier in a chain of ownership described in section 958(a) does not of itself change such classifications. For example, earnings and profits of a foreign corporation attributable to amounts of previously excluded subpart F income withdrawn from investment in less developed countries (or from investments in export trade assets or foreign base company shipping operations) shall be reclassified as amounts to which subparagraph (2), rather than subparagraph (3), of this paragraph applies for purposes of determining priority of distribution, and such earnings and profits shall be considered attributable to the taxable year in which the withdrawal occurs.

This paragraph shall apply to distributions by one foreign corporation to another foreign corporation and by a foreign corporation to a United States person. The application of this paragraph may be illustrated by the following example:

Example. (a) M, a controlled foreign corporation is organized on January 1, 1963, and is 100-percent owned by A, a United States shareholder. Both A and M Corporation use the calendar year as a taxable year, and M Corporation is a controlled foreign corporation throughout the period here involved. As of December 31, 1966, M Corporation's accumulated earnings and profits of $450 (before taking into account distributions made in 1966) applicable to A's interest in such corporation are classified for purposes of section 959(c) as follows:

Year	Classification of earnings and profits for purposes of sec. 959		
	(c)(1)	(c)(2)	(c)(3)
1963	$100		
1964	100	$75	
1965		75	$50
1966			50

(b) During 1966, M Corporation makes three separate distributions to A of $150 each, and the source of such distributions under section 959(c) is as follows:

	Amount	Year	Allocation of distributions under sec. 959
Distribution # 1:	$100	1964	(c)(1)
	50	1963	(c)(1)
	150		
Distribution # 2:	$50	1963	(c)(1)
	75	1965	(c)(2)
	25	1964	(c)(2)
	150		
Distribution # 3:	$50	1964	(c)(2)
	50	1966	(c)(3)
	50	1965	(c)(3)
	150		

(c) If, in addition to the above facts—

(1) M Corporation owns throughout the period here involved 100 percent of the only class of stock of N Corporation, a controlled foreign corporation which uses the calendar year as a taxable year,

(2) Corporation N derives $60 of subpart F income for 1963 which A includes in his gross income for such year under section 951(a)(1)(A)(i),

(3) Corporation N has earnings and profits for 1963 of $60 but has neither earnings or profits nor a deficit in earnings and profits for 1964, 1965, or 1966, and

(4) During 1966, N Corporation invests $20 in tangible property (not described in section 956(b)(2)) located in the United States and distributes $45 to M Corporation,

the $20 investment of earnings in United States property is excludable from A's gross income for 1966, under section 959(a)(2) and paragraph (c) of § 1.959-1, with respect to N Corporation and the $45 dividend received by M Corporation does not, under section 959(b) and § 1.959-2, constitute gross income of M Corporation for 1966 for purposes of determining amounts includible in A's gross income under section 951(a)(1)(A)(i) with respect to M Corporation. However, the $45 dividend paid by N Corporation to M Corporation is allocated under section 959(c) and this paragraph to the earnings and profits of N Corporation as follows: $20 to 1963 earnings described in section 959(c)(1) and $25 to 1963 earnings described in section 959(c)(2). In such case, M Corporation's earnings and profits of $495 (before taking into account distributions made in 1966) would be classified as follows for purposes of section 959(c):

Year	Classification of earnings and profits for purposes of sec. 959		
	(c)(1)	(c)(2)	(c)(3)
1963	$120	$25	
1964	100	$75	
1965		75	$50
1966			50

Reg. § 1.959-3(b)(3)

(d) The three distributions to A in 1966 of $150 each would then have the following source under section 959(c):

	Amount	Year	Allocation of distributions under sec. 959
Distribution # 1:	$100	1964	(c)(1)
	50	1963	(c)(1)
	150		
Distribution # 2:	$70	1963	(c)(1)
	75	1965	(c)(2)
	5	1964	(c)(2)
	150		
Distribution # 3:	$70	1964	(c)(2)
	25	1963	(c)(2)
	50	1966	(c)(3)
	5	1965	(c)(3)
	150		

(c) *Treatment of deficits in earnings and profits.*—For purposes of this section, a United States shareholder's pro rata share (determined in accordance with the principles of paragraph (e) of § 1.951-1) of a foreign corporation's deficit in earnings and profits, determined under section 964(a) and § 1.964-1, for any taxable year shall be applied only to earnings and profits described in paragraph (b)(3) of this section.

(d) *Treatment of certain foreign taxes.*—For purposes of this section, any amount described in subparagraph (1), (2), or (3) of paragraph (b) of this section which is distributed by a foreign corporation through a chain of ownership described in section 958(a)(2) shall be reduced by any income, war profits, or excess profits taxes imposed on or with respect to such distribution by any foreign country or possession of the United States.

Example. (a) Domestic corporation M owns 100 percent of the only class of stock of foreign corporation A, which is incorporated under the laws of foreign country X and which, in turn, owns 100 percent of the only class of stock of foreign corporation B, which is incorporated under the laws of foreign country Y. All corporations use the calendar year as a taxable year and corporations A and B are controlled foreign corporations throughout the period here involved.

(b) During 1963, B Corporation (a less developed country corporation for 1963 within the meaning of § 1.955-5) derives $90 of subpart F income, after incurring $10 of foreign income tax allocable to such income under paragraph (c) of § 1.954-1, has earnings and profits in excess of $90, and makes no distributions. Corporation M must include $90 in its gross income for 1963 under section 951(a)(1)(A)(i). As of December 31, 1963, with respect to M Corporation, B Corporation has earnings and profits for 1963 described in section 959(c)(2) of $90.

(c) During 1964, B Corporation has neither earnings and profits nor a deficit in earnings and profits but distributes $90 to A Corporation, and, by reason of section 959(b) and § 1.959-2, such amount is not includible in the gross income of M Corporation for 1964 under section 951(a) with respect to A Corporation. Corporation A incurs a withholding tax of $13.50 on the $90 dividend distributed from B Corporation (15 percent of $90) and an additional foreign income tax of 10 percent or $7.65 by reason of the inclusion of the net distribution of $76.50 ($90 minus $13.50) in its taxable income for 1964. As of December 31, 1964, with respect to M Corporation, B Corporation's earnings and profits for 1963 described in section 959(c)(2) amount to zero ($90 minus $90); and A Corporation's earnings and profits for 1963 described in section 959(c)(2) amount to $68.85 ($90 minus $13.50 minus $7.65).

(e) *Determination of foreign tax credit.*—For purposes of applying section 902 and section 960 in determining the foreign tax credit allowable under section 901 in a case in which distributions are made by a second-tier corporation or a first-tier corporation, as the case may be, from its earnings and profits for a taxable year which are attributable to an amount included in the gross income of a United States shareholder under section 951(a) or which are attributable to amounts excluded from the gross income of such foreign corporation under section 959(b) and § 1.959-2 with respect to a United States shareholder, the rules of paragraph (b) of this section shall apply except that in applying subparagraph (1) or (2) of such paragraph—

(1) Distributions from the earnings and profits for such taxable year of the second-tier corporation shall be considered first attributable to its earnings and profits attributable to distributions from the earnings and profits of the foreign corporation, if any, next lower in the chain of ownership described in section 958(a), to the extent of such earnings and profits of the second-tier corporation, and then to the other earnings and profits of such second-tier corporation, and

(2) Distributions from the earnings and profits for such taxable year of the first-tier corporation shall be considered first attributable to its earnings and profits attributable to distributions from the earnings and profits of the second-tier corporation, to the extent of such earnings and profits of the first-tier corporation, and then to the other earnings and profits of such first-tier corporation.

For purposes of this paragraph, a second-tier corporation is a foreign corporation referred to in section 960(a)(1)(B), and a first-tier corporation is a foreign corporation referred to in section 960(a)(1)(A). The application of this paragraph may be illustrated by the following examples:

Example (1). (a) Domestic corporation A, a United States shareholder, owns 100 percent of the only class of stock of foreign corporation R which, in turn, owns 100 percent of the only class of stock of foreign corporation S. All corporations use the calendar year as a taxable year, and corporations R and S are controlled foreign corporations throughout the period here involved.

(b) Neither R Corporation nor S Corporation has subpart F income for 1963. During 1963, S Corporation increases by $100 its investment in tangible property (not described in section 956(b)(2)) located in the United States, makes no distributions, and has earnings and profits of $100. Corporation A must include $100 in its gross income for 1963 under section 951(a)(1)(B) with respect to S Corporation. During 1963, R Corporation also increases by $100 its investment in tangible property (not described in section 956(b)(2)) located in the United States, makes no distributions, and has earnings and profits of $100. Corporation A must include $100 in its gross income for 1963 under section 951(a)(1)(B) with respect to R Corporation.

(c) During 1964, S Corporation distributes $100 to R Corporation, and R Corporation distributes $100 to A Corporation. Neither corporation has any earnings or profits or deficit in earnings and profits for such year. At December 31, 1964, R Corporation has earnings and profits (computed before distributions to A Corporation made for the year) of $200, consisting of $100 of section 959(c)(1) amounts of R Corporation for 1963 and of $100 of section 959(c)(1) amounts of S Corporation for 1963. For purposes of determining the foreign tax credit under section 960 and the regulations thereunder, the $100 distribution by R Corporation shall be considered attributable to S Corporation's earnings and profits for 1963 described in section 959(c)(1).

Example (2). (a) Domestic corporation A, a United States shareholder, owns 100 percent of the only class of stock of foreign corporation T which, in turn, owns 100 percent of the only class of stock of foreign corporation U. All corporations use the calendar year as a taxable year, and corporations T and U are controlled foreign corporations throughout the period here involved.

(b) During 1964, T Corporation invests $100 in tangible property (not described in section 956(b)(2)) located in the United States. For 1964, T Corporation has no subpart F income and makes no distributions; A must include $100 in its gross income for 1964 under section 951(a)(1)(B) with respect to T Corporation. For 1964, U Corporation has no subpart F income or investment of earnings in United States property but U Corporation has $100 of earnings and profits which it distributes to T Corporation. At December 31, 1964, T Corporation has earnings and profits of $300, consisting of operating income of $100 for each of the years 1963 and 1964 and $100 in dividends received from the earnings and profits of U Corporation for 1964. These earnings and profits are classified as follows under section 959(c): $100 of section 959(c)(1) amounts of T Corporation for 1964, $100 of section 959(c)(3) amounts of U Corporation for 1964, and $100 of section 959(c)(3) amounts of T Corporation for 1963.

(c) During 1965 neither T Corporation nor U Corporation has any earnings and profits or deficit in earnings and profits or investment of earnings in United States property, but T Corporation distributes $100 to A Corporation. For purposes of determining the foreign tax credit under section 960 and the regulations thereunder, the $100 distribution of T Corporation shall be considered attributable to T Corporation's earnings and profits for 1964 described in section 959(c)(1).

Reg. §1.959-3(e)(2)

(f) *Illustration.*—The application of this section may be illustrated by the following example:

Example. (a) M, a controlled foreign corporation is organized on January 1, 1963, and is wholly owned by A, a United States shareholder. Both A and Corporation M use the calendar year as a taxable year.

(b) Corporation M's earnings and profits (before distributions) for 1963 are $200, $100 of which is attributable to subpart F income. Corporation M's earnings and profits for such year also include $25 attributable to subpart F income which is excluded from M Corporation's foreign base company income under section 954(b)(1) as dividends, interest, and gains invested in qualified investments in less developed countries. Corporation M's increase in earnings invested in tangible property (not described in section 956(b)(2)) located in the United States for 1963, is $50, and M Corporation makes a distribution of such property during such year of $20. For purposes of section 959, A's interest in M Corporation's earnings and profits as of December 31, 1963, determined after the distribution of $20, is classified as follows:

Sec. 959(c)(1) amounts:
    Earnings for 1963 attributable to increased investment in United States property which would have been included in A's gross income but for application of sec. 959(a)(2) and § 1.959-1(c) $50
    Less: Distribution for 1963 allocated under sec. 959(c)(1) and paragraph (b)(1) of this section to such amounts 20 $30

Sec. 959(c)(2) amounts:
    Earnings for 1963 attributable to subpart F income included in A's gross income under sec. 951(a)(1)(A)(i) $100
    Less: Earnings for 1963 attributable to increased investment in United States property which would have been included in A's gross income but for application of sec. 959(a)(2) and § 1.959-1(c) 50 $50

Sec. 959(c)(3) amounts:
    Predistribution earnings for 1963 .... $200
    Less: Earnings for 1963 classified as:
        Sec. 959(c)(1) amounts $50
        Sec. 959(c)(2) amounts 50   100 $100

A's total interest in M Corporation's earnings and profits $180

For 1963, A is required to include $100 of subpart F income in his gross income under section 951(a)(1)(A)(i). He would have been required to include $50 in his gross income under section 951(a)(1)(B) as M Corporation's increase in earnings invested in United States property, except that section 959(a)(2) and paragraph (c) of § 1.959-1 provide in effect that earnings and profits taxed to A under section 951(a)(1)(A) with respect to M Corporation (whether in the current taxable year or in prior years) may be invested in United States property without again being included in gross income under section 951(a). The $20 dividend from M Corporation is excluded from A's gross income under section 959(a)(1) and paragraph (b) of § 1.959-1, since such distribution is allocated under section 959(c)(1) and paragraph (b)(1) of this section to amounts described in section 959(c)(1).

(c) During 1964, M Corporation's earnings and profits (before distributions) are $300, $75 of which is attributable to subpart F income. Corporation M has no change in investments in United States property during such year and withdraws $15 of previously excluded subpart F income from investment in less developed countries. Corporation M makes a cash distribution of $250 to A during 1964. For purposes of section 959, A's interest in M Corporation's earnings and profits as of December 31, 1964, determined after the distribution of $250, is classified as follows:

Sec. 959(c)(1) amounts:
    Sec. 959(c)(1) net amount for 1963 (as determined under paragraph (b) of this example) $30
    Less: Distribution for 1964 allocated under sec. 959(c)(1) and paragraph (b)(1) of this section to such amount 30 $0

Sec. 959(c)(2) amounts:
    Sec. 959(c)(2) net amount for 1963 (as determined under paragraph (b) of this example) $50

Plus: Earnings for 1964 attributable to:				
Subpart F income for 1964 included in A's gross income under sec. 951(a)(1)(A)(i)			75	
Previously excluded subpart F income withdrawn in 1964 from investment in less developed countries and included in A's gross income under sec. 951(a)(1)(A)(ii)			15	
			$140	
Less: Distribution for 1964 allocated under sec. 959(c)(2) and paragraph (b)(2) of this section to such amounts			$140	0
Sec. 959(c)(3) amounts:				
Sec. 959(c)(3) net amount for 1963 (as determined under paragraph (b) of this example)			$100	
Plus: Sec. 959(c)(3) net amount for 1964:				
Predistribution earnings for 1964		$300		
Less:				
Earnings for 1964 classified as sec. 959(c)(1) amounts ($0) and as sec. 959(c)(2) amounts ($75 + $15)		$90		
Distributions for 1964 allocated under sec. 959(c)(3) and paragraph (b)(3) of this section	$80	$170	$130	$230
A's total interest in M Corporation's earnings and profits				$230

For 1964, A is required to include in his gross income under section 951(a)(1)(A)(i) $75 of subpart F income, and under section 951(a)(1)(A)(ii) $15 of previously excluded subpart F income withdrawn from investment in less developed countries. Of the $250 cash distribution, A may exclude $170 from his gross income under section 959(a)(1) and paragraph (b) of § 1.959-1 and $80 is includible in his gross income as a dividend.

(d) The source under section 959(c) of the 1964 distribution of $250 to A is as follows:

Year	Amount	
1963	$30	(c)(1)
1964	90	(c)(2)
1963	50	(c)(2)
1964	80	(c)(3)
Total	$250	

[Reg. § 1.959-3.]

☐ [*T.D.* 6795, 1-28-65. *Amended by T.D.* 7334, 12-20-74; *T.D.* 7545, 5-5-78 *and T.D.* 7893, 5-11-83.]

§ 1.959-4. Distributions to United States persons not counting as dividends.—Except as provided in section 960(a)(3) and § 1.960-1 any distribution to a United States person which is excluded from the gross income of such person under section 959(a)(1) and § 1.959-1 shall be treated for purposes of chapter 1 (relating to normal taxes and surtaxes) of subtitle A (relating to income taxes) of the Code as a distribution which is not a dividend. However, see paragraph (b)(1) of § 1.956-1, relating to the dividend limitation on the amount of a controlled foreign corporation's investment of earnings in United States property. [Reg. § 1.959-4.]

☐ [*T.D.* 6795, 1-28-65. *Amended by T.D.* 7120, 6-3-71.]

§ 1.960-1. Foreign tax credit with respect to taxes paid on earnings and profits of controlled foreign corporations.—(a) *Scope of regulations under section 960.*—This section prescribes rules for determining the foreign income taxes deemed paid under section 960(a)(1) by a domestic corporation which is required under section 951 to include in gross income an amount attributable to a first-, second-, or third-tier corporation's earnings and profits. Section 1.960-2 prescribes rules for applying section 902 to dividends paid by a third-, second-, or first-tier corporation from earnings and profits attributable to an amount which is, or has been, included in gross income under section 951. Section 1.960-3 provides special rules for the application of the gross-up provisions of section 78 where an amount is included in gross income under section 951. Section 1.960-4 prescribes rules for increasing the applicable foreign tax credit limitation under section 904(a) of the domestic corporation for the taxable year in which it receives a distribution of earnings and profits in respect of which it was required under section 951 to include an amount in its gross income for a prior taxable year. Section 1.960-5 prescribes rules for disallowing a deduction for foreign income taxes for such taxable year of receipt where the domestic corporation received the benefits of the foreign tax credit for such previous taxable year of inclusion. Section 1.960-6 provides that the excess of such an increase in the applicable limitation under section 904(a) over the tax liability of the domestic corporation for such taxable year of receipt results in an overpayment of tax. Section 1.960-7 prescribes the effective dates for application of these rules.

(b) *Definitions.*—For purposes of section 960 and §§ 1.960-1 through 1.960-7—

(1) *First-tier corporation.*—The term "first-tier corporation" means a foreign corporation at least 10 percent of the voting stock of which is owned by the domestic corporation described in paragraph (a) of this section.

(2) *Second-tier corporation.*—In the case of amounts included in the gross income of the taxpayer under section 951—

(i) For taxable years beginning before January 1, 1977, the term "second-tier corporation" means a foreign corporation at least 50 percent of the voting stock of which is owned by such first-tier corporation.

(ii) For taxable years beginning after December 31, 1976, the term "second-tier corporation" means a foreign corporation at least 10 percent of the voting stock of which is owned by such first-tier corporation.

(3) *Third-tier corporation.*—In the case of amounts included in the gross income of a domestic shareholder under section 951 for taxable years beginning after December 31, 1976, the term "third-tier corporation" means a foreign corporation at least 10 percent of the voting stock of which is owned by such second-tier corporation.

(4) *Immediately lower-tier corporation.*—In the case of a first-tier corporation the term "immediately lower-tier corporation" means a second-tier corporation. In the case of a second-tier corporation, the term "immediately lower-tier corporation" means a third-tier corporation. In the case of a third-tier corporation, the term "immediately lower-tier corporation" means a fourth-tier corporation.

(5) *Foreign income taxes.*—The term "foreign income taxes" means income, war profits, and excess profits taxes, and taxes included in the term "income, war profits, and excess profits taxes" by reason of section 903, imposed by a foreign country or a possession of the United States.

(c) *Amount of foreign income taxes deemed paid by domestic corporation in respect of earnings and profits of foreign corporation attributable to amount included in income under section 951.*—(1) *In general.*—For purposes of section 901—

(i) If for the taxable year there is included in the gross income of a domestic corporation under section 951 an amount attributable to the earnings and profits of a first- or second-tier corporation for any taxable year, the domestic corporation shall be deemed to have paid the same proportion of the total foreign income taxes paid, accrued, or deemed (in accordance with paragraph (b) of § 1.960-2) to be paid by such foreign corporation on or with respect to its earnings and profits for its taxable year as the amount (in the case of a first-tier corporation, determined without regard to section 958(a)(2); in the case of a second-tier corporation, determined without regard to section 958(a)(1)(A) and, to the extent that stock of such second-tier corporation is owned by the domestic corporation through a foreign corporation other than the first-tier corporation, determined without regard to section 958(a)(2)) so included in the gross income of the domestic corporation under section 951 with respect to such foreign corporation bears to the total earnings and profits of such foreign corporation for its taxable year. This paragraph (c)(1)(i) shall not apply to amounts included in the gross income of the domestic corporation under section 951 with respect to the second-tier corporation unless the percentage-of-voting-stock requirement of section 902(b)(3)(A) is satisfied.

(ii) If for the taxable year there is included in the gross income of a domestic corporation under section 951 an amount attributable to the earnings and profits of a third-tier corporation for any taxable year, the domestic corporation shall be deemed to have paid the same proportion of the total foreign income taxes paid or accrued by such foreign corporation on or with respect to its earnings and profits for its taxable year as the amount (determined without regard to section 958(a)(1)(A) and, to the extent that stock of such third-tier corporation is owned by the domestic corporation through a foreign corporation other than the second-tier corporation, determined without regard to section 958(a)(2)) so included in the gross income of the domestic corporation under section 951 with respect to such foreign corporation bears to the total earnings and profits of such foreign corporation. This paragraph (c)(1)(ii) shall not apply unless the percentage-of-voting-stock requirement of section 902(b)(3)(B) is satisfied.

(iii) In applying paragraph (c)(1)(i) or (c)(1)(ii) of this section to a first-, second-, or third-tier corporation which for the taxable year has income excluded under section 959(b), paragraph (c)(3) of this section shall apply for purposes of excluding certain earnings and profits of such foreign corporation and foreign income taxes, if any, attributable to such excluded income.

(iv) This paragraph (c)(1) applies whether or not the first-, second-, or third-tier corporation makes a distribution for the taxable year of its earnings and profits which are attributable to the amount included in the gross income of the domestic corporation under section 951.

(v) This paragraph (c)(1) does not apply to an increase in current earnings invested in United States property which, but for paragraph (e) of § 1.963-3 (applied as if section 963 had not been repealed by the Tax Reduction Act of 1975), would be included in the gross income of the domestic corporation under section 951(a)(1)(B) but which, pursuant to such paragraph, counts toward a minimum distribution for the taxable year. This subdivision shall apply in taxable years subsequent to the Tax Reduction Act of 1975 only in those cases where an adjustment is required as a result of an election made under section 963 prior to the Act.

(2) *Taxes paid or accrued on or with respect to earnings and profits of foreign corporation.*— For purposes of paragraph (c)(1) of this section, the foreign income taxes paid or accrued by a first-, second-, or third-tier corporation on or with respect to its earnings and profits for its taxable year shall be the total amount of the foreign income taxes paid or accrued by such foreign corporation for such taxable year.

(3) *Exclusion of earnings and profits and taxes of a first-, second-, or third-tier corporation having income excluded under section 959(b).*— If in the case of a first-, second-, or third-tier corporation to which paragraph (c)(1)(i) or (c)(1)(ii) of this section is applied—

(i) The earnings and profits of such foreign corporation for its taxable year consist of (A) earnings and profits attributable to dividends received from an immediately lower-tier corporation which are attributable to amounts included in the gross income of a domestic corporation under section 951 with respect to the immediately lower- or lower-tier corporations, and (B) other earnings and profits, and

(ii) The effective rate of foreign income taxes paid or accrued by such foreign corporation in respect to the dividends to which its earnings and profits described in paragraph (c)(3)(i)(A) of this section are attributable is higher or lower than the effective rate of foreign income taxes paid or accrued by such foreign corporation in respect to the income to which its earnings and profits described in paragraph (c)(3)(i)(B) of this section are attributable,

then, for purposes of applying paragraph (c)(1)(i) or (c)(1)(ii) of this section to the foreign income taxes paid, accrued, or deemed to be paid, by such foreign corporation on or with respect to its earnings and profits for such taxable year, the earnings and profits of such foreign corporation for such taxable year shall be considered not to include the earnings and profits described in paragraph (c)(3)(i)(A) of this section and only the foreign income taxes paid, accrued, or deemed to be paid, by such foreign corporation in respect to the income to which its earnings and profits described in paragraph (c)(3)(i)(B) of this section are attributable shall be taken into account. For purposes of applying this paragraph (c)(3), the effective rate of foreign income taxes paid or accrued in respect to income shall be determined consistently with the principles of paragraphs (b)(3)(iv) and (viii) and (c) of § 1.954-1. Thus, for example, the effective rate of foreign income taxes paid or accrued in respect to dividends received by such foreign corporation shall be determined by taking into account any intercorporate dividends received deduction allowed to such corporation for such dividends.

(4) *Illustrations.*—The application of this paragraph may be illustrated by the following examples:

Example (1). Domestic corporation N owns all the one class of stock of controlled foreign corporation A. Both corporations use the calendar year as the taxable year. For 1978, N Corporation is required under section 951 to include in gross income $50 attributable to the earnings and profits of A Corporation for such year, but A Corporation does not distribute any earnings and profits for such year. The foreign income taxes paid by A Corporation for 1978 which are deemed paid by N Corporation for such year under section 960(a)(1) are determined as follows upon the basis of the facts assumed:

Pretax earnings and profits of A Corporation	$100.00
Foreign income taxes (20%)	20.00
Earnings and profits	80.00
Amount required to be included in N Corporation's gross income under sec. 951	50.00
Dividends paid to N Corporation	none
Foreign income taxes paid on or with respect to earnings and profits of A Corporation	20.00
Foreign income taxes of A Corporation deemed paid by N Corporation under sec. 960(a)(1) ($50/$80 × $20)	12.50

Example (2). Domestic corporation N owns all the one class of stock of controlled foreign corporation A, which owns all the one class of stock of controlled foreign corporation B. All such corporations use the calendar year as the taxable year. For 1978, N Corporation is required under section 951 to include in gross income $45 attributable to the earnings and profits of B Corporation for such year, but is not required to include any amount in gross income under section 951 attributable to the earnings and profits of A Corporation for such year. Neither B Corporation nor A Corporation distributes any earnings and profits for 1978. The foreign income taxes paid by B Corporation for 1978 which are deemed paid by N Corporation for such year under section 960(a)(1) are determined as follows upon the basis of the facts assumed:

Pretax earnings and profits of B Corporation	$100.00
Foreign income taxes (40%)	40.00
Earnings and profits	60.00
Amount required to be included in N Corporation's gross income under sec. 951 with respect to B Corporation	45.00
Dividends paid	none
Foreign income taxes paid on or with respect to earnings and profits of B Corporation	40.00
Foreign income taxes of B Corporation deemed paid by N Corporation under sec. 960(a)(1) ($45/$60 × $40)	30.00

Example (3). Domestic corporation N owns all the one class of stock of controlled foreign corporation A, which owns all the one class of stock of controlled foreign corporation B, which owns all the one class of stock of foreign corporation C. All such corporations use the calendar year as the taxable year. For 1978, N Corporation is required under section 951 to include the gross income $80 attributable to the earnings and profits of C Corporation for such year, $45 attributable to the earnings and profits of B Corporation for such year and $50 attributable to the earnings and profits of A Corporation for such year. Neither C Corporation nor B Corporation distributes any earnings and profits for 1978. The foreign income taxes which are deemed paid by N Corporation for such year under section 960(a)(1) are determined as follows upon the basis of the facts assumed:

C Corporation (third-tier corporation):

Pretax earnings of C Corporation	$150.00
Foreign income taxes (40%)	60.00
Earnings and profits	90.00
Amounts required to be included in N Corporation's gross income under section 951	80.00
Dividends paid to B Corporation	0
Foreign income taxes paid on or with respect to earnings and profits of C Corporation	60.00

B Corporation (second-tier corporation):

Pretax earnings of B Corporation	$100.00
Foreign income taxes (40%)	40.00
Earnings and profits	60.00
Amount required to be included in N Corporation's gross income under section 951	45.00
Dividends paid to A Corporation	0
Foreign income taxes paid on or with respect to earnings and profits of B Corporation	40.00

A Corporation (first-tier corporation):

Pretax earnings and profits of A Corporation	$100.00
Foreign income taxes (20%)	20.00
Earnings and profits	80.00
Amount required to be included in N Corporation's gross income under section 951	50.00
Dividends paid to N Corporation	0
Foreign income taxes paid on or with respect to earnings and profits of A Corporation	20.00

N Corporation (domestic corporation):

Foreign income taxes deemed paid by N Corporation under section 960(a)(1):	
Taxes of C Corporation $80/$90 × $60	$53.33
Taxes of B Corporation $45/$60 × $40	30.00
Taxes of A Corporation $50/$80 × $20	12.50
Total taxes deemed paid under section 960(a)(1)	$95.83

Example (4). Domestic corporation N owns all the one class of stock of controlled foreign corporation A, which owns 5 percent of the one class of stock of controlled foreign corporation B. N Corporation also directly owns 95 percent of the one class of stock of B Corporation. (Under these facts, B Corporation is only a first-tier corporation with respect to N Corporation.) All such corporations use the calendar year as the taxable year. For 1978, N Corporation is required under section 951 to include in gross income $60 attributable to the earnings and profits of B Corporation and $79.20 attributable to the earnings and profits of A Corporation. For 1978, B Corporation distributes $19 to N Corporation and $1 to A Corporation, but A Corporation makes no distribution to N Corporation. The foreign income taxes paid by N Corporation for such year under section 960(a)(1) are determined as follows upon the basis of the facts assumed in accordance with § 1.960-1(c)(1)(i):

B Corporation (first-tier corporation):

Pretax earnings and profits	$100.00
Foreign income taxes (40%)	40.00
Earnings and profits	60.00

Amount required to be included in N Corporation's gross income under section 951 with respect to B Corporation	60.00
A Corporation (first-tier corporation):	
Pretax earnings and profits (including $1 dividend from B Corporation)	$100.00
Foreign income taxes (20%)	20.00
Earnings and profits	80.00
Amount required to be included in N Corporation's gross income with respect to A Corporation ($99 − [$99 × 0.20])	79.20
N Corporation (domestic corporation):	
Foreign income taxes deemed paid by N Corporation under section 960(a)(1) with respect to—	
B Corporation ([$60 × 0.95/$60] × $40)	$38.00
A Corporation ($79.20/$80 × $20)	19.80
Total taxes deemed paid under section 960(a)(1)	$57.80

Example (5). Domestic corporation N owns all the one class of stock of controlled foreign corporation A, which owns all the one class of stock of controlled foreign corporation B. All such corporations use the calendar year as the taxable year. For 1978, N Corporation is required under section 951 to include in gross income $175 attributable to the earnings and profits of A Corporation for such year. For 1978, B Corporation has earnings and profits of $225, on which it pays foreign income taxes of $75. In 1978, B Corporation distributes $150, which, under paragraph (b) of §1.960-2, consists of $100 to which section 902(b)(1) does not apply (from B Corporation's earnings and profits attributable to an amount required under section 951 to be included in N Corporation's gross income with respect to B Corporation) and $50 to which section 902(b)(1) applies (from B Corporation's other earnings and profits). The country under the laws of which A Corporation is incorporated imposes an income tax of 40 percent on all income but exempts from tax dividends received from a subsidiary corporation. A Corporation makes no distribution for 1978. Under paragraph (b) of §1.960-2, A Corporation is deemed to have paid $25 ($50/$150 × $75) of the $75 foreign income taxes paid by B Corporation on its pretax earnings and profits of $225. The foreign income taxes deemed paid by N Corporation for 1978 under section 960(a)(1) with respect to A Corporation are determined as follows upon the basis of the following assumed facts:

Pretax earnings and profits of A Corporation:			
Dividends received from B Corporation		$150.00	
Other income		250.00	
Total pretax earnings and profits			$400.00
Foreign income taxes:			
On dividends received from B Corporation		0	
On other income ($250 × 0.40)		$100.00	
Total foreign income taxes			$100.00
Earnings and profits:			
Attributable to dividends received from B Corporation which are attributable to amounts included in N Corporation's gross income under section 951 with respect to B Corporation		100.00	
Attributable to other income:			
Attributable to dividends received from B Corporation which are attributable to amounts not included in N Corporation's gross income under 951 with respect to B Corporation	$50.00		
Attributable to other income ($250 − $100 [$250 × 0.40])	150.00	200.00	
Total earnings and profits			300.00
Foreign income taxes deemed paid by N Corporation under sec. 960(a)(1) with respect to A Corporation:			
Tax paid by A Corporation in respect to its income other than dividends received from B Corporation attributable to amounts included in N Corporation's gross income under section 951 with respect to B Corporation ($175/$200 × $100)			87.50
Tax of B Corporation deemed paid by A Corporation under sec. 902(b)(1) in respect to such income ($175/$200 × $25)			21.88
Total foreign income taxes deemed paid by N Corporation under sec. 960(a)(1) with respect to A Corporation			$109.38

(d) *Time for meeting stock ownership requirements.*—(1) *In general.*—For the purposes of applying paragraph (c) of this section to amounts included in the gross income of a domestic corporation attributable to the earnings and profits of a first-, second-, or third-tier corporation, the stock ownership requirements of paragraph (b)(1), (2), and (3) of this section and the percentage of voting stock requirements of paragraph (c)(1)(i) and (ii) of this section, if applicable, must be satisfied on the last day in the taxable year of such first-, second-, or third-tier corporation, as the case may be, on which such foreign corporation is a controlled foreign corporation. For paragraph (c) to apply to amounts included in a domestic corporation's gross income attributable to the earnings and profits of a second-tier corporation, the requirements of paragraph (b)(1) and (2) of this section and the percentage of voting stock requirement of paragraph (c)(1)(i) of this section must be met on such date. For paragraph (c) to apply to amounts included in a domestic corporation's gross income attributable to the earnings and profits of a third-tier corporation, the requirements of paragraph (b)(1), (2), and (3) of this section and the percentage of voting stock requirement of paragraph (c)(1)(ii) of this section must be met on such date.

(2) *Illustrations.*—The application of this paragraph may be illustrated by the following examples:

Example (1). Domestic corporation N is required for its taxable year ending June 30, 1978, to include in gross income under section 951 an amount attributable to the earnings and profits of controlled foreign corporation A for 1977 and another amount attributable to the earnings and profits of controlled foreign corporation B for such year. Corporations A and B use the calendar year as the taxable year. Such amounts are required to be included in N Corporation's gross income by reason of its ownership of stock in A Corporation and in turn by A Corporation's ownership of stock in B Corporation. Corporation A is a controlled foreign corporation throughout 1977, but B Corporation is a controlled foreign corporation only from January 1, 1977, through September 30, 1977. Corporation N may obtain credit under section 960(a)(1) for the year ending June 30, 1978, for foreign income taxes paid by A Corporation for 1977, only if N Corporation owns at least 10 percent of the voting stock of A Corporation on December 31, 1977. Corporation N may obtain credit under section 960(a)(1) for the year ending June 30, 1978, for foreign income taxes paid by B Corporation for 1977, only if on September 30, 1977, N Corporation owns at least 10 percent of the voting stock of A Corporation, A Corporation owns at least 10 percent of the voting stock of B Corporation, and the percentage of voting stock requirement of paragraph (c)(1)(i) of this section is met.

Example (2). The facts are the same as in example (1), except that A Corporation is a controlled foreign corporation only from January 1, 1977, through March 31, 1977. Corporation N may obtain credit under section 960(a)(1) for the year ending June 30, 1978, for foreign income taxes paid by A Corporation for 1977, only if N Corporation owns at least 10 percent of the voting stock of A Corporation on March 31, 1977. Corporation N may obtain credit under section 960(a)(1) for the year ending June 30, 1978, for foreign income taxes paid by B Corporation for 1977, only if on September 30, 1977, N Corporation owns at least 10 percent of the voting stock of A Corporation, A Corporation owns at least 10 percent of the voting stock of B Corporation, and the percentage of voting stock requirement of paragraph (c)(1)(i) of this section is met.

Example (3). Domestic Corporation N owns 100 percent of the stock of controlled foreign corporation A. A Corporation owns 20 percent of the stock of controlled foreign corporation B. B Corporation owns 10 percent of the voting stock of controlled foreign corporation C. For calendar year 1983, N Corporation is required to include amounts in its gross income attributable to the earnings and profits of A, B, and C Corporations. A, B, and C Corporations were all controlled foreign corporations throughout their respective taxable years ending as follows: A Corporation, December 31, 1983; B Corporation, November 30, 1983; and C Corporation, August 31, 1983. Paragraph (c) of this section applies to amounts included in gross income of N Corporation with respect to the earnings and profits of A Corporation because the 10 percent ownership requirement of paragraph (b)(1) of this section is met on December 31, 1983. Paragraph (c) of this section applies to amounts included in the gross income of N Corporation with respect to the earnings and profits of B Corporation because the 10 percent stock ownership requirements of paragraph (b)(1) and (2) of this section are met on November 30, 1983, and the percentage of voting stock requirement of paragraph (c)(1)(i) of this section (5 percent) is also met on such date. The percentage of voting stock in A Corporation owned by N Corporation (100 percent) multiplied by the percentage of voting stock in B Corporation owned by A Corporation (20 percent) is 20 percent. Paragraph (c) of this section will not apply to amounts included in N Corporation's gross income attributable to the earnings and profits of C Corporation even though on August 31, 1983, the 10 percent stock ownership requirements of paragraph (b)(1), (2), and (3) of this section are met, because the percentage of voting stock requirement of paragraph (c)(1)(ii) of this section (5 percent) is not met on such date. The percentage of voting stock of C Corporation owned by B Corporation (10 percent) multiplied by 20 percent (the percentage of voting stock of A Corporation owned by N Corporation multiplied by the percentage of voting stock of B Corporation owned by A Corporation) is 2 percent.

(e) *Information to be furnished.*—If the credit for foreign income taxes claimed under section 901 includes taxes deemed paid under section 960(a)(1), the domestic corporation must furnish the same information with respect to the taxes so deemed paid as it is required to furnish with respect to the taxes actually paid or accrued by it and for which credit is claimed. See § 1.905-2. For other information required to be furnished by the domestic corporation for the annual accounting period of certain foreign corporations ending with or within such corporation's taxable year, see section 6038(a) and the regulations thereunder.

(f) *Reduction of foreign income taxes paid or deemed paid.*—For reduction of the amount of foreign income taxes paid or deemed paid by a foreign corporation for purposes of section 960, see section 6038(c) (as amended by section 338 of the Tax Equity and Fiscal Responsibility Act of 1982) and the regulations thereunder, relating to failure to furnish information with respect to certain foreign corporations. For reduction of the foreign income taxes deemed paid by a domestic corporation under section 960 with respect to foreign oil and gas extraction income, see section 907(a).

(g) *Amounts under section 951 treated as distributions for purposes of applying effective dates.*—For purposes of applying section 902 in determining the amount of credit allowed under section 960(a)(1) and paragraph (c) of this section, the effective date provisions of the regulations under section 902 shall apply, and for purposes of so applying the regulations under section 902, any amount attributable to the earnings and profits for the taxable year of a first-, second-, or third-tier corporation which is included in the gross income of a domestic corporation under section 951 shall be treated as a distribution received by such domestic corporation on the last day in such taxable year on which such foreign corporation is a controlled foreign corporation.

(h) *Source of income and country to which tax is deemed paid.*—(1) *Source of income.*—For purposes of section 904—

(i) The amount included in gross income of a domestic corporation under section 951 for the taxable year with respect to a first-, second-, or third-tier corporation, plus

(ii) Any section 78 dividend to which such section 951 amount gives rise by reason of taxes deemed paid by such domestic corporation under section 960(a)(1),

shall be deemed to be derived from sources within the foreign country or possession of the United States under the laws of which such first-tier corporation, or the first-tier corporation in the same chain of ownership as such second- or third-tier corporation, is created or organized.

(2) *Country to which taxes deemed paid.*—For purposes of section 904, the foreign income taxes paid by the first-, second-, or third-tier corporation and deemed to be paid by the domestic corporation under section 960(a)(1) by reason of the inclusion of the amount described in paragraph (h)(1)(i) of this section in the gross income of such domestic corporation shall be deemed to be paid to the foreign country or possession of the United States under the laws of which such first-tier corporation, or the first-tier corporation in the same chain of ownership as such second- or third-tier corporation, is created or organized.

(3) *Illustration.*—The application of this paragraph may be illustrated by the following example:

Example. Domestic corporation N owns all the one class of stock of controlled foreign corporation A, incorporated under the laws of foreign country X, which owns all the one class of stock of controlled foreign corporation B, incorporated under the laws of foreign country Y. All such corporations use the calendar year as the taxable year. For 1978, N Corporation is required under section 951 to include in gross income $45 attributable to the earnings and profits of B Corporation for such year and $50 attributable to the earnings and profits of A Corporation for such year. For 1978, because of the inclusion of such amounts in gross income, N Corporation is deemed under section 960(a)(1) and paragraph (c) of this section to have paid $15 of foreign income taxes paid by B Corporation for such year and $10 of foreign income taxes paid by A Corporation for such year. For purposes of section 904, the amount ($95) included in N Corporation's gross income under section 951 attributable to the earnings and profits of corporations A and B is deemed to be derived from sources within country X, and the section 78 dividend consisting of the foreign income taxes ($25) deemed paid by N Corporation under section 960(a)(1) with respect to such $95 is deemed to be derived from sources within country X. The $25 of foreign income taxes so deemed paid by N Corporation are deemed to be paid to country X for purposes of section 904.

(i) *Computation of deemed-paid taxes in post-1986 taxable years.*—(1) *General rule.*—If a domestic corporation is eligible to compute deemed-paid taxes under section 960(a)(1) with respect to an amount included in gross income under section 951(a), then, such domestic corporation shall be deemed to have paid a portion of the foreign corporation's post-1986 foreign income taxes determined under section 902 and the regulations under that section in the same manner as if the amount so included were a dividend paid by such foreign corporation (determined by applying section 902(c) in accordance with section 904(d)(3)(B)).

(2) *Ordering rule for computing deemed-paid taxes under sections 902 and 960.*—If a domestic corporation computes deemed-paid taxes under both sections 902 and 960 in the same taxable year, section 960 shall be applied first. After the deemed-paid taxes are computed under section 960 with respect to a deemed income inclusion, post-1986 undistributed earnings and post-1986 foreign income taxes in each separate category shall be reduced by the appropriate amounts before deemed-paid taxes are computed under section 902 with respect to a dividend distribution.

(3) *Computation of post-1986 undistributed earnings.*—Post-1986 undistributed earnings (or an accumulated deficit in post-1986 undistributed earnings) are computed under section 902 and the regulations under that section.

(4) *Allocation of accumulated deficits.*—For purposes of computing post-1986 undistributed earnings under sections 902 and 960, a post-1986 accumulated deficit in a separate category shall be allocated proportionately to reduce post-1986 undistributed earnings in the other separate categories. However, a deficit in any separate category shall not permanently reduce earnings in other separate categories, but after the deemed-paid taxes are computed the separate limitation deficit shall be carried forward in the same separate category in which it was incurred. In addition, because deemed-paid taxes may not exceed taxes paid or accrued by the controlled foreign corporation, in computing deemed-paid taxes with respect to an inclusion out of a separate category that exceeds post-1986 undistributed earnings in that separate category, the numerator of the deemed-paid credit fraction (deemed inclusion from the separate category) may not exceed the denominator (post-1986 undistributed earnings in the separate category).

(5) *Examples.*—The application of this paragraph (i) may be illustrated by the following examples. See § 1.952-1(f)(4) for additional illustrations of these rules.

Example 1. (i) A, a U.S. person, is the sole shareholder of CFC, a controlled foreign corporation formed on January 1, 1998, whose functional currency is the u. In 1998 CFC earns 100u of general limitation income described in section 904(d)(1)(I) that is not subpart F income and 100u of foreign personal holding company income that is passive income described in section 904(d)(1)(A). In 1998 CFC also incurs a (50u) loss in the shipping category described in section 904(d)(1)(D). CFC's subpart F income for 1998, 100u, does not exceed CFC's current earnings and profits of 150u. Accordingly, all 100u of CFC's subpart F income is included in A's gross income under section 951(a)(1)(A). Under section 904(d)(3)(B) of the Internal Revenue Code and paragraph (i)(1) of this section, A includes 100u of passive limitation income in gross income for 1998.

(ii) For purposes of computing post-1986 undistributed earnings under sections 902, 904(d) and 960 with respect to the subpart F inclusion, the shipping limitation deficit of (50u) is allocated proportionately to reduce general limitation earnings of 100u and passive limitation earnings of 100u. Thus, general limitation earnings are reduced by 25u to 75u (100u general limitation earnings/200u total earnings in positive separate categories x (50u) shipping deficit = 25u reduction), and passive limitation earnings are reduced by 25u to 75u (100u passive earnings/200u total earnings in positive separate categories x (50u) shipping deficit = 25u reduction). All of CFC's post-1986 foreign income taxes with respect to passive limitation earnings are deemed paid by A under section 960 with respect to the 100u subpart F inclusion of passive income (75u inclusion (numerator limited to denominator under paragraph (i)(4) of this section)/75u passive earnings). After the inclusion and deemed-paid taxes are computed, at the close of 1998 CFC has 100u of general limitation earnings, 0 of passive limitation earnings (100u of foreign personal holding company income - 100u inclusion), and a (50u) deficit in shipping limitation earnings.

Example 2. (i) The facts are the same as in *Example 1* with the addition of the following facts. In 1999, CFC distributes 150u to A. CFC has 100u of previously-taxed earnings and profits described in section 959(c)(2) attributable to 1998, all of which is passive limitation earnings and profits. Under section 959(c), 100u of the 150u distribution is deemed to be made from earnings and profits described in section 959(c)(2). The remaining 50u is deemed to be made from earnings and profits described in section 959(c)(3). The entire dividend distribution of 50u is treated as made out of CFC's general limitation earnings and profits. See section 904(d)(3)(D).

(ii) For purposes of computing post-1986 undistributed earnings under section 902 with respect to the 1999 dividend of 50u, the shipping limitation accumulated deficit of (50u) reduces general limitation earnings and profits of 100u to 50u. Thus, 100% of CFC's post-1986 foreign income taxes with respect to general limitation earnings are deemed paid by A under section 902 with respect to the 1999 dividend of 50u (50u dividend/50u general limitation earnings). After the deemed-paid taxes are computed, at the close of 1999 CFC has 50u of general limitation earnings (100u opening balance - 50u distribution), 0 of passive limitation earnings, and a (50u) deficit in shipping limitation earnings.

(6) *Effective date.*—This paragraph (i) applies to taxable years of a controlled foreign corporation beginning after March 3, 1997. [Reg. § 1.960-1.]

☐ [T.D. 7120, 6-3-71. *Amended by* T.D. 7334, 12-20-74; T.D. 7481, 4-15-77; T.D. 7545, 5-5-78; T.D. 7649, 10-17-79; T.D. 7843, 11-5-82; T.D. 7961, 6-27-84 *and* T.D. 8704, 12-31-96.]

§ 1.960-2. Interrelation of section 902 and section 960 when dividends are paid by third-, second-, or first-tier corporation.

—(a) *Scope of this section.*—This section prescribes rules for the application of section 902 in a case where dividends are paid by a third-, second-, or first-tier corporation, as the case may be, from its earnings and profits for a taxable year when an amount attributable to such earnings and profits is included in the gross income of a domestic corporation under section 951, or when such earnings and profits are attributable to an amount excluded from the gross income of such foreign corporation under section 959(b) and § 1.959-2, with respect to the domestic corporation. In making determinations under this section, any portion of a distribution received from a first-tier corporation by the domestic corporation which is excluded from the domestic corporation's gross income under section 959(a) and § 1.959-1, or any portion of a distribution received from an immediately lower-tier corporation by the third-, second-, or first-tier corporation which is excluded from such foreign corporation's gross income under section 959(b) and § 1.959-2, shall be treated as a dividend for purposes of taking into account under section 902 any foreign income taxes paid by such third-, second-, or first-tier corporation which are not deemed paid by the domestic corporation under section 960(a)(1) and § 1.960-1.

(b) *Application of section 902(b) to dividends received from an immediately lower-tier corporation.*—For purposes of paragraph (a) of this section and paragraph (c)(1)(i) of § 1.960-1, section 902(b) shall apply to all dividends received by the first- or second-tier corporation from the immediately lower-tier corporation other than dividends attributable to earnings and profits of such immediately lower-tier corporation in respect of which an amount is, or has been, included in the gross income of a domestic corporation under section 951 with respect to such immediately lower-tier corporation.

(c) *Application of section 902(a) to dividends received by domestic corporation from first-tier corporation.*—For purposes of paragraph (a) of this section, section 902(a) shall apply to all dividends received by the domestic corporation for its taxable year from the first-tier corporation other than dividends attributable to earnings and profits of such first-tier corporation in respect of which an amount is, or has been, included in the gross income of a domestic corporation under section 951 with respect to such first-tier corporation.

(d) *Allocation of earnings and profits of a first-or second-tier corporation having income excluded under section 959(b).*—(1) *First-tier corporations.*—If the first-tier corporation for its taxable year receives dividends from the second-tier corporation to which in accordance with paragraph (b) of this section 902(b)(1) or section 902(b)(2) applies and other dividends from the second-tier corporation to which such sections do not apply, then in applying section 902(a) pursuant to this section and in applying section 960(a)(1) pursuant to § 1.960-1(c)(1)(i), with respect to the foreign income taxes paid and deemed paid by the second-tier corporation which are deemed paid by the first-tier corporation for such taxable year under section 902(b)(1)—

(i) The earnings and profits of the first-tier corporation for such taxable year shall be considered not to include its earnings and profits which are attributable to the dividends to which section 902(b)(1) does not apply (in determining the domestic corporation's credit for the taxes paid by the second-tier corporation) or which are attributable to the dividends to which sections 902(b)(1) and 902(b)(2) do not apply (in determining the domestic corporation's credit for taxes deemed paid by the second-tier corporation) and

(ii) For the purposes of so applying section 902(a), distributions to the domestic corporation from such earnings and profits which are attributable to the dividends to which section 902(b)(1) does not apply (in determining the domestic corporation's credit for taxes paid by the second-tier corporation) or which are attributable to the dividends to which sections 902(b)(1) and 902(b)(2) do not apply (in determining the domestic corporation's credit for taxes deemed paid by the second-tier corporation) shall not be treated as a dividend.

(2) *Second-tier corporations.*—If the second-tier corporation for its taxable year receives dividends from the third-tier corporation to which, in accordance with paragraph (b) of this section, section 902(b)(2) applies and other dividends from the third-tier corporation to which such section does not apply, then in applying section 902(b)(1) pursuant to this section, and in applying section 960(a)(1) pursuant to paragraph (c)(1)(i) of § 1.960-1, with respect to the foreign taxes deemed paid by the second-tier corporation for such taxable year under section 902(b)(2)—

(i) The earnings and profits of the second-tier corporation for such taxable year shall be considered not to include its earnings and profits which are attributable to such other dividends from the third-tier corporation, and

(ii) For the purposes of so applying section 902(b)(1), distributions to the first-tier corporation from such earnings and profits which are attributable to such other dividends from the third-tier corporation shall not be treated as a dividend.

(e) *Separate determinations under sections 902(a), 902(b)(1), and 902(b)(2) in the case of a first-, second-, or third-tier corporation having income excluded under section 959(b).*—If in the case of a first-, second-, or third-tier corporation to which paragraph (b) or (c) of this section is applied—

(1) The earnings and profits of such foreign corporation for its taxable year consist of—

(i) Dividends received from an immediately lower-tier corporation which are attributable to amounts included in the gross income of a domestic corporation under section 951 with respect to the immediately lower- or lower-tier corporations, and

(ii) Other earnings and profits, and

(2) The effective rate of foreign income taxes paid or accrued by such foreign corporation on the dividends described in paragraph (e)(1)(i) of this section is higher or lower than the effective rate of foreign income taxes attributable to its earnings and profits described in paragraph (e)(1)(ii) of this section,

then, for purposes of applying paragraphs (b) or (c) of this section to dividends paid by such foreign corporation to the domestic corporation or the first- or second-tier corporation, sections 902(a), 902(b)(1), and 902(b)(2) shall be applied separately to the portion of the dividend which is attributable to the earnings and profits described in paragraph (e)(1)(i) of this section and separately to the portion of the dividend which is attributable to the earnings and profits described in paragraph (e)(1)(ii) of this section. In making a separate determination with respect to the earnings and profits described in paragraph (e)(1)(i) or (e)(1)(ii) of this section, only the foreign income taxes paid or accrued (or, in the case of earnings and profits of a first- or second-tier corporation described in paragraph (e)(1)(ii) of this section, deemed to be paid) by such foreign corporation on the income attributable to such earnings and profits shall be taken into account. For purposes of applying this paragraph (e), no part of the foreign income taxes paid, accrued, or deemed to be paid which are attributable to the earnings and profits described in paragraph (e)(1)(ii) of this section shall be attributed to the dividend described in paragraph (e)(1)(i) of this section; and no part of the foreign income taxes paid or accrued on the dividend described in paragraph (e)(1)(i) of this section shall be attributed to the earnings and profits described in paragraph (e)(1)(ii) of this section. Furthermore, the effective rate of foreign income taxes paid or accrued shall be determined consistently with the principles of paragraph (b)(3)(iv) and (viii) and (c) of § 1.954-1. Thus, for example, the effective rate of foreign income taxes on dividends received by such foreign corporation shall be determined by taking into account any intercorporate dividends received deduction allowed to such corporation for such dividends.

(f) *Illustrations.*—The application of this section may be illustrated by the following examples. In all of the examples other than examples (6), (7), (9) and (10), it is assumed that the effective rate of foreign income taxes paid or accrued by the first- or second-tier corporation, as the case may be, in respect to dividends received from the immediately lower-tier corporation is the same as the effective rate of foreign income taxes paid or accrued by the first- or second-tier corporation with respect to its other income:

Example (1). Domestic corporation N owns all the one class of stock of controlled foreign corporation A, which owns all the one class of stock of controlled foreign corporation B. All such corporations use the calendar year as the taxable year. For 1978, N Corporation is required under section 951 to include $50 in gross income attributable to the earnings and profits of A Corporation for such year, but is not required to include any amount in gross income under section 951 attributable to the earnings and profits of B Corporation. For such year, B Corporation distributes a dividend of $45, but A Corporation does not make any distributions. The foreign income taxes deemed paid by N Corporation for 1978 under section 960(a)(1), after applying section 902(b)(1) for such year of A Corporation, are determined as follows upon the basis of the facts assumed:

B Corporation (second-tier corporation):
Pretax earnings and profits	$100.00
Foreign income taxes (40%)	40.00
Earnings and profits	60.00
Dividends paid to A Corporation	45.00
Foreign income taxes paid by B Corporation on or with respect to its accumulated profits	40.00
Foreign income taxes of B Corporation deemed paid by A Corporation for 1978 under sec. 902(b)(1) ($45/$60 × $40)	30.00

A Corporation (first-tier corporation):
Pretax earnings and profits:
Dividends from B Corporation	$45.00	
Other income	100.00	
Total pretax earnings and profits		$145.00
Foreign income taxes (20%)		29.00
Earnings and profits		116.00
Foreign income taxes paid, and deemed to be paid, by A Corporation on or with respect to its earnings and profits ($29 + $30)		59.00
Amount required to be included in N Corporation's gross income under sec. 951 with respect to A Corporation		$50.00
Dividends paid to N Corporation		none

N Corporation (domestic corporation):
Foreign income taxes of A Corporation deemed paid by N Corporation for 1965 under sec. 960(a)(1) ($50/$116 × $59)	$25.43

Example (2). Domestic corporation N owns all the one class of stock of controlled foreign corporation A, which owns all the one class of stock of controlled foreign corporation B. All such corporations use the calendar year as the taxable year. For 1978, N Corporation is required under section 951 to include in gross income $150 attributable to the earnings and profits of B Corporation for such year, which B Corporation distributes during such year. Corporation N is not required for 1978 to include any amount in gross income under section 951 attributable to the earnings and profits of A Corporation, but A Corporation distributes for such year $135 from its earnings and profits attributable to B Corporation's dividend. The foreign income taxes deemed paid by N Corporation for 1978 under section 960(a)(1) and section 902(a) are determined as follows upon the basis of the facts assumed:

B Corporation (second-tier corporation):
Pretax earnings and profits	$250.00
Foreign income taxes (20%)	50.00
Earnings and profits	200.00
Amounts required to be included in N Corporation's gross income under sec. 951 with respect to B Corporation	150.00
Dividends paid to A Corporation	150.00
Foreign income taxes paid on or with respect to earnings and profits of B Corporation	50.00

A Corporation (first-tier corporation):
Pretax earnings and profits:
Dividends from B Corporation	$150.00	
Other income	200.00	
Total pretax earnings and profits		$350.00
Foreign income taxes (10%)		35.00
Earnings and profits		315.00
Dividends paid to N Corporation		135.00
Foreign income taxes paid by A Corporation on or with respect to its accumulated profits		35.00

N Corporation (domestic corporation):
Foreign income taxes of B Corporation deemed paid by N Corporation for 1978 under sec. 960(a)(1) ($150/$200 × $50)	$37.50
Foreign income taxes of A Corporation deemed paid by N Corporation for 1978 under sec. 902(a) ($135/$315 × $35)	15.00
Total foreign income taxes deemed paid by N Corporation under sec. 901	$52.50

Reg. § 1.960-2(f)

Example (3). Domestic corporation N owns all the one class of stock of controlled foreign corporation A, which owns all the one class of stock of controlled foreign corporation B. All such corporations use the calendar year as the taxable year. For 1978, N Corporation is required under section 951 to include $180 in gross income attributable to the earnings and profits of A Corporation for such year, but is not required to include any amount in gross income under section 951 attributable to the earnings and profits of B Corporation. Corporation B distributes from its earnings and profits for 1978 a dividend of $50. For 1978, A Corporation distributes $180 from its earnings and profits attributable to the amount required under section 951 to be included in N Corporation's gross income for such year with respect to A Corporation and $20 from its other earnings and profits. The foreign income taxes deemed paid by N Corporation for 1978 under section 960(a)(1) and section 902(a) are determined as follows upon the basis of the facts assumed:

B Corporation (second-tier corporation):
Pretax earnings and profits	$100.00
Foreign income taxes (40%)	40.00
Earnings and profits	60.00
Dividends paid to A Corporation	50.00
Foreign income taxes paid by B Corporation on or with respect to its accumulated profits	40.00
Foreign income taxes of B Corporation deemed paid by A Corporation for 1978 under sec. 902(b)(1) ($50/$60 × $40)	33.33

A Corporation (first-tier corporation):
Pretax earnings and profits:

Dividends from B Corporation	$50.00	
Other income	200.00	
Total pretax earnings and profits		250.00
Foreign income taxes (10%)		25.00
Earnings and profits		225.00
Foreign income taxes paid, and deemed to be paid, by A Corporation on or with respect to its earnings and profits ($25.00 + $33.33)		58.33
Amounts required to be included in N Corporation's gross income for 1978 under sec. 951 with respect to A Corporation		180.00

Dividends paid to N Corporation:

Dividends to which sec. 902(a) does not apply (from A Corporation's earnings and profits in respect of which an amount is required under sec. 951 to be included in N Corporation's gross income with respect to A Corporation)	$180.00	
Dividends to which sec. 902(a) applies (from A Corporation's other earnings and profits)	20.00	
Total dividends paid to N Corporation		200.00

N Corporation (domestic corporation):
Foreign income taxes of corporations A and B deemed paid by N Corporation under sec. 960(a)(1) ($180/$225 × $58.33)	46.66
Foreign income taxes of corporations A and B deemed paid by N Corporation under sec. 902(a) ($20/$225 × $58.33)	5.18
Total foreign income taxes deemed paid by N Corporation under sec. 901	$51.84

Example (4). Domestic corporation N owns all the one class of stock of controlled foreign corporation A, which owns all the one class of stock of controlled foreign corporation B. All such corporations use the calendar year as the taxable year. For 1978, N Corporation is required under section 951 to include in gross income $150 attributable to the earnings and profits of B Corporation for such year and $22.50 attributable to the earnings and profits of A Corporation for such year. For 1978, B Corporation distributes $175, consisting of $150 from its earnings and profits attributable to amounts required under section 951 to be included in N Corporation's gross income with respect to B Corporation and $25 from its other earnings and profits. Corporation A does not distribute any dividends for 1978. The foreign income taxes deemed paid by N Corporation for 1978 under section 960(a)(1) are determined as follows upon the basis of the facts assumed:

B Corporation (second-tier corporation):
Pretax earnings and profits	$250.00
Foreign income taxes (20%)	50.00
Earnings and profits	200.00

Controlled Foreign Corporations

Amounts required to be included in N Corporation's gross income under sec. 951 for 1978 with respect to B Corporation		150.00
Dividends paid by B Corporation:		
Dividends to which sec. 902(b) does not apply (from B Corporation's earnings and profits in respect of which an amount is required under sec. 951 to be included in N Corporation gross income with respect to B Corporation)	$150.00	
Dividends to which sec. 902(b)(1) applies (from B Corporation's other earnings and profits)	25.00	
Total dividends paid to A Corporation		175.00
Foreign income taxes paid by B Corporation on or with respect to its accumulated profits		50.00
Foreign income taxes of B Corporation deemed paid by A Corporation for 1978 under sec. 902(b)(1) ($25/$200 × $50)		6.25

A Corporation (first-tier corporation):

Pretax earnings and profits	$175.00
Foreign income tax (10%)	17.50
Earnings and profits	157.50
Earnings and profits after exclusion of amounts attributable to dividends to which sec. 902(b) does not apply ($157.50 less [$150 − ($150 × .10)])	22.50
Amount required to be included in N Corporation's gross income for 1978 under sec. 951 with respect to A Corporation	22.50
Dividends paid to N Corporation	0

N Corporation (domestic corporation):

Foreign income taxes deemed paid by N Corporation under sec. 960(a)(1) with respect to A Corporation:		
Tax actually paid by A Corporation ($22.50/$157.50 × $17.50) ..	$2.50	
Tax of B Corporation deemed paid by A Corporation under sec. 902(b)(1) ($22.50/$22.50 × $6.25)	6.25	
		$8.75
Foreign income taxes deemed paid by N Corporation under sec. 960(a)(1)(C) with respect to B Corporation ($150/$200 × $50)		37.50
Total taxes deemed paid under sec. 960(a)(1)		$46.25

Example (5). Domestic corporation N owns all the one class of stock of controlled foreign corporation A, which owns all the one class of stock of controlled foreign corporation B. All such corporations use the calendar year as the taxable year. For 1978, N Corporation is required under section 951 to include in gross income $150 attributable to the earnings and profits of B Corporation for such year and $22.50 attributable to the earnings and profits of A Corporation for such year. For 1978, B Corporation distributes $175, consisting of $150 from its earnings and profits attributable to amounts required under section 951 to be included in N Corporation's gross income with respect to B Corporation and $25 from its other earnings and profits. For 1978, A Corporation distributes $225, consisting of $135 from its earnings and profits attributable to the amount required under section 951 to be included in N Corporation's gross income with respect to B Corporation, $22.50 from its earnings and profits attributable to the amount required under section 951 to be included in N Corporation's gross income with respect to A Corporation, and $67.50 from its other earnings and profits. The foreign income taxes deemed paid by N Corporation for 1978 under section 960(a)(1) and section 902(a) are determined as follows upon the basis of the facts assumed:

B Corporation (second-tier corporation):

Pretax earnings and profits		$250.00
Foreign income taxes (20%)		50.00
Earnings and profits		200.00
Amounts required to be included in N Corporation's gross income for 1978 under sec. 951 with respect to B Corporation		150.00
Dividends paid by B Corporation:		
Dividends to which sec. 902(b) does not apply (from B Corporation's earnings and profits in respect of which an amount is required under sec. 951 to be included in N Corporation's gross income with respect to B Corporation)	$150.00	
Dividends to which sec. 902(b)(1) applies (from B Corporation's other earnings and profits)	25.00	
Total dividends paid to A Corporation		175.00

Reg. §1.960-2(f)

Foreign income taxes paid by B Corporation on or with respect to its accumulated profits		50.00
Foreign income taxes of B Corporation deemed paid by A Corporation for 1978 under sec. 902(b)(1) ($25/$200 × $50)		6.25

A Corporation (first-tier corporation):

Pretax earnings and profits:		
Dividends received from B Corporation	$175.00	
Other income	100.00	
Total pretax earnings and profits		$275.00
Foreign income taxes (10%)		27.50
Earnings and profits		247.50
Earnings and profits after exclusion of amounts attributable to dividends to which sec. 902(b) does not apply ($247.50 less [$150 − ($150 × .10)])		112.50
Amount required to be included in N Corporation's gross income for 1978 under sec. 951 with respect to A Corporation		22.50
Distributions paid by A Corporation:		
Dividends to which sec. 902(a) does not apply (from A Corporation's earnings and profits in respect of which an amount is required under sec. 951 to be included in N Corporation's gross income with respect to A Corporation)	$22.50	
Dividends to which sec. 902(a) applies (from A Corporation's other earnings and profits)	202.50	
Total dividends paid to N Corporation	$225.00	

N Corporation (domestic corporation):

Foreign income taxes deemed paid by N Corporation under sec. 960(a)(1) with respect to—			
B Corporation ($150/$200 × $50)			$37.50
A Corporation:			
Tax paid by A Corporation ($22.50/$247.50 × $27.50)	$2.50		
Tax of B Corporation deemed paid by A Corporation under sec. 902(b)(1) ($22.50/$112.50 × $6.25)	1.25	3.75	
Total taxes deemed paid under sec. 960(a)(1)			$41.25
Foreign income taxes deemed paid by N Corporation under sec. 902(a) with respect to A Corporation:			
Tax paid by A Corporation ($202.50/$247.50 × $27.50)	$22.50		
Tax of B Corporation deemed paid by A Corporation ($67.50/$112.50 × $6.25)	3.75		
Total taxes deemed paid under sec. 902(a)			$26.25
Total foreign income taxes deemed paid by N Corporation under sec. 901			$67.50

Example (6). Domestic corporation N owns all the one class of stock of controlled foreign corporation A, which owns all the one class of stock of controlled foreign corporation B. All such corporations use the calendar year as the taxable year. A and B corporations are organized under the laws of foreign country X. All of B corporation's assets used in a trade or business are located in country X. Country X imposes an income tax of 20 percent on B corporation's income. For 1978, N Corporation is required under section 951 to include in gross income $100 attributable to the earnings and profits of B Corporation for such year. For 1978, B Corporation distributes $150, consisting of $100 from its earnings and profits attributable to the amount required under section 951 to be included in N Corporation's gross income with respect to B Corporation and $50 from its other earnings and profits. Country X imposes an income tax of 10 percent on A Corporation's income but exempts from tax dividends received from B Corporation. N is not required to include any amount in gross income under section 951 for 1978 attributable to the earnings and profits of A Corporation for such year. For 1978, A Corporation distributes $175, consisting of $100 from its earnings and profits attributable to the amount required under section 951 to be included in N Corporation's gross income with respect to B Corporation, and $75 from its other earnings and profits. The foreign income taxes deemed paid by N Corporation for 1978 under section 960(a)(1) and section 902(a) are determined as follows on the basis of the facts assumed:

B Corporation (second-tier corporation):

Pretax earnings and profits	$200.00
Foreign income taxes (20%)	40.00
Earnings and profits	160.00

Amount required to be included in N Corporation's gross income for 1978 under sec. 951 with respect to B Corporation		100.00
Dividends paid by B Corporation:		
Dividends to which sec. 902(b) does not apply (from B Corporation's earnings and profits in respect of which an amount is required under sec. 951 to be included in N Corporation's gross income with respect to B Corporation)	$100.00	
Dividends to which sec. 902(b)(1) applies (from B Corporation's other earnings and profits)	50.00	
Total dividends paid to A Corporation		$150.00
Foreign income taxes of B Corporation deemed paid by A Corporation for 1978 under sec. 902(b)(1) ($50/$160 × $40)		$12.50

A Corporation (first-tier corporation):

Pretax earnings and profits:		
Dividends received from B Corporation	$150.00	
Other income	100.00	
Total pretax earnings and profits		$250.00
Foreign income taxes:		
On dividends received from B Corporation	none	
On other income ($100 × .10)	$10.00	
Total foreign income taxes		$10.00
Earnings and profits:		
Attributable to dividends received from B Corporation to which sec. 902(b) does not apply		$100.00
Attributable to other income:		
Attributable to dividends received from B Corporation to which sec. 902(b)(1) applies ..	$50.00	
Attributable to other income ($100 – $10) ...	90.00	140.00
Total earnings and profits		$240.00
Earnings and profits after exclusion of amounts attributable to dividends to which sec. 902(b) does not apply ($240 – $100)		$140.00
Amount required to be included in N Corporation's gross income for 1978 under sec. 951 with respect to A Corporation		none
Dividends paid by A Corporation:		
Dividends to which sec. 902(a) does not apply (from A Corporation's earnings and profits in respect of which an amount is required under sec. 951 to be included in N Corporation's gross income with respect to A Corporation)	none	
Dividends to which sec. 902(a) applies (from A Corporation's other earnings and profits)	$175.00	
Total dividends paid to N Corporation		$175.00

N Corporation (domestic corporation):

Foreign income taxes deemed paid by N Corporation under sec. 960(a)(1) with respect to B Corporation ($100/$160 × $40)		$25.00
Foreign income taxes deemed paid by N Corporation under sec. 902(a) with respect to A Corporation (allocation of earnings and profits being made under pars. (c)(2) and (d) of this section):		
Tax paid by A Corporation in respect to dividends received from B Corporation to which sec. 902(b) does not apply ($100/$100 × $0)	none	
Tax paid by A Corporation in respect to its other income ($75/$140 × $10)	$5.36	
Tax of B Corporation in respect to such other income ($75/$140 × $12.50)	6.70	
Total taxes deemed paid under sec. 902(a)		$12.06
Total foreign income taxes deemed paid by N Corporation under sec. 901		$37.06

Example (7). Domestic corporation N owns all the one class of stock of controlled foreign corporation A, which owns all the one class of stock of controlled foreign corporation B. All such corporations use the calendar year as the taxable year. For 1978, N Corporation is required under section 951 to include in gross income $150 attributable to the earnings and profits of B Corporation for such year and $47.50 attributable to the earnings and profits of A Corporation for such year. For 1978, B Corporation distributes $200, consisting of $150 from its earnings and profits attributable to the amount required under section 951 to be included in N Corporation's gross income with respect to B Corporation and $50 from its other earnings and profits. The country under the laws of which A Corporation is incorporated imposes an income tax of 5 percent on dividends received from a subsidiary corporation and 20 percent on other income. For 1978, A Corporation distributes $100 from its earnings and profits to N Corporation, such amount being attributable under paragraph (e) of § 1.959-3 to the amount required under section 951 to be included in N Corporation's gross income with respect to B Corporation. The foreign income taxes deemed paid by N Corporation for 1978 under section 960(a)(1) and section 902(a) are determined as follows on the basis of the facts assumed:

B Corporation (second-tier corporation):
- Pretax earnings and profits $250.00
- Foreign income taxes (20 percent) 50.00
- Earnings and profits 200.00
- Amount required to be included in N Corporation's gross income for 1978 under sec. 951 with respect to B Corporation 150.00
- Dividends paid by B Corporation:
  - Dividends to which sec. 902(b) does not apply (from B Corporation's earnings and profits in respect of which an amount is required under sec. 951 to be included in N Corporation's gross income with respect to B Corporation) $150.00
  - Dividends to which sec. 902(b)(1) applies (from B Corporation's other earnings and profits) 50.00
    - Total dividends paid to A Corporation 200.00
- Foreign income taxes of B Corporation deemed paid by A Corporation for 1978 under sec. 902(b)(1) ($50/$200 × $50) 12.50

A Corporation (first-tier corporation):
- Pretax earnings and profits:
  - Dividends received from B Corporation $200.00
  - Other income 100.00
    - Total pretax earnings and profits $300.00
- Foreign income taxes:
  - On dividends received from B Corporation to which sec. 902(b) does not apply ($150 × .05) $7.50
  - On other income:
    - Dividends received from B Corporation to which sec. 902(b)(1) applies ($50 × .05) $2.50
    - Other income of A Corporation ($100 × .20) .. 20.00   22.50
      - Total foreign income taxes 30.00
- Earnings and Profits:
  - Attributable to dividends received from B Corporation to which sec. 902(b) does not apply ($150 − $7.50) $142.50
  - Attributable to other income:
    - Attributable to dividends received from B Corporation to which sec. 902(b)(1) applies ($50 − $2.50) $47.50
    - Attributable to other income ($100 − $20) ... 80.00   127.50
      - Total earnings and profits $270.00
- Earnings and profits after exclusion of amounts attributable to dividends to which sec. 902(b) does not apply ($270 less $142.50) $127.50
- Amount required to be included in N Corporation's gross income for 1978 under sec. 951 with respect to A Corporation 47.50
- Dividends paid by A Corporation:
  - Dividends to which sec. 902(a) does not apply (from A Corporation's earnings and profits in respect of which an amount is required under sec. 951 to be included in N Corporation's gross income with respect to A Corporation) .... none
  - Dividends to which sec. 902(a) applies (from A Corporation's other earnings and profits) $100.00
    - Total dividends paid to N Corporation 100.00

N Corporation (domestic corporation):

Foreign income taxes deemed paid by N Corporation under sec. 960(a)(1) with respect to—

B Corporation ($150/$200 × $50)		37.50
A Corporation (allocation of earnings and profits being made under § 1.960-1(c)(3) and par. (d) of this sec.):		
Tax paid by A Corporation ($47.50/$127.50 × $22.50)	$8.38	
Tax of B Corporation deemed paid by A Corporation under sec. 902(b)(1) ($47.50/$127.50 × $12.50) . .	4.66	$13.04
Total taxes deemed paid under sec. 960(a)(1)(C)		50.54
Foreign income taxes deemed paid by N Corporation under sec. 902(a) with respect to A Corporation (allocations of earnings and profits being made under pars. (c)(2) and (d) of this sec.) ($100/$142.50 × $7.50)		5.26
Total foreign income taxes deemed paid by N Corporation under sec. 901		**$55.80**

Example (8). Domestic corporation N owns all the one class of stock of controlled foreign corporation A, which owns all the one class of stock of controlled foreign corporation B, which owns all the one class of controlled foreign corporation C. All such corporations use the calendar year as the taxable year. For 1978, N Corporation is required under section 951 to include $50 attributable to the earnings and profits of C Corporation and $15 attributable to the earnings and profits of B Corporation in its gross income. N Corporation is not required to include any amount in its gross income with respect to A Corporation under section 951 in 1978. For such year, C Corporation distributes $75 to B Corporation. B Corporation in turn distributes $60 of its earnings and profits to A Corporation. A Corporation has no other earnings and profits for 1978 and distributes $45 of its earnings and profits to N Corporation. The foreign income taxes deemed paid by N Corporation under section 960(a)(1) and section 902(a) are determined as follows on the basis of the facts assumed:

C Corporation (third-tier corporation):

Pretax earnings and profits		$150.00
Foreign income taxes paid by C Corporation (30%)		45.00
Earnings and profits		105.00
Amount required to be included in gross income of N Corporation under section 951 with respect to C Corporation		50.00
Dividend to B Corporation		75.00
Dividend from earnings and profits to which section 902(b)(2) does not apply (attributable to amounts included in N Corporation's gross income under section 951 with respect to C Corporation)	$50.00	
Dividend from earnings and profits to which section 902(b)(2) applies (attributable to amounts not included in N Corporation's gross income with respect to C Corporation)	25.00	

Amount of foreign income taxes of C Corporation deemed paid by B Corporation under section 902(b)(2) and § 1.960-2(b):

$$\frac{\text{Dividend to B Corporation less portion of dividend from earnings included in N Corporation's gross income under section 951 with respect to C Corporation}}{\text{Earnings and profits of C Corporation}} \times \text{Taxes paid by C Corporation}$$

($25/$105 × $45) $10.71

B Corporation (second-tier corporation):

Pretax earnings and profits:		
Dividend from C Corporation	$75.00	
Other earnings and profits	225.00	
Total pretax earnings and profits		300.00
Foreign income taxes paid by B Corporation (40%)		120.00
Earnings and profits		180.00

Reg. §1.960-2(f)

Earnings and profits attributable to amounts to which section 902(b)(2) does not apply (amounts included in N Corporation's gross income under section 951 with respect to C Corporation) ($50 − ($50 × .40)) 30.00
Other earnings and profits 150.00
Earnings and profits of B Corporation after exclusion for amounts to which section 902(b)(2) does not apply (amounts attributable to earnings and profits which are included in N Corporation's gross income under section 951 with respect to C Corporation) ($180 − $30) . . . 150.00
Amount to be included in gross income under section 951 of N Corporation with respect to B Corporation 15.00
Amount of dividend to A Corporation 60.00
    Dividend from earnings and profits to which section 902(b)(2) does not apply (attributable to amounts included in N Corporation's gross income under section 951 with respect to C Corporation) 30.00
    Dividend from earnings and profits to which section 902(b)(1) does not apply (attributable to amounts included in N Corporation's gross income under section 951 with respect to B Corporation) 15.00
    Dividend from other earnings and profits (attributable to amounts not included in N Corporation's gross income under section 951 with respect to B or C Corporation) 15.00

Foreign income taxes of B Corporation deemed paid by A Corporation under section 902(b)(1) and § 1.960-2(b):

$$\frac{\text{Dividend to A Corporation less portion of dividend from earnings included in N Corporation's gross income under section 951 with respect to B Corporation}}{\text{Earnings and profits of B Corporation}} \times \text{Taxes paid by B Corporation}$$

($45/$180 × $120) 30.00

Foreign income taxes (of C Corporation) deemed paid by B Corporation deemed paid by A Corporation under section 902(b)(1) in accordance with § 1.960-2(b) and § 1.960-2(d)(2)(i) and (ii):

$$\frac{\text{Dividend to A Corporation less portion of dividend from earnings included in N Corporation's gross income under section 951 with respect to B Corporation and C Corporation}}{\text{Earnings and profits of B Corporation less earnings and profits attributable to amounts included in N Corporation's gross income with respect to C Corporation}} \times \text{Taxes paid by C Corporation which are deemed paid by B Corporation}$$

($15/$150 × $10.71) $1.07

A Corporation (first-tier corporation):
Pretax earnings and profits:
    Dividend from B Corporation $60.00
    Other earnings and profits 0

Total pretax earnings and profits 60.00
Foreign income taxes paid by A Corporation (10%) 6.00
Earnings and profits 54.00
    Earnings and profits attributable to amounts to which section 902(b)(2) does not apply (attributable to amounts previously included in N Corporation's gross income under section 951 with respect to C Corporation) ($30 − ($30 × .10)) . . $27.00
    Earnings and profits attributable to amounts to which section 902(b)(1) does not apply (attributable to amounts included in N Corporation's gross income under section 951 with respect to B Corporation) ($15 − ($15 × .10)) 13.50
    Other earnings and profits ($15 − ($15 × .10)) 13.50
Earnings and profits of A Corporation after exclusion for amounts to which section 902(b)(1) does not apply (attributable to amounts included in N Corporation's gross income under section 951 with respect to B Corporation) ($54.00 − $13.50) $40.50

Earnings and profits of A Corporation after exclusion for amounts to which sections 902(b)(1) and (2) do not apply (attributable to amounts included in N Corporation's gross income under section 951 with respect to B or C Corporation) ($40.50 − $27.00) 13.50

Dividend to N Corporation 45.00

 Dividend from earnings and profits to which section 902(b)(2) does not apply (attributable to amounts included in N Corporation's gross income under section 951 with respect to C Corporation) 27.00

 Dividend from earnings and profits to which section 902(b)(1) does not apply (attributable to amounts included in N Corporation's gross income under section 951 with respect to B Corporation) 13.50

 Dividend from earnings and profits to which section 902(a) does not apply (attributable to amounts included in N Corporation's gross income under section 951 with respect to A Corporation) 0

 Dividend from other earnings and profits (attributable to amounts not included in N Corporation's gross income under section 951 with respect to A, B, or C Corporation) $4.50

N Corporation (domestic corporation):

Foreign income taxes deemed paid by N Corporation under section 960(a)(1) and § 1.960-1(c)(1)(ii) with respect to C Corporation:

$$\frac{\text{Amount included in N Corporation's gross income under section 951 with respect to C Corporation}}{\text{Earnings and profits of C Corporation}} \times \text{Taxes paid by C Corporation}$$

($50/$105 × $45.00) $21.43

Foreign income taxes deemed paid by N Corporation under section 960(a)(1) and § 1.960-1(c)(1)(i) with respect to B Corporation 11.07

 Taxes paid by B Corporation:

$$\frac{\text{Amount included in N Corporation's gross income under section 951 with respect to B Corporation}}{\text{Earnings and profits of B Corporation}} \times \text{Taxes paid by B Corporation}$$

($15/$180 × $120) $10.00

Taxes deemed paid by B Corporation in accordance with § 1.960-2(d)(2)(i):

$$\frac{\text{Amount included in N Corporation's gross income under section 951 with respect to B Corporation}}{\text{Earnings and profits of B Corporation less earnings and profits attributable to amounts included in N Corporation's gross income with respect to C Corporation}} \times \text{Taxes paid by C Corporation which are deemed paid by B Corporation}$$

($15/$150 × $10.71) 1.07

Total taxes deemed paid by N Corporation under section 960(a)(1) $32.50

Foreign income taxes deemed paid by N Corporation under section 902(a):

 Taxes paid by A Corporation in accordance with § 1.960-2(c):

$$\frac{\text{Dividend to N Corporation less portion of dividend from earnings included in N Corporation's gross income under section 951 with respect to A Corporation}}{\text{Earnings and profits of A Corporation}} \times \text{Taxes paid by A Corporation}$$

($45/$54 × $6) 5.00

Taxes paid by B Corporation deemed paid by A Corporation in accordance with §§ 1.960-2(c) and 1.960-2(d)(1)(i) and (ii):

$$\frac{\text{Dividend to N Corporation less portion of dividend from earnings included in N Corporation's gross income under section 951 with respect to A and B Corporations}}{\text{Earnings and profits of A Corporation less earnings and profits attributable to amounts included in N Corporation's gross income under section 951 with respect to B Corporation}} \times \begin{array}{l}\text{Taxes paid by B} \\ \text{Corporation} \\ \text{which are} \\ \text{deemed paid by} \\ \text{A Corporation}\end{array}$$

($31.50/$40.50 × $30.00) 23.33

Taxes (of C Corporation) deemed paid by B Corporation deemed paid by A Corporation in accordance with §§ 1.960-2(c) and 1.960-2(d)(1)(i) and (ii):

$$\frac{\text{Dividend to N Corporation less portion of dividend from earnings included in N Corporation's gross income under section 951 with respect to A, B, and C Corporations}}{\text{Earnings and profits of A Corporation less earnings and profits attributable to amounts included in N Corporation's gross income under section 951 with respect to B and C Corporations}} \times \begin{array}{l}\text{Taxes deemed} \\ \text{paid by B} \\ \text{Corporation} \\ \text{which are} \\ \text{deemed paid by} \\ \text{A Corporation}\end{array}$$

($4.50/$13.50 × $1.07) .... .36

Total taxes deemed paid by N Corporation under section 902(a) $28.69

Total foreign income taxes deemed paid by N Corporation under section 901 .... $61.19

Example (9). Domestic corporation N owns all the one class of stock of controlled foreign corporation A, which owns all the one class of stock of controlled foreign corporation B, which owns all the one class of controlled foreign corporation C. A and B Corporations are organized under the laws of foreign country X. C Corporation is organized under the laws of foreign country Y. All of B Corporation's assets used in a trade or business are located in country X. All such corporations use the calendar year as the taxable year. For 1978, N Corporation is required to include in its gross income under section 951, $50 attributable to the earnings and profits of C Corporation and $100 attributable to the earnings and profits of B Corporation. N Corporation is not required to include any amount in its gross income under section 951 with respect to A Corporation. Country X imposes an income tax of 10 percent on dividends from foreign subsidiaries, 20 percent on dividends from domestic subsidiaries, and 40 percent on other earnings and profits. For 1978, C Corporation distributes $75 to B Corporation. For such year, B Corporation distributes $175 of its earnings and profits to A Corporation. A Corporation has no other earnings and profits for 1978 and distributes $130 of its earnings and profits of N Corporation. The foreign income taxes deemed paid by N Corporation under sections 960(a)(1) and 902(a) are determined as follows on the basis of the facts assumed:

C Corporation (third-tier corporation):
Pretax earnings and profits $150.00
Foreign income taxes paid by C Corporation (30%) 45.00
Earnings and profits 105.00
Amount required to be included in gross income of N Corporation under section 951 with respect to C Corporation $50.00
Dividend to B Corporation 75.00
Dividend to which section 902(b)(2) does not apply (attributable to amounts included in N Corporation's gross income under section 951 with respect to C Corporation) $50.00

Dividend to which section 902(b)(2) applies (attributable to amounts not included in N Corporation's gross income under section 951 with respect to C Corporation) 25.00
Amount of foreign income taxes of C Corporation deemed paid by B Corporation under section 902(b)(2) and § 1.960-2(b)
($25/$105 × $45) 10.71
(for formula see § 1.960-2(g)(1)(i)(A))

B Corporation (second-tier corporation):
    Pretax earnings and profits:
        Dividend from C Corporation 75.00
        Other earnings and profits 225.00
    Total pretax earnings and profits 300.00
    Foreign income taxes paid by B Corporation 97.50
    On dividends received from C Corporation to which section 902(b)(2) does not apply (attributable to amounts included in N Corporation's gross income under section 951 with respect to C Corporation) ($50 × .10) 5.00
    On dividend from C Corporation to which section 902(b)(2) applies (attributable to amounts not included in N Corporation's gross income under section 951 with respect to C Corporation) ($25 × .10) $2.50
    On other income of B Corporation ($225 × .40) 90.00
    Earnings and profits $202.50
    Attributable to dividend to which section 902(b)(2) does not apply (attributable to amounts included in N Corporation's gross income under section 951 with respect to C Corporation) ($50 − $5) 45.00
    Attributable to dividend from C Corporation to which section 902(b)(2) applies (attributable to amounts not included in N Corporation's gross income under section 951 with respect to C Corporation) ($25 − $2.50) 22.50
    Attributable to other income of B Corporation ($225 − $90) ... 135.00
    Earnings and profits after exclusion of amounts attributable to dividend to which section 902(b)(2) does not apply (attributable to amounts included in N Corporation's gross income under section 951 with respect to C Corporation) ($202.50 − $45) 157.50
    Amount required to be included in N Corporation's gross income under section 951 with respect to B Corporation 100.00
    Dividend paid by B Corporation $175.00
    Dividend to which section 902(b)(2) does not apply (attributable to amounts included in N Corporation's gross income under section 951 with respect to C Corporation) $45.00
    Dividend to which section 902(b)(1) does not apply (attributable to amounts included in N Corporation's gross income under section 951 with respect to B Corporation) 100.00
    Dividend from other earnings and profits (attributable to amounts not included in N Corporation's gross income with respect to B or C Corporation) 30.00

    Foreign income taxes of B Corporation deemed paid by A Corporation under section 902(b)(1) (separate tax rate applicable to dividend received by B Corporation allocation in accordance with § 1.960-2(e)) (for formula see § 1.960-2(g)(1)(ii)(A)(2)(*i*) and (*ii*)):

    Tax paid by B Corporation on earnings previously taxed with respect to C Corporation or lower-tiers which is deemed paid by A Corporation:

$$\frac{\text{Portion of dividend to A Corporation from earnings included in N Corporation's gross income under section 951 with respect to C Corporation or lower-tiers}}{\text{Earnings and profits of B Corporation included in N Corporation's gross income under section 951 with respect to C Corporation or lower-tiers}} \times \text{Tax paid by B Corporation on dividend received by B Corporation from earnings included in N Corporation's gross income with respect to C Corporation or lower-tiers}$$

($45/$45 × $5) $5.00

Tax paid by B Corporation on earnings not previously taxed with respect to C Corporation or lower-tiers which is deemed paid by A Corporation:

$$\frac{\text{Portion of dividend to A Corporation which is from earnings not included in N Corporation's gross income under section 951 with respect to B Corporation or lower-tiers}}{\text{Earnings and profits of B Corporation not included in N Corporation's gross income under section 951 with respect to C Corporation or lower-tiers}} \times \text{Tax paid by B Corporation on earnings not included in N Corporation's gross income with respect to C Corporation or lower-tiers}$$

($30/$157.50 × $92.50) 17.62

Foreign income taxes (of C Corporation) deemed paid by B Corporation deemed paid by A Corporation under section 902(b)(1)
 ($30/$157.50 × $10.71) 2.04
 (for formula see § 1.960-2(g)(1)(ii)(B)(*1*))

A Corporation (first-tier corporation):
 Pretax earnings and profits:
  Dividend from B Corporation $175.00
  Other income 0
 Total pretax earnings and profits 175.00
 Foreign income taxes paid by A Corporation (20%) 35.00
 Earnings and profits 140.00
  Attributable to dividend to which section 902(b)(2) does not apply (attributable
   to amounts included in N Corporation's gross income under section 951 with
   respect to C Corporation) ($45 − ($45 × .20)) $36.00
  Attributable to amounts to which section 902(b)(1) does not apply (attributable
   to amounts included in N Corporation's gross income under section 951 with
   respect to B Corporation) ($100 − ($100 × .20)) 80.00
  Attributable to other earnings and profits (attributable to amounts not included
   in N Corporation's gross income with respect to B or C Corporation) 24.00
  Earnings and profits after exclusion for amounts to which section 902(b)(1) does not apply
   (attributable to amounts included in N Corporation's gross income under section 951 with
   respect to B Corporation) ($140 − $80) 60.00
  Earnings and profits after exclusion for amounts to which sections 902(b)(1) and
   902(b)(2) do not apply (attributable to amounts included in N Corporation's gross income
   under section 951 with respect to B or C Corporation) ($60 − $36) 24.00
  Amount required to be included in N Corporation's gross income under section 951 with
   respect to A Corporation .... None
  Dividend to N Corporation 130.00
  Dividend to which section 902(b)(2) does not apply (attributable to amounts
   included in N Corporation's gross income under section 951 with respect to C
   Corporation) $36.00
  Dividend to which section 902(b)(1) does not apply (attributable to amounts
   included in N Corporation's gross income under section 951 with respect to B
   Corporation) 80.00
  Dividend to which section 902(a) does not apply (attributable to amounts
   included in N Corporation's gross income under section 951 with respect to A
   Corporation) 0
  Dividend from other earnings and profits (attributable to amounts not included
   in N Corporation's gross income with respect to A,B, or C Corporation) 14.00

N Corporation (domestic corporation):
 Foreign income taxes deemed paid by N Corporation under section 960(a)(1) and
  § 1.960-1(c) with respect to C Corporation ($50/$105 × $45) 21.43
  (for formula see § 1.960-2(g)(2)(i)(A))
 Foreign income taxes deemed paid by N Corporation under section 960(a)(1) with respect
  to B Corporation (allocation of earnings and profits being made in accordance with
  § 1.960-1(c)(3) and § 1.960-2(e)) (Separate tax rate applicable to dividend received by B
  Corporation) 65.53

Taxes paid by B corporation (for formula see § 1.960-2(g)(2)(ii)(A)(*2*))

$$\frac{\text{Amount included in N Corporation's gross income under section 951 with respect to B Corporation}}{\text{Earnings and profits of B Corporation not included in N Corporation's gross income under section 951 with respect to C Corporation or lower tiers}} \times \text{Tax paid by B Corporation on earnings not included in N Corporation's gross income with respect to C Corporation or lower tiers}$$

($100/$157.50 × $92.50) $58.73

Taxes (of C Corporation) deemed paid by B Corporation under section 902(b)(2) which are deemed paid by N Corporation under section 960(a)(1) ($100/$157.50 × $10.71) 6.80
(for formula see § 1.960-2(g)(2)(ii)(B)(*1*))
Total taxes deemed paid by N Corporation under section 960(a)(1) $86.96
Foreign income taxes deemed paid by N Corporation under section 902(a):
Taxes paid by A Corporation ($130/$140 × $35) 32.50
(for formula see § 1.960-2(g)(1)(iii)(A)(*1*))
Taxes paid by B Corporation deemed paid by A Corporation (Separate tax rate applicable to dividend received by B Corporation allocation required by § 1.960-2(e)) (for formula see § 1.960-2(g)(1)(iii)(B)(*2*)(*i*) and (*ii*))

Tax paid by B Corporation on earnings previously taxed with respect to C Corporation or lower tiers which is deemed paid by N Corporation:

$$\frac{\text{Portion of dividend to N Corporation which is from earnings included in N Corporation's gross income under section 951 with respect to C Corporation or lower tiers}}{\text{Earnings and profits of A Corporation included in N Corporation's gross income under section 951 with respect to C Corporation or lower tiers}} \times \text{Tax paid by B Corporation on earnings previously taxed with respect to C Corporation or lower tiers which is deemed paid by A Corporation}$$

($36/$36 × $5) $5.00

Tax paid by B corporation on earnings not previously taxed with respect to C corporation or lower tiers which is deemed paid by N Corporation:

$$\frac{\text{Portion of dividend to N Corporation which is from earnings not included in N Corporation's gross income under section 951 with respect to A Corporation or lower tiers}}{\text{Earnings and profits of A Corporation not included in N Corporation's gross income under section 951 with respect to B Corporation or lower tiers}} \times \text{Tax paid by B Corporation on earnings not previously taxed with respect to C Corporation or lower tiers which is deemed paid by A Corporation}$$

($14/$24 × $17.62) $10.28
Taxes (of C corporation) deemed paid by B Corporation deemed paid by A Corporation
($14/$24 × $2.04) 1.19
(for formula see § 1.960-2(g)(1)(iii)(C)(*1*))
Total taxes deemed paid by N Corporation under section 902(a) 48.97

Total foreign income taxes deemed paid by N Corporation under section 901 .... $135.93

Reg. § 1.960-2(f)

Example (10). The facts are the same as in example (9) except that A Corporation has other earnings and profits of $200 in 1978 and country X imposes a tax of 50 percent on A Corporation's other earnings and profits. A Corporation distributes $200 of its earnings and profits to N Corporation in 1978. The foreign income taxes paid by N Corporation under sections 960(a)(1) and 902(a) are determined as follows on the basis of the facts assumed:

C Corporation (third-tier corporation):

Pretax earnings and profits		$150.00
Foreign incomes taxes paid by C Corporation (30%)		45.00
Earnings and profits		105.00
Amount required to be included in gross income of N Corporation under section 951 with respect to C Corporation		50.00
Dividend to B Corporation		75.00
Dividend to which section 902(b)(2) does not apply (attributable to amounts included in N Corporation's gross income under section 951 with respect to C Corporation)	$50.00	
Dividend to which section 902(b)(2) applies attributable to amounts not included in N Corporation's gross income under section 951 with respect to C Corporation	$25.00	
Amount of foreign income taxes of C Corporation deemed paid by B Corporation under section 902(b)(2) and § 1.960-2(b) ($25/$105 × $45)		10.71
(for formula see § 1.960-2(g)(1)(i)(A))		

B Corporation (second-tier corporation):

Pretax earnings and profits:		
Dividend from C Corporation	75.00	
Other earnings and profits	225.00	
Total pretax earnings and profits		300.00
Foreign income taxes of B Corporation		97.50
On dividends received from C Corporation to which section 902(b)(2) does not apply (attributable to amounts included in N Corporation's gross income under section 951 with respect to C Corporation) ($50 × .10)	$5.00	
On dividend from C Corporation to which section 902(b)(2) applies (attributable to amounts not included in N Corporation's gross income under section 951 with respect to C Corporation) ($25 × .10)	2.50	
On other income of B Corporation ($225 × .40)	90.00	
Earnings and profits		202.50
Attributable to dividend to which section 902(b)(2) does not apply (attributable to amounts included in N Corporation's gross income under section 951 with respect to C Corporation) ($50 − $5)	45.00	
Attributable to dividend from C Corporation to which section 902(b)(2) applies (attributable to amounts not included in N Corporation's gross income under section 951 with respect to C Corporation) ($25 − $2.50)	22.50	
Attributable to other income of B Corporation ($225 − $90)	135.00	
Earnings and profits after exclusion of amounts attributable to dividend to which section 902(b)(2) does not apply (attributable to amounts included in N Corporation's gross income under section 951 with respect to C Corporation) ($202.50 − $45)		157.50
Amount required to be included in N Corporation's gross income under section 951 with respect to B Corporation		100.00
Dividend paid by B Corporation		175.00
Dividend to which section 902(b)(2) does not apply (attributable to amounts included in N Corporation's gross income under section 951 with respect to C Corporation)	$45.00	
Dividend to which section 902(b)(1) does not apply (attributable to amounts included in N Corporation's gross income under section 951 with respect to B Corporation)	100.00	
Dividend from other earnings and profits (attributable to amounts not included in N Corporation's gross income with respect to B or C Corporation)	30.00	
Foreign income taxes of B Corporation deemed paid by A Corporation under section 902(b)(1) with allocation required by § 1.960-2(e):		
($45/$45 × $5)		5.00
($30/$157.50 × $92.50)		17.62
(for formula see § 1.960-2(g)(1)(ii)(A)(2)(i) and (ii))		
Foreign income taxes (of C Corporation) deemed paid by B Corporation deemed paid by A Corporation under section 902(b)(1) ($30/$157.50 × $10.71)		2.04
(for formula see § 1.960-2(g)(1)(ii)(B)(1))		

Controlled Foreign Corporations

A Corporation (first-tier corporation):

Pretax earnings and profits:
- Dividend from B Corporation $175.00
- Other earnings and profits 200.00

Total pretax earnings and profits $375.00

Foreign income taxes paid by A Corporation 135.00
- On dividend received from B Corporation to which section 902(b)(2) does not apply (attributable to amounts included in N Corporation's gross income under section 951 with respect to C Corporation) ($45 × .20) .... $ 9.00
- On dividend received from B Corporation to which section 902(b)(1) does not apply (attributable to amounts included in N Corporation's gross income under section 951 with respect to B Corporation) ($100 × .20) 20.00
- On dividend from B Corporation attributable to B Corporation's other earnings and profits (attributable to amounts not included in N Corporation's gross income with respect to B or C Corporation) ($30 × .20) 6.00
- On other income of A Corporation ($200 × .50) 100.00

Earnings and profits $240.00
- Attributable to dividend to which section 902(b)(2) does not apply (attributable to amounts included in N Corporation's gross income under section 951 with respect to C Corporation) ($45 – $9) 36.00
- Attributable to dividend to which section 902(b)(1) does not apply (attributable to amounts included in N Corporation's gross income with respect to B Corporation) ($100 – $20) 80.00
- Attributable to other earnings and profits of A Corporation (attributable to amounts not included in N Corporation's gross income with respect to A, B, or C Corporation) [($30 – $6) + ($200 – $100)] $124.00
- Amount required to be included in N Corporation's gross income under section 951 with respect to A Corporation .... None

Earnings and profits after exclusion of amounts attributable to dividend to which section 902(b)(1) does not apply (attributable to amounts included in N Corporation's gross income under section 951 with respect to B Corporation) $160.00

Earnings and profits after exclusion of amounts attributable to dividend to which sections 902(b)(1) and 902(b)(2) do not apply (attributable to amounts included in N Corporation's gross income under section 951 with respect to B and C Corporation) 124.00

Dividend to N Corporation 200.00
- Dividend attributable to amounts to which section 902(b)(2) does not apply (attributable to amounts included in N Corporation's gross income under section 951 with respect to C Corporation) 36.00
- Dividend attributable to amounts to which section 902(b)(1) does not apply (attributable to amounts included in N Corporation's gross income with respect to B Corporation) 80.00
- Dividend attributable to amounts to which section 902(a) does not apply (attributable to amounts included in N Corporation's gross income under section 951 with respect to A Corporation) 0
- Dividend attributable to A Corporation's other earnings and profits (attributable to amounts not included in N Corporation's gross income under section 951 with respect to A, B, or C Corporation) .... $ 84.00

N Corporation (domestic corporation)

Foreign income taxes deemed paid by N Corporation under section 960(a)(1) and § 1.960-1(c) with respect to C Corporation ($50/$150 × $45) .... $ 21.43
(for formula see § 1.960-2(g)(2)(i)(A))

Foreign income taxes deemed paid by N Corporation under section 960(a)(1) with respect to B Corporation (allocation of earning and profits being made in accordance with § 1.960-1(c)(3) and § 1.960-2(e)) 65.53
- Taxes paid by B Corporation ($100/$157.50 × $92.50) 58.73
  (for formula see § 1.960-2(g)(2)(ii)(A)(*2*))
- Taxes deemed paid by B Corporation ($100/$157.50 × $10.71) 6.80
  (for formula see § 1.960-2(g)(2)(ii)(B)(*1*))

Total taxes deemed paid by N Corporation under section 960(a)(1) ... 86.96

Foreign income taxes deemed paid by N Corporation under section 902(a) (separate tax rate applicable to dividends received by A Corporation allocation required by § 1.960-2(e)) (for formula see § 1.960-2(g)(1)(iii)(A)(*2*)(*i*) and (*ii*)):

Tax paid by A Corporation on earnings previously taxed with respect to B Corporation or lower tiers which is deemed paid by N Corporation:

Reg. § 1.960-2(f)

$$\frac{\text{Portion of dividend to N Corporation which is from earnings included in N Corporation's gross income under section 951 with respect to B Corporation or lower tiers}}{\text{Earnings and profits of A Corporation included in N Corporation's gross income under section 951 with respect to B Corporation or lower tiers}} \times \begin{array}{l}\text{Tax paid by A Corporation on}\\ \text{dividends received by A}\\ \text{Corporation from earnings}\\ \text{included in N Corporation's}\\ \text{gross income with respect to B}\\ \text{Corporation or lower tiers}\end{array}$$

($116/$116 × $29) .... $ 29.00

Tax paid by A Corporation on earnings not previously taxed with respect to B Corporation or lower tiers which is deemed paid by N Corporation:

$$\frac{\text{Portion of dividend to N Corporation which is from earnings not included in N Corporation's gross income under section 951 with respect to A Corporation or lower tiers}}{\text{Earnings and profits of A Corporation not included in N Corporation's gross income under section 951 with respect to B Corporation or lower tiers}} \times \begin{array}{l}\text{Tax paid by A Corporation on}\\ \text{earnings not included in N}\\ \text{Corporation's gross income}\\ \text{with respect to B Corporation}\\ \text{or lower tiers}\end{array}$$

    ($84/$124 × $106) .... $ 71.81

Taxes (paid by B Corporation) deemed paid by A Corporation allocation required by § 1.960-2(e):
    $36/$36 × $5) .... $ 5.00
    ($84/$124 × $17.62) 11.94
    (for formula see § 1.960-2(g)(1)(iii)(B)(2)(i) and (ii))

Taxes (of C Corporation) deemed paid by B Corporation deemed paid by A Corporation
    ($84/$124 × $2.04) 1.38
    (for formula see § 1.960-2(g)(1)(iii)(C)(1))

Total taxes deemed paid by N Corporation under section 902(a) credit $119.13

Total foreign income taxes deemed paid by N Corporation under section 901 .... $206.09

(g) *Formulas.*—This paragraph contains formulas for determining a domestic corporation's section 902 and 960 credits when amounts distributed through a chain of ownership have been included in whole or in part in the gross income of a domestic corporation under section 951 with respect to first-, second-, third-, or lower-tier corporations.

(1) *Determination of the section 902 credit.*—(i) *Section 902(b)(2) credit.*—If the second-tier corporation receives a dividend from a third-tier corporation attributable in whole or in part to amounts included in a domestic corporation's gross income under section 951 with respect to the third- or lower-tier corporations, the second-tier corporation's credit for taxes paid by the third-tier corporation under section 902(b)(2) is determined as follows:

(A) If the effective rate of tax on dividends received by the third-tier corporation is the same as the effective rate of tax on its other earnings and profits—

$$\frac{\text{Dividend to second-tier corporation less portion of dividend from earnings included in domestic corporation's gross income under section 951 with respect to third-tier corporation}}{\text{Earnings and profits of third-tier corporation}} \times \text{Taxes paid by third-tier corporation}$$

(B) If the effective rate of tax on dividends received by the third-tier corporation is higher or lower than the effective rate of tax on its other earnings and profits—

(1) Credit for tax paid by third-tier corporation on earnings included in domestic corporation's gross income with respect to fourth- or lower-tier corporations—

Portion of dividends to second-tier corporation which is from earnings included in domestic corporation's gross income under section 951 with respect to fourth-or lower-tier corporations

―――――――――――――――――――――――――

Earnings and profits of third-tier corporation included in domestic corporation's gross income under section 951 with respect to fourth- or lower-tier corporations

× Tax paid by third-tier corporation on dividend received by third-tier corporation from earnings included in domestic corporation's gross income with respect to fourth- or lower-tier corporations

(2) Credit for tax paid by third-tier corporation on earnings not included in domes-tic corporation's gross income with respect to fourth-or lower-tier corporations—

Portion of dividend to second-tier corporation which is from earnings not included in domestic corporation's gross income under section 951 with respect to third- or lower-tier corporations

―――――――――――――――――――――――――

Earnings and profits of third-tier corporation not included in domestic corporation's gross income under section 951 with respect to fourth- or lower-tier corporations

× Tax paid by third-tier corporation on earnings not included in domestic corporation's gross income with respect to fourth- or lower-tier corporations

(ii) Section 902(b)(1) credit.—If the first-tier corporation receives a dividend from a second-tier corporation attributable in a whole or in part to amounts included in a domestic corporation's gross income under section 951 with respect to the second- or lower-tier corporations, the first-tier corporation's credit for taxes paid and deemed paid by the second-tier corporation under section 902(b)(1) is determined as follows:

(A) *Taxes paid by the second-tier corporation which are deemed paid by the first-tier corporation.*

(1) If the effective rate of tax on dividends received by the second-tier corporation is the same as the effective rate of tax on its other earnings and profits—

Dividend to first-tier corporation less portion of dividend from earnings included in domestic corporation's gross income under section 951 with respect to second-tier corporation

―――――――――――――――――――――――――

Earnings and profits of second-tier corporation

× Taxes paid by second-tier corporation

(2) If the effective rate of tax on dividends received by the second-tier corporation is higher or lower than the effective rate of tax on its other earnings and profits—

(i) Credit for tax paid by second-tier corporation on earnings previously taxed with respect to third- or lower-tier corporations—

Portion of dividend to first-tier corporation which is from earnings included in domestic corporation's gross income under section 951 with respect to third- or lower-tier corporations

―――――――――――――――――――――――――

Earnings and profits of second-tier corporation included in domestic corporation's gross income under section 951 with respect to third- or lower-tier corporations

× Tax paid by second-tier corporation on dividend received by second-tier corporation from earnings included in domestic corporation's gross income with respect to third- or lower-tier corporations

(ii) Credit for tax paid by second-tier corporation on earnings not previously taxed with respect to third- or lower-tier corporations—

Portion of dividend to first-tier corporation which is from earnings not included in domestic corporation's gross income under section 951 with respect to second-or lower-tier corporations

―――――――――――――――――――――――――

Earnings and profits of second-tier corporation not included in domestic corporation's gross income under section 951 with respect to third- or lower-tier corporations

× Tax paid by second-tier corporation on earnings not included in domestic corporation's gross income with respect to third- or lower-tier corporations

Reg. §1.960-2(g)(1)(ii)(A)(2)(ii)

(B) *Taxes deemed paid by the second-tier corporation which are deemed paid by the first-tier corporation.*

(1) If the effective rate of tax on dividends received by the third-tier corporation is the same as the effective rate of tax on its other earnings and profits—

$$\frac{\text{Dividend to first-tier corporation less portion of dividend from earnings included in domestic corporation's gross income under section 951 with respect to second- and third-tier corporations}}{\text{Earnings and profits of second-tier corporation less earnings and profits attributable to amounts included in domestic corporation's gross income under section 951 with respect to third-tier corporation}} \times \text{Taxes paid by third-tier corporation which are deemed paid by second-tier corporation}$$

(2) If the effective rate of tax on dividends received by the third-tier corporation is higher or lower than the effective rate of tax on its other earnings and profits—

(i) Credit for tax paid by third-tier corporation on earnings previously taxed with respect to fourth- or lower-tier corporations—

$$\frac{\text{Portion of dividend to first-tier corporation which is from earnings included in domestic corporation's gross income under section 951 with respect to fourth-or lower-tier corporations}}{\text{Earnings and profits of second-tier corporations included in domestic corporation's gross income under section 951 with respect to fourth- or lower-tier corporations}} \times \text{Tax paid by third-tier corporation on earnings previously taxed with respect to fourth-or lower-tier corporations which is deemed paid by second-tier corporation}$$

(ii) Credit for tax paid by third-tier corporation on earnings not previously taxed with respect to fourth-or lower-tier corporations—

$$\frac{\text{Portion of dividend to first-tier corporation which is from earnings not included in domestic corporation's gross income under section 951 with respect to second-or lower-tier corporations}}{\text{Earnings and profits of second-tier corporation not included in domestic corporation's gross income under section 951 with respect to third- or lower-tier corporations}} \times \text{Tax paid by third-tier corporation on earnings not previously taxed with respect to fourth-or lower-tier corporations which is deemed paid by second-tier corporation}$$

(iii) *Section 902(a) credit.*—If the domestic corporation receives a dividend from a first-tier corporation attributable in whole or in part to amounts included in a domestic corporation's gross income under section 951 with respect to the first- or lower-tier corporations, the domestic corporation's credit for taxes paid and deemed paid by the first-tier corporation under section 902(a) is determined as follows:

$$\frac{\text{Dividend to domestic corporation less portion of dividend from earnings included in domestic corporation's gross income under section 951 with respect to first-tier corporation}}{\text{Earnings and profits of first-tier corporation}}$$

(2) If the effective rate of tax on dividends received by the first-tier corporation is higher or lower than the effective rate of tax on its other earnings and profits—

(A) *Taxes paid by the first-tier corporation which are deemed paid by domestic corporation.*

(1) If the effective rate of tax on dividends received by the first-tier corporation is the same as the effective rate of tax on its other earnings and profits—

$$\times \text{Taxes paid by first-tier corporation}$$

(i) Credit for tax paid by first-tier corporation on earnings previously taxed with respect to second- or lower-tier corporations—

Portion of dividend to domestic corporation which is from earnings included in domestic corporation's gross income under section 951 with respect to second-or lower-tier corporations
─────────────────────────────────────
Earnings and profits of first-tier corporation included in domestic corporation's gross income under section 951 with respect to second- or lower-tier corporations

× Tax paid by first-tier corporation on dividends received by first-tier corporation from earnings included in domestic corporation's gross income with respect to second- or lower-tier corporations

(ii) Credit for tax paid by first-tier corporation on earnings not previously taxed with respect to second- or lower-tier corporations—

Portion of dividend to domestic corporation which is from earnings not included in domestic corporation's gross income under section 951 with respect to first- or lower-tier corporations
─────────────────────────────────────
Earnings and profits of first-tier corporation not included in domestic corporation's gross income under section 951 with respect to second- or lower-tier corporations

× Tax paid by first-tier corporation on earnings not included in domestic corporation's gross income with respect to second- or lower-tier corporations

(B) *Taxes (paid by second-tier corporation) deemed paid by first-tier corporation which are deemed paid by domestic corporation.*

(1) If the effective rate of tax on dividends received by the second-tier corporation is the same as its tax rate on other earnings and profits—

Dividend to domestic corporation less portion of dividend from earnings included in domestic corporation's gross income under section 951 with respect to first- and second-tier corporations
─────────────────────────────────────
Earnings and profits of first-tier corporation less earnings and profits attributable to amounts included in domestic corporation's gross income under section 951 with respect to second-tier corporation

× Taxes paid by second-tier corporation which are deemed paid by first-tier corporation

(2) If the effective rate of tax on dividends received by the second-tier corporation is higher or lower than the effective rate of tax on its other earnings and profits—

(i) Credit for tax paid by second-tier corporation on earnings previously taxed with respect to third-tier or lower-tier corporations—

Portion of dividend to domestic corporation which is from earnings included in domestic corporation's gross income under section 951 with respect to third- or lower-tier corporations
─────────────────────────────────────
Earnings and profits of first-tier corporation included in domestic corporation's gross income under section 951 with respect to third- or lower-tier corporations

× Tax paid by second-tier corporation on earnings previously taxed with respect to third- or lower-tier corporations which is deemed paid by first-tier corporation

(ii) Credit for tax paid by second-tier corporation on earnings not previously taxed with respect to third- or lower-tier corporations—

Portion of dividend to domestic corporation which is from earnings not included in domestic corporation's gross income under section 951 with respect to first- or lower-tier corporations
─────────────────────────────────────
Earnings and profits of first-tier corporation not included in domestic corporation's gross income under section 951 with respect to second- or lower-tier corporations

× Tax paid on second-tier corporation on earnings not previously taxed with respect to third- or lower-tier corporations which is deemed paid by first-tier corporation

Reg. § 1.960-2(g)(1)(iii)(B)(2)(ii)

(C) *Taxes (of a third-tier corporation) deemed paid by first-tier corporation which are deemed paid by domestic corporation.*

(1) If the effective rate of tax on dividends received by the third-tier corporation is the same as the effective rate of tax on its other earnings and profits—

$$\frac{\text{Dividend to domestic corporation less portion of dividend from earnings included in domestic corporation's gross income under section 951 with respect to first-, second- and third-tier corporations}}{\text{Earnings and profits of first-tier corporation less earnings and profits attributable to amounts included in domestic corporation's gross income with respect to second- and third-tier corporations}} \times \text{Taxes deemed paid by second-tier corporation which are deemed paid by first-tier corporation}$$

(2) If the effective rate of tax on dividends received by the third-tier corporation is higher or lower than the effective rate of tax on its other earnings and profits—

(i) Credit for tax (of third-tier corporation) deemed paid by second-tier corporation on earnings previously taxed with respect to fourth- or lower-tier corporation—

$$\frac{\text{Portion of dividend to domestic corporation which is from earnings included in domestic corporation's gross income under section 951 with respect to fourth-or lower-tier corporations}}{\text{Earnings and profits of first-tier corporation included in domestic corporation's gross income under section 951 with respect to fourth- or lower-tier corporations}} \times \text{Tax deemed paid by second-tier corporation on earnings previously taxed with respect to fourth- or lower-tier corporations which is deemed paid by first-tier corporation}$$

(ii) Credit for tax (of third-tier corporation) deemed paid by second-tier on earnings not previously taxed with respect to fourth- or lower-tier corporations—

$$\frac{\text{Portion of dividend to domestic corporation which is from earnings not included in domestic corporation's gross income under section 951 with respect to first- or lower-tier corporations}}{\text{Earnings and profits of first-tier corporation not included in domestic corporation's gross income under section 951 with respect to second- or lower-tier corporations}} \times \text{Tax deemed paid by second-tier corporation on earnings not previously taxed with respect to fourth- or lower-tier corporations which is deemed paid by first-tier corporation}$$

(2) Determination of domestic corporation's section 960 credit for amounts included in its gross income with respect to a first-, second-, or third-tier corporation which has received a distribution previously included in the gross income of a domestic corporation under section 951.—
(i) *Third-tier credit.*—If a domestic corporation is required to include an amount in its gross income under section 951 with respect to a third-tier corporation which has received a distribution from a fourth-tier corporation of amounts included in a domestic corporation's gross income under section 951 with respect to the fourth- or lower-tier corporations, the domestic corporation's credit for taxes paid by the third-tier corporation under section 960(a)(1) is determined as follows:

(A) If the effective rate of tax on dividends received by the third-tier corporation is the same as the effective rate of tax on its other earnings and profits—

$$\frac{\text{Amount included in domestic corporation's gross income under section 951 with respect to third-tier corporation}}{\text{Earnings and profits of third-tier corporation}} \times \text{Taxes paid by third-tier corporation}$$

(B) If the effective rate of tax on dividends received by the third-tier corporation is higher or lower than the effective rate of tax on its other earnings and profits—

$$\frac{\text{Amount included in domestic corporation's gross income under section 951 with respect to third-tier corporation}}{\text{Earnings and profits of third-tier corporation not included in domestic corporation's gross income under section 951 with respect to fourth- or lower-tier corporations}} \times \text{Tax paid by third-tier corporation on earnings not included in domestic corporation's gross income with respect to fourth- or lower-tier corporations}$$

(ii) *Second-tier credit.*—If a domestic corporation is required to include an amount in its gross income under section 951 with respect to a second-tier corporation which has received a distribution from a third-tier corporation of amounts included in a domestic corporation's gross income under section 951 with respect to the third- or lower-tier corporations, the domestic corporation's credit for taxes paid and deemed paid by the second-tier corporation under section 960(a)(1) is determined as follows:

(A) *Credit for taxes paid by the second-tier corporation which are deemed paid by the domestic corporation.*

(1) If the effective rate of tax on dividends received by the second-tier corporation is the same as the effective rate of tax on its other earnings and profits—

$$\frac{\text{Amount included in domestic corporation's gross income under section 951 with respect to second-tier corporation}}{\text{Earnings and profits of second-tier corporation}} \times \text{Taxes paid by second-tier corporation}$$

(2) If the effective rate of tax on dividends received by the second-tier is higher or lower than the effective rate of tax on its other earnings and profits—

$$\frac{\text{Amount included in domestic corporation's gross income under section 951 with respect to second-tier corporation}}{\text{Earnings and profits of second-tier corporation not included in domestic corporation's gross income under section 951 with respect to third- or lower-tier corporations}} \times \text{Tax paid by second-tier corporation on earnings not included in domestic corporation's gross income with respect to third- or lower-tier corporations}$$

(B) *Credit for taxes (of the third-tier corporation) deemed paid by the second-tier corporation under section 902(b)(2).*

(1) If the effective rate of tax on dividends received by the third-tier corporation is the same as the effective rate of tax on its other earnings and profits—

$$\frac{\text{Amount included in domestic corporation's gross income under section 951 with respect to second-tier corporation}}{\text{Earnings and profits of second-tier corporation less earnings and profits attributable to amounts included in domestic corporation's gross income with respect to third-tier corporation}} \times \text{Taxes paid by third-tier corporation which are deemed paid by second-tier corporation}$$

(2) If the effective rate of tax on dividends received by the third-tier corporation is higher or lower than the effective rate of tax on its other earnings and profits—

$$\frac{\text{Amount included in domestic corporation's gross income under section 951 with respect to second-tier corporation}}{\text{Earnings and profits of second-tier corporation not included in domestic corporation's gross income under section 951 with respect to third- or lower-tier corporations}} \times \text{Tax paid by third-tier corporation on earnings not previously taxed with respect to fourth- or lower-tier corporations which is deemed paid by second-tier corporation}$$

Reg. §1.960-2(g)(2)(ii)(B)(2)

(iii) *First-tier credit.*—If a domestic corporation is required to include amounts in its gross income under section 951 with respect to a first-tier corporation which has received a distribution from a second-tier corporation of amounts included in a domestic corporation's gross income under section 951 with respect to the second- or lower-tier corporations, the domestic corporation's credit for taxes paid and deemed paid by the first-tier corporation under section 960(a)(1) shall be determined as follows:

(A) *Credit for taxes paid by the first-tier corporation.*

(1) If the effective rate of tax on dividends received by the first-tier corporation is the same as the effective rate of tax on its other earnings and profits—

$$\frac{\text{Amount included in domestic corporation's gross income under section 951 with respect to first-tier corporation}}{\text{Earnings and profits of first-tier corporation}} \times \text{Taxes paid by first-tier corporation}$$

(2) If the effective rate of tax on dividends received by the first-tier corporation is higher or lower than the effective rate of tax on its other earnings and profits—

$$\frac{\text{Amount included in domestic corporation's gross income under section 951 with respect to first-tier corporation}}{\text{Earnings and profits of first-tier corporation not included in domestic corporation's gross income under section 951 with respect to second- or lower-tier corporations}} \times \text{Tax paid by first-tier corporation on earnings not included in domestic corporation's gross income with respect to second- or lower-tier corporations}$$

(B) *Credit for taxes paid by the second-tier corporation deemed paid by the first-tier corporation under section 902(b)(1).*

(1) If the effective rate of tax on dividends received by the second-tier corporation is the same as the effective rate of tax on its other earnings and profits—

$$\frac{\text{Amount included in domestic corporation's gross income under section 951 with respect to first-tier corporation}}{\text{Earnings and profits of first-tier corporation less earnings and profits attributable to amounts included in domestic corporation's gross income under section 951 with respect to second-tier corporation}} \times \text{Taxes paid by second-tier corporation which are deemed paid by first-tier corporation}$$

(2) If the effective rate of tax on dividends received by the second-tier corporation is higher or lower than the effective rate of tax on its other earnings and profits—

$$\frac{\text{Amount included in domestic corporation's gross income under section 951 with respect to first-tier corporation}}{\text{Earnings and profits of first-tier corporation not included in domestic corporation's gross income under section 951 with respect to second- or lower-tier corporations}} \times \text{Tax paid by second-tier corporation on earnings not previously taxed with respect to third- or lower-tier corporations which is deemed paid by first-tier corporation}$$

(C) *Credit for taxes (of the third-tier corporation) deemed paid by the second-tier corporation which are deemed paid by first-tier corporation under section 902(b)(1).*

(1) If the effective rate of tax on dividends received by the third-tier corporation

$$\frac{\text{Amount included in domestic corporation's gross income under section 951 with respect to first-tier corporation}}{\text{Earnings and profits of first-tier corporation less earnings and profits attributable to amounts included in domestic corporation's gross income with respect to second- and third-tier corporation}}$$

is the same as the effective rate of tax on its other earnings and profits—

× Taxes deemed paid by second-tier corporation which are deemed paid by first-tier corporation

(2) If the effective rate of tax on dividends received by the third-tier corporation

$$\frac{\text{Amount included in domestic corporation's gross income under section 951 with respect to first-tier corporation}}{\text{Earnings and profits of first-tier corporation not included in domestic corporation's gross income under section 951 with respect to second- or lower-tier corporation}}$$

is higher or lower than the effective rate of tax on its other earnings and profits—

× Tax deemed paid by second-tier corporation on earnings not previously taxed with respect to fourth- or lower-tier corporations which is deemed paid by first-tier corporation

[Reg. § 1.960-2.]

☐ [*T.D.* 7120, 6-3-71. *Amended by T.D.* 7334, 12-20-74; *T.D.* 7649, 10-17-79 *and T.D.* 7843, 11-3-82.]

§ 1.960-3. Gross-up of amounts included in income under section 951.— (a) *General rule for including taxes in income.—*Any taxes deemed paid by a domestic corporation for the taxable year pursuant to section 960(a)(1) shall, except as provided in paragraph (b) of this section, be included in the gross income of such corporation for such year as a dividend pursuant to section 78 and § 1.78-1. See also paragraph (a)(8) of § 1.902-3.

(b) *Certain taxes not included in income.—* Any taxes deemed paid by a domestic corporation for the taxable year pursuant to section 902(a) or section 960(a)(1) shall not be included in the gross income of such corporation for such year as a dividend pursuant to section 78 and § 1.78-1 to the extent that such taxes are paid or accrued by the first-, second-, or third-tier corporation, as the case may be, on or with respect to an amount which is excluded from the gross income of such foreign corporation under section 959(b) and § 1.959-2 as distributions from the earnings and profits of another controlled foreign corporation attributable to an amount which is, or has been, required to be included in the gross income of the domestic corporation under section 951.

(c) *Illustrations.—*The application of this section may be illustrated by the following examples:

Example (1). Domestic corporation N owns all the one class of stock of controlled foreign corporation A which owns all the one class of stock of controlled foreign corporation B. All such corporations use the calendar year as the taxable year. For 1978, B Corporation, after having paid $20 of foreign income taxes, has $80 in earnings and profits, which are attributable to the amount required to be included in N Corporation's gross income for such year under section 951 with respect to B Corporation and all of which are distributed to A Corporation in such year. The dividend so received from B Corporation is excluded from A Corporation's gross income under section 959(b) and § 1.959-2. An income tax of 10 percent is required to be withheld from such dividend by the foreign country under the laws of which B Corporation is created, and the foreign country under the laws of which A Corporation is created imposes an income tax of $22 on the dividend received from B Corporation. For 1978, A Corporation's earnings and profits are $50 ($80 − [.10 × $80] − $22), which it distributes in such year to N Corporation. For 1978, N Corporation is required under section 951 to include $80 in gross income with respect to B Corporation and also is required under the gross-up provisions of section 78 to include in gross income $20 ($80/$80 × $20), the amount equal to the foreign income taxes of B Corporation which are deemed paid by N Corporation under section 960(a)(1). Under paragraph (b) of this section N Corporation is not required to include in gross income the $30 ($8 + $22) of foreign income taxes which are paid by A Corporation in connection with the dividend received from B Corporation and which are deemed paid by N Corporation under section 902(a) and paragraph (c) of §1.960-2.

Example (2). Domestic corporation N owns all the one class of stock of controlled foreign corporation A which owns all the one class of stock of controlled foreign corporation B, which in turn owns all the one class of stock of controlled foreign corporation C. All such corporations use the calendar year as the taxable year. For 1978, C Corporation, after having paid $20 of foreign income taxes, has $80 in earnings and profits, which are attributable to the amount required to be included in N Corporation's gross income for such year under section 951 with respect to C Corporation and all of which are distributed to B Corporation in such year. After having paid foreign income taxes of $10 on the dividend received from C Corporation, B Corporation distributes the balance of $70 to A Corporation. After having paid foreign income taxes of $5 on the dividend received from B Corporation, A Corporation distributes the balance of $65 to N Corporation. The dividend so received by B Corporation, and in turn by A Corporation, is excluded from the gross income of such corporations under section 959(b) and §1.959-2. [Reg. §1.960-3.]

☐ [*T.D.* 7120, 6-3-71. *Amended by T.D.* 7481, 4-15-77; *T.D.* 7649, 10-17-79 *and T.D.* 7843, 11-3-82.]

§1.960-4. Additional foreign tax credit in year of receipt of previously taxed earnings and profits.—(a) *Increase in section 904(a) limitation for the taxable year of exclusion.*—(1) *In general.*—The applicable limitation under section 904(a) for a taxpayer's taxable year (hereinafter in this section referred to as the "taxable year of exclusion") in which he receives an amount which is excluded from gross income under section 959(a)(1) and which is attributable to a controlled foreign corporation's earnings and profits in respect of which an amount was required to be included in the gross income of such taxpayer under section 951(a) for a taxable year (hereinafter in this section referred to as the "taxable year of inclusion") previous to the taxable year of exclusion shall be increased under section 960(b)(1) by the amount described in paragraph (b) of this section if the conditions described in subparagraph (2) of this paragraph are satisfied.

(2) *Conditions under which increase in limitation is allowed for the taxable year of exclusion.*—The increase in limitation described in subparagraph (1) of this paragraph for the taxable year of exclusion shall be made only if the taxpayer—

(i) For the taxable year of inclusion either chose to claim a foreign tax credit as provided in section 901 or did not pay or accrue any foreign income taxes,

(ii) Chooses to claim a foreign tax credit as provided in section 901 for the taxable year of exclusion, and

(iii) For the taxable year of exclusion pays, accrues, or is deemed to have paid foreign income taxes with respect to the amount, described in subparagraph (1) of this paragraph, which is excluded from his gross income for such year under section 959(a)(1).

For purposes of determining the source of distributions in determining the foreign tax credit under section 960(b) and this section, see also paragraph (e) of §1.959-3.

(b) *Amount of increase in limitation for the taxable year of exclusion.*—The amount of increase under section 960(b)(1) in the applicable limitation under section 904(a) for the taxable year of exclusion shall be—

(1) The amount by which the applicable section 904(a) limitation for the taxable year of inclusion was increased, determined as provided in paragraph (c) of this section, by reason of the inclusion of the amount in the taxpayer's income for such year under section 951(a), reduced by

(2) The amount of foreign income taxes allowed as a credit under section 901 for such taxable year of inclusion and which were allowable to such taxpayer solely by reason of the inclusion of such amount in his gross income under section 951(a), as determined under paragraph (d) of this section, and then by

(3) The additional reduction for such taxable year of inclusion arising by reason of increases in limitation under section 960(b)(1) for taxable years intervening between such taxable year of inclusion and such taxable year of exclusion, as determined under paragraph (e) of this section in respect of such inclusion under section 951(a),

except that the amount of increase determined under this paragraph for the taxable year of exclusion shall in no case exceed the amount of foreign income taxes paid, accrued, or deemed to be paid by such taxpayer for such taxable year of exclusion with respect to the amount, described in paragraph (a)(1) of this section, which is excluded from gross income for such year under section 959(a)(1).

(c) *Determination of increase in limitation for the taxable year of inclusion.*—The amount of the increase in the applicable limitation under section 904(a) for the taxable year of inclusion which arises by reason of the inclusion of the amount in gross income under section 951(a) shall be the amount of the applicable limitation under section 904(a) for such year reduced by the amount which would have been the applicable limitation under section 904(a) for such year if the amount had not been included in gross income for such year under section 951(a).

(d) *Determination of foreign income taxes allowed for taxable year of inclusion by reason of section 951(a) amount.*—The amount of foreign income taxes allowed as a credit under section 901 for the taxable year of inclusion which were allowable solely by reason of the inclusion of the amount in gross income for such year under section 951(a) shall be the amount of foreign income taxes allowed as a credit under section 901 for such year reduced by the amount of foreign income taxes which would have been allowed as a credit under section 901 for such year if the amount had not been included in gross income for such year under section 951(a). For purposes of this paragraph, the term "foreign income taxes" includes foreign income taxes paid or accrued, and foreign income taxes deemed paid under section 902, section 904(d), and section 960(a), for the taxable year of inclusion.

(e) *Additional reduction for the taxable year of inclusion arising by reason of increases in limitation for intervening years.*—The amount of increase in the applicable limitation under section 904(a) for the taxable year of inclusion shall also be reduced, after first deducting the foreign income taxes described in paragraph (b)(2) of this section, by any increases in limitation which arise under section 960(b)(1)—by reason of any earlier exclusions under section 959(a)(1) in respect of the same inclusion under section 951(a) for such taxable year of inclusion—for the first, second, third, fourth, etc., succeeding taxable years of exclusion, in that order, which follow such taxable year of inclusion and precede the taxable year of exclusion in respect of which the increase in limitation under section 960(b)(1) and paragraph (b) of this section is being determined. The amount of any increase in limitation which arises under section 960(b)(1) for any such succeeding taxable year of exclusion shall be the amount of foreign income taxes allowed as a credit under section 901 for each such taxable year reduced by the amount of foreign income taxes which would have been allowed as a credit under section 901 for each such year if the limitation for each such year were not increased under section 960(b)(1). For any such succeeding taxable year of exclusion for which the taxpayer does not choose to claim a foreign tax credit as provided in section 901, the same increase in limitation under section 960(b)(1) shall be treated as having been made, for purposes of this paragraph, which would have been made for such taxable year if the taxpayer had chosen to claim the foreign tax credit for such year.

(f) *Illustrations.*—The application of this section may be illustrated by the following examples:

Example (1). Domestic corporation N owns all of the one class of stock of controlled foreign corporation A. Corporation A, after paying foreign income taxes of $30, has earnings and profits for 1978 of $70, all of which are attributable to an amount required under section 951(a) to be included in N Corporation's gross income for 1978. Both corporations use the calendar year as the taxable year. For 1979 and 1980, A Corporation has no earnings and profits attributable to an amount required to be included in N Corporation's gross income under section 951(a); for each such year it makes a distribution of $35 (from its earnings and profits for 1978) from which a foreign income tax of $6 is withheld. For each of 1978, 1979, and 1980, N Corporation derives taxable income of $50 from sources within the United States and claims a foreign tax credit under section 901, determined by applying the overall limitation under section 904(a)(2). The United States tax payable by N Corporation is determined as follows, assuming a corporate tax rate of 48 percent:

1978

Taxable income of N Corporation:		
U.S. sources		$ 50.00
Sources without the U.S.:		
Amount required to be included in N Corporation's gross income under sec. 951(a)	$70.00	
Foreign income taxes deemed paid by N Corporation under sec. 960(a)(1) and included in N Corporation's gross income under sec. 78 ($30 × $70/$70)	30.00	100.00
Total taxable income		$150.00
U.S. tax payable for 1978:		
U.S. tax before credit ($150 × .48)		$ 72.00
Credit: Foreign income taxes of $30, but not to exceed overall limitation of $48 for 1965 ($100/$150 × $72)		30.00
U.S. tax payable		$ 42.00

Reg. §1.960-4(f)

1979

Taxable income of N Corporation, consisting of income from U.S. sources		$ 50.00
U.S. tax before credit ($50 × .48)		24.00
Section 904(a)(2) overall limitation for 1966:		
Limitation for 1966 before increase under sec. 960(b)(1) ($24 × $0/$50)		0
Plus: Increase in overall limitation for 1979 under sec. 960(b)(1):		
Amount by which 1978 overall limitation was increased by reason of inclusion in N Corporation's gross income under sec. 951(a) for 1978 ($48 − [($50 × .48) × $0/$50])	$48.00	
Less: Foreign income taxes allowed as a credit for 1978 which were allowable solely by reason of such sec. 951(a) inclusion ($30 − $0)	30.00	
Balance	18.00	
But: Such balance not to exceed foreign income taxes paid by N Corporation for 1979 with respect to $35 distribution excluded under sec. 959(a)(1) ($6 tax withheld)	6.00	$6.00
Overall limitation for 1979		$ 6.00
U.S. tax payable for 1979:		
U.S. tax before credit ($50 × .48)		$ 24.00
Credit: Foreign income taxes of $6, but not to exceed overall limitation of $6 for 1966		6.00
U.S. tax payable		$18.00

1980

Taxable income of N Corporation, consisting of income from U.S. sources		$ 50.00
U.S. tax before credit ($50 × .48)		24.00
Section 904(a)(2) overall limitation for 1980:		
Limitation for 1980 before increase under sec. 960(b)(1) ($24 × $0/$50)		0
Plus: Increase in overall limitation for 1980 under sec. 960(b)(1):		
Amount by which 1978 overall limitation was increased by reason of inclusion in N Corporation's gross income under sec. 951(a) for 1978 ($48 − [($50 × .48) × $0/$50])	$48.00	
Less: Foreign income taxes allowed as a credit for 1978 which were allowable solely by reason of such sec. 951(a) inclusion ($30 − $0)	30.00	
Tentative balance	18.00	
Less: Increase in overall limitation under sec. 960(b)(1) for 1979 by reason of such sec. 951(a) inclusion	$ 6.00	
Balance	12.00	
But: Such balance not to exceed foreign income taxes paid by N Corporation for 1980 with respect to $35 distribution excluded under sec. 959(a)(1) ($6 tax withheld)	6.00	$ 6.00
Overall limitation for 1980		$ 6.00
U.S. tax payable for 1980:		
U.S. tax before credit ($50 × .48)		$ 24.00
Credit: Foreign income taxes of $6, but not to exceed overall limitation of $6 for 1980		6.00
U.S. tax payable		$ 18.00

Example (2). The facts for 1978, 1979, and 1980, are the same as in example (1), except that in 1977, to which the section 904(a)(2) overall limitation applies, N Corporation pays $18 of foreign income taxes in excess of the overall limitation and that such excess is not absorbed as a carryback to 1975 or 1976 under section 904(c). Therefore, there is no increase under section 960(b)(1) in the overall limitation for 1979 or 1980 since the amount ($48) by which the 1978 overall limitation was increased by reason of the inclusion in N Corporation's gross income for 1978 under section 951(a), less the foreign income taxes ($48) allowed as a credit which were allowable solely by reason of such inclusion, is zero. The foreign income taxes so allowed as a credit for 1978 which were allowable solely by reason of such section 951(a) inclusion consist of the $30 of foreign income taxes deemed paid for 1978 under section 960(a)(1) and the $18 of foreign income taxes for 1977 carried over and deemed paid for 1965 under section 904(c).

Example (3). (a) Domestic corporation N owns all the one class of stock of controlled foreign corporation A, which in turn owns all the one class of stock of controlled foreign corporation B. All corporations use the calendar year as the taxable year. Corporation B, after paying foreign income taxes of $30, has earnings and profits for 1978 of $70, all of which is attributable to an amount required under section 951(a) to be included in N Corporation's gross income for 1978, and $35 of which it distributes in such year to A Corporation. For 1978, A Corporation, after paying foreign income taxes of $5 on such dividend from B Corporation, has total earnings and profits of $30, all of which it distributes in such year to N Corporation, a foreign income tax of $3 being withheld therefrom.

(b) For 1966, B Corporation has no earnings and profits, but distributes in such year to A Corporation the $35 remaining of its earnings and profits for 1978. For 1979, A Corporation, after paying foreign income taxes of $5 on such dividend from B Corporation, has total earnings and profits of $30, all of which it distributes to N Corporation, a foreign income tax of $3 being withheld therefrom.

(c) For each of 1978 and 1979, N Corporation has taxable income of $100 from United States sources and claims a foreign tax credit under section 901, determined by applying the overall limitation under section 904(a)(2). The United States tax payable by N Corporation is determined as follows, assuming a corporate tax rate of 48 percent:

1978

Taxable income of N Corporation:		
U.S. sources		$100
Sources without the U.S.:		
Amount required to be included in N Corporation's gross income under sec. 951(a) with respect to B Corporation	$70	
Foreign income taxes deemed paid by N Corporation under sec. 960(a)(1) and included in N Corporation's gross income under sec. 78 ($30 × $70/$70)	30	100
Total taxable income		$200
U.S. tax payable for 1978:		
U.S. tax before credit ($200 × .48)		$96
Credit: Foreign income taxes of $38 ([$30 × $70/$70] + [$5 × $30/$30] + $3), but not to exceed overall limitation of $48 ($96 × $100/$200)		38
U.S. tax payable		$58

1979

Taxable income of N Corporation, consisting of income from U.S. sources		$100
U.S. tax before credit ($100 × .48)		48
Section 904(a)(2) overall limitation for 1979:		
Limitation for 1979 before increase under sec. 960(b)(1) ($48 × $0/$100)		0
Plus: Increase in overall limitation for 1979 under sec. 960(b)(1):		
Amount by which 1978 overall limitation was increased by reason of inclusion in N Corporation's gross income under sec. 951(a) for 1978 ($48 − [($100 × .48) × $0/$100])	$48	
Less: Foreign income taxes allowed as a credit for 1965 which were allowable solely by reason of such sec. 951(a) inclusion ($38 − $0)	38	
Balance	10	
But: Such balance not to exceed foreign income taxes paid and deemed paid by N Corporation for 1979 with respect to $30 distribution excluded under sec. 959(a)(1) ([$5 × $30/$30] + $3)	$8	$8
Overall limitation for 1979		$8
U.S. tax payable for 1979:		
U.S. tax before credit ($100 × .48)		$48
Credit: Foreign income taxes of $8 ($3 + $5), but not to exceed overall limitation of $8 for 1979		8
U.S. tax payable		$40

[Reg. § 1.960-4.]

☐ [*T.D. 7120, 6-3-71. Amended by T.D. 7649, 10-17-79.*]

§ 1.960-5. Credit for taxable year of inclusion binding for taxable year of exclusion.—(a) *Taxes not allowed as a deduction for taxable year of exclusion.*—In the case of any taxpayer who—

(1) Chooses to claim a foreign tax credit as provided in section 901 for the taxable year for which he is required to include in gross income under section 951(a) an amount attributable to the earnings and profits of a controlled foreign corporation, and

(2) Does not choose to claim a foreign tax credit as provided in section 901 for a taxable year in which he receives an amount which is excluded from gross income under section

959(a)(1) and which is attributable to such earnings and profits of such controlled foreign corporation,

no deduction shall be allowed under section 164 for the taxable year of such exclusion for any foreign income taxes paid or accrued on or with respect to such excluded amount.

(b) *Illustration.*—The application of this section may be illustrated by the following example:

Example. Domestic corporation N owns all the one class of stock of controlled foreign corporation A. Both corporations use the calendar year as the taxable year. All of A Corporation's earnings and profits of $80 for 1978 (after payment of foreign income taxes of $20 on its total income of $100 for such year) are attributable to an amount required under section 951(a) to be included in N Corporation's gross income for 1978. For 1978, N Corporation chooses to claim a foreign tax credit for the $20 of foreign income taxes which for such year are paid by A Corporation and deemed paid by N Corporation under section 960(a)(1) and paragraph (c)(1) of § 1.960-1. For 1979, A Corporation distributes the entire $80 of 1978 earnings and profits, a foreign income tax of $8 being withheld therefrom. Although N Corporation does not choose to claim a foreign tax credit for 1966, it may not deduct such $8 of foreign income taxes under section 164. Corporation N may, however, deduct under such section a foreign income tax of $4 which is withheld from a distribution of $40 by A Corporation during 1979 from its 1979 earnings and profits. [Reg. § 1.960-5.]

☐ [*T.D.* 7120, 6-3-71. *Amended by T.D.* 7649, 10-17-79.]

§ 1.960-6. Overpayments resulting from increase in limitation for taxable year of exclusion.—(a) *Amount of overpayment.*—If an increase in the limitation under section 960(b)(1) and § 1.960-4 for a taxable year of exclusion exceeds the tax (determined before allowance of any credits against tax) imposed by chapter 1 of the Code for such year, the amount of such excess shall be deemed an overpayment of tax for such year and shall be refunded or credited to the taxpayer in accordance with chapter 65 (section 6401 and following) of the Code.

(b) *Illustration.*—The application of this section may be illustrated by the following example:

Example. Domestic corporation N owns all the one class of stock of controlled foreign corporation A. Both corporations use the calendar year as the taxable year. For 1978, A Corporation has total income of $100,000 on which it pays foreign income taxes of $20,000. All of A Corporation's earnings and profits for 1978 of $80,000 are attributable to an amount which is required under section 951(a) to be included in N Corporation's gross income for 1978. By reason of such income inclusion N Corporation is deemed for 1978 to have paid under section 960(a)(1), and is required under section 78 to include in gross income for such year, the $20,000 ($20,000 × $80,000/$80,000) of foreign income taxes paid by A Corporation for such year. Corporation N also derives $100,000 taxable income from sources within the United States for 1978. For 1979 N Corporation has $25,000 of taxable income, all of which is derived from sources within the United States. No part of A Corporation's earnings and profits for 1979 is attributable to an amount required under section 951(a) to be included in N Corporation's gross income. During 1979, A Corporation makes one distribution consisting of its $80,000 earnings and profits for 1978, all of which is excluded under section 959(a)(1) from N Corporation's gross income for 1979, and from which distribution foreign income taxes of $10,000 are withheld. For 1978 and 1979, N Corporation claims the foreign tax credit under section 901, determined by applying the overall limitation under section 904(a)(2). The United States tax of N Corporation is determined as follows for such years:

1978

Taxable income of N Corporation:		
U.S. sources		$100,000
Sources without the U.S.:		
Amount required to be included in N Corporation's gross income under sec. 951(a)	$80,000	
Foreign income taxes deemed paid by N Corporation under sec. 960(a)(1) and included in N Corporation's gross income under sec. 78 ($20,000 × $80,000/$80,000)	20,000	100,000
Total taxable income		$200,000
U.S. tax payable for 1978:		
U.S. tax before credit ([$200,000 × .22] + [$175,000 × .26])		$89,500
Credit: Foreign income taxes of $20,000, but not to exceed overall limitation of $44,750 ($89,500 × $100,000/$200,000)		20,000
U.S. tax payable		$69,500

1979

Taxable income of N Corporation, consisting of income from U.S. sources	$ 25,000
U.S. tax before credit ($25,000 × .22)	5,500
Section 904(a)(2) overall limitation for 1979:	
Limitation for 1979 before increase under sec. 960(b)(1) ($5,500 × $0/25,000)	0
Plus: Increase in overall limitation for 1979 under sec. 960(b)(1):	
Amount by which 1978 overall limitation was increased by reason of inclusion in N Corporation's gross income under sec. 951(a) for 1965 ($44,750 – [$41,500 × $0/$100,000]) $44,750	
Less: Foreign income taxes allowed as a credit for 1965 which were allowable solely by reason of such sec. 951(a) inclusion ($20,000 – $0) 20,000	
Balance $24,750	
But: Such balance not to exceed foreign income taxes paid by N Corporation for 1966 with respect to $80,000 distribution excluded under sec. 959(a)(1) ($10,000 tax withheld) $10,000	$ 10,000
Overall limitation for 1979	$ 10,000
U.S. tax payable for 1979:	
U.S. tax before credit ($25,000 × .22)	$ 5,500
Credit: Foreign income taxes of $10,000, but not to exceed overall limitation of $10,000 for 1979	10,000
U.S. tax payable	none
Overpayment of tax for 1979:	
Increase in limitation under sec. 960(b)(1) for 1979	$ 10,000
Less: Tax imposed for 1979 under chapter 1 of the Code	5,500
Excess treated as overpayment	$ 4,500

[Reg. § 1.960-6.]

☐ [*T.D.* 7120, 6-3-71. *Amended by T.D.* 7649, 10-17-79.]

§ 1.961-1. Increase in basis of stock in controlled foreign corporations and of other property.—(a) *Increase in basis.*—(1) *In general.*—Except as provided in subparagraph (2) of this paragraph, the basis of a United States shareholder's—

    (i) Stock in a controlled foreign corporation; or

    (ii) Property (as defined in paragraph (b)(1) of this section) by reason of the ownership of which he is considered under section 958(a)(2) as owning stock in a controlled foreign corporation

shall be increased under section 961(a), as of the last day in the taxable year of such corporation on which it is a controlled foreign corporation, by the amount required to be included with respect to such stock or such property in such shareholder's gross income under section 951(a) for his taxable year in which or with which such taxable year of such corporation ends. The increase in basis provided by the preceding sentence shall be made only to the extent to which such amount required to be included in gross income under section 951(a) was so included in gross income.

(2) *Limitation on amount of increase in case of election under section 962.*—In the case of a United States shareholder who makes the election under section 962 for the taxable year, the amount of the increase in basis provided by subparagraph (1) of this paragraph shall not exceed the amount of United States tax paid in accordance with such election with respect to the amounts included in such shareholder's gross income under section 951(a) for such year (as determined under § 1.962-1).

(b) *Rules of application.*—(1) *Property defined.*—The property of a United States shareholder referred to in paragraph (a)(1)(ii) of this section shall consist of—

    (i) Stock in a foreign corporation;

    (ii) An interest in a foreign partnership; or

    (iii) A beneficial interest in a foreign estate or trust (as defined in section 7701(a)(31)).

(2) *Increase with respect to each share of stock.*—Any increase under paragraph (a) of this section in the basis of a United States shareholder's stock in a foreign corporation shall be made in the amount included in gross income under section 951(a) or in the amount of United States tax paid in accordance with an election under section 962, as the case may be, with respect to each share of such stock.

(c) *Illustration.*—The application of this section may be illustrated by the following examples:

Example (1). Domestic corporation M owns 800 of the 1,000 shares of the one class of stock in controlled foreign corporation R which owns all of the one class of stock in controlled foreign corporation S. Corporations M, R, and S use the calendar year as a taxable year. In 1964, S Corporation has $100,000 of earnings and profits after the payment of $11,250 of foreign income taxes, and $100,000 of subpart F income. Corporation R has no earnings and profits. With respect to S Corporation, M Corporation is required to include in gross income $80,000 (800/1,000 × $100,000) under section 951(a), and $9,000 ($80,000/$100,000 × $11,250) under section 78. On December 31, 1964, M Corporation must increase the basis of each share of its stock in R Corporation by $100 ($80,000/800).

Example (2). A, an individual United States shareholder, owns all of the 1,000 shares of the one class of stock in controlled foreign corporation T. Corporation T and A use the calendar year as a taxable year. In 1964, T Corporation has $80,000 of earnings and profits after the payment of $20,000 of foreign income taxes, and $80,000 of subpart F income. A makes the election under section 962 for 1964 and in accordance with such election pays a United States tax of $23,000 with respect to the $80,000 included in his gross income under section 951(a). On December 31, 1964, A must increase the basis of each share of his stock in T Corporation by $23 ($23,000/1,000). [Reg. § 1.961-1.]

☐ [T.D. 6850, 9-15-65.]

§ 1.961-2. Reduction in basis of stock in foreign corporations and of other property.

—(a) *Reduction in basis.*—(1) *In general.*—Except as provided in subparagraph (2) of this paragraph, the adjusted basis of a United States person's—

(i) Stock in a foreign corporation;

(ii) Interest in a foreign partnership; or

(iii) Beneficial interest in a foreign estate or trust (as defined in section 7701(a)(31)),

with respect to which such United States person receives an amount which is excluded from gross income under section 959(a), shall be reduced under section 961(b), as of the time such person receives such excluded amount, by the sum of the amount so excluded and any income, war profits, or excess profits taxes imposed by any foreign country or possession of the United States on or with respect to the earnings and profits attributable to such excluded amount when such earnings and profits were actually distributed directly or indirectly through a chain or ownership described in section 958(a)(2).

(2) *Limitation on amount of reduction in case of election under section 962.*—In the case of a distribution of earnings and profits attributable to amounts with respect to which an election under section 962 has been made, the amount of the reduction in basis provided by subparagraph (1) of this paragraph shall not exceed the sum of—

(i) The amount of such distribution which is excluded from gross income under section 959(a) after the application of section 962(d) and § 1.962-3; and

(ii) Any income, war profits, or excess profits taxes imposed by any foreign country or possession of the United States on or with respect to the earnings and profits attributable to such excluded amount when such earnings and profits were actually distributed directly or indirectly through a chain of ownership described in section 958(a)(2).

(b) *Reduction with respect to each share of stock.*—Any reduction under paragraph (a) of this section in the adjusted basis of a United States person's stock in a foreign corporation shall be made with respect to each share of such stock in the sum of—

(1)(i) The amount excluded from gross income under section 959(a); or

(ii) The amount excluded from gross income under section 959(a) after the application of section 962(d) and § 1.962-3; and

(2) The amount of any income, war profits, or excess profits taxes imposed by any foreign country or possession of the United States on or with respect to the earnings and profits attributable to such excluded amount when such earnings and profits were actually distributed directly or indirectly through a chain of ownership described in section 958(a)(2).

(c) *Amount in excess of basis.*—To the extent that the amount of the reduction in the adjusted basis of property provided by paragragh (a) of this section exceeds such adjusted basis, the amount shall be treated as gain from the sale or exchange of property.

(d) *Illustration.*—The application of this section may be illustrated by the following examples:

Example (1). (a) Domestic corporation M owns all of the 1,000 shares of the one class of stock in controlled foreign corporation R, which owns all of the 500 shares of the one class of stock in controlled foreign corporation S. Each share of M Corporation's stock in R

Corporation has a basis of $200. Corporations M, R, and S use the calendar year as a taxable year. In 1963, S Corporation has $100,000 of earnings and profits after the payment of $50,000 of foreign income taxes and $100,000 of subpart F income. For 1963, M Corporation includes $100,000 in gross income under section 951(a) with respect to S Corporation. In accordance with the provisions of §1.961-1, M Corporation increases the basis of each of its 1,000 shares of stock in R Corporation to $300 ($200 + $100,000/1,000) as of December 31, 1963.

(b) On July 31, 1964, M Corporation sells 250 of its shares of stock in R Corporation to domestic corporation N at a price of $350 per share. Corporation N satisfies the requirements of paragraph (d) of §1.959-1 so as to qualify as M Corporation's successor in interest. On September 30, 1964, the earnings and profits attributable to the $100,000 included in M Corporation's gross income under section 951(a) for 1963 are distributed to R Corporation which incurs a withholding tax of $10,000 on such distribution (10 percent of $100,000) and an additional foreign income tax of 33⅓ percent or $30,000 by reason of the inclusion of the net distribution of $90,000 ($100,000 minus $10,000) in its taxable income for 1964. On June 30, 1965, R Corporation distributes the remaining $60,000 of such earnings and profits to corporations M and N: Corporation M receives $45,000 (750/1000 × $60,000) and excludes such amount from gross income under section 959(a); Corporation N receives $15,000 (250/1,000 × $60,000) and, as M Corporation's successor in interest, excludes such amount from gross income under section 959(a). As of June 30, 1965, M Corporation must reduce the adjusted basis of each of its 750 shares of stock in R Corporation to $200 ($300 minus ($45,000/750 + $10,000/1,000 + $30,000/1,000)); and N Corporation must reduce the basis of each of its 250 shares of stock in R Corporation to $250 ($350 minus ($15,000/250 + $10,000/1,000 + $30,000/1,000)).

Example (2). The facts are the same as in paragraph (a) of example (1), except that in addition, on July 31, 1964, R Corporation sells its 500 shares of stock in S Corporation to domestic corporation P at a price of $600 per share. Corporation P satisfies the requirements of paragraph (d) of §1.959-1 so as to qualify as M Corporation's successor in interest. On September 30, 1964, S Corporation distributes $100,000 of earnings and profits to P Corporation, which earnings and profits are attributable to the $100,000 included in M Corporation's gross income under section 951(a) for 1963. Corporation P incurs a withholding tax of $10,000 on the distribution from S Corporation (10 percent of $100,000). As M Corporation's successor in interest, P Corporation excludes the $90,000 it receives from gross income under section 959(a). As of September 30, 1964, P Corporation must reduce the basis of each of its 500 shares of stock in S Corporation to $400 ($600 minus ($90,000/500 + $10,000/500)). [Reg. §1.961-2.]

☐ [*T.D.* 6850, 9-15-65.]

§1.962-1. Limitation of tax for individuals on amounts included in gross income under section 951(a).—(a) *In general.*—An individual United States shareholder may, in accordance with §1.962-2, elect to have the provisions of section 962 apply for his taxable year. In such case—

(1) The tax imposed under chapter 1 of the Internal Revenue Code on all amounts which are included in his gross income for such taxable year under section 951(a) shall (in lieu of the tax determined under section 1) be an amount equal to the tax which would be imposed under section 11 if such amounts were received by a domestic corporation (determined in accordance with paragraph (b)(1) of this section), and

(2) For purposes of applying section 960(a)(1) (relating to foreign tax credit) such amounts shall be treated as if received by a domestic corporation (as provided in paragraph (b)(2) of this section).

Thus, an individual United States shareholder may elect to be subject to tax at corporate rates on amounts included in his gross income under section 951(a) and to have the benefit of a credit for certain foreign tax paid with respect to the earnings and profits attributable to such amounts. Section 962 also provides rules for the treatment of an actual distribution of earnings and profits previously taxed in accordance with an election of the benefits of this section. See §1.962-3. For transitional rules for certain taxable years, see §1.962-4.

(b) *Rules of application.*—For purposes of this section—

(1) *Application of section 11.*—For purposes of applying section 11 for a taxable year as provided in paragraph (a)(1) of this section in the case of an electing United States shareholder—

(i) *Determination of taxable income.*—The term "taxable income" as used in section 11 shall mean the sum of—

(a) All amounts required to be included in his gross income under section 951(a) for such taxable year; plus

(b) All amounts which would be required to be included in his gross income under section 78 for such taxable year with respect to the amounts referred to in *(a)* of this subdivision if such shareholder were a domestic corporation.

For purposes of this section, such sum shall not be reduced by any deduction of the United States shareholder even if such shareholder's deductions exceed his gross income.

(ii) *Limitation on surtax exemption.*— The surtax exemption provided by section 11(c) shall not exceed an amount which bears the same ratio to $25,000 ($50,000 in the case of a taxable year ending after December 31, 1974, and before January 1, 1976) as the amounts included in his gross income under section 951(a) for the taxable year bear to his pro rata share of the earnings and profits for the taxable year of all controlled foreign corporations with respect to which such United States shareholder includes any amount in his gross income under section 951(a) for the taxable year.

(2) *Allowance of foreign tax credit.*—(i) *In general.*—Subject to the applicable limitation of section 904 and to the provisions of this subparagraph, there shall be allowed as a credit against the United States tax on the amounts described in subparagraph (1)(i) of this paragraph the foreign income, war profits, and excess profits taxes deemed paid under section 960(a)(1) by the electing United States shareholder with respect to such amounts.

(ii) *Application of section 960(a)(1).*— In applying section 960(a)(1) for purposes of this subparagraph in the case of an electing United States shareholder, the term "domestic corporation" as used in sections 960(a)(1) and 78, and the term "corporation" as used in section 901, shall be treated as referring to such shareholder with respect to the amounts described in subparagraph (1)(i) of this paragraph.

(iii) *Carryback and carryover of excess tax deemed paid.*—For purposes of this subparagraph, any amount by which the foreign income, war profits, and excess profits taxes deemed paid by the electing United States shareholder for any taxable year under section 960(a)(1) exceed the limitation determined under subdivision (iv) *(a)* of this subparagraph shall be treated as a carryback and carryover of excess tax paid under section 904(d), except that in no case shall excess tax paid be deemed paid in a taxable year if an election under section 962 by such shareholders does not apply for such taxable year. Such carrybacks and carryovers shall be applied only against the United States tax on amounts described in subparagraph (1)(i) of this paragraph.

(iv) *Limitation on credit.*—For purposes of determining the limitation under section 904 on the amount of the credit for foreign income, war profits, and excess profit taxes—

(a) Deemed paid with respect to amounts described in subparagraph (1)(i) of this paragraph, the electing United States shareholder's taxable income shall be considered to consist only of the amounts described in such subparagraph (1)(i), and

(b) Paid with respect to amounts other than amounts described in subparagraph (1)(i) of this paragraph, the electing United States shareholder's taxable income shall be considered to consist only of amounts other than the amounts described in such subparagraph (1)(i).

(v) *Effect of choosing benefits of sections 901 to 905.*—The provisions of this subparagraph shall apply for a taxable year whether or not the electing United States shareholder chooses the benefits of subpart A of part III of subchapter N of chapter 1 (sections 901 to 905) of the Internal Revenue Code for such year.

(c) *Illustration.*—The application of this section may be illustrated by the following example:

Example. Throughout his taxable year ending December 31, 1964, A, an unmarried individual who is not the head of a household, owns 60 of the 100 shares of the one class of stock in foreign corporation M and 80 of the 100 shares of the one class of stock in foreign corporation N. A and corporations M and N use the calendar year as a taxable year, corporations M and N are controlled foreign corporations throughout the period here involved, and neither corporation is a less developed country corporation. The earnings and profits and subpart F income of, and the foreign income taxes paid by, such corporations for 1964 are as follows:

Reg. § 1.962-1(b)(1)(i)(b)

	M	N
Pretax earnings and profits	$500,000	$1,200,000
Foreign income taxes	200,000	400,000
Earnings and profits	300,000	800,000
Subpart F income	150,000	750,000

Apart from his section 951(a) income, A has gross income of $200,600 and $100,000 of deductions attributable to such income. He is required to include $90,000 (.60 × $150,000) in gross income under section 951(a) with respect to M Corporation and $600,000 (.80 × $750,000) with respect to N Corporation. A elects to have the provisions of section 962 apply for 1964 and computes his tax as follows:

Tax on amounts included under sec. 951(a):			
Income under sec. 951(a) from M Corporation	$ 90,000		
Gross-up under secs. 960(a)(1) and 78 ($90,000/$300,000 × $200,000)	60,000		
Income under sec. 951(a) from N Corporation	$ 600,000		
Gross-up under secs. 960(a)(1) and 78 ($600,000/$800,000 × $400,000)	300,000		
Taxable income under sec. 11	$1,050,000		
Normal tax (.22 × $1,050,000)		$231,000	
Surtax exemption ([$90,000+$600,000]/[.60 × $300,000 + (.80 × $800,000)] × $25,000)	21,036		
Subject to surtax under sec. 11 ($1,050,000 − $21,036)	1,028,964		
Surtax (.28 × $1,028,964)		288,110	
Tentative U.S. tax		$519,110	
Foreign tax credit ($60,000 + $300,000)		360,000	
Total U.S. tax payable on amounts included under sec. 951(a)			$159,110
Tax with respect to other income:			
Gross income		200,600	
Less:			
Personal exemption	$ 600		
Deductions	100,000	100,600	
Taxable income		$100,000	
Tax with respect to such other taxable income			59,340
Total tax ($159,110 + $59,340)			$218,450

[Reg. § 1.962-1.]

☐ [*T.D.* 6858, 10-27-65. *Amended by T.D.* 7413, 3-25-76.]

§ 1.962-2. Election of limitation of tax for individuals.—(a) *Who may elect.*—The election under section 962 may be made only by a United States shareholder who is an individual (including a trust or estate).

(b) *Time and manner of making election.*—Except as provided in § 1.962-4, a United States shareholder shall make an election under this section by filing a statement to such effect with his return for the taxable year with respect to which the election is made. The statement shall include the following information:

(1) The name, address, and taxable year of each controlled foreign corporation with respect to which the electing shareholder is a United States shareholder and of all other corporations, partnerships, trusts, or estates in any applicable chain of ownership described in section 958(a);

(2) The amounts, on a corporation-by-corporation basis, which are included in such shareholder's gross income for his taxable year under section 951(a);

(3) Such shareholder's pro rata share of the earnings and profits (determined under § 1.964-1) of each such controlled foreign corporation with respect to which such shareholder includes any amount in gross income for his taxable year under section 951(a) and the foreign income, war profits, excess profits, and similar taxes paid on or with respect to such earnings and profits;

(4) The amount of distributions received by such shareholder during his taxable year from each controlled foreign corporation referred to in subparagraph (1) of this paragraph from excludable section 962 earnings and profits (as defined in paragraph (b)(1)(i) of § 1.962-3), from taxable section 962 earnings and profits (as defined in paragraph (b)(1)(ii) of § 1.962-3), and from earnings and profits other than section 962 earnings and profits, showing the source of such amounts by taxable year; and

(5) Such further information as the Commissioner may prescribe by forms and accompanying instructions relating to such election.

(c) *Effect of election.*—(1) *In general.*—Except as provided in subparagraph (2) of this paragraph and § 1.962-4, an election under this section by a United States shareholder for a taxable year shall be applicable to all controlled foreign corporations with respect to which such shareholder includes any amount in gross income for his taxable year under section 951(a) and shall be binding for the taxable year for which such election is made.

(2) *Revocation.*—Upon application by the United States shareholder, an election made under this election may, subject to the approval of the Commissioner, be revoked. Approval will not be granted unless a material and substantial change in circumstances occurs which could not have been anticipated when the election was made. The application for consent to revocation shall be made by the United States shareholder's mailing a letter for such purpose to Commissioner of Internal Revenue, Attention: T.R., Washington, D.C. 20224 containing a statement of the facts upon which such shareholder relies in requesting such consent. [Reg. § 1.962-2.]

☐ [T.D. 6858, 10-27-65.]

§ 1.962-3. Treatment of actual distributions.

—(a) *In general.*—Section 962(d) provides that the earnings and profits of a foreign corporation attributable to amounts which are, or have been, included in the gross income of an individual United States shareholder under section 951(a) by reason of such shareholder's ownership (within the meaning of section 958(a)) of stock in such corporation and with respect to which amounts an election under § 1.962-2 applies or applied shall, when such earnings and profits are distributed to such shareholder with respect to such stock, notwithstanding the provisions of section 959(a)(1), be included in his gross income to the extent that such earnings and profits exceed the amount of income tax paid by such shareholder under this chapter on the amounts to which such election applies or applied. Thus, when such shareholder receives an actual distribution of section 962 earnings and profits (as defined in paragraph (b)(1) of this section) from a foreign corporation, only the excludable section 962 earnings and profits (as defined in paragraph (b)(1)(i) of this section) may be excluded from his gross income.

(b) *Rules of application.*—For purposes of this section—

(1) *Section 962 earnings and profits defined.*—With respect to an individual United States shareholder, the term "section 962 earnings and profits" means the earnings and profits of a foreign corporation referred to in paragraph (a) of this section. Such earnings and profits include—

(i) *Excludable section 962 earnings and profits.*—Excludable section 962 earnings and profits which are the amount of the section 962 earnings and profits equal to the amount of income tax paid under this chapter by such shareholder on the amounts included in his gross income under section 951(a); and

(ii) *Taxable section 962 earnings and profits.*—Taxable section 962 earnings and profits which are the excess of section 962 earnings and profits over the amount described in subdivision (i) of this subparagraph.

(2) *Determinations made separately for each taxable year.*—If section 962 earnings and profits attributable to more than one taxable year are distributed by a foreign corporation, the determinations under this section shall be made separately with respect to each such taxable year.

(3) *Source of distributions.*—(i) *In general.*—Except as otherwise provided in this subparagraph, the provisions of paragraphs (a) through (d) of § 1.959-3 shall apply in determining the source of distributions of earnings and profits by a foreign corporation.

(ii) *Treatment of section 962 earnings and profits under § 1.959-3.*—For purposes of a section 959(c) amount and year classification under paragraph (b) of § 1.959-3, a distribution of earnings and profits by a foreign corporation shall be first allocated to earnings and profits other than section 962 earnings and profits (as defined in subparagraph (1) of this paragraph) and then to section 962 earnings and profits. Thus, distributions shall be considered first attributable to amounts described in paragraph (b)(1) of § 1.959-3 which are not section 962 earnings and profits and then to amounts described in such paragraph (b)(1) which are section 962 earnings and profits (first for the current taxable year and then for prior taxable years beginning with the most recent prior taxable year), secondly to amounts described in paragraph (b)(2) of § 1.959-3 which are not section 962 earnings and profits and then to amounts described in such paragraph (b)(2) which are section 962 earnings and profits (first for the current taxable year and then for prior taxable years beginning with the most recent prior taxable year), and finally to the amounts described in paragraph (b)(3) of § 1.959-3 (first for the current taxable year and then for prior taxable years beginning with the most recent prior taxable year).

(iii) *Allocation to excludable section 962 earnings and profits.*—A distribution of section

962 earnings and profits by a foreign corporation for any taxable year shall be considered first attributable to the excludable section 962 earnings and profits (as defined in subparagraph (1)(i) of this paragraph) and then to taxable section 962 earnings and profits.

(iv) *Allocation of deficits in earnings and profits.*—A United States shareholder's pro rata share (determined in accordance with the principles of paragraph (e) of § 1.951-1) of a foreign corporation's deficit in earnings and profits (determined under § 1.964-1) for any taxable year shall be applied in accordance with the provisions of paragraph (c) of § 1.959-3 except that such deficit shall also be applied to taxable section 962 earnings and profits (as defined in subparagraph (1)(ii) of this paragraph).

(4) *Distribution in exchange for stock.*—The provisions of this section shall not apply to a distribution of section 962 earnings and profits which is treated as in part or full payment in exchange for stock under subchapter C of chapter 1 of the Internal Revenue Code. The application of this subparagraph may be illustrated by the following example:

Example. Individual United States shareholder A owns 60 percent of the only class of stock in foreign corporation M, the basis of which is $10,000. Both A and M Corporation use the calendar year as a taxable year. In each of the taxable years 1964, 1965, and 1966, M Corporation has $1,000 of earnings and profits and $1,000 of subpart F income. With respect to each such amount, A includes $600 in gross income under section 951(a), makes the election under section 962, and pays a United States tax of $132 (22 percent of $600). Accordingly, A increases the basis of his stock in M Corporation under section 961(a) by $132 in each of the years 1964, 1965, and 1966, and thus on December 31, 1966, the adjusted basis for A's stock in M Corporation is $10,396. In 1967, M Corporation is completely liquidated (in a transaction described in section 331) and A receives $13,800, consisting of $1,800 of earnings and profits attributable to the amounts which A included in gross income under section 951(a) in 1964, 1965, and 1966, and $12,000 attributable to the other assets of M Corporation. No amount of the $3,404 gain realized by A on such distribution ($13,800 minus $10,396) may be excluded from gross income under section 959(a)(1). However, section 962(d) will not prevent any part of such $3,404 from being treated as a capital gain under section 331.

(5) *Illustration.*—The application of this paragraph may be illustrated by the following example:

Example. (a) M, a controlled foreign corporation is organized on January 1, 1963; A and B, individual United States shareholders, own 50 percent and 25 percent, respectively, of the only class of stock in M Corporation. Corporation M, A, and B use the calendar year as a taxable year, and M Corporation is a controlled foreign corporation throughout the period here involved. For the taxable years 1963, 1964, 1965, and 1966, A and B must include amounts in gross income under section 951(a) with respect to M Corporation. For the years 1963, 1965, and 1966, A makes the election under section 962. On January 1, 1967, B sells his 25-percent interest in M Corporation to A; A satisfies the requirements of paragraph (d) of § 1.959-1 so as to qualify as B's successor in interest. As of December 31, 1967, M Corporation's accumulated earnings and profits of $675 (before taking into account distributions made in 1967) applicable to A's interest (including his interest as B's successor in interest) in such corporation are classified under § 1.959-3 and this section for purposes of section 962(d) as follows:

Classification of earnings and profits for purposes of § 1.962-3.

Year	Sec. 959(c)(1)			Sec. 959(c)(2)			Sec. 959(c)(3)
	Non-sec. 962 earnings and profits	Excludable sec. 962 earnings and profits	Taxable sec. 962 earnings and profits	Non-sec. 962 earnings and profits	Excludable sec. 962 earnings and profits	Taxable sec. 962 earnings and profits	
1963	$25	$11	$39	...	...	...	...
1964	75	...	...	$60	...	...	$15
1965	...	...	...	75	$33	$117	...
1966	...	...	...	50	22	78	...
1967	...	...	...	...	...	...	75

(b) During 1967, M Corporation makes three separate distributions to A of $200, $208, and $267. The source of such distributions under § 1.959-3 and this section is as follows:

Reg. § 1.962-3(b)(5)

Distribution	Amount	Year	Classification of distributions under secs. 959 and 962(d)
No. 1	$75	1964	(c)(1) non-sec. 962
	25	1963	(c)(1) non-sec. 962
	11	1963	(c)(1) excludable sec. 962
	39	1963	(c)(1) taxable sec. 962
	50	1966	(c)(2) non-sec. 962
	200		
No. 2	$22	1966	(c)(2) excludable sec. 962
	78	1966	(c)(2) taxable sec. 962
	75	1965	(c)(2) non-sec. 962
	33	1965	(c)(2) excludable sec. 962
	208		
No. 3	$117	1965	(c)(2) taxable sec. 962
	60	1964	(c)(2) non-sec. 962
	75	1967	(c)(3)
	15	1964	(c)(3)
	267		

(c) A must include $324 in his gross income for 1967. The source of these amounts is as follows:

Distribution	Amount	Year	Classification
No. 1	$39	1963	(c)(1) taxable sec. 962
No. 2	78	1966	(c)(2) taxable sec. 962
No. 3	117	1965	(c)(2) taxable sec. 962
	75	1967	(c)(3)
	15	1964	(c)(3)
Total	$324		

(c) *Treatment of shareholder's successor in interest.*—(1) *In general.*—If a United States person (as defined in § 1.957-4) acquires from any person any portion of the interest in the foreign corporation of a United States shareholder referred to in this section, the rules of paragraphs (a) and (b) of this section shall apply to such acquiring person. However, no exclusion of section 962 earnings and profits under paragraph (a) of this section shall be allowed unless such acquiring person establishes to the satisfaction of the district director his right to such exclusion. The information to be furnished by the acquiring person to the district director with his return for the taxable year to support such exclusion shall include:

(i) The name, address, and taxable year of the foreign corporation from which a distribution of section 962 earnings and profits is received and of all other corporations, partnerships, trusts, or estates in any applicable chain of ownership described in section 958(a);

(ii) The name and address of the person from whom the stock interest was acquired;

(iii) A description of the stock interest acquired and its relation, if any, to a chain of ownership described in section 958(a);

(iv) The amount for which an exclusion under paragraph (a) of this section is claimed; and

(v) Evidence showing that the section 962 earnings and profits for which an exclusion is claimed are attributable to amounts which were included in the gross income of a United States shareholder under section 951(a) subject to an election under § 1.962-2, that such amounts were not previously excluded from the gross income of a United States person, and the identity of the United States shareholder including such amount.

The acquiring person shall also furnish to the district director such other information as may be required by the district director in support of the exclusion.

(2) *Taxes previously deemed paid by an individual United States shareholder.*—If a corporate successor in interest of an individual United States shareholder receives a distribution of section 962 earnings and profits, the income, war profits, and excess profits taxes paid to any foreign country or to any possession of the United States in connection with such earnings and profits shall not be taken into account for purposes of section 902, to the extent such taxes were deemed paid by such individual United States shareholder under paragraph (b)(2) of § 1.962-1 and section 960(a)(1) for any prior taxable year. [Reg. § 1.962-3.]

☐ [*T.D.* 6858, 10-27-65.]

Earnings and Profits of Foreign Corporations

§ 1.964-1. Determination of the earnings and profits of a foreign corporation.—(a) *In general.*—For purposes of sections 951 through 964, the earnings and profits (or deficit in earnings and profits) of a foreign corporation for its taxable year shall, except as provided in paragraph (f) of this section, be computed substantially as if such corporation were a domestic corporation by—

(1) Preparing a profit and loss statement with respect to such year from the books of account regularly maintained by the corporation for the purpose of accounting to its shareholders;

(2) Making the adjustments necessary to conform such statement to the accounting principles described in paragraph (b) of this section;

(3) Making the further adjustments necessary to conform such statement to the tax accounting standards described in paragraph (c) of this section;

(4) Translating the amounts shown on such adjusted statement into United States dollars in accordance with paragraph (d) of this section; and

(5) Adjusting the amount of profit or loss shown on such translated and adjusted statement in accordance with paragraph (e) of this section to reflect any exchange gain or loss determined thereunder.

The computation described in the preceding sentence may be made by following the procedures described in subparagraphs (1) through (5) of this paragraph in an order other than the one listed, as long as the result so obtained would be the same. In determining earnings and profits, or the deficit in earnings and profits, of a foreign corporation under section 964, the amount of any illegal bribe, kickback, or other payment (within the meaning of section 162(c), as amended by section 288 of the Tax Equity and Fiscal Responsibility Act of 1982 in the case of payments made after September 3, 1982, and the regulations thereunder) paid after November 3, 1976, by or on behalf of the corporation during the taxable year of the corporation directly or indirectly to an official, employee, or agent in fact of a government shall not be taken into account to decrease such earnings and profits or to increase such deficit. No adjustment shall be required under subparagraph (2) or (3) of this paragraph unless it is material. Whether an adjustment is material depends on the facts and circumstances of the particular case, including the amount of the adjustment, its size relative to the general level of the corporation's total assets and annual profit or loss, the consistency with which the practice has been applied, and whether the item to which the adjustment relates is of a recurring or merely a nonrecurring nature. For the treatment of earnings and profits whose distribution is prevented by restrictions and limitations imposed by a foreign government, see section 964(b) and the regulations thereunder.

(b) *Accounting adjustments.*—(1) *In general.*—The accounting principles to be applied in making the adjustments required by paragraph (a)(2) of this section shall be those accounting principles generally accepted in the United States for purposes of reflecting in the financial statements of a domestic corporation the operations of its foreign affiliates, including the following:

(i) *Clear reflection income.*—Any accounting practice designed for purposes other than the clear reflection on a current basis of income and expense for the taxable year shall not be given effect. For example, an adjustment will be required where an allocation is made to an arbitrary reserve out of current income.

(ii) *Physical assets, depreciation, etc.*—All physical assets (as defined in paragraph (e)(5)(ii) of this section), including inventory when reflected at cost, shall be taken into account at historical cost computed either for individual assets or groups of similar assets. The historical cost of such an asset shall not reflect any appreciation or depreciation in its value or in the relative value of the currency in which its cost was incurred. Depreciation, depletion, and amortization allowances shall be based on the historical cost of the underlying asset and no effect shall be given to any such allowance determined on the basis of a factor other than historical cost. For special rules for determining historical cost where assets are acquired during a taxable year beginning before January 1, 1950, or a majority interest in the foreign corporation is acquired after December 31, 1949, but before October 27, 1964, see subparagraph (2) of this paragraph.

(iii) *Valuation of assets and liabilities.*—Any accounting practice which results in the systematic undervaluation of assets or overvaluation of liabilities shall not be given effect, even though expressly permitted or required under foreign law, except to the extent allowa-

Reg. § 1.964-1(b)(1)(iii)

ble under paragraph (c) of this section. For example, an adjustment will be required where inventory is written down below market value. For the definition of market value, see paragraph (a) of § 1.471-4.

(iv) *Income equalization.*—Income and expense shall be taken into account without regard to equalization over more than one accounting period; and any equalization reserve or similar provision affecting income or expense shall not be given effect, even though expressly permitted or required under foreign law, except to the extent allowable under paragraph (c) of this section.

(v) *Foreign currency.*—If transactions effected in a foreign currency other than that in which the books of the corporation are kept are translated into the foreign currency reflected in the books, such translation shall be made in a manner substantially similar to that prescribed by paragraph (d) of this section for the translation of foreign currency amounts into United States dollars.

(2) *Historical cost.*—For purposes of this section, the historical cost of an asset acquired by the foreign corporation during a taxable year beginning before January 1, 1963, shall be determined, if it is so elected by or on behalf of such corporation—

(i) In the event that the foreign corporation became a majority owned subsidiary of a United States person (within the meaning of section 7701(a)(30)) after December 31, 1949, but before October 27, 1964, and the asset was held by such foreign corporation at that time, as though the asset was purchased on the date during such period the foreign corporation first became a majority owned subsidiary at a price equal to its then fair market value, or

(ii) In the event that subdivision (i) of this subparagraph is inapplicable but the asset was acquired by the foreign corporation during a taxable year beginning before January 1, 1950, as though the asset were purchased on the first day of the first taxable year of the foreign corporation beginning after December 31, 1949, at a price equal to the undepreciated cost (cost or other basis minus book depreciation) of that asset as of that date as shown on the books of account of such corporation regularly maintained for the purpose of accounting to its shareholders.

For purposes of this subparagraph, a foreign corporation shall be considered a majority owned subsidiary of a United States person if, taking into account only stock acquired by purchase (as defined in section 334(b)(3)), the United States person owns (within the meaning of section 958(a)) more than 50 percent of the total combined voting power of all classes of stock of the foreign corporation entitled to vote. The election under this subparagraph shall be made for the first taxable year beginning after December 31, 1962, in which the foreign corporation is a controlled foreign corporation (within the meaning of section 957), or for which it is included in a chain or group under section 963(c)(2)(B) of 1975, (applied as if section 963 had not been repealed by the Tax Reduction Act of 1975) or has a deficit in earnings and profits sought to be taken into account under section 952(d), or pays a dividend that is included in the foreign base company shipping income of a controlled foreign corporation under § 1.954-6(f). Once made, such an election shall be irrevocable. For the time and manner in which an election may be made on behalf of a foreign corporation, see paragraph (c)(3) of this section.

(3) *Illustrations.*—The application of this paragraph may be illustrated by the following examples:

Example (1). Corporation M is a controlled foreign corporation which regularly maintains books of account for the purpose of accounting to its shareholders in accordance with the accounting practices prevalent in country X, the country in which it operates. As a consequence of those practices, the profit and loss statement prepared from these books of account reflects an allocation to an arbitrary reserve out of current income and depreciation allowances based on replacement values which are greater than historical cost. Adjustments are necessary to conform such statement to accounting principles generally accepted in the United States. Assuming these adjustments to be material, the unacceptable practices will have to be eliminated from the statement, an increase in the amount of profit (or a decrease in the amount of loss) thereby resulting.

Example (2). In 1973, Corporation N is a foreign corporation which is not a controlled foreign corporation but which is included in a chain, for minimum distribution purposes, under section 963(c)(2)(B). Corporation N regularly maintains books of account for the purpose of accounting to its shareholders in accordance with the accounting practices of country Y, the country in which it operates. As a consequence of those practices, the profit and loss statement prepared from these books of account reflects the inclusion in income of stock dividends and of corporate distributions representing a return of capital. Adjustments are necessary to conform such statement to accounting principles generally accepted in the United States. Assuming these adjustments to be material, the unacceptable practices will have to be eliminated from the statement, a decrease in the amount of profit (or increase in the amount of loss) thereby resulting.

(c) *Tax adjustments.*—(1) *In general.*—The tax accounting standards to be applied in making the adjustments required by paragraph (a)(3) of this section shall be the following:

(i) *Accounting methods.*—The method of accounting shall reflect the provisions of section 446 and the regulations thereunder.

(ii) *Inventories.*—Inventories shall be taken into account in accordance with the provisions of sections 471 and 472 and the regulations thereunder.

(iii) *Depreciation.*—Depreciation shall be computed as follows:

(a) For any taxable year beginning before July 1, 1972, depreciation shall be computed in accordance with section 167 and the regulations thereunder.

(b) If, for any taxable year beginning after June 30, 1972, 20 percent or more of the gross income from all sources of the corporation is derived from sources within the United States, then depreciation shall be computed in accordance with the provisions of § 1.312-15.

(c) If, for any taxable year beginning after June 30, 1972, less than 20 percent of the gross income from all sources of the corporation is derived from sources within the United States, then depreciation shall be computed in accordance with section 167 and the regulations thereunder.

(iv) *Elections.*—Effect shall be given to any election made in accordance with an applicable provision of the Code and the regulations thereunder and these regulations.

Except as provided in subparagraphs (2) and (3) of this paragraph, any requirements imposed by the Code or applicable regulations with respect to making an election or adopting or changing a method of accounting must be satisfied by or on behalf of the foreign corporation just as though it were a domestic corporation if such election or such adoption or change of method is to be taken into account in the computation of its earnings and profits.

(2) *Adoption of method.*—For the first taxable year beginning after December 31, 1962, in which the foreign corporation is a controlled foreign corporation (within the meaning of section 957), or for which it is included in a chain or group under section 963(c)(2)(B) of 1975, (applied as if section 963 had not been repealed by the Tax Reduction Act of 1975) or has a deficit in earnings and profits sought to be taken into account under section 952(d), or pays a dividend that is included in the foreign base company shipping income of a controlled foreign corporation under § 1.954-6(f), there may be adopted or made by such corporation or on its behalf any method of accounting or election allowable under this section notwithstanding that, in previous years, its earnings and profits were computed, or its books or financial statements prepared, on a different basis and notwithstanding that such election is required by the Code or regulations to be made in a prior taxable year. For purposes of determining the amount of a deficit in earnings and profits taken into account pursuant to section 952(c)(1)(B), if a different basis is used in previous years, ratable adjustments shall be made in the earnings and profits attributable to such previous years to prevent any duplication or omission of amounts that would otherwise result from the adoption of such method or the making of such election. See subparagraph (3) of this paragraph for the manner in which a method of accounting or an election may be adopted or made on behalf of the foreign corporation.

(3) *Action on behalf of corporation.*—(i) *In general.*—An election shall be deemed made, or an adoption or change in method of accounting deemed effectuated, on behalf of the foreign corporation only if its controlling United States shareholders (as defined in subparagraph (5) of this paragraph)—

(a) Satisfy for such corporation any requirements imposed by the Code or applicable regulations with respect to such election or such adoption or change in method, such as the filing of forms, the execution of consents, securing the permission of the Commissioner, or maintaining books and records in a particular manner.

(b) File the written statement described in subdivision (ii) of this subparagraph at the time and in the manner prescribed therein, and

(c) Provide the written notice required by subdivision (iii) of this subparagraph at the time and in the manner prescribed therein.

For purposes of the preceding sentence, the books of the foreign corporation shall be considered to be maintained in a particular manner if the controlling United States shareholders or the foreign corporation regularly keep the records and accounts required by section 964(c) and the regulations thereunder in that manner. Any election required to be made or information required to be filed with a tax return shall be deemed made or furnished on behalf of the foreign corporation if its controlling United States shareholders file the written statement described in subdivision (ii) of this subparagraph with respect to such election within the period specified therein. For a special rule postponing the time for taking action by or on behalf of a foreign corporation until the amount of its earnings and profits becomes significant, see subparagraph (6) of this paragraph.

(ii) *Written statement.*—The written statement required by subdivision (i) of this subparagraph shall be jointly executed by the controlling United States shareholders, shall be filed with the Director of Internal Revenue Service Center, 11601 Roosevelt Blvd., Philadelphia, Pennsylvania 19155, within 180 days after the close of the taxable year of the foreign corporation with respect to which the election is made or the adoption or change of method effected, or before May 1, 1965, whichever is later, and shall set forth the name and country of organization of the foreign corporation, the names, addresses, taxpayer identification numbers (in the case of statements required to be filed after June 20, 1983), and stock interests of the controlling United States shareholders, the nature of the action taken, the names, addresses, and (in the case of statements required to be filed after June 20, 1983) taxpayer identification numbers of all other United States shareholders notified of the election or adoption or change of method, and such other information as the Commissioner may by forms require.

(iii) *Notice.*—Prior to the filing of the written statement described in subdivision (ii) of this subparagraph, the controlling United States shareholders shall provide written notice of the election made or the adoption or change of method effected to all other persons known by them to be United States shareholders who own (within the meaning of section 958(a)) stock of the foreign corporation. Such notice shall set forth the name and country of organization of the foreign corporation, the names, addresses, and stock interests of the controlling United States shareholders, the nature of the action taken, and such other information as the Commissioner may by forms require. However, the failure of the controlling United States shareholders to provide such notice to a person required to be notified thereunder shall not invalidate the election made or the adoption or change of method effected, if it is established to the satisfaction of the Commissioner that reasonable cause existed for such failure.

(4) *Effect of action by controlling United States shareholders.*—Any action taken by the controlling United States shareholders on behalf of the foreign corporation pursuant to subparagraph (3) of this paragraph shall be reflected in the computation of the earnings and profits of such corporation under this section to the extent that it bears upon the tax liability of a United States shareholder who either—

(i) Was a controlling United States shareholder with respect to the action taken;

(ii) Received the written notice provided by subparagraph (3)(iii) of this paragraph;

(iii) Failed to file any of the returns required by section 6046 and the regulations thereunder within the period prescribed by section 6046(d); or

(iv) Was notified by the Director of the Philadelphia Service Center of the action taken—

(a) Within 61 days after the last day (including extensions of time) prescribed with respect to the taxable year of the foreign corporation by subparagraph (3)(ii) of this paragraph for filing the written statement described in such subparagraph, or

(b) Within 180 days after the close of the first taxable year in which such shareholder becomes a United States shareholder,

whichever is later.

To the extent that the computation of the earnings and profits of the foreign corporation bears upon the tax liability of any United States shareholder other than those enumerated in the preceding sentence, the computation shall reflect the action taken only if such shareholder assents to such treatment. Such assent may be given at any time, but not later than 90 days after the shareholder is first apprised of such action by the Director of the Philadelphia Service Center. The shareholder shall signify his assent by filing a written statement with the Director of the Internal Revenue Service Center, 11601 Roosevelt Blvd., Philadelphia, Pennsylvania 19155, setting forth the name and country of organization of the foreign corporation, his own name, address, and stock interest in the corporation, the nature of the action being assented to, and such other information as the Commissioner may by forms require.

(5) *Controlling United States shareholders.*—For purposes of this paragraph the controlling United States shareholders of a foreign corporation shall be those United States shareholders (as defined in section 951(b)), who, in the aggregate, own (within the meaning of section 958(a)) more than 50 percent of the total combined voting power of all classes of the stock of such corporation entitled to vote and who undertake to act on its behalf. In the event that the foreign corporation is not a controlled foreign corporation but is included in a chain or group under section 963(c)(2)(B) or (3)(B), the controlling United States shareholder with respect to such foreign corporation shall be deemed to be the domestic corporation which

elects to receive the minimum distribution from such chain or group. In the event that the foreign corporation is neither a controlled foreign corporation nor included in a chain or group under section 963(c)(2)(B) or (3)(B) but has a deficit in earnings and profits sought to be taken into account under section 952(d), the controlling United States shareholder with respect to such foreign corporation shall be the shareholder seeking to take such deficit into account. In the event that the foreign corporation is a controlled foreign corporation but the United States shareholders (as defined in section 951(b)) do not, in the aggregate, own (within the meaning of section 958(a)) more than 50 percent of the total combined voting power of all classes of the stock of such corporation entitled to vote, the controlling United States shareholders of the foreign corporation shall be all those United States shareholders who own (within the meaning of section 958(a)) stock of such corporation. In the event that a foreign corporation is not a controlled foreign corporation but pays a dividend to a controlled foreign corporation that is attributable to foreign base company shipping income under § 1.954-6(f), the controlling United States shareholders (as defined in this subparagraph) of the controlled foreign corporation shall be considered the controlling United States shareholders of the foreign corporation.

(6) *Action not required until significant.*—Notwithstanding any other provision of this paragraph, action by or on behalf of a foreign corporation (other than a foreign corporation subject to tax under section 882) to make an election or to adopt a method of accounting shall not be required until 180 days after the close of the first taxable year for which—

(i) An amount is includible in gross income with respect to such corporation under section 951(a);

(ii) It is sought to be established that such corporation is a less developed country corporation (within the meaning of section 955(c), as in effect before the enactment of the Tax Reduction Act of 1975);

(iii) An amount is excluded from subpart F income (within the meaning of section 952) by section 952(c), section 952(d), or section 970(a);

(iv) Such corporation is the subject of an election to secure an exclusion under section 963 (applied as if section 963 had not been repealed by the Tax Reduction Act of 1975); or

(v) It is sought to be established that the corporation has foreign base company shipping income (within the meaning of section 954(f)).

In the event that action by or on behalf of the foreign corporation is not undertaken by the time specified in the preceding sentence and such failure is shown to the satisfaction of the Commissioner to be due to inadvertence or a reasonable cause, such action may be undertaken during any period of at least 30 days occurring after such showing is made which the Commissioner may specify as appropriate for this purpose. Where the action necessary to make an election or to adopt a method of accounting is undertaken by or on behalf of the foreign corporation in accordance with this subparagraph, such election shall be deemed to have been made, or such adoption of accounting method effected, for the first taxable year of the foreign corporation beginning after December 31, 1962, in which such corporation is a controlled foreign corporation (within the meaning of section 957) or for which it is included in a chain or group under section 963(c)(2)(B) or (3)(B) (applied as if section 963 had not been repealed by the Tax Reduction Act of 1975) or has a deficit in earnings and profits sought to be taken into account under section 952(d), or pays a dividend that is included in the foreign base company shipping income of a controlled foreign corporation under § 1.954-6(f). For special rules for computing earnings and profits for purposes of section 1248 or income for purposes of applying an exclusion set forth in section 954(b) where the taxable year of the foreign corporation occurs prior to the making of elections or the adoption of methods of accounting under this subparagraph, see the regulations under section 952 and section 1248.

(7) *Revocation of election.*—Notwithstanding any other provision of this section, any election made by or on behalf of a foreign corporation (other than a foreign corporation subject to tax under section 882) may be modified or revoked by or on behalf of such corporation for the taxable year for which made whenever the consent of the Commissioner is secured for such modification or revocation, even though such election would be irrevocable but for this subparagraph.

(8) *Illustrations.*—The application of this paragraph may be illustrated by the following examples:

Example (1). X Corporation is a controlled foreign corporation which maintains its books, in accordance with the laws of the country in which it operates, by taking inventoriable items into account under the "first-in, first-out" method. A, B, and C, the United States shareholders of X Corporation, own 45 percent, 30 percent, and 25 percent of its voting stock, respectively. For the first taxable year of X Corporation beginning after December 31, 1962, B and C adopt on its behalf the "last-in, first-out" inventory method, notifying A of the action taken. Even though A may object to such action, adjustments must be made to reflect the use of the LIFO method of inventorying in the computation of the earnings and profits of X Corporation with respect to him as well as with respect to B and C.

Example (2). Y Corporation is a controlled foreign corporation which maintains its books, in accordance with the laws of the country in which it operates, by employing the straight-line method of depreciation. D and E, the United States shareholders of Y Corporation, own 51 percent and 10 percent of its voting stock, respectively. For the first taxable year of Y Corporation beginning after December 31, 1962, D adopts on its behalf the declining balance method of depreciation. However, not knowing that E is a United States shareholder of the company, D fails to provide him with notice of the action taken. Assuming that E has filed the return required by section 6046 and the regulations thereunder within the period prescribed by section 6046(d), adjustments in the computation of earnings and profits will not be required with respect to him unless the Director of International Operations notifies him of the action taken within 240 days after the close of Y's taxable year. If notice is not provided to E within this period, he will not be compelled to make the adjustments. At his option, however, he may accept the action taken by assenting thereto not later than 90 days after he is first apprised of such action by the Director of International Operations.

(d) *Translation into United States dollars.*—(1) *In general.*—(i) *General rule.*—Except as provided in subdivisions (ii), (iii), and (iv) of this subparagraph, the amounts to be shown on the profit and loss statement, adjusted pursuant to paragraphs (b) and (c) of this section, shall be translated into United States dollars (as required by paragraph (a)(4) of this section) at the appropriate exchange rate for the translation period (as defined in subparagraph (6) of this paragraph) to which they relate.

(ii) *Cost of goods sold.*—Amounts representing items of inventory reflected in the cost of goods sold shall be translated—

(a) To the extent that such amounts represent items included in the opening inventory balance, so as to obtain the same amount of United States dollars which represented (after translation and adjustment) such items in the closing inventory balance for the preceding taxable year,

(b) To the extent that such amounts represent items purchased or otherwise first included in inventory during the taxable year, at the appropriate exchange rate for the translation period in which the historical cost of such items was incurred, and

(c) To the extent that such amounts represent items included in the closing inventory balance, at the appropriate exchange rate for the translation period in which the historical cost of such items was incurred, except that, if such amounts are written down to market value, such market value shall be determined at the year-end rate. Notwithstanding the preceding sentence, amounts representing items of inventory included in the closing inventory balance may be translated at the year-end rate even though not written down to market value; however, once such a rate is employed under those circumstances, translation may not be made for subsequent taxable years at the appropriate exchange rate for the translation period in which the historical cost of the items of inventory was incurred unless the permission of the Commissioner is secured.

(iii) *Depreciation, depletion, and amortization.*—Amounts representing allowances for depreciation, depletion, or amortization shall be translated at the appropriate exchange rate for the translation period in which the historical cost of the underlying asset was incurred or is deemed to have been incurred. For purposes of this subdivision, if the historical cost of an asset is determined under paragraph (b)(2) of this section, such cost shall be deemed to have been incurred on the date the asset is considered to have been purchased under that paragraph.

(iv) *Prepaid expenses or income.*—Amounts representing expenses or income paid or received in a prior taxable year shall be translated at the appropriate exchange rate for the translation period during which they were paid or received. Notwithstanding the preceding sentence, amounts representing such prepaid income or expenses may be translated at the year-end rate; however, once such a rate is employed, translation may not be made for subsequent taxable years at the appropriate exchange rate for the translation period during which such income or expenses were paid or received unless the permission of the Commissioner is secured.

(2) *Appropriate exchange rate.*—(i) *In general.*—Where the value of the foreign currency relative to the United States dollar does not fluctuate substantially during a translation period, a single exchange rate shall be appropriate for all amounts representing classes of items which relate to such period, such rate to be a simple average determined by dividing the sum of the closing rates for each of the calendar months ending with or within such period by the number of such months. On the other

hand, where the value of the foreign currency relative to the United States dollar does fluctuate substantially during a translation period, the exchange rate appropriate to an amount representing a class of items which relates to such period shall be either *(a)* a simple average determined in accordance with the preceding sentence, or *(b)* a weighted average taking into account the volume of transactions (reflected by the amount being translated) for the calendar months ending with or within such period, depending upon which average would produce a result more representative of that which would have been obtained by translating the individual transactions reflected by that amount at the closing rate for the month to which each such transaction relates. Whether the value of the foreign currency relative to the United States dollar fluctuates substantially during the translation period is a question of fact, depending upon, among other things, the extent to which the volume of transactions varies from month to month. In general, however, the degree of fluctuation will be considered substantial if the closing rate for any calendar month ending with or within the translation period varies by more than 10 percent from the closing rate for any preceding calendar month ending within that period.

(ii) *Monthly rate.*—Notwithstanding subdivision (i) of this subparagraph, if it is so elected by or on behalf of the foreign corporation, and if the closing rate for any calendar month ending with or within a translation period does not vary by more than 3 percent from the closing rate for any preceding calendar month ending within that period, the appropriate exchange rate for amounts representing all classes of items relating to such period shall be any exchange rate which is designated in the election and which does not vary by more than 3 percent from the closing rate for any calendar month ending with or within such period. An election under this subdivision may be made with respect to any translation period of any taxable year of the foreign corporation beginning after December 31, 1962. Such election shall be effective only with respect to the translation period for which it is made, and once made shall be irrevocable with respect to that period. See paragraph (c)(3) of this section for the time and manner in which an election may be made on behalf of the foreign corporation.

(iii) *Class of items.*—For purposes of this subparagraph, the term "class of items" means any category which is reflected separately on books of account or financial statements. For example, sales is a class of items which is reflected separately on the profit and loss statement, and accounts receivable is a class of items which is reflected separately on the balance sheet.

(3) *Closing rate.*—The closing rate for any calendar month shall be the exchange rate on the last day of that month determined by reference to a qualified source of exchange rates within the meaning of subparagraph (5) of this paragraph.

(4) *Year-end rate.*—The year-end rate shall be the closing rate for the last calendar month of the taxable year.

(5) *Qualified source of exchange rates.*—A qualified source of exchange rates shall be any source which is demonstrated to the satisfaction of the district director to reflect actual transactions conducted in a free market and involving representative amounts. In the absence of such a demonstration, the exchange rates taken into account in the computation of the earnings and profits of the foreign corporation shall be determined by reference to the free market rate set forth in the pertinent monthly issue of "International Financial Statistics" or a successor publication of the International Monetary Fund, or such other source of exchange rates reflecting actual transactions conducted in a free market and involving representative amounts as the Commissioner may designate as appropriate for this purpose.

(6) *Translation period.*—(i) *In general.*—Except as provided in subdivision (ii) of this subparagraph, the translation period shall be a taxable year.

(ii) *Currency fluctuations.*—If it is so elected by or on behalf of the foreign corporation, the taxable year shall be divided into groups consisting of a calendar month or consecutive calendar months as specified in the election, each such group constituting a separate translation period. Where the value of the foreign currency relative to the United States dollar fluctuates substantially during the taxable year, the use of the weighted average referred to in subparagraph (2)(i) of this paragraph ordinarily may be avoided by dividing the taxable year into translation periods so that the first translation period begins with the first day of such year and each subsequent translation period begins with the first day of the first calendar month thereafter ending with or within such year for which the closing rate varies by more than 10 percent from the closing rate for any month in the preceding translation period. An election under this subdivision may be made with respect to any taxable year of the foreign corporation beginning after December 31, 1962. Such an election shall be effective only with respect to the taxable year for which it is made, and once made shall be irrevocable with respect to such year. For the time and manner in which an election may be made on behalf of the foreign corporation, see paragraph (c)(3) of this section.

(7) *Actual transactions.*—Notwithstanding any other provisions of this paragraph—

(i) *Dollar transactions.*—Any transaction involving the payment or receipt of United States dollars shall be reflected in the profit and loss statement by the amount of United States dollars involved in such transaction.

(ii) *Conversion transactions.*—Any transaction involving the conversion of a foreign currency into United States dollars, or the conversion of United States dollars into a foreign currency, shall be reflected in the profit and loss statement by an amount expressed in United States dollars and determined by translation at the exchange rate which conversion was effected if the foreign corporation knows, or reasonably should know, that exchange rate.

(iii) *Daily rate.*—Any transaction other than one described in subdivision (i) or (ii) may be translated into United States dollars at the exchange rate for the day on which that transaction occurred, such rate to be determined by reference to a qualified source of exchange rates within the meaning of subparagraph (5) of this paragraph.

No transaction shall be required to be taken into account under subdivision (i) or (ii) unless the United States dollars involved are material in amount.

(8) *Other methods.*—Notwithstanding the other provisions of this paragraph, translation into United States dollars may be made in accordance with a system or method not otherwise described in this paragraph, provided that such system or method (i) was employed by the corporation for purposes of accounting to its shareholders prior to January 1, 1963, and (ii) is shown to the satisfaction of the Commissioner to clearly reflect the earnings and profits of the corporation.

(9) *Illustrations.*—The application of this paragraph may be illustrated by the following examples:

Example (1). M Corporation, a controlled foreign corporation organized on January 1, 1963, employs the calendar year as its taxable year and maintains its books of account in abbas, the currency of the country in which it operates. During 1963 M Corporation's monthly sales amounted to 100,000 abbas per month, its total payroll and other expenses for the year amounted to 180,000 abbas, and its total inventory purchases amounted to 1,050,000 abbas. Also during 1963, M Corporation purchased depreciable assets for 1,000,000 abbas. The value of the abba relative to the United States dollar fluctuated only slightly in 1963; the monthly closing rate moved between 19.8 abbas and 20.2 abbas per United States dollar and stood at 19.9 abbas per United States dollar for most of the year and at year-end. An election under subparagraph (2)(ii) of this paragraph is made on behalf of M Corporation to use the par rate of 20 abbas per United States dollar as the exchange rate appropriate for 1963. Assuming that none of the amounts shown therein reflects a transaction described in subparagraph (7) of this paragraph, M Corporation's adjusted profit and loss statement for 1963 would be translated into United States dollars as follows:

	Local Currency	Exchange Rate	U.S. Dollars
Sales	1,200,000	20:1	$60,000
Cost of Goods Sold:			
Purchases	1,050,000	20:1	52,500
Less—Closing Inventory	(350,000)	20:1	(17,500)
	700,000		35,000
Wages and Other Expenses	180,000	20:1	9,000
Depreciation	200,000	20:1	10,000
Total Costs and Expenses	1,080,000		54,000
Operating Profit	120,000		6,000

Example (2). The facts are the same as in example (1) and in addition during 1964 M Corporation had annual sales of 1,470,000 abbas, annual wages and other expenses of 252,000 abbas, and inventory purchases of 910,000 abbas. Also during 1964, M Corporation purchased additional depreciable assets for 430,000 abbas, the bulk of such purchases being made in the last half of the year. The value of the abba relative to the United States dollar gradually declined in 1964, the monthly closing rate moving from 19.9 abbas per United States dollar down to 22 abbas per United States dollar. For most classes of items, the appropriate exchange rate is a simple average of monthly closing rates or 21 abbas per United States dollar. However, since the bulk of the depreciable asset purchases were made in the last half of the year, the rate representative of those transactions is a weighted average of 21.5 abbas per United States dollar. Assuming that none of the amounts shown therein reflects a transaction described in subparagraph (7) of this paragraph and that closing inventory is translated at historical rates, M Corporation's adjusted profit and loss statement for 1964 would be translated into United States dollars as follows:

	Local Currency	Exchange Rate	U.S. Dollars
Sales	1,470,000	21:1	$70,000
Cost of Goods Sold:			
Opening Inventory	350,000	20:1	17,500
Purchases	910,000	21:1	43,333
Less—Closing Inventory	(418,000)	21:1	(19,905)
	842,000		40,928
Wages and Other Expenses	252,000	21:1	12,000
Depreciation (1963 assets)	150,000	20:1	7,500
Depreciation (1964 assets)	86,000	21.5:1	4,000
Total Costs and Expenses	1,330,000		64,428
Operating Profit	140,000		5,572

Example (3). The facts are the same as in examples (1) and (2) except that the 1964 sales of M Corporation amounted to 1,260,000 abbas plus $10,500 in United States dollars. Assuming that closing inventory is translated at historical rates, M Corporation's adjusted profit and loss statement for 1964 would be translated as follows:

	Local Currency	Exchange Rate	U.S. Dollars
Sales—Abbas	1,260,000	21:1	$60,000
Sales—U.S. Dollars	215,250	Transaction	10,500
Total Sales	1,475,250		70,500
Cost of Goods Sold:			
Opening Inventory	350,000	20:1	17,500
Purchases	910,000	21:1	43,333
Less—Closing Inventory	(418,000)	21:1	19,905
	842,000		40,928
Wages and Other Expenses	252,000	21:1	12,000
Depreciation (1963 assets)	150,000	20:1	7,500
Depreciation (1964 assets)	86,000	21.5:1	4,000
Total Costs and Expenses	1,330,000		64,428
Operating Profit	$ 145,250		$ 6,072

Example (4). The facts are the same as in examples (1) and (2). M Corporation continues to operate during 1965 and the value of the abba relative to the United States dollar declines materially during that year; the monthly closing rate drops from 22 abbas per United States dollar to 26 abbas per United States dollar, a decrease of more than 10 percent. An election under subparagraph (6)(ii) of this paragraph is made on behalf of M Corporation to divide the year into translation periods, the applicable periods being January 1 through July 31 and August 1 through December 31. For most classes of items, the appropriate exchange rate for each of these translation periods is a simple average of monthly closing rates, or 23 abbas and 25 abbas per United States dollar, respectively. However, all of the depreciable asset purchases were made at the end of the first translation period—January 1 through July 31—and, therefore, the rate representative of those transactions is a weighted average of 24 abbas per United States dollar. The classes of items reflecting M Corporation's 1965 financial transactions and the representative rates of exchange for such classes of items are as follows:

	Local Currency	Exchange Rate
Sales (Jan. 1—July 31)	1,000,000	23:1
(Aug. 1—Dec. 31)	500,000	25:1
Inventory Purchases:		
(Jan. 1—July 31)	559,000	23:1
(Aug. 1—Dec. 31)	361,000	25:1

Reg. §1.964-1(d)(9)

	Local Currency	Exchange Rate
Expenses (Jan. 1—July 31)	115,000	23:1
(Aug. 1—Dec. 31)	145,000	25:1
Fixed Asset Purchases	216,000	24:1
Closing Inventory	430,000	Historical

Assuming that M Corporation uses the first-in, first-out method of inventory valuation, the closing inventory is assumed in normal circumstances to consist of purchases made during the most recent translation period as follows:

	Local Currency	Exchange Rate	U.S. Dollars
All of the August-December Purchases	361,000	25:1	$14,440
Balance from January-July Purchases	69,000	23:1	3,000
Total Closing Inventory	430,000		$17,440

Assuming that none of the amounts shown therein reflects a transaction described in subparagraph (7) of this paragraph, and that closing inventory is translated at historical rates, M Corporation's adjusted profit and loss statement for 1965 would be translated into United States dollars as follows:

	Local Currency	Exchange Rate	U.S. Dollars
Sales (Jan. 1—July 31)	1,000,000	23:1	$43,478
(Aug. 1—Dec. 31)	500,000	25:1	20,000
	1,500,000		$63,478
Cost of Goods Sold:			
Opening Inventory			
Purchases	418,000	21:1	19,905
(Jan. 1—July 31)	559,000	23:1	24,304
(Aug. 1—Dec. 31)	361,000	25:1	14,440
Less—Closing Inventory	(430,000)	Historical	(17,440)
	908,000		41,209
Wages and Other Expenses			
(Jan. 1—July 31)	115,000	23:1	5,000
(Aug. 1—Dec. 31)	145,000	25:1	5,800
Depreciation (1963 assets)	120,000	20:1	6,000
(1964 assets)	64,500	21.5:1	3,000
(1965 assets)	43,200	24:1	1,800
Total Costs and Expenses	1,395,700		62,809
Operating Profit	104,300		669

(e) *Exchange gain or loss.*—(1) *In general.*—The exchange gain or loss determined in accordance with subparagraph (2) of this paragraph shall be applied against and reduce, or applied to and increase, as the case may be, the amount of profit or loss shown on the profit and loss statement prepared pursuant to paragraph (a)(1) of this section, as adjusted and translated pursuant to paragraph (a)(2), (3), and (4) of this section. For the manner in which the exchange gain or loss is to be allocated to or applied against subpart F income, see section 952 and the regulations thereunder.

(2) *Determination of exchange gain or loss.*—The exchange gain (or loss) for the taxable year shall be the amount which equals—

(i) The retained earnings for the taxable year as determined under subparagraph (3) of this paragraph, plus

(ii) The amount of any distributions made during the taxable year translated at the exchange rate appropriate to the translation period during which such distributions were made (or taken into account in accordance with paragraph (d)(7) of this section, if applicable), minus

(iii) The amount representing retained earnings for the preceding taxable year as determined under subparagraph (3) of this paragraph, minus

(iv) The amount of profit (or plus the amount of any loss) shown on the profit and loss statement for the taxable year prepared pursuant to paragraph (a)(1) of this section and adjusted and translated pursuant to paragraph (a)(2), (3), and (4) of this section.

(3) *Retained earnings.*—The retained earnings for any taxable year shall be determined by first—

Reg. §1.964-1(e)(1)

(i) Preparing a balance sheet as of the end of such year from the books of account regularly maintained by the foreign corporation for the purpose of accounting to its shareholders;

(ii) Making the adjustments necessary to conform such balance sheet to the accounting principles described in paragraph (b) of this section;

(iii) Making the further adjustments necessary to conform such balance sheet to the tax accounting standards described in paragraph (c) of this section; and

(iv) Translating the amounts shown on the balance sheet (other than amounts representing retained earnings) into United States dollars in accordance with subparagraph (4) of this paragraph.

The retained earnings shall be an amount equal to the excess of the aggregate amount representing assets on the balance sheet (as adjusted and translated under this subparagraph) over the aggregate amount representing liabilities, reserves (other than reserves out of current or accumulated earnings), and paid-in capital on the balance sheet (as adjusted and translated under this subparagraph).

(4) *Translation of balance sheet.*—Amounts shown on the balance sheet as adjusted pursuant to subparagraph (3)(ii) and (iii) of this paragraph (other than amounts representing retained earnings) shall be translated into United States dollars as follows:

(i) *Financial assets.*—Amounts representing financial assets shall be translated at the year-end rate.

(ii) *Physical assets.*—Amounts representing physical assets (other than inventory) shall be translated at the appropriate exchange rate for the translation period in which the historical cost of the asset was incurred or is deemed to have been incurred. For special rules for determining date on which the historical cost of certain assets acquired during taxable years beginning before January 1, 1950, or owned at the time a majority interest in the corporation was acquired after December 31, 1949, but before October 27, 1964, is deemed to have been incurred, see paragraph (b)(2) of this section.

(iii) *Depreciation and similar reserves.*—Amounts representing depreciation, depletion, and amortization reserves shall be translated at the appropriate exchange rate for the translation period in which the historical cost of the underlying asset was incurred or is deemed to have been incurred.

(iv) *Inventory.*—Amounts representing items of inventory included in the closing inventory balance shall be translated in accordance with paragraph (d)(1)(ii) of this section.

(v) *Bad debt reserves.*—Amounts representing bad debt reserves shall be translated at the year-end rate.

(vi) *Prepaid income or expense.*—Amounts representing expenses or income paid or received in a prior taxable year shall be translated in accordance with paragraph (d)(1)(iv) of this section.

(vii) *Short-term liabilities.*—Amounts representing short-term liabilities shall be translated at the year-end rate.

(viii) *Long-term liabilities.*—Amounts representing long-term liabilities shall be translated at the appropriate exchange rate for the translation period in which such liabilities were incurred.

(ix) *Paid-in capital.*—Amounts representing paid-in capital shall be translated at the appropriate exchange rate for the translation period in which such capital was paid in.

Notwithstanding any other provisions of this subparagraph, where the amount representing an item shown on the balance sheet reflects a transaction described in paragraph (d)(7) of this section, such transaction shall be taken into account in accordance with that paragraph.

(5) *Definitions.*—For purposes of this paragraph—

(i) *Financial assets.*—A financial asset shall be any asset reflecting a fixed amount of foreign currency, such as cash on hand, bank deposits, and loans and accounts receivable. Securities (within the meaning of section 1236(c)) shall be considered physical assets if they have been or are reasonably expected to be held for at least six months; if not they shall be considered financial assets whether or not they reflect a fixed amount of foreign currency. Moreover, advances on open account to any corporation in which the foreign corporation and any related persons (within the meaning of section 954(d)(3) and the regulations thereunder) with respect thereto own at least 10 percent of the combined voting power of all classes of stock entitled to vote shall not be considered financial assets if such advances have remained open for more than one year.

(ii) *Physical assets.*—A physical asset shall be any asset other than a financial asset and shall include goodwill, patents, and other intangibles.

(iii) *Short-term liabilities.*—A short-term liability shall be any indebtedness of the foreign corporation which is due or overdue as of the date of the balance sheet or which will become due within one year thereafter.

(iv) *Long-term liabilities.*—A long-term liability is any indebtedness of the foreign corporation other than a short-term liability.

For the definition of "appropriate exchange rate," "year-end rate," and "translation period," see paragraph (d)(2), (4) and (6), respectively, of this section.

(6) *Illustrations.*—The application of this paragraph may be illustrated by the following examples:

Example (1). N Corporation is a controlled foreign corporation which uses the calendar year as its taxable year and which maintains its books in yuccas, the currency of the country in which it operates. For 1963, its operating profit is 140,000 yuccas or $55,720. At the end of the year, its balance sheet, as translated and adjusted pursuant to subparagraph (3) of this paragraph, is as follows:

	Local Currency	Exchange Rate	U.S. Dollars
Cash	77,000	2.20:1	$ 35,000
Accounts Receivable	209,000	2.20:1	95,000
Inventory	418,000	Historical	199,050
Fixed Assets	1,430,000	Historical	700,000
Less—Accumulated Depreciation	(436,000)	Historical	(215,000)
Total Assets	1,698,000		814,050
Current Liabilities	338,000	2.20:1	$153,640
Long-term Liabilities	300,000	Historical	150,000
Paid-in Capital	800,000	Historical	400,000
Retained Earnings	260,000		110,410
Total Liabilities and Net Worth	1,698,000		814,050

N Corporation's retained earnings for 1962 are determined on the basis of its balance sheet as of the end of that year, translated as follows:

	Local Currency	Exchange Rate	U.S. Dollars
Cash	70,000	2.00:1	$ 35,000
Accounts Receivable	180,000	2.00:1	90,000
Inventory	350,000	Historical	175,000
Fixed Assets	1,000,000	Historical	500,000
Less—Accumulated Depreciation	(200,000)	Historical	(100,000)
Total Assets	1,400,000		700,000
Current Liabilities	180,000	2.00:1	$ 90,000
Long-term Liabilities	300,000	Historical	150,000
Paid-in Capital	800,000	Historical	400,000
Retained Earnings	120,000		60,000
Total Liabilities and Net Worth	1,400,000		700,000

The exchange gain or loss of N Corporation for 1963 may be computed as follows:

Retained Earnings—1963		$110,410
Less—Retained Earnings—1962	$60,000	
Operating Profit—1963	55,720	115,720
Exchange Loss		(5,310)

Example (2). Assume the same facts as in example (1). For 1964, N Corporation's operating profit is 104,300 yuccas or $15,740. It pays a dividend of 26,000 yuccas during a translation period when the appropriate exchange rate is 2.60 yuccas per United States dollar. At year-end, its balance sheet, as translated and adjusted pursuant to subparagraph (3) of this paragraph, is as follows:

	Local Currency	Exchange Rate	U.S. Dollars
Cash	91,000	2.60:1	$ 35,000
Accounts Receivable	260,000	2.60:1	100,000
Inventory	430,000	Historical	174,400
Fixed Assets	1,646,000	Historical	790,000
Less—Accumulated Depreciation	(663,700)	Historical	(323,000)
Total Assets	1,763,300		776,400
Current Liabilities	325,000	2.60:1	$125,000
Long-term Liabilities	300,000	Historical	150,000
Paid-in Capital	800,000	Historical	400,000
Retained Earnings	338,300		101,400
Total Liabilities and Net Worth	1,763,300		776,400

The exchange gain or loss of N Corporation for 1964 would be computed as follows:

Retained Earnings—1964		$101,400
Add—Dividends—1964		10,000
Predistribution earnings		111,400
Less—Retained Earnings—1963	$110,410	
Operating Profit—1964	15,740	126,150
Exchange Loss		(14,750)

(f) *Determination of earnings and profits as if a domestic corporation.*—(1) *In general.*—If the books of account regularly maintained by a foreign corporation for the purpose of accounting to its shareholders are kept in U.S. dollars and in accordance with accounting principles generally accepted in the United States, and if it is so elected by or on behalf of such corporation, the earnings and profits of the foreign corporation for a taxable year shall, except as otherwise provided in paragraph (f)(2) of this section, be determined in every respect as if it were a domestic corporation. Such election shall be effective only for the taxable year with respect to which the election is made. Once made, such election shall be irrevocable. See paragraph (c)(3) of this section for the time and manner in which an election may be made on behalf of a foreign corporation.

(2) *Illegal payments.*—The amount of any illegal bribe, kickback, or other payment (within the meaning of section 162(c), as amended by section 288 of the Tax Equity and Fiscal Responsibility Act of 1982 in the case of payments made after September 3, 1982, and the regulations thereunder) paid after November 3, 1976, by or on behalf of the corporation during the taxable year of the corporation directly or indirectly to an official, employee, or agent in fact of a government shall not be taken into account to decrease earnings and profits or increase the deficit in earnings and profits otherwise determined under paragraph (f)(1) of this section. [Reg. § 1.964-1.]

☐ [*T.D.* 6764, 10-26-64. *Amended by T.D.* 6787, 12-28-64; *T.D.* 6829, 6-22-65; *T.D.* 6995, 1-17-69; *T.D.* 7221, 11-20-72; *T.D.* 7322, 8-23-74; *T.D.* 7545, 5-5-78; *T.D.* 7862, 12-16-82 *and T.D.* 7893, 5-11-83.]

§ 1.964-1T. Special rules for computing earnings and profits of controlled foreign corporations in taxable years beginning after December 31, 1986 (temporary).—

(a)-(f) [Reserved]

(g)(1) *Earnings and profits computed in functional currency.*—(i) *Rule.*—For taxable years of a controlled foreign corporation (within the meaning of section 957) beginning after December 31, 1986, earnings and profits shall be computed in the controlled foreign corporation's functional currency (determined under section 985 and the regulations thereunder) in accordance with § 1.964-1 as modified by this paragraph (g). Accordingly, § 1.964-1 (d), (e), and (f) and (to the extent inconsistent with this paragraph (g)) § 1.964-1(c) do not apply for taxable years of a controlled foreign corporation beginning after December 31, 1986. For purposes of this section, the term "earnings and profits" includes a deficit in earnings and profits.

(ii) *Cross reference.*—In the case of a controlled foreign corporation with a functional currency other than the United States dollar (dollar), see sections 986(b) and 989(b) for rules regarding the time and manner of translating distributions or inclusions of the controlled foreign corporation's earnings and profits into dollars.

(2) *Election required when first significant.*—Tax accounting methods or elections may be adopted or made by, or on behalf of, a controlled foreign corporation in the manner

prescribed by the Code and regulations no later than 180 days after the close of the first taxable year of the controlled foreign corporation in which the computation of its earnings and profits is significant for United States income tax purposes with respect to its controlling United States shareholders (as defined in § 1.964-1(c)(5)). For taxable years of a controlled foreign corporation beginning before January 1, 1989, only the events listed in § 1.964-1(c)(6) are considered to cause a controlled foreign corporation's earnings and profits to have United States tax significance. For taxable years of a controlled foreign corporation beginning after December 31, 1988, events that cause a controlled foreign corporation's earnings and profits to have United States tax significance include, without limitation—

(i) The events listed in § 1.964-1(c)(6),

(ii) A distribution from the controlled foreign corporation to its shareholders with respect to their stock,

(iii) Any event making the controlled foreign corporation subject to tax under section 882,

(iv) An election by the controlled foreign corporation's controlling United States shareholders to use the tax book value method of allocating interest expense under section 864(e)(4), and

(v) A sale or exchange of the controlled foreign corporation's stock by the controlling United States shareholders.

The filing of the information return required by section 6038 shall not itself constitute a significant event.

(3) *Effect of failure to make required election.*—If an accounting method or election is not timely adopted or made by, or on behalf of, a controlled foreign corporation, and such failure is not shown to the satisfaction of the Commissioner to be due to reasonable cause under § 1.964-1(c)(6), earnings and profits shall be computed in accordance with this section. Such computation shall be made as if no elections had been made and any permissible accounting methods not requiring an election and reflected in the books of account regularly maintained by the controlled foreign corporation for the purpose of accounting to its shareholders had been adopted. Thereafter, any change in a particular accounting method or methods may be made by, or on behalf of, the controlled foreign corporation only with the Commissioner's consent.

(4) *Computation of earnings and profits by a minority shareholder prior to majority election or significant event.*—A minority United States shareholder (as defined in section 951(b)) of a controlled foreign corporation may be required to compute a controlled foreign corporation's earnings and profits before the controlled foreign corporation or its controlling United States shareholders make, or are required under this section to make, an election or adopt a method of accounting for United States tax purposes. In such a case, the minority United States shareholder must compute earnings and profits in accordance with this section. Such computation shall be made as if no elections had been made and any permissible accounting methods not requiring an election and reflected in the books of account regularly maintained by the controlled foreign corporation for the purpose of accounting to its shareholders had been adopted. However, a later, properly filed, and timely election or adoption of method by, or on behalf of, the controlled foreign corporation shall not be treated as a change in accounting method.

(5) *Binding effect.*—For taxable years beginning after December 31, 1986, except as otherwise provided in the Code or regulations, earnings and profits of a controlled foreign corporation shall be computed consistently under the rules of sections 964(a) and 986(b) for all federal income tax purposes. An election or adoption of a method of accounting for United States tax purposes by a controlled foreign corporation, or on its behalf pursuant to § 1.964-1(c) or any other provision of the regulations (*e.g.,* § 1.985-2(c)(3)), shall bind both the controlled foreign corporation and its United States shareholders as to the computation of the controlled foreign corporation's earnings and profits under section 964 (a) for the year of the election or adoption and in subsequent taxable years unless the Commissioner consents to a change. The preceding sentence shall apply regardless of—

(i) Whether the election or adoption of a method of accounting was made in a pre-1987 or a post-1986 taxable year;

(ii) Whether the controlled foreign corporation was a controlled foreign corporation at the time of the election or adoption of method;

(iii) When ownership was acquired; or

(iv) Whether the United States shareholder received the written notice required by § 1.964-1(c)(3).

Adjustments to the appropriate separate category (as defined in § 1.904-5(a)(1)) of earnings and profits and income of the controlled foreign corporation shall be required using the principles of section 481 to prevent any duplication or omission of amounts attributable to previous years that would otherwise result from any such election or adoption.

(6) *Examples.*—The following examples illustrate the rules of this section.

Example (1)—(i) P, a calendar year domestic corporation, owns all of the outstanding stock of *FX*, a calendar year controlled foreign corporation. None of the significant events specified in § 1.964-1(c)(6) or this section has occurred. In addition, neither *P* nor *FX* has ever made or adopted, or been required to make or adopt, an election or method of accounting for United States tax purposes with respect to *FX*. On June 1, 1990, *FX* makes a distribution to *P*. *FX* does not act to make any election or adopt a method of accounting for United States tax purposes.

(ii) *P* must compute *FX*'s earnings and profits in order to determine if any portion of the distribution is taxable as a dividend and to determine *P*'s foreign tax credit on such portion under section 902. *P* must satisfy the requirements of § 1.964-1(c)(3) and file the written statement and notice described therein within 180 days after the close of *FX*'s 1990 taxable year in order to make an election or to adopt a method of accounting on behalf of *FX*. Any such election or adoption will govern the computation of earnings and profits of *FX* for all federal income tax purposes (including, *e.g.,* the determination of foreign tax credits on subpart F inclusions) in 1990 and subsequent taxable years unless the Commissioner consents to a change.

(iii) If *P* fails to satisfy the regulatory requirements in a timely manner and such failure is not shown to the satisfaction of the Commissioner to be due to reasonable cause, the earnings and profits of *FX* shall be computed as if no elections were made and any permissible methods of accounting not requiring an election and reflected in its books were adopted. Any subsequent attempt by *FX* or *P* to change an accounting method shall be effective only if the Commissioner consents to the change.

Example (2)—(i) The facts are the same as in *Example (1),* except that *P* elects to allocate its interest expense under section 864(e)(4) for its 1989 taxable year under the tax book value method of § 1.861-12T(c) of the Temporary Income Tax Regulations.

(ii) *P* must compute the earnings and profits of *FX* in order to determine the adjustment to *P*'s basis in the stock of *FX* for *P*'s 1989 taxable year. *P* must satisfy the requirements of § 1.964-1(c)(3) and file the written statement and notice described therein within 180 days after the close of *FX*'s 1989 taxable year in order to make an election or to adopt a method of accounting on behalf of *FX*. Any such election or adoption will govern the computation of *FX*'s earnings and profits in 1989 and subsequent taxable years for all federal income tax purposes (including, *e.g.,* the characterization of the June 1, 1990 distribution and the determination of *P*'s foreign tax credit, if any, with respect thereto) unless the Commissioner consents to a change.

(iii) If *P* fails to satisfy the regulatory requirements in a timely manner and such failure is not shown to the satisfaction of the Commissioner to be due to reasonable cause, the earnings and profits of *FX* shall be computed as if no elections were made and any permissible methods of accounting not requiring an election and reflected in its books were adopted. Any subsequent attempt by *FX* or *P* to change an accounting method shall be effective only if the Commissioner consents to the change.

Example (3)—(i) The facts are the same as in *Example (2),* except that *P* elects to allocate its interest expense under section 864(e)(4) for its 1988 taxable year under the tax book value method of § 1.861-12T(c) of the Temporary Income Tax Regulations.

(ii) *P* must compute the earnings and profits of *FX* in order to determine the adjustment to *P*'s basis in the stock of *FX* for *P*'s 1988 taxable year. *P* must satisfy the requirements of § 1.964-1(c)(3) and file the written statement and notice described therein within 180 days after the close of *FX*'s 1988 taxable year in order to make an election or to adopt a method of accounting on behalf of *FX*. Any such election or adoption will govern the computation of *FX*'s earnings and profits in 1988 and subsequent taxable years for all federal income tax purposes (including, *e.g., P*'s basis adjustment for purposes of section 864(e)(4) in 1989 and the characterization of the June 1, 1990 distribution and the determination of *P*'s foreign tax credit, if any, with respect thereto) unless the Commissioner consents to a change.

(iii) If *P* fails to satisfy the regulatory requirements in a timely manner and such failure is not shown to the satisfaction of the Commissioner to be due to reasonable cause, the earnings and profits of *FX* for 1988 shall be computed as if no elections were made and any permissible methods of accounting not requiring an election and reflected in its books were adopted. However, a properly filed, timely election or adoption of method by, or on behalf of, *FX* with respect to its 1989 taxable year, when *P*'s basis adjustment for purposes of section 864(e)(4) first constitutes a significant event, shall not be treated as a change in accounting method. No recomputation of *P*'s basis adjustment for 1988 shall be required by reason of any such election or adoption of method with respect to *FX*'s 1989 taxable year, but prospective adjustments to *FX*'s earnings and profits and income shall be made to the extent required by § 1.964-1T(g)(5).

Example (4)—(i) The facts are the same as in *Example (3),* except that *FX* had subpart F income taxable to *P* in 1986, and *P* computed *FX*'s earnings and profits for purposes of determining the amount of the inclusion and the foreign taxes deemed paid by *P* in 1986 under section 960 pursuant to § 1.964-1(a) through (e).

(ii) Any election made or method of accounting adopted on behalf of *FX* by *P* pursuant to § 1.964-1(c) in 1986 is binding on *P* and *FX* for purposes of computing *FX*'s earnings and profits in 1986 and subsequent taxable years. Thus, in determining *P*'s basis adjustment for purposes of section 864(e)(4) in 1988 and 1989 and its deemed-paid credit with respect to the 1990 dividend, *FX*'s earnings and profits must be computed consistently with the method used by *P* with regard to the 1986 subpart F inclusion. (However, § 1.964-1(d), (e), and (f) do not apply in computing *FX*'s earnings and profits in post-1986 taxable years.)

Example (5)—(i) The facts are the same as in *Example (4)*, except that *FX* made a dividend distribution to *P* on June 1, 1985, and *P* computed *FX*'s earnings and profits for purposes of computing the foreign taxes deemed paid by *P* in 1985 under section 902 with respect to the distribution under § 1.964-1 exclusive of paragraphs (d), (e), and (f) pursuant to a timely election under § 1.902-1(g)(1).

(ii) Any election made or method of accounting adopted on behalf of *FX* by *P* pursuant to § 1.964-1(c) in 1985 is binding on *P* and *FX* for purposes of computing *FX*'s earnings and profits in 1985 and subsequent taxable years. Thus, in determining *P*'s basis adjustment for purposes of section 864(e)(4) in 1988 and 1989 and its deemed-paid credit with respect to the 1986 subpart F inclusion and the 1990 dividend, *FX*'s earnings and profits must be computed consistently with the method used by *P* with regard to the 1985 dividend. If, rather than choosing under § 1.902-1(g)(1) to use the section 964 rules, *P* computed *FX*'s earnings and profits for purposes of section 902 in 1985 in all respects as if *FX* were a domestic corporation, then *P* would have been free to make elections or adopt a method of accounting on behalf of *FX* under § 1.964-1(c) with respect to the subpart F inclusion in 1986. Any such election or adoption would be binding on *P* and *FX* as to the computation of *FX*'s earnings and profits in 1986 and subsequent taxable years. [Temporary Reg. § 1.964-1T.]

☐ [T.D. 8283, 1-24-90.]

§ 1.964-2. Treatment of blocked earnings and profits.—(a) *General rule.*—If, in accordance with paragraph (d) of this section, it is established to the satisfaction of the district director that any amount of the earnings and profits of a controlled foreign corporation for the taxable year (determined under § 1.964-1) was subject to a currency or other restriction or limitation imposed under the laws of any foreign country (within the meaning of paragraph (b) of this section) on its distribution to United States shareholders who own (within the meaning of section 958(a)) stock of such corporation, such amount shall not be included in earnings and profits for purposes of sections 952, 955 (as in effect both before and after the enactment of the Tax Reduction Act of 1975), and 956 for such taxable year. For rules governing the treatment of amounts with respect to which such restriction or limitation is removed, see paragraph (c) of this section.

(b) *Rules of application.*—For purposes of paragraph (a) of this section—

(1) *Period of restriction or limitation.*—An amount of earnings and profits of a controlled foreign corporation for any taxable year shall not be included in earnings and profits for purposes of sections 952, 955 (as in effect both before and after the enactment of the Tax Reduction Act of 1975), and 956 only if such amount of earnings and profits is subject to a currency or other restriction or limitation (within the meaning of subparagraph (2) of this paragraph) throughout the 150-day period beginning 90 days before the close of the taxable year and ending 60 days after the close of such taxable year.

(2) *Restriction or limitation defined.*— Whether earnings and profits of a controlled foreign corporation are subject to a currency or other restriction or limitation imposed under the laws of a foreign country must be determined on the basis of all the facts and circumstances in each case. Generally, such a restriction or limitation must prevent—

(i) The ready conversion (directly or indirectly) of such currency into United States dollars or into property of a type normally owned by such corporation in the operation of its business or other money which is readily convertible into United States dollars; or

(ii) The distribution of dividends by such corporation to its United States shareholders.

For purposes of this subparagraph, if a United States shareholder owns (within the meaning of section 958(a)), or is considered as owning by applying the rules of ownership of section 958(b), 80 percent or more of the total combined voting power of all classes of stock of a foreign corporation in a chain of ownership described in section 958(a), the distribution of dividends by such corporation to such shareholder will not be considered prevented solely by reason of the existence of a currency or other restriction or limitation at an intermediate tier in such chain if dividends may be distributed directly to such shareholders.

(3) *Foreign laws.*—A currency or other restriction or limitation on the distribution of earnings and profits may be imposed in a foreign country by express statutory provisions, executive orders or decrees, rules or regulations of a governmental agency, court decisions, the actions of appropriate officials who are acting within the scope of their authority, or by any similar official action. A currency restriction will not be considered to exist unless export restrictions are also imposed which prevent the exportation of property of a type normally owned by the controlled foreign corporation in the operation of its business which could be readily converted into United States dollars.

(4) *Voluntary restriction or limitation.*—A currency or other restriction or limitation arising from the voluntary act of the controlled foreign corporation or its United States shareholders during a taxable year beginning after December 31, 1962, will not be taken into account. For example, if a controlled foreign corporation—

(i) Issues a stock dividend which has the effect of capitalizing earnings and profits;

(ii) Elects to restrict its earnings and profits or to make certain investments as a means of avoiding current tax or securing a reduced rate of tax; or

(iii) Allocates earnings and profits to an optional or arbitrary reserve;

such restriction is voluntary and will not be taken into account.

(5) *Treatment of earnings and profits in cases of certain mandatory reserves.*—(i) *In general.*—If a controlled foreign corporation is required under the laws of a foreign country to establish a reserve out of earnings and profits for the taxable year, such earnings and profits shall be considered subject to a restriction or limitation by reason of such requirement only to the extent that the amount required to be included in such reserve at the close of the taxable year exceeds the accumulated earnings and profits (determined in accordance with subdivision (ii) of this subparagraph) of such corporation at the close of the preceding taxable year,

(ii) *Determination of earnings and profits.*—For purposes of determining the accumulated earnings and profits of a controlled foreign corporation under subdivision (i) of this subparagraph, such earnings and profits shall not include any amounts which are attributable to—

(a) Amounts which, for any prior taxable year, have been included in the gross income of a United States shareholder under section 951(a) and have not been distributed;

(b) Amounts which, for any prior taxable year, have been included in the gross income of a United States shareholder of such foreign corporation under section 551(b) and have not been distributed; or

(c) Amounts which become subject to a voluntary restriction or limitation (within the meaning of subparagraph (4) of this paragraph) during a taxable year beginning before January 1, 1963.

The rules of this subdivision apply only in determining the accumulated earnings and profits of a controlled foreign corporation for purposes of this subparagraph. See section 959 and the regulations thereunder for limitations on the exclusion from gross income of previously taxed earnings and profits.

(6) *Exhaustion of procedures for distributing earnings and profits.*—Earnings and profits of a controlled foreign corporation for a taxable year will not be considered subject to a currency or other restriction or limitation on their distribution unless the United States shareholders of such corporation demonstrate either that the available procedures for distributing such earnings and profits have been exhausted or that the use of such procedures will be futile. As a general rule, such procedures will be considered to have been exhausted if the foreign corporation applies for dollars (or foreign currency readily convertible into dollars) at the appropriate rate of exchange and complies with the applicable laws and regulations governing the acquisition and transfer of such currency including submission of the necessary documentation to the exchange authority. The fact that available procedures for distributing earnings and profits were exhausted without success with respect to a prior year is not, of itself, sufficient evidence that such procedures would not be successful with respect to the current taxable year.

(c) *Removal of restriction or limitation.*—(1) *In general.*—If, during any taxable year, a currency or other restriction or limitation (within the meaning of paragraph (b) of this section) imposed under the laws of a foreign country on the distribution of earnings and profits of a controlled foreign corporation to its United States shareholders is removed—

(i) *Treatment of deferred income.*—Each United States shareholder of such corporation on the last day in such year that such corporation is a controlled foreign corporation shall include in his gross income for such taxable year the amounts attributable to such earnings and profits which would have been includible in his gross income under section 951(a) for

Reg. §1.964-2(c)(1)(i)

prior taxable years but for the existence of the currency or other restriction or limitation except that the amounts included under this subdivision (i) shall not exceed his pro rata share of—

(a) The earnings and profits upon which the restriction was removed determined on the basis of his stock ownership on the last day of the immediately preceding taxable year, and

(b) The applicable limitations under paragraph (c) of § 1.952-1, paragraph (b)(2) of § 1.955-1, paragraph (b)(2) of § 1.955A-1, or paragraph (b) of § 1.956-1, determined as of the last day of the immediately preceding taxable year, taking into account the provisions of subdivision (ii) of this subparagraph.

(ii) *Treatment of earnings and profits.*—For purposes of sections 952, 955 (as in effect both before and after the enactment of the Tax Reduction Act of 1975), and 956, the earnings and profits which are no longer subject to a currency or other restriction or limitation shall be treated as included in the corporation's earnings and profits for the year in which such earnings and profits were derived.

Amounts with respect to which a currency or other restriction or limitation is removed shall be translated into United States dollars at the appropriate exchange rate for the translation period during which such currency or other restriction or limitation is removed. See paragraph (d) of § 1.964-1. Amounts with respect to which a currency or other restriction or limitation is removed shall not be taken into account in determining whether a deficiency distribution (within the meaning of § 1.963-6 (applied as if section 963 had not been repealed by the Tax Reduction Act of 1975)) is required to be made for the year in which such earnings and profits were derived.

(2) *Removal of restriction or limitation defined.*—An amount of earnings and profits shall be considered no longer subject to a limitation or restriction if and to the extent that—

(i) Money or property in such foreign country is readily convertible into United States dollars, or into other money or property of a type normally owned by such corporation in the operation of its business which is readily convertible into United States dollars;

(ii) Notwithstanding the existence of any laws or regulations forbidding the exchange of money or property into United States dollars, conversion is actually made into United States dollars, or other money or property of a type normally owned by such corporation in the operation of its business which is readily convertible into United States dollars; or

(iii) A mandatory reserve requirement (described in paragraph (b)(5) of this section) is removed either by a change in law of the foreign country imposing such requirement or by an accumulation of earnings and profits not subject to such requirement.

(3) *Distribution in foreign country.*—If, during any taxable year, earnings and profits previously subject to a currency or other restriction or limitation are distributed in a foreign country to one or more United States shareholders of a controlled foreign corporation directly, or indirectly through a chain of ownership described in section 958(a), such earnings and profits shall be considered no longer subject to a restriction or limitation. However, distributed amounts may be excluded from such shareholder's gross income for the taxable year of receipt if such shareholder elects a method of accounting under which the reporting of blocked foreign income is deferred until the income ceases to be blocked.

(4) *Source of distribution.*—If, during any taxable year, earnings and profits previously subject to a currency or other restriction or limitation are distributed to one or more United States shareholders of a controlled foreign corporation directly, or indirectly through a chain of ownership described in section 958(a), the source of such distribution shall be determined in accordance with the rules of § 1.959-3.

(5) *Illustration.*—The provisions of this paragraph may be illustrated by the following example:

Example. (a) M, a United States person, owns all of the only class of stock of A Corporation, a foreign corporation incorporated under the laws of foreign country X on January 1, 1963. Both M and A Corporations use the calendar year as a taxable year and A Corporation is a controlled foreign corporation throughout the period here involved.

(b) During 1963, A Corporation derives income of $100,000 all of which is subpart F income and has earnings and profits of $100,000. Under the laws of X Country, currency cannot be exported without a license. During the last 90 days of 1963 and the first 60 days of 1964, A Corporation can obtain a license to distribute only an amount equivalent to $10,000. M must include $10,000 in his gross income for 1963 under section 951(a)(1)(A)(i) and $90,000 of A Corporation's earnings and profits for 1963 are not taken into account for purposes of sections 952, 955, and 956.

(c) During 1964, A Corporation has no income and no earnings and profits. On June 1, 1964, A Corporation converts an amount equivalent to $20,000 into property of a type normally owned by such corporation in the operation of its business which is readily convertible into United States dollars but does not distribute such amount. Corporation A must include $20,000 in its earnings and profits for 1963 for purposes of sections 952, 955, and 956. M must include $20,000 in his gross income for 1964.

(d) During 1965, A Corporation has no income and no earnings and profits. On December 15, 1965, A Corporation distributes an amount equivalent to $15,000 to M in X Country. Neither M nor A Corporation can obtain a license to export currency from X Country. In his return for the taxable year 1965, M elects a method of accounting under which the reporting of blocked foreign income is deferred until the income ceases to be blocked. Accordingly, M does not include the $15,000 in his gross income for 1965.

(e) During 1966, A Corporation has no income and no earnings and profits. On February 1, 1966, notwithstanding the laws and regulations of X Country which forbid the exchange of X Country's currency into United States dollars, M converts an amount equivalent to $15,000 into a currency which is readily convertible into United States dollars. Since the income has ceased to be blocked, M must include $15,000 in his gross income for 1966.

(d) *Manner of claiming existence of restriction or limitation on distribution of earnings and profits.*—A United States shareholder claiming that an amount of the earnings and profits of a controlled foreign corporation for the taxable year was subject to a currency or other restriction or limitation imposed under the laws of a foreign country on its distribution shall file a statement with his return for the taxable year with or within which the taxable year of the foreign corporation ends which shall include—

(1) The name and address of the foreign corporation,

(2) A description of the classes of stock of the foreign corporation and a statement of the number of shares of each class owned (within the meaning of section 958(a)) or considered as owned (by applying the rules of ownership of section 958(b)) by the United States shareholder,

(3) A description of the currency or other restriction or limitation on the distribution of earnings and profits,

(4) The total earnings and profits of the foreign corporation for the taxable year (before any amount is excluded from earnings and profits under this section) and the United States shareholder's pro rata share of such total earnings and profits,

(5) The United States shareholder's pro rata share of the amount of earnings and profits subject to a restriction or limitation on distribution,

(6) The amounts which would be includible in the United States shareholder's gross income under section 951(a) but for the existence of the currency or other restriction or limitation,

(7) A description of the available procedures for distributing earnings and profits and a statement setting forth the steps taken to exhaust such procedures or a statement setting forth the reasons that the use of such procedures would be futile, and

(8) The amount of distributions made in a foreign country and a statement as to whether a method of accounting has been elected under which the reporting of blocked income is deferred until such income ceases to be blocked, including an identification of the taxable year and place of filing of such election.

In addition, such United States shareholder shall furnish to the district director such other information as he may require to verify the status of a currency or other restriction or limitation. [Reg. § 1.964-2.]

☐ [*T.D. 6892, 8-22-66. Amended by T.D. 7545, 5-5-78 and T.D. 7893, 5-11-83.*]

§ 1.964-3. Records to be provided by United States shareholders.—(a) *Shareholder's responsibility for providing records.*—For purposes of verifying his income tax liability in respect of amounts includible in income under section 951 for the taxable year of a controlled foreign corporation each United States shareholder (as defined in section 951(b)) who owns (within the meaning of section 958(a)) stock of such corporation shall, within a reasonable time after demand by the district director, provide the district director—

(1) Such permanent books of account or records as are sufficient to satisfy the requirements of section 6001 and section 964(c), or true copies thereof, as are reasonably demanded, and

(2) If such books or records are not maintained in the English language, either (i) an accurate English translation of such books or records or (ii) the services of a qualified interpreter satisfactory to the district director. If such books or records are being used by another district director, the United States shareholder upon whom the district director has made a demand to provide such books or records shall file a statement of such fact with his district director, indicating the location of such books or records. For the length of time the United States shareholder of a controlled foreign corporation must cause such books or records as are under his control to be retained, see paragraph (e) of § 1.6001-1.

(b) *Records to be provided.*—Except as otherwise provided in paragraph (c) of this section, the requirements of section 6001 and section 964(c) for record keeping shall be considered satisfied if the books or records produced are sufficient to verify for the taxable year—

(1) The subpart F income of the controlled foreign corporation and, if any part of such income is excluded from the income of the United States shareholder under section 963 or section 970(a), the application of such exclusion,

(2) The previously excluded subpart F income of such corporation withdrawn from investment in less developed countries,

(3) The previously excluded subpart F income of such corporation withdrawn from investment in foreign base company shipping operations,

(4) The previously excluded export trade income of such corporation withdrawn from investment, and

(5) The increase in earnings invested by such corporation in United States property.

(c) *Special rules.*—Verification of the subpart F income of the controlled foreign corporation for the taxable year shall not be required if—

(1) It can be demonstrated to the satisfaction of the district director that—

(i) The locus and nature of such corporation's activities were such as to make it unlikely that the foreign base company income of such corporation (determined in accordance with paragraph (c)(3) of § 1.952-3) exceeded 5 percent of its gross income (determined in accordance with paragraph (b)(1) of § 1.952-3) for the taxable year (For taxable years to which § 1.952-3 does not apply, such amounts shall be determined under 26 CFR § § 1.954-1(d)(3)(i) and (ii) (Rev. as of April 1, 1975)), and

(ii) If such corporation reinsures or issues insurance or annuity contracts in connection with United States risks, the 5-percent minimum premium requirement prescribed in paragraph (b) of § 1.953-1 has not been exceeded for the taxable year, or

(2) The United States shareholder's pro rata share of such subpart F income is excluded in full from his income under section 963 and the books or records verify the application of such exclusion. [Reg. § 1.964-3.]

☐ [*T.D.* 6824, 5-10-65. *Amended by T.D.* 7893, 5-11-83.]

Foreign Currency

§ 1.985-1. Functional currency.—(a) *Applicability and effective date.*—(1) *Purpose and scope.*—These regulations provide guidance with respect to defining the functional currency of a taxpayer and each qualified business unit (QBU), as defined in section 989 (a). Generally, a taxpayer and each QBU must make all determinations under subtitle A of the Code (relating to income taxes) in its respective functional currency. This section sets forth rules for determining when the functional currency is the United States dollar (dollar) or a currency other than the dollar. Section 1.985-2 provides an election to use the dollar as the functional currency for certain QBUs that absent the election would have a functional currency that is a hyperinflationary currency, and explains the effect of making the election. Section 1.985-3 sets forth the dollar approximate separate transactions method that certain QBUs must use to compute their income or loss or earnings and profits. Section 1.985-4 provides that the adoption of a functional currency is a method of accounting and sets forth conditions for a change in functional currency. Section 1.985-5 provides adjustments that are required to be made upon a change in functional currency. Finally, § 1.985-6 provides transition rules for a QBU that uses the dollar approximate separate transactions method for its first taxable year beginning after December 31, 1986.

(2) *Effective date.*—These regulations apply to taxable years beginning after December 31, 1986. However, any taxpayer desiring to apply temporary Income Tax Regulations § 1.985-0T through § 1.985-4T in lieu of these regulations to all taxable years beginning after December 31, 1986, and on or before OCT 20, 1989 may (on a consistent basis) so choose. For the text of the temporary regulations, see 53 Fed. Reg. 20308 (1988).

(b) *Dollar functional currency.*—(1) *In general.*—The dollar shall be the functional currency of a taxpayer or QBU described in paragraph (b)(1)(i) through (v) of this section regardless of the currency used in keeping its books and records (as defined in § 1.989(a)-1(d)). The dollar shall be the functional currency of—

(i) A taxpayer that is not a QBU (e.g., an individual);

(ii) A QBU that conducts its activities primarily in dollars. A QBU conducts its activities primarily in dollars if the currency of the economic environment in which the QBU conducts its activities is primarily the dollar. The facts and circumstances test set forth in paragraph (c)(2) of this section shall apply in making this determination;

(iii) Except as otherwise provided by ruling or administrative pronouncement, a QBU that has the United States, or any possession or territory of the United States where the dollar is the standard currency, as its residence (as defined in section 988(a)(3)(B));

(iv) A QBU that does not keep books and records in the currency of any economic environment in which a significant part of its activities is conducted. Whether a QBU keeps such books and records is determined in accordance with paragraph (c)(3) of this section; or

(v) A QBU that produces income or loss that is, or is treated as, effectively connected with the conduct of a trade or business within the United States.

(2) *QBUs operating in a hyperinflationary environment.*—(i) *Taxable years beginning on or before August 24, 1994.*—For taxable years beginning on or before August 24, 1994, see § 1.985-2 with respect to a QBU that elects to use, or is otherwise required to use, the dollar as its functional currency.

(ii) *Taxable years beginning after August 24, 1994.*—(A) *In general.*—For taxable years beginning after August 24, 1994, except as otherwise provided in paragraph (b)(2)(ii)(B) of this section, any QBU that otherwise would be required to use a hyperinflationary currency as its functional currency must use the dollar as its functional currency and compute income or loss or earnings and profits under the rules of § 1.985-3.

(B) *Exceptions.*—(1) *Certain QBU branches.*—The functional currency of a QBU that otherwise would be required to use a hyperinflationary currency as its functional currency and that is a branch of a foreign corporation having a non-dollar functional currency that is not hyperinflationary shall be the functional currency of the foreign corporation. Such QBU's income or loss or earnings and profits shall be determined under § 1.985-3 by substituting the functional currency of the foreign corporation for the dollar.

(2) *Corporation that is not a controlled foreign corporation.*—A foreign corporation (or its QBU branch) operating in a hyperinflationary environment is not required to use the dollar as its functional currency pursuant to paragraph (b)(2)(ii)(A) of this section if that foreign corporation is not a controlled foreign corporation as defined in section 957 or 953(c)(1)(B). However, a noncontrolled section 902 corporation, as defined in section 904(d)(2)(E), may elect to use the dollar (or, if appropriate, the currency specified in paragraph (b)(2)(ii)(B)(*1*) of this section) as its (or its QBU branch's) functional currency under the procedures set forth in § 1.985-2(c)(3).

(C) *Change in functional currency.*—(1) *In general.*—If a QBU is required to change its functional currency to the dollar under paragraph (b)(2)(ii)(A) of this section, or chooses or is required to change its functional currency to the dollar for any open taxable year (and all subsequent taxable years) under § 1.985-3(a)(2)(ii), the change is considered to be made with the consent of the Commissioner for purposes of § 1.985-4. A QBU changing functional currency must make adjustments described in § 1.985-7 if the year of change (as defined in § 1.481-1(a)(1)) begins after 1987, or the adjustments described in § 1.985-6 if the year of change begins in 1987. No adjustments under section 481 are required solely because of a change in functional currency described in this paragraph (b)(2)(ii)(C).

(2) *Effective date.*—This paragraph (b)(2)(ii)(C) applies to taxable years beginning after April 6, 1998. However, a taxpayer may choose to apply this paragraph (b)(2)(ii)(C) to all open years after December 31, 1986, provided each person, and each QBU branch of a person, that is related (within the meaning of § 1.985-2(d)(3)) also applies to this paragraph (b)(2)(ii)(C).

(D) *Hyperinflationary currency.*—For purposes of sections 985 through 989, the term hyperinflationary currency means the currency of a country in which there is cumulative inflation during the base period of at least 100 percent as determined by reference to the consumer price index of the country listed in the monthly issues of the "International Financial Statistics" or a successor publication of the International Monetary Fund. If a country's currency is not listed in the monthly issues of "International Financial Statistics," a QBU may use any other reasonable method consistently applied for determining the country's consumer price index. Base period means, with respect to any taxable year, the thirty-six calendar months immediately preceding the first day of the current calendar year. For this purpose, the cumulative inflation rate for the base period is based on compounded inflation rates. Thus, if for 1991, 1992, and 1993, a country's annual inflation rates are 29 percent, 25 percent, and 30 percent, respectively, the cumulative inflation rate for the three-year base period is 110 percent [((1.29 × 1.25 × 1.3) − 1.0 = 1.10) × 100 = 110%] and the currency of the country for the QBU's 1994 year is considered hyperinflationary. In making the determination whether a currency is hyperinflationary, the determination for purposes of United States generally

Reg. § 1.985-1(b)(2)(ii)(D)

accepted accounting principles may be used for income tax purposes provided the determination is based on criteria that is substantially similar to the rules previously set forth in this paragraph (b)(2)(ii)(D), the method of determination is applied consistently from year to year, and the same method is applied to all related persons as defined in § 1.985-3(e)(2)(vi).

(E) *Change in functional currency when currency ceases to be hyperinflationary.*—(1) *In general.*—A QBU that has been required to use the dollar as its functional currency under paragraph (b)(2) of this section, or has elected to use the dollar as its functional currency under paragraph (b)(2)(ii)(B)(2) of this section or § 1.985-2, must change its functional currency as of the first day of the first taxable year that follows three consecutive taxable years in which the currency of its economic environment, determined under paragraph (c)(2) of this section, is not a hyperinflationary currency. The functional currency of the QBU for such year shall be determined in accordance with paragraph (c) of this section. For purposes of § 1.985-4, the change is considered to be made with the consent of the Commissioner. See § 1.985-5 for adjustments that are required upon a change in functional currency.

(2) *Effective date.*—This paragraph (b)(2)(ii)(E) of this section applies to taxable years beginning after April 6, 1998.

(c) *Functional currency of a QBU that is not required to use the dollar.*—(1) *General rule.*—The functional currency of a QBU that is not required to use the dollar under paragraph (b) of this section shall be the currency of the economic environment in which a significant part of the QBU's activities is conducted, if the QBU keeps, or is presumed under paragraph (c)(3) of this section to keep, its books and records in such currency.

(2) *Economic environment.*—For purposes of section 985 and the regulations thereunder, the economic environment in which a significant part of a QBU's activities is conducted shall be determined by taking into account all the facts and circumstances.

(i) *Facts and circumstances.*—The facts and circumstances that are considered in determining the economic environment in which a significant part of a QBU's activities is conducted include, but are not limited to, the following:

(A) The currency of the country in which the QBU is a resident as determined under section 988 (a)(3)(B);

(B) The currencies of the QBU's cash flows;

(C) The currencies in which the QBU generates revenues and incurs expenses;

(D) The currencies in which the QBU borrows and lends;

(E) The currencies of the QBU's sales markets;

(F) The currencies in which pricing and other financial decisions are made;

(G) The duration of the QBU's business operations; and

(H) The significance and/or volume of the QBU's independent activities.

(ii) *Rate of inflation.*—The rate of inflation (regardless of how it is determined) shall not be a factor used to determine a QBU's economic environment.

(iii) *Consistency.*—A taxpayer must consistently apply the facts and circumstances test set forth in this paragraph (c)(2) in evaluating the economic environment of its QBUs, *e.g.,* its branches, that engage in the same or similar trades or businesses.

(3) *Books and records presumption.*—A QBU shall be presumed to keep books and records in the currency of the economic environment in which a significant part of its activities are conducted. The presumption may be overcome only if the QBU can demonstrate to the satisfaction of the district director that a substantial nontax purpose exists for not keeping any books and records in such currency. A taxpayer may not use this presumption affirmatively in determining a QBU's functional currency.

(4) *Multiple currencies.*—If a QBU has more than one currency that satisfies the requirements of paragraph (c)(1) of this section, the QBU may choose any such currency as its functional currency.

(5) *Relationship of United States accounting principles.*—In making the functional currency determination under this paragraph (c), the currency of the QBU for purposes of United States generally accepted accounting principles (GAAP) will ordinarily be accepted as the functional currency of the QBU for income tax purposes, provided that the GAAP determination is based on facts and circumstances substantially similar to those set forth in paragraph (c)(2) of this section.

(6) *Effect of changed circumstances.*—Regardless of any change in circumstances, a QBU may change its functional currency determined under this paragraph (c) only if the QBU complies with § 1.985-4 or the Commis-

sioner's consent is considered to have been granted under § 1.985-2(d)(4) or § 1.985-3(a)(2)(ii). For special rules relating to the conversion to the euro, see § 1.985-8.

(d) *Single functional currency for a foreign corporation.*—(1) *General rule.*—This paragraph (d) applies to a foreign corporation that has two or more QBUs that do not have the same functional currency. The foreign corporation shall be treated as having a single functional currency for the corporation as a whole that is different from the functional currency of one or more of its QBUs. The determination of a foreign corporation's functional currency shall be made by first applying paragraph (d) (1) (i) and then paragraph (d) (1) (ii) of this section.

(i) *Step 1.*—Each QBU of the foreign corporation determines its functional currency in accordance with the rules set forth in paragraphs (b) and (c) of this section and § 1.985-2.

(ii) *Step 2.*—The foreign corporation determines its functional currency applying the principles of paragraphs (b) and (c) of this section to the corporation's activities as a whole. Thus, if a foreign corporation has two branches, the corporation shall determine its functional currency by applying the principles of paragraphs (b) and (c) of this section to the combined activities of the corporation and the branches.

For purposes of this paragraph (d)(1), if a QBU of a foreign corporation has the dollar as its functional currency under paragraph (b)(2) of this section, the QBU's activities shall be considered dollar activities of the corporation.

(2) *Translation of income or loss of QBUs having different functional currencies than the foreign corporation as a whole.*—Where the functional currency of a foreign corporation as a whole differs from the functional currency of one or more of its QBUs, each such QBU shall determine the amount of its income or loss or earnings and profits (or deficit in earnings and profits) in its functional currency under the principles of section 987 (relating to branch transactions). The amount of income or loss or earnings and profits (or deficit in earnings and profits) of each QBU in its functional currency shall then be translated into the foreign corporation's functional currency using the appropriate exchange rate as defined in section 989 (b) (4) for purposes of determining the corporation's income or loss or earnings and profits (or deficit in earnings and profits).

(e) *Translation of nonfunctional currency transactions.*—Except for a QBU using the dollar approximate separate transactions method described in § 1.985-3, *see* section 988 and the regulations thereunder for the treatment of nonfunctional currency transactions.

(f) *Examples.*—The provisions of this section are illustrated by the following examples:

Example (1). P, a domestic corporation, operates exclusively through foreign branch X in Country A. X is a QBU within the meaning of section 989 (a) and its residence is Country A as determined under section 988 (a) (3) (B). The currency of Country A is the LC. All of X's purchases, sales, and expenses are in the LC. The laws of A require X to keep books and records in the LC. It is determined that the LC is the currency of X under United States generally accepted accounting principles. This determination is based on facts and circumstances substantially similar to those set forth in paragraph (c) (2) of this section. Under these facts, while the functional currency of P is the dollar since its residence is the United States, the functional currency of X is the LC.

Example (2). P, a publicly-held domestic regulated investment company (as defined under section 851), operates exclusively through foreign branch B in Country R. B is a QBU within the meaning of section 989 (a) and its residence is Country R as determined under section 988 (a) (3) (B). The currency of Country R is the LC. B's principal activities consist of purchasing and selling stock and securities of Country R companies and securities issued by Country R. It is determined that the dollar is the currency of B under United States generally accepted accounting principles. This determination is not based on facts and circumstances substantially similar to those set forth in paragraph (c) (2) of this section. Under these facts, while the functional currency of P is the dollar since its residence is the United States, B may choose the LC as its functional currency because it has significant activities in the LC provided it keeps books and records in the LC. The fact that the dollar is the currency of B under generally accepted accounting principles is irrelevant for purposes of determining B's functional currency because the GAAP determination was not based on factors similar to those set forth in paragraph (c) (2) of this section.

Example (3). P, a domestic bank, operates through foreign branch X in Country R. X is a QBU within the meaning of section 989 (a) and its residence is Country R as determined under section 988 (a) (3) (B). The currency of Country R is the LC. The laws of R require X to keep books and records in the LC. The branch customarily loans dollars and LCs. In the case of its LC loans, X ordinarily fixes the terms of the loans by reference to a contemporary London

Inter-Bank Offered Rate (LIBOR) on dollar deposits. For instance, the interest on the amount of the outstanding LC loan principal might equal LIBOR plus 2 percent and the amount of the outstanding LC loan principal would be adjusted to reflect changes in the dollar value of the LC. X is primarily funded with dollar-denominated funds borrowed from related and unrelated parties. X's only LC activities are paying local taxes, employee wages, and local expenses such as rent and electricity. Under these facts, X's activities are primarily conducted in dollars. Thus, although X keeps its books and records in LCs, X's functional currency is the dollar.

Example (4). S, a foreign corporation organized in Country U, is wholly-owned by P, a domestic corporation. The currency of Country U is the LC. S's sole function is acting as a financing vehicle for P and domestic corporations that are affiliated with P. All borrowing and lending transactions between S and P and its domestic affiliates are in dollars. Furthermore, primarily all of S's other borrowings are dollar-denominated or based on a dollar index. S's only LC activities are paying local taxes, employee wages, and local expenses such as rent and electricity. S keeps its books and records in the LC. Under these facts, S's activities are primarily conducted in dollars. Thus, although S keeps its books and records in LCs, S's functional currency is the dollar.

Example (5). D is a domestic corporation whose primary activity is the extraction of natural gas and oil through foreign branch X in Country Y. X is a QBU within the meaning of section 989 (a) and its residence is Country Y as determined under section 988 (a) (3) (B). The currency of Country Y is the LC. X bills a significant amount of its natural gas and oil sales in dollars and a significant amount in LCs. X also incurs significant LC and dollar expenses and liabilities. The laws of Country Y require X to keep its books and records in the LC. It is determined that the LC is the currency of X under United States generally accepted accounting principles. This determination is based on facts and circumstances substantially similar to those set forth in paragraph (c) (2) of this section. Absent other factors indicating that K primarily conducts its activities in the dollar, D could choose either the dollar or the LC as X's functional currency because X has significant activities in both the dollar and the LC, provided the books and records requirement is satisfied. If, instead, X's activities were determined to be primarily in the dollar, then X would have to use the dollar as its functional currency.

Example (6). S, a foreign corporation organized in Country U, is wholly-owned by P, a domestic corporation. The currency of U is the LC. S purchases the products it sells from related and unrelated parties, including P. These purchases are made in the LC. In addition, most of S's gross receipts are generated by transactions denominated in the LC. S attempts to determine its LC price for goods sold in such a manner as to obtain an LC equivalent of a certain dollar amount after reduction for all LC costs. However, local market conditions sometimes result in pricing adjustments. Thus, changes in the LC-dollar exchange rate from period to period generally result in corresponding changes in the LC price of S's products. S pays local taxes, employee wages, and other local expenses in the LC. It is determined that the dollar is the currency of S under United States generally accepted accounting principles. This determination is not based on facts and circumstances substantially similar to those set forth in paragraph (c) (2) of this section. Under these facts, S could choose either the dollar or the LC as its functional currency because S has significant activities in both the dollar and the LC, provided that the books and records requirement is satisfied.

Example (7). S, a foreign corporation organized in Country X, is wholly-owned by P, a domestic corporation. S conducts all of its operations through two branches. Branch A is located in Country F and branch B is located in Country G. S, A, and B are QBUs within the meaning of section 989 (a). Branch A's and branch B's residences are Country F and Country G respectively as determined under section 988 (a) (3) (B). The currency of Country F is the FC and the currency of Country G is the LC. The functional currencies of S, A, and B are determined in a two step procedure.

Step 1: The functional currency of branches A and B. Branch A and branch B both conduct all activities in their respective local currencies. The FC is the currency of branch A and the LC is the currency of branch B under United States generally accepted accounting principles. This determination is based on facts and circumstances substantially similar to those set forth in paragraph (c) (2) of this section. Under these facts, the functional currency of branch A is the FC and the functional currency of branch B is the LC.

Step 2: The functional currency of S. S's functional currency is determined by disregarding the fact that A and B are branches. When A's activities and B's activities are viewed as a whole, S determines that it only conducts significant activities in the LC. Therefore, S's functional currency is the LC. See Examples (9), (10), and (11) for how the earnings and profits of a foreign corporation, which has branches with different functional currencies, are determined.

Example (8). Assume the same facts as in Example (7), except that S does not exist and P conducts all of its operations through branch A and branch B. In this instance P's functional currency in Step 2 is the dollar, regardless of the fact that its branches' activities viewed as a whole are in the LC, because P is a taxpayer whose residence is the United States under section 988 (a) (3) (B) (i). Therefore, while the functional currency of branch A is the FC and the functional currency of branch B is the LC, the functional currency of P is the dollar because its residence is the United States.

Example (9). The facts are the same as in Example (7). In addition, assume that in 1987 branch A has earnings of 100 FC and branch B has earnings of 100 LC as determined under section 987. The weighted average exchange rate for the year is 1 FC/2 LC. Branch A's earnings are translated into 200 LC for purposes of computing S's earnings and profits in 1987. Thus, the total earnings and profits of S from branch A and branch B for 1987 is 300 LC.

Example (10). (i) X, a foreign corporation organized in Country W, is wholly-owned by P, a domestic corporation. Both X and P are calendar year taxpayers that began business during 1987. X operates exclusively through two branches, A and B both of which are located outside of Country W. The functional currency of X and A is the LC, while the functional currency of B is the DC as determined under section 985 and §1.985-1. The earnings of B must be computed under section 987, relating to branch transactions. In 1987, A earns 900 LCs of nonsubpart F income and B earns 200 DCs of nonsubpart F income. Under section 904 (d) (2), A's income is financial service income and B's income is general limitation income. In order to determine X's earnings and profits, B's income must be translated into LCs (the functional currency of X). The weighted average exchange rate for 1987 is 1 LC/2 DC. Thus, in 1987 X's current earnings and profits (and its post-1986 undistributed earnings) are 1000 LCs consisting of 900 LCs of financial services income earned by A and 100 LCs (200 DC/2) of general limitation income earned by B. Neither A nor B makes any remittances during 1987.

(ii) In 1988, neither A nor B earns any income or generates any loss. On December 31, 1988, A remits 50 LCs directly to P. The remittance to P is considered to be remitted by A to X and then immediately distributed by X as a dividend. The 50 LC remittance does not result in an exchange gain or loss under section 987 to X because the functional currency of X and A is the LC. See section 987 (3). Under section 904 (d) (3) (D), the 50 LC dividend is treated as income in a separate category to the extent of the dividend's pro rata share of X's earnings and profits in each separate limitation category. Thus, 90 percent, or 45 LCs, is treated as financial services income, and 10 percent, or 5 LCs, is treated as general limitation income. After the dividend distribution, X has 950 LCs of accumulated earnings and profits (and post-1986 undistributed earnings) consisting of 855 LCs of financial service limitation income and 95 LCs of general limitation income.

Example (11). The facts are the same as in Example (10), except that A makes no remittance during 1988 but B remits 120 DCs to X on December 31, 1988, which X immediately converts into LCs, and X makes no dividend distribution during 1988. Assume that the appropriate exchange rate for the remittance is 1 LC/3 DCs. B's remittance triggers exchange loss to X. See section 987 (3). Under section 987, the exchange loss on the remittance is 20 LCs calculated as follows: 40 LCs, which is the LC value of the 120 DC remittance (120 DCs/3), less 60 LCs, their LC basis (120 DCs/2). This loss is sourced and characterized under section 987 and regulations thereunder.

Example (12). F, a foreign corporation, has gain from the disposition of a United States real property interest (as defined in section 897 (c)). The gain is taken into account as if F were engaged in a trade or business within the United States during the taxable year and as if such gain were effectively connected with such trade or business. F's disposition activity shall be treated as a separate QBU with a dollar functional currency because such activity produced income that is treated as effectively connected with a trade or business within the United States. Therefore, F must compute its gain from the disposition by giving the United States real property interest an historic dollar basis. [Reg. § 1.985-1.]

☐ [*T.D.* 8263, 9-19-89. *Amended by T.D.* 8556, 7-22-94; *T.D.* 8765, 3-4-98 (*corrected* 3-31-98); *T.D.* 8776, 7-28-98 *and T.D.* 8927, 1-10-2001.]

§ 1.985-2. Election to use the United States dollar as the functional currency of a QBU.—(a) *Background and scope.*—(1) *In general.*—This section permits an eligible QBU to elect to use the dollar as its functional currency for taxable years beginning on or before August 24, 1994. An election to use a dollar functional currency is not permitted for a QBU other than an eligible QBU. Paragraph (b) of this section defines an eligible QBU. Paragraph (c) of this section describes the time and manner for making the dollar election and paragraph (d) of this section describes the effect of making the election. For the definition of a QBU, see section 989(a). See § 1.985-1(b) (2) (ii) for rules requiring a QBU to use the dollar as its functional currency in taxable years beginning after August 24, 1994.

(2) *Exception.*—Pursuant to § 1.985-1(b)(2)(ii)(B)(2), the rules of paragraph (c)(3) of this section shall apply with respect to the procedure required to be followed by a noncontrolled section 902 corporation as defined in section 904(d)(2)(E) to elect the dollar as its (or its QBU branch's) functional currency and the application of § 1.985-3.

(b) *Eligible QBU.*—(1) *In general.*—The term "eligible QBU" means a QBU that could have used a hyperinflationary currency as its functional currency absent the dollar election. See § 1.985-1 for how a QBU determines its functional currency absent the dollar election.

(2) *Hyperinflationary currency.*—See § 1.985-1(b)(2)(ii)(D) for the definition of hyperinflationary currency.

(c) *Time and manner for dollar election.*—(1) *QBUs that are branches of United States persons.*—(i) *Rule.*—If an eligible QBU is a branch of a United States person, the dollar election shall be made by attaching a completed Form 8819 to the United States person's timely filed (taking extensions into account) tax return for the first taxable year for which the election is to be effective.

(ii) *Procedure prior to the issuance of Form 8819.*—In the absence of Form 8819, the election shall be made in accordance with § 1.985-2T(c)(1). Failure to file an amended return within the time period prescribed in § 1.985-2T(c)(1) shall not invalidate the dollar election if it is established to the satisfaction of the district director that reasonable cause existed for such failure. A subsequent election for 1988 will not prejudice the taxpayer with respect to such reasonable cause determination. Nevertheless, each United States person making an election under the § 1.985-2T(c)(1) must file a Form 8819 in the time and manner provided in the Form's instructions.

(2) *Eligible QBUs that are controlled foreign corporations or branches of controlled foreign corporations.*—(i) *Rule.*—If an eligible QBU is a controlled foreign corporation (as described in section 957), or a branch of a controlled foreign corporation, the election may be made either by the foreign corporation or by the controlling United States shareholders on behalf of the foreign corporation by—

(A) Filing a completed Form 8819 in the time and manner provided in the Form's instructions, and

(B) Providing the written notice required by paragraph (c)(2)(ii) of this section at the time and in the manner prescribed therein.

The term "controlling United States shareholders" means those United States shareholders (as defined in section 951(b)) who, in the aggregate, own (within the meaning of section 958(a)) greater than 50 percent of the total combined voting power of all classes of stock of the foreign corporation entitled to vote. If the foreign corporation is a controlled foreign corporation (as described in section 957) but the United States shareholders do not, in the aggregate, own the requisite voting power, the term "controlling United States shareholders" means all the United States shareholders (as defined in section 951(b)) who own (within the meaning of section 958(a)) stock of the controlled foreign corporation.

(ii) *Notice.*—Prior to filing Form 8819, the controlling United States shareholders (or the foreign corporation, if the dollar election is made by the corporation) shall provide written notice that the dollar election will be made to all United States persons known to be shareholders who own (within the meaning of section 958(a)) stock of the foreign corporation. Such notice shall also include all information required in Form 8819.

(iii) *Reasonable cause exception.*—Failure of the controlling United States shareholders (or the foreign corporation, if the dollar election is made by the corporation) to timely file Form 8819 or provide written notice to a United States person required to be notified by paragraph (c)(2)(ii) of this section shall not invalidate the dollar election, if it is established to the satisfaction of the district director that reasonable cause existed for such failure.

(iv) *Procedure prior to the issuance of Form 8819.*—In the absence of Form 8819, an eligible QBU described in paragraph (c)(2)(i) of this section shall make the dollar election in accordance with § 1.985-2T(c)(2). Nevertheless, the person or persons that made such election must file a Form 8819 in the time and manner provided in the Form's instructions.

(3) *Eligible QBUs that are noncontrolled foreign corporations or branches of noncontrolled foreign corporations.*—(i) *Rule.*—If an eligible QBU is a noncontrolled foreign corporation (a foreign corporation not described in section 957), or a branch of a noncontrolled foreign corporation, the dollar election must be made by the corporation or the majority domestic corporate shareholders on behalf of the corporation by applying the rules provided in paragraph (c)(2)(i)(A) and (B), (ii), (iii), and (iv) of this section substituting "majority domestic corporate shareholders" for "controlling United States shareholders" wherever it appears therein. The term "majority domestic corporate shareholders" means those domestic corporate shareholders (as described in section 902(a))

who, in the aggregate, own (within the meaning of section 958(a) greater than 50 percent of the total combined voting stock of all classes of stock of the noncontrolled foreign corporation entitled to vote that is owned (within the meaning of section 958(a)) by all the domestic corporate shareholders.

(ii) *Procedure prior to the issuance of Form 8819.* In the absence of Form 8819, an eligible QBU described in paragraph (c)(3)(i) of this section shall make the dollar election in accordance with § 1.985-2T(c)(3). Nevertheless, the person or persons that made such election must file a Form 8819 in the time and manner provided in the Form's instructions.

(4) *Others.*—Any other person making a dollar election under this section shall elect by filing Form 8819 and fulfilling any other notice requirements that may be required by the Commissioner.

(d) *Effect of dollar election.*—(1) *General rule.*—If a dollar election is made (or considered made under paragraph (d)(3) of this section) by or on behalf of an eligible QBU, the QBU shall be deemed to have the dollar as its functional currency. Each United States person that owns (within the meaning of section 958(a)) stock of a foreign corporation which has the dollar as its functional currency under § 1.985-2 must make all of its federal income tax calculations with respect to the foreign corporation using the dollar as the corporation's functional currency (regardless of when ownership was acquired or whether the United States person received the written notice required by paragraph (c)(2)(i)(B) of this section).

(2) *Computation.*—(i) *In general.*—Except as provided in paragraph (d)(2)(ii) of this section, any eligible QBU that pursuant to this § 1.985-2 has a dollar functional currency must compute income or loss or earnings and profits (or deficit in earnings and profits) in dollars using the dollar approximate separate transactions method described in § 1.985-3.

(ii) *Alternative method.*—An eligible QBU that has a dollar functional currency pursuant to this § 1.985-2 may use a method other than the dollar approximate separate transactions method described in § 1.985-3 only if the QBU demonstrates to the satisfaction of the Commissioner that it can properly employ such method. Generally, the QBU must show that it could compute foreign currency gain or loss under the principles of section 988 with respect to each of its section 988 transactions. If subsequently the QBU can no longer demonstrate to the satisfaction of the district director that it can properly employ such an alternative method, then the QBU will be deemed to have changed its method of accounting to the dollar approximate separate transactions method described in § 1.985-3. This change in accounting will be treated as having been made with the consent of the Commissioner. No adjustments under either § 1.985-5T (or any succeeding final regulation) or section 481(a) shall be required solely because of the change. Rather the QBU shall begin accounting for its operations under § 1.985-3 based on its dollar books and records as of the time of the change.

(3) *Conformity.*—(i) *General rule.*—If a dollar election is made under this § 1.985-2 for an eligible QBU ("electing QBU"), then the dollar shall be the functional currency of any related person (regardless of when such person became related to the electing QBU) that is an eligible QBU, or any branch of any such related person that is an eligible QBU. For purposes of the preceding sentence, the term "related person" means any person with a relationship defined in section 267(b) to the electing QBU (or to the United States or foreign person of which the electing QBU is a part). In determining whether two or more corporations are members of the same controlled group under section 267(b)(3), a person is considered to own stock owned directly by such person, stock owned with the application of section 1563(e)(1), and stock owned with the application of section 267(c).

(ii) *Branches of United States and foreign persons.*—If a dollar election is made for a QBU branch of any person, each eligible QBU branch of such person shall have the dollar as its functional currency.

(4) *Required adjustments.*—If an eligible QBU's functional currency changes due to a dollar election, or due to the conformity requirements of paragraph (d)(3) of this section, such change shall be deemed for purposes of § 1.985-4 to be consented to by the Commissioner. No adjustments under section 481(a) shall be required solely because of the change. However, the QBU must make those adjustments required by § 1.985-5T (or any succeeding final regulation).

(5) *Taxable year conformity required.*— Generally, the adjustments required by paragraph (d)(4) of this section shall be made for a related person's taxable year—

(i) that includes the date in which the electing QBU made the dollar election if the person was related to such electing QBU at any time during the QBU's taxable year that includes such date, or

(ii) during which the person first becomes related to any electing QBU, in all other cases.

For purposes of this paragraph (d)(5), the date in which the electing QBU makes the dollar election shall be the last day of the electing QBU's taxable year. The district director may permit the related party to make such adjustments beginning one taxable year later if, in the district director's sole judgment, reasonable cause exists for the related party not being able to make the required adjustments for the earlier year.

(6) *Availability of election.*—A dollar election may be made by or on behalf of a QBU, or considered made under the conformity rule of paragraph (d)(3), in any year in which the QBU is an eligible QBU. If a dollar election is not made by or on behalf of a QBU for its first taxable year beginning after December 31, 1986 in which it is an eligible QBU, then any dollar election made by or on behalf of the QBU, or considered made under the conformity rules of paragraph (d)(3) of this section, that results in a change in the QBU's functional currency shall be treated as having been made with the consent of the Commissioner. In such a case, however, the taxpayer must make those adjustments required by § 1.985-5T (or any succeeding final regulation).

(7) *Effect of changed circumstances.*—Regardless of any change in circumstances (e.g., a currency ceases to qualify as hyperinflationary), a QBU whose functional currency is the dollar under this section may change its functional currency only if the QBU complies with § 1.985-4.

(8) *Examples.*—The provisions of this section are illustrated by the following examples.

Example (1). X is a calendar year domestic corporation that in 1987 establishes a branch, A, in Country Z. A's functional currency under section 985(b)(1) and and § 1.985-1 is the "h", the currency of Country Z. The cumulative inflation in Country Z exceeds 100 percent for the thirty-six months prior to January 1987, as measured by the consumer price index of Country Z listed in the monthly issues of the "International Financial Statistics". Accordingly, A is an eligible QBU in 1987 because the h is a hyperinflationary currency. Thus, X may elect the dollar as the functional currency of A for 1987.

Example (2). The facts are the same as in Example (1). X does not elect the dollar as the functional currency of A for 1987. Rather, X elects the dollar as the functional currency of A for 1991, a year A is an eligible QBU. The election constitutes a change in A's functional currency that is made with the consent of the Commissioner. However, A must make the adjustments required under § 1.985-5T (or any succeeding final regulation).

Example (3). X is a domestic corporation that establishes A, an eligible QBU branch. X is wholly owned by domestic corporation Y. Y has an eligible QBU branch, B. Both X and Y are calendar year taxpayers. X makes a dollar election for A in 1987. Thus, A is an electing QBU. X and Y are related persons as defined in section 267(b) (*i.e.,* Y has a relationship under section 267(b)(3) to X, the corporation of which A is a part). Therefore, the dollar election by X for A in 1987 results in B, the eligible QBU branch of Y, also having the dollar as its functional currency for 1987.

Example (4). The facts are the same as in Example (3), except that Y does not have an eligible QBU branch but owns all the stock of C, a calendar year controlled foreign corporation, which is not itself an eligible QBU but which has an eligible QBU branch, D. X and C are related persons as defined in section 267(b) (*i.e.,* C has a relationship under section 267(b)(3) to X, the corporation of which A is a part). Therefore, the dollar election by X for A in 1987 results in D, the eligible QBU branch of C, also having the dollar as its functional currency for 1987.

Example (5). X, whose taxable year ends September 30, is an eligible QBU that does not use the dollar as its functional currency. X is wholly-owned by domestic corporation W. On January 1, 1989, X acquires all the stock of Y, an unrelated eligible QBU that made the dollar election under § 1.985-2. Y is a calendar year taxpayer. After the stock purchase, X and Y are related persons as defined in section 267(b). Under § 1.985-2(d)(3) and (5), the dollar shall be the functional currency of X, any person related to X, and any branch of such related person that is an eligible QBU beginning with the taxable year that includes December 31, 1989. Thus, X must change to the dollar for its taxable year beginning October 1, 1988. However, the district director may allow X to change to the dollar for its taxable year beginning October 1, 1989, provided reasonable cause exists. Those QBUs changing to the dollar as their functional currency as the result of the conformity requirements must make the adjustments required under § 1.985-5T (or any succeeding final regulation).

Example (6). The facts are the same as in Example (5), except that before X purchased the Y stock, X made the dollar election under § 1.985-2 but Y did not use the dollar as its functional currency. Under § 1.985-2(d)(3) and (5) the dollar shall be the functional currency of Y, any person related to Y, and any branch of such related person that is an eligible QBU beginning with the taxable year that includes September 30, 1989. Thus, Y must change to the dollar for its taxable year beginning January 1, 1989. However the district director may allow Y to change to the dollar for its taxable year beginning January 1, 1990, provided reasonable cause exists. Those QBUs changing to the dollar as their functional currency as the result of the conformity requirements must make the adjustments required under § 1.985-5T (or any succeeding final regulation). [Reg. § 1.985-2.]

☐ [T.D. 8263, 9-19-89. Amended by T.D. 8556, 7-22-94.]

§ 1.985-3. United States dollar approximate separate transactions method.— (a) *Scope and effective date.—*(1) *Scope.—*This section describes the United States dollar (dollar) approximate separate transactions method of accounting (DASTM). For all purposes of subtitle A, this method of accounting must be used to compute the gross income, taxable income or loss, or earnings and profits (or deficit in earnings and profits) of a QBU (as defined in section 989(a)) that has the dollar as its functional currency pursuant to § 1.985-1(b)(2).

(2) *Effective date.—*(i) *In general.—*This section is effective for taxable years beginning after August 24, 1994.

(ii) *DASTM prior-year election.—*A taxpayer may elect to apply this section to any open taxable year beginning after December 31, 1986 (whether or not DASTM has been previously elected for some or all of those years). In order to make this election, the taxpayer must apply § 1.985-3 to that year and all subsequent years. In addition, each person that is related (within the meaning of § 1.985-3(e)(2)(vi)) to the taxpayer on the last day of any taxable year for which the election is effective and that would have been eligible to elect DASTM must also apply these rules to that year and all subsequent years. A taxpayer that has not previously elected to apply DASTM to its prior taxable years may make the DASTM election for the pertinent years by filing amended returns and complying with the applicable election procedures of § 1.985-2. Form 8819 shall be attached to the return for the first year for which the election is to be effective. A taxpayer that has elected DASTM for prior taxable years and applied the rules under § 1.985-3 (as contained in the April 1, 1994 edition of 26 CFR part 1 (1.908 to 1.1000)) may amend its returns to apply the rules of this § 1.985-3. In either case, the DASTM election for prior taxable years shall be deemed to be made with the consent of the Commissioner.

(b) *Statement of method.—*Under DASTM, income or loss or earnings and profits (or a deficit in earnings and profits) of a QBU for its taxable year shall be determined in dollars by—

(1) Preparing an income or loss statement from the QBU's books and records (within the meaning of § 1.989(a)-1(d)) as recorded in the QBU's hyperinflationary currency (as defined in § 1.985-1(b)(2)(ii)(D));

(2) Making the adjustments necessary to conform such statement to United States generally accepted accounting principles and tax accounting principles (including reversing monetary correction adjustments required by local accounting principles);

(3) Translating the amounts of hyperinflationary currency as shown on such adjusted statement into dollars in accordance with paragraph (c) of this section; and

(4) Adjusting the resulting dollar income or loss or earnings and profits (or deficit in earnings and profits) and, where necessary, particular items of gross income, deductible expense or other amounts, in accordance with paragraph (e) of this section to reflect the amount of DASTM gain or loss as determined under paragraph (d) of this section.

(c) *Translation into United States dollars.—*(1) *In general.—*Except as otherwise provided in this paragraph (c), the amounts shown on the income or loss statement, as adjusted under paragraph (b)(2) of this section, shall be translated into dollars at the exchange rate (as defined in paragraph (c)(6) of this section) for the translation period (as defined in paragraph (c)(7) of this section) to which they relate. However, if the QBU previously changed its functional currency to the dollar, and the rules of § 1.985-5 (or, if applicable, § 1.985-5T, as contained in the April 1, 1993 edition of 26 CFR part 1 (1.908 to 1.1000)) applied in translating its balance sheet amounts into dollars, then the spot exchange rate applied under those rules shall be used to translate any amount that would otherwise be translated at a rate determined by reference to a translation period prior to the change in functional currency. For example, depreciation with respect to an asset acquired while the QBU had a nondollar functional currency shall be translated into dollars at the spot rate on the last day of the taxable year before the year of change to a dollar functional currency, rather than at the rate for the period in which the asset was acquired.

(2) *Cost of goods sold.—*The dollar value of cost of goods sold shall equal the sum of the dollar values of beginning inventory and purchases less the dollar value of closing inventory as these amounts are determined under paragraph (c)(3) of this section.

(3) *Beginning inventory, purchases, and closing inventory.*—(i) *Beginning inventory.*—Amounts representing beginning inventory shall be translated so as to obtain the same amount of dollars which represented such items in the closing inventory balance for the preceding taxable year.

(ii) *Purchases.*—Amounts representing items purchased or otherwise first included in inventory during the taxable year shall be translated at the exchange rate for the translation period in which the cost of such items was incurred.

(iii) *Closing inventory.*—(A) *In general.*—Amounts representing items included in the closing inventory balance shall be translated at the exchange rate for the translation period in which the cost of such items was incurred. However, if amounts representing items included in the closing inventory balance are either valued at market or written down to market value, they shall be translated at the exchange rate existing on the last day of the taxable year. For purposes of determining lower of cost or market, items of inventory included in the closing inventory balance shall be translated into dollars at the exchange rate for the translation period in which the cost of such items was incurred and compared with market as determined in the QBU's hyperinflationary currency translated into dollars at the exchange rate existing on the last day of the taxable year.

(B) *Determination of translation period.*—The method used to determine the translation period of amounts representing items of closing inventory for purposes of paragraph (c)(3)(iii)(A) of this section may be based upon reasonable approximations and averages, including rates of turnover, provided that the method is used consistently from year to year.

(4) *Depreciation, depletion, and amortization.*—Amounts representing allowances for depreciation, depletion, or amortization shall be translated at the exchange rate for the translation period in which the cost of the underlying asset was incurred, except as provided in paragraph (c)(1) of this section.

(5) *Prepaid expenses or income.*—Amounts representing expense or income paid or received in a prior taxable year shall be translated at the exchange rate for the translation period during which they were paid or received.

(6) *Exchange rate.*—The exchange rate for a translation period may be determined under any reasonable method, provided that the method is consistently applied to all translation periods and conforms to the taxpayer's method of financial accounting. Reasonable methods include the average of beginning and ending exchange rates for the translation period and the spot rate on the last day of the translation period. Once chosen, a method for determining an exchange rate can be changed only with the consent of the district director.

(7) *Translation period.*—(i) *In general.*—Except as provided in paragraphs (c)(3)(iii)(B) and (c)(7)(ii) of this section, a translation period shall be each month within a QBU's taxable year.

(ii) *Exception.*—A taxpayer may divide its taxable year into translation periods of equal length (with not more than one short period annually) that are less than one month. Once such a translation period is established, it may not be changed without the consent of the district director.

(8) *Dollar transactions.*—(i) *In general.*—Except as provided in paragraph (c)(8)(ii) of this section, no DASTM gain or loss is realized with respect to dollar transactions since the dollar is the functional currency of the QBU. Thus, the amount of any payment or receipt of dollars shall be reflected in the income or loss statement by the amount of such dollars. Also, the income or loss attributable to any transaction in which the amount that a QBU is entitled to receive (or is required to pay) by reason of such transaction is denominated in terms of the dollar, or is determined by reference to the value of the dollar, must be computed transaction by transaction. For example, if a foreign corporation lends 20 LC when 20 LC = $20 and is entitled to receive the LC equivalent of $20 at maturity plus a market rate of interest in dollars (or its LC equivalent), the loan is a dollar transaction. Similarly, this paragraph applies to any transaction that is determined to be a dollar transaction under section 988.

(ii) *Non-dollar functional currency.*—If pursuant to § 1.985-1(b)(2)(ii)(B)(*1*), a QBU is required to use a functional currency other than the dollar, then that currency shall be substituted for the dollar in applying paragraph (c)(8)(i) of this section.

(9) *Third currency transactions.*—A taxpayer may use any reasonable method of accounting for transactions described in section 988(c)(1)(B) and (C) that are denominated in, or determined by reference to, a currency other than the QBU's hyperinflationary currency or the dollar (third currency transactions) so long as such method is consistent with its method of financial accounting.

(10) *Examples.*—The provisions of this paragraph (c) are illustrated by the following examples:

Example 1. S is an accrual basis QBU that is required to use the dollar as its functional currency for its first taxable year beginning in 1994. S's hyperinflationary currency is the "h." During 1994, S accrues 100 dollars attributable to dollar-denominated sales. Because this is a dollar transaction under paragraph (c)(8) of this section, S's income or loss for 1994 shall reflect the 100 dollars (not the hyperinflationary value of such dollars when accrued).

Example 2. (i) S is an accrual basis QBU that is required to use the dollar as its functional currency for its first taxable year beginning in 1994. S's hyperinflationary currency is the "h." During 1994, S's sales amounted to 240,000,000h, its currently deductible expenses were 26,000,000h, and its total inventory purchases amounted to 100,000,000h. During January and February of 1994, S purchased depreciable assets for 80,000,000h and was allowed depreciation of 4,000,000h. At the end of 1994, S's closing inventory was 23,000,000h. No election to use a translation period other than the month is made, S had no transactions described in paragraph (c)(8) or (c)(9) of this section, and S's closing inventory was computed on the first-in, first-out inventory method. S's adjusted income or loss statement for 1994 is translated into dollars as follows:

	Hyperinflationary Currency	Exchange Rate	United States Dollars
Sales			
(Jan-Feb)	10,000,000 h	20:1 [1]	$500,000
(Mar-Apr)	20,000,000	21:1	952,381
(May-June)	50,000,000	22:1	2,272,727
(July)	50,000,000	23:1	2,173,913
(August)	20,000,000	26:1	769,231
(Sept.)	20,000,000	28:1	714,286
(Oct.)	20,000,000	29:1	689,655
(Nov.)	20,000,000	30:1	666,667
(Dec.)	30,000,000	31:1	967,742
Total	240,000,000 h		$9,706,602
Cost of Goods Sold:			
Opening Inventory	-0-		-0-
Purchases:			
(Jan-Feb)	15,000,000 h	20:1	$750,000
(Mar-Apr)	10,000,000	21:1	476,190
(May-June)	30,000,000	22:1	1,363,636
(July)	20,000,000	23:1	869,565
(August)	10,000,000	26:1	384,615
(Sept.)	5,000,000	28:1	178,571
(Oct.)	5,000,000	29:1	172,414
(Nov.)	2,500,000	30:1	83,333
(Dec.)	2,500,000	31:1	80,645
Less Closing Inventory	(23,000,000)	[2]	(822,655)
	77,000,000 h		$3,536,314

[1] Where multiple months are indicated, the exchange rate applies for all months.
[2] See paragraph (ii) for this *Example*.

(ii) Since S uses the first-in, first-out inventory method, the closing inventory is assumed to consist of purchases made during the most recent translation period as follows:

	Hyperinflationary Currency	Exchange Rate	United States Dollars
December	2,500,000 h	31:1	$80,645
November	2,500,000	30:1	83,333
October	5,000,000	29:1	172,414
September	5,000,000	28:1	178,571
August	8,000,000	26:1	307,692
Total	23,000,000 h		$822,655

	Hyperinflationary Currency	Exchange Rate	United States Dollars
Non-Capitalized Expenses:			
(Jan-Feb)	4,000,000 h	20:1	$200,000
(Mar-Apr)	2,500,000	21:1	119,048
(May-June)	2,500,000	22:1	113,636
(July)	2,000,000	23:1	86,957
(August)	3,000,000	26:1	115,385
(Sept.)	3,000,000	28:1	107,143
(Oct.)	2,000,000	29:1	68,966
(Nov.)	3,000,000	30:1	100,000
(Dec.)	4,000,000	31:1	129,032
Total	26,000,000 h		$1,040,167
Depreciation	4,000,000 h	20:1	$200,000
Total Cost & Expenses	107,000,000 h		$4,776,481
Operating Profit	133,000,000 h		$4,930,121

(d) *Computation of DASTM gain or loss.*—(1) *Rule.*—DASTM gain or loss of a QBU equals—

(i) The net worth of the QBU (as determined under paragraph (d)(2) of this section) at the end of the taxable year minus the net worth of the QBU at the end of the preceding taxable year; plus

(ii) The dollar amount of the items described in paragraph (d)(3) of this section and minus the dollar amount of the items described in paragraph (d)(4) of this section; minus

(iii) The amount of dollar income or earnings and profits (or plus the amount of any dollar loss or deficit in earnings and profits) as determined for the taxable year pursuant to paragraphs (b)(1) through (b)(3) of this section.

(2) *Net worth.*—Net worth of a QBU at the end of any taxable year equals the aggregate dollar amount representing assets on the QBU's balance sheet at the end of the taxable year less the aggregate dollar amount representing liabilities on the balance sheet. Notwithstanding any other provision in this paragraph (d)(2), the district director may adjust the amount of any asset or liability if a purpose for acquiring (or disposing of) the asset or incurring (or discharging) the liability is to manipulate the composition of the balance sheet for any period during the taxable year in order to avoid tax. The taxpayer shall determine net worth by—

(i) Preparing a balance sheet as of the end of the taxable year from the QBU's books and records (within the meaning of § 1.989(a)-1(d)) as recorded in the QBU's hyperinflationary currency;

(ii) Making adjustments necessary to conform such balance sheet to United States generally accepted accounting principles and tax accounting principles (including reversing monetary correction adjustments required by local accounting principles); and

(iii) Translating the asset and liability amounts shown on the balance sheet into United States dollars in accordance with paragraph (d)(5) of this section.

(3) *Positive adjustments.*—The items described in this paragraph (d)(3) are dividend distributions for the taxable year and any items that decrease net worth for the taxable year but that generally do not affect income or loss or earnings and profits (or a deficit in earnings and profits). Such items include a transfer to the home office of a QBU branch and a return of capital. Except as otherwise provided by ruling or administrative pronouncement, the amount of a transfer to the home office of a QBU branch, a dividend, or a distribution that is a return of capital shall be translated into dollars at the exchange rate on the date the amount is paid.

(4) *Negative adjustments.*—The items described in this paragraph (d)(4) are items that increase net worth for the taxable year but that generally do not affect income or loss or earnings and profits (or a deficit in earnings and profits). Such items include a capital contribution or a transfer from a home office to a QBU branch. Except as otherwise provided by ruling or administrative pronouncement, if the contribution or transfer is not in dollars, the amount of a capital contribution or transfer shall be translated into dollars at the exchange rate on the date made.

(5) *Translation of balance sheet.*—Asset and liability amounts shown on the balance sheet in hyperinflationary currency (adjusted pursuant to paragraph (d)(2)(ii) of this section) shall be translated into dollars as provided in this paragraph (d)(5). However, if the QBU previously changed its functional currency to the dollar and the rules of § 1.985-5 (or, if appli-

cable, § 1.985-5T, as contained in the April 1, 1993 edition of 26 CFR part 1 (1.908 to 1.1000)) applied in translating its balance sheet amounts into dollars, then the spot exchange rate applied under those rules shall be used to translate any amount that would otherwise be translated at a rate determined by reference to a translation period prior to the change in functional currency. For example, the basis of real property acquired while the QBU had a nondollar functional currency shall be translated into dollars at the spot rate on the last day of the taxable year before the year of change to a dollar functional currency, rather than at the rate for the period in which the cost was incurred.

(i) *Closing inventory.*—Amounts representing items of inventory included in the closing inventory balance shall be translated in accordance with paragraph (c)(3)(iii) of this section.

(ii) *Bad debt reserves.*—Amounts representing bad debt reserves shall be translated at the exchange rate for the last translation period for the taxable year.

(iii) *Prepaid income or expense.*—Amounts representing expenses or income paid or received in a prior taxable year shall be translated in accordance with paragraph (c)(5) of this section.

(iv) *Hyperinflationary currency.*—Amounts of the hyperinflationary currency and hyperinflationary demand deposit balances shall be translated at the exchange rate for the last translation period of the taxable year.

(v) *Certain assets.*—(A) *In general.*—Amounts representing plant, real property, equipment, goodwill, and patents and other intangibles shall be translated at the exchange rate for the translation period in which the cost of the asset was incurred.

(B) *Adjustment to certain assets.*—Amounts representing depreciation, depletion, and amortization reserves shall be translated in accordance with paragraph (c)(4) of this section.

(vi) *Hyperinflationary debt obligations.*—Except as provided in paragraph (d)(5)(vii) of this section, amounts representing a hyperinflationary debt obligation (including accounts receivable and payable) shall be translated at the exchange rate for the last translation period for the taxable year.

(vii) *Accrued foreign income taxes.*—Amounts representing an accrued but unpaid foreign income tax shall be translated at the exchange rate on the last day of the last translation period of the taxable year of accrual.

(viii) *Certain hyperinflationary financial instruments.*—Amounts representing any item described in section 988(c)(1)(B)(iii) (relating to forward contracts, futures contracts, options, or similar financial instruments) denominated in or determined by reference to the hyperinflationary currency shall be translated at the exchange rate for the last translation period for the taxable year.

(ix) *Other assets and liabilities.*—Amounts representing assets and liabilities, other than those described in paragraphs (d)(5)(i) through (viii) of this section, shall be translated at the exchange rate for the translation period in which the cost of the asset or the amount of the liability was incurred.

(6) *Dollar transactions.*—Notwithstanding any other provisions of this paragraph (d), where the amount representing an item shown on the balance sheet reflects a dollar transaction (described in paragraph (c)(8) of this section), the transaction shall be taken into account in accordance with that paragraph.

(7) *Third currency transactions.*—A taxpayer may use any reasonable method of accounting for transactions described in section 988(c)(1)(B) and (C) that are denominated in, or determined by reference to, a currency other than the QBU's hyperinflationary currency or the dollar (third currency transactions), so long as such method is consistent with its method of financial accounting.

(8) *Character.*—The amount of DASTM gain or loss determined under paragraph (d)(1) of this section shall be ordinary income or loss.

(9) *Example.*—The provisions of this paragraph (d) are illustrated by the following example:

Example. (i) S, an accrual method calendar year foreign corporation, uses DASTM. S's hyperinflationary currency is the "h." S's net worth at December 31, 1993 was $3,246,495. For 1994, S's operating profit is 81,340,000h, or $2,038,200. S made a 5,000,000h distribution in April and again in December of 1994. S's translation period is the month. None of S's assets or liabilities reflect a dollar or third currency transaction described in paragraph (c)(8) or (c)(9) of this section, respectively. The exchange rate for each month in 1994 is as follows:

January	32h:$1	Nov.	39:1
Feb.-Mar.	33:1	Dec.	40:1
April-May	34:1		
June	35:1		
July	36:1		
Aug.-Sept.	37:1		
Oct.	38:1		

(ii) At the end of 1994, S's assets and liabilities, as adjusted and translated pursuant to paragraphs (d)(2) and (d)(5) of this section, are as follows:

	Hyper-inflationary	Exchange Rate	U.S.-Dollar
Hyperinflationary cash on hand	40,000 h	40:1	$1,000
Checking account	400,000	40:1	10,000
Accounts Receivable- 30 Day Accounts	20,000,000	40:1 [1]	500,000
60 Day Accounts	25,000,000	40:1	625,000
Inventory	65,000,000	[2]	2,500,000
Fixed assets—Property	90,000,000	27:1	3,333,333
Plant	190,000,000	[3]	6,785,714
Accumulated Depreciation	(600,000)	[3]	(21,428)
Equipment	10,000,000	[4]	340,000
Accumulated Depreciation	(400,000)	[4]	(13,333)
Common Stock—Stock A	500,000	34:1	14,706
Stock B	400,000	26:1	15,385
Preferred Stock	1,000,000	32:1	31,250
C.D.s	5,000,000	40:1	125,000
Total Assets	406,340,000		14,246,627
Accounts Payable	35,000,000	40:1	875,000
Long-term liabilities:			
Liability A	150,000,000	40:1	3,750,000
Liability B	80,000,000	40:1	2,000,000
Liability C	30,000,000	40:1	750,000
Total Liabilities	295,000,000 h		$7,375,000

[1] S ages its accounts receivable and groups them into two categories - those outstanding for 30 days and those outstanding for 60 days.
[2] Translated the same as closing inventory under paragraph (c)(3)(iii).
[3] The cost of S's plant was incurred in several translation periods. Therefore, the dollar cost and dollar depreciation reflect several translation rates.
[4] S has a variety of equipment.

(iii) The DASTM gain of S for 1994 is computed as follows:

Net worth — 1994	. . . .	$6,871,627
Less — Net worth — 1993	. . . .	$3,246,495
Plus — 1994 Dividends:		
April	$149,254	
December	126,582 [1]	275,836
Less Operating Profit — 1994	. . . .	2,038,200
DASTM Gain	. . . .	$1,862,768

[1] The exchange rates on the date of the April and December dividends were 33.5h:$1 and 39.5h:$1, respectively.

Reg. § 1.985-3(d)(9)

(iv) Thus, total profit = $2,038,200 + $1,862,768 = *$3,900,968*.

(e) *Effect of DASTM gain or loss on gross income, taxable income, or earnings and profits.*—(1) *In general.*—For all purposes of subtitle A, the amount of DASTM gain or loss of a QBU determined under paragraph (d) of this section is taken into account by the QBU for purposes of determining the amount of its gross income, taxable income or loss, earnings and profits (or deficit in earnings and profits), and, where necessary, particular items of income, expense or other amounts. DASTM gain or loss is allocated under one of two methods. Certain small QBUs may elect the small QBU DASTM allocation described in paragraph (e)(2) of this section. All other QBUs must use the 9-step procedure described in paragraph (e)(3) of this section.

(2) *Small QBU DASTM allocation.*—(i) *Election threshold.*—A taxpayer may elect to use the small QBU DASTM allocation described in paragraph (e)(2)(iv) of this section with respect to a QBU that has an adjusted basis in assets (translated as provided in paragraph (d)(5) of this section) of $10 million or less at the end of any taxable year. In calculating the $10 million threshold, a QBU shall be treated as owning all of the assets of each related QBU (as defined in paragraph (e)(2)(vi) of this section) having its residence (as defined in section 988(a)(3)(B)) in the QBU's country of residence (related same-country QBU). For this purpose, appropriate adjustment shall be made to eliminate the double counting of assets created in transactions between related QBUs resident in the same country. For example, assume QBU-1, resident in country X, sells inventory to related QBU-2, also resident in country X, in exchange for an account receivable. For purposes of determining the assets of QBU-1 under this paragraph (e)(2)(i), the taxpayer shall take into account either the inventory shown on the books of QBU-2 or QBU-1's receivable from QBU-2 (but not both).

(ii) *Consent to election.*—The election of the small QBU DASTM allocation or subsequent application of the rules of paragraph (e)(3) of this section due to an increase in the adjusted basis of the QBU's assets shall be deemed to have been made with the consent of the Commissioner. Once the election under paragraph (e)(2)(iii) of this section is made, it shall apply for all years in which the adjusted basis of the assets of the QBU (and any related same-country QBU) is $10 million or less, unless revoked with the Commissioner's consent. If the adjusted basis of the assets of the QBU (and any related same-country QBU) exceeds $10 million at the end of any taxable year, the rules of paragraph (e)(3) of this section shall apply to that QBU (and any related same-country QBU) for such year and each subsequent year unless such QBU again qualifies, and applies for and obtains the Commissioner's consent, to use the small QBU DASTM allocation. However, if a QBU acquires assets with a principal purpose of avoiding the application of paragraph (e)(2)(iv) of this section, the Commissioner may disregard the acquisition of such assets.

(iii) *Manner of making election.*—(A) *QBUs that are branches of United States persons.*—For the first year in which this election is effective, in the case of a QBU branch of a United States person, a statement shall be attached to the United States person's timely filed Federal income tax return (taking extensions into account). The statement shall identify the QBU (or QBUs) for which the election is being made by describing its business and its country of residence, state the adjusted basis of the assets of the QBU (and any related same-country QBUs) to which the election applies, and include a statement that the election is being made pursuant to § 1.985-3(e)(2).

(B) *Other QBUs.*—In the case of a QBU other than one described in paragraph (e)(2)(iii)(A) of this section, an election must be made in the manner prescribed in § 1.964-1. The statement filed with the Internal Revenue Service as required under § 1.964-1 must include the information required under paragraph (e)(2)(iii)(A) of this section.

(iv) *Effect of election.*—If a taxpayer elects under this paragraph (e)(2) to use the small QBU DASTM allocation, DASTM gain or loss, as determined under paragraph (d) of this section, of a small QBU shall be allocated ratably to all items of the QBU's gross income (determined prior to adjustment for DASTM gain or loss). Therefore, for purposes of the foreign tax credit, DASTM gain or loss shall be allocated on the basis of the relative amounts of gross income in each separate category as defined in § 1.904-5(a)(1). In the case of a controlled foreign corporation (within the meaning of section 957 or 953(c)(1)(B)), for purposes of section 952, DASTM gain or loss shall be allocated to subpart F income in a separate category in the same ratio that the gross subpart F income in that category for the taxable year bears to its total gross income in that category for the taxable year.

(v) *Conformity.*—If a person (or a QBU of such person) makes an election under this paragraph (e)(2) to use the small QBU DASTM allocation, then each QBU of any related person (as defined in paragraph (e)(2)(vi) of this section) that satisfies the threshold requirement of paragraph (e)(2)(i) of this section (after application of the aggregation rule of paragraph (e)(2)(i) of this section) shall be deemed to have made the election.

(vi) *Related person.*—The term related person means any person with a relationship to the QBU (or to the United States or foreign person of which the electing QBU is a part) that is defined in section 267(b) or section 707(b).

(3) *DASTM 9-step procedure.*—(i) *Step 1—prepare balance sheets.*—The taxpayer shall prepare an opening and a closing balance sheet for the QBU for each balance sheet period during the taxable year. The balance sheet period is the most frequent period for which balance sheet data are reasonably available (but in no event less frequently than quarterly). The balance sheet period may not be changed without the consent of the district director. The balance sheets must be prepared under the principles of paragraph (d)(2) of this section.

(ii) *Step 2—identify certain assets and liabilities.*—The taxpayer shall identify each item on the balance sheet that is described in section 988(c)(1)(B) or (C) and that would have been translated under paragraph (d)(5) of this section into dollars at the exchange rate for the last translation period for the taxable year (or the exchange rate on the last day of the last translation period of the taxable year in the case of an accrued foreign income tax liability).

(iii) *Step 3—characterize the assets.*—The taxpayer shall characterize and group the assets identified in paragraph (e)(3)(ii) of this section (Step 2) according to the source and the type of income that they generate, have generated, or may reasonably be expected to generate by applying the principles of § 1.861-9T(g)(3) or its successor regulation (relating to characterization of assets for purposes of interest expense allocation). If a purpose for a taxpayer's business practices is to manipulate asset characterization or groupings, the district director may allocate or apportion DASTM gain or loss attributable to the assets. Thus, if a taxpayer that previously did not separately state interest on accounts receivable begins to impose an interest charge and a purpose for the change was to manipulate tax characterizations or groupings, then the district director may require that none of the DASTM gain or loss attributable to those receivables be allocated or apportioned to interest income.

(iv) *Step 4—determine DASTM gain or loss attributable to certain assets.*—(A) *General rule.*—The taxpayer shall determine the dollar amount of DASTM gain or loss attributable to assets in each group identified in paragraph (e)(3)(iii) of this section (Step 3) as follows:

$$[(bb + eb) \div 2] \times [er - br]$$

where

bb = the hyperinflationary currency adjusted basis of the assets in the group at the beginning of the balance sheet period.

eb = the hyperinflationary currency adjusted basis of the assets in the group at the end of the balance sheet period.

er = one dollar divided by the number of hyperinflationary currency units that equal one dollar at the end of the balance sheet period.

br = one dollar divided by the number of hyperinflationary currency units that equal one dollar at the beginning of the balance sheet period.

(B) *Weighting to prevent distortion.*—If averaging the adjusted basis of assets in a group at the beginning and end of a balance sheet period results in an allocation of DASTM gain or loss that does not clearly reflect income, as might be the case in the event of a purchase or disposition of an asset that is not in the normal course of business, the taxpayer must use a weighting method that reflects the time the assets are held by the QBU during the translation period.

(C) *Example.*—The provisions of this paragraph (e)(3)(iv) are illustrated by the following example:

Example. S is a foreign corporation that operates in the hyperinflationary currency "h" and computes its income or loss or earnings and profits under DASTM. S's adjusted basis in a group of assets described in section 988(c)(1)(B) or (C) that generate general limitation foreign source income (as characterized under paragraph (e)(3)(iii) of this section) at the beginning of the balance sheet period is 750,000h. S's basis in such assets at the end of the balance sheet period is 1,250,000h. The exchange rate at the beginning of the balance sheet period is $1 = 200h. The exchange rate at the end of the balance sheet period is $1 = 500h. The DASTM loss attributable to the assets described above is $3,000, determined as follows:

$$[(750{,}000h + 1{,}250{,}000h) \div 2] \times [(\$1 \div 500h) - (\$1 \div 200h)] = (\$3000)$$

(v) *Step 5—adjust dollar gross income by DASTM gain or loss from assets.*—The taxpayer shall adjust the dollar amount of the QBU's gross income (computed under paragraphs (b)(1) through (b)(3) of this section) generated by each group of assets characterized in paragraph (e)(3)(iii) of this section (Step 3) by the amount of DASTM gain or loss attributable to those assets computed under paragraph (e)(3)(iv) of this section (Step 4). Thus, if a group of assets, such as accounts receivable, generates both a category of income described in section 904(d)(1)(I) (relating to general limitation income) that is not foreign base company income as defined in section 954 and a DASTM loss under paragraph (e)(3)(iv) of this section (Step 4), the amount of the DASTM loss would reduce the amount of the QBU's gross income in that category. Similarly, if a group of assets, such as short-term bank deposits, generates both foreign personal holding company income that is passive income (described in sections 954(c)(1)(A) and 904(d)(1)(A)) and a DASTM loss under paragraph (e)(3)(iv) of this section (Step 4), the amount of the DASTM loss would reduce the amount of the QBU's foreign personal holding company income and passive income. See section 904(f) and the regulations thereunder in the case where that section would apply and DASTM loss attributable to a group of assets exceeds the income generated by such assets.

(vi) *Step 6—determine DASTM gain or loss attributable to liabilities.*—(A) *General rule.*—The taxpayer shall determine the dollar amount of DASTM gain or loss attributable to liabilities identified in paragraph (e)(3)(ii) of this section (Step 2), and described in paragraph (e)(3)(vi)(B) of this section as follows:

$$[(bl + el) \div 2] \times [br - er]$$

where

bl = the hyperinflationary currency amount of liabilities at the beginning of the balance sheet period.

el = the hyperinflationary currency amount of liabilities at the end of the balance sheet translation period.

br = one dollar divided by the number of hyperinflationary currency units that equal one dollar at the beginning of the balance sheet period.

er = one dollar divided by the number of hyperinflationary currency units that equal one dollar at the end of the balance sheet period.

(B) *Separate calculation.*—The calculation shall be made separately for interest-bearing liabilities described in paragraph (e)(3)(vii) of this section (Step 7) and for each of the classes of non-interest-bearing liabilities described in paragraph (e)(3)(viii) of this section (Step 8).

(C) *Weighting to prevent distortion.*—Where a distortion would result from averaging the amount of liabilities at the beginning and end of a balance sheet period, as might be the case where a taxpayer incurs or retires a substantial liability, the taxpayer must use a different method that more clearly reflects the average amount of liabilities weighted to reflect the time the liability was outstanding during the balance sheet period.

(vii) *Step 7—adjust dollar income and expense by DASTM gain or loss from interest-bearing liabilities.*—(A) *In general.*—The taxpayer shall apply the amount of DASTM gain on interest-bearing liabilities computed under paragraph (e)(3)(vi) of this section (Step 6) to reduce interest expense generated by such liabilities (*e.g.*, prior to the application of § 1.861-9T or its successor regulation). To the extent DASTM gain on such liabilities exceeds interest expense, it shall be sourced or otherwise classified in the same manner that interest expense is allocated and apportioned under § 1.861-9T or its successor regulation. The amount of DASTM loss on interest-bearing liabilities computed under paragraph (e)(3)(vi) of this section (Step 6) shall be allocated and apportioned in the same manner that interest expense is allocated and apportioned under § 1.861-9T or its successor regulation (without regard to the exceptions to fungibility in § 1.861-10T or its successor regulation). For purposes of this section, an interest-bearing liability is a liability that requires payment of periodic interest (whether fixed or variable), has original issue discount, or would have interest imputed under subtitle A.

(B) *Allocation of DASTM gain or loss from interest-bearing liabilities that generate related person interest expense.*—DASTM gain or loss from interest-bearing liabilities that generate related person interest expense (as provided in section 954(b)(5)) shall be allocated for purposes of subtitle A (including sections 904 and 952) in the same manner that the related person interest expense of that debt is required to be allocated under the rules of section 954(b)(5) and § 1.904-5(c)(2).

(C) *Modified gross income method.*—In applying the modified gross income method described in § 1.861-9T(j) or its successor regulation, gross income shall be adjusted for any DASTM gain or loss from assets as provided in paragraph (e)(3)(v) of this section (Step 5) and

Reg. § 1.985-3(e)(3)(vii)(C)

any DASTM gain or loss with respect to short-term, non-interest-bearing trade payables as provided in paragraph (e)(3)(viii)(A) of this section.

(viii) *Step 8—adjust dollar income and expense by DASTM gain or loss from non-interest bearing liabilities.*—(A) *Short-term, non-interest-bearing trade payables.*—The taxpayer shall allocate DASTM gain or loss on short-term non-interest-bearing trade payables for purposes of subtitle A (including sections 904 and 952) to the same category or type of gross income as the cost or expense to which the trade payable relates. For this purpose, a short-term, non-interest-bearing trade payable is a non-interest-bearing liability with a term of 183 days or less that is incurred to purchase property or services to be used by the obligor in an active trade or business.

(B) *Excise tax payables.*—The taxpayer shall allocate DASTM gain or loss on excise tax payables for purposes of subtitle A (including sections 904 and 952) to the same category or type of gross income as would be derived from the activity to which the excise tax relates.

(C) *Other non-interest-bearing liabilities.*—(*1*) *In general.*—Except as provided in paragraphs (e)(3)(viii)(A), (e)(3)(viii)(B), and (e)(3)(viii)(C)(*2*) of this section, DASTM gain or loss on non-interest-bearing liabilities shall be allocated under paragraph (e)(3)(ix) of this section (Step 9).

(*2*) *Tracing if substantial distortion of income.*—DASTM gains and losses on liabilities described in paragraph (e)(3)(viii)(C)(*1*) of this section may be attributed to the same section 904(d) separate category or subpart F category as the transaction to which the liability relates if the taxpayer demonstrates to the satisfaction of the district director, or it is determined by the district director, that application of paragraph (e)(3)(viii)(C)(*1*) of this section results in a substantial distortion of income.

(ix) *Step 9—allocate residual DASTM gain or loss.*—If there is a difference between the net DASTM gain or loss determined under paragraphs (e)(3)(i) through (viii) of this section (Steps 1 through 8) and the DASTM gain or loss determined under paragraph (d) of this section, the amount of the difference must be allocated for purposes of subtitle A (including sections 904 and 952) to the QBU's gross income (computed under paragraphs (b)(1) through (3) of this section, as adjusted under paragraphs (e)(3)(i) through (viii) of this section (Steps 1 through 8)) on the basis of the relative amounts of each category or type of gross income. [Reg. § 1.985-3.]

☐ [*T.D.* 8263, 9-19-89. *Amended by T.D.* 8556, 7-22-94.]

§ 1.985-4. Method of accounting.—(a) *Adoption or election.*—The adoption of, or the election to use, a functional currency shall be treated as a method of accounting. The functional currency shall be used for the year of adoption (or election) and for all subsequent taxable years unless permission to change is granted, or considered to be granted under § 1.985-2 or 1.985-8, by the Commissioner.

(b) *Condition for changing functional currencies.*—Generally, permission to change functional currencies shall not be granted unless significant changes in the facts and circumstances of the QBU's economic environment occur. If the determination of the functional currency of the QBU for purposes of United States generally accepted accounting principles (GAAP) is based on facts and circumstances substantially similar to those set forth in § 1.985-1(c)(2), then ordinarily the Commissioner will grant a taxpayer's request to change its functional currency (or the functional currency of its branch that is a QBU) to a new functional currency only if the taxpayer (or its QBU) also changes to the new functional currency for purposes of GAAP. However, permission to change will not necessarily be granted merely because the new functional currency will conform to the taxpayer's GAAP functional currency.

(c) *Relationship to certain other sections of the Code.*—Nothing in this section shall be construed to override the provisions of any other sections of the Code or regulations that require the use of consistent accounting methods. Such provisions must be independently satisfied separate and apart from the identification of a functional currency. For instance, while separate geographical divisions of a taxpayer's trade or business may have different functional currencies, such geographical divisions may nevertheless be required to consistently use other methods of accounting. [Reg. § 1.985-4.]

☐ [*T.D.* 8263, 9-19-89. *Amended by T.D.* 8776, 7-28-98 *and T.D.* 8927, 1-10-2001.]

§ 1.985-5. Adjustments required upon change in functional currency.—(a) *In general.*—This section applies in the case of a QBU that changes from one functional currency (old functional currency) to another functional currency (new functional currency). A taxpayer or QBU subject to the rules of this section shall make the adjustments set forth in the 3-step procedure described in paragraphs (b) through (e) of this section. The adjustments shall be made on the last day of the taxable year ending before the year of change as defined in

§ 1.481-1(a)(1). Gain or loss required to be recognized under paragraphs (b), (d)(2), and (e)(2) of this section is not subject to section 481 and, therefore, the full amount of the gain or loss must be included in income or earnings and profits on the last day of the taxable year ending before the year of change. Except as provided in § 1.985-6, a QBU with a functional currency for its first taxable year beginning in 1987 that is different from the currency in which it had kept its books and records for United States accounting and tax accounting purposes for its prior taxable year shall apply the principles of this § 1.985-5 for purposes of computing the relevant functional currency items, such as earnings and profits, basis of an asset, and amount of a liability, as of the first day of a taxpayer's first taxable year beginning in 1987. However, a QBU that changes to the dollar pursuant to § 1.985-1(b)(2) after 1987 shall apply § 1.985-7.

(b) *Step 1—Taking into account exchange gain or loss on certain section 988 transactions.*—The QBU shall recognize or otherwise take into account for all purposes of the Code the amount of any unrealized exchange gain or loss attributable to a section 988 transaction (as defined in section 988(c)(1)(A), (B), and (C)) that, after applying section 988(d), is denominated in terms of or determined by reference to the new functional currency. The amount of such gain or loss shall be determined without regard to the limitations of section 988(b) (*i.e.*, whether any gain or loss would be realized on the transaction as a whole). The character and source of such gain or loss shall be determined under section 988.

(c) *Step 2—Determining the new functional currency basis of property and the new functional currency amount of liabilities and any other relevant items.*—The new functional currency adjusted basis of property and the new functional currency amount of liabilities and any other relevant items (*e.g.*, items described in section 988(c)(1)(B)(iii)) shall equal the product of the amount of the old functional currency adjusted basis or amount multiplied by the new functional currency/old functional currency spot exchange rate on the last day of the taxable year ending before the year of change (spot rate).

(d) *Step 3A—Additional adjustments that are necessary when a branch changes functional currency.*—(1) *Branch changing to a functional currency other than the taxpayer's functional currency.*—(i) *Rule.*—If a QBU that is a branch of a taxpayer changes to a functional currency other than the taxpayer's functional currency, the branch shall make the adjustments set forth in either paragraph (d)(1)(ii) or (d)(1)(iii) of this section for purposes of section 987. See § 1.987-5(d) for rules for computing the branch's equity pool and basis pool.

(ii) *Where prior to the change the branch and taxpayer had different functional currencies.*—If the branch and the taxpayer had different functional currencies prior to the change, the branch's new functional currency equity pool shall equal the product of the old functional currency amount of the equity pool multiplied by the spot rate. No adjustment to the basis pool is necessary.

(iii) *Where prior to the change the branch and taxpayer had the same functional currency.*—If the branch and the taxpayer had the same functional currency prior to the change, the branch's basis pool shall equal the difference between the branch's total old functional currency basis of its assets and its total old functional currency amount of its liabilities. The branch's equity pool shall equal the product of the basis pool multiplied by the spot rate.

(2) *Branch changing to the taxpayer's functional currency.*—If a branch changes its functional currency to the taxpayer's functional currency, the branch shall be treated as if it terminated on the last day of the taxable year ending before the year of change. In such a case, the taxpayer shall realize gain or loss attributable to the branch's equity pool under the principles of section 987.

(e) *Step 3B—Additional adjustments that are necessary when a taxpayer changes functional currency.*—(1) *Corporations.*—The amount of a corporation's new functional currency earnings and profits and the amount of its new functional currency paid-in capital shall equal the product of the old functional currency amounts of such items multiplied by the spot rate. The foreign income taxes and accumulated profits or deficits in accumulated profits of a foreign corporation that were maintained in foreign currency for purposes of section 902 and that are attributable to taxable years of the foreign corporation beginning before January 1, 1987, also shall be translated into the new functional currency at the spot rate.

(2) *Collateral consequences to a United States shareholder of a corporation changing to the United States dollar as its functional currency.*—A United States shareholder (within the meaning of section 951(b) or section 953(c)(1)(A)) of a controlled foreign corporation (within the meaning of section 957 or section 953(c)(1)(B)) changing its functional currency to the dollar shall recognize foreign currency gain or loss computed under section 986(c) as if all previously taxed earnings and profits, if any, (including amounts attributable

to pre-1987 taxable years that were translated from dollars into functional currency in the foreign corporation's first post-1986 taxable year) were distributed immediately prior to the change. Such a shareholder shall also recognize gain or loss attributable to the corporation's paid-in capital to the same extent, if any, that such gain or loss would be recognized under the regulations under section 367(b) if the corporation was liquidated completely.

(3) *Taxpayers that are not corporations.*—[Reserved]

(4) *Adjustments to a branch's accounts when a taxpayer changes functional currency.*—(i) *Taxpayer changing to a functional currency other than the branch's functional currency.*—If a taxpayer changes to a functional currency that differs from the functional currency of a branch of the taxpayer, the branch shall adjust its basis pool in the manner prescribed in paragraph (d)(1)(ii) of this section for adjusting the equity pool, if the taxpayer's old functional currency was different from the branch's functional currency. If the taxpayer's old functional currency was the same as the branch's functional currency, the branch shall determine its equity pool and basis pool in the manner set forth in paragraph (d)(1)(iii) of this section for determining the basis pool and equity pool, respectively.

(ii) *Taxpayer changing to the same functional currency as the branch.*—If a taxpayer changes to the same functional currency as a branch of the taxpayer, the taxpayer shall realize gain or loss as set forth in paragraph (d)(2) of this section.

(f) *Examples.*—The provisions of this section are illustrated by the following examples.

Example 1. S, a calendar year foreign corporation, is wholly owned by domestic corporation P. The Commissioner granted permission to change S's functional currency from the LC to the FC beginning January 1, 1993. The LC/FC exchange rate on December 31, 1992 is 1 LC/2 FC. The following shows how S must convert the items on its balance sheet from the LC to the FC.

	LC	1:2	FC
Assets:			
Cash on hand	40,000		80,000
Accounts Receivable	10,000		20,000
Inventory	100,000		200,000
100,000 FC Bond (100,000 LC historical basis)	50,000 [1]		100,000
Fixed assets:			
Property	200,000		400,000
Plant	500,000		1,000,000
Accumulated Depreciation	(200,000)		(400,000)
Equipment	1,000,000		2,000,000
Accumulated Depreciation	(400,000)		(800,000)
Total Assets	1,300,000		2,600,000
Liabilities:			
Accounts Payable	50,000		100,000
Long-term Liabilities	400,000		800,000
Paid-in-Capital	800,000		1,600,000
Retained Earnings	50,000 [2]		100,000
Total Liabilities and Equity	1,300,000		2,600,000

Example 2. P, a domestic corporation, operates a foreign branch, S. The Commissioner granted permission to change S's functional currency from the LC to the FC beginning January 1, 1993. As of December 31, 1992, S's equity pool was 2,000 LC and its basis pool was $4,000. The LC/FC exchange rate on December 31, 1992 is 1 LC/2 FC. On January 1, 1993, the new functional currency amount of S's equity pool is 4,000 FC. The basis pool is not affected. [Reg. § 1.985-5.]

☐ [T.D. 8464, 12-31-92. Amended by T.D. 8765, 3-4-98.]

§ 1.985-6. Transition rules for a QBU that uses the dollar approximate separate transactions method for its first taxable year beginning in 1987.

—(a) *In general.*—This section sets forth transition rules for a QBU that used the dollar approximate separate transactions method of accounting set forth in § 1.985-3 or § 1.985-3T (as contained in the April 1, 1989 edition of 26 CFR part 1 (1.908 to 1.1000)) for its first taxable year beginning in 1987 (DASTM QBU). A DASTM QBU must determine the dollar and hyperinflationary currency basis of its assets and the dollar and hyperinflationary currency amount of its liabilities that were acquired or incurred in taxable years beginning before January 1, 1987. In addition, a DASTM QBU must determine its net worth, including its retained earnings, at the end of the QBU's last taxable year beginning before January 1, 1987. This section provides rules for controlled foreign corporations (as defined in section 957 or section 953(c)(1)(B)), other foreign corporations, and branches of United States persons that must make these determinations.

---

[1] Under § 1.985-5(b), S will recognize a 50,000 LC loss (100,000 LC basis − 50,000 LC value) on the bond resulting from the change in functional currency. Thus, immediately before the change, S's basis in the PC bond (taking into account the loss) is 50,000 LC.

[2] The amount of S's LC retained earnings reflects the 50,000 LC loss on the bond.

(b) *Certain controlled foreign corporations.*—If a DASTM QBU was a controlled foreign corporation for its last taxable year beginning before January 1, 1987, and it had a significant event as described in § 1.964-1(c)(6) in a taxable year beginning before January 1, 1987, then the rules of this paragraph (b) shall apply.

(1) *Basis in assets and amount of liabilities.*—The hyperinflationary currency adjusted basis of the QBU's assets and the hyperinflationary currency amount of the QBU's liabilities acquired or incurred by the QBU in a taxable year beginning before January 1, 1987, shall be the basis or the amount as determined under § 1.964-1(e) prior to translation under § 1.964-1(e)(4). The dollar adjusted basis of such assets and the dollar amount of such liabilities shall be the adjusted basis or the amount as determined under the rules of § 1.964-1(e) after translation under § 1.964-1(e)(4).

(2) *Retained earnings.*—The dollar amount of the QBU's retained earnings at the end of its last taxable year beginning before January 1, 1987, shall be the dollar amount determined under § 1.964-1(e)(3).

(c) *All other foreign corporations.*—If a foreign corporation is a DASTM QBU that is not described in paragraph (b) of this section, then the hyperinflationary currency and dollar adjusted basis in the QBU's assets acquired in taxable years beginning before January 1, 1987, the hyperinflationary currency and dollar amount of the QBU's liabilities acquired or incurred in taxable years beginning before January 1, 1987, and the dollar amount of the QBU's net worth, including its retained earnings, at the end of its last taxable year beginning before January 1, 1987, shall be determined by applying the principles of § 1.985-3T or § 1.985-3. Thus, for example, the dollar basis of plant and equipment shall be determined using the appropriate historical exchange rate.

(d) *Pre-1987 section 902 amounts.*—(1) *Translation of pre-1987 section 902 accumulated profits and taxes into United States dollars.*—The foreign income taxes and accumulated profits or deficits in accumulated profits of a foreign corporation that were maintained in foreign currency for purposes of section 902 and that are attributable to taxable years of the foreign corporation beginning before January 1, 1987, shall be translated into dollars at the spot exchange rate on the first day of its first taxable year beginning after December 31, 1986. Once translated into dollars, these accumulated profits and taxes shall (absent a change in functional currency) remain in dollars for all federal income tax purposes.

(2) *Carryforward of accumulated deficits in accumulated profits from pre-1987 taxable years to post-1986 taxable years.*—For purposes of sections 902 and 960, the post-1986 undistributed earnings of a foreign corporation that is subject to the rules of this section shall be reduced by the dollar amount of the corporation's deficit in accumulated profits, if any, determined under section 902 and the regulations thereunder, that was accumulated at the end of the corporation's last taxable year beginning before January 1, 1987. The dollar amount of the accumulated deficit shall be determined by multiplying the foreign currency amount of such deficit by the spot exchange rate on the last day of the corporation's last taxable year beginning before January 1, 1987, and shall be taken into account on the first day of the corporation's first taxable year beginning after December 31, 1986. Post-1986 undistributed earnings may not be reduced by the dollar amount of a pre-1987 deficit in retained earnings determined under § 1.964-1(e).

(e) *Net worth branch.*—If a DASTM QBU is a branch of a United States person and the QBU used a net worth method of accounting for its last taxable year beginning before January 1, 1987, then the rules of this paragraph (e) shall apply. A net worth method of accounting is any method of accounting under which the taxpayer calculates the taxable income of a QBU based on the net change in the dollar value of the QBU's equity (assets minus liabilities) during the course of a taxable year, taking into account any contributions or remittances made during the year. *See, e.g.,* Rev. Rul. 75-106, 1975-1 C.B. 31. (See § 601.601(d)(2)(ii)(*b*) of this chapter).

(1) *Basis in assets and amount of liabilities.*—(i) *Hyperinflationary amounts.*—For the first taxable year beginning in 1987, the hyperinflationary currency adjusted basis of a QBU's assets or the hyperinflationary currency amounts of its liabilities acquired or incurred in a taxable year beginning before January 1, 1987 is the hyperinflationary currency basis or amount at the date when acquired or incurred, as adjusted according to United States generally accepted accounting and tax accounting principles. If a hyperinflationary currency basis or amount was not determined at such date, the dollar basis or amount, as adjusted according to United States generally accepted accounting and tax accounting principles, shall be translated into hyperinflationary currency at the spot exchange rate on the date when the asset or liability was acquired or incurred.

Reg. § 1.985-6(e)(1)(i)

(ii) *Dollar amounts.*—For the first taxable year beginning in 1987, the dollar adjusted basis of the QBU's assets and the amounts of its liabilities shall be those amounts reflected on the QBU's dollar books and records at the end of the taxpayer's last taxable year beginning before January 1, 1987, after adjusting the books and records according to United States generally accepted accounting and tax accounting principles.

(2) *Ending net worth.*—The dollar amount of the QBU's net worth at the end of its last taxable year beginning before January 1, 1987 shall equal the QBU's net worth at that date as determined under paragraph (e)(1)(ii) of this section.

(f) *Profit and loss branch.*—If a DASTM QBU is a branch of a United States person and the QBU used a profit and loss method of accounting for its last taxable year beginning before January 1, 1987, then the United States person shall first apply the transition rules of § 1.987-5 in order to determine the beginning amount and dollar basis of the branch's EQ pool, the hyperinflationary currency basis of the branch's assets, and the hyperinflationary currency amounts of its liabilities. A profit and loss method of accounting is any method of accounting under which the taxpayer calculates the profits of a QBU by computing the QBU's profits in its functional currency and translating the net result into dollars. *See, e.g.*, Rev. Rul. 75-107, 1975-1 C.B. 32. (See § 601.601(d)(2)(ii)(*b*) of this chapter). The QBU and the taxpayer must then make the adjustments required by § 1.985-5, *e.g.*, the QBU must take into account unrealized exchange gain or loss on dollar-denominated section 988 transactions, the taxpayer must account for the deemed termination of the branch, and the taxpayer must translate the QBU's balance sheet items from hyperinflationary currency into dollars at the spot rate. [Reg. § 1.985-6.]

☐ [*T.D.* 8464, 12-31-92.]

§ 1.985-7. Adjustments required in connection with a change to DASTM.—(a) *In general.*—If a QBU begins to use the dollar approximate separate transactions method of accounting set forth in § 1.985-3 (DASTM) in a taxable year beginning after April 6, 1998, adjustments shall be made as provided by this section. For the rules with respect to foreign corporations, see paragraph (b) of this section. For the rules with respect to adjustments to the income of United States shareholders of controlled foreign corporations, see paragraph (c) of this section. For the rules with respect to adjustments relating to QBU branches, see paragraph (d) of this section. For the effective date of this section, see paragraph (e). For purposes of applying this section, the look-back period shall be the period beginning with the first taxable year after the transition date and ending on the last day prior to the taxable year of change. The term transition date means the later of the last day of the last taxable year ending before the base period as defined in § 1.985-1(b)(2)(ii)(D) or the last day of the taxable year in which the QBU last applied DASTM. The taxable year of change shall mean the taxable year of change as defined in § 1.481-1(a)(1). The application of this paragraph may be illustrated by the following examples:

Example 1. A calendar year QBU that has not previously used DASTM operates in a country in which the functional currency of the country is hyperinflationary as defined under § 1.985-1(b)(2)(ii)(D) for the QBU's 1999 tax year. The look-back period is the period from January 1, 1996 through December 31, 1998, the transition date is December 31, 1995, and the taxable year of change is the taxable year beginning January 1, 1999.

Example 2. A QBU that has not previously used DASTM with a taxable year ending June 30, operates in a country in which the functional currency of the country is hyperinflationary for the QBU's tax year beginning July 1, 1999 as defined under § 1.985-1(b)(2)(ii)(D) (where the base period is the thirty-six calendar months immediately preceding the first day of the current calendar year 1999). The look-back period is the period from July 1, 1995 through June 30, 1999, the transition date is June 30, 1995, and the taxable year of change is the taxable year beginning July 1, 1999.

(b) *Adjustments to foreign corporations.*—(1) *In general.*—In the case of a foreign corporation, the corporation shall make the adjustments set forth in paragraphs (b)(2) through (4) of this section. The adjustments shall be made on the first day of the taxable year of change.

(2) *Treatment of certain section 988 transactions.*—(i) *Exchange gain or loss from section 988 transactions unrealized as of the transition date.*—A foreign corporation shall adjust earnings and profits by the amount of any unrealized exchange gain or loss that was attributable to a section 988 transaction (as defined in sections 988(c)(1)(A), (B), and (C)) that was denominated in terms of (or determined by reference to) the dollar and was held by the corporation on the transition date. Such gain or loss shall be computed as if recognized on the transition date and shall be reduced by any gain and increased by any loss recognized by the corporation with respect to such transac-

tion during the look-back period. The amount of such gain or loss shall be determined without regard to the limitations of section 988(b) (i.e., whether any gain or loss would be realized on the transaction as a whole). The character and source of such gain or loss shall be determined under section 988. Proper adjustments shall be made to account for gain or loss taken into account by reason of this paragraph (b)(2). See § 1.985-5(f) *Example 1, footnote 1.*

(ii) *Treatment of a section 988 transaction entered into and terminated during the look-back period.*—A foreign corporation shall reduce earnings and profits by the amount of any gain, and increase earnings and profits by the amount of any loss, that was recognized with respect to any dollar denominated section 988 transactions entered into and terminated during the look-back period.

(3) *Opening balance sheet.*—The opening balance sheet of a foreign corporation for the taxable year of change shall be determined as if the corporation had changed its functional currency to the dollar by applying § 1.985-5(c) on the transition date and had translated its assets and liabilities acquired and incurred during the look-back period under § 1.985-3.

(4) *Earnings and profits adjustments.*—(i) *Pre-1987 accumulated profits.*—The foreign income taxes and accumulated profits or deficits in accumulated profits of a foreign corporation that are attributable to taxable years beginning before January 1, 1987, as stated on the transition date, and that were maintained for purposes of section 902 in the old functional currency, shall be translated into dollars at the spot rate in effect on the transition date. The applicable accumulated profits shall be reduced on a last-in, first-out basis by the aggregate dollar amount (translated from functional currency in accordance with the rules of section 989(b)) attributable to earnings and profits that were distributed (or treated as distributed) during the look-back period to the extent such amounts distributed exceed the earnings and profits calculated under (b)(4)(ii) or (b)(4)(iii), as applicable. See § 1.902-1(b)(2)(ii). Once translated into dollars, these pre-1987 taxes and accumulated profits or deficits in accumulated profits shall (absent a change in functional currency) remain in dollars for all federal income tax purposes.

(ii) *Post-1986 undistributed earnings of a CFC.*—In the case of a controlled foreign corporation (within the meaning of section 957 or section 953(c)(1)(B)) (CFC) or a foreign corporation subject to the rules of § 1.904-6(a)(2), the corporation's post-1986 undistributed earnings in each separate category as defined in § 1.904-5(a)(1) as of the first day of the taxable year of change (and prior to adjustment under paragraph (c)(1) of this section) shall equal the sum of—

(A) The corporation's post-1986 undistributed earnings and profits (or deficit in earnings and profits) in each separate category as defined in § 1.904-5(a)(1) as stated on the transition date translated into dollars at the spot rate in effect on the transition date; and

(B) The sum of the earnings and profits (or deficit in earnings and profits) in each separate category determined under § 1.985-3 for each post-transition date taxable year prior to the taxable year of change.

Such amount shall be reduced by the aggregate dollar amount (translated from functional currency in accordance with the rules of section 989(b)) attributable to earnings and profits that were distributed (or treated as distributed) during the look-back period out of post-1986 earnings and profits in such separate category. For purposes of applying this paragraph (b)(4)(ii)(B), the opening balance sheet for calculating earnings and profits under § 1.985-3 for the first post-transition year shall be translated into dollars pursuant to § 1.985-5(c).

(iii) *Post-1986 undistributed earnings of other foreign corporations.*—In the case of a foreign corporation that is not a CFC or subject to the rules of § 1.904-6(a)(2), the corporation's post-1986 undistributed earnings shall equal the sum of—

(A) The corporation's post-1986 undistributed earnings (or deficit) on the transition date translated into dollars at the spot rate in effect on the transition date; and

(B) The sum of the earnings and profits (or deficit in earnings and profits) determined under § 1.985-3 for each post-transition date taxable year (or such later year determined under section 902(c)(3)(A)) prior to the taxable year of change.

Such amount shall be reduced by the aggregate dollar amount (translated from functional currency in accordance with the rules of section 989(b)) that was distributed (or treated as distributed) during the look-back period out of post-1986 earnings and profits. For purposes of applying this paragraph (b)(4)(iii)(B), the opening balance sheet for calculating earnings and profits under § 1.985-3 for the first post-transition year shall be translated into dollars pursuant to § 1.985-5(c).

(c) *United States shareholders of controlled foreign corporations.*—(1) *In general.*—A United States shareholder (within the meaning of section 951(b) or section 953(c)(1)(B)) of a CFC that changes to DASTM shall make the adjustments set forth in paragraphs (c)(2) through (5) of this section on the first day of the taxable year of change. Adjustments under this section shall be taken into account by the shareholder (or such shareholder's successor in interest) ratably over four taxable years beginning with the taxable year of change. Similar rules shall apply in determining adjustments to income of United States persons who have made an election under section 1295 to treat a passive foreign investment company as a qualified electing fund.

(2) *Treatment under subpart F of income recognized on section 988 transactions.*—The character of amounts taken into account under paragraph (b)(2) of this section for purposes of sections 951 through 964, shall be determined on the transition date and to the extent characterized as subpart F income shall be taken into account in accordance with the rules of paragraph (c)(1) of this section. Such amounts shall retain their character for all federal income tax purposes (including sections 902, 959, 960, 961, 1248, and 6038).

(3) *Recognition of foreign currency gain or loss on previously taxed earnings and profits on the transition date.*—Gain or loss is recognized under section 986(c) as if all previously taxed earnings and profits as determined on the transition date, if any, were distributed on such date. Such gain or loss shall be reduced by any foreign currency gain and increased by any foreign currency loss that was recognized under section 986(c) with respect to distributions of previously taxed earnings and profits during the look-back period. Such amount shall be characterized in accordance with section 986(c) and taken into account in accordance with the rules of paragraph (c)(1) of this section.

(4) *Subpart F income adjustment.*—Subpart F income in a separate category shall be determined under § 1.985-3 for each look-back year. For this purpose, the opening DASTM balance sheet shall be determined under § 1.985-5. The sum of the difference (positive or negative) between the amount computed pursuant to § 1.985-3 and amount that was included in income for each year shall be taken into account in the taxable year of change pursuant to paragraph (c)(1) of this section. Such amounts shall retain their character for all federal income tax purposes (including sections 902, 959, 960, 961, 1248, and 6038). For rules applicable if an adjustment under this section results in a loss for the taxable year in a separate category, see section 904(f) and the regulations thereunder. The amount of previously taxed earnings and profits as determined under section 959(c)(2) shall be adjusted (positively or negatively) by the amount taken into account under this paragraph (c)(4) as of the first day of the taxable year of change.

(5) *Foreign tax credit.*—A United States shareholder of a CFC shall compute an amount of foreign taxes deemed paid under section 960 with respect to any positive adjustments determined under paragraph (c) of this section. The amount of foreign tax deemed paid shall be computed with reference to the full amount of the adjustment and to the post-1986 undistributed earnings determined under paragraph (b)(4)(i) and (ii) of this section and the post-1986 foreign income taxes of the CFC on the first day of the taxable year of change (i.e., without taking into account earnings and taxes for the taxable year of change). For purposes of section 960, the associated taxes in each separate category shall be allocated pro rata among, and deemed paid in, the shareholder's taxable years in which the income is taken into account. (No adjustment to foreign taxes deemed paid in prior years is required solely by reason of a negative adjustment to income under paragraph (c)(1) of this section).

(d) *QBU branches.*—(1) *In general.*—In the case of a QBU branch, the taxpayer shall make the adjustments set forth in paragraphs (d)(2) through (d)(4) of this section. Adjustments under this section shall be taken into account by the taxpayer ratably over four taxable years beginning with the taxable year of change.

(2) *Treatment of certain section 988 transactions.*—(i) *Exchange gain or loss from section 988 transactions unrealized as of the transition date.*—A QBU branch shall adjust income by the amount of any unrealized exchange gain or loss that was attributable to a section 988 transaction (as defined in sections 988(c)(1)(A), (B), and (C)) that was denominated in terms of (or determined by reference to) the dollar and was held by the QBU branch on the transition date. Such gain or loss shall be computed as if recognized on the transition date and shall be reduced by any gain and increased by any loss recognized by the QBU branch with respect to such transaction during the look-back period. The amount of such gain or loss shall be determined without regard to the limitations of section 988(b) (i.e., whether any gain or loss would be realized on the transaction as a whole). The character and source of such gain or loss shall be determined under section 988. Proper adjustments shall be made to account for gain or loss taken into account by reason of this paragraph (d)(2). See § 1.985-5(f) *Example 1, footnote 1.*

(ii) *Treatment of a section 988 transaction entered into and terminated during the look-back period.*—A QBU branch shall reduce income by the amount of any gain, and increase income by the amount of any loss, that was recognized with respect to any dollar denominated section 988 transactions entered into and terminated during the look-back period.

(3) *Deemed termination income adjustment.*—The taxpayer shall realize gain or loss attributable to the QBU branch's equity pool (as stated on the transition date) under the principles of section 987, computed as if the branch terminated on the transition date. Such amount shall be reduced by section 987 gain and increased by section 987 loss that was recognized by such taxpayer with respect to remittances during the look-back period.

(4) *Branch income adjustment.*—Branch income in a separate category shall be determined under § 1.985-3 for each look-back year. For this purpose, the opening DASTM balance sheet shall be determined under § 1.985-5. The sum of the difference (positive or negative) between the amount computed pursuant to § 1.985-3 and amount taken into account for each year shall be taken into account in the taxable year of change pursuant to paragraph (d)(1) of this section. Such amounts shall retain their character for all federal income tax purposes.

(5) *Opening balance sheet.*—The opening balance sheet of a QBU branch for the taxable year of change shall be determined as if the branch had changed its functional currency to the dollar by applying § 1.985-5(c) on the transition date and had translated its assets and liabilities acquired and incurred during the look-back period under § 1.985-3.

(e) *Effective date.*—This section is effective for taxable years beginning after April 6, 1998. However, a taxpayer may choose to apply this section to all open taxable years beginning after December 31, 1986, provided each person, and each QBU branch of a person, that is related (within the meaning of § 1.985-2(d)(3)) to the taxpayer also applies this section. [Reg. § 1.985-7.]

☐ [*T.D.* 8765, 3-4-98 (*corrected* 3-31-98).]

§ 1.985-8. Special rules applicable to the European Monetary Union (conversion to euro).

—(a) *Definitions.*—(1) *Legacy currency.*—A legacy currency is the former currency of a Member State of the European Community which is substituted for the euro in accordance with the Treaty establishing the European Community signed February 7, 1992. The term legacy currency shall also include the European Currency Unit.

(2) *Conversion rate.*—The conversion rate is the rate at which the euro is substituted for a legacy currency.

(b) *Operative rules.*—(1) *Initial adoption.*—A QBU (as defined in § 1.989(a)-1(b)) whose first taxable year begins after the euro has been substituted for a legacy currency may not adopt a legacy currency as its functional currency.

(2) *QBU with a legacy currency as its functional currency.*—(i) *Required change.*—A QBU with a legacy currency as its functional currency is required to change its functional currency to the euro beginning the first day of the first taxable year—

(A) That begins on or after the day that the euro is substituted for that legacy currency (in accordance with the Treaty on European Union); and

(B) In which the QBU begins to maintain its books and records (as described in § 1.989(a)-1(d)) in the euro.

(ii) Notwithstanding paragraph (b)(2)(i) of this section, a QBU with a legacy currency as its functional currency is required to change its functional currency to the euro no later than the last taxable year beginning on or before the first day such legacy currency is no longer valid legal tender.

(3) *QBU with a non-legacy currency as its functional currency.*—(i) *In general.*—A QBU with a non-legacy currency as its functional currency may change its functional currency to the euro pursuant to this § 1.985-8 if—

(A) Under the rules set forth in § 1.985-1(c), the euro is the currency of the economic environment in which a significant part of the QBU's activities are conducted;

(B) After conversion, the QBU maintains its books and records (as described in § 1.989(a)-1(d)) in the euro; and

(C) The QBU is not required to use the dollar as its functional currency under § 1.985-1(b).

(ii) *Time period for change.*—A QBU with a non-legacy currency as its functional currency may change its functional currency to the euro under this section only if it does so within the period set forth in paragraph (b)(2) of this section as if the functional currency of the QBU was a legacy currency.

(4) *Consent of Commissioner.*—A change made pursuant to paragraph (b) of this section shall be deemed to be made with the consent of the Commissioner for purposes of § 1.985-4. A QBU changing its functional currency to the euro pursuant to paragraph (b)(2) of this section must make adjustments as provided in

paragraph (c) of this section. A QBU changing its functional currency to the euro pursuant to paragraph (b)(3) must make adjustments as provided in § 1.985-5.

(5) *Statement to file upon change.*—With respect to a QBU that changes its functional currency to the euro under paragraph (b) of this section, an affected taxpayer shall attach to its return for the taxable year of change a statement that includes the following: "TAXPAYER CERTIFIES THAT A QBU OF THE TAXPAYER HAS CHANGED ITS FUNCTIONAL CURRENCY TO THE EURO PURSUANT TO TREAS. REG. § 1.985-8." For purposes of this paragraph (b)(5), an affected taxpayer shall be in the case where the QBU is: a QBU of an individual U.S. resident (as a result of the activities of such individual), the individual; a QBU branch of a U.S. corporation, the corporation; a controlled foreign corporation (as described in section 957) (or QBU branch thereof), each United States shareholder (as described in section 951(b)); a partnership, each partner separately; a noncontrolled section 902 corporation (as described in section 904(d)(2)(E)) (or branch thereof), each domestic shareholder as described in § 1.902-1(a)(1); or a trust or estate, the fiduciary of such trust or estate.

(c) *Adjustments required when a QBU changes its functional currency from a legacy currency to the euro pursuant to paragraph (b)(2) of this section.*—(1) *In general.*—A QBU that changes its functional currency from a legacy currency to the euro pursuant to paragraph (b)(2) of this section must make the adjustments described in paragraphs (c)(2) through (5) of this section. Section 1.985-5 shall not apply.

(2) *Determining the euro basis of property and the euro amount of liabilities and other relevant items.*—The euro basis in property and the euro amount of liabilities and other relevant items shall equal the product of the legacy functional currency adjusted basis or amount of liabilities multiplied by the applicable conversion rate.

(3) *Taking into account exchange gain or loss on legacy currency section 988 transactions.*—(i) *In general.*—Except as provided in paragraphs (c)(3)(iii) and (iv) of this section, a legacy currency denominated section 988 transaction (determined after applying section 988(d)) outstanding on the last day of the taxable year immediately prior to the year of change shall continue to be treated as a section 988 transaction after the change and the principles of section 988 shall apply.

(ii) *Examples.*—The application of this paragraph (c)(3) may be illustrated by the following examples:

Example 1. X, a calendar year QBU on the cash method of accounting, uses the deutschmark as its functional currency. X is not described in section 1281(b). On July 1, 1998, X converts 10,000 deutschmarks (DM) into Dutch guilders (fl) at the spot rate of fl1 = DM1 and loans the 10,000 guilders to Y (an unrelated party) for one year at a rate of 10% with principal and interest to be paid on June 30, 1999. On January 1, 1999, X changes its functional currency to the euro pursuant to this section. Assume that the euro/deutschmark conversion rate is set by the European Council at €1 = DM2. Assume further that the euro/guilder conversion rate is set at €1 = fl2.25. Accordingly, under the terms of the note, on June 30, 1999, X will receive €4444.44 (fl10,000/2.25) of principal and €4444.44 (fl1,000/2.25) of interest. Pursuant to this paragraph (c)(3), X will realize an exchange loss on the principal computed under the principles of § 1.988-2(b)(5). For this purpose, the exchange rate used under § 1.988-2(b)(5)(i) shall be the guilder/euro conversion rate. The amount under § 1.988-2(b)(5)(ii) is determined by translating the fl10,000 at the guilder/deutschmark spot rate on July 1, 1998, and translating that deutschmark amount into euros at the deutschmark/euro conversion rate. Thus, X will compute an exchange loss for 1999 of €555.56 determined as follows: [€4444.44 (fl10,000/2.25) − €5000 ((fl10,000/1) /2) = −€555.56]. Pursuant to this paragraph (c)(3), the character and source of the loss are determined pursuant to section 988 and regulations thereunder. Because X uses the cash method of accounting for the interest on this debt instrument, X does not realize exchange gain or loss on the receipt of that interest.

Example 2. (i) X, a calendar year QBU on the accrual method of accounting, uses the deutschmark as its functional currency. On February 1, 1998, X converts 12,000 deutschmarks into Dutch guilders at the spot rate of fl1 = DM1 and loans the 12,000 guilders to Y (an unrelated party) for one year at a rate of 10% with principal and interest to be paid on January 31, 1999. In addition, assume the average rate (deutschmark/guilder) for the period from February 1, 1998, through December 31, 1998 is fl1.07 = DM1. Pursuant to § 1.988-2(b)(2)(ii)(C), X will accrue eleven months of interest on the note and recognize interest income of DM1028.04 (fl1100/1.07) in the 1998 taxable year.

(ii) On January 1, 1999, the euro will replace the deutschmark as the national currency of Germany pursuant to the Treaty on European Union signed February 7, 1992. Assume that on January 1, 1999, X changes its functional currency to the euro pursuant to this section. Assume that the euro/deutschmark conversion rate is set by the European Council at €1 = DM2. Assume further that the euro/guilder conversion rate is set at €1 = fl2.25. In 1999, X will accrue one month of interest equal to €44.44 (fl100/2.25). On January 31, 1999, pursuant to the note, X will receive interest denominated in euros of €533.33 (fl1200/2.25). Pursuant to this paragraph (c)(3), X will realize an exchange loss in the 1999 taxable year with respect to accrued interest computed under the principles of §1.988-2(b)(3). For this purpose, the exchange rate used under §1.988-2(b)(3)(i) is the guilder/euro conversion rate and the exchange rate used under §1.988-2(b)(3)(ii) is the deutschmark/euro conversion rate. Thus, with respect to the interest accrued in 1998, X will realize exchange loss of €25.13 under §1.988-2(b), (3) as follows: [€488.89 (fl1100/2.25) − €514.02 (DM1028.04/2) = −€25.13]. With respect to the one month of interest accrued in 1999, X will realize no exchange gain or loss since the exchange rate when the interest accrued and the spot rate on the payment date are the same.

(iii) X will realize exchange loss of €666.67 on repayment of the loan principal computed in the same manner as in Example 1 [€5333.33 (fl12,000/2.25) − €6000 fl12,000/1)/2)]. The losses with respect to accrued interest and principal are characterized and sourced under the rules of section 988.

(iii) *Special rule for legacy nonfunctional currency.*—The QBU shall realize or otherwise take into account for all purposes of the Internal Revenue Code the amount of any unrealized exchange gain or loss attributable to nonfunctional currency (as described in section 988(c)(1)(C)(ii)) that is denominated in a legacy currency as if the currency were disposed of on the last day of the taxable year immediately prior to the year of change. The character and source of the gain or loss are determined under section 988.

(iv) *Legacy currency denominated accounts receivable and payable.*—(A) *In general.*—A QBU may elect to realize or otherwise take into account for all purposes of the Internal Revenue Code the amount of any unrealized exchange gain or loss attributable to a legacy currency denominated item described in section 988(c)(1)(B)(ii) as if the item were terminated on the last day of the taxable year ending prior to the year of change.

(B) *Time and manner of election.*—With respect to a QBU that makes an election described in paragraph (c)(3)(iv)(A) of this section, an affected taxpayer (as described in paragraph (b)(5) of this section) shall attach a statement to its tax return for the taxable year ending immediately prior to the year of change which includes the following: "TAXPAYER CERTIFIES THAT A QBU OF THE TAXPAYER HAS ELECTED TO REALIZE CURRENCY GAIN OR LOSS ON LEGACY CURRENCY DENOMINATED ACCOUNTS RECEIVABLE AND PAYABLE UPON CHANGE OF FUNCTIONAL CURRENCY TO THE EURO." A QBU making the election must do so for all legacy currency denominated items described in section 988(c)(1)(B)(ii).

(4) *Adjustments when a branch changes its functional currency to the euro.*—(i) *Branch changing from a legacy currency to the euro in a taxable year during which taxpayer's functional currency is other than the euro.*—If a branch changes its functional currency from a legacy currency to the euro for a taxable year during which the taxpayer's functional currency is other than the euro, the branch's euro equity pool shall equal the product of the legacy currency amount of the equity pool multiplied by the applicable conversion rate. No adjustment to the basis pool is required.

(ii) *Branch changing from a legacy currency to the euro in a taxable year during which taxpayer's functional currency is the euro.*—If a branch changes its functional currency from a legacy currency to the euro for a taxable year during which the taxpayer's functional currency is the euro, the taxpayer shall realize gain or loss attributable to the branch's equity pool under the principles of section 987, computed as if the branch terminated on the last day prior to the year of change. Adjustments under this paragraph (c)(4)(ii) shall be taken into account by the taxpayer ratably over four taxable years beginning with the taxable year of change.

(5) *Adjustments to a branch's accounts when a taxpayer changes to the euro.*—(i) *Taxpayer changing from a legacy currency to the euro in a taxable year during which a branch's functional currency is other than the euro.*—If a taxpayer changes its functional currency to the euro for a taxable year during which the functional currency of a branch of the taxpayer is other than the euro, the basis pool shall equal the product of the legacy currency amount of the basis pool multiplied by the applicable conversion rate. No adjustment to the equity pool is required.

(ii) *Taxpayer changing from a legacy currency to the euro in a taxable year during which a branch's functional currency is the euro.*—If a taxpayer changes its functional currency from a legacy currency to the euro for a taxable year during which the functional currency of a branch of the taxpayer is the euro, the taxpayer shall take into account gain or loss as determined under paragraph (c)(4)(ii) of this section.

(6) *Additional adjustments that are necessary when a corporation changes its functional currency to the euro.*—The amount of a corporation's euro currency earnings and profits and the amount of its euro paid-in capital shall equal the product of the legacy currency amounts of these items multiplied by the applicable conversion rate. The foreign income taxes and accumulated profits or deficits in accumulated profits of a foreign corporation that were maintained in foreign currency for purposes of section 902 and that are attributable to taxable years of the foreign corporation beginning before January 1, 1987, also shall be translated into the euro at the conversion rate.

(d) *Treatment of legacy currency section 988 transactions with respect to a QBU that has the euro as its functional currency.*—(1) *In general.*—This § 1.985-8(d) applies to a QBU that has the euro as its functional currency and that holds a section 988 transaction denominated in, or determined by reference to, a currency that is substituted by the euro. For example, this paragraph (d) will apply to a German QBU with the euro as its functional currency if the QBU is holding Country X currency or other section 988 transactions denominated in such currency on the day in the year 2005 when the euro is substituted for the Country X currency.

(2) *Principles of paragraph (c)(3) of this section shall apply.*—With respect to a QBU described in paragraph (d) of this section, the principles of paragraph (c)(3) of this section shall apply. For example, if a German QBU with the euro as its functional currency is holding a Country X currency denominated debt instrument on the day in the year 2005 when the euro is substituted for the Country X currency, the instrument shall continue to be treated as a section 988 transaction pursuant to the principles of paragraph (c)(3)(i) of this section. However, if such QBU holds Country X currency, the QBU shall take into account any unrealized exchange gain or loss pursuant to the principles of paragraph (c)(3)(iii) of this section as if the currency was disposed of on the day prior to the day the euro is substituted for the Country X currency. Similarly, if the QBU makes an election under the principles of paragraph (c)(3)(iv) of this section, the QBU shall take into account for all purposes of the Internal Revenue Code the amount of any unrealized exchange gain or loss attributable to a legacy currency denominated item described in section 988(c)(1)(B)(ii) as if the item were terminated on the day prior to the day the euro is substituted for the Country X currency.

(e) *Effective date.*—This section applies to tax years ending after July 29, 1998. [Reg. § 1.985-8.]

☐ [T.D. 8927, 1-10-2001.]

§ 1.988-1. Certain definitions and special rules.—(a) *Section 988 transaction.*—(1) *In general.*—The term "section 988 transaction" means any of the following transactions—

(i) A disposition of nonfunctional currency as defined in paragraph (c) of this section;

(ii) Any transaction described in paragraph (a)(2) of this section if any amount which the taxpayer is entitled to receive or is required to pay by reason of such transaction is denominated in terms of a nonfunctional currency or is determined by reference to the value of one or more nonfunctional currencies.

A transaction described in this paragraph (a) need not require or permit payment with a nonfunctional currency as long as any amount paid or received is determined by reference to the value of one or more nonfunctional currencies. The acquisition of nonfunctional currency is treated as a section 988 transaction for purposes of establishing the taxpayer's basis in such currency and determining exchange gain or loss thereon.

(2) *Description of transactions.*—The following transactions are described in this paragraph (a)(2).

(i) *Debt instruments.*—Acquiring a debt instrument or becoming an obligor under a debt instrument. The term "debt instrument" means a bond, debenture, note, certificate or other evidence of indebtedness.

(ii) *Payables, receivables, etc.*—Accruing, or otherwise taking into account, for purposes of subtitle A of the Internal Revenue Code, any item of expense or gross income or receipts which is to be paid or received after the date on which so accrued or taken into account. A payable relating to cost of goods sold, or a payable or receivable relating to a capital expenditure or receipt, is within the meaning of this paragraph (a)(2)(ii). Generally, a payable relating to foreign taxes (whether or not claimed as a credit under section 901) is within the meaning of this paragraph (a)(2)(ii). However, a payable of a domestic person relating to accrued foreign taxes of its qualified business unit (QBU branch) is not within the meaning of this paragraph (a)(2)(ii) if the QBU branch's functional currency is the U.S. dollar and the foreign taxes are claimed as a credit under section 901.

(iii) *Forward contract, futures contract, option contract, or similar financial instrument.*—Except as otherwise provided in this paragraph (a)(2)(iii) and paragraph (a)(4)(i) of this section, entering into or acquiring any forward contract, futures contract, option, warrant, or similar financial instrument.

(A) *Limitation for certain derivative instruments.*—A forward contract, futures contract, option, warrant, or similar financial instrument is within this paragraph (a)(2)(iii) only if the underlying property to which the instrument ultimately relates is a nonfunctional currency or is otherwise described in paragraph (a)(1)(ii) of this section. Thus, if the underlying property of an instrument is another financial instrument (*e.g.*, an option on a futures contract), then the underlying property to which such other instrument (*e.g.*, the futures contract) ultimately relates must be a nonfunctional currency. For example, a forward contract to purchase wheat denominated in a nonfunctional currency, an option to enter into a forward contract to purchase wheat denominated in a nonfunctional currency, or a warrant to purchase stock denominated in a nonfunctional currency is not described in this paragraph (a)(2)(iii). On the other hand, a forward contract to purchase a nonfunctional currency, an option to enter into a forward contract to purchase a nonfunctional currency, an option to purchase a bond denominated in or the payments of which are determined by reference to the value of a nonfunctional currency, or a warrant to purchase nonfunctional currency is described in this paragraph (a)(2)(iii).

(B) *Nonfunctional currency notional principal contracts.*—(1) *In general.*—The term "similar financial instrument" includes a notional principal contract only if the payments required to be made or received under the contract are determined with reference to a nonfunctional currency.

(2) *Definition of notional principal contract.*—The term "notional principal contract" means a contract (*e.g.*, a swap, cap, floor or collar) that provides for the payment of amounts by one party to another at specified intervals calculated by reference to a specified index upon a notional principal amount in exchange for specified consideration or a promise to pay similar amounts. For this purpose, a "notional principal contract" shall only include an instrument where the underlying property to which the instrument ultimately relates is money (*e.g.*, functional currency), nonfunctional currency, or property the value of which is determined by reference to an interest rate. Thus, the term "notional principal contract" includes a currency swap as defined in § 1.988-2(e)(2)(ii), but does not include a swap referenced to a commodity or equity index.

(C) *Effective date with respect to certain contracts.*—This paragraph (a)(2)(iii) does not apply to any forward contract, futures contract, option, warrant, or similar financial instrument entered into or acquired on or before October 21, 1988, if such instrument would have been marked to market under section 1256 if held on the last day of the taxable year.

(3)-(5) [Reserved]

(6) *Examples.*—The following examples illustrate the application of paragraph (a) of this section. The examples assume that X is a U.S. corporation on an accrual method with the calendar year as its taxable year. Because X is a U.S. corporation the U.S. dollar is its functional currency under section 985. The examples also assume that section 988(d) does not apply.

Example 1. On January 1, 1989, X acquires 10,000 Canadian dollars. On January 15, 1989, X uses the 10,000 Canadian dollars to purchase inventory. The acquisition of the 10,000 Canadian dollars is a section 988 transaction for purposes of establishing X's basis in such Canadian dollars. The disposition of the 10,000 Canadian dollars is a section 988 transaction pursuant to paragraph (a)(1) of this section.

Example 2. On January 1, 1989, X acquires 10,000 Canadian dollars. On January 15, 1989, X converts the 10,000 Canadian dollars to U.S. dollars. The acquisition of the 10,000 Canadian dollars is a section 988 transaction for purposes of establishing X's basis in such Canadian dollars. The conversion of the 10,000 Canadian dollars to U.S. dollars is a section 988 transaction pursuant to paragraph (a)(1) of this section.

Example 3. On January 1, 1989, X borrows 100,000 British pounds (£) for a period of 10 years and issues a note to the lender with a face amount of £100,000. The note provides for payments of interest at an annual rate of 10% paid quarterly in pounds and has a stated redemption price at maturity of £100,000. X's becoming the obligor under the note is a section 988 transaction pursuant to paragraphs (a)(1)(ii) and (2)(i) of this section. Because X is an accrual basis taxpayer, the accrual of interest expense under X's note is a section 988 transaction pursuant to paragraphs (a)(1)(ii) and (2)(ii) of this section. In addition, the acquisition of the British pounds to make payments under the note is a section 988 transaction for purposes of establishing X's basis in such pounds, and the disposition of such pounds is a section 988 transaction under paragraph (a)(1)(i) of this section. See §1.988-2(b) with respect to the translation of accrued interest expense and the determination of exchange gain or loss upon payment of accrued interest expense.

Example 4. On January 1, 1989, X purchases at original issue for 74,621.54 British pounds (£) a 3-year bond maturing on December 31, 1991, at a stated redemption price of £100,000. The bond provides for no stated interest. The bond has a yield to maturity of 10% compounded semiannually and has £25,378.46 of original issue discount. The acquisition of the bond is a section 988 transaction as provided in paragraphs (a)(1)(ii) and (2)(i) of this section. The accrual of original issue discount with respect to the bond is a section 988 transaction under paragraphs (a)(1)(ii) and (2)(ii) of this section. See §1.988-2(b) with respect to the translation of original issue discount and the determination of exchange gain or loss upon receipt of such amounts.

Example 5. On January 1, 1989, X sells and delivers inventory to Y for 10,000,000 Italian lira for payment on April 1, 1989. Under X's method of accounting, January 1, 1989 is the accrual date. Because X is an accrual basis taxpayer, the accrual of a nonfunctional currency denominated item of gross receipts on January 1, 1989, for payment after the date of accrual is a section 988 transaction under paragraphs (a)(1)(ii) and (2)(ii) of this section.

Example 6. On January 1, 1989, X agrees to purchase a machine from Y for delivery on March 1, 1990 for 1,000,000 yen. The agreement calls for X to pay Y for the machine on June 1, 1990. Under X's method of accounting, the expenditure for the machine does not accrue until delivery on March 1, 1990. The agreement to purchase the machine is not a section 988 transaction. In particular, the agreement to purchase the machine is not described in paragraph (a)(2)(ii) of this section because the agreement is not an item of expense taken into account under subtitle A (but rather is an agreement to purchase a capital asset in the future). However, the payable that will arise on the delivery date is a section 988 transaction under paragraphs (a)(1)(ii) and (2)(ii) of this section even though the payable relates to a capital expenditure. In addition, the disposition of yen to satisfy the payable on June 1, 1990, is a section 988 transaction under paragraph (a)(1)(i) of this section.

Example 7. On January 1, 1989, X purchases and takes delivery of inventory for 10,000 French francs with payment to be made on April 1, 1989. Under X's method of accounting, the expense accrues on January 1, 1989. On January 1, 1989, X also enters into a forward contract with a bank to purchase 10,000 French francs for $2,000 on April 1, 1989. Because X is an accrual basis taxpayer, the accrual of a nonfunctional currency denominated item of expense on January 1, 1989, for payment after the date of accrual is a section 988 transaction under paragraphs (a)(1)(ii) and (2)(ii) of this section. Entering into the forward contract to purchase the 10,000 French francs is a section 988 transaction under paragraphs (a)(1)(ii) and (2)(iii) of this section.

Example 8. On January 1, 1989, X acquires 100,000 Norwegian krone. On January 15, 1989, X purchases and takes delivery of 1,000 shares of common stock with the 100,000 krone acquired on January 1, 1989. On August 1, 1989, X sells the 1,000 shares of common stock and receives 120,000 krone in payment. On August 30, 1989, X converts the 120,000 krone to U.S. dollars. The acquisition of the 100,000 krone on January 1, 1989, and the acquisition of the 120,000 krone on August 1, 1989, are section 988 transactions for purposes of establishing the basis of such krone. The disposition of the 100,000 krone on January 15, 1989, and the 120,000 krone on August 30, 1989, are section 988 transactions as provided in paragraph (a)(1)(i) of this section. Neither the acquisition on January 15, 1989, nor the disposition on August 1, 1989, of the stock is a section 988 transaction.

Example 9. On May 11, 1989, X purchases a one year note at original issue for its issue price of $1,000. The note pays interest in dollars at the rate of 4 percent compounded semiannually. The amount of principal received by X upon maturity is equal to $1,000 plus the equivalent of the excess, if any, of (a) the Financial Times One Hundred Stock Index (an index of stocks traded on the London Stock Exchange hereafter referred to as the FT100) determined and translated into dollars on the last business day prior to the maturity date, over (b) £2,150, the "stated value" of the FT100, which is equal to 110% of the average value of the index for the six months prior to the issue date, translated at the exchange rate of £1 = $1.50. The purchase by X of the instrument described above is not a section 988 transaction because the index used to compute the principal amount received upon maturity is determined with reference to the value of stock and not nonfunctional currency.

Example 10. On April 9, 1989, X enters into an interest rate swap that provides for the payment of amounts by X to its counterparty based on 4% of a 10,000 yen principal amount in exchange for amounts based on yen LIBOR rates. Pursuant to paragraphs (a)(1)(ii) and (2)(iii) of this section, this yen for yen interest rate swap is a section 988 transaction.

Example 11. On August 11, 1989, X enters into an option contract for sale of a group of stocks traded on the Japanese Nikkei exchange. The contract is not a section 988 transaction within the meaning of §1.988-1(a)(2)(iii) because the underlying property to which the option relates is a group of stocks and not nonfunctional currency.

(7) *Special rules for regulated futures contracts and non-equity options.*—(i) *In general.*—Except as provided in paragraph (a)(7)(ii) of this section, paragraph (a)(2)(iii) of this section shall not apply to any regulated futures contract or non-equity option which would be marked to market under section 1256 if held on the last day of the taxable year.

(ii) *Election to have paragraph (a)(2)(iii) of this section apply.*—Notwithstanding paragraph (a)(7)(i) of this section, a taxpayer may elect to have paragraph (a)(2)(iii) of this section apply to regulated futures contracts and non-equity options as provided in paragraph (a)(7)(iii) and (iv) of this section.

(iii) *Procedure for making the election.*—A taxpayer shall make the election provided in paragraph (a)(7)(ii) of this section by sending to the Internal Revenue Service Center, Examination Branch, Stop Number 92, Kansas City, MO 64999 a statement titled "ELECTION TO TREAT REGULATED FUTURES CONTRACTS AND NON-EQUITY OPTIONS AS SECTION 988 TRANSACTIONS UNDER SECTION 988(c)(1)(D)(ii)" that contains the following:

(A) The taxpayer's name, address, and taxpayer identification number;

(B) The date the notice is mailed or otherwise delivered to the Internal Revenue Service Center;

(C) A statement that the taxpayer (including all members of such person's affiliated group as defined in section 1504 or in the case of an individual all persons filing a joint return with such individual) elects to have section 988(c)(1)(D)(i) and §1.988-1(a)(7)(i) not apply;

(D) The date of the beginning of the taxable year for which the election is being made;

(E) If the election is filed after the first day of the taxable year, a statement regarding whether the taxpayer has previously held a contract described in section 988(c)(1)(D)(i) or §1.988-1(a)(7)(i) during such taxable year, and if so, the first date during the taxable year on which such contract was held; and

(F) The signature of the person making the election (in the case of individuals filing a joint return, the signature of all persons filing such return).

The election shall be made by the following persons: in the case of an individual, by such individual; in the case of a partnership, by each partner separately; effective for taxable years beginning after March 17, 1992, in the case of tiered partnerships, each ultimate partner; in the case of an S corporation, by each shareholder separately; in the case of a trust (other than a grantor trust) or estate, by the fiduciary of such trust or estate; in the case of any corporation other than an S corporation, by such corporation (in the case of a corporation that is a member of an affiliated group that files a consolidated return, such election shall be valid and binding only if made by the common parent, as that term is used in §1.1502-77(a)); in the case of a controlled foreign corporation, by its controlling United States shareholders under §1.964-1(c)(3). With respect to a corporation (other than an S corporation), the election, when made by the common parent, shall be binding on all members of such corporation's affiliated group as defined in section 1504 that file a consolidated return. The election shall be binding on any income or loss derived from the partner's share (determined under the principles of section 702(a)) of all contracts described in section 988(c)(1)(D)(i) or paragraph (a)(7)(i) of this section in which the taxpayer holds a direct interest or indirect interest through a partnership or S corporation; however, the election shall not apply to any income or loss of a partnership for any taxable year if such partnership made an election under section 988(c)(1)(E)(iii)(V) for such year or any preceding year. Generally, a copy of the election must be attached to the taxpayer's income tax return for the first year it is effective. It is not required to be attached to subsequent returns. However, in the case of a partner, a copy of the election must be attached to the taxpayer's income tax return for every year during which the taxpayer is a partner in a partnership that engages in a transaction that is subject to the election.

(iv) *Time for making the election.*—(A) *In general.*—Unless the requirements for making a late election described in paragraph (a)(7)(iv)(B) of this section are satisfied, an election under section 988(c)(1)(D)(ii) and paragraph (a)(7)(ii) of this section for any taxable year shall be made on or before the first day of the taxable year or, if later, on or before the first day during such taxable year on which the taxpayer holds a contract described in section 988(c)(1)(D)(ii) and paragraph (a)(7)(ii) of this section. The election under section 988(c)(1)(D)(ii) and paragraph (a)(7)(ii) of this section shall apply to contracts entered into or acquired after October 21, 1988, and held on or after the effective date of the election. The election shall be effective as of the beginning of the taxable year and shall be binding with respect to all succeeding taxable years unless revoked with the prior consent of the Commissioner. In determining whether to grant revocation of the election, recapture of the tax benefit derived from the election in previous taxable years will be considered.

(B) *Late elections.*—A taxpayer may make an election under section 988(c)(1)(D)(ii) and paragraph (a)(7)(ii) of this section within 30 days after the time prescribed in the first sentence of paragraph (a)(7)(iv)(A) of this section. Such a late election shall be effective as of the beginning of the taxable year; however, any losses recognized during the taxable year with respect to contracts described in section 988(c)(1)(D)(ii) or paragraph (a)(7)(ii) of this section which were entered into or acquired after October 21, 1988, and held on or before the date on which the late election is mailed or otherwise delivered to the Internal Revenue Service Center shall not be treated as derived from a section 988 transaction. A late election must comply with the procedures set forth in paragraph (a)(7)(iii) of this section.

(v) *Transition rule.*—An election made prior to September 21, 1989 which satisfied the requirements of Notice 88-124, 1988-51 I.R.B. 6, shall be deemed to satisfy the requirements of paragraphs (a)(7)(iii) and (iv) of this section.

(vi) *General effective date provision.*—This paragraph (a)(7) shall apply with respect to futures contracts and options entered into or acquired after October 21, 1988.

(8) *Special rules for qualified funds.*—(i) *Definition of qualified fund.*—The term "qualified fund" means any partnership if—

(A) At all times during the taxable year (and during each preceding taxable year to which an election under section 988(c)(1)(E)(iii)(V) applied) such partnership has at least 20 partners and no single partner owns more than 20 percent of the interests in the capital or profits of the partnership;

(B) The principal activity of such partnership for such taxable year (and each such preceding taxable year) consists of buying and selling options, futures, or forwards with respect to commodities;

(C) At least 90 percent of the gross income of the partnership for the taxable year (and each such preceding year) consists of income or gains described in subparagraph (A), (B), or (G) of section 7704(d)(1) or gain from the sale or disposition of capital assets held for the production of interest or dividends;

(D) No more than a de minimis amount of the gross income of the partnership for the taxable year (and each such preceding taxable year) was derived from buying and selling commodities; and

(E) An election under section 988(c)(1)(E)(iii)(V) as provided in paragraph (a)(8)(iv) of this section applies to the taxable year.

(ii) *Special rules relating to paragraph (a)(8)(i)(A) of this section.*—(A) *Certain general partners.*—The interest of a general partner in the partnership shall not be treated as failing to meet the 20 percent ownership requirement of paragraph (a)(8)(i)(A) of this section for any taxable year of the partnership if, for the taxable year of the partner in which such partnership's taxable year ends, such partner (and each corporation filing a consolidated return with such partner) had no ordinary income or loss from a section 988 transaction (other than income from the partnership) which is exchange gain or loss (as the case may be).

(B) *Treatment of incentive compensation.*—For purposes of paragraph (a)(8)(i)(A) of this section, any income allocable to a general partner as incentive compensation based on profits rather than capital shall not be taken into account in determining such partner's interest in the profits of the partnership.

(C) *Treatment of tax exempt partners.*—The interest of a partner in the partnership shall not be treated as failing to meet the 20 percent ownership requirements of paragraph (a)(5)(8)(A) of this section if none of the income of such partner from such partnership is subject to tax under chapter 1 of subtitle A of the Internal Revenue Code (whether directly or through one or more pass-through entities).

(D) *Look-through rule.*—In determining whether the 20% ownership requirement of paragraph (a)(8)(i)(A) of this section is met with respect to any partnership, any interest in such partnership held by another partnership shall be treated as held proportionately by the partners in such other partnership.

(iii) *Other special rules.*—(A) *Related persons.*—Interests in the partnership held by persons related to each other (within the meaning of section 267(b) or 707(b)) shall be treated as held by one person.

(B) *Predecessors.*—Reference to any partnership shall include a reference to any predecessor thereof.

(C) *Treatment of certain debt instruments.*—Solely for purposes of paragraph (a)(8)(i)(D) of this section, any debt instrument which is described in both paragraph (a)(1)(ii) and (2)(i) of this section shall be treated as a commodity.

(iv) *Procedure for making the election provided in section 988(c)(1)(E)(iii)(V).*—A partnership shall make the election provided in section 988(c)(1)(E)(iii)(V) by sending to the Internal Revenue Service Center, Examination Branch, Stop Number 92, Kansas City, MO 64999 a statement titled "QUALIFIED FUND ELECTION UNDER SECTION 988(c)(1)(E)(iii)(V)" that contains the following:

(A) The partnership's name, address, and taxpayer identification number;

(B) The name, address and taxpayer identification number of the general partner making the election on behalf of the partnership;

(C) The date the notice is mailed or otherwise delivered to the Internal Revenue Service Center;

(D) A brief description of the activity of the partnership;

(E) A statement that the partnership is making the election provided in section 988(c)(1)(E)(iii)(V);

(F) The date of the beginning of the taxable year for which the election is being made;

(G) If the election is filed after the first day of the taxable year, then a statement regarding whether the partnership previously held an instrument referred to in section 988(c)(1)(E)(i) during such taxable year and, if so, the first date during the taxable year on which such contract was held; and

(H) The signature of the general partner making the election.

The election shall be made by a general partner with management responsibility of the partnership's activities and a copy of such election shall be attached to the partnership's income tax return (Form 1065) for the first taxable year it is effective. It is not required to be attached to subsequent returns.

(v) *Time for making the election.*—The election under section 988(c)(1)(E)(iii)(V) for any taxable year shall be made on or before the first day of the taxable year or, if later, on or before the first day during such year on which the partnership holds an instrument described in section 988(c)(1)(E)(i). The election under section 988(c)(1)(E)(iii)(V) shall apply to the taxable year for which made and all succeeding taxable years. Such election may only be revoked with the consent of the Commissioner. In determining whether to grant revocation of the election, recapture by the partners of the tax benefit derived from the election in previous taxable years will be considered.

(vi) *Operative rules applicable to qualified funds.*—(A) *In general.*—In the case of a qualified fund, any bank forward contract or any foreign currency futures contract traded on a foreign exchange which is not otherwise a section 1256 contract shall be treated as a section 1256 contract for purposes of section 1256.

(B) *Gains and losses treated as short-term.*—In the case of any instrument treated as a section 1256 contract under paragraph (a)(8)(vi)(A) of this section, subparagraph (A) of section 1256(a)(3) shall be applied by substituting "100 percent" for "40 percent" (and subparagraph (B) of such section shall not apply).

(vii) *Transition rule.*—An election made prior to September 21, 1989, which satisfied the requirements of Notice 88-124, 1988-51 I.R.B. 6, shall be deemed to satisfy the requirements of § 1.988-1(a)(8)(iv) and (v).

(viii) *General effective date rules.*—(A) The requirements of subclause (IV) of section 988(c)(1)(E)(iii) shall not apply to contracts entered into or acquired on or before October 21, 1988.

(B) In the case of any partner in an existing partnership, the 20 percent ownership requirements of subclause (I) of section 988(c)(1)(E)(iii) shall be treated as met during any period during which such partner does not own a percentage interest in the capital or profits of such partnership greater than 33 1/3 percent (or, if lower, the lowest such percentage interest of such partner during any period after October 21, 1988, during which such partnership is in existence). For purposes of the preceding sentence, the term "existing partnership" means any partnership if—

(1) such partnership was in existence on October 21, 1988, and principally engaged on such date in buying and selling options, futures, or forwards with respect to commodities; or

(2) a registration statement was filed with respect to such partnership with the Securities and Exchange Commission on or before such date and such registration statement indicated that the principal activity of such partnership will consist of buying and selling instruments referred to in paragraph (a)(8)(viii)(B)(*1*) of this section.

(9) *Exception for certain transactions entered into by an individual.*—(i) *In general.*—A transaction entered into by an individual which otherwise qualifies as a section 988 transaction shall be considered a section 988 transaction only to the extent expenses properly allocable to such transaction meet the requirements of section 162 or 212 (other than the part of sec-

tion 212 dealing with expenses incurred in connection with taxes).

(ii) *Examples.*—The following examples illustrate the application of paragraph (a)(9) of this section.

Example 1. X is a U.S. citizen who therefore has the U.S. dollar as his functional currency. On January 1, 1990, X enters into a spot contract to purchase 10,000 British pounds (£) for $15,000 for delivery on January 3, 1990. Immediately upon delivery, X acquires at original issue a pound denominated bond with an issue price of £ 10,000. The bond matures on January 3, 1993, pays interest in pounds at a rate of 10% compounded semiannually, and has no original issue discount. Assume that all expenses properly allocable to these transactions would meet the requirements of section 212. Under § 1.988-2(d)(1)(ii), entering into the spot contract on January 1, 1990, is not a section 988 transaction. The acquisition of the pounds on January 3, 1990, under the spot contract is a section 988 transaction for purposes of establishing X's basis in the pounds. The disposition of the pounds and the acquisition of the bond by X are section 988 transactions. These transactions are not excluded from the definition of a section 988 transaction under paragraph (a)(9) of this section because expenses properly allocable to such transactions meet the requirements of section 212.

Example 2. X is a U.S. citizen who therefore has the dollar as his functional currency. In preparation for X's vacation, X purchases 1,000 British pounds (£) from a bank on June 1, 1989. During the period of X's vacation in the United Kingdom beginning June 10, 1989, and ending June 20, 1989, X spends £500 for hotel rooms, £ 300 for food and £200 for miscellaneous vacation expenses. The expenses properly allocable to such dispositions do not meet the requirements of section 162 or 212. Thus, the disposition of the pounds by X on his vacation are not section 988 transactions.

(10) *Intra-taxpayer transactions.*—(i) *In general.*—Except as provided in paragraph (a)(10)(ii) of this section, transactions between or among the taxpayer and/or qualified business units of that taxpayer ("intra-taxpayer transactions") are not section 988 transactions. See section 987 and the regulations thereunder.

(ii) *Certain transfers.*—Exchange gain or loss with respect to nonfunctional currency or any item described in paragraph (a)(2) of this section entered into with another taxpayer shall be realized upon an intra-taxpayer transfer of such currency or item where as the result of the transfer the currency or other such item—

(A) Loses its character as nonfunctional currency or an item described in paragraph (a)(2) of this section; or

(B) Where the source of the exchange gain or loss could be altered absent the application of this paragraph (a)(10)(ii).

Such exchange gain or loss shall be computed in accordance with § 1.988-2 (without regard to § 1.988-2(b)(8)) as if the nonfunctional currency or item described in paragraph (a)(2) of this section had been sold or otherwise transferred at fair market value between unrelated taxpayers. For purposes of the preceding sentence, a taxpayer must use the translation rate that it uses for purposes of computing section 987 gain or loss with respect to the QBU branch that makes the transfer. In the case of a gain or loss incurred in a transaction described in this paragraph (a)(10)(ii) that does not have a significant business purpose, the Commissioner, may defer such gain or loss.

(iii) *Example.*—The following example illustrates the provisions of this paragraph (a)(10).

Example. (A) X, a corporation with the U.S. dollar as its functional currency, operates through foreign branches Y and Z. Y and Z are qualified business units as defined in section 989(a) with the LC as their functional currency. X computes Y's and Z's income under section 987 (relating to branch transactions). On November 12, 1988, Y transfers $25 to the home office of X when the fair market value of such amount equals LC120. Y has a basis of LC100 in the $25. Under paragraph (a)(10)(ii) of this section, Y realizes foreign source exchange gain of LC20 (LC120 - LC100) as the result of the $25 transfer. For purposes of determining whether the transfer is a remittance resulting in additional gain or loss, see section 987 and the regulations thereunder.

(B) If instead Y transfers the $25 to Z, exchange gain is not realized because the $25 is nonfunctional currency with respect to Z and if Z were to immediately convert the $25 into LCs, the gain would be foreign source. For purposes of determining whether the transfer is a remittance resulting in additional gain or loss, see section 987 and the regulations thereunder.

(11) *Authority to include or exclude transactions from section 988.*—(i) *In general.*—The Commissioner may recharacterize a transaction (or series of transactions) in whole or in part as a section 988 transaction if the effect of such transaction (or series of transactions) is to avoid section 988. In addition, the Commissioner may exclude a transaction (or series of transactions) which in form is a section 988 transaction from the provisions of section 988 if

the substance of the transaction (or series of transactions) indicates that it is not properly considered a section 988 transaction.

(ii) *Example.*—The following example illustrates the provisions of this paragraph (a)(11).

Example. B is an individual with the U.S. dollar as its functional currency. B holds 500,000 Swiss francs which have a basis of $100,000 and a fair market value of $400,000 as of October 15, 1989. On October 16, 1989, B transfers the 500,000 Swiss francs to a newly formed U.S. corporation, X, with the dollar as its functional currency. On October 16, 1989, B sells the stock of X for $400,000. Assume the transfer to X qualified for nonrecognition under section 351. Because the sale of the stock of X is a substitute for the disposition of an asset subject to section 988, the Commissioner may recharacterize the sale of the stock as a section 988 transaction. The same result would obtain if B transferred the Swiss francs to a partnership and then sold the partnership interest.

(b) *Spot contract.*—A spot contract is a contract to buy or sell nonfunctional currency on or before two business days following the date of the execution of the contract. See § 1.988-2(d)(1)(ii) for operative rules regarding spot contracts.

(c) *Nonfunctional currency.*—The term "nonfunctional currency" means with respect to a taxpayer or a qualified business unit (as defined in section 989(a)) a currency (including the European Currency Unit) other than the taxpayer's or the qualified business unit's functional currency as defined in section 985 and the regulations thereunder. For rules relating to nonrecognition of exchange gain or loss with respect to certain dispositions of nonfunctional currency, see § 1.988-2(a)(1)(iii).

(d) *Spot rate.*—(1) *In general.*—Except as otherwise provided in this paragraph, the term "spot rate" means a rate demonstrated to the satisfaction of the District Director or the Assistant Commissioner (International) to reflect a fair market rate of exchange available to the public for currency under a spot contract in a free market and involving representative amounts. In the absence of such a demonstration, the District Director or the Assistant Commissioner (International), in his or her sole discretion, shall determine the spot rate from a source of exchange rate information reflecting actual transactions conducted in a free market. For example, the taxpayer or the District Director or the Assistant Commissioner (International) may determine the spot rate by reference to exchange rates published in the pertinent monthly issue of "International Financial Statistics" or a successor publication of the International Monetary Fund; exchange rates published by the Board of Governors of the Federal Reserve System pursuant to 31 U.S.C. section 5151; exchange rates published in newspapers, financial journals or other daily financial news sources; or exchange rates quoted by electronic financial news services.

(2) *Consistency required in valuing transactions subject to section 988.*—If the use of inconsistent sources of spot rate quotations results in the distortion of income, the District Director or the Assistant Commissioner (International) may determine the appropriate spot rate.

(3) *Use of certain spot rate conventions for payables and receivables denominated in nonfunctional currency.*—If consistent with the taxpayer's financial accounting, a taxpayer may utilize a spot rate convention determined at intervals of one quarter year or less for purposes of computing exchange gain or loss with respect to payables and receivables denominated in a nonfunctional currency that are incurred in the ordinary course of business with respect to the acquisition or sale of goods or the obtaining or performance of services. For example, if consistent with the taxpayer's financial accounting, a taxpayer may accrue all payables and receivables incurred during the month of January at the spot rate on December 31 or January 31 (or at an average of any spot rates occurring between these two dates) and record the payment or receipt of amounts in satisfaction of such payables and receivables consistent with such convention. The use of a spot rate convention cannot be changed without the consent of the Commissioner.

(4) *Currency where an official government established rate differs from a free market rate.*—(i) *In general.*—If a currency has an official government established rate that differs from a free market rate, the spot rate shall be the rate which most clearly reflects the taxpayer's income. Generally, this shall be the free market rate.

(ii) *Examples.*—The following examples illustrate the application of this paragraph (d)(4).

Example 1. X is an accrual method U.S. corporation with the dollar as its functional currency. X owns all the stock of a Country L subsidiary, CFC. CFC has the currency of Country L, the LC, as its functional currency. Country L imposes restrictions on the remittance of dividends. On April 1, 1990, CFC pays a dividend to X in the amount of LC100. Assume that the official government established rate is $1 = LC1 and the free market rate, which takes into account the remittance restrictions and which is the rate that most clearly reflects income, is $1 = LC4. On April 1, 1990, X donates the LC100 in a transaction that otherwise qualifies as a charitable contribution under section 170(c). Both the amount of the dividend income and the deduction under section 170 is $25 (LC100 × the free market rate, $.25).

Example 2. X, a corporation with the U.S. dollar as its functional currency, operates in foreign country L through branch Y. Y is a qualified business unit as defined in section 989(a). X computes Y's income under the dollar approximate separate transactions method as described in § 1.985-3. The currency of L is the LC. X can purchase legally United States dollars ($) in L only from the L government. In order to take advantage of an arbitrage between the official and secondary dollar to LC exchange rates in L:

(i) X purchases LC100 for $60 in L on the secondary market when the official exchange rate is $1 = LC1;

(ii) X transfers the LC100 to Y;

(iii) Y purchases $100 for LC100; and

(iv) Y transfers $65 ($100 less an L tax withheld of $35 on the transfer) to the home office of X.

Under paragraph (a)(7) of this section, the transfer of the LC100 by X to Y is a realization event. X has a basis of $60 in the LC100. Under these facts, the appropriate dollar to LC exchange rate for computing the amount realized by X is the official exchange rate. Therefore, X realizes $40 ($100 − $60) of U.S. source gain from the transfer to Y. The same result would obtain if Y rather than X purchased the LC100 on the secondary market in L with $60 supplied by X, because the substance of this transaction is that X is performing the arbitrage.

(e) *Exchange gain or loss.*—The term "exchange gain or loss" means the amount of gain or loss realized as determined in § 1.988-2 with respect to a section 988 transaction. Except as otherwise provided in these regulations (*e.g.,* § 1.988-5), the amount of exchange gain or loss from a section 988 transaction shall be separately computed for each section 988 transaction, and such amount shall not be integrated with gain or loss recognized on another transaction (whether or not such transaction is economically related to the section 988 transaction). See § 1.988-2(b)(8) for a special rule with respect to debt instruments.

(f) *Hyperinflationary currency.*—(1) *Definition.*—(i) *General rule.*—For purposes of section 988, a hyperinflationary currency means a currency described in § 1.985-1(b)(2)(ii)(D). Unless otherwise provided, the currency in any example used in § § 1.988-1 through 1.988-5 is not a hyperinflationary currency.

(ii) *Special rules for determining base period.*—In determining whether a currency is hyperinflationary under § 1.985-1(b)(2)(ii)(D) for purposes of this paragraph (f), the following rules will apply:

(A) The base period means the thirty-six calendar month period ending on the last day of the taxpayer's (or qualified business unit's) current taxable year. Thus, for example, if for 1996, 1997, and 1998, a country's annual inflation rates are 6 percent, 11 percent, and 90 percent, respectively, the cumulative inflation rate for the three-year base period is 124% [((1.06 × 1.11 × 1.90) − 1.0 = 1.24) × 100 = 124%]. Accordingly, assuming the QBU has a calendar year as its taxable year, the currency of the country is hyperinflationary for the 1998 taxable year. This change in the § 1.985-1(b)(2)(ii)(D) base period shall not apply to any section 988 transaction of an entity described in section 851 (regulated investment company (RIC)) or section 856 (real estate investment trust (REIT)). The Service may, by notice, provide that the foregoing change in the § 1.985-1(b)(2)(ii)(D) base period does not apply to any section 988 transaction of an entity with distribution requirements similar to a RIC or REIT.

(B) The last sentence of § 1.985-1(b)(2)(ii)(D) shall not apply to alter the base period for purposes of this paragraph (f) in determining whether a currency is hyperinflationary for purposes of section 988. Accordingly, generally accepted accounting principles may not apply to alter the base period for purposes of this paragraph (f).

(2) *Effective date.*—Paragraph (f)(1) of this section shall apply to transactions entered into after February 14, 2000.

(g) *Fair market value.*—The fair market value of an item shall, where relevant, reflect an appropriate premium or discount for the time value of money (*e.g.,* the fair market value of a forward contract to buy or sell nonfunctional currency shall reflect the present value of the difference between the units of nonfunctional currency times the market forward rate at the time of valuation and the units of nonfunctional currency times the forward rate set forth in the contract). However, if consistent with the taxpayer's method of financial accounting (and consistently applied from year to year), the preceding sentence shall not apply to a financial instrument that matures within one year from the date of issuance or acquisition. Unless otherwise provided, the fair market value given in any example used in § § 1.988-1 through 1.988-5 is deemed to reflect appropriately the time value of money. If the use of inconsistent sources of forward or other market rate quotations results in the distortion of income, the District Director or the Assistant Commissioner (International) may determine the appropriate rate.

(h) *Interaction with sections 1092 and 1256.*—Unless otherwise provided, it is assumed for purposes of §§ 1.988-1 through 1.988-5 that any contract used in any example is not a section 1256 contract and is not part of a straddle as defined in section 1092. No inference is intended regarding the application of section 1092 or 1256 unless expressly stated.

(i) *Effective date.*—Except as otherwise provided in this section, this section shall be effective for taxable years beginning after December 31, 1986. Thus, except as otherwise provided in this section, any payments made or received with respect to a section 988 transaction in taxable years beginning after December 31, 1986, are subject to this section. [Reg. § 1.988-1.]

☐ [*T.D.* 8400, 3-16-92. *Amended by T.D.* 8914, 12-29-2000.]

§ 1.988-2. Recognition and computation of exchange gain or loss.—(a) *Disposition of nonfunctional currency.*—(1) *Recognition of exchange gain or loss.*—(i) *In general.*—Except as otherwise provided in this section, § 1.988-1(a)(7)(ii), and § 1.988-5, the recognition of exchange gain or loss upon the sale or other disposition of nonfunctional currency shall be governed by the recognition provisions of the Internal Revenue Code which apply to the sale or disposition of property (*e.g.*, section 1001 or, to the extent provided in regulations, section 1092). The disposition of nonfunctional currency in settlement of a forward contract, futures contract, option contract, or similar financial instrument is considered to be a sale or disposition of the nonfunctional currency for purposes of the preceding sentence.

(ii) *Clarification of section 1031.*—An amount of one nonfunctional currency is not "property of like kind" with respect to an amount of a different nonfunctional currency.

(iii) *Coordination with section 988(c)(1)(C)(ii).*—No exchange gain or loss is recognized with respect to the following transactions—

(A) An exchange of units of nonfunctional currency for different units of the same nonfunctional currency;

(B) The deposit of nonfunctional currency in a demand or time deposit or similar instrument (including a certificate of deposit) issued by a bank or other financial institution if such instrument is denominated in such currency;

(C) The withdrawal of nonfunctional currency from a demand or time deposit or similar instrument issued by a bank or other financial institution if such instrument is denominated in such currency;

(D) The receipt of nonfunctional currency from a bank or other financial institution from which the taxpayer purchased a certificate of deposit or similar instrument denominated in such currency by reason of the maturing or other termination of such instrument; and

(E) The transfer of nonfunctional currency from a demand or time deposit or similar instrument issued by a bank or other financial institution to another demand or time deposit or similar instrument denominated in the same nonfunctional currency issued by a bank or other financial institution.

The taxpayer's basis in the units of nonfunctional currency or other property received in the transaction shall be the adjusted basis of the units of nonfunctional currency or other property transferred. See paragraph (b) of this section with respect to the timing of interest income or expense and the determination of exchange gain or loss thereon.

(iv) *Example.*—The following example illustrates the provisions of paragraph (a)(1)(iii) of this section.

Example. X is a corporation on the accrual method of accounting with the U.S. dollar as its functional currency. On January 1, 1989, X acquires 1,500 British pounds (£) for $2,250 (£1 = $1.50). On January 3, 1989, when the spot rate is £ 1 = $1.49, X deposits the £1,500 with a British financial institution in a non-interest bearing demand account. On February 1, 1989, when the spot rate is £1 = $1.45, X withdraws the £1,500. On February 5, 1989, when the spot rate is £1 = $1.42, X purchases inventory in the amount of £ 1,500. Pursuant to paragraph (a)(1)(iii) of this section, no exchange loss is realized until February 5, 1989, when X disposes of the £1,500 for inventory. At that time, X realizes exchange loss in the amount of $120 computed under paragraph (a)(2) of this section. The loss is not an adjustment to the cost of the inventory.

(2) *Computation of gain or loss.*—(i) *In general.*—Exchange gain realized from the sale or other disposition of nonfunctional currency shall be the excess of the amount realized over the adjusted basis of such currency, and exchange loss realized shall be the excess of the adjusted basis of such currency over the amount realized.

(ii) *Amount realized.*—(A) *In general.*—The amount realized from the disposition of nonfunctional currency shall be determined under section 1001(b). A taxpayer that uses a spot rate convention under §1.988-1(d)(3) to determine exchange gain or loss with respect to a payable shall determine the amount realized upon the disposition of nonfunctional currency paid in satisfaction of the payable in a manner consistent with such convention.

(B) *Exchange of nonfunctional currency for property.*—For purpose of paragraph (a)(2) of this section, the exchange of nonfunctional currency for property (other than nonfunctional currency) shall be treated as—

(1) An exchange of the units of nonfunctional currency for units of functional currency at the spot rate on the date of the exchange, and

(2) The purchase or sale of the property for such units of functional currency.

(C) *Example.*—The following example illustrates the provisions of paragraph (a)(2)(ii)(B) of this section.

Example. G is a U.S. corporation with the U.S. dollar as its functional currency. On January 1, 1989, G enters into a contract to purchase a paper manufacturing machine for 10,000,000 British pounds (£) for delivery on January 1, 1991. On January 1, 1991, when G exchanges £10,000,000 (which G purchased for $12,000,000) for the machine, the fair market value of the machine is £17,000,000. On January 1, 1991, the spot exchange rate is £1 = $1.50. Under paragraph (a)(2)(ii)(B) of this section, the transaction is treated as an exchange of £10,000,000 for $15,000,000 and the purchase of the machine for $15,000,000. Accordingly, in computing G's exchange gain of $3,000,000 on the disposition of the £10,000,000, the amount realized is $15,000,000. G's basis in the machine is $15,000,000. No gain is recognized on the bargain purchase of the machine.

(iii) *Adjusted basis.*—(A) *In general.*—Except as provided in paragraph (a)(2)(iii)(B) of this section, the adjusted basis of nonfunctional currency is determined under the applicable provisions of the Internal Revenue Code (*e.g.*, sections 1011 through 1023). A taxpayer that uses a spot rate convention under §1.988-1(d)(3) to determine exchange gain or loss with respect to a receivable shall determine the basis of nonfunctional currency received in satisfaction of such receivable in a manner consistent with such convention.

(B) *Determination of the basis of nonfunctional currency withdrawn from an account with a bank or other financial institution.*—

(1) *In general.*—The basis of nonfunctional currency withdrawn from an account with a bank or other financial institution shall be determined under any reasonable method that is consistently applied from year to year by the taxpayer to all accounts denominated in a nonfunctional currency. For example, a taxpayer may use a first in first out method, a last in first out method, a prorata method (as illustrated in the example below), or any other reasonable method that is consistently applied. However, a method that consistently results in units of nonfunctional currency with the highest basis being withdrawn first shall not be considered reasonable.

(2) *Example.*—The following example illustrates the provisions of this paragraph (a)(2)(iii)(B).

Example. (i) X, a cash basis individual with the dollar as his functional currency, opens a demand account with a Swiss bank. Assume expenses associated with the demand account are deductible under section 212. The following chart indicates Swiss franc deposits to the account, Swiss franc interest credited to the account, the dollar basis of each deposit, and the determination of the aggregate dollar basis of all Swiss francs in the account. Assume that the taxpayer has properly translated all the amounts specified in the chart and that all transactions are subject to section 988.

Date	Swiss francs Deposited	Interest Received	U.S. dollar Basis	Aggregate U.S. dollar Basis
1/01/89	1000 Sf		$500	$500
3/31/89		50 Sf	$25	$525
6/30/89		50 Sf	$24	$549
9/30/89		50 Sf	$25	$574
12/31/89		50 Sf	$26	$600

(ii) On January 1, 1990, X withdraws 500 Swiss francs from the account. X may determine his basis in the Swiss francs by multiplying the aggregate U.S. dollar basis of Swiss francs in the account by a fraction the numerator of which is the number of Swiss francs withdrawn from the account and the denominator is the total number of Swiss francs in the account. Under this method, X's basis in the 500 Swiss francs is $250 computed as follows:

$$\frac{500 \text{ Sf}}{1200 \text{ Sf}} \times \$600 = \$250$$

(iii) X's basis in the Swiss francs remaining in the account is $350 ($600 − $250). X must use this method consistently from year to year with respect to withdrawals of nonfunctional currency from all of X's accounts.

(iv) *Purchase and sale of stock or securities traded on an established securities market by cash basis taxpayer.*—(A) *Amount realized.*—If stock or securities traded on an established securities market are sold by a cash basis taxpayer for nonfunctional currency, the amount realized with respect to the stock or securities (as determined on the trade date) shall be computed by translating the units of nonfunctional currency received into functional currency at the spot rate on the settlement date of the sale. This rule applies notwithstanding that the stock or securities are treated as disposed of on a date other than the settlement date under another section of the Code. See section 453(k).

(B) *Basis.*—If stock or securities traded on an established securities market are purchased by a cash basis taxpayer for nonfunctional currency, the basis of the stock or securities shall be determined by translating the units of nonfunctional currency paid into functional currency at the spot rate on the settlement date of the purchase.

(C) *Example.*—The following example illustrates the provisions of this paragraph (a)(2)(iv).

Example. On November 1, 1989 (the trade date), X, a calendar year cash basis U.S. individual, purchases stock for £100 for settlement on November 5, 1989. On November 1, 1989, the spot value of the £100 is $140. On November 5, 1989, X purchases £100 for $141 which X uses to pay for the stock. X's basis in the stock is $141. On December 30, 1990 (the trade date), X sells the stock for £110 for settlement on January 5, 1991. On December 30, 1990, the spot value of £110 is $165. On January 5, 1991, X transfers the stock and receives £110 which, translated at the spot rate, equal $166. Under section 453(k), the stock is considered disposed of on December 30, 1990. The amount realized with respect to such disposition is the value of the £110 on January 5, 1991 ($166). Accordingly, X's gain realized on December 30, 1990, from the disposition of the stock is $25 ($166 amount realized less $141 basis). X's basis in the £110 received from the sale of the stock is $166.

(v) *Purchase and sale of stock or securities traded on an established securities market by accrual basis taxpayer.*—For taxable years beginning after March 17, 1992, an accrual basis taxpayer may elect to apply the rules of paragraph (a)(2)(iv) of this section. The election shall be made by filing a statement with the taxpayer's first return in which the election is effective clearly indicating that the election has been made. A method so elected must be applied consistently from year to year and cannot be changed without the consent of the Commissioner.

(b) *Translation of interest income or expense and determination of exchange gain or loss with respect to debt instruments.*—(1) *Translation of interest income received with respect to a nonfunctional currency demand account.*—Interest income received with respect to a demand account with a bank or other financial institution which is denominated in (or the payments of which are determined by reference to) a nonfunctional currency shall be translated into functional currency at the spot rate on the date received or accrued or pursuant to any reasonable spot rate convention consistently applied by the taxpayer to all taxable years and to all accounts denominated in nonfunctional currency in the same financial institution. For example, a taxpayer may translate interest income received with respect to a demand account on the last day of each month of the taxable year, on the last day of each quarter of the taxable year, on the last day of each half of the taxable year, or on the last day of the taxable year. No exchange gain or loss is realized upon the receipt or accrual of interest income with respect to a demand account subject to this paragraph (b)(1).

(2) *Translation of nonfunctional currency interest income or expense received or paid with respect to a debt instrument described in § 1.988-1(a)(1)(ii) and (2)(i).*—(i) *Scope.*—(A) *In general.*—Paragraph (b) of this section only applies to debt instruments described in § 1.988-1(a)(1)(ii) and (2)(i) where all payments are denominated in, or determined with reference to, a single nonfunctional currency. Except as provided in paragraph (b)(2)(i)(B) of this section, this paragraph (b) shall not apply to contingent payment debt instruments.

(B) *Nonfunctional currency contingent payment debt instruments.*—(1) *Operative rules.*—See § 1.988-6 for rules applicable to contingent payment debt instruments for which one or more payments are denominated in, or determined by reference to, a nonfunctional currency.

(2) *Certain instruments are not contingent payment debt instruments.*—For purposes of sections 163(e) and 1271 through 1275 and the regulations thereunder, a debt instrument does not provide for contingent payments merely because the instrument is denominated in, or all payments of which are determined with reference to, a single nonfunctional currency. See § 1.988-6 for the treatment of nonfunctional currency contingent payment debt instruments.

(ii) *Determination and translation of interest income or expense.*—(A) *In general.*—Interest income or expense on a debt instrument described in paragraph (b)(2)(i) of this section (including original issue discount determined in accordance with sections 1271 through 1275 and 163(e) as adjusted for acquisition premium under section 1272(a)(7), and acquisition discount determined in accordance with sections 1281 through 1283) shall be determined in units of nonfunctional currency and translated into functional currency as provided in paragraphs (b)(2)(ii)(B) and (C) of this section. For purposes of sections 483, 1273(b)(5) and 1274, the nonfunctional currency in which an instrument is denominated (or by reference to which payments are determined) shall be considered money.

(B) *Translation of interest income or expense that is not required to be accrued prior to receipt or payment.*—With respect to an instrument described in paragraph (b)(2)(i) of this section, interest income or expense received or paid that is not required to be accrued by the taxpayer prior to receipt or payment shall be translated at the spot rate on the date of receipt or payment. No exchange gain or loss is realized with respect to the receipt or payment of such interest income or expense (other than the exchange gain or loss that might be realized under paragraph (a) of this section upon the disposition of the nonfunctional currency so received or paid).

(C) *Translation of interest income or expense that is required to be accrued prior to receipt or payment.*—With respect to an instrument described in paragraph (b)(2)(i) of this section, interest income or expense that is required to be accrued prior to receipt or payment (*e.g.,* under section 1272, 1281 or 163(e) or because the taxpayer uses an accrual method of accounting) shall be translated at the average rate (or other rate specified in paragraph (b)(2)(iii)(B) of this section) for the interest accrual period or, with respect to an interest accrual period that spans two taxable years, at the average rate (or other rate specified in paragraph (b)(2)(iii)(B) of this section) for the partial period within the taxable year. See paragraphs (b)(3) and (4) of this section for the determination of exchange gain or loss on the receipt or payment of accrued interest income or expense.

(iii) *Determination of average rate or other accrual convention.*—(A) *In general.*—For purposes of this paragraph (b), the average rate for an accrual period (or partial period) shall be a simple average of the spot exchange rates for each business day of such period or other average exchange rate for the period reasonably derived and consistently applied by the taxpayer.

(B) *Election to use spot accrual convention.*—For taxable years beginning after March 17, 1992, a taxpayer may elect to translate interest income and expense at the spot rate on the last day of the interest accrual period (and in the case of a partial accrual period, the spot rate on the last day of the taxable year). If the last day of the interest accrual period is within five business days of the date of receipt or payment, the taxpayer may translate interest income or expense at the spot rate on the date of receipt or payment. The election shall be made by filing a statement with the taxpayer's first return in which the election is effective clearly indicating that the election has been made. A method so elected must be applied consistently to all debt instruments from year to year and cannot be changed without the consent of the Commissioner.

(3) *Exchange gain or loss recognized by the holder with respect to accrued interest income.*—The holder of a debt instrument described in paragraph (b)(2)(i) of this section shall realize exchange gain or loss with respect to accrued interest income on the date such accrued interest income is received or the instrument is disposed of (including a deemed disposition under section 1001 that results from a material change in terms of the instrument). Except as otherwise provided in this paragraph (b) (*e.g.,* paragraph (b)(8) of this section), exchange gain or loss realized with respect to accrued interest income shall be recognized in accordance with the applicable recognition provisions of the Internal Revenue Code. The amount of exchange gain or loss so realized with respect to accrued interest income is determined for each accrual period by—

(i) Translating the units of nonfunctional currency interest income received with respect to such accrual period (as determined under the ordering rules of paragraph (b)(7) of this section) into functional currency at the spot rate on the date the interest income is received or the instrument is disposed of (or deemed disposed of), and

(ii) Subtracting from such amount the amount computed by translating the units of nonfunctional currency interest income accrued with respect to such income received at the average rate (or other rate specified in paragraph (b)(2)(iii)(B) of this section) for the accrual period.

(4) *Exchange gain or loss recognized by the obligor with respect to accrued interest expense.*—The obligor under a debt instrument described in paragraph (b)(2)(i) of this section shall realize exchange gain or loss with respect to accrued interest expense on the date such

accrued interest expense is paid or the obligation to make payments is transferred or extinguished (including a deemed disposition under section 1001 that results from a material change in terms of the instrument). Except as otherwise provided in this paragraph (b) (*e.g.*, paragraph (b)(8) of this section), exchange gain or loss realized with respect to accrued interest expense shall be recognized in accordance with the applicable recognition provisions of the Internal Revenue Code. The amount of exchange gain or loss so realized with respect to accrued interest expense is determined for each accrual period by—

(i) Translating the units of nonfunctional currency interest expense accrued with respect to the amount of interest paid into functional currency at the average rate (or other rate specified in paragraph (b)(2)(iii)(B) of this section) for such accrual period; and

(ii) Subtracting from such amount the amount computed by translating the units of nonfunctional currency interest paid (or, if the obligation to make payments is extinguished or transferred, the units accrued) with respect to such accrual period (as determined under the ordering rules in paragraph (b)(7) of this section) into functional currency at the spot rate on the date payment is made or the obligation is transferred or extinguished (or deemed extinguished).

(5) *Exchange gain or loss recognized by the holder of a debt instrument with respect to principal.*—The holder of a debt instrument described in paragraph (b)(2)(i) of this section shall realize exchange gain or loss with respect to the principal amount of such instrument on the date principal (determined under the ordering rules of paragraph (b)(7) of this section) is received from the obligor or the instrument is disposed of (including a deemed disposition under section 1001 that results from a material change in terms of the instrument). For purposes of computing exchange gain or loss, the principal amount of a debt instrument is the holder's purchase price in units of nonfunctional currency. See paragraph (b)(10) of this section for rules regarding the amortization of that part of the principal amount that represents bond premium and the computation of exchange gain or loss thereon. If, however, the holder acquired the instrument in a transaction in which exchange gain or loss was realized but not recognized by the transferor, the nonfunctional currency principal amount of the instrument with respect to the holder shall be the same as that of the transferor. Except as otherwise provided in this paragraph (b) (*e.g.*, paragraph (b)(8) of this section), exchange gain or loss realized with respect to such principal amount shall be recognized in accordance with the applicable recognition provisions of the Internal Revenue Code. The amount of exchange gain or loss so realized by the holder with respect to principal is determined by—

(i) Translating the units of nonfunctional currency principal at the spot rate on the date payment is received or the instrument is disposed of (or deemed disposed of); and

(ii) Subtracting from such amount the amount computed by translating the units of nonfunctional currency principal at the spot rate on the date the holder (or a transferor from whom the nonfunctional principal amount is carried over) acquired the instrument (is deemed to acquire the instrument).

(6) *Exchange gain or loss recognized by the obligor of a debt instrument with respect to principal.*—The obligor under a debt instrument described in paragraph (b)(2)(i) of this section shall realize exchange gain or loss with respect to the principal amount of such instrument on the date principal (determined under the ordering rules of paragraph (b)(7) of this section) is paid or the obligation to make payments is transferred or extinguished (including a deemed disposition under section 1001 that results from a material change in terms of the instrument). For purposes of computing exchange gain or loss, the principal amount of a debt instrument is the amount received by the obligor for the debt instrument in units of nonfunctional currency. See paragraph (b)(10) of this section for rules regarding the amortization of that part of the principal amount that represents bond premium and the computation of exchange gain or loss thereon. If, however, the obligor became the obligor in a transaction in which exchange gain or loss was realized but not recognized by the transferor, the nonfunctional currency principal amount of the instrument with respect to such obligor shall be the same as that of the transferor. Except as otherwise provided in this paragraph (b) (*e.g.*, paragraph (b)(8) of this section), exchange gain or loss realized with respect to such principal shall be recognized in accordance with the applicable recognition provisions of the Internal Revenue Code. The amount of exchange gain or loss so realized by the obligor is determined by—

(i) Translating the units of nonfunctional currency principal at the spot rate on the date the obligor (or a transferor from whom the principal amount is carried over) became the obligor (or is deemed to have become the obligor); and

(ii) Subtracting from such amount the amount computed by translating the units of nonfunctional currency principal at the spot rate on the date payment is made or the obliga-

Reg. § 1.988-2(b)(6)(ii)

tion is transferred or extinguished (or deemed extinguished).

(7) *Payment ordering rules.*—(i) *Debt instruments subject to the rules of sections 163(e), or 1271 through 1288.*—In the case of a debt instrument described in paragraph (b)(2)(i) of this section that is subject to the rules of sections 163(e), or 1272 through 1288, units of nonfunctional currency (or an amount determined with reference to nonfunctional currency) received or paid with respect to such debt instrument shall be treated first as a receipt or payment of periodic interest under the principles of section 1273 and the regulations thereunder, second as a receipt or payment of original issue discount to the extent accrued as of the date of the receipt or payment, and finally as a receipt or payment of principal. Units of nonfunctional currency (or an amount determined with reference to nonfunctional currency) treated as a receipt or payment of original issue discount under the preceding sentence are attributed to the earliest accrual period in which original issue discount has accrued and to which prior receipts or payments have not been attributed. No portion thereof shall be treated as prepaid interest. These rules are illustrated by *Example 10* of paragraph (b)(9) of this section.

(ii) *Other debt instruments.*—In the case of a debt instrument described in paragraph (b)(2)(i) of this section that is not subject to the rules of section 163(e) or 1272 through 1288, whether units of nonfunctional currency (or an amount determined with reference to nonfunctional currency) received or paid with respect to such debt instrument are treated as interest or principal shall be determined under section 163 or other applicable section of the Code.

(8) *Limitation of exchange gain or loss on payment or disposition of a debt instrument.*—When a debt instrument described in paragraph (b)(2)(i) of this section is paid or disposed of, or when the obligation to make payments thereunder is satisfied by another person, or extinguished or assumed by another person, exchange gain or loss is computed with respect to both principal and any accrued interest (including original issue discount), as provided in paragraph (b)(3) through (7) of this section. However, pursuant to section 988(b)(1) and (2), the sum of any exchange gain or loss with respect to the principal and interest of any such debt instrument shall be realized only to the extent of the total gain or loss realized on the transaction. The gain or loss realized shall be recognized in accordance with the general principles of the Code. See *Examples 3, 4* and *6* of paragraph (b)(9) of this section.

(9) *Examples.*—The preceding provisions are illustrated in the following examples. The examples assume that any transaction involving an individual is a section 988 transaction.

Example 1. (i) X is an individual on the cash method of accounting with the dollar as his functional currency. On January 1, 1992, X converts $13,000 to 10,000 British pounds (£) at the spot rate of £1 = $1.30 and loans the £10,000 to Y for 3 years. The terms of the loan provide that Y will make interest payments of £1,000 on December 31 of 1992, 1993, and 1994, and will repay X's £10,000 principal on December 31, 1994. Assume the spot rates for the pertinent dates are as follows:

Date	Spot rate (pounds to dollars)
January 1, 1992	£1 = $1.30
December 31, 1992	£1 = $1.35
December 31, 1993	£1 = $1.40
December 31, 1994	£1 = $1.45

(ii) Under paragraph (b)(2)(ii)(B) of this section, X will translate the £1,000 interest payments at the spot rate on the date received. Accordingly, X will have interest income of $1,350 in 1992, $1,400 in 1993, and $1,450 in 1994. Because X is a cash basis taxpayer, X does not realize exchange gain or loss on the receipt of interest income.

(iii) Under paragraph (b)(5) of this section, X will realize exchange gain upon repayment of the £10,000 principal amount determined by translating the £10,000 at the spot rate on the date it is received (£10,000 × $1.45 = $14,500) and subtracting from such amount, the amount determined by translating the £10,000 at the spot rate on the date the loan was made (£10,000 × $1.30 = $13,000). Accordingly, X will realize an exchange gain of $1,500 on the repayment of the loan on December 31, 1994.

Example 2. (i) Assume the same facts as in *Example 1* except that X is an accrual method taxpayer and that average rates are as follows:

Accrual Period	Average rate (pounds to dollars)
1992	£1 = $1.32
1993	£1 = $1.37
1994	£1 = $1.42

(ii) Under paragraph (b)(2)(ii)(C) of this section, X will accrue the £1,000 interest payments at the average rate for the accrual period. Accordingly, X will have interest income of $1,320 in 1992, $1,370 in 1993, and $1,420 in 1994. Because X is an accrual basis taxpayer, X determines exchange gain or loss for each interest accrual period by translating the units of nonfunctional currency interest income received with respect to such accrual period at the spot rate on the date received and subtracting the amounts of interest income accrued for such period. Thus, X will realize $90 of exchange gain with respect to interest received under the loan, computed as follows:

Year	Spot Value Interest Received	Accrued Interest @ Avg. Rate	Exch. Gain
1992	$1,350	$1,320	$30
1993	$1,400	$1,370	$30
1994	$1,450	$1,420	$30
TOTAL			$90

(iii) Under paragraph (b)(5) of this section, X will realize exchange gain upon repayment of the £10,000 loan principal determined in the same manner as in *Example 1*. Accordingly, X will realize an exchange gain of $1,500 on the repayment of the loan principal on December 31, 1994.

Example 3. Assume the same facts as in *Example 1* except that X is a calendar year taxpayer on the accrual method of accounting that elects to use a spot rate convention to translate interest income as provided in § 1.988-2(b)(2)(iii)(B). Interest income is received by X on the last day of each accrual period. Under paragraph (b)(2)(ii)(C), X will translate the interest income at the spot rate on the last day of each interest accrual period. Accordingly, X will have interest income of $1,350 in 1992, and $1,400 in 1993, $1,450 in 1994. Because the rate at which the interest income is translated is the same as the rate on the day of receipt, X will not realize any exchange gain or loss with respect to the interest income. Under paragraph (b)(5) of this section, X will realize exchange gain upon repayment of the £10,000 loan principal determined in the same manner as in *Example 1*. Accordingly, X will realize an exchange gain of $1,500 on the repayment of the loan principal on December 31, 1994.

Example 4. Assume the same facts as in *Example 1* except that on December 31, 1993, X sells Y's note for 9,821.13 British pounds (£) after the interest payment. Under paragraph (b)(8) of this section, X will compute exchange gain on the £10,000 principal. The exchange gain is $1,000 [(£10,000 × $1.40) - (£10,000 × $1.30)]. This exchange gain, however, is only realized to the extent of the total gain on the disposition. X's total gain is $749.58 [(£9,821.13 ×$1.40) - (£10,000 × $1.30)]. Thus, X will realize $749.58 of exchange gain (and will realize no market loss).

Example 5. (i) The facts are the same as in *Example 1* except that Y becomes insolvent and fails to repay the full £10,000 principal when due. Instead, X and Y agree to compromise the debt for a payment of £8,000 on December 31, 1994. Under paragraph (b)(8) of this section, X will compute exchange gain on the £10,000 originally booked. The exchange gain is $1,500 [(£10,000 × $1.45) - (£10,000 × $1.30) = $1,500]. This exchange gain, however, is only realized to the extent of the total gain on the disposition. X realizes an overall loss on the disposition of $1,400 [(£8,000 × $1.45) - (£10,000 × $1.30) = ($1,400)]. Thus, X will realize no exchange gain (and a $1400 market loss).

(ii) If the exchange rate on December 31, 1994, were £1 = $1.25, rather than £1 = $1.45, X would compute exchange loss under paragraph (b)(8) of this section, on the £10,000 originally booked. The exchange loss would be $500 [(£10,000 × $1.25) - (£10,000 × $1.30) = ($500)]. X's total loss on the disposition would be $3,000 [(£8,000 × $1.25) - (£10,000 × $1.30) = ($3,000)]. Thus, X would realize $500 of exchange loss and a $2,500 market loss on the disposition.

Example 6. (i) X is an individual with the dollar as his functional currency. X is on the cash method of accounting. On January 1, 1989, X borrows 10,000 British pounds (£) from Y, an unrelated person. The terms of the loan provide that X will make interest payments of £1,200 on December 31 of 1989 and 1990 and will repay Y's £10,000 principal on December 31, 1990. The spot rates for the pertinent dates are as follows:

DATE	SPOT RATE (pounds to dollars)
January 1, 1989	1 = $1.50
December 31, 1989	1 = $1.60
December 31, 1990	1 = $1.70

Assume that the basis of the £1,200 paid as interest by X on December 31, 1989 is $2,000, the basis of the £1,200 paid as interest by X on December 31, 1990, is $2,020 and the basis of the £10,000 principal paid by X on December 31, 1990 is $16,000.

(ii) Under paragraph (b)(2)(ii)(B) of this section, X translates the £1,200 interest payments at the spot rate on the day paid. Thus, X paid $1,920 (£1,200 × $1.60) of interest on December 31, 1989 and $2,040 (£1,200 × $1.70) of interest on December 31, 1990. In addition, X will realize exchange gain or loss on the disposition of the £1,200 on December 31, 1989 and 1990, under paragraph (a) of this section. Pursuant to paragraph (a)(2) of this section, X will realize an exchange loss of $80 [(£1,200 × $1.60) - $2,000] on December 31, 1989 and exchange gain of $20 [(£1,200 × $1.70) - $2,020] on December 31, 1990.

(iii) Under paragraph (b)(6) of this section, X will realize exchange loss on December 31, 1990 upon repayment of the £10,000 principal amount determined by translating the £10,000 received at the spot rate on January 1,

1989 (£10,000 × $1.50 = $15,000) and subtracting from such amount, the amount determined by translating the £10,000 paid at the spot rate on December 31, 1990 (£10,000 × $1.70 = $17,000). Thus, under paragraph (b)(6) of this section, X has an exchange loss with respect to the £10,000 principal of $2,000. Further, under paragraph (a)(2) of this section, X will realize an exchange gain upon disposition of the £10,000 on December 31, 1990. Under paragraph (a)(2) of this section, X will subtract his adjusted basis in the £10,000 ($16,000) from the amount realized upon the disposition of the £10,000 (£10,000 × $1.70 = $17,000) resulting in a gain of $1,000. Accordingly, X's combined exchange gain and loss realized on December 31, 1990 with respect to the repayment of the £10,000 is a $1,000 exchange loss.

Example 7. (i) X is a calendar year corporation on the accrual method of accounting and with the dollar as its functional currency. On January 1, 1989, X purchases at original issue for 82.64 Canadian dollars (C$) M corporation's 2 year note maturing on December 31, 1990, at a stated redemption price of C$ 100. The yield to maturity in Canadian dollars is 10 percent and the accrual period is the one year period beginning January 1 and ending December 31. The note has C$17.36 of original issue discount. Assume that the spot rates are as follows: C$1 = U.S.$.72 on January 1, 1989; C$1 = U.S.$.80 on January 1, 1990; C$1 = U.S.$.82 on December 31, 1990. Assume further that the average rate for 1989 is C$1 = U.S.$.76 and for 1990 is C$1 = U.S.$.81.

(ii) Under paragraph (b)(2)(ii)(A) of this section, X will determine its interest income in Canadian dollars. Accordingly, under section 1272, X must take into account original issue discount in the amount of C$8.26 on December 31, 1989 and C$9.10 on December 31, 1990. Pursuant to paragraph (b)(2)(ii)(C) of this section, X will translate these amounts into U.S. dollars at the average exchange rate for the relevant accrual period. Thus, the amount of interest income taken into account in 1989 is U.S.$6.28 (C$8.26 × U.S.$.76) and in 1990 is U.S.$7.37 (C$9.10 × U.S.$.81). Pursuant to paragraph (b)(3)(ii) of this section, X will realize exchange gain or loss with respect to the accrued interest determined for each accrual period by translating the Canadian dollars received with respect to such accrual period into U.S. dollars at the spot rate on the date the interest is received and subtracting from that amount the amount accrued in U.S. dollars. Thus, the amount of exchange gain realized on December 31, 1990, is U.S.$.58 (U.S.$.49 from 1989 + U.S.$.09 from 1990). Pursuant to paragraph (b)(5) of this section, X shall realize exchange gain or loss with respect to the principal (C$82.64) on December 31, 1990, computed by translating the C$82.64 at the spot rate on December 31, 1990 (U.S.$67.76) and subtracting the C$82.64 translated at the spot rate on January 1, 1989 (U.S.$59.50) for an exchange gain of U.S.$8.26. Thus, X's combined exchange gain is U.S.$8.84 (U.S.$.49 + U.S.$.09 + U.S.$8.26).

(iii) Assume instead that on January 1, 1990, X sells the note for C$86.95, which it immediately converts to U.S. dollars. X's exchange gain is computed under paragraph (b)(8) of this section with reference to the nonfunctional currency denominated principal amount (C$82.64) and the nonfunctional currency denominated accrued original issue discount (C$8.26). X will compute an exchange gain of U.S.$6.61 with respect to the issue price [(C$82.64 × U.S.$.80) – (C$82.64 × U.S.$.72)] and an exchange gain of U.S.$.33 with respect to the accrued original issue discount [(C$8.26 ×U.S.$.80) – (C$8.26 × U.S.$.76)]. Accordingly, prior to the application of paragraph (b)(8) of this section, X's total exchange gain is U.S.$6.94 (U.S.$6.61 + U.S.$.33), and X's market loss is U.S.$3.16 [(C$90.90 – C$86.95) × U.S.$.80]. Pursuant to paragraph (b)(8) of this section, however, X's market loss on the note of U.S.$3.16 is netted against X's exchange gain of U.S.$6.94, resulting in a realized exchange gain of U.S.$3.78 and no market loss.

Example 8. (i) The facts are the same as in *Example 7* (i) except that on January 1, 1990, X contributes the M corporation note to Y, a wholly-owned U.S. subsidiary of X with the dollar as its functional currency, and Y collects C$100 from M corporation at maturity on December 31, 1990, when the spot rate is C$1= U.S.$.82. The transfer of the note from X to Y qualifies for nonrecognition of gain under section 351(a). On December 31, 1990, Y includes C$9.10 of accrued interest in income which translated at the average exchange rate of C$1 = U.S.$.81 for the year results in U.S.$7.37 of interest income.

(ii) Y's exchange gain is computed under paragraph (b)(3) of this section with respect to accrued interest income and paragraph (b)(5) of this section with respect to the nonfunctional currency principal amount. Under paragraph (b)(3) of this section, Y will realize exchange gain or loss for each accrual period computed by translating the units of nonfunctional currency interest income received with respect to such accrual period at the spot rate on the day received and subtracting the amounts of interest income accrued for such period. Thus, Y will realize $.49 of exchange gain with respect to original issue discount accrued in 1989 [(C$8.26 × U.S.$.82) – (C$8.26 × U.S.$.76) = U.S.$.49] and $.09 of exchange gain with respect to original issue discount accrued in 1990

[(C$9.10 × U.S.$.82) − (C$9.10 × U.S.$.81) = $.09].

(iii) Pursuant to paragraph (b)(5) of this section, the nonfunctional currency principal amount of the M bond in the hands of Y is C$82.64, the amount carried over from X, the transferor. Y's exchange gain with respect to the nonfunctional currency principal amount is $8.26 [(C$82.64 × U.S.$.82) − (C$82.64 × U.S.$.72) = U.S.$8.26]. Accordingly, Y's combined exchange gain is U.S.$8.84 ($.49 + $.09 + $8.26). Because the amount realized in Canadian dollars equals the adjusted issue price (C$100) on retirement of the M note, there is no market loss, and the netting rule of paragraph (b)(8) of this section does not limit realization of the exchange gain.

Example 9. (i) X is a calendar year corporation on the accrual method of accounting and with the dollar as its functional currency. X elects to use the spot rate convention to translate interest income as provided in paragraph (b)(2)(iii)(B) of this section. On January 31, 1992, X loans £1000 to Y, an unrelated person. Under the terms of the loan, Y will pay X interest of £50 on July 31, 1992, and January 31, 1993, and will repay the £1000 principal on January 31, 1993. Assume the following spot exchange rates:

DATE	SPOT RATE (pounds to dollars)
January 31, 1992	£1 = $1.50
July 31, 1992	£1 = $1.55
December 31, 1992	£1 = $1.60
January 31, 1993	£1 = $1.61

(ii) Under paragraph (b)(2)(ii)(C) of this section, X will translate the interest income at the spot rate on the last day of each interest accrual period (and in the case of a partial accrual period, at the spot rate on the last day of the taxable year). Accordingly, X will have interest income of $77.50 (£50 × $1.55) on July 31, 1992. Assuming under X's method of accounting that interest is accrued daily, X will accrue $66.50 (153/184 × £50) × $1.60) of interest income on December 31, 1992. On January 31, 1993, X will have interest income of $13.60 ((31/184 × £50) × $1.61). Because the rate at which the interest income is translated is the same as the rate on the day of receipt, X will not realize any exchange gain or loss with respect to the interest income received on July 31, 1992. However, X will realize exchange gain on the £41.50 (153/184 × £50) of accrued interest income of $.41 [(£41.50 × $1.61) − (£41.50 × $1.60) = $.41].

(iii) Under paragraph (b)(5) of this section, X will realize exchange gain upon repayment of the £100 principal amount determined by translating the £100 at the spot rate on the date it is received (£100 × $1.61 = $161.00) and subtracting from such amount, the amount determined by translating the £100 at the spot rate on the date the loan was made (£100 × $1.50 = $150.00). Accordingly, X will realize an exchange gain of $11 on the repayment of the loan on January 31, 1993.

Example 10. (i) X, a cash basis taxpayer with the dollar as its functional currency, has the calendar year as its taxable year. On January 1, 1992, X purchases at original issue for 65.88 British pounds (£) M corporation's 5-year bond maturing on December 31, 1996, having a stated redemption price at maturity of £100. The bond provides for annual payments of interest in pounds of 1 pound per year on December 31 of each year. The bond has 34.12 British pounds of original issue discount. The yield to maturity is 10 percent in British pounds and the accrual period is the one year period beginning January 1 and ending December 31 of each calendar year. The amount of original issue discount is determined in pounds for each accrual period by multiplying the adjusted issue price expressed in pounds by the yield and subtracting from such amount the periodic interest payments expressed in pounds for such period. The periodic interest payments are translated at the spot rate on the payment date (December 31 of each year). The original issue discount is translated at the average rate for the accrual period (January 1 through December 31). The following chart describes the determination of interest income with respect to the facts presented and provides other pertinent information.

Table 1

1	2	3	4	5	6	7	8	9	10
Year (Dec. 31)	Periodic interest payments in pounds for the accrual period	Original issue discount in pounds for the accrual period	Issue price or adjusted issue price in pounds	Assumed spot rate on Dec. 31 (pounds to dollars)	Assumed average rate for accrual period (pounds to dollars)	Periodic interest payments in pounds multiplied by spot rate on the date of payment (column 2 times column 5)	Original issue discount in pounds multiplied by the average rate for the accrual period (column 3 times column 6)	Total interest income in dollars (column 7 plus column 8)	Adjusted issue price in dollars
Issue Date			65.88	1 = $1.20					$79.06
1992	1	5.59	71.47	1 = $1.30	1 = $1.25	$1.30	$6.99	$8.29	$86.05
1993	1	6.15	77.62	1 = $1.40	1 = $1.35	$1.40	$8.30	$9.70	$94.35
1994	1	6.76	84.38	1 = $1.50	1 = $1.45	$1.50	$9.80	$11.30	$104.15
1995	1	7.44	91.82	1 = $1.60	1 = $1.55	$1.60	$11.53	$13.13	$115.68
1996	1	8.18	100.00	1 = $1.70	1 = $1.65	$1.70	$13.50	$15.20	$129.18

(ii) Because X is a cash basis taxpayer, X does not realize exchange gain or loss on the receipt of the £1 periodic interest payments. However, X will realize exchange gain on December 31, 1996 totaling $7.88 with respect to the original issue discount. Exchange gain is determined for each interest accrual period by translating the units of nonfunctional currency interest income received with respect to such accrual period at the spot rate on the date received and subtracting from such amount, the amount computed by translating the units of nonfunctional currency interest income accrued for such period at the average rate for the period. The following chart illustrates this computation:

Table 2

1	2	3	4	5	6	7
Year	OID accrued in pounds for each accrual period	Assumed spot rate on date payment received (pounds to dollars)	Interest received times spot rate on the date received (col. 2 times col. 3)	Assumed average rate for accrual period (pounds to dollars)	OID in pounds times the average rate for the accrual period (col. 2 times col. 5)	Exchange gain or loss (col. 4 less col. 6)
1992	5.59	1 = $1.70	$9.50	1 = $1.25	$6.99	$2.51
1993	6.15	1 = $1.70	$10.46	1 = $1.35	$8.30	$2.16
1994	6.76	1 = $1.70	$11.49	1 = $1.45	$9.80	$1.69
1995	7.44	1 = $1.70	$12.65	1 = $1.55	$11.53	$1.12
1996	8.18	1 = $1.70	$13.90	1 = $1.65	$13.50	$.40
					TOTAL	$7.88

(iii) X will also realize exchange gain with respect to the principal of the loan (*i.e.*, the issue price of 65.88 British pounds) on December 31, 1996 computed by translating the units of nonfunctional currency principal received at the spot rate on the date principal is received (65.88 British pounds × $1.70 = $112.00) and subtracting from such amount, the units of nonfunctional currency principal received translated at the spot rate on the date the instrument was acquired (65.88 British pounds × $1.20 = $79.06). Accordingly, X's exchange gain on the principal is $32.94 and X's total exchange gain with respect to the accrued interest and principal is $40.82. It should be noted that, under this fact pattern, the total exchange gain may be determined in an alternative fashion. Exchange gain may be computed by subtracting the adjusted issue price in dollars at maturity ($129.18—see column 10 of Table 1) from the amount computed by multiplying the stated redemption price at maturity in pounds times the spot rate on the maturity date (£100 × $1.70 = $170), which equals $40.82.

Example 11. (i) The facts are the same as in *Example 10* except that X makes an election under paragraph (b)(2)(iii) of this section to translate accrued interest on the last day of the accrual period. Accordingly, columns 8, 9 and 10 in Table 1 would change as follows:

1 Year (Dec. 31)	8 Original issue discount in pounds multiplied by the spot rate on last day of accrual period (Dec. 31)	9 Total interest income in dollars (column 7 plus column 8)	10 Adjusted issue price in dollars
1992	$ 7.27	$ 8.57 $ 79.06	$ 87.63
1993	$ 8.61	$10.01	$ 97.64
1994	$10.14	$11.64	$109.28
1995	$11.90	$13.50	$122.78
1996	$13.91	$15.61	$138.39

(ii) Because X is a cash basis taxpayer, X does not realize exchange gain or loss on the receipt of the £1 periodic interest payments. However, X will realize exchange gain on December 31, 1993 totaling $6.18 with respect to the original issue discount. Exchange gain is determined for each interest accrual period by translating the units of nonfunctional currency interest income received with respect to such accrual period at the spot rate on the date received and subtracting from such amount, the amount computed by translating the units of nonfunctional currency interest income accrued for such period at the spot rate on the last day of the accrual period. Accordingly, columns 5, 6 and 7 of Table 2 would change as follows:

1 Year	5 Spot rate on last day of accrual period	6 OID in pounds times the spot rate on the last day of the accrual period (col. 2 times col. 3)	7 Exchange gain or loss (col. 4 less col. 6)
1992	$1.30	$ 7.27	$2.23
1993	$1.40	$ 8.61	$1.85
1994	$1.50	$10.14	$1.35
1995	$1.60	$11.90	$0.75
1996	$1.70	$13.90	$0.00
		$6.18	

(iii) X will realize exchange gain with respect to the principal amount of the loan as provided in the preceding example.

Example 12. (i) C is a corporation that is a calendar year accrual method taxpayer with the dollar as its functional currency. On January 1, 1989, C lends 100 British pounds (£) in exchange for a note under the terms of which C will receive two equal payments of £57.62 on December 31, 1989, and December 31, 1990. Each payment of £57.62 represents the annual payment necessary to amortize the £100 principal amount at a rate of 10% compounded annually over a two year period. The following tables reflect the amounts of principal and interest that compose each payment and assumptions as to the relevant exchange rates:

Date	Principal	Interest
12/31/89	£47.62	£10.00
12/31/90	£52.38	£ 5.24

Date	Spot Rate £1 =	Average Rate for Year Ending
1/01/89	$1.30	
12/31/89	$1.40	$1.35
12/31/90	$1.50	$1.45

(ii) Because each interest payment is equal to the product of the outstanding principal balance of the obligation and a single fixed rate of interest, each stated interest payment constitutes periodic interest under the principles of section 1273. Accordingly, there is no original issue discount.

(iii) Because C is an accrual basis taxpayer, C will translate the interest income at the average rate for the annual accrual period pursuant to paragraph (b)(2)(ii)(C) of this section. Thus, C's interest income is $13.50 (£10.00 × $1.35) in 1989, and $7.60 (£5.24 × $1.45) in 1990. C will realize exchange gain or loss upon receipt of accrued interest computed in accordance with paragraph (b)(3) of this section. Thus, C will realize exchange gain in the amount of $ .50 [(£10.00 × $1.40) - $13.50] in 1989, and $ .26 [(£5.24 × $1.50) - $7.60] in 1990.

(iv) In addition, C will realize exchange gain or loss upon the receipt of principal each year computed under paragraph (b)(5) of this section. Thus, C will realize exchange gain in the amount of $4.76 [(£47.62 × $1.40) - (£47.62 × $1.30)] in 1989, and $10.48 [(£52.38 × $1.50) - (£52.38 × $1.30)] in 1990.

(10) *Treatment of bond premium.*—(i) *In general.*—Amortizable bond premium on a bond described in paragraph (b)(2)(i) of this section shall be computed in the units of nonfunctional currency in which the bond is denominated (or in which the payments are determined). Amortizable bond premium properly taken into account under section 171 or § 1.61-12 (or the successor provision thereof) shall reduce interest income or expense in units of nonfunctional currency. Exchange gain or loss is realized with respect to bond pre-

mium described in the preceding sentence by treating the portion of premium amortized with respect to any period as a return of principal. With respect to a holder that does not elect to amortize bond premium under section 171, the amount of bond premium will constitute a market loss when the bond matures. See paragraph (b)(8) of this section. The principles set forth in this paragraph (b)(10) shall apply to determine the treatment of acquisition premium described in section 1272(a)(7).

(ii) *Example.*—The following example illustrates the provisions of this paragraph (b)(10).

Example. (A) X is an individual on the cash method of accounting with the dollar as his functional currency. On January 1, 1989, X purchases Y corporation's note for 107.99 British pounds (£) from Z, an unrelated party. The note has an issue price of £100, a stated redemption price at maturity of £100, pays interest in pounds at the rate of 10% compounded annually, and matures on December 31, 1993. X elects to amortize the bond premium of £7.99 under the rules of section 171. Pursuant to paragraph (b)(10)(i) of this section, bond premium is determined and amortized in British pounds. Assume the amortization schedule is as follows:

Year Ending 12/31	Bond Premium Amortized	Unamortized Premium Plus Principal	Interest
		£107.99	
1989	£1.36	£106.63	£8.64
1990	£1.47	£105.16	£8.53
1991	£1.59	£103.57	£8.41
1992	£1.71	£101.86	£8.29
1993	£1.85	£100.00	£8.25

(B) The bond premium reduces X's pound interest income under the note. For example, the £10 stated interest payment made in 1989 is reduced by £1.36 of bond premium, and the resulting £8.64 interest income is translated into dollars at the spot rate on December 31, 1989. Exchange gain or loss is realized on the £1.36 bond premium based on the difference between the spot rates on January 1, 1989, the date the premium is paid to acquire the bond, and December 31, 1989, the date the bond premium is returned as part of the stated interest. The £1.36 bond premium reduces the unamortized premium plus principal to £106.63 (£107.99 − £1.36). On December 31, 1993, when the bond matures and the £7.99 of bond premium has been fully amortized, X will realize exchange gain or loss with respect to the remaining purchase price of £100.

(11) *Market discount.*—(i) *In general.*—Market discount as defined in section 1278(a)(2) shall be determined in units of nonfunctional currency in which the market discount bond is denominated (or in which the payments are determined). Accrued market discount (other than market discount currently included in income pursuant to section 1278(b)) shall be translated into functional currency at the spot rate on the date the market discount bond is disposed of. No part of such accrued market discount is treated as exchange gain or loss. Accrued market discount currently includible in income pursuant to section 1278(b) shall be translated into functional currency at the average exchange rate for the accrual period. Exchange gain or loss with respect to accrued market discount currently includible in income under section 1278(b) shall be determined in accordance with paragraph (b)(3) of this section relating to accrued interest income.

(ii) *Example.*—The following example illustrates the provisions of this paragraph (b)(11).

Example—(A) X is a calendar year corporation with the U.S. dollar as its functional currency. On January 1, 1990, X purchases a bond of M corporation for 96,530 British pounds (£). The bond, which was issued on January 1, 1989, has an issue price of £100,000, a stated redemption price at maturity of £100,000, and provides for annual pound payments of interest at 8 percent. The bond matures on December 31, 1991. X purchased the bond at a market discount of 3,470 pounds and did not elect to include the market discount currently in income under section 1278(b). X holds the bond to maturity and on December 31, 1991, receives payment of £100,000 (plus £8,000 interest) when the exchange rate is £1 = $1.50.

(B) Pursuant to paragraph (b)(11) of this section, X computes market discount in units of nonfunctional currency. Thus, the market discount as defined under section 1278(a)(2) is £3,470. Accrued market discount (other than market discount currently included in income pursuant to section 1278(b)) is translated at the spot rate on the date the market discount bond is disposed of. Accordingly, X will translate the accrued market discount of £3,470 at the spot rate on December 31, 1991 (£3,470 × $1.50 = $5,205). No exchange gain or loss is realized with respect to the £3,470 of accrued market discount. See paragraphs (b)(3) and (5) of this section for the realization and recognition of exchange gain or loss with respect to accrued interest and principal.

(12) *Tax exempt bonds.*—See § 1.988-3(c)(2), which characterizes exchange loss realized with respect to a nonfunctional currency tax exempt bond as a reduction of interest income.

(13) *Nonfunctional currency debt exchanged for stock of obligor.*—(i) *In general.*—Notwithstanding any other section of the Code other than section 267, 1091 or 1092, exchange

gain or loss shall be realized and recognized by the holder and the obligor in accordance with the rules of paragraphs (b)(3) through (7) of this section with respect to the principal and accrued interest of a debt instrument described in paragraph (b)(2)(i) of this section that is acquired by the obligor in exchange for its stock, provided however, that such gain or loss shall be recognized only to the extent of the total gain or loss on the exchange (regardless of whether such gain or loss would otherwise be recognized). This rule shall apply whether the debt instrument is converted into stock according to its terms or exchanged pursuant to a separate agreement between the obligor and the holder. A debt instrument that is acquired by the obligor from a shareholder as a contribution to capital shall be treated for purposes of this section as exchanged for stock, whether or not additional stock is issued.

(ii) *Coordination with section 108.*—Section 988 and this section shall apply before section 108. Exchange gain realized by the obligor on an exchange described in paragraph (b)(13)(i) of this section shall not be treated as discharge of indebtedness income, but shall be considered to reduce the amount of the liability for purposes of computing the obligor's income on the exchange under section 108(e)(4), section 108(e)(6) or section 108(e)(10).

(iii) *Effective date.*—This paragraph (b)(13) shall be effective for exchanges of debt for stock effected after September 21, 1989.

(iv) *Examples.*—The following examples illustrate the operation of this paragraph (b)(13). In each such example, assume that sections 267, 1091 and 1092 do not apply.

Example 1. (i) X is a calendar year U.S. corporation with the U.S. dollar as its functional currency. On January 1, 1990 (the issue date), X acquired a convertible bond maturing on December 31, 1998, issued by Y corporation, a U.K. corporation with the British pound (£) as its functional currency. The issue price of the bond is £100,000, the stated redemption price at maturity is £100,000, and the bond provides for annual pound interest payments at the rate of 10%. The terms of the bond also provide that at any time prior to December 31, 1998, the holder may surrender all of his interest in the bond in exchange for 20 shares of Y common stock. On January 1, 1994, X surrenders his interest in the bond for 20 shares of Y common stock. Assume the following: (a) The spot rate on January 1, 1990, is £1 = $1.30, (b) The spot rate on January 1, 1994, is £1 = $1.50, and (c) The 20 shares of Y common stock have a market value of £200,000 on January 1, 1994.

(ii) Pursuant to paragraph (b)(13) of this section, X will realize and recognize exchange gain with respect to the issue price (£100,000) of the bond on January 1, 1994, when the bond is converted to stock. X will compute exchange gain pursuant to paragraph (b)(5) of this section by translating the issue price at the spot rate on the conversion date (£100,000 × $1.50 = $150,000) and subtracting from such amount the issue price translated at the spot rate on the date X acquired the bond (£100,000 × $1.30 = $130,000). Thus, X will realize and recognize $20,000 of exchange gain. X's basis in the 20 shares of Y common stock is $150,000 ($130,000 substituted basis + $20,000 recognized gain).

Example 2. (i) X, a foreign corporation with the British pound (£) as its functional currency, lends £100 at a market rate of interest to Y, its wholly-owned U.S. subsidiary, on January 1, 1990, on which date the spot exchange rate is £1 = $1. Y's functional currency is the U.S. dollar. On January 1, 1992, when the spot exchange rate is £1 = $.50, X cancels the debt as a contribution to capital. Pursuant to paragraph (b)(13) of this section, Y will realize and recognize exchange gain with respect to the £100 issue price of the debt instrument on January 1, 1992. Y will compute exchange gain pursuant to paragraph (b)(6) of this section by translating the issue price at the spot rate on the date Y became the obligor (£100 × $1 = $100) and subtracting from such amount the issue price translated at the spot rate on the date of extinguishment (£100 × $.50 = $50). Thus, Y will realize and recognize $50 of exchange gain.

(ii) Under section 108(e)(6), on the acquisition of its indebtedness from X as a contribution to capital Y is treated as having satisfied the debt with an amount of money equal to X's adjusted basis in the debt (£100). For purposes of section 108(e)(6), X's adjusted basis is translated into United States dollars at the spot rate on the date Y acquires the debt (£1 = $.50). Therefore, Y is treated as having satisfied the debt for $50. Pursuant to paragraph (b)(13) of this section, for purposes of section 108 the amount of the indebtedness is considered to be reduced by the exchange gain from $100 to $50. Accordingly, Y recognizes $50 of exchange gain and no discharge of indebtedness income on the extinguishment of its debt to X.

(iii) If X were a United States taxpayer with a dollar functional currency and a $100 basis in Y's obligation, X would realize and recognize an exchange loss of $50 under paragraph (b)(5) of this section on the contribution of the debt to Y. The recognized loss would reduce X's adjusted basis in the debt from $100 to $50, so that for purposes of applying section 108(e)(6) Y is treated as having satisfied the debt for $50. Accordingly, under these facts as well Y would recognize $50 of exchange gain and no discharge of indebtedness income.

Example 3. (i) X and Y are unrelated calendar year U.S. corporations with the U.S. dollar as their functional currency. On January 1, 1990 (the issue date), X acquires Y's bond maturing on December 31, 1999. The issue price of the bond is £100,000, the stated redemption price at maturity is £100,000, and the bond provides for annual pound interest payments at the rate of 10%. On January 1, 1994, X and Y agree that Y will redeem its bond from X in exchange for 20 shares of Y common stock. Assume the following:

(a) The spot rate on January 1, 1990, is £1 = $1.00,

(b) The spot rate on January 1, 1994, is £1 = $.50,

(c) Interest rates on equivalent bonds have increased so that as of January 1, 1994, the value of Y's bond has declined to £90,000, and

(d) The 20 shares of Y common stock have a market value of £90,000 as of January 1, 1994.

(ii) Pursuant to paragraph (b)(13) of this section, X will realize and recognize exchange loss with respect to the issue price (£100,000) of the bond on January 1, 1994, when the bond is exchanged for stock. X will compute exchange loss pursuant to paragraph (b)(5) of this section by translating the issue price at the spot rate on the exchange date (£100,000 × $.50 = $50,000) and subtracting from such amount the issue price translated at the spot rate on the date X acquired the bond (£100,000 × $1.00 = $100,000). Thus, X will compute $50,000 of exchange loss, all of which will be realized and recognized because it does not exceed the total $55,000 realized loss on the exchange ($45,000 worth of stock received less $100,000 basis in the exchanged bond).

(iii) Pursuant to paragraph (b)(13) of this section, Y will realize and recognize exchange gain with respect to the issue price, computed under paragraph (b)(6) of this section by translating the issue price at the spot rate on the date Y became the obligor (£100,000 × $1.00 = $100,000) and subtracting from such amount the issue price translated at the spot rate on the exchange date (£100,000 × $.50 = $50,000). Thus, Y will realize and recognize $50,000 of exchange gain. Under section 108(e)(10), on the transfer of stock to X in satisfaction of its indebtedness Y is treated as having satisfied the indebtedness with an amount of money equal to the fair market value of the stock (£90,000 × $.50 = $45,000). Pursuant to paragraph (b)(13) of this section, for purposes of section 108 the amount of the indebtedness is considered to be reduced by the recognized exchange gain from $100,000 to $50,000. Accordingly, Y recognizes an additional $5,000 of discharge of indebtedness income on the exchange.

Example 4. (i) The facts are the same as in *Example 3* except that interest rates on equivalent bonds have declined, rather than increased, so that the value of Y's bond on January 1, 1994, has risen to £112,500; and X and Y agree that Y will redeem its bond from X on that date in exchange for 25 shares of Y common stock worth £112,500. Pursuant to paragraphs (b)(13) and (b)(5) of this section, X will compute $50,000 of exchange loss on the exchange with respect to the £100,000 issue price of the bond. See Example 3. However, because X's total loss on the exchange is only $43,750 ($56,250 worth of stock received less $100,000 basis in the exchanged bond), under the netting rule of paragraph (b)(13) of this section the realized exchange loss is limited to $43,750.

(ii) Pursuant to paragraphs (b)(13) and (b)(6) of this section, Y will compute $50,000 of exchange gain with respect to the issue price. See *Example 3*. Under section 108(e)(10), Y is treated as having satisfied the $100,000 indebtedness with an amount of money equal to the fair market value of the stock (£112,500 × $.50 =$56,250), resulting in a total gain on the exchange of $43,750. Accordingly, under paragraph (b)(13) of this section Y's realized (and recognized) exchange gain on the exchange is limited to $43,750. Also pursuant to paragraph (b)(13) of this section, for purposes of section 108 the amount of the indebtedness is considered to be reduced by the recognized exchange gain from $100,000 to $56,250. Accordingly, Y recognizes no discharge of indebtedness income on the exchange.

(14) [Reserved]

(15) *Debt instruments and deposits denominated in hyperinflationary currencies.*—(i) *In general.*—If a taxpayer issues, acquires, or otherwise enters into or holds a hyperinflationary debt instrument (as defined in paragraph (b)(15)(vi)(A) of this section) or a hyperinflationary deposit (as defined in paragraph (b)(15)(vi)(B) of this section) on which interest is paid or accrued that is denominated in (or determined by reference to) a nonfunctional currency of the taxpayer, then the taxpayer shall realize exchange gain or loss with respect to such instrument or deposit for its taxable year determined by reference to the change in exchange rates between—

(A) The later of the first day of the taxable year, or the date the instrument was entered into (or an amount deposited); and

(B) The earlier of the last day of the taxable year, or the date the instrument (or deposit) is disposed of or otherwise terminated.

(ii) *Only exchange gain or loss is realized.*—No gain or loss is realized under paragraph (b)(15)(i) by reason of factors other than movement in exchange rates, such as the creditworthiness of the debtor.

(iii) *Special rule for synthetic, non-hyperinflationary currency debt instruments.*—(A) *General rule.*—Paragraph (b)(15)(i) does not apply to a debt instrument that has interest and principal payments that are to be made by reference to a currency or item that does not reflect hyperinflationary conditions in a country (within the meaning of § 1.988-1(f)).

(B) *Example.*—Paragraph (b)(15)(iii)(A) is illustrated by the following example:

Example. When the Turkish lira (TL) is a hyperinflationary currency, A, a U.S. corporation with the U.S. dollar as its functional currency, makes a 5 year, 100,000 TL-denominated loan to B, an unrelated corporation, at a 10% interest rate when 1,000 TL equals $1. Under the terms of the debt instrument, B must pay interest annually to A in an amount of Turkish lira that is equal to $100. Also under the terms of the debt instrument, B must pay A upon maturity of the debt instrument an amount of Turkish lira that is equal to $1,000. Although the principal and interest are payable in a hyperinflationary currency, the debt instrument is a synthetic dollar debt instrument and is not subject to paragraph (b)(15)(i) of this section.

(iv) *Source and character of gain or loss.*—(A) *General rule for hyperinflationary conditions.*—The rules of this paragraph (b)(15)(iv)(A) shall apply to any taxpayer that is either an issuer of (or obligor under) a hyperinflationary debt instrument or deposit and has currency gain on such debt instrument or deposit, or a holder of a hyperinflationary debt instrument or deposit and has currency loss on such debt instrument or deposit. For purposes of subtitle A of the Internal Revenue Code, any exchange gain or loss realized under paragraph (b)(15)(i) of this section is directly allocable to the interest expense or interest income, respectively, from the debt instrument or deposit (computed under this paragraph (b)), and therefore reduces or increases the amount of interest income or interest expense paid or accrued during that year with respect to that instrument or deposit. With respect to a debt instrument or deposit during a taxable year, to the extent exchange gain realized under paragraph (b)(15)(i) of this section exceeds interest expense of an issuer, or exchange loss realized under paragraph (b)(15)(i) of this section exceeds interest income of a holder or depositor, the character and source of such excess amount shall be determined under §§ 1.988-3 and 1.988-4.

(B) *Special rule for subsiding hyperinflationary conditions.*—If the taxpayer is an issuer of (or obligor under) a hyperinflationary debt instrument or deposit and has currency loss, or if the taxpayer is a holder of a hyperinflationary debt instrument or deposit and has currency gain, then for purposes of subtitle A of the Internal Revenue Code, the character and source of the currency gain or loss is determined under §§ 1.988-3 and 1.988-4. Thus, if an issuer has both interest expense and currency loss, the currency loss is sourced and characterized under section 988, and does not affect the determination of interest expense.

(v) *Adjustment to principal or basis.*—Any exchange gain or loss realized under paragraph (b)(15)(i) of this section is an adjustment to the functional currency principal amount of the issuer, functional currency basis of the holder, or the functional currency amount of the deposit. This adjusted amount or basis is used in making subsequent computations of exchange gain or loss, computing the basis of assets for purposes of allocating interest under §§ 1.861-9T through 1.861-12T and 1.882-5, or making other determinations that may be relevant for computing taxable income or loss.

(vi) *Definitions.*—(A) *Hyperinflationary debt instrument.*—A hyperinflationary debt instrument is a debt instrument that provides for—

(1) Payments denominated in or determined by reference to a currency that is hyperinflationary (as defined in § 1.988-1(f)) at the time the taxpayer enters into or otherwise acquires the debt instrument; or

(2) Payments denominated in or determined by reference to a currency that is hyperinflationary (as defined in § 1.988-1(f)) during the taxable year, and the terms of the instrument provide for the adjustment of principal or interest payments in a manner that reflects hyperinflation. For example, a debt instrument providing for a variable interest rate based on local conditions and generally responding to changes in the local consumer price index will reflect hyperinflation.

(B) *Hyperinflationary deposit.*—A hyperinflationary deposit is a demand or time deposit or similar instrument issued by a bank or other financial institution that provides for—

(1) Payments denominated in or determined by reference to a currency that is hyperinflationary (as defined in § 1.988-1(f)) at

Reg. § 1.988-2(b)(15)(vi)(B)(1)

the time the taxpayer enters into or otherwise acquires the deposit; or

(2) Payments denominated in or determined by reference to a currency that is hyperinflationary (as defined in § 1.988-1(f)) during the taxable year, and the terms of the deposit provide for the adjustment of the deposit amount or interest payments in a manner that reflects hyperinflation.

(vii) *Interaction with other provisions.*—(A) *Interest allocation rules.*—In determining the amount of interest expense, this paragraph (b)(15) applies before §§ 1.861-9T through 1.861-12T, and 1.882-5.

(B) *DASTM.*—With respect to a qualified business unit that uses the United States dollar approximate separate transactions method of accounting described in § 1.985-3, paragraph (b)(15)(i) of this section does not apply.

(C) *Interaction with section 988(a)(3)(C).*—Section 988(a)(3)(C) does not apply to a debt instrument subject to the rules of paragraph (b)(15)(i) of this section.

(D) *Hedging rules.*—To the extent § 1.446-4 or 1.988-5 apply, the rules of paragraph (b)(15)(i) of this section will not apply. This paragraph (b)(15)(vii)(D) does not apply if the application of § 1.988-5 results in hyperinflationary debt instrument or deposit described in paragraph (b)(15)(vi)(A) or (B) of this section.

(viii) *Effective date.*—This paragraph (b)(15) applies to transactions entered into after February 14, 2000.

(16) *Coordination with section 267 regarding debt instruments.*—(i) *Treatment of a creditor.*—For rules applicable to a corporation included in a controlled group that is a creditor under a debt instrument see § 1.267(f)-1(h).

(ii) *Treatment of a debtor.*—[Reserved]

(17) *Coordination with installment method under section 453.*—[Reserved]

(18) *Interaction of section 988 and § 1.1275-2(g).*—(i) *In general.*—If a principal purpose of structuring a debt instrument subject to section 988 and any related hedges is to achieve a result that is unreasonable in light of the purposes of section 163(e), section 988, sections 1271 through 1275, or any related section of the Internal Revenue Code, the Commissioner can apply or depart from the regulations under the applicable sections as necessary or appropriate to achieve a reasonable result. For example, if this paragraph (b)(18) applies to a multicurrency debt instrument and a hedge or hedges, the Commissioner can wholly or partially integrate transactions or treat portions of the debt instrument as separate instruments where appropriate. See also § 1.1275-2(g).

(ii) *Unreasonable result.*—Whether a result is unreasonable is determined based on all the facts and circumstances. In making this determination, a significant fact is whether the treatment of the debt instrument is expected to have a substantial effect on the issuer's or a holder's U.S. tax liability. Another significant fact is whether the result is obtainable without the application of § 1.988-6 and any related provisions (e.g., if the debt instrument and the contingency were entered into separately). A result will not be considered unreasonable, however, in the absence of an expected substantial effect on the present value of a taxpayer's tax liability.

(iii) *Effective date.*—This paragraph (b)(18) shall apply to debt instruments issued on or after October 29, 2004.

(c) *Item of expense or gross income or receipts which is to be paid or received after the date accrued.*—(1) *In general.*—Except as provided in § 1.988-5, exchange gain or loss with respect to an item described in § 1.988-1(a)(1)(ii) and (2)(ii) (other than accrued interest income or expense subject to paragraph (b) of this section) shall be realized on the date payment is made or received. Except as provided in the succeeding sentence, such exchange gain or loss shall be recognized in accordance with the applicable recognition provisions of the Internal Revenue Code. If the taxpayer's right to receive income, or obligation to pay an expense, is transferred or modified in a transaction in which gain or loss would otherwise be recognized, exchange gain or loss shall be realized and recognized only to the extent of the total gain or loss on the transaction.

(2) *Determination of exchange gain or loss with respect to an item of gross income or receipts.*—Exchange gain or loss realized on an item of gross income or receipts described in paragraph (c)(1) of this section shall be determined by multiplying the units of nonfunctional currency received by the spot rate on the payment date, and subtracting from such amount the amount determined by multiplying the units of nonfunctional currency received by the spot rate on the booking date. The term "spot rate on the payment date" means the spot rate determined under § 1.988-1(d) on the date payment is received or otherwise taken into account. Pursuant to § 1.988-1(d)(3), a taxpayer may use a spot rate convention for purposes of determining the spot rate on the payment date. The term "spot rate on the booking date"

means the spot rate determined under § 1.988-1(d) on the date the item of gross income or receipts is accrued or otherwise taken into account. Pursuant to § 1.988-1(d)(3), a taxpayer may use a spot rate convention for purposes of determining the spot rate on the booking date.

(3) *Determination of exchange gain or loss with respect to an item of expense.*—Exchange gain or loss realized on an item of expense described in paragraph (c)(1) of this section shall be determined by multiplying the units of nonfunctional currency paid by the spot rate on the booking date and subtracting from such amount the amount determined by multiplying the units of nonfunctional currency paid by the spot rate on the payment date. The term "spot rate on the booking date" means the spot rate determined under § 1.988-1(d) on the date the item of expense is accrued or otherwise taken into account. Pursuant to § 1.988-1(d)(3), a taxpayer may use a spot rate convention for purposes of determining the spot rate on the booking date. The term "spot rate on the payment date" means the spot rate determined under § 1.988-1(d) on the date payment is made or otherwise taken into account. Pursuant to § 1.988-1(d)(3), a taxpayer may use a spot rate convention for purposes of determining the spot rate on the payment date.

(4) *Examples.*—The following examples illustrate the application of paragraph (c) of this section.

Example 1. X is a calendar year corporation with the dollar as its functional currency. X is on the accrual method of accounting. On January 15, 1989, X sells inventory for 10,000 Canadian dollars (C$). The spot rate on January 15, 1989, is C$1 = U.S. $.55. On February 23, 1989, when X receives payment of the C$10,000, the spot rate is C$1 = U.S. $.50. On February 23, 1989, X will realize exchange loss. X's loss is computed by multiplying the C$10,000 by the spot rate on the date the C$10,000 are received (C$10,000 × .50 = U.S. $5,000) and subtracting from such amount, the amount computed by multiplying the C$10,000 by the spot rate on the booking date (C$10,000 × .55 = U.S. $5,500). Thus, X's exchange loss on the transaction is U.S. $500 (U.S. $5,000 − U.S. $5,500).

Example 2. The facts are the same as in *Example 1* except that X uses a spot rate convention to determine the spot rate as provided in § 1.988-1(d)(3). Pursuant to X's spot rate convention, the spot rate at which a payable or receivable is booked is determined monthly for each nonfunctional currency payable or receivable by adding the spot rate at the beginning of the month and the spot rate at the end of the month and dividing by two. All payables and receivables in a nonfunctional currency booked during the month are translated into functional currency at the rate described in the preceding sentence. Further, the translation of nonfunctional currency paid with respect to a payable, and nonfunctional currency received with respect to a receivable, is also performed pursuant to the spot rate convention. Assume the spot rate determined under the spot rate convention for the month of January is C$1 = U.S. $.54 and for the month of February is C$1 = U.S. $.51. On the last date in February, X will realize exchange loss. X's loss is computed by multiplying the C$10,000 by the spot rate convention for the month of February (C$10,000 × U.S. $.51 = U.S. $5,100) and subtracting from such amount, the amount computed by multiplying the C$10,000 by the spot rate convention for the month of January (C$10,000 × U.S. $.54 =$5,400). Thus, X's exchange loss on the transaction is U.S. $300 (U.S. $5,100 − U.S. $5,400). X's basis in the C$10,000 is U.S. $5,400.

Example 3. The facts are the same as in *Example 2* except that X has a standing order with X's bank for the bank to convert any nonfunctional currency received in satisfaction of a receivable into U.S. dollars on the day received and to deposit those U.S. dollars in X's U.S. dollar bank account. X may use its convention to translate the amount booked into U.S. dollars, but must use the U.S. dollar amounts received from the bank with respect to such receivables to determine X's exchange gain or loss. Thus, if X receives payment of the C$10,000 on February 23, 1989, when the spot rate is C$1 = U.S.$ .50, X determines exchange gain or loss by subtracting the amount booked under X's convention (U.S.$5,400) from the amount of U.S. dollars received from the bank under the standing conversion order (assume $5,000). X's exchange loss is U.S.$400.

(d) *Exchange gain or loss with respect to forward contracts, futures contracts and option contracts.*—(1) *Scope.*—(i) *In general.*—This paragraph (d) applies to forward contracts, futures contracts and option contracts described in § 1.988-1(a)(1)(ii) and (2)(iii). For rules applicable to currency swaps and notional principal contracts described in § 1.988-1(a)(1)(ii) and (2)(iii), see paragraph (e) of this section.

(ii) *Treatment of spot contracts.*—Solely for purposes of this paragraph (d), a spot contract as defined in § 1.988-1(b) to buy or sell nonfunctional currency is not considered a forward contract or similar transaction described in § 1.988-1(a)(2)(iii) unless such spot contract is disposed of (or otherwise terminated) prior to making or taking delivery of the currency. For example, if a taxpayer with the dollar as its functional currency enters into a spot contract to purchase British pounds, and takes delivery of such pounds under the contract, the delivery of the pounds is not a realization event under section 988(c)(5) and paragraph (e)(4)(ii) of this section because the contract is not considered a forward contract or similar transaction described in § 1.988-1(a)(2)(iii). However, if the taxpayer sells or otherwise terminates the contract before taking delivery of the pounds, exchange gain or loss shall be realized and recognized in accordance with paragraphs (d)(2) and (3) of this section.

(2) *Realization of exchange gain or loss.*— (i) *In general.*—Except as provided in § 1.988-5, exchange gain or loss on a contract described in § 1.988-2(d)(1) shall be realized in accordance with the applicable realization section of the Internal Revenue Code (*e.g.*, sections 1001, 1092, and 1256). See also section 988(c)(5). For purposes of determining the timing of the realization of exchange gain or loss, sections 1092 and 1256 shall take precedence over section 988(c)(5).

(ii) *Realization by offset.*—(A) *In general.*—Except as provided in paragraphs (d)(2)(ii)(B) and (C) of this section, exchange gain or loss with respect to a transaction described in § 1.988-1(a)(1)(ii) and (2)(iii) shall not be realized solely because such transaction is offset by another transaction (or transactions).

(B) *Exception where economic benefit is derived.*—If a transaction described in § 1.988-1(a)(1)(ii) and (2)(iii) is offset by another transaction or transactions, exchange gain shall be realized to the extent the taxpayer derives, by pledge or otherwise, an economic benefit (*e.g.*, cash, property or the proceeds from a borrowing) from any gain inherent in such offsetting positions. Proper adjustment shall be made in the amount of any gain or loss subsequently realized for gain taken into account by reason of the preceding sentence. This paragraph (d)(2)(ii)(B) shall apply to transactions creating an offset after September 21, 1989.

(C) *Certain contracts traded on an exchange.*—If a transaction described in § 1.988-1(a)(1)(ii) and (2)(iii) is traded on an exchange and it is the general practice of the exchange to terminate offsetting contracts, entering into an offsetting contract shall be considered a termination of the contract being offset.

(iii) *Clarification of section 988(c)(5).*— If the delivery date of a contract subject to section 988(c)(5) and paragraph (d)(4)(ii) of this section is different than the date the contract expires, then for purposes of determining the date exchange gain or loss is realized, the term delivery date shall mean expiration date.

(iv) *Examples.*—The following examples illustrate the rules of this paragraph (d)(1) and (2).

Example 1. On August 1, 1989, X, a calendar year corporation with the dollar as its functional currency, enters into a forward contract with Bank A to buy 100 New Zealand dollars for $80 for delivery on January 31, 1990. (The forward purchase contract is not a section 1256 contract.) On November 1, 1989, the market price for the purchase of 100 New Zealand dollars for delivery on January 31, 1990, is $76. On November 1, 1989, X cancels its obligation under the forward purchase contract and pays Bank A $3.95 (the present value of $4 discounted at 12% for the period) in cancellation of such contract. Under section 1001(a), X realizes an exchange loss of $3.95 on November 1, 1989, because cancellation of the forward purchase contract for cash results in the termination of X's contract.

Example 2. X is a corporation with the dollar as its functional currency. On January 1, 1989, X enters into a currency swap contract with Bank A under which X is obligated to make a series of Japanese yen payments in exchange for a series of dollar payments. On February 21, 1992, X has a gain of $100,000 inherent in such contract as a result of interest rate and exchange rate movements. Also on February 21, 1992, X enters into an offsetting swap with Bank A to lock in such gain. If on February 21, 1992, X pledges the gain inherent in such offsetting positions as collateral for a loan, X's initial swap contract is treated as being terminated on February 21, 1992, under paragraph (d)(2)(ii)(B) of this section. Proper adjustment is made in the amount of any gain or loss subsequently realized for the gain taken into account by reason of paragraph (d)(2)(ii)(B) of this section.

Example 3. X is a calendar year corporation with the dollar as its functional currency. On October 1, 1989, X enters into a forward contract to buy 100,000 Swiss francs (Sf) for delivery on March 1, 1990, for $51,220. Assume that the contract is a section 1256 contract under section 1256(g)(2) and that section 1256(e) does not apply. Pursuant to section 1256(a)(1), the forward contract is treated as sold for its fair market value on December 31, 1989. Assume that the fair market value of the contract is $1,000 determined under § 1.988-1(g). Thus X will realize an exchange gain of $1,000 on December 31, 1989. Such gain is subject to the character rules of § 1.988-3 and the source rules of § 1.988-4.

(v) *Extension of the maturity date of certain contracts.*—An extension of time for making or taking delivery under a contract described in paragraph (d)(1) of this section (*e.g.*, a historical rate rollover as defined in § 1.988-5(b)(2)(iii)(C)) shall be considered a sale or exchange of the contract for its fair market value on the date of the extension and the establishment of a new contract on such date. If, under the terms of the extension, the time value of any gain or loss recognized pursuant to the preceding sentence adjusts the price of the currency to be bought or sold under the new contract, the amount attributable to such time value shall be treated as interest income or expense for all purposes of the Code. However, the preceding sentence shall not apply and the amount attributable to the time value of any gain or loss recognized shall be treated as exchange gain or loss if the period beginning on the first date the contract is rolled over and ending on the date payment is ultimately made or received with respect to such contract does not exceed 183 days.

(3) *Recognition of exchange gain or loss.*—Except as provided in § 1.988-5 (relating to section 988 hedging transactions), exchange gain or loss realized with respect to a contract described in paragraph (d)(1) of this section shall be recognized in accordance with the applicable recognition provisions of the Internal Revenue Code. For example, a loss realized with respect to a contract described in paragraph (d)(1) of this section which is part of a straddle shall be recognized in accordance with the provisions of section 1092 to the extent such section is applicable.

(4) *Determination of exchange gain or loss.*—(i) *In general.*—Exchange gain or loss with respect to a contract described in § 1.988-2(d)(1) shall be determined by subtracting the amount paid (or deemed paid), if any, for or with respect to the contract (including any amount paid upon termination of the contract) from the amount received (or deemed received), if any, for or with respect to the contract (including any amount received upon termination of the contract). Any gain or loss determined according to the preceding sentence shall be treated as exchange gain or loss.

(ii) *Special rules where taxpayer makes or takes delivery.*—If the taxpayer makes or takes delivery in connection with a contract described in paragraph (d)(1) of this section, any gain or loss shall be realized and recognized in the same manner as if the taxpayer sold the contract (or paid another person to assume the contract) on the date on which he took or made delivery for its fair market value on such date. See paragraph (d)(2)(iii) of this section regarding the definition of the term "delivery date." This paragraph (d)(4)(ii) shall not apply in any case in which the taxpayer makes or takes delivery before June 11, 1987.

(iii) *Examples.*—The following examples illustrate the application of paragraph (d)(4) of this section.

Example 1. X is a calendar year corporation with the dollar as its functional currency. On October 1, 1989, when the six month forward rate is $.4907, X enters into a forward contract to buy 100,000 New Zealand dollars (NZD) for delivery on March 1, 1990. On March 1, 1990, when X takes delivery of the 100,000 NZD, the spot rate is 1NZD equals $.48. Pursuant to section 988(c)(5) and paragraph (d)(4)(ii) of this section, a taxpayer that takes delivery of nonfunctional currency under a forward contract that is subject to section 988 is treated as if the taxpayer sold the contract for its fair market value on the date delivery is taken. If X sold the contract on March 1, 1990, the transferee would require a payment of $1,070 [($.48 × 100,000NZD) − ($.4907 × 100,000NZD)] to compensate him for the loss in value of the 100,000NZD. Therefore, X realizes an exchange loss of $1,070. X has a basis in the 100,000NZD of $48,000.

Example 2. Assume the same facts as in *Example 1* except that the contract is for Swiss francs and is a section 1256 contract. Assume further that on December 31, 1989, the value to X of the contract as marked to market is $1,000. Pursuant to section 1256(a), X realizes an exchange gain of $1,000. Such gain, however, is characterized as ordinary income under § 1.988-3 and will be sourced under § 1.988-4.

Example 3. X is a calendar year corporation with the dollar as its functional currency. On May 2, 1989, X enters into an option contract with Bank A to purchase 50,000 Canadian dollars (C$) for U.S. $42,500 (C$1 = U.S. $.85) for delivery on or before September 18, 1989. X pays a $285 premium to Bank A to obtain the option contract. On September 18, 1989, when X exercises the option and takes delivery of the C$50,000, the spot rate is C$1 equals U.S. $.90. Pursuant to section 988(c)(5) and paragraph (d)(4)(ii) of this section, a taxpayer that takes delivery under an option contract that is subject to section 988 is treated as if the taxpayer sold the contract for its fair market value on the date delivery is taken. If X sold the contract for its fair market value on September 18, 1989, X would receive U.S. $2,500 [(C$50,000 × U.S. $.90) − (C$50,000 × U.S. $.85)]. Accordingly, X is deemed to have received U.S. $2,500 on the sale of the contract at its fair market value. X will realize U.S. $2,215 ($2,500 deemed received less $285 paid) of exchange gain with respect to the delivery of Canadian dollars under the option contract. X's basis in the 50,000 Canadian dollars is U.S. $45,000.

(5) *Hyperinflationary contracts.*—(i) *In general.*—If a taxpayer acquires or otherwise enters into a hyperinflationary contract (as defined in paragraph (d)(5)(ii) of this section) that has payments to be made or received that are denominated in (or determined by reference to) a nonfunctional currency of the taxpayer, then the taxpayer shall realize exchange gain or loss with respect to such contract for its taxable year determined by reference to the change in exchange rates between—

(A) The later of the first day of the taxable year, or the date the contract was acquired or entered into; and

(B) The earlier of the last day of the taxable year, or the date the contract is disposed of or otherwise terminated.

(ii) *Definition of hyperinflationary contract.*—A hyperinflationary contract is a contract described in paragraph (d)(1) of this section that provides for payments denominated in or determined by reference to a currency that is hyperinflationary (as defined in § 1.988-1(f)) at the time the taxpayer acquires or otherwise enters into the contract.

(iii) *Interaction with other provisions.*— (A) *DASTM.*—With respect to a qualified business unit that uses the United States dollar approximate separate transactions method of accounting described in § 1.985-3, this paragraph (d)(5) does not apply.

(B) *Hedging rules.*—To the extent § 1.446-4 or 1.988-5 apply, this paragraph (d)(5) does not apply.

(C) *Adjustment for subsequent transactions.*—Proper adjustments must be made in the amount of any gain or loss subsequently realized for gain or loss taken into account by reason of this paragraph (d)(5).

(iv) *Effective date.*—This paragraph (d)(5) is applicable to transactions acquired or otherwise entered into after February 14, 2000.

(e) *Currency swaps and other notional principal contracts.*—(1) *In general.*—Except as provided in paragraph (e)(2) of this section or in § 1.988-5, the timing of income, deduction and loss with respect to a notional principal contract that is a section 988 transaction shall be governed by section 446 and the regulations thereunder. Such income, deduction and loss is characterized as exchange gain or loss (except as provided in another section of the Internal Revenue Code (or regulations thereunder), § 1.988-5, or in paragraph (f) of this section).

(2) *Special rules for currency swaps.*— (i) *In general.*—Except as provided in paragraph (e)(2)(iii)(B) of this section, the provisions of this paragraph (e)(2) shall apply solely for purposes of determining the realization, recognition and amount of exchange gain or loss with respect to a currency swap contract, and not for purposes of determining the source of such gain or loss, or characterizing such gain or loss as interest. Except as provided in § 1.988-3(c), any income or loss realized with respect to a currency swap contract shall be characterized as exchange gain or loss (and not as interest income or expense). Any exchange gain or loss realized in accordance with this paragraph (e)(2) shall be recognized unless otherwise provided in an applicable section of the Code. For purposes of this paragraph (e)(2), a currency swap contract is a contract defined in paragraph (e)(2)(ii) of this section. With respect to a contract which requires the payment of swap principal prior to maturity of such contract, see paragraph (f) of this section. For purposes of this paragraph (e), the rules of paragraph (d)(2)(ii) of this section (regarding realization by offset) apply. See Example 2 of paragraph (d)(2)(iv) of this section.

(ii) *Definition of currency swap contract.*—(A) *In general.*—A currency swap contract is a contract involving different currencies between two or more parties to—

(1) Exchange periodic interim payments, as defined in paragraph (e)(2)(ii)(C) of this section, on or prior to maturity of the contract; and

(2) Exchange the swap principal amount upon maturity of the contract.

A currency swap contract may also require an exchange of the swap principal amount upon commencement of the agreement.

(B) *Swap principal amount.*—The swap principal amount is an amount of two different currencies which, under the terms of the currency swap contract, is used to determine the periodic interim payments in each currency and which is exchanged upon maturity of the contract. If such amount is not clearly set forth in the contract, the Commissioner may determine the swap principal amount.

(C) *Exchange of periodic interim payments.*—An exchange of periodic interim payments is an exchange of one or more payments in one currency specified by the contract for one or more payments in a different currency specified by the contract where the payments in each currency are computed by reference to an interest index applied to the swap principal amount. A currency swap contract must clearly indicate the periodic interim payments, or the

Reg. § 1.988-2(d)(5)(i)

interest index used to compute the periodic interim payments, in each currency.

(iii) *Timing and computation of periodic interim payments.*—(A) *In general.*—Except as provided in paragraph (e)(2)(iii)(B) of this section and § 1.988-5, the timing and computation of the periodic interim payments provided in a currency swap agreement shall be determined by treating—

(1) Payments made under the swap as payments made pursuant to a hypothetical borrowing that is denominated in the currency in which payments are required to be made (or are determined with reference to) under the swap, and

(2) Payments received under the swap as payments received pursuant to a hypothetical loan that is denominated in the currency in which payments are received (or are determined with reference to) under the swap.

Except as provided in paragraph (e)(2)(v) of this section, the hypothetical issue price of such hypothetical borrowing and loan shall be the swap principal amount. The hypothetical stated redemption price at maturity is the total of all payments (excluding any exchange of the swap principal amount at the inception of the contract) provided under the hypothetical borrowing or loan other than periodic interest payments under the principles of section 1273. For purposes of determining economic accrual under the currency swap, the number of hypothetical interest compounding periods of such hypothetical borrowing and loan shall be determined pursuant to a semiannual compounding convention unless the currency swap contract indicates otherwise. For purposes of determining the timing and amount of the periodic interim payments, the principles regarding the amortization of interest (see generally, sections 1272 through 1275 and 163(e)) shall apply to the hypothetical interest expense and income of such hypothetical borrowing and loan. However, such principles shall not apply to determine the time when principal is deemed to be paid on the hypothetical borrowing and loan. See paragraph (d)(2)(iii) of this section and *Example 2* of paragraph (d)(5) of this section with respect to the time when principal is deemed to be paid. With respect to the translation and computation of exchange gain or loss on any hypothetical interest income or expense, see § 1.988-2(b). The amount treated as exchange gain or loss by the taxpayer with respect to the periodic interim payments for the taxable year shall be the amount of hypothetical interest income and exchange gain or loss attributable to such interest income from the hypothetical borrowing and loan for such year less the amount of hypothetical interest expense and exchange gain or loss attributable to the interest expense from such hypothetical borrowing and loan for such year.

(B) *Effect of prepayment for purposes of section 956.*—For purposes of section 956, the Commissioner may treat any prepayment of a currency swap as a loan.

(iv) *Timing and determination of exchange gain or loss with respect to the swap principal amount.*—Exchange gain or loss with respect to the swap principal amount shall be realized on the day the units of swap principal in each currency are exchanged. (See paragraph (e)(2)(ii)(A)(*2*) of this section which requires that the entire swap principal amount be exchanged upon maturity of the contract.) Such gain or loss shall be determined on the date of the exchange by subtracting the value (on such date) of the units of swap principal paid from the value of the units of swap principal received. This paragraph (e)(2)(iv) does not apply to an equal exchange of the swap principal amount at the commencement of the agreement at a market exchange rate.

(v) *Anti-abuse rules.*—(A) *Method of accounting does not clearly reflect income.*—If the taxpayer's method of accounting for income, expense, gain or loss attributable to a currency swap does not clearly reflect income, or if the present value of the payments to be made is not equivalent to that of the payments to be received (including the swap premium or discount, as defined in paragraph (e)(3)(ii) of this section) on the day the taxpayer enters into or acquires the contract, the Commissioner may apply principles analogous to those of section 1274 or such other rules as the Commissioner deems appropriate to clearly reflect income. For example, in order to clearly reflect income the Commissioner may determine the hypothetical issue price, the hypothetical stated redemption price at maturity, and the amounts required to be taken into account within a taxable year. Further, if the present value of the payments to be made is not equivalent to that of the payments to be received (including the swap premium or discount, as defined in paragraph (e)(3)(ii) of this section) on the day the taxpayer enters into or acquires the contract, the Commissioner may integrate the swap with another transaction (or transactions) in order to clearly reflect income.

(B) *Terms must be clearly stated.*—If the currency swap contract does not clearly set forth the swap principal amount in each currency, and the periodic interim payments in each currency (or the interest index used to compute the periodic interim payments in each currency), the Commissioner may defer any income, deduction, gain or loss with respect to such contract until termination of the contract.

(3) *Amortization of swap premium or discount in the case of off-market currency swaps.*— (i) *In general.*—An "off-market currency swap" is a currency swap contract under which the present value of the payments to be made is not equal to that of the payments to be received on the day the taxpayer enters into or acquires the contract (absent any swap premium or discount, as defined in paragraph (e)(3)(ii) of this section). Generally, such present values may not be equal if the swap exchange rate (as defined in paragraph (e)(3)(iii) of this section) is not the spot rate, or the interest indices used to compute the periodic interim payments do not reflect current values, on the day the taxpayer enters into or acquires the currency swap.

(ii) *Treatment of taxpayer entering into or acquiring an off-market currency swap.*—If a taxpayer that enters into or acquires a currency swap makes a payment (that is, the taxpayer pays a premium, "swap premium," to enter into or acquire the currency swap) or receives a payment (that is, the taxpayer enters into or acquires the currency swap at a discount, "swap discount") in order to make the present value of the amounts to be paid equal the amounts to be received, such payment shall be amortized in a manner which places the taxpayer in the same position it would have been in had the taxpayer entered into a currency swap contract under which the present value of the amounts to be paid equal the amounts to be received (absent any swap premium or discount). Thus, swap premium or discount shall be amortized as follows—

(A) The amount of swap premium or discount that is attributable to the difference between the swap exchange rate (as defined in paragraph (e)(3)(iii) of this section) and the spot rate on the date the contract is entered into or acquired shall be taken into account as income or expense on the date the swap principal amounts are taken into account; and

(B) The amount of swap premium or discount attributable to the difference in values of the periodic interim payments shall be amortized in a manner consistent with the principles of economic accrual. *Cf.*, section 171.

Any amount taken into account pursuant to this paragraph (e)(3)(ii) shall be treated as exchange gain or loss.

(iii) *Definition of swap exchange rate.*— The swap exchange rate is the single exchange rate set forth in the contract at which the swap principal amounts are determined. If the swap exchange rate is not clearly set forth in the contract, the Commissioner may determine such rate.

(iv) *Coordination with §1.446-3(g)(4) regarding swaps with significant nonperiodic payments.*—The rules of §1.446-3(g)(4) apply to any currency swap with a significant nonperiodic payment. Section 1.446-3(g)(4) applies before this paragraph (e)(3). Thus, if §1.446-3(g)(4) applies, currency gain or loss may be realized on the loan. This paragraph (e)(3)(iv) applies to transactions entered into after February 14, 2000.

(4) *Treatment of taxpayer disposing of a currency swap.*—Any gain or loss realized on the disposition or the termination of a currency swap is exchange gain or loss.

(5) *Examples.*—The following examples illustrate the application of this paragraph (e).

Example 1. (i) C is an accrual method calendar year corporation with the dollar as its functional currency. On January 1, 1989, C enters into a currency swap with J with the following terms:

(1) the principal amount is $150 and 100 British pounds (£) (the equivalent of $150 on the effective date of the contract assuming a spot rate of £1 = $1.50 on January 1, 1989);

(2) C will make payments equal to 10% of the dollar principal amount on December 31, 1989, and December 31, 1990;

(3) J will make payments equal to 12% of the pound principal amount on December 31, 1989, and December 31, 1990; and

(4) on December 31, 1990, C will pay to J the $150 principal amount and J will pay to C the £100 principal amount.

Assume that the spot rate is £1 = $1.50 on January 1, 1989, £1 = $1.40 on December 31, 1989, and £1 = $1.30 on December 31, 1990. Assume further that the average rate for 1989 is £1 = $1.45 and for 1990 is £1 = $1.35.

(ii) Solely for determining the realization of gain or loss in accordance with paragraph (e)(2) of this section (and not for purposes of determining whether any payments are treated as interest), C will treat the dollar payments made by C as payments made pursuant to a dollar borrowing with an issue price of $150, a stated redemption price at maturity of $150, and yield to maturity of 10%. C will treat the pound payments received as payments received pursuant to a pound loan with an issue price of £100, a stated redemption price at maturity of £100, and a yield of 12% to maturity. Pursuant to §1.988-2(b), C is required to compute hypothetical accrued pound interest income at the average rate for the accrual period and then determine exchange gain or loss on the day payment is received with respect to such accrued amount. Accordingly, C will accrue $17.40 (£12 × $1.45) in 1989 and $16.20 (£12 × $1.35) in 1990. C also will compute hypothetical exchange loss of $.60 on December 31, 1989 [(£12 × $1.40) – (£12 × $1.45)] and hypothetical exchange loss of $.60 on December 31, 1990 [£12 × $1.30) – (£12 × $1.35)]. All such hypothetical interest income and exchange loss are characterized and sourced as exchange gain and loss. Further, C is treated as having paid $15 ($150 × 10%) of hypothetical interest on December 31, 1989, and again on December 31, 1990. Such hypothetical interest expense is characterized and sourced as exchange loss. Thus, C will have a net exchange gain of $1.80 ($17.40 – $.60 – $15.00) with respect to the periodic interim payments in 1989 and a net exchange gain of $.60 ($16.20 – $.60 – $15.00) with respect to the periodic interim payments in 1990. Finally, C will realize an exchange loss on December 31, 1990 with respect to the exchange of the swap principal amount. This loss is determined by subtracting the value of the units of swap principal paid ($150) from the value of the units of swap principal received (£100 × $1.30 = $130) resulting in a $20 exchange loss.

Example 2. (i) C is an accrual method calendar year corporation with the dollar as its functional currency. On January 1, 1989, when the spot rate is £1 = $1.50, C enters into a currency swap contract with J under which C agrees to make and receive the following payments:

Date	C Pays	J Pays
December 31, 1989	$15.00	£12.00
December 31, 1990	$41.04	£12.00
December 31, 1991	$0.00	£12.00
December 31, 1992	$150.00	£112.00

(ii) Under paragraph (e)(2)(iii) of this section, C must treat the dollar periodic interim payments under the swap as made pursuant to a hypothetical dollar borrowing. The hypothetical issue price is $150 and the stated redemption price at maturity is $206.04. The amount of hypothetical interest expense must be amortized in accordance with economic accrual. Thus J must include and C must deduct periodic interim payment amounts as follows:

	Amount Taken into Account	Adjusted Issue Price
December 31, 1989	$15.00	150.00
December 31, 1990	$15.00	123.96
December 31, 1991	$12.40	136.36
December 31, 1992	$13.64	

(iii) Gain or loss with respect to the periodic interim payments of the currency swap is determined under paragraph (e)(2)(iii)(A) of this section with respect to the dollar cash flow amortized as set forth above and the corresponding pound cash flow as stated in the currency swap contract. Gain or loss with respect to the principal payments (*i.e.*, $150 and £100) exchanged on December 31, 1992, is determined under paragraph (e)(2)(iv) of this section on December 31, 1992, notwithstanding that under the principles regarding amortization of interest $26.04 would have been regarded as a payment of principal on December 31, 1990.

Example 3. (i) X is a corporation on the accrual method of accounting with the dollar as its functional currency and the calendar year as its taxable year. On January 1, 1989, X enters into a three year currency swap contract with Y with the following terms. The swap principal amount is $100 and the Swiss franc (Sf) equivalent of such amount which equals Sf200 translated at the swap exchange rate of $1 = Sf2. There is no initial exchange of the swap principal amount. The interest rates used to compute the periodic interim payments are 10% compounded annually for U.S. dollar payments and 5% compounded annually for Swiss franc payments. Thus, under the currency swap, X agrees to pay Y $10 (10% × $100) on December 31st of 1989, 1990 and 1991 and to pay Y the swap principal amount of $100 on December 31, 1991. Y agrees to pay X Sf10 (5% × Sf200) on December 31st of 1989, 1990 and 1991 and to pay X the swap principal amount of Sf200 on December 31, 1991. Assume that the average rate for 1989 and the spot rate on December 31, 1989, is $1 = Sf2.5.

(ii) Under paragraph (e)(2)(iii) of this section, on December 31, 1989, X will realize an exchange loss of $6 (the sum of $10 of loss by reason of the $10 periodic interim payment paid to Y and $4.00 of gain, the value of Sf10 on December 31, 1989, from the receipt of Sf10 on such date).

(iii) On January 1, 1990, X transfers its rights and obligations under the swap contract to Z, an unrelated corporation. Z has the dollar as its functional currency, is on the accrual method of accounting, and has the calendar year as its taxable year. On January 1, 1990, the exchange rate is $1 = Sf2.50. The relevant dollar interest rate is 8% compounded annually and the relevant Swiss franc interest rate is 5% compounded annually. Because of the movement in exchange and interest rates, the agreement between X and Z to transfer the currency swap requires X to pay Z $23.56 (the swap discount as determined under paragraph (e)(3) of this section).

(iv) Pursuant to paragraph (e)(4) of this section, X may deduct the loss of $23.56 in 1990. The loss is characterized under § 1.988-3 and sourced under § 1.988-4.

(v) Pursuant to paragraph (e)(3)(ii) of this section, Z is required to amortize the $23.56 received as follows. The amount of the $23.56 payment that is attributable to movements in exchange rates ($20) is taken into account on December 31, 1991, the date the swap principal amounts are exchanged, under paragraph (e)(3)(ii)(A) of this section. This amount is the present value (discounted at 10%, the rate under the currency swap contract used to compute the dollar periodic interim payments) of the financial asset required to compensate Z for the loss in value of the hypothetical Swiss franc loan resulting from movements in exchange rates between January 1, 1989 and January 1, 1990. This amount is determined by assuming that interest rates did not change from the date the swap originally was entered into (January 1, 1989), but that the exchange rate is $1 = Sf2.50. Under this assumption, a taxpayer undertaking the obligation to pay dollars under the currency swap on January 1, 1990, would only agree to pay $8 for Sf10 on December 31, 1990 and $88 for Sf210 on December 31, 1991, because the exchange rates have moved from $1 = Sf2 to $1 = Sf2.50. Thus, Z requires $2 on December 31, 1990 and $22 on December 31, 1991 to compensate for the amount of dollar payments Z is required to make in exchange for the Swiss francs received on December 31, 1990 and 1991. The present value of $2 on December 31, 1990 and $22 on December 31, 1991 discounted at the rate for U.S. dollar payments of 10% is $20 ($1.82 + $18.18). This amount is discounted at the rate for U.S. dollar payments (i.e., at the historic rate) because the amount of the $23.56 payment received by Z that is attributable to movements in interest rates is computed and amortized separately as provided in the following paragraph.

(vi) Pursuant to paragraph (e)(3)(ii)(B) of this section, Z is required to amortize the portion of the $23.56 payment attributable to movements in interest rates under principles of economic accrual over the term of the currency swap agreement. The amount of the $23.56 payment that is attributable to movements in interest rates (assuming that exchange rates have not changed) is the present value ($3.56) of the excess ($2.00 in 1990 and $2.00 in 1991) of the periodic interim payments Z is required to pay under the currency swap agreement ($10 in 1990 and $10 in 1991) over the amount Z would be required to pay if the currency swap agreement reflected current interest rates on the day Z acquired the swap contract ($8 in 1990 and $8 in 1991) discounted at the appropriate dollar interest rate on January 1, 1990. Thus, under principles of economic accrual (e.g., see section 171 of the Code), Z will include in income $1.72 on December 31, 1990, the amount that, when added to the interest ($.28) on the $3.56 computed at the 8% rate on the date Z acquired the currency swap contract, will equal the $2.00 needed to compensate Z for the movement in interest rates between January 1, 1989 and January 1, 1990. Z also will include in income $1.85 on December 31, 1991, the amount that, when added to the interest ($.15) on the $1.85 (the remaining balance of the $3.56 payment) computed at the 8% rate on the date Z acquired the currency swap contract, will equal the $2.00 needed to compensate Z for the movement in interest rates between January 1, 1990 and January 1, 1991. This amount is computed assuming exchange rates have not changed because the amount attributable to movements in exchange rates is computed and amortized separately under the preceding paragraph.

(6) *Special effective date for rules regarding currency swaps.*—Paragraph (e)(3) of this section regarding amortization of swap premium or discount in the case of off-market currency swaps shall be effective for transactions entered into after September 21, 1989, unless such swap premium or discount was paid or received pursuant to a binding contract with an unrelated party that was entered into prior to such date. For transactions entered into prior to this date, see Notice 89-21, 1989-8 I.R.B. 23.

(7) *Special rules for currency swap contracts in hyperinflationary currencies.*—(i) *In general.*—If a taxpayer enters into a hyperinflationary currency swap (as defined in paragraph (e)(7)(iv) of this section), then the taxpayer realizes exchange gain or loss for its taxable year with respect to such instrument determined by reference to the change in exchange rates between—

(A) The later of the first day of the taxable year, or the date the instrument was entered into (by the taxpayer); and

(B) The earlier of the last day of the taxable year, or the date the instrument is disposed of or otherwise terminated.

(ii) *Adjustment to principal or basis.*—Proper adjustments are made in the amount of any gain or loss subsequently realized for gain or loss taken into account by reason of this paragraph (e)(7).

(iii) *Interaction with DASTM.*—With respect to a qualified business unit that uses the United States dollar approximate separate transactions method of accounting described in § 1.985-3, this paragraph (e)(7) does not apply.

(iv) *Definition of hyperinflationary currency swap contract.*—A hyperinflationary currency swap contract is a currency swap contract that provides for—

(A) Payments denominated in or determined by reference to a currency that is hyperinflationary (as defined in § 1.988-1(f)) at the time the taxpayer enters into or otherwise acquires the currency swap; or

(B) Payments that are adjusted to take into account the fact that the currency is hyperinflationary (as defined in § 1.988-1(f)) during the current taxable year. A currency swap contract that provides for periodic payments determined by reference to a variable interest rate based on local conditions and generally responding to changes in the local consumer price index is an example of this latter type of currency swap contract.

(v) *Special effective date for nonfunctional hyperinflationary currency swap contracts.*—This paragraph (e)(7) applies to

Date	
1/1/90	....
12/31/90	....
12/31/91	....
12/31/92	....

(ii) X and Y designate this contract as a "currency swap." Notwithstanding this designation, for purposes of determining the timing, source, and character with respect to the transaction, the transaction is characterized by the Commissioner in accordance with its substance. Thus, the January 1, 1990, exchange by X of $100 for LC 100 is treated as a spot purchase of LCs by X and the December 31, 1992, exchange by X at 109.3 LC for $133 is treated as a forward sale of LCs by X. Under such treatment there would be no tax consequences to X under paragraph (e)(2) of this section in 1990, 1991, and 1992 with respect to this transaction other than the realization of exchange gain or loss on the sale of the LC109.3 on December 31, 1992. Calculation of such gain or loss would be governed by the rules of paragraph (d) of this section.

(g) *Effective date.*—Except as otherwise provided in this section, this section shall be effective for taxable years beginning after December 31, 1986. Thus, except as otherwise provided in this section, any payments made or received with respect to a section 988 transactions entered into after February 14, 2000.

(f) *Substance over form.*—(1) *In general.*—If the substance of a transaction described in § 1.988-1(a)(1) differs from its form, the timing, source, and character of gains or losses with respect to such transaction may be recharacterized by the Commissioner in accordance with its substance. For example, if a taxpayer enters into a transaction that it designates a "currency swap contract" that requires the prepayment of all payments to be made or to be received (but not both), the Commissioner may recharacterize the contract as a loan. In applying the substance over form principle, separate transactions may be integrated where appropriate. See also § 1.861-9T(b)(1).

(2) *Example.*—The following example illustrates the provisions of this paragraph (f).

Example. (i) On January 1, 1990, X, a U.S. corporation with the dollar as its functional currency, enters into a contract with Y under which X will pay Y $100 and Y will pay X LC100 on January 1, 1990, and X will pay Y LC109.3 and Y will pay X $133 on December 31, 1992. On January 1, 1990, the spot exchange rate is LC1 = $1 and the 3 year forward rate is LC1 = $.8218. X's cash flows are summarized below:

Dollar	LC
(100)	100
0	0
0	0
133	(109.3)

tion in taxable years beginning after December 31, 1986, are subject to this section.

(h) *Timing of income and deductions from notional principal contracts.*—Except as otherwise provided (e.g., in § 1.988-5 or 1.446-3(g)), income or loss from a notional principal contract described in § 1.988-1(a)(2)(iii)(B) (other than a currency swap) is exchange gain or loss. For the rules governing the timing of income and deductions with respect to notional principal contracts, see § 1.446-3. See paragraph (e)(2) of this section with respect to currency swaps. [Reg. § 1.988-2.]

☐ [*T.D.* 8400, 3-16-92. *Amended by T.D.* 8491, 10-8-93; *T.D.* 8860, 1-12-2000 *and T.D.* 9157, 8-27-2004.]

§ 1.988-3. Character of exchange gain or loss.—(a) *In general.*—The character of exchange gain or loss recognized on a section 988 transaction is governed by section 988 and this section. Except as otherwise provided in section 988(c)(1)(E), section 1092, § 1.988-5 and this section, exchange gain or loss realized with respect to a section 988 transaction (including a section 1256 contract that is also a section 988 transaction) shall be characterized as ordinary gain or loss. Accordingly, unless a valid election is made under paragraph (b) of this section, any section providing special rules for capital gain or loss treatment, such as sections 1233, 1234, 1234A, 1236 and 1256(f)(3), shall not apply.

(b) *Election to characterize exchange gain or loss on certain identified forward contracts, futures contracts and option contracts as capital gain or loss.*—(1) *In general.*—Except as provided in paragraph (b)(2) of this section, a taxpayer may elect, subject to the requirements of paragraph (b)(3) of this section, to treat any gain or loss recognized on a contract described in § 1.988-2(d)(1) as capital gain or loss, but only if the contract—

(i) Is a capital asset in the hands of the taxpayer;

(ii) Is not part of a straddle within the meaning of section 1092(c) (without regard to subsections (c)(4) or (e)); and

(iii) Is not a regulated futures contract or nonequity option with respect to which an election under section 988(c)(1)(D)(ii) is in effect.

If a valid election under this paragraph (b) is made with respect to a section 1256 contract, section 1256 shall govern the character of any gain or loss recognized on such contract.

(2) *Special rule for contracts that become part of a straddle after an election is made.*—If a contract which is the subject of an election under paragraph (b)(1) of this section becomes part of a straddle within the meaning of section 1092(c) (without regard to subsections (c)(4) or (e)) after the date of the election, the election shall be invalid with respect to gains from such contract and the Commissioner, in his sole discretion, may invalidate the election with respect to losses.

(3) *Requirements for making the election.*— A taxpayer elects to treat gain or loss on a transaction described in paragraph (b)(1) of this section as capital gain or loss by clearly identifying such transaction on its books and records on the date the transaction is entered into. No specific language or account is necessary for identifying a transaction referred to in the preceding sentence. However, the method of identification must be consistently applied and must clearly identify the pertinent transaction as subject to the section 988(a)(1)(B) election. The Commissioner, in his sole discretion, may invalidate any purported election that does not comply with the preceding sentence.

(4) *Verification.*—A taxpayer that has made an election under § 1.988-3(b)(3) must attach to his income tax return a statement which sets forth the following:

(i) A description and the date of each election made by the taxpayer during the taxpayer's taxable year;

(ii) A statement that each election made during the taxable year was made before the close of the date the transaction was entered into;

(iii) A description of any contract for which an election was in effect and the date such contract expired or was otherwise sold or exchanged during the taxable year;

(iv) A statement that the contract was never part of a straddle as defined in section 1092; and

(v) A statement that all transactions subject to the election are included on the statement attached to the taxpayer's income tax return.

In addition to any penalty that may otherwise apply, the Commissioner, in his sole discretion, may invalidate any or all elections made during the taxable year under § 1.988-3(b)(1) if the taxpayer fails to verify each election as provided in this § 1.988-3(b)(4). The preceding sentence shall not apply if the taxpayer's failure to verify each election was due to reasonable cause or bona fide mistake. The burden of proof to show reasonable cause or bona fide mistake made in good faith is on the taxpayer.

(5) *Independent verification.*—(i) *Effect of independent verification.*—If the taxpayer receives independent verification of the election in paragraph (b)(3) of this section, the taxpayer shall be presumed to have satisfied the requirements of paragraphs (b)(3) and (4) of this section. A contract that is a part of a straddle as defined in section 1092 may not be independently verified and shall be subject to the rules of paragraph (b)(2) of this section.

(ii) *Requirements for independent verification.*—A taxpayer receives independent verification of the election in paragraph (b)(3) of this section if—

(A) The taxpayer establishes a separate account(s) with an unrelated broker(s) or dealer(s) through which all transactions to be independently verified pursuant to this paragraph (b)(5) are conducted and reported.

(B) Only transactions entered into on or after the date the taxpayer establishes such account may be recorded in the account.

(C) Transactions subject to the election of paragraph (b)(3) of this section are entered into such account on the date such transactions are entered into.

(D) The broker or dealer provides the taxpayer a statement detailing the transactions conducted through such account and includes on such statement the following: "Each transaction identified in this account is subject to the election set forth in section 988(a)(1)(B)."

(iii) *Special effective date for independent verification.*—The rules of this paragraph (b)(5) shall be effective for transactions entered into after March 17, 1992.

(6) *Effective date.*—Except as otherwise provided, this paragraph (b) is effective for taxable years beginning on or after September 21, 1989. For prior taxable years, any reasonable contemporaneous election meeting the requirements of section 988(a)(1)(B) shall satisfy this paragraph (b).

(c) *Exchange gain or loss treated as interest.*—(1) *In general.*—Except as provided in this paragraph (c)(1), exchange gain or loss realized on a section 988 transaction shall not be treated as interest income or expense. Exchange gain or loss realized on a section 988 transaction shall be treated as interest income or expense as provided in paragraph (c)(2) of this section with regard to tax exempt bonds, § 1.988-2(e)(2)(ii)(B), § 1.988-5, and in administrative pronouncements. See § 1.861-9T(b), providing rules for the allocation of certain items of exchange gain or loss in the same manner as interest expense.

(2) *Exchange loss realized by the holder on nonfunctional currency tax exempt bonds.*—Exchange loss realized by the holder of a debt instrument the interest on which is excluded from gross income under section 103(a) or any similar provision of law shall be treated as an offset to and reduce total interest income received or accrued with respect to such instrument. Therefore, to the extent of total interest income, no exchange loss shall be recognized. This paragraph (c)(2) shall be effective with respect to debt instruments acquired on or after June 24, 1987.

(d) *Effective date.*—Except as otherwise provided in this section, this section shall be effective for taxable years beginning after December 31, 1986. Thus, except as otherwise provided in this section, any payments made or received with respect to a section 988 transaction in taxable years beginning after December 31, 1986, are subject to this section. Thus, for example, a payment made prior to January 1, 1987, under a forward contract that results in the deferral of a loss under section 1092 to a taxable year beginning after December 31, 1986, is not characterized as an ordinary loss by virtue of paragraph (a) of this section because payment was made prior to January 1, 1987. [Reg. § 1.988-3.]

☐ [*T.D.* 8400, 3-16-92.]

§ 1.988-4. Source of gain or loss realized on a section 988 transfer.—(a) *In general.*—Except as otherwise provided in § 1.988-5 and this section, the source of exchange gain or loss shall be determined by reference to the residence of the taxpayer. This rule applies even if the taxpayer has made an election under § 1.988-3(b) to characterize exchange gain or loss as capital gain or loss. This section takes precedence over section 865.

(b) *Qualified business unit.*—(1) *In general.*—The source of exchange gain or loss shall be determined by reference to the residence of the qualified business unit of the taxpayer on whose books the asset, liability, or item of income or expense giving rise to such gain or loss is properly reflected.

(2) *Proper reflection on the books of the taxpayer or qualified business unit.*—(i) *In general.*—Whether an asset, liability, or item of income or expense is properly reflected on the books of a qualified business unit is a question of fact.

(ii) *Presumption if booking practices are inconsistent.*—It shall be presumed that an asset, liability, or item of income or expense is not properly reflected on the books of the qualified business unit if the taxpayer and its qualified business units employ inconsistent booking practices with respect to the same or similar assets, liabilities, or items of income or expense. If not properly reflected on the books, the Commissioner may allocate any asset, liability, or item of income or expense between or among the taxpayer and its qualified business units to properly reflect the source (or realization) of exchange gain or loss.

(c) *Effectively connected exchange gain or loss.*—Notwithstanding paragraphs (a) and (b) of this section, exchange gain or loss that under principles similar to those set forth in § 1.864-4(c) arises from the conduct of a United States trade or business shall be sourced in the United States and such gain or loss shall be treated as effectively connected to the conduct of a United States trade or business for purposes of sections 871(b) and 882(a)(1).

(d) *Residence.*—(1) *In general.*—Except as otherwise provided in this paragraph (d), for purposes of sections 985 through 989, the residence of any person shall be—

(i) In the case of an individual, the country in which such individual's tax home (as defined in section 911(d)(3)) is located;

(ii) In the case of a corporation, partnership, trust or estate which is a United States person (as defined in section 7701(a)(30)), the United States; and

(iii) In the case of a corporation, partnership, trust or estate which is not a United States person, a country other than the United States.

If an individual does not have a tax home (as defined in section 911(d)(3)), the residence of such individual shall be the United States if such individual is a United States citizen or a resident alien and shall be a country other than the United States if such individual is not a United States citizen or resident alien. If the taxpayer is a U.S. person and has no principal place of business outside the United States, the residence of the taxpayer is the United States. Notwithstanding paragraph (d)(1)(ii) of this section, if a partnership is formed or availed of to avoid tax by altering the source of exchange gain or loss, the source of such gain or loss shall be determined by reference to the residence of the partners rather than the partnership.

(2) *Exception.*—In the case of a qualified business unit of any taxpayer (including an individual), the residence of such unit shall be the country in which the principal place of business of such qualified business unit is located.

(3) *Partner in a partnership not engaged in a U.S. trade or business under section 864(b)(2).*—The determination of residence shall be made at the partner level (without regard to whether the partnership is a qualified business unit of the partners) in the case of partners in a partnership that are not engaged in a U.S. trade or business by reason of section 864(b)(2).

(e) *Special rule for certain related party loans.*—(1) *In general.*—In the case of a loan by a United States person or a related person to a 10 percent owned foreign corporation, or a corporation that meets the 80 percent foreign business requirements test of section 861(c)(1), other than a corporation subject to § 1.861-11T(e)(2)(i), which is denominated in, or determined by reference to, a currency other than the U.S. dollar and bears interest at a rate at least 10 percentage points higher than the Federal mid-term rate (as determined under section 1274(d)) at the time such loan is entered into, the following rules shall apply—

(i) For purposes of section 904 only, such loan shall be marked to market annually on the earlier of the last business day of the United States person's (or related person's) taxable year or the date the loan matures; and

(ii) Any interest income earned with respect to such loan for the taxable year shall be treated as income from sources within the United States to the extent of any notional loss attributable to such loan under paragraph (d)(1)(i) of this section.

(2) *United States person.*—For purposes of this paragraph (e), the term "United States person" means a person described in section 7701(a)(30).

(3) *Loans by related foreign persons.*—(i) *In general.*—[Reserved]

(ii) *Definition of related person.*—For purposes of this paragraph (e), the term "related person" has the meaning given such term by section 954(d)(3) except that such section shall be applied by substituting "United States person" for "controlled foreign corporation" each place such term appears.

(4) *10 percent owned foreign corporation.*—For purposes of this paragraph (e), the term "10 percent owned foreign corporation" means any foreign corporation in which the United States person owns directly or indirectly (within the meaning of section 318(a)) at least 10 percent of the voting stock.

(f) *Exchange gain or loss treated as interest under § 1.988-3.*—Notwithstanding the provisions of this section, any gain or loss realized on a section 988 transaction that is treated as interest income or expense under § 1.988-3(c)(1) shall be sourced or allocated and apportioned pursuant to section 861(a)(1), 862(a)(1), or 864(e) as the case may be.

(g) *Exchange gain or loss allocated in the same manner as interest under § 1.861-9T.*—The allocation and apportionment of exchange gain or loss under § 1.861-9T shall not affect the source of exchange gain or loss for purposes of sections 871(a), 881, 1441, 1442 and 6049.

(h) *Effective date.*—This section shall be effective for taxable years beginning after December 31, 1986. Thus, any payments made or received with respect to a section 988 transaction in taxable years beginning after December 31, 1986, are subject to this section. [Reg. § 1.988-4.]

☐ [*T.D.* 8400, 3-16-92.]

§ 1.988-5. Section 988(d) hedging transactions.—(a) *Integration of a nonfunctional currency debt instrument and a § 1.988-5(a) hedge.*—(1) *In general.*—This paragraph (a) applies to a qualified hedging transaction as defined in this paragraph (a)(1). A qualified hedging transaction is an integrated economic transaction, as provided in paragraph (a)(5) of this section, consisting of a qualifying debt instrument as defined in paragraph (a)(3) of this section and a § 1.988-5(a) hedge as defined in paragraph (a)(4) of this section. If a taxpayer enters into a transaction that is a qualified hedging transaction, no exchange gain or loss is recognized by the taxpayer on the qualifying debt instrument or on the § 1.988-5(a) hedge for the period that either is part of a qualified hedging transaction, and the transactions shall be integrated as provided in paragraph (a)(9) of this section. However, if the qualified hedging transaction results in a synthetic nonfunctional currency denominated debt instrument, such instrument shall be subject to the rules of § 1.988-2(b).

(2) *Exception.*—This paragraph (a) does not apply with respect to a qualified hedging transaction that creates a synthetic asset or liability denominated in, or determined by reference to, a currency other than the U.S. dollar if the rate that approximates the Federal short-term rate in such currency is at least 20 percentage points higher than the Federal short term rate (determined under section 1274(d)) on the date the taxpayer identifies the transaction as a qualified hedging transaction.

(3) *Qualifying debt instrument.*—(i) *In general.*—A qualifying debt instrument is a debt instrument described in § 1.988-1(a)(2)(i), regardless of whether denominated in, or determined by reference to, nonfunctional currency (including dual currency debt instruments, multi-currency debt instruments and contingent payment debt instruments). A qualifying debt instrument does not include accounts payable, accounts receivable or similar items of expense or income.

(ii) *Special rule for debt instrument of which all payments are proportionately hedged.*—If a debt instrument satisfies the requirements of paragraph (a)(3)(i) of this section, and all principal and interest payments under the instrument are hedged in the same proportion, then for purposes of this paragraph (a), that portion of the instrument that is hedged is eligible to be treated as a qualifying debt instrument, and the rules of this paragraph (a) shall apply separately to such qualifying debt instrument. See Example 8 in paragraph (a)(9)(iv) of this section.

(4) *Section 1.988-5(a) hedge.*—(i) *In general.*—A § 1.988-5(a) hedge (hereinafter referred to in this paragraph (a) as a "hedge") is a spot contract, futures contract, forward contract, option contract, notional principal contract, currency swap contract, similar financial instrument, or series or combination thereof, that when integrated with a qualifying debt instrument permits the calculation of a yield to maturity (under principles of section 1272) in the currency in which the synthetic debt instrument is denominated (as determined under paragraph (a)(9)(ii)(A) of this section).

(ii) *Retroactive application of definition of currency swap contract.*—A taxpayer may apply the definition of currency swap contract set forth in § 1.988-2(e)(2)(ii) in lieu of the definition of swap agreement in section 2(e)(5) of Notice 87-11, 1987-1 C.B. 423 to transactions entered into after December 31, 1986 and before September 21, 1989.

(5) *Definition of integrated economic transaction.*—A qualifying debt instrument and a hedge are an integrated economic transaction if all of the following requirements are satisfied—

(i) All payments to be made or received under the qualifying debt instrument (or amounts determined by reference to a nonfunctional currency) are fully hedged on the date the taxpayer identifies the transaction under paragraph (a) of this section as a qualified hedging transaction such that a yield to maturity (under principles of section 1272) in the currency in which the synthetic debt instrument is denominated (as determined under paragraph (a)(9)(ii)(A) of this section) can be calculated. Any contingent payment features of the qualifying debt instrument must be fully offset by the hedge such that the synthetic debt instrument is not classified as a contingent payment debt instrument. See *Examples 6* and *7* of paragraph (a)(9)(iv) of this section.

(ii) The hedge is identified in accordance with paragraph (a)(8) of this section on or before the date the acquisition of the financial instrument (or instruments) constituting the hedge is settled or closed.

(iii) None of the parties to the hedge are related. The term "related" means the relationships defined in section 267(b) or section 707(b).

(iv) In the case of a qualified business unit with a residence, as defined in section 988(a)(3)(B), outside of the United States, both the qualifying debt instrument and the hedge are properly reflected on the books of such qualified business unit throughout the term of the qualified hedging transaction.

(v) Subject to the limitations of paragraph (a)(5) of this section, both the qualifying debt instrument and the hedge are entered into by the same individual, partnership, trust, estate, or corporation. With respect to a corporation, the same corporation must enter into both the qualifying debt instrument and the hedge whether or not such corporation is a member of an affiliated group of corporations that files a consolidated return.

(vi) With respect to a foreign person engaged in a U.S. trade or business that enters into a qualifying debt instrument or hedge through such trade or business, all items of income and expense associated with the quali-

Reg. § 1.988-5(a)(5)(vi)

fying debt instrument and the hedge (other than interest expense that is subject to § 1.882-5), would have been effectively connected with such U.S. trade or business throughout the term of the qualified hedging transaction had this paragraph (a) not applied.

(6) *Special rules for legging in and legging out of integrated treatment.*—(i) *Legging in.*—"Legging in" to integrated treatment under this paragraph (a) means that a hedge is entered into after the date the qualifying debt instrument is entered into or acquired, and the requirements of this paragraph (a) are satisfied on the date the hedge is entered into ("leg in date"). If a taxpayer legs into integrated treatment, the following rules shall apply—

(A) Exchange gain or loss shall be realized with respect to the qualifying debt instrument determined solely by reference to changes in exchange rates between—

(1) The date the instrument was acquired by the holder, or the date the obligor assumed the obligation to make payments under the instrument; and

(2) The leg in date.

(B) The recognition of such gain or loss will be deferred until the date the qualifying debt instrument matures or is otherwise disposed of.

(C) The source and character of such gain or loss shall be determined on the leg in date as if the qualifying debt instrument was actually sold or otherwise terminated by the taxpayer.

(ii) *Legging out.*—With respect to a qualifying debt instrument and hedge that are properly identified as a qualified hedging transaction, "legging out" of integrated treatment under this paragraph (a) means that the taxpayer disposes of or otherwise terminates all or a part of the qualifying debt instrument or hedge prior to maturity of the qualified hedging transaction, or the taxpayer changes a material term of the qualifying debt instrument (*e.g.*, exercises an option to change the interest rate or index, or the maturity date) or hedge (*e.g.*, changes the interest or exchange rates underlying the hedge, or the expiration date) prior to maturity of the qualified hedging transaction. A taxpayer that disposes of or terminates a qualified hedging transaction (*i.e.*, disposes of or terminates both the qualifying transaction and the hedge on the same day) shall be considered to have disposed of or otherwise terminated the synthetic debt instrument rather than as legging out. If a taxpayer legs out of integrated treatment, the following rules shall apply—

(A) The transaction will be treated as a qualified hedging transaction during the time the requirements of this paragraph (a) were satisfied.

(B) If the hedge is disposed of or otherwise terminated, the qualifying debt instrument shall be treated as sold for its fair market value on the date the hedge is disposed of or otherwise terminated (the "leg-out date"), and any gain or loss (including gain or loss resulting from factors other than movements in exchange rates) from the identification date to the leg-out date is realized and recognized on the leg-out date. The spot rate on the leg-out date shall be used to determine exchange gain or loss on the debt instrument for the period beginning on the leg-out date and ending on the date such instrument matures or is disposed of or otherwise terminated. Proper adjustment to the principal amount of the debt instrument must be made to reflect any gain or loss taken into account. The netting rule of § 1.988-2(b)(8) shall apply.

(C) If the qualifying debt instrument is disposed of or otherwise terminated, the hedge shall be treated as sold for its fair market value on the date the qualifying debt instrument is disposed of or otherwise terminated (the "leg-out date"), and any gain or loss from the identification date to the leg-out date is realized and recognized on the leg-out date. The spot rate on the leg-out date shall be used to determine exchange gain or loss on the hedge for the period beginning on the leg-out date and ending on the date such hedge is disposed of or otherwise terminated.

(D) Except as provided in paragraph (a)(8)(iii) of this section (regarding identification by the Commissioner), that part of the qualified hedging transaction that has not been terminated (*i.e.*, the remaining debt instrument in its entirety even if partially hedged, or hedge) cannot be part of a qualified hedging transaction for any period subsequent to the leg out date.

(E) If a taxpayer legs out of a qualified hedging transaction and realizes a gain with respect to the terminated instrument, then paragraph (a)(6)(ii)(B) or (C) of this section, as appropriate, shall not apply if during the period beginning 30 days before the leg-out date and ending 30 days after that date the taxpayer enters into another transaction that hedges at least 50% of the remaining currency flow with respect to the qualifying debt instrument which was part of the qualified hedging transaction (or, if appropriate, an equivalent amount under the § 1.988-5 hedge which was part of the qualified hedging transaction).

(7) *Transactions part of a straddle.*—At the discretion of the Commissioner, a transaction shall not satisfy the requirements of paragraph (a)(5) of this section if the debt instrument

making up the qualified hedging transaction is part of a straddle as defined in section 1092(c) prior to the time the qualified hedging transaction is identified.

(8) *Identification requirements.*—(i) *Identification by the taxpayer.*—A taxpayer must establish a record and before the close of the date the hedge is entered into, the taxpayer must enter into the record for each qualified hedging transaction the following information—

(A) The date the qualifying debt instrument and hedge were entered into;

(B) The date the qualifying debt instrument and the hedge are identified as constituting a qualified hedging transaction;

(C) The amount that must be deferred, if any, under paragraph (a)(6) of this section and the source and character of such deferred amount;

(D) A description of the qualifying debt instrument and the hedge; and

(E) A summary of the cash flow resulting from treating the qualifying debt instrument and the hedge as a qualified hedging transaction.

(ii) *Identification by trustee on behalf of beneficiary.*—A trustee of a trust that enters into a qualified hedging transaction may satisfy the identification requirements described in paragraph (a)(8)(i) of this section on behalf of a beneficiary of such trust.

(iii) *Identification by the Commissioner.*—If—

(A) A taxpayer enters into a qualifying debt instrument and a hedge but fails to comply with one or more of the requirements of this paragraph (a), and

(B) On the basis of all the facts and circumstances, the Commissioner concludes that the qualifying debt instrument and the hedge are, in substance, a qualified hedging transaction,

then the Commissioner may treat the qualifying debt instrument and the hedge as a qualified hedging transaction. The Commissioner may identify a qualifying debt instrument and a hedge as a qualified hedging transaction regardless of whether the qualifying debt instrument and the hedge are held by the same taxpayer.

(9) *Taxation of qualified hedging transactions.*—(i) *In general.*—(A) *General rule.*—If a transaction constitutes a qualified hedging transaction, the qualifying debt instrument and the hedge are integrated and treated as a single transaction with respect to the taxpayer that has entered into the qualified hedging transaction during the period that the transaction qualifies as a qualified hedging transaction. Neither the qualifying debt instrument nor the hedge that makes up the qualified hedging transaction shall be subject to section 263(g), 1092 or 1256 for the period such transactions are integrated. However, the qualified hedging transaction may be subject to section 263(g) or 1092 if such transaction is part of a straddle.

(B) *Special rule for income or expense of foreign persons effectively connected with a U.S. trade or business.*—Interest income of a foreign person resulting from a qualified hedging transaction entered into by such foreign person that satisfies the requirements of paragraph (a)(5)(vii) of this section shall be treated as effectively connected with a U.S. trade or business. Interest expense of a foreign person resulting from a qualified hedging transaction entered into by such foreign person that satisfies the requirements of paragraph (a)(5)(vii) of this section shall be allocated and apportioned under § 1.882-5 of the regulations.

(C) *Special rule for foreign persons that enter into qualified hedging transactions giving rise to U.S. source income not effectively connected with a U.S. trade or business.*—If a foreign person enters into a qualified hedging transaction that gives rise to U.S. source interest income (determined under the source rules for synthetic asset transactions as provided in this section) not effectively connected with a U.S. trade or business of such foreign person, for purposes of sections 871(a), 881, 1441, 1442 and 6049, the provisions of this paragraph (a) shall not apply and such sections of the Internal Revenue Code shall be applied separately to the qualifying debt instrument and the hedge. To the extent relevant to any foreign person, if the requirements of this paragraph (a) are otherwise met, the provisions of this paragraph (a) shall apply for all other purposes of the Internal Revenue Code (*e.g.*, for purposes of calculating the earnings and profits of a controlled foreign corporation that enters into a qualified hedging transaction through a qualified business unit resident outside the United States, income or expense with respect to such qualified hedging transaction shall be calculated under the provisions of this paragraph (a)).

(ii) *Income tax effects of integration.*—The effect of integrating and treating a transaction as a single transaction is to create a synthetic debt instrument for income tax purposes, which is subject to the original issue discount provisions of sections 1272 through 1288 and 163(e), the terms of which are determined as follows:

Reg. § 1.988-5(a)(9)(ii)

(A) *Denomination of synthetic debt instrument.*—In the case where the qualifying debt instrument is a borrowing, the denomination of the synthetic debt instrument is the same as the currency paid under the terms of the hedge to acquire the currency used to make payments under the qualifying debt instrument. In the case where the qualifying debt instrument is a lending, the denomination of the synthetic debt instrument is the same as the currency received under the terms of the hedge in exchange for amounts received under the qualifying debt instrument. For example, if the hedge is a forward contract to acquire British pounds for dollars, and the qualifying debt instrument is a borrowing denominated in British pounds, the synthetic debt instrument is considered a borrowing in dollars.

(B) *Term and accrual periods.*—The term of the synthetic debt instrument shall be the period beginning on the identification date and ending on the date the qualifying debt instrument matures or such earlier date that the qualifying debt instrument or hedge is disposed of or otherwise terminated. Unless otherwise clearly indicated by the payment interval under the hedge, the accrual period shall be a six month period which ends on the dates determined under section 1272(a)(5).

(C) *Issue price.*—The issue price of the synthetic debt instrument is the adjusted issue price of the qualifying debt instrument translated into the currency in which the synthetic debt instrument is denominated at the spot rate on the identification date.

(D) *Stated redemption price at maturity.*—In the case where the qualifying debt instrument is a borrowing, the stated redemption price at maturity shall be determined under section 1273(a)(2) on the identification date by reference to the amounts to be paid under the hedge to acquire the currency necessary to make interest and principal payments on the qualifying debt instrument. In the case where the qualifying debt instrument is a lending, the stated redemption price at maturity shall be determined under section 1273(a)(2) on the identification date by reference to the amounts to be received under the hedge in exchange for the interest and principal payments received pursuant to the terms of the qualifying debt instrument.

(iii) *Source of interest income and allocation of expense.*—Interest income from a synthetic debt instrument described in paragraph (a)(9)(ii) of this section shall be sourced by reference to the source of income under sections 861(a)(1) and 862(a)(1) of the qualifying debt instrument. The character for purposes of section 904 of interest income from a synthetic debt instrument shall be determined by reference to the character of the interest income from qualifying debt instrument. Interest expense from a synthetic debt instrument described in paragraph (a)(9)(ii) of this section shall be allocated and apportioned under §§ 1.861-8T through 1.861-12T or the successor sections thereof or under § 1.882-5.

(iv) *Examples.*—The following examples illustrate the application of this paragraph (a)(9).

Example 1. (i) K is a U.S. corporation with the U.S. dollar as its functional currency. On December 24, 1989, K agrees to close the following transaction on December 31, 1989. K will borrow from an unrelated party on December 31, 1989, 100 British pounds (£) for 3 years at a 10 percent rate of interest, payable annually, with no principal payment due until the final installment. K will also enter into a currency swap contract with an unrelated counterparty under the terms of which—

(a) K will swap, on December 31, 1989, the £100 obtained from the borrowing for $100; and

(b) K will exchange dollars for pounds pursuant to the following table in order to obtain the pounds necessary to make payments on the pound borrowing:

DATE	U.S. Dollars	Pounds
December 31, 1990	8	10
December 31, 1991	8	10
December 31, 1992	108	110

(ii) The interest rate on the borrowing is set and the exchange rates on the swap are fixed on December 24, 1989. On December 31, 1989, K borrows the £100 and swaps such pounds for $100. Assume K has satisfied the identification requirements of paragraph (a)(8) of this section.

(iii) The pound borrowing (which constitutes a qualifying debt instrument under paragraph (a)(3) of this section) and the currency swap contract (which constitutes a hedge under paragraph (a)(4) of this section) are a qualified hedging transaction as defined in paragraph (a)(1) of this section. Accordingly, the pound borrowing and the swap are integrated and treated as one transaction with the following consequences:

(A) The integration of the pound borrowing and the swap results in a synthetic dollar borrowing with an issue price of $100 under section 1273(b)(2).

(B) The total amount of interest and principal of the synthetic dollar borrowing is equal to the dollar payments made by K under the currency swap contract (i.e., $8 in 1990, $8 in 1991, and $108 in 1992).

(C) The stated redemption price at maturity (defined in section 1273(a)(2)) is $100. Because the stated redemption price equals the issue price, there is no OID on the synthetic dollar borrowing.

(D) K may deduct the annual interest payments of $8 under section 163(a) (subject to any limitations on deductibility imposed by other provisions of the Code) according to its regular method of accounting. K has also paid $100 as a return of principal in 1992.

(E) K must allocate and apportion its interest expense with respect to the synthetic dollar borrowing under the rules of §§ 1.861-8T through 1.861-12T.

Example 2. (i) K, a U.S. corporation, has the U.S. dollar as its functional currency. On December 24, 1989, when the spot rate for Swiss francs (Sf) is Sf1 = $1, K enters into a forward contract to purchase Sf100 in exchange for $100.04 for delivery on December 31, 1989. The Sf100 are to be used for the purchase of a franc denominated debt instrument on December 31, 1989. The instrument will have a term of 3 years, an issue price of Sf100, and will bear interest at 6 percent, payable annually, with no repayment of principal until the final installment. On December 24, 1989, K also enters into a series of forward contracts to sell the franc interest and principal payments that will be received under the terms of the franc denominated debt instrument for dollars according to the following schedule:

DATE	U.S. Dollars	Francs
December 31, 1990	6.12	6
December 31, 1991	6.23	6
December 31, 1992	112.16	106

(ii) On December 31, 1989, K takes delivery of the Sf100 and purchases the franc denominated debt instrument. Assume K satisfies the identification requirements of paragraph (a)(8) of this section. The purchase of the franc debt instrument (which constitutes a qualifying debt instrument under paragraph (a)(3) of this section) and the series of forward contracts (which constitute a hedge under paragraph (a)(4) of this section) are a qualified hedging transaction under paragraph (a)(1) of this section. Accordingly, the franc debt instrument and all the forward contracts are integrated and treated as one transaction with the following consequences:

(A) The integration of the franc debt instrument and the forward contracts results in a synthetic dollar debt instrument in an amount equal to the dollars exchanged under the forward contract to purchase the francs necessary to acquire the franc debt instrument. Accordingly, the issue price is $100.04 (section 1273(b)(2) of the Code).

(B) The total amount of interest and principal received by K with respect to the synthetic dollar debt instrument is equal to the dollars received under the forward sales contracts (i.e., $6.12 in 1990, $6.23 in 1991, and $112.16 in 1992).

(C) The synthetic dollar debt instrument is an installment obligation and its stated redemption price at maturity is $106.15 (i.e., $6.12 of the payments in 1990, 1991, and 1992 are treated as periodic interest payments under the principles of section 1273). Because the stated redemption price at maturity exceeds the issue price, under section 1273(a)(1) the synthetic dollar debt instrument has OID of $6.11.

(D) The yield to maturity of the synthetic dollar debt instrument is 8.00 percent, compounded annually. Assuming K is a calendar year taxpayer, it must include interest income of $8.00 in 1990 (of which $1.88 constitutes OID), $8.15 in 1991 (of which $2.03 constitutes OID), and $8.32 in 1992 (of which $2.20 constitutes OID). The amount of the final payment received by K in excess of the interest income includible is a return of principal and a payment of previously accrued OID.

(E) The source of the interest income shall be determined by applying sections 861(a)(1) and 862(a)(1) with reference to the franc interest income that would have been received had the transaction not been integrated.

Example 3. (i) K is an accrual method U.S. corporation with the U.S. dollar as its functional currency. On January 1, 1992, K borrows 100 British pounds (£) for 3 years at a 10% rate of interest payable on December 31 of each year with no principal payment due until the final installment. The spot rate on January 1, 1992, is £1 = $1.50. On January 1, 1993, when the spot rate is £1 = $1.60, K enters into a currency swap contract with an unrelated counterparty under the terms of which K will exchange dollars for pounds pursuant to the following table in order to obtain the pounds necessary to make the remaining payments on the pound borrowing:

Reg. § 1.988-5(a)(9)(iv)

DATE	U.S. Dollars	Pounds
December 31, 1993	12.80	10
December 31, 1994	12.80	10
December 31, 1994	160.00	100

(ii) Assume that British pound interest rates are still 10% and that K properly identifies the pound borrowing and the currency swap contract as a qualified hedging transaction as provided in paragraph (a)(8) of this section. Under paragraph (a)(6)(i) of this section, K must realize exchange gain or loss with respect to the pound borrowing determined solely by reference to changes in exchange rates between January 1, 1992 and January 1, 1993. (Thus, gain or loss from other factors such as movements in interest rates or changes in credit quality of K are not taken into account). Recognition of such gain or loss is deferred until K terminates its pound borrowing. Accordingly, K must defer exchange loss in the amount of $10 [(£100 × 1.50) - (£100 × 1.60)].

(iii) Additionally, the qualified hedging transaction is treated as a synthetic U.S. dollar debt instrument with an issue date of January 1, 1993, and a maturity date of December 31, 1994. The issue price of the synthetic debt instrument is $160 (£100 × 1.60, the spot rate on January 1, 1993) and the total amount of interest and principal is $185.60. The accrual period is the one year period beginning on January 1 and ending December 31 of each year. The stated redemption price at maturity is $160. Thus, K is treated as paying $12.80 of interest in 1993, $12.80 of interest in 1994, and $160 of principal in 1994. The interest expense from the synthetic instrument is allocated and apportioned in accordance with the rules of §§ 1.861-8T through 1.861-12T. Sections 263(g), 1092, and 1256 do not apply to the positions comprising the synthetic dollar borrowing.

Example 4. (i) K is an accrual method U.S. corporation with the U.S. dollar as its functional currency. On January 1, 1990, K borrows 100 British pounds (£) for 3 years at a 10% rate of interest payable on December 31 of each year with no principal payment due until the final installment. The spot rate on January 1, 1990, is £1 = $1.50. Also on January 1, 1990, K enters into a currency swap contract with an unrelated counterparty under the terms of which K will exchange dollars for pounds pursuant to the following table in order to obtain the pounds necessary to make the remaining payments on the pound borrowing:

DATE	U.S. Dollars	Pounds
December 31, 1990	12.00	10
December 31, 1991	12.00	10
December 31, 1992	162.00	110

(ii) Assume that K properly identifies the pound borrowing and the currency swap contract as a qualified hedging transaction as provided in paragraph (a)(1) of this section.

(iii) The pound borrowing (which constitutes a qualifying debt instrument under paragraph (a)(3) of this section) and the currency swap contract (which constitutes a hedge under paragraph (a)(4) of this section) are a qualified hedging transaction as defined in paragraph (a)(1) of this section. Accordingly, the pound borrowing and the swap are integrated and treated as one transaction with the following consequences:

(A) The integration of the pound borrowing and the swap results in a synthetic dollar borrowing with an issue price of $150 under section 1273(b)(2).

(B) The total amount of interest and principal of the synthetic dollar borrowing is equal to the dollar payments made by K under the currency swap contract (i.e., $12 in 1990, $12 in 1991, and $162 in 1992).

(C) The stated redemption price at maturity (defined in section 1273(a)(2)) is $150. Because the stated redemption price equals the issue price, there is no OID on the synthetic dollar borrowing.

(D) K may deduct the annual interest payments of $12 under section 163(a) (subject to any limitations on deductibility imposed by other provisions of the Code) according to its regular method of accounting. K has also paid $150 as a return of principal in 1992.

(E) K must allocate and apportion its interest expense from the synthetic instrument under the rules of §§ 1.861-8T through 1.861-12T.

(iv) Assume that on January 1, 1991, the spot exchange rate is £1 = $1.60, interest rates have not changed since January 1, 1990, (accordingly, assume that the market value of K's bond in pounds has not changed) and that K transfers its rights and obligations under the currency swap contract in exchange for $10. Under § 1.988-2(e)(3)(iii), K will include in income as exchange gain $10 on January 1, 1991. Pursuant to paragraph (a)(6)(ii) of this section, the pound borrowing and the currency swap contract are treated as a qualified hedging transaction for 1990. The loss inherent in the pound borrowing from January 1, 1990, to January 1, 1991, is realized and recognized on Janu-

Reg. § 1.988-5(a)(9)(iv)

ary 1, 1991. Such loss is exchange loss in the amount of $10.00 [(£100 × $1.50, the spot rate on January 1, 1990) − (£100 × $1.60, the spot rate on January 1, 1991)]. For purposes of determining exchange gain or loss on the £100 principal amount of the debt instrument for the period January 1, 1991, to December 31, 1992, the spot rate on January 1, 1991 is used rather than the spot rate on the issue date. Thus, assuming that the spot rate on December 31, 1992, the maturity date, is £1 = $1.80, K realizes exchange loss in the amount of $20 [(£100 × $1.60) − (£100 × $1.80)]. Except as provided in paragraph (a)(8)(iii) (regarding identification by the Commissioner), the pound borrowing cannot be part of a qualified hedging transaction for any period subsequent to the leg out date.

Example 5. (i) K, a U.S. corporation, has the U.S. dollar as its functional currency. On January 1, 1990, when the spot rate for Swiss francs (Sf) is Sf1 = $.50, K converts $100 to Sf200 and purchases a franc denominated debt instrument. The instrument has a term of 3 years, an adjusted issue price of Sf200, and will bear interest at 5 percent, payable annually, with no repayment of principal until the final installment. The U.S. dollar interest rate on an equivalent instrument is 8% on January 1, 1990, compounded annually. On January 1, 1990, K also enters into a series of forward contracts to sell the franc interest and principal payments that will be received under the terms of the franc denominated debt instrument for dollars according to the following schedule:

DATE	U.S. Dollars	Francs
December 31, 1990	5.14	10
December 31, 1991	5.29	10
December 31, 1992	114.26	210

(ii) Assume K satisfies the identification requirements of paragraph (a)(8) of this section. Assume further that on January 1, 1991, the spot exchange rate is Sf1 = U.S.$ .5143, the U.S. dollar interest rate is 10%, compounded annually, and the Swiss franc interest rate is the same as on January 1, 1990 (5%, compounded annually). On January 1, 1991, K disposes of the forward contracts that were to mature on December 31, 1991, and December 31, 1992 and incurs a loss of $3.62 (the present value of $.10 with respect to the 1991 contract and $4.27 with respect to the 1992 contract).

(iii) The purchase of the franc debt instrument (which constitutes a qualifying debt instrument under paragraph (a)(3) of this section) and the series of forward contracts (which constitute a hedge under paragraph (a)(4) of this section) are a qualified hedging transaction under paragraph (a)(1) of this section. Accordingly, the franc debt instrument and all the forward contracts are integrated for the period beginning January 1, 1990, and ending January 1, 1991.

(A) The integration of the franc debt instrument and the forward contracts results in a synthetic dollar debt instrument with an issue price of $100.

(B) The total amount of interest and principal to be received by K with respect to the synthetic dollar debt instrument is equal to the dollars to be received under the forward sales contracts (i.e., $5.14 in 1990, $5.29 in 1991, and $114.26 in 1992).

(C) The synthetic dollar debt instrument is an installment obligation and its stated redemption price at maturity is $109.27 (i.e., $5.14 of the payments in 1990, 1991, and 1992 is treated as periodic interest payments under the principles of section 1273). Because the stated redemption price at maturity exceeds the issue price, under section 1273(a)(1) the synthetic dollar debt instrument has OID of $9.27.

(D) The yield to maturity of the synthetic dollar debt instrument is 8.00 percent, compounded annually. Assuming K is a calendar year taxpayer, it must include interest income of $8.00 in 1990 (of which $2.86 constitutes OID).

(E) The source of the interest income is determined by applying sections 861(a)(1) and 862(a)(1) with reference to the franc interest income that would have been received had the transaction not been integrated.

(iv) Because K disposed of the forward contracts on January 1, 1991, the rules of paragraph (a)(6)(ii) of this section shall apply. Accordingly, the $3.62 loss from the disposition of the forward contracts is realized and recognized on January 1, 1991. Additionally, K is deemed to have sold the franc debt instrument for $102.86, its fair market value in dollars on January 1, 1991. K will compute gain or loss with respect to the deemed sale of the franc debt instrument by subtracting its adjusted basis in the instrument ($102.86—the value of the Sf200 issue price at the spot rate on the identification date plus $2.86 of original issue discount accrued on the synthetic dollar debt instrument for 1990) from the amount realized on the deemed sale of $102.86. Thus K realizes and recognizes no gain or loss from the deemed sale of the debt instrument. The dollar amount used to determine exchange gain or loss with respect to the franc debt instrument is the Sf200 issue price on January 1, 1991, translated into dollars at the spot rate on January 1, 1991, of Sf1 = U.S.$ .5143. Except as provided in

Reg. § 1.988-5(a)(9)(iv)

paragraph (a)(8)(iii) of this section (regarding identification by the Commissioner), the franc borrowing cannot be part of a qualified hedging transaction for any period subsequent to the leg out date.

Example 6. (i) K is a U.S. corporation with the dollar as its functional currency. On January 1, 1992, K issues a debt instrument with the following terms: the issue price is $1,000, the instrument pays interest annually at a rate of 8% on the $1,000 principal amount, the instrument matures on December 31, 1996, and the amount paid at maturity is the greater of zero or $2,000 less the U.S. dollar value (determined on December 31, 1996) of 150,000 Japanese yen.

(ii) Also on January 1, 1992, K enters into the following hedges with respect to the instrument described in the preceding paragraph: a forward contract under which K will sell 150,000 yen for $1,000 on December 31, 1996 (note that this forward rate assumes that interest rates in yen and dollars are equal); and an option contract that expires on December 31, 1996, under which K has the right (but not the obligation) to acquire 150,000 yen for $2,000. K will pay for the option by making payments to the writer of the option equal to $5 each December 31 from 1992 through 1996.

(iii) The net economic effect of these transactions is that K has created a liability with a principal amount and amount paid at maturity of $1,000, with an interest cost of 8.5% (8% on debt instrument, 0.5% option price) compounded annually. For example, if on December 31, 1996, the spot exchange rate is $1 = 100 yen, K pays $500 on the bond [$2,000 − (150,000 yen/$100)], and $500 in satisfaction of the forward contract [$1,000 − (150,000 yen/$100)]. If instead the spot exchange rate on December 31, 1996 is $1 = 200 yen, K pays $1,250 on the bond [$2,000 − (150,000 yen/$200)] and K receives $250 in satisfaction of the forward contract [$1,000 − (150,000 yen/$200)]. Finally, if the spot exchange rate on December 31, 1996 is $1 = 50 yen, K pays $0 on the bond [$2,000 − (150,000 yen/$50), but the bond holder is not required under the terms of the instrument to pay additional principal]; K exercises the option to buy 150,000 yen for $2,000; and K then delivers the 150,000 yen as required by the forward contract in exchange for $1,000.

(iv) Assume K satisfies the identification requirements of paragraph (a)(8) of this section. The debt instrument described in paragraph (i) of this *Example 6* (which constitutes a qualifying debt instrument under paragraph (a)(3) of this section) and the forward contract and option contract described in paragraph (ii) of this example (which constitute a hedge under paragraph (a)(4) of this section and are collectively referred to hereafter as "the contracts") together are a qualified hedging transaction under paragraph (a)(1) of this section. Accordingly, with respect to K, the debt instrument and the contracts are integrated, resulting in a synthetic dollar debt instrument with an issue price of $1000, a stated redemption price at maturity of $1000 and a yield to maturity of 8.5% compounded annually (with no original issue discount). K must allocate and apportion its annual interest expense of $85 under the rules of §§ 1.861-8T through 1.861-12T.

Example 7. (i) R is a U.S. corporation with the dollar as its functional currency. On January 1, 1995, R issues a debt instrument with the following terms: the issue price is 504 British pounds (£), the instrument pays interest at a rate of 3.7% (compounded semi-annually) on the £504 principal amount, the instrument matures on December 31, 1999, with a repayment at maturity of the £ 504 principal plus the proportional gain, if any, in the "Financial Times" 100 Stock Exchange (FTSE) index (determined by the excess of the value of the FTSE index on the maturity date over the value of the FTSE on the issue date, divided by the value of the FTSE index on the issue date, multiplied by the number of FTSE index contracts that could be purchased on the issue date for £504).

(ii) Also on January 1, 1995, R enters into a contract with a bank under which on January 1, 1995, R will swap the £504 for $1,000 (at the current spot rate). R will make U.S. dollar payments to the bank equal to 8.15% on the notional principal amount of $1,000 (compounded semiannually) for the period beginning January 1, 1995 and ending December 31, 1999. R will receive pound payments from the bank equal to 3.7% on the notional principal amount of £504 (compounded semi-annually) for the period beginning January 1, 1995 and ending December 31, 1999. On December 31, 1999, R will swap with the bank $1,000 for £504 plus the proportional gain, if any, in the FTSE index (computed as provided above).

(iii) Economically, both the indexed debt instrument and the hedging contract are hybrid instruments with the following components. The indexed debt instrument is composed of a par pound debt instrument that is assumed to have a 10.85% coupon (compounded semi-annually) plus an embedded FTSE equity index option for which the investor pays a premium of 7.15% (amortized semi-annually) on the pound principal amount. The combined effect is that the premium paid by the investor partially offsets the coupon payments resulting in a return of 3.7% (10.85% − 7.15%). Similarly, the dollar payments under the hedging contract to be made by R are computed by multiplying the dollar notional principal amount by an 8.00% rate (compounded semi-annually) which the facts assume would be the rate paid on a conventional currency swap plus a premium of 0.15% (amortized semi-annually) on the dollar notional principal amount for an embedded FTSE equity index option.

(iv) Assume R satisfies the identification requirements of paragraph (a)(8) of this section. The indexed debt instrument described in paragraph (i) of this *Example 7* constitutes a qualifying debt instrument under paragraph (a)(3) of this section. The hedging contract described in paragraph (ii) of this *Example 7* constitutes a hedge under paragraph (a)(4) of this section. Since both the pound exposure of the indexed debt instrument and the exposure to movements of the FTSE embedded in the indexed debt instrument are hedged such that a yield to maturity can be determined in dollars, the transaction satisfies the requirement of paragraph (a)(5)(i) of this section. Assuming the transactions satisfy the other requirements of paragraph (a)(5) of this section, the indexed debt instrument and hedge are a qualified hedging transaction under paragraph (a)(1) of this section. Accordingly, with respect to R, the debt instrument and the contracts are integrated, resulting in a synthetic dollar debt instrument with an issue price of $1000, a stated redemption price at maturity of $1000 and a yield to maturity of 8.15% compounded semi-annually (with no original issue discount). K must allocate and apportion its interest expense from the synthetic instrument under the rules §§ 1.861-8T through 1.861-12T.

Example 8. (i) K is a U.S. corporation with the U.S. dollar as its functional currency. On December 24, 1992, K agrees to close the following transaction on December 31, 1992. K will borrow from an unrelated party on December 31, 1992, 200 British pounds (£) for 3 years at a 10 percent rate of interest, payable annually, with no principal payment due until the final installment. K will also enter into a currency swap contract with an unrelated counterparty under the terms of which—

(A) K will swap, on December 31, 1992, £ 100 obtained from the borrowing for $100; and

(B) K will exchange dollars for pounds pursuant to the following table:

DATE	U.S. Dollars	Pounds
December 31, 1993	8	10
December 31, 1994	8	10
December 31, 1995	108	110

(ii) The interest rate on the borrowing is set and the exchange rates on the swap are fixed on December 24, 1992. On December 31, 1992, K borrows the £200 and swaps £100 for $100. Assume K has satisfied the identification requirements of paragraph (a)(8) of this section.

(iii) The £200 debt instrument satisfies the requirements of paragraph (a)(3)(i) of this section. Because all principal and interest payments under the instrument are hedged in the same proportion (50% of all interest and principal payments are hedged), 50% of the payments under the £200 instrument (principal amount of £100 and annual interest of £10) are treated as a qualifying debt instrument for purposes of paragraph (a) of this section. Thus, the distinct £100 borrowing and the currency swap contract (which constitutes a hedge under paragraph (a)(4) of this section) are a qualified hedging transaction as defined in paragraph (a)(1) of this section. Accordingly, £100 of the pound borrowing and the swap are integrated and treated as one synthetic dollar transaction with the following consequences:

(A) The integration of £100 of the pound borrowing and the swap results in a synthetic dollar borrowing with an issue price of $100 under section 1273(b)(2).

(B) The total amount of interest and principal of the synthetic dollar borrowing is equal to the dollar payments made by K under the currency swap contract (i.e., $8 in 1993, $8 in 1994, and $108 in 1995).

(C) The stated redemption price at maturity (defined in section 1273(a)(2)) is $100. Because the stated redemption price equals the issue price, there is no OID on the synthetic dollar borrowing.

(D) K may deduct the annual interest payments of $8 under section 163(a) (subject to any limitations on deductibility imposed by other provisions of the Code) according to its regular method of accounting. K has also paid $100 as a return of principal in 1995.

(E) K must allocate and apportion its interest expense from the synthetic instrument under the rules of §§ 1.861-8T through 1.861-12T.

That portion of the £200 pound debt instrument that is not hedged (*i.e.*, £100) is treated as a separate debt instrument subject to the rules of § 1.988-2(b) and §§ 1.861-8T through 1.861-12T.

Example 9. (i) K is an accrual method U.S. corporation with the U.S. dollar as its functional currency. On January 1, 1992, K borrows 100 British pounds (£) for 3 years at a 10% rate of interest payable on December 31 of each year with no principal payment due until the final installment. On the same day, K enters into a currency swap agreement with an unre-

Reg. § 1.988-5(a)(9)(iv)

lated bank under which K agrees to the following:

(A) On January 1, 1992, K will exchange the £100 borrowed for $150.

(B) For the period beginning January 1, 1992 and ending December 31, 1994, K will pay at the end of each month an amount determined by multiplying $150 by one month LIBOR less 65 basis points and receive from the bank on December 31st of 1992, 1993, and 1994, £10.

(C) On December 31, 1994, K will exchange $150 for £100.

Assume K satisfies the identification requirements of paragraph (a)(8) of this section.

(ii) The pound borrowing (which constitutes a qualifying debt instrument under paragraph (a)(3) of this section) and the currency swap contract (which constitutes a hedge under paragraph (a)(4) of this section) are a qualified hedging transaction as defined in paragraph (a)(1) of this section. Accordingly, the pound borrowing and the swap are integrated and treated as one transaction with the following consequences:

(A) The integration of the pound borrowing and the swap results in a synthetic dollar borrowing with an issue price of $150 under section 1273(b)(2).

DATE	
December 31, 1992	
December 31, 1993	
December 31, 1994	

(ii) Assume that K properly identifies the pound borrowing and the currency swap contract as a qualified hedging transaction as provided in paragraph (a)(1) of this section.

(iii) The pound loan (which constitutes a qualifying debt instrument under paragraph (a)(3) of this section) and the currency swap contract (which constitutes a hedge under paragraph (a)(4) of this section) are a qualified hedging transaction as defined in paragraph (a)(1) of this section. Accordingly, the pound loan and the swap are integrated and treated as one transaction with the following consequences:

(A) The integration of the pound loan and the swap results in a synthetic dollar loan with an issue price of $150 under section 1273(b)(2).

(B) The total amount of interest and principal of the synthetic dollar loan is equal to the dollar payments received by K under the currency swap contract (i.e., $12 in 1992, $12 in 1993, and $162 in 1994).

(C) The stated redemption price at maturity (defined in section 1273(a)(2)) is $150. Because the stated redemption price equals the

(B) The total amount of interest and principal of the synthetic dollar borrowing is equal to the dollar payments made by K under the currency swap contract.

(C) The stated redemption price at maturity (defined in section 1273(a)(2)) is $150. Because the stated redemption price equals the issue price, there is no OID on the synthetic dollar borrowing.

(D) K may deduct the monthly variable interest payments under section 163(a) (subject to any limitations on deductibility imposed by other provisions of the Code) according to its regular method of accounting. K has also paid $150 as a return of principal in 1994.

(E) K must allocate and apportion its interest expense from the synthetic instrument under the rules of §§ 1.861-8T through 1.861-12T.

Example 10. (i) K is an accrual method U.S. corporation with the U.S. dollar as its functional currency. On January 1, 1992, K loans 100 British pounds (£) for 3 years at a 10% rate of interest payable on December 31 of each year with no principal payment due until the final installment. The spot rate on January 1, 1992, is £1 = $1.50. Also on January 1, 1992, K enters into a currency swap contract with an unrelated counterparty under the terms of which K will exchange pounds for dollars pursuant to the following table:

	Pounds	Dollars
December 31, 1992	10	12
December 31, 1993	10	12
December 31, 1994	110	162

issue price, there is no OID on the synthetic dollar loan.

(D) K must include in income as interest $12 in 1992, 1993, and 1994.

(E) The source of the interest income shall be determined by applying sections 861(a)(1) and 862(a)(1) with reference to the pound interest income that would have been received had the transaction not been integrated.

(iv) On January 1, 1993, K transfers both the pound loan and the currency swap to B, its wholly owned U.S. subsidiary, in exchange for B stock in a transfer that satisfies the requirements of section 351. Under paragraph (a)(6) of this section, the transfer of both instruments is not "legging out." Rather, K is considered to have transferred the synthetic dollar loan to B in a transaction in which gain or loss is not recognized. B's basis in the loan under section 362 is $100.

(10) *Transition rules and effective dates for certain provisions.*—(i) *Coordination with Notice 87-11.*—Any transaction entered into prior to September 21, 1989 which satisfied the re-

quirements of Notice 87-11, 1987-1 C.B. 423, shall be deemed to satisfy the requirements of paragraph (a) of this section.

(ii) *Prospective application to contingent payment debt instruments.*—In the case of a contingent payment debt instrument, the definition of qualifying debt instrument set forth in paragraph (a)(3)(i) of this section applies to transactions entered into after March 17, 1992.

(iii) *Prospective application of partial hedging rule.*—Paragraph (a)(3)(ii) of this section is effective for transactions entered into after March 17, 1992.

(iv) *Effective date for paragraph (a)(6)(i) of this section.*—The rules of paragraph (a)(6)(i) of this section are effective for qualified hedging transactions that are legged into after March 17, 1992.

(b) *Hedged executory contracts.*—(1) *In general.*—If the taxpayer enters into a hedged executory contract as defined in paragraph (b)(2) of this section, the executory contract and the hedge shall be integrated as provided in paragraph (b)(4) of this section.

(2) *Definitions.*—(i) *Hedged executory contract.*—A hedged executory contract is an executory contract as defined in paragraph (b)(2)(ii) of this section that is the subject of a hedge as defined in paragraph (b)(2)(iii) of this section, provided that the following requirements are satisfied—

(A) The executory contract and the hedge are identified as a hedged executory contract as provided in paragraph (b)(3) of this section.

(B) The hedge is entered into (*i.e.*, settled or closed, or in the case of nonfunctional currency deposited in an account with a bank or other financial institution, such currency is acquired and deposited) on or after the date the executory contract is entered into and before the accrual date as defined in paragraph (b)(2)(iv) of this section.

(C) The executory contract is hedged in whole or in part throughout the period beginning with the date the hedge is identified in accordance with paragraph (b)(3) of this section and ending on or after the accrual date.

(D) None of the parties to the hedge are related. The term related means the relationships defined in section 267(b) and section 707(c)(1).

(E) In the case of a qualified business unit with a residence, as defined in section 988(a)(3)(B), outside of the United States, both the executory contract and the hedge are properly reflected on the books of the same qualified business unit.

(F) Subject to the limitations of paragraph (b)(2)(i)(E) of this section, both the executory contract and the hedge are entered into by the same individual, partnership, trust, estate, or corporation. With respect to a corporation, the same corporation must enter into both the executory contract and the hedge whether or not such corporation is a member of an affiliated group of corporations that files a consolidated return.

(G) With respect to a foreign person engaged in a U.S. trade or business that enters into an executory contract or hedge through such trade or business, all items of income and expense associated with the executory contract and the hedge would have been effectively connected with such U.S. trade or business throughout the term of the hedged executory contract had this paragraph (b) not applied.

(ii) *Executory contract.*—(A) *In general.*—Except as provided in paragraph (b)(2)(ii)(B) of this section, an executory contract is an agreement entered into before the accrual date to pay nonfunctional currency (or an amount determined with reference thereto) in the future with respect to the purchase of property used in the ordinary course of the taxpayer's business, or the acquisition of a service (or services), in the future, or to receive nonfunctional currency (or an amount determined with reference thereto) in the future with respect to the sale of property used or held for sale in the ordinary course of the taxpayer's business, or the performance of a service (or services), in the future. Notwithstanding the preceding sentence, a contract to buy or sell stock shall be considered an executory contract. (Thus, for example, a contract to sell stock of an affiliate is an executory contract for this purpose.) On the accrual date, such agreement ceases to be considered an executory contract and is treated as an account payable or receivable.

(B) *Exceptions.*—An executory contract does not include a section 988 transaction. For example, a forward contract to purchase nonfunctional currency is not an executory contract. An executory contract also does not include a transaction described in paragraph (c) of this section.

(C) *Effective date for contracts to buy or sell stock.*—That part of paragraph (b)(2)(ii)(A) of this section which provides that a contract to buy or sell stock shall be considered an executory contract applies to contracts to buy or sell stock entered into on or after March 17, 1992.

(iii) *Hedge.*—(A) *In general.*—For purposes of this paragraph (b), the term hedge means a deposit of nonfunctional currency in a hedging account (as defined in paragraph (b)(3)(iii)(D) of this section), a forward or futures contract described in § 1.988-1(a)(1)(ii) and (2)(iii), or combination thereof, which reduces the risk of exchange rate fluctuations by reference to the taxpayer's functional currency with respect to nonfunctional currency payments made or received under an executory contract. The term hedge also includes an option contract described in § 1.988-1(a)(1)(ii) and (2)(iii), but only if the option's expiration date is on or before the accrual date. The premium paid for an option that lapses shall be integrated with the executory contract.

(B) *Special rule for series of hedges.*—A series of hedges as defined in paragraph (b)(3)(iii)(A) of this section shall be considered a hedge if the executory contract is hedged in whole or in part throughout the period beginning with the date the hedge is identified in accordance with paragraph (b)(3)(i) of this section and ending on or after the accrual date. A taxpayer that enters into a series of hedges will be deemed to have satisfied the preceding sentence if the hedge that succeeds a hedge that has been terminated is entered into no later than the business day following such termination.

(C) *Special rules for historical rate rollovers.*—*(1) Definition.*—A historical rate rollover is an extension of the maturity date of a forward contract where the new forward rate is adjusted on the rollover date to reflect the taxpayer's gain or loss on the contract as of the rollover date plus the time value of such gain or loss through the new maturity date.

(2) Certain historical rate rollovers considered a hedge.—A historical rate rollover is considered a hedge if the rollover date is before the accrual date.

(3) Treatment of time value component of certain historical rate rollovers that are hedges.—Interest income or expense determined under § 1.988-2(d)(2)(v) with respect to a historical rate rollover shall be considered part of a hedge if the period beginning on the first date a hedging contract is rolled over and ending on the date payment is made or received under the executory contract does not exceed 183 days. Such interest income or expense shall not be recognized and shall be an adjustment to the income from, or expense of, the services performed or received under the executory contract, or to the amount realized or basis of the property sold or purchased under the executory contract. For the treatment of such interest income or expense that is not considered part of a hedge, see § 1.988-2(d)(2)(v).

(D) *Special rules regarding deposits of nonfunctional currency in a hedging account.*—A hedging account is an account with a bank or other financial institution used exclusively for deposits of nonfunctional currency used to hedge executory contracts. For purposes of determining the basis of units in such account that comprise the hedge, only those units in the account as of the accrual date shall be taken into consideration. A taxpayer may adopt any reasonable convention (consistently applied to all hedging accounts) to determine which units comprise the hedge as of the accrual date and the basis of the units as of such date.

(E) *Interest income on deposit of nonfunctional currency in a hedging account.*—Interest income on a deposit of nonfunctional currency in a hedging account may be taken into account for purposes of determining the amount of a hedge if such interest is accrued on or before the accrual date. However, such interest income shall be included in income as provided in section 61. For example, if a taxpayer with the dollar as its functional currency enters into an executory contract for the purchase and delivery of a machine in one year for 100 British pounds (£), and on such date deposits £90.91 in a properly identified bank account that bears interest at the rate of 10%, the interest that accrues prior to the accrual date shall be included in income and may be considered a hedge.

(iv) *Accrual date.*—The accrual date is the date when the item of income or expense (including a capital expenditure) that relates to an executory contract is required to be accrued under the taxpayer's method of accounting.

(v) *Payment date.*—The payment date is the date when payment is made or received with respect to an executory contract or the subsequent corresponding account payable or receivable.

(3) *Identification rules.*—(i) *Identification by the taxpayer.*—A taxpayer must establish a record and before the close of the date the hedge is entered into, the taxpayer must enter into the record a clear description of the executory contract and the hedge and indicate that the transaction is being identified in accordance with paragraph (b)(3) of this section.

(ii) *Identification by the Commissioner.*—If a taxpayer enters into an executory contract and a hedge but fails to satisfy one or more of the requirements of paragraph (b) of this section and, based on the facts and circumstances, the Commissioner concludes that the executory contract in substance is hedged, then the Commissioner may apply the provisions of paragraph (b) of this section as if the taxpayer had satisfied all of the requirements therein, and may make appropriate adjustments. The Commissioner may apply the provisions of paragraph (b) of this section regardless of whether the executory contract and the hedge are held by the same taxpayer.

(4) *Effect of hedged executory contract.*—(i) *In general.*—If a taxpayer enters into a hedged executory contract, amounts paid or received under the hedge by the taxpayer are treated as paid or received by the taxpayer under the executory contract, or any subsequent account payable or receivable, or that portion to which the hedge relates. Also, the taxpayer recognizes no exchange gain or loss on the hedge. If an executory contract, on the accrual date, becomes an account payable or receivable, the taxpayer recognizes no exchange gain or loss on such payable or receivable for the period covered by the hedge.

(ii) *Partially hedged executory contracts.*—The effect of integrating an executory contract and a hedge that partially hedges such contract is to treat the amounts paid or received under the hedge as paid or received under the portion of the executory contract being hedged, or any subsequent account payable or receivable. The income or expense of services performed or received under the executory contract, or the amount realized or basis of property sold or purchased under the executory contract, that is attributable to that portion of the executory contract that is not hedged shall be translated into functional currency on the accrual date. Exchange gain or loss shall be realized when payment is made or received with respect to any payable or receivable arising on the accrual date with respect to such unhedged amount.

(iii) *Disposition of a hedge or executory contract prior to the accrual date.*—(A) *In general.*—If a taxpayer identifies an executory contract as part of a hedged executory contract as defined in paragraph (b)(2) of this section, and disposes of (or otherwise terminates) the executory contract prior to the accrual date, the hedge shall be treated as sold for its fair market value on the date the executory contract is disposed of and any gain or loss shall be realized and recognized on such date. Such gain or loss shall be an adjustment to the amount received or expended with respect to the disposition or termination, if any. The spot rate on the date the hedge is treated as sold shall be used to determine subsequent exchange gain or loss on the hedge. If a taxpayer identifies a hedge as part of a hedged executory contract as defined in paragraph (b)(2) of this section, and disposes of the hedge prior to the accrual date, any gain or loss realized on such disposition shall not be recognized and shall be an adjustment to the income from, or expense of, the services performed or received under the executory contract, or to the amount realized or basis of the property sold or purchased under the executory contract.

(B) *Certain events in a series of hedges treated as a termination of the hedged executory contract.*—If the rules of paragraph (b)(2)(iii)(B) of this section are not satisfied, the hedged executory contract shall be terminated and the provisions of paragraph (b)(4)(iii)(A) of this section shall apply to any gain or loss previously realized with respect to such hedge. Any subsequent hedging contracts entered into to reduce the risk of exchange rate movements with respect to such executory contract shall not be considered a hedge as defined in paragraph (b)(2)(iii) of this section.

(C) *Executory contracts between related persons.*—If an executory contract is between related persons as defined in section 267(b) and 707(b), and the taxpayer disposes of the hedge or terminates the executory contract prior to the accrual date, the Commissioner may redetermine the timing, source, and character of gain or loss from the hedge or the executory contract if he determines that a significant purpose for disposing of the hedge or terminating the executory contract prior to the accrual date was to affect the timing, source, or character of income, gain, expense, or loss for Federal income tax purposes.

(iv) *Disposition of a hedge on or after the accrual date.*—If a taxpayer identifies a hedge as part of a hedged executory contract as defined in paragraph (b)(2) of this section, and disposes of the hedge on or after the accrual date, no gain or loss is recognized on the hedge and the booking date as defined in § 1.988-2(c)(2) of the payable or receivable for purposes of computing exchange gain or loss shall be the date such hedge is disposed of. See *Example 3* of paragraph (b)(4)(iv) of this section.

(v) *Sections 263(g), 1092, and 1256 do not apply.*—Sections 263(g), 1092, and 1256 do not apply with respect to an executory contract or hedge which comprise a hedged executory contract as defined in paragraph (b)(2) of this section. However, sections 263(g), 1092 and 1256 may apply to the hedged executory contract if such transaction is part of a straddle.

(vi) *Examples.*—The principles set forth in paragraph (b) of this section are illustrated in the following examples. The examples assume that K is an accrual method, calendar year U.S. corporation with the dollar as its functional currency.

Example 1. (i) On January 1, 1992, K enters into a contract with JPF, a Swiss machine manufacturer, to pay 500,000 Swiss francs for delivery of a machine on June 1, 1993. Also on January 1, 1992, K enters into a foreign currency forward agreement to purchase 500,000 Swiss francs for $250,000 for delivery on June 1, 1993. K properly identifies the executory contract and the hedge in accordance with paragraph (b)(3)(i) of this section. On June 1, 1993, K takes delivery of the 500,000 Swiss francs (in exchange for $250,000) under the forward contract and makes payment of 500,000 Swiss francs to JPF in exchange for the machine. Assume that the accrual date is June 1, 1993.

(ii) Under paragraph (b)(1) of this section, the hedge is integrated with the executory contract. Therefore, K is deemed to have paid $250,000 for the machine and there is no exchange gain or loss on the foreign currency forward contract. K's basis in the machine is $250,000. Section 1256 does not apply to the forward contract.

Example 2. (i) On January 1, 1992, K enters into a contract with S, a Swiss machine manufacturer, to pay 500,000 Swiss francs for delivery of a machine on June 1, 1993. Under the contract, K is not obligated to pay for the machine until September 1, 1993. On February 1, 1992, K enters into a foreign currency forward agreement to purchase 500,000 Swiss francs for $250,000 for delivery on September 1, 1993. K properly identifies the executory contract and the hedge in accordance with paragraph (b)(3) of this section. On June 1, 1993, K takes delivery of [the] machine. Assume that under K's method of accounting the delivery date is the accrual date. On September 1, 1993, K takes delivery of the 500,000 Swiss francs (in exchange for $250,000) under the forward contract and makes payment of 500,000 Swiss francs to S.

(ii) Under paragraph (b)(1) of this section, the hedge is integrated with the executory contract. Therefore K is deemed to have paid $250,000 for the machine and there is no exchange gain or loss on the foreign currency forward contract. Thus K's basis in the machine is $250,000. In addition, no exchange gain or loss is recognized on the payable in existence from June 1, 1993, to September 1, 1993. Section 1256 does not apply to the forward contract.

Example 3. The facts are the same as in *Example 2* except that K disposed of the forward contract on August 1, 1993 for $10,000.

Pursuant to paragraph (b)(4)(iv) of this section, K does not recognize the $10,000 gain. K's basis in the machine is $250,000 (the amount fixed by the forward contract), regardless of the amount in dollars that K actually pays to acquire the Sf500,000 when K pays for the machine. K has a payable with a booking date of August 1, 1993, payable on September 1, 1993 for 500,000 Swiss francs. Thus, K will realize exchange gain or loss on the difference between the amount booked on August 1, 1993 and the amount paid on September 1, 1993 under § 1.988-2(c).

Example 4. (i) On January 1, 1992, K enters into a contract with S, a Swiss machine repair firm, to pay 500,000 Swiss francs for repairs to be performed on June 1, 1992. Under the contract, K is not obligated to pay for the repairs until September 1, 1992. On February 1, 1992, K enters into a foreign currency forward agreement to purchase 500,000 Swiss francs for $250,000 for delivery on August 1, 1992. K properly identifies the executory contract and the hedge in accordance with paragraph (b)(3) of this section. On June 1, 1992, S performs the repair services. Assume that under K's method of accounting this date is the accrual date. On August 1, 1992, K takes delivery of the 500,000 Swiss francs (in exchange for $250,000) under the forward contract. On the same day, K deposits the Sf500,000 in a separate account with a bank and properly identifies the transaction as a continuation of the hedged executory contract. On September 1, 1992, K makes payment of the Sf500,000 in the account to S.

(ii) Under paragraph (b)(1) of this section, the hedge is integrated with the executory contract. Therefore K is deemed to have paid $250,000 for the services and there is no exchange gain or loss on the foreign currency forward contract or on the disposition of Sf500,000 in the account. Any interest on the Swiss francs in the account is included in income but is not considered part of the hedge (because the amount paid for the services must be set on or before the accrual date). In addition, no exchange gain or loss is recognized on the payable in existence from June 1, 1992, to September 1, 1992. Section 1256 does not apply to the forward contract.

Example 5. (i) On January 1, 1992, K enters into a contract with S, a Swiss machine manufacturer, to pay 500,000 Swiss francs for delivery of a machine on June 1, 1993. Under the contract, K is not obligated to pay for the machine until September 1, 1993. On February 1, 1992, K enters into a foreign currency forward agreement to purchase 250,000 Swiss francs for $125,000 for delivery on September 1, 1993. K properly identifies the executory contract and the hedge in accordance with paragraph (b)(3) of this section. On June 1, 1993,

K takes delivery of the machine. Assume that under K's method of accounting the delivery date is the accrual date. Assume further that the exchange rate is Sf1 = $.50 on June 1, 1993. On August 30, 1993, K purchases Sf250,000 for $135,000. On September 1, 1993, K takes delivery of the 250,000 Swiss francs (in exchange for $125,000) under the forward contract and makes payment of 500,000 Swiss francs (the Sf250,000 received under the contract plus the Sf250,000 purchased on August 30, 1993) to S. Assume the spot rate on September 1, 1993, is 1 Sf1 = $.5420 (Sf250,000 equal $135,500).

(ii) Under paragraph (b)(1) of this section, the partial hedge is integrated with the executory contract. K is deemed to have paid $250,000 for the machine [$125,000 on the hedged portion of the Sf500,000 and $125,000 ($.50, the spot rate on June 1, 1993, times Sf250,000) on the unhedged portion of the Sf500,000]. K's basis in the machine therefore is $250,000. K recognizes no exchange gain or loss on the foreign currency forward contract but K will realize exchange gain of $500 on the disposition of the Sf250,000 purchased on August 30, 1993 under § 1.988-2(a). In addition, exchange loss is realized on the unhedged portion of the payable in existence from June 1, 1993, to September 1, 1993. Thus, K will realize exchange loss of $10,500 ($125,000 booked less $135,500 paid) under § 1.988-2 (c) on the payable. Section 1256 does not apply to the forward contract.

Example 6. (i) On January 1, 1990, K enters into a contract with S, a Swiss steel manufacturer, to buy steel for 1,000,000 Swiss francs (Sf) for delivery and payment on December 31, 1990. On January 1, 1990, the spot rate is Sf1 = $.50, the U.S. dollar interest rate is 10% compounded annually, and the Swiss franc rate is 5% compounded annually. Under K's method of accounting, the delivery date is the accrual date.

(ii) Assume that on January 1, 1990, K enters into a foreign currency forward contract to buy Sf1,000,000 for $523,800 for delivery on December 31, 1990. K properly identifies the executory contract and the hedge in accordance with paragraph (b)(3) of this section. Pursuant to paragraph (b)(2)(iii) of this section, the forward contract constitutes a hedge. Assuming that the requirements of paragraph (b)(2)(i) of this section are satisfied, the executory contract to buy steel and the forward contract are integrated under paragraph (b)(1) of this section. Thus, K is deemed to have paid $523,800 for the steel and will have a basis in the steel of $523,800. No gain or loss is realized with respect to the forward contract and section 1256 does not apply to such contract.

(iii) Assume instead that on January 1, 1990, K enters into a foreign currency forward contract to buy Sf1,000,OOO for $512,200 for delivery on July 1, 1990. K properly identifies the executory contract and the hedge in accordance with paragraph (b)(3) of this section. On July 1, 1990, when the spot rate is Sf1 = $.53, K cancels the forward contract in exchange for $17,800 ($530,000 - $512,200). On July 1, 1990, K enters into a second forward agreement to buy Sf1,000,000 for $542,900 for delivery on December 31, 1990. K properly identifies the second forward agreement as a hedge in accordance with paragraph (b)(3) of this section. Pursuant to paragraph (b)(2)(iii) of this section, the forward contract entered into on January 1, 1990, and the forward contract entered into on July 1, 1990, constitute a hedge. Assuming that the requirements of paragraph (b)(2)(i) of this section are satisfied, the executory contract to buy steel and the forward agreements are integrated under paragraph (b)(1) of this section. Thus, K is deemed to have paid $525,100 for the steel (the forward price in the second forward agreement of $542,900 less the gain on the first forward agreement of $17,800) and will have a basis in the steel of $525,100. No gain is realized with respect to the forward contracts and section 1256 does not apply to such contracts.

(iv) Assume instead that on January 1, 1990, K enters into a foreign currency forward contract to buy Sf1,000,000 for $512,200 for delivery on July 1, 1990. K properly identifies the executory contract and the hedge in accordance with paragraph (b)(3) of this section. On July 1, 1990, when the spot rate is Sf1 = $.53, K enters into a historical rate rollover of its $17,800 gain ($530,000 - $512,200) on the forward agreement. Thus, K enters into a second foreign currency forward agreement to buy Sf1,000,000 for $524,210 for delivery on December 31, 1990. (The forward price of $524,210 is the market forward price on July 1, 1990 for the purchase of Sf1,000,000 for delivery on December 31, 1990 of $542,900 less the $17,800 gain on January 1, 1990 contract and less the time value of such gain of $890.) K properly identifies the second forward agreement as a hedge in accordance with paragraph (b)(3) of this section. On December 31, 1990, when the spot rate is Sf1 = $.54, K takes delivery of the Sf1,000,000 (in exchange for $524,210) and purchases the steel for Sf1,000,000. Pursuant to paragraph (b)(2)(iii) of this section, the forward contract entered into on January 1, 1990, and the forward contract entered into on July 1, 1990, which incorporates the rollover of K's gain on the January 1, 1990 contract, constitute a hedge. Assuming that the requirements of paragraph (b)(2)(i) of this section are satisfied, the executory contract to buy steel and the forward agreements are integrated under paragraph (b)(1) of this section. Because the period

Reg. § 1.988-5(b)(4)(vi)

from the rollover date to the date payment is made under the executory contract does not exceed 183 days, the $890 of interest income is considered part of the hedge and is not recognized. Thus, K is deemed to have paid $524,210 for the steel and will have a basis in the steel of $524,210. No gain is realized with respect to the forward contracts and section 1256 does not apply to such contracts.

(v) Assume instead that on January 1, 1990, K purchases Sf952,380.95 (the present value of Sf1,000,000 to be paid on December 31, 1990) for $476,190.48 and on the same day deposits the Swiss francs in a separate bank account that bears interest at a rate of 5%, compounded annually. K properly identifies the transaction as a hedged executory contract. Over the period beginning January 1, 1990, and ending December 31, 1990, K receives Sf47,619.05 in interest on the account that is included in income and that has a basis of $25,714.29. (Assume that under § 1.988-2(b)(1), K uses the spot rate of Sf1 = $.54 to translate the interest income). On December 31, 1990, K makes payment of the Sf1,000,000 principal and accrued interest in the account to S. Pursuant to paragraph (b)(2)(iii) of this section, the principal in the bank account and the interest constitute a hedge. Under paragraph (b)(1) of this section, the hedge is integrated with the executory contract. Therefore K is deemed to have paid $501,904.77 (the basis of the principal deposited plus the basis of the interest) for the steel and there is no exchange gain or loss on the disposition of the Sf1,000,000. K's basis in the steel therefore is $501,904.77.

(5) *References to this paragraph (b).*—If the rules of this paragraph (b) are referred to in another paragraph of this section (*e.g.*, paragraph (c) of this section), then the rules of this paragraph (b) shall be applied for purposes of such other paragraph by substituting terms appropriate for such other paragraph. For example, paragraph (c)(2) of this section refers to the identification rules of paragraph (b)(3) of this section. Accordingly, for purposes of paragraph (c)(2), the rules of paragraph (b)(3) will be applied by substituting the term "stock or security" for "executory contract".

(c) *Hedges of period between trade date and settlement date on purchase or sale of publicly traded stock or security.*—If a taxpayer purchases or sells stocks or securities which are traded on an established securities market and—

(1) Hedges all or part of such purchase or sale for any part of the period beginning on the trade date and ending on the settlement date; and

(2) Identifies the hedge and the underlying stock or securities as an integrated transaction under the rules of paragraph (b)(3) of this section;

then any gain or loss on the hedge shall be an adjustment to the amount realized or the adjusted basis of the stock or securities sold or purchased (and shall not be taken into account as exchange gain or loss). The term hedge means a deposit of nonfunctional currency in a hedging account (within the meaning of paragraph (b)(2)(iii)(D) of this section), or a forward or futures contract described in § 1.988-1(a)(1)(ii) and (2)(iii), or combination thereof, which reduces the risk of exchange rate fluctuations for any portion of the period beginning on the trade date and ending on the settlement date. The provisions of paragraphs (b)(2)(i)(D) through (G), and (b)(2)(iii)(D) and (E) of this section shall apply. Sections 263(g), 1092, and 1256 do not apply with respect to stock or securities and a hedge which are subject to this paragraph (c).

(d) [Reserved]

(e) *Advance rulings regarding net hedging and anticipatory hedging systems.*—In his sole discretion, the Commissioner may issue an advance ruling addressing the income tax consequences of a taxpayer's system of hedging either its net nonfunctional currency exposure or anticipated nonfunctional currency exposure. The ruling may address the character, source, and timing of both the section 988 transaction(s) making up the hedge and the underlying transactions being hedged. The procedures for obtaining a ruling shall be governed by such pertinent revenue procedures and revenue rulings as the Commissioner may provide. The Commissioner will not issue a ruling regarding hedges of a taxpayer's investment in a foreign subsidiary.

(f) [Reserved]

(g) *General effective date.*—Except as otherwise provided in this section, the rules of this section shall apply to qualified hedging transactions, hedged executory contracts and transactions described in paragraph (c) of this section entered into on or after September 21, 1989. This section shall apply even if the transaction being hedged (*e.g.*, the debt instrument) was entered into or acquired prior to such date. The effective date regarding advance rulings for net and anticipatory hedging shall be governed by such revenue procedures that the Commissioner may publish. [Reg. § 1.988-5.]

☐ [*T.D.* 8400, 3-16-92.]

§ 1.988-6. Nonfunctional currency contingent payment debt instruments.—(a) *In general.*—(1) *Scope.*—This section determines the accrual of interest and the amount, timing, source, and character of any gain or loss on nonfunctional currency contingent payment debt instruments described in this paragraph (a)(1) and to which § 1.1275-4(a) would otherwise apply if the debt instrument were denominated in the taxpayer's functional currency. Except as provided by the rules in this section, the rules in § 1.1275-4 (relating to contingent payment debt instruments) apply to the following instruments—

(i) A debt instrument described in § 1.1275-4(b)(1) for which all payments of principal and interest are denominated in, or determined by reference to, a single nonfunctional currency and which has one or more non-currency related contingencies;

(ii) A debt instrument described in § 1.1275-4(b)(1) for which payments of principal or interest are denominated in, or determined by reference to, more than one currency and which has no non-currency related contingencies;

(iii) A debt instrument described in § 1.1275-4(b)(1) for which payments of principal or interest are denominated in, or determined by reference to, more than one currency and which has one or more non-currency related contingencies; and

(iv) A debt instrument otherwise described in paragraph (a)(1)(i), (ii) or (iii) of this section, except that the debt instrument is described in § 1.1275-4(c)(1) rather than § 1.1275-4(b)(1) (e.g., the instrument is issued for non-publicly traded property).

(2) *Exception for hyperinflationary currencies.*—(i) *In general.*—Except as provided in paragraph (a)(2)(ii) of this section, this section shall not apply to an instrument described in paragraph (a)(1) of this section if any payment made under such instrument is determined by reference to a hyperinflationary currency, as defined in § 1.985-1(b)(2)(ii)(D). In such case, the amount, timing, source and character of interest, principal, foreign currency gain or loss, and gain or loss relating to a non-currency contingency shall be determined under the method that reflects the instrument's economic substance.

(ii) *Discretion as to method.*—If a taxpayer does not account for an instrument described in paragraph (a)(2)(i) of this section in a manner that reflects the instrument's economic substance, the Commissioner may apply the rules of this section to such an instrument or apply the principles of § 1.988-2(b)(15), reasonably taking into account the contingent feature or features of the instrument.

(b) *Instruments described in paragraph (a)(1)(i) of this section.*—(1) *In general.*—Paragraph (b)(2) of this section provides rules for applying the noncontingent bond method (as set forth in § 1.1275-4(b)) in the nonfunctional currency in which a debt instrument described in paragraph (a)(1)(i) of this section is denominated, or by reference to which its payments are determined (the denomination currency). Paragraph (b)(3) of this section describes how amounts determined in paragraph (b)(2) of this section shall be translated from the denomination currency of the instrument into the taxpayer's functional currency. Paragraph (b)(4) of this section describes how gain or loss (other than foreign currency gain or loss) shall be determined and characterized with respect to the instrument. Paragraph (b)(5) of this section describes how foreign currency gain or loss shall be determined with respect to accrued interest and principal on the instrument. Paragraph (b)(6) of this section provides rules for determining the source and character of any gain or loss with respect to the instrument. Paragraph (b)(7) of this section provides rules for subsequent holders of an instrument who purchase the instrument for an amount other than the adjusted issue price of the instrument. Paragraph (c) of this section provides examples of the application of paragraph (b) of this section. See paragraph (d) of this section for the determination of the denomination currency of an instrument described in paragraph (a)(1)(ii) or (iii) of this section. See paragraph (e) of this section for the treatment of an instrument described in paragraph (a)(1)(iv) of this section.

(2) *Application of noncontingent bond method.*—(i) *Accrued interest.*—Interest accruals on an instrument described in paragraph (a)(1)(i) of this section are initially determined in the denomination currency of the instrument by applying the noncontingent bond method, set forth in § 1.1275-4(b), to the instrument in its denomination currency. Accordingly, the comparable yield, projected payment schedule, and comparable fixed rate debt instrument, described in § 1.1275-4(b)(4), are determined in the denomination currency. For purposes of applying the noncontingent bond method to instruments described in this paragraph, the applicable Federal rate described in § 1.1275-4(b)(4)(i) shall be the rate described in § 1.1274-4(d) with respect to the denomination currency.

(ii) *Net positive and negative adjustments.*—Positive and negative adjustments, and net positive and net negative adjustments, with respect to an instrument described in paragraph (a)(1)(i) of this section are determined by applying the rules of § 1.1275-4(b)(6) (and § 1.1275-4(b)(9)(i) and (ii), if applicable) in the denomination currency. Accordingly, a net positive adjustment is treated as additional interest (in the denomination currency) on the instrument. A net negative adjustment first reduces interest that otherwise would be accrued by the taxpayer during the current tax year in the denomination currency. If a net negative adjustment exceeds the interest that would otherwise be accrued by the taxpayer during the current tax year in the denomination currency, the excess is treated as ordinary loss (if the taxpayer is a holder of the instrument) or ordinary income (if the taxpayer is the issuer of the instrument). The amount treated as ordinary loss by a holder with respect to a net negative adjustment is limited, however, to the amount by which the holder's total interest inclusions on the debt instrument (determined in the denomination currency) exceed the total amount of the holder's net negative adjustments treated as ordinary loss on the debt instrument in prior taxable years (determined in the denomination currency). Similarly, the amount treated as ordinary income by an issuer with respect to a net negative adjustment is limited to the amount by which the issuer's total interest deductions on the debt instrument (determined in the denomination currency) exceed the total amount of the issuer's net negative adjustments treated as ordinary income on the debt instrument in prior taxable years (determined in the denomination currency). To the extent a net negative adjustment exceeds the current year's interest accrual and the amount treated as ordinary loss to a holder (or ordinary income to the issuer), the excess is treated as a negative adjustment carryforward, within the meaning of § 1.1275-4(b)(6)(iii)(C), in the denomination currency.

(iii) *Adjusted issue price.*—The adjusted issue price of an instrument described in paragraph (a)(1)(i) of this section is determined by applying the rules of § 1.1275-4(b)(7) in the denomination currency. Accordingly, the adjusted issue price is equal to the debt instrument's issue price in the denomination currency, increased by the interest previously accrued on the debt instrument (determined without regard to any net positive or net negative adjustments on the instrument) and decreased by the amount of any noncontingent payment and the projected amount of any contingent payment previously made on the instrument. All adjustments to the adjusted issue price are calculated in the denomination currency.

(iv) *Adjusted basis.*—The adjusted basis of an instrument described in paragraph (a)(1)(i) of this section is determined by applying the rules of § 1.1275-4(b)(7) in the taxpayer's functional currency. In accordance with those rules, a holder's basis in the debt instrument is increased by the interest previously accrued on the debt instrument (translated into functional currency), without regard to any net positive or net negative adjustments on the instrument (except as provided in paragraph (b)(7) or (8) of this section, if applicable), and decreased by the amount of any noncontingent payment and the projected amount of any contingent payment previously made on the instrument to the holder (translated into functional currency). See paragraph (b)(3)(iii) of this section for translation rules.

(v) *Amount realized.*—The amount realized by a holder and the repurchase price paid by the issuer on the scheduled or unscheduled retirement of a debt instrument described in paragraph (a)(1)(i) of this section are determined by applying the rules of § 1.1275-4(b)(7) in the denomination currency. For example, with regard to a scheduled retirement at maturity, the holder is treated as receiving the projected amount of any contingent payment due at maturity, reduced by the amount of any negative adjustment carryforward. For purposes of translating the amount realized by the holder into functional currency, the rules of paragraph (b)(3)(iv) of this section shall apply.

(3) *Treatment and translation of amounts determined under noncontingent bond method.*—(i) *Accrued interest.*—The amount of accrued interest, determined under paragraph (b)(2)(i) of this section, is translated into the taxpayer's functional currency at the average exchange rate, as described in § 1.988-2(b)(2)(iii)(A), or, at the taxpayer's election, at the appropriate spot rate, as described in § 1.988-2(b)(2)(iii)(B).

(ii) *Net positive and negative adjustments.*—(A) *Net positive adjustments.*—A net positive adjustment, as referenced in paragraph (b)(2)(ii) of this section, is translated into the taxpayer's functional currency at the spot rate on the last day of the taxable year in which the adjustment is taken into account under § 1.1275-4(b)(6), or, if earlier, the date the instrument is disposed of or otherwise terminated.

(B) *Net negative adjustments.*—A net negative adjustment is treated and, where necessary, is translated from the denomination currency into the taxpayer's functional currency under the following rules:

(1) The amount of a net negative adjustment determined in the denomination currency that reduces the current year's interest in that currency shall first reduce the current year's accrued but unpaid interest, and then shall reduce the current year's interest which was accrued and paid. No translation is required.

Reg. § 1.988-6(b)(2)(iii)

(2) The amount of a net negative adjustment treated as ordinary income or loss under § 1.1275-4(b)(6)(iii)(B) first is attributable to accrued but unpaid interest accrued in prior taxable years. For this purpose, the net negative adjustment shall be treated as attributable to any unpaid interest accrued in the immediately preceding taxable year, and thereafter to unpaid interest accrued in each preceding taxable year. The amount of the net negative adjustment applied to accrued but unpaid interest is translated into functional currency at the same rate used, in each of the respective prior taxable years, to translate the accrued interest.

(3) Any amount of the net negative adjustment remaining after the application of paragraphs (b)(3)(ii)(B)(1) and (2) of this section is attributable to interest accrued and paid in prior taxable years. The amount of the net negative adjustment applied to such amounts is translated into functional currency at the spot rate on the date the debt instrument was issued or, if later, acquired.

(4) Any amount of the net negative adjustment remaining after application of paragraphs (b)(3)(ii)(B)(1), (2) and (3) of this section is a negative adjustment carryforward, within the meaning of § 1.1275-4(b)(6)(iii)(C). A negative adjustment carryforward is carried forward in the denomination currency and is applied to reduce interest accruals in subsequent years. In the year in which the instrument is sold, exchanged or retired, any negative adjustment carryforward not applied to interest reduces the holder's amount realized on the instrument (in the denomination currency). An issuer of a debt instrument described in paragraph (a)(1)(i) of this section who takes into income a negative adjustment carryforward (that is not applied to interest) in the year the instrument is retired, as described in § 1.1275-4(b)(6)(iii)(C), translates such income into functional currency at the spot rate on the date the instrument was issued.

(iii) *Adjusted basis.*—(A) *In general.*—Except as otherwise provided in this paragraph and paragraph (b)(7) or (8) of this section, a holder determines and maintains adjusted basis by translating the denomination currency amounts determined under § 1.1275-4(b)(7)(iii) into functional currency as follows:

(1) The holder's initial basis in the instrument is determined by translating the amount paid by the holder to acquire the instrument (in the denomination currency) into functional currency at the spot rate on the date the instrument was issued or, if later, acquired.

(2) An increase in basis attributable to interest accrued on the instrument is translated at the rate applicable to such interest under paragraph (b)(3)(i) of this section.

(3) Any noncontingent payment and the projected amount of any contingent payments determined in the denomination currency that decrease the holder's basis in the instrument under § 1.1275-4(b)(7)(iii) are translated as follows:

(i) The payment first is attributable to the most recently accrued interest to which prior amounts have not already been attributed. The payment is translated into functional currency at the rate at which the interest was accrued.

(ii) Any amount remaining after the application of paragraph (b)(3)(iii)(A)(3)(i) of this section is attributable to principal. Such amounts are translated into functional currency at the spot rate on the date the instrument was issued or, if later, acquired.

(B) *Exception for interest reduced by a negative adjustment carryforward.*—Solely for purposes of this § 1.988-6, any amounts of accrued interest income that are reduced as a result of a negative adjustment carryforward shall be treated as principal and translated at the spot rate on the date the instrument was issued or, if later, acquired.

(iv) *Amount realized.*—(A) *Instrument held to maturity.*—(1) *In general.*—With respect to an instrument held to maturity, a holder translates the amount realized by separating such amount in the denomination currency into the component parts of interest and principal that make up adjusted basis prior to translation under paragraph (b)(3)(iii) of this section, and translating each of those component parts of the amount realized at the same rate used to translate the respective component parts of basis under paragraph (b)(3)(iii) of this section. The amount realized first shall be translated by reference to the component parts of basis consisting of accrued interest during the taxpayer's holding period as determined under paragraph (b)(3)(iii) of this section and ordering such amounts on a last in first out basis. Any remaining portion of the amount realized shall be translated by reference to the rate used to translate the component of basis consisting of principal as determined under paragraph (b)(3)(iii) of this section.

(2) *Subsequent purchases at discount and fixed but deferred contingent payments.*—For purposes of this paragraph (b)(3)(iv) of this section, any amount which is required to be added to adjusted basis under paragraph (b)(7) or (8) of this section shall be treated as additional interest which was accrued on the date the amount was added to adjusted basis. To the extent included in

amount realized, such amounts shall be translated into functional currency at the same rates at which they were translated for purposes of determining adjusted basis. See paragraphs (b)(7)(iv) and (b)(8) of this section for rules governing the rates at which the amounts are translated for purposes of determining adjusted basis.

(B) *Sale, exchange, or unscheduled retirement.*—*(1) Holder.*—In the case of a sale, exchange, or unscheduled retirement, application of the rule stated in paragraph (b)(3)(iv)(A) of this section shall be as follows. The holder's amount realized first shall be translated by reference to the principal component of basis as determined under paragraph (b)(3)(iii) of this section, and then to the component of basis consisting of accrued interest as determined under paragraph (b)(3)(iii) of this section and ordering such amounts on a first in first out basis. Any gain recognized by the holder (i.e., any excess of the sale price over the holder's basis, both expressed in the denomination currency) is translated into functional currency at the spot rate on the payment date.

(2) Issuer.—In the case of an unscheduled retirement of the debt instrument, any excess of the adjusted issue price of the debt instrument over the amount paid by the issuer (expressed in denomination currency) shall first be attributable to accrued unpaid interest, to the extent the accrued unpaid interest had not been previously offset by a negative adjustment, on a last-in-first-out basis, and then to principal. The accrued unpaid interest shall be translated into functional currency at the rate at which the interest was accrued. The principal shall be translated at the spot rate on the date the debt instrument was issued.

(C) *Effect of negative adjustment carryforward with respect to the issuer.*—Any amount of negative adjustment carryforward treated as ordinary income under § 1.1275-4(b)(6)(iii)(C) shall be translated at the exchange rate on the day the debt instrument was issued.

(4) *Determination of gain or loss not attributable to foreign currency.*—A holder of a debt instrument described in paragraph (a)(1)(i) of this section shall recognize gain or loss upon sale, exchange, or retirement of the instrument equal to the difference between the amount realized with respect to the instrument, translated into functional currency as described in paragraph (b)(3)(iv) of this section, and the adjusted basis in the instrument, determined and maintained in functional currency as described in paragraph (b)(3)(iii) of this section.

The amount of any gain or loss so determined is characterized as provided in § 1.1275-4(b)(8), and sourced as provided in paragraph (b)(6) of this section.

(5) *Determination of foreign currency gain or loss.*—(i) *In general.*—Other than in a taxable disposition of the debt instrument, foreign currency gain or loss is recognized with respect to a debt instrument described in paragraph (a)(1)(i) of this section only when payments are made or received. No foreign currency gain or loss is recognized with respect to a net positive or negative adjustment, as determined under paragraph (b)(2)(ii) of this section (except with respect to a positive adjustment described in paragraph (b)(8) of this section). As described in this paragraph (b)(5), foreign currency gain or loss is determined in accordance with the rules of § 1.988-2(b).

(ii) *Foreign currency gain or loss attributable to accrued interest.*—The amount of foreign currency gain or loss recognized with respect to payments of interest previously accrued on the instrument is determined by translating the amount of interest paid or received into functional currency at the spot rate on the date of payment and subtracting from such amount the amount determined by translating the interest paid or received into functional currency at the rate at which such interest was accrued under the rules of paragraph (b)(3)(i) of this section. For purposes of this paragraph, the amount of any payment that is treated as accrued interest shall be reduced by the amount of any net negative adjustment treated as ordinary loss (to the holder) or ordinary income (to the issuer), as provided in paragraph (b)(2)(ii) of this section. For purposes of determining whether the payment consists of interest or principal, see the payment ordering rules in paragraph (b)(5)(iv) of this section.

(iii) *Principal.*—The amount of foreign currency gain or loss recognized with respect to payment or receipt of principal is determined by translating the amount paid or received into functional currency at the spot rate on the date of payment or receipt and subtracting from such amount the amount determined by translating the principal into functional currency at the spot rate on the date the instrument was issued or, in case of the holder, if later, acquired. For purposes of determining whether the payment consists of interest or principal, see the payment ordering rules in paragraph (b)(5)(iv) of this section.

(iv) *Payment ordering rules.*—(A) *In general.*—Except as provided in paragraph (b)(5)(iv)(B) of this section, payments with respect to an instrument described in paragraph (a)(1)(i) of this section shall be treated as follows:

(*1*) A payment shall first be attributable to any net positive adjustment on the instrument that has not previously been taken into account.

(*2*) Any amount remaining after applying paragraph (b)(5)(iv)(A)(*1*) of this section shall be attributable to accrued but unpaid interest, remaining after reduction by any net negative adjustment, and shall be attributable to the most recent accrual period to the extent prior amounts have not already been attributed to such period.

(*3*) Any amount remaining after applying paragraphs (b)(5)(iv)(A)(*1*) and (*2*) of this section shall be attributable to principal. Any interest paid in the current year that is reduced by a net negative adjustment shall be considered a payment of principal for purposes of determining foreign currency gain or loss.

(B) *Special rule for sale or exchange or unscheduled retirement.*—Payments made or received upon a sale or exchange or unscheduled retirement shall first be applied against the principal of the debt instrument (or in the case of a subsequent purchaser, the purchase price of the instrument in denomination currency) and then against accrued unpaid interest (in the case of a holder, accrued while the holder held the instrument).

(C) *Subsequent purchaser that has a positive adjustment allocated to a daily portion of interest.*—A positive adjustment that is allocated to a daily portion of interest pursuant to paragraph (b)(7)(iv) of this section shall be treated as interest for purposes of applying the payment ordering rule of this paragraph (b)(5)(iv).

(6) *Source of gain or loss.*—The source of foreign currency gain or loss recognized with respect to an instrument described in paragraph (a)(1)(i) of this section shall be determined pursuant to §1.988-4. Consistent with the rules of §1.1275-4(b)(8), all gain (other than foreign currency gain) on an instrument described in paragraph (a)(1)(i) of this section is treated as interest income for all purposes. The source of an ordinary loss (other than foreign currency loss) with respect to an instrument described in paragraph (a)(1)(i) of this section shall be determined pursuant to §1.1275-4(b)(9)(iv). The source of a capital loss with respect to an instrument described in paragraph (a)(1)(i) of this section shall be determined pursuant to §1.865-1(b)(2).

(7) *Basis different from adjusted issue price.*—(i) *In general.*—The rules of §1.1275-4(b)(9)(i), except as set forth in this paragraph (b)(7), shall apply to an instrument described in paragraph (a)(1)(i) of this section purchased by a subsequent holder for more or less than the instrument's adjusted issue price.

(ii) *Determination of basis.*—If an instrument described in paragraph (a)(1)(i) of this section is purchased by a subsequent holder, the subsequent holder's initial basis in the instrument shall equal the amount paid by the holder to acquire the instrument, translated into functional currency at the spot rate on the date of acquisition.

(iii) *Purchase price greater than adjusted issue price.*—If the purchase price of the instrument (determined in the denomination currency) exceeds the adjusted issue price of the instrument, the holder shall, consistent with the rules of §1.1275-4(b)(9)(i)(B), reasonably allocate such excess to the daily portions of interest accrued on the instrument or to a projected payment on the instrument. To the extent attributable to interest, the excess shall be reasonably allocated over the remaining term of the instrument to the daily portions of interest accrued and shall be a negative adjustment on the dates the daily portions accrue. On the date of such adjustment, the holder's adjusted basis in the instrument is reduced by the amount treated as a negative adjustment under this paragraph (b)(7)(iii), translated into functional currency at the rate used to translate the interest which is offset by the negative adjustment. To the extent related to a projected payment, such excess shall be treated as a negative adjustment on the date the payment is made. On the date of such adjustment, the holder's adjusted basis in the instrument is reduced by the amount treated as a negative adjustment under this paragraph (b)(7)(iii), translated into functional currency at the spot rate on the date the instrument was acquired.

(iv) *Purchase price less than adjusted issue price.*—If the purchase price of the instrument (determined in the denomination currency) is less than the adjusted issue price of the instrument, the holder shall, consistent with the rules of §1.1275-4(b)(9)(i)(C), reasonably allocate the difference to the daily portions of interest accrued on the instrument or to a projected payment on the instrument. To the extent attributable to interest, the difference shall be reasonably allocated over the remaining term of the instrument to the daily portions of interest accrued and shall be a positive adjustment on the dates the daily portions accrue. On the date of such adjustment, the holder's adjusted basis in the instrument is increased by

Reg. §1.988-6(b)(7)(iv)

the amount treated as a positive adjustment under this paragraph (b)(7)(iv), translated into functional currency at the rate used to translate the interest to which it relates. For purposes of determining adjusted basis under paragraph (b)(3)(iii) of this section, such increase in adjusted basis shall be treated as an additional accrual of interest during the period to which the positive adjustment relates. To the extent related to a projected payment, such difference shall be treated as a positive adjustment on the date the payment is made. On the date of such adjustment, the holder's adjusted basis in the instrument is increased by the amount treated as a positive adjustment under this paragraph (b)(7)(iv), translated into functional currency at the spot rate on the date the adjustment is taken into account. For purposes of determining the amount realized on the instrument in functional currency under paragraph (b)(3)(iv) of this section, amounts attributable to the excess of the adjusted issue price of the instrument over the purchase price of the instrument shall be translated into functional currency at the same rate at which the corresponding adjustments are taken into account under this paragraph (b)(7)(iv) for purposes of determining the adjusted basis of the instrument.

(8) *Fixed but deferred contingent payments.*—In the case of an instrument with a contingent payment that becomes fixed as to amount before the payment is due, the rules of § 1.1275-4(b)(9)(ii) shall be applied in the denomination currency of the instrument. For this purpose, foreign currency gain or loss shall be recognized on the date payment is made or received with respect to the instrument under the principles of paragraph (b)(5) of this section. Any increase or decrease in basis required under § 1.1275-4(b)(9)(ii)(D) shall be taken into account at the same exchange rate as the corresponding net positive or negative adjustment is taken into account.

(c) *Examples.*—The provisions of paragraph (b) of this section may be illustrated by the following examples. In each example, assume that the instrument described is a debt instrument for federal income tax purposes. No inference is intended, however, as to whether the instrument is a debt instrument for federal income tax purposes. The examples are as follows:

Example 1. Treatment of net positive adjustment—(i) *Facts.* On December 31, 2004, Z, a calendar year U.S. resident taxpayer whose functional currency is the U.S. dollar, purchases from a foreign corporation, at original issue, a zero-coupon debt instrument with a non-currency contingency for £1000. All payments of principal and interest with respect to the instrument are denominated in, or determined by reference to, a single nonfunctional currency (the British pound). The debt instrument would be subject to § 1.1275-4(b) if it were denominated in dollars. The debt instrument's comparable yield, determined in British pounds under paragraph (b)(2)(i) of this section and § 1.1275-4(b), is 10 percent, compounded annually, and the projected payment schedule, as constructed under the rules of § 1.1275-4(b), provides for a single payment of £1210 on December 31, 2006 (consisting of a noncontingent payment of £975 and a projected payment of £235). The debt instrument is a capital asset in the hands of Z. Z does not elect to use the spot-rate convention described in § 1.988-2(b)(2)(iii)(B). The payment actually made on December 31, 2006, is £1300. The relevant pound/dollar spot rates over the term of the instrument are as follows:

Date	Spot rate (pounds to dollars)
Dec. 31, 2004	£1.00 = $1.00
Dec. 31, 2005	£1.00 = $1.10
Dec. 31, 2006	£1.00 = $1.20

Accrual period	Average rate (pounds to dollars)
2005	£1.00 = $1.05
2006	£1.00 = $1.15

(ii) *Treatment in 2005*—(A) *Determination of accrued interest.* Under paragraph (b)(2)(i) of this section, and based on the comparable yield, Z accrues £100 of interest on the debt instrument for 2005 (issue price of £1000 × 10 percent). Under paragraph (b)(3)(i) of this section, Z translates the £100 at the average exchange rate for the accrual period ($1.05 × £100 = $105). Accordingly, Z has interest income in 2005 of $105.

(B) *Adjusted issue price and basis.* Under paragraphs (b)(2)(iii) and (iv) of this section, the adjusted issue price of the debt instrument determined in pounds and Z's adjusted basis in dollars in the debt instrument are increased by the interest accrued in 2005. Thus, on January 1, 2006, the adjusted issue price of the debt instrument is £1100. For purposes of determining Z's dollar basis in the debt instrument, the $1000 basis ($1.00 × £1000 original cost basis) is increased by the £100 of accrued interest, translated at the rate at which interest was accrued for 2005. See paragraph (b)(3)(iii) of this section. Accordingly, Z's adjusted basis in the debt instrument as of January 1, 2006, is $1105.

(iii) *Treatment in 2006*—(A) *Determination of accrued interest.* Under paragraph (b)(2)(i) of this section, and based on the comparable yield, Z accrues £110 of interest on the debt instrument for 2006 (adjusted issue price of

£1100 × 10 percent). Under paragraph (b)(3)(i) of this section, Z translates the £110 at the average exchange rate for the accrual period ($1.15 × £110 = $126.50). Accordingly, Z has interest income in 2006 of $126.50.

(B) *Effect of net positive adjustment.* The payment actually made on December 31, 2006, is £1300, rather than the projected £1210. Under paragraph (b)(2)(ii) of this section, Z has a net positive adjustment of £90 on December 31, 2006, attributable to the difference between the amount of the actual payment and the amount of the projected payment. Under paragraph (b)(3)(ii)(A) of this section, the £90 net positive adjustment is treated as additional interest income and is translated into dollars at the spot rate on the last day of the year ($1.20 × £90 = $108). Accordingly, Z has a net positive adjustment of $108 resulting in a total interest inclusion for 2006 of $234.50 ($126.50 + $108 = $234.50).

(C) *Adjusted issue price and basis.* Based on the projected payment schedule, the adjusted issue price of the debt instrument immediately before the payment at maturity is £1210 (£1100 plus £110 of accrued interest for 2006). Z's adjusted basis in dollars, based only on the noncontingent payment and the projected amount of the contingent payment to be received, is $1231.50 ($1105 plus $126.50 of accrued interest for 2006).

(D) *Amount realized.* Even though Z receives £1300 at maturity, for purposes of determining the amount realized, Z is treated under paragraph (b)(2)(v) of this section as receiving the projected amount of the contingent payment on December 31, 2006. Therefore, Z is treated as receiving £1210 on December 31, 2006. Under paragraph (b)(3)(iv) of this section, Z translates its amount realized into dollars and computes its gain or loss on the instrument (other than foreign currency gain or loss) by breaking the amount realized into its component parts. Accordingly, £100 of the £1210 (representing the interest accrued in 2005) is translated at the rate at which it was accrued (£1 = $1.05), resulting in an amount realized of $105; £110 of the £1210 (representing the interest accrued in 2006) is translated into dollars at the rate at which it was accrued (£1 = $1.15), resulting in an amount realized of $126.50; and £1000 of the £1210 (representing a return of principal) is translated into dollars at the spot rate on the date the instrument was purchased (£1 = $1), resulting in an amount realized of $1000. Z's total amount realized is $1231.50, the same as its basis, and Z recognizes no gain or loss (before consideration of foreign currency gain or loss) on retirement of the instrument.

(E) *Foreign currency gain or loss.* Under paragraph (b)(5) of this section Z recognizes foreign currency gain under section 988 on the instrument with respect to the consideration actually received at maturity (except for the net positive adjustment), £1210. The amount of recognized foreign currency gain is determined based on the difference between the spot rate on the date the instrument matures and the rates at which the principal and interest were taken into account. With respect to the portion of the payment attributable to interest accrued in 2005, the foreign currency gain is $15 [£100 ×($1.20 − $1.05)]. With respect to interest accrued in 2006, the foreign currency gain equals $5.50 [£110 × ($1.20 − $1.15)]. With respect to principal, the foreign currency gain is $200 [£1000 × ($1.20 − $1.00)]. Thus, Z recognizes a total foreign currency gain on December 31, 2006, of $220.50.

(F) *Source.* Z has interest income of $105 in 2005, interest income of $234.50 in 2006 (attributable to £110 of accrued interest and the £90 net positive adjustment), and a foreign currency gain of $220.50 in 2006. Under paragraph (b)(6) of this section and section 862(a)(1), the interest income is sourced by reference to the residence of the payor and is therefore from sources without the United States. Under paragraph (b)(6) of this section and §1.988-4, Z's foreign currency gain of $220.50 is sourced by reference to Z's residence and is therefore from sources within the United States.

Example 2. Treatment of net negative adjustment—(i) *Facts.* Assume the same facts as in *Example 1*, except that Z receives £975 at maturity instead of £1300.

(ii) *Treatment in 2005.* The treatment of the debt instrument in 2005 is the same as in Example 1. Thus, Z has interest income in 2005 of $105. On January 1, 2006, the adjusted issue price of the debt instrument is £1100, and Z's adjusted basis in the instrument is $1105.

(iii) *Treatment in 2006*—(A) *Determination of accrued interest.* Under paragraph (b)(2)(i) of this section and based on the comparable yield, Z's accrued interest for 2006 is £110 (adjusted issue price of £1100 × 10 percent). Under paragraph (b)(3)(i) of this section, the £110 of accrued interest is translated at the average exchange rate for the accrual period ($1.15 × £110 = $126.50).

(B) *Effect of net negative adjustment.* The payment actually made on December 31, 2006, is £975, rather than the projected £1210. Under paragraph (b)(2)(ii) of this section, Z has a net negative adjustment of £235 on December 31, 2006, attributable to the difference between the amount of the actual payment and the amount of the projected payment. Z's accrued interest income of £110 in 2006 is reduced to zero by the net negative adjustment. Under paragraph (b)(3)(ii)(B)(*1*) of this section the net negative adjustment which reduces the current year's is not translated into functional cur- Under paragraph (b)(2)(ii) of this sec- treats the remaining £125 net negative ient as an ordinary loss to the extent of the £100 previously accrued interest in 2005. This £100 ordinary loss is attributable to interest accrued but not paid in the preceding year. Therefore, under paragraph (b)(3)(ii)(B)(2) of this section, Z translates the loss into dollars at the average rate for such year (£1 = $1.05). Accordingly, Z has an ordinary loss of $105 in 2006. The remaining £25 of net negative adjustment is a negative adjustment carryforward under paragraph (b)(2)(ii) of this section.

(C) *Adjusted issue price and basis.* Based on the projected payment schedule, the adjusted issue price of the debt instrument immediately before the payment at maturity is £1210 (£1100 plus £110 of accrued interest for 2006). Z's adjusted basis in dollars, based only on the noncontingent payments and the projected amount of the contingent payments to be received, is $1231.50 ($1105 plus $126.50 of accrued interest for 2006).

(D) *Amount realized.* Even though Z receives £975 at maturity, for purposes of determining the amount realized, Z is treated under paragraph (b)(2)(v) of this section as receiving the projected amount of the contingent payment on December 31, 2006, reduced by the amount of Z's negative adjustment carryforward of £25. Therefore, Z is treated as receiving £1185 (£1210 − £25) on December 31, 2006. Under paragraph (b)(3)(iv) of this section, Z translates its amount realized into dollars and computes its gain or loss on the instrument (other than foreign currency gain or loss) by breaking the amount realized into its component parts. Accordingly, £100 of the £1185 (representing the interest accrued in 2005) is translated at the rate at which it was accrued (£1 = $1.05), resulting in an amount realized of $105; £110 of the £1185 (representing the interest accrued in 2006) is translated into dollars at the rate at which it was accrued (£1 = $1.15), resulting in an amount realized of $126.50; and £975 of the £1185 (representing a return of principal) is translated into dollars at the spot rate on the date the instrument was purchased (£1 = $1), resulting in an amount realized of $975. Z's amount realized is $1206.50 ($105 + $126.50 + $975 = $1206.50), and Z recognizes a capital loss (before consideration of foreign currency gain or loss) of $25 on retirement of the instrument ($1206.50 − $1231.50 = −$25).

(E) *Foreign currency gain or loss.* Z recognizes foreign currency gain with respect to the consideration actually received at maturity, £975. Under paragraph (b)(5)(ii) of this section, no foreign currency gain or loss is recognized with respect to unpaid accrued interest reduced to zero by the net negative adjustment resulting in 2006. In addition, no foreign currency gain or loss is recognized with respect to unpaid accrued interest from 2005, also reduced to zero by the ordinary loss. Accordingly, Z recognizes foreign currency gain with respect to principal only. Thus, Z recognizes a total foreign currency gain on December 31, 2006, of $195 [£975 × ($1.20 − $1.00)].

(F) *Source.* In 2006, Z has an ordinary loss of $105, a capital loss of $25, and a foreign currency gain of $195. Under paragraph (b)(6) of this section and § 1.1275-4(b)(9)(iv), the $105 ordinary loss generally reduces Z's foreign source passive income under section 904(d) and the regulations thereunder. Under paragraph (b)(6) of this section and § 1.865-1(b)(2), the $25 capital loss is sourced by reference to how interest income on the instrument would have been sourced. Therefore, the $25 capital loss generally reduces Z's foreign source passive income under section 904(d) and the regulations thereunder. Under paragraph (b)(6) of this section and § 1.988-4, Z's foreign currency gain of $195 is sourced by reference to Z's residence and is therefore from sources within the United States.

Example 3. Negative adjustment and periodic interest payments—(i) *Facts.* On December 31, 2004, Z, a calendar year U.S. resident taxpayer whose functional currency is the U.S. dollar, purchases from a foreign corporation, at original issue, a two-year debt instrument with a non-currency contingency for £1000. All payments of principal and interest with respect to the instrument are denominated in, or determined by reference to, a single nonfunctional currency (the British pound). The debt instrument would be subject to § 1.1275-4(b) if it were denominated in dollars. The debt instrument's comparable yield, determined in British pounds under §§ 1.988-2(b)(2) and 1.1275-4(b), is 10 percent, compounded semiannually. The debt instrument provides for semiannual interest payments of £30 payable each June 30, and December 31, and a contingent payment at maturity on December 31, 2006, which is projected to equal £1086.20 (consisting of a noncontingent payment of £980 and a projected payment of £106.20) in addition to the interest payable at maturity. The debt instrument is a capital asset in the hands of Z. Z does not elect to use the spot-rate convention described in § 1.988-2(b)(2)(iii)(B). The payment actually made on December 31, 2006, is £981.00. The relevant pound/dollar spot rates over the term of the instrument are as follows:

Date	Spot rate (pounds to dollars)
Dec. 31, 2004	£1.00 = $1.00
June 30, 2005	£1.00 = $1.20
Dec. 31, 2005	£1.00 = $1.40
June 30, 2006	£1.00 = $1.60
Dec. 31, 2006	£1.00 = $1.80

Accrual period	Average rate (pounds to dollars)
Jan. – June 2005	£1.00 = $1.10
July – Dec. 2005	£1.00 = $1.30
Jan. – June 2006	£1.00 = $1.50
July – Dec. 2006	£1.00 = $1.70

(ii) *Treatment in 2005*—(A) *Determination of accrued interest.* Under paragraph (b)(2)(i) of this section, and based on the comparable yield, Z accrues £50 of interest on the debt instrument for the January-June accrual period (issue price of £1000 × 10 percent/2). Under paragraph (b)(3)(i) of this section, Z translates the £50 at the average exchange rate for the accrual period ($1.10 × £50 = $55.00). Similarly, Z accrues £51 of interest in the July-December accrual period [(£1000 + £50 – £30) × 10 percent/2], which is translated at the average exchange rate for the accrual period ($1.30 × £51 = $66.30). Accordingly, Z accrues $121.30 of interest income in 2005.

(B) *Adjusted issue price and basis*—(*1*) *January-June accrual period.* Under paragraphs (b)(2)(iii) and (iv) of this section, the adjusted issue price of the debt instrument determined in pounds and Z's adjusted basis in dollars in the debt instrument are increased by the interest accrued, and decreased by the interest payment made, in the January-June accrual period. Thus, on July 1, 2005, the adjusted issue price of the debt instrument is £1020 (£1000 + £50 – £30 = £1020). For purposes of determining Z's dollar basis in the debt instrument, the $1000 basis is increased by the £50 of accrued interest, translated, under paragraph (b)(3)(iii) of this section, at the rate at which interest was accrued for the January-June accrual period ($1.10 × £50 = $55). The resulting amount is reduced by the £30 payment of interest made during the accrual period, translated, under paragraph (b)(3)(iii) of this section and § 1.988-2(b)(7), at the rate applicable to accrued interest ($1.10 × £30 = $33). Accordingly, Z's adjusted basis as of July 1, 2005, is $1022 ($1000 + $55 – $33).

(*2*) *July-December accrual period.* Under paragraphs (b)(2)(iii) and (iv) of this section, the adjusted issue price of the debt instrument determined in pounds and Z's adjusted basis in dollars in the debt instrument are increased by the interest accrued, and decreased by the interest payment made, in the July-December accrual period. Thus, on January 1, 2006, the adjusted issue price of the instrument is £1041 (£1020 + £51 – £30 = £1041). For purposes of determining Z's dollar basis in the debt instrument, the $1022 basis is increased by the £51 of accrued interest, translated, under paragraph (b)(3)(iii) of this section, at the rate at which interest was accrued for the July-December accrual period ($1.30 × £51 = $66.30). The resulting amount is reduced by the £30 payment of interest made during the accrual period, translated, under paragraph (b)(3)(iii) of this section and § 1.988-2(b)(7), at the rate applicable to accrued interest ($1.30 × £30 = $39). Accordingly, Z's adjusted basis as of January 1, 2006, is $1049.30 ($1022 + $66.30 – $39).

(C) *Foreign currency gain or loss.* Z will recognize foreign currency gain on the receipt of each £30 payment of interest actually received during 2005. The amount of foreign currency gain in each case is determined, under paragraph (b)(5)(ii) of this section, by reference to the difference between the spot rate on the date the £30 payment was made and the average exchange rate for the accrual period during which the interest accrued. Accordingly, Z recognizes $3 of foreign currency gain on the January-June interest payment [£30 × ($1.20 – $1.10)], and $3 of foreign currency gain on the July-December interest payment [£30 × ($1.40 – $1.30)]. Z recognizes in 2005 a total of $6 of foreign currency gain.

(D) *Source.* Z has interest income of $121.30 and a foreign currency gain of $6. Under paragraph (b)(6) of this section and section 862(a)(1), the interest income is sourced by reference to the residence of the payor and is therefore from sources without the United States. Under paragraph (b)(6) of this section and § 1.988-4, Z's foreign currency gain of $6 is sourced by reference to Z's residence and is therefore from sources within the United States.

(iii) *Treatment in 2006*—(A) *Determination of accrued interest.* Under paragraph (b)(2)(i) of this section, and based on the comparable yield, Z's accrued interest for the January-June accrual period is £52.05 (adjusted issue price of £1041 × 10 percent/2). Under paragraph (b)(3)(i) of this section, Z translates the £52.05 at the average exchange rate for the accrual period ($1.50 × £52.05 = $78.08). Similarly, Z accrues £53.15 of interest in the July-December accrual period [(£1041 + £52.05 – £30) × 10 percent/2], which is translated at the average exchange rate for the accrual period ($1.70 × £53.15 = $90.35). Accordingly, Z accrues £105.20, or $168.43, of interest income in 2006.

(B) *Effect of net negative adjustment.* The payment actually made on December 31, 2006, is £981.00, rather than the projected £1086.20. Under paragraph (b)(2)(ii)(B) of this section, Z has a net negative adjustment of £105.20 on December 31, 2006, attributable to the difference between the amount of the actual payment and the amount of the projected payment. Z's accrued interest income of £105.20 in 2006 is reduced to zero by the net negative adjustment. Elimination of the 2006 accrued interest fully utilizes the net negative adjustment.

(C) *Adjusted issue price and basis*—(*1*) *January-June accrual period.* Under paragraphs (b)(2)(iii) and (iv) of this section, the adjusted issue price of the debt instrument determined in pounds and Z's adjusted basis in dollars in the debt instrument are increased by the interest accrued, and decreased by the interest payment made, in the January-June accrual period. Thus, on July 1, 2006, the adjusted issue price of the debt instrument is £1063.05 (£1041 + £52.05 – £30 = £1063.05). For purposes of determining Z's dollar basis in the debt instrument, the $1049.30 adjusted basis is increased by the £52.05 of accrued interest, translated, under paragraph (b)(3)(iii) of this section, at the rate at which interest was accrued for the January-June accrual period ($1.50 × £52.05 = $78.08). The resulting amount is reduced by the £30 payment of interest made during the accrual period, translated, under paragraph (b)(3)(iii) of this section and § 1.988-2(b)(7), at the rate applicable to accrued interest ($1.50 × £30 = $45). Accordingly, Z's adjusted basis as of July 1, 2006, is $1082.38 ($1049.30 + $78.08 – $45).

(*2*) *July-December accrual period.* Under paragraphs (b)(2)(iii) and (iv) of this section, the adjusted issue price of the debt instrument determined in pounds and Z's adjusted basis in dollars in the debt instrument are increased by the interest accrued, and decreased by the interest payment made, in the July-December accrual period. Thus, immediately before maturity on December 31, 2006, the adjusted issue price of the instrument is £1086.20 (£1063.05 + £53.15 – £30 = £1086.20). For purposes of determining Z's dollar basis in the debt instrument, the $1082.38 adjusted basis is increased by the £53.15 of accrued interest, translated, under paragraph (b)(3)(iii) of this section, at the rate at which interest was accrued for the July-December accrual period ($1.70 × £53.15 = $90.36). The resulting amount is reduced by the £30 payment of interest made during the accrual period, translated, under paragraph (b)(3)(iii) of this section and § 1.988-2(b)(7), at the rate applicable to accrued interest ($1.70 × £30 = $51). Accordingly, Z's adjusted basis on December 31, 2006, immediately prior to maturity is $1121.74 ($1082.38 + $90.36 – $51).

(D) *Amount realized.* Even though Z receives £981.00 at maturity, for purposes of determining the amount realized, Z is treated under paragraph (b)(2)(v) of this section as receiving the projected amount of the contingent payment on December 31, 2006. Therefore, Z is treated as receiving £1086.20 on December 31, 2006. Under paragraph (b)(3)(iv) of this section, Z translates its amount realized into dollars and computes its gain or loss on the instrument (other than foreign currency gain or loss) by breaking the amount realized into its component parts. Accordingly, £20 of the £1086.20 (representing the interest accrued in the January-June 2005 accrual period, less £30 interest paid) is translated into dollars at the rate at which it was accrued (£1 = $1.10), resulting in an amount realized of $22; £21 of the £1086.20 (representing the interest accrued in the July-December 2005 accrual period, less £30 interest paid) is translated into dollars at the rate at which it was accrued (£1 = $1.30), resulting in an amount realized of $27.30; £22.05 of the £1086.20 (representing the interest accrued in the January-June 2006 accrual period, less £30 interest paid) is translated into dollars at the rate at which it was accrued (£1 = $1.50), resulting in an amount realized of $33.08; £23.15 of the £1086.20 (representing the interest accrued in the July 1-December 31, 2006 accrual period, less the £30 interest payment) is translated into dollars at the rate at which it was accrued (£1 = $1.70), resulting in an amount realized of $39.36; and £1000 (representing principal) is translated into dollars at the spot rate on the date the instrument was purchased (£1 = $1), resulting in an amount realized of $1000. Accordingly, Z's total amount realized is $1121.74 ($22 + $27.30 + $33.08 + $39.36 + $1000), the same as its basis, and Z recognizes no gain or loss (before consideration of foreign currency gain or loss) on retirement of the instrument.

(E) *Foreign currency gain or loss.* Z recognizes foreign currency gain with respect to each £30 payment actually received during 2006. These payments, however, are treated as payments of principal for this purpose because all 2006 accrued interest is reduced to zero by the net negative adjustment. See paragraph (b)(5)(iv)(A)(*3*) of this section. The amount of foreign currency gain in each case is determined, under paragraph (b)(5)(iii) of this section, by reference to the difference between the spot rate on the date the £30 payment is made and the spot rate on the date the debt instrument was issued. Accordingly, Z recognizes $18 of foreign currency gain on the January-June 2006 interest payment [£30 × ($1.60 – $1.00)], and $24 of foreign currency gain on the July-December 2006 interest payment [£30 × ($1.80 – $1.00)]. Z separately recognizes foreign currency gain with respect to the consideration actually received at maturity, £981.00. The amount of such gain is determined based on the difference between the spot rate on the date the instrument matures and the rates at which the principal and interest were taken into account. With respect to the portion of the payment attributable to interest accrued in January-June 2005 (other than the £30 payments), the foreign currency gain is $14 [£20 × ($1.80 − $1.10)]. With respect to the portion of the payment attributable to interest accrued in July-December 2005 (other than the £30 payments), the foreign currency gain is $10.50 [£21 × ($1.80 − $1.30)]. With respect to the portion of the payment attributable to interest accrued in 2006 (other than the £30 payments), no foreign currency gain or loss is recognized under paragraph (b)(5)(ii) of this section because such interest was reduced to zero by the net negative adjustment. With respect to the portion of the payment attributable to principal, the foreign currency gain is $752 [£940 × ($1.80 − $1.00)]. Thus, Z recognizes a foreign currency gain of $42 on receipt of the two £30 payments in 2006, and $776.50 ($14 + $10.50 + $752) on receipt of the payment at maturity, for a total 2006 foreign currency gain of $818.50.

(F) *Source.* Under paragraph (b)(6) of this section and § 1.988-4, Z's foreign currency gain of $818.50 is sourced by reference to Z's residence and is therefore from sources within the United States.

Example 4. Purchase price greater than adjusted issue price—(i) *Facts.* On July 1, 2005, Z, a calendar year U.S. resident taxpayer whose functional currency is the U.S. dollar, purchases a debt instrument with a non-currency contingency for £1405. All payments of principal and interest with respect to the instrument are denominated in, or determined by reference to, a single nonfunctional currency (the British pound). The debt instrument would be subject to § 1.1275-4(b) if it were denominated in dollars. The debt instrument was originally issued by a foreign corporation on December 31, 2003, for an issue price of £1000, and matures on December 31, 2006. The debt instrument's comparable yield, determined in British pounds under §§ 1.988-2(b)(2) and 1.1275-4(b), is 10.25 percent, compounded semiannually, and the projected payment schedule for the debt instrument (determined as of the issue date under the rules of § 1.1275-4(b)) provides for a single payment at maturity of £1349.70 (consisting of a noncontingent payment of £1000 and a projected payment of £349.70). At the time of the purchase, the adjusted issue price of the debt instrument is £1161.76, assuming semiannual accrual periods ending on June 30 and December 31 of each year. The increase in the value of the debt instrument over its adjusted issue price is due to an increase in the expected amount of the contingent payment. The debt instrument is a capital asset in the hands of Z. Z does not elect to use the spot-rate convention described in § 1.988-2(b)(2)(iii)(B). The payment actually made on December 31, 2006, is £1400. The relevant pound/dollar spot rates over the term of the instrument are as follows:

Date	Spot rate (pounds to dollars)
July 1, 2005	£1.00 = $1.00
Dec. 31, 2006	£1.00 = $2.00

Accrual period	Average rate (pounds to dollars)
July 1 – December 31, 2005	£1.00 = $1.50
January 1 – June 30, 2006	£1.00 = $1.50
July 1 – December 31, 2006	£1.00 = $1.50

(ii) *Initial basis.* Under paragraph (b)(7)(ii) of this section, Z's initial basis in the debt instrument is $1405, Z's purchase price of £1405, translated into functional currency at the spot rate on the date the debt instrument was purchased (£1 = $1).

(iii) *Allocation of purchase price differential.* Z purchased the debt instrument for £1405 when its adjusted issue price was £1161.76. Under paragraph (b)(7)(iii) of this section, Z allocates the £243.24 excess of purchase price over adjusted issue price to the contingent payment at maturity. This allocation is reasonable because the excess is due to an increase in the expected amount of the contingent payment and not, for example, to a decrease in prevailing interest rates.

(iv) *Treatment in 2005*—(A) *Determination of accrued interest.* Under paragraph (b)(2)(i) of this section, and based on the comparable yield, Z accrues £59.54 of interest on the debt instrument for the July-December 2005 accrual period (issue price of £1161.76 × 10.25 percent/2). Under paragraph (b)(3)(i) of this section, Z translates the £59.54 of interest at the average exchange rate for the accrual period ($1.50 × £59.54 = $89.31). Accordingly, Z has interest income in 2005 of $89.31.

(B) *Adjusted issue price and basis.* Under paragraphs (b)(2)(iii) and (iv) of this section, the adjusted issue price of the debt instrument determined in pounds and Z's adjusted basis in dollars in the debt instrument are increased by the interest accrued in July-December 2005. Thus, on January 1, 2006, the adjusted issue price of the debt instrument is £1221.30 (£1161.76 + £59.54). For purposes of determining Z's dollar basis in the debt instrument on January 1, 2006, the $1405 basis is increased by the £59.54 of accrued interest, translated at the rate at which interest was accrued for the July-December 2005 accrual period. Paragraph (b)(3)(iii) of this section. Accordingly, Z's adjusted basis in the instrument, as of January 1, 2006, is $1494.31 [$1405 + (£59.54 × $1.50)].

(v) *Treatment in 2006*—(A) *Determination of accrued interest.* Under paragraph (b)(2)(i) of this section, and based on the comparable yield, Z accrues £62.59 of interest on the debt instrument for the January-June 2006 accrual period (issue price of £1221.30 × 10.25 percent/2). Under paragraph (b)(3)(i) of this sec-

Reg. § 1.988-6(c)

tion, Z translates the £62.59 of accrued interest at the average exchange rate for the accrual period ($1.50 × £62.59 = $93.89). Similarly, Z accrues £65.80 of interest in the July-December 2006 accrual period [(£1221.30 + £62.59) × 10.25 percent/2], which is translated at the average exchange rate for the accrual period ($1.50 × £65.80 = $98.70). Accordingly, Z accrues £128.39, or $192.59, of interest income in 2006.

(B) *Effect of positive and negative adjustments*—(*1*) *Offset of positive adjustment.* The payment actually made on December 31, 2006, is £1400, rather than the projected £1349.70. Under paragraph (b)(2)(ii) of this section, Z has a positive adjustment of £50.30 on December 31, 2006, attributable to the difference between the amount of the actual payment and the amount of the projected payment. Under paragraph (b)(7)(iii) of this section, however, Z also has a negative adjustment of £243.24, attributable to the excess of Z's purchase price for the debt instrument over its adjusted issue price. Accordingly, Z will have a net negative adjustment of £192.94 (£50.30 − £243.24 = −£192.94) for 2006.

(*2*) *Offset of accrued interest.* Z's accrued interest income of £128.39 in 2006 is reduced to zero by the net negative adjustment. The net negative adjustment which reduces the current year's interest is not translated into functional currency. Under paragraph (b)(2)(ii) of this section, Z treats the remaining £64.55 net negative adjustment as an ordinary loss to the extent of the £59.54 previously accrued interest in 2005. This £59.54 ordinary loss is attributable to interest accrued but not paid in the preceding year. Therefore, under paragraph (b)(3)(ii)(B)(*2*) of this section, Z translates the loss into dollars at the average rate for such year (£1 = $1.50). Accordingly, Z has an ordinary loss of $89.31 in 2006. The remaining £5.01 of net negative adjustment is a negative adjustment carryforward under paragraph (b)(2)(ii) of this section.

(C) *Adjusted issue price and basis*—(*1*) *January-June accrual period.* Under paragraph (b)(2)(iii) of this section, the adjusted issue price of the debt instrument on July 1, 2006, is £1283.89 (£1221.30 + £62.59 = £1283.89). Under paragraphs (b)(2)(iv) and (b)(3)(iii) of this section, Z's adjusted basis as of July 1, 2006, is $1588.20 ($1494.31 + $93.89).

(*2*) *July-December accrual period.* Based on the projected payment schedule, the adjusted issue price of the debt instrument immediately before the payment at maturity is £1349.70 (£1283.89 + £65.80 accrued interest for July-December). Z's adjusted basis in dollars, based only on the noncontingent payments and the projected amount of the contingent payments to be received, is $1686.90 ($1588.20 plus $98.70 of accrued interest for July-December).

(*3*) *Adjustment to basis upon contingent payment.* Under paragraph (b)(7)(iii) of this section, Z's adjusted basis in the debt instrument is reduced at maturity by £243.24, the excess of Z's purchase price for the debt instrument over its adjusted issue price. For this purpose, the adjustment is translated into functional currency at the spot rate on the date the instrument was acquired (£1 = $1). Accordingly, Z's adjusted basis in the debt instrument at maturity is $1443.66 ($1686.90 − $243.24).

(D) *Amount realized.* Even though Z receives £1400 at maturity, for purposes of determining the amount realized, Z is treated under paragraph (b)(2)(v) of this section as receiving the projected amount of the contingent payment on December 31, 2006, reduced by the amount of Z's negative adjustment carryforward of £5.01. Therefore, Z is treated as receiving £1344.69 (£1349.70 − £5.01) on December 31, 2006. Under paragraph (b)(3)(iv) of this section, Z translates its amount realized into dollars and computes its gain or loss on the instrument (other than foreign currency gain or loss) by breaking the amount realized into its component parts. Accordingly, £59.54 of the £1344.69 (representing the interest accrued in 2005) is translated at the rate at which it was accrued (£1 = $1.50), resulting in an amount realized of $89.31; £62.59 of the £1344.69 (representing the interest accrued in January-June 2006) is translated into dollars at the rate at which it was accrued (£1 = $1.50), resulting in an amount realized of $93.89; £65.80 of the £1344.69 (representing the interest accrued in July-December 2006) is translated into dollars at the rate at which it was accrued (£1 = $1.50), resulting in an amount realized of $98.70; and £1156.76 of the £1344.69 (representing a return of principal) is translated into dollars at the spot rate on the date the instrument was purchased (£1 = $1), resulting in an amount realized of $1156.76. Z's amount realized is $1438.66 ($89.31 + $93.89 + $98.70 + $1156.76), and Z recognizes a capital loss (before consideration of foreign currency gain or loss) of $5 on retirement of the instrument ($1438.66 − $1443.66 = −$5).

(E) *Foreign currency gain or loss.* Z recognizes foreign currency gain under section 988 on the instrument with respect to the entire consideration actually received at maturity, £1400. While foreign currency gain or loss ordinarily would not have arisen with respect to £50.30 of the £1400, which was initially treated as a positive adjustment in 2006, the larger negative adjustment in 2006 reduced this positive adjustment to zero. Accordingly, foreign currency gain or loss is recognized with respect to the entire £1400. Under paragraph

Reg. § 1.988-6(c)

(b)(5)(ii) of this section, however, no foreign currency gain or loss is recognized with respect to unpaid accrued interest reduced to zero by the net negative adjustment resulting in 2006, and no foreign currency gain or loss is recognized with respect to unpaid accrued interest from 2005, also reduced to zero by the ordinary loss. Therefore, the entire £1400 is treated as a return of principal for the purpose of determining foreign currency gain or loss, and Z recognizes a total foreign currency gain on December 31, 2001, of $1400 [£1400 × ($2.00 – $1.00)].

(F) *Source.* Z has an ordinary loss of $89.31, a capital loss of $5, and a foreign currency gain of $1400. Under paragraph (b)(6) of this section and §1.1275-4(b)(9)(iv), the $89.31 ordinary loss generally reduces Z's foreign source passive income under section 904(d) and the regulations thereunder. Under paragraph (b)(6) of this section and §1.865-1(b)(2), the $5 capital loss is sourced by reference to how interest income on the instrument would have been sourced. Therefore, the $5 capital loss generally reduces Z's foreign source passive income under section 904(d) and the regulations thereunder. Under paragraph (b)(6) of this section and §1.988-4, Z's foreign currency gain of $1400 is sourced by reference to Z's residence and is therefore from sources within the United States.

Example 5. Sale of an instrument with a negative adjustment carryforward—(i) *Facts.* On December 31, 2003, Z, a calendar year U.S. resident taxpayer whose functional currency is the U.S. dollar, purchases at original issue a debt instrument with non-currency contingencies for £1000. All payments of principal and interest with respect to the instrument are denominated in, or determined by reference to, a single nonfunctional currency (the British pound). The debt instrument would be subject to §1.1275-4(b) if it were denominated in dollars. The debt instrument's comparable yield, determined in British pounds under §§1.988-2(b)(2) and 1.1275-4(b), is 10 percent, compounded annually, and the projected payment schedule for the debt instrument provides for payments of £310 on December 31, 2005 (consisting of a noncontingent payment of £50 and a projected amount of £260) and £990 on December 31, 2006 (consisting of a noncontingent payment of £940 and a projected amount of £50). The debt instrument is a capital asset in the hands of Z. Z does not elect to use the spot-rate convention described in §1.988-2(b)(2)(iii)(B). The payment actually made on December 31, 2005, is £50. On December 30, 2006, Z sells the debt instrument for £940. The relevant pound/dollar spot rates over the term of the instrument are as follows:

Date	Spot rate (pounds to dollars)
Dec. 31, 2003	£1.00 = $1.00
Dec. 31, 2005	£1.00 = $2.00
Dec. 30, 2006	£1.00 = $2.00

Accrual period	Average rate (pounds to dollars)
January 1 –December 31, 2004	£1.00 = $2.00
January 1 –December 31, 2005	£1.00 = $2.00
January 1 –December 31, 2006	£1.00 = $2.00

(ii) *Treatment in 2004*—(A) *Determination of accrued interest.* Under paragraph (b)(2)(i) of this section, and based on the comparable yield, Z accrues £100 of interest on the debt instrument for 2004 (issue price of £1000 × 10 percent). Under paragraph (b)(3)(i) of this section, Z translates the £100 at the average exchange rate for the accrual period ($2.00 × £100 = $200). Accordingly, Z has interest income in 2004 of $200.

(B) *Adjusted issue price and basis.* Under paragraphs (b)(2)(iii) and (iv) of this section, the adjusted issue price of the debt instrument determined in pounds and Z's adjusted basis in dollars in the debt instrument are increased by the interest accrued in 2004. Thus, on January 1, 2005, the adjusted issue price of the debt instrument is £1100. For purposes of determining Z's dollar basis in the debt instrument, the $1000 basis ($1.00 × £1000 original cost basis) is increased by the £100 of accrued interest, translated at the rate at which interest was accrued for 2004. See paragraph (b)(3)(iii) of this section. Accordingly, Z's adjusted basis in the debt instrument as of January 1, 2005, is $1200 ($1000 + $200).

(iii) *Treatment in 2005*—(A) *Determination of accrued interest.* Under paragraph (b)(2)(i) of this section, and based on the comparable yield, Z's accrued interest for 2005 is £110 (adjusted issue price of £1100 × 10 percent). Under paragraph (b)(3)(i) of this section, the £110 of accrued interest is translated at the average exchange rate for the accrual period ($2.00 × £110 = $220).

(B) *Effect of net negative adjustment.* The payment actually made on December 31, 2005, is £50, rather than the projected £310. Under paragraph (b)(2)(ii) of this section, Z has a net negative adjustment of £260 on December 31, 2005, attributable to the difference between the amount of the actual payment and the amount of the projected payment. Z's accrued interest income of £110 in 2005 is reduced to zero by the net negative adjustment. Under paragraph (b)(3)(ii)(B)(*1*) of this section, the net negative adjustment which reduces the current year's interest is not translated into functional currency. Under paragraph (b)(2)(ii) of this section, Z treats the remaining £150 net negative adjustment as an ordinary loss to the extent of the £100 previously accrued interest in 2004. This £100 ordinary loss is attributable to interest accrued but not paid in the preceding year. Therefore, under paragraph (b)(3)(ii)(B)(*2*) of this section, Z translates the loss into dollars at the average rate for such year (£1 = $2.00). Accordingly, Z has an ordinary loss of $200 in 2005. The remaining £50 of net negative adjustment is a negative adjustment carryforward under paragraph (b)(2)(ii) of this section.

(C) *Adjusted issue price and basis.* Based on the projected payment schedule, the adjusted issue price of the debt instrument on January 1, 2006 is £900, i.e., the adjusted issue price of the debt instrument on January 1, 2005 (£1100), increased by the interest accrued in 2005 (£110), and decreased by the projected amount of the December 31, 2005, payment (£310). See paragraph (b)(2)(iii) of this section. Z's adjusted basis on January 1, 2006 is Z's adjusted basis on January 1, 2005 ($1200), increased by the functional currency amount of interest accrued in 2005 ($220), and decreased by the amount of the payments made in 2005, based solely on the projected payment schedule, (£310). The amount of the projected payment is first attributable to the interest accrued in 2005 (£110), and then to the interest accrued in 2004 (£100), and the remaining amount to principal (£100). The interest component of the projected payment is translated into functional currency at the rates at which it was accrued, and the principal component of the projected payment is translated into functional currency at the spot rate on the date the instrument was issued. See paragraph (b)(3)(iii) of this section. Accordingly, Z's adjusted basis in the debt instrument, following the increase of adjusted basis for interest accrued in 2005 ($1200 + $220 = $1420), is decreased by $520 ($220 + $200 + $100 = $520). Z's adjusted basis on January 1, 2006 is therefore, $900.

(D) *Foreign currency gain or loss.* Z will recognize foreign currency gain on the receipt of the £50 payment actually received on December 31, 2005. Based on paragraph (b)(5)(iv) of this section, the £50 payment is attributable to principal since the accrued unpaid interest was completely eliminated by the net negative adjustment. The amount of foreign currency gain is determined, under paragraph (b)(5)(iii) of this section, by reference to the difference between the spot rate on the date the £50 payment was made and the spot rate on the date the debt instrument was issued. Accordingly, Z recognizes $50 of foreign currency gain on the £50 payment. [($2.00 − $1.00) × £50 = $50]. Under paragraph (b)(6) of this section and § 1.988-4, Z's foreign currency gain of $50 is sourced by reference to Z's residence and is therefore from sources within the United States.

(iv) *Treatment in 2006*—(A) *Determination of accrued interest.* Under paragraph (b)(2)(i) of this section, and based on the comparable yield, Z accrues £90 of interest on the debt instrument for 2006 (adjusted issue price of £900 × 10 percent). Under paragraph (b)(3)(i) of this section, Z translates the £90 at the average exchange rate for the accrual period ($2.00 × £90 = $180). Accordingly, prior to taking into account the 2005 negative adjustment carryforward, Z has interest income in 2006 of $180.

(B) *Effect of net negative adjustment.* The £50 negative adjustment carryforward from 2005 is a negative adjustment for 2006. Since there are no other positive or negative adjustments, there is a £50 negative adjustment in 2006 which reduces Z's accrued interest income by £50. Accordingly, after giving effect to the £50 negative adjustment carryforward, Z will accrue $80 of interest income. [(£90 − £50) × $2.00 = $80].

(C) *Adjusted issue price.* Under paragraph (b)(2)(iii) of this section, the adjusted issue price of the debt instrument determined in pounds is increased by the interest accrued in 2006 (prior to taking into account the negative adjustment carryforward). Thus, on December 30, 2006, the adjusted issue price of the debt instrument is £990.

(D) *Adjusted basis.* For purposes of determining Z's dollar basis in the debt instrument, Z's $900 adjusted basis on January 1, 2006, is increased by the accrued interest, translated at the rate at which interest was accrued for 2006. See paragraph (b)(3)(iii)(A) of this section. Note, however, that under paragraph (b)(3)(iii)(B) of this section the amount of accrued interest which is reduced as a result of the negative adjustment carryforward, i.e., £50, is treated for purposes of this section as principal, and is translated at the spot rate on the date the instrument was issued, i.e., £1.00 = $1.00. Accordingly, Z's adjusted basis in the debt instrument as of December 30, 2006, is $1030 ($900 + $50 + $80).

(E) *Amount realized.* Z's amount realized in denomination currency is £940, i.e., the amount of pounds Z received on the sale of the debt instrument. Under paragraph (b)(3)(iv)(B)(*1*) of this section, Z's amount realized is first translated by reference to the principal component of basis (including the amount which is treated as principal under paragraph (b)(3)(iii)(B) of this section) and then the remaining amount realized, if any, is translated by reference to the accrued unpaid interest component of adjusted basis. Thus, £900 of Z's amount realized is translated by reference to the principal component of adjusted basis. The remaining £40 of Z's amount realized is treated as principal under paragraph (b)(3)(iii)(B) of this section, and is also is translated by reference to the principal component of adjusted basis. Accordingly, Z's amount realized in functional currency is $940. (No part of Z's amount realized is attributable to the interest accrued on the debt instrument.) Z realizes a loss of $90 on the sale of the debt instrument ($1030 basis − $940 amount realized). Under paragraph (b)(4) of this section and § 1.1275-4(b)(8), $80 of the loss is characterized as ordinary loss, and the remaining $10 of loss is characterized as capital loss. Under § § 1.988-6(b)(6) and 1.1275-4(b)(9)(iv) the $80 ordinary loss is treated as a deduction that is definitely related to the interest income accrued on the debt instrument. Similarly, under § § 1.988-6(b)(6) and 1.865-1(b)(2) the $10 capital loss is also allocated to the interest income from the debt instrument.

(F) *Foreign currency gain or loss.* Z recognizes foreign currency gain with respect to the £940 he received on the sale of the debt instrument. Under paragraph (b)(5)(iv) of this section, the £940 Z received is attributable to principal (and the amount which is treated as principal under paragraph (b)(3)(iii)(B) of this section). Thus, Z recognizes foreign currency gain on December 31, 2006, of $940. [($2.00 − $1.00) × £940]. Under paragraph (b)(6) of this section and § 1.988-4, Z's foreign currency gain of $940 is sourced by reference to Z's residence and is therefore from sources within the United States.

(d) *Multicurrency debt instruments.*—(1) *In general.*—Except as provided in this paragraph (d), a multicurrency debt instrument described in paragraph (a)(1)(ii) or (iii) of this section shall be treated as an instrument described in paragraph (a)(1)(i) of this section and shall be accounted for under the rules of paragraph (b) of this section. Because payments on an instrument described in paragraph (a)(1)(ii) or (iii) of this section are denominated in, or determined by reference to, more than one currency, the issuer and holder or holders of the instrument are required to determine the denomination currency of the instrument under paragraph (d)(2) of this section before applying the rules of paragraph (b) of this section.

(2) *Determination of denomination currency.*—(i) *In general.*—The denomination currency of an instrument described in paragraph (a)(1)(ii) or (iii) of this section shall be the predominant currency of the instrument. Except as otherwise provided in paragraph (d)(2)(ii) of this section, the predominant currency of the instrument shall be the currency with the greatest value determined by comparing the functional currency value of the noncontingent and projected payments denominated in, or determined by reference to, each currency on the issue date, discounted to present value (in each relevant currency), and translated (if necessary) into functional currency at the spot rate on the issue date. For this purpose, the applicable discount rate may be determined using any method, consistently applied, that reasonably reflects the instrument's economic substance. If a taxpayer does not determine a discount rate using such a method, the Commissioner may choose a method for determining the discount rate that does reflect the instrument's economic substance. The predominant currency is determined as of the issue date and does not change based on subsequent events (e.g., changes in value of one or more currencies).

(ii) *Difference in discount rate of greater than 10 percentage points.*—This § 1.988-6(d)(2)(ii) applies if no currency has a value determined under paragraph (d)(2)(i) of this section that is greater than 50% of the total value of all payments. In such a case, if the difference between the discount rate in the denomination currency otherwise determined under (d)(2)(i) of this section and the discount rate determined under paragraph (d)(2)(i) of this section with respect to any other currency in which payments are made (or determined by reference to) pursuant to the instrument is greater than 10 percentage points, then the Commissioner may determine the predominant currency under any reasonable method.

(3) *Issuer/holder consistency.*—The issuer determines the denomination currency under the rules of paragraph (d)(2) of this section and provides this information to the holders of the instrument in a manner consistent with the issuer disclosure rules of § 1.1275-2(e). If the issuer does not determine the denomination currency of the instrument, or if the issuer's determination is unreasonable, the holder of the instrument must determine the denomination currency under the rules of paragraph (d)(2) of this section. A holder that determines the denomination currency itself must explicitly disclose this fact on a statement attached to the holder's timely filed federal income tax return for the taxable year that includes the acquisition date of the instrument.

(4) *Treatment of payments in currencies other than the denomination currency.*—For purposes of applying the rules of paragraph (b) of this section to debt instruments described in paragraph (a)(1)(ii) or (iii) of this section, payments not denominated in (or determined by reference to) the denomination currency shall be treated as non-currency-related contingent payments. Accordingly, if the denomination currency of the instrument is determined to be the taxpayer's functional currency, the instrument shall be accounted for under § 1.1275-4(b) rather than under this section.

(e) *Instruments issued for nonpublicly traded property.*—(1) *Applicability.*—This paragraph (e) applies to debt instruments issued for nonpublicly traded property that would be described in paragraph (a)(1)(i), (ii), or (iii) of this section, but for the fact that such instruments are described in § 1.1275-4(c)(1) rather than § 1.1275-4(b)(1). For example, this paragraph (e) generally applies to a contingent payment debt instrument denominated in a nonfunctional currency that is issued for nonpublicly traded property. Generally the rules of § 1.1275-4(c) apply except as set forth by the rules of this paragraph (e).

(2) *Separation into components.*—An instrument described in this paragraph (e) is not accounted for using the noncontingent bond method of § 1.1275-4(b) and paragraph (b) of this section. Rather, the instrument is separated into its component payments. Each noncontingent payment or group of noncontingent payments which is denominated in a single currency shall be considered a single component treated as a separate debt instrument denominated in the currency of the payment or group of payments. Each contingent payment shall be treated separately as provided in paragraph (e)(4) of this section.

(3) *Treatment of components consisting of one or more noncontingent payments in the same currency.*—The issue price of each component treated as a separate debt instrument which consists of one or more noncontingent payments is the sum of the present values of the noncontingent payments contained in the separate instrument. The present value of any noncontingent payment shall be determined under § 1.1274-2(c)(2), and the test rate shall be determined under § 1.1274-4 with respect to the currency in which each separate instrument is considered denominated. No interest payments on the separate debt instrument are qualified stated interest payments (within the meaning of § 1.1273-1(c)) and the de minimis rules of section 1273(a)(3) and § 1.1273-1(d) do not apply to the separate debt instrument. Interest income or expense is translated, and exchange gain or loss is recognized on the separate debt instrument as provided in § 1.988-2(b)(2), if the instrument is denominated in a nonfunctional currency.

(4) *Treatment of components consisting of contingent payments.*—(i) *General rule.*—A component consisting of a contingent payment shall generally be treated in the manner provided in § 1.1275-4(c)(4). However, except as provided in paragraph (e)(4)(ii) of this section, the test rate shall be determined by reference to the U.S. dollar unless the dollar does not reasonably reflect the economic substance of the contingent component. In such case, the test rate shall be determined by reference to the currency which most reasonably reflects the economic substance of the contingent component. Any amount received in nonfunctional currency from a component consisting of a contingent payment shall be translated into functional currency at the spot rate on the date of receipt. Except in the case when the payment becomes fixed more than six months before the payment is due, no foreign currency gain or loss shall be recognized on a contingent payment component.

(ii) *Certain delayed contingent payments.*—(A) *Separate debt instrument relating to the fixed component.*—The rules of § 1.1275-4(c)(4)(iii) shall apply to a contingent component the payment of which becomes fixed more than 6 months before the payment is due. For this purpose, the denomination currency of the separate debt instrument relating to the fixed payment shall be the currency in which payment is to be made and the test rate for such separate debt instrument shall be determined in the currency of that instrument. If the separate debt instrument relating to the fixed payment is denominated in nonfunctional currency, the rules of § 1.988-2(b)(2) shall apply to that instrument for the period beginning on the date the payment is fixed and ending on the payment date.

(B) *Contingent component.*—With respect to the contingent component, the issue price considered to have been paid by the issuer to the holder under § 1.1275-4(c)(4)(iii)(A) shall be translated, if necessary, into the functional currency of the issuer or holder at the spot rate on the date the payment becomes fixed.

(5) *Basis different from adjusted issue price.*—The rules of § 1.1275-4(c)(5) shall apply to an instrument subject to this paragraph (e).

(6) *Treatment of a holder on sale, exchange, or retirement.*—The rules of § 1.1275-4(c)(6) shall apply to an instrument subject to this paragraph (e).

(f) *Rules for nonfunctional currency tax exempt obligations described in § 1.1275-4(d).*—(1) *In general.*—Except as provided in paragraph (f)(2) of this section, section 1.988-6 shall not apply to a debt instrument the interest on which is excluded from gross income under section 103(a).

(2) *Operative rules.*—[RESERVED].

(g) *Effective date.*—This section shall apply to debt instruments issued on or after October 29, 2004. [Reg. § 1.988-6.]

☐ [*T.D.* 9157, 8-27-2004.]

§ 1.989(a)-1. Definition of a Qualified Business Unit.—(a) *Applicability.*—(1) *In general.*—This section provides rules relating to the definition of the term "qualified business unit" (QBU) within the meaning of section 989.

(2) *Effective date.*—These rules shall apply to taxable years beginning after December 31, 1986. However, any person may apply on a consistent basis § 1.989(a)-IT(c) of the Temporary Income Tax Regulations in lieu of § 1.989(a)-1(c) to all taxable years beginning after December 31, 1986, and on or before February 3, 1990. For the text of the temporary regulation, see 53 FR 20612 (June 8, 1988).

(b) *Definition of a qualified business unit.*—(1) *In general.*—A QBU is any separate and clearly identified unit of a trade or business of a taxpayer provided that separate books and records are maintained.

(2) *Application of the QBU definition.*—

(i) *Persons.*—A corporation is a QBU. An individual is not a QBU. A partnership, trust, or estate is a QBU of a partner or beneficiary.

(ii) *Activities.*—Activities of a corporation, partnership, trust, estate, or individual qualify as a QBU if—

(A) The activities constitute a trade or business; and

(B) A separate set of books and records is maintained with respect to the activities.

(3) *Special rule.*—Any activity (wherever conducted and regardless of its frequency) that produces income or loss that is, or is treated as, effectively connected with the conduct of a trade or business within the United States shall be treated as a separate QBU, provided the books and records requirement of paragraph (d)(2) of this section is satisfied.

(c) *Trade or business.*—The determination as to whether activities constitute a trade or business is ultimately dependent upon an examination of all the facts and circumstances. Generally, a trade or business for purposes of section 989(a) is a specific unified group of activities that constitutes (or could constitute) an independent economic enterprise carried on for profit, the expenses related to which are deductible under section 162 or 212 (other than that part of section 212 dealing with expenses incurred in connection with taxes). To constitute a trade or business, a group of activities must ordinarily include every operation which forms a part of, or a step in, a process by which an enterprise may earn income or profit. Such group of activities must ordinarily include the collection of income and the payment of expenses. It is not necessary that the activities carried out by a QBU constitute a different trade or business from those carried out by other QBUs of the taxpayer. A vertical, functional, or geographic division of the same trade or business may be a trade or business for this purpose provided that the activities otherwise qualify as a trade or business under this paragraph (c). However, activities that are merely ancillary to a trade or business will not constitute a trade or business under this paragraph (c). Activities of an individual as an employee are not considered by themselves to constitute a trade or business under this paragraph (c).

(d) *Separate books and records.*—(1) *General rule.*—Except as provided in paragraph (d)(2) of this section, a separate set of books and records shall include books of original entry and ledger accounts, both general and subsidiary, or similar records. For example, in the case of a taxpayer using the cash receipts and disbursements method of accounting, the books of original entry include a cash receipts and disbursements journal where each receipt and each disbursement is recorded. Similarly, in the case of a taxpayer using an accrual method of accounting, the books of original entry include a journal to record sales (accounts receivable) and a journal to record expenses incurred (accounts payable). In general, a journal represents a chronological account of all transactions entered into by an entity for an accounting period. A ledger account, on the other hand, chronicles the impact during an accounting period of the specific transactions recorded in the journal for that period upon the various items shown on the entity's balance sheet (*i.e.*, assets, liabilities, and capital accounts) and income statement (*i.e.*, revenues and expenses).

(2) *Special rule.*—For purposes of paragraph (b)(3) of this section, books and records include books and records used to determine income or loss that is, or is treated as, effectively connected with the conduct of a trade or business within the United States.

(e) *Examples.*—The provisions of this section may be illustrated by the following examples:

Example (1). Corporation X is a domestic corporation. Corporation X manufactures widgets in the U.S. for export. Corporation X sells widgets in the United Kingdom through a branch office in London. The London office has its own employees and solicits and processes orders. Corporation X maintains in the U.S. a separate set of books and records for all transactions conducted by the London office. Corporation X is a QBU under paragraph (b)(2)(i) of this section because of its corporate status. The London branch office is a QBU under paragraph (b)(2)(ii) of this section because (1) the sale of widgets is a trade or business as defined in paragraph (c) of this section; and (2) a complete and separate set of books and records (as described in paragraph (d) of this section) is maintained with respect to its sales operations.

Example (2). A domestic corporation incorporates a wholly-owned subsidiary in Switzerland. The domestic corporation is a manufacturer that markets its product abroad primarily through the Swiss subsidiary. To facilitate sales of the parent's product in Europe, the Swiss subsidiary has branch offices in France and West Germany that are responsible for all marketing operations in those countries. Each branch has its own employees, solicits and processes orders, and maintains a separate set of books and records. The domestic corporation and the Swiss subsidiary are both QBUs under paragraph (b)(2)(i) of this section because of their corporate status. The French and West German branches are QBUs of the Swiss subsidiary. They satisfy paragraph (b)(2)(ii) because each constitutes a trade or business (as defined in paragraph (c) of this section) and because separate sets of books and records (as described in paragraph (d) of this section) of their respective operations is maintained. Each branch is considered to have a trade or business although each is a geographical division of the same trade or business.

Example (3). W is a domestic corporation that manufactures product X in the United States for sale worldwide. All of W's sales functions are conducted exclusively in the United States. W employs individual Q to work in France. Q's sole function is to act as a courier to deliver sales documents to customers in France. With respect to Q's activities in France, a separate set of books and records as described in paragraph (d) is maintained. Under paragraph (c) of this section, Q's activities in France do not constitute a QBU since they are merely ancillary to W's manufacturing and selling business. Q is not considered to have a QBU because an individual's activities as an employee are not considered to constitute a trade or business of the individual under paragraph (c).

Example (4). The facts are the same as in example (3) except that the courier function is the sole activity of a wholly-owned French subsidiary of W. Under paragraph (b)(2)(i) of this section, the French subsidiary is considered to be a QBU.

Example (5). A corporation incorporated in the Netherlands is a subsidiary of a domestic corporation and a holding company for the stock of one or more subsidiaries incorporated in other countries. The Dutch corporation's activities are limited to paying its directors and its administrative expenses, receiving capital contributions from its United States parent corporation, contributing capital to its subsidiaries, receiving dividend distributions from its subsidiaries, and distributing dividends to its domestic parent corporation. Under paragraph (b)(2)(i) of this section, the Netherlands corporation is considered to be a QBU.

Example (6). Taxpayer A, an individual resident of the United States, is engaged in a trade or business wholly unrelated to any type of investment activity. A also maintains a portfolio of foreign currency-denominated investments through a foreign broker. The broker is responsible for all activities necessary to the management of A's investments and maintains books and records as described in paragraph (d) of this section, with respect to all investment activities of A. A's investment activities qualify as a QBU under paragraph (b)(2)(ii) of this section to the extent the activities engaged in by A generate expenses that are deductible under section 212 (other than that part of section 212 dealing with expenses incurred in connection with taxes).

Example (7). Taxpayer A, an individual resident of the United States, is the sole shareholder of foreign corporation (FC) whose activities are limited to trading in stocks and securities. FC is a QBU under paragraph (b)(2)(i) of this section.

Example (8). Taxpayer A, an individual resident of the United States, markets and sells in Spain and in the United States various products produced by other United States manufacturers. A has an office and employs a salesman to manage A's activities in Spain, maintains a separate set of books and records with respect to his activities in Spain, and is engaged in a trade or business as defined in paragraph (c) of this section. Therefore, under paragraph (b)(2)(ii) of this section, the activities of A in Spain are considered to be a QBU.

Example (9). Foreign corporation FX is incorporated in Mexico and is wholly owned by a domestic corporation. The domestic corporation elects to treat FX as a domestic corporation under section 1504(d). FX operates entirely in Mexico and maintains a separate set of books and records with respect to its activities in Mexico. FX is a QBU under paragraph (b)(2)(i) of this section. The activities of FX in Mexico also constitute a QBU under paragraph (b)(2)(ii) of this section.

Example (10). F, a foreign corporation, computes a gain of $100 from the disposition of a United States real property interest (as defined in section 897(c)). The gain is taken into account as if F were engaged in a trade or business in the United States and as if such gain were effectively connected with such trade or business. F is a QBU under paragraph (b)(2)(i) of this section because of its corporate status. F's disposition activity constitutes a separate QBU under paragraph (b)(3) of this section. [Reg. § 1.989(a)-1.]

☐ [T.D. 8279, 1-3-90.]

§ 1.989(b)-1. Definition of weighted average exchange rate.

—For purposes of section 989(b)(3) and (4), the term "weighted average exchange rate" means the simple average of the daily exchange rates (determined by reference to a qualified source of exchange rates within the meaning of § 1.964-1(d)(5)), excluding weekends, holidays and any other nonbusiness days for the taxable year. [Reg. § 1.989(b)-1.]

☐ [T.D. 8263, 9-19-89. Amended by T.D. 8367, 9-24-91.]

§ 1.989(c)-1. Transition rules for certain branches of United States persons using a net worth method of accounting for taxable years beginning before January 1, 1987.

—(a) *Applicability.*—(1) *In general.*—This section applies to qualified business units (QBU) branches of United States persons, whose functional currency (as defined in section 985 of the Code and regulations issued thereunder) is other than the United States dollar (dollar) and that used a net worth method of accounting for their last taxable year beginning before January 1, 1987. Generally, a net worth method of accounting is any method of accounting under which the taxpayer calculates the taxable income of a QBU branch based on the net change in the dollar value of the QBU branch's equity over the course of a taxable year, taking into account any remittance made during the year. QBU branch equity is the excess of QBU branch assets over QBU branch liabilities. For all taxable years beginning after December 31, 1986, such QBU branches must use the profit and loss method of accounting as described in section 987, except to the extent otherwise provided in regulations under section 985 or any other provision of the Code.

(2) *Insolvent QBU branches.*—A taxpayer may apply the principles of this section to a QBU branch that used a net worth method of accounting for its last taxable year beginning before January 1, 1987, whose $E pool (as defined in paragraph (d)(3)(i) of this section) is negative. For taxable years beginning on or after October 25, 1991 the principles of this section shall apply to insolvent QBU branches.

(b) *General rules.*—For the general rules, see § 1.987-5(b).

(c) *Determining the pool(s) from which a remittance is made.*—To determine from which pool(s) a remittance is made, see § 1.987-5(c).

(d) *Calculation of Section 987 gain or loss.*—(1) *In general.*—See § 1.987-5(d)(1) for rules to make this calculation.

(2) *Step 1—Calculate the amount of the functional currency pools.*—For calculation of the amount of the functional currency pools, see § 1.987-5(d)(2).

(3) *Step 2—Calculate the dollar basis pools.*—(i) *Dollar basis of the EQ pool.*—(A) *Beginning dollar basis.*—The beginning dollar basis of the EQ pool (hereinafter referred to as the $E pool) equals the final net worth of the QBU branch. Final net worth of the QBU branch equals the QBU branch's equity value (assets less liabilities) measured in dollars at the end of the taxpayer's last taxable year beginning before January 1, 1987, determined on the basis of the QBU branch's books and records as adjusted according to United States tax principles.

(B) *Adjusting the $E pool.*—For adjustments to be made to the $E pool, see § 1.987-5(d)(3)(i)(B).

(ii) *Dollar basis of the post-86 profits pool.*—To calculate the dollar basis of the post-86 profits pool, see § 1.987-5(d)(3)(ii).

(iii) *Dollar basis of the equity pool.*—To calculate the dollar basis of the equity pool, see § 1.987-5(d)(3)(iii).

(4) *Step 3—Calculation of the dollar basis of a remittance.*—To calculate the dollar basis of the EQ remitted, see § 1.987-5(d)(4).

(5) *Step 4—Calculation of the section 987 gain or loss on a remittance.*—To calculate 987 gain or loss determined on a remittance, see § 1.987-5(d)(5).

(e) *Functional currency adjusted basis of QBU branch assets acquired in taxable years beginning before January 1, 1987.*—To determine the functional currency adjusted basis of QBU branch assets acquired in taxable years beginning before January 1, 1987, see § 1.987-5(e).

(f) *Functional currency amount of QBU branch liabilities acquired in taxable years beginning before January 1, 1987.*—To determine the functional currency amount of QBU branch liabilities acquired in taxable years beginning before January 1, 1987, see § 1.987-5(f). [Reg. § 1.989(c)-1.]

☐ [T.D. 8367, 9-24-91.]

Domestic International Sales Corporations

§ 1.994-1. Inter-company pricing rules for DISC's.—

* * *

(e) *Methods of applying paragraphs (c) and (d) of this section.*—(1) *Limitation on DISC income ("no loss" rule).*—(i) *In general.*—Except as otherwise provided in this subparagraph, neither the gross receipts method nor the combined taxable income method may be applied to cause in any taxable year a loss to the related supplier, but either method may be applied to the extent it does not cause a loss. A loss to a related supplier would result if the taxable income of the DISC would exceed the combined taxable income of the related supplier and the DISC. If, however, there is no combined taxable income of the DISC and the related supplier (because, for example, a combined loss is incurred), a transfer price (or commission) will not be deemed to cause a loss to the related supplier if it allows the DISC to recover an amount not in excess of its costs (if any).

* * *

[Reg. § 1.994-1.]

☐ [*T.D. 7364, 7-15-75. Amended by T.D. 7435, 9-29-76; T.D. 7854, 11-6-82 and T.D. 7984, 10-11-84.*]

International Boycott Determinations

§ 7.999-1. Computation of the international boycott factor (Temporary).—(a) *In general.*—Sections 908(a), 952(a)(3), and 995(b)(1)(F) provide that certain benefits of the foreign tax credit, deferral of earnings of foreign corporations, and DISC are denied if a person or a member of a controlled group (within the meaning of section 993(a)(3)) that includes that person participates in or cooperates with an international boycott (within the meaning of section 999(b)(3)). The loss of tax benefits may be determined by multiplying the otherwise allowable tax benefits by the "international boycott factor." Section 999(c)(1) provides that the international boycott factor is to be determined under regulations prescribed by the Secretary. The method of computing the international boycott factor is set forth in paragraph (c) of this section. A special rule for computing the international boycott factor of a person that is a member of two or more controlled groups is set forth in paragraph (d). Transitional rules for making adjustments to the international boycott factor for years affected by the effective dates are set forth in paragraph (e). The definitions of the terms used in this section are set forth in paragraph (b).

(b) *Definitions.*—For purposes of this section:

(1) *Boycotting country.*—In respect of a particular international boycott, the term "boycotting country" means any country described in section 999(a)(1)(A) or (B) that requires participation in or cooperation with that particular international boycott.

(2) *Participation in or cooperation with an international boycott.*—For the definition of the term "participation in or cooperation with an international boycott", see section 999(b)(3) and Parts H through M of the Treasury Department's International Boycott Guidelines.

(3) *Operations in or related to a boycotting country.*—For the definitions of the terms "operations", "operations in a boycotting country", "operations related to a boycotting country", and "operations with the government, a company, or a national of a boycotting country", see Part B of the Treasury Department's International Boycott Guidelines.

(4) *Clearly demonstrating clearly separate and identifiable operations.*—For the rules for "clearly demonstrating clearly separate and identifiable operations", see Part D of the Treasury Department's International Boycott Guidelines.

(5) *Purchase made from a country.*—The terms "purchase made from a boycotting country" and "purchases made from any country other than the United States" mean, in respect of any particular country, the gross amount paid in connection with the purchase of, the use of, or the right to use:

(i) Tangible personal property (including money) from a stock of goods located in that country,

(ii) Intangible property (other than securities) in that country,

(iii) Securities by a dealer to a beneficial owner that is a resident of that country (but only if the dealer knows or has reason to know the country of residence of the beneficial owner),

(iv) Real property located in that country, or

(v) Services performed in, and the end product of services performed in, that country (other than payroll paid to a person that is an officer or employee of the payor).

(6) *Sales made to a country.*—The terms "sales made to a boycotting country" and "sales made to any country other than the United States" mean, in respect of any particular country, the gross receipts from the sale, exchange, other disposition, or use of:

(i) Tangible personal property (including money) for direct use, consumption, or disposition in that country,

(ii) Services performed in that country.

(iii) The end product of services (wherever performed) for direct use, consumption, or disposition in that country,

(iv) Intangible property (other than securities) in that country,

(v) Securities by a dealer to a beneficial owner that is a resident of the country (but only if the dealer knows or has reason to know the country of residence of the beneficial owner), or

(vi) Real property located in that country.

To determine the country of direct use, consumption, or disposition of tangible personal property and the end product of services, see paragraph (b)(10) of this section.

(7) *Sales made from a country.*—The terms "sales made from a boycotting country" and "sales made from any country other than the United States" mean, in respect of a particular country, the gross receipts from the sale, exchange, other disposition, or use of:

(i) Tangible personal property (including money) from a stock of goods located in that country,

(ii) Intangible property (other than securities) in that country, or

(iii) Services performed in, and the end product of services performed in, that country.

However, gross receipts from any such sale, exchange, other disposition, or use by a person that are included in the numerator of that person's international boycott factor by reason of paragraph (b)(6) of this section shall not again be included in the numerator by reason of this subparagraph.

(8) *Payroll paid or accrued for services performed in a country.*—The terms "payroll paid or accrued for services performed in a boycotting country" and "payroll paid or accrued for services performed in any country other than the United States" mean, in respect of a particular country, the total amount paid or accrued as compensation to officers and employees, including wages, salaries, commissions, and bonuses, for services performed in that country.

(9) *Services performed partly within and partly without a country.*—(i) *In general.*—Except as provided in paragraph (b)(9)(ii) of this section, for purposes of allocating to a particular country:

(A) The gross amount paid in connection with the purchase or use of,

(B) The gross receipts from the sale, exchange, other disposition or use of, and

(C) The payroll paid or accrued

for services performed, or the end product of services performed, partly within and partly without that country, the amount paid, received, or accrued to be allocated to that country, unless the facts and circumstances of a particular case warrant a different amount, will be that amount that bears the same relation to the total amount paid, received, or accrued as the number of days of performance of the services within that country bears to the total number of days of performance of services for which the total amount is paid, received, or accrued.

(ii) *Transportation, telegraph, and cable services.*—Transportation, telegraph, and cable services performed partly within one country and partly within another country are allocated between the two countries as follows:

(A) In the case of a purchase of such services performed from Country A to Country B, fifty percent of the gross amount paid is deemed to be a purchase made from Country A and the remaining fifty percent is deemed to be a purchase made from Country B.

(B) In the case of a sale of such services performed from Country A to Country B, fifty percent of the gross receipts is deemed to be a sale made from Country B and the remaining fifty percent is deemed to be a sale made to Country B.

(10) *Country of use, consumption, or disposition.*—As a general rule, the country of use, consumption, or disposition of tangible personal property (including money) and the end product of services (wherever performed) is deemed to be the country of destination of the tangible personal property or the end product of the services. (Thus, if legal services are performed in one country and an opinion is given for use by a client in a second country, the end product of the legal services is used, consumed, or disposed of in the second country.) The occurrence in a country of a temporary interruption in the shipment of the tangible personal property or the delivery of the end product of services shall not constitute such country the country of destination. However, if at the time of the transaction the person providing the tangible personal property or the end product of services knew, or should have known from the facts and circumstances surrounding the transaction, that the tangible personal property or the end product of services

Reg. §7.999-1(b)(10)

probably would not be used, consumed, or disposed of in the country of destination, that person must determine the country of ultimate use, consumption or disposition of the tangible personal property or the end product of services. Notwithstanding the preceding provisions of this subparagraph, a person that sells, exchanges, otherwise disposes of, or makes available for use, tangible personal property to any person all of whose business except for an insubstantial part consists of selling from inventory to retail customers at retail outlets all within one country may assume at the time of such sale to such person that the tangible personal property will be used, consumed, or disposed of within such country.

(11) *Controlled group taxable year.*—The term "controlled group taxable year" means the taxable year of the controlled group's common parent corporation. In the event that no common parent corporation exists, the members of the group shall elect the taxable year of one of the members of the controlled group to serve as the controlled group taxable year. The taxable year election is a binding election to be changed only with the approval of the Secretary or his delegate. The election is to be made in accordance with the procedures set forth in the instructions to Form 5713, the International Boycott Report.

(c) *Computation of international boycott factor.*—(1) *In general.*—The method of computing the international boycott factor of a person that is not a member of a controlled group is set forth in paragraph (c)(2) of this section. The method of computing the international boycott factor of a person that is a member of a controlled group is set forth in paragraph (c)(3) of this section. For purposes of paragraphs (c)(2) and (3), purchases and sales made by, and payroll paid or accrued by, a partnership are deemed to be made or paid or accrued by a partner in that proportion that the partner's distributive share bears to the purchases and sales made by, and the payroll paid or accrued by, the partnership. Also for purposes of paragraphs (c)(2) and (3), purchases and sales made by, and payroll paid or accrued by, a trust referred to in section 671 are deemed to be made both by the trust (for purposes of determining the trust's international boycott factor), and by a person treated under section 671 as the owner of the trust (but only in that proportion that the portion of the trust that such person is considered as owning under sections 671 through 679 bears to the purchases and sales made by, and the payroll paid and accrued by, the trust).

(2) *International boycott factor of a person that is not a member of a controlled group.*—The international boycott factor to be applied by a person that is not a member of a controlled group (within the meaning of section 993(a)(3)) is a fraction.

(i) The numerator of the fraction is the sum of the—

(A) Purchases made from all boycotting countries associated in carrying out a particular international boycott,

(B) Sales made to or from all boycotting countries associated in carrying out a particular international boycott, and

(C) Payroll paid or accrued for services performed in all boycotting countries associated in carrying out a particular international boycott by that person during that person's taxable year, minus the amount of such purchases, sales, and payroll that is clearly demonstrated to be attributable to clearly separate and identifiable operations in connection with which there was no participation in or cooperation with that international boycott.

(ii) The denominator of the fraction is the sum of the—

(A) Purchases made from any country other than the United States,

(B) Sales made to or from any country other than the United States, and

(C) Payroll paid or accrued for services performed in any country other than the United States

by that person during that person's taxable year.

(3) *International boycott factor of a person that is a member of a controlled group.*—The international boycott factor to be applied by a person that is a member of a controlled group (within the meaning of section 993(a)(3)) shall be computed in the manner described in paragraph (c)(2) of this section, except that there shall be taken into account the purchases and sales made by, and the payroll paid or accrued by, each member of the controlled group during each member's own taxable year that ends with or within the controlled group taxable year that ends with or within that person's taxable year.

(d) *Computation of the international boycott factor of a person that is a member of two or more controlled groups.*—The international boycott factor to be applied under sections 908(a), 953(a)(3), and 995(b)(1)(F) by a person that is a member of two or more controlled groups shall be determined in the manner described in paragraph (c)(3), except that the purchases, sales, and payroll included in the numerator and denominator shall include the purchases, sales, and payroll of that person and of all other members of the two or more controlled groups of which that person is a member.

(e) *Transitional rules.*—(1) *Pre-November 3, 1976 boycotting operations.*—The international boycott factor to be applied under sections 908(a), 952(a)(3), and 995(b)(1)(F) by a person that is not a member of a controlled group, for that person's taxable year that includes November 3, 1976, or a person that is a member of a controlled group, for the controlled group taxable year that includes November 3, 1976, shall be computed in the manner described in paragraphs (c)(2) and (c)(3), respectively, of this section. However, that the following adjustments shall be made:

(i) There shall be excluded from the numerators described in paragraphs (c)(2)(i) and (c)(3)(i) of this section purchases, sales, and payroll clearly demonstrated to be attributable to clearly separate and identifiable operations—

(A) That were completed on or before November 3, 1976, or

(B) In respect of which it is demonstrated that the agreements constituting participation in or cooperation with the international boycott were renounced, the renunciations were communicated on or before November 3, 1976, to the governments or persons with which the agreements were made, and the agreements have not been reaffirmed after November 3, 1976, and

(ii) The international boycott factor resulting after the numerator has been modified in accordance with paragraph (e)(1)(i) of this section shall be further modified by multiplying it by a fraction. The numerator of that fraction shall be the number of days in that person's taxable year (or, if applicable, in that person's controlled group taxable year) remaining after November 3, 1976, and the denominator shall be 366.

The principles of this subparagraph are illustrated in the following example:

Example. Corporation A, a calendar year taxpayer, is not a member of a controlled group. During the 1976 calendar year, Corporation A had three operations in a boycotting country under three separate contracts, each of which contained agreements constituting participation in or cooperation with an international boycott. Each contract was entered into on or after September 2, 1976. Operation (1) was completed on November 1, 1976. The sales made to a boycotting country in connection with Operation (1) amounted to $10. Operation (2) was not completed during the taxable year, but on November 1, 1976, Corporation A communicated a renunciation of the boycott agreement covering that operation to the government of the boycotting country. The sales made to a boycotting country in connection with Operation (2) amounted to $40. Operation (3) was not completed during the taxable year, nor was any renunciation of the boycott agreement made. The sales made to a boycotting country in connection with Operation (3) amounted to $25. Corporation A had no purchases made from, sales made from, or payroll paid or accrued for services performed in, a boycotting country. Corporation A had $500 of purchases made from, sales made from, sales made to, and payroll paid or accrued for services performed in, countries other than the United States. Company A's boycott factor for 1976, computed under paragraph (c)(2) of this section (before the application of this subparagraph) would be:

$$\frac{\$10 + \$40 + \$25}{\$500} = \frac{\$75}{\$500}$$

However, the $10 is eliminated from the numerator by reason of paragraph (e)(j)(1)(A) of this section, and the $40 is eliminated from the numerator by reason of paragraph (e)(j)(1)(B) of this section. Thus, before the application of paragraph (e)(1)(ii) of this section, Corporation A's international boycott factor is $25/$500. After the application of paragraph (e)(1)(ii), Corporation A's international boycott factor is:

$$\frac{\$25}{\$500} \times \frac{58}{366}$$

(2) *Pre-December 31, 1977 boycotting operations.*—The international boycott factor to be applied under sections 908(a), 952(a)(3), and 995(b)(1)(P) by a person that is not a member of a controlled group, for that person's taxable year that includes December 31, 1977, or by a person that is a member of a controlled group, for the controlled group taxable year that includes December 31, 1977, shall be computed in the manner described in paragraphs (c)(2) and (c)(3), respectively, of this section. However, the following adjustments shall be made:

(i) There shall be excluded from the numerators described in paragraphs (c)(2)(i) and (c)(3)(i) of this section purchases, sales, and payroll clearly demonstrated to be attributable to clearly separate and identifiable operations that were carried out in accordance with the terms of binding contracts entered into before September 3, 1976, and—

(A) That were completed on or before December 31, 1977, or

(B) In respect of which it is demonstrated that the agreements constituting participation in or cooperation with the international boycott were renounced, the renunciations were communicated on or before December 31, 1977, to the governments or persons with which the agreements were made, and the agreements were not reaffirmed after December 31, 1977, and

(ii) In the case of clearly separate and identifiable operations that are carried out in accordance with the terms of binding contracts entered into before September 2, 1976, but that do not meet the requirements of paragraph (e)(2)(i) of this section, the numerators described in paragraphs (e)(2)(i) and (e)(3)(i) of this section shall be adjusted by multiplying the purchases, sales, and payroll clearly demonstrated to be attributable to those operations by a fraction, the numerator of which is the number of days in such person's taxable year (or, if applicable, in such person's controlled group taxable year) remaining after December 31, 1977, and the denominator of which is 365.

The principles of this subparagraph are illustrated in the following example:

Example. Corporation A is not a member of a controlled group and reports on the basis of a July 1-June 30 fiscal year. During the 1977-1978 fiscal year, Corporation A had 2 operations carried out pursuant to the terms of separate contracts, each of which had a clause that constituted participation in or cooperation with an international boycott. Neither operation was completed during the fiscal year, nor were either of the boycotting clauses renounced. Operation (1) was carried out in accordance with the terms of a contract entered into on November 15, 1976. Operation (2) was carried out in accordance with the terms of a binding contract entered into before September 2, 1976. Corporation A had sales made to a boycotting country in connection with Operation (1) in the amount of $50, and in connection with Operation (2) in the amount of $100. Corporation A had sales made to countries other than the United States in the amount of $500. Corporation A had no purchases made from, sales made from, or payroll paid or accrued for services performed in, any country other than the United States. In the absence of this subparagraph, Corporation A's international boycott factor would be

$$\frac{\$50 + \$100}{\$500}$$

However, by reason of the application of this subparagraph, Corporation A's international boycott factor is reduced to

$$\frac{[(\$50 + \$100)(181/365)]}{\$500}$$

(3) *Incomplete controlled group taxable year.*—If, at the end of the taxable year of a person that is a member of a controlled group, the controlled group taxable year that includes November 3, 1976 has not ended, or the taxable year of one or more members of the controlled group that includes November 3, 1976 has not ended, then the international boycott factor to be applied under sections 908(a), 952(a)(3) and 955(b)(1)(P) by such person for the taxable year shall be computed in the manner described in paragraph (c)(3) of this section. However, the numerator and the denominator in that paragraph shall include only the purchases, sales, and payroll of those members of the controlled group whose taxable years ending after November 3, 1976 have ended as the end of the taxable year of such person.

(f) *Effective date.*—This section applies to participation in or cooperation with an international boycott after November 3, 1976. In the case of operations which constitute participation in or cooperation with an international boycott and which are carried out in accordance with the terms of a binding contract entered into before September 2, 1976, this section applies to such participation or cooperation after December 31, 1977. [Temporary Reg. § 7.999-1.]

☐ [*T.D.* 7467, 2-24-77.]

Sales of Controlled Foreign Corporation Stock

§ 1.1248-1. Treatment of gain from certain sales or exchanges of stock in certain foreign corporations.—(a) *In general.*—(1) If a United States person (as defined in section 7701(a)(30)) recognizes gain on a sale or exchange after December 31, 1962, of stock in a foreign corporation, and if in respect of such person the conditions of subparagraph (2) of this paragraph are satisfied, then the gain shall be included in the gross income of such person as a dividend to the extent of the earnings and profits of such corporation attributable to such stock under § 1.1248-2 or 1.1248-3, whichever is applicable, which were accumulated in taxable years of such foreign corporation beginning after December 31, 1962, during the period or periods such stock was held (or was considered as held by reason of the application of section 1223) by such person while such corporation was a controlled foreign corporation. See section 1248(a). For computation of earnings and profits attributable to such stock if there are any "lower tier" corporations, see paragraph (a)(3) and (4) of § 1.1248-2 or paragraph (a) of § 1.1248-3, whichever is applicable. In general, the amount of gain to be included in a person's gross income as a dividend under section 1248(a) shall be determined separately for each share of stock sold or exchanged. However, such determination may be made in respect of a block of stock if earnings and profits attributable to the block are computed under § 1.1248-2 or 1.1248-3. See paragraph (b) of § 1.1248-2 and paragraph (a)(5) of § 1.1248-3. For the limitation on the tax attributable to an amount included in an individual's gross income as a dividend under section 1248(a), see section 1248(b) and § 1.1248-4. For the treatment, under certain circumstances, of the sale or exchange of stock in a domestic corporation as the sale or exchange of stock held by the domestic corporation in a foreign corporation, see section 1248(e) and § 1.1248-6. For the nonapplication of section 1248 in certain circumstances, see section 1248(f) and paragraph (e) of this section. For the requirement that the person establish the amount of earnings and profits attributable to the stock sold or exchanged and, for purposes of section 1248(b), the amount of certain taxes, see section 1248(g) and § 1.1248-7.

(2) In respect of a United States person who sells or exchanges stock in a foreign corporation, the conditions referred to in subparagraph (1) of this paragraph are satisfied only if (i) such person owned, within the meaning of section 958(a), or was considered as owning by applying the rules of ownership of section 958(b), 10 percent or more of the total combined voting power of all classes of stock entitled to vote of such foreign corporation at any time during the 5-year period ending on the date of the sale or exchange, and (ii) at such time such foreign corporation was a controlled foreign corporation (as defined in section 957).

(3) For purposes of subparagraph (2) of this paragraph, (i) a foreign corporation shall not be considered to be a controlled foreign corporation at any time before the first day of its first taxable year beginning after December 31, 1962, and (ii) the percentage of the total combined voting power of stock of a foreign corporation owned (or considered as owned) by a United States person shall be determined in accordance with the principles of section 951(b) and the regulations thereunder.

(4) The application of this paragraph may be illustrated by the following examples:

Example (1). Corporation F is a foreign corporation which has outstanding 100 shares of one class of stock. F was a controlled foreign corporation for the period beginning on January 1, 1963, and ending on June 30, 1965, but was not a controlled foreign corporation at any time thereafter. On December 31, 1965, Brown, a United States person who has owned 15 shares of F stock since 1962, sells 7 of his 15 shares and recognizes gain with respect to each share sold. Since Brown owned stock representing at least 10 percent of the total combined voting power of F at a time during the 5-year period ending on December 31, 1965, while F was a controlled foreign corporation, the conditions of subparagraph (2) of this paragraph are satisfied. Therefore, section 1248(a) applies to the gain recognized by Brown to the extent of the earnings and profits attributable under § 1.1248-3 to such shares.

Example (2). Assume the same facts as in example (1). Assume further that on February 1, 1970, Brown sells the remainder of his shares in F Corporation and recognizes gain with respect to each share sold. Even though Brown did not own stock representing at least 10 percent of the total combined voting power of F on February 1, 1970, nevertheless, in respect of each of the 8 shares of F stock which he sold on such date, the conditions of subparagraph (2) of this paragraph are satisfied since Brown owned stock representing at least 10 percent of such voting power at a time during the 5-year period ending on February 1, 1970, while F was a controlled foreign corporation. Therefore, section 1248(a) applies to the gain recognized by Brown to the extent of the earnings and profits attributable under § 1.1248-3 to such shares. If, however, Brown had sold the remainder of his shares in F on July 1, 1970, since the last date on which Brown owned stock representing at least 10 percent of the total combined voting power of F while F was a controlled foreign corporation was June 30, 1965, a date which is not within the 5-year period ending July 1, 1970, the conditions of subparagraph (2) of this paragraph would not be satisfied and section 1248(a) would not apply.

Example (3). Corporation G, a foreign corporation created in 1950, has outstanding 100 shares of one class of stock and uses the calendar year as its taxable year. Corporation X, a United States person, owns 60 shares of G stock and has owned such stock since G was created. Corporation Y, a United States person, owned 15 shares of the G stock from 1950 until December 1, 1962, on which date it sold 10 of such shares. On December 31, 1963, Y sells its remaining 5 shares of the G stock and recognizes gain on the sale. Since G is not considered to be a controlled foreign corporation at any time before January 1, 1963, and since Y did not own stock representing at least 10 percent of the total combined voting power of G at any time on or after such date, the conditions of subparagraph (2) of this paragraph are not satisfied and section 1248(a) does not apply.

(b) *Sale or exchange.*—For purposes of this section and §§ 1.1248-2 through 1.1248-7, the term "sale or exchange" includes the receipt of a distribution which is treated as in exchange for stock under section 302(a) (relating to distributions in redemption of stock), section 331(a)(1) (relating to distributions in complete

Reg. § 1.1248-1(b)

liquidation of a corporation), or section 331(a)(2) (relating to distributions in partial liquidation of a corporation).

(c) *Gain recognized.*—Section 1248(a) applies to a sale or exchange of stock in a foreign corporation only if gain is recognized in whole or in part upon such sale or exchange. Thus, for example, if a United States person exchanges stock in a foreign corporation, and if under section 332, 351, 354, 355, or 361 no gain is recognized as a result of a determination by the Commissioner under section 367 that the exchange is not in pursuance of a plan having as one of its principal purposes the avoidance of Federal income taxes, then no amount is includible in the gross income of such person as a dividend under section 1248(a).

(d) *Credit for foreign taxes.*—(1) If a domestic corporation includes an amount in its gross income as a dividend under section 1248(a) upon a sale or exchange of stock in a foreign corporation (referred to as a "first tier" corporation), and if on the date of the sale or exchange the domestic corporation owns directly at least 10 percent of the voting stock of the first tier corporation—

(i) The foreign tax credit provisions of sections 901 through 908 shall apply in the same manner and subject to the same conditions and limitations as if the first tier corporation on such date distributed to the domestic corporation as a dividend that portion of the amount included in gross income under section 1248(a) which does not exceed the earnings and profits of the first tier corporation attributable to the stock under § 1.1248-2 or § 1.1248-3, as the case may be, and

(ii) If on such date such first tier corporation owns directly 50 percent or more of the voting stock of a "lower tier" corporation described in paragraph (a)(3) of § 1.1248-2 or paragraph (a)(3) of § 1.1248-3, as the case may be (referred to as a "second tier" corporation), then the foreign tax credit provisions of sections 901 through 905 shall apply in the same manner and subject to the same conditions and limitations as if on such date (*a*) the domestic corporation owned directly that percentage of the stock in the second tier corporation which such domestic corporation is considered to own by reason of the application of section 958(a)(2), and (*b*) the second tier corporation had distributed to the domestic corporation as a dividend that portion of the amount included in gross income under section 1248(a) which does not exceed the earnings and profits of the second tier corporation attributable to such stock under § 1.1248-2 or § 1.1248-3, as the case may be.

(2) A credit shall not be allowed under subparagraph (1) of this paragraph in respect of taxes which are not actually paid or accrued. For the inclusion as a dividend in the gross income of a domestic corporation of an amount equal to the taxes deemed paid by such corporation under section 902(a)(1), see section 78.

(3) If subparagraph (1)(ii) of this paragraph applies, and if the amount included in gross income under section 1248(a) upon the sale or exchange of the stock in a first tier corporation described in subparagraph (1)(ii) of this paragraph is less than the sum of the earnings and profits of the first tier corporation attributable to such stock under § 1.1248-2 or § 1.1248-3, as the case may be, plus the earnings and profits of the second tier corporation attributable to such stock under § 1.1248-2 or 1.1248-3, as the case may be, then the amount considered distributed to the domestic corporation as a dividend shall be determined by multiplying the amount included in gross income under section 1248(a) by—

(i) For purposes of applying subparagraph (1)(i) of this paragraph, the percentage that (*a*) the earnings and profits of the first tier corporation attributable to such stock under § 1.1248-2 or § 1.1248-3, as the case may be, bears to (*b*) the sum of the earnings and profits of the first tier corporation attributable to such stock under § 1.1248-2 or § 1.1248-3, as the case may be, plus the earnings and profits of the second tier corporation attributable to such stock under § 1.1248-2 or § 1.1248-3, as the case may be, and

(ii) For purposes of applying subparagraph (1)(ii) of this paragraph, the percentage that (*a*) the earnings and profits of the second tier corporation attributable to such stock under § 1.1248-2 or 1.1248-3, as the case may be, bears to (*b*) the sum referred to in subdivision (i)(*b*) of this subparagraph.

(4) The provisions of this paragraph may be illustrated by the following examples:

Example (1). On June 30, 1964, domestic corporation D owns 10 percent of the voting stock of controlled foreign corporation X. On such date, D sells a share of X stock and includes $200 of the gain on the sale in its gross income as a dividend under section 1248(a). X does not own any stock of a lower tier corporation referred to in paragraph (a)(3) of § 1.1248-3. D uses the calendar year as its taxable year and instead of deducting foreign taxes under section 164, D chooses the benefits of the foreign tax credit provisions for 1964. If D had included $200 in its gross income as a dividend with respect to a distribution from X on June 30, 1964, the amount of the foreign income taxes paid by X which D would be deemed to have paid under section 902(a) in respect of such distribution would be $60. Thus, in respect of the $200 included in D's gross income as a dividend under section 1248(a), and subject to the applicable limitations and conditions of sections 901 through 905, D is entitled under this paragraph to a foreign tax credit of $60 for 1964.

Example (2). On June 30, 1965, domestic corporation D owns all of the voting stock of foreign corporation Y, and Y (the first tier corporation) owns all of the voting stock of foreign corporation Z (a second tier corporation). On such date, D sells a block of Y stock and includes $400 of the gain on the sale in its gross income as a dividend under section 1248(a). The earnings and profits attributable under § 1.1248-3 to the block are $600 from Y and $1,800 from Z. D uses the calendar year as its taxable year and instead of deducting foreign taxes under section 164, D chooses the benefits of the foreign tax credit provisions for 1965. For purposes of applying the foreign tax credit provisions, Y is considered under subparagraph (3) of this paragraph to have distributed to D a dividend of $100 ($400 × 600/2400) and Z is considered to have so distributed to D a dividend of $300 ($400 × 1800/2400). If D had included $100 in its gross income as a dividend with respect to a distribution from Y on June 30, 1965, the amount of foreign income taxes paid by Y which D would be deemed to have paid under section 902(a) in respect of such distribution is $80. If D had owned the stock in Z directly, and if D had included $300 in its gross income as a dividend with respect to a distribution from Z, the amount of foreign income taxes paid by Z which D would be deemed to have paid under section 902(a) in respect of such distribution is $120. Thus, in respect of the $400 included in D's gross income as a dividend under section 1248(a), and subject to the applicable limitations and conditions of sections 901 through 905, D is entitled under this paragraph to a foreign tax credit of $200 ($80 plus $120) for 1965.

(e) *Exceptions.*—Under section 1248(f), this section and §§ 1.1248-2 through 1.1248-7 shall not apply to—

(1) Distributions to which section 303 (relating to distributions in redemption of stock to pay death taxes) applies;

(2) Gain realized on exchanges to which section 356 (relating to receipt of additional consideration in certain reorganizations) applies; or

(3) Any amount to the extent that such amount is, under any other provision of the Code, treated as (i) a dividend, (ii) gain from the sale of an asset which is not a capital asset, or (iii) gain from the sale of an asset held for not more than 1 year (6 months for taxable years beginning before 1977; 9 months for taxable years beginning in 1977).

(f) *Installment method.*—(1) Gain from a sale or exchange to which section 1248 applies may be reported under the installment method if such method is otherwise available under section 453 of the Code. In such case, the income (other than interest) in each installment payment shall be deemed to consist of gain which is included in gross income under section 1248 as a dividend until all such gain has been reported, and the remaining portion (if any) of such income shall be deemed to consist of gain to which section 1248 does not apply. For treatment of amounts as interest on certain deferred payments, see section 483.

(2) The application of this paragraph may be illustrated by the following example:

Example. Jones contracts to sell stock in a controlled foreign corporation for $5,000 to be paid in 10 equal payments of $500 each, plus a sufficient amount of interest so that section 483 does not apply. He properly elects under section 453 to report under the installment method gain of $1,000 which is includible in gross income under section 1248 as a dividend and gain of $500 which is a long-term capital gain. Accordingly, $150 of each of the first 6 installment payments and $100 of the seventh installment payment are included in gross income under section 1248 as a dividend, and $50 of the seventh installment payment and $150 of each of the last 3 installment payments are long-term capital gain. [Reg. § 1.1248-1.]

☐ [T.D. 6779, 12-21-64. *Amended by* T.D. 7728, 10-31-80 *and* T.D. 7961, 6-20-84.]

§ 1.1248-2. Earnings and profits attributable to a block of stock in simple cases.— (a) *General.*—(1) *Manner of computation.*—For purposes of paragraph (a)(1) of § 1.1248-1, if a United States person sells or exchanges a block of stock (as defined in paragraph (b) of this section) in a foreign corporation, and if the conditions of paragraph (c) of this section are satisfied in respect of the block, then the earnings and profits attributable to the block which were accumulated in taxable years of the corporation beginning after December 31, 1962, during the period such block was held (or was considered to be held by reason of the application of section 1223) by such person while such corporation was a controlled foreign corporation, shall be computed in accordance with the steps set forth in subparagraphs (2), (3), and (4) of this paragraph.

(2) *Step 1.*—(i) For each taxable year of the corporation beginning after December 31, 1962, the earnings and profits accumulated for each such taxable year by the corporation shall

be computed in the manner prescribed in paragraph (d) of this section, and

(ii) for the period the person held (or is considered to have held by reason of the application of section 1223) the block, the amount of earnings and profits attributable to the block shall be computed in the manner prescribed in paragraph (e) of this section.

(3) *Step 2.*—If the conditions of paragraph (c)(5)(ii) of this section must be satisfied in respect of stock in a "lower tier" foreign corporation which such person owns within the meaning of section 958(a)(2), then (i) the earnings and profits accumulated for each such taxable year by such lower tier corporation shall be computed in the manner prescribed in paragraph (d) of this section, and (ii) for the period the person held (or is considered to have held by reason of the application of section 1223) the block, the amount of earnings and profits of the lower tier corporation attributable to the block shall be computed in the manner prescribed in paragraph (e) of this section applied as if such person owned directly the percentage of such stock in such lower tier corporation which such person owns within the meaning of section 958(a)(2).

(4) *Step 3.*—The amount of earnings and profits attributable to the block shall be the sum of the amounts computed under steps 1 and 2.

(b) *Block of stock.*—For purposes of this section, the term "block of stock" means a group of shares sold or exchanged in one transaction, but only if—

(1) The amount realized, basis, and holding period are identical for each such share, and

(2) In case, during the period the person held (or is considered to have held by reason of the application of section 1223) such shares, any amount was included under section 951 in the gross income of the person (or another person) in respect of the shares, the excess under paragraph (e)(3)(ii) of this section (computed as if each share were a block) is identical for each such share.

(c) *Conditions to application.*—This section shall apply only if the following conditions are satisfied:

(1)(i) On each day of the period during which the block of stock was held (or is considered as held by reason of the application of section 1223) by the person during taxable years of the corporation beginning after December 31, 1962, the corporation is a controlled foreign corporation, and

(ii) on no such day is the corporation a foreign personal holding company (as defined in section 552) or a foreign investment company (as defined in section 1246(b)).

(2) The corporation had only one class of stock, and the same number of shares of such stock were outstanding, on each day of each taxable year of the corporation beginning after December 31, 1962, any day of which falls within the period referred to in subparagraph (1) of this paragraph.

(3) For each taxable year referred to in subparagraph (2) of this paragraph, the corporation is not a less developed country corporation (as defined in section 902(d)).

(4) For each taxable year referred to in subparagraph (2) of this paragraph, the corporation does not make any distributions out of its earnings and profits other than distributions which, under section 316 (as modified by section 959), are considered to be out of earnings and profits accumulated in taxable years beginning after December 31, 1962, during the period such person held (or is considered to have held by reason of the application of section 1223) the block while such corporation was a controlled foreign corporation.

(5)(i) If (*a*) on the date of the sale or exchange such person, by reason of his ownership of such block, owns within the meaning of section 958(a)(2) stock in another foreign corporation (referred to as a "lower tier" corporation), and (*b*) the conditions of paragraph (a)(2) of § 1.1248–1 would be satisfied by such person in respect of such stock in the lower tier corporation if such person were deemed to have sold or exchanged such stock in the lower tier corporation on the date he actually sold or exchanged such block in the first tier corporation, then the conditions of subdivision (ii) of this subparagraph must be satisfied.

(ii) In respect of stock in such lower tier corporation, (*a*) the conditions set forth in subparagraphs (1) through (4) of this paragraph (applied as if such person owned directly such stock in such lower tier corporation) must be met and (*b*) such person must own within the meaning of section 958(a)(2) the same percentage of the shares of such stock on each day which falls within the period referred to in subparagraph (1) of this paragraph.

(d) *Earnings and profits accumulated for a taxable year.*—(1) *General.*—For purposes of this section, the earnings and profits accumulated for a taxable year of a foreign corporation shall be the earnings and profits for such year computed in accordance with the rules prescribed in § 1.964–1 (relating to determination of earnings and profits for a taxable year of a controlled foreign corporation) and reduced by any distributions therefrom. If the stock in the corporation is sold or exchanged before any action is taken by or on behalf of the corporation under paragraph (c) of § 1.964-1, the computation of earnings and profits under § 1.964-1 for purposes of this section shall be made as if no elections had been made and no accounting method had been adopted.

(2) *Special rules.*—(i) The earnings and profits of the corporation accumulated—

(a) For any taxable year beginning before January 1, 1967 (computed without any reduction for distributions), shall not include the excess of any item includible in gross income of the foreign corporation under section 882(b) as gross income derived from sources within the United States, and

(b) For any taxable year beginning after December 31, 1966 (computed without any reduction for distributions), shall not include the excess of any item includible in gross income of the foreign corporation under section 882(b)(2) as income effectively connected for that year with the conduct by such corporation of a trade or business in the United States, whether derived from sources within or from sources without the United States,

over any deductions allocable to such item under section 882(c). However, if the sale or exchange of stock in the foreign corporation by the United States person occurs before January 1, 1967, the provisions of (a) of this subdivision apply with respect to such sale or exchange even though the taxable year begins after December 31, 1966. See section 1248(d)(4). Any item which is required to be excluded from gross income, or which is taxed at a reduced rate, under an applicable treaty obligation of the United States shall not be excluded under this subdivision from earnings and profits accumulated for a taxable year (computed without any reduction for distributions).

(ii) If a foreign corporation adopts a plan of complete liquidation in a taxable year of the corporation beginning after December 31, 1962, and if because of the application of section 337(a) gain or loss would not be recognized by the corporation from the sale or exchange of property if the corporation were a domestic corporation, then the earnings and profits of the corporation accumulated for the taxable year (computed without any reduction for distributions) shall be determined without regard to the amount of such gain or loss. See section 1248(d)(2). For the nonapplication of section 337(a) to a liquidation by a collapsible corporation (as defined in section 341) and to certain other liquidations, see section 337(c).

(e) *Earnings and profits attributable to block.*—(1) *General.*—Except as provided in subparagraph (3) of this paragraph, the earnings and profits attributable to a block of stock of a controlled foreign corporation for the period a United States person held (or is considered to have held by reason of the application of section 1223) the block are an amount equal to—

(i) The sum of the earnings and profits accumulated for each taxable year of the corporation beginning after December 31, 1962 (computed under paragraph (d) of this section) during such period, multiplied by

(ii) The percentage that (a) the number of shares in the block, bears to (b) the total number of shares of the corporation outstanding during such period.

(2) *Special rule.*—For purposes of computing the sum referred to in subparagraph (1)(i) of this paragraph, in case the block was held (or is considered as held by reason of the application of section 1223) during a taxable year beginning after December 31, 1962, but not on each day of such taxable year, there shall be included in such sum only that portion which bears the same ratio to (i) the total earnings and profits for such taxable year computed under paragraph (d) of this section), as (ii) the number of days during such taxable year the block was held (or is considered as so held), bears to (iii) the total number of days in such taxable year.

(3) *Amounts included in gross income under section 951.*—(i) If, during the period the person held (or is considered to have held by reason of the application of section 1223) the block, any amount was included under section 951 in the gross income of such person (or of another person whose holding of the stock sold or exchanged is, by reason of the application of section 1223, attributed to such person) in respect of the block, then the earnings and profits attributable to the block for such period shall be an amount equal to (a) the earnings and profits attributable to the block which would have been computed under subparagraph (1) of this paragraph if this subparagraph did not apply, reduced by (b) the excess computed under subdivision (ii) of this subparagraph. See section 1248(d)(1).

(ii) The excess computed under this subdivision is the excess (if any) of (a) amounts included under section 951 in the gross income of such person (or such other person) in respect of the block during such period, over (b) the portion of such amounts which, in any taxable year of such person (or such other person), resulted in an exclusion from the gross income of such person (or such other person) under section 959(a)(1) (relating to exclusion from gross income of distributions of previously taxed earnings and profits).

(iii) This subparagraph shall apply notwithstanding an election under section 962 by such person to be subject to tax at corporate rates.

(4) *Example.*—The application of this paragraph may be illustrated by the following examples:

Example (1). On May 26, 1965, Green, a United States person, purchases at its fair market value a block of 25 of the 100 outstanding shares of the only class of stock of controlled foreign corporation F. He sells the block on January 1, 1968. In respect of the block, Green did not include any amount in his gross income under section 951. F uses the calendar year as its taxable year and does not own stock in any lower tier corporation referred to in paragraph (c)(5)(i) of this section. All of the conditions of paragraph (c) of this section are satisfied in respect of the block. The earnings and profits accumulated by F (computed under paragraph (d) of this section) are $10,000 for 1965, $13,000 for 1966, and $11,000 for 1967. The earnings and profits of F attributable to the block are $7,500, determined as follows:

Sum of earnings and profits accumulated by F during period block was held:

For 1965 (219/365 × $10,000)	$6,000
For 1966	13,000
For 1967	11,000
Sum	$30,000
Multiplied by:	
Number of shares in block (25), divided by total number of shares outstanding (100)	25%
Earnings and profits attributable to block	$7,500

Example (2). Assume the same facts as in example (1) except that in respect of the block Green includes in his gross income under section 951 the total amount of $2,800 for 1965 and 1966, and because of such inclusion the amount of $2,300 which was distributed to Green by F on January 15, 1967, is excluded from his gross income under section 959(a)(1). Accordingly, the earnings and profits of F attributable to the block are $7,000, determined as follows:

Earnings and profits attributable to the block, as computed in example (1)	$7,500
Minus:	
Excess of amount included in Green's gross income under section 951 ($2,800), over portion thereof which resulted in an exclusion under section 959(a)(1) ($2,300)	$500
Earnings and profits attributable to block	$7,000

Example (3). Assume the same facts as in example (1) except that on each day beginning on January 1, 1966 (the date controlled foreign corporation G was organized) through January 1, 1968, F owns 80 of the 100 outstanding shares of the only class of G stock. Since, by reason of his ownership of 25 shares of F stock, Green owns within the meaning of section 958(a)(2) the equivalent of 20 shares of G stock (25/100 of 80 shares), G is a lower tier corporation referred to in paragraph (c)(5)(i)(*a*) of this section. If Green had sold the 20 shares of G stock on January 1, 1968, the date he actually sold the block of F stock, the conditions of paragraph (a)(2) of §1.1248-1 would be satisfied in respect of the G stock, and, accordingly, the conditions of paragraph (c)(5)(ii) of this section must be satisfied. Assume further that such conditions are satisfied, that G uses the calendar year as its taxable year, and that the earnings and profits accumulated by G (computed under paragraph (d) of this section) are $19,000 for 1966 and $21,000 for 1967. The earnings and profits of F and of G attributable to the block are $15,500, determined as follows:

Sum of earnings and profits accumulated by G for period Green owned G stock within the meaning of section 958(a)(2) ($19,000 plus $21,000)	$40,000
Multiplied by:	
Number of G shares deemed owned within the meaning of section 958(a)(2) by Green (20), divided by total number of G shares outstanding (100)	20%
Earnings and profits of G attributable to block	$8,000
Earnings and profits of F attributable to block, as determined in example (1)	7,500
Total earnings and profits attributable to block	$15,500

[Reg. §1.1248-2.]

☐ [*T.D.* 6779, 12-21-64. *Amended by T.D.* 7293, 11-27-73.]

§1.1248-3. Earnings and profits attributable to stock in complex cases.—(a) *General.*—(1) *Manner of computation.*—For purposes of paragraph (a)(1) of §1.1248-1, if a United States person sells or exchanges stock in a foreign corporation, and if the provisions of §1.1248-2 do not apply, then the earnings and profits attributable to the stock which were accumulated in taxable years of the corporation beginning after December 31, 1962, during the period or periods such stock was held (or was considered to be held by reason of the application of section 1223) by such person while such corporation was a controlled foreign corporation, shall be computed in accordance with the steps set forth in subparagraphs (2), (3), and (4) of this paragraph.

(2) *Step 1.*—For each taxable year of the corporation beginning after December 31, 1962, (i) the earnings and profits accumulated for such taxable year by the corporation shall be computed in the manner prescribed in paragraph (b) of this section, (ii) the person's "tentative ratable share" of such earnings and profits shall be computed in the manner prescribed in paragraph (c) or (d) (whichever is applicable) of this section, and (iii) the person's "ratable share" of such earnings and profits shall be computed by adjusting the tentative ratable share in the manner prescribed in paragraph (e) of this section.

(3) *Step 2.*—If the provisions of paragraph (f) of this section (relating to earnings and profits of "lower tier" foreign corporations) apply, the amount of the person's ratable share of the earnings and profits accumulated by each "lower tier" corporation attributable to any such taxable year (i) shall be computed in the manner prescribed by paragraph (f) of this section,, and (ii) shall be added to such person's ratable share for such taxable year determined in step 1.

(4) *Step 3.*—The amount of earnings and profits attributable to the share shall be the sum of the ratable shares computed for each such taxable year in the manner prescribed in steps 1 and 2.

(5) *Share or block.*—In general, the computation under this paragraph shall be made separately for each share of stock sold or exchanged, except that if a group of shares constitute a block of stock the computation may be made in respect of the block. For purposes of this section, the term "block of stock" means a group of shares sold or exchanged in one transaction, but only if (i) the amount realized, basis, and holding period are identical for each such share, and (ii) the adjustments (if any) under paragraphs (e) and (f)(5) of this section of the tentative ratable shares would be identical for each such share if such adjustments were computed separately for each such share.

(6) *Deficit in earnings and profits.*—For purposes of this section and §§ 1.1248-4 through 1.1248-7, in respect of a taxable year, the term "earnings and profits accumulated" for a taxable year (but only if computed under paragraph (b) of this section) includes a deficit in earnings and profits accumulated for such taxable year. Similarly, a tentative ratable share, or a ratable share, may be a deficit.

(7) *Examples.*—The application of the provisions of this paragraph may be illustrated by the following examples:

Example (1). On December 31, 1967, Brown sells 10 shares of stock in foreign corporation X, which uses the calendar year as its taxable year. The 10 shares constitute a block of stock under subparagraph (5) of this paragraph. Under step 1, Brown's ratable shares of the earnings and profits of X attributable to the block are as follows:

Taxable year of X	Ratable shares
1963	$100
1964	150
1965	−50 (deficit)
1966	50
1967	100
Sum	$350

The amount of the earnings and profits attributable to such block under step 3 is $350.

Example (2). Assume the same facts as in example (1), except that in respect of X there are "lower tier" corporations Y and Z to which the provisions of paragraph (f) of this section apply. Brown's ratable shares of the earnings and profits of X, Y, and Z attributable to the block under steps 1 and 2 for each taxable year of X are as follows:

Taxable year of X	X	Y	Z	Total
		Ratable shares		
1963	$100	$40	$20	$160
1964	150	40	−60	130
1965	−50	30	50	30
1966	50	50	30	130
1967	100	−40	40	100
Sum	$350	$120	$80	$550

The amount of the earnings and profits attributable to such block under step 3 is $550.

(b) *Earnings and profits accumulated for a taxable year.*—(1) *General.*—For purposes of this section, the earnings and profits accumulated for a taxable year of a foreign corporation shall be the earnings and profits for such year, computed in accordance with the rules prescribed in § 1.964-1 (relating to determination of earnings and profits for a taxable year of a controlled foreign corporation), except that (i) the special rules of subparagraph (2) of this paragraph shall apply, and (ii) adjustments shall be made under subparagraph (3) of this paragraph for distributions made by the corporation during such taxable year. If the stock in the corporation is sold or exchanged before any action is taken by or on behalf of the

Reg. § 1.1248-3(b)(1)

corporation under paragraph (c) of § 1.964-1, the computation of earnings and profits under § 1.964-1 for purposes of this section shall be made as if no elections had been made and no accounting method had been adopted. The amount of earnings and profits accumulated for a taxable year of a foreign corporation, as computed under this paragraph, is not necessarily the same amount as the earnings and profits of the taxable year computed under section 316(a)(2) or paragraph (d) of § 1.1248-2. Thus, for example, if a distribution with respect to stock is in excess of the amount of earnings and profits of the taxable year computed under section 316(a)(2), such excess is treated under section 316(a)(1) or paragraph (d) of § 1.1248-2 as made out of any earnings and profits accumulated in prior taxable years, whereas the amount of such excess may create, or increase, a deficit in the earnings and profits accumulated for the taxable year as computed under this paragraph. See subparagraph (3) of this paragraph.

(2) *Special rules.*—(i) The earnings and profits of the corporation accumulated—

(a) For any taxable year beginning before January 1, 1967, shall not include the excess of any item includible in gross income of the foreign corporation under section 882(b) as gross income derived from sources within the United States, and

(b) For any taxable year beginning after December 31, 1966, shall not include the excess of any item includible in gross income of the foreign corporation under section 882(b)(2) as income effectively connected for that year with the conduct by such corporation of a trade or business in the United States, whether derived from sources within or from sources without the United States,

over any deductions allocable to such item under section 882(c). However, if the sale or exchange of stock in the foreign corporation by the U.S. person occurs before January 1, 1967, the provisions of (a) of this subdivision apply with respect to such sale or exchange even though the taxable year begins after December 31, 1966. See section 1248(d)(4). Any item which is required to be excluded from gross income, or which is taxed at a reduced rate, under an applicable treaty obligation of the United States shall not be excluded under this subdivision from earnings and profits accumulated for a taxable year.

(ii) If a foreign corporation adopts a plan of complete liquidation in a taxable year of the corporation beginning after December 31, 1962, and if because of the application of section 337(a) gain or loss would not be recognized by the corporation from the sale or exchange of property if the corporation were a domestic corporation, then the earnings and profits of the corporation accumulated for the taxable year shall be determined without regard to the amount of such gain or loss. See section 1248(d)(2). For the nonapplication of section 337(a) to a liquidation by a collapsible corporation (as defined in section 341) and to certain other liquidations, see section 337(c).

(3) *Adjustment for distributions.*—(i) The earnings and profits of a foreign corporation accumulated for a taxable year (computed without regard to this subparagraph) shall be reduced (if necessary below zero so as to create a deficit), or a deficit in such earnings and profits shall be increased, by the amount of the distributions (other than in redemption of stock under section 302(a) or 303) made by the corporation in respect of its stock during such taxable year *(a)* out of such earnings and profits, or *(b)* out of earnings and profits accumulated for prior taxable years beginning after December 31, 1962 (computed under this paragraph). Except for purposes of applying this subparagraph, the application of the preceding sentence shall not affect the amount of earnings and profits accumulated for any such prior taxable year.

(ii) The application of this subparagraph may be illustrated by the following examples:

Example (1). X Corporation, which uses the calendar year as its taxable year, was organized on January 1, 1965, and was a controlled foreign corporation on each day of 1965. The amount of X's earnings and profits accumulated for 1965 (computed under this paragraph without regard to the adjustment for distributions under this subparagraph) is $400,000, of which $100,000 is distributed by X as dividends during 1965. The amount of X's earnings and profits accumulated for 1965 (computed under this paragraph) is $300,000 (that is, $400,000 minus $100,000). The result would be the same even if X was not a controlled foreign corporation on each day of 1965.

Example (2). Assume the same facts as in example (1). Assume further that the amount of X's earnings and profits accumulated for 1966 (computed under this paragraph without regard to the adjustment for distributions under this subparagraph) is $150,000, and that X distributes the amount of $260,000 as dividends during 1966. Since $150,000 of the distribution is from earnings and profits accumulated for 1966 (computed without regard to the adjustment for distributions under this subparagraph), and since $110,000 is from earnings and profits accumulated for 1965, the earnings and profits of X accumulated for 1966 are a deficit of $110,000 (that is, $150,000 minus $260,000). However, the earnings and profits accumulated for 1965 are still $300,000 for purposes of computing in the manner prescribed in paragraph (c) of this section a person's tentative ratable share.

(c) *Tentative ratable share if earnings and profits accumulated for a taxable year not less than zero.*—(1) *General rule.*—For purposes of paragraph (a)(2)(ii) of this section, in respect of a share (or block) of stock in a foreign corporation, if the amount of the earnings and profits accumulated for a taxable year of the corporation (computed under paragraph (b) of this section), beginning after December 31, 1962, is not less than zero, then the person's tentative ratable share for such taxable year shall be equal to—

(i) *(a)* Such amount (if the computation is made in respect of a block, multiplied by the number of shares in the block), divided by *(b)* the number of shares in the corporation outstanding, or deemed under subparagraph (2) of this paragraph to be outstanding, on each day of such taxable year, multiplied by

(ii) The percentage that *(a)* the number of days in such taxable year of the corporation during the period the person held (or was considered to have held by reason of the application of section 1223) the share (or block) while the corporation was a controlled foreign corporation, bears to *(b)* the total number of days in such taxable year.

(2) *Shares deemed outstanding for a taxable year.*—For purposes of this section and §§ 1.1248-4 through 1.1248-7, if the number of shares of stock in a foreign corporation outstanding on each day of a taxable year of the corporation is not constant, then the number of such shares deemed outstanding on each such day shall be the sum of the fractional amounts in respect of each share outstanding on any day of the taxable year. The fractional amount in respect of a share shall be determined by dividing (i) the number of days in the taxable year during which such share was outstanding (excluding the day the share became outstanding, but including the day the share ceased to be outstanding), by (ii) the total number of days in such taxable year.

(3) *Examples.*—The application of subparagraphs (1) and (2) of this paragraph may be illustrated by the following examples:

Example (1). On each day of 1964, S owns a block consisting of 30 of the 100 shares of the only class of stock outstanding in F Corporation, and on each such day F is a controlled foreign corporation. F uses the calendar year as its taxable year and F's earnings and profits accumulated for 1964 (computed under paragraph (b) of this section) are $10,000. S's tentative ratable share with respect to the block is $3,000, computed as follows:

Earnings and profits accumulated for taxable year	$10,000
Multiplied by:	
Number of shares in block (30), divided by number of shares outstanding (100)	30%
Multiplied by:	
Number of days in 1964 S held block while F was a controlled foreign corporation (365), divided by number of days in 1964 (365)	100%
Tentative ratable share for block	$3,000

Example (2). On December 31, 1964, X Corporation, a controlled foreign corporation which uses the calendar year as its taxable year, had 100 shares of one class of stock outstanding, 15 of which were owned by T. T's 15 shares were redeemed by X on March 14, 1965. On December 31, 1965, in addition to the remaining 85 shares, 10 new shares of stock (which were issued on May 26, 1965) were outstanding. Thus, during 1965, 15 shares were outstanding for 73 days, 10 for 219 days, and 85 for 365 days. The earnings and profits (computed under paragraph (b) of this section) accumulated for X's taxable year ending on December 31, 1965, are $18,800. T's tentative ratable share with respect to one share of stock is $40, computed as follows:

Earnings and profits accumulated for taxable year		$18,800
Divided by:		
Number of shares deemed outstanding on each day of 1965:		
15 for 73 days (15 × 73/365)	3	
10 for 219 days (10 × 219/365)	6	
85 for 365 days (85 × 365/365)	85	
Total number of shares deemed outstanding each day of 1965		94
Earnings and profits accumulated per share		$200
Multiplied by:		
Number of days in 1965 T held his share while X was a controlled foreign corporation (73), divided by number of days in 1965 (365)		20%
T's tentative ratable share per share of stock		$40

Example (3). Assume the same facts as in example (2) except that X was not a controlled foreign corporation after January 31, 1965. T's tentative ratable share with respect to one share of stock for 1965 is $17, computed as follows:

Reg. § 1.1248-3(c)(3)

Earnings and profits accumulated per share, determined in example (2)	$200
Multiplied by:	
Number of days in 1965 T held X stock while X was a controlled foreign corporation (31), divided by number of days in 1965 (365)	8.5%
Tentative ratable share	$17

(4) *More than one class of stock.*—If a foreign corporation for a taxable year has more than one class of stock outstanding, then before applying subparagraphs (1) and (2) of this paragraph the earnings and profits accumulated for the taxable year of the corporation (computed under paragraph (b) of this section) shall be allocated to each class of stock in accordance with the principles of paragraph (e)(2) and (3) of §1.951-1, applied as if the corporation were a controlled foreign corporation on each day of such taxable year.

(d) *Tentative ratable share if deficit in earnings and profits accumulated for taxable year.*—(1) *General rule.*—For purposes of paragraph (a)(2)(ii) of this section, in respect of a share (or block) of stock in a foreign corporation, if there is a deficit in the earnings and profits accumulated for a taxable year of the corporation (computed under paragraph (b) of this section) beginning after December 31, 1962, the person's tentative ratable share for such taxable year shall be an amount equal to the sum of the partial tentative ratable shares computed under subparagraphs (2) and (3) of this paragraph.

(2) *Operating deficit.*—The partial tentative ratable share under this subparagraph is computed in 2 steps. First, compute (under paragraph (b) of this section without regard to the adjustment for distributions under subparagraph (3) thereof) the deficit (if any) in earnings and profits accumulated for such taxable year. Second, compute the partial tentative ratable share in the same manner as the tentative ratable share for such taxable year would be computed under paragraph (c) of this section if such deficit were the amount referred to in paragraph (c)(1)(i) *(a)* of this section.

(3) *Deficit from distributions.*—The partial tentative ratable share under this subparagraph is computed in 2 steps. First, compute and treat as a deficit only that portion of the adjustment for distributions under paragraph (b)(3) of this section for such taxable year which is attributable under subparagraph (4) of this paragraph to distributions out of earnings and profits accumulated during prior taxable years of the corporation beginning after December 31, 1962, during the period or periods the corporation was a controlled foreign corporation and the share (or block) of stock was owned by a United States shareholder (as defined in section 951(b) and the regulations thereunder). Second, compute the partial tentative ratable share for such taxable year in the same manner as the tentative ratable share for such taxable year would be computed under paragraph (c) of this section if (i) such deficit were the amount referred to in paragraph (c)(1)(i) *(a)* of this section, and (ii) the corporation were a controlled foreign corporation on each day of such taxable year.

(4) *Order of distributions.*—For purposes of applying subparagraph (3) of this paragraph only, the adjustment for distributions under paragraph (b)(3) of this section for a taxable year of a foreign corporation shall be treated as attributable first to distributions of earnings and profits for the taxable year (computed under paragraph (b) of this section without regard to such adjustment) to the extent thereof, and then to distributions out of the most recent of earnings and profits accumulated during prior taxable years beginning after December 31, 1962 (computed under paragraph (b) of this section). If the foreign corporation was a controlled foreign corporation during a prior taxable year for a period or periods which was only part of such prior taxable year, then for purposes of the preceding sentence (i) such taxable year shall be divided into periods the corporation was or was not a controlled foreign corporation, (ii) distributions of the earnings and profits accumulated during such prior taxable year shall be considered made from the most recent period first, and (iii) the earnings and profits accumulated during such prior taxable year shall be allocated to a period during such year in the same proportion as the number of days in the period bears to the number of days in such year. Except for purposes of applying subparagraph (3) of this paragraph, the application of this subparagraph shall not affect the amount of earnings and profits accumulated for any such prior taxable year (computed under paragraph (b) of this section).

(5) *Examples.*—The application of this paragraph may be illustrated by the following examples:

Example (1). On each day of 1965 X Corporation, which uses the calendar year as its taxable year, was a controlled foreign corporation having 100 shares of one class of stock outstanding, a block of 25 of which were owned by T, who acquired them in 1962 and sold them in 1967. The deficit in X's earnings and profits accumulated for 1965 (computed under paragraph (b) of this section without regard to the adjustment for distributions under subparagraph (3) thereof) is $100,000, and thus in respect of the block T's partial tentative ratable share computed under subparagraph (2) of this paragraph is a deficit of $25,000 (that is, $100,000 × 25/100). During 1965 X does not make any distributions in respect of its stock, and thus in respect of the block T's partial tentative ratable share computed under subparagraph (3) of this paragraph is zero. Accordingly, T's tentative ratable share in respect of the block of X stock for 1965 is a deficit of $25,000. If, however, X was a controlled foreign corporation for only 292 days during 1965, T's tentative ratable share in respect of the block for 1965 would be a deficit of $20,000 (that is, $25,000 × 292/365).

Example (2). (i) Assume the same facts as in example (1) except that at no time during 1965 is X a controlled foreign corporation and that during 1965 X distributes $80,000 with respect to its stock. Assume further that X was a controlled foreign corporation on each day of 1964, but only for the first 146 days of 1963, and that X's earnings and profits accumulated for prior taxable years computed under paragraph (b) of this section are $70,000 for 1964 and $20,000 for 1963.

(ii) Since X was not a controlled foreign corporation on any day of 1965, in respect of the block T's partial tentative ratable share computed under subparagraph (2) of this paragraph is zero.

(iii) The partial tentative ratable share under subparagraph (3) of this paragraph is computed in the following manner: For 1965 the adjustment for distributions under paragraph (b)(3) of this section is $80,000. Under subparagraph (4) of this paragraph $70,000 of such adjustment is attributable to the distribution of all of the earnings and profits accumulated during 1964, on every day of which X was a controlled foreign corporation, and $10,000 of the adjustment is attributable to the distribution of $10,000 of the earnings and profits accumulated for 1963. The portion of the earnings and profits accumulated by X in 1963 attributable to the first 146 days in 1963 during which X was a controlled foreign corporation is $8,000 (that is, $20,000 × 146/365), and the portion attributable to the period in 1963 during which X was not a controlled foreign corporation is $12,000 (that is, $20,000 × 219/365). Under subparagraph (4)(ii) of this paragraph, the distribution in 1965 of $10,000 of earnings and profits accumulated during 1963 is attributable to the more recent period in 1963, that is, the period X was not a controlled foreign corporation. Accordingly, the portion of the adjustment for distributions under paragraph (b)(3) of this section attributable to earnings and profits accumulated during periods X was a controlled foreign corporation is $70,000, and in respect of the block T's partial tentative ratable share under subparagraph (3) of this paragraph is a deficit of $17,500 (that is, $70,000 × 25/100).

(iv) T's tentative ratable share in respect of the block of X stock for 1965 is a deficit of $17,500 (that is, the sum of the partial tentative ratable share for the block computed under subparagraph (2) of this paragraph, zero, plus the partial tentative ratable share for the block computed under subparagraph (3) of this paragraph, a deficit of $17,500).

(v) Assume that X had 100 shares of one class of stock outstanding on each day of 1964 and 1963. Notwithstanding the distributions in 1965 of earnings and profits accumulated during 1964 and 1963 (computed under paragraph (b) of this section), nevertheless, in respect of the block T's tentative ratable share for 1964 is $17,500 (that is, earnings and profits accumulated during 1964 so computed of $70,000, multiplied by 25 shares/100 shares) and in respect of the block T's tentative ratable share for 1963 is $2,000 (that is, earnings and profits accumulated during 1963 so computed of $20,000, multiplied by 25 shares/100 shares, and multiplied by the percentage that the number of days in 1963 on which X was a controlled foreign corporation bears to the total number of days in 1963, 146/365).

Example (3). Assume the same facts as in example (2) except that X was a controlled foreign corporation on each day of 1965. The tentative ratable share with respect to the block of stock for 1965 is a deficit of $42,500, that is, the sum of the partial tentative ratable share under subparagraph (2) of this paragraph (as determined in example (1)), a deficit of $25,000, plus the partial tentative ratable share under subparagraph (3) of this paragraph (as determined in example (2)), a deficit of $17,500.

(6) *More than one class of stock.*—If a foreign corporation for a taxable year has more than one class of stock outstanding, then before applying subparagraph (1) of this paragraph the earnings and profits accumulated for the taxable year of the corporation (computed under paragraph (b) of this section) shall be allocated to each class of stock in accordance with the principles of paragraph (e)(2) and (3) of § 1.951-1, applied as if the corporation were a controlled foreign corporation on each day of such taxable year.

(e) *Ratable share of earnings and profits accumulated for a taxable year.*—(1) *In general.*— For purposes of paragraph (a)(2)(iii) of this section, in respect of a share (or block) of stock in a foreign corporation, the person's ratable share of the earnings and profits accumulated for a taxable year beginning after December 31, 1962, shall be an amount equal to the tentative ratable share computed under paragraph (c) or (d) (as the case may be) of this section, adjusted in the manner prescribed in subparagraphs (2) through (6) of this paragraph.

(2) *Amounts included in gross income under section 951.*—(i) In respect of a share (or block) of stock in a foreign corporation, a person's tentative ratable share for a taxable year of the corporation (computed under paragraph (c) of this section) shall be reduced (but not below zero) by the excess of *(a)* the amount, if any, included (in respect of such corporation for such taxable year) under section 951 in the gross income of such person or (during the period such share, or block, was considered to be held by such person by reason of the application of section 1223) in the gross income of any other person who held such share (or block), over *(b)* the portion of such amount which, in any taxable year of such person or such other person, resulted in an exclusion from the gross income of such person or such other person of an amount under section 959(a)(1) (relating to exclusion from gross income of distributions of previously taxed earnings and profits). See section 1248(d)(1). This subdivision shall apply notwithstanding an election under section 962 by such person to be subject to tax at corporate rates.

(ii) The application of this subparagraph may be illustrated by the following example:

Example. On December 31, 1975, Brown sells one share of stock in X Corporation, a controlled foreign corporation which has never been a less developed country corporation (as defined in section 902(d)). Both Brown and X use the calendar year as the taxable year. In respect of his share, Brown's tentative ratable share for 1971 (computed under paragraph (c) of this section) is $35. In respect of his share, Brown included $4 in his gross income for 1971 under section 951, and the amount of $3, which was distributed to him by X on January 15, 1972, is excluded from Brown's gross income under section 959(a)(1). In respect of the stock, Brown's ratable share for 1971 is $34, determined as follows:

Tentative ratable share	$35
Minus:	
Excess of amount of tentative ratable share included in Brown's gross income under section 951 ($4), over portion thereof which resulted in exclusion under section 959(a)(1) ($3)	1
Ratable share	$34

(3) *Amounts included in gross income under section 551.*—In respect of a share (or block) of stock in a foreign corporation, a person's tentative ratable share for a taxable year of the corporation (computed under paragraph (c) of this section) shall be reduced (but not below zero) by the amount, if any, included (in respect of such corporation for such taxable year) under section 551 in the gross income of such person or (during the period such share, or block, was considered to be held by such person by reason of the application of section 1223) in the gross income of any other person who held such share (or block).

(4) *Less developed country corporations.*—(i) If the foreign corporation was a less developed country corporation as defined in section 902(d) for a taxable year of the corporation, and if the person who sold or exchanged a share (or block) of stock in such corporation satisfies the requirements of paragraph (a) of § 1.1248-5 in respect of such stock, then his ratable share for such taxable year shall be zero. See section 1248(d)(3).

(ii) The application of this subparagraph may be illustrated by the following example:

Example. Assume the same facts as in the example in subparagraph (2)(ii) of this paragraph except that X was a less developed country corporation for 1971. Assume further that Brown satisfies the requirements of paragraph (a) of § 1.1248-5. Brown's ratable share in respect of the stock for 1971 is zero.

(5) *Qualified shareholder of foreign investment company.*—In respect of a share (or block) of stock in a foreign corporation which was a foreign investment company described in section 1246(b)(1), if the election under section 1247(a) to distribute income currently was in effect for a taxable year of the company, and if the person who sold or exchanged the stock (or another person who actually owned the stock during such taxable year and whose holding of the stock is attributed by reason of the application of section 1223 to the person who sold or exchanged the stock) was a qualified shareholder (as defined in section 1247(c)) for his taxable year in which or with which such taxable year of the company ends, then the ratable share in respect of the share (or block) for such taxable year of the company shall be zero. See section 1248(d)(5). In case gain is recognized under section 1246 in respect of a share (or block), see section 1248(f)(3)(B).

(6) *Adjustment for certain distributions.*—If (i) the person who sold or exchanged the share or block (or another person who actually owned the share or block and whose holding of the share or block is attributed by reason of the application of section 1223 to such person) received a distribution during a taxable year of the corporation, and (ii) such distribution was not included in the gross income of such person (or such other person) by reason of the

application of section 959(a)(1) to amounts which were included under section 951(a)(1) in the gross income of a United States shareholder whose holding of the share or block is not attributed by reason of the application of section 1223 to such person (or such other person), then the amount of such distribution shall be added to such person's tentative ratable share for such taxable year. Thus, for example, such tentative ratable share may be increased, or a deficit reduced, by the amount of such distribution.

(f) *Earnings and profits of subsidiaries of foreign corporations.*—(1) *Application of paragraph.*—(i) In respect of a person who sells or exchanges stock in a foreign corporation (referred to as a "first tier" corporation), the provisions of this paragraph shall apply if the following 3 conditions exist:

(a) The conditions of paragraph (a)(2) of §1.1248-1 are satisfied by the person in respect of such stock;

(b) By reason of his ownership of such stock, on the date of such sale or exchange such person owned, within the meaning of section 958(a)(2), stock in another foreign corporation (referred to as a "lower tier" corporation); and

(c) The conditions of paragraph (a)(2) of §1.1248-1 would be satisfied by such person in respect of such stock in the lower tier corporation if such person were deemed to have sold or exchanged such stock in the lower tier corporation on the date he actually sold or exchanged such stock in the first tier corporation.

(ii) If the provisions of this paragraph apply, *(a)* the person's tentative ratable share (or shares) of the earnings and profits accumulated by the lower tier corporation attributable to a taxable year of the first tier corporation shall be computed under subparagraph (2) or (4) of this paragraph, whichever is applicable, and *(b)* such person's ratable share (or shares) for the lower tier corporation attributable to a taxable year of the first tier corporation shall be computed under subparagraph (5) of this paragraph. For the manner of taking into account the ratable share for a lower tier corporation, see paragraph (a)(3) of this section.

(iii) The application of this subparagraph may be illustrated by the following example:

Example. On each day of 1964 and 1965 corporations X and Y are controlled foreign corporations, and each has outstanding 100 shares of one class of stock. On January 15, 1965, T, a United States person, owns one share of stock in X and X directly owns 20 shares of stock in Y. Thus, T owns, within the meaning of section 958(a)(2), stock in Y. On that date, T sells his share in X and satisfies the conditions of paragraph (a)(2) of §1.1248-1 in respect of his stock in X. Assuming that the conditions of paragraph (a)(2) of §1.1248-1 would be satisfied by T in respect of the stock he indirectly owns in Y if, on January 15, 1965, he were deemed to have sold such stock in Y, the provisions of this paragraph apply.

(2) *Tentative ratable share (of lower tier corporation attributable to a taxable year of first tier corporation) not less than zero.*—If the provisions of this paragraph apply to a sale or exchange by a United States person of a share (or block) of stock in a first tier corporation, and if the amount of earnings and profits accumulated (computed under paragraph (b) of this section) for a taxable year (beginning after December 31, 1962) of the lower tier corporation is not less than zero, then in respect of the share (or block) such person's tentative ratable share of the earnings and profits accumulated for such taxable year of the lower tier corporation attributable to any taxable year (beginning after December 31, 1962) of such first tier corporation shall be an amount equal to—

(i) *(a)* Such amount of earnings and profits accumulated for such taxable year of the lower tier corporation (if the computation is made in respect of a block in the first tier corporation, multiplied by the number of shares in the block), divided by *(b)* the number of shares in the first tier corporation outstanding, or deemed under paragraph (c)(2) of this section to be outstanding, on each day of such taxable year of the first tier corporation, multiplied by

(ii) The percentage that *(a)* the number of days during the period or periods in such taxable year of the first tier corporation on which such person held (or was considered to have held by reason of the application of section 1223) the share (or block) in the first tier corporation while the first tier corporation owned (within the meaning of section 958(a)) stock of such lower tier corporation at times while such lower tier corporation was a controlled foreign corporation, bears to *(b)* the total number of days in such taxable year of the first tier corporation, multiplied by

(iii) The percentage that *(a)* the average number of shares in the lower tier corporation which were owned within the meaning of section 958(a) by the first tier corporation during such period or periods (referred to in subdivision (ii)*(a)* of this subparagraph), bears to *(b)* the total number of such shares outstanding, or deemed under the principles of paragraph (c)(2) of this section to be outstanding, during such period or periods, multiplied by

(iv) The percentage that *(a)* the number of days in such taxable year of the lower tier corporation which fall within the taxable year of the first tier corporation, bears to *(b)* the total number of days in such taxable year of the lower tier corporation.

(3) *Examples.*—The application of subparagraph (2) of this paragraph may be illustrated by the following examples:

Example (1). In a year subsequent to 1969, Brown, a United States person, sells 5 of his shares of stock in X Corporation in a transaction as to which the provisions of this paragraph apply. Brown had purchased the 5 shares prior to 1969. On each day of 1969 X Corporation actually had 100 shares of one class of stock outstanding. On each such day X Corporation directly owned all of the shares of stock in Y Corporation, and Y Corporation directly owned all of the shares of stock in Z Corporation. Z Corporation on each such day was a controlled foreign corporation. Both X and Z use the calendar year as the taxable year. Z's earnings and profits accumulated for 1969 (computed under paragraph (b) of this section) are $2,000. Brown's tentative ratable share of the earnings and profits accumulated by Z attributable to the 1969 calendar year of X is $20 per share, computed as follows:

(i) Z's earnings and profits for 1969 ($2,000), divided by the number of shares in X deemed outstanding each day of 1969 (100) $20

Multiplied by:

(ii) Since on each day of 1969 Brown (by reason of owning directly his shares in X) owned, within the meaning of section 958(a)(2), stock in Z while Z was a controlled foreign corporation, the percentage determined under subparagraph (2)(ii) of this paragraph equals 100%

Multiplied by:

(iii) Since on each day of 1969 X owned 100 percent of the stock of Y while Y owned 100 percent of the stock in Z, the percentage determined under subparagraph (2)(iii) equals 100%

Multiplied by:

(iv) Since X and Z each use the same taxable year, the percentage determined under subparagraph (2)(iv) of this paragraph equals 100%

Total $20

Example (2). Assume the same facts as in example (1), except that Brown sold his stock in X on October 19, 1969. Brown's tentative ratable share of the earnings and profits accumulated by Z attributable to the 1969 calendar year of X is $16 per share, computed as follows:

(i) The amount determined in subdivision (i) of example (1)	$20
Multiplied by:	
(ii) The number of days in the period during 1969 Brown (by reason of owning directly his stock in X) owned, within the meaning of section 958(a)(2), his stock in Z while Z was a controlled foreign corporation (292), divided by the number of days in 1969 (365), equals	80%
Multiplied by:	
(iii) The percentage determined in subdivision (iii) of example (1)	100%
Multiplied by:	
(iv) The percentage determined in subdivision (iv) of example (1)	100%
Total	$16

Example (3). Assume the same facts as in examples (1) and (2), except that on each day during 1969 Y owned (within the meaning of section 958(a)(2)) 81 of the 100 shares of Z's outstanding stock. Brown's tentative ratable share of the earnings and profits accumulated by Z attributable to the 1969 calendar year of X is $12.96 per share, computed as follows:

(i) The amount determined in subdivision (i) of example (1)	$20
Multiplied by:	
(ii) The percentage determined in subdivision (ii) of example (2)	80%
Multiplied by:	
(iii) The average number of shares in Z which were owned (within the meaning of section 958(a)) by X during the applicable period (81), divided by the total number of shares in Z during such period (100)	81%
Multiplied by:	
(iv) The percentage determined in subdivision (iv) of example (1)	100%
Total	$12.96

The result would be the same if X owned (within the meaning of section 958(a)(2)) 81 percent of the stock in Y while Y so owned 100 percent of the stock in X, or if X so owned 90 percent of the stock in Y while Y so owned 90 percent of the stock in Z.

Reg. §1.1248-3(f)(3)

Example (4). Assume the same facts as in example (3), except that Z Corporation uses a fiscal year ending June 30 as its taxable year. Assume further that Z's earnings and profits accumulated for its fiscal year ending June 30, 1969, and for its fiscal year ending June 30, 1970, are $3,000 and $2,000, respectively. Brown's tentative ratable share of the earnings and profits accumulated by Z attributable to the 1969 calendar year of X is $16.17 per share, computed as follows:

	In respect of Z's taxable year ending	
	June 30, 1969	June 30, 1970
(i) Z's earnings and profits, divided by the number of shares in X deemed outstanding on each day of 1969:		
$3,000/100	$30	
$2,000/100		$20
Multiplied by:		
(ii) The percentage determined in subdivision (ii) of example (2)	80%	80%
Multiplied by:		
(iii) The percentage determined in subdivision (iii) of example (3)	81%	81%
Multiplied by:		
(iv) Number of days in Z's taxable year which fall within 1969, divided by total number of days in Z's taxable year:		
181/365	49.6%	
184/365		50.4%
Totals	$9.64	$6.53

(v) Sum of tentative ratable shares of Z attributable to X's 1969 calendar year:

For Z's taxable year ending
June 30, 1969 .... $ 9.64
June 30, 1970 ....   6.53
Sum $16.17

(4) *Deficit in tentative ratable share of lower tier corporation attributable to a taxable year of first tier corporation.*—(i) If there is a deficit in the earnings and profits accumulated for a taxable year of a lower tier corporation beginning after December 31, 1962 (computed under paragraph (b) of this section), the person's tentative ratable share for such taxable year of such lower tier corporation attributable to a taxable year of a first tier corporation shall not be computed under subparagraph (2) of this paragraph but shall be an amount equal to the sum of the partial tentative ratable shares computed under subdivisions (ii) and (iii) of this subparagraph.

(ii) The partial tentative ratable share under this subdivision is computed in 2 steps. First, compute (under paragraph (b) of this section without regard to the adjustments for distributions under subparagraph (3) thereof) the deficit (if any) in earnings and profits accumulated for such taxable year of such lower tier corporation. Second, compute the partial tentative ratable share in the same manner as such tentative ratable share would be computed under subparagraph (2) of this paragraph if such deficit were the amount referred to in subparagraph (2)(i)(a) of this paragraph.

(iii) The partial tentative ratable share under this subdivision is computed in 2 steps. First, compute and treat as a deficit the portion of the adjustment for distributions under paragraph (b)(3) of this section for such taxable year which is attributable under paragraph (d)(4) of this section to distributions of earnings and profits accumulated during prior taxable years of the lower tier corporation beginning after December 31, 1962, during the period or periods such lower tier corporation was a controlled foreign corporation and the percentage of the stock of such lower tier corporation (which the person owns within the meaning of section 958(a)(2)) was owned within the meaning of section 958(a) by a United States shareholder (as defined in section 951(b) and the regulations thereunder). Second, compute the partial tentative ratable share in the same manner as such tentative ratable share would be computed under subparagraph (2) of this paragraph if (a) such deficit were the amount referred to in subparagraph (2)(i)(a) of this paragraph, and (b) such lower tier corporation were a controlled foreign corporation on each day of such taxable year.

(5) *Ratable share of lower tier corporation attributable to a first tier corporation.*—(i) If the provisions of this paragraph apply in respect of

a share of stock in a first tier corporation, a person's ratable share of the earnings and profits accumulated by the lower tier corporation attributable to a taxable year of the first tier corporation shall be an amount equal to the tentative ratable share computed under subparagraph (2) or (4) of this paragraph, adjusted in the manner prescribed in this subparagraph.

(ii) If the first tier corporation and the lower tier corporation use the same taxable year, then in respect of a share (or block) of stock in the first tier corporation the person's tentative ratable share of the accumulated earnings and profits of the lower tier corporation attributable to the taxable year of the first tier corporation (computed under subparagraph (2) of this paragraph) shall be reduced (but not below zero) by the excess of *(a)* the amount, if any, included (in respect of such lower tier corporation for its taxable year) under section 951 in the gross income of such person or (during the period such stock was considered to be held by such person by reason of the application of section 1223) in the gross income of any other person who held such stock, over *(b)* the portion of such amount which, in any taxable year of such person or such other person, resulted in an exclusion from the gross income of such person or such other person of an amount under section 959(a)(1). For an illustration of the principles in the preceding sentence, see the example in paragraph (e)(2)(ii) of this section.

(iii) If the first tier corporation and the lower tier corporation do not use the same taxable year, and if there would be an excess computed under subdivision (ii) of this subparagraph in respect of a taxable year of the lower tier corporation (were the taxable years of such corporations the same), then such person's tentative ratable share of the accumulated earnings and profits for a taxable year of the lower tier corporation attributable to such taxable year of the first tier corporation shall be reduced (but not below zero) by an amount which bears the same ratio to *(a)* such excess, as *(b)* the number of days in the taxable year of the lower tier corporation which fall within the taxable year of the first tier corporation, bears to *(c)* the total number of days in the taxable year of the first tier corporation.

(iv) If the first tier corporation and the lower tier corporation use the same taxable year, then in respect of a share (or block) of stock in the first tier corporation the person's tentative ratable share of the accumulated earnings and profits of the lower tier corporation attributable to the taxable year of the first tier corporation (computed under subparagraph (2) of this paragraph) shall be reduced (but not below zero) by the amount, if any, included (in respect of such corporation for such taxable year) under section 551, by reason of the application of section 555(b), in the gross income of such person or (during the period such share (or block) was considered to be held by such person by reason of the application of section 1223) in the gross income of any other person who held such share (or block).

(v) If the first tier corporation and the lower tier corporation do not use the same taxable year, and if there would be a reduction in the person's tentative ratable share of the accumulated earnings and profits of the lower tier corporation attributable to the taxable year of the first tier corporation by an amount computed under subdivision (iv) of this subparagraph in respect of a taxable year of the lower tier corporation (were the taxable years of such corporations the same), then such person's tentative ratable share of the accumulated earnings and profits for a taxable year of the lower tier corporation attributable to such taxable year of the first tier corporation shall be reduced by an amount which bears the same ratio to *(a)* such amount, as *(b)* the number of days in the taxable year of the lower tier corporation which fall within the taxable year of the first tier corporation, bears to *(c)* the total number of days in the taxable year of the first tier corporation.

(vi) If the lower tier corporation was a less developed country corporation as defined in section 902(d) for a taxable year of the corporation, see paragraph (g) of this section.

(g) *Lower tier corporation a less developed country corporation.*—(1) *General.*—If the lower tier corporation was a less developed country corporation as defined in section 902(d) for a taxable year of such corporation, and if the person who sold or exchanged a share (or block) of stock in the first tier corporation satisfies on the date of such sale or exchange—

(i) The requirements of paragraph (a)(1) of §1.1248-5 with respect to such stock, and

(ii) The requirements of paragraph (d)(1) of §1.1248-5 with respect to any stock of the lower tier corporation which such person, by reason of his direct ownership of such stock in the first tier corporation, owned within the meaning of section 958(a)(2),

then such person's ratable share (or a deficit in such ratable share) for such taxable year of the lower tier corporation attributable to a taxable year of the first tier corporation (determined without regard to this paragraph) shall be reduced by an amount computed by multiplying such ratable share (so determined without regard to this paragraph) by the percentage computed under either subparagraph

(2) or (4) of this paragraph, whichever is applicable.

(2) *Percentage for second tier corporation.*—For purposes of subparagraph (1) of this paragraph, if stock of a lower tier corporation (hereinafter referred to as a "second tier" corporation) is owned directly by the first tier corporation on the date of the sale or exchange referred to in such subparagraph (1), the percentage under this subparagraph shall be computed by dividing (i) the number of shares of stock of the second tier corporation which the first tier corporation has owned directly for an uninterrupted 10-year period ending on such date, by (ii) the total number of shares of the stock of such second tier corporation owned directly by such first tier corporation on such date.

(3) *Examples.*—The provisions of subparagraph (2) of this paragraph may be illustrated by the following examples:

Example (1). On January 1, 1966, Smith, a United States person, recognizes gain upon the sale of one share of the only class of stock of F Corporation, which he has owned continuously since 1955. He includes a portion of the gain in his gross income as a dividend under section 1248(a). On January 1, 1966, F owns directly 60 shares of the 100 outstanding shares of the only class of stock of G Corporation, which F acquired in 1955 and owned continuously until such sale. F uses a taxable year ending June 30, and G uses the calendar year as the taxable year. For 1964, G was a less developed country corporation, and on each day of 1964 G was a controlled foreign corporation. Smith's ratable share for G's taxable year ending December 31, 1964, attributable to F's taxable year ending June 30, 1965 (determined without regard to this paragraph) is $6.00. Since the percentage computed under subparagraph (2) of this paragraph is 100 percent (60 shares divided by 60 shares), Smith's ratable share for G's taxable year ending December 31, 1964, attributable to F's taxable year ending June 30, 1965 (after the application of subparagraph (2) of this paragraph) is zero (that is, $6.00 reduced by 100 percent of $6.00).

Example (2). Assume the same facts as in example (1) except that of the 60 shares of G Corporation which F Corporation owned on January 1, 1966, 20 shares were acquired in 1961. The percentage computed under subparagraph (2) of this paragraph is 66⅔ percent (40 shares divided by 60 shares). Accordingly, Smith's ratable share for G's taxable year ending December 31, 1964, attributable to F's taxable year ending June 30, 1965 (after the application of subparagraph (2) of this paragraph) is $2.00 (that is, $6.00 reduced by 66⅔ percent of $6.00).

(4) *Percentage for lower tier corporations other than second tier corporation.*—For purposes of subparagraph (1) of this paragraph, if stock of a lower tier corporation (other than a second tier corporation) is owned within the meaning of section 958(a)(2) by the first tier corporation on the date of the sale or exchange referred to in such subparagraph (1), the percentage under this subparagraph shall be computed in the following manner:

(i) First, determine the percentage for the second tier corporation in accordance with subparagraph (2) of this paragraph.

(ii) Second, determine a partial percentage for each other lower tier corporation in the same manner as the percentage for the second tier corporation is determined. Thus, for example, the partial percentage for a third tier corporation is determined by dividing *(a)* the number of shares of stock of the third tier corporation which the second tier corporation has owned directly for an uninterrupted 10-year period ending on the date of the sale or exchange referred to in subparagraph (1) of this paragraph, by *(b)* the total number of shares of stock of such third tier corporation owned directly by such second tier corporation on such date.

(iii) Third, the percentage for a third tier corporation is the percentage for the second tier corporation multiplied by the partial percentage for the third tier corporation. The percentage for a fourth tier corporation is the percentage for the third tier corporation (as determined in the preceding sentence) multiplied by the partial percentage for the fourth tier corporation. In a similar manner, the percentage for any other lower tier corporation may be determined.

(5) *Example.*—The application of subparagraph (4) of this paragraph may be illustrated by the following example:

Example. On January 1, 1967, Brown, a United States person recognizes gain upon the sale of one share of the only class of stock of W Corporation, which he has owned continuously since 1955. He includes a portion of the gain in his gross income as a dividend under section 1248(a). W is the first tier corporation of a chain of foreign corporations W, X, Y, and Z. W and Z each use the calendar year as the taxable year. For 1964, Z was a less developed country corporation and on each day of 1964 Z was a controlled foreign corporation. Additional facts are set forth in the table below:

(1) Corporation	(2) Shares directly owned by preceding tier		(3)	(4) Col. (2) divided by Col. (3) (percent)
	For uninterrupted 10-year period ending 1/1/67		on 1/1/67	
X	40		60	66⅔
Y	30		40	75
Z	20		30	66⅔

For 1964, the percentage referred to in subparagraph (4) of this paragraph for Z is 33⅓ percent (66⅔% × 75% × 66⅔%).

(6) *Special rule.*—For purposes of applying the provisions of this paragraph, a lower tier corporation may be treated as a second tier corporation with respect to any of its stock which is owned directly by a first tier corporation whereas such lower tier corporation may be treated as a lower tier corporation other than a second tier corporation with respect to other stock in such lower tier corporation which is owned (within the meaning of section 958(a)(2)) by such first tier corporation. Thus, for example, if corporations X, Y, and Z are foreign corporations, X is a first tier corporation owning directly 100 percent of the stock of Y and 40 percent of the stock of Z, and in addition Y owns directly 60 percent of the stock of Z, then the 40 percent of the Z stock (which X owns directly) is considered to be stock in a second tier corporation and the 60 percent of the Z stock (which Y owns directly and which X is considered to own within the meaning of section 958(a)(2)) is considered to be stock in a third tier corporation. [Reg. § 1.1248-3.]

☐ [T.D. 6779, 12-21-64. Amended by T.D. 7293, 11-27-73 and T.D. 7545, 5-5-78.]

§ 1.1248-4. Limitation on tax applicable to individuals.—(a) *General rule.*—(1) *Limitation on tax.*—Under section 1248(b), if during a taxable year an individual sells or exchanges stock in a foreign corporation, then in respect of the stock the increase in the individual's income tax liability for such taxable year which is attributable (under paragraph (b) of this section) to the amount included in his gross income as a dividend under section 1248(a) shall not be greater than an amount equal to the sum of—

(i) The excess, computed under paragraph (c) of this section in respect of the stock, of the United States taxes which would have been paid by the corporation over the taxes (including United States taxes) actually paid by the corporation, plus

(ii) An amount equal to the increase in the individual's income tax liability which would be attributable to the inclusion in his gross income for such taxable year, as long-term capital gain, of an amount equal to the excess of *(a)* the amount included in the individual's gross income as a dividend under section 1248(a) in respect of such stock, over *(b)* the excess referred to in subdivision (i) of this subparagraph.

(2) *Share or block.*—In general, the limitation on tax attributable (under paragraph (b) of this section) to the amount included in an individual's gross income as a dividend under section 1248(a) shall be determined separately for each share of stock sold or exchanged. However, such determination may be made in respect of a block of stock if earnings and profits attributable to the block are computed under § 1.1248-2 or 1.1248-3. See paragraph (b) of § 1.1248-2 and paragraph (a)(5) of § 1.1248-3.

(3) *Application of limitation.*—The provisions of subparagraph (1) of this paragraph shall not apply unless the individual establishes—

(i) In the manner prescribed in § 1.1248-7, the amount of the earnings and profits of the corporation attributable under paragraph (a)(1) of § 1.1248-2 or under paragraph (a)(1) of § 1.1248-3, whichever is applicable, to the stock, and

(ii) The amount equal to the sum described in subparagraph (1) of this paragraph, computed in accordance with the provisions of this section.

(4) *Example.*—The provisions of this paragraph may be illustrated by the following example:

Example. On December 31, 1966, Smith, a United States person, sells a share of stock of X Corporation which he has owned continuously since December 31, 1965, and includes $100 of the gain on the sale in his gross income as a dividend under section 1248(a). Both X and Smith use the calendar year as the taxable year. The increase in Smith's income tax liability for 1966 which is attributable (under paragraph (b) of this section) to the inclusion of the $100 in his gross income as a dividend is $70. X was a controlled foreign corporation on each day of 1966. The excess, computed under paragraph (c) of this section in respect of the share, of the United States taxes which X would have paid over the taxes (including United States taxes) actually paid by X is $49. Under section 1248(b), the limitation on the tax attributable to the $100 included by Smith in his gross income as a dividend under section 1248(a) is $61.75, computed as follows:

(i) Excess, computed under paragraph (c) of this section, of United States taxes which X Corporation would have paid in 1966 over the taxes actually paid by X in 1966		$49.00
(ii) The amount determined under subparagraph (1)(ii) of this paragraph:		
The amount Smith included in his gross income as a dividend under section 1248(a)	$100.00	
Less the excess referred to in subdivision (i) of this example	$49.00	
Difference	$51.00	
Increase in Smith's tax liability attributable to including $51 in his gross income as long-term capital gain (25 percent of $51)		$12.75
(iii) Limitation on tax		$61.75

(b) *Tax attributable to amount treated as dividend.*—(1) *General.*—For purposes of paragraph (a)(1) of this section, in respect of a share (or block) of stock in a foreign corporation sold or exchanged by an individual during a taxable year, the tax attributable to the amount included in his gross income as a dividend under section 1248(a) shall be the amount which bears the same ratio to (i) the excess of *(a)* his income tax liability for the taxable year determined without regard to section 1248(b) over *(b)* such tax liability determined as if the portion of the total gain recognized during the taxable year which is treated as a dividend under section 1248(a) had not been recognized, as (ii) the amount included as a dividend under section 1248(a) in respect of the share (or block), bears to (iii) the total amount included as a dividend under section 1248(a) in the individual's gross income for such taxable year.

(2) *Examples.*—The application of this paragraph may be illustrated by the following examples:

Example (1). (i) During 1963, Brown, an unmarried United States person, sells a block of stock in a controlled foreign corporation. On the sale, he recognizes $22,000 gain, of which $18,000 is treated as a dividend under section 1248(a) and $4,000 as long-term capital gain. Brown computes his income tax liability for his taxable year ending December 31, 1963, under section 1201 (relating to alternative tax) in accordance with the additional facts assumed in the following table:

	Computation of income tax liability without regard to section 1248(b)	Computation of income tax liability as if the gain treated as a dividend under section 1248(a) had not been recognized
Income from salary	$300,000	$300,000
Long-term capital gain resulting from sale of stock, less deduction for capital gains under section 1202 ($4,000 less $2,000)	2,000	2,000
Amount treated as a dividend under section 1248(a)	$18,000	0
Adjusted gross income	$320,000	$302,000
Charitable contribution of $100,000 to church (limited under section 170(b) to 30 percent of adjusted gross income)	(96,000)	(90,600)
Other itemized deductions and personal exemption .	(7,700)	(7,700)
Taxable income	$216,300	$203,700
Less 50 percent of $4,000	2,000	2,000
Amount subject to partial tax under section 1201(b)(1)	$214,300	$201,700
Partial tax	$169,833	$158,367
25 percent of $4,000	1,000	1,000
Tax liability	$170,833	$159,367

(ii) The tax attributable to the $18,000 treated as a dividend under section 1248(a) is $11,466 ($170,833 minus $159,367).

Example (2). Assume the same facts as in example (1) except that the $18,000 treated as a dividend under section 1248(a) is attributable

Reg. §1.1248-4(b)(2)

to the sale of a block of stock in X Corporation and a block of stock in Y Corporation. Assume further that $10,000 of the gain on the block of X stock was treated as a dividend and that $8,000 of the gain on the block of Y stock was treated as a dividend. Thus, the tax attributable to the amount treated as a dividend in respect of the block of X stock is $6,370 ($10,000/$18,000 of $11,466) and the amount in respect of the block of Y stock is $5,096 ($8,000/$18,000 of $11,466). The result would be the same if both blocks of stock were blocks of stock in the same corporation.

(c) *Excess (of United States taxes which would have been paid over taxes actually paid) attributable to a share.*—(1) *General.*—For purposes of paragraph (a)(1)(i) of this section—

(i) The term "taxes" means income, war profits, or excess profits taxes, and

(ii) The excess (and the portion of such excess attributable to an individual's share or block of stock in a foreign corporation) of the United States taxes which would have been paid by the corporation over the taxes (including United States taxes) actually paid by the corporation, for the period or periods the stock was held (or was considered to be held by reason of the application of section 1223) by the individual in taxable years of the corporation beginning after December 31, 1962, while the corporation was a controlled foreign corporation, shall be computed in accordance with the steps set forth in subparagraphs (2), (3), and (4) of this paragraph.

(2) *Step 1.*—For each taxable year of the corporation beginning after December 31, 1962, in respect of the individual's share (or block) of such stock (i) the taxable income of the corporation shall be computed in the manner prescribed in paragraph (d) of this section, and (ii) the excess (and the portion of such excess attributable to the stock) of the United States taxes which would have been paid by the corporation on such taxable income over the taxes (including United States taxes) actually paid by the corporation shall be computed in the manner prescribed in paragraph (e) of this section.

(3) *Step 2.*—If during such taxable year the corporation is a first tier corporation to which paragraph (f) of this section applies, (i) the excess (and the portion of such excess attributable to the individual's share, or block, of stock in the first tier corporation) of the United States taxes which would have been paid by any lower tier corporation over the taxes (including United States taxes) actually paid by such lower tier corporation shall be computed under paragraph (f) of this section, and (ii) such portion shall be added to the portion of the excess attributable to the individual's share (or block) of such stock as determined in step 1 for such taxable year.

(4) *Step 3.*—The excess, in respect of the individual's share (or block), of the United States taxes which would have been paid by the corporation over the taxes actually paid by the corporation shall be the sum of the portions computed for each such taxable year in the manner prescribed in steps 1 and 2.

(d) *Taxable income.*—For purposes of paragraph (c)(2)(i) of this section, taxable income shall be computed in respect of an individual's share (or block) in accordance with the following rules:

(1) *Application of principles of § 1.952-2.*—Except as otherwise provided in this paragraph, the principles of paragraphs (a)(1), (b)(1), and (c) of § 1.952-2 (other than subparagraphs (2)(iii) *(b)*, (2)(v), (5)(i), and (6) of such paragraph (c)) shall apply.

(2) *Effect of elections.*—In respect of a taxable year of a foreign corporation, no effect shall be given to an election or an adoption of accounting method unless for such taxable year effect is given to such election or adoption of accounting method under paragraph (d)(1) of § 1.1248-2 or paragraph (b)(1) of § 1.1248-3, whichever is applicable.

(3) The deductions for certain dividends received provided in sections 243, 244, and 245 shall not be allowed.

(4) *Deduction for taxes.*—In computing the amount of the deduction allowed under section 164, there shall be excluded income, war profits, or excess profits taxes paid or accrued which are imposed by the authority of any foreign country or possession of the United States.

(5) *Capital loss carryover.*—In determining the amount of a net capital loss to be carried forward under section 1212 to the taxable year—

(i) No net capital loss shall be carried forward from a taxable year beginning before January 1, 1963.

(ii) The portion of a net capital loss or a capital gain net income (net capital gain for taxable years beginning before January 1, 1977) for a taxable year beginning after December 31, 1962, which shall be taken into account shall be the amount of such loss or gain (as the case may be), multiplied by the percentage which *(a)* the number of days in such taxable year during which the individual held (or was considered to have held by reason of the application of section 1223) the share (or block) of stock sold or exchanged while the corporation was a controlled foreign corporation, bears to *(b)* the total number of days in such taxable year.

(iii) The application of this subparagraph may be illustrated by the following examples:

Example (1). Corporation X is a foreign corporation which was created on January 1, 1963, and which uses the calendar year as its taxable year. X was a controlled foreign corporation on each day of the period March 15, 1963, through December 31, 1965, but was not a controlled foreign corporation on any day during the period January 1, 1963, through March 14, 1963. On December 31, 1965, Smith, a United States person, sells a share of X stock which he has owned continuously since January 1, 1963. A portion of the gain recognized on the sale is includible in Smith's gross income as a dividend under section 1248(a). X had a net capital loss (determined without regard to subchapter N, chapter 1 of the Code) of $200 for 1963. Since, however, X was a controlled foreign corporation for only 292 days in 1963, for purposes of determining the net capital loss carryover to 1964 the portion of the net capital loss of $200 for 1963 which Smith takes into account under subdivision (ii) of this subparagraph is $160 (292/365 of $200), and, accordingly, the amount of the net capital loss carryover to 1964 is $160.

Example (2). Assume the same facts as in example (1), except that X was not a controlled foreign corporation on any day of the period May 26, 1964, through June 30, 1965. Assume further that X had a net capital gain (capital gain net income for taxable years beginning after December 31, 1976) (determined without regard to subchapter N, chapter 1, of the Code) of $160 for 1964. In computing X's taxable income for 1964 under this paragraph, Smith applies the net capital loss carryover of $160 from 1963 to reduce the net capital gain (capital gain net income for taxable years beginning after December 31, 1976) of $160 for 1964 to zero. Since, however, X was a controlled foreign corporation for only 146 days in 1964, for purposes of computing the portion of the 1963 capital loss of $160 which is a net capital loss carryover to 1965, the portion of the 1964 capital gain which Smith takes into account under subdivision (ii) of this subparagraph is $63.83 (146/366 of $160). Thus, the net capital loss carryover to 1965 is $96.17 ($160 minus $63.83).

(6) *Net operating loss deduction.*—(i) The individual shall reduce the taxable income (computed under subparagraphs (1) through (5) of this paragraph) of the corporation for the taxable year by the amount of the net operating loss deduction of the corporation computed under section 172, as modified in the manner prescribed in this subparagraph.

(ii) The rules of subparagraphs (1) through (5) of this paragraph shall apply for purposes of determining the excess referred to in section 172(c) and the taxable income referred to in section 172(b)(2).

(iii) A net operating loss shall not be carried forward from, or carried back to, a taxable year beginning before January 1, 1963.

(iv) The portion of a net operating loss incurred, or of taxable income earned, in a taxable year beginning after December 31, 1962, which shall be taken into account under section 172(b)(2) shall be the amount of such loss or income (as the case may be), multiplied by the percentage which *(a)* the number of days in such taxable year during which the individual held (or was considered to have held by reason of the application of section 1223) the share (or block) of stock sold or exchanged while the corporation was a controlled foreign corporation, bears to *(b)* the total number of days in such taxable year.

(v) For illustrations of the principles of this subparagraph, see the examples relating to net capital loss carryovers in subparagraph (5)(iii) of this paragraph.

(7) *Adjustment for amount previously included in gross income of United States shareholders.*—In respect of the individual's share (or block) of stock sold or exchanged, the taxable income of the corporation for the taxable year (determined without regard to this subparagraph and subparagraph (8) of this paragraph) shall be reduced (but not below zero) by an amount equal to the sum of the amounts included under section 951 in the gross income of United States shareholders (as defined in section 951(b)) of the corporation for the taxable year.

(8) *Adjustment for distributions.*—In respect of the individual's share (or block) of stock sold or exchanged, the taxable income of the corporation for the taxable year (determined without regard to this subparagraph) shall be reduced (but not below zero) by the amount of the distributions (other than in redemption of stock under section 302(a) or 303) made by the corporation out of earnings and profits of such taxable year (within the meaning of section 316(a)(2)). For purposes of the preceding sentence, distributions shall be taken into account only to the extent not excluded from the gross income of the United States shareholders of the corporation under section 959.

(e) *Excess attributable to a share (or block) of stock.*—(1) *Excess of United States taxes which would have been paid over taxes actually paid.*—

For purposes of paragraph (c)(2)(ii) of this section, in respect of a taxable year of a foreign corporation, the portion of the excess under this subparagraph which is attributable to an individual's share (or block) of such stock shall be an amount equal to—

(i) The excess (if any) of *(a)* the United States taxes which would have been paid by the corporation on its taxable income (computed under paragraph (d) of this section) for the taxable year had it been taxed as a domestic corporation under chapter 1 of the Code (but without regard to subchapters F, G, H, L, M, N, S, and T thereof) for such taxable year, over *(b)* the income, war profits, or excess profits taxes actually paid by the corporation during such taxable year (including such taxes paid to the United States),

(ii) Multiplied by the percentage that *(a)* the number of days in such taxable year of the corporation during the period or periods the share (or block) was held (or was considered as held by reason of the application of section 1223) by the individual while the corporation was a controlled foreign corporation, bears to *(b)* the total number of days in such taxable year,

(iii) If the computation is made in respect of a block, multiplied by the number of shares in the block, and

(iv) Divided by the number of shares in the corporation outstanding, or deemed under paragraph (c)(2) of § 1.1248-3 to be outstanding, on each day of such taxable year.

(2) *Example.*—The provisions of this paragraph may be illustrated by the following example:

Example. (i) Jones, a United States person, owns on each day of 1963 10 shares of the 100 shares of the only class of outstanding stock of X Corporation. He sells one of such shares on December 31, 1963. X Corporation is a controlled foreign corporation on each day of 1963 and Jones and X each use the calendar year as the taxable year. For 1963, the excess of the United States taxes which would have been paid by X had it been taxable as a domestic corporation over the taxes (including United States taxes) actually paid by X is $23,500, computed as follows:

Amount subject to partial tax under section 1201 (a)(1), as computed by Jones:		
Taxable income		$300,000
Less excess of net long-term capital gain over net short-term capital loss		100,000
Amount subject to partial tax		$200,000
Excess determined under subparagraph (1)(i) of this paragraph:		
30 percent × $25,000	$7,500	
52 percent × $175,000	91,000	
Partial tax		$98,500
25 percent × $100,000		25,000
United States taxes X would have paid (alternative tax computed under section 1201(a))		$123,500
Less income taxes X actually paid to: United States	$10,000	
foreign countries	90,000	
Total		$100,000
Excess		$23,500
Multiplied by:		
Percentage determined under subparagraph (1)(ii) of this paragraph:		
Since on each day of 1963, Jones held the share of X stock while X was a controlled foreign corporation, the percentage equals		100 %
Total		$23,500

(ii) The portion of the excess determined in subdivision (i) of this example which is attributable to the share held by Jones is $235, that is, the amount of such excess ($23,500), divided by the number of shares of X deemed to be outstanding on each day of 1963 (100).

(3) *More than one class of stock.*—If a foreign corporation for a taxable year has more than one class of stock outstanding, then before applying subparagraph (1) of this paragraph the excess (if any) which would be determined under subparagraph (1)(i) of this paragraph shall be allocated to each class of stock in accordance with the principles of paragraph (e)(2) and (3) and § 1.951-1, applied as if the corporation were a controlled foreign corporation on each day of such taxable year.

(f) *Subsidiaries of foreign corporations.*—(1) *Excess for lower tier corporation attributable to taxable year of first tier corporation.*—For purposes of paragraph (c)(3) of this section, if the provisions of paragraph (a)(3) of § 1.1248-2 or paragraph (f) of § 1.1248-3 apply in the case of the sale or exchange by an individual of a share (or block) of stock in a first tier corporation, then in respect of a taxable year of a lower tier corporation (beginning after December 31, 1962) which includes at least one day which falls within a taxable year of the first tier corporation (beginning after December 31, 1962), the portion of the excess under this subparagraph attributable to the share shall be an amount equal to—

(i) The excess (if any) of *(a)* the United States taxes which would have been paid by the lower tier corporation on its taxable income (computed under paragraph (g) of this section) for such taxable year of the lower tier corporation had it been taxed as a domestic corporation under chapter 1 of the Code (but without regard to subchapters F, G, H, L, M, N, and T thereof) for such taxable year of the lower tier corporation, over *(b)* the income, war profits, or excess profits taxes actually paid by the lower tier corporation during such taxable year (including such taxes paid to the United States),

(ii) Multiplied by each of the percentages described under paragraph (f)(2)(ii), (iii), and (iv) of § 1.1248-3 in respect of such taxable year of the first tier corporation,

(iii) If the computation is made in respect of a block of stock, multiplied by the number of shares in the block, and

(iv) Divided by the number of shares in the first tier corporation outstanding, or deemed under paragraph (c)(2) of § 1.1248-3 to be outstanding, on each day of such taxable year of the first tier corporation.

(2) *More than one class of stock.*—If a foreign corporation for a taxable year has more than one class of stock outstanding, then before applying subparagraph (1) of this paragraph the principles of paragraph (e)(3) of this section shall apply.

(g) *Taxable income of lower tier corporations.*—(1) *General.*—For purposes of paragraph (f)(1)(i) of this section, in respect of the individual's share (or block) the taxable income of a lower tier corporation shall be computed in the manner provided in paragraph (d) of this section, except as provided in this paragraph.

(2) *Capital loss carryover.*—For purposes of subparagraph (1) of this paragraph, the provisions of paragraph (d)(5)(ii) of this section shall not apply. In determining the amount of a net capital loss to be carried forward under section 1212 to the taxable year of a lower tier corporation, the portion of a net capital loss or a capital gain net income (net capital gain for taxable years beginning before January 1, 1977) for a taxable year of the lower tier corporation beginning after December 31, 1962, which shall be taken into account shall be the amount of such loss or gain (as the case may be), multiplied by the percentage which (i) the number of days in such taxable year during the period or periods the individual held (or was considered to have held by reason of the application of section 1223) the share (or block) of stock in the first tier corporation sold or exchanged while the first tier corporation owned (within the meaning of section 958(a)) stock in the lower tier corporation while the lower tier corporation was a controlled foreign corporation, bears to (ii) the total number of days in such taxable year.

(3) *Net operating loss deduction.*—For purposes of subparagraph (1) of this paragraph, the provisions of paragraph (d)(6)(iv) of this section shall not apply. In determining the amount of the net operating loss deduction for a taxable year of a lower tier corporation, the portion of a net operating loss incurred, or of taxable income earned, in a taxable year of the lower tier corporation beginning after December 31, 1962, which shall be taken into account under section 172(b)(2) shall be the amount of such loss or income (as the case may be) multiplied by the percentage described in subparagraph (2) of this paragraph for such taxable year. [Reg. § 1.1248-4.]

☐ [T.D. 6779, 12-21-64. Amended by T.D. 7545, 5-5-78 and T.D. 7728, 10-31-80.]

§ 1.1248-5. Stock ownership requirements for less developed country corporations.—(a) *General rule.*—(1) *Requirements.*—For purposes of paragraph (e)(4) of § 1.1248-3, a United States person shall be considered as satisfying the requirements of this paragraph with respect to a share (or block) of stock of a foreign corporation if on the date he sells or exchanges such share (or block)—

(i) The 10-year stock ownership requirement of paragraph (b) of this section is met with respect to such share (or block), and

(ii) In the case of a United States person which is a domestic corporation, the requirement of paragraph (c) of this section, if applicable, is met.

(2) *Ownership of stock.*—For purposes of this section—

(i) The rules for determining ownership of stock prescribed by section 958(a) and (b) shall apply.

(ii) Stock owned by a United States person who is an individual, estate, or trust which was acquired by reason of the death of the predecessor in interest of such United States person shall be considered as owned by such United States person during the period such stock was owned by such predecessor in interest, and during the period such stock was owned by any other predecessor in interest if between such United States person and such other predecessor in interest there was no transfer other than by reason of the death of an individual.

(b) *10-year stock ownership requirement.*—(1) *General.*—A United States person meets the 10-year stock ownership requirement with respect to a share (or block) of stock in a foreign corporation which he sells or exchanges only if the share (or block) was owned (under the rules of paragraph (a)(2) of this section) by such person for a continuous period of at least 10 years ending on the date of the sale or exchange. See the first sentence of section 1248(d)(3). Thus, for example, if Jones, a United States person, sells a share of stock in a foreign corporation on January 1, 1965, the 10-year stock ownership requirement is met with respect to the share only if the share was owned (under the rules of paragraph (a)(2) of this section) by Jones continuously from January 1, 1955, to January 1, 1965. If a foreign corporation has not been in existence for at least 10 years on the date of the sale or exchange of the share, the 10-year stock ownership requirement cannot be met.

(2) *Special rule.*—For purposes of this paragraph, a United States person shall be considered to have owned stock during the period he was considered to have held the stock by reason of the application of section 1223.

(c) *Disqualification of domestic corporation as a result of changes in ownership of its stock.*—(1) *General.*—(i) For purposes of paragraph (a)(1)(ii) of this section, the requirement of this paragraph must be met only if, on at least one day during the 10-year period ending on the date of the sale or exchange by a domestic corporation of a share of stock in a foreign corporation, one or more noncorporate United States shareholders (as defined in subdivision (iii) of this subparagraph) own more than 50 percent of the total combined voting power of all classes of stock entitled to vote of the domestic corporation.

(ii) The requirement of this paragraph is that if one or more persons are noncorporate United States shareholders on the first such day (referred to in subdivision (i) of this subparagraph), such person or persons continue after such first day, at all times during the remainder of such 10-year period, to own in the aggregate more than 50 percent of the total combined voting power of all classes of stock entitled to vote of the domestic corporation. For purposes of determining whether a domestic corporation meets the requirement of this paragraph, the stock owned by a United States person who is a noncorporate United States shareholder of a domestic corporation on such first day shall not be counted at any time after he ceases during such ten-year period to be a noncorporate United States shareholder of such corporation.

(iii) For purposes of this paragraph, the term "noncorporate United States shareholder" means, with respect to a domestic corporation, a United States person who is an individual, estate, or trust and who owns 10 percent or more of the total combined voting power of all classes of stock of such domestic corporation.

(iv) For purposes of this paragraph, the percentage of the total combined voting power of stock of a foreign corporation owned by a United States person shall be determined in accordance with the principles of section 951(b) and the regulations thereunder.

(2) *Examples.*—The application of this paragraph may be illustrated by the following examples:

Example (1). During the entire period beginning December 31, 1954, and ending December 31, 1964, domestic corporation N owns all the stock of controlled foreign corporation X, a less developed country corporation. On December 31, 1964, N recognizes gain upon the sale of all its X stock. A, B, and C, who are unrelated individuals, were the only United States persons owning, or considered as owning, 10 percent or more of the total combined voting power of all classes of stock entitled to vote of N at any time during the 10-year period December 31, 1954, through December 31, 1964. The percentages of the total combined voting power in N, which A, B, and C owned during such 10-year period, are as follows:

Owner	Dec. 31, 1954-Apr. 1, 1957 Percent	Apr. 2, 1957-Oct. 1, 1959 Percent	Oct. 2, 1959-Dec. 31, 1964 Percent
A	20	20	20
B	9	30	30
C	30	15	9

Domestic corporation N does not meet the requirement of this paragraph with respect to the stock of controlled foreign corporation X for the following reasons:

(i) April 2, 1957, is the first day (during the 10-year period ending on December 31, 1964, the date N sells the X stock) on which noncorporate United States shareholders of N own more than 50 percent of the total combined voting power in N, and thus the requirement of this paragraph must be met. See subparagraph (1)(i) of this paragraph. Although A, B, and C did own, in the aggregate, more than 50 percent of such voting power before April 2, 1957, the voting power owned by B is not counted because B was not a noncorporate United States shareholder of N before such date.

(ii) Although C is a noncorporate United States shareholder on April 2, 1957, C ceases to own 10 percent or more of the total combined voting power in N on October 2, 1959. Thus, after October 1, 1959, the N stock which C owns is not counted for purposes of determining whether the more-than-50-percent stock ownership test is met. See subparagraph (1)(ii) of this paragraph. Accordingly, after October 1, 1959, the requirement of this paragraph is not met.

Example (2). Assume the same facts as in example (1), except that B's wife owns directly 5 percent of the total combined voting power in N from December 31, 1954, to December 31, 1964. On the basis of the assumed facts, N meets the requirement of this paragraph with respect to the stock of controlled foreign corporation X for the following reasons:

(i) December 31, 1954, is the first day (of the 10-year period ending on the date N sells the X stock) on which noncorporate United States shareholders of N own more than 50 percent of the total combined voting power in N. B is a noncorporate United States shareholder on such date because he owns, and is considered as owning, 14 percent of the total combined voting power in N (9 percent directly, and, under section 958(b), 5 percent constructively). Thus, on December 31, 1954, noncorporate United States shareholders A, B, and C own, in the aggregate, more than 50 percent of the total combined voting power in N.

(ii) A, B, and C, the noncorporate United States shareholders of N on December 31, 1954, own, and are considered as owning, more than 50 percent of the total voting power of N from December 31, 1954, to October 1, 1959. Since beginning on October 2, 1959, A owns 20 percent and B owns, and is considered as owning, 35 percent of the total combined voting power in N, A and B own, and are considered as owning, more than 50 percent of the total combined voting power in N from October 2, 1959, to December 31, 1964. Therefore, the requirement of this paragraph is met.

(d) *Application of section to lower tier corporation.*—(1) *General.*—For purposes of paragraph (g)(1)(ii) of §1.1248-3, a United States person satisfies the requirements of this subparagraph in respect of stock of a lower tier corporation which such person, by reason of his direct ownership of the share (or block) of the first tier corporation sold or exchanged, owned within the meaning of section 958(a)(2) on the date he sold or exchanged such share (or block), if on such date—

(i) The 10-year stock ownership requirement of paragraph (b) of this section is met by such person with respect to any stock in the lower tier corporation which such person so owned, and

(ii) In the case of a United States person which is a domestic corporation, the requirement of paragraph (c) of this section, if applicable, is met.

(2) *Special rule.*—For purposes of this paragraph, in applying paragraphs (b) and (c) of this section, the sale or exchange of a share (or block) of stock in a first tier corporation by a United States person shall be deemed to be the sale or exchange of any stock in a lower tier corporation which the person, by reason of his direct ownership of such share (or block) of the first tier corporation, owned within the meaning of section 958(a)(2) on the date he actually sold or exchanged such share (or block) in the first tier corporation. [Reg. §1.1248-5.]

☐ [*T.D.* 6779, 12-21-64.]

§1.1248-6. Sale or exchange of stock in certain domestic corporations.—(a) *General rule.*—If a United States person recognizes gain upon the sale or exchange of a share (or block) of stock of a domestic corporation which was formed or availed of principally for the holding, directly or indirectly, of stock of one or more foreign corporations, and if the conditions of paragraph (a)(2) of §1.1248-1 would be met by such person in respect of the share (or block) if the domestic corporation were a foreign corporation, then section 1248 shall apply in respect of such gain in accordance with the rules provided in paragraph (b) of this section.

(b) *Application.*—(1) The gain referred to in paragraph (a) of this section shall be included in the gross income of the United States person as a dividend under section 1248(a) to the extent of the earnings and profits attributable under §1.1248-2 or §1.1248-3, whichever is applicable, to the share (or block), computed, however, in accordance with the following rules:

(i) The domestic corporation shall be treated as if it were a first tier foreign corporation;

(ii) If, after the application of subdivision (i) of this subparagraph, the provisions of paragraph (a)(3) of §1.1248-2 or paragraph (f) of § 1.1248-3 (as the case may be) would apply in respect of a foreign corporation the stock of which is owned (within the meaning of section 958(a)) by the domestic corporation treated as the first tier corporation, such foreign corporation shall be considered a lower tier corporation;

(iii) Except to the extent provided in subdivision (iv) of this subparagraph, the earnings and profits of the domestic corporation treated as the first tier corporation accumulated for a taxable year, as computed under paragraph (d) of § 1.1248-2 or paragraph (b) of § 1.1248-3 (as the case may be), shall be considered to be zero; and

(iv) If, during a taxable year, a domestic corporation treated as the first tier corporation realizes gain upon the sale or exchange of stock in a foreign corporation, and solely by reason of the application of section 337 (relating to certain liquidations) the gain was not recognized, then the earnings and profits of such domestic corporation accumulated for the taxable year as computed under paragraph (d) of § 1.1248-2 or paragraph (b) of § 1.1248-3 (as the case may be), shall be considered to be an amount equal to the portion of such gain realized during the taxable year which, if section 337 had not applied, would have been treated as a dividend under section 1248(a).

(2) If the person selling or exchanging the stock in the domestic corporation is an individual, the limitation on tax attributable to the amount included in his gross income as a dividend under subparagraph (1) of this paragraph shall be determined, in accordance with the principles of paragraph (f) of § 1.1248-4, by treating the domestic corporation as a first tier corporation.

(3)(i) If the earnings and profits of the foreign corporation or corporations (or of the domestic corporation treated as a first tier corporation) to be taken into account under subparagraph (1) of this paragraph are not established in the manner provided in paragraph (a)(1) of § 1.1248-7, all of the gain from the sale or exchange of the share (or block) of the domestic corporation shall be treated as a dividend.

(ii) To the extent that the person does not establish, in the manner provided in paragraph (c) of § 1.1248-7, the foreign taxes paid by such foreign corporation or corporations to be taken into account for purposes of computing the limitation on tax attributable to a share, such foreign taxes shall not be taken into account for purposes of such computation.

(c) *Corporation formed or availed of principally for holding stock of foreign corporations.*— Whether or not a domestic corporation is formed or availed of principally for the holding, directly or indirectly, of stock of one or more foreign corporations shall be determined on the basis of all the facts and circumstances of each particular case. [Reg. § 1.1248-6.]

☐ [T.D. 6779, 12-21-64.]

§ 1.1248-7. Taxpayer to establish earnings and profits and foreign taxes.—(a) *In general.*—(1) *Earnings and profits.*—If a taxpayer sells or exchanges stock in a foreign corporation which was a controlled foreign corporation and the Commissioner determines that the taxpayer has not established the amount of the earnings and profits of the corporation attributable to the stock under § 1.1248-2 or § 1.1248-3, whichever is applicable, all the gain from such sale or exchange shall be treated as a dividend under section 1248(a). See section 1248(g). A taxpayer shall be considered to have established such amount if—

(i) He attaches to his income tax return, filed on or before the last day prescribed by law (including extensions thereof) for his taxable year in which he sold or exchanged the stock, the schedule prescribed by paragraph (b) of this section or, if such last day is before April 1, 1965, he files such schedule before such date with the district director with whom such return was filed, and

(ii) He establishes in the manner prescribed by paragraph (d) of this section the correctness of each amount shown on such schedule.

(2) Notwithstanding an omission of information from, or an error with respect to an amount shown on, the schedule referred to in subparagraph (1)(i) of this paragraph, a taxpayer shall be considered to have complied with such subparagraph (1)(i) if—

(i) He establishes that such omission or error was inadvertent, or due to reasonable cause and not due to willful neglect, and that he has substantially complied with the requirements of this section, and

(ii) The taxpayer corrects such omission or error at the time when he complies with paragraph (d) of this section.

(3) For the requirement to establish the amount of foreign taxes to be taken into account for purposes of section 1248(b), see paragraph (c) of this section.

(b) *Schedule attached to return.*—(1) The taxpayer shall attach to his income tax return for his taxable year in which he sold or exchanged the stock, a schedule showing his name, address, and identifying number. Except to the extent provided in paragraph (e) of this section, the schedule shall also show the amount of the earnings and profits attributable under paragraph (a) of § 1.1248-2 or paragraph (a) of § 1.1248-3 (as the case may be) to the stock, and, in order to support the computation of such amount, any additional information required by subparagraphs (2), (3), (4), and (5) of this paragraph.

(2) The schedule shall also show for the first tier corporation, and for each lower tier corporation as to which information is required under subparagraph (4) of this paragraph, (i) the name of the corporation, (ii) the country under whose laws the corporation is created or organized, and (iii) the last day of the taxable year which the corporation regularly uses in computing its income.

(3) If the amount of earnings and profits attributable to a block of stock sold or exchanged are computed under § 1.1248-2, the schedule shall also show—

(i) For each taxable year of the corporation, beginning after December 31, 1962, during the period the taxpayer held (or was considered to have held by reason of the application of section 1223) the block, (*a*) the earnings and profits accumulated for each such taxable year computed under paragraph (d) of § 1.1248-2, and (*b*) the sum thereof computed under paragraph (e)(1)(i) and (2) of § 1.1248-2,

(ii) The number of shares in the block and the total number of shares of the corporation outstanding during such period,

(iii) If during the period the person held (or is considered to have held by reason of the application of section 1223) the block any amount was included under section 951 in the gross income of such person (or another person) in respect of the block, the computation of the excess referred to in paragraph (e)(3)(ii) of § 1.1248-2, and

(iv) If the amount of earnings and profits of a lower tier corporation attributable to the block are computed under paragraph (a)(3) of § 1.1248-2, (*a*) the number of shares in the lower tier corporation which the taxpayer owns within the meaning of section 958(a)(2), (*b*) the total number of shares of such lower tier corporation outstanding during such period, and (*c*) in respect of such lower tier corporation, the information prescribed in subdivisions (i) and (iii) of this subparagraph.

(4) If the amount of earnings and profits attributable to a share (or block) sold or exchanged are computed under § 1.1248-3, the schedule shall also show for each taxable year of the corporation beginning after December 31, 1962, any day of which falls in a period or periods the taxpayer held (or was considered to have held by reason of the application of section 1223) the stock while the corporation was a controlled foreign corporation—

(i) The number of days in such period or periods, but only if such number is less than the total number of days in such taxable year,

(ii) The earnings and profits accumulated for the taxable year computed under paragraph (b) of § 1.1248-3,

(iii) The number of shares in the corporation outstanding, or deemed under paragraph (c)(2) of § 1.1248-3 to be outstanding, on each day of the taxable year,

(iv) The taxpayer's tentative ratable share computed under paragraph (c) or (d) (as the case may be) of § 1.1248-3,

(v) The amount of, and a short description of each adjustment to, the tentative ratable share under paragraph (e) of § 1.1248-3, and

(vi) The amount of the ratable share referred to in paragraph (e)(1) of § 1.1248-3.

(5) In respect of a taxable year referred to in subparagraph (4) of this paragraph of a first tier corporation, if the taxpayer is required to compute under paragraph (f)(5) of § 1.1248-3 his ratable share of the earnings and profits for a taxable year of the lower tier corporation attributable to such taxable year of such first tier corporation, then for such taxable year of the lower tier corporation the schedule shall show—

(i) The earnings and profits accumulated for the taxable year of the lower tier corporation, computed under paragraph (b) of § 1.1248-3,

(ii) Each percentage described in paragraph (f)(2)(ii), (iii), and (iv) of § 1.1248-3,

(iii) The amount of the taxpayer's tentative ratable share computed under paragraph (f)(2) or (4) (as the case may be) of § 1.1248-3,

(iv) The amount of, and a short description of each adjustment to, the tentative ratable share under paragraph (f)(5) of § 1.1248-3, and

(v) The amount of the ratable share referred to in paragraph (f)(5)(i) of § 1.1248-3.

(c) *Foreign taxes.*—(1) If the taxpayer fails to establish any portion of the amount of any foreign taxes which he is required to establish by subparagraph (2) of this paragraph, then such portion shall not be taken into account under section 1248(b)(1)(B).

(2) The taxpayer shall establish in respect of the stock he sells or exchanges the amount of the foreign taxes described in section 1248(b)(1)(B) paid by the first tier corporation for each taxable year of such corporation for which the information is required under paragraph (b)(3) or (4) of this section, and the amount of such taxes paid by each lower tier corporation for each taxable year (as to which information is required under paragraph (b)(3)(iv) or (5) of this section) of each such lower tier corporation. A taxpayer shall be considered to have established the amount of such foreign taxes if—

(i) He attaches to the schedule described in paragraph (b) of this section a sup-

Reg. § 1.1248-7(c)(2)(i)

plementary schedule which, except to the extent provided in paragraph (e) of this section, sets forth the amount of such foreign taxes for each taxable year (of the first tier corporation and of each such lower tier corporation) as to which such amount must be established under this subparagraph, and

(ii) He establishes in the manner prescribed by paragraph (d)(2) of this section the correctness of each amount shown on such supplementary schedule.

(d) *Establishing amounts on schedules.*—(1) A taxpayer shall be considered to have established, in respect of the stock he sold or exchanged, the correctness of an amount shown on a schedule described in paragraph (b) of this section only if he produces or provides within 180 days after demand by the district director (or within such longer period to which such director consents)—

(i) The books of original entry, or similar systematic accounting records maintained by any person or persons on a current basis as supplements to such books, which establish to the satisfaction of the district director the correctness of each such amount, and

(ii) In respect of any such books or records which are not in the English language, either an accurate English translation of any such records as are demanded, or the services of a qualified interpreter satisfactory to such director.

(2) A shareholder shall be considered to have established in respect of such stock the correctness of an amount shown on a supplementary schedule described in paragraph (c) of this section only if he produces or provides within 180 days after demand by the district director (or within such longer period to which such director consents)—

(i) Evidence described in paragraph (a)(2) of § 1.905-2 of such amount, or

(ii) Secondary evidence of such amount, in the same manner and to the same extent as would be permissible under paragraph (b) of § 1.905-2 in the case of a taxpayer who claimed the benefits of the foreign tax credit in respect of such amount.

(e) *Insufficient information at time return is filed.*—If stock in a foreign corporation, which was a controlled foreign corporation, is sold or exchanged by a taxpayer during a taxable year of the corporation (or of a lower tier corporation) which ends after the last day of the taxpayer's taxable year in which the sale or exchange occurs, and if—

(1) For the taxpayer's taxable year, the last day referred to in paragraph (a)(1) of this section for filing his income tax return with a schedule prescribed in paragraph (b) of this section, and, if applicable, with a supplemental schedule prescribed in paragraph (c) of this section, or

(2) The last day referred to in paragraph (a)(1) of this section (that is, April 1, 1965) for filing any such schedule or schedules with the district director with whom such return was filed,

is not later than 90 days after the close of such taxable year of any such corporation, then such return with such schedule or schedules may be filed, or any such schedule or schedules may be filed, on the basis of estimates of amounts or percentages (for any such taxable year of any such corporation) required to be shown on any such schedule or schedules. If any such estimate differs from the actual amount or percentage, the taxpayer shall, within 90 days after the close of any such taxable year of any such corporation, file (or attach to a claim for refund or amended return filed) at the office of the district director with whom he filed the return a new schedule or schedules showing the actual amounts or percentages. [Reg. § 1.1248-7.]

☐ [*T.D.* 6779, 12-21-64.]

§ 1.1249-1. **Gain from certain sales or exchanges of patents, etc., to foreign corporations.**—(a) *General rule.*—Section 1249 provides that if gain is recognized from the sale or exchange after December 31, 1962, of a patent, an invention, model, or design (whether or not patented), a copyright, a secret formula or process, or any other similar property right (not including property such as goodwill, a trademark, or a trade brand) to any foreign corporation by any United States person (as defined in section 7701(a)(30)) which controls such foreign corporation, and if such gain would (but for the provisions of section 1249) be gain from the sale or exchange of a capital asset or of property described in section 1231, then such gain shall be considered as gain from the sale or exchange of property which is neither a capital asset nor property described in section 1231. Section 1249 applies only to gain recognized in taxable years beginning after December 31, 1962.

(b) *Control.*—For purposes of paragraph (a) of this section, the term "control" means, with respect to any foreign corporation, the ownership, directly or indirectly, of stock possessing more than 50 percent of the total combined voting power of all classes of stock entitled to vote. For purposes of the preceding sentence, the rules for determining ownership of stock provided by section 958(a) and (b), and the principles for determining percentage of total combined voting power owned by United States shareholders provided by paragraphs (b) and (c) of § 1.957-1, shall apply. [Reg. § 1.1249-1.]

☐ [*T.D.* 6765, 11-2-64.]

Passive Foreign Investment Companies

§ 1.1291-1. Taxation of U.S. persons that are shareholders of section 1291 funds.—(a) and (b) [Reserved].

(c) *Coordination with other PFIC rules.*

(1) and (2) [Reserved].

(3) *Coordination with section 1296: distributions and dispositions.*—If PFIC stock is marked to market under section 1296 for any taxable year, then, except as provided in § 1.1296-1(i), section 1291 and the regulations thereunder shall not apply to any distribution with respect to section 1296 stock (as defined in § 1.1296-1(a)(2)), or to any disposition of such stock, for such taxable year.

(4) *Coordination with mark to market rules under chapter 1 of the Internal Revenue Code other than section 1296.*—(i) *In general.*—If PFIC stock is marked to market for any taxable year under section 475 or any other provision of chapter 1 of the Internal Revenue Code, other than section 1296, regardless of whether the application of such provision is mandatory or results from an election by the taxpayer or another person, then, except as provided in paragraph (c)(4)(ii) of this section, section 1291 and the regulations thereunder shall not apply to any distribution with respect to such PFIC stock or to any disposition of such PFIC stock for such taxable year. See §§ 1.1295-1(i)(3) and 1.1296-1(h)(3)(i) for rules regarding the automatic termination of an existing election under section 1295 or section 1296 when a taxpayer marks to market PFIC stock under section 475 or any other provision of chapter 1 of the Internal Revenue Code.

(ii) *Coordination rule.*—(A) Notwithstanding any provision in this section to the contrary, the rule of paragraph (c)(4)(ii)(B) of this section shall apply to the first taxable year in which a United States person marks to market its PFIC stock under a provision of chapter 1 of the Internal Revenue Code, other than section 1296, if such foreign corporation was a PFIC for any taxable year, prior to such first taxable year, during the United States person's holding period (as defined in section 1291(a)(3)(A) and § 1.1296-1(f)) in such stock, and for which such corporation was not treated as a QEF with respect to such United States person.

(B) For the first taxable year of a United States person that marks to market its PFIC stock under any provision of chapter 1 of the Internal Revenue Code, other than section 1296, such United States person shall, in lieu of the rules under which the United States person marks to market, apply the rules of § 1.1296-1(i)(2) and (3) as if the United States person had made an election under section 1296 for such first taxable year.

(d) [Reserved].

(e) *Exempt organization as shareholder.*—(1) *In general.*—If the shareholder of a PFIC is an organization exempt from tax under this chapter, section 1291 and these regulations apply to such shareholder only if a dividend from the PFIC would be taxable to the organization under subchapter F.

(2) *Effective date.*—Paragraph (e)(1) of this section is applicable on and after April 1, 1992.

(f) through (i) [Reserved].

(j) *Effective dates.*—This section applies for taxable years beginning on or after May 3, 2004, except as otherwise provided in paragraph (e)(2) of this section. [Reg. § 1.1291-1.]

☐ [T.D. 8750, 12-31-97. *Redesignated by T.D. 8870, 2-4-2000. Amended by T.D. 9123, 4-30-2004.*]

Proposed Regulation

§ 1.1291-1. Taxation of U.S. persons that are shareholders of section 1291 funds.—(a) *In general.*—A U.S. person that is a shareholder (within the meaning of paragraph (b)(7) of this section) of a section 1291 fund (as defined in paragraph (b)(2)(v) of this section) is subject to the special rules under section 1291 and these regulations with respect to gain recognized on direct and indirect dispositions of stock of the section 1291 fund and upon certain direct and indirect distributions by the section 1291 fund. This section provides definitions and rules applicable to all PFICs and their shareholders. For rules governing the taxation of distributions and dispositions, *see* §§ 1.1291-2 and 1.1291-3, respectively. For rules governing the determination of the deferred tax amount, *see* § 1.1291-4. For rules governing the determination of the foreign tax credit that a shareholder of a section 1291 fund may claim on distributions and certain dispositions, *see* § 1.1291-5. For rules governing the recognition of gain on a direct or indirect disposition of stock of a section 1291 fund notwithstanding an otherwise applicable nonrecognition provision, *see* § 1.1291-6. For guidance for regulated investment companies making a mark-to-market election, *see* § 1.1291-8. For the time and manner of making the deemed sale and dividend elections under section 1291(d)(2), *see* §§ 1.1291-9 and 1.1291-10, respectively.

(b) *Definitions.*—(1) *PFIC.*—(i) *In general.*—A passive foreign investment company (PFIC) is a foreign corporation that satisfies either the income test of section 1296(a)(1) or the asset test of section 1296(a)(2). A corporation will not be treated as a PFIC with respect to a shareholder for those days included in the shareholder's holding period before the shareholder became a United States person within the meaning of section 7701(a)(30).

(ii) *PFIC characterization continued.*—A corporation will be treated as a PFIC with respect to a shareholder even if the corporation satisfies neither the income test nor the asset test of section 1296(a), if the corporation (or its predecessor in a reorganization described in section 368(a)(1)(F)) was a section 1291 fund with respect to the shareholder at any time during the shareholder's holding period of the corporation's stock.

(2) *Types of PFICs.*—(i) *QEF.*—A PFIC is a qualified electing fund (QEF) with respect to a shareholder that has elected under section 1295 to be taxed currently on its share of the PFIC's earnings and profits pursuant to section 1293.

(ii) *Pedigreed QEF.*—A PFIC is a pedigreed QEF with respect to a shareholder if the PFIC has been a QEF with respect to the shareholder for all taxable years that are included wholly or partly in the shareholder's holding period of the PFIC stock and during which the corporation was a PFIC.

(iii) *Unpedigreed QEF.*—A PFIC is an unpedigreed QEF for a taxable year if—

(A) An election under section 1295 is in effect for that year;

(B) The PFIC has been a QEF with respect to the shareholder for at least one, but not all, of the taxable years that are included wholly or partly in the shareholder's holding period of the PFIC stock and during which the corporation was a PFIC; and

(C) The shareholder has not made an election under section 1291(d)(2) and § 1.1291-9 or 1.1291-10 with respect to the PFIC to purge the prior PFIC years from the shareholder's holding period.
For the effect on a shareholder's holding period of an election under section 1291(d)(2), *see* §§ 1.1291-9(f) and 1.1291-10(f).

(iv) *Nonqualified fund.*—A PFIC is a nonqualified fund with respect to a shareholder if the shareholder has not elected under section 1295 to treat the PFIC as a QEF.

(v) *Section 1291 fund.*—A section 1291 fund is an unpedigreed QEF or a nonqualified fund.

(3) *PrePFIC year and day.*—A prePFIC year is a taxable year (or portion thereof) of the shareholder, included in its holding period of the stock of a corporation, during which the corporation was not a PFIC within the meaning of paragraph (b)(1) of this section. A prePFIC day is a day in a prePFIC year of the shareholder. Thus, the days in a taxable year of a shareholder beginning after 1986 that are included in a taxable year of the corporation that began before 1987 are prePFIC days.

(4) *Prior PFIC year and day.*—A prior PFIC year is a taxable year (or portion thereof) of a shareholder, other than the current shareholder year, included in its holding period of stock of a corporation during which the corporation was a section 1291 fund. A prior PFIC day is a day in a prior PFIC year of a shareholder.

(5) *Current shareholder year.*—The current shareholder year is the taxable year of the shareholder in which occurs a distribution by, or disposition of stock of, a section 1291 fund.

(6) *Stock.*—The term stock includes any equity interest in a corporation, without regard to whether there is a certificate or other representation of the equity interest in the corporation. For a rule that treats an option holder as a shareholder of a section 1291 fund, *see* § 1.1291-1(d).

(7) *Shareholder.*—A shareholder is a U.S. person that directly owns stock (as defined in paragraph (b)(6) of this section) of a PFIC, or that is an indirect shareholder (as defined in paragraph (b)(8)(i) of this section). For purposes of these regulations, a partnership or S corporation is treated as a shareholder of a PFIC only for purposes of the information reporting requirements of §§ 1.1291-1(i), 1.1291-2(f)(2)(ii), 1.1291-3(e)(5)(iii), and 1.1291-6(g).

(8) *Indirect shareholder.*—(i) *In general.*—An indirect shareholder of a PFIC is a U.S. person that indirectly owns stock of a PFIC. A person indirectly owns stock if it is treated as owning stock of a corporation owned by another person (the actual owner) under this paragraph (b)(8). In applying this paragraph (b)(8), the determination of a person's indirect ownership is made on the basis of all the facts and circumstances in each case; the substance rather than the form of ownership is controlling, taking into account the purpose of section 1291. *Cf.* § 1.958-1(c)(2).

(ii) *Ownership through a corporation.*—(A) *Ownership through a nonPFIC.*—A person that directly or indirectly owns 50 percent or more in value of the stock of a foreign corporation that is not a PFIC is considered to own a proportionate amount (by value) of any stock owned directly or indirectly by that foreign corporation.

(B) *Ownership through a PFIC.*—A person that directly or indirectly owns stock of a PFIC is considered to own a proportionate amount (by value) of any stock owned directly or indirectly by the PFIC.

(C) *Ownership through a domestic corporation.*—If stock of a section 1291 fund is not treated as owned indirectly by a U.S. person under the rules of paragraph (b)(8) of this section (determined without regard to this paragraph (b)(8)(ii)(C)), but would be treated as owned by a U.S. person if paragraph (b)(8)(ii)(A) of this section applied to domestic corporations as well as foreign corporations, then such stock is considered owned by such U.S. person.

(iii) *Ownership through pass-through entities.*—(A) *Partnerships.*—If a partnership directly or indirectly owns stock, the partners of the partnership are considered to own a proportion of such stock in accordance with their ownership interests in the partnership.

(B) *S corporations.*—If an S corporation directly or indirectly owns stock, each S corporation shareholder is considered to own a proportion of such stock equal to the proportion of the S corporation stock owned by that shareholder.

(C) *Estates and trusts.*—If an estate or trust (other than an employees' trust described in section 401(a) that is exempt from tax under section 501(a)) directly or indirectly owns stock, the beneficiaries of such estate or trust will be considered to own a proportionate amount of such stock.

(c) *Coordination with QEF rules.*—(1) *Pedigreed QEFs.*—Section 1291 and these regulations do not apply to direct and indirect distributions by, and direct and indirect dispositions of stock of, a PFIC that, with respect to the shareholder, is a pedigreed QEF as defined in paragraph (b)(2)(ii) of this section.

(2) *Unpedigreed QEFs.*—Section 1291 and these regulations apply to direct and indirect distributions by, and direct and indirect dispositions of stock of, a PFIC that, with respect to the shareholder, is an unpedigreed QEF, as defined in paragraph (b)(2)(iii) of this section. For the treatment under section 1291 and these regulations of inclusions in income under section 1293(a) and distributions of amounts not includible in income by reason of section 1293(c), *see* § 1.1291-2(b)(2).

(d) *Option holder as shareholder.*—If a U.S. person has an option to acquire stock of a PFIC (other than stock with respect to which the PFIC is a pedigreed QEF), such option is considered to be stock of a section 1291 fund for purposes of applying section 1291 and these regulations to a disposition of the option. For purposes of this paragraph (d), the exercise of an option is not a disposition to which section 1291 applies. For purposes of this paragraph (d), an option to acquire an option, and each one of a series of such options, are considered an option to acquire stock. For the holding period of stock acquired upon the exercise of an option, *see* § 1.1291-1(h)(3).

(e) *Exempt organization as shareholder.*—If the shareholder of a section 1291 fund is an organization exempt from tax under this chapter, section 1291 and these regulations apply to such shareholder only if a dividend from the section 1291 fund would be taxable to the organization under subchapter F.

(f) *Excess distribution from sources within Puerto Rico.*—A deferred tax amount, as defined in § 1.1291-4, will be determined under section 1291 and these regulations on amounts derived from sources within Puerto Rico (within the meaning of section 933(1)) by an individual shareholder who is a bona fide resident of Puerto Rico, but only to the extent such amounts are allocated under § 1.1291-2(e)(2) to a taxable year in the shareholder's holding period during which the shareholder was not entitled to the benefits of section 933.

(g) *Regulated investment companies and real estate investment trusts.*—A regulated investment company, as defined in section 851, and a real estate investment trust, as defined in section 856, that are shareholders of a section 1291 fund are taxable under section 1291 and these regulations on direct or indirect distributions from a section 1291 fund and on direct or indirect dispositions of the stock of a section 1291 fund, and are therefore liable for the deferred tax amount, as defined in section 1291(c) and § 1.1291-4. For a mark-to-market election that may be made by a regulated investment company that is a shareholder of a section 1291 fund, *see* § 1.1291-8.

(h) *Holding period.*—(1) *In general.*—Except as otherwise provided in this paragraph (h), § 1.1291-6(b)(5), 1.1291-9(f), or 1.1291-10(f), a shareholder's holding period of stock of a PFIC is determined under the general rules of the Code and regulations concerning the holding period of stock. The following example illustrates the rule of this paragraph (h)(1).

Example. T purchased the stock of FC, a foreign corporation, on December 31, 1985. FC has qualified as a PFIC since its taxable year beginning January 1, 1987. For purposes of sections 1291 through 1297 and the regulations under those sections, as well as other provisions of the Code and regulations, T's holding period of the FC stock began on January 1, 1986.

(2) *Stock acquired from U.S. decedent or domestic estate.*—For purposes of section 1291 and these regulations, a shareholder's holding period of a share of stock of a PFIC includes the period the share was held by another U.S. person if the shareholder acquired the share by reason of the death of that other U.S. person (the decedent), the PFIC was a section 1291 fund with respect to the decedent, and the decedent did not recognize gain pursuant to § 1.1291-6(c)(2)(iii) (or would not have recognized gain had there been any) on the transfer to the shareholder.

(3) *Stock acquired upon exercise of option.*—The holding period of a share of stock of a PFIC acquired upon the exercise of an option includes the period the option was held. The following example illustrates the rule of this paragraph (h)(3).

Example. X is a domestic corporation that owns all of the stock of Y, a PFIC. On January 1, 1993, X issues a debt instrument to G, a U.S. person. Under the terms of the instrument, G may convert the debt instrument into 20 shares of the stock of Y on any date prior to the maturity date of December 31, 2002. On August 14, 1997, G exercises the conversion right and receives 20 shares of Y stock. Pursuant to § 1.1291-1(h)(3), G's holding period of the Y stock begins at the time of the acquisition of the debt instrument, not at the time of acquisition of the Y stock.

(4) *Stock owned directly and indirectly.*—(i) *In general.*—Except as provided in paragraph (h)(2), (3), (4)(ii), (5), or (6) of this section, 1.1291-6(b)(5), 1.1291-9(f), or 1.1291-10(f), a shareholder's holding period of stock of a PFIC owned indirectly begins on the first day that a shareholder is considered to own stock of the PFIC (or of another PFIC that was a predecessor of that PFIC) under § 1.1291-1(b)(8). If a shareholder has owned a share of stock of a PFIC both directly and indirectly, the shareholder's holding period of that share begins on the earlier of—

(A) The first day that the shareholder owned the stock of the PFIC directly; or

(B) The first day that the shareholder was an indirect shareholder with respect to the share of stock of the PFIC (or of another PFIC that was a predecessor of that PFIC).

(ii) *Examples.*—The following examples illustrate the operation of the rule of paragraph (h)(4)(i) of this section.

Example 1. A's holding period of stock of X began on August 14, 1990. X is a corporation that always has been an S corporation. At the time A acquired the X stock, X held stock of FC, a PFIC. For purposes of sections 1291 through 1297, A's holding period of the FC stock began on August 14, 1990, even though X's holding period of that stock began on an earlier day.

Example 2. B, a U.S. person, owns all the stock of FP, a foreign corporation that is not a PFIC; under section 1223, B's holding period of the FP stock began on August 1, 1987. FP owns 50 percent of the stock of FS, a foreign corporation that is not a PFIC; FP's holding period of the FS stock began on December 13, 1987. FS owns 10 percent of FC, a PFIC; under section 1223, FS's holding period of the FC stock began on November 20, 1986. For purposes of section 1291, B's holding period of the FC stock began on December 13, 1987, the first day that ownership of the FC stock is attributed to B under § 1.1291-1(b)(8).

(iii) *Section 1291 fund stock held by former C corporation.*—For purposes of § 1.1291-2(e)(2)(i), if an S corporation's holding period of stock of a section 1291 fund includes any period during which the S corporation was a C corporation, the S corporation shareholder's holding period is the S corporation's holding period of such stock.

(5) *New holding period.*—If a shareholder recognizes all of the gain realized on a direct or indirect disposition of stock of a section 1291 fund, within the meaning of § 1.1291-3(c), (d), or (e), but continues to be a shareholder with respect to such stock immediately after such disposition, the shareholder's holding period for such stock will be treated as beginning on the day after the disposition. For an illustration of this rule as applied to a disposition pursuant to § 1.1291-3(d) (regarding pledged stock), *see* § 1.1291-3(d)(7), *Example 1.*

(6) *Stock transferred to a member of a consolidated return group.*—For the holding period of stock of a section 1291 fund transferred from one member of a consolidated return group to

another member of the group for purposes of § 1.1291-2(e)(2)(i), see § 1.1291-3(f).

(7) *PFIC character of holding period.*—(i) *In general.*—If a shareholder's holding period of stock of a PFIC includes a period described in section 1223(1), the character of the days in such latter period as prePFIC or prior PFIC days is determined by reference to the character of those days in the shareholder's holding period immediately prior to the exchange. If a shareholder's holding period of stock of a PFIC includes a period described in section 1223(2), the character of the days in such latter period as prePFIC or prior PFIC days is determined by reference to the character, immediately prior to the transfer, of those days in the holding period of the person from whom the stock was acquired.

(ii) *Anti-avoidance rule.*—If a shareholder's holding period of stock of a PFIC includes a period described in section 1223(1), the character of the days in such latter period will be deemed to be prior PFIC days if a purpose for the exchange described in section 1223(1) was avoidance of the interest charge rules under section 1291.

(i) *Annual reporting requirements.*—Except as otherwise provided in this paragraph (i), a U.S. person must file annually, with its federal income tax return for that year, a separate Form 8621, Return by a Shareholder of a Passive Foreign Investment Company or Qualified Electing Fund, for each PFIC of which the person is a shareholder during the taxable year. Generally, an S corporation and its shareholders, a domestic partnership and its partners that are U.S. persons, and a domestic trust or estate and its beneficiaries that are U.S. persons considered to own stock of a PFIC under § 1.1291-1(b)(8)(iii)(C), must file Form 8621 annually. However, an S corporation shareholder, a partner, or beneficiary is not required to file Form 8621 for its taxable year in which ends the taxable year of the S corporation, partnership, trust or estate if—

(1) The S corporation, partnership, trust or estate files Form 8621; and

(2) The S corporation shareholder, partner, or beneficiary does not have to include any amount in income under section 1291 or 1293, report a nonrecognition transfer pursuant to § 1.1291-6(g), or report the status of a section 1294 election.

If a U.S. person is not required to file an income tax return or other return for the taxable year during which it was a direct or indirect shareholder of a PFIC, the shareholder files Form 8621 with the Philadelphia Service Center, P.O. 21086, Philadelphia, PA 19114, on or before the 15th day of the fourth month after the close of the shareholder's taxable year. For special reporting requirements for direct and indirect dispositions entitled to nonrecognition treatment under § 1.1291-6, see § 1.1291-6(g).

(j) *Effective date.*—(1) *In general.*—Except as otherwise provided in this paragraph (j), §§ 1.1291-1 through 1.1291-9 and the new parts of § 1.1291-10 are effective on April 11, 1992. However, sections 1291 through 1297, inclusive, are effective for taxable years of foreign corporations beginning after December 31, 1986. Accordingly, shareholders of PFICs are subject to sections 1291 through 1297 with respect to transactions occurring within those taxable years. Shareholders of section 1291 funds, in determining their liability under sections 1291 through 1297 during those years, must apply reasonable interpretations of the statute and legislative history and employ reasonable methods to preserve the interest charge.

(2) *Section 1.1291-3(d)(6).*—For purposes of applying section 1297(b)(6), concerning a disposition resulting from the use of PFIC stock as security for a loan, the transition rule provided in § 1.1291-3(d)(6) is effective for taxable years of foreign corporations beginning after 1986.

(3) *Section 1.1291-8.*—Section 1.1291-8 is effective for taxable years of RICs ending after [*INSERT DATE OF PUBLICATION OF THIS DOCUMENT AS A FINAL REGULATION*].
[Prop. Reg. § 1.1291-1.]

[Proposed 4-1-92.]

Proposed Regulation

§ 1.1291-2. Taxation of distributions by section 1291 funds.—(a) *In general.*—Notwithstanding section 301 and the regulations under that section, a shareholder is subject to the rules of section 1291, this section, and § 1.1291-4 with respect to a distribution (including an indirect distribution as defined in paragraph (f) of this section) by a section 1291 fund, if any portion of such distribution is an excess distribution. An excess distribution is defined in paragraph (c)(1) of this section. Under paragraph (e)(2)(i) of this section, the excess distribution is allocated ratably over the shareholder's holding period of the stock of the section 1291 fund. The portions of the excess distribution allocated to the current shareholder year and to prePFIC years are included in the shareholder's gross income as ordinary income in the current shareholder year under paragraph (e)(2)(ii) of this section. The portions of the excess distribution allocated to prior PFIC years are not included in the shareholder's gross income pursuant to paragraph (e)(2)(iii) of this section. Instead, the shareholder incurs tax plus interest (the deferred tax amount) on those portions of the excess distribution, as provided in § 1.1291-4.

(b) *Distribution.*—(1) *In general.*—For purposes of section 1291 and these regulations, unless otherwise provided in this paragraph (b), a distribution is any actual or constructive transfer of money or property by a section 1291 fund with respect to its stock. For example, a distribution includes a transfer of stock taxable pursuant to section 305(b) and (c), a transfer in redemption of stock taxable under section 301 pursuant to section 302(d), and an amount treated as a dividend under section 78. A distribution, however, does not include a transfer that qualifies under section 305(a) or 355(a). Transfers with respect to stock that are treated as dispositions of the stock under § 1.1291-3 are not treated as distributions under this section. For transfers with respect to stock (including transfers that qualify under section 355(a)) that are treated as dispositions, *see* § 1.1291-3.

(2) *Coordination with current inclusion rules.*—(i) *Deemed dividend or income inclusions; distributions of previously taxed amounts.*—Amounts included in gross income under section 551(a), 951(a), or 1293(a), and transfers of amounts not included in gross income by reason of section 551(d), 959, or 1293(c), are not treated as distributions for purposes of this section. The following example illustrates the rule of this paragraph (b)(2)(i).

Example. USP, a domestic corporation, purchased in 1989 10 percent of the stock of FC, a section 1291 fund that also is a CFC. Both USP and FC use the calendar year as their taxable year. In 1989, USP, pursuant to section 951(a)(1), included in income $100 of subpart F income of FC, none of which was distributed in 1989. The $100 of subpart F income is not treated as a distribution taxable under section 1291. In 1990, FC did not have any subpart F income. In that year, FC distributed $200 to USP. Of the $200 distribution, $100 had been previously taxed to USP. Because $100 of the $200 distribution is not included in gross income by reason of section 959, pursuant to § 1.1291-2(b)(2) that amount is not treated as a distribution for purposes of § 1.1291-2(c)(2)(i). Therefore, the total distribution, for purposes of calculating the excess distribution for 1990, is $100.

(ii) *Other rules.*—For treatment of amounts that would be taxable in the same taxable year under section 951(a) or 1293(a) and section 1291, *see* §§ 1.1291-2(f)(3) and 1.1291-3(e)(4)(ii).

(3) *Section 304 transactions.*—(i) *In general.*—If, in a transaction described in section 304(a), the issuing corporation is a section 1291 fund, any amount treated as paid out of the earnings and profits of such section 1291 fund by virtue of section 304(b)(2) is treated as an excess distribution by such fund for purposes of section 1291 and this section. In addition, the transfer of the stock of such fund will be treated as a disposition to which §§ 1.1291-3 and 1.1291-6 apply. If, in a transaction described in section 304(a), the acquiring corporation is a section 1291 fund, any amount paid by such corporation to the transferor is treated as a distribution by such fund (notwithstanding the provisions of section 304(b)(2)), and the transferor is treated for purposes of section 1291 and this section as the owner of any stock of the fund that it owns directly or constructively under section 304(c). The following example illustrates the rule of this paragraph (b)(3)(i).

Example. USP, a domestic corporation, owns all the stock of FS1 and FS2. FS1 and FS2 each have accumulated earnings and profits of $100 that were not previously taxed under any other section of the Code. FS1, but not FS2, is a PFIC. USP has not elected under section 1295 to treat FS1 as a QEF. However, USP plans to make a section 1295 election to treat FS1 as a QEF, as well as the deemed dividend election under section 1291(d)(2)(B) to purge USP's holding period of the FS1 stock of its prior PFIC years. Before it makes those elections, USP plans to sell the stock of FS1 to FS2 for its fair market value of $200. The transfer of the FS1 stock to FS2 is a transaction to which section 304 applies. Section 304(b)(2) provides that $100 of the $200 payment to USP is treated as paid directly by FS1 out of its earnings and profits. Pursuant to § 1.1291-2(b)(3)(i), the $100 distribution to USP is taxable as an excess distribution. The transfer will not be a taxable disposition under § 1.1291-3 because USP's interest in FS1 is not reduced as a result of the transfer. *See* section 304(a)(1) and § 1.1291-6(c)(1)(i).

(ii) *Limitation.*—[Reserved]

(c) *Excess distribution and nonexcess distribution.*—(1) *Excess distribution.*—An excess distribution is that portion of any direct or indirect distribution with respect to a share of stock of a section 1291 fund during the current shareholder year that is the ratable portion (as defined in paragraph (c)(4) of this section) of the total excess distribution (as defined in paragraph (c)(3) of this section), if any. Except as provided in § 1.1291-5, an excess distribution and the taxation thereof are determined without regard to the amount or character of the earnings and profits of the section 1291 fund. Except as provided in paragraph (d)(2) of this section (concerning shares of stock having the same holding period), the excess distribution is calculated separately for each share of stock held.

(2) *Nonexcess distribution.*—(i) *In general.*—A nonexcess distribution with respect to a share of section 1291 stock is the portion of the total amount of all distributions during the current shareholder year with respect to the share that does not exceed 125 percent of the average amount of the distributions with respect to the share during the three taxable years of the shareholder's holding period (or during the lesser number of taxable years in the shareholder's holding period) that immediately precede the current shareholder year. Distributions in any of the preceding three (or fewer) taxable years of the shareholder included in the shareholder's holding period that began before 1987 are included in determining the nonexcess distribution.

(ii) *Amount not included in income.*—The portion of an excess distribution in a prior taxable year that was not included in income pursuant to § 1.1291-2 (e)(2)(iii) is not treated as a distribution in that prior year for purposes of paragraph (c)(2)(i) or (iii) of this section. For an illustration of the rule of this paragraph (c)(2)(ii), *see* paragraph (e)(4), *Example 1*, of this section.

(iii) *Distributions received by predecessors.*—If a shareholder's holding period of the stock of a section 1291 fund includes the period the stock was held by another person, distributions made during the holding period of such other person with respect to the stock will be treated as if they had been received by the shareholder for purposes of paragraph (c)(2)(i) of this section.

(3) *Total excess distribution.*—(i) *In general.*—The total excess distribution with respect to a share of stock of a section 1291 fund is the excess, if any, of—

(A) The total amount of all distributions during the current shareholder year with respect to the share, over

(B) The nonexcess distribution with respect to that stock.

(ii) *Exception.*—Notwithstanding paragraph (c)(3)(i) of this section, the total excess distribution is zero for the taxable year of the shareholder in which the shareholder's holding period of the stock begins. The following example illustrates the rule of this paragraph (c)(3)(ii).

Example. On January 1, 1989, X, a U.S. person, gave his son Y, also a U.S. person, one share of stock of FC, a section 1291 fund, that X had purchased in 1986. Y purchased another share of FC stock on January 3, 1989. Y did not make the section 1295 election with respect to FC. In 1989, FC distributed $100 for each outstanding share of its stock. Pursuant to § 1.1291-2(c)(3)(ii), no portion of the distribution in respect of the share Y purchased in 1989 is treated as an excess distribution. However, the distribution paid to Y with respect to the stock given to him by his father may be wholly or partly an excess distribution. Although Y first held that share of FC stock in 1989, Y's holding period includes the period X held that share of stock, as provided in section 1223(2), and therefore does not begin in 1989.

(4) *Ratable portion.*—The total excess distribution is allocated ratably to each distribution received with respect to a share of stock during the current shareholder year. A distribution's ratable portion of the total excess distribution is the product of the total excess distribution and the ratio of the distribution to the total distribution with respect to the share of stock during the current shareholder year. Each ratable portion of the total excess distribution is an excess distribution.

(d) *Special rules.*—The following rules apply for purposes of calculating the nonexcess distribution and the total excess distribution—

(1) *Stock acquired during the year.*—In general, a distribution in a prior taxable year with respect to a share of stock may only be taken into account in determining a nonexcess distribution under paragraph (c)(2)(i) of this section if the shareholder was a shareholder at the time of such distribution, or the distribution was received by a person whose holding period of the stock is included in the shareholder's holding period. However, with respect to a prior taxable year during which a person became a shareholder, the shareholder may instead take into account the total amount (or portion thereof) that the shareholder determines was actually paid by the section 1291 fund with respect to that share of stock during that taxable year. No other annualization rule will apply under section 1291(b)(3)(C). The following example illustrates the rule of this paragraph (d)(1).

Example. R, a U.S. person, became an indirect shareholder of one share of FC stock on August 1, 1991. R did not elect under section 1295 to treat FC, a PFIC, as a QEF. R and FC both use the calendar year as their taxable years. R determines, based on dividend information provided in FC's 1991 annual report, that FC distributed $100 with respect to each outstanding share of its stock at the end of each quarter during that year. For purposes of calculating nonexcess distributions in 1992, 1993, and 1994, R may treat $400 as the amount received in 1991. If R had been unable to determine the amount distributed in 1991 before August 1, the 1991 distribution would have been limited to the $200 actually distributed after August 1 with respect to the one share of FC stock attributed to R.

(2) *Calculations for shares with same holding period.*—The calculation of the nonexcess distribution and the total excess distribution may be made on an aggregate basis for shares of stock having the same holding period (block of stock). The following example illustrates the rule of this paragraph (d)(2).

Example. (i) *Facts.* X, a U.S. person that is a calendar year taxpayer, owns 12 shares of stock of FC, a PFIC. X has not elected under section 1295 to treat FC as a QEF. X acquired two of the 12 shares on December 31, 1986 (Block #1), four shares on December 31, 1987 (Block #2), and six shares on December 31, 1988 (Block #3). On June 30 of 1987 and 1988, FC distributed $10 in respect of each outstanding share of its stock; no portion of either distribution was an excess distribution. On June 30, 1989, FC distributed $30 in respect of each outstanding share of its stock. For purposes of determining the taxation of the 1989 distribution, the excess distribution may be calculated for each of the three blocks of stock held by X instead of on a share-by-share basis.

(ii) *Block #1 excess distribution.* The nonexcess distribution for Block #1 is $25 (125% times $20 [($20 + $20)/2]). The total excess distribution for Block #1 is $35 ($60 - $25).

(iii) *Block #2 excess distribution.* The nonexcess distribution for Block #2 is $50 (125% × $40, the distribution made in the only preceding taxable year in the holding period of the Block #2 shares). The total excess distribution for Block #2 is $70 ($120 - $50).

(iv) *Block #3.* There is no excess distribution with respect to the Block #3 stock because the first taxable year of the holding period of that block of stock is 1989, the taxable year of the distribution.

(3) *Effect of nontaxable distribution or exchange.*—(i) *Tax-free distributions of stock.*—A distribution with respect to a share of stock, made during the shareholder's holding period for the share but before a distribution of stock under section 305(a) with respect to that share, will be treated ratably as a distribution with respect to the shares in the block of stock composed of the original share and the shares distributed with respect to that share pursuant to the stock distribution.

(ii) *Nontaxable exchange of stock.*—Distributions with respect to stock include distributions with respect to stock exchanged therefor in a nonrecognition transfer in which gain was not recognized pursuant to § 1.1291-6(c).

(iii) *Example.*—The following example illustrates the rule of paragraph (d)(3) of this section.

Example. On December 31, 1985, X, a U.S. person, purchased one share of stock of FC, a corporation. FC has been a section 1291 fund with respect to X since FC's taxable year that began January 1, 1987. In both 1986 and 1987, FC distributed $6 with respect to each share of its stock. FC transferred all its assets and liabilities to F, a PFIC, in a transaction that qualified as a reorganization defined in section 368(a)(1)(C) and that was effective on January 1, 1988. X exchanged his share of FC stock for one share of stock of F in an exchange to which section 354 applied and no gain was recognized pursuant to § 1.1291-6(c)(1). On December 31, 1988, F distributed $3 with respect to each share of its stock. No part of the 1986, 1987, and 1988 distributions was an excess distribution. On December 31, 1989, F distributed $10 with respect to each share of its stock. In calculating the total excess distribution for 1989, the $6 distributions paid in 1986 and 1987 by FC with respect to the FC stock held by X, as well as the $3 distribution paid by F in 1988 on the F stock received in exchange for the FC stock, are taken into account. Accordingly, the total excess distribution for 1989 is $3.75 ($10 - [125% × $5 (the average distribution for the three preceding taxable years)]).

(4) *Distributions in a foreign currency.*—(i) *In general.*—Except as provided in paragraph (d)(4)(ii) of this section, the nonexcess distribution and the total excess distribution are determined in U.S. dollars. Each distribution that must be taken into account for purposes of the calculation is translated into the U.S. dollar at the spot rate (within the meaning of § 1.988-1T (d)) on the date on which such distribution was made. The following example illustrates the rule of this paragraph (d)(4)(i).

Example. USP, a domestic corporation, purchased on December 31, 1986, five percent of the stock of FC, a country X corporation that is a section 1291 fund with respect to USP. The functional currency of FC is the "LC", the currency of country X. FC made no distributions during 1987. FC distributed $100 to USP on August 1, 1988; LC20 on November 20, 1989; and 100 units of country Y currency on December 13, 1990. In order to calculate the 1989 and 1990 excess distributions, USP must convert the 1989 distribution of LC20 into U.S. dollars at the spot rate on November 20, 1989, and the 1990 distribution of 100 units of country Y cur-

Prop. Reg. § 1.1291-2(d)(2)

rency into U.S. dollars at the spot rate on December 13, 1990.

(ii) *Exception.*—If all distributions that must be taken into account for purposes of calculating the nonexcess distribution and the total excess distribution for the current shareholder year were made in a single currency (other than the U.S. dollar), the nonexcess distribution and total excess distribution will be determined in the currency in which the distributions were made. Each ratable portion of a total excess distribution determined in a foreign currency is translated into U.S. dollars at the spot rate on the date of the distribution to which the ratable portion is allocated.

(5) *Adjustments for section 642(c) charitable deduction.*—(i) *In general.*—A trust that is permitted to deduct the amount of its fixed annual charitable obligation from gross income pursuant to section 642(c)(1) (the section 642(c) deduction) generally may adjust an excess distribution from a section 1291 fund as provided in this paragraph (d)(5) by the amount of the section 642(c) deduction. Except as otherwise provided in this paragraph (d)(5), the trust may adjust an excess distribution if, in satisfaction of its fixed annual obligation, it distributes—

(A) amounts received from the section 1291 fund;

(B) the stock of a section 1291 fund; or

(C) the proceeds from the sale thereof, to an organization described in section 170(c), as required under the terms of the governing instrument of the trust.

The adjustment provided in this paragraph (d)(5) is limited to the amount of the trust's fixed annual charitable obligation.

(ii) *Exception.*—This paragraph (d)(5) does not apply to a grantor of a trust if the grantor deducted from income, as provided in section 170(f)(2)(B), the value of an interest in any share of stock of the section 1291 fund upon its transfer to the trust.

(iii) *Adjustments.*—(A) *Corpus consisting only of section 1291 fund stock.*—Where the assets of the trust consist only of stock of one or more section 1291 funds, the section 642(c) deduction first reduces the nonexcess distributions, if any, determined under paragraph (c)(2)(i) of this section. The amount of the section 642(c) deduction remaining after reduction of the nonexcess distributions reduces the portions of the excess distributions allocated to the prePFIC and current shareholder years. Finally, the amount of the section 642(c) deduction remaining after the prior two reductions reduces pro rata the portions of the excess distributions allocated to the prior PFIC years. The deferred tax amount, as defined in §1.1291-4, is determined with respect to the adjusted allocations of the excess distributions.

(B) *Corpus consisting of section 1291 fund stock and other property.*—(1) *Income from both section 1291 fund stock and other property.*—A distribution of income in satisfaction of a fixed annual charitable obligation is treated as distributed out of income, if any, derived from the trust property other than the stock of a section 1291 fund to the extent thereof, before being treated as distributed out of amounts received from a section 1291 fund. An adjustment will be permitted in the manner provided in paragraph (d)(5)(iii)(A) of this section only after the deduction permitted under section 642(c) has reduced income from other property to zero.

(2) *Use of corpus to satisfy obligation.*—The trust will not be entitled to the adjustment permitted under this paragraph (d)(5) if the trust uses stock of a section 1291 fund instead of its other property to satisfy its fixed annual charitable obligation.

(6) *PFIC for part of current shareholder year.*—This paragraph (d)(6) applies if the section 1291 fund first qualified as a PFIC for its taxable year beginning after the first day of the current shareholder year and therefore is a section 1291 fund for only a portion of the current shareholder year. Distributions during the portion of the current shareholder year before the corporation qualified as a PFIC are taken into account for purposes of calculating the nonexcess distribution and the total excess distribution. However, those distributions are taxable under the general rules applicable to distributions by a corporation to its shareholder with respect to its stock, notwithstanding that a ratable portion thereof may be an excess distribution within the meaning of paragraph (c)(1) of this section. The following example illustrates the rule of this paragraph (d)(6).

Example. X, a U.S. person, purchased one share of stock of FC, a corporation, on December 31, 1986. X uses the calendar year as its taxable year; FC's taxable year ends November 30. FC first qualified as a PFIC for its taxable year that began December 1, 1990. X did not elect under section 1295 to treat FC as a QEF. X received a distribution of $100 in 1987, but did not receive another distribution from FC until August 1, 1990, when FC distributed $100 per share. On December 13, 1990, FC made another $100 per share distribution. The August distribution is taken into account for purposes of calculating the nonexcess distribution and total excess distribution for 1990 and the ratable portion of the December 13 distribution that is an excess distribution. However, pursuant to § 1.1291-2(d)(6), the August distribution is not subject to section 1291 notwithstanding that a ratable portion of that distribution is an excess distribution within the meaning of § 1.1291-2(c)(1). The August distribution is included in X's 1990 gross income to the extent provided in section 301(c).

(e) *Taxation of a distribution and effect on earnings and profits.*—(1) *Nonexcess distribution.*—A nonexcess distribution, as defined in paragraph (c)(2)(i) of this section, is taxable to a shareholder according to the general rules of taxation applicable to distributions made by a corporation to a shareholder with respect to its stock. *See, e.g.*, section 301 and the regulations under that section.

(2) *Excess distribution.*—(i) *In general.*—To determine the taxation of an excess distribution, the excess distribution is first allocated pro rata to each day in the shareholder's holding period (as determined under § 1.1291-1(h)) of the share of stock with respect to which the distribution was made. The holding period of a share of stock of a section 1291 fund is treated as ending on (and including) the date of each excess distribution solely for purposes of allocating the excess distribution.

(ii) *Allocations included in income.*—The portions of an excess distribution allocated to prePFIC years and the current shareholder year are included in the shareholder's gross income for the current shareholder year as ordinary income.

(iii) *Allocations not included in income.*—The portions of an excess distribution allocated to prior PFIC years are not included in the shareholder's gross income for purposes of this title. These amounts are subject to the deferred tax amount. The deferred tax amount is an additional liability of the shareholder for tax and interest for the current shareholder year. For the calculation of the deferred tax amount and the foreign tax credit that may be taken to reduce the deferred tax amount, *see* §§ 1.1291-4 and 1.1291-5.

(3) *Allocation of earnings and profits.*—For purposes of determining the taxation of a nonexcess distribution and calculating the foreign tax credit under § 1.1291-5, the earnings and profits of a section 1291 fund are allocated proportionately between the nonexcess distribution (as defined in paragraph (c)(2)(i) of this section) and the total excess distribution (as defined in paragraph (c)(3) of this section) and reduced (but not below zero) by the amounts thereof.

(4) *Examples.*—The following examples illustrate the operation of paragraphs (c), (d), and (e) of this section.

Example 1. (i) *Facts.* X, a U.S. person, purchased a share of stock of FC, a corporation, on December 31, 1985. FC has been a section 1291 fund since its taxable year that began January 1, 1987. X received distributions from FC of $50 on December 31, 1987, $80 on December 31, 1988, and $150 on December 31, 1989. FC made no distributions in 1986.

(ii) *1987 excess distribution.* Because X did not receive a distribution from FC during 1986, the only preceding taxable year in its holding period, the total distribution of $50 is the total excess distribution for 1987. That amount is allocated pro rata over X's two-year holding period, as provided in § 1.1291-2(e)(2)(i): $25 is allocated to 1986, a prePFIC year, and $25 to 1987, the current shareholder year. The entire $50 therefore is included in X's gross income for 1987 as ordinary income.

(iii) *1988 excess distribution.* In 1988, of the $80 total distribution, $31.25 (125% × $25 [(0 + $50) / 2]) is the nonexcess distribution, and is taxable as a corporate distribution as provided in section 301(c). The total excess distribution for 1988, $48.75 ($80 − $31.25), is allocated over X's three-year holding period; $16.25 is allocated to each year. The portions of the excess distribution allocated to the prePFIC year (1986) and the current shareholder year (1988) total $32.50; that amount is included in X's gross income as ordinary income. The $16.25 portion of the excess distribution allocated to 1987, the prior PFIC year, is not included in X's gross income, but is subject to the deferred tax amount. Of the $80 distribution, $63.75 ($31.25 +$32.50) is included in X's gross income in 1988.

(iv) *1989 excess distribution.* In 1989, of the $150 total distribution, $47.40 (125% × $37.90 [(0 + $50 + $63.75) / 3]) is the nonexcess distribution, and is taxable as a corporate distribution as provided in section 301(c). The total excess distribution for 1989, $102.60 ($150 −$47.40), is allocated over X's four-year holding period; $25.65 is allocated to each year. The portions of the excess distribution allocated to the prePFIC year (1986) and the current shareholder year (1989) total $51.30; that amount is included in X's gross income as ordinary income. The portions of the excess distribution allocated to the prior PFIC years (1987 and 1988) total $51.30; that amount is not included in X's gross income but is subject to the deferred tax amount. Of the total $150 distribution, $98.70 ($47.40 + $51.30) is included in X's gross income in 1989.

Example 2. (i) *Facts.* X, a U.S. person with a calendar taxable year, purchased 1,000

Prop. Reg. § 1.1291-2(e)

shares of stock of FC, a corporation, on December 31, 1985. FC has been a section 1291 fund since its taxable year that began January 1, 1987. FC distributed $100,000 to X on January 31, 1989, and $200,000 to X on July 31, 1989. X determined the total excess distribution for 1989 to be $150,000.

(ii) *January 31 distribution.* The excess distribution allocated to the January 31 distribution, which is the ratable portion of the total excess distribution allocated to the $100,000 distribution made on that date, is $50,000 [$150,000 × ($100,000 / $300,000)]. For purposes of allocating the $50,000 excess distribution over X's holding period, X's holding period is treated as ending on (and including) January 31, 1989. X thus held the stock for 1,127 days (365 days in both 1986 and 1987, 366 days in 1988, and 31 days in 1989) at the time of the January 31 distribution. The $50,000 excess distribution allocated to the January 31 distribution is allocated pro rata to the 1,127 days; approximately $44.37 is allocated to each day in the holding period. The total allocations to each of the taxable years in X's holding period are as follows:

TAXABLE YEAR	TOTAL ALLOCATION PER YEAR
1986	$16,193.70
1987	$16,193.70
1988	$16,237.70
1989	$ 1,374.90
Excess distribution:	$50,000.00

The allocation to 1986, the prePFIC year, and the allocation to 1989, the current shareholder year, are included in X's gross income for 1989 as ordinary income. The allocations to 1987 and 1988, the prior PFIC years, are not included in X's gross income in 1989, but are subject to the deferred tax amount.

(iii) *July 31 distribution.* The excess distribution allocated to the July 31 distribution, which is the ratable portion of the total excess distribution allocated to the distribution made on that date, is $100,000 [$150,000 × ($200,000 / $300,000)]. For purposes of the allocation of this excess distribution, X's holding period is treated as ending on July 31, 1989. X thus held the stock for 1,308 days (365 days in both 1986 and 1987, 366 days in 1988, and 212 days in 1989) at the time of the July 31 distribution. The $100,000 excess distribution allocated to the July 31 excess distribution is allocated pro rata to the 1,308 days; approximately $76.45 is allocated to each day in the holding period. The total allocations of the July 31 excess distribution to each of the taxable years in X's holding period are as follows:

TAXABLE YEAR	TOTAL ALLOCATION PER YEAR
1986	$ 27,905.20
1987	$ 27,905.20
1988	$ 27,981.65
1989	$ 16,207.95
Excess distribution:	$100,000.00

The portions of the excess distribution allocated to 1986, the prePFIC year, and to 1989, the current shareholder year, are included as ordinary income in X's gross income for 1989. The portions of the excess distribution allocated to 1987 and 1988, the prior PFIC years, are not included in X's gross income in 1989, but are subject to the deferred tax amount.

Example 3. (i) *Facts.* X, a U.S. person, holds six shares of the stock of FC, a section 1291 fund. Two shares were purchased on December 31, 1986 (Block #1), and four shares were purchased on December 31, 1987 (Block #2). On June 30 of 1987 and 1988, FC distributed $10,000 in respect of each outstanding share of its stock. No portion of the distributions in either year was an excess distribution. On June 30, 1989, FC distributed $30,000 in respect of each outstanding share of its stock.

(ii) *Calculation of the 1989 excess distributions.* The excess distribution is determined separately for each block of stock.

(A) *Block #1 excess distribution.* The nonexcess distribution for Block #1 is $25,000 [125% times ($20,000 + $20,000) / 2]. The total excess distribution for Block #1 is $35,000 ($60,000 – $25,000).

(B) *Block #2 excess distribution.* The nonexcess distribution for Block #2 is $50,000 [125% times $40,000 (the distribution received in the only preceding taxable year included in X's holding period]. The total excess distribution for Block #2 is $70,000 ($120,000 – $50,000).

(iii) *Block #1 allocation.* The holding period of the Block #1 stock began on January 1, 1987, and ended, for purposes of section 1291, on June 30, 1989, for a total of 912 days (365 days in 1987, 366 days in 1988 and 181 days in 1989). The $35,000 excess distribution for Block #1 is allocated pro rata to each of the 912 days. Accordingly, approximately $38.38 is allocated to each day. The total allocations to each of the taxable years in X's holding period are as follows:

TAXABLE YEAR	TOTAL ALLOCATION PER YEAR
1987	$14,007.70
1988	$14,046.10
1989	$ 6,946.20
Excess distribution:	$35,000.00

The portion of the excess distribution allocated to 1989, the current shareholder year, of $6,946.20, is included as ordinary income in X's gross income for 1989. The portions of the excess distribution allocated to the prior PFIC years, 1987 and 1988, an aggregate of $28,053.80, are not included in X's gross income in 1989, but are subject to the deferred tax amount.

(iv) *Block #2 allocation.* The holding period of the Block #2 stock began on January 1, 1988, and ended, for purposes of section 1291, on June 30, 1989, for a total of 547 days (366 days in 1988 and 181 days in 1989). The excess distribution of $70,000 in respect of the Block #2 stock is allocated pro rata to each of the 547 days. Accordingly, approximately $127.97 is allocated to each day. The total allocations to each of the taxable years in X's holding period are as follows:

TAXABLE YEAR	TOTAL ALLOCATION PER YEAR
1988	$46,837.40
1989	$23,162.60
Excess distribution:	$70,000.00

The portion of the excess distribution allocated to 1989, the current shareholder year, of $23,162.60, is included as ordinary income in X's gross income for 1989. The portion of the excess distribution allocated to 1988, $46,837.40, is not included in X's gross income in 1989, but is subject to the deferred tax amount.

Example 4. X is a U.S. person that owns all the stock of FC, a section 1291 fund. At the end of its 1991 taxable year, FC has accumulated earnings and profits, before reduction for distributions made during the year, of $100, none of which was previously taxed to X under section 951 or 1293. FC distributes $200 to X on the last day of FC's taxable year. X determines that, of the $200 distribution, $50 is a nonexcess distribution, and $150 is the total excess distribution. FC's earnings and profits of $100 are allocated proportionately between the nonexcess distribution of $50 and the excess distribution of $150, and reduced to zero. Accordingly, $25 of FC's earnings and profits are allocated to the nonexcess distribution and $75 of FC's earnings and profits are allocated to the excess distribution. Therefore, $25 of the $50 nonexcess distribution is taxable as a dividend under section 301(c)(1), and the remaining $25 is taxable to the extent provided in section 301(c)(2) and (3). The excess distribution of $150 is taxable as provided in § 1.1291-2(e)(2).

(f) *Indirect distributions.*—(1) *In general.*— A distribution (as defined in § 1.1291-2(b)) by a section 1291 fund to the actual owner of stock of the section 1291 fund is an indirect distribution if such stock is considered owned by a U.S. person pursuant to § 1.1291-1(b)(8). Except as otherwise provided in this paragraph (f), an indirect shareholder is taxable on the total distribution paid by the section 1291 fund with respect to the stock attributed to the indirect shareholder, as if the indirect shareholder had actually received that amount. The following example illustrates the rule of this paragraph (f)(1).

Example. (i) X, an S corporation under section 1361, purchased 100 shares of stock of FC, a corporation, on December 31, 1985. FC has been a section 1291 fund since its taxable year that began January 1, 1987. A purchased 10 percent of the stock of X on December 31, 1986, and thus became an indirect shareholder of 10 shares of FC stock. Pursuant to § 1.1291-1(h)(4)(i), A's holding period of the FC stock began on January 1, 1987.

(ii) FC distributed $5 per share of stock to its shareholders in 1986, and $8 per share in 1987. In 1987 A is treated as receiving a distribution of $80 from FC. A did not have a total excess distribution in 1987, the taxable year in which A's holding period of the FC stock began.

(iii) FC distributed $12 per share in 1988, all of which was paid on June 30, 1988. A therefore is treated as receiving a distribution of $120 from FC. The nonexcess distribution is $100 [125% times $80]. Accordingly, the excess distribution is $20 ($120 − $100). That amount is allocated under § 1.1291-2(e)(2)(i) to each day in A's holding period of the FC stock, which began on January 1, 1987, and ended, for purposes of the allocation of the excess distribution, on June 30, 1988.

(2) *Pass-through entities.*—(i) *Taxation of trusts, estates, and their beneficiaries.*—[Reserved]

(ii) *Information reporting.*—(A) *In general.*—A domestic partnership that is a direct or indirect shareholder of a section 1291 fund must separately state the total distribution as a distribution from a section 1291 fund on its federal income tax return (if any) and on any Schedule K-1 filed by the partnership or provided to a partner to which a distributive share of the distribution from the section 1291 fund is allocated pursuant to section 704. In addition, the partnership must state on the Schedule K-1 the information needed by the partner to compute its excess distribution with respect to such total distribution, and provide the name, address and stock basis, where appropriate, of the actual owner of the section 1291 fund that paid the distribution (or whose stock was transferred in an indirect disposition). Any partner receiving such a Schedule K-1 that is itself a domestic partnership is in turn obligated to separately state such information according to the same rules. Similar rules apply to S corporations.

(B) *Trusts and estates.*—[Reserved]

(3) *Coordination with subpart F.*—If, but for this paragraph (f)(3), an indirect distribution would be taxable to an indirect shareholder under this section and also included in the gross income of the indirect shareholder under section 551(a), 951(a)(1), or 1293(a), the indirect distribution is taxable only under this section.

(4) *Exceptions.*—(i) *Distribution to sole shareholder.*—A distribution by a section 1291 fund (distributing fund) to another section 1291 fund (distributee fund) will not be taxable to the direct shareholder of the distributee fund if—

(A) The distributee fund owns all the stock of the distributing fund; and

(B) The distributing fund distributed all its earnings and profits in the current shareholder year and annually distributed all its earnings and profits for each year that is included in the shareholder's holding period of the distributing fund.

(ii) *Other exceptions.*—[Reserved]

(5) *Adjustment to basis.*—The shareholder's adjusted basis of the stock or other property that is owned directly by the shareholder and through which ownership of the section 1291 fund is attributed to the shareholder is increased by the amount of the indirect distribution taxed to the shareholder pursuant to paragraph (f)(1) of this section.

(6) *Treatment of previously taxed amounts.*—The principles of sections 959 and 961 apply with respect to amounts previously taxed under this paragraph (f). The following example illustrates the rule of this paragraph (f)(6).

Example. USP owns 50% of CFC1. CFC1 and its wholly owned subsidiary, CFC2, are both controlled foreign corporations within the meaning of section 957(a), but are not PFICs. CFC2 owns 10% of the stock of NQF, a PFIC. USP is an indirect shareholder of NQF pursuant to § 1.1291-1(b)(8)(ii). USP has not elected to treated NQF as a QEF. In 1992, NQF distributes $100 to CFC2, and CFC1 distributes $100 to USP, but CFC2 makes no distributions to CFC1. At the end of 1992, CFC1 has accumulated earnings and profits of $200, none of which was previously taxed to USP under section 951(a)(1). USP is taxable pursuant to § 1.1291-2(f) on its pro rata share of the indirect distribution paid to CFC2, and also is taxable on CFC1's distribution pursuant to section 301(c). No part of the distribution by CFC1 to USP is attributable to the amount taxed to USP under § 1.1291-2(f) because no part of the distribution can be attributed to NQF's distribution to CFC2. [Prop. Reg. § 1.1291-2.]

[Proposed 4-1-92.]

Proposed Regulation

§ 1.1291-3. Dispositions.—(a) *Purpose and scope.*—Any direct or indirect disposition of stock of a section 1291 fund within the meaning of paragraphs (b), (c), (d), and (e) of this section is taxable to the extent provided in section 1291, this section, and § 1.1291-6. For dispositions of stock of a section 1291 fund that qualify for nonrecognition treatment, *see* § 1.1291-6. Gain is determined on a share-by-share basis and is taxed as an excess distribution as provided in § 1.1291-2(e)(2). Unless otherwise provided under another provision of the Code, a loss realized on a disposition of stock of a section 1291 fund is not recognized.

(b) *Disposition.*—(1) *In general.*—For purposes of this section, a disposition is any transaction or event that constitutes an actual or deemed transfer of property for any purpose of the Code and the regulations thereunder, including (but not limited to) a sale, exchange, gift, or transfer at death, an exchange pursuant to a liquidation or section 302(a) redemption, or a distribution described in section 311, 336, 337, 355(c) or 361(c). For purposes of this paragraph (b), any person receiving a distribution that qualifies under section 355 will be treated as disposing of all of its stock in the distributing corporation (whether or not there is an actual disposition of such stock) in exchange for stock of the distributing corporation, the controlled corporation, or both, as the case may be.

(2) *Change of U.S. residence or citizenship.*—If a shareholder of a section 1291 fund becomes a nonresident alien for U.S. tax purposes, the shareholder will be treated as having disposed of the shareholder's stock in the section 1291 fund for purposes of section 1291 on the last day that the shareholder is a U.S. person. Termination of an election under section 6013(g) is treated as a change of residence (within the meaning of this paragraph (b)(2)) of the spouse who was a resident solely by reason of the section 6013(g) election.

(c) *Direct disposition of stock of a section 1291 fund.*—Except to the extent provided in § 1.1291-6, a direct shareholder of a section 1291 fund recognizes all gain that it realizes on a disposition of the stock of such fund.

(d) *Stock of a section 1291 fund used as security for an obligation.*—(1) *In general.*—Except to the extent provided in paragraphs (d)(3) and (6) of this section, the use of stock of a section 1291 fund as security for the performance of an obligation of a direct or indirect shareholder (or of a person related within the meaning of section 267(b) to that shareholder), in connection with a loan, guarantee, margin account, or otherwise (a pledge of stock), is a transaction that results in a disposition of the stock of the section 1291 fund within the meaning of paragraph (b) of this section. Such pledged stock will be treated as having been disposed of on the later of the date when such stock is first used as security with respect to such obligation, or the first day of the first taxable year of the foreign corporation as a PFIC. Such pledged stock will be treated as having been disposed of for consideration equal to the lesser of—

(i) The unpaid principal of the obligation secured by the stock on the date of disposition; or

(ii) The fair market value of the stock immediately before such disposition.

(2) *Indirect pledge.*—A pledge of stock of a section 1291 fund, as described in paragraph (d)(1) of this section, will be deemed to occur if such stock serves indirectly as security for the performance of an obligation described in that paragraph, and a principal purpose for the structure of the security arrangement was to avoid the rule of that paragraph.

(3) *Requirement of gain realized.*—This paragraph (d) does not apply if the shareholder would realize a loss on an actual disposition of the stock of the section 1291 fund at the time the obligation was secured by the stock.

(4) *Increase in value of pledged stock.*—An increase in the value of stock being used to secure the performance of an obligation will not be treated as a disposition of the stock unless the pledged stock is used to secure additional principal or new indebtedness.

(5) *Adjustment to basis; holding period.*—If stock of a section 1291 fund is treated as disposed of under this paragraph (d), adjustments to basis will be made in accordance with rules similar to those in § 1.1291-6(b)(4). For the holding period of pledged stock, *see* § 1.1291-1(h)(5).

(6) *Transition rule.*—Stock of a section 1291 fund that secured an obligation within the meaning of paragraph (d)(1) of this section as of the effective date of section 1297(b)(6) is not treated as disposed of as of the first day of the first taxable year of the foreign corporation as a PFIC, unless such stock continued to secure such obligation 180 days after the effective date. For a special effective date pertaining to this rule, *see* § 1.1291-1(j)(2).

(7) *Examples.*—The following examples illustrate the operation of this paragraph (d).

Example 1. On November 20, 1995, X, a U.S. person that was a shareholder of FC, a section 1291 fund, used its stock in FC, valued immediately before the loan at $120,000, as security for a $100,000 loan. X's basis in the stock is $70,000. The pledge is treated as a disposition of the stock for $100,000, which is the lesser of the loan principal secured by the stock and the fair market value of the stock. S recognizes $30,000 on the disposition, which gain is taxed as an excess distribution under section 1291 and § 1.1291-2(e)(2). X's basis in the FC stock is increased by $30,000, the amount of gain recognized on the deemed disposition. The holding period of the pledged stock is not adjusted to reflect the disposition because the full amount of the gain inherent in the stock was not recognized (*see* § 1.1291-1(h)(5)).

Example 2. The facts are the same as in *Example 1.* In addition, on August 12, 1996, X borrows an additional $30,000 (for a total outstanding loan balance on that day of $130,000). The value of the FC stock immediately before the additional loan is $130,000. Pursuant to § 1.1291-3(d)(4), there is a disposition within the meaning of § 1.1291-3(d)(1) to the extent the value of the FC stock secures additional indebtedness. The FC stock first secured a loan of $100,000, which was less than its full value. The second loan results in a disposition to the extent that the previously unrecognized appreciation and any additional appreciation secure additional indebtedness. Accordingly, there is an excess distribution of $30,000. X's basis in its FC stock is increased by $30,000, the amount of gain recognized. X's holding period in the FC stock for section 1291 purposes is treated as beginning on the day after the effective date of the second borrowing (see § 1.1291-1(h)(5)).

(e) *Indirect dispositions.*—(1) *In general.*—Except as otherwise provided in this paragraph (e) and § 1.1291-6, an indirect shareholder of a section 1291 fund is taxable under section 1291 and this section on an indirect disposition of stock of the section 1291 fund.

(2) *Indirect disposition defined.*—An indirect disposition is—

(i) Any disposition of stock of a section 1291 fund by its actual owner if such stock is attributed to an indirect shareholder under § 1.1291-1(b)(8);

(ii) Any disposition, by an indirect shareholder or any other person, of any interest in a person, if by virtue of such interest the indirect shareholder was treated as owning stock of a section 1291 fund under § 1.1291-1(b)(8); or

(iii) Any other transaction as a result of which an indirect shareholder's ownership of a section 1291 fund is reduced or terminated.

Paragraph (e)(2)(i) of this section applies without regard to whether the indirect shareholder's ownership of a section 1291 fund is changed by the disposition. However, paragraph (e)(2)(ii) of this section does not apply if the disposition does not result in a reduction in the indirect shareholder's ownership of the fund or an increase in the basis of the stock of the fund in the hands of the actual owner.

(3) *Examples.*—The following examples illustrate paragraph (e)(2) of this section.

Example 1. T, a U.S. person, and M, a foreign person, are equal partners of FP, a foreign partnership that owns 10 shares of stock of FC, a PFIC. Pursuant to § 1.1291-1(b)(8)(iii), T is an indirect shareholder of one-half of the shares of FC stock held by FP. T did not elect under section 1295 to treat FC as a QEF. On August 14, 1994, H, a U.S. person, joins the partnership as an equal partner. As a result of H's acquisition of one-third of FP, H is an indirect shareholder of one-third of the FC stock held by FP. H's acquisition of the FP interest is a disposition pursuant to § 1.1291-3(e)(2)(iii), taxable to T, of one-third of T's interest in the FC stock.

Example 2. E, a U.S. person, and R, a foreign person, each own 50% of the outstanding stock of Distributing, a foreign corporation that is not a PFIC or a controlled foreign corporation within the meaning of section 957(a). Distributing owns all the stock of Controlled, a PFIC. Pursuant to § 1.1291-1(b)(8)(ii)(A), E is an indirect shareholder of Controlled. E did not elect under section 1295 to treat Controlled as a QEF. In a transaction that qualifies under section 355(a), Distributing distributes all the Controlled stock to R. As a result of the distribution, E's interest in Controlled is terminated. The distribution is an indirect disposition of E's ownership of Controlled, within the meaning of § 1.1291-3(e)(2)(i), taxable to E under § 1.1291-3(e).

Example 3. C, a U.S. person, owns 51% of the stock of CFC, a foreign corporation that is not a PFIC. Several foreign persons own the remaining 49% of CFC. CFC owns 100 shares of FYZ, a PFIC. Pursuant to § 1.1291-1(b)(8)(ii)(A), C is an indirect shareholder of 51 shares of the FYZ stock held by CFC. C did not elect under section 1295 to treat FYZ as a QEF. To raise capital, CFC makes a public offering of its stock. After the offering, C owns only 35% of the CFC stock. The reduction of C's ownership of CFC terminated C's indirect ownership of the FYZ stock, and therefore is an indirect disposition of the FYZ stock, pursuant to § 1.1291-3(e)(2)(iii), taxable to C under § 1.1291-3(e).

(4) *General rules.*—(i) *Amount and treatment of gain.*—If a shareholder with respect to a share of stock of a section 1291 fund is taxable on an indirect disposition of that share, the shareholder is treated as recognizing an amount of gain with respect to that share equal to the shareholder's pro rata share of the gain realized by the actual owner of that share (in the case of a disposition described in paragraph (e)(2)(i) of this section), or the gain the actual owner would have realized on an actual disposition of such stock (in the case of other dispositions). The gain taxable to the shareholder is an excess distribution, taxable in the manner provided in § 1.1291-2(e)(2). The gain is allocated over the shareholder's holding period of the stock of the section 1291 fund as determined in § 1.1291-1(h)(4).

(ii) *Coordination with current inclusion rules.*—If gain from an indirect disposition would be taxable to a shareholder under this section, and would, but for this paragraph (e)(4)(ii), also be included in the gross income of the shareholder under section 551(a), 951(a)(1), or 1293(a), the indirect disposition is taxable only under this section.

(iii) *Adjustment to basis; holding period.*—The shareholder's adjusted basis of the stock or other property that is owned directly by the shareholder and through which ownership of the section 1291 fund is attributed to the shareholder is increased by the amount of gain recognized by the shareholder pursuant to par-

Prop. Reg. § 1.1291-3(e)(4)(iii)

agraph (e)(4)(i) of this section. In addition, solely for purposes of determining the subsequent treatment under the Code of a direct or indirect shareholder of the stock of the section 1291 fund treated as transferred in an indirect disposition, the adjusted basis of the actual owner of the stock of the section 1291 fund is increased by the amount of gain recognized by the shareholder. For the holding period rule for stock that is treated as disposed of under paragraph (e)(2) of this section, see § 1.1291-1(h)(5).

(iv) *Treatment of previously taxed amounts.*—The principles of sections 959 and 961 apply with respect to distributions by a foreign corporation through which a shareholder was considered to own stock of a section 1291 fund, to the extent that such distributions are attributable to amounts previously taxed under this paragraph (e) on a disposition of the stock of such fund.

(5) *Pass-through entities.*—(i) *Section 1291 fund stock held by former C corporation.*—Solely for purposes of calculating the aggregate amount of interest under § 1.1291-4(d)(1), the S corporation shareholder's gain is determined without regard to section 1366(f)(2). Accordingly, the excess distribution for this purpose includes the amount of the S corporation's liability for tax attributable to the built-in gain in the stock of the section 1291 fund pursuant to section 1374. For an illustration of the rule of this paragraph (e)(5)(i), see § 1.1291-4(e), *Example 2*. For the taxation of the S corporation on the disposition of the stock of a section 1291 fund, *see* section 1374.

(ii) *Taxation of trusts, estates, and their beneficiaries.*—[Reserved]

(iii) *Information reporting.*—The information reporting obligations to which pass-through entities are subject with respect to indirect distributions also apply with respect to indirect dispositions. See § 1.1291-2(f)(2)(ii).

(6) *Exceptions.*—(i) *Disposition of PFIC's wholly-owned PFIC.*—A direct shareholder of a section 1291 fund (first-tier fund) will not be taxable on an indirect disposition of a section 1291 fund (second-tier fund) that is a wholly owned subsidiary of the first-tier fund if the second-tier fund annually distributed all its earnings and profits for each year that is included in the shareholder's holding period of the second-tier fund.

(ii) *Other exceptions.*—[Reserved]

(f) *Transfers within a consolidated group.*—For purposes of applying sections 1291 through 1297 to the stock of a PFIC, transfers by one member of a consolidated group to another member are ignored. Thus, the basis of the transferred stock in the hands of the transferee is the adjusted basis of such stock in the hands of the transferor, and the holding period of such stock held by a member of the consolidated group includes the holding period of all members of the group that have transferred the stock.

(g) *Installment sales.*—If the gain from a disposition of a share of stock of a section 1291 fund is reported on the installment basis, there is an excess distribution on the receipt of each installment or portion thereof in the amount of the gain to be reported in accordance with section 453 with respect to such share. For purposes of allocating each excess distribution under § 1.1291-2(e)(2)(i), the holding period of the transferred stock, which begins on the date determined under § 1.1291-1(h), is treated as ending on the date of each installment.

(h) *Series of liquidation distributions.*—For purposes of allocating the gain recognized on a distribution of property that is one of a series of distributions in liquidation of a section 1291 fund, the holding period of the stock of the liquidating corporation, which begins on the date determined under § 1.1291-1(h), is treated as ending on the date of each liquidation distribution with respect to which gain is recognized.

(i) *Sections 1246 and 1248 inapplicable.*—Sections 1246 and 1248 do not apply to the disposition of stock of a section 1291 fund that is taxable under section 1291. *See* sections 1246(g) and 1248(g)(2).

(j) *Estate tax deduction.*—If a shareholder acquired the stock of a section 1291 fund from a decedent (other than a decedent who was a nonresident alien at all times during the holding period of the stock), and the decedent did not recognize any gain on the transfer of his or her stock at death pursuant to § 1.1291-6(c)(2)(iii)(A), the shareholder may deduct from gross income, for the taxable year of the disposition of the stock of the section 1291 fund that is taxable to the shareholder, an amount equal to that portion of the decedent's estate tax deemed paid which is attributable to the excess of (A) the value at which such stock was taken into account for purposes of determining the value of the decedent's gross estate, over (B) the value at which it would have been so taken into account if such value had been the basis of the stock in the hands of the shareholder determined under § 1.1291-6(b)(4)(iii). [Prop. Reg. § 1.1291-3.]

[Proposed 4-1-92.]

Proposed Regulation

§ 1.1291-4. The deferred tax amount.— (a) *In general.*—The deferred tax amount is the sum of the aggregate increases in taxes (defined in paragraph (c)(5) of this section) and the aggregate amount of interest (defined in paragraph (d) of this section) determined with respect to the aggregate increases in taxes. The deferred tax amount is computed for the portions of each excess distribution allocated to different prior PFIC years, as defined in § 1.1291-1(b)(4).

(b) *Character of deferred tax amount.*—The aggregate increases in taxes are an additional amount of tax imposed on the shareholder for the current shareholder year. The aggregate increases in taxes are treated as an income tax for purposes of subtitle F (Procedure and Administration), and therefore will be assessed, collected, paid, and subject to penalties and interest in the same manner as other taxes on income. The aggregate amount of interest is treated as interest under section 6601. To determine the extent to which such interest may be deducted for federal income tax purposes, *see* section 163 and the regulations under that section.

(c) *Increase in tax.*—(1) *In general.*—An increase in tax is determined for each portion of an excess distribution allocated to a prior PFIC year. Each increase in tax is determined by multiplying the amount of the excess distribution allocated to the prior PFIC year by the highest statutory rate of tax in effect under either section 1 or section 11, as applicable, for that prior PFIC year.

(2) *Rate of tax in effect.*—The highest statutory rate of tax is determined without regard to the actual rate of tax to which the shareholder was subject in that prior PFIC year. The rate of tax in effect in the case of a distribution or disposition taxable to an indirect shareholder is the rate in effect for the indirect shareholder. For taxable years of the shareholder beginning after 1987 and before January 1, 1991, the highest statutory rate of tax in effect under section 1 is 28 percent. If there was a change of tax rates during a taxable year, the highest rate of tax is determined in the manner described in section 15(e) using the highest statutory rates of tax in effect before and after the change of rates.

(3) *Reduction for foreign taxes.*—To the extent provided in section 1291(g) and § 1.1291-5, each increase in tax is reduced by the foreign tax credit calculated with respect to the increase in tax.

(4) *Net increase in tax.*—The net increase in tax is the amount of the increase in tax after reduction for creditable foreign taxes. *See* paragraph (d) of this section.

(5) *Aggregate increases in taxes.*—The term aggregate increases in taxes means the sum of all net increases in tax calculated for an excess distribution.

(d) *Aggregate amount of interest.*—(1) *In general.*—The aggregate amount of interest is the sum of the interest charges computed on all net increases in tax calculated for an excess distribution. An interest charge is computed separately for the interest period of each net increase in tax by using the applicable rates and method under section 6621. The interest period for a net increase in tax is the period beginning on the due date of the income tax return for the prior PFIC year for which the net increase in tax was computed and ending on the due date for the income tax return for the current shareholder year. For purposes of this paragraph, the term due date means the date prescribed by law, determined without regard to extensions, for filing the income tax return for the taxable year of the shareholder.

(2) *Reduction for interest paid under section 453A(c).*—A disposition may be subject to both sections 1291 and 453A(c). The aggregate amount of interest determined in paragraph (d)(1) of this section is reduced by the amount of interest paid under section 453A(c) that is attributable to an excess distribution arising from the disposition. The shareholder may use any reasonable method of determining the amount of the reduction.

(e) *Examples.*—The following examples illustrate the rules of this section.

Example 1. (i) *Facts.* X is a domestic corporation that is a calendar year taxpayer. The due date (without regard to extensions) for its federal income tax return is March 15. X acquired a share of stock of FC, a corporation, on December 31, 1986, for $500. FC has been a section 1291 fund with respect to X since FC's taxable year that began January 1, 1987. On December 31, 1990, X sold the FC stock for $1000. X did not incur any foreign tax on the disposition of the FC stock. X's gain on the sale, $500, is taxed as an excess distribution. The excess distribution is allocated pro rata over X's four-year holding period. Accordingly, $125 is allocated to each year in X's holding period. The $125 allocated to 1990, the current shareholder year, is included in X's ordinary income for that year. The allocations to 1987, 1988 and 1989, the prior PFIC years, are subject to the deferred tax amount under § 1.1291-4.

Prop. Reg. § 1.1291-4(e)

(ii) *Calculation of the 1987 increase in tax.* The increase in tax for the $125 allocated to 1987 is determined in the manner described in section 15(e) by using a weighted average rate. The weighted average rate is 40 percent:

$$
\begin{aligned}
46\% \text{ rate: } 181/365 \times 46\% &= 22.81\% \\
34\% \text{ rate: } 184/365 \times 34\% &= 17.14\% \\
&\ 39.95\%
\end{aligned}
$$

The increase in tax for 1987 is $49.94 ($125 × 39.95%).

(iii) *Calculation of the other increases in tax.* The highest statutory rate of tax applicable to X that was in effect for both 1988 and 1989 was 34 percent. The increase in tax for each of 1988 and 1989 is $42.50 ($125 × 34%).

(iv) *Aggregate increases in taxes.* The aggregate increases in taxes are $134.94 ($49.94 + $42.50 + $42.50).

(v) *Interest charge.* Interest on each of the three increases in tax ($49.94, $42.50, and $42.50) is computed using the rates and method provided in section 6621 for the respective interest period. The following are the interest periods:

| Year of Allocation | Increase in Tax | Interest Period | |
		Beginning on	Ending on
1987	$49.94	March 15, 1988	March 15, 1991
1988	42.50	March 15, 1989	March 15, 1991
1989	42.50	March 15, 1990	March 15, 1991

Example 2. (i) *Facts.* The facts are the same as in *Example 1* except that X was a C corporation until it elected to be treated as an S corporation effective for its taxable year beginning January 1, 1988. A is a U.S. person who has been a shareholder of X since January 1, 1988. A's holding period of the FC stock began on January 1, 1988, pursuant to § 1.1291-1(h)(4)(i). As of January 1, 1988, the FC stock had appreciated in value to $800; X therefore had $300 of built-in gain within the meaning of section 1374. Assume X pays a built-in gain tax of $102 because of the sale of the FC stock in 1990.

(ii) *Calculation of the aggregate increases in taxes owed by A.* The $500 gain recognized, reduced as provided in section 1366(f)(2) by the amount of built-in gain tax of $102 paid by X pursuant to section 1374 to $398, is taxable to A as an excess distribution as provided in § 1.1291-2(e)(2). The $398 excess distribution is allocated pro rata over X's four-year holding period (not A's three-year holding period) as provided in § 1.1291-3(e)(5). The allocation of $99.50 to 1990, the current shareholder year, is included in A's ordinary income. The allocations of $99.50 to 1987, 1988, and 1989 are not included in income, but are subject to the deferred tax amount. The aggregate increases in taxes are determined based on those $99.50 allocations.

(A) *Calculation of the 1987 increase in tax.* The highest statutory rate of tax applicable to A that was in effect in 1987 was 38.5 percent. The increase in tax for the portion of the excess distribution allocated to 1987 is $38.31 ($99.50 × 38.5%).

(B) *Calculation of the other increases in tax.* The highest statutory rate of tax applicable to A that was in effect for both 1988 and 1989 is 28 percent. The increase in tax for each of 1988 and 1989 is $27.86 ($99.50 × 28%).

(C) *Calculation of the aggregate increases in taxes.* The aggregate increases in taxes are $94.03 ($38.31 + 27.86 + 27.86).

(iii) *Calculation of the aggregate amount of interest.* For purposes of calculating the aggregate amount of interest, the reduction provided under section 1366(f)(2) is disregarded and the excess distribution is $500. Accordingly, for purposes of calculating the aggregate amount of interest, $125 is allocated to 1987, 1988, and 1989.

(A) *Calculation of the 1987 hypothetical increase in tax.* The highest statutory rate of tax applicable to A that was in effect in 1987 was 38.5 percent. The hypothetical increase in tax for the portion of the excess distribution allocated to 1987 is $48.12 ($125 × 38.5%).

(B) *Calculation of the other hypothetical increases in tax.* The highest statutory rate of tax applicable to A that was in effect for both 1988 and 1989 is 28 percent. The hypothetical increase in tax for each of 1988 and 1989 is $35.00 ($125 × 28%).

(C) *Interest charge.* Interest on each of the three hypothetical increases in tax ($48.12, $35, and $35) is computed using the rates and method provided in section 6621 for the respective interest period. The following are the interest periods:

Year of Allocation	Increase in Tax	Interest Period	
		Beginning on	Ending on
1987	$48.12	April 15, 1988	April 15, 1991
1988	35.00	April 15, 1989	April 15, 1991
1989	35.00	April 15, 1990	April 15, 1991

(iv) *The deferred tax amount.* The deferred tax amount is the sum of the aggregate increases in taxes determined in (ii) and the aggregate amount of interest determined in (iii). [Prop. Reg. § 1.1291-4.]

[Proposed 4-1-92.]

Proposed Regulation

§ 1.1291-5. Coordination with the foreign tax credit rules.—(a) *Scope.*—This section provides rules for determining the amount of foreign tax credit that a shareholder may claim on a distribution from a section 1291 fund, and in certain cases, on a disposition of stock of a section 1291 fund. This section applies to a shareholder that has chosen under section 901 for the current shareholder year to claim a credit for foreign taxes paid. The rules of this section apply separately with respect to each section 1291 fund in which the shareholder directly or indirectly owns stock. For purposes of this section, an S corporation is treated as a partnership, and its shareholders as partners of the partnership. *See* section 1373.

(b) *Distributions from section 1291 funds to shareholders that are not entitled to a foreign tax credit for foreign taxes deemed paid.*—(1) *Rule.*—If a section 1291 fund makes a distribution with respect to which a shareholder (other than a shareholder described in paragraph (c) of this section) is subject to tax under § 1.1291-2, and the shareholder would be entitled to a foreign tax credit for foreign taxes paid (including withholding taxes) with respect to such distribution, but not for foreign taxes deemed paid with respect to such distribution (determined in both cases without regard to section 1291 and this section), the foreign tax credit with respect to that distribution is determined under the steps provided in this paragraph (b). The excess distribution is treated as foreign source income described in section 904(d)(1)(A).

(i) *Step 1.*—The shareholder determines the total excess distribution under § 1.1291-2 (c)(3), and the excess distribution taxes. The excess distribution taxes are the creditable foreign taxes (within the meaning of section 1291(g)(2)(A)), paid or accrued with respect to the total distribution for the current shareholder year, allocated to the total excess distribution as follows:

$$\text{Foreign taxes paid with respect to the total distribution} \times \frac{\text{Total excess distribution}}{\text{Total distribution}}$$

The remainder of the creditable foreign taxes are allocated to the nonexcess distribution.

(ii) *Step 2.*—The shareholder allocates the total excess distribution and the excess distribution taxes ratably to each distribution received during the shareholder's taxable year in the manner provided in § 1.1291-2 (c)(4). The shareholder then allocates each excess distribution and the excess distribution taxes allocated to that distribution to each taxable year included in the shareholder's holding period based on the number of days in each such taxable year.

(iii) *Step 3.*—The shareholder determines the tentative increase in tax for each prior PFIC year. The term tentative increase in tax means the increase in tax determined in the manner provided in § 1.1291-4(c) for each prior PFIC year. The tentative increase in tax for a prior PFIC year is the foreign tax credit limitation for the excess distribution taxes allocated to that prior PFIC year.

(iv) *Step 4.*—The shareholder claims as a foreign tax credit with respect to an increase in tax for a prior PFIC year the lesser of the tentative increase in tax for that year determined in *Step 3* or the excess distribution taxes allocated to that prior PFIC year in *Step 2*.

(v) *Step 5.*—The shareholder determines the net increase in tax for each prior PFIC year by reducing the tentative increase in tax for a prior PFIC year determined in *Step 3* by the foreign tax credit determined for that year in *Step 4*. For the calculation of the interest charge for each net increase in tax, *see* § 1.1291-4(d).

(vi) *Step 6.*—The portions of the excess distribution and excess distribution taxes allocated to the current shareholder year and pre-PFIC years, if any, as well as the creditable foreign taxes allocated to the nonexcess distribution, are taken into account in the current shareholder year under the general foreign tax credit rules.

(2) *Carryovers disallowed.*—The amount by which the excess distribution taxes allocated to a prior PFIC year exceed the tentative increase in tax for that year may not be claimed as a foreign tax credit against any federal income tax.

(c) *Distributions from section 1291 funds that are CFCs.*—(1) *Rule.*—If a controlled foreign corporation (CFC) (as defined in section 904(d)(4)) that is a section 1291 fund makes a distribution with respect to which a United States shareholder (also as defined in section 904(d)(4)) is subject to tax under §1.1291-2, the foreign tax credit with respect to that excess distribution is determined by applying the rules of section 1291(g) on a separate category basis within the meaning of section 904. *See* section 904(d)(3)(A) and the regulations under that section. A distribution described in this paragraph (c) from a section 1291 fund is foreign source income except to the extent the distribution is determined to be derived from U.S. sources pursuant to section 904(g). The foreign tax credit of a United States shareholder with respect to a distribution by a CFC that is taxable as an excess distribution to the shareholder under §1.1291-2(e)(2) is determined according to the following steps.

(i) *Step 1.*—The shareholder determines—

(A) The separate category or categories (as defined in §1.904-5(a)(1)) to which the total distribution (including the amount of the gross-up determined under section 78) for the taxable year is allocable under the rules of section 904(d)(3) and the regulations under that section (*see* §1.904-5(c)(4));

(B) The creditable foreign taxes, which are the foreign taxes paid or deemed paid on the distribution (determined without regard to section 1291 and this section) with respect to each separate category under the rules of sections 901, 902, 904, and 960 and the regulations under those sections (*see* §1.904-6(b)(3)); and

(C) The portion of the total distribution (including the gross-up) in each separate category that is from U.S. sources pursuant to section 904(g) (*see* §1.904-5(m)(4) and (6)).

Solely for purposes of section 1291, any portion of the total excess distribution that would not be allocated to a separate category under normally applicable rules because it exceeds the fund's earnings and profits is deemed to be foreign source income allocated to the separate category defined in section 904(d)(1)(A).

(ii) *Step 2.*—The shareholder determines—

(A) The total excess distribution under §1.1291-2(c)(3) with respect to the total distribution (including the gross-up); and

(B) The portion of the total excess distribution allocable to each separate category (the separate category excess distribution). Each separate category excess distribution is calculated as follows:

$$\frac{\text{Distribution allocable to a separate category (including gross-up) } (Step\ 1\ (A))}{\text{Total distribution (including gross-up)}} \times \text{Total excess distribution } (Step\ 2\ (A))$$

(iii) *Step 3.*—The shareholder determines the U.S. source portion of each separate category excess distribution as follows:

$$\frac{\text{U.S. source portion of distribution allocable to a separate category } (Step\ 1\ (C))}{\text{Total distribution allocable to that category } (Step\ 1\ (A))} \times \text{Separate category excess distribution } (Step\ 2\ (B))$$

(iv) *Step 4.*—The shareholder determines the excess distribution taxes with respect to each separate category (separate category excess distribution taxes) as follows:

$$\frac{\text{Creditable foreign taxes with respect to the distribution and allocable to the separate category } (Step\ 1\ (B))}{} \times \frac{\text{Separate category excess distribution } (Step\ 2\ (B))}{\text{Total distribution allocable to that category } (Step\ 1\ (A))}$$

(v) *Step 5.*—(A) The shareholder allocates—

(*1*) The separate category excess distribution;

(*2*) The separate category excess distribution taxes; and

(*3*) The U.S. source portion of the separate category excess distribution ratably to each distribution received during the shareholder's taxable year in the manner provided in §1.1291-2(c)(4).

(B) The shareholder then allocates—

(1) The amount determined in *Step 5* (A)*(1)* for each distribution to each taxable year included in the shareholder's holding period based on the number of days in each such taxable year;

(2) The amount determined in *Step 5* (A)*(2)* for each distribution to each taxable year included in the shareholder's holding period based on the number of days in each such taxable year; and

(3) The amount determined in *Step 5* (A)*(3)* for each distribution to each taxable year included in the shareholder's holding period based on the number of days in each such taxable year.

Solely for purposes of determining the foreign tax credit limitation for the current shareholder year, the portion of an excess distribution that is allocated to the current shareholder year and prePFIC years, and included in income, is treated as a dividend from a CFC that is not a PFIC. The excess distribution taxes allocated to that portion of the excess distribution are treated as foreign taxes paid with respect to a dividend from a CFC that is not a PFIC and taken into account in the current shareholder year under general foreign tax credit rules.

(vi) *Step 6.*—The shareholder determines a tentative increase in tax for each prior PFIC year for each allocation of a separate category excess distribution determined under *Step 5* (B)*(1)* (separate category tentative increase in tax).

(vii) *Step 7.*—The shareholder determines a foreign tax credit limitation for each prior PFIC year to which the separate category excess distribution is allocated. The limitation is determined as follows:

Separate category tentative increase in tax for prior PFIC year (*Step 6*) × $\dfrac{\text{Foreign source separate category excess distribution allocated to that prior PFIC year } (Step\ 5(B)(1) - Step\ 5(B)(3))}{\text{Separate category excess distribution allocated to that prior PFIC year } (Step\ 5(B)(1))}$

(viii) *Step 8.*—The shareholder may claim a foreign tax credit for each separate category tentative increase in tax. The foreign tax credit for a prior PFIC year is the lesser of the foreign tax credit limitation determined in *Step 7* for the prior PFIC year or the amount of the separate category excess distribution taxes allocated to that prior PFIC year under *Step 5* (B)*(2)*.

(ix) *Step 9.*—The shareholder determines the separate category net increase in tax for each prior PFIC year by reducing the separate category tentative increase in tax determined for that year in *Step 6* by the amount of the foreign tax credit determined for that year in *Step 8*. For the calculation of the interest charge on each net increase in tax, see §1.1291-4(d).

(2) *Carryovers disallowed.*—The amount by which the excess distribution taxes allocated to a prior PFIC year exceed the separate category tentative increase in tax for that year may not be claimed as a foreign tax credit against any federal income tax.

(3) *Example.*—The following example illustrates the rules of paragraph (c) of this section.

Example. (i) *Facts.* USP, a domestic corporation, has been a United States shareholder of FC, a CFC that is a section 1291 fund, since December 31, 1986. USP and FC both use the calendar year as their taxable year. USP has not included any amount in income under section 951 with respect to FC. On March 31, 1989, FC distributed $1000 to USP. As of that date, USP had held the FC stock for 821 days (365 days in 1987, 366 days in 1988, and 90 days in 1989). USP elects to credit foreign taxes for 1989, and determines the total creditable taxes with respect to the distribution from FC to be $485, $425 of which are deemed paid taxes and $60 of which are withholding taxes. The total distribution for 1989, including the section 78 gross-up, is $1425.

(ii) *Step 1: Determination of separate category income, U.S. source portions, and foreign taxes.* Applying the look through rules of section 904(d)(3), USP determines that $1125 of the total distribution of $1425 is allocable to distributions from a noncontrolled section 902 corporation, and that the remaining $300 is allocable to general limitation income. USP determines that $390 of creditable foreign taxes were paid and deemed paid with respect to the distributions from the noncontrolled section 902 corporation, and $95 were paid and deemed paid with respect to the general limitation income. USP determines that the distributions from the noncontrolled section 902 corporation and the general limitation income are from foreign sources. Accordingly, *Steps 3* and *5* (A)*(3)* will not be performed.

(iii) *Step 2: Calculation of total excess distribution and separate category excess distributions.* USP determines, based on FC distributions during the preceding three taxable years, that the total excess distribution for the current taxable year is $800. Of that amount, $631.58

[[$1125 (distribution allocable to distributions from a noncontrolled section 902 corporation)/ $1425 (total distribution)] × $800 (total excess distribution)] is allocable to distributions from a noncontrolled section 902 corporation, and $168.42 [[$300 (distribution allocable to general limitation income)/$1425 (total distribution)] × $800 (total excess distribution)] is allocable to general limitation income.

(iv) *Step 4: Calculation of separate category excess distribution taxes.* USP calculates the excess distribution taxes (EDT) allocable to the separate category excess distributions. The noncontrolled section 902 corporation excess distribution taxes are $218.95 [$390 (creditable foreign taxes paid and deemed paid with respect to distributions from a noncontrolled section 902 corporation) × [$631.58 (noncontrolled section 902 corporation excess distribution)/ $1125 (distribution from noncontrolled section 902 corporation)]], and the general limitation excess distribution taxes are $53.33 [$95 (creditable foreign taxes paid and deemed paid with respect to general limitation income) × [$168.42 (general limitation income excess distribution)/$300 (distribution allocable to general limitation income)]].

(v) *Step 5: Allocations of separate category excess distributions and excess distribution taxes over holding period.* The separate category excess distributions and the separate category EDT are allocated to each taxable year in USP's holding period based on the number of days in each such taxable year. (Discrepancies may be observed in the following presentation. These discrepancies reflect rounding to the nearest penny of the different calculations performed.)

(A) *Noncontrolled section 902 corporation excess distribution:* $.77 of the noncontrolled section 902 corporation excess distribution ($631.58/821 days) and $.27 of EDT ($218.95/821 days) are allocated to each day. The allocations to each taxable year are as follows:

Taxable year in holding period	Allocations to taxable year	
	Excess distribution	EDT
1987 (365 days)	$281.05	$98.55
1988 (366 days)	281.82	98.82
1989 (90 days)	69.30	24.30

(B) *General limitation excess distribution:* $.21 of the general limitation excess distribution ($168.42/821 days) and $.065 of EDT ($53.33/821 days) are allocated to each day. The allocations to each taxable year are as follows:

Taxable year in holding period	Allocations to taxable year	
	Excess distribution	EDT
1987 (365 days)	$76.65	$23.73
1988 (366 days)	76.86	23.79
1989 (90 days)	18.90	5.85

(vi) *Step 6: Calculation of separate category tentative increases in taxes.* USP determines the tentative increases in tax (TIIT) for the allocations of each separate category excess distribution to 1987 and 1988, the prior PFIC years in USP's holding period. The noncontrolled section 902 corporation excess distribution TIIT for 1987 is $112.28 [$281.05 (allocation of noncontrolled section 902 corporation excess distribution to 1987) × 39.95% (the highest corporate tax rate in effect in 1987)], and for 1988, $95.82 [$281.82 (allocation of noncontrolled section 902 corporation excess distribution to 1988) × 34% (highest corporate tax rate in effect in 1988)]. The general limitation excess distribution TIIT for 1987 is $30.62 [$76.65 (allocation of general limitation income excess distribution to 1987) × 39.95% (highest corporate tax rate in effect in 1987)], and for 1988, $26.13 [$76.86 (allocation of general limitation income excess distribution to 1988) × 34% (highest corporate tax rate in effect in 1988)].

(vii) *Step 7: Calculation of the foreign tax credit limitations.* USP determines the foreign tax credit (FTC) limitations for each prior PFIC year on a separate category basis. The FTC limitations are the same as the tentative increases in tax because none of the separate category distributions are from U.S. sources. Therefore, the FTC limitation for the noncontrolled section 902 corporation excess distribution for 1987 is $112.28, and for 1988, $95.82. The FTC limitation for the general limitation excess distribution for 1987 is $30.62, and for 1988, $26.13.

(viii) *Step 8: Calculation of the foreign tax credit.* The FTC for the noncontrolled section 902 corporation excess distribution for 1987 is $98.55 [lower of $112.28 (1987 noncontrolled section 902 corporation FTC limitation) and $98.55 (1987 noncontrolled section 902 corporation EDT)], and for 1988, $95.82 [lower of $95.82 (1988 noncontrolled section 902 corporation FTC limitation) and $98.82 (1988 noncontrolled section 902 corporation EDT)]. The FTC for the general limitation excess distribution for 1987 is $23.73 [lower of $30.62 (1987 general limitation FTC limitation) and $23.73 (1987 general limitation income EDT)], and for 1988 is $23.79 [lower of $26.13 (1988 general limitation income FTC limitation) and $23.79 (1988 general limitation EDT)].

(ix) *Step 9: Calculation of the separate category net increases in taxes.* As provided in § 1.1291-4(c)(3), USP determines the net increase in tax (NIIT) for each separate category excess distribution allocated to a prior PFIC year. The noncontrolled section 902 corporation NIIT for 1987 is $13.73 [$112.28 (1987 noncontrolled section 902 corporation TIIT) less $98.55 (1987 noncontrolled section 902 corporation FTC)], and the noncontrolled section 902 corporation NIIT for 1988 is 0 [$95.82 (1988 noncontrolled section 902 corporation TIIT) less $95.82 (1988 noncontrolled section 902 corporation FTC)]. The general limitation income NIIT for 1987 is $6.89 [$30.62 (1987 general limitation income TIIT) less $23.73 (1987 general limitation income FTC)], and the general limitation NIIT for 1988 is $2.34 [$26.13 (1988 general limitation income TIIT) less $23.79 (1988 general limitation income FTC)]. An interest charge is calculated for each NIIT as provided in § 1.1291-4(d). The $3 excess of noncontrolled section 902 EDT allocated to 1988 ($98.82) over the FTC limitation calculated for the 1988 allocation of the noncontrolled section 902 excess distribution ($95.82) may not be used to reduce any federal income tax. The calculations of *Steps 5* through *9* are summarized as follows:

(A) *Noncontrolled section 902 corporation excess distribution:*

Taxable year (days) in holding period	Allocations to taxable year—Step 5 Excess distribution	EDT	Step 6 TIIT	Step 8 FTC	Step 9 NIIT
1987 (365)	$281.05	$98.55	$112.28	$98.55	$13.73
1988 (366)	281.82	98.82	95.82	95.82	0
1989 (90)	69.30	24.30			

(B) *General limitation income excess distribution:*

Taxable year (days) in holding period	Allocations to taxable year—Step 5 Excess distribution	EDT	Step 6 TIIT	Step 8 FTC	Step 9 NIIT
1987 (365)	$76.65	$23.73	$30.62	$23.73	$6.89
1988 (366)	76.86	23.79	26.13	23.79	2.34
1989 (90)	69.30	24.30			

(x) *Current shareholder year foreign tax credit.* The allocations of the separate category excess distributions to 1989, the current shareholder year, are included in USP's ordinary income. Such income is treated as a dividend from a CFC that is not a PFIC, and the EDT allocated to that income are treated as foreign taxes paid with respect to a dividend from a CFC that is not a PFIC.

(d) *Distributions from section 1291 funds that are noncontrolled section 902 corporations.*—If a noncontrolled section 902 corporation (as defined in section 904(d)(2)(E) and the regulations under that section) that is a section 1291 fund makes a distribution with respect to which a domestic shareholder (as defined in section 902 and the regulations under that section) is subject to tax under § 1.1291-2, the rules of paragraph (c) of this section apply for purposes of determining the amount of the foreign tax credit with respect to that distribution; however, the only separate category is described in section 904(d)(1)(E). This paragraph (d) does not apply to a United States shareholder of a CFC to whom paragraph (c) of this section applies.

(e) *Section 1248 gain.*—For purposes of determining the foreign tax credit under this section, a shareholder treats gain from a disposition of stock of a section 1291 fund as a distribution only to the extent that the gain would be, but for section 1291, includible in gross income as a dividend under section 1248. [Prop. Reg. § 1.1291-5.]

[Proposed 4-1-92.]

Proposed Regulation

§ 1.1291-6. Nonrecognition transfers of stock of section 1291 funds.—(a) *In general.*—(1) *Scope.*—This section provides rules concerning the recognition of gain by a shareholder on a direct or indirect disposition of stock of a section 1291 fund that results from a transaction in which, but for section 1291 and these regulations, there would not be full recognition of gain under the Code and regulations (the transaction hereinafter referred to as a nonrecognition transfer). This section also provides coordination between section 1291 and other provisions of the Code and regulations under which gain must be recognized in transactions that would otherwise be entitled to nonrecognition.

(2) *Nonrecognition transfers.*—A nonrecognition transfer includes, but is not limited to, a gift, a transfer by reason of death, a distribution to a beneficiary by a trust or estate (other than a distribution to which section 643(e)(3) applies), and a transfer in which gain or loss is not fully recognized pursuant to any of the following provisions: Sections 311(a), 332, 336(e), 337, 351, 354, 355, 361, 721, 731, 852(b)(6), 1036, and 1041.

(3) *Application of section to transfer of stock of a pedigreed QEF.*—This section does not apply to a nonrecognition transfer of stock of a pedigreed QEF. The following example illustrates the rule of this paragraph (a)(3).

Example. X is a U.S. person that is a shareholder of FC, a corporation. FC owns all the stock of FS. Both FC and FS are pedigreed QEFs with respect to X. Pursuant to a plan of complete liquidation, satisfying the requirements of section 332, FS distributes all its assets and liabilities to FC. No gain or loss will be recognized to FC, FS, or X under section 1291(f) or 1297(b)(5).

(b) *Recognition of gain or loss.*—(1) *In general.*—Unless otherwise provided in paragraph (c) of this section, a shareholder recognizes gain on any direct or indirect disposition of stock of a section 1291 fund in accordance with the rules of § 1.1291-3, without regard to whether the disposition is a result of a nonrecognition transfer as defined in paragraph (a)(2) of this section.

(2) *Coordination with other recognition provisions.*—A direct or indirect disposition of stock to which an exception to the gain recognition rule of paragraph (b)(1) of this section applies will nevertheless be a disposition taxable under § 1.1291-3 if the gain must be recognized pursuant to another provision of the Code or regulations. For coordination with section 367, *see* paragraph (d)(1) of this section.

(3) *No recognition of loss.*—This section does not permit or require the recognition of loss on a direct or indirect disposition of stock of a section 1291 fund if such loss would not otherwise be recognized under another section of the Code or regulations. For the effect on the holding period of a disposition resulting from a nonrecognition transfer that would be subject to the gain recognition rule but for the fact that a loss is realized, *see* paragraph (b)(5) of this section.

(4) *Special basis rules.*—(i) *Direct shareholders.*—If the gain recognition rule of paragraph (b)(1) of this section applies to a nonrecognition transfer in which a direct shareholder transfers stock of a section 1291 fund, proper adjustment is made to the basis of such stock in the hands of the transferee, as well as to the basis of the property, if any, received by the shareholder in the transaction.

(ii) *Indirect shareholders.*—If the gain recognition rule of paragraph (b)(1) of this section applies to a disposition by an indirect shareholder that results from a nonrecognition transfer, the shareholder's adjusted basis of the stock or other property owned directly by the shareholder through which ownership of the section 1291 fund is attributed to the shareholder is increased by the amount of gain recognized by the shareholder. In addition, solely for purposes of determining the subsequent treatment under the Code and regulations of a direct or indirect shareholder of the stock of the section 1291 fund treated as disposed of, the adjusted basis of the actual owner of the stock of the section 1291 fund is increased by the amount of gain recognized by the shareholder.

(iii) *Stock acquired by reason of death.*—Unless all of the gain is recognized to a shareholder (the decedent) pursuant to paragraph (c)(2)(iii)(B) of this section, the basis of stock received on the death of the decedent by the decedent's estate (other than a foreign estate within the meaning of section 7701(a)(31)), or directly by another U.S. person, is the lower of the fair market value or adjusted basis of the transferred stock in the hands of the shareholder immediately before death. If gain is recognized by the decedent, the decedent's adjusted basis of the stock of the section 1291 fund is increased by the gain recognized with respect thereto.

(iv) *Assets distributed in certain subsidiary liquidations.*—The bases of the assets of a section 1291 fund distributed to an 80 percent corporate distributee (within the meaning of section 337(c)), in complete liquidation of the section 1291 fund pursuant to section 332, is increased by the amount by which the gain recognized by the shareholder exceeds the amount that would have been taxed as a dividend under section 367(b). Except as otherwise provided in this paragraph (b)(4)(iv), the adjusted basis of each distributed asset is increased (but not in excess of its fair market value) by a pro rata portion of the excess described in the preceding sentence, based on the realized but unrecognized gain with respect to such asset relative to the realized but unrecognized gain with respect to all distributed assets. For purposes of the preceding sentence, money is not treated as an asset. The adjusted basis of a receivable may not be increased pursuant to this paragraph (b)(4)(iv) to an amount that exceeds the receivable's face amount.

Prop. Reg. § 1.1291-6(a)(2)

(5) *Special holding period rule for transfers subject to gain recognition rule.*—If a loss is realized on a direct or indirect disposition of stock of a section 1291 fund in a transaction in which any gain, if realized, would have been recognized under this section, the shareholder's holding period for stock received in the transaction, if any, as well as the transferee's holding period of the transferred stock, begins on the day after the disposition, but only for purposes of applying sections 1291 through 1297 to the shareholder or the transferee with respect to such stock, as appropriate.

(c) *Exceptions to general rule.*—(1) *Transfer of section 1291 fund stock for PFIC stock.*—Gain is not recognized on a direct or indirect disposition of stock of a section 1291 fund that results from a nonrecognition transfer if in the transfer, stock of the section 1291 fund, or an interest in another person that causes the shareholder to be an indirect shareholder, is exchanged solely for either—

(i) Stock of the same or another corporation that either qualifies under section 1296(a) as a PFIC for its taxable year that includes the day after the nonrecognition transfer or is the acquiring foreign corporation in a section 368(a)(1)(F) reorganization; or

(ii) An interest in another person that owns directly or indirectly stock of the transferred section 1291 fund or of another PFIC, but only to the extent (by value) that the shareholder is treated under §1.1291-1(b)(8) as owning after the transfer at least as great an interest in the section 1291 fund or other PFIC that the indirect shareholder owned before the transfer. Stock in another PFIC owned before the transfer is not taken into account for purposes of the preceding sentence. For the definition of an indirect disposition, *see* generally §1.1291-3(e)(2).

(2) *Transfer to U.S. person.*—(i) *In general.*—Unless otherwise provided, a shareholder does not recognize gain on a direct or indirect disposition of stock of a section 1291 fund that results from a nonrecognition transfer if immediately after the transfer such stock is owned or considered owned by a U.S. person (U.S. transferee), provided that—

(A) The basis of the stock that is the subject of the disposition, in the hands of its actual owner immediately after the transfer, is no greater than the basis of such stock in the hands of its actual owner immediately before the transfer;

(B) The U.S. transferee's holding period for the transferred stock is at least as long as the holding period of the shareholder immediately before the transfer; and

(C) The aggregate ownership (determined under §1.1291-1(b)(8)) of the shareholder and the U.S. transferee immediately after the transfer (determined without regard to stock held by the U.S. transferee prior to the transfer) is the same as or greater than the shareholder's proportionate ownership immediately before the transfer.

This paragraph (c)(2)(i) does not apply to a transfer to a partnership, S corporation, trust or estate. For those rules, *see* paragraph (c)(3) of this section.

(ii) *Transitory ownership.*—Gain is not recognized to a domestic corporation that is a party to a reorganization within the meaning of section 368(b) if, pursuant to a plan of reorganization, the corporation acquires stock of a PFIC that is a party to the reorganization in exchange for the domestic corporation's assets, and transfers the PFIC stock under section 361(c) to a shareholder that is a U.S. person in exchange for the shareholder's stock of the domestic corporation.

(iii) *Transfer by reason of death.*—(A) *In general.*—Except as provided in paragraph (c)(2)(iii)(B) of this section, gain is not recognized to a shareholder upon a disposition of stock of a section 1291 fund that results from a nonrecognition transfer to the shareholder's domestic estate or directly to another U.S. person upon the death of the shareholder.

(B) *Exception.*—Gain is recognized to a shareholder on the transfer of stock of a section 1291 fund to the shareholder's domestic estate if, pursuant to the terms of the will, the section 1291 fund stock may be transferred to either a foreign beneficiary or a trust established in the will.

(iv) *Section 355 distribution of stock of section 1291 fund.*—Gain is not recognized to a shareholder that is the distributing corporation upon a direct or indirect disposition of stock of a section 1291 fund that results from the distribution of stock of a controlled corporation to another U.S. person (the distributee) in a transaction qualifying under section 355(a) if the distributee is a shareholder with respect to such stock immediately after the distribution. The distributee in such a transaction takes a holding period in the stock of the controlled corporation equal to the longer of the holding period determined under section 1223(1) or the distributing corporation's holding period of the stock of the controlled corporation. If the controlled corporation is itself the section 1291 fund, the distributee in such a transaction takes a basis in the stock of the controlled corporation equal to the lesser of the adjusted basis determined under section 358 or the distributing corporation's adjusted basis of the stock of the controlled corporation immediately prior to the distribution.

(v) *Gifts incurring gift tax.*—If a shareholder makes a gift of stock of a section 1291 fund to a U.S. person and thereby incurs gift tax, the shareholder will not recognize gain, but will be liable for the deferred tax amount as if the shareholder recognized gain in the amount of the gift tax that is added to the basis of the transferred stock under section 1015(d). The adjusted basis of the transferred stock may only be increased, to the extent provided in section 1015(d), by the amount of gift tax paid. The following example illustrates the rule of this paragraph (c)(2)(v).

Example. M, a U.S. person, purchased 1,000 shares of NQF, a PFIC, on December 31, 1989. M did not elect to treat NQF as a QEF. M gave the NQF stock to her daughter, H, also a U.S. person, on December 31, 1993. M paid $100x of gift tax. As provided in section 1015(a) and (d)(6), H's adjusted basis in the NQF stock is M's adjusted basis, increased by $60x of gift tax paid. As a result, pursuant to § 1.1291-6(c)(2)(v), M is liable for the deferred tax amount that M would have owed if M recognized $60x of gain on a taxable transfer of the NQF stock. For purposes of calculating the deferred tax amount, the $60x is allocated over M's four-year holding period, with the deferred tax amount calculated with respect to the $45x allocated to 1991, 1992, and 1993. Other than for the $60x of gift tax paid, there are no further adjustments to H's basis in the NQF.

(vi) *Exception inapplicable.*—Paragraph (c)(2) of this section does not apply to a disposition of stock of a section 1291 fund that results from a nonrecognition transfer of stock of a section 1291 fund if the U.S. transferee is—

(A) An organization that will not be subject to section 1291 and these regulations pursuant to § 1.1291-1(e) with respect to that section 1291 fund; or

(B) A trust, including a testamentary trust or other irrevocable trust, that is not a grantor trust or beneficiary-owned section 678 trust to which paragraph (c)(3)(iv) of this section applies.

(3) *Transfers involving pass-through entities.*—(i) *Section 721 transfer to partnership.*—Gain is not recognized to a shareholder on a disposition of stock of a section 1291 fund that results from a transfer to a partnership under section 721, but only to the extent that the shareholder is treated as owning such stock immediately after the transfer pursuant to § 1.1291-1(b)(8)(iii)(A).

(ii) *Section 731 distribution by partnership.*—Gain is not recognized to a partner on a disposition of stock of a section 1291 fund that results from a distribution under section 731, but only to the extent that the partner is treated as owning such stock immediately after the distribution pursuant to § 1.1291-1(b)(8).

(iii) *Transfer to S corporation.*—Gain is not recognized to a shareholder on a disposition of stock of a section 1291 fund that results from a transfer to an S corporation under section 351, but only to the extent that the shareholder is treated as owning such stock immediately after the transfer pursuant to § 1.1291-1(b)(8)(iii)(B).

(iv) *Transfer to grantor trust.*—Gain is not recognized on a disposition of stock of a section 1291 fund that results from a nonrecognition transfer to a trust by the grantor of the trust if the grantor is treated as owning the portion of the trust that includes both the income and corpus portions of the stock that is disposed of. If a person other than the grantor is treated as the owner of the portion of a beneficiary-owned section 678 trust that includes the income and corpus portions of the stock transferred to the trust, that person is treated as acquiring the stock by gift from the grantor, which is a transfer subject to the general rules of this section. Stock owned directly or indirectly by a grantor of a grantor trust or by a beneficiary of a beneficiary-owned section 678 trust will be treated as transferred by the grantor or other person considered the owner thereof for purposes of this section at the time the grantor or beneficiary is no longer considered the owner of both the income and corpus portions of the stock of the section 1291 fund. For special rules applicable to a grantor or beneficiary-owned section 678 trust, *see* sections 671 through 679 and the regulations under those sections.

(4) *Transfer to nonresident alien spouse who files joint return.*—Gain is not recognized on a disposition of stock of a section 1291 fund that results from a nonrecognition transfer to the shareholder's nonresident alien spouse who has made the election under section 6013(g) and is treated as a resident for purposes of chapter 1 of the Code. A termination of the election pursuant to section 6013(g)(4) will be treated as a disposition of the stock by the transferee spouse as provided in § 1.1291-3(b)(2).

(d) *Special rules.*—(1) *Section 367 or 1492 transfer.*—(i) *Gain recognition transfer.*—If the gain recognition rule of paragraph (b)(1) of this section applies to a disposition of stock of a section 1291 fund that results from a transfer with respect to which section 367 or 1492 requires the shareholder to recognize gain or include an amount in income as a distribution under section 301, the gain realized on the transfer is taxable as an excess distribution as provided in § 1.1291-2(e)(2). The excess, if any, of the amount to be included in income pursuant to section 367(b) over the gain realized is taxable as provided in the regulations under section 367(b).

(ii) *Disposition to which exception applies.*—If an exception to the gain recognition rule of paragraph (b)(1) of this section applies to a disposition to which section 367(b) applies, and section 367(b) requires the shareholder to include an amount in income as a distribution taxable under section 301, that amount is an excess distribution taxable as provided in § 1.1291-2(e)(2).

(2) *Taxable year of disposition by reason of death.*—A disposition of stock of a section 1291 fund by reason of a shareholder's death, to which the gain recognition rule of paragraph (b)(1) or (c)(2)(iii)(B) of this section applies, will be treated as a disposition by the shareholder effected immediately before death and taxable to the shareholder in the shareholder's last taxable year.

(3) *Section 643(e)(3) election.*—An election by a foreign estate or trust under section 643(e)(3) will not apply to stock of a section 1291 fund distributed to a U.S. person if the gain recognized by reason of the election is not taxable in the United States.

(e) *Receipt of nonqualifying property.*—If a nonrecognition transfer results in a disposition of stock of a section 1291 fund to which an exception to the gain recognition rule of paragraph (b)(1) of this section would apply but for the fact that the property received in the transfer includes money or property (nonqualifying property) in addition to property permitted to be received pursuant to paragraph (c) of this section, gain is recognized only to the extent of the nonqualifying property. If such nonqualifying property is treated as a distribution by the section 1291 fund under otherwise applicable provisions of the Code, the distribution will be taxable on an excess distribution as provided in § 1.1291-2(e)(2).

(f) *Examples.*—The following examples illustrate the operation of this section.

Example 1. A is a shareholder of PFIC, a corporation organized under the laws of Country X. PFIC is a section 1291 fund with respect to A. To avoid expropriation of the assets of PFIC by the government of Country X, PFIC's management has decided to relocate to Country Y. To effect the relocation, PFIC adopted a plan of reorganization pursuant to which PFIC will transfer all of its assets to Newco, a newly organized Country Y corporation, in exchange for Newco stock and the assumption of PFIC's liabilities in a transaction that will qualify as a reorganization described in section 368(a)(1)(F). PFIC will distribute the Newco stock to its shareholders in exchange for its stock. A will transfer all of its PFIC stock in exchange for Newco stock of equal value. A will not recognize gain on the transfer of PFIC stock in exchange for Newco stock pursuant to section 354 and § 1.1291-6(c)(1)(i), and the days in A's holding period of the Newco stock will retain the prePFIC and prior PFIC character of the days in A's holding period of the PFIC stock pursuant to § 1.1291-1(h)(7). See § 1.1291-1(b)(1)(ii).

Example 2. X is a domestic corporation that owns 75 percent of F, a foreign corporation that is not a PFIC. F owns 100 percent of the stock of FS, a PFIC. X is treated under § 1.1291-1(b)(8)(ii)(A) as owning 75 percent of the stock of FS. X has not elected under section 1295 to treat FS as a QEF. FC, a foreign corporation, will acquire substantially all the assets of F in exchange for FC stock and the assumption of the liabilities of F in a transaction that will qualify as a reorganization described in section 368(a)(1)(C). FC never qualified as a PFIC and will not qualify as a PFIC at the beginning of the day after the transaction. F will distribute the FC stock to its shareholders in exchange for their F stock. X will transfer all its F stock to F in exchange for FC stock of equal value. After the reorganization, X will hold 49 percent of the outstanding FC stock, and therefore will no longer be treated under § 1.1291-1(b)(8)(ii)(A) as owning stock of FS. Pursuant to §§ 1.1291-6(b)(1) and 1.1291-3(e)(1), X will be taxed on the indirect disposition of the FS stock.

Example 3. X, a domestic corporation, owns stock of PFIC, a corporation that is a section 1291 fund with respect to X. Pursuant to a plan of reorganization, X will transfer to FC, a foreign corporation, substantially all of its assets in exchange for FC voting stock and FC's assumption of the liabilities of X in a transaction that will qualify as a reorganization described in section 368(a)(1)(C). It is assumed that the transaction is not taxable under section 367(a) (including section 367(a)(5)). X will distribute the FC stock to its shareholders in exchange for their X stock. FC is not a PFIC and will not qualify as a PFIC for the taxable year that includes the day after the transfer. In addition, after the reorganization, no U.S. person will own 50 percent or more of FC. Pursuant to § 1.1291-6(b)(1), section 361(a) will not apply to X's transfer of the PFIC stock to FC. X therefore will recognize the gain realized on the transfer of the stock of PFIC. The gain will be taxed to X as an excess distribution pursuant to § 1.1291-3.

Example 4. X, a domestic corporation, satisfies the stock ownership requirements specified in section 332(b) with respect to PFIC, a corporation that is a section 1291 fund with respect to X. Pursuant to a plan of complete liquidation, PFIC will distribute all its assets and liabilities to X in exchange for its stock and liquidate. Pursuant to § 1.1291-6(b)(1) and (d)(1)(i), section 332(a) will not apply to the complete liquidation of PFIC. X therefore will recognize gain on the disposition of the stock of PFIC, which gain will be taxed as an excess distribution pursuant to § 1.1291-3. The adjusted basis of the assets of X will be increased as provided in § 1.1291-6(b)(4)(iv).

Example 5. USP, a domestic corporation, owns all the stock of USS, also a domestic corporation. USS owns stock of FS, a corporation that is a section 1291 fund with respect to USS. Pursuant to a plan of reorganization that will qualify under section 368(a)(1)(C), USS will transfer substantially all its assets to FC, a PFIC, in exchange for FC stock and the assumption by FC of the liabilities of USS. USS will transfer the FC stock to USP in exchange for its stock. Pursuant to § 1.1291-6(c)(1), section 361 applies to USS's transfer to FC of the FS stock. As provided in § 1.1291-6(c)(2)(ii), USS will not recognize any gain on the transfer of the FC stock to USP in exchange for its stock.

Example 6. A, a U.S. person, owns all the stock of FC, a corporation that is both a controlled foreign corporation and a section 1291 fund with respect to A. Pursuant to a reorganization plan, FC will transfer all its assets to F, a foreign corporation that is a PFIC but not a controlled foreign corporation after the transfer, in exchange for F stock and the assumption of FC's liabilities in a transaction that will qualify as a reorganization described in section 368(a)(1)(C). FC will distribute the F stock to A in exchange for A's FC stock. A will not recognize gain on the transfer of FC stock in exchange for F stock pursuant to section 354 and § 1.1291-6(c)(1). However, the regulations under section 367(b) require A to include a certain amount in gross income as a distribution taxable under section 301. As provided in § 1.1291-6(d)(1)(ii), A will treat that amount as an excess distribution taxable as provided in § 1.1291-2(e)(2).

Example 7. M, a U.S. person, purchased 100 shares of the stock of NQF on December 31, 1989, for $100. NQF is a corporation that is a section 1291 fund with respect to M. On January 1, 1992, when the 100 shares of NQF stock had a fair market value of $200, M transferred its NQF stock to P, a domestic partnership, of which M and N, also a U.S. person, are equal partners. After the transfer to P, M will be considered to own only 50 shares of the NQF stock pursuant to § 1.1291-1(b)(8)(iii)(A), notwithstanding that gain recognized with respect to all 100 shares would be allocated to M pursuant to section 704(c). M therefore is taxable on the disposition of 50 shares of NQF stock in accordance with § 1.1291-6(c)(3)(i).

(g) *Reporting requirements for transfers entitled to nonrecognition treatment under this section.*—If an exception to the gain recognition rule of paragraph (b)(1) of this section applies wholly or partly to a disposition of stock of a section 1291 fund that results from a nonrecognition transfer, the shareholder must provide the following information in an attachment to Form 8621, which must be filed with the shareholder's federal income tax return for the taxable year in which the transfer occurs:

(1) A complete description of the transfer, including a complete description of the stock, securities or other property received directly or indirectly in the transfer.

(2) The name, address, and taxpayer identification number (if available) of the transferor and transferee of the transferred property.

(3) A statement citing the applicable exception to the gain recognition rule and stating why the exception is applicable.

(h) *Transfers involving QEF stock.*—For rules concerning the effect of a transfer of stock of a QEF on the section 1295 election, see § 1.1295-1. [Prop. Reg. § 1.1291-6.]

[Proposed 4-1-92.]

Proposed Regulation

§ 1.1291-7. Section 1291(e) rules similar to section 1246.—[Reserved]

[Proposed 4-1-92.]

§ 1.1291-9. Deemed dividend election.—(a) *Deemed dividend election.*—(1) *In general.*—This section provides rules for making the election under section 1291(d)(2)(B) (deemed dividend election). Under that section, a shareholder (as defined in paragraph (j)(3) of this section) of a PFIC that is an unpedigreed QEF may elect to include in income as a dividend the shareholder's pro rata share of the post-1986 earnings and profits of the PFIC attributable to the stock held on the qualification date (as defined in paragraph (e) of this section), provided the PFIC is a controlled foreign corporation (CFC) within the meaning of section 957(a) for the taxable year for which the shareholder elects under section 1295 to treat the PFIC as a QEF (section 1295 election). If the shareholder makes the deemed dividend election, the PFIC will become a pedigreed QEF with respect to the shareholder. The deemed dividend is taxed under section 1291 as an excess distribution received on the qualification date. The excess distribution determined under this paragraph (a) is allocated under section 1291(a)(1)(A) only to those days in the shareholder's holding period during which the foreign corporation qualified as a PFIC. For purposes of the preceding sentence, the holding period of the PFIC stock with respect to which the election is made ends on the day before the qualification date. For the definitions of PFIC, QEF, unpedigreed QEF, and pedigreed QEF, see paragraph (j)(1) and (2) of this section.

(2) *Post-1986 earnings and profits defined.*—(i) *In general.*—For purposes of this section, the term post-1986 earnings and profits means the undistributed earnings and profits, within the meaning of section 902(c)(1), as of the day before the qualification date, that were accumulated and not distributed in taxable years of the PFIC beginning after 1986 and during which it was a PFIC, but without regard to whether the earnings relate to a period during which the PFIC was a CFC.

(ii) *Pro rata share of post-1986 earnings and profits attributable to shareholder's stock.*— (A) *In general.*—A shareholder's pro rata share of the post-1986 earnings and profits of the PFIC attributable to the stock held by the shareholder on the qualification date is the amount of post-1986 earnings and profits of the PFIC accumulated during any portion of the shareholder's holding period ending at the close of the day before the qualification date and attributable, under the principles of section 1248 and the regulations under that section, to the PFIC stock held on the qualification date.

(B) *Reduction for previously taxed amounts.*—A shareholder's pro rata share of the post-1986 earnings and profits of the PFIC does not include any amount that the shareholder demonstrates to the satisfaction of the Commissioner (in the manner provided in paragraph (d)(2) of this section) was, pursuant to another provision of the law, previously included in the income of the shareholder, or of another U.S. person if the shareholder's holding period of the PFIC stock includes the period during which the stock was held by that other U.S. person.

(b) *Who may make the election.*—A shareholder of an unpedigreed QEF that is a CFC for the taxable year of the PFIC for which the shareholder makes the section 1295 election may make the deemed dividend election provided the shareholder held stock of that PFIC on the qualification date. A shareholder is treated as holding stock of the PFIC on the qualification date if its holding period with respect to that stock under section 1223 includes the qualification date. A shareholder may make the deemed dividend election without regard to whether the shareholder is a United States shareholder within the meaning of section 951(b). A deemed dividend election may be made by a shareholder whose pro rata share of the post-1986 earnings and profits of the PFIC attributable to the PFIC stock held on the qualification date is zero.

(c) *Time for making the election.*—The shareholder makes the deemed dividend election in the shareholder's return for the taxable year that includes the qualification date. If the shareholder and the PFIC have the same taxable year, the shareholder makes the deemed dividend election in either the original return for the taxable year for which the shareholder makes the section 1295 election, or in an amended return for that year. If the shareholder and the PFIC have different taxable years, the deemed dividend election must be made in an amended return for the taxable year that includes the qualification date. If the deemed dividend election is made in an amended return, the amended return must be filed by a date that is within three years of the due date, as extended under section 6081, of the original return for the taxable year that includes the qualification date.

(d) *Manner of making the election.*—(1) *In general.*—A shareholder makes the deemed dividend election by filing Form 8621 and the attachment to Form 8621 described in paragraph (d)(2) of this section with the return for the taxable year of the shareholder that includes the qualification date, reporting the deemed dividend as an excess distribution pursuant to section 1291(a)(1), and paying the tax and interest due on the excess distribution. A shareholder that makes the deemed dividend election after the due date of the return (determined without regard to extensions) for the taxable year that includes the qualification date must pay additional interest, pursuant to section 6601, on the amount of the underpayment of tax for that year.

(2) *Attachment to Form 8621.*—The shareholder must attach a schedule to Form 8621 that demonstrates the calculation of the shareholder's pro rata share of the post-1986 earnings and profits of the PFIC that is treated as distributed to the shareholder on the qualification date pursuant to this section. If the shareholder is claiming an exclusion from its pro rata share of the post-1986 earnings and profits for an amount previously included in its income or the income of another U.S. person, the

shareholder must include the following information:

(i) The name, address, and taxpayer identification number of each U.S. person that previously included an amount in income, the amount previously included in income by each such U.S. person, the provision of the law pursuant to which the amount was previously included in income, and the taxable year or years of inclusion of each amount; and

(ii) A description of the transaction pursuant to which the shareholder acquired, directly or indirectly, the stock of the PFIC from another U.S. person, and the provisions of law pursuant to which the shareholder's holding period includes the period the other U.S. person held the CFC stock.

(e) *Qualification date.*—(1) *In general.*—Except as otherwise provided in this paragraph (e), the qualification date is the first day of the PFIC's first taxable year as a QEF (first QEF year).

(2) *Elections made after March 31, 1995, and before January 27, 1997.*—(i) *In general.*—The qualification date for deemed dividend elections made after March 31, 1995, and before January 27, 1997, is the first day of the shareholder's election year. The shareholder's election year is the taxable year of the shareholder for which it made the section 1295 election.

(ii) *Exception.*—A shareholder who made the deemed dividend election after May 1, 1992, and before January 27, 1997, may elect to change its qualification date to the first day of the first QEF year, provided the periods of limitations on assessment for the taxable year that includes that date and for the shareholder's election year have not expired. A shareholder changes the qualification date by filing amended returns, with revised Forms 8621 and the attachments described in paragraph (d)(2) of this section, for the shareholder's election year and the shareholder's taxable year that includes the first day of the first QEF year, and making all appropriate adjustments and payments.

(3) *Examples.*—The rules of this paragraph (e) are illustrated by the following examples:

Example 1—(i) *Eligibility to make deemed dividend election.* A is a U.S. person who files its income tax return on a calendar year basis. On January 2, 1994, A purchased one percent of the stock of M, a PFIC with a taxable year ending November 30. M was both a CFC and a PFIC, but not a QEF, for all of its taxable years. On December 3, 1996, M made a distribution to its shareholders. A received $100, all of which A reported in its 1996 return as an excess distribution as provided in section 1291(a)(1). A decides to make the section 1295 election in A's 1997 taxable year to treat M as a QEF effective for M's taxable year beginning December 1, 1996. Because A did not make the section 1295 election in 1994, the first year in its holding period of M stock that M qualified as a PFIC, M would be an unpedigreed QEF and A would be subject to both sections 1291 and 1293. A, however, may elect under section 1291(d)(2) to purge the years M was not a QEF from A's holding period. If A makes the section 1291(d)(2) election, the December 3 distribution will not be taxable under section 1291(a). Because M is a CFC, even though A is not a U.S. shareholder within the meaning of section 951(b), A may make the deemed dividend election under section 1291(d)(2)(B).

(ii) *Making the election.* Under paragraph (e)(1) of this section, the qualification date, and therefore the date of the deemed dividend, is December 1, 1996. Accordingly, to make the deemed dividend election, A must file an amended return for 1996, and include the deemed dividend in income in that year. As a result, M will be a pedigreed QEF as of December 1, 1996, and the December 3, 1996, distribution will not be taxable as an excess distribution. Therefore, in its amended return, A may report the December 3, 1996, distribution consistent with section 1293 and the general rules applicable to corporate distributions.

Example 2. X, a U.S. person, owned a five percent interest in the stock of FC, a PFIC with a taxable year ending June 30. X never made the section 1295 election with respect to FC. X transferred her interest in FC to her granddaughter, Y, a U.S. person, on February 14, 1996. The transfer qualified as a gift for federal income tax purposes, and no gain was recognized on the transfer (see Regulation Project INTL-656-87, published in 1992-1 C.B. 1124; see § 601.601(d)(2)(ii)(*b*) of this chapter). As provided in section 1223(2), Y's holding period includes the period that X held the FC stock. Y decides to make the section 1295 election in her 1996 return to treat FC as a QEF for its taxable year beginning July 1, 1995. However, because Y's holding period includes the period that X held the FC stock, and FC was a PFIC but not a QEF during that period, FC will be an unpedigreed QEF with respect to Y unless Y makes a section 1291(d)(2) election. Although Y did not actually own the stock of FC on the qualification date (July 1, 1995), Y's holding period includes that date. Therefore, provided FC is a CFC for its taxable year beginning July 1, 1995, Y may make a section 1291(d)(2)(B) election to treat FC as a pedigreed QEF.

(f) *Adjustment to basis.*—A shareholder that makes the deemed dividend election increases its adjusted basis of the stock of the PFIC owned directly by the shareholder by the amount of the deemed dividend. If the shareholder makes the deemed dividend election with respect to a PFIC of which it is an indirect shareholder, the shareholder's adjusted basis of the stock or other property owned directly by the shareholder, through which ownership of the PFIC is attributed to the shareholder, is increased by the amount of the deemed dividend. In addition, solely for purposes of determining the subsequent treatment under the Code and regulations of a shareholder of the stock of the PFIC, the adjusted basis of the direct owner of the stock of the PFIC is increased by the amount of the deemed dividend.

(g) *Treatment of holding period.*—For purposes of applying sections 1291 through 1297 to the shareholder after the deemed dividend, the shareholder's holding period of the stock of the PFIC begins on the qualification date. For other purposes of the Code and regulations, this holding period rule does not apply.

(h) *Coordination with section 959(e).*—For purposes of section 959(e), the entire deemed dividend is treated as included in gross income under section 1248(a).

(i) *Election inapplicable to shareholder of former PFIC.*—(1) [Reserved].

(2) *Former PFIC.*—A shareholder may not make the section 1295 and deemed dividend elections if the foreign corporation is a former PFIC (as defined in paragraph (j)(2)(iv) of this section) with respect to the shareholder. For the rules regarding the election by a shareholder of a former PFIC, see § 1.1297-3T.

(j) *Definitions.*—(1) *Passive foreign investment company (PFIC).*—A passive foreign investment company (PFIC) is a foreign corporation that satisfies either the income test of section 1296(a)(1) or the asset test of section 1296(a)(2). A corporation will not be treated as a PFIC with respect to a shareholder for those days included in the shareholder's holding period when the shareholder, or a person whose holding period of the stock is included in the shareholder's holding period, was not a United States person within the meaning of section 7701(a)(30).

(2) *Types of PFICs.*—(i) *Qualified electing fund (QEF).*—A PFIC is a qualified electing fund (QEF) with respect to a shareholder that has elected, under section 1295, to be taxed currently on its share of the PFIC's earnings and profits pursuant to section 1293.

(ii) *Pedigreed QEF.*—A PFIC is a pedigreed QEF with respect to a shareholder if the PFIC has been a QEF with respect to the shareholder for all taxable years during which the corporation was a PFIC that are included wholly or partly in the shareholder's holding period of the PFIC stock.

(iii) *Unpedigreed QEF.*—A PFIC is an unpedigreed QEF for a taxable year if—

(A) An election under section 1295 is in effect for that year;

(B) The PFIC has been a QEF with respect to the shareholder for at least one, but not all, of the taxable years during which the corporation was a PFIC that are included wholly or partly in the shareholder's holding period of the PFIC stock; and

(C) The shareholder has not made an election under section 1291(d)(2) and this section or § 1.1291-10 with respect to the PFIC to purge the nonQEF years from the shareholder's holding period.

(iv) *Former PFIC.*—A foreign corporation is a former PFIC with respect to a shareholder if the corporation satisfies neither the income test of section 1296(a)(1) nor the asset test of section 1296(a)(2), but whose stock, held by that shareholder, is treated as stock of a PFIC, pursuant to section 1297(b)(1), because at any time during the shareholder's holding period of the stock the corporation was a PFIC that was not a QEF.

(3) *Shareholder.*—A shareholder is a U.S. person that is a direct or indirect shareholder as defined in Regulation Project INTL-656-87 published in 1992-1 C.B. 1124; see § 601.601(d)(2)(ii)(*b*) of this chapter.

(k) *Effective date.*—The rules of this section are applicable as of April 1, 1995. [Reg. § 1.1291-9.]

☐ [*T.D.* 8701, 12-26-96. *Amended by T.D.* 8750, 12-31-97.]

§ 1.1291-10. Deemed sale election.— (a) *Deemed sale election.*—This section provides rules for making the election under section 1291(d)(2)(A) (deemed sale election). Under that section, a shareholder (as defined in § 1.1291-9(j)(3)) of a PFIC that is an unpedigreed QEF may elect to recognize gain with respect to the stock of the unpedigreed QEF held on the qualification date (as defined in paragraph (e) of this section). If the shareholder makes the deemed sale election, the PFIC will become a pedigreed QEF with respect to the shareholder. A shareholder that makes the deemed sale election is treated as having sold, for its fair market value, the stock of the PFIC that the shareholder held on the qualification date. The gain recognized on the deemed sale is taxed under section 1291 as an excess distribution received on the qualification date. In the case of an election made by an indirect shareholder, the amount of gain to be recognized and taxed as an excess distribution is the amount of gain that the direct owner of the stock of the PFIC would have realized on an actual sale or other disposition of the stock of the PFIC indirectly owned by the shareholder. Any loss realized on the deemed sale is not recognized. For the definitions of PFIC, QEF, unpedigreed QEF, and pedigreed QEF, see § 1.1291-9(j)(1) and (2).

(b) *Who may make the election.*—A shareholder of an unpedigreed QEF may make the deemed sale election provided the shareholder held stock of that PFIC on the qualification date. A shareholder is treated as holding stock of the PFIC on the qualification date if its holding period with respect to that stock under section 1223 includes the qualification date. A deemed sale election may be made by a shareholder that would realize a loss on the deemed sale.

(c) *Time for making the election.*—The shareholder makes the deemed sale election in the shareholder's return for the taxable year that includes the qualification date. If the shareholder and the PFIC have the same taxable year, the shareholder makes the deemed sale election in either the original return for the taxable year for which the shareholder makes the section 1295 election, or in an amended return for that year. If the shareholder and the PFIC have different taxable years, the deemed sale election must be made in an amended return for the taxable year that includes the qualification date. If the deemed sale election is made in an amended return, the amended return must be filed by a date that is within three years of the due date, as extended under section 6081, of the original return for the taxable year that includes the qualification date.

(d) *Manner of making the election.*—A shareholder makes the deemed sale election by filing Form 8621 with the return for the taxable year of the shareholder that includes the qualification date, reporting the gain as an excess distribution pursuant to section 1291(a), and paying the tax and interest due on the excess distribution. A shareholder that makes the deemed sale election after the due date of the return (determined without regard to extensions) for the taxable year that includes the qualification date must pay additional interest, pursuant to section 6601, on the amount of the underpayment of tax for that year. A shareholder that realizes a loss on the deemed sale reports the loss on Form 8621, but does not recognize the loss.

(e) *Qualification date.*—(1) *In general.*—Except as otherwise provided in this paragraph (e), the qualification date is the first day of the PFIC's first taxable year as a QEF (first QEF year).

(2) *Elections made after March 31, 1995, and before January 27, 1997.*—(i) *In general.*—The qualification date for deemed sale elections made after March 31, 1995, and before January 27, 1997, is the first day of the shareholder's election year. The shareholder's election year is the taxable year of the shareholder for which it made the section 1295 election.

(ii) *Exception.*—A shareholder who made the deemed sale election after May 1, 1992, and before January 27, 1997, may elect to change its qualification date to the first day of the first QEF year, provided the periods of limitations on assessment for the taxable year that includes that date and for the shareholder's election year have not expired. A shareholder changes the qualification date by filing amended returns, with revised Forms 8621, for the shareholder's election year and the shareholder's taxable year that includes the first day of the first QEF year, and making all appropriate adjustments and payments.

(f) *Adjustments to basis.*—(1) *In general.*—A shareholder that makes the deemed sale election increases its adjusted basis of the PFIC stock owned directly by the amount of gain recognized on the deemed sale. If the shareholder makes the deemed sale election with respect to a PFIC of which it is an indirect shareholder, the shareholder's adjusted basis of the stock or other property owned directly by the shareholder, through which ownership of the PFIC is attributed to the shareholder, is increased by the amount of gain recognized by the shareholder. In addition, solely for purposes of determining the subsequent treatment under the Code and regulations of a shareholder of the stock of the PFIC, the adjusted basis of the direct owner of the stock of the PFIC is increased by the amount of gain recognized on the deemed sale. A shareholder shall not adjust the basis of any stock with respect to which the shareholder realized a loss on the deemed sale.

(2) *Adjustment of basis for section 1293 inclusion with respect to deemed sale election made after March 31, 1995, and before January 27, 1997.*—For purposes of determining the amount of gain recognized with respect to a deemed sale election made after March 31, 1995, and before January 27, 1997, by a shareholder that treats the first day of the share-

holder's election year as the qualification date, the adjusted basis of the stock deemed sold includes the shareholder's section 1293(a) inclusion attributable to the period beginning with the first day of the PFIC's first QEF year and ending on the day before the qualification date.

(g) *Treatment of holding period.*—For purposes of applying sections 1291 through 1297 to the shareholder after the deemed sale, the shareholder's holding period of the stock of the PFIC begins on the qualification date, without regard to whether the shareholder recognized gain on the deemed sale. For other purposes of the Code and regulations, this holding period rule does not apply.

(h) *Election inapplicable to shareholder of former PFIC.*—A shareholder may not make the section 1295 and deemed sale elections if the foreign corporation is a former PFIC (as defined in § 1.1291-9(j)(2)(iv)) with respect to the shareholder. For the rules regarding the election by a shareholder of a former PFIC, see 1.1297-3T.

(i) *Effective date.*—The rules of this section are applicable as of April 1, 1995. [Reg. § 1.1291-10.]

☐ [*T.D.* 8701, 12-26-96.]

§ 1.1293-1. Current taxation of income from qualified electing funds.—(a) *In general.*—[Reserved].

(1) *Other rules.*—[Reserved].

(2) *Net capital gain defined.*—(i) *In general.*—This paragraph (a)(2) defines the term net capital gain for purposes of sections 1293 and 1295 and the regulations under those sections. The QEF, as defined in § 1.1291-9(j)(2)(i), in determining its net capital gain for a taxable year, may either—

(A) Calculate and report the amount of each category of long-term capital gain provided in section 1(h) that was recognized by the PFIC in the taxable year;

(B) Calculate and report the amount of net capital gain recognized by the PFIC in the taxable year, stating that that amount is subject to the highest capital gain rate of tax applicable to the shareholder; or

(C) Calculate its earnings and profits for the taxable year and report the entire amount as ordinary earnings.

(ii) *Effective date.*—Paragraph (a)(2)(i) of this section is applicable to sales by QEFs during their taxable years ending on or after May 7, 1997.

(b) *Other rules.*—[Reserved].

(c) *Application of rules of inclusion with respect to stock held by a pass through entity.*—(1) *In general.*—If a domestic pass through entity makes a section 1295 election, as provided in paragraph (d)(2) of this section, with respect to the PFIC shares that it owns, directly or indirectly, the domestic pass through entity takes into account its pro rata share of the ordinary earnings and net capital gain attributable to the QEF shares held by the pass through entity. A U.S. person that indirectly owns QEF shares through the domestic pass through entity accounts for its pro rata shares of ordinary earnings and net capital gain attributable to the QEF shares according to the general rules applicable to inclusions of income from the domestic pass through entity. For the definition of pass through entity, see § 1.1295-1(j).

(2) *QEF stock transferred to a pass through entity.*—(i) *Pass through entity makes a section 1295 election.*—If a shareholder transfers stock subject to a section 1295 election to a domestic pass through entity of which it is an interest holder and the pass through entity makes a section 1295 election with respect to that stock, as provided in § 1.1295-1(d)(2), the shareholder takes into account its pro rata shares of the ordinary earnings and net capital gain attributable to the QEF shares under the rules applicable to inclusions of income from the pass through entity.

(ii) *Pass through entity does not make a section 1295 election.*—If the pass through entity does not make a section 1295 election with respect to the PFIC, the shares of which were transferred to the pass through entity subject to the 1295 election of the shareholder, the shareholder continues to be subject, in its capacity as an indirect shareholder, to the income inclusion rules of section 1293 and reporting rules required of shareholders of QEFs. Proper adjustments to reflect an inclusion in income under section 1293 by the indirect shareholder must be made, under the principles of § 1.1291-9(f), to the basis of the indirect shareholder's interest in the pass through entity.

(3) *Effective date.*—Paragraph (c) of this section is applicable to taxable years of shareholders beginning after December 31, 1997. [Reg. § 1.1293-1.]

☐ [*T.D.* 8750, 12-31-97. *Redesignated and amended by T.D. 8870, 2-4-2000.*]

Proposed Regulations

§ 1.1293-1. Current taxation of income from qualified electing funds.—(a) *In general.*—Pursuant to section 1293(a)(1), every U.S. person that is a direct or indirect shareholder of a PFIC during a taxable year of the PFIC for which the shareholder has in effect a section 1295 election (within the meaning of § 1.1295-1(a)) includes in gross income the shareholder's pro rata share of the ordinary earnings and net capital gain of such fund for that taxable year. Such amounts are included in income in the taxable year of the shareholder in which or with which the taxable year of the PFIC ends. Section 1293 applies to a shareholder of a pedigreed QEF (as defined in § 1.1291-1(b)(2)(ii)) only for those taxable years during which the corporation qualifies as a PFIC under section 1296(a). Section 1293 applies to a shareholder of an unpedigreed QEF (as defined in § 1.1291-1(b)(2)(iii)) for those taxable years during which the corporation is a PFIC (as defined in § 1.1291-1(b)(1)).

(b) *Other rules.*—[Reserved] [Prop. Reg. § 1.1293-1.]

[Proposed 4-1-92.]

Proposed Regulation

§ 1.1293-2. Special inclusion rules for special preferred QEF election.—(a) *In general.*—A shareholder (including a shareholder that is a pass-through entity, as described in § 1.1295-2(c)(1)) that makes a special preferred QEF election under § 1.1295-2 must, regardless of the shareholder's method of accounting, include in income in respect of each share subject to the election, an annual amount (preferred QEF amount) determined according to the rules of paragraph (b) of this section. A shareholder that makes a special preferred QEF election must include the preferred QEF amount in income under this section for each year in which the taxpayer continues to hold a share that is subject to the election. The rules of this section apply in lieu of the general rules of section 1293 and § 1.1293-1.[1]

(b) *Preferred QEF amount.*—(1) *In general.*—The preferred QEF amount for any share subject to a special preferred QEF election is the sum of the ratable daily portion of each periodic dividend amount (as described in paragraph (b)(2) of this section) on the share for the taxable year of the shareholder to which that portion relates, plus the preferred discount amount (as defined below), if any, for the taxable year. For purposes of this section, the preferred discount amount for a taxable year is the amount that bears the same ratio to the total amount of preferred discount (as described in § 1.1295-2(b)(2)(i)) on the share as the number of days that the taxpayer held the share in the taxable year bears to the number of days after the date the taxpayer acquired the share and up to (and including) the share's redemption date as established under the principles of § 1.305-5(b). Notwithstanding the preceding sentence, the preferred discount amount for a taxable year is zero if the preferred discount on the share at the time of its acquisition by the shareholder was less than an amount equal to ¼ of 1 percent of the redemption price of the stock, multiplied by the number of complete years from the date of acquisition of the stock to the redemption date of the stock.

(2) *Periodic dividend amount.*—A periodic dividend amount is the amount payable with respect to a share, whether on a cumulative or noncumulative basis, for a period (wholly or partly within the shareholder's taxable year) for which dividends on the share are calculated based upon the redemption or liquidation price of the share multiplied by a fixed percentage rate.

(c) *Special rules of application.*—(1) *Earnings and profits disregarded.*—The amounts to be included in income pursuant to this section are determined without regard to the earnings and profits of the foreign corporation with respect to which the special preferred QEF election applies.

(2) *Year of inclusion.*—The shareholder includes the preferred QEF amount in its taxable year without regard to the taxable year of the foreign corporation with respect to which the special preferred QEF election applies.

(3) *Character of inclusions.*—The shareholder includes all preferred QEF amounts in income as ordinary earnings.

(4) *Treatment of distributions.*—Distributions received by a shareholder on shares subject to a special preferred QEF election that are paid out of earnings and profits of the foreign corporation are not included in gross income of the shareholder to the extent the distributions do not exceed the preferred QEF amounts (other than any portion of preferred QEF amounts consisting of preferred discount amounts) previously includible in income pursuant to this section. These distributions will, however, be treated as dividends for all other purposes of the Code and regulations. Amounts distributed to a shareholder with respect to shares subject to a special preferred QEF election that exceed amounts previously included in income under this section with respect to such shares are treated for all purposes of the Code and regulations as a distribution of property subject to the rules of section 301.

---

[1] This proposed regulation was published on April 1, 1992, at 57 Fed. Reg. 11024.

(5) *Basis adjustment rules.*—The adjusted basis of a shareholder in shares that are subject to a special preferred QEF election shall be—

(i) Increased by any amount that is included in the gross income of the shareholder under paragraph (a) of this section; and

(ii) Decreased by any dividends (not to exceed the amount included in gross income under paragraph (a) of this section) actually paid to the shareholder in respect of such shares.

(6) *Effect limited to electing shareholder.*—This section does not apply to the foreign corporation with respect to which a special preferred QEF election applies. Accordingly, the provisions of this section will not affect the foreign corporation's calculation of its earnings and profits for any purpose of the Code or regulations. In addition, the rules of this section apply only for purposes of determining the tax consequences for holders of shares subject to the election. Thus, the election shall have no effect on the application of the Code or regulations with respect to the tax consequences of the ownership of shares that are not subject to the election, including for purposes of determining whether any distributions from the foreign corporation with respect to such shares should be treated as having been included in the income of any United States person pursuant to section 1293(c) or section 959.

(d) *Examples.*—The following examples illustrate the rules of paragraphs (a), (b) and (c) of this section. Although these examples assume a 30-day month, 360-day year, any reasonable counting method may be used to compute the length of accrual periods. For purposes of simplicity, the relevant amounts as stated are rounded to two decimal places. However, the computations do not reflect any such rounding convention. The examples are as follows:

Example 1. Preferred QEF amount—(i) *Facts.* (A) On May 1, 1998, A, an individual who files his returns on a calendar year basis, purchased for $10,000 in a single secondary market transaction 100 shares of nonconvertible Class A $100 par value preferred stock (the Class A Stock) of FC, a foreign corporation with a taxable year ending on March 31.

(B) The terms of the Class A Stock provide for a mandatory redemption of the Class A Stock by the issuer at par on June 1, 2012. The Class A Stock is not redeemable pursuant to an issuer call or holder put on any other date. Each share of Class A Stock provides for a semi-annual cumulative distribution payable in dollars on June 1 and December 1 equal to one-half the product of the par value of the Class A Stock and the applicable annual dollar LIBOR in effect on the distribution date immediately prior to the relevant distribution date. The shares of the Class A stock are qualified preferred shares in the hands of A. A purchases no other qualified preferred shares of FC during its 1998 or 1999 taxable years.

(C) A made a special preferred QEF election for A's taxable year ended December 31, 1998, which applies to the Class A Stock acquired by A on May 1, 1998. FC is a PFIC under section 1296 for its taxable year ending March 31, 1999, but FC is not a PFIC for its taxable year ending March 31, 2000. FC paid no current dividends on June 1, 1998, and December 1, 1998, paid the June 1, 1999, dividend currently on June 1, 1999, together with accumulated distributions from June 1, 1998, and December 1, 1998, and paid the December 1, 1999, dividend currently on December 1, 1999. The applicable annual LIBOR is 8 percent on December 1, 1997, 7 percent on June 1, 1998, 9 percent on December 1, 1998, 10 percent on June 1, 1999, and 9 percent on December 1, 1999. FC had sufficient earnings and profits, within the meaning of section 312, for its taxable year ending on March 31, 2000, so that actual distributions to all shareholders of Class A Stock in that year were treated as paid out of earnings and profits of FC.

(ii) *Tax consequences to A for A's taxable year ending December 31, 1998.* As required under paragraph (a) of this section, A must include in gross income for its 1998 taxable year the 1998 preferred QEF amount. The preferred QEF amount, as determined under paragraph (b) of this section, for A's 1998 taxable year is the ratable portion of each periodic dividend amount for that year. For 1998, there are three periodic dividend amounts: The periodic dividend amount for the period from December 1, 1997, to June 1, 1998 (periodic dividend amount 1), the periodic dividend amount for the period from June 1, 1998, to December 1, 1998 (periodic dividend amount 2), and the periodic dividend amount for the period from December 1, 1998, to June 1, 1999 (periodic dividend amount 3). Periodic dividend amount 1 in respect of each share owned by A is $4 (1/2 multiplied by the applicable annual LIBOR of 8 percent set on December 1, 1997, multiplied by the $100 amount payable on redemption). Because A acquired the shares on May 1, 1998, A's ratable portion of periodic dividend amount 1 for 1998 is approximately $.67 (30/180 multiplied by $4) per share. Periodic dividend amount 2 in respect of each share owned by A is $3.50 (1/2 multiplied by the applicable annual LIBOR of 7 percent set on June 1, 1998, multiplied by $100). Because A owned the shares for the entire period associated with periodic dividend amount 2, A's ratable portion of periodic dividend amount 2 for 1998 is the full $3.50 per share. Periodic dividend amount 3 in respect of

Prop. Reg. §1.1293-2(d)

each share owned by A is $4.50 (1/2 multiplied by the applicable annual LIBOR of 9 percent set on December 1, 1998, multiplied by $100). Because the portion of 1998 associated with periodic dividend amount 3 is only the month of December, 1998, A's ratable portion of periodic dividend amount 3 for 1998 is approximately $.75 (30/180 multiplied by $4.50). Accordingly, A's preferred QEF amount for 1998 is approximately $4.92 ($.67 + $3.5 + $.75) per share. A must include approximately $492 (approximately $4.92 per share, multiplied by 100 shares) in income as ordinary earnings for its 1998 tax year even though FC paid no actual dividend to shareholders of Class A Stock for the period in 1998 during which A held the Class A Stock.

(iii) *Tax consequences to A for A's taxable year ending December 31, 1999.* As required under paragraph (a) of this section, A includes in gross income for its 1999 taxable year its preferred QEF amount for 1999. The preferred QEF amount, as determined under paragraph (b) of this section, for A's 1999 taxable year is the ratable portion of each periodic dividend amount for that year. For 1999, there are three periodic dividend amounts: The periodic dividend amount for the period from December 1, 1998, to June 1, 1999 (periodic dividend amount 1), the periodic dividend amount for the period from June 1, 1999, to December 1, 1999 (periodic dividend amount 2), and the periodic dividend amount for the period from December 1, 1999, to June 1, 2000 (periodic dividend amount 3). Periodic dividend amount 1 in respect of each share owned by A is $4.50 (1/2 multiplied by the applicable annual LIBOR of 9 percent set on December 1, 1998, multiplied by $100). Because A held each share of Class A Stock for five months in 1999 for the period associated with periodic dividend amount 1, A's ratable portion of periodic dividend amount 1 for 1999 is approximately $3.75 (150/180 multiplied by $4.50). Periodic dividend amount 2 in respect of each share owned by A is $5 (1/2 multiplied by the applicable annual LIBOR of 10 percent set on June 1, 1999, multiplied by $100). Because A owned the share for the entire period associated with periodic dividend amount 2, A's ratable portion of periodic dividend amount 2 for 1999 is the full $5. Periodic dividend amount 3 in respect of each share owned by A is $4.50 (1/2 multiplied by the applicable annual LIBOR of 9 percent set on December 1, 1999, multiplied by $100). Because A held each share of Class A Stock for one month in 1999 for the period associated with periodic dividend amount 3, A's ratable portion of periodic dividend amount 3 for 1999 is approximately $.75 (30/180 multiplied by $4.50). Accordingly, A's preferred QEF amount for 1998 is approximately $9.50 ($3.75 + $5 + $.75). A must include approximately $950 ($9.50 per share, multiplied by 100 shares) in income as ordinary income for its 1999 taxable year even though FC was not a PFIC for FC's taxable year ending in 2000. The current distributions and arrearages actually paid to A with respect to the Class A Stock are not includible in income by A under paragraph (c)(4) of this section because they constitute amounts previously included in income.

Example 2. Preferred Discount—(i) *Facts.* The facts are the same as in *Example 1* except that A acquired the 100 shares of Class A Stock for $9000.

(ii) *Tax Consequences to A for A's taxable year ending December 31, 1998.* (A) Because the Class A Stock is fixed term preferred stock (as described in § 1.1295-2(b)(1)(vii)) and A acquired each share of the Class A stock with $10 of preferred discount, as described in § 1.1295-2(b)(2), A's preferred QEF amount to be included by A for the taxable year consists of the sum of the ratable daily portion of each periodic dividend amount, as calculated in paragraph (d)(ii) of *Example 1* of this section, plus the preferred discount amount described in paragraph (b)(1) of this section.

(B) The preferred discount amount with respect to each share is approximately $.47 ($10 multiplied by 240 days/5070 days to maturity). A must include approximately $47 ($.47 per share, multiplied by 100 shares), together with the amount calculated in paragraph (d)(ii) of *Example 1* of this section, in income as ordinary earnings for its 1998 tax year even though FC paid no actual dividend to shareholders of Class A Shares for the period in 1998 during which A held the Class A Stock.

(iii) *Tax consequences to A for A's taxable year ending December 31, 1999.* The portion of the preferred discount on each share includible under paragraph (a) of this section is approximately $.71 ($10 multiplied by 360 days/5070 days to maturity). A must include this amount, together with the amount calculated in paragraph (d)(iii) of *Example 1* of this section, in income as ordinary earnings for its 1999 tax year even though FC was not a PFIC for FC's taxable year ending in 2000. The current distributions and arrearages actually paid to A in 1999 with respect to the Class A Stock are not includible in income by A under paragraph (c)(4) of this section, because they constitute amounts previously included in income.

(e) *Effective date.*—The rules under this section apply with respect to qualified preferred stock subject to a special preferred QEF election made after the date that is 30 days after the date of publication of this document as a final regulation. [Prop. Reg. § 1.1293-2.]

[Proposed 12-24-96.]

§ 1.1294-1T. **Election to extend the time for payment of tax on undistributed earnings of a qualified electing fund (Temporary).**—(a) *Purpose and scope.*—This section provides rules for making the annual election under section 1294. Under that section, a U.S. person that is a shareholder in a qualified electing fund (QEF) may elect to extend the time for payment of its tax liability which is attributable to its share of the undistributed earnings of the QEF. In general, a QEF is a passive foreign investment company (PFIC), as defined in section 1296, that makes the election under section 1295. Under section 1293, a U.S. person that owns, or is treated as owning, stock of a QEF at any time during the taxable year of the QEF shall include in gross income, as ordinary income, its pro rata share of the ordinary earnings of the QEF for the taxable year and, as long-term capital gain, its pro rata share of the net capital gain of the QEF for the taxable year. The shareholder's share of the earnings shall be included in the shareholder's taxable year in which or with which the taxable year of the QEF ends.

(b) *Election to extend time for payment.*—(1) *In general.*—A U.S. person that is a shareholder of a QEF on the last day of the QEF's taxable year may elect under section 1294 to extend the time for payment of that portion of its tax liability which is attributable to the inclusion in income pursuant to section 1293 of the shareholder's share of the QEF's undistributed earnings. The election under section 1294 may be made only with respect to undistributed earnings, and interest is imposed under section 6601 on the amount of the tax liability which is subject to the extension. This interest must be paid on the termination of the election.

(2) *Exception.*—An election under this § 1.1294-1T cannot be made for a taxable year of the shareholder if any portion of the QEF's earnings is includible in the gross income of the shareholder for such year under either section 551 (relating to foreign personal holding companies) or section 951 (relating to controlled foreign corporations).

(3) *Undistributed earnings.*—(i) *In general.*—For purposes of this § 1.1294-1T the term "undistributed earnings" means the excess, if any, of the amount includible in gross income by reason of section 1293(a) for the shareholder's taxable year (the includible amount) over the sum of (A) the amount of any distribution to the shareholder during the QEF's taxable year and (B) the portion of the includible amount that is attributable to stock in the QEF that the shareholder transferred or otherwise disposed of before the end of the QEF's year. For purposes of this paragraph, a distribution will be treated as made from the most recently accumulated earnings and profits.

(ii) *Effect of a loan, pledge or guarantee.*—A loan, pledge, or guarantee described in § 1.1294-1T(e)(2) or (4) will be treated as a distribution of earnings for purposes of paragraph (b)(3)(i)(A). If earnings are treated as distributed in a taxable year by reason of a loan, pledge or guarantee described in § 1.1294-1T(e)(2) or (4), but the amount of the deemed distribution resulting therefrom was less than the amount of the actual loan by the QEF (or the amount of the loan secured by the pledge or guarantee), earnings derived by the QEF in a subsequent taxable year will be treated as distributed in such subsequent year to the shareholder for purposes of paragraph (b)(3)(i)(A) by virtue of such loan, but only to the extent of the difference between the outstanding principal balance on the loan in such subsequent year and the prior years' deemed distributions resulting from the loan. For this purpose, the outstanding principal balance on a loan in a taxable year shall be treated as equal to the greatest amount of the outstanding balance at any time during such year.

Example (1). (i) *Facts.* FC is a PFIC that made the election under section 1295 to be a QEF for its taxable year beginning January 1, 1987. S owned 500 shares, or 50 percent, of FC throughout the first six months of 1987, but on June 30, 1987 sold 10 percent, or 50 shares, of the FC stock that it held. FC had $100,000x of ordinary earnings but no net capital gain in 1987. No part of FC's earnings is includible in S's income under either section 551 or 951. FC made no distributions to its shareholders in 1987. S's pro rata share of income is determined by attributing FC's income ratably to each day in FC's year. Accordingly, FC's daily earnings are $274x ($100,000x/365). S's share of the earnings of FC is $47,484x, determined as follows.

FC's daily earnings × number of days percentage held by S × percentage of ownership in FC.

Accordingly, S's pro rata share of FC's earnings for the first six months of FC's year deemed earned while S held 50 percent of FC's stock is $24,797x ($274x × 181 days × 50%). S's pro rata share of FC's earnings for the remainder of FC's year deemed earned while S held 45 percent of FC's stock is $22,687x ($274x × 184 days ×45%). Therefore, S's total share of FC's earnings to be included in income under section 1293 is $47,484x$ ($24,797x + $22,687x$).

(ii) *Election.* S intends to make the election under section 1294 to defer the payment of its tax liability that is attributable to the undistributed earnings of FC. The amount of current year undistributed earnings as defined in § 1.1294-1T(b)(3) with respect to which S can make the election is the excess of S's inclusion in gross income under section 1293(a) for the taxable year over the sum of (1) the cash and other property distributed to S during FC's tax year out of earnings included in income pursuant to section 1293(a), and (2) the earnings attributable to stock disposed of during FC's tax year. Because S sold 10 percent, or 50 shares, of the FC stock that it held during the first six months of the year, 10 percent of its share of the earnings for that part of the year, which is $2,480x$ ($24,797x \times 10\%$), is attributable to the shares sold. S therefore cannot make the election under section 1294 to extend the time for payment of its tax liability on that amount. Accordingly, S can make the election under section 1294 with respect to its tax on $45,004x$ ($47,484x$ less $2,480x$), which is its pro rata share of FC's earnings, reduced by the earnings attributable to the stock disposed of during the year.

Example (2). (i) *Facts.* The facts are the same as in Example (1) with the following exceptions. S did not sell any FC stock during 1987. Therefore, because S held 50 percent of the FC stock throughout 1987, S's pro rata share of FC's ordinary earnings was $50,000x$, no part of which was includible in S's income under either section 551 or 951. There were no actual distributions of earnings to S in 1988. On December 31, 1987, S pledged the FC stock as security for a bank loan of $75,000x$. The pledge is treated as a disposition of the FC stock and therefore a distribution of S's share of the undistributed earnings of FC up to the amount of the loan principal. S's entire share of the undistributed earnings of FC are deemed distributed as a result of the pledge of the FC stock. S therefore cannot make the election under section 1294 to extend the time for payment of its tax liability on its share of FC's earnings for 1987.

(ii) *Deemed distribution.* In 1988, FC has ordinary earnings of $100,000x$ but no net capital gain. S's pro rata share of FC's 1988 ordinary earnings was $50,000x$. S's loan remained outstanding throughout 1988; the highest loan balance during 1988 was $74,000x$. Of S's share of the ordinary earnings of FC of $50,000x$, $24,000x$ is deemed distributed to S. This is the amount by which the highest loan balance for the year ($74,000x$) exceeds the portion of the undistributed earnings of FC deemed distributed to S in 1987 by reason of the pledge ($50,000x$). S may make the election under section 1294 to extend the time for payment of its tax liability on $26,000x$, which is the amount by which S's includible amount for 1988 exceeds the amount deemed distributed to S during 1988.

(c) *Time for making the election.*—(1) *In general.*—An election under this § 1.1294-1T may be made for any taxable year in which a shareholder reports income pursuant to section 1293. Except as provided in paragraph (c)(2), the election shall be made by the due date, as extended, of the tax return for the shareholder's taxable year for which the election is made.

(2) *Exception.*—An election under this section may be made within 60 days of receipt of notification from the QEF of the shareholder's pro rata share of the ordinary earnings and net capital gain if notification is received after the time for filing the election provided in paragraph (c)(1) (and requires the filing of an amended return to report income pursuant to section 1293). If the notification reports an increase in the shareholder's pro rata share of the earnings previously reported to the shareholder by the QEF, the shareholder may make the election under this paragraph (c)(2) only with respect to the amount of such increase.

(d) *Manner of making the election.*—(1) *In general.*—A shareholder shall make the election by (i) attaching to its return for the year of the election Form 8621 or a statement containing the information and representations required by this section and (ii) filing a copy of Form 8621 or the statement with the Internal Revenue Service Center, P.O. Box 21086, Philadelphia, Pennsylvania 19114.

(2) *Information to be included in the election statement.*—If a statement is used in lieu of Form 8621, the statement should be identified, in a heading, as an election under section 1294 of the Code. The statement must include the following information and representations:

(i) The name, address, and taxpayer identification number of the electing shareholder and the taxable year of the shareholder for which the election is being made;

(ii) The name, address and taxpayer identification number of the QEF if provided to the shareholder;

(iii) A statement that the shareholder is making the election under section 1294 of the Code;

(iv) A schedule containing the following information:

(A) the ordinary earnings and net capital gain for the current year included in the shareholder's income under section 1293;

(B) the amount of cash and other property distributed by the QEF during its taxable year with respect to stock held directly or indirectly by the shareholder during that year, identifying the amount of such distributions that is paid out of current earnings and profits and the amount paid out of each prior year's earnings and profits; and

(C) the undistributed PFIC earnings tax liability (as defined in paragraph (f) of this section) for the taxable year, payment of which is being deferred by reason of the election under section 1294;

(v) The number of shares of stock held in the QEF during the QEF's taxable year which gave rise to the section 1293 inclusion and the number of such shares transferred, deemed transferred or otherwise disposed of by the electing shareholder before the end of the QEF's taxable year, and the date of transfer; and

(vi) The representations of the electing shareholder that—

(A) No part of the QEF's earnings for the taxable year is includible in the electing shareholder's gross income under either section 551 or 951 of the Code;

(B) The election is made only with respect to the shareholder's pro rata share of the undistributed earnings of the QEF; and

(C) The electing shareholder, upon termination of the election to extend the date for payment, shall pay the undistributed PFIC earnings tax liability attributable to those earnings to which the termination applies as well as interest on such tax liability pursuant to section 6601. Payment of this tax and interest must be made by the due date (determined without extensions) of the tax return for the taxable year in which the termination occurs.

(e) *Termination of the extension.*—The election to extend the date for payment of tax will be terminated in whole or in part upon the occurrence of any of the following events:

(1) The QEF's distribution of earnings to which the section 1294 extensic pay tax is attributable; the extension will terminate only with respect to the tax attributable to the earnings that were distributed.

(2) The electing shareholder's transfer of stock in the QEF (or use thereof as security for a loan) with respect to which an election under this § 1.1294-1T was made. The election will be terminated with respect to the undistributed earnings attributable to the shares of the stock transferred. In the case of a pledge of the stock, the election will be terminated with respect to undistributed earnings equal to the amount of the loan for which the stock is pledged.

(3) Revocation of the QEF's election as a QEF or cessation of the QEF's status as a PFIC. A revocation of the QEF election or cessation of PFIC status will result in the complete termination of the extension.

(4) A loan of property by the QEF directly or indirectly to the electing shareholder or related person, or a pledge or guarantee by the QEF with respect to a loan made by another party to the electing shareholder or related person. The election will be terminated with respect to undistributed earnings in an amount equal to the amount of the loan, pledge, or guarantee.

(5) A determination by the District Director pursuant to section 1294(c)(3) that collection of the tax is in jeopardy. The amount of undistributed earnings with respect to which the extension is terminated under this paragraph (d)(5) will be left to the discretion of the District Director.

(f) *Undistributed PFIC earnings tax liability.*—The electing shareholder's tax liability attributable to the ordinary earnings and net capital gain included in gross income under section 1293 shall be the excess of the tax imposed under chapter 1 of the Code for the taxable year over the tax that would be imposed for the taxable year without regard to the inclusion in income under section 1293 of the undistributed earnings as defined in paragraph (b)(3) of this section.

Example. The facts are the same as in § 1.1294-1T(b)(3), *Example (1),* with the following exceptions. S, a domestic corporation, did not dispose of any FC stock in 1987. Therefore, because S held 50 percent of the FC stock throughout 1987, S's pro rata share of FC's ordinary earnings was $50,000x$. In addition to $50,000x$ of ordinary earnings from FC, S had $12,500x$ of domestic source income and $6,000x$ of expenses (other than interest expense) not definitely related to any gross income. These expenses are apportioned, pursuant to § 1.861-8(c)(2), on a pro rata basis between the domestic and foreign source income—$1,200x$ of expenses, or one-fifth, to domestic source income, and $4,800x$ of expenses, or four-fifths, to the section 1293 inclusion. FC paid foreign taxes of $25,000x$ in 1987. Accordingly, S is entitled to claim as an indirect foreign tax credit pursuant to section 1293(f) a proportionate amount of the foreign taxes paid by FC, which is $12,500x$ ($25,000x \times 50,000x / 100,000x$). S is taxed in the U.S. at the rate of 34 percent. The amount for payment is determined as follows:

Reg. § 1.1294-1T(f)

1987 Tax Liability (with section 1293 inclusion)

Source	U.S.	Foreign
Income	12,500x	0
Section 1293	0	50,000x
Expenses	–1,200x	–4,800x
Taxable income	11,300x	45,200x
Total taxable income	56,500x	
U.S. income tax rate	×34%	
Pre-credit U.S. tax	19,210x	
Foreign tax credit	–12,500x	
1987 Tax Liability	6,710x	

1987 Tax Liability (without section 1293 inclusion)

Source	U.S.	Foreign
Income	12,500x	0
Expenses	–6,000x	
Taxable income	6,500x	
U.S. tax rate	×34%	
U.S. tax	2,210x	
Foreign tax credit	0	
Hypothetical 1987 Tax Liability	2,210x	

The amount of tax, payment of which S may defer pursuant to section 1294, is $4,500x ($6,710x less $2,210x).

(g) *Authority to require a bond.*—Pursuant to the authority granted in section 6165 and in the manner provided therein, and subject to notification, the District Director may require the electing shareholder to furnish a bond to secure payment of the tax, the time for payment of which is extended under this section. If the electing shareholder does not furnish the bond within 60 days after receiving a request from the District Director, the election will be revoked.

(h) *Annual reporting requirement.*—The electing shareholder must attach Form 8621 or a statement to its income tax return for each year during which an election under this section is outstanding. The statement must contain the following information: (1) the total amount of undistributed earnings as of the end of the taxable year to which the outstanding elections apply; (2) the total amount of the undistributed PFIC earnings tax liability and accrued interest charge as of the end of the year; (3) the total amount of distributions received during the taxable year; and (4) a description of the occurrence of any other termination event described in paragraph (e) of this section that occurred during the taxable year. The electing shareholder also shall file by the due date, as extended, for its return a copy of Form 8621 or the statement with the Philadelphia Service Center, P.O. Box 21086, Philadelphia, Pennsylvania 19114. [Temporary Reg. § 1.1294-1T.]

☐ [*T.D.* 8178, 2-26-88.]

§ 1.1295-1. Qualified electing funds.—
(a) *In general.*—[Reserved].

(b) *Application of section 1295 election.*—[Reserved].

(1) *Election personal to shareholder.*—[Reserved].

(2) *Election applicable to specific corporation only—*

(i) *In general.*—[Reserved].

(ii) *Stock of QEF received in a nonrecognition transfer.*—[Reserved].

(iii) *Exception for options.*—A shareholder's section 1295 election does not apply to any option to buy stock of the PFIC.

(3) *Application of general rules to stock held by a pass through entity.*—(i) *Stock subject to a section 1295 election transferred to a pass through entity.*—A shareholder's section 1295 election will not apply to a domestic pass through entity to which the shareholder transfers stock subject to a section 1295 election, or to any other U.S. person that is an interest holder or beneficiary of the domestic pass through entity. However, as provided in paragraph (c)(2)(iv) of this section (relating to a transfer to a domestic pass through entity of stock subject to a section 1295 election), a shareholder that transfers stock subject to a section 1295 election to a pass through entity will continue to be subject to the section 1295 election with respect to the stock indirectly owned through the pass through entity and any

other stock of that PFIC owned by the shareholder.

(ii) *Limitation on application of pass through entity's section 1295 election.*—Except as provided in paragraph (c)(2)(iv) of this section, a section 1295 election made by a domestic pass through entity does not apply to other stock of the PFIC held directly or indirectly by the interest holder or beneficiary.

(iii) *Effect of partnership termination on section 1295 election.*—Termination of a section 1295 election made by a domestic partnership by reason of the termination of the partnership under section 708(b) will not terminate the section 1295 election with respect to partners of the terminated partnership that are partners of the new partnership. Except as otherwise provided, the stock of the PFIC of which the new partners are indirect shareholders will be treated as stock of a QEF only if the new domestic partnership makes a section 1295 election with respect to that stock.

(iv) *Characterization of stock held through a pass through entity.*—Stock of a PFIC held through a pass through entity will be treated as stock of a pedigreed QEF with respect to an interest holder or beneficiary only if—

(A) In the case of PFIC stock acquired (other than in a transaction in which gain is not recognized pursuant to regulations under section 1291(f) with respect to that stock) and held by a domestic pass through entity, the pass through entity makes the section 1295 election and the PFIC has been a QEF with respect to the pass through entity for all taxable years that are included wholly or partly in the pass through entity's holding period of the PFIC stock and during which the foreign corporation was a PFIC within the meaning of § 1.1291-9(j)(1); or

(B) In the case of PFIC stock transferred by an interest holder or beneficiary to a pass through entity in a transaction in which gain is not fully recognized (including pursuant to regulations under section 1291(f)), the pass through entity makes the section 1295 election with respect to the PFIC stock transferred for the taxable year in which the transfer was made. The PFIC stock transferred will be treated as stock of a pedigreed QEF by the pass through entity, however, only if that stock was treated as stock of a pedigreed QEF with respect to the interest holder or beneficiary at the time of the transfer, and the PFIC has been a QEF with respect to the pass through entity for all taxable years of the PFIC that are included wholly or partly in the pass through entity's holding period of the PFIC stock during which the foreign corporation was a PFIC within the meaning of § 1.1291-9(j).

(v) *Characterization of stock distributed by a partnership.*—In the case of PFIC stock distributed by a partnership to a partner in a transaction in which gain is not fully recognized, the PFIC stock will be treated as stock of a pedigreed QEF by the partners only if that stock was treated as stock of a pedigreed QEF with respect to the partnership for all taxable years of the PFIC that are included wholly or partly in the partnership's holding period of the PFIC stock during which the foreign corporation was a PFIC within the meaning of § 1.1291-9(j), and the partner has a section 1295 election in effect with respect to the distributed PFIC stock for the partner's taxable year in which the distribution was made. If the partner does not have a section 1295 election in effect, the stock shall be treated as stock in a section 1291 fund. See paragraph (k) of this section for special applicability date of paragraph (b)(3)(v) of this section.

(4) *Application of general rules to a taxpayer filing a joint return under section 6013.*—A section 1295 election made by a taxpayer in a joint return, within the meaning of section 6013, will be treated as also made by the spouse that joins in the filing of that return. See paragraph (k) of this section for special applicability date of paragraph (b)(4) of this section.

(c) *Effect of section 1295 election.*—(1) *In general.*—Except as otherwise provided in this paragraph (c), the effect of a shareholder's section 1295 election is to treat the foreign corporation as a QEF with respect to the shareholder for each taxable year of the foreign corporation ending with or within a taxable year of the shareholder for which the election is effective. A section 1295 election is effective for the shareholder's election year and all subsequent taxable years of the shareholder unless invalidated, terminated or revoked as provided in paragraph (i) of this section. The terms shareholder and shareholder's election year are defined in paragraph (j) of this section.

(2) *Years to which section 1295 election applies.*—(i) *In general.*—Except as otherwise provided in this paragraph (c), a foreign corporation with respect to which a section 1295 election is made will be treated as a QEF for its taxable year ending with or within the shareholder's election year and all subsequent taxable years of the foreign corporation that are included wholly or partly in the shareholder's holding period (or periods) of stock of the foreign corporation.

(ii) *Effect of PFIC status on election.*—A foreign corporation will not be treated as a QEF for any taxable year of the foreign corporation that the foreign corporation is not a PFIC under section 1297(a) and is not treated as a PFIC under section 1298(b)(1). Therefore, a shareholder shall not be required to include pursuant to section 1293 the shareholder's pro rata share of ordinary earnings and net capital gain for such year and shall not be required to satisfy the section 1295 annual reporting requirement of paragraph (f)(2) of this section for such year. Cessation of a foreign corporation's status as a PFIC will not, however, terminate a section 1295 election. Thus, if the foreign corporation is a PFIC in any taxable year after a year in which it is not treated as a PFIC, the shareholder's original election under section 1295 continues to apply and the shareholder must take into account its pro rata share of ordinary earnings and net capital gain for such year and comply with the section 1295 annual reporting requirement.

(iii) *Effect on election of complete termination of a shareholder's interest in the PFIC.*—Complete termination of a shareholder's direct and indirect interest in stock of a foreign corporation will not terminate a shareholder's section 1295 election with respect to the foreign corporation. Therefore, if a shareholder reacquires a direct or indirect interest in any stock of the foreign corporation, that stock is considered to be stock for which an election under section 1295 has been made and the shareholder is subject to the income inclusion and reporting rules required of a shareholder of a QEF.

(iv) *Effect on section 1295 election of transfer of stock to a domestic pass through entity.*—The transfer of a shareholder's direct or indirect interest in stock of a foreign corporation to a domestic pass through entity (as defined in paragraph (j) of this section) will not terminate the shareholder's section 1295 election with respect to the foreign corporation, whether or not the pass through entity makes a section 1295 election. For the rules concerning the application of section 1293 to stock transferred to a domestic pass through entity, see § 1.1293–1(c).

(v) *Examples.*—The following examples illustrate the rules of this paragraph (c)(2).

Example 1. In 1998, C, a U.S. person, purchased stock of FC, a foreign corporation that is a PFIC. Both FC and C are calendar year taxpayers. C made a timely section 1295 election to treat FC as a QEF in C's 1998 return, and FC was therefore a pedigreed QEF. C included its shares of FC's 1998 ordinary earnings and net capital gain in C's 1998 income and did not make a section 1294 election to defer the time for payment of tax on that income. In 1999, 2000, and 2001, FC did not satisfy either the income or asset test of section 1296(a), and therefore was neither a PFIC nor a QEF. C therefore did not have to include its pro rata shares of the ordinary earnings and net capital gain of FC pursuant to section 1293, or satisfy the section 1295 annual reporting requirements for any of those years. FC qualified as a PFIC again in 2002. Because C had made a section 1295 election in 1998, and the election had not been invalidated, terminated, or revoked, within the meaning of paragraph (i) of this section, C's section 1295 election remains in effect for 2002. C therefore is subject in 2002 to the income inclusion and reporting rules required of shareholders of QEFs.

Example 2. The facts are the same as in Example (1) except that FC did not lose PFIC status in any year and C sold all the FC stock in 1999 and repurchased stock of FC in 2002. Because C had made a section 1295 election in 1998 with respect to stock of FC, and the election had not been invalidated, terminated, or revoked, within the meaning of paragraph (i) of this section, C's section 1295 election remained in effect and therefore applies to the stock of FC purchased by C in 2002. C therefore is subject in 2002 to the income inclusion and reporting rules required of shareholders of QEFs.

Example 3. The facts are the same as in Example (2) except that C is a partner in domestic partnership P and C transferred its FC stock to P in 1999. Because C had made a section 1295 election in 1998 with respect to stock of FC, and the election had not been invalidated, terminated, or revoked, within the meaning of paragraph (i) of this section, C's section 1295 election remains in effect with respect to its indirect interest in the stock of FC. If P does not make the section 1295 election with respect to the FC stock, C will continue to be subject, in C's capacity as an indirect shareholder of FC, to the income inclusion and reporting rules required of shareholders of QEFs in 1999 and subsequent years for that portion of the FC stock C is treated as owning indirectly through the partnership. If P makes the section 1295 election, C will take into account its pro rata shares of the ordinary earnings and net capital gain of the FC under the rules applicable to inclusions of income from P.

(d) *Who may make a section 1295 election.*—(1) *General rule.*—Except as otherwise provided in this paragraph (d), any U.S. person that is a shareholder (as defined in paragraph (j) of this section) of a PFIC, including a shareholder that holds stock of a PFIC in bearer form, may make a section 1295 election with respect to that PFIC. The shareholder need not own directly or indirectly any stock of the PFIC at the time the shareholder makes the section 1295 election provided the shareholder is a shareholder of the PFIC during the taxable year of the PFIC that ends with or within the taxable year of the shareholder for which the section 1295 election is made. Except in the case of a shareholder that is an exempt organization that may not make a section 1295 election, as provided in paragraph (d)(6) of this section, in a chain of ownership only the first U.S. person that is a shareholder of the PFIC may make the section 1295 election.

(2) *Application of general rule to pass through entities.*—(i) *Partnerships.*—(A) *Domestic partnership.*—A domestic partnership that holds an interest in stock of a PFIC makes the section 1295 election with respect to that PFIC. The partnership election applies only to the stock of the PFIC held directly or indirectly by the partnership and not to any other stock held directly or indirectly by any partner. As provided in § 1.1293-1(c)(1), shareholders owning stock of a QEF by reason of an interest in the partnership take into account the section 1293 inclusions with respect to the QEF shares owned by the partnership under the rules applicable to inclusions of income from the partnership.

(B) *Foreign partnership.*—A U.S. person that holds an interest in a foreign partnership that, in turn, holds an interest in stock of a PFIC makes the section 1295 election with respect to that PFIC. A partner's election applies to the stock of the PFIC owned directly or indirectly by the foreign partnership and to any other stock of the PFIC owned by that partner. A section 1295 election by a partner applies only to that partner.

(ii) *S corporation.*—An S corporation that holds an interest in stock of a PFIC makes the section 1295 election with respect to that PFIC. The S corporation election applies only to the stock of the PFIC held directly or indirectly by the S corporation and not to any other stock held directly or indirectly by any S corporation shareholder. As provided in § 1.1293-1(c)(1), shareholders owning stock of a QEF by reason of an interest in the S corporation take into account the section 1293 inclusions with respect to the QEF shares under the rules applicable to inclusions of income from the S corporation.

(iii) *Trust or estate.*—(A) *Domestic trust or estate.*—(1) *Nongrantor trust or estate.*—A domestic nongrantor trust or a domestic estate that holds an interest in stock of a PFIC makes the section 1295 election with respect to that PFIC. The trust or estate's election applies only to the stock of the PFIC held directly or indirectly by the trust or estate and not to any other stock held directly or indirectly by any beneficiary. As provided in § 1.1293-1(c)(1), shareholders owning stock of a QEF by reason of an interest in a domestic trust or estate take into account the section 1293 inclusions with respect to the QEF shares under the rules applicable to inclusions of income from the trust or estate.

(2) *Grantor trust.*—A U.S. person that is treated under sections 671 through 678 as the owner of the portion of a domestic trust that owns an interest in stock of a PFIC makes the section 1295 election with respect to that PFIC. If that person ceases to be treated as the owner of the portion of the trust that owns an interest in the PFIC stock and is a beneficiary of the trust, that person's section 1295 election will continue to apply to the PFIC stock indirectly owned by that person under the rules of paragraph (c)(2)(iv) of this section as if the person had transferred its interest in the PFIC stock to the trust. However, the stock will be treated as stock of a PFIC that is not a QEF with respect to other beneficiaries of the trust, unless the trust makes the section 1295 election as provided in paragraph (d)(2)(iii)(A)(*1*) of this section.

(B) *Foreign trust or estate.*—(1) *Nongrantor trust or estate.*—A U.S. person that is a beneficiary of a foreign nongrantor trust or estate that holds an interest in stock of a PFIC makes the section 1295 election with respect to that PFIC. A beneficiary's section 1295 election applies to all the PFIC stock owned directly and indirectly by the trust or estate and to the other PFIC stock owned directly or indirectly by the beneficiary. A section 1295 election by a beneficiary applies only to that beneficiary.

(2) *Grantor trust.*—A U.S. person that is treated under sections 671 through 679 as the owner of the portion of a foreign trust that owns an interest in stock of a PFIC stock makes the section 1295 election with respect to that PFIC. If that person ceases to be treated as the owner of the portion of the trust that owns an interest in the PFIC stock and is a beneficiary of the trust, that person's section 1295 election will continue to apply to the PFIC stock indirectly owned by that person under the rules of paragraph (c)(2)(iv) of this section. However, as provided in paragraph (d)(2)(iii)(B)(*1*) of this section, any other shareholder that is a beneficiary of the trust and that wishes to treat the PFIC as a QEF must make the section 1295 election.

(iv) *Indirect ownership of the pass through entity or the PFIC.*—The rules of this paragraph (d)(2) apply whether or not the shareholder holds its interest in the pass through entity directly or indirectly and whether or not the pass through entity holds its interest in the PFIC directly or indirectly.

(3) *Indirect ownership of a PFIC through other PFICs.*—(i) *In general.*—An election under section 1295 shall apply only to the foreign corporation for which an election is made. Therefore, if a shareholder makes an election under section 1295 to treat a PFIC as a QEF, that election applies only to stock in that foreign corporation and not to the stock in any other corporation which the shareholder is treated as owning by virtue of its ownership of stock in the QEF.

(ii) *Example.*—The following example illustrates the rules of paragraph (d)(3)(i) of this section:

Example. In 1988, T, a U.S. person, purchased stock of FC, a foreign corporation that is a PFIC. FC also owns the stock of SC, a foreign corporation that is a PFIC. T makes an election under section 1295 to treat FC as a QEF. T's section 1295 election applies only to the stock T owns in FC, and does not apply to the stock T indirectly owns in SC.

(4) *Member of consolidated return group as shareholder.*—Pursuant to § 1.1502-77(a), the common parent of an affiliated group of corporations that join in filing a consolidated income tax return makes a section 1295 election for all members of the affiliated group. An election by a common parent will be effective for all members of the affiliated group with respect to interests in PFIC stock held at the time the election is made or at any time thereafter. A separate election must be made by the common parent for each PFIC of which a member of the affiliated group is a shareholder.

(5) *Option holder.*—A holder of an option to acquire stock of a PFIC may not make a section 1295 election that will apply to the option or to the stock subject to the option.

(6) *Exempt organization.*—A tax-exempt organization that is not taxable under section 1291, pursuant to § 1.1291-1(e), with respect to a PFIC may not make a section 1295 election with respect to that PFIC. In addition, such an exempt organization will not be subject to any section 1295 election made by a domestic pass through entity.

(e) *Time for making a section 1295 election.*—(1) *In general.*—Except as provided in § 1.1295-3, a shareholder making the section 1295 election must make the election on or before the due date, as extended under section 6081 (election due date), for filing the shareholder's income tax return for the first taxable year to which the election will apply. The section 1295 election must be made in the original return for that year, or in an amended return, provided the amended return is filed on or before the election due date.

(2) *Examples.*—The following examples illustrate the rules of paragraph (e)(1) of this section:

Example 1. In 1998, C, a domestic corporation, purchased stock of FC, a foreign corporation that is a PFIC. Both C and FC are calendar year taxpayers. C wishes to make the section 1295 election for its taxable year ended December 31, 1998. The section 1295 election must be made on or before March 15, 1999, the due date of C's 1998 income tax return as provided by section 6072(b). On March 14, 1999, C files a request for a three-month extension of time to file its 1998 income tax return under section 6081(b). C's time to file its 1998 income tax return and to make the section 1295 election is thereby extended to June 15, 1999.

Example 2. The facts are the same as in *Example 1* except that on May 1, 1999, C filed its 1998 income tax return and failed to include the section 1295 election. C may file an amended income tax return for 1998 to make the section 1295 election provided the amended return is filed on or before the extended due date of June 15, 1999.

(f) *Manner of making a section 1295 election and the annual election requirements of the shareholder.*—(1) *Manner of making the election.*—A shareholder must make a section 1295 election by—

(i) Completing Form 8621 in the manner required by that form and this section for making the section 1295 election;

(ii) Attaching Form 8621 to its federal income tax return filed by the election due date for the shareholder's election year; and

(iii) Receiving and reflecting in Form 8621 the information provided in the PFIC Annual Information Statement described in paragraph (g)(1) of this section, the Annual Intermediary Statement described in paragraph (g)(3) of this section, or the applicable combined statement described in paragraph (g)(4) of this section, for the taxable year of the PFIC ending with or within the taxable year for which Form 8621 is being filed. If the PFIC Annual Information Statement contains a statement described in paragraph (g)(1)(ii)(C) of this section, the shareholder must attach a statement to Form 8621 that indicates that the shareholder rather than the PFIC calculated the PFIC's ordinary earnings and net capital gain.

(2) *Annual election requirements.*—(i) *In general.*—A shareholder that makes a section 1295 election with respect to a PFIC held directly or indirectly, for each taxable year to which the section 1295 election applies, must—

(A) Complete Form 8621 in the manner required by that form and this section;

(B) Attach Form 8621 to its federal income tax return filed by the due date of the return, as extended; and

(C) Receive and reflect in Form 8621 the PFIC Annual Information Statement described in paragraph (g)(1) of this section, the Annual Intermediary Statement described in paragraph (g)(3) of this section, or the applicable combined statement described in paragraph (g)(4) of this section, for the taxable year of the PFIC ending with or within the taxable year for which Form 8621 is being filed. If the PFIC Annual Information Statement contains a statement described in paragraph (g)(1)(ii)(C) of this section, the shareholder must attach a statement to its Form 8621 that the shareholder rather than the PFIC provided the calculations of the PFIC's ordinary earnings and net capital gain.

(ii) *Retention of documents.*—For all taxable years subject to the section 1295 election, the shareholder must retain copies of all Forms 8621, with their attachments, and PFIC Annual Information Statements or Annual Intermediary Statements. Failure to produce those documents at the request of the Commissioner in connection with an examination may result in invalidation or termination of the shareholder's section 1295 election.

(3) *Effective date.*—See paragraph (k) of this section for special applicability date of paragraph (f) of this section.

(g) *Annual election requirements of the PFIC or intermediary.*—(1) *PFIC Annual Information Statement.*—For each year of the PFIC ending in a taxable year of a shareholder to which the shareholder's section 1295 election applies, the PFIC must provide the shareholder with a PFIC Annual Information Statement. The PFIC Annual Information Statement is a statement of the PFIC, signed by the PFIC or an authorized representative of the PFIC, that contains the following information and representations—

(i) The first and last days of the taxable year of the PFIC to which the PFIC Annual Information Statement applies;

(ii) Either—

(A) The shareholder's pro rata shares of the ordinary earnings and net capital gain (as defined in § 1.1293-1(a)(2)) of the PFIC for the taxable year indicated in paragraph (g)(1)(i) of this section; or

(B) Sufficient information to enable the shareholder to calculate its pro rata shares of the PFIC's ordinary earnings and net capital gain, for that taxable year; or

(C) A statement that the foreign corporation has permitted the shareholder to examine the books of account, records, and other documents of the foreign corporation for the shareholder to calculate the amounts of the PFIC's ordinary earnings and the net capital gain according to federal income tax accounting principles and to calculate the shareholder's pro rata shares of the PFIC's ordinary earnings and net capital gain;

(iii) The amount of cash and the fair market value of other property distributed or deemed distributed to the shareholder during the taxable year of the PFIC to which the PFIC Annual Information Statement pertains; and

(iv) Either—

(A) A statement that the PFIC will permit the shareholder to inspect and copy the PFIC's permanent books of account, records, and such other documents as may be maintained by the PFIC to establish that the PFIC's ordinary earnings and net capital gain are computed in accordance with U.S. income tax principles, and to verify these amounts and the shareholder's pro rata shares thereof; or

(B) In lieu of the statement required in paragraph (g)(1)(iv)(A) of this section, a description of the alternative documentation requirements approved by the Commissioner, with a copy of the private letter ruling and the closing agreement entered into by the Commissioner and the PFIC pursuant to paragraph (g)(2) of this section.

(2) *Alternative documentation.*—In rare and unusual circumstances, the Commissioner will consider alternative documentation requirements necessary to verify the ordinary earnings and net capital gain of a PFIC other than the documentation requirements described in paragraph (g)(1)(iv)(A) of this section. Alternative documentation requirements will be allowed only pursuant to a private letter ruling and a closing agreement entered into by the Commissioner and the PFIC describing an alternative method of verifying the PFIC's ordinary earnings and net capital gain. If the PFIC has not obtained a private letter ruling from the Commissioner approving an alternative method of verifying the PFIC's ordinary earnings and net capital gain by the time a shareholder is required to make a section 1295 election, the shareholder may not use an alternative method for that taxable year.

(3) *Annual Intermediary Statement.*—In the case of a U.S. person that is an indirect shareholder of a PFIC that is owned through an intermediary, as defined in paragraph (j) of this section, an Annual Intermediary Statement issued by an intermediary containing the information described in paragraph (g)(1) of this section and reporting the indirect shareholder's pro rata share of the ordinary earnings and net capital gain of the QEF as described in paragraph (g)(1)(ii)(A) of this section, may be provided to the indirect shareholder in lieu of the PFIC Annual Information Statement if the following conditions are satisfied—

(i) The intermediary receives a copy of the PFIC Annual Information Statement or the intermediary receives an annual intermediary statement from another intermediary which contains a statement that the other intermediary has received a copy of the PFIC Annual Information Statement and represents that the conditions of paragraphs (g)(3)(ii) and (g)(3)(iii) of this section are met;

(ii) The representations and information contained in the Annual Intermediary Statement reflect the representations and information contained in the PFIC Annual Information Statement; and

(iii) The PFIC Annual Information Statement issued to the intermediary contains either the representation set forth in paragraph (g)(1)(iv)(A) of this section, or, if alternative documentation requirements were approved by the Commissioner pursuant to paragraph (g)(2) of this section, a copy of the private letter ruling and closing agreement between the Commissioner and the PFIC, agreeing to an alternative method of verifying PFIC ordinary earnings and net capital gain as described in paragraph (g)(2) of this section;

(4) *Combined statements.*—(i) *PFIC Annual Information Statement.*—A PFIC that owns directly or indirectly any stock of one or more PFICs with respect to which a shareholder may make the section 1295 election may prepare a PFIC Annual Information Statement that combines with its own information and representations the information and representations of all the PFICs. The PFIC may use any format for a combined PFIC Annual Information Statement provided the required information and representations are separately stated and identified with the respective corporations.

(ii) *Annual Intermediary Statement.*— An intermediary described in paragraph (g)(3) of this section that owns directly or indirectly stock of one or more PFICs with respect to which an indirect shareholder may make the section 1295 election may prepare an Annual Intermediary Statement that combines with its own information and representations the information and representations with respect to all the PFICs. The intermediary may use any format for a combined Annual Intermediary Statement provided the required information and representations are separately stated and identified with the intermediary and the respective corporations.

(5) *Effective date.*—See paragraph (k) of this section for special applicability date of paragraph (g) of this section.

(h) *Transition rules.*—Taxpayers may rely on Notice 88-125 (1988-2 C.B. 535) (see § 601.601(d)(2) of this chapter), for rules on making and maintaining elections for shareholder election years (as defined in paragraph (j) of this section) beginning after December 31, 1986, and before January 1, 1998. Elections made under Notice 88-125 must be maintained as provided in § 1.1295-1 for taxable years beginning after December 31, 1997. A section 1295 election made prior to February 2, 1998, that was intended to be effective for the taxable year of the PFIC that began during the shareholder's election year will be effective for that taxable year of the foreign corporation provided that it is clear from all the facts and circumstances that the shareholder intended the election to be effective for that taxable year of the foreign corporation.

(i) *Invalidation, termination, or revocation of section 1295 election.*—(1) *Invalidation or termination of election at the discretion of the Commissioner.*—(i) *In general.*—The Commissioner, in the Commissioner's discretion, may invalidate or terminate a section 1295 election applicable to a shareholder if the shareholder, the PFIC, or any intermediary fails to satisfy the requirements for making a section 1295 election or the annual election requirements of this section to which the shareholder, PFIC, or intermediary is subject, including the requirement to provide, on request, copies of the books and records of the PFIC or other documentation substantiating the ordinary earnings and net capital gain of the PFIC.

(ii) *Deferral of section 1293 inclusion.*— The Commissioner may invalidate any pass through entity section 1295 election with respect to an interest holder or beneficiary if the section 1293 inclusion with respect to that interest holder or beneficiary is not included in the gross income of either the pass through entity, an intermediate pass through entity, or the interest holder or beneficiary within two years of the end of the PFIC's taxable year due to nonconforming taxable years of the interest holder and the pass through entity or any intermediate pass through entity.

(iii) *When effective.*—Termination of a shareholder's section 1295 election will be effective for the taxable year of the PFIC determined by the Commissioner in the Commissioner's discretion. An invalidation of a shareholder's section 1295 election will be effective for the first taxable year to which the section 1295 election applied, and the shareholder whose election is invalidated will be treated as if the section 1295 election was never made.

(2) *Shareholder revocation.*—(i) *In general.*—In the Commissioner's discretion, upon a finding of a substantial change in circumstances, the Commissioner may consent to a shareholder's request to revoke a section 1295 election. Request for revocation must be made by the shareholder that made the election and at the time and in the manner provided in paragraph (i)(2)(ii) of this section.

(ii) *Time for and manner of requesting consent to revoke.*—(A) *Time.*—The shareholder must request consent to revoke the section 1295 election no later than 12 calendar months after the discovery of the substantial change of circumstances that forms the basis for the shareholder's request to revoke the section 1295 election.

(B) *Manner of making request.*—A shareholder requests consent to revoke a section 1295 election by filing a ruling request with the Office of the Associate Chief Counsel (International). The ruling request must satisfy the requirements, including payment of the user fee, for filing ruling requests with that office.

(iii) *When effective.*—Unless otherwise determined by the Commissioner, revocation of a section 1295 election will be effective for the first taxable year of the PFIC beginning after the date the Commissioner consents to the revocation.

(3) *Automatic termination.*—If a United States person, or the United States shareholder on behalf of a controlled foreign corporation, makes an election pursuant to section 1296 and the regulations thereunder with respect to PFIC stock for which a QEF election is in effect, or marks to market such stock under another provision of chapter 1 of the Internal Revenue Code, the QEF election is automatically terminated with respect to such stock that is marked to market under section 1296 or another provision of chapter 1 of the Internal Revenue Code. Such termination shall be effective on the last day of the shareholder's taxable year preceding the first taxable year for which the section 1296 election is in effect or such stock is marked to market under another provision of chapter 1 of the Internal Revenue Code.

Example. Corp Y, a domestic corporation, owns directly 100 shares of marketable stock in foreign corporation FX, a PFIC. Corp Y also owns a 50 percent interest in FP, a foreign partnership that owns 200 shares of FX stock. Accordingly, under section 1298(a)(3) and §1.1296-1(e)(1), Corp Y is treated as indirectly owning 100 shares of FX stock. Corp Y also owns 100 percent of the stock of FZ, a foreign corporation that is not a PFIC. FZ owns 100 shares of FX stock, and therefore under section 1298(a)(2)(A), Corp Y is treated as owning the 100 shares of FX stock owned by FZ. For taxable year 2005, Corp Y has a QEF election in effect with respect to all 300 shares of FX stock that it owns directly or indirectly. See generally §1.1295-1(c)(1). For taxable year 2006, Corp Y makes a timely election pursuant to section 1296 and the regulations thereunder. For purposes of section 1296, Corp Y is treated as owning stock held indirectly through a partnership, but not through a foreign corporation. Section 1296(g); §1.1296-1(e)(1). Accordingly, Corp Y's section 1296 election covers the 100 shares it owns directly and the 100 shares it owns indirectly through FP, but not the 100 shares owned by FZ. With respect to the first 200 shares, Corp Y's QEF election is automatically terminated effective December 31, 2005. With respect to the 100 shares Corp Y owns through foreign FZ, Corp Y's QEF election remains in effect unless invalidated, terminated, or revoked pursuant to this paragraph (i).

(4) *Effect of invalidation, termination, or revocation.*—An invalidation, termination, or revocation of a section 1295 election—

(i) Terminates all section 1294 elections, as provided in §1.1294-1T(e), and the undistributed PFIC earnings tax liability and interest thereon are due by the due date, without regard to extensions, for the return for the last taxable year of the shareholder to which the section 1295 election applies;

(ii) In the Commissioner's discretion, results in a deemed sale of the QEF stock on the last day of the PFIC's last taxable year as a QEF, in which gain, but not loss, will be recognized and with respect to which appropriate basis and holding period adjustments will be made; and

(iii) Subjects the shareholder to any other terms and conditions that the Commissioner determines are necessary to ensure the shareholder's compliance with sections 1291 through 1298 or any other provisions of the Code.

Reg. §1.1295-1(i)(4)(iii)

(5) *Effect after invalidation, termination, or revocation.*—(i) *In general.*—Without the Commissioner's consent, a shareholder whose section 1295 election was invalidated, terminated, or revoked under this paragraph (i) may not make the section 1295 election with respect to the PFIC before the sixth taxable year in which the invalidation, termination, or revocation became effective.

(ii) *Special rule.*—Notwithstanding paragraph (i)(5)(i) of this section, a shareholder whose section 1295 election was terminated pursuant to paragraph (i)(3) of this section, and either whose section 1296 election has subsequently been terminated because its PFIC stock ceased to be marketable or who no longer marks to market such stock under another provision of chapter 1 of the Internal Revenue Code, may make a section 1295 election with respect to its PFIC stock before the sixth taxable year in which its prior section 1295 election was terminated.

(j) *Definitions.*—For purposes of this section—

Intermediary is a nominee or shareholder of record that holds stock on behalf of the shareholder or on behalf of another person in a chain of ownership between the shareholder and the PFIC, and any direct or indirect beneficial owner of PFIC stock (including a beneficial owner that is a pass through entity) in the chain of ownership between the shareholder and the PFIC.

Pass through entity is a partnership, S corporation, trust, or estate.

Shareholder has the same meaning as the term shareholder in § 1.1291-9(j)(3), except that for purposes of this section, a partnership and an S corporation also are treated as shareholders. Furthermore, unless otherwise provided, an interest holder of a pass through entity, which is treated as a shareholder of a PFIC, also will be treated as a shareholder of the PFIC.

Shareholder's election year is the taxable year of the shareholder for which it made the section 1295 election.

(k) *Effective dates.*—Except as otherwise provided, paragraphs (b)(2)(iii), (b)(3), (b)(4), and (c) through (j) of this section are applicable to taxable years of shareholders beginning after December 31, 1997. However, taxpayers may apply the rules under paragraphs (b)(4), (f) and (g) of this section to a taxable year beginning before January 1, 1998, provided the statute of limitations on the assessment of tax has not expired as of April 27, 1998, and, in the case of paragraph (b)(4) of this section, the taxpayers who filed the joint return have consistently applied the rules of that section to all taxable years following the year the election was made. Paragraph (b)(3)(v) of this section is applicable as of February 7, 2000, however, a taxpayer may apply the rules to a taxable year prior to the applicable date provided the statute of limitations on the assessment of tax for that taxable year has not expired. Paragraphs (i)(3) and (i)(5)(ii) of this section are applicable for taxable years beginning on or after May 3, 2004. [Reg. § 1.1295-1.]

☐ [*T.D.* 8750, 12-31-97. *Redesignated and amended by T.D.* 8870, 2-4-2000. *Amended by T.D.* 9123, 4-30-2004.]

Proposed Regulation

§ 1.1295-1. Qualified electing funds.—(a) *In general.*—This section provides certain rules under section 1295 applicable to a U.S. person that has elected to treat a PFIC (as defined in § 1.1291-1(b)(1)) as a QEF (as defined in § 1.1291-1(b)(2)(i)). A U.S. person that has elected to treat a PFIC as a QEF is taxable annually, pursuant to section 1293, on its pro rata share of the ordinary earnings and net capital gain of the QEF.

(b) *Application of section 1295 election.*—(1) *Election personal to shareholder.*—An election under section 1295 and this section (section 1295 election) applies only to the shareholder that makes the election. Accordingly, a shareholder's section 1295 election will not apply to a U.S. transferee (as defined in § 1.1291-6(c)(2)(i)) of stock of a PFIC with respect to which the shareholder made a section 1295 election. A section 1295 election made by a common parent of a consolidated group as agent for members of the group is considered made by each member of the group that owns stock of the PFIC at the time of the election and at any time thereafter.

(2) *Election applicable to specific corporation only.*—(i) *In general.*—Only a corporation with respect to which a shareholder makes a section 1295 election is a QEF. The shareholder's section 1295 election applies to all the stock of the QEF that the shareholder owns at the time of the election or acquires thereafter. Except as provided in paragraph (b)(2)(ii) of this section, if a shareholder transfers stock of a QEF in exchange for stock of another PFIC, the latter PFIC is not a QEF unless the shareholder makes a section 1295 election to treat it as a QEF. If a shareholder disposes of stock of a QEF in exchange for stock of another PFIC in a nonrecognition transfer (as defined in § 1.1291-6(a)(2)) effected prior to April 1, 1992, and the shareholder has consistently treated the other PFIC as a QEF, the shareholder may make a section 1295 election with respect to the other PFIC whose stock was received for

the taxable year of the PFIC that includes the day the transfer was effected. Such election must be made by the later of—

(A) The due date provided in section 1295(b); or

(B) The due date for the return for the taxable year of the shareholder that includes April 1, 1992.

For the deadline for making the section 1295 election in the case of nonrecognition transfers effected after April 1, 1992, *see* section 1295(b).

(ii) *Stock of QEF received in a nonrecognition transfer.*—If a U.S. person is a U.S. transferee (as defined in § 1.1291-6(c)(2)(i)) of stock of a PFIC in a nonrecognition transfer in which the shareholder disposing of such stock does not fully recognize the gain with respect to such stock, and the U.S. transferee, at the time of the transaction, has in effect a section 1295 election with respect to that PFIC, the section 1295 election will apply to the newly acquired stock on the day after the transaction. The newly acquired stock will be treated as stock of an unpedigreed QEF for which an election under section 1291(d)(2) and § 1.1291-9 or 1.1291-10 may be made. For purposes of making a section 1291(d)(2) election pursuant to this paragraph (b)(2)(ii), the qualification date is the day after the nonrecognition transaction. The following example illustrates the rule of this paragraph (b)(2)(ii).

Example. (i) X, a domestic corporation, owns stock of NQF, a section 1291 fund with respect to X, and stock of FC, a pedigreed QEF with respect to X. Pursuant to a plan of reorganization, X and the other shareholders of NQF exchange their NQF stock for voting stock of FC in a transaction that qualifies as a reorganization described in section 368(a)(1)(C). Pursuant to § 1.1291-6(c)(1), the gain recognition rule of § 1.1291-6(b)(1) does not apply to X's disposition of NQF stock. X therefore does not recognize gain on the exchange of NQF stock for FC stock. X's adjusted basis in the FC stock received in the reorganization is equal to X's adjusted basis in the NQF stock immediately prior to the transfer. The holding period of the FC stock received includes the period during which X held the NQF stock, and, as provided in § 1.1291-1(h)(7), the character of the days during that period as prePFIC and prior PFIC carry over to the FC stock.

(ii) As provided in § 1.1295-1(b)(2)(ii), the section 1295 election that X made with respect to FC applies to the FC stock received in the reorganization. However, because the holding period of the FC stock received in exchange for the NQF stock includes days that are treated as prior PFIC days, the FC stock received in the reorganization is treated as stock of an unpedigreed QEF. X may make an election under section 1291(d)(2) to purge the holding period of the FC stock received of the prior PFIC days carried over with the NQF holding period.

[Prop. Reg. § 1.1295-1.]

[Proposed 4-1-92.]

Proposed Regulation

§ 1.1295-2. Special preferred QEF election.—(a) *In general.*—This section provides rules permitting certain shareholders to make a special election under section 1295 (special preferred QEF election) in lieu of the election described in § 1.1295-1[1] and Notice 88-125, 1988-2 C.B. 535 (see § 601.601(d)(2)(ii)(*b*) of this chapter), with respect to certain preferred shares (qualified preferred shares) of a foreign corporation that certifies either that it is a PFIC (as defined in § 1.1291-1(b)(1)(i))[1] or that it reasonably believes that it is a PFIC. In order to make a special preferred QEF election, a shareholder must satisfy the stock ownership requirement of paragraph (c)(2) of this section. A special preferred QEF election of a shareholder applies only to those qualified preferred shares acquired and held directly by the shareholder in the taxable year of the shareholder for which the election is made. A shareholder making a special preferred QEF election must account for dividend income on shares subject to the election under the special income inclusion rules described in § 1.1293-2, rather than under the general income inclusion rules of section 1293 and § 1.1293-1. In addition, for purposes of determining the tax consequences of owning shares subject to the special preferred QEF election, an electing shareholder must treat the foreign corporation as a PFIC for the entire period during which the shareholder continues to hold any of such shares. Paragraph (b) of this section defines qualified preferred share. Paragraph (c) of this section provides rules for determining who may make the special preferred QEF election. Paragraph (d) of this section provides rules concerning the effect of the election. Paragraph (e) of this section provides rules for the time and manner of making the election. Paragraph (f) of this section sets forth the annual reporting requirement for the election. Paragraph (g) of this section provides rules concerning the possible termination or invalidation of the election. For the applicability date of this section, see paragraph (h) of this section.

---

[1] This proposed regulation was published on April 1, 1992, at 57 Fed. Reg. 11024.

(b) *Qualified preferred share defined.*—(1) *In general.*—For purposes of this section, a share of a foreign corporation is a qualified preferred share only if—

(i) The share was originally issued for cash or in exchange for qualified preferred shares of the foreign corporation in a transaction to which section 354(a)(1) applied;

(ii) If the share were to constitute a debt obligation, the share would be in registered form within the meaning of § 5f.103-1(c) of this chapter;

(iii) All amounts payable with respect to the share are denominated in U.S. dollars and are not determined by reference to the value of a currency other than the U.S. dollar;

(iv) The share is limited and preferred as to dividends and does not participate in corporate growth to any significant extent within the meaning of section 1504(a)(4)(B);

(v) The share has a fixed redemption or liquidation price;

(vi) The share provides for cumulative or noncumulative dividend rights that are limited to an annual (or shorter period) amount computed by multiplying either the redemption or liquidation price of the share by a specified index described in § 1.446-3(c)(2)(i), (iii), or (iv) (specified index), or by a specified index periodically re-established pursuant to an auction reset mechanism, set in advance of the period with respect to which the specified index applies;

(vii) If the share may be redeemed under circumstances described in § 1.305-5(b) such that redemption premium (as described in § 1.305-5(b)) could be treated under section 305(c) as a constructive distribution (fixed term preferred stock), the share was not issued with redemption premium exceeding the de minimis amount described in section 305(c)(1) and § 1.305-5(b)(1);

(viii) If the share may not be redeemed under circumstances described in § 1.305-5(b) such that redemption premium would not be treated under section 305 as a constructive distribution (perpetual preferred stock), the share does not provide shareholders with the right to receive an amount upon liquidation or redemption that exceeds the issue price of the share (as determined under the principles of section 1273(b)) by an amount in excess of 5 percent of such liquidation or redemption amount;

(ix) If redeemable, the share is redeemable only in whole and not in part and is not subject to mandatory redemption within five years of the issue date of the share. Further, the share is not subject to a holder put or issuer call that, based on all the facts and circumstances as of the issue date of the share, is more likely than not to be exercised at a time within five years of the issue date;

(x) If convertible, the share is not convertible into a share other than a share meeting all the conditions set forth in paragraphs (b)(1)(i) through (b)(1)(ix) of this section; and

(xi) The issuer of the share has indicated in an offering document relating to the original issuance of the share or in a written statement available to U.S. holders that the issuer has no current intention or belief that it will not pay dividends on the share on a current basis and that the share meets the conditions set forth in paragraphs (b)(1)(i) through (b)(1)(x) of this section and this paragraph (b)(1)(xi).

(2) *Special rules for shares acquired in secondary market transactions.*—(i) *Fixed term preferred stock.*—A share of fixed term preferred stock (as described in paragraph (b)(1)(vii) of this section) that satisfies the conditions set forth in paragraph (b)(1) of this section and that is acquired in a transaction other than in connection with the initial issuance of the share (a secondary market transaction), shall constitute a qualified preferred share with respect to a shareholder, but only if the shareholder acquires the share for cash and the share has preferred discount (as defined below) that is less than or equal to an amount equal to 1 percent of the redemption price, multiplied by the number of complete years from the date of acquisition of the share to the redemption date as established under the principles of § 1.305-5(b). Sales of shares to bond houses, brokers, or similar persons or organizations acting in the capacity as underwriters, placement agents, or wholesalers are ignored for purposes of determining whether a share is acquired in connection with the initial issuance of the share. For purposes of this section, the preferred discount for a share is the excess of the redemption price of the share payable on the redemption date over the shareholder's acquisition cost for the share.

(ii) *Perpetual preferred stock.*—A share of perpetual preferred stock, within the meaning of paragraph (b)(1)(viii) of this section, that satisfies the conditions set forth in paragraph (b)(1) of this section and that is acquired in a secondary market transaction, shall constitute a qualified preferred share with respect to the shareholder, but only if the shareholder acquires the share for cash and the amount payable upon liquidation of the share exceeds the shareholder's acquisition cost for the share by an amount less than or equal to 10 percent of such liquidation amount.

Prop. Reg. § 1.1295-2(b)(1)

(iii) *Examples.*—The following examples illustrate the rules of this paragraph (b)(2).

Example 1—(i) *Facts.* On May 1, 1998, A, an individual who files her return on a calendar year basis, purchases for $9000 cash in a single secondary market transaction (as defined in paragraph (b)(2)(i) of this section) 100 shares of nonconvertible Class A $100 par value preferred stock (Class A Stock) of FC, a foreign corporation with a taxable year ending March 31. The terms of the Class A Stock satisfy all the conditions described in paragraph (b)(1) of this section and provide for a mandatory redemption of the Class A Stock by the issuer in U.S. dollars at par on June 1, 2012. The Class A Stock is not redeemable pursuant to an issuer call or holder put on any other date.

(ii) *Analysis.* In order for A to make a special preferred QEF election with respect to the Class A Stock acquired by A, the Class A Stock acquired must constitute qualified preferred shares. Although the Class A Stock meets the requirements for qualified preferred shares set forth in paragraph (b)(1) of this section, the stock also must satisfy the requirements described in paragraph (b)(2) because A acquired the stock in a secondary market transaction. Because the terms of the Class A Stock provide that the stock will be redeemed by the issuer on June 1, 2012, the stock constitutes fixed term preferred stock within the meaning of paragraph (b)(1)(vii) of this section. A purchased the Class A Stock for $90 per share, representing a $10 discount ($100 June 1, 2012, per share redemption price less $90 acquisition cost). Because this $10 discount, which constitutes preferred discount within the meaning of paragraph (b)(2)(i) of this section, is less than $14 (1 percent of the redemption price multiplied by 14 (the number of complete years until the mandatory redemption date)), the Class A Stock acquired by A satisfies the conditions of paragraph (b)(2)(i) of this section and therefore constitutes qualified preferred shares.

Example 2—(i) *Facts.* The facts are the same as in *Example 1*, except that A acquires the 100 shares of Class A Stock for $8000.

(ii) *Analysis.* In this case, A purchased the Class A Stock for $80 per share, representing a $20 discount ($100 June 1, 2012, redemption price less $80 acquisition cost). Because this $20 of preferred discount is greater than $14 (1 percent of the redemption price multiplied by 14 (the number of complete years until the mandatory redemption date)), the Class A Stock fails to satisfy the conditions of paragraph (b)(2)(i) of this section and therefore fails to qualify as qualified preferred shares.

(c) *Who may make the election.*—(1) *In general.*—A U.S. person that acquires qualified preferred shares for cash or in a nonrecognition transaction described in § 1.1291-6(a)[2] (nonrecognition transaction) and that holds such shares directly may make a special preferred QEF election, provided that, in the case of shares acquired in a nonrecognition transaction, either the qualified preferred shares are treated as stock of a pedigreed QEF, as defined in § 1.1291-1(b)(2)(ii), immediately prior to the nonrecognition transaction, or the gain, if any, realized on the transaction would be recognized under § 1.1291-6(b) with respect to the nonrecognition transaction. A special preferred QEF election will not apply to any shares with respect to which the electing shareholder is an indirect shareholder, within the meaning of § 1.1291-1(b)(8). Solely for purposes of this section, partnerships, S corporations, trusts and estates (pass-through entities) that directly own qualified preferred shares are treated as shareholders that may make a special preferred QEF election. A shareholder may not make a special preferred QEF election if at any time the shareholder made a section 1295 election (other than a special preferred QEF election) with respect to the foreign corporation. A shareholder may not make a special preferred QEF election unless the shareholder satisfies the stock ownership requirements set forth in paragraph (c)(2) of this section, and the shareholder receives from the foreign corporation the statement described in paragraph (c)(3) of this section.

(2) *Ownership requirement.*—A holder of qualified preferred shares of a foreign corporation may make a special preferred QEF election only if, at all times during the taxable year of the shareholder, the shareholder does not own, directly, indirectly, or constructively, within the meaning of section 958, five percent or more of the vote or value of any class of stock of the foreign corporation. The five percent vote or value limitation must be satisfied for each taxable year of the shareholder during which the shareholder continues to hold shares subject to the special preferred QEF election.

(3) *Statement from corporation.*—A shareholder may make the special preferred QEF election only if the foreign corporation has provided a written statement relating to the taxable year of the corporation that ends with or within the taxable year of the shareholder for

---

[2] This proposed regulation was published on April 1, 1992, at 57 Fed. Reg. 11024.

which the election is made certifying either that the foreign corporation is, or that it reasonably believes that it is, a PFIC, and that it is not a controlled foreign corporation within the meaning of section 957(a) for such taxable year of the corporation. The statement must be provided directly to the electing shareholder or in a disclosure or other document generally available to all U.S. holders. Electing shareholders must retain a copy of the statement for their records.

(d) *Effect of election.*—(1) *In general.*—Unless terminated or invalidated pursuant to paragraph (g) of this section, shares subject to a special preferred QEF election will be treated as shares of a pedigreed QEF (as defined in § 1.1291-1(b)(2)(ii)) for all taxable years of the foreign corporation that are included wholly or partly in the shareholder's holding period of the shares. A special preferred QEF election applies to all qualified preferred shares owned directly by the shareholder that are acquired in the taxable year of the election. Separate special preferred QEF elections may be made for qualified preferred shares acquired in other taxable years of the taxpayer. A special preferred QEF election is personal to the shareholder that made the election and does not apply to a transferee of the shares. A shareholder that has made a special preferred QEF election may not make, with respect to the foreign corporation, any other election permitted under sections 1291 through 1297 and the regulations under those sections, including a section 1295 election as described in § 1.1295-1 and Notice 88-125, 1988-2 C.B. 535 (see § 601.601(d)(2)(ii)(*b*) of this chapter), for any period during which the special preferred QEF election remains in effect with respect to any shares of the shareholder.

(2) *Continued PFIC Characterization.*—By making the special preferred QEF election, the shareholder agrees to treat the foreign corporation as a PFIC with respect to qualified preferred shares subject to the election at all times during its holding period for such shares, without regard to whether the foreign corporation is a PFIC for any taxable year of the foreign corporation during which the preferred QEF election remains in effect.

(3) *Section 1293 inclusions.*—For each taxable year of the shareholder to which an election under this section applies, the shareholder must include in income the preferred QEF amount, as defined in § 1.1293-2, in the manner and under the rules provided in that section.

(e) *Time for and manner of making the special preferred QEF election.*—(1) *Time for making the election.*—A special preferred QEF election must be made on or before the due date, as extended, for filing the shareholder's return for the taxable year during which the shareholder acquired the qualified preferred shares for which the election is being made. A special preferred QEF election may not be made for those shares at any other time pursuant to any other provision of the Code or regulations.

(2) *Manner of making the election.*—(i) *In general.*—A shareholder makes the special preferred QEF election under this section for all qualified preferred shares of a foreign corporation acquired during the shareholder's taxable year by checking the appropriate box in Form 8621 (Return by a Shareholder of a Passive Foreign Investment Company or Qualified Electing Fund), Part I, for making the section 1295 election, and indicating in the margin of Part I that the shareholder is making a special preferred QEF election with respect to certain specified shares. The shareholder also must report the preferred QEF amount for the taxable year of the election on Line 6a of Part II of Form 8621. In addition, the shareholder must attach to Form 8621 the statement (preferred QEF statement) described in paragraph (e)(2)(ii) of this section, signed by the shareholder under penalties of perjury, stating that the information and representations provided in the preferred QEF statement are true, correct, and complete to the best of the shareholder's knowledge and belief.

(ii) *Preferred QEF statement contents.*—The preferred QEF statement must include the following information and representations:

(A) The first taxable year of the shareholder for which the special preferred QEF election is made;

(B) The number of shares subject to the election, their acquisition date(s) and acquisition price(s), and the class designation(s) of the shares;

(C) A representation by the shareholder that it did not at any time during its taxable year own directly, indirectly, or constructively, within the meaning of section 958, five percent or more of the vote or value of any class of stock of the foreign corporation with respect to which the election applies;

(D) A representation by the shareholder that it has obtained the written statement described in paragraph (c)(3) of this section; and

(E) A representation by the shareholder that it has never made a section 1295 election other than a special preferred QEF election with respect to the foreign corporation.

(f) *Annual reporting requirement.*—For each taxable year of a shareholder during which the shareholder holds shares of a foreign corporation subject to one or more special preferred QEF elections, the shareholder must file Form 8621 with respect to the foreign corporation regardless of whether the foreign corporation is or is not a PFIC under section 1296 during any portion of the taxable year. The shareholder must indicate in the margin of Part I of Form 8621 the number of special preferred QEF elections of the shareholder that remain in effect with respect to the foreign corporation. In addition, the shareholder must report, on Line 6a of Part II of Form 8621, the aggregate of the preferred QEF amounts for all relevant special preferred QEF elections in effect for the taxable year.

(g) *Termination or invalidation of election.*—(1) *In general.*—A sale, exchange or other disposition of a share that is subject to a special preferred QEF election will terminate the special preferred QEF election with respect to that share. In addition, the Commissioner may, in the Commissioner's discretion, terminate or invalidate a special preferred QEF election if a shareholder that made the election fails to satisfy the initial or ongoing requirements of the election. Once made, a special preferred QEF election may not be terminated or invalidated by the shareholder.

(2) *Effect of termination or invalidation.*—Termination of a special preferred QEF election by the Commissioner will be effective on the first day of the shareholder's first taxable year following the last taxable year of the shareholder for which the requirements of the election are satisfied. For purposes of sections 1291 through 1297 and the regulations thereunder, the holding period of qualified preferred shares subject to an election that has been terminated will be treated as beginning on the effective date of the termination. A shareholder that has made an election that is invalidated by the Commissioner will be treated for purposes of sections 1291 through 1297 and the regulations thereunder as if the shareholder never made the election.

(h) *Effective date.*—An election under this section may only be made with respect to qualified preferred shares that are issued after the date that is 30 days after the date of publication of this document as a final regulation. [Prop. Reg. § 1.1295-2.]

[Proposed 12-24-96.]

§ 1.1295-3. Retroactive elections.—(a) *In general.*—This section prescribes the exclusive rules under which a shareholder, as defined in § 1.1295-1(j), may make a section 1295 election for a taxable year after the election due date, as defined in § 1.1295-1(e) (retroactive election). Therefore, a shareholder may not seek such relief under any other provision of the law, including § 301.9100 of this chapter. Paragraph (b) of this section describes the general rules for a shareholder to preserve the ability to make a retroactive election. These rules require that the shareholder possess reasonable belief as of the election due date that the foreign corporation was not a PFIC for its taxable year that ended in the shareholder's taxable year to which the election due date pertains, and that the shareholder file a Protective Statement to preserve its ability to make a retroactive election. Paragraph (c) of this section establishes the terms, conditions and other requirements with respect to a Protective Statement required to be filed under the general rules. Paragraph (d) of this section sets forth factors that establish a shareholder's reasonable belief that a foreign corporation was not a PFIC. Paragraph (e) of this section prescribes special rules for certain shareholders that are deemed to satisfy the reasonable belief requirement and therefore are not required to file a Protective Statement. Paragraph (f) of this section describes the limited circumstances under which the Commissioner may permit a shareholder that lacked the requisite reasonable belief or failed to satisfy the requirements of paragraph (b) or (e) of this section to make a retroactive election. Paragraph (g) of this section provides the time for and manner of making a retroactive election. Paragraph (h) of this section provides the effective date of this section.

(b) *General rule.*—Except as provided in paragraphs (e) and (f) of this section, a shareholder may make a retroactive election for a taxable year of the shareholder (retroactive election year) only if the shareholder—

(1) Reasonably believed, within the meaning of paragraph (d) of this section, that as of the election due date, as defined in § 1.1295-1(e), the foreign corporation was not a PFIC for its taxable year that ended during the retroactive election year;

(2) Filed a Protective Statement with respect to the foreign corporation, applicable to the retroactive election year, in which the shareholder described the basis for its reasonable belief and extended, in the manner provided in paragraph (c)(4) of this section, the periods of limitations on the assessment of taxes determined under sections 1291 through 1298 with respect to the foreign corporation (PFIC related taxes) for all taxable years of the shareholder to which the Protective Statement applies; and

(3) Complied with the other terms and conditions of the Protective Statement.

(c) *Protective Statement.*—(1) *In general.*—A Protective Statement is a statement executed under penalties of perjury by the shareholder, or a person authorized to sign a federal income tax return on behalf of the shareholder, that preserves the shareholder's ability to make a retroactive election. To file a Protective Statement that applies to a taxable year of the shareholder, the shareholder must reasonably believe as of the election due date that the foreign corporation was not a PFIC for the foreign corporation's taxable year that ended during the retroactive election year. The Protective Statement must contain—

(i) The shareholder's reasonable belief statement, as described in paragraph (c)(2) of this section;

(ii) The shareholder's agreement extending the periods of limitations on the assessment of PFIC related taxes for all taxable years to which the Protective Statement applies, as provided in paragraph (c)(4) of this section; and

(iii) The following information and representations—

(A) The shareholder's name, address, taxpayer identification number, and the shareholder's first taxable year to which the Protective Statement applies;

(B) The foreign corporation's name, address, and taxpayer identification number, if any; and

(C) The highest percentage of shares of each class of stock of the foreign corporation held directly or indirectly by the shareholder during the shareholder's first taxable year to which the Protective Statement applies.

(2) *Reasonable belief statement.*—The Protective Statement must contain a reasonable belief statement, as described in paragraph (c)(1) of this section. The reasonable belief statement is a description of the shareholder's basis for its reasonable belief that the foreign corporation was not a PFIC for its taxable year that ended with or within the shareholder's first taxable year to which the Protective Statement applies. If the Protective Statement applies to a taxable year or years described in paragraph (c)(5)(ii) of this section, the reasonable belief statement must describe the shareholder's basis for its reasonable belief that the foreign corporation was not a PFIC for the foreign corporation's taxable year or years that ended in such taxable year or years of the shareholder. The reasonable belief statement must discuss the application of the income and asset tests to the foreign corporation and the factors, including those stated in paragraph (d) of this section, that affect the results of those tests.

(3) *Who executes and files the Protective Statement.*—The person that executes and files the Protective Statement is the person that makes the section 1295 election, as provided in § 1.1295-1(d).

(4) *Waiver of the periods of limitations.*—(i) *Time for and manner of extending periods of limitations.*—(A) *In general.*—A shareholder that files the Protective Statement with the Commissioner must extend the periods of limitations on the assessment of all PFIC related taxes for all of the shareholder's taxable years to which the Protective Statement applies, as provided in this paragraph (c)(4). The shareholder is required to execute the waiver on such form as the Commissioner may prescribe for purposes of this paragraph (c)(4). Until that form is published, the shareholder must execute a statement in which the shareholder agrees to extend the periods of limitations on the assessment of all PFIC related taxes for all the shareholder's taxable years to which the Protective Statement applies, as provided in this paragraph (c)(4), and agrees to the restrictions in paragraph (c)(4)(ii)(A) of this section. The shareholder or a person authorized to sign the shareholder's federal income tax return must sign the form or statement. A properly executed form or statement authorized by this paragraph (c)(4) will be deemed consented to and signed by a Service Center Director or the Assistant Commissioner (International) for purposes of § 301.6501(c)-1(d) of this chapter.

(B) *Application of general rule to domestic partnerships.*—(*1*) *In general.*—A domestic partnership that holds an interest in stock of a PFIC satisfies the waiver requirement of paragraph (c)(4) of this section pursuant to the rules of this paragraph (c)(4)(i)(B)(*1*). The partnership must file one or more waivers obtained or arranged under this paragraph (c)(4)(i)(B) as part of the Protective Statement, as provided in paragraph (c)(1) of this section. The partnership must either—

(*i*) Obtain from each partner the partner's waiver of the periods of limitations;

(*ii*) Obtain from each partner a duly executed power of attorney under § 601.501 of this chapter authorizing the partnership to extend that partner's periods of limitations, and execute a waiver on behalf of the partners; or

(*iii*) In the case of a domestic partnership governed by the unified audit and litigation procedures of sections 6221 through 6233 (TEFRA partnership), arrange for the tax matters partner (or any other person authorized to enter into an agreement to extend the periods of limitations), as provided in section 6229(b), to execute a waiver on behalf of all the partners.

(2) Special rules.—(i) Addition of partner to non-TEFRA partnership.—In the case of any individual who becomes a partner in a domestic partnership other than a TEFRA partnership (non-TEFRA partnership) in a taxable year subsequent to the year in which the partnership filed a Protective Statement, the partner and the partnership must comply with the rules applicable to non-TEFRA partnerships, as provided in paragraph (c)(4)(i)(B)(*1*) of this section, by the due date, as extended, for the federal income tax return of the partnership for the taxable year during which the individual became a partner. Failure to so comply will render the Protective Statement invalid with respect to the partnership and partners.

(ii) Change in status from non-TEFRA partnership to TEFRA partnership.—If a partnership is a non-TEFRA partnership in one taxable year but becomes a TEFRA partnership in a subsequent taxable year, the partnership must file one or more waivers obtained or arranged under this paragraph (c)(4)(i)(B)(*2*)(*ii*), as part of the Protective Statement, as provided in paragraph (c)(1) of this section. The partnership must either obtain from any new partner the partner's waiver described in this paragraph (c)(4); obtain from the new partner a duly executed power of attorney under § 601.501 of this chapter authorizing the partnership to extend the partner's periods of limitations, and execute a waiver on behalf of the new partner; or arrange for the tax matters partner (or any other person authorized to enter into an agreement to extend the periods of limitations) to execute a waiver on behalf of all the partners. In each case, the partnership must attach any new waiver of a partner's periods of limitations, and a copy of the Protective Statement to its federal income tax return for that taxable year.

(C) *Application of general rule to domestic nongrantor trusts and domestic estates.*—A domestic nongrantor trust or a domestic estate that holds an interest in stock of a PFIC satisfies the waiver requirement of this paragraph (c)(4) at the entity level. For this purpose, such entity must comply with rules similar to those applicable to non-TEFRA partnerships, as provided in paragraph (c)(4)(i)(B)(*1*) of this section.

(D) *Application of general rule to S corporations.*—An S corporation that holds an interest in stock of a PFIC satisfies the waiver requirement of this paragraph (c)(4) at the S corporation level. For this purpose, the S corporation must comply with rules similar to those applicable to non-TEFRA partnerships, as provided in paragraph (c)(4)(i)(B)(*1*) of this section. However, in the case of an S corporation that was governed by the unified audit corporate proceedings of sections 6241 through 6245 for any taxable year to which a Protective Statement applies (former TEFRA S corporation), the tax matters person (or any other person authorized to enter into such an agreement), as was provided in sections 6241 through 6245, may execute a waiver described in this paragraph (c)(4) that applies to such taxable year; for any other taxable year, the former TEFRA S corporation must comply with rules similar to those applicable to non-TEFRA partnerships.

(E) *Effect on waiver of complete termination of a pass through entity or pass through entity's business.*—The complete termination of a pass through entity described in paragraphs (c)(4)(i)(B) through (D) of this section, or a pass through entity's trade or business, will not terminate a waiver that applies to a partner, shareholder, or beneficiary.

(F) *Application of general rule to foreign partnerships, foreign trusts, domestic or foreign grantor trusts, and foreign estates.*—A U.S. person that is a partner or beneficiary of a foreign partnership, foreign trust, or foreign estate that holds an interest in stock of a PFIC satisfies the waiver requirement of this paragraph (c)(4) at the partner or beneficiary level. A U.S. person that is treated under sections 671 through 679 as the owner of the portion of a domestic or foreign trust that owns an interest in PFIC stock also satisfies the waiver requirement at the owner level. A waiver by a partner or beneficiary applies only to that partner or beneficiary, and is not affected by a complete termination of the entity or the entity's trade or business.

(ii) *Terms of waiver.*—(A) *Scope of waiver.*—The waiver of the periods of limitations is limited to the assessment of PFIC related taxes. If the period of limitations for a taxable year affected by a retroactive election has expired with respect to the assessment of other non-PFIC related taxes, no adjustments, other than consequential changes, may be made by the Internal Revenue Service or by the shareholder to any other items of income, deduction, or credit for that year. If the period of limitations for refunds or credits for a taxable year affected by a retroactive election is open only by virtue of the assessment period extension and section 6511(c), no refund or credit is allowable on grounds other than adjustments to PFIC related taxes and consequential changes.

Reg. § 1.1295-3(c)(4)(ii)(A)

(B) *Period of waiver.*—The extension of the periods of limitations on the assessment of PFIC related taxes will be effective for all of the shareholder's taxable years to which the Protective Statement applies. In addition, the waiver, to the extent it applies to the period of limitations for a particular year, will terminate with respect to that year no sooner than three years from the date on which the shareholder files an amended return, as provided in paragraph (g) of this section, for that year. For the suspension of the running of the period of limitations for the collection of taxes for which a shareholder has elected under section 1294 to extend the time for payment, as provided in paragraph (g)(3)(ii) of this section, see sections 6503(i) and 6229(h).

(5) *Time of and manner for filing a Protective Statement.*—(i) *In general.*—Except as provided in paragraph (c)(5)(ii) of this section, a Protective Statement must be attached to the shareholder's federal income tax return for the shareholder's first taxable year to which the Protective Statement will apply. The shareholder must file its return and the copy of the Protective Statement by the due date, as extended under section 6081, for the return.

(ii) *Special rule for taxable years ended before January 2, 1998.*—A shareholder may file a Protective Statement that applies to the shareholder's taxable year or years that ended before January 2, 1998, provided the period of limitations on the assessment of taxes for any such year has not expired (open year). The shareholder must file the Protective Statement applicable to such open year or years, as provided in paragraph (c)(5)(i) of this section, by the due date, as extended, for the shareholder's return for the first taxable year ending after January 2, 1998.

(6) *Applicability of the Protective Statement.*—(i) *In general.*—Except as otherwise provided in this paragraph (c)(6), a Protective Statement applies to the shareholder's first taxable year for which the Protective Statement was filed and to each subsequent taxable year. The Protective Statement will not apply to any taxable year of the shareholder during which the shareholder does not own any stock of the foreign corporation or to any taxable year thereafter. Accordingly, if the shareholder has not made a retroactive election with respect to the previously owned stock by the time the shareholder reacquires stock of the foreign corporation, the shareholder must file another Protective Statement to preserve its right to make a retroactive election with respect to the later acquired stock. For the rule that provides that a section 1295 election made with respect to a foreign corporation applies to stock of that corporation acquired after a lapse in ownership, see § 1.1295-1(c)(2)(iii).

(ii) *Invalidity of the Protective Statement.*—A shareholder will be treated as if it never filed a Protective Statement if—

(A) The shareholder failed to make a retroactive election by the date prescribed for making the retroactive election in paragraph (g)(1) of this section; or

(B) The waiver of the periods of limitations terminates (by reason of a court decision or other determination) with respect to any taxable year before the expiration of three years from the date of filing of an amended return for that year pursuant to paragraph (g) of this section.

(7) *Retention of Protective Statement and information demonstrating reasonable belief.*—A shareholder that files a Protective Statement must retain a copy of the Protective Statement and its attachments and must, for each taxable year of the shareholder to which the Protective Statement applies, retain information sufficient to demonstrate the shareholder's reasonable belief that the foreign corporation was not a PFIC for the taxable year of the foreign corporation ending during each such taxable year of the shareholder.

(d) *Reasonable belief.*—(1) *In general.*—A foreign corporation is a PFIC for a taxable year if the foreign corporation satisfies either the income or asset test of section 1297(a). To determine whether a shareholder had reasonable belief that the foreign corporation is not a PFIC under section 1297(a), the shareholder must consider all relevant facts and circumstances. Reasonable belief may be based on a variety of factors, including reasonable asset valuations as well as reasonable interpretations of the applicable provisions of the Code, regulations, and administrative guidance regarding the direct or indirect ownership of the income or assets of the foreign corporation, the proper character of that income or those assets, and similar issues. Reasonable belief may be based on reasonable predictions regarding income to be earned and assets to be owned in subsequent years where qualification of the foreign corporation as a PFIC for the current taxable year will depend on the qualification of the corporation as a PFIC in a subsequent year. Reasonable belief may be based on an analysis of generally available financial information of the foreign corporation. To determine whether a shareholder had reasonable belief that the foreign corporation was not a PFIC, the Commissioner may consider the size of the shareholder's interest in the foreign corporation.

(2) *Knowledge of law required.*—Reasonable belief must be based on a good faith effort to apply the Code, regulations, and related administrative guidance. Any person's failure to know or apply these provisions will not form the basis of reasonable belief.

(e) *Special rules for qualified shareholders.*—(1) *In general.*—A shareholder that is a qualified shareholder, as defined in paragraph (e)(2) of this section, for a taxable year of the shareholder is not required to satisfy the reasonable belief requirement of paragraph (b)(1) of this section or file a Protective Statement to preserve its ability to make a retroactive election with respect to such taxable year. Accordingly, a qualified shareholder may make a retroactive election for any open taxable year in the shareholder's holding period. The retroactive election will be treated as made in the earliest taxable year of the shareholder during which the foreign corporation qualified as a PFIC (including a taxable year ending prior January 2, 1998) and the shareholder will be treated as a shareholder of a pedigreed QEF, as defined in § 1.1291-9(j)(2)(ii), provided the shareholder—

(i) Has been a qualified shareholder with respect to the foreign corporation for all taxable years of the shareholder included in the shareholder's holding period during which the foreign corporation was a PFIC, or in the case of taxable years ending before January 2, 1998, the shareholder satisfies the criteria of a qualified shareholder, for all such years; or

(ii) Has been a qualified shareholder, or in the case of taxable years ending before January 2, 1998, satisfies the criteria of a qualified shareholder, for all taxable years in its holding period before it filed a Protective Statement, which Protective Statement is applicable to all subsequent years, beginning with the first taxable year in which the shareholder is not a qualified shareholder.

(2) *Qualified shareholder.*—A shareholder will be treated as a qualified shareholder for a taxable year if the shareholder did not file a Protective Statement applicable to an earlier taxable year included in the shareholder's holding period of the stock of the foreign corporation currently held and—

(i) At all times during the taxable year the shareholder owned, within the meaning of section 958, directly, indirectly, or constructively, less than two percent of the vote and value of each class of stock of the foreign corporation; and

(ii) With respect to the taxable year of the foreign corporation ending within the shareholder's taxable year, the foreign corporation or U.S. counsel for the foreign corporation indicated in a public filing, disclosure statement or other notice provided to U.S. persons that are shareholders of the foreign corporation (corporate filing) that the foreign corporation—

(A) Reasonably believes that it is not or should not constitute a PFIC for the corporation's taxable year; or

(B) Is unable to conclude that it is not or should not be a PFIC (due to certain asset valuation or interpretation issues, or because PFIC status will depend on the income or assets of the foreign corporation in the corporation's subsequent taxable years) but reasonably believes that, more likely than not, it ultimately will not be a PFIC.

(3) *Exceptions.*—Notwithstanding paragraph (e)(2)(ii) of this section, a shareholder will not be treated as a qualified shareholder for a taxable year of the shareholder if the shareholder knew or had reason to know that a corporate filing regarding the foreign corporation's PFIC status was inaccurate, or knew that the foreign corporation was a PFIC for the taxable year of the foreign corporation ending with or within such taxable year of the shareholder. For purposes of this paragraph, a shareholder will be treated as knowing that a foreign corporation was a PFIC if the principal activity of the foreign corporation, directly or indirectly, is owning or trading a diversified portfolio of stock, securities, or other financial contracts.

(f) *Special consent.*—(1) *In general.*—A shareholder that has not satisfied the requirements of paragraph (b) or (e) of this section may request the consent of the Commissioner to make a retroactive election for a taxable year of the shareholder provided the shareholder satisfies the requirements set forth in this paragraph (f). The Commissioner will grant relief under this paragraph (f) only if—

(i) The shareholder reasonably relied on a qualified tax professional, within the meaning of paragraph (f)(2) of this section;

(ii) Granting consent will not prejudice the interests of the United States government, as provided in paragraph (f)(3) of this section;

(iii) The shareholder requests consent under paragraph (f) of this section before a representative of the Internal Revenue Service raises upon audit the PFIC status of the corporation for any taxable year of the shareholder; and

(iv) The shareholder satisfies the procedural requirements set forth in paragraph (f)(4) of this section.

(2) *Reasonable reliance on a qualified tax professional.*—(i) *In general.*—Except as provided in paragraph (f)(2)(ii) of this section, a

Reg. § 1.1295-3(f)(2)(i)

shareholder is deemed to have reasonably relied on a qualified tax professional only if the shareholder reasonably relied on a qualified tax professional (including a tax professional employed by the shareholder) who failed to identify the foreign corporation as a PFIC or failed to advise the shareholder of the consequences of making, or failing to make, the section 1295 election. A shareholder will not be considered to have reasonably relied on a qualified tax professional if the shareholder knew, or reasonably should have known, that the foreign corporation was a PFIC and of the availability of a section 1295 election, or knew or reasonably should have known that the qualified tax professional—

(A) Was not competent to render tax advice with respect to the ownership of shares of a foreign corporation; or

(B) Did not have access to all relevant facts and circumstances.

(ii) *Shareholder deemed to have not reasonably relied on a qualified tax professional.*—For purposes of this paragraph (f)(2), a shareholder is deemed to have not reasonably relied on a qualified tax professional if the shareholder was informed by the qualified tax professional that the foreign corporation was a PFIC and of the availability of the section 1295 election and related tax consequences, but either chose not to make the section 1295 election or was unable to make a valid section 1295 election.

(3) *Prejudice to the interests of the United States government.*—(i) *General rule.*—Except as otherwise provided in paragraph (f)(3)(ii) of this section, the Commissioner will not grant consent under paragraph (f) of this section if doing so would prejudice the interests of the United States government. The interests of the United States government are prejudiced if granting relief would result in the shareholder having a lower tax liability, taking into account applicable interest charges, in the aggregate for all years affected by the retroactive election (other than by a de minimis amount) than the shareholder would have had if the shareholder had made the section 1295 election by the election due date. The time value of money is taken into account for purposes of this computation.

(ii) *Elimination of prejudice to the interests of the United States government.*—Notwithstanding the general rule of paragraph (f)(3)(i) of this section, if granting relief would prejudice the interests of the United States government, the Commissioner may, in the Commissioner's sole discretion, grant consent to make the election provided the shareholder enters into a closing agreement with the Commissioner that requires the shareholder to pay an amount sufficient to eliminate any prejudice to the United States government as a consequence of the shareholder's inability to file amended returns for closed taxable years.

(4) *Procedural requirements.*—(i) *Filing instructions.*—A shareholder requests consent under paragraph (f) of this section to make a retroactive election by filing with the Office of the Associate Chief Counsel (International) a ruling request that includes the affidavits required by this paragraph (f)(4). The ruling request must satisfy the requirements, including payment of the user fee, for ruling requests filed with that office.

(ii) *Affidavit from shareholder.*—The shareholder, or a person authorized to sign a federal income tax return on behalf of the shareholder, must submit a detailed affidavit describing the events that led to the failure to make a section 1295 election by the election due date, and to the discovery thereof. The shareholder's affidavit must describe the engagement and responsibilities of the qualified tax professional as well as the extent to which the shareholder relied on the tax professional. The shareholder must sign the affidavit under penalties of perjury. An individual who signs for an entity must have personal knowledge of the facts and circumstances at issue.

(iii) *Affidavits from other persons.*—The shareholder must submit detailed affidavits from individuals having knowledge or information about the events that led to the failure to make a section 1295 election by the election due date, and to the discovery thereof. These individuals must include the qualified tax professional upon whose advice the shareholder relied, as well as any individual (including an employee of the shareholder) who made a substantial contribution to the return's preparation, and any accountant or attorney, knowledgeable in tax matters, who advised the shareholder with regard to its ownership of the stock of the foreign corporation. Each affidavit must describe the individual's engagement and responsibilities as well as the advice concerning the tax treatment of the foreign corporation that the individual provided to the shareholder. Each affidavit also must include the individual's name, address, and taxpayer identification number, and must be signed by the individual under penalties of perjury.

(iv) *Other information.*—In connection with a request for consent under this paragraph (f), a shareholder must provide any additional information requested by the Commissioner.

(v) *Notification of Internal Revenue Service.*—The shareholder must notify the branch of the Associate Chief Counsel (International) considering the request for relief under this paragraph (f) if, while the shareholder's request for consent is pending, the Internal Revenue Service begins an examination of the shareholder's return for the retroactive election year or for any subsequent taxable year during which the shareholder holds stock of the foreign corporation.

(vi) *Who requests special consent under this paragraph (f) and who enters into a closing agreement.*—The person that requests consent under this paragraph (f) is the person that makes the section 1295 election, as provided in § 1.1295-1(d). If a shareholder is required to enter into a closing agreement with the Commissioner, as described in paragraph (f)(3)(ii) of this section, rules similar to those under paragraphs (c)(4)(i)(B) through (E) of this section apply for purposes of determining the person that enters into the closing agreement.

(g) *Time for and manner of making a retroactive election.*—(1) *Time for making a retroactive election.*—(i) *In general.*—Except as otherwise provided in paragraph (g)(1)(ii) of this section, a shareholder must make a retroactive election, in the manner provided in paragraph (g)(2) of this section, on or before the due date, as extended, for the shareholder's return—

(A) In the case of a shareholder that makes a retroactive election pursuant to paragraph (b) or (e) of this section, for the taxable year in which the shareholder determines or reasonably should have determined that the foreign corporation was a PFIC; or

(B) In the case of a shareholder that obtains the consent of the Commissioner pursuant to paragraph (f) of this section, for the taxable year in which such consent is granted.

(ii) *Transition rule.*—A shareholder that files a Protective Statement for a taxable year described in paragraph (c)(5)(ii) of this section may make a retroactive election by the due date, as extended, for the return for the first taxable year ended after January 2, 1998, even if the shareholder determined or should have determined that the foreign corporation was a PFIC for a year described in paragraph (c)(5)(ii) of this section at any time on or before January 2, 1998.

(iii) *Ownership not required at time retroactive election is made.*—The shareholder need not own shares of the foreign corporation at the time the shareholder makes a retroactive election with respect to the foreign corporation.

(2) *Manner of making a retroactive election.*—A shareholder that has satisfied the requirements of paragraph (b) or (e) of this section, or a shareholder that has been granted consent under paragraph (f) of this section, must make a retroactive election in the manner provided in Form 8621 for making a section 1295 election, and must attach Form 8621 to an amended return for the later of the retroactive election year or the earliest open taxable year of the shareholder. The shareholder also must file an amended return for each of its subsequent taxable years affected by the retroactive election. In each amended return the shareholder must redetermine its income tax liability for that year to take into account the assessment of PFIC related taxes. If the period of limitations for the assessment of taxes for a taxable year affected by the retroactive election has expired except to the extent the waiver of limitations, described in paragraph (c)(4) of this section, has extended such period, no adjustments, other than consequential changes, may be made to any other items of income, deduction, or credit in that year. In addition, the shareholder must pay all taxes and interest owing by reason of the PFIC and QEF status of the foreign corporation in those years (except to the extent a section 1294 election extends the time to pay the taxes and interest). A shareholder that filed a Protective Statement must attach to Form 8621 filed with each amended return a representation that the shareholder, until the taxable year in which it determined or reasonably should have determined that the foreign corporation was a PFIC, reasonably believed, within the meaning of paragraph (d) of this section, that the foreign corporation was not a PFIC in the taxable year for which the amended return is filed, and in all other taxable years to which the Protective Statement applies. A shareholder that entered into a closing agreement must comply with the terms of that agreement, as provided in paragraph (f)(3)(ii) of this section, to eliminate any prejudice to the United States government's interests, as described in paragraph (f)(3) of this section.

(3) *Who makes the retroactive election.*—The person that makes the retroactive election is the person that makes the section 1295 election, as provided in § 1.1295-1(d). A partner, shareholder, or beneficiary for which a pass through entity, as described in paragraphs (c)(4)(i)(B) through (D) of this section, filed a Protective Statement may make a retroactive election, if the pass through entity completely terminates its business or otherwise ceases to exist.

(4) *Other elections.*—(i) *Section 1291(d)(2) election.*—If the foreign corporation for which the shareholder makes a retroactive election will be treated as an unpedigreed QEF, as defined in § 1.1291-9(j)(2)(iii), with respect to the shareholder, the shareholder may make an election under section 1291(d)(2) to

purge its holding period of the years or parts of years before the effective date of the retroactive election. If the qualification date, within the meaning of § 1.1291-9(e) or 1.1291-10(e), falls in a taxable year for which the period of limitations has expired, the shareholder may treat the first day of the retroactive election year as the qualification date. The shareholder may make a section 1291(d)(2) election at the time that it makes the retroactive election, but no later than two years after the date that the amended return in which the retroactive election is made is filed. For the requirements for making a section 1291(d)(2) election, see §§ 1.1291-9 and 1.1291-10.

(ii) *Section 1294 election.*—A shareholder may make an election under section 1294 to extend the time for payment of tax on the shareholder's pro rata shares of the ordinary earnings and net capital gain of the foreign corporation reported in the shareholder's amended return, and section 6621 interest attributable to such tax, but only to the extent the tax and interest are attributable to earnings that have not been distributed to the shareholder. The shareholder must make a section 1294 election for a taxable year at the time that it files its amended return for that year, as provided in paragraph (g)(1) of this section. For the requirements for making a section 1294 election, see § 1.1294-1T.

(h) *Effective date.*—The rules of this section are effective as of January 2, 1998. [Reg. § 1.1295-3.]

☐ [*T.D. 8750, 12-31-97. Redesignated and amended by T.D. 8870, 2-4-2000.*]

§ 1.1296-1. Mark to market election for marketable stock.—(a) *Definitions.*—(1) *Eligible RIC.*—An *eligible RIC* is a regulated investment company that offers for sale, or has outstanding, any stock of which it is the issuer and which is redeemable at net asset value, or that publishes net asset valuations at least annually.

(2) *Section 1296 stock.*—The term *section 1296 stock* means marketable stock in a passive foreign investment company (PFIC), including any PFIC stock owned directly or indirectly by an eligible RIC, for which there is a valid section 1296 election. Section 1296 stock does not include stock of a foreign corporation that previously had been a PFIC, and for which a section 1296 election remains in effect.

(3) *Unreversed inclusions.*—(i) *General rule.*—The term *unreversed inclusions* means with respect to any section 1296 stock, the excess, if any, of—

(A) The amount of mark to market gain included in gross income of the United States person under paragraph (c)(1) of this section with respect to such stock for prior taxable years; over

(B) The amount allowed as a deduction to the United States person under paragraph (c)(3) of this section with respect to such stock for prior taxable years.

(ii) *Section 1291 adjustment.*—The amount referred to in paragraph (a)(3)(i)(A) of this section shall include any amount subject to section 1291 under the coordination rule of paragraph (i)(2)(ii) of this section.

(iii) *Example.*—An example of the computation of unreversed inclusions is as follows:

Example. A, a United States person, acquired stock in Corp X, a foreign corporation, on January 1, 2005 for $150. At such time and at all times thereafter, Corp X was a PFIC and A's stock in Corp X was marketable. For taxable years 2005 and 2006, Corp X was a nonqualified fund subject to taxation under section 1291. A made a timely section 1296 election with respect to the X stock, effective for taxable year 2007. The fair market value of the X stock was $200 as of December 31, 2006, and $240 as of December 31, 2007. Additionally, Corp X made no distribution with respect to its stock for the taxable years at issue. In 2007, pursuant to paragraph (i)(2)(ii) of this section, A must include the $90 gain in the X stock in accordance with the rules of section 1291 for purposes of determining the deferred tax amount and any applicable interest. Nonetheless, for purposes of determining the amount of the unreversed inclusions pursuant to paragraph (a)(3)(ii) of this section, A will include the $90 of gain that was taxed under section 1291 and not the interest thereon.

(iv) *Special rule for regulated investment companies.*—In the case of a regulated investment company which had elected to mark to market the PFIC stock held by such company as of the last day of the taxable year preceding such company's first taxable year for which such company makes a section 1296 election, the amount referred to in paragraph (a)(3)(i)(A) of this section shall include amounts previously included in gross income by the company pursuant to such mark to market election with respect to such stock for prior taxable years. For further guidance, see Notice 92-53 (1992-2 C.B. 384) (see also 601.601(d)(2) of this chapter).

(b) *Application of section 1296 election.*—(1) *In general.*—Any United States person and any controlled foreign corporation (CFC) that owns directly, or is treated as owning under this section, marketable stock, as defined in § 1.1296-2, in a PFIC may make an election to mark to market such stock in accordance with the provisions of section 1296 and this section.

(2) *Election applicable to specific United States person.*—A section 1296 election applies only to the United States person (or CFC that is treated as a U.S. person under paragraph (g)(2) of this section) that makes the election. Accordingly, a United States person's section 1296 election will not apply to a transferee of section 1296 stock.

(3) *Election applicable to specific corporation only.*—A section 1296 election is made with respect to a single foreign corporation, and thus a separate section 1296 election must be made for each foreign corporation that otherwise meets the requirements of this section. A United States persons section 1296 election with respect to stock in a foreign corporation applies to all marketable stock of the corporation that the person owns directly, or is treated as owning under paragraph (e) of this section, at the time of the election or that is subsequently acquired.

(c) *Effect of election.*—(1) *Recognition of gain.*—If the fair market value of section 1296 stock on the last day of the United States person's taxable year exceeds its adjusted basis, the United States person shall include in gross income for its taxable year the excess of the fair market value of such stock over its adjusted basis (mark to market gain).

(2) *Character of gain.*—Mark to market gain, and any gain on the sale or other disposition of section 1296 stock, shall be treated as ordinary income.

(3) *Recognition of loss.*—If the adjusted basis of section 1296 stock exceeds its fair market value on the last day of the United States persons taxable year, such person shall be allowed a deduction for such taxable year equal to the lesser of the amount of such excess or the unreversed inclusions with respect to such stock (mark to market loss).

(4) *Character of loss.*—(i) *Losses not in excess of unreversed inclusions.*—Any mark to market loss allowed as a deduction under paragraph (c)(3) of this section, and any loss on the sale or other disposition of section 1296 stock, to the extent that such loss does not exceed the unreversed inclusions attributable to such stock, shall be treated as an ordinary loss, deductible in computing adjusted gross income.

(ii) *Losses in excess of unreversed inclusions.*—Any loss recognized on the sale or other disposition of section 1296 stock in excess of any prior unreversed inclusions will be subject to the rules generally applicable to losses provided elsewhere in the Internal Revenue Code and the regulations thereunder.

(5) *Application of election to separate lots of stock.*—In the case in which a United States person purchased or acquired shares of stock in a PFIC at different prices, the rules of this section shall be applied in a manner consistent with the rules of § 1.1012-1.

(6) *Source rules.*—The source of any amount included in gross income under paragraph (c)(1) of this section, or the allocation and apportionment of any amount allowed as a deduction under paragraph (c)(3) of this section, shall be determined in the same manner as if such amounts were gain or loss (as the case may be) from the sale of stock in the PFIC.

(7) *Examples.*—The following examples illustrate this paragraph (c):

Example 1. Treatment of gain as ordinary income. A, a United States individual, purchases stock in FX, a foreign corporation that is not a PFIC, in 1990 for $1,000. On January 1, 2005, when the fair market value of the FX stock is $1,100, FX becomes a PFIC. A makes a timely section 1296 election for taxable year 2005. On December 31, 2005, the fair market value of the FX stock is $1,200. For taxable year 2005, A includes $200 of mark to market gain (the excess of the fair market value of FX stock ($1,200) over A's adjusted basis ($1,000)) in gross income as ordinary income and pursuant to paragraph (d)(1) of this section increases his basis in the FX stock by that amount.

Example 2. Treatment of gain as capital gain. The facts are the same as in *Example 1.* For taxable year 2006, FX does not satisfy either the asset test or the income test of section 1297(a). A does not revoke the section 1296 election it made with respect to the FX stock. On December 1, 2006, A sells the FX stock when the fair market value of the stock is $1,500. For taxable year 2006, A includes $300 of gain (the excess of the fair market value of FX stock ($1,500) over A's adjusted basis ($1,200)) in gross income as long-term capital gain because at the time of sale of the FX stock by A, FX did not qualify as a PFIC, and, therefore, the FX stock was not section 1296 stock at the time of the disposition. Further, A's holding period for non-PFIC purposes was more than one year.

Example 3. Treatment of losses as ordinary where they do not exceed unreversed inclusions. The facts are the same as in *Example 1.* On December 1, 2006, A sells the stock in FX for

$1,100. At that time, A's unreversed inclusions (the amount A included in income as mark to market gain) with respect to the stock in FX are $200. Accordingly, for taxable year 2006, A recognizes a loss on the sale of the FX stock of $100, (the fair market value of the FX stock ($1,100) minus A's adjusted basis ($1,200) in the stock) that is treated as an ordinary loss because the loss does not exceed the unreversed inclusions attributable to the stock of FX.

Example 4. Treatment of losses as long-term capital losses. The facts are the same as in *Example 3*, except that FX does not satisfy either the asset test or the income test of section 1297(a) for taxable year 2006. For taxable year 2006, A's $100 loss from the sale of the FX stock is treated as long-term capital loss because at the time of the sale of the FX stock by A FX did not qualify as a PFIC, and, therefore, the FX stock was not section 1296 stock at the time of the disposition. Further, A's holding period in the FX stock for non-PFIC purposes was more than one year.

Example 5. Long-term capital loss treatment of losses in excess of unreversed inclusions. The facts are the same as in *Example 3*, except that A sells his FX stock for $900. At the time of A's sale of the FX stock on December 1, 2006, A's unreversed inclusions with respect to the FX stock are $200. Accordingly, the $300 loss recognized by A on the disposition is treated as an ordinary loss to the extent of his unreversed inclusions ($200). The amount of the loss in excess of A's unreversed inclusions ($100) will be treated as a long-term capital loss because A's holding period in the FC stock for non-PFIC purposes was more than one year.

Example 6. Application of section 1296 election to separate lots of stock. On January 1, 2005, Corp A, a domestic corporation, purchased 100 shares (first lot) of stock in FX, a PFIC, for $500 ($5 per share). On June 1, 2005, Corp A purchased 100 shares (second lot) of FX stock for $1,000 ($10 per share). Corp A made a timely section 1296 election with respect to its FX stock for taxable year 2005. On December 31, 2005, the fair market value of FX stock was $8 per share. For taxable year 2005, Corp A includes $300 of gain in gross income as ordinary income under paragraph (c)(1) of this section with respect to the first lot, and adjusts its basis in that lot to $800 pursuant to paragraph (d)(1) of this section. With respect to the second lot, Corp A is not permitted to recognize a loss under paragraph (c)(3) of this section for taxable year 2005. Although Corp A's adjusted basis in that stock exceeds its fair market value by $200, Corp A has no unreversed inclusions with respect to that particular lot of stock. On July 1, 2006, Corp A sells 100 shares of FX stock for $900. Assuming that Corp A adequately identifies (in accordance with the rules of § 1.1012-1(c)) the shares of FX stock sold as being from the second lot, Corp A recognizes $100 of long term capital loss pursuant to paragraph (c)(4)(ii) of this section.

(d) *Adjustment to basis.*—(1) *Stock held directly.*—The adjusted basis of the section 1296 stock shall be increased by the amount included in the gross income of the United States person under paragraph (c)(1) of this section with respect to such stock, and decreased by the amount allowed as a deduction to the United States person under paragraph (c)(3) of this section with respect to such stock.

(2) *Stock owned through certain foreign entities.*—(i) In the case of section 1296 stock that a United States person is treated as owning through certain foreign entities pursuant to paragraph (e) of this section, the basis adjustments under paragraph (d)(1) of this section shall apply to such stock in the hands of the foreign entity actually holding such stock, but only for purposes of determining the subsequent treatment under chapter 1 of the Internal Revenue Code of the United States person with respect to such stock. Such increase or decrease in the adjusted basis of the section 1296 stock shall constitute an adjustment to the basis of partnership property only with respect to the partner making the section 1296 election. Corresponding adjustments shall be made to the adjusted basis of the United States person's interest in the foreign entity and in any intermediary entity described in paragraph (e) of this section through which the United States person holds the PFIC stock.

(ii) *Example.*—The following example illustrates this paragraph (d)(2):

Example. FP is a foreign partnership. Corp A, a domestic corporation, owns a 20 percent interest in FP. Corp B, a domestic corporation, owns a 30 percent interest in FP. Corp C, a foreign corporation, with no direct or indirect shareholders that are U.S. persons, owns a 50% interest in FP. Corp A, Corp B, and FP all use a calendar year for their taxable year. In 2005, FP purchases stock in FX, a foreign corporation and a PFIC, for $1,000. Corp A makes a timely section 1296 election for taxable year 2005. On December 31, 2005, the fair market value of the PFIC stock is $1,100. Corp A includes $20 of ordinary income in taxable year 2005 under paragraphs (c)(1) and (2) of this section. Corp A increases its basis in its FP partnership interest by $20. FP increases its basis in the FX stock to $1,020 solely for purposes of determining the subsequent treatment of Corp A, under chapter 1 of the Internal Revenue Code, with respect to such stock. In 2006, FP sells the FX stock for $1,200. For purposes of determining the amount of gain of Corp A, FP will be treated as having $180 in gain of which $20 is allocated to Corp A. Corp A's $20 of gain will be treated as ordinary income under paragraph (c)(2) of this section. For purposes of determining the amount of gain attributable to Corp B, FP will be treated as having $200 gain, $60 of which will be allocated to Corp B.

(3) *Stock owned indirectly by an eligible RIC.*—Paragraph (d)(2) of this section shall also apply to an eligible RIC which is an indirect shareholder under §1.1296-2(f) of stock in a PFIC and has a valid section 1296 election in effect with respect to the PFIC stock.

(4) *Stock acquired from a decedent.*—In the case of stock of a PFIC which is acquired by bequest, devise, or inheritance (or by the decedent's estate) and with respect to which a section 1296 election was in effect as of the date of the decedent's death, notwithstanding section 1014, the basis of such stock in the hands of the person so acquiring it shall be the adjusted basis of such stock in the hands of the decedent immediately before his death (or, if lesser, the basis which would have been determined under section 1014 without regard to this paragraph).

(5) *Transition rule for individuals becoming subject to United States income taxation.*—(i) *In general.*—If any individual becomes a United States person in a taxable year beginning after December 31, 1997, solely for purposes of this section, the adjusted basis, before adjustments under this paragraph (d), of any section 1296 stock owned by such individual on the first day of such taxable year shall be treated as being the greater of its fair market value or its adjusted basis on such first day.

(ii) An example of the transition rule for individuals becoming subject to United States income taxation is as follows:

Example. A, a nonresident alien individual, purchases marketable stock in FX, a PFIC, for $50 in 1995. On January 1, 2005, A becomes a United States person and makes a timely section 1296 election with respect to the stock in accordance with paragraph (h) of this section. The fair market value of the FX stock on January 1, 2005, is $100. The fair market value of the FX stock on December 31, 2005, is $110. Under paragraph (d)(5)(i) of this section, A computes the amount of mark to market gain or loss for the FX stock in 2005 by reference to an adjusted basis of $100, and therefore A includes $10 in gross income as mark to market gain under paragraph (c)(1) of this section. Additionally, under paragraph (d)(1) of this section, A's adjusted basis in the FX stock for purposes of this section is increased to $110 (and to $60 for all other tax purposes). A sells the FX stock in 2006 for $120. For purposes of applying section 1001, A must use its original basis of $50, with any adjustments under paragraph (d)(1) of this section, $10 in this case, and therefore A recognizes $60 of gain. Under paragraph (c)(2) of this section (which is applied using an adjusted basis of $110), $10 of such gain is treated as ordinary income. The remaining $50 of gain from the sale of the FX stock is long term capital gain because A held such stock for more than one year.

(e) *Stock owned through certain foreign entities.*—(1) *In general.*—Except as provided in paragraph (e)(2) of this section, the following rules shall apply in determining stock ownership for purposes of this section. PFIC stock owned, directly or indirectly, by or for a foreign partnership, foreign trust (other than a foreign trust described in sections 671 through 679), or foreign estate shall be considered as being owned proportionately by its partners or beneficiaries. PFIC stock owned, directly or indirectly, by or for a foreign trust described in sections 671 through 679 shall be considered as being owned proportionately by its grantors or other persons treated as owners under sections 671 through 679 of any portion of the trust that includes the stock. The determination of a person's proportionate interest in a foreign partnership, foreign trust or foreign estate will be made on the basis of all the facts and circumstances. Stock considered owned by reason of this paragraph shall, for purposes of applying the rules of this section, be treated as actually owned by such person.

(2) *Stock owned indirectly by eligible RICs.*—The rules for attributing ownership of stock contained in §1.1296-2(f) will apply to determine the indirect ownership of PFIC stock by an eligible RIC.

(f) *Holding period.*—Solely for purposes of sections 1291 through 1298, if section 1296 applied to stock with respect to the taxpayer for any prior taxable year, the taxpayer's holding period in such stock shall be treated as beginning on the first day of the first taxable year beginning after the last taxable year for which section 1296 so applied.

(g) *Special rules.*—(1) *Certain dispositions of stock.*—To the extent a United States person is treated as actually owning stock in a PFIC under paragraph (e) of this section, any disposition which results in the United States person being treated as no longer owning such stock, and any disposition by the person owning such stock, shall be treated as a disposition by the United States person of the stock in the PFIC.

(2) *Treatment of CFC as a United States person.*—In the case of a CFC that owns, or is treated as owning under paragraph (e) of this section, section 1296 stock:

(i) Other than with respect to the sourcing rules in paragraph (c)(6) of this section, this section shall apply to the CFC in the same manner as if such corporation were a United States person. The CFC will be treated as a foreign person for purposes of applying the source rules of paragraph (c)(6).

(ii) For purposes of subpart F of part III of subchapter N of the Internal Revenue Code—

(A) Amounts included in the CFC's gross income under paragraph (c)(1) or (i)(2)(ii) of this section shall be treated as foreign personal holding company income under section 954(c)(1)(A); and

(B) Amounts allowed as a deduction under paragraph (c)(3) of this section shall be treated as a deduction allocable to foreign personal holding company income for purposes of computing net foreign base company income under § 1.954-1(c).

(iii) A United States shareholder, as defined in section 951(b), of the CFC shall not be subject to section 1291 with respect to any stock of the PFIC for the period during which the section 1296 election is in effect for that stock, and the holding period rule of paragraph (f) of this section shall apply to such United States shareholder.

(iv) The rules of this paragraph (g)(2) shall not apply to a United States person that is a shareholder of the PFIC for purposes of section 1291, but is not a United States shareholder under section 951(b) with respect to the CFC making a section 1296 election.

(3) *Timing of inclusions for stock owned through certain foreign entities.*—In the case of section 1296 stock that a United States person is treated as owning through certain foreign entities pursuant to paragraph (e) of this section, the mark to market gain or mark to market loss is determined in accordance with paragraphs (c) and (i)(2)(ii) of this section as of the last day of the taxable year of the foreign partnership, foreign trust or foreign estate and then included in the taxable year of such United States person that includes the last day of the taxable year of the entity.

(h) *Elections.*—(1) *Timing and manner for making a section 1296 election.*—(i) *United States persons.*—A United States person that owns marketable stock in a PFIC, or is treated as owning marketable stock under paragraph (e) of this section, on the last day of the taxable year of such person, and that wants to make a section 1296 election, must make a section 1296 election for such taxable year on or before the due date (including extensions) of the United States person's income tax return for that year. The section 1296 election must be made on the Form 8621, "Return by a Shareholder of a Passive Foreign Investment Company or Qualified Electing Fund", included with the original tax return of the United States person for that year, or on an amended return, provided that the amended return is filed on or before the election due date.

(ii) *Controlled foreign corporations.*—A section 1296 election by a CFC shall be made by its controlling United States shareholders, as defined in § 1.964-1(c)(5), and shall be included with the Form 5471, "Information Return of U.S. Persons With Respect To Certain Foreign Corporations", for that CFC by the due date (including extensions) of the original income tax returns of the controlling United States shareholders for that year. A section 1296 election by a CFC shall be binding on all United States shareholders of the CFC.

(iii) *Retroactive elections for PFIC stock held in prior years.*—A late section 1296 election may be permitted only in accordance with § 301.9100 of this chapter.

(2) *Effect of section 1296 election.*—(i) A section 1296 election will apply to the taxable year for which such election is made and remain in effect for each succeeding taxable year unless such election is revoked or terminated pursuant to paragraph (h)(3) of this section.

(ii) *Cessation of a foreign corporation as a PFIC.*—A United States person will not include mark to market gain or loss pursuant to paragraph (c) of this section with respect to any stock of a foreign corporation for any taxable year that such foreign corporation is not a PFIC under section 1297 or treated as a PFIC under section 1298(b)(1) (taking into account the holding period rule of paragraph (f) of this section). Cessation of a foreign corporation's status as a PFIC will not, however, terminate a section 1296 election. Thus, if a foreign corporation is a PFIC in a taxable year after a year in which it is not treated as a PFIC, the United States person's original election (unless revoked or terminated in accordance with paragraph (h)(3) of this section) continues to apply and the shareholder must include any mark to market gain or loss in such year.

(3) *Revocation or termination of election.*—(i) *In general.*—A United States person's section 1296 election is terminated if the section 1296 stock ceases to be marketable; if the United States person elects, or is required, to mark to market the section 1296 stock under another provision of chapter 1 of the Internal

Revenue Code; or if the Commissioner, in the Commissioner's discretion, consents to the United States person's request to revoke its section 1296 election upon a finding of a substantial change in circumstances. A substantial change in circumstances for this purpose may include a foreign corporation ceasing to be a PFIC.

(ii) *Timing of termination or revocation.*—Where a section 1296 election is terminated automatically (e.g., the stock ceases to be marketable), section 1296 will cease to apply beginning with the taxable year in which such termination occurs. Where a section 1296 election is revoked with the consent of the Commissioner, section 1296 will cease to apply beginning with the first taxable year of the United States person after the revocation is granted unless otherwise provided by the Commissioner.

(4) *Examples.*—The operation of the rules of this paragraph (h) is illustrated by the following examples:

Example 1. A, a United States person, owns stock in FX, a PFIC. A makes a QEF election in 1996 with respect to the FX stock. For taxable year 2005, A makes a timely section 1296 election with respect to its stock, and thus its QEF election is automatically terminated pursuant to § 1.1295-1(i)(3). In 2006, A's stock in FX ceases to be marketable, and therefore its section 1296 election is automatically terminated under paragraph (h)(3) of this section. Beginning with taxable year 2006, A is subject to the rules of section 1291 with respect to its FX stock unless it makes a new QEF election. See § 1.1295-1(i)(5).

Example 2. The facts are the same as in *Example 1*, except that A's stock in FX becomes marketable again in 2007. A may make a new section 1296 election with respect to the FX stock for its taxable year 2007, or thereafter. A will be subject to the coordination rules under paragraph (i) of this section unless it made a new QEF election in 2006.

(i) *Coordination rules for first year of election.*—(1) *In general.*—Notwithstanding any provision in this section to the contrary, the rules of this paragraph (i) shall apply to the first taxable year in which a section 1296 election is effective with respect to marketable stock of a PFIC if such foreign corporation was a PFIC for any taxable year, prior to such first taxable year, during the United States person's holding period (as defined in paragraph (f) of this section) in such stock, and for which such corporation was not treated as a QEF with respect to such United States person.

(2) *Shareholders other than regulated investment companies.*—For the first taxable year of a United States person (other than a regulated investment company) for which a section 1296 election is in effect with respect to the stock of a PFIC, such United States person shall, in lieu of the rules of paragraphs (c) and (d) of this section—

(i) Apply the rules of section 1291 to any distributions with respect to, or disposition of, section 1296 stock;

(ii) Apply section 1291 to the amount of the excess, if any, of the fair market value of such section 1296 stock on the last day of the United States person's taxable year over its adjusted basis, as if such amount were gain recognized from the disposition of stock on the last day of the taxpayer's taxable year; and

(iii) Increase its adjusted basis in the section 1296 stock by the amount of excess, if any, subject to section 1291 under paragraph (i)(2)(ii) of this section.

(3) *Shareholders that are regulated investment companies.*—For the first taxable year of a regulated investment company for which a section 1296 election is in effect with respect to the stock of a PFIC, such regulated investment company shall increase its tax under section 852 by the amount of interest that would have been imposed under section 1291(c)(3) for such taxable year if such regulated investment company were subject to the rules of paragraph (i)(2) of this section, and not this paragraph (i)(3). No deduction or increase in basis shall be allowed for the increase in tax imposed under this paragraph (i)(3).

(4) The operation of the rules of this paragraph (i) is illustrated by the following examples:

Example (1). A, a United States person and a calendar year taxpayer, owns marketable stock in FX, a PFIC that it acquired on January 1, 1992. At all times, A's FX stock was a nonqualified fund subject to taxation under section 1291. A made a timely section 1296 election effective for taxable year 2005. At the close of taxable year 2005, the fair market value of A's FX stock exceeded its adjusted basis by $10. Pursuant to paragraph (i)(2)(ii) of this section, A must treat the $10 gain under section 1291 as if the FX stock were disposed of on December 31, 2005. Further, A increases its adjusted basis in the FX stock by the $10 in accordance with paragraph (i)(2)(iii) of this section.

Example (2). Assume the same facts as in *Example (1)*, except that A is a RIC that had not made an election prior to 2005 to mark to market the PFIC stock. In taxable year 2005, A includes $10 of ordinary income under paragraph (c)(1) of this section, and such amount is not subject to section 1291. A also increases its tax imposed under section 852 by the amount of interest that would have been determined under section 1291(c)(3), and no deduction is permitted for such amount. Finally, under paragraph (d)(1) of this section, A increases its adjusted basis in the FX stock by $10.

(j) *Effective date.*—The provisions in this section are applicable for taxable years beginning on or after May 3, 2004. [Reg. § 1.1296-1.]

☐ [T.D. 9123, 4-30-2004.]

§ 1.1296-2. Definition of marketable stock.—(a) *General rule.*—For purposes of section 1296, the term *marketable stock* means—

(1) Passive foreign investment company (PFIC) stock that is regularly traded, as defined in paragraph (b) of this section, on a qualified exchange or other market, as defined in paragraph (c) of this section;

(2) Stock in certain PFICs, as described in paragraph (d) of this section; and

(3) Options on stock that is described in paragraph (a)(1) or (2) of this section, to the extent provided in paragraph (e) of this section.

(b) *Regularly traded.*—(1) *General rule.*—For purposes of paragraph (a)(1) of this section, a class of stock that is traded on one or more qualified exchanges or other markets, as defined in paragraph (c) of this section, is regularly traded on such exchanges or markets for any calendar year during which such class of stock is traded, other than in de minimis quantities, on at least 15 days during each calendar quarter.

(2) *Special rule for year of initial public offering.*—For the calendar year in which a corporation initiates a public offering of a class of stock for trading on one or more qualified exchanges or other markets, as defined in paragraph (c) of this section, such class of stock meets the requirements of paragraph (b)(1) of this section for such year if the stock is regularly traded on such exchanges or markets, other than in de minimis quantities, on 1/6 of the days remaining in the quarter in which the offering occurs, and on at least 15 days during each remaining quarter of the taxpayer's calendar year. In cases where a corporation initiates a public offering of a class of stock in the fourth quarter of the calendar year, such class of stock meets the requirements of paragraph (b)(1) of this section in the calendar year of the offering if the stock is regularly traded on such exchanges or markets, other than in de minimis quantities, on the greater of 1/6 of the days remaining in the quarter in which the offering occurs, or 5 days.

(3) *Anti-abuse rule.*—Trades that have as one of their principal purposes the meeting of the trading requirements of paragraph (b)(1) or (2) of this section shall be disregarded. Further, a class of stock shall not be treated as meeting the trading requirement of paragraph (b)(1) or (2) of this section if there is a pattern of trades conducted to meet the requirement of paragraph (b)(1) or (2) of this section. Similarly, paragraph (b)(2) of this section shall not apply to a public offering of stock that has as one of its principal purposes to avail itself of the reduced trading requirements under the special rule for the calendar year of an initial public offering. For purposes of applying the immediately preceding sentence, consideration will be given to whether the trading requirements of paragraph (b)(1) of this section are satisfied in the subsequent calendar year.

(c) *Qualified exchange or other market.*—(1) *General rule.*—For purposes of paragraph (a)(1) of this section, the term *qualified exchange or other market* means, for any calendar year—

(i) A national securities exchange that is registered with the Securities and Exchange Commission or the national market system established pursuant to section 11A of the Securities Exchange Act of 1934 (15 U.S.C. 78f); or

(ii) A foreign securities exchange that is regulated or supervised by a governmental authority of the country in which the market is located and which has the following characteristics—

(A) The exchange has trading volume, listing, financial disclosure, surveillance, and other requirements designed to prevent fraudulent and manipulative acts and practices, to remove impediments to and perfect the mechanism of a free and open, fair and orderly, market, and to protect investors; and the laws of the country in which the exchange is located and the rules of the exchange ensure that such requirements are actually enforced; and

(B) The rules of the exchange effectively promote active trading of listed stocks.

(2) *Exchange with multiple tiers.*—If an exchange in a foreign country has more than one tier or market level on which stock may be separately listed or traded, each such tier shall be treated as a separate exchange.

(d) *Stock in certain PFICs.*—(1) *General rule.*—Except as provided in paragraph (d)(2) of this section, a foreign corporation is a corporation described in section 1296(e)(1)(B), and paragraph (a)(2) of this section, if the foreign corporation offers for sale or has outstanding stock of which it is the issuer and which is redeemable at its net asset value and if the foreign corporation satisfies the following conditions with respect to the class of shares held by the electing taxpayer—

(i) At all times during the calendar year, the foreign corporation has more than one hundred shareholders with respect to the class, other than shareholders who are related under section 267(b);

(ii) At all times during the calendar year, the class of shares of the foreign corporation is readily available for purchase by the general public at its net asset value and the foreign corporation does not require a minimum initial investment of greater than $10,000 (U.S.);

(iii) At all times during the calendar year, quotations for the class of shares of the foreign corporation are determined and published no less frequently than on a weekly basis in a widely-available permanent medium not controlled by the issuer of the shares, such as a newspaper of general circulation or a trade publication;

(iv) No less frequently than annually, independent auditors prepare financial statements of the foreign corporation that include balance sheets (statements of assets, liabilities, and net assets) and statements of income and expenses, and those statements are made available to the public;

(v) The foreign corporation is supervised or regulated as an investment company by a foreign government or an agency or instrumentality thereof that has broad inspection and enforcement authority and effective oversight over investment companies;

(vi) At all times during the calendar year, the foreign corporation has no senior securities authorized or outstanding, including any debt other than in de minimis amounts;

(vii) Ninety percent or more of the gross income of the foreign corporation for its taxable year is passive income, as defined in section 1297(a)(1) and the regulations thereunder; and

(viii) The average percentage of assets held by the foreign corporation during its taxable year which produce passive income or which are held for the production of passive income, as defined in section 1297(a)(2) and the regulations thereunder, is at least 90 percent.

(2) *Anti-abuse rule.*—If a foreign corporation undertakes any actions that have as one of their principal purposes the manipulation of the net asset value of a class of its shares, for the calendar year in which the manipulation occurs, the shares are not marketable stock for purposes of paragraph (d)(1) of this section.

(e) [Reserved]

(f) *Special rules for regulated investment companies (RICs).*—(1) *General rule.*—In the case of any RIC that is offering for sale, or has outstanding, any stock of which it is the issuer and which is redeemable at net asset value, if the RIC owns directly or indirectly, as defined in section 1298(a), stock in any passive foreign investment company, that stock will be treated as marketable stock owned by that RIC for purposes of section 1296. Except as provided in paragraph (f)(2) of this section, in the case of any other RIC that publishes net asset valuations at least annually, if the RIC owns directly or indirectly, as defined in section 1298(a), stock in any passive foreign investment company, that stock will be treated as marketable stock owned by that RIC for purposes of section 1296.

(2) [Reserved]

(g) *Effective date.*—This section applies to shareholders whose taxable year ends on or after January 25, 2000 for stock in a foreign corporation whose taxable year ends with or within the shareholder's taxable year. In addition, shareholders may elect to apply these regulations to any taxable year beginning after December 31, 1997, for stock in a foreign corporation whose taxable year ends with or within the shareholder's taxable year. [Reg. § 1.1296-2.]

☐ [*T.D.* 8867, 1-25-2000. *Redesignated and amended by T.D.* 9123, 4-30-2004.]

§ 1.1297-3T. Deemed sale election by a United States person that is a shareholder of a passive foreign investment company (Temporary).—(a) *In general.*—Except as indicated below, a shareholder of a foreign corporation that no longer qualifies as a passive foreign investment company (PFIC) shall be treated for tax purposes as holding stock in a PFIC and therefore continue to be subject to taxation under section 1291 unless the shareholder makes the election under section 1297(b)(1). This continuing PFIC taint shall not apply to stock in a PFIC for which an election under section 1295 to be a qualified electing fund (QEF) has been in effect throughout that portion of the shareholder's holding period during which the PFIC qualified as a PFIC. A U.S. person making the election under section 1297(b)(1) shall be treated as having sold its stock in the PFIC on the last day of the last taxable year of the foreign corporation during which it qualified as a PFIC (termination date). The shareholder thereafter shall not be treated as holding stock in a PFIC and shall not be subject to taxation under section 1291. The deemed sale is taxed as a disposition under section 1291. Pursuant to that section, the gain, if any, is considered earned pro rata over the shareholder's holding period in the stock and is taxed as ordinary income. The tax on the gain is based on the value of the tax deferral and includes an interest charge. Any loss realized in the deemed sale may not be recognized. This section provides rules for making the election under section 1297(b)(1). The election is available to a U.S. person that is a shareholder of a foreign corporation if—

(1) The foreign corporation was a PFIC at any time during the period the U.S. person held the stock;

(2) At any one time during the U.S. person's holding period, the foreign corporation qualified as a PFIC but was not a QEF; and

(3) The foreign corporation is no longer a PFIC within the meaning of section 1296.

(b) *Time and manner of making the election.*—(1) *In general.*—The shareholder shall make the election under this section and section 1297(b)(1) by filing an amended income tax return for its taxable year that includes the termination date within three years of the due date, as extended, for the shareholder's tax return for such taxable year. The shareholder must attach to the amended return either Form 8621 or a statement, prepared in accordance with paragraph (c)(2) of this section, reporting the gain on the deemed sale of the stock as required by section 1291(a)(2) (as if such deemed sale occurred under section 1291(d)(2)), and by paying the tax on the gain as required by section 1291 (including the payment of the deferred tax amount required under sections 1291(a)(1)(C) and 1291(c)). The electing shareholder also shall pay interest, pursuant to section 6601, on the underpayment of tax for the taxable year of termination. An electing shareholder that realizes a loss shall report the loss on Form 8621, but shall not recognize the loss.

(2) *Information to be included in the election.*—If a statement is used, the statement should be identified, in a heading, as an election under section 1297(b)(1). The statement must include the following information and representations:

(i) The name, address and taxpayer identification number of the electing shareholder;

(ii) The name, address and taxpayer identification number, if any, of the PFIC;

(iii) A statement that the shareholder is making the election under section 1297(b)(1);

(iv) The period in the electing shareholder's holding period in the stock during which the foreign corporation was a PFIC, the period during which it was a QEF (and whether the shareholder elected under section 1294 to defer payment of its tax liability attributable to any portion of such period), and the termination date;

(v) The manner in which the PFIC lost the characteristics of a PFIC;

(vi) A schedule listing the shares in the PFIC held by the electing shareholder on the termination, listing the date(s) each share or block of shares acquired, the number of shares acquired on each date listed, and the tax basis of each share;

(vii) The fair market value of the stock in the PFIC on the termination date; for this purpose, the fair market value of the stock shall be determined according to the rules of § 1.1295-1T(b)(9); and

(viii) A schedule showing the computation of the gain recognized on the deemed sale, and a calculation of the deferred tax amount, as defined in section 1291(c).

(3) *Adjustment to basis; treatment of holding period.*—An electing shareholder that recognizes gain on the deemed sale of stock shall increase its adjusted basis in the stock by the amount of gain recognized. An electing shareholder shall not adjust the basis in stock with respect to which the shareholder realized a loss on the deemed sale. An electing shareholder shall thereafter treat its holding period in the stock, for purposes of sections 1291 through 1297, as beginning on the day following the termination date without regard to whether it recognized gain on the deemed sale; for section 1223 purposes, the holding period in the stock in the PFIC shall include the period prior to the deemed sale.

(c) *Application of deemed dividend election rules.*—(1) *In general.*—A shareholder of a former PFIC, within the meaning of § 1.1291-9(j)(2)(iv), that was a controlled foreign corporation, within the meaning of section 957(a) (CFC), during its last taxable year as a PFIC under section 1296(a), may apply the rules of section 1291(d)(2)(B) and § 1.1291-9 to an election under section 1297(b)(1) and this section made by the time and in the manner provided in paragraph (b) of this section.

(2) *Transition rule.*—If the time for making an election under this section, as provided in paragraph (b) of this section, expired before January 2, 1998, a shareholder that applied rules similar to the rules of section 1291(d)(2)(A) and § 1.1291-10 to an election under this section made with respect to a corporation that was a CFC during its last taxable year as a PFIC under section 1296(a) may file an amended return for the taxable year that includes the termination date, as defined in paragraph (a) of this section, and apply the rules of section 1291(d)(2)(B) and § 1.1291-9 at any time before the expiration of the period of limitations for the assessment of taxes for that taxable year.

Reg. § 1.1297-3T(a)(1)

(3) *Effective date.*—The rules of this paragraph are effective as of January 2, 1998. [Temporary Reg. § 1.1297-3T.]

☐ [*T.D.* 8178, 2-26-88. Amended by *T.D.* 8750, 12-31-97.]

Withholding Taxes

§ 1.1441-1. Requirement for the deduction and withholding of tax on payments to foreign persons.—(a) *Purpose and scope.*— This section, §§ 1.1441-2 through 1.1441-9, and 1.1443-1 provide rules for withholding under sections 1441, 1442, and 1443 when a payment is made to a foreign person. This section provides definitions of terms used in chapter 3 of the Internal Revenue Code (Code) and regulations thereunder. It prescribes procedures to determine whether an amount must be withheld under chapter 3 of the Code and documentation that a withholding agent may rely upon to determine the status of a payee or a beneficial owner as a U.S. person or as a foreign person and other relevant characteristics of the payee that may affect a withholding agent's obligation to withhold under chapter 3 of the Code and the regulations thereunder. Special procedures regarding payments to foreign persons that act as intermediaries are also provided. Section 1.1441-2 defines the income subject to withholding under section 1441, 1442, and 1443 and the regulations under these sections. Section 1.1441-3 provides rules regarding the amount subject to withholding. Section 1.1441-4 provides exemptions from withholding for, among other things, certain income effectively connected with the conduct of a trade or business in the United States, including certain compensation for the personal services of an individual. Section 1.1441-5 provides rules for withholding on payments made to flow-through entities and other similar arrangements. Section 1.1441-6 provides rules for claiming a reduced rate of withholding under an income tax treaty. Section 1.1441-7 defines the term *withholding agent* and provides due diligence rules governing a withholding agent's obligation to withhold. Section 1.1441-8 provides rules for relying on claims of exemption from withholding for payments to a foreign government, an international organization, a foreign central bank of issue, or the Bank for International Settlements. Sections 1.1441-9 and 1.1443-1 provide rules for relying on claims of exemption from withholding for payments to foreign tax exempt organizations and foreign private foundations.

(b) *General rules of withholding.*—(1) *Requirement to withhold on payments to foreign persons.*—A withholding agent must withhold 30-percent of any payment of an amount subject to withholding made to a payee that is a foreign person unless it can reliably associate the payment with documentation upon which it can rely to treat the payment as made to a payee that is a U.S. person or as made to a beneficial owner that is a foreign person entitled to a reduced rate of withholding. However, a withholding agent making a payment to a foreign person need not withhold where the foreign person assumes responsibility for withholding on the payment under chapter 3 of the Code and the regulations thereunder as a qualified intermediary (see paragraph (e)(5) of this section), as a U.S. branch of a foreign person (see paragraph (b)(2)(iv) of this section), as a withholding foreign partnership (see § 1.1441-5(c)(2)(i)), or as an authorized foreign agent (see § 1.1441-7(c)(1)). This section (dealing with general rules of withholding and claims of foreign or U.S. status by a payee or a beneficial owner), and §§ 1.1441-4, 1.1441-5, 1.1441-6, 1.1441-8, 1.1441-9, and 1.1443-1 provide rules for determining whether documentation is required as a condition for reducing the rate of withholding on a payment to a foreign beneficial owner or to a U.S. payee and if so, the nature of the documentation upon which a withholding agent may rely in order to reduce such rate. Paragraph (b)(2) of this section prescribes the rules for determining who the payee is, the extent to which a payment is treated as made to a foreign payee, and reliable association of a payment with documentation. Paragraph (b)(3) of this section describes the applicable presumptions for determining the payee's status as U.S. or foreign and the payee's other characteristics (i.e., as an owner or intermediary, as an individual, partnership, corporation, etc.). Paragraph (b)(4) of this section lists the types of payments for which the 30-percent withholding rate may be reduced. Because the treatment of a payee as a U.S. or a foreign person also has consequences for purposes of making an information return under the provisions of chapter 61 of the Code and for withholding under other provisions of the Code, such as sections 3402, 3405 or 3406, paragraph (b)(5) of this section lists applicable provisions outside chapter 3 of the Code that require certain payees to establish their foreign status (e.g., in order to be exempt from information reporting). Paragraph (b)(6) of this section describes the withholding obligations of a foreign person making a payment that it has received in its capacity as an intermediary. Paragraph (b)(7) of this section describes the liability of a withholding agent that fails to withhold at the required 30-percent rate in the absence of documentation. Paragraph (b)(8) of this section deals with adjustments and refunds in the case of overwithholding. Paragraph (b)(9) of this section deals with determining the status of the payee when the payment is jointly owned. See paragraph (c)(6) of this section for a definition of beneficial owner. See § 1.1441-7(a) for a definition of withholding agent. See § 1.1441-2(a) for the determination of an amount subject to withholding. See § 1.1441-2(e) for the definition of a payment and when it is considered made. Except as otherwise provided, the provisions of this section apply only for purposes of determining a withholding agent's obligation to withhold under chapter 3 of the Code and the regulations thereunder.

(2) *Determination of payee and payee's status.*—(i) *In general.*—Except as otherwise provided in this paragraph (b)(2) and § 1.1441-5(c)(1) and (e)(3), a payee is the person to whom a payment is made, regardless of whether such person is the beneficial owner of the amount (as defined in paragraph (c)(6) of this section). A foreign payee is a payee who is a foreign person. A U.S. payee is a payee who is a U.S. person. Generally, the determination by a withholding agent of the U.S. or foreign status of a payee and of its other relevant characteristics (e.g., as a beneficial owner or intermediary, or as an individual, corporation, or flow-through entity) is made on the basis of a withholding certificate that is a Form W-8 or a Form 8233 (indicating foreign status of the payee or beneficial owner) or a Form W-9 (indicating U.S. status of the payee). The provisions of this paragraph (b)(2), paragraph (b)(3) of this section, and § 1.1441-5(c), (d), and (e) dealing with determinations of payee and applicable presumptions in the absence of documentation, apply only to payments of amounts subject to withholding under chapter 3 of the Code (within the meaning of § 1.1441-2(a)). Similar payee and presumption provisions are set forth under § 1.6049-5(d) for payments of amounts that are not subject to withholding under chapter 3 of the Code (or the regulations thereunder) but that may be reportable under provisions of chapter 61 of the Code (and the regulations thereunder). See paragraph (d) of this section for documentation upon which the withholding agent may rely in order to treat the payee or beneficial owner as a U.S. person. See paragraph (e) of this section for documentation upon which the withholding agent may rely in order to treat the payee or beneficial owner as a foreign person. For applicable presumptions of status in the absence of documentation, see paragraph (b)(3) of this section and § 1.1441-5(d). For definitions of a foreign person and U.S. person, see paragraph (c)(2) of this section.

(ii) *Payments to a U.S. agent of a foreign person.*—A withholding agent making a payment to a U.S. person (other than to a U.S. branch that is treated as a U.S. person pursuant to paragraph (b)(2)(iv) of this section) and who has actual knowledge that the U.S. person receives the payment as an agent of a foreign person must treat the payment as made to the foreign person. However, the withholding agent may treat the payment as made to the U.S. person if the U.S. person is a financial institution and the withholding agent has no reason to believe that the financial institution will not comply with its obligation to withhold. See paragraph (c)(5) of this section for the definition of a financial institution.

(iii) *Payments to wholly-owned entities.*—(A) *Foreign-owned domestic entity.*—A payment to a wholly-owned domestic entity that is disregarded for federal tax purposes under § 301.7701-2(c)(2) of this chapter as an entity separate from its owner and whose single owner is a foreign person shall be treated as a payment to the owner of the entity, subject to the provisions of paragraph (b)(2)(iv) of this section. For purposes of this paragraph (b)(2)(iii)(A), a domestic entity means a person that would be treated as a U.S. person if it had an election in effect under § 301.7701-3(c)(1)(i) of this chapter to be treated as a corporation. For example, a limited liability company, A, organized under the laws of the State of Delaware, opens an account at a U.S. bank. Upon opening of the account, the bank requests A to furnish a Form W-9 as required under section 6049(a) and the regulations under that section. A does not have an election in effect under § 301.7701-3(c)(1)(i) of this chapter and, therefore, is not treated as an organization taxable as a corporation, including for purposes of the exempt recipient provisions in § 1.6049-4(c)(1). If A has a single owner and the owner is a foreign person (as defined in paragraph (c)(2) of this section), then A may not furnish a Form W-9 because it may not represent that it is a U.S. person for purposes of the provisions of chapters 3 and 61 of the Code, and section 3406. Therefore, A must furnish a Form W-8 with the name, address, and taxpayer identifying number (TIN) (if required) of the foreign person who is the single owner in the same manner as if the account were opened directly by the foreign single owner. See §§ 1.894-1T(d) and 1.1441-6(b)(2) for special rules where the entity's owner is claiming a reduced rate of withholding under an income tax treaty.

(B) *Foreign entity.*—A payment to a wholly-owned foreign entity that is disregarded under § 301.7701-2(c)(2) of this chapter as an entity separate from its owner shall be treated as a payment to the single owner of the entity, subject to the provisions of paragraph (b)(2)(iv) of this section if the foreign entity has a U.S. branch in the United States. For purposes of this paragraph (b)(2)(iii)(B), a foreign entity means a person that would be treated as a foreign person if it had an election in effect under § 301.7701-3(c)(1)(i) of this chapter to be treated as a corporation. See §§ 1.894-1T(d) and 1.1441-6(b)(2) for special rules where the foreign entity or its owner is claiming a reduced rate of withholding under an income tax treaty. Thus, for example, if the foreign entity's single owner is a U.S. person, the payment shall be treated as a payment to a U.S. person. Therefore, based on the saving clause in U.S. income tax treaties, such an entity may not claim benefits under an income tax treaty even if the entity is organized in a country with which the United States has an income tax treaty in effect and treats the entity as a non-fiscally transparent entity. See § 1.894-1T(d)(6), *Example 10.* Unless it has actual knowledge or reason to know that the foreign entity to whom the payment is made is disregarded under § 301.7701-2(c)(2) of this chapter, a withholding agent may treat a foreign entity as an entity separate from its owner unless it can reliably associate the payment with a withholding certificate from the entity's owner.

(iv) *Payments to a U.S. branch of certain foreign banks or foreign insurance companies.*—(A) *U.S. branch treated as a U.S. person in certain cases.*—A payment to a U.S. branch of a foreign person is a payment to a foreign person. However, a U.S. branch described in this paragraph (b)(2)(iv)(A) and a withholding agent (including another U.S. branch described in this paragraph (b)(2)(iv)(A)) may agree to treat the branch as a U.S. person for purposes of withholding on specified payments to the U.S. branch. Notwithstanding the preceding sentence, a withholding agent making a payment to a U.S. branch treated as a U.S. person under this paragraph (b)(2)(iv)(A) shall not treat the branch as a U.S. person for purposes of reporting the payment made to the branch. Therefore, a payment to such U.S. branch shall be reported on Form 1042-S under § 1.1461-1(c). Further, a U.S. branch that is treated as a U.S. person under this paragraph (b)(2)(iv)(A) shall not be treated as a U.S. person for purposes of the withholding certificate it may provide to a withholding agent. Therefore, the U.S. branch must furnish a U.S. branch withholding certificate on Form W-8 as provided in paragraph (e)(3)(v) of this section and not a Form W-9. An agreement to treat a U.S. branch as a U.S. person must be evidenced by a U.S. branch withholding certificate described in paragraph (e)(3)(v) of this section furnished by the U.S. branch to the withholding agent. A U.S. branch described in this paragraph (b)(2)(iv)(A) is any U.S. branch of a foreign bank subject to regulatory supervision by the Federal Reserve Board or a U.S. branch of a foreign insurance company required to file an annual statement on a form approved by the National Association of Insurance Commissioners with the Insurance Department of a State, a Territory, or the District of Columbia. The Internal Revenue Service (IRS) may approve a list of U.S. branches that may qualify for treatment as a U.S. person under this paragraph (b)(2)(iv)(A) (see § 601.601(d)(2) of this chapter). See § 1.6049-5(c)(5)(vi) for the treatment of U.S. branches as U.S. payors if they make a payment that is subject to reporting under chapter 61 of the Internal Revenue Code. Also see § 1.6049-5(d)(1)(ii) for the treatment of U.S. branches as foreign payees under chapter 61 of the Internal Revenue Code.

(B) *Consequences to the withholding agent.*—Any person that is otherwise a withholding agent regarding a payment to a U.S. branch described in paragraph (b)(2)(iv)(A) of this section shall treat the payment in one of the following ways—

(1) As a payment to a U.S. person, in which case the withholding agent is not responsible for withholding on such payment to the extent it can reliably associate the payment with a withholding certificate described in paragraph (e)(3)(v) of this section that has been furnished by the U.S. branch under its agreement with the withholding agent to be treated as U.S. person;

(2) As a payment directly to the persons whose names are on withholding certificates or other appropriate documentation forwarded by the U.S. branch to the withholding agent when no agreement is in effect to treat the U.S. branch as a U.S. person for such payment, to the extent the withholding agent can reliably associate the payment with such certificates or documentation; or

(3) As a payment to a foreign person of income that is effectively connected with the conduct of a trade or business in the United States if the withholding agent cannot reliably associate the payment with a withholding certificate from the U.S. branch or any other certificate or other appropriate documentation from another person. See § 1.1441-4(a)(2)(ii).

Reg. § 1.1441-1(b)(2)(iv)(B)(3)

(C) *Consequences to the U.S. branch.*—A U.S. branch that is treated as a U.S. person under paragraph (b)(2)(iv)(A) of this section shall be treated as a separate person solely for purposes of section 1441(a) and all other provisions of chapter 3 of the Internal Revenue Code and the regulations thereunder (other than for purposes of reporting the payment to the U.S. branch under § 1.1461-1(c) or for purposes of the documentation such a branch must furnish under paragraph (e)(3)(v) of this section) for any payment that it receives as such. Thus, the U.S. branch shall be responsible for withholding on the payment in accordance with the provisions under chapter 3 of the Internal Revenue Code and the regulations thereunder and other applicable withholding provisions of the Internal Revenue Code. For this purpose, it shall obtain and retain documentation from payees or beneficial owners of the payments that it receives as a U.S. person in the same manner as if it were a separate entity. For example, if a U.S. branch receives a payment on behalf of its home office and the home office is a qualified intermediary, the U.S. branch must obtain a qualified intermediary withholding certificate described in paragraph (e)(3)(ii) of this section from its home office. In addition, a U.S. branch that has not provided documentation to the withholding agent for a payment that is, in fact, not effectively connected income is a withholding agent with respect to that payment. See paragraph (b)(6) of this section and § 1.1441-4(a)(2)(ii).

(D) *Definition of payment to a U.S. branch.*—A payment is treated as a payment to a U.S. branch of a foreign bank or foreign insurance company if the payment is credited to an account maintained in the United States in the name of a U.S. branch of the foreign person, or the payment is made to an address in the United States where the U.S. branch is located and the name of the U.S. branch appears on documents (in written or electronic form) associated with the payment (e.g., the check mailed or a letter addressed to the branch).

(E) *Payments to other U.S. branches.*—Similar withholding procedures may apply to payments to U.S. branches that are not described in paragraph (b)(2)(iv)(A) of this section to the extent permitted by the district director or the Assistant Commissioner (International). Any such branch must establish that its situation is analogous to that of a U.S. branch described in paragraph (b)(2)(iv)(A) of this section regarding its registration with, and regulation by, a U.S. governmental institution, the type and amounts of assets it is required to, or actually maintains in the United States, and the personnel who carry out the activities of the branch in the United States. In the alternative, the branch must establish that the withholding and reporting requirements under chapter 3 of the Code and the regulations thereunder impose an undue administrative burden and that the collection of the tax imposed by section 871(a) or 881(a) on the foreign person (or its members in the case of a foreign partnership) will not be jeopardized by the exemption from withholding. Generally, an undue administrative burden will be found to exist in a case where the person entitled to the income, such as a foreign insurance company, receives from the withholding agent income on securities issued by a single corporation, some of which is, and some of which is not, effectively connected with conduct of a trade or business within the United States and the criteria for determining the effective connection are unduly difficult to apply because of the circumstances under which such securities are held. No exemption from withholding shall be granted under this paragraph (b)(2)(iv)(E) unless the person entitled to the income complies with such other requirements as may be imposed by the district director or the Assistant Commissioner (International) and unless the district director or the Assistant Commissioner (International) is satisfied that the collection of the tax on the income involved will not be jeopardized by the exemption from withholding. The IRS may prescribe such procedures as are necessary to make these determinations (see § 601.601(d)(2) of this chapter).

(v) *Payments to a foreign intermediary.*—(A) *Payments treated as made to persons for whom the intermediary collects the payment.*—Except as otherwise provided in paragraph (b)(2)(v)(B) of this section, the payee of a payment to a person that the withholding agent may treat as a foreign intermediary in accordance with the provisions of paragraph (b)(3)(ii)(C) or (b)(3)(v)(A) of this section is the person or persons for whom the intermediary collects the payment. Thus, for example, the payee of a payment that the withholding agent can reliably associate with a withholding certificate from a qualified intermediary (defined in paragraph (e)(5)(ii) of this section) that does not assume primary withholding responsibility or a payment to a nonqualified intermediary are the persons for whom the qualified intermediary or nonqualified intermediary acts and not to the intermediary itself. See paragraph (b)(3)(v) of this section for presumptions that apply if the payment cannot be reliably associated with valid documentation. For similar rules for payments to flow-through entities, see § 1.1441-5(c)(1) and (e)(3).

(B) *Payments treated as made to foreign intermediary.*—The payee of a payment to a person that the withholding agent may treat as a qualified intermediary is the qualified intermediary to the extent that the qualified intermediary assumes primary withholding responsibility under paragraph (e)(5)(iv) of this section for the payment. For example if a qualified intermediary assumes primary withholding responsibility under chapter 3 of the Internal Revenue Code but does not assume primary reporting or withholding responsibility under chapter 61 or section 3406 of the Internal Revenue Code and therefore provides Forms W-9 for U.S. non-exempt recipients, the qualified intermediary is the payee except to the extent the payment is reliably associated with a Form W-9 from a U.S. non-exempt recipient.

(vi) *Other payees.*—A payment to a person described in §1.6049-4(c)(1)(ii) that the withholding agent would treat as a payment to a foreign person without obtaining documentation for purposes of information reporting under section 6049 (if the payment were interest) is treated as a payment to a foreign payee for purposes of chapter 3 of the Code and the regulations thereunder (or to a foreign beneficial owner to the extent provided in paragraph (e)(1)(ii)(A)(6) or (7) of this section). Further, payments that the withholding agent can reliably associate with documentary evidence described in §1.6049-5(c)(1) relating to the payee is treated as a payment to a foreign payee. A payment that the withholding agent may treat as a payment to an authorized foreign agent (as defined in §1.1441-7(c)(2)) is treated as a payment to the agent and not to the persons for whom the agent collects the payment. See §1.1441-5(b)(1) and (c)(1) for payee determinations for payments to partnerships. See §1.1441-5(e) for payee determinations for payments to foreign trusts or foreign estates.

(vii) *Rules for reliably associating a payment with a withholding certificate or other appropriate documentation.*—(A) *Generally.*—The presumption rules of paragraph (b)(3) of this section and §§1.1441-5(d) and (e)(6) and 1.6049-5(d) apply to any payment, or portion of a payment, that a withholding agent cannot reliably associate with valid documentation. Generally, a withholding agent can reliably associate a payment with valid documentation if, prior to the payment, it holds valid documentation (either directly or through an agent), it can reliably determine how much of the payment relates to the valid documentation, and it has no actual knowledge or reason to know that any of the information, certifications, or statements in, or associated with, the documentation are incorrect. Special rules apply for payments made to intermediaries, flow-through entities, and certain U.S. branches. See paragraph (b)(2)(vii)(B) through (F) of this section. The documentation referred to in this paragraph (b)(2)(vii) is documentation described in paragraphs (c)(16) and (17) of this section upon which a withholding agent may rely to treat the payment as a payment made to a payee or beneficial owner, and to ascertain the characteristics of the payee or beneficial owner that are relevant to withholding or reporting under chapter 3 of the Internal Revenue Code and the regulations thereunder. For purposes of this paragraph (b)(2)(vii), documentation also includes the agreement that the withholding agent has in effect with an authorized foreign agent in accordance with §1.1441-7(c)(2)(i). A withholding agent that is not required to obtain documentation with respect to a payment is considered to lack documentation for purposes of this paragraph (b)(2)(vii). For example, a withholding agent paying U.S. source interest to a person that is an exempt recipient, as defined in §1.6049-4(c)(1)(ii), is not required to obtain documentation from that person in order to determine whether an amount paid to that person is reportable under an applicable information reporting provision under chapter 61 of the Internal Revenue Code. The withholding agent must, however, treat the payment as made to an undocumented person for purposes of chapter 3 of the Internal Revenue Code. Therefore, the presumption rules of paragraph (b)(3)(iii) of this section apply to determine whether the person is presumed to be a U.S. person (in which case, no withholding is required under this section), or whether the person is presumed to be a foreign person (in which case 30-percent withholding is required under this section). See paragraph (b)(3)(v) of this section for special reliance rules in the case of a payment to a foreign intermediary and §1.1441-5(d) and (e)(6) for special reliance rules in the case of a payment to a flow-through entity.

(B) *Special rules applicable to a withholding certificate from a nonqualified intermediary or flow-through entity.*—(1) In the case of a payment made to a nonqualified intermediary, a flow-through entity (as defined in paragraph (c)(23) of this section), and a U.S. branch described in paragraph (b)(2)(iv) of this section (other than a branch that is treated as a U.S. person), a withholding agent can reliably associate the payment with valid documentation only to the extent that, prior to the payment, the withholding agent can allocate the payment to a valid nonqualified intermediary, flow-through, or U.S. branch withholding certificate; the withholding agent can reliably determine how much of the payment relates to valid docu-

Reg. §1.1441-1(b)(2)(vii)(B)(1)

mentation provided by a payee as determined under paragraph (c)(12) of this section (i.e., a person that is not itself an intermediary, flow-through entity, or U.S. branch); and the withholding agent has sufficient information to report the payment on Form 1042-S or Form 1099, if reporting is required. See paragraph (e)(3)(iii) of this section for the requirements of a nonqualified intermediary withholding certificate, paragraph (e)(3)(v) of this section for the requirements of a U.S. branch certificate, and §§ 1.1441-5(c)(3)(iii) and (e)(5)(iii) for the requirements of a flow-through withholding certificate. Thus, a payment cannot be reliably associated with valid documentation provided by a payee to the extent such documentation is lacking or unreliable, or to the extent that information required to allocate and report all or a portion of the payment to each payee is lacking or unreliable. If a withholding certificate attached to an intermediary, U.S. branch, or flow-through withholding certificate is another intermediary, U.S. branch, or flow-through withholding certificate, the rules of this paragraph (b)(2)(vii)(B) apply by treating the share of the payment allocable to the other intermediary, U.S. branch, or flow-through entity as if the payment were made directly to such other entity. See paragraph (e)(3)(iv)(D) of this section for rules permitting information allocating a payment to documentation to be received after the payment is made.

(2) The rules of paragraph (b)(2)(vii)(B)(1) of this section are illustrated by the following examples:

Example 1. WH, a withholding agent, makes a payment of U.S. source interest to NQI, an intermediary that is a nonqualified intermediary. NQI provides a valid intermediary withholding certificate under paragraph (e)(3)(iii) of this section. NQI does not, however, provide valid documentation from the persons on whose behalf it receives the interest payment, and, therefore, the interest payment cannot be reliably associated with valid documentation provided by a payee. WH must apply the presumption rules of paragraph (b)(3)(v) of this section to the payment.

Example 2. The facts are the same as in *Example 1*, except that NQI does attach valid beneficial owner withholding certificates (as defined in paragraph (e)(2)(i) of this section) from A, B, C, and D establishing their status as foreign persons. NQI does not, however, provide WH with any information allocating the payment among A, B, C, and D and, therefore, WH cannot determine the portion of the payment that relates to each beneficial owner withholding certificate. The interest payment cannot be reliably associated with valid documentation from a payee and WH must apply the presumption rules of paragraph (b)(3)(v) of this section to the payment. See, however, paragraph (e)(3)(iv)(D) of this section providing special rules permitting allocation information to be received after a payment is made.

Example 3. The facts are the same as in *Example 2*, except that NQI does provide allocation information associated with its intermediary withholding certificate indicating that 25 percent of the interest payment is allocable to A and 25 percent to B. NQI does not provide any allocation information regarding the remaining 50 percent of the payment. WH may treat 25 percent of the payment as made to A and 25 percent as made to B. The remaining 50 percent of the payment cannot be reliably associated with valid documentation from a payee, however, since NQI did not provide information allocating the payment. Thus, the remaining 50 percent of the payment is subject to the presumption rules of paragraph (b)(3)(v) of this section.

Example 4. WH makes a payment of U.S. source interest to NQI1, an intermediary that is not a qualified intermediary. NQI1 provides WH with a valid nonqualified intermediary withholding certificate as well a valid beneficial owner withholding certificates from A and B and a valid nonqualified intermediary withholding certificate from NQI2. NQI2 has provided valid beneficial owner documentation from C sufficient to establish C's status as a foreign person. Based on information provided by NQI1, WH can allocate 20 percent of the interest payment to A, and 20 percent to B. Based on information that NQI2 provided NQI1 and that NQI1 provides to WH, WH can allocate 60 percent of the payment to NQI 2, but can only allocate one half of that payment (30 percent) to C. Therefore, WH cannot reliably associate 30 percent of the payment made to NQI2 with valid documentation and must apply the presumption rules of paragraph (b)(3)(v) of this section to that portion of the payment.

(C) *Special rules applicable to a withholding certificate provided by a qualified intermediary that does not assume primary withholding responsibility.*—(1) If a payment is made to a qualified intermediary that does not assume primary withholding responsibility under chapter 3 of the Internal Revenue Code or primary Form 1099 reporting and backup withholding responsibility under chapter 61 and section 3406 of the Internal Revenue Code for the payment, a withholding agent can reliably associate the payment with valid documentation only to the extent that, prior to the payment, the withholding agent has received a valid qualified intermediary withholding certificate and the withholding agent can reliably determine the portion of the payment that relates to a withholding rate pool, as defined in paragraph (e)(5)(v)(C) of this section. In the case of a withholding rate pool attributable to a U.S. non-exempt recipient, a payment cannot be reliably associated with valid documentation unless, prior to the payment, the qualified intermediary has provided the U.S. person's Form W-9 (or, in the absence of the form, the name, address, and TIN, if available, of the U.S. person) and sufficient information for the withholding agent to report the payment on Form 1099. See paragraph (e)(5)(v)(C)(2) of this section for special rules regarding allocation of payments among U.S. non-exempt recipients.

(2) The rules of this paragraph (b)(2)(vii)(C) are illustrated by the following examples:

Example 1. WH, a withholding agent, makes a payment of U.S. source dividends to QI. QI provides WH with a valid qualified intermediary withholding certificate on which it indicates that it does not assume primary withholding responsibility under chapter 3 of the Internal Revenue Code or primary Form 1099 reporting and backup withholding responsibility under chapter 61 and section 3406 of the Internal Revenue Code. QI does not provide any information allocating the dividend to withholding rate pools. WH cannot reliably associate the payment with valid payee documentation and therefore must apply the presumption rules of paragraph (b)(3)(v) of this section.

Example 2. WH makes a payment of U.S. source dividends to QI. QI has 5 customers: A, B, C, D, and E. QI has obtained documentation from A and B establishing their entitlement to a 15 percent rate of tax on U.S. source dividends under an income tax treaty. C is a U.S. person that is an exempt recipient as defined in paragraph (c)(20) of this section. D and E are U.S. non-exempt recipients who have provided Forms W-9 to QI. A, B, C, D, and E are each entitled to 20 percent of the dividend payment. QI provides WH with a valid qualified intermediary withholding certificate as described in paragraph (e)(2)(ii) of this section with which it associates the Forms W-9 from D and E. QI associates the following allocation information with its qualified intermediary withholding certificate: 40 percent of the payment is allocable to the 15 percent withholding rate pool, and 20 percent is allocable to each of D and E. QI does not provide any allocation information regarding the remaining 20 percent of the payment. WH cannot reliably associate 20 percent of the payment with valid documentation and, therefore, must apply the presumption rules of paragraph (b)(3)(v) of this section to that portion of the payment. The 20 percent of the payment allocable to the 15 percent withholding rate pool, and the portion of the payments allocable to D and E are payments that can be reliably associated with documentation.

(D) *Special rules applicable to a withholding certificate provided by a qualified intermediary that assumes primary withholding responsibility under chapter 3 of the Internal Revenue Code.*—(*1*) In the case of a payment made to a qualified intermediary that assumes primary withholding responsibility under chapter 3 of the Internal Revenue Code with respect to that payment (but does not assume primary Form 1099 reporting and backup withholding responsibility under chapter 61 and section 3406 of the Internal Revenue Code), a withholding agent can reliably associate the payment with valid documentation only to the extent that, prior to the payment, the withholding agent has received a valid qualified intermediary withholding certificate and the withholding agent can reliably determine the portion of the payment that relates to the withholding rate pool for which the qualified intermediary assumes primary withholding responsibility under chapter 3 of the Internal Revenue Code and the portion of the payment attributable to withholding rate pools for each U.S. non-exempt recipient for whom the qualified intermediary has provided a Form W-9 (or, in absence of the form, the name, address, and TIN, if available, of the U.S. non-exempt recipient). See paragraph (e)(5)(v)(C)(2) of this section for alternative allocation procedures for payments made to U.S. persons that are not exempt recipients.

(*2*) *Examples.*—The following examples illustrate the rules of paragraph (b)(2)(vii)(D)(*1*) of this section:

Example 1. WH makes a payment of U.S. source interest to QI, a qualified intermediary. QI provides WH with a withholding certificate that indicates that QI will assume primary withholding responsibility under chapter 3 of the Internal Revenue Code with respect to the payment. In addition, QI attaches a Form W-9 from A, a U.S. nonexempt recipient, as defined in paragraph (c)(21) of this section, and provides the name, address, and TIN of B, a U.S. person that is also a non-exempt recipient but who has not provided a Form W-9. QI associates a withholding statement with its qualified intermediary withholding certificate indicating that 10 percent of the payment is attributable to A, and 10 percent to B, and that QI will assume primary withholding responsibility with respect to the remaining 80 percent of the payment. WH can reliably associate the entire payment with valid documentation. Although under the presumption rule of paragraph (b)(3)(v) of this section, an undocumented person receiving U.S. source interest is generally presumed to be a foreign person, WH has actual knowledge that B is a U.S. non-exempt recipient and therefore must report the payment on Form 1099 and backup withhold on the interest payment under section 3406.

Example 2. The facts are the same as in *Example 1*, except that no Forms W-9 or other information have been provided for the 20 percent of the payment that is allocable to A and B. Thus, QI has accepted withholding responsibility for 80 percent of the payment, but has provided no information for the remaining 20 percent. In this case, 20 percent of the payment cannot be reliably associated with valid documentation, and WH must apply the presumption rule of paragraph (b)(3)(v) of this section.

(E) *Special rules applicable to a withholding certificate provided by a qualified intermediary that assumes primary Form 1099 reporting and backup withholding responsibility but not primary withholding under chapter 3.*— *(1)* If a payment is made to a qualified intermediary that assumes primary Form 1099 reporting and backup withholding responsibility for the payment (but does not assume primary withholding responsibility under chapter 3 of the Internal Revenue Code), a withholding agent can reliably associate the payment with valid documentation only to the extent that, prior to the payment, the withholding agent has received a valid qualified intermediary withholding certificate and the withholding agent can reliably determine the portion of the payment that relates to a withholding rate pool or pools provided as part of the qualified intermediary's withholding statement and the portion of the payment for which the qualified intermediary assumes primary Form 1099 reporting and backup withholding responsibility.

(2) The following example illustrates the rules of paragraph (b)(2)((vii)(D)(*1*) of this section:

Example. WH makes a payment of U.S. source dividends to QI, a qualified intermediary. QI has provided WH with a valid qualified intermediary withholding certificate. QI states on its withholding statement accompanying the certificate that it assumes primary Form 1099 reporting and backup withholding responsibility but does not assume primary withholding responsibility under chapter 3 of the Internal Revenue Code. QI represents that 15 percent of the dividend is subject to a 30 percent rate of withholding, 75 percent of the dividend is subject to a 15 percent rate of withholding, and that QI assumed primary Form 1099 reporting and backup withholding for the remaining 10 percent of the payment. The entire payment can be reliably associated with valid documentation.

(F) *Special rules applicable to a withholding certificate provided by a qualified intermediary that assumes primary withholding responsibility under chapter 3 and primary Form 1099 reporting and backup withholding responsibility and a withholding certificate provided by a withholding foreign partnership.*—If a payment is made to a qualified intermediary that assumes both primary withholding responsibility under chapter 3 of the Internal Revenue Code and primary Form 1099 reporting and backup withholding responsibility under chapter 61 and section 3406 of the Internal Revenue Code for the payment, a withholding agent can reliably associate a payment with valid documentation provided that it receives a valid qualified intermediary withholding certificate as described in paragraph (e)(3)(ii) of this section. In the case of a payment made to a withholding foreign partnership, the withholding agent can reliably associate the payment with valid documentation to the extent it can associate the payment with a valid withholding certificate described in § 1.1441-5(c)(2)(iv).

(3) *Presumptions regarding payee's status in the absence of documentation.*—(i) *General rules.*—A withholding agent that cannot, prior to the payment, reliably associate (within the meaning of paragraph (b)(2)(vii) of this section) a payment of an amount subject to withholding (as described in § 1.1441-2(a)) with valid documentation may rely on the presumptions of this paragraph (b)(3) to determine the status of the payee as a U.S. or a foreign person and the payee's other relevant characteristics (e.g., as an owner or intermediary, as an individual, trust, partnership, or corporation). The determination of withholding and reporting requirements applicable to payments to a person presumed to be a foreign person is governed only by the provisions of chapter 3 of the Code and the regulations thereunder. For the determination of withholding and reporting requirements applicable to payments to a person presumed to be a U.S. person, see chapter 61 of the Code, sections 3402, 3405, or 3406, and the regulations under these provisions. A presumption that a payee is a foreign payee is not a presumption that the payee is a foreign beneficial owner. Therefore, the provisions of this paragraph (b)(3) have no effect for purposes of reducing the withholding rate if associating the payment with documentation of foreign beneficial ownership is required as a condition for such rate reduction. See paragraph (b)(3)(ix) of this section for consequences to a withholding agent that fails to withhold in accordance with the presumptions set forth in this paragraph (b)(3) or if the withholding agent has

actual knowledge or reason to know of facts that are contrary to the presumptions set forth in this paragraph (b)(3). See paragraph (b)(2)(vii) of this section for rules regarding the extent which a withholding agent can reliably associate a payment with documentation.

(ii) *Presumptions of classification as individual, corporation, partnership, etc.*—(A) *In general.*—A withholding agent that cannot reliably associate a payment with a valid withholding certificate or that has received valid documentary evidence under §§ 1.1441-1(e)(1)(ii)(*2*) and 1.6049-5(c)(1) or (4) but cannot determine a payee's classification from the documentary evidence must apply the rules of this paragraph (b)(3)(ii) to determine the payee's classification as an individual, trust, estate, corporation, or partnership. The fact that a payee is presumed to have a certain status under the provisions of this paragraph (b)(3)(ii) does not mean that it is excused from furnishing documentation if documentation is otherwise required to obtain a reduced rate of withholding under this section. For example, if, for purposes of this paragraph (b)(3)(ii), a payee is presumed to be a tax-exempt organization based on § 1.6049-4(c)(1)(ii)(B), the withholding agent cannot rely on this presumption to reduce the rate of withholding on payments to such person (if such person is also presumed to be a foreign person under paragraph (b)(3)(iii)(A) of this section) because a reduction in the rate of withholding for payments to a foreign tax-exempt organization generally requires that a valid Form W-8 described in § 1.1441-9(b)(2) be furnished to the withholding agent.

(B) *No documentation provided.*—If the withholding agent cannot reliably associate a payment with a valid withholding certificate or valid documentary evidence, it must presume that the payee is an individual, a trust, or an estate, if the payee appears to be such person (e.g., based on the payee's name or other indications). In the absence of reliable indications that the payee is an individual, trust, or an estate, the withholding agent must presume that the payee is a corporation or one of the persons enumerated under § 1.6049-4(c)(1)(ii)(B) through (Q) if it can be so treated under § 1.6049-4(c)(1)(ii)(A)(*1*) or any one of the paragraphs under § 1.6049-4(c)(1)(ii)(B) through (Q) without the need to furnish documentation. If the withholding agent cannot treat a payee as a person described in § 1.6049-4(c)(1)(ii)(A)(*1*) through (Q), then the payee shall be presumed to be a partnership. If such a partnership is presumed to be foreign, it is not the beneficial owner of the income paid to it. See paragraph (c)(6) of this section. If such a partnership is presumed to be domestic, it is a U.S. non-exempt recipient for purposes of chapter 61 of the Internal Revenue Code.

(C) *Documentary evidence furnished for offshore account.*—If the withholding agent receives valid documentary evidence, as described in § 1.6049-5(c)(1) or (4), with respect to an offshore account from an entity but the documentary evidence does not establish the entity's classification as a corporation, trust, estate, or partnership, the withholding agent may presume (in the absence of actual knowledge otherwise) that the entity is the type of person enumerated under § 1.6049-4(c)(1)(ii)(B) through (Q) if it can be so treated under any one of those paragraphs without the need to furnish documentation. If the withholding agent cannot treat a payee as a person described in § 1.6049-4(c)(1)(ii)(B) through (Q), then the payee shall be presumed to be a corporation unless the withholding agent knows, or has reason to know, that the entity is not classified as a corporation for U.S. tax purposes. If a payee is, or is presumed to be, a corporation under this paragraph (b)(3)(ii)(C) and a foreign person under paragraph (b)(3)(iii) of this section, a withholding agent shall not treat the payee as the beneficial owner of income if the withholding agent knows, or has reason to know, that the payee is not the beneficial owner of the income. For this purpose, a withholding agent shall have reason to know that the payee is not a beneficial owner if the documentary evidence indicates that the payee is a bank, broker, intermediary, custodian, or other agent, or is treated under § 1.6049-4(c)(1)(ii)(B) through (Q) as such a person. A withholding agent may, however, treat such a person as a beneficial owner if the foreign person provides a statement, in writing and signed by a person with authority to sign the statement, that is attached to the documentary evidence stating it is the beneficial owner of the income.

(iii) *Presumption of U.S. or foreign status.*—A payment that the withholding agent cannot reliably associate with documentation is presumed to be made to a U.S. person, except as otherwise provided in this paragraph (b)(3)(iii), in paragraphs (b)(3)(iv) and (v) of this section, or in § 1.1441-5(d) or (e).

(A) *Payments to exempt recipients.*—If a withholding agent cannot reliably associate a payment with documentation from the payee and the payee is an exempt recipient (as determined under the provisions of § 1.6049-4(c)(1)(ii) in the case of interest, or under similar provisions under chapter 61 of the Code applicable to the type of payment involved, but not including a payee that the withholding agent may treat as a foreign intermediary in accordance with paragraph (b)(3)(v) of this section), the payee is presumed to be a foreign person and not a U.S. person—

(1) If the withholding agent has actual knowledge of the payee's employer identification number and that number begins with the two digits "98";

(2) If the withholding agent's communications with the payee are mailed to an address in a foreign country;

(3) If the name of the payee indicates that the entity is the type of entity that is on the per se list of foreign corporations contained in § 301.7701-2(b)(8)(i) of this chapter; or

(4) If the payment is made outside the United States (as defined in § 1.6049-5(e)).

(B) *Scholarships and grants.*—A payment representing taxable scholarship or fellowship grant income that does not represent compensation for services (but is not excluded from tax under section 117) and that a withholding agent cannot reliably associate with documentation is presumed to be made to a foreign person if the withholding agent has a record that the payee has a U.S. visa that is not an immigrant visa. See section 871(c) and § 1.1441-4(c) for applicable tax rate and withholding rules.

(C) *Pensions, annuities, etc.*—A payment from a trust described in section 401(a), an annuity plan described in section 403(a), a payment with respect to any annuity, custodial account, or retirement income account described in section 403(b), or a payment from an individual retirement account or individual retirement annuity described in section 408 that a withholding agent cannot reliably associate with documentation is presumed to be made to a U.S. person only if the withholding agent has a record of a Social Security number for the payee and relies on a mailing address described in the following sentence. A mailing address is an address used for purposes of information reporting or otherwise communicating with the payee that is an address in the United States or in a foreign country with which the United States has an income tax treaty in effect and the treaty provides that the payee, if an individual resident in that country, would be entitled to an exemption from U.S. tax on amounts described in this paragraph (b)(3)(iii)(C). Any payment described in this paragraph (b)(3)(iii)(C) that is not presumed to be made to a U.S. person is presumed to be made to a foreign person. A withholding agent making a payment to a person presumed to be a foreign person may not reduce the 30-percent amount of withholding required on such payment unless it receives a withholding certificate described in paragraph (e)(2)(i) of this section furnished by the beneficial owner. For reduction in the 30-percent rate, see §§ 1.1441-4(e) or 1.1441-6(b).

(D) *Certain payments to offshore accounts.*—A payment is presumed made to a foreign payee if the payment is made outside the United States (as defined in § 1.6049-5(e)) to an offshore account (as defined in § 1.6049-5(c)(1)) and the withholding agent does not have actual knowledge that the payee is a U.S. person. See § 1.6049-5(d)(2) and (3) for exceptions to this rule.

(iv) *Grace period.*—A withholding agent may choose to apply the provisions of § 1.6049-5(d)(2)(ii) regarding a 90-day grace period for purposes of this paragraph (b)(3) (by applying the term *withholding agent* instead of the term *payor*) to amounts described in § 1.1441-6(c)(2) and to amounts covered by a Form 8233 described in § 1.1441-4(b)(2)(ii). Thus, for these amounts, a withholding agent may choose to treat an account holder as a foreign person and withhold under chapter 3 of the Internal Revenue Code (and the regulations thereunder) while awaiting documentation. For purposes of determining the rate of withholding under this section, the withholding agent must withhold at the unreduced 30-percent rate at the time that the amounts are credited to an account. However, a withholding agent who can reliably associate the payment with a withholding certificate that is otherwise valid within the meaning of the applicable provisions except for the fact that it is transmitted by facsimile may rely on that facsimile form for purposes of withholding at the claimed reduced rate. For reporting of amounts credited both before and after the grace period, see § 1.1461-1(c)(4)(i)(A). The following adjustments shall be made at the expiration of the grace period:

(A) If, at the end of the grace period, the documentation is not furnished in the manner required under this section and the account holder is presumed to be a U.S. nonexempt recipient, then backup withholding applies to amounts credited to the account after the expiration of the grace period only. Amounts credited to the account during the grace period shall be treated as owned by a foreign payee and adjustments must be made to correct any underwithholding on such amounts in the manner described in § 1.1461-2.

(B) If, at the end of the grace period, the documentation is not furnished in the manner required under this section, or if documentation is furnished that does not support the claimed rate reduction, and the account holder is presumed to be a foreign person then adjustments must be made to correct any underwithholding on amounts credited to the account during the grace period, based on the adjustment procedures described in § 1.1461-2.

(v) *Special rules applicable to payments to foreign intermediaries.*—(A) *Reliance on claim of status as foreign intermediary.*—The presumption rules of paragraph (b)(3)(v)(B) of this section apply to a payment made to an intermediary (whether the intermediary is a qualified or nonqualified intermediary) that has provided a valid withholding certificate under paragraph (e)(3)(ii) or (iii) of this section (or has provided documentary evidence described in paragraph (b)(3)(ii)(C) of this section that indicates it is a bank, broker, custodian, intermediary, or other agent) to the extent the withholding agent cannot treat the payment as being reliably associated with valid documentation under the rules of paragraph (b)(2)(vii) of this section. For this purpose, a U.S. person's foreign branch that is a qualified intermediary defined in paragraph (e)(5)(ii) of this section shall be treated as a foreign intermediary. A payee that the withholding agent may not reliably treat as a foreign intermediary under this paragraph (b)(3)(v)(A) is presumed to be a payee other than an intermediary whose classification as an individual, corporation, partnership, etc., must be determined in accordance with paragraph (b)(3)(ii) of this section to the extent relevant. In addition, such payee is presumed to be a U.S. or a foreign payee based upon the presumptions described in paragraph (b)(3)(iii) of this section. The provisions of paragraph (b)(3)(v)(B) of this section are not relevant to a withholding agent that can reliably associate a payment with a withholding certificate from a person representing to be a qualified intermediary to the extent the qualified intermediary has assumed primary withholding responsibility in accordance with paragraph (e)(5)(iv) of this section.

(B) *Beneficial owner documentation or allocation information is lacking or unreliable.*—Any portion of a payment that the withholding agent may treat as made to a foreign intermediary (whether a nonqualified or a qualified intermediary) but that the withholding agent cannot treat as reliably associated with valid documentation under the rules of paragraph (b)(2)(vii) of this section is presumed made to an unknown, undocumented foreign payee. As a result, a withholding agent must deduct and withhold 30 percent from any payment of an amount subject to withholding. If a withholding certificate attached to an intermediary certificate is another intermediary withholding certificate or a flow-through withholding certificate, the rules of this paragraph (b)(3)(v)(B) (or § 1.1441-5(d)(3) or (e)(6)(iii)) apply by treating the share of the payment allocable to the other intermediary or flow-through entity as if it were made directly to the other intermediary or flow-through entity. Any payment of an amount subject to withholding that is presumed made to an undocumented foreign person must be reported on Form 1042-S. See § 1.1461-1(c). See § 1.6049-5(d) for payments that are not subject to withholding.

(vi) *U.S. branches.*—The rules of paragraph (b)(3)(v)(B) of this section shall apply to payments to a U.S. branch described in paragraph (b)(2)(iv)(A) of this section that has provided a withholding certificate as described in paragraph (e)(3)(v) of this section on which it has not agreed to be treated as a U.S. person.

(vii) *Joint payees.*—(A) *In general.*—Except as provided in paragraph (b)(3)(vii)(B) of this section, if a withholding agent makes a payment to joint payees and cannot reliably associate a payment with valid documentation from all payees, the payment is presumed made to an unidentified U.S. person. However, if one of the joint payees provides a Form W-9 furnished in accordance with the procedures described in §§ 31.3406(d)-1 through 31.3406(d)-5 of this chapter, the payment shall be treated as made to that payee. See § 31.3406(h)-2 of this chapter for rules to determine the relevant payee if more than one Form W-9 is provided. For purposes of applying this paragraph (b)(3), the grace period rules in paragraph (b)(3)(iv) of this section shall apply only if each payee meets the conditions described in paragraph (b)(3)(iv) of this section.

(B) *Special rule for offshore accounts.*—If a withholding agent makes a payment to joint payees and cannot reliably associate a payment with valid documentation from all payees, the payment is presumed made to an unknown foreign payee if the payment is made outside the United States (as defined in § 1.6049-5(e)) to an offshore account (as defined in § 1.6049-5(c)(1)).

(viii) *Rebuttal of presumptions.*—A payee or beneficial owner may rebut the presumptions described in this paragraph (b)(3) by providing reliable documentation to the withholding agent or, if applicable, to the IRS.

(ix) *Effect of reliance on presumptions and of actual knowledge or reason to know otherwise.*—(A) *General rule.*—Except as otherwise provided in paragraph (b)(3)(ix)(B) of this section, a withholding agent that withholds on a payment under section 3402, 3405 or 3406 in accordance with the presumptions set forth in this paragraph (b)(3) shall not be liable for withholding under this section even it is later established that the beneficial owner of the payment is, in fact, a foreign person. Similarly, a withholding agent that withholds on a payment under this section in accordance with the presumptions set forth in this paragraph (b)(3) shall not be liable for withholding under section 3402 or 3405 or for backup withholding under section 3406 even if it is later established that the payee or beneficial owner is, in fact, a U.S. person. A withholding agent that, instead of relying on the presumptions described in this paragraph (b)(3), relies on its own actual knowledge to withhold a lesser amount, not withhold, or not report a payment, even though reporting of the payment or withholding a greater amount would be required if the withholding agent relied on the presumptions described in this paragraph (b)(3) shall be liable for tax, interest, and penalties to the extent provided under section 1461 and the regulations under that section. See paragraph (b)(7) of this section for provisions regarding such liability if the withholding agent fails to withhold in accordance with the presumptions described in this paragraph (b)(3).

(B) *Actual knowledge or reason to know that amount of withholding is greater than is required under the presumptions or that reporting of the payment is required.*—Notwithstanding the provisions of paragraph (b)(3)(ix)(A) of this section, a withholding agent may not rely on the presumptions described in this paragraph (b)(3) to the extent it has actual knowledge or reason to know that the status or characteristics of the payee or of the beneficial owner are other than what is presumed under this paragraph (b)(3) and, if based on such knowledge or reason to know, it should withhold (under this section or another withholding provision of the Code) an amount greater than would be the case if it relied on the presumptions described in this paragraph (b)(3) or it should report (under this section or under another provision of the Code) an amount that would not otherwise be reportable if it relied on the presumptions described in this paragraph (b)(3). In such a case, the withholding agent must rely on its actual knowledge or reason to know rather than on the presumptions set forth in this paragraph (b)(3). Failure to do so and, as a result, failure to withhold the higher amount or to report the payment, shall result in liability for tax, interest, and penalties to the extent provided under sections 1461 and 1463 and the regulations under those sections.

(x) *Examples.*—The provisions of this paragraph (b)(3) are illustrated by the following examples:

Example 1. A withholding agent, W, makes a payment of U.S. source dividends to person X, Inc. at an address outside the United States. W cannot reliably associate the payment to X with documentation. Under §§ 1.6042-3(b)(1)(vii) and 1.6049-4(c)(1)(ii)(A)(*1*), W may treat X as a corporation. Thus, under the presumptions described in paragraph (b)(3)(iii) of this section, W must presume that X is a foreign person (because the payment is made outside the United States). However, W knows that X is a U.S. person who is an exempt recipient. W may not rely on its actual knowledge to not withhold under this section. If W's knowledge is, in fact, incorrect, W would be liable for tax, interest, and, if applicable, penalties, under section 1461. W would be permitted to reduce or eliminate its liability for the tax by establishing, in accordance with paragraph (b)(7) of this section, that the tax is not due or has been satisfied. If W's actual knowledge is, in fact, correct, W may nevertheless be liable for tax, interest, or penalties under section 1461 for the amount that W should have withheld based upon the presumptions. W would be permitted to reduce or eliminate its liability for the tax by establishing, in accordance with paragraph (b)(7) of this section, that its actual knowledge was, in fact, correct and that no tax or a lesser amount of tax was due.

Example 2. A withholding agent, W, makes a payment of U.S. source dividends to Y who does not qualify as an exempt recipient under §§ 1.6042-3(b)(1)(vii) and 1.6049-4(c)(1)(ii). W cannot reliably associate the payment to Y with documentation. Under the presumptions described in paragraph (b)(3)(iii) of this section, W must presume that Y is a U.S. person who is not an exempt recipient for purposes of section 6042. However, W knows that Y is a foreign person. W may not rely on its actual knowledge to withhold under this section rather than backup withhold under section 3406. If W's knowledge is, in fact, incorrect, W would be liable for tax, interest, and, if applicable, penalties, under section 3403. If W's actual knowledge is, in fact, correct, W may nevertheless be liable for tax, interest, or penalties under section 3403 for the amount that W should have withheld based upon the presumptions. Paragraph (b)(7) of this section does not apply to provide relief from liability under section 3403.

Example 3. A withholding agent, W, makes a payment of U.S. source dividends to X, Inc. W cannot reliably associate the payment to X, Inc. with documentation. X, Inc. presents none of the indicia of foreign status described in paragraph (b)(3)(iii)(A) of this section, but W has actual knowledge that X, Inc. is a foreign corporation. W may treat X, Inc. as an exempt recipient under § 1.6042-3(b)(1)(vii). Because there are no indicia of foreign status, W would, absent actual knowledge or reason to know otherwise, be permitted to treat X, Inc. as a domestic corporation in accordance with the presumptions of paragraph (b)(3)(iii) of this section. However, under paragraph (b)(3)(ix)(B) of this section, W may not rely on the presumption of U.S. status since reliance on its actual knowledge requires that it withhold an amount greater than would be the case under the presumptions.

Example 4. A withholding agent, W, is a plan administrator who makes pension payments to person X with a mailing address in a foreign country with which the United States has an income tax treaty in effect. Under that treaty, the type of pension income paid to X is taxable solely in the country of residence. The plan administrator has a record of X's U.S. social security number. W has no actual knowledge or reason to know that X is a foreign person. W may rely on the presumption of paragraph (b)(3)(iii)(C) of this section in order to treat X as a U.S. person. Therefore, any withholding and reporting requirements for the payment are governed by the provisions of section 3405 and the regulations under that section.

(4) *List of exemptions from, or reduced rates of, withholding under chapter 3 of the Code.*—A withholding agent that has determined that the payee is a foreign person for purposes of paragraph (b)(1) of this section must determine whether the payee is entitled to a reduced rate of withholding under section 1441, 1442, or 1443. This paragraph (b)(4) identifies items for which a reduction in the rate of withholding may apply and whether the rate reduction is conditioned upon documentation being furnished to the withholding agent. Documentation required under this paragraph (b)(4) is documentation that a withholding agent must be able to associate with a payment upon which it can rely to treat the payment as made to a foreign person that is the beneficial owner of the payment in accordance with paragraph (e)(1)(ii) of this section. This paragraph (b)(4) also cross-references other sections of the Code and applicable regulations in which some of these exceptions, exemptions, or reductions are further explained. See, for example, paragraph (b)(4)(viii) of this section, dealing with effectively connected income, that cross-references § 1.1441-4(a); see paragraph (b)(4)(xv) of this section, dealing with exemptions from, or reductions of, withholding under an income tax treaty, that cross-references § 1.1441-6. This paragraph (b)(4) is not an exclusive list of items to which a reduction of the rate of withholding may apply and, thus, does not preclude an exemption from, or reduction in, the rate of withholding that may otherwise be allowed under the regulations under the provisions of chapter 3 of the Code for a particular item of income identified in this paragraph (b)(4).

(i) Portfolio interest described in section 871(h) or 881(c) and substitute interest payments described in § 1.871-7(b)(2) or 1.881-2(b)(2) are exempt from withholding under section 1441(a). See § 1.871-14 for regulations regarding portfolio interest and section 1441(c)(9) for exemption from withholding. Documentation establishing foreign status is required for interest on an obligation in registered form to qualify as portfolio interest. See section 871(h)(2)(B)(ii) and § 1.871-14(c)(1)(ii)(C). For special documentation rules regarding foreign-targeted registered obligations described in § 1.871-14(e)(2), see § 1.871-14(e)(3) and (4) and, in particular, § 1.871-14(e)(4)(i)(A) and (ii)(A) regarding the time when the withholding agent must receive the documentation. The documentation furnished for purposes of qualifying interest as portfolio interest serves as the basis for the withholding exemption for purposes of this section and for purposes of establishing foreign status for purposes of section 6049. See § 1.6049-5(b)(8). Documentation establishing foreign status is not required for qualifying interest on an obligation in bearer form described in § 1.871-14(b)(1) as portfolio interest. However, in certain cases, documentation for portfolio interest on a bearer obligation may have to be furnished in order to establish foreign status for purposes of the information reporting provisions of section 6049 and backup withholding under section 3406. See § 1.6049-5(b)(7).

(ii) Bank deposit interest and similar types of deposit interest (including original issue discount) described in section 871(i)(2)(A) or 881(d) that are from sources within the United States are exempt from withholding under section 1441(a). See section 1441(c)(10). Documentation establishing foreign status is not required for purposes of this withholding exemption but may have to be furnished for purposes of the information reporting provisions of section 6049 and backup withholding under section 3406. See § 1.6049-5(d)(3)(iii) for exceptions to the foreign payee and exempt recipient rules regarding this type of income. See also § 1.6049-5(b)(11) for applicable documentation exemptions for certain bank deposit interest paid on obligations in bearer form.

(iii) Bank deposit interest (including original issue discount) described in section 861(a)(1)(B) is exempt from withholding under sections 1441(a) as income that is not from U.S. sources. Documentation establishing foreign status is not required for purposes of this withholding exemption but may have to be furnished for purposes of the information reporting provisions of section 6049 and backup withholding under section 3406. Reporting requirements for payments of such interest are governed by section 6049 and the regulations under that section. See § 1.6049-5(b)(12) and alternative documentation rules under § 1.6049-5(c)(1).

(iv) Interest or original issue discount from sources within the United States on certain short-term obligations described in section 871(g)(1)(B) or 881(a)(3) is exempt from withholding under sections 1441(a). Documentation establishing foreign status is not required for purposes of this withholding exemption but may have to be furnished for purposes of the information reporting provisions of section 6049 and backup withholding under section 3406. See § 1.6049-5(b)(12) for applicable documentation for establishing foreign status and § 1.6049-5(d)(3)(iii) for exceptions to the foreign payee and exempt recipient rules regarding this type of income. See also § 1.6049-5(b)(10) for applicable documentation exemptions for certain obligations in bearer form.

(v) Income from sources without the United States is exempt from withholding under sections 1441(a). Documentation establishing foreign status is not required for purposes of this withholding exemption but may have to be furnished for purposes of the information reporting provisions of section 6049 or other applicable provisions of chapter 61 of the Code and backup withholding under section 3406. See, for example, § 1.6049-5(b)(6) and (12) and alternative documentation rules under § 1.6049-5(c). See also paragraph (b)(5) of this section for cross references to other applicable provisions of the regulations under chapter 61 of the Code.

(vi) Distributions from certain domestic corporations described in section 871(i)(2)(B) or 881(d) are exempt from withholding under section 1441(a). See section 1441(c)(10). Documentation establishing foreign status is not required for purposes of this withholding exemption but may have to be furnished for purposes of the information reporting provisions of section 6042 and backup withholding under section 3406. See § 1.6042-3(b)(1)(iii) through (vi).

(vii) Dividends paid by certain foreign corporations that are treated as income from sources within the United States by reason of section 861(a)(2)(B) are exempt from withholding under section 884(e)(3) to the extent that the distributions are paid out of earnings and profits in any taxable year that the corporation was subject to branch profits tax for that year. Documentation establishing foreign status is not required for purposes of this withholding exemption but may have to be furnished for purposes of the information reporting provisions of section 6042 and backup withholding under section 3406. See § 1.6042-3(b)(1)(iii) through (vii).

(viii) Certain income that is effectively connected with the conduct of a U.S. trade or business is exempt from withholding under section 1441(a). See section 1441(c)(1). Documentation establishing foreign status and status of the income as effectively connected must be furnished for purposes of this withholding exemption to the extent required under the provisions of § 1.1441-4(a). Documentation furnished for this purpose also serves as documentation establishing foreign status for purposes of applicable information reporting provisions under chapter 61 of the Code and for backup withholding under section 3406. See, for example, § 1.6041-4(a)(1).

(ix) Certain income with respect to compensation for personal services of an individual that are performed in the United States is exempt from withholding under section 1441(a). See section 1441(c)(4) and § 1.1441-4(b). However, such income may be subject to withholding as wages under section 3402. Documentation establishing foreign status must be furnished for purposes of any withholding exemption or reduction to the extent required under § 1.1441-4(b) or 31.3401(a)(6)-1(e) and (f) of this chapter. Documentation furnished for this purpose also serves as documentation establishing foreign status for purposes of information reporting under section 6041. See § 1.6041-4(a)(1).

(x) Amounts described in section 871(f) that are received as annuities from certain qualified plans are exempt from withholding under section 1441(a). See section 1441(c)(7). Documentation establishing foreign status must be furnished for purposes of the withholding exemption as required under § 1.1441-4(d). Documentation furnished for this purpose also serves as documentation establishing foreign status for purposes of information reporting under section 6041. See § 1.6041-4(a)(1).

(xi) Payments to a foreign government (including a foreign central bank of issue) that are excludable from gross income under section 892(a) are exempt from withholding under section 1442. See § 1.1441-8(b). Documentation establishing status as a foreign government is required for purposes of this withholding exemption. Payments to a foreign government are exempt from information reporting under chapter 61 of the Code (see § 1.6049-4(c)(1)(ii)(F)).

(xii) Payments of certain interest income to a foreign central bank of issue or the Bank for International Settlements that are exempt from tax under section 895 are exempt from withholding under section 1442. Documentation establishing eligibility for such exemption is required to the extent provided in § 1.1441-8(c)(1). Payments to a foreign central bank of issue or to the Bank for International Settlements are exempt from information reporting under chapter 61 of the Code (see § 1.6049-4(c)(1)(ii)(H) and (M)).

(xiii) Amounts derived by a foreign central bank of issue from bankers' acceptances described in section 871(i)(2)(C) or 881(d) are exempt from tax and, therefore, from withholding. See section 1441(c)(10). Documentation establishing foreign status is not required for purposes of this withholding exemption if the name of the payee and other facts surrounding the payment reasonably indicate that the beneficial owner of the payment is a foreign central bank of issue as defined in § 1.861-2(b)(4). See § 1.1441-8(c)(2) for withholding procedures. See also §§ 1.6049-4(c)(1)(ii)(H) and 1.6041-3(q)(8) for a similar exemption from information reporting.

(xiv) Payments to an international organization from investments in the United States of stocks, bonds, or other domestic securities or from interest on deposits in banks in the United States of funds belonging to such international organization are exempt from tax under section 892(b) and, thus, from withholding. Documentation establishing status as an international organization is not required if the name of the payee and other facts surrounding the payment reasonably indicate that the beneficial owner of the payment is an international organization within the meaning of section 7701(a)(18). See § 1.1441-8(d). Payments to an international organization are exempt from information reporting under chapter 61 of the Code (see § 1.6049-4(c)(1)(ii)(G)).

(xv) Amounts may be exempt from, or subject to a reduced rate of, withholding under an income tax treaty. Documentation establishing eligibility for benefits under an income tax treaty is required for this purpose as provided under §§ 1.1441-6. Documentation furnished for this purpose also serves as documentation establishing foreign status for purposes of applicable information reporting provisions under chapter 61 of the Code and for backup withholding under section 3406. See, for example, § 1.6041-4(a)(1).

(xvi) Amounts of scholarships and grants paid to certain exchange or training program participants that do not represent compensation for services but are not excluded from tax under section 117 are subject to a reduced rate of withholding of 14-percent under section 1441(b). Documentation establishing foreign status is required for purposes of this reduction in rate as provided under § 1.1441-4(c). This income is not subject to information reporting under chapter 61 of the Code nor to backup withholding under section 3406. The compensatory portion of a scholarship or grant is reportable as wage income. See § 1.6041-3(o).

(xvii) Amounts paid to a foreign organization described in section 501(c) are exempt from withholding under section 1441 to the extent that the amounts are not income includible under section 512 in computing the organization's unrelated business taxable income and are not subject to the tax imposed by section 4948(a). Documentation establishing status as a tax-exempt organization is required for purposes of this exemption to the extent provided in § 1.1441-9. Amounts includible under section 512 in computing the organization's unrelated business taxable income are subject to withholding to the extent provided in section 1443(a) and § 1.1443-1(a). Gross investment income (as defined in section 4940(c)(2)) of a private foundation is subject to withholding at a 4-percent rate to the extent provided in section 1443(b) and § 1.1443-1(b). Payments to a tax-exempt organization are exempt from information reporting under chapter 61 of the Code and the regulations thereunder (see § 1.6049-4(c)(1)(ii)(B)(*1*)).

(xviii) Per diem amounts for subsistence paid by the U.S. government to a nonresident alien individual who is engaged in any program of training in the United States under the Mutual Security Act of 1954 are exempt from withholding under section 1441(a). See section 1441(c)(6). Documentation of foreign status is not required under § 1.1441-4(e) for purposes of establishing eligibility for this exemption. See § 1.6041-3(p).

(xix) Interest with respect to tax-free covenant bonds issued prior to 1934 is subject to special withholding procedures set forth in § 1.1461-1 in effect prior to January 1, 2001 (see § 1.1461-1 as contained in 26 CFR part 1, revised April 1, 1999).

(xx) Income from certain gambling winnings of a nonresident alien individual is exempt from tax under section 871(j) and from withholding under section 1441(a). See section 1441(c)(11). Documentation establishing foreign status is not required for purposes of this exemption but may have to be furnished for purposes of the information reporting provisions of section 6041 and backup withholding under section 3406. See §§ 1.6041-1 and 1.6041-4(a)(1).

(xxi) Any payments not otherwise mentioned in this paragraph (b)(4) shall be subject to withholding at the rate of 30-percent if it is an amount subject to withholding (as defined in § 1.1441-2(a)) unless and to the extent the IRS may otherwise prescribe in published guidance (see § 601.601(d)(2) of this chapter) or unless otherwise provided in regulations under chapter 3 of the Code.

(5) *Establishing foreign status under applicable provisions of chapter 61 of the Code.*—This paragraph (b)(5) identifies relevant provisions of the regulations under chapter 61 of the Code that exempt payments from information reporting, and therefore, from backup withholding under section 3406, based on the payee's status as a foreign person. Many of these exemptions require that the payee's foreign status be established in order for the exemption to apply. The regulations under applicable provisions of chapter 61 of the Code generally provide that the documentation described in this section may be relied upon for purposes of determining foreign status.

(i) Payments to a foreign person that are governed by section 6041 (dealing with certain trade or business income) are exempt from information reporting under § 1.6041-4(a).

(ii) Payments to a foreign person that are governed by section 6041A (dealing with remuneration for services and certain sales) are exempt from information reporting under § 1.6041A-1(d)(3).

(iii) Payments to a foreign person that are governed by section 6042 (dealing with dividends) are exempt from information reporting under § 1.6042-3(b)(1)(iii) through (vi).

(iv) Payments to a foreign person that are governed by section 6044 (dealing with patronage dividends) are exempt from information reporting under § 1.6044-3(c)(1).

(v) Payments to a foreign person that are governed by section 6045 (dealing with broker proceeds) are exempt from information reporting under § 1.6045-1(g).

(vi) Payments to a foreign person that are governed by section 6049 (dealing with interest) to a foreign person are exempt from information reporting under § 1.6049-5(b)(6) through (15).

(vii) Payments to a foreign person that are governed by section 6050N (dealing with royalties) are exempt from information reporting under § 1.6050N-1(c).

(viii) Payments to a foreign person that are governed by section 6050P (dealing with income from cancellation of debt) are exempt from information reporting under section 6050P or the regulations under that section except to the extent provided in Notice 96-61 (1996-2 C.B. 227); see also § 601.601(b)(2) of this chapter.

(6) *Rules of withholding for payments by a foreign intermediary or certain U.S. branches.*—
(i) *In general.*—A foreign intermediary described in paragraph (e)(3)(i) of this section or a U.S. branch described in paragraph (b)(2)(iv) of this section that receives an amount subject to withholding (as defined in § 1.1441-2(a)) shall be required to withhold (if another withholding agent has not withheld the full amount required) and report such payment under chapter 3 of the Internal Revenue Code and the regulations thereunder except as otherwise provided in this paragraph (b)(6). A nonqualified intermediary or U.S. branch described in paragraph (b)(2)(iv) of this section (other than a branch that is treated as a U.S. person) shall not be required to withhold or report if it has provided a valid nonqualified intermediary withholding certificate or a U.S. branch withholding certificate, it has provided all of the information required by paragraph (e)(3)(iv) of this section (withholding statement), and it does not know, and has no reason to know, that another withholding agent failed to withhold the correct amount or failed to report the payment correctly under § 1.1461-1(c). A qualified intermediary's obligations to withhold and report shall be determined in accordance with its qualified intermediary withholding agreement.

(ii) *Examples.*—The following examples illustrate the rules of paragraph (b)(6)(i) of this section:

Example 1. FB, a foreign bank, acts an intermediary for five different persons, A, B, C, D, and E, each of whom owns U.S. securities that generate U.S. source dividends. The dividends are paid by USWA, a U.S. withholding agent. FB furnished USWA with a nonqualified intermediary withholding certificate, described in paragraph (e)(3)(iii) of this section, to which it attached the withholding certificates of each of A, B, C, D, and E. The withholding certificates from A and B claim a 15 percent reduced rate of withholding under an income tax treaty. C, D, and E claim no reduced rate of withholding. FB provides a withholding statement that meets all of the requirements of paragraph (e)(3)(iv) of this section, including information allocating 20 percent of each dividend payment to each of A, B, C, D, and E. FB does not have actual knowledge or reason to know that USWA did not withhold the correct amounts or report the dividends on Forms 1042-S to each of A, B, C, D, and E. FB is not required to withhold or to report the dividends to A, B, C, D, and E.

Example 2. The facts are the same as in *Example 1*, except that FB did not provide any information for USWA to determine how much of the dividend payments were made to A, B, C, D, and E. Because USWA could not reliably associate the dividend payments with documentation under paragraph (b)(2)(vii) of this section, USWA applied the presumption rules of paragraph (b)(3)(v) of this section and withheld 30 percent from all dividend payments. In addition, USWA filed a single Form 1042-S reporting the payment to an unknown foreign payee. FB is deemed to know that USWA did not report the payment to A, B, C, D, and E because it did not provide all of the information required on a withholding statement under paragraph (e)(3)(iv) of this section (i.e., allocation information). Although FB is not required to withhold on the payment because the full 30 percent withholding was imposed by USWA, it is required to report the payments on Forms 1042-S to A, B, C, D, and E. FB's intentional failure to do so will subject it to intentional disregard penalties under sections 6721 and 6722.

(7) *Liability for failure to obtain documentation timely or to act in accordance with applicable presumptions.*—(i) *General rule.*—A withholding agent that cannot reliably associate a payment with documentation on the date of payment and that does not withhold under this section, or withholds at less than the 30-percent rate prescribed under section 1441(a) and paragraph (b)(1) of this section, is liable under section 1461 for the tax required to be withheld under chapter 3 of the Code and the regulations thereunder, without the benefit of a reduced rate unless—

(A) The withholding agent has appropriately relied on the presumptions described in paragraph (b)(3) of this section (including the grace period described in paragraph (b)(3)(iv) of this section) in order to treat the payee as a U.S. person or, if applicable, on the presumptions described in § 1.1441-4(a)(2)(ii) or (3)(i) to treat the payment as effectively connected income; or

(B) The withholding agent can demonstrate to the satisfaction of the district director or the Assistant Commissioner (International) that the proper amount of tax, if any, was in fact paid to the IRS; or

(C) No documentation is required under section 1441 or this section in order for a reduced rate of withholding to apply.

(D) The withholding agent has complied with the provisions of § 1.1441-6(c) or (g).

(ii) *Proof that tax liability has been satisfied.*—Proof of payment of tax may be established for purposes of paragraph (b)(7)(i)(B) of this section on the basis of a Form 4669 (or such other form as the IRS may prescribe in published guidance (see § 601.601(d)(2) of this chapter)), establishing the amount of tax, if any, actually paid by or for the beneficial owner on the income. Proof that a reduced rate of withholding was, in fact, appropriate under the provisions of chapter 3 of the Code and the regulations thereunder may also be established after the date of payment by the withholding agent on the basis of a valid withholding certificate or other appropriate documentation furnished after that date. However, in the case of a withholding certificate or other appropriate documentation received after the date of payment (or after the grace period specified in paragraph (b)(3)(iv) of this section), the district director or the Assistant Commissioner (International) may require additional proof if it is determined that the delays in obtaining the withholding certificate affect its reliability.

(iii) *Liability for interest and penalties.*—A withholding agent that has failed to withhold other than based on appropriate reliance on the presumptions described in paragraph (b)(3) of this section or in § 1.1441-4(a)(2)(ii) or (3)(i) is not relieved from liability for interest under section 6601. Such liability exists even if there is no underlying tax liability due. The interest on the amount that should have been withheld shall be imposed as prescribed under section 6601 beginning on the last date for paying the tax due under section 1461 (which, under section 6601, is the due date for filing the withholding agent's return of tax). The interest shall stop accruing on the earlier of the date that the required withholding certificate or other documentation is provided to the withholding agent and to the extent of the amount of tax that is determined not to be due based on documentation provided, or the date, and to the extent, that the unpaid tax liability under section 871, 881 or under section 1461 is satisfied. Further, in the event that a tax liability is assessed against the beneficial owner under section 871, 881, or 882 and interest under section 6601(a) is assessed against, and collected from, the beneficial owner, the interest charge imposed on the withholding agent shall be abated to that extent so as to avoid the imposition of a double interest charge. However, the withholding agent is not relieved of any applicable penalties. See section 1464.

(iv) *Special effective date.*—See paragraph (f)(2)(ii) of this section for the special effective date applicable to this paragraph (b)(7).

(v) *Examples.*—The provisions of paragraph (b)(7) of this section are illustrated by the following examples:

Example 1. On June 15, 2001, a withholding agent pays U.S. source interest on an obligation in registered form (issued after July 18, 1984) to a foreign corporation that it cannot reliably associate with a Form W-8 or other appropriate documentation upon which to rely to treat the beneficial owner as a foreign person. The withholding agent does not withhold from the payment. On September 30, 2003, the withholding agent receives from the foreign corporation a valid Form W-8 described in paragraph (e)(2)(ii) of this section. Thus, the interest qualifies as portfolio interest retroactively to June 15, 2001 (the date of payment). See § 1.871-14(c)(3). The foreign corporation does not file a U.S. federal income tax return and does not pay the tax owed. The withholding agent is not liable under section 1461 for the 30-percent tax on the interest income because the receipt of the Form W-8 exempts the interest from tax for purposes of sections 881(a) and 1461. The withholding agent, however, is liable for interest on the amount of withholding that should have been deducted from the payment on June 15, 2001 and deposited. Under paragraph (b)(7)(iii) of this section, the period during which interest may be assessed against the withholding agent runs from March 15, 2002 (the due date for the Form 1042 relating to the payment) until September 30, 2003 (i.e., the date that appropriate documentation is furnished to the withholding agent).

Example 2. On June 15, 2001, a withholding agent pays U.S. source dividends to a foreign corporation that it cannot reliably associate with a Form W-8 or other appropriate documentation upon which to rely to treat the beneficial owner as a foreign person. The withholding agent does not withhold from the payment. On September 30, 2003, the withholding agent receives from the foreign corporation a valid Form W-8 described in paragraph (e)(2)(ii) of this section claiming a reduced 15-percent rate of withholding under a U.S. income tax treaty. The dividend qualifies for the reduced treaty rate retroactively to June 15, 2001, (the date of payment). The foreign corporation does not file a U.S. federal income tax return and does not pay the tax owed. Under section 1461, the withholding agent is liable only for a 15-percent tax on the dividend income because the receipt of the Form W-8 allows the tax rate to be reduced for purposes of sections 881(a) and 1461 from 30-percent to 15-percent. The withholding agent, however, is liable for interest on the full 30-percent amount that should have been deducted and withheld from the payment on June 15, 2001, and deposited, over a period running from March 15, 2002, (the due date for the Form 1042 relating to the payment) until September 30, 2003, (the date that the appropriate documentation is furnished to the withholding agent supporting a reduction in rate under a tax treaty). Additional interest may be assessed relating to the outstanding 15-percent tax liability (i.e., the portion of the 30-percent total tax liability that is not reduced under the treaty). Such additional interest runs from March 15, 2002, until such date as that 15-percent tax liability is satisfied by the withholding agent or the taxpayer (subject to abatement in order to avoid a double interest charge).

(8) *Adjustments, refunds, or credits of overwithheld amounts.*—If the amount withheld under section 1441, 1442, or 1443 is greater than the tax due by the withholding agent or the taxpayer, adjustments may be made in accordance with the procedures described in § 1.1461-2(a). Alternatively, refunds or credits may be claimed in accordance with the procedures described in § 1.1464-1, relating to refunds or credits claimed by the beneficial owner, or § 1.6414-1, relating to refunds or credits claimed by the withholding agent. If an amount was withheld under section 3406 or is subsequently determined to have been paid to a foreign person, see paragraph (b)(3)(vii) of this section and § 31.6413(a)-3(a)(1) of this chapter.

(9) *Payments to joint owners.*—A payment to joint owners that requires documentation in order to reduce the rate of withholding under chapter 3 of the Code and the regulations thereunder does not qualify for such reduced rate unless the withholding agent can reliably associate the payment with documentation from each owner. Notwithstanding the preceding sentence, a payment to joint owners qualifies as a payment exempt from withholding under this section if any one of the owners provides a certificate of U.S. status on a Form W-9 in accordance with paragraph (d)(2) or (3) of this section or the withholding agent can associate the payment with an intermediary or flow-through withholding certificate upon which it can rely to treat the payment as made to a U.S. payee under paragraph (d)(4) of this section. See § 31.3406(h)-2(a)(3)(i)(B) of this chapter.

(c) *Definitions.*—(1) *Withholding.*—The term *withholding* means the deduction and withholding of tax at the applicable rate from the payment.

(2) *Foreign and U.S. person.*—The term *foreign person* means a nonresident alien individual, a foreign corporation, a foreign partnership, a foreign trust, a foreign estate, and any other person that is not a U.S. person described in the next sentence. Solely for purposes of the regulations under chapter 3 of the Internal Revenue Code, the term *foreign person* also means, with respect to a payment by a withholding agent, a foreign branch of a U.S. person that furnishes an intermediary withholding certificate described in paragraph (e)(3)(ii) of this section. Such a branch continues to be a U.S. payor for purposes of chapter 61 of the Internal Revenue Code. See

§ 1.6049-5(c)(4). A U.S. person is a person described in section 7701(a)(30), the U.S. government (including an agency or instrumentality thereof), a State (including an agency or instrumentality thereof), or the District of Columbia (including an agency or instrumentality thereof).

(3) *Individual.*—(i) *Alien individual.*—The term *alien individual* means an individual who is not a citizen or a national of the United States. See § 1.1-1(c).

(ii) *Nonresident alien individual.*—The term *nonresident alien individual* means a person described in section 7701(b)(1)(B), an alien individual who is a resident of a foreign country under the residence article of an income tax treaty and § 301.7701(b)-7(a)(1) of this chapter, or an alien individual who is a resident of Puerto Rico, Guam, the Commonwealth of Northern Mariana Islands, the U.S. Virgin Islands, or American Samoa as determined under § 301.7701(b)-1(d) of this chapter. An alien individual who has made an election under section 6013(g) or (h) to be treated as a resident of the United States is nevertheless treated as a nonresident alien individual for purposes of withholding under chapter 3 of the Code and the regulations thereunder.

(4) *Certain foreign corporations.*—For purposes of this section, a corporation created or organized in Guam, the Commonwealth of Northern Mariana Islands, the U.S. Virgin Islands, and American Samoa, is not treated as a foreign corporation if the requirements of sections 881(b)(1)(A), (B), and (C) are met for such corporation. Further, a payment made to a foreign government or an international organization shall be treated as a payment made to a foreign corporation for purposes of withholding under chapter 3 of the Code and the regulations thereunder.

(5) *Financial institution and foreign financial institution.*—For purposes of the regulations under chapter 3 of the Code, the term *financial institution* means a person described in § 1.165-12(c)(1)(iv) (not including a person providing pension or other similar benefits or a regulated investment company or other mutual fund, unless otherwise indicated) and the term *foreign financial institution* means a financial institution that is a foreign person, as defined in paragraph (c)(2) of this section.

(6) *Beneficial owner.*—(i) *General rule.*—This paragraph (c)(6) defines the term *beneficial owner* for payments of income other than a payment for which a reduced rate of withholding is claimed under an income tax treaty. The term *beneficial owner* means the person who is the owner of the income for tax purposes and who beneficially owns that income. A person shall be treated as the owner of the income to the extent that it is required under U.S. tax principles to include the amount paid in gross income under section 61 (determined without regard to an exclusion or exemption from gross income under the Internal Revenue Code). Beneficial ownership of income is determined under the provisions of section 7701(l) and the regulations under that section and any other applicable general U.S. tax principles, including principles governing the determination of whether a transaction is a conduit transaction. Thus, a person receiving income in a capacity as a nominee, agent, or custodian for another person is not the beneficial owner of the income. In the case of a scholarship, the student receiving the scholarship is the beneficial owner of that scholarship. In the case of a payment of an amount that is not income, the beneficial owner determination shall be made under this paragraph (c)(6) as if the amount were income.

(ii) *Special rules.*—(A) *General rule.*—The beneficial owners of income paid to an entity described in this paragraph (c)(6)(ii) are those persons described in paragraphs (c)(6)(ii)(B) through (D) of this section.

(B) *Foreign partnerships.*—The beneficial owners of income paid to a foreign partnership (whether a nonwithholding or a withholding foreign partnership) are the partners in the partnership, unless they themselves are not the beneficial owners of the income under this paragraph (c)(6). For example, a partnership (first tier) that is a partner in another partnership (second tier) is not the beneficial owner of income paid to the second tier partnership since the first tier partnership is not the owner of the income under U.S. tax principles. Rather, the partners of the first tier partnership are the beneficial owners (to the extent they are not themselves persons that are not beneficial owners under this paragraph (c)(6)). See § 1.1441-5(b) for applicable withholding procedures for payments to a domestic partnership. See also § 1.1441-5(c)(3)(ii) for applicable withholding procedures for payments to a foreign partnership where one of the partners (at any level in the chain of tiers) is a domestic partnership.

(C) *Foreign simple trusts and foreign grantor trusts.*—The beneficial owners of income paid to a foreign simple trust, as described in paragraph (c)(23) of this section, are the beneficiaries of the trust, unless they themselves are not the beneficial owners of the income under this paragraph (c)(6). The beneficial owners of income paid to a foreign grantor trust, as described in paragraph (c)(26) of this section, are the persons treated as the owners of the trust, unless they themselves are not the beneficial owners of the income under this paragraph (c)(6).

(D) *Other foreign trusts and foreign estates.*—The beneficial owner of income paid to a foreign complex trust as defined in paragraph (c)(25) of this section or to a foreign estate is the foreign complex trust or estate itself.

(7) *Withholding agent.*—For a definition of the term *withholding agent* and applicable rules, see § 1.1441-7.

(8) *Person.*—For purposes of the regulations under chapter 3 of the Code, the term *person* shall mean a person described in section 7701(a)(1) and the regulations under that section and a U.S. branch to the extent treated as a U.S. person under paragraph (b)(2)(iv) of this section. For purposes of the regulations under chapter 3 of the Code, the term *person* does not include a wholly-owned entity that is disregarded for federal tax purposes under § 301.7701-2(c)(2) of this chapter as an entity separate from its owner. See paragraph (b)(2)(iii) of this section for procedures applicable to payments to such entities.

(9) *Source of income.*—The source of income is determined under the provisions of part I (section 861 and following), subchapter N, chapter 1 of the Code and the regulations under those provisions.

(10) *Chapter 3 of the Code.*—For purposes of the regulations under sections 1441, 1442, and 1443, any reference to chapter 3 of the Code shall not include references to sections 1445 and 1446, unless the context indicates otherwise.

(11) *Reduced rate.*—For purposes of regulations under chapter 3 of the Code, and other withholding provisions of the Code, the term *reduced rate*, when used in regulations under chapter 3 of the Code, shall include an exemption from tax.

(12) *Payee.*—For purposes of chapter 3 of the Internal Revenue Code, the term *payee* of a payment is determined under paragraph (b)(2) of this section, § 1.1441-5(c)(1) (relating to partnerships), and § 1.1441-5(e)(2) and (3) (relating to trusts and estates) and includes foreign persons, U.S. exempt recipients, and U.S. nonexempt recipients. A nonqualified intermediary and a qualified intermediary (to the extent it does not assume primary withholding responsibility) are not payees if they are acting as intermediaries and not the beneficial owner of income. In addition, a flow-through entity is not a payee unless the income is (or is deemed to be) effectively connected with the conduct of a trade or business in the United States. See § 1.6049-5(d)(1) for rules to determine the payee for purposes of chapter 61 of the Internal Revenue Code. See § § 1.1441-1(b)(3), 1.1441-5(d), and (e)(6) and 1.6049-5(d)(3) for presumption rules that apply if a payee's identity cannot be determined on the basis of valid documentation.

(13) *Intermediary.*—An *intermediary* means, with respect to a payment that it receives, a person that, for that payment, acts as a custodian, broker, nominee, or otherwise as an agent for another person, regardless of whether such other person is the beneficial owner of the amount paid, a flow-through entity, or another intermediary.

(14) *Nonqualified intermediary.*—A *nonqualified intermediary* means any intermediary that is not a U.S. person and not a qualified intermediary, as defined in paragraph (e)(5)(ii) of this section, or a qualified intermediary that is not acting in its capacity as a qualified intermediary with respect to a payment. For example, to the extent an entity that is a qualified intermediary provides another withholding agent with a foreign beneficial owner withholding certificate as defined in paragraph (e)(2)(i) of this section, the entity is not acting in its capacity as a qualified intermediary. Notwithstanding the preceding sentence, a qualified intermediary is acting as a qualified intermediary to the extent it provides another withholding agent with Forms W-9, or other information regarding U.S. non-exempt recipients pursuant to its qualified intermediary agreement with the IRS.

(15) *Qualified intermediary.*—The term *qualified intermediary* is defined in paragraph (e)(5)(ii) of this section.

(16) *Withholding certificate.*—The term *withholding certificate* means a Form W-8 described in paragraph (e)(2)(i) of this section (relating to foreign beneficial owners), paragraph (e)(3)(i) of this section (relating to foreign intermediaries), § 1.1441-5(c)(2)(iv), (c)(3)(iii), and (e)(3)(iv) (relating to flow-through entities), a Form 8233 described in § 1.1441-4(b)(2), a Form W-9 as described in paragraph (d) of this section, a statement described in § 1.871-14(c)(2)(v) (relating to portfolio interest), or any other certificates that under the Internal Revenue Code or regulations certifies or establishes the status of a payee or beneficial owner as a U.S. or a foreign person.

(17) *Documentary evidence: other appropriate documentation.*—The terms *documentary evidence* or *other appropriate documentation* re-

fer to documents other than a withholding certificate that may be provided for payments made outside the United States to offshore accounts or any other evidence that under the Internal Revenue Code or regulations certifies or establishes the status of a payee or beneficial owner as a U.S. or foreign person. See §§ 1.1441-6(b)(2), (c)(3) and (4) (relating to treaty benefits), and 1.6049-5(c)(1) and (4) (relating to chapter 61 reporting). Also see § 1.1441-4(a)(3)(ii) regarding documentary evidence for notional principal contracts.

(18) *Documentation.*—The term *documentation* refers to both withholding certificates, as defined in paragraph (c)(16) of this section, and documentary evidence or other appropriate documentation, as defined in paragraph (c)(17) of this section.

(19) *Payor.*—The term *payor* is defined in § 31.3406(a)-2 of this chapter and § 1.6049-4(a)(2) and generally includes a withholding agent, as defined in § 1.1441-7(a). The term also includes any person that makes a payment to an intermediary, flow-through entity, or U.S. branch that is not treated as a U.S. person to the extent the intermediary, flow-through, or U.S. branch provides a Form W-9 or other appropriate information relating to a payee so that the payment can be reported under chapter 61 of the Internal Revenue Code and, if required, subject to backup withholding under section 3406. This latter rule does not preclude the intermediary, flow-through entity, or U.S. branch from also being a payor.

(20) *Exempt recipient.*—The term *exempt recipient* means a person that is exempt from reporting under chapter 61 of the Internal Revenue Code and backup withholding under section 3406 and that is described in §§ 1.6041-3(q), 1.6045-2(b)(2)(i), and 1.6049-4(c)(1)(ii), and § 5f.6045-1(c)(3)(i)(B) of this chapter. Exempt recipients are not exempt from withholding under chapter 3 of the Internal Revenue Code unless they are U.S. persons or foreign persons entitled to an exemption from withholding under chapter 3.

(21) *Non-exempt recipient.*—A *non-exempt recipient* is any person that is not an exempt recipient under paragraph (c)(20) of this section.

(22) *Reportable amounts.*—*Reportable amounts* are defined in paragraph (e)(3)(vi) of this section.

(23) *Flow-through entity.*—A *flow-through entity* means any entity that is described in this paragraph (c)(23) and that may provide documentation on behalf of others to a withholding agent. The entities described in this paragraph are a foreign partnership (other than a withholding foreign partnership), a foreign simple trust (other than a withholding foreign trust) that is described in paragraph (c)(24) of this section, a foreign grantor trust (other than a withholding foreign trust) that is described in paragraph (c)(25) of this section, or, for any payments for which a reduced rate of withholding under an income tax treaty is claimed, any entity to the extent the entity is considered to be fiscally transparent under section 894 with respect to the payment by an interest holder's jurisdiction.

(24) *Foreign simple trust.*—A *foreign simple trust* is a foreign trust that is described in section 651(a).

(25) *Foreign complex trust.*—A *foreign complex trust* is a foreign trust other than a trust described in section 651(a) or sections 671 through 679.

(26) *Foreign grantor trust.*—A *foreign grantor trust* is a foreign trust but only to the extent all or a portion of the income of the trust is treated as owned by the grantor or another person under sections 671 through 679.

(27) *Partnership.*—The term *partnership* means any entity treated as a partnership under § 301.7701-2 or -3 of this chapter.

(28) *Nonwithholding foreign partnership.*—A *nonwithholding foreign partnership* is a foreign partnership that is not a withholding foreign partnership, as defined in § 1.1441-5(c)(2)(i).

(29) *Withholding foreign partnership.*—A withholding foreign partnership is defined in § 1.1441-5(c)(2)(i).

(d) *Beneficial owner's or payee's claim of U.S. status.*—(1) *In general.*—Under paragraph (b)(1) of this section, a withholding agent is not required to withhold under chapter 3 of the Code on payments to a U.S. payee, to a person presumed to be a U.S. payee in accordance with the provisions of paragraph (b)(3) of this section, or to a person that the withholding agent may treat as a U.S. beneficial owner of the payment. Absent actual knowledge or reason to know otherwise, a withholding agent may rely on the provisions of this paragraph (d) in order to determine whether to treat a payee or beneficial owner as a U.S. person.

(2) *Payments for which a Form W-9 is otherwise required.*—A withholding agent may treat as a U.S. payee any person who is required to furnish a Form W-9 and who furnishes it in accordance with the procedures described in §§ 31.3406(d)-1 through 31.3406(d)-5 of this chapter (including the re-

quirement that the payee furnish its taxpayer identifying number (TIN)) if the withholding agent meets all the requirements described in § 31.3406(h)-3(e) of this chapter regarding reliance by a payor on a Form W-9. Providing a Form W-9 or valid substitute form shall serve as a statement that the person whose name is on the form is a U.S. person. Therefore, a foreign person, including a U.S. branch treated as a U.S. person under paragraph (b)(2)(iv) of this section, shall not provide a Form W-9. A U.S. branch of a foreign person may establish its status as a foreign person exempt from reporting under chapter 61 and backup withholding under section 3406 by providing a withholding certificate on Form W-8.

(3) *Payments for which a Form W-9 is not otherwise required.*—In the case of a payee who is not required to furnish a Form W-9 under section 3406 (e.g., a person exempt from reporting under chapter 61 of the Internal Revenue Code), the withholding agent may treat the payee as a U.S. payee if the payee provides the withholding agent with a Form W-9 or a substitute form described in § 31.3406(h)-3(c)(2) of this chapter (relating to forms for exempt recipients) that contains the payee's name, address, and TIN. The form must be signed under penalties of perjury by the payee if so required by the form or by § 31.3406(h)-3 of this chapter. Providing a Form W-9 or valid substitute form shall serve as a statement that the person whose name is on the certificate is a U.S. person. A Form W-9 or valid substitute form shall not be provided by a foreign person, including any U.S. branch of a foreign person whether or not the branch is treated as a U.S. person under paragraph (b)(2)(iv) of this section. See paragraph (e)(3)(v) of this section for withholding certificates provided by U.S. branches described in paragraph (b)(2)(iv) of this section. The procedures described in § 31.3406(h)-2(a) of this chapter shall apply to payments to joint payees. A withholding agent that receives a Form W-9 to satisfy this paragraph (d)(3) must retain the form in accordance with the provisions of § 31.3406(h)-3(g) of this chapter, if applicable, or of paragraph (e)(4)(iii) of this section (relating to the retention of withholding certificates) if § 31.3406(h)-3(g) of this chapter does not apply. The rules of this paragraph (d)(3) are only intended to provide a method by which a withholding agent may determine that a payee is a U.S. person and do not otherwise impose a requirement that documentation be furnished by a person who is otherwise treated as an exempt recipient for purposes of the applicable information reporting provisions under chapter 61 of the Internal Revenue Code (e.g., § 1.6049-4(c)(1)(ii) for payments of interest).

(4) *When a payment to an intermediary or flow-through entity may be treated as made to a U.S. payee.*—A withholding agent that makes a payment to an intermediary (whether a qualified intermediary or nonqualified intermediary), a flow-through entity, or a U.S. branch described in paragraph (b)(2)(iv) of this section may treat the payment as made to a U.S. payee to the extent that, prior to the payment, the withholding agent can reliably associate the payment with a Form W-9 described in paragraph (d)(2) or (3) of this section attached to a valid intermediary, flow-through, or U.S. branch withholding certificate described in paragraph (e)(3)(i) of this section or to the extent the withholding agent can reliably associate the payment with a Form W-8 described in paragraph (e)(3)(v) of this section that evidences an agreement to treat a U.S. branch described in paragraph (b)(2)(iv) of this section as a U.S. person. In addition, a withholding agent may treat the payment as made to a U.S. payee only if it complies with the electronic confirmation procedures described in paragraph (e)(4)(v) of this section, if required, and it has not been notified by the IRS that any of the information on the withholding certificate or other documentation is incorrect or unreliable. In the case of a Form W-9 that is required to be furnished for a reportable payment that may be subject to backup withholding, the withholding agent may be notified in accordance with section 3406(a)(1)(B) and the regulations under that section. See applicable procedures under section 3406(a)(1)(B) and the regulations under that section for payors who have been notified with regard to such a Form W-9. Withholding agents who have been notified in relation to other Forms W-9, including under section 6724(b) pursuant to section 6721, may rely on the withholding certificate or other documentation only to the extent provided under procedures as prescribed by the IRS (see § 601.601(d)(2) of this chapter).

(e) *Beneficial owner's claim of foreign status.*—(1) *Withholding agent's reliance.*—(i) *In general.*—Absent actual knowledge or reason to know otherwise, a withholding agent may treat a payment as made to a foreign beneficial owner in accordance with the provisions of paragraph (e)(1)(ii) of this section. See paragraph (e)(4)(viii) of this section for applicable reliance rules. See paragraph (b)(4) of this section for a description of payments for which a claim of foreign status is relevant for purposes of claiming a reduced rate of withholding for purposes of section 1441, 1442, or 1443. See paragraph (b)(5) of this section for a list of payments for which a claim of foreign status is relevant for other purposes, such as claiming an exemption from information reporting under chapter 61 of the Code.

(ii) *Payments that a withholding agent may treat as made to a foreign person that is a beneficial owner.*—(A) *General rule.*—The withholding agent may treat a payment as made to a foreign person that is a beneficial owner if it complies with the requirements described in paragraph (e)(1)(ii)(B) of this section and, then, only to the extent—

(1) That the withholding agent can reliably associate the payment with a beneficial owner withholding certificate described in paragraph (e)(2) of this section furnished by the person whose name is on the certificate or attached to a valid foreign intermediary, flow-through, or U.S. branch withholding certificate;

(2) That the payment is made outside the United States (within the meaning of § 1.6049-5(e)) to an offshore account (within the meaning of § 1.6049-5(c)(1)) and the withholding agent can reliably associate the payment with documentary evidence described in §§ 1.1441-6(c)(3) or (4), or 1.6049-5(c)(1) relating to the beneficial owner;

(3) That the withholding agent can reliably associate the payment with a valid qualified intermediary withholding certificate, as described in paragraph (e)(3)(ii) of this section, and the qualified intermediary has provided sufficient information for the withholding agent to allocate the payment to a withholding rate pool other than a withholding rate pool or pools established for U.S. non-exempt recipients;

(4) That the withholding agent can reliably associate the payment with a withholding certificate described in § 1.1441-5(c)(3)(iii) or (e)(5)(iii) from a flow-through entity claiming the income is effectively connected income;

(5) That the withholding agent identifies the payee as a U.S. branch described in paragraph (b)(2)(iv) of this section, the payment to which it treats as effectively connected income in accordance with § 1.1441-4(a)(2)(ii) or (3);

(6) That the withholding agent identifies the payee as an international organization (or any wholly-owned agency or instrumentality thereof) as defined in section 7701(a)(18) that has been designated as such by executive order (pursuant to 22 U.S.C. 288 through 288(f)); or

(7) That the withholding agent pays interest from bankers' acceptances and identifies the payee as a foreign central bank of issue (as defined in § 1.861-2(b)(4)).

(B) *Additional requirements.*—In order for a payment described in paragraph (e)(1)(ii)(A) of this section to be treated as made to a foreign beneficial owner, the withholding agent must hold the documentation (if required) prior to the payment, comply with the electronic confirmation procedures described in paragraph (e)(4)(v) of this section (if required), and must not have been notified by the IRS that any of the information on the withholding certificate or other documentation is incorrect or unreliable. If the withholding agent has been so notified, it may rely on the withholding certificate or other documentation only to the extent provided under procedures prescribed by the IRS (see § 601.601(d)(2) of this chapter). See paragraph (b)(2)(vii) of this section for rules regarding reliable association of a payment with a withholding certificate or other appropriate documentation.

(2) *Beneficial owner withholding certificate.*—(i) *In general.*—A beneficial owner withholding certificate is a statement by which the beneficial owner of the payment represents that it is a foreign person and, if applicable, claims a reduced rate of withholding under section 1441. A separate withholding certificate must be submitted to each withholding agent. If the beneficial owner receives more than one type of payment from a single withholding agent, the beneficial owner may have to submit more than one withholding certificate to the single withholding agent for the different types of payments as may be required by the applicable forms and instructions, or as the withholding agent may require (such as to facilitate the withholding agent's compliance with its obligations to determine withholding under this section or the reporting of the amounts under § 1.1461-1(b) and (c)). For example, if a beneficial owner claims that some but not all of the income it receives is effectively connected with the conduct of a trade or business in the United States, it may be required to submit two separate withholding certificates, one for income that is not effectively connected and one for income that is so connected. See § 1.1441-6(b)(2) for special rules for determining who must furnish a beneficial owner withholding certificate when a benefit is claimed under an income tax treaty. See paragraph (e)(4)(ix) of this section for reliance rules in the case of certificates held by another person or at a different branch location of the same person.

(ii) *Requirements for validity of certificate.*—A beneficial owner withholding certificate is valid only if it is provided on a Form W-8, or a Form 8233 in the case of personal services income described in § 1.1441-4(b) or certain scholarship or grant amounts described in § 1.1441-4(c) (or a substitute form described in paragraph (e)(4)(vi) of this section, or such other form as the IRS may prescribe). A Form

W-8 is valid only if its validity period has not expired, it is signed under penalties of perjury by the beneficial owner, and it contains all of the information required on the form. The required information is the beneficial owner's name, permanent residence address, and TIN (if required), the country under the laws of which the beneficial owner is created, incorporated, or governed (if a person other than an individual), the classification of the entity, and such other information as may be required by the regulations under section 1441 or by the form or accompanying instructions in addition to, or in lieu of, the information described in this paragraph (e)(2)(ii). A person's permanent residence address is an address in the country where the person claims to be a resident for purposes of that country's income tax. In the case of a certificate furnished in order to claim a reduced rate of withholding under an income tax treaty, the residence must be determined in the manner prescribed under the applicable treaty. See § 1.1441-6(b). The address of a financial institution with which the beneficial owner maintains an account, a post office box, or an address used solely for mailing purposes is not a residence address for this purpose. If the beneficial owner is an individual who does not have a tax residence in any country, the permanent residence address is the place at which the beneficial owner normally resides. If the beneficial owner is not an individual and does not have a tax residence in any country, then the permanent residence address is the place at which the person maintains its principal office. See paragraph (e)(4)(vii) of this section for circumstances in which a TIN is required on a beneficial owner withholding certificate. See paragraph (f)(2)(i) of this section for continued validity of certificates during a transition period.

(3) *Intermediary, flow-through, or U.S. branch withholding certificate.*—(i) *In general.*—An intermediary withholding certificate is a Form W-8 by which a payee represents that it is a foreign person and that it is an intermediary (whether a qualified or nonqualified intermediary) with respect to a payment and not the beneficial owner. See paragraphs (e)(3)(ii) and (iii) of this section. A flow-through withholding certificate is a Form W-8 used by a flow-through entity as defined in paragraph (c)(23) of this section. See § 1.1441-5(c)(3)(iii) (a nonwithholding foreign partnership), § 1.1441-5(e)(5)(iii) (a foreign simple trust or foreign grantor trust) or § 1.1441-6(b)(2) (foreign entity presenting claims on behalf of its interest holders for a reduced rate of withholding under an income tax treaty). A U.S. branch certificate is a Form W-8 furnished under paragraph (e)(3)(v) of this section by a U.S. branch described in paragraph (b)(2)(iv) of this section. See paragraph (e)(4)(viii) of this section for applicable reliance rules.

(ii) *Intermediary withholding certificate from a qualified intermediary.*—A qualified intermediary shall provide a qualified intermediary withholding certificate for reportable amounts received by the qualified intermediary. See paragraph (e)(3)(vi) of this section for the definition of reportable amount. A qualified intermediary-withholding certificate is valid only if it is furnished on a Form W-8, an acceptable substitute form, or such other form as the IRS may prescribe, it is signed under penalties of perjury by a person with authority to sign for the qualified intermediary, its validity has not expired, and it contains the following information, statement, and certifications—

(A) The name, permanent residence address (as described in paragraph (e)(2)(ii) of this section), qualified intermediary employer identification number (QI-EIN), and the country under the laws of which the intermediary is created, incorporated, or governed. A qualified intermediary that does not act in its capacity as a qualified intermediary must not use its QI-EIN. Rather the intermediary should provide a nonqualified intermediary withholding certificate, if it is acting as an intermediary, and should use the taxpayer identification number, if any, that it uses for all other purposes;

(B) A certification that, with respect to accounts it identifies on its withholding statement (as described in paragraph (e)(5)(v) of this section), the qualified intermediary is not acting for its own account but is acting as a qualified intermediary;

(C) A certification that the qualified intermediary has provided, or will provide, a withholding statement as required by paragraph (e)(5)(v) of this section; and

(D) Any other information, certifications, or statements as may be required by the form or accompanying instructions in addition to, or in lieu of, the information and certifications described in this paragraph (e)(3)(ii) or paragraph (e)(3)(v) of this section. See paragraph (e)(5)(v) of this section for the requirements of a withholding statement associated with the qualified intermediary withholding certificate.

(iii) *Intermediary withholding certificate from a nonqualified intermediary.*—A nonqualified intermediary shall provide a nonqualified intermediary withholding certificate for reportable amounts received by the nonqualified intermediary. See paragraph (e)(3)(vi) of this section for the definition of reportable amount. A nonqualified intermediary withholding certificate is valid only to the extent it is furnished on a Form W-8, an acceptable substitute form, or such other form as the IRS may prescribe, it is signed under penalties of perjury by a person authorized to sign for the nonqualified intermediary, it contains the information, statements, and certifications described in this paragraph (e)(3)(iii) and paragraph (e)(3)(iv) of this section, its validity has not expired, and the withholding certificates and other appropriate documentation for all persons to whom the certificate relates are associated with the certificate. Withholding certificates and other appropriate documentation consist of beneficial owner withholding certificates described in paragraph (e)(2)(i) of this section, intermediary and flow-through withholding certificates described in paragraph (e)(3)(i) of this section, withholding foreign partnership certificates described in § 1.1441-5(c)(2)(iv), documentary evidence described in §§ 1.1441-6(c)(3) or (4) and 1.6049-5(c)(1), and any other documentation or certificates applicable under other provisions of the Internal Revenue Code or regulations that certify or establish the status of the payee or beneficial owner as a U.S. or a foreign person. If a nonqualified intermediary is acting on behalf of another nonqualified intermediary or a flow-through entity, then the nonqualified intermediary must associate with its own withholding certificate the other nonqualified intermediary withholding certificate or the flow-through withholding certificate and separately identify all of the withholding certificates and other appropriate documentation that are associated with the withholding certificate of the other nonqualified intermediary or flow-through entity. Nothing in this paragraph (e)(3)(iii) shall require an intermediary to furnish original documentation. Copies of certificates or documentary evidence may be transmitted to the U.S. withholding agent, in which case the nonqualified intermediary must retain the original documentation for the same time period that the copy is required to be retained by the withholding agent under paragraph (e)(4)(iii) of this section and must provide it to the withholding agent upon request. For purposes of this paragraph (e)(3)(iii), a valid intermediary withholding certificate also includes a statement described in § 1.871-14(c)(2)(v) furnished for interest to qualify as portfolio interest for purposes of sections 871(h) and 881(c). The information and certifications required on a Form W-8 described in this paragraph (e)(3)(iii) are as follows—

(A) The name and permanent resident address (as described in paragraph (e)(2)(ii) of this section) of the nonqualified intermediary, and the country under the laws of which the nonqualified intermediary is created, incorporated, or governed;

(B) A certification that the nonqualified intermediary is not acting for its own account;

(C) If the nonqualified intermediary withholding certificate is used to transmit withholding certificates or other appropriate documentation for more than one person on whose behalf the nonqualified intermediary is acting, a withholding statement associated with the Form W-8 that provides all the information required by paragraph (e)(3)(iv) of this section; and

(D) Any other information, certifications, or statements as may be required by the form or accompanying instructions in addition to, or in lieu of, the information, certifications, and statements described in this paragraph (e)(3)(iii) or paragraph (e)(5)(iv) of this section.

(iv) *Withholding statement provided by nonqualified intermediary.*—(A) *In general.*—A nonqualified intermediary shall provide a withholding statement required by this paragraph (e)(3)(iv) to the extent the nonqualified intermediary is required to furnish, or does furnish, documentation for payees on whose behalf it receives reportable amounts (as defined in paragraph (e)(3)(vi) of this section) or to the extent it otherwise provides the documentation of such payees to a withholding agent. A nonqualified intermediary is not required to disclose information regarding persons for whom it collects reportable amounts unless it has actual knowledge that any such person is a U.S. non-exempt recipient as defined in paragraph (c)(21) of this section. Information regarding U.S. non-exempt recipients required under this paragraph (e)(3)(iv) must be provided irrespective of any requirement under foreign law that prohibits the disclosure of the identity of an account holder of a nonqualified intermediary or financial information relating to such account holder. Although a nonqualified intermediary is not required to provide documentation and other information required by this paragraph (e)(3)(iv) for persons other than U.S. non-exempt recipients, a withholding agent that does not receive documentation and such information must apply the presumption rules of paragraph (b) of this section, §§ 1.1441-5(d) and (e)(6) and 1.6049-5(d) or the withholding agent shall be liable for tax, interest, and penalties. A withholding agent must apply the presumption rules even if it is not required under chapter 61 of the Internal Revenue Code to obtain documentation to treat a payee as an exempt recipient and even though it has actual knowledge that the payee is a U.S. person. For example, if a nonqualified intermediary fails to provide a withholding agent with a Form W-9 for an account holder

Reg. § 1.1441-1(e)(3)(iv)(A)

that is a U.S. exempt recipient, the withholding agent must presume (even if it has actual knowledge that the account holder is a U.S. exempt recipient), that the account holder is an undocumented foreign person with respect to amounts subject to withholding. See paragraph (b)(3)(v) of this section for applicable presumptions. Therefore, the withholding agent must withhold 30 percent from the payment even though if a Form W-9 had been provided, no withholding or reporting on the payment attributable to a U.S. exempt recipient would apply. Further, a nonqualified intermediary that fails to provide the documentation and the information under this paragraph (e)(3)(iv) for another withholding agent to report the payments on Forms 1042-S and Forms 1099 is not relieved of its responsibility to file information returns. See paragraph (b)(6) of this section. Therefore, unless the nonqualified intermediary itself files such returns and provides copies to the payees, it shall be liable for penalties under sections 6721 (failure to file information returns), and 6722 (failure to furnish payee statements), including the penalties under those sections for intentional failure to file information returns. In addition, failure to provide either the documentation or the information required by this paragraph (e)(3)(iv) results in a payment not being reliably associated with valid documentation. Therefore, the beneficial owners of the payment are not entitled to reduced rates of withholding and if the full amount required to be held under the presumption rules is not withheld by the withholding agent, the nonqualified intermediary must withhold the difference between the amount withheld by the withholding agent and the amount required to be withheld. Failure to withhold shall result in the nonqualified intermediary being liable for tax under section 1461, interest, and penalties, including penalties under section 6656 (failure to deposit) and section 6672 (failure to collect and pay over tax).

(B) *General requirements.*—A withholding statement must be provided prior to the payment of a reportable amount and must contain the information specified in paragraph (e)(3)(iv)(C) of this section. The statement must be updated as often as required to keep the information in the withholding statement correct prior to each subsequent payment. The withholding statement forms an integral part of the withholding certificate provided under paragraph (e)(3)(iii) of this section, and the penalties of perjury statement provided on the withholding certificate shall apply to the withholding statement. The withholding statement may be provided in any manner the nonqualified intermediary and the withholding agent mutually agree, including electronically. If the withholding statement is provided electronically, there must be sufficient safeguards to ensure that the information received by the withholding agent is the information sent by the nonqualified intermediary and all occasions of user access that result in the submission or modification of the withholding statement information must be recorded. In addition, an electronic system must be capable of providing a hard copy of all withholding statements provided by the nonqualified intermediary. A withholding agent will be liable for tax, interest, and penalties in accordance with paragraph (b)(7) of this section to the extent it does not follow the presumption rules of paragraph (b)(3) of this section or §§1.1441-5(d) and (e)(6), and 1.6049-5(d) for any payment of a reportable amount, or portion thereof, for which it does not have a valid withholding statement prior to making a payment.

(C) *Content of withholding statement.*—The withholding statement provided by a nonqualified intermediary must contain the information required by this paragraph (e)(3)(iv)(C).

(1) The withholding statement must contain the name, address, TIN (if any) and the type of documentation (documentary evidence, Form W-9, or type of Form W-8) for every person from whom documentation has been received by the nonqualified intermediary and provided to the withholding agent and whether that person is a U.S. exempt recipient, a U.S. non-exempt recipient, or a foreign person. See paragraphs (c)(2), (20), and (21) of this section for the definitions of foreign person, U.S. exempt recipient, and U.S. non-exempt recipient. In the case of a foreign person, the statement must indicate whether the foreign person is a beneficial owner or an intermediary, flow-through entity, or U.S. branch described in paragraph (b)(2)(iv) of this section and include the type of recipient, based on recipient codes used for filing Forms 1042-S, if the foreign person is a recipient as defined in §1.1461-1 (c)(1)(ii).

(2) The withholding statement must allocate each payment, by income type, to every payee (including U.S. exempt recipients) for whom documentation has been provided. Any payment that cannot be reliably associated with valid documentation from a payee shall be treated as made to an unknown payee in accordance with the presumption rules of paragraph (b) of this section and §§1.1441-5(d) and (e)(6) and 1.6049-5(d). For this purpose, a type of income is determined by the types of income required to be reported on Forms 1042-S or 1099, as appropriate. Notwithstanding the preceding sentence, deposit interest (including original issue discount) described in section

871(i)(2)(A) or 881(d) and interest or original issue discount on short-term obligations as described in section 871(g)(1)(B) or 881(e) is only required to be allocated to the extent it is required to be reported on Form 1099 or Form 1042-S. See § 1.6049-8 (regarding reporting of bank deposit interest to certain foreign persons). If a payee receives income through another nonqualified intermediary, flow-through entity, or U.S. branch described in paragraph (e)(2)(iv) of this section (other than a U.S. branch treated as a U.S. person), the withholding statement must also state, with respect to the payee, the name, address, and TIN, if known, of the other nonqualified intermediary or U.S. branch from which the payee directly receives the payment or the flow-through entity in which the payee has a direct ownership interest. If another nonqualified intermediary, flow-through entity, or U.S. branch fails to allocate a payment, the name of the nonqualified intermediary, flow-through entity, or U.S. branch that failed to allocate the payment shall be provided with respect to such payment.

(3) If a payee is identified as a foreign person, the nonqualified intermediary must specify the rate of withholding to which the payee is subject, the payee's country of residence and, if a reduced rate of withholding is claimed, the basis for that reduced rate (e.g., treaty benefit, portfolio interest, exempt under section 501(c)(3), 892, or 895). The allocation statement must also include the taxpayer identification numbers of those foreign persons for whom such a number is required under paragraph (e)(4)(vii) of this section or § 1.1441-6(b)(1) (regarding claims for treaty benefits). In the case of a claim of treaty benefits, the nonqualified intermediary's withholding statement must also state whether the limitation on benefits and section 894 statements required by § 1.1441-6(c)(5) have been provided, if required, in the beneficial owner's Form W-8 or associated with such owner's documentary evidence.

(4) The withholding statement must also contain any other information the withholding agent reasonably requests in order to fulfill its obligations under chapter 3, chapter 61 of the Internal Revenue Code, and section 3406.

(D) *Alternative procedures.*—(*1*) *In general.*—Under the alternative procedures of this paragraph (e)(3)(iv)(D), a nonqualified intermediary may provide information allocating a payment of a reportable amount to each payee (including U.S. exempt recipients) otherwise required under paragraph (e)(3)(iv)(B)(*2*) of this section after a payment is made. To use the alternative procedure of this paragraph (e)(3)(iv)(D), the nonqualified intermediary must inform the withholding agent on a statement associated with its nonqualified intermediary withholding certificate that it is using the procedure under this paragraph (e)(3)(iv)(D) and the withholding agent must agree to the procedure. If the requirements of the alternative procedure are met, a withholding agent, including the nonqualified intermediary using the procedures, can treat the payment as reliably associated with documentation and, therefore, the presumption rules of paragraph (b)(3) of this section and §§ 1.1441-5(d) and (e)(6) and 1.6049-5(d) do not apply even though information allocating the payment to each payee has not been received prior to the payment. See paragraph (e)(3)(iv)(D)(*7*) of this section, however, for a nonqualified intermediary's liability for tax and penalties if the requirements of this paragraph (e)(3)(iv)(D) are not met. These alternative procedures shall not be used for payments that are allocable to U.S. non-exempt recipients. Therefore, a nonqualified intermediary is required to provide a withholding agent with information allocating payments of reportable amounts to U.S. non-exempt recipients prior to the payment being made by the withholding agent.

(*2*) *Withholding rate pools.*—In place of the information required in paragraph (e)(3)(iv)(C)(*2*) of this section allocating payments to each payee, the nonqualified intermediary must provide a withholding agent with withholding rate pool information prior to the payment of a reportable amount. The withholding statement must contain all other information required by paragraph (e)(3)(iv)(C) of this section. Further, each payee listed in the withholding statement must be assigned to an identified withholding rate pool. To the extent a nonqualified intermediary is required to, or does provide, documentation, the alternative procedures do not relieve the nonqualified intermediary from the requirement to provide documentation prior to the payment being made. Therefore, withholding certificates or other appropriate documentation and all information required by paragraph (e)(3)(iv)(C) of this section (other than allocation information) must be provided to a withholding agent before any new payee receives a reportable amount. In addition, the withholding statement must be updated by assigning a new payee to a withholding rate pool prior to the payment of a reportable amount. A withholding rate pool is a payment of a single type of income, determined in accordance with the categories of income used to file Form 1042-S, that is subject to a single rate of withholding. A withholding rate pool may be established by any reasonable method to which the nonqualified intermediary

Reg. § 1.1441-1(e)(3)(iv)(D)(2)

and a withholding agent agree (e.g., by establishing a separate account for a single withholding rate pool, or by dividing a payment made to a single account into portions allocable to each withholding rate pool). The nonqualified intermediary shall determine withholding rate pools based on valid documentation or, to the extent a payment cannot be reliably associated with valid documentation, the presumption rules of paragraph (b)(3) of this section and §§ 1.1441-5(d) and (e)(6) and 1.6049-5(d).

(3) *Allocation information.*—The nonqualified intermediary must provide the withholding agent with sufficient information to allocate the income in each withholding rate pool to each payee (including U.S. exempt recipients) within the pool no later than January 31 of the year following the year of payment. Any payments that are not allocated to payees for whom documentation has been provided shall be allocated to an undocumented payee in accordance with the presumption rules of paragraph (b)(3) of this section and §§ 1.1441-5(d) and (e)(6) and 1.6049-5(d). Notwithstanding the preceding sentence, deposit interest (including original issue discount) described in section 871(i)(2)(A) or 881(d) and interest or original issue discount on short-term obligations as described in section 871(g)(1)(B) or 881(e) is not required to be allocated to a U.S. exempt recipient or a foreign payee, except as required under § 1.6049-8 (regarding reporting of deposit interest paid to certain foreign persons).

(4) *Failure to provide allocation information.*—If a nonqualified intermediary fails to provide allocation information, if required, by January 31 for any withholding rate pool, a withholding agent shall not apply the alternative procedures of this paragraph (e)(3)(iv)(D) to any payments of reportable amounts paid after January 31 in the taxable year following the calendar year for which allocation information was not given and any subsequent taxable year. Further, the alternative procedures shall be unavailable for any other withholding rate pool even though allocation information was given for that other pool. Therefore, the withholding agent must withhold on a payment of a reportable amount in accordance with the presumption rules of paragraph (b)(3) of this section, and §§ 1.1441-5(d) and (e)(6) and 1.6049-5(d), unless the nonqualified intermediary provides all of the information, including information sufficient to allocate the payment to each specific payee, required by paragraph (e)(3)(iv)(A) through (C) of this section prior to the payment. A nonqualified intermediary must allocate at least 90 percent of the income required to be allocated for each withholding rate pool or the nonqualified intermediary will be treated as having failed to provide allocation information for purposes of this paragraph (e)(3)(iv)(D). See paragraph (e)(3)(iv)(D)(7) of this section for liability for tax and penalties if a nonqualified intermediary fails to provide allocation information in whole or in part.

(5) *Cure provision.*—A nonqualified intermediary may cure any failure to provide allocation information by providing the required allocation information to the withholding agent no later than February 14 following the calendar year of payment. If the withholding agent receives the allocation information by that date, it may apply the adjustment procedures of § 1.1461-2 to any excess withholding for payments made on or after February 1 and on or before February 14. Any nonqualified intermediary that fails to cure by February 14, may request the ability to use the alternative procedures of this paragraph (e)(3)(iv)(D) by submitting a request, in writing, to the Assistant Commissioner (International). The request must state the reason that the nonqualified intermediary did not comply with the alternative procedures of this paragraph (e)(3)(iv)(D) and steps that the nonqualified intermediary has taken, or will take, to ensure that no failures occur in the future. If the Assistant Commissioner (International) determines that the alternative procedures of this paragraph (e)(3)(iv)(D) may apply, a determination to that effect will be issued by the IRS to the nonqualified intermediary.

(6) *Form 1042-S reporting in case of allocation failure.*—If a nonqualified intermediary fails to provide allocation information by February 14 following the year of payment for a withholding rate pool, the withholding agent must file Forms 1042-S for payments made to each payee in that pool (other than U.S. exempt recipients) in the prior calendar year by pro rating the payment to each payee (including U.S. exempt recipients) listed in the withholding statement for that withholding rate pool. If the nonqualified intermediary fails to allocate 10 percent or less of an amount required to be allocated for a withholding rate pool, a withholding agent shall report the unallocated amount as paid to a single unknown payee in accordance with the presumption rules of paragraph (b) of this section and §§ 1.1441-5(d) and (e)(6) and 1.6049-5(d). The portion of the payment that can be allocated to specific recipients, as defined in § 1.1461-1(c)(1)(ii), shall be reported to each recipient in accordance with the rules of § 1.1461-1(c).

(7) *Liability for tax, interest, and penalties.*—If a nonqualified intermediary fails to provide allocation information by February

14 following the year of payment for all or a portion of the payments made to any withholding rate pool, the withholding agent from whom the nonqualified intermediary received payments of reportable amounts shall not be liable for any tax, interest, or penalties, due solely to the errors or omissions of the nonqualified intermediary. See § 1.1441-7(b)(2) through (10) for the due diligence requirements of a withholding agent. Because failure by the nonqualified intermediary to provide allocation information results in a payment not being reliably associated with valid documentation, the beneficial owners for whom the nonqualified intermediary acts are not entitled to a reduced rate of withholding. Therefore, the nonqualified intermediary, as a withholding agent, shall be liable for any tax not withheld by the withholding agent in accordance with the presumption rules, interest on the under withheld tax if the nonqualified intermediary fails to pay the tax timely, and any applicable penalties, including the penalties under sections 6656 (failure to deposit), 6721 (failure to file information returns) and 6722 (failure to file payee statements). Failure to provide allocation information for more than 10 percent of the payments made to a particular withholding rate pool will be presumed to be an intentional failure within the meaning of sections 6721(e) and 6722(c). The nonqualified intermediary may rebut the presumption.

(8) Applicability to flow-through entities and certain U.S. branches.—See paragraph (e)(3)(v) of this section and § 1.1441-5(c)(3)(iv) and (e)(5)(iv) for the applicability of this paragraph (e)(3)(iv) to U.S. branches described in paragraph (b)(2)(iv) of this section (other than U.S. branches treated as U.S. persons) and flow-through entities.

(E) *Notice procedures.*—The IRS may notify a withholding agent that the alternative procedures of paragraph (e)(3)(iv)(D) of this section are not applicable to a specified nonqualified intermediary, a U.S. branch described in paragraph (b)(2)(iv) of this section, or a flow-through entity. If a withholding agent receives such a notice, it must commence withholding in accordance with the presumption rules of paragraph (b)(3) of this section and §§ 1.1441-5(d) and (e)(6) and 1.6049-5(d) unless the nonqualified intermediary, U.S. branch, or flow-through entity complies with the procedures in paragraphs (e)(3)(iv)(A) through (C) of this section. In addition, the IRS may notify a withholding agent, in appropriate circumstances, that it must apply the presumption rules of paragraph (b)(3) of this section and §§ 1.1441-5(d) and (e)(6) and 1.6049-5(d) to payments made to a nonqualified intermediary, a U.S. branch, or a flow-through entity even if the nonqualified intermediary, U.S. branch or flow-through entity provides allocation information prior to the payment. A withholding agent that receives a notice under this paragraph (e)(3)(iv)(E) must commence withholding in accordance with the presumption rules within 30 days of the date of the notice. The IRS may withdraw its prohibition against using the alternative procedures of paragraph (e)(3)(iv)(D) of this section, or its requirement to follow the presumption rules, if the nonqualified intermediary, U.S. branch, or flow-through entity can demonstrate to the satisfaction of the Assistant Commissioner (International) or his delegate that it is capable of complying with the rules under chapter 3 of the Internal Revenue Code and any other conditions required by the Assistant Commissioner (International).

(v) *Withholding certificate from certain U.S. branches.*—A U.S. branch certificate is a withholding certificate provided by a U.S. branch described in paragraph (b)(2)(iv) of this section that is not the beneficial owner of the income. The withholding certificate is provided with respect to reportable amounts and must state that such amounts are not effectively connected with the conduct of a trade or business in the United States. The withholding certificate must either transmit the appropriate documentation for the persons for whom the branch receives the payment (i.e., as an intermediary) or be provided as evidence of its agreement with the withholding agent to be treated as a U.S. person with respect to any payment associated with the certificate. A U.S. branch withholding certificate is valid only if it is furnished on a Form W-8, an acceptable substitute form, or such other form as the IRS may prescribe, it is signed under penalties of perjury by a person authorized to sign for the branch, its validity has not expired, and it contains the information, statements, and certifications described in this paragraph (e)(3)(v). If the certificate is furnished to transmit withholding certificates and other documentation, it must contain the information, certifications, and statements described in paragraphs (e)(3)(v)(A) through (C) of this section and in paragraphs (e)(3)(iii) and (iv) (alternative procedures) of this section, applying the term *U.S. branch* instead of the term *nonqualified intermediary*. If the certificate is furnished pursuant to an agreement to treat the U.S. branch as a U.S. person, the information and certifications required on the withholding certificate are limited to the following—

(A) The name of the person of which the branch is a part and the address of the branch in the United States;

(B) A certification that the payments associated with the certificate are not effec-

Reg. § 1.1441-1(e)(3)(v)(B)

tively connected with the conduct of its trade or business in the United States; and

(C) Any other information, certifications, or statements as may be required by the form or accompanying instructions in addition to, or in lieu of, the information and certification described in this paragraph (e)(3)(v).

(vi) *Reportable amounts.*—For purposes of chapter 3 of the Internal Revenue Code, a nonqualified intermediary, qualified intermediary, flow-through entity, and U.S. branch described in paragraph (b)(2)(iv) of this section (other than a U.S. branch that agrees to be treated as a U.S. person) must provide a withholding certificate and associated documentation and other information with respect to reportable amounts. For purposes of the regulations under chapter 3 of the Internal Revenue Code, the term reportable amount means an amount subject to withholding within the meaning of § 1.1441-2(a), bank deposit interest (including original issue discount) and similar types of deposit interest described in section 871(i)(2)(A) or 881(d) that are from sources within the United States, and any amount of interest or original issue discount from sources within the United States on the redemption of certain short-term obligations described in section 871(g)(1)(B) or 881(e). Reportable amounts shall not include amounts received on the sale or exchange (other than a redemption) of an obligation described in section 871(g)(1)(B) or 881(e) that is effected at an office outside the United States. See § 1.6045-1(g)(3) to determine whether a sale is effected at an office outside the United States. Reportable amounts also do not include payments with respect to deposits with banks and other financial institutions that remain on deposit for a period of two weeks or less, to amounts of original issue discount arising from a sale and repurchase transaction that is completed within a period of two weeks or less, or to amounts described in § 1.6049-5(b)(7), (10) or (11) (relating to certain obligations issued in bearer form). While short-term OID and bank deposit interest are not subject to withholding under chapter 3 of the Internal Revenue Code, such amounts may be subject to information reporting under section 6049 if paid to a U.S. person who is not an exempt recipient described in § 1.6049-4(c)(1)(ii) and to backup withholding under section 3406 in the absence of documentation. See § 1.6049-5(d)(3)(iii) for applicable procedures when such amounts are paid to a foreign intermediary.

(4) *Applicable rules.*—The provisions in this paragraph (e)(4) describe procedures applicable to withholding certificates on Form W-8 or Form 8233 (or a substitute form) or documentary evidence furnished to establish foreign status. These provisions do not apply to Forms W-9 (or their substitutes). For corresponding provisions regrading Form W-9 (or a substitute form), see section 3406 and the regulations under that section.

(i) *Who may sign the certificate.*—A withholding certificate (or other acceptable substitute) may be signed by any person authorized to sign a declaration under penalties of perjury on behalf of the person whose name is on the certificate as provided in section 6061 and the regulations under that section (relating to who may sign generally for an individual, estate, or trust, which includes certain agents who may sign returns and other documents), section 6062 and the regulations under that section (relating to who may sign corporate returns), and section 6063 and the regulations under that section (relating to who may sign partnership returns).

(ii) *Period of validity.*—(A) *Three-year period.*—A withholding certificate described in paragraph (e)(2)(i) of this section, or a certificate described in § 1.871-14(c)(2)(v) (furnished to qualify interest as portfolio interest for purposes of sections 871(h) and 881(c)), shall remain valid until the earlier of the last day of the third calendar year following the year in which the withholding certificate is signed or the day that a change in circumstances occurs that makes any information on the certificate incorrect. For example, a withholding certificate signed on September 30, 2001, remains valid through December 31, 2004, unless circumstances change that make the information on the form no longer correct. Documentary evidence described in §§ 1.1441-6(c)(3) or (4) or 1.6049-5(c)(1) shall remain valid until the earlier of the last day of the third calendar year following the year in which the documentary evidence is provided to the withholding agent or the day that a change in circumstances occurs that makes any information on the documentary evidence incorrect.

(B) *Indefinite validity period.*—Notwithstanding paragraph (e)(4)(ii)(A) of this section, the following certificates or parts of certificates shall remain valid until the status of the person whose name is on the certificate is changed in a way relevant to the certificate or circumstances change that make the information on the certificate no longer correct:

(1) A withholding certificate described in paragraph (e)(2)(ii) of this section that is furnished with a TIN, provided that the withholding agent reports at least one payment annually to the beneficial owner under § 1.1461-1(c) or the TIN furnished on the certificate is reported to the IRS under the procedures described in § 1.1461-1(d). For example,

assume a withholding agent receives a Form W-8 in 2001 from a beneficial owner with respect to an account that contains bonds, the interest on which must be reported on Form 1042-S under § 1.1461-1(c). The Form W-8 contains a valid TIN and the withholding agent reports on Forms 1042-S interest to the beneficial owner for 2001 through 2005. In 2005, the beneficial owner sells some of the bonds. For purposes of the exemption from Form 1099 reporting under § 1.6045-1(g), the withholding agent may consider the Form W-8 as valid, even though the payment of the sales proceeds is not reportable on Form 1042-S under § 1.1461-1(c) and even though the Form W-8 was provided more than three years previously.

(2) certificate described in paragraph (e)(3)(ii) of this section (a qualified intermediary withholding certificate) but not including the withholding certificates, documentary evidence, statements or other information associated with the certificate.

(3) A certificate described in paragraph (e)(3)(iii) of this section (a nonqualified intermediary certificate), but not including the withholding certificates, documentary evidence, statements or other information associated with the certificate.

(4) A certificate described in paragraph (e)(3)(v) of this section (a U.S. branch withholding certificate), but not including the withholding certificates, documentary evidence, statements or other information associated with the certificate.

(5) A certificate described in § 1.1441-5(c)(2)(iv) (dealing with a certificate from a person representing to be a withholding foreign partnership).

(6) A certificate described in § 1.1441-5(c)(3)(iii) (a withholding certificate from a nonwithholding foreign partnership) but not including the withholding certificates, documentary evidence, statements or other information required to be associated with the certificate.

(7) A certificate furnished by a person representing to be an integral part of a foreign government (within the meaning of § 1.892-2T(a)(2)) in accordance with § 1.1441-8(b), or by a person representing to be a foreign central bank of issue (within the meaning of § 1.861-2(b)(4)) or the Bank for International Settlements in accordance with § 1.1441-8(c)(1).

(8) A withholding certificate described in § 1.1441-5(e)(5)(iii) provided by a foreign simple trust or a foreign grantor trust to transmit documentation of beneficiaries or owners, but not including the withholding certificates, documentary evidence, statements or other information associated with the certificate.

(C) *Withholding certificate for effectively connected income.*—Notwithstanding paragraph (e)(4)(ii)(B)*(1)* of this section, the period of validity of a withholding certificate furnished to a withholding agent to claim a reduced rate of withholding for income that is effectively connected with the conduct of a trade or business within the United States shall be limited to the three-year period described in paragraph (e)(4)(ii)(A) of this section.

(D) *Change in circumstances.*—If a change in circumstances makes any information on a certificate or other documentation incorrect, then the person whose name is on the certificate or other documentation must inform the withholding agent within 30 days of the change and furnish a new certificate or new documentation. A certificate or documentation becomes invalid from the date that the withholding agent holding the certificate or documentation knows or has reason to know that circumstances affecting the correctness of the certificate or documentation have changed. However, a withholding agent may choose to apply the provisions of paragraph (b)(3)(iv) of this section regarding the 90-day grace period as of that date while awaiting a new certificate or documentation or while seeking information regarding changes, or suspected changes, in the person's circumstances. If an intermediary (including a U.S. branch described in paragraph (b)(2)(iv)(A) of this section that passes through certificates to a withholding agent) or a flow-through entity becomes aware that a certificate or other appropriate documentation it has furnished to the person from whom it collects the payment is no longer valid because of a change in the circumstances of the person who issued the certificate or furnished the other appropriate documentation, then the intermediary or flow-through entity must notify the person from whom it collects the payment of the change of circumstances. It must also obtain a new withholding certificate or new appropriate documentation to replace the existing certificate or documentation whose validity has expired due to the change in circumstances. If a beneficial owner withholding certificate is used to claim foreign status only (and not, also, residence in a particular foreign country for purposes of an income tax treaty), a change of address is a change in circumstances for purposes of this paragraph (e)(4)(ii)(D) only if it changes to an address in the United States. Further, a change of address within the same foreign country is not a change in circumstances for purposes of this paragraph (e)(4)(ii)(D). A change in the circumstances affecting the withholding information provided to the withholding agent in accordance with the provisions in paragraph (e)(3)(iv) or (5)(v) of this section or in § 1.1441-5(c)(3)(iv) shall terminate the validity of the withholding certificate with respect to the information that is no longer reliable unless the information is updated. A withholding agent may rely on a certificate without having to inquire into possible changes of circumstances that may affect the validity of the statement, unless it knows or has reason to know that circumstances have changed. A withholding agent may require a new certificate at any time prior to a payment, even though the withholding agent has no actual knowledge or reason to know that any information stated on the certificate has changed.

(iii) *Retention of withholding certificate.*—A withholding agent must retain each withholding certificate and other documentation for as long as it may be relevant to the determination of the withholding agent's tax liability under section 1461 and § 1.1461-1.

(iv) *Electronic transmission of information.*—(A) *In general.*—A withholding agent may establish a system for a beneficial owner or payee to electronically furnish a Form W-8, an acceptable substitute Form W-8, or such other form as the Internal Revenue Service may prescribe. The system must meet the requirements described in paragraph (e)(4)(iv)(B) of this section. A withholding agent may accept Forms W-8 that are furnished electronically on or after January 1, 2000, provided the requirements of paragraph (e)(4)(iv)(B) of this section are met.

(B) *Requirements.*—(1) *In general.*—The electronic system must ensure that the information received is the information sent, and must document all occasions of user access that result in the submission renewal, or modification of a Form W-8. In addition, the design and operation of the electronic system, including access procedures, must make it reasonably certain that the person accessing the system and furnishing Form W-8 is the person named in the Form.

(2) *Same information as paper Form W-8.*—The electronic transmission must provide the withholding agent or payor with exactly the same information as the paper Form W-8.

(3) *Perjury statement and signature requirements.*—The electronic transmission must contain an electronic signature by the person whose name is on the Form W-8 and the signature must be under penalties of perjury in the manner described in this paragraph (e)(4)(iv)(B)(3).

(i) *Perjury statement.*—The perjury statement must contain the language that appears on the paper Form W-8. The electronic system must inform the person whose name is on the Form W-8 that the person must make the declaration contained in the perjury statement and that the declaration is made by signing the Form W-8. The instructions and the language of the perjury statement must immediately follow the person's certifying statements and immediately precede the person's electronic signature.

(ii) *Electronic signature.*—The act of the electronic signature must be effected by the person whose name is on the electronic Form W-8. The signature must also authenticate and verify the submission. For this purpose, the terms *authenticate* and *verify* have the same meanings as they do when applied to a written signature on a paper Form W-8. An electronic signature can be in any form that satisfies the foregoing requirements. The electronic signature must be the final entry in the person's Form W-8 submission.

(4) *Requests for electronic Form W-8 data.*—Upon request by the Internal Revenue Service during an examination, the withholding agent must supply a hard copy of the electronic Form W-8 and a statement that, to the best of the withholding agent's knowledge, the electronic Form W-8 was filed by the person whose name is on the form. The hard copy of the electronic Form W-8 must provide exactly the same information as, but need not be identical to, the paper Form W-8.

(C) *Special requirements for transmission of Forms W-8 by an intermediary.*—[Reserved]

(v) *Electronic confirmation of taxpayer identifying number on withholding certificate.*—The Commissioner may prescribe procedures in a revenue procedure (see § 601.601(d)(2) of this chapter) or other appropriate guidance to require a withholding agent to confirm electronically with the IRS information concerning any TIN stated on a withholding certificate.

(vi) *Acceptable substitute form.*—A withholding agent may substitute its own form instead of an official Form W-8 or 8233 (or such other official form as the IRS may prescribe). Such a substitute for an official form will be acceptable if it contains provisions that are substantially similar to those of the official form, it contains the same certifications relevant to the transactions as are contained on the official form and these certifications are clearly set forth, and the substitute form includes a signature-under-penalties-of-perjury statement identical to the one stated on the official form. The substitute form is acceptable even if it does not contain all of the provisions contained on the official form, so long as it contains those provisions that are relevant to the transaction for which it is furnished. For example, a withholding agent that pays no income for which treaty benefits are claimed may develop a substitute form that is identical to the official form, except that it does not include information regarding claim of benefits under an income tax treaty. A withholding agent who uses a substitute form must furnish instructions relevant to the substitute form only to the extent and in the manner specified in the instructions to the official form. A withholding agent may refuse to accept a certificate from a payee or beneficial owner (including the official Form W-8 or 8233) if the certificate is not provided on the acceptable substitute form provided by the withholding agent. However, a withholding agent may refuse to accept a certificate provided by a payee or beneficial owner only if the withholding agent furnishes the payee or beneficial owner with an acceptable substitute form immediately upon receipt of an unacceptable form or within 5 business days of receipt of an unacceptable form from the payee or beneficial owner. In that case, the substitute form is acceptable only if it contains a notice that the withholding agent has refused to accept the form submitted by the payee or beneficial owner and that the payee or beneficial owner must submit the acceptable form provided by the withholding agent in order for the payee or beneficial owner to be treated as having furnished the required withholding certificate.

(vii) *Requirement of taxpayer identifying number.*—A TIN must be stated on a withholding certificate when required by this paragraph (e)(4)(vii). A TIN is required to be stated on—

(A) A withholding certificate on which a beneficial owner is claiming the benefit of a reduced rate under an income tax treaty (other than for amounts described in § 1.1441-6(c)(2);

(B) A withholding certificate on which a beneficial owner is claiming exemption from withholding because income is effectively connected with a U.S. trade or business;

(C) A withholding certificate on which a beneficial owner is claiming exemption from withholding under section 871(f) for certain annuities received under qualified plans;

(D) A withholding certificate on which a beneficial owner is claiming an exemption based solely on a foreign organization's claim of tax exempt status under section 501(c) or private foundation status (however, a TIN is not required from a foreign private foundation that is subject to the 4-percent tax under section 4948(a) on income if that income would be exempt from withholding but for section 4948(a) (e.g., portfolio interest));

(E) A withholding certificate from a person representing to be a qualified intermediary described in paragraph (e)(5)(ii) of this section;

(F) A withholding certificate from a person representing to be a withholding foreign partnership described in § 1.1441-5(c)(2)(i));

(G) A withholding certificate from a person representing to be a foreign grantor trust with 5 or fewer grantors;

(H) A withholding certificate provided by a foreign organization that is described in section 501(c);

(I) A withholding certificate from a person representing to be a U.S. branch described in paragraph (b)(2)(iv) of this section.

(viii) *Reliance rules.*—A withholding agent may rely on the information and certifications stated on withholding certificates or other documentation without having to inquire into the truthfulness of this information or certification, unless it has actual knowledge or reason to know that the same is untrue. In the case of amounts described in § 1.1441-6(c)(2), a withholding agent described in § 1.1441-7(b)(2)(ii) has reason to know that the information or certifications on a certificate are untrue only to the extent provided in § 1.1441-7(b)(2)(ii). See § 1.1441-6(b)(1) for reliance on representations regarding eligibility for a reduced rate under an income tax treaty. Paragraphs (e)(4)(viii)(A) and (B) of this section provide examples of such reliance.

(A) *Classification.*—A withholding agent may rely on the claim of entity classification indicated on the withholding certificate that it receives from or for the beneficial owner, unless it has actual knowledge or reason to know that the classification claimed is incorrect. A withholding agent may not rely on a person's claim of classification other than as a corporation if the name of the corporation indicates that the person is a per se corporation described in § 301.7701-2(b)(8)(i) of this chapter unless the certificate contains a statement that the person is a grandfathered per se corporation described in § 301.7701-2(b)(8) of this chapter and that its grandfathered status has not been terminated. In the absence of reliable representation or information regarding the classification of the payee or beneficial owner, see § 1.1441-1(b)(3)(ii) for applicable presumptions.

(B) *Status of payee as an intermediary or as a person acting for its own account.*—A withholding agent may rely on the type of cer-

Reg. § 1.1441-1(e)(4)(viii)(B)

tificate furnished as indicative of the payee's status as an intermediary or as an owner, unless the withholding agent has actual knowledge or reason to know otherwise. For example, a withholding agent that receives a beneficial owner withholding certificate from a foreign financial institution may treat the institution as the beneficial owner, unless it has information in its records that would indicate otherwise or the certificate contains information that is not consistent with beneficial owner status (e.g., sub-account numbers or names). If the financial institution also acts as an intermediary, the withholding agent may request that the institution furnish two certificates, i.e., a beneficial owner certificate described in paragraph (e)(2)(i) of this section for the amounts that it receives as a beneficial owner, and an intermediary withholding certificate described in paragraph (e)(3)(i) of this section for the amounts that it receives as an intermediary. In the absence of reliable representation or information regarding the status of the payee as an owner or as an intermediary, see paragraph (b)(3)(v)(A) for applicable presumptions.

(ix) *Certificates to be furnished for each account unless exception applies.*—Unless otherwise provided in this paragraph (e)(4)(ix), a withholding agent that is a financial institution with which a customer may open an account shall obtain withholding certificates or other appropriate documentation on an account-by-account basis.

(A) *Coordinated account information system in effect.*—A withholding agent may rely on the withholding certificate or other appropriate documentation furnished by a customer for a pre-existing account under any one or more of the circumstances described in this paragraph (e)(4)(ix)(A).

(*1*) A withholding agent may rely on documentation furnished by a customer for another account if all such accounts are held at the same branch location.

(*2*) A withholding agent may rely on documentation furnished by a customer for an account held at another branch location of the same withholding agent or at a branch location of a person related to the withholding agent if the withholding agent and the related person are part of a universal account system that uses a customer identifier that can be used to retrieve systematically all other accounts of the customer. See § 31.3406(c)-1(c)(3)(ii) and (iii)(C) of this chapter for an identical procedure for purposes of backup withholding. For purposes of this paragraph (e)(4)(ix)(A), a withholding agent is related to another person if it is related within the meaning of section 267(b) or 707(b).

(*3*) A withholding agent may rely on documentation furnished by a customer for an account held at another branch location of the same withholding agent or at a branch location of a person related to the withholding agent if the withholding agent and the related person are part of an information system other than a universal account system and the information system is described in this paragraph (e)(4)(ix)(A)(*3*). The system must allow the withholding agent to easily access data regarding the nature of the documentation, the information contained in the documentation, and its validity status, and must allow the withholding agent to easily transmit data into the system regarding any facts of which it becomes aware that may affect the reliability of the documentation. The withholding agent must be able to establish how and when it has accessed the data regarding the documentation and, if applicable, how and when it has transmitted data regarding any facts of which it became aware that may affect the reliability of the documentation. In addition, the withholding agent or the related party must be able to establish that any data it has transmitted to the information system has been processed and appropriate due diligence has been exercised regarding the validity of the documentation.

(*4*) A withholding agent may rely on documentation furnished by a beneficial owner or payee to an agent of the withholding agent. The agent may retain the documentation as part of an information system maintained for a single or multiple withholding agents provided that the system permits any withholding agent that uses the system to easily access data regarding the nature of the documentation, the information contained in the documentation, and its validity, and must allow the withholding agent to easily transmit data into the system regarding any facts of which it becomes aware that may affect the reliability of the documentation. The withholding agent must be able to establish how and when it has accessed the data regarding the documentation and, if applicable, how and when it has transmitted data regarding any facts of which it became aware that may affect the reliability of the documentation. In addition, the withholding agent must be able to establish that any data it has transmitted to the information system has been processed and appropriate due diligence has been exercised regarding the validity of the documentation.

(B) *Family of mutual funds.*—An interest in a mutual fund that has a common investment advisor or common principal underwriter with other mutual funds (within the same family of funds) may, in the discretion of the mutual fund, be represented by one single withholding certificate where shares are acquired or owned in any of the funds. See § 31.3406(h)-3(a)(2) of this chapter for an identical procedures for purposes of backup withholding.

(C) *Special rule for brokers.—(1) In general.*—A withholding agent may rely on the certification of a broker that the broker holds a valid beneficial owner withholding certificate described in paragraph (e)(2)(i) of this section or other appropriate documentation for that beneficial owner with respect to any readily tradable instrument, as defined in § 31.3406(h)-1(d) of this chapter, if the broker is a United States person (including a U.S. branch treated as a U.S. person under paragraph (b)(2)(iv) of this section) that is acting as the agent of a beneficial owner and the U.S. broker has been provided a valid Form W-8 or other appropriate documentation. The certification must be in writing or in electronic form and contain all of the information required of a nonqualified intermediary under paragraphs (e)(3)(iv)(B) and (C) of this section. If a U.S. broker chooses to use this paragraph (e)(4)(ix)(C), that U.S. broker will be solely responsible for applying the rules of § 1.1441-7(b) to the withholding certificates or other appropriate documentation. For purposes of this paragraph (c)(4)(ix)(C), the term broker means a person treated as a broker under § 1.6045-1(a).

(2) The following example illustrates the rules of this paragraph (e)(4)(ix)(C):

Example. SCO is a U.S. securities clearing organization that provides clearing services for correspondent broker, CB, a U.S. corporation. Pursuant to a fully disclosed clearing agreement, CB fully discloses the identity of each of its customers to SCO. Part of SCO's clearing duties include the crediting of income and gross proceeds of readily tradeable instruments (as defined in § 31.3406(h)-1(d)) to each customer's account. For each disclosed customer that is a foreign beneficial owner, CB provides SCO with information required under paragraphs (e)(3)(iv)(B) and (C) of this section that is necessary to apply the correct rate of withholding and to file Forms 1042-S. SCO may use the representations and beneficial owner information provided by CB to determine the proper amount of withholding and to file Forms 1042-S. CB is responsible for determining the validity of the withholding certificates or other appropriate documentation under § 1.1441-1(b).

(5) *Qualified intermediaries.*—(i) *General rule.*—A qualified intermediary, as defined in paragraph (e)(5)(ii) of this section, may furnish a qualified intermediary withholding certificate to a withholding agent. The withholding certificate provides certifications on behalf of other persons for the purpose of claiming and verifying reduced rates of withholding under section 1441 or 1442 and for the purpose of reporting and withholding under other provisions of the Internal Revenue Code, such as the provisions under chapter 61 and section 3406 (and the regulations under those provisions). Furnishing such a certificate is in lieu of transmitting to a withholding agent withholding certificates or other appropriate documentation for the persons for whom the qualified intermediary receives the payment, including interest holders in a qualified intermediary that is fiscally transparent under the regulations under section 894. Although the qualified intermediary is required to obtain withholding certificates or other appropriate documentation from beneficial owners, payees, or interest holders pursuant to its agreement with the IRS, it is generally not required to attach such documentation to the intermediary withholding certificate. Notwithstanding the preceding sentence a qualified intermediary must provide a withholding agent with the Forms W-9, or disclose the names, addresses, and taxpayer identifying numbers, if known, of those U.S. non-exempt recipients for whom the qualified intermediary receives reportable amounts (within the meaning of paragraph (e)(3)(vi) of this section) to the extent required in the qualified intermediary's agreement with the IRS. A person may claim qualified intermediary status before an agreement is executed with the IRS if it has applied for such status and the IRS authorizes such status on an interim basis under such procedures as the IRS may prescribe.

(ii) *Definition of qualified intermediary.*—With respect to a payment to a foreign person, the term *qualified intermediary* means a person that is a party to a withholding agreement with the IRS and such person is—

(A) A foreign financial institution or a foreign clearing organization (as defined in § 1.163-5(c)(2)(i)(D)*(8)*, without regard to the requirement that the organization hold obligations for members), other than a U.S. branch or U.S. office of such institution or organization;

(B) A foreign branch or office of a U.S. financial institution or a foreign branch or office of a U.S. clearing organization (as defined in § 1.163-5(c)(2)(i)(D)*(8)*, without regard to the requirement that the organization hold obligations for members);

(C) A foreign corporation for purposes of presenting claims of benefits under an income tax treaty on behalf of its shareholders; or

(D) Any other person acceptable to the IRS.

(iii) *Withholding agreement.*—(A) *In general.*—The IRS may, upon request, enter into a withholding agreement with a foreign person described in paragraph (e)(5)(ii) of this section pursuant to such procedures as the IRS may prescribe in published guidance (see § 601.601(d)(2) of this chapter). Under the withholding agreement, a qualified intermediary shall generally be subject to the applicable withholding and reporting provisions applicable to withholding agents and payors under chapters 3 and 61 of the Internal Revenue Code, section 3406, the regulations under those provisions, and other withholding provisions of the Internal Revenue Code, except to the extent provided under the agreement.

(B) *Terms of the withholding agreement.*—Generally, the agreement shall specify the type of certifications and documentation upon which the qualified intermediary may rely to ascertain the classification (e.g., corporation or partnership) and status (i.e., U.S. or foreign) of beneficial owners and payees who receive payments collected by the qualified intermediary and, if necessary, entitlement to the benefits of a reduced rate under an income tax treaty. The agreement shall specify if, and to what extent, the qualified intermediary may assume primary withholding responsibility in accordance with paragraph (e)(5)(iv) of this section. It shall also specify the extent to which applicable return filing and information reporting requirements are modified so that, in appropriate cases, the qualified intermediary may report payments to the IRS on an aggregated basis, without having to disclose the identity of beneficial owners and payees. However, the qualified intermediary may be required to provide to the IRS the name and address of those foreign customers who benefit from a reduced rate under an income tax treaty pursuant to the qualified intermediary arrangement for purposes of verifying entitlement to such benefits, particularly under an applicable limitation on benefits provision. Under the agreement, a qualified intermediary may agree to act as an acceptance agent to perform the duties described in § 301.6109-1(d)(3)(iv)(A) of this chapter. The agreement may specify the manner in which applicable procedures for adjustments for underwithholding and overwithholding, including refund procedures, apply in the context of a qualified intermediary arrangement and the extent to which applicable procedures may be modified. In particular, a withholding agreement may allow a qualified intermediary to claim refunds of overwithheld amounts. If relevant, the agreement shall specify the manner in which the qualified intermediary may deal with payments to other intermediaries and flow-through entities. In addition, the agreement shall specify the manner in which the IRS will verify compliance with the agreement. In appropriate cases, the IRS may agree to rely on audits performed by an intermediary's approved auditor. In such a case, the IRS's audit may be limited to the audit of the auditor's records (including work papers of the auditor and reports prepared by the auditor indicating the methodology employed to verify the entity's compliance with the agreement). For this purpose, the agreement shall specify the auditor or class of auditors that are approved. Generally, an auditor will not be approved if the auditor is not subject to laws, regulations, or rules that impose sanctions for failure to exercise its independence and to perform the audit competently. The agreement may include provisions for the assessment and collection of tax in the event that failure to comply with the terms of the agreement results in the failure by the withholding agent or the qualified intermediary to withhold and deposit the required amount of tax. Further, the agreement may specify the procedures by which deposits of amounts withheld are to be deposited, if different from the deposit procedures under the Internal Revenue Code and applicable regulations. To determine whether to enter a qualified intermediary withholding agreement and the terms of any particular withholding agreement, the IRS will consider appropriate factors including whether or not the foreign person agrees to assume primary withholding responsibility, the type of local know-your-customer laws and practices to which it is subject, the extent and nature of supervisory and regulatory control exercised under the laws of the foreign country over the foreign person, the volume of investments in U.S. securities (determined in dollar amounts and number of account holders), the financial condition of the foreign person, and whether the qualified intermediary is a resident of a country with which the United States has an income tax treaty.

(iv) *Assignment of primary withholding responsibility.*—Any person who meets the definition of a withholding agent under § 1.1441-7(a) (whether a U.S. person or a foreign person) is required to withhold and deposit any amount withheld under § 1.1461-1(a) and to make the returns prescribed by § 1.1461-1(b) and (c). If permitted by its qualified intermediary agreement, a qualified intermediary agreement may, however, inform a withholding agent from which it receives a payment that it will assume the primary obligation to withhold, deposit, and report amounts under chapter 3 of the Internal Revenue Code and/or under chapter 61 of the Internal Revenue Code and section 3406. If a withholding agent makes a payment of an amount subject to withholding, as defined in § 1.1441-2(a), or a reportable payment, as defined in section 3406(b), to a qualified intermediary that represents to the withholding agent that it has assumed primary withholding responsibility for the payment, the withholding agent is not required to withhold on the payment. The withholding agent is not required to determine that the qualified intermediary agreement actually permits the qualified intermediary to assume primary withholding responsibility. A qualified intermediary that assumes primary withholding responsibility under chapter 3 of the Internal Revenue Code or primary reporting and backup withholding responsibility under chapter 61 and section 3406 is not required to assume primary withholding responsibility for all accounts it has with a withholding agent but must assume primary withholding responsibility for all payments made to any one account that it has with the withholding agent. A qualified intermediary may agree with the withholding agent to assume primary withholding responsibility under chapter 3 and section 3406, only if expressly permitted to do so under its agreement with the IRS.

(v) *Withholding statement.*—(A) *In general.*—A qualified intermediary must provide each withholding agent from which it receives reportable amounts, as defined in paragraph (e)(3)(vi) of this section, as a qualified intermediary with a written statement (the withholding statement) containing the information specified in paragraph (e)(5)(v)(B) of this section. A withholding statement is not required, however, if all of the information a withholding agent needs to fulfill its withholding and reporting requirements is contained in the withholding certificate. The qualified intermediary agreement may require, in appropriate circumstances, the qualified intermediary to include information in its withholding statement relating to payments other than payments of reportable amounts. The withholding statement forms an integral part of the qualified intermediary's qualified intermediary withholding certificate and the penalties of perjury statement provided on the withholding certificate shall apply to the withholding statement as well. The withholding statement may be provided in any manner, and in any form, to which qualified intermediary and the withholding agent mutually agree, including electronically. If the withholding statement is provided electronically, there must be sufficient safeguards to ensure that the information received by the withholding agent is the information sent by qualified intermediary and must also document all occasions of user access that result in the submission or modification of withholding statement information. In addition, the electronic system must be capable of providing a hard copy of all withholding statements provided by the qualified intermediary. The withholding statement shall be updated as often as necessary for the withholding agent to meet its reporting and withholding obligations under chapters 3 and 61 of the Internal Revenue Code and section 3406. A withholding agent will be liable for tax, interest, and penalties in accordance with paragraph (b)(7) of this section to the extent it does not follow the presumption rules of paragraph (b)(3) of this section, §§ 1.1441-5(d) and (e)(6), and 1.6049-5(d) for any payment, or portion thereof, for which it does not have a valid withholding statement prior to making a payment.

(B) *Content of withholding statement.*—The withholding statement must contain sufficient information for a withholding agent to apply the correct rate of withholding on payments from the accounts identified on the statement and to properly report such payments on Forms 1042-S and Forms 1099, as applicable. The withholding statement must—

(1) Designate those accounts for which the qualified intermediary acts as a qualified intermediary;

(2) Designate those accounts for which qualified intermediary assumes primary withholding responsibility under chapter 3 of the Internal Revenue Code and/or primary reporting and backup withholding responsibility under chapter 61 and section 3406; and

(3) Provide information regarding withholding rate pools, as described in paragraph (e)(5)(v)(C) of this section.

(C) *Withholding rate pools.*—*(1) In general.*—Except to the extent it has assumed both primary withholding responsibility under chapter 3 of the Internal Revenue Code and primary reporting and backup withholding responsibility under chapter 61 and section 3406 with respect to a payment, a qualified intermediary shall provide as part of its withholding statement the withholding rate pool information that is required for the withholding agent to meet its withholding and reporting obligations under chapters 3 and 61 of the Internal Revenue Code and section 3406. A withholding rate pool is a payment of a single type of income, determined in accordance with the categories of income reported on Form 1042-S or Form 1099, as applicable, that is subject to a single rate of withholding. A withholding rate pool may be established by any reasonable method on which the qualified intermediary and a withholding agent agree (e.g., by establishing a separate account for a single withholding rate pool, or by dividing a payment made to a single account into portions allocable to each withholding rate pool). To the extent a qualified intermediary does not assume primary reporting and backup withholding responsibility under chapter 61 and section 3406, a qualified intermediary's withholding statement must establish a separate withholding rate pool for each U.S. non-exempt recipient account holder that the qualified intermediary has disclosed to the withholding agent unless the qualified intermediary uses the alternative procedures in paragraph (e)(5)(v)(C)(2) of this section. A qualified intermediary shall determine withholding rate pools based on valid documentation that it obtains under its withholding agreement with the IRS, or if a payment cannot be reliably associated with valid documentation, under the applicable presumption rules. If a qualified intermediary has an account holder that is another intermediary (whether a qualified intermediary or a nonqualified intermediary) or a flow-through entity, the qualified intermediary may combine the account holder information provided by the intermediary or flow-through entity with the qualified intermediary's direct account holder information to determine the qualified intermediary's withholding rate pools.

(2) Alternative procedure for U.S. non-exempt recipients.—If permitted under its agreement with the IRS, a qualified intermediary may, by mutual agreement with a withholding agent, establish a single zero withholding rate pool that includes U.S. non-exempt recipient account holders for whom the qualified intermediary has provided Forms W-9 prior to the withholding agent paying any reportable payments, as defined in the qualified intermediary agreement, and a separate withholding rate pool (subject to 31-percent withholding) that includes only U.S. non-exempt recipient account holders for whom a qualified intermediary has not provided Forms W-9 prior to the withholding agent paying any reportable payments. If a qualified intermediary chooses the alternative procedure of this paragraph (e)(5)(v)(C)(2), the qualified intermediary must provide the information required by its qualified intermediary agreement to the withholding agent no later than January 15 of the year following the year in which the payments are paid. Failure to provide such information will result in the application of penalties to the qualified intermediary under sections 6721 and 6722, as well as any other applicable penalties, and may result in the termination of the qualified intermediary's withholding agreement with the IRS. A withholding agent shall not be liable for tax, interest, or penalties for failure to backup withhold or report information under chapter 61 of the Internal Revenue Code due solely to the errors or omissions of the qualified intermediary. If a qualified intermediary fails to provide the allocation information required by this paragraph (e)(5)(v)(C)(2), with respect to U.S. non-exempt recipients, the withholding agent shall report the unallocated amount paid from the withholding rate pool to an unknown recipient, or otherwise in accordance with the appropriate Form 1099 and the instructions accompanying the form.

(f) *Effective date.*—(1) *In general.*—This section applies to payments made after December 31, 2000.

(2) *Transition rules.*—(i) *Special rules for existing documentation.*—For purposes of paragraphs (d)(3) and (e)(2)(i) of this section, the validity of a withholding certificate (namely, Form W-8, 8233, 1001, 4224, or 1078, or a statement described in § 1.1441-5 in effect prior to January 1, 2001 (see § 1.1441-5 as contained in 26 CFR part 1, revised April 1, 1999)) that was valid on January 1, 1998 under the regulations in effect prior to January 1, 2001 (see 26 CFR parts 1 and 35a, revised April 1, 1999) and expired, or will expire, at any time during 1998, is extended until December 31, 1998. The validity of a withholding certificate that is valid on or after January 1, 1999, remains valid until its validity expires under the regulations in effect prior to January 1, 2001 (see 26 CFR parts 1 and 35a, revised April 1, 1999) but in no event will such withholding certificate remain valid after December 31, 2000. The rule in this paragraph (f)(2)(i), however, does not apply to extend the validity period of a withholding certificate that expires solely by reason of changes in the circumstances of the person whose name is on the certificate. Notwithstanding the first three sentences of this paragraph (f)(2)(i), a withholding agent may choose to not take advantage of the transition rule in this paragraph (f)(2)(i) with respect to one or more withholding certificates valid under the regulations in effect prior to January 1, 2001 (see 26 CFR parts 1 and 35a, revised April 1, 1999) and, therefore, to require withholding certificates conforming to the requirements described in this section (new withholding certificates). For purposes of this section, a new withholding certificate is deemed to satisfy the documentation requirement under the regulations in effect prior to January 1, 2001 (see 26 CFR parts 1 and 35a, revised April 1, 1999). Further, a new withholding certificate remains valid for the period specified in paragraph (e)(4)(ii) of this section, regardless of when the certificate is obtained.

(ii) *Lack of documentation for past years.*—A taxpayer may elect to apply the provisions of paragraphs (b)(7)(i)(B), (ii), and (iii) of this section, dealing with liability for failure to obtain documentation timely, to all of its open tax years, including tax years that are currently under examination by the IRS. The election is made by simply taking action under those provisions in the same manner as the taxpayer would take action for payments made after December 31, 2000. [Reg. § 1.1441-1.]

☐ [*T.D.* 6187, 7-5-56. *Amended by T.D.* 6592, 2-27-62; *T.D.* 6908, 12-30-66; *T.D.* 7157, 12-29-71; *T.D.* 7385, 10-28-75; *T.D.* 7670, 1-30-80; *T.D.* 8734, 10-6-97; *T.D.* 8804, 12-30-98; *T.D.* 8856, 12-29-99 (*corrected* 3-27-2000); *T.D.* 8881, 5-15-2000 (*corrected* 4-5-2001) *and T.D.* 9023, 11-21-2002.]

§ 1.1441-2. Amounts subject to withholding.—(a) *In general.*—For purposes of the regulations under chapter 3 of the Internal Revenue Code, the term *amounts subject to withholding* means amounts from sources within the United States that constitute either fixed or determinable annual or periodical income described in paragraph (b) of this section or other amounts subject to withholding described in paragraph (c) of this section. For purposes of this paragraph (a), an amount shall be treated as being from sources within the United States if the source of the amount cannot be determined at the time of payment. See § 1.1441-3(d)(1) for determining the amount to be withheld from a payment in the absence of information at the time of payment regarding the source of the amount. Amounts subject to withholding include amounts that are not fixed or determinable annual or periodical income and upon which withholding is specifically required under a provision of this section or another section of the regulations under chapter 3 of the Internal Revenue Code (such as corporate distributions upon which withholding is required under § 1.1441-3(c)(1) that do not constitute dividend income). Amounts subject to withholding do not include—

(1) Amounts described in § 1.1441-1(b)(4)(i) to the extent they involve interest on obligations in bearer form or on foreign-targeted registered obligations (but, in the case of a foreign-targeted registered obligation, only to the extent of those amounts paid to a registered owner that is a financial institution within the meaning of section 871(h)(5)(B) or a member of a clearing organization which member is the beneficial owner of the obligation);

(2) Amounts described in § 1.1441-1(b)(4)(ii) (dealing with bank deposit interest and similar types of interest (including original issue discount) described in section 871(i)(2)(A) or 881(d));

(3) Amounts described in § 1.1441-1(b)(4)(iv) (dealing with interest or original issue discount on certain short-term obligations described in section 871(g)(1)(B) or 881(e));

(4) Amounts described in § 1.1441-1(b)(4)(xx) (dealing with income from certain gambling winnings exempt from tax under section 871(j));

(5) Amounts paid as part of the purchase price of an obligation sold or exchanged between interest payment dates, unless the sale or exchange is part of a plan the principal purpose of which is to avoid tax and the withholding agent has actual knowledge or reason to know of such plan;

(6) Original issue discount paid as part of the purchase price of an obligation sold or exchanged in a transaction other than a redemption of such obligation, unless the purchase is part of a plan the principal purpose of which is to avoid tax and the withholding agent has actual knowledge or reason to know of such plan; and

(7) Insurance premiums paid with respect to a contract that is subject to the section 4371 excise tax.

(b) *Fixed or determinable annual or periodical income.*—(1) *In general.*—(i) *Definition.*—For purposes of chapter 3 of the Internal Revenue Code and the regulations thereunder, fixed or determinable annual or periodical income includes all income included in gross income under section 61 (including original issue discount) except for the items specified in paragraph (b)(2) of this section. Items of income that are excluded from gross income under a provision of law without regard to the U.S. or foreign status of the owner of the income, such as interest excluded from gross income under section 103(a) or qualified scholarship income under section 117, shall not be treated as fixed or determinable annual or periodical income under chapter 3 of the Internal Revenue Code. Income excluded from gross income under section 892 (income of foreign governments) or section 115 (income of a U.S. possession) is fixed or determinable annual or periodical income since the exclusion from gross income under those sections is dependent on the foreign status of the owner of the income. See § 1.306-3(h) for treating income from the disposition of section 306 stock as fixed or determinable annual or periodical income.

(ii) *Manner of payment.*—The term *fixed or determinable annual or periodical* is merely descriptive of the character of a class of income. If an item of income falls within the class of income contemplated in the statute and described in paragraph (a) of this section, it is immaterial whether payment of that item is made in a series of payments or in a single lump sum. Further, the income need not be paid annually if it is paid periodically; that is to say, from time to time, whether or not at regular intervals. The fact that a payment is not made annually or periodically does not, however, prevent it from being fixed or determinable annual or periodical income (e.g., a lump sum payment). In addition, the fact that the length of time during which the payments are to be made may be increased or diminished in accordance with someone's will or with the happening of an event does not disqualify the payment as determinable or periodical. For this purpose, the share of the fixed or determinable annual or periodical income of an estate or trust from sources within the United States which is required to be distributed currently, or which has been paid or credited during the taxable year, to a nonresident alien beneficiary of such estate or trust constitutes fixed or determinable annual or periodical income.

(iii) *Determinability of amount.*—An item of income is fixed when it is to be paid in amounts definitely pre-determined. An item of income is determinable if the amount to be paid is not known but there is a basis of calculation by which the amount may be ascertained at a later time. For example, interest is determinable even if it is contingent in that its amount cannot be determined at the time of payment of an amount with respect to a loan because the calculation of the interest portion of the payment is contingent upon factors that are not fixed at the time of the payment. For purposes of this section, an amount of income does not have to be determined at the time that the payment is made in order to be determinable. An amount of income described in paragraph (a) of this section which the withholding agent knows is part of a payment it makes but which it cannot calculate exactly at the time of payment, is nevertheless determinable if the determination of the exact amount depends upon events expected to occur at a future date. In contrast, a payment which may be income in the future based upon events that are not anticipated at the time the payment is made is not determinable. For example, loan proceeds may become income to the borrower when and to the extent the loan is canceled without repayment. While the cancellation of the debt is income to the borrower when it occurs, it is not determinable at the time the loan proceeds are disbursed to the borrower if the lack of repayment leading to the cancellation of part or all of the debt was not anticipated at the time of disbursement. The fact that the source of an item of income cannot be determined at the time that the payment is made does not render a payment not determinable. See § 1.1441-3(d)(1) for determining the amount to be withheld from a payment in the absence of information at the time of payment regarding the source of the amount.

(2) *Exceptions.*—For purposes of chapter 3 of the Code and the regulations thereunder, the items of income described in this paragraph (b)(2) are not fixed or determinable annual or periodical income—

(i) Gains derived from the sale of property (including market discount and option premiums), except for gains described in paragraph (b)(3) or (c) of this section; and

(ii) Any other income that the Internal Revenue Service (IRS) may determine, in published guidance (see § 601.601(d)(2) of this chapter), is not fixed or determinable annual or periodical income.

(3) *Original issue discount.*—(i) *Amount subject to tax.*—An amount representing original issue discount is fixed or determinable annual or periodical income that is subject to tax under sections 871(a)(1)(C) and 881(a)(3) to the extent provided in those sections and this paragraph (b)(3) if not otherwise excluded under paragraph (a) of this section. An amount of original issue discount is subject to tax with respect to a foreign beneficial owner of an obligation carrying original issue discount upon a sale or exchange of the obligation or when a payment is made on such obligation. The amount taxable is the amount of original issue discount that accrued while the foreign person held the obligation up to the time that the obligation is sold or exchanged or that a payment is made on the obligation, reduced by any amount of original issue discount that was taken into account prior to that time (due to a payment made on the obligation). In the case of a payment made on the obligation, the tax due on the amount of original issue discount may not exceed the amount of the payment reduced by the tax imposed on any portion of the payment that is qualified stated interest.

(ii) *Amounts subject to withholding.*—A withholding agent must withhold on the taxable amount of original issue discount paid on the redemption of an original issue discount obligation unless an exception to withholding applies (e.g., portfolio interest or treaty exception). In addition, withholding is required on the taxable amount of original issue discount upon the sale or exchange of an original issue discount obligation, other than in a redemption, to the extent the withholding agent has actual knowledge or reason to know that the sale or exchange is part of a plan the principal purpose of which is to avoid tax. If a withholding agent cannot determine the taxable amount of original issue discount on the redemption of an original issue discount obligation (or on the sale or exchange of such an obligation if the principal purpose of the sale is to avoid tax), then it must withhold on the entire amount of original issue discount accrued from the date of issue until the date of redemption (or the date the obligation is sold or exchanged) determined on the basis of the most recently published "List of Original Issue Discount Instruments" (IRS Publication 1212, available from the IRS Forms Distribution Center) or similar list published by the IRS as if the beneficial owner of the obligation had held the obligation since its original issue.

(iii) *Exceptions to withholding.*—To the extent that this paragraph (b)(3) applies to require withholding by a person other than an issuer of an original issue discount obligation, or the issuer's agent, it shall apply only to obligations issued after December 31, 2000.

(4) *Securities lending transactions and equivalent transactions.*—See §§ 1.871-7(b)(2) and 1.881-2(b)(2) regarding the character of substitute payments as fixed and determinable annual or periodical income. Such amounts constitute income subject to withholding to the extent they are from sources within the United States, as determined under section §§ 1.861-2(a)(7) and 1.861-3(a)(6). See §§ 1.6042-3(a)(2) and 1.6049-5(a)(5) for reporting requirements applicable to substitute dividend and interest payments, respectively.

(c) *Other income subject to withholding.*—Withholding is also required on the following items of income—

(1) Gains described in sections 631(b) or (c), relating to treatment of gain on disposal of timber, coal, or domestic iron ore with a retained economic interest; and

(2) Gains subject to the 30-percent tax under section 871(a)(1)(D) or 881(a)(4), relating to contingent payments received from the sale or exchange of patents, copyrights, and similar intangible property.

(d) *Exceptions to withholding where no money or property is paid or lack of knowledge.*—(1) *General rule.*—A withholding agent who is not related to the recipient or beneficial owner has an obligation to withhold under section 1441 only to the extent that, at any time between the date that the obligation to withhold would arise (but for the provisions of this paragraph (d)) and the due date for the filing of return on Form 1042 (including extensions) for the year in which the payment occurs, it has control over, or custody of money or property owned by the recipient or beneficial owner from which to withhold an amount and has knowledge of the facts that give rise to the payment. The exemption from the obligation to withhold under this paragraph (d) shall not apply, however, to distributions with respect to stock or if the lack of control or custody of money or property from which to withhold is part of a pre-arranged plan known to the withholding agent to avoid withholding under section 1441, 1442, or 1443. For purposes of this paragraph (d), a withholding agent is related to the recipient or beneficial owner if it is related within the meaning of section 482. Any exemption from withholding pursuant to this paragraph (d) applies without a requirement that documentation be furnished to the withholding agent. However, documentation may have to be furnished for purposes of the information reporting provisions under chapter 61 of the Code and backup withholding under section 3406. The exemption from withholding under this paragraph (d) is not a determination that the amounts are not fixed or determinable annual or periodical income, nor does it constitute an exemption from reporting the amount under § 1.1461-1(b) and (c).

(2) *Cancellation of debt.*—A lender of funds who forgives any portion of the loan is deemed to have made a payment of income to the borrower under § 1.61-12 at the time the event of forgiveness occurs. However, based on the rules of paragraph (d)(1) of this section, the lender shall have no obligation to withhold on such amount to the extent that it does not have custody or control over money or property of the borrower at any time between the time that the loan is forgiven and the due date (including extensions) of the Form 1042 for the year in which the payment is deemed to occur. A payment received by the lender from the borrower in partial settlement of the debt obligation does not, for this purpose, constitute an amount of money or property belonging to the borrower from which the withholding tax liability can be satisfied.

(3) *Satisfaction of liability following underwithholding by withholding agent.*—A withholding agent who, after failing to withhold the proper amount from a payment, satisfies the underwithheld amount out of its own funds may cause the beneficial owner to realize income to the extent of such satisfaction or may be considered to have advanced funds to the beneficial owner. Such determination depends upon the contractual arrangements governing the satisfaction of such tax liability (e.g., arrangements in which the withholding agent agrees to pay the amount due under section 1441 for the beneficial owner) or applicable laws governing the transaction. If the satisfaction of the tax liability is considered to constitute an advance of funds by the withholding agent to the beneficial owner and the withholding agent fails to collect the amount from the

Reg. § 1.1441-2(d)(3)

beneficial owner, a cancellation of indebtedness may result, giving rise to income to the beneficial owner under § 1.61-12. While such income is annual or periodical fixed or determinable, the withholding agent shall have no liability to withhold on such income to the extent the conditions set forth in paragraphs (d)(1) and (2) of this section are satisfied with respect to this income. Contrast the rules of this paragraph (d)(3) with the rules in § 1.1441-3(f)(1) dealing with a situation in which the satisfaction of the beneficial owner's tax liability itself constitutes additional income to the beneficial owner. See, also, § 1.1441-3(c)(2)(ii)(B) for a special rule regarding underwithholding on corporate distributions due to underestimating an amount of earnings and profits.

(e) *Payment.*—(1) *General rule.*—A payment is considered made to a person if that person realizes income whether or not such income results from an actual transfer of cash or other property. For example, realization of income from cancellation of debt results in a deemed payment. A payment is considered made when the amount would be includible in the income of the beneficial owner under the U.S. tax principles governing the cash basis method of accounting. A payment is considered made whether it is made directly to the beneficial owner or to another person for the benefit of the beneficial owner (e.g., to the agent of the beneficial owner). Thus, a payment of income is considered made to a beneficial owner if it is paid in complete or partial satisfaction of the beneficial owner's debt to a creditor. In the event of a conflict between the rules of this paragraph (e)(1) governing whether a payment has occurred and its timing and the rules of § 31.3406(a)-4 of this chapter, the rules in § 31.3406(a)-4 of this chapter shall apply to the extent that the application of section 3406 is relevant to the transaction at issue.

(2) *Income allocated under section 482.*—A payment is considered made to the extent income subject to withholding is allocated under section 482. Further, income arising as a result of a secondary adjustment made in conjunction with a reallocation of income under section 482 from a foreign person to a related U.S. person is considered paid to a foreign person unless the taxpayer to whom the income is reallocated has entered into a repatriation agreement with the IRS and the agreement eliminates the liability for withholding under this section. For purposes of determining the liability for withholding, the payment of income is deemed to have occurred on the last day of the taxable year in which the transactions that give rise to the allocation of income and the secondary adjustments, if any, took place.

(3) *Blocked income.*—Income is not considered paid if it is blocked under executive authority, such as the President's exercise of emergency power under the Trading with the Enemy Act (50 U.S.C. App. 5), or the International Emergency Economic Powers Act (50 U.S.C. 1701 et seq).. However, on the date that the blocking restrictions are removed, the income that was blocked is considered constructively received by the beneficial owner (and therefore paid for purposes of this section) and subject to withholding under § 1.1441-1. Any exemption from withholding pursuant to this paragraph (e)(3) applies without a requirement that documentation be furnished to the withholding agent. However, documentation may have to be furnished for purposes of the information reporting provisions under chapter 61 of the Code and backup withholding under section 3406. The exemption from withholding granted by this paragraph (e)(3) is not a determination that the amounts are not fixed or determinable annual or periodical income.

(4) *Special rules for dividends.*—For purposes of sections 1441 and 6042, in the case of stock for which the record date is earlier than the payment date, dividends are considered paid on the payment date. In the case of a corporate reorganization, if a beneficial owner is required to exchange stock held in a former corporation for stock in a new corporation before dividends that are to be paid with respect to the stock in the new corporation will be paid on such stock, the dividend is considered paid on the date that the payee or beneficial owner actually exchanges the stock and receives the dividend. See § 31.3406(a)-4(a)(2) of this chapter.

(5) *Certain interest accrued by a foreign corporation.*—For purposes of sections 1441 and 6049, a foreign corporation shall be treated as having made a payment of interest as of the last day of the taxable year if it has made an election under § 1.884-4(c)(1) to treat accrued interest as if it were paid in that taxable year.

(6) *Payments other than in U.S. dollars.*—For purposes of section 1441, a payment includes amounts paid in a medium other than U.S. dollars. See § 1.1441-3(e) for rules regarding the amount subject to withholding in the case of such payments.

(f) *Effective date.*—This section applies to payments made after December 31, 2000. [Reg. § 1.1441-2.]

☐ [*T.D. 6187, 7-5-56. Amended by T.D.* 6464, 5-11-60; *T.D.* 6592, 2-27-62; *T.D.* 6841, 7-26-65; *T.D.* 6873, 1-24-66; *T.D.* 6908, 12-30-66; *T.D.* 7977, 9-19-84; *T.D.* 8734, 10-6-97; *T.D.* 8804,

12-30-98; *T.D. 8856,* 12-29-99 *and T.D. 8881,* 5-15-2000.]

§ 1.1441-3. Determination of amounts to be withheld.—(a) *Withholding on gross amount.*—Except as otherwise provided in regulations under section 1441, the amount subject to withholding under § 1.1441-1 is the gross amount of income subject to withholding that is paid to a foreign person. The gross amount of income subject to withholding may not be reduced by any deductions, except to the extent that one or more personal exemptions are allowed as provided under § 1.1441-4(b)(6).

(b) *Withholding on payments on certain obligations.*—(1) *Withholding at time of payment of interest.*—When making a payment on an interest-bearing obligation, a withholding agent must withhold under § 1.1441-1 upon the gross amount of stated interest payable on the interest payment date, regardless of whether the payment constitutes a return of capital or the payment of income within the meaning of section 61. To the extent an amount was withheld on an amount of capital rather than interest, see the rules for adjustments, refunds, or credits under § 1.1441-1(b)(8).

(2) *No withholding between interest payment dates.*—(i) *In general.*—A withholding agent is not required to withhold under § 1.1441-1 upon interest accrued on the date of a sale or exchange of a debt obligation when that sale occurs between two interest payment dates (even though the amount is treated as interest under § 1.61-7(c) or (d) and is subject to tax under section 871 or 881). See § 1.6045-1(c) for reporting requirements by brokers with respect to sale proceeds. See § 1.61-7(c) regarding the character of payments received by the acquirer of an obligation subsequent to such acquisition (that is, as a return of capital or interest accrued after the acquisition). Any exemption from withholding pursuant to this paragraph (b)(2)(i) applies without a requirement that documentation be furnished to the withholding agent. However, documentation may have to be furnished for purposes of the information reporting provisions under section 6045 or 6049 and backup withholding under section 3406. The exemption from withholding granted by this paragraph (b)(2) is not a determination that the accrued interest is not fixed or determinable annual or periodical income under section 871 (a) or 881(a).

(ii) *Anti-abuse rule.*—The exemption in paragraph (b)(2)(i) of this section does not apply if the sale of securities is part of a plan the principal purpose of which is to avoid tax by selling and repurchasing securities and the withholding agent has actual knowledge or reason to know of such plan.

(c) *Corporate distributions.*—(1) *General rule.*—A corporation making a distribution with respect to its stock or any intermediary (described in § 1.1441-1(c)(13)) making a payment of such a distribution is required to withhold under section 1441, 1442, or 1443 on the entire amount of the distribution, unless it elects to reduce the amount of withholding under the provisions of this paragraph (c). Any exceptions from withholding provided by this paragraph (c) apply without any requirement to furnish documentation to the withholding agent. However, documentation may have to be furnished for purposes of the information reporting provisions under section 6042 or 6045 and backup withholding under section 3406. See § 1.1461-1(c) to determine whether amounts excepted from withholding under this section are considered amounts that are subject to reporting.

(2) *Exception to withholding on distributions.*—(i) *In general.*—An election described in paragraph (c)(1) of this section is made by actually reducing the amount of withholding at the time that the payment is made. An intermediary that makes a payment of a distribution is not required to reduce the withholding based on the distributing corporation's estimates under this paragraph (c)(2), even if the distributing corporation itself elects to reduce the withholding on payments of distributions that it itself makes to foreign persons. Conversely, an intermediary may elect to reduce the amount of withholding with respect to the payment of a distribution even if the distributing corporation does not so elect for the payments of distributions that it itself makes of distributions to foreign persons. The amounts with respect to which a distributing corporation or intermediary may elect to reduce the withholding are as follows:

(A) A distributing corporation or intermediary may elect to not withhold on a distribution to the extent it represents a nontaxable distribution payable in stock or stock rights.

(B) A distributing corporation or intermediary may elect to not withhold on a distribution to the extent it represents a distribution in part or full payment in exchange for stock.

(C) A distributing corporation or intermediary may elect to not withhold on a distribution (actual or deemed) to the extent it is not paid out of accumulated earnings and profits or current earnings and profits, based on a reasonable estimate determined under paragraph (c)(2)(ii) of this section.

(D) A regulated investment company or intermediary may elect to not withhold on a distribution representing a capital gain dividend (as defined in section 852(b)(3)(C)) or an exempt interest dividend (as defined in section 852(b)(5)(A)) based on the applicable procedures described under paragraph (c)(3) of this section.

(E) A U.S. Real Property Holding Corporation (defined in section 897(c)(2)) or a real estate investment trust (defined in section 856) or intermediary may elect to not withhold on a distribution to the extent it is subject to withholding under section 1445 and the regulations under that section. See paragraph (c)(4) of this section for applicable procedures.

(ii) *Reasonable estimate of accumulated and current earnings and profits on the date of payment.*—(A) *General rule.*—A reasonable estimate for purposes of paragraph (c)(2)(i)(C) of this section is a determination made by the distributing corporation at a time reasonably close to the date of payment of the extent to which the distribution will constitute a dividend, as defined in section 316. The determination is based upon the anticipated amount of accumulated earnings and profits and current earnings and profits for the taxable year in which the distribution is made, the distributions made prior to the distribution for which the estimate is made and all other relevant facts and circumstances. A reasonable estimate may be made based on the procedures described in § 31.3406(b)(2)-4(c)(2) of this chapter.

(B) *Procedures in case of underwithholding.*—A distributing corporation or intermediary that is a withholding agent with respect to a distribution and that determines at the end of the taxable year in which the distribution is made that it underwithheld under section 1441 on the distribution shall be liable for the amount underwithheld as a withholding agent under section 1461. However, for purposes of this section and § 1.1461-1, any amount underwithheld paid by a distributing corporation, its paying agent, or an intermediary shall not be treated as income subject to additional withholding even if that amount is treated as additional income to the shareholders unless the additional amount is income to the shareholder as a result of a contractual arrangement between the parties regarding the satisfaction of the shareholder's tax liabilities. In addition, no penalties shall be imposed for failure to withhold and deposit the tax if—

(1) The distributing corporation made a reasonable estimate as provided in paragraph (c)(2)(ii)(A) of this section; and

(2) Either—

(i) The corporation or intermediary pays over the underwithheld amount on or before the due date for filing a Form 1042 for the calendar year in which the distribution is made, pursuant to § 1.1461-2(b); or

(ii) The corporation or intermediary is not a calendar year taxpayer and it files an amended return on Form 1042X (or such other form as the Commissioner may prescribe) for the calendar year in which the distribution is made and pays the underwithheld amount and interest within 60 days after the close of the taxable year in which the distribution is made.

(C) *Reliance by intermediary on reasonable estimate.*—For purposes of determining whether the payment of a corporate distribution is a dividend, a withholding agent that is not the distributing corporation may, absent actual knowledge or reason to know otherwise, rely on representations made by the distributing corporation regarding the reasonable estimate of the anticipated accumulated and current earnings and profits made in accordance with paragraph (c)(2)(ii)(A) of this section. Failure by the withholding agent to withhold the required amount due to a failure by the distributing corporation to reasonably estimate the portion of the distribution treated as a dividend or to properly communicate the information to the withholding agent shall be imputed to the distributing corporation. In such a case, the Internal Revenue Service (IRS) may collect from the distributing corporation any underwithheld amount and subject the distributing corporation to applicable interest and penalties as a withholding agent.

(D) *Example.*—The rules of this paragraph (c)(2) are illustrated by the following example:

Example. (i) *Facts.* Corporation X, a publicly traded corporation with both U.S. and foreign shareholders and a calendar year taxpayer, has an accumulated deficit in earnings and profits at the close of 2000. In 2001, Corporation X generates $1 million of current earnings and profits each month and makes an $18 million distribution, resulting in a $12 million dividend. Corporation X plans to make an additional $18 million distribution on October 1, 2002. Approximately one month before that date, Corporation X's management receives an internal report from its legal and accounting department concerning Corporation X's estimated current earnings and profits. The report states that Corporation X should generate only $5.1 million of current earnings and profits by the close of the third quarter due to costs relating to substantial organizational and product changes, but these changes will enable Corporation X to generate $1.3 million of earnings and profits monthly for the last quarter of the 2002 fiscal year. Thus, the total amount of current and earnings and profits for 2002 is estimated to be $9 million.

(ii) *Analysis.* Based on the facts in paragraph (i) of this *Example*, including the fact that earnings and profits estimate was made within a reasonable time before the distribution, Corporation X can rely on the estimate under paragraph (c)(2)(ii)(A) of this section. Therefore, Corporation X may treat $9 million of the $18 million of the October 1, 2002, distribution to foreign shareholders as a non-dividend distribution.

(3) *Special rules in the case of distributions from a regulated investment company.*—(i) *General rule.*—If the amount of any distributions designated as being subject to section 852(b)(3)(C) or (5)(A) exceeds the amount that may be designated under those sections for the taxable year, then no penalties will be asserted for any resulting underwithholding if the designations were based on a reasonable estimate (made pursuant to the same procedures as are described in paragraph (c)(2)(ii)(A) of this section) and the adjustments to the amount withheld are made within the time period described in paragraph (c)(2)(ii)(B) of this section. Any adjustment to the amount of tax due and paid to the IRS by the withholding agent as a result of underwithholding shall not be treated as a distribution for purposes of section 562(c) and the regulations thereunder. Any amount of U.S. tax that a foreign shareholder is treated as having paid on the undistributed capital gain of a regulated investment company under section 852(b)(3)(D) may be claimed by the foreign shareholder as a credit or refund under § 1.1464-1.

(ii) *Reliance by intermediary on reasonable estimate.*—For purposes of determining whether a payment is a distribution designated as subject to section 852(b)(3)(C) or (5)(A), a withholding agent that is not the distributing regulated investment company may, absent actual knowledge or reason to know otherwise, rely on the designations that the distributing company represents have been made in accordance with paragraph (c)(3)(i) of this section. Failure by the withholding agent to withhold the required amount due to a failure by the regulated investment company to reasonably estimate the required amounts or to properly communicate the relevant information to the withholding agent shall be imputed to the distributing company. In such a case, the IRS may collect from the distributing company any underwithheld amount and subject the company to applicable interest and penalties as a withholding agent.

(4) *Coordination with withholding under section 1445.*—(i) *In general.*—A distribution from a U.S. Real Property Holding Corporation (USRPHC) (or from a corporation that was a USRPHC at any time during the five-year period ending on the date of distribution) with respect to stock that is a U.S. real property interest under section 897(c) or from a Real Estate Investment Trust (REIT) with respect to its stock is subject to the withholding provisions under section 1441 (or section 1442 or 1443) and section 1445. A USRPHC making a distribution shall be treated as satisfying its withholding obligations under both sections if it withholds in accordance with one of the procedures described in either paragraph (c)(4)(i)(A) or (B) of this section. A USRPHC must apply the same withholding procedure to all the distributions made during the taxable year. However, the USRPHC may change the applicable withholding procedure from year to year. For rules regarding distributions by REITs, see paragraph (c)(4)(i)(C) of this section.

(A) *Withholding under section 1441.*—The USRPHC may choose to withhold on a distribution only under section 1441 (or 1442 or 1443) and not under section 1445. In such a case, the USRPHC must withhold under section 1441 (or 1442 or 1443) on the full amount of the distribution, whether or not any portion of the distribution represents a return of basis or capital gain. If a reduced tax rate under an income tax treaty applies to the distribution by the USRPHC, then the applicable rate of withholding on the distribution shall be no less than 10-percent, unless the applicable treaty specifies an applicable lower rate for distributions from a USRPHC, in which case the lower rate may apply.

(B) *Withholding under both sections 1441 and 1445.*—As an alternative to the procedure described in paragraph (c)(4)(i)(A) of this section, a USRPHC may choose to withhold under both sections 1441 (or 1442 or 1443) and 1445 under the procedures set forth in this paragraph (c)(4)(i)(B). The USRPHC must make a reasonable estimate of the portion of the distribution that is a dividend under paragraph (c)(2)(ii)(A) of this section, and must—

(1) Withhold under section 1441 (or 1442 or 1443) on the portion of the distribution that is estimated to be a dividend under paragraph (c)(2)(ii)(A) of this section; and

(2) Withhold under section 1445(e)(3) and § 1.1445-5(e) on the remainder of the distribution or on such smaller portion

Reg. § 1.1441-3(c)(4)(i)(B)(2)

based on a withholding certificate obtained in accordance with § 1.1445-5(e)(2)(iv).

(C) *Coordination with REIT withholding.*—Withholding is required under section 1441 (or 1442 or 1443) on the portion of a distribution from a REIT that is not designated as a capital gain dividend, a return of basis, or a distribution in excess of a shareholder's adjusted basis in the stock of the REIT that is treated as a capital gain under section 301(c)(3). A distribution in excess of a shareholder's adjusted basis in the stock of the REIT is, however, subject to withholding under section 1445, unless the interest in the REIT is not a U.S. real property interest (e.g., an interest in a domestically controlled REIT under section 897(h)(2)). In addition, withholding is required under section 1445 on the portion of the distribution designated by a REIT as a capital gain dividend. See § 1.1445-8.

(ii) *Intermediary reliance rule.*—A withholding agent that is not the distributing USRPHC must withhold under paragraph (c)(4)(i) of this section, but may, absent actual knowledge or reason to know otherwise, rely on representations made by the USRPHC regarding the determinations required under paragraph (c)(4)(i) of this section. Failure by the withholding agent to withhold the required amount due to a failure by the distributing USRPHC to make these determinations in a reasonable manner or to properly communicate the determinations to the withholding agent shall be imputed to the distributing USRPHC. In such a case, the IRS may collect from the distributing USRPHC any underwithheld amount and subject the distributing USRPHC to applicable interest and penalties as a withholding agent.

(d) *Withholding on payments that include an undetermined amount of income.*—(1) *In general.*—Where the withholding agent makes a payment and does not know at the time of payment the amount that is subject to withholding because the determination of the source of the income or the calculation of the amount of income subject to tax depends upon facts that are not known at the time of payment, then the withholding agent must withhold an amount under § 1.1441-1 based on the entire amount paid that is necessary to assure that the tax withheld is not less than 30 percent (or other applicable percentage) of the amount that will subsequently be determined to be from sources within the United States or to be income subject to tax. The amount so withheld shall not exceed 30 percent of the amount paid. In the alternative, the withholding agent may make a reasonable estimate of the amount from U.S. sources or of the taxable amount and set aside a corresponding portion of the amount due under the transaction and hold such portion in escrow until the amount from U.S. sources or the taxable amount can be determined, at which point withholding becomes due under § 1.1441-1. See § 1.1441-1(b)(8) regarding adjustments in the case of overwithholding. The provisions of this paragraph (d)(1) shall not apply to the extent that other provisions of the regulations under chapter 3 of the Internal Revenue Code (Code) specify the amount to be withheld, if any, when the withholding agent lacks knowledge at the time of payment (e.g., lack of reliable knowledge regarding the status of the payee or beneficial owner, addressed in § 1.1441-1(b)(3), or lack of knowledge regarding the amount of original issue discount under § 1.1441-2(b)(3)).

(2) *Withholding on certain gains.*—Absent actual knowledge or reason to know otherwise, a withholding agent may rely on a claim regarding the amount of gain described in § 1.1441-2(c) if the beneficial owner withholding certificate, or other appropriate withholding certificate, states the beneficial owner's basis in the property giving rise to the gain. In the absence of a reliable representation on a withholding certificate, the withholding agent must withhold an amount under § 1.1441-1 that is necessary to assure that the tax withheld is not less than 30 percent (or other applicable percentage) of the recognized gain. For this purpose, the recognized gain is determined without regard to any deduction allowed by the Code from the gains. The amount so withheld shall not exceed 30 percent of the amount payable by reason of the transaction giving rise to the recognized gain. See § 1.1441-1(b)(8) regarding adjustments in the case of overwithholding.

(e) *Payments other than in U.S. dollars.*—(1) *In general.*—The amount of a payment made in a medium other than U.S. dollars is measured by the fair market value of the property or services provided in lieu of U.S. dollars. The withholding agent may liquidate the property prior to payment in order to withhold the required amount of tax under section 1441 or obtain payment of the tax from an alternative source. However, the obligation to withhold under section 1441 is not deferred even if no alternative source can be located. Thus, for purposes of withholding under chapter 3 of the Code, the provisions of § 31.3406(h)-2(b)(2)(ii) of this chapter (relating to backup withholding from another source) shall not apply. If the withholding agent satisfies the tax liability related to such payments, the rules of paragraph (f) of this section apply.

(2) *Payments in foreign currency.*—If the amount subject to withholding tax is paid in a currency other than the U.S. dollar, the amount of withholding under section 1441 shall be determined by applying the applicable rate of withholding to the foreign currency amount and converting the amount withheld into U.S. dollars on the date of payment at the spot rate (as defined in § 1.988-1(d)(1)) in effect on that date. A withholding agent making regular or frequent payments in foreign currency may use a month-end spot rate or a monthly average spot rate. A spot rate convention must be used consistently for all non-dollar amounts withheld and from year to year. Such convention cannot be changed without the consent of the Commissioner. The U.S. dollar amount so determined shall be treated by the beneficial owner as the amount of tax paid on the income for purposes of determining the final U.S. tax liability and, if applicable, claiming a refund or credit of tax.

(f) *Tax liability of beneficial owner satisfied by withholding agent.*—(1) *General rule.*—In the event that the satisfaction of a tax liability of a beneficial owner by a withholding agent constitutes income to the beneficial owner and such income is of a type that is subject to withholding, the amount of the payment deemed made by the withholding agent for purposes of this paragraph (f) shall be determined under the gross-up formula provided in this paragraph (f)(1). Whether the payment of the tax by the withholding agent constitutes a satisfaction of the beneficial owner's tax liability and whether, as such, it constitutes additional income to the beneficial owner, must be determined under all the facts and circumstances surrounding the transaction, including any agreements between the parties and applicable law. The formula described in this paragraph (f)(1) is as follows:

$$\text{Payment} = \frac{\text{Gross payment without withholding}}{1 - (\text{tax rate})}$$

(2) *Example.*—The following example illustrates the provisions of this paragraph (f):

Example. College X awards a qualified scholarship within the meaning of section 117(b) to foreign student, FS, who is in the United States on an F visa. FS is a resident of a country that does not have an income tax treaty with the United States. The scholarship is $20,000 to be applied to tuition, mandatory fees and books, plus benefits in kind consisting of room and board and roundtrip air transportation. College X agrees to pay any U.S. income tax owed by FS with respect to the scholarship. The fair market value of the room and board measured by the amount College X charges non-scholarship students is $6,000. The cost of the roundtrip air transportation is $2,600. Therefore, the total fair market value of the scholarship received by FS is $28,600. However, the amount taxable is limited to the fair market value of the benefits in kind ($8,600) because the portion of the scholarship amount for tuition, fees, and books is not included in gross income under section 117. The applicable rate of withholding is 14 percent under section 1441(b). Therefore, under the gross-up formula, College X is deemed to make a payment of $10,000 ($8,600 divided by (1 − .14). The U.S. tax that must be deducted and withheld from the payment under section 1441(b) is $1,400 (.14 × $10,000). College X reports scholarship income of $30,000 and $1,400 of U.S. tax withheld on Forms 1042 and 1042-S.

(g) *Conduit financing arrangements.*—(1) *Duty to withhold.*—A financed entity or other person required to withhold tax under section 1441 with respect to a financing arrangement that is a conduit financing arrangement within the meaning of § 1.881-3(a)(2)(iv) shall be required to withhold under section 1441 as if the district director had determined, pursuant to § 1.881-3(a)(3), that all conduit entities that are parties to the conduit financing arrangement should be disregarded. The amount of tax required to be withheld shall be determined under § 1.881-3(d). The withholding agent may withhold tax at a reduced rate if the financing entity establishes that it is entitled to the benefit of a treaty that provides a reduced rate of tax on a payment of the type deemed to have been paid to the financing entity. Section 1.881-3(a)(3)(ii)(E) shall not apply for purposes of determining whether any person is required to deduct and withhold tax pursuant to this paragraph (g), or whether any party to a financing arrangement is liable for failure to withhold or entitled to a refund of tax under sections 1441 or 1461 to 1464 (except to the extent the amount withheld exceeds the tax liability determined under § 1.881-3(d)). See § 1.1441-7(f) relating to withholding tax liability of the withholding agent in conduit financing arrangements subject to § 1.881-3.

(2) *Effective date.*—This paragraph (g) is effective for payments made by financed entities on or after September 11, 1995. This paragraph shall not apply to interest payments covered by section 127(g)(3) of the Tax Reform Act of 1984, and to interest payments with respect to other debt obligations issued prior to October 15, 1984 (whether or not such debt was issued by a Netherlands Antilles corporation).

(h) *Effective date.*—Except as otherwise provided in paragraph (g) of this section, this section applies to payments made after December 31, 2000. [Reg. § 1.1441-3.]

☐ [*T.D.* 6187, 7-5-56. *Amended by T.D.* 6592, 2-27-62; *T.D.* 6636, 2-25-63; *T.D.* 6669, 8-26-63; *T.D.* 6777, 12-15-64; *T.D.* 6908, 12-30-66; *T.D.* 7378, 9-29-75; *T.D.* 7977, 9-19-84; *T.D.* 8611, 8-10-95; *T.D.* 8734, 10-6-97; *T.D.* 8804, 12-30-98; *T.D.* 8856, 12-29-99 *and T.D.* 8881, 5-15-2000.]

§ 1.1441-4. Exemptions from withholding for certain effectively connected income and other amounts.—(a) *Certain income connected with a U.S. trade or business.*—(1) *In general.*—No withholding is required under section 1441 on income otherwise subject to withholding if the income is (or is deemed to be) effectively connected with the conduct of a trade or business within the United States and is includible in the beneficial owner's gross income for the taxable year. For purposes of this paragraph (a), an amount is not deemed to be includible in gross income if the amount is (or is deemed to be) effectively connected with the conduct of a trade or business within the United States and the beneficial owner claims an exemption from tax under an income tax treaty because the income is not attributable to a permanent establishment in the United States. To claim a reduced rate of withholding because the income is not attributable to a permanent establishment, see § 1.1441-6(b)(1). This paragraph (a) does not apply to income of a foreign corporation to which section 543(a)(7) applies for the taxable year or to compensation for personal services performed by an individual. See paragraph (b) of this section for compensation for personal services performed by an individual.

(2) *Withholding agent's reliance on a claim of effectively connected income.*—(i) *In general.*—Absent actual knowledge or reason to know otherwise, a withholding agent may rely on a claim of exemption based upon paragraph (a)(1) of this section if, prior to the payment to the foreign person, the withholding agent can reliably associate the payment with a Form W-8 upon which it can rely to treat the payment as made to a foreign beneficial owner in accordance with § 1.1441-1(e)(1)(ii). For purposes of this paragraph (a), a withholding certificate is valid only if, in addition to other applicable requirements, it includes the taxpayer identifying number of the person whose name is on the Form W-8 and represents, under penalties of perjury, that the amounts for which the certificate is furnished are effectively connected with the conduct of a trade or business in the United States and is includable in the beneficial owner's gross income for the taxable year. In the absence of a reliable claim that the income is effectively connected with the conduct of a trade or business in the United States, the income is presumed not to be effectively connected, except as otherwise provided in paragraph (a)(2)(ii) or (3) of this section. See § 1.1441-1(e)(4)(ii)(C) for the period of validity applicable to a certificate provided under this section and § 1.1441-1(e)(4)(ii)(D) for changes in circumstances arising during the taxable year indicating that the income to which the certificate relates is not, or is no longer expected to be, effectively connected with the conduct of a trade or business within the United States. A withholding certificate shall be effective only for the item or items of income specified therein. The provisions of § 1.1441-1(b)(3)(iv) dealing with a 90-day grace period shall apply for purposes of this section.

(ii) *Special rules for U.S. branches of foreign persons.*—(A) *U.S. branches of certain foreign banks or foreign insurance companies.*—A payment to a U.S. branch described in § 1.1441-1(b)(2)(iv)(A) is presumed to be effectively connected with the conduct of a trade or business in the United States without the need to furnish a certificate, unless the U.S. branch provides a U.S. branch withholding certificate described in § 1.1441-1(e)(3)(v) that represents otherwise. If no certificate is furnished but the income is not, in fact, effectively connected income, then the branch must withhold whether the payment is collected on behalf of other persons or on behalf of another branch of the same entity. See § 1.1441-1(b)(2)(iv) and (6) for general rules applicable to payments to U.S. branches of foreign persons.

(B) *Other U.S. branches.*—See § 1.1441-1(b)(2)(iv)(E) for similar procedures for other U.S. branches to the extent provided in a determination letter from the district director or the Assistant Commissioner (International).

(3) *Income on notional principal contracts.*—(i) *General rule.*—A withholding agent that pays amounts attributable to a notional principal contract described in § 1.863-7(a) or 1.988-2(e) shall have no obligation to withhold on the amounts paid under the terms of the notional principal contract regardless of whether a withholding certificate is provided. However, a withholding agent must file returns under § 1.1461-1(b) and (c) reporting the income that it must treat as effectively connected with the conduct of a trade or business in the United States under the provisions of this paragraph (a)(3). Except as otherwise provided in paragraph (a)(3)(ii) of this section, a withholding agent must treat the income as effectively connected with the conduct of a U.S. trade or business if the income is paid to, or to the account of, a qualified business unit of a foreign person located in the United States or, if the

payment is paid to, or to the account of, a qualified business unit of a foreign person located outside the United States, the withholding agent knows, or has reason to know, the payment is effectively connected with the conduct of a trade or business within the United States. Income on a notional principal contract does not include the amount characterized as interest under the provisions of § 1.446-3(g)(4).

(ii) *Exception for certain payments.*—A payment shall not be treated as effectively connected with the conduct of a trade or business within the United States for purposes of paragraph (a)(3)(i) of this section even if no withholding certificate is furnished if the payee provides a representation in a master agreement that governs the transactions in notional principal contracts between the parties (for example an International Swaps and Derivatives Association (ISDA) Agreement, including the Schedule thereto) or in the confirmation on the particular notional principal contract transaction that the payee is a U.S. person or a non-U.S. branch of a foreign person.

(b) *Compensation for personal services of an individual.*—(1) *Exemption from withholding.*—Withholding is not required under § 1.1441-1 from salaries, wages, remuneration, or any other compensation for personal services of a nonresident alien individual if such compensation is effectively connected with the conduct of a trade or business within the United States and—

(i) Such compensation is subject to withholding under section 3402 (relating to withholding on wages) and the regulations under that section;

(ii) Such compensation would be subject to withholding under section 3402 but for the provisions of section 3401(a) (not including section 3401(a)(6)) and the regulations under that section. This paragraph (b)(1)(ii) does not apply to payments to a nonresident alien individual from any trust described in section 401(a), any annuity plan described in section 403(a), any annuity, custodial account, or retirement income account described in section 403(b), or an individual retirement account or individual retirement annuity described in section 408. Instead, these payments are subject to withholding under this section to the extent they are exempted from the definition of wages under section 3401(a)(12) or to the extent they are from an annuity, custodial account, or retirement income account described in section 403(b), or an individual retirement account or individual retirement annuity described in section 408. Thus, for example, payments to a nonresident alien individual from a trust described in section 401 (a) are subject to withholding under section 1441 and not under section 3405 or section 3406;

(iii) Such compensation is for services performed by a nonresident alien individual who is a resident of Canada or Mexico and who enters and leaves the United States at frequent intervals;

(iv) Such compensation is, or will be, exempt from the income tax imposed by chapter 1 of the Code by reason of a provision of the Internal Revenue Code or a tax treaty to which the United States is a party;

(v) Such compensation is paid after January 3, 1979 as a commission or rebate paid by a ship supplier to a nonresident alien individual, who is employed by a nonresident alien individual, foreign partnership, or foreign corporation in the operation of a ship or ships of foreign registry, for placing orders for supplies to be used in the operation of such ship or ships with the supplier. See section 162(c) and the regulations thereunder for denial of deductions for illegal bribes, kickbacks, and other payments; or

(vi) Compensation that is exempt from withholding under section 3402 by reason of section 3402(e), provided that the employee and his employer enter into an agreement under section 3402(p) to provide for the withholding of income tax upon payments of amounts described in § 31.3401(a)-3(b)(1) of this chapter. An employee who desires to enter into such an agreement should furnish his employer with Form W-4 (withholding exemption certificate) (or such other form as the Internal Revenue Service (IRS) may prescribe). See section 3402(f) and the regulations thereunder and § 31.3402(p)-1 of this chapter.

(2) *Manner of obtaining withholding exemption under tax treaty.*—(i) *In general.*—In order to obtain the exemption from withholding by reason of a tax treaty, provided by paragraph (b)(1)(iv) of this section, a nonresident alien individual must submit a withholding certificate (described in paragraph (b)(2)(ii) of this section) to each withholding agent from whom amounts are to be received. A separate withholding certificate must be filed for each taxable year of the alien individual. If the withholding agent is satisfied that an exemption from withholding is warranted (see paragraph (b)(2)(iii) of this section), the withholding certificate shall be accepted in the manner set forth in paragraph (b)(2)(iv) of this section. The exemption from withholding becomes effective for payments made at least ten days after a copy of the accepted withholding certificate is forwarded to the Assistant Commissioner (International). The withholding agent may rely on an accepted withholding certificate only if the IRS has not objected to the certifi-

cate. For purposes of this paragraph (b)(2)(i), the IRS will be considered to have not objected to the certificate if it has not notified the withholding agent within a 10-day period beginning from the date that the withholding certificate is forwarded to the IRS pursuant to paragraph (b)(2)(v) of this section. After expiration of the 10-day period, the withholding agent may rely on the withholding certificate retroactive to the date of the first payment covered by the certificate. The fact that the IRS does not object to the withholding certificate within the 10-day period provided in this paragraph (b)(2)(i) shall not preclude the IRS from examining the withholding agent at a later date in light of facts that the withholding agent knew or had reason to know regarding the payment and eligibility for a reduced rate and that were not disclosed to the IRS as part of the 10-day review process.

(ii) *Withholding certificate claiming withholding exemption.*—The statement claiming an exemption from withholding shall be made on Form 8233 (or an acceptable substitute or such other form as the IRS may prescribe). Form 8233 shall be dated, signed by the beneficial owner under penalties of perjury, and contain the following information—

(A) The individual's name, permanent residence address, taxpayer identifying number (or a copy of a completed Form W-7 or SS-5 showing that a number has been applied for), and the U.S. visa number, if any;

(B) The individual's current immigration status and visa type;

(C) The individual's original date of entry into the United States;

(D) The country that issued the individual's passport and the number of such passport, or the individual's permanent address if a citizen of Canada or Mexico;

(E) The taxable year, for which the statement is to apply the compensation to which it relates, and the amount (or estimated amount if exact amount not known) of such compensation;

(F) A statement that the individual is not a citizen or resident of the United States;

(G) The number of personal exemptions claimed by the individual;

(H) A statement as to whether the compensation to be paid to him or her during the taxable year is or will be exempt from income tax and the reason why the compensation is exempt;

(I) If the compensation is exempt from withholding by reason of an income tax treaty to which the United States is a party, the tax treaty and provision under which the exemption from withholding is claimed and the country of which the individual is a resident;

(J) Sufficient facts to justify the claim in exemption from withholding; and

(K) Any other information as may be required by the form or accompanying instructions in addition to, or in lieu of, the information described in this paragraph (b)(2)(ii).

(iii) *Review by withholding agent.*—The exemption from withholding provided by paragraph (b)(1)(iv) of this section shall not apply unless the withholding agent accepts (in the manner provided in paragraph (b)(2)(iv) of this section) the statement on Form 8233 supplied by the nonresident alien individual. Before accepting the statement the withholding agent must examine the statement. If the withholding agent knows or has reason to know that any of the facts or assertions on Form 8233 may be false or that the eligibility of the individual's compensation for the exemption cannot be readily determined, the withholding agent may not accept the statement on Form 8233 and is required to withhold under this section. If the withholding agent accepts the statement and subsequently finds that any of the facts or assertions contained on Form 8233 may be false or that the eligibility of the individual's compensation for the exemption can no longer be readily determined, then the withholding agent shall promptly so notify the Assistant Commissioner (International) by letter, and the withholding agent is not relieved of liability to withhold on any amounts still to be paid. If the withholding agent is notified by the Assistant Commissioner (International) that the eligibility of the individual's compensation for the exemption is in doubt or that such compensation is not eligible for the exemption, the withholding agent is required to withhold under this section. The rules of this paragraph are illustrated by the following examples.

Example 1. C, a nonresident alien individual, submits Form 8233 to W, a withholding agent. The statement on Form 8233 does not include all the information required by paragraph (b)(2)(ii) of this section. Therefore, W has reason to know that he or she cannot readily determine whether C's compensation for personal services is eligible for an exemption from withholding and, therefore, W must withhold.

Example 2. D, a nonresident alien, is performing services for W, a withholding agent. W has accepted a statement on Form 8233 submitted by D, according to the provisions of this section. W receives notice from the Internal Revenue Service that the eligibility of D's compensation for a withholding exemption is in doubt. Therefore, W has reason to know that the eligibility of the compensation for a withholding exemption cannot be readily determined, as of the date W receives the notification, and W must withhold tax under section 1441 on amounts paid after receipt of the notification.

Example 3. E, a nonresident alien individual, submits Form 8233 to W, a withholding agent for whom E is to perform personal services. The statement contains all the information requested on Form 8233. E claims an exemption from withholding based on a personal exemption amount computed on the number of days E will perform personal services for W in the United States. If W does not know or have reason to know that any statement on the Form 8233 is false or that the eligibility of E's compensation for the withholding exemption cannot be readily determined, W can accept the statement on Form 8233 and exempt from withholding the appropriate amount of E's income.

(iv) *Acceptance by withholding agent.*—If after the review described in paragraph (b)(2)(iii) of this section the withholding agent is satisfied that an exemption from withholding is warranted, the withholding agent may accept the statement by making a certification, verified by a declaration that it is made under the penalties of perjury, on Form 8233. The certification shall be—

(A) That the withholding agent has examined the statement,

(B) That the withholding agent is satisfied that an exemption from withholding is warranted, and

(C) That the withholding agent does not know or have reason to know that the individual's compensation is not entitled to the exemption or that the eligibility of the individual's compensation for the exemption cannot be readily determined.

(v) *Copies of Form 8233.*—The withholding agent shall forward one copy of each Form 8233 that is accepted under paragraph (b)(2)(iv) of this section to the Assistant Commissioner (International), within five days of such acceptance. The withholding agent shall retain a copy of Form 8233.

(3) *Withholding agreements.*—Compensation for personal services of a nonresident alien individual who is engaged during the taxable year in the conduct of a trade or business within the United States may be wholly or partially exempted from the withholding required by § 1.1441-1 if an agreement is reached between the Assistant Commissioner (International) and the alien individual with respect to the amount of withholding required. Such agreement shall be available in the circumstances and in the manner set forth by the Internal Revenue Service, and shall be effective for payments covered by the agreement that are made after the agreement is executed by all parties. The alien individual must agree to timely file an income tax return for the current taxable year.

(4) *Final payment exemption.*— (i) *General rule.*—Compensation for independent personal services of a nonresident alien individual who is engaged during the taxable year in the conduct of a trade or business within the United States may be wholly or partially exempted from the withholding required by § 1.1441-1 from the final payment of compensation for independent personal services. This exemption does not apply to wages. This exemption from withholding is available only once during an alien individual's taxable year and is obtained by the alien individual presenting to the withholding agent a letter in duplicate from a district director stating the amount of compensation subject to the exemption and the amount that would otherwise be withheld from such final payment under section 1441 that shall be paid to the alien individual due to the exemption. The alien individual shall attach a copy of the letter to his or her income tax return for the taxable year for which the exemption is effective.

(ii) *Final payment of compensation for personal services.*—For purposes of this paragraph, final payment of compensation for personal services means the last payment of compensation, other than wages, for personal services rendered within the United States that the individual expects to receive from any withholding agent during the taxable year.

(iii) *Manner of applying for final payment exemption.*—In order to obtain the final payment exemption provided by paragraph (b)(4)(i) of this section, the nonresident alien individual (or his or her agent) must file the forms and provide the information required by the district director. Ordinary and necessary business expenses may be taken into account if substantiated to the satisfaction of the district director. The alien individual must submit a statement, signed by him or her and verified by a declaration that it is made under the penalties of perjury, that all the information provided is true and that to his or her knowledge no relevant information has been omitted. The information required to be submitted includes, but is not limited to—

(A) A statement by each withholding agent from whom amounts of gross income effectively connected with the conduct of a trade or business within the United States have been received by the alien individual during the taxable year, of the amount of such income paid and the amount of tax withheld, signed

Reg. § 1.1441-4(b)(4)(iii)(A)

and verified by a declaration that it is made under penalties of perjury;

(B) A statement by the withholding agent from whom the final payment of compensation for personal services will be received, of the amount of such final payment and the amount which would be withheld under § 1.1441-1 if a final payment exemption under paragraph (b)(4)(i) of this section is not granted, signed and verified by a declaration that it is made under penalties of perjury;

(C) A statement by the individual that he or she does not intend to receive any other amounts of gross income effectively connected with the conduct of a trade or business within the United States during the current taxable year;

(D) The amount of tax which has been withheld (or paid) under any other provision of the Code or regulations with respect to any income effectively connected with the conduct of a trade or business within the United States during the current taxable year;

(E) The amount of any outstanding tax liabilities (and interest and penalties relating thereto) from the current taxable year or prior taxable periods; and

(F) The provision of any income tax treaty under which a partial or complete exemption from withholding may be claimed, the country of the individual's residence, and a statement of sufficient facts to justify an exemption pursuant to such treaty.

(iv) *Letter to withholding agent.*—If the district director is satisfied that the information provided under paragraph (b)(4)(iii) of this section is sufficient, the district director will, after coordination with the Director of the Foreign Operations District, ascertain the amount of the alien individual's tentative income tax for the taxable year with respect to gross income that is effectively connected with the conduct of a trade or business within the United States. After the tentative tax has been ascertained, the district director will provide the alien individual with a letter to the withholding agent stating the amount of the final payment of compensation for personal services that is exempt from withholding, and the amount that would otherwise be withheld under section 1441 that shall be paid to the alien individual due to the exemption. The amount of compensation for personal services exempt from withholding under this paragraph (b)(4) shall not exceed $5,000.

Example 1. On July 15, 1983, B, a nonresident alien individual, appears before a district director with the information required by paragraph (b)(4)(iii) of this section. B has received personal service income in 1983 from which $3,000 has been withheld under section 1441. On August 1, 1983, B will receive $5,000 in personal service income from W. B does not intend to receive any other income subject to U.S. tax during 1983. Taking into account B's substantiated deductible business expenses, the district director computes the tentative tax liability on B's income effectively connected with the conduct of a trade or business in the United States during 1983 (including the $5,000 payment to be made on August 1, 1983) to be $3,300. B does not owe U.S. tax for any other taxable periods. The amount of B's final payment exemption is determined as follows:

(1) The amount of total withholding is $4,500 ($3,000 previously withheld plus $1,500, 30% of the $5,000 final payment);

(2) The amount of tentative excess withholding is $1,200 (total withholding of $4,500 minus B's tentative tax liability of $3,300); and

(3) To allow B to receive $1,200 of the amount which would otherwise have been withheld from the final payment, the district director allows a withholding exemption for $4,000 of B's final payment. W must withhold $300 from the final payment.

Example 2. The facts are the same as in Example 1 except B will receive a final payment of compensation on August 1, 1983, in the amount of $10,000 and B's tentative tax liability is $3,900. The amount of B's final payment exemption is determined as follows:

(1) The amount of total withholding is $6,000 ($3,000 previously withheld plus $3,000, 30% of the $10,000 final payment);

(2) The amount of tentative excess withholding is $2,100 (total withholding of $6,000 minus B's tentative tax liability of $3,900); and

(3) To allow B to receive $2,100 of the amount which would otherwise be withheld from the final payment, $7,000 of the final payment would have to be exempt from withholding; however, as no more than $5,000 of the final payment can be exempt from withholding under this paragraph (b)(4), the district director allows a withholding exemption for $5,000 of B's final payment. B must file a claim for refund at the end of the taxable year to obtain a refund of $600. W must withhold $1,500 from the final payment.

(5) *Requirement of return.*—The tentative tax determined by the district director under paragraph (b)(4)(iv) of this section or by the Director of the Foreign Operations District under the withholding agreement procedure of paragraph (b)(3) of this section shall not constitute a final determination of the income tax liability of the nonresident alien individual, nor shall such determination constitute a tax return of the nonresident alien individual for any taxable period. An alien individual who applies for or obtains an exemption from withholding

under the procedures of paragraphs (b)(2), (3), or (4) of this section is not relieved of the obligation to file a return of income under section 6012.

(6) *Personal exemption.*—(i) *In general.*—To determine the tax to be withheld at source under § 1.1441-1 from remuneration paid for personal services performed within the United States by a nonresident alien individual and from scholarship and fellowship income described in paragraph (c) of this section, a withholding agent may take into account one personal exemption pursuant to sections 873(b)(3) and 151 regardless of whether the income is effectively connected. For purposes of withholding under section 1441 on remuneration for personal services, the exemption must be prorated upon a daily basis for the period during which the personal services are performed within the United States by the nonresident alien individual by dividing by 365 the number of days in the period during which the individual is present in the United States for the purpose of performing the services and multiplying the result by the amount of the personal exemption in effect for the taxable year. See § 31.3402(f)(6)-1 of this chapter.

(ii) *Multiple exemptions.*—More than one personal exemption may be claimed in the case of a resident of a contiguous country or a national of the United States under section 873(b)(3). In addition, residents of a country with which the United States has an income tax treaty in effect may be eligible to claim more than one personal exemption if the treaty so provides. Claims for more than one personal exemption shall be made on the withholding certificate furnished to the withholding agent. The exemption must be prorated on a daily basis in the same manner as described in paragraph (b)(6)(i) of this section.

(iii) *Special rule where both certain scholarship and compensation income are received.*—The fact that both non-compensatory scholarship income and compensation income (including compensatory scholarship income) are received during the taxable year does not entitle the taxpayer to claim more than one personal exemption amount (or more than the additional amounts permitted under paragraph (b)(6)(ii) of this section). Thus, if a nonresident alien student receives non-compensatory taxable scholarship income from one withholding agent and compensation income from another withholding agent, no more than the total personal exemption amount permitted under the Internal Revenue Code or under an income tax treaty may be taken into account by both withholding agents. For this purpose, the withholding agent may rely on a representation from the beneficial owner that the exemption amount claimed does not exceed the amount permissible under this section.

* * *

(f) *Failure to receive withholding certificates timely or to act in accordance with applicable presumptions.*—See applicable procedures described in § 1.1441-1(b)(7) in the event the withholding agent does not hold an appropriate withholding certificate or other appropriate documentation at the time of payment or does not act in accordance with applicable presumptions described in paragraph (a)(2)(i), (2)(ii), or (3) of this section.

(g) *Effective date.*—(1) *General rule.*—This section applies to payments made after December 31, 2000.

(2) *Transition rules.*—The validity of a Form 4224 or 8233 that was valid on January 1, 1998, under the regulations in effect prior to January 1, 2001 (see 26 CFR part 1, revised April 1, 1999) and expired, or will expire, at any time during 1998, is extended until December 31, 1998. The validity of a Form 4224 or 8233 that is valid on or after January 1, 1999, remains valid until its validity expires under the regulations in effect prior to January 1, 2001 (see 26 CFR part 1, revised April 1, 1999) but in no event will such form remain valid after December 31, 2000. The rule in this paragraph (g)(2), however, does not apply to extend the validity period of a Form 4224 or 8223 that expires solely by reason of changes in the circumstances of the person whose name is on the certificate. Notwithstanding the first three sentences of this paragraph (g)(2), a withholding agent may choose to not take advantage of the transition rule in this paragraph (g)(2) with respect to one or more withholding certificates valid under the regulations in effect prior to January 1, 2001 (see 26 CFR part 1, revised April 1, 1999) and, therefore, to require withholding certificates conforming to the requirements described in this section (new withholding certificates). For purposes of this section, a new withholding certificate is deemed to satisfy the documentation requirement under the regulations in effect prior to January 1, 2001 (see 26 CFR part 1, revised April 1, 1999). Further, a new withholding certificate remains valid for the period specified in § 1.1441-1(e)(4)(ii), regardless of when the certificate is obtained. [Reg. § 1.1441-4.]

☐ [*T.D.* 6187, 7-5-56. *Amended by T.D.* 6229, 4-22-57; *T.D.* 6592, 2-27-62; *T.D.* 6908, 12-30-66; *T.D.* 6922, 6-16-67; *T.D.* 7378, 9-29-75; *T.D.* 7582, 1-2-79; *T.D.* 7777, 5-18-81; *T.D.* 7842, 11-2-82; *T.D.* 7977, 9-19-84; *T.D.* 8015, 3-25-85; *T.D.* 8288, 2-2-90; *T.D.* 8734, 10-6-97; *T.D.* 8804,

12-30-98; *T.D.* 8856, 12-29-99 *and T.D.* 8881, 5-15-2000.]

§ 1.1441-5. Withholding on payments to partnerships, trusts, and estates.—(a) *In general.*—This section describes the rules that apply to payments made to partnerships, trusts, and estates. Paragraph (b) of this section prescribes the rules that apply to a withholding agent making a payment to a U.S. partnership, trust, or estate. It also prescribes the obligations of a U.S. partnership, trust, or estate that makes a payment to a foreign partner, beneficiary, or owner. Paragraph (c) of this section prescribes rules that apply to a withholding agent that makes a payment to a foreign partnership. Paragraph (d) of this section provides presumption rules that apply to payments made to foreign partnerships. Paragraph (e) of this section prescribes rules, including presumption rules, that apply to a withholding agent that makes a payment to a foreign trust or foreign estate.

(b) *Rules applicable to U.S. partnerships, trusts, and estates.*—(1) *Payments to U.S. partnerships, trusts, and estates.*—No withholding is required under section 1.1441-1(b)(1) on a payment of an amount subject to withholding (as defined in § 1.1441-2(a)) that a withholding agent may treat as made to a U.S. payee. Therefore, if a withholding agent can reliably associate (within the meaning of § 1.1441-2(b)(vii)) a Form W-9 provided in accordance with § 1.1441-1(d)(2) or (4) by a U.S. partnership, U.S. trust, or a U.S. estate the withholding agent may treat the payment as made to a U.S. payee and the payment is not subject to withholding under section 1441 even though the partnership, trust, or estate may have foreign partners, beneficiaries, or owners. A withholding agent is also not required to withhold under section 1441 on a payment it makes to an entity presumed to be a U.S. payee under paragraphs (d)(2) and (e)(6)(ii) of this section.

(2) *Withholding by U.S. payees.*—(i) *U.S. partnerships.*—(A) *In general.*—A U.S. partnership is required to withhold under § 1.1441-1 as a withholding agent on an amount subject to withholding (as defined in § 1.1441-2(a)) that is includible in the gross income of a partner that is a foreign person. Subject to paragraph (b)(2)(v) of this section, a U.S. partnership shall withhold when any distributions that include amounts subject to withholding (including guaranteed payments made by a U.S. partnership) are made. To the extent a foreign partner's distributive share of income subject to withholding has not actually been distributed to the foreign partner, the U.S. partnership must withhold on the foreign partner's distributive share of the income on the earlier of the date that the statement required under section 6031(b) is mailed or otherwise provided to the partner or the due date for furnishing the statement.

(B) *Effectively connected income of partners.*—Withholding on items of income that are effectively connected income in the hands of the partners who are foreign persons is governed by section 1446 and not by this section. In such a case, partners in a domestic partnership are not required to furnish a withholding certificate in order to claim an exemption from withholding under section 1441(c)(1) and § 1.1441-4.

(ii) *U.S. simple trusts.*—A U.S. trust that is described in section 651(a) (a U.S. simple trust) is required to withhold under chapter 3 of the Internal Revenue Code as a withholding agent on the distributable net income includible in the gross income of a foreign beneficiary to the extent the distributable net income is an amount subject to withholding (as defined in § 1.1441-2(a)). A U.S. simple trust shall withhold when a distribution is made to a foreign beneficiary. The U.S. trust may make a reasonable estimate of the portion of the distribution that constitutes distributable net income consisting of an amount subject to withholding and apply the appropriate rate of withholding to the estimated amount. If, at the end of the taxable year in which the distribution is made, the U.S. simple trust determines that it underwithheld under section 1441 or 1442, the trust shall be liable as a withholding agent for the amount under withheld under section 1461. No penalties shall be imposed for failure to withhold and deposit the tax if the U.S. simple trust's estimate was reasonable and the trust pays the underwithheld amount on or before the due date of Form 1042 under section 1461. Any payment of underwithheld amounts by the U.S. simple trust shall not be treated as income subject to additional withholding even if that amount is treated as additional income to the foreign beneficiary, unless the additional amount is income to the foreign beneficiary as a result of a contractual arrangement between the parties regarding the satisfaction of the foreign beneficiary's tax liability. To the extent a U.S. simple trust is required to, but does not, distribute such income to a foreign beneficiary, the U.S. trust must withhold on the foreign beneficiary's allocable share at the time the income is required (without extension) to be reported on Form 1042-S under § 1.1461-1(c).

(iii) *U.S. complex trusts and U.S. estates.*—A U.S. trust that is not a trust described in section 651(a) (a U.S. complex trust) is required to withhold under chapter 3 of the Internal Revenue Code as a withholding agent on the distributable net income includible in the gross income of a foreign beneficiary to the extent the distributable net income consists of an amount subject to withholding (as defined in § 1.1441-2(a)) that is, or is required to be, distributed currently. The U.S. complex trust shall withhold when a distribution is made to a foreign beneficiary. The trust may use the same procedures regarding an estimate of the amount subject to withholding as a U.S. simple trust under paragraph (b)(2)(ii) of this section. To the extent an amount subject to withholding is required to be, but is not actually distributed, the U.S. complex trust must withhold on the foreign beneficiary's allocable share at the time the income is required to be reported on Form 1042-S under § 1.1461-1(c), without extension. A U.S. estate is required to withhold under chapter 3 of the Internal Revenue Code on the distributable net income includible in the gross income of a foreign beneficiary to the extent the distributable net income consists of an amount subject to withholding (as defined in § 1.1441-2(a)) that is actually distributed. A U.S. estate may also use the reasonable estimate procedures of paragraph (b)(2)(ii) of this section. However, those procedures apply to an estate that has a taxable year other than a calendar year only if the estate files an amended return on Form 1042 for the calendar year in which the distribution was made and pays the underwithheld tax and interest within 60 days after the close of the taxable year in which the distribution was made.

(iv) *U.S. grantor trusts.*—A U.S. trust that is described in section 671 through 679 (a U.S. grantor trust) must withhold on any income includible in the gross income of a foreign person that is treated as an owner of the grantor trust to the extent the amount includible consists of an amount that is subject to withholding (as described in § 1.1441-2(a)). The withholding must occur at the time the income is received by, or credited to, the trust.

(v) *Subsequent distribution.*—If a U.S. partnership or U.S. trust withholds on a foreign partner, beneficiary, or owner's share of an amount subject to withholding before the amount is actually distributed to the partner, beneficiary, or owner, withholding is not required when the amount is subsequently distributed.

(c) *Foreign partnerships.*—(1) *Determination of payee.*—(i) *Payments treated as made to partners.*—Except as otherwise provided in paragraph (c)(1)(ii) of this section, the payees of a payment to a person that the withholding agent may treat as a nonwithholding foreign partnership under paragraph (c)(3)(i) or (d)(2) of this section are the partners (looking through partners that are foreign intermediaries or flow-through entities) as follows—

(A) If the withholding agent can reliably associate a partner's distributive share of the payment with a valid Form W-9 provided under § 1.1441-1 (d), the partner is a U.S. payee;

(B) If the withholding agent can reliably associate a partner's distributive share of the payment with a valid Form W-8, or other appropriate documentation, provided under § 1.1441-1 (e)(1)(ii), the partner is a payee that is a foreign beneficial owner;

(C) If the withholding agent can reliably associate a partner's distributive share of the payment with a qualified intermediary withholding certificate under § 1.1441-1(e)(3)(ii), a nonqualified intermediary withholding certificate under § 1.1441-1(e)(3)(iii), or a U.S. branch certificate under § 1.1441-1(e)(3)(v), then the rules of § 1.1441-1(b)(2)(v) shall apply to determine who the payee is in the same manner as if the partner's distributive share of the payment had been paid directly to such intermediary or U.S. branch;

(D) If the withholding agent can reliably associate the partner's distributive share with a withholding foreign partnership certificate under paragraph (c)(2)(iv) of this section or a nonwithholding foreign partnership certificate under paragraph (c)(3)(iii) of this section, then the rules of this paragraph (c)(1)(i) or paragraph (c)(1)(ii) of this section shall apply to determine whether the payment is treated as made to the partners of the higher-tier partnership under this paragraph (c)(1)(i) or to the higher-tier partnership itself (under the rules of paragraph (c)(1)(ii) of this section) in the same manner as if the partner's distributive share of the payment had been paid directly to the higher-tier foreign partnership;

(E) If the withholding agent can reliably associate the partner's distributive share with a withholding certificate described in paragraph (e) of this section regarding a foreign trust or estate, then the rules of paragraph (e) of this section shall apply to determine who the payees are; and

(F) If the withholding agent cannot reliably associate the partner's distributive share with a withholding certificate or other appropriate documentation, the partners are considered to be the payees and the presumptions described in paragraph (d)(3) of this section shall apply to determine their classification and status.

(ii) *Payments treated as made to the partnership.*—A payment to a person that the withholding agent may treat as a foreign partnership is treated as a payment to the foreign partnership and not to its partners only if—

(A) The withholding agent can reliably associate the payment with a withholding certificate described in paragraph (c)(2)(iv) of this section (withholding certificate of a withholding foreign partnership);

(B) The withholding agent can reliably associate the payment with a withholding certificate described in paragraph (c)(3)(iii) of this section (nonwithholding foreign partnership) certifying that the payment is income that is effectively connected with the conduct of a trade or business in the United States; or

(C) The withholding agent can treat the income as effectively connected income under the presumption rules of § 1.1441-4(a)(2)(ii) or (3)(i).

(iii) *Rules for reliably associating a payment with documentation.*—For rules regarding the reliable association of a payment with documentation, see § 1.1441-1(b)(2)(vii). In the absence of documentation, see §§ 1.1441-1(b)(3) and 1.6049-5(d) and paragraphs (d) and (e)(6) of this section for applicable presumptions.

(iv) *Examples.*—The rules of paragraphs (c)(1)(i) and (ii) of this section are illustrated by the following examples:

Example 1. FP is a nonwithholding foreign partnership organized in Country X. FP has two partners, FC, a foreign corporation, and USP, a U.S. partnership. USWH, a U.S. withholding agent, makes a payment of U.S. source interest to FP. FP has provided USWH with a valid nonwithholding foreign partnership certificate, as described in paragraph (c)(3)(iii) of this section, with which it associates a beneficial owner withholding certificate from FC and a Form W-9 from USP together with the withholding statement required by paragraph (c)(3)(iv) of this section. USWH can reliably associate the payment of interest with the withholding certificates from FC and USP. Under paragraph (c)(1)(i) of this section, the payees of the interest payment are FC and USP.

Example 2. The facts are the same as in *Example 1*, except that FP1, a nonwithholding foreign partnership, is a partner in FP rather than USP. FP1 has two partners, A and B, both foreign persons. FP provides USWH with a valid nonwithholding foreign partnership certificate, as described in paragraph (c)(3)(iii) of this section, with which it associates a beneficial owner withholding certificate from FC and a nonwithholding foreign partnership certificate from FP1. In addition, foreign beneficial owner withholding certificates from A and B are associated with the nonwithholding foreign partnership withholding certificate from FP1. FP also provides the withholding statement required by paragraph (c)(3)(iv) of this section. USWH can reliably associate the interest payment with the withholding certificates provided by FC, A, and B. Therefore, under paragraph (c)(1)(i) of this section, the payees of the interest payment are FC, A, and B.

Example 3. USWH makes a payment of U.S. source dividends to WFP, a withholding foreign partnership. WFP has two partners, FC1 and FC2, both foreign corporations. USWH can reliably associate the payment with a valid withholding foreign partnership withholding certificate from WFP. Therefore, under paragraph (c)(1)(ii)(A) of this section, WFP is the payee of the dividends.

Example 4. USWH makes a payment of U.S. source royalties to FP, a foreign partnership. USWH can reliably associate the royalties with a valid withholding certificate from FP on which FP certifies that the income is effectively connected with the conduct of a trade or business in the United States. Therefore, under paragraph (c)(1)(ii)(B) of this section, FP is the payee of the royalties.

(2) *Withholding foreign partnerships.*—(i) *Reliance on claim of withholding foreign partnership status.*—A withholding foreign partnership is a foreign partnership that has entered into an agreement with the Internal Revenue Service (IRS), as described in paragraph (c)(2)(ii) of this section, with respect to distributions and guaranteed payments it makes to its partners. A withholding agent that can reliably associate a payment with a certificate described in paragraph (c)(2)(iv) of this section may treat the person to whom it makes the payment as a withholding foreign partnership for purposes of withholding under chapter 3 of the Internal Revenue Code, information reporting under chapter 61 of the Internal Revenue Code, backup withholding under section 3406, and withholding under other provisions of the Internal Revenue Code. Furnishing such a certificate is in lieu of transmitting to a withholding agent withholding certificates or other appropriate documentation for its partners. Although the withholding foreign partnership generally will be required to obtain withholding certificates or other appropriate documentation from its partners pursuant to its agreement with the IRS, it will generally not be required to attach such documentation to its withholding foreign partnership withholding certificate. A foreign partnership may act as a qualified intermediary under § 1.1441-1(e)(5) with respect to payments it makes to persons other than its partners. In addition, the IRS may permit a foreign partnership to act as a qualified intermediary under § 1.1441-1(e)(5)(ii)(D) with respect to its partners in appropriate circumstances.

Reg. § 1.1441-5(c)(1)(ii)(A)

(ii) *Withholding agreement.*—The IRS may, upon request, enter into a withholding agreement with a foreign partnership pursuant to such procedures as the IRS may prescribe in published guidance (see § 601.601(d)(2) of this chapter). Under the withholding agreement, a foreign partnership shall generally be subject to the applicable withholding and reporting provisions applicable to withholding agents and payors under chapters 3 and 61 of the Internal Revenue Code, section 3406, the regulations under those provisions, and other withholding provisions of the Internal Revenue Code, except to the extent provided under the agreement. Under the agreement, a foreign partnership may agree to act as an acceptance agent to perform the duties described in § 301.6109-1(d)(3)(iv)(A) of this chapter. The agreement may specify the manner in which applicable procedures for adjustments for underwithholding and overwithholding, including refund procedures, apply to the withholding foreign partnership and its partners and the extent to which applicable procedures may be modified. In particular, a withholding agreement may allow a withholding foreign partnership to claim refunds of overwithheld amounts on behalf of its customers. In addition, the agreement must specify the manner in which the IRS will audit the foreign partnership's books and records in order to verify the partnership's compliance with its agreement. A withholding foreign partnership must file a return on Form 1042 and information returns on Form 1042-S. The withholding foreign partnership agreement may also require a withholding foreign partnership to file a partnership return under section 6031(a) and partner statements under 6031(b).

(iii) *Withholding responsibility.*—A withholding foreign partnership must assume primary withholding responsibility under chapter 3 of the Internal Revenue Code. It is not required to provide information to the withholding agent regarding each partner's distributive share of the payment. The withholding foreign partnership will be responsible for reporting the payments under § 1.1461-1(c) and chapter 61 of the Internal Revenue Code. A withholding agent making a payment to a withholding foreign partnership is not required to withhold any amount under chapter 3 of the Internal Revenue Code on a payment to the withholding foreign partnership, unless it has actual knowledge or reason to know that the foreign partnership is not a withholding foreign partnership. The withholding foreign partnership shall withhold the payments under the same procedures and at the same time as prescribed for withholding by a U.S. partnership under paragraph (b)(2) of this section, except that, for purposes of determining the partner's status, the provisions of paragraph (d)(4) of this section shall apply.

(iv) *Withholding certificate from a withholding foreign partnership.*—The rules of § 1.1441-1(e)(4) shall apply to withholding certificates described in this paragraph (c)(2)(iv). A withholding certificate furnished by a withholding foreign partnership is valid with regard to any partner on whose behalf the certificate is furnished only if it is furnished on a Form W-8, an acceptable substitute form, or such other form as the IRS may prescribe, it is signed under penalties of perjury by a partner with authority to sign for the partnership, its validity has not expired, and it contains the information, statement, and certifications described in this paragraph (c)(2)(iv) as follows—

(A) The name, permanent residence address (as described in § 1.1441-1(e)(2)(ii)), and the employer identification number of the partnership, and the country under the laws of which the partnership is created or governed;

(B) A certification that the partnership is a withholding foreign partnership within the meaning of paragraph (c)(2)(i) of this section; and

(C) Any other information, certifications or statements as may be required by the withholding foreign partnership agreement with the IRS or the form or accompanying instructions in addition to, or in lieu of, the information, statements, and certifications described in this paragraph (c)(2)(iv).

(3) *Nonwithholding foreign partnerships.*—(i) *Reliance on claim of foreign partnership status.*—A withholding agent may treat a person as a nonwithholding foreign partnership if it receives from that person a nonwithholding foreign partnership withholding certificate as described in paragraph (c)(3)(iii) of this section. A withholding agent that does not receive a nonwithholding foreign partnership withholding certificate, or does not receive a valid withholding certificate, from an entity it knows, or has reason to know, is a foreign partnership, must apply the presumption rules of §§ 1.1441-1(b)(3) and 1.6049-5(d) and paragraphs (d) and (e)(6) of this section. In addition, to the extent a withholding agent cannot, prior to a payment, reliably associate the payment with valid documentation from a payee that is associated with the nonwithholding foreign partnership withholding certificate or has insufficient information to report the payment on Form 1042-S or Form 1099, to the extent reporting is required, must also apply the presumption rules. See § 1.1441-1(b)(2)(vii)(A) and (B) for rules regarding reliable association. See paragraph

Reg. § 1.1441-5(c)(3)(i)

(c)(3)(iv) of this section and § 1.1441-1(e)(3)(iv) for alternative procedures permitting allocation information to be received after a payment is made.

(ii) *Reliance on claim of reduced withholding by a partnership for its partners.*—This paragraph (c)(3)(ii) describes the manner in which a withholding agent may rely on a claim of reduced withholding when making a payment to a nonwithholding foreign partnership. To the extent that a withholding agent treats a payment to a nonwithholding foreign partnership as a payment to the nonwithholding foreign partnership's partners (whether direct or indirect) in accordance with paragraph (c)(1)(i) of this section, it may rely on a claim for reduced withholding by the partner if, prior to the payment, the withholding agent can reliably associate the payment (within the meaning of § 1.1441-1(b)(2)(vii)) with a valid withholding certificate or other appropriate documentation from the partner that establishes entitlement to a reduced rate of withholding. A withholding certificate or other appropriate documentation that establishes entitlement to a reduced rate of withholding is a beneficial owner withholding certificate described in § 1.1441-1(e)(2)(i), documentary evidence described in § 1.1441-6(c)(3) or (4) or 1.6049-5(c)(1) (for a partner claiming to be a foreign person and a beneficial owner, determined under the provisions of § 1.1441-1(c)(6)), a Form W-9 described in § 1.1441-1(d) (for a partner claiming to be a U.S. payee), or a withholding foreign partnership withholding certificate described in paragraph (c)(2)(iv) of this section. Unless a nonwithholding foreign partnership withholding certificate is provided for income claimed to be effectively connected with the conduct of a trade or business in the United States, a claim must be presented for each portion of the payment that represents an item of income includible in the distributive share of a partner as required under paragraph (c)(3)(iii)(C) of this section. When making a claim for several partners, the partnership may present a single nonwithholding foreign partnership withholding certificate to which the partners' certificates or other appropriate documentation are associated. Where the nonwithholding foreign partnership withholding certificate is provided for income claimed to be effectively connected with the conduct of a trade or business in the United States under paragraph (c)(3)(iii)(D) of this section, the claim may be presented without having to identify any partner's distributive share of the payment.

(iii) *Withholding certificate from a nonwithholding foreign partnership.*—A nonwithholding foreign partnership shall provide a nonwithholding foreign partnership withholding certificate with respect to reportable amounts received by the nonwithholding foreign partnership. A nonwithholding foreign partnership withholding certificate is valid only to the extent it is furnished on a Form W-8 (or an acceptable substitute form or such other form as the IRS may prescribe), it is signed under penalties of perjury by a partner with authority to sign for the partnership, its validity has not expired, and it contains the information, statements, and certifications described in this paragraph (c)(3)(iii) and paragraph (c)(3)(iv) of this section, and the withholding certificates and other appropriate documentation for all the persons to whom the certificate relates are associated with the certificate. The rules of § 1.1441-1(e)(4) shall apply to withholding certificates described in this paragraph (c)(3)(iii). No withholding certificates or other appropriate documentation from persons who derive income through a partnership (whether or not U.S. exempt recipients) are required to be associated with the nonwithholding foreign partnership withholding certificate if the certificate is furnished solely for income claimed to be effectively connected with the conduct of a trade or business in the United States. Withholding certificates and other appropriate documentation that may be associated with the nonwithholding foreign partnership withholding certificate consist of beneficial owner withholding certificates under § 1.1441-1(e)(2)(i), intermediary withholding certificates under § 1.1441-1(e)(3)(i), withholding foreign partnership withholding certificates under paragraph (c)(2)(iv) of this section, nonwithholding foreign partnership withholding certificates under this paragraph (c)(3)(iii), withholding certificates from foreign trusts or estates under paragraph (e) of this section, documentary evidence described in § 1.1441-6(c)(3) or (4) or documentary evidence described in § 1.6049-5(c)(1), and any other documentation or certificates applicable under other provisions of the Internal Revenue Code or regulations that certify or establish the status of the payee or beneficial owner as a U.S. or a foreign person. Nothing in this paragraph (c)(3)(iii) shall require a nonwithholding foreign partnership to furnish original documentation. Copies of certificates or documentary evidence may be transmitted to the U.S. withholding agent, in which case the nonwithholding foreign partnership must retain the original documentation for the same time period that the copy is required to be retained by the withholding agent under § 1.1441-1(e)(4)(iii) and must provide it to the withholding agent upon request. The information, statement, and certifications required on the withholding certificate are as follows—

(A) The name, permanent residence address (as described in § 1.1441-1(e)(2)(ii)), and the employer identification number of the partnership, if any, and the country under the laws of which the partnership is created or governed;

(B) A certification that the person whose name is on the certificate is a foreign partnership;

(C) A withholding statement associated with the nonwithholding foreign partnership withholding certificate that provides all of the information required by paragraph (c)(3)(iv) of this section and § 1.1441-1(e)(3)(iv). No withholding statement is required, however, for a nonwithholding foreign partnership withholding certificate furnished for income claimed to be effectively connected with the conduct of a trade or business in the United States;

(D) A certification that the income is effectively connected with the conduct of a trade or business in the United States, if applicable; and

(E) Any other information, certifications, or statements required by the form or accompanying instructions in addition to, or in lieu of, the information and certifications described in this paragraph (c)(3)(iii).

(iv) *Withholding statement provided by nonwithholding foreign partnership.*—The provisions of § 1.1441-1(e)(3)(iv) (regarding a withholding statement) shall apply to a nonwithholding foreign partnership by substituting the term nonwithholding foreign partnership for the term nonqualified intermediary.

(v) *Withholding and reporting by a foreign partnership.*—A nonwithholding foreign partnership described in this paragraph (c)(3) that receives an amount subject to withholding (as defined in § 1.1441-2(a)) shall be required to withhold and report such payment under chapter 3 of the Internal Revenue Code and the regulations thereunder except as otherwise provided in this paragraph (c)(3)(v). A nonwithholding foreign partnership shall not be required to withhold and report if it has provided a valid nonwithholding foreign partnership withholding certificate, it has provided all of the information required by paragraph (c)(3)(iv) of this section (withholding statement), and it does not know, and has no reason to know, that another withholding agent failed to withhold the correct amount or failed to report the payment correctly under § 1.1461-1(c). A withholding foreign partnership's obligations to withhold and report shall be determined in accordance with its withholding foreign partnership agreement.

(d) *Presumption rules.*—(1) *In general.*—This paragraph (d) contains the applicable presumptions for a withholding agent (including a partnership) to determine the classification and status of a partnership and its partners in the absence of documentation. The provisions of § 1.1441-1(b)(3)(iv) (regarding the 90-day grace period) and § 1.1441-1(b)(3)(vii) through (ix) shall apply for purposes of this paragraph (d).

(2) *Determination of partnership status as U.S. or foreign in the absence of documentation.*—In the absence of a valid representation of U.S. partnership status in accordance with paragraph (b)(1) of this section or of foreign partnership status in accordance with paragraph (c)(2)(i) or (3)(i) of this section, the withholding agent shall determine the classification of the payee under the presumptions set forth in § 1.1441-1(b)(3)(ii). If the withholding agent treats the payee as a partnership under § 1.1441-1(b)(3)(ii), the withholding agent shall presume the partnership to be a U.S. partnership unless there are indicia of foreign status. If there are indicia of foreign status, the withholding agent may presume the partnership to be foreign. Indicia of foreign status exist only if the withholding agent has actual knowledge of the payee's employer identification number and that number begins with the two digits "98," the withholding agent's communications with the payee are mailed to an address in a foreign country, or the payment is made outside the United States (as defined in § 1.6049-5(e)). For rules regarding reliable association with a withholding certificate from a domestic or a foreign partnership, see § 1.1441-1(b)(2)(vii).

(3) *Determination of partners' status in the absence of certain documentation.*—If a nonwithholding foreign partnership has provided a nonwithholding foreign partnership withholding certificate under paragraph (c)(3)(iii) of this section that would be valid except that the withholding agent cannot reliably associate all or a portion of the payment with valid documentation from a partner of the partnership, then the withholding agent may apply the presumption rule of this paragraph (d)(3) with respect to all or a portion of the payment for which documentation has not been received. See § 1.1441-1(b)(2)(vii)(A) and (B) for rules regarding reliable association. The presumption rule of this paragraph (d)(3) also applies to a person that is presumed to be a foreign partnership under the rule of paragraph (d)(2) of this section. Any portion of a payment that the withholding agent cannot treat as reliably associated with valid documentation from a partner may be presumed made to a foreign payee. As a result, any payment of an amount subject to withholding is subject to withholding

Reg. § 1.1441-5(d)(3)

at a rate of 30 percent. Any payment that is presumed to be made to an undocumented foreign payee must be reported on Form 1042-S. See § 1.1461-1(c).

(4) *Determination by a withholding foreign partnership of the status of its partners.*—A withholding foreign partnership shall determine whether the partners or some other persons are the payees of the partners' distributive shares of any payment made by a withholding foreign partnership by applying the rules of § 1.1441-1(b)(2), paragraph (c)(1) of this section (in the case of a partner that is a foreign partnership), and paragraph (e)(3) of this section (in the case of a partner that is a foreign estate or a foreign trust). Further, the provisions of paragraph (d)(3) of this section shall apply to determine the status of partners and the applicable withholding rates to the extent that, at the time the foreign partnership is required to withhold on a payment, it cannot reliably associate the amount with documentation for any one or more of its partners.

(e) *Foreign trusts and estates.*—(1) *In general.*—This paragraph (e) provides rules applicable to payments of amounts subject to withholding (as defined in § 1.1441-2(a)) that a withholding agent may treat as made to any foreign trust or a foreign estate. For rules relating to payments to a U.S. trust or a U.S. estate, see paragraph (b) of this section. For the definitions of foreign simple trust, foreign complex trust, and foreign grantor trust, see § 1.1441-1(c)(24), (25), and (26).

(2) *Payments to foreign complex trusts and foreign estates.*—Under § 1.1441-1(c)(6)(ii)(D), a foreign complex trust or foreign estate is generally considered to be the beneficial owner of income paid to the foreign complex trust or foreign estate. See paragraph (e)(4) of this section for rules describing when a withholding agent may treat a payment as made to a foreign complex trust or a foreign estate.

(3) *Payees of payments to foreign simple trusts and foreign grantor trusts.*—(i) *Payments for which beneficiaries and owners are payees.*—For purposes of the regulations under chapters 3 and 61 of the Internal Revenue Code and section 3406, a foreign simple trust is not a beneficial owner or a payee of a payment. Also, a foreign grantor trust (or a portion of a trust that is a foreign grantor trust) is not considered a beneficial owner or a payee of a payment. Except as otherwise provided in paragraph (e)(3)(ii) of this section, the payees of a payment made to a person that the withholding agent may treat as a foreign simple trust or a foreign grantor trust (or a portion of a trust that is a foreign grantor trust) are determined under the rules of this paragraph (e)(3)(i). The payees shall be treated as the beneficial owners if they may be so treated under § 1.1441-1(c)(6)(ii)(C) and they provide documentation supporting their status as the beneficial owners. The payees of a payment to a foreign simple trust or foreign grantor trust are determined as follows—

(A) If the withholding agent can reliably associate a payment with a valid Form W-9 provided under § 1.1441-1(d) from a beneficiary or owner of the foreign trust, then the beneficiary or owner is a U.S. payee;

(B) If the withholding agent can reliably associate a payment with a valid Form W-8, or other appropriate documentation, provided under § 1.1441-1(e)(1)(ii) from a beneficiary or owner of the foreign trust, then the beneficiary or owner is a payee that is a foreign beneficial owner;

(C) If the withholding agent can reliably associate a payment with a qualified intermediary withholding certificate under § 1.1441-1(e)(3)(ii), a nonqualified intermediary withholding certificate under § 1.1441-1(e)(3)(ii), or a U.S. branch withholding certificate under § 1.1441-1(e)(3)(v), then the rules of § 1.1441-1(b)(2)(v) shall apply to determine the payee in the same manner as if the payment had been paid directly to such intermediary or U.S. branch;

(D) If the withholding agent can reliably associate a payment with a withholding foreign partnership withholding certificate under paragraph (c)(2)(iv) of this section or a nonwithholding foreign partnership withholding certificate under paragraph (c)(3)(iii) of this section, then the rules of paragraph (c)(1)(i) or (ii) of this section shall apply to determine the payee;

(E) If the withholding agent can reliably associate the payment with a foreign simple trust withholding certificate or a foreign grantor trust withholding certificate (both described in paragraph (e)(5)(iii) of this section) from a second or higher-tier foreign simple trust or foreign grantor trust, then the rules of this paragraph (e)(3)(i) or paragraph (e)(3)(ii) of this section shall apply to determine whether the payment is treated as made to a beneficiary or owner of the higher-tier trust or to the trust itself in the same manner as if the payment had been made directly to the higher-tier trust; and

(F) If the withholding agent cannot reliably associate a payment with a withholding certificate or other appropriate documentation, the payees shall be determined by applying the presumptions described in paragraph (e)(6) of this section.

(ii) *Payments for which trust is payee.*—A payment to a person that the withholding agent may treat as made to a foreign trust under paragraph (e)(5)(iii) of this section is treated as a payment to the trust, and not to a beneficiary of the trust, only if—

(A) The withholding agent can reliably associate the payment with a foreign complex trust withholding certificate under paragraph (e)(4) of this section;

(B) The withholding agent can reliably associate the payment with a foreign simple trust withholding certificate under paragraph (e)(5)(iii) of this section certifying that the payment is income that is treated as effectively connected with the conduct of a trade or business in the United States; or

(C) The withholding agent can treat the income as effectively connected income under the presumption rules of § 1.1441-4(a)(3)(i).

(4) *Reliance on claim of foreign complex trust or foreign estate status.*—A withholding agent may treat a payment as made to a foreign complex trust or a foreign estate if the withholding agent can reliably associate the payment with a beneficial owner withholding certificate described in § 1.1441-1(e)(2)(i) or other documentary evidence under § 1.1441-6(c)(3) or (4) (regarding a claim for treaty benefits) or § 1.6049-5(c)(1) (regarding documentary evidence to establish foreign status for purposes of chapter 61 of the Internal Revenue Code) that establishes the foreign complex trust or foreign estate's status as a beneficial owner. See paragraph (e)(6) of this section for presumption rules if documentation is lacking.

(5) *Foreign simple trust and foreign grantor trust.*—(i) *Reliance on claim of foreign simple trust or foreign grantor trust status.*—A withholding agent may treat a person as a foreign simple trust or foreign grantor trust if it receives from that person a foreign simple trust or foreign grantor trust withholding certificate as described in paragraph (e)(5)(iii) of this section. A withholding agent must apply the presumption rules of §§ 1.1441-1(b)(3) and 1.6049-5(d) and paragraphs (d) and (e)(6) of this section to the extent it cannot, prior to the payment, reliably associate a payment (within the meaning of § 1.1441-1(b)(2)(vii)) with a valid foreign simple trust or foreign grantor trust withholding certificate, it cannot reliably determine how much of the payment relates to valid documentation provided by a payee (e.g., a person that is not itself a nonqualified intermediary, flow-through entity, or U.S. branch) associated with the foreign simple trust or foreign grantor trust withholding certificate, or it does not have sufficient information to report the payment on Form 1042-S or Form 1099, if reporting is required. See § 1.1441-1(b)(2)(vii)(A) and (B).

(ii) *Reliance on claim of reduced withholding by a foreign simple trust or foreign grantor trust for its beneficiaries or owners.*—This paragraph (e)(5)(ii) describes the manner in which a withholding agent may rely on a claim of reduced withholding when making a payment to a foreign simple trust or foreign grantor trust. To the extent that a withholding agent treats a payment to a foreign simple trust or foreign grantor trust as a payment to payees other than the trust in accordance with paragraph (e)(3)(i) of this section, it may rely on a claim for reduced withholding by a beneficiary or owner if, prior to the payment, the withholding agent can reliably associate the payment (within the meaning of § 1.1441-1(b)(2)(vii)) with a valid withholding certificate or other appropriate documentation from a payee or beneficial owner that establishes entitlement to a reduced rate of withholding. A withholding certificate or other appropriate documentation that establishes entitlement to a reduced rate of withholding is a beneficial owner withholding certificate described in § 1.1441-1(e)(2)(i) or documentary evidence described in § 1.1441-6(c)(3) or (4) or in § 1.6049-5(c)(1) (for a beneficiary or owner claiming to be a foreign person and a beneficial owner, determined under the provisions of § 1.1441-1(c)(6)), a Form W-9 described in § 1.1441-1(d) (for a beneficiary or owner claiming to be a U.S. payee), or a withholding foreign partnership withholding certificate described in paragraph (c)(2)(iv) of this section. Unless a foreign simple trust or foreign grantor trust withholding certificate is provided for income treated as income effectively connected with the conduct of a trade or business in the United States, a claim must be presented for each payee's portion of the payment. When making a claim for several payees, the trust may present a single foreign simple trust or foreign grantor trust withholding certificate with which the payees' certificates or other appropriate documentation are associated. Where the foreign simple trust or foreign grantor trust withholding certificate is provided for income that is treated as effectively connected with the conduct of a trade or business in the United States under paragraph (e)(5)(iii)(D) of this section, the claim may be presented without having to identify any beneficiary's or grantor's distributive share of the payment.

(iii) *Withholding certificate from foreign simple trust or foreign grantor trust.*—A withholding certificate furnished by a foreign simple trust or a foreign grantor trust that is not a withholding foreign trust (within the meaning of paragraph (e)(5)(v) of this section) is valid only if it is furnished on a Form W-8, an acceptable substitute form, or such other form as the IRS may prescribe, it is signed under penalties of perjury by a trustee, its validity has not expired, it contains the information, statements, and certifications required by this paragraph (e)(5)(iii) and §1.1441-1(e)(3)(iv), and the withholding certificates or other appropriate documentation for all of the payees (as determined under paragraph (e)(3)(i) of this section) to whom the certificate relates are associated with the foreign simple trust or foreign grantor trust withholding certificate. The rules of §1.1441-1(e)(4) shall apply to withholding certificates described in this paragraph (e)(5)(iii). No withholding certificates or other appropriate documentation from persons who derive income through a foreign simple trust or a foreign grantor trust (whether or not U.S. exempt recipients) are required to be associated with the foreign simple trust or foreign grantor trust withholding certificate if the certificate is furnished solely for income that is treated as effectively connected with the conduct of a trade or business in the United States. Withholding certificates and other appropriate documentation (as determined under paragraph (e)(3)(i) of this section) that may be associated with a foreign simple trust or foreign grantor trust withholding certificate consist of beneficial owner withholding certificates under §1.1441-1(e)(2)(i), intermediary withholding certificates under §1.1441-1(e)(3)(i), withholding foreign partnership withholding certificates under paragraph (c)(2)(iv) of this section, nonwithholding foreign partnership withholding certificates under paragraph (c)(3)(iii) of this section, withholding certificates from foreign trusts or estates under paragraph (e)(4) or (5)(iii) of this section, documentary evidence described in §§1.1441-6(c)(3) or (4), or 1.6049-5(c)(1), and any other documentation or certificates applicable under other provisions of the Internal Revenue Code or regulations that certify or establish the status of the payee or beneficial owner as a U.S. or a foreign person. Nothing in this paragraph (e)(5)(iii) shall require a foreign simple trust or foreign grantor trust to provide original documentation. Copies of certificates or documentary evidence may be passed up to the U.S. withholding agent, in which case the foreign simple trust or foreign grantor trust must retain the original documentation for the same time period that the copy is required to be retained by the withholding agent under §1.1441-1(e)(4)(iii) and must provide it to the withholding agent upon request. The information, statement, and certifications required on a foreign simple trust or foreign grantor trust withholding certificate are as follows—

(A) The name, permanent residence address (as described in §1.1441-1(e)(2)(ii)), and the employer identification number, if required, of the trust and the country under the laws of which the trust is created;

(B) A certification that the person whose name is on the certificate is a foreign simple trust or a foreign grantor trust;

(C) A withholding statement associated with the foreign simple trust or foreign grantor trust withholding certificate that provides all of the information required by paragraph (e)(5)(iv) of this section. No withholding statement is required, however, for a foreign simple trust withholding certificate furnished for income that is treated as effectively connected with the conduct of a trade or business in the United States;

(D) A certification on a foreign simple trust withholding certificate that the income is treated as effectively connected with the conduct of a trade or business in the United States, if applicable; and

(E) Any other information, certifications, or statements required by the form or accompanying instructions in addition to, or in lieu of, the information, certifications, and statements described in this paragraph (e)(5)(iii);

(iv) *Withholding statement provided by a foreign simple trust or foreign grantor trust.*— The provisions of §1.1441-1(e)(3)(iv) (regarding a withholding statement) shall apply to a foreign simple trust or foreign grantor trust by substituting the term foreign simple trust or foreign grantor trust for the term nonqualified intermediary.

(v) *Withholding foreign trusts.*—The IRS may enter an agreement with a foreign trust to treat the trust or estate as a withholding foreign trust. Such an agreement shall generally follow the same principles as an agreement with a withholding foreign partnership under paragraph (c)(2)(ii) of this section. A withholding agent may treat a payment to a withholding foreign trust in the same manner the withholding agent would treat a payment to a withholding foreign partnership. The IRS may also enter an agreement to treat a trust as a qualified intermediary in appropriate circumstances. See §1.1441-1(e)(5)(ii)(D).

(6) *Presumption rules.*—(i) *In general.*— This paragraph (e)(6) contains the applicable presumptions for a withholding agent (including a trust or estate) to determine the classification and status of a trust or estate and its beneficiaries or owners in the absence of valid documentation. The provisions of §1.1441-1(b)(3)(iv) (regarding the 90-day grace period) and §1.1441-1(b)(3)(vii) through

(ix) shall apply for purposes of this paragraph (e)(6).

(ii) *Determination of status as U.S. or foreign trust or estate in the absence of documentation.*—In the absence of valid documentation that establishes the U.S. status of a trust or estate under paragraph (b)(1) of this section and of documentation that establishes the foreign status of a trust or estate under paragraph (e)(4) or (5)(iii) of this section, the withholding agent shall determine the classification of the payee based upon the presumptions set forth in § 1.1441-1(b)(3)(ii). If, based upon those presumptions, the withholding agent classifies the payee as a trust or estate, the trust or estate shall be presumed to be a U.S. trust or U.S. estate unless there are indicia of foreign status, in which case the trust or estate shall be presumed to be foreign. Indicia of foreign status exists if the withholding agent has actual knowledge of the payee's employer identification number and that number begins with the two digits "98," the withholding agent's communications with the payee are mailed to an address in a foreign country, or the payment is made outside the United States (as defined in § 1.6049-5(e)). If an undocumented payee is presumed to be a foreign trust it shall be presumed to be a foreign complex trust. If a withholding agent has documentary evidence that establishes that an entity is a foreign trust, but the withholding agent cannot determine whether the foreign trust is a complex trust, a simple trust, or foreign grantor trust, the withholding agent may presume that the trust is a foreign complex trust.

(iii) *Determination of beneficiary or owner's status in the absence of certain documentation.*—If a foreign simple trust or foreign grantor trust has provided a foreign simple trust or foreign grantor trust withholding certificate under paragraph (e)(5)(iii) of this section but the payment to such trust cannot be reliably associated with valid documentation from a specific beneficiary or owner of the trust, then any portion of a payment that a withholding agent cannot treat as reliably associated with valid documentation from a beneficiary or owner may be presumed made to a foreign payee. As a result, any payment of an amount subject to withholding is subject to withholding at a rate of 30 percent. Any such payment that is presumed to be made to an undocumented foreign person must be reported on Form 1042-S. See § 1.1461-1(c).

(f) *Failure to receive withholding certificate timely or to act in accordance with applicable presumptions.*—See applicable procedures described in § 1.1441-1(b)(7) in the event the withholding agent does not hold an appropriate withholding certificate or other appropriate documentation at the time of payment or fails to rely on the presumptions set forth in § 1.1441-1(b)(3) or in paragraph (d) or (e) of this section.

(g) *Effective date.*—(1) *General rule.*—This section applies to payments made after December 31, 2000.

(2) *Transition rules.*—The validity of a withholding certificate that was valid on January 1, 1998, under the regulations in effect prior to January 1, 2001 (see 26 CFR parts 1 and 35a, revised April 1, 1999) and expired, or will expire, at any time during 1998, is extended until December 31, 1998. The validity of a withholding certificate that is valid on or after January 1, 1999, remains valid until its validity expires under the regulations in effect prior to January 1, 2001 (see 26 CFR parts 1 and 35a, revised April 1, 1999) but in no event will such a withholding certificate remain valid after December 31, 2000. The rule in this paragraph (g)(2), however, does not apply to extend the validity period of a withholding certificate that expires solely by reason of changes in the circumstances of the person whose name is on the certificate. Notwithstanding the first three sentences of this paragraph (g)(2), a withholding agent may choose to not take advantage of the transition rule in this paragraph (g)(2) with respect to one or more withholding certificates valid under the regulations in effect prior to January 1, 2001 (see 26 CFR parts 1 and 35a, revised April 1, 1999) and, therefore, to require withholding certificates conforming to the requirements described in this section (new withholding certificates). For purposes of this section, a new withholding certificate is deemed to satisfy the documentation requirement under the regulations in effect prior to January 1, 2001 (see 26 CFR parts 1 and 35a, revised April 1, 1999). Further, a new withholding certificate remains valid for the period specified in § 1.1441-1(e)(4)(ii), regardless of when the certificate is obtained. [Reg. § 1.1441-5.]

☐ [*T.D.* 6187, 7-5-56. *Amended by T.D.* 6238, 6-10-57; *T.D.* 6908, 12-30-66; *T.D.* 7277, 5-14-73; *T.D.* 7842, 11-2-82; *T.D.* 7977, 9-19-84; *T.D.* 8160, 9-8-87; *T.D.* 8411, 4-24-92; *T.D.* 8734, 10-6-97; *T.D.* 8804, 12-30-98; *T.D.* 8856, 12-29-99 and *T.D.* 8881, 5-15-2000 (*corrected* 4-5-2001).]

§ 1.1441-6. Claim of reduced withholding under an income tax treay.—(a) *In general.*—The rate of withholding on a payment of income subject to withholding may be reduced to the extent provided under an income tax treaty in effect between the United States and a foreign country. Most benefits under income tax treaties are to foreign persons who reside in the treaty country. In some cases, benefits are available under an income tax treaty to U.S. citizens or U.S. residents or to residents of a third country. See paragraph (b)(5) of this section for claims of benefits by U.S. persons. If the requirements of this section are met, the amount withheld from the payment may be reduced at source to account for the treaty benefit. See also § 1.1441-4(b)(2) for rules regarding claims of reduced rate of withholding under an income tax treaty in the case of compensation from personal services.

(b) *Reliance on claim of reduced withholding under an income tax treaty.*—(1) *In general.*—The withholding imposed under section 1441, 1442, or 1443 on any payment to a foreign person is eligible for reduction under the terms of an income tax treaty only to the extent that such payment is treated as derived by a resident of an applicable treaty jurisdiction, such resident is a beneficial owner, and all other requirements for benefits under the treaty are satisfied. See section 894 and the regulations thereunder to determine whether a resident of a treaty country derives the income. Absent actual knowledge or reason to know otherwise, a withholding agent may rely on a claim that a beneficial owner is entitled to a reduced rate of withholding based upon an income tax treaty if, prior to the payment, the withholding agent can reliably associate the payment with a beneficial owner withholding certificate, described in § 1.1441-1(e)(2), that contains the information necessary to support the claim, or, in the case of a payment of income described in paragraph (c)(2) of this section made outside the United States with respect to an offshore account, documentary evidence described in paragraphs (c)(3), (4) and (5) of this section. See §§ 1.6049-5(e) for the definition of payments made outside the United States and 1.6049-5(c)(1) for the definition of offshore account. For purposes of this paragraph (b)(1), a beneficial owner withholding certificate described in § 1.1441-1(e)(2)(i) contains information necessary to support the claim for a treaty benefit only if it includes the beneficial owner's taxpayer identifying number (except as otherwise provided in paragraph (c)(1) of this section and § 1.1441-6(g)) and the representations that the beneficial owner derives the income under section 894 and the regulations thereunder, if required, and meets the limitation on benefits provisions of the treaty, if any. The withholding certificate must also contain any other representations required by this section and any other information, certifications, or statements as may be required by the form or accompanying instructions in addition to, or in place of, the information and certifications described in this section. Absent actual knowledge or reason to know that the claims are incorrect (and subject to the standards of knowledge in § 1.1441-7(b)), a withholding agent may rely on the claims made on a withholding certificate or on documentary evidence. A withholding agent may also rely on the information contained in a withholding statement provided under §§ 1.1441-1(e)(3)(iv) and 1.1441-5(c)(3)(iv) and (e)(5)(iv) to determine whether the appropriate statements regarding section 894 and limitation on benefits have been provided in connection with documentary evidence. If the beneficial owner is a person related to the withholding agent within the meaning of section 482, the withholding certificate must also contain a representation that the beneficial owner will file the statement required under § 301.6114-1(d) of this chapter (if applicable). The requirement to file an information statement under section 6114 for income subject to withholding applies only to amounts received during the calendar year that, in the aggregate, exceed $500,000. See § 301.6114-1(d) of this chapter. The Internal Revenue Service (IRS) may apply the provisions of § 1.1441-1(e)(1)(ii)(B) to notify the withholding agent that the certificate cannot be relied upon to grant benefits under an income tax treaty. See § 1.1441-1(e)(4)(viii) regarding reliance on a withholding certificate by a withholding agent. The provisions of § 1.1441-1(b)(3)(iv) dealing with a 90-day grace period shall apply for purposes of this section.

(2) *Payment to fiscally transparent entity.*—(i) *In general.*—If the person claiming a reduced rate of withholding under an income tax treaty is the interest holder of an entity that is considered to be fiscally transparent (as defined in the regulations under section 894) by the interest holder's jurisdiction with respect to an item of income, then, with respect to such income derived by that person through the entity, the entity shall be treated as a flow-through entity and may provide a flow-through withholding certificate with which the withholding certificate or other documentary evidence of the interest holder that supports the claim for treaty benefits is associated. For purposes of the preceding sentence, interest holders do not include any direct or indirect interest holders that are themselves treated as fiscally transparent entities with respect to that income by the interest holder's jurisdiction. See § 1.1441-1(c)(23) and (e)(3)(i) for the definition of flow-through entity and flow-through withholding certificate. The entity may provide a beneficial owner withholding certificate, or beneficial owner documentation, with respect to any remaining portion of the income to the extent the entity is receiving income and is not treated as fiscally transparent by its own jurisdiction. Further, the entity may claim a re-

duced rate of withholding with respect to the portion of a payment for which it is not treated as fiscally transparent if it meets all the requirements to make such a claim and, in the case of treaty benefits, it provides the documentation required by paragraph (b)(1) of this section. If dual claims, as described in paragraph (b)(2)(iii) of this section, are made, multiple withholding certificates may have to be furnished. Multiple withholding certificates may also have to be furnished if the entity receives income for which a reduction of withholding is claimed under a provision of the Internal Revenue Code (e.g., portfolio interest) and income for which a reduction of withholding is claimed under an income tax treaty.

(ii) *Certification by qualified intermediary.*—Notwithstanding paragraph (b)(2)(i) of this section, a foreign entity that is fiscally transparent, as defined in the regulations under section 894, that is also a qualified intermediary for purposes of claiming a reduced rate of withholding under an income tax treaty for its interest holders (who are deriving the income paid to the entity as residents of an applicable treaty jurisdiction) may furnish a single qualified intermediary withholding certificate, as described in § 1.1441-1(e)(3)(ii), for amounts for which it claims a reduced rate of withholding under an income tax treaty on behalf of its interest holders.

(iii) *Dual treatment.*—Under paragraph (b)(2)(i) of this section, a withholding agent may make a payment to a foreign entity that is simultaneously claiming to be the beneficial owner of a portion of the income (whether or not it is also claiming a reduced rate of tax on its own behalf) and a reduced rate on behalf of persons in their capacity as interest holders in the entity with respect to the same, or a different, portion of the income. If the same portion of a payment may be reliably associated with both the entity's claim and an interest holder's claim, the withholding agent may choose to reject both claims and request new documentation and information allocating the payment among the beneficial owners of the payment or the withholding agent may choose which claim to apply. If the entity and the interest holder's claims are reliably associated with separate portions of the payment, the withholding agent may, at its option, accept such dual claims based on withholding certificates or other appropriate documentation furnished by the entity and its interest holders with respect to their respective shares of the payment even though this will result in the withholding agent treating the entity differently with respect to different portions of the same payment. Alternatively, the withholding agent may choose to apply only the claim made by the entity, provided the entity may be treated as a beneficial owner of the income. If the withholding agent does not accept claims for a reduced rate of withholding presented by any one or more of the interest holders, or by the entity, any interest holder or the entity may subsequently claim a refund or credit of any amount so withheld to the extent the interest holder's or entity's share of such withholding exceeds the amount of tax due.

(iv) *Examples.*—The following examples illustrate the rules of this paragraph (b)(2):

Example 1. (i) *Facts.* Entity E is a business organization formed under the laws of country Y. Country Y has an income tax treaty with the United States. The treaty contains a limitation on benefits provision. E receives U.S. source royalties from withholding agent W and claims a reduced rate of withholding under the U.S.-Y tax treaty on its own behalf (rather than on behalf of its interest holders). E furnishes a beneficial owner withholding certificate described in paragraph (b)(1) of this section that represents that E is a resident of country Y (within the meaning of the U.S.-Y tax treaty), is the beneficial owner of the income, derives the income under section 894 and the regulations thereunder, and is not precluded from claiming benefits by the treaty's limitation on benefits provision.

(ii) *Analysis.* Absent actual knowledge or reason to know otherwise, W may rely on the representations made by E to apply a reduced rate of withholding.

Example 2. (i) *Facts.* The facts are the same as under *Example 1*, except that one of E's interest holders, H, is an entity organized in country Z. The U.S.-Z tax treaty reduces the rate on royalties to zero whereas the rate on royalties under the U.S.-Y tax treaty applicable to E is 5 percent. H is not fiscally transparent under country Z's tax law with respect to such income. H furnishes a beneficial owner withholding certificate to E that represents that H derives, within the meaning of section 894 and the regulations thereunder, its share of the royalty income paid to E as a resident of country Z, is the beneficial owner of the royalty income, and is not precluded from claiming treaty benefits by virtue of the limitation on benefits provision in the U.S.-Z treaty. E furnishes to W a flow-through withholding certificate described in § 1.1441-1(e)(3)(i) to which it attaches H's beneficial owner withholding certificate and a withholding statement for the portion of the payment that H claims as its distributive share of the royalty income. E also furnishes to W a beneficial owner withholding certificate for itself for the portion of the payment that H does not claim as its distributive share.

(ii) *Analysis.* Absent actual knowledge or reason to know otherwise, W may rely on the documentation furnished by E to treat the royalty payment to a single foreign entity (E) as derived by different residents of tax treaty countries as a result of the claims presented under different treaties. W may, at its option, grant dual treatment, that is, a reduced rate of zero percent under the U.S.-Z treaty on the portion of the royalty payment that H claims to derive as a resident of country Z and a reduced rate of 5 percent under the U.S.-Y treaty for the balance. However, under paragraph (b)(2)(iii) of this section, W may, at its option, treat E as the only relevant person deriving the royalty and grant benefits under the U.S.-Y treaty only.

Example 3. (i) *Facts.* E is a business organization formed under the laws of country X. Country X has an income tax treaty with the United States. E has two interest holders, H1, organized in country Y, and H2, organized in country Z. E receives from W, a U.S. withholding agent, U.S. source royalties and interest that is eligible for the portfolio interest exception under sections 871(h) and 881(c), provided W receives the appropriate beneficial owner statement required under section 871(h)(5). E is classified as a corporation under U.S. tax law principles. Country X, E's country of organization, treats E as an entity that is not fiscally transparent with respect to items of income under the regulations under section 894. Under the U.S.-X income tax treaty, royalties are subject to 5 percent rate of withholding. Country Y, H1's country of organization, treats E as fiscally transparent with respect to items of income under section 894 and H1 as not fiscally transparent with respect to items of income. Under the country Y-U.S. income tax treaty, royalties are exempt from U.S. tax. Country Z, H2's country of organization, treats E as not fiscally transparent under section 894 with respect to items of income. E provides W with a flow-through beneficial owner withholding certificate with which it associates a beneficial owner withholding certificate from H1. H1's withholding certificate states that H1 is a resident of country Y, derives the royalty income under section 894, meets the applicable limitations on benefits provisions of the U.S.-Y treaty, and is the beneficial owner of the income. The withholding statement attached to E's flow-through withholding certificate allocates one-half of the royalty payment to H1. E also provides W with a beneficial owner withholding certificate for the interest income and the remaining one-half of the royalty income. The withholding certificate states that E is a resident of country X, derives the royalty income under section 894, meets the limitation on benefits provisions of the U.S.-X treaty, and is the beneficial owner of the income.

(ii) *Analysis.* Absent actual knowledge or reason to know that the claims are incorrect, W may treat one-half of the royalty derived by E as subject to a 5 percent withholding rate and one-half of the royalty as derived by H1 and subject to no withholding. Further, it may treat all of the interest as being paid to E and as qualifying for the portfolio interest exception. W can, at its option, treat the entire royalty as paid to E and subject it to withholding at a 5 percent rate of withholding. In that case, H1 would be entitled to claim a refund with respect to its one-half of the royalty.

(3) *Certified TIN.*—The IRS may issue guidance requiring a foreign person claiming treaty benefits and for whom a TIN is required to establish with the IRS, at the time the TIN is requested or after the TIN is issued, that the person is a resident in a treaty country and meets other conditions (such as limitation on benefits provisions) of the treaty. See § 601.601(d)(2) of this chapter.

(4) *Claim of benefits under an income tax treaty by a U.S. person.*—In certain cases, a U.S. person may claim the benefit of an income tax treaty. For example, under certain treaties, a U.S. citizen residing in the treaty country may claim a reduced rate of U.S. tax on certain amounts representing a pension or an annuity from U.S. sources. Claims of treaty benefits by a U.S. person may be made by furnishing a Form W-9 to the withholding agent or such other form as the IRS may prescribe in published guidance (see § 601.601(d)(2) of this chapter).

(c) *Exemption from requirement to furnish a taxpayer identifying number and special documentary evidence rules for certain income.*—(1) *General rule.*—In the case of income described in paragraph (c)(2) of this section, a withholding agent may rely on a beneficial owner withholding certificate described in paragraph (b)(1) of this section without regard to the requirement that the withholding certificate include the beneficial owner's taxpayer identifying number. In the case of payments of income described in paragraph (c)(2) of this section made outside the United States (as defined in § 1.6049-5(e)) with respect to an offshore account (as defined in § 1.6049-5(c)(1)), a withholding agent may, as an alternative to a withholding certificate described in paragraph (b)(1) of this section, rely on a certificate of residence described in paragraph (c)(3) of this section or documentary evidence described in paragraph (c)(4) of this section, relating to the beneficial owner, that the withholding agent has reviewed and maintains in its records in accordance with § 1.1441-1(e)(4)(iii). In the case of a payment to a person other than an individual, the certificate of residence or documentary evidence must be accompanied by the statements described in paragraphs (c)(5)(i) and (ii) of this section regarding limitation on benefits and whether the amount paid is derived by such person or by one of its interest holders. The withholding agent maintains the reviewed documents by retaining either the documents viewed or a photocopy thereof and noting in its records the date on which, and by whom, the documents were received and reviewed. This paragraph (c)(1) shall not apply to amounts that are exempt from withholding based on a claim that the income is effectively connected with the conduct of a trade or business in the United States.

(2) *Income to which special rules apply.*—The income to which paragraph (c)(1) of this section applies is dividends and interest from stocks and debt obligations that are actively traded, dividends from any redeemable security issued by an investment company registered under the Investment Company Act of 1940 (15 U.S.C. 80a-1), dividends, interest, or royalties from units of beneficial interest in a unit investment trust that are (or were upon issuance) publicly offered and are registered with the Securities and Exchange Commission under the Securities Act of 1933 (15 U.S.C. 77a) and amounts paid with respect to loans of securities described in this paragraph (c)(2). For purposes of this paragraph (c)(2), a stock or debt obligation is actively traded if it is actively traded within the meaning of section 1092(d) and §1.1092(d)-1 when documentation is provided.

(3) *Certificate of residence.*—A certificate of residence referred to in paragraph (c)(1) of this section is a certification issued by an appropriate tax official of the treaty country of which the taxpayer claims to be a resident that the taxpayer has filed its most recent income tax return as a resident of that country (within the meaning of the applicable tax treaty). The certificate of residence must have been issued by such official within three years prior to its being presented to the withholding agent, or such other period as the IRS may prescribe in published guidance (see §601.601(d)(2) of this chapter). See §1.1441-1(e)(4)(ii)(A) for the period during which a withholding agent may rely on a certificate of residence. The competent authorities may agree to a different procedure for certifying residence, in which case such procedure shall govern for payments made to a person claiming to be a resident of the country with which such an agreement is in effect.

(4) *Documentary evidence establishing residence in the treaty country.*—(i) *Individuals.*—For an individual, the documentary evidence referred to in paragraph (c)(1) of this section is any documentation that includes the individuals name, address, and photograph, is an official document issued by an authorized governmental body (i.e., a government or agency thereof, or a municipality), and has been issued no more than three years prior to presentation to the withholding agent. A document older than three years may be relied upon as proof of residence only if it is accompanied by additional evidence of the person's residence in the treaty country (e.g., a bank statement, utility bills, or medical bills). Documentary evidence must be in the form of original documents or certified copies thereof.

(ii) *Persons other than individuals.*—For a person other than an individual, the documentary evidence referred to in paragraph (c)(1) of this section is any documentation that includes the name of the entity and the address of its principal office in the treaty country, and is an official document issued by an authorized governmental body (e.g., a government or agency thereof, or a municipality).

(5) *Statements regarding entitlement to treaty benefits.*—(i) *Statement regarding conditions under a limitation on benefits provision.*—In addition to the documentary evidence described in (c)(4)(ii) of this section, a taxpayer that is not an individual must provide a statement that it meets one or more of the conditions set forth in the limitation on benefits article (if any, or in a similar provision) contained in the applicable tax treaty.

(ii) *Statement regarding whether the taxpayer derives the income.*—A taxpayer that is not an individual must also provide, in addition to the documentary evidence and the statement described in paragraph (c)(5)(i) of this section, a statement that any income for which it intends to claim benefits under an applicable income tax treaty is income that will properly be treated as derived by itself as a resident of the applicable treaty jurisdiction within the meaning of section 894 and the regulations thereunder. This requirement does not apply if the taxpayer furnishes a certificate of residence that certifies that fact.

(d) *Joint owners.*—In the case of a payment to joint owners, each owner must furnish a withholding certificate or, if applicable, documentary evidence or a certificate of residence. The applicable rate of withholding on a payment of income to joint owners shall be the highest applicable rate.

(e) *Competent authority.*—The procedures described in this section may be modified to the extent the U.S. competent authority may agree with the competent authority of a country with which the United States has an income tax treaty in effect.

(f) *Failure to receive withholding certificate timely.*—See applicable procedures described in § 1.1441-1(b)(7) in the event the withholding agent does not hold an appropriate withholding certificate or other appropriate documentation at the time of payment.

(g) *Special taxpayer identifying number rule for certain foreign individuals claiming treaty benefits.*—(1) *General rule.*—Except as provided in paragraph (c) or (g)(2) of this section, for purposes of paragraph (b)(1) of this section, a withholding agent may not rely on a beneficial owner withholding certificate, described in paragraph (b)(1) of this section, that does not include the beneficial owner's taxpayer identifying number (TIN).

(2) *Special rule.*—For purposes of satisfying the TIN requirement of paragraph (b)(1) of this section, a withholding agent may rely on a beneficial owner withholding certificate, described in such paragraph, without regard to the requirement that the withholding certificate include the beneficial owner's TIN, if—

(i) A withholding agent, who is also an acceptance agent, as defined in § 301.6109-1(d)(3)(iv) of this chapter (the payor), has entered into an acceptance agreement that permits the acceptance agent to request an individual taxpayer identification number (ITIN) on an expedited basis because of the circumstances of payment or unexpected nature of payments required to be made by the payor;

(ii) The payor was required to make an unexpected payment to the beneficial owner who is a foreign individual;

(iii) An ITIN for the beneficial owner cannot be received by the payor from the Internal Revenue Service (IRS) because the IRS is not issuing ITINs at the time of payment or any time prior to the time of payment when the payor has knowledge of the unexpected payment;

(iv) The unexpected payment to the beneficial owner could not be reasonably delayed to permit the payor to obtain an ITIN for the beneficial owner on an expedited basis; and

(v) The payor satisfies the provisions of paragraph (g)(3) of this section.

(3) *Requirement that an ITIN be requested during the first business day following payment.*—The payor must submit a beneficial owner payee application for an ITIN (Form W-7 "Application for IRS Individual Taxpayer Identification Number") that complies with the requirements of § 301.6109-1(d)(3)(ii) of this chapter, and also the certification described in § 301.6109-1(d)(3)(iv)(A)(*4*) of this chapter, to the IRS during the first business day after payment is made.

(4) *Definition of unexpected payment.*—For purposes of this section, an *unexpected payment* is a payment that, because of the nature of the payment or the circumstances in which it is made, could not reasonably have been anticipated by the payor or beneficial owner during a time when the payor or beneficial owner could obtain an ITIN from the IRS. For purposes of this paragraph (g)(4), a payor or beneficial owner will not lack the requisite knowledge of the forthcoming payment solely because the amount of the payment is not fixed.

(5) *Examples.*—The rules of this paragraph (g) are illustrated by the following examples:

Example 1. G, a citizen and resident of Country Y, a country with which the United States has an income tax treaty that exempts U.S. source gambling winnings from U.S. tax, is visiting the United States for the first time. During his visit, G visits Casino B, a casino that has entered into a special acceptance agent agreement with the IRS that permits Casino B to request an ITIN on an expedited basis. During that visit, on a Sunday, G wins $5000 in slot machine play at Casino B and requests immediate payment from Casino B. ITINs are not available from the IRS on Sunday and would not again be available until Monday. G, who does not have an individual taxpayer identification number, furnishes a beneficial owner withholding certificate, described in § 1.1441-1(e)(2), to the Casino upon winning at the slot machine. The beneficial owner withholding certificate represents that G is a resident of Country Y (within the meaning of the U.S.—Y tax treaty) and meets all applicable requirements for claiming benefits under the U.S.—Y tax treaty. The beneficial owner withholding certificate does not, however, contain an ITIN for G. On the following Monday, Casino B faxes a completed Form W-7, including the required certification, for G, to the IRS for an expedited ITIN. Pursuant to paragraph (b) and (g)(2) of this section, absent actual knowledge or reason to know otherwise, Casino B, may rely on the documentation furnished by G at the time of payment and pay the $5000 to G without withholding U.S. tax based on the treaty exemption.

Example 2. The facts are the same as *Example 1*, except G visits Casino B on Monday. G requests payment Monday afternoon. In order to pay the winnings to G without withholding the 30 percent tax, Casino B must apply for and obtain an ITIN for G because an expedited

ITIN is available from the IRS at the time of the $5000 payment to G.

Example 3. The facts are the same as *Example 1*, except G requests payment fifteen minutes before the time when the IRS begins issuing ITINs. Under these facts, it would be reasonable for Casino B to delay payment to G. Therefore, Casino B must apply for and obtain an ITIN for G if G wishes to claim an exemption from U.S. withholding tax under the U.S.—Y tax treaty at the time of payment.

Example 4. P, a citizen and resident of Country Z, is a lawyer and a well-known expert on real estate transactions. P is scheduled to attend a three-day seminar on complex real estate transactions, as a participant, at University U, a U.S. university, beginning on a Saturday and ending on the following Monday, which is a holiday. University U has entered into a special acceptance agent agreement with the IRS that permits University U to request an ITIN on an expedited basis. Country Z is a country with which the United States has an income tax treaty that exempts certain income earned from the performance of independent personal services from U.S. tax. It is P's first visit to the United States. On Saturday, prior to the start of the seminar, Professor Q, one of the lecturers at the seminar, cancels his lecture. That same day the Dean of University U offers P $5000, to replace Professor Q at the seminar, payable at the conclusion of the seminar on Monday. P agrees. P gives her lecture Sunday afternoon. ITINs are not available from the IRS on that Saturday, Sunday, or Monday. After the seminar ends on Monday, P, who does not have an ITIN, requests payment for her teaching. P furnishes a beneficial owner withholding certificate, described in § 1.1441-1(e)(2), to University U that represents that P is a resident of Country Z (within the meaning of the U.S.—Z tax treaty) and meets all applicable requirements for claiming benefits under the U.S.—Z tax treaty. The beneficial owner withholding certificate does not, however, contain an ITIN for P. On Tuesday, University U faxes a completed Form W-7, including the required certification, for P, to the IRS for an expedited ITIN. Pursuant to paragraph (b) and (g)(2) of this section, absent actual knowledge or reason to know otherwise, University U may rely on the documentation furnished by P and pay $5000 to P without withholding U.S. tax based on the treaty exemption.

(h) *Effective dates.*—(1) *General rule.*—This section applies to payments made after December 31, 2000, except for paragraph (g) of this section which applies to payments made after December 31, 2001.

(2) *Transition rules.*—For purposes of this section, the validity of a Form 1001 or 8233 that was valid on January 1, 1998, under the regulations in effect prior to January 1, 2001 (see 26 CFR parts 1 and 35a, revised April 1, 1999) and expired, or will expire, at any time during 1998, is extended until December 31, 1998. The validity of a Form 1001 or 8233 that is valid on or after January 1, 1999, remains valid until its validity expires under the regulations in effect prior to January 1, 2001 (see 26 CFR parts 1 and 35a, revised April 1, 1999) but in no event will such a form remain valid after December 31, 2000. The rule in this paragraph (h)(2), however, does not apply to extend the validity period of a Form 1001 or 8233 that expires solely by reason of changes in the circumstances of the person whose name is on the certificate or in interpretation of the law under the regulations under § 1.894-1T(d). Notwithstanding the first three sentences of this paragraph (h)(2), a withholding agent may choose to not take advantage of the transition rule in this paragraph (h)(2) with respect to one or more withholding certificates valid under the regulations in effect prior to January 1, 2001 (see 26 CFR parts 1 and 35a, revised April 1, 1999) and, therefore, to require withholding certificates conforming to the requirements described in this section (new withholding certificates). For purposes of this section, a new withholding certificate is deemed to satisfy the documentation requirement under the regulations in effect prior to January 1, 2001 (see 26 CFR parts 1 and 35a, revised April 1, 1999). Further, a new withholding certificate remains valid for the period specified in § 1.1441-1(e)(4)(ii), regardless of when the certificate is obtained. [Reg. § 1.1441-6.]

☐ [*T.D.* 7157, 12-29-71. *Amended by T.D.* 7842, 11-2-82; *T.D.* 7977, 9-19-84; *T.D.* 8734, 10-6-97; *T.D.* 8804, 12-30-98; *T.D.* 8856, 12-29-99 (*corrected* 3-27-2000); *T.D.* 8881, 5-15-2000; *T.D.* 8977, 1-16-2002 *and T.D.* 9023, 11-21-2002.]

§ 1.1441-7. General provisions relating to withholding agents.—(a) *Withholding agent defined.*—(1) *In general.*—For purposes of chapter 3 of the Internal Revenue Code and the regulations under such chapter, the term *withholding agent* means any person, U.S. or foreign, that has the control, receipt, custody, disposal, or payment of an item of income of a foreign person subject to withholding, including (but not limited to) a foreign intermediary described in § 1.1441-1(e)(3)(i), a foreign partnership, or a U.S. branch described in § 1.1441-1(b)(2)(iv)(A) or (E). See §§ 1.1441-1(b)(2) and (3) and 1.1441-5(c), (d), and (e), for rules to determine whether a payment is considered made to a foreign person. Any person who meets the definition of a withholding agent is required to deposit any tax withheld under §1.1461-1(a) and to make the returns prescribed by §1.1461-1(b) and (c), except as otherwise may be required by a qualified intermediary withholding agreement, a withholding foreign partnership agreement, or a withholding foreign trust agreement. When several persons qualify as withholding agents with respect to a single payment, only one tax is required to be withheld and deposited. See §1.1461-1. A person who, as a nominee described in §1.6031(c)-1T, has furnished to a partnership all of the information required to be furnished under §1.6031(c)-1T(a) shall not be treated as a withholding agent if it has notified the partnership that it is treating the provision of information to the partnership as a discharge of its obligations as a withholding agent.

(2) *Examples.*—The following examples illustrate the rules of paragraph (a)(1) of this section:

Example 1. USB is a broker organized in the United States. USB pays U.S. source dividends and interest, which are amounts subject to withholding under §1.1441-2(a), to FC, a foreign corporation that has an investment account with USB. USB is a withholding agent as defined in paragraph (a)(1) of this section.

Example 2. USB is a bank organized in the United States. FB is a bank organized in country X. X has an omnibus account with USB through which FB invests in debt and equity instruments that pay amounts subject to withholding as defined in §1.1441-2(a). FB is a nonqualified intermediary, as defined in §1.1441-1(c)(14). Both USB and FB are withholding agents as defined in paragraph (a)(1) of this section.

Example 3. The facts are the same as in *Example 2*, except that FB is a qualified intermediary. Both USB and FB are withholding agents as defined in paragraph (a)(1) of this section.

Example 4. FB is a bank organized in country X. FB has a branch in the United States. FB's branch has customers that are foreign persons who receive amounts subject to withholding, as defined in §1.1441-2(a). FB is a withholding agent under paragraph (a)(1) of this section and is required to withhold and report payments of amounts subject to withholding in accordance with chapter 3 of the Internal Revenue Code.

Example 5. X is a foreign corporation. X pays dividends to shareholders who are foreign persons. Under section 861(a)(2)(B), a portion of the dividends are from sources within the United States and constitute amounts subject to withholding within the meaning of §1.1441-2(a). The dividends are not subject to tax under section 884(a). See 884(e)(3). X is a withholding agent under paragraph (a)(1) of this section.

(b) *Standards of knowledge.*—(1) *In general.*—A withholding agent must withhold at the full 30-percent rate under section 1441, 1442, or 1443(a) or at the full 4-percent rate under section 1443(b) if it has actual knowledge or reason to know that a claim of U.S. status or of a reduced rate of withholding under section 1441, 1442, or 1443 is unreliable or incorrect. A withholding agent shall be liable for tax, interest, and penalties to the extent provided under sections 1461 and 1463 and the regulations under those sections if it fails to withhold the correct amount despite its actual knowledge or reason to know the amount required to be withheld. For purposes of the regulations under sections 1441, 1442, and 1443, a withholding agent may rely on information or certifications contained in, or associated with, a withholding certificate or other documentation furnished by or for a beneficial owner or payee unless the withholding agent has actual knowledge or reason to know that the information or certifications are incorrect or unreliable and, if based on such knowledge or reason to know, it should withhold (under chapter 3 of the Code or another withholding provision of the Code) an amount greater than would be the case if it relied on the information or certifications, or it should report (under chapter 3 of the Code or under another provision of the Code) an amount that would not otherwise be reportable if it relied on the information or certifications. See §1.1441-1(e)(4)(viii) for applicable reliance rules. A withholding agent that has received notification by the Internal Revenue Service (IRS) that a claim of U.S. status or of a reduced rate is incorrect has actual knowledge beginning on the date that is 30 calendar days after the date the notice is received. A withholding agent that fails to act in accordance with the presumptions set forth in §§1.1441-1(b)(3), 1.1441-4(a), 1.1441-5(d) and (e), or 1.1441-9(b)(3) may also be liable for tax, interest, and penalties. See §1.1441-1(b)(3)(ix) and (7).

(2) *Reason to know.*—A withholding agent shall be considered to have reason to know if its knowledge of relevant facts or of statements contained in the withholding certificates or other documentation is such that a reasonably prudent person in the position of the withholding agent would question the claims made.

(3) *Financial institutions—limits on reason to know.*—For purposes of this paragraph (b)(3) and paragraphs (b)(4) through (b)(10) of this section, the terms *withholding certificate*,

documentary evidence, and *documentation* are defined in § 1.1441-1(c)(16), (17) and (18). Except as otherwise provided in paragraphs (b)(4) through (b)(9) of this section, a withholding agent that is a financial institution (including a regulated investment company) that has a direct account relationship with a beneficial owner (a direct account holder) has a reason to know, with respect to amounts described in § 1.1441-6(c)(2), that documentation provided by the direct account holder is unreliable or incorrect only if one or more of the circumstances described in paragraphs (b)(4) through (b)(9) of this section exist. If a direct account holder has provided documentation that is unreliable or incorrect under the rules of paragraph (b)(4) through (b)(9) of this section, the withholding agent may require new documentation. Alternatively, the withholding agent may rely on the documentation originally provided if the rules of paragraphs (b)(4) through (b)(9) of this section permit such reliance based on additional statements and documentation. Paragraph (b)(10) of this section provides limits on reason to know for financial institutions that receive beneficial owner documentation from persons (indirect account holders) that have an account relationship with, or an ownership interest in, a direct account holder. For rules regarding reliance on Form W-9, see § 31.3406(g)-3(e)(2) of this chapter.

(4) *Rules applicable to withholding certificates.*—(i) *In general.*—A withholding agent has reason to know that a beneficial owner withholding certificate provided by a direct account holder in connection with a payment of an amount described in § 1.1441-6(c)(2) is unreliable or incorrect if the withholding certificate is incomplete with respect to any item on the certificate that is relevant to the claims made by the direct account holder, the withholding certificate contains any information that is inconsistent with the direct account holder's claim, the withholding agent has other account information that is inconsistent with the direct account holder's claim, or the withholding certificate lacks information necessary to establish entitlement to a reduced rate of withholding. For purposes of establishing a direct account holder's status as a foreign person or resident of a treaty country a withholding certificate shall be considered unreliable or inconsistent with an account holder's claims only if it is not reliable under the rules of paragraphs (b)(5) and (6) of this section. A withholding agent that relies on an agent to review and maintain a withholding certificate is considered to know or have reason to know the facts within the knowledge of the agent.

(ii) *Examples.*—The rules of paragraph (b)(4) of this section are illustrated by the following examples:

Example 1. F, a foreign person that has a direct account relationship with USB, a bank that is a U.S. person, provides USB with a beneficial owner withholding certificate for the purpose of claiming a reduced rate of withholding on U.S. source dividends. F resides in a treaty country that has a limitation on benefits provision in its income tax treaty with the United States. The withholding certificate, however, does not contain a statement regarding limitations on benefits or deriving the income under section 894 as required by § 1.1441-6(b)(1). USB cannot rely on the withholding certificate to grant a reduced rate of withholding because it is incomplete with respect to the claim made by F.

Example 2. F, a foreign person that has a direct account relationship with USB, a broker that is a U.S. person, provides USB with a withholding certificate for the purpose of claiming the portfolio interest exception under section 881(c), which applies to foreign corporations. F indicates on its withholding certificate, however, that it is a partnership. USB may not treat F as a beneficial owner of the interest for purposes of the portfolio interest exception because F has indicated on its withholding certificate that it is a foreign partnership, and therefore under § 1.1441-1(c)(6)(ii) it is not the beneficial owner of the interest payment.

(5) *Withholding certificate—establishment of foreign status.*—A withholding agent has reason to know that a beneficial owner withholding certificate (as defined in § 1.1441-1(e)(2)) provided by a direct account holder in connection with a payment of an amount described in § 1.1441-6(c)(2) is unreliable or incorrect for purposes of establishing the account holder's status as a foreign person if the certificate is described in paragraph (b)(5)(i) or (ii) of this section.

(i) A withholding certificate is unreliable or incorrect if the withholding certificate has a permanent residence address (as defined in § 1.1441-1(e)(2)(ii)) in the United States, the withholding certificate has a mailing address in the United States, the withholding agent has a residence or mailing address as part of its account information that is an address in the United States, or the direct account holder notifies the withholding agent of a new residence or mailing address in the United States (whether or not provided on a withholding certificate). A withholding agent may, however, rely on the beneficial owner withholding certificate as establishing the account holder's for-

Reg. § 1.1441-7(b)(5)(i)

eign status if it may do so under the provisions of paragraph (b)(5)(i)(A) or (B) of this section.

(A) A withholding agent may treat a direct account holder as a foreign person if the beneficial owner withholding certificate has been provided by an individual and—

(1) The withholding agent has in its possession or obtains documentary evidence (which does not contain a U.S. address) that has been provided within the past three years, was valid at the time it was provided, the documentary evidence supports the claim of foreign status, and the direct account holder provides the withholding agent with a reasonable explanation, in writing, supporting the account holder's foreign status; or

(2) The account is maintained at an office of the withholding agent outside the United States and the withholding agent is required to report annually a payment to the direct account holder on a tax information statement that is filed with the tax authority of the country in which the office is located and that country has an income tax treaty in effect with the United States.

(B) A withholding agent may treat an account holder as a foreign person if the beneficial owner withholding certificate has been provided by an entity that the withholding agent does not know, or does not have reason to know, is a flow-through entity and—

(1) The withholding agent has in its possession, or obtains, documentation that substantiates that the entity is actually organized or created under the laws of a foreign country; or

(2) The account is maintained at an office of the withholding agent outside the United States and the withholding agent is required to report annually a payment to the direct account holder on a tax information statement that is filed with the tax authority of the country in which the office is located and that country has an income tax treaty in effect with the United States.

(ii) A beneficial owner withholding certificate is unreliable or incorrect if it is provided with respect to an offshore account (as defined in § 1.6049-5(c)(1)) and the direct account holder has standing instructions directing the withholding agent to pay amounts from its account to an address or an account maintained in the United States. The withholding agent may treat the direct account holder as a foreign person, however, if the direct account holder provides a reasonable explanation in writing that supports its foreign status.

(6) *Withholding certificate—claim of reduced rate of withholding under treaty.*—A withholding agent has reason to know that a withholding certificate (other than Form W-9) provided by a direct account holder in connection with a payment of an amount described in § 1.1441-6(c)(2) is unreliable or incorrect for purposes of establishing that the direct account holder is a resident of a country with which the United States has an income tax treaty if it is described in paragraphs (b)(6)(i) through (iii) of this section.

(i) A beneficial owner withholding certificate is unreliable or incorrect if the permanent residence address on the beneficial owner withholding certificate is not in the country whose treaty is invoked, or the direct account holder notifies the withholding agent of a new permanent residence address that is not in the treaty country. A withholding agent may, however, treat a direct account holder as entitled to a reduced rate of withholding under an income tax treaty if the direct account holder provides a reasonable explanation for the permanent residence address outside the treaty country (e.g., the address is the address of a branch of the beneficial owner located outside the treaty country in which the entity is a resident) or the withholding agent has in its possession, or obtains, documentary evidence that establishes residency in a treaty country.

(ii) A beneficial owner withholding certificate is unreliable or incorrect if the permanent residence address on the withholding certificate is in the applicable treaty country but the withholding certificate contains a mailing address outside the treaty country or the withholding agent has a mailing address as part of its account information that is outside the treaty country. A mailing address that is a P.O. Box, in-care-of address, or address at a financial institution (if the financial institution is not a beneficial owner) shall not preclude a withholding agent from treating the direct account holder as a resident of a treaty country if such address is in the treaty country. If a withholding agent has a mailing address (whether or not contained on the withholding certificate) outside the applicable treaty country, the withholding agent may nevertheless treat a direct account holder as a resident of an applicable treaty country if—

(A) The withholding agent has in its possession, or obtains, additional documentation supporting the direct account holder's claim of residence in the applicable treaty country (and the additional documentation does not contain an address outside the treaty country);

(B) The withholding agent has in its possession, or obtains, documentation that establishes that the direct account holder is an entity organized in a treaty country (or an entity managed and controlled in a treaty country, if the applicable treaty so requires);

(C) The withholding agent knows that the address outside the applicable treaty country (other than a P.O. box, or in-care-of address) is a branch of a bank or insurance company that is a resident of the applicable treaty country; or

(D) The withholding agent obtains a written statement from the direct account holder that reasonably establishes entitlement to treaty benefits.

(iii) A beneficial owner withholding certificate is unreliable or incorrect to establish entitlement to a reduced rate of withholding under an income tax treaty if the direct account holder has standing instructions for the withholding agent to pay amounts from its account to an address or an account outside the treaty country unless the direct account holder provides a reasonable explanation, in writing, establishing the direct account holder's residence in the applicable treaty country.

(7) *Documentary evidence.*—A withholding agent shall not treat documentary evidence provided by a direct account holder as valid if the documentary evidence does not reasonably establish the identity of the person presenting the documentary evidence. For example, documentary evidence is not valid if it is provided in person by a direct account holder that is a natural person and the photograph or signature on the documentary evidence, if any, does not match the appearance or signature of the person presenting the document. A withholding agent shall not rely on documentary evidence to reduce the rate of withholding that would otherwise apply under the presumption rules of §§ 1.1441-1(b)(3), 1.1441-5(d) and (e)(6), and 1.6049-5(d) if the documentary evidence contains information that is inconsistent with the direct account holder's claim of a reduced rate of withholding, the withholding agent has other account information that is inconsistent with the direct account holder's claim, or the documentary evidence lacks information necessary to establish entitlement to a reduced rate of withholding. For example, if a direct account holder provides documentary evidence to claim treaty benefits and the documentary evidence establishes the direct account holder's status as a foreign person and a resident of a treaty country, but the account holder fails to provide the treaty statements required by § 1.1441-6(c)(5), the documentary evidence does not establish the direct account holder's entitlement to a reduced rate of withholding. For purposes of establishing a direct account holder's status as a foreign person or resident of a country with which the United States has an income tax treaty with respect to income described in § 1.1441-6(c)(2), documentary evidence shall be considered unreliable or incorrect only if it is not reliable under the rules of paragraph (b)(8) and (9) of this section.

(8) *Documentary evidence—establishment of foreign status.*—A withholding agent has reason to know that documentary evidence provided in connection with a payment of an amount described in § 1.1441-6(c)(2) is unreliable or incorrect for purposes of establishing the direct account holder's status as a foreign person if the documentary evidence is described in paragraphs (b)(8)(i), (ii), (iii) or (iv) of this section.

(i) A withholding agent shall not treat documentary evidence provided by an account holder after December 31, 2000, as valid for purposes of establishing the direct account holder's foreign status if the only mailing or residence address that is available to the withholding agent is an address at a financial institution (unless the financial institution is a beneficial owner of the income), an in-care-of address, or a P.O. box. In this case, the withholding agent must obtain additional documentation that is sufficient to establish the direct account holder's status as a foreign person. A withholding agent shall not treat documentary evidence provided by an account holder before January 1, 2001, as valid for purposes of establishing a direct account holder's status as a foreign person if it has actual knowledge that the direct account holder is a U.S. person or if it has a mailing or residence address for the direct account holder in the United States. If a withholding agent has an address for the direct account holder in the United States, the withholding agent may nevertheless treat the direct account holder as a foreign person if it can so treat the direct account holder under the rules of paragraph (b)(8)(ii) of this section.

(ii) Documentary evidence is unreliable or incorrect to establish a direct account holder's status as a foreign person if the withholding agent has a mailing or residence address (whether or not on the documentation) for the direct account holder in the United States or if the direct account holder notifies the withholding agent of a new address in the United States. A withholding agent may, however, rely on documentary evidence as establishing the direct account holder's foreign status if it may do so under the provisions of paragraph (b)(8)(ii)(A) or (B) of this section.

(A) A withholding agent may treat a direct account holder that is an individual as a foreign person even if it has a mailing or residence address for the direct account holder in the United States if the withholding agent—

(1) Has in its possession or obtains additional documentary evidence (which does not contain a U.S. address) supporting the claim of foreign status and a reasonable expla-

Reg. § 1.1441-7(b)(8)(ii)(A)(1)

nation in writing supporting the account holder's foreign status;

(2) Has in its possession or obtains a valid beneficial owner withholding certificate on Form W-8 and the Form W-8 contains a permanent residence address outside the United States and a mailing address outside the United States (or if a mailing address is inside the United States the direct account holder provides a reasonable explanation in writing supporting the direct account holder's foreign status); or

(3) The account is maintained at an office of the withholding agent outside the United States and the withholding agent is required to report annually a payment to the direct account holder on a tax information statement that is filed with the tax authority of the country in which the office is located and that country has an income tax treaty in effect with the United States.

(B) A withholding agent may treat a direct account holder that is an entity (other than a flow-through entity) as a foreign person even if it has a mailing or residence address for the direct account holder in the United States if the withholding agent—

(1) Has in its possession, or obtains, documentation that substantiates that the entity is actually organized or created under the laws of a foreign country;

(2) Obtains a valid beneficial owner withholding certificate on Form W-8 and the Form W-8 contains a permanent residence address outside the United States and a mailing address outside the United States (or if a mailing address is inside the United States the direct account holder provides additional documentary evidence sufficient to establish the direct account holder's foreign status); or

(3) The account is maintained at an office of the withholding agent outside the United States and the withholding agent is required to report annually a payment to the direct account holder on a tax information statement that is filed with the tax authority of the country in which the office is located and that country has an income tax treaty in effect with the United States.

(iii) Documentary evidence is unreliable or incorrect if the direct account holder has standing instructions directing the withholding agent to pay amounts from its account to an address or an account maintained in the United States. The withholding agent may treat the direct account holder as a foreign person, however, if the account holder provides a reasonable explanation in writing that supports its foreign status.

(9) *Documentary evidence—claim of reduced rate of withholding under treaty.*—A with-holding agent has reason to know that documentary evidence provided in connection with a payment of an amount described in § 1.1441-6(c)(2) is unreliable or incorrect for purposes of establishing that a direct account holder is a resident of a country with which the United States has an income tax treaty if it is described in paragraph (b)(9)(i) or (ii) of this section.

(i) Documentary evidence is unreliable or incorrect if the withholding agent has a mailing or residence address for the direct account holder (whether or not on the documentary evidence) that is outside the applicable treaty country, or the only address that the withholding agent has (whether in or outside of the applicable treaty country) is a P.O. box, an in-care-of address, or the address of a financial institution (if the financial institution is not the beneficial owner). If a withholding agent has a mailing or residence address for the direct account holder outside the applicable treaty country, the withholding agent may nevertheless treat a direct account holder as a resident of an applicable treaty country if the withholding agent—

(A) Has in its possession, or obtains, additional documentary evidence supporting the direct account holder's claim of residence in the applicable treaty country (and the documentary evidence does not contain an address outside the applicable treaty country, a P.O. box, an in-care-of address, or the address of a financial institution);

(B) Has in its possession, or obtains, documentary evidence that establishes the direct account holder is an entity organized in a treaty country (or an entity managed and controlled in a treaty country, if the applicable treaty so requires); or

(C) Obtains a valid beneficial owner withholding certificate on Form W-8 that contains a permanent residence address and a mailing address in the applicable treaty country.

(ii) Documentary evidence is unreliable or incorrect if the direct account holder has standing instructions directing the withholding agent to pay amounts from its account to an address or an account maintained outside the treaty country unless the direct account holder provides a reasonable explanation, in writing, establishing the direct account holder's residence in the applicable treaty country.

(10) *Limits on reason to know—indirect account holders.*—A financial institution that receives documentation from a payee through a nonqualified intermediary, a flow-through entity, or a U.S. branch described in § 1.1441-1(b)(2)(iv) (other than a U.S. branch that is treated as a U.S. person) with respect to

a payment of an amount described in § 1.1441-6(c)(2) has reason to know that the documentation is unreliable or incorrect if a reasonably prudent person in the position of a withholding agent would question the claims made. This standard requires, but is not limited to, a withholding agent's compliance with the rules of paragraphs (b)(10)(i) through (iii).

(i) The withholding agent must review the withholding statement described in § 1.1441-1(e)(3)(iv) and may not rely on information in the statement to the extent the information does not support the claims made for any payee. For this purpose, a withholding agent may not treat a payee as a foreign person if an address in the United States is provided for such payee and may not treat a person as a resident of a country with which the United States has an income tax treaty if the address for that person is outside the applicable treaty country. Notwithstanding a U.S. address or an address outside a treaty country, the withholding agent may treat a payee as a foreign person or a foreign person as a resident of a treaty country if a reasonable explanation is provided, in writing, by the nonqualified intermediary, flow-through entity, or U.S. branch supporting the payee's foreign status or the foreign person's residency in a treaty country.

(ii) The withholding agent must review each withholding certificate in accordance with the requirements of paragraphs (b)(5) and (6) of this section and verify that the information on the withholding certificate is consistent with the information on the withholding statement required under § 1.1441-1(e)(3)(iv). If there is a discrepancy between the withholding certificate and the withholding statement, the withholding agent may choose to rely on the withholding certificate, if valid, and instruct the nonqualified intermediary, flow-through entity, or U.S. branch to correct the withholding statement or apply the presumption rules of §§ 1.1441-1(b), 1.1441-5(d) and (e)(6), and 1.6049-5(d) to the payment allocable to the payee who provided the withholding certificate. A withholding agent that receives a withholding certificate before December 31, 2001, is not required to review the information on withholding certificates or determine if it is consistent with the information on the withholding statement until December 31, 2001. A withholding agent may withhold and report in accordance with a withholding statement until December 31, 2001, unless it has actually performed the verification procedures required by this paragraph (b)(10)(ii) and determined that the withholding statement is inaccurate with respect to a particular payee.

(iii) The withholding agent must review the documentary evidence provided by the nonqualified intermediary, flow-through entity, or U.S. branch to determine that there is no obvious indication that the payee is a U.S. non-exempt recipient or that the documentary evidence does not establish the identity of the person who provided the documentation (e.g., the documentary evidence does not appear to be an identification document).

(11) *Additional guidance.*—The IRS may prescribe other circumstances for which a withholding certificate or documentary evidence is unreliable or incorrect in addition to the circumstances described in paragraph (b) of this section to establish an account holder's status as a foreign person or a beneficial owner entitled to a reduced rate of withholding in published guidance (see § 601.601(d)(2) of this chapter).

(c) *Authorized agent.*—(1) *In general.*—The acts of an agent of a withholding agent (including the receipt of withholding certificates, the payment of amounts of income subject to withholding, and the deposit of tax withheld) are imputed to the withholding agent on whose behalf it is acting. However, if the agent is a foreign person, a withholding agent that is a U.S. person may treat the acts of the foreign agent as its own for purposes of determining whether it has complied with the provisions of this section, but only if the agent is an authorized foreign agent, as defined in paragraph (c)(2) of this section. An authorized foreign agent cannot apply the provisions of this paragraph (c) to appoint another person its authorized foreign agent with respect to the payments it receives from the withholding agent.

(2) *Authorized foreign agent.*—An agent is an authorized foreign agent only if—

(i) There is a written agreement between the withholding agent and the foreign person acting as agent;

(ii) The notification procedures described in paragraph (c)(3) of this section have been complied with;

(iii) Books and records and relevant personnel of the foreign agent are available (on a continuous basis, including after termination of the relationship) for examination by the IRS in order to evaluate the withholding agent's compliance with the provisions of chapters 3 and 61 of the Code, section 3406, and the regulations under those provisions; and

(iv) The U.S. withholding agent remains fully liable for the acts of its agent and does not assert any of the defenses that may otherwise be available, including under common law principles of agency in order to avoid tax liability under the Internal Revenue Code.

(3) *Notification.*—A withholding agent that appoints an authorized agent to act on its

behalf for purposes of § 1.871-14(c)(2), the withholding provisions of chapter 3 of the Code, section 3406 or other withholding provisions of the Internal Revenue Code, or the reporting provisions of chapter 61 of the Code, is required to file notice of such appointment with the Office of the Assistant Commissioner (International). Such notice shall be filed before the first payment for which the authorized agent acts as such. Such notice shall acknowledge the withholding agent liability as provided in paragraph (c)(2)(iv) of this section.

(4) *Liability of U.S. withholding agent.*—An authorized foreign agent is subject to the same withholding and reporting obligations that apply to any withholding agent under the provisions of chapter 3 of the Code and the regulations thereunder. In particular, an authorized foreign agent does not benefit from the special procedures or exceptions that may apply to a qualified intermediary. A withholding agent acting through an authorized foreign agent is liable for any failure of the agent, such as failure to withhold an amount or make payment of tax, in the same manner and to the same extent as if the agent's failure had been the failure of the U.S. withholding agent. For this purpose, the foreign agent's actual knowledge or reason to know shall be imputed to the U.S. withholding agent. The U.S. withholding agent's liability shall exist irrespective of the fact that the authorized foreign agent is also a withholding agent and is itself separately liable for failure to comply with the provisions of the regulations under section 1441, 1442, or 1443. However, the same tax, interest, or penalties shall not be collected more than once.

(5) *Filing of returns.*—See § 1.1461-1(b)(2)(iii) and (c)(4)(iii) regarding returns required to be made where a U.S. withholding agent acts through an authorized foreign agent.

(d) *United States obligations.*—If the United States is a withholding agent for an item of interest, including original issue discount, on obligations of the United States or of any agency or instrumentality thereof, the withholding obligation of the United States is assumed and discharged by—

(1) The Commissioner of the Public Debt, for interest paid by checks issued through the Bureau of the Public Debt;

(2) The Treasurer of the United States, for interest paid by him or her, whether by check or otherwise;

(3) Each Federal Reserve Bank, for interest paid by it, whether by check or otherwise; or

(4) Such other person as may be designated by the IRS.

(e) *Assumed obligations.*—If, in connection with the sale of a corporation's property, payment on the bonds or other obligations of the corporation is assumed by a person, then that person shall be a withholding agent to the extent amounts subject to withholding are paid to a foreign person. Thus, the person shall withhold such amounts under § 1.1441-1 as would be required to be withheld by the seller or corporation had no such sale or assumption been made.

(f) *Conduit financing arrangements.*—(1) *Liability of withholding agent.*—Subject to paragraph (f)(2) of this section, any person that is required to deduct and withhold tax under § 1.1441-3(g) is made liable for that tax by section 1461. A person that is required to deduct and withhold tax but fails to do so is liable for the payment of the tax and any applicable penalties and interest.

(2) *Exception for withholding agents that do not know of conduit financing arrangement.*—(i) *In general.*—A withholding agent will not be liable under paragraph (f)(1) of this section for failing to deduct and withhold with respect to a conduit financing arrangement unless the person knows or has reason to know that the financing arrangement is a conduit financing arrangement. This standard shall be satisfied if the withholding agent knows or has reason to know of facts sufficient to establish that the financing arrangement is a conduit financing arrangement, including facts sufficient to establish that the participation of the intermediate entity in the financing arrangement is pursuant to a tax avoidance plan. A withholding agent that knows only of the financing transactions that comprise the financing arrangement will not be considered to know or have reason to know of facts sufficient to establish that the financing arrangement is a conduit financing arrangement.

(ii) *Examples.*—The following examples illustrate the operation of paragraph (d)(2) of this section.

Example 1. (i) DS is a U.S. subsidiary of FP, a corporation organized in Country N, a country that does not have an income tax treaty with the United States. FS is a special purpose subsidiary of FP that is incorporated in Country T, a country that has an income tax treaty with the United States that prohibits the imposition of withholding tax on payments of interest. FS is capitalized with $10,000,000 in debt from BK, a Country N bank, and $1,000,000 in capital from FS.

(ii) On May 1, 1995, C, a U.S. person, purchases an automobile from DS in return for an installment note. On July 1, 1995, DS sells a number of installment notes, including C's, to

FS in exchange for $10,000,000. DS continues to service the installment notes for FS and C is not notified of the sale of its obligation and continues to make payments to DS. But for the withholding tax on payments of interest by DS to BK, DS would have borrowed directly from BK, pledging the installment notes as collateral.

(iii) The C installment note is a financing transaction, whether held by DS or by FS, and the FS note held by BK also is a financing transaction. After FS purchases the installment note, and during the time the installment note is held by FS, the transactions constitute a financing arrangement, within the meaning of § 1.881-3(a)(2)(i). BK is the financing entity, FS is the intermediate entity, and C is the financed entity. Because the participation of FS in the financing arrangement reduces the tax imposed by section 881 and because there was a tax avoidance plan, FS is a conduit entity.

(iv) Because C does not know or have reason to know of the tax avoidance plan (and by extension that the financing arrangement is a conduit financing arrangement), C is not required to withhold tax under section 1441. However, DS, who knows that FS's participation in the financing arrangement is pursuant to a tax avoidance plan and is a withholding agent for purposes of section 1441, is not relieved of its withholding responsibilities.

Example 2. Assume the same facts as in *Example 1*, except that C receives a new payment booklet on which DS is described as "agent". Although C may deduce that its installment note has been sold, without more C has no reason to know of the existence of a financing arrangement. Accordingly, C is not liable for failure to withhold, although DS still is not relieved of its withholding responsibilities.

Example 3. (i) DC is a U.S. corporation that is in the process of negotiating a loan of $10,000,000 from BK1, a bank located in Country N, a country that does not have an income tax treaty with the United States. Before the loan agreement is signed, DC's tax lawyers point out that interest on the loan would not be subject to withholding tax if the loan were made by BK2, a subsidiary of BK1 that is incorporated in Country T, a country that has an income tax treaty with the United States that prohibits the imposition of withholding tax on payments of interest. BK1 makes a loan to BK2 to enable BK2 to make the loan to DC. Without the loan from BK1 to BK2, BK2 would not have been able to make the loan to DC.

(ii) The loan from BK1 to BK2 and the loan from BK2 to DC are both financing transactions and together constitute a financing arrangement within the meaning of § 1.881-3(a)(2)(i). BK1 is the financing entity, BK2 is the intermediate entity, and DC is the financed entity. Because the participation of BK2 in the financing arrangement reduces the tax imposed by section 881 and because there is a tax avoidance plan, BK2 is a conduit entity.

(iii) Because DC is a party to the tax avoidance plan (and accordingly knows of its existence), DC must withhold tax under section 1441. If DC does not withhold tax on its payment of interest, BK2, a party to the plan and a withholding agent for purposes of section 1441, must withhold tax as required by section 1441.

Example 4. (i) DC is a U.S. corporation that has a long-standing banking relationship with BK2, a U.S. subsidiary of BK1, a bank incorporated in Country N, a country that does not have an income tax treaty with the United States. DC has borrowed amounts of as much as $75,000,000 from BK2 in the past. On January 1, 1995, DC asks to borrow $50,000,000 from BK2. BK2 does not have the funds available to make a loan of that size. BK2 considers asking BK1 to enter into a loan with DC but rejects this possibility because of the additional withholding tax that would be incurred. Accordingly, BK2 borrows the necessary amount from BK1 with the intention of on-lending to DC. BK1 does not make the loan directly to DC because of the withholding tax that would apply to payments of interest from DC to BK1. DC does not negotiate with BK1 and has no reason to know that BK1 was the source of the loan.

(ii) The loan from BK2 to DC and the loan from BK1 to BK2 are both financing transactions and together constitute a financing arrangement within the meaning of § 1.881-3(a)(2)(i). BK1 is the financing entity, BK2 is the intermediate entity, and DC is the financed entity. The participation of BK2 in the financing arrangement reduces the tax imposed by section 881. Because the participation of BK2 in the financing arrangement reduces the tax imposed by section 881 and because there was a tax avoidance plan, BK2 is a conduit entity.

(iii) Because DC does not know or have reason to know of the tax avoidance plan (and by extension that the financing arrangement is a conduit financing arrangement), DC is not required to withhold tax under section 1441. However, BK2, who is also a withholding agent under section 1441 and who knows that the financing arrangement is a conduit financing arrangement, is not relieved of its withholding responsibilities.

(3) *Effective date.*—This paragraph (f) is effective for payments made by financed entities on or after September 11, 1995. This paragraph shall not apply to interest payments

Reg. § 1.1441-7(f)(3)

covered by section 127(g)(3) of the Tax Reform Act of 1984, and to interest payments with respect to other debt obligations issued prior to October 15, 1984 (whether or not such debt was issued by a Netherlands Antilles corporation).

(g) *Effective date.*—Except as otherwise provided in paragraph (f)(3) of this section, this section applies to payments made after December 31, 2000. [Reg. § 1.1441-7.]

☐ [*T.D. 7977, 9-19-84. Amended by T.D. 8611, 8-10-95; T.D. 8734, 10-6-97; T.D. 8804, 12-30-98; T.D. 8856, 12-29-99 and T.D. 8881, 5-15-2000 (corrected 4-5-2001).*]

§ 1.1441-8. Exemption from withholding for payments to foreign governments, international organizations, foreign central banks of issue, and the Bank for International Settlements.—(a) *Foreign governments.*—Under section 892, certain specific types of income received by foreign governments are excluded from gross income and are exempt from taxation, unless derived from the conduct of a commercial activity or received from or by a controlled commercial entity. Accordingly, withholding is not required under § 1.1441-1 with regard to any item of income which is exempt from taxation under section 892.

(b) *Reliance on claim of exemption by foreign government.*—Absent actual knowledge or reason to know otherwise, the withholding agent may rely upon a claim of exemption made by the foreign government if, prior to the payment, the withholding agent can reliably associate the payment with documentation upon which it can rely to treat the payment as made to a beneficial owner in accordance with § 1.1441-1(e)(1)(ii). A Form W-8 furnished by a foreign government for purposes of claiming an exemption under this paragraph (b) is valid only if, in addition to other applicable requirements, it certifies that the income is, or will be, exempt from taxation under section 892 and the regulations under that section and whether the person whose name is on the certificate is an integral part of a foreign government (as defined in § 1.892-2T(a)(2)) or a controlled entity (as defined in § 1.892-2T(a)(3)).

(c) *Income of a foreign central bank of issue or the Bank for International Settlements.*—(1) *Certain interest income.*—Section 895 provides for the exclusion from gross income of certain income derived by a foreign central bank of issue, or by the Bank for International Settlements, from obligations of the United States or of any agency or instrumentality thereof or from interest on deposits with persons carrying on the banking business if the bank is the owner of the obligations or deposits and does not hold the obligations or deposits for, or use them in connection with, the conduct of a commercial banking function or other commercial activity by such bank. See § 1.895-1. Absent actual knowledge or reason to know that a foreign central bank of issue, or the Bank for International Settlements, is operating outside the scope of the exclusion granted by section 895 and the regulations under that section, the withholding agent may rely on a claim of exemption if, prior to the payment, the withholding agent can reliably associate the payment with documentation upon which it can rely to treat the foreign central bank of issue or the Bank for International Settlements as the beneficial owner of the payment in accordance with § 1.1441-1(e)(1)(ii). A Form W-8 furnished by a foreign central bank of issue or the Bank for International Settlements for purposes of claiming an exemption under this paragraph (c)(1) is valid only if, in addition to other applicable requirements, it certifies that the person whose name is on the certificate is a foreign central bank of issue, or the Bank for International Settlements, and that the bank does not, and will not, hold the obligations or the bank deposits covered by the Form W-8 for, or use them in connection with, the conduct of a commercial banking function or other commercial activity.

(2) *Bankers' acceptances.*—Interest derived by a foreign central bank of issue from bankers' acceptances is exempt from tax under sections 871(i)(2)(C) and 881(d) and § 1.861-2(b)(4). With respect to bankers' acceptances, a withholding agent may treat a payee as a foreign central bank of issue without requiring a withholding certificate if the name of the payee and other facts surrounding the payment reasonably indicate that the payee or beneficial owner is a foreign central bank of issue, as defined in § 1.861-2(b)(4).

(d) *Exemption for payments to international organizations.*—A payment to an international organization (within the meaning of section 7701(a)(18)) is exempt from withholding on any payment. A withholding agent may treat a payee as an international organization without requiring a withholding certificate if the name of the payee is one that is designated as an international organization by executive order (pursuant to 22 U.S.C. 288 through 288(f)) and other facts surrounding the transaction reasonably indicate that the international organization is the beneficial owner of the payment.

(e) *Failure to receive withholding certificate timely and other applicable procedures.*—See applicable procedures described in § 1.1441-1(b)(7) in the event the withholding agent does not hold a valid withholding certificate described in paragraph (b) or (c)(1) of this section or other appropriate documentation at the time of payment. Further, the provisions of § 1.1441-1(e)(4) shall apply to withholding certificates and other documents related thereto furnished under the provisions of this section.

(f) *Effective date.*—(1) *In general.*—This section applies to payments made after December 31, 2000.

(2) *Transition rules.*—For purposes of this section, the validity of a Form 8709 that was valid on January 1, 1998, under the regulations in effect prior to January 1, 2001 (see 26 CFR part 1, revised April 1, 1999) and expired, or will expire, at any time during 1998, is extended until December 31, 1998. The validity of a Form 8709 that is valid on or after January 1, 1999, remains valid until its validity expires under the regulations in effect prior to January 1, 2001 (see 26 CFR part 1, revised April 1, 1999) but in no event shall such a form remain valid after December 31, 2000. The rule in this paragraph (f)(2), however, does not apply to extend the validity period of a Form 8709 that expires solely by reason of changes in the circumstances of the person whose name is on the certificate. Notwithstanding the first three sentences of this paragraph (f)(2), a withholding agent may choose to not take advantage of the transition rule in this paragraph (f)(2) with respect to one or more withholding certificates valid under the regulations in effect prior to January 1, 2001 (see 26 CFR part 1, revised April 1, 1999) and, therefore, to require withholding certificates conforming to the requirements described in this section (new withholding certificates). For purposes of this section, a new withholding certificate is deemed to satisfy the documentation requirement under the regulations in effect prior to January 1, 2001 (see 26 CFR part 1, revised April 1, 1999). Further, a new withholding certificate remains valid for the period specified in § 1.1441-1(e)(4)(ii), regardless of when the certificate is obtained. [Reg. § 1.1441-8.]

☐ [*T.D.* 8211, 6-24-88. *Redesignated and amended by T.D.* 8734, 10-6-97 *and amended by T.D.* 8804, 12-30-98 *and T.D.* 8856, 12-29-99.]

§ 1.1441-9. Exemption from withholding on exempt income of a foreign tax-exempt organization, including foreign private foundations.—(a) *Exemption from withholding for exempt income.*—No withholding is required under section 1441(a) or 1442, and the regulations under those sections, on amounts paid to a foreign organization that is described in section 501(c) to the extent that the amounts are not income includible under section 512 in computing the organization's unrelated business taxable income. See, however, § 1.1443-1 for withholding on payments of unrelated business income to foreign tax-exempt organizations and on payments subject to tax under section 4948. For a foreign organization to claim an exemption from withholding under section 1441(a) or 1442 based on its status as an organization described in section 501(c), it must furnish the withholding agent with a withholding certificate described in paragraph (b)(2) of this section. A foreign organization described in section 501(c) may choose to claim a reduced rate of withholding under the procedures described in other sections of the regulations under section 1441 and not under this section. In particular, if an organization chooses to claim benefits under an income tax treaty, the withholding procedures applicable to claims of such a reduced rate are governed solely by the provisions of § 1.1441-6 and not of this section.

(b) *Reliance on foreign organization's claim of exemption from withholding.*—(1) *General rule.*—A withholding agent may rely on a claim of exemption under this section only if, prior to the payment, the withholding agent can reliably associate the payment with a valid withholding certificate described in paragraph (b)(2) of this section.

(2) *Withholding certificate.*—A withholding certificate under this paragraph (b)(2) is valid only if it is a Form W-8 and if, in addition to other applicable requirements, the Form W-8 includes the taxpayer identifying number of the organization whose name is on the certificate, and it certifies that the Internal Revenue Service (IRS) has issued a favorable determination letter (and the date thereof) that is currently in effect, what portion, if any, of the amounts paid constitute income includible under section 512 in computing the organization's unrelated business taxable income, and, if the organization is described in section 501(c)(3), whether it is a private foundation described in section 509. Notwithstanding the preceding sentence, if the organization cannot certify that it has been issued a favorable determination letter that is still in effect, its withholding certificate is nevertheless valid under this paragraph (b)(2) if the organization attaches to the withholding certificate an opinion that is acceptable to the withholding agent from a U.S. counsel (or any other person as the IRS may prescribe in published guidance (see § 601.601(d)(2) of this chapter)) concluding that the organization is described in section 501(c). If the determination letter or opinion of counsel to which the withholding certificate refers concludes that the organization is described in section 501(c)(3), and the certificate further certifies that the organization is not a private foundation described in section

509, an affidavit of the organization setting forth sufficient facts concerning the operations and support of the organization for the Internal Revenue Service (IRS) to determine that such organization would be likely to qualify as an organization described in section 509(a)(1), (2), (3), or (4) must be attached to the withholding certificate. An organization that provides an opinion of U.S. counsel or an affidavit may provide the same opinion or affidavit to more than one withholding agent provided that the opinion is acceptable to each withholding agent who receives it in conjunction with a withholding certificate. Any such opinion of counsel or affidavit must be renewed whenever there is a change in facts or circumstances that are relevant to determine the organization's status under section 501(c) or, if relevant, that the organization is or is not a private foundation described in section 509.

(3) *Presumptions in the absence of documentation.*—Notwithstanding paragraph (b)(1) of this section, if the organization's certification with respect to whether amounts paid constitute income includible under section 512 in computing the organization's unrelated business taxable income is not reliable or is lacking but all other certifications are reliable, the withholding agent may rely on the certificate but the amounts paid are presumed to be income includible under section 512 in computing the organization's unrelated business taxable income. If the certification regarding private foundation status is not reliable, the withholding agent may rely on the certificate but the amounts paid are presumed to be paid to a foreign beneficial owner that is a private foundation.

(4) *Reason to know.*—Reliance by a withholding agent on the information and certifications stated on a withholding certificate is subject to the agent's actual knowledge or reason to know that such information or certification is incorrect as provided in § 1.1441-7(b). For example, a withholding agent must cease to treat a foreign organization's claim for exemption from withholding based on the organization's tax-exempt status as valid beginning on the earlier of the date on which such agent knows that the IRS has given notice to such foreign organization that it is not an organization described in section 501(c) or the date on which the IRS gives notice to the public that such foreign organization is not an organization described in section 501(c). Similarly, a withholding agent may no longer rely on a certification that an amount is not subject to tax under section 4948 beginning on the earlier of the date on which such agent knows that the IRS has given notice to such foreign organization that it is subject to tax under section 4948 or the date on which the IRS gives notice that such foreign organization is a private foundation within the meaning of section 509(a).

(c) *Failure to receive withholding certificate timely and other applicable procedures.*—See applicable procedures described in § 1.1441-1(b)(7) in the event the withholding agent does not hold a valid withholding certificate or other appropriate documentation at the time of payment. Further, the provisions of § 1.1441-1(e)(4) shall apply to withholding certificates and other documents related thereto furnished under the provisions of this section.

* * *

[Reg. § 1.1441-9.]

☐ [*T.D.* 8734, 10-6-97. *Amended by T.D.* 8804, 12-30-98; *T.D.* 8856, 12-29-99 *and T.D.* 8881, 5-15-2000.]

§ 1.1442-3. Tax exempt income of a foreign tax-exempt corporation.—For regulations providing for a claim of exemption for income exempt from tax under section 501(a) of a foreign tax-exempt corporation, see § 1.1441-9. See § 1.1443-1 for withholding rules applicable to foreign private foundations and to the unrelated business income of foreign tax-exempt organizations. [Reg. § 1.1442-3.]

☐ [*T.D.* 8734, 10-6-97 (T.D. 8804 delayed the effective date of T.D. 8734 from January 1, 1999, to January 1, 2000; T.D. 8856 further delayed the effective date of T.D. 8734 until January 1, 2001).]

§ 1.1445-1. Withholding on dispositions of U.S. real property interests by foreign persons: In general.—(a) *Purpose and scope of regulations.*—These regulations set forth rules relating to the withholding requirements of section 1445. In general, section 1445(a) provides that any person who acquires a U.S. real property interest from a foreign person must withhold a tax of 10 percent from the amount realized by the transferor foreign person (or a lesser amount established by agreement with the Internal Revenue Service). Section 1445(e) provides special rules requiring withholding on distributions and certain other transactions by corporations, partnerships, trusts, and estates. This § 1.1445-1 provides general rules concerning the withholding requirement of section 1445(a), as well as definitions applicable under both sections 1445(a) and 1445(e). Section 1.1445-2 provides for various situations in which withholding is not required under section 1445(a). Section 1.1445-3 provides for adjustments to the amount required to be withheld by transferees under section 1445(a). Section 1.1445-4 prescribes the duties of agents in transactions subject to withholding under either section 1445(a) or 1445(e). Section

1.1445-5 provides rules concerning the withholding required under section 1445(e), while § 1.1445-6 provides for adjustments to the amount required to be withheld under section 1445(e). Finally, § 1.1445-7 provides rules concerning the treatment of a foreign corporation that has made an election under section 897(i) to be treated as a domestic corporation.

(b) *Duty to withhold.*—(1) *In general.*—Transferees of U.S. real property interests are required to deduct and withhold a tax equal to 10 percent of the amount realized by the transferor, if the transferor is a foreign person and the disposition takes place on or after January 1, 1985. Neither the transferee's duty to withhold nor the amount required to be withheld is affected by the amount of cash to be paid by the transferee. Amounts withheld must be reported and paid over in accordance with the requirements of paragraph (c) of this section. Failures to withhold and pay over are subject to the liabilities set forth in paragraph (e) of this section. If two or more persons are joint transferees of a U.S. real property interest, each such person is subject to the obligation to withhold. That obligation is fulfilled with respect to each such person if any one of them withholds and pays over the required amount in accordance with the rules of this section. If the amount realized (as defined in paragraph (g)(5) of this section) by the transferor is zero, then no withholding is required. For example, if a real property interest is transferred as a gift (i.e., the recipient does not assume any liabilities or furnish any other consideration to the transferor) then no withholding is required. Withholding is not required with respect to dispositions that take place before January 1, 1985, even if the first payment of consideration is made after December 31, 1984.

(2) *U.S. real property interest owned jointly by foreign and non-foreign transferors.*—The amount subject to withholding under paragraph (b)(1) of this section with respect to the transfer of a U.S. real property interest owned by one or more foreign persons (as defined in § 1.897-1(k)) and one or more non-foreign persons shall be determined by allocating the amount realized from the transfer between (or among) such transferors based upon the capital contribution of each transferor with respect to the property and by aggregating the amounts allocated to any foreign person (or persons). For this purpose, a husband and wife will each be deemed to have contributed 50 percent of the aggregate capital contributed by such husband and wife. See § 1.1445-1(f)(3)(iv) with respect to the crediting of the amount withheld between or among joint foreign transferors.

(3) *Options to acquire a U.S. real property interest.*—(i) *No withholding on grant of option.*—No withholding is required under section 1445 with respect to any amount realized by the grantor on the grant of an option to acquire a U.S. real property interest.

(ii) *No withholding upon lapse of option.*—No withholding is required under section 1445 with respect to any amount realized by the grantor upon the lapse of an option to acquire a U.S. real property interest.

(iii) *Withholding required upon the sale or exchange of option.*—A transferee of an option to acquire a U.S. real property interest must deduct and withhold a tax equal to 10 percent of the amount realized by the transferor upon the disposition. This § 1.1445-1(b)(3)(iii) does not apply to require withholding upon the initial grant of an option.

(iv) *Withholding required on exercise of option.*—If the holder exercises an option to purchase a U.S. real property interest, the amount paid for the option shall be considered an amount realized by the grantor/transferor upon the transfer of the property with respect to which the option was granted, and shall thus be subject to withholding on the day that such underlying property is transferred. The preceding sentence applies regardless of whether or not the terms of the option specifically provide that the option price is applied to the purchase price.

(4) *Exceptions and modifications.*—The duty to withhold under section 1445(a) is subject to the exceptions and modifications contained in §§ 1.1445-2 and 1.1445-3. Generally, § 1.1445-2 provides rules for determining that withholding is not required because either the transferor is not a foreign person or the interest transferred is not a U.S. real property interest. In addition, § 1.1445-2 provides exceptions to the withholding requirement, including a rule that exempts from withholding any person who acquires a U.S. real property interest for use as a residence for a contract price of $300,000 or less. If withholding is required under section 1445(a), § 1.1445-3 allows the amount withheld to be modified pursuant to a withholding certificate issued by the Internal Revenue Service. If a transferee cannot withhold the full amount required because the first payment of consideration for the transfer does not involve sufficient cash (or other liquid assets convertible into cash, such as foreign currency), then a withholding certificate must be obtained pursuant to § 1.1445-3.

(c) *Reporting and paying over of withheld amounts.*—(1) *In general.*—A transferee must report and pay over any tax withheld by the

Reg. § 1.1445-1(c)(1)

20th day after the date of the transfer. Forms 8288 and 8288-A are used for this purpose, and must be filed at the location as provided in the instructions to Forms 8288 and 8288-A. Pursuant to section 7502 and regulations thereunder, the timely mailing of Forms 8288 and 8288-A will be treated as their timely filing. Form 8288-A will be stamped by the IRS to show receipt, and a stamped copy will be mailed by the IRS to the transferor (at the address reported on the form) for the transferor's use. See §§ 1.1445-1(f) and 1.1445-3(f). Forms 8288 and 8288-A are required to include the identifying numbers of both the transferor and the transferee, as provided in paragraph (d) of this section. If any identifying number as required by such forms is not provided, the transferee must still report and pay over any tax withheld on Form 8288, although the transferor cannot obtain a credit or refund of tax on the basis of a Form 8288-A that does not include the transferor's identifying number (see paragraph (f)(2) of this section).

(2) *Pending application for withholding certificate.*—(i) *In general.*—(A) *Delayed reporting and payment with respect to application submitted by transferee.*—If an application for a withholding certificate with respect to a transfer of a U.S. real property interest is submitted to the Internal Revenue Service by the transferee on the day of or at any time prior to the transfer, the transferee must withhold 10 percent of the amount realized as required by paragraph (b) of this section. However, the amount withheld, or a lesser amount as determined by the Service, need not be reported and paid over to the Service until the 20th day following the Service's final determination with respect to the application for a withholding certificate. For this purpose, the Service's final determination occurs on the day when the withholding certificate is mailed to the transferee by the Service or when a notification denying the request for a withholding certificate is mailed to the transferee by the Service. An application is submitted to the Service on the day it is actually received by the Service at the address provided in § 1.1445-1(g)(10) or, under the rules of section 7502, on the day it is mailed to the Service at the address provided in § 1.1445-1(g)(10).

(B) *Delayed reporting and payment with respect to application submitted by transferor.*—If an application for a withholding certificate with respect to a transfer of a U.S. real property interest is submitted to the Internal Revenue Service by the transferor on the day of or any time prior to the transfer, such transferor must provide notice to the transferee prior to the transfer. No particular form is required but the notice must set forth the name, address, and taxpayer identification number of the transferor, a brief description of the property which is the subject of the application, and the date the application was submitted to the Service. The transferee must withhold 10 percent of the amount realized as required in paragraph (b) of this section but need not report or pay over to the Service such amount (or a lesser amount as determined by the Service) until the 20th day following the Service's final determination with respect to the application. The Service will send a copy of the withholding certificate or copy of the notification denying the request for a withholding certificate to the transferee. For this purpose, the Service's final determination will be deemed to occur on the day when the copy of the withholding certificate or the copy of the notification denying the request for a withholding certificate is mailed by the Service to the transferee (or transferees). An application is submitted to the Service on the day it is actually received by the Service at the address provided in § 1.1445-1(g)(10) or, under the rules of § 7502, on the day it is mailed to the Service at the address provided in § 1.1445-1(g)(10).

(ii) *Anti-abuse rule.*—(A) *In general.*—A transferee that in reliance upon the rules of this paragraph (c)(2) fails to report and pay over amounts withheld by the 20th day following the date of the transfer, shall be subject to the payment of interest and penalties if the relevant application for a withholding certificate (or an amendment to the application for a withholding certificate) was submitted for a principal purpose of delaying the transferee's payment to the IRS of the amount withheld. Interest and penalties shall be assessed on the amount that is ultimately paid over (or collected pursuant to the agreement) with respect to the period between the 20th day after the date of the transfer and the date on which payment is made (or collected).

(B) *Presumption.*—A principal purpose of delaying payment of the amount withheld shall be presumed if—

(*1*) The transferee applies for a withholding certificate pursuant to § 1.1445-3(c) based on a determination of the transferor's maximum tax liability, and

(*2*) Such liability is ultimately determined to be equal to 90 percent or more of the amount that was otherwise required to be withheld and paid over.

However, the presumption created by the previous sentence may be rebutted by evidence establishing that delaying payment of the amount withheld was not a principal purpose of the transaction.

(d) *Contents of Forms 8288 and 8288-A.*—(1) *Transactions subject to section 1445(a).*—

Any person that is required to file Forms 8288 and 8288-A pursuant to section 1445(a) and the rules of this section must set forth thereon the following information:

(i) The name, identifying number, and home address (in the case of an individual) or office address (in the case of any entity) of the transferee(s) filing the return;

(ii) The name, identifying number, and home address (in the case of an individual) or office address (in the case of any entity) of the transferor(s);

(iii) A brief description of the U.S. real property interest transferred, including its location and the nature of any substantial improvements in the case of real property, and the class or type and amount of interests transferred in the case of interests in a corporation that constitute U.S. real property interests;

(iv) The date of the transfer;

(v) The amount realized by the transferor, as defined in paragraph (g)(5) of this section;

(vi) The amount withheld by the transferee and whether withholding is at the statutory or reduced rate; and

(vii) Such other information as the Commissioner may require.

For purposes of paragraph (d)(1)(i) and (ii), mailing addresses may be provided in addition to, but not in lieu of, home addresses or office addresses.

(2) *Transactions subject to section 1445(e).*—Any person that is required to file Forms 8288 and 8288-A pursuant to the rules of § 1.1445-5 must set forth thereon the following information:

(i) The name, identifying number, and office address of the entity or fiduciary filing the return;

(ii) The amount withheld by the entity or fiduciary;

(iii) The date of the transfer;

(iv) In the case of a transaction subject to withholding pursuant to section 1445(e)(1) and § 1.1445-5(c):

(A) A brief description of the U.S. real property interest transferred, as described in paragraph (d)(1)(iii) of this section;

(B) The name, identifying number, and home address (in the case of an individual) or office address (in the case of an entity) of each holder of an interest in the entity that is a foreign person; and

(C) Each such interest-holder's pro rata share of the amount withheld;

(v) In the case of a distribution subject to withholding pursuant to section 1445(e)(2) and § 1.1445-5(d):

(A) A brief description of the U.S. real property interest transferred, as described in paragraph (d)(1)(iii) of this section; and

(B) The amount of gain recognized upon the distribution by the corporation.

(vi) In the case of a distribution subject to withholding pursuant to section 1445(e)(3) and § 1.1445-5(e):

(A) A brief description of the property distributed by the corporation;

(B) The name, identifying number, and home address (in the case of an individual) or office address (in the case of an entity) of each holder of an interest in the entity that is a foreign person;

(C) The amount realized upon the distribution by each such foreign interest holder; and

(D) Each foreign interest-holder's pro rata share of the amount withheld; and

(vii) Such other information as the Commissioner may require.

(e) *Liability of transferee upon failure to withhold.*—(1) *In general.*—Every person required to deduct and withhold tax under section 1445 is made liable for that tax by section 1461. Therefore, a person that is required to deduct and withhold tax but fails to do so may be held liable for the payment of the tax and any applicable penalties and interest.

(2) *Transferor's liability not otherwise satisfied.*—(i) *Tax and penalties.*—Except as provided in paragraph (e)(3) of this section, if a transferee is required to deduct and withhold tax under section 1445 but fails to do so, then the tax shall be assessed against and collected from that transferee. Such person may also be subject to any of the civil and criminal penalties that apply. Corporate officers or other responsible persons may be subject to a civil penalty under section 6672 equal to the amount that should have been withheld and paid over.

(ii) *Interest.*—If a transferee is required to deduct and withhold tax under section 1445 but fails to do so, then such transferee shall be liable for the payment of interest pursuant to section 6601 and the regulations thereunder. Interest shall be payable with respect to the period between—

(A) The last date on which the tax imposed under section 1445 was required to be paid over by the transferee, and

(B) The date on which such tax is actually paid. Interest shall be payable with respect to the entire amount that is required to be deducted and withheld. However, if the Service issues a withholding certificate providing for withholding of a reduced amount, then, for the period after the issuance of the certificate, interest shall be payable with respect to that reduced amount.

(3) *Transferor's liability otherwise satisfied.*—(i) *Tax and penalties.*—If a transferee is required to deduct and withhold tax under section 1445 but fails to do so, and the transferor's tax liability with respect to the transfer was satisfied (or was established to be zero) by—

(A) The transferor's filing of an income tax return (and payment of any tax due) with respect to the transfer, or

(B) The issuance of a withholding certificate by the Internal Revenue Service establishing that the transferor's maximum tax liability is zero,

then the tax required to be withheld under section 1445 shall not be collected from the transferee. Such transferee's liability for tax, and the requirement that such person file Forms 8288 and 8288-A, shall be deemed to have been satisfied as of the date on which the transferor's income tax return was filed or the withholding certificate was issued. No penalty shall be imposed on or collected from such person for failure to return or pay the tax, unless such failure was fraudulent and for the purpose of evading payment. A transferee that seeks to avoid liability for tax and penalties pursuant to the rule of paragraph (e)(3)(i) must provide sufficient information for the Service to determine whether the transferor's tax liability was satisfied (or was established to be zero).

(ii) *Interest.*—If a transferee is required to deduct and withhold tax under section 1445 but fails to do so, then such person shall be liable for the payment of interest under section 6601 and regulations thereunder. Such transferee's liability for the payment of interest shall not be excused by reason of the deemed satisfaction, pursuant to subdivision (i) of this paragraph (e)(3), of the transferee's liability under section 1445, because the deemed satisfaction of that liability is the equivalent of the late payment of a liability, on which interest must be paid. Interest shall be payable with respect to the period between—

(A) The last date on which the tax imposed under section 1445 was required to be paid over, and

(B) The date (established from information supplied to the Service by the transferee) on which any tax due is paid with respect to the transferor's relevant income tax return, or the date the withholding certificate is issued establishing that the transferor's maximum tax liability is zero.

Interest shall be payable with respect to the entire amount that is required to be deducted and withheld. However, if the Service issues a withholding certificate providing for withholding of a reduced amount, then for the period after the issuance of the certificate interest shall be payable with respect to that reduced amount.

(4) *Coordination with entity withholding rules.*—For purposes of section 1445(e) and §§ 1.1445-5, 1.1445-6, 1.1445-7, and 1.1445-8T, the rules of this paragraph (e) shall be applied by—

(i) Substituting the words "person required to withhold" for the word "transferee" each place it appears in this paragraph (e), and

(ii) Substituting the words "person subject to withholding" for the word "transferor" each place it appears in this paragraph (e).

(f) *Effect of withholding on transferor.*—(1) *In general.*—The withholding of tax under section 1445(a) does not excuse a foreign person that disposes of a U.S. real property interest from filing a U.S. tax return with respect to the income arising from the disposition. Form 1040NR, 1041, or 1120F, as appropriate, must be filed, and any tax due must be paid, by the filing deadline generally applicable to such person. (The return may be filed by such later date as is provided in an extension granted by the Internal Revenue Service.) Any tax withheld under section 1445(a) shall be credited against the amount of income tax as computed in such return.

(2) *Manner of obtaining credit or refund.*—A stamped copy of Form 8288-A will be provided to the transferor by the Service (under paragraph (c) of this section) if the Form 8288-A is complete, including the transferor's identifying number. Except as provided in paragraph (f)(3) of this section, a stamped copy of Form 8288-A must be attached to the transferor's return to establish the amount withheld that is available as a credit. If the amount withheld under section 1445(a) constitutes less than the full amount of the transferor's U.S. tax liability for that taxable year, then a payment of estimated tax may be required to be made pursuant to section 6154 or 6654 prior to the filing of the income tax return for that year. Alternatively, if the amount withheld under section 1445(a) exceeds the transferor's maximum tax liability with respect to the disposition (as determined by the IRS), then the transferor may seek an early refund of the excess pursuant to § 1.1445-3T(g), or a normal refund upon filing of a tax return.

(3) *Special rules.*—(i) *Failure to receive Form 8288-A.*—If a stamped copy of Form 8288-A has not been provided to the transferor by the Service, the transferor may establish the amount of tax withheld by the transferee by

attaching to its return substantial evidence (*e.g.,* closing documents) of such amount. Such a transferor must attach to its return a statement which supplies all of the information required by § 1.1445-1(d), including the transferor's identifying number.

(ii) *U.S. persons subjected to withholding.*—If a transferee withholds tax under section 1445(a) with respect to a person who is not a foreign person, such person may credit the amount of any tax withheld against his income tax liability in accordance with the provisions of this § 1.1445-1(f) or apply for an early refund under § 1.1445-3(g).

(iii) *Refund in case of installment sale.*—A transferor that takes gain into account in accordance with the provisions of section 453 shall not be entitled to a refund of the amount withheld, unless a withholding certificate providing for such a refund is obtained from the Internal Revenue Service pursuant to the provisions of § 1.1445-3.

(iv) *Joint foreign transferors.*—If two or more foreign persons jointly transfer a U.S. real property interest, each transferor shall be credited with such portion of the amount withheld as such transferors mutually agree. Such transferors must request that the transferee reflect the agreed-upon crediting of the amount withheld on the Forms 8288-A filed by the transferee. If the foreign transferors fail to request that the transferee reflect the agreed-upon crediting of the amount withheld by the 10th day after the date of transfer, the transferee must credit the amount withheld equally between (or among) the foreign transferors. In such case, the transferee is indemnified pursuant to section 1461 against any claim by a transferor objecting to the resulting division of credits. For rules regarding the amount realized allocated to joint foreign and non-foreign transferors, see § 1.1445-1(b)(2).

(g) *Definitions.*—(1) *In general.*—Unless otherwise specified, the definitions of terms provided in § 1.897-1 shall apply for purposes of this section and §§ 1.1445-2 through 1.1445-7. For purposes of section 1445 and the regulations thereunder, definitions of other relevant terms are provided in this paragraph (g). In addition, the term "residence" is defined in § 1.1445-2(d)(1), the terms "transferor's agent" and "transferee's agent" are defined in § 1.1445-4(f), and the term "relevant taxpayer" is defined in § 1.1445-6(a)(2).

(2) *Transfer.*—The term "transfer" means any transaction that would constitute a disposition for any purpose of the Internal Revenue Code and regulations thereunder. For purposes of §§ 1.1445-5 and 1.1445-6, the term includes distributions to shareholders of a corporation, partners of a partnership, and beneficiaries of a trust or estate.

(3) *Transferor.*—The term "transferor" means any person, foreign or domestic, that disposes of a U.S. real property interest by sale, exchange, gift or any other transfer. The term "U.S. real property interest" is defined in § 1.897-1(c).

(4) *Transferee.*—The term "transferee" means any person, foreign or domestic, that acquires a U.S. real property interest by purchase, exchange, gift, or any other transfer.

(5) *Amount realized.*—The amount realized by the transferor for the transfer of a U.S. real property interest is the sum of:

(i) The cash paid, or to be paid,

(ii) The fair market value of other property transferred, or to be transferred, and

(iii) The outstanding amount of any liability assumed by the transferee or to which the U.S. real property interest is subject immediately before and after the transfer. The term "cash paid or to be paid" does not include stated or unstated interest or original issue discount (as determined under the rules of sections 1271 through 1275).

(6) *Contract price.*—The contract price of a U.S. real property interest is the sum that is agreed to by the transferee and transferor as the total amount of consideration to be paid for the property. That amount will generally be equal to the amount realized by the transferor, as defined in paragraph (b)(5) of this section.

(7) *Fair market value.*—The fair market value of property means the price at which the property would change hands between an unrelated willing buyer and willing seller, neither being under any compulsion to buy or to sell and both having reasonable knowledge of all relevant facts.

(8) *Date of transfer.*—The date of transfer of a U.S. real property interest is the first date on which consideration is paid (or a liability assumed) by the transferee. However, for purposes of section 1445(e)(2), (3), and (4) and § 1.1445-5(c)(1)(iii) and 1.1445-5(c)(3) only, the date of transfer is the date of the distribution that gives rise to the obligation to withhold. For purposes of this paragraph (g)(8), the payment of consideration does not include the payment, prior to the passage of legal or equitable title (other than pursuant to an initial contract for purchase), of earnest money, a good-faith deposit, or any similar sum that is primarily intended to bind the transferee or transferor to the entering or performance of a contract. Such a payment will not constitute a payment of

Reg. § 1.1445-1(g)(8)

consideration solely because it may ultimately be applied against the amount owed to the transferor by the transferee. Such a payment is presumed to be earnest money, a good faith deposit, or a similar sum if it is subject to forfeiture in the event of a failure to enter into a contract or a breach of contract. However, a payment that is not forfeitable may nevertheless be found to constitute earnest money, a good faith deposit, or a similar sum.

(9) *Identifying number.*—Pursuant to § 1.897-1(p), an individual's identifying number is the social security number or the identification number assigned by the Internal Revenue Service (see § 301.6109-1 of this chapter). The identifying number of any other person is its United States employer identification number.

(10) *Address of the Director, Philadelphia Service Center.*—Any written communication directed to the Director, Philadelphia Service Center is to be addressed as follows: P.O. Box 21086, Drop Point 8731, FIRPTA Unit, Philadelphia, PA 19114-0586.

(h) *Effective date for taxpayer identification numbers.*—The requirement in paragraphs (c)(2)(i)(B), (d)(1)(i) and (ii), (d)(2)(i), (d)(2)(iv)(B), and (d)(2)(vi)(B) of this section that taxpayer identification numbers be provided (in all cases) is applicable for dispositions of U.S. real property interests occurring after November 3, 2003. [Reg. § 1.1445-1.]

☐ [*T.D. 8113, 12-18-86. Amended by T.D. 8647, 12-20-95 and T.D. 9082, 8-4-2003.*]

§ 1.1445-2. Situations in which withholding is not required under section 1445(a).—(a) *Purpose and scope of section.*— This section provides rules concerning various situations in which withholding is not required under section 1445(a). In general, a transferee has a duty to withhold under section 1445(a) only if both of the following are true:

(1) The transferor is a foreign person; and

(2) The transferee is acquiring a U.S. real property interest.

Thus, paragraphs (b) and (c) of this section provide rules under which a transferee of property can ascertain that he has no duty to withhold because one or the other of the two key elements is missing. Under paragraph (b), a transferee may determine that no withholding is required because the transferor is not a foreign person. Under paragraph (c), a transferee may determine that no withholding is required because the property acquired is not a U.S. real property interest. Finally, paragraph (d) of this section provides rules concerning exceptions to the withholding requirement.

(b) *Transferor not a foreign person.*—(1) *In general.*—No withholding is required under section 1445 if the transferor of a U.S. real property interest is not a foreign person. Therefore, paragraph (b)(2) of this section provides rules pursuant to which the transferor can provide a certification of non-foreign status to inform the transferee that withholding is not required. A transferee that obtains such a certification must retain that document for five years, as provided in paragraph (b)(3) of this section. Except to the extent provided in paragraph (b)(4) of this section, the obtaining of this certification excuses the transferee from any liability otherwise imposed by section 1445 and § 1.1445-1(e). However, section 1445 and the rules of this section do not impose any obligation upon a transferee to obtain a certification from the transferor; thus, a transferee may instead rely upon other means to ascertain the non-foreign status of the transferor. If, however, the transferee relies upon other means and the transferor was, in fact, a foreign person, then the transferee is subject to the liability imposed by section 1445 and § 1.1445-1(e).

A transferee is in no event required to rely upon other means to ascertain the non-foreign status of the transferor and may demand a certification of non-foreign status. If the certification is not provided, the transferee may withhold tax under section 1445 and will be considered, for purposes of sections 1461 through 1463, to have been required to withhold such tax.

(2) *Transferor's certification of non-foreign status.*—(i) *In general.*—A transferee of a U.S. real property interest is not required to withhold under section 1445(a) if, prior to or at the time of the transfer, the transferor furnishes to the transferee a certification that—

(A) States that the transferor is not a foreign person,

(B) Sets forth the transferor's name, identifying number and home address (in the case of an individual) or office address (in the case of an entity), and

(C) Is signed under penalties of perjury.

In general, a foreign person is a nonresident alien individual, foreign corporation, foreign partnership, foreign trust, or foreign estate, but not a resident alien individual. In this regard, see § 1.897-1(k). However, a foreign corporation that has made a valid election under section 897(i) is generally not treated as a foreign person for purposes of section 1445. In this regard, see § 1.1445-7. Pursuant to § 1.897-1(p), an individual's identifying number is the individual's Social Security number and any other person's identifying number is its U.S. employer identification number. A certification pursuant to this paragraph (b) must be verified as true and signed under penalties of perjury by a responsible officer in the case of a corporation, by a general partner in the case of a partnership, and by a trustee, executor, or equivalent fiduciary in the case of a trust or estate. No particular form is needed for a certification pursuant to this paragraph (b), nor is any particular language required, so long as the document meets the requirements of this paragraph (b)(2)(i). Samples of acceptable certifications are provided in paragraph (b)(2)(iii) of this section.

(ii) *Foreign corporation that has made election under section 897(i).*—A foreign corporation that has made a valid election under section 897(i) to be treated as a domestic corporation for purposes of section 897 may provide a certification of non-foreign status pursuant to this paragraph (b)(2). However, an electing foreign corporation must attach to such certification a copy of the acknowledgment of the election provided to the corporation by the Internal Revenue Service pursuant to § 1.897-3(d)(4). An acknowledgement is valid for this purpose only if it states that the information required by § 1.897-3 has been determined to be complete.

(iii) *Disregarded entities.*—A disregarded entity may not certify that it is the transferor of a U.S. real property interest, as the disregarded entity is not the transferor for U.S. tax purposes, including sections 897 and 1445. Rather, the owner of the disregarded entity is treated as the transferor of property and must provide a certificate of non-foreign status to avoid withholding under section 1445. A disregarded entity for these purposes means an entity that is disregarded as an entity separate from its owner under § 301.7701-3 of this chapter, a qualified REIT subsidiary as defined in section 856(i), or a qualified subchapter S subsidiary under section 1361(b)(3)(B). Any domestic entity must include in its certification of non-foreign status with respect to the transfer a certification that it is not a disregarded entity. This paragraph (b)(2)(iii) and the sample certification provided in paragraph (b)(2)(iv)(B) of this section (to the extent it addresses disregarded entities) is applicable for dispositions occurring [after] September 4, 2003.

(iv) *Sample certifications.*—
(A) *Individual transferor.*—"Section 1445 of the Internal Revenue Code provides that a transferee (buyer) of a U.S. real property interest must withhold tax if the transferor (seller) is a foreign person. To inform the transferee (buyer) that withholding of tax is not required upon my disposition of a U.S. real property interest, I, [*name of transferor*], hereby certify the following:

    1. I am not a nonresident alien for purposes of U.S. income taxation;

    2. My U.S. taxpayer identifying number (Social Security number) is ____; and

    3. My home address is
_____
_____

I understand that this certification may be disclosed to the Internal Revenue Service by the transferee and that any false statement I have made here could be punished by fine, imprisonment, or both.

Under penalties of perjury I declare that I have examined this certification and to the best of my knowledge and belief it is true, correct, and complete.
[Signature and Date]"

(B) *Entity transferor.*—"Section 1445 of the Internal Revenue Code provides that a transferee of a U.S. real property interest must withhold tax if the transferor is a foreign person. For U.S. tax purposes (including section 1445), the owner of a disregarded entity (which has legal title to a U.S. real property interest under local law) will be the transferor of the property and not the disregarded entity. To inform the transferee that withholding of tax is not required upon the disposition of a U.S. real property interest by [name of transferor], the undersigned hereby certifies the following on behalf of [name of the transferor]:

    1. [Name of transferor] is not a foreign corporation, foreign partnership, foreign trust, or foreign estate (as those terms are defined in the Internal Revenue Code and Income Tax Regulations);

    2. [Name of transferor] is not a disregarded entity as defined in § 1.1445-2(b)(2)(iii);

    3. [Name of transferor]'s U.S. employer identification number is ____; and

    4. [Name of transferor]'s office address is _____.

[Name of transferor] understands that this certification may be disclosed to the Internal Revenue Service by transferee and that any false statement contained herein could be punished by fine, imprisonment, or both.

Under penalties of perjury I declare that I have examined this certification and to the best of my knowledge and belief it is true, correct, and complete, and I further declare that I have authority to sign this document on behalf of [name of transferor].
[Signature(s) and date]
[Title(s)]"

(3) *Transferee must retain certification.*—If a transferee obtains a transferor's certification

Reg. § 1.1445-2(b)(3)

pursuant to the rules of this paragraph (b), then the transferee must retain that certification until the end of the fifth taxable year following the taxable year in which the transfer takes place. The transferee must retain the certification, and make it available to the Internal Revenue Service when requested in accordance with the requirements of section 6001 and regulations thereunder.

(4) *Reliance upon certification not permitted.*—(i) *In general.*—A transferee may not rely upon a transferor's certification pursuant to this paragraph (b) under the circumstances set forth in either subdivision (ii) or (iii) of this paragraph (b)(4). In either of those circumstances, a transferee's withholding obligation shall apply as if a certification had never been obtained, and the transferee is fully liable pursuant to section 1445 and § 1445-1(e) for any failure to withhold.

(ii) *Failure to attach IRS acknowledgment of election.*—A transferee that knows that the transferor is a foreign corporation may not rely upon a certification of non-foreign status provided by the corporation on the basis of election under section 897(i), unless there is attached to the certification a copy of the acknowledgment by the Internal Revenue Service of the corporation's election, as required by paragraph (b)(2)(ii) of this section.

(iii) *Knowledge of falsity.*—A transferee is not entitled to rely upon a transferor's certification if prior to or at the time of the transfer the transferee either—

(A) Has actual knowledge that the transferor's certification is false; or

(B) Receives a notice that the certification is false from a transferor's or transferee's agent, pursuant to § 1.1445-4.

(iv) *Belated notice of false certification.*— If after the date of the transfer a transferee receives a notice that a certification is false, then that transferee is entitled to rely upon the certification only with respect to consideration that was paid prior to receipt of the notice. Such a transferee is required to withhold a full 10 percent of the amount realized from the consideration that remains to be paid to the transferor if possible. Thus, if 10 percent or more of the amount realized remains to be paid to the transferor then the transferee is required to withhold and pay over the full 10 percent. The transferee must do so by withholding and paying over the entire amount of each successive payment of consideration to the transferor until the full 10 percent of the amount realized has been withheld and paid over. Amounts so withheld must be reported and paid over by the 20th day following the date on which each such payment of consideration is made. A transferee that is subject to the rules of this paragraph (b)(4)(iv) may not obtain a withholding certificate pursuant to § 1.1445-3, but must instead withhold and pay over the amounts required by this paragraph.

(c) *Transferred property not a U.S. real property interest.*—(1) *In general.*—No withholding is required under section 1445 if the transferee acquires only property that is not a U.S. real property interest. As defined in section 897(c) and § 1.897-1(c), a U.S. real property interest includes certain interests in U.S. corporations, as well as direct interests in real property and certain associated personal property. This paragraph (c) provides rules pursuant to which a person acquiring an interest in a U.S. corporation may determine that withholding is not required because that interest is not a U.S. real property interest. To determine whether an interest in tangible property constitutes a U.S. real property interest the acquisition of which would be subject to withholding, see § 1.897-1(b) and (c).

(2) *Interests in publicly traded entities.*— No withholding is required under section 1445(a) upon the acquisition of an interest in a domestic corporation if any class of stock of the corporation is regularly traded on an established securities market. This exemption shall apply if the disposition is incident to an initial public offering of stock pursuant to a registration statement filed with the Securities and Exchange Commission. Similarly, no withholding is required under section 1445(a) upon the acquisition of an interest in a publicly traded partnership or trust. However, the rule of this paragraph (c)(2) shall not apply to the acquisition, from a single transferor (or related transferors as defined in § 1.897-1(i)) in a single transaction (or related transactions), of an interest described in § 1.897-1(c)(2)(iii)(B) (relating to substantial amounts of non-publicly traded interests in publicly traded corporations) or to similar interests in publicly traded partnerships or trusts. The person making an acquisition described in the preceding sentence must otherwise determine whether withholding is required, pursuant to section 1445 and the regulations thereunder. Transactions shall be deemed to be related if they are undertaken within 90 days of one another or if it can otherwise be shown that they were undertaken in pursuance of a prearranged plan.

(3) *Transferee receives statement that interest in corporation is not a U.S. real property interest.*—(i) *In general.*—No withholding is required under section 1445(a) upon the acquisition of an interest in a domestic corporation, if the transferor provides the transferee with a

copy of a statement, issued by the corporation pursuant to §1.897-2(h), certifying that the interest is not a U.S. real property interest. In general, a corporation may issue such a statement only if the corporation was not a U.S. real property holding corporation at any time during the previous five years (or the period in which the interest was held by its present holder, if shorter) or if interests in the corporation ceased to be United States real property interests under section 897(c)(1)(B). (A corporation may not provide such a statement based on its determination that the interest in question is an interest solely as a creditor.) See §1.897-2(f) and (h). The corporation may provide such a statement directly to the transferee at the transferor's request. The transferor must request such a statement prior to the transfer, and shall, to the extent possible, specify the anticipated date of the transfer. A corporation's statement may be relied upon for purposes of this paragraph (c)(3) only if the statement is dated not more than 30 days prior to the date of the transfer. A transferee may also rely upon a corporation's statement that is voluntarily provided by the corporation in response to a request from the transferee, if that statement otherwise complies with the requirements of this paragraph (c)(3) and §1.897-2(h).

(ii) *Reliance on statement not permitted.*—A transferee is not entitled to rely upon a statement that a corporation is not a U.S. real property holding corporation if, prior to or at the time of the transfer, the transferee either—

(A) Has actual knowledge that the statement is false, or

(B) Receives a notice that the statement is false from a transferor's or transferee's agent, pursuant to §1.1445-4.

Such a transferee's withholding obligations shall apply as if a statement had never been given, and such a transferee may be held fully liable pursuant to §1.1445-1(e) for any failure to withhold.

(iii) *Belated notice of false statement.*—If after the date of the transfer, a transferee receives notice that a statement provided under §1.1445-2(c)(3)(i) (that an interest in a corporation is not a U.S. real property interest) is false, then such transferee may rely on the statement only with respect to consideration that was paid prior to the receipt of the notice. Such a transferee is required to withhold a full 10 percent of the amount realized from the consideration that remains to be paid to the transferor, if possible. Thus, if 10 percent or more of the amount realized remains to be paid to the transferor, then the transferee is required to withhold any pay over the full 10 percent. The transferee must do so by withholding and paying over the entire amount of each successive payment of consideration to the transferor, until the full 10 percent of the amount realized has been withheld and paid over. Amounts so withheld must be reported and paid over by the 20th day following the date on which each such payment of consideration is made. A transferee that is subject to the rules of this paragraph 1.1445-2(c)(3)(iii) may not obtain a withholding certificate pursuant to §1.1445-3, but must instead withhold and pay over the amounts required by this paragraph.

(d) *Exceptions to requirement of withholding.*—(1) *Purchase of residence for $300,000 or less.*—No withholding is required under section 1445(a) if one or more individual transferees acquire a U.S. real property interest for use as a residence and the amount realized on the transaction is $300,000 or less. For purposes of this section, a U.S. real property interest is acquired for use as a residence if on the date of the transfer the transferee (or transferees) has definite plans to reside at the property for at least 50 percent of the number of days that the property is used by any person during each of the first two 12-month periods following the date of the transfer. The number of days that the property will be vacant is not taken into account in determining the number of days such property is used by any person. A transferee shall be considered to reside at a property on any day on which a member of the transferee's family, as defined in section 267(c)(4), resides at the property. No form or other document need be filed with the Internal Revenue Service to establish a transferee's entitlement to rely upon the exception provided by this paragraph (d)(1). A transferee who fails to withhold in reliance upon this exception, but who does not in fact reside at the property for the minimum number of days set forth above, shall be liable for the failure to withhold (if the transferor was a foreign person and did not pay the full U.S. tax due on any gain recognized upon the transfer). However, if the transferee establishes that the failure to reside the minimum number of days was caused by a change in circumstances that could not reasonably have been anticipated at the time of the transfer, then the transferee shall not be liable for the failure to withhold. The exception provided by paragraph (d)(1) does not apply in any case where the transferee is other than an individual even if the property is acquired for or on behalf of an individual who will use the property as a residence. However, this exception applies regardless of the organizational structure of the transferor (i.e., regardless of whether the transferor is an individual, partnership, trust, corporation, etc.).

(2) *Coordination with nonrecognition provisions.*—(i) *In general.*—A transferee shall not be required to withhold under section 1445(a) with respect to the transfer of a U.S. real property interest if—

(A) The transferor notifies the transferee, in the manner described in paragraph (d)(2)(iii) of this section, that by reason of the operation of a nonrecognition provision of the Internal Revenue Code or the provisions of any United States treaty the transferor is not required to recognize any gain or loss with respect to the transfer; and

(B) By the 20th day after the date of the transfer the transferee provides a copy of the transferor's notice to the Director, Philadelphia Service Center, at the address provided in § 1.1445-1(g)(10), together with a cover letter setting forth the name, identifying number, and home address (in the case of an individual) or office address (in the case of an entity) of the transferee providing the notice to the Service.

The rule of this paragraph (d)(2)(i) is subject to the exceptions set forth in paragraph (d)(2)(ii). For purposes of this paragraph (d)(2) a nonrecognition provision is any provision of the Internal Revenue Code for not recognizing gain or loss.

(ii) *Exceptions.*—A transferee may not rely upon the rule of paragraph (d)(2)(i) of this section, and must therefore withhold under section 1445(a) with respect to the transfer of a U.S. real property interest, if either:

(A) The transferor qualifies for nonrecognition treatment with respect to part, but not all, of the gain realized by the transferor upon the transfer; or

(B) The transferee knows or has reason to know that the transferor is not entitled to the nonrecognition treatment claimed by the transferor.

In either of the above circumstances the transferee or transferor may request a withholding certificate from the Internal Revenue Service pursuant to the rules of § 1.1445-3.

(iii) *Contents of the notice.*—No particular form is required for a transferor's notice to a transferee that the transferor is not required to recognize gain or loss with respect to a transfer. The notice must be verified as true and signed under penalties of perjury by the transferor, by a responsible officer in the case of a corporation, by a general partner in the case of a partnership, and by a trustee or equivalent fiduciary in the case of a trust or estate. The following information must be set forth in paragraphs labeled to correspond with the designation set forth as follows—

(A) A statement that the document submitted constitutes a notice of a nonrecognition transaction or a treaty provision pursuant to the requirements of § 1.1445-2(d)(2);

(B) The name, identifying number, and home address (in the case of an individual) or office address (in the case of an entity) of the transferor submitting the notice;

(C) A statement that the transferor is not required to recognize any gain or loss with respect to the transfer;

(D) A brief description of the transfer; and

(E) A brief summary of the law and facts supporting the claim that recognition of gain or loss is not required with respect to the transfer.

(iv) *No notice allowed.*—The provisions of this paragraph (d)(2) do not apply to exclusions from income under section 121, to simultaneous like-kind exchanges under section 1031 that do not qualify for nonrecognition treatment in their entirety (see paragraph (d)(2)(ii)(A) of this section), and to non-simultaneous like-kind exchanges under section 1031 where the transferee cannot determine that the exchange has been completed and all the conditions for nonrecognition have been satisfied at the time it is otherwise required to pay the section 1445 withholding tax and file the withholding tax return (Form 8288, "U.S. Withholding Tax Return for Dispositions by Foreign Persons of U.S. Real Property Interests"). In these cases, the transferee is excused from withholding only upon the timely application for and receipt of a withholding certificate under § 1.1445-3 (see § 1.1445-3(b)(5) and (6) for specific rules applicable to transactions under sections 121 and 1031). This paragraph (d)(2)(iv) is applicable for dispositions and exchanges occurring [after] September 4, 2003.

(3) *Special procedural rules applicable to foreclosures.*—(i) *Amount to be withheld.*—(A) *Foreclosures.*—A transferee that acquires a U.S. real property interest pursuant to a repossession or foreclosure on such property under a mortgage, security agreement, deed of trust or other instrument securing a debt must withhold tax under section 1445(a) equal to 10 percent of the amount realized on such sale. Such amount must be reported and paid over to the Service under the general rules of § 1.1445-1. However, if the transferee complies with the notice requirements of § 1.1445-2(d)(3)(ii) and (iii), such transferee may report and pay over to the Service on or before the 20th day following the final determination by a court or trustee with jurisdiction over the foreclosure action, the lesser of:

(1) the amount otherwise required to be withheld under section 1445(a), or

(2) the "alternative amount" as defined in the succeeding sentence.

The alternative amount is the entire amount, if any, determined by a court or trustee with jurisdiction over the matter, that accrues to the debtor/transferor out of the amount realized from the foreclosure sale. The amount of any mortgage, lien, or other security agreement secured by the property, that is terminated, assumed by another person, or otherwise extinguished (as to the debtor/transferor) shall not be treated as an amount that accrues to the debtor/transferor for purposes of this § 1.1445-2(d)(3)(i)(A). If the alternative amount is zero, no withholding is required. Any difference between the amount withheld at the time of the foreclosure sale and the amount to be reported and paid over to the Service must be transferred to the court or trustee with jurisdiction over the foreclosure action. Amounts withheld, if any, are to be reported and paid over to the Service by using Forms 8288 and 8288-A in conformity with § 1.1445-1(d).

(B) Deeds in lieu of foreclosures.—A transferee of a U.S. real property interest pursuant to a deed in lieu of foreclosure must withhold tax equal to 10 percent of the amount realized by the debtor/transferor on the transfer. However, no withholding is required if:

(1) The transferee is the only person with a security interest in the property,

(2) No cash or other property (other than incidental fees incurred with respect to the transfer) is paid, directly or indirectly, to any person with respect to the transfer, and

(3) The notice requirements of § 1.1445-2(d)(3) are satisfied.

The amount withheld, if any, must be reported and paid over to the Service not later than the 20th day following the date of transfer. In a case where withholding would otherwise be required, a withholding certificate may be requested in accordance with § 1.1445-3.

(ii) *Notice to the court or trustee in a foreclosure action.*—(A) *Notice on day of purchase.*—A transferee in a foreclosure sale that chooses to use the special rules applicable to foreclosures must provide notice to the court or trustee with jurisdiction over the foreclosure action on the day the property is transferred with respect to such transferee's withholding obligation. No particular form is necessary but the notice must set forth the transferee's name, home address in the case of an individual, office address in the case of an entity, a brief description of the property, the date of the transfer, the amount realized on the sale of the foreclosed property and the amount withheld under section 1445(a).

(B) *Notice whether amount withheld or alternative amount is reported and paid over the Service.*—A purchaser/transferee in a foreclosure that chooses to use the special rules applicable to foreclosures must provide notice to the court or trustee with jurisdiction over the foreclosure action regarding whether the amount withheld or the alternative amount will be (or has been) reported and paid over to the Service. The notice should set forth all the information required by the preceding paragraph (d)(3)(ii)(A), the amount withheld or alternative amount that will be (or has been) reported and paid over to the Service, and the amount that will be (or has been) paid over to the court or trustee.

(iii) *Notice to the Service.*—(A) *General rule.*—A transferee that in reliance upon the rules of this paragraph (d)(3) withholds an alternative amount (or does not withhold because the alternative amount is zero) must, on or before the 20th day following the final determination by a court or trustee in a foreclosure action or on or before the 20th day following the date of the transfer with respect to a transfer pursuant to a deed in lieu of foreclosure, provide notice thereof to the Assistant Commissioner (International) at the address provided in § 1.1445-1(g)(10). (The filing of such a notice shall not relieve a creditor of any obligation it may have to file a notice pursuant to section 6050J and the regulations thereunder.) No particular form is required but the following information must be set forth in paragraphs labelled to correspond with the numbers set forth below.

(1) A statement that the notice constitutes a notice of foreclosure action or transfer pursuant to a deed in lieu of foreclosure under § 1.1445-2(d)(3).

(2) The name, identifying number, and home address (in the case of an individual) or office address (in the case of an entity) of the purchaser/transferee.

(3) The name, identifying number, and home address (in the case of an individual) or office address (in the case of an entity) of the debtor/transferor.

(4) In a foreclosure action, the date of the final determination by a court or trustee regarding the distribution of the amount realized from the foreclosure sale. In a transfer pursuant to a deed in lieu of foreclosure, the date the property is transferred to the purchaser/transferee.

(5) A brief description of the property.

(6) The amount realized from the foreclosure sale or with respect to the transfer pursuant to a deed in lieu of foreclosure.

(7) The alternative amount.

(B) *Special rule for lenders required to file Form 1099-A where the alternative amount is zero.*—A person required under section 6050J to file Form 1099-A does not have to comply with the notice requirement of § 1.1445-2(d)(3)(iii)(A) if the alternative amount is zero. In such case, the filing of the Form 1099-A will be deemed to satisfy the notice requirement of § 1.1445-2(d)(3)(iii)(A).

(iv) *Requirements not applicable.*—A transferee is not required to withhold tax or provide notice pursuant to the rules of this paragraph (d)(3) if no substantive withholding liability applies to the transfer of the property by the debtor/transferor. For example, if the debtor/transferor provides the transferee with a certification of non-foreign status pursuant to paragraph (b) of this section, then no substantive withholding liability would exist with respect to the acquisition of the property from the debtor transferor. In such a case, no withholding of tax or notice to the Internal Revenue Service is required of the transferee with respect to the repossession or foreclosure.

(v) *Anti-abuse rule.*—If a U.S. real property interest is transferred in foreclosure or pursuant to a deed in lieu of foreclosure for a principal purpose of avoiding the requirements of section 1445(a), then the provisions of this paragraph (d)(3) shall not apply to the transfer and the transferee shall be fully liable for any failure to withhold with respect to the transfer. A principal purpose to avoid section 1445(a) will be presumed (subject to rebuttal on the basis of all relevant facts and circumstances) if:

(A) The transferee acquires property in which it, or a related party, has a security interest;

(B) The security interest did not arise in connection with the debtor/transferor's or a related party's or predecessor in interest's acquisition, improvement, or maintenance of the property; and

(C) The total amount of all debts secured by the property exceeds 90 percent of the fair market value of the property.

(4) *Installment payments.*—A transferee of a U.S. real property interest is not required to withhold under section 1445 when making installment payments on an obligation arising out of a disposition that took place before January 1, 1985. With respect to dispositions that take place after December 31, 1984, the transferee shall be required to satisfy its entire withholding obligation within the time specified in § 1.1445-1(c) regardless of the amount actually paid by the transferee. Thereafter, no withholding is required upon further installment payments on an obligation arising out of the transfer. A transferee that is unable to satisfy its entire withholding obligation within the time specified in § 1.1445-1(c) may request a withholding certificate pursuant to § 1.1445-3.

(5) *Acquisitions by governmental bodies.*—No withholding of tax is required under section 1445 with respect to any acquisition of property by the United States, a state or possession of the United States, a political subdivision thereof, or the District of Columbia.

(6) [Reserved.]

(7) *Withholding certificate obtained by transferee or transferor.*—No withholding is required under section 1445(a) if the transferee is provided with a withholding certificate that so specifies. Either the transferor or the transferee may seek a withholding certificate from the Internal Revenue Service, pursuant to the provisions of § 1.1445-3.

(8) *Amount realized by transferor is zero.*—If the amount realized by the transferor on a transfer of a U.S. real property interest is zero, no withholding is required.

(e) *Effective date for taxpayer identification numbers.*—The requirement in paragraphs (d)(2)(i)(B), (d)(2)(iii)(B), and (d)(3)(iii)(A)(*2*) and (*3*) of this section that taxpayer identification numbers be provided (in all cases) is applicable for dispositions of U.S. real property interests occurring after November 3, 2003. [Reg. § 1.1445-2.]

☐ [*T.D.* 8113, 12-18-86. *Amended by T.D.* 8198, 5-4-88 *and T.D.* 9082, 8-4-2003.]

§ 1.1445-3. Adjustments to amount required to be withheld pursuant to withholding certificate.—(a) *In general.*—Withholding under section 1445(a) may be reduced or eliminated pursuant to a withholding certificate issued by the Internal Revenue Service in accordance with the rules of this section. A withholding certificate may be issued by the Service in cases where reduced withholding is appropriate (see paragraph (c) of this section), where the transferor is exempt from U.S. tax (see paragraph (d) of this section), or where an agreement for the payment of tax is entered into with the Service (see paragraph (e) of this section). A withholding certificate that is obtained prior to a transfer notifies the transferee that no withholding is required. A withholding certificate that is obtained after a transfer has been made may authorize a normal refund or an early refund pursuant to paragraph (g) of this section. Either a transferee or transferor may apply for a withholding certificate. The Internal Revenue Service will act upon an application for a withholding certificate not later than the 90th day after it is received. Solely for this purpose (i.e., determining the day upon which the 90-day period commences), an application is received by the Service on the date that all information necessary for the Service to make a determination is provided by the applicant. In no event, however, will a withholding certificate be issued without the transferor's identifying number. (For rules regarding whether an application for a withholding certificate has been timely submitted, see § 1.1445-1(c)(2).) The Service may deny a request for a withholding certificate where, after due notice, an applicant fails to provide information necessary for the Service to make a determination. The Service will act upon an application for an early refund not later than the 90th day after it is received. An application for an early refund must either (1) include a copy of a withholding certificate issued by the Service with respect to the transaction, or (2) be combined with an application for a withholding certificate. Where an application for an early refund is combined with an application for a withholding certificate, the Service will act upon both applications not later than the 90th day after receipt. In the case of an application for a certificate based on nonconforming security under paragraph (e)(3)(v) of this section, and in unusually complicated cases, the Service may be unable to provide a final withholding certificate by the 90th day. In such a case the Service will notify the applicant, by the 45th day after receipt of the application, that additional processing time will be necessary. The Service's notice may request additional information or explanation concerning particular aspects of the application, and will provide a target date for final action (contingent upon the applicant's timely submission of any requested information). A withholding certificate issued pursuant to the provisions of this section serves to fulfill the requirements of section 1445(b)(4) concerning qualifying statements, section 1445(c)(1) concerning the transferor's maximum tax liability, or section 1445(c)(2) concerning the Secretary's authority to prescribe reduced withholding.

(b) *Applications for withholding certificates.*—(1) *In general.*—An application for a withholding certificate must be submitted to the Director, Philadelphia Service Center, at the address provided in § 1.1445-1(g)(10). An application for a withholding certificate must be signed by a responsible officer in the case of a corporation, by a general partner in the case of a partnership, by a trustee, executor, or equivalent fiduciary in the case of a trust or estate, and in the case of an individual by the individual himself. A duly authorized agent may sign the application but the application must contain a valid power of attorney authorizing the agent to sign the application on behalf of the applicant. The person signing the application must verify under penalties of perjury that all representations made in connection with the application are true, correct, and complete to his knowledge and belief. No particular form is required for an application, but the application must set forth the information described in paragraphs (b)(2), (3), and (4), and to the extent applicable, paragraph (b)(5) or (6) of this section.

(2) *Parties to the transaction.*—The application must set forth the name, address, and identifying number of the person submitting the application (specifying whether that person is the transferee or transferor), and the name, address, and identifying number of other parties to the transaction (specifying whether each such party is a transferee or transferor). The Service will deny the application if complete information, including the identifying numbers of all the parties, is not provided. Thus, for example, the applicant should determine if an identifying number exists for each party, and, if none exists for a particular party, the applicant should notify the particular party of the obligation to get an identifying number before the application can be submitted to the Service. The address provided in the case of an individual must be that individual's home address, and the address provided in the case of an entity must be that entity's office address. A mailing address may be provided in addition to, but not in lieu of, a home address or office address.

(3) *Real property interest to be transferred.*—The application must set forth information concerning the U.S. real property interest with respect to which the withholding certificate is sought, including the type of interest, the contract price, and, in the case of an interest in real property, its location and general description, or in the case of an interest in a U.S. real property holding corporation, the class or type and amount of the interest.

(4) *Basis for certificate.*—(i) *Reduced withholding.*—If a withholding certificate is sought on the basis of a claim that reduced withholding is appropriate, the application must include:

(A) A calculation of the maximum tax that may be imposed on the disposition in accordance with paragraph (c)(2) of this section. Such calculation must be accompanied by a copy of the relevant contract and depreciation schedules or other evidence that confirms the contract price and adjusted basis of the property. If no depreciation schedules are provided, the application must state the nature of the use of the property and why depreciation was not allowable. Evidence that supports any claimed adjustment to the maximum tax on the disposition must also be provided;

Reg. § 1.1445-3(b)(4)(i)(A)

(B) A calculation of the transferor's unsatisfied withholding liability, or evidence supporting the claim that no such liability exists, in accordance with paragraph (c)(3) of this section; and

(C) In the case of a request for a special reduction of withholding pursuant to paragraph (c)(4) of this section, a statement of law and facts in support of the request.

(ii) *Exemption.*—If a withholding certificate is sought on the basis of the transferor's exemption from U.S. tax, the application must set forth a brief statement of the law and facts that support the claimed exemption. In this regard, see paragraph (d) of this section.

(iii) *Agreement.*—If a withholding certificate is sought on the basis of an agreement for the payment of tax, the application must include a signed copy of the agreement proposed by the applicant and a copy of the security instrument (if any) proposed by the applicant. In this regard, see paragraph (e) of this section.

(5) *Special rule for exclusions from income under section 121.*—A withholding certificate may be sought on the basis of a section 121 exclusion as a reduction in the amount of tax due under paragraph (c)(2)(v) of this section. The application must include information establishing that the transferor, who is a nonresident alien individual at the time of the sale (and is therefore subject to sections 897 and 1445) is entitled to claim the benefits of section 121. For example, a claim for reduced withholding as a result of section 121 must include information that the transferor occupied the U.S. real property interest as his or her personal residence for the required period of time.

(6) *Special rule for like-kind exchanges under Section 1031.*—A withholding certificate may be requested with respect to a like-kind exchange under section 1031 as a transaction subject to a nonrecognition provision under paragraph (c)(2)(ii) of this section. The application must include information substantiating the requirements of section 1031. The IRS may require additional information during the course of the application process to determine that the requirements of section 1031 are satisfied. In the case of a deferred like-kind exchange, the withholding agent is excused from reporting and paying the withholding tax to the IRS within 20 days after the transfer only if an application for a withholding certificate is submitted prior to or on the date of transfer. See § 1.1445-1(c)(2) for rules concerning delayed reporting and payment where an application for a withholding certificate has been submitted to the IRS prior to or on the date of transfer.

(c) *Adjustment of amount required to be withheld.*—(1) *In general.*—The Internal Revenue Service may issue a withholding certificate that excuses withholding or that permits the transferee to withhold an adjusted amount reflecting the transferor's maximum tax liability. The transferor's maximum tax liability is the sum of—

(i) The maximum amount which could be imposed as tax under section 871 or 882 upon the transferor's disposition of the subject real property interest, as determined under paragraph (c)(2) of this section, and

(ii) The transferor's unsatisfied withholding liability with respect to the subject real property interest, as determined under paragraph (c)(3) of this section.

In addition, the Internal Revenue Service may issue a withholding certificate that permits the transferee to withhold a reduced amount if the Service determines pursuant to paragraph (c)(4) of this section that reduced withholding will not jeopardize the collection of tax.

(2) *Maximum tax imposed on disposition.*—The first element of the transferor's maximum tax liability is the maximum amount which the transferor could be required to pay as tax upon the disposition of the subject real property interest. In the case of an individual transferor that amount will generally be the contract price of the property minus its adjusted basis, multiplied by the maximum individual income tax rate applicable to long-term capital gain. In the case of a corporate transferor, that amount will generally be the contract price of the property minus its adjusted basis, multiplied by the maximum corporate income tax rate applicable to long-term capital gain. However, that amount must be adjusted to take into account the following:

(i) Any reduction of tax to which the transferor is entitled under the provisions of a U.S. income tax treaty;

(ii) The effect of any nonrecognition provision that is applicable to the transaction;

(iii) Any losses realized and recognized upon the previous disposition of U.S. real property interests during the taxable year;

(iv) Any amount that is required to be treated as ordinary income; and

(v) Any other factor that may increase or reduce the tax upon the disposition.

(3) *Transferor's unsatisfied withholding liability.*—(i) *In general.*—The second element of the transferor's maximum tax liability is the transferor's unsatisfied withholding liability. That liability is the amount of any tax that the transferor was required to but did not withhold and pay over under section 1445 upon the ac-

quisition of the subject U.S. real property interest or a predecessor interest. The transferor's unsatisfied withholding liability is included in the calculation of maximum tax liability so that such prior withholding liability can be satisfied by the transferee's withholding upon the current transfer. Alternatively, the transferor's unsatisfied withholding liability may be disregarded for purposes of calculating the maximum tax liability, if either—

(A) Such prior withholding liability is fully satisfied by a payment that is made with the application submitted pursuant to this section; or

(B) An agreement is entered into for the payment of that liability pursuant to the rules of paragraph (e) of this section. Because section 1445 only requires withholding after December 31, 1984, no transferor's unsatisfied withholding liability can exist unless the transferor acquired the subject or predecessor real property interest after that date. For purposes of this paragraph (c), a predecessor interest is one that was exchanged for the subject U.S. real property interest in a transaction in which the transferor was not required to recognize the full amount of the gain or loss realized upon the transfer.

(ii) *Evidence that no unsatisfied withholding liability exists.*—For purposes of paragraph (b)(4)(i)(B) of this section (concerning information that must be submitted with an application for a withholding certificate), evidence that the transferor has no unsatisfied withholding liability includes any one of the following documents:

(A) Evidence that the transferor acquired the subject or predecessor real property interest prior to January 1, 1985;

(B) A copy of the Form 8288 that was filed by the transferor, and proof of payment of the amount shown due thereon, with respect to the transferor's acquisition of the subject or predecessor real property interest;

(C) A copy of a withholding certificate with respect to the transferor's acquisition of the subject or predecessor real property interest, plus a copy of Form 8288 and proof of payment with respect to any withholding required under that certificate;

(D) A copy of the non-foreign certification furnished by the person from whom the subject or predecessor U.S. real property interest was acquired, executed at the time of that acquisition;

(E) Evidence that the transferor purchased the subject or predecessor real property for $300,000 or less, and a statement, signed by the transferor under penalties of perjury, that the transferor purchased the property for use as a residence within the meaning of §1.1445-2(d)(1);

(F) Evidence that the person from whom the transferor acquired the subject or predecessor U.S. real property interest fully paid any tax imposed on that transaction pursuant to section 897;

(G) A copy of a notice of nonrecognition treatment provided to the transferor pursuant to §1.1445-2(d)(2) by the person from whom the transferor acquired the subject or predecessor U.S. real property interest; and

(H) A statement, signed by the transferor under penalties of perjury, setting forth the facts and circumstances that supported the transferor's conclusion that no withholding was required under section 1445(a) with respect to the transferor's acquisition of the subject or predecessor real property interest.

(4) *Special reduction of amount required to be withheld.*—The Internal Revenue Service may, in its discretion, issue a withholding certificate that permits the transferee to withhold a reduced amount based upon a determination that reduced withholding will not jeopardize the collection of tax. A transferor that requests a withholding certificate pursuant to this paragraph (c)(4) is required pursuant to paragraph (b)(4)(i)(C) of this section to submit a statement of law and facts in support of the request. That statement must explain why the transferor is unable to enter into an agreement for the payment of tax pursuant to paragraph (e) of this section.

(d) *Transferor's exemption from U.S. tax.*— (1) *In general.*—The Internal Revenue Service will issue a withholding certificate that excuses all withholding by a transferee if it is established that:

(i) The transferor's gain from the disposition of the subject U.S. real property interest will be exempt from U.S. tax, and

(ii) The transferor has no unsatisfied withholding liability.

For the available exemptions, see paragraph (d)(2) of this section. The transferor's unsatisfied withholding liability shall be determined in accordance with the provisions of paragraph (c)(3) of this section. A transferor that is entitled to a reduction of (rather than an exemption from) U.S. tax may obtain a withholding certificate to that effect pursuant to the provisions of paragraph (c) of this section.

(2) *Available exemptions.*—A transferor's gain from the disposition of a U.S. real property interest may be exempt from U.S. tax because either:

(i) The transferor is an integral part or controlled entity of a foreign government and the disposition of the subject property is not a commercial activity, as determined pursuant to section 892 and the regulations thereunder; or

(ii) The transferor is entitled to the benefits of an income tax treaty that provides for such an exemption (subject to the limitations imposed by section 1125(c) of Pub. L. 96-499, which, in general, overrides such benefits as of January 1, 1985).

(e) *Agreement for the payment of tax.*—(1) *In general.*—The Internal Revenue Service will issue a withholding certificate that excuses withholding or that permits a transferee to withhold a reduced amount, if either the transferee or the transferor enters into an agreement for the payment of tax pursuant to the provisions of this paragraph (e). An agreement for the payment of tax is a contract between the Service and any other person that consists of two necessary elements. Those elements are—

(i) A contract between the Service and the other person, setting forth in detail the rights and obligations of each; and

(ii) A security instrument or other form of security acceptable to the Director, Foreign Operations District.

(2) *Contents of agreement.*—(i) *In general.*—An agreement for the payment of tax must cover an amount described in subdivision (ii) or (iii) of this paragraph (e)(2). The agreement may either provide adequate security for the payment of the chosen amount in accordance with paragraph (e)(3) of this section, or provide for the payment of that amount through a combination of security and withholding of tax by the transferee.

(ii) *Tax that would otherwise be withheld.*—An agreement for the payment of tax may cover the amount of tax that would otherwise be required to be withheld pursuant to section 1445(a). In addition to the amount computed pursuant to section 1445(a), the applicant must agree to pay interest upon that amount, at the rate established under section 6621, with respect to the period between the date on which the tax imposed by section 1445(a) would otherwise be due (*i.e.*, the 20th day after the date of transfer) and the date on which the transferor's payment of tax with respect to the disposition will be due under the agreement. The amount of interest agreed upon must be paid by the applicant regardless of whether or not the Service is required to draw upon any security provided pursuant to the agreement. The interest may be paid either with the return or by the Service drawing upon the security.

(iii) *Maximum tax liability.*—An agreement for the payment of tax may cover the transferor's maximum tax liability, determined in accordance with paragraph (c) of this section. The agreement must also provide for the payment of an additional amount equal to 25 percent of the amount determined under paragraph (c) of this section. This additional amount secures the interest and penalties that would accrue between the date of a failure to file a return and pay tax with respect to the disposition, and the date on which the Service collects upon that liability pursuant to the agreement. Such additional amount will only be collected if the Service finds it necessary to draw upon any security provided due to the transferor's failure to file a return and pay tax with respect to the relevant disposition.

(3) *Major types of security.*—(i) *In general.*—The following are the major types of security acceptable to the Service. Further details with respect to the terms and conditions of each type may be specified by Revenue Procedure.

(ii) *Bond with surety or guarantor.*—The Service may accept as security with respect to a transferor's tax liability a bond that is executed with a satisfactory surety or guarantor. Only the following persons may act as surety or guarantor for this purpose:

(A) A surety company holding a certificate of authority from the Secretary as an acceptable surety on Federal bonds, as listed in Treasury Department Circular No. 570, published annually in the Federal Register on the first working day of July;

(B) A person that is engaged within or without the United States in the conduct of a banking, financing, or similar business under the principles of § 1.864-4(c)(5) and that is subject to U.S. or foreign local or national regulation of such business, if that person is otherwise acceptable to the Service; and

(C) A person that is engaged within or without the United States in the conduct of an insurance business that is subject to U.S. or foreign local or national regulation, if that person is otherwise acceptable to the Service.

(iii) *Bond with collateral.*—The Service may accept as security with respect to a transferor's tax liability a bond that is secured by acceptable collateral. All collateral must be deposited with a responsible financial institution acting as escrow agent or, in the Service's discretion, with the Service. Only the following types of collateral are acceptable:

(A) Bonds, notes, or other public debt obligations of the United States, in accordance with the rules of 31 CFR Part 225; and

(B) A certified cashier's, or treasurer's check, drawn on an entity acceptable to the Service that is engaged within or without the United States in the conduct of a banking, financing, or similar business under the principles of § 1.864-4(c)(5) and that is subject to U.S. or foreign local or national regulation of such business.

(iv) *Letter of credit.*—The Service may accept as security with respect to a transferor's tax liability an irrevocable letter of credit. The Service may accept a letter of credit issued by an entity acceptable to the Service that is engaged within or without the United States in the conduct of a banking, financing or similar business under the principles of § 1.884-4(c)(5) and that is subject to U.S. or foreign local or national regulation of such business. However, the Director will accept a letter of credit from an entity that is not engaged in trade or business in the United States only if such letter may be drawn on an advising bank within the United States.

(v) *Guarantees and other nonconforming security.*—(A) *Guarantee.*—The Service may in its discretion accept as security with respect to a transferor's tax liability the applicant's guarantee that it will pay such liability. The Service will in general accept such a guarantee only from a corporation, foreign or domestic, any class of stock of which is regularly traded on an established securities market on the date of the transfer.

(B) *Other forms of security.*—The Service may in unusual circumstances and at its discretion accept any form of security that it finds to be adequate. An application for a withholding certificate that proposes a form of security that does not conform with any of the preferred types set forth in paragraph (e)(3)(ii) through (iv) of this section or any relevant Revenue Procedure must include:

(1) A detailed statement of the facts and circumstances supporting the use of the proposed form of security, and

(2) A memorandum of law concerning the validity and enforceability of the proposed form of security.

(4) *Terms of security instrument.*—Any security instrument that is furnished pursuant to this section must provide that—

(i) The amount of each deposit of estimated tax that will be required with respect to the gain realized on the subject disposition may be collected by levy upon the security as of the date following the date on which each such deposit is due (unless such deposit is timely made);

(ii) The entire amount of the liability may be collected by levy upon the security at any time during the nine months following the date on which the payment of tax with respect to the subject disposition is due, subject to release of the security upon the full payment of the tax and any interest and penalties due. If the transferor requests an extension of time to file a return with respect to the disposition, then the Director may require that the term of the security instrument be extended until the date that is nine months after the filing deadline as extended.

(f) *Amendments to application for withholding certificate.*—(1) *In general.*—An applicant for a withholding certificate may amend an otherwise complete application by submitting an amending statement to the Director, Philadelphia Service Center, at the address provided in § 1.1445-1(g)(10). The amending statement shall provide the information required by § 1.1445-3(f)(3) and must be signed and accompanied by a penalties of perjury statement in accordance with § 1.1445-3(b)(1).

(2) *Extension of time for the Service to process requests for withholding certificates.*—(i) *In general.*—If an amending statement is submitted, the time in which the Internal Revenue Service must act upon the amended application shall be extended by 30 days.

(ii) *Substantial amendments.*—If an amending statement is submitted and the Service finds that the statement substantially amends the facts of the underlying application or substantially alters the terms of the withholding certificate as requested in the initial application, the time within which the Service must act upon the amended application shall be extended by 60 days. The applicant shall be so notified.

(iii) *Amending statement received after the requested withholding certificate has been signed by the Director, Philadelphia Service Center.*—If an amending statement is received after the withholding certificate, drafted in response to the underlying application, has been signed by the Director, Philadelphia Service Center, or his delegate and prior to the day such certificate is mailed to the applicant, the time in which the Service must act upon the amended application shall be extended by 90 days. The applicant will be so notified.

(3) *Information required to be submitted.*—No particular form is required for an amending statement but the statement must provide the following information:

(i) *Identification of applicant.*—The amending statement must set forth the name, address and identifying number of the person submitting the amending statement (specifying whether that person is the transferee or transferor).

Reg. § 1.1445-3(f)(3)(i)

(ii) *Date of underlying application.*—The amending statement must set forth the date of the underlying application for a withholding certificate.

(iii) *Real property interest to be (or that has been) transferred.*—The amending statement must set forth a brief description of the real property interest with respect to which the underlying application for a withholding certificate was submitted.

(iv) *Amending information.*—The amending statement must fully set forth the basis for the amendment including any modification of the facts supporting the application for a withholding certificate and any change sought in the terms of the withholding certificate.

(g) *Early refund of overwithheld amounts.*—If a transferor receives a withholding certificate pursuant to this section, and an amount greater than that specified in the certificate was withheld by the transferee, then pursuant to the rules of this paragraph (g) the transferor may apply for a refund (without interest) of the excess amount prior to the date on which the transferor's tax return is due (without extensions). (Any interest payable on refunds issued after the filing of a tax return shall be determined in accordance with the provisions of section 6611 and regulations thereunder.) An application for an early refund must be addressed to the Director, Philadelphia Service Center, at the address provided in § 1.1445-1(g)(10). No particular form is required for the application, but the following information must be set forth in separate paragraphs numbered to correspond with the number given below:

(1) Name, address, and identifying number of the transferor seeking the refund;

(2) Amount required to be withheld pursuant to the withholding certificate issued by Internal Revenue Service;

(3) Amount withheld by the transferee (attach a copy of Form 8288-A stamped by IRS pursuant to § 1.1445-1(c));

(4) Amount to be refunded to the transferor. An application for an early refund cannot be processed unless the required copy of Form 8288-A (or substantial evidence of the amount withheld in the case of a failure to receive Form 8288-A as provided in § 1.1445-1(f)(3)) is attached to the application. If an application for a withholding certificate based upon the transferor's maximum tax liability is submitted after the transfer takes place, then that application may be combined with an application for an early refund. The Service will act upon a claim for refund within the time limits set forth in paragraph (a) of this section.

(h) *Effective date for taxpayer identification numbers.*—The requirement in paragraphs (b)(2), (f)(3)(i), and (g)(1) of this section that taxpayer identification numbers be provided (in all cases) is applicable for dispositions of U.S. real property interests occurring after November 3, 2003. [Reg. § 1.1445-3.]

☐ [T.D. 8113, 12-18-86. Amended by T.D. 9082, 8-4-2003.]

§ 1.1445-4. Liability of agents.—(a) *Duty to provide notice of false certification or statement to transferee.*—A transferee's or transferor's agent must provide notice to the transferee if either—

(1) The transferee is furnished with a non-U.S. real property interest statement pursuant to § 1.1445-2(c)(3) and the agent knows that the statement is false; or

(2) The transferee is furnished with a non-foreign certification pursuant to § 1.1445-2(b)(2) and either (i) the agent knows that the certification is false, or (ii) the agent represents a transferor that is a foreign corporation.

An agent that represents a transferor that is a foreign corporation is not required to provide notice to the transferee if the foreign corporation provided a nonforeign certification to the transferee prior to such agent's employment and the agent does not know that the corporation did so.

(b) *Duty to provide notice of false certification or statement to entity or fiduciary.*—A transferee's or transferor's agent must provide notice to an entity or fiduciary that plans to carry out a transaction described in section 1445(e)(1), (2), (3), or (4) if either—

(1) The entity or fiduciary is furnished with a non-U.S. real property interest statement pursuant to § 1.1445-5(b)(4)(iii) and the agent knows that such statement is false; or

(2) The entity or fiduciary is furnished with a non-foreign certification pursuant to § 1.1445-5(b)(3)(ii) and either (i) the agent knows that such certification is false, or (ii) the agent represents a foreign corporation that made such a certification.

(c) *Procedural requirements.*—(1) *Notice to transferee, entity, or fiduciary.*—An agent who is required by this section to provide notice must do so in writing as soon as possible after learning of the false certification or statement, but not later than the date of the transfer (prior to the transferee's payment of consideration). If an agent first learns of a false certification or statement after the date of the transfer, notice must be given by the third day following that discovery. The notice must state that the certification or statement is false and may not be relied upon. The notice must also explain the possible consequences to the recipient of a failure to withhold. The notice need not disclose the information on which the agent's statement is based. The following is an example of an acceptable notice: "This is to notify you that you may be required to withhold tax in connection with *(describe transaction)*. You have been provided with a certification of nonforeign status (or a non-U.S. real property interest statement) in connection with that transaction. I have learned that that document is false. Therefore, you may not rely upon it as a basis for failing to withhold under section 1445 of the Internal Revenue Code. Section 1445 provides that any person who acquires a U.S. real property interest from a foreign person must withhold a tax equal to 10 percent of the total purchase price. (The term 'U.S. real property interest' includes real property, stock in U.S. corporations whose assets are primarily real property, and some personal property associated with realty.) Any person who is required to withhold but fails to do so can be held liable for the tax. Thus, if you do not withhold the 10 percent tax from the total that you pay on this transaction, you could be required to pay the tax yourself, if what you are acquiring is a U.S. real property interest and the transferor is a foreign person. Tax that is withheld must be promptly paid over to the IRS using Form 8288. For further information see sections 897 and 1445 of the Internal Revenue Code and the related regulations."

(2) *Notice to be filed with IRS.*—An agent who is required by paragraph (a) or (b) of this section to provide notice to a transferee, entity, or fiduciary must furnish a copy of that notice to the Internal Revenue Service by the date on which the notice is required to be given to the transferee, entity, or fiduciary. The copy of the notice must be delivered to the Director, Philadelphia Service Center, at the address provided in § 1.1445-1(g)(10), and must be accompanied by a cover letter stating that the copy is being filed pursuant to the requirements of this § 1.1445-4(c)(2).

(d) *Effect on recipient.*—A transferee, entity, or fiduciary that receives a notice pursuant to this section prior to the date of the transfer from any agent of the transferor or transferee may not rely upon the subject certification or statement for purposes of excusing withholding pursuant to § 1.1445-2 or § 1.1445-5. Therefore, the recipient of a notice may be held liable for any failure to deduct and withhold tax under section 1445 as if such certification or statement had never been given. For special rules concerning the effect of the receipt of a notice after the date of the transfer, see §§ 1.1445-2(b)(4)(iv) and 1.1445-5(c), (d) and (e).

(e) *Failure to provide notice.*—Any agent who is required to provide notice but who fails to do so in the manner required by paragraph (a) or (b) of this section shall be held liable for the tax that the recipient of the notice would have been required to withhold under section 1445 if such notice had been given. However, an agent's liability under this paragraph (e) is limited to the amount of compensation that that agent derives from the transaction. In addition, an agent who assists in the preparation of, or fails to disclose knowledge of, a false certification or statement may be liable for civil or criminal penalties.

(f) *Definition of transferor's or transferee's agent.*—(1) *In general.*—For purposes of this section, the terms "transferor's agent" and "transferee's agent" mean any person who represents the transferor or transferee (respectively)—

(i) In any negotiation with another person (or another person's agent) relating to the transaction; or

(ii) In settling the transaction.

(2) *Transactions subject to section 1445(e).*—In the case of transactions subject to section 1445(e), the following definitions apply.

(i) The term "transferor's agent" means any person that represents or advises an entity or fiduciary with respect to the planning, arrangement, or consummation by the entity of a transaction described in section 1445(e)(1), (2), (3), or (4).

(ii) The term "transferee's agent" means any person that represents or advises the holder of an interest in an entity with respect to the planning, arrangement or consummation by the entity of a transaction described in section 1445(e)(1), (2), (3), or (4).

(3) *Exclusion of settlement officers and clerical personnel.*—For purposes of this section, a person shall not be treated as a transferor's agent or transferee's agent with respect to any transaction solely because such person performs one or more of the following activities:

(i) The receipt and disbursement of any portion of the consideration for the transaction;

(ii) The recording of any document in connection with the transaction; or

(iii) Typing, copying, and other clerical tasks;

(iv) The obtaining of title insurance reports and reports concerning the condition of the real property that is the subject of the transaction; or

Reg. § 1.1445-4(f)(3)(iv)

(v) The transmission or delivery of documents between the parties.

(4) *Exclusion for governing body of a condominium association and the board of directors of a cooperative housing corporation.*—The members of a board, committee or other governing body of a condominium association and the board of directors and officers of a cooperative housing corporation will not be deemed agents of the transferor or transferee if such individuals function exclusively in their capacity as representatives of such association or corporation with respect to the transaction. In addition, the managing agent of a cooperative housing corporation or condominium association will not be deemed to be an agent of the transferee or transferor if such person functions exclusively in its capacity as a managing agent. If a person's activities include advising the transferee or transferor with respect to the transfer, this exclusion shall not apply. [Reg. § 1.1445-4.]

☐ [*T.D.* 8113, 12-18-86. *Amended by T.D.* 9082, 8-4-2003.]

§ 1.1445-5. Special rules concerning distributions and other transactions by corporations, partnerships, trusts, and estates.—(a) *Purpose and scope.*—This section provides special rules concerning the withholding that is required under section 1445(e) upon distributions and other transactions involving domestic or foreign corporations, partnerships, trusts, and estates. Paragraph (b) of this section provides rules that apply generally to the various withholding requirements set forth in this section. Under section 1445(e)(1) and paragraph (c) of this section, a domestic partnership or the fiduciary of a domestic trust or estate is required to withhold tax upon the entity's disposition of a U.S. real property interest if any foreign persons are partners or beneficiaries of the entity. Paragraph (d) provides rules concerning the requirement of section 1445(e)(2) that a foreign corporation withhold tax upon its distribution of a U.S. real property interest to its interest-holders. Finally, under section 1445(e)(3) and paragraph (e) of this section a domestic U.S. real property holding corporation is required to withhold tax upon certain distributions to interest-holders that are foreign persons. Paragraphs (f) and (g) of this section are reserved to provide rules concerning transactions involving interests in partnerships, trusts, and estates that will be subject to withholding pursuant to section 1445(e)(4) and (5).

(b) *Rules of general application.*—(1) *Double withholding not required.*—If tax is required to be withheld with respect to a transfer of property in accordance with the rules of this section, then no additional tax is required to be withheld by the transferee of the property with respect to that transfer pursuant to the general rules of section 1445(a) and § 1.1445-1. For rules coordinating the withholding under section 1441 (or section 1442 or 1443) and under section 1445 on distributions from a corporation, see § 1.1441-3(b)(4). If a transfer of a U.S. real property interest described in section 1445(e) is exempt from withholding under the rules of this section, then no withholding is required under the general rules of section 1445(a) and § 1.1445-1.

(2) *Coordination with nonrecognition provisions.*—(i) *In general.*—Withholding shall not be required under the rules of this section with respect to a transfer described in section 1445(e) of a U.S. real property interest if—

(A) By reason of the operation of a nonrecognition provision of the Internal Revenue Code or the provisions of any treaty of the United States no gain or loss is required to be recognized by the foreign person with respect to which withholding would otherwise be required; and

(B) The entity or fiduciary that is otherwise required to withhold complies with the notice requirements of paragraph (b)(2)(ii) of this section. The entity or fiduciary must determine whether gain or loss is required to be recognized pursuant to the rules of section 897 and the applicable nonrecognition provisions of the Internal Revenue Code. An entity or fiduciary may obtain a withholding certificate from the Internal Revenue Service that confirms the applicability of a nonrecognition provision, but is not required to do so. For purposes of this paragraph (b)(2), a nonrecognition provision is any provision of the Internal Revenue Code for not recognizing gain or loss. If nonrecognition treatment is available only with respect to part of the gain realized on a transfer, the exemption from withholding provided by this paragraph (b)(2) shall not apply. In such cases a withholding certificate may be sought pursuant to the provisions of § 1.1445-6.

(ii) *Notice of nonrecognition transfer.*—An entity or fiduciary that fails to withhold tax with respect to a transfer in reliance upon the rules of this paragraph (b)(2) must by the 20th day after the date of the transfer deliver a notice thereof to the Director, Philadelphia Service Center, at the address provided in § 1.1445-1(g)(10). No particular form is required for a notice of transfer, but the following information must be set forth in paragraphs labelled to correspond with the letter set forth below:

(A) A statement that the document submitted constitutes a notice of a nonrecognition transfer pursuant to the requirements of § 1.1445-5(b)(2)(ii);

(B) The name, office address, and identifying number of the entity of fiduciary submitting the notice;

(C) The name, identifying number, and home address (in the case of an individual) or office address (in the case of an entity) of each foreign person with respect to which withholding would otherwise be required;

(D) A brief description of the transfer; and

(E) A brief statement of the law and facts supporting the claim that recognition of gain or loss is not required with respect to the transfer.

(3) *Interest-holder not a foreign person.*—(i) *In general.*—Pursuant to the provisions of paragraphs (c) and (e) of this section, an entity or fiduciary is required to withhold with respect to certain transfers of property if a holder of an interest in the entity is a foreign person. For purposes of determining whether a holder of an interest is a foreign person, an entity or fiduciary may rely upon a certification of non-foreign status provided by that person in accordance with paragraph (b)(3)(ii) of this section. Except to the extent provided in paragraph (b)(3)(iii) of this section, such a certification excuses the entity or fiduciary from any liability otherwise imposed pursuant to section 1445(e) and regulations thereunder. However, no obligation is imposed upon an entity or fiduciary to obtain certifications from interest-holders; an entity or fiduciary may instead rely upon other means to ascertain the non-foreign status of an interest-holder. If the entity or fiduciary does rely upon other means but the interest-holder proves, in fact, to be a foreign person, then the entity or fiduciary is subject to any liability imposed pursuant to section 1445 and regulations thereunder. An entity or fiduciary is not required to rely upon other means to ascertain the non-foreign status of an interest-holder and may demand a certification of non-foreign status. If the certification is not provided, the entity or fiduciary may withhold tax under section 1445 and will be considered, for purposes of sections 1461 through 1463, to have been required to withhold such tax.

(ii) *Interest-holder's certification of non-foreign status.*—(A) *In general.*—For purposes of this section, an entity or fiduciary may treat any holder of an interest in the entity as a U.S. person if that interest-holder furnishes to the entity or fiduciary a certification stating that the interest-holder is not a foreign person, in accordance with the provisions of paragraph (b)(3)(ii)(B) of this section. In general, a foreign person is a nonresident alien individual, foreign corporation, foreign partnership, foreign trust, or foreign estate, but not a resident alien individual. In this regard, see § 1.897-1(k).

(B) *Procedural rules.*—An interest-holder's certification of non-foreign status must—

(1) State that the interest-holder is not a foreign person;

(2) Set forth the interest-holder's name, identifying number, home address (in the case of an individual) or office address (in the case of an entity), and place of incorporation (in the case of a corporation); and

(3) Be signed under penalties of perjury.

Pursuant to § 1.897-1(p), an individual's identifying number is the individual's Social Security number and any other person's identifying number is its U.S. employer identification number. The certification must be signed by a responsible officer in the case of a corporation, by a general partner in the case of a partnership, and by a trustee, executor, or equivalent fiduciary in the case of a trust or estate. No particular form is needed for a certification pursuant to this paragraph (b)(3)(ii)(B), nor is any particular language required, so long as the document meets the requirements of this paragraph. Samples of acceptable certifications are provided in paragraph (b)(3)(ii)(D) of this section. An entity may rely upon a certification pursuant to this paragraph (b)(3)(ii)(B) for a period of two calendar years following the close of the calendar year in which the certification was given. If an interest holder becomes a foreign person within the period described in the preceding sentence, the interest holder must notify the entity prior to any further dispositions or distributions and upon receipt of such notice (or any other notification of the foreign status of the interest holder) the entity may no longer rely upon the prior certification. An entity that obtains and relies upon a certification must retain that certification with its books and records for a period of three calendar years following the close of the last calendar year in which the entity relied upon the certification.

(C) *Foreign corporation that has made an election under section 897(i).*—A foreign corporation that has made a valid election under section 897(i) to be treated as a domestic corporation for purposes of section 897 may provide a certifi-cation of non-foreign status pursuant to this paragraph (b)(3)(ii). However, an electing foreign corporation must attach to such certification a copy of the acknowledgment of the election provided to the corporation by the Internal Revenue Service pursuant to § 1.897-3(d)(4).

Reg. § 1.1445-5(b)(3)(ii)(C)

An acknowledgment is valid for this purpose only if it states that the information required by § 1.897-3 has been determined to be complete.

(D) *Sample certifications.*—(1) *Individual interest-holder.*—"Under section 1445(e) of the Internal Revenue Code, a corporation, partnership, trust or estate must withhold tax with respect to certain transfers of property if a holder of an interest in the entity is a foreign person. To inform [name of entity] that no withholding is required with respect to my interest in it, I, [name of interest-holder], hereby certify the following:

    1. I am not a nonresident alien for purposes of U.S. income taxation;

    2. My U.S. taxpayer identifying number (Social Security number) is _____; and

    3. My home address is _____

I agree to inform [name of entity] promptly if I become a nonresident alien at any time during the three years immediately following the date of this notice.

I understand that this certification may be disclosed to the Internal Revenue Service by [name of entity] and that any false statement I have made here could be punished by fine, imprisonment, or both.

Under penalties of perjury I declare that I have examined this certification and to the best of my knowledge and belief it is true, correct, and complete.
[Signature and date]"

    (2) *Entity interest-holder.*—"Under section 1445(e) of the Internal Revenue Code, a corporation, partnership, trust, or estate must withhold tax with respect to certain transfers of property if a holder of an interest in the entity is a foreign person. To inform [name of entity] that no withholding is required with respect to [name of interest-holder]'s interest in it, the undersigned hereby certifies the following on behalf of [name of interest-holder]:

    1. [Name of interest-holder] is not a foreign corporation, foreign partnership, foreign trust, or foreign estate (as those terms are defined in the Internal Revenue Code and Income Tax Regulations);

    2. [Name of interest-holder]'s U.S. employer identification number is _____; and

    3. [Name of interest-holder]'s office address is _____

and place of incorporation (if applicable) is _____

[Name of interest-holder] agrees to inform [name of entity] if it becomes a foreign person at any time during the three year period immediately following the date of this notice.

[Name of interest-holder] understands that this certification may be disclosed to the Internal Revenue Service by [name of entity] and that any false statement contained herein could be punished by fine, imprisonment, or both.

Under penalties of perjury I declare that I have examined this certification and to the best of my knowledge and belief it is true, correct, and complete, and I further declare that I have authority to sign this document on behalf of [name of interest-holder].
[Signature and date]
[Title]"

    (iii) *Reliance upon certification not permitted.*—An entity or fiduciary may not rely upon an interest-holder's certification of non-foreign status if, prior to or at the time of the transfer with respect to which withholding would be required, the entity or fiduciary either—

    (A) Has actual knowledge that the certification is false;

    (B) Has received a notice that the certification is false from a transferor's or transferee's agent, pursuant to § 1.1445-4; or

    (C) Has received from a corporation that it knows to be a foreign corporation a certification that does not have attached to it a copy of the IRS acknowledgment of the corporation's election under section 897(i), as required by paragraph (b)(3)(ii)(C) of this section.

Such an entity's or fiduciary's withholding obligations shall apply as if a statement had never been given, and such an entity or fiduciary may be held fully liable pursuant to § 1.1445-1(e) for any failure to withhold. For special rules concerning an entity's belated receipt of a notice concerning a false certification, see paragraphs (c)(2)(ii) and (e)(2)(iii) of this section.

    (4) *Property transferred not a U.S. real property interest.*—(i) *In general.*—Pursuant to the provisions of paragraphs (c) and (d) of this section, an entity or fiduciary is required to withhold with respect to certain transfers of property, if the property transferred is a U.S. real property interest. (In addition, taxable distributions of U.S. real property interests by domestic or foreign partnerships, trusts, and estates will be subject to withholding pursuant to section 1445(e)(4) and paragraph (f) of this section after publication of a Treasury decision under sections 897(e)(2) and (g).) As defined in section 897(c) and § 1.897-1(c), a U.S. real

property interest includes certain interests in U.S. corporations, as well as direct interests in real property and certain associated personal property. This paragraph (b)(4) provides rules pursuant to which an entity (or fiduciary thereof) that transfers an interest in a U.S. corporation may determine that withholding is not required because the interest transferred is not a U.S. real property interest. To determine whether an interest in tangible property constitutes a U.S. real property interest the transfer of which would be subject to withholding, see § 1.897-1(b) and (c).

(ii) *Interests in publicly traded entities.*—Withholding is not required under paragraph (c) or (d) of this section upon an entity's transfer of an interest in a domestic corporation if any class of stock of the corporation is regularly traded on an established securities market. This exemption shall apply to a disposition incident to an initial public offering of stock pursuant to a registration statement filed with the Securities and Exchange Commission. Similarly, no withholding is required under paragraph (c) or (d) of this section upon an entity's transfer of an interest in a publicly traded partnership or trust. However, the rule of this paragraph (b)(4)(ii) shall not apply to the transfer, to a single transferee (or related transferees as defined in § 1.897-1(i)) in a single transaction (or related transactions), of an interest described in § 1.897-1(c)(2)(iii)(B) (relating to substantial amounts of non-publicly traded interests in publicly traded corporations) or of similar interests in publicly traded partnerships or trusts. The entity making a transfer described in the preceding sentence must otherwise determine whether withholding is required, pursuant to section 1445(e) and the regulations thereunder. Transactions shall be deemed to be related if they are undertaken within 90 days of one another or if if can otherwise be shown that they were undertaken in pursuance of a prearranged plan.

(iii) *Corporation's statement that interest is not a U.S. real property interest.*—(A) *In general.*—No withholding is required under paragraph (c) or (d) of this section upon an entity's transfer of an interest in a domestic corporation if, prior to the transfer, the entity or fiduciary obtains a statement, issued by the corporation pursuant to § 1.897-2(h), certifying that the interest is not a U.S. real property interest. In general, a corporation may issue such a statement only if the corporation was not a U.S. real property holding corporation at any time during the previous five years (or the period in which the interest was held by its present holder, if shorter) or if interests in the corporation ceased to be United States real property interests under section 897(c)(1)(B). (A corporation may not provide such a statement based on its determination that the interest in question is an interest solely as a creditor.) See § 1.897-2(f) and (h). A corporation's statement may be relied upon for purposes of this paragraph (b)(4)(iii) only if the statement is dated not more than 30 days prior to the date of the transfer.

(B) *Reliance on statement not permitted.*—An entity or fiduciary is not entitled to rely upon a statement that an interest in a corporation is not a U.S. real property interest if, prior to or at the time of the transfer, the entity or fiduciary either—

(1) Has actual knowledge that the statement is false, or

(2) Receives a notice that the statement is false from a transferor's or transferee's agent, pursuant to § 1.1445-4.

Such an entity's or fiduciary's withholding obligations shall apply as if a statement had never been given, and such an entity or fiduciary may be held fully liable pursuant to § 1.1445-1(e) for any failure to withhold. For special rules concerning an entity's belated receipt of a notice concerning a false statement, see paragraphs (c)(2)(iii) and (d)(2)(i) of this section.

(5) *Reporting and paying over of withheld amounts.*—(i) *In general.*—An entity or fiduciary must report and pay over to the Internal Revenue Service any tax withheld pursuant to section 1445(e) and this section by the 20th day after the date of the transfer (as defined in § 1.1445-1(g)(8)). Forms 8288 and 8288-A are used for this purpose and must be filed at the location as provided in the instructions to Forms 8288 and 8288-A. The contents of Forms 8288 and 8288-A are described in § 1.1445-1(d). Pursuant to section 7502 and regulations thereunder, the timely mailing of Forms 8288 and 8288-A by U.S. mail will be treated as their timely filing. Form 8288-A will be stamped by the Internal Revenue Service to show receipt, and a stamped copy will be mailed by the Service to the interest holder if the Form 8288 is complete, including the transferor's identifying number, at the address shown on the form, for the interest-holder's use. See paragraph (b)(7) of this section.

If an application for a withholding certificate with respect to a transfer of a U.S. real property interest was submitted to the Internal Revenue Service on the day of or at any time prior to the transfer, the entity or fiduciary must withhold the amount required under section 1445(e) and the rules of this section. However, the amount withheld, or a lesser amount as determined by the Service, need not be reported and paid over to the Service until the 20th day following the Service's final determination. For this purpose,

Reg. § 1.1445-5(b)(5)(i)

the Service's final determination occurs on the day when the withholding certificate is mailed to the applicant by the Service or when notification denying the request for a withholding certificate is mailed to the applicant by the Service. An application is submitted to the Service on the day it is actualy received by the Service at the address provided in § 1.1445-1(g)(10) or, under the rules of section 7502, on the day it is mailed to the Service at the address provided in § 1.1445-1(g)(10), concerning the issuance of withholding certificates see § 1.1445-6.

(ii) *Anti-abuse rule.*—An entity or fiduciary that in reliance upon the rules of this paragraph (b)(5)(ii) fails to report and pay over amounts withheld by the 20th day following the date of the transfer, shall be subject to the payment of interest and penalties if the relevant application for a withholding certificate (or an amendment of the application for a withholding certificate) was submitted for a principle purpose of delaying the payment to the IRS of the amount withheld. Interest and penalties shall be assessed on the amount that is ultimately paid over with respect to the period between the 20th day after the date of the transfer and the date on which payment is made.

(6) *Liability upon failure to withhold.*—For rules regarding liability upon failure to withhold under section 1445(e) and this § 1.1445-5, see § 1.1445-1(e).

* * *

(c) *Dispositions of U.S. real property interests by domestic partnerships, trusts, and estates.*— (1) *Withholding required.*—(i) *In general.*—If a domestic partnership, trust, or estate disposes of a U.S. real property interest and any partner, beneficiary, or owner of the entity is a foreign person, then the partnership or the trustee, executor, or equivalent fiduciary of the trust or estate must withhold tax with respect to each such foreign person in accordance with the provisions of subdivision (ii), (iii), or (iv) of this paragraph (c)(1) (as applicable). The withholding obligation imposed by this paragraph (c) applies to the fiduciary of a trust even if the grantor of the trust or another person is treated as the owner of the trust or any portion thereof for purposes of the Internal Revenue Code. Thus, the withholding obligation imposed by this paragraph (c) applies to the trustee of a land trust or similar arrangement, even if such a trustee is not ordinarily treated under the applicable provisions of local law as a true fiduciary.

(ii) *Disposition by partnership.*—A partnership must withhold a tax equal to 35 percent (or the highest rate specified in section 1445(e)(1)) of each foreign partner's distributive share of the gain realized by the partnership upon the disposition of each U.S. real property interest. Such distributive share of the gain must be determined pursuant to the principles of section 704 and the regulations thereunder. For the rules applicable to partnerships, interests in which are regularly traded on an established securities market, see § 1.1445-8.

(iii) *Disposition by trust or estate.*— (A) *In general.*—A trustee, fiduciary, executor or equivalent fiduciary (hereafter collectively referred to as the fiduciary) of a trust or estate having one or more foreign beneficiaries must withhold tax in accordance with the rules of this § 1.1445-5(c)(1)(iii). Such a fiduciary must establish a U.S. real property interest account and must enter in such account all gains and losses realized during the taxable year of the trust or estate from dispositions of U.S. real property interests. The fiduciary must withhold 35 percent (or the highest rate specified in section 1445(e)(1)) of any distribution to a foreign beneficiary that is attributable to the balance in the U.S. real property interest account on the day of the distribution. A distribution from a trust or estate to a beneficiary (domestic or foreign) shall, solely for purposes of section 1445(e)(1), be deemed to be attributable first to any balance in the U.S. real property interest account and then to other amounts. However, a distribution that occurs prior to the transfer of a U.S. real property interest in a taxable year or at any other time when the amount contained in the U.S. real property interest account is zero, is not subject to withholding under this § 1.1445-5(c)(1)(iii). The U.S. real property interest account is reduced by the amount distributed to all beneficiaries (domestic and foreign) attributable to such account during the taxable year of the trust or estate. Any ending balance of the U.S. real property interest account not distributed by the close of the taxable year of the trust or estate is cancelled and is not carried over (or carried back) to any other year. Thus, the beginning balance of such account in any taxable year of the trust or estate is always zero. For rules applicable to grantor trusts see § 1.1445-5(c)(1)(iv). For rules applicable to trusts, interests in which are regularly traded on an established securities market and real estate investment trusts, see § 1.1445-8.

(B) *Example.*—The following example illustrates the rules of paragraph (c)(1)(iii)(A) of this section.

On January 1, 1994, A establishes a domestic trust (which has as its taxable year, the calendar year) for the benefit of B, a nonresident alien, and C, a U.S. citizen. The trust is not a trust subject to sections 671 through 679. Under the terms of the trust, the trustee, T, is given discretion to distribute income and corpus of the trust to provide for the reasonable needs of B and C. During the trust's 1994 tax year, T disposes of three parcels of vacant land located in the United States. The following chart illustrates the computation of the amount subject to withholding under section 1445 with respect to distributions made by T to B and C during 1994.

Date	Parcel sold	Gains or (loss) realized	Distributions to C	Distributions to B (before withholding)	Section 1445 withholding (35% rate)	U.S. real property interest account
1/01/94						–0–
3/01/94	Parcel 1	140,000				140,000
3/05/94			5,000	10,000	3,500	125,000
3/15/94			10,000	5,000	1,750	110,000
5/01/94	Parcel 2	300,000				410,000
5/15/94	Parcel 3	(50,000)				360,000
12/01/94			170,000	170,000	59,500	20,000
1/01/95						–0–

(iv) *Disposition by grantor trust.*—The trustee or equivalent fiduciary of a trust that is subject to the provisions of subpart E of part I of subchapter J (sections 671 through 679) must withhold a tax equal to 35 percent (or the highest rate specified in section 1445(e)(1)) of the gain realized from each disposition of a U.S. real property interest to the extent such gain is allocable to a portion of the trust treated as owned by a foreign person under subpart E of part I of subchapter J.

(2) *Withholding not required under paragraph (c).*—(i) [Removed]

(ii) *Interest-holder not a foreign person.*—(A) *In general.*—A domestic partnership, trust, or estate that disposes of a U.S. real property interest shall not be required to withhold with respect to any partner or beneficiary that it determines, pursuant to the rules of paragraph (b)(3) of this section, not to be a foreign person.

(B) *Belated notice of false certification.*—If after the date of the transfer a partnership or fiduciary learns that a partner's or beneficiary's certification of non-foreign status is false, then that partnership or fiduciary shall be required to withhold, with respect to the foreign partner or beneficiary that gave the false certification, the lesser of—

(1) The amount otherwise required to be withheld under the rules of this paragraph (c), or

(2) An amount equal to that partner's or beneficiary's remaining interests in the income or assets of the partnership, trust, or estate.

Amounts so withheld must be reported and paid over by the 60th day following the date on which the partnership or fiduciary learns that the certification is false. For rules concerning the notifications of false certifications that may be required to be given to partnerships and fiduciaries, see § 1.1445-4(b).

(iii) *Property disposed of not a U.S. real property interest.*—(A) *In general.*—No withholding is required under this paragraph (c) if a domestic partnership, trust, or estate that disposes of property determines pursuant to the rules of paragraph (b)(4) of this section that the property disposed of is not a U.S. real property interest.

(B) *Belated notice of false statement.*—If after the date of the transfer a partnership or fiduciary learns that a corporation's statement (that an interest in the corporation is not a U.S. real property interest) is false, then that partnership or fiduciary shall be required to withhold, with respect to each foreign partner or beneficiary, the lesser of—

(1) The amount otherwise required to be withheld under the rules of this paragraph (c), or

(2) An amount equal to that partner's or beneficiary's remaining interests in the income or assets of the partnership, trust, or estate.

Amounts so withheld must be reported and paid over by the 60th day following the date on which the partnership or fiduciary learns that the statement is false. For rules concerning the notifications of false statements that may be required to be given to partnerships or fiduciaries, see § 1.1445-4(b).

(iv) *Withholding certificate.*—No withholding is required under this paragraph (c) with respect to the transfer of a U.S. real property interest if the Internal Revenue Service issues a withholding certificate that so provides. For rules concerning the issuance of withholding certificates, see § 1.1445-6.

(v) *Nonrecognition transactions.*—For special rules concerning transactions entitled to nonrecognition of gain or loss, see paragraph (b)(2) of this section.

(3) *Large partnerships or trusts.*—(i) *In general.*—If a partnership or trust has more

than 100 partners or beneficiaries, then the partnership or fiduciary of the trust may elect to withhold in accordance with the provisions of this § 1.1445-5(c)(3) in lieu of withholding in the manner required by § 1.1445-5(c)(1). However, the rules of this § 1.1445-5(c)(3) shall not apply to any partnership or trust interests in which are regularly traded on an established securities market except as described in § 1.1445-8(c)(1). The rules of this § 1.1445-5(c)(3) shall not apply to any real estate investment trust. See § 1.1445-8.

(ii) *Amount to be withheld.*—A partnership or trust electing to withhold under this § 1.1445-5(c)(3) shall withhold from each distribution to a foreign person an amount equal to 35 percent (or the highest rate specified in section 1445(e)(1)) of the amount attributable to section 1445(e)(1) transfers.

(iii) *Amounts attributable to section 1445(e)(1) transfers.*—A distribution is attributable to section 1445(e)(1) transfers to the extent of the partner's or beneficiary's proportionate share of the current balance of the entity's section 1445(e)(1) account. A distribution from a partnership or trust that has made an election under this § 1.1445-5(c)(3) shall be deemed first to be attributable to a section 1445(e)(1) transfer to the extent of the balance in the section 1445(e)(1) account. An entity's section 1445(e)(1) account shall be equal to—

(A) The total amount of net gain realized by the entity upon all transfers of U.S. real property interests carried out by the entity after the date of its election under this § 1.1445-5(c)(3); minus

(B) The total amount of all distributions by the entity to domestic and foreign distributees from such account.

(iv) *Special rules for entities that make recurring sales of growing crops and timber.*—An entity that makes an election under § 1.1445-5(c)(3) and that makes recurring sales of growing crops and timber may further elect to determine the amount subject to withholding under the rules of this § 1.1445-5(c)(3)(iv). Such an entity must withhold from each distribution to a foreign partner or beneficiary an amount equal to 10 percent of such partner's or beneficiary's proportionate share of the current balance of the entity's gross section 1445(e)(1) account. An entity's gross section 1445(e)(1) account equals—

(A) The total amount realized by the entity upon all transfers of U.S. real property interests carried out by the entity after the date of its election under this § 1.1445-5(c)(3)(iv); minus

(B) The total amount of all distributions to domestic and foreign distributees from such account.

An entity that elects to compute the amount subject to withholding under this § 1.1445-5(c)(3)(iv), shall make such election in accordance with § 1.1445-5(c)(3)(vi) and shall be subject to the provisions otherwise applicable under § 1.1445-5(c)(3).

(v) *Procedural rules.*—An election under paragraph (c)(3) may be made by filing a notice thereof with the Director, Philadelphia Service Center, at the address provided in § 1.1445-1(g)(10). The notice must be submitted by a general partner (in the case of a partnership) or the trustee or equivalent fiduciary (in the case of a trust). The notice must set forth the name, office address, and identifying number of the partnership or fiduciary making the election, and, in the case of a partnership, must include the name, office address, and identifying number of the general partner submitting the election. An election under this paragraph (c)(3) may be revoked only with the consent of the Internal Revenue Service. Consent of the Service may be requested by filing an application to revoke the election with the Director, Philadelphia Service Center, at the address stated above. This application must include all information provided to the Service with the election notice and must provide an explanation of the reasons for revoking the election. The application to revoke an election must also specify the amount remaining to be distributed in the section 1445(e)(1) account or the gross section 1445(e)(1) account. An entity that ceases to qualify under section 1.1445-5(c)(3) because such entity does not have more than 100 partners or beneficiaries may revoke its election only with the consent of the Internal Revenue Service.

(d) *Distributions of U.S. real property interests by foreign corporations.*—(1) *In general.*—A foreign corporation that distributes a U.S. real property interest must deduct and withhold a tax equal to 35 percent (or the rate specified in section 1445(e)(2)) of the amount of gain recognized by the corporation on the distribution. The amount of gain required to be recognized by the corporation must be detemined pursuant to the rules of section 897 and any other applicable section. For special rules concerning the applicability of a nonrecognition provision to a distribution, see paragraph (b)(2) of this section. The withholding liability imposed by this paragraph (d) applies to the same taxpayer that owes the related substantive income tax liability pursuant to the operation of section 897. Only one such liability will be assessed and collected from a foreign corporation, but separate penalties for failures to comply with the two requirements will be asserted.

(2) *Withholding not required.*—(i) *Property distributed not a U.S. real property interest.*—(A) *In general.*—No withholding is required under this paragraph (d) if a foreign corporation that distributes property determines pursuant to the rules of paragraph (b)(3) of this section that the property distributed is not a U.S. real property interest.

(B) *Belated notice of false statement.*—If after the date of a distribution described in paragraph (d)(1) of this section a foreign corporation learns that another corporation's statement (that an interest in that other corporation is not a U.S. real property interest) is false, then the foreign corporation may not rely upon that statement for any purpose. Such a foreign corporation's withholding obligations under this paragaph (d) shall apply as if a statement had never been given, and such a corporation may be held fully liable pursuant to § 1.1445-5(b)(5) for any failure to withhold. Amounts withheld pursuant to the rule of this paragraph (d)(2)(i)(B) must be reported and paid over by the 60th day following the date on which the foreign corporation learns that the statement is false. No penalties or interest will be assessed for failures to withhold prior to that date. For rules concerning the notifications of false statements that may be required to be given to foreign corporations, see § 1.1445-4(b).

(ii) *Withholding certificate.*—No withholding is required under this paragraph (d) with respect to a foreign corporation's distribution of a U.S. real property interest if the distributing corporation obtains a withholding certificate from the Internal Revenue Service that so provides. For rules concerning the issuance of withholding certificates, see § 1.1445-6.

(e) *Distributions to foreign persons by U.S. real property holding corporations.*—(1) *In general.*—A domestic corporation that distributes any property to a foreign person that holds an interest in the corporation must deduct and withhold a tax equal to 10 percent of the fair market value of the property distributed to the foreign person, if—

(i) The foreign person's interest in the corporation constitutes a U.S. real property interest under the provisions of section 897 and regulations thereunder; and

(ii) There is a distribution of property in redemption of stock treated as an exchange under section 302(a), in liquidation of the corporation pursuant to the provisions of Part II of subchapter C of the Internal Revenue Code (sections 331 through section 346), or with respect to stock under section 301 that is not made out of earnings and profits of the corporation.

(2) *Coordination rules for Section 301 distributions.*—If a domestic corporation makes a distribution of property under section 301 to a foreign person whose interest in such corporation constitutes a U.S. real property interest under the provisions of section 897 and the regulations thereunder, then see § 1.1441-3(c)(4) for rules coordinating withholding obligations under sections 1445 and 1441 (or 1442 or 1443)).

(3) *Withholding not required.*—(i) *Foreign person's interest not a U.S. real property interest.*—Withholding is required under this paragraph (e) only with respect to distributions to foreign persons holding interests in the corporation that constitute U.S. real property interests. In general, a foreign person's interest in a domestic corporation constitutes a U.S. real property interest if the corporation was a U.S. real property holding corporation at any time during the shorter of (A) the period in which the foreign person held the interest or (B) the previous five years (but not earlier than June 19, 1980). See section 897(c) and §§ 1.897-1(c) and 1.897-2(b) and (h). However, an interest in such a corporation ceases to be a U.S. real property interest after all of the U.S. real property interests held by the corporation itself are disposed of in transactions on which gain or loss is recognized. See section 897(c)(1)(B) and § 1.897-2(f)(2). Thus, if a U.S. real property holding corporation in the process of liquidation does not elect section 337 nonrecognition treatment upon its sale of all U.S. real property interests held by the corporation, and recognizes gain or loss upon such sales, interests in that corporation cease to be U.S. real property interests. Therefore, no withholding would be required with respect to that corporation's subsequent liquidating distribution to a foreign shareholder of property other than a U.S. real property interest.

(ii) *Nonrecognition transactions.*—For special rules concerning the applicability of a nonrecognition provision to a distribution described in paragraph (e)(1) of this section, see paragraph (b)(2) of this section.

(iii) *Interest-holder not a foreign person.*—(A) *In general.*—A domestic corporation shall not be required to withhold under this paragraph (e) with respect to a distribution of property to any distributee that it determines, pursuant to the rules of paragraph (b)(3) of this section, not to be a foreign person.

(B) *Belated notice of false certification.*—If after the date of a distribution described in paragraph (e)(1) of this section a domestic corporation learns that an interest-holder's certification of non-foreign status is false, then the corporation may rely upon that certification only if the person providing the false certification holds (or held) less than 10 percent of the value of the outstanding stock of the corporation. With respect to less than 10 percent interest-holders, no withholding is required under this paragraph (e) upon receipt of a belated notice of false certification. With respect to 10 percent or greater interest-holders, the corporation's withholding obligations under this paragraph (e) shall apply as if a certification had never been given, and such a corporation may be held fully liable pursuant to § 1.1445-5(b)(6) for any failure to withhold as of the date specified in this § 1.1445-5(e)(3)(iii)(B). Amounts withheld pursuant to the rule of this paragraph (e)(3)(iii)(B) must be reported and paid over by the 60th day following the date on which the corporation learns that the certification is false. No penalties or interest for failures to withhold will be assessed prior to that date. For rules concerning the notifications of false certifications that may be required to be given to U.S. real property holding corporations, see § 1.1445-4(b).

(iv) *Withholding certificate.*—No withholding, or reduced withholding, is required under this paragraph (e) with respect to a domestic corporation's distribution of property if the distributing corporation obtains a withholding certificate from the Internal Revenue Service that so provides. For rules concerning the issuance of withholding certificates, see § 1.1445-6.

(f) *Taxable distributions by domestic or foreign partnerships, trusts, or estates.*—[Reserved]

(g) *Dispositions of interests in partnerships, trusts, and estates.*—[Reserved]

(h) *Effective date for taxpayer identification numbers.*—The requirement in paragraphs (b)(2)(ii)(B) and (C) of this section that taxpayer identification numbers be provided (in all cases) is is applicable for dispositions of U.S. real property interests occurring after November 3, 2003. [Reg. § 1.1445-5.]

☐ [*T.D.* 8113, 12-18-86. *Amended by T.D.* 8198, 5-4-88; *T.D.* 8321, 12-6-90; *T.D.* 8647, 12-20-95; *T.D.* 8734, 10-6-97 (T.D. 8804 delayed the effective date of T.D. 8734 from January 1, 1999, to January 1, 2000; T.D. 8856 further delayed the effective date of T.D. 8734 until January 1, 2001) *and T.D.* 9082, 8-4-2003.]

§ 1.1445-6. Adjustments pursuant to withholding certificate of amount required to be withheld under section 1445(e).—
(a) *Withholding certificate for purposes of section 1445(e).*—(1) *In general.*—Pursuant to the provisions of § 1.1445-5(c)(2)(iv), (d)(2)(ii), and (e)(2)(iv), withholding under section 1445(e) may be reduced or eliminated pursuant to a withholding certificate issued by the Internal Revenue Service in accordance with the rules of this § 1.1445-6. A withholding certificate may be issued in cases where adjusted withholding is appropriate (e.g., because of the applicability of a nonrecognition provision—see paragraph (c) of this section), where the relevant taxpayers are exempt from U.S. tax (see paragraph (d) of this section), or where an agreement for the payment of tax is entered into with the Service (see paragraph (e) of this section). A withholding certificate that is obtained prior to a transfer allows the entity or fiduciary to withhold a reduced amount or excuses withholding entirely. A withholding certificate that is obtained after a transfer has been made may authorize a normal refund or an early refund pursuant to paragraph (g) of this section. The Internal Revenue Service will act upon an application for a withholding certificate not later than the 90th day after it is received. (The Service may deny a request for a withholding certificate where, after due notice, an applicant fails to provide the information necessary to make a determination.) Solely for this purpose (i.e., determining the day upon which the 90 day period commences), an application is received by the Service on the date when all information necessary for the Service to make a determination is provided by the applicant. In no event, however, will a withholding certificate be issued without the transferor's identifying number. (For rules regarding whether an application has been timely submitted, see § 1.1445-5(b)(5).) The Internal Revenue Service will act upon an application for an early refund not later than the 90th day after it is received. An application for an early refund must either (i) include a copy of a withholding certificate issued by the Service with respect to the transaction, or (ii) be combined with an application for a withholding certificate. Where an application for an early refund is combined with an application for a withholding certificate, the Service will act upon both applications not later than the 90th day after receipt. Either an entity, a fiduciary, or a relevant taxpayer (as defined in paragraph (a)(2) of this section) may apply for a withholding certificate. An entity or fiduciary may apply for a withholding certificate with respect to all or less than all relevant taxpayers. For special rules concerning the issuance of a withholding certificate to a foreign corporation that has made an election under section 897(i), see § 1.1445-7(d).

(2) *Relevant taxpayer.*—For purposes of this section, the term "relevant taxpayer" means any foreign person that will bear sub-

stantive income tax liability by reason of the operation of section 897 with respect to a transaction upon which withholding is required under section 1445(e).

(b) *Applications for withholding certificates.*—(1) *In general.*—An application for a withholding certificate pursuant to this § 1.1445-6 must be submitted in the manner provided in § 1.1445-3(b). However, in lieu of the information required to be submitted pursuant to § 1.1445-3(b)(4), the applicant must provide the information required by paragraph (b)(2) of this section. In addition, the information required by paragraph (b)(3) of this section must be submitted with the application.

(2) *Basis for certificate.*—(i) *Adjusted withholding.*—If a withholding certificate is sought on the basis of a claim that adjusted withholding is appropriate, the application must include a calculation, in accordance with paragraph (c) of this section, of the maximum tax that may be imposed on each relevant taxpayer with respect to which adjusted withholding is sought. The application must also include all evidence necessary to substantiate the claimed calculation, such as records of adjustments to basis or appraisals of fair market value.

(ii) *Exemption.*—If a withholding certificate is sought on the basis of a relevant taxpayer's exemption from U.S. tax, the application must set forth a brief statement of the law and facts that support the claimed exemption. See paragraph (d) of this section.

(iii) *Agreement.*—If a withholding certificate is sought on the basis of an agreement for the payment of tax, the application must include a copy of the agreement proposed by the applicant and a copy of the security instrument (if any) proposed by the applicant. In this regard, see paragraph (e) of this section.

(3) *Relevant taxpayers.*—An application for withholding certificate pursuant to this section must include all of the following information: the name, identifying number, and home address (in the case of an individual) or office address (in the case of an entity) of each relevant taxpayer with respect to which adjusted withholding is sought.

(c) *Adjustment of amount required to be withheld.*—The Internal Revenue Service may issue a withholding certificate that excuses withholding, or that permits an entity or fiduciary to withhold an adjusted amount reflecting the relevant taxpayers' maximum tax liability. A relevant taxpayer's maximum tax liability is the maximum amount which that taxpayer could be required to pay as tax by reason of the transaction upon which withholding is required. In the case of an individual taxpayer that amount will generally be the gain realized by the individual, multiplied by the maximum individual income tax rate applicable to long term capital gain. In the case of a corporate taxpayer, that amount will generally be the gain realized by the corporation, multiplied by the maximum corporate income tax rate applicable to long term capital gain. However, that amount must be adjusted to take into account the following:

(1) Any reduction of tax to which the relevant taxpayer is entitled under the provisions of a U.S. income tax treaty;

(2) The effect of any nonrecognition provision that is applicable to the transaction;

(3) Any losses previously realized and recognized by the relevant taxpayer during the taxable year by reason of the operation of section 897;

(4) Any amount realized upon the subject transfer by the relevant taxpayer that is required to be treated as ordinary income under any provision of the Code; and

(5) Any other factor that may increase or reduce the tax upon the transaction.

(d) *Relevant taxpayer's exemption from U.S. tax.*—(1) *In general.*—The Internal Revenue Service will issue a withholding certificate that excuses withholding by an entity or fiduciary if it is established that a relevant taxpayer's income from the transaction will be exempt from U.S. tax. For the available exemptions, see paragraph (d)(2) of this section. If a relevant taxpayer is entitled to a reduction of (rather than an exemption from) U.S. tax, then the entity or fiduciary may obtain a withholding certificate to that effect pursuant to the provisions of paragraph (c) of this section.

(2) *Available exemptions.*—A relevant taxpayer's income from a transaction with respect to which withholding is required under section 1445(e) may be exempt from U.S. tax because either:

(i) The relevant taxpayer is an integral part or controlled entity of a foreign government and the subject income is exempt from U.S. tax pursuant to section 892 and the regulations thereunder; or

(ii) The relevant taxpayer is entitled to the benefits of an income tax treaty that provides for such an exemption (subject to the limitations imposed by section 1125(c) of Pub. L. 96-499, which, in general, overrides such benefits as of January 1, 1985).

(e) *Agreement for the payment of tax.*—(1) *In general.*—The Internal Revenue Service will issue a withholding certificate that excuses withholding or that permits an entity or fiduciary to withhold a reduced amount, if the entity, fiduciary, or a relevant taxpayer enters into an agreement for the payment of tax pursuant to the provisions of this paragraph (e). An agreement for the payment of tax is a contract between the Service and the entity, fiduciary, or relevant taxpayer that consists of two necessary elements. Those elements are—

(i) A contract between the Service and the other person, setting forth in detail the rights and obligations of each; and

(ii) A security instrument or other form of security acceptable to the Assistant Commissioner (International).

(2) *Contents of agreement.*—(i) *In general.*—An agreement for the payment of tax must cover an amount described in subdivision (ii) or (iii) of this paragraph (e)(2). The agreement may either provide adequate security for the payment of the chosen amount with respect to the relevant taxpayer in accordance with paragraph (e)(3) of this section, or provide for the payment of that amount through a combination of security and withholding of tax by the entity or fiduciary.

(ii) *Tax that would otherwise be withheld.*—An agreement for the payment of tax may cover the amount of tax that would otherwise be required to be withheld with respect to the relevant taxpayer pursuant to section 1445(e). In addition to the amount computed pursuant to section 1445(e), the applicant must agree to pay interest upon that amount, at the rate established under section 6621, with respect to the period between the date on which withholding tax under section 1445(e) would otherwise be due and the date on which the relevant taxpayer's payment of tax with respect to the disposition will be due. The amount of interest agreed upon must be paid by the applicant regardless of whether or not the Service is required to draw upon any security provided pursuant to the agreement. The interest may be paid either with the return or by the Service drawing upon the security.

(iii) *Maximum tax liability.*—An agreement for the payment of tax may cover the relevant taxpayer's maximum tax liability, determined in accordance with paragraph (c) of this section. The agreement must also provide for the payment of an additional amount equal to 25 percent of the amount determined under paragraph (c) of this section. This additional amount secures the interest and penalties that would accrue between the date of the relevant taxpayer's failure to file a return and pay tax with respect to the disposition, and the date on which the Service collects upon that liability pursuant to the agreement.

(iv) *Allocation of payment.*—An agreement for the payment of tax pursuant to this section must set forth an allocation of the payment provided for by the agreement among the relevant taxpayers with respect to which the withholding certificate is sought. In the case of an agreement that covers an amount described in subdivision (ii) of this paragraph (e)(2), such allocation must be based upon the amount that would otherwise be required to be withheld with respect to each relevant taxpayer. In the case of an agreement that covers an amount described in subdivision (iii) of this paragraph (e)(2), such allocation must be based upon each relevant taxpayer's maximum tax liability.

(3) *Major types of security.*—The major types of security that are acceptable to the Internal Revenue Service for purposes of this section are described in § 1.1445-3(e)(3).

(4) *Terms of security instrument.*—Any security instrument that is furnished pursuant to this section must contain the terms described in § 1.1445-3(e)(4).

(f) *Amendments to application for withholding certificates.*—(1) *In general.*—An applicant for a withholding certificate may amend an otherwise complete application by submitting an amending statement to the Director, Philadelphia Service Center, at the address provided in § 1.1445-1(g)(10). The amending statement shall provide the information required by § 1.1445-6(f)(3) and must be signed and accompanied by a penalties of perjury statement in accordance with § 1.1445-6(b).

(2) *Extension of time for the Service to process requests for withholding certificates.*—(i) *In general.*—If an amending statement is submitted, the time in which the Internal Revenue Service must act upon the amended application shall be extended by 30 days.

(ii) *Substantial amendments.*—If an amending statement is submitted and the Service finds that the statement substantially amends to the facts of the underlying application or substantially alters the terms of the withholding certificate as requested in the initial application, the time within which the Service must act upon the amended application shall be extended by 60 days. The applicant shall be so notified.

(iii) *Amending statement received after the requested withholding certificate has been signed by the Director, Philadelphia Service Center.*—If an amending statement is received after the withholding certificate, drafted in response to the underlying application, has been signed by the Director, Philadelphia Service

Center, or his delegate and prior to the day such certificate is mailed to the applicant, the time in which the Service must act upon the amended application shall be extended by 90 days.

(3) *Information required to be submitted.*—No particular form is required for an amending statement but the statement must provide the following information:

(i) *Identification of applicant.*—The amending statement must set forth the name, address, and identifying number of the person submitting the amending statement.

(ii) *Date of application.*—The amending statement must set forth the date of the underlying application for a withholding certificate.

(iii) *Real property interest to be (or that has been) transferred.*—The amending statement must set forth a brief description of the real property interest with respect to which the underlying application for a withholding certificate was submitted.

(iv) *Amending information.*—The amending statement must fully set forth the basis for the amendment including any modification of the facts supporting the application for a withholding certificate and any change sought in the terms of the withholding certificate.

(g) *Early refund of overwithheld amounts.*—If the Internal Revenue Service issues a withholding certificate pursuant to this section, and an amount greater than that specified in the certificate was withheld by the entity or fiduciary, then pursuant to the rules of this paragraph (g) a relevant taxpayer may apply for an early refund of a proportionate share of the excess amount (without interest) prior to the date on which the relevant taxpayer's return is due (without extensions). An application for an early refund must be addressed to the Director, Philadelphia Service Center, at the address provided in § 1.1445-1(g)(10). No particular form is required for the application, but the following information must be set forth in separate paragraphs numbered to correspond with the numbers given below:

(1) Name, address, and identifying number of the relevant taxpayer seeking the refund;

(2) Amount required to be withheld pursuant to withholding certificate;

(3) Amount withheld by entity or fiduciary (attach a copy of Form 8388-A stamped by IRS pursuant to § 1.1445-5(b)(4) or provide substantial evidence of the amount withheld in the case of a failure to receive Form 8288-A, as provided in § 1.1445-5(b)(7));

(4) Amount to be refunded to the relevant taxpayer.

An application for an early refund cannot be processed unless the required copy of Form 8288-A or substantial evidence of the amount withheld in the case of a failure to receive Form 8288-A (as provided in § 1.1445-5(b)(7)) is attached to the application. If an application for a withholding certificate is submitted after the transfer takes place, then that application may be combined with an application for an early refund. The Service will act upon a claim for refund within the time limits set forth in § 1.1445-6(a)(1).

(h) *Effective date for taxpayer identification numbers.*—The requirement in paragraphs (b)(3), (f)(3)(i), and (g)(1) of this section that taxpayer identification numbers be provided (in all cases) is applicable for dispositions of U.S. real property interests occurring after November 3, 2003. [Reg. § 1.1445-6.]

☐ [T.D. 8113, 12-18-86. Amended by T.D. 9082, 8-4-2003.]

§ 1.1445-7. Treatment of foreign corporation that has made an election under section 897(i) to be treated as a domestic corporation.—(a) *In general.*—Pursuant to section 897(i) a foreign corporation may elect to be treated as a domestic corporation for purposes of sections 897 and 6039C. A foreign corporation that has made such an election shall also be treated as a domestic corporation for purposes of the withholding required under section 1445, in accordance with the provisions of this section.

(b) *Withholding under section 1445(a).*—(1) *Dispositions by corporation.*—A foreign corporation that has made an election under section 897(i) may provide a transferee with a certification of non-foreign status in connection with the corporation's disposition of a U.S. real property interest. However, in accordance with the provisions of §§ 1.1445-2(b)(2)(ii) and 1.1445-5(b)(3)(ii)(C), such an electing foreign corporation must attach to such certification a copy of the acknowledgment of the election provided to the corporation by the Internal Revenue Service pursuant to § 1.897-3(d)(4) which states that the information required by § 1.897-3 has been determined to be complete.

(2) *Dispositions of interests in corporation.*—Dispositions of interests in electing foreign corporations shall be subject to the withholding requirements of section 1445(a) and the rules of §§ 1.1445-1 through 1.1445-4. Therefore, if a foreign person disposes of an interest in such a corporation, and that interest is a U.S. real property interest under the provisions of section 897 and regulations thereun-

der, then the transferee is required to withhold under section 1445(a).

(c) *Withholding under section 1445(e).*—Because a foreign corporation that has made an election under section 897(i) is treated as a domestic corporation for purposes of determining withholding obligations under section 1445, such a corporation is not subject to the requirement of section 1445(e)(2) that a foreign corporation withhold at the corporate capital gain rate from the gain recognized upon the distribution of a U.S. real property interest. Such a corporation is subject to the provisions of section 1445(e)(3). Thus, if interests in an electing corporation constitute U.S. real property interests, then the corporation is required to withhold with respect to the non-dividend distribution of any property to an interestholder that is a foreign person. See § 1.1445-5(e). Dividend distributions (distributions that are described in section 301) shall be treated as provided in sections 897(f), 1441 and 1442. In addition, if interests in an electing foreign corporation do not constitute U.S. real property interests, then distributions by such corporation shall be treated as provided in sections 897(f) (if applicable), 1441 and 1442. Approved by the Office of Management and Budget under control number 545-0902. [Reg. § 1.1445-7.]

☐ [*T.D.* 8113, 12-18-86.]

§ 1.1445-8. Special rules regarding publicly traded partnerships, publicly traded trusts and real estate investment trusts (REITS).—(a) *Entities to which this section applies.*—The rules of this section apply to—

(1) Any partnership or trust, interests in which are regularly traded on an established securities market (regardless of the number of its partners or beneficiaries), and

(2) Any REIT (regardless of the form of its organization).

For purposes of paragraph (a)(1) of this section, the rules of section 1445(e)(1) and this section shall not apply to a publicly traded partnership (as defined in section 7704) which is treated as a corporation under section 7704(a), or to those entities that are classified as "associations" and taxed as corporations. See § 301.7701-2.

(b) *Obligation to withhold.*—(1) *In general.*—An entity described in paragraph (a) of this section is not required to withhold under the provisions of § 1.1445-5(c), which states the withholding requirements of domestic partnerships, trusts and estates upon the disposition of U.S. real property interests. Except as otherwise provided in this paragraph (b), an entity described in paragraph (a) of this section shall be liable to withhold tax upon the distribution of any amount attributable to the disposition of a U.S. real property interest, with respect to each holder of an interest in the entity that is a foreign person. The amount to be withheld is described in paragraph (c) of this section.

(2) *Publicly traded partnerships.*—Publicly traded partnerships which comply with the withholding procedures under section 1446 will be deemed to have satisfied their withholding obligations under this paragraph (b).

(3) *Special rule for certain distributions to nominees.*—In the case of a person that—

(i) Is a nominee (as defined in paragraph (d) of this section),

(ii) Receives a distribution attributable to the disposition of a U.S. real property interest directly from an entity described in paragraph (a) of this section or indirectly from such entity through a nominee,

(iii) Receives the distribution for payment to any foreign person, or the account of any foreign person, and

(iv) Receives a qualified notice pursuant to paragraph (f) of this section,

then the obligation to withhold in accordance with the general rules of section 1445(e)(1) and this paragraph (b) shall be imposed solely on that person to the extent of the amount specified by the qualified notice. A person obligated to withhold by reason of this paragraph (b)(3) is referred to as a withholding agent.

(4) *Person designated to act for withholding agent.*—The rules stated in § 1.1441-7(b)(1) and (2) regarding a person designated to act for a withholding agent shall apply for purposes of this section.

(5) *Effect of withholding exemption granted under § 1.1441-4(f).*—A letter issued by a district director under the provisions of § 1.1441-4(f), which exempts a person from withholding under section 1441 or section 1442, shall also exempt that person from withholding under this paragraph (b), if—

(i) The letter identifies another person as the withholding agent for purposes of section 1441 or 1442, and

(ii) Such other person enters into a written agreement, with the district director who issued the letter, to be the withholding agent for purposes of this paragraph (b).

The exemption granted, and the corresponding withholding obligation imposed, by this paragraph (b)(5) shall apply with respect to the first distribution made after execution of the agreement described in the preceding sentence and shall continue to apply to all distributions made during the period in which the exemption granted under § 1.1441-4(f) is in effect.

(6) *Payment other than in money.*—The rule stated in § 1.1441-7(c) regarding payment other than in money shall apply for purposes of this section.

(c) *Amount to be withheld.*—(1) *Distribution from a publicly traded partnership or publicly traded trust.*—The amount to be withheld under this section with respect to a distribution by a publicly traded partnership or publicly traded trust shall be computed in the manner described in § 1.1445-5(c)(3)(ii) and (iii), subject to the rules of this section.

(2) *REITs.*—(i) *In general.*—The amount to be withheld with respect to a distribution by a REIT, under this section shall be equal to 35 percent (or the highest rate specified in section 1445(e)(1)) of the amount described in paragraph (c)(2)(ii) of this section.

(ii) *Amount subject to withholding.*—(A) *In general.*—Except as otherwise provided in paragraph (c)(2)(ii)(C) of this section, the amount subject to withholding is the amount of any distribution, determined with respect to each share or certificate of beneficial interest, designated by a REIT as a capital gain dividend, multiplied by the number of shares or certificates of beneficial interest owned by the foreign person. Solely for purposes of this paragraph, the largest amount of any distribution occurring after March 7, 1991 that could be designated as a capital gain dividend under section 857(b)(3)(C) shall be deemed to have been designated by a REIT as a capital gain dividend regardless of the amount actually designated.

(B) *Distribution attributable to net short-term capital gain from the disposition of a U.S. real property interest.*—[Reserved]

(C) *Designation of prior distribution as capital gain dividend.*—If a REIT makes an actual designation of a prior distribution, in whole or in part, as a capital gain dividend, such prior distribution shall not be subject to withholding under this section. Rather, a REIT must characterize and treat as a capital gain dividend distribution (solely for purposes of section 1445(e)(1)) each distribution, determined with respect to each share or certificate of beneficial interest, made on the day of, or any time subsequent to, such designation as a capital gain dividend until such characterized amounts equal the amount of the prior distribution designated as a capital gain dividend. The provisions of this paragraph shall not be applicable in any taxable year in which the REIT adopts a formal or informal resolution or plan of complete liquidation.

(iii) *Example.*—The following example illustrates the rules of paragraph (c)(2)(ii)(C) of this section.

In the first quarter of 1988, XYZ REIT makes a dividend distribution of $2X. In the second quarter of 1988, XYZ sells real property, recognizing a long term capital gain of $15X, and makes a dividend distribution of $5X. In the third quarter of 1988, XYZ makes a distribution of $3X. In the fourth quarter of 1988, XYZ sells real property recognizing a long term capital loss of $2X. Within 30 days after the close of the taxable year, XYZ designates a capital gain dividend for the year of $13X. It subsequently makes a fourth quarter distribution of $7X. Since XYZ has made an actual designation of prior distributions during the taxable year as capital gain dividends, withholding on those prior distributions will not be required. However, the REIT must characterize, solely for purposes of § 1445(e)(1), a total amount of $13X of dividend distributions as capital gain dividends. Therefore, the fourth quarter dividend distribution of $7X must be characterized as a capital gain dividend subject to withholding under this section. In addition, XYZ will be required to characterize an additional $6X of subsequent dividend distributions as capital gain dividends.

(d) *Definition of nominee.*—For purposes of this section, the term "nominee" means a domestic person that holds an interest in an entity described in paragraph (a) of this section on behalf of another domestic or foreign person.

(e) *Determination of non-foreign status by withholding agent.*—A withholding agent may rely on a certificate of non-foreign status pursuant to § 1.1445-2(b) or on the statements and address provided to it on Form W-9 or a form that is substantially similar to such form, to determine whether an interest holder is a domestic person. Reliance on these documents will excuse the withholding agent from liability imposed under section 1445(e)(1) in the absence of actual knowledge that the interest holder is a foreign person. A withholding agent may also employ other means to determine the status of an interest holder, but, if the agent relies on such other means and the interest holder proves, in fact, to be a foreign person, then the withholding agent is subject to any liability imposed pursuant to section 1445 and the regulations thereunder for failure to withhold.

(f) *Qualified notice.*—A qualified notice for purposes of paragraph (b)(3)(iv) of this section is a notice given by a partnership, trust or REIT regarding a distribution that is attributable to the disposition of a U.S. real property interest in accordance with the notice requirements with respect to dividends described in 17 C.F.R. 240.10b-17(b)(1) or (3) issued pursuant to the Securities Exchange Act of 1934, 15 U.S.C. § 78a *et seq.* In the case of a REIT, a qualified notice is only a notice of a distribution, all or any portion of which the REIT actually designates, or characterizes in accordance with paragraph (c)(2)(ii)(C) of this section, as a capital gain dividend in accordance with 17 C.F.R. 240.10b-17(b)(1) or (3), with respect to each share or certificate of beneficial interest. A deemed designation under paragraph (c)(2)(ii)(A) of this section may not be the subject of a qualified notice under this paragraph (f). A person described in paragraph (b)(3) of this section shall be treated as receiving a qualified notice at the time such notice is published in accordance with 17 C.F.R. 240.10b-17(b)(1) or (3).

(g) *Reporting and paying over withheld amounts.*—With respect to an amount withheld under this section, a withholding agent is not required to conform to the requirements of § 1.1445-5(b)(5) but is required to report and pay over to the Internal Revenue Service any amount required to be withheld pursuant to the rules and procedures of section 1461, the regulations thereunder and § 1.6302-2. Forms 1042 and 1042S are to be used for this purpose.

(h) *Early refund procedure not available.*—The early refund procedure set forth in § 1.1445-6(g) shall not apply to amounts withheld under the rules of this section. For adjustment of over-withheld amounts, see § 1.1461-4.

(i) *Liability upon failure to withhold.*—For rules regarding liability upon failure to withhold under § 1445(e) and this section, see § 1.1445-1(e). [Reg. § 1.1445-8.]

☐ [*T.D.* 8321, 12-6-90. *Amended by T.D.* 8647, 12-20-95.]

§ 1.1445-10T. Special rule for foreign governments (Temporary).—(a) This section provides a temporary regulation that, if and when adopted as a final regulation, will add a new paragraph (d)(6) to § 1.1445-2. Paragraph (b) of this section would then appear as paragraph (d)(6) of § 1.1445-2.

(b) *Foreign government.*—(1) *As transferor.*—A foreign government is subject to U.S. taxation under section 897 on the disposition of a U.S. real property interest except to the extent specifically otherwise provided in the regulations issued under section 892. A foreign government that disposes of a U.S. real property interest that is not subject to taxation as specifically provided by the regulations under section 892 may present a notice of nonrecognition treatment pursuant to paragraph (d)(2) of this section that specifically cites the provision of such regulation, and thereby avoids withholding by the transferee of the property. A foreign government that disposes of a U.S. real property interest or the transferee of the property may obtain a withholding certificate from the Internal Revenue Service that confirms the applicability of section 892, but neither is required to do so. Rules concerning the issuance of withholding certificates are provided in § 1.1445-3.

(2) *As transferee.*—A foreign government or international organization that acquires a U.S. real property interest is fully subject to section 1445 and the regulations thereunder. Therefore, such an entity is required to withhold tax upon the acquisition of a U.S. real property interest from a foreign person.

(c) *Effective date.*—The rules of this section shall be effective for transfers, exchanges, distributions and other dispositions occurring on or after June 6, 1988. [Temporary Reg. § 1.1445-10T.]

☐ [*T.D.* 8198, 5-4-88.]

§ 1.1445-11T. Special rules requiring withholding under § 1.1445-5 (Temporary).—(a) *Purpose and scope.*—This section provides temporary regulations that, if and when adopted as a final regulation, will add certain new paragraphs within § 1.1445-5(b) and (c). The paragraphs of this section would then appear as set forth below. Paragraph (b) of this section would then appear as paragraph (b)(8)(v) of § 1.1445-5. Paragraph (c) of this section would then appear as paragraph (c)(2)(i) of § 1.1445-5. Paragraph (d) of this section would then appear as paragraph (g) of § 1.1445-5.

(b) *Disposition of interests in partnerships, trusts, and estates.*—The provisions of section 1445(e)(5), requiring withholding upon certain dispositions of interests in partnerships, trusts, and estates, that own directly or indirectly a U.S. real property interest shall apply to dispositions on or after the effective date of a later Treasury decision under section 897(g) of the Code except in the case of dispositions of interests in partnerships in which fifty percent of the value of the gross assets consist of U.S. real property interests and ninety percent or more of the value of the gross assets consist of U.S. real property interests plus any cash or cash equivalents. The provisions of section 1445(e)(5), shall apply, however, to dispositions after June 6, 1988, of interests in partnerships in which fifty percent or more of the value of the gross assets consist of U.S. real property interests, and ninety percent or more of the value of the gross assets consist of U.S.

real property interests plus any cash or cash equivalents. See paragraph (d) of this section.

(c) *Transactions covered elsewhere.*—No withholding is required under this paragraph (c) with respect to the distribution of a U.S. real property interest by a partnership, trust, or estate. Such distributions shall be subject to withholding under section 1445(e)(4) and paragraph (f) of this § 1.1445-5 on the effective date of a later Treasury decision published under section 897(g) of the Code. No withholding is required at this time for distributions described in the preceding sentence. See paragraph (b)(8)(iv) of this § 1.1445-5. No withholding is required under this paragraph with respect to the disposition of an interest in a trust, estate, or partnership except in the case of a partnership in which fifty percent or more of the value of the gross assets consist of U.S. real property interests, and ninety percent or more of the value of the gross assets consist of U.S. real property interests plus any cash or cash equivalents. See paragraph (b)(8)(v) of § 1.1445-5. Withholding shall be required as provided in section 1445(e)(5) and paragraph (g) of this section with respect to the disposition after June 6, 1988, of an interest in a partnership in which fifty percent or more of the value of the gross assets consist of U.S. real property interests, and ninety percent or more of the value of the gross assets consist of U.S. real property interests plus any cash or cash equivalents.

(d) *Dispositions of interests in partnerships, trusts, and estates.*—(1) *Withholding required on disposition of certain partnership interests.*—Withholding is required under section 1445(e)(5) and this paragraph with respect to the disposition by a foreign partner of an interest in a domestic or foreign partnership in which fifty percent or more of the value of the gross assets consist of U.S. real property interests, and ninety percent or more of the value of the gross assets consist of U.S. real property interests plus any cash or cash equivalents. For purposes of this paragraph cash equivalents means any asset readily convertible into cash (whether or not denominated in U.S. dollars), including, but not limited to, bank accounts, certificates of deposit, money market accounts, commercial paper, U.S. and foreign treasury obligations and bonds, corporate obligations and bonds, precious metals or commodities, and publicly traded instruments. The taxpayer on filing an income tax return for the year of the disposition may demonstrate the extent to which the gain on the disposition of the interest is not attributable to U.S. real property interests. A taxpayer is also permitted by § 1.1445-3 to apply for a withholding certificate in instances where reduced withholding is appropriate.

(2) *Withholding not required.*—(i) *Transferee receives statement that interest in partnership is not described in paragraph (d)(1).*—No withholding is required under paragraph (d)(1) of this section upon the disposition of a partnership interest otherwise described in that paragraph if the transferee is provided a statement, issued by the partnership and signed by a general partner under penalties of perjury no earlier than 30 days before the transfer, certifying that fifty percent or more of the value of the gross assets does not consist of U.S. real property interests, or that ninety percent or more of the value of the gross assets of the partnership does not consist of U.S. real property interests plus cash or cash equivalents.

(ii) *Reliance on statement not permitted.*—A transferee is not entitled to rely upon a statement described in paragraph (d)(2)(i) of this section if, prior to or at the time of the transfer, the transferee either—

(A) Has actual knowledge that the statement is false, or

(B) Receives a notice, pursuant to § 1.1445-4.

Such a transferee's withholding obligations shall apply as if the statement had never been given, and such a transferee may be held fully liable pursuant to § 1.1445-1(e) for any failure to withhold.

(iii) *Belated notice of false statement.*—If, after the date of the transfer, a transferee receives notice that a statement provided under paragraph (d)(2)(i) of this section is false, then such transferee may rely on the statement only with respect to consideration that was paid prior to the receipt of the notice. Such a transferee is required to withhold a full 10 percent of the amount realized from the consideration that remains to be paid to the transferor. Thus, if 10 percent or more of the amount realized remains to be paid to the transferor, then the transferee is required to withhold and pay over the full 10 percent. The transferee must do so by withholding and paying over the entire amount of each successive payment of consideration to the transferor, until the full 10 percent of the amount realized has been withheld and paid over. Amounts so withheld must be reported and paid over by the 20th day following the date on which each such payment of consideration is made. A transferee that is subject to the rules of this § 1.1445-10T(d)(2)(iii) may not obtain a withholding certificate pursuant to § 1.1445-3, but must instead withhold and pay over the amounts required by this paragraph.

Reg. § 1.1445-11T(d)(2)(iii)

(e) *Effective date.*—The rules of this section are effective for transactions after June 6, 1988. [Temporary Reg. § 1.1445-11T.]

☐ [*T.D.* 8198, 5-4-88.]

Application of Withholding Provisions

§ 1.1462-1. Withheld tax as credit to recipient of income.—(a) *Creditable tax.*—The entire amount of the income from which the tax is required to be withheld (including amounts calculated under the gross-up formula in § 1.1441-3(f)(1)) shall be included in gross income in the return required to be made by the beneficial owner of the income, without deduction for the amount required to be or actually withheld, but the amount of tax actually withheld shall be allowed as a credit against the total income tax computed in the beneficial owner's return.

* * *

(c) *Effective date.*—Unless otherwise provided in this section, this section applies to payments made after December 31, 2000. [Reg. § 1.1462-1.]

☐ [*T.D.* 6187, 7-5-56. *Amended by T.D.* 7977, 9-19-84; *T.D.* 8734, 10-6-97; *T.D.* 8804, 12-30-98; *T.D.* 8856, 12-29-99 *and T.D.* 9200, 5-13-2005.]

Tax on Transfers to Avoid Income Tax

§ 1.1494-1. Returns; payment and collection of tax.—(a) *Returns and payment.*—Every person making a transfer described in section 1491 shall make a return to the district director on the day on which the transfer is made and, unless the transfer is nontaxable under section 1492, pay the tax due on such transfer. This return, which shall contain, or be verified by, a written declaration that it is made under the penalties of perjury, shall be made on Form 926 and shall be filed with the district director to whom the transferor's return of income is required to be made. The return shall set forth in detail the following information:

(1) Name and address of transferor, and place of organization or creation, if a corporation, partnership, or trust.

(2) Name and address of transferee, place of organization or creation, and whether the transferee is a foreign corporation, a foreign trust, or a foreign partnership. If the transferee is a foreign trust or a foreign partnership, the name and address of the fiduciary and each beneficiary, in the case of a trust, or of each partner, in the case of a partnership, must be shown.

(3) Description and amount of stock or securities transferred, the date of transfer, and a complete statement showing all the facts relating to the transfer, accompanied by a copy of the plan under which the transfer was made.

(4) The fair market value of the stock or securities transferred as of the date of transfer, and the adjusted basis provided in section 1011 for determining gain in the hands of the transferor.

(5) Whether the transfer was made in pursuance of a plan submitted to and approved by the Commissioner as not having as one of its principal purposes the avoidance of Federal income taxes. If the plan has been so approved, a copy of the Commissioner's letter approving the plan shall accompany the return.

(6) Such other information as may be required by the return form.

(b) *Certificate.*—(1) If the transferee of the stock or securities, the transfer of which is reported in the return, is a foreign organization meeting the tests of exemption from income tax provided in part I (section 501 and following), subchapter F, chapter 1 of the Code, and the transferor on that account claims that no liability for tax is imposed by section 1491, such transferor must file with Form 926 a certificate establishing the exemption of the transferee under such part I. This certificate, which shall contain, or be verified by, a written declaration that it is made under the penalties of perjury, shall contain complete information showing the character of the transferee, the purpose for which it was organized, its actual activities, the source of its income and the disposition of such income, whether or not any of its income is credited to surplus or may inure to the benefit of any private shareholder or individual, and in general all facts relating to its operations which affect its right to exemption. To such certificate shall be attached a copy of the charter or articles of incorporation, the by-laws of the organzation, and the latest financial statement showing the assets, liabilities, receipts, and disbursements of the organization.

(2) If the transferee is a foreign organization which has been held to be exempt from income tax under such part I (or corresponding provisions of prior law), a copy of the Commissioner's letter so holding shall be filed with Form 926 in lieu of the above certificate and attachments.

(c) *Assessment and collection.*—The determination, assessment, and collection of the tax and the examination of returns and claims filed pursuant to chapter 5 of the Code will be made under such procedure as may be prescribed from time to time by the Commissioner. [Reg. § 1.1494-1.]

☐ [*T.D.* 6127, 3-17-55.]

§ 1.1494-2. Effective date.—Chapter 5 (section 1491 and following) of the Internal Revenue Code of 1954 and the regulations prescribed thereunder apply with respect to transfers occurring after December 31, 1954. * * * [Reg. § 1.1494-2.]

☐ [*T.D.* 6127, 3-17-55.]

Consolidated Returns

§ 1.1502-4. Consolidated foreign tax credit.—(a) *In general.*—The credit under section 901 for taxes paid or accrued to any foreign country or possession of the United States shall be allowed to the group only if the common parent corporation chooses to use such credit in the computation of the tax liability of the group for the consolidated return year. If this choice is made, no deduction may be taken on the consolidated return for such taxes paid or accrued by any member of the group. See section 275(a)(4).

(b) *Limitation effective under section 904(a) for the group.*—(1) *Common parent's limitation effective for group.*—The determination of whether the overall limitation or the per-country limitation applies for a consolidated return year shall be made by reference to the limitation effective with respect to the common parent corporation for such year. If the limitation effective with respect to a member for its immediately preceding separate return year differs from the limitation effective with respect to the common parent corporation for the consolidated return year, then such member shall, if the overall limitation is effective with respect to the common parent, be deemed to have made an election to use such overall limitation, or, if the per-country limitation is effective with respect to the common parent, be deemed to have revoked its election to use the overall limitation. Consent of the Secretary or his delegate (if otherwise required) is hereby given to such member for such election or revocation. Any such election or revocation shall apply only prospectively beginning with such consolidated return year.

(2) *Limitation effective for subsequent years.*—The limitation effective with respect to a member for the last year for which it joins in the filing of a consolidated return with a group shall remain in effect for a subsequent separate return year and may be changed by such corporation for such subsequent year only in accordance with the provisions of section 904(b) (and this paragraph if it joins in the filing of a consolidated return with another group). Any retroactive change in the limitation by the common parent corporation for such member's last consolidated return year shall change the election effective with respect to such member for such last period. Thus, if the common parent (P) elects the overall limitation with respect to calendar year 1966, such election would be effective with respect to its subsidiary S for 1966. If S leaves the group at the beginning of calendar year 1967, such election shall be effective for 1967 with respect to S (unless S revokes such election for 1967 or a subsequent year in accordance with section 904(b), or this paragraph if it joins in the filing of a consolidated return with another group). However, if P retroactively changes back to the per-country limitation with respect to 1966, such limitation would be effective with respect to S for 1966 and subsequent years (unless S elects the overall limitation for any such subsequent year).

(c) *Computation of consolidated foreign tax credit.*—The foreign tax credit for the consolidated return year shall be determined on a consolidated basis under the principles of sections 901 through 905 and section 960. For example, if the per-country limitation applies to the consolidated return year, taxes paid or accrued for such year (including those deemed paid or accrued under sections 902 and 960(a) and paragraph (e) of this section) to each foreign country or possession by the members of the group shall be aggregated. If the overall limitation applies, taxes paid or accrued for such year (including those deemed paid or accrued) to all foreign countries and possessions by members of the group shall be aggregated. If the overall limitation applies and a member of the group qualifies as a Western Hemisphere trade corporation, see section 1503(b).

(d) *Computation of limitation on credit.*—For purposes of computing the group's applicable limitation under section 904(a), the following rules shall apply:

(1) *Computation of taxable income from foreign sources.*—The numerator of the applicable limiting fraction under section 904(a) shall be an amount (not in excess of the amount determined under subparagraph (2) of this paragraph) equal to the aggregate of the separate taxable incomes of the members from sources within each foreign country or possession of the United States (if the per-country limitation is applicable), or from sources without the

United States (if the overall limitation is applicable), determined under § 1.1502-12, adjusted for the following items taken into account in the computation of consolidated taxable income:

(i) The portion of the consolidated net operating loss deduction, the consolidated charitable contributions deduction, the consolidated dividends received deduction, and the consolidated section 922 deduction, attributable to such foreign source income;

(ii) Any such foreign source capital gain net income (net capital gain for taxable years beginning before January 1, 1977) (determined without regard to any net capital loss carryover or carryback);

(iii) Any such foreign source net capital loss and section 1231 net loss, reduced by the portion of the consolidated net capital loss attributable to such foreign source loss; and

(iv) The portion of any consolidated net capital loss carryover or carryback attributable to such foreign source income which is absorbed in the taxable year.

(2) *Computation of entire taxable income.*—The denominator of the applicable limiting fraction under section 904(a) (that is, the entire taxable income of the group) shall be the consolidated taxable income of the group computed in accordance with § 1.1502-11.

(3) *Computation of tax against which credit is taken.*—The tax against which the limiting fraction under section 904(a) is applied shall be the consolidated tax liability of the group determined under § 1.1502-2, but without regard to paragraphs (b), (c), (d), and (j) thereof, and without regard to any credit against such liability.

(e) *Carryover and carryback of unused foreign tax.*—(1) *Allowance of unused foreign tax as consolidated carryover or carryback.*—The aggregate of the consolidated unused foreign tax carryovers and carrybacks to the taxable year, to the extent absorbed for such year under the principles of section 904(d), shall be deemed to be paid or accrued to a foreign country or possession for such year. The consolidated unused foreign tax carryovers and carrybacks to the taxable year shall consist of any consolidated unused foreign tax, plus any unused foreign tax of members for separate return years of such members, which may be carried over or back to the taxable year under the principles of section 904(d) and (e). However, such consolidated carryovers and carrybacks shall not include any consolidated unused foreign taxes apportioned to a corporation for a separate return year pursuant to § 1.1502-79(d) and shall be subject to the limitations contained in paragraphs (f) and (g) of this section. A consolidated unused foreign tax is the excess of the foreign taxes paid or accrued by the group (or deemed paid or accrued by the group, other than by reason of section 904(d)) over the applicable limitation for the consolidated return year.

(2) *Absorption rules.*—For purposes of determining the amount, if any, of an unused foreign tax (consolidated or separate) which can be carried to a taxable year (consolidated or separate), the amount of such unused tax which is absorbed in a prior consolidated return year under section 904(d) shall be determined by—

(i) Applying all unused foreign taxes which can be carried to such prior year in the order of the taxable years in which such unused taxes arose, beginning with the taxable year which ends earliest, and

(ii) Applying all such unused taxes which can be carried to such prior year from taxable years ending on the same date on a pro rata basis.

(f) *Limitation on unused foreign tax carryover or carryback from separate return limitation years.*—(1) *General rule.*—In the case of an unused foreign tax of a member of the group arising in a separate return limitation year (as defined in paragraph (f) of § 1.1502-1) of such member, the amount which may be included under paragraph (e) of this section (computed without regard to the limitation contained in paragraph (g) of this section) shall not exceed the amount determined under subparagraph (2) of this paragraph.

(2) *Computation of limitation.*—The amount referred to in subparagraph (1) of this paragraph with respect to a member of the group is the excess, if any, of—

(i) The section 904(a) limitation of the group, minus such limitation recomputed by excluding the items of income and deduction of such member, over

(ii) The sum of (*a*) the foreign taxes paid (or deemed paid, other than be reason of section 904(d)) by such member for the consolidated return year, and (*b*) the unused foreign tax attributable to such member which may be carried to such consolidated return year arising in taxable years ending prior to the particular separate return limitation year.

(3) *Limitation on unused foreign tax credit carryover or carryback from separate return limitation years.*—Paragraphs (f)(1) and (2) of this section do not apply for consolidated return years for which the due date of the income tax return (without extensions) is after March 13, 1998. For consolidated return years for which the due date of the income tax return (without

extensions) is after March 13, 1998, a group shall include an unused foreign tax of a member arising in a SRLY without regard to the contribution of the member to consolidated tax liability for the consolidated return year. See also § 1.1502-3(d)(4) for an optional effective date rule (generally making the rules of paragraphs (f)(1) and (2) of this section also inapplicable to a consolidated return year beginning on or after January 1, 1997, if the due date of the income tax return (without extensions) for such year is on or before March 13, 1998).

(g) *Limitation on unused foreign tax carryover where there has been a consolidated return change of ownership.*—(1) *General rule.*—If a consolidated return change of ownership (as defined in paragraph (g) of § 1.1502-1) occurs during the taxable year or an earlier taxable year, the amount which may be included under paragraph (e) of this section in the consolidated unused foreign tax carryovers to the taxable year with respect to the aggregate unused credits attributable to the old members of the group (as defined in paragraph (g)(3) of § 1.1502-1) arising in taxable years (consolidated or separate) ending on the same day and before the taxable year in which the consolidated return change of ownership occurred shall not exceed the amount determined under subparagraph (2) of this paragraph.

(2) *Computation of limitation.*—The amount referred to in subparagraph (1) of this paragraph shall be the excess of the section 904(a) limitation of the group for the taxable year, recomputed by including only the items of income and deduction of the old members of the group, over the sum of—

(i) The aggregate foreign taxes paid (or deemed paid, other than by reason of section 904(d)) by the old members for the taxable year, and

(ii) The aggregate unused foreign tax attributable to the old members which can be carried to the taxable year arising in taxable years ending prior to the particular unused foreign tax year or years.

(3) *Special effective date for CRCO limitation.*—Paragraphs (g)(1) and (2) of this section apply only to a consolidated return change of ownership that occurred during a consolidated return year for which the due date of the income tax return (without extensions) is on or before March 13, 1998. See also § 1.1502-3(d)(4) for an optional effective date rule (generally making the rules of paragraph (g)(1) and (2) of this section also inapplicable if the consolidated return change of ownership occurred on or after January 1, 1997, and during a consolidated return year for which the due date of the income tax return (without extensions) is on or before March 13, 1998).

(h) *Amount of credit with respect to interest income.*—If any member of the group has interest income described in section 904(f)(2) (for a year for which it filed on a consolidated or separate basis), the group's foreign tax credit with respect to such interest shall be computed separately in accordance with the principles of section 904(f) and this section.

(i) [Reserved]

(j) *Examples.*—The provisions of this section may be illustrated by the following examples:

Example (1). Domestic corporation P is incorporated on January 1, 1966. On that same day it also incorporates domestic corporations S and T, wholly owned subsidiaries. P, S, and T file consolidated returns for 1966 and 1967 on the basis of a calendar year. T engages in business solely in country A. S transacts business solely in countries A and B. P does business solely in the United States. During 1966 T sold an item of inventory to P at a profit of $2,000. Under § 1.1502-13 (as contained in the 26 CFR part 1 edition revised as of April 1, 1995) such profit is deferred and none of the circumstances of restoration contained in paragraph (d), (e), or (f) of § 1.1502-13 have occurred as of the close of 1966. The taxable income for 1966 from foreign and United States sources, and the foreign taxes paid on such foreign income are as follows:

Corporation	U.S. Taxable income	Country A Taxable income	Country A Foreign tax paid	Country B Taxable income	Country B Foreign tax paid	Total Taxable income
P	$40,000	.....	.....	.....	.....	$40,000
T	.....	$20,000	$12,000	.....	.....	20,000
S	.....	10,000	6,000	$10,000	$3,000	20,000
						$80,000

Such taxable income was computed by taking into account the rules provided in § 1.1502-12. Thus, the $2,000 deferred profit is not included in T's taxable income for 1966 (but will be included for the taxable year for which one of the events specified in paragraph (d), (e), or (f) of § 1.1502-13 occurs). The consolidated taxable income of the group (computed in accordance with § 1.1502-11 is $80,000. The consolidated tax liability against which the credit may be taken (computed in accordance with paragraph (d)(3) of this section) is $31,900.

(i) Assuming P chooses to use the foreign taxes paid as a credit and the group is subject to the per-country limitation, the group may take as a credit against the consolidated tax liability $11,962.50 of the amount paid to country A, plus the $3,000 paid to country B. Such amounts are computed as follows: The aggregate taxes paid to country A of $18,000 is limited to $11,962.50 ($31,900 times $30,000/$80,000). The unused foreign tax with respect to country A is $6,037.50 ($18,000 less $11,962.50), and is a consolidated unused foreign tax which shall be carried to the years prescribed by section 904(d). A credit of $3,000 is available with respect to the taxes paid to country B since such amount is less than the limitation of $3,987.50 ($31,900 times $10,000/$80,000).

(ii) Assuming the overall limitation is in effect for the taxable year, the group may take $15,950 as a credit, computed as follows: The aggregate taxes paid to all foreign countries of $21,000 is limited to $15,950 ($31,900 times $40,000/$80,000). The unused foreign tax is $5,050 ($21,000 less $15,950), and is a consolidated unused foreign tax which shall be carried to the years prescribed by section 904(d).

Example (2). Assume the same facts as in example (1), except that T has a $10,000 long-term capital gain (derived from a sale to a nonmember in country A) and P has a $10,000 long-term capital loss (derived from a sale to a nonmember in the United States). Notwithstanding that the consolidated net capital gain (capital gain net income for taxable years beginning after December 31, 1976) of the group is zero, T's capital gain shall be reflected in full in the computation of taxable income from foreign sources.

Example (3). Assume the same facts as in example (1), except that the group had a consolidated section 172 deduction of $8,000 which is attributable to a net operating loss sustained by T. The $8,000 consolidated net operating loss deduction is offset against T's income from country A, thus reducing T's taxable income from country A to $12,000. [Reg. § 1.1502-4.]

☐ [T.D. 6894, 9-7-66. *Amended by* T.D. 7637, 8-6-79; T.D. 7728, 10-31-80; T.D. 8597, 7-12-95; T.D. 8751, 1-9-98; T.D. 8766, 3-13-98 *and* T.D. 8884, 5-24-2000.]

§ 1.1502-9. Consolidated overall foreign losses and separate limitation losses.— (a) *In general.*—This section provides rules for applying section 904(f) (including its definitions and nomenclature) to a group and its members. Generally, section 904(f) concerns rules relating to overall foreign losses (OFLs) and separate limitation losses (SLLs) and the consequences of such losses. As provided in section 904(f)(5), losses are computed separately in each category of income described in section 904(d)(1) (basket). Paragraph (b) of this section defines terms and provides computational and accounting rules, including rules regarding recapture. Paragraph (c) of this section provides rules that apply to OFLs and SLLs when a member becomes or ceases to be a member of a group. Paragraph (d) of this section provides a predecessor and successor rule. Paragraph (e) of this section provides effective dates.

(b) *Consolidated application of section 904(f).*—A group applies section 904(f) for a consolidated return year in accordance with that section, subject to the following rules:

(1) *Computation of CSLI or CSLL and consolidated U.S. source income or loss.*—The group computes its consolidated separate limitation income (CSLI) or consolidated separate limitation loss (CSLL) for each basket under the principles of § 1.1502-11 by aggregating each member's foreign-source taxable income or loss in such basket computed under the principles of § 1.1502-12, and taking into account the foreign portion of the consolidated items described in § 1.1502-11(a)(2) through (8) for such basket. The group computes its consolidated U.S.-source taxable income or loss under similar principles.

(2) *Netting CSLLs, CSLIs, and consolidated U.S. source taxable income or loss.*—The group applies section 904(f)(5) to determine the extent to which a CSLL for a basket reduces CSLI for another basket or consolidated U.S.-source taxable income.

(3) *CSLL and COFL accounts.*—To the extent provided in section 904(f), the amount by which a CSLL for a basket (the loss basket) reduces CSLI for another basket (the income basket) shall result in the creation of (or addition to) a CSLL account for the loss basket with respect to the income basket. Likewise, the amount by which a CSLL for a loss basket reduces consolidated U.S.-source income will create (or add to) a consolidated overall foreign loss account (a COFL account).

(4) *Recapture of COFL and CSLL accounts.*—In the case of a COFL account for a loss basket, section 904(f)(1) and (3) recharacterizes some or all of the foreign-source income in the loss basket as U.S.-source income. In the case of a CSLL account for a loss basket with respect to an income basket, section 904(f)(5)(C) and (F) recharacterizes some or all of the foreign-source income in the loss basket as foreign-source income in the

income basket. The COFL account or CSLL account is reduced to the extent amounts are recharacterized with respect to such account.

(5) *Intercompany transactions.*—(i) *Nonapplication of section 904(f) disposition rules.*—Neither section 904(f)(3) (in the case of a COFL account) nor (5)(F) (in the case of a CSLL account) applies at the time of a disposition that is an intercompany transaction to which § 1.1502-13 applies. Instead, section 904(f)(3) and (5)(F) applies only at such time and only to the extent that the group is required under § 1.1502-13 (without regard to section 904(f)(3) and (5)(F)) to take into account any intercompany items resulting from the disposition, based on the COFL or CSLL account existing at the end of the consolidated return year during which the group takes the intercompany items into account.

(ii) *Example.*—Paragraph (b)(5)(i) of this section is illustrated by the following examples. The identity of the parties and the basic assumptions set forth in § 1.1502-13(c)(7)(i) apply to the examples. Except as otherwise stated, assume further that the consolidated group recognizes no foreign-source income other than as a result of the transactions described. The examples are as follows:

Example 1. (i) On June 10, Year 1, S transfers nondepreciable property with a basis of $100 and a fair market value of $250 to B in a transaction to which section 351 applies. The property was predominantly used without the United States in a trade or business, within the meaning of section 904(f)(3). B continues to use the property without the United States. The group has a COFL account in the relevant loss basket of $120 as of December 31, Year 1.

(ii) Because the contribution from S to B is an intercompany transaction, section 904(f)(3) does not apply to result in any gain recognition in Year 1. See paragraph (b)(5)(i) of this section.

(iii) On January 10, Year 4, B ceases to be a member of the group. Because S did not recognize gain in Year 1 under section 351, no gain is taken into account in Year 4 under § 1.1502-13(d). Thus, no portion of the group's COFL account is recaptured in Year 4. For rules requiring apportionment of a portion of the COFL account to B, see paragraph (c)(2) of this section.

Example 2. (i) The facts are the same as in paragraph (i) of *Example 1.* On January 10, Year 4, B sells the property to X for $300. As of December 31, Year 4, the group's COFL account is $40. (The COFL account was reduced between Year 1 and Year 4 due to unrelated foreign-source income taken into account by the group.)

(ii) B takes into account gain of $200 in Year 4. The $40 COFL account in Year 4 recharacterizes $40 of the gain as U.S. source. See section 904(f)(3).

Example 3. (i) On June 10, Year 1, S sells nondepreciable property with a basis of $100 and a fair market value of $250 to B for $250 cash. The property was predominantly used without the United States in a trade or business, within the meaning of section 904(f)(3). The group has a COFL account in the relevant loss basket of $120 as of December 31, Year 1. B predominately uses the property in a trade or business without the United States.

(ii) Because the sale is an intercompany transaction, section 904(f)(3) does not require the group to take into account any gain in Year 1. Thus, under paragraph (b)(5)(i) of this section, the COFL account is not reduced in Year 1.

(iii) On January 10, Year 4, B sells the property to X for $300. As of December 31, Year 4, the group's COFL account is $60. (The COFL account was reduced between Year 1 and Year 4 due to unrelated foreign-source income taken into account by the group.)

(iv) In Year 4, S's $150 intercompany gain and B's $50 corresponding gain are taken into account to produce the same effect on consolidated taxable income as if S and B were divisions of a single corporation. See § 1.1502-13(c). All of B's $50 corresponding gain is recharacterized under section 904(f)(3). If S and B were divisions of a single corporation and the intercompany sale were a transfer between the divisions, B would succeed to S's $100 basis in the property and would have $200 of gain ($60 of which would be recharacterized under section 904(f)(3)), instead of a $50 gain. Consequently, S's $150 intercompany gain and B's $50 corresponding gain are taken into account, and $10 of S's gain is recharacterized under section 904(f)(3) as U.S. source to reflect the $10 difference between B's $50 recharacterized gain and the $60 recomputed gain that would have been recharacterized.

(c) *Becoming or ceasing to be a member of a group.*—(1) *Adding separate accounts on becoming a member.*—At the time that a corporation becomes a member of a group (a new member), the group adds to the balance of its COFL or CSLL account the balance of the new member's corresponding OFL account or SLL account. A new member's OFL account corresponds to a COFL account if the account is for the same loss basket. A new member's SLL account corresponds to a CSLL account if the account is for the same loss basket and with respect to the same income basket. If the group does not have a COFL or CSLL account corresponding to the new member's account, it creates a COFL or CSLL account with a balance equal to the balance of the member's account.

(2) *Apportionment of consolidated account to departing member.*—(i) *In general.*—A group apportions to a member that ceases to be a member (a departing member) a portion of each COFL and CSLL account as of the end of the year during which the member ceases to be a member and after the group makes the additions or reductions to such account required under paragraphs (b)(3), (b)(4) and (c)(1) of this section (other than an addition under paragraph (c)(1) of this section attributable to a member becoming a member after the departing member ceases to be a member). The group computes such portion under paragraph (c)(2)(ii) of this section, as limited by paragraph (c)(2)(iii) of this section. The departing member carries such portion to its first separate return year after it ceases to be a member. Also, the group reduces each account by such portion and carries such reduced amount to its first consolidated return year beginning after the year in which the member ceases to be a member. If two or more members cease to be members in the same year, the group computes the portion allocable to each such member (and reduces its accounts by such portion) in the order that the members cease to be members.

(ii) *Departing member's portion of group's account.*—A departing member's portion of a group's COFL or CSLL account for a loss basket is computed based upon the member's share of the group's assets that generate income subject to recapture at the time that the member ceases to be a member. Under the characterization principles of §§ 1.861-9T(g)(3) and 1.861-12T, the group identifies the assets of the departing member and the remaining members that generate foreign-source income (foreign assets) in each basket. The assets are characterized based upon the income that the assets are reasonably expected to generate after the member ceases to be a member. The member's portion of a group's COFL or CSLL account for a loss basket is the group's COFL or CSLL account, respectively, multiplied by a fraction, the numerator of which is the value of the member's foreign assets for the loss basket and the denominator of which is the value of the foreign assets of the group (including the departing member) for the loss basket. The value of the foreign assets is determined under the asset valuation rules of § 1.861-9T(g)(1) and (2) using either tax book value or fair market value under the method chosen by the group for purposes of interest apportionment as provided in § 1.861-9T(g)(1)(ii). For purposes of this paragraph (c)(2)(ii), § 1.861-9T(g)(2)(iv) (assets in intercompany transactions) shall apply, but § 1.861-9T(g)(2)(iii) (adjustments for directly allocated interest) shall not apply. If the group uses the tax book value method, the member's portions of COFL and CSLL accounts are limited by paragraph (c)(2)(iii) of this section. In addition, for purposes of this paragraph (c)(2)(ii), the tax book value of assets transferred in intercompany transactions shall be determined without regard to previously deferred gain or loss that is taken into account by the group as a result of the transaction in which the member ceases to be a member. The assets should be valued at the time the member ceases to be a member, but values on other dates may be used unless this creates substantial distortions. For example, if a member ceases to be a member in the middle of the group's consolidated return year, an average of the values of assets at the beginning and end of the year (as provided in § 1.861-9T(g)(2)) may be used or, if a member ceases to be a member in the early part of the group's consolidated return year, values at the beginning of the year may be used, unless this creates substantial distortions.

(iii) *Limitation on member's portion for groups using tax book value method.*—If a group uses the tax book value method of valuing assets for purposes of paragraph (c)(2)(ii) of this section and the aggregate of a member's portions of COFL and CSLL accounts for a loss basket (with respect to one or more income baskets) determined under paragraph (c)(2)(ii) of this section exceeds 150 percent of the actual fair market value of the member's foreign assets in the loss basket, the member's portion of the COFL or CSLL accounts for the loss basket shall be reduced (proportionately, in the case of multiple accounts) by such excess. This rule does not apply if the departing member and all other members that cease to be members as part of the same transaction own all (or substantially all) the foreign assets in the loss basket.

(iv) *Determination of values of foreign assets binding on departing member.*—The group's determination of the value of the member's and the group's foreign assets for a loss basket is binding on the member, unless the Commissioner concludes that the determination is not appropriate. The common parent of the group must attach a statement to the return for the taxable year that the departing member ceases to be a member of the group that sets forth the name and taxpayer identification number of the departing member, the amount of each COFL or CSLL for each loss basket that is apportioned to the departing member under this paragraph (c)(2), the method used to determine the value of the member's and the group's foreign assets in each such loss basket, and the value of the member's and the group's foreign assets in each such loss basket. The common parent must also furnish a copy of the statement to the departing member.

(v) *Anti-abuse rule.*—If a corporation becomes a member and ceases to be a member, and a principal purpose of the corporation becoming and ceasing to be a member is to transfer the corporation's OFL account or SLL account to the group or to transfer the group's COFL or CSLL account to the corporation, appropriate adjustments will be made to eliminate the benefit of such a transfer of accounts. Similarly, if any member acquires assets or disposes of assets (including a transfer of assets between members of the group and the departing member) with a principal purpose of affecting the apportionment of accounts under paragraph (c)(2)(i) of this section, appropriate adjustments will be made to eliminate the benefit of such acquisition or disposition.

(vi) *Examples.*—The following examples illustrate this paragraph (c):

Example 1. (i) On November 6, Year 1, S, a member of the P group, a consolidated group with a calendar consolidated return year, ceases to be a member of the group. On December 31, Year 1, the P group has a $40 COFL account for the general limitation basket, a $20 CSLL account for the general limitation basket (i.e., the loss basket) with respect to the passive basket (i.e., the income basket), and a $10 CSLL account for the shipping income basket (i.e., the loss basket) with respect to the passive basket (i.e., the income basket). No member of the group has foreign-source income or loss in Year 1. The group apportions its interest expense according to the tax book value method.

(ii) On November 6, Year 1, the group identifies S's assets and its own assets (including S's assets) expected to produce foreign general limitation income. Use of end-of-the-year values will not create substantial distortions in determining the relative values of S's and the group's relevant assets on November 6, Year 1. The group determines that S's relevant assets have a tax book value of $2,000 and a fair market value of $2,200. Also, the group's relevant assets (including S's assets) have a tax book value of $8,000. On November 6, Year 1, S has no assets expected to produce foreign shipping income.

(iii) Under paragraph (c)(2)(ii) of this section, S takes a $10 COFL account for the general limitation basket ($40 × $2000/$8000) and a $5 CSLL account for the general limitation basket with respect to the passive basket ($20 × $2000/$8000). S does not take any portion of the shipping income basket CSLL account. The limitation described in paragraph (c)(2)(iii) of this section does not apply because the aggregate of the COFL and CSLL accounts for the general limitation basket that are apportioned to S ($15) is less than 150 percent of the actual fair market value of S's general limitation foreign assets ($2,200 × 150%).

Example 2. (i) Assume the same facts as in *Example 1*, except that the fair market value of S's general limitation foreign assets is $4 as of November 6, Year 1.

(ii) Under paragraph (c)(2)(iii) of this section, S's COFL and CSLL accounts for the general limitation basket must be reduced by $9, which is the excess of $15 (the aggregate amount of the accounts apportioned under paragraph (c)(2)(ii) of this section) over $6 (150 percent of the $4 actual fair market value of S's general limitation foreign assets). S thus takes a $4 COFL account for the general limitation basket ($10 − ($9 × $10/$15)) and a $2 CSLL account for the general limitation basket with respect to the passive basket ($5 − ($9 × $5/$15)).

(d) *Predecessor and successor.*—A reference to a member includes, as the context may require, a reference to a predecessor or successor of the member. See § 1.1502-1(f).

(e) *Effective dates.*—This section applies to consolidated return years for which the due date of the income tax return (without extensions) is after August 11, 1999. However, paragraph (b)(5) of this section (intercompany transactions) is not applicable for intercompany transactions that occur before January 28, 1999. A group applies the principles of § 1.1502-9A(e) to a disposition which is an intercompany transaction to which § 1.1502-13 applies and that occurs before January 28, 1999. Also, paragraph (c)(2) of this section (apportionment of consolidated account to departing member) is not applicable for members ceasing to be members of a group before January 28, 1999. A group applies the principles of § 1.1502-9A (rather than paragraph (c)(2) of this section) to determine the amount of a consolidated account that is apportioned to a member that ceases to be a member of the group before January 28, 1999 (and reduces its consolidated account by such apportioned amount) before applying paragraph (c)(2) of this section to members that cease to be members on or after January 28, 1999. [Reg. § 1.1502-9.]

☐ [*T.D.* 8833, 8-10-99.]

§ 1.1503-2. Dual consolidated loss.—
(a) *Purpose and scope.*—This section provides rules for the application of section 1503(d),

concerning the determination and use of dual consolidated losses. Paragraph (b) of this section provides a general rule prohibiting a dual consolidated loss from offsetting the taxable income of a domestic affiliate. Paragraph (c) of this section provides definitions of the terms used in this section. Paragraph (d) of this section provides rules for calculating the amount of a dual consolidated loss and for adjusting the basis of stock of a dual resident corporation. Paragraph (e) of this section contains an anti-avoidance provision. Paragraph (f) of this section applies the rules of paragraph (d) of this section to the computation of foreign tax credit limitations. Paragraph (g) of this section provides certain exceptions to the limitation rule of paragraph (b) of this section. Finally, paragraph (h) of this section provides the effective date of the regulations and a provision for the retroactive application of the regulations to qualifying taxpayers.

(b) *In general.*—(1) *Limitation on the use of a dual consolidated loss to offset income of a domestic affiliate.*—Except as otherwise provided in this section, a dual consolidated loss of a dual resident corporation cannot offset the taxable income of any domestic affiliate in the taxable year in which the loss is recognized or in any other taxable year, regardless of whether the loss offsets income of another person under the income tax laws of a foreign country and regardless of whether the income that the loss may offset in the foreign country is, has been, or will be subject to tax in the United States. Pursuant to paragraph (c)(1) and (2) of this section, the same limitation shall apply to a dual consolidated loss of a separate unit of a domestic corporation as if the separate unit were a wholly owned subsidiary of such corporation.

(2) *Limitation on the use of a dual consolidated loss to offset income of a successor-in-interest.*—A dual consolidated loss of a dual resident corporation also cannot be used to offset the taxable income of another corporation by means of a transaction in which the other corporation succeeds to the tax attributes of the dual resident corporation under section 381 of the Code. Similarly, a dual consolidated loss of a separate unit of a domestic corporation cannot be used to offset income of the domestic corporation following the termination, liquidation, sale, or other disposition of the separate unit. However, if a dual resident corporation transfers its assets to another corporation in a transaction subject to section 381, and the acquiring corporation is a dual resident corporation of the same foreign country of which the transferor dual resident corporation is a resident, or a domestic corporation that carries on the business activities of the transferor dual resident corporation as a separate unit, then income generated by the transferee dual resident corporation, or separate unit, may be offset by the carryover losses of the transferor dual resident corporation. In addition, if a domestic corporation transfers a separate unit to another domestic corporation in a transaction subject to section 381, the income generated by the separate unit following the transfer may be offset by the carryover losses of the separate unit.

(3) *Application of rules to multiple tiers of separate units.*—If a separate unit of a domestic corporation is owned indirectly through another separate unit, the principles of paragraph (b)(1) and (2) of this section shall apply as if the upper-tier separate unit were a subsidiary of the domestic corporation and the lower-tier separate unit were a lower-tier subsidiary.

(4) *Examples.*—The following examples illustrate the application of this paragraph (b).

Example 1. P, a domestic corporation, owns all of the outstanding stock of DRC, a domestic corporation. P and DRC file a consolidated U.S. income tax return. DRC is managed and controlled in Country W, a country that determines the tax residence of corporations according to their place of management and control. Therefore, DRC is a dual resident corporation and any net operating loss it incurs is a dual consolidated loss. In Years 1 through 3, DRC incurs dual consolidated losses. Under this paragraph (b), the dual consolidated losses may not be used to offset P's income on the group's consolidated U.S. income tax return. At the end of Year 3, DRC sells all of its assets and discontinues its business operations. DRC is then liquidated into P, pursuant to the provisions of section 332. Normally, under section 381, P would succeed to, and be permitted to utilize, DRC's net operating loss carryovers. However, this paragraph (b) prohibits the dual consolidated losses of DRC from reducing P's income for U.S. tax purposes. Therefore, DRC's net operating loss carryovers will not be available to offset P's income.

Example 2. The facts are the same as in *Example 1,* except that DRC does not sell its assets and, following the liquidation of DRC, P continues to operate DRC's business as a separate unit (*e.g.,* a branch). DRC's loss carryovers are available to offset P's income generated by the assets previously owned by DRC and now held by the separate unit.

(c) *Definitions.*—The following definitions shall apply for purposes of this section.

(1) *Domestic corporation.*—The term "domestic corporation" has the meaning assigned to it by section 7701(a)(3) and (4). The term

also includes any corporation otherwise treated as a domestic corporation by the Code, including, but not limited to, sections 269B, 953(d), and 1504(d). For purposes of this section, any separate unit of a domestic corporation, as defined in paragraph (c)(3) and (4) of this section, shall be treated as a separate domestic corporation.

(2) *Dual resident corporation.*—A dual resident corporation is a domestic corporation that is subject to the income tax of a foreign country on its worldwide income or on a residence basis. A corporation is taxed on a residence basis if it is taxed as a resident under the laws of the foreign country. An S corporation, as defined in section 1361, is not a dual resident corporation. For purposes of this section, any separate unit of a domestic corporation, as defined in paragraph (c)(3) and (4) of this section, shall be treated as a dual resident corporation. Unless otherwise indicated, any reference in this section to a dual resident corporation refers also to a separate unit.

(3) *Separate unit.*—(i) The term "separate unit" shall mean any of the following:

(A) A foreign branch, as defined in § 1.367(a)-6T(g) (or a successor regulation), that is owned either directly by a domestic corporation or indirectly by a domestic corporation through ownership of a partnership or trust interest (regardless of whether the partnership or trust is a United States person);

(B) an interest in a partnership; or

(C) an interest in a trust.

(ii) If two or more foreign branches located in the same foreign country are owned by a single domestic corporation and the losses of each branch are made available to offset the income of the other branches under the tax laws of the foreign country, within the meaning of paragraph (c)(15)(ii) of this section, then the branches shall be treated as one separate unit.

(4) *Hybrid entity separate unit.*—The term "separate unit" includes an interest in an entity that is not taxable as an association for U.S. income tax purposes but is subject to income tax in a foreign country as a corporation (or otherwise at the entity level) either on its worldwide income or on a residence basis.

(5) *Dual consolidated loss.*—(i) *In general.*—The term "dual consolidated loss" means the net operating loss (as defined in section 172(c) and the regulations thereunder) of a domestic corporation incurred in a year in which the corporation is a dual resident corporation. The dual consolidated loss shall be computed under paragraph (d)(1) of this section. The fact that a particular item taken into account in computing a dual resident corporation's net operating loss is not taken into account in computing income subject to a foreign country's income tax shall not cause such item to be excluded from the calculation of the dual consolidated loss.

(ii) *Exceptions.*—A dual consolidated loss shall not include the following—

(A) A net operating loss incurred by a dual resident corporation in a foreign country whose income tax laws—

(1) Do not permit the dual resident corporation to use its losses, expenses or deductions to offset the income of any other person that is recognized in the same taxable year in which the losses, expenses or deductions are incurred; and

(2) Do not permit the losses, expenses or deductions of the dual resident corporation to be carried over or back to be used, by any means, to offset the income of any other person in other taxable years; or

(B) A net operating loss incurred during that portion of the taxable year prior to the date on which the domestic corporation becomes a dual resident corporation or subsequent to the date on which the domestic corporation ceases to be a dual resident corporation. For purposes of determining the amount of the net operating loss incurred in that portion of the taxable year prior to the date on which the domestic corporation becomes a dual resident corporation or subsequent to the date on which the domestic corporation ceases to be a dual resident corporation, in no event shall more than the aggregate of the equal daily portion of the net operating loss commensurate with the portion of the taxable year during which the domestic corporation was not a dual resident corporation be allocated to that portion of the taxable year in which the domestic corporation was not a dual resident corporation.

(iii) *Dual consolidated losses of separate units that are partnership interests, including interests in hybrid entities.*—[Reserved]

(6) *Subject to tax.*—For purposes of determining whether a domestic corporation is subject to the income tax of a foreign country on its income, the fact that the corporation has no actual income tax liability to the foreign country for a particular taxable year shall not be taken into account.

(7) *Foreign country.*—For purposes of this section, possessions of the United States shall be considered foreign countries.

(8) *Consolidated group.*—The term "consolidated group" means an affiliated group, as defined in section 1504(a), with which a dual

resident corporation or domestic owner files a consolidated U.S. income tax return.

(9) *Domestic owner.*—The term "domestic owner" means a domestic corporation that owns one or more separate units.

(10) *Affiliated dual resident corporation or affiliated domestic owner.*—The term "affiliated dual resident corporation" or "affiliated domestic owner" means a dual resident corporation or domestic owner that is a member of a consolidated group.

(11) *Unaffiliated dual resident corporation or unaffiliated domestic owner.*—The term "unaffiliated dual resident corporation" or "unaffiliated domestic owner" means a dual resident corporation or domestic owner that is an unaffiliated domestic corporation.

(12) *Successor-in-interest.*—The term "successor-in-interest" means an acquiring corporation that succeeds to the tax attributes of an acquired corporation by means of a transaction subject to section 381.

(13) *Domestic affiliate.*—The term "domestic affiliate" means any member of an affiliated group, without regard to the exceptions contained in section 1504(b) (other than section 1504(b)(3)) relating to includible corporations.

(14) *Unaffiliated domestic corporation.*—The term "unaffiliated domestic corporation" means a domestic corporation that is not a member of an affiliated group.

(15) *Use of loss to offset income of a domestic affiliate or another person.*—(i) A dual consolidated loss shall be deemed to offset income of a domestic affiliate in the year it is included in the computation of the consolidated taxable income of a consolidated group. The fact that no tax benefit results from the inclusion of the dual consolidated loss in the computation of the group's consolidated taxable income in the taxable year shall not be taken into account.

(ii) Except as provided in paragraph (c)(15)(iii) of this section, a loss, expense, or deduction taken into account in computing a dual consolidated loss shall be deemed to offset income of another person under the income tax laws of a foreign country in the year it is made available for such offset. The fact that the other person does not have sufficient income in that year to benefit from such an offset shall not be taken into account. However, where the laws of a foreign country provide an election that would enable a dual resident corporation or separate unit to use its losses, expenses, or deductions to offset income of another person, the losses, expenses, or deductions shall be considered to offset such income only if the election is made.

(iii) The losses, expenses, or deductions taken into account in computing a dual resident corporation's or separate unit's dual consolidated loss shall not be deemed to offset income of another person under the income tax laws of a foreign country for purposes of this section, if under the laws of the foreign country the losses, expenses, or deductions of the dual resident corporation or separate unit are used to offset the income of another dual resident corporation or separate unit within the same consolidated group (or income of another separate unit that is owned by the unaffiliated domestic owner of the first separate unit). If the losses, expenses, or deductions of a dual resident corporation or separate unit are made available under the laws of a foreign country to offset the income of other dual resident corporations or separate units within the same consolidated group (or other separate units owned by the unaffiliated domestic owner of the first separate unit), as well as the income of another person, and the laws of the foreign country do not provide applicable rules for determining which person's income is offset by the losses, expenses, or deductions, then for purposes of this section, the losses, expenses or deductions shall be deemed to offset the income of the other dual resident corporations or separate units, to the extent of such income, before being considered to offset the income of the other person.

(iv) Except to the extent paragraph (g)(1) of this section applies, where the income tax laws of a foreign country deny the use of losses, expenses, or deductions of a dual resident corporation to offset the income of another person because the dual resident corporation is also subject to income taxation by another country on its worldwide income or on a residence basis, the dual resident corporation shall be treated as if it actually had offset its dual consolidated loss against the income of another person in such foreign country.

(16) *Examples.*—The following examples illustrate this paragraph (c).

Example 1. X, a member of a consolidated group, conducts business through a branch in Country Y. Under Country Y's income tax laws, the branch is taxed as a permanent establishment and its losses may be used under the Country Y form of consolidation to offset the income of Z, a Country Y affiliate of X. In Year 1, the branch of X incurs an overall loss that would be treated as a net operating loss if the branch were a separate domestic corporation. Under paragraph (c)(3) of this section, the branch of X is treated as a separate domestic corporation and a dual resident corporation.

Thus, under paragraph (c)(5), its loss constitutes a dual consolidated loss. Unless X qualifies for an exception under paragraph (g) of this section, paragraph (b) of this section precludes the use of the branch's loss to offset any income of X not derived from the branch operations or any income of a domestic affiliate of X.

Example 2. A and B are members of a consolidated group. FC is a Country X corporation that is wholly owned by B. A and B organize a partnership, P, under the laws of Country X. P conducts business in Country X and its business activity constitutes a foreign branch within the meaning of paragraph (c)(3)(i)(A) of this section. P also earns U.S. source income that is unconnected with the branch operations and, therefore, is not subject to tax by Country X. Under the laws of Country X, the branch can consolidate with FC. The interests in P held by A and B are each treated as a dual resident corporation. The branch is also treated as a separate dual resident corporation. Unless an exception under paragraph (g) of this section applies, any dual consolidated loss incurred by P's branch cannot offset the U.S. source income earned by P or any other income of A or B.

Example 3. X is classified as a partnership for U.S. income tax purposes. A, B and C are the sole partners of X. A and B are domestic corporations and C is a Country Y corporation. For U.S. income tax purposes, each partner has an equal interest in each item of partnership profit or loss. Under Country Y's law, X is classified as a corporation and its income and losses may be used under the Country Y form of consolidation to offset the income of companies that are affiliates of X. Under paragraph (c)(3) and (4) of this section, the partnership interests held by A and B are treated as separate domestic corporations and as dual resident corporations. Unless an exception under paragraph (g) of this section applies, losses allocated to A and B can only be used to offset profits of X allocated to A and B, respectively.

Example 4. P, a domestic corporation, files a consolidated U.S. income tax return with its two wholly-owned domestic subsidiaries, DRC1 and DRC2. Each subsidiary is also treated as a Country Y resident for Country Y tax purposes. Thus, DRC1 and DRC2 are dual resident corporations. DRC1 owns FC, a Country Y corporation. Country Y's tax laws permit affiliated resident corporations to file a form of consolidated return. In Year 1, DRC1 incurs a $200 net operating loss for both U.S. and Country Y tax purposes, while DRC2 recognizes $200 of income under the tax laws of each country. FC also earns $200 of income for Country Y tax purposes. DRC1, DRC2, and FC file a Country Y consolidated return. However, Country Y has no applicable rules for determining which income is offset by DRC1's $200 loss. Under paragraph (c)(15)(iii) of this section, the loss shall be treated as offsetting DRC2's $200 of income. Because DRC1 and DRC2 are members of the same consolidated group, for purposes of this section, the offset of DRC1's loss against the income of DRC2 is not considered a use of the loss against the income of another person under the laws of a foreign country.

Example 5. DRC, a domestic corporation, files a consolidated U.S. income tax return with its parent, P. DRC is also subject to tax in Country Y on its worldwide income. Therefore, DRC is a dual resident corporation and any net operating loss incurred by DRC is a dual consolidated loss. Country Y's tax laws permit corporations that are subject to tax on their worldwide income to use the Country Y form of consolidation, thus enabling eligible corporations to use their losses to offset income of affiliates. However, to prevent corporations like DRC from offsetting losses against income of affiliates in Country Y and then again offsetting the losses against income of foreign affiliates under the tax laws of another country, Country Y prevents a corporation that is also subject to the income tax of another country on its worldwide income or on a residence basis from using the Country Y form of consolidation. There is no agreement, as described in paragraph (g)(1) of this section, between the United States and Country Y. Because of Country Y's statute, DRC will be treated as having actually offset its losses against the income of affiliates in Country Y under paragraph (c)(15)(iv) of this section. Therefore, DRC will not be able to file an agreement described in paragraph (g)(2) of this section and offset its losses against the income of P or any other domestic affiliate.

(d) *Special rules for accounting for dual consolidated losses.*—(1) *Determination of amount of dual consolidated loss.*—(i) *Dual resident corporation that is a member of a consolidated group.*—For purposes of determining whether a dual resident corporation that is a member of a consolidated group has a dual consolidated loss for the taxable year, the dual resident corporation shall compute its taxable income (or loss) in accordance with the rules set forth in the regulations under section 1502 governing the computation of consolidated taxable income, taking into account only the dual resident corporation's items of income, gain, deduction, and loss for the year. However, for purposes of this computation, the following items shall not be taken into account:

(A) Any net capital loss of the dual resident corporation; and

(B) Any carryover or carryback losses.

(ii) *Dual resident corporation that is a separate unit of a domestic corporation.*—For purposes of determining whether a separate unit has a dual consolidated loss for the taxable year, the separate unit shall compute its taxable income (or loss) as if it were a separate domestic corporation and a dual resident corporation in accordance with the provisions of paragraph (d)(1)(i) of this section, using only those items of income, expense, deduction, and loss that are otherwise attributable to such separate unit.

(2) *Effect of a dual consolidated loss.*—For any taxable year in which a dual resident corporation or separate unit has a dual consolidated loss to which paragraph (b) of this section applies, the following rules shall apply.

(i) If the dual resident corporation is a member of a consolidated group, the group shall compute its consolidated taxable income without taking into account the items of income, loss, or deduction taken into account in computing the dual consolidated loss. The dual consolidated loss may be carried over or back for use in other taxable years as a separate net operating loss carryover or carryback of the dual resident corporation arising in the year incurred. It shall be treated as a loss incurred by the dual resident corporation in a separate return limitation year and (without regard to whether the dual resident corporation is a common parent) shall be subject to all of the limitations of §1.1502-21A(c) or 1.1502-21(c), as appropriate (relating to limitations on net operating loss carryovers and carrybacks from separate return limitation years).

(ii) The unaffiliated domestic owner of a separate unit, or the consolidated group of an affiliated domestic owner, shall compute its taxable income without taking into account the items of income, loss or deduction taken into account in computing the separate unit's dual consolidated loss. The dual consolidated loss shall be treated as a loss incurred by a separate corporation and its use shall be subject to all of the limitations of §1.1502-21A(c) or 1.1502-21(c), as appropriate, as if the separate unit were filing a consolidated return with the unaffiliated domestic owner or with the consolidated group of the affiliated domestic owner.

(3) *Basis adjustments for dual consolidated losses.*—(i) *Dual resident corporation that is a member of an affiliated group.*—When a dual resident corporation is a member of a consolidated group, each other member owning stock in the dual resident corporation shall adjust the basis of the stock in the following manner.

(A) *Positive adjustments.*—Positive adjustments shall be made in accordance with the principles of §1.1502-32(b)(1), except that there shall be no positive adjustment under §1.1502-32(b)(1)(ii) for any amount of the dual consolidated loss that is not absorbed as a result of the application of paragraph (b) of this section. In addition, there shall be no positive adjustment for any amount included in income pursuant to paragraph (g)(2)(vii) of this section.

(B) *Negative adjustments.*—Negative adjustments shall be made in accordance with the principles of §1.1502-32(b)(2), except that there shall be no negative adjustment under §1.1502-32(b)(2)(ii) for the amount of the dual consolidated loss subject to paragraph (b) of this section that is absorbed in a carryover year.

(ii) *Dual resident corporation that is a separate unit arising from an interest in a partnership.*—Where a separate unit is an interest in a partnership, the domestic owner shall adjust its basis in the separate unit in accordance with section 705, except that no increase in basis shall be permitted for any amount included as income pursuant to paragraph (g)(2)(vii) of this section.

(4) *Examples.*—The following examples illustrate this paragraph (d).

Example 1. (i) P, S1, S2, and T are domestic corporations. P owns all of the stock of S1 and S2. S2 owns all of the stock of T. T is a resident of Country FC for Country FC income tax purposes. Therefore, T is a dual resident corporation. P, S1, S2, and T file a consolidated U.S. income tax return. X and Y are corporations that are not members of the consolidated group.

(ii) At the beginning of Year 1, P has a basis of $1,000 in the stock of S2. S2 has a $500 basis in the stock of T.

(iii) In Year 1, T incurs interest expense in the amount of $100. In addition, T sells a noncapital asset, u, in which it has a basis of $10, to S1 for $50. T also sells a noncapital asset, v, in which it has a basis of $200, to S1 for $100. The sales of u and v are intercompany transactions described in §1.1502-13. T also sells a capital asset, z, in which it has a basis of $180, to Y for $90. In Year 1, S1 earns $200 of separate taxable income, calculated in accordance with §1.1502-12, as well as $90 of capital gain from a sale of an asset to X. P and S2 have no items of income, loss, or deduction for Year 1.

(iv) In Year 1, T has a dual consolidated loss of $100 (attributable to its interest expense). T's $90 capital loss is not included in the computation of the dual consolidated loss. Instead, T's capital loss is included in the computation of the consolidated group's capital gain net income under §1.1502-22(c) and is used to offset S1's $90 capital gain.

(v) No elective agreement, as described in paragraph (g)(1) of this section, exists between the United States and Country FC. For Country FC tax purposes, T's $100 loss is offset against the income of a Country FC affiliate. Therefore, T is not eligible for the exception provided in paragraph (g)(2) of this section.

(vi) Because T has a dual consolidated loss for the year, the consolidated taxable income of the consolidated group is calculated without regard to T's items of income, loss or deduction taken into account in computing the dual consolidated loss. Therefore, the consolidated taxable income of the consolidated group is $200 (the sum of $200 of separate taxable income earned by S1 plus $90 of capital gain earned by S1 minus $90 of capital loss incurred by T). The $40 gain recognized by T upon the sale of item u to S1 and the $100 loss recognized by T upon the sale of Item v to S1 are deferred pursuant to §1.1502-13(c)(1).

(vii) S2 may not make the positive adjustment provided for in §1.1502-32(b)(1)(ii) to its basis in the stock of T for the $100 dual consolidated loss incurred by T. In addition, no positive adjustment in the basis of the stock is required for T's $90 capital loss because the loss has been absorbed by the consolidated group. S2, however, must make the negative adjustment provided for in §1.1502-32(b)(2)(i) for its allocable part of T's deficit in earnings and profits for the taxable year attributable to both T's $100 dual consolidated loss and T's $90 capital loss. Thus, as provided in §1.1502-32(e)(1), S2 must make a $190 net negative adjustment to its basis in the stock of T, reducing its basis to $310. As provided in §1.1502-33(c)(4)(ii)(a), S2's earnings and profits for Year 1 will reflect S2's decrease in its basis in T stock for the taxable year. Since S2 has no other earnings and profits for the taxable year, S2 has a $190 deficit in earnings and profits for the year. As provided in §1.1502-32(b)(2)(i), P must make a negative adjustment to its basis in the stock of S2 for its allocable part of S2's deficit in earnings and profits for the taxable year. Thus, P must make a $190 net negative adjustment to its basis in S2 stock, reducing its basis to $810.

Example 2. (i) The facts are the same as in *Example 1,* except that in Year 2, S1 sells items u and v to X for no gain or loss. The disposition of items u and v outside of the consolidated group restores the deferred loss and gain to T. T also incurs $100 of interest expense in Year 2. In addition, T sells a noncapital asset, r, in which it has a basis of $100, to Y for $300. P and S2 have no items of income, loss, or deduction for Year 2.

(ii) T has $40 of separate taxable income in Year 2, computed as follows:

($100)	interest expense
($100)	sale of item v to S1
$40	sale of item u to S1
$200	sale of item r to Y
$40	

Thus, T has no dual consolidated loss for the year.

(iii) Since T does not have a dual consolidated loss for the taxable year, the group's consolidated taxable income is calculated in accordance with the general rule of §1.1502-11 and not in accordance with paragraph (d)(2) of this section. T is the only member of the consolidated group that has any income or loss for the taxable year. Thus, the consolidated taxable income of the group, computed without regard to T's dual consolidated loss carryover, is $40.

(iv) As provided by §1.1502-21A(c), the amount of the dual consolidated loss arising in Year 1 that is included in the group's consolidated net operating loss deduction for Year 2 is $40 (that is, the consolidated taxable income computed without regard to the consolidated net operating loss deduction minus such consolidated taxable income recomputed by excluding the items of income and deduction of T). Thus, the group has no consolidated taxable income for the year.

(v) S2 must make the positive adjustment provided for in §1.1502-32(b)(1)(i) to its basis in T stock for its allocable part of T's undistributed earnings and profits for the taxable year. S2 cannot make the negative adjustment provided for in §1.1502-32(b)(2)(ii) for the dual consolidated loss of T incurred in Year 1 and absorbed in Year 2. Thus, as provided in §1.1502-32(e)(2), S2 must make a $40 net positive adjustment to its basis in T stock, increasing its basis to $350. As provided in §1.1502-33(c)(4)(ii)(a), S2's earnings and profits for Year 2 will reflect S2's increase in its basis in T stock for the taxable year. Since S2 has no other earnings and profits for the taxable year, S2 has $40 of earnings and profits for the year. As provided in §1.1502-32(b)(1)(i), P must make a positive adjustment to its basis in the stock of S2 for its allocable part of the undistributed earnings and profits of S2 for the taxable year. Thus, P must make a $40 net positive adjustment to its basis in S2 stock, increasing its basis to $850.

(e) *Special rule for use of dual consolidated loss to offset tainted income.*—(1) *In general.*—The dual consolidated loss of any dual resident corporation that ceases to be a dual resident corporation shall not be used to offset income of such corporation to the extent that such income is tainted income, as defined in paragraph (e)(2) of this section.

Reg. §1.1503-2(e)(1)

(2) *Tainted income defined.*—Tainted income is any income derived from tainted assets, as defined in paragraph (e)(3) of this section, beginning on the date such assets are acquired by the dual resident corporation. In the absence of evidence establishing the actual amount of income that is attributable to the tainted assets, the portion of a corporation's income in a particular taxable year that is treated as tainted income shall be an amount equal to the corporation's taxable income for the year multiplied by a fraction, the numerator of which is the fair market value of the tainted asset at the end of the taxable year and the denominator of which is the fair market value of the total assets owned by the corporation at the end of the taxable year. Documentation submitted to establish the actual amount of income that is attributable to the tainted assets must be attached to the consolidated group's or unaffiliated dual resident corporation's timely filed tax return for the taxable year in which the income is recognized.

(3) *Tainted assets defined.*—Tainted assets are any assets acquired by a dual resident corporation in a nonrecognition transaction, as defined in section 7701(a)(45), or any assets otherwise transferred to the corporation as a contribution to capital, at any time during the three taxable years immediately preceding the taxable year in which the corporation ceases to be a dual resident corporation or at any time thereafter. Tainted assets shall not include assets that were acquired by such dual resident corporation on or before December 31, 1986.

(4) *Exceptions.*—Income derived from assets acquired by a dual resident corporation shall not be subject to the limitation described in paragraph (e)(1) of this section, if—

(i) For the taxable year in which the assets were acquired, the corporation did not have a dual consolidated loss (or a carry forward of a dual consolidated loss to such year); or

(ii) The assets were acquired as replacement property in the ordinary course of business.

(f) *Computation of foreign tax credit limitations.*—If a dual resident corporation or separate unit is subject to paragraph (d)(2) of this section, the consolidated group or unaffiliated domestic owner shall compute its foreign tax credit limitation by applying the limitations of paragraph (d)(2). Thus, the dual consolidated loss is not taken into account until the year in which it is absorbed.

(g) *Exception.*—(1) *Elective agreement in place between the United States and a foreign country.*—Paragraph (b) of this section shall not apply to a dual consolidated loss to the extent the dual resident corporation, or domestic owner of a separate unit, elects to deduct the loss in the United States pursuant to an agreement entered into between the United States and a foreign country that puts into place an elective procedure through which losses offset income in only one country.

(2) *Elective relief provision.*—(i) [Reserved].—For further guidance, see § 1.1503-2T(g)(2)(i).

(ii) *Consistency rule.*—(A) If any loss, expense, or deduction taken into account in computing the dual consolidated loss of a dual resident corporation or separate unit is used under the laws of a foreign country to offset the income of another person, then the following other dual consolidated losses (if any) shall be treated as also having been used to offset income of another person under the laws of such foreign country, but only if the income tax laws of the foreign country permit any loss, expense, or deduction taken into account in computing the other dual consolidated loss to be used to offset the income of another person in the same taxable year:

(1) Any dual consolidated loss of a dual resident corporation that is a member of the same consolidated group of which the first dual resident corporation or domestic owner is a member, if any loss, expense, or deduction taken into account in computing such dual consolidated loss is recognized under the income tax laws of such country in the same taxable year; and

(2) Any dual consolidated loss of a separate unit that is owned by the same domestic owner that owns the first separate unit, or that is owned by any member of the same consolidated group of which the first dual resident corporation or domestic owner is a member, if any loss, expense, or deduction taken into account in computing such dual consolidated loss is recognized under the income tax laws of such country in the same taxable year.

(B) The following examples illustrate the application of this paragraph (g)(2)(ii).

Example 1. P, a domestic corporation, owns A and B, which are domestic corporations, and C, a Country X corporation. A is subject to the income tax laws of Country X on a residence basis and, thus, is a dual resident corporation. B conducts business in Country X through a branch, which is a separate unit under paragraph (c)(3) of this section. The income tax laws of Country X permit branches of foreign corporations to elect to file consolidated returns with Country X affiliates. In Year 1, A incurs a dual consolidated loss, which is used to offset the income of C under the Country X form of consolidation. The branch of B also incurs a net operating loss. However, B elects not to use the loss on a Country X consolidated return to offset the income of foreign affiliates. The use of A's loss to offset the income of C in Country X will cause the separate unit of B to be treated as if it too had used its dual consolidated loss to offset the income of an affiliate in Country X. Therefore, an election and agreement under this paragraph (g)(2) cannot be made with respect to the separate unit's dual consolidated loss.

Example 2. The facts are the same as in *Example 1,* except that the income tax laws of Country X do not permit branches of foreign corporations to file consolidated income tax returns with Country X affiliates. Therefore, an election and agreement described in this paragraph (g)(2) may be made for the dual consolidated loss incurred by the separate unit of B.

(iii) *Triggering events requiring the recapture of dual consolidated losses.*—(A) The consolidated group, unaffiliated dual resident corporation, or unaffiliated domestic owner must agree that, if there is a triggering event described in this paragraph (g)(2)(iii), and no exception applies under paragraph (g)(2)(iv) of this section, the consolidated group, unaffiliated dual resident corporation, or unaffiliated domestic owner will recapture and report as income the amount of the dual consolidated loss provided in paragraph (g)(2)(vii) of this section on its tax return for the taxable year in which the triggering event occurs (or, when the triggering event is a use of the loss for foreign purposes, the taxable year that includes the last day of the foreign tax year during which such use occurs). In addition, the consolidated group, unaffiliated dual resident corporation, or unaffiliated domestic owner must pay any applicable interest charge required by paragraph (g)(2)(vii) of this section. For purposes of this section, any of the following events shall constitute a triggering event:

(1) In any taxable year up to and including the 15th taxable year following the year in which the dual consolidated loss that is the subject of the agreement filed under this paragraph (g)(2) was incurred, any portion of the losses, expenses, or deductions taken into account in computing the dual consolidated loss is used by any means to offset the income of any other person under the income tax laws of a foreign country;

(2) An affiliated dual resident corporation or affiliated domestic owner ceases to be a member of the consolidated group that filed the election. For purposes of this paragraph (g)(2)(iii)(A)(2), a dual resident corporation or domestic owner shall be considered to cease to be a member of the consolidated group if it is no longer a member of the group within the meaning of §1.1502-1(b), or if the group ceases to exist because the common parent is no longer in existence or is no longer a common parent or the group no longer files on the basis of a consolidated return. Such disaffiliation, however, shall not constitute a triggering event if the taxpayer demonstrates, to the satisfaction of the Commissioner, that the dual resident corporation's or separate unit's losses, expenses, or deductions cannot be used to offset income of another person under the laws of a foreign country at any time after the affiliated dual resident corporation or affiliated domestic owner ceases to be a member of the consolidated group;

(3) An unaffiliated dual resident corporation or unaffiliated domestic owner becomes a member of a consolidated group. Such affiliation of the dual resident corporation or domestic owner, however, shall not constitute a triggering event if the taxpayer demonstrates, to the satisfaction of the Commissioner, that the losses, expenses, or deductions of the dual resident corporation or separate unit cannot be used to offset the income of another person under the laws of a foreign country at any time after the dual resident corporation or domestic owner becomes a member of the consolidated group.

(4) A dual resident corporation transfers assets in a transaction that results, under the laws of a foreign country, in a carryover of its losses, expenses, or deductions. For purposes of this paragraph (g)(2)(iii)(A)(4), a transfer, either in a single transaction or a series of transactions within a twelve-month period, of 50% or more of the dual resident corporation's assets (measured by the fair market value of the assets at the time of such transfer (or for multiple transactions, at the time of the first transfer)) shall be deemed a triggering event, unless the taxpayer demonstrates, to the satisfaction of the Commissioner, that the transfer of assets did not result in a carryover under foreign law of the dual resident corporation's losses, expenses, or deductions to the transferee of the assets;

(5) A domestic owner of a separate unit transfers assets of the separate unit in a transaction that results, under the laws of a foreign country, in a carryover of the separate unit's losses, expenses, or deductions. For purposes of this paragraph (g)(2)(iii)(A)(5), a transfer, either in a single transaction or a series of transactions over a twelve-month period, of 50% or more of the separate unit's assets (measured by the fair market value of the assets at the time of the transfer (or for multiple transfers, at the time of the first transfer)), shall be deemed a triggering event, unless the taxpayer demonstrates, to the satisfaction of

Reg. §1.1503-2(g)(2)(iii)(A)(5)

the Commissioner, that the transfer of assets did not result in a carryover under foreign law of the separate unit's losses, expenses, or deductions to the transferee of the assets;

(6) An unaffiliated dual resident corporation or unaffiliated domestic owner becomes a foreign corporation by means of a transaction (*e.g.,* a reorganization) that, for foreign tax purposes, is not treated as involving a transfer of assets (and carryover of losses) to a new entity. Such a transaction, however, shall not constitute a triggering event if the taxpayer demonstrates, to the satisfaction of the Commissioner, that the dual resident corporation's or separate unit's losses, expenses, or deductions cannot be used to offset income of another person under the laws of the foreign country at any time after the unaffiliated dual resident corporation or unaffiliated domestic owner becomes a foreign corporation.

(7) A domestic owner of a separate unit, either in a single transaction or a series of transactions within a twelve-month period, sells, or otherwise disposes of, 50% or more of the interest in the separate unit (measured by voting power or value) owned by the domestic owner on the last day of the taxable year in which the dual consolidated loss was incurred. For purposes of this paragraph (g)(2)(iii)(A)(7), the domestic owner shall be deemed to have disposed of its entire interest in a hybrid entity separate unit if such hybrid entity becomes classified as a foreign corporation for U.S. tax purposes. The disposition of 50% or more of the interest in a separate unit, however, shall not constitute a triggering event if the taxpayer demonstrates, to the satisfaction of the Commissioner, that the losses, expenses, or deductions of the separate unit cannot be used to offset income of another person under the laws of the foreign country at any time after the disposition of the interest in the separate unit; or

(8) The consolidated group, unaffiliated dual resident corporation, or unaffiliated domestic owner fails to file a certification required under paragraph (g)(2)(vi)(B) of this section.

(B) A taxpayer wishing to rebut the presumption of a triggering event described in paragraphs (g)(2)(iii)(A) (2) through (7) of this section, by demonstrating that the losses, expenses, or deductions of the dual resident corporation or separate unit cannot be carried over or otherwise used under the laws of the foreign country, must attach documents demonstrating such facts to its timely filed U.S. income tax return for the year in which the presumed triggering event occurs.

(C) The following example illustrates this paragraph (g)(2)(iii).

Example. DRC, a domestic corporation, is a member of CG, a consolidated group. DRC is a resident of Country Y for Country Y income tax purposes. Therefore, DRC is a dual resident corporation. In Year 1, DRC incurs a dual consolidated loss of $100. CG files an agreement described in paragraph (g)(2) of this section and, thus, the $100 dual consolidated loss is included in the computation of CG's consolidated taxable income. In Year 6, all of the stock of DRC is sold to P, a domestic corporation that is a member of NG, another consolidated group. The sale of DRC to P is a triggering event under paragraph (g)(2)(iii)(A) of this section, requiring the recapture of the dual consolidated loss. However, the laws of Country Y provide for a five-year carryover period for losses. At the time of DRC's disaffiliation from CG, the losses, expenses and deductions that were included in the computation of the dual consolidated loss had expired for Country Y purposes. Therefore, upon adequate documentation that the losses, expenses, or deductions have expired for Country Y purposes, CG can rebut the presumption that a triggering event has occurred.

(iv) *Exceptions.*—(A) *Acquisition by a member of the consolidated group.*—The following events shall not constitute triggering events, requiring the recapture of the dual consolidated loss under paragraph (g)(2)(vii) of this section:

(1) An affiliated dual resident corporation or affiliated domestic owner ceases to be a member of a consolidated group solely by reason of a transaction in which a member of the same consolidated group succeeds to the tax attributes of the dual resident corporation or domestic owner under the provisions of section 381;

(2) Assets of an affiliated dual resident corporation or assets of a separate unit of an affiliated domestic owner are acquired by a member of its consolidated group in any other transaction; or

(3) An affiliated domestic owner of a separate unit transfers its interest in the separate unit to another member of its consolidated group.

(B) *Acquisition by an unaffiliated domestic corporation or a new consolidated group.*—*(1)* If all the requirements of paragraph (g)(2)(iv)(B)(3) of this section are met, the following events shall not constitute triggering events requiring the recapture of the dual consolidated loss under paragraph (g)(2)(vii) of this section:

(i) An affiliated dual resident corporation or affiliated domestic owner becomes an unaffiliated domestic corporation or a

member of a new consolidated group (other than in a transaction described in paragraph (g)(2)(iv)(B)(*2*)(*ii*) of this section);

(*ii*) Assets of a dual resident corporation or a separate unit are acquired by an unaffiliated domestic corporation or a member of a new consolidated group; or

(*iii*) A domestic owner of a separate unit transfers its interest in the separate unit to an unaffiliated domestic corporation or to a member of a new consolidated group.

(*2*) If the requirements of paragraph (g)(2)(iv)(B)(*3*)(*iii*) of this section are met, the following events shall not constitute triggering events requiring the recapture of the dual consolidated loss under paragraph (g)(2)(vii) of this section—

(*i*) An unaffiliated dual resident corporation or unaffiliated domestic owner becomes a member of a consolidated group;

(*ii*) A consolidated group that filed an agreement under this paragraph (g)(2) ceases to exist as a result of a transaction described in § 1.1502-13(j)(5)(i) (other than a transaction in which any member of the terminating group, or the successor-in-interest of such member, is not a member of the surviving group immediately after the terminating group ceases to exist).

(*3*) If the following requirements (as applicable) are satisfied, the events listed in paragraphs (g)(2)(iv)(B)(*1*) and (*2*) of this section shall not constitute triggering events requiring recapture under paragraph (g)(2)(vii) of this section.

(*i*) The consolidated group, unaffiliated dual resident corporation, or unaffiliated domestic owner that filed the agreement under this paragraph (g)(2) and the unaffiliated domestic corporation or new consolidated group must enter into a closing agreement with the Internal Revenue Service providing that the consolidated group, unaffiliated dual resident corporation, or unaffiliated domestic owner and the unaffiliated domestic corporation or new consolidated group will be jointly and severally liable for the total amount of the recapture of dual consolidated loss and interest charge required in paragraph (g)(2)(vii) of this section, if there is a triggering event described in paragraph (g)(2)(iii) of this section;

(*ii*) The unaffiliated domestic corporation or new consolidated group must agree to treat any potential recapture amount under paragraph (g)(2)(vii) of this section as unrealized built-in gain for purposes of section 384(a), subject to any applicable exceptions thereunder;

(*iii*) [Reserved]. For further guidance, see § 1.1503-2T(g)(2)(iv)(B)(*3*)(*iii*).

(C) *Subsequent triggering events.*—Any triggering event described in paragraph (g)(2)(iii) of this section that occurs subsequent to one of the transactions described in paragraph (g)(2)(iv)(A) or (B) of this section and does not fall within the exceptions provided in paragraph (g)(2)(iv)(A) or (B) of this section shall require recapture under paragraph (g)(2)(vii) of this section.

(D) Example. The following example illustrates the application of paragraph (g)(2)(iv)(B)(*2*)(*ii*) of this section:

Example. (i) Facts. C is the common parent of a consolidated group (the C Group) that includes DRC, a domestic corporation. DRC is a dual resident corporation and incurs a dual consolidated loss in its taxable year ending December 31, Year 1. The C Group elects to be bound by the provisions of this paragraph (g)(2) with respect to the Year 1 dual consolidated loss. No member of the C Group incurs a dual consolidated loss in Year 2. On December 31, Year 2, stock of C is acquired by D in a transaction described in § 1.1502-13(j)(5)(i). As a result of the acquisition, all the C Group members, including DRC, become members of a consolidated group of which D is the common parent (the D Group).

(ii) Acquisition not a triggering event. Under paragraph (g)(2)(iv)(B)(*2*)(*ii*) of this section, the acquisition by D of the C Group is not an event requiring the recapture of the Year 1 dual consolidated loss of DRC, or the payment of an interest charge, as described in paragraph (g)(2)(vii) of this section, provided that the D Group files the new (g)(2)(i) agreement described in paragraph (g)(2)(iv)(B)(*3*)(*iii*) of this section.

(iii) Subsequent event. A triggering event occurs on December 31, Year 3, that requires recapture by the D Group of the dual consolidated loss that DRC incurred in Year 1, as well as the payment of an interest charge, as provided in paragraph (g)(2)(vii) of this section. Each member of the D Group, including DRC and the other former members of the C Group, is severally liable for the additional tax (and the interest charge) due upon the recapture of the dual consolidated loss of DRC.

(v) *Ordering rules for determining the foreign use of losses.*—If the laws of a foreign country provide for the use of losses of a dual resident corporation to offset the income of another person but do not provide applicable rules for determining the order in which such losses are used to offset the income of another person in a taxable year, then for purposes of this section, the following rules shall govern:

(A) If under the laws of the foreign country the dual resident corporation has losses from different taxable years, the dual resident corporation shall be deemed to use first the losses from the earliest taxable year from which a loss may be carried forward or back for foreign law purposes.

(B) Any net loss, or income, that the dual resident corporation has in a taxable year shall first be used to offset net income, or loss, recognized by affiliates of the dual resident corporation in the same taxable year before any carryover of the dual resident corporation's losses is considered to be used to offset any income from the taxable year.

(C) Where different losses, expenses, or deductions (*e.g.,* capital losses and ordinary losses) of a dual resident corporation incurred in the same taxable year are available to offset the income of another person, the different losses shall be deemed to offset such income on a pro rata basis.

Example. DRC, a domestic corporation, is taxed as a resident under the tax laws of Country Y. Therefore, DRC is a dual resident corporation. FA is a Country Y affiliate of DRC. Country Y's tax laws permit affiliated corporations to file a form of consolidated return. In Year 1, DRC incurs a capital loss of $80 which, for Country Y purposes, offsets completely $30 of capital gain recognized by FA. Neither corporation has any other taxable income or loss for the year. In Year 1 (and in other years), DRC recognizes the same amount of income for U.S. purposes as it does for Country Y purposes. Under paragraph (d)(1)(i) of this section, however, DRC's $80 capital loss is not a dual consolidated loss. In Year 2, DRC incurs a net operating loss of $100, while FA incurs a net operating loss of $50. DRC's $100 loss is a dual consolidated loss. Since the dual consolidated loss is not used to offset the income of another person under Country Y law, DRC is permitted to file an agreement described in this paragraph (g)(2). In Year 3, DRC has a net operating loss of $10 and FA has capital gains of $60. For Country Y purposes, DRC's $10 net operating loss is used to offset $10 of FA's $60 capital gain. DRC's $10 loss is a dual consolidated loss. Because the loss is used to offset FA's income, DRC will not be able to file an agreement under this paragraph (g)(2) with respect to the loss. Country Y permits FA's remaining $50 of Year 3 income to be offset by carryover losses. However, Country Y has no applicable rules for determining which carryover losses from Years 1 and 2 are used to offset such income. Under the ordering rules of paragraph (g)(2)(v)(A) of this section, none of DRC's $100 Year 2 loss will be deemed to offset FA's remaining $50 of Year 3 income. Instead, the $50 of capital loss carryover from Year 1 will be considered to offset the income.

(vi) *Reporting requirements.*—(A) *In general.*—The consolidated group, unaffiliated dual resident corporation, or unaffiliated domestic owner must answer the applicable questions regarding dual consolidated losses on its U.S. income tax return filed for the year in which the dual consolidated loss is incurred and for each of the following fifteen taxable years.

(B) [Reserved]. For further guidance, see § 1.1503-2T(g)(2)(vi)(B).

(C) *Exception.*—A consolidated group or unaffiliated domestic owner is not required to file annual certifications under paragraph (g)(2)(vi)(B) of this section with respect to a dual consolidated loss of any separate unit other than a hybrid entity separate unit.

(vii) *Recapture of loss and interest charge.*—(A) *Presumptive rule.*—*(1) Amount of recapture.*—Except as otherwise provided in this paragraph (g)(2)(vii), upon the occurrence of a triggering event described in paragraph (g)(2)(iii) of this section, the taxpayer shall recapture and report as gross income the total amount of the dual consolidated loss to which the triggering event applies on its income tax return for the taxable year in which the triggering event occurs (or, when the triggering event is a use of the loss for foreign tax purposes, the taxable year that includes the last day of the foreign tax year during which such use occurs).

(2) Interest charge.—In connection with the recapture, the taxpayer shall pay an interest charge. Except as otherwise provided in this paragraph (g)(2)(vii), such interest shall be determined under the rules of section 6601(a) as if the additional tax owed as a result of the recapture had accrued and been due and owing for the taxable year in which the losses, expenses, or deductions taken into account in computing the dual consolidated loss gave rise to a tax benefit for U.S. income tax purposes. For purposes of this paragraph (g)(2)(vii)(A)(*2*), a tax benefit shall be considered to have arisen in a taxable year in which such losses, expenses or deductions reduced U.S. taxable income.

(B) *Rebuttal of presumptive rule.*—*(1) Amount of recapture.*—The amount of dual consolidated loss that must be recaptured under this paragraph (g)(2)(vii) may be reduced if the taxpayer demonstrates, to the satisfaction of the Commissioner, the offset permitted by this paragraph (g)(2)(vii)(B). The reduction in the amount of recapture is the amount by which the dual consolidated loss would have offset other taxable income reported on a timely filed U.S. income tax return for any taxable year up to and including the year of the triggering event if such loss had been subject to the restrictions of paragraph (b) of this section (and therefore had been subject to the separate return limitation year restrictions of §1.1502-21A(c) or 1.1502-21(c) (as appropriate)) commencing in the taxable year in which the loss was incurred. A taxpayer utilizing this rebuttal rule must attach to its timely filed U.S. income tax return a separate accounting showing that the income for each year that offsets the dual resident corporation's or separate unit's recapture amount is attributable only to the dual resident corporation or separate unit.

(2) Interest charge.—The interest charge imposed under this paragraph (g)(2)(vii) may be appropriately reduced if the taxpayer demonstrates, to the satisfaction of the Commissioner, that the net interest owed would have been less than that provided in paragraph (g)(2)(vii)(A)(2) of this section if the taxpayer had filed an amended return for the year in which the loss was incurred, and for any other affected years up to and including the year of recapture, treating the dual consolidated loss as a loss subject to the restrictions of paragraph (b) of this section (and therefore subject to the separate return limitation year restrictions of §1.1502-21A(c) or 1.1502-21(c) (as appropriate)). A taxpayer utilizing this rebuttal rule must attach to its timely filed U.S. income tax return a computation demonstrating the reduction in the net interest owed as a result of treating the dual consolidated loss as a loss subject to the restrictions of paragraph (b) of this section.

(C) *Computation of taxable income in year of recapture.*—*(1) Presumptive rule.*—Except as otherwise provided in paragraph (g)(2)(vii)(C)(2) of this section, for purposes of computing the taxable income for the year of recapture, no current, carryover or carryback losses of the dual resident corporation or separate unit, of other members of the consolidated group, or of the domestic owner that are not attributable to the separate unit, may offset and absorb the recapture amount.

(2) Rebuttal of presumptive rule.—The recapture amount included in gross income may be offset and absorbed by that portion of the taxpayer's (consolidated or separate) net operating loss carryover that is attributable to the dual consolidated loss being recaptured, if the taxpayer demonstrates, to the satisfaction of the Commissioner, the amount of such portion of the carryover. A taxpayer utilizing this rebuttal rule must attach to its timely filed U.S. income tax return a computation demonstrating the amount of net operating loss carryover that, under this paragraph (g)(2)(vii)(C)(2), may absorb the recapture amount included in gross income.

(D) *Character and source of recapture income.*—The amount recaptured under this paragraph (g)(2)(vii) shall be treated as ordinary income in the year of recapture. The amount recaptured shall be treated as income having the same source and falling within the same separate category for purposes of section 904 as the dual consolidated loss being recaptured.

(E) *Reconstituted net operating loss.*—Commencing in the taxable year immediately following the year in which the dual consolidated loss is recaptured, the dual resident corporation or separate unit shall be treated as having a net operating loss in an amount equal to the amount actually recaptured under paragraph (g)(2)(vii)(A) or (B) of this section. This reconstituted net operating loss shall be subject to the restrictions of paragraph (b) of this section (and therefore, the separate return limitation year restrictions of §§1.1502-21A(c) or 1.1502-21T(c) (as appropriate)). The net operating loss shall be available only for carryover, under section 172(b), to taxable years following the taxable year of recapture. For purposes of determining the remaining carryover period, the loss shall be treated as if it had been recognized in the taxable year in which the dual consolidated loss that is the basis of the recapture amount was incurred.

(F) *Consequences of failing to comply with recapture provisions.*—*(1) In general.*—If the taxpayer fails to comply with the recapture provisions of this paragraph (g)(2)(vii) upon the occurrence of a triggering event, then the dual resident corporation or separate unit that incurred the dual consolidated loss (or a successor-in-interest) shall not be eligible for the relief provided in paragraph (g)(2) of this section with respect to any dual consolidated losses incurred in the five taxable years beginning with the taxable year in which recapture is required.

(2) Exceptions.—In the case of a triggering event other than a use of the losses, expenses, or deductions taken into account in computing the dual consolidated loss to offset income of another person under the income tax laws of a foreign country, this rule shall not apply in the following circumstances:

(i) The failure to recapture is due to reasonable cause; or

(ii) A taxpayer seeking to rebut the presumption of a triggering event satisfies the filing requirements of paragraph (g)(2)(iii)(B) of this section.

Reg. §1.1503-2(g)(2)(vii)(F)(2)(ii)

(G) *Examples.*—The following examples illustrate this paragraph (g)(2)(vii).

Example 1. P, a domestic corporation, files a consolidated return with DRC, a dual resident corporation. In Year 1, DRC incurs a dual consolidated loss of $100 and P earns $100. P files an agreement under this paragraph (g)(2). Therefore, the consolidated group is permitted to offset P's $100 of income with DRC's $100 loss. In Year 2, DRC earns $30, which is completely offset by a $30 net operating loss incurred by P. In Year 3, DRC earns income of $25 while P recognizes no income or loss. In addition, there is a triggering event in Year 3. Therefore, under the presumptive rule of paragraph (g)(2)(vii)(A) of this section, DRC must recapture $100. However, the $100 recapture amount may be reduced by $25 (the amount by which the dual consolidated loss would have offset other taxable income if it had been subject to the separate return limitation year restrictions from Year 1) upon adequate documentation of such offset under paragraph (g)(2)(vii)(B)(*1*) of this section. Commencing in Year 4, the $100 (or $75) recapture amount is treated as a loss incurred by DRC in a separate return limitation year, subject to the restrictions of § 1.1502-21A(c) or 1.1502-21(c), as appropriate. The carryover period of the loss, for purposes of section 172(b), will start from Year 1, when the dual consolidated loss was incurred.

Example 2. The facts are the same as in *Example 1,* except that in Year 2, DRC earns $75 and P earns $50. In Year 3, DRC earns $25 while P earns $30. A triggering event occurs in Year 3. The $100 presumptive amount of recapture can be reduced to zero by the $75 and $25 earned by DRC in Years 2 and 3, respectively, upon adequate documentation of such offset under paragraph (g)(2)(vii)(B)(*1*) of this section. Nevertheless, an interest charge will be owed. Under the presumptive rule of paragraph (g)(2)(vii)(A)(*2*) of this section, interest will be charged on the additional tax owed on the $100 of recapture income as if the tax had accrued in Year 1 (the year in which the dual consolidated loss reduced the income of P). However, the net interest will be reduced to the amount that would have been owed if the consolidated group had filed amended returns, treating the dual consolidated loss as a loss subject to the separate return limitation year restrictions of § 1.1502-21A(c) or 1.1502-21(c), as appropriate, upon adequate documentation of such reduction of interest under paragraph (g)(2)(vii)(B)(*2*) of this section.

Example 3. P, a domestic corporation, owns DRC, a domestic corporation that is subject to the income tax laws of Country Z on a residence basis. DRC owns FE, a Country Z corporation. In Year 1, DRC incurs a net operating loss for U.S. tax purposes. Under the tax laws of Country Z, the loss is not recognized until Year 3. The Year 1 net operating loss is a dual consolidated loss under paragraph (c)(5) of this section. The consolidated group elects relief under paragraph (g)(2) of this section by filing the appropriate agreement and uses the dual consolidated loss on its U.S. income tax return. In Year 3, the dual consolidated loss is used under the laws of Country Z to offset the income of FE, which is a triggering event under paragraph (g)(2)(iii) of this section. However, the consolidated group does not recapture the dual consolidated loss. The consolidated group's failure to comply with the recapture provisions of this paragraph (g)(2)(vii) prevents DRC from being eligible for the relief provided under paragraph (g)(2) of this section for any dual consolidated losses incurred in Years 3 through 7, inclusive.

(h) *Effective date.*—(1) *In general.*—These regulations are effective for taxable years beginning on or after October 1, 1992. Section 1.1503-2A is effective for taxable years beginning after December 31, 1986, and before October 1, 1992. Paragraph (g)(2)(iv)(B)(*2*) of this section shall apply with respect to transactions otherwise constituting triggering events occurring on or after January 1, 2002.

(2) *Taxpayers that have filed for relief under § 1.1503-2A.*—(i) *In general.*—Except as provided in paragraph (h)(ii)(b) of this section, taxpayers that have filed agreements described in § 1.1503-2A(c)(3) or certifications described in § 1.1503-2A(d)(3) shall continue to be subject to the provisions of such agreements or certifications, including the amended return or recapture requirements applicable in the event of a triggering event, for the remaining term of such agreements or certifications.

(ii) *Special transition rule.*—A taxpayer that has filed an agreement described in § 1.1503-2A(c)(3) or a certification described in § 1.1503-2A(d)(3) and that is in compliance with the provisions of § 1.1503-2A may elect to replace such agreement or certification with an agreement described in paragraph (g)(2)(i) of this section. However, a taxpayer making this election must replace all agreements and certifications filed under § 1.1503-2A. If the taxpayer is a consolidated group, the election must be made with respect to all dual resident corporations or separate units within the group. Likewise, if the taxpayer is an unaffiliated domestic owner, the election must be made with respect to all separate units of the domestic owner. The taxpayer must file the replacement agreement with its timely filed income tax return for its first taxable year commencing on or after October 1, 1992, stating that such agreement is a replacement for the agreement filed under § 1.1503-2A(c)(3) or the certification filed under § 1.1503-2A(d)(3) and identifying the taxable year for which the original agreement or certification was filed. A single agreement described in paragraph (g)(2)(i) of this section may be filed to replace more than one agreement or certification filed under § 1.1503-2A; however, each dual consolidated loss must be separately identified. A taxpayer may also elect to apply § 1.1503-2 for all open years, with respect to agreements filed under § 1.1503-2A(c)(3) or certifications filed under § 1.1503-2A(d)(3), in cases where the agreement or certification is no longer in effect and the taxpayer has complied with the provisions of § 1.1503-2A. For example, a taxpayer may have had a triggering event under § 1.1503-2A that is not a triggering event under § 1.1503-2. If the taxpayer fully complied with the requirements of the agreement entered into under § 1.1503-2A(c)(3) and filed amended U.S. income tax returns within the time required under § 1.1503-2A(c)(3), the taxpayer may file amended U.S. income tax returns consistent with the position that the earlier triggering event is no longer a triggering event.

(3) *Taxpayers that are in compliance with § 1.1503-2A but have not filed for relief thereunder.*—A taxpayer that is in compliance with the provisions of § 1.1503-2A but has not filed an agreement described in § 1.1503-2A(c)(3) or a certification described in § 1.1503-2A(d)(3) may elect to have the provisions of § 1.1503-2 apply for any open year. In particular, a taxpayer may elect to apply the provisions of § 1.1503-2 in a case where the dual consolidated loss has been subjected to the separate return limitation year restrictions of § 1.1502-21A(c) or 1.1502-21(c) (as appropriate) but the losses, expenses, or deductions taken into account in computing the dual consolidated loss have not been used to offset the income of another person for foreign tax purposes. However, if a taxpayer is a consolidated group, the election must be made with respect to all dual resident corporations or separate units within the group. Likewise, if the taxpayer is an unaffiliated domestic owner, the election must be made with respect to all separate units of the domestic owner. [Reg. § 1.1503-2.]

☐ [*T.D.* 8434, 9-4-92. *Amended by T.D.* 8597, 7-12-95; *T.D.* 8677, 6-26-96; *T.D.* 8823, 6-25-99; *T.D.* 9084, 7-29-2003 *and T.D.* 9100, 12-18-2003.]

§ 1.1503-2T. Dual consolidated loss (temporary).—(a) through (g)(1) [Reserved]. For further guidance, see § 1.1503-2(a) through (g)(1).

(2) *Elective relief provision.*—(i) *In general.*—Paragraph (b) of this section shall not apply to a dual consolidated loss if the consolidated group, unaffiliated dual resident corporation, or unaffiliated domestic owner elects to be bound by the provisions of § 1.1503-2(g)(2) and this paragraph (g)(2). In order to elect relief under § 1.1503-2(g)(2) and this paragraph (g)(2), the consolidated group, unaffiliated dual resident corporation, or unaffiliated domestic owner must attach to its timely filed U.S. income tax return for the taxable year in which the dual consolidated loss is incurred an agreement described in paragraph (g)(2)(i)(A) of this section. The agreement must be signed under penalties of perjury by the person who signs the return. For taxable years beginning after December 31, 2002, the agreement attached to the income tax return of the consolidated group, unaffiliated dual resident corporation or unaffiliated domestic owner pursuant to the preceding sentence may be an unsigned copy. If an unsigned copy is attached to the return, the consolidated group, unaffiliated dual resident corporation, or unaffiliated domestic owner must retain the original in its records in the manner specified by § 1.6001-1(e). The agreement must include the following items, in paragraphs labeled to correspond with the items set forth in paragraphs (g)(2)(i)(A) through (F) of this section:

(A) A statement that the document submitted is an election and an agreement under the provisions of § 1.1503-2(g)(2) of the Income Tax Regulations.

(B) The name, address, identifying number, and place and date of incorporation of the dual resident corporation, and the country or countries that tax the dual resident corporation on its worldwide income or on a residence basis, or, in the case of a separate unit, identification of the separate unit, including the name under which it conducts business, its principal activity, and the country in which its principal place of business is located.

(C) An agreement by the consolidated group, unaffiliated dual resident corporation, or unaffiliated domestic owner to comply with all of the provisions of paragraphs (g)(2)(iii) through (vii) of § 1.1503-2 and this section.

(D) A statement of the amount of the dual consolidated loss covered by the agreement.

(E) A certification that no portion of the dual resident corporation's or separate unit's losses, expenses, or deductions taken into account in computing the dual consolidated loss has been, or will be, used to offset the income of any other person under the income tax laws of a foreign country.

(F) A certification that arrangements have been made to ensure that no portion of the dual consolidated loss will be used to offset the income of another person under the laws of a foreign country and that the consolidated group, unaffiliated dual resident corporation, or unaffiliated domestic owner will be informed of any such foreign use of any portion of the dual consolidated loss.

(g)(2)(ii) through (iv)(B)(3)(ii) [Reserved] For further guidance, see § 1.1503-2(g)(2)(ii) through (iv)(B)(3)(ii).

(g)(2)(iv)(B)(3)(iii) The unaffiliated domestic corporation or new consolidated group must file, with its timely filed income tax return for the taxable year in which the event described in § 1.1503-2(g)(2)(iv)(B)(1) or (2) occurs, an agreement described in paragraph (g)(2)(i) of this section (new (g)(2)(i) agreement), whereby it assumes the same obligations with respect to the dual consolidated loss as the corporation or consolidated group that filed the original (g)(2)(i) agreement with respect to that loss. The new (g)(2)(i) agreement must be signed under penalties of perjury by the person who signs the return and must include a reference to § 1.1503-2(g)(2)(iv)(B)(3)(iii) or this paragraph (g)(2)(iv)(B)(3)(iii). For taxable years beginning after December 31, 2002, the agreement attached to the return pursuant to the preceding sentence may be an unsigned copy. If an unsigned copy is attached to the return, the corporation or consolidated group must retain the original in its records in the manner specified by § 1.6001-1(e).

(g)(2)(iv)(C) through (vi)(A) [Reserved]. For further guidance, see § 1.1503-2(g)(2)(iv)(C) through (vi)(A).

(B) *Annual certification.*—Except as provided in § 1.1503-2(g)(2)(vi)(C), until and unless Form 1120 or the Schedules thereto contain questions pertaining to dual consolidated losses, the consolidated group, unaffiliated dual resident corporation, or unaffiliated domestic owner must file with its income tax return for each of the 15 taxable years following the taxable year in which the dual consolidated loss is incurred a certification that the losses, expenses, or deductions that make up the dual consolidated loss have not been used to offset the income of another person under the tax laws of a foreign country. For taxable years beginning before January 1, 2003, the annual certification must be signed under penalties of perjury by a person authorized to sign the agreement described in paragraph (g)(2)(i) of this section. For taxable years beginning after December 31, 2002, the certification is verified by signing the return with which the certification is filed. The certification for a taxable year must identify the dual consolidated loss to which it pertains by setting forth the taxpayer's year in which the loss was incurred and the amount of such loss. In addition, the certification must warrant that arrangements have been made to ensure that the loss will not be used to offset the income of another person under the laws of a foreign country and that the taxpayer will be informed of any such foreign use of any portion of the loss. If dual consolidated losses of more than one taxable year are subject to the rules of this paragraph (g)(2)(vi)(B), the certifications for those years may be combined in a single document but each dual consolidated loss must be separately identified.

(g)(2)(vii) [(g)(2)(vi)(C)] through (h) [Reserved]. For further guidance, see § 1.1503-2(g)(2)(vi)[(C)] through (h). [Temporary Reg. § 1.1503-2T.]

☐ [T.D. 9100, 12-18-2003.]

Proposed Regulation

§ 1.1503(d)-1. Definitions and special rules for filings under section 1503(d).—(a) *In general.*—This section and §§ 1.1503(d)-2 through 1.1503(d)-6 provide general rules concerning the determination and use of dual consolidated losses pursuant to section 1503(d). This section provides definitions that apply for purposes of this section and §§ 1.1503(d)-2 through 1.1503(d)-6. This section also provides a reasonable cause exception and a signature requirement for filings under this section and §§ 1.1503(d)-2 through 1.1503(d)-4.

(b) *Definitions.*—The following definitions apply for purposes of this section and §§ 1.1503(d)-2 through 1.1503(d)-6:

(1) *Domestic corporation.*—The term *domestic corporation* means an entity classified as a domestic corporation under section 7701(a)(3) and (4) or otherwise treated as a domestic corporation by the Internal Revenue Code, including, but not limited to, sections 269B, 953(d), and 1504(d). However, solely for purposes of Section 1503(d), the term domestic corporation does not include an S corporation, as defined in section 1361.

(2) *Dual resident corporation.*—The term *dual resident corporation* means a domestic corporation that is subject to an income tax of a foreign country on its worldwide income or on a residence basis. A corporation is taxed on a residence basis if it is taxed as a resident under the laws of the foreign country. The term *dual resident corporation* also means a foreign insurance company that makes an election to be treated as a domestic corporation pursuant to

section 953(d) and is treated as a member of an affiliated group for purposes of chapter 6, even if such company is not subject to an income tax of a foreign country on its worldwide income or on a residence basis. See section 953(d)(3).

(3) *Hybrid entity.*—The term *hybrid entity* means an entity that is not taxable as an association for U.S. income tax purposes but is subject to an income tax of a foreign country as a corporation (or otherwise at the entity level) either on its worldwide income or on a residence basis.

(4) *Separate unit.*—(i) *In general.*—The term *separate unit* means either of the following that is owned, directly or indirectly, by a domestic corporation—

(A) A foreign branch, as defined in § 1.367(a)-6T(g) (foreign branch separate unit); or

(B) An interest in a hybrid entity (hybrid entity separate unit).

(ii) *Separate unit combination rule.*—If two or more separate units (individual separate units) are owned, directly or indirectly, by a single domestic corporation, and the losses of each individual separate unit are made available to offset the income of the other individual separate units under the income tax laws of a single foreign country, then such individual separate units shall be treated as one separate unit (combined separate unit), provided that—

(A) If the individual separate unit is a foreign branch separate unit, it is located in such foreign country; and

(B) If the individual separate unit is a hybrid entity separate unit, the hybrid entity (an interest in which is the hybrid entity separate unit) is subject to an income tax of such foreign country either on its worldwide income or on a residence basis. See § 1.1503(d)-5(c) *Example 1.*

(iii) *Indirectly.*—The term *indirectly*, when used in reference to ownership of a separate unit, means ownership through a separate unit, through an entity classified as a partnership under §§ 301.7701-1 through -3 of this chapter, or through a grantor trust (as defined in paragraph (b)(15) of this section), regardless of whether the partnership or grantor trust is a U.S. person.

(5) *Dual consolidated loss.*—The term *dual consolidated loss* means—

(i) In the case of a dual resident corporation, the net operating loss (as defined in section 172(c) and the regulations thereunder) incurred in a year in which the corporation is a dual resident corporation; and

(ii) In the case of a separate unit, the net loss attributable to, or taken into account by, the separate unit under § 1.1503(d)-3(b)(2).

(6) *Subject to tax.*—For purposes of determining whether a domestic corporation or hybrid entity is subject to an income tax of a foreign country on its income, the fact that it has no actual income tax liability to the foreign country for a particular taxable year shall not be taken into account.

(7) *Foreign country.*—The term *foreign country* includes any possession of the United States.

(8) *Consolidated group.*—The term *consolidated group* means a consolidated group, as defined in § 1.1502-1(h), that includes either a dual resident corporation or a domestic owner.

(9) *Domestic owner.*—The term *domestic owner* means a domestic corporation that owns, directly or indirectly, one or more separate units.

(10) *Affiliated dual resident corporation and affiliated domestic owner.*—The terms *affiliated dual resident corporation* and *affiliated domestic owner* mean a dual resident corporation and a domestic owner, respectively, that is a member of a consolidated group.

(11) *Unaffiliated dual resident corporation, unaffiliated domestic corporation, and unaffiliated domestic owner.*—The terms *unaffiliated dual resident corporation, unaffiliated domestic corporation,* and *unaffiliated domestic owner* mean a dual resident corporation, domestic corporation, and domestic owner, respectively, that is not a member of a consolidated group.

(12) *Domestic affiliate.*—The term *domestic affiliate* means—

(i) A member of an affiliated group, without regard to the exceptions contained in section 1504(b) (other than section 1504(b)(3)) relating to includible corporations;

(ii) A domestic owner; or

(iii) A separate unit.

(13) *Domestic use.*—A *domestic use* of a dual consolidated loss shall be deemed to occur when the dual consolidated loss is made available to offset, directly or indirectly, the taxable income of any domestic affiliate of the dual resident corporation or separate unit (that incurred the dual consolidated loss) in the taxable year in which the dual consolidated loss is recognized, or in any other taxable year, regardless of whether the dual consolidated loss offsets income under the income tax laws of a foreign country and regardless of whether any income that the dual consolidated loss may

Prop. Reg. § 1.1503(d)-1(b)(13)

offset in the foreign country is, has been, or will be subject to tax in the United States. A domestic use shall be deemed to occur in the year the dual consolidated loss is included in the computation of the taxable income of a consolidated group or an unaffiliated domestic owner, even if no tax benefit results from such inclusion in that year. See § 1.1503(d)-5(c) *Examples 2* through *5*.

(14) *Foreign use.*—(i) *In general.*—A foreign use of a dual consolidated loss shall be deemed to occur when any portion of a loss or deduction taken into account in computing the dual consolidated loss is made available under the income tax laws of a foreign country to offset or reduce, directly or indirectly, any item that is recognized as income or gain under such laws and that is considered under U.S. tax principles to be an item of—

(A) A foreign corporation as defined in section 7701(a)(3) and (a)(5); or

(B) A direct or indirect owner of an interest in a hybrid entity, provided such interest is not a separate unit. See § 1.1503(d)-5(c) *Examples 6* through *11*.

(ii) *Available for use.*—A foreign use shall be deemed to occur in the year in which any portion of a loss or deduction taken into account in computing the dual consolidated loss is made available for an offset described in paragraph (b)(14)(i) of this section, regardless of whether it actually offsets or reduces any items of income or gain under the income tax laws of the foreign country in such year and regardless of whether any of the items that may be so offset or reduced are regarded as income under U.S. tax principles.

(iii) *Exceptions.*—(A) *No election to enable foreign use.*—Where the laws of a foreign country provide an election that would enable a foreign use, a foreign use shall be considered to occur only if the election is made.

(B) *Presumed use where no foreign country rule for determining use.*—If the losses or deductions composing the dual consolidated loss are made available under the laws of a foreign country both to offset income that would constitute a foreign use and to offset income that would not constitute a foreign use, and the laws of the foreign country do not provide applicable rules for determining which income is offset by the losses or deductions, then for purposes of paragraph (b)(14) of this section, the losses or deductions shall be deemed to be made available to offset income that does not constitute a foreign use, to the extent of such income, before being considered to be made available to offset the income that does constitute a foreign use. See § 1.1503(d)-5(c) *Examples 12* and *14*.

(C) *No dilution of an interest in a separate unit.*—(*1*) *General rules.*—(*i*) *Interest in a hybrid entity partnership or hybrid entity grantor trust.*—Except as provided in paragraph (b)(14)(iii)(C)(*2*) of this section, no foreign use shall be considered to occur with respect to a dual consolidated loss attributable to an interest in a hybrid entity partnership or a hybrid entity grantor trust, solely because an item of deduction or loss taken into account in computing such dual consolidated loss is made available, under the income tax laws of a foreign country, to offset or reduce, directly or indirectly, any item that is recognized as income or gain under such laws and, that is considered under U.S. tax principles, to be an item of the direct or indirect owner of an interest in such hybrid entity that is not a separate unit. See § 1.1503(d)-5(c) *Examples 8* and *14* through *16*.

(*ii*) *Indirectly owned separate units.*—Except as provided in paragraph. (b)(14)(iii)(C)(*2*) of this section, no foreign use shall be considered to occur with respect to a dual consolidated loss attributable to or taken into account by a separate unit owned indirectly through a partnership or grantor trust solely because an item of deduction or loss taken into account in computing such dual consolidated loss is made available, under the income tax laws of a foreign country, to offset or reduce, directly or indirectly, any item that is recognized as income or gain under such laws, and that is considered under U.S. tax principles, to be an item of a direct or indirect owner of an interest in such partnership or trust. See § 1.1503(d)-5(c) *Examples 17* and *18*.

(*iii*) *Combined separate unit.*—This paragraph (b)(14)(iii)(C)(*1*)(*iii*) applies to a dual consolidated loss attributable to or taken into account by a combined separate unit that includes an individual separate unit to which paragraph (b)(14)(iii)(C)(*1*)(*i*) or (*ii*) of this section would apply, but for the application of the separate unit combination rule provided under § 1.1503(d)-1(b)(4)(ii). Except as provided in paragraph (b)(14)(iii)(C)(*2*) of this section, paragraph (b)(14)(iii)(C)(*1*)(*i*) or (*ii*), as applicable, shall apply to the portion of the dual consolidated loss of such combined separate unit that is attributable, as provided under § 1.1503(d)-3(b)(2)(vii)(*B*)(*1*), to the individual separate unit (otherwise described in paragraph (b)(14)(iii)(C)(*1*)(*i*) or (*ii*) of this section) that is a component of the combined separate unit. See § 1.1503(d)-5(c) *Example 19*.

(*2*) *Exceptions.*—(*i*) *Dilution of an interest in a separate unit.*—Paragraph (b)(14)(iii)(C)(*1*) of this section shall not apply with respect to any item of deduction or loss that is taken into account in computing a dual consolidated loss attributable to or taken into account by a separate unit if during any taxable year the domestic owner's percentage interest in such separate unit, as compared to its interest in the separate unit as of the last day of the taxable year in which such dual consolidated loss was incurred, is reduced as a result of another person acquiring through sale, exchange, contribution or other means, an interest in the partnership or grantor trust. The previous sentence shall not apply, however, if the unaffiliated domestic owner or consolidated group, as the case may be, demonstrates, to the satisfaction of the Commissioner, that the other person that acquired the interest in the partnership or grantor trust was a domestic corporation. Such demonstration must be made on a statement that is attached to, and filed by the due date (including extensions) of, its U.S. income tax return for the taxable year in which the ownership interest of the domestic owner is reduced. See § 1.1503(d)-5(c) *Examples 14* through *16* and *19*.

(*ii*) *Consolidation and other prohibited uses.*—Paragraph (b)(14)(iii)(C)(*1*) of this section shall not apply if the availability described in such section does not arise solely from the ownership in such partnership or grantor trust and the allocation of the item of deduction or loss, or the offsetting by such deduction or loss, of an item of income or gain of the partnership or trust. For example, paragraph (b)(14)(iii)(C)(*1*) of this section shall not apply in the case where the item of loss or deduction is made available through a foreign consolidation regime. See § 1.1503(d)-5(c) *Examples 17* and *18*.

(*iv*) *Ordering rules for determining the foreign use of losses.*—If the laws of a foreign country provide for the foreign use of a dual consolidated loss, but do not provide applicable rules for determining the order in which such losses are used in a taxable year, the following rules shall govern—

(A) Any net loss, or net income, that the dual resident corporation or separate unit has in a taxable year shall first be used to offset net income, or loss, recognized by its affiliates in the same taxable year before any carryover of its losses is considered to be used to offset any income from the taxable year;

(B) If under the laws of the foreign country the dual resident corporation or separate unit has losses from different taxable years, it shall be deemed to use first the losses from the earliest taxable year from which a loss may be carried forward or back for foreign law purposes; and

(C) Where different losses or deductions (for example, capital losses and ordinary losses) of a dual resident corporation or separate unit incurred in the same taxable year are available for foreign use, the different losses shall be deemed to be used on a pro rata basis. See § 1.1503(d)-5(c) *Example 13*.

(v) *Mirror legislation rule.*—Except to the extent § 1.1503(d)-4(b) applies, and other than for purposes of the consistency rule under § 1.1503(d)-4(d)(2), a foreign use shall be deemed to occur if and when the income tax laws of a foreign country deny any opportunity for the foreign use of the dual consolidated loss for any of the following reasons—

(A) The loss is incurred by a dual resident corporation or separate unit that is subject to income taxation by another country on its worldwide income or on a residence basis;

(B) The loss may be available to offset income (other than income of the dual resident corporation or separate unit) under the laws of another country; or

(C) The deductibility of any portion of a loss or deduction taken into account in computing the dual consolidated loss depends on whether such amount is deductible under the laws of another country. See § 1.1503(d)-5(c) *Examples 20* through *23*.

(15) *Grantor trust.*—The term *grantor trust* means a trust, any portion of which is treated as being owned by the grantor or another person under subpart E of subchapter J of this chapter.

(c) *Special rules for filings under section 1503(d).*—(1) *Reasonable cause exception.*—If a person that is permitted or required to file an election, agreement, statement, rebuttal, computation, or other information under the provisions of this section or §§ 1.1503(d)-2 through 1.1503(d)-4 and that fails to make such filing in a timely manner, shall be considered to have satisfied the timeliness requirement with respect to such filing if the person is able to demonstrate, to the Director of Field operations having jurisdiction of the taxpayer's tax return for the taxable year, that such failure was due to reasonable cause and not willful neglect. The previous sentence shall only apply if, once the person becomes aware of the failure, the person attaches all documents that should have been filed previously, as well as a written statement setting forth the reasons for the failure to timely comply, to an amended income tax return that amends the return to which the documents should have been attached under the rules of this section or

Prop. Reg. § 1.1503(d)-1(c)(1)

§§ 1.1503(d)-2 through 1.1503(d)-4. In determining whether the taxpayer has reasonable cause, the Director of Field Operations shall consider whether the taxpayer acted reasonably and in good faith. Whether the taxpayer acted reasonably and in good faith will be determined after considering all the facts and circumstances. The Director of Field Operations shall notify the person in writing within 120 days of the filing if it is determined that the failure to comply was not due to reasonable cause, or if additional time will be needed to make such determination.

(2) *Signature requirement.*—When an election, agreement, statement, rebuttal, computation, or other information is required under this section or §§ 1.1503(d)-2 through 1.1503(d)-4 to be attached to and filed by the due date (including extensions) of a U.S. tax return and signed under penalties of perjury by the person who signs the return, the attachment and filing of an unsigned copy is considered to satisfy such requirement, provided the taxpayer retains the original in its records in the manner specified by § 1.6001-1(e). [Prop. Reg. § 1.1503(d)-1.]

[Proposed 5-24-2005.]

Proposed Regulation

§ 1.1503(d)-2. Operating rules.—(a) *In general.*—This section provides operating rules relating to dual consolidated losses, including a general rule prohibiting the domestic use of a dual consolidated loss, a rule that eliminates a dual consolidated loss following certain transactions, an anti-abuse rule for tainted income, and rules for computing foreign tax credit limitations.

(b) *Limitation on domestic use of a dual consolidated loss.*—Except as provided in § 1.1503(d)-4, the domestic use of a dual consolidated loss is not permitted. See § 1.1503(d)-5(c) *Examples 2* through *4* and *5*.

(c) *Elimination of a dual consolidated loss after certain transactions.*—(1) *General rules.*— (i) *Dual resident corporation.*—Except as provided in paragraph (c)(2) of this section, a dual consolidated loss of a dual resident corporation shall not carry over to another corporation in a transaction described in section 381(a) and, as a result, shall be eliminated. See § 1.1503(d)-5(c) *Example 24.*

(ii) *Separate unit.*—(A) *General rule.*— Except as provided in paragraph (c)(2) of this section, a dual consolidated loss of a separate unit shall not carry over as a result of a transaction in which the separate unit ceases to be a separate unit of its domestic owner (for example, as a result of a termination, dissolution, liquidation, sale or other disposition of the separate unit) and, as a result, shall be eliminated.

(B) *Combined separate unit.*— This paragraph (c)(1)(ii)(B) applies to an individual separate unit that is a component of a combined separate unit that would, but for the separate unit combination rule, cease to be a separate unit of its domestic owner. In such a case, and except as provided in paragraph (c)(2) of this section, the portion of the dual consolidated loss of the combined separate unit that is attributable to, or taken into account by, as provided under § 1.1503(d)-3 (b)(2)(vii)(B)(*1*), such individual separate unit shall not carry over and, as a result, shall be eliminated.

(2) *Exceptions.*—(i) *Certain section 368(a)(1)(F) reorganizations.*—Paragraph (c)(1)(i) of this section shall not apply to a reorganization described in section 368(a)(1)(F) in which the resulting corporation is a domestic corporation.

(ii) *Acquisition of a dual resident corporation by another dual resident corporation.*—If a dual resident corporation transfers its assets to another dual resident corporation in a transaction described in section 381(a), and the transferee corporation is a resident of (or is taxed on its worldwide income by) the same foreign country of which the transferor was a resident (or was taxed on its worldwide income), then income generated by the transferee may be offset by the carryover dual consolidated losses of the transferor, subject to the limitations of § 1.1503(d)-3(c) applied as if the transferee generated the dual consolidated loss. Dual consolidated losses of the transferor may not, however, be used to offset income of separate units owned by the transferee because such separate units constitute domestic affiliates of the transferee as provided under § 1.1503(d)-1(b)(12)(iii).

(iii) *Acquisition of a separate unit by a domestic corporation.*—If a domestic owner transfers ownership of a separate unit to a domestic corporation in a transaction described in section 381(a), and the transferee is a domestic owner of the separate unit immediately following the transfer, then income generated by the separate unit following the transfer may be offset by the carryover dual consolidated losses of the separate unit, subject to the limitations of § 1.1503(d)-3(c) applied as if the separate unit of the transferee generated the dual consolidated loss. In addition, if a domestic owner transfers ownership of a separate unit to a domestic corporation in a transaction described in section 381(a), the transferee is a domestic owner of the separate unit immediately following the transfer, and the transferred separate unit is combined with another separate unit of the transferee immediately after the transfer as provided under § 1.1503(d)-1(b)(4)(ii), then income generated by the combined separate unit may be offset by the carryover dual consolidated losses of the transferred separate unit, subject to the limitations of § 1.1503(d)-3(c) applied as if the combined separate unit of the transferee generated the dual consolidated loss. See § 1.1503(d)-5(c) *Example 25*.

(d) *Special rule denying the use of a dual consolidated loss to offset tainted income.*—(1) *In general.*—Dual consolidated losses incurred by a dual resident corporation shall not be used to offset income it earns after it ceases to be a dual resident corporation to the extent that such income is tainted income.

(2) *Tainted income.*—(i) *Definition.*—For purposes of paragraph (d)(1) of this section, the term *tainted income* means—

(A) Income or gain recognized on the sale or other disposition of tainted assets; and

(B) Income derived as a result of holding tainted assets.

(ii) *Income presumed to be derived from holding tainted assets.*—In the absence of evidence establishing the actual amount of income that is attributable to holding tainted assets, the portion of a corporation's income in a particular taxable year that is treated as tainted income derived as a result of holding tainted assets shall be an amount equal to the corporation's taxable income for the year (other than income described in paragraph (d)(2)(i)(A) of this section) multiplied by a fraction, the numerator of which is the fair market value of all tainted assets acquired by the corporation (determined at the time such assets were so acquired) and the denominator of which is the fair market value of the total assets owned by the corporation at the end of such taxable year. To establish the actual amount of income that is attributable to holding tainted assets, documentation must be attached to, and filed by the due date (including extensions) of, the domestic corporation's tax return or the consolidated tax return of an affiliated group of which it is a member, as the case may be, for the taxable year in which the income is generated. See § 1.1503(d)-5(c) *Example 26*.

(3) *Tainted assets defined.*—For purposes of paragraph (d)(2) of this section, tainted assets are any assets acquired by a domestic corporation in a nonrecognition transaction, as defined in section 7701(a)(45), or any assets otherwise transferred to the corporation as a contribution to capital, at any time during the three taxable years immediately preceding the taxable year in which the corporation ceases to be a dual resident corporation or at any time thereafter.

(4) *Exceptions.*—Income derived from assets acquired by a domestic corporation shall not be subject to the limitation described in paragraph (d)(1) of this section, if—

(i) For the taxable year in which the assets were acquired, the corporation did not have a dual consolidated loss (or a carryforward of a dual consolidated loss to such year); or

(ii) The assets were acquired as replacement property in the ordinary course of business.

(e) *Computation of foreign tax credit limitation.*—If a dual resident corporation or separate unit is subject to § 1.1503(d)-3(c) (addressing the effect of a dual consolidated loss on a domestic affiliate), the consolidated group or unaffiliated domestic owner shall compute its foreign tax credit limitation by applying the limitations of § 1.1503(d)-3(c). Thus, the items constituting the dual consolidated loss are not taken into account until the year in which such items are absorbed. [Prop. Reg. § 1.1503(d)-2.]

[Proposed 5-24-2005.]

Proposed Regulation

§ 1.1503(d)-3. Special rules for accounting for dual consolidated losses.—(a) *In general.*—This section provides special rules for determining the amount of income or loss of a dual resident corporation or separate unit for purposes of section 1503(d). In addition, this section provides rules for determining the effect of a dual consolidated loss on domestic affiliates and for making special basis adjustments.

(b) *Determination of amount of dual consolidated loss.*—(1) *Affiliated dual resident corporation.*—For purposes of determining whether an affiliated dual resident corporation has a dual consolidated loss for the taxable year, the dual resident corporation shall compute its taxable income (or loss) in accordance with the rules set forth in the regulations under section 1502 governing the computation of consolidated taxable income, taking into account only the dual resident corporation's items of income, gain, deduction, and loss for the year. However, for purposes of this computation, the following items shall not be taken into account—

(i) Any net capital loss of the dual resident corporation; and

(ii) Any carryover or carryback losses.

(2) *Separate unit.*—(i) *General rules.*—Paragraph (b)(2) of this section applies for pur-

Prop. Reg. § 1.1503(d)-3(b)(2)(i)

poses of determining whether a separate unit has a dual consolidated loss for the taxable year. The taxable income (or loss) in U.S. dollars of a separate unit shall be computed as if it were a separate domestic corporation and a dual resident corporation in accordance with the provisions of paragraph (b)(1) of this section, using only those existing items of income, gain, deduction, and loss (translated into U.S. dollars) that are attributable to or taken into account by such separate unit. Treating a separate unit as a separate domestic corporation of the domestic owner under this paragraph shall not cause items of income, gain, deduction and loss that are otherwise disregarded for U.S. Federal tax purposes to be regarded for purposes of calculating a dual consolidated loss. Paragraph (b)(2) of this section shall apply separately to each separate unit and an item of income, gain, deduction, or loss shall not be considered attributable to or taken into account by more than one separate unit. Items of income, gain, deduction, and loss of one separate unit shall not offset items of income, gain, deduction, and loss, or otherwise be taken into account by, another separate unit for purposes of calculating a dual consolidated loss. But see the separate unit combination rule in § 1.1503(d)-1(b)(4)(ii). See also § 1.1503(d)-5(c) *Example 27*.

(ii) *Foreign branch separate unit.*—(A) *In general.*—For purposes of determining the items of income, gain, deduction (other than interest), and loss that are taken into account in determining the taxable income or loss of a foreign branch separate unit, the principles of section 864(c)(2) and (c)(4) as set forth in § 1.864-4(c) and § 1.864-6 shall apply. The principles apply without regard to limitations imposed on the effectively connected treatment of income, gain or loss under the trade or business safe harbors in section 864(b) and the limitations for treating foreign source income as effectively connected under section 864(c)(4)(D). For purposes of determining the interest expense that is taken into account in determining the taxable income or loss of a foreign branch separate unit, the principles of § 1.882-5, subject to paragraph (b)(2)(ii)(B) of this section, shall apply. When applying the principles of section 864(c) and § 1.882-5 (subject to paragraph (b)(2)(ii)(B) of this section), the domestic corporation that owns, directly or indirectly, the foreign branch separate unit shall be treated as a foreign corporation, the foreign branch separate unit shall be treated as a trade or business within the United States, and the other assets of the domestic corporation shall be treated as assets that are not U.S. assets.

(B) *Principles of § 1.882-5.*—For purposes of paragraph (b)(2)(ii)(A) of this section, the principles of § 1.882-5 shall be applied subject to the following:

(1) Except as otherwise provided in this section, only the assets, liabilities and interest expense of the domestic owner shall be taken into account in the § 1.882-5 formula;

(2) Except as provided under paragraph (b)(2)(ii)(B)(3) of this section, a taxpayer may use the alternative tax book value method under § 1.861-9T(i) for purposes of determining the value of its U.S. assets pursuant to § 1.882-5(b)(2) and its worldwide assets pursuant to § 1.882-5(c)(2);

(3) For purposes of determining the value of a U.S. asset pursuant to § 1.882-5(b)(2), and worldwide assets pursuant to § 1.882-5(c)(2), the taxpayer must use the same methodology under § 1.861-9T(g) (that is, tax book value, alternative tax book value, or fair market value) that the taxpayer uses for purposes of allocating and apportioning interest expense for the taxable year under section 864(e);

(4) Asset values shall be determined pursuant to § 1.861-9T(g)(2); and

(5) For purposes of determining the step-two U.S. connected liabilities, the amounts of worldwide assets and liabilities under § 1.882-5(c)(2)(iii) and (iv), must be determined in accordance with U.S. tax principles rather than substantially in accordance with U.S. tax principles.

(iii) *Hybrid entity.*—(A) *General rule.*—The items of income, gain, deduction and loss attributable to a hybrid entity are those items that are properly reflected on its books and records under the principles of § 1.988-4(b)(2), to the extent consistent with U.S. tax principles. See § 1.1503(d)-5(c) *Example 28*.

(B) *Interest in a non-hybrid partnership and a non-hybrid grantor trust.*—If a hybrid entity owns, directly or indirectly (other than through a hybrid entity separate unit), an interest in either a partnership that is not a hybrid entity or a grantor trust that is not a hybrid entity, items of income, gain, deduction or loss that are properly reflected on the books and records of such partnership or grantor trust (under the principles of § 1.988-4(b)(2), to the extent consistent with U.S. tax principles), to the extent provided under paragraphs (b)(2)(v) or (b)(2)(vi) of this section, respectively, shall be treated as being properly reflected on the books and records of the hybrid entity for purposes of paragraph (b)(2)(iii)(A) of this section. See § 1.1503(d)-5(c) *Example 30*.

(iv) *Interest in a disregarded hybrid entity.*—Except as provided in paragraph (b)(2)(vii) of this section, for purposes of determining the items of income, gain, deduction and loss that are attributable to an interest in a hybrid entity that is disregarded as an entity separate from its owner (for example, as a result of an election made pursuant to § 301.7701-3(c) of this chapter), those items described in paragraph (b)(2)(iii) of this section shall be taken into account. See § 1.1503(d)-5(c) *Example 30.*

(v) *Items attributable to an interest in a hybrid entity partnership and a separate unit owned indirectly through a partnership.*—(A) This paragraph (b)(2)(v) applies for purposes of determining—

(1) The extent to which the items of income, gain, deduction and loss attributable to a hybrid entity that is a partnership (as provided in paragraph (b)(2)(iii) of this section) are attributable to an interest in such hybrid entity partnership; and

(2) The extent to which items of income, gain, deduction and loss of a separate unit that is owned indirectly through a partnership are taken into account by a partner in such partnership.

(B) Items of income, gain, deduction and loss are taken into account by the owner of such interest, or separate unit, to the extent such items are includible in the owner's distributive share of the partnership income, gain, deduction and loss, as determined under the rules and principles of subchapter K of this chapter. See § 1.1503(d)-5(c) *Example 30.*

(vi) *Items attributable to an interest in a hybrid entity grantor trust and a separate unit owned indirectly through a grantor trust.*—(A) This paragraph (b)(2)(vi) applies for purposes of determining—

(1) The extent to which items of income, gain, deduction and loss attributable to a hybrid entity that is a grantor trust (as provided in paragraph (b)(2)(iii) of this section) are attributable to an interest in such grantor trust; and

(2) The extent to which the items of income, gain, deduction and loss of a separate unit owned indirectly through a grantor trust are taken into account by an owner of such grantor trust.

(B) Items of income; gain, deduction and loss are taken into account to the extent such items are attributable to trust property that the holder of the trust interest is treated as owning under the rules and principles of subpart E of subchapter J of this chapter.

(vii) *Special rules.*—The following special rules shall apply for purposes of attributing items under paragraphs (b)(2)(i) through (vi) of this section:

(A) *Allocation of items between certain tiered separate units.*—(1) When a hybrid entity owns, directly or indirectly (other than through a hybrid entity separate unit), a foreign branch separate unit, for purposes of determining items of income, gain, deduction and loss that are taken into account in determining the taxable income or loss of such foreign branch separate unit, only items of income, gain, deduction and loss that are attributable to the hybrid entity as provided in paragraph (b)(2)(iii) of this section (and intervening entities, if any, that are not themselves separate units) shall be taken into account. Items of the hybrid entity (including assets and liabilities) are taken into account for purposes of determining the taxable income or loss of the foreign branch separate unit pursuant to paragraph (b)(2)(ii) of this section. See § 1.1503(d)-5(c) *Example 30.*

(2) For purposes of determining items of income, gain, deduction and loss that are attributable to an interest in the hybrid entity described in paragraph (b)(2)(vii)(A)(*1*) of this section, the items attributable to the hybrid entity in paragraph (b)(2)(iii) of this section shall not be taken into account to the extent they are also taken into account in determining, under the rules of paragraph (b)(2)(ii) of this section, the taxable income or loss of a foreign branch separate unit that is owned, directly or indirectly (other than through a hybrid entity separate unit), by the hybrid entity separate unit. See § 1.1503(d)-5(c) *Example 30.*

(B) *Combined separate unit.*—If two or more separate units defined in § 1.1503(d)-1(b)(4)(i) are treated as one combined separate unit pursuant to § 1.1503(d)-1(b)(4)(ii), the items of income, gain, deduction and loss that are attributable to or taken into account in determining the taxable income of the combined separate unit shall be determined as follows—

(1) Items of income, gain, deduction and loss are first attributed to, or taken into account by, each individual separate unit, as defined in § 1.1503(d)-1(b)(4)(i) without regard to § 1.1503(d)-1(b)(4)(ii), pursuant to the rules of paragraph (b)(2) of this section; and

(2) The combined separate unit then takes into account all of the items of income, gain, deduction and loss attributable to, or taken into account by, the individual separate units pursuant to paragraph (b)(2)(vii)(B)(*1*) of this section. See § 1.1503(d)-5(c) *Example 30.*

Prop. Reg. § 1.1503(d)-3(b)(2)(vii)(B)(2)

(C) *Gain or loss on the direct or indirect disposition of a separate unit.*—For purposes of calculating a dual consolidated loss of a separate unit, items of income or gain (including loss recapture income or gain under section 367(a)(3)(C) or 904(f)(3)), deduction and loss recognized on the sale, exchange or other disposition of a separate unit (or an interest in a partnership or grantor trust that owns, directly or indirectly, a separate unit), are attributable to or taken into account by the separate unit to the extent of the gain or loss that would have been recognized had such separate unit sold all its assets in a taxable exchange, immediately before the disposition of the separate unit, for an amount equal to their fair market value. If, as a result of the sale, exchange or other disposition of a separate unit (or interest in a partnership or grantor trust) more than one separate unit is, directly or indirectly, disposed of, items of income, gain, deduction, and loss recognized on such disposition are attributable to or taken into account by each such separate unit (under the rules of this paragraph (b)(2)(vii)(C)) based on the gain or loss that would have been recognized by each separate unit if it had sold all of its assets in a taxable exchange, immediately before the disposition of the separate unit, for an amount equal to their fair market value. See § 1.1503(d)-5(c) *Examples 31* through *34.*

(D) *Income inclusion on stock.*—Any amount included in income of a U.S. person arising from ownership of stock in a foreign corporation (for example, under section 951) through a separate unit shall be taken into account for purposes of calculating the dual consolidated loss of the separate unit if an actual dividend from such foreign corporation would have been so taken into account. See § 1.1503(d)-5(c) *Example 29.*

(3) *Foreign tax treatment disregarded.*—The fact that a particular item taken into account in computing a dual resident corporation's net operating loss, or a separate unit's loss, is not taken into account in computing income subject to a foreign country's income tax shall not cause such item to be excluded from the calculation of the dual consolidated loss.

(4) *Items generated or incurred while a dual resident corporation or a separate unit.*—For purposes of determining the amount of the dual consolidated loss of a dual resident corporation or a separate unit for the taxable year, only the items of income, gain, deduction and loss generated or incurred during the period the dual resident corporation or separate unit qualified as such shall be taken into account.

The allocation of items to such period shall be made under the principles of § 1.1502-76(b).

(c) *Effect of a dual consolidated loss on a domestic affiliate.*—For any taxable year in which a dual resident corporation or separate unit has a dual consolidated loss to which § 1.1503(d)-2(b) applies, the following rules shall apply:

(1) *Dual resident corporation.*—If the dual resident corporation is a member of a consolidated group, the group shall compute its consolidated taxable income (or loss) by taking into account the dual resident corporation's items of gross income, gain, deduction, or loss taken into account in computing the dual consolidated loss, other than those items of deduction and loss that compose the dual resident corporation's dual consolidated loss. The dual consolidated loss shall be treated as composed of a pro rata portion of each item of deduction and loss of the dual resident corporation taken into account in calculating the dual consolidated loss. The dual consolidated loss is subject to the limitations on its use contained in paragraph (c)(3) of this section and, subject to such limitation, may be carried over or back for use in other taxable years as a separate net operating loss carryover or carryback of the dual resident corporation arising in the year incurred.

(2) *Separate unit.*—The unaffiliated domestic owner of a separate unit, or the consolidated group of an affiliated domestic owner of a separate unit, shall compute its taxable income (or loss) by taking into account the separate unit's items of gross income, gain, deduction and loss taken into account in computing the dual consolidated loss, other than those items of deduction and loss that compose the separate unit's dual consolidated loss. The dual consolidated loss shall be treated as composed of a pro rata portion of each item of deduction and loss of the separate unit taken into account in calculating the dual consolidated loss. The dual consolidated loss is subject to the limitations contained in paragraph (c)(3) of this section as if the separate unit that generated the dual consolidated loss were a separate domestic corporation that filed a consolidated return with its unaffiliated domestic owner or with the consolidated group of its affiliated domestic owner. Subject to such limitation, the dual consolidated loss may be carried over or back for use in other taxable years as a separate net operating loss carryover or carryback of the separate unit arising in the year incurred.

(3) *SRLY limitation.*—The dual consolidated loss shall be treated as a loss incurred by the dual resident corporation or separate unit

in a separate return limitation year and shall be subject to all of the limitations of § 1.1502-21(c) (SRLY limitation), subject to the following:

(i) Notwithstanding § 1.1502-1(f)(2)(i), the SRLY limitation is applied to any dual consolidated loss of a common parent;

(ii) The SRLY limitation is applied without regard to § 1.1502-21(c)(2) (SRLY subgroup limitation) and 1.1502-21(g) (overlap with section 382);

(iii) For purposes of calculating the general SRLY limitation under § 1.1502-21(c)(1)(i), the calculation of aggregate consolidated taxable income shall only include items of income, gain, deduction or loss generated—

(A) In the case of a dual resident corporation or hybrid entity separate unit, in years in which the dual resident corporation or hybrid entity (whose interest constitutes the separate unit) is resident (or is taxed on its worldwide income) in the same foreign country in which it was resident (or was taxed on its worldwide income) during the year in which the dual consolidated loss was generated; and

(B) In the case of a foreign branch separate unit, items of income, gain, deduction or loss generated in years in which the foreign branch qualified as a separate unit; and

(iv) For purposes of calculating the general SRLY limitation under § 1.1502-21(c)(1)(i), the calculation of aggregate consolidated taxable income shall not include any amount included in income pursuant to § 1.1503(d)-4(h) (relating to the recapture of a dual consolidated loss).

(4) *Items of a dual consolidated loss used in other taxable years.*—A pro rata portion of each item of deduction or loss that composes the dual consolidated loss shall be considered to be used when the dual consolidated loss is used in other taxable years. See § 1.1503(d)-5(c) *Example 35.*

(d) *Special basis adjustments.*—(1) *Affiliated dual resident corporation or affiliated domestic owner.*—If a dual resident corporation or domestic owner is a member of a consolidated group, each other member owning stock in the dual resident corporation or domestic owner shall adjust the basis of the stock in accordance with the principles of § 1.1502-32(b), subject to the following:

(i) *Dual consolidated loss subject to domestic use limitation.*—There shall be a negative adjustment under § 1.1502-32(b)(2) for any amount of a dual consolidated loss of the dual resident corporation (or, in the case of a domestic owner, of separate units of such domestic owner) that is not absorbed as a result of the application of §§ 1.1503(d)-2(b) and 3(c).

(ii) *Dual consolidated loss absorbed in carryover or carryback year.*—There shall be no negative adjustment under § 1.1502-32(b)(2) for the amount of a dual consolidated loss of the dual resident corporation (or, in the case of a domestic owner, of separate units of such domestic owner) subject to §§ 1.1503(d)-2(b) and 1.1503(d)-3(c) that is absorbed in a carryover or carryback taxable year.

(iii) *Recapture income.*—There shall be no positive adjustment under § 1.1502-32(b)(2) for any amount included in income by the dual resident corporation or domestic owner pursuant to § 1.1503(d)-4(h).

(2) *Interests in hybrid entities that are partnerships or interests in partnerships through which a separate unit is owned indirectly.*—(i) *Scope.*—This paragraph (d)(2) applies for purposes of determining the adjusted basis of an interest in:

(A) A hybrid entity that is a partnership; and

(B) A partnership through which a domestic owner indirectly owns a separate unit.

(ii) *Determination of basis of partner's interest.*—The adjusted basis of an interest in a hybrid entity that is a partnership, or a partnership through which a domestic owner indirectly owns a separate unit, shall be adjusted in accordance with section 705 of this chapter, except as otherwise provided in this paragraph (d)(2)(ii).

(A) *Dual consolidated loss subject to domestic use limitation.*—The adjusted basis shall be decreased for any amount of the dual consolidated loss that is not absorbed as a result of the application of §§ 1.1503(d)-2(b) and 1.1503(d)-3(c).

(B) *Dual consolidated loss absorbed in carryover or carryback year.*—The adjusted basis shall not be decreased for the amount of a dual consolidated loss subject to §§ 1.1503(d)-2(b) and 1.1503(d)-3(c) that is absorbed in a carryover or carryback taxable year.

(C) *Recapture income.*—The adjusted basis shall not be increased for any amount included in income pursuant to § 1.1503(d)-4(h).

(3) *Examples.*—See § 1.1503(d)-5(c) *Examples 36* and *37.*

[Prop. Reg. § 1.1503(d)-3.]

[Proposed 5-24-2005.]

Proposed Regulation

§ 1.1503(d)-4. Exceptions to the domestic use limitation rule.—(a) *In general.*—This section provides certain exceptions to the domestic use limitation rule of § 1.1503(d)-2(b).

(b) *Elective agreement in place between the United States and a foreign country.*—The domestic use limitation rule of § 1.1503(d)-2(b) shall not apply to a dual consolidated loss to the extent the consolidated group, unaffiliated dual resident corporation, or unaffiliated domestic owner, as the case may be, elects to deduct the loss in the United States pursuant to an agreement entered into between the United States and a foreign country that puts into place an elective procedure through which losses offset income in only one country.

(c) *No possibility of foreign use.*—(1) *In general.*—The domestic use limitation rule of § 1.1503(d)-2(b) shall not apply to a dual consolidated loss if the consolidated group, unaffiliated dual resident corporation, or unaffiliated domestic owner, as the case may be—

(i) Demonstrates, to the satisfaction of the Commissioner, that no foreign use of the dual consolidated loss occurred in the year in which it was incurred, and no such use can occur in any other year by any means; and

(ii) Prepares a statement described in paragraph (c)(2) of this section that is attached to, and filed by the due date (including extensions) of, its U.S. income tax return for the taxable year in which the dual consolidated loss is incurred. See § 1.1503(d)-5(c) *Examples 38* through *40.*

(2) *Statement.*—The statement described in this section must be signed under penalties of perjury by the person who signs the tax return. The statement must be labeled No Possibility of Foreign Use of Dual Consolidated Loss Statement at the top of the page and must include the following items, in paragraphs labeled to correspond with the items set forth in paragraphs (c)(2)(i) through (iv) of this section:

(i) A statement that the document is submitted under the provisions of § 1.1503(d)-4(c);

(ii) The name, address, tax identification number, and place and date of incorporation of the dual resident corporation, and the country or countries that tax the dual resident corporation on its worldwide income or on a residence basis, or, in the case of a separate unit, identification of the separate unit, including the name under which it conducts business, its principal activity, and the country in which its principal place of business is located;

(iii) A statement of the amount of the dual consolidated loss at issue; and

(iv) An analysis, in reasonable detail and specificity, supported with official or certified English translations of the relevant provisions of foreign law, of the treatment of the losses and deductions composing the dual consolidated loss under the laws of the foreign jurisdiction and the reasons supporting the conclusion that no foreign use of the dual consolidated loss occurred in the year in which it was incurred, and no such use can occur in any other year by any means.

(d) *Domestic use election.*—(1) *In general.*—The domestic use limitation rule of § 1.1503(d)-2(b) shall not apply to a dual consolidated loss if an election to be bound by the provisions of this paragraph (d) of this section (domestic use election) is made by the consolidated group, unaffiliated dual resident corporation, or unaffiliated domestic owner, as the case may be (elector). In order to elect relief under this paragraph (d) of this section, an agreement described in this paragraph (d)(1) of this section (domestic use agreement) must be attached to, and filed by the due date (including extensions) of, the U.S. income tax return of the elector for the taxable year in which the dual consolidated loss is incurred. The domestic use agreement must be signed under penalties of perjury by the person who signs the return. If dual consolidated losses of more than one dual resident corporation or separate unit are subject to the rules of this paragraph (d) which requires the filing of domestic use agreements by the same elector, the agreements may be combined in a single document, but the information required by paragraphs (d)(1)(ii) and (iv) of this section must be provided separately with respect to each dual consolidated loss. The domestic use agreement must be labeled Domestic Use Election and Agreement at the top of the page and must include the following items, in paragraphs labeled to correspond with the following:

(i) A statement that the document submitted is an election and an agreement under the provisions of § 1.1503(d)-4(d);

(ii) The name, address, tax identification number, and place and date of incorporation of the dual resident corporation, and the country or countries that tax the dual resident corporation on its worldwide income or on a residence basis, or, in the case of a separate unit, identification of the separate unit, including the name under which it conducts business, its principal activity, and the country in which its principal place of business is located;

(iii) An agreement by the elector to comply with all of the provisions of paragraphs (d) through (h) of this section, as applicable;

(iv) A statement of the amount of the dual consolidated loss covered by the agreement;

(v) A certification that there has not been, and will not be, a foreign use of the dual consolidated loss in any taxable year up to and including the seventh taxable year following the year in which the dual consolidated loss that is the subject of the agreement filed under paragraph (d) of this section was incurred (certification period);

(vi) A certification that arrangements have been made to ensure that there will be no foreign use of the dual consolidated loss during the certification period, and that the elector will be informed of any such foreign use of the dual consolidated loss during such period;

(vii) If applicable, a notification that an excepted triggering event under paragraph (f)(2)(i) of this section has occurred with respect to the dual consolidated loss within the taxable year covered by the elector's tax return and providing the name, taxpayer identification number, and address of the subsequent elector (within the meaning of paragraph (f)(2)(iii)(A) of this section) that will be filing future certifications with respect to such dual consolidated loss.

(2) *Consistency rule.*—If under the laws of a particular foreign country there is a foreign use of a dual consolidated loss of a dual resident corporation or separate unit that is subject to a domestic use agreement (but not a new domestic use agreement, defined in paragraph (f)(2)(iii)(A) of this paragraph), then a foreign use shall be deemed to occur for the following other dual consolidated losses (if any), but only if the income tax laws of the foreign country permit a foreign use of such other dual consolidated losses in the same taxable year—

(i) Any dual consolidated loss of a dual resident corporation that is a member of the same consolidated group of which the first dual resident corporation or domestic owner is a member, if any deduction or loss taken into account in computing such dual consolidated loss is recognized under the income tax laws of such foreign country in the same taxable year; and

(ii) Any dual consolidated loss of a separate unit that is owned directly or indirectly by the same domestic owner that owns the first separate unit, or that is owned directly or indirectly by any member of the same consolidated group of which the first dual resident corporation or domestic owner is a member, if any deduction or loss taken into account in computing such dual consolidated loss is recognized under the income tax laws of such foreign country in the same taxable year. See § 1.1503(d)-5(c) *Examples 41* and *42.*

(3) *Restrictions on domestic use election.*—(i) *Triggering event in year of dual consolidated loss.*—Except as otherwise provided in this section, if an event described in paragraphs (e)(1)(i) through (vii) of this section occurs during the year in which a dual resident corporation or separate unit incurs a dual consolidated loss (including a dual consolidated loss resulting, in whole or in part, from the occurrence of the triggering event itself), the consolidated group, unaffiliated dual resident corporation, or unaffiliated domestic owner, as the case may be, may not make a domestic use election with respect to the dual consolidated loss and such loss therefore is subject to the domestic use limitation rule of § 1.1503(d)-2(b). See § 1.1503(d)-5(c) *Example 32.* See also § 1.1503(d)-2(c) for rules that eliminate a dual consolidated loss after certain transactions.

(ii) *Losses of a foreign insurance company treated as a domestic corporation.*—A foreign insurance company that has elected to be treated as a domestic corporation pursuant to section 953(d) may not make a domestic use election. See section 953(d)(3).

(e) *Triggering events requiring the recapture of a dual consolidated loss.*—(1) *Events.*—The elector must agree that, except as provided under paragraphs (e)(2) and (f) of this section, if there is a triggering event described in this paragraph (e) during the certification period, the elector will recapture and report as income the amount of the dual consolidated loss as provided in paragraph (h) of this section on its tax return for the taxable year in which the triggering event occurs (or, when the triggering event is a foreign use of the dual consolidated loss, the taxable year that includes the last day of the foreign tax year during which such use occurs). In addition, the elector must pay any applicable interest charge required by paragraph (h) of this section. For purposes of this section, except as provided under paragraphs (e)(2) and (f) of this section, any of the following events shall constitute a triggering event:

(i) *Foreign use.*—A foreign use of the dual consolidated loss (including a deemed foreign use pursuant to the mirror legislation rule set forth in § 1.1503(d)-1(b)(13)(ii)(D) or the consistency rule set forth in paragraph (d)(2) of this section).

(ii) *Disaffiliation.*—An affiliated dual resident corporation or affiliated domestic owner ceases to be a member of the consolidated group that made the domestic use election. For purposes of this paragraph (e)(1)(ii), a dual resident corporation or domestic owner shall be considered to cease to be a member of the consolidated group if it is no longer a member of the group within the meaning of § 1.1502-1(b), or if the group ceases to exist (for example, when the group no longer files a consolidated return). See § 1.1503(d)-5(c) *Example 47.*

(iii) *Affiliation.*—An unaffiliated dual resident corporation or unaffiliated domestic owner becomes a member of a consolidated group. Any consequences resulting from this triggering event (for example, recapture of a dual consolidated loss) shall be taken into account in the tax return of the unaffiliated dual resident corporation or unaffiliated domestic owner for the taxable year that ends immediately before the taxable year in which the unaffiliated dual resident corporation or unaffiliated domestic owner becomes a member of the consolidated group.

(iv) *Transfer of assets.*—Fifty percent or more of the dual resident corporation's or separate unit's gross assets (measured by the fair market value of the assets at the time of such transfer (or for multiple transactions, at the time of the first transfer)) are sold or otherwise disposed of in either a single transaction or a series of transactions within a twelve-month period. For purposes of this paragraph, the interest in a separate unit and the shares of a dual resident corporation shall not be treated as assets of a dual resident corporation or a separate unit.

(v) *Transfer of an interest in a separate unit.*—Fifty percent or more of the interest in a separate unit (measured by voting power or value) owned directly or indirectly by the domestic owner on the last day of the taxable year in which the dual consolidated loss was incurred is sold or otherwise disposed of either in a single transaction or a series of transactions within a twelve-month period.

(vi) *Conversion to a foreign corporation.*—An unaffiliated dual resident corporation, unaffiliated domestic owner, or hybrid entity an interest in which is a separate unit, becomes a foreign corporation by means of a transaction (for example, a reorganization, or an election to be classified as a corporation under § 301.7701-3(c) of this chapter) that, for foreign tax purposes, is not treated as involving a transfer of assets (and carryover of losses) to a new entity.

(vii) *Conversion to an S corporation.*—An unaffiliated dual resident corporation or unaffiliated domestic owner elects to be an S corporation pursuant to section 1362(a).

(viii) *Failure to certify.*—The elector fails to file a certification required under paragraph (g) of this section.

(2) *Rebuttal.*—An event described in paragraphs (e)(1)(ii) through (viii) of this section shall not constitute a triggering event if the elector demonstrates, to the satisfaction of the Commissioner, that there can be no foreign use of the dual consolidated loss at any time during the remaining certification period. The elector must prepare a statement, labeled Rebuttal of Triggering Event at the top of the page, that indicates that it is submitted under the provisions of this section § 1.1503(d)-4(e)(2). The statement must set forth an analysis, in reasonable detail and specificity, supported with official or certified English translations of the relevant provisions of foreign law, of the treatment of the losses and deductions composing the dual consolidated loss under the facts of the event in question. The statement must be attached to, and filed by the due date (including extensions) of, the elector's income tax return for the taxable year in which the presumed triggering event occurs. See § 1.1503(d)-5(c) *Examples 43* through *45.*

(f) *Exceptions.*—(1) *Acquisition by a member of the consolidated group.*—The following events shall not constitute triggering events, requiring the recapture of the dual consolidated loss under paragraph (h) of this section—

(i) An affiliated dual resident corporation or affiliated domestic owner ceases to be a member of a consolidated group solely by reason of a transaction in which a member of the same consolidated group succeeds to the tax attributes of the dual resident corporation or domestic owner under the provisions of section 381.

(ii) Assets of an affiliated dual resident corporation or assets of a separate unit owned by an affiliated domestic owner are acquired in any other transaction by—

(A) One or more members of its consolidated group; or

(B) A partnership, a grantor trust, or a hybrid entity, but only if 100 percent of such entity's interests are owned, directly or indirectly, by such affiliated dual resident corporation or affiliated domestic owner, as the case may be, or by members of its consolidated group.

(iii) Assets of a separate unit are acquired in any other transaction by its domestic owner or by a hybrid entity or grantor trust, but only if 100 percent of such entity's interest is owned by the domestic owner.

(iv) The interest of a hybrid entity separate unit, or an indirectly owned separate unit, owned by an affiliated domestic owner, is transferred to—

(A) A member of its consolidated group; or

(B) (B) A partnership, a grantor trust, or a hybrid entity, but only if 100 percent of such entity's interests are owned, directly or indirectly, by such affiliated domestic owner, or by members of its consolidated group.

(2) *Acquisition by an unaffiliated domestic corporation or a new consolidated group.*— (i) *Subsequent elector events.*—If all the requirements of paragraph (f)(2)(iii) of this section are met, the following events shall not constitute triggering events requiring the recapture of the dual consolidated loss under paragraph (h) of this section—

(A) An affiliated dual resident corporation or affiliated domestic owner becomes an unaffiliated domestic corporation or a member of a new consolidated group (other than in a transaction described in paragraph (f)(2)(ii)(B) of this section);

(B) Assets of a dual resident corporation or a separate unit are acquired by—

(1) An unaffiliated domestic corporation;

(2) One or more members of a new consolidated group; or

(3) A partnership, a grantor trust, or a hybrid entity, but only if 100 percent of such entity's interests are owned, directly or indirectly, by members of a new consolidated group.

(C) The interest of a hybrid entity separate unit, or an indirectly owned separate unit, owned by a domestic owner is transferred to—

(1) An unaffiliated domestic corporation;

(2) One or more members of a new consolidated group; or

(3) A partnership, a grantor trust, or a hybrid entity, but only if 100 percent of such entity's interests is owned, directly or indirectly, by members of a new consolidated group.

(ii) *Non-subsequent elector events.*—If the requirements of paragraph (f)(2)(iii)(A) of this section are met, the following events also shall not constitute triggering events requiring the recapture of the dual consolidated loss under paragraph (h) of this section—

(A) An unaffiliated dual resident corporation or unaffiliated domestic owner becomes a member of a consolidated group; or

(B) A consolidated group that filed a domestic use agreement ceases to exist as a result of a transaction described in § 1.1502-13(j)(5)(i) (other than a transaction in which any member of the terminating group, or the successor-in-interest of such member, is not a member of the surviving group immediately after the terminating group ceases to exist). See § 1.1503(d)-5(c) *Example 46.*

(iii) *Requirements.*—(A) *New domestic use agreement.*—The unaffiliated domestic corporation or new consolidated group (subsequent elector) must file an agreement described in paragraph (d)(1) of this section (new domestic use agreement). The new domestic use agreement must be labeled New Domestic Use Agreement at the top of the page, and must be attached to and filed by the due date (including extensions) of, the subsequent elector's income tax return for the taxable year in which the event described in paragraph (f)(2)(i) or (f)(2)(ii) of this section occurs. The new domestic use agreement must be signed under penalties of perjury by the person who signs the return and must include the following items—

(1) A statement that the document submitted is an election and agreement under the provisions of § 1.1503(d)-4(f)(2);

(2) An agreement to assume the same obligations with respect to the dual consolidated loss as the corporation or consolidated group that filed the original domestic use agreement (original elector) with respect to that loss;

(3) An agreement to treat any potential recapture amount under paragraph (h) of this section with respect to the dual consolidated loss as unrealized built-in gain for purposes of section 384(a), subject to any applicable exceptions thereunder;

(4) An agreement to be subject to the successor elector rules as provided in paragraph (h)(3) of this section; and

(5) The name, U.S. taxpayer identification number, and address of the original elector and prior subsequent electors with respect to the dual consolidated losses, if any.

(B) *Statement filed by original elector.*—The original elector must file a statement that is attached to and filed by the due date (including extensions) of its income tax return for the taxable year in which the event described in paragraph (f)(2)(i) of this section occurs. The statement must be labeled Original Elector Statement at the top of the page, must be signed under penalties of perjury by the person who signs the tax return, and must include the following items—

(1) A statement that the document submitted is an election and agreement under the provisions of § 1.1503(d)-4(f)(2);

Prop. Reg. § 1.1503(d)-4(f)(2)(iii)(B)(1)

(2) An agreement to be subject to the successor elector rules as provided in paragraph (h)(3) of this section; and

(3) The name, U.S. taxpayer identification number, and address of the subsequent elector.

(3) *Subsequent triggering events.*—Any triggering event described in paragraph (e) of this section that occurs subsequent to one of the transactions described in paragraph (f)(1) or (2) of this section, and that itself does not fall within the exceptions provided in paragraph (f)(1) or (2) of this section, shall require recapture under paragraph (h) of this section.

(g) *Annual certification reporting requirement.*—Except as provided in paragraph (i) of this section, the elector must file a certification, labeled Certification of Dual Consolidated Loss at the top of the page, that is attached to, and filed by the due date (including extensions) of, its income tax return for each taxable year during the certification period. The certification must certify that there has been no foreign use of such dual consolidated loss. The certification must identify the dual consolidated loss to which it pertains by setting forth the elector's year in which the loss was incurred and the amount of such loss. In addition, the certification must warrant that arrangements have been made to ensure that there will be no foreign use of the dual consolidated loss and that the elector will be informed of any such foreign use. If dual consolidated losses of more than one taxable year are subject to the rules of this paragraph (g) of this section, the certification for those years may be combined in a single document but each dual consolidated loss must be separately identified.

(h) *Recapture of dual consolidated loss and interest charge.*—(1) *Presumptive rules.*— (i) *Amount of recapture.*—Except as otherwise provided in this section, upon the occurrence of a triggering event described in paragraph (e)(1) of this section that falls outside the exceptions provided in paragraph (f)(1) or (2) of this section, the dual resident corporation or separate unit shall recapture, and the elector shall report, as gross income the total amount of the dual consolidated loss to which the triggering event applies on its income tax return for the taxable year in which the triggering event occurs (or, when the triggering event is a foreign use of the dual consolidated loss, the taxable year that includes the last day of the foreign tax year during which such foreign use occurs).

(ii) *Interest charge.*—In connection with the recapture, the elector shall pay an interest charge. Except as otherwise provided in this section, such interest shall be determined under the rules of section 6601(a) as if the additional tax owed as a result of the recapture had accrued and been due and owing for the taxable year in which the losses or deductions taken into account in computing the dual consolidated loss gave rise to a tax benefit for U.S. income tax purposes. For purposes of this paragraph (h)(1)(ii), a tax benefit shall be considered to have arisen in a taxable year in which such losses or deductions reduced U.S. taxable income. See § 1.1503(d)-5(c) *Example 51.*

(2) *Reduction of presumptive recapture amount and presumptive interest charge.*— (i) *Amount of recapture.*—The amount of dual consolidated loss that must be recaptured under paragraph (h) of this section may be reduced if the elector demonstrates, to the satisfaction of the Commissioner, the offset permitted by this paragraph (h)(2)(i). The reduction in the amount of recapture is the amount by which the dual consolidated loss would have offset other taxable income reported on a timely filed U.S. income tax return for any taxable year up to and including the taxable year of the triggering event if such loss had been subject to the restrictions of § 1.1503(d)-2(b) (and therefore subject to the limitation under § 1.1503(d)-3(c)(3)). In the case of a separate unit, the prior sentence is applied as if the separate unit were a separate domestic corporation that filed a consolidated return with its unaffiliated domestic owner or with the consolidated group of its affiliated domestic owner. For purposes of determining the reduction in the amount of recapture pursuant to this paragraph, the rules under § 1.1503(d)-3(b) shall apply. Any reduction to recapture pursuant to this paragraph that is attributable to income generated in taxable years prior to the year in which the dual consolidated loss was generated, subject to the restrictions of § 1.1503(d)-2(b) (and therefore subject to the limitation under § 1.1503(d)-3(c)(3)), shall be permitted only if the elector demonstrates to the satisfaction of the Commissioner that the dual resident corporation or separate unit, as the case may be, qualified as such (with respect to the same foreign country in which the dual consolidated loss was generated) in the taxable years such income was generated. An elector utilizing this rebuttal rule must prepare a separate accounting showing that the income for each year that offsets the dual resident corporation or separate unit's recapture amount is attributable only to the dual resident corporation or separate unit. The separate accounting must be signed under penalties of perjury by the person who signs the elector's tax return, must be labeled Reduction of Recapture Amount at the top of

the page, and must indicate that it is submitted under the provisions of paragraph (h)(2)(i) of this section. The accounting must be attached to, and filed by the due date (including extensions) of, the elector's income tax return for the taxable year in which the triggering event occurs.

(ii) *Interest charge.*—The interest charge imposed under this section may be appropriately reduced if the elector demonstrates, to the satisfaction of the Commissioner, that the net interest owed would have been less than that provided in paragraph (h)(1)(ii) of this section if the elector had filed an amended return for the taxable year in which the loss was incurred, and for any other affected taxable years up to and including the taxable year of recapture, treating the dual consolidated loss as a loss subject to the restrictions of §1.1503(d)-2(b) (and therefore subject to the limitations under §1.1503(d)-3(c)(3)). In the case of a separate unit, the prior sentence is applied as if the separate unit were a separate domestic corporation that filed a consolidated return with its unaffiliated domestic owner. An elector utilizing this rebuttal rule must prepare a computation demonstrating the reduction in the net interest owed as a result of treating the dual consolidated loss as a loss subject to the restrictions of §1.1503(d)-2(b) (and therefore subject to the limitations under §1.1503(d)-3(c)(3)). The computation must be labeled Reduction of Interest Charge at the top of the page and must indicate that it is submitted under the provisions of paragraph (h)(2)(ii) of this section. The computation must be signed under penalties of perjury by the person who signs the elector's tax return, and must be attached to, and filed by the due date (including extensions) of, the elector's income tax return for the taxable year in which the triggering event occurs. See §1.1503(d)-5(c) *Examples 51* and *52.*

(3) *Rules regarding subsequent electors.*—(i) *In general.*—The rules of this paragraph (h)(3) apply when, subsequent to an event described in paragraph (e)(1) of this section with respect to which the requirements of paragraph (f)(2)(i) of this section were met (excepted event), a triggering event under paragraph (e) of this section occurs, and no exception applies to such triggering event under paragraph (f) of this section (subsequent triggering event).

(ii) *Original elector and prior subsequent electors not subject to recapture or interest charge.*—(A) Except to the extent provided in paragraph (h)(3) of this section, neither the original elector nor any prior subsequent elector shall be subject to the rules of paragraph (h) of this section with respect to dual consolidated losses subject to the original domestic use agreement.

(B) In the case of a dual consolidated loss with respect to which multiple excepted events have occurred, only the subsequent elector that owns the dual resident corporation or separate unit at the time of the subsequent triggering event shall be subject to the recapture rules of paragraph (h) of this section. For purposes of paragraph (h) of this section, the term *prior subsequent elector* refers to all other subsequent electors.

(iii) *Recapture tax amount and required statement.*—(A) *In general.*—If a subsequent triggering event occurs, the subsequent elector must prepare a statement that computes the recapture tax amount, as provided under paragraph (h)(3)(iii)(B) of this section, with respect to the dual consolidated loss subject to the new domestic use agreement. This statement must be attached to, and filed by the due date (including extensions) of, the subsequent elector's income tax return for the taxable year in which the subsequent triggering event occurs. The statement must be signed under penalties of perjury by the person who signs the return. The statement must be labeled Statement Identifying Secondary Liability at the top and, in addition to the calculation of the recapture tax amount, must include the following items, in paragraphs labeled to correspond with the items set forth in paragraphs (h)(3)(iii)(A)(*1*) through (*3*) of this section:

(*1*) A statement that the document is submitted under the provisions of §1.1503(d)-4(h)(3)(iii);

(*2*) A statement identifying the amount of the dual consolidated losses at issue and the taxable year in which they were used;

(*3*) The name, address, and tax identification number of the original elector and all prior subsequent electors.

(B) *Recapture tax amount.*—The *recapture tax amount* equals the excess (if any) of—

(*1*) The income tax liability of the subsequent elector for the taxable year of the subsequent triggering event; over

(*2*) The income tax liability of the subsequent elector for the taxable year of the subsequent triggering event, computed by excluding the amount of recapture and related interest charge with respect to the dual consolidated losses that are recaptured as a result of the subsequent triggering event, as provided under paragraphs (h)(1) and (h)(2) of this section.

Prop. Reg. §1.1503(d)-4(h)(3)(iii)(B)(2)

(iv) *Tax assessment and collection procedures.*—(A) *In general.*—(1) *Subsequent elector.*—An assessment identifying an income tax liability of the subsequent elector is considered an assessment of the recapture tax amount where the recapture tax amount is part of the income tax liability being assessed and the recapture tax amount is reflected in a statement attached to the subsequent elector's income tax return as provided under paragraph (h)(3)(iii) of this section.

(2) *Original elector and prior subsequent electors.*—The assessment of the recapture tax amount as set forth in paragraph (h)(3)(iv)(A)(1) of this section shall be considered as having been properly assessed as an income tax liability of the original elector and of each prior subsequent elector, if any. The date of such assessment shall be the date the income tax liability of the subsequent elector was properly assessed. The Commissioner may collect all or a portion of such recapture tax amount from the original elector and/or the prior subsequent electors under the circumstances set forth in paragraph (h)(3)(iv)(B) of this section.

(B) *Collection from original elector and prior subsequent electors; joint and several liability.*—If the subsequent elector does not pay in full any of the income tax liability that includes a recapture tax amount, the Commissioner may collect that portion of the unpaid balance of such income tax liability attributable to the recapture tax amount in full or in part from the original elector and/or from any prior subsequent elector, provided that the following conditions are satisfied with respect to such elector—

(1) The Commissioner properly has assessed the recapture tax amount pursuant to paragraph (h)(3)(iv)(A)(*1*) of this section;

(2) The Commissioner has issued a notice and demand for payment of the recapture tax amount to the subsequent elector in accordance with § 301.6303-1 of this chapter;

(3) The subsequent elector has failed to pay all of the recapture tax amount by the date specified in such notice and demand; and

(4) The Commissioner has issued a notice and demand for payment of the unpaid portion of the recapture tax amount to the original elector, or prior subsequent elector (as the case may be), in accordance with § 301.6303-1 of this chapter. The liability imposed under this paragraph (h)(3)(iv)(B) on the original elector and each prior subsequent elector shall be joint and several.

(C) *Allocation of partial payments of tax.*—If the subsequent elector's income tax liability for a taxable period includes a recapture tax amount, and if such income tax liability is satisfied in part by payment, credit, or offset, such payment, credit or offset shall be allocated first to that portion of the income tax liability that is not attributable to the recapture tax amount, and then to that portion of the income tax liability that is attributable to the recapture tax amount.

(D) *Refund.*—If the Commissioner makes a refund of any income tax liability that includes a recapture tax amount, the Commissioner shall allocate and pay the refund to each elector who paid a portion of such income tax liability as follows:

(*1*) The Commissioner shall first determine the total amount of recapture tax paid by and/or collected from the original elector and from any prior subsequent elector(s). The Commissioner shall then allocate and pay such refund to the original elector and prior subsequent elector(s), with each such elector receiving an amount of such refund on a pro rata basis, not to exceed the amount of recapture tax paid by and/or collected from such elector.

(*2*) The Commissioner shall pay any balance of such refund, if any, to the subsequent elector.

(v) *Definition of income tax liability.*—Solely for purposes of paragraph (h)(3) of this section, the term *income tax liability* means the income tax liability imposed on a domestic corporation under Title 26 of the United States Code for a taxable year, including additions to tax, additional amounts, penalties, and any interest charge related to such income tax liability.

(vi) *Example.*—See § 1.1503(d)-5(c) *Example 49.*

(4) *Computation of taxable income in year of recapture.*—(i) *Presumptive rule.*—Except to the extent provided in paragraph (h)(4)(ii) of this section, for purposes of computing the taxable income for the year of recapture, no current, carryover or carryback losses of the dual resident corporation or separate unit, of other members of the consolidated group, or of the domestic owner that are not attributable to the separate unit, may offset and absorb the recapture amount.

(ii) *Rebuttal of presumptive rule.*—The recapture amount included in gross income may be offset and absorbed by that portion of the elector's (consolidated or separate) net operating loss carryover that is attributable to the dual consolidated loss being recaptured, if the elector demonstrates, to the satisfaction of the Commissioner, the amount of such portion of the carryover. An elector utilizing this rebuttal rule must prepare a computation demonstrating the amount of net operating loss carryover that, under this paragraph (h)(4)(ii) of this section, may absorb the recapture amount included in gross income. Such computation must be signed under penalties of perjury and attached to and filed by the due date (including extensions) of, the income tax return for the taxable year in which the triggering event occurs.

(5) *Character and source of recapture income.*—The amount recaptured under paragraph (h) of this section shall be treated as ordinary income. Except as provided in the prior sentence, such income shall be treated, as applicable, as income from the same source, having the same character, and falling within the same separate category, for all purposes of the Internal Revenue Code, including sections 856(c)(2) and (3), 904(d), and 907, to which the items of deduction or loss composing the dual consolidated loss were allocated and apportioned, as provided under sections 861(b), 862(b), 863(a), 864(e), 865 and the regulations thereunder. See § 1.1503(d)-5(c) *Example 50.*

(6) *Reconstituted net operating loss.*—Commencing in the taxable year immediately following the year in which the dual consolidated loss is recaptured, the dual resident corporation or separate unit (but only if such separate unit is owned, directly or indirectly, by a domestic corporation) shall be treated as having a net operating loss in an amount equal to the amount actually recaptured under paragraph (h) of this section. This reconstituted net operating loss shall be subject to the restrictions of § 1.1503(d)-2(b) (and therefore, the restrictions of § 1.1503(d)-3(c)(3)), without regard to the exceptions contained in paragraphs (b) through (d) of this section. The net operating loss shall be available only for carryover, under section 172(b), to taxable years following the taxable year of recapture. For purposes of determining the remaining carryover period, the loss shall be treated as if it had been recognized in the taxable year in which the dual consolidated loss that is the basis of the recapture amount was incurred. See § 1.1503(d)-5(c) *Example 52.*

(i) *Termination of domestic use agreement and annual certifications.*—(1) *Rebuttal of triggering event.*—If, pursuant to paragraph (e)(2) of this section, an elector is able to rebut the presumption of a triggering event described in paragraphs (e)(1)(ii) through (ix) of this section, including complying with the related reporting requirements, then the domestic use agreement filed with respect to any dual consolidated losses that would have been recaptured as a result of the event, but for the rebuttal, shall terminate and have no further effect. See § 1.1503(d)-5(c) *Example 43.*

(2) *Exception to triggering event.*—If an event described in paragraph (e)(1) of this section is not a triggering event as a result of the application of paragraph (f)(2)(i) or (ii) of this section, then the domestic use agreement filed with respect to any dual consolidated losses that would have been recaptured as a result of the event, but for the application of paragraph (f)(2)(i) or (f)(2)(ii) of this section, shall terminate and have no further effect. See § 1.1503(d)-5(c) *Examples 46* and *49.*

(3) *Recapture of dual consolidated loss.*—If a dual consolidated loss is recaptured pursuant to paragraph (h) of this section, then the domestic use agreement filed with respect to such recaptured dual consolidated loss shall terminate and have no further effect. See § 1.1503(d)-5(c) *Examples 49* through *52.*

(4) *Termination of ability for foreign use.*—(i) *In general.*—A domestic use agreement filed with respect to a dual consolidated loss shall terminate and have no further effect as of the end of a taxable year if the elector—

(A) Demonstrates, to the satisfaction of the Commissioner, that as of the end of such taxable year no foreign use of the dual consolidated loss can occur in any year by any means; and

(B) Prepares a statement described in paragraph (i)(4)(ii) of this section that is attached to, and filed by the due date (including extensions) of, its U.S. income tax return for such taxable year.

(ii) *Statement.*—The statement described in this paragraph (i)(4)(ii) must be signed under penalties of perjury by the person who signs the return. The statement must be labeled Termination of Ability for Foreign Use at the top of the page and must include the following items, in paragraphs labeled to correspond with the following:

(A) A statement that the document is submitted under the provisions of § 1.1503(d)-4(i)(4).

(B) The name, address, tax identification number, and place and date of incorporation of the dual resident corporation, and the country or countries that tax the dual resident corporation on its worldwide income or on a residence basis, or, in the case of a separate unit, identification of the separate unit, including the name under which it conducts business, its principal activity, and the country in which its principal place of business is located.

(C) A statement of the amount of the dual consolidated loss at issue and the year in which such dual consolidated loss was incurred.

(D) An analysis, in reasonable detail and specificity, supported with official or certified English translations of the relevant provisions of foreign law, of the treatment of the losses and deductions composing the dual consolidated loss under the laws of the foreign jurisdiction and the reasons supporting the conclusion that no foreign use of the dual consolidated loss can occur in any year by any means. [Prop. Reg. § 1.1503(d)-4.]

[Proposed 5-24-2005.]

Proposed Regulation

§ 1.1503(d)-5. Examples.—(a) *In general.*—This section provides examples that illustrate the application of §§ 1.1503(d)-1 through 1.1503(d)-4. This section also provides facts that are presumed for such examples.

(b) *Presumed facts for examples.*—For purposes of the examples in this section, unless otherwise indicated, the following facts are presumed:

(1) Each entity has only a single class of equity outstanding, all of which is held by a single owner.

(2) P, a domestic corporation and the common parent of the P consolidated group, owns S, a domestic corporation and a member of the P consolidated group.

(3) DRC_X, a domestic corporation, is subject to Country X tax on its worldwide income or on a residence basis, and is a dual resident corporation.

(4) $DE1_X$ and $DE2_X$ are both Country X entities, subject to Country X tax on their worldwide income or on a residence basis, and disregarded as entities separate from their owners for U.S. tax purposes. $DE3_Y$ is a Country Y entity, subject to Country Y tax on its worldwide income or on a residence basis, and disregarded as an entity separate from its owner for U.S. tax purposes. The interests in $DE1_X$, $DE2_X$, and $DE3_Y$ constitute hybrid entity separate units.

(5) FB_X is a foreign branch, as defined in § 1.367(a)-6T(g), and is a Country X foreign branch separate unit.

(6) Neither the assets nor the activities of an entity constitutes a foreign branch separate unit.

(7) FS_X is a Country X entity that is subject to Country X tax on its worldwide income or on a residence basis and is classified as a foreign corporation for U.S. tax purposes.

(8) The applicable foreign jurisdiction has a consolidation regime that—

(i) Includes as members of a consolidated group any commonly controlled branches and permanent establishments in such jurisdiction, and entities that are subject to tax in such jurisdiction on their worldwide income or on a residence basis; and

(ii) Allows the losses of members of consolidated groups to offset income of other members.

(9) There is no mirror legislation, within the meaning of § 1.1503(d)-1(b)(14)(v), in the applicable foreign jurisdiction.

(10) There is no elective agreement described in § 1.1503(d)-4(b) between the United States and the applicable foreign jurisdiction.

(11) If a domestic use election, within the meaning of § 1.1503(d)-4(d), is made, all the necessary filings related to such election are properly completed on a timely basis.

(12) If there is a triggering event requiring recapture of a dual consolidated loss, the amount of recapture is not reduced pursuant to § 1.1503(d)-4(h)(2).

(c) *Examples.*—The following examples illustrate the application of §§ 1.1503(d)-1 through 1.1503(d)-4:

Example 1. Separate unit combination rule. (i) *Facts.* P owns $DE3_Y$ which, in turn, owns $DE1_X$. $DE1_X$ owns FB_X. Domestic partnership PRS, owned 50% by P and 50% by an unrelated foreign person, conducts operations in Country X that constitute a foreign branch within the meaning of § 1.367(a)-6T(g). S owns $DE2_X$.

(ii) *Result.* Pursuant to § 1.1503(d)-1(b)(4)(ii), the interest in $DE1_X$, FB_X, and P's share of the Country X branch owned by PRS, which is owned by P indirectly through its interest in PRS, are combined and treated as one separate unit owned by P. P's interest in $DE3_Y$, however, is another separate unit because it is subject to tax in Country Y, rather than Country X. S's interest in $DE2_X$ also is another separate unit because it is owned by S, a different domestic corporation.

Example 2. Domestic use limitation—foreign branch separate unit. (i) *Facts.* P conducts operations in Country X that constitute a permanent establishment under the Country X income tax laws. In Year 1, P's Country X permanent establishment has a loss, as determined under § 1.1503(d)-3(b)(2).

(ii) *Result.* Under § 1.1503(d)-1(b)(4)(i) and § 1.367(a)-6T(g)(1), P's Country X permanent establishment constitutes a foreign branch separate unit. Therefore, the Year 1 loss of the foreign branch separate unit constitutes a dual consolidated loss pursuant to § 1.1503(d)-1(b)(5)(ii). The dual consolidated loss rules apply even though there is no affiliate of the foreign branch separate unit in Country X because it is still possible that all or a portion of the dual consolidated loss can be put to a foreign use. For example, there may be a foreign use with respect to an affiliate acquired in a year subsequent to the year in which the dual consolidated loss was generated. Accordingly, unless an exception under § 1.1503(d)-4 applies (such as a domestic use election), the Year 1 dual consolidated loss of P's Country X permanent establishment is subject to the domestic use limitation rule of § 1.1503(d)-2(b). As a result, the Year 1 dual consolidated loss cannot offset income of P that is not from its Country X foreign branch separate unit, or income from any other domestic affiliate of such foreign branch separate unit.

Example 3. Domestic use limitation—no foreign consolidation regime. (i) *Facts.* The facts are the same as in *Example 2*, except that Country X does not have a consolidation regime that includes as members of consolidated groups Country X branches or permanent establishments.

(ii) *Result.* The result is the same as *Example 2*. The dual consolidated loss rules apply even in the absence of a consolidation regime in the foreign country because it is possible that all or a portion of a dual consolidated loss can be put to a foreign use by other means, such as through an acquisition or similar transaction.

Example 4. Domestic use limitation—foreign branch separate unit owned through a partnership. (i) *Facts.* P and S organize a partnership, PRS_X, under the laws of Country X. PRS_X is treated as a partnership for both U.S. and Country X income tax purposes. PRS_X owns FB_X. PRS_X earns U.S. source income that is unconnected with its FB_X branch operations and such income, therefore, is not subject to tax by Country X.

(ii) *Result.* Under § 1.1503(d)-1(b)(4)(i), P's and S's shares of FB_X owned indirectly through their interests in PRS_X are foreign branch separate units. Unless an exception under § 1.1503(d)-4 applies, any dual consolidated loss incurred by FB_X cannot offset income of P or S (other than income attributable to FB_X), including their distributive share of the U.S. source income earned through their interests in PRS_X, or income of any other domestic affiliates of FB_X.

Example 5. Domestic use limitation—interest in hybrid entity partnership and indirectly owned foreign branch separate unit. (i) *Facts.* HPS_X is a Country X entity that is subject to Country X tax on its worldwide income. HPS_X is classified as a partnership for U.S. tax purposes. P, S, and F_X, an unrelated Country X corporation, are the sole partners of HPS_X. For U.S. tax purposes, P, S, and F_X each has an equal interest in each item of HPS_X's profit or loss. HPS_X conduct operations in Country Y that, if carried on by a U.S. person, would constitute a foreign branch within the meaning of § 1.367(a)-6T(g).

(ii) *Result.* Under § 1.1503(d)-1(b)(4)(i), the partnership interests in HPS_X held by P and S are hybrid entity separate units. In addition, P's and S's share of the Country Y branch owned indirectly through their interests in HPS_X are foreign branch separate units. Unless an exception under § 1.1503(d)-4 applies, dual consolidated losses attributable to P's and S's interests in HPS_X can only be used to offset income attributable to their respective interests in HPS_X (other than income of HPS_X's Country Y foreign branch separate unit). Similarly, dual consolidated losses of P's and S's interests in the Country Y branch of HPS_X can only be used to offset income attributable to their respective interests in the Country Y branch.

Example 6. Foreign use—general rule. (i) *Facts.* P owns $DE1_X$. $DE1_X$ owns FS_X. In Year 1, $DE1_X$ incurs a $100x net operating loss for both U.S. and Country X tax purposes. The $100x Year 1 loss of $DE1_X$ is attributable to P's interest in $DE1_X$ and is a dual consolidated loss. FS_X earns $200x of income in Year 1 for Country X tax purposes. $DE1_X$ and FS_X file a Country X consolidated tax return. For Country X purposes, the Year 1 $100x loss of $DE1_X$ is used to offset $100x of Year 1 income generated by FS_X.

(ii) *Result.* $DE1_X$'s $100x loss offsets FS_X's income under the laws of Country X. In addition, under U.S. tax principles, such income is an item of FS_X, a foreign corporation. As a result, under § 1.1503(d)-1(b)(14)(i), there has been a foreign use of the Year 1 dual consolidated loss attributable to P's interest in $DE1_X$. Therefore, P cannot make a domestic use election with respect to the Year 1 dual consolidated loss of $DE1_X$ as provided under § 1.1503(d)-4(d)(3)(i), and such loss will be subject to the domestic use limitation rule of § 1.1503(d)-2(b). The result would be the same even if FS_X, under Country X laws, had no income against which the dual consolidated loss of $DE1_X$ could be offset (unless FS_X's ability to use the loss under Country X laws requires an election, and no such election is made).

Example 7. Foreign use—foreign reverse hybrid structure. (i) *Facts.* P owns $DE1_X$. $DE1_X$ owns 99% and S owns 1% of FRH_X, a Country X partnership that elected to be treated as a corporation for U.S. tax purposes. FRH_X conducts an active business in Country X. The 99% interest in FRH_X is the only asset owned by $DE1_X$. $DE1_X$'s sole item of income, gain, deduction, or loss in Year 1 for purposes of calculating a dual consolidated loss attributable to P's interest in

Prop. Reg. § 1.1503(d)-5(c)

$DE1_X$ is interest expense incurred on a loan from an unrelated party. $DE1_X$'s Year 1 interest expense constitutes a dual consolidated loss. In Year 1, for Country X income tax purposes, $DE1_X$ took into account its distributive share of income generated by FRH_X and offset such income with its interest expense.

(ii) *Result.* In year 1, the dual consolidated loss attributable to P's interest in $DE1_X$, offsets income recognized in Country X and under U.S. tax principles the income is considered to be income of FRH_X, a foreign corporation. Accordingly, pursuant to § 1.1503(d)-1(b)(14)(i), there is a foreign use of the dual consolidated loss. Therefore, P cannot make a domestic use election with respect to $DE1_X$'s Year 1 dual consolidated loss, as provided under § 1.1503(d)-4(d)(3)(i), and such loss will be subject to the domestic use limitation rule of § 1.1503(d)-2(b).

Example 8. Foreign use—inapplicability of no dilution exception to foreign reverse hybrid structure. (i) *Facts.* The facts are the same as in *Example 7*, except as follows. Instead of owning $DE1_X$, P owns 75% of HPS_X, a Country X entity subject to Country X tax on its worldwide income. F_X, an unrelated foreign corporation, owns the remaining 25% of HPS_X. HPS_X is classified as a partnership for U.S. income tax purposes. HPS_X owns 99% and S owns 1% of FRH_X. HPS_X incurs the Year 1 interest expense and P's interest in HPS_X, therefore, has a dual consolidated loss in Year 1.

(ii) *Result.* In year 1, the dual consolidated loss attributable to P's interest in HPS_X offsets income recognized under Country X law and under U.S. tax principles the income is considered to be income of FRH_X, a foreign corporation. Accordingly, pursuant to § 1.1503(d)-1(b)(14)(i), there is a foreign use of the dual consolidated loss. In addition, the exception to foreign use under § 1.1503(d)-1(b)(14)(iii)(C)(*1*)(*i*) does not apply because the foreign use is not solely the result of the dual consolidated loss being made available under Country X laws to offset an item of income or gain recognized under Country X laws that is considered, under U.S. tax principles, to be an item of F_X. Instead, the income that is offset is, under U.S. tax principles, income of FRH_X, a foreign corporation. Therefore, P cannot make a domestic use election with respect to the Year 1 dual consolidated loss attributable to its interest in HPS_X, and such loss will be subject to the domestic use limitation rule of § 1.1503(d)-2(b).

Example 9. Foreign use—dual resident corporation with hybrid entity joint venture. (i) *Facts.* P owns DRC_X, a member of the P consolidated group. DRC_X owns 80% of HPS_X, a Country X entity that is subject to Country X tax on its worldwide income. HPS_X is classified as a partnership for U.S. tax purposes. F_X, an unrelated foreign corporation, owns the remaining 20% of HPS_X. In Year 1, DRC_X generates a $100x net operating loss. Also in Year 1, HPS_X generates $100x of income for Country X tax purposes. DRC_X and HPS_X file a consolidated tax return for Country X tax purposes, and HPS_X offsets its $100x of income with the $100x loss generated by DRC_X.

(ii) *Result.* The $100x Year 1 net operating loss incurred by DRC_X is a dual consolidated loss. In addition, HPS_X is a hybrid entity and DRC_X's interest in HPS_X is a hybrid entity separate unit; however, there is no dual consolidated loss attributable to such separate unit in Year 1. DRC_X's Year 1 dual consolidated loss offsets $100x of income for Country X purposes, and $20x of such amount is (under U.S. tax principles) income of F_X, which owns an interest in HPS_X that is not a separate unit. As a result, pursuant to § 1.1503(d)-1(b)(14)(i), there is a foreign use of the Year 1 dual consolidated loss of DRC_X, and P cannot make a domestic use election with respect to such loss pursuant to § 1.1503(d)-4(d)(3)(i). Therefore, such loss will be subject to the domestic use limitation rule of § 1.1503(d)-2(b).

Example 10. Foreign use—foreign parent corporation. (i) *Facts.* F1 and F2, nonresident alien individuals, each own 50% of FP_X, a Country X entity that is subject to Country X tax on its worldwide income. FP_X is classified as a corporation for U.S. tax purposes. FP_X owns DRC_X. DRC_X is the parent of a consolidated group that includes as a member DS, a domestic corporation. In Year 1, DRC_X generates a dual consolidated loss of $100x and, for Country X tax purposes, FP_X generates $100x of income. In Year 1, FP_X elects to consolidate with DRC_X, and the $100x Year 1 loss of DRC_X is used to offset the income of FP_X under the laws of Country X. For U.S. tax purposes, the items of FP_X do not constitute items of income in Year 1.

(ii) *Result.* The Year 1 dual consolidated loss of DRC_X offsets the income of FP_X under the laws of Country X. Pursuant to § 1.1503(d)-1(b)(14)(i), the offset constitutes a foreign use because the items constituting such income are considered under U.S. tax principles to be items of a foreign corporation. This is the case even though the United States does not recognize such items as income in Year 1. Therefore, DRC_X cannot make a domestic use election with respect to its Year 1 dual consolidated loss pursuant to § 1.1503(d)-4(d)(3)(i). As a result, such loss will be subject to the domestic use limitation rule of § 1.1503(d)-2(b).

Example 11. Foreign use—parent hybrid entity. (i) *Facts.* The facts are the same as *Exam-*

ple 10, except that FP_X is classified as a partnership for U.S. tax purposes.

(ii) *Result.* The dual consolidated loss of DRC_X offsets the income of FP_X under the laws of Country X. Pursuant to § 1.1503(d)-1(b)(14)(i), such offset constitutes a foreign use because the items constituting such income are considered under U.S. tax principles to be items of F1 and F2, the owners of interests in FP_X (a hybrid entity), that are not separate units. Therefore, DRC_X cannot make a domestic use election with respect to its Year 1 dual consolidated loss pursuant to § 1.1503(d)-4(d)(3)(i). As a result, such loss will be subject to the domestic use limitation rule of § 1.1503(d)-2(b). The result would be the same if F1 and F2 owned their interests in FP_X indirectly through another partnership.

Example 12. No foreign use—absence of foreign loss allocation rules. (i) *Facts.* P owns $DE1_X$ and DRC_X. DRC_X is a member of the P consolidated group and owns FS_X. In Year 1, DRC_X incurs a $200x net operating loss for both U.S. and Country X tax purposes, while $DE1_X$ recognizes $200x of income in Year 1 under the laws of each country. The $200x loss of DRC_X is a dual consolidated loss. FS_X also earns $200x of income in Year 1 for Country X tax purposes. DRC_X, $DE1_X$, and FS_X file a Country X consolidated tax return. However, Country X has no applicable rules for determining which income is offset by DRC_X's Year 1 $200x loss.

(ii) *Result.* Under § 1.1503(d)-1 (b)(14)(iii)(B), DRC_X's $200x loss shall be treated as having been made available to offset $DE1_X$'s $200x of income. $DE1_X$ is not, under U.S. tax principles, a foreign corporation, and there is no interest in $DE1_X$ that is not a separate unit. As a result, DRC_X's loss being made available to offset the income of $DE1_X$ is not considered a foreign use of such loss. Therefore, P can make a domestic use election with respect to DRC_X's Year 1 dual consolidated loss.

Example 13. No foreign use—absence of foreign loss usage ordering rules. (i) *Facts.* (A) P owns DRC_X, a member of the P consolidated group. DRC_X owns FS_X. Under the Country X consolidation regime, a consolidated group may elect in any given year to use all or a portion of the losses of one consolidated group member to offset income of other consolidated group members. If no such election is made in a year in which losses are generated by a consolidated member, such losses carry forward and are available, at the election of the consolidated group, to offset income of consolidated group members in subsequent tax years. Country X law does not provide ordering rules for determining when a loss from a particular tax year is used because, under Country X law, losses never expire. Similarly, Country X law does not provide ordering rules for determining when a particular type of loss (for example, capital or ordinary) is used. The United States and Country X recognize the same items of income, gain, deduction and loss in each year. In addition, neither DRC_X nor FS_X has items of income or loss for the taxable year other than those stated below.

(B) In Year 1, DRC_X incurs a capital loss of $80x which, under § 1.1503(d)-3(b)(1), is not a dual consolidated loss. DRC_X also incurs a net operating loss of $80x in Year 1. FS_X generates $60x of capital gain in Year 1 which, for Country X purposes, can be offset by capital losses and net operating losses. DRC_X elects to use $60x of its total Year 1 loss of $160x to offset the $60x of capital gain generated by FS_X in Year 1; the remaining $100x of Year 1 loss carries forward. In Year 2, DRC_X incurs a net operating loss of $100x, while FS_X incurs a net operating loss of $50x. DRC_X's $100x loss is a dual consolidated loss. Because DRC_X does not elect under the laws of Country X to use all or a portion of its Year 2 net operating loss of $100x to offset the income of other members of the Country X consolidated group, P is permitted to make (and in fact does make) a domestic use election with respect to the Year 2 dual consolidated loss of DRC_X. In Year 3, DRC_X has a net operating loss of $10x and FS_X generates $60x of capital gains. Country X law permits, upon an election, FS_X's $60x of capital gain generated in Year 3 to be offset by losses (including carryover losses from prior years) of other group members. Accordingly, in Year 3, DRC_X elects to use $60x of its accumulated losses to offset the $60x of Year 3 capital gain generated by FS_X.

(ii) *Result.* (A) DRC_X's $80x Year 1 net operating loss is a dual consolidated loss. Under the ordering rules of § 1.1503(d)-1(b)(14)(iv)(C), a pro rata amount of DRC_X's Year 1 net operating loss ($30x) and capital loss ($30x) is considered to be used to offset FS_X's Year 1 $60x capital gain. As a result, P will not be able to make a domestic use election with respect to DRC_X's Year 1 $80x dual consolidated loss.

(B) DRC_X's $10x Year 3 net operating loss is also a dual consolidated loss. Under the ordering rules of § 1.1503(d)-1(b)(14)(iv)(A), such loss is considered to be used to offset $10x of FS_X's Year 3 $60x capital gain. Consequently, P will not be able to make a domestic use election with respect to such loss. Under the ordering rules of § 1.1503(d)-1(b)(14)(iv)(B), $50x of loss carryover from Year 1 will be considered to offset the remaining $50x of Year 3 income because the income is deemed to have been offset by losses from the earliest taxable year from which a loss can be carried forward or back for foreign law purposes. Thus, none of DRC_X's $100x Year 2 net operating loss will be

Prop. Reg. § 1.1503(d)-5(c)

deemed to offset FS$_X$'s remaining $50x of Year 3 income. As a result, such offset will not constitute a foreign use of DRC$_X$'s Year 2 dual consolidated loss.

Example 14. No foreign use—no dilution of an interest in a separate unit. (i) *Facts.* (A) P owns 50% of HPS$_X$, a Country X entity subject to Country X tax on its worldwide income. F$_X$, an unrelated foreign corporation, owns the remaining 50% of HPS$_X$. HPS$_X$ is classified as a partnership for U.S. income tax purposes.

(B) The United States and Country X recognize the same items of income, gain, deduction and loss in Years 1 and 2. In Year 1, HPS$_X$ incurs a loss of $100x. Under § 1.1503(d)-1(b)(4)(i)(B), P's interest in HPS$_X$ is a separate unit and P's interest in HPS$_X$ has a dual consolidated loss of $50x in Year 1. P makes a domestic use election with respect to such dual consolidated loss. In Year 2, HPS$_X$ generates $50x of income. Under Country X income tax laws, the $100x of Year 1 loss incurred by HPS$_X$ is carried forward and offsets the $50x of income generated by HPS$_X$ in Year 2; the remaining $50x of loss is carried forward and is available to offset income generated by HPS$_X$ in subsequent years. P and F$_X$ maintain their 50% ownership interests in HPS$_X$ throughout Years 1 and 2.

(ii) *Result.* In Year 2, under the laws of Country X, the $100x of Year 1 loss, which includes the $50x dual consolidated loss attributable to P's interest in HPS$_X$, is made available to offset income of HPS$_X$. Such income would be attributable to P's interest in HPS$_X$, which is a separate unit. Such income would also be income of F$_X$, an owner of an interest in HPS$_X$, which is not a separate unit. Under § 1.1503(d)-1(b)(14)(iii)(B), because Country X does not have applicable rules for determining which Year 2 income of HPS$_X$ is offset by the $100x loss carried forward from year 1, the $50x dual consolidated loss is deemed to first have been made available to offset the $25x of income attributable to P's interest in HPS$_X$. However, because only $25x of income is attributable to P's interest in HPS$_X$, a portion of the remaining $25x of the dual consolidated loss is made available (under U.S. tax principles) to offset income of F$_X$. As a result, a portion of the $50x dual consolidated loss is made available to offset income of the owner of an interest in a hybrid entity that is not a separate unit and, under the general rule of § 1.1503(d)-1(b)(14)(i), there would be a foreign use of P's $50x Year 1 dual consolidated loss (there would also be a foreign use in this case because F$_X$ is a foreign corporation). However, pursuant to the exception to foreign use under § 1.1503(d)-1(b)(14)(iii)(C)(1)(i), there is no foreign use of the Year 1 dual consolidated loss in Year 2. In addition, the exceptions under § 1.1503(d)-1(b)(14)(iii)(C)(2) do not apply because P's interest in HPS$_X$ as of the end of Year 1 has not been reduced, and the portion of the $50x dual consolidated loss was made available for a foreign use in Year 2 solely as a result of F$_X$'s ownership in HPS$_X$ and by the offsetting of income attributable to HPS$_X$, the partnership in which F$_X$ holds an interest. Therefore, there is no foreign use of the Year 1 dual consolidated loss in Year 2. The result would be the same if F$_X$ owned its interest in HPS$_X$ indirectly through a partnership.

Example 15. Foreign use—dilution of an interest in a separate unit. (i) *Facts.* The facts are the same as *Example 14*, except that at the beginning of Year 2, F$_X$ contributes cash to HPS$_X$ in exchange for additional equity of HPS$_X$. As a result of the contribution, F$_X$'s interest in HPS$_X$ increases from 50% to 60%, and P's interest in HPS$_X$ decreases from 50% to 40%.

(ii) *Result.* At the beginning of Year 2, P's interest in HPS$_X$ has been reduced as a result of a person other than a domestic corporation acquiring an interest in HPS$_X$. Accordingly, pursuant to § 1.1503(d)-1(b)(14)(iii)(C)(2)(i), the exception to foreign use provided under § 1.1503(d)-1(b)(14)(iii)(C)(1)(i) does not apply. Therefore, in Year 2 there is a foreign use of the $50x Year 1 dual consolidated loss attributable to P's interest in HPS$_X$. Such foreign use constitutes a triggering event and the $50x Year 1 dual consolidated loss is recaptured.

Example 16. No foreign use—dilution by a domestic corporation. (i) *Facts.* The facts are the same as *Example 14*, except that at the beginning of Year 2, instead of F$_X$ contributing cash to HPS$_X$, S purchases 20% of P's interest in HPS$_X$. As a result of the purchase, P's interest in HPS$_X$ decreases from 50% to 40%.

(ii) *Result.* At the beginning of Year 2, P's interest in HPS$_X$ has been reduced as a result of a person acquiring an interest in HPS$_X$. Accordingly, § 1.1503(d)-1(b)(14)(iii)(C)(1)(i) generally does not apply, and there would be a foreign use of the $50x Year 1 dual consolidated loss attributable to P's interest in HPS$_X$. However, if P demonstrates, to the satisfaction of the Commissioner, that S is a domestic corporation in a statement attached to, and filed by the due date (including extensions) of P's U.S. income tax return for the taxable year in which the ownership interest of P was reduced, the exception to foreign use under § 1.1503-1(b)(14)(iii)(C)(1)(i) will apply. In such a case, there will be no foreign use of the $50x Year 1 dual consolidated loss attributable to P's interest in HPS$_X$. The result would be the same if S were unrelated to P, or if S acquired its interest in HPS$_X$ through the contribution of property to HPS$_X$ in exchange for equity (rather than as a purchase of a portion of P's interest).

Example 17. Foreign use—foreign consolidation. (i) *Facts.* (A) P and F_X, an unrelated Country X corporation, organize HPS_Y. P owns 20% of HPS_Y and F_X owns 80% of HPS_Y. HPS_Y is classified as a partnership for U.S. income tax purposes and is a Country Y entity subject to Country Y tax on its worldwide income. HPS_Y conducts operations in Country X that, if carried on by a U.S. person, would constitute a foreign branch within the meaning of § 1.367(a)-6T(g).

(B) In Year 1, the Country X branch of HPS_Y has a loss of $100x as determined under § 1.1503(d)-3(b)(2). Under § 1.1503(d)-1(b)(4)(i), P's interest in HPS_Y is a separate unit, and P's indirect interest in a portion of the Country X branch of HPS_Y is also a separate unit. As a result, P has a dual consolidated loss of $20x in Year 1 attributable to its interest in the Country X branch owned indirectly through HPS_Y. HPS_Y conducts no other activities in Year 1 and has no other items of income, gain, deduction or loss. Accordingly, there is no dual consolidated loss attributable to P's interest in HPS_Y. Under Country X income tax laws, F_X elects to consolidate with the Country X branch of HPS_Y. As a result, the $100x Year 1 loss of the Country X branch of HPS_Y is available to offset the income of F_X under the laws of Country X through consolidation.

(ii) *Result.* Pursuant to § 1.1503(d)-1(b)(14)(iii)(C)(*1*)(*ii*), P's Year 1 $20x dual consolidated loss attributable to its indirect ownership of the Country X branch of HPS_Y would not generally be considered to be made available, under the laws of Country X, to reduce or offset an item of income or gain that is considered under U.S. tax principles to be income of F_X. However, F_X elected to consolidate with the Country X branch under Country X law such that the $20x dual consolidated loss attributable to P's interest in such separate unit is available to offset income under the laws of Country X as described in § 1.1503(d)-1(b)(14)(iii)(C)(*2*)(*ii*). As a result, the exception under § 1.1503(d)-1(b)(14)(iii)(C)(*1*)(*ii*) shall not apply and there is a foreign use of the $20x Year 1 dual consolidated loss attributable to P's interest in the Country X branch of HPS_Y.

Example 18. No foreign use—no election to consolidate under foreign law. (i) *Facts.* The facts are the same as in *Example 17*, except that F_X does not elect under Country X law to consolidate with the Country X branch of HPS_Y.

(ii) *Result.* Because F_X does not elect to consolidate under foreign law, P's dual consolidated loss of $20x is not made available to offset F_X's income, other than as a result of F_X's ownership of HPS_Y. Accordingly, because there has been no dilution of P's interest in the Country X branch of HPS_Y, there has been no foreign use of P's $20x Year 1 dual consolidated loss pursuant § 1.1503(d)-1(b)(14)(iii)(C)(*1*)(*ii*).

Example 19. No foreign use—combination rule. (i) *Facts.* (A) P and F_X, an unrelated foreign corporation, form PRS_X. P and F_X each own 50 percent of PRS_X throughout Years 1 and 2. PRS_X is treated as a partnership for both U.S. and Country X income tax purposes. PRS_X owns DE_Y. DE_Y is a Country Y entity subject to Country Y tax on its worldwide income and disregarded as an entity separate from its owner for U.S. tax purposes. PRS_X does not have any items of income, gain, deduction, or loss from sources other than DE_Y. P also owns FB_Y, a Country Y foreign branch separate unit. Pursuant to Country Y law, the losses of DE_Y are available to offset the income of FB_Y, and vice versa. Under § 1.1503(d)-1(b)(4)(i), P's interest in DE_Y, owned indirectly through PRS_X, is a hybrid entity separate unit. In addition, under § 1.1503(d)-1(b)(4)(ii), FB_Y and P's indirect interest in DE_Y are treated as a combined separate unit.

(B) The United States and Country Y recognize the same items of income, gain, deduction and loss in Years 1 and 2. In year 1, DE_Y incurs a $100x loss and FB_Y incurs a $200x loss. Under § 1.1503(d)-3(b)(vii)(B), the dual consolidated loss attributable to P's combined separate unit is $250x ($50x loss attributable to P's indirect interest in DE_Y plus $200x loss of FB_Y). In Year 2, DE_Y generates no income or loss.

(ii) *Result.* Under Country Y law, the $100x of Year 1 loss incurred by DE_Y is carried forward and is available to offset income of DE_Y in Year 2. As a result, a portion of such loss will be available to offset income of DE_Y that is attributable to P's interest in DE_Y owned indirectly through PRS_X. A portion of such loss will also be available to offset income of DE_Y that is attributable to F_X's indirect ownership of DE_Y. Accordingly, under § 1.1503(d)-1(b)(14)(i), there would be a foreign use of a portion of P's $250x Year 1 dual consolidated loss because it is available to offset an item of income of the owner of an interest in a hybrid entity, which is not a separate unit (there would also be a foreign use in this case because F_X is a foreign corporation). However, under § 1.1503(d)-1(b)(14)(iii)(C)(*1*)(*ii*) and (*iii*), and because there has been no dilution of P's interest in DE_Y (and no consolidation of DE_Y), no foreign use occurs as a result of the carryforward.

Example 20. Mirror legislation rule—dual resident corporation. (i) *Facts.* P owns DRC_X, a member of the P consolidated group. DRC_X owns FS_X. In Year 1, DRC_X generates a $100x net operating loss that is a dual consolidated loss. To prevent corporations like DRC_X from offsetting losses both against income of affiliates in Country X and against income of foreign affiliates under the tax laws of another country, Country X mirror legislation prevents a corporation that is subject to the income tax of another country on its worldwide income or on a residence basis from using the Country X form of consolidation. Accordingly, the Country X mirror legislation prevents the loss of DRC_X from being made available to offset income of FS_X.

(ii) *Result.* Under § 1.1503(d)-1(b)(14)(v), because the losses of DRC_X are subject to Country X's mirror legislation, there shall, other than for purposes of the consistency rule under § 1.1503(d)-4(d)(2), be a deemed foreign use of DRC_X's Year 1 dual consolidated loss. Therefore, P will not be able to make a domestic use election with respect to DRC_X's Year 1 dual consolidated loss pursuant to § 1.1503(d)-4(d)(3)(i).

Example 21. Mirror legislation rule—standalone foreign branch separate unit. (i) *Facts.* P owns FB_X. In Year 1, FB_X incurs a dual consolidated loss of $100x. Under Country X tax laws, FB_X also generates a loss. Country X enacted mirror legislation to prevent Country X branches of nonresident corporations from offsetting losses both against income of Country X affiliates and against other income of its owner (or foreign affiliate thereof) under the tax laws of another country. The Country X mirror legislation prevents a Country X branch of a nonresident corporation from offsetting its losses against the income of Country X affiliates if such losses may be deductible against income (other than income of the Country X branch) under the laws of another country.

(ii) *Result.* Under § 1.1503(d)-1(b)(14)(v), because the losses of FB_X are subject to Country X's mirror legislation, there shall, other than for purposes of the consistency rule under § 1.1503(d)-4(d)(2), be a deemed foreign use of FB_X's Year 1 dual consolidated loss. This is the result even though P has no Country X affiliates. Therefore, P cannot make a domestic use election with respect to the Year 1 dual consolidated loss of FB_X pursuant to § 1.1503(d)-4(d)(3)(i).

Example 22. Mirror legislation rule—absence of election to file consolidated return under local law. (i) *Facts.* The facts are the same as in *Example 21*, except that P also owns FS_X and no election is made under Country X law to consolidate FB_X and FS_X.

(ii) *Result.* The result is the same as *Example 21*, even though FB_X has a Country X affiliate and no election is made under Country X law to consolidate FB_X and FS_X.

Example 23. Mirror legislation rule—inapplicability to particular dual resident corporation or separate unit. (i) *Facts.* The facts are the same as in *Example 21*, except as follows. Rather than conducting operations in Country X through a foreign branch, P owns $DE1_X$. In Year 1, $DE1_X$ incurs a loss of $100x and also generates a loss for Country X tax purposes. The $100x Year 1 loss of $DE1_X$ is a dual consolidated loss attributable to P's interest in $DE1_X$.

(ii) *Result.* The Country X mirror legislation only applies to Country X branches owned by non-resident corporations and therefore does not apply to losses generated by $DE1_X$. Thus, if $DE1_X$ had a Country X affiliate, it would be permitted under the laws of Country X to use its loss to offset income of such affiliate, notwithstanding the Country X mirror legislation. As a result, the mirror legislation rule under § 1.1503(d)-1(b)(14)(v) does not apply with respect to the Year 1 dual consolidated loss of P's interest in $DE1_X$. Therefore, a domestic use election can be made with respect to such loss (provided the conditions for such an election are otherwise satisfied).

Example 24. Dual consolidated loss limitation after section 381 transaction—disposition of assets and subsequent liquidation of dual resident corporation. (i) *Facts.* P owns DRC_X, a member of the P consolidated group. In Year 1, DRC_X incurs a dual consolidated loss and P does not make a domestic use election with respect to such loss. Under § 1.1503(d)-2(b), DRC_X's Year 1 dual consolidated loss may not be used to offset the income of P or S (or the income of any other domestic affiliate of DRC_X) on the group's consolidated U.S. income tax return. At the beginning of Year 2, DRC_X sells all of its assets and discontinues its business operations. DRC_X is then liquidated into P pursuant to section 332.

(ii) *Result.* Typically, under section 381, P would succeed to, and be permitted to utilize, DRC_X's net operating loss carryover. However, § 1.1503(d)-2(c)(1)(i) prohibits the dual consolidated loss of DRC_X from carrying over to P. Therefore, DRC_X's Year 1 net operating loss carryover is eliminated.

Example 25. Dual consolidated loss limitation after section 381 transaction—liquidation of dual resident corporation. (i) *Facts.* The facts are the same as in *Example 24*, except as follows. DRC_X's activities constitute a foreign branch within the meaning of § 1.367(a)-6T(g) and therefore are a foreign branch separate unit. In addition, DRC_X's foreign branch separate unit incurs the Year 1 dual consolidated loss, rather than DRC_X itself. Finally, DRC_X does not sell its assets and, following the liquidation of DRC_X, P continues to operate DRC_X's business as a foreign branch separate unit.

(ii) *Result.* Pursuant to § 1.1503(d)-2(c)(2)(iii), DRC_X's Year 1 loss carryover is available to offset P's income generated by the foreign branch separate unit previously owned by DRC_X (and now owned by P), subject to the limitations of §1.1503(d)-3(c) applied as if the separate unit of P generated the dual consolidated loss.

Example 26. Tainted income. (i) *Facts.* P owns 100% of DRC_Z, a domestic corporation that is included as a member of the P consolidated group. The P consolidated group uses the calendar year as its taxable year. During Year 1, DRC_Z was managed and controlled in Country Z and therefore was subject to tax as a resident of Country Z and was a dual resident corporation. In Year 1, DRC_Z generated a dual consolidated loss of $200x, and P did not make a domestic use election with respect to such loss. As a result, such loss is subject to the domestic use limitation rule of §1.1503(d)-2(b). At the end of Year 1, DRC_Z moved its management and control from Country Z to the United States and therefore ceased being a dual resident corporation. At the beginning of Year 2, P transferred asset A, a non-depreciable asset, to DRC_Z in exchange for common stock in a transaction that qualified for nonrecognition under section 351. At the time of the transfer, P's tax basis in asset A equaled $50x and the fair market value of asset A equaled $100x. The tax basis of asset A in the hands of DRC_Z immediately after the transfer equaled $50x pursuant to section 362. Asset A did not constitute replacement property acquired in the ordinary course of business. DRC_Z did not generate income or gain during Years 2, 3 or 4. On June 30, Year 5, DRC_Z sold asset A to a third party for $100x, its fair market value at the time of the sale, and recognized $50x of income on such sale. In addition to the $50x income generated on the sale of asset A, DRC_Z generated $100x of operating income in Year 5. At the end of Year 5, the fair market value of all the assets of DRC_Z was $400x.

(ii) *Result.* DRC_Z ceased being a dual resident corporation at the end of Year 1. Therefore, its Year 1 dual consolidated loss cannot be offset by tainted income. Asset A is a tainted asset because it was acquired in a nonrecognition transaction after DRC_Z ceased being a dual resident corporation (and was not replacement property acquired in the ordinary course of business). As a result, the $50x of income recognized by DRC_Z on the disposition of asset A is tainted income and cannot be offset by the Year 1 dual consolidated loss of DRC_Z. In addition, absent evidence establishing the actual amount of tainted income, $25x of the $100x Year 5 operating income of DRC_Z (($100x/$400x) × $100x) also is treated as tainted income and cannot be offset by the Year 1 dual consolidated loss of DRC_Z under §1.1503(d)-2(d)(2)(ii). Therefore, $75x of the $150x Year 5 income of DRC_Z constitutes tainted income and may not be offset by the Year 1 dual consolidated loss of DRC_Z; however, the remaining $75x of Year 5 income of DRC_Z may be offset by such dual consolidated loss.

Example 27. Treatment of disregarded item. (i) *Facts.* P owns $DE1_X$. In Year 1, $DE1_X$ incurs interest expense attributable to a loan made from P to $DE1_X$. $DE1_X$ has no other items of income, gain, deduction, or loss in Year 1. Because $DE1_X$ is disregarded as an entity separate from its owner, however, the interest expense is disregarded for federal tax purposes.

(ii) *Result.* Even though $DE1_X$ is treated as a separate domestic corporation for purposes of determining the amount of dual consolidated loss pursuant to §1.1503(d)-3 (b)(2)(i), such treatment does not cause the interest expense incurred on the loan from P to $DE1_X$ that is disregarded for federal tax purposes to be regarded for purposes of calculating the Year 1 dual consolidated loss, if any, of $DE1_X$. Therefore, P's interest in $DE1_X$ does not have a dual consolidated loss in Year 1.

Example 28. Hybrid entity books and records. (i) *Facts.* P owns $DE1_X$. In Year 1, P incurs interest expense attributable to a loan from a third party. The third party loan and related interest expense are properly recorded on the books and records of P (and not on the books and records of $DE1_X$).

(ii) *Result.* The interest expense on P's loan from the third party is not properly recorded on the books and records of $DE1_X$. No portion of the interest expense on such loan is attributable to $DE1_X$ pursuant to §1.1503(d)-3(b)(2)(iii) and (iv). Therefore, no portion of the interest expense is taken into account for purposes of calculating the Year 1 dual consolidated loss, if any, attributable to P's interest in $DE1_X$ pursuant to §1.1503(d)-3(b)(2).

Example 29. Dividend income attributable to a separate unit. (i) *Facts.* P owns $DE1_X$. $DE1_X$ owns $DE3_Y$. $DE3_Y$ owns CFC, a controlled foreign corporation. P's interest in $DE1_X$ would otherwise have a dual consolidated loss of $75x (without regard to Year 1 dividend income or section 78 gross-up received from CFC) in Year 1. In Year 1, CFC distributes $50x to $DE3_Y$ that is taxable as a dividend. $DE3_Y$ distributes the same amount to $DE1_X$. P computes foreign taxes deemed paid on the dividend under section 902 of $25x and includes that amount in gross income under section 78 as a dividend.

(ii) *Result.* The $75x of dividend income ($50x distribution plus $25x section 78 gross-up) is properly recorded on the books and records of $DE3_Y$, as adjusted to conform to U.S. tax principles. Accordingly, for purposes of determining whether the interest in $DE3_Y$ has a dual consolidated loss, the $75x dividend in-

Prop. Reg. §1.1503(d)-5(c)

come from CFC is an item of income attributable to $DE3_Y$, a disregarded entity, and therefore is an item attributable to the interest in $DE3_Y$. The distribution of $50x from $DE3_Y$ to $DE1_X$ is generally not regarded for tax purposes and therefore does not give rise to an item that is taken into account for purposes of calculating a dual consolidated loss. As a result, the dual consolidated loss of $75x attributable to P's interest in $DE1_X$ in Year 1 is not reduced by the amount of dividend income attributable to the interest in $DE3_Y$.

Example 30. Items attributable to a combined separate unit. (i) *Facts.* P owns $DE1_X$. $DE1_X$ owns a 50% interest in PRS_Z, a Country Z entity that is classified as a partnership both for Country Z tax purposes and for U.S. tax purposes. F_Z, a Country Z corporation unrelated to P, owns the remaining 50% interest in PRS_Z. PRS_Z conducts operations in Country X that, if owned by a U.S. person, would constitute a foreign branch as defined in § 1.367(a)-6T(g). Therefore, P's share of the Country X branch owned by PRS_Z constitutes a foreign branch separate unit. PRS_Z also owns assets that do not constitute a part of its Country X branch.

(ii) *Result.* (A) Pursuant to § 1.1503(d)-1(b)(4)(ii), P's interest in $DE1_X$, and P's indirect ownership of a portion of the Country X branch of PRS_Z, are combined and treated as one Country X separate unit. Pursuant to § 1.1503(d)-3(b)(2)(vii)(B)(*1*), for purposes of determining P's items of income, gain, deduction and loss taken into account by its combined separate unit, the items of P are first attributed to each separate unit that compose the combined Country X separate unit.

(B) Pursuant to § 1.1503(d)-3(b)(2)(ii)(A), the principles of section 864(c)(2), as modified, apply for purposes of determining P's items of income, gain, deduction (other than interest expense) and loss that are taken into account in determining the taxable income or loss of P's indirect interest in the Country X foreign branch owned by PRS_Z. For purposes of determining interest expense taken into account in determining the taxable income or loss of P's indirect interest in the Country X foreign branch owned by PRS_Z, the principles of § 1.882-5, subject to § 1.1503(d)-3(b)(2)(ii)(B), shall apply. For purposes of applying the principles of section 864(c) and § 1.882-5, P is treated as a foreign corporation, the Country X branch of PRS_Z is treated as a trade or business within the United States, and the assets of P (other than those of FB_X) are treated as assets that are not U.S. assets. In addition, pursuant to § 1.1503(d)-3(b)(2)(vii)(A)(*1*), only the items of $DE1_X$ and PRS_Z are taken into account for purposes of this determination.

(C) For purposes of determining the items of income, gain, deduction and loss that are attributable to $DE1_X$ and, therefore, attributable to P's interest in $DE1_X$, only those items that are properly reflected on the books and records of $DE1_X$, as adjusted to conform to U.S. tax principles, are taken into account. For this purpose, $DE1_X$'s distributive share of the items of income, gain, deduction and loss that are properly reflected on the books and records of PRS_Z, as adjusted to conform to U.S. tax principles, are treated as being reflected on the books and records of $DE1_X$, except to the extent such items are taken into account by the Country X branch of PRS_Z, as provided above.

(D) Pursuant to § 1.1503(d)-3(b)(2)(vii)(B)(*2*), the combined Country X separate unit of P calculates its dual consolidated loss by taking into account all the items of income, gain deduction and loss that were separately taken into account by P's interest in $DE1_X$ and the Country X branch of PRS_Z owned indirectly by P.

Example 31. Sale of branch by domestic owner. (i) *Facts.* P owns FB_X. FB_X has a $100x dual consolidated loss in Year 1. P makes a domestic use election with respect to such dual consolidated loss. In Year 2, P sells FB_X and recognizes $75x of gain as a result of such sale. The sale is a triggering event of the Year 1 dual consolidated loss under § 1.1503(d)-4(e)(1).

(ii) *Result.* Pursuant to § 1.1503(d)-3(b)(2)(vii)(C), the gain on the sale of FB_X is attributable to FB_X for purposes of calculating the Year 2 dual consolidated loss (if any) of FB_X, and for purposes of determining FB_X's Year 2 taxable income for purposes of rebutting the amount of the Year 1 dual consolidated loss to be recaptured pursuant to § 1.1503(d)-4(h)(2)(i). Assuming FB_X has no other items of income, gain, deduction and loss in Year 2, only $25x of the Year 1 dual consolidated loss must be recaptured.

Example 32. Sale of separate unit by another separate unit. (i) *Facts.* P owns $DE1_X$. $DE1_X$ owns $DE3_Y$. $DE1_X$ sells its interest in $DE3_Y$ at the end of Year 1 to an unrelated third party. The sale resulted in an ordinary loss of $30x. Without regard to the sale of $DE3_Y$, no items of income, gain, deduction or loss are attributable to the interest of $DE3_Y$ in Year 1.

(ii) *Result.* Pursuant to § 1.1503(d)-3(b)(2)(vii)(C), the $30x loss recognized on the sale is attributable to the interest in $DE3_Y$, and not the interest in $DE1_X$. In addition, the loss attributable to the sale creates a Year 1 dual consolidated loss attributable to the interest in $DE3_Y$. Pursuant to § 1.1503(d)-4(d)(3)(i), P cannot make a domestic use election with respect to the Year 1 dual consolidated loss attributable to the interest in $DE3_Y$ because the sale of the interest in $DE3_Y$ is described in § 1.1503(d)-4(e)(1). As a result, although the

Year 1 dual consolidated loss would otherwise be subject to the domestic use limitation rule of § 1.1503(d)-2(b), it is eliminated pursuant to § 1.1503(d)-2(c)(1)(ii).

Example 33. Gain and loss on sale of tiered separate units. (i) *Facts.* P owns $DE1_X$. $DE1_X$ owns $DE3_Y$. P sells its interest in $DE1_X$ to an unrelated third party. As a result of this sale, P recognizes $25x of net gain, consisting of $75 of income and $50 of loss. If $DE1_X$ sold its assets in a taxable transaction immediately before the sale of P's interest in $DE1_X$, $DE1_X$ would have recognized $75x of income. In addition, if $DE3_Y$ had sold its assets in a taxable transaction immediately before the sale of P's interest in $DE1_X$, $DE3_Y$ would have recognized a $50x loss.

(ii) *Result.* Pursuant to § 1.1503(d)-3(b)(2)(vii)(C), the $75x of income and $50x of loss must be allocated to the interests of $DE1_X$ and $DE3_Y$ based on the amount of gain or loss that would be recognized if such entities sold their assets in a taxable exchange for an amount equal to their fair market value immediately before P sold its interest in $DE1_X$. Therefore, $75x of gain and $50x of loss recognized by P on the sale of its interest $DE1_X$ are attributable to the interests in $DE1_X$ and $DE3_Y$, respectively. As a result, such items will be taken into account in determining whether an interest in either entity has a dual consolidated loss in the year of the sale and for purposes of rebutting the amount of recapture of any dual consolidated loss (for which a domestic use election was made) of $DE1_X$ from a prior year, if any, pursuant to § 1.1503(d)-4(h)(2)(i).

Example 34. Gain on sale of tiered separate units. (i) *Facts.* P owns 75% of HPS_X, a Country X entity subject to Country X tax on its worldwide income. F_X, a an unrelated foreign corporation, owns the remaining 25% of HPS_X. HPS_X is classified as a partnership for U.S. income tax purposes. HPS_X owns operations in Country Y that, if owned by a U.S. person, would constitute a foreign branch within the meaning of § 1.367(a)-6T(g). HPS_X also owns assets that do not constitute a part of its Country Y branch. P's indirect interest in the Country Y branch owned by HPS_X, and P's interest in HPS_X, are each separate units. P sells its interest in HPS_X and recognizes a gain of $150x on such sale. Immediately prior to P's sale of its interest in HPS_X, P's indirect interest in HPS_X's Country Y branch had a net built-in gain of $200x, and P's pro rata portion of HPS_X's other assets had a net built-in gain of $100x.

(ii) *Result.* Pursuant to § 1.1503(d)-3(b)(2)(vii)(C), $100x of the total $150x of gain recognized ($200x/$300x × $150x) is taken into account for purposes of determining the taxable income of P's indirect interest in its share of the Country Y branch owned by HPS_X. Thus, such amount will be taken into account in determining whether it has a dual consolidated loss in the year of the sale and for purposes of rebutting the amount of dual consolidated loss recapture, if any, pursuant to § 1.1503(d)-4(h)(2)(i). Similarly, $50x of such gain ($100x/$300x × $150x) is attributable to P's interest in HPS_X and will be taken into account in determining whether it has a dual consolidated loss in the year of sale, and for purposes of rebutting the amount of recapture, if any, pursuant to § 1.1503(d)-4(h)(2)(i).

Example 35. Effect on domestic affiliate. (i) *Facts.* (A) P owns $DE1_X$. In Years 1 and 2, the items of income, gain, deduction, and loss that are attributable to P's interest in $DE1_X$ for purposes of determining whether such interest has a dual consolidated loss for each year, pursuant to § 1.1503(d)-3(b)(2), are as follows:

Item	Year 1	Year 2
Sales income	$100x	$160x
Salary expense	($75x)	($75x)
Research and experimental expense	($50x)	($50x)
Interest expense	($25x)	($25x)
Income/(dual consolidated loss)	($50x)	$10x

(B) P does not make a domestic use election with respect to $DE1_X$'s Year 1 dual consolidated loss. Pursuant to §§ 1.1503(d)-2(b) and 1.1503(d)-3(c)(2), $DE1_X$'s Year 1 dual consolidated loss of $50x is treated as a loss incurred by a separate corporation and is subject to the limitations under § 1.1503(d)-3(c)(3).

(ii) *Result.* (A) P must compute its taxable income for Year 1 without taking into account the $50x dual consolidated loss attributable to P's interest in $DE1_X$. Such amount consists of a pro rata portion of the expenses that were taken into account by $DE1_X$ in calculating its Year 1 dual consolidated loss. Thus, the items of the dual consolidated loss that are not taken into account by P in computing its taxable income are as follows: $25x of salary expense ($75x/$150x × $50x); $16.67x of research and experimental expense ($50x/$150x × $50x); and $8.33x of interest expense ($25x/$150x × $50x). The remaining amounts of each of these items, together with the $100x of sales income, are taken into account by P in computing its taxable income for Year 1 as follows: $50x of salary expense ($75x - $25x); $33.33x of research and experimental expense ($50x - $16.67x); and $16.67x of interest expense ($25x -$8.33x).

(B) Subject to the limitations provided under § 1.1503(d)-3(c)(3), the $50x dual consolidated loss generated by $DE1_X$ in Year 1 is carried forward and is available to offset the $10x of income generated by $DE1_X$ in Year 2. A pro rata portion of each item of deduction or loss included in such dual consolidated loss is considered to be used to offset the $10x of income, as follows: $5x of salary expense ($25x/$50x × $10x); $3.33x of research and experimental expense ($16.67x/$50x × $10x); and $1.67x of interest expense ($8.33x/$50x × $10x). The remaining amount of each item shall continue to be subject to the limitations under § 1.1503(d)-3(c)(3).

Example 36. Basis adjustment rule—year of dual consolidated loss. (i) *Facts.* (A) In addition to S, P owns S1, a domestic corporation. S owns DRC_X and DRC_X, in turn, owns FS_X. S, S1 and DRC_X are each members of the P consolidated group. W and Y are unrelated corporations that are not members of the P consolidated group.

(B) At the beginning of Year 1, P has a basis of $1,000_X$ in the stock of S. S has a $500x basis in the stock of DRC_X.

(C) In Year 1, DRC_X incurs interest expense in the amount of $100x. In addition, DRC_X sells a noncapital asset, u, in which it has a basis of $10x, to S1 for $50x. DRC_X also sells a noncapital asset, v, in which it has a basis of $200x, to S1 for $100x. The sales of u and v are intercompany transactions described in § 1.1502-13. DRC_X also sells a capital asset, z, in which it has a basis of $180x, to Y for $90x. In Year 1, S1 earns $200x of separate taxable income, calculated in accordance with § 1.1502-12, as well as $90x of capital gain from a sale of an asset to W. P and S have no items of income, gain, deduction or loss for Year 1.

(D) In Year 1, DRC_X has a dual consolidated loss of $100x (attributable to its interest expense). The sale of non-capital assets u and v to S1, which are intercompany transactions, are not taken into account in calculating DRC_X's dual consolidated loss. Pursuant to § 1.1503(d)-3(b)(1), DRC_X's $90x capital loss also is not included in the computation of the dual consolidated loss. Instead, DRC_X's capital loss is included in the computation of the consolidated group's capital gain net income under § 1.1502-22(c) and is used to offset S1's $90x capital gain.

(E) For Country X tax purposes, DRC_X's $100x loss is available to offset the income of FS_X, a foreign corporation, and therefore constitutes a foreign use. As a result, DRC_X is not eligible to make a domestic use election pursuant to § 1.1503(d)-4(d), and the $100x Year 1 dual consolidated loss of DRC_X is subject to the domestic use limitation rule of § 1.1503(d)-2(b).

(ii) *Result.* (A) Because DRC_X has a dual consolidated loss for the year, the consolidated taxable income of the consolidated group is calculated without regard to DRC_X's items of loss or deduction taken into account in computing its dual consolidated loss (that is, the $100x of interest expense). Therefore, the consolidated taxable income of the consolidated group is $200x (the sum of $200x of separate taxable income earned by S1, plus $90x of capital gain earned by S1, minus $90x of capital loss incurred by DRC_X). The $40x gain of DRC_X upon the sale of item u to S1, and the $100x loss of DRC_X upon the sale of item v to S1, are deferred pursuant to § 1.1502-13(c).

(B) Pursuant to § 1.1503(d)-3(d)(1)(i), S must make a negative adjustment under § 1.1502-32(b)(2) to its basis in the stock of DRC_X for the $100x dual consolidated loss incurred by DRC_X. In addition, S must make a negative adjustment under § 1.1502-32(b)(2) in the basis of the DRC_X stock for DRC_X's $90x capital loss because the loss has been absorbed by the consolidated group. Thus, S must make a $190x net negative adjustment to its basis in the stock of DRC_X, reducing its basis from $500x to $310x. As provided in § 1.1502-32(a)(3)(iii), the adjustments in the DRC_X stock made by S are taken into account in determining P's basis in its S stock. Since S has no items of income, gain, deduction or loss for the taxable year, P must only make a negative adjustment to its basis in the stock of S to account for the tiering-up of adjustments for the taxable year pursuant to § 1.1502-32(a)(3)(iii). Thus, P must make a $190x net negative adjustment to its basis in S stock, reducing its basis from $1,000x to $810x.

Example 37. Basis adjustment rule—subsequent income of dual resident corporation. (i) *Facts.* (A) The facts are the same as in *Example 36*, except as follows. In Year 2, S1 sells items u and v to W for no gain or loss. The disposition of items u and v outside of the P consolidated group causes the intercompany gain and loss of DRC_X attributable to u and v to be taken into account pursuant to § 1.1502-13(c). DRC_X also incurs $100x of interest expense in Year 2. In addition, DRC_X sells a noncapital asset, r, in which it has a basis of $100x, to Y for $300x. P and S have no items of income, loss, or deduction for Year 2.

(B) DRC_X has $40x of separate taxable income in Year 2, computed as follows:

Interest Expense	($100x)
Sale of Item v to S1	($100x)
Sale of Item u to S1	$40x
Sale of Item r to Y	$200x
Net Income/(Loss)	$40x

(C) Since DRC_X does not have a dual consolidated loss for Year 2, the group's consolidated taxable income for the year is calculated in accordance with the general rule of § 1.1502-11, and not in accordance with § 1.1503(d)-3(c). In addition, DRC_X is the only member of the consolidated group that has any income or loss for the taxable year. Thus, the consolidated taxable income of the group, computed without regard to DRC$_X$'s dual consolidated loss carryover, is $40x.

(ii) *Result.* (A) As provided under § 1.1503(d)-3(c), the portion of the $100x dual consolidated loss arising in Year 1 that is included in the group's consolidated net operating loss deduction for Year 2 is $40x. Thus, the P group has no consolidated taxable income for the year.

(B) Pursuant to § 1.1503(d)-3(d)(1)(ii), S does not make a negative adjustment to its basis in DRC$_X$ stock for the $40x of Year 1 dual consolidated loss that is absorbed in Year 2. However, pursuant to § 1.1502-32(b), S does make a $40x net positive adjustment to its basis in DRC$_X$ stock, increasing its basis from $310x to $350x. In addition, as provided in § 1.1502-32(a)(3)(iii), the adjustments in the DRC$_X$ stock made by S are taken into account in determining P's basis in its S stock. Since S has no other items of income, gain, deduction or loss for the taxable year, P must only make a positive adjustment to its basis in the stock of S for to account for the tiering-up of adjustments for the taxable year pursuant to § 1.1502-32(a)(3)(iii). Thus, P must make a $40x net positive adjustment to its basis in S stock, increasing its basis from $810x to $850x.

Example 38. Exception to domestic use limitation—no possibility of foreign use because items are not deducted or capitalized under foreign law. (i) *Facts.* P owns DE1$_X$. In Year 1, the sole item of income, gain, deduction or loss attributable to P's interest in DE1$_X$ as provided under § 1.1503(d)-3(b)(2) is $100x of interest expense. For Country X tax purposes, the $100x interest expense attributable to P's interest in DE1$_X$ in Year 1 is treated as a repayment of principal and therefore cannot be deducted (at any time) or capitalized.

(ii) *Result.* The $100x of interest expense attributable to P's interest in DE1$_X$ constitutes a dual consolidated loss. However, because the sole item constituting the dual consolidated loss cannot be deducted or capitalized for Country X tax purposes, P can demonstrate that there can be no foreign use of the dual consolidated loss at any time. As a result, pursuant to § 1.1503(d)-4(c)(1), if P prepares a statement described in § 1.1503(d)-4(c)(2) and attaches it to its timely filed tax return, the Year 1 dual consolidated loss of DE1$_X$ will not be subject to the domestic use limitation rule of § 1.1503(d)-2(b).

Example 39. No exception to domestic use limitation—inability to demonstrate no possibility of foreign use because items are deferred under foreign law. (i) *Facts.* P owns DE1$_X$. In Year 1, the sole items of income, gain, deduction or loss attributable to P's interest in DE1$_X$ as provided under § 1.1503(d)-3(b)(2) are $75x of sales income and $100x of depreciation expense. For Country X tax purposes, DE1$_X$ also generates $75x of sales income in Year 1, but the $100x of depreciation expense is not deductible in Year 1. Instead, for Country X tax purposes the $100x of depreciation expense is deductible in Year 2. P does not make a domestic use election with respect to the Year 1 dual consolidated loss attributable to P's interest in DE1$_X$.

(ii) *Result.* The Year 1 $25x net loss of DE1$_X$ constitutes a dual consolidated loss attributable to P's interest in DE1$_X$. In addition, even though DE1$_X$ has positive income in Year 1 for Country X tax purposes, P cannot demonstrate that there is no possibility of foreign use of its dual consolidated loss as provided under § 1.1503(d)-4(c)(1)(i). P cannot make such a demonstration because the depreciation expense, an item composing the Year 1 dual consolidated loss, is deductible (in a later year) for Country X tax purposes and, therefore, may be available to offset or reduce income for Country X purposes that would constitute a foreign use. For example, if DE1$_X$ elected to be classified as a corporation pursuant to § 301.7701-3(c) of this chapter effective as of the end of Year 1, and the deferred depreciation expense were available for Country X tax purposes to offset Year 2 income of DE1$_X$, an entity treated as a foreign corporation in Year 2 for U.S. tax purposes, there would be a foreign use. P could, however, make a domestic use election pursuant to § 1.1503(d)-4(d) with respect to the Year 1 dual consolidated loss.

Example 40. No exception to domestic use limitation—inability to demonstrate no possibility of foreign use because items are deferred and not deducted or capitalized under foreign law. (i) *Facts.* P owns DE1$_X$. In Year 1, the sole items of income, gain, deduction or loss attributable to P's interest in DE1$_X$ as provided in § 1.1503(d)-3(b)(2) are $75x of sales income, $100x of interest expense and $25x of depreciation expense. For Country X tax purposes, DE1$_X$ generates $75x of sales income in Year 1, but the $100x interest expense is treated as a repayment of principal and therefore cannot be deducted (at any time) or capitalized. In addition, for Country X tax purposes the $25x of depreciation expense is not deductible in Year 1, but is deductible in Year 2.

(ii) *Result.* The Year 1 $50x net loss of DE1$_X$ constitutes a dual consolidated loss attributable to P's interest in DE1$_X$. Even though the $100x interest expense, a nondeductible and noncapital item for Country X tax purposes, exceeds the $50x Year 1 dual consolidated loss of DE1$_X$, P cannot demonstrate that there is no possibility of foreign use of the dual consolidated loss as provided under § 1.1503(d)-4(c)(1)(i). P cannot make such a demonstration because the

$25x depreciation expense, an item of deduction or loss composing the Year 1 dual consolidated loss, is deductible under Country X law (in Year 2) and, therefore, may be available to offset or reduce income for Country X purposes that would constitute a foreign use. P could, however, make a domestic use election pursuant to § 1.1503(d)-4(d) with respect to the Year 1 dual consolidated loss.

Example 41. Consistency rule—deemed foreign use. (i) *Facts.* P owns DRC_X, a member of the P consolidated group, FBx, and FSx. In Year 1, DRC_X incurs a dual consolidated loss, which is used to offset the income of FSx under the Country X form of consolidation. FB_X also incurs a dual consolidated loss in Year 1. However, P elects not to use the FB_X loss on a Country X consolidated return to offset the income of Country X affiliates.

(ii) *Result.* The use of DRC_X's dual consolidated loss to offset the income of FS_X for Country X purposes constitutes a foreign use. Pursuant to § 1.1503(d)-4(d)(2), this foreign use results in a foreign use of the dual consolidated loss of FBx. Therefore, the dual consolidated loss attributable to FBx is subject to the domestic use limitation rule of § 1.1503(d)-2(b), and P cannot make a domestic use election with respect to such loss.

Example 42. Consistency rule—no foreign use permitted. (i) *Facts.* The facts are the same as in *Example 41*, except that the income tax laws of Country X do not permit Country X branches of foreign corporations to file consolidated income tax returns with Country X affiliates.

(ii) *Result.* The consistency rule does not apply with respect to the dual consolidated loss of FBx because the income tax laws of Country X do not permit a foreign use for such dual consolidated loss. Therefore, P may make a domestic use election for the dual consolidated loss attributable to FB_X.

Example 43. Triggering event rebuttal—expiration of losses in foreign country. (i) *Facts.* P owns DRC_X, a member of the P consolidated group. In Year 1, DRC_X incurs a dual consolidated loss of $100x. P makes a domestic use election with respect to DRC_X's Year 1 dual consolidated loss and such loss therefore is included in the computation of the P group's consolidated taxable income. DRC_X has no income or loss in Year 2 through Year 6. In Year 7, P sells the stock of DRC_X to an unrelated party. At the time of the sale of the stock of DRC_X, all of the losses and deductions that were included in the computation of the Year 1 dual consolidated loss of DRC_X had expired for Country X purposes because the laws of Country X only provide for a five year carryover period of such items.

(ii) *Result.* The sale of DRC_X to the unrelated party generally would be a triggering event under § 1.1503(d)-4(e)(1)(ii), which would require the recapture of the Year 1 dual consolidated loss (and an applicable interest charge). However, upon adequate documentation that the losses and deductions have expired for Country X purposes, P can rebut the presumption that a triggering event has occurred pursuant to § 1.1503(d)-4(e)(2). Pursuant to § 1.1503(d)-4(i)(1), if the triggering event presumption is rebutted, the domestic use agreement filed by the P consolidated group with respect to the Year 1 dual consolidated loss of DRC_X is terminated and has no further effect (absent a rebuttal, the domestic use agreement would terminate pursuant to § 1.1503(d)-4(i)(3)).

Example 44. Inability to rebut triggering event-tax basis carryover transaction. (i) *Facts.* (A) P owns $DE1_X$. $DE1_X$'s sole asset is A, which it acquired at the beginning of Year 1 for $100x. $DE1_X$ does not have any liabilities. For U.S. tax purposes, $DE1_X$'s tax basis in A at the beginning of Year 1 is $100x and $DE1_X$'s sole item of income, gain, deduction and loss for Year 1 is a $20x depreciation deduction attributable to A. As a result, $DE1_X$'s Year 1 $20x depreciation deduction constitutes a dual consolidated loss attributable to P's interest in $DE1_X$. P makes a domestic use election with respect to $DE1_X$'s Year 1 dual consolidated loss.

(B) For Country X tax purposes, $DE1_X$ has a $100x tax basis in A at the beginning of Year 1, but A is not a depreciable asset. As a result, $DE1_X$ does not have any items of income, gain, deduction or loss in Year 1 for Country X tax purposes.

(C) At the beginning of Year 2, P sells its interest in $DE1_X$ to F, an unrelated foreign person, for $80x. P's disposition of its interest in $DE1_X$ constitutes a presumptive triggering event under § 1.1503(d)-4(e)(1) requiring the recapture of the $20x dual consolidated loss (plus the applicable interest charge). For Country X tax purposes, $DE1_X$ retains its tax basis of $100x in A following the sale.

(ii) *Result.* The Year 1 dual consolidated loss is a result of the $20x depreciation deduction attributable to A. Although no item of loss or deduction was recognized by $DE1_X$ by the time of the sale for Country X tax purposes, the deduction composing the dual consolidated loss was retained by $DE1_X$ after the sale in the form of tax basis in A. As a result, a portion of the dual consolidated loss may offset income for Country X purposes in a manner that would constitute a foreign use. For example, if $DE1_X$ were to dispose of A, the amount of gain recognized by $DE1_X$ would be reduced and, therefore, an item composing the dual consolidated loss would reduce foreign income of an owner of an interest in a hybrid entity that is not a separate unit. Thus, P cannot demonstrate pursuant to § 1.1503(d)-4(e)(2) that there can be no foreign use of the Year 1 dual consolidated loss following the triggering event and must recapture the Year 1 dual consolidated loss. Pursuant to § 1.1503(d)-4(i)(3), the domestic use agreement filed by the P consolidated group with respect to the Year 1 dual consolidated of $DE1_X$ is terminated and has no further effect.

Example 45. Ability to rebut triggering event—taxable asset sale. (i) *Facts.* The facts are the same as *Example 44*, except that instead of P selling its interests in $DE1_X$ to F, $DE1_X$ sells asset A to F for $80x. Such sale constitutes a presumptive triggering event under § 1.1503(d)-4(e)(1). For Country X tax purposes, F's tax basis in A is $80x.

(ii) *Result.* The Year 1 dual consolidated loss attributable to P's interest in $DE1_X$ is a result of the $20x depreciation deduction attributable to A. For Country X tax purposes, however, F's tax basis in A was not determined, in whole or in part, by reference to the basis of A in the hands of $DE1_X$. As a result, the deduction composing the dual consolidated loss will not give rise to an item of deduction or loss in the form of tax basis for Country X purposes (for example, when F disposes of A). Therefore, P may be able to demonstrate pursuant to § 1.1503(d)-4(e)(2) that there can be no foreign use of the Year 1 dual consolidated loss and, thus, may not be required to recapture the Year 1 dual consolidated loss. Pursuant to § 1.1503(d)-4(i)(1), if such a demonstration is made, the domestic use agreement filed by the P consolidated group with respect to the Year 1 dual consolidated loss of $DE1_X$ is terminated pursuant to § 1.1503(d)-4(i)(1) and has no further effect (absent a rebuttal, the domestic use agreement would terminate pursuant to § 1.1503(d)-4(i)(3)).

Example 46. Termination of consolidated group not a triggering event if acquirer files a new domestic use agreement. (i) *Facts.* P owns DRC_X, a member of the P consolidated group. The P consolidated group uses the calendar year as its taxable year. In Year 1, DRC_X incurs a dual consolidated loss and P makes a domestic use election with respect to such loss. No member of the P consolidated group incurs a dual consolidated loss in Year 2. On December 31, Year 2, T, the parent of the T consolidated group acquires all the stock of P, and all the members of the P group, including DRC_X, become members of a consolidated group of which T is the common parent.

(ii) *Result.* (A) Under § 1.1503(d)-4 (f)(2)(ii)(B), the acquisition by T of the P consolidated group is not an event described in § 1.1503(d)-4(e)(1) requiring the recapture of the Year 1 dual consolidated loss of DRC_X (and the payment of an interest charge), provided that the T consolidated group files a new domestic use agreement described in § 1.1503(d)-4(f)(2)(iii)(A). If a new domestic use agreement is filed, then pursuant to § 1.1503(d)-4(i)(2), the domestic use agreement filed by the P consolidated group with respect to the Year 1 dual consolidated loss of DRC_X is terminated and has no further effect.

(iii) If a triggering event occurs on December 31, Year 3, the T consolidated group must recapture the dual consolidated loss that DRC_X incurred in Year 1 (and pay an interest charge), as provided in § 1.1503(d)-4(h). Each member of the T consolidated group, including DRC_X and any former members of the P consolidated group, is severally liable for the additional tax (and the interest charge) due upon the recapture of the dual consolidated loss of DRC_X. In addition, pursuant to § 1.1503(d)-4(i)(3), the new domestic use agreement filed by the T group with respect to the Year 1 dual consolidated loss of DRC_X is terminated and has no further effect.

Example 47. No triggering event if consolidated group remains in existence in connection with a reverse acquisition. (i) *Facts.* S owns FB_X. FB_X incurs a dual consolidated loss of $100x in Year 1 and P makes a domestic use election with respect to such loss. At the end of Year 2, P merges into T, the common parent of the T consolidated group, which includes U as a member. The shareholders of P immediately before the merger, as a result of owning stock in P, own 60% of the fair market value of T's stock immediately after the merger.

(ii) *Result.* The P group is treated as continuing in existence under § 1.1502-75(d)(3) with T and U being added as members of the P group, and T taking the place of P as the common parent. The merger of P into T does not constitute a triggering event with respect to the dual consolidated loss in Year 1 pursuant to § 1.1503(d)-4(e)(1)(ii) because the P consolidated group, which owned FB_X, continues to exist.

Example 48. Triggering event exception—acquisition of assets by domestic owner. (i) *Facts.* P owns $DE1_X$. In Year 1, $DE1_X$ incurs a loss of $100x and, as a result, P's interest in $DE1_X$ has a Year 1 dual consolidated loss of $100x. P makes a domestic use election with respect to the Year 1 dual consolidated loss and such loss therefore is included in the computation of the P group's consolidated taxable income. In Year 3, $DE1_X$ dissolves and surrenders its Country X corporate charter. Pursuant to its dissolution, $DE1_X$ distributes its assets and liabilities to P and the shares of $DE1_X$ are cancelled.

Prop. Reg. § 1.1503(d)-5(c)

(ii) *Result.* The disposition of the assets of $DE1_X$ (and the disposition of P's interest in $DE1_X$) as a result of the dissolution generally would be a triggering event under § 1.1503(d)-4(e)(1). However, because the assets of $DE1_X$ are acquired by P, its domestic owner, as a result of the dissolution, the dissolution does not constitute a triggering event under § 1.1503(d)-4(f)(1).

Example 49. Subsequent elector rules. (i) *Facts.* P owns DRC_X, a member of the P consolidated group. The P consolidated group uses the calendar year as its taxable year. In Year 1, DRC_X incurs a dual consolidated loss and P makes a domestic use election with respect to such loss. No member of the P consolidated group incurs a dual consolidated loss in Year 2. On December 31, Year 2, T, the parent of the T consolidated group that also uses the calendar year as its taxable year, acquires all the stock of DRC_X for cash.

(ii) *Result.* (A) Under § 1.1503(d)-4 (f)(2)(i)(A), the acquisition by T of DRC_X is not an event described in § 1.1503(d)-4(e)(1) requiring the recapture of the Year 1 dual consolidated loss of DRC_X (and the payment of an interest charge), provided: (1) the T consolidated group files a new domestic use agreement described in § 1.1503(d)-4 (f)(2)(iii)(A) with respect to the Year 1 dual consolidated loss of DRC_X; and (2) the P consolidated group files a statement described in § 1.1503(d)-4(f)(2)(iii)(B) with respect to the Year 1 dual consolidated loss of DRC_X. If these requirements are satisfied, then pursuant to § 1.1503(d)-4(i)(2) the domestic use agreement filed by the P consolidated group with respect to the Year 1 dual consolidated loss of DRC_X is terminated and has no further effect (if such requirements are not satisfied, the domestic use agreement would terminate pursuant to § 1.1503(d)-4(i)(3).

(B) Assume a triggering event occurs on December 31, Year 3, that requires recapture by the T consolidated group of the dual consolidated loss that DRC_X incurred in Year 1, as well as the payment of an interest charge, as provided in § 1.1503(d)-4(h). In that case, each member of the T consolidated group, including DRC_X, is severally liable for the additional tax (and the interest charge) due upon the recapture of the Year 1 dual consolidated loss of DRC_X. The T consolidated group must prepare a statement that computes the recapture tax amount as provided under § 1.1503(d)-4(h)(3)(iii). Pursuant to § 1.1503(d)-4(h)(3)(iv)(A), the recapture tax amount is assessed as an income tax liability of the T consolidated group and is considered as having been properly assessed as an income tax liability of the P consolidated group. If the T consolidated group does not pay in full the income tax liability attributable to the recapture tax amount, the unpaid balance of such recapture tax amount may be collected from the P consolidated group in accordance with the provisions of § 1.1503(d)-4(h)(3)(iv)(B). Pursuant to § 1.1503(d)-4(i)(3), the new domestic use agreement filed by the T consolidated group is terminated and has no further effect.

Example 50. Character and source of recapture income. (i) *Facts.* (A) P owns $DE1_X$. In Year 1, the items of income, gain, deduction, and loss that are attributable to P's interest in $DE1_X$ for purposes of determining whether such interest has a dual consolidated loss are as follows:

Sales income	$100x
Salary expense	($75x)
Interest expense	($50x)
Dual consolidated loss	($25x)

(B) P makes a domestic use election with respect to the Year 1 dual consolidated loss attributable to P's interest in $DE1_X$ and, thus, the $25x dual consolidated loss is included in the computation of P's taxable income.

(C) Pursuant to § 1.861-8, the $75x of salary expense incurred by $DE1_X$ is allocated and apportioned entirely to foreign source general limitation income. Pursuant to § 1.861-9T, $25x of the $50x interest expense attributable to $DE1_X$ is allocated and apportioned to domestic source income, $15x of such interest expense is allocated and apportioned to foreign source general limitation income, and the remaining $10x of such interest expense is allocated and apportioned to foreign source passive income.

(D) During Year 2, $DE1_X$ generates $5x of income, an amount which the $25x dual consolidated loss generated by $DE1_X$ in Year 1 would have offset if such loss had been subject to the separate return limitation year restrictions as provided under § 1.1503(d)-3(c)(3).

(E) At the beginning of Year 3, $DE1_X$ undergoes a triggering event within the meaning of § 1.1503(d)-4(e)(1). Pursuant to § 1.1503(d)-4(h)(2)(i), P demonstrates, to the satisfaction of the Commissioner, that the $5x generated by $DE1_X$ in Year 2 qualifies to reduce the amount that P must recapture as a result of the triggering event.

(ii) *Result.* P must recapture and report as income $20x ($25x − $5x) of $DE1_X$'s Year 1 dual consolidated loss, plus applicable interest, on its Year 3 tax return. Pursuant to § 1.1503(d)-4(h)(5), the recapture income is treated as ordinary income whose source and character (including section 904 separate limitation character) is determined by reference to the manner in which the recaptured items of expense or loss taken into account in calculating the dual consolidated loss were allocated and apportioned. Accordingly, P's $20x of recapture income is characterized and sourced as follows: $4x of domestic source income (($25x/$125x) × $20x); $14.4x of foreign source general limitation income (($75x + $15x)/$125x) × $20x); and $1.6x of foreign source passive income (($10x/$125x) × $20x). Pursuant to §1.1503(d)-4(i)(3), the domestic use agreement filed by the P consolidated group with respect to the Year 1 dual consolidated of $DE1_X$ is terminated and has no further effect.

Example 51. Interest charge without recapture. (i) *Facts.* P owns $DE1_X$. In Year 1, a dual consolidated loss of $100x is attributable to P's interest in $DE1_X$. P makes a domestic use election with respect to the Year 1 dual consolidated loss and uses the loss to offset the P group's consolidated taxable income. $DE1_X$ earns income of $100x in Year 2. At the end of Year 2, $DE1_X$ undergoes a triggering event within the meaning of §1.1503(d)-4(e)(1). P demonstrates, to the satisfaction of the Commissioner, that taking into the limitation of §1.1503(d)-3(c)(3) (modified SRLY limitation), the Year 1 $100x dual consolidated loss would have been offset by the $100x Year 2 income.

(ii) *Result.* There is no recapture of the Year 1 dual consolidated loss attributable to P's interest in DE1 because it is reduced to zero under §1.1503(d)-4(h)(2)(i). However, P is liable for one year of interest charge under §1.1503(d)-4(h)(1)(ii), even though P's recapture amount is zero. Pursuant to §1.1503(d)-4(i)(3), the domestic use agreement filed by the P consolidated group with respect to the Year 1 dual consolidated of $DE1_X$ is terminated and has no further effect.

Example 52. Reduced recapture and interest charge, and reconstituted dual consolidated loss. (i) *Facts.* P owns DRC_X, a member of the P consolidated group. In Year 1, DRC_X incurs a dual consolidated loss of $100x and P earns $100x. P makes a domestic use election with respect to DRC_X's Year 1 dual consolidated loss. Therefore, the consolidated group is permitted to offset P's $100x of income with DRC_X's $100x loss. In Year 2, DRC_X earns $30x, which is completely offset by a $30x net operating loss incurred by P in Year 2. In Year 3, DRC_X earns income of $25x, while P recognizes no income or loss. In addition, there is a triggering event at the end of Year 3.

(ii) *Result.* (A) Under the presumptive rule of §1.1503(d)-4(h)(1)(i), DRC_X must recapture $100x. However, the $100x recapture amount may be reduced by the amount by which the dual consolidated loss would have offset other taxable income if it had been subject to the limitation under §1.1503(d)-3(c)(3), upon adequate documentation of such offset under §1.1503(d)-4(h)(2)(i).

(B) Although DRC_X earned $30x of income in Year 2, there was no consolidated taxable income in such year. As a result, the $100x of recapture income cannot be reduced by the $30x earned in Year 2, but such amount can be carried forward to subsequent taxable years and be used to the extent of consolidated taxable income generated in such years. In Year 3, DRC_X earns $25x of income and the P consolidated group has $25 of consolidated taxable income in such year. As a result, the $100x of recapture income can be reduced by the $25x. The $30x generated in Year 2 cannot be used in Year 3 because there is insufficient consolidated taxable income in such year.

(C) Commencing in Year 4, the $75x recapture amount ($100x − $25x) is reconstituted and treated as a loss incurred by DRC_X in a separate return limitation year, subject to the limitation under §1.1503(d)-2(b) (and therefore subject to the restrictions of §1.1503(d)-3(c)(3)). The carryover period of the loss, for purposes of section 172(b), will start from Year 1, when the dual consolidated loss was incurred. Pursuant to §1.1503(d)-4(i)(3), the domestic use agreement filed by the P consolidated group with respect to the Year 1 dual consolidated of $DE1_X$ is terminated and has no further effect.

[Prop. Reg. §1.1503(d)-5.]

[Proposed 5-24-2005.]

Proposed Regulation

§1.1503(d)-6. Effective date.—Sections 1.1503(d)-1 through 1.1503(d)-5 shall apply to dual consolidated losses incurred in taxable years beginning after the date that these regulations are published as final regulations in the Federal Register. [Prop. Reg. §1.1503(d)-6.]

[Proposed 5-24-2005.]

Information Returns

§1.6031(a)-1. Return of partnership income.—(a) *Domestic partnerships.*—(1) *Return required.*—Except as provided in paragraphs (a)(3) and (c) of this section, every domestic partnership must file a return of partnership income under section 6031 (partnership return) for each taxable year on the form prescribed for the partnership return. The partnership return must be filed for the taxable year of the partnership regardless of the taxable years of the partners. For taxable years of a partnership and of a partner, see section 706 and §1.706-1. For the rules governing partnership statements to partners and nominees, see §1.6031(b)-1T. For the rules requiring the disclosure of certain transactions, see §1.6011-4T.

(2) *Content of return.*—The partnership return must contain the information required by the prescribed form and the accompanying instructions.

(3) *Special rule.*—(i) A partnership that has no income, deductions, or credits for federal income tax purposes for a taxable year is not required to file a partnership return for that year.

(ii) The Commissioner may, in guidance published in the Internal Revenue Bulletin (see § 601.601(d)(2)(ii)(*b*) of this chapter), provide for an exception to partnership reporting under section 6031 and for conditions for the exception, if all or substantially all of a partnership's income is derived from the holding or disposition of tax-exempt obligations (as defined in section 1275(a)(3) and § 1.1275-1(e)) or shares in a regulated investment company (as defined in section 851(a)) that pays exempt-interest dividends (as defined in section 852(b)(5)).

(4) *Failure to file.*—For the consequences of a failure to comply with the requirements of section 6031(a) and this paragraph (a), see sections 6229(a), 6231(f), 6698, and 7203.

(b) *Foreign partnerships.*—(1) *General rule.*—(i) *Filing requirement.*—A foreign partnership is not required to file a partnership return, if the foreign partnership does not have gross income that is (or is treated as) effectively connected with the conduct of a trade or business within the United States (ECI) and does not have gross income (including gains) derived from sources within the United States (U.S.-source income). Except as provided in paragraphs (b)(2) and (3) of this section, a foreign partnership that has ECI or has U.S.-source income that is not ECI must file a partnership return for its taxable year in accordance with the rules for domestic partnerships in paragraph (a) of this section.

(ii) *Special rule.*—For purposes of this paragraph (b)(1) and paragraph (b)(3)(iii) of this section, a foreign partnership will not be considered to have derived income from sources within the United States solely because a U.S. partner marks to market his pro rata share of PFIC stock held by the foreign partnership pursuant to an election under section 1296.

(2) *Foreign partnerships with de minimis U.S.-source income and de minimis U.S. partners.*—A foreign partnership (other than a withholding foreign partnership, as defined in § 1.1441-5(c)(2)(i)) that has $20,000 or less of U.S.-source income and has no ECI during its taxable year is not required to file a partnership return if, at no time during the partnership taxable year, one percent or more of any item of partnership income, gain, loss, deduction, or credit is allocable in the aggregate to direct United States partners. The United States partners must directly report their shares of the allocable items of partnership income, gain, loss, deduction, and credit.

(3) *Filing obligations for certain other foreign partnerships with no ECI.*—(i) *General requirements for modified filing obligations.*—A foreign partnership will be subject to the modified filing obligations in paragraphs (b)(3)(ii) and (iii) of this section if, in addition to satisfying the requirements contained in paragraph 5(b)(3)(ii) and (iii) of this section—

(A) The partnership is not a withholding foreign partnership as defined in § 1.1441-5(c)(2)(i);

(B) Forms 1042 and 1042-S are filed by the partnership with respect to the amounts subject to reporting under § 1.1461-1(b) and (c), unless the partnership is not required to file such returns under § 1.1461-1(b)(2) and (c)(4), in which case Forms 1042 and 1042-S must be filed by another withholding agent or agents; and

(C) The tax liability of the partners with respect to such amounts has been fully satisfied by the withholding of tax at the source, if applicable, under chapter 3 of the Internal Revenue Code.

(ii) *Foreign partnerships with U.S.-source income but no U.S. partners.*—A foreign partnership that has U.S.-source income is not required to file a partnership return if the partnership has no ECI and no United States partners at any time during the partnership's taxable year.

(iii) *Foreign partnerships with U.S.-source income and U.S. partners.*—Except as provided in paragraph (b)(2) of this section, a foreign partnership with one or more United States partners that has U.S.-source income but no ECI must file a partnership return. However, such a foreign partnership need not file Statements of Partner's Share of Income, Credit, Deduction, Etc. (Schedules K-1) for any partners other than its direct United States partners and its passthrough partners (whether U.S. or foreign) through which United States partners hold an interest in the foreign partnership. Schedules K-1 that are not excepted from filing under this paragraph (b)(3)(iii) must contain the same information required of a domestic partnership filing under paragraph (a) of this section.

(4) *Information or returns required of partners who are United States persons.*—(i) *In general.*—If a United States person is a partner in a

partnership that is not required to file a partnership return, the district director or director of the relevant service center may require that person to render the statements or provide the information necessary to verify the accuracy of the reporting by that person of any items of partnership income, gain, loss, deduction, or credit.

(ii) *Controlled foreign partnerships.*—Certain United States persons who are partners in a foreign partnership controlled (within the meaning of section 6038(e)(1)) by United States persons may be required to provide information with respect to the partnership under section 6038.

(5) *Certain partnership elections.*—For a partnership that is not otherwise required to file a partnership return, if an election that can only be made by the partnership under section 703 (affecting the computation of taxable income derived from a partnership) is to be made by or for the partnership, a return on the form prescribed for the partnership return must be filed for the partnership. Unless otherwise provided in the form or the accompanying instructions, a return filed solely to make an election need only contain a written statement citing paragraph (b)(5)(ii) of this section, listing the name and address of the partnership making the election, and clearly identifying the specific election being made. A return filed under paragraph (b)(5)(ii) of this section solely to make an election is not a partnership return. Thus, such a return is not a return filed under section 6031(a) for purposes of sections 6501 (except regarding the specific election issue), 6231(a)(1)(A), and 6233. The return must be signed by—

(i) Each partner that is a partner in the partnership at the time the election is made; or

(ii) Any partner of the partnership who is authorized (under local law or the partnership's organizational documents) to make the election and who represents to having such authorization under penalties of perjury.

(6) *Exclusion for certain organizations.*—The return requirement of section 6031 and this section does not apply to the International Telecommunications Satellite Organization, the International Maritime Satellite Organization, or any organization that is a successor of either.

(c) *Partnerships excluded from the application of subchapter K of the Internal Revenue Code.*—(1) *Wholly excluded.*—(i) *Year of election.*—An eligible partnership as described in § 1.761-2(a) that elects to be excluded from all the provisions of subchapter K of chapter 1 of the Internal Revenue Code in the manner specified by § 1.761-2(b)(2)(i) must timely file the form prescribed for the partnership return for the taxable year for which the election is made. In lieu of the information otherwise required, the return must contain or be accompanied by the information required by § 1.761-2(b)(2)(i).

(ii) *Subsequent years.*—Except as otherwise provided in paragraph (c)(1)(i) of this section, an eligible partnership that elects to be wholly excluded from the application of subchapter K is not required to file a partnership return.

(2) *Deemed excluded.*—An eligible partnership that is deemed to have elected exclusion from the application of subchapter K beginning with its first taxable year, as specified in § 1.761-2(b)(2)(ii), is not required to file a partnership return.

(d) *Definitions.*—(1) *Partnership.*—For the meaning of the term *partnership*, see § 1.761-1(a).

(2) *United States person.*—In applying this section, a United States person is a person described in section 7701(a)(30); the government of the United States, a State, or the District of Columbia (including an agency or instrumentality thereof); or a corporation created or organized in Guam, the Commonwealth of Northern Mariana Islands, the U.S. Virgin Islands, and American Samoa, if the requirements of section 881(b)(1)(A), (B), and (C) are met for such corporation. The term does not include an alien individual who is a resident of Puerto Rico, Guam, the Commonwealth of Northern Mariana Islands, the U.S. Virgin Islands, or American Samoa, as determined under § 301.7701(b)-1(d) of this chapter.

(3) *United States partner.*—In applying this section, a United States partner is any United States person who holds a direct or indirect interest in the partnership.

(4) *Indirect interest.*—An indirect interest is any interest held through one or more passthrough partners, as defined in section 6231(a)(9).

(e) *Procedural requirements.*—(1) *Place for filing.*—The return of a partnership must be filed with the service center prescribed in the relevant IRS revenue procedure, publication, form, or instructions to the form (see § 601.601(d)(2)).

(2) *Time for filing.*—The return of a partnership must be filed on or before the fifteenth day of the fourth month following the close of the taxable year of the partnership.

(3) *Magnetic media filing.*—For magnetic media filing requirements with respect to partnerships, see section 6011(e)(2) and the regulations thereunder.

(f) *Effective dates.*—This section applies to taxable years of a partnership beginning after December 31, 1999, except that—

(1) Paragraph (b)(3) of this section applies to taxable years of a foreign partnership beginning after December 31, 2000; and

(2) Paragraph (a)(3)(ii) of this section applies to taxable years of a partnership beginning on or after November 5, 2003. [Reg. § 1.6031(a)-1.]

☐ [T.D. 8841, 11-10-99. Amended by T.D. 9000, 6-14-2002; T.D. 9094, 11-5-2003; T.D. 9123, 4-30-2004 and T.D. 9177, 2-10-2005.]

§ 1.6035-1. Returns of U.S. officers, directors and 10-percent shareholders of foreign personal holding companies for taxable years beginning after September 3, 1982.—(a) *Requirement of returns.*—(1) *In general.*—For taxable years of a foreign personal holding company beginning after September 3, 1982, each United States citizen or resident who is an officer, director, or 10-percent shareholder of the foreign personal holding company (as defined in section 552) shall file with his income tax return, on or before the date that return is due, Form 5471 and the applicable schedules to be completed in accordance with the instructions setting forth corporate, shareholder, and income information for the foreign personal holding company's annual accounting period that ends with or within the officer's, director's, or shareholder's taxable year. In the case of a foreign personal holding company which is a specified foreign corporation (as defined in section 898), the taxable year of such corporation shall be treated as its annual accounting period.

(2) *General corporate information.*—The general foreign personal holding company information required by this section with respect to each taxable year is as follows:

(i) The name and address and employer identification number (if any) of the corporation;

(ii) The kind of business in which the corporation is engaged;

(iii) The date of its incorporation;

(iv) The country under the laws of which the corporation is incorporated;

(v) A description of each class of stock issued and outstanding by the corporation for the beginning and end of the annual accounting period;

(vi) The number of shares and par value of common stock of the corporation issued and outstanding as of the beginning and end of the taxable year;

(vii) The number of shares and par value of preferred stock of the corporation issued and outstanding as of the beginning and end of the taxable year, the rate of dividend on such stock and whether such dividend is cumulative or noncumulative; and

(viii) Any other information required by the appropriate form and its instructions.

For purposes of this paragraph, the term "share" includes any security convertible into a share in the corporation and any option granted by the corporation with respect to any share in the corporation.

(3) *Shareholder information.*—The shareholder information required by this section is as follows:

(i) The name, address and taxpayer identification number (if any) of each person, whether foreign or U.S., who was a shareholder during the taxable year and the class and number of shares held by each, together with an explanation of any changes in stock holdings during the taxable year;

(ii) The name and address of each holder during the taxable year of securities convertible into stock of the corporation and the class, number, and face value of the securities held by each, together with an explanation of any changes in the holdings of such securities during the taxable year;

(iii) The name and address of each holder during the taxable year of any option granted by the corporation with respect to any share in the corporation, and a full description of the options held by each, together with an explanation of any changes in the holdings of such options during the taxable year; and

(iv) Any other information required by the appropriate form and its instructions.

(4) *Income information.*—The income information required by this section is the gross income, deductions and credits, taxable income, foreign personal holding company income, and undistributed foreign personal holding company income for the taxable year and other information required by the appropriate form and its instructions.

(b) *Persons required to file return.*—(1) *In general.*—The determination of whether a United States citizen or resident is a person who is an officer, director, or 10-percent shareholder required to file a return with respect to any foreign corporation is made as of the date that Form 5471 is required to be filed. If there is no such person required to file on that date (because, for example, the corporation has been dissolved), then filing is required of the persons who were officers, directors or 10-percent shareholders on the last day of the most recent taxable year of the corporation for which there was such a person who was a United States citizen or resident.

(2) *10-percent shareholder.*—(i) The term "10-percent shareholder" means any individual who owns directly or indirectly (within the meaning of section 554) 10 percent or more in value of the outstanding stock of a foreign corporation.

(ii) An individual who does not own 10 percent or more in value of the outstanding stock directly but is required to file solely by attribution of another United States person's stock ownership is excused from filing if the direct owner that is an individual furnishes all the information required.

(3) *Two or more persons required to submit the same information.*—If two or more persons are required to furnish the information for the same foreign personal holding company for the same period, one person may make one return on Form 5471. The single Form 5471 may be filed with the income tax return of any one of the persons and shall disclose the name, address, and identifying number of each other person or persons on whose behalf the return is filed. Each person on whose behalf the return if filed remains liable for any penalties imposed under sections 6679, 7203, 7206, and 7207.

(4) *Statement required.*—Any United States citizen or resident required to furnish information under this section with his return who does not do so by reason of the provisions of subparagraph (2)(ii) or (3) of this paragraph shall file a statement with his income tax return indicating that such requirement has been or will be satisfied and identifying the return with which the information was or will be filed and the place of filing.

(c) *Separate returns for each corporation.*—If a person is required to file returns under section 6035 and this section with respect to more than one foreign personal holding company, separate returns must be filed with respect to each company.

(d) *Corrective filing.*—If an information return with respect to a taxable year of a foreign personal holding company beginning after September 3, 1982, is filed before July 5, 1985, and that return does not contain all of the information required by this section, then the filer of the return shall file an amended information return containing all of such information within 90 days after June 4, 1985.

(e) *Penalties.*—(1) *Criminal penalties.*—For criminal penalties for failure to file a return and filing a false or fraudulent return, see sections 7203, 7206, and 7207.

(2) *Civil penalties.*—For civil penalties for failure to file a proper foreign personal holding company information return, see section 6679 and the regulations thereunder. [Reg. § 1.6035-1.]

☐ [*T.D.* 6364, 2-13-59. *Amended by T.D.* 7322, 8-23-74; *T.D.* 7517, 11-11-77; *T.D.* 7557, 8-4-78; *T.D.* 8028, 6-3-85 *and T.D.* 8573, 12-13-94.]

§ 1.6038-2. Information returns required of United States persons with respect to annual accounting periods of certain foreign corporations beginning after December 31, 1962.—(a) *Requirement of return.*—Every U.S. person shall make a separate annual information return with respect to each annual accounting period (described in paragraph (e) of this section) beginning after December 31, 1962, of each foreign corporation which that person controls (as defined in paragraph (b) of this section) for an uninterrupted period of 30 days or more during such annual accounting period. Such information shall not be required to be furnished, however, with respect to a corporation defined in section 1504(d) of the Code which makes a consolidated return for the taxable year. The return shall be made, with respect to annual accounting periods ending with or within the United States person's taxable year, on—

(1) Form 2952 if such taxable year ends before December 31, 1982,

(2) Form 5471 if such taxable year ends on or after December 31, 1983, or

(3) Either Form 5471 or Form 2952 if such taxable year ends on or after December 31, 1982 and before December 31, 1963.

(b) *Control.*—A person shall be deemed to be in control of a foreign corporation if at any time during that person's taxable year it owns stock possessing more than 50 percent of the total combined voting power of all classes of stock entitled to vote, or more than 50 percent of the total value of shares of all classes of stock of the foreign corporation. A person in control of a corporation which, in turn, owns more than 50 percent of the combined voting power, or of the value, of all classes of stock of another corporation is also treated as being in control of such other corporation. The provisions of this paragraph may be illustrated by the following example:

Example. Corporation A owns 51 percent of the voting stock in Corporation B. Corporation B owns 51 percent of the voting stock in Corporation C. Corporation C in turn owns 51 percent of the voting stock in Corporation D. Corporation D is controlled by Corporation A.

(c) *Attribution rules.*—For the purpose of determining control of domestic or foreign corporations the constructive ownership rules of section 318(a) shall apply except that:

(1) Stock owned by or for a partner or a beneficiary of an estate or trust shall not be considered owned by the partnership, estate, or trust when the effect is to consider a United States person as owning stock owned by a person who is not a United States person;

(2) A corporation will not be considered as owning stock owned by or for a 50 percent or more shareholder when the effect is to consider a United States person as owning stock owned by a person who is not a United States person; and

(3) If 10 percent or more in value of the stock in a corporation is owned, directly or indirectly, by or for any person, section 318(a)(2)(C) shall apply.

The constructive ownership rules of section 318(a) apply only for purposes of determining control as defined in paragraph (b) of this section.

(d) [Reserved].—For further guidance, see § 1.6038-2T(d).

(e) *Period covered by return.*—The information required under paragraphs (f) and (g) of this section with respect to a foreign corporation shall be furnished for the annual accounting period of the foreign corporation ending with or within the United States person's taxable year. For purposes of this section, the annual accounting period of a foreign corporation is the annual period on the basis of which that corporation regularly computes its income in keeping its books. In the case of a specified foreign corporation (as defined in section 898), the taxable year of such corporation shall be treated as its annual accounting period. The term *annual accounting period* may refer to a period of less than one year, where, for example, the foreign income, war profits, and excess profits taxes are determined on the basis of an accounting period of less than one year as described in section 902(c)(5). If more than one annual accounting period ends with or within the United States person's taxable year, separate annual information returns shall be submitted for each annual accounting period.

(f) *Contents of return.*—The return on Form 2952 or Form 5471 shall contain so much of the following information, and in such form or manner, as the form shall prescribe with respect to each foreign corporation:

(1) The name, address, and employer identification number, if any, of the corporation;

(2) The principal place of business of the corporation;

(3) The date of incorporation and the country under whose laws incorporated;

(4) The name and address of the foreign corporation's statutory or resident agent in the country of incorporation;

(5) The name, address, and identifying number of any branch office or agent of the foreign corporation located in the United States;

(6) The name and address of the person (or persons) having custody of the books of account and records of the foreign corporation, and the location of such books and records if different from such address;

(7) The nature of the corporation's business and the principal places where conducted;

(8) As regards the outstanding stock of the corporation—

(i) A description of each class of the corporation's stock, and

(ii) The number of shares of each class outstanding at the beginning and end of the annual accounting period;

(9) A list showing the name, address, and identifying number of, and the number of shares of each class of the corporation's stock held by, each United States person who is a shareholder owning at any time during the annual accounting period 5 percent or more in value of any class of the corporation's outstanding stock;

(10) For the annual accounting period, the amount of the corporation's:

(i) Current earnings and profits;

(ii) Foreign income, war profits, and excess profits taxes paid or accrued;

(iii) Distributions out of current earnings and profits for the period;

(iv) Distributions other than those described in paragraph (f)(10)(iii) of this section and the source thereof; and

(v) For Forms 5471 filed for taxable years ending after December 15, 1990, such earnings and profits information as the form shall prescribe, including post-1986 undistributed earnings described in section 902(c)(1), pre-1987 amounts, total earnings and profits, and previously taxed earnings and profits described in section 959(c); and

(11) A summary showing the total amount of each of the following types of transactions of the corporation, which took place during the annual accounting period, with the person required to file this return, any other corporation controlled by that person, or any United States

person owning at the time of the transaction 10 percent or more in value of any class of stock outstanding of the foreign corporation, or of any corporation controlling that foreign corporation:

(i) Sales and purchases of stock in trade;

(ii) Purchases of tangible property other than stock in trade;

(iii) Sales and purchases of patents, inventions, models, or designs (whether or not patented), copyrights, trademarks, secret formulas or processes, or any other similar property rights;

(iv) Compensation paid and compensation received for the rendition of technical, managerial, engineering, construction, scientific, or like services;

(v) Commission paid and commissions received;

(vi) Rents and royalties paid and rents and royalties received;

(vii) Amount loaned and amounts borrowed (except open accounts resulting from sales and purchases reported under other items listed in this paragraph (f)(11) that arise and are collected in full in the ordinary course of business);

(viii) Dividends paid and dividends received;

(ix) Interest paid and interest received; and

(x) Premiums received for insurance or reinsurance.

For purposes of paragraph (f)(11) of this section, if the United States person is a bank as defined in section 581, or is controlled within the meaning of section 368(c) by a bank, the term "transactions" shall not, as to a corporation with respect to which a return is filed, include banking transactions entered into on behalf of customers; in any event, however, deposits in accounts between a foreign corporation, controlled (within the meaning of paragraph (b) of this section) by a United States person, and a person described in paragraph (f)(11) of this section and withdrawals from such accounts shall be summarized by reporting end-of-month balances.

(g) *Financial statements.*—The following information with respect to the foreign corporation shall be attached to and filed as part of the return required by this section. Forms 5471 filed after September 30, 1991, shall contain this information in such form or manner as the form shall prescribe with respect to each foreign corporation:

(1) A statement of the corporation's profit and loss for the annual accounting period;

(2) A balance sheet as of the end of the annual accounting period of the corporation showing—

(i) The corporation's assets;

(ii) The corporation's liabilities; and

(iii) The corporation's net worth; and

(3) An analysis of changes in the corporation's surplus accounts during the annual accounting period including both opening and closing balances.

The information listed in this paragraph (g) shall be prepared in conformity with generally accepted accounting principles, and in such detail as is customary for the corporation's accounting records.

(h) *Method of reporting.*—Except as provided in this paragraph (h), all amounts furnished under paragraphs (f) and (g) of this section shall be expressed in United States dollars with a statement of the exchange rates used. The following rules shall apply for taxable years ending after December 31, 1994, with respect to returns filed after December 31, 1995. All amounts furnished under paragraph (g) of this section shall be expressed in United States dollars computed and translated in conformity with United States generally accepted accounting principles. Amounts furnished under paragraph (g)(1) of this section shall also be furnished in the foreign corporation's functional currency as required on the form. Earnings and profits amounts furnished under paragraphs (f)(10)(i), (iii), (iv), and (v) of this section shall be expressed in the foreign corporation's functional currency except to the extent the form requires specific items to be translated into United States dollars. Tax amounts furnished under paragraph (f)(10)(ii) of this section shall be furnished in the foreign currency in which the taxes are payable and in United States dollars translated in accordance with section 986(a). All amounts furnished under paragraph (f)(11) of this section shall be expressed in U.S. dollars translated from functional currency at the weighted average exchange rate for the year as defined in §1.989(b)-1. The foreign corporation's functional currency is determined under section 985. All statements submitted on or with the return required under this section shall be rendered in the English language.

(i) *Time and place for filing return.*—Returns on Form 2952 or Form 5471 required under paragraph (a) of this section shall be filed with the United States person's income tax return on or before the date required by law for the filing of that person's income tax return. District directors and directors of service centers are authorized to grant reasonable extensions of time for filing returns on Form 2952 or Form

5471 in accordance with the applicable provisions of § 1.6081-1 of this chapter. An application for an extension of time for filing a return of income shall also be considered as an application for an extension of time for filing returns on Form 2952 or Form 5471.

(j) *Two or more persons required to submit the same information.*—(1) *Return jointly made.*— If two or more persons are required to furnish information with respect to the same foreign corporation for the same period, such persons may, in lieu of making separate returns, jointly make one return. Such joint return shall be filed with the income tax return of any one of the persons making such joint return.

(2) *Persons excepted from furnishing information.*—(i) *Conditions.*—Any person required to furnish information under this section with respect to a foreign corporation need not furnish that information provided all of the following conditions are met:

(A) Such person does not directly own an interest in the foreign corporation;

(B) Such person is required to furnish the information solely by reason of attribution of stock ownership from a United States person under paragraph (c) of this section; and

(C) The person from whom the stock ownership is attributed furnishes all of the information required under this section of the person to whom the stock ownership is attributed. (For a rule regarding attribution from a nonresident alien, see paragraph (l) of this section).

(ii) If an individual who is a United States person required to furnish information with respect to a foreign corporation under section 6038 is entitled under a treaty to be treated as a nonresident of the United States, and if the individual claims this treaty benefit, and if there are no other United States persons that are required to furnish information under section 6038 with respect to the foreign corporation, then the individual may satisfy the requirements of paragraphs (f)(10), (f)(11), (g), and (h) of this section by filing the audited foreign financial statements of the foreign corporation with the individual's return required under section 6038.

(iii) *Illustrations.*—The rule of this paragraph (j)(2) is illustrated by the following examples:

Example (1). A, a U.S. person owns 100 percent of the stock of M, a domestic corporation. A also owns 100 percent of the stock of N, a foreign corporation organized under the laws of foreign country Y. A, in filing the information return required by this section with respect to N Corporation, in fact furnishes all of the information required of M Corporation with respect to N Corporation. M Corporation need not file the information.

Example (2). X, a domestic corporation owns 100 percent of the stock of Y, a domestic corporation, Y Corporation owns 100 percent of the stock of Z, a foreign corporation. X Corporation is not excused by this paragraph (j)(2) from filing information with respect to Z Corporation because X Corporation is deemed to control Z Corporation under the provisions of paragraph (b) of this section without recourse to the attribution rules in paragraph (c) of this section.

(3) *Statement required.*—Any United States person required to furnish information under this section with his return who does not do so by reason of the provisions of paragraph (j)(1) or (j)(2) of this section shall file a statement with his income tax return indicating that such liability has been (or, in the case of a joint return made under paragraph (j)(1) of this section, will be) satisfied and identifying the return with which the information was or will be filed and the place of filing.

(k) *Failure to furnish information.*—(1) *Dollar amount penalty.*—(i) *In general.*—If any person required to file Form 2952 or Form 5471 under section 6038 and this section fails to furnish any information described in paragraphs (f) and (g) of this section within the time prescribed by paragraph (i) of this section, such person shall pay a penalty of $1,000 for each annual accounting period of each foreign corporation with respect to which such failure occurs.

(ii) *Increase in penalty for continued failure after notification.*—If a failure described in paragraph (k)(1)(i) of this section continues for more than 90 days after the date on which the district director mails notice of such failure to the person required to file Form 2952 or Form 5471, such person shall pay a penalty of $1,000, in addition to the penalty imposed by section 6038(b)(1) and paragraph (k)(1)(i) of this section, for each 30-day period (or fraction thereof) during which such failure continues after such 90-day period has expired. The additional penalty imposed by section 6038(b)(2) and this paragraph (k)(1)(ii) shall be limited to a maximum of $24,000 for each failure.

(iii) *Effective date.*—The penalty imposed by section 6038(b) and this paragraph (k)(1) shall apply with respect to information for annual accounting periods ending after September 3, 1982.

(2) *Penalty of reducing foreign tax credit.*— (i) *Effect on foreign tax credit.*—Failure of a United States person to furnish, in accordance

with the provisions of this section, any return of any information in any return, required to be filed for a taxable year under authority of section 6038 on or before the date prescribed in paragraph (i) of this section may affect the application of section 901 as provided in paragraph (k)(2)(ii) of this section and may affect the application of sections 902 and 960 as provided in paragraph (k)(2)(iii) of this section. Such failure may affect the application of sections 902 and 960 to any such United States person which is a corporation or to any person who acquires from any other person any portion (but only to the extent of such portion) of the interest of such other person in any such foreign corporation.

(ii) *Application of section 901.*—In the application of section 901 to a United States person referred to in paragraph (k)(2)(i) of this section, the amount of taxes paid or deemed paid by such person for any taxable year, with or within which the annual accounting period of a foreign corporation for which such person failed to furnish information required under this section ended, may be reduced by 10 percent. However, no tax reduced under paragraph (k)(2)(iii) of this section or deemed paid under section 904(c) shall be reduced under the provisions of this paragraph (k)(2)(ii).

(iii) *Application of sections 902 and 960.*—In the application of sections 902 and 960 to a United States person referred to in paragraph (k)(2)(i) of this section for any taxable year, the amount of taxes paid or deemed paid by each foreign corporation for the accounting period or periods for which such person was required for the taxable year of the failure to furnish information under this section may be reduced by 10 percent. The 10-percent reduction is not limited to the taxes paid or deemed paid by the foreign corporation with respect to which there is a failure to file information but may apply to the taxes paid or deemed paid by all foreign corporations controlled by that person. In applying subsections (a) and (b) of section 902, and in applying subsection (a) of section 960, the reduction provided by this paragraph (k)(2) shall not apply for purposes of determining the amount of accumulated profits in excess of income, war profits, and excess profits taxes.

(iv) *Reduction for continued failure after notice.*—(A) If the failure referred to in paragraph (k)(2)(i) of this section continues for more than 90 days after the date on which the district director mails notice of such failure to such United States person, then the amount of the reduction referred to in paragraph (k)(2)(ii) and (iii) of this section may be 10 percent plus an additional 5 percent for each 3-month period, or fraction thereof, during which such failure continues after the expiration of such 90-day period.

(B) No taxes shall be reduced under this paragraph (k)(2) more than once for the same failure. Taxes paid by a foreign corporation when once reduced for a failure shall not be reduced again for the same failure in their status as taxes deemed paid by a corporate shareholder. Where a failure continues, each additional periodic 5-percent reduction, referred to in paragraph (k)(2)(iv)(A) of this section, shall be considered as part of the one reduction.

(v) *Limitation on reduction of foreign tax credit.*—The amount of the reduction under this paragraph (k)(2) for each failure to furnish information with respect to a foreign corporation as required under this section shall not exceed the greater of:

(A) $10,000, or

(B) The income of the foreign corporation for its annual accounting period with respect to which the failure occurs. For purposes of this section if a person is required to furnish information with respect to more than one foreign corporation, controlled (within the meaning of paragraph (b) of this section) by that person, each failure to submit information for each such corporation constitutes a separate failure.

(vi) *Offset for dollar amount penalty imposed.*—The total amount of the reduction or reductions which, but for this paragraph (k)(2)(vi), may be made under this paragraph (k)(2) with respect to any separate failure, shall not exceed the maximum amount of such reductions which may be imposed, reduced (but not below zero) by the amount of the dollar amount penalty imposed by paragraph (k)(1) of this section with respect to such separate failure.

(3) *Reasonable cause.*—(i) For purposes of section 6038(b) and (c) and this section, the time prescribed for furnishing information under paragraph (i) of this section, and the beginning of the 90-day period after mailing of notice by the district director under paragraph (k)(1)(ii) and (k)(2)(iv)(A) of this section, shall be treated as being not earlier than the last day on which reasonable cause existed for failure to furnish the information.

(ii) To show that reasonable cause existed for failure to furnish information as required by section 6038 and this section, the person required to report such information must make an affirmative showing of all facts alleged as reasonable cause for such failure in a written statement containing a declaration that it is made under the penalties of perjury. The statement must be filed with the district director for the district or the director of the service center where the return is required to be filed. The district director or the director of the service center shall determine whether the failure to furnish information was due to reasonable cause, and if so, the period of time for which such reasonable cause existed. In the case of a return that has been filed as required by this section except for an omission of, or error with respect to, some of the information required, if the person who filed the return establishes to the satisfaction of the district director or the director of the service center that the person has substantially complied with this section, then the omission or error shall not constitute a failure under this section.

(4) *Other penalties.*—The information required by section 6038 and this section must be furnished even though there are no foreign taxes which would be reduced under the provisions of this section, and even though the information required may not affect the amount of any tax due under the Internal Revenue Code. For criminal penalties for failure to file a return and filing a false or fraudulent return, see sections 7203, 7206, and 7207 of the Code.

(5) *Illustrations.*—The provisions of this paragraph may be illustrated by the following examples.

Example (1). M, a domestic corporation owns 100 percent of the stock of N, a foreign corporation. Both M and N use the calendar year as a taxable year and annual accounting period, and all of the following events occur in or with respect to the 1980 taxable year. The dividend from N is the only dividend from a foreign corporation received by M during the taxable year, and the foreign taxes listed are the only foreign taxes paid or deemed paid by M and N for the taxable year. On March 15, 1981, M filed its income tax return and paid its income tax, but M did not file Form 2952 with respect to N's 1980 annual accounting period. On June 1, 1961, the district director mailed notice to M of M's failure to file Form 2952 with respect to N. On November 30, 1981, M filed a complete Form 2952 with respect to N's 1980 annual accounting period.

(a)	Gains, profits, and income of N	$100,000
(b)	Foreign tax paid by N with respect to such gains, profits, and income	40,000
(c)	Deduction of foreign tax paid by N (for purposes of M's section 902 deemed paid credit) resulting from M's failure to file information with respect to N as required under section 6038(a) and this section: failure to file within the time prescribed in paragraph (i) of this section, 10-percent reduction; continued failure for one additional 3-month period after 90-day period after notice mailed, 5-percent reduction; total reduction, 15 percent ($40,000 times 15 percent)	6,000
(d)	Foreign tax paid by N after section 6038(c)(1)(B) reduction	34,000
(e)	Dividend paid by N to M	45,000
(f)	Accumulated profits of N as defined in section 902(c)(1) (determined without regard to the section 6038(c)(1)(B) reduction)	100,000
(g)	Accumulated profits of N as described in section 902(a) (determined without regard to the section 6038(c)(1)(B) reduction)	60,000
(h)	For purposes of section 902 credit, M is deemed to have paid the same proportion of foreign taxes paid (reduced as provided under section 6038(c)) with respect to the accumulated profits described in section 902(a) (determined without regard to the reduction provided under section 6038(c)) as the amount of the dividend (determined without regard to section 78) bears to such amount of accumulated profits	25,500

$(45,000 \div 60,000) \times 34,000 = 25,500$

M must include $25,500 in gross income as a dividend under the provisions of section 78 of the Code. This example illustrates that the reductions in foreign taxes paid by the foreign corporation provided under section 8038(c) are taken into account in determining the amount included in gross income of the domestic corporation under section 78 of the Code as foreign taxes deemed paid, but such reductions are not taken into account in computing accumulated profits for purposes of determining the portion of foreign taxes deemed paid with respect to a particular dividend. The dollar amount penalty imposed by section 8038(b) and paragraph (k)(1) of this section does not apply with respect to information for annual accounting periods ending before September 4, 1982, and therefore does not apply to M with respect to M's failure to file Form 2952 in this example.

Example (2). The facts are the same as in example (1) except that all of the events occur in or with respect to the 1982 taxable year. On March 15, 1983, M filed its income tax return and paid its income tax, but M did not file Form 2952 or Form 5471 with respect to N's 1982 annual accounting period. On June 1, 1983, the district director mailed notice to M of M's failure to file Form 2952 or Form 5471 with respect to N. On November 30, 1983, M filed a complete Form 5471 with respect to N's 1982 annual accounting period. Under paragraph (k)(1)(i) of this section, M is subject to a penalty of $1,000. Under paragraph (k)(1)(ii) of this section, that penalty is increased by $4,000 because the failure continued for 92 days (three full 30-day periods and a fraction of a fourth 30-day period) after the end of the 90-day period following mailing of the notice by the district director, bringing M's dollar amount penalty under paragraph (k)(1) of this section to $5,000. For purpose of determining the foreign tax credit available to M, there may be imposed a reduction of foreign tax paid by N of $6,000, which would be the total of reductions under paragraph (k)(2) of this section with respect to M's failure to file under section 6038 for N's 1982 annual accounting period, before application of paragraph (k)(2)(vi) of this section. Under said paragraph (k)(2)(vi), the amount of the foreign tax reduction imposed is reduced by the amount of the dollar amount penalty, leaving a foreign tax reduction penalty of $1,000 which may be imposed in addition to the $5,000 dollar amount penalty. If imposed, the $1,000 tax reduction would then be applied in the calculation of taxes deemed paid by M under section 902 as in example (1), item (c), (d), and (h).

(l) *Other persons excepted from filing.*—For tax years of foreign corporations ending on or after December 29, 1999, any person required to furnish information under this section with respect to a foreign corporation does not have to furnish that information if the following conditions are met—

(1) Such person does not own a direct or indirect interest in the foreign corporation; and

(2) Such person is required to furnish information solely by reason of attribution of stock ownership from a nonresident alien(s) under paragraph (c) of this section. [Reg. § 1.6038-2.]

☐ [*T.D.* 6621, 11-30-62. *Amended by T.D.* 6969, 8-22-68; *T.D.* 6997, 1-17-69; *T.D.* 8040, 7-23-85; *T.D.* 8573, 12-13-94; *T.D.* 8733, 10-6-97; *T.D.* 8850, 12-27-99 *and T.D.* 9194, 4-6-2005.]

§ 1.6038-2T. Information returns required of United States persons with respect to annual accounting periods of certain foreign corporations (temporary).—
(a) through (c) [Reserved] For further guidance, see § 1.6038-2(a) through (c).

(d) *U.S. person.*—(1) *In general.*—For purposes of section 6038 and this section, the term *United States person* has the meaning assigned to it by section 7701(a)(30), except as provided in paragraphs (d)(2) and (3) of this section.

(2) *Special rule for individuals residing in certain possessions.*—With respect to individuals who are bona fide residents of Puerto Rico or any section 931 possession, as defined in § 1.931-1T(c)(1), the term United States person has the meaning assigned to it by § 1.957-3T.

(3) *Special rule for certain nonresident aliens.*—An individual for whom an election under section 6013(g) or (h) is in effect shall, subject to the exceptions contained in paragraph (d)(2) of this section, be considered a United States person for purposes of section 6038 and this section.

(e) through (l)(2) [Reserved] For further guidance, see § 1.6038-2(e) through (l)(2).

(m) *Effective date.*—This section shall apply for taxable years ending after October 22, 2004. [Temporary Reg. § 1.6038-2T.]

☐ [*T.D.* 9194, 4-6-2005.]

§ 1.6038-3. Information returns required of certain United States persons with respect to controlled foreign partnerships (CFPs).—(a) *Persons required to make return.*—(1) *Controlling fifty-percent partners.*—The term *controlling fifty-percent partner* means a United States person that controlled (as defined in paragraph (b)(1) of this section) the foreign partnership at any time during the partnership's tax year (as defined in paragraph (b)(8) of this section). Except as provided in paragraph (c), (d), or (e) of this section, for each tax year of a foreign partnership during which the partnership has one or more controlling fifty-percent partners, each controlling fifty-percent partner must complete and file Form 8865, "Return of U.S. Persons With Respect To Certain Foreign Partnerships," containing the information described in paragraph (g) of this section.

(2) *Controlling ten-percent partners.*—If at any point during a foreign partnership's tax year (as defined in paragraph (b)(8) of this section) a United States person owned a ten-percent or greater interest in the partnership while the partnership was controlled by United States persons owning ten-percent or greater interests, such United States person is a controlling ten-percent partner. See paragraph (b)(1) of this section for the definition of control. However, a United States person is not a controlling ten-percent partner with respect to a particular foreign partnership for a particular tax year of the foreign partnership if at any point during that year the partnership had a controlling fifty-percent partner, as defined in paragraph (a)(1) of this section. Except as provided in paragraph (c), (d), or (e) of this section, for each tax year of a partnership during which the partnership has controlling ten-percent partners, each controlling ten-percent partner must complete and file Form 8865

containing the information described in paragraph (g)(1) of this section.

(3) *Separate returns for each partnership.*—A United States person required to report under this paragraph (a) must file a separate Form 8865 for each foreign partnership with respect to which the person is a controlling fifty-percent partner or a controlling ten-percent partner.

(b) *Ownership determinations and definitions.*—(1) *Control.*—Control of a foreign partnership is ownership of more than a fifty-percent interest in the partnership.

(2) *Fifty-percent interest.*—A fifty-percent interest in a partnership is an interest equal to fifty percent of the capital interest in such partnership, an interest equal to fifty percent of the profits interest in such partnership, or an interest to which fifty percent of the deductions or losses of such partnership are allocated.

(3) *Ten-percent interest.*—A ten-percent interest in a partnership is an interest equal to ten percent of the capital interest in such partnership, an interest equal to ten percent of the profits interest in such partnership, or an interest to which ten percent of the deductions or losses of such partnership are allocated.

(4) *Constructive ownership rules.*—For purposes of determining an interest in a partnership, the constructive ownership rules of section 267(c) (other than section 267(c)(3)) apply, taking into account that such rules refer to corporations and not to partnerships. However, an interest will be attributed from a nonresident alien under the family attribution rules of section 267(c)(2) and (4) only if the person to whom the interest is attributed owns a direct or indirect (under the rules of 267(c)(1) or (5)) interest in the foreign partnership.

(5) *Determination of amount of interest.*—Whether a person owns a fifty-percent interest, or a ten-percent interest, as described in paragraphs (b)(2) and (3) of this section, is determined for each tax year of the foreign partnership by reference to the agreement of the partners relating to such interests during that tax year.

(6) *Definition of United States person.*—The term *United States person* is defined in section 7701(a)(30).

(7) *Definition of a foreign partnership.*—A foreign partnership is a partnership described in section 7701(a)(5).

(8) *Tax year of a foreign partnership.*—The tax year of a foreign partnership is determined under section 706.

(9) *Examples.*—The rules of paragraph (a) of this section and this paragraph (b) are illustrated by the following examples:

Example 1. Sole U.S. partner does not own more than a fifty-percent interest. No United States person owns any interest (directly or constructively) in *FPS*, a foreign partnership whose tax year under section 706 is the calendar year. On January 1, 2001, *US*, a United States person with the calendar year as its tax year, contributes property to *FPS* in exchange for a 40% interest in a section 721 transaction. No United States persons acquire directly or constructively any other interests in *FPS* during *FPS*'s 2001 tax year. *US* is not a controlling fifty-percent partner during *FPS*'s 2001 tax year. *US* did not own during that tax year, either directly or constructively, more than a 50% interest in the partnership under paragraphs (b)(2) and (4) of this section. Also, *US* is not a controlling ten-percent partner; although *US* owned a 10% or greater interest, *US* persons owning at least 10% interests did not control *FPS*. Therefore, *US* does not have to file with its 2001 income tax return a Form 8865 with respect to *FPS* under section 6038. (But see section 6038B for the reporting obligations of *US* with respect to its transfer of property to *FPS* and section 6046A for the reporting obligation of *US* with respect to its acquisition of an interest in *FPS*. See also §1.6046A-1(f)(1) regarding the overlap between sections 6038B and 6046A).

Example 2. Controlling ten-percent partners. Assume the same facts as in *Example 1*. In addition, on January 1, 2002, *US1*, a United States person unrelated to *US* and a calendar year taxpayer, purchases a 15% interest in *FPS* from a foreign partner of *FPS*. Neither *US* nor *US1* is a controlling fifty-percent partner during *FPS*'s 2002 tax year because neither one owns more than a 50% percent interest in *FPS* during that year. However, *US* and *US1* are controlling ten-percent partners for that year because each owns at least a 10% interest (*US* owns a 40% interest and *US1* owns a 15% interest) and together they control *FPS* because collectively they own more than a 50% interest in *FPS*. As controlling ten-percent partners, under section 6038, each is required to file a Form 8865 with its 2002 income tax return. (*US1* must also report its acquisition of the 15% interest in *FPS* under section 6046A on its Form 8865 filed with its 2002 income tax return.)

Example 3. Constructive ownership rules. Assume the same facts as in *Example 2*. In addition, on January 1, 2003, *US2*, a United States person and the brother of *US*, purchases 50% of the stock of *FC*, a foreign corporation. *FC* owns a 20% interest in *FPS*. Thus, under sections 6038(e)(3) and 267(c)(1), *US2* indirectly owns a 10% interest in *FPS* (10% is *US2*'s proportionate share of *FC*'s 20% interest in *FPS*), and under sections 6038(e)(3) and 267(c)(2), *US2* is attributed *US*'s 40% interest. Additionally, *US* directly owns a 40% interest in *FPS* and is attributed *US2*'s 10% interest pursuant to section 6038(e)(3) and section 267(c)(2). Therefore, *US2* is considered to own a 50% interest (10% indirectly and 40% from *US*) in *FPS*, and *US* is considered to own a 50% interest in *FPS* (40% directly and 10% from *US2*). *FPS* has no controlling fifty-percent partners, because neither *US*, *US1*, nor *US2*, owns a greater than 50% interest. However, *US*, *US1*, and *US2* are each controlling ten-percent partners and each must file Form 8865 pursuant to section 6038 for *FPS*'s 2003 tax year ending December 31, 2003. Each must attach Form 8865 to its tax return for its 2003 tax year.

Example 4. Controlling fifty-percent partners. Assume the same facts as in *Example 3*. In addition, on June 1, 2004, *US* acquires an additional 1% direct interest in *FPS*. *US* is now a controlling fifty-percent partner of *FPS*, because *US* owns a 41% interest directly and a 10% interest constructively from *US2*. *US2* is also a controlling fifty-percent partner, because *US2* owns 10% indirectly and 41% constructively from *US*. Both *US* and *US2* are required to file Form 8865 containing all the information required to be submitted by controlling fifty-percent partners. (But see paragraph (c)(1) of this section, which contains filing exceptions when there are multiple controlling fifty-percent partners). *US1* is no longer a controlling ten-percent partner because *FPS* now has at least one controlling fifty-percent partner, and *US1* does not qualify as a controlling fifty-percent partner. Therefore, *US1* is not required to file Form 8865 under section 6038.

Example 5. Constructive ownership from a nonresident alien. *US*, a United States person, does not own directly or constructively an interest in *FPS*, a foreign partnership. The tax year of *FPS* is the calendar year. *NRA*, a nonresident alien, is the mother of *US*. In 2002, *NRA* acquires a 55% interest in *FPS*. Because *US* owns neither a direct nor a constructive interest in *FPS* under sections 6038(e)(3) and 267(c)(1) or (5), *NRA*'s interest is not attributed to *US* under sections 6038(e)(3) and 267(c)(2). If in 2003 *NRA* becomes a United States person, *NRA*'s interest will be attributed to *US*. However, *US* is excused from filing Form 8865 if *US* satisfies the requirements of the constructive owners exception in paragraph (c)(2) of this section. In 2003, *NRA* is a controlling fifty-percent partner and must file a Form 8865 under section 6038 for *FPS*'s 2003 tax year.

(c) *Exceptions when more than one United States person is required to file Form 8865 pursuant to section 6038.*—(1) *Multiple controlling fifty-percent partners.*—(i) *In general.*—If, with respect to the same foreign partnership for the same tax year, more than one United States person is a controlling fifty-percent partner, then in lieu of each controlling fifty-percent partner filing a separate Form 8865, only one Form 8865 from one of the controlling fifty-percent partners is required, provided all of the requirements of paragraph (c)(1)(ii) of this section are satisfied. A person that is a controlling fifty-percent partner solely because of an interest to which deductions or losses are allocated may file the single return only if there is no United States person that is a controlling fifty-percent partner by reason of an interest in capital or profits.

(ii) *Requirements.*—(A) The person undertaking the filing obligation must file Form 8865 with that person's income tax return in the manner provided by Form 8865 and the accompanying instructions. The return must contain all of the information that would have been required to be reported by this section if each controlling fifty-percent partner had filed its own Form 8865.

(B) Any controlling fifty-percent partner not filing Form 8865 must file with its income tax return a statement titled "Controlled Foreign Partnership Reporting" containing the following information—

(1) A statement that the person qualified as a controlling fifty-percent partner, but is not submitting Form 8865 pursuant to the multiple controlling fifty-percent partners exception;

(2) The name, address, and taxpayer identification number (if any) of the foreign partnership of which the person qualified as a controlling fifty-percent partner;

(3) A representation that the filing requirement has been or will be satisfied;

(4) The name and address of the person filing the single return;

(5) The Internal Revenue Service Center where the single return is required to be filed; and

(6) Any additional information that Form 8865 and the accompanying instructions require.

(iii) *Penalties.*—If the requirements listed in paragraph (c)(1)(ii) of this section are not satisfied, a United States person that did not file a Form 8865 pursuant to this paragraph will be subject to the penalties in paragraph (k) of this section, unless the reasonable cause provision in paragraph (k)(4) of this section is satisfied.

(2) *Certain constructive owners excepted from furnishing information.*—(i) *In general.*—

Reg. §1.6038-3(c)(2)(i)

A United States person that does not own a direct interest in the foreign partnership and that is required to file Form 8865 under this section solely by reason of constructive ownership from a United States person(s) pursuant to paragraph (b)(4) of this section (an indirect partner) is not required to file Form 8865 if all of the requirements listed in paragraph (c)(2)(ii) of this section are met.

(ii) *Requirements.*—(A) The United States person(s) whose interest the indirect partner constructively owns reports all the information such person(s) is required to submit under this section, unless such person also is required to file solely by reason of constructive ownership from a United States person(s) pursuant to paragraph (b)(4) of this section, or another person reports the information pursuant to paragraph (c)(1) of this section.

(B) The indirect partner files with its income tax return a statement titled "Controlled Foreign Partnership Reporting" containing the following information—

(*1*) A representation that the indirect partner was required to file Form 8865, but is not doing so pursuant to the constructive owners exception;

(*2*) The names and addresses of the United States persons whose interests the indirect partner constructively owns;

(*3*) The name and address of the foreign partnership with respect to which the indirect partner would have had to have filed Form 8865 but for this exception; and

(*4*) Any additional information that Form 8865 and the accompanying instructions require.

(iii) *Penalties.*—A United States person that pursuant to this paragraph (c)(2) does not file a return will be subject to the penalties in paragraph (k) of this section if the requirements listed in paragraph (c)(2)(ii) of this section are not satisfied, unless such failure is due to reasonable cause, as defined in paragraph (k)(4) of this section.

(iv) *Overlap with multiple controlling fifty-percent partners exception.*—(A) If a United States person qualifies for both the exception in paragraph (c)(1) of this section and the exception in this paragraph (c)(2), such person may only utilize the multiple controlling fifty-percent partners exception in paragraph (c)(1) of this section to avoid filing Form 8865.

(B) *Example.*—The following example illustrates the operation of this paragraph (c)(2)(iv):

Example. US is a U.S. citizen. *US* owns 100% of the stock of *DC,* a domestic corporation. *DC* owns a 60% direct interest in *FPS,* a foreign partnership. *DC* and *US* are the only U.S. persons that own interests directly or constructively in *FPS. DC* owns directly a greater than 50% interest in *FPS. US* constructively owns *DC*'s interest pursuant to sections 6038(e)(3) and 267(c)(1). Therefore, both *DC* and *US* are controlling fifty-percent partners. *US* qualifies for both the exception in paragraph (c)(1) of this section (multiple controlling fifty-percent partners) and the exception in paragraph (c)(2) of this section (constructive owner exception). *US* may only utilize the paragraph (c)(1) exception to avoid its filing obligation. Accordingly, *DC* may file a single Form 8865 on behalf of *US* and itself. However, that form must contain all the information that would have been submitted had *DC* and *US* each submitted a separate Form 8865.

(3) *Members of an affiliated group of corporations filing a consolidated return.*—If one or more members of an affiliated group of corporations filing a consolidated return are required under section 6038 to file a Form 8865 for a particular foreign partnership, the common parent corporation may file one Form 8865 on behalf of all of the members of the group required to report under section 6038. Except with respect to group members who also qualify under the exception in paragraph (c)(2) of this section, the Form 8865 must contain all the information that would have been required to be submitted if each group member were required to file its own Form 8865.

(d) *Exception for certain trusts.*—Trusts relating to state and local government employee retirement plans are not required to report under this section, unless the instructions to Form 8865 provide otherwise.

(e) *Reporting under this section not required with respect to partnerships excluded from the application of subchapter K.*—The reporting requirements of this section will not apply to any United States person in respect of an eligible partnership as described in § 1.761-2(a) if such partnership has validly elected to be excluded from all of the provisions of subchapter K of chapter 1 of the Internal Revenue Code in the manner specified in § 1.761-2(b)(2)(i), or such partnership is deemed to have elected to be excluded from all of the provisions of subchapter K of chapter 1 of the Internal Revenue Code in accordance with the provisions of § 1.761-2(b)(2)(ii).

(f) *Period covered by return.*—The information required under this section must be furnished for the tax year of the foreign partnership ending with or within the United States person's tax year. See section 706 for rules regarding tax years of partnerships.

Reg. § 1.6038-3(c)(2)(ii)(A)

(g) *Contents of return.*—(1) *Information required to be submitted by controlling fifty-percent partners and controlling ten-percent partners.*— All controlling fifty-percent partners and all controlling ten-percent partners must submit the following information on Form 8865 in the form and manner and to the extent prescribed by Form 8865 and its instructions—

(i) The name, address, and taxpayer identification number (if any) of the foreign partnership of which the person qualified as a controlling fifty-percent partner or a controlling ten-percent partner;

(ii) A statement of the income, gain, losses, deductions and credits allocated to the direct interest in the partnership of the person reporting under section 6038;

(iii) A list of all partnerships (foreign or domestic) in which the foreign partnership owned a direct interest, or owned a constructive interest of ten percent of more under the rules of section 267(c)(1) or (5), during the partnership's tax year for which the Form 8865 is being filed;

(iv) Information about all foreign entities that were disregarded as entities separate from their owner under §§ 301.7701-2 and 301.7701-3 that were owned by the foreign partnership during the partnership's tax year for which the Form 8865 is being filed;

(v) A summary of the transactions that took place during the partnership's tax year between the partnership and the person filing the return, between the partnership and any other partnership of which the person filing the return is a controlling fifty-percent partner, and between the partnership and any corporation controlled (under section 6038(e)(2) and the regulations thereunder) by the person filing the return; and

(vi) Any other information that Form 8865 or its accompanying instructions require to be submitted.

(2) *Additional information required to be submitted by controlling fifty-percent partners.*— In addition to the information required pursuant to paragraph (g)(1) of this section, controlling fifty-percent partners must also submit the following information in the form and manner and to the extent required by Form 8865 and its instructions—

(i) A list of the names, addresses and tax identification numbers (if any) of each United States person that owned a direct interest of ten percent or more in the partnership during the partnership's tax year, and of each United States and foreign person whose interests in the partnership the controlling fifty-percent partner constructively owned under paragraph (b)(4) of this section during the partnership's tax year;

(ii) A list of transactions between the partnership and any United States person owning at the time of the transaction at least a 10-percent direct interest (as defined in paragraph (b)(3) of this section) in the foreign partnership;

(iii) A statement of the aggregate of the partners' distributive shares of items of income, gain, losses, deductions and credits;

(iv) A statement of income, gain, losses, deductions and credits allocated to each United States person holding a direct interest in the foreign partnership of ten percent or more; and

(v) Any other information Form 8865 or its accompanying instructions require controlling fifty-percent partners to submit.

(h) *Method of reporting.*—Except as otherwise provided on Form 8865 or the accompanying instructions, all amounts required to be furnished on Form 8865 must be expressed in United States dollars. All statements required on or with Form 8865 pursuant to this section must be in English.

(i) *Time and place for filing return.*—(1) *In general.*—Form 8865 must be filed with the United States person's income tax return on or before the due date (including extensions) of that return. If the United States person is not required to file an income tax return for its tax year with which or within which the foreign partnership's tax year ends, but is required to file an information return for that year (for example, Form 1065, "U.S. Partnership Return of Income," or Form 990, "Return of Organization Exempt from Income Tax"), the Form 8865 must be filed with the United States person's information return filed on or before the due date (including extensions) of that return.

(2) *Duplicate return.*—If required by the instructions to Form 8865, a duplicate Form 8865 (including attachments and schedules) must also be filed.

(j) *Overlap with section 6031.*—A partner may be required to file Form 8865 under this section and the foreign partnership in which it is a partner may also be required to file a Form 1065 or Form 1065-B under section 6031(e) for the same partnership tax year. For cases where a United States person is a controlling fifty-percent partner or a controlling ten-percent partner with respect to a foreign partnership, and that foreign partnership completes and files Form 1065 or Form 1065-B, the instructions for Form 8865 will specify the filing requirements that address this overlap in reporting obligations.

(k) *Failure to comply with reporting requirement.*—(1) *In general.*—Any United States person required to file Form 8865 under Section 6038 and this section that fails to comply (as defined in paragraph (k)(2) of this section) with the reporting requirements of this section, will be subject to the penalties described in paragraph (k)(3) of this section.

(2) *Failure to comply.*—A failure to comply is separately determined for each foreign partnership for which a United States person has a section 6038 reporting obligation. A failure to comply with the requirements of section 6038 includes the following—

(i) The failure to report at the proper time and in the proper manner any information required to be reported under the rules of this section; or

(ii) The provision of false or inaccurate information in purported compliance with the requirements of this section.

(3) *Penalties.*—A United States person that fails to comply (as defined in paragraph (k)(2) of this section) with the reporting requirements of this section must pay the following penalties, subject to the reasonable cause exception in paragraph (k)(4) of this section:

(i) *Dollar amount penalty.*— (A) *$10,000 penalty.*—A penalty of $10,000 shall be imposed for each tax year of each foreign partnership with respect to which a failure to comply occurs.

(B) *Increase in penalty.*—If a failure to comply with the applicable reporting requirements of section 6038 and this section continues for more than 90 days after the date on which the Commissioner or the Commissioner's delegate mails notice of the failure to the United States person required to file Form 8865, the person must pay an additional penalty of $10,000 for each 30-day period (or fraction thereof) during which the failure continues after the 90-day period has expired.

(C) *Limitation.*—The additional penalty imposed on any United States person by section 6038(b)(2) and paragraph (k)(3)(i)(B) of this section is limited to a maximum of $50,000 for each partnership for each tax year with respect to which the failure occurs.

(ii) *Penalty of reducing foreign tax credit.*—(A) *Effect on foreign tax credit.*—Failure to comply with the reporting requirements of section 6038 and this section may cause a reduction of foreign tax credits under section 901 (taxes of foreign countries and of possessions of the United States). In applying section 901 to a United States person for any tax year with or within which its foreign partnership's tax year ended, the amount of taxes paid (and deemed paid under sections 902 and 960) by the United States person will be reduced by 10 percent if the person fails to comply. However, no tax deemed paid under section 904(c) will be reduced under the provisions of this paragraph (k)(3)(ii).

(B) *Reduction for continued failure.*— If a failure to comply with the reporting requirements of section 6038 and this section continues for more than 90 days after the date on which the Commissioner or the Commissioner's delegate mails notice of the failure to the person required to file Form 8865, then the amount of the reduction in paragraph (k)(3)(ii)(A) of this section will be 10 percent, plus an additional 5 percent for each 3-month period (or fraction thereof) during which the failure continues after the 90-day period has expired.

(C) *Limitation on reduction.*—The amount of the reduction under paragraphs (k)(3)(ii)(A) and (B) of this section for each failure to furnish information required under this section will not exceed the greater of $10,000, or the gross income of the foreign partnership for its tax year with respect to which the failure occurred.

(D) *Offset for dollar amount penalty imposed.*—The total amount of the reduction which, but for this paragraph (k)(3)(ii)(D), may be made under this paragraph (k)(3)(ii) with respect to any separate failure, may not exceed the maximum amount of the reductions that may be imposed, reduced (but not below zero) by the dollar amount penalty imposed by paragraph (k)(3)(i) of this section with respect to the failure.

(4) *Reasonable cause limitation.*—The time prescribed for filing a complete Form 8865, and the beginning of the 90-day period after the Commissioner or the Commissioner's delegate mails notice under paragraphs (k)(3)(i)(B) and (ii)(B) of this section, will be treated as being not earlier than the last day on which reasonable cause existed for failure to furnish the information. The United States person may show reasonable cause by providing a written statement to the Commissioner's delegate having jurisdiction over the person's return to which the Form 8865 should have been attached, setting forth the reasons for the failure to comply. Whether a failure to comply was due to reasonable cause will be determined by the Commissioner, or the Commissioner's delegate, under all the facts and circumstances.

(5) *Statute of limitations.*—For exceptions to the limitations on assessment in the event of a failure to provide information under section 6038, see section 6501(c)(8).

(l) *Effective date.*—Except as otherwise provided, this section shall apply for tax years of a foreign partnership ending on or after December 31, 2000. For tax years of a foreign partnership ending before December 23, 2002, see § 1.6038-3(j) in effect prior to the amendments made by T.D. 9033 (see 26 CFR part 1 revised April 1, 2002). [Reg. § 1.6038-3.]

☐ [*T.D.* 8850, 12-27-99. *Amended by T.D.* 9033, 12-20-2002 *and T.D.* 9065, 6-30-2003.]

§ 1.6038A-1. General requirements and definitions.—(a) *Purpose and scope.*—This section and §§ 1.6038A-2 through 1.6038A-7 provide rules for certain foreign-owned U.S. corporations and foreign corporations engaged in trade or business within the United States (reporting corporations) relating to information that must be furnished, records that must be maintained, and the authorization of the reporting corporation to act as agent for related foreign persons for purposes of sections 7602, 7603, and 7604 that must be executed. Section 6038A(a) and this section require that a reporting corporation furnish certain information annually and maintain certain records relating to transactions between the reporting corporation and certain related parties. This section also provides definitions of terms used in section 6038A. Section 1.6038A-2 provides guidance concerning the information to be submitted and the filing of the required return. Section 1.6038A-3 provides guidance concerning the maintenance of records. Section 1.6038A-4 provides guidance concerning the application of the monetary penalty for the failure either to furnish information or to maintain records. Section 1.6038A-5 provides guidance concerning the authorization of an agent for purposes of sections 7602, 7603, and 7604. Section 1.6038A-6 provides guidance concerning the failure to furnish information requested by a summons. Finally, § 1.6038A-7 provides guidance concerning the application of the noncompliance penalty for failure by the related party to authorize an agent or by the reporting corporation to substantially comply with a summons.

(b) *In general.*—A reporting corporation must furnish the information described in § 1.6038A-2 by filing an annual information return (Form 5472 or any successor), and must maintain records as described in § 1.6038A-3.

(c) *Reporting corporation.*—(1) *In general.*—For purposes of section 6038A, a reporting corporation is either a domestic corporation that is 25-percent foreign-owned as defined in paragraph (c)(2) of this section, or a foreign corporation that is 25-percent foreign-owned and engaged in trade or business within the United States. After November 4, 1990, a foreign corporation engaged in a trade or business within the United States at any time during a taxable year is a reporting corporation. *See* section 6038C.

(2) *25-percent foreign-owned.*—A corporation is 25-percent foreign-owned if it has at least one direct or indirect 25-percent foreign shareholder at any time during the taxable year.

(3) *25-percent foreign shareholder.*—(i) *In general.*—A foreign person is a 25-percent foreign shareholder of a corporation if the person owns at least 25 percent of—

(A) The total voting power of all classes of stock of the corporation entitled to vote, or

(B) The total value of all classes of stock of the corporation.

(ii) *Total voting power and value.*—In determining whether one foreign person owns 25 percent of the total voting power of all classes of stock of a corporation entitled to vote or 25 percent of the total value of all classes of stock of a corporation, consideration will be given to all the facts and circumstances of each case, under principles similar to § 1.957-1(b)(2) (consideration of arrangements to shift formal voting power away from a foreign person).

(iii) *Direct 25-percent foreign shareholder.*—A foreign person is a direct 25-percent foreign shareholder if it owns directly at least 25 percent of the stock of the reporting corporation, either by vote or by value.

(iv) *Indirect 25-percent foreign shareholder.*—A foreign person is an indirect 25-percent foreign shareholder if it owns indirectly (or under the attribution rules of section 318 is considered to own indirectly) at least 25 percent of the stock of the reporting corporation, either by vote or by value.

(4) *Application to prior open years.*—For taxable years beginning before July 11, 1989, the definition of a reporting corporation under this paragraph applies in determining whether a foreign-owned corporation is a reporting corporation. An examination may be reopened if the statute of limitations period for that taxable year has not expired. A taxable year may not be reopened under section 6038A for examination purposes if the taxable year is open under section 6511 only for purposes of the carryback of net operating losses or net capital losses.

(5) *Exceptions.*—(i) *Treaty country residents having no permanent establishment.*—A foreign corporation that has no permanent establishment in the United States under an applicable income tax convention is not a reporting corporation for purposes of section 6038A and this section. Accordingly, such a foreign corpo-

ration is not subject to §§ 1.6038A-2, 1.6038A-3, and 1.6038A-5. It must timely and fully provide the required notice to the Commissioner under section 6114. See section 6114 and the regulations thereunder for the notice that such a corporation must file and the applicable penalties for failure to file such notice.

(ii) *Qualified exempt shipping income.*—A foreign corporation whose gross income is exempt from U.S. taxation under section 883 is not a reporting corporation provided that it timely and fully complies with the reporting requirements required to claim such exemption. In the event that such a corporation does not timely and fully comply with the reporting requirements under sections 887 and 883, it will be a reporting corporation subject to section 6038A, including the application of the monetary penalty for failure to file required information.

(iii) *Status as foreign related party.*—Nothing in this paragraph affects the determination of whether a person is a foreign related party as defined in paragraph (g) of this section.

(d) *Related party.*—The term "related party" means—

(1) Any direct or indirect 25-percent foreign shareholder of the reporting corporation,

(2) Any person who is related within the meaning of sections 267(b) or 707(b)(1) to the reporting corporation or to a 25-percent foreign shareholder of the reporting corporation, or

(3) Any other person who is related to the reporting corporation within the meaning of section 482 and the regulations thereunder.

However, the term "related party" does not include any corporation filing a consolidated federal income tax return with the reporting corporation.

(e) *Attribution rules.*—(1) *Attribution under section 318.*—For purposes of determining whether a corporation is 25-percent foreign-owned and whether a person is a related party under section 6038A, the constructive ownership rules of section 318 shall apply, and the attribution rules of section 267(c) also shall apply to the extent they attribute ownership to persons to whom section 318 does not attribute ownership. However, "10 percent" shall be substituted for "50 percent" in section 318(a)(2)(C), and section 318(a)(3)(A), (B), and (C) shall not be applied so as to consider a U.S. person as owning stock that is owned by a person who is not a U.S. person. Additionally, section 318(a)(3)(C) and § 1.318-1(b) shall not be applied so as to consider a U.S. corporation as being a reporting corporation if, but for the application of such sections, the U.S. corporation would not be 25-percent foreign owned.

(2) *Attribution of transactions with related parties engaged in by a partnership.*—The transactions in which a domestic or foreign partnership engages shall be attributed to any reporting corporation whose interest in the capital or profits of the partnership, either directly or indirectly, combined with the interests of all related parties of the reporting corporation partner, equals 25 percent or more of the total partnership interests. Attribution of such transactions shall be made only to the extent of the partnership interest held by that reporting corporation partner. See sections 875 and 702(a) and the regulations thereunder. (Attribution shall not be made, however, of transactions directly between the partnership and a reporting corporation.) Accordingly, a reporting corporation partner that is deemed to engage in transactions with related parties under this rule is subject to the information reporting requirements of § 1.6038A-2, to the record maintenance requirements of § 1.6038A-3, to the monetary penalty under § 1.6038A-4, to the requirement of authorization of agent under § 1.6038A-5, to the rules of § 1.6038A-6 relating to the requirement to produce records, and to the noncompliance penalty adjustment under § 1.6038A-7.

(f) *Foreign person.*—For purposes of section 6038A, a foreign person is—

(1) Any individual who is not a citizen or resident of the United States, but not including any individual for whom an election under section 6013(g) or (h) (relating to an election to file a joint return) is in effect;

(2) Any individual who is a citizen of any possession of the United States and who is not otherwise a citizen or resident of the United States;

(3) Any partnership, association, company, or corporation that is not created or organized in the United States or under the law of the United States or any State thereof;

(4) Any foreign trust or foreign estate, as defined in section 7701(a)(31); or

(5) Any foreign government (or agency or instrumentality thereof). To the extent that a foreign government is engaged in the conduct of commercial activity as defined under section 892 and the regulations thereunder, it will be treated as a foreign person under section 6038A and this section only for purposes of the information reporting requirements of § 1.6038A-2. A foreign government will not be treated as a foreign related party for purposes of §§ 1.6038A-3 and 1.6038A-5.

For purposes of section 6038A, a possession of the United States shall be considered to be a foreign country.

(g) *Foreign related party.*—A foreign related party is a foreign person as defined under paragraph (f) of this section that is also a related party as defined under paragraph (d) of this section.

(h) *Small corporation exception.*—A reporting corporation that has less than $10,000,000 in U.S. gross receipts for a taxable year is not subject to §§ 1.6038A-3 and 1.6038A-5 for that taxable year. Such a corporation, however, remains subject to the information reporting requirements of § 1.6038A-2 and the general record maintenance requirements of section 6001. For purposes of this paragraph, U.S. gross receipts includes all amounts received or accrued to the extent that such amounts are taken into account for the determination and computation of the gross income of the corporation. For purposes of this test, the U.S. gross receipts of all related reporting corporations shall be aggregated.

(i) *Safe harbor for reporting corporations with related party transactions of de minimis value.*—(1) *In general.*—A reporting corporation is not subject to §§ 1.6038A-3 and 1.6038A-5 for any taxable year in which the aggregate value of all gross payments it makes to and receives from foreign related parties with respect to related party transactions (including monetary consideration, nonmonetary consideration, and the value of transactions involving less than full consideration), is not more than $5,000,000 and is less than 10 percent of its U.S. gross income. Such a corporation, however, remains subject to the information reporting requirements of § 1.6038A-2 and the general record maintenance requirements of section 6001. For purposes of this paragraph, U.S. gross income means the gross income reportable by the reporting corporation (or the aggregate gross income reportable by all related reporting corporations) for U.S. income tax purposes. Gross payments made to or received from foreign related parties cannot be netted; rather, the gross payments made to and received from foreign related parties are to be aggregated. Thus, for example, if a reporting corporation receives $4,700,000 of gross payments from a related party and makes $500,000 of gross payments to the same related party, it has aggregate gross payments of $5,200,000, and, therefore, does not qualify for the safe harbor under this paragraph.

(2) *Aggregate value of gross payments made or received.*—The aggregate value of gross payments made to (or received from) a foreign related party with respect to foreign related party transactions is determined by totaling the dollar amounts of foreign related party transactions as described in § 1.6038A-2(b)(3) and (4) on all Forms 5472 filed by the reporting corporation or related reporting corporations.

(j) *Related reporting corporations.*—A reporting corporation is related to another reporting corporation if it is related to that other reporting corporation under the principles described in paragraphs (d) and (e) of this section.

(k) *Consolidated return groups.*—(1) *Required information.*—If a reporting corporation is a member of an affiliated group for which a U.S. consolidated income tax return is filed, the return requirement of § 1.6038A-2 may be satisfied by filing a consolidated Form 5472. The common parent, as identified on Form 851, must attach a schedule to the consolidated Form 5472 stating which members of the U.S. affiliated group are reporting corporations under section 6038A, and which of those are joining in the consolidated Form 5472. The schedule must provide the name, address, and taxpayer identification number of each member whose transactions are included on the consolidated Form 5472. A member is not required to join in filing a consolidated Form 5472 merely because other members of the group choose to file one or more Forms 5472 on a consolidated basis.

(2) *Maintenance of records and authorization of agent.*—Either the common parent or the principal operating company of an affiliated group filing a consolidated income tax return may be authorized under § 1.6038A-5 to act as the agent for foreign related persons engaged in transactions with members of the group solely for purposes of section 7602, 7603, and 7604 under section 6038A(e)(1) and § 1.6038A-5. Each member of the group, however, must maintain the records required under section 6038A(a) and § 1.6038A-3 relating to its related party transactions.

(3) *Monetary penalties.*—The common parent (or principal operating company) and all reporting corporations that join in the filing of a consolidated Form 5472 are liable jointly and severally for penalties for failure to file Form 5472 and for failure to maintain records under section 6038A(d) and § 1.6038A-4(e). See § 1.1502-77(a) regarding the scope of agency of the common parent corporation.

(l) *District Director.*—For purposes of the regulations under section 6038A, the term "District Director" means any District Director, or the Assistant Commissioner (International) when performing duties similar to those of a District Director with respect to any person over which the Assistant Commissioner (International) has appropriate jurisdiction.

(m) *Examples.*—The following examples illustrate the rules of this section.

Example 1. P, a U.S. partnership that is engaged in a U.S. trade or business, is 75 percent owned by FC1, a foreign corporation that, in turn, is wholly owned by another foreign corporation, FC2. The remaining 25 percent of P is owned by Corp, a domestic corporation, that is wholly owned by FC3. P engages in transactions solely with FC2 and FC3. These transactions are attributed to FC1 and Corp. Under section 875, FC1 is considered as being engaged in a U.S. trade or business. For purposes of section 6038A and this section, FC1 and Corp are reporting corporations and must report their pro rata shares of the value of the transactions with FC2 and FC3. Thus, Corp must report 25 percent of P's transactions with FC3 and FC1 must report 75 percent of P's transactions with FC2.

Example 2. FC2 and FC3 are both foreign corporations that are wholly owned by FC1, also a foreign corporation. FC2 engages in a trade or business in the United States through a branch. The branch engages in related party transactions with FC1. FC2 is a reporting corporation. FC3 is a foreign related party. FC1 is a direct 25-percent foreign shareholder of both FC2 and FC3. Neither FC1 nor FC3 is a reporting corporation.

Example 3. FC1 owns 25 percent of total voting power in each of FC2 and FC3. FC2 and FC3 each own 20 percent of the total voting power of Corp, a domestic corporation. The remaining stock of Corp is owned by an unrelated domestic corporation. Neither FC2 nor FC3 is engaged in a U.S. trade or business. Under section 318(a)(2)(C) and paragraph (e) of this section, FC1 constructively owns its proportionate share of the stock of Corp owned directly by FC2 and FC3. Thus, FC1 is treated as constructively owning five percent of Corp through each of FC2 and FC3 or a total of 10 percent of the Corp stock. Consequently, Corp is not a reporting corporation because no 25 percent shareholder exists.

Example 4. FP owns 100 percent of FC1 which, in turn, owns 100 percent of FC2. FC2 owns 100 percent of FC3 which owns 100 percent of RC. FP, FC1, and FC2 are indirect 25-percent foreign shareholders of RC, and FC3 is a direct 25-percent foreign shareholder.

Example 5. FP owns 100 percent of USS, a U.S. corporation, and 25 percent of FS, a foreign corporation. The remaining 75 percent of FS is publicly owned by numerous small shareholders. Sales transactions occur between USS and FS. Applying the rules of this section, USS is a reporting corporation. It is determined that USS and FS are each controlled by FP under section 482 and the regulations thereunder. Therefore, FS is related to USS within the meaning of section 482 and is a related party to USS. Accordingly, the sales transactions between USS and FS are subject to section 6038A.

Example 6. The facts are the same as in *Example 5*, except that the remaining 75 percent of FS is owned by one shareholder that is unrelated to the FP group and it is determined that FS is not controlled by FP for purposes of section 482. Under these facts, FS is not a related party of either FP or USS. Accordingly, section 6038A does not apply to the sales transactions between FS and USS.

Example 7. P, a U.S. multinational, is a holding company that wholly owns X, a U.S. operating company, which in turn wholly owns FS, a controlled foreign corporation. Applying the rule of section 318(a)(3)(C), FS is deemed to own the stock of X that is actually held by P. However, under the rules of paragraph (e) of this section, X will not be a reporting corporation by reason of section 318.

(n) *Effective dates.*—(1) *Section 1.6038A-1.*—Paragraphs (c) (relating to the definition of a reporting corporation), (d) (relating to the definition of a related party), (e)(1) (relating to the application of section 318), and (f) (relating to the definition of a foreign person) of this section are effective for taxable years beginning after July 10, 1989. The remaining paragraphs of this section are effective December 10, 1990, without regard to when the taxable year began.

(2) *Section 1.6038A-2.*—Section 1.6038A-2 (relating to the requirement to file Form 5472) generally applies for taxable years beginning after July 10, 1989. However, § 1.6038A-2 as it applies to reporting corporations whose sole trade or business in the United States is a banking, financing, or similar business as defined in § 1.864-4(c)(5)(i) applies for taxable years beginning after December 10, 1990. The final sentence of § 1.6038A-2(d) applies for taxable years ending on or after January 1, 2003. For taxable years ending prior to January 1, 2003, see § 1.6038A-2(d) in effect prior to January 1, 2003 (see 26 CFR part 1 revised as of April 1, 2002).

(3) *Section 1.6038A-3.*—Section 1.6038A-3 (relating to the record maintenance requirement) is generally effective December 10, 1990. However, records described in § 1.6038A-3 in existence on or after March 20, 1990, must be maintained, without regard to when the taxable year to which the records relate began.

(4) *Section 1.6038A-4.*—Section 1.6038A-4 (relating to the monetary penalty) is generally

effective for taxable years beginning after July 10, 1989, for the failure to file Form 5472. For the failure to maintain records or the failure to produce documents under § 1.6038A-4(f)(2), the section is effective December 10, 1990, without regard to when the taxable year to which the records relate began.

(5) *Section 1.6038A-5.*—Section 1.6038A-5 (relating to the authorization of agent requirement) is effective December 10, 1990, without regard to when the taxable year to which the records relate began.

(6) *Section 1.6038A-6.*—Section 1.6038A-6 (relating to the failure to furnish information under a summons) is effective November 6, 1990, without regard to when the taxable year to which the summons relates began.

(7) *Section 1.6038A-7.*—Section 1.6038A-7 (relating to the noncompliance penalty adjustment) is effective December 10, 1990, without regard to when the taxable year began. [Reg. § 1.6038A-1.]

☐ [T.D. 8353, 6-14-91. *Amended by T.D.* 9161, 9-14-2004.]

§ 1.6038A-2. Requirement of return.—(a) *Form 5472 required.*—(1) *In general.*—Each reporting corporation as defined in § 1.6038A-1(c) (or members of an affiliated group filing together as described in § 1.6038A-1(k)) shall make a separate annual information return on Form 5472 with respect to each related party as defined in § 1.6038A-1(d) with which the reporting corporation (or any group member joining in a consolidated Form 5472) has had any reportable transaction during the taxable year. The information required by section 6038A and this section must be furnished even though it may not affect the amount of any tax due under the Code.

(2) *Reportable transaction.*—A reportable transaction is any transaction of the types listed in paragraphs (b)(3) and (4) of this section. However, if neither party to the transaction is a United States person as defined in section 7701(a)(30) and the transaction—

(i) Will not generate in any taxable year gross income from sources within the United States or income effectively connected, or treated as effectively connected, with the conduct of a trade or business within the United States, and

(ii) Will not generate in any taxable year any expense, loss, or other deduction that is allocable or apportionable to such income, the transaction is not a reportable transaction.

(b) *Contents of return.*—(1) *Reporting corporation.*—Form 5472 must provide the following information in the manner the form prescribes with respect to each reporting corporation:

(i) Its name, address (including mailing code), and U.S. taxpayer identification number; each country in which the reporting corporation files an income tax return as a resident under the tax laws of that country; its country or countries of organization, and incorporation; its total assets for U.S. reporting corporation; the places where it conducts its business; and its principal business activity.

(ii) The name, address, and U.S. taxpayer identification number, if applicable, of all its direct and indirect 25-percent foreign shareholders (for an indirect 25-percent foreign shareholder, explain the attribution of ownership); each country in which each 25-percent foreign shareholder files an income tax return as a resident under the tax laws of that country; the places where each 25-percent shareholder conducts its business; and the country or countries of organization, citizenship, and incorporation of each 25-percent foreign shareholder.

(iii) The number of Forms 5472 filed for the taxable year and the aggregate value in U.S. dollars of gross payments as defined in § 1.6038A-1(h)(2) made with respect to all foreign related party transactions reported on all Forms 5472.

(2) *Related party.*—The reporting corporation must provide information on Form 5472, set forth in the manner the form prescribes, about each related party, whether foreign or domestic, with which the reporting corporation had a transaction of the types described in paragraphs (b)(3) and (4) of this section during its taxable year, including the following information:

(i) The name, U.S. taxpayer identification number, if applicable, and address of the related party.

(ii) The nature of the related party's business and the principal place or places where it conducts its business.

(iii) Each country in which the related party files an income tax return as a resident under the tax laws of that country.

(iv) The relationship of the reporting corporation to the related party.

(3) *Foreign related party transactions for which only monetary consideration is paid or received by the reporting corporation.*—If the related party is a foreign person, the reporting corporation must set forth on Form 5472 the dollar amounts of all reportable transactions for which monetary consideration (including U.S. and foreign currency) was the sole consideration paid or received during the taxable year of the reporting corporation. The total amount of such transactions, as well as the separate

amounts for each type of transaction described below, must be reported on Form 5472, in the manner the form prescribes. Where actual amounts are not determinable, a reasonable estimate (as described in paragraph (b)(6) of this section) is permitted. The types of transactions described in this paragraph are:

(i) Sales and purchases of stock in trade (inventory);

(ii) Sales and purchases of tangible property other than stock in trade;

(iii) Rents and royalties paid and received (other than amounts reported under paragraph (b)(3)(iv) of this section);

(iv) Sales, purchases, and amounts paid and received as consideration for the use of all intangible property, including (but not limited to) copyrights, designs, formulas, inventions, models, patents, processes, trademarks, and other similar intangible property rights;

(v) Consideration paid and received for technical, managerial, engineering, construction, scientific, or other services;

(vi) Commissions paid and received;

(vii) Amounts loaned and borrowed (except open accounts resulting from sales and purchases reported under other items listed in this paragraph (b)(3) that arise and are collected in full in the ordinary course of business);

(viii) Interest paid and received;

(ix) Premiums paid and received for insurance and reinsurance; and

(x) Other amounts paid or received not specifically identified in this paragraph (b)(3) to the extent that such amounts are taken into account for the determination and computation of the taxable income of the reporting corporation.

Amounts required to be reported under paragraph (b)(3)(vii) of this section shall be reported as monthly averages or outstanding balances at the beginning and end of the taxable year, as the form shall prescribe.

(4) *Foreign related party transactions involving nonmonetary consideration or less than full consideration.*—If the related party is a foreign person, the reporting corporation must provide on Form 5472 a description of any reportable transaction, or group of reportable transactions, listed in paragraph (b)(3) of this section, for which any part of the consideration paid or received was not monetary consideration, or for which less than full consideration was paid or received. A description required under paragraph (b)(4) of this section shall include sufficient information from which to determine the nature and approximate monetary value of the transaction or group of transactions, and shall include:

(i) A description of all property (including monetary consideration), rights, or obligations transferred from the reporting corporation to the foreign related party and from the foreign related party to the reporting corporation;

(ii) A description of all services performed by the reporting corporation for the foreign related party and by the foreign related party for the reporting corporation; and

(iii) A reasonable estimate of the fair market value of all properties and services exchanged, if possible, or some other reasonable indicator of value.

If, for any transaction, the entire consideration received includes both tangible and intangible property and the consideration paid is solely monetary consideration, the transaction should be reported under paragraph (b)(3) of this section if the intangible property was related and incidental to the transfer of the tangible property (for example, a right to warranty services.)

(5) *Additional information.*—In addition to the information required under paragraphs (b)(3) and (4) of this section, a reporting corporation must provide on Form 5472, in the manner the form prescribes, the following information:

(i) If the reporting corporation imports goods from a foreign related party, whether the costs taken into account in computing the basis or inventory cost of such goods are greater than the costs taken into account in computing the valuation of the goods for customs purposes, adjusted pursuant to section 1059A and the regulations thereunder, and if so, the reasons for the difference.

(ii) If the costs taken into account in computing the basis or inventory cost of such goods are greater than the costs taken into account in computing the valuation of the goods for customs purposes, whether the documents supporting the reporting corporation's treatment of the items set forth in paragraph (b)(5)(i) of this section are in existence and available in the United States at the time Form 5472 is filed.

(6) *Reasonable estimate.*—(i) *Estimate within 25 percent of actual amount.*—Any amount reported under this section is considered to be a reasonable estimate if it is at least 75 percent and not more than 125 percent of the actual amount.

(ii) *Other estimates.*—If any amount reported under this paragraph (b) of this section fails to meet the reasonable estimate test of paragraph (b)(6)(i) of this section, the reporting corporation nevertheless may show that such amount is a reasonable estimate by making an affirmative showing of relevant facts and circumstances in a written statement containing a declaration that it is made under the penalties of perjury. The District Director shall determine whether the amount reported was a reasonable estimate.

(7) *Small amounts.*—If any actual amount required under this section does not exceed $50,000, the amount may be reported as "$50,000 or less."

(8) *Accrued payments and receipts.*—For purposes of this section, in the case of an accrual basis taxpayer, the terms "paid" and "received" shall include accrued payments and receipts, respectively.

(c) *Method of reporting.*—All statements required on or with the Form 5472 under this section and §1.6038A-5 shall be in the English language. All amounts required to be reported under paragraph (b) of this section shall be expressed in United States currency, with a statement of the exchange rates used.

(d) *Time and place for filing returns.*—A Form 5472 required under this section shall be filed with the reporting corporation's income tax return for the taxable year by the due date (including extensions) of that return. A duplicate Form 5472 (including any attachments and schedules) shall be filed at the same time with the Internal Revenue Service Center, Philadelphia, PA 19255. A Form 5472 that is timely filed electronically satisfies the duplicate filing requirement.

(e) *Untimely filed return.*—If the reporting corporation's income tax return is untimely filed, Form 5472 (with a duplicate to Philadelphia) nonetheless shall be timely filed at the service center where the return is due. When the income tax return is ultimately filed, a copy of Form 5472 must be attached.

(f) *Exceptions.*—(1) *No reportable transactions.*—A reporting corporation is not required to file Form 5472 if it has no transactions of the types listed in paragraphs (b)(3) and (4) of this section during the taxable year with any related party.

(2) *Transactions solely with a domestic reporting corporation.*—If all of a foreign reporting corporation's reportable transactions are with one or more related domestic reporting corporations that are not members of the same affiliated group, the foreign reporting corporation shall furnish on Form 5472 only the information required under paragraphs (b)(1) and (2) of this section, if the domestic reporting corporations provide the information required under paragraphs (b)(3) through (5) of this section. Such a foreign reporting corporation nonetheless is subject to the record maintenance requirements of §1.6038A-3 and the requirements of §§1.6038A-5 and 1.6038A-6. The name, address, and taxpayer identification number of each domestic reporting corporation that provided such information must be indicated on Form 5472 in the space provided for the information under paragraphs (b)(1) and (2) of this section.

(3) *Transactions with a corporation subject to reporting under section 6038.*—A reporting corporation is not required to make a return of information on Form 5472 with respect to a related foreign corporation for a taxable year for which a U.S. person that controls the foreign related corporation makes a return of information on Form 5471 that is required under section 6038 and this section, if that return contains information required under §1.6038-2(f)(11) with respect to the reportable transactions between the reporting corporation and the related corporation for that taxable year. Such a reporting corporation also is not subject to §§1.6038A-3 and 1.6038A-5. It remains subject to the general record maintenance requirements of section 6001.

(4) *Transactions with a foreign sales corporation.*—A reporting corporation is not required to make a return of information on Form 5472 with respect to a related corporation that qualifies as a foreign sales corporation for a taxable year for which the foreign sales corporation files Form 1120-FSC.

(g) *Filing Form 5472 when transactions with related parties engaged in by a partnership are attributed to a reporting corporation.*—If transactions engaged in by a partnership are attributed under §1.6038A-1(e)(2) to a reporting corporation, the reporting corporation need report on Form 5472 only the percentage of the value of the transaction or transactions equal to the percentage of its partnership interest. Thus, for example, if a partnership buys $1000 of widgets from the foreign parent of a reporting corporation whose partnership interest in the partnership equals 50 percent of the partnership interests (and the remaining 50 percent is held by unrelated parties), the reporting corporation must report $500 of purchases from a foreign related party on Form 5472.

(h) *Effective dates for certain reporting corporations.*—For effective dates for this section, see §1.6038A-1(n). [Reg. §1.6038A-2.]

□ [*T.D. 8353, 6-14-91. Amended by T.D. 9113, 2-6-2004 and T.D. 9161, 9-14-2004.*]

§1.6038A-3. Record maintenance.—(a) *General maintenance requirements.*—(1) *Section 6001 and section 6038A.*—A report-

Reg. §1.6038A-3(a)(1)

ing corporation must keep the permanent books of account or records as required by section 6001 that are sufficient to establish the correctness of the federal income tax return of the corporation, including information, documents, or records ("records") to the extent they may be relevant to determine the correct U.S. tax treatment of transactions with related parties. Under section 6001, the District Director may require any person to make such returns, render such statements, or keep such specific records as will enable the District Director to determine whether or not that person is liable for any of the taxes to which the regulations under Part I have application. *See* section 6001 and the regulations thereunder. Such records must be permanent, accurate, and complete, and must clearly establish income, deductions, and credits. Additionally, in appropriate cases, such records include sufficient relevant cost data from which a profit and loss statement may be prepared for products or services transferred between a reporting corporation and its foreign related parties. This requirement includes records of the reporting corporation itself, as well as to records of any foreign related party that may be relevant to determine the correct U.S. tax treatment of transactions between the reporting corporation and foreign related parties. The relevance of such records with respect to related party transactions shall be determined upon the basis of all the facts and circumstances. Section 6038A and this section provide detailed guidance regarding the required maintenance of records with respect to such transactions and specify penalties for noncompliance. Banks and other financial institutions shall follow the specific record maintenance rules described in paragraph (h) of this section.

(2) *Safe harbor.*—A safe harbor for record maintenance is provided under paragraph (c) of this section, which sets forth detailed guidance concerning the types of records to be maintained with respect to related party transactions. The safe harbor consists of an all-inclusive list of record types that could be relevant to different taxpayers under a variety of facts and circumstances. It does not constitute a checklist of records that every reporting corporation must maintain or that generally should be requested by the Service. A specific reporting corporation is required to maintain, and the Service will request, only those records enumerated in the safe harbor (including material profit and loss statements) that may be relevant to its business or industry and to the correct U.S. tax treatment of its transactions with its foreign related parties. Accordingly, not every item listed in the safe harbor must be maintained by every reporting corporation. A corporation that maintains or causes another person to maintain the records listed in paragraph (c)(2) of this section that may be relevant to its foreign related party transactions and to its business or industry will be deemed to have met the record maintenance requirements of section 6038A.

(3) *Examples.*—The following examples illustrate the rules of this paragraph.

Example 1. RC, a U.S. reporting corporation, is owned by two shareholders, F and P. F is a foreign corporation that owns 30 percent of the stock of RC. P is a domestic corporation that owns the remaining 70 percent. RC purchases tangible property from F; however, the only potential audit issue with respect to these transactions is their treatment under section 482. It is determined that F does not in fact control RC and the two corporations do not constitute a group of "controlled taxpayers" for purposes of section 482 and the regulations thereunder. There are no other reportable transactions between RC and F. Under § 1.6038A-1(g), F is a foreign related party with respect to RC. Accordingly, RC is required to report its purchases of property from F under the reporting requirements of § 1.6038A-2. Nevertheless, because section 482 is not applicable to the transactions between RC and F, the records created by F with respect to its sales to RC are not relevant for purposes of determining the correct tax treatment of these transactions. RC is required to maintain its own records of these transactions under the requirements of section 6001, but the transactions are not subject to the record maintenance requirements of this section. If, however, on audit it is determined that F does control RC, all records relevant to determining the arm's length consideration for the tangible property under section 482 will be subject to these requirements.

Example 2. FP, a foreign person, owns 30 percent of the stock of RC, a reporting corporation. The remaining 70 percent of RC stock is held by persons that are not 25-percent foreign shareholders. It is determined that FP is related to RC within the meaning of section 482 and the regulations thereunder. The only transactions between FP and RC are FP's capital contributions, dividends paid from RC to FP, and loans from FP to RC. Under section 6001, RC is required to maintain all documentation necessary to establish the U.S. tax treatment of the capital contributions, dividends, and loans. RC is not required to maintain records in other categories listed in paragraph (c)(3) of this section because they are not relevant to the transactions between FP and RC. Records of FP not related to these transactions are not subject to the record maintenance requirements under section 6038A(a) and this section.

Example 3. G, a foreign multinational group, creates Sub, a wholly-owned U.S. subsidiary, in order to purchase tangible property from unrelated parties in the United States and resell such property to G. The property purchased by Sub is either used in G's business or resold to other unrelated parties by G. Sub's sole function is to act as a buyer for G and these purchases are the only transactions that G has with any U.S. affiliates. Under all the facts and circumstances of this case, it is determined that an analysis of the group's worldwide profit attributable to the property it purchases from Sub is not relevant for purposes of determining the tax treatment of the sales from Sub to G. Therefore, the records with respect to the profitability of G are not subject to the record maintenance requirements of this section. However, all records related to the appropriate method under section 482 for determining an arm's-length consideration for the property sold by Sub to G are subject to the record maintenance requirements of this section.

Example 4. S, a U.S. reporting corporation, is the purchasing agent for its multinational parent group. It arranges for the purchase and export of miscellaneous tangible property to X, Y, and Z, each of which is a foreign related party. The miscellaneous tangible property is purchased from unrelated third parties for resale to X, Y, and Z. These resales of miscellaneous tangible property constitute the sole transactions between S and X, Y, and Z. The purchasing agent activity of S is not an integral part of the business activity of S or of any beneficiary of the purchasing agent services provided by S as defined in § 1.482-2(b)(7). Under § 1.482-2(b)(7), the arm's-length charge is deemed to be equal to the costs or deductions incurred with respect to the provision of the purchasing agent services. S is required to maintain records to permit verification upon audit of such costs or deductions. The records of X, Y, and Z are not relevant to the costs or deductions incurred by S with respect to its purchasing agent activities. Therefore, under section 6038A and this section, only the records maintained by S that permit verification of the costs and deductions of the purchasing agent services are relevant. Accordingly, solely with respect to these transactions, records of X, Y, and Z need not be maintained under section 6038A or this section. If, however, upon audit, it is determined that S is not merely engaging in services not integral to its business as defined in § 1.482-2(b)(7), the record maintenance requirements under section 6038A(a) and this section will be applicable to the records of S, X, Y and Z to the extent that such records are relevant for determining the correct tax treatment of transactions engaged in by X, Y, or Z with S. If S has other transactions with X, S must maintain or cause to be maintained records that may be relevant with respect to those transactions.

(b) *Other maintenance requirements.*—(1) *Indirectly related records.*—This section applies to records that are directly or indirectly related to transactions between the reporting corporation and any foreign related parties. An example of records that are indirectly related to such transactions is records possessed by a foreign subsidiary of a foreign related party that document the raw material or component costs of a product that is manufactured or assembled by the subsidiary and sold as a finished product by the foreign related party to the reporting corporation.

(2) *Foreign related party or third-party maintenance.*—If records that are required to be maintained under this section are in the control of a foreign related party, the records may be obtained or compiled (if not already in the possession of the foreign related party or already compiled) under the direction of the reporting corporation and then maintained by the reporting corporation, the foreign related party, or a third party. Thus, for example, a foreign related party may either itself maintain such records outside the United States or permit a third party to maintain such records outside the United States, provided that the conditions described in paragraph (f) of this section are met. Upon a request for such records by the Service, a foreign related party or third party may make arrangements with the District Director to furnish the records directly, rather than through the reporting corporation.

(3) *Translation of records.*—When records are provided to the Service under a request for production, any portion of such records must be translated into the English language within 30 days of a request for translation of that portion by the District Director. To the extent that any requested documents are identical to documents that have already been translated, an explanation of how such documents are identical instead may be provided. An extension of this time period may be requested under paragraph (f)(4) of this section. Appropriate extensions will be liberally granted for translation requests where circumstances warrant. If a good faith effort is made to translate accurately the requested documents within the specified time period, the reporting corporation will not be subject to the penalties in §§ 1.6038A-4 and 1.6038A-7.

Reg. § 1.6038A-3(b)(3)

(4) *Exception for foreign governments.*—A foreign government is not subject to the obligation to maintain records under this section.

(5) *Records relating to conduit financing arrangements.*—See §1.881-4 relating to conduit financing arrangements.

(c) *Specific records to be maintained for safe harbor.*—(1) *In general.*—A reporting corporation that maintains or causes another person to maintain the records specified in this paragraph (c) that are relevant to its business or industry and to the correct U.S. tax treatment of its transactions with its foreign related parties will be deemed to have met the record maintenance requirements of this section. This paragraph provides general descriptions of the categories of records to be maintained; the particular title or label applied by a reporting corporation or related party does not control. Functional equivalents of the specified documents are acceptable. Record maintenance in accordance with this safe harbor, however, requires only the maintenance of types of documents described in paragraph (c)(2) of this section that are directly or indirectly related to transactions between the reporting corporation and any foreign related party. Additionally, to the extent the reporting corporation establishes that records in a particular category are not applicable to the industry or business of the reporting corporation and any foreign related party, maintenance of such records is not required under this paragraph. Record maintenance in accordance with this paragraph (c) generally does not require the original creation of records that are ordinarily not created by the reporting corporation or its related parties. (If, however, a document that is actually created is described in this paragraph (c), it is to be maintained even if the document is not of the type ordinarily created by the reporting corporation or its related parties.) There are two exceptions to the rule. First, basic accounting records that are sufficient to document the U.S. tax effects of transactions between related parties must be created and retained, if they do not otherwise exist. Second, records sufficient to produce material profit and loss statements as described in paragraphs (c)(2)(ii) and (3) of this section that are relevant for determining the U.S. tax treatment of transactions between the reporting corporation and foreign related parties must be created if such records are not ordinarily maintained. All internal records storage and retrieval systems used for each taxable year must be retained.

(2) *Descriptions of categories of documents to be maintained.*—The following records must be maintained in order to satisfy this paragraph (c) to the extent they may be relevant to determine the correct U.S. tax treatment of transactions between the reporting corporation and any foreign related party.

(i) *Original entry books and transaction records.*—This category includes books and records of original entry or their functional equivalents, however designated or labelled, that are relevant to transactions between any foreign related party and the reporting corporation. Examples include, but are not limited to, general ledgers, sales journals, purchase order books, cash receipts books, cash disbursement books, canceled checks and bank statements, workpapers, sales contracts, and purchase invoices. Descriptive material to explicate entries in the foregoing types of records, such as a chart of accounts or an accounting policy manual, is included in this category.

(ii) *Profit and loss statements.*—This category includes records from which the reporting corporation can compile and supply, within a reasonable time, material profit and loss statements of the reporting corporation and all related parties as defined in §1.6038A-1(d) the "related party group") that reflect profit or loss of the related party group attributable to U.S.-connected products or services as defined in paragraph (c)(7)(i) of this section. The determination of whether a profit and loss statement is material is made under the rules provided in paragraph (c)(3) of this section. The material profit and loss statements described in this paragraph (c)(2)(ii) must reflect the consolidated revenue and expenses of all members of the related party group. Thus, records in this category include the documentation of the cost of raw materials used by a related party to manufacture finished goods that are then sold by another related party to the reporting corporation. The records should be kept under U.S. generally accepted accounting principles if they are ordinarily maintained in such manner; if not, an explanation of the material differences between the accounting principles used and U.S. generally accepted accounting principles must be made available. The statements need not reflect tracing of the actual costs borne by the group with respect to its U.S.-connected products or services; rather, any reasonable method may be used to allocate the group's worldwide costs to the revenues generated by the sales of those products or services. An explanation of the methods used to allocate specific items to a particular profit and loss statement must be made available. The explanation of material differences between accounting principles and the explanation of allocation methods must be sufficient to permit a comparison of the profitability of the group to that of the reporting corporation attributable to the provision of U.S.-connected products or services.

(iii) *Pricing documents.*—This category includes all documents relevant to establishing the appropriate price or rate for transactions between the reporting corporation and any foreign related party. Examples include, but are not limited to, documents related to transactions involving the same or similar products or services entered into by the reporting corporation or a foreign related party with related and unrelated parties; shipping and export documents; commission agreements; documents relating to production or assembly facilities; third-party and intercompany purchase invoices; manuals, specifications, and similar documents relating to or describing the performance of functions conducted at particular locations; intercompany correspondence discussing any instructions or assistance relating to such transactions provided to the reporting corporations by the related foreign person (or vice versa); intercompany and intracompany correspondence concerning the price or the negotiation of the price used in such transactions; documents related to the value and ownership of intangibles used or developed by the reporting corporation or the foreign related party; documents related to cost of goods sold and other expenses; and documents related to direct and indirect selling, and general and administrative expenses (for example, relating to advertising, sales promotions, or warranties).

(iv) *Foreign country and third party filings.*—This category includes financial and other documents relevant to transactions between a reporting corporation and any foreign related party filed with or prepared for any foreign government entity, any independent commission, or any financial institution.

(v) *Ownership and capital structure records.*—This category includes records or charts showing the relationship between the reporting corporation and the foreign related party; the location, ownership, and status (for example, joint venture, partnership, branch, or division) of all entities and offices directly or indirectly involved in the transactions between the reporting corporation and any foreign related party; a worldwide organization chart; records showing the management structure of all foreign affiliates; and loan documents, agreements, and other documents relating to any transfer of the stock of the reporting corporation that results in the change of the status of a foreign person as a foreign related party.

(vi) *Records of loans, services, and other non-sales transactions.*—This category includes relevant documents relating to loans (including all deposits by one foreign related party or reporting corporation with an unrelated party and a subsequent loan by that unrelated party to a foreign related party or reporting corporation that is in substance a direct loan between a reporting corporation and a foreign related party); guarantees of a foreign related party of debts of the reporting corporation, and vice versa; hedging arrangements or other risk shifting or currency risk shifting arrangements involving the reporting corporation and any foreign related party; security agreements between the reporting corporation and any foreign related party; research and development expense allocations between any foreign related party and the reporting corporation; service transactions between any foreign related party and the reporting corporation, including, for example, a description of the allocation of charges for management services, time or travel records, or allocation studies; import and export transactions between a reporting corporation and any foreign related party; the registration of patents and copyrights with respect to transactions between the reporting corporation and any foreign related party; and documents regarding lawsuits in foreign countries that relate to such transactions between a reporting corporation and any foreign related party (for example, product liability suits for U.S. products).

(vii) *Records relating to conduit financing arrangements.*—See § 1.881-4 relating to conduit financing arrangements.

(3) *Material profit and loss statements.*—For purposes of paragraph (c)(2)(ii) of this section, the determination of whether a profit and loss statement is material will be made according to the following rules. An agreement between the reporting corporation and the District Director as described in paragraph (e) of this section may identify material profit and loss statements of the related party group and describe the items to be included in any profit and loss statements for which records are to be maintained to satisfy the requirements of paragraph (c)(2)(ii) of this section. In the absence of such an agreement, a profit and loss statement will be material if it meets any of the following tests: the existing records test described in paragraph (c)(4) of this section, the significant industry segment test described in paragraph (c)(5) of this section, or the high profit test described in paragraph (c)(6) of this section.

(4) *Existing records test.*—A profit and loss statement is material under the existing records test described in this paragraph (c)(4) if any member of the related party group cre-

ates or compiles such statement in the course of its business operations and the statement reflects the profit or loss of the related party group attributable to the provision of U.S.-connected products or services (regardless of whether the profit and loss attributable to U.S.-connected products or services is shown separately or included within the calculation of aggregate figures on the statement). For example, a profit and loss statement is described in this paragraph if it was produced for internal accounting or management purposes, or for disclosure to shareholders, financial institutions, government agencies, or any other persons. Such existing statements and the records from which they were compiled (to the extent such records relate to profit and loss attributable to U.S.-connected products or services) are subject to the record maintenance requirements described in paragraph (c)(2)(ii) of this section.

(5) *Significant industry segment test.*—
(i) *In general.*—A profit and loss statement is material under the significant industry segment test described in this paragraph (c)(5) if—

(A) The statement reflects the profit or loss of the related party group attributable to the group's provision of U.S.-connected products or services within a single industry segment (as defined in paragraph (c)(7)(ii) of this section);

(B) The worldwide gross revenue attributable to such industry segment is 10 percent or more of the worldwide gross revenue attributable to the group's combined industry segments; and

(C) The amount of gross revenue earned by the group from the provision of U.S.-connected products or services within such industry segment is $25 million or more in the taxable year.

(ii) *Form of the statements.*—Profit and loss statements compiled for the group's provision of U.S.-connected products or services in each significant industry segment must reflect revenues and expenses attributable to the operations in such segment by all members of the related party group. Statements may show each related party's revenues and expenses separately, or may be prepared in a consolidated format. Any reasonable method may be used to allocate the group's worldwide costs within the industry segment to the U.S.-connected products or services within that segment. An explanation of the methods used to prepare consolidated statements and to allocate specific items to a particular profit and loss statement must be made available, and the records from which the consolidations and allocations were prepared must be maintained.

(iii) *Special rule for component sales.*—Where the U.S.-connected products or services consist of components that are incorporated into other products or services before sale to customers, the portion of the total gross revenue derived from sales of the finished products or services attributable to the components may be determined on the basis of relative costs of production. Thus, where relevant for determining whether the $25 million threshold in paragraph (c)(5)(i)(C) of this section has been met, the amount of gross revenue derived by the related party group from the provision of the finished products or services may be reduced by multiplying it by a fraction, the numerator of which is the costs of production of the related party group attributable to the component products or services that constitute U.S.-connected products or services and the denominator of which is the costs of production of the related party group attributable to the finished products in which such components are incorporated.

(iv) *Level of specificity required.*—In applying the significant industry segment test of this paragraph (c)(5), groups of related products and services must be chosen to provide a reasonable level of specificity that results in the greatest number of separate significant industry segments in comparison to other possible classifications. This determination must be made on the basis of the particular facts presented by the operations of the related party group. The following rules, however, provide general guidelines for making such classifications. First, the related party group's operations that involve the provision of U.S.-connected products should be grouped into product lines. The rules of this paragraph (c)(5) should then be applied to determine if any such product line would, standing alone, constitute a significant industry segment when compared to the related party group's operations as a whole. Any significant industry segments determined at the level of product lines should be further segregated, and tested for significant industry segments, at the level of separate products. Finally, any significant industry segments determined at the level of separate products should be segregated, and tested for significant industry segments, at the level of separate models. Similar principles should be applied in classifying and testing types of services. A profit and loss statement reflecting the related party group's provision of any product or service (or group of products or services as classified under these rules) that constitutes a significant industry segment will be considered material for purposes of this paragraph (c)(5). For definitions of the terms "product", "related products or services", "model", and "product line", see paragraph (c)(7) of this section.

(v) *Examples.*—The rules for determining reasonable levels of specificity for significant industry segments may be illustrated by the following examples.

Example 1. A related party group is engaged in the manufacture and worldwide sales of automobiles and aftermarket parts. The group's operations within the categories of "automobiles" and "aftermarket parts" are each sufficient to constitute significant industry segments for the group under the rules of this paragraph (c)(5). No narrower classification of aftermarket parts results in any significant industry segments. Automobiles produced by the group are generally classified for marketing purposes by trade names; aggregating groups of automobiles by these trade names results in three significant industry segments, those for trade names A, B, and C. Finally, two car models sold under the trade name A ("A1" and "A2") and one car model sold under the trade name B ("B3"), produce sufficient revenue to constitute significant industry segments. Such classifications into trade names and car models are generally used in the related party group's industry; moreover, different types of classifications would produce fewer significant industry segments. Accordingly, a reasonable level of specificity for this related party group's industry segments would be eight categories of products consisting of "automobiles", "aftermarket parts", "A", "B", "C", "A1", "A2", and "B3".

Example 2. A related party group is engaged in manufacturing electronic goods that are distributed at retail in the United States by the reporting corporation. The group sells three types of products in the United States: televisions, radios, and video cassette recorders (VCRs). Each of these three broad product areas constitutes a significant industry segment for the group as a whole. VCRs can be further segregated by price into high-end and low-end models, and the provision of each constitutes a significant industry segment for the group. Revenues from only one VCR model, model number VCRX-10, are sufficiently large to make the provision of that model a significant industry segment. With respect to televisions, the group normally accounts for these products by size. Using this classification, portable televisions, medium-sized televisions, and consoles each constitute significant industry segments. Narrower classifications by television model numbers result in no additional significant industry segments. Finally, a single radio product line, those sold under the trade name R, produces sufficient revenue to constitute a significant industry segment, but no other radio models or product groups are large enough to constitute a significant industry segment. In each case, these classifications conform to normal business practices in the industry and result in the greatest possible number of significant industry segments for this related party group. Accordingly, a reasonable level of specificity for this related party group's industry segments would include the ten categories consisting of "VCRs", "high-end VCRs", "low-end VCRs", "model number VCRX-10", "televisions", "portable televisions", "medium-sized televisions", "console televisions", "radios", and "radio trade name R".

(6) *High profit test.*—(i) *In general.*—A profit and loss statement is material under the high profit test described in this paragraph (c)(6) if—

(A) The statement reflects the profit or loss of the related party group attributable to the group's provision of U.S.-connected products or services within a single industry segment (as defined in paragraph (c)(7)(ii) of this section);

(B) The amount of gross revenue earned by the group from the provision of U.S.-connected products or services within such industry segment is $100 million or more in the taxable year; and

(C) The return on assets test described in paragraph (c)(6)(ii) of this section is satisfied with respect to the products and services attributable to such segment.

Accordingly, a significant industry segment (as determined under paragraph (c)(5) of this section) must be divided into any narrower industry segments that meet the high profit test of this paragraph (c)(6), even if such narrower segments would not, standing alone, meet the significant industry segment test of paragraph (c)(5) of this section.

(ii) *Return on assets test.*—An industry segment meets the return on assets test if the rate of return on assets earned by the related party group on its worldwide operations within this industry segment exceeds 15 percent, and is at least 200 percent of the return on assets earned by the group in all industry segments combined. For purposes of this paragraph, the rate of return on assets earned by an industry segment is determined by dividing that segment's operating profit (as defined in paragraph (c)(7)(v) of this section) by its identifiable assets (as defined in paragraph (c)(7)(iv) of this section).

(iii) *Additional rules.*—The rules in paragraphs (c)(5)(ii) through (iv) of this section describing the application of the significant industry segment test shall apply in a similar manner for purposes of the high profit test.

(7) *Definitions.*—The following definitions apply for purposes of paragraphs (c)(2)(ii), (c)(5), and (c)(6) of this section.

(i) *U.S.-connected products or services.*—The term "U.S.-connected products or services" means products or services that are imported to or exported from the United States by transfers between the reporting corporation and any of its foreign related parties.

(ii) *Industry segment.*—An industry segment is a segment of the related party group's combined operations that is engaged in providing a product or service or a group of related products or services (as defined in paragraph (c)(7)(vii) of this section) primarily to customers that are not members of the related party group.

(iii) *Gross revenue of an industry segment.*—Gross revenue of an industry segment includes receipts (prior to reduction for cost of goods sold) both from sales to customers outside of the related party group and from sales or transfers to other industry segments within the related party group (but does not include sales or transfers between members of the related party group within the same industry segment). Interest from sources outside the related party group and interest earned on trade receivables between industry segments is included in gross revenue if the asset on which the interest is earned is included among the industry segment's identifiable assets, but interest earned on advances or loans to other industry segments is not included.

(iv) *Identifiable assets of an industry segment.*—The identifiable assets of an industry segment are those tangible and intangible assets of the related party group that are used by the industry segment, including assets that are used exclusively by that industry segment and an allocated portion of assets used jointly by two or more industry segments. The value of an identifiable asset may be determined using any reasonable method (such as book value or fair market value) applied consistently. Any allocation of assets among industry segments must be made on a reasonable basis, and a description of such basis must be provided. Assets of an industry segment that transfers products or services to another industry segment shall not be allocated to the receiving segment. Assets that represent part of the related party group's investment in an industry segment, such as goodwill, shall be included in the industry segment's identifiable assets. Assets maintained for general corporate purposes (that is, those not used in the operations of any industry segment) shall not be allocated to industry segments.

(v) *Operating profit of an industry segment.*—The operating profit of an industry segment is its gross revenue (as defined in paragraph (c)(7)(iii) of this section) minus all operating expenses. None of the following shall be added or deducted in computing the operating profit of an industry segment: revenue earned at the corporate level and not derived from the operations of any industry segment; general corporate expenses; interest expense; domestic and foreign income taxes; and other extraordinary items not reflecting the ongoing business operations of the industry segment.

(vi) *Product.*—The term "product" means an item of property (or combination of component parts) that is the result of a production process, is primarily sold to unrelated parties (or incorporated by the related party group into other products sold to unrelated parties), and performs a specific function.

(vii) *Related products or services.*—The term "related products or services" means groupings of products and types of services that reflect reasonable accounting, marketing, or other business practices within the industries in which the related party group operates.

(viii) *Model.*—The term "model" means a classification of products that incorporate particular components, options, styles, and any other unique features resulting in product differentiation. Examples of models are electronic products that are sold or accounted for under a single model number and automobiles sold under a single model name.

(ix) *Product line.*—The term "product line" means a group of products that are aggregated into a single classification for accounting, marketing, or other business purposes. Examples of product lines are groups of products that perform similar functions; products that are marketed under the same trade names, brand names, or trademarks; and products that are related economically (that is, having similar rates of profitability, similar degrees of risk, and similar opportunities for growth).

(8) *Example.*—The application of the rules for determining material profit and loss statements under paragraphs (c)(4) through (7) of this section is illustrated by the following example.

Example. (i) *Facts.* A multinational enterprise manufactures 50 different agricultural and chemical products that are sold through Sub1, its wholly owned U.S. subsidiary, and other subsidiaries located in foreign countries. The parent company of the enterprise, P, is a foreign corporation. The corporations participating in the enterprise form a related party group, and Sub1 is a reporting corporation for purposes of section 6038A. Under the facts and circumstances of this case, an analysis of the group's worldwide profit attributable to its products sold in the U.S. is relevant for determining an arm's length consideration under section 482 for the transfers of goods between Sub1 and its foreign affiliates.

(ii) *Existing records test.* For management purposes, the group prepares profit and loss statements that are segmented by sales in different geographic markets. One of these statements shows the combined worldwide profitability of the group. Another statement shows the profitability of the group attributable to its North American sales. Both of these profit and loss statements reflect aggregate figures that include sales to unrelated parties of products that have been transferred from P and other group members to Sub1 (that is, the group's "U.S.-connected products"). The two statements meet the existing records test described in paragraph (c)(4) of this section.

(iii) *Significant industry segments.* The group's worldwide gross revenue in all industry segments is $2 billion. An analysis of the group's 50 products demonstrates that they are reasonably grouped into eight industry segments (each of which earns roughly $250 million in worldwide gross revenue). Segments 1 through 6 relate to agricultural products and Segments 7 and 8 relate to other chemical products. More specific categories would result in groupings that generate less than 10 percent of the group's worldwide gross revenue (that is, less than $200 million each); these narrower categories would thus fail the gross revenue percentage test of paragraph (c)(5)(i)(B) of this section. The gross revenue in each of the eight segments from the sale to unrelated parties of U.S.-connected products is as follows: $180 million for Segment 1; $30 million for Segment 2; and less than $25 million for each of Segments 3 through 8. Under the $25 million threshold test of paragraph (c)(5)(i)(C) of this section, the group's significant industry segments are thus limited to Segments 1 and 2. In addition, the combined operations of the group related to agricultural products (encompassing Segments 1 through 6 on an aggregated basis), constitute a single significant industry segment.

(iv) *High profit test.* One highly profitable product line within Segment 1, HPPL, accounts for $120 million gross revenue from Sub1's domestic sales of U.S.-connected products (and thus exceeds the $100 million gross revenue threshold in paragraph (c)(6)(i)(B) of this section). The return on the identifiable assets attributable to the HPPL product line is 85 percent, which is more than 15 percent and more than twice the return on assets earned by the group from its worldwide operations in its combined industry segments. The group's industry segment for HPPL thus meets the high profit test described in paragraph (c)(6) of this section.

(v) *Material Profit and Loss Statements.* The group's material profit and loss statements consist of statements for combined worldwide sales and North American sales (under the existing records test); Segment 1, Segment 2, and aggregated Segments 1-6 (under the significant industry segment test); and HPPL (under the high profit test). Under paragraph (c) of this section, Sub1 is required to retain the combined worldwide sales and North American sales profit and loss statements and to maintain sufficient records so that it can compile and supply upon request statements of the group's profitability from sales of its U.S.-connected products within Segment 1, Segment 2, aggregated Segments 1-6, and HPPL. These records need not be in the possession of Sub1 and may be kept under the control of and produced by P or any third party. The statements for Segment 1, Segment 2, aggregated Segments 1-6, and HPPL do not require tracing of actual costs to the U.S.-connected products; rather, these statements may be prepared by using any reasonable method to allocate a portion of the industry segment's overall operating costs to the sales of U.S.-connected products within that segment.

(d) *Liability for certain partnership record maintenance.*—A reporting corporation to which transactions engaged in by a partnership are attributed under §1.6038A-1(e)(2) is subject to the record maintenance requirements of this section to the extent of the transactions so attributed.

(e) *Agreements with the District Director.*— (1) *In general.*—The District Director who has audit jurisdiction over the reporting corporation may negotiate and enter into an agreement with a reporting corporation that establishes the records the reporting corporation must maintain or cause another to maintain, how the records must be maintained, the period of retention for the records, and by whom the records must be maintained in order to satisfy the reporting corporation's obligations under this section.

(2) *Content of agreement.*—(i) *In general.*—The agreement may include provisions relating to the authorization of agent requirement, the record maintenance requirement, and the production and translation time periods that vary the rules contained in these regulations under section 6038A. The District Director will generally require a reporting corporation to maintain only those records specified under the safe harbor provisions of

paragraph (c) of this section that permit an adequate audit of the income tax return of the reporting corporation and to provide such authorizations of agent that permit adequate access to such records. In most instances, required record maintenance for a particular reporting corporation under a negotiated agreement will be less than the broad range of records described under the safe harbor provisions. Additionally, a provision specifying the effective date and the expiration date of the agreement that may vary the effective date of the regulations may be included.

(ii) *Significant industry segment test.*—A District Director may determine which industry segment profit and loss statements are material for purposes of requiring the maintenance of records (under either paragraph (a)(1) of this section or the safe harbor described in paragraph (a)(2) of this section). The industry segments that the District Director determines are material need not be the industry segments that meet the significant industry segment test under paragraph (c)(5) of this section or the high profit test under paragraph (c)(6) of this section. For this purpose, a reporting corporation will be required to maintain only those records from which profit and loss statements for the related party group may be constructed with respect to industry segments identified by the District Director. To the extent that existing profit and loss statements are similar in scope and level of detail to statements for industry segments that would otherwise be described under the tests of paragraphs (c)(5) and (6) of this section, the District Director shall accept the existing statements instead of the statements that would otherwise be required under paragraphs (c)(5) and (6) of this section.

(iii) *Example.*—The following example illustrates the rules of paragraph (e)(2)(ii) of this section.

Example. The District Director determines that RC, a reporting corporation that is a manufacturer of related chemical products, has two industry segments, Segment 1 and Segment 2. While both industry segments meet the significant industry segment test of paragraph (c)(5) of this section, Segment 1 has a relatively low volume of sales to foreign related parties. Additionally, Segment 1 consists of products that produce only a small profit margin because the product is generic and other companies also sell the product. The District Director enters into an agreement with RC that requires only records from which a profit and loss statement for the related party group can be constructed for Segment 2. Therefore, RC is not required to maintain records for Segment 1 from which a profit and loss statement for the related party group can be constructed. The other record maintenance requirements under this section apply, however.

(3) *Circumstances of agreement.*—The District Director generally will enter into an agreement under this paragraph (e) upon request by the reporting corporation when the District Director believes that the District has or can obtain sufficient knowledge of the business or industry of the reporting corporation to limit the record maintenance requirement to particular documents.

(4) *Agreement as part of APA process.*—An agreement with a reporting corporation under this paragraph (e) may be entered into as a part of the Advance Pricing Agreement (APA) process at any time during the APA process, insofar as the agreement relates to the subject matter of the APA.

(f) *U.S. maintenance.*—(1) *General rule.*—Records that must be maintained under this section must be maintained within the United States, unless the conditions described in paragraph (f)(2) of this section are met.

(2) *Non-U.S. maintenance requirements.*—A reporting corporation may maintain outside the United States records not ordinarily maintained in the United States but required to be maintained in the United States under this section. However, the reporting corporation must either:

(i) Deliver to the Service the original documents (or duplicates) requested within 60 days of the request by the Service for such records and provide translations of such documents within 30 days of a request for translations of specific documents; or

(ii) Move the original documents (or duplicates) requested to the United States within 60 days of the request of the Service for such records; provide the Service with an index to the requested records, the name and address of a custodian located within the United States having control over the records, and the address where the records are located within 60 days of the Service's request for the records; and continue to maintain the records within the United States throughout the period of retention described in paragraph (g) of this section. For summons procedures with respect to records that have been moved to the United States, see sections 6038A(e), 7602, 7603, and 7604.

With respect to any material profit and loss statements required to be created (either under paragraph (c) of this section or under an agreement with the District Director), unless otherwise specified, "120 days" shall be substituted for "60 days" in this paragraph (f)(2), and labels and text with respect to such statements must be in the English language.

(3) *Prior taxable years.*—The non-U.S. maintenance requirements described in paragraph (f)(2) of this section apply to records located outside the United States that were in existence on or after March 20, 1990, without regard to the taxable year to which such records relate.

(4) *Scheduled production for high volume or other reasons.*—Upon a written request, for good cause shown, the District Director may grant an extension of the time for the production or translation of the requested documents. Such requests should be made within 30 days of the request for records by the Service. If an extension is needed because of the volume of records requested or the amount of translation requested, the District Director may allow production or translation to be scheduled over a period of time so that not all records need be produced or translated at the same time.

(5) *Required U.S. maintenance.*—The District Director (with the concurrence of the Assistant Commissioner (International)), may require, for cause, the maintenance within the United States of any records specified in paragraph (f)(1) of this section. Such a requirement will be imposed only if there exists a clear pattern of failure to maintain or timely produce the required records. The assessment of a monetary penalty under section 6038A(d) and § 1.6038A-4 for failure to maintain records is not necessarily sufficient to require the maintenance of records within the United States.

(g) *Period of retention.*—Records required to be maintained by section 6038A(a) and this section shall be kept as long as they may be relevant or material to determining the correct tax treatment of any transaction between the reporting corporation and a related party, but in no case less than the applicable statute of limitations on assessment and collection with respect to the taxable year in which the transaction or item to which the records relate affects the U.S. tax liability of the reporting corporation. *See* section 6001 and the regulations thereunder.

(h) *Application of record maintenance rules to banks and other financial institutions.*—[Reserved].

(i) *Effective dates.*—For effective dates for this section, see § 1.6038A-1(n). [Reg. § 1.6038A-3.]

☐ [*T.D.* 8353, 6-14-91. *Amended by T.D.* 8611, 8-10-95.]

Proposed Amendments to Regulation

§ 1.6038A-3. Record maintenance.

(a) * * *

(3) * * *

Example 4. S, a U.S. reporting corporation, provides computer consulting services for its foreign parent, X. Based on the application of section 482 and the regulations thereunder, it is determined that the cost of services plus method, as described in § 1.482-9(d), will provide the most reliable measure of an arm's length result, based on the facts and circumstances of the controlled transaction between S and X. S is required to maintain records to permit verification upon audit of the comparable transactional costs (as described in § 1.482-9(d)(2)(iii)) used to calculate the arm's length price. Based on the facts and circumstances, if it is determined that X's records are relevant to determine the correct U.S. tax treatment of the controlled transaction between S and X, the record maintenance requirements under section 6038A(a) and this section will be applicable to the records of X.

* * *

[Prop. Reg. § 1.6038A-3.]

[Proposed 9-10-2003.]

§ 1.6038A-4. Monetary penalty.—(a) *Imposition of monetary penalty.*—(1) *In general.*—If a reporting corporation fails to furnish the information described in § 1.6038A-2 within the time and manner prescribed in § 1.6038A-2(d) and (e), fails to maintain or cause another to maintain records as required by § 1.6038A-3, or (in the case of records maintained outside the United States) fails to meet the non-U.S. record maintenance requirements within the applicable time prescribed in § 1.6038A-3(f), a penalty of $10,000 shall be assessed for each taxable year with respect to which such failure occurs. Such a penalty may be imposed by the District Director or the Director of the Internal Revenue Service Center where the Form 5472 is filed. The filing of a substantially incomplete Form 5472 constitutes a failure to file Form 5472. Where, however, the information described in § 1.6038A-2(b)(3) through (5) is not required to be reported, a Form 5472 filed without such information is not a substantially incomplete Form 5472.

(2) *Liability for certain partnership transactions.*—A reporting corporation to which transactions engaged in by a partnership are attributed under § 1.6038A-1(e)(2) is subject to the rules of this section to the extent failures occur with respect to the partnership transactions so attributed.

(3) *Calculation of monetary penalty.*—If a reporting corporation fails to maintain records as required by § 1.6038A-3 of transactions with multiple related parties, the monetary penalty may be assessed for each failure to maintain records with respect to each related party. The monetary penalty, however, shall be imposed on a reporting corporation only once for a taxable year with respect to each related party for a failure to furnish the information required on Form 5472, for a failure to maintain or cause another to maintain records, or for a failure to comply with the non-U.S. maintenance requirements described in § 1.6038A-3(f). An additional penalty for another failure may be imposed, however, under the rules of paragraph (d)(2) of this section. Thus, unless such failures continue after notification as described in paragraph (d) of this section, the maximum penalty under this paragraph with respect to each related party for all such failures in a taxable year is $10,000. The members of a group of corporations filing a consolidated return are jointly and severally liable for any monetary penalty that may be imposed under this section.

(b) *Reasonable cause.*—(1) *In general.*—Certain failures may be excused for reasonable cause, including not timely filing Form 5472, not maintaining or causing another to maintain records as required by § 1.6038A-3, and not complying with the non-U.S. maintenance requirements described in § 1.6038A-3(f). If an affirmative showing is made that the taxpayer acted in good faith and there is reasonable cause for a failure that results in the assessment of the monetary penalty, the period during which reasonable cause exists shall be treated as beginning on the day reasonable cause is established and ending not earlier than the last day on which reasonable cause existed for any such failure. Additionally, the beginning of the 90-day period after mailing of a notice by the District Director or the Director of an Internal Revenue Service Center of a failure described in paragraph (d) of this section shall be treated as not earlier than the last day on which reasonable cause existed.

(2) *Affirmative showing required.*—(i) *In general.*—To show that reasonable cause exists for purposes of paragraph (b)(1) of this section, the reporting corporation must make an affirmative showing of all the facts alleged as reasonable cause for the failure in a written statement containing a declaration that it is made under penalties of perjury. The statement must be filed with the District Director (in the case of failure to maintain or furnish requested information permitted to be maintained outside the United States within the time required under § 1.6038A-3(f) or a failure to file Form 5472) or the Director of the Internal Revenue Service Center where the Form 5472 is required to be filed (in the case of failure to file Form 5472). The District Director or the Director of the Internal Revenue Service Center where the Form 5472 is required to be filed, as appropriate, shall determine whether the failure was due to reasonable cause, and if so, the period of time for which reasonable cause existed. If a return has been filed as required by § 1.6038A-2 or records have been maintained as required by § 1.6038A-3, except for an omission of, or error with respect to, some of the information required or a record to be maintained, the omission or error shall not constitute a failure for purposes of section 6038A(d) if the reporting corporation that filed the return establishes to the satisfaction of the District Director or the Director of the Internal Revenue Service Center that it has substantially complied with the filing of Form 5472 or the requirement to maintain records.

(ii) *Small corporations.*—The District Director shall apply the reasonable cause exception liberally in the case of a small corporation that had no knowledge of the requirements imposed by section 6038A; has limited presence in and contact with the United States; and promptly and fully complies with all requests by the District Director to file Form 5472, and to furnish books, records, or other materials relevant to the reportable transaction. A small corporation is a corporation whose gross receipts for a taxable year are $20,000,000 or less.

(iii) *Facts and circumstances taken into account.*—The determination of whether a taxpayer acted with reasonable cause and in good faith is made on a case-by-case basis, taking into account all pertinent facts and circumstances. Circumstances that may indicate reasonable cause and good faith include an honest misunderstanding of fact or law that is reasonable in light of the experience and knowledge of the taxpayer. Isolated computational or transcriptional errors generally are not inconsistent with reasonable cause and good faith. Reliance upon an information return or on the advice of a professional (such as an attorney or accountant) does not necessarily demonstrate reasonable cause and good faith. Similarly, reasonable cause and good faith is not necessarily indicated by reliance on facts that, unknown to the taxpayer, are incorrect. Reliance on an information return, professional advice or other facts, however, constitutes reasonable cause and good faith if, under all the circumstances, the reliance was reasonable. A taxpayer, for example, may have reasonable cause for not filing a Form 5472 or for not maintaining records under section 6038A if the taxpayer has a reasonable belief that it is not owned by a 25-percent foreign shareholder. A reasonable belief means that the taxpayer does not know or has no reason to know that it is owned by a 25-percent foreign shareholder. For example, a reporting corporation would not know or have reason to know that it is owned by a 25-percent foreign shareholder if its belief that it is not so owned is consistent with other information reported or otherwise furnished to or known by the reporting corporation. A taxpayer may have reasonable cause for not treating a foreign corporation as a related party for purposes of section 6038A where the foreign corporation is a related party solely by reason of §1.6038A-1(d)(3) (under the principles of section 482), and the taxpayer had a reasonable belief that its relationship with the foreign corporation did not meet the standards for related parties under section 482.

(c) *Failure to maintain records or to cause another to maintain records.*—A failure to maintain records or to cause another to maintain records is determined by the District Director upon the basis of the reporting corporation's overall compliance (including compliance with the non-U.S. maintenance requirements under §1.6038A-3(f)(2)) with the record maintenance requirements. It is not an item-by-item determination. Thus, for example, a failure to maintain a single or small number of items may not constitute a failure for purposes of section 6038A(d), unless the item or items are essential to the correct determination of transactions between the reporting corporation and any foreign related parties. The District Director shall notify the reporting corporation in writing of any determination that it has failed to comply with the record maintenance requirement.

(d) *Increase in penalty where failure continues after notification.*—(1) *In general.*—If any failure described in this section continues for more than 90 days after the day on which the District Director or the Director of the Internal Revenue Service Center where the Form 5472 is required to be filed mails notice of the failure to the reporting corporation, the reporting corporation shall pay a penalty (in addition to the penalty described in paragraph (a) of this section) of $10,000 with respect to each related party for which a failure occurs for each 30-day period during which the failure continues after the expiration of the 90-day period. Any uncompleted fraction of a 30-day period shall count as a 30-day period for purposes of this paragraph (d).

(2) *Additional penalty for another failure.*—An additional penalty for a taxable year may be imposed, however, if at a time subsequent to the time of the imposition of the monetary penalty described in paragraph (a) of this section, a second failure is determined and the second failure continues after notification under paragraph (d)(1) of this section. Thus, if a taxpayer fails to file Form 5472 and is assessed a monetary penalty and later, upon audit, is determined to have failed to maintain records, an additional penalty for the failure to maintain records may be assessed under the rules of this paragraph if the failure to maintain records continues after notification under this paragraph.

(3) *Cessation of accrual.*—The monetary penalty will cease to accrue if the reporting corporation either files Form 5472 (in the case of a failure to file Form 5472), furnishes information to substantially complete Form 5472, or demonstrates compliance with respect to the maintenance of records (in the case of a failure to maintain records) for the taxable year in which the examination occurs and subsequent years to the satisfaction of the District Director. The monetary penalty also will cease to accrue if requested information, documents, or records, kept outside the United States under the requirements of §1.6038A-3(f) and not produced within the time specified are produced or moved to the United States under the rules of paragraph (f)(2)(ii) of this section.

(4) *Continued failures.*—If a failure under this section relating to a taxable year beginning before July 11, 1989 occurs, and if the failure continues following 90 days after the notice of failure under this paragraph is sent, the amount of the additional penalty to be assessed under this paragraph is $10,000 for each 30-day period beginning after November 5, 1990, during which the failure continues. There is no limitation on the amount of the monetary penalty that may be assessed after November 5, 1990.

(e) *Other penalties.*—For criminal penalties for failure to file a return and filing a false or fraudulent return, see sections 7203 and 7206 of the Code. For the penalty relating to an underpayment of tax, see section 6662.

(f) *Examples.*—The following examples illustrate the rules of this section.

Example 1—Failure to file Form 5472. Corp X, a U.S. reporting corporation, engages in related party transactions with FC. Corp X does not timely file a Form 5472 or maintain records relating to the transactions with FC for Year 1 or subsequent years. The Service Center with which Corp X files its income tax return imposes a $10,000 penalty for each of Years 1, 2, and 3 under section 6038A(d) and this section for failure to provide information as required on Form 5472 and mails a notice of failure to provide information. Corp X does not file Form

5472. Ninety days following the mailing of the notice of failure to Corp X an additional penalty of $10,000 is imposed. On the 135th day following the mailing of the notice of failure, Corp X files Form 5472 for Years 1, 2, and 3. The total penalty owed by Corp X for Year 1 is $30,000 ($10,000 for not timely filing Form 5472, $10,000 for the first 30-day period following the expiration of the 90-day period, and $10,000 for the fraction of the second 30-day period). The penalty for Years 2 and 3 for the failure to file Form 5472 is also $30,000 for each year, calculated in the same manner as for Year 1. The total penalty for failure to file Form 5472 for Years 1, 2, and 3 is $90,000.

Example 2—Failure to maintain records. Assume the same facts as in *Example 1.* In Year 5, Corp X is audited for Years 1 through 3. Corp X has not been maintaining records relating to the transactions with FC. The District Director issues a notice of failure to maintain records. Corp X has already been subject to the monetary penalty of $10,000 for each of Years 1, 2, and 3 for failure to file Form 5472 and, therefore, a monetary penalty under paragraph (a) of this section for failure to maintain records is not assessed. However, an additional penalty is assessed after the 90th day following the mailing of the notice of failure to maintain records. Corp X develops a record maintenance system as required by section 6038A and § 1.6038A-3. On the 180th day following the mailing of the notice of failure to maintain records, Corp X demonstrates to the satisfaction of the District Director that the newly developed record maintenance system will comply with the requirements of § 1.6038A-3 and the increase in the monetary penalty after notification ceases to accrue. The additional penalty for failure to maintain records is $30,000. An additional penalty of $30,000 per year is assessed for each of years 2 and 3 for the failure to maintain records for a total of $90,000.

(g) *Effective dates.*—For effective dates for this section, see § 1.6038A-1(n). [Reg. § 1.6038A-4.]

☐ [*T.D.* 8353, 6-14-91.]

§ 1.6038A-5. Authorization of agent.—
(a) *Failure to authorize.*—The rules of § 1.6038A-7 shall apply to any transaction between a foreign related party and a reporting corporation (including any transaction engaged in by a partnership that is attributed to the reporting corporation under § 1.6038A-1(e)(2)), unless the foreign related party authorizes (in the manner described in paragraph (b) of this section) the reporting corporation to act as its limited agent solely for purposes of sections 7602, 7603, and 7604 with respect to any request by the Service to examine records or produce testimony that may be relevant to the tax treatment of such a transaction or with respect to any summons by the Service for such records or testimony. The fact that a reporting corporation is authorized to act as an agent for a foreign related party is to be disregarded for purposes of determining whether the foreign related party either has a trade or business in the United States for purposes of the Code or a permanent establishment or fixed base in the United States for purposes of an income tax treaty.

(b) *Authorization by related party.*—(1) *In general.*—Upon request by the Service, a foreign related party shall authorize as its agent (solely for purposes of sections 7602, 7603, and 7604) the reporting corporation with which it engages in transactions. The authorization must be signed by the foreign related party or an officer of the foreign related party possessing the authority to authorize an agent for purposes of Rule 4 of the Federal Rules of Civil Procedure. The reporting corporation will accept this appointment by providing a statement to that effect, signed by an officer of the reporting corporation possessing the authority to accept such an appointment. The agency shall be effective at all times. For taxable years beginning after July 10, 1989, the authorization and acceptance must be provided to the Service within 30 days of a request by the Service to the reporting corporation for such an authorization. The authorization must contain a heading and statement as set forth below. A foreign government is not subject to the authorization of agent requirement.

AUTHORIZATION OF AGENT

"[Name of foreign related party] hereby expressly authorizes [name of reporting corporation] to act as its agent solely for purposes of sections 7602, 7603, and 7604 of the Internal Revenue Code with respect to any request to examine records or produce testimony that may be relevant to the U.S. income tax treatment of any transaction between [name of the above-named foreign related party] and [name of reporting corporation] or with respect to any summons for such records or testimony.

_____   _____   _____
Signature of or for   (Title)   (Date)
[name of foreign related party]

(If signed by a corporate officer, partner, or fiduciary on behalf of a foreign related party: I certify that I have the authority to execute this authorization of agent to act on behalf of [name of foreign related party]).

_____

Type or print your name below if signing for a foreign related party that is not an individual.

_____

[Name of reporting corporation] accepts this appointment to act as agent for [name of foreign related party] for the above purpose.

_____ _____ _____
Signature for   (Title)   (Date)
[Name of Reporting Corporation]

I certify that I have the authority to accept this appointment to act as agent on behalf of [name of foreign related party] and agree to accept service of process for the above purposes.

Type or print your name below.

_____

(2) *Authorization for prior years.*—A foreign related party shall authorize a reporting corporation to act as its agent with respect to taxable years for which a Form 5472 is required to be filed prior to the date on which the final regulations under section 6038A are published by providing the above executed authorization of agent within 30 days of a request by the Service for such an authorization.

(c) *Foreign affiliated groups.*—(1) *In general.*—A foreign corporation that has effective legal authority to make the authorization of agent under paragraph (b) of this section on behalf of any group of foreign related parties may execute such an authorization for any members of the group. A single authorization may be made on a consolidated basis. In such a case, the common parent must attach a schedule to the authorization of agent stating which members of the group would otherwise be required to separately authorize the reporting corporation as agent. The schedule must provide the name, address, relationship to the reporting corporation, and U.S. taxpayer identification number, if applicable, of each member.

(2) *Application of noncompliance penalty adjustment.*—In circumstances where a consolidated authorization of agent has been executed, if the agency authorization for any member of the group is not legally effective for purposes of sections 7602, 7603, and 7604, the noncompliance penalty adjustment under section 6038A(e) and § 1.6038A-7 shall apply.

(d) *Legal effect of authorization of agent.*—The legal consequences of a foreign related party authorizing a reporting corporation to act as its agent for purposes of sections 7602, 7603, and 7604 of the Code are as follows.

(1) *Agent for purposes of commencing judicial proceedings.*—A reporting corporation that is authorized by a foreign related party to act as its agent for purposes of sections 7602, 7603, and 7604 (including service of process) is also the agent of the foreign related party for purposes of—

(i) The filing of a petition to quash under section 6038A(e)(4)(A) or a petition to review an Internal Revenue Service determination of noncompliance under section 6038A(e)(4)(B), and

(ii) The commencement of a judicial proceeding to enforce a summons under section 7604, whether commenced in conjunction with a petition to quash under section 6038A(e)(4)(A) or commenced as a separate proceeding in the federal district court for the district in which the person to whom the summons is issued resides or is found.

(2) *Foreign related party found where reporting corporation found.*—For any purposes relating to sections 7602, 7603, or 7604 (including service of process), a foreign related party that authorizes a reporting corporation to act on its behalf under section 6038A(e)(1) and this section may be found anywhere where the reporting corporation has residence or is found.

Reg. § 1.6038A-5(d)(2)

(e) *Successors in interest.*—A successor in interest to a related party must execute the authorization of agent as described in paragraph (b) of this section.

(f) *Deemed compliance.*—(1) *In general.*—In exceptional circumstances, the District Director may treat a reporting corporation as authorized to act as agent for a related party for purposes of sections 7602, 7603, and 7604 in the absence of an actual agency appointment by the foreign related party, in circumstances where the actual absence of an appointment is reasonable. Factors to be considered include—

(i) If neither the reporting corporation nor the other party to the transaction knew or had reason to know that the two parties were related at the time of the transaction, and

(ii) The extent to which the taxpayer establishes to the satisfaction of the District Director that all transactions between the reporting corporation and the related party were on arm's length terms and did not involve the participation of any known related party.

(2) *Reason to know.*—Whether the reporting corporation or other party had reason to know that the two parties were related at the time of the transaction will be determined by all the facts and circumstances.

(3) *Effect of deemed compliance.*—If a reporting corporation is deemed under this paragraph (f) to have been authorized to act as an agent for a foreign related party for purposes of section 7602, 7603, and 7604, such deemed compliance is applicable only for that particular transaction and other reportable transactions entered into prior to the time when the reporting corporation knew or had reason to know that the related party, in fact, was related. The noncompliance rule of §1.6038A-7 shall apply to any transaction subsequent to that time with the same related party, unless the related party actually authorizes the reporting corporation to act as its agent under paragraph (a) of this section. In addition, the record maintenance requirements of §1.6038A-3 will apply to all subsequent transactions and, with respect to prior transactions, will apply to relevant records in existence at the time the relationship was discovered.

(g) *Effective dates.*—For effective dates for this section, see §1.6038A-1(n). [Reg. §1.6038A-5.]

☐ [*T.D.* 8353, 6-14-91.]

§1.6038A-6. Failure to furnish information.

—(a) *In general.*—The rules of §1.6038A-7 may be applied with respect to a transaction between a foreign related party and the reporting corporation (including any transaction engaged in by a partnership that is attributed to the reporting corporation under §1.6038A-1(e)(2)) if a summons is issued to the reporting corporation to produce any records or testimony, either directly or as agent for such related party, to determine the correct treatment under Title 1 of the Code of such a transaction between the reporting corporation and the related party; and if—

(1)(i) The summons is not quashed in a proceeding, if any, begun under section 6038A(e)(4) and is not determined to be invalid in a proceeding, if any, begun under section 7604 to enforce such summons; and

(ii) The reporting corporation does not substantially and timely comply with the summons, and the District Director has sent by certified or registered mail a notice under section 6038A(e)(2)(C) to the reporting corporation that it has not so complied; or

(2) The reporting corporation fails to maintain or to cause another to maintain records as required by §1.6038A-3, and by reason of that failure, the summons is quashed in a proceeding under section 6038A(e)(4) or in a proceeding begun under section 7604 to enforce the summons, or the reporting corporation is not able to provide the records requested in the summons.

(b) *Coordination with treaties.*—Where records of a related party are obtainable on a timely and efficient basis under information exchange procedures provided under a tax treaty or tax information exchange agreement (TIEA), the Service generally will make use of such procedures before issuing a summons. The absence or pendency of a treaty or TIEA request may not be asserted as grounds for refusing to comply with a summons or as a defense against the assertion of the noncompliance penalty adjustment under §1.6038A-7. For purposes of this paragraph, information is available on a timely and efficient basis if it can be obtained within 180 days of the request.

(c) *Enforcement proceeding not required.*—The District Director is not required to begin an enforcement proceeding to enforce the summons in order to apply the rules of §1.6038A-7.

(d) *De minimis failure.*—Where a reporting corporation's failure to comply with the requirement to furnish information under this section is *de minimis*, the District Director, in the exercise of discretion, may choose not to apply the noncompliance penalty. Thus, for example, in cases where a particular document or group of documents is not furnished upon request or summons, the District Director (in the District Director's sole discretion), may choose not to apply the noncompliance penalty if the District Director deems the document or documents not to have significant or sufficient value in the determination of the correctness of the tax treatment of the related party transaction.

(e) *Suspension of statute of limitations.*—If the reporting corporation brings an action under section 6038A(e)(4)(A) (proceeding to quash) or (e)(4)(B) (review of secretarial determination of noncompliance), the running of any period of limitation under section 6501 (relating to assessment and collection of tax) or under section 6531 (relating to criminal prosecutions) for the taxable year or years to which the summons that is the subject of such proceeding relates shall be suspended for the period during which such proceeding, and appeals therein, are pending. In no event shall any such period expire before the 90th day after the day on which there is a final determination in such proceeding.

(f) *Effective dates.*—For effective dates for this section, see § 1.6038A-1(n). [Reg. § 1.6038A-6.]

☐ [*T.D.* 8353, 6-14-91.]

§ 1.6038B-1. Reporting of certain transfers to foreign corporations.—(a) *Purpose and scope.*—This section sets forth information reporting requirements under section 6038B concerning certain transfers of property to foreign corporations. Paragraph (b) of this section provides general rules explaining when and how to carry out the reporting required under section 6038B with respect to the transfers to foreign corporations. Paragraph (c) of this section and § 1.6038B-1T(d) specify the information that is required to be reported with respect to certain transfers of property that are described in section 6038B(a)(1)(A) and 367(d), respectively. Section 1.6038B-1(e) describes the filing requirements for property transfers described in section 367(e). Paragraph (f) of this section sets forth the consequences of a failure to comply with the requirements of section 6038B and this section. For effective dates, see paragraph (g) of this section. For rules regarding transfers to foreign partnerships, see section 6038B(a)(1)(B) and any regulations thereunder.

(b)(1)(i) and (ii) [Reserved]. For further guidance, see § 1.6038B-1T(b)(1)(i) and (ii).

(iii) *Transfers of jointly-owned property.*—If two or more persons transfer jointly-owned property to a foreign corporation in a transfer with respect to which a notice is required under this section, then each person must report with respect to the particular interest transferred, specifying the nature and extent of the interest. However, a husband and wife who jointly file a single Federal income tax return may file a single Form 926 with their tax return.

(2) *Exceptions and special rules for transfers of stock or securities under section 367(a).*—
(i) *Transfers on or after July 20, 1998.*—A U.S. person that transfers stock or securities on or after July 20, 1998 in a transaction described in section 6038B(a)(1)(A) will be considered to have satisfied the reporting requirement under section 6038B and paragraph (b)(1) of this section if either—

(A) The U.S. transferor owned less than 5 percent of both the total voting power and the total value of the transferee foreign corporation immediately after the transfer (taking into account the attribution rules of section 318 as modified by section 958(b)), and either:

(1) The U.S. transferor qualified for nonrecognition treatment with respect to the transfer (i.e., the transfer was not taxable under §§ 1.367(a)-3(b) or (c)); or

(2) The U.S. transferor is a tax-exempt entity and the income was not unrelated business income; or

(3) The transfer was taxable to the U.S. transferor under § 1.367(a)-3(c), and such person properly reported the income from the transfer on its timely-filed (including extensions) Federal income tax return for the taxable year that includes the date of the transfer; or

(4) The transfer is considered to be to a foreign corporation solely by reason of § 1.83-6(d)(1) and the fair market value of the property transferred did not exceed $100,000; or

(B) The U.S. transferor owned 5 percent or more of the total voting power or the total value of the transferee foreign corporation immediately after the transfer (taking into account the attribution rules of section 318 as modified by section 958(b)) and either:

(1) The transferor (or one or more successors) properly entered into a gain recognition agreement under § 1.367(a)-8; or

(2) The transferor is a tax-exempt entity and the income was not unrelated business income; or

(3) The transferor properly reported the income from the transfer on its timely-filed (including extensions) Federal income tax return for the taxable year that includes the date of the transfer; or

(4) The transfer is considered to be to a foreign corporation solely by reason of § 1.83-6(d)(1) and the fair market value of the property transferred did not exceed $100,000.

(ii) *Transfers before July 20, 1998.*—With respect to transfers occurring after December 16, 1987, and prior to July 20, 1998, a

U.S. transferor that transferred U.S. or foreign stock or securities in a transfer described in section 367(a) is not subject to section 6038B if such person is described in paragraph (b)(2)(i)(A) of this section.

(3) *Special rule for transfers of cash.*—A U.S. person that transfers cash to a foreign corporation in a transfer described in section 6038B(a)(1)(A) must report the transfer if—

(i) Immediately after the transfer such person holds directly, indirectly, or by attribution (determined under the rules of section 318(a), as modified by section 6038(e)(2)) at least 10 percent of the total voting power or the total value of the foreign corporation; or

(ii) The amount of cash transferred by such person or any related person (determined under section 267(b)(1) through (3) and (10) through (12)) to such foreign corporation during the 12-month period ending on the date of the transfer exceeds $100,000.

(4) [Reserved]. For further guidance, see § 1.6038B-1T(b)(4).

(c) *Information required with respect to transfers described in section 6038B(a)(1)(A).*—A United States person that transfers property to a foreign corporation in an exchange described in section 6038B(a)(1)(A) (including cash transferred in taxable years beginning after February 5, 1999, and other unappreciated property) must provide the following information, in paragraphs labeled to correspond with the number or letter set forth in this paragraph (c) and § 1.6038B-1T(c)(1) through (5). If a particular item is not applicable to the subject transfer, the taxpayer must list its heading and state that it is not applicable. For special rules applicable to transfers of stock or securities, see paragraph (b)(2)(ii) of this section.

(1) through (5) [Reserved]. For further guidance, see § 1.6038B-1T(c)(1) through (5).

(6) *Application of section 367(a)(5).*—If the asset is transferred in an exchange described in section 361(a) or (b), a statement that the conditions set forth in the second sentence of section 367(a)(5) and any regulations under that section have been satisfied, and an explanation of any basis or other adjustments made pursuant to section 367(a)(5) and any regulations thereunder.

(d) [Reserved]. For further guidance, see § 1.6038B-1T(d).

(e) *Transfers subject to section 367(e).*—(1) *In general.*—If a domestic corporation (distributing corporation) makes a distribution described in section 367(e)(1) or section 367(e)(2), the distributing corporation must comply with the reporting requirements of this paragraph (e). Unless otherwise provided in this section, a distributing corporation making a distribution described in sections 367(e)(1) or 367(e)(2) must file a Form 926, "Return by a U.S. Transferor of Property to a Foreign Corporation (under section 367)," as amended and modified by this section.

(2) *Reporting requirements for section 367(e)(1) distributions of domestic controlled corporations.*—A domestic distributing corporation making a distribution of the stock or securities of a domestic corporation under section 355 is not required to file a Form 926, as described in paragraph (e)(1) of this section, and shall have no other reporting requirements under section 6038B.

(3) *Reporting requirements for section 367(e)(1) distributions of foreign controlled corporations.*—If the distributing corporation makes a section 355 distribution of the stock or securities of a foreign controlled corporation to distributee shareholders who are not qualified U.S. persons, as defined in § 1.367(e)-1(b)(1), then the distributing corporation shall complete Part 1 of the Form 926 and attach a signed copy of such form to its U.S. income tax return for the year of the distribution. The distributing corporation shall also attach to its U.S. income tax return for the year of distribution a statement signed under the penalties of perjury entitled, "Addendum to Form 926." The addendum shall contain a brief description of the transaction, state the number of shares distributed to distributees who are not qualified U.S. persons (applying the rules contained in § 1.367(e)-1(d)), and state the basis and fair market value of the distributed stock or securities (including a list stating the amounts that were distributed to distributees who were not qualified U.S. persons and distributees who were qualified U.S. persons).

(4) *Reporting rules for section 367(e)(2) distributions by domestic liquidating corporations.*—If the distributing corporation makes a distribution of property in complete liquidation under section 332 to a foreign distributee corporation that meets the stock ownership requirements of section 332(b) with respect to the stock of the distributing corporation, then the distributing corporation shall complete a Form 926 and attach a signed copy of such form to its U.S. income tax return for the year of the distribution. The property description contained in Part III of the Form 926 shall contain a description of all property distributed by the liquidating corporation (regardless of whether the property qualifies for nonrecognition). The description shall also identify the property excepted from gain recognition under § 1.367(e)-2(b)(2)(ii) and (iii). If the distributing corporation distributes property that will be

used by the foreign distributee corporation in a U.S. trade or business and the distributing corporation does not recognize gain on such distribution under § 1.367(e)-2(b)(2)(i), then the distributing corporation may satisfy the requirements of this section by completing Part 1 of the Form 926, noting thereon that the information required by the Form 926 is contained in the statement required by § 1.367(e)-2(b)(2)(i)(C)(*2*), and attaching a signed copy of the Form 926 to its U.S. income tax return for the year of the distribution.

(f) *Failure to comply with reporting requirements.*—(1) *Consequences of failure.*—If a U.S. person is required to file a notice (or otherwise comply) under paragraph (b) of this section and fails to comply with the applicable requirements of section 6038B and this section, then with respect to the particular property as to which there was a failure to comply—

(i) That property shall not be considered to have been transferred for use in the active conduct of a trade or business outside of the United States for purposes of section 367(a) and the regulations thereunder;

(ii) The U.S. person shall pay a penalty under section 6038B(b)(1) equal to 10 percent of the fair market value of the transferred property at the time of the exchange, but in no event shall the penalty exceed $100,000 unless the failure with respect to such exchange was due to intentional disregard (described under paragraph (g)(4) of this section); and

(iii) The period of limitations on assessment of tax upon the transfer of that property does not expire before the date which is 3 years after the date on which the Secretary is furnished the information required to be reported under this section. See section 6501(c)(8) and any regulations thereunder.

(2) *Failure to comply.*—A failure to comply with the requirements of section 6038B is—

(i) The failure to report at the proper time and in the proper manner any material information required to be reported under the rules of this section; or

(ii) The provision of false or inaccurate information in purported compliance with the requirements of this section. Thus, a transferor that timely files Form 926 with the attachments required under the rules of this section shall, nevertheless, have failed to comply if, for example, the transferor reports therein that property will be used in the active conduct of a trade or business outside of the United States, but in fact the property continues to be used in a trade or business within the United States.

(3) *Reasonable cause exception.*—The provisions of paragraph (f)(1) of this section shall not apply if the transferor shows that a failure to comply was due to reasonable cause and not willful neglect. The transferor may do so by providing a written statement to the district director having jurisdiction of the taxpayer's return for the year of the transfer, setting forth the reasons for the failure to comply. Whether a failure to comply was due to reasonable cause shall be determined by the district director under all the facts and circumstances.

(4) *Definition of intentional disregard.*—If the transferor fails to qualify for the exception under paragraph (f)(3) of this section and if the taxpayer knew of the rule or regulation that was disregarded, the failure will be considered an intentional disregard of section 6038B, and the monetary penalty under paragraph (f)(1)(ii) of this section will not be limited to $100,000. See § 1.6662-3(b)(2).

(g) [*Effective dates.*] This section applies to transfers occurring on or after July 20, 1998, except for transfers of cash made in tax years beginning on or before February 5, 1999, which are not required to be reported under section 6038B, and except for paragraph (e) of this section, which applies to transfers that are subject to §§ 1.367(e)-1(f) and 1.367(e)-2(e). See § 1.6038B-1T for transfers occurring prior to July 20, 1998. See also § 1.6038B-1T(e) in effect prior to August 9, 1999, (as contained in 26 CFR part 1 revised April 1, 1999) for transfers described in section 367(e) that are not subject to §§ 1.367(e)-1(f) and 1.367(e)-2(e). [Reg. § 1.6038B-1.]

☐ [*T.D.* 8770, 6-18-98 (*corrected* 3-31-99). *Amended by T.D.* 8817, 2-4-99 (*corrected* 3-31-99); *T.D.* 8834, 8-6-99; *T.D.* 8850, 12-27-99 *and T.D.* 9100, 12-18-2003.]

§ 1.6038B-1T. Reporting of certain transactions to foreign corporations (temporary).—(a) [Reserved]. For further guidance, see § 1.6038B-1(a).

(b) *Time and manner of reporting.*—(1) *In general.*—(i) *Reporting procedure.*—Except for stock or securities qualifying under the special reporting rule of § 1.6038B-1(b)(2), and certain exchanges described in section 354 (listed below), any U.S. person that makes a transfer described in section 6038B(a)(1)(A), 367(d) or (e), is required to report pursuant to section 6038B and the rules of § 1.6038B-1 and this section and must attach the required information to Form 926, "Return by a U.S. Transferor of Property to a Foreign Corporation." For special rules regarding cash transfers made in tax years beginning after February 5, 1999, see § 1.6038B-1(b)(3) and (g). For purposes of determining a U.S. transferor that is subject to section 6038B, the rules of § 1.367(a)-1T(c) and § 1.367(a)-3(d) shall apply with respect to a transfer described in section 367(a), and the rules of § 1.367(a)-1T(c) shall apply with respect to a transfer described in section 367(d). Additionally, if in an exchange described in section 354, a U.S. person exchanges stock of a foreign corporation in a reorganization described in section 368(a)(1)(E), or a U.S. person exchanges stock of a domestic or foreign corporation for stock of a foreign corporation pursuant to an asset reorganization described in section 368(a)(1)(C), (D), or (F), that is not treated as an indirect stock transfer under section 367(a), then the U.S. person exchanging stock is not required to report under section 6038B. Notwithstanding any statement to the contrary on Form 926, the form and attachments must be attached to, and filed by the due date (including extensions) of the transferor's income tax return for the taxable year that includes the date of the transfer (as defined in § 1.6038B-1T(b)(4)). For taxable years beginning before January 1, 2003, any attachment to Form 926 required under the rules of this section is filed subject to the transferor's declaration under penalties of perjury on Form 926 that the information submitted is true, correct and complete to the best of the transferor's knowledge and belief. For taxable years beginning after December 31, 2002, Form 926 and any attachments shall be verified by signing the income tax return with which the form and attachments are filed.

(ii) *Reporting by corporate transferor.*— For transfers by corporations in taxable years beginning before January 1, 2003, Form 926 must be signed by an authorized officer of the corporation if the transferor is not a member of an affiliated group under section 1504(a)(1) that files a consolidated Federal income tax return and by an authorized officer of the common parent corporation if the transferor is a member of such an affiliated group. For transfers by corporations in taxable years beginning after December 31, 2002, Form 926 shall be verified by signing the income tax return to which the form is attached.

(b)(2) through (b)(3) [Reserved]. For further guidance, see § 1.6038B-1(b)(2) through (b)(3).

(4) *Date of transfer.*—(i) *In general.*—For purposes of this section, the date of a transfer described in section 367 is the first date on which title to, possession of, or rights to the use of stock, securities, or other property passes pursuant to the plan for purposes of subtitle A of the Internal Revenue Code. A transfer will not be considered to begin with a decision of a board of directors or similar action unless the transaction otherwise takes effect for purposes of subtitle A of the Internal Revenue Code on that date.

(ii) *Termination of section 1504(d) election.*—A transfer deemed to occur as a result of the termination of an election under section 1504(d) will be considered to occur on the date the contiguous country corporation first fails to continue to qualify for the election under section 1504(d). The rule of this paragraph (b)(3)(ii) is illustrated by the following example.

Example. Domestic corporation W previously made a valid election under section 1504(d) to have its Mexican subsidiary S treated as a domestic corporation. On August 1, 1986, W disposes of its right, title, and interest in 10 percent of the stock of S by selling such stock to an unrelated United States person who is not a director of S. S first fails to continue to qualify for the election under section 1504(d) on August 1, 1986, since on such date it ceases to be directly or indirectly wholly owned or controlled by W. The constructive transfer of assets from "domestic" corporation S to Mexican corporation S is considered to occur on that date.

(iii) *Change in classification.*—A transfer deemed to occur as a result of a change in classification of an entity caused by a change in the governing documents, articles, or agreements of the entity (as described in § 1.367(a)-1T(c)(6)) will be considered to occur on the date that such changes take effect for purposes of subtitle A of the Internal Revenue Code.

(iv) *U.S. resident under section 6013(g) or (h).*—A transfer made by an alien individual who is considered to be a U.S resident by reason of a timely election under section 6013(g) or (h) will be considered to occur, for purposes of this section (but not for purposes of section 367), on the later of—

(A) The date on which the election under section 6013(g) or (h) is made; or

(B) The date on which the transfer would otherwise be considered to occur under the rules of this paragraph (b)(3).

The rule of this paragraph (b)(3)(iv) is illustrated by the following example.

Example. D is a nonresident alien individual who is married to a United States citizen. On March 1, 1986, D transfers property to a foreign corporation in an exchange described in section 351. On April 15, 1987, D and the spouse timely file with their tax return for the taxable year ended December 31, 1986, an election under section 6013(g) for D to be treated as a United States resident. The election is effective on January 1, 1986. For purposes of section 6038B, the transfer described in section 367(a) made by D in connection with the section 351 exchange is considered to occur on

April 15, 1987, the date on which the timely election was made under section 6013(g).

(c) Introductory text [Reserved]. For further guidance, see § 1.6038B-1(c).

(1) *Transferor.*—Provide the name, U.S. taxpayer identification number, and address of the U.S. person making the transfer.

(2) *Transfer.*—Provide the following information concerning the transfer:

(i) Name, U.S. taxpayer identification number (if any), address, and country of incorporation of transferee foreign corporation;

(ii) A general description of the transfer, and any wider transaction of which it forms a part, including a chronology of the transfers involved and an identification of the other parties to the transaction to the extent known.

(3) *Consideration received.*—Provide a description of the consideration received by the U.S. person making the transfer, including its estimated fair market value and, in the case of stock or securities, the class or type, amount, and characteristics of the interest received.

(4) *Property transferred.*—Provide a description of the property transferred. The description must be divided into the following categories, and must include the estimated fair market value and adjusted basis of the property, as well as any additional information specified below.

(i) *Active business property.*—Describe any transferred property (other than stock or securities) to be used in the active conduct of a trade or business outside of the United States. Provide here a general description of the business conducted (or to be conducted) by the transferee, including the location of the business, the number of its employees, the nature of the business, and copies of the most recently prepared balance sheet and profit and loss statement. Property listed within this category may be identified by general type. For example, upon the transfer of the assets of a manufacturing operation, a reasonable description of the property to be used in the business might include the categories of office equipment and supplies, computers and related equipment, motor vehicles, and several major categories of manufacturing equipment. However, any property that is includible both in this subdivision (i) and in subdivision (iii) of this paragraph (c)(4) (property subject to depreciation recapture under § 1.367(a)-4T(b)) must be identified in the manner required in subdivision (iii). If property is considered to be transferred for use in the active conduct of a trade or business under a special rule in § 1.367(a)-4T, specify the applicable rule and provide information supporting the application of the rule. If property is subject to section 367(a)(1) regardless of its use in a trade or business under the rules of §§ 1.367(a)-4T or 1.367(a)-5T, list the property only in response to subdivision (vii) of this paragraph (c)(4).

(ii) *Stock or securities.*—Describe any transferred stock or securities, including the class or type, amount, and characteristics of the transferred stock or securities, as well as the name, address, place of incorporation, and general description of the corporation issuing the stock. In addition, provide the following information if applicable:

(A) *Active trade or business stock.*—If the stock or securities are considered to be transferred for use in the active conduct of a trade or business outside of the United States under the rules of § 1.367(a)-3T(d)(2), provide information supporting the application of the rule.

(B) *Application of special rules.*—If any provision of § 1.367(a)-3T applies to except the transfer of stock or securities from the rule of section 367(a)(1), provide information supporting the claimed application of such provision (including information supporting the nonapplicability of either anti-abuse rule under § 1.367(a)-3T(h)). If the transferor is entering into an agreement to recognize gain upon a later disposition of the transferred stock by the transferee foreign corporation under § 1.367(a)-3T(g), attach the agreement and waiver as required by the rules of that paragraph.

(iii) *Depreciated property.*—Describe any property that is subject to depreciation recapture under the rules of § 1.367(a)-4T(b). Property within this category must be separately identified to the same extent as was required for purposes of the previously claimed depreciation deduction. Specify with respect to each such asset the relevant recapture provision, the number of months in which such property was in use within the United States, the total number of months the property was in use, the fair market value of the property, a schedule of the depreciation deduction taken with respect to the property, and a calculation of the amount of depreciation required to be recaptured.

(iv) *Property to be leased.*—Describe any property to be leased to other persons by the transferee foreign corporation (unless such property is considered to be transferred for use in the active conduct of a trade or business and was thus listed under subdivision (i) of this paragraph (c)(4)). If the rules of § 1.367(a)-4T(c)(2) apply to except the transfer from the rule of section 367(a)(1), provide information supporting the claimed application of such provision.

(v) *Property to be sold.*—Describe any transferred property that is to be sold or otherwise disposed of by the transferee foreign corporation, as described in § 1.367(a)-4T(d).

(vi) *Transfers to FSCs.*—Describe any property that is subject to the special rule of § 1.367(a)-4T(g) for transfers to FSCs. Provide information supporting the claimed application of that rule.

(vii) *Tainted property.*—Describe any property that is subject to § 1.367(a)-5T (concerning property that is subject to the rule of section 367(a)(1) regardless of whether it is transferred for use in the active conduct of a trade or business outside of the United States). Such description must be divided into the relevant categories, as follows:

(A) *Inventory, etc.*—Property described in § 1.367(a)-5T(b);

(B) *Installment obligations, etc.*—Property described in § 1.367(a)-5T(c);

(C) *Foreign currency, etc.*—Property described in § 1.367(a)-5T(d);

(D) *Intangible property.*—Property described in § 1.367(a)-5T(e); and

(E) *Leased property.*—Property described in § 1.367(a)-4T(f).

If any exception provided in § 1.367(a)-5T applies to the transferred property (making section 367(a)(1) not applicable to the transfer), provide information supporting the claimed application of such exception.

(viii) *Foreign loss branch.*—Provide the information specified in paragraph (c)(5) of this section.

(ix) *Other intangibles.*—Describe any intangible property sold or licensed by the transferor to the transferee foreign corporation, and set forth the general terms of each sale or license.

(5) *Transfer of foreign branch with previously deducted losses.*—If the property transferred is property of a foreign branch with previously deducted losses subject to the rules of § 1.367(a)-6T, provide the following information:

(i) *Branch operation.*—Describe the foreign branch the property of which is transferred, in accordance with the definition of § 1.367(a)-6T(g).

(ii) *Branch property.*—Describe the property of the foreign branch, including its adjusted basis and fair market value. For this purpose property must be identified with reasonable particularity, but may be identified by category rather than listing every asset separately. Substantially similar property may be listed together for this purpose, and property of minor value may be grouped into functional categories. For example, a reasonable description of the property of a business office might include the following categories: word processing or data processing equipment, other office equipment and furniture, and office supplies.

(iii) *Previously deducted losses.*—Set forth a detailed calculation of the sum of the losses incurred by the foreign branch before the transfer, and a detailed calculation of any reduction of such losses, in accordance with § 1.367(a)-6T(d) and (e).

(iv) *Character of gain.*—Set forth a statement of the character of the gain required to be recognized, in accordance with § 1.367(a)-6T(c)(1).

(6) [Reserved]. For further guidance, see § 1.6038B-1(c)(6).

(d) *Transfers subject to section 367(d).*—(1) *Initial transfer.*—A U.S. person that transfers intangible property to a foreign corporation in an exchange described in section 351 or 361 must provide the following information in paragraphs labelled to correspond with the number or letter set forth below. If a particular item is not applicable to the subject transfer, list its heading and state that it is not applicable. The information required by subdivisions (i) through (iii) need only be provided if such information was not otherwise provided under paragraph (c) of this section. (Note that the U.S. transferor may subsequently be required to file another return under paragraph (d)(2) of this section.)

(i) *Transferor.*—Provide the name, U.S. taxpayer identification number, and address of the U.S. person making the transfer.

(ii) *Transfer.*—Provide information concerning the transfer, including:

(A) Name, U.S. taxpayer identification number (if any), address, and country of incorporation of the transferee foreign corporation;

(B) A general description of the transfer, and any wider transaction of which it forms a part, including a chronology of the transfers involved and an identification of the other parties to the transaction to the extent known.

(iii) *Consideration received.*—Provide a description of the consideration received by the U.S. person making the transfer, including its estimated fair market value and, in the case of stock or securities, the class or type, amount, and characteristics of the interest received.

(iv) *Intangible property transferred.*—Provide a description of the intangible property transferred, including its adjusted basis. Generally, each intangible asset must be separately identified. Operating intangibles and foreign goodwill or going concern value, as defined in § 1.367(a)-1T(d)(5)(ii) and (iii), should be so identified and classified.

(v) *Annual payment.*—Provide and explain the calculation of the annual deemed payment for the use of the intangible property required to be recognized by the transferor under the rules of section 367(d).

(vi) *Election to treat as sale.*—List any intangible with respect to which an election is being made under § 1.367(d)-1T(g)(2) to treat the transfer as a sale. Include the fair market value of the intangible on the date of the transfer and a calculation of the gain required to be recognized in the year of the transfer by reason of the election.

(vii) *Coordination with loss rules.*—List any intangible property subject to section 367(d) the transfer of which also gives rise to the recognition of gain under section 904(f)(3) or § 1.367(a)-6T. Provide a calculation of the gain required to be recognized with respect to such property, in accordance with the provisions of § 1.367(d)-1T(g)(4).

(viii) *Other intangibles.*—Describe any intangible property sold or licensed by the transferor to the transferee foreign corporation, and set forth the general terms of each sale or license.

(2) *Subsequent transfers.*—If a U.S. person transfers intangible property to a foreign corporation in an exchange described in section 351 or 361, and at any time thereafter (within the useful life of the intangible property) either that U.S. person disposes of the stock of the transferee foreign corporation or the transferee foreign corporation disposes of the transferred intangible, then the U.S. person must provide the following information in paragraphs labelled to correspond with the number or letter set forth below. The information required by subdivisions (i) and (ii) need only be provided if such information was not otherwise provided in the same return, pursuant to paragraph (c) or (d)(1) of this section. For purposes of determining the date on which a return under this subparagraph (2) is required to be filed, the date of transfer is the date of the subsequent transfer of stock or intangible property.

(i) *Transferor.*—Provide the name, U.S. taxpayer identification number, and address of the U.S. person making the transfer.

(ii) *Initial transfer.*—Provide the following information concerning the initial transfer:

(A) The date of the transfer;

(B) The name, U.S. taxpayer identification number (if any), address, and country of incorporation of the transferee foreign corporation; and

(C) A general description of the transfer and any wider transaction of which it formed a part.

(iii) *Subsequent transfer.*—Provide the following information concerning the subsequent transfer:

(A) A general description of the subsequent transfer and any wider transaction of which it forms a part;

(B) A calculation of any gain required to be recognized by the U.S. person under the rules of § 1.367(d)-1T(d) through (f); and

(C) The name, address, and identifying number of each person that under the rules of § 1.367(d)-1T(e) or (f) will be considered to receive contingent annual payments for the use of the intangible property.

(e) [Reserved] For further guidance, see § 1.6038B-1(e).

(f) [Reserved]. For further guidance, see § 1.6038B-1(f).

(g) *Effective date.*—This section applies to transfers occurring after December 31, 1984. See § 1.6038B-1T(a) through (b)(2), (c) introductory text, and (f) (26 CFR part 1, revised April 1, 1998) for transfers occurring prior to July 20, 1998. See § 1.6038B-1 for transfers occurring on or after July 20, 1998. [Temporary Reg. § 1.6038B-1T.]

☐ [*T.D. 8087, 5-15-86. Amended by T.D. 8682, 8-9-96; T.D. 8770, 6-18-98; T.D. 8834, 8-6-99 and T.D. 9100, 12-18-2003 (corrected 2-2-2004).*]

§ 1.6038B-2. Reporting of certain transfers to foreign partnerships.—(a) *Reporting requirements.*—(1) *Requirement to report transfers.*—A United States person that transfers property to a foreign partnership in a contribution described in section 721 (including section 721(b)) must report that transfer on Form 8865 "Information Return of U.S. Persons With Respect To Certain Foreign Partnerships" pursuant to section 6038B and the rules of this section, if—

(i) Immediately after the transfer, the United States person owns, directly, indirectly, or by attribution, at least a 10-percent interest in the partnership, as defined in section 6038(e)(3)(C) and the regulations thereunder; or

(ii) The value of the property transferred, when added to the value of any other property transferred in a section 721 contribution by such person (or any related person) to such partnership during the 12-month period ending on the date of the transfer, exceeds $100,000.

(2) *Indirect transfer through a domestic partnership.*—For purposes of this section, if a domestic partnership transfers property to a foreign partnership in a section 721 transaction, the domestic partnership's partners shall be considered to have transferred a proportionate share of the property to the foreign partnership. However, if the domestic partnership properly reports all of the information required under this section with respect to the contribution, no partner of the transferor partnership, whether direct or indirect (through tiers of partnerships), is also required to report under this section. For illustrations of this rule, see *Examples 4* and *5* of paragraph (a)(7) of this section.

(3) *Indirect transfer through a foreign partnership.*—[Reserved]

(4) *Requirement to report dispositions.*—(i) *In general.*—If a United States person was required to report a transfer to a foreign partnership of appreciated property under paragraph (a)(1) or (2) of this section, and the foreign partnership disposes of the property while such United States person remains a direct or indirect partner, that United States person must report the disposition by filing Form 8865. The form must be attached to, and filed by the due date (including extensions) of, the United States person's income tax return for the year in which the disposition occurred.

(ii) *Disposition of contributed property in nonrecognition transaction.*—If a foreign partnership disposes of contributed appreciated property in a nonrecognition transaction and substituted basis property is received in exchange, and the substituted basis property has built-in gain under § 1.704-3(a)(8), the original transferor is not required to report the disposition. However, the transferor must report the disposition of the substituted basis property in the same manner as provided for the contributed property.

(5) *Time for filing Form 8865.*—The Form 8865 on which a transfer is reported must be attached to the transferor's timely filed (including extensions) income tax return for the tax year that includes the date of the transfer. If the person required to report under this section is not required to file an income tax return for its tax year during which the transfer occurred, but is required to file an information return for that year (for example, Form 1065, "U.S. Partnership Return of Income," or Form 990, "Return of Organization Exempt from Income Tax"), the person should attach the Form 8865 to its information return.

(6) *Returns to be made.*—(i) *Separate returns for each partnership.*—If a United States person transfers property reportable under this section to more than one foreign partnership in a taxable year, the United States person must submit a separate Form 8865 for each partnership.

(ii) *Duplicate form to be filed.*—If required by the instructions accompanying Form 8865, a duplicate Form 8865 (including attachments and schedules) must also be filed by the due date for submitting the original Form 8865 under paragraph (a)(5)(i) or (ii) of this section, as applicable.

(7) *Examples.*—The application of this paragraph (a) may be illustrated by the following examples:

Example 1. On November 1, 2001, *US*, a United States person that uses the calendar year as its taxable year, contributes $200,000 to *FP*, a foreign partnership, in a transaction subject to section 721. After the contribution, *US* owns a 5% interest in *FP*. *US* must report the contribution by filing Form 8865 for its taxable year ending December 31, 2001. On March 1, 2002, *US* makes a $40,000 section 721 contribution to *FP*, after which *US* owns a 6% interest in *FP*. *US* must report the $40,000 contribution by filing Form 8865 for its taxable year ending December 31, 2002, because the contribution, when added to the value of the other property contributed by *US* to *FP* during the 12-month period ending on the date of the transfer, exceeds $100,000.

Example 2. *F*, a nonresident alien, is the brother of *US*, a United States person. *F* owns a 15% interest in *FP*, a foreign partnership. *US* contributes $99,000 to *FP*, in exchange for a 1-percent partnership interest. Under sections 6038(e)(3)(C) and 267(c)(2), *US* is considered to own at least a 10-percent interest in *FP* and, therefore, *US* must report the $99,000 contribution under this section.

Example 3. *US*, a United States person, owns 40 percent of *FC*, a foreign corporation. *FC* owns a 20-percent interest in *FP*, a foreign partnership. Under section 267(c)(1), *US* is considered to own 8 percent of *FP* due to its ownership of *FC*. *US* contributes $50,000 to *FP* in exchange for a 5-percent partnership interest. Immediately after the contribution, *US* is considered to own at least a 10-percent interest in *FP* and, therefore, must report the $50,000 contribution under this section.

Example 4. *US*, a United States person, owns a 60-percent interest in *USP*, a domestic partnership. On March 1, 2001, *USP* contributes $200,000 to *FP*, a foreign partnership, in exchange for a 5-percent partnership interest. Under paragraph (a)(2) of this section, *US* is considered as having contributed $120,000 to *FP* ($200,000 × 60%). However, under paragraph (a)(2), if *USP* properly reports the contribution to *FP*, *US* is not required to report its $120,000 contribution. If *US* directly contributes $5,000 to *FP* on June 10, 2001, *US* must report the $5,000 contribution because *US* is considered to have contributed more than $100,000 to *FP* in the 12-month period ending on the date of the $5,000 contribution.

Example 5. *US*, a United States person, owns an 80-percent interest in *USP*, a domestic partnership. USP owns an 80-percent interest in *USP1*, a domestic partnership. On March 1, 2001, *USP1* contributes $200,000 to *FP*, a foreign partnership, in exchange for a 3-percent partnership interest. Under paragraph (a)(2) of this section, *USP* is considered to have contributed $160,000 ($200,000 × 80%) to *FP*. *US* is considered to have contributed $128,000 to *FP* ($200,000 × 80% × 80%). However, if *USP1* reports the transfer of the $200,000 to *FP*, neither *US* nor *USP* are required to report under this section the amounts they are considered to have contributed. Additionally, regardless of whether *USP1* reports the $200,000 contribution, if *USP* reports the $160,000 contribution it is considered to have made, *US* does not have to report under this section the $128,000 contribution *US* is considered to have made.

(b) *Transfers by trusts relating to state and local government employee retirement plans.*—Trusts relating to state and local government employee retirement plans are not required to report transfers under this section, unless otherwise specified in the instructions to Form 8865.

(c) *Information required with respect to transfers of property.*—With respect to transfers required to be reported under paragraph (a)(1) or (2) of this section, the return must contain information in such form or manner as Form 8865 (and its accompanying instructions) prescribes with respect to reportable events, including—

(1) The name, address, and U.S. taxpayer identification number of the United States person making the transfer;

(2) The name, U.S. taxpayer identification number (if any), and address of the transferee foreign partnership, and the type of entity and country under whose laws the partnership was created or organized;

(3) A general description of the transfer, and of any wider transaction of which it forms a part, including the date of transfer;

(4) The names and addresses of the other partners in the foreign partnership, unless the transfer is solely of cash and the transferor holds less than a ten-percent interest in the transferee foreign partnership immediately after the transfer. However, for tax years of U.S. persons beginning on or after January 1, 2000, the person reporting pursuant to section 6038B (the transferor) must provide the names and addresses of each United States person that owned a ten-percent or greater direct interest in the foreign partnership during the transferor's tax year in which the transfer occurred, and the names and addresses of any other United States or foreign persons that were direct partners in the foreign partnership during that tax year and that were related to the transferor during that tax year. See paragraph (i)(4) of this section for the definition of a related person;

(5) A description of the partnership interest received by the United States person, including a change in partnership interest;

(6) A separate description of each item of contributed property that is appreciated property subject to the allocation rules of section 704(c) (except to the extent that the property is permitted to be aggregated in making allocations under section 704(c)), or is intangible property, including its estimated fair market value and adjusted basis; and

(7) A description of other contributed property, not specified in paragraph (c)(6) of this section, aggregated by the following categories (with, in each case, a brief description of the property)—

(i) Stock in trade of the transferor (inventory);

(ii) Tangible property (other than stock in trade) used in a trade or business of the transferor;

(iii) Cash;

(iv) Stock, notes receivable and payable, and other securities; and

(v) Other property.

(d) *Information required with respect to dispositions of property.*—In respect of dispositions required to be reported under paragraph (a)(4) of this section, the return must contain information in such form or manner as Form 8865 (and its accompanying instructions) prescribes with respect to reportable events, including—

(1) The date and manner of disposition;

(2) The gain and depreciation recapture amounts, if any, realized by the partnership; and

(3) Any such amounts allocated to the United States person.

(e) *Method of reporting.*—Except as otherwise provided on Form 8865, or the accompanying instructions, all amounts reported as required under this section must be expressed in United States currency, with a statement of the exchange rates used. All statements required on or with Form 8865 pursuant to this section must be in the English language.

(f) *Reporting under this section not required of partnerships excluded from the application of subchapter K.*—(1) *Election to be wholly excluded.*—The reporting requirements of this section will not apply to any United States person in respect of an eligible partnership as described in §1.761-2(a), if such partnership has validly elected to be excluded from all of the provisions of subchapter K of chapter 1 of the Internal Revenue Code in the manner specified in §1.761-2(b)(2)(i).

(2) *Deemed excluded.*—The reporting requirements of this section will not apply to any United States person in respect of an eligible partnership as described in §1.761-2(a), if such partnership is validly deemed to have elected to be excluded from all of the provisions of subchapter K of chapter 1 of the Internal Revenue Code in accordance with the provisions of §1.761-2(b)(2)(ii).

(g) *Deemed contributions.*—Deemed contributions resulting from IRS-initiated section 482 adjustments are not required to be reported under section 6038B. However, taxpayers must report deemed contributions resulting from taxpayer-initiated adjustments. Such information will be furnished timely if filed by the due date, including extensions, for filing the taxpayer's income tax return for the year in which the adjustment is made.

(h) *Failure to comply with reporting requirements.*—(1) *Consequences of failure.*—If a United States person is required to file a return under paragraph (a) of this section and fails to comply with the reporting requirements of section 6038B and this section, then such person is subject to the following penalties:

(i) The United States person is subject to a penalty equal to 10 percent of the fair market value of the property at the time of the contribution. Such penalty with respect to a particular transfer is limited to $100,000, unless the failure to comply with respect to such transfer was due to intentional disregard.

(ii) The United States person must recognize gain (reduced by the amount of any gain recognized, with respect to that property, by the transferor after the transfer) as if the contributed property had been sold for fair market value at the time of the contribution. Adjustments to the basis of the partnership's assets and any relevant partner's interest as a result of gain being recognized under this provision will be made as though the gain was recognized in the year in which the failure to report was finally determined.

(2) *Failure to comply.*—A failure to comply with the requirements of section 6038B includes—

(i) The failure to report at the proper time and in the proper manner any information required to be reported under the rules of this section; and

(ii) The provision of false or inaccurate information in purported compliance with the requirements of this section.

(3) *Reasonable cause exception.*—Under section 6038B(c)(2) and this section, the provisions of paragraph (h)(1) of this section will not apply if the transferor shows that a failure to comply was due to reasonable cause and not willful neglect. The transferor may attempt to do so by providing a written statement to the district director having jurisdiction of the taxpayer's return for the year of the transfer, setting forth the reasons for the failure to comply. Whether a failure to comply was due to reasonable cause will be determined by the district director under all the facts and circumstances.

(4) *Statute of limitations.*—For exceptions to the limitations on assessment in the event of a failure to provide information under section 6038B, see section 6501(c)(8).

(i) *Definitions.*—(1) *Appreciated property.*—Appreciated property is property that has a fair market value in excess of basis.

(2) *Domestic partnership.*—A domestic partnership is a partnership described in section 7701(a)(4).

(3) *Foreign partnership.*—A foreign partnership is a partnership described in section 7701(a)(5).

(4) *Related person.*—Persons are related persons if they bear a relationship described in section 267(b)(1) through (3) or (10) through (12), after application of section 267(c) (except for (c)(3)), or in section 707(b)(1)(B).

(5) *Substituted basis property.*—Substituted basis property is property described in section 7701(a)(42).

(6) *Taxpayer-initiated adjustment.*—A taxpayer-initiated adjustment is a section 482 adjustment that is made by the taxpayer pursuant to § 1.482-1(a)(3).

(7) *United States person.*—A United States person is a person described in section 7701(a)(30).

(j) *Effective dates.*—(1) *In general.*—Except as otherwise provided in this section, this section applies to transfers made on or after January 1, 1998. However, for a transfer made on or after January 1, 1998, but before January 1, 1999, the filing requirements of this section may be satisfied by—

(i) Filing a Form 8865 with the taxpayer's income tax return (including a partnership return of income) for the first taxable year beginning on or after January 1, 1999; or

(ii) Filing a Form 926 (modified to reflect that the transferee is a partnership, not a corporation) with the taxpayer's income tax return (including a partnership return of income) for the taxable year in which the transfer occurred.

(2) *Transfers made between August 5, 1997 and January 1, 1998.*—A United States person that made a transfer of property between August 5, 1997, and January 1, 1998, that is required to be reported under section 6038B may satisfy its reporting requirement by reporting in accordance with the provisions of this section or in accordance with the provisions of Notice 98-17 (1998-11 IRB 6) (see § 601.601(d)(2) of this chapter).

(3) *Special rule for transfers made before January 1, 2000.*—Even if not reported in accordance with the rules provided in paragraph (a)(5) of this section, or paragraph (j)(1) or (2) of this section, a transfer that occurred before January 1, 2000 will nevertheless be considered timely reported if the transferor reports it on a Form 8865 attached to an amended tax return for the transferor's tax year in which the transfer occurred, provided such amended return is filed no later than September 15, 2000. [Reg. § 1.6038B-2.]

☐ [*T.D.* 8817, 2-4-99 (*corrected* 3-31-99). Amended by *T.D.* 8850, 12-27-99.]

§ 1.6046-1. Returns as to organization or reorganization of foreign corporations and as to acquisitions of their stock.—

(a) *Officers or directors.*—(1) *When liability arises on January 1, 1963.*—Each United States citizen or resident who is on January 1, 1963, an officer or director of a foreign corporation shall make a return on Form 959 showing the name, address, and identifying number of each United States person who, on January 1, 1963, owns 5 percent or more in value of the outstanding stock of such foreign corporation.

(2) *When liability arises after January 1, 1963.*—(i) *Requirement of return.*—Each United States citizen or resident who is at any time after January 1, 1963, an officer or director of a foreign corporation shall make a return on Form 959 setting forth the information described in subdivision (ii) of this subparagraph with respect to each United States person who, during the time such citizen or resident is such an officer or director—

(a) Acquires (whether in one or more transactions) outstanding stock of such corporation which has, or which when added to any such stock then owned by him (excluding any stock owned by him on January 1, 1963, if on that date he owned 5 percent or more in value of such stock) has, a value equal to 5 percent or more in value of the outstanding stock of such foreign corporation, or

(b) Acquires (whether in one or more transactions) an additional 5 percent or more in value of the outstanding stock of such foreign corporation.

(ii) *Information required to be shown on return.*—The return required under subdivision (i) of this subparagraph shall contain the following information:

(a) Name, address, and identifying number of each shareholder with respect to whom the return is filed;

(b) A statement showing that the shareholder is either described in subdivision (i)(a) or (i)(b) of this subparagraph; and

(c) The date on which the shareholder became a person described in subdivision (i)(a) or (i)(b) of this subparagraph.

(3) *Application of rules.*—The provisions of this paragraph may be illustrated by the following examples:

Example (1). A, a United States citizen, is, on January 1, 1963, a director of M, a foreign corporation. X, on January 1, 1963, is a United States person owning 5 percent in value of the outstanding stock of M Corporation. A must file a return under the provisions of subparagraph (1) of this paragraph.

Example (2). The facts are the same as in Example (1) except that X owns only 2 percent in value of the outstanding stock of M Corporation on January 1, 1963. On July 1, 1963, X acquires 2 percent in value of the outstanding stock of M Corporation and on September 1, 1963, he acquires an additional 2 percent in value of such stock. The July 1, 1963, transaction does not give rise to liability to file a return; however, A must file a return as a result of the September 1, 1963, transaction because X's holdings now exceed 5 percent.

Example (3). The facts are the same as in Example (2) and, on September 15, 1963, X acquires an additional 4 percent in value of the outstanding stock of M Corporation (X's total holdings are now 10 percent). On November 1, 1963, X acquires an additional 2 percent in value of the outstanding stock of M Corporation. The September 15, 1963, transaction does not give rise to liability to file a return since X has not acquired 5 percent in value of the outstanding stock of M Corporation since A last became liable to file a return. However, A must file a return as a result of the November 1, 1963, transaction because X has now acquired an additional 5 percent in value of the outstanding stock of M Corporation.

Example (4). The facts are the same as in Examples (2) and (3) and, in addition, B, a United States citizen, becomes an officer of M Corporation on October 1, 1963. B is not required to file a return either as a result of the facts set forth in Example (2) or as a result of the September 15, 1963, transaction described in Example (3). However, B is required to file a return as a result of the November 1, 1963, transaction described in Example (3) because X has acquired an additional 5 percent in value of the outstanding stock of M Corporation while B is an officer or director.

(b) *Returns required of United States persons when liability to file arises on January 1, 1963.*— Each United States person who, on January 1, 1963, owns 5 percent or more in value of the outstanding stock of a foreign corporation, shall make a return on Form 959 with respect to such foreign corporation setting forth the following information:

(1) The name, address, and identifying number of the shareholder (or shareholders) filing the return, and the internal revenue district in which such shareholder filed his most recent United States income tax return;

(2) The name, business address, and employer identification number, if any, of the foreign corporation, the name of the country under the laws of which it is incorporated, and the name of the country in which is located its principal place of business;

(3) The date of organization and, if any, of each reorganization of the foreign corporation if such reorganization occurred on or after January 1, 1960, while the shareholder owned 5 percent or more in value of the outstanding stock of such corporation;

(4) The name and address of the foreign corporation's statutory or resident agent in the country of incorporation;

(5) The name, address, and identifying number of any branch office or agent of the foreign corporation located in the United States;

(6) If the foreign corporation has filed a United States income tax return, or participated in the filing of a consolidated return, for any of its last three calendar or fiscal years immediately preceding January 1, 1963, state each year for which a return was filed (including, in the case of a consolidated return, the name of the corporation filing such return), the type of form used, the internal revenue office to which it was sent, and the amount of tax, if any, paid;

(7) The name and address of the person (or persons) having custody of the books of account and records of the foreign corporation, and the location of such books and records if different from such address;

(8) The names, addresses, and identifying numbers of all United States persons who are principal officers (for example, president, vice president, secretary, treasurer, and comptroller) or members of the board of directors of the foreign corporation as of January 1, 1963;

(9) A complete description of the principal business activities in which the foreign corporation is actually engaged and, if the foreign corporation is a member of a group constituting a chain of ownership with respect to each unit of which the shareholder owns 5 percent or more in value of the outstanding stock, a chart showing the foreign corporation's position in the chain of ownership and the percentages of ownership;

(10) The following information prepared in accordance with generally accepted accounting principles and in such detail as is customary for the corporation's accounting records:

(i) The corporation's profit and loss statement for the most recent complete annual accounting period; and

(ii) The corporation's balance sheet as of the end of the most recent complete annual accounting period;

(11) A statement showing as of January 1, 1963, the amount and type of any indebtedness of the foreign corporation—

(i) To any United States person owning 5 percent or more in value of its stock, or

(ii) To any other foreign corporation owning 5 percent or more in value of the outstanding stock of the foreign corporation with respect to which the return is filed provided that the shareholder filing the return owns 5 percent or more in value of the outstanding stock of such other foreign corporation,

together with the name, address, and identifying number, if any, of each such shareholder or entity;

(12) A statement, as of January 1, 1963, showing the name, address, and identifying number, if any, of each person who is, on Janu-

ary 1, 1963, a subscriber to the stock of the foreign corporation, and the number of shares subscribed to by each;

(13) A statement showing the number of shares of each class of stock of the foreign corporation owned by each shareholder filing the return and—

(i) If such stock was acquired after December 31, 1953, the dates of acquisition, the amounts paid or value given therefor, the method of acquisition, i.e., by original issue, purchase on open market, direct purchase, gift, inheritance, etc., and from whom acquired; or

(ii) If such stock was acquired before January 1, 1954, a statement that such stock was acquired before such date, and the value at which such stock is carried on the books of such shareholder;

(14) A statement showing as of January 1, 1963, the name, address, and identifying number of each United States person who owns 5 percent or more in value of the outstanding stock of the foreign corporation, the classes of stock held, the number of shares of each class held, including the name, address, and identifying number, if any, of each actual owner if such person is different from the shareholder of record and a statement of the nature and amount of the interests of each such actual owner; and

(15) The total number of shares of each class of outstanding stock of the foreign corporation (or other data indicating the shareholder's percentage of ownership).

(c) *Returns required of United States persons when liability to file arises after January 1, 1963.*—(1) *United States persons required to file.*—A return on Form 959, containing the information required by subparagraph (3) of this paragraph, shall be made by each United States person when at any time after January 1, 1963—

(i) Such person acquires (whether in one or more transactions) outstanding stock of such foreign corporation which has, or which when added to any such stock then owned by him (excluding any stock owned by him on January 1, 1963, if on that date he owned 5 percent or more in value of such stock) has, a value equal to 5 percent or more in value of the outstanding stock of such foreign corporation, or

(ii) Such person, having already acquired the interest referred to in paragraph (b) of this section or in subdivision (i) of this subparagraph—

(a) Acquires (whether in one or more transactions) an additional 5 percent or more in value of the outstanding stock of such foreign corporation,

(b) Owns 5 percent or more in value of the outstanding stock of such foreign corporation when such foreign corporation is reorganized (as defined in paragraph (f)), or

(c) Disposes of sufficient stock in such foreign corporation to reduce his interest to less than 5 percent in value of the outstanding stock of such foreign corporation.

The provisions of this subparagraph may be illustrated by the following examples:

Example (1). On January 15, 1963, A, a United States person, acquires 5 percent in value of the outstanding stock of M, a foreign corporation. A must file a return under the provisions of this subparagraph.

Example (2). On January 1, 1963, B, a United States person, owns 2 percent in value of the outstanding stock of M, a foreign corporation. B is not required to file a return under the provisions of this section because he does not own 5 percent or more in value of the outstanding stock of M Corporation. On February 1, 1963, B acquires an additional 3 percent in value of the outstanding stock of M Corporation. B must file a return under the provisions of this subparagraph.

Example (3). On January 1, 1963, C, a United States person, owns 6 percent in value of the outstanding stock of M, a foreign corporation. C must file a return under the provisions of paragraph (b) of this section. On February 1, 1963, C acquires an additional 2 percent in value of the outstanding stock of M Corporation in a transaction not involving a reorganization. C is not required to file a return under the provisions of this subparagraph.

Example (4). The facts are the same as in Example (3) except that, in addition, on April 1, 1963, C acquires 2 percent in value of the outstanding stock of M Corporation in a transaction not involving a reorganization. (C's total holdings are now 10 percent.) C is not required to file a return under the provisions of this subparagraph because he has not acquired 5 percent or more in value of the outstanding stock of M Corporation since he last became liable to file a return. On May 1, 1963, C acquires 1 percent in value of the outstanding stock of M Corporation. C must file a return under the provisions of this subparagraph.

Example (5). On June 1, 1963, D, a United States person, owns 12 percent in value of the outstanding stock of M, a foreign corporation. Also, on June 1, 1963, M Corporation is reorganized and, as a result of such reorganization, D owns only 6 percent of the outstanding stock of such foreign corporation. D must file a return under the provisions of this subparagraph.

Example (6). The facts are the same as in Example (5) except that, in addition, on

November 1, 1970, D donates 2 percent of the outstanding stock of M Corporation to a charity. Since D has disposed of sufficient stock to reduce his interest in M Corporation to less than 5 percent in value of the outstanding stock of such corporation, D must file a return under the provisions of this subparagraph.

(2) *Shareholders who become United States persons.*—A return on Form 959, containing the information required by subparagraph (3) of this paragraph, shall be made by each person who at any time after January 1, 1963, becomes a United States person while owning 5 percent or more in value of the outstanding stock of such foreign corporation.

(3) *Information required to be shown on return.*—(i) *In general.*—The return on Form 959, required to be filed by persons described in subparagraph (1) or (2) of this paragraph, shall set forth the same information as is required by the provisions of paragraph (b) of this section except that where such provisions require information with respect to January 1, 1963, such information shall be furnished with respect to the date on which liability arises to file the return required under this paragraph.

(ii) *Additional information.*—In addition to the information required under subdivision (i) of this subparagraph, the following information shall also be furnished in the return required under this paragraph:

(a) The date on or after January 1, 1963, if any, on which such shareholder (or shareholders) last filed a return under this section with respect to the corporation;

(b) If a return is filed by reason of becoming a United States person, the date the shareholder became a United States person;

(c) If a return is filed by reason of the disposition of stock, the date and method of such disposition and the person to whom such disposition was made; and

(d) If a return is filed by reason of the organization or reorganization of the foreign corporation on or after January 1, 1963, the following information with respect to such organization or reorganization:

(1) A statement showing a detailed list of the classes and kinds of assets transferred to the foreign corporation including a description of the assets (such as a list of patents, copyrights, stock, securities, etc.), the fair market value of each asset transferred (and, if such asset is transferred by a United States person, its adjusted basis), the date of transfer, the name, address, and identifying number, if any, of the owner immediately prior to the transfer, and the consideration paid by the foreign corporation for such transfer;

(2) A statement showing the assets transferred and the notes or securities issued by the foreign corporation, the name, address, and identifying number, if any, of each person to whom such transfer or issue was made, and the consideration paid to the foreign corporation for such transfer or issue; and

(3) An analysis of the changes in the corporation's surplus accounts occurring on or after January 1, 1963.

(iii) *Exclusion of information previously furnished.*—In any case where any identical item of information required to be filed under this paragraph by a shareholder with respect to a foreign corporation has previously been furnished by such shareholder in any return made in accordance with the provisions of this section, such shareholder may satisfy the requirements of this paragraph by filing Form 959, identifying such item of information, the date furnished, and stating that it is unchanged.

(d) *Associations, etc.*—Returns are required to be filed in accordance with the provisions of this section with respect to any foreign association, foreign joint-stock company, or foreign insurance company, etc., which would be considered to be a corporation under § 301.7701-2 of this chapter (Regulations on Procedure and Administration). Persons who would qualify by the nature of their functions and ownership in such associations, etc., as officers, directors, or shareholders thereof will be treated as such for purposes of this section without regard to their designations under local law.

(e) *Special provisions.*—(1) *Return jointly made.*—Any two or more persons required under paragraph (a) of this section to make a return with respect to one or more shareholders of the same corporation, or under paragraph (b) or (c) of this section to make a return with respect to the same corporation, may in lieu of making several returns, jointly make one return.

(2) *Separate return for each corporation.*—When returns are required with respect to more than one foreign corporation, a separate return must be made for each corporation.

(3) *Use of power of attorney by officers or directors.*—(i) *In general.*—Any two or more persons required under paragraph (a) of this section to make a return with respect to one or more shareholders of the same corporation may, by means of one or more duly executed powers of attorney, constitute one of their number as attorney in fact for the purpose of making such returns or for the purpose of making a joint return under subparagraph (1) of this paragraph.

Reg. § 1.6046-1(c)(2)

(ii) *Nature of power of attorney.*—The power of attorney referred to in subdivision (i) of this subparagraph shall be limited to the making of returns required under paragraph (a) of this section and shall be limited to a single calendar year with respect to which such returns are required.

(iii) *Manner of execution of power of attorney.*—The use of technical language in the preparation of the power of attorney referred to in subdivision (i) of this subparagraph is not necessary. Such power of attorney shall be signed by the individual United States citizen or resident required to file a return or returns under paragraph (a) of this section. Such power of attorney must be acknowledged before a notary public or, in lieu thereof, witnessed by two disinterested persons. The notarial seal must be affixed unless such seal is not required under the laws of the state or country wherein such power of attorney is executed.

(iv) *Manner of execution of return under authority of power of attorney.*—A return made under authority of one or more powers of attorney referred to in subdivision (i) of this subparagraph shall be signed by the attorney in fact for each principal for which such attorney in fact is acting. A copy of such one or more powers of attorney shall be kept at a convenient and safe location accessible to internal revenue officers, and shall at all times be available for inspection by such officers.

(v) *Effect on penalties.*—The fact that a return is made under authority of a power of attorney referred to in subdivision (i) of this subparagraph shall not affect the principal's liability for penalties provided for failure to file a return required under paragraph (a) of this section or for filing a false or fraudulent return.

(4) *Persons excepted from filing returns.*— (i) *Return required of officer or director under paragraph (a)(1).*—Notwithstanding paragraph (a)(1) of this section, any United States citizen or resident required to make a return under such paragraph with respect to shareholders of a foreign corporation, need not make such return if, on January 1, 1963, three or fewer United States persons own 95 percent or more in value of the outstanding stock of such foreign corporation and file a return or returns with respect to such corporation under paragraph (b) of this section.

(ii) *Return required of officer or director under paragraph (a)(2).*—Notwithstanding paragraph (a)(2) of this section, any United States citizen or resident required to make a return under such paragraph with respect to a person acquiring stock of a foreign corporation in an acquisition described in subdivision (i)(*a*) or (*b*) of such paragraph need not make such return, if—

(*a*) As a result of such acquisition of stock of such foreign corporation, a United States person files a return as a shareholder under paragraph (c)(1) of this section, and

(*b*) Immediately after such acquisition of stock, three or fewer United States persons own 95 percent or more in value of the outstanding stock of such foreign corporation.

(iii) *Return required by reason of attribution rules.*—Notwithstanding paragraph (b) or (c) of this section, any person required to make a return under such paragraph with respect to a foreign corporation need not make such return, if—

(*a*) Such person does not directly own an interest in the foreign corporation,

(*b*) Such person is required to furnish the information solely by reason of attribution of stock ownership from a United States person under paragraph (i) of this section, and

(*c*) The person from whom the stock ownership is attributed furnishes all of the information required under paragraph (b) or (c) of this section of the person to whom such stock ownership is attributed.

(iv) *Return required of officer or director with respect to person described in subdivision (iii).*—Notwithstanding paragraph (a) of this section, any United States citizen or resident required to make a return under such paragraph with respect to a person exempted under subdivision (iii) of this subparagraph from making a return need not make a return with respect to such person.

(5) *Persons excepted from furnishing items of information.*—Any person required to furnish any item of information under paragraph (b) or (c) of this section with respect to a foreign corporation may, if such item of information is furnished by another person having an equal or greater stock interest (measured in terms of value of such stock) in such foreign corporation, satisfy such requirement by filing a statement with his return on Form 959 indicating that such liability has been satisfied and identifying the return in which such item of information was included.

(f) *Meaning of terms.*—For purposes of this section—

(1) *Acquisition.*—Stock in a foreign corporation shall be considered acquired when a person has an unqualified right to receive such stock, even though such stock is not actually issued. For example, when under the law of a foreign country, all the necessary steps for incorporation are completed but stock in the cor-

poration will not be issued within 30 days, every United States citizen or resident who is an officer or a director of such corporation, provided a United States person has an interest of 5 percent or more in such corporation, and every such United States person shall, within 90 days of the date of incorporation, file the returns required under section 6046 and this section. In the case of a reorganization, new stock may be acquired, depending on the type of reorganization, whether or not any stock certificates are surrendered or exchanged or the designation of such stock is altered.

(2) *Reorganization.*—With respect to a foreign corporation, the term "reorganization" shall mean not only a transaction described in section 368(a)(1) and the regulations thereunder but also any other transaction or series of transactions which has the same effect.

(3) [Reserved] For further guidance, see § 1.6046-1T(f)(3).

(4) *Applicable Form 959.*—The Form 959 which shall be used for purposes of this section is Form 959. (Rev. Jan. 1963) or such subsequent revision of such form as may be in use at the time the liability to file a return on Form 959 arises.

(5) *Accounting period and taxable year.*—In the case of a specified foreign corporation (as defined in section 898), the taxable year of such corporation shall be treated as its annual accounting period.

(g) *Method of reporting.*—All amounts furnished in returns prescribed under this section shall be expressed in United States currency with a statement of the exchange rates used. All statements required to be submitted on or with returns under this section shall be rendered in the English language. For taxable years ending after December 31, 1994, with respect to returns filed after December 31, 1995, all amounts furnished under paragraph (c) of this section shall be expressed in United States dollars computed and translated in conformity with United States generally accepted accounting principles. Amounts furnished under paragraph (c)(3)(i) of this section shall also be furnished in the foreign corporation's functional currency as required on the form. Information described in paragraphs (b)(10) and (c)(3) of this section shall be submitted in such form or manner as the form shall prescribe. If an individual who is a United States person required to make a return with respect to a foreign corporation under section 6046 is entitled under a treaty to be treated as a nonresident of the United States, and if the individual claims this treaty benefit, and if there are no other United States persons that are required to furnish information under section 6046 with respect to the foreign corporation, then the individual may satisfy the requirements of paragraphs (b)(10), (11) and (12), (c)(3)(ii)(d), and (g) of this section by filing the audited foreign financial statements of the foreign corporation with the individual's return required under section 6046.

(h) *Actual ownership of stock.*—If any shareholder, referred to in this section, is not the actual owner of the stock of the foreign corporation, the information required under this section shall be furnished in the name of and by such actual owner. For example, in the case of stock held by a nominee, the information required under this section shall be furnished by the actual owner of such stock.

(i) *Constructive ownership of stock.*—(1) *In general.*—Stock owned directly or indirectly by or for a foreign corporation or a foreign partnership shall be considered as being owned proportionately by its shareholders or partners. Thus, any United States person who is a member of a nonresident foreign partnership which becomes a shareholder in a foreign corporation shall be considered to be a shareholder in such foreign corporation to the extent of his proportionate share in such partnership.

(2) *Members of family.*—An individual shall be considered as owning the stock owned directly or indirectly by or for his brothers and sisters (whether by the whole or half blood), his spouse, his ancestors, and his lineal descendants. However, when stock is treated as owned by an individual under the rule provided in this subparagraph, it shall not be treated as owned by him for the purpose of again applying such rule in order to make another the constructive owner of such stock. The provisions of this subparagraph may be illustrated by the following example:

Example. H, W, and HF are United States citizens. W, wife of H, owns 20 percent of the value of the outstanding stock of X, a foreign corporation. X Corporation owns 90 percent of the value of the outstanding stock of Y Corporation, a foreign corporation. Y Corporation becomes the owner of 50 percent of the value of the outstanding stock of each of two newly organized foreign corporations, M and N. In applying the "members of family" rule, H is considered to own 20 percent of the value of the outstanding stock of X Corporation, and 18 percent of the value of the outstanding stock of Y Corporation, and 9 percent of M Corporation and N Corporation. However, HF, the father of H, is not considered to own stock of X, Y, M, or N since his son, H, is not treated as the owner of such stock for purposes of again applying the "members of family" rule.

(j) *Time and place for filing return.*—(1) *Time for filing.*—Any return required by section 6046 and this section shall be filed on or before the 90th day after the date on which a United States citizen, resident, or person becomes liable to file such return under any provision of section 6046(a) and of paragraph (a), (b), or (c) of this section. With respect to returns filed after September 3, 1982, such return shall be filed on or before such later date (if any) as may be authorized by the return form. The Director of the Internal Revenue Service Center where the return is required to be filed is authorized to grant reasonable extensions of time for filing returns under section 6046 and this section in accordance with the applicable provisions of section 6081(a) and § 1.6081-1.

(2) *Place for filing.*—Returns required by section 6046 and this section shall be filed with the Internal Revenue Service Center designated in the instructions of the applicable form.

(k) *Penalties.*—(1) For criminal penalties for failure to file a return and filing a false or fraudulent return, see sections 7203, 7206, and 7207.

(2) For civil penalty for failure to file return, or failure to show information required on a return, under this section, see section 6679. [Reg. § 1.6046-1.]

☐ [*T.D.* 6623, 11-30-62. Amended by *T.D.* 6997, 1-17-69; *T.D.* 7322, 8-23-74; *T.D.* 7925, 12-12-83; *T.D.* 8573, 12-13-94; *T.D.* 8733, 10-6-97 and *T.D.* 9194, 4-6-2005.]

§ 1.6046-1T. Returns as to organization or reorganization of foreign corporations and as to acquisitions of their stock (temporary).

—(a) through (f)(2) [Reserved] For further guidance, see § 1.6046-1(a) through (f)(2).

(f)(3) *U.S. person.*—(i) *In general.*—For purposes of section 6046 and this section, the term *United States person* has the meaning assigned to it by section 7701(a)(30), except as provided in paragraphs (f)(3)(ii) and (iii) of this section.

(ii) *Special rule for individuals residing in certain possessions.*—With respect to individuals who are bona fide residents of Puerto Rico or any section 931 possession, as defined in § 1.931-1T(c)(1), the term United States person has the meaning assigned to it by § 1.957-3T.

(iii) *Special rule for certain nonresident aliens.*—An individual for whom an election under section 6013(g) or (h) is in effect shall, subject to the exceptions contained in paragraph (f)(3)(ii) of this section, be considered a United States person for purposes of section 6046 and this section.

(f)(4) through (k) [Reserved] For further guidance, see § 1.6046-1(f)(4) through (k).

(l) *Effective date.*—This section shall apply for taxable years ending after October 22, 2004. [Temporary Reg. § 1.6046-1T.]

☐ [*T.D.* 9194, 4-6-2005.]

§ 1.6046A-1. Return requirement for United States persons who acquire or dispose of an interest in a foreign partnership, or whose proportional interest in a foreign partnership changes substantially.

—(a) *Return requirement.*—(1) *General rule.*—If a United States person has a reportable event (as defined in paragraph (b)(1) of this section) during the person's tax year, then, except as provided in paragraph (f) of this section, the United States person is required to complete and file Form 8865, "Return of U.S. Persons With Respect To Certain Foreign Partnerships," containing the information described in paragraph (c) of this section.

(2) *Separate return for each partnership.*—If a United States person has a reportable event with respect to an interest in more than one foreign partnership, the United States person must file a separate Form 8865 for each foreign partnership.

(b) *Definitions.*—(1) *Reportable event.*—There are three categories of reportable events under section 6046A: acquisitions, dispositions, and changes in proportional interests.

(i) *Acquisitions.*—A United States person that acquires a foreign partnership interest has a reportable event if—

(A) The person did not own a ten-percent or greater direct interest in the partnership and as a result of the acquisition the person owns a ten-percent or greater direct interest in the partnership. For purposes of this paragraph (b)(1)(i)(A), an acquisition includes an increase in a person's direct proportional interest; or

(B) Subject to paragraph (b)(2) of this section, compared to the person's direct interest when the person last had a reportable event, after the acquisition the person's direct interest has increased by at least a ten-percent interest.

(ii) *Dispositions.*—A United States person that disposes of a foreign partnership interest has a reportable event if—

(A) The person owned a ten-percent or greater direct interest in the partnership before the disposition and as a result of the disposition the person owns less than a ten-percent direct interest. For purposes of this paragraph (b)(1)(ii)(A), a disposition includes a decrease in a person's direct proportional interest; or

(B) Subject to paragraph (b)(2) of this section, compared to the person's direct interest when the person last had a reportable event, after the disposition the person's direct interest has decreased by at least a ten-percent interest.

(iii) *Changes in proportional interests not otherwise reportable as acquisitions or dispositions under paragraph (b)(1)(i)(A) or (b)(1)(ii)(A) of this section.*—A United States person has a reportable event if, subject to paragraph (b)(2) of this section, compared to the person's direct proportional interest the last time the person had a reportable event, the person's direct proportional interest has increased or decreased by at least the equivalent of a ten-percent interest.

(2) *Special rule for foreign partnership interests owned on December 31, 1999.*—If a United States person owned a ten-percent or greater direct interest in a foreign partnership on December 31, 1999, then to determine whether the person has a reportable event under paragraph (b)(1)(i)(B), (b)(1)(ii)(B), or (b)(1)(iii) of this section, the comparison should be made to the person's direct interest on December 31, 1999. Once the person has a reportable event after December 31, 1999, future comparisons should be made by reference to the last reportable event.

(3) *Change in a proportional interest.*—A partner's proportional interest in a foreign partnership may change for a number of reasons, for example, the change may be caused by changes in other partners' interests resulting from a partner withdrawing from the partnership. A proportional change may also occur by operation of the partnership agreement, for example, if the partnership agreement provides that a partner's interest in profits will change on a set date or when the partnership has earned a specified amount of profits and one of those events occurs.

(4) *Ten-percent interest.*—Under section 6046A(d) and this section, a *ten-percent interest* in a foreign partnership, as described in section 6038(e)(3)(C) and the regulations thereunder, means an interest equal to ten percent of the capital interest in such partnership, an interest equal to ten percent of the profits interest in such partnership, or an interest to which ten percent of the deductions or losses of such partnership are allocated.

(5) *United States person.*—*United States person* means a person described in section 7701(a)(30).

(6) *Foreign partnership.*—*Foreign partnership* means any partnership that is a foreign partnership under sections 7701(a)(2) and (5).

(7) *Examples.*—The rules of paragraph (a) of this section and this paragraph (b) are illustrated by the following examples:

Example 1. Acquisition of an indirect interest. FP, a foreign partnership, has two partners, FC1 and FC2, both foreign corporations. FC1 owns a 40% interest in FP, and FC2 owns a 60% interest in FP. No United States person owns an interest in FP, either directly, or constructively under section 6038(e)(3)(C) and section 267(c). On January 1, 2001, US, a United States person and calendar year taxpayer, acquires by purchase 100% of FC2's stock. US has acquired an indirect interest of 60% in FP. See sections 6038(e)(3)(C) and 267(c)(1). However, US is not required to report the January 1, 2001 indirect acquisition under section 6046A. US did not own a 10% or greater direct interest in FP before the acquisition, and US does not own a 10% or greater direct interest as a result of the acquisition. (US must, however, comply with the reporting requirements under section 6038 (controlled foreign corporation and controlled foreign partnership reporting) with respect to FC2 and FP.)

Example 2. Acquisition of direct interests. (i) Assume the same facts as *Example 1*. In addition, on June 1, 2001, US purchases a 5% direct interest in FP from FC1. US did not own a 10% or greater direct interest in FP before the acquisition. After the acquisition, US does not own a direct interest of 10% or more. US owns a 10% or greater total interest (direct and indirect), but only a 5% direct interest. Therefore, US is not required to report the June 1, 2001, acquisition under section 6046A.

(ii) On September 1, 2001, US purchases a 7% direct interest in FP from FC1. The September 1, 2001 acquisition constitutes a reportable event under paragraph (b)(1)(i)(A) of this section. Before the September 1 acquisition, US did not own a 10% or greater direct interest in FP. After the September 1 acquisition, US owns a 12% direct interest, and therefore, as a result of the September 1 acquisition, US now owns a 10% or greater direct interest in FP. Consequently, US must report its September 1 acquisition under section 6046A on Form 8865 filed with US's 2001 income tax return.

(iii) On December 1, 2001, US acquires an additional 4% direct interest in FP from FC1, so that US's total direct interest has increased from 12% to 16%. This acquisition does not constitute a reportable event. Compared to US's direct interest when US last had a reportable event (12% on September 1, 2001), after acquiring the 4% interest US's direct interest has not increased by at least a 10% direct interest (i.e., its direct interest increased by only 4%). Therefore, US does not have to report the December 1, 2001, acquisition under section 6046A. On April 1, 2002, FC2 distributes a 6% direct interest in FP to US. US now owns a 22% direct interest in FP. Compared to US's direct interest when US last had a reportable event (12% on September 1, 2001), after the April 1 acquisition US's direct interest has increased by at least a 10% interest (12% to 22%). US must report the April 1, 2002 acquisition on a Form 8865 attached to US's 2002 income tax return.

Example 3. Change in proportional interest resulting from withdrawal of a partner. Assume the same facts as *Example 3.* In addition, on January 5, 2003, FC2 withdraws entirely from FP. As a result, the direct interests of US and FC1 in FP each increase by at least the equivalent of 10% interests. Compared to US's direct interest the last time US had a reportable event (22% on April 1, 2002), US's direct interest has increased by at least the equivalent of a ten percent interest. Therefore, US has had a reportable event pursuant to paragraph (b)(1)(iii) of this section, and US must report the change in its interest resulting from FC2's withdrawal from the partnership on US's Form 8865 filed with US's 2003 tax year income tax return.

Example 4. Change in proportional interest constituting an acquisition. FP is a foreign partnership that has no United States persons as direct or constructive partners. US is a United States person and a calendar year taxpayer. On January 1, 2001, US purchases an 8% direct interest in FP. US is not required to report this acquisition. US did not own a 10% or greater direct interest in FP, and US does not own a 10% or greater direct interest as a result of the acquisition. On March 1, 2001, FC, a foreign partner of FP, withdraws from FP, and as result, US's direct interest in FP increases by a 7% interest. The increase in US's direct interest is considered an acquisition of an interest under paragraph (b)(1)(i)(A) of this section. US did not own a 10% or greater direct interest in FP before FC withdrew, and as a result of the increase in US's direct interest because of FC's withdrawal from FP, US now owns a 10% or greater direct interest in FP. Therefore, US must report under section 6046A the increase in US's direct interest resulting from the withdrawal of FC from FP on Form 8865 filed with US's tax return for US's 2001 tax year.

(c) *Content of return.*—The Form 8865 that must be filed under paragraph (a)(1) of this section must contain the following information in such form and manner and to the extent that Form 8865 and its instructions prescribe—

(1) The name, address, and taxpayer identification number of the United States person required to file the return;

(2) Information about other persons (foreign or domestic) whose interests in the foreign partnership the person reporting under section 6046A is considered to own under section 6038(e)(3)(C) and section 267(c);

(3) Information about all foreign entities that were disregarded as entities separate from their owners under "301.7701-2 and 301.7701-3 of this chapter that were owned by the foreign partnership during the partnership's tax year ending with or within the tax year of the person filing Form 8865 pursuant to section 6046A;

(4) For each reportable event, the date of the event, the type of event (acquisition, disposition, or change in proportional interest), and the United States person's direct percentage interest in the foreign partnership immediately before and immediately after the event;

(5) The fair market value of the interest acquired or disposed of;

(6) Information about partnerships (foreign and domestic) in which the foreign partnership owned a direct interest, or a constructive interest of ten percent or more under sections section 267(c)(1) and (5) and the regulations thereunder, during the partnership's tax year ending with or within the tax year of the person filing Form 8865 pursuant to section 6046A; and

(7) Any other information required to be submitted by Form 8865 and its instructions.

(d) *Time and manner for filing returns.*—The Form 8865 must be filed with the timely filed (including extensions) income tax return of the United States person for the tax year in which the reportable event occurs. If the United States person is not required to file an income tax return for its tax year in which the reportable event occurs, but is required to file an information return for that year (for example, Form 1065, "U.S. Partnership Return of Income," or Form 990, "Return of Organization Exempt from Income Tax"), the United States person should attach the Form 8865 to its information return filed for that tax year.

(e) *Duplicate returns.*—If required by the instructions to Form 8865, a duplicate Form 8865 (including attachments and schedules) must also be filed.

(f) *Persons excepted from filing return.*—(1) *Section 6038B overlap.*—If a United States person acquires an interest in a foreign partnership as a result of a section 721 contribution required to be reported under section 6038B, and the person properly reports the contribution under section 6038B, then the United

States person is not required to report the acquisition of the partnership interest under section 6046A(a) should it constitute a reportable event under paragraph (b)(1) of this section. The acquisition will still constitute a reportable event for purposes of making future comparisons pursuant to paragraphs (b)(1)(i)(B), (b)(1)(ii)(B) and (b)(1)(iii) of this section. A person that fails to properly report the section 721 contribution under section 6038B and the regulations thereunder and that fails to properly report the acquisition of the partnership interest under section 6046A may be subject to the penalties applicable to a failure to comply with the requirements of section 6038B, as well as the penalties applicable for a failure to comply with the requirements of section 6046A. See paragraph (h) of this section for more information about the penalties for failure to comply with the requirements of section 6046A.

(2) *Trusts relating to state and local government employee retirement plans.*—The return requirement of section 6046A does not apply to trusts relating to state and local government employee retirement plans, unless the instructions to Form 8865 provide otherwise.

(3) *Reporting under this section not required of partnerships excluded from the application of subchapter K.*—The reporting requirements of this section will not apply to any United States person in respect of an eligible partnership as described in §1.761-2(a) in which that United States person is a partner, if such partnership has validly elected to be excluded from all of the provisions of subchapter K of chapter 1 of the Internal Revenue Code in the manner specified in §1.761-2(b)(2)(i), or is deemed to have elected to be excluded from all of the provisions of subchapter K of chapter 1 of the Internal Revenue Code in accordance with the provisions of §1.761-2(b)(2)(ii).

(4) *Exclusion for satellite organizations.*—The return requirement of section 6046A does not apply to the International Telecommunications Satellite Organization (or a successor organization) or the International Maritime Satellite Organization (or a successor organization).

(g) *Method of reporting.*—Except as otherwise provided on Form 8865, or the accompanying instructions, any amounts required to be reported under section 6046A and this section must be expressed in United States dollars, with a statement of the exchange rates used. All statements required on or with Form 8865 pursuant to this section must be in English.

(h) *Penalties for violating section 6046A.*—For penalties for violating section 6046A, see sections 6679 and 7203.

(i) *Statute of limitations.*—For exceptions to the limitations on assessment in the event of a failure to provide information under section 6046A, see section 6501(c)(8).

(j) *Effective date.*—This section applies to reportable events occurring after December 31, 1999. No reporting under section 6046A is required for reportable events occurring on or before December 31, 1999. [Reg. §1.6046A-1.]

☐ [*T.D.* 8851, 12-27-99.]

§301.6111-1T. Questions and answers relating to tax shelter registration (Temporary).—The following questions and answers relate to the tax shelter registration requirements of section 6111 of the Internal Revenue Code of 1954, as added by section 14-1(a) of the Tax Reform Act of 1984 (Pub. L. 98-369, 98 Stat. 678).

Table of Contents

The following table of contents is provided as part of these temporary regulations to help the reader locate relevant provisions. The headings are to be used only as a matter of convenience and have no substantive effect.

In general
Overview of tax shelter registration . . . A-1
Overview of applicable penalties . . . A-2
Effect of registration A-3
Tax shelter defined
Definition of tax shelter A-4
Tax shelter ratio
Definition of tax shelter ratio A-5
Deductions and credits represented as potentially allowable
Definition of amount of deductions and credits A-6
Definition of year A-7
Definition of explicit representation . . A-8
Definition of inferred representation . . A-9
Effect of qualified representation . . . A-10
Representation regarding interest deduction A-11
Representation regarding unintended events A-12
Investment Base
Definition of investment base A-13
Amounts eliminated from investment base A-14
Tax Shelter Ratio—Miscellaneous
Effect of different ratios for different investors A-15
Effect of alternate financing arrangements A-16
Investments subject to securities regulation
Federal law regulating securities . . . A-17
State law regulating securities A-18
Exemptions from federal securities registration A-19
Exemptions from state securities registration A-20
Substantial Investment
Definition of substantial investment . A-21

Reg. §1.6046A-1(f)(2)

Aggregation rules	A-22—A-23
Exceptions from tax shelter registration	
Investments excepted from tax shelter registration	A-24
Certain persons not treated as investors	A-24A
Persons required to register a tax shelter	
Tax shelter organizer	A-25—A-26
Principal organizer	A-27
Participant in the organization	A-28
Manager	A-29
Exception for certain unrelated persons	A-30
Sellers	A-31
Absence of representations by organizer	A-32
Exception for support services	A-33
Circumstances under which tax shelter organizers are required to register a tax shelter	
Principal organizer and a participant in the organization	A-34
Manager who has not signed designation agreement	A-35
Seller who has not signed designation agreement	A-36
Person acting in multiple capacities .	A-37
Designation agreement (designated organizer)	A-38
Person who has signed designation agreement	A-39
Registration—General Rules	
Date registration is required	A-40
Requirement to provide registration notice to sellers and others	A-41
Definition of sale of an interest . . .	A-42
Definition of offering for sale	A-43
No requirement to submit revised registration form	A-44—A-45
Effect of resale of an asset	A-46
When registration is complete	A-47
Separate forms required for certain aggregated investments	A-48
Applicability of section 7502	A-49
Required investor disclaimer	A-50
Furnishing tax shelter registration numbers to investors	
Who must furnish number	A-51
When number must be furnished . . .	A-52
Form required to furnish number . . .	A-53—A-54
Including the registration number on tax returns	
Requirement to include registration number on investor's return . . .	A-55—A-57
Projected income investments	
Special rules for projected income investments	A-57A
Definitions relating to projected income investments	A-57B—A-57D
Tax shelters ineligible for the special rules	A-57E
Consequences of bad faith or unreasonable projections	A-57F
When a tax shelter ceases to be a projected income investment . .	A-57G
Special rule for registration	A-57H
Special rule for furnishing registration number	A-57I
Special rule for including registration number on tax return	A-57J
Effective Dates	
Effective dates	A-58—A-60

In general

Q-1. What is tax shelter registration?

A-1. Tax shelter registration is a new provision of the Internal Revenue Code that affects organizers, sellers, investors and certain other persons associated with investments that are considered tax shelters. The new provision imposes the following three requirements. First, a tax shelter must be registered by the tax shelter organizer. (See A-4 of this section for the definition of a tax shelter. See A-25 through A-39 of this section for rules relating to tax shelter organizers. See A-26 of this section for rules regarding when the seller of an interest in a tax shelter is treated as the tax shelter organizer.) Registration is accomplished by filing a properly completed Form 8264 with the Internal Revenue Service. The Internal Revenue Service will assign a registration number to each tax shelter that is registered. Second, any person who sells or otherwise transfers an interest in a tax shelter must furnish the registration number of the tax shelter to the purchaser or transferee of the interest. (See A-51 through A-54 of this section for the time and manner in which the number must be furnished.) Third, any person who claims a deduction, loss, credit, or other tax benefit or reports any income from the tax shelter must report the registration number of the tax shelter on any return on which the deduction, loss, credit, benefit, or income is included. (See A-55 through A-57 of this section for rules relating to the reporting of tax shelter registration numbers.)

Q-2. Are penalties provided for failure to comply with the requirements of tax shelter registration?

A-2. Yes. Separate penalties are provided for failure to satisfy any of the requirements set forth in A-1 of this section. See A-1 of § 301.6707-1T for the penalty for failure to register a tax shelter and A-8 of § 301.6707-1T for the penalty for filing false or incomplete information with respect to the registration of a tax shelter. See A-12 of § 301.6707-1T for the penalty for failure to furnish the tax shelter registration number to purchasers or transferees.

Reg. § 301.6111-1T

See A-13 of §301.6707-1T for the penalty for failure to report the tax shelter registration number on a tax return on which a deduction, loss, credit, income, or other tax benefit is included. In addition, criminal penalties may be imposed for willful noncompliance with the requirements of tax shelter registration. See, for example, section 7203, relating to willful failure to supply information, and section 7206, relating to fraudulent and false statements.

Q-3. Does registration of a tax shelter with the Internal Revenue Service indicate that the Internal Revenue Service has reviewed, examined, or approved the tax shelter or the claimed tax benefits?

A-3. No. Moreover, any representation to prospective investors that states that a tax shelter is registered with the Internal Revenue Service (or that registration is being sought) must include a legend stating that registration does not indicate that the Internal Revenue Service has reviewed, examined or approved the tax shelter or any of the claimed tax benefits. (See A-50 of this section for the form and content of the legend.)

Tax shelter defined

Q-4. What investments are tax shelters that are required to be registered with the Internal Revenue Service?

A-4. A tax shelter is any investment that meets the following two requirements:

(I) The investment must be one with respect to which a person could reasonably infer, from the representations made or to be made in connection with any offer for sale of any interest in the investment, that the tax shelter ratio for any investor may be greater than 2 to 1 as of the close of any of the first 5 years ending after the date on which the investment is offered for sale.

(II) The investment must be (i) required to be registered under a federal or state law regulating securities, (ii) sold pursuant to an exemption from registration requiring the filing of a notice with a federal or state agency regulating the offering or sale of securities, or (iii) a substantial investment. An investment that satisfies these two requirements is considered a tax shelter for registration purposes regardless of whether it is marketed or customarily designated as a tax shelter. See A-5 of this section for the definition of tax shelter ratio. See A-17 and A-18 of this section for the definition of an investment required to be registered under a federal or state law regulating securities. See A-19 and A-20 of this section for the definition of an investment sold pursuant to an exemption from registration requiring the filing of a notice. See A-21 of this section for the definition of a substantial investment.

Reg. §301.6111-1T

Tax shelter ratio

Q-5. What does the term "tax shelter ratio" mean?

A-5. The term "tax shelter ratio" means, with respect to any year, the ratio that the aggregate amount of deductions and 200 percent of the credits that are or will be represented as potentially allowable to an investor under subtitle A of the Internal Revenue Code for all periods up to (and including) the close of such year, bears to the investment base for such investor as of the close of such year.

Deductions and credits represented as potentially allowable

Q-6. What do the terms "amount of deductions" and "credits" mean?

A-6. The term "amount of deductions" means the amount of gross deductions and other similar tax benefits potentially allowable with respect to the investment. The gross deductions are not to be offset by any gross income to be derived or potentially derived from the investment. Thus, the term "amount of deductions" is not equivalent to the net loss, if any, attributable to the investment. The term "credits" means the gross amount of credits potentially allowable with respect to the investment without regard to any possible tax liability resulting from the investment or any potential recapture of the credits.

Q-7. What does the term "year" mean for purposes of determining the tax shelter ratio?

A-7. The term "year" means the taxable year of a tax shelter, or if the tax shelter has no taxable year, the calendar year.

Q-8. Under what circumstances is a deduction or credit considered to be represented as being potentially allowable to an investor?

A-8. A deduction or credit is considered to be represented as being potentially allowable to an investor if any statement is made (or will be made) in connection with the offering for sale of an interest in an investment indicating that a tax deduction or credit is available or may be used to reduce federal income tax or federal taxable income. Representations of tax benefits may be oral or written and include those made at the time of the initial offering for sale of interests in the investment, such as advertisements, written offering materials, prospectuses, or tax opinions, and those that are expected to be made subsequent to the initial offering. Representations are not confined solely to statements regarding actual dollar amounts of tax benefits, but also include general representations that tax benefits are available with respect to an investment. Thus, for example, an advertisement stating that "purchase of restaurant includes trade fixtures (5-year write-off and investment tax credit)" constitutes an explicit representation of tax benefits.

Q-9. If a deduction or credit is not explicitly represented as being potentially allowable to an investor may it be inferred as a represented tax benefit that is includible in the tax shelter ratio?

A-9. Yes. Although some explicit representation concerning tax benefits is necessary before an investment may be considered a tax shelter, once an explicit representation is made (or will be made) regarding any tax benefit, all deductions or credits typically associated with the investment will be inferred to have been represented as potentially allowable. Thus, the tax shelter ratio will be determined with reference to those tax benefits that are explicitly represented as being potentially allowable as well as all other tax benefits that are typically associated with the investment. The amount of each deduction or credit that is includible in the tax shelter ratio, if not specifically represented as to amount, should be reasonably estimated based on representations of economic value or economic projections, if any, or on any other information available to the tax shelter organizer. Reasonable estimates of deductions or credits may take into account past experience with similar investments. Reasonable estimates must assume use of the most accelerated allowable basis for cost recovery deductions.

As an example of the application of this A-9, assume that an advertisement explicitly states that a building is eligible for the investment tax credit for rehabilitation of a certified historic structure, but makes no mention of cost recovery deductions, amortization deductions for construction period interest and taxes, real estate taxes after construction, ongoing maintenance expenses, or other deductions or credits typically associated with a building. Reasonable estimates of all such deductions and credits must be included with the investment tax credit explicitly represented in determining the tax shelter ratio associated with any investor's acquisition of an interest in the building.

Q-10. Does the fact that representations are made (or to be made) indicating that a deduction may be offset by income from the investment or that a deduction or credit may be subject to recapture or may be disallowed on audit affect the computation of the tax shelter ratio?

A-10. No. Deductions and credits represented as being potentially allowable are taken into account in computing the tax shelter ratio regardless of whether any qualifying statements are made.

Q-11. Is interest to be paid by an investor with respect to a debt obligation incurred in connection with the acquisition of an interest in the tax shelter included in the aggregate amount of deductions?

A-11. If a deduction for such interest is explicitly represented (or will be represented) as being potentially allowable, the interest is includible in the aggregate amount of the deductions. In addition, any interest to be paid with respect to a debt obligation the proceeds of which reduce the investment base (see A-14 of this section), regardless of whether a deduction for such interest is explicitly represented as being allowable, will be considered a deduction typically associated with the investment (see A-9 of this section). Accordingly, such interest will be considered to be represented as being potentially allowable and must be taken into account in computing the tax shelter ratio. If interest to be paid with respect to a debt obligation the proceeds of which do not reduce the investment base (see A-14 of this section) is not explicitly represented as being potentially allowable, however, such interest will not be considered typically associated with the investment and will not be taken into account in computing the tax shelter ratio.

Q-12. If representations are made that part or all of an amount invested in a tax shelter will be deductible upon the occurrence of an unintended event, will the deduction be included in the aggregate amount of deductions?

A-12. No. Thus, for example, if representations are made that a person's investment in a tax shelter may give rise to a loss deduction if the investment becomes worthless, the amount of the loss deduction will not be included in the aggregate amount of deductions and will not be taken into account in computing the tax shelter ratio. Similarly, if representations are made that the costs of acquiring oil and gas lease interests may be deductible if the lease is proved worthless by abandonment, the amount of any loss deduction will not be included in the aggregate amount of deductions.

Investment base

Q-13. What does the term "investment base" mean?

A-13. The term "investment base" means, with respect to any year (as defined in A-7 of this section), the cumulative amount of money and the adjusted basis of other property (reduced by any liability to which such other property is subject) that is unconditionally required to be contributed or paid directly to the tax shelter on or before the close of such year by an investor.

Q-14. What amounts must be eliminated from the investment base?

A-14. The investment base must be reduced by the following amounts:

(1) Any amount borrowed by the investor, even if borrowed on a recourse basis, from any person who participated in the organization, sale, or management of the investment or who

Reg. §301.6111-1T

has an interest (other than an interest as a creditor) in the investment ("a participating person") or from any person who is related (as defined in section 168(e)(4)) to a participating person, unless the amount is unconditionally required to be repaid by the investor before the close of the year for which the determination is being made. An amount will be considered unconditionally required to be repaid by the investor only if any offering material in which the borrowed amount is described and any agreement to be entered into between a participating (or related) person and the investor provide that the amount must be repaid (without exception) by the end of the year for which the determination is being made. An amount that is to be repaid only from earnings of the investment is not an amount that is unconditionally required to be repaid and is thus excluded from the investment base. In addition, an amount is not unconditionally required to be repaid if the amount will be (or is expected to be) reloaned to the investor during the 5-year period ending after the date the investment is offered for sale.

(2) Any amount borrowed by the investor, even if borrowed on a recourse basis, from any person, if the loan is arranged by a participating (or related) person, unless the amount is unconditionally required to be repaid by the investor before the close of the year for which the determination is being made. Any borrowing that is represented (orally or in writing) as being available from a specific source will be treated as arranged by a participating (or related) person, if the participating (or related) person provides a list of investors, or information relating to the investment, to the lender or otherwise informs the lender about the investment. However, in the case of an amount borrowed on a recourse basis, the mere fact that a lender who is actively and regularly engaged in the business of lending money obtained information relating to the investment, from a participating (or related) person, solely in response to a lender's request made in connection with such borrowing or a prior loan to the investment, a participating (or related) person, or an investor, will not, by itself, result in a determination that the loans are arranged by a participating (or related) person. Financing may be treated as arranged by a participating (or related) person regardless of whether a commitment to provide the financing is made by the lender to the participating or related person.

For example, assume that a tax shelter organizer represents that the purchase of an interest in a tax shelter may be financed with the proceeds of a revolving loan, and the tax shelter organizer provides investors with the names of several banks or other lending institutions to which the tax shelter organizer has provided information about the investment. Assume further that the information was not provided in response to requests from such lending institutions made in connection with prior loans. The proceeds of the revolving loan will be excluded from the investment base because the loan is not unconditionally required to be repaid and it is treated as having been arranged by the tax shelter organizer.

(3) Any amount borrowed, directly or indirectly, from a lender located outside the United States ("foreign-connected financing"), of which a participating (or related) person knows or has reason to know.

(4) Any amounts to be held for the benefit of investors in cash, cash equivalents, or marketable securities. An amount is to be held in cash equivalents if the amount is to be held in a checking account, savings account, mutual fund, certificate of deposit, book entry government obligation, or any other similar account or arrangement. Marketable securities are any securities that are part of an issue any portion of which is traded on an established securities market and any securities that are regularly quoted by brokers or dealers making a market.

(5) Any distributions (whether of cash or property) that will be made without regard to the income of the tax shelter, but only to the extent such distributions exceed the amount to be held as of the close of the year in cash, cash equivalents, or marketable securities.

Tax shelter ratio—Miscellaneous

Q-15. Does an investment satisfy the requirement in A-4(I) of this section ("the tax shelter ratio requirement") if it may be inferred from the representations made or to be made to investors that the tax shelter ratio for some, but not all, of the investors may be greater than 2 to 1 as of the close of any one of the first five years?

A-15. Yes. If the tax shelter ratio for any one investor may be greater than 2 to 1, the investment satisfies the tax shelter ratio requirement and is a tax shelter if it also meets the requirement in A-4 (II) of this section. Moreover, an investment will satisfy the tax shelter ratio requirement even if the tax shelter ratio for a single investor exceeds 2 to 1 as of the close of only one of the first five years.

For purposes of computing the tax shelter ratio for a year, all persons with interests in the investment are considered investors, except that general partners in a limited partnership will not be treated as investors in the partnership if the general partners' aggregate interest in each item of partnership income, gain, loss, deduction, and credit for such year is not expected to exceed 2 percent. In determining the general partners' interest in such items, limited partnership interests owned by general partners shall not be taken into account. For purposes other than the computation of the tax shelter ratio, however, all general partners will be treated as investors. Thus, for example, a general partner with a 1 percent interest in a limited partnership will be treated as an investor for the purpose of determining whether the partnership is a substantial investment.

Q-16. If a person could reasonably infer from the representations made or to be made about an investment that the tax shelter ratio for the investment may be greater than 2 to 1 under one arrangement for financing the purchase of an interest by an investor, but would be 2 to 1 or less under an alternative financing arrangement, does the investment satisfy the tax shelter ratio requirement of A-4(I) of this section?

A-16. Yes. An investment satisfies the tax shelter ratio requirement of A-4(I) of this section if a person could reasonably infer from the representations made or to be made that the tax shelter ratio for any person may be greater than 2 to 1 as of the close of any one of the first five years. The tax shelter ratio requirement is met if the tax shelter ratio may exceed 2 to 1 under any type of financing arrangement that is or will be represented as being available to investors.

Investments subject to securities regulation

Q-17. What is an investment that is required to be registered under a federal law regulating securities?

A-17. An investment required to be registered under a federal law regulating securities is any public offering of an investment that is required to be registered under the Securities Act of 1933 (1933 Act), the Investment Company Act of 1940, or any other federal law regulating securities. An investment is required to be registered under the 1933 Act, the Investment Company Act, or any other federal law regulating securities, if failure to register the investment would result in a violation of the applicable federal law, whether or not the investment has in fact been registered and, if proper notice has not been filed, whether or not the investment could have been sold pursuant to an exemption listed in A-19 of this section if such notice had been filed.

Q-18. What is an investment required to be registered under a state law regulating securities?

A-18. An investment required to be registered under a state law regulating securities is any investment required to be registered under a blue sky law or other similar state statute regulating securities. The term "state" includes the 50 states, the District of Columbia, and possessions of the United States.

Q-19. What is an investment sold pursuant to an exemption from registration requiring the filing of a notice with a federal agency regulating the offering or sale of securities?

A-19. An investment sold pursuant to an exemption from registration requiring the filing of a notice with such a federal agency is any investment that is sold pursuant to an exemption from registration requiring the filing or submission of a notice or other document with the Securities and Exchange Commission or any other federal agency regulating the offering or sale of securities, including the following exemptions (and applicable filing):

(1) Regulation A, as promulgated under section (3)(b) of the 1933 Act (Form 1(A)),

(2) Regulation B, as promulgated under section 3(b) of the 1933 Act (Schedules A through F),

(3) Regulation D, as promulgated under sections (3)(b) and 4(2) of the 1933 Act (Form D), and

(4) Any other statutory or regulatory exemption from registration requiring the filing or submission of a notice or other document.

Q-20. What is an investment sold pursuant to an exemption from registration requiring the filing of a notice with a state agency regulating the offering or sale of securities?

A-20. An investment sold pursuant to an exemption from registration requiring the filing of a notice with such a state agency is any investment sold pursuant to an exemption under a blue sky law or other similar state statutory or regulatory scheme that requires the filing or submission of a notice or other document with such a state agency. See A-18 of this section for the definition of state.

Substantial investments

Q-21. What is a substantial investment?

A-21. An investment is a substantial investment if the aggregate amount that may be offered for sale to all investors exceeds $250,000 and 5 or more investors are expected. The aggregate amount offered for sale is the aggregate amount to be received from the sale of interests in the investment and includes all cash, the fair market value of all property contributed, and the principal amount of all indebtedness received in exchange for interests in the investment, regardless of whether the proceeds of the indebtedness are included in the investment base under A-14 of this section.

For purposes of determining whether 5 or more investors are expected in an investment involving real property (and related personal property) that is used as a farm (as defined in section 2032A(e)(4)) for farming purposes (as defined in section 2032A(e)(5)), interests in the investment expected to be held by a husband and wife, their children and parents, and the spouses of their children (or any of them) will be treated as if the interests were to be held by

Reg. §301.6111-1T

one investor. Thus, for example, interests in a farm that are offered to two brothers and their wives would be treated as interests offered to one investor. Such an investment could be a substantial investment only if four or more persons who were not members of the family were expected to be investors in the farm.

Q-22. Will an investment be considered a substantial investment if the investment involves a number of parts each including fewer than 5 investors or an aggregate amount of $250,000 or less?

A-22. Yes, under the circumstances described in this A-22. For purposes of determining whether investments are parts of a substantial investment, similar investments offered by the same person or related persons (as defined in section 168(e)(4)) are aggregated together. Investments are considered similar if they involve similar principal business assets and similar plans or arrangements. Investments that include no business assets will be considered similar if they involve similar plans or arrangements.

Similar investments are aggregated solely for the purpose of determining whether investments involving fewer than 5 investors or an aggregate amount of $250,000 or less are substantial investments. For this purpose, similar investments are aggregated even though some, but not all, of the investments are (i) required to be registered under a federal or state law regulating securities or are sold pursuant to an exemption from securities registration requiring the filing of a notice with a federal or state agency regulating the offering or sale of securities (*i.e.*, required to be registered as tax shelters whether or not a substantial investment) or (ii) substantial investments without regard to aggregation.

Assume, for example, that a person develops similar arrangements involving 8 different partnerships, each investing in a separate but similar asset (such as a separate master recording or separate piece of similar real estate), each with a different general partner and each with 3 different limited partners. Assume further that the arrangements of all of the partnerships are similar. These partnerships involving similar arrangements and similar assets would be aggregated together. Thus, if each partner is expected to invest $11,000, there will be 32 investors (1 general partner plus 3 limited partners times 8 partnerships) and an aggregate investment of $352,000 (32 partners times $11,000). Accordingly, each partnership will constitute part of a substantial investment. If representations are made that $1,000 in tax credits and $3,000 in deductions are available to each limited partner in the first year and $10,000 of the cash invested was expected to be the proceeds of a loan arranged by the organizer, the tax shelter ratio as of the close of the first year (assuming there are no deductions or credits typically associated with such investment, as described in A-9 of this section) would be 5 to 1 ($5,000 in total tax benefits and $1,000 investment base). Accordingly, the organizer would be required to register the partnerships with the Internal Revenue Service.

Q-23. If an investment involving fewer than 5 investors or an aggregate amount of $250,000 or less is offered for sale and, at the time of the offering, it is not known (and there is no reason to know) that subsequent similar investments will be offered by the person who made the first offering (or a related person), will subsequent similar investments offered by that person (or a related person) be aggregated with the first investment for purposes of determining whether the investments constitute a substantial investment?

A-23. No. However, a tax shelter organizer will be presumed to have known of any similar investments (as defined in A-22 of this section) offered during the 12 months following the first offering of an investment.

Exceptions from tax shelter registration

Q-24. Are there any investments that will not be subject to tax shelter registration even if they satisfy the requirements of a tax shelter (as defined in A-4 of this section)?

A-24. Yes. The following investments are not subject to tax shelter registration:

(1) Sales of residences primarily to persons who are expected to use the residences as their principal place of residence,

(2) Sales or leases of tangible personal property (other than master sound recordings, motion picture or television films, videotapes, lithograph plates, or other property relating to a literary, musical, or artistic composition) by the manufacturer (or a member of an affiliated group, within the meaning of section 1502, including the manufacturer) of the property primarily to persons who are expected to use the property in their principal active trade or business (see, however, A-32 and A-46 of this section for the additional rules applicable to a purchaser of property described in this A-24 who organizes an investment involving the property),

(3) Any other investment as specified by the Secretary in a rule-related notice published in the Federal Register.

Q-24A. Under what other circumstances are particular sales or leases of tangible personal property to certain persons or the performance of particular services for certain persons exempt from tax shelter registration?

A-24A. A person who, in the ordinary course of a trade or business, sells or leases tangible personal property (other than collectibles (as defined in section 408(m)(2)), master sound recordings, motion picture or television films, videotapes, lithograph plates, or other property that includes or relates to a literary, musical or artistic composition) to a purchaser or lessee who is reasonably expected to use the property either for a personal use or in the purchaser's or lessee's principal active trade or business is not required for any purpose to treat such a purchaser or lessee as an investor in a tax shelter. Property may be reasonably expected to be used by a purchaser or lessee for personal use only if sold or leased to the purchaser or lessee in a quantity that is customary for such use. Similarly, a person who performs services for another person in connection with the principal active trade or business of the recipient of the services or for the recipient's personal use is not required to treat the recipient as an investor in a tax shelter. Persons who are not reasonably expected to use property or services either in their principal active trade or business or for personal use must be treated as tax shelter investors in the event the sales, leases, or performance of services otherwise constitute a tax shelter.

Assume, for example, that an organizer forms Z corporation to feed cattle and to provide services in connection with the cattle feeding operations. Z will agree to serve customers with a minimum of 200 head of cattle. The fee for the services is $20 per head. Feed for the cattle will cost $280 per head. Z represents that the service fee and the cost of the feed may be financed by $5,000 of cash and $55,000 of proceeds of a revolving recourse note that Z has arranged to be available. Z provides its services to 100 customers. Ninety-five of the customers are persons whose principal active trade or business is reasonably expected to be farming (as defined in section 464(e)(1)). Five of the customers are not reasonably expected to engage in farming as their principal active trade or business. Although all the individual investments involve similar principal business assets and similar plans or arrangements, only the 5 customers who are not reasonably expected to be in the principal active trade or business of farming will be treated as investors in a tax shelter and aggregated to determine whether a substantial investment exists. Thus, there will be 5 investors and an aggregate investment of $300,000. If representations are made that the service fee and the cost of the feed are tax deductible, the tax shelter ratio (assuming there are no deductions or credits typically associated with such an investment, as described in A-9 of this section) would be 12 to 1 ($60,000 in total tax benefits and $5,000 investment base) and the organizer would be required to register the five aggregated feeding arrangements as a tax shelter. The registration number of the tax shelter must be provided to the five customers treated as investors in the tax shelter, but would not be required to be furnished to the customers whose principal active trade or business is reasonably expected to be farming.

Persons required to register a tax shelter.

Q-25. Who has the legal obligation to register a tax shelter?

A-25. A tax shelter organizer is obligated to register the tax shelter.

Q-26. What is the definition of tax shelter organizer?

A-26. Several categories of persons may be tax shelter organizers. In general, the term tax shelter organizer means a person principally responsible for organizing a tax shelter. If a person principally responsible for organizing a tax shelter has not registered the tax shelter by the day on which interests in the shelter are first offered for sale, any other person who participated in the organization of the tax shelter will be treated as a tax shelter organizer. If neither a person principally responsible for organizing the tax shelter nor any other person who participated in the organization of tax shelter has registered the tax shelter by the day on which interests in the tax shelter are first offered for sale, then any person who participates in the management of the tax shelter at a time when the tax shelter is not registered will be treated as a tax shelter organizer. Finally, if a person participates in the sale of a tax shelter at a time when the person knows or has reason to know that a tax shelter has not been registered, that person will be treated as a tax shelter organizer. See A-38 of this section for rules relating to the execution of an agreement among persons who may be treated as tax shelter organizers to designate one person to register a tax shelter.

Q-27. Who is a person principally responsible for organizing a tax shelter?

A-27. A person principally responsible for organizing a tax shelter ("principal organizer") is any person who discovers, creates, investigates, or initiates the investment, devises the business or financial plans for the investment, or carries out those plans through negotiations or transactions with others.

Q-28. What constitutes participation in the organization of a tax shelter?

A-28. Participation in the organization of a tax shelter includes the performance of any act (directly or through an agent) related to the establishment of the tax shelter, including the following:

(1) Preparation of any document establishing the tax shelter (for example, articles of incorporation, a trust instrument, or a partnership agreement);

Reg. §301.6111-1T

(2) Preparation of any document in connection with the registration (or exemption from registration) of the tax shelter with any federal, state, or local government body;

(3) Preparation of a prospectus, offering memorandum, financial statement, or other statement describing the tax shelter;

(4) Preparation of a tax or other legal opinion relating to the tax shelter;

(5) Preparation of an appraisal relating to the tax shelter;

(6) Negotiation or other participation on behalf of the tax shelter in the purchase of any property relating to the tax shelter.

Q-29. What constitutes participation in the management of a tax shelter?

A-29. Participation in the management of a tax shelter includes managing the assets of the tax shelter, directing the business activity of the tax shelter, or, depending on the form of the tax shelter, acting as a general partner who actively participates in the management of a partnership, a trustee of a trust, a director or an officer of a corporation (including a corporate general partner of a partnership), or performing activities similar to those performed by such a general partner, a trustee, a director, or an officer.

Q-30. Will the performance of any act described in A-27 through A-29 of this section constitute participation in the organization or management of a tax shelter if the person performing the act is unrelated to the tax shelter (or any principal organizer of the tax shelter) and does not participate in the entrepreneurial risks or benefits of the tax shelter?

A-30. No. The performance of an act described in A-27 through A-29 of this section will not constitute participation in the organization or management of a tax shelter unless the person performing the act is related to the tax shelter (or a principal organizer of the tax shelter) or the person participates in the entrepreneurial risks or benefits of the tax shelter. A person will be considered related to a tax shelter if the person is related to the tax shelter or a principal organizer of the tax shelter within the meaning of section 168(e)(4) or is employed by the tax shelter or a principal organizer of the tax shelter or has an interest (other than an interest as a creditor) in the tax shelter. A person will be considered a participant in the entrepreneurial risks or benefits of a tax shelter if the person's compensation for performing an act described in A-27 through A-29 of this section is contingent on any matter relating to the tax shelter (*e.g.,* the compensation is based in whole or in part upon (i) whether interests in the tax shelter are actually sold or (ii) the number or value of the units in the tax shelter that are sold), or if the person will receive an interest in the tax shelter as part or all of the person's compensation.

For example, assume that A forms Z partnership, a tax shelter for which registration is required. Z hires the X law firm, none of the partners of which is related to the tax shelter, to prepare the documents necessary to register the offering of Z securities with the Securities and Exchange Commission. X charges $100 an hour for its services in connection with the preparation of the necessary documents, and payment of the fee is not contingent. X will not be treated as a participant in the organization of the tax shelter. If, however, X were to charge a fee equal to 1 percent of the value of the units in the tax shelter that are sold, X would be considered a participant in the organization of the shelter.

As another example, assume that individual C is an attorney employed by W corporation, the corporate general partner and principal organizer of Z, and that C prepares the documents necessary to register the tax shelter with the Securities and Exchange Commission. C will be treated as having participated in the organization of the tax shelter regardless of the way in which C's compensation is structured, because C, as an employee, is related to the principal organizer of the tax shelter.

Q-31. What constitutes participation in the sale of a tax shelter?

A-31. Participation in the sale of a tax shelter includes any marketing activities (directly or through an agent) with respect to an investment, including the following:

(1) Direct contact with a prospective purchaser of an interest, or with a representative or agent of a prospective purchaser, but only if the contact relates to the possible purchase of an interest in the tax shelter;

(2) Solicitation of investors using the mail, telephone, or other means, or by placing an advertisement for the tax shelter in a newspaper, magazine, or other publication or medium;

(3) Instructing or advising salespersons regarding the tax shelter or sales presentations.

Q-32. May persons be treated as tax shelter organizers if such persons do not make any representations of tax benefits to investors?

A-32. Yes. If a person described in A-26 of this section knows or has reason to know that representations of tax benefits have been made, that person may be treated as a tax shelter organizer. For example, a participant in the sale of a tax shelter may know or have reason to know that representations of tax benefits have been made by the principal organizer or others who participate in the organization of the tax shelter. In addition, a person who acquires property from a manufacturer in a transaction exempt from tax shelter registration under A-24 of this section and who organizes an investment involving the property may know or have reason to know of any representation of tax benefits made by the manufacturer.

Q-33. If a person performs support services such as typing, photocopying, or printing for a tax shelter (or a tax shelter organizer) or performs other ministerial functions for the tax shelter (or a tax shelter organizer), may the person be considered to have participated in the organization, management, or sale of the tax shelter?

A-33. No. Merely performing support services or ministerial functions will not be considered participation in the organization, management, or sale of a tax shelter.

Circumstances under which tax shelter organizers are required to register a tax shelter

Q-34. When is a principal organizer or a person who participates in the organization of a tax shelter required to register a tax shelter?

A-34. A principal organizer or a person who participates in the organization of a tax shelter (*i.e.*, a person who could be treated as a tax shelter organizer within the meaning of A-26 of this section) is required to register the tax shelter by the day on which the first offering for sale of interests in the tax shelter occurs, unless the person has signed a designation agreement pursuant to A-38 of this section. If a group of persons who could be treated as tax shelter organizers has signed a designation agreement pursuant to A-38 of this section, the designated organizer is required to register the tax shelter by the day on which the first offering for sale of interests in the tax shelter occurs. See A-39 of this section for additional rules applicable to tax shelter organizers (other than a designated organizer) who have signed a designation agreement.

Q-35. When is a person who participates in the management of a tax shelter ("manager") required to register a tax shelter?

A-35. A manager who has not signed a designation agreement pursuant to A-38 of this section must register the tax shelter if the manager participates in the management of the tax shelter on or after the first offering for sale of interests in the tax shelter at a time when the tax shelter has not been properly registered (*i.e.*, the manager is treated as a tax shelter organizer within the meaning of A-26 of this section). Such a manager must register the tax shelter by the day on which the first offering for sale of interests in the tax shelter occurs, or by the day on which the manager's participation in the management of the tax shelter commences, whichever is later. See A-39 of this section for rules applicable to a manager who has signed a designation agreement.

Q-36. When is a person who participates in the sale of a tax shelter ("seller") required to register the tax shelter?

A-36. A seller who has not signed a designation agreement pursuant to A-38 of this section must register the tax shelter if the seller participates in the sale of the tax shelter at a time when the seller knows or has reason to know that the tax shelter has not been properly registered (*i.e.*, the seller is treated as a tax shelter organizer within the meaning of A-26 of this section). A seller who has not signed a designation agreement will be deemed to have reason to know that the tax shelter has not been properly registered if the seller does not receive a copy of the Internal Revenue Service tax shelter registration notice containing the registration number within the 30-day period after the seller first offers interests in the tax shelter for sale. A seller must register the tax shelter as soon as practicable after the seller first knows or has reason to know that the tax shelter has not been properly registered. See A-39 of this section for rules applicable to a seller who has signed a designation agreement.

Q-37. When is a person who acts in more than one capacity with respect to a tax shelter required to register the shelter?

A-37. A person who acts in more than one capacity with respect to a tax shelter (*i.e.*, as two or more of the following: principal organizer, participant in the organization, manager, or seller) must register the tax shelter by the earliest day on which a tax shelter organizer acting in any of the person's several capacities would be required to register the tax shelter.

Q-38. May a group of persons who could be treated as tax shelter organizers under A-26 of this section designate one person to register the tax shelter?

A-38. Yes. A group of persons who could be treated as tax shelter organizers under A-26 of this section may enter into a written agreement designating one person as the tax shelter organizer responsible for registering the tax shelter ("designated organizer"). The designated organizer should ordinarily be a person principally responsible for organizing the tax shelter, but may be any person who participates in the organization of the tax shelter. Although persons who participate only in the sale or management of a tax shelter may sign a designation agreement, they may not be the designated organizer. In addition, the designated organizer may not be a person who is resident in a country other than the United States. Any person who signs a designation agreement, other than the designated organizer, will not be liable for failing to register the tax shelter and will not be subject to a penalty, even if the designated organizer fails to register the tax shelter, un-

Reg. §301.6111-1T

less the person fails to register the tax shelter when such registration is required under A-39 of this section. See A-7 of § 301.6707-1T for additional rules relating to the reasonable cause exception applicable to persons who sign a designation agreement.

Q-39. Is a tax shelter organizer who has signed a designation agreement and who is not the designated organizer required to register the tax shelter under any circumstances?

A-39. Yes. If a tax shelter organizer who has signed a designation agreement pursuant to A-38 of this section knows or has reason to know on or after the day on which the first offering for sale of interests in a tax shelter occurs that the designated organizer failed to register the tax shelter, such tax shelter organizer must register the tax shelter as soon as practicable after he first knows or has reason to know of the failure. A tax shelter organizer who has signed a designation agreement is deemed to have reason to know that the designated organizer has failed to register the tax shelter if the tax shelter organizer does not receive a copy of the Internal Revenue Service registration notice containing the registration number from the designated organizer within the 60-day period after the day on which the first offering for sale of interests in the tax shelter occurs (or the person signs the designation agreement, if later). See A-41 of this section for the requirement that the designated organizer provide a copy of the registration notice and number to persons who have signed the designation agreement.

Registration—General Rules

Q-40. By what date must a tax shelter be registered?

A-40. A tax shelter must be registered not later than the day on which the first offering for sale of an interest in the tax shelter occurs.

Q-41. Is a tax shelter organizer (including a designated organizer) who registers a tax shelter responsible for performing any act with respect to tax shelter registration other than registering the tax shelter?

A-41. Yes. A tax shelter organizer (including a designated organizer) who registers a tax shelter must provide a copy of the Internal Revenue Service registration notice, containing the registration number within 7 days after the notice is received from the Internal Revenue Service to the principal organizer (if a different person) and to any persons who the tax shelter organizer knows or has reason to know are participating in the sale of interests in the tax shelter (if such persons begin to participate after the registration number is received, they must be provided the notice within 7 days after they commence their participation). In addition, a designated organizer must provide a copy of the notice within 7 days after it is received to all persons who have signed the designation agreement.

Q-42. What is the sale of an interest in a tax shelter?

A-42. The sale of an interest in a tax shelter includes the sale of property, or any interest in property, the entry into a leasing arrangement, a consulting, management or other agreement for the performance of services, or the sale or entry into any other plan, investment, or arrangement.

Q-43. What does the term "offering for sale" mean?

A-43. The term "offering for sale" means making any representation, whether oral or written, relating to participation in a tax shelter as an investor. The term includes any advertisement relating to the tax shelter and any mail, telephonic, or other contact with prospective investors. A representation relating to participation in a tax shelter will be considered an offering for sale of an interest in the tax shelter even though there is included in the representation an explicit statement that the representation does not constitute an offer to sell or a solicitation of an offer to buy an interest in the tax shelter. In determining whether an offering for sale of an interest has occurred, federal and state laws regulating securities are not controlling.

Q-44. After a tax shelter has been registered, must it be registered again each year that it continues to be offered for sale?

A-44. No. Registration is effective for the year in which first accomplished and all subsequent years.

Q-45. If the facts relating to a tax shelter change after the tax shelter has been registered, must the tax shelter be registered again or must an amended application for registration be filed by the tax shelter organizer?

A-45. No. The tax shelter organizer, however, is permitted to file an amended application if a material change in facts occurs after the initial registration. A material change in facts is—

(1) A change in the identifying information relating to the tax shelter or tax shelter organizer,

(2) The acquisition or construction of a principal asset not reported on the initial application for registration,

(3) A change in the method of financing a minimum investment unit, or

(4) A change in the principal business activity.

In addition, a change in any tax shelter ratio reported on the initial application for registration that increases or decreases the reciprocal of the tax shelter ratio (*i.e.,* the fraction in which the amount of the applicable investment base is the numerator and the amount of the applicable deductions and credits is the denominator) by 50 percent or more is a material change in facts. For example, if the tax shelter ratio increases from 2 to 1 to 4 to 1, the reciprocal of the tax shelter ratio decreases from $\frac{1}{2}$ to $\frac{1}{4}$, a 50-percent decrease. Similarly, if the tax shelter ratio decreases from 6 to 1 to 4 to 1, the reciprocal of the tax shelter ratio increases from $\frac{1}{6}$ to $\frac{1}{4}$, a 50-percent increase. In either case, there is a material change in facts and an amended application could be filed.

Q-45A. What information should be included on an amended application for registration?

A-45A. The tax shelter organizer must include the identifying information requested on Form 8264, Application for Registration of a Tax Shelter, and the tax shelter registration number that has been assigned to the tax shelter. In addition, the tax shelter organizer should include any other information requested on Form 8264 (1) that has changed since the tax shelter was registered, or (2) that the tax shelter organizer did not know at the time the tax shelter was registered but has learned of since the registration.

For example, assume that A organizes partnership L, a blind pool that will invest in real estate. Before the real estate is identified or acquired, interests in L will be offered to the public in an offering that must be registered with the Securities and Exchange Commission. Although A does not know what real estate L will acquire and therefore is unable to calculate the tax shelter ratio with certainty, A concludes (based on representations made or to be made) that the tax shelter ratio will exceed 2 to 1 as to some of the investors. Accordingly, A registers L as a tax shelter. A attaches a statement to the application for registration, explaining that L is a blind pool organized to invest in real estate, but that L has not yet acquired any real estate. In addition, A attaches a statement explaining that although the tax shelter ratio is expected to exceed 2 to 1, A cannot compute the tax shelter ratio with certainty because L has not yet acquired any real estate. Several months after L is registered, L acquires a shopping center. A may file an amended application for registration. In addition to reporting the identifying information and the tax shelter registration number on the amended application, A should report the shopping center as the principal asset and the recomputed tax shelter ratio.

As another example, assume that C organizes a limited partnership that is a tax shelter. On the application for registration, C reports that the tax shelter ratio is 2.2 to 1. After the partnership has been registered, C finds that the partnership is unable to attract sufficient investors. To make investing in the partnership more attractive, C decides to offer financing for the purchase of interests in the partnership. As a result of the change in financing, the tax shelter ratio will be 5 to 1. Because there is a change in financing and a change in the tax shelter ratio that decreases the reciprocal of the tax shelter ratio by 50 percent or more, C may file an amended application for registration. In addition to reporting the identifying information and the tax shelter registration number on the amended application, C should report the recomputed tax shelter ratio and information relating to the change in financing.

Q-46. If assets constituting a tax shelter are sold ("original sale") and, subsequently, either the assets or interests in the assets are offered for sale by the purchaser ("resale"), must the purchaser file a new application for registration if the resale is an offering or sale of interests in a tax shelter?

A-46. If the resale constitutes a tax shelter, the purchaser must file a new application for registration, unless the tax shelter organizer with respect to the original sale is also the tax shelter organizer with respect to the resale and the facts pertaining to the resale were reflected in the application for registration filed with respect to the original sale. For example, assume that A intends to sell a building with an estimated fair market value of $2.5 million to a group of 5 investors (*i.e.,* a substantial investment, as defined in A-21 of this section). A also intends to make representations of tax benefits attributable to an investment in the building. Based on these representations and the investment base, the tax shelter ratio attributable to an investment in the building may be greater than 2 to 1. A therefore files an application for registration relating to the building with the Internal Revenue Service. The Internal Revenue Service issues a registration number for the investment, and A furnishes the registration number to each of the 5 investors in accordance with A-53 of this section. In an unrelated transaction, the 5 investors decide to syndicate the building and to offer interests in the syndicate to approximately 500 investors. In connection with this offer, the investors expect to make representations concerning tax benefits with respect to the syndication. If based on these representations and the investment base, the tax shelter ratio may be greater than 2 to 1 for an investor in the syndicate, the 5 investors must file an application for registration for the syndicate before interests in the syndicate may be offered for sale. The investors in the syndicate must be furnished with the new registration number and not the registration number issued with respect to A. On the other hand, if the original sale and the syndication were part of A's plan to sell interests in the building, A is

Reg. §301.6111-1T

a tax shelter organizer with respect to the syndication. If the facts pertaining to the syndication were reflected on A's application for registration with respect to the original sale, a second application for registration would not be required with respect to the syndication. However, the investors in the syndicate would have to be furnished with the tax shelter registration number issued to A.

Q-47. When is a tax shelter considered registered?

A-47. A tax shelter is considered registered when a properly completed Form 8264, Application for Registration of a Tax Shelter, is filed with the appropriate Internal Revenue Service Center. See A-7 of § 301.6111-2T for rules relating to the information required to be included on the form, and A-8 of § 301.6707-1T for rules relating to the penalty for filing incomplete information.

Q-48. Must a person registering a tax shelter that is a substantial investment only by reason of an aggregation of multiple investments under A-22 of this section complete a separate Form 8264 for each investment constituting part of the substantial investment?

A-48. A separate Form 8264 must be completed for each investment that differs from the other investments in a substantial investment with respect to any of the following:

(1) Principal asset,

(2) Accounting methods,

(3) Federal or state agencies with which the investment is registered or with which an exemption notice is filed,

(4) Methods of financing the purchase of an interest in the investment,

(5) Tax shelter ratio.

Such aggregated investments, however, are part of a single tax shelter.

Q-49. Do the rules of section 7502 of the Internal Revenue Code, regarding timely mailing, apply to the filing of registration forms?

A-49. Yes.

Q-50. After a tax shelter has been registered, may representations that the investment has been registered with the Internal Revenue Service be made to potential investors?

A-50. Investors may be informed that the investment has been registered with the Internal Revenue Service. Investors also must be informed, however, that registration does not imply that the Internal Revenue Service has reviewed, examined, or approved the investment or the claimed tax benefits. The disclaimer must be substantially in the form provided below:

Issuance of a registration number does not indicate that this investment or the claimed tax benefits have been reviewed, examined, or approved by the Internal Revenue Service.

See A-53 of this section for rules relating to the legend that must be included on any statement on which the tax shelter registration number is furnished to investors.

Furnishing tax shelter registration numbers

Q-51. Who must furnish investors in a tax shelter with the registration number of the tax shelter?

A-51. Any person who sells (or otherwise transfers) an interest in a tax shelter is required to furnish the registration number assigned to that tax shelter to each person who purchases (or otherwise acquires) an interest in that tax shelter from the seller or transferor. For example, X, a tax shelter organizer, sells an interest in a tax shelter to A. One year later A sells A's interest in the shelter to B. X must furnish the tax shelter registration number to A, and A must furnish the number to B. If B sells or otherwise transfers the interest (by gift, for example), B must furnish the number to the purchaser or transferee of B's interest in the tax shelter.

Q-52. When must the registration number be furnished to purchasers of interests in the tax shelter?

A-52. The person who sells (or otherwise transfers) an interest in a tax shelter must furnish the registration number to the purchaser (or transferee) at the time of sale (or transfer) of the interest (or, if later, within 20 days after the seller or transferor receives the registration number). If the registration number is not furnished at the time of the sale (or other transfer), the seller (or transferor) must furnish the statement described in A-54 to the purchaser (or transferee) at the time of the sale (or other transfer). If interests in a tax shelter were sold before September 1, 1984, all investors who acquired their interests in the tax shelter before September 1, 1984, must be furnished with the registration number of the tax shelter by December 31, 1984. The registration number will be considered furnished to the investor if it is mailed to the investor at the last address of the investor known to the person required to furnish the number.

Q-53. How is a seller or transferor of an interest in a tax shelter required to furnish the registration number to investors?

A-53. The person who sells (or otherwise transfers) an interest in a tax shelter must furnish the registration number of the tax shelter to the purchaser (or transferee) on a written statement. The written statement shall show the name, registration number, and taxpayer identification number of the tax shelter, and include a prominent legend in bold and conspicuous type stating that the registration number must be included on any return on which the investor claims any deduction, loss, credit, or other tax benefit, or reports any income, by reason of the tax shelter. The statement must also include a prominent legend in bold and conspicuous type stating that the issuance of the registration number does not indicate that the Internal Revenue Service has reviewed, examined, or approved the investment or the claimed tax benefits. The statement shall be substantially in the form provided below:

You have acquired an interest in [name and address of tax shelter] whose taxpayer identification number is [if any]. The Internal Revenue Service has issued [name of tax shelter] the following tax shelter registration number: [Number]

You must report this registration number to the Internal Revenue Service, if you claim any deduction, loss, credit, or other tax benefit or report any income by reason of your investment in [name of tax shelter].

You must report the registration number (as well as the name, and taxpayer identification number of [name of tax shelter]) on Form 8271.

Form 8271 must be attached to the return on which you claim the deduction, loss, credit, or other tax benefit or report any income.

Issuance of a registration number does not indicate that this investment or the claimed tax benefits have been reviewed, examined, or approved by the Internal Revenue Service.

This statement may be modified as necessary if the tax shelter is not a separate entity (*e.g.*, certain Schedule F or Schedule C activities) or has no name or taxpayer identification number.

Q-54. If a registration number has not been received by a seller (or transferor) from the person who registered the tax shelter by the time interests in the tax shelter are sold (or otherwise transferred), must the seller (or transferor) of the interests furnish the purchaser (or transferee) with any information regarding the registration?

A-54. Yes. At the time of the sale (or other transfer) the seller (or other transferor) must furnish the purchaser (or transferee) with a written statement in substantially the form prescribed in A-53 of this section, except that the second sentence of the form prescribed in A-53 shall be replaced by a statement in the form provided below:

On behalf of [name of tax shelter], [name of tax shelter organizer who has applied for registration] has applied to the Internal Revenue Service for a tax shelter registration number. The number will be furnished to you when it is received.

Including the registration number on tax returns

Q-55. Is an investor required to report the registration number of a tax shelter in which the investor has acquired an interest to the Internal Revenue Service?

A-55. Yes. Any person claiming any deduction, loss, credit, or other tax benefit by reason of a tax shelter must report the registration number of the tax shelter on Form 8271, Investor Reporting of Tax Shelter Registration Number, which must be attached to the return on which any deduction, loss, credit, or other tax benefit attributable to the tax shelter is claimed. For purposes of determining whether the tax shelter registration number must be reported by an investor, income attributable to an investment, such as a partner's distributive share of income, constitutes a deduction or tax benefit that is claimed, because gross deductions and other tax benefits are included in the net income reported by the investor. Thus, the registration number also must be reported on any return on which an investor reports any income attributable to a tax shelter.

Q-56. What should the investor do if the investor has received a notice that a registration number for the tax shelter has been applied for, but the investor has not received the registration number by the time the investor files a return on which a deduction, loss, credit, other tax benefit, or income attributable to the tax shelter is included?

A-56. The investor must attach to the return a Form 8271 with the words "Applied For" written in the space for the registration number and must include on the Form 8271 the name and taxpayer identification number (if any) of the tax shelter and the name of the person who has applied for registration of the tax shelter.

Q-57. Does the requirement to include the tax shelter registration number on a return apply to applications for tentative refund (Form 1045 and Form 1139) and amended returns (Form 1040X, Form 1120X)?

A-57. Yes. A completed Form 8271 must be attached to any such return on which any deduction, loss, credit, other tax benefit, or income relating to a tax shelter is included.

Projected income investments

Q-57A. Are the registration requirements suspended with respect to any tax shelters?

A-57A. Yes. If a tax shelter is a projected income investment, it is not required to be registered before the first offering for sale of an interest in the tax shelter occurs, but is subject only to the registration requirements set forth in A-57H through A-57J of this section. A tax shelter is a projected income investment if—

(a) The tax shelter is not expected to reduce the cumulative tax liability of any investor for

Reg. §301.6111-1T

any year during the 5-year period described in A-4(I) of this section; and

(b) The assets of the tax shelter do not include or relate to any property described in A-57E of this section.

Q-57B. Under what circumstances does a tax shelter satisfy the requirement of paragraph (a) of A-57A of this section?

A-57B. A tax shelter is not expected to reduce the cumulative tax liability of an investor for any year during the 5-year period described in A-4(I) of this section only if—

(a) A written financial projection or other written representation that is provided to investors before the sale of interests in the investment states (or leads a reasonable investor to believe) that the investment will not reduce the cumulative tax liability of any investor with respect to any year (within the meaning of A-7 of this section) in such 5-year period; and

(b) No written or oral projections or representations, other than those related to circumstances that are highly unlikely to occur, state (or lead a reasonable investor to believe) that the investment may reduce the cumulative tax liability of any investor with respect to any such year.

Thus, a tax shelter for which there are multiple written or oral financial projections or other representations is not a projected income investment if any such projection or representation that relates to circumstances that are not highly unlikely to occur states (or leads a reasonable investor to believe) that the investment may reduce the cumulative tax liability of any investor. See A-57D and A-57F of this section for rules relating to financial projections or other representations that are not made in good faith, that are not based on reasonable economic and business assumptions, or that relate to circumstances that are highly unlikely.

Q-57C. When does an investment reduce the cumulative tax liability of an investor?

A-57C. (a) An investment reduces the cumulative tax liability of an investor with respect to a year during the 5-year period described in A-4(I) of this section if, as of the close of such year, (i) cumulative projected deductions for the investor exceed cumulative projected income for the investor, or (ii) cumulative projected credits for the investor exceed cumulative projected tax liability (without regard to credits) for the investor.

(b) The cumulative projected deductions for an investor as of the close of a year are the gross deductions of the investor with respect to the investment, for all periods up to (and including) the end of such year, that are included in the financial projection or upon which the representation is based. The deductions with respect to an investment include all deductions explicitly represented as being allowable and all deductions typically associated (within the meaning of A-9 of this section) with the investment. Therefore, interest to be paid by the investor that is taken into account in determining the tax shelter ratio of the investment (see A-11 of this section) is treated as a deduction with respect to the investment.

(c) The cumulative projected income for an investor as of the close of a year is the gross income of the investor with respect to the investment, for all periods up to (and including) the end of such year, that is included in the financial projection or upon which the representation is based. For this purpose, income attributable to cash, cash equivalents, or marketable securities (within the meaning of A-14(4) of this section) may not be treated as income from the investment.

(d) The cumulative projected credits for an investor as of the close of a year are the gross credits of the investor with respect to the investment, for all periods up to (and including) the close of such year, that are included in the financial projection or upon which the representation is based. The credits with respect to an investment include all credits explicitly represented as being allowable and all credits typically associated (within the meaning of A-9 of this section) with the investment.

(e) The cumulative projected tax liability (without regard to credits) for an investor as of the close of a year is 50 percent of the excess of cumulative projected income for the investor over cumulative projected deductions for the investor with respect to the investment as of the close of such year.

(f) The following examples illustrate the application of the principles of this A-57C:

Example (1). The promotional material with respect to a tax shelter includes a written financial projection indicating that the expected income of the investment in each of its first 5 years is $800,000. In subsequent oral discussions, investors are advised that, in certain circumstances that are not highly unlikely, the income expected from the investment may be as little as $500,000 per year. The subsequent oral discussions are taken into account in determining whether any projections or representations state or lead a reasonable investor to believe that the investment may reduce the cumulative tax liability of any investor. Thus, if the written financial projections indicate that the gross deductions attributable to the investment in each of its first 5 years are expected to be $600,000 and the subsequent oral discussions do not indicate that the amount of those deductions will change under the circumstances in which the income expected may be as little as $500,000, the subsequent oral discussions taken together with the written financial projections state (or lead a reasonable investor to believe) that the cumulative tax liability of an investor may be reduced (*i.e.,* the subsequent oral discussions (taken together with the projections) state or lead a reasonable investor to believe that cumulative projected deductions may exceed cumulative projected income under circumstances that are not highly unlikely). Accordingly, under paragraph (b) of A-57B of this section, the tax shelter would not qualify as a projected income investment.

Example (2). The written promotional material with respect to a tax shelter states that certain deductions are allowable to an investor (without specifying their amount), but there is no written statement relating to the amount of income expected from the investment. Because there is no written financial projection or other written representation that states or leads a reasonable investor to believe that the investment will not reduce the investor's cumulative tax liability (*i.e.,* the cumulative projected deductions, although not specified in the projections, may exceed the cumulative projected income (0)), the requirement of paragraph (a) of A-57B of this section would not be satisfied. The result in this example would be the same if there were only oral representations that the income to be derived from the investment would exceed the deductions with respect to the investment, because there would be no written statement as required by paragraph (a) of A-57B of this section. The tax shelter in this case would qualify as a projected income investment, however, if the written promotional material contains good-faith representations based on reasonable economic and business assumptions that state or lead reasonable investors to believe that the cumulative projected income from the investment will exceed the cumulative projected deductions allowable with respect to the investment for each year in the 5-year period, even though the amounts of income and deductions are not specified.

Example (3). The written promotional material with respect to a tax shelter includes a good-faith financial projection for the first 5 years of the investment. Based on reasonable economic and business assumptions, the projection indicates that the expected net income of the investment in each of its first 4 years is $100,000 ($500,000 of gross income and $400,000 of gross deductions), but as a result of the anticipated acquisition of new business assets a loss of $20,000 is expected in the fifth year of the investment ($500,000 of gross income and $520,000 of gross deductions). The projection also indicates that a credit of $50,000 is expected in the fifth year of the investment. Such a written financial projection would be considered to state that the investment will not reduce the cumulative tax liability of any investor with respect to any year in the 5-year period described in A-4(I) of this section. Although a loss and a credit are projected in the fifth year of the investment, as of the close of such year, cumulative projected income ($2,500,000) exceeds cumulative projected deductions ($2,120,000), and cumulative projected tax liability (without regard to credits) ($380,000 × 50 percent = $190,000) exceeds cumulative projected credits ($50,000). Assuming no contrary oral or written projections or representations are made, the tax shelter would thus be a projected income investment.

Example (4). The written promotional material with respect to a tax shelter states that an investor will be entitled to a "1.5 to 1 write-off" in the year of investment. This statement is a representation that the investment will reduce the cumulative tax liability of an investor with respect to the first year of the investment and, accordingly, the investment is not a projected income investment. The result in this example would be the same if any "write-off" were represented, even if the write-off were less than 1.5 to 1.

Q-57D. Are all financial projections and representations relating to the cumulative tax liability of an investor taken into account for purposes of A-57B of this section?

A-57D. (a) No. A financial projection or other representation relating to the cumulative tax liability of an investor is not taken into account for purposes of A-57B of this section unless it is made in good faith and is based on reasonable economic and business assumptions. In addition, a financial projection or other representation is not taken into account if it relates to circumstances that are highly unlikely. Moreover, a general statement or disclaimer indicating that projected income is not guaranteed or otherwise assured, standing alone, is not a projection or representation for purposes of paragraph (b) of A-57B of this section.

(b) The following example illustrates the application of the principles of this A-57D:

Example. The written promotional material with respect to a tax shelter contains a representation stating that the investment is projected to produce net income for all investors in each of its first five years and there are no credits potentially allowable with respect to the investment. This statement is based on reasonable economic and business assumptions. Such a written representation, if made in good faith, would be considered under paragraph (a) of A-57B of this section to state that the investment will not reduce the cumulative tax liability of any investor with respect to any year in the 5-year period described in A-4(I) of this section.

Reg. §301.6111-1T

In addition, no oral or written statements or representations are communicated to investors that would indicate under paragraph (b) of A-57B of this section that the investment might reduce the cumulative tax liability of any investor with respect to any year in the 5-year period.

Assume the tax shelter organizer has knowledge of certain other facts that lead the tax shelter organizer to believe that it is more likely than not that the investment will produce a net loss in the first year. The representation projecting net income is thus contrary to the tax shelter organizer's belief that it is more likely than not that the investment will produce a net loss in the first year. Therefore, the representation is not made in good faith. Since representations not made in good faith are ignored under A-57D, the tax shelter would not be a projected income investment. If, on the other hand, the tax shelter organizer did not know of the other facts so that the tax shelter organizer did not believe that the investment would produce a net loss in the first year, the representation projecting income is made in good faith. In that case, the tax shelter would be a projected income investment.

Q-57E. What assets may not be held by a projected income investment?

A-57E. A tax shelter is not a projected income investment if more than an incidental amount of its assets include or relate to any interest in a collectible (as defined in section 408(m)(2)), a master sound recording, motion picture or television film, videotape, lithograph plate, copyright, or a literary, musical, or artistic composition.

Q-57F. What are the consequences if financial projections or other representations are not made in good faith or are not based on reasonable economic and business assumptions?

A-57F. If a tax shelter is not a projected income investment because the financial projections or other representations are not made in good faith or are not based on reasonable economic and business assumptions, it must be registered not later than the day on which the first offering for sale of an interest in the tax shelter occurs. If the tax shelter is not registered timely, the tax shelter organizer may be subject to a penalty. (See A-1 of §301.6707-1T.)

Q-57G. When does a tax shelter cease to be a projected income investment?

A-57G. A tax shelter ceases to be a projected income investment on the last day of the first year (as defined in A-7 of this section) in the 5-year period described in A-4(I) of this section for which, for any investor, (i) the gross deductions allocable to the investor for that year and prior years exceed the gross income allocable to the investor for such years, or (ii) the credits allocable to the investor for that year and prior years exceed 50 percent of the amount by which gross income allocable to the investor exceeds gross deductions allocable to the investor for such years. For purposes of determining when a tax shelter ceases to be a projected income investment, the tax shelter organizer is not required to take into account interest that may be incurred by an investor with respect to debt described in A-14(2) or (3) of this section, but is required to take into account interest incurred by an investor with respect to debt described in A-14(1) of this section. In addition, the tax shelter organizer may not take into account income attributable to cash, cash equivalents, or marketable securities (within the meaning of A-14(4) of this section).

Q-57H. How does the requirement to register apply with respect to a tax shelter that is a projected income investment?

A-57H. In the case of a tax shelter that is a projected income investment, registration is not required unless the tax shelter ceases to be a projected income investment under A-57G of this section. If the tax shelter ceases to be a projected income investment, the tax shelter organizer must register the tax shelter in accordance with the rules set forth in A-1 through A-39 and A-41 through A-50 of this section. The tax shelter must be registered—

(a) Within 30 days after the date on which the tax shelter ceases to be a projected income investment, and

(b) Before the date on which the tax shelter or a tax shelter organizer sends the investor any schedule of profit or loss, or income, deduction, or credit that may be used in preparing the investor's income tax return for the taxable year that includes the date on which the tax shelter ceases to be a projected income investment. If a tax shelter organizer fails to register timely as required by this A-57H, the tax shelter organizer may be subject to a penalty. (See A-1 of §301.6707-1T.) For example, assume that C is the principal organizer and general partner of a limited partnership. Interests in the partnership will be offered for sale in a public offering required to be registered with the Securities and Exchange Commission. C knows that the tax shelter ratio (as defined in A-5 of this section) for the limited partners will be 5 to 1. Although C knows the partnership is a tax shelter, C does not register the partnership by the day on which the first offering for sale of an interest occurs because C believes the partnership is a projected income investment. In the second year of the partnership, the gross deductions allocable to each of the limited partners for the first two years of the partnership exceed the gross income allocable to the limited partners in such years. Thus, the partnership ceases to be a projected income investment under A-57G of this section. Assuming further that C continues as the general partner and knowingly fails to register the partnership as a tax shelter within the time prescribed in this A-57H, C will be subject to a penalty of 1 percent of the aggregate amount invested in the partnership. Because there is an intentional disregard of the registration requirements, the $10,000 limitation will not apply.

Q-57I. How does the requirement to furnish registration numbers (A-51 through A-54 of this section) apply in the case of a tax shelter that is a projected income investment?

A-57I. In the case of a tax shelter that is a projected income investment, a person who sells or transfers an interest in the tax shelter is not required to furnish a registration number under A-51 of this section or a notice under A-54 of this section unless the tax shelter ceases to be a projected income investment. If the tax shelter ceases to be a projected income investment, the tax shelter organizer who registers the tax shelter is required to furnish the registration number to all persons who the tax shelter organizer knows or has reason to know are participating in the sale of interests in the tax shelter and to all persons who the tax shelter organizer knows or has reason to know have acquired interests in the tax shelter. A person who sold (or otherwise transferred) an interest in the tax shelter before the date on which the tax shelter ceased to be a projected income investment is required to furnish the registration number to the purchaser or transferee as provided in A-51 of this section only if the seller or transferor knows or has reason to know that the tax shelter has ceased to be a projected income investment and that the tax shelter organizer who registered the tax shelter has not provided a registration number to such purchaser or transferee. In the case of persons who acquired interests in the tax shelter before the date on which the tax shelter ceased to be a projected income investment, the registration number must be provided not later than the date described in paragraph (b) of A-57H of this section or, if the tax shelter does not provide any schedule described in paragraph (b) of A-57H of this section, within 60 days after the date on which the tax shelter ceases to be a projected income investment. Thus, for example, if a tax shelter that ceases to be a projected income investment is a partnership, the tax shelter organizer would be required to provide the registration number to each partner not later than the date the Schedule K-1 for the year in which the tax shelter ceases to be a projected income investment is provided to each partner.

The registration number must be provided in accordance with A-51 and A-52 of this section and must be accompanied by a statement explaining that the tax shelter has ceased to be a projected income investment and instructing the recipient to furnish the registration number to any persons to whom the recipient has sold or otherwise transferred interests in the tax shelter. A tax shelter organizer who fails to provide the registration number as provided in this A-57I may be subject to penalties. (See A-12 of § 301.6707-1T.)

Q-57J. How does the requirement to include the registration number on tax returns (A-55 through A-57 of this section) apply in the case of a tax shelter that is a projected income investment?

A-57J. In the case of a tax shelter that is a projected income investment, an investor is not required to report a registration number on the investor's tax return unless the tax shelter ceases to be a projected income investment. If the tax shelter ceases to be a projected income investment, the requirements of A-55 through A-57 apply with respect to returns for taxable years ending on or after the date on which the tax shelter ceases to be a projected income investment.

Effective dates

Q-58. On what date does the requirement to register a tax shelter become effective?

A-58. In general, a tax shelter must be registered if any interest in the tax shelter (other than an interest previously sold to an investor) is sold on or after September 1, 1984 (whether or not interests in the tax shelter were sold or offered for sale before September 1, 1984). The tax shelter must be registered with the Internal Revenue Service not later than the first day after August 31, 1984 on which an interest in the tax shelter is offered for sale.

Q-59. By what date must the tax shelter registration number be furnished to investors who acquired interests before September 1, 1984 in a tax shelter that is required to be registered.

A-59. All investors who acquired their interests in a tax shelter before September 1, 1984 must be supplied with the tax shelter registration number by December 31, 1984. See A-52 of this section for the date by which registration numbers must be furnished to investors who acquire their interests on or after September 1, 1984.

Q-60. What interests will be taken into account in determining whether an investment in which interests were sold before September 1, 1984, is a substantial investment?

A-60. The determination of whether an investment is a substantial investment will be made by taking into account only the interests that are offered for sale on or after September 1, 1984. An investment will be considered a substantial investment if there are expected to be 5 or more investors on or after September 1, 1984, and the aggregate amount offered for sale on or after September 1, 1984 is expected to exceed $250,000. Amounts received from the sale of interests before September 1, 1984, however, are taken into account in computing the amount of the penalty for failure to register. [Temporary Reg. § 301.6111-1T.]

☐ [T.D. 7964, 8-13-84. *Amended by* T.D. 7990, 10-26-84 *and* T.D. 8078, 3-3-86.]

§ 301.6111-2. Confidential corporate tax shelters.—(a) *In general.*—(1) Under section 6111(d) and this section, a confidential corporate tax shelter is treated as a tax shelter subject to the requirements of sections 6111(a) and (b).

(2) A confidential corporate tax shelter is any transaction—

(i) A significant purpose of the structure of which is the avoidance or evasion of Federal income tax, as described in paragraph (b) of this section, for a direct or indirect corporate participant;

(ii) That is offered to any potential participant under conditions of confidentiality, as described in paragraph (c) of this section; and

(iii) For which the tax shelter promoters may receive fees in excess of $100,000 in the aggregate, as described in paragraph (d) of this section.

(3) For purposes of this section, references to the term *transaction* include all of the factual elements relevant to the expected tax treatment of any investment, entity, plan, or arrangement, and include any series of steps carried out as part of a plan. For purposes of this section, the term *substantially similar* includes any transaction that is expected to obtain the same or similar types of tax consequences and that is either factually similar or based on the same or similar tax strategy. Receipt of an opinion regarding the tax consequences of the transaction is not relevant to the determination of whether the transaction is the same as or substantially similar to another transaction. Further, the term *substantially similar* must be broadly construed in favor of registration. For examples, see § 1.6011-4(c)(4) of this chapter.

(4) A transaction described in paragraph (b) of this section is for a direct or an indirect corporate participant if it is expected to provide Federal income tax benefits to any corporation (U.S. or foreign) whether or not that corporation participates directly in the transaction.

(b) *Transactions structured for avoidance or evasion of Federal income tax.*—(1) *In general.*—The avoidance or evasion of Federal income tax will be considered a significant purpose of the structure of a transaction if the transaction is described in paragraph (b)(2) or (3) of this section. However, a transaction described in paragraph (b)(3) of this section need not be registered if the transaction is described in paragraph (b)(4) of this section. For purposes of this section, Federal income tax benefits include deductions, exclusions from gross income, nonrecognition of gain, tax credits, adjustments (or the absence of adjustments) to the basis of property, status as an entity exempt from Federal income taxation, and any other tax consequences that may reduce a taxpayer's Federal income tax liability by affecting the amount, timing, character, or source of any item of income, gain, expense, loss, or credit.

(2) *Listed transactions.*—A transaction is described in this paragraph (b)(2) if the transaction is the same as or substantially similar to one of the types of transactions that the Internal Revenue Service (IRS) has determined to be a tax avoidance transaction and identified by notice, regulation, or other form of published guidance as a listed transaction. If a transaction becomes a listed transaction after the date on which registration would otherwise be required under this section, and if the transaction otherwise satisfies the confidentiality and fee requirements of paragraphs (a)(2)(ii) and (iii) of this section, registration shall in all events be required with respect to any interests in the transaction that are offered for sale after the transaction becomes a listed transaction. However, because a transaction identified as a listed transaction is generally considered to have been structured for a significant tax avoidance purpose, such a transaction ordinarily will have been subject to registration under this section before becoming a listed transaction if the transaction previously satisfied the confidentiality and fee requirements of paragraphs (a)(2)(ii) and (iii) of this section.

(3) *Other tax-structured transactions.*—A transaction is described in this paragraph (b)(3) if it has been structured to produce Federal income tax benefits that constitute an important part of the intended results of the transaction and the tax shelter promoter (or other person who would be responsible for registration under this section) reasonably expects the transaction to be presented in the same or substantially similar form to more than one potential participant, unless the promoter reasonably determines that—

(i) The potential participant is expected to participate in the transaction in the ordinary course of its business in a form consistent with customary commercial practice (a transaction involving the acquisition, disposition, or restructuring of a business, including the acquisition, disposition, or other change in the ownership or control of an entity that is engaged in a business, or a transaction involving a recapitalization or an acquisition of capital for use in the taxpayer's business, shall be considered a transaction carried out in the ordinary course of a taxpayer's business); and

(ii) There is a generally accepted understanding that the expected Federal income tax benefits from the transaction (taking into account any combination of intended tax consequences) are properly allowable under the Internal Revenue Code for substantially similar transactions. There is no minimum period of time for which such a generally accepted understanding must exist. In general, however, a tax shelter promoter (or other person who would be responsible for registration under this section) cannot reasonably determine whether the intended tax treatment of a transaction has become generally accepted unless information relating to the tax treatment and tax structure of such transactions has been in the public domain (e.g., rulings, published articles, etc.) and widely known for a sufficient period of time (ordinarily a period of years) to provide knowledgeable tax practitioners and the IRS reasonable opportunity to evaluate the intended tax treatment. The mere fact that one or more knowledgeable tax practitioners have provided an opinion or advice to the effect that the intended tax treatment of the transaction should or will be sustained, if challenged by the IRS, is not sufficient to satisfy the requirements of this paragraph (b)(3)(ii).

(4) *Excepted transactions.*—The avoidance or evasion of Federal income tax will not be considered a significant purpose of the structure of a transaction if the transaction is described in either paragraph (b)(4)(i), (ii), or (iii) of this section.

(i) In the case of a transaction other than a transaction described in paragraph (b)(2) of this section, the tax shelter promoter (or other person who would be responsible for registration under this section) reasonably determines that there is no reasonable basis under Federal tax law for denial of any significant portion of the expected Federal income tax benefits from the transaction. This paragraph (b)(4)(i) applies only if the tax shelter promoter (or other person who would be responsible for registration under this section) reasonably determines that there is no basis that would meet the standard applicable to taxpayers under §1.6662-3(b)(3) of this chapter under which the IRS could disallow any significant portion of the expected Federal income tax benefits of the transaction. Thus, the reasonable basis standard is not satisfied by an IRS position that would be merely arguable or that would constitute merely a colorable claim. However, the determination of whether the IRS would or would not have a reasonable basis for such a position must take into account the entirety of the transaction and any combination of tax consequences that are expected to result from any component steps of the transaction, must not be based on any unreasonable or unrealistic factual assumptions, and must take into account all relevant aspects of Federal tax law, including the statute and legislative history, treaties, administrative guidance, and judicial decisions that establish principles of general application in the tax law (e.g., *Gregory v. Helvering*, 293 U.S. 465 (1935)). The determination of whether the IRS would or would not have such a reasonable basis is qualitative in nature and does not depend on any percentage or other quantitative assessment of the likelihood that the taxpayer would ultimately prevail if a significant portion of the expected tax benefits were disallowed by the IRS.

(ii) The IRS makes a determination by published guidance that the transaction is not subject to the registration requirements of this section.

(iii) The IRS makes a determination by individual ruling under paragraph (b)(5) of this section that a specific transaction is not subject to the registration requirements of this section for the taxpayer requesting the ruling.

(5) *Requests for ruling.*—If a tax shelter promoter (or other person who would be responsible for registration under this section) is uncertain whether a transaction is properly classified as a confidential corporate tax shelter or is otherwise uncertain whether registration is required under this section, that person may, on or before the date that registration would otherwise be required under this section, submit a request to the IRS for a ruling as to whether the transaction is subject to the registration requirements of this section. If the request fully discloses all relevant facts relating to the transaction, that person's potential obligation to register the transaction will be suspended during the period that the ruling request is pending and, if the IRS subsequently concludes that the transaction is a confidential corporate tax shelter subject to registration under this section, until the sixtieth day after the issuance of the ruling (or, if the request is withdrawn, sixty days from the date that the request is withdrawn). In the alternative, that person may register the transaction in accordance with the requirements of this section and append a statement to the Form 8264, "Application for Registration of a Tax Shelter," which states that the person is uncertain whether the transaction is required to be registered as a

Reg. §301.6111-2(b)(5)

confidential corporate tax shelter, and that the Form 8264 is being filed on a protective basis.

(6) *Example.*—The following example illustrates the application of paragraphs (b)(1) through (4) of this section. Assume, for purposes of the example, that the transaction is not the same as or substantially similar to any of the types of transactions that the IRS has identified as listed transactions under section 6111 and, thus, is not described in paragraph (b)(2) of this section. The example is as follows:

Example. (i) *Facts.* Y has designed a combination of financial instruments to be issued as a package by corporations. The financial instruments are expected to be treated as equity for financial accounting purposes and as debt giving rise to allowable interest deductions for Federal income tax purposes. Y reasonably expects to present this method of raising capital to more than one potential corporate participant. Assume that, because of the unusual nature of the combination of financial instruments, Y cannot conclude either that the transaction represented by the financial instruments is in customary commercial form or that there is a generally accepted understanding that interest deductions are available to issuers of substantially similar combinations of financial instruments. Further, assume that Y cannot reasonably determine that the IRS would have no reasonable basis to deny the deductions.

(ii) *Analysis.* The transaction represented by this combination of financial instruments is a transaction described in paragraph (b)(3) of this section. However, if Y is uncertain whether this transaction is described in paragraph (b)(3) of this section, or is otherwise uncertain whether registration is required, Y may apply for a ruling under paragraph (b)(5) of this section, and Y will not be required to register the transaction while the ruling is pending or for sixty days thereafter.

(c) *Conditions of confidentiality.*—(1) *In general.*—All the facts and circumstances relating to the transaction will be considered when determining whether an offer is made under conditions of confidentiality as described in section 6111(d)(2), including prior conduct of the parties. Pursuant to section 6111(d)(2)(A), if an offeree's disclosure of the tax treatment or tax structure of the transaction is limited in any manner by an express or implied understanding or agreement with or for the benefit of any tax shelter promoter, an offer is considered made under conditions of confidentiality, whether or not such understanding or agreement is legally binding. The tax treatment of a transaction is the purported or claimed Federal income tax treatment of the transaction. The tax structure of a transaction is any fact that may be relevant to understanding the purported or claimed Federal income tax treatment of the transaction. Pursuant to section 6111(d)(2)(B), an offer will also be considered made under conditions of confidentiality in the absence of any such understanding or agreement if any tax shelter promoter knows or has reason to know that the offeree's use or disclosure of information relating to the tax treatment or tax structure of the transaction is limited for the benefit of any person other than the offeree in any other manner, such as where the transaction is claimed to be proprietary or exclusive to the tax shelter promoter or any party other than the offeree.

(2) *Exceptions.*—(i) *Securities law.*—An offer is not considered made under conditions of confidentiality if disclosure of the tax treatment or tax structure of the transaction is subject to restrictions reasonably necessary to comply with securities laws and such disclosure is not otherwise limited.

(ii) *Mergers and acquisitions.*—In the case of a proposed taxable or tax-free acquisition of historic assets of a corporation (other than an investment company, as defined in section 351(e), that is not publicly traded) that constitute an active trade or business the acquirer intends to continue, or a proposed taxable or tax-free acquisition of more than 50 percent of the stock of a corporation (other than an investment company, as defined in section 351(e), that is not publicly traded) that owns historic assets used in an active trade or business the acquirer intends to continue, the transaction is not considered offered under conditions of confidentiality under paragraph (c)(1) of this section if the offeree is permitted to disclose the tax treatment and tax structure of the transaction no later than the earlier of the date of the public announcement of discussions relating to the transaction, the date of the public announcement of the transaction, or the date of the execution of an agreement (with or without conditions) to enter into the transaction. However, this exception is not available where the offeree's ability to consult any tax advisor (including a tax advisor independent from all other entities involved in the transaction) regarding the tax treatment or tax structure of the transaction is limited in any way.

(3) *Presumption.*—Unless facts and circumstances indicate otherwise, an offer is not considered made under conditions of confidentiality if the tax shelter promoter provides express written authorization to each offeree permitting the offeree (and each employee, representative, or other agent of such offeree) to disclose to any and all persons, without limita-

tion of any kind, the tax treatment and tax structure of the transaction, and all materials of any kind (including opinions or other tax analyses) that are provided to the offeree related to such tax treatment and tax structure. Except as provided in paragraph (c)(2) of this section, this presumption is available only in cases in which each written authorization permits the offeree to disclose the tax treatment and tax structure of the transaction immediately upon commencement of discussions with the tax shelter promoter providing the authorization and each written authorization is given no later than 30 days from the day the tax shelter promoter commenced discussions with the offeree. A transaction that is exclusive or proprietary to any party other than the offeree will not be considered offered under conditions of confidentiality if written authorization to disclose is provided to the offeree in accordance with this paragraph (c)(3) and the transaction is not otherwise confidential.

(d) *Determination of fees.*—All the facts and circumstances relating to the transaction will be considered when determining the amount of fees, in the aggregate, that the tax shelter promoters may receive. For purposes of this paragraph (d), all consideration that tax shelter promoters may receive is taken into account, including contingent fees, fees in the form of equity interests, and fees the promoters may receive for other transactions as consideration for promoting the tax shelter. For example, if a tax shelter promoter may receive a fee for arranging a transaction that is a confidential corporate tax shelter and a separate fee for another transaction that is not a confidential corporate tax shelter, part or all of the fee paid with respect to the other transaction may be treated as a fee paid with respect to the confidential corporate tax shelter if the facts and circumstances indicate that the fee paid for the other transaction is in consideration for the confidential corporate tax shelter. For purposes of determining whether the tax shelter promoters may receive fees in excess of $100,000, the fees from all substantially similar transactions are considered part of the same tax shelter and must be aggregated.

(e) *Registration.*—(1) *Time for registering.*—(i) *In general.*—A tax shelter must be registered not later than the day on which the first offering for sale of interests in the shelter occurs. An offer to participate in a confidential corporate tax shelter shall be treated as an offer for sale. If interests in a confidential corporate tax shelter were first offered for sale on or before February 28, 2000, the first offer for sale of interests in the shelter that occurs after February 28, 2000 shall be considered the first offer for sale under this section.

(ii) *Special rule.*—If a transaction becomes a confidential corporate tax shelter (e.g., because of a change in the law or factual circumstances, or because the transaction becomes a listed transaction) subsequent to the first offering for sale after February 28, 2000, and the transaction was not previously required to be registered as a confidential corporate tax shelter under this section, the transaction must be registered under this section if interests are offered for sale after the transaction becomes a confidential corporate tax shelter. The transaction must be registered by the next offering for sale of interests in the shelter. If, subsequent to the first offering for sale, a transaction becomes a confidential corporate tax shelter because the transaction becomes a listed transaction on or after February 28, 2003, and the transaction was not previously required to be registered as a confidential corporate tax shelter under this section, the transaction must be registered under this section within 60 days after the transaction becomes a listed transaction/confidential corporate tax shelter if any interests were offered for sale within the previous six years.

(2) *Procedures for registering.*—To register a confidential corporate tax shelter, the person responsible for registering the tax shelter must file Form 8264, "Application for Registration of a Tax Shelter." (Form 8264 is also used to register tax shelters defined in section 6111(c).) Similar to the treatment provided under Q&A-22 and Q&A-48 of §301.6111-1T, transactions involving similar business assets and similar plans or arrangements that are offered to corporate taxpayers by the same person or related persons are aggregated and considered part of a single tax shelter. However, in contrast with the requirement of Q&A-48 of §301.6111-1T, the tax shelter promoter may file a single Form 8264 with respect to any such aggregated tax shelter, provided an amended Form 8264 is filed to reflect any material changes and to include any additional or revised written materials presented in connection with an offer to participate in the shelter. Furthermore, all transactions that are part of the same tax shelter and that are to be carried out by the same corporate participant (or one or more other members of the same affiliated group within the meaning of section 1504) must be registered on the same Form 8264.

(f) *Definition of tax shelter promoter.*—For purposes of section 6111(d)(2) and this section, the term *tax shelter promoter* includes a tax shelter organizer and any other person who participates in the organization, management or sale of a tax shelter (as those persons are described in section 6111(e)(1) and §301.6111-1T (Q&A-26 through Q&A-33) or any person related (within the meaning of section 267 or 707) to such tax shelter organizer or such other person.

(g) *Person required to register.*—(1) *Tax shelter promoters.*—The rules in section 6111(a) and (e) and §301.6111-1T (Q&A-34 through Q&A-39) determine who is required to register a confidential corporate tax shelter. A promoter of a confidential corporate tax shelter must register the tax shelter only if it is a person required to register under the rules in section 6111(a) and (e) and §301.6111-1T (Q&A-34 through Q&A-39).

(2) *Persons who discuss the transaction; all promoters are foreign persons.*—(i) *In general.*—If all of the tax shelter promoters of a confidential corporate tax shelter are foreign persons, any person who discusses participation in the transaction must register the shelter under this section within 90 days after beginning such discussions.

(ii) *Exceptions.*—Registration by a person discussing participation in a transaction is not required if either—

(A) The person does not participate, directly or indirectly, in the shelter and notifies the tax shelter promoter in writing, within 90 days of beginning such discussions, that the person will not participate; or

(B) Within 90 days after beginning such discussions, the person obtains and reasonably relies on both—

(1) A written statement from one of the tax shelter promoters that such promoter has registered the tax shelter under this section; and

(2) A copy of the registration.

(iii) *Determination of foreign status.*—For purposes of this paragraph (g)(2), a person must presume that all tax shelter promoters are foreign persons unless the person either—

(A) Discusses participation in the tax shelter with a promoter that is a United States person; or

(B) Obtains and reasonably relies on a written statement from one of the promoters that at least one of the promoters is a United States person.

(iv) *Discussion.*—Discussing participation in a transaction includes discussing such participation with any person that conveys the tax shelter promoter's proposal. For purposes of this paragraph (g)(2), any person that participates directly or indirectly in a transaction will be treated as having discussed participation in the transaction not later than the date of the agreement to participate. Thus, a tax shelter participant will be treated as having discussed participation in the transaction even if all discussions were conducted by an intermediary and the agreement to participate was made indirectly through another person acting on the participant's behalf (for example, through an intermediary empowered to commit the participant to participate in the shelter).

(v) *Special rule for controlled entities.*—A person (first person) will be treated as participating indirectly in a confidential corporate tax shelter if a foreign person controlled by the first person participates in the shelter, and a significant purpose of the shelter is the avoidance or evasion of the first person's Federal income tax. For purposes of this paragraph (g)(2)(v), control of a foreign corporation or partnership will be determined under the rules of section 6038(e)(2) and (3), except that such section shall be applied by substituting "10" for "50" each place it appears and "at least" for "more than" each place it appears. In addition, section 6038(e)(2) shall be applied for these purposes without regard to the constructive ownership rules of section 318 and by treating stock as owned if it is owned directly or indirectly. Section 6038(e)(3) shall be applied for these purposes without regard to the last sentence of section 6038(e)(3)(B). Any beneficiary with a 10 percent or more interest in a foreign trust or estate shall be treated as controlling that trust or estate for purposes of this paragraph (g)(2)(v).

(vi) *Other rules.*—(A) For purposes of the registration requirements under section 6111(d)(3), it is presumed that the tax shelter promoters will receive fees in excess of $100,000 in the aggregate unless the person responsible for registering the tax shelter can show otherwise.

(B) Any person treated as a tax shelter promoter under section 6111(d) solely by reason of being related (within the meaning of section 267 or 707) to a foreign promoter will be treated as a foreign promoter for purposes of this paragraph (g)(2).

(h) *Effective dates.*—This section applies to confidential corporate tax shelters in which any interests are offered for sale after February 28, 2000. If an interest is sold after February 28, 2000, it is treated as offered for sale after February 28, 2000, unless the sale was pursuant to a written binding contract entered into on or before February 28, 2000. However, paragraphs (a) through (g) of this section apply to confidential corporate tax shelters in which any interests are offered for sale on or after February 28, 2003, and to transactions described in paragraph (e)(1)(ii) of this section. The rules that apply to confidential corporate tax shelters in which any interests are offered for sale after

February 28, 2000, and before February 28, 2003, are contained in §301.6111-2T in effect prior to February 28, 2003 (see 26 CFR part 301 revised as of April 1, 2002, 2002-28 I.R.B 91, and 2002-45 I.R.B. 823 (see §601.601(d)(2) of this chapter)). [Reg. §301.6111-2.]

☐ [*T.D.* 9046, 2-28-2003.]

§301.6114-1. Treaty-based return positions.—(a) *Reporting requirement.*—(1) *General rule.*—(i) Except as provided in paragraph (c) of this section, if a taxpayer takes a return position that any treaty of the United States (including, but not limited to, an income tax treaty, estate and gift tax treaty, or friendship, commerce and navigation treaty) overrules or modifies any provision of the Internal Revenue Code and thereby effects (or potentially effects) a reduction of any tax incurred at any time, the taxpayer shall disclose such return position on a statement (in the form required in paragraph (d) of this section) attached to such return.

(ii) If a return of tax would not otherwise be required to be filed, a return must nevertheless be filed for purposes of making the disclosure required by this section. For this purpose, such return need include only the taxpayer's name, address, taxpayer identifying number, and be signed under penalties of perjury (as well as the subject disclosure). Also, the taxpayer's taxable year shall be deemed to be the calendar year (unless the taxpayer has previously established, or timely chooses for this purpose to establish, a different taxable year). In the case of a disclosable return position relating solely to income subject to withholding (as defined in §1.1441-2(a) of this chapter), however, the statement required to be filed in paragraph (d) of this section must instead be filed at times and in accordance with procedures published by the Internal Revenue Service.

(2) *Application.*—(i) A taxpayer is considered to adopt a return position when the taxpayer determines its tax liability with respect to a particular item of income, deduction or credit. A taxpayer may be considered to adopt a return position whether or not a return is actually filed. To determine whether a return position is a "treaty-based return position" so that reporting is required under this paragraph (a), the taxpayer must compare:

(A) The tax liability (including credits, carrybacks, carryovers, and other tax consequences or attributes for the current year as well as for any other affected tax years) to be reported on a return of the taxpayer, and

(B) The tax liability (including such credits, carrybacks, carryovers, and other tax consequences or attributes) that would be reported if the relevant treaty provision did not exist.

If there is a difference (or potential difference) in these two amounts, the position taken on a return is a treaty-based return position that must be reported.

(ii) In the event a taxpayer's return position is based on a conclusion that a treaty provision is consistent with a Code provision, but the effect of the treaty provision is to alter the scope of the Code provision from the scope that it would have in the absence of the treaty, then the return position is a treaty-based return position that must be reported.

(iii) A return position is a treaty-based return position unless the taxpayer's conclusion that no reporting is required under paragraphs (a)(2)(i) and (ii) of this section has a substantial probability of successful defense if challenged.

(3) *Examples.*—The application of section 6114 and paragraph (a)(2) of this section may be illustrated by the following examples:

Example (1). X, a Country A corporation, claims the benefit of a provision of the income tax treaty between the United States and Country A that modifies a provision of the Code. This position does not result in a change of X's U.S. tax liability for the current tax year but does give rise to, or increases, a net operating loss which may be carried back (or forward) such that X's tax liability in the carryback (or forward) year may be affected by the position taken by X in the current year. X must disclose this treaty-based return position with its tax return for the current tax year.

Example (2). Z, a domestic corporation, is engaged in a trade or business in Country B. Country B imposes a tax on the income from certain of Z's petroleum activities at a rate significantly greater than the rate applicable to income from other activities. Z claims a foreign tax credit for this tax on its tax return. The tax imposed on Z is specifically listed as a creditable tax in the income tax treaty between the United States and Country B; however, there is no specific authority that such tax would otherwise be a creditable tax for U.S. purposes under sections 901 or 903 of the Code. Therefore, in the absence of the treaty, the creditability of this petroleum tax would lack a substantial probability of successful defense if challenged, and Z must disclose this treaty-based return position (see also paragraph (b)(7) of this section).

(b) *Reporting specifically required.*—Reporting is required under this section except as expressly waived under paragraph (c) of this section. The following list is not a list of all positions for which reporting is required under this section but is a list of particular positions for which reporting is specifically required. These positions are as follows:

(1) That a nondiscrimination provision of a treaty precludes the application of any otherwise applicable Code provision, other than with respect to the making of or the effect of an election under section 897 (i);

(2) That a treaty reduces or modifies the taxation of gain or loss from the disposition of a United States real property interest;

(3) That a treaty exempts a foreign corporation from (or reduces the amount of tax with respect to) the branch profits tax (section 884(a)) or the tax on excess interest (section 884(f)(1)(B));

(4) That, notwithstanding paragraph (c)(1)(i) of this section,

(i) A treaty exempts from tax, or reduces the rate of tax on, interest or dividends paid by a foreign corporation that are from sources within the United States by reason of section 861(a)(2)(B) or section 884(f)(1)(A); or

(ii) A treaty exempts from tax, or reduces the rate of tax on, fixed or determinable annual or periodical income subject to withholding under section 1441 or 1442 that a foreign person receives from a U.S. person, but only if described in paragraphs (b)(4)(ii)(A) and (B) of this section, or in paragraph (b)(4)(ii)(C) or (D) of this section as follows—

(A) The payment is not properly reported to the Service on a Form 1042S; and

(B) The foreign person is any of the following:

(1) A controlled foreign corporation (as defined in section 957) in which the U.S. person is a U.S. shareholder within the meaning of section 951(b);

(2) A foreign corporation that is controlled within the meaning of section 6038 by the U.S. person;

(3) A foreign shareholder of the U.S. person that, in the case of tax years beginning on or before July 10, 1989, is controlled within the meaning of section 6038A by the foreign shareholder, or, in the case of tax years beginning after July 10, 1989, is 25-percent owned within the meaning of section 6038A by the foreign shareholder; or

(4) With respect to payments made after October 10, 1990, a foreign related party, as defined in section 6038A(c)(2)(B), to the U.S. person; or

(C) For payments made after December 31, 2000, with respect to a treaty that contains a limitation on benefits article, that—

(1) The treaty exempts from tax, or reduces the rate of tax on income subject to withholding (as defined in § 1.1441-2(a) of this chapter) that is received by a foreign person (other than a State, including a political subdivision or local authority) that is the beneficial owner of the income and the beneficial owner is related to the person obligated to pay the income within the meaning of sections 267(b) and 707(b), and the income exceeds $500,000; and

(2) A foreign person (other than an individual or a State, including a political subdivision or local authority) meets the requirements of the limitation on benefits article of the treaty; or

(D) For payments made after December 31, 2000, with respect to a treaty that imposes any other conditions for the entitlement of treaty benefits, for example as a part of the interest, dividends, or royalty article, that such conditions are met;

(5) That, notwithstanding paragraph (c)(1)(i) of this section, under a treaty—

(i) Income that is effectively connected with a U.S. trade or business of a foreign corporation or a nonresident alien is not attributable to a permanent establishment or a fixed base of operations in the United States and, thus, is not subject to taxation on a net basis, or that

(ii) Expenses are allowable in determining net business income so attributable, notwithstanding an inconsistent provision of the Code;

(6) Except as provided in paragraph (c)(1)(iv) of this section, that a treaty alters the source of any item of income or deduction;

(7) That a treaty grants a credit for a specific foreign tax for which a foreign tax credit would not be allowed by the Code; or

(8) For returns relating to taxable years for which the due date for filing returns (without extensions) is after December 15, 1997, that residency of an individual is determined under a treaty and apart from the Internal Revenue Code.

(c) *Reporting requirement waived.*—(1) Pursuant to the authority contained in section 6114(b), reporting is waived under this section with respect to any of the following return positions taken by the taxpayer:

(i) Notwithstanding paragraph (b)(4) or (5) of this section, that a treaty has reduced the rate of withholding tax otherwise applicable to a particular type of fixed or determinable annual or periodical income subject to withholding under section 1441 or 1442, such as dividends, interest, rents, or royalties to the extent such income is beneficially owned by an individual or a State (including a political subdivision or local authority);

(ii) For returns relating to taxable years for which the due date for filing returns (without extensions) is on or before December 15, 1997, that residency of an individual is determined under a treaty and apart from the Internal Revenue Code.

(iii) That a treaty reduces or modifies the taxation of income derived from dependent personal services, pensions, annuities, social security and other public pensions, or income derived by artistes, athletes, students, trainees or teachers;

(iv) That income of an individual is resourced (for purposes of applying the foreign tax credit limitation) under a treaty provision relating to elimination of double taxation;

(v) That a nondiscrimination provision of a treaty allows the making of an election under section 897 (i);

(vi) That a Social Security Totalization Agreement or a Diplomatic or Consular Agreement reduces or modifies the taxation of income derived by the taxpayer; or

(vii) That a treaty exempts the taxpayer from the excise tax imposed by section 4371, but only if:

(A) The person claiming such treaty-based return position is an insured, as defined in section 4372(d) (without the limitation therein referring to section 4371(1)), or a U.S. or foreign broker of insurance risks,

(B) Reporting under this section that would otherwise be required to be made by foreign insurers or reinsurers on a Form 720 on a quarterly basis is made on an annual basis on a Form 720 by a date no later than the date on which the return is due for the first quarter after the end of the calendar year, or

(C) A closing agreement relating to entitlement to the exemption from the excise tax has been entered into with the Service by the foreign insurance company that is the beneficial recipient of the premium that is subject to the excise tax.

(2) Reporting is waived for an individual if payments or income items otherwise reportable under this section (other than by reason of paragraph (b)(8) of this section), received by the individual during the course of the taxable year do not exceed $10,000 in the aggregate or, in the case of payments or income items reportable only by reason of paragraph (b)(8) of this section, do not exceed $100,000 in the aggregate.

(3) Reporting with respect to payments or income items the treatment of which is mandated by the terms of a closing agreement with the Internal Revenue Service, and that would otherwise be subject to the reporting requirements of this section, is also waived.

(4) If a partnership, trust, or estate that has the taxpayer as a partner or beneficiary discloses on its information return a position for which reporting is otherwise required by the taxpayer, the taxpayer (partner or beneficiary) is then excused from disclosing that position on a return.

(5) This section does not apply to a withholding agent with respect to the performance of its withholding functions.

(6) This section does not apply to amounts required to be reported under section 6038A on a Form 5472 (or successor form) to the extent permitted under the form or accompanying instructions.

(d) *Information to be reported.*—(1) *Returns due after December 15, 1997.*—When reporting is required under this section for a return relating to a taxable year for which the due date (without extensions) is after December 15, 1997, the taxpayer must furnish, in accordance with paragraph (a) of this section, as an attachment to the return, a fully completed Form 8833 (Treaty-Based Return Position Disclosure Under Section 6114 or 7701(b)) or appropriate successor form.

(2) *Earlier returns.*—For returns relating to taxable years for which the due date for filing returns (without extensions) is on or before December 15, 1997, the taxpayer must furnish information in accordance with paragraph (d) of this section in effect prior to December 15, 1997 (see §301.6114-1(d) as contained in 26 CFR part 301, revised April 1, 1997).

(3) *In general.*—(i) *Permanent establishment.*—For purposes of determining the nature and amount (or reasonable estimate thereof) of gross receipts, if a taxpayer takes a position that it does not have a permanent establishment or a fixed base in the United States and properly discloses that position, it need not separately report its payment of actual or deemed dividends or interest exempt from tax by reason of a treaty (or any liability for tax imposed by reason of section 884).

(ii) *Single income item.*—For purposes of the statement of facts relied upon to support each separate Treaty-Based Return Position taken, a taxpayer may treat payments or income items of the same type (e.g., interest items) received from the same ultimate payor (e.g., the obligor on a note) as a single separate payment or income item.

(iii) *Foreign source effectively connected income.*—If a taxpayer takes the return position that, under the treaty, income that would be income effectively connected with a U.S. trade or business is not subject to U.S. taxation because it is income treated as derived from sources outside the United States, the taxpayer may treat payments or income items of the same type (e.g., interest items) as a single separate payment or income item.

(iv) *Sales or services income.*—Income from separate sales or services, whether or not made or preformed by an agent (independent or dependent), to different U.S. customers on behalf of a foreign corporation not having a permanent establishment in the United States may be treated as a single payment or income item.

(v) *Foreign insurers or reinsurers.*—For purposes of reporting by foreign insurers or reinsurers, as described in paragraph (c)(1)(vii)(B) of this section, such reporting must separately set forth premiums paid with respect to casualty insurance and indemnity bonds (subject to section 4371(1)); life insurance, sickness and accident policies, and annuity contracts (subject to section 4371(2)); and reinsurance (subject to section 4371(3)). All premiums paid with respect to each of these three categories may be treated as a single payment or income item within that category. For reports first due before May 1, 1991, the report may disclose, for each of the three categories, the total amount of premiums derived by the foreign insurer or reinsurer in U.S. dollars (even if a portion of these premiums relate to risks that are not U.S. situs). Reasonable estimates of the amounts required to be disclosed will satisfy these reporting requirements.

(e) *Effective date.*—This section is effective for taxable years of the taxpayer for which the due date for filing returns (without extensions) occurs after December 31, 1988. However, if—

(1) A taxpayer has filed a return for such a taxable year, without complying with the reporting requirement of this section, before November 13, 1989, or

(2) A taxpayer is not otherwise than by paragraph (a) of this section required to file a return for a taxable year before November 13, 1989,

such taxpayer must file (apart from any earlier filed return) the statement required by paragraph (d) of this section before June 12, 1990, by mailing the required statement to the Internal Revenue Service, P. O. Box 21086, Philadelphia, PA 19114. Any such statement filed apart from a return must be dated, signed and sworn to by the taxpayer under the penalties of perjury. In addition, with respect to any return due (without extensions) on or before March 10, 1990, the reporting required by paragraph (a) of this section must be made no later than June 12, 1990. If a taxpayer files or has filed a return on or before November 13, 1989, that provides substantially the same information required by paragraph (d) of this section, no additional submission will be required. Foreign insurers and reinsurers subject to reporting described in paragraph (c)(7)(ii) of this section must so report for calendar years 1988 and 1989 no later than August 15, 1990.

(f) *Cross reference.*—For the provisions concerning penalties for failure to disclose a treaty-based return position, see section 6712 and § 301.6712-1. [Reg. § 301.6114-1.]

☐ [*T.D.* 8292, 3-13-90. *Amended by T.D.* 8305, 7-11-90; *T.D.* 8733, 10-6-97; *T.D.* 8734, 10-6-97; *T.D.* 8804, 12-30-98 *and T.D.* 8856, 12-29-99.]

Accuracy-Related and Fraud Penalties

§ 1.6662-1. Overview of the accuracy-related penalty.—Section 6662 imposes an accuracy-related penalty on any portion of an underpayment of tax required to be shown on a return that is attributable to one or more of the following:

(a) Negligence or disregard of rules or regulations;

(b) Any substantial understatement of income tax;

(c) Any substantial valuation misstatement under chapter 1;

(d) Any substantial overstatement of pension liabilities; or

(e) Any substantial estate or gift tax valuation understatement.

Sections 1.6662-1 through 1.6662-5 address only the first three components of the accuracy-related penalty, *i.e.*, the penalties for negligence or disregard of rules or regulations, substantial understatements of income tax, and substantial (or gross) valuation misstatements under chapter 1. The penalties for disregard of rules or regulations and for a substantial understatement of income tax may be avoided by adequately disclosing certain information as provided in § 1.6662-3(c) and § § 1.6662-4(e) and (f), respectively. The penalties for negligence and for a substantial (or gross) valuation misstatement under chapter 1 may not be avoided by disclosure. No accuracy-related penalty may be imposed on any portion of an underpayment if there was reasonable cause for, and the taxpayer acted in good faith with respect to, such portion. The reasonable cause and good faith exception to the accuracy-related penalty is set forth in § 1.6664-4. [Reg. § 1.6662-1.]

☐ [*T.D.* 8381, 12-30-91. *Amended by T.D.* 8617, 8-31-95.]

§ 1.6662-2. Accuracy-related penalty.

(a) *In general.*—Section 6662(a) imposes an accuracy-related penalty on any portion of an underpayment of tax (as defined in section 6664(a) and § 1.6664-2) required to be shown on a return if such portion is attributable to one or more of the following types of misconduct:

(1) Negligence or disregard of rules or regulations (see § 1.6662-3);

(2) Any substantial understatement of income tax (see § 1.6662-4); or

(3) Any substantial (or gross) valuation misstatement under chapter 1 ("substantial valuation misstatement" or "gross valuation misstatement"), provided the applicable dollar limitation set forth in section 6662(e)(2) is satisfied (see § 1.6662-5).

The accuracy-related penalty applies only in cases in which a return of tax is filed, except that the penalty does not apply in the case of a return prepared by the Secretary under the authority of section 6020(b). The accuracy-related penalty under section 6662 and the penalty under section 6651 for failure to timely file a return of tax may both be imposed on the same portion of an underpayment if a return is filed, but is filed late. The fact that a return is filed late, however, is not taken into account in determining whether an accuracy-related penalty should be imposed. No accuracy-related penalty may be imposed on any portion of an underpayment of tax on which the fraud penalty set forth in section 6663 is imposed.

(b) *Amount of penalty.*—(1) *In general.*—The amount of the accuracy-related penalty is 20 percent of the portion of an underpayment of tax required to be shown on a return that is attributable to any of the types of misconduct listed in paragraphs (a)(1) through (a)(3) of this section, except as provided in paragraph (b)(2) of this section.

(2) *Increase in penalty for gross valuation misstatement.*—In the case of a gross valuation misstatement, as defined in section 6662(h)(2) and § 1.6662-5(e)(2), the amount of the accuracy-related penalty is 40 percent of the portion of an underpayment of tax required to be shown on a return that is attributable to the gross valuation misstatement, provided the applicable dollar limitation set forth in section 6662(e)(2) is satisfied.

(c) *No stacking of accuracy-related penalty components.*—The maximum accuracy-related penalty imposed on a portion of an underpayment may not exceed 20 percent of such portion (40 percent of the portion attributable to a gross valuation misstatement), notwithstanding that such portion is attributable to more than one of the types of misconduct described in paragraph (a) of this section. For example, if a portion of an underpayment of tax required to be shown on a return is attributable both to negligence and a substantial understatement of income tax, the maximum accuracy-related penalty is 20 percent of such portion. Similarly, the maximum accuracy-related penalty imposed on any portion of an underpayment that is attributable both to negligence and a gross valuation misstatement is 40 percent of such portion.

(d) *Effective dates.*—(1) *Returns due before January 1, 1994.* Section 1.6662-3(c) and §§ 1.6662-4(e) and (f) (relating to methods of making adequate disclosure) (as contained in 26 CFR part 1 revised April 1, 1995) apply to returns the due date of which (determined without regard to extensions of time for filing) is after December 31, 1991, but before January 1, 1994. Except as provided in the preceding sentence and in paragraphs (d)(2), (3), and (4) of this section, §§ 1.6662-1 through 1.6662-5 apply to returns the due date of which (determined without regard to extensions of time for filing) is after December 31, 1989, but before January 1, 1994. To the extent the provisions of these regulations were not reflected in the statute as amended by the Omnibus Budget Reconciliation Act of 1989 (OBRA 1989), in Notice 90-20, 1990-1 C.B. 328, or in rules and regulations in effect prior to March 4, 1991 (to the extent not inconsistent with the statute as amended by OBRA 1989), these regulations will not be adversely applied to a taxpayer who took a position based upon such prior rules on a return filed before January 1, 1992.

(2) *Returns due after December 31, 1993.*—Except as provided in paragraphs (d)(3), (4) and (5) of this section and the last sentence of this paragraph (d)(2), the provisions of §§ 1.6662-1 through 1.6662-4 and § 1.6662-7 (as revised to reflect the changes made to the accuracy-related penalty by the Omnibus Budget Reconciliation Act of 1993) and of § 1.6662-5 apply to returns the due date of which (determined without regard to extensions of time for filing) is after December 31, 1993. These changes include raising the disclosure standard for the penalties for disregarding rules or regulations and for a substantial understatement of income tax from not frivolous to reasonable basis, eliminating the disclosure exception for the negligence penalty, and providing guidance on the meaning of reasonable basis. The Omnibus Budget Reconciliation Act of 1993 changes relating to the penalties for negligence or disregard of rules or regulations will not apply to returns (including qualified amended returns) that are filed on or before March 14, 1994, but the provisions of §§ 1.6662-1 through 1.6662-3 (as contained in

26 CFR part 1 revised April 1, 1995) relating to those penalties will apply to such returns.

(3) *Special rules for tax shelter items.*—Sections 1.6662-4(g)(1) and 1.6662-4(g)(4) apply to returns the due date of which (determined without regard to extensions of time for filing) is after September 1, 1995. Except as provided in the last sentence of this paragraph (d)(3), §§ 1.6662-4(g)(1) and 1.6662-4(g)(4) (as contained in 26 CFR part 1 revised April 1, 1995) apply to returns the due date of which (determined without regard to extensions of time for filing) is on or before September 1, 1995, and after December 31, 1989. For transactions occurring after December 8, 1994, §§ 1.6662-4(g)(1) and 1.6662-4(g)(2) (as contained in 26 CFR part 1 revised April 1, 1995) are applied taking into account the changes made to section 6662(d)(2)(C) (relating to the substantial understatement penalty for tax shelter items of corporations) by section 744 of Title VII of the Uruguay Round Agreements Act, Pub. L. 103-465 (108 Stat. 4809).

(4) *Special rules for reasonable basis.*—Section 1.6662-3(b)(3) applies to returns filed on or after December 2, 1998.

(5) *For returns filed after December 31, 2002.*—Sections 1.6662-3(a), 1.6662-3(b)(2) and 1.6662-3(c)(1) (relating to adequate disclosure) apply to returns filed after December 31, 2002, with respect to transactions entered into on or after January 1, 2003. Except as provided in paragraph (d)(1) of this section, §§ 1.6662-3(a), 1.6662-3(b)(2) and 1.6662-3(c)(1) (as contained in 26 CFR part 1 revised April 1, 2003) apply to returns filed with respect to transactions entered into prior to January 1, 2003. [Reg. § 1.6662-2.]

☐ [*T.D.* 8381, 12-30-91. *Amended by T.D.* 8617, 8-31-95; *T.D.* 8790, 12-1-98 *and T.D.* 9109, 12-29-2003.]

§ 1.6662-3. Negligence or disregard of rules or regulations.—(a) *In general.*—If any portion of an underpayment, as defined in section 6664(a) and § 1.6664-2, of any income tax imposed under subtitle A of the Internal Revenue Code that is required to be shown on a return is attributable to negligence or disregard of rules or regulations, there is added to the tax an amount equal to 20 percent of such portion. The penalty for disregarding rules or regulations does not apply, however, if the requirements of paragraph (c)(1) of this section are satisfied and the position in question is adequately disclosed as provided in paragraph (c)(2) of this section (and, if the position relates to a reportable transaction as defined in § 1.6011-4(b) (or § 1.6011-4T(b), as applicable), the transaction is disclosed in accordance with § 1.6011-4 (or § 1.6011-4T, as applicable)), or to the extent that the reasonable cause and good faith exception to this penalty set forth in § 1.6664-4 applies. In addition, if a position with respect to an item (other than with respect to a reportable transaction, as defined in § 1.6011-4(b) or § 1.6011-4T(b), as applicable) is contrary to a revenue ruling or notice (other than a notice of proposed rulemaking) issued by the Internal Revenue Service and published in the Internal Revenue Bulletin (see § 601.601(d)(2) of this chapter), this penalty does not apply if the position has a realistic possibility of being sustained on its merits. See § 1.6694-2(b) of the income tax return preparer penalty regulations for a description of the realistic possibility standard.

(b) *Definitions and rules.*—(1) *Negligence.*—The term "negligence" includes any failure to make a reasonable attempt to comply with the provisions of the internal revenue laws or to exercise ordinary and reasonable care in the preparation of a tax return. "Negligence" also includes any failure by the taxpayer to keep adequate books and records or to substantiate items properly. A return position that has a reasonable basis as defined in paragraph (b)(3) of this section is not attributable to negligence. Negligence is strongly indicated where—

(i) A taxpayer fails to include on an income tax return an amount of income shown on an information return, as defined in section 6724(d)(1);

(ii) A taxpayer fails to make a reasonable attempt to ascertain the correctness of a deduction, credit or exclusion on a return which would seem to a reasonable and prudent person to be "too good to be true" under the circumstances;

(iii) A partner fails to comply with the requirements of section 6222, which requires that a partner treat partnership items on its return in a manner that is consistent with the treatment of such items on the partnership return (or notify the Secretary of the inconsistency); or

(iv) A shareholder fails to comply with the requirements of section 6242, which requires that an S corporation shareholder treat subchapter S items on its return in a manner that is consistent with the treatment of such items on the corporation's return (or notify the Secretary of the inconsistency).

(2) *Disregard of rules or regulations.*—The term "disregard" includes any careless, reckless or intentional disregard of rules or regulations. The term "rules or regulations" includes the provisions of the Internal Revenue Code, temporary or final Treasury regulations issued under the Code, and revenue rulings or notices

(other than notices of proposed rulemaking) issued by the Internal Revenue Service and published in the Internal Revenue Bulletin. A disregard of rules or regulations is "careless" if the taxpayer does not exercise reasonable diligence to determine the correctness of a return position that is contrary to the rule or regulation. A disregard is "reckless" if the taxpayer makes little or no effort to determine whether a rule or regulation exists, under circumstances which demonstrate a substantial deviation from the standard of conduct that a reasonable person would observe. A disregard is "intentional" if the taxpayer knows of the rule or regulation that is disregarded. Nevertheless, a taxpayer who takes a position (other than with respect to a reportable transaction, as defined in §1.6011-4(b) or §1.6011-4T(b), as applicable) contrary to a revenue ruling or notice has not disregarded the ruling or notice if the contrary position has a realistic possibility of being sustained on its merits.

(3) *Reasonable basis.*—Reasonable basis is a relatively high standard of tax reporting, that is, significantly higher than not frivolous or not patently improper. The reasonable basis standard is not satisfied by a return position that is merely arguable or that is merely a colorable claim. If a return position is reasonably based on one or more of the authorities set forth in §1.6662-4(d)(3)(iii) (taking into account the relevance and persuasiveness of the authorities, and subsequent developments), the return position will generally satisfy the reasonable basis standard even though it may not satisfy the substantial authority standard as defined in §1.6662-4(d)(2). (See §1.6662-4(d)(3)(ii) for rules with respect to relevance, persuasiveness, subsequent developments, and use of a well-reasoned construction of an applicable statutory provision for purposes of the substantial understatement penalty.) In addition, the reasonable cause and good faith exception in §1.6664-4 may provide relief from the penalty for negligence or disregard of rules or regulations, even if a return position does not satisfy the reasonable basis standard.

(c) *Exception for adequate disclosure.*—(1) *In general.*—No penalty under section 6662(b)(1) may be imposed on any portion of an underpayment that is attributable to a position contrary to a rule or regulation if the position is disclosed in accordance with the rules of paragraph (c)(2) of this section (and, if the position relates to a reportable transaction as defined in §1.6011-4(b) (or §1.6011-4T(b), as applicable), the transaction is disclosed in accordance with §1.6011-4 (or §1.6011-4T, as applicable)) and, in case of a position contrary to a regulation, the position represents a good faith challenge to the validity of the regulation. This disclosure exception does not apply, however, in the case of a position that does not have a reasonable basis or where the taxpayer fails to keep adequate books and records or to substantiate items properly.

(2) *Method of disclosure.*—Disclosure is adequate for purposes of the penalty for disregarding rules or regulations if made in accordance with the provisions of §§1.6662-4(f)(1), (3), (4) and (5), which permit disclosure on a properly completed and filed Form 8275 or 8275-R, as appropriate. In addition, the statutory or regulatory provision or ruling in question must be adequately identified on the Form 8275 or 8275-R, as appropriate. The provisions of §1.6662-4(f)(2), which permit disclosure in accordance with an annual revenue procedure for purposes of the substantial understatement penalty, do not apply for purposes of this section.

(d) *Special rules in the case of carrybacks and carryovers.*—(1) *In general.*—The penalty for negligence or disregard of rules or regulations applies to any portion of an underpayment for a year to which a loss, deduction or credit is carried, which portion is attributable to negligence or disregard of rules or regulations in the year in which the carryback or carryover of the loss, deduction or credit arises (the "loss or credit year").

(2) *Transition rule for carrybacks to pre-1990 years.*—A 20 percent penalty under section 6662(b)(1) is imposed on any portion of an underpayment for a carryback year, the return for which is due (without regard to extensions) before January 1, 1990, if—

(i) That portion is attributable to negligence or disregard of rules or regulations in a loss or credit year; and

(ii) The return for the loss or credit year is due (without regard to extensions) after December 31, 1989.

(3) *Example.*—The following example illustrates the provisions of paragraph (d) of this section. This example does not take into account the reasonable cause exception under §1.6664-4.

Example. Corporation M is a C corporation. In 1990, M had a loss of $200,000 before taking into account a deduction of $350,000 that M claimed as an expense in careless disregard of the capitalization requirements of section 263 of the Code. M failed to make adequate disclosure of the item for 1990. M reported a $550,000 loss for 1990 and carried back the loss to 1987 and 1988. M had reported taxable income of $400,000 for 1987 and $200,000 for 1988, before application of the carryback. The carryback eliminated all of M's taxable income for 1987 and $150,000 of taxable income for 1988. After disallowance of the $350,000 expense deduction and allowance of a $35,000 depreciation deduction with respect to the capitalized amount, the correct loss for 1990 was determined to be $235,000. Because there is no underpayment for 1990, the penalty for negligence or disregard of rules or regulations does not apply for 1990. However, as a result of the 1990 adjustments, the loss carried back to 1987 is reduced from $550,000 to $235,000. After application of the $235,000 carryback, M has taxable income of $165,000 for 1987 and $200,000 for 1988. This adjustment results in underpayments for 1987 and 1988 that are attributable to the disregard of rules or regulations on the 1990 return. Therefore, the 20 percent penalty rate applies to the 1987 and 1988 underpayments attributable to the disallowed carryback. [Reg. § 1.6662-3.]

☐ [T.D. 8381, 12-30-91. Amended by T.D. 8617, 8-31-95; T.D. 8790, 12-1-98 and T.D. 9109, 12-29-2003.]

§ 1.6662-4. Substantial understatement of income tax.—(a) *In general.*—If any portion of an underpayment, as defined in section 6664(a) and § 1.6664-2, of any income tax imposed under subtitle A of the Code that is required to be shown on a return is attributable to a substantial understatement of such income tax, there is added to the tax an amount equal to 20 percent of such portion. Except in the case of any item attributable to a tax shelter (as defined in paragraph (g)(2) of this section), an understatement is reduced by the portion of the understatement that is attributable to the tax treatment of an item for which there is substantial authority, or with respect to which there is adequate disclosure. General rules for determining the amount of an understatement are set forth in paragraph (b) of this section and more specific rules in the case of carrybacks and carryovers are set forth in paragraph (c) of this section. The rules for determining when substantial authority exists are set forth in § 1.6662-4(d). The rules for determining when there is adequate disclosure are set forth in § 1.6662-4(e) and (f). This penalty does not apply to the extent that the reasonable cause and good faith exception to this penalty set forth in § 1.6664-4 applies.

(b) *Definitions and computational rules.*—(1) *Substantial.*—An understatement (as defined in paragraph (b)(2) of this section) is "substantial" if it exceeds the greater of—

(i) 10 percent of the tax required to be shown on the return for the taxable year (as defined in paragraph (b)(3) of this section); or

(ii) $5,000 ($10,000 in the case of a corporation other than an S corporation (as defined in section 1361(a)(1)) or a personal holding company (as defined in section 542)).

(2) *Understatement.*—Except as provided in paragraph (c)(2) of this section (relating to special rules for carrybacks), the term "understatement" means the excess of—

(i) The amount of the tax required to be shown on the return for the taxable year (as defined in paragraph (b)(3) of this section), over

(ii) The amount of the tax imposed which is shown on the return for the taxable year (as defined in paragraph (b)(4) of this section), reduced by any rebate (as defined in paragraph (b)(5) of this section).

The definition of understatement also may be expressed as—

$$Understatement = X - (Y - Z)$$

where X = the amount of the tax required to be shown on the return; Y = the amount of the tax imposed which is shown on the return; and Z = any rebate.

(3) *Amount of the tax required to be shown on the return.*—The "amount of the tax required to be shown on the return" for the taxable year has the same meaning as the "amount of income tax imposed" as defined in § 1.6664-2(b).

(4) *Amount of the tax imposed which is shown on the return.*—The "amount of the tax imposed which is shown on the return" for the taxable year has the same meaning as the "amount shown as the tax by the taxpayer on his return," as defined in § 1.6664-2(c), except that—

(i) There is no reduction for the excess of the amount described in § 1.6664-2(c)(1)(i) over the amount described in § 1.6664-2(c)(1)(ii), and

(ii) The tax liability shown by the taxpayer on his return is recomputed as if the following items had been reported properly:

(A) Items (other than tax shelter items as defined in § 1.6662-4(g)(3)) for which there is substantial authority for the treatment claimed (as provided in § 1.6662-4(d)).

(B) Items (other than tax shelter items as defined in § 1.6662-4(g)(3)) with respect to which there is adequate disclosure (as provided in § 1.6662-4(e) and (f)).

(C) Tax shelter items (as defined in § 1.6662-4(g)(3)) for which there is substantial authority for the treatment claimed (as provided in § 1.6662-4(d)), and with respect to which the taxpayer reasonably believed that the tax treatment of the items was more likely than not the proper tax treatment (as provided in § 1.6662-4(g)(4)).

(5) *Rebate.*—The term "rebate" has the meaning set forth in § 1.6664-2(e), except that—

(i) "Amounts not so shown previously assessed (or collected without assessment)" includes only amounts not so shown previously assessed (or collected without assessment) as a deficiency, and

(ii) The amount of the rebate is determined as if any items to which the rebate is attributable that are described in paragraph (b)(4) of this section had received the proper tax treatment.

(6) *Examples.*—The following examples illustrate the provisions of paragraph (b) of this section. These examples do not take into account the reasonable cause exception under § 1.6664-4:

Example 1. In 1990, Individual A, a calendar year taxpayer, files a return for 1989, which shows taxable income of $18,200 and tax liability of $2,734. Subsequent adjustments on audit for 1989 increase taxable income to $51,500 and tax liability to $12,339. There was substantial authority for an item resulting in an adjustment that increases taxable income by $5,300. The item is not a tax shelter item. In computing the amount of the understatement, the amount of tax shown on A's return is determined as if the item for which there was substantial authority had been given the proper tax treatment. Thus, the amount of tax that is treated as shown on A's return is $4,176, i.e., the tax on $23,500 ($18,200 taxable income actually shown on A's return plus $5,300, the amount of the adjustment for which there was substantial authority). The amount of the understatement is $8,163, i.e., $12,339 (the amount of tax required to be shown) less $4,176 (the amount of tax treated as shown on A's return after adjustment for the item for which there was substantial authority). Because the $8,163 understatement exceeds the greater of 10 percent of the tax required to be shown on the return for the year, i.e., $1,234 ($12,339 × .10) or $5,000, A has a substantial understatement of income tax for the year.

Example 2. Individual B, a calendar year taxpayer, files a return for 1990 that fails to include income reported on an information return, Form 1099, that was furnished to B. The Service detects this omission through its document matching program and assesses $3,000 in unreported tax liability. B's return is later examined and as a result of the examination the Service makes an adjustment to B's return of $4,000 in additional tax liability. Assuming there was neither substantial authority nor adequate disclosure with respect to the items adjusted, there is an understatement of $7,000 with respect to B's return. There is also an underpayment of $7,000. (See § 1.6664-2.) The amount of the understatement is not reduced by imposition of a negligence penalty on the $3,000 portion of the underpayment that is attributable to the unreported income. However, if the Service does impose the negligence penalty on this $3,000 portion, the Service may only impose the substantial understatement penalty on the remaining $4,000 portion of the underpayment. (See § 1.6662-2(c), which prohibits stacking of accuracy-related penalty components.)

(c) *Special rules in the case of carrybacks and carryovers.*—(1) *In general.*—The penalty for a substantial understatement of income tax applies to any portion of an underpayment for a year to which a loss, deduction or credit is carried that is attributable to a "tainted item" for the year in which the carryback or carryover of the loss, deduction or credit arises (the "loss or credit year"). The determination of whether an understatement is substantial for a carryback or carryover year is made with respect to the return of the carryback or carryover year. "Tainted items" are taken into account with items arising in a carryback or carryover year to determine whether the understatement is substantial for that year.

(2) *Understatements for carryback years not reduced by amount of carrybacks.*—The amount of an understatement for a carryback year is not reduced on account of a carryback of a loss, deduction or credit to that year.

(3) *Tainted items defined.*—(i) *In general.*—Except in the case of a tax shelter item (as defined in paragraph (g)(3) of this section), a "tainted item" is any item for which there is neither substantial authority nor adequate disclosure with respect to the loss or credit year.

(ii) *Tax shelter items.*—In the case of a tax shelter item (as defined in paragraph (g)(3) of this section), a "tainted item" is any item for which there is not, with respect to the loss or credit year, both substantial authority and a reasonable belief that the tax treatment is more likely than not the proper treatment.

(4) *Transition rule for carrybacks to pre-1990 years.*—A 20 percent penalty under section 6662(b)(2) is imposed on any portion of an underpayment for a carryback year, the return for which is due (without regard to extensions) before January 1, 1990, if—

(i) That portion is attributable to one or more "tainted items" (as defined in paragraph (c)(3) of this section) arising in a loss or credit year; and

Reg. § 1.6662-4(c)(4)(i)

(ii) The return for the loss or credit year is due (without regard to extensions) after December 31, 1989.

The preceding sentence applies only if the understatement in the carryback year is substantial. See *Example 2* in paragraph (c)(5) of this section.

(ii) During 1990, N files Form 1139, Corporation Application for Tentative Refund, to carry back the NOL generated in 1989 (NOLCB). N received refunds of $4,575 for 1987 and $22,250 for 1988.

(iii) For tax year 1990, N carries over $50,000 of the 1989 loss to offset $50,000 of income earned in 1990 and reduce taxable in-

(v) There was not substantial authority for N's treatment of the items comprising the 1989 adjustment and N did not make adequate disclosure.

(vi) As a result of the adjustment to the 1989 return, N had an understatement of $4,575 for tax year 1987; an understatement of $22,250 for tax year 1988; an understatement of $1,500 for tax year 1989; and an understatement of $7,500 for tax year 1990. Only the $22,250 understatement for 1988 is a substantial understatement, i.e., it exceeds the greater of (a) $2,225 (10 percent of the tax required to be shown on the return for the taxable year (.10 × $22,250)) or (b) $10,000. The underpayment for 1988 is subject to a penalty rate of 20 percent.

Example 2. The facts are the same as in *Example 1*, except that in addition to examining the 1989 return, the Service also examines the 1987 return and makes an adjustment that results in an understatement. (This adjustment is unrelated to the adjustment on the 1987 return for the disallowance of the NOLCB from 1989.) If the understatement resulting from the adjustment to the 1987 return, when combined with the understatement resulting from the disallowance of the NOLCB from 1989, exceeds the greater of (a) 10 percent of the tax required to be shown on the return for 1987 or (b) $10,000, the underpayment for 1987 will also be subject to a substantial understatement penalty. The

(5) *Examples.*—The following examples illustrate the rules of paragraph (c) of this section regarding carrybacks and carryovers. These examples do not take into account the reasonable cause exception under § 1.6664-4.

Example 1. (i) Corporation N, a calendar year taxpayer, is a C corporation. N was formed on January 1, 1987, and timely filed the following income tax returns:

Tax Year	1987	1988	1989	1990
Taxable Income	$30,000	$100,000	($300,000)	$50,000 (Before NOLCO)
Tax Liability	$4,575	$22,250	–0–	$7,500 (Before NOLCO)

come to zero. N would have reported $7,500 of tax liability for 1990 if it were not for use of the net operating loss carryover (NOLCO). N assumes there is a remaining NOLCO of $120,000 to be applied for tax year 1991.

(iv) In June 1991, the Service completes its examination of the 1989 loss year return and makes the following adjustment:

Taxable income per 1989 return	($300,000)
Adjustment: Unreported income	310,000
Corrected taxable income	$ 10,000
Corrected tax liability	$1,500

portion of the underpayment attributable to the adjustment unrelated to the disallowance of the NOLCB will be subject to a penalty rate of 25 percent under former section 6661. The portion of the underpayment attributable to the disallowance of the NOLCB will be subject to a penalty rate of 20 percent under section 6662.

Example 3. Individual P, a calendar year single taxpayer, files his 1990 return reporting taxable income of $10,000 and a tax liability of $1,504. An examination of the 1990 return results in an adjustment for unreported income of $25,000. There was not substantial authority for P's failure to report the income, and P did not make adequate disclosure with respect to the unreported income. P's correct tax liability for 1990 is determined to be $7,279, resulting in an understatement of $5,775 (the difference between the amount of tax required to be shown on the return ($7,279) and the tax shown on the return ($1,504)). Because the understatement exceeds the greater of (a) $728 (10 percent of the tax required to be shown on the return (.10 × $7,279)) or (b) $5,000, the understatement is substantial. Subsequently, P files his 1993 return showing a net operating loss. The loss is carried back to his 1990 return, reducing his taxable income for 1990 to zero. However, the amount of the understatement for 1990 is not reduced on account of the NOLCB to that year. P is subject to the 20 percent penalty rate under section 6662 on the underpayment attributable to the substantial understatement for 1990, notwithstanding that the tax required to be shown on the return for that year, after application of the NOLCB, is zero.

(d) *Substantial authority.*—(1) *Effect of having substantial authority.*—If there is substantial authority for the tax treatment of an item, the item is treated as if it were shown properly on the return for the taxable year in computing the amount of the tax shown on the return. Thus, for purposes of section 6662(d), the tax attributable to the item is not included in the understatement for that year. (For special rules relating to tax shelter items see § 1.6662-4(g).)

(2) *Substantial authority standard.*—The substantial authority standard is an objective standard involving an analysis of the law and application of the law to relevant facts. The substantial authority standard is less stringent than the more likely than not standard (the standard that is met when there is a greater than 50-percent likelihood of the position being upheld), but more stringent than the reasonable basis standard as defined in § 1.6662-3(b)(3). The possibility that a return will not be audited or, if audited, that an item will not be raised on audit, is not relevant in determining whether the substantial authority standard (or the reasonable basis standard) is satisfied.

(3) *Determination of whether substantial authority is present.*—(i) *Evaluation of authorities.*—There is substantial authority for the tax treatment of an item only if the weight of the authorities supporting the treatment is substantial in relation to the weight of authorities supporting contrary treatment. All authorities relevant to the tax treatment of an item, including the authorities contrary to the treatment, are taken into account in determining whether substantial authority exists. The weight of authorities is determined in light of the pertinent facts and circumstances in the manner prescribed by paragraph (d)(3)(ii) of this section. There may be substantial authority for more than one position with respect to the same item. Because the substantial authority standard is an objective standard, the taxpayer's belief that there is substantial authority for the tax treatment of an item is not relevant in determining whether there is substantial authority for that treatment.

(ii) *Nature of analysis.*—The weight accorded an authority depends on its relevance and persuasiveness, and the type of document providing the authority. For example, a case or revenue ruling having some facts in common with the tax treatment at issue is not particularly relevant if the authority is materially distinguishable on its facts, or is otherwise inapplicable to the tax treatment at issue. An authority that merely states a conclusion ordinarily is less persuasive than one that reaches its conclusion by cogently relating the applicable law to pertinent facts. The weight of an authority from which information has been deleted, such as a private letter ruling, is diminished to the extent that the deleted information may have affected the authority's conclusions. The type of document also must be considered. For example, a revenue ruling is accorded greater weight than a private letter ruling addressing the same issue. An older private letter ruling, technical advice memorandum, general counsel memorandum or action on decision generally must be accorded less weight than a more recent one. Any document described in the preceding sentence that is more than 10 years old generally is accorded very little weight. However, the persuasiveness and relevance of a document, viewed in light of subsequent developments, should be taken into account along with the age of the document. There may be substantial authority for the tax treatment of an item despite the absence of certain types of authority. Thus, a taxpayer may have substantial authority for a position that is supported only by a well-reasoned construction of the applicable statutory provision.

(iii) *Types of authority.*—Except in cases described in paragraph (d)(3)(iv) of this section concerning written determinations, only the following are authority for purposes of determining whether there is substantial authority for the tax treatment of an item: applicable provisions of the Internal Revenue Code and other statutory provisions; proposed, temporary and final regulations construing such statutes; revenue rulings and revenue procedures; tax treaties and regulations thereunder, and Treasury Department and other official explanations of such treaties; court cases; congressional intent as reflected in committee reports, joint explanatory statements of managers included in conference committee reports, and floor statements made prior to enactment by one of a bill's managers; General Explanations of tax legislation prepared by the Joint Committee on Taxation (the Blue Book); private letter rulings and technical advice memoranda issued after October 31, 1976; actions on decisions and general counsel memoranda issued after March 12, 1981 (as well as general counsel memoranda published in pre-1955 volumes of the Cumulative Bulletin); Internal Revenue Service information or press releases; and notices, announcements and other administrative pronouncements published by the Service in the Internal Revenue Bulletin. Conclusions

Reg. §1.6662-4(d)(3)(iii)

reached in treatises, legal periodicals, legal opinions or opinions rendered by tax professionals are not authority. The authorities underlying such expressions of opinion where applicable to the facts of a particular case, however, may give rise to substantial authority for the tax treatment of an item. Notwithstanding the preceding list of authorities, an authority does not continue to be an authority to the extent it is overruled or modified, implicitly or explicitly, by a body with the power to overrule or modify the earlier authority. In the case of court decisions, for example, a district court opinion on an issue is not an authority if overruled or reversed by the United States Court of Appeals for such district. However, a Tax Court opinion is not considered to be overruled or modified by a court of appeals to which a taxpayer does not have a right of appeal, unless the Tax Court adopts the holding of the court of appeals. Similarly, a private letter ruling is not authority if revoked or if inconsistent with a subsequent proposed regulation, revenue ruling or other administrative pronouncement published in the Internal Revenue Bulletin.

(iv) *Special rules.*—(A) *Written determinations.*—There is substantial authority for the tax treatment of an item by a taxpayer if the treatment is supported by the conclusion of a ruling or a determination letter (as defined in § 301.6110-2(d) and (e)) issued to the taxpayer, by the conclusion of a technical advice memorandum in which the taxpayer is named, or by an affirmative statement in a revenue agent's report with respect to a prior taxable year of the taxpayer ("written determinations"). The preceding sentence does not apply, however, if—

(*1*) There was a misstatement or omission of a material fact or the facts that subsequently develop are materially different from the facts on which the written determination was based, or

(*2*) The written determination was modified or revoked after the date of issuance by—

(*i*) A notice to the taxpayer to whom the written determination was issued,

(*ii*) The enactment of legislation or ratification of a tax treaty,

(*iii*) A decision of the United States Supreme Court,

(*iv*) The issuance of temporary or final regulations, or

(*v*) The issuance of a revenue ruling, revenue procedure, or other statement published in the Internal Revenue Bulletin.

Except in the case of a written determination that is modified or revoked on account of § 1.6662-4(d)(3)(iv)(A)(*1*), a written determination that is modified or revoked as described in § 1.6662-4(d)(3)(iv)(A)(*2*) ceases to be authority on the date, and to the extent, it is so modified or revoked. See section 6404(f) for rules which require the Secretary to abate a penalty that is attributable to erroneous written advice furnished to a taxpayer by an officer or employee of the Internal Revenue Service.

(B) *Taxpayer's jurisdiction.*—The applicability of court cases to the taxpayer by reason of the taxpayer's residence in a particular jurisdiction is not taken into account in determining whether there is substantial authority for the tax treatment of an item. Notwithstanding the preceding sentence, there is substantial authority for the tax treatment of an item if the treatment is supported by controlling precedent of a United States Court of Appeals to which the taxpayer has a right of appeal with respect to the item.

(C) *When substantial authority determined.*—There is substantial authority for the tax treatment of an item if there is substantial authority at the time the return containing the item is filed or there was substantial authority on the last day of the taxable year to which the return relates.

(v) *Substantial authority for tax returns due before January 1, 1990.*—There is substantial authority for the tax treatment of an item on a return that is due (without regard to extensions) after December 31, 1982 and before January 1, 1990, if there is substantial authority for such treatment under either the provisions of paragraph (d)(3)(iii) of this section (which set forth an expanded list of authorities) or of § 1.6661-3(b)(2) (which set forth a narrower list of authorities). Under either list of authorities, authorities both for and against the position must be taken into account.

(e) *Disclosure of certain information.*—(1) *Effect of adequate disclosure.*—Items for which there is adequate disclosure as provided in this paragraph (e) and in paragraph (f) of this section are treated as if such items were shown properly on the return for the taxable year in computing the amount of the tax shown on the return. Thus, for purposes of section 6662(d), the tax attributable to such items is not included in the understatement for that year.

(2) *Circumstances where disclosure will not have an effect.*—The rules of paragraph (e)(1) of this section do not apply where the item or position on the return —

(i) Does not have a reasonable basis (as defined in § 1.6662-3(b)(3));

(ii) Is attributable to a tax shelter (as defined in section 6662(d)(2)(C)(iii) and paragraph (g)(2) of this section); or

(iii) Is not properly substantiated, or the taxpayer failed to keep adequate books and records with respect to the item or position.

(3) *Restriction for corporations.*—For purposes of paragraph (e)(2)(i) of this section, a corporation will not be treated as having a reasonable basis for its tax treatment of an item attributable to a multi-party financing transaction entered into after August 5, 1997, if the treatment does not clearly reflect the income of the corporation.

(f) *Method of making adequate disclosure.*—(1) *Disclosure statement.*—Disclosure is adequate with respect to an item (or group of similar items, such as amounts paid or incurred for supplies by a taxpayer engaged in business) or a position on a return if the disclosure is made on a properly completed form attached to the return or to a qualified amended return (as defined in § 1.6664-2(c)(3)) for the taxable year. In the case of an item or position other than one that is contrary to a regulation, disclosure must be made on Form 8275 (Disclosure Statement); in the case of a position contrary to a regulation, disclosure must be made on Form 8275-R (Regulation Disclosure Statement).

(2) *Disclosure on return.*—The Commissioner may by annual revenue procedure (or otherwise) prescribe the circumstances under which disclosure of information on a return (or qualified amended return) in accordance with applicable forms and instructions is adequate. If the revenue procedure does not include an item, disclosure is adequate with respect to that item only if made on a properly completed Form 8275 or 8275-R, as appropriate, attached to the return for the year or to a qualified amended return.

(3) *Recurring item.*—Disclosure with respect to a recurring item, such as the basis of recovery property, must be made for each taxable year in which the item is taken into account.

(4) *Carrybacks and carryovers.*—Disclosure is adequate with respect to an item which is included in any loss, deduction or credit that is carried to another year only if made in connection with the return (or qualified amended return) for the taxable year in which the carryback or carryover arises (the "loss or credit year"). Disclosure is not also required in connection with the return for the taxable year in which the carryback or carryover is taken into account.

(5) *Pass-through entities.*—Disclosure in the case of items attributable to a pass-through entity (pass-through items) is made with respect to the return of the entity, except as provided in this paragraph (f)(5). Thus, disclosure in the case of pass-through items must be made on a Form 8275 or 8275-R, as appropriate, attached to the return (or qualified amended return) of the entity, or on the entity's return in accordance with the revenue procedure described in paragraph (f)(2) of this section, if applicable. A taxpayer (i.e., partner, shareholder, beneficiary, or holder of a residual interest in a REMIC) also may make adequate disclosure with respect to a pass-through item, however, if the taxpayer files a properly completed Form 8275 or 8275-R, as appropriate, in duplicate, one copy attached to the taxpayer's return (or qualified amended return) and the other copy filed with the Internal Revenue Service Center with which the return of the entity is required to be filed. Each Form 8275 or 8275-R, as appropriate, filed by the taxpayer should relate to the pass-through items of only one entity. For purposes of this paragraph (f)(5), a pass-through entity is a partnership, S corporation (as defined in section 1361(a)(1)), estate, trust, regulated investment company (as defined in section 851(a)), real estate investment trust (as defined in section 856(a)), or real estate mortgage investment conduit ("REMIC") (as defined in section 860D(a)).

(g) *Items relating to tax shelters.*—(1) *In general.*—(i) *Noncorporate taxpayers.*—Tax shelter items (as defined in paragraph (g)(3) of this section) of a taxpayer other than a corporation are treated for purposes of this section as if such items were shown properly on the return for a taxable year in computing the amount of the tax shown on the return, and thus the tax attributable to such items is not included in the understatement for the year, if—

(A) There is substantial authority (as provided in paragraph (d) of this section) for the tax treatment of that item; and

(B) The taxpayer reasonably believed at the time the return was filed that the tax treatment of that item was more likely than not the proper treatment.

(ii) *Corporate taxpayers.*—(A) *In general.*—Except as provided in paragraph (g)(1)(ii)(B) of this section, all tax shelter items (as defined in paragraph (g)(3) of this section) of a corporation are taken into account in computing the amount of any understatement.

(B) *Special rule for transactions occurring prior to December 9, 1994.*—The tax shelter items of a corporation arising in connection with transactions occurring prior to December

9, 1994 are treated for purposes of this section as if such items were shown properly on the return if the requirements of paragraph (g)(1)(i) are satisfied with respect to such items.

(iii) *Disclosure irrelevant.*—Disclosure made with respect to a tax shelter item of either a corporate or noncorporate taxpayer does not affect the amount of an understatement.

(iv) *Cross-reference.*—See § 1.6664-4(f) for certain rules regarding the availability of the reasonable cause and good faith exception to the substantial understatement penalty with respect to tax shelter items of corporations.

(2) *Tax shelter.*—(i) *In general.*—For purposes of section 6662(d), the term "tax shelter" means—

(A) A partnership or other entity (such as a corporation or trust),

(B) An investment plan or arrangement, or

(C) Any other plan or arrangement,

if the principal purpose of the entity, plan or arrangement, based on objective evidence, is to avoid or evade Federal income tax. The principal purpose of an entity, plan or arrangement is to avoid or evade Federal income tax if that purpose exceeds any other purpose. Typical of tax shelters are transactions structured with little or no motive for the realization of economic gain, and transactions that utilize the mismatching of income and deductions, overvalued assets or assets with values subject to substantial uncertainty, certain nonrecourse financing, financing techniques that do not conform to standard commercial business practices, or the mischaracterization of the substance of the transaction. The existence of economic substance does not of itself establish that a transaction is not a tax shelter if the transaction includes other characteristics that indicate it is a tax shelter.

(ii) *Principal purpose.*—The principal purpose of an entity, plan or arrangement is not to avoid or evade Federal income tax if the entity, plan or arrangement has as its purpose the claiming of exclusions from income, accelerated deductions or other tax benefits in a manner consistent with the statute and Congressional purpose. For example, an entity, plan or arrangement does not have as its principal purpose the avoidance or evasion of Federal income tax solely as a result of the following uses of tax benefits provided by the Internal Revenue Code: the purchasing or holding of an obligation bearing interest that is excluded from gross income under section 103; taking an accelerated depreciation allowance under section 168; taking the percentage depletion allowance under section 613 or section 613A; deducting intangible drilling and development costs as expenses under section 263(c); establishing a qualified retirement plan under sections 401-409; claiming the possession tax credit under section 936; or claiming tax benefits available by reason of an election under section 992 to be taxed as a domestic international sales corporation ("DISC"), under section 927(f)(1) to be taxed as a foreign sales corporation ("FSC"), or under section 1362 to be taxed as an S corporation.

(3) *Tax shelter item.*—An item of income, gain, loss, deduction or credit is a "tax shelter item" if the item is directly or indirectly attributable to the principal purpose of a tax shelter to avoid or evade Federal income tax. Thus, if a partnership is established for the principal purpose of avoiding or evading Federal income tax by acquiring and overstating the basis of property for purposes of claiming accelerated depreciation, the depreciation with respect to the property is a tax shelter item. However, a deduction claimed in connection with a separate transaction carried on by the same partnership is not a tax shelter item if the transaction does not constitute a plan or arrangement the principal purpose of which is to avoid or evade tax.

(4) *Reasonable belief.*—(i) *In general.*—For purposes of section 6662(d) and paragraph (g)(1)(i)(B) of this section (pertaining to tax shelter items of noncorporate taxpayers), a taxpayer is considered reasonably to believe that the tax treatment of an item is more likely than not the proper tax treatment if (without taking into account the possibility that a return will not be audited, that an issue will not be raised on audit, or that an issue will be settled)—

(A) The taxpayer analyzes the pertinent facts and authorities in the manner described in paragraph (d)(3)(ii) of this section, and in reliance upon that analysis, reasonably concludes in good faith that there is a greater than 50-percent likelihood that the tax treatment of the item will be upheld if challenged by the Internal Revenue Service; or

(B) The taxpayer reasonably relies in good faith on the opinion of a professional tax advisor, if the opinion is based on the tax advisor's analysis of the pertinent facts and authorities in the manner described in paragraph (d)(3)(ii) of this section and unambiguously states that the tax advisor concludes that there is a greater than 50-percent likelihood that the tax treatment of the item will be upheld if challenged by the Internal Revenue Service.

(ii) *Facts and circumstances; reliance on professional tax advisor.*—All facts and circumstances must be taken into account in determining whether a taxpayer satisfies the requirements of paragraph (g)(4)(i) of this section. However, in no event will a taxpayer be considered to have reasonably relied in good faith on the opinion of a professional tax advisor for purposes of paragraph (g)(4)(i)(B) of this section unless the requirements of § 1.6664-4(c)(1) are met. The fact that the requirements of § 1.6664-4(c)(1) are satisfied will not necessarily establish that the taxpayer reasonably relied on the opinion in good faith. For example, reliance may not be reasonable or in good faith if the taxpayer knew, or should have known, that the advisor lacked knowledge in the relevant aspects of Federal tax law.

(5) *Pass-through entities.*—In the case of tax shelter items attributable to a pass-through entity, the actions described in paragraphs (g)(4)(i)(A) and (B) of this section, if taken by the entity, are deemed to have been taken by the taxpayer and are considered in determining whether the taxpayer reasonably believed that the tax treatment of an item was more likely than not the proper tax treatment. [Reg. § 1.6662-4.]

☐ [*T.D.* 8381, 12-30-91. *Amended by T.D.* 8617, 8-31-95; *T.D.* 8790, 12-1-98 *and T.D.* 9109, 12-29-2003.]

§ 1.6662-5. Substantial and gross valuation misstatements under chapter 1.—

(a) *In general.*—If any portion of an underpayment, as defined in section 6664(a) and § 1.6664-2, of any income tax imposed under chapter 1 of subtitle A of the Code that is required to be shown on a return is attributable to a substantial valuation misstatement under chapter 1 ("substantial valuation misstatement"), there is added to the tax an amount equal to 20 percent of such portion. Section 6662(h) increases the penalty to 40 percent in the case of a gross valuation misstatement under chapter 1 ("gross valuation misstatement"). No penalty under section 6662(b)(3) is imposed, however, on a portion of an underpayment that is attributable to a substantial or gross valuation misstatement unless the aggregate of all portions of the underpayment attributable to substantial or gross valuation misstatements exceeds the applicable dollar limitation ($5,000 or $10,000), as provided in section 6662(e)(2) and paragraphs (b) and (f)(2) of this section. This penalty also does not apply to the extent that the reasonable cause and good faith exception to this penalty set forth in § 1.6664-4 applies. There is no disclosure exception to this penalty.

(b) *Dollar limitation.*—No penalty may be imposed under section 6662(b)(3) for a taxable year unless the portion of the underpayment for that year that is attributable to substantial or gross valuation misstatements exceeds $5,000 ($10,000 in the case of a corporation other than an S corporation (as defined in section 1361(a)(1)) or a personal holding company (as defined in section 542)). This limitation is applied separately to each taxable year for which there is a substantial or gross valuation misstatement.

(c) *Special rules in the case of carrybacks and carryovers.*—(1) *In general.*—The penalty for a substantial or gross valuation misstatement applies to any portion of an underpayment for a year to which a loss, deduction or credit is carried that is attributable to a substantial or gross valuation misstatement for the year in which the carryback or carryover of the loss, deduction or credit arises (the "loss or credit year"), provided that the applicable dollar limitation set forth in section 6662(e)(2) is satisfied in the carryback or carryover year.

(2) *Transition rule for carrybacks to pre-1990 years.*—The penalty under section 6662(b)(3) is imposed on any portion of an underpayment for a carryback year, the return for which is due (without regard to extensions) before January 1, 1990, if—

(i) That portion is attributable to a substantial or gross valuation misstatement for a loss or credit year; and

(ii) The return for the loss or credit year is due (without regard to extensions) after December 31, 1989.

The preceding sentence applies only if the underpayment for the carryback year exceeds the applicable dollar limitation ($5,000, or $10,000 for most corporations). See *Example 3* in paragraph (d) of this section.

(d) *Examples.*—The following examples illustrate the provisions of paragraphs (b) and (c) of this section. These examples do not take into account the reasonable cause exception under § 1.6664-4.

Example 1. Corporation Q is a C corporation. In 1990, the first year of its existence, Q had taxable income of $200,000 without considering depreciation of a particular asset. On its calendar year 1990 return, Q overstated its basis in this asset by an amount that caused a substantial valuation misstatement. The overstated basis resulted in depreciation claimed of $350,000, which was $250,000 more than the $100,000 allowable. Thus, on its 1990 return, Q showed a loss of $150,000. In 1991, Q had taxable income of $450,000 before application of the loss carryover, and Q claimed a carryover loss deduction under section 172 of $150,000, resulting in taxable income of $300,000 for 1991. Upon audit of the 1990 return, the basis of the asset was corrected, resulting in an adjustment of $250,000. For 1990, the underpayment resulting from the $100,000 taxable income (−$150,000 + $250,000) is attributable to the valuation misstatement. Assuming the underpayment resulting from the $100,000 taxable income exceeds the $10,000 limitation, the penalty will be imposed in 1990. For 1991, the elimination of the loss carryover results in additional taxable income of $150,000. The underpayment for 1991 resulting from that adjustment is also attributable to the substantial valuation misstatement on the 1990 return. Assuming the underpayment resulting from the $150,000 additional taxable income for 1991 exceeds the $10,000 limitation, the substantial valuation misstatement penalty also will be imposed for that year.

Example 2. (i) Corporation T is a C corporation. In 1990, the first year of its existence, T had a loss of $3,000,000 without considering depreciation of its major asset. On its calendar year 1990 return, T overstated its basis in this asset in an amount that caused a substantial valuation misstatement. This overstatement resulted in depreciation claimed of $3,500,000, which was $2,500,000 more than the $1,000,000 allowable. Thus, on its 1990 return, T showed a loss of $6,500,000. In 1991, T had taxable income of $4,500,000 before application of the carryover loss, but claimed a carryover loss deduction under section 172 in the amount of $4,500,000, resulting in taxable income of zero for that year and leaving a $2,000,000 carryover available. Upon audit of the 1990 return, the basis of the asset was corrected, resulting in an adjustment of $2,500,000.

(ii) For 1990, the underpayment is still zero (−$6,500,000 + $2,500,000 = −$4,000,000). Thus, the penalty does not apply in 1990. The loss for 1990 is reduced to $4,000,000.

(iii) For 1991, there is additional taxable income of $500,000 as a result of the reduction of the carryover loss ($4,500,000 reported income before carryover loss minus corrected carryover loss of $4,000,000 = $500,000). The underpayment for 1991 resulting from reduction of the carryover loss is attributable to the valuation misstatement on the 1990 return. Assuming the underpayment resulting from the $500,000 additional taxable income exceeds the $10,000 limitation, the substantial valuation misstatement penalty will be imposed in 1991.

Example 3. Corporation V is a C corporation. In 1990, V had a loss of $100,000 without considering depreciation of a particular asset which it had fully depreciated in earlier years. V had a depreciable basis in the asset of zero, but on its 1990 calendar year return erroneously claimed a basis in the asset of $1,250,000 and depreciation of $250,000. V reported a $350,000 loss for the year 1990, and carried back the loss to the 1987 and 1988 tax years. V had reported taxable income of $300,000 in 1987 and $200,000 in 1988, before application of the carryback. The $350,000 carryback eliminated all taxable income for 1987, and $50,000 of the taxable income for 1988. After disallowance of the $250,000 depreciation deduction for 1990, V still had a loss of $100,000. Because there is no underpayment for 1990, no valuation misstatement penalty is imposed for 1990. However, as a result of the 1990 depreciation adjustment, the carryback to 1987 is reduced from $350,000 to $100,000. After absorption of the $100,000 carryback, V has taxable income of $200,000 for 1987. This adjustment results in an underpayment for 1987 that is attributable to the valuation misstatement on the 1990 return. The valuation misstatement for 1990 is a gross valuation misstatement because the correct adjusted basis of the depreciated asset was zero. (See paragraph (e)(2) of this section.) Therefore, the 40 percent penalty rate applies to the 1987 underpayment attributable to the 1990 misstatement, provided that this underpayment exceeds $10,000. The adjustment also results in the elimination of any loss carryback to 1988 resulting in an increase in taxable income for 1988 of $50,000. Assuming the underpayment resulting from this additional $50,000 of income exceeds $10,000, the gross valuation misstatement penalty is imposed on the underpayment for 1988.

(e) *Definitions.*—(1) *Substantial valuation misstatement.*—There is a substantial valuation misstatement if the value or adjusted basis of any property claimed on a return of tax imposed under chapter 1 is 200 percent or more of the correct amount.

(2) *Gross valuation misstatement.*—There is a gross valuation misstatement if the value or adjusted basis of any property claimed on a return of tax imposed under chapter 1 is 400 percent or more of the correct amount.

(3) *Property.*—For purposes of this section, the term "property" refers to both tangible and intangible property. Tangible property includes property such as land, buildings, fixtures and inventory. Intangible property includes property such as goodwill, covenants not to compete, leaseholds, patents, contract rights, debts and choses in action.

(f) *Multiple valuation misstatements on a return.*—(1) *Determination of whether valuation misstatements are substantial or gross.*—The determination of whether there is a substantial or gross valuation misstatement on a return is made on a property-by-property basis. Assume, for example, that property A has a value of 60 but a taxpayer claims a value of 110, and that property B has a value of 40 but the taxpayer claims a value of 100. Because the claimed and correct values are compared on a property-by-property basis, there is a substantial valuation misstatement with respect to property B, but not with respect to property A, even though the claimed values (210) are 200 percent or more of the correct values (100) when compared on an aggregate basis.

(2) *Application of dollar limitation.*—For purposes of applying the dollar limitation set forth in section 6662(e)(2), the determination of the portion of an underpayment that is attributable to a substantial or gross valuation misstatement is made by aggregating all portions of the underpayment attributable to substantial or gross valuation misstatements. Assume, for example, that the value claimed for property C on a return is 250 percent of the correct value, and that the value claimed for property D on the return is 400 percent of the correct value. Because the portions of an underpayment that are attributable to a substantial or gross valuation misstatement on a return are aggregated in applying the dollar limitation, the dollar limitation is satisfied if the portion of the underpayment that is attributable to the misstatement of the value of property C, when aggregated with the portion of the underpayment that is attributable to the misstatement of the value of property D, exceeds $5,000 ($10,000 in the case of most corporations).

(g) *Property with a value or adjusted basis of zero.*—The value or adjusted basis claimed on a return of any property with a correct value or adjusted basis of zero is considered to be 400 percent or more of the correct amount. There is a gross valuation misstatement with respect to such property, therefore, and the applicable penalty rate is 40 percent.

(h) *Pass-through entities.*—(1) *In general.*—The determination of whether there is a substantial or gross valuation misstatement in the case of a return of a pass-through entity (as defined in §1.6662-4(f)(5)) is made at the entity level. However, the dollar limitation ($5,000 or $10,000, as the case may be) is applied at the taxpayer level (*i.e.,* with respect to the return of the shareholder, partner, beneficiary, or holder of a residual interest in a REMIC).

(2) *Example.*—The rules of paragraph (h)(1) of this section may be illustrated by the following example.

Example. Partnership P has two partners, individuals A and B. P claims a $40,000 basis in a depreciable asset which, in fact, has a basis of $15,000. The determination that there is a substantial valuation misstatement is made solely with reference to P by comparing the $40,000 basis claimed by P with P's correct basis of $15,000. However, the determination of whether the $5,000 threshold for application of the penalty has been reached is made separately for each partner. With respect to partner A, the penalty will apply if the portion of A's underpayment attributable to the passthrough of the depreciation deduction, when aggregated with any other portions of A's underpayment also attributable to substantial or gross valuation misstatements, exceeds $5,000 (assuming there is not reasonable cause for the misstatements (*see* §1.6664-4(c)).

(i) [Reserved]

(j) *Transactions between persons described in section 482 and net section 482 transfer price adjustments.*—[Reserved]

(k) *Returns affected.*—Except in the case of rules relating to transactions between persons described in section 482 and net section 482 transfer price adjustments, the provisions of section 6662(b)(3) apply to returns due (without regard to extensions of time to file) after December 31, 1989, notwithstanding that the original substantial or gross valuation misstatement occurred on a return that was due (without regard to extensions) before January 1, 1990. Assume, for example, that a calendar year corporation claimed a deduction on its 1990 return for depreciation of an asset with a basis of X. Also assume that it had reported the same basis for computing depreciation on its returns for the preceding 5 years and that the basis shown on the return each year was 200 percent or more of the correct basis. The corporation may be subject to a penalty for substantial valuation misstatements on its 1989 and 1990 returns, even though the original misstatement occurred prior to the effective date of sections 6662(b)(3) and (e). [Reg. §1.6662-5.]

☐ [*T.D.* 8381, 12-30-91.]

§1.6662-5T. Substantial and gross valuation misstatements under chapter 1 (Temporary).—(a) through (e)(3) [Reserved]. For further information, see §1.6662-5(a) through (e)(3).

(e)(4) *Tests related to section 482.*—(i) *Substantial valuation misstatement.*—There is a substantial valuation misstatement if there is a misstatement described in §1.6662-6(b)(1) or (c)(1) (concerning substantial valuation misstatements pertaining to transactions between related persons).

(ii) *Gross valuation misstatement.*—There is a gross valuation misstatement if there is a misstatement described in §1.6662-6(b)(2) or (c)(2) (concerning gross valuation misstatements pertaining to transactions between related persons).

(iii) *Property.*—For purposes of this section, the term *property* refers to both tangible and intangible property. Tangible property includes property such as money, land, buildings, fixtures and inventory. Intangible property includes property such as goodwill, covenants not to compete, leaseholds, patents, contract rights, debts, choses in action, and any other item of intangible property described in § 1.482-4(b).

(f) through (h) [Reserved] For further information, see § 1.6664-5(f) through (h).

(i) [Reserved].

(j) *Transactions between persons described in section 482 and net section 482 transfer price adjustments.*—For rules relating to the penalty imposed with respect to a substantial or gross valuation misstatement arising from a section 482 allocation, see § 1.6662-6. [Temporary Reg. § 1.6662-5T.]

☐ [*T.D.* 8519, 1-27-94. *Amended by T.D.* 8656, 2-8-96.]

§ 1.6662-6. Transactions between persons described in section 482 and net section 482 transfer price adjustments.— (a) *In general.*—(1) *Purpose and scope.*—Pursuant to section 6662(e) a penalty is imposed on any underpayment attributable to a substantial valuation misstatement pertaining to either a transaction between persons described in section 482 (the transactional penalty) or a net section 482 transfer price adjustment (the net adjustment penalty). The penalty is equal to 20 percent of the underpayment of tax attributable to that substantial valuation misstatement. Pursuant to section 6662(h) the penalty is increased to 40 percent of the underpayment in the case of a gross valuation misstatement with respect to either penalty. Paragraph (b) of this section provides specific rules related to the transactional penalty. Paragraph (c) of this section provides specific rules related to the net adjustment penalty, and paragraph (d) of this section describes amounts that will be excluded for purposes of calculating the net adjustment penalty. Paragraph (e) of this section sets forth special rules in the case of carrybacks and carryovers. Paragraph (f) of this section provides coordination rules between penalties. Paragraph (g) of this section provides the effective date of this section.

(2) *Reported results.*—Whether an underpayment is attributable to a substantial or gross valuation misstatement must be determined from the results of controlled transactions that are reported on an income tax return, regardless of whether the amount reported differs from the transaction price initially reflected in the taxpayer's books and records. The results of controlled transactions that are reported on an amended return will be used only if the amended return is filed before the Internal Revenue Service has contacted the taxpayer regarding the corresponding original return. A written statement furnished by a taxpayer subject to the Coordinated Examination Program or a written statement furnished by the taxpayer when electing Accelerated Issue Resolution or similar procedures will be considered an amended return for purposes of this section if it satisfies either the requirements of a qualified amended return for purposes of § 1.6664-2(c)(3) or such requirements as the Commissioner may prescribe by revenue procedure. In the case of a taxpayer that is a member of a consolidated group, the rules of this paragraph (a)(2) apply to the consolidated income tax return of the group.

(3) *Identical terms used in the section 482 regulations.*—For purposes of this section, the terms used in this section shall have the same meaning as identical terms used in regulations under section 482.

(b) *The transactional penalty.*—(1) *Substantial valuation misstatement.*—In the case of any transaction between related persons, there is a substantial valuation misstatement if the price for any property or services (or for the use of property) claimed on any return is 200 percent or more (or 50 percent or less) of the amount determined under section 482 to be the correct price.

(2) *Gross valuation misstatement.*—In the case of any transaction between related persons, there is a gross valuation misstatement if the price for any property or services (or for the use of property) claimed on any return is 400 percent or more (or 25 percent or less) of the amount determined under section 482 to be the correct price.

(3) *Reasonable cause and good faith.*—Pursuant to section 6664(c), the transactional penalty will not be imposed on any portion of an underpayment with respect to which the requirements of § 1.6664-4 are met. In applying the provisions of § 1.6664-4 in a case in which the taxpayer has relied on professional analysis in determining its transfer pricing, whether the professional is an employee of, or related to, the taxpayer is not determinative in evaluating whether the taxpayer reasonably relied in good faith on advice. A taxpayer that meets the requirements of paragraph (d) of this section with respect to an allocation under section 482 will be treated as having established that there was reasonable cause and good faith with respect to that item for purposes of § 1.6664-4. If a substantial or gross valuation misstatement under the transactional penalty also constitutes (or is part of) a substantial or gross valuation misstatement under the net adjustment penalty, then the rules of paragraph (d) of this section (and not the rules of § 1.6664-4) will be applied to determine whether the adjustment is

excluded from calculation of the net section 482 adjustment.

(c) *Net adjustment penalty.*—(1) *Net section 482 adjustment.*—For purposes of this section, the term *net section 482 adjustment* means the sum of all increases in the taxable income of a taxpayer for a taxable year resulting from allocations under section 482 (determined without regard to any amount carried to such taxable year from another taxable year) less any decreases in taxable income attributable to collateral adjustments as described in § 1.482-1(g). For purposes of this section, amounts that meet the requirements of paragraph (d) of this section will be excluded from the calculation of the net section 482 adjustment. Substantial and gross valuation misstatements that are subject to the transactional penalty under paragraph (b)(1) or (2) of this section are included in determining the amount of the net section 482 adjustment. See paragraph (f) of this section for coordination rules between penalties.

(2) *Substantial valuation misstatement.*—There is a substantial valuation misstatement if a net section 482 adjustment is greater than the lesser of 5 million dollars or ten percent of gross receipts.

(3) *Gross valuation misstatement.*—There is a gross valuation misstatement if a net section 482 adjustment is greater than the lesser of 20 million dollars or twenty percent of gross receipts.

(4) *Setoff allocation rule.*—If a taxpayer meets the requirements of paragraph (d) of this section with respect to some, but not all of the allocations made under section 482, then for purposes of determining the net section 482 adjustment, setoffs, as taken into account under § 1.482-1(g)(4), must be applied ratably against all such allocations. The following example illustrates the principle of this paragraph (c)(4):

Example. (i) The Internal Revenue Service makes the following section 482 adjustments for the taxable year:

(1) Attributable to an increase in gross income because of an increase in royalty payments . . . $9,000,000
(2) Attributable to an increase in sales proceeds due to a decrease in the profit margin of a related buyer . 6,000,000
(3) Because of a setoff under § 1.482-1(g)(4) . . . . (5,000,000)

Total section 482 adjustments 10,000,000

(ii) The taxpayer meets the requirements of paragraph (d) with respect to adjustment number one, but not with respect to adjustment number two. The five million dollar setoff will be allocated ratably against the nine million dollar adjustment ($9,000,000/$15,000,000 x $5,000,000 = $3,000,000) and the six million dollar adjustment ($6,000,000/$15,000,000 x $5,000,000 = $2,000,000). Accordingly, in determining the net section 482 adjustment, the nine million dollar adjustment is reduced to six million dollars ($9,000,000 -$3,000,000) and the six million dollar adjustment is reduced to four million dollars ($6,000,000 -$2,000,000). Therefore, the net section 482 adjustment equals four million dollars.

(5) *Gross receipts.*—For purposes of this section, gross receipts must be computed pursuant to the rules contained in § 1.448-1T(f)(2)(iv), as adjusted to reflect allocations under section 482.

(6) *Coordination with reasonable cause exception under section 6664(c).*—Pursuant to section 6662(e)(3)(D), a taxpayer will be treated as having reasonable cause under section 6664(c) for any portion of an underpayment attributable to a net section 482 adjustment only if the taxpayer meets the requirements of paragraph (d) of this section with respect to that portion.

(7) *Examples.*—The principles of this paragraph (c) are illustrated by the following examples:

Example 1. (i) The Internal Revenue Service makes the following section 482 adjustments for the taxable year:

(1) Attributable to an increase in gross income because of an increase in royalty payments $2,000,000
(2) Attributable to an increase in sales proceeds due to a decrease in the profit margin of a related buyer . . 2,500,000
(3) Attributable to a decrease in the cost of goods sold because of a decrease in the cost plus mark-up of a related seller 2,000,000

Total section 482 adjustments 6,500,000

(ii) None of the adjustments are excluded under paragraph (d) of this section. The net section 482 adjustment ($6.5 million) is greater than five million dollars. Therefore, there is a substantial valuation misstatement.

Example 2. (i) The Internal Revenue Service makes the following section 482 adjustments for the taxable year:

(1) Attributable to an increase in gross income because of an increase in royalty payments . .	$11,000,000
(2) Attributable to an increase in sales proceeds due to a decrease in the profit margin of a related buyer	2,000,000
(3) Because of a setoff under § 1.482-1(g)(4)	(9,000,000)
Total section 482 adjustments	$4,000,000

(ii) The taxpayer has gross receipts of sixty million dollars after taking into account all section 482 adjustments. None of the adjustments are excluded under paragraph (d) of this section. The net section 482 adjustment ($4 million) is less than the lesser of five million dollars or ten percent of gross receipts ($60 million × 10% = $6 million). Therefore, there is no substantial valuation misstatement.

Example 3. (i) The Internal Revenue Service makes the following section 482 adjustments to the income of an affiliated group that files a consolidated return for the taxable year:

(1) Attributable to Member A . .	$1,500,000
(2) Attributable to Member B . .	1,000,000
(3) Attributable to Member C . .	2,000,000
Total section 482 adjustments	4,500,000

(ii) Members A, B, and C have gross receipts of 20 million dollars, 12 million dollars, and 11 million dollars, respectively. Thus, the total gross receipts are 43 million dollars. None of the adjustments are excluded under paragraph (d) of this section. The net section 482 adjustment ($4.5 million) is greater than the lesser of five million dollars or ten percent of gross receipts ($43 million × 10% = $4.3 million). Therefore, there is a substantial valuation misstatement.

Example 4. (i) The Internal Revenue Service makes the following section 482 adjustments to the income of an affiliated group that files a consolidated return for the taxable year:

(1) Attributable to Member A	$1,500,000
(2) Attributable to Member B	3,000,000
(3) Attributable to Member C	2,500,000
Total section 482 adjustments	7,000,000

(ii) Members A, B, and C have gross receipts of 20 million dollars, 35 million dollars, and 40 million dollars, respectively. Thus, the total gross receipts are 95 million dollars. None of the adjustments are excluded under paragraph (d) of this section. The net section 482 adjustment (7 million dollars) is greater than the lesser of five million dollars or ten percent of gross receipts ($95 million × 10% = $9.5 million). Therefore, there is a substantial valuation misstatement.

Example 5. (i) The Internal Revenue Service makes the following section 482 adjustments to the income of an affiliated group that files a consolidated return for the taxable year:

(1) Attributable to Member A . . .	$2,000,000
(2) Attributable to Member B . . .	1,000,000
(3) Attributable to Member C . . .	1,500,000
Total section 482 adjustments	4,500,000

(ii) Members A, B, and C have gross receipts of 10 million dollars, 35 million dollars, and 40 million dollars, respectively. Thus, the total gross receipts are 85 million dollars. None of the adjustments are excluded under paragraph (d) of this section. The net section 482 adjustment ($4.5 million) is less than the lesser of five million dollars or ten percent of gross receipts ($85 million × 10% = $8.5 million). Therefore, there is no substantial valuation misstatement even though individual member A's adjustment ($2 million) is greater than ten percent of its individual gross receipts ($10 million × 10% = $1 million).

(d) *Amounts excluded from net section 482 adjustments.*—(1) *In general.*—An amount is excluded from the calculation of a net section 482 adjustment if the requirements of paragraph (d)(2), (3), or (4) of this section are met with respect to that amount.

(2) *Application of a specified section 482 method.*—(i) *In general.*—An amount is excluded from the calculation of a net section 482 adjustment if the taxpayer establishes that both the specified method and documentation requirements of this paragraph (d)(2) are met with respect to that amount. For purposes of this paragraph (d), a method will be considered a specified method if it is described in the regulations under section 482 and the method applies to transactions of the type under review. A qualified cost sharing arrangement is considered a specified method. See § 1.482-7. An unspecified method is not considered a specified method. See §§ 1.482-3(e) and 1.482-4(d).

(ii) *Specified method requirement.*—The specified method requirement is met if the taxpayer selects and applies a specified method in a reasonable manner. The taxpayer's selection and application of a specified method is reasonable only if, given the available data and the applicable pricing methods, the taxpayer reasonably concluded that the method (and its application of that method) provided the most reliable measure of an arm's length result under the principles of the best method rule of § 1.482-1(c). A taxpayer can reasonably conclude that a specified method provided the most reliable measure of an arm's length result only if it has made a reasonable effort to evaluate the potential applicability of the other specified methods in a manner consistent with the principles of the best method rule. The extent of this evaluation generally will depend on the nature of the available data, and it may vary from case to case and from method to method. This evaluation may not entail an exhaustive analysis or detailed application of each method. Rather, after a reasonably thorough search for relevant data, the taxpayer should consider which method would provide the most reliable measure of an arm's length result given that data. The nature of the available data may enable the taxpayer to conclude reasonably that a particular specified method provides a more reliable measure of an arm's length result than one or more of the other specified methods, and accordingly no further consideration of such other specified methods is needed. Further, it is not necessary for a taxpayer to conclude that the selected specified method provides a more reliable measure of an arm's length result than any unspecified method. For examples illustrating the selection of a specified method consistent with this paragraph (d)(2)(ii), see § 1.482-8. Whether the taxpayer's conclusion was reasonable must be determined from all the facts and circumstances. The factors relevant to this determination include the following:

(A) The experience and knowledge of the taxpayer, including all members of the taxpayer's controlled group.

(B) The extent to which reliable data was available and the data was analyzed in a reasonable manner. A taxpayer must engage in a reasonably thorough search for the data necessary to determine which method should be selected and how it should be applied. In determining the scope of a reasonably thorough search for data, the expense of additional efforts to locate new data may be weighed against the likelihood of finding additional data that would improve the reliability of the results and the amount by which any new data would change the taxpayer's taxable income. Furthermore, a taxpayer must use the most current reliable data that is available before the end of the taxable year in question. Although the taxpayer is not required to search for relevant data after the end of the taxable year, the taxpayer must maintain as a principal document described in paragraph (d)(2)(iii)(B)(9) of this section any relevant data it obtains after the end of the taxable year but before the return is filed, if that data would help determine whether the taxpayer has reported its true taxable income.

(C) The extent to which the taxpayer followed the relevant requirements set forth in regulations under section 482 with respect to the application of the method.

(D) The extent to which the taxpayer reasonably relied on a study or other analysis performed by a professional qualified to conduct such a study or analysis, including an attorney, accountant, or economist. Whether the professional is an employee of, or related to, the taxpayer is not determinative in evaluating the reliability of that study or analysis, as long as the study or analysis is objective, thorough, and well reasoned. Such reliance is reasonable only if the taxpayer disclosed to the professional all relevant information regarding the controlled transactions at issue. A study or analysis that was reasonably relied upon in a prior year may reasonably be relied upon in the current year if the relevant facts and circumstances have not changed or if the study or analysis has been appropriately modified to reflect any change in facts and circumstances.

(E) If the taxpayer attempted to determine an arm's length result by using more than one uncontrolled comparable, whether the taxpayer arbitrarily selected a result that corresponds to an extreme point in the range of results derived from the uncontrolled comparables. Such a result generally would not likely be closest to an arm's length result. If the uncontrolled comparables that the taxpayer uses to determine an arm's length result are described in § 1.482-1(e)(2)(ii)(B), one reasonable method of selecting a point in the range would be that provided in § 1.482-1(e)(3).

(F) The extent to which the taxpayer relied on a transfer pricing methodology developed and applied pursuant to an Advance Pricing Agreement for a prior taxable year, or specifically approved by the Internal Revenue Service pursuant to a transfer pricing audit of the transactions at issue for a prior taxable year, provided that the taxpayer applied the approved method reasonably and consistently with its prior application, and the facts and circumstances surrounding the use of the method have not materially changed since the time of the IRS's action, or if the facts and circumstances have changed in a way that materially affects the reliability of the results, the taxpayer makes appropriate adjustments to reflect such changes.

(G) The size of a net transfer pricing adjustment in relation to the size of the controlled transaction out of which the adjustment arose.

(iii) *Documentation requirement.*—(A) *In general.*—The documentation requirement of this paragraph (d)(2)(iii) is met if the taxpayer maintains sufficient documentation to establish that the taxpayer reasonably concluded that, given the available data and the applicable pricing methods, the method (and its application of that method) provided the most reliable measure of an arm's length result under the principles of the best method rule in

§ 1.482-1(c), and provides that documentation to the Internal Revenue Service within 30 days of a request for it in connection with an examination of the taxable year to which the documentation relates. With the exception of the documentation described in paragraphs (d)(2)(iii)(B)(9) and (10) of this section, that documentation must be in existence when the return is filed. The district director may, in his discretion, excuse a minor or inadvertent failure to provide required documents, but only if the taxpayer has made a good faith effort to comply, and the taxpayer promptly remedies the failure when it becomes known. The required documentation is divided into two categories, principal documents and background documents as described in paragraphs (d)(2)(iii)(B) and (C) of this section.

(B) *Principal documents.*—The principal documents should accurately and completely describe the basic transfer pricing analysis conducted by the taxpayer. The documentation must include the following—

(1) An overview of the taxpayer's business, including an analysis of the economic and legal factors that affect the pricing of its property or services;

(2) A description of the taxpayer's organizational structure (including an organization chart) covering all related parties engaged in transactions potentially relevant under section 482, including foreign affiliates whose transactions directly or indirectly affect the pricing of property or services in the United States;

(3) Any documentation explicitly required by the regulations under section 482;

(4) A description of the method selected and an explanation of why that method was selected;

(5) A description of the alternative methods that were considered and an explanation of why they were not selected;

(6) A description of the controlled transactions (including the terms of sale) and any internal data used to analyze those transactions. For example, if a profit split method is applied, the documentation must include a schedule providing the total income, costs, and assets (with adjustments for different accounting practices and currencies) for each controlled taxpayer participating in the relevant business activity and detailing the allocations of such items to that activity;

(7) A description of the comparables that were used, how comparability was evaluated, and what (if any) adjustments were made;

(8) An explanation of the economic analysis and projections relied upon in developing the method. For example, if a profit split method is applied, the taxpayer must provide an explanation of the analysis undertaken to determine how the profits would be split;

(9) A description or summary of any relevant data that the taxpayer obtains after the end of the tax year and before filing a tax return, which would help determine if a taxpayer selected and applied a specified method in a reasonable manner; and

(10) A general index of the principal and background documents and a description of the recordkeeping system used for cataloging and accessing those documents.

(C) *Background documents.*—The assumptions, conclusions, and positions contained in principal documents ordinarily will be based on, and supported by, additional background documents. Documents that support the principal documentation may include the documents listed in § 1.6038A-3(c) that are not otherwise described in paragraph (d)(2)(iii)(B) of this section. Every document listed in those regulations may not be relevant to pricing determinations under the taxpayer's specific facts and circumstances and, therefore, each of those documents need not be maintained in all circumstances. Moreover, other documents not listed in those regulations may be necessary to establish that the taxpayer's method was selected and applied in the way that provided the most reliable measure of an arm's length result under the principles of the best method rule in § 1.482-1(c). Background documents need not be provided to the Internal Revenue Service in response to a request for principal documents. If the Internal Revenue Service subsequently requests background documents, a taxpayer must provide that documentation to the Internal Revenue Service within 30 days of the request. However, the district director may, in his discretion, extend the period for producing the background documentation.

(3) *Application of an unspecified method.*—(i) *In general.*—An adjustment is excluded from the calculation of a net section 482 adjustment if the taxpayer establishes that both the unspecified method and documentation requirements of this paragraph (d)(3) are met with respect to that amount.

(ii) *Unspecified method requirement.*—(A) *In general.*—If a method other than a specified method was applied, the unspecified method requirement is met if the requirements of paragraph (d)(3)(ii)(B) or (C) of this section, as appropriate, are met.

(B) *Specified method potentially applicable.*—If the transaction is of a type for which methods are specified in the regulations under section 482, then a taxpayer will be considered to have met the unspecified method requirement if the taxpayer reasonably concludes, given the available data, that none of the specified methods was likely to provide a reliable measure of an arm's length result, and that it selected and applied an unspecified method in a way that would likely provide a reliable measure of an arm's length result. A taxpayer can reasonably conclude that no specified method was likely to provide a reliable measure of an arm's length result only if it has made a reasonable effort to evaluate the potential applicability of the specified methods in a manner consistent with the principles of the best method rule. However, it is not necessary for a taxpayer to conclude that the selected method provides a more reliable measure of an arm's length result than any other unspecified method. Whether the taxpayer's conclusion was reasonable must be determined from all the facts and circumstances. The factors relevant to this conclusion include those set forth in paragraph (d)(2)(ii) of this section.

(C) *No specified method applicable.*—If the transaction is of a type for which no methods are specified in the regulations under section 482, then a taxpayer will be considered to have met the unspecified method requirement if it selected and applied an unspecified method in a reasonable manner. For purposes of this paragraph (d)(3)(ii)(C), a taxpayer's selection and application is reasonable if the taxpayer reasonably concludes that the method (and its application of that method) provided the most reliable measure of an arm's length result under the principles of the best method rule in § 1.482-1(c). However, it is not necessary for a taxpayer to conclude that the selected method provides a more reliable measure of an arm's length result than any other unspecified method. Whether the taxpayer's conclusion was reasonable must be determined from all the facts and circumstances. The factors relevant to this conclusion include those set forth in paragraph (d)(2)(ii) of this section.

(iii) *Documentation requirement.*—(A) *In general.*—The documentation requirement of this paragraph (d)(3) is met if the taxpayer maintains sufficient documentation to establish that the unspecified method requirement of paragraph (d)(3)(ii) of this section is met and provides that documentation to the Internal Revenue Service within 30 days of a request for it. That documentation must be in existence when the return is filed. The district director may, in his discretion, excuse a minor or inadvertent failure to provide required documents, but only if the taxpayer has made a good faith effort to comply, and the taxpayer promptly remedies the failure when it becomes known.

(B) *Principal and background documents.*—See paragraphs (d)(2)(iii)(B) and (C) of this section for rules regarding these two categories of required documentation.

(4) *Certain foreign to foreign transactions.*—For purposes of calculating a net section 482 adjustment, any increase in taxable income resulting from an allocation under section 482 that is attributable to any controlled transaction solely between foreign corporations will be excluded unless the treatment of that transaction affects the determination of either corporation's income from sources within the United States or taxable income effectively connected with the conduct of a trade or business within the United States.

(5) *Special rule.*—If the regular tax (as defined in section 55(c)) imposed on the taxpayer is determined by reference to an amount other than taxable income, that amount shall be treated as the taxable income of the taxpayer for purposes of section 6662(e)(3). Accordingly, for taxpayers whose regular tax is determined by reference to an amount other than taxable income, the increase in that amount resulting from section 482 allocations is the taxpayer's net section 482 adjustment.

(6) *Examples.*—The principles of this paragraph (d) are illustrated by the following examples:

Example 1. (i) The Internal Revenue Service makes the following section 482 adjustments for the taxable year:

(1)	Attributable to an increase in gross income because of an increase in royalty payments . .	$9,000,000
(2)	Not a 200 percent or 400 percent adjustment	2,000,000
(3)	Attributable to a decrease in the cost of goods sold because of a decrease in the cost plus mark-up of a realted seller	9,000,000
	Total section 482 adjustments	$20,000,000

(ii) The taxpayer has gross receipts of 75 million dollars after all section 482 adjustments. The taxpayer establishes that for adjustments number one and three, it applied a transfer pricing method specified in section 482, the selection and application of the method was reasonable, it documented the pricing analysis, and turned that documentation over to the IRS within 30 days of a request. Accordingly, eighteen million dollars is excluded from the calculation of the net section 482 adjustment. Because the net section 482 adjustment is two million dollars, there is no substantial valuation misstatement.

Reg. § 1.6662-6(d)(6)

Example 2. (i) The Internal Revenue Service makes the following section 482 adjustments for the taxable year:

(1)	Attributable to an increase in gross income because of an increase in royalty payments . .	$9,000,000
(2)	Attributable to an adjustment that is 200 percent or more of the correct section 482 price)	2,000,000
(3)	Attributable to a decrease in the cost of goods sold because of a decrease in the cost plus mark-up of a related seller	9,000,000
	Total section 482 adjustments	$20,000,000

(ii) The taxpayer has gross receipts of 75 million dollars after all section 482 adjustments. The taxpayer establishes that for adjustments number one and three it applied a transfer pricing method specified in section 482, the selection and application of the method was reasonable, it documented that analysis, and turned the documentation over to the IRS within 30 days. Accordingly, eighteen million dollars is excluded from the calculation of the section 482 transfer pricing adjustments for purposes of applying the five million dollar or 10% of gross receipts test. Because the net section 482 adjustment is only two million dollars, the taxpayer is not subject to the net adjustment penalty. However, the taxpayer may be subject to the transactional penalty on the underpayment of tax attributable to the two million dollar adjustment.

Example 3. CFC1 and CFC2 are controlled foreign corporations within the meaning of section 957. Applying section 482, the IRS disallows a deduction for 25 million dollars of the interest that CFC1 paid to CFC2, which results in CFC1's U.S. shareholder having a subpart F inclusion in excess of five million dollars. No other adjustments under section 482 are made with respect to the controlled taxpayers. However, the increase has no effect upon the determination of CFC1's or CFC2's income from sources within the United States or taxable income effectively connected with the conduct of a trade or business within the United States. Accordingly, there is no substantial valuation misstatement.

(e) *Special rules in the case of carrybacks and carryovers.*—If there is a substantial or gross valuation misstatement for a taxable year that gives rise to a loss, deduction or credit that is carried to another taxable year, the transactional penalty and the net adjustment penalty will be imposed on any resulting underpayment of tax in that other taxable year. In determining whether there is a substantial or gross valuation misstatement for a taxable year, no amount carried from another taxable year shall be included. The following example illustrates the principle of this paragraph (e):

Example. The Internal Revenue Service makes a section 482 adjustment of six million dollars in taxable year 1, no portion of which is excluded under paragraph (d) of this section. The taxpayer's income tax return for year 1 reported a loss of three million dollars, which was carried to taxpayer's year 2 income tax return and used to reduce income taxes otherwise due with respect to year 2. A determination is made that the six million dollar allocation constitutes a substantial valuation misstatement, and a penalty is imposed on the underpayment of tax in year 1 attributable to the substantial valuation misstatement and on the underpayment of tax in year 2 attributable to the disallowance of the net operating loss in year 2. For purposes of determining whether there is a substantial or gross valuation misstatement for year 2, the three million dollar reduction of the net operating loss will not be added to any section 482 adjustments made with respect to year 2.

(f) *Rules for coordinating between the transactional penalty and the net adjustment penalty.*— (1) *Coordination of a net section 482 adjustment subject to the net adjustment penalty and a gross valuation misstatement subject to the transactional penalty.*—In determining whether a net section 482 adjustment exceeds five million dollars or 10 percent of gross receipts, an adjustment attributable to a substantial or gross valuation misstatement that is subject to the transactional penalty will be taken into account. If the net section 482 adjustment exceeds five million dollars or ten percent of gross receipts, any portion of such amount that is attributable to a gross valuation misstatement will be subject to the transactional penalty at the forty percent rate, but will not also be subject to net adjustment penalty at a twenty percent rate. The remaining amount is subject to the net adjustment penalty at the twenty percent rate, even if such amount is less than the lesser of five million dollars or ten percent of gross receipts.

(2) *Coordination of net section 482 adjustment subject to the net adjustment penalty and substantial valuation misstatements subject to the transactional penalty.*—If the net section 482 adjustment exceeds twenty million dollars or 20 percent of gross receipts, the entire amount of the adjustment is subject to the net adjustment penalty at a forty percent rate. No portion of the adjustment is subject to the transactional penalty at a twenty percent rate.

(3) *Examples.*—The following examples illustrate the principles of this paragraph (f):

Example 1. (i) Applying section 482, the Internal Revenue Service makes the following adjustments for the taxable year:

(1)	Attributable to an adjustment that is 400 percent or more of the correct section 482 arm's length result) . .	$2,000,000
(2)	Not a 200 or 400 percent adjustment)	2,500,000
	Total	$4,500,000

(ii) The taxpayer has gross receipts of 75 million dollars after all section 482 adjustments. None of the adjustments is excluded under paragraph (d) (Amounts excluded from net section 482 adjustments) of this section, in determining the five million dollar or 10% of gross receipts test under section 6662(e)(1)(B)(ii). The net section 482 adjustment (4.5 million dollars) is less than the lesser of five million dollars or ten percent of gross receipts ($75 million x 10% = $7.5 million). Thus, there is no substantial valuation misstatement. However, the two million dollar adjustment is attributable to a gross valuation misstatement. Accordingly, the taxpayer may be subject to a penalty, under section 6662(h), equal to 40 percent of the underpayment of tax attributable to the gross valuation misstatement of two million dollars. The 2.5 million dollar adjustment is not subject to a penalty under section 6662(b)(3).

Example 2. The facts are the same as in *Example 1*, except the taxpayer has gross receipts of 40 million dollars. The net section 482 adjustment ($4.5 million) is greater than the lesser of five million dollars or ten percent of gross receipts ($40 million x 10% – $4 million). Thus, the five million dollar or 10% of gross receipts test has been met. The two million dollar adjustment is attributable to a gross valuation misstatement. Accordingly, the taxpayer is subject to a penalty, under section 6662(h), equal to 40 percent of the underpayment of tax attributable to the gross valuation misstatement of two million dollars. The 2.5 million dollar adjustment is subject to a penalty under sections 6662(a) and 6662(b)(3), equal to 20 percent of the underpayment of tax attributable to the substantial valuation misstatement.

Example 3. (i) Applying section 482, the Internal Revenue Service makes the following transfer pricing adjustments for the taxable year:

(1)	Attributable to an adjustment that is 400 percent or more of the correct section 482 arm's length result) . .	$6,000,000
(2)	Not a 200 or 400 percent adjustment	15,000,000
	Total	21,000,000

(ii) None of the adjustments are excluded under paragraph (d) (Amounts excluded from net section 482 adjustments) in determining the twenty million dollar or 20% of gross receipts test under section 6662(h). The net section 482 adjustment (21 million dollars) is greater than twenty million dollars and thus constitutes a gross valuation misstatement. Accordingly, the total adjustment is subject to the net adjustment penalty equal to 40 percent of the underpayment of tax attributable to the 21 million dollar gross valuation misstatement. The six million dollar adjustment will not be separately included for purposes of any additional penalty under section 6662.

(g) *Effective date.*—This section is effective February 9, 1996. However, taxpayers may elect to apply this section to all open taxable years beginning after December 31, 1993. [Reg. § 1.6662-6.]

☐ [*T.D.* 8656, 2-8-96.]

Proposed Amendments to Regulation

☐ Section 1.6662-6 is amended by:

1. Redesignating paragraphs (d)(2)(ii)(A) through (d)(2)(ii)(G) as paragraphs (d)(2)(ii)(A)(*1*) through (d)(2)(ii)(A)(*7*), respectively and redesignating paragraph (d)(2)(ii) introductory text as paragraph (d)(2)(ii)(A).

2. Adding a new paragraph (d)(2)(ii)(B).

3. Revising paragraphs (d)(2)(iii)(B)(*4*) and (d)(2)(iii)(B)(*6*).

4. Adding a third sentence to paragraph (g).

The revisions and additions read as follows:

§ 1.6662-6. Transactions between persons described in section 482 and net section 482 transfer price adjustments.

* * *

(d) * * *

(2) * * *

(ii) * * *

(B) *Simplified cost-based method.*—A taxpayer's selection of the simplified cost-based method for certain services, described in § 1.482-9(f), and its application of that method to a controlled services transaction will be considered reasonable for purposes of the specified method requirement only if the taxpayer reasonably concluded that the controlled services transaction meets the conditions of § 1.482-9(f)(3) and is not described in paragraphs § 1.482-9(f)(2)(iii) or (f)(4). Whether the taxpayer's conclusion was reasonable must be determined from all the facts and circumstances. The factors relevant to this determination include those described in paragraph (d)(2)(ii)(A) of this section, to the extent applicable.

(iii) * * *

(B) * * *

(*4*) A description of the method selected and an explanation of why that method was selected, including an evaluation of whether the regulatory conditions and requirements for application of that method, if any, were met;

* * *

(6) A description of the controlled transactions (including the terms of sale) and any internal data used to analyze those transactions. For example, if a profit split method is applied, the documentation must include a schedule providing the total income, costs, and assets (with adjustments for different accounting practices and currencies) for each controlled taxpayer participating in the relevant business activity and detailing the allocations of such items to that activity. Similarly, if a cost-based method (such as the cost plus method, the simplified cost-based method for certain services, or a comparable profits method with a cost-based profit level indicator) is applied, the documentation must include a description of the manner in which relevant costs are determined and are allocated and apportioned to the relevant controlled transaction.

* * *

(g) * * * Paragraphs (d)(2)(ii)(B), (iii)(B)(4) and (iii)(B)(6) of this section are applicable for taxable years beginning after the date the final regulations are published in the Federal Register. [Prop. Reg. § 1.6662-6.]

[Proposed 9-10-2003.]

§ 1.6662-7. Omnibus Budget Reconciliation Act of 1993 changes to the accuracy-related penalty.—(a) *Scope.*—The Omnibus Budget Reconciliation Act of 1993 made certain changes to the accuracy-related penalty in section 6662. This section provides rules reflecting those changes.

(b) *No disclosure exception for negligence penalty.*—The penalty for negligence in section 6662(b)(1) may not be avoided by disclosure of a return position.

(c) *Disclosure standard for other penalties is reasonable basis.*—The penalties for disregarding rules or regulations in section 6662(b)(1) and for a substantial understatement of income tax in section 6662(b)(2) may be avoided by adequate disclosure of a return position only if the position has at least a reasonable basis. See § 1.6662-3(c) and § § 1.6662-4(e) and (f) for other applicable disclosure rules.

(d) *Reasonable basis.*—For purposes of § § 1.6662-3(c) and 1.6662-4(e) and (f) (relating to methods of making adequate disclosure), the provisions of § 1.6662-3(b)(3) apply in determining whether a return position has a reasonable basis. [Reg. § 1.6662-7.]

☐ [*T.D.* 8617, 8-31-95. *Amended by T.D.* 8790, 12-1-98.]

§ 1.6664-4T. Reasonable cause and good faith exception to section 6662 penalties.—(a) through (e) [Reserved].

(f) *Transactions between persons described in section 482 and net section 482 transfer price adjustments.*—For purposes of applying the reasonable cause and good faith exception of section 6664(c) to net section 482 adjustments, the rules of § 1.6662-6(d) apply. A taxpayer that does not satisfy the rules of § 1.6662-6(d) for a net section 482 adjustment cannot satisfy the reasonable cause and good faith exception under section 6664(c). The rules of this section apply to underpayments subject to the transactional penalty in § 1.6662-6(b). If the standards of the net section 482 penalty exclusion provisions under § 1.6662-6(d) are met with respect to such underpayments, then the taxpayer will be considered to have acted with reasonable cause and good faith for purposes of this section. [Temporary Reg. § 1.6664-4T.]

☐ [*T.D.* 8519, 1-27-94. *Amended by T.D.* 8656, 2-8-96.]

Departing Aliens

§ 1.6851-2. Certificates of compliance with income tax laws by departing aliens.—(a) *In general.*—(1) *Requirement.*—The rules of this section are applicable, except as otherwise expressly provided, to any alien who departs from the United States or any of its possessions after January 20, 1961. Except as provided in subparagraph (2) of this paragraph, no such alien, whether resident or nonresident, may depart from the United States unless he first procures a certificate that he has complied with all of the obligations imposed upon him by the income tax laws. In order to procure such a certificate, an alien who intends to depart from the United States (i) must file with the district director for the internal revenue district in which he is located the statements or returns required by paragraph (b) of this section to be filed before obtaining such certificate, (ii) must appear before such district director if the district director deems it necessary, and (iii) must pay any taxes required under paragraph (b) of this section to be paid before obtaining the certificate. Either such certificate of compliance, properly executed, or evidence that the alien is excepted under subparagraph (2) of this paragraph from obtaining the certificate must be presented at the point of departure. An alien who presents himself at the point of departure without a certificate of compliance, or evidence establishing that such a certificate is not required, will be subject at such departure point to examination by an internal revenue officer or employee and to the completion of returns and statements and payment of taxes as required by paragraph (b) of this section.

(2) *Exceptions.*—(i) *Employees of foreign governments or international organizations.*—(a) *Diplomatic representatives, their families and servants.*—*(1)* Representatives of foreign governments bearing diplomatic passports, whether accredited to the United States or other countries, and members of their households shall not, upon departure from the United States or any of its possessions, be examined as to their liability for United States income tax or be required to obtain a certificate of compliance. If a foreign government does not issue diplomatic passports but merely indicates on passports issued to members of its diplomatic service the status of the bearer as a member of such service, such passports are considered as diplomatic passports for income tax purposes.

(2) Likewise, the servant of a diplomatic representative who accompanies any individual bearing a diplomatic passport upon departure from the United States or any of its possessions shall not be required, upon such departure, to obtain a certificate of compliance or to submit to examination as to his liability for United States income tax. If the departure of such a servant from the United States or any of its possessions is not made in the company of an individual bearing a diplomatic passport, the servant is required to obtain a certificate of compliance. However, such certificate will be issued to him on Form 2063 without examination as to his income tax liability upon presentation to the district director for the internal revenue district in which the servant is located of a letter from the chief of the diplomatic mission to which the servant is attached certifying *(i)* that the name of the servant appears on the "White List," a list of employees of diplomatic missions, and *(ii)* that the servant is not obligated to the United States for any income tax, and will not be so obligated up to and including the intended date of departure.

(b) Other employees.—Any employee of an international organization or of a foreign government (other than a diplomatic representative to whom *(a)* of this subdivision applies) whose compensation for official services rendered to such organization or government is excluded from gross income under section 893 and who has received no gross income from sources within the United States, and any member of his household who has received no gross income from sources within the United States, shall not, upon departure from the United States or any of its possessions after November 30, 1962 be examined as to his liability for United States income tax or be required to obtain a certificate of compliance.

(c) Effect of waiver.—An alien who has filed with the Attorney General the waiver provided for under section 247(b) of the Immigration and Nationality Act (8 U.S.C. 1257(b)) is not entitled to the exception provided by this subdivision.

(ii) *Alien students, industrial trainees, and exchange visitors.*—A certificate of compliance shall not be required, and examination as to United States income tax liability shall not be made, upon the departure from the United States or any of its possessions of—

(A) An alien student, industrial trainee, or exchange visitor, and any spouse and children of that alien, admitted solely on an F-1, F-2, H-3, H-4, J-1 or J-2 visa, who has received no gross income from sources inside the United States other than—

(1) Allowances to cover expenses incident to study or training in the United States (including expenses for travel, maintenance, and tuition);

(2) The value of any services or accommodations furnished incident to such study or training;

(3) Income derived in accordance with the employment authorizations in 8 CFR 274a.12(b) and (c) that apply to the alien's visa; or

(4) Interest on deposits described in section 871(i)(2)(A); or

(B) An alien student, and any spouse or children of that alien admitted solely on an M-1 or M-2 visa, who has received no gross income from sources inside the United States other than income derived in accordance with the employment authorization in 8 CFR 274a.12(c)(6) or interest on deposits described in section 871(i)(2)(A).

(b) *Issuance of certificate of compliance.*—(1) *In general.*—(i) Upon the departure of an alien required to secure a certificate of compliance under paragraph (a) of this section, the district director shall determine whether the departure of such alien jeopardizes the collection of any income tax for the current or the preceding taxable year, but the district director may determine that jeopardy does not exist in some cases. If the district director finds that the departure of such an alien results in jeopardy, the taxable period of the alien will be terminated, and the alien will be required to file returns and make payment of tax in accordance with subparagraph (3)(iii) of this paragraph. On the other hand, if the district director finds that the departure of the alien does not result in jeopardy, the alien will be required to file the statement on returns required by subparagraph (2) or (3)(ii) of this paragraph, but will not be required to pay income tax before the usual time for payment.

(ii) The departure of an alien who is a resident of the United States or a possession thereof (or treated as a resident under section 6013(g) or (h)) and who intends to continue such residence (or treatment as a resident) shall be treated as not resulting in jeopardy, and thus not requiring termination of his taxable period, except when the district director has information indicating that the alien intends by such departure to avoid the payment of his income tax. In the case of a nonresident alien (including a resident alien discontinuing residence), the fact that the alien intends to depart from the United States will justify termination of his taxable period unless the alien establishes to the satisfaction of the district director that he intends to return to the United States and that his departure will not jeopardize collection of the tax. The determination of whether the departure of the alien results in jeopardy will be made on examination of all the facts in the case. Evidence tending to establish that jeopardy does not result from the departure of the alien may be provided, for example, by information showing that the alien is engaged in trade or business in the United States or that he leaves sufficient property in the United States to secure payment of his income tax for the taxable year and of any income tax for the preceding year which remains unpaid.

(2) *Alien having no taxable income and resident alien whose taxable period is not terminated.*—A statement on Form 2063 shall be filed with the district director by every alien required to obtain a certificate of compliance—

(i) Who is a resident of the United States and whose taxable period is not terminated either because he has had no taxable income for the taxable year up to and including the date of his departure (and for the preceding taxable year where the period for making the income tax return for such year has not expired) or because, although he has had taxable income for such period or periods, the district director has not found that his departure jeopardizes collection of the tax on such income; or

(ii) Who is not a resident of the United States and who has had no taxable income for the taxable year up to and including the date of his departure (and for the preceding taxable year where the period for making the income tax return for such year has not expired).

Any alien described in subdivision (i) or (ii) of this subparagraph who is in default in making return of, or paying, income tax for any taxable year shall, in addition, file with the district director any returns which have not been made as required and pay to the district director the amount of any tax for which he is in default. Upon compliance by an alien with the foregoing requirements of this subparagraph, the district director shall execute and issue to the alien the certificate of compliance attached to Form 2063. The certificate of compliance so issued shall be effective for all departures of the alien during his current taxable year, subject to revocation upon any subsequent departure should the district director have reason to believe that such subsequent departure would result in jeopardy. The statement required of a resident alien under this subparagraph, if made before January 21, 1961, with respect to a departure after January 20, 1961, may be made on a Form 1040C in lieu of a Form 2063.

(3) *Nonresident alien having taxable income and resident alien whose taxable period is terminated.*—(i) *Nonresident alien having taxable income.*—Every nonresident alien required to obtain a certificate of compliance (but not described in subparagraph (2) of this paragraph) who wishes to establish that his departure does not result in jeopardy shall furnish to the district director such information as may be required for the purpose of determining whether the departure of the alien jeopardizes collection of the income tax and thus requires termination of his taxable period.

(ii) *Nonresident alien whose taxable period is not terminated.*—Every nonresident alien described in subdivision (i) of this subparagraph whose taxable period is not terminated upon departure shall file with the district director—

(a) A return in duplicate on Form 1040C for the taxable year of his intended departure, showing income received, and reasonably expected to be received, during the entire taxable year within which the departure occurs; and

(b) Any income tax returns which have not been filed as required.

Upon compliance by the alien with the foregoing requirements of this subdivision, and the payment of any income tax for which he is in default, the district director shall execute and issue to the alien the certificate of compliance on the duplicate copy of Form 1040C. The certificate of compliance so issued shall be effective for all departures of the alien during his current taxable year, subject to revocation by the district director upon any subsequent departure if the taxable period of the alien is terminated on such subsequent departure.

(iii) *Alien (whether resident or nonresident) whose taxable period is terminated.*—

Reg. § 1.6851-2(b)(1)(ii)

Every alien required to obtain a certificate of compliance, whether resident or nonresident, whose taxable period is terminated upon departure shall file with the district director—

(a) A return in duplicate on Form 1040C for the short taxable period resulting from such termination, showing income received, and reasonably expected to be received, during the taxable year up to and including the date of departure;

(b) Where the period for filing has not expired, the return required under section 6012 and § 1.6012-1 for the preceding taxable years; and

(c) Any other income tax returns which have not been filed as required.

Upon compliance with the foregoing requirements of this subdivision, and payment of the income tax required to be shown on the returns filed pursuant to *(a)* and *(b)* of this subdivision and of any income tax due and owing for prior years, the departing alien will be issued the certificate of compliance on the duplicate copy of Form 1040C. The certificate of compliance so issued shall be effective only for the specific departure with respect to which it is issued. A departing alien may postpone payment of the tax required to be shown on the returns filed in accordance with *(a)* and *(b)* of this subdivision until the usual time of payment by furnishing a bond as provided in § 301.6863-1 of this chapter (regulations on procedure and administration).

(4) *Joint return on Form 1040C.*—A departing alien may not file a joint return on Form 1040C unless—

(i) Such alien and his spouse may reasonably be expected to be eligible to file a joint return at the normal close of their taxable periods for which the return is made; and

(ii) If the taxable period of such alien is terminated, the taxable periods of both spouses are so terminated as to end at the same time.

(5) *Annual return.*—Notwithstanding that Form 1040C has been filed for either the entire taxable year of departure or for a terminated period, the return required under section 6012 and § 1.6012-1 for such taxable year shall be filed. Any income tax paid on income shown on the return on Form 1040C shall be applied against the tax determined to be due on the income required to be shown on the subsequent return under section 6012 and § 1.6012-1. [Reg. § 1.6851-2.]

☐ [T.D. 6426, 11-30-59. *Amended by T.D.* 6537, 1-19-61; *T.D.* 6620, 11-29-62; *T.D.* 7575, 12-15-78; *T.D.* 7670, 1-30-80; *T.D.* 8332, 1-25-91 *and T.D.* 8526, 3-2-94.]

Definitions

§ 301.7701-1. Classification of organizations for federal tax purposes.—(a) *Organizations for federal tax purposes.*—(1) *In general.*—The Internal Revenue Code prescribes the classification of various organizations for federal tax purposes. Whether an organization is an entity separate from its owners for federal tax purposes is a matter of federal tax law and does not depend on whether the organization is recognized as an entity under local law.

(2) *Certain joint undertakings give rise to entities for federal tax purposes.*—A joint venture or other contractual arrangement may create a separate entity for federal tax purposes if the participants carry on a trade, business, financial operation, or venture and divide the profits therefrom. For example, a separate entity exists for federal tax purposes if co-owners of an apartment building lease space and in addition provide services to the occupants either directly or through an agent. Nevertheless, a joint undertaking merely to share expenses does not create a separate entity for federal tax purposes. For example, if two or more persons jointly construct a ditch merely to drain surface water from their properties, they have not created a separate entity for federal tax purposes. Similarly, mere co-ownership of property that is maintained, kept in repair, and rented or leased does not constitute a separate entity for federal tax purposes. For example, if an individual owner, or tenants in common, of farm property lease it to a farmer for a cash rental or a share of the crops, they do not necessarily create a separate entity for federal tax purposes.

(3) *Certain local law entities not recognized.*—An entity formed under local law is not always recognized as a separate entity for federal tax purposes. For example, an organization wholly owned by a State is not recognized as a separate entity for federal tax purposes if it is an integral part of the State. Similarly, tribes incorporated under section 17 of the Indian Reorganization Act of 1934, as amended, 25 U.S.C. 477, or under section 3 of the Oklahoma Indian Welfare Act, as amended, 25 U.S.C. 503, are not recognized as separate entities for federal tax purposes.

(4) *Single owner organizations.*—Under §§ 301.7701-2 and 301.7701-3, certain organizations that have a single owner can choose to be recognized or disregarded as entities separate from their owners.

(b) *Classification of organizations.*—The classification of organizations that are recognized as separate entities is determined under §§ 301.7701-2, 301.7701-3, and 301.7701-4 unless a provision of the Internal Revenue Code (such as section 860A addressing Real Estate Mortgage Investment Conduits (REMICs)) provides for special treatment of that organization. For the classification of organizations as trusts, see § 301.7701-4. That section provides that trusts generally do not have associates or an objective to carry on business for profit. Sections 301.7701-2 and 301.7701-3 provide rules for classifying organizations that are not classified as trusts.

(c) *Qualified cost sharing arrangements.*—A qualified cost sharing arrangement that is described in § 1.482-7 of this chapter and any arrangement that is treated by the Commissioner as a qualified cost sharing arrangement under § 1.482-7 of this chapter is not recognized as a separate entity for purposes of the Internal Revenue Code. See § 1.482-7 of this chapter for the proper treatment of qualified cost sharing arrangements.

(d) *Domestic and foreign business entities.*—[Reserved]. For further guidance, see § 301.7701-1T.

(e) *State.*—For purposes of this section and § 301.7701-2, the term *State* includes the District of Columbia.

(f) *Effective date.*—The rules of this section are effective as of January 1, 1997. [Reg. § 301.7701-1.]

☐ [*T.D.* 6503, 11-15-80. *Amended by T.D.* 6797, 2-2-65; *T.D.* 7515, 10-17-77; *T.D.* 8697, 12-17-96 *and T.D.* 9153, 8-11-2004.]

§ 301.7701-1T. Classification of organizations for federal tax purposes (temporary).—

* * *

(d) *Domestic and foreign entities.*—See § 301.7701-5T for the rules that determine whether a business entity is domestic or foreign.

(e) through (f) [Reserved]. [Temporary Reg. § 301.7701-1T.]

☐ [*T.D.* 9153, 8-11-2004.]

§ 301.7701-2. Business entities; definitions.—(a) *Business entities.*—For purposes of this section and § 301.7701-3, a *business entity* is any entity recognized for federal tax purposes (including an entity with a single owner that may be disregarded as an entity separate from its owner under § 301.7701-3) that is not properly classified as a trust under § 301.7701-4 or otherwise subject to special treatment under the Internal Revenue Code. A business entity with two or more members is classified for federal tax purposes as either a corporation or a partnership. A business entity with only one owner is classified as a corporation or is disregarded; if the entity is disregarded, its activities are treated in the same manner as a sole proprietorship, branch, or division of the owner.

(b) *Corporations.*—For federal tax purposes, the term *corporation* means—

(1) A business entity organized under a Federal or State statute, or under a statute of a federally recognized Indian tribe, if the statute describes or refers to the entity as incorporated or as a corporation, body corporate, or body politic;

(2) An association (as determined under § 301.7701-3);

(3) A business entity organized under a State statute, if the statute describes or refers to the entity as a joint-stock company or joint-stock association;

(4) An insurance company;

(5) A State-chartered business entity conducting banking activities, if any of its deposits are insured under the Federal Deposit Insurance Act, as amended, 12 U.S.C. 1811 et seq., or a similar federal statute;

(6) A business entity wholly owned by a State or any political subdivision thereof, or a business entity wholly owned by a foreign government or any other entity described in § 1.892-2T;

(7) A business entity that is taxable as a corporation under a provision of the Internal Revenue Code other than section 7701(a)(3); and

(8) *Certain foreign entities.*—(i) *In general.*—Except as provided in paragraphs (b)(8)(ii) and (d) of this section, the following business entities formed in the following jurisdictions:

    American Samoa, Corporation
    Argentina, Sociedad Anonima
    Australia, Public Limited Company
    Austria, Aktiengesellschaft
    Barbados, Limited Company
    Belgium, Societe Anonyme
    Belize, Public Limited Company
    Bolivia, Sociedad Anonima
    Brazil, Sociedade Anonima
    Canada, Corporation and Company
    Chile, Sociedad Anonima
    People's Republic of China, Gufen Youxian Gongsi
    Republic of China (Taiwan), Ku-fen Yu-hsien Kung-szu
    Colombia, Sociedad Anonima

Costa Rica, Sociedad Anonima
Cyprus, Public Limited Company
Czech Republic, Akciova Spolecnost
Denmark, Aktieselskab
Ecuador, Sociedad Anonima or Compania Anonima
Egypt, Sharikat Al-Mossahamah
El Salvador, Sociedad Anonima
Finland, Julkinen Osakeyhtio/Publikt Aktiebolag
France, Societe Anonyme
Germany, Aktiengesellschaft
Greece, Anonymos Etairia
Guam, Corporation
Guatemala, Sociedad Anonima
Guyana, Public Limited Company
Honduras, Sociedad Anonima
Hong Kong, Public Limited Company
Hungary, Reszvenytarsasag
Iceland, Hlutafelag
India, Public Limited Company
Indonesia, Perseroan Terbuka
Ireland, Public Limited Company
Israel, Public Limited Company
Italy, Societa per Azioni
Jamaica, Public Limited Company
Japan, Kabushiki Kaisha
Kazakstan, Ashyk Aktsionerlik Kogham
Republic of Korea, Chusik Hoesa
Liberia, Corporation
Luxembourg, Societe Anonyme
Malaysia, Berhad
Malta, Public Limited Company
Mexico, Sociedad Anonima
Morocco, Societe Anonyme
Netherlands, Naamloze Vennootschap
New Zealand, Limited Company
Nicaragua, Compania Anonima
Nigeria, Public Limited Company
Northern Mariana Islands, Corporation
Norway, Allment Aksjeselskap
Pakistan, Public Limited Company
Panama, Sociedad Anonima
Paraguay, Sociedad Anonima
Peru, Sociedad Anonima
Philippines, Stock Corporation
Poland, Spolka Akcyjna
Portugal, Sociedade Anonima
Puerto Rico, Corporation
Romania, Societe pe Actiuni
Russia, Otkrytoye Aktsionernoy Obshchestvo
Saudi Arabia, Sharikat Al-Mossahamah
Singapore, Public Limited Company
Slovak Republic, Akciova Spolocnost
South Africa, Public Limited Company
Spain, Sociedad Anonima
Surinam, Naamloze Vennootschap
Sweden, Publika Aktiebolag
Switzerland, Aktiengesellschaft
Thailand, Borisat Chamkad (Mahachon)
Trinidad and Tobago, Limited Company
Tunisia, Societe Anonyme
Turkey, Anonim Sirket
Ukraine, Aktsionerne Tovaristvo Vidkritogo Tipu
United Kingdom, Public Limited Company
United States Virgin Islands, Corporation
Uruguay, Sociedad Anonima
Venezuela, Sociedad Anonima or Compania Anonima

(ii) *Clarification of list of corporations in paragraph (b)(8)(i) of this section.*—(A) *Exceptions in certain cases.*—The following entities will not be treated as corporations under paragraph (b)(8)(i) of this section:

(1) With regard to Canada, a Nova Scotia Unlimited Liability Company (or any other company or corporation all of whose owners have unlimited liability pursuant to federal or provincial law).

(2) With regard to India, a company deemed to be a public limited company solely by operation of Section 43A(1) (relating to corporate ownership of the company), section 43A(1A) (relating to annual average turnover), or section 43A(1B) (relating to ownership interests in other companies) of the Companies Act, 1956 (or any combination of these), provided that the organizational documents of such deemed public limited company continue to meet the requirements of section 3(1)(iii) of the Companies Act, 1956.

(3) With regard to Malaysia, a Sendirian Berhad.

(B) *Inclusions in certain cases.*—With regard to Mexico, the term Sociedad Anonima includes a Sociedad Anonima that chooses to apply the variable capital provision of Mexican corporate law (Sociedad Anonima de Capital Variable).

(iii) *Public companies.*—For purposes of paragraph (b)(8)(i) of this section, with regard to Cyprus, Hong Kong, and Jamaica, the term Public Limited Company includes any Limited Company that is not defined as a private company under the corporate laws of those jurisdictions. In all other cases, where the term Public Limited Company is not defined, that term shall include any Limited Company defined as a public company under the corporate laws of the relevant jurisdiction.

(iv) *Limited companies.*—For purposes of this paragraph (b)(8), any reference to a Limited Company includes, as the case may be, companies limited by shares and companies limited by guarantee.

(v) *Multilingual countries.*—Different linguistic renderings of the name of an entity listed in paragraph (b)(8)(i) of this section shall be disregarded. For example, an entity formed under the laws of Switzerland as a Societe Anonyme will be a corporation and treated in the same manner as an Aktiengesellschaft.

(vi) *Certain European entities.*—[Reserved]. For further guidance, see § 301.7701-2T.

(9) [Reserved]. For further guidance, see § 301.7701-2T(b)(9).

(c) *Other business entities.*—For federal tax purposes—

(1) The term *partnership* means a business entity that is not a corporation under paragraph (b) of this section and that has at least two members.

(2) *Wholly owned entities.*—(i) *In general.*—A business entity that has a single owner and is not a corporation under paragraph (b) of this section is disregarded as an entity separate from its owner.

(ii) *Special rule for certain business entities.*—If the single owner of a business entity is a bank (as defined in section 581, or, in the case of a foreign bank, as defined in section 585(a)(2)(B) without regard to the second sentence thereof), then the special rules applicable to banks under the Internal Revenue Code will continue to apply to the single owner as if the wholly owned entity were a separate entity. For this purpose, the special rules applicable to banks under the Internal Revenue Code do not include the rules under sections 864(c), 882(c), and 884.

(iii) *Tax liabilities of certain disregarded entities.*—(A) *In general.*—An entity that is otherwise disregarded as separate from its owner is treated as an entity separate from its owner for purposes of:

(1) Federal tax liabilities of the entity with respect to any taxable period for which the entity was not disregarded.

(2) Federal tax liabilities of any other entity for which the entity is liable.

(3) Refunds or credits of Federal tax.

(B) *Examples.*—The following examples illustrate the application of paragraph (c)(2)(iii)(A) of this section:

Example 1. In 2001, X, a domestic corporation that reports its taxes on a calendar year basis, merges into Z, a domestic LLC wholly owned by Y that is disregarded as an entity separate from Y, in a state law merger. X was not a member of a consolidated group at any time during its taxable year ending in December 2000. Under the applicable state law, Z is the successor to X and is liable for all of X's debts. In 2004, the Internal Revenue Service (IRS) seeks to extend the period of limitations on assessment for X's 2000 taxable year. Because Z is the successor to X and is liable for X's 2000 taxes that remain unpaid, Z is the proper party to sign the consent to extend the period of limitations.

Example 2. The facts are the same as in *Example 1*, except that in 2002, the IRS determines that X miscalculated and underreported its income tax liability for 2000. Because Z is the successor to X and is liable for X's 2000 taxes that remain unpaid, the deficiency may be assessed against Z and, in the event that Z fails to pay the liability after notice and demand, a general tax lien will arise against all of Z's property and rights to property.

(d) *Special rule for certain foreign business entities.*—(1) *In general.*—Except as provided in paragraph (d)(3) of this section, a foreign business entity described in paragraph (b)(8)(i) of this section will not be treated as a corporation under paragraph (b)(8)(i) of this section if—

(i) The entity was in existence on May 8, 1996;

(ii) The entity's classification was relevant (as defined in § 301.7701-3(d)) on May 8, 1996;

(iii) No person (including the entity) for whom the entity's classification was relevant on May 8, 1996, treats the entity as a corporation for purposes of filing such person's federal income tax returns, information returns, and withholding documents for the taxable year including May 8, 1996;

(iv) Any change in the entity's claimed classification within the sixty months prior to May 8, 1996, occurred solely as a result of a change in the organizational documents of the entity, and the entity and all members of the entity recognized the federal tax consequences of any change in the entity's classification within the sixty months prior to May 8, 1996;

(v) A reasonable basis (within the meaning of section 6662) existed on May 8, 1996, for treating the entity as other than a corporation; and

(vi) Neither the entity nor any member was notified in writing on or before May 8, 1996, that the classification of the entity was under examination (in which case the entity's classification will be determined in the examination).

(2) *Binding contract rule.*—If a foreign business entity described in paragraph (b)(8)(i) of this section is formed after May 8, 1996, pursuant to a written binding contract (including an accepted bid to develop a project) in effect on May 8, 1996, and all times thereafter, in which the parties agreed to engage (directly or indirectly) in an active and substantial business operation in the jurisdiction in which the entity is formed, paragraph (d)(1) of this section will be applied to that entity by substituting the date of the entity's formation for May 8, 1996.

(3) *Termination of grandfather status.*—(i) *In general.*—An entity that is not treated as a corporation under paragraph (b)(8)(i) of this section by reason of paragraph (d)(1) or (d)(2) of this section will be treated permanently as a corporation under paragraph (b)(8)(i) of this section from the earliest of:

(A) The effective date of an election to be treated as an association under § 301.7701-3;

(B) A termination of the partnership under section 708(b)(1)(B) (regarding sale or exchange of 50 percent or more of the total interest in an entity's capital or profits within a twelve month period);

(C) A division of the partnership under section 708(b)(2)(B); or

(D) The date any person or persons, who were not owners of the entity as of November 29, 1999, own in the aggregate a 50 percent or greater interest in the entity.

(ii) *Special rule for certain entities.*—For purposes of paragraph (d)(2) of this section, paragraph (d)(3)(i)(B) of this section shall not apply if the sale or exchange of interests in the entity is to a related person (within the meaning of sections 267(b) and 707(b)) and occurs no later than twelve months after the date of the formation of the entity.

(e) *Effective date.*—(1) Except as otherwise provided in this paragraph (e), the rules of this section apply as of January 1, 1997, except that paragraph (b)(6) of this section applies on or after January 14, 2002, to a business entity wholly owned by a foreign government regardless of any prior entity classification, and paragraph (c)(2)(ii) of this section applies to taxable years beginning after January 12, 2001. The reference to the Finnish, Maltese, and Norwegian entities in paragraph (b)(8)(i) of this section is applicable on November 29, 1999. The reference to the Trinidadian entity in paragraph (b)(8)(i) of this section applies to entities formed on or after November 29, 1999. Any Maltese or Norwegian entity that becomes an eligible entity as a result of paragraph (b)(8)(i) of this section in effect on November 29, 1999, may elect by February 14, 2000, to be classified for Federal tax purposes as an entity other than a corporation retroactive to any period from and including January 1, 1997. Any Finnish entity that becomes an eligible entity as a result of paragraph (b)(8)(i) of this section in effect on November 29, 1999, may elect by February 14, 2000, to be classified for Federal tax purposes as an entity other than a corporation retroactive to any period from and including September 1, 1997. However, paragraph (d)(3)(i)(D) of this section applies on or after October 22, 2003.

(2) Paragraph (c)(2)(iii) of this section applies on or after April 1, 2004. [Reg. § 301.7701-2.]

☐ [*T.D.* 6503, 11-15-60. *Amended by T.D.* 6797, 2-2-65; *T.D.* 7515, 10-17-77; *T.D.* 7889, 4-25-83; *T.D.* 8475, 5-13-93; *T.D.* 8697, 12-17-96; *T.D.* 8844, 11-26-99; *T.D.* 9012, 7-31-2002; *T.D.* 9093, 10-21-2003; *T.D.* 9153, 8-11-2004; *T.D.* 9183, 2-24-2005 *and T.D.* 9197, 4-13-2005.]

§ 301.7701-3. Classification of certain business entities.—(a) *In general.*—A business entity that is not classified as a corporation under § 301.7701-2(b)(1), (3), (4), (5), (6), (7), or (8) (an *eligible entity*) can elect its classification for federal tax purposes as provided in this section. An eligible entity with at least two members can elect to be classified as either an association (and thus a corporation under § 301.7701-2(b)(2)) or a partnership, and an eligible entity with a single owner can elect to be classified as an association or to be disregarded as an entity separate from its owner. Paragraph (b) of this section provides a default classification for an eligible entity that does not make an election. Thus, elections are necessary only when an eligible entity chooses to be classified initially as other than the default classification or when an eligible entity chooses to change its classification. An entity whose classification is determined under the default classification retains that classification (regardless of any changes in the members' liability that occurs at any time during the time that the entity's classification is relevant as defined in paragraph (d) of this section) until the entity makes an election to change that classification under paragraph (c)(1) of this section. Paragraph (c) of this section provides rules for making express elections. Paragraph (d) of this section provides special rules for foreign eligible entities. Paragraph (e) of this section provides special rules for classifying entities resulting from partnership terminations and divisions under section 708(b). Paragraph (f) of this section sets forth the effective date of this section and a special rule relating to prior periods.

(b) *Classification of eligible entities that do not file an election.*—(1) *Domestic eligible entities.*—Except as provided in paragraph (b)(3) of this section, unless the entity elects otherwise, a domestic eligible entity is—

(i) A partnership if it has two or more members; or

(ii) Disregarded as an entity separate from its owner if it has a single owner.

(2) *Foreign eligible entities.*—(i) *In general.*—Except as provided in paragraph (b)(3) of this section, unless the entity elects otherwise, a foreign eligible entity is—

(A) A partnership if it has two or more members and at least one member does not have limited liability;

(B) An association if all members have limited liability; or

(C) Disregarded as an entity separate from its owner if it has a single owner that does not have limited liability.

(ii) *Definition of limited liability.*—For purposes of paragraph (b)(2)(i) of this section, a member of a foreign eligible entity has limited liability if the member has no personal liability for the debts of or claims against the entity by reason of being a member. This determination is based solely on the statute or law pursuant to which the entity is organized, except that if the underlying statute or law allows the entity to specify in its organizational documents whether the members will have limited liability, the organizational documents may also be relevant. For purposes of this section, a member has personal liability if the creditors of the entity may seek satisfaction of all or any portion of the debts or claims against the entity from the member as such. A member has personal liability for purposes of this paragraph even if the member makes an agreement under which another person (whether or not a member of the entity) assumes such liability or agrees to indemnify that member for any such liability.

(3) *Existing eligible entities.*—(i) *In general.*—Unless the entity elects otherwise, an eligible entity in existence prior to the effective date of this section will have the same classification that the entity claimed under §§ 301.7701-1 through 301.7701-3 as in effect on the date prior to the effective date of this section; except that if an eligible entity with a single owner claimed to be a partnership under those regulations, the entity will be disregarded as an entity separate from its owner under this paragraph (b)(3)(i). For special rules regarding the classification of such entities prior to the effective date of this section, see paragraph (h)(2) of this section.

(ii) *Special rules.*—For purposes of paragraph (b)(3)(i) of this section, a foreign eligible entity is treated as being in existence prior to the effective date of this section only if the entity's classification was relevant (as defined in paragraph (d) of this section) at any time during the sixty months prior to the effective date of this section. If an entity claimed different classifications prior to the effective date of this section, the entity's classification for purposes of paragraph (b)(3)(i) of this section is the last classification claimed by the entity. If a foreign eligible entity's classification is relevant prior to the effective date of this section, but no federal tax or information return is filed or the federal tax or information return does not indicate the classification of the entity, the entity's classification for the period prior to the effective date of this section is determined under the regulations in effect on the date prior to the effective date of this section.

(c) *Elections.*—(1) *Time and place for filing.*—(i) *In general.*—Except as provided in paragraphs (c)(1)(iv) and (v) of this section, an eligible entity may elect to be classified other than as provided under paragraph (b) of this section, or to change its classification, by filing Form 8832, Entity Classification Election, with the service center designated on Form 8832. An election will not be accepted unless all of the information required by the form and instructions, including the taxpayer identifying number of the entity, is provided on Form 8832. See § 301.6109-1 for rules on applying for and displaying Employer Identification Numbers.

(ii) [Reserved]. For further guidance, see § 301.7701-3T(c)(1)(ii).

(iii) *Effective date of election.*—An election made under paragraph (c)(1)(i) of this section will be effective on the date specified by the entity on Form 8832 or on the date filed if no such date is specified on the election form. The effective date specified on Form 8832 can not be more than 75 days prior to the date on which the election is filed and can not be more than 12 months after the date on which the election is filed. If an election specifies an effective date more than 75 days prior to the date on which the election is filed, it will be effective 75 days prior to the date it was filed. If an election specifies an effective date more than 12 months from the date on which the election is filed, it will be effective 12 months after the date it was filed. If an election specifies an effective date before January 1, 1997, it will be effective as of January 1, 1997. If a purchasing corporation makes an election under section 338 regarding an acquired subsidiary, an election under paragraph (c)(1)(i) of this section for the acquired subsidiary can be effective no earlier than the day after the acquisition date (within the meaning of section 338(h)(2)).

(iv) *Limitation.*—If an eligible entity makes an election under paragraph (c)(1)(i) of this section to change its classification (other than an election made by an existing entity to change its classification as of the effective date of this section), the entity cannot change its classification by election again during the sixty months succeeding the effective date of the election. However, the Commissioner may permit the entity to change its classification by election within the sixty months if more than fifty percent of the ownership interests in the entity as of the effective date of the subsequent election are owned by persons that did not own any interests in the entity on the filing date or on the effective date of the entity's prior election. An election by a newly formed eligible entity that is effective on the date of formation is not considered a change for purposes of this paragraph (c)(1)(iv).

(v) *Deemed elections.*—(A) *Exempt organizations.*—An eligible entity that has been determined to be, or claims to be, exempt from taxation under section 501(a) is treated as having made an election under this section to be classified as an association. Such election will be effective as of the first day for which exemption is claimed or determined to apply, regardless of when the claim or determination is made, and will remain in effect unless an election is made under paragraph (c)(1)(i) of this section after the date the claim for exempt status is withdrawn or rejected or the date the determination of exempt status is revoked.

(B) *Real estate investment trusts.*—An eligible entity that files an election under section 856(c)(1) to be treated as a real estate investment trust is treated as having made an election under this section to be classified as an association. Such election will be effective as of the first day the entity is treated as a real estate investment trust.

(C) *S corporations.*—An eligible entity that timely elects to be an S corporation under section 1362(a)(1) is treated as having made an election under this section to be classified as an association, provided that (as of the effective date of the election under section 1362(a)(1)) the entity meets all other requirements to qualify as a small business corporation under section 1361(b). Subject to § 301.7701-3(c)(1)(iv), the deemed election to be classified as an association will apply as of the effective date of the S corporation election and will remain in effect until the entity makes a valid election, under § 301.7701-3(c)(1)(i), to be classified as other than an association.

(vi) *Examples.*—The following examples illustrate the rules of this paragraph (c)(1):

Example 1. On July 1, 1998, X, a domestic corporation, purchases a 10% interest in Y, an eligible entity formed under Country A law in 1990. The entity's classification was not relevant to any person for federal tax or information purposes prior to X's acquisition of an interest in Y. Thus, Y is not considered to be in existence on the effective date of this section for purposes of paragraph (b)(3) of this section. Under the applicable Country A statute, all members of Y have limited liability as defined in paragraph (b)(2)(ii) of this section. Accordingly, Y is classified as an association under paragraph (b)(2)(i)(B) of this section unless it elects under this paragraph (c) to be classified as a partnership. To be classified as a partnership as of July 1, 1998, Y must file a Form 8832 by September 14, 1998. See paragraph (c)(1)(i) of this section. Because an election cannot be effective more than 75 days prior to the date on which it is filed, if Y files its Form 8832 after September 14, 1998, it will be classified as an association from July 1, 1998, until the effective date of the election. In that case, it could not change its classification by election under this paragraph (c) during the sixty months succeeding the effective date of the election.

Example 2. (i) Z is an eligible entity formed under Country B law and is in existence on the effective date of this section within the meaning of paragraph (b)(3) of this section. Prior to the effective date of this section, Z claimed to be classified as an association. Unless Z files an election under this paragraph (c), it will continue to be classified as an association under paragraph (b)(3) of this section.

(ii) Z files a Form 8832 pursuant to this paragraph (c) to be classified as a partnership, effective as of the effective date of this section. Z can file an election to be classified as an association at any time thereafter, but then would not be permitted to change its classification by election during the sixty months succeeding the effective date of that subsequent election.

(2) *Authorized signatures.*—(i) *In general.*—An election made under paragraph (c)(1)(i) of this section must be signed by—

(A) Each member of the electing entity who is an owner at the time the election is filed; or

(B) Any officer, manager, or member of the electing entity who is authorized (under local law or the entity's organizational documents) to make the election and who represents to having such authorization under penalties of perjury.

(ii) *Retroactive elections.*—For purposes of paragraph (c)(2)(i) of this section, if an election under paragraph (c)(1)(i) of this section is to be effective for any period prior to the time that it is filed, each person who was an owner between the date the election is to be effective and the date the election is filed, and who is not an owner at the time the election is filed, must also sign the election.

(iii) *Changes in classification.*—For paragraph (c)(2)(i) of this section, if an election under paragraph (c)(1)(i) of this section is made to change the classification of an entity, each person who was an owner on the date that any transactions under paragraph (g) of this section are deemed to occur, and who is not an owner at the time the election is filed, must also sign the election. This paragraph (c)(2)(iii) applies to elections filed on or after November 29, 1999.

(d) *Special rules for foreign eligible entities.*—(1) *Definition of relevance.*—(i) *General rule.*—For purposes of this section, a foreign eligible entity's classification is relevant when its classification affects the liability of any person for federal tax or information purposes. For example, a foreign entity's classification would be relevant if U.S. income was paid to the entity and the determination by the withholding agent of the amount to be withheld under chapter 3 of the Internal Revenue Code (if any) would vary depending upon whether the entity is classified as a partnership or as an association. Thus, the classification might affect the documentation that the withholding agent must receive from the entity, the type of tax or information return to file, or how the return must be prepared. The date that the classification of a foreign eligible entity is relevant is the date an event occurs that creates an obligation to file a federal tax return, information return, or statement for which the classification of the entity must be determined. Thus, the classification of a foreign entity is relevant, for example, on the date that an interest in the entity is acquired which will require a U.S. person to file an information return on Form 5471.

(ii) *Deemed relevance.*—(A) *General rule.*—For purposes of this section, except as provided in paragraph (d)(1)(ii)(B) of this section, the classification for Federal tax purposes of a foreign eligible entity that files Form 8832, "Entity Classification Election", shall be deemed to be relevant only on the date the entity classification election is effective.

(B) *Exception.*—If the classification of a foreign eligible entity is relevant within the meaning of paragraph (d)(1)(i) of this section, then the rule in paragraph (d)(1)(ii)(A) of this section shall not apply.

(2) *Entities the classification of which has never been relevant.*—If the classification of a foreign eligible entity has never been relevant (as defined in paragraph (d)(1) of this section), then the entity's classification will initially be determined pursuant to the provisions of paragraph (b)(2) of this section when the classification of the entity first becomes relevant (as defined in paragraph (d)(1)(i) of this section).

(3) *Special rule when classification is no longer relevant.*—If the classification of a foreign eligible entity is not relevant (as defined in paragraph (d)(1) of this section) for 60 consecutive months, then the entity's classification will initially be determined pursuant to the provisions of paragraph (b)(2) of this section when the classification of the foreign eligible entity becomes relevant (as defined in paragraph (d)(1)(i) of this section). The date that the classification of a foreign entity is not relevant is the date an event occurs that causes the classification to no longer be relevant, or, if no event occurs in a taxable year that causes the classification to be relevant, then the date is the first day of that taxable year.

(4) *Effective date.*—Paragraphs (d)(1)(ii), (d)(2), and (d)(3) of this section apply on or after October 22, 2003.

(e) *Coordination with section 708(b).*—Except as provided in §301.7701-2(d)(3) (regarding termination of grandfather status for certain foreign business entities), an entity resulting from a transaction described in section 708(b)(1)(B) (partnership termination due to sales or exchanges) or section 708(b)(2)(B) (partnership division) is a partnership.

(f) *Changes in number of members of an entity.*—(1) *Associations.*—The classification of an eligible entity as an association is not affected by any change in the number of members of the entity.

(2) *Partnerships and single member entities.*—An eligible entity classified as a partnership becomes disregarded as an entity separate from its owner when the entity's membership is reduced to one member. A single member entity disregarded as an entity separate from its owner is classified as a partnership when the entity has more than one member. If an elective classification change under paragraph (c) of this section is effective at the same time as a membership change described in this paragraph (f)(2), the deemed transactions in paragraph (g) of this section resulting from the

elective change preempt the transactions that would result from the change in membership.

(3) *Effect on sixty month limitation.*—A change in the number of members of an entity does not result in the creation of a new entity for purposes of the sixty month limitation on elections under paragraph (c)(1)(iv) of this section.

(4) *Examples.*—The following examples illustrate the application of this paragraph (f):

Example 1. A, a U.S. person, owns a domestic eligible entity that is disregarded as an entity separate from its owner. On January 1, 1998, B, a U.S. person, buys a 50 percent interest in the entity from A. Under this paragraph (f), the entity is classified as a partnership when B acquires an interest in the entity. However, A and B elect to have the entity classified as an association effective on January 1, 1998. Thus, B is treated as buying shares of stock on January 1, 1998. (Under paragraph (c)(1)(iv) of this section, this election is treated as a change in classification so that the entity generally cannot change its classification by election again during the sixty months succeeding the effective date of the election.) Under paragraph (g)(1) of this section, A is treated as contributing the assets and liabilities of the entity to the newly formed association immediately before the close of December 31, 1997. Because A does not retain control of the association as required by section 351, A's contribution will be a taxable event. Therefore, under section 1012, the association will take a fair market value basis in the assets contributed by A, and A will have a fair market value basis in the stock received. A will have no additional gain upon the sale of stock to B, and B will have a cost basis in the stock purchased from A.

Example 2. (i) On April 1, 1998, A and B, U.S. persons, form X, a foreign eligible entity. X is treated as an association under the default provisions of paragraph (b)(2)(i) of this section, and X does not make an election to be classified as a partnership. A subsequently purchases all of B's interest in X.

(ii) Under paragraph (f)(1) of this section, X continues to be classified as an association. X, however, can subsequently elect to be disregarded as an entity separate from A. The sixty month limitation of paragraph (c)(1)(iv) of this section does not prevent X from making an election because X has not made a prior election under paragraph (c)(1)(i) of this section.

Example 3. (i) On April 1, 1998, A and B, U.S. persons, form X, a foreign eligible entity. X is treated as an association under the default provisions of paragraph (b)(2)(i) of this section, and X does not make an election to be classified as a partnership. On January 1, 1999, X elects to be classified as a partnership effective on that date. Under the sixty month limitation of paragraph (c)(1)(iv) of this section, X cannot elect to be classified as an association until January 1, 2004 (i.e., sixty months after the effective date of the election to be classified as a partnership).

(ii) On June 1, 2000, A purchases all of B's interest in X. After A's purchase of B's interest, X can no longer be classified as a partnership because X has only one member. Under paragraph (f)(2) of this section, X is disregarded as an entity separate from A when A becomes the only member of X. X, however, is not treated as a new entity for purposes of paragraph (c)(1)(iv) of this section. As a result, the sixty month limitation of paragraph (c)(1)(iv) of this section continues to apply to X, and X cannot elect to be classified as an association until January 1, 2004 (i.e., sixty months after January 1, 1999, the effective date of the election by X to be classified as a partnership).

(5) *Effective date.*—This paragraph (f) applies as of November 29, 1999.

(g) *Elective changes in classification.*—(1) *Deemed treatment of elective change.*—(i) *Partnership to association.*—If an eligible entity classified as a partnership elects under paragraph (c)(1)(i) of this section to be classified as an association, the following is deemed to occur: The partnership contributes all of its assets and liabilities to the association in exchange for stock in the association, and immediately thereafter, the partnership liquidates by distributing the stock of the association to its partners.

(ii) *Association to partnership.*—If an eligible entity classified as an association elects under paragraph (c)(1)(i) of this section to be classified as a partnership, the following is deemed to occur: The association distributes all of its assets and liabilities to its shareholders in liquidation of the association, and immediately thereafter, the shareholders contribute all of the distributed assets and liabilities to a newly formed partnership.

(iii) *Association to disregarded entity.*—If an eligible entity classified as an association elects under paragraph (c)(1)(i) of this section to be disregarded as an entity separate from its owner, the following is deemed to occur: The association distributes all of its assets and liabilities to its single owner in liquidation of the association.

(iv) *Disregarded entity to an association.*—If an eligible entity that is disregarded as an entity separate from its owner elects under paragraph (c)(1)(i) of this section to be classified as an association, the following is deemed to occur: The owner of the eligible entity contributes all of the assets and liabilities of the entity to the association in exchange for stock of the association.

(2) *Effect of elective changes.*—(i) *In general.*—The tax treatment of a change in the classification of an entity for federal tax purposes by election under paragraph (c)(1)(i) of this section is determined under all relevant provisions of the Internal Revenue Code and general principles of tax law, including the step transaction doctrine.

(ii) *Adoption of plan of liquidation.*—For purposes of satisfying the requirement of adoption of a plan of liquidation under section 332, unless a formal plan of liquidation that contemplates the election to be classified as a partnership or to be disregarded as an entity separate from its owner is adopted on an earlier date, the making, by an association, of an election under paragraph (c)(1)(i) of this section to be classified as a partnership or to be disregarded as an entity separate from its owner is considered to be the adoption of a plan of liquidation immediately before the deemed liquidation described in paragraph (g)(1)(ii) or (iii) of this section. This paragraph (g)(2)(ii) applies to elections filed on or after December 17, 2001. Taxpayers may apply this paragraph (g)(2)(ii) retroactively to elections filed before December 17, 2001, if the corporate owner claiming treatment under section 332 and its subsidiary making the election take consistent positions with respect to the federal tax consequences of the election.

(3) *Timing of election.*—(i) *In general.*—An election under paragraph (c)(1)(i) of this section that changes the classification of an eligible entity for federal tax purposes is treated as occurring at the start of the day for which the election is effective. Any transactions that are deemed to occur under this paragraph (g) as a result of a change in classification are treated as occurring immediately before the close of the day before the election is effective. For example, if an election is made to change the classification of an entity from an association to a partnership effective on January 1, the deemed transactions specified in paragraph (g)(1)(ii) of this section (including the liquidation of the association) are treated as occurring immediately before the close of December 31 and must be reported by the owners of the entity on December 31. Thus, the last day of the association's taxable year will be December 31 and the first day of the partnership's taxable year will be January 1.

(ii) *Coordination with section 338 election.*—A purchasing corporation that makes a qualified stock purchase of an eligible entity taxed as a corporation may make an election under section 338 regarding the acquisition if it satisfies the requirements for the election, and may also make an election to change the classification of the target corporation. If a taxpayer makes an election under section 338 regarding its acquisition of another entity taxable as a corporation and makes an election under paragraph (c) of this section for the acquired corporation (effective at the earliest possible date as provided by paragraph (c)(1)(iii) of this section), the transactions under paragraph (g) of this section are deemed to occur immediately after the deemed asset purchase by the new target corporation under section 338.

(iii) *Application to successive elections in tiered situations.*—When elections under paragraph (c)(1)(i) of this section for a series of tiered entities are effective on the same date, the eligible entities may specify the order of the elections on Form 8832. If no order is specified for the elections, any transactions that are deemed to occur in this paragraph (g) as a result of the classification change will be treated as occurring first for the highest tier entity's classification change, then for the next highest tier entity's classification change, and so forth down the chain of entities until all the transactions under this paragraph (g) have occurred. For example, Parent, a corporation, wholly owns all of the interest of an eligible entity classified as an association (S1), which wholly owns another eligible entity classified as an association (S2), which wholly owns another eligible entity classified as an association (S3). Elections under paragraph (c)(1)(i) of this section are filed to classify S1, S2, and S3 each as disregarded as an entity separate from its owner effective on the same day. If no order is specified for the elections, the following transactions are deemed to occur under this paragraph (g) as a result of the elections, with each successive transaction occurring on the same day immediately after the preceding transaction: S1 is treated as liquidating into Parent, then S2 is treated as liquidating into Parent, and finally S3 is treated as liquidating into Parent.

(4) *Effective date.*—Except as otherwise provided in paragraph (g)(2)(ii) of this section, this paragraph (g) applies to elections that are filed on or after November 29, 1999. Taxpayers may apply this paragraph (g) retroactively to elections filed before November 29, 1999 if all taxpayers affected by the deemed transactions file consistently with this paragraph (g).

(h) *Effective date.*—(1) *In general.*—Except as otherwise provided in this section, the rules of this section are applicable as of January 1, 1997.

(2) *Prior treatment of existing entities.*—In the case of a business entity that is not described in § 301.7701-2(b)(1), (3), (4), (5), (6), or (7), and that was in existence prior to January 1, 1997, the entity's claimed classification(s) will be respected for all periods prior to January 1, 1997, if—

(i) The entity had a reasonable basis (within the meaning of section 6662) for its claimed classification;

(ii) The entity and all members of the entity recognized the federal tax consequences of any change in the entity's classification within the sixty months prior to January 1, 1997; and

(iii) Neither the entity nor any member was notified in writing on or before May 8, 1996, that the classification of the entity was under examination (in which case the entity's classification will be determined in the examination).

(3) *Deemed elections for S corporations.*—Paragraph (c)(1)(v)(C) of this section applies to timely S corporation elections under section 1362(a) filed on or after July 20, 2004. Eligible entities that filed timely S elections before July 20, 2004 may also rely on the provisions of the regulation. [Reg. § 301.7701-3.]

☐ [*T.D.* 6503, 11-15-60. *Amended by T.D.* 8632, 12-19-95; *T.D.* 8697, 12-17-96; *T.D.* 8767, 3-23-98; *T.D.* 8827, 7-12-99 (*corrected* 10-29-99); *T.D.* 8844, 11-26-99; *T.D.* 8970, 12-14-2001; *T.D.* 9093, 10-21-2003; *T.D.* 9100, 12-18-2003; *T.D.* 9139, 7-19-200; *T.D.* 9153, 8-11-2004 *and T.D.* 9203, 5-20-2005.]

§ 301.7701-5. Domestic and foreign business entities.—[Reserved]. For further guidance, see § 301.7701-5T. [Reg. § 301.7701-5.]

☐ [*T.D.* 6503, 11-15-60. *Amended by T.D.* 8813, 2-1-99 *and T.D.* 9153, 8-11-2004.]

§ 301.7701-5T. Domestic and foreign business entities (temporary).—(a) *Domestic and foreign entities.*—A business entity (including an entity that is disregarded as separate from its owner) is domestic if it is created or organized as any type of entity (including, but not limited to, a corporation, unincorporated association, general partnership, limited partnership, and limited liability company) in the United States, or under the law of the United States or of any State. Accordingly, a business entity that is created or organized both in the United States and in a foreign jurisdiction is a domestic entity. A business entity (including an entity that is disregarded as separate from its owner) is foreign if it is not domestic. (The determination of whether an entity is domestic is made independently of the determination of its classification for Federal tax purposes. See §§ 301.7701-2, 301.7701-2T, and 301.7701-3 for the rules governing the classification of entities.)

(b) *Examples.*—The following examples illustrate the rules of this section:

Example 1. (i) *Facts.* Y is an entity that is created or organized under the laws of Country A as a public limited company. It is also an entity that is organized as a limited liability company (LLC) under the laws of State B. Y has been classified as a corporation for Federal tax purposes under the rules of §§ 301.7701-2, 301.7701-2T, and 301.7701-3.

(ii) *Result.* Y is a domestic corporation because it is an entity that is classified as a corporation and it is organized as an entity under the laws of State B.

Example 2. (i) *Facts.* P is an entity with more than one owner organized under the laws of Country A as an unlimited company. It is also an entity that is organized as a general partnership under the laws of State B. P has been classified as a partnership for Federal tax purposes under the rules of §§ 301.7701-2, 301.7701-2T, and 301.7701-3.

(ii) *Result.* P is a domestic partnership because it is an entity that is classified as a partnership and it is organized as an entity under the laws of State B.

(c) *Effective date.*—The rules of this section apply as of August 12, 2004 to all business entities existing on or after that date. [Temporary Reg. § 301.7701-5T.]

☐ [*T.D.* 9153, 8-11-2004.]

§ 301.7701(b)-1. Resident alien.—(a) *Scope.*—Section 301.7701(b)-1(b) provides rules for determining whether an alien individual is a lawful permanent resident of the United States. Section 301.7701(b)-1(c) provides rules for determining if an alien individual satisfies the substantial presence test. Section 301.7701(b)-2 provides rules for determining when an alien individual will be considered to maintain a tax home in a foreign country and to have a closer connection to that foreign country. Section 301.7701(b)-3 provides rules for determining if an individual is an exempt individual because of his or her status as a foreign government-related individual, teacher, trainee, student, or professional athlete. Section 301.7701(b)-3 also provides rules for determining whether an individual may exclude days of presence in the United States because the individual was unable to leave the United States because of a medical condition. Section 301.7701(b)-4 provides rules for determining an individual's residency starting and termination dates. Section 301.7701(b)-5 provides rules for applying section 877 to a nonresident alien individual. Section 301.7701(b)-6 provides rules for determining the taxable year of an alien. Section 301.7701(b)-7 provides rules for determining the effect of these regulations on rules in tax conventions to which the United States is a party. Section 301.7701(b)-8 provides procedural rules for establishing that an individual is a nonresident alien. Section 301.7701(b)-9 provides the effective dates of section 7701(b) and the regulations under that section. Unless the context indicates otherwise, the regulations under §§ 301.7701(b)-1 through 301.7701(b)-9 apply for purposes of determining whether a United States citizen is also a resident of the United States. (This determination may be relevant, for example, to the application of section 861(a)(1) which treats income from interest-bearing obligations of residents as income from sources within the United States.) The regulations do not apply and §§ 1.871-2 and 1.871-5 of this chapter continue to apply for purposes of the bona fide residence test of section 911. See § 1.911-2(c) of this chapter. For purposes of determining whether an individual is a resident of the United States for estate and gift tax purposes, see § 20.0-1(b)(1) and (2) and § 25.2501-1(b) of this chapter, respectively.

(b) *Lawful permanent resident.*—(1) *Green card test.*—An alien is a resident alien with respect to a calendar year if the individual is a lawful permanent resident at any time during the calendar year. A lawful permanent resident is an individual who has been lawfully granted the privilege of residing permanently in the United States as an immigrant in accordance with the immigration laws. Resident status is deemed to continue unless it is rescinded or administratively or judicially determined to have been abandoned.

(2) *Rescission of resident status.*—Resident status is considered to be rescinded if a final administrative or judicial order of exclusion or deportation is issued regarding the alien individual. For purposes of this paragraph, the term "final judicial order" means an order that is no longer subject to appeal to a higher court of competent jurisdiction.

(3) *Administrative or judicial determination of abandonment of resident status.*—An administrative or judicial determination of abandonment of resident status may be initiated by the alien individual, the Immigration and Naturalization Service (INS), or a consular officer. If the alien initiates this determination, resident status is considered to be abandoned when the individual's application for abandonment (INS Form I-407) or a letter stating the alien's intent to abandon his or her resident status, with the Alien Registration Receipt Card (INS Form I-151 or Form I-551) enclosed, is filed with the INS or a consular officer. If INS replaces any of the form numbers referred to in this paragraph or § 301.7701(b)-2(f), refer to the comparable INS replacement form number. For purposes of this paragraph, an alien individual shall be considered to have filed a letter stating the intent to abandon resident status with the INS or a consular office if such letter is sent by certified mail, return receipt requested (or a foreign country's equivalent thereof). A copy of the letter, along with proof that the letter was mailed and received, should be retained by the alien individual. If the INS or a consular officer initiates this determination, resident status will be considered to be abandoned upon the issuance of a final administrative order of abandonment. If an individual is granted an appeal to a federal court of competent jurisdiction, a final judicial order is required.

(c) *Substantial presence test.*—(1) *In general.*—An alien individual is a resident alien if the individual meets the substantial presence test. An individual satisfies this test if he or she has been present in the United States on at least 183 days during a three year period that includes the current year. For purposes of this test, each day of presence in the current year is counted as a full day. Each day of presence in the first preceding year is counted as one-third of a day and each day of presence in the second preceding year is counted as one-sixth of a day. For purposes of this paragraph, any fractional days resulting from the above calculations will not be rounded to the nearest whole number. (See § 301.7701(b)-9(b)(2) for transitional rules for calendar years 1985 and 1986.)

(2) *Determination of presence.*— (i) *Physical presence.*—For purposes of the substantial presence test, an individual shall be treated as present in the United States on any day that he or she is physically present in the United States at any time during the day. (But see § 301.7701(b)-3 relating to days of presence that may be excluded.)

(ii) *United States.*—For purposes of section 7701(b) and the regulations thereunder, the term "United States" when used in a geographical sense includes the states and the District of Columbia. It also includes the territorial waters of the United States and the seabed and subsoil of those submarine areas which are adjacent to the territorial waters of the United States and over which the United States has exclusive rights, in accordance with international law, with respect to the exploration and exploitation of natural resources. It does not include the possessions and territories of the United States or the air space over the United States.

(3) *Current year.*—The term "current year" means any calendar year for which an alien individual is determining his or her resident status.

(4) *Thirty-one day minimum.*—If an individual is not physically present for more than 30 days during the current year, the substantial presence test will not be applied for that year even if the three-year total is 183 or more days. For purposes of the substantial presence test, it is irrelevant that an individual was not present for more than 30 days in the first or second year preceding the current year.

(d) [Reserved].—For further guidance, see §301.7701(b)-1T(d).

(e) *Examples.*—This section may be illustrated by the following examples:

Example 1. B, an alien individual, is present in the United States for 122 days in the current year. He was present in the United States for 122 days in the first preceding calendar year and for 122 days in the second preceding calendar year. In determining his status for the current year, B counts all 122 days in the United States in the current year plus ⅓ of the 122 days in the United States in the first preceding calendar year (40 ⅔ days) and ⅙ of the 122 days in the United States during the second preceding calendar year (20 ⅓ days). The total of 122 + 40 ⅔ + 20 ⅓ equals 183 days. B meets the substantial presence test and is a resident alien for the current year.

Example 2. C, an alien individual, is present in the United States for 25 days during the current year. She was present in the United States for 365 days during the first preceding year and 365 days during the second preceding year. The substantial presence test does not apply because C is present in the United States for fewer than 31 days during the current year.

Example 3. D, an alien individual, is present in the United States for 170 days during the current year. He was present in the United States for 30 days during the first preceding year and 30 days during the second preceding year. In determining his status for the current year, D counts all 170 days in the United States in the current year plus ⅓ of the 30 days in the United States in the first preceding calendar year (10 days) and ⅙ of the 30 days in the United States during the second preceding calendar year (5 days). The total of 170 + 10 + 5 equals 185 days. D meets the substantial presence test and is a resident alien for the current year notwithstanding the fact that he was present in the United States for fewer than 31 days in each of the two preceding years. [Reg. §301.7701(b)-1.]

☐ [*T.D.* 8411, 4-24-92. *Amended by T.D.* 9194, 4-6-2005.]

§301.7701(b)-1T. Resident alien (temporary).—(a) through (c) [Reserved] For further guidance, see §301.7701(b)-1(a) through (c).

(d) *Application of section 7701(b) to the possessions and territories.*—(1) *Application to aliens for purposes of mirror systems.*—Section 7701(b) provides the basis for determining whether an alien individual is a resident of a United States possession or territory that administers income tax laws that are identical (except for the substitution of the name of the possession or territory for the term United States where appropriate) to those in force in the United States, for purposes of applying such laws with respect to income tax liability incurred to such possession or territory.

(2) *Non-application for bona fide resident determination.*—Section 7701(b) does not provide the basis for determining whether an individual (including an alien individual) is a bona fide resident of a United States possession or territory for U.S. Federal income tax purposes. For the applicable rules for making this determination, see section 937(a) and the regulations thereunder.

(e) [Reserved].—For further guidance, see §301.7701(b)-1(e).

(f) *Effective date.*—This section shall apply for taxable years ending after October 22, 2004. [Temporary Reg. §301.7701(b)-1T.]

☐ [*T.D.* 9194, 4-6-2005 (*corrected* 6-2-2005).]

§301.7701(b)-2. Closer connection exception.—(a) *In general.*—An alien individual who meets the substantial presence test may nevertheless be considered a nonresident alien for the current year if the following conditions are satisfied—

(1) The individual is present in the United States for fewer than 183 days in the current year;

(2) The individual maintains a tax home in a foreign country during the current year; and

(3) Except as provided in paragraph (e) of this section, the individual has a closer connection during the current year to a single foreign country in which he or she maintains a tax home than to the United States.

(b) *Foreign country.*—For purposes of section 7701(b) and the regulations thereunder, the term "foreign country" when used in a geographical sense includes any territory under the sovereignty of the United Nations or a government other than that of the United States. It includes the territorial waters of the foreign country (determined in accordance with the laws of the United States), and the seabed and subsoil of those submarine areas which are adjacent to the territorial waters of the foreign country and over which the foreign country has exclusive rights, in accordance with international law, with respect to the exploration and exploitation of natural resources. It also includes the possessions and territories of the United States.

(c) *Tax home.*—(1) *Definition.*—For purposes of section 7701(b) and the regulations under that section, the term "tax home" has the same meaning that it has for purposes of section 162(a)(2) (relating to travel expenses while away from home). Thus, an individual's tax home is considered to be located at the individual's regular or principal (if more than one regular) place of business. If the individual has no regular or principal place of business because of the nature of the business, or because the individual is not engaged in carrying on any trade or business within the meaning of section 162(a), then the individual's tax home is the individual's regular place of abode in a real and substantial sense.

(2) *Duration and nature of tax home.*—The tax home maintained by the alien individual must be in existence for the entire current year. The tax home must be located in the same foreign country for which the individual is claiming to have the closer connection described in paragraph (d) of this section.

(d) *Closer connection to a foreign country.*—(1) *In general.*—For purposes of section 7701(b) and the regulations under that section, an alien individual will be considered to have a closer connection to a foreign country than the United States if the individual or the Commissioner establishes that the individual has maintained more significant contacts with the foreign country than with the United States. In determining whether an individual has maintained more significant contacts with a foreign country than the United States, the facts and circumstances to be considered include, but are not limited to, the following—

(i) The location of the individual's permanent home;

(ii) The location of the individual's family;

(iii) The location of personal belongings, such as automobiles, furniture, clothing and jewelry owned by the individual and his or her family;

(iv) The location of social, political, cultural or religious organizations with which the individual has a current relationship;

(v) The location where the individual conducts his or her routine personal banking activities;

(vi) The location where the individual conducts business activities (other than those that constitute the individual's tax home);

(vii) The location of the jurisdiction in which the individual holds a driver's license;

(viii) The location of the jurisdiction in which the individual votes;

(ix) The country of residence designated by the individual on forms and documents; and

(x) The types of official forms and documents filed by the individual, such as Form 1078 (Certificate of Alien Claiming Residence in the United States), Form W-8 (Certificate of Foreign Status) or Form W-9 (Payee's Request for Taxpayer Identification Number).

(2) *Permanent home.*—For purposes of paragraph (d)(1)(i) of this section, it is immaterial whether a permanent home is a house, an apartment, or a furnished room. It is also immaterial whether the home is owned or rented by the alien individual. It is material, however, that the dwelling be available at all times, continuously, and not solely for stays of short duration.

(e) *Special rule.*—An alien individual may demonstrate in one year that he or she has a closer connection to two foreign countries (but no more than two) if he or she satisfies all of the following conditions—

(1) The individual maintains a tax home beginning on the first day of the current year in one foreign country;

(2) The individual changes his or her tax home during the current year to a second foreign country;

(3) The individual continues to maintain his or her tax home in the second foreign country for the remainder of the current year;

(4) The individual has a closer connection to each foreign country than to the United States for the period during which the individual maintains a tax home in that foreign country; and

(5) The individual is subject to taxation as a resident pursuant to the internal laws of either foreign country for the entire year or subject to taxation as a resident in both foreign countries for the period during which the individual maintains a tax home in each foreign country.

(f) *Closer connection exception unavailable.*—An alien individual who has personally applied, or taken other affirmative steps, to change his or her status to that of a permanent resident during the current year or has an application pending for adjustment of status during the current year will not be eligible for the closer connection exception. Affirmative steps to change status to that of a permanent resident include, but are not limited to, the following—

(1) The filing of Immigration and Naturalization Form I-508 (Waiver of Immunities) by the alien;

(2) The filing of Immigration and Naturalization Form I-485 (Application for Status as Permanent Resident) by the alien;

(3) The filing of Immigration and Naturalization Form I-130 (Petition for Alien Relative) on behalf of the alien;

(4) The filing of Immigration and Naturalization Form I-140 (Petition for Prospective Immigrant Employee) on behalf of the alien;

(5) The filing of Department of Labor Form ETA-750 (Application for Alien Employment Certification) on behalf of the alien; or

(6) The filing of Department of State Form OF-230 (Application for Immigrant Visa and Alien Registration) by the alien.

(g) *Filing requirements.*—See § 301.7701(b)-8 with regard to the statement that must be filed by an alien individual claiming the closer connection exception. [Reg. § 301.7701(b)-2.]

□ [*T.D.* 8411, 4-24-92.]

§ 301.7701(b)-3. Days of presence in the United States that are excluded for purposes of section 7701(b).—(a) *In general.*—In computing days of presence in the United States, an alien is considered to be present if the individual is physically present in the United States at any time during the day (see § 301.7701(b)-1(c)(2)(i)). However, for purposes of section 7701(b) and the regulations under that section, the following days shall be excluded and will not count as days of presence in the United States—

(1) Any day that an individual is present in the United States as an exempt individual;

(2) Any day that an individual is prevented from leaving the United States because of a medical condition that arose while the individual was present in the United States—

(3) Any day that an individual is in transit between two points outside the United States; and

(4) Any day on which a regular commuter residing in Canada or Mexico commutes to and from employment in the United States.

(b) *Exempt individuals.*—(1) *In general.*—An exempt individual is an individual who is either a—

(i) Foreign government-related individual as defined in paragraph (b)(2) of this section;

(ii) Teacher or trainee as defined in paragraph (b)(3) of this section;

(iii) Student as defined in paragraph (b)(4) of this section; or

(iv) Professional athlete as defined in paragraph (b)(5) of this section.

(2) *Foreign government-related individual.*—(i) *In general.*—A foreign government-related individual is an individual (and that individual's immediate family) who is temporarily present in the United States—

(A) as a full-time employee of an international organization;

(B) by reason of diplomatic status; or

(C) by reason of a visa that the Secretary of the Treasury or his or her delegate (after consultation with the Secretary of State when appropriate) determines represents full-time diplomatic or consular status. An individual described in this paragraph shall be considered to be temporarily present in the United States if the individual is not a lawful permanent resident as described in § 301.7701(b)-1(b)(1), regardless of the actual amount of time that the individual is present in the United States.

(ii) *Definition of international organization.*—The term "international organization" means any public international organization that has been designated by the President by Executive Order as being entitled to enjoy the privileges, exemptions, and immunities provided for in the International Organizations Act (22 U.S.C. 288). An individual described in paragraph (b)(2)(i) of this section will be a full-time employee of an international organization if that individual's employment with the organization is consistent with an employment schedule of a person with a standard full-time work schedule with the organization.

(iii) *Full-time diplomatic or consular status.*—An individual is considered to have full-time diplomatic or consular status if—

(A) The individual has been accredited by a foreign government recognized de jure or de facto by the United States;

(B) The individual intends to engage primarily in official activities for that foreign government while in the United States; and

(C) The individual has been recognized by the President, or by the Secretary of State, or by a consular officer acting on behalf of the Secretary of State, as being entitled to such status.

(3) *Teacher or trainee.*—A teacher or trainee includes any individual (and that individual's immediate family), other than a student, who is admitted temporarily to the United

States as a nonimmigrant under section 101(a)(15)(J) (relating to the admission of teachers and trainees into the United States) or section 101(a)(15)(Q) (relating to the admission of participants in international cultural exchange programs) of the Immigration and Nationality Act (8 U.S.C. 1101(a)(15)(J), (Q)) and who substantially complies with the requirements of being admitted.

(4) *Student.*—A student is any individual (and that individual's immediate family) who is admitted temporarily to the United States as a nonimmigrant under section 101(a)(15)(F) or (M) (relating to the admission of students into the United States) or as a student under section 101(a)(15)(J) (relating to the admission of teachers and trainees into the United States) or section 101(a)(15)(Q) (relating to the admission of participants in international cultural exchange programs) of the Immigration and Nationality Act (8 U.S.C. 1101(a)(15)(F), (J), (M), (Q)) who substantially complies with the requirements of being admitted. For rules concerning taxation of certain nonresident students or trainees, see section 871(c) and § 1.871-9(a) of this chapter.

(5) *Professional athlete.*—A professional athlete is an individual who is temporarily present in the United States to compete in a charitable sports event described in section 274(l)(1)(B). For purposes of computing the days of presence in the United States, only days on which the athlete actually competes in a charitable sports event described in section 274(l)(1)(B) shall be excluded. Thus, days on which the individual is present to practice for the event, to perform promotional or other activities related to the event, or to travel between events shall be included for purposes of the substantial presence test.

(6) *Substantial compliance.*—An individual described in paragraph (b)(3) or (4) of this section will be deemed to comply substantially with the visa requirements relevant to residence for tax purposes if the individual has not engaged in activities that are prohibited by the Immigration and Nationality Act and the regulations thereunder and could result in the loss of F, J or M visa status. An individual will not be deemed to comply substantially with the visa requirements relevant to residence for tax purposes merely by showing that the individual's visa has not been revoked. An independent determination of substantial compliance may be made by the Internal Revenue Service for any individual claiming to be an exempt individual under paragraph (b)(3) or (4) of this section. For example, if an individual with an F visa (student visa) is found to have accepted unauthorized employment or to have maintained a course of study that is not considered by the Internal Revenue Service to be full-time, the individual will not be considered to comply substantially with the individual's visa requirements regardless of whether the individual's visa has been revoked.

(7) *Limitation on teacher or trainee and student exemptions.*—(i) *Teacher or trainee limitation in general.*—Except as otherwise provided, an individual shall not exclude days of presence as a teacher or trainee if the individual has been exempt as a teacher, trainee, or student for any part of two of the six preceding calendar years.

(ii) *Special teacher or trainee limitation for section 872 (b) (3) compensation.*—If—

(A) A teacher or trainee receives compensation in the current year and all of that compensation is described in section 872(b)(3);

(B) That individual was present in the United States as a teacher or trainee in any prior year within the last 6 years; and

(C) During each prior year (within the 6 year period) in which the individual was present as a teacher or trainee, the individual received compensation all of which was described in section 872(b)(3);

then that individual shall include days of presence as a teacher or trainee in the current year only if the individual has been exempt as a teacher, trainee, or student for any part of four of the six preceding calendar years.

(iii) *Limitation on student exemption.*—An individual will not be able to exclude days of presence as a student if the individual has been exempt as a teacher, trainee, or student for any part of more than five calendar years, unless it is established to the satisfaction of the district director that the individual does not intend to reside permanently in the United States and has substantially complied with the requirements of the student visa providing for the individual's temporary presence in the United States. For purposes of this paragraph (b)(7), the facts and circumstances to be considered in determining if an individual has demonstrated an intent to reside permanently in the United States include (but are not limited to)—

(A) Whether the individual has maintained a closer connection with a foreign country as described in § 301.7701(b)-2; and

(B) Whether the individual has taken affirmative steps within the meaning of paragraph (f) of § 301.7701(b)-2 to adjust the individual's status from nonimmigrant to lawful permanent resident.

(iv) *Transition rule.*—The rules in this paragraph (b)(7) relating to stated periods of exempt status apply only for those stated periods that occur after 1984. Thus, for example, an alien who is present as a student during the calendar years 1982-1990 will not be subject to the five year rule for students until 1990.

(v) *Examples.*—The following examples illustrate the application of paragraphs (b)(7)(i) and (ii) of this section:

Example 1. B is temporarily present in the United States during the current year as a teacher, within the meaning of section 101(a)(15)(J) of the Immigration and Nationality Act. B does not receive compensation described in section 872(b)(3) in the current year. B has been treated as an exempt student for the past three years. Although this is the first year that B is seeking to be exempt as a teacher, he will not be considered an exempt individual for the year because he has been exempt as a student for at least two of the past six years.

Example 2. C is temporarily present in the United States during the current year as a teacher and receives compensation described in section 872(b)(3) in the current year. C has been treated as an exempt teacher for the past two years but C's compensation for those years was not described in section 872(b)(3). C will not be considered an exempt individual for the current year because she has been exempt as a teacher for at least two of the past six years.

Example 3. The facts are the same as in *Example 2*, except that all of C's compensation for the two preceding years was described in section 872(b)(3). C will be considered to be an exempt individual for the current year because she has not been exempt as a student, teacher or trainee for four of the six preceding calendar years.

Example 4. D is temporarily present in the United States during the current year as a teacher, within the meaning of section 101(a)(15)(J) of the Immigration and Nationality Act. D does not receive compensation described in section 872(b)(3) in the current year. D entered the United States in December of the second preceding year and intends to remain in the United States until June of the current year. D will not be considered an exempt individual for the current year because he has been exempt as a teacher for at least two of the past six years.

(8) *Immediate family.*—The immediate family of an exempt individual includes the individual's spouse and unmarried children (whether by blood or adoption) but only if the spouse's or unmarried children's visa status are derived from and dependent on the visa classification of the exempt individual. For the purposes of this paragraph, the term "unmarried children" means those children who are under 21 years of age, who reside regularly in the household of the exempt individual, and who are not members of some other household. The immediate family of an exempt individual does not include the attendants, servants, and personal employees of that individual.

(c) *Medical condition.*—(1) *In general.*—An individual will not be considered present on any day that the individual intends to leave and is unable to leave the United States because of a medical condition or medical problem that arose while the individual was present in the United States. A day of presence will not be excluded if the individual, who was initially prevented from leaving, is subsequently able to leave the United States and then remains in the United States beyond a reasonable period for making arrangements to leave the United States. A day will also not be excluded if the medical condition arose during a prior stay in the United States (whether or not days of presence during the prior stay were excluded) and the alien returns to the United States for treatment of the medical condition or medical problem that arose during the prior stay.

(2) *Intent to leave the United States.*—For purposes of paragraph (c)(1) of this section, whether an individual intends to leave the United States on a particular day will be determined based on all the facts and circumstances. Thus, if at the time an individual's medical condition or medical problem arose, the individual was present in the United States for a definite purpose which by its nature could be accomplished within the United States during a period of time that would not cause the individual to be a resident under the substantial presence test, the individual may be able to establish that he or she intended to leave the United States. However, if the individual's purpose is of such a nature that an extended period of time would be required for its accomplishment (sufficient to cause the individual to be a resident under the substantial presence test), the individual would not be able to establish the requisite intent to leave the United States. If the individual is present in the United States for no particular purpose or a purpose by its nature that does not require a specific period of time to accomplish, the determination of whether the individual has the requisite intent to leave the United States will depend on all the surrounding facts and circumstances. In the case of an individual adjudicated mentally incompetent, proof of intent to leave the United States may be determined by analyzing the incompetent's pattern of behavior prior to the adjudication of incompetence. Generally, an individual will be presumed to have intended to leave during a period of illness if the individual leaves the United States within a

reasonable period of time (time to make arrangements to leave) after becoming physically able to leave.

(3) *Pre-existing medical condition.*—A medical condition or problem will not be considered to arise while the individual is present in the United States, if the condition or problem existed prior to the individual's arrival in the United States, and the individual was aware of the condition or problem, regardless of whether the individual required treatment for the condition or problem when the individual entered the United States.

(4) *Examples.*—The following examples illustrate the application of this paragraph (c):

Example 1. B is in a serious automobile accident in the United States on March 25. B intended to leave the United States on March 31 (as evidenced by an airline ticket), but was unable to leave on that date as a result of the injuries suffered in the accident. B recovered from the injuries and was able to leave and did leave the United States on May 31. B's presence in the United States during the period from April 1 through May 31 will not be counted as days of presence in the United States.

Example 2. The facts are the same as in *Example 1*, except that B's return flight (as evidenced by an airline ticket) was scheduled for May 31. Because B did not intend to leave the United States until May 31, B may not exclude any days of presence in the United States.

(d) *Days in transit.*—An alien individual may exclude days of presence in the United States if the individual is in transit between two foreign points, and is physically present in the United States for fewer than 24 hours. For purposes of this paragraph, an individual will be considered to be in transit if the individual pursues activities that are substantially related to completing his or her travel to a foreign point of destination. For example, an alien who travels between airports in the United States in order to change planes en route to the individual's destination will be considered to be in transit. However, if the individual attends a business meeting while he or she is present in the United States, whether or not that meeting is within the confines of the airport, the individual will not be considered to be in transit. For purposes of this paragraph, the term "foreign point" means any areas that are not included within the definition of the term "United States" provided in § 301.7701(b)-1(c)(2)(ii).

(e) *Regular commuters from Mexico or Canada.*—(1) *General rule.*—An alien individual will not be considered to be present in the United States on days that the individual commutes to the United States from the individual's residence in Mexico or Canada if the individual regularly commutes from Mexico or Canada. An alien individual will be considered to commute regularly if the individual commutes to the individual's location of employment or self-employment in the United States from his or her residence in Mexico or Canada on more than 75% of the workdays during the working period.

(2) *Definitions.*—(i) The term "commutes" means to travel to employment or self-employment and to return to one's residence within a 24-hour period.

(ii) The term "workdays" means days on which the individual works in the United States or Canada or Mexico.

(iii) The term "working period" means the period beginning with the first day in the current year on which the individual is physically present in the United States for purposes of engaging in employment or self-employment and ending on the last day in the current year on which the individual is physically present in the United States for purposes of engaging in that employment or self-employment. If the nature of the employment or self-employment is such that it requires the individual to be present in the United States only on a seasonal or cyclical basis, the working period will begin with the first day of the season or cycle on which the individual is present in the United States for purposes of engaging in that employment or self-employment and end on the last day of the season or cycle on which the individual is present in the United States for the purpose of engaging in that employment or self-employment. Thus, there may be more than one working period in a calendar year and a working period may begin in one calendar year and end in the following calendar year.

(3) *Examples.*—The following examples illustrate the operation of this paragraph (e):

Example 1. B lives in Mexico and is employed by Corporation X in its office in Mexico. B was temporarily assigned to X's office in the United States. B's employment in the United States office began on February 1, 1988, and continued through June 1, 1988. On June 2, B resumed his employment in Mexico. On 59 days in the period beginning on February 1, 1988, and ending on June 1, 1988, B travelled each morning from his residence in Mexico to X Corporation's United States office for the purpose of engaging in his employment with X Corporation. B returned to his residence in Mexico on each of those evenings. On seven days in the period from February 1, 1988, through June 1, 1988, B worked in X's Mexico office. B is not considered to have been present in the United States on any of the days that he travelled to X's United States office for the purpose of engaging in employment with Corporation X because he commuted to his place of employment within the United States on more than 75% of the workdays during the working period (59 workdays in the United States/66 workdays in the working period = 89.4%).

Example 2. C, who lives in Canada, contracted with a resort located in the United States to provide snow-skiing instructions for the resort's customers for two skiing seasons, the first beginning on November 15, 1987, and ending on March 15, 1988, and the second beginning on November 15, 1988, and ending on March 15, 1989. On 90 days in each of the two skiing seasons, C travelled in the morning from Canada to the resort to provide skiing instructions pursuant to the contract. C returned to Canada on each of those evenings. On 20 days during each of the two skiing seasons, C worked in Canada. C is not considered to have been present in the United States on any of the days that she travelled to the United States to provide ski instructions in either the first working period beginning on November 15, 1987, and ending on March 15, 1988, or the second working period beginning on November 15, 1988, and ending on March 15, 1989, because she commuted to her employment within the United States on more than 75% of the workdays during each of the working periods (90 workdays in the United States / 110 workdays in the working period = 81.8%).

Example 3. D, who lives in Canada, is the sole proprietor of a wholesale lumber business with offices in both the United States and Canada. Beginning on January 4, 1988, and ending on February 12, 1988, D commuted to work in his United States office on 30 days. Beginning on February 15, 1988, and ending on March 25, 1988, D commuted to work in his Canadian office on 30 days. Beginning on March 28, 1988, and ending on May 27, 1988, D commuted to work in his United States office on 45 days. Subsequent to May 27, D did not commute to the United States on any other days in 1988. D is considered to have been present in the United States on each day that he travelled to his office in the United States because D did not commute to the United States office on more than 75% of the workdays during the working period beginning on January 4, 1988, and ending on May 27, 1988 (75 workdays in the United States / 105 workdays in the working period = 71.4%).

(f) *Determination of excluded days applies beyond year of determination.*—If a day of presence is excluded under this section, then that day shall not be taken into account in the current year or the first or second preceding year. [Reg. § 301.7701(b)-3.]

☐ [*T.D.* 8411, 4-24-92. *Amended by T.D.* 8733, 10-6-97.]

§ 301.7701(b)-4. Residency time periods.—(a) *First year of residency.*—An alien individual who was not a United States resident during the preceding calendar year and who is a United States resident for the current year will begin to be a resident for tax purposes on the alien's residency starting date. The residency starting date for an alien who meets the substantial presence test is the first day during the calendar year on which the individual is present in the United States. The residency starting date for an alien who meets the lawful permanent resident test (green card test), described in paragraph (b)(1) of § 301.7701(b)-1, is the first day during the calendar year in which the individual is physically present in the United States as a lawful permanent resident. The residency starting date for an alien who satisfies both the substantial presence test and the green card test will be the earlier of the first day the individual is physically present in the United States as a lawful permanent resident of the United States or the first day during the year that the individual is present for purposes of the substantial presence test. (See § 301.7701(b)-9(b)(1) for the transitional rule relating to the residency starting date of an alien individual who was a lawful permanent resident in 1984. See also § 301.7701(b)-3 for days that may be excluded.)

(b) *Last year of residency.*—(1) *General rule.*—An alien individual who is a United States resident during the current year but who is not a United States resident at any time during the following calendar year will cease to be a resident for tax purposes on the individual's residency termination date. Generally, the residency termination date will be the last day of the calendar year.

(2) *Exceptions.*—Notwithstanding paragraph (b)(1) of this section, the residency termination date for an alien individual who meets the substantial presence test is the last day during the calendar year that the individual is physically present in the United States if the individual establishes that, for the remainder of the calendar year, the individual's tax home was in a foreign country and he or she maintained a closer connection (within the meaning of § 301.7701(b)-2(d)) to that foreign country than to the United States. Similarly, the residency termination date for an alien who meets the green card test is the first day during the calendar year that the alien is no longer a lawful permanent resident if the individual es-

tablishes that, for the remainder of the calendar year, his or her tax home was in a foreign country and he or she maintained a closer connection to that foreign country than to the United States. The residency termination date for an alien who satisfies both the substantial presence test and the green card test for the current year, will be the later of the first day the individual is no longer a lawful permanent resident of the United States or the last day the individual was physically present in the United States if the alien establishes that, for the remainder of the calendar year, his or her tax home was in a foreign country and he or she maintained a closer connection to that foreign country than to the United States. It is immaterial whether the individual's tax home was in the United States, or that the individual had a closer connection to the United States than to the foreign country, prior to the date of his or her departure from the United States or the date on which the individual was no longer a lawful permanent resident, whichever is applicable.

(c) *Rules relating to residency starting date and residency termination date.*—(1) *De minimis presence.*—An alien individual may be present in the United States for up to 10 days without triggering the residency starting date (for purposes of the substantial presence test) or extending the residency termination date (for purposes of the substantial presence test) if the individual is able to establish that, during that period, the individual's tax home was in a foreign country and he or she maintained a closer connection to that foreign country than to the United States. Days from more than one period of presence may be disregarded for purposes of determining an individual's residency starting date or termination date so long as the total is not more than 10 days. However, an individual may not disregard any days that occur in a period of consecutive days of presence, if all the days that occur during that period cannot be excluded. An individual must include days of presence for purposes of determining whether the individual meets the substantial presence test even though the days may be disregarded for purposes of determining the individual's residency starting date or residency termination date.

(2) *Proration.*—If an individual's residency starting date does not fall on the first day of the tax year, or the individual's residency termination date does not fall on the last day of the tax year, the individual's income tax liability should be calculated in accordance with § 1.871-13 of this chapter dealing with the taxation of individuals who change residence status during the taxable year.

(3) *Residency starting date for certain individuals.*—(i) *In general.*—If an alien individual (who otherwise does not meet the substantial presence test or the green card test for the current year) is physically present in the United States for at least 31 consecutive days during the current year, and also for a period of continuous presence beginning with the first day of that thirty-one day period (see paragraph (c)(3)(iii) of this section), then the individual may elect to be treated as a resident during the current year. The individual's residency starting date shall be the first day of that thirty-one day period, if—

(A) The individual was not a resident of the United States under the substantial presence test or the green card test in the year preceding the current year; and

(B) The individual is a resident of the United States in the subsequent year under the substantial presence test (whether or not the individual is also a resident of the United States under the green card test).

(ii) *Determination of presence.*—Except as otherwise provided in paragraph (c)(3)(iii) of this section, an individual shall be treated as present in the United States on any day that the individual is physically present in the United States at any time during the day.

(iii) *Thirty-one day period.*—For purposes of this paragraph (c)(3), the term "thirty-one day period" means any period of 31 consecutive days during which an individual is physically present in the United States during each day of the period.

(iv) *Period of continuous presence.*—For purposes of this paragraph (c)(3), the term "continuous presence" means a period of presence in the United States that includes 75 percent of the days in the current year beginning with (and including) the first day of the individual's thirty-one day period of presence. Only for purposes of the continuous presence requirement, an individual will be deemed to be present in the United States for up to 5 days on which the individual is absent from the United States. These days will not be deemed to be days of presence for purposes of the thirty-one day period of presence requirement. If an individual is present for more than one thirty-one day period of presence and satisfies the continuous presence requirement with regard to each period, the individual's residency starting date shall be the first day of the first thirty-one day period of presence. If an individual is present for more than one thirty-one day period of presence but satisfies the continuous presence requirement only for a later thirty-one day period, the individual's residency starting date shall be the first day of the later thirty-one day period of

Reg. § 301.7701(b)-4(c)

presence. For purposes of this paragraph (c)(3), days of presence that are otherwise excluded under section 7701(b)(3)(D)(i) and § 301.7701(b)-3(a)(1) (exempt individual), (a)(2) (medical condition), (a)(3) (in transit between two foreign points), and (a)(4) (regular commuter) shall not be counted as days of presence for purposes of either the thirty-one day period or continuous presence requirement.

(v) *Election procedure.*—(A) *Filing requirements.*—An alien individual shall make an election to be treated as a resident under paragraph (c)(3) of this section by attaching a statement (described in paragraph (c)(3)(v)(C) of this section) to the individual's income tax return (Form 1040) for the taxable year for which the election is to be in effect (the election year). The alien individual may not make this election until such time as he has satisfied the substantial presence test for the year following the election year. If an alien individual has not satisfied the substantial presence test for the year following the election year as of the due date (not including extensions) of the tax return for the election year, the alien individual may request an extension of time for filing the return until a reasonable period after he or she has satisfied such test, provided that the individual pays with his or her extension application the amount of tax he or she expects to owe for the election year computed as if he or she were a nonresident alien throughout the election year. An election made under paragraph (c)(3) of this section may not be revoked without the approval of the Commissioner or his delegate.

(B) *Election on behalf of a dependent child.*—An individual may make an election on behalf of a dependent child (as defined in paragraphs (1) and (2) of section 152(a), without regard to section 152(b)(3)) if the individual is qualified to make an election on his or her own behalf, the child qualifies to make an election under this paragraph (c)(3), and the child is not required by section 6012 to file a United States income tax return for the year for which the election is to be effective.

(C) *Statement.*—The statement required by paragraph (c)(3)(v)(A) of this section shall include the name and address of the alien individual and contain a signed declaration that the election is being made. If the individual is also making an election on behalf of any dependent children, then the statement must include the required information with respect to those children. The statement must specify—

(1) That the alien individual was not a resident in the year immediately preceding the election year;

(2) That the alien individual is a resident under the substantial presence test in the year following the election year;

(3) The individual's number of days of presence in the United States during the year following the election year;

(4) The date or dates of the alien individual's thirty-one day period of presence and period of continuous presence in the United States during the election year; and

(5) The date or dates of absence from the United States during the election year that are deemed to be days of presence.

(vi) *Penalty for failure to comply with filing requirements.*—(A) *General rule.*—If an individual fails to comply with the election procedure of paragraph (c)(3)(v) of this section, the individual must file his or her income tax return for the current year as a nonresident alien.

(B) *Exception.*—The penalty described in paragraph (c)(3)(vi)(A) of this section shall not apply if the individual can show by clear and convincing evidence that he or she took reasonable actions to become aware of the filing requirements and significant affirmative steps to comply with the requirements. An individual who requests an extension of time to file his or her income tax return pursuant to paragraph (c)(3)(v) of this section will be considered to have taken significant affirmative steps to comply with the requirement that the individual pay his or her tax determined as if the individual were a nonresident alien if the individual paid with his or her extension application at least 90 percent of the amount of the tax the individual actually owed for the election year computed as if he or she were a nonresident alien throughout the election year.

(d) *Examples.*—The following examples illustrate the operation of this section:

Example 1. B, a citizen of foreign country X, is an alien who has never before been a United States resident for tax purposes. B comes to the United States on January 6, 1985, to attend a business meeting and returns to country X on January 10, 1985. B is able to establish a closer connection to country X for the period January 6-10. On March 1, 1985, B moves to the United States and resides here until August 20, 1985, when he returns to country X. On December 12, 1985, B comes to the United States for pleasure and stays here until December 16, 1985 when he returns to country X. B is able to establish a closer connection to country X for the period December 12-16. B is not a United

States resident for tax purposes during the following year and can establish a closer connection to country X for the remainder of calendar year 1985. B is a resident of the United States under the substantial presence test because B is present in the United States for 183 days (5 days in January plus 173 days for the period March 1-August 20 plus 5 days in December). B's residency starting date is March 1, 1985, and his residency termination date is August 20, 1985.

Example 2. The facts are the same as in *Example 1,* except that B remains in the United States until December 17, 1985, and is able to establish a closer connection to country X for the period December 18 through 31. B's residency termination date is December 17, 1985.

Example 3. C, a citizen of foreign country Y, is an alien who has never before been a United States resident for tax purposes. C comes to the United States for the first time on February 10, 1985, and attends a business conference until February 24, 1985, when she returns to country Y. On April 20, 1985, C enters the United States as a lawful permanent resident. On November 10, 1985, C ceases to be a lawful permanent resident but stays on in the United States until November 20, 1985 when she returns to country Y. On December 8, 1985, C comes to the United States and stays here until December 17, 1985 when she returns to country Y. She can establish a closer connection to country Y for that period. C is not a resident of the United States during the following calendar year and can establish a closer connection to country Y for the remainder of calendar year 1985. C qualifies as a United States resident under both the green card test and the substantial presence test. C's residency starting date under the green card test is April 20, 1985. Under the substantial presence test, C's residency starting date is February 10, 1985, because she is present for more than ten days in February and cannot take advantage of the de minimis presence rule. Therefore, C's residency starting date is February 10, 1985. C's residency termination date under the green card test is November 10, 1985. Her residency termination date under the substantial presence test is November 20, because B can disregard ten days of presence in December. Thus, her residency termination date is November 20, 1985, the later of her residency termination date under the substantial presence test or the green card test.

Example 4. The facts are the same as in *Example 3,* except that C is initially present in the United States on business from February 5 to February 9, 1985. C is able to establish a closer connection to country Y for that period. C may take advantage of only ten days of de minimis presence and may exclude days from a continuous period of presence only if she can exclude all the days that occur during that period. Thus, C may choose either of the following periods of residency: residency starting date February 5, 1985, and residency termination date November 20, 1985, or residency starting date April 20, 1985, and residency termination date December 17, 1985.

Example 5. D, a citizen of foreign country Z, is an alien who has never before been a United States resident for tax purposes. D comes to the United States on November 1, 1985 and is present in the United States on 31 consecutive days (from November 1 through December 1, 1985). D returns to country Z on December 1 and does not come back to the United States until December 17, 1985. He remains in the United States for the rest of the year. During 1986, D is a resident of the United States under the substantial presence test. D may elect to be treated as a resident of the United States for 1985 because he was present in the United States in 1985 for a 31 consecutive day period of presence (November 1 through December 1, 1985) and for at least 75 percent of the days following (and including) the first day of D's 31 consecutive day period of presence (46 total days of presence in the United States/61 days in the period from November 1 through December 31 = 75.4%). If D makes the election to be treated as a resident, his residency starting date will be November 1, 1985.

Example 6. The facts are the same as in *Example 5,* except that D is absent from the United States on December 24, 25, 29, 30 and 31. D may make the election to be treated as a resident for 1985 because up to five days of absence will be deemed to be days of presence for purposes of the continuous presence requirement.

Example 7. F, a citizen of foreign country M, is an alien individual who has never before been a United States resident for tax purposes. F comes to the United States on January 1, 1985 and remains in the United States through January 31, 1985, when she returns to country M. F comes back to the United States on October 1, 1985 and is present in the United States through November 1, 1985. From November 1, 1985 through December 31, 1985, F is present in the United States for 38 days. Although F satisfies two 31 consecutive day periods of presence, (January 1 through January 31 and October 1 through November 1), she satisfies the continuous presence requirement only with regard to the later period of presence (69 total days of presence/92 days in the period from October 1 through December 31 = 75%). Thus, if F makes the election to be treated as a resident, his residency starting date is October 1, 1985.

(e) *No lapse.*—(1) *Residency in prior year.*—An alien individual who was a United States resident during any part of the preceding calendar year and who is a United States resident for any part of the current year will be considered to be taxable as a resident at the beginning of the current year. For purposes of this paragraph (e)(1), it is immaterial whether an individual is considered to be a resident under the substantial presence test or the green card test.

(2) *Residency in following year.*—An alien individual who is a United States resident for any part of the current year and who is also a United States resident for any part of the following year (regardless of whether the individual has a closer connection to a foreign country than the United States during the current year) will be taxable as a resident through the end of the current year. For purposes of this paragraph (e)(2), it is immaterial whether an individual is considered to be a resident under the substantial presence test or the green card test.

(3) *Special rule.*—If an individual meets the green card test for the current year but is not physically present in the United States during the current year, then the individual's residency starting date shall be the first day of the following year.

(4) *Example.*—The following example illustrates the application of this paragraph (e).

Example. B, an alien individual who is a citizen of foreign country M, comes to the United States for the first time on May 1, 1985, and remains in the United States until November 5, 1985, when he returns to country M. B comes back to the United States on March 5, 1986 as a lawful permanent resident and remains in the United States until September 10, 1986, when he ceases to be a lawful permanent resident and returns to country M. B is not a resident in calendar year 1987. B's United States residency in calendar year 1985 continues through December 31, 1985, because he is a United States resident in the following calendar year. In calendar year 1986, B's United States residency is deemed to begin on January 1, 1986 because B qualified as a resident in the preceding calendar year. Thus, B's residency period in the United States begins on May 1, 1985, and ends on September 10, 1986. [Reg. § 301.7701(b)-4.]

☐ [*T.D.* 8411, 4-24-92.]

§ 301.7701(b)-5. Coordination with section 877.—(a) *General rule.*—An alien individual will be subject to United States income tax in the manner provided by section 877, regardless of whether the individual has a tax avoidance motive, if—

(1) The alien individual is a resident alien of the United States for at least three consecutive calendar years (the initial residency period) beginning after December 31, 1984;

(2) The period of residence for each of the three consecutive calendar years includes at least 183 days;

(3) The alien is once again taxed as a nonresident (including an individual taxed as a nonresident under § 301.7701(b)-7(a)(1); and

(4) The alien then becomes a resident of the United States before the close of the third calendar year beginning after the individual's residency termination date in the initial residency period.

(b) *Tax imposed.*—The tax provided for under paragraph (a) of this section will be imposed for the intervening period of nonresidency only if the amount of tax would exceed the amount of tax that would be imposed under section 871, relating to the taxation of nonresident aliens.

(c) *Example.*—The following example illustrates the application of this section.

Example. B, a citizen of foreign country F, enters the United States on April 1, 1985, as a lawful permanent resident. On August 1, 1987, B ceases to be a lawful permanent resident and returns to country F. B meets the initial residency period requirement because he is a resident of the United States for at least 183 days in each of three consecutive years (1985, 1986 and 1987). B returns to the United States on October 5, 1990, as a lawful permanent resident. Because B became a resident of the United States before the close of the third calendar year (1990) beginning after the close of the initial residency period (August 1, 1987), he is subject to tax under section 877(b) for the intervening period of nonresidency, August 2, 1987 through October 4, 1990, if the amount of the tax imposed under section 877 is more than the tax imposed under section 871. [Reg. § 301.7701(b)-5.]

☐ [*T.D.* 8411, 4-24-92.]

§ 301.7701(b)-6. Taxable year.—(a) *In general.*—An alien individual who has not established a fiscal year as his or her taxable year prior to the period that the individual is subject to United States income tax as a resident or a nonresident shall adopt the calendar year as his or her taxable year. An alien who has established a fiscal year in a foreign country prior to the period that the individual is subject to United States income tax may adopt the calendar year as his or her taxable year for United States income tax purposes without requesting a change in accounting period. An individual will be considered to have established a fiscal year (whether in the United States or a foreign country) if the annual accounting period on which the individual computes his or her income is a fiscal year, the individual keeps his or her books in accordance with that fiscal year, and the requirements of section 441 and § 1.441-1(b) of this chapter are otherwise satisfied. An alien who has established a fiscal year and is a resident alien during the calendar year will be treated as a resident alien with respect to any portion of his or her taxable year (beginning with the individual's residency starting date and ending with the individual's residency termination date) that falls within such calendar year. Once the individual has established either a fiscal or calendar year taxable year for any period for which the individual is subject to United States income tax, the individual may not change that taxable year without the approval of the Secretary. See section 442.

(b) *Examples.*—The following examples illustrate the operation of this section:

Example 1. B, a citizen and resident of foreign country F, was engaged in a United States business during 1982 and filed a return on a fiscal year basis. B's fiscal year runs from October 1 to September 30. B comes to the United States on March 8, 1985 and remains in the United States until October 10, 1985, when he returns to country F. B maintains a closer connection to and his tax home in Country F for the remainder of calendar year 1985. B, who is not a United States resident at any time in 1986, is a United States resident for the period that begins on March 8, 1985, and ends on October 10, 1985. B has adopted a fiscal year taxable year for purposes of computing his United States income tax liability. For his fiscal year that ends on September 30, 1985, B will be taxed as a United States resident for the period that begins on March 8, 1985 and ends on September 30, 1985. For his fiscal year that ends on September 30, 1986, B will only be taxed as a United States resident for the period that begins on October 1, 1985 and ends on October 10, 1985.

Example 2. The facts are the same as in *Example 1,* except that B's 1982 business was a country F business established on a fiscal year basis and at no time prior to 1985 was B subject to United States income tax. B may adopt a calendar year as his taxable year for United States income tax purposes without requesting a change of accounting period. B continues to use a fiscal year as his taxable year. For his fiscal year that ends on September 30, 1985, B will be taxed as a United States resident for the period that begins on March 8, 1985 and ends September 30, 1985. For his fiscal year that ends on September 30, 1986, B will be taxed as a United States resident for the period that begins on October 1, 1985 and ends on October 10, 1985.

Example 3. The facts are the same as in *Example 1,* except that B's 1982 business was a country F business established on a fiscal year basis and at no time prior to 1985 was B subject to United States income tax. B may adopt a calendar year as his taxable year for United States income tax purposes without requesting a change of accounting period. B adopts a calendar year as his taxable year for 1985. For his calendar year taxable year ending on December 31, 1985, B will be taxed as a United States resident for the period that begins on March 8, 1985, and ends on October 10, 1985. [Reg. § 301.7701(b)-6.]

☐ [*T.D. 8411, 4-24-92. Amended by T.D. 8996, 5-16-2002.*]

§ 301.7701(b)-7. Coordination with income tax treaties.—(a) *Consistency requirement.*—(1) *Application.*—The application of this section shall be limited to an alien individual who is a dual resident taxpayer pursuant to a provision of a treaty that provides for resolution of conflicting claims of residence by the United States and its treaty partner. A "dual resident taxpayer" is an individual who is considered a resident of the United States pursuant to the internal laws of the United States and also a resident of a treaty country pursuant to the treaty partner's internal laws. If the alien individual determines that he or she is a resident of the foreign country for treaty purposes, and the alien individual claims a treaty benefit (as a nonresident of the United States) so as to reduce the individual's United States income tax liability with respect to any item of income covered by an applicable tax convention during a taxable year in which the individual was considered a dual resident taxpayer, then that individual shall be treated as a nonresident alien of the United States for purposes of computing that individual's United States income tax liability under the provisions of the Internal Revenue Code and the regulations thereunder (including the withholding provisions of section 1441 and the regulations under that section in cases in which the dual resident taxpayer is the recipient of income subject to withholding) with respect to that portion of the taxable year the individual was considered a dual resident taxpayer.

(2) *Computation of tax liability.*—If an alien individual is a dual resident taxpayer, then the rules on residency provided in the convention shall apply for purposes of determining the individual's residence for all purposes of that treaty.

(3) *Other Code purposes.*—Generally, for purposes of the Internal Revenue Code other

than the computation of the individual's United States income tax liability, the individual shall be treated as a United States resident. Therefore, for example, the individual shall be treated as a United States resident for purposes of determining whether a foreign corporation is a controlled foreign corporation under section 957 or whether a foreign corporation is a foreign personal holding company under section 552. In addition, the application of paragraph (a)(2) of this section does not affect the determination of the individual's residency time periods under § 301.7701(b)-4.

(4) *Special rules for S corporations.*—[Reserved]

(b) *Filing requirements.*—An alien individual described in paragraph (a) of this section who determines his or her U.S. tax liability as if he or she were a nonresident alien shall make a return on Form 1040NR on or before the date prescribed by law (including extensions) for making an income tax return as a nonresident. The individual shall prepare a return and compute his or her tax liability as a nonresident alien. The individual shall attach a statement (in the form required in paragraph (c) of this section) to the Form 1040NR. The Form 1040NR and the attached statement, shall be filed with the Internal Revenue Service Center, Philadelphia, PA 19255. The filing of a Form 1040NR by an individual described in paragraph (a) of this section may affect the determination by the Immigration and Naturalization Service as to whether the individual qualifies to maintain a residency permit.

(c) *Contents of statement.*—(1) *In general.*—(i) *Returns due after December 15, 1997.*—The statement filed by an individual described in paragraph (a)(1) of this section, for a return relating to a taxable year for which the due date (without extensions) is after December 15, 1997, must be in the form of a fully completed Form 8833 (Treaty-Based Return Position Disclosure Under Section 6114 or 7701(b)) or appropriate successor form. See section 6114 and § 301.6114-1 for rules relating to other treaty-based return positions taken by the same taxpayer.

(ii) *Earlier returns.*—For returns relating to taxable years for which the due date for filing returns (without extensions) is on or before December 15, 1997, the statement filed by the individual described in paragraph (a)(1) of this section must contain the information in accordance with paragraph (c)(1) of this section in effect prior to December 15, 1997 (see § 301.7701(b)(-7(c)(1) as contained in 26 CFR part 301, revised April 1, 1997).

(2) *Controlled foreign corporation shareholders.*—If the taxpayer who claims a treaty benefit as a nonresident of the United States is a United States shareholder in a controlled foreign corporation (CFC), as defined in section 957 or section 953(c), and there are no other United States shareholders in that CFC, then for purposes of paragraph (c)(1) of this section, the approximate amount of subpart F income (as defined in section 952) that would have been included in the taxpayer's income may be determined based on the audited foreign financial statements of the CFC.

(3) *S corporation shareholders.*—[Reserved]

(d) *Relationship to section 6114(a) treaty-based return positions.*—The statement required by paragraph (b) of this section will be considered disclosure for purposes of section 6114 and § 301.6114-1(a), but only if the statement is in the form required by paragraph (c) of this section. If the taxpayer fails to file the statement required by paragraph (b) of this section on or before the date prescribed in paragraph (b) of this section, the taxpayer will be subject to the penalties imposed by section 6712. See section 6712 and § 301.6712-1.

(e) *Examples.*—The following examples illustrate the application of this section:

Example 1. B, an alien individual, is a resident of foreign country X, under X's internal law. Country X is a party to an income tax convention with the United States. B is also a resident of the United States under the Internal Revenue Code. B is considered to be a resident of country X under the convention. The convention does not specifically deal with characterization of foreign corporations as controlled foreign corporations or the taxability of United States shareholders on inclusions of subpart F income, but it provides, in an "Other Income" article similar to Article 21 of the 1981 draft of the United States Model Income Tax Convention (U.S. Model), that items of income of a resident of country X that are not specifically dealt with in the convention shall be taxable only in country X. B owns 80% of the one class of stock of foreign corporation R. The remaining 20% is owned by C, a United States citizen who is unrelated to B. In 1985, corporation R's only income is interest that is foreign personal holding company income under § 1.954A-2 of this chapter. Because the United States-X income tax convention does not deal with characterization of foreign corporations as controlled foreign corporations, United States internal income tax law applies. Therefore, B and C are United States shareholders within the meaning of § 1.951-1(g) of this chapter, corporation R is a controlled foreign corporation within the meaning of §1.957-1 of this chapter, and corporation R's income is included in C's income as subpart F income under §1.951-1 of this chapter. B may avoid current taxation on his share of the subpart F inclusion by filing as a nonresident (*i.e.*, by following the procedure in §301.7701(b)-7(b)).

Example 2. The facts are the same as in *Example 1*, except that B also earns United States source dividend income. The United States-X income tax convention provides that the rate of United States tax on United States source dividends paid to residents of country X shall not exceed 15 percent of the gross amount of the dividends. B's United States tax liability with respect to the dividends would be smaller if he were treated as a resident alien, subject to tax on a net basis (*i.e.*, after the allowance of deductions) than if he were treated as a nonresident alien. If, however, B chooses to file as a nonresident in order to claim treaty benefits with respect to his share of R's subpart F income, his overall United States tax liability, including the portion attributable to the dividends, must be determined as if he were a nonresident alien.

Example 3. C, a married alien individual with three children, is a resident of foreign country Y, under Y's internal law. Country Y is a party to an income tax convention with the United States. C is also a resident of the United States under the Internal Revenue Code. C is considered to be a resident of country Y under the convention. The convention specifically covers, among other items of income, personal services income, dividends and interest. C is sent by her country Y employer to work in the United States from January 1, 1985 until December 31, 1985. During 1985, C also earns United States source dividends and interest and incurs mortgage interest expenses on her personal residence. The United States-Y treaty provides that remuneration for personal services performed in the United States by a country Y resident is exempt from United States tax if, among other things, the individual performing such services is present in the United States for a period that is not in excess of 183 days. The treaty provides that the rate of United States tax on United States source dividends paid to residents of Y shall not exceed 15 percent of the gross amount of the dividends and it exempts residents of Y from United States tax on United States source interest. In filing her 1985 tax return, C may choose to file either as a resident alien without claiming any treaty benefits or as a nonresident alien if she desires to claim any treaty benefit. C files as a nonresident (*i.e.*, by following the procedure described in §301.7701(b)-7(b)). Because C does not satisfy the requirements of the United States-Y treaty with regard to exempting personal services income from United States tax, C will be taxed on her personal services income at graduated rates under section 1 of the Code pursuant to section 871(b) of the Code. She will not be entitled to deduct her mortgage interest expenses or to claim more than one personal exemption because she is taxed as a nonresident alien under the Code by virtue of her decision to claim treaty benefits, and section 873 of the Code denies nonresidents the deduction for personal residence mortgage interest expense and generally limits them to only one personal exemption. C will be subject to a tax of 15 percent of the gross amount of her dividend income under section 871(a) of the Code as modified by the treaty, and she will be exempt from tax on her interest income. C is not entitled to file a joint return with her spouse even if he is a resident alien under the Code for 1985.

Example 4. The facts are the same as in *Example 3*, except that C does not choose to claim treaty benefits with respect to any items of income covered by the treaty (*i.e.*, she files as a resident). Therefore, she is taxed as a resident under the Code and pays tax at graduated rates on her personal services income, dividends, and interest. In addition, she is entitled to deduct her mortgage interest expenses and to take personal exemptions for her spouse and three children. C will be entitled to file a joint return with her spouse if he is a resident alien for 1985 or, if he is a nonresident alien, C and her spouse may elect to file a joint return pursuant to section 6013. [Reg. §301.7701(b)-7.]

☐ [T.D. 8411, 4-24-92. Amended by T.D. 8733, 10-6-97.]

§301.7701(b)-8. Procedural rules.— (a) *Who must file.*—(1) *Closer connection exception.*—An alien individual who otherwise meets the substantial presence test must file a statement to explain the basis of the individual's claim that he or she is able to satisfy the closer connection exception described in §301.7701(b)-2.

(2) *Exempt individuals and individuals with a medical condition.*—An alien individual must file a statement to explain the basis of the individual's claim that he or she is able to exclude days of presence in the United States because the individual—

(i) Is an exempt individual as described in §301.7701(b)-3(b)(3) (teacher/trainee) or (b)(4) (student);

(ii) Is an exempt individual described in §301.7701(b)-3(b)(5) (professional athlete); or

(iii) Has a medical condition or problem as described in §301.7701(b)-3(c).

(3) *De minimis presence and residency starting and termination dates.*—A statement must be filed by an individual who is seeking to establish—

(i) That a period of de minimis presence of ten or fewer days should be disregarded for purposes of the individual's residency starting or termination date; or

(ii) A residency termination date.

(b) *Contents of statement.*—(1) *Closer connection exception.*—(i) *Returns due after December 15, 1997.*—The statement filed by an individual described in paragraph (a)(1) of this section, for a return relating to a taxable year for which the due date (without extensions) is after December 15, 1997, must be in the form of a fully completed Form 8840 (Closer Connection Exception Statement) or appropriate successor form.

(ii) *Earlier returns.*—For returns relating to taxable years for which the due date for filing returns (without extensions) is on or before December 15, 1997, the statement filed by the individual described in paragraph (a)(1) of this section must contain the information in accordance with paragraph (b)(1) of this section in effect prior to December 15, 1997 (see § 301.7701(b)-8(b)(1) as contained in 26 CFR Part 301, revised April 1, 1997).

(2) *Exempt individuals and individuals with a medical condition.*—(i) *Returns due after December 15, 1997.*—The statement filed by an individual described in paragraph (a)(2) of this section, for a return relating to a taxable year for which the due date (without extensions) is after December 15, 1997, must be in the form of a fully completed Form 8843 (Statement for Exempt Individuals and Individuals with a Medical Condition) or appropriate successor form.

(ii) *Earlier returns.*—For returns relating to taxable years for which the due date for filing returns (without extensions) is on or before December 15, 1997, the statement filed by the individual described in paragraph (a)(2) of this section must contain the information in accordance with paragraph (b)(2) of this section in effect prior to December 15, 1997 (see § 301.7701(b)-8(b)(2) as contained in 26 CFR Part 301, revised April 1, 1997).

(3) *De minimis presence and residency starting and termination dates.*—The statement filed by an individual described in paragraph (a)(3) of this section shall be dated, signed by the individual seeking to exclude de minimis presence for purposes of the individual's residency starting or termination date or to establish a residency termination date, and verified by a declaration that the statement is made under the penalty of perjury. The statement shall contain the information described in paragraphs (b)(1)(i), (ii) and (iii) of this section and the following information (as applicable)—

(i) The first day that the individual was present in the United States during the current year;

(ii) The last day that the individual was present in the United States during the current year;

(iii) Dates of de minimis presence that the individual is seeking to exclude from his or her residency starting or termination dates;

(iv) Sufficient facts to establish that the individual has maintained his or her tax home in and a closer connection to a foreign country during a period of de minimis presence;

(v) Sufficient facts to establish that the individual has maintained his or her tax home in and a closer connection to a foreign country following the individual's last day of presence in the United States during the current year or following the abandonment or rescission of the individual's status as a lawful permanent resident during the current year;

(vi) Date that the individual's status as a lawful permanent resident was abandoned or rescinded; and

(vii) Sufficient facts (including copies of relevant documents) to establish that the individual's status as lawful permanent resident has been abandoned or rescinded.

(c) *How to file.*—Individuals described in paragraph (a) of this section who are required to make a return on Form 1040 or 1040NR pursuant to paragraph (a) or (b) of § 1.6012-1 of this chapter must attach the statement described in paragraph (b) of this section to their return for the taxable year for which the statement is relevant. An individual who is not required to file either Form 1040 or 1040NR must file the statement with the Internal Revenue Service Center, Philadelphia, PA 19255 on or before the date prescribed by law (including extensions) for making an income tax return as a nonresident for the calendar year for which the statement applies. The statement may be signed and filed for the taxpayer by the taxpayer's agent in accordance with § 1.6061-1 of this chapter.

(d) *Penalty for failure to file statement.*—(1) *General rule.*—If an individual is required to file a statement pursuant to paragraph (a)(1), (a)(2)(ii), (a)(2)(iii) or (a)(3) of this section and fails to file such statement on or before the date prescribed by paragraph (c) of this section, the individual will not be eligible for the closer connection exception described in

§ 301.7701(b)-2 and will be required to include all days of presence in the United States (calculated without the benefit of §§ 301.7701(b)-3(b)(5), 301.7701(b)-3(c), and 301.7701(b)-4(c)(1)) for purposes of the substantial presence test and for determining the individual's residency starting and termination dates. If an individual is considered to be a resident because of this paragraph and the individual is also a resident of a country with which the United States has an income tax convention pursuant to that convention, the individual shall be treated in the manner provided in § 301.7701(b)-7(a) (relating to the treatment of individuals who are dual residents).

(2) *Exception.*—The penalty described in paragraph (d)(1) of this section shall not apply if the individual can show by clear and convincing evidence that he or she took reasonable actions to become aware of the filing requirements and significant affirmative steps to comply with those requirements.

(e) *Filing requirement disregarded.*—Notwithstanding paragraph (d) of this section, the Secretary or his or her delegate may in their sole discretion, when it is in the best interest of the government to do so and based on all of the facts and circumstances, disregard the individual's failure to file timely the statement described in paragraph (a) of this section in determining the individual's days of presence in the United States. [Reg. § 301.7701(b)-8.]

☐ [*T.D.* 8411, 4-24-92. *Amended by T.D.* 8733, 10-6-97.]

§ 1.7701(l)-1. Conduit financing arrangements.—Section 7701(l) authorizes the issuance of regulations that recharacterize any multiple-party financing transaction as a transaction directly among any two or more of such parties where the Secretary determines that such recharacterization is appropriate to prevent avoidance of any tax imposed by title 26 of the United States Code. [Reg. § 1.7701(l)-1.]

☐ [*T.D.* 8611, 8-10-95. *Amended by T.D.* 8735, 10-6-97.]

INDEX TO CODE

References are to Code Section numbers.

A

Accelerated cost recovery system
. alternative system . . . 168(g)
. imported property . . . 168(g)
. property used predominantly outside U.S. . . . 168(g)

Accounting methods—see also Accounting periods . . . 446—482
. change of . . . 446(e)
. different businesses . . . 446(d)
. excise taxes collected . . . 7512
. hybrid methods . . . 446(c)
. securities dealers
. . mark-to-market method . . . 475

Accounting periods—see also Accounting methods . . . 441
. change of
. . personal holding company tax computation not affected . . . 546

Accrual basis of accounting
. election of method . . . 446(c)
. foreign tax credit . . . 905

Accumulated earnings credit . . . 535(c)

Accumulated earnings tax . . . 531—537
. accumulated taxable income . . . 535
. . income distributed to U.S.-owned foreign corporation . . . 535(d)
. burden of proof . . . 534
. dividends paid deduction . . . 563(a)
. evidence of purpose to avoid income tax . . . 533
. imposition of tax . . . 531
. income not placed on annual basis . . . 536
. liability for tax . . . 532
. rate of tax . . . 531
. reasonable needs of the business, accumulations of surplus to meet . . . 537

Accumulated taxable income . . . 535

Accumulation trusts
. distribution . . . 904(f)(4)

Accuracy-related penalty . . . 6662
. gross valuation misstatements, increase in penalty . . . 6662(h)
. substantial underpayment of tax . . . 6662(d)
. substantial valuation misstatement . . . 6662(e)
. tax shelters, corporations . . . 6662(d)(2)(C)

Acquiring corporations
. assets of target corporations . . . 338(e)
. stock purchases as asset acquisitions . . . 338(a)

Acquisitions made to evade or avoid tax . . . 269

Adjusted basis
. controlled foreign corporation's stock . . . 961

Affiliated corporations
. consolidated returns . . . 1501—1504
. dividends paid deduction . . . 562(d)
. dividends received deduction . . . 243
. intragroup transactions
. . basis of stock . . . 358(g)
. possessions of the U.S., corporations in . . . 936(h)
. retirement plans, service group . . . 414(m)(5)
. service group, employees of . . . 414(m)

Affiliated group defined . . . 1504(a)

Aircraft, foreign, earnings exempt . . . 872(b)(2); 883(a)(2)

Aircraft, leased, income from . . . 861

Aliens
. reciprocal penalty tax for discriminatory tax by foreign country . . . 891; 896

Alimony and separate maintenance
. inclusion in gross income of amounts received . . . 61(a)(8)

Allocation
. basis for gain or loss . . . 358(b)
. income and deductions, related taxpayers . . . 482
. principal and interest, deferred payment sales . . . 483
. travel expenses . . . 274(c)

Alternative minimum tax . . . 55—59
. adjustments based on adjusted current earnings . . . 56(g)
. alternative minimum taxable income . . . 55
. corporations
. . small . . . 55(e)
. definitions and special rules . . . 59
. imposition of . . . 55
. noncorporate taxpayers . . . 55(b)(3)
. tentative minimum tax . . . 55(b)

American Samoa
. coordination of individual income tax . . . 7654
. foreign corporations . . . 881(b)
. income from sources within . . . 931
. residents of, tax on . . . 876

Amortization
. goodwill and certain other intangibles . . . 197

Annualizing income
. accumulated earnings tax computation . . . 536
. personal holding companies . . . 546

Annuities and annuity contracts
. amounts received as annuities, inclusion in gross income . . . 61(a)(9)
. gross income . . . 61(a)(9)

Appreciated property
. distribution by corporation
. . recognition of gain or loss . . . 311(b)

Artistic work of invention, capital asset status . . . 1221; 1231(b)(1)(C)

Assessable penalties . . . 6672—6689

Assessment of tax
. jeopardy assessments . . . 534(d)
. suspension of running of period of limitation . . . 6503

Asset acquistions
. stock purchases treated as . . . 338(a)

Association, corporate status . . . 7701(a)(3)

Audit standards, selection of returns
. protection from disclosure . . . 6103(b)

Authors, sale of literary property . . . 1221

Away from home expenses . . . 162(a)(2); 274(c)

B

Backup withholding . . . 3406

Bad debts
. deduction . . . 166(b)

Banks
. exclusion from definition of personal holding company . . . 542(c)(2)
. foreign central banks, interest from obligations of the U. S. . . . 895

Basis
. allocation of . . . 358(b)
. limitation on
. . related persons, property imported from . . . 1059A
. liquidation distributions . . . 334
. . subsidiary . . . 334(b)
. paid-in surplus, property acquired as . . . 362
. property acquired by issuance of stock or as paid-in surplus . . . 362(a)
. property distributions . . . 301(d)
. property received in liquidations . . . 334
. reorganizations
. . basis to corporations . . . 362
. . basis to distributees . . . 358

Beneficiaries of estates and trusts
. nonresident aliens . . . 875

Blocked foreign income, controlled foreign corporation . . . 964(b)

Board and lodging . . . 119

Bona fide resident of a foreign country defined . . . 911(d)(5)

Bond discount . . . 6049

Bonds
. losses
. . nonregistered form . . . 165(j)
. premiums
. . unamortized, cancellation of debt
. registered form requirement . . . 163(f)
. . unregistered, capital gains treatment denied . . . 1287
. registration . . . 149

Books and records
. controlled foreign corporations . . . 964(c)
. foreign corporations engaged in U.S. business . . . 6038C

Boot received in nontaxable exchange . . . 356

Branch profits tax
. foreign corporations . . . 884

Bribes . . . 162(c)
. foreign government officials, to . . . 162(c)(1)

Building improvement costs . . . 263(a)

Burden of proof
. accumulated earnings tax . . . 534
. assumption of liability in connection with certain exchanges . . . 357(b)(2)

Business expenses . . . 162
. accelerated cost recovery system . . . 168
. bad debts . . . 166
. election to expense certain depreciable assets
. . installment method of accounting . . . 453(i)
. foreign advertising broadcast to U.S. . . . 162(j)

Business expenses—continued
. illegal payments, foreign government officials . . . 952(a)
. interest paid . . . 163
. losses . . . 165
. related taxpayers, transactions between . . . 267
. taxes paid . . . 164
. unpaid within 2 1/2 months after close of taxable year, disallowance . . . 267(a)(2)

Business needs, corporation . . . 537

Business outside U. S., foreign corporations . . . 881

C

Capital assets
. defined . . . 1221

Capital expenditures . . . 263

Capital gains and losses . . . 1221—1253
. capital asset defined . . . 1221
. capital gain net income defined . . . 1222(9)
. capital gains rate, maximum . . . 1(h)
. casualty losses . . . 1231(a)
. coal disposal . . . 631(c)
. dealers in securities . . . 1236
. determination of . . . 1221
. dividend income . . . 1(h)(11)
. foreign service gains
. . limitation computation . . . 904(b)(3)(C)
. franchises . . . 1253
. involuntary conversions . . . 1231(a)
. long-term capital gain defined . . . 1222(3)
. long-term capital loss defined . . . 1222(4)
. net capital gain defined . . . 1222(11)
. net capital loss defined . . . 1222(10)
. net long-term capital gain defined . . . 1222(7)
. net long-term capital loss defined . . . 1222(8)
. net Sec. 1201 gain defined . . . 1222(11)
. net short-term capital gain defined . . . 1222(5)
. net short-term capital loss defined . . . 1222(6)
. patents . . . 1235
. property used in trade or business . . . 1231
. reduction in rates for individuals . . . 1(h)(1)
. related taxpayers, transactions between . . . 1239
. securities dealers . . . 1236
. short-term capital gain defined . . . 1222(1)
. short-term capital loss defined . . . 1222(2)
. timber . . . 631
. trade or business property sold or exchanged . . . 1231
. trademarks and trade names . . . 1253
. unregistered obligations, sale or disposition . . . 1287

Caribbean basin
. conventions, deductibility of expenses . . . 274(h)(6)

Carrybacks and carryovers
. dividend carryover, personal holding companies . . . 564(b)
. foreign tax credits unused . . . 904(c)

Cash method of accounting . . . 446(c)

Casualty losses
. personal property, netting . . . 1231(a)

Charitable contributions
. nonresident aliens . . . 873(b)(2)

Citizens
. expatriation to avoid tax . . . 877

Index to Code

References are to Code Section numbers.

Citizens—continued
. foreign income . . . 911
. foreign tax credit . . . 901—908
. individuals losing citizenship, information returns . . . 6039G
. nonresident alien married to, community income of . . . 879

Claims
. deficiency dividends deduction . . . 547(e)

Clifford rule . . . 679

Coal
. royalties . . . 631(c)

Collection
. failure to make, penalties . . . 7202
. limitations period . . . 6501—6503
. suspension of running of period of limitations . . . 6503
. withholding on wages . . . 3402

Communications satellite system, foreign corporation operating . . . 883(b)

Community income
. nonresident aliens . . . 879
. U.S. resident or citizen married to nonresident alien . . . 879

Compensation from services
. gross income . . . 61(a)(1)

Compensation paid
. information returns . . . 6041(a)
. social security coverage for employees of foreign subsidiary . . . 176

Compensation received
. foreign government employees, exempt income . . . 893
. international organization employees, exemption . . . 893

Condemnation of property, gain or loss . . . 1231(a)

Congress
. members of
.. expenses of . . . 162

Consent dividends, dividends paid deduction . . . 565

Consent stock defined . . . 565(f)

Consolidated returns . . . 1501—1504

Constructive ownership of stock
. losses nondeductible . . . 267(c)
. personal holding company status determination . . . 544(a)

Continental shelf areas . . . 638

Contributions to capital
. partnerships . . . 721

Control defined, reorganizations . . . 368(c)

Controlled corporations
. acquisition to evade or avoid tax . . . 269
. allocation of income and deductions among . . . 482
. distribution
.. additional consideration received . . . 356(b)
.. special rules . . . 355(e)(4)
.. stock or obligations . . . 355
. foreign corporations . . . 951—964
.. accounts of United States shareholders . . . 964(c)
.. blocked foreign income . . . 964(b)

Controlled corporations—continued
. foreign corporations—continued
.. definition . . . 957(a)
.. dividends received deduction . . . 965
.. earnings and profits . . . 964(a)
.. earnings invested in United States property . . . 956
.. earnings previously taxed, exclusion from gross income . . . 959
.. export trade corporation status . . . 971(a)(3)
.. foreign tax credit for domestic corporation shareholder . . . 960
.. individual shareholders, election to be taxed at corporate rates . . . 962
.. insurance income . . . 953; 957(b)
.. records of United States shareholders . . . 964(c)
.. related person factoring income . . . 864(d)
.. stock ownership rules . . . 958
.. Subpart F income . . . 952(a)
.. taxable year . . . 898(c)(1)
.. United States person defined . . . 957(c)
.. United States shareholders, inclusions in gross income . . . 951(a)

Convenience of employer, exclusion of value of meals or lodging furnished for . . . 119

Conventions
. cruise ships, costs incurred
.. deductibility of . . . 274(h)(2)
.. reporting requirements . . . 274(h)(5)
. foreign, expenses incurred . . . 274(h)(1)
.. Caribbean basin countries . . . 274(h)(6)

Convertible securities, personal holding companies . . . 544(b)

Copyrights
. royalties, personal holding company income . . . 543(a)(4)
. sales to foreign corporations, nature of gain . . . 1249

Corporations
. accumulated earnings tax . . . 531—537
.. accumulated taxable income . . . 535
.. burden of proof . . . 534
.. evidence of purpose to avoid income tax . . . 533
.. income not placed on annual basis . . . 536
.. liability for tax . . . 532
.. rate of tax . . . 531
.. reasonable needs of the business, accumulations of surplus to meet . . . 537
. avoidance of tax on stockholders . . . 531—565
. business deductions . . . 162
. deductions . . . 162—176
. definition . . . 7701(a)(3)
. export trade corporations . . . 970—971
. foreign ownership, information returns . . . 6038A
. foreign tax credit . . . 901(b)(1)
. interests in, treatment as stock or indebtedness . . . 385
. normal tax . . . 11(b)
. organization of
.. transfer to corporation controlled by transferor . . . 351
. rate of tax on . . . 11(b)
.. exceptions . . . 11(c)
. reasonable accumulations . . . 537
. related, stock redemption through use of . . . 304
. returns
.. consolidated returns . . . 1501—1504
.. foreign shareholders . . . 6039C(a)

Corporations—continued
  returns—continued
    information . . . 6041—6046
  tax shelters, substantial understatement penalty . . . 6662(d)(2)(C)
  Virgin Islands
    intangible property income . . . 934(e)
Cost, basis of property . . . 1012
Cost-of-living allowances, foreign service employees . . . 912(2)
Credits against tax
  nonresident aliens . . . 33; 874
  partners . . . 702
  Puerto Rican economic activity credit . . . 30A
  withheld tax on nonresident aliens, foreign partnerships, and foreign corporations . . . 1462
Criminal penalties . . . 7201—7203

D

Debt-financed acquisitions
  corporate interests, treatment as stock or indebtedness . . . 385
Debt instruments
  issued for property
    determination of issue price . . . 1274
  retirement, sale, or exchange
    original issue discount rules . . . 1271
Deductions . . . 162—275
  allocation among related taxpayers . . . 482
  dividends received by corporations . . . 243—246
  foreign corporations . . . 882(c)
  nondeductible items . . . 263—269B
  taxes paid . . . 164
Deferred payment sales, allocation of payments to interest . . . 483
Deficiency dividends deduction
  personal holding companies . . . 547
Definitions . . . 7701
  affiliated group . . . 1504(a)
  bona fide resident of foreign country . . . 911(d)(5)
  capital asset . . . 1221
  capital gain net income . . . 1222(9)
  complete liquidation . . . 346(a)
  consent stock . . . 565(f)(1)
  control . . . 368(c)
  corporation . . . 7701(a)(3)
  deficiency dividends . . . 547(d)
  dividend . . . 316; 6042(b)
  dividends paid deduction . . . 561
  fiscal year . . . 7701(a)(24)
  foreign corporation . . . 901(d); 7701(a)(5)
  foreign earned income . . . 911(b)
  foreign partnership . . . 7701(a)(5)
  holder . . . 1235(b)
  includible corporation . . . 1504(b)
  interest . . . 6049(b)
  international organization . . . 7701(a)(18)
  long-term capital gain . . . 1222(3)
  long-term capital loss . . . 1222(4)
  material advisor . . . 6111(b)(1)
  net capital gain . . . 1222(11)
  net capital loss . . . 1222(10)
  net long-term capital gain . . . 1222(7)
  net long-term capital loss . . . 1222(8)

Definitions—continued
  net short-term capital gain . . . 1222(5)
  net short-term capital loss . . . 1222(6)
  nonresident alien . . . 7701(b)
  partial liquidation . . . 302(e); 346
  partner . . . 7701(a)(2)
  partnership . . . 7701(a)(2)
  party to a reorganization . . . 368(b)
  person . . . 7701(a)(1)
  personal holding company . . . 542
    income . . . 543
  possessions corporations . . . 367(d)(2)
  preferred dividends . . . 565(f)(2)
  property
    used in the trade or business . . . 1231(b)
  reorganization . . . 368
  resident alien . . . 7701(b)
  securities . . . 1236(c)
  short-term capital gain . . . 1222(1)
  short-term capital loss . . . 1222(2)
  state . . . 7701(a)(10)
  taxable income . . . 63
  taxable year . . . 7701(a)(23)
  undistributed personal holding company income . . . 545
  United States person . . . 957(c)
  United States property . . . 956(d)
  wages . . . 3401(a)
Depreciation
  earnings and profits, effect on . . . 312(k)
Development expenditures
  oil and gas wells, intangible expenses . . . 263(c)
Discharge of debt
  income from . . . 61(a)(12)
Disclosure of returns and information . . . 6103
Distributions by corporations . . . 301—368
  additional consideration received . . . 356
  basis to distributees . . . 358
    property distributions . . . 301(d)
  controlled corporation's stock and securities . . . 355
    additional consideration received . . . 356(b)
  earnings and profits, effect on . . . 312
  gain or loss to corporation . . . 311
    appreciated property distributed . . . 311(b)
  property . . . 301
    earnings and profits, effect on . . . 312
  redemption of stock . . . 302—304
Distributions by partnerships
  share of partner . . . 704
Dividend carryover, personal holding companies . . . 564
Dividend income, corporations
  dividends received deduction . . . 243—246
  domestic corporation recipient of dividends from foreign corporation . . . 902
  deficiency, deduction for
    personal holding companies . . . 547
  defined . . . 316
  information returns . . . 6042
  paid, deduction . . . 561—565
  preferential dividends, dividends paid deduction . . . 562(c)
  withholding of tax at source
    nonresident aliens and foreign corporations . . . 1441(b); 1442

Dividend income, individuals ... 61(a)(7)
. capital gains treatment ... 1(h)(11)

Dividends
. taxed as net capital gain ... 1(h)(11)

Dividends in kind ... 301
. gain or loss to corporation ... 311

Dividends paid deduction ... 561—565
. accumulated earnings tax ... 563(a)
. affiliated corporations ... 562(d)
. consent dividends ... 565
. definition ... 561
. eligible dividends ... 562
.. payment on last day of year ... 563(c)
. liquidation distributions ... 562(b)
. payment of dividends after close of taxable year ... 563
. personal holding companies
.. computation of personal holding company tax ... 563(b)
.. dividend carryover ... 564
. preferential dividends ... 562(c)
. real estate investment trusts ... 562(e)

Dividends received deduction ... 243—246
. temporary
.. controlled foreign corporation ... 965

Domestic defined ... 7701(a)(4)

Domestic International Sales Corporations ... 991—997
. actual distributions
.. adjustments to basis of shareholder's stock ... 996(e)
.. disqualification ... 995(b)(2)
.. dividends received deduction ... 246(d)
.. earnings and profits ... 996(f)
.. failure to qualify ... 995(b)(2)
.. foreign shareholders ... 996(g)
.. order of absorption ... 996(a)
.. order of application ... 996(c)
.. property ... 997
.. qualification requirements, distributions to meet ... 992(c)
.. revocation of election ... 995(b)(2)
. affiliated corporations, consolidated returns ... 1504(b)
. assets, transfers of ... 995(e)
. conditions for qualification ... 992(c)
. consolidated returns ... 1504(b)
. constructive distributions ... 995(b)
.. adjustments to basis of shareholder's stock ... 996(e)
.. disqualification ... 995(b)(2)
.. dividends received deduction ... 246(d)
.. 50% rule ... 995(b)(1)(D)
.. foreign investment attributable to producer's loans ... 995(b)(1)(G); 995(d)
.. foreign tax credit ... 904(f)
.. interest on producer's loans ... 993(d)
.. qualification requirements, distributions to meet ... 992(c)
.. revocation of election ... 995(b)(2)
.. sales or exchanges, gain from ... 995(b)(1)(B)
. disqualification, constructive dividends ... 995(b)(2)
. dividends received deduction ... 246(d)
. earnings and profits
.. actual distributions ... 996(f)

Domestic International Sales Corporations—continued
. earnings and profits—continued
.. measure of tax ... 995(a)
.. ordering rules for losses ... 996(b)
. election ... 992(b)
. 50% rule, constructive distributions ... 995(b)(1)(D)
. foreign investment attributable to producer's loans, constructive distributions ... 995(b)(1)(G); 995(d)
. foreign shareholders, distributions to ... 996(g)
. foreign tax credit for distributions ... 901(d)
. information requirements
.. failure to meet, penalties ... 6686
. intercompany pricing, measure of tax ... 994
. interest on DISC-related deferred tax liability ... 995(f)
. interest on producer's loans, constructive distributions ... 993(d); 995(b)(1)(A)
. measure of tax
.. earnings and profits ... 995(a)
.. intercompany pricing ... 994
.. taxable income ... 994
. minimum capital requirement ... 992(a)(1)(C)
. non-DISC treated as DISC ... 992(a)(2)
. nonqualifying corporations ... 992(d)
. one class of stock requirement ... 992(a)
. order of absorption, actual distributions ... 996(a)
. order of application, actual distributions ... 996(c)
. personal holding companies ... 992(e)
. possession tax credit and Puerto Rico ... 936(f)
. pricing rules ... 994
. property distributions ... 997
. qualified export assets ... 993(b); 993(c)
. qualified export receipts ... 993(a)
. qualifying corporations ... 992(a)
. revocation of election, constructive distributions ... 995(b)(2)
. sales or exchanges, gain as constructive distributions ... 995(b)(1)(B); 995(b)(1)(C)
. shareholder, tax on ... 991
. stock transfers ... 995(c)
.. redemptions, adjustments ... 996(d)
.. sales ... 996(d)
. taxable income, measure of tax ... 994

Domestic production activities
. deduction for income attributable to ... 199
.. phase-in ... 199(a)(2)

Drilling and development costs, oil and gas wells ... 263(c)

Dual consolidated loss, consolidated returns ... 1503(c)

E

Earned income credit
. earned income defined ... 911(d)(2)

Earnings and profits
. accumulated earnings tax ... 531—537
. basis adjustment, investment tax credit ... 312(k)
. depreciation affecting ... 312(k)
.. exception for recovery and section 179 property ... 312(k)(3)
. distributions by corporations affecting ... 312
. information returns as to ... 6042
. property distributions affecting ... 312

Employees
. meals and lodging furnished for convenience of employer . . . 119

Endowment insurance
. income . . . 61(a)(10)

Entertainment expenses, substantiation . . . 274
. convention expenses, cruise ships . . . 274(h)(2)
. foreign conventions . . . 274(h)(1)

Estates and trusts
. expatriation to avoid tax . . . 2107
. foreign
. . recognition of gain on transfers to . . . 684
. income from interest in . . . 61(a)(15)
. rates of tax . . . 1(e)

Estimated tax, estates and trusts
. payments treated as paid by beneficiary . . . 643(g)

Evasion or avoidance of tax
. acquisitions made for purpose of . . . 269
. corporations used to avoid income tax on shareholders . . . 531—565
. liability assumed for purpose of . . . 357(b)
. penalties . . . 7201

Exchanges of property
. assumption of liability . . . 357
. basis to distributees . . . 358
. investment property . . . 1031
. nontaxable . . . 1031
. productive use or investment property . . . 1031
. securities transferred under certain agreements . . . 1058
. tax-free . . . 1031

Exempt income
. citizens of United States residing in foreign country . . . 911; 912
. cost of living allowances . . . 912(2)
. extraterritorial income . . . 114
. foreign central banks of issue . . . 861; 895
. foreign corporations . . . 883
. . employees of . . . 893
. foreign governments . . . 892
. international organizations . . . 892
. . employees of . . . 893
. lodging furnished for convenience of employer . . . 119
. meals furnished for convenience of employer . . . 119
. Peace Corps members . . . 912(3)
. qualifying foreign trade income . . . 941

Exempt organizations
. exclusion from definition of personal holding company . . . 542(c)(1)
. foreign tax-exempts, withholding on income
. . payment of withheld tax . . . 1461

Exemptions
. withholding . . . 3402(f)

Expatriated entities . . . 7874
. stock compensation of insiders . . . 4985

Expatriation
. avoidance of tax . . . 877
. . estate tax . . . 2107
. entities
. . stock compensation of insiders . . . 4985
. information returns . . . 6039G

Expenses
. export promotion . . . 971(d)

Export promotion expenses defined . . . 971(d)

Export trade assets
. defined . . . 971(c)

Export trade corporations . . . 970—971
. controlled foreign corporations . . . 971(a)(3)
. definition . . . 971(a)

Export trade income
. defined . . . 971(b)

Expropriation losses
. recoveries . . . 1351

Extraterritorial income . . . 114

F

Family members
. losses of . . . 267(b)

Finance companies, exception from definition of personal holding company . . . 542(c)(6)

Fines, deductibility . . . 162(f)

FIRPTA (Foreign Investment in Real Property Tax Act of 1980) . . . 861(a)(5); 897; 6039C

FISC . . . 993(e)

Foreign areas allowances . . . 912(1)

Foreign base company income . . . 954
. exclusions . . . 954(b)
. export trade . . . 970(a)
. sales income . . . 954(d)
. services income . . . 954(e)
. shipping income . . . 954(f)
. shipping operations, qualified investment in . . . 955(b)

Foreign capital gains and losses, limitation computations . . . 904(b)(3)(C)

Foreign central banks, interest from obligations of the U. S. . . . 895

Foreign conventions
. entertainment expense deduction
. . Caribbean basin countries . . . 274(h)(6)
. . substantiation . . . 274(h)(1)

Foreign corporations . . . 881—887
. accumulated earnings tax . . . 535(d)
. acquiring stock
. . target affiliate . . . 338(h)
. branch profits tax . . . 884
. consent dividends . . . 565(e)
. credits . . . 33; 882(c)(3)
. definition . . . 901(d); 7701(a)(5)
. dividends received from
. . corporate deduction . . . 243(e); 245
. . domestic corporation recipient . . . 861(a)(2)(B); 902
. . gross-up . . . 78
. domestic corporation, treatment as . . . 897(i)
. exempt income . . . 883
. export trade corporations . . . 970—971
. failure to file returns . . . 6679
. foreign base company income . . . 954(g)
. foreign ownership, information returns . . . 6038A
. foreign tax credit . . . 901(b)(4); 906
. formation of, information returns . . . 6046
. Guam and Mariana Islands corporations . . . 881(b)
. imposition of tax on
. . nonresident foreign corporations . . . 881
. . resident foreign corporations . . . 882

EMP

Foreign corporations—continued
. information returns . . . 6038; 6046
. . engaged in U.S. business . . . 6038C
. interest received, portfolio debt investments . . . 881(c)
. original issue discount . . . 881(a)(3)
. real property in U.S. owned by
. . sale or exchange . . . 861(a)(5); 897; 1445; 6039C
. reciprocal penalty tax for discriminatory tax by foreign country . . . 891; 896
. reorganizations . . . 367
. . information returns . . . 6046
. similar credit requirement, alien residents . . . 901(c)
. stapled stock . . . 269B
. stock sold or exchanged, gain . . . 1248
. taxable year . . . 898
. transportation income, tax on . . . 887
. Virgin Islands and American Samoa corporations . . . 881(b)

Foreign countries
. discriminatory taxes, reprisal . . . 891; 896
. taxes imposed by, credit . . . 27; 702; 874; 882(c)(3); 901—908

Foreign currency, payment of tax in . . . 6316

Foreign currency contracts . . . 1256(g)

Foreign currency transactions . . . 985—989

Foreign expropriation losses
. defined . . . 1351(b)

Foreign governments
. bribe payments to officials and employees . . . 162(c)(1)
. discriminatory taxes imposed, reciprocal penalty tax . . . 891
. exempt income . . . 892
. . compensation of foreign government employees . . . 893
. expropriation of property, loss deduction
. . recoveries . . . 1351; 6167
. improper payments to officials of . . . 162(c)

Foreign income . . . 901—943
. election to exclude from gross income . . . 911(e)

Foreign items
. collection of, information returns . . . 6041(b)

Foreign loss, overall, recapture . . . 904(f)

Foreign officials, improper payments to . . . 162(c)

Foreign oil related income . . . 907(c)

Foreign oil related loss . . . 907(c)
. defined . . . 907(f)(2)
. recapture of . . . 907(f)

Foreign organizations
. private foundations, taxes on . . . 4948

Foreign parents
. expatriated entities . . . 7874

Foreign partnership
. definition . . . 7701(a)(5)
. interests . . . 6046A

Foreign personal holding companies
. controlled foreign corporations, income . . . 954(c)
. information returns . . . 6046
. reorganizations, information returns . . . 6046
. taxable year . . . 898(c)(2)

Foreign Sales Corporations
. information requirements
. . failure to meet, penalties . . . 6686

Foreign service allowances . . . 912

Foreign shareholders
. domestic corporation . . . 6039C(a)

Foreign sources, information returns from . . . 982

Foreign students and exchange visitors
. compensation . . . 872(b)(3)
. rates of tax . . . 871(c)
. scholarships . . . 1441(b)

Foreign subsidiaries, credit for taxes of . . . 902

Foreign tax credit . . . 27; 901—908
. adjustments on payment of accrued taxes . . . 905(c)
. allowance of credit . . . 901(a)
. amount allowed . . . 901(b)
. controlled foreign corporations . . . 960
. . stock sale . . . 964(e)
. coordination with nonrefundable personal credits . . . 904(i)
. corporate stockholder in foreign corporation . . . 902
. corporations treated as foreign . . . 901(d)
. deconsolidation, avoidance of limitations by . . . 904(j)
. deemed paid credit . . . 902
. definitions and special rules . . . 902(c)
. denial of credit . . . 901(j)
. dividends received by domestic corporations from foreign corporations . . . 902
. foreign mineral income . . . 901(e)
. foreign subsidiary of second and third tier foreign corporation . . . 902(b)
. foreign trade income, taxes paid on . . . 901(h)
. international boycott, reduction for participation in . . . 908
. limitations on credit . . . 904
. minimum holding period for certain taxes . . . 901(k)
. nonresident aliens . . . 874(c)
. oil and gas income, foreign . . . 907(a)
. oil and gas properties
. . carryback or carryover of credit . . . 907(f)
. oil and gas purchases and sales . . . 901(f); 907
. overall limitation . . . 904(a); 904(b)
. . certain income, separate application of provision . . . 904(d)
. per-country limitation . . . 904(a)
. possessions corporation . . . 901(g)
. proof of credits . . . 905(b)
. reduction of
. . penalty . . . 6038(c)
. stockholder in foreign corporation . . . 902
. subsidies, taxes used to provide . . . 901(i)
. taxes in lieu of income, war profits, and excess profits taxes . . . 903
. year in which credit taken . . . 905(a)

Foreign tax credit
. domestic loss
. . recharacterization . . . 904(g)

Foreign taxes
. discriminatory, reciprocal penalty . . . 891; 896
. oil and gas properties . . . 907(b)
. redetermination, failure to notify . . . 6689(a)

Foreign trade income . . . 941—943
. definitions and special rules . . . 943
. foreign trading gross receipts . . . 942
. qualifying foreign trade income . . . 941

Foreign trusts ... 904(f)(4)
. creation of or transfers to, information returns ... 6048
.. failure to file returns ... 6677
. one or more U.S. beneficiaries ... 679

Franchises
. capital gains and losses ... 1253

Fraud
. deficiency dividends deduction disallowed because of ... 547(g)
. penalties for ... 6674; 7201—7203

G

Gain or loss
. appreciated property distributed by corporation ... 311(b)
. coal sold ... 631
. condemnation of property ... 1231(a)
. contributions to capital of partnership ... 721
. involuntary conversions ... 1231(a)
. liquidations ... 331—346
. natural resources sold ... 631
.. shareholder ... 331(a)
. partnerships
.. capital contribution of partner to ... 721
. real property, U.S. ... 897
. stock disposed of
.. controlled corporations ... 355(e)
. timber sold ... 631

Gambling
. winnings
.. nonresident aliens ... 871(j)

Gas royalties, personal holding company income ... 543(a)(3)

Gasoline taxes
. state
.. deductibility ... 164(b)(4)

Gift tax
. imposition of tax ... 2501

Goodwill
. amortization ... 197

Grantor trusts ... 679

Gross income
. controlled taxpayers, allocation among ... 482
. defined ... 61(a)
. nonresident aliens ... 872

Gross income requirement, personal holding companies ... 542(a)(1)

Guam
. coordination of individual income tax ... 7654
.. penalties for failure to furnish information ... 6688
. foreign corporations, exception ... 881(b)
. income from sources within ... 931
. residents of, tax on ... 876

H

Head of household
. rate of tax ... 1(b); 1(l)

Husband and wife
. joint returns ... 6013

I

Illegal payments ... 162(c)
. foreign government officials, payments to ... 952(a)

Imported property
. alternative depreciation ... 168(g)

Improvements
. capital expenditures ... 263

Imputed interest, deferred payment sales ... 483

Income
. allocation among related taxpayers ... 482
. foreign, tax-exempt, withholding on
.. payment of withheld tax ... 1461
. partners ... 702
. possessions of the United States, income from sources within ... 931
. Puerto Rican sources ... 933
. sources outside United States ... 901—943
. sources partly within and partly without United States ... 863
.. international communications income ... 863(e)
.. space and ocean activities ... 863(d)
.. transportation income ... 863(c)
. sources within the United States ... 861
. sources without the United States ... 862

Income in respect of a decedent ... 61(a)(14)

Indexing of taxes
. income tax brackets ... 1(f)

Individuals
. foreign tax credit ... 901(b)(1)
. head-of-household rates ... 1(b)
. rates of tax ... 1—2
.. head of household ... 1(b)
.. indexing income tax brackets ... 1(f)
.. phaseout of marriage penalty ... 1(f)
.. rate reductions after 2000 ... 1(i)
. unmarried, rates of tax ... 1(c)

Information returns ... 6038—6049
. address and phone number of information contact ... 6041(d)
. citizenship, individuals losing ... 6039G
. corporations
.. foreign ownership ... 6038A
. dividend payments ... 6042
. foreign corporations ... 6038
.. engaged in U.S. business ... 6038C
. foreign partnership interests ... 6046A
. foreign persons holding United States property interests ... 6039C
. foreign sources, request for ... 982
. foreign trusts, creation of or transfers to ... 6048
. information contact, address and phone number of ... 6041(d)
. interest payments ... 6049
. partnership ... 6031
. payments of $600 or more ... 6041(a)
. resident status ... 6039E
. $10 or more in dividends, payments of ... 6042(a)(1)(A)
. transfers to foreign persons ... 6038B

Inspection of returns ... 6103

Inspection of written determinations ... 6110

Index to Code
References are to Code Section numbers.

Installment sales
. imputed interest . . . 483
. . related parties . . . 483(f)

Intangible assets (Sec. 197 intangibles)
. amortization . . . 197

Intangible drilling and development costs
. oil and gas wells . . . 263(c)
. . incurrence outside the United States . . . 263(i)

Interest paid
. deduction . . . 163
. . registered obligations . . . 163(f)
. deferred payment . . . 483
. information returns . . . 6049
. original issue discount . . . 163(e)
. . high yield obligations . . . 163(e)(5); 163(i)
. related person, limitation . . . 163(j)
. related taxpayers, transactions between . . . 267

Interest received . . . 61(a)(4)
. allocation, rules for . . . 864(e)
. backup withholding . . . 3406
. portfolio debt investments
. . foreign corporations . . . 881(c)
. . nonresident aliens . . . 871(h)

Internal Revenue Service
. audit standards, selection of returns
. . protection from disclosure . . . 6103(b)

International boycotts
. determination as to particular operations . . . 999(d)
. factor . . . 999(c)
. foreign tax credit reduction for participation in . . . 908
. participation in or cooperation . . . 999(b)
. . related persons . . . 999(e)
. reports by taxpayers . . . 999(a)
. . failure to make . . . 999(f)

International organizations
. compensation of employees, exempt income . . . 893

Inventories
. costs, limitation on
. . related persons, property imported from . . . 1059A

Investment companies
. exchanges between . . . 368(a)(2)(F)(vii)

Investment property, exchange of . . . 1031

Investment tax credit
. earnings and profit . . . 312(k)

Involuntary conversions
. capital gains and losses . . . 1231

Iron ore royalties
. royalties, capital gains treatment . . . 631

Itemized deductions
. income attributable to domestic production activities . . . 199

J

Joint returns . . . 6013
. rate of tax . . . 1(a)

K

Kickbacks to foreign officials . . . 162(c)

L

Letters, capital asset status . . . 1221

Liabilities assumed
. corporate distributions and adjustments . . . 301(b)(2); 357; 358(d)
. incorporation of a business . . . 357(c)(3)

Liability for tax
. gift tax . . . 2501

Life insurance
. income from life insurance contracts . . . 61(a)(10)

Life insurance companies
. exclusion from definition of personal holding company . . . 542(c)(3)

Liquidations
. basis of property received . . . 334
. complete, definition . . . 346(a)
. distributing corporation, effects on . . . 336—338
. dividends
. . basis . . . 334
. . dividends paid deduction . . . 562(b)
. . partial liquidation defined . . . 346
. gain or loss to shareholders . . . 331
. partial liquidation
. . definition . . . 302(e); 346
. . noncorporate shareholder . . . 302(b)(4)
. recipients of distributions, effects on . . . 331—334
. subsidiaries . . . 332; 337
. . basis of property received . . . 334

Literary property, sale . . . 1221

Livestock
. holding period . . . 1231(b)(3)
. property used in trade or business . . . 1231(b)(3)

Loan companies, exception from definition of personal holding company . . . 542(c)(6)

Lodging . . . 119

Long-term capital gain defined . . . 1222(3)

Long-term capital loss defined . . . 1222(4)

Losses . . . 165
. expropriation by foreign government
. . recoveries . . . 1351
. nonregistered obligations . . . 165(j)
. nonresident aliens . . . 873(b)
. related taxpayers, transactions between . . . 267

Lump-sum distributions, retirement plans
. nonresident aliens, tax imposed . . . 871(b)

M

Mark-to-market method
. passive foreign investment companies (PFICs) . . . 1296
. securities dealers . . . 475

Marriage penalty phaseout . . . 1(f)(8)

Meals and lodging . . . 119

Medical referral payments . . . 162(c)

Memorandums, capital asset status . . . 1221

N

Natural resources
. continental shelf areas . . . 638

NAT

Net capital gain defined ... 1222(11)
Net capital loss
. definitions ... 1222(10)
Net long-term capital gain defined ... 1222(7)
Net long-term capital loss defined ... 1222(8)
Net short-term capital gain defined ... 1222(5)
Net short-term capital loss defined ... 1222(6)
Netting of casualty losses ... 1231(a)
Nonbusiness debts ... 166(d)
Nondeductibles ... 263—269B
Nonresident aliens ... 871—879
. charitable contributions ... 873(b)(2)
. community income treatment ... 879
. consent dividends ... 565(e)
. credits ... 33
. deductions ... 873; 874
. defined ... 7701(b)
. foreign tax credit ... 901(b)(4); 906
. gambling winnings ... 871(j)
. gross income ... 872
. imposition of tax on ... 871
. interest received, portfolio debt investments ... 871(h)
. losses ... 873(b)
. original issue discount ... 871(g)
. partnerships ... 875
. personal exemption ... 873(b)(3)
. real property in U.S. owned by
.. sale or exchange ... 861(a)(5); 897; 1445; 6039C
. Social Security benefits, taxation of ... 871(a)(3)
. tax on, scope
.. certain interest and dividends ... 871(i)
. transportation income, tax on ... 887
. U.S. resident or citizen married to, community income of ... 879
. withholding of tax on ... 1441; 3401(a)(6)
.. overwithheld tax, refunds and credits ... 1464
.. payment of withheld tax ... 1461
.. recipient of income paying tax, recollection from withholding agent ... 1463
Nonresident citizens
. exclusions
.. definitions ... 911(d)
.. election ... 911(e)
.. foreign earned income ... 911(b)
.. housing cost amount ... 911(c)
.. residence requirement ... 911(d)(5)
.. special rules ... 911(d)
.. waiver of period of stay in foreign country ... 911(d)(4)
Nontaxable exchanges ... 1031
Northern Mariana Islands, U.S. income tax
. coordination of individual income tax ... 7654
. foreign corporations ... 881(b)
. income from sources within ... 931
. residents of, tax on ... 876

O

Obligations
. registered form requirement ... 163(f)
.. unregistered, capital gains treatment denied ... 1287

Oil and gas properties
. carryback and carryover of disallowed credits ... 907(f)
. extraction taxes ... 907(c)(5)
. foreign base company ... 954(g)
. foreign taxes paid ... 907(b)
. foreign, credit against tax for income from ... 907
. producers, gases from nonconventional sources ... 29(e)
. purchase or sale, foreign, foreign tax credit ... 901(f); 907
Oil royalties, personal holding company income ... 543(a)(3)
Original issue discount ... 1271—1274
. debt instruments—retirement, sale, or exchange ... 1271
. determination of amount ... 1273
. determination of issue price
.. debt instruments issued for property ... 1274
. foreign corporations ... 881(a)(3)
. inclusion in income, current ... 1272
. interest paid ... 163(e)
.. high yield obligations ... 163(e)(5); 163(i)
. nonresident aliens ... 871(g)
Overall limitation on foreign tax credit ... 904(a); 904(b)
Overseas allowances ... 912
Ownership of stock, rules in determining personal holding company status ... 544

P

Paid-in surplus, basis of property acquired as ... 362(a)
Partial liquidation
. definition ... 346
. gain or loss to shareholders ... 331
Partners and partnerships ... 701
. adoption of taxable year ... 706(b)
. computation of taxable income ... 703
. contributions to capital ... 721
. credits of partner ... 702
. distributive shares ... 704
. foreign partners' share of effectively connected income
.. withholding at source ... 1446
. foreign partnership interests ... 6046A
. foreign tax credit ... 901(b)(5)
. gross income, distribution of share of ... 61(a)(13)
. income of partner ... 702
. information returns ... 6031
. liability for tax ... 701
. taxable income, computation ... 703
. taxable years ... 706(b)
. transactions between
.. losses disallowed ... 707(b)
. year in which partnership income is includible ... 706(a)
Party to a reorganization, defined ... 368(b)
Passive foreign investment companies (PFICs) ... 1291—1298
. election of mark-to-market for stock ... 1296

Index to Code
References are to Code Section numbers.

Patents
. sale or exchange of . . . 1235
. . foreign corporation purchaser, nature of gain . . . 1249

Patronage dividends
. backup withholding . . . 3406

Payment of tax
. consolidated returns . . . 1503
. extension of time . . . 6167
. foreign currency . . . 6316
. withheld tax on nonresident aliens, foreign partnerships, and foreign corporations . . . 1461

Peace Corps, allowances for volunteers and volunteer members
. exempt status . . . 912(3)

Penalties
. accuracy-related penalty . . . 6662
. assessable . . . 6672—6689
. evasion of tax . . . 6672; 7201
. failure to disclose treaty-based return positions . . . 6712
. failure to file returns . . . 6652
. failure to pay tax . . . 7202; 7203
. foreign tax redetermination, notification of . . . 6689(a)
. fraud . . . 6663
. Guam-U.S. tax coordination, failure to furnish information . . . 6688
. information returns
. . failure to file . . . 6652
. . foreign corporate shareholders . . . 6038(b)
. reasonable cause exception . . . 6664(c)

Pensions
. gross income . . . 61(a)(11)

Personal deductions
. bad debts . . . 166
. interest paid . . . 163
. losses . . . 165
. taxes paid . . . 164

Personal exemptions
. nonresident aliens . . . 873(b)(3)

Personal holding companies . . . 541—547
. annualization of income . . . 546
. corporations filing consolidated returns . . . 542(b)
. deduction for deficiency dividends . . . 547
. deficiency dividends, deduction . . . 547
. defined . . . 542
. dividends paid deduction, dividends paid after close of taxable year . . . 563
. Domestic International Sales Corporation status . . . 992(d)
. finance companies, exception from definition . . . 542(c)(6)
. imposition of tax on . . . 541
. liquidating distributions, denial of dividends-paid deduction . . . 562(b)
. personal holding company income . . . 543
. 60% of adjusted ordinary gross income requirement . . . 542(a)(1)
. small business investment companies . . . 542(c)(8)
. special rules . . . 542(d)
. stock ownership . . . 544
. undistributed personal holding company income . . . 545

Personal service corporations
. graduated rates . . . 11(b)

Possessions corporations
. foreign tax credit . . . 901(g)
. sales of assets, possessions tax credit, exception . . . 936(d)(3)

Possessions corporations, Domestic International Sales Corporation status
. definitions . . . 367(d)(2)
. intangibles, transfer of . . . 367(d)

Possessions of the United States
. credit
. . intangible property income . . . 936(h)

Possessions tax credit . . . 27
. Caribbean Basin countries, qualified, investment in . . . 936(d)(4)
. Puerto Rico . . . 936

Preferential dividends, dividends paid deduction . . . 562(c)

Preferred dividends, defined . . . 565(f)(2)

Product liability losses
. accumulated earnings tax . . . 537(b)(4)

Property
. dividends paid in . . . 301
. . gain or loss to corporation . . . 311

Puerto Rico
. economic activity credit . . . 30A
. income from sources within . . . 933
. possession tax credit . . . 936
. residents of, tax on . . . 876
. . foreign tax credit . . . 901(b)(2); 901(b)(3)

R

Railroads
. rolling stock
. . rentals, sources of income . . . 861(e)

Rates of tax
. alternative minimum tax . . . 55
. corporations . . . 11(a)
. . accumulated earnings tax . . . 531
. estates . . . 1(e)
. head of household . . . 1(b)
. husband and wife . . . 1(a); 1(d)
. indexing income tax brackets . . . 1(f)
. individuals . . . 1—2
. personal holding company tax . . . 541
. trusts . . . 1(e)

Real estate
. effectively connected with U.S. trade or business, disposition . . . 897(a)
. foreign corporation owning U.S.
. . sale or exchange . . . 861(a)(5); 897; 1445; 6039C
. nonresident alien owning U.S.
. . sale or exchange . . . 861(a)(5); 897; 1445; 6039C
. taxes . . . 164(a)(1)
. . deduction . . . 164

Real estate investment trusts
. dividends paid deduction . . . 562(e)
. nonresident, disposition of interest in . . . 897(h)

Reasonable accumulations by corporations . . . 537

Recapture
. foreign losses . . . 904(f)

Receipt, payment of tax . . . 6316

Recordkeeping, charged tips . . . 6041(e)

Redemption of stock, distributions by corporations
in . . . 302—304
. partial liquidation
. . noncorporate shareholder . . . 302(b)(4)
. related taxpayers . . . 304

Refunds and credits
. limitations on . . . 6511
. overwithheld taxes on nonresident aliens, foreign partnerships, and foreign corporations . . . 1464

Related person
. interest paid, limitation . . . 163(j)

Related taxpayers
. allocation of income and deductions among . . . 482
. installment sales
. . rate of imputed interest, special rule . . . 483(f)
. redemption of stock . . . 304
. transactions between
. . capital gains and losses . . . 1239
. . controlled groups . . . 267(f)
. . deductions disallowed . . . 267(a)
. . pass-through entities . . . 267(e)

Rent
. income . . . 61(a)(5)
. information return . . . 6041(a)

Reorganizations . . . 351—385
. assumption of liability . . . 357
. basis to corporations . . . 362
. basis to distributees . . . 358
. control defined . . . 368(c)
. definition . . . 368
. effects on corporations that are parties to . . . 361
. effects on transferor corporation . . . 362
. exchanges of stock and securities . . . 354
. foreign corporations . . . 367
. . information returns . . . 6046
. liabilities assumed . . . 357
. merger . . . 368(a)
. nonrecognition of gain or loss to corporations . . . 361
. party to a reorganization defined . . . 368(b)
. stock and securities exchanged in . . . 354
. . additional consideration received . . . 356
. stock-for-stock . . . 368(a)(1)

Reportable transactions
. disclosure . . . 6111

Resident alien
. defined . . . 7701(b)

Retail sales tax, deduction for . . . 164(b)(4)

Returns . . . 6011—6049
. consolidated returns . . . 1501—1504
. corporation
. disclosure of . . . 6103
. . domestic, foreign shareholders . . . 6039C(a)
. failure to file
. . additions to tax . . . 6652
. . fraud penalty . . . 7203
. . international boycotts . . . 999(a)
. . failure to report . . . 999(f)
. real property in U.S., substantial investor . . . 6039C(b)
. treaty-based return positions, disclosure . . . 6114
. . failure to disclose, penalty . . . 6712

Royalties
. coal . . . 631(c)
. income . . . 61(a)(6)
. iron ore . . . 631

Royalties—continued
. patents, treatment in case of sale or exchange . . . 1235
. personal holding company income . . . 543(a)(1)

S

S corporations
. related taxpayers . . . 267

Sales of property
. foreign corporation stock, character of gain . . . 1248
. inventory property . . . 861(a)(6)
. natural resources . . . 631
. patents and copyrights, foreign corporation purchaser . . . 1249
. source of income . . . 861(a)(5)
. timber . . . 631

Sales taxes, deductibility . . . 164(b)(4), 164(b)(5)

Sec. 197 intangibles
. amortization . . . 197

Securities
. controlled corporation's, distribution of . . . 355
. . additional consideration received . . . 356(b)
. dealers
. . capital gains and losses . . . 1236
. . mark-to-market method . . . 475
. exchange in reorganization . . . 354

Separate returns
. rates of tax . . . 1(d)

Shareholders
. controlled foreign corporations
. . inclusions for U.S. shareholders, special rules . . . 956(b)
. foreign corporation, foreign tax credit . . . 902
. liquidations . . . 331(a)

Shipping activities, international
. alternative tax . . . 1352
. . election . . . 1354
. . revocation . . . 1354
. . termination . . . 1354
. credits, allocation . . . 1358
. deductions, allocation . . . 1358
. definitions . . . 1355
. depreciation . . . 1357
. election to detemine corporate tax using per ton rate . . . 1352—1359
. income, allocation . . . 1358
. interest . . . 1357
. items not subject to regular tax . . . 1357
. notional shipping income . . . 1353
. qualifying . . . 1356
. qualifying vessels, disposition . . . 1359
. special rules . . . 1355

Ships
. foreign, earnings exempt income to foreign corporation . . . 883(a)(1)
. leased, income from . . . 861

Short-term capital gain defined . . . 1222(1)

Short-term capital loss defined . . . 1222(2)

Single persons, tax rate . . . 1(c)

Small business corporations
. investment companies, losses
. . personal holding company provisions excepting . . . 542(c)(8)

Index to Code
References are to Code Section numbers.

Social security benefits
. nonresident aliens, taxation of . . . 871(a)(3)

Social security taxes (FICA)
. employees of foreign subsidiary, deduction for payments in behalf of . . . 176

Sources of income . . . 861—864
. interest . . . 864(e)
. . election to allocate . . . 864(f)
. personal property, sales of . . . 865
. railroad rolling stock . . . 861(e)
. within United States . . . 861
. without United States . . . 862

Splitting of income . . . 1(a)

Standard deduction
. income from sources outside United States . . . 862(b)
. income from sources within United States . . . 861(b)

Stapled stock . . . 269B

Statements to payees of dividends and interest . . . 6049(c)

Statements, false and fraudulent . . . 7206; 7211

States
. defined . . . 7701(a)(10)
. gasoline taxes, deductibility . . . 164(b)(4)
. sales taxes, deductibility . . . 164(b)(4)

Statute of limitations
. assessment and collection of tax . . . 6503
. collection of tax . . . 6503
. levy and distraint . . . 6503
. refunds and credits . . . 6511
. suspension of running . . . 6503

Statutory merger or consolidation as reorganization . . . 368(a)

Stock
. consent stock . . . 565(f)(1)
. controlled corporation's, distribution of . . . 355
. . additional consideration received . . . 356(b)
. . recognition of gain . . . 355(e)
. exchange of, gain or loss recognition
. . reorganization . . . 354
. ownership rule
. . affiliated corporations . . . 1504(a)
. . controlled foreign corporations . . . 958
. . nondeductible losses . . . 267(c)
. . personal holding companies . . . 542(a)(2); 544
. property acquired by issuance of, basis . . . 362
. stapled . . . 269B

Stock distributions
. excess, passive foreign investment companies . . . 1291

Subpart F income . . . 952
. export trade corporations . . . 970
. withdrawal of previously excluded income from qualified investment . . . 955

Subsidiaries
. foreign subsidiary of domestic parent
. . consolidated returns . . . 1504(d)
. . social security coverage for employees . . . 176
. foreign subsidiary of second and third tier foreign corporation, foreign tax credit . . . 902(b)
. liquidation of . . . 332; 337
. . basis of property received . . . 334

Surplus, improper accumulations . . . 531—537

T

Tax-free dividends, effect of depreciation on earnings and profits . . . 312(k)

Tax-free exchanges . . . 1031
. investment property . . . 1031

Tax rates
. individuals
. . long-term capital gains rates . . . 1(h); 55(b)(3)
. long-term capital gains
. . revised holding periods and tax rates . . . 1(h)
. ten-percent rate bracket . . . 1(i)

Tax shelters
. corporations, substantial understatement penalty . . . 6662(d)(2)(C)

Taxable income
. computation . . . 61—275
. . partnership . . . 703
. . period for . . . 441
. defined . . . 63

Taxable year
. controlled foreign corporations . . . 898(c)(1)
. defined . . . 7701(a)(23)
. foreign corporations . . . 898
. foreign personal holding companies . . . 898(c)(2)
. personal service corporation . . . 280H

Taxes
. deductibility . . . 164; 275

Timber
. capital gains and losses . . . 631

Tips
. charged, employer's reporting requirements . . . 6041(e)

Trade or business
. gross income from . . . 61(a)(2)
. property used in . . . 1231
. within the U.S. defined . . . 864(b)

Trademark and trade name expenditures
. capital gains and losses . . . 1253

Transfers
. intangibles, possessions corporations . . . 367(d)
. possessions corporations, by
. . intangibles . . . 367(d)

Traveling expenses . . . 162(a)(2)
. foreign travel, repeal of allocation requirement . . . 274(c)
. substantiation . . . 274

Treaties
. disclosure of return positions based on . . . 6114
. . failure to disclose, penalty . . . 6712
. income affected by . . . 894

Trusts
. accumulation distributions . . . 904(f)(4)
. alternative minimum tax . . . 55
. Clifford rule . . . 679
. foreign
. . creation of or transfers to, information returns . . . 6048
. . distributions by . . . 901(b)(5)
. grantor trusts . . . 679
. grantors and others treated as substantial owners . . . 679
. rates of tax . . . 1(e)

TRU

Trusts—continued
. transfers to
.. recognition of gain . . . 684

U

Undistributed personal holding company income . . . 545

United States nationals . . . 873(b)(3)

United States person defined . . . 957(c); 7701(a)(30)

United States property
. controlled foreign corporations
.. inclusions for U.S. shareholders, special rules . . . 956(b)

United States real property
. controlled foreign corporations
.. inclusions for U.S. shareholders, special rules . . . 956(b)
. disposition . . . 897
.. withholding of tax at source . . . 1445
. interests held by foreign persons, information returns . . . 6039C

Unmarried individuals, rates of tax . . . 1(c)

V

Virgin Islands
. coordination of individual income tax . . . 7654

Virgin Islands—continued
. corporations
.. intangible property income . . . 934(e)
. foreign corporations, exception . . . 881(b)
. income taxes, coordination with U.S. . . . 932
. reduction of tax liability to, limitations . . . 934
. withholding of tax on income sourced within Virgin Islands . . . 1444

W

Waivers
. family attribution rules . . . 302(c)

Withholding of tax at source . . . 1441—1464
. credit to recipient of income . . . 1462
. credits against income tax . . . 31; 33
. foreign corporations . . . 1441(b); 1442
.. dispositions of U.S. property interests . . . 1445
. nonresident aliens
.. dispositions of U.S. property interests . . . 1445
. overwithheld tax, refunds and credits . . . 1464
. partnerships
.. foreign partners' share of effectively connected income . . . 1446
. payment . . . 1461
. recipient paying tax, re-collection from withholding agent . . . 1463
. Virgin Islands, income sourced within . . . 1444

Written determinations, inspection of . . . 6110

INDEX TO REGULATIONS

References are to Reg. § numbers; boldface references are to proposed Reg. § numbers.

A

Accounting methods
. allocation of income and deductions
. . controlled services transactions . . . **1.482-1**, **1.482-2**, **1.482-6**, **1.6038A-3**, **1.6662-6**
. . global dealing operation . . . **1.482-1**, **1.482-2**, **1.482-8**
. . intangible property transfers . . . **1.482-4**
. . cost-sharing . . . 1.482-1
. . stock-based compensation . . . 1.482-7
. dollar approximate separate transactions method
. . characterization of income and earnings . . . 1.954-2, 1.985-1—1.985-3
. . gain or loss . . . 1.904-4
. foreign currency
. . functional currency . . . 1.985-4
. foreign tax credit . . . 1.901-1—1.905-4T
. intercompany transfer pricing . . . 1.482-1, 1.482-2, 1.482-6, 1.482-8
. qualified business units
. . change to dollar approximate separate transactions method . . . 1.985-7

Accumulated earnings tax . . . 1.532-1—1.535-2
. adjustments to taxable income . . . 1.535-2
. corporations subject to . . . 1.532-1

Adjusted basis
. controlled foreign corporation stock . . . 1.961-1, 1.961-2

Adjustments
. taxable income . . . 1.535-2

Affiliated group
. dual consolidated loss . . . 1.1503-2, 1.1503-2T
. . reduction of taxable income . . . **1.1503(d)-1—1.1503(d)-6**
. expense allocation and apportionment . . . 1.861-9, 1.861-9T, 1.861-11, 1.861-11T, 1.861-14, 1.861-14T, 1.904-4, 1.904-5
. foreign tax credit limitation . . . 1.861-9, 1.861-11, 1.861-14, 1.904-5, 1.904(i)-1

Aliens . . . 1.871-1
. definition . . . 301.7701(b)-1—301.7701(b)-8
. employer's duty to determine status of . . . 1.871-6
. income tax compliance
. . certificates . . . 1.6851-2
. multiple-party financing and conduit arrangements . . . 1.871-1, 1.881-3, 1.881-4, 1.7701(l)-1
. . withholding . . . 1.1441-3, 1.1441-7
. proof of residence . . . 1.871-4
. residence
. . determination of . . . 1.871-2
. . loss of . . . 1.871-5
. . proof of . . . 1.871-4
. . seamen . . . 1.871-3

Allocation
. cost-sharing
. . stock-based compensation . . . 1.482-7
. foreign taxes . . . 1.904-6
. income
. . comparable profits method . . . 1.482-5
. . property transfers, intangible . . . 1.482-4

Allocation—continued
. income—continued
. . property transfers, tangible . . . 1.482-3
. income and deductions
. . controlled services transactions . . . **1.482-1**, **1.482-2**, **1.482-6**, **1.6038A-3**, **1.6662-6**
. . global dealing operation . . . **1.482-1**, **1.482-2**, **1.482-8**, **1.863-3**, **1.863-7**
. . intangible property transfers . . . **1.482-4**
. income from within and without U.S.
. . natural resources . . . 1.863-1—1.863-4
. research and experimental expenditures . . . 1.861-17
. shared inventory costs . . . 1.482-7
. stock dispositions . . . 1.865-1, 1.865-2

Asset acquisitions
. allocation of purchase price . . . 1.338-1, 1.338-2, 1.338-4, 1.338-8, 1.338-9
. international aspects . . . 1.338-1, 1.338-4

Associations, corporate status . . . 301.7701-2

B

Basis
. adjustments to
. . dual consolidated losses . . . 1.1503-2, 1.1503-2T

Blocked foreign income
. controlled foreign corporations . . . 1.964-2

Bond for payment of tax . . . 1.6851-2

Books and records
. foreign corporations . . . 1.6038A-3

C

Capital gains and losses
. income from sources outside the United States . . . 1.904(b)-1

Carryovers
. unused foreign tax credit . . . 1.904-2

Charitable contributions
. allocation and apportionment . . . **1.861-8**
. limitations on deductions
. . partnerships . . . 1.702-1(b)

Check-the-box regulations
. entity classification . . . 301.7701-1, 301.7701-1T, 301.7701-2, 301.7701-3, 301.7701-5T
. . foreign entities . . . 301.7701-2, 301.7701-3, 301.7701-5T

Citizen defined . . . 1.1-1

Compensation received
. foreign government employees
. . exempt income . . . 1.893-1

Computer programs
. transfers, transaction classification . . . 1.861-18

Conduit financing arrangements . . . 1.7701(l)-1

Consolidated returns
. consolidated groups
. . intercompany transactions . . . **1.861-9T**
. corporations exempt from tax
. . dual consolidated loss . . . 1.1503-2, 1.1503-2T

Consolidated returns—continued
. dual consolidated losses
.. reduction of taxable income ... **1.1503(d)-1—1.1503(d)-6**
. foreign loss recapture rules ... 1.1502-9
.. SRLY limitation ... 1.1502-9
. foreign tax credit ... 1.1502-4, 1.1502-4T

Constructive ownership
. stock
.. controlled foreign corporations ... 1.958-2

Controlled corporate groups
. intercompany transactions ... **1.861-9T**

Controlled corporations
. taxable income determination ... 1.482-1, 1.482-3
.. controlled services transactions ... **1.482-1, 1.482-2, 1.482-6, 1.6038A-3, 1.6662-6**

Controlled foreign corporations
. base company service income ... 1.954-4
. basis of stock adjustments to ... 1.961-1, 1.961-2
. definition ... 1.957-1
. earnings and profits
.. allocation of distributions to ... 1.959-3
.. previously taxed, exclusion from gross income ... 1.959-1, 1.959-2
.. special rules, years after December 1986 ... 1.964-1T
. earnings invested in U. S. property, shareholder's pro rata share ... 1.956-1, 1.956-1T
. election of shareholders to be taxed
.. corporate rates ... 1.962-1—1.962-3
. foreign base company income ... 1.954-1
. foreign tax credit ... 1.952-1, 1.952-2, 1.954-2, 1.960-1—1.960-6
. functional currency ... 1.985-1—1.985-4
.. weighted average exchange rate ... 1.989(b)-1
. gross income exclusions
.. international operation of ships or aircraft ... 1.883-1, 1.883-3
. gross income of United States shareholders
.. inclusions ... 1.951-1—1.951-3
.. shareholder's pro rata share of subpart F income ... **1.951-1**
. hybrid branches
.. separate entity treatment ... **1.954-9**
.. subpart F income ... **1.954-2, 1.954-9**
. nonfunctional currency ... 1.988-1—1.988-6
. partnerships
.. subpart F income ... 1.952-1, 1.954-1, 1.954-2, 1.954-3, 1.954-4, **1.954-9**
. qualified election fund ... 1.1291-1, 1.1291-9, 1.1291-10
. qualified investments in less developed countries ... 1.954-5
. records of U.S. shareholders ... 1.964-3
. sales income ... 1.954-3
. services income ... 1.954-4
. shareholders, inclusions in gross income ... 1.951-1—1.951-3
. stock ownership ... 1.958-1, 1.958-2
. subpart F income defined ... 1.952-1
. trade or service receivables ... 1.956-3T
. U.S. property defined ... 1.956-2

Copyrights
. sales
.. foreign corporations ... 1.871-11
.. nonresident aliens ... 1.871-11

Corporations
. associations, taxable as ... 301.7701-2
. consolidated returns
.. dual consolidated losses ... 1.1503-2, 1.1503-2T
. distributions and adjustments
.. passive foreign investment companies ... 1.367(e)-1, **1.1291-1—1.1291-7, 1.1293-1, 1.1295-1**
. dual consolidated losses ... 1.1503-2, 1.1503-2T
.. reduction of taxable income ... **1.1503(d)-1—1.1503(d)-6**
. dual resident corporations
.. dual consolidated losses ... **1.1503(d)-1—1.1503(d)-6**
. earnings and profits
.. interest paid to related persons ... **1.163(j)-1—1.163(j)-8**
.. strippings limitations ... **1.163(j)-1—1.163(j)-8**
. entity classification
.. election to change to partnership or disregarded entity ... 301.7701-3
. publicly traded
.. U.S. real estate interests ... 1.897-9T
. rate of tax ... 1.11-1
. real estate distributions by domestic corporations ... 1.897-5T
. reorganizations
.. foreign corporations involved ... **1.367(a)-3, 1.367(b)-4, 1.367(b)-6**
. stapled foreign corporation
.. definition and tax treatment ... **1.269B-1**
. stock transfers involving foreign corporations ... **1.367(a)-3, 1.367(b)-4, 1.367(b)-6**
. surtax, rate ... 1.11-1
. tax shelters
.. registration ... 301.6111-2

Credits against tax
. foreign corporations ... 1.882-4
. foreign tax credit limitation ... **1.904-5**
. foreign taxes paid ... 1.902-1—1.902-3
.. exemption from limitation ... 1.904(j)-1
. nonresident aliens ... 1.874-1
. partners ... 1.702-1
. withheld tax ... 1.1462-1

D

Deductions
. allocation among taxpayers ... 1.482-1
.. controlled services transactions ... **1.482-1, 1.482-2, 1.482-6, 1.6038A-3, 1.6662-6**
. corporate
.. foreign corporations paying dividends ... 1.245-1
. foreign corporations ... 1.882-4
. nonresident aliens ... 1.873-1, 1.874-1
. qualified business unit (QBU)
.. weighted average exchange rate ... 1.989(b)-1

Definitions
. business entities classification ... 301.7701-1—301.7701-3, 301.7701-5T
.. wholly owned by a foreign government or foreign bank ... 301.7701-2
. controlled foreign corporation ... 1.957-1
. less developed country corporation ... 1.902-4
. resident aliens ... 1.871-9
. stapled foreign corporation ... **1.269B-1**
. United States person ... 1.957-3T

Index to Regulations

References are to Reg. § numbers; boldface references are to proposed Reg. § numbers.

Definitions—continued
. United States property . . . 1.956-2

Distributive share of partners
. character of items constituting . . . 1.702-1(b)
. contributed property . . . 1.704-1, 1.704-1T
. determined by income or loss ratio . . . 1.704-1
. effect of partnership agreement . . . 1.704-1
. limitation on allowance of losses . . . 1.704-1, 1.704-1T

District Director of Internal Revenue
. returns for nonresident aliens . . . 1.874-1

Dividends
. DISC or former DISC . . . 1.861-3
. foreign corporation payor . . . 1.78-1
. . gross-up . . . 1.902-1, 1.902-3
. received, income
. . foreign corporation payor, domestic gross-up . . . 1.902-1—1.902-4
. source of income . . . 1.861-3

Domestic International Sales Corporations (DISCs)
. dividends . . . 1.861-3
. inter-company pricing rules . . . 1.994-1

E

Earned income
. foreign income . . . 1.911-7
. sources without the United States . . . 1.911-1, 1.911-2
. . community income . . . 1.911-5
. . deductions disallowed . . . 1.911-6
. . qualifying earned income . . . 1.911-3

Earnings and profits
. corporations
. . interest paid to related persons . . . **1.163(j)-1—1.163(j)-8**
. earnings strippings limitations . . . **1.163(j)-1—1.163(j)-8**
. foreign corporation . . . 1.964-1
. . sale or exchange of stock in . . . 1.1248-7
. foreign corporation stock . . . 1.1248-2, 1.1248-3
. foreign personal holding company income . . . 1.954-2
. inventories
. . subpart F . . . 1.952-1

Elections
. foreign earned income . . . 1.911-7
. functional currency, use of . . . 1.985-1—1.985-4
. nonfunctional currency . . . 1.988-1
. notional principal contract income . . . 1.863-7
. . defined . . . 1.988-1
. partnership making . . . 1.704-1, 1.704-1T

Employers and employees
. duty of employer to determine status of alien . . . 1.871-6

Engaged in U.S. business
. nonresident alien students or trainees . . . 1.871-9

Euro
. conversion to the euro
. . special rules . . . 1.985-8

Exchanges
. nonrecognition
. . U.S. real property interests . . . 1.897-6T

Exempt income
. compensation received, employees of foreign governments and international organizations . . . 1.893-1
. foreign corporations
. . international operation of ships or aircraft by foreign corporations . . . 1.883-1—1.883-5
. foreign governments . . . 1.892-1T—1.892-7T
. . controlled commercial entity excluded . . . 1.892-5
. international organizations
. . controlled commercial entity excluded . . . 1.892-5

Exempt organizations
. foreign corporations . . . 1.1442-3
. foreign organizations and foundations . . . 1.1441-9
. international organizations . . . 1.892-1T—1.892-6T
. shareholder of PFIC . . . 1.1291-1

F

Family members, transactions between . . . 1.267(a)-3

Family partnerships
. income, allocation of . . . 1.704-1
. ownership tests . . . 1.704-1
. purchased interest . . . 1.704-1
. recognition of . . . 1.704-1

Foreign base companies . . . 1.952-1, 1.952-2, 1.954-1, **1.954-1**, 1.954-2, **1.954-2**, 1.960-1

Foreign controlled corporations
. information returns . . . 1.6038A-1—1.6038A-6
. repeal of Code Sec. 963 . . . 1.954-1

Foreign corporations
. allocation of income and deductions . . . 1.482-1
. base company income . . . 1.954-1
. branch profits tax . . . 1.884-1
. . branch level interest tax . . . 1.884-4
. . incorporation, termination and liquidation . . . 1.884-2, 1.884-2T
. . qualified residents . . . 1.884-5
. branch transactions
. . foreign base company income . . . 1.954-1
. . personal holding company income . . . 1.954-2
. deductions . . . 1.874-1, 1.882-3, 1.882-4
. definition . . . 1.367(b)-2, **1.367(b)-2**
. less developed country corporation . . . 1.902-4
. determination of earnings and profits . . . 1.964-1
. directors, returns . . . 1.6035-1
. dispositions of U.S. real property interests . . . 1.897-1—1.897-3
. . TINs required . . . 1.1445-1
. distributions, dividend status . . . 1.78-1
. dividends received from . . . 1.78-1
. . deduction by recipient . . . 1.245-1
. . dividends-received deduction . . . 1.245-1
. dual consolidated losses
. . reduction of taxable income . . . **1.1503(d)-1—1.1503(d)-6**
. earnings and profits accounts . . . 1.243-3
. . complex cases . . . 1.1248-3
. . simple cases . . . 1.1248-2
. exchanges
. . carryover of earnings and taxes . . . **1.367(b)-1—1.367(b)-3, 1.367(b)-5—1.367(b)-9, 1.367(e)-1**
. exempt foreign corporations . . . 1.1442-3
. foreign base company sales income . . . 1.954-3
. . deductions . . . **1.954-1**

Foreign corporations—continued
  foreign insurance companies
    determination of income effectively connected with U.S. trade or business . . . **1.864-4**
  gross income . . . 1.882-2
    exclusions from . . . 1.883-1
  gross income exclusions
    international operation of ships or aircraft . . . 1.883-1—1.883-5
  income effectively connected with U.S. trade or business . . . 1.864-3, 1.864-4, 1.864-5
    income attributable to place of business in U.S. . . . 1.864-6, 1.864-7
  information returns . . . 1.6038A-1, 1.6046-1, 1.6046-1T
    agent authorization . . . 1.6038A-5
    annual accounting periods . . . 1.6035-1, 1.6038-2, 1.6038-2T, 1.6046-1, 1.6046-1T
    failure to furnish information . . . 1.6038A-6
    penalties . . . 1.6038A-4
    recordkeeping . . . 1.6038A-3
    reporting requirements . . . 1.6038A-2
  interest deduction . . . 1.882-5
  interest expense . . . **1.882-5**
    affiliated group . . . 1.861-11
  interest on portfolio debt investments . . . 1.871-14
  international operation of ships or aircraft
    gross income exclusions . . . 1.883-1—1.883-5
  liquidations . . . 1.367(e)-1, 1.367(e)-2
    outbound transfers to, anti-abuse rule . . . 1.367(e)-2
  manner of taxing . . . 1.881-1—1.894-1
  nonresident . . . 1.874-1, 1.881-2
  officers, returns . . . 1.6035-1
  real property in U.S.
    corporate distributions . . . 1.897-5, 1.897-5T
  resident . . . 1.882-1
  sale or exchange of stock . . . 1.1248-1
    securities transfers . . . 1.367(a)-3
    gain recognition . . . 1.367(a)-8
  stock sold or exchanged
    limitation on individual's tax . . . 1.1248-4
  stock transfers . . . 1.367(a)-3, **1.367(a)-3**, 1.367(b)-4, 1.367(b)-6
    gain recognition . . . 1.367(a)-8
  trade or business in United States defined . . . 1.864-2
  transfers . . . 1.367(a)-1T—1.367(a)-6T, 1.367(b)-1—1.367(b)-6, 1.367(b)-12, 1.367(d)-1T
    carryover of earnings and taxes . . . **1.367(b)-1**—**1.367(b)-3, 1.367(b)-5**—**1.367(b)-9, 1.367(e)-1**
    information returns . . . 1.6038B-1, 1.6038B-1T
  transfers to, by U.S. persons
    cash, reporting of . . . 1.6038B-1, 1.6038B-1T
    reporting requirements . . . 1.6038B-1, 1.6038B-1T
  treaties exempting income from tax . . . 1.894-1

Foreign currency transactions
  conversion to the euro
    special rules . . . 1.985-8
  functional currency . . . 1.985-1—1.985-3
    accounting methods . . . 1.985-4
    adjustments required upon change in . . . 1.985-5
    approximate separate transactions method . . . 1.985-3
    transition rules for QBUs . . . 1.985-6
    U.S. dollar, election to use . . . 1.985-2
  nonfunctional currency . . . 1.988-1—1.988-6
    contingent payment debt instruments . . . 1.988-6

Foreign currency transactions—continued
  qualified business unit
    defined . . . 1.989(a)-1
  transition rules
    net worth method . . . 1.989(c)-1
Foreign earned income . . . 1.911-1, 1.911-2
  community income . . . 1.911-4
  procedural rules . . . 1.911-7
Foreign entities
  classification . . . 301.7701-2, 301.7701-3
Foreign governments
  exempt income . . . 1.892-1T—1.892-7T
    controlled commercial entity excluded . . . 1.892-5
Foreign investment companies
  exceptions to passive income . . . **1.1293-2**, **1.1295-2**
Foreign mineral income . . . 1.901-2
Foreign personal holding companies
  dollar approximate separate transactions method
    characterization of income and earnings . . . 1.954-2
  foreign tax credit . . . 1.952-1, 1.952-2, 1.954-2, 1.960-1
  income . . . 4.954-2
  returns of officers, shareholders and directors . . . 1.6035-1
Foreign persons
  related taxpayers
    deductible amount . . . 1.267(a)-3
  transfers to
    information returns . . . 1.6038B-1T
Foreign private foundations . . . 1.1441-9
Foreign tax credit . . . 1.901-1—1.905-4T
  affiliated groups . . . 1.861-9, 1.861-11, 1.861-14, 1.904-4, 1.904-5
  allocation and apportionment of taxes . . . 1.904-6
  allowance of credit . . . 1.901-1, 1.901-1T
  alternative minimum tax . . . 1.904(b)-2
  amount of tax available as basis for . . . 1.902-1, 1.902-3
  conditions of allowance . . . 1.905-2
  consolidated returns . . . 1.1502-4, 1.1502-4T
  controlled foreign corporations . . . 1.952-1, 1.952-2, 1.960-1—1.960-6
    definition . . . 1.957-1
    look-through rules . . . 1.904-5
  credit for taxes in lieu of income taxes . . . 1.903-1
  definitions . . . 1.901-2
  dividends received from foreign corporations . . . 1.78-1
  domestic corporation owning stock of foreign corporation . . . 1.902-1, 1.902-3
  dual capacity taxpayers . . . 1.901-2A
  foreign base companies . . . 1.952-1, 1.952-2, 1.954-2, 1.960-1
  foreign oil-related income . . . 1.901-1, 1.901-1T
  foreign personal holding companies . . . 1.952-1, 1.952-2, 1.954-2, 1.960-1
  foreign tax redetermination
    notification and redetermination of U.S. tax . . . 1.905-4T
    required adjustments to pools . . . 1.905-3T
  functional currency . . . 1.985-1—1.985-4
  gross-up, controlled foreign corporations . . . 1.902-3, 1.960-1—1.960-6
  international boycott factor . . . 7.999-1

Index to Regulations

References are to Reg. § numbers; boldface references are to proposed Reg. § numbers.

Foreign tax credit—continued
. limitation on . . . 1.861-9, 1.861-11, 1.861-14, 1.904-1, 1.904-4, 1.904-5, **1.904-5**
. . capital gain . . . 1.904(b)-1
. . deconsolidation . . . 1.904(i)-1
. . exemption for certain individuals . . . 1.904(j)-1
. . look-through rules . . . 1.904-5
. . nonfunctional currency . . . 1.988-1—1.988-6
. . overall foreign loss . . . 1.904(f)-1
. . recapture of foreign losses . . . 1.904(f)-2
. . consolidated returns . . . 1.1502-9
. separate limitation for Sec. 904 interest . . . 1.904-4
. tier corporations . . . 1.960-1, 1.960-2
. when credit may be taken . . . 1.905-1, 1.905-2

Foreign taxpayers
. dispositions of U.S. real property interests
. . TINs required . . . 1.1445-1
. United States real property
. . corporate distributions . . . 1.897-5, 1.897-5T
. . corporate reorganizations . . . 1.897-6T
. . partnership interests . . . 1.897-7T

Foreign trusts
. transfers of property by U.S. persons
. . recognition of gain . . . 1.684-1—1.684-4
. U.S. beneficiaries . . . 1.679-1—1.679-6

Functional currency . . . 1.985-1—1.985-5
. transition rules . . . 1.985-6
. weighted average exchange rate . . . 1.989(b)-1

G

Gain or loss
. nonfunctional currency, foreign tax credit . . . 1.988-2
. stock dispositions . . . 1.865-1, 1.865-2

Global dealing operations
. allocation of income and deductions . . . **1.482-1, 1.482-8, 1.863-3, 1.863-7, 1.894-1**
. U.S. source income . . . **1.864-4**

Governmental obligations
. source . . . 1.863-1

Gross income
. exclusions
. . international operation of ships or aircraft by foreign corporations . . . 1.883-1—1.883-5
. natural resources, allocation of . . . 1.863-1
. partner . . . 1.702-1(c)
. scholarships and fellowships . . . 1.863-1
. shareholders, controlled foreign corporations . . . **1.951-1**

I

Income . . . 1.861-1—1.894-1
. affiliated groups
. . expense allocation . . . 1.861-14, 1.861-14T
. allocation
. . apportionment of interest expense . . . 1.861-9, 1.861-9T
. . comparable profits method . . . 1.482-5
. allocation among taxpayers . . . 1.482-1
. . controlled services transactions . . . **1.482-1, 1.482-2, 1.482-6, 1.6038A-3, 1.6662-6**
. . optional application . . . 1.861-13T
. allocation and apportionment of charitable deductions . . . **1.861-8**

Income—continued
. allocation and apportionment of interest expense
. . FASIT interest expense . . . **1.861-9T**
. assets
. . characterization rules . . . 1.861-12T
. computation of income from sources within or without United States . . . 1.861-1, 1.861-8, **1.861-8**, 1.861-8T
. . compensation for labor or services . . . **1.861-4**
. foreign taxes
. . undistributed earnings . . . 1.902-1, 1.902-2
. income from sources partly within and partly without United States . . . 1.863-2
. . communication activity . . . **1.863-9**
. . space and ocean activities . . . **1.863-8**
. . transportation service . . . 1.863-4
. income from sources within United States
. . allocation . . . 1.863-1
. . compensation for labor or services . . . **1.861-4**
. . definitions . . . 1.864-1—1.864-7
. . dividends . . . 1.861-3
. . interest . . . 1.861-2
. . personal property sold . . . 1.861-6
. . real property sold . . . 1.861-6
. . rentals . . . 1.861-5
. . royalties . . . 1.861-5
. . taxable income, computation . . . 1.861-8, **1.861-8**
. income from sources without United States . . . 1.861-1, 1.862-1
. . allocation . . . 1.863-1
. . earned income . . . 1.911-1, 1.911-2
. interest expense
. . allocation . . . 1.861-9—1.861-11, 1.861-9T—1.861-11T
. . FASIT interest expense . . . **1.861-9T**
. . transition rules . . . 1.861-13
. interest received . . . 1.861-2
. lease income
. . vessels, aircraft, spacecraft . . . 1.862-1
. research and experimental expenditures
. . allocation and apportionment . . . 1.861-8
. U.S. source income
. . global dealing operation . . . **1.864-4**

Information returns—see also Returns
. controlled foreign partnerships
. . U.S. persons owning interests in . . . 1.6038-3
. foreign controlled corporations . . . 1.6038A-1
. foreign corporations . . . 1.6035-1, 1.6038-2, 1.6038-2T, 1.6038A-1, 1.6046-1, 1.6046-1T
. . agent authorization . . . 1.6038A-5
. . failure to furnish information . . . 1.6038A-6
. . penalties . . . 1.6038A-4
. . recordkeeping . . . 1.6038A-3
. . reporting requirements . . . 1.6038A-2
. . transfers to . . . 1.6038B-1, 1.6038B-1T
. foreign partnerships
. . transfers to . . . 1.6038B-2
. . U.S. persons owning interests in . . . 1.6038-3, 1.6046A-1
. foreign personal holding company officers, shareholders and directors . . . 1.6035-1
. foreign persons
. . transfers to . . . 1.6038B-1T

Insurance companies
. foreign insurance companies
. . determination of income effectively connected with U.S. trade or business . . . **1.864-4**

INS

Intangible drilling costs
. transfers . . . 1.367(a)-4T

Intangible property
. allocation of income from transfers of . . . 1.482-4

Interest paid
. foreign corporations . . . 1.882-5
. . interest expense deduction . . . **1.882-5**
. registration-required obligations . . . 1.163-5

Interest received
. registration-required obligations . . . 5f.163-1
. United States obligations
. . withholding on nonresident aliens . . . 1.1441-3

International boycott factor . . . 7.999-1

International organizations
. exempt income . . . 1.892-1T
. U.S. sourced income . . . 1.892-6T

Inventories
. cost
. . shared cost allocation . . . 1.482-7
. sales of . . . 1.863-3

L

Less developed country corporation
. defined . . . 1.902-4
. stock ownership requirements . . . 1.1248-5

Liability for tax
. accumulated earnings tax . . . 1.532-1

Liquidations
. foreign corporations . . . 1.367(e)-2
. . carryover of earnings and taxes . . . **1.367(b)-1—1.367(b)-3, 1.367(b)-5—1.367(b)-9, 1.367(e)-1**
. . outbound transfers to, anti-abuse rule . . . 1.367(e)-2
. . stock or securities transfers . . . 1.367(a)-3, 1.367(a)-8
. stock and asset consistency rules . . . 1.367(a)-4T

M

Mark-to-market activities
. passive foreign investment company
. . mark-to-market election for marketable stock . . . 1.1291-1, 1.1295-1, 1.1296-1, 1.1296-2

Multiple-party financing and conduit arrangements . . . 1.7701(l)-1

N

Natural resources
. allocation of income . . . 1.863-1
. income from sources partly within and partly without United States . . . 1.863-1—1.863-4

Nonfunctional currency . . . 1.988-1—1.988-6
. contingent payment debt instruments . . . 1.988-6

Nonresident aliens
. classes of . . . 1.871-7
. computation of taxable income . . . 1.861-8
. deductions allowable . . . 1.873-1, 1.874-1
. dispositions of U.S. real property interests . . . 1.897-1—1.897-3
. "engaging in trade or business within the United States" defined . . . 1.871-8, 1.871-9

Nonresident aliens—continued
. gross income of . . . 1.872-1
. . exclusions from . . . 1.872-2
. income effectively connected with U.S. trade or business . . . 1.864-3, 1.864-4, 1.864-5
. . income attributable to place of business in U.S. . . . 1.864-6, 1.864-7
. income factoring, related person . . . 1.864-8T
. interest expense
. . allocation . . . 1.861-9, 1.861-9T, 1.861-10
. . optional application . . . 1.861-13T
. . transitional rules . . . 1.861-13T
. multiple-party financing and conduit arrangements . . . 1.871-1, 1.881-3, 1.881-4, 1.7701(l)-1
. . withholding . . . 1.1441-3, 1.1441-7
. resident alien, treatment as
. . defined . . . 1.871-9
. returns . . . 1.874-1
. students or trainees engaged in U.S. business . . . 1.871-9
. trade or business in the U.S. . . . 1.864-2
. withholding of taxes
. . exemption claim . . . 1.1441-5

Nonresident citizens
. foreign income . . . 1.911-1

P

Partners and partnerships
. anti-abuse rule
. . subchapter K . . . 1.701-2
. built-in gains or losses
. . property contributions by partner . . . 1.704-1, 1.704-1T
. business entity classification . . . 301.7701-3
. change in taxable year . . . 1.706-1
. controlled foreign corporations as partner
. . distributive share of income . . . 1.954-1, 1.954-2, 1.954-3, 1.954-4
. . hybrid branches . . . 1.954-1, **1.954-9**
. . subpart F income . . . 1.952-1
. controlled partnerships, taxable income determination . . . 1.482-1
. credits of partner . . . 1.702-1
. defined . . . 301.7701-3
. distributive share of partners
. . character of items constituting . . . 1.702-1(b)
. . determination of . . . 1.704-1, 1.704-1T
. . partnership agreement . . . 1.704-1
. entertainment expenses, separate accounting . . . 1.702-1
. foreign partnerships
. . information returns required of U.S. persons . . . 1.6038-3, 1.6046A-1
. . transfers to . . . 1.6038B-2
. gross income of partner . . . 1.702-1(c)
. income and credits of partner
. . distributive share . . . 1.702-1
. . subpart F income . . . 1.952-1
. meal expenses
. . separate accounting . . . 1.702-1
. property contributions by partner
. . built-in gains or losses . . . 1.704-1, 1.704-1T
. returns . . . 1.6031(a)-1
. subchapter K
. . anti-abuse rule . . . 1.701-2

Partners and partnerships—continued
. taxable years . . . 1.706-1
. . tax-exempt partners disregarded . . . 1.706-1
. travel expenses, separate accounting . . . 1.702-1

Passive foreign investment company
. deemed sale election . . . 1.1297-3T
. exempt organization as shareholder . . . 1.1291-1
. marketable stock
. . definition . . . 1.1296-2
. . mark-to-market election . . . 1.1291-1, 1.1295-1, 1.1296-1, 1.1296-2
. mark-to-market election of marketable stock . . . 1.1296-2
. qualified electing funds . . . 1.1295-1
. . shareholder taxation . . . 1.367(e)-1, **1.1291-1—1.1291-7, 1.1293-1, 1.1293-2, 1.1295-1, 1.1295-2**
. retroactive elections . . . 1.1295-3

Payment of tax
. stock transfer excise tax . . . 1.1494-1

Penalties
. accuracy-related . . . 1.6662-1—1.6662-7
. . allocation of income and deductions . . . 1.6662-5T
. . negligence or disregard . . . 1.6662-1—1.6662-5
. returns
. . accuracy-related . . . 1.6662-1—1.6662-5
. valuation misstatements . . . 1.6662-5T, 1.6664-4T

Personal property
. sale of
. . income from sources within United States . . . 1.861-7
. . income from sources without United States . . . 1.861-7
. . sources of income . . . 1.863-1

Private foundations
. foreign foundations
. . exempt status . . . 1.1441-9

Proprietorships
. controlled, taxable income determination . . . 1.482-1

Q

Qualified business units (QBUs)
. change in accounting method
. . dollar approximate separate transactions method . . . 1.985-7
. functional currency . . . 1.985-1—1.985-4
. . transition rules . . . 1.985-6
. . weighted average exchange rate . . . 1.989(b)-1
. net worth method of accounting . . . 1.989(c)-1

Qualified electing funds (QEFs) . . . 1.1295-1
. current inclusion of income . . . 1.1293-1
. dividend election by shareholder . . . 1.1291-9
. election by passive foreign investment company . . . **1.1293-2, 1.1295-1, 1.1295-2**
. election to recognize gain . . . 1.1291-10
. exempt organization as shareholder . . . 1.1291-1
. net capital gain defined . . . 1.1293-1
. pass-through entities . . . 1.1293-1, 1.1295-1
. retroactive elections . . . 1.1295-3
. undistributed earnings, election to extend time for tax payment on . . . 1.1294-1T

R

Real estate
. income
. . election to treat as connected to U.S. business . . . 1.871-10

Registration-required obligations
. interest on . . . 5f.103-1

Related taxpayers
. foreign persons
. . deductible amount . . . 1.267(a)-3
. transactions between . . . 1.267(a)-3, **1.861-9T**

Reorganizations
. foreign corporations
. . carryover of earnings and taxes . . . **1.367(b)-1—1.367(b)-3, 1.367(b)-5—1.367(b)-9, 1.367(e)-1**
. statutory merger or consolidation . . . **1.367(a)-3, 1.367(b)-4, 1.367(b)-6**

Reporting requirements
. foreign corporations
. . transfers to . . . 1.6038B-1, 1.6038B-1T
. foreign partnerships
. . transfers to . . . 1.6038B-2

Research and experimental expenditures
. domestic and foreign source income
. . allocation and apportionment . . . 1.861-8

Returns—see also Information returns
. business organizations, classification . . . 301.7701-1—301.7701-3, 301.7701-5T
. foreign corporations . . . 1.6038A-2
. . officers and directors . . . 1.6035-1
. partnership income . . . 1.6031(a)-1
. penalties
. . accuracy-related . . . 1.6662-1—1.6662-5
. stock transfers . . . 1.1494-1

S

Sales or exchanges
. foreign corporations
. . carryover of earnings and taxes . . . **1.367(b)-1—1.367(b)-3, 1.367(b)-5—1.367(b)-9, 1.367(e)-1**
. gain from sale of stock . . . 1.1248-1
. stock
. . domestic corporation "principally availed" for holding foreign company stock . . . 1.1248-6

Shareholders
. corporate
. . foreign tax credit . . . 1.902-1, 1.902-3

Small business corporations
. stock
. . space and ocean activities . . . **1.863-8**

Sources of income
. within and without U.S.
. . communication activity . . . 1.863-9
. . compensation for labor or services . . . **1.861-4**
. . global dealing operation . . . **1.863-3, 1.864-4**

Stock
. dispositions . . . 1.865-1, 1.865-2
. ownership
. . controlled foreign corporations . . . 1.958-2
. passive foreign investment company
. . definition of marketable stock . . . 1.1296-2

STO

Stock—continued
. reorganization distributions
.. foreign corporations . . . **1.367(b)-1—1.367(b)-3**, **1.367(b)-5—1.367(b)-9, 1.367(e)-1**
. transfer of assets
.. consistency . . . 1.338-4
. transfers involving foreign corporations . . . **1.367(a)-3, 1.367(b)-4, 1.367(b)-6**

Subpart F income
. definition . . . 1.952-1
. limitation on U.S. shareholder's pro rata share . . . **1.951-1**

T

Tax shelters
. registration
.. confidential corporate tax shelters . . . 301.6111-2
. questions and answers
.. registration . . . 301.6111-1T

Tax treaties
. income
.. global dealing operation . . . **1.894-1**
. payments to entities
.. determination of tax . . . 1.894-1
.. eligibility for benefits . . . 1.894-1

Taxable income
. adjustments to . . . 1.535-2

Taxable year
. change of U.S. citizenship or residence . . . 1.871-13
. partnerships . . . 1.706-1

Transfers
. computer programs . . . 1.861-18
. foreign corporations . . . 1.367(a)-1T—1.367(a)-6T, 1.367(b)-1—1.367(b)-6, 1.367(b)-12, 1.367(d)-1T, 1.6038B-1, 1.6038B-1T
.. carryover of earnings and taxes . . . **1.367(b)-1—1.367(b)-3, 1.367(b)-5—1.367(b)-9, 1.367(e)-1**
. foreign partnerships . . . 1.6038B-2
. intangible property
.. allocation of income . . . **1.482-4**
.. controlled transactions, taxable income . . . 1.482-4
. tangible property
.. controlled transactions, taxable income . . . 1.482-3

Transportation service, income from sources partly within and partly without United States . . . 1.863-4

Treaty-based return positions . . . 301.6114-1

Treaty income
. determination of tax . . . 1.871-12
.. income paid to entities . . . 1.894-1

Treaty income—continued
. exemptions . . . 1.894-1

Trusts
. foreign trusts
.. recognition of gain on transfers by U.S. persons . . . 1.684-1—1.684-4
.. U.S. beneficiaries . . . 1.679-1—1.679-6

U

United States real property
. disposition of investment in . . . 1.897-1—1.897-3
.. TINs required . . . 1.1445-1

United States real property, foreign owned
. corporate distributions . . . 1.897-5, 1.897-5T
. corporations, publicly traded . . . 1.897-9T
. exchanges, nonrecognition of . . . 1.897-6T
. partnership interests, treatment of . . . 1.897-7T
. withholding . . . 1.1445-11T

W

Withholding agents . . . 1.1441-7

Withholding of tax
. foreign taxpayers
.. dispositions of U.S. real property interests, TINs required . . . 1.1445-1

Withholding of tax at source
. dispositions by foreign persons
.. certain partnerships and trusts . . . 1.1445-8
.. U.S. real property interests . . . 1.1445-1—1.1445-8
. reduced treaty rate . . . 1.1441-6
.. special taxpayer identifying number rule . . . 1.1441-1, 1.1441-6
. requirement for withholding
.. foreign persons . . . 1.1441-1
. U.S. source income
.. exemption . . . 1.1441-4

Withholding of tax on foreign governments
. exempt income . . . 1.1441-8

Withholding of tax on nonresident aliens
. agents . . . 1.1441-7
. exemption from withholding . . . 1.1441-4
. income exempt from withholding . . . 1.1441-3
. income subject to withholding . . . 1.1441-2
. interest on government obligations . . . 1.1441-3
. per diem of alien trainees . . . 1.1441-4
. rate of withholding . . . 1.1441-1
. requirement for withholding . . . 1.1441-1

Withholding of tax on wages
. reduced treaty rate . . . 1.1441-6